PRESENTED TO

_____

BY

_____

ON THE OCCASION OF

_____

DATE

_____

The grass withers
and the flowers fade,
but the word of our
God stands forever.

ISAIAH 40:8

In this space, write or illustrate the story of how you met Jesus so that you will remember it and can share it with others.

— SIGNIFICANT MOMENTS IN YOUR STORY —

Event
....

Place .... Date ....

Event
....

Place .... Date ....

Event
....

Place .... Date ....

Event
....

Place .... Date ....

Event
....

Place .... Date ....

Blessed are those who trust in
the LORD and have made the
LORD their hope and confidence.

JEREMIAH 17:7

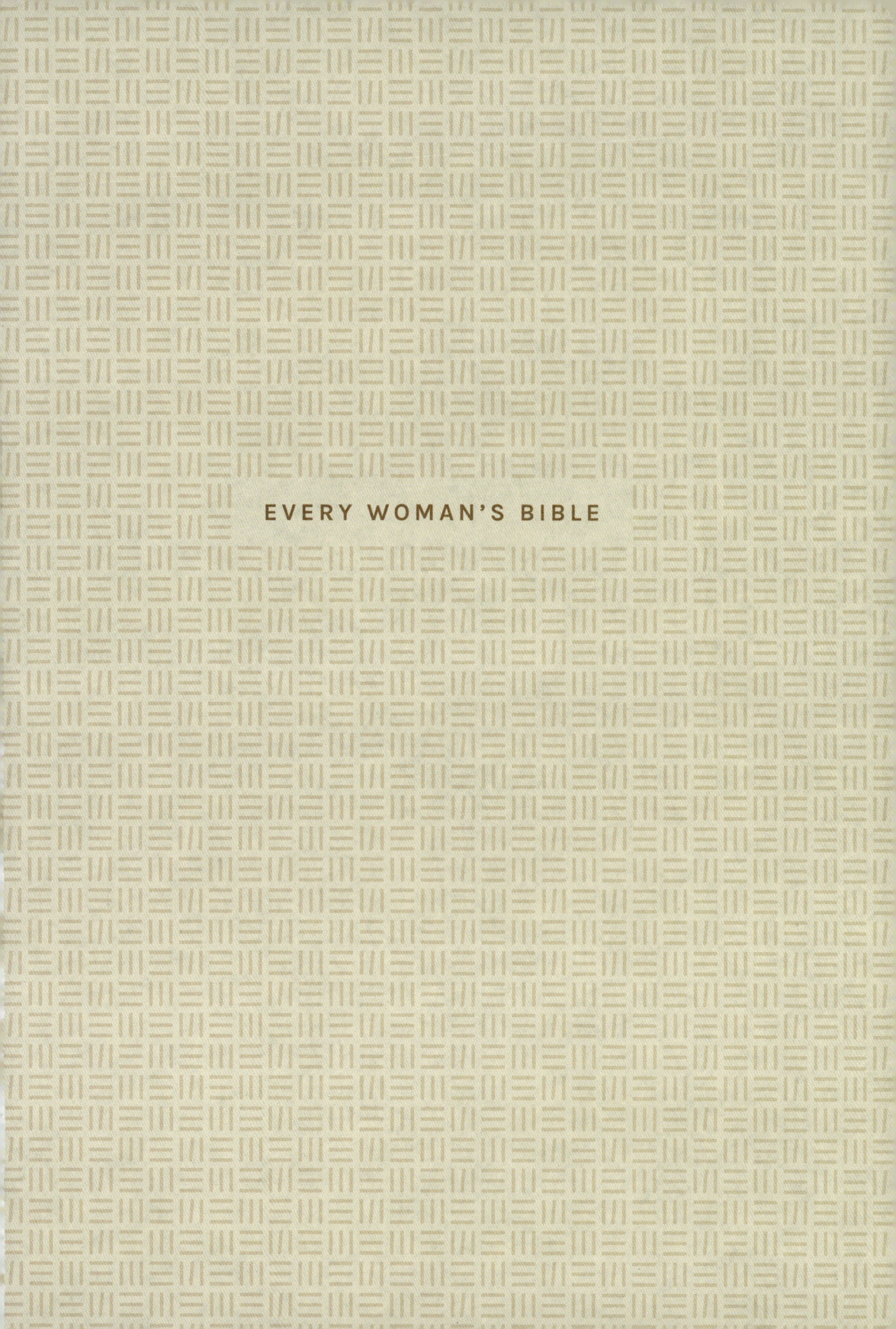
EVERY WOMAN'S BIBLE

Visit Tyndale online at newlivingtranslation.com and tyndale.com.

Visit the Every Woman's Bible online at EveryWomansBible.com.

Filament-enabled Bibles and the Filament Bible app are protected by US Patent 10,896,235.

Every Woman's Bible copyright © 2024 by Naomi Cramer Overton and Misty Arterburn. All rights reserved.

Every Woman's Bible features and Bible helps copyright © 2024 by Naomi Cramer Overton and Misty Arterburn. All rights reserved.

Insight features on pages 22, 47, 83, 109, 185, 268, 444, 578, 615, 977, 1036, 1081, 1098, 1212-13, 1354, 1403, 1452, 1632 copyright © 2004 by Stephen Arterburn and Dean Merrill. All rights reserved. Insight features on pages 72, 387, 472 copyright © Naomi Cramer Overton and Stephen Arterburn. All rights reserved. Insight features on pages 6, 14, 18, 38, 53, 89, 93, 113, 136, 143, 169, 191, 237, 455, 339, 359, 376, 378-79, 420, 496, 522-23, 620, 652, 656-57, 680, 709, 775, 845, 870-71, 1022-23, 1054-55, 1192, 1196, 1244, 1264, 1292, 1334-35, 1360, 1378, 1409, 1433, 1566, 1641, 1652 copyright © 2024 by Tyndale House Publishers. All rights reserved.

The One Year Bible Reading Plan copyright © 1985, 1996 by Tyndale House Publishers. All rights reserved.

Authors are represented by the literary agency of WordServe Literary, www.wordserveliterary.com.

NLT Dictionary/Concordance copyright © 2007 by Tyndale House Publishers. All rights reserved.

Color maps copyright © 2018 by Tyndale House Publishers. All rights reserved.

Every Woman's Bible is an edition of the *Holy Bible*, New Living Translation.

Holy Bible, New Living Translation, copyright © 1996, 2004, 2015 by Tyndale House Foundation. All rights reserved.

The text of the *Holy Bible*, New Living Translation, may be quoted in any form (written, visual, electronic, or audio) up to and inclusive of five hundred (500) verses without express written permission of the publisher, provided that the verses quoted do not account for more than twenty-five percent (25%) of the work in which they are quoted, and provided that a complete book of the Bible is not quoted.

When the *Holy Bible*, New Living Translation, is quoted, one of the following credit lines must appear on the copyright page or title page of the work:

Scripture quotations are taken from the *Holy Bible*, New Living Translation, copyright © 1996, 2004, 2015 by Tyndale House Foundation. Used by permission of Tyndale House Publishers, Carol Stream, Illinois 60188. All rights reserved.

Unless otherwise indicated, all Scripture quotations are taken from the *Holy Bible*, New Living Translation, copyright © 1996, 2004, 2015 by Tyndale House Foundation. Used by permission of Tyndale House Publishers, Carol Stream, Illinois 60188. All rights reserved.

Scripture quotations marked *NLT* are taken from the *Holy Bible*, New Living Translation, copyright © 1996, 2004, 2015 by Tyndale House Foundation. Used by permission of Tyndale House Publishers, Carol Stream, Illinois 60188. All rights reserved.

When quotations from the NLT text are used in nonsalable media, such as church bulletins, orders of service, newsletters, transparencies, or similar media, a complete copyright notice is not required, but the initials *NLT* must appear at the end of each quotation.

Quotations in excess of five hundred (500) verses or twenty-five percent (25%) of the work, or other permission requests, must be approved in writing by Tyndale House Publishers. Send requests by email to permission@tyndale.com.

Publication of any commentary or other Bible reference work produced for commercial sale that uses the New Living Translation requires written permission for use of the NLT text.

Designed and typeset using Bible Serif and Bible Sans Next by 2k/denmark, Højbjerg, Denmark

Scripture quotations marked AMPC are taken from the Amplified® Bible (AMPC), copyright © 1954, 1958, 1962, 1964, 1965, 1987 by The Lockman Foundation. Used by permission. www.lockman.org.

Scripture quotations marked NASB are taken from the (NASB®) New American Standard Bible,® copyright © 1960, 1971, 1977, 1995, 2020 by The Lockman Foundation. Used by permission. All rights reserved. www.lockman.org.

Scripture quotations marked NET are taken from the New English Translation, NET Bible,® copyright ©1996–2006 by Biblical Studies Press, L.L.C. http://netbible.com. All rights reserved.

Scripture quotations marked NIV are taken from the Holy Bible, New International Version.® NIV.® Copyright © 1973, 1978, 1984, 2011 by Biblica, Inc.® Used by permission. All rights reserved worldwide.

Tyndale, *New Living Translation*, *NLT*, the New Living Translation logo, *Filament*, and *LeatherLike* are registered trademarks of Tyndale House Ministries. *Every Woman's* and the Every Woman's logo are trademarks of Tyndale House Ministries.

For information about special discounts for bulk purchases, please contact Tyndale House Publishers at csresponse@tyndale.com, or call 1-855-277-9400.

ISBN 978-1-4964-5299-3	Hardcover
ISBN 978-1-4964-5300-6	Hardcover Indexed
ISBN 978-1-4964-5301-3	LeatherLike Soft Gold
ISBN 978-1-4964-5302-0	LeatherLike Soft Gold Indexed
ISBN 978-1-4964-8438-3	LeatherLike Sky Blue
ISBN 978-1-4964-8439-0	LeatherLike Sky Blue Indexed

Printed in China

30	29	28	27	26	25	24
8	7	6	5	4	3	2

filament ENABLED

EVERY WOMAN'S BIBLE

NLT.

TYNDALE HOUSE PUBLISHERS
CAROL STREAM, ILLINOIS

CONTENTS

Welcome to Your Filament-Enabled Bible! A6
Canonical Listing of Bible Books A7
Alphabetical Listing of Bible Books A8
Welcome to the *Every Woman's Bible* A9
Every Woman's Bible User's Guide A10
How to Explore a Relationship with God A14
Where to Start Reading the Bible A16
Basic Bible Helps A17
Bible Reading Worksheet A18
Meet Our Contributors A19
A Note to Readers A25
New Living Translation: Our Choice for You A26
Introduction to the New Living Translation A27

THE OLD TESTAMENT 1
What Is My Purpose? 1170
THE NEW TESTAMENT 1187

The One Year Bible Reading Plan 1655
What Do We Learn About God's Mission and Ours? 1669
Image Index 1672
Identity Index 1675
Come Close Index 1678
Perspective Index 1680
What the Bible Says About... Index 1682
Insight Index 1683
She Says Index 1685
Scripture Pause Index 1689
Contributors Index 1690
NLT Dictionary/Concordance 1693
Image Credits 1777

filament®

WELCOME TO YOUR FILAMENT-ENABLED BIBLE!
This Bible works with the Filament Bible app, which uses your phone or tablet to enhance this Bible with even more powerful study and devotional content.

WHY USE THE FILAMENT BIBLE APP?
The Filament Bible app illuminates and amplifies this Bible. By simply scanning Filament-enabled page numbers, it instantly delivers helpful, in-depth content centered on the passage you are reading. Study notes, devotionals, videos, profiles, interactive maps, and more enable you to get the most out of your time in God's Word.

HOW TO GET STARTED WITH FILAMENT:

1. Grab your device, and open the App Store or Google Play.
2. Search for "Filament Bible," and install the app.
3. Follow the prompts to learn how it works, and enjoy exploring!

TO LEARN MORE ABOUT FILAMENT, GO TO FILAMENTBIBLES.COM

CANONICAL LISTING OF BIBLE BOOKS

OLD TESTAMENT

Genesis...............3	2 Chronicles.........515	Daniel.............1033
Exodus 79	Ezra................557	Hosea.............1057
Leviticus.............131	Nehemiah 573	Joel 1071
Numbers 167	Esther..............593	Amos..............1079
Deuteronomy 217	Job.................607	Obadiah...........1093
Joshua..............257	Psalms 649	Jonah..............1097
Judges..............289	Proverbs............753	Micah 1105
Ruth 323	Ecclesiastes.........793	Nahum 1117
1 Samuel 333	Song of Songs......809	Habakkuk..........1125
2 Samuel 371	Isaiah 821	Zephaniah 1131
1 Kings..............407	Jeremiah............895	Haggai 1139
2 Kings 441	Lamentations........961	Zechariah..........1145
1 Chronicles........477	Ezekiel 973	Malachi............1161

NEW TESTAMENT

Matthew...........1189	Ephesians..........1489	Hebrews...........1559
Mark...............1239	Philippians 1501	James 1579
Luke 1271	Colossians 1511	1 Peter.............1587
John................1319	1 Thessalonians 1519	2 Peter 1597
Acts................1357	2 Thessalonians.....1527	1 John 1605
Romans 1407	1 Timothy 1533	2 John 1615
1 Corinthians 1435	2 Timothy..........1541	3 John 1619
2 Corinthians.......1461	Titus 1549	Jude...............1623
Galatians 1479	Philemon 1555	Revelation 1627

ALPHABETICAL LISTING OF BIBLE BOOKS

Acts 1357	James 1579	Nehemiah 573
Amos 1079	Jeremiah 895	Numbers 167
1 Chronicles 477	Job 607	Obadiah 1093
2 Chronicles 515	Joel 1071	1 Peter 1587
Colossians 1511	John 1319	2 Peter 1597
1 Corinthians 1435	1 John 1605	Philemon 1555
2 Corinthians 1461	2 John 1615	Philippians 1501
Daniel 1033	3 John 1619	Proverbs 753
Deuteronomy 217	Jonah 1097	Psalms 649
Ecclesiastes 793	Joshua 257	Revelation 1627
Ephesians 1489	Jude 1623	Romans 1407
Esther 593	Judges 289	Ruth 323
Exodus 79	1 Kings 407	1 Samuel 333
Ezekiel 973	2 Kings 441	2 Samuel 371
Ezra 557	Lamentations 961	Song of Songs 809
Galatians 1479	Leviticus 131	1 Thessalonians 1519
Genesis 3	Luke 1271	2 Thessalonians 1527
Habakkuk 1125	Malachi 1161	1 Timothy 1533
Haggai 1139	Mark 1239	2 Timothy 1541
Hebrews 1559	Matthew 1189	Titus 1549
Hosea 1057	Micah 1105	Zechariah 1145
Isaiah 821	Nahum 1117	Zephaniah 1131

WELCOME TO THE
Every Woman's Bible

Welcome. You belong here.

I am so glad you opened these pages to see what we have prepared for you, a Bible that invites every woman to explore her story through God's story. Here, in this Bible, I hope you can shed every expectation, role, and fear and hear God's deep, authentic call to extraordinary purpose.

You may be wondering, "How will this Bible live up to the name, *Every Woman's Bible*?" What you hold in your hands is an answer the Lord gave me in prayer: "By having as many women as possible tell their own stories and inviting you to tell your story too." In this Bible, you'll meet a global sisterhood of more than one hundred voices (see the contributors' map, page A19). Each woman tells her story alongside God's story, and these women reflect the diversity of God's creation in their cultures, faces, races, ages, gifts, and vocations. Each book benefits from globally respected women Bible scholars who wrote study notes adding women's perspectives.

When it comes to living our stories, some days we soar toward a great, life-giving mission. On other days we struggle to get off the ground, fighting against our burdens. Sometimes we struggle with our faith or just with ourselves, and other times we feel sure, confident. In many, many ways, each of us is "every woman." We are all these women, just on different days.

As we open this Bible, we might fear we'll meet women who are nothing like us. We fear feeling different, divided by political convictions, social issues, bank accounts, facial lines, or body sizes. But God's love letter for us, the Bible, speaks life to our social-media-airbrushed anxieties. God's love letter is for every woman. When we open this Bible, we hear God through his story and through others' stories.

I pray the Bible's story and these women's stories cheer you on to live abundantly and serve extravagantly. I pray they help you go deeper in God's story—available to all of us, new every day, no matter what our stories have been before.

Additionally, in the middle of this Bible (page 1170), you'll find a unique section that walks you through a proven journey to find your purpose in God's purpose, your story in God's story.

As you journey through these pages, we want to be right alongside so you come to say, "I'm living what God made me for, alongside other women who make me strong." We want you to feel guided toward action! We want you to feel rooted in God, strengthened in your relationships, and activated in God's calling, his world-renewing cause.

Sister, you have a story. A story that matters. I can't wait to hear your voice.

With my ordinary and God's extraordinary,
DR. NAOMI CRAMER OVERTON
GENERAL EDITOR

Every Woman's Bible

USER'S GUIDE

The *Every Woman's Bible* focuses on what hundreds of women say they desire from a Bible: great study notes and information from maps and charts, clarity on their calling, insights from others' stories, and help for their needs. This begins with the clear and trusted New Living Translation, which communicates the Bible's message in language that meets us where we are today.

Globally respected Bible scholars, who also happen to be women, provide the study notes and walk alongside you on your journey through God's story and your story. This Bible contains an array of illustrations and charts, including original ones written by women. This Bible also offers writings by women from many places, stages, and walks of life.

For a full list of each of these writings, see the indexes beginning on page 1669.

INTRODUCTION

Before each of the Bible's sixty-six books you will find:

BEAUTY To help you prepare visually for what you'll read, a full-page image draws on the themes and feel of each book.

MISSION To help you consider what each book has to say about God's purposes and your own, look for a key takeaway on *God's mission and ours*.

HISTORY Who, When, and How questions orient you to each book. Timelines give you further historical context, showing what events were happening at the time.

ESTIMATED READING TIMES To show you how much time to budget, these estimates are divided into thirty-minute segments.

FEATURE HIGHLIGHTS A sampling of articles on purpose and calling, identity, needs, and wonderings. They spotlight topics you've told us you care about, illuminating the Bible's story through the lens of women scholars and writers who make Scripture more relatable.

STUDY NOTES Each respected Bible scholar—all of whom are women—applied her research and cultural understanding of the ancient world to craft these notes. The scholars particularly focused the notes and additional commentary on portions of Scripture which address topics women might find relevant, fascinating, and helpful and zeroed in on aspects that women might silently struggle with but that are rarely addressed. These notes clarify the cultural, historical, and literary context we all need so we can read the Bible with greater understanding.

IMAGE
Discover your purpose and how to make the most of God's designs for your four core relationships. We find our purpose and calling as we relate to (1) God; (2) our family and friends; (3) our communities, including our workplaces, neighborhoods, schools, and churches; and (4) the unique ways God has made each of us to bring more goodness to God's world.

Learn more on page 13.

IDENTITY
These articles showcase both stories of Bible people and stories of God's character to shed light on who they were, their role in God's mission, and what their lives can teach us. Many of these explore stories through imaginative, first-person narrative based on what the Bible suggests the woman might tell us herself if she could. Learning about these women's hopes, struggles, failures, and victories can help us grow in our own God-given identities.

COME CLOSE
These devotionals address real-life emotions and needs that invite us to draw near to God. For some, it's pain or a problem. For others, it's a life season or a startling opportunity. Each includes a quote from someone who has faced a similar need, a relevant Bible quote, and a prayer.

PERSPECTIVE
Have you ever encountered something in the Bible and thought, "Wait, what?" Here, we dig into questions we'd like to ask but may not have thought we could. The Perspective articles take a deep look at these passages rather than giving us pat answers. They highlight each passage's language, meaning, and context to provide deeper wisdom from God's Word. These focus especially on aspects of the Bible that may unsettle us.

USER'S GUIDE   A11

WHAT THE BIBLE SAYS ABOUT…

Sometimes it helps to look at the big picture. This feature illuminates key themes throughout the Bible, especially themes of interest to women, by gathering key verses all in one place. Consider these pages to be a starting place for your study of each topic.

INSIGHT

These charts, maps, graphs, and illustrations help us understand the Bible beyond what words alone may offer. You'll find these where an illustration, more information, or a cultural insight can help you see beyond the pages themselves to the real world of the Bible.

SHE SAYS

Throughout the Bible, you'll find powerful quotes that capture the voices of Christian women across history. These quotes show us how they lived out their faith across many cultures and places. We gain inspiration from their words as we hear from leaders of movements and church denominations, singers and writers and artists, and missionaries and theologians. We find strength from the variety of voices, reminding us that women throughout history and from many walks of life have much to say about how God is with us today, where we are.

SCRIPTURE PAUSE

Throughout this Bible, you'll find full-page script lettering of Bible verses that inspire us. We hope these pages give you space to take a breath, spend a moment reflecting on a brief Bible verse, and experience the peace God's Word gives.

WORDS TO REMEMBER

You will find highlighted portions of Scripture throughout the Bible. We've spotlighted these frequently cited passages so you can see what verses draw the most interest from other readers. And you may want to take some of these with you into your days by committing them to memory.

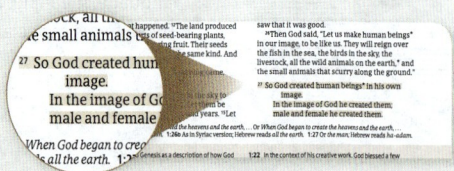

DIGGING DEEPER INTO IMAGE
LIVING GOD'S MISSION THROUGH OUR FOUR CORE RELATIONSHIPS

We are made for relationships—with God, our family and friends, our communities, and our own place of unique influence. Our relationships form us at least as much as we shape them! Understanding these relationships, and how we can invest in their health and purpose, allows us to thrive and live out our God-given callings. Through these relationships, we see how those around us and we ourselves are made in the image of God and how to share that with the world.

THEOS MY STORY WITH GOD

The Greek word *Theos* means "God," and in this sphere we can discover our extraordinary purpose in the God whose faithful love defines each of us. This place of relationship is just for you and God. One central way we get to know God is through his Word, the Bible—and he invites us to join his mission.

OIKOS MY STORY WITH FAMILY & FRIENDS

The Greek word *Oikos* means "home" or "household." But this sphere, so dear to many of us, can consume us, bringing us comfort and life or struggle and grief (often both). The Bible shows us complicated family and friend dynamics, where God can reveal how he wants us to relate to each other in ways that yield life.

KOINONIA MY STORY WITH COMMUNITY, WORKPLACE & CHURCH

The Greek word *Koinonia* means "fellowship," and this sphere comes naturally to some. It's a place we can find fulfillment. And yet, these relationships can also develop places of deep hurt, burnout, and avoidance. God can show us how to develop this sphere intentionally so that our neighborhoods, workplaces or schools, and churches thrive. And we thrive, too.

SHALOM MY STORY OF MY UNIQUE INFLUENCE

The Hebrew word *Shalom*, at its simplest, means "peace." However, this word carries an even greater depth of meaning beyond our language. This sphere relates to our contentment, completeness, wholeness, well-being, and harmony, which come from expressing our unique calling in God's mission.

HOW TO EXPLORE
A RELATIONSHIP WITH GOD

When I (Naomi) was a little girl, I wanted to know God. So I grabbed the little Bible someone at church had handed me, and at night, I'd open it up and read it all alone. One time, I remember praying one enormously powerful prayer in my dark room: "God, if you're real, I am desperate to know you. Will you help me?" He did by showing me in the Bible how I didn't live up to the good ways God asked me to live, particularly that part about loving others as myself.

Thankfully, in college, my friend Beth invited me to a group where I heard about how to know God in a way I never had before. I told Beth, "I'm a Christian, but I don't understand why so many people always talk about Jesus." Beth explained that the gap between how I wanted to live and the way I really did live was a gap Jesus came to fill.

The diagram below shows how Jesus and his death on the cross bridges the gap between our problem with sin and being with God. God's greatest act of drawing close to us is in his Son, Jesus. Sin, or falling short of living and loving perfectly, separates us from God (Genesis 3:1-24; Romans 5:12), but Jesus came to earth and lived a perfectly loving and just life so he could draw us to God.

Jesus paid for our wrongdoing by dying in our place on the cross, but he did not stay dead! He returned to life forever and now offers us forgiveness for our sins and new life, too. Jesus is alive today and wants to give us a new life:

"This means that anyone who belongs to Christ has become a new person. The old life is gone; a new life has begun!"
2 CORINTHIANS 5:17

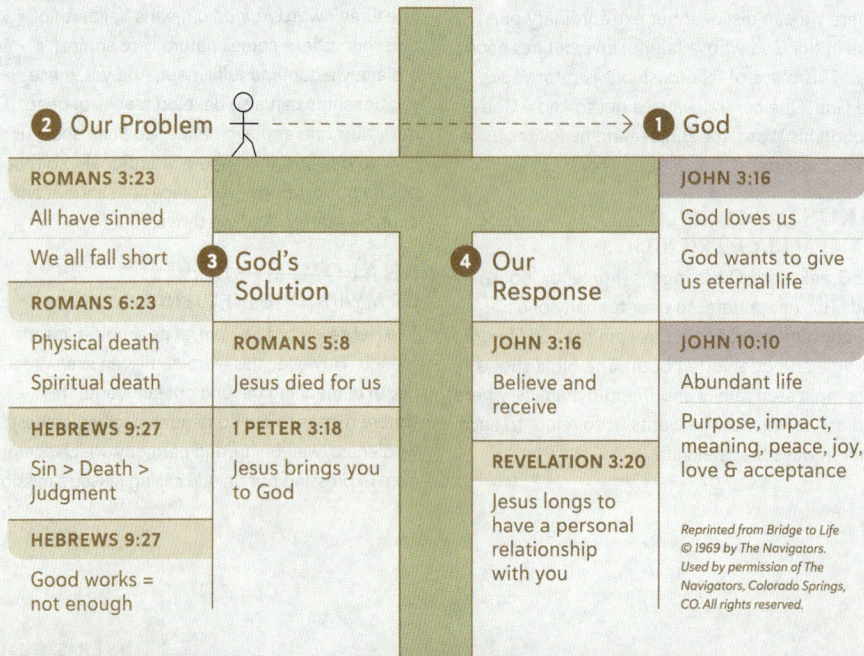

2 Our Problem → **1 God**

ROMANS 3:23
All have sinned
We all fall short

ROMANS 6:23
Physical death
Spiritual death

HEBREWS 9:27
Sin > Death > Judgment

HEBREWS 9:27
Good works = not enough

3 God's Solution

ROMANS 5:8
Jesus died for us

1 PETER 3:18
Jesus brings you to God

4 Our Response

JOHN 3:16
Believe and receive

REVELATION 3:20
Jesus longs to have a personal relationship with you

JOHN 3:16
God loves us
God wants to give us eternal life

JOHN 10:10
Abundant life
Purpose, impact, meaning, peace, joy, love & acceptance

Reprinted from Bridge to Life © 1969 by The Navigators. Used by permission of The Navigators, Colorado Springs, CO. All rights reserved.

Do you ever feel like I felt, like you long to be close to God but don't know how that can happen? What will you do with the God who pursues you, covers your wrongs, heals your heart, and invites you to new life now and forever? How do we begin this new life he offers? By trusting Jesus. If you're ready to believe in God's good purpose for you and your story, you can begin by telling him so in prayer. Here's a simple and memorable way to pray:

> **CONFESS:** We confess that we have fallen short of living a perfectly loving and just life. We tell God that we cannot earn his forgiveness, cannot be good enough on our own, and are ready to stop trying. We accept the free gift of our new life and ask God to give us the Holy Spirit to lead our life. **ROMANS 10:9-13, PAGE 1422**
>
> **BELIEVE:** We believe that God loves us so much that he gave what he loved most—his Son, Jesus—to pay the life sentence for our sin. **JOHN 3:16, PAGE 1324** We agree that he saves us not because of good things we have done but because of his undeserved kindness. Because of God's kindness and love, we have confidence that God makes us new from the inside out in this life and gives us everlasting life with him after we die. **TITUS 3:4-7, PAGE 1552**
>
> **ACCEPT:** We accept that God forgave us and brought us close when we confessed and believed. We accept that we can't take credit for it. We accept that we are God's masterpiece, now living with new life thanks to Jesus. And we embrace the good things God has planned for us to do. **EPHESIANS 2:8-10, PAGE 1490**

When we believe in and trust Jesus, he pens new stories for us. God retitled mine from "She Is Striving and Stuck" to "She Is Accepted and Free." Do you want to begin this new story, this new life? You might pray something like this:

> *Father, I confess I fall short of being perfectly loving and just, as you are. I believe you sent your Son, Jesus, to die on the cross and pay entirely for all my sin. I call on Jesus as Lord and accept your gift of life now, with your Spirit living in me, and life with you forever in your Kingdom. I pray this in your Son's name, Jesus. Amen (an affirmation that means "So be it!").*

So, sister, I don't want you to do what I did—read this book alone in the dark. Don't wait to feel close to the Author of the story and the Creator of you. You can know God now by asking him to forgive you and give you new life. If you've done so, then you are a child of God (1 John 3:1) and you have become a new person. You are never alone because God is always with you.

Turn to page A16 for more help getting started reading your Bible!

WHERE TO START
READING THE BIBLE

Opening the Bible can be intimidating or confusing. It's hard to know exactly where to start! And not every way of reading the Bible works for everyone in every life season. It's good to try different ways, and it's okay to try a new one if you get stuck. Below are some ideas for how to get started.

START WITH A SIMPLE READING PLAN

We've provided a daily Bible reading plan that helps you read the whole Bible in one year (see page 1655). Each day offers portions from the Old Testament, the New Testament, Psalms, and Proverbs. If you'd like to follow along, the readings might take you about ten to twenty minutes a day.

START WITH JESUS

Each of the four Gospels—Matthew, Mark, Luke, and John—tells the story of the life of Jesus from a different perspective. These books are a good place to start because they show us who Jesus is and what his plans are for the world. Choose any one and get started: Matthew begins on page 1189; Mark begins on page 1239; Luke begins on page 1271; and John begins on page 1319.

START WITH WHERE YOU ARE AND WHERE YOU WANT TO GO

Turn to "What Is My Purpose?" on page 1170. This is a guide to help you know where you are right now in your story with God and discover where you want to go next. This guide focuses especially on your four core relationships (see page A13): your relationship with God, your relationship with family and friends, your relationship with community, workplace, and church, and your unique influence.

START WITH CORE RELATIONSHIPS AND WHAT YOU HOPE FOR

If you want to see how the Bible can guide your relationships, check out the Image articles and use the Scripture passages they cover and their devotionals as a place to begin reading. You can explore the topics within each sphere by turning to page 1672.

START WITH A BIBLE WOMAN YOU'D LIKE TO KNOW MORE ABOUT

The Identity articles help you learn from others' stories. Each Identity article pairs with the Bible references where that woman is mentioned or her story is told. See page 1675 for a full list of these women and where you can find their features.

START WITH HOW YOU ARE FEELING RIGHT NOW

The Come Close articles tend to your heart. Those times we feel uncomfortable can offer us good opportunities for God to make us stronger. Turn to page 1678 and look for a topic or theme that speaks to you.

START WITH YOUR TOUGH QUESTIONS

God is not afraid of your most challenging questions, and the Perspective articles show how the Bible can answer them too. Go to page 1680 for a list of these questions and the Bible verses they cover, and take on some of the big ones you wonder about. We didn't shy away from hard passages. We purposely asked knowledgeable scholars and writers to dive into every bit that could put a woman off from reading the Bible.

BASIC BIBLE HELPS

THE DIFFERENCE BETWEEN THE OLD TESTAMENT AND THE NEW TESTAMENT

The Old Testament and the New Testament are separated by time, and each focuses on different eras in God's story. See page A7 for a list of which books are in each group.

The Old Testament takes place between Creation and 445 BC. It includes historical narratives like the creation account, the Flood account, the origin of the Israelites (God's chosen people group), chronologies of Israel's rulers and records of political changes. It also includes poetry and wise sayings in books like Psalms and Proverbs. God's encouragements and warnings to his people from his prophets also appear in the Old Testament.

Between the Old Testament and New Testament, there is a gap in the Biblical record of about four hundred years.

The New Testament takes place between approximately 7 BC and AD 100. It includes books about the life of Jesus, the historical account of the beginning of the Christian church, letters to early churches about their new life in Jesus Christ, and the apocalyptic book of Revelation, describing John's vision about Jesus' final return.

HOW TO LOOK UP A VERSE

Bible verse references are a human-made system for navigating the Bible. The first part is the Bible book name (either from the Old Testament or the New Testament). The second part is the chapter number (the number before the colon). And the third part is the verse number or span (the number[s] after the colon).

JOHN 3:16

BOOK JOHN	New Testament book, found toward the back of the Bible
CHAPTER 3	The third chapter of the Gospel of John
VERSE 16	The verse labeled 16 within that chapter

See page A7 for a list of the Bible books in the order they appear and the page numbers they start on.

See page A8 for an alphabetical list of the Bible books and the page numbers they start on. Once you've found the book, then turn to the chapter, and finally the verse.

BIBLE READING WORKSHEET

Taking notes while reading the Bible can help us remember what we've learned, come back to it later, and see how we are growing in knowing—and living from—God's story. Here is an example page you can use to take notes. You can also find a downloadable version of this on our website EveryWomansBible.com that you can use time and again.

DATE

BIBLE PASSAGE

WHO IS THIS ABOUT?

WHEN & WHERE IS THIS HAPPENING?

WHAT DO I UNDERSTAND?

WHAT DO I NOT UNDERSTAND?

Is there a study note or article that helps me? *See indexes on page 1669.*

WHAT CAN I ACT ON TODAY?

MEET OUR CONTRIBUTORS

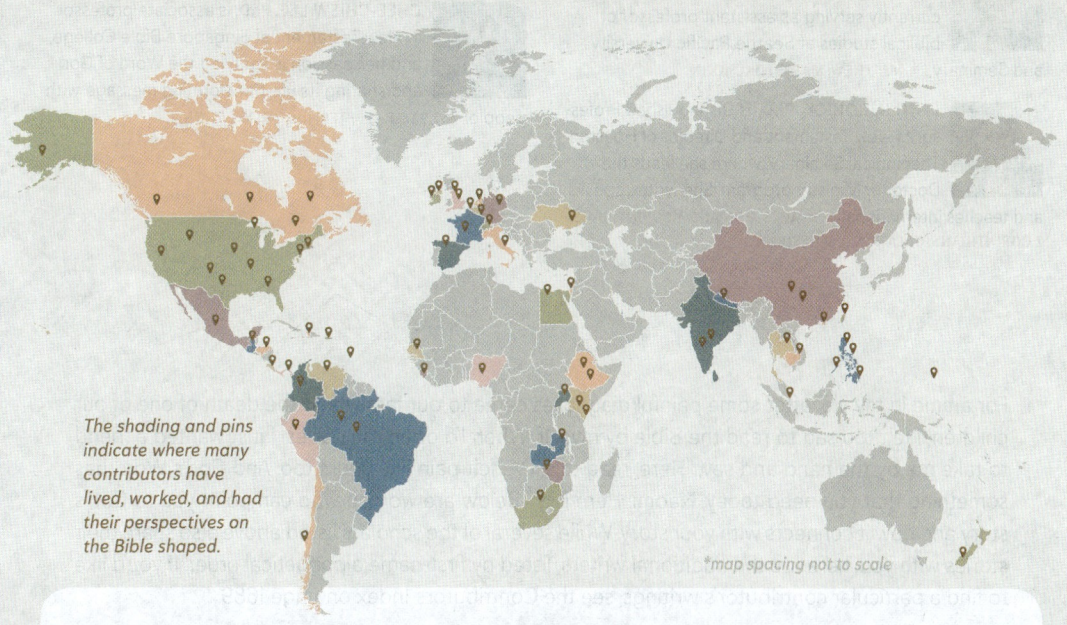

The shading and pins indicate where many contributors have lived, worked, and had their perspectives on the Bible shaped.

*map spacing not to scale

I (Naomi) am most excited about inviting you to discover God's story and your story alongside others who help you know you're not alone. Let's begin by meeting the scholars who wrote the study notes and some of the other articles (especially Perspective articles, see page 1680 for a full list) to help answer our difficult questions.

CARMEN JOY IMES, PhD, is an author, speaker, blogger, YouTuber, and serves as associate professor of Old Testament at Biola University in California. ◆ **GENESIS, EXODUS**

JENNIFER BROWN JONES, PhD, is an author, speaker, and instructor of Old Testament for Liberty University's PhD of Bible Exposition program. She loves helping others see how God speaks to them through the Bible today. ◆ **LEVITICUS, NUMBERS, DEUTERONOMY, JOB, PSALMS, PROVERBS**

SHIRLEY SIONG SHU HO, PhD, is assistant professor of Old Testament at China Evangelical School of Theology in Taiwan. She loves teaching and mentoring students. She is a Langham scholar. ◆ **JOSHUA**

HAVILAH DHARAMRAJ, PhD, serves at South Asia Institute of Advanced Christian Studies, Bangalore, India. Her research interests include biblical narrative and comparative literature. She encourages her students to retrieve traditional storytelling methods for ministry. ◆ **JUDGES, OBADIAH, JONAH, ZEPHANIAH, HAGGAI, ZECHARIAH, MALACHI**

ALEXIANA FRY, MDiv, PhD, is a devoted academic in the Hebrew Bible. She is a professor, wife, and pug mom who is working on her first book post-dissertation. ◆ **RUTH, 1 SAMUEL 2 SAMUEL**

JENNIFER M. MATHENY, PhD, is associate professor of Old Testament at Nazarene Theological Seminary, Missouri, and director of the Wynkoop Center for Women in Leadership. She enjoys speaking engagements and research. ◆ **1 KINGS, 2 KINGS, 1 CHRONICLES, 2 CHRONICLES, EZRA, NEHEMIAH, ESTHER, ECCLESIASTES, SONG OF SONGS, ISAIAH, JEREMIAH**

CATHERINE L. McDOWELL, PhD, is associate professor of Old Testament at Gordon-Conwell Theological Seminary. She has authored several books and articles on Bible backgrounds, Genesis, Isaiah, and Biblical Hebrew. ◆ **LAMENTATIONS, HOSEA, JOEL, AMOS, NAHUM, HABAKKUK, MALACHI**

CHRISTINE WALKER, MDiv, is a spiritual director who facilitates spiritual formation sessions for people desiring to grow their relationship with Christ. She loves ancient languages and teaches Biblical Hebrew and Koine Greek. ◆ EZEKIEL, DANIEL, MICAH

ESTHER G. CEN, MDiv, PhD, is a follower of Christ and multilingual writer and teacher, currently serving as assistant professor of biblical studies at Seattle Pacific University and Seminary. ◆ MATTHEW, MARK, LUKE, JOHN

LYNN H. COHICK, PhD, is Distinguished Professor of New Testament and Director of Houston Theological Seminary, where she leads the Doctor of Ministry program. She writes, speaks, and teaches internationally. ◆ ACTS, ROMANS, 1 CORINTHIANS, 2 CORINTHIANS, GALATIANS, EPHESIANS

SARAH HARRIS, PhD, lectures in New Testament at Carey Baptist College, Auckland, New Zealand. She is a scholar who specializes in the Gospel of Luke. She loves to teach, preach, and encourage women in their callings. ◆ PHILIPPIANS, COLOSSIANS, 1 THESSALONIANS, 2 THESSALONIANS, 1 TIMOTHY, 2 TIMOTHY, TITUS, PHILEMON, HEBREWS, JAMES, 1 JOHN, 2 JOHN, 3 JOHN

CHEE-CHIEW LEE, PhD, is associate professor in New Testament at Singapore Bible College, and her passion is studying the Word of God and sharing its life-transforming message with people. ◆ 1 PETER, 2 PETER, JUDE, REVELATION

For a time in my life, after some painful diagnoses came to our family and the death of one of our children, I felt too sad to read the Bible by myself. When I'd open the pages, I just wanted a friend to take me by the hand and say, "Here, read this. I've felt pain like yours too. And God's Word has something that you need today, Naomi. Here it is." Below are women who can point you to God's story and how it connects with your story. While several of the scholars listed above also share their stories with you, here are the additional writers, listed by first-name alphabetical order. If you'd like to find a particular contributor's writings, see the Contributors Index on page 1689.

ADELAIDE MANYARA MUCHETU shares true life experiences with many women and believes in relational evangelism. Discipleship is her mantra with exhortation being her greatest strength.

ALEXANDRA KUYKENDALL is a cofounder of The Open Door Sisterhood and author of several books, including *Seeking Out Goodness: Finding the True and Beautiful All around You.*

ALICE PATTERSON, JD, is an associate court attorney in New York who has a fondness for teaching the Old Testament. She encourages everyone to put down the world's lies and put on God's truth.

AMANDA AZADIAN is a Christ follower on a mission to bridge traditional medicine and modern innovation. She is a doctoral student of acupuncture, a senior product manager in digital health strategy, and a lover of adventure.

AMY SIMPSON, MBA, is the Bible publisher at Tyndale House Publishers, and she can't think of a better job than making God's Word available and accessible around the world.

ANDREA GIBSON is a certified coach and trainer. She and her husband spent seventeen years church planting. Her deepest desire now is to mentor and train women in the art of wise, godly leadership.

ANGELA TKACHENKO is an evangelist, worshiper, and leader of Steiger Ukraine mission. She is passionate to see this generation love the Bible.

NO PHOTO **AVA JAMES** is an editor who advocates for living with compassion and respect.

BELÉN PETERS is a mobilizer with Scatter Global. Since 2002, she has been mobilizing mission-minded Latinos to take their passion and profession to places where Christ is unknown.

BRENDA GARCIA de BRIZENDINE is the former communications manager for Compassion International's Guatemala office. She works with Iron Rose Sister Ministries and also interprets Spanish for CPCD-Head Start in Colorado Springs, CO.

BRENDA L. YODER, MA, LMHC, is a licensed mental health counselor and school counselor whose passion is encouraging others when life doesn't fit the storybook image.

 **CARA DAY** is a writer and illustrator. She has served with Stonecroft Ministries helping women live "extraordinary."

 **CATHY SCRIVNER** has twenty-five years of experience as a diversity, equity, and inclusion consultant. She is a devoted Christian who believes in loving people to Christ.

 **DAISY ASIIMWE BYARUGABA** is a learning and development professional passionate about empowering people to become the most productive version of themselves that God intended. She and her husband minister at Church of the Resurrection, Bugolobi, in Kampala, Uganda.

 **DEBORA DA SILVA** is from Brazil and found release from poverty through Compassion International. She works with Facebook in Colombia and lives to serve as she tries to be a channel—not only a recipient—of God's goodness.

 **DELANEY OVERTON** develops programs and business strategies for impact-oriented organizations in education, food access, environmentalism, and other sectors. She experiences God's love and glory through creation, especially the seemingly unending ocean.

 DONNA LEE LAMOTHE, MA, is executive director and founder of inSPIRE Channels at RSVP Ministries. She teaches and guides all to find wholeness through faith in Jesus.

 **ELISA MORGAN, MDiv,** speaks, writes, and cohosts podcasts for Our Daily Bread Ministries. For twenty years, she served as president of MOPS International, now as president emerita. Her motto is "Living really ... Really living."

 **ELISABETH SELZER ROGERS, MDiv, MA, PhD,** is a passionate believer and follower of Christ, bringing his love to the secular world through mentoring, coaching, and modeling his unconditional love.

 **ELIZA CORTÉS BAST, DEd candidate,** is senior director of programs with Stonecroft. She is a pastor, professor, wife, mom, and mentor. She believes in passionately pursuing God and people by developing talent, asking strategic questions, and amplifying the good.

 **ELIZABETH GLANVILLE, PhD,** is retired faculty from Fuller Theological Seminary, School of Mission and Theology. She is an international teacher on missions and leadership and chaplain for a local police department and her retirement community.

 ELLEN RICHARD VOSBURG, MA, is a Bible editor for Tyndale House Publishers. She studied Greek and Hebrew and lives to lead others into God's deep love by getting to know him through his Word.

 **EMILY SARMIENTO** is a wife and mom of two school-aged children and serves as president and CEO of Tearfund USA, based in Denver, CO.

 ESTHER FLEECE ALLEN is an international speaker and bestselling author of *No More Faking Fine: Ending the Pretending* and *Your New Name: Saying Goodbye to the Labels That Limit*.

 **EVIE POLSLEY, MS,** loves stories of how God uses everyday people. A digital communications manager at Tyndale, her favorite roles are wife to the good doctor and mom to two girls who will one day change the world.

 **GABRIELA MAGAÑA BANKS, PhD,** is an author, teacher, and certified HeartSync inner healing prayer minister who facilitates freedom. Biblical principles and powerful moves of the Holy Spirit are her passion.

 HÉLÈNE M. DALLAIRE, PhD, serves as Earl S. Kalland Professor of Old Testament and Semitic Languages at Denver Seminary. She is deeply involved in the Messianic movement, serving in worship, prayer, teaching, and preaching.

 **IRENE PACE** trusts the Lord Jesus Christ and believes his life-changing message of salvation. She writes about God's lessons learned through adversity; she speaks with gratitude and joy.

 JANICE MAYO MATHERS is author of multiple books and Bible studies, including *Every Season: Embracing a Forever Kind of Purpose* (Stonecroft) and *Mothers-in-Law vs. Daughters-in-Law: Let There Be Peace*. She helps women see adverse circumstances as godly challenges.

 JENNIFER KELLER, MA Min, is a pastor at a multisite church in Central Indiana and has self-published three Bible studies. She is a devoted Christ-follower, wife, and mom of four.

 **JENNIFER ROSNER, PhD,** is a writer and Messianic Jewish theologian currently serving as Affiliate Assistant Professor at Fuller Theological Seminary. Much of her work focuses on the relationship between Judaism and Christianity.

 JULIE WRIGHT is author of *Redeeming Eve: When a Woman Lives Loved* and founder of Live Loved Ministry. Her passion is for women to embrace God's love and cultivate an authentic relationship with Jesus.

 **KARA POWELL, PhD,** is the executive director of the Fuller Youth Institute and chief of leadership formation at Fuller Theological Seminary. Kara speaks and has authored numerous books, including *3 Big Questions That Change Every Teenager*.

 **KAT ARMSTRONG, MA,** is a Bible teacher, preacher, coach, and ministry leader. She cofounded the Polished Network and authored *No More Holding Back*, *The In-Between Place*, and the Storyline Bible Studies series.

 **KATHERINE LEARY ALSDORF** founded and directed Redeemer Church's Center for Faith & Work. She co-authored *Every Good Endeavor: Connecting Your Work to God's Work* with Timothy Keller.

 **KATHERINE WOLF** is a communicator, author, and advocate. She leverages her redemptive story to encourage those with broken bodies, broken brains, and broken hearts.

 **KATRIEL OVERTON** is a Christian with autism who experiences and believes all people can feel and know God's love if they choose. She sees God helping her love people, including herself.

 **KRISTEN CARY, CPSAS,** cofounded Living Truth with her husband. She guides women toward hope and healing after the devastating impact of sexual betrayal in their marriage.

 **LILLIAN GITAU** is a lifelong learner and an advocate for the marginalized. She finds satisfaction from seeing others realize their full potential. She is the author of *You Are Special* and *Pia Was Different*.

 **LISA D. EDMONDS** is mother of two daughters, a Stonecroft Ministries speaker and speaker trainer, worship leader, and constituent care director for The Dr. James Dobson Family Institute.

 **LISA WHITTLE** is a sought-out Bible teacher, podcast host, and bestselling author whose works include *Jesus Over Everything*. She is the founder of the online communities Ministry Strong and Called Creatives. She's a wife, mom, and a self-professed feisty work in progress.

 **LOIS NANGUDI, MA,** studied spiritual formation and discipleship at Moody Seminary. She served as an advocate with Compassion International, founded Awaken To Follow, and is currently serving in the Pastors Discipleship Network.

 **LORINA AVENIDO, BEEd with CAR,** has served for thirty-seven years as a full-time pastor/missionary of Philippine Good News International Inc. She is a licensed minister of Worldwide Impact Group, preaching the gospel and empowering women leaders.

 **LYNN LONG** has studied at National Louis University and is completing her doctorate at Wheaton College. Lynn is a Native American writer and speaker with Stonecroft Ministries.

 MANDY ARIOTO is the president and CEO of MOPS International, influencing millions of moms around the world every year. She is a scholar of Greek, author, and speaker who believes in the transformational power of Scripture.

 **MARGARET FITZWATER, MS, MBA,** is a Navigator and life and leadership coach. Her passion is helping others live and lead from the Word to thrive in their lives and ministries.

 **MARY SCHALLER, MDiv,** is the former president of Q Place and coauthor of *The 9 Arts of Spiritual Conversations*. Her life mission is to build and nurture Christ-centered communities.

 **MAY YOUNG, MDiv, PhD,** is an associate professor of biblical studies at Taylor University, with a passion for discipleship, teaching, and writing.

 **MEGAN C. ROBERTS, PhD,** teaches Old Testament at Prairie College in Three Hills, Alberta, Canada. She loves mountains, music, and the unending joy of discovering the depths of the gospel in Scripture and the church.

 MELISSA HOUDMANN is the cofounder of GotQuestions Ministries, a website dedicated to answering Bible questions. She also wrote Stonecroft Ministries' *Why Believe* study.

 **MENCHIT WONG, MBA,** is a Gallup-certified Strengths Coach and leadership consultant. She also serves on the leadership of global mission movements that enable children to be disciples of Jesus.

 MILLIE SERRANO is a faithful follower of Jesus Christ devoted to supporting women in their pursuit of growing a biblical, strong, and fruitful relationship with God through his Son, Jesus.

 **MINDY CALIGUIRE** is founder and president of Soul Care, dedicated to increasing soul health in the Body of Christ. Her books include *Discovering Soul Care* and *Spiritual Friendships*.

 MISTY ARTERBURN is an author and speaker, contributing to Bible projects, devotionals, and recovery materials for over twenty years. Wife and mom to five, Misty is the founder of Recovery Girls and the general editor of *The One Year Bible for Women*.

 **NANCY CHAMBERLIN SPROWLS** is a devotional writer, mother, and grandmother. She encourages women to have a passion for God's Word and to leave a spiritual legacy for their families.

 **NAOMI CRAMER OVERTON, MBA, DIS,** lives to realize beauty-filled visions that lift us to flourishing, with our families and beyond. Naomi has been CEO for Stonecroft and MOPS, director with Compassion International and World Vision, and General Editor for this Bible.

 **PATRICIA RAYBON** is an award-winning Colorado author, essayist, and novelist who writes top-rated books and stories at the daring intersection of faith, race, and mystery—including the Annalee Spain mystery series.

 **QUANTRILLA ARD, PhD,** is a faith-based personal and spiritual development author, speaker, Bible teacher, and literary agent who believes in the power of collective strength, community, and fellowship.

 **RACHEL LINDSAY McCANTS** is an author, speaker, and founder of R. Lindsay Unlimited, which encourages, inspires, and challenges ladies to raise their self-worth and standards and to walk in God's will, in Jesus' name.

 ROBIN REESE is a volunteer leader with Stonecroft Ministries. She and her husband, Terry, love to travel, enjoy the company of their son and two corgis, and live life to the fullest!

 **SARA HALL** is a professional marathon runner and cofounder of the Hall Steps Foundation. She has been competing professionally for seventeen years in various distances and using her platform to bring aid to orphaned children in Ethiopia.

 **SARAH OVERTON, MA,** is a researcher specializing in refugee and asylum policy. She has worked in the UK Parliament, public-policy think tanks, and at Lambeth Palace.

 **SHARON WILHARM** is the host of the *All God's Women* podcast and internationally syndicated radio show. She loves bringing to life stories of Bible women and providing takeaways for modern women.

 **STEPHANIE THOMAS** is a follower of Jesus Christ. She is the coordinator and a contributing author at Pruned Life. She is also a gospel singer.

 **SUSAN I. BUBBERS, MDiv, DMin, PhD,** is the Dean of the Center for Anglican Theology in Orlando, FL. She is a professor, Anglican priest, spiritual director, and a Fellow of the Oxford Centre for Animal Ethics.

 **SUSAN M. JONES** is a US Army veteran, native Alaskan, wife, mother, and follower of Jesus Christ. She shares her testimony with Stonecroft Ministries. Sprinkling the love of Jesus is her joy.

 SUSIE GAMEZ, MA, is a teaching pastor at Midtown Covenant Church in Sacramento, CA, and preaches across the country, making the reconciling love of Jesus come alive through the Scriptures.

 **SUZY SHEPHERD** is the founder of SHINE, creator of Stonecroft's Where Love Lives outreach experience, and mom to a blended tribe of nine. She finds great joy in creating experiences for people to know God's love.

 **TAMI HEIM** is president and CEO of Christian Leadership Alliance and serves on many nonprofit boards. She and her husband lead mission teams to Haiti to love and disciple orphans.

 **TONI J. COLLIER** is a speaker, the founder of Broken Crayons Still Color, the host of the *Still Coloring* podcast, and the author of *Brave Enough to Be Broken: How to Embrace Your Pain and Discover Hope and Healing*.

 TRACI CROWDER is a joyful, energetic, Jesus-following wife, mom, and pastor. She serves with Stonecroft and deeply longs for every person to experience God's extraordinary in their ordinary, together in community.

 **VALERIE BELL** is an author of several books on children, including *RESILIENT: Child Discipleship and the Fearless Future of the Church*. Valerie serves as Awana's CEO emerita and 2050 vision caster.

 **VANEETHA RENDALL RISNER** is the author of *Walking Through Fire*. She and her family live in North Carolina, where she writes and speaks about how God meets us in suffering.

 VIRGINIA WARD, MA, DMin, serves as the Dean of the Boston Campus for Gordon-Conwell Theological Seminary. She is a wife, a mother, and an associate pastor at Abundant Life Church in Cambridge, MA.

 **VIVIAN MABUNI** is a national speaker, author of *Open Hands, Willing Heart*, and podcast host of *Someday Is Here* for AAPI Christians, with over thirty years of ministry experience.

WHITNEY PUTNAM is the senior director of women's events and marketing at New Life Ministries. She is an overall joy-chaser and is often found dancing in her kitchen.

ADDITIONAL CONTRIBUTORS

GENERAL EDITOR
Dr. Naomi Cramer Overton

ASSOCIATE EDITOR
Misty Arterburn

PROJECT DEVELOPER & EDITORIAL CONSULTANT
Stephen Arterburn

PUBLISHER
Amy Simpson

TYNDALE HOUSE EDITOR
Ellen Richard Vosburg

DEVELOPMENTAL EDITORS
Mark R. Norton
Jonathan Bryant

COPY EDITORS
Ava James
Leanne F. Rolland
Susan F. Tristano
Charles E. Cruise

PROOFREADING
Peachtree Publishing Services

DESIGNER
Jennifer L. Phelps

TYPESETTING
Laura Cruise

A NOTE TO READERS

The *Holy Bible,* New Living Translation, was first published in 1996. It quickly became one of the most popular Bible translations in the English-speaking world. While the NLT's influence was rapidly growing, the Bible Translation Committee determined that an additional investment in scholarly review and text refinement could make it even better. So shortly after its initial publication, the committee began an eight-year process with the purpose of increasing the level of the NLT's precision without sacrificing its easy-to-understand quality. This second-generation text was completed in 2004, with minor changes subsequently introduced in 2007, 2013, and 2015.

The goal of any Bible translation is to convey the meaning and content of the ancient Hebrew, Aramaic, and Greek texts as accurately as possible to contemporary readers. The challenge for our translators was to create a text that would communicate as clearly and powerfully to today's readers as the original texts did to readers and listeners in the ancient biblical world. The resulting translation is easy to read and understand, while also accurately communicating the meaning and content of the original biblical texts. The NLT is a general-purpose text especially good for study, devotional reading, and reading aloud in worship services.

We believe that the New Living Translation—which combines the latest biblical scholarship with a clear, dynamic writing style—will communicate God's word powerfully to all who read it. We publish it with the prayer that God will use it to speak his timeless truth to the church and the world in a fresh, new way.

THE PUBLISHERS

A complete list of the translators can be found at tyndale.com/nlt/scholars.

NEW LIVING TRANSLATION: OUR CHOICE FOR YOU

I (Naomi) love the New Living Translation because the brilliant people who translated it used simple, understandable words that we use in our everyday lives. Have you ever found that writing a simple sentence is harder than a long, complicated one? I love this translation because it serves *you*—the woman we most want to help find her story in God's story. I want the language to be an invitation—not a barrier—for you. It's easy to read, and the language draws us in.

> *Here is one of my favorites:*
>
> Don't be afraid, for I am with you.
> Don't be discouraged, for I am your God.
> I will strengthen you and help you.
> I will hold you up with my victorious right hand.
>
> ISAIAH 41:10

I prayed this verse while in labor with my twins, one of whom I knew I would deliver stillborn. The other, I wasn't sure how she would be when I finally saw her after such a stressful, high-risk pregnancy. I held these simple words on a 3x5 index card and sensed God's victorious right hand strengthening me to breathe, bear the pain, and set aside my fear of the future.

Isaiah is a big book with lofty ideas. It's also full of gems like this one that feel like God is speaking straight to us amid our everyday lives, full of stresses and anxieties. And the New Living Translation reads in a way our hearts can hear.

We believe you will experience this, too, as you move through the Bible with the help of our sisterhood of contributors. We all experience times when we read the Bible and need a little help understanding, but the more straightforward the language, the more our hearts and minds can absorb the words.

For more about this translation, see the Introduction to the New Living Translation on the following page.

INTRODUCTION TO THE
NEW LIVING TRANSLATION

TRANSLATION PHILOSOPHY AND METHODOLOGY

English Bible translations tend to be governed by one of two general translation theories. The first theory has been called "formal-equivalence," "literal," or "word-for-word" translation. According to this theory, the translator attempts to render each word of the original language into English and seeks to preserve the original syntax and sentence structure as much as possible in translation. The second theory has been called "dynamic-equivalence," "functional-equivalence," or "thought-for-thought" translation. The goal of this translation theory is to produce in English the closest natural equivalent of the message expressed by the original-language text, both in meaning and in style.

Both of these translation theories have their strengths. A formal-equivalence translation preserves aspects of the original text—including ancient idioms, term consistency, and original-language syntax—that are valuable for scholars and professional study. It allows a reader to trace formal elements of the original-language text through the English translation. A dynamic-equivalence translation, on the other hand, focuses on translating the message of the original-language text. It ensures that the meaning of the text is readily apparent to the contemporary reader. This allows the message to come through with immediacy, without requiring the reader to struggle with foreign idioms and awkward syntax.

The pure application of either of these translation philosophies would create translations at opposite ends of the translation spectrum. But in reality, all translations contain a mixture of these two philosophies. A purely formal-equivalence translation would be unintelligible in English, and a purely dynamic-equivalence translation would risk being unfaithful to the original. That is why translations shaped by dynamic-equivalence theory are usually quite literal when the original text is relatively clear, and the translations shaped by formal-equivalence theory are sometimes quite dynamic when the original text is obscure.

The translators of the New Living Translation set out to render the message of the original texts of Scripture into clear, contemporary English. As they did so, they kept the concerns of both formal-equivalence and dynamic-equivalence in mind. On the one hand, they translated as simply and literally as possible when that approach yielded an accurate, clear, and natural English text. Many words and phrases were rendered literally and consistently into English, preserving essential literary and rhetorical devices, ancient metaphors, and word choices that give structure to the text and provide echoes of meaning from one passage to the next.

On the other hand, the translators rendered the message more dynamically when the literal rendering was hard to understand, was misleading, or yielded archaic or foreign wording. They clarified difficult metaphors and terms to aid in the reader's understanding. The translators first struggled with the meaning of the words and phrases in the ancient context; then they rendered the message into clear, natural English. Their goal was to be both faithful to the ancient texts and eminently readable.

TRANSLATION PROCESS AND TEAM

To produce an accurate translation of the Bible into contemporary English, the translation team needed the skills necessary to enter into the thought patterns of the ancient authors and then to render their ideas, connotations, and effects into clear, contemporary English. To begin this process, qualified biblical scholars were needed to interpret the meaning of the original text and to check it against our base English translation. In order to guard against personal and theological biases, the scholars needed to represent a diverse group of evangelicals who would employ the best exegetical tools. Then to work alongside the scholars, skilled English stylists were needed to shape the text into clear, contemporary English.

With these concerns in mind, the Bible Translation Committee recruited teams of scholars that represented a broad spectrum of denominations, theological perspectives, and backgrounds within the worldwide evangelical community. (A list of these scholars can be found online.) Each book of the Bible was assigned to three different scholars with proven expertise in the book or group of books to be reviewed. Each of these scholars made a thorough review of a base translation and submitted suggested revisions to the appropriate Senior Translator. The Senior Translator then reviewed and summarized these suggestions and proposed a first-draft revision of the base text. This draft served as the basis for several additional phases of exegetical and stylistic committee review. Then the Bible Translation Committee jointly reviewed and approved every verse of the final translation.

Throughout the translation and editing process, the Senior Translators and their scholar teams were given a chance to review the editing done by the team of stylists. This ensured that exegetical errors would not be introduced late in the process and that the entire Bible Translation Committee was happy with the final result. By choosing a team of qualified scholars and skilled stylists and by setting up a process that allowed their interaction throughout the process, the New Living Translation has been refined to preserve the essential formal elements of the original biblical texts, while also creating a clear, understandable English text.

The New Living Translation was first published in 1996. Shortly after its initial publication, the Bible Translation Committee began a process of further committee review and translation refinement. The purpose of this continued revision was to increase the level of precision without sacrificing the text's easy-to-understand quality. This second-edition text was completed in 2004, with minor changes subsequently introduced in 2007, 2013, and 2015.

WRITTEN TO BE READ ALOUD

It is evident in Scripture that the biblical documents were written to be read aloud, often in public worship (see Nehemiah 8; Luke 4:16-20; 1 Timothy 4:13; Revelation 1:3). It is still the case today that more people will hear the Bible read aloud in church than are likely to read it for themselves. Therefore, a new translation must communicate with clarity and power when it is read publicly. Clarity was a primary goal for the NLT translators, not only to facilitate private reading and understanding, but also to ensure that it would be excellent for public reading and make an immediate and powerful impact on any listener.

THE TEXTS BEHIND THE NEW LIVING TRANSLATION

The Old Testament translators used the Masoretic Text of the Hebrew Bible as represented in *Biblia Hebraica Stuttgartensia* (1977), with its extensive system of textual notes. The translators also further compared the Dead Sea Scrolls, the Septuagint and other Greek manuscripts, the Samaritan Pentateuch, the Syriac Peshitta, the Latin Vulgate, and any other versions or manuscripts that shed light on the meaning of difficult passages.

The New Testament translators used the two standard editions of the Greek New Testament: the *Greek New Testament,* published by the United Bible Societies (UBS, fourth revised edition, 1993), and *Novum Testamentum Graece,* edited by Nestle and Aland (NA, twenty-seventh edition, 1993). These two editions, which have the same text but differ in punctuation and textual notes, represent, for the most part, the best in modern textual scholarship. However, in cases where strong textual or other scholarly evidence supported the decision, the translators sometimes chose to differ from the UBS and NA Greek texts and followed variant readings found in other ancient witnesses. Significant textual variants of this sort are always noted in the textual notes of the New Living Translation.

TRANSLATION ISSUES

The translators have made a conscious effort to provide a text that can be easily understood by the typical reader of modern English. To this end, we sought to use only vocabulary and language structures in common use today. We avoided using language likely to become quickly dated or that reflects only a narrow subdialect of English, with the goal of making the New Living Translation as broadly useful and timeless as possible.

But our concern for readability goes beyond the concerns of vocabulary and sentence structure. We are also concerned about historical and cultural barriers to understanding the Bible, and we have sought to translate terms shrouded in history and culture in ways that can be immediately understood. To this end:

- We have converted ancient weights and measures (for example, "ephah" [a unit of dry volume] or "cubit" [a unit of length]) to modern English (American) equivalents, since the ancient measures are not generally meaningful to today's readers. Then in the textual footnotes we offer the literal Hebrew, Aramaic, or Greek measures, along with modern metric equivalents.
- Instead of translating ancient currency values literally, we have expressed them in common terms that communicate the message. For example, in the Old Testament, "ten shekels of silver" becomes "ten pieces of silver" to convey the intended message.
- Since the names of Hebrew months are unknown to most contemporary readers, and since the Hebrew lunar calendar fluctuates from year to year in relation to the solar calendar used today, we have looked for clear ways to communicate the time of year the Hebrew months (such as Abib) refer to. Where it is possible to define a specific ancient date in terms of our modern calendar, we use modern dates in the text. A textual footnote then gives the literal Hebrew date and states the rationale for our rendering.
- Since ancient references to the time of day differ from our modern methods of denoting time, we have used renderings that are instantly understandable to the modern reader. Accordingly, we have rendered specific times of day by using approximate equivalents in terms of our common "o'clock" system.
- When the meaning of a proper name (or a wordplay inherent in a proper name) is relevant to the message of the text, its meaning is often illuminated with a textual footnote. For example, in Exodus 2:10 the text reads: "The princess named him Moses, for she explained, 'I lifted him out of the water.'"

Sometimes, when the actual meaning of a name is clear, that meaning is included in parentheses within the text itself. For example, the text at Genesis 16:11 reads: "You are to name him Ishmael *(which means 'God hears'),* for the LORD has heard your cry of distress." Since the original hearers and readers would have instantly understood the meaning of the name "Ishmael," we have provided modern readers with the same information so they can experience the text in a similar way.

- Many words and phrases carry a great deal of cultural meaning that was obvious to the original readers but needs explanation in our own culture. For example, the phrase "they beat their breasts" (Luke 23:48) in ancient times meant that people were very upset, often in mourning. In our translation we chose to translate this phrase dynamically for clarity: "They went home *in deep sorrow*."

- Metaphorical language is sometimes difficult for contemporary readers to understand, so at times we have chosen to translate or illuminate the meaning of a metaphor. For example, the ancient poet writes, "Your neck is *like* the tower of David" (Song of Songs 4:4). We have rendered it "Your neck is *as beautiful as* the tower of David" to clarify the intended positive meaning of the simile.
- When the content of the original language text is poetic in character, we have rendered it in English poetic form. Hebrew poetry often uses parallelism, a literary form where a second phrase (or in some instances a third or fourth) echoes the initial phrase in some way. Whenever possible, we sought to represent these parallel phrases in natural poetic English.
- The Greek term *hoi Ioudaioi* is literally translated "the Jews" in many English translations. In the Gospel of John, however, this term doesn't always refer to the Jewish people generally. In some contexts, it refers more particularly to the Jewish religious leaders. We have attempted to capture the meaning in these different contexts by using terms such as "the people" (with a footnote: Greek *the Jewish people*) or "the Jewish leaders," where appropriate.
- One challenge we faced was how to translate accurately the ancient biblical text that was originally written in a context where male-oriented terms were used to refer to humanity generally. We needed to respect the nature of the ancient context while also trying to make the translation clear to a modern audience that tends to read male-oriented language as applying only to males. Often the original text, though using masculine nouns and pronouns, clearly intends that the message be applied to both men and women. A typical example is found in the New Testament letters, where the believers are called "brothers" (*adelphoi*). Yet it is clear

from the content of these letters that they were addressed to all the believers—male and female. Thus, we have usually translated this Greek word as "brothers and sisters" in order to represent the historical situation more accurately.

We have also been sensitive to passages where the text applies generally to human beings or to the human condition. In some instances we have used plural pronouns (they, them) in place of the masculine singular (he, him). For example, a traditional rendering of Proverbs 22:6 is: "Train up a child in the way he should go, and when he is old he will not turn from it." We have rendered it: "Direct your children onto the right path, and when they are older, they will not leave it." At times, we have also replaced third person pronouns with the second person to ensure clarity. A traditional rendering of Proverbs 26:27 is: "He who digs a pit will fall into it, and he who rolls a stone, it will come back on him." We have rendered it: "If you set a trap for others, you will get caught in it yourself. If you roll a boulder down on others, it will crush you instead."

We should emphasize that all masculine nouns and pronouns used to represent God (for example, "Father") have been maintained without exception. All decisions of this kind have been driven by the concern to reflect accurately the intended meaning of the original texts of Scripture.

LEXICAL CONSISTENCY IN TERMINOLOGY

For the sake of clarity, we have translated certain original-language terms consistently, especially within synoptic passages and for commonly repeated rhetorical phrases, and within certain word categories such as divine names and non-theological technical terminology (e.g., liturgical, legal, cultural, zoological, and botanical terms). For theological terms, we have allowed a greater semantic range of acceptable English words or phrases for a single Hebrew or Greek word. We have avoided some theological terms that are not readily understood by many

modern readers. For example, we avoided using words such as "justification" and "sanctification," which are carryovers from Latin translations. In place of these words, we have provided renderings such as "made right with God" and "made holy."

THE SPELLING OF PROPER NAMES

Many individuals in the Bible, especially the Old Testament, are known by more than one name (e.g., Uzziah/Azariah). For the sake of clarity, we have tried to use a single spelling for any one individual, footnoting the literal spelling whenever we differ from it. This is especially helpful in delineating the kings of Israel and Judah. King Joash/Jehoash of Israel has been consistently called Jehoash, while King Joash/Jehoash of Judah is called Joash. A similar distinction has been used to distinguish between Joram/Jehoram of Israel and Joram/Jehoram of Judah. All such decisions were made with the goal of clarifying the text for the reader. When the ancient biblical writers clearly had a theological purpose in their choice of a variant name (e.g., Esh-baal/Ishbosheth), the different names have been maintained with an explanatory footnote.

For the names Jacob and Israel, which are used interchangeably for both the individual patriarch and the nation, we generally render it "Israel" when it refers to the nation and "Jacob" when it refers to the individual. When our rendering of the name differs from the underlying Hebrew text, we provide a textual footnote, which includes this explanation: "The names 'Jacob' and 'Israel' are often interchanged throughout the Old Testament, referring sometimes to the individual patriarch and sometimes to the nation."

THE RENDERING OF DIVINE NAMES

In the Old Testament, all appearances of *'el*, *'elohim*, or *'eloah* have been translated "God," except where the context demands the translation "god(s)." We have generally rendered the tetragrammaton (YHWH) consistently as "the LORD," utilizing a form with small capitals that is common among English translations. This will distinguish it from the name *'adonai*, which we render "Lord." When *'adonai* and *YHWH* appear together, we have rendered it "Sovereign LORD." This also distinguishes *'adonai YHWH* from cases where *YHWH* appears with *'elohim*, which is rendered "LORD God." When *YH* (the short form of *YHWH*) and *YHWH* appear together, we have rendered it "LORD GOD." When *YHWH* appears with the term *tseba'oth*, we have rendered it "LORD of Heaven's Armies" to translate the meaning of the name. In a few cases, we have utilized the transliteration, *Yahweh*, when the personal character of the name is being invoked in contrast to another divine name or the name of some other god (for example, see Exodus 3:15; 6:2-3).

In the Gospels and Acts, the Greek word *christos* has normally been translated as "Messiah" when the context assumes a Jewish audience. When a Gentile audience can be assumed (which is consistently the case in the Epistles and Revelation), *christos* has been translated as "Christ." The Greek word *kurios* is consistently translated "Lord," except that it is translated "LORD" wherever the New Testament text explicitly quotes from the Old Testament, and the text there has it in small capitals.

TEXTUAL FOOTNOTES

The New Living Translation provides several kinds of textual footnotes, all designated in the text with an asterisk:

- When for the sake of clarity the NLT renders a difficult or potentially confusing phrase dynamically, we generally give the literal rendering in a textual footnote. This allows the reader to see the literal source of our dynamic rendering and how our translation relates to other more literal translations. These notes are prefaced with "Hebrew," "Aramaic," or "Greek," identifying the language of the underlying source text. For example, in Acts 2:42 we translated the literal "breaking of bread" (from the Greek) as "the Lord's Supper" to clarify that this verse refers to the ceremonial practice of the church rather than just an ordinary meal. Then we attached a footnote to "the Lord's Supper," which reads: "Greek *the breaking of bread*."
- Textual footnotes are also used to show alternative renderings, prefaced with the word "Or." These normally occur for passages where an aspect of the meaning is debated. On occasion, we also provide notes on words or phrases that represent a departure from long-standing tradition. These notes are prefaced with "Traditionally rendered." For example, the footnote to the translation "serious skin disease" at Leviticus 13:2 says: "Traditionally rendered *leprosy*. The Hebrew word used throughout this passage is used to describe various skin diseases."
- When our translators follow a textual variant that differs significantly from our standard Hebrew or Greek texts (listed earlier), we document that difference with a footnote. We also footnote cases when the NLT excludes a passage that is included in the Greek text known as the *Textus Receptus* (and familiar to readers through its translation in the King James Version). In such cases, we offer a translation of the excluded text in a footnote, even though it is generally recognized as a later addition to the Greek text and not part of the original Greek New Testament.
- All Old Testament passages that are quoted in the New Testament are identified by a textual footnote at the New Testament location. When the New Testament clearly quotes from the Greek translation of the Old Testament, and when it differs significantly in wording from the Hebrew text, we also place a textual footnote at the Old Testament location. This note includes a rendering of the Greek version, along with a cross-reference to the New Testament passage(s) where it is cited (for example, see notes on Psalms 8:2; 53:3; Proverbs 3:12).
- Some textual footnotes provide cultural and historical information on places, things, and people in the Bible that are probably obscure to modern readers. Such notes should aid the reader in understanding the message of the text. For example, in Acts 12:1, "King Herod" is named in this translation as "King Herod Agrippa" and is identified in a footnote as being "the nephew of Herod Antipas and a grandson of Herod the Great."
- When the meaning of a proper name (or a wordplay inherent in a proper name) is relevant to the meaning of the text, it is either illuminated with a textual footnote or included within parentheses in the text itself. For example, the footnote concerning the name "Eve" at Genesis 3:20 reads: "*Eve* sounds like a Hebrew term that means 'to give life.'" This wordplay in the Hebrew illuminates the meaning of the text, which goes on to say that Eve "would be the mother of all who live."

AS WE SUBMIT this translation for publication, we recognize that any translation of the Scriptures is subject to limitations and imperfections. Anyone who has attempted to communicate the richness of God's word into another language will realize it is impossible to make a perfect translation. Recognizing these limitations, we sought God's guidance and wisdom throughout this project. Now we pray that he will accept our efforts and use this translation for the benefit of the church and of all people.

We pray that the New Living Translation will overcome some of the barriers of history, culture, and language that have kept people from reading and understanding God's word. We hope that readers unfamiliar with the Bible will find the words clear and easy to understand and that readers well versed in the Scriptures will gain a fresh perspective. We pray that readers will gain insight and wisdom for living, but most of all that they will meet the God of the Bible and be forever changed by knowing him.

THE BIBLE
TRANSLATION
COMMITTEE

Genesis

WHAT DO WE LEARN ABOUT GOD'S MISSION AND OURS?
God made women and men in God's image, to be like God, and reign over creation.

WHO WROTE IT? Moses, according to Jewish and Christian traditions.

WHEN DID IT HAPPEN? The events of Genesis stretch from the beginning of time through the 1800s BC.

HOW IS IT ORGANIZED?

- 1–5: God creates the world; humans sin
- 6–11: Flood destroys the world; Noah's family rebuilds
- 12–25: God provides for Abraham and Sarah and for Hagar and Ishmael
- 25–35: Isaac and Rebekah's lives; Jacob meets Leah and Rachel and builds their family
- 36: Esau's many descendants
- 37–50: Jacob's family suffers betrayal and famine and moves to Egypt

FEATURE HIGHLIGHTS

+ *Being God's Image* (5)
+ *Days of Creation* (6)
+ *Why Would God Punish Eve Like That?* (8)
+ *Eve: Ruined to Redeemed* (9)
+ *Needing Favor: Finding God's Gift* (13)
+ *Image* (43)

Words to Remember are highlighted throughout this book

HOW LONG DOES IT TAKE TO READ? 3:00

Timeline

BC	Event
	CREATION — Adam and Eve made by God; Eve bears Cain and Abel, then Seth
NOT DATED	**FLOOD** — Noah's wife, sons, and daughters-in-law survive
2166	ABRAM BORN
2156	SARAI BORN
c. 2100	HAGAR BORN
2091	ABRAM AND SARAI ENTER CANAAN
2066	SARAH GIVES BIRTH TO ISAAC
c. 2069	HAGAR AND ISHMAEL RESCUED BY "THE GOD WHO SEES"
c. 2050	REBEKAH BORN
2006	REBEKAH GIVES BIRTH TO JACOB AND ESAU
c. 1940	LEAH BORN, RACHEL BORN
1929	JACOB FLEES TO HARAN
c. 1918	LEAH GIVES BIRTH TO JUDAH
1915	RACHEL GIVES BIRTH TO JOSEPH
1898	JOSEPH SOLD INTO SLAVERY
c. 1890	TAMAR BECOMES PREGNANT BY JUDAH
1885	JOSEPH RULES EGYPT
1805	JOSEPH DIES

The Account of Creation

1 In the beginning God created the heavens and the earth.* ²The earth was formless and empty, and darkness covered the deep waters. And the Spirit of God was hovering over the surface of the waters.

³Then God said, "Let there be light," and there was light. ⁴And God saw that the light was good. Then he separated the light from the darkness. ⁵God called the light "day" and the darkness "night."

And evening passed and morning came, marking the first day.

⁶Then God said, "Let there be a space between the waters, to separate the waters of the heavens from the waters of the earth." ⁷And that is what happened. God made this space to separate the waters of the earth from the waters of the heavens. ⁸God called the space "sky."

And evening passed and morning came, marking the second day.

⁹Then God said, "Let the waters beneath the sky flow together into one place, so dry ground may appear." And that is what happened. ¹⁰God called the dry ground "land" and the waters "seas." And God saw that it was good. ¹¹Then God said, "Let the land sprout with vegetation—every sort of seed-bearing plant, and trees that grow seed-bearing fruit. These seeds will then produce the kinds of plants and trees from which they came." And that is what happened. ¹²The land produced vegetation—all sorts of seed-bearing plants, and trees with seed-bearing fruit. Their seeds produced plants and trees of the same kind. And God saw that it was good.

¹³And evening passed and morning came, marking the third day.

¹⁴Then God said, "Let lights appear in the sky to separate the day from the night. Let them be signs to mark the seasons, days, and years. ¹⁵Let these lights in the sky shine down on the earth." And that is what happened. ¹⁶God made two great lights—the larger one to govern the day, and the smaller one to govern the night. He also made the stars. ¹⁷God set these lights in the sky to light the earth, ¹⁸to govern the day and night, and to separate the light from the darkness. And God saw that it was good.

¹⁹And evening passed and morning came, marking the fourth day.

²⁰Then God said, "Let the waters swarm with fish and other life. Let the skies be filled with birds of every kind." ²¹So God created great sea creatures and every living thing that scurries and swarms in the water, and every sort of bird—each producing offspring of the same kind. And God saw that it was good. ²²Then God blessed them, saying, "Be fruitful and multiply. Let the fish fill the seas, and let the birds multiply on the earth."

²³And evening passed and morning came, marking the fifth day.

²⁴Then God said, "Let the earth produce every sort of animal, each producing offspring of the same kind—livestock, small animals that scurry along the ground, and wild animals." And that is what happened. ²⁵God made all sorts of wild animals, livestock, and small animals, each able to produce offspring of the same kind. And God saw that it was good.

²⁶Then God said, "Let us make human beings* in our image, to be like us. They will reign over the fish in the sea, the birds in the sky, the livestock, all the wild animals on the earth,* and the small animals that scurry along the ground."

²⁷ So God created human beings* in his own image.
In the image of God he created them;
male and female he created them.

1:1 Or *In the beginning when God created the heavens and the earth,...* Or *When God began to create the heavens and the earth,...* **1:26a** Or *man;* Hebrew reads *adam.* **1:26b** As in Syriac version; Hebrew reads *all the earth.* **1:27** Or *the man;* Hebrew reads *ha-adam.*

1:1 Some Christians read Genesis as a description of how God made the world. Other Christians see it as a poetic celebration of creation that unveils God's intentions without revealing his methods. Whatever you conclude about the way God made the world, Genesis leaves no room to see our world as an accident. Other biblical accounts of creation agree (for example, Job 38; Psalm 104).

1:11-12 The focus of the creation week is fertility. God told the residents of creation to "be fruitful and multiply" and to "fill the earth" (1:22, 28). He repeatedly emphasized the fruitfulness of plants (1:11-12, 29-30) and made each living thing "able to produce offspring of the same kind" (1:11-12, 21, 25). Like animals, people are residents of the world God made, but unlike animals, people were made in God's likeness, according to his image.

1:22 In the context of his creative work, God blessed a few specific things: fish and birds (1:21-22), animals and humans (1:25-28), and the seventh day (2:3)—later called the Sabbath. This trilogy of blessings highlights the Creator's plan: God made humankind in his image to exercise stewardship over the creatures of the earth and to participate in God's Sabbath rest.

1:26-27 Humans are not divine, but we share kinship with our creator as the only creature made in his image. "Image of God" is our human identity, expressed through the loving rule of creation on God's behalf (see Psalm 8:5-8). Men and women share this role. Together we participate in the human task of creating culture, maintaining order, and ensuring the flourishing of the natural world. Male and female sexuality is central to what it means to be human because the perpetuation of the human race depends on it.

Being God's Image—Finding Our Human Identity and Vocation

SCRIPTURE CONNECTION: GENESIS 1:1-31

When I was twenty, I had my first chance to teach in a college classroom under the supervision of my professor. I was hooked. I knew instantly that this is what I was born to do.

You and I are different people. We each possess unique talents and interests and participate in a unique sphere of relationships. The fact that humans have been created as God's image-bearers means that every life is precious—yours, mine, our neighbors, even our enemies (see 9:6). And because we reflect God's image, each of us is needed for the world to be what God intended.

Genesis 1 is a beautifully structured account of God's creative work. At the beginning of the chapter, the earth was "formless and empty" (1:2). Step by step, God created the framework in which life could flourish. On days one to three, God formed three domains, preparing each for inhabitants—light and darkness, water and sky, and dry land. On days four to six, God populated those domains with residents—heavenly lights, fish and birds, and animals and humans. By the end of creation week, the earth was no longer "formless and empty," but organized and filled with life.

The Bible imagines creation as a cosmic temple in which all creatures worship God. Unlike other ancient temples, the Israelite temple lacked a statue or idol of God as a symbol of divine presence in the central sanctuary. God prohibited such images because, as we see in the creation account, humans fill the role of representing him. This mission to represent him, which arises from this crucial chapter, requires every one of us—in a wide variety of ways, in every corner of the globe. Both men and women are essential workers in this task.

> Our mission is to represent God on earth.

Genesis 1:28-30 hints at one particular task envisioned by God. We represent the Creator by being responsible stewards of the world he made. Edible plants are to be food for both humans and animals. This human stewardship does not imply unlimited resources for people or free and unlimited enterprise. Part of our job is to ensure equitable access to the world's resources for both humans and animals. If we pollute the natural world and endanger animal or human habitats, then we are not fulfilling our God-given roles. If each of us leans into our roles as God's image-bearers, his glory will be evident over the whole earth.

IMAGINE

How does it feel to know you are God's appointed representative?

In what ways might God be calling you to care for some part of the earth?

> "My mom and I have very different gifts. While I teach in a college classroom, my mom works in her sewing room, using her skills to make feminine hygiene products to ensure that teenage girls in Africa can stay in school."

CARMEN JOY IMES, PhD, is an author, speaker, blogger, YouTuber, and serves as associate professor of Old Testament at Biola University in California.

Insight — DAYS OF CREATION

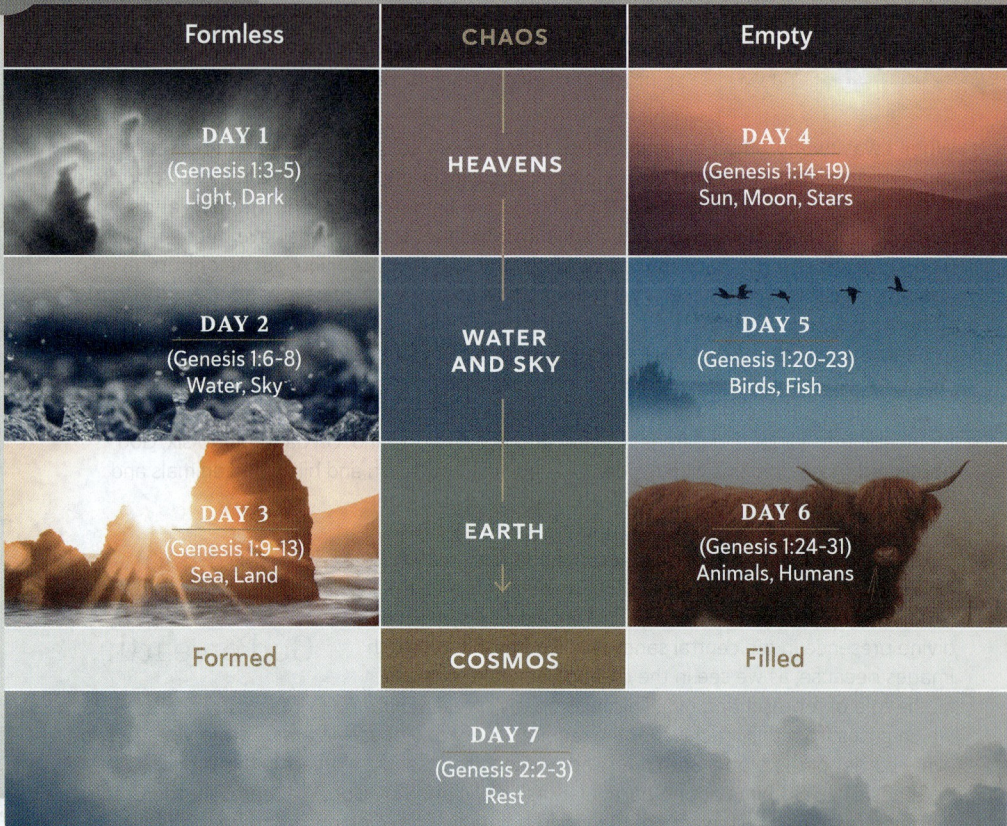

²⁸Then God blessed them and said, "Be fruitful and multiply. Fill the earth and govern it. Reign over the fish in the sea, the birds in the sky, and all the animals that scurry along the ground."

²⁹Then God said, "Look! I have given you every seed-bearing plant throughout the earth and all the fruit trees for your food. ³⁰And I have given every green plant as food for all the wild animals, the birds in the sky, and the small animals that scurry along the ground— everything that has life." And that is what happened.

³¹Then God looked over all he had made, and he saw that it was very good!

And evening passed and morning came, marking the sixth day.

2 So the creation of the heavens and the earth and everything in them was completed. ²On the seventh day God had finished his work of creation, so he rested* from all his work. ³And God blessed the seventh day and declared it holy, because it was the day when he rested from all his work of creation.

⁴This is the account of the creation of the heavens and the earth.

The Man and Woman in Eden

When the LORD God made the earth and the heavens, ⁵neither wild plants nor grains were growing on the earth. For the LORD God had not yet sent rain to water the earth, and there were no people to cultivate the soil. ⁶Instead, springs* came up from the

2:2 Or *ceased;* also in 2:3.   2:6 Or *mist.*

2:2 God did not rest because he was tired. He rested because his creative work was finished. He rested the way a king rests on his throne when his dominion is at peace. The creation week is a model for us to emulate. None of us can work nonstop. We need regular periods of rest. Genesis 1:1–2:3 invites us to pattern our work week after God's.

ground and watered all the land. ⁷Then the LORD God formed the man from the dust of the ground. He breathed the breath of life into the man's nostrils, and the man became a living person.

⁸Then the LORD God planted a garden in Eden in the east, and there he placed the man he had made. ⁹The LORD God made all sorts of trees grow up from the ground—trees that were beautiful and that produced delicious fruit. In the middle of the garden he placed the tree of life and the tree of the knowledge of good and evil.

¹⁰A river flowed from the land of Eden, watering the garden and then dividing into four branches. ¹¹The first branch, called the Pishon, flowed around the entire land of Havilah, where gold is found. ¹²The gold of that land is exceptionally pure; aromatic resin and onyx stone are also found there. ¹³The second branch, called the Gihon, flowed around the entire land of Cush. ¹⁴The third branch, called the Tigris, flowed east of the land of Asshur. The fourth branch is called the Euphrates.

¹⁵The LORD God placed the man in the Garden of Eden to tend and watch over it. ¹⁶But the LORD God warned him, "You may freely eat the fruit of every tree in the garden—¹⁷except the tree of the knowledge of good and evil. If you eat its fruit, you are sure to die."

¹⁸Then the LORD God said, "It is not good for the man to be alone. I will make a helper who is just right for him." ¹⁹So the LORD God formed from the ground all the wild animals and all the birds of the sky. He brought them to the man* to see what he would call them, and the man chose a name for each one. ²⁰He gave names to all the livestock, all the birds of the sky, and all the wild animals. But still there was no helper just right for him.

²¹So the LORD God caused the man to fall into a deep sleep. While the man slept, the LORD God took out one of the man's ribs* and closed up the opening. ²²Then the LORD God made a woman from the rib, and he brought her to the man.

²³"At last!" the man exclaimed.

"This one is bone from my bone,
 and flesh from my flesh!
She will be called 'woman,'
 because she was taken from 'man.'"

²⁴This explains why a man leaves his father and mother and is joined to his wife, and the two are united into one.

²⁵Now the man and his wife were both naked, but they felt no shame.

The Man and Woman Sin

3 The serpent was the shrewdest of all the wild animals the LORD God had made. One day he asked the woman, "Did God really say you must not eat the fruit from any of the trees in the garden?"

²"Of course we may eat fruit from the trees in the garden," the woman replied. ³"It's only the fruit from the tree in the middle of the garden that we are not allowed to eat. God said, 'You must not eat it or even touch it; if you do, you will die.'"

⁴"You won't die!" the serpent replied to the woman. ⁵"God knows that your eyes will be opened as soon as you eat it, and you will be like God, knowing both good and evil."

⁶The woman was convinced. She saw that the tree

2:19 Or *Adam*, and so throughout the chapter.   2:21 Or *took a part of the man's side.*

2:7 God personally formed the first human (*adam* in Hebrew) from the dust of the ground (*adamah* in Hebrew) and brought him to life with divine breath. This description emphasizes God's personal attention, and it reinforces the representative role of humans as God's image. In ancient Mesopotamia, artisans would craft an idol (or "image") and wash the statue's mouth in a garden ritual, preparing it to be inhabited by the divine presence. Similarly, God placed the first human in a garden and breathed life into him so that he could carry out his role as God's representative (2:15), a fitting role for someone made in God's image (1:27).

2:18-20 For the first time, something in creation was "not good," namely, the lack of a partner for the human. The man could not carry out all his work alone. He needed "a helper . . . just right for him." The Hebrew word *ezer*, translated "helper" here, is not a term of subservience, as though the man needed a servant. In fact, the term *ezer* most often describes God as Israel's helper (see Genesis 49:25; Exodus 18:4; Deuteronomy 33:7; Psalm 146:5). The human needed a true partner who would be just like him.

2:21-22 While the first human came from the ground, the second human came from the first. This origin emphasizes their essential unity. They are "of the same kind." The word "rib" may be misleading. The Hebrew term (*tsela*) denotes the "side" of something or a "supporting beam" (see Exodus 25:12). The verbal form of the word (*tsala*) means "to limp" (Genesis 32:31). One might even imagine that God divided the first human in half, making each half into a whole.

2:23-25 Woman (*ishah* in Hebrew) was from man (*ish*) just like human (*adam*) was from the ground (*adamah*). The wordplays in Hebrew underscore the connectedness of humans to the earth and to each other. Unity in marriage is possible because man and woman share the essential characteristics of humanity, including the status as God's image-bearer and representative (1:27). Their relationship began in mutual trust and honor.

3:1-7 Did the serpent ask the woman because she would be more easily deceived? She was not present when God instructed Adam. This may explain Paul's instruction in 1 Timothy 2:11-14 that women be allowed to learn so that they will not be easily deceived. But even though the woman is the first to appear in this scene, the man was clearly present and culpable as well. Neither resisted the temptation to define good and evil for themselves. Every temptation begins with casting doubt on the goodness of God. Cultivating trust in him is the surest defense against temptation.

Perspective

Why would God punish Eve like that?

SCRIPTURE CONNECTION: GENESIS 3:1-19

Why would God impose such consequences for Eve's one wayward choice? After all, when she decided to take and eat, she did not yet know good and evil. Though adult in form, Eve was young in creation and unwise to the serpent's shrewdness.

When a toddler plays with fire, will the parent discipline for spite? Or to protect? Banning Adam and Eve was God's rescue. In their fallen state, eating of the tree of life would tragically seal them in sin's aftermath.

Eve bore some of God's own torment. Her pain in bringing forth life would compel her toward the Creator, and she would begin to understand how a loving parent chooses pain to give life. Eve's love for Adam would also bear pain, requiring a lifetime of learning what it means to partner in the mystery of marriage.

Our pain compels our outreach for God, and therein lies the gift.

Eve's consequences led to another sacred tree, the Cross, from which we now partake. This time, the body and blood of Christ and the pain he bore delivers us into life everlasting, restoring our perfect communion with God. As Paul says,

> Yes, Adam's one sin brings condemnation for everyone, but Christ's one act of righteousness brings a right relationship with God and new life for everyone. (Romans 5:18)

VIEWPOINTS

HERS: *Perhaps unaware of what her choice would mean, how was Eve's perspective limited? How did Eve's understanding grow?*
MINE: *"We do not get to choose results, only our actions. We can practice choosing wisely and entrusting results to God."*
YOURS: *Even in pain, how might we trust God as a loving parent?*

MISTY ARTERBURN is an author and speaker, contributing to Bible projects, devotionals, and recovery materials for over twenty years. Wife and mom to five, Misty is the founder of Recovery Girls and the general editor of *The One Year Bible for Women*.

---

was beautiful and its fruit looked delicious, and she wanted the wisdom it would give her. So she took some of the fruit and ate it. Then she gave some to her husband, who was with her, and he ate it, too. ⁷At that moment their eyes were opened, and they suddenly felt shame at their nakedness. So they sewed fig leaves together to cover themselves.

⁸When the cool evening breezes were blowing, the man* and his wife heard the Lord God walking about in the garden. So they hid from the Lord God among the trees. ⁹Then the Lord God called to the man, "Where are you?"

¹⁰He replied, "I heard you walking in the garden, so I hid. I was afraid because I was naked."

¹¹"Who told you that you were naked?" the Lord God asked. "Have you eaten from the tree whose fruit I commanded you not to eat?"

¹²The man replied, "It was the woman you gave me who gave me the fruit, and I ate it."

¹³Then the Lord God asked the woman, "What have you done?"

"The serpent deceived me," she replied. "That's why I ate it."

¹⁴Then the Lord God said to the serpent,

"Because you have done this, you are cursed
    more than all animals, domestic and wild.
You will crawl on your belly,
    groveling in the dust as long as you live.
¹⁵ And I will cause hostility between you and the woman,
    and between your offspring and her offspring.
He will strike* your head,
    and you will strike his heel."

¹⁶Then he said to the woman,

"I will sharpen the pain of your pregnancy,
    and in pain you will give birth.
And you will desire to control your husband,
    but he will rule over you.*"

3:8 Or *Adam*, and so throughout the chapter. **3:15** Or *bruise*; also in 3:15b. **3:16** Or *And though you will have desire for your husband, / he will rule over you.*

3:11-13 Rather than confessing, the man blamed the woman for giving him the fruit and God for giving him the woman. The woman followed suit, accusing the serpent. The serpent played a role and would be punished (3:14), but that did not release the woman or the man from their guilt.
3:16-19 The consequences of human rebellion complicated human vocation. Pain in childbirth would make it more difficult to fill the earth. The partnership God intended between man and woman would become antagonistic, so that rather than ruling the earth, they would seek to dominate each other. Fruitful cultivation of the land would prove difficult. Although humans do far more than have babies and plant crops, these activities bear the brunt of the consequences of sin because they are essential to the fulfillment of the creation blessing (1:26-28).

Eve
IDENTITY — Ruined to Redeemed

Eve remembers…

The fruit looked *so* good. It was so beautiful I could almost taste it before I bit into it. The serpent promised that good things would come from it: I would be wise and know everything. That first bite was so sweet…

And then everything changed, dramatically.

If I had only known. I didn't really understand the consequences. Adam was right there, and he didn't stop me either. In fact, he later blamed me. Wasn't he to blame too? Oh, God, now what?

The consequences: pain in childbirth, desire to control my husband. What does that even mean?

A promise: A descendant of mine will one day crush the head of the serpent? When? How?

Life became painful. We were driven out of the Garden, never to reenter. God gave us clothes, but we had to learn how to survive. We lost two sons—Cain killed Abel, then Cain was banished from our presence. Oh, the pain of loss!

Yet in the pain, God provided. He gave us Seth, a son to carry on life. We learned to trust that God is still in charge.

EVE'S STORY IS TOLD IN GENESIS 2:19–4:26.

> God is bigger than our missteps and our pain. He is always ready to restore and provide.

IDENTIFY

What life-changing events have you experienced?

Where do you find God in them?

> "I miscarried my second child, propelling me into early menopause. Then, God opened doors to counsel grieving women and to a new career in academia, which I may not have pursued if I had a small child at home."

ELIZABETH GLANVILLE, PhD, is retired faculty from Fuller Theological Seminary, School of Mission and Theology. She is an international teacher on missions and leadership and chaplain for a local police department and her retirement community.

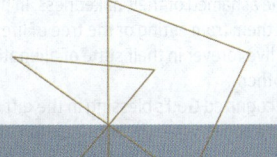

[17] And to the man he said,

> "Since you listened to your wife and ate from the tree
> whose fruit I commanded you not to eat,
> the ground is cursed because of you.
> All your life you will struggle to scratch a living from it.
> [18] It will grow thorns and thistles for you,
> though you will eat of its grains.
> [19] By the sweat of your brow
> will you have food to eat
> until you return to the ground
> from which you were made.
> For you were made from dust,
> and to dust you will return."

Paradise Lost: God's Judgment

[20] Then the man—Adam—named his wife Eve, because she would be the mother of all who live.* [21] And the LORD God made clothing from animal skins for Adam and his wife.

[22] Then the LORD God said, "Look, the human beings* have become like us, knowing both good and evil. What if they reach out, take fruit from the tree of life, and eat it? Then they will live forever!" [23] So the LORD God banished them from the Garden of Eden, and he sent Adam out to cultivate the ground from which he had been made. [24] After sending them out, the LORD God stationed mighty cherubim to the east of the Garden of Eden. And he placed a flaming sword that flashed back and forth to guard the way to the tree of life.

Cain and Abel

4 Now Adam* had sexual relations with his wife, Eve, and she became pregnant. When she gave birth to Cain, she said, "With the LORD's help, I have produced* a man!" [2] Later she gave birth to his brother and named him Abel.

When they grew up, Abel became a shepherd, while Cain cultivated the ground. [3] When it was time for the harvest, Cain presented some of his crops as a gift to the LORD. [4] Abel also brought a gift—the best portions of the firstborn lambs from his flock. The LORD accepted Abel and his gift, [5] but he did not accept Cain and his gift. This made Cain very angry, and he looked dejected.

[6] "Why are you so angry?" the LORD asked Cain. "Why do you look so dejected? [7] You will be accepted if you do what is right. But if you refuse to do what is right, then watch out! Sin is crouching at the door, eager to control you. But you must subdue it and be its master."

[8] One day Cain suggested to his brother, "Let's go out into the fields."* And while they were in the field, Cain attacked his brother, Abel, and killed him.

[9] Afterward the LORD asked Cain, "Where is your brother? Where is Abel?"

"I don't know," Cain responded. "Am I my brother's guardian?"

[10] But the LORD said, "What have you done? Listen! Your brother's blood cries out to me from the ground! [11] Now you are cursed and banished from the ground, which has swallowed your brother's blood. [12] No longer will the ground yield good crops for you, no matter how hard you work! From now on you will be a homeless wanderer on the earth."

[13] Cain replied to the LORD, "My punishment* is too great for me to bear! [14] You have banished me from the land and from your presence; you have made me a homeless wanderer. Anyone who finds me will kill me!"

[15] The LORD replied, "No, for I will give a sevenfold punishment to anyone who kills you." Then the LORD put a mark on Cain to warn anyone who might try to kill him. [16] So Cain left the LORD's presence and settled in the land of Nod,* east of Eden.

The Descendants of Cain

[17] Cain had sexual relations with his wife, and she became pregnant and gave birth to Enoch. Then Cain founded a city, which he named Enoch, after his son. [18] Enoch had a son named Irad. Irad became the father of* Mehujael. Mehujael became the father of Methushael. Methushael became the father of Lamech.

3:20 *Eve* sounds like a Hebrew term that means "to give life." **3:22** Or *the man;* Hebrew reads *ha-adam.* **4:1a** Or *the man;* also in 4:25. **4:1b** Or *I have acquired. Cain* sounds like a Hebrew term that can mean "produce" or "acquire." **4:8** As in Samaritan Pentateuch, Greek and Syriac versions, and Latin Vulgate; Masoretic Text lacks *"Let's go out into the fields."* **4:13** Or *My sin.* **4:16** *Nod* means "wandering." **4:18** Or *the ancestor of,* and so throughout the verse.

3:20-24 God graciously clothed Adam and Eve since they had become ashamed of their nakedness. In his mercy, God prevented them from eating of the tree of life, so that they would not live forever in their state of alienation from God and each other.
4:1 Eve recognized God's blessing in the gift of children. The birth of a son ensured the continuation of the family line. However, the tragic consequences of sin threatened her family's survival. Cain did not offer God his best, and his jealousy toward Abel drove him to kill his own brother.
4:17 Where did Cain find a wife? If Adam and Eve were the only people, then he would have to have married his sister. However, Genesis does not specifically claim that Adam and Eve were the only humans created. It's possible that their story is an archetype of the human experience. The existence of other humans seems to be implied in Cain's fear that others would kill him if he wandered alone (4:14-15). In 1 Corinthians 15:22, the apostle Paul speaks of Adam's representative role for humanity. Some believe Adam's role requires him to be the genetic parent of all humans, while others do not.

¹⁹Lamech married two women. The first was named Adah, and the second was Zillah. ²⁰Adah gave birth to Jabal, who was the first of those who raise livestock and live in tents. ²¹His brother's name was Jubal, the first of all who play the harp and flute. ²²Lamech's other wife, Zillah, gave birth to a son named Tubal-cain. He became an expert in forging tools of bronze and iron. Tubal-cain had a sister named Naamah. ²³One day Lamech said to his wives,

"Adah and Zillah, hear my voice;
  listen to me, you wives of Lamech.
I have killed a man who attacked me,
  a young man who wounded me.
²⁴ If someone who kills Cain is punished
    seven times,
  then the one who kills me will be punished
    seventy-seven times!"

4:19 Lamech was the first polygamist mentioned in the Bible. Marrying two women is contrary to God's pattern for marriage (2:24) and might have been a manifestation of the rebellion of Cain's descendants. Lamech later boasted to his wives about his vengeful spirit, revealing his violent nature. Genesis certainly does not present him as a role model. For other negative examples related to polygamy, see 28:6-9; 29:14–30:24.

MY STORY WITH FAMILY & FRIENDS

Seeing Our Families Shine

SCRIPTURE CONNECTION: GENESIS 4:1-12

Have you ever had a rock hit your windshield while driving? The sound may startle you, and at first you might not see any damage. Then a few days later, you notice a tiny chip. Then the chip becomes a crack, and soon there's a line across the windshield you can no longer ignore.

Isn't that how brokenness works in our families? Cain's sin starts so small—unjustified anger—and only he knows about it. In the end, his selfishness and jealousy break the entire family.

Abel loses life.

Cain loses community.

Eve and Adam lose two sons.

Has your family experienced loss because sin caused a fracture? Divorce was ours. As we meet families in the Bible and consider our own families, we see that every family member has flaws. And our failures hurt us and others.

But that's not the end of the story.

Family is God's idea. He longs to see whole, healthy, joy-filled homes that display his love. Just as an intact windshield helps us see and protects those in the car, asking God to show us what's broken can make us a blessing to our families—and make our families a blessing to others.

Through divorce, I lost much. But God restored. He redeemed. He also stretched my previously limited view of family. When we come to the end of denial and invite God's intervention, he responds. For every crack, his love restores.

> God's love brings blessings, sparkling through our family's shattered places.

IMAGINE

Consider your best and highest dream for your family. How has God positioned you to help lead them there?

What conversations or actions of love need to happen?

"I pray God helps me see my own faults and be courageous enough to address them before they splinter and grow."

SUZY SHEPHERD is the founder of SHINE, creator of Stonecroft's Where Love Lives outreach experience, and mom to a blended tribe of nine. She finds great joy in creating experiences for people to know God's love.

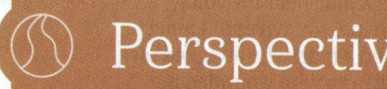

Perspective

Does God okay the "forcible taking" of women?

SCRIPTURE CONNECTION: GENESIS 6:1-8

What "sons of God" would forcibly take any women they wanted to be their wives? This doesn't sound very godly at all.

Many scholars resolve this by concluding that the "sons of God" phrasing refers to spiritual or angelic beings who had rebelled against God. Others suggest that it refers to human rulers who married commoners. Still others argue that it refers to descendants of Seth who married the female descendants of Cain.

Regardless, we recognize that the sexual arena has been a favorite playground for the enemy from the time man and woman first knew their nakedness (3:7). At the birth of their shame, they covered their sexual bodies with fig leaves.

This passage from Genesis 6 conceals whether the human women were consenting to these unions or were taken against their will. But one thing is clear: This sexual deviancy wreaked havoc.

VIEWPOINTS

HERS: *What does the phrase "took any they wanted" suggest about how these "sons of God" esteemed women and interacted with them?*

MINE: *"I am not a fan of the word victim—at least with respect to many of my own experiences. While I acknowledge its appropriate use when I have been deceived, used, or harmed, I don't want to downplay any part of choice I may have had in a matter: how I show up, how I respond, what resources I turn to, whether an incident defines or grows me, whether I reach for God or reject him. I am not responsible for others' choices, and sometimes I may not have a choice, but when I do, I can ask, What choices will I make today?"*

YOURS: *How might you guard against sexual trouble and champion sexual responsibility today?*

MISTY ARTERBURN is an author and speaker, contributing to Bible projects, devotionals, and recovery materials for over twenty years. Wife and mom to five, Misty is the founder of Recovery Girls and the general editor of *The One Year Bible for Women*.

The Birth of Seth

²⁵Adam had sexual relations with his wife again, and she gave birth to another son. She named him Seth,* for she said, "God has granted me another son in place of Abel, whom Cain killed." ²⁶When Seth grew up, he had a son and named him Enosh. At that time people first began to worship the LORD by name.

The Descendants of Adam

5 This is the written account of the descendants of Adam. When God created human beings,* he made them to be like himself. ²He created them male and female, and he blessed them and called them "human."

³When Adam was 130 years old, he became the father of a son who was just like him—in his very image. He named his son Seth. ⁴After the birth of Seth, Adam lived another 800 years, and he had other sons and daughters. ⁵Adam lived 930 years, and then he died.

⁶When Seth was 105 years old, he became the father of* Enosh. ⁷After the birth of* Enosh, Seth lived another 807 years, and he had other sons and daughters. ⁸Seth lived 912 years, and then he died.

⁹When Enosh was 90 years old, he became the father of Kenan. ¹⁰After the birth of Kenan, Enosh lived another 815 years, and he had other sons and daughters. ¹¹Enosh lived 905 years, and then he died.

¹²When Kenan was 70 years old, he became the father of Mahalalel. ¹³After the birth of Mahalalel, Kenan lived another 840 years, and he had other sons and daughters. ¹⁴Kenan lived 910 years, and then he died.

¹⁵When Mahalalel was 65 years old, he became the father of Jared. ¹⁶After the birth of Jared, Mahalalel lived another 830 years, and he had other sons and daughters. ¹⁷Mahalalel lived 895 years, and then he died.

¹⁸When Jared was 162 years old, he became the father of Enoch. ¹⁹After the birth of Enoch, Jared lived another 800 years, and he had other sons and daughters. ²⁰Jared lived 962 years, and then he died.

²¹When Enoch was 65 years old, he became the father of Methuselah. ²²After the birth of Methuselah, Enoch lived in close fellowship with God for another 300 years, and he had other

4:25 *Seth* probably means "granted"; the name may also mean "appointed." **5:1** Or *man;* Hebrew reads *adam;* similarly in 5:2. **5:6** Or *the ancestor of;* also in 5:9, 12, 15, 18, 21, 25. **5:7** Or *the birth of this ancestor of;* also in 5:10, 13, 16, 19, 22, 26.

5:1-3 This second biblical mention of the image of God helps to define it. God made humans to be like him. Similarly, Adam fathered a son who was just like him—in his very image. Our identity as God's image implies kinship. We are related to God in a way analogous to a human family. This passage also affirms that the human status as God's image was not lost when Adam and Eve sinned.

sons and daughters. ²³Enoch lived 365 years, ²⁴walking in close fellowship with God. Then one day he disappeared, because God took him.

²⁵When Methuselah was 187 years old, he became the father of Lamech. ²⁶After the birth of Lamech, Methuselah lived another 782 years, and he had other sons and daughters. ²⁷Methuselah lived 969 years, and then he died.

²⁸When Lamech was 182 years old, he became the father of a son. ²⁹Lamech named his son Noah, for he said, "May he bring us relief* from our work and the painful labor of farming this ground that the LORD has cursed." ³⁰After the birth of Noah, Lamech lived another 595 years, and he had other sons and daughters. ³¹Lamech lived 777 years, and then he died.

³²After Noah was 500 years old, he became the father of Shem, Ham, and Japheth.

A World Gone Wrong

6 Then the people began to multiply on the earth, and daughters were born to them. ²The sons of God saw the beautiful women* and took any they wanted as their wives. ³Then the LORD said, "My Spirit will not put up with* humans for such a long time, for they are only mortal flesh. In the future, their normal lifespan will be no more than 120 years."

⁴In those days, and for some time after, giant Nephilites lived on the earth, for whenever the sons of God had intercourse with women, they gave birth to children who became the heroes and famous warriors of ancient times.

5:29 *Noah* sounds like a Hebrew term that can mean "relief" or "comfort." **6:2** Hebrew *daughters of men;* also in 6:4. **6:3** Greek version reads *will not remain in.*

6:1-4 Obviously the birth of daughters was nothing new, but in this passage, the daughters take center stage. Their stunning beauty attracted some unlikely suitors. Scholars have suggested three possibilities for the identity of the "sons of God" in this passage: angelic beings who left their stations to cohabit with women, royalty who intermarried with commoners, or members of Seth's family who married women from Cain's family. Language reminiscent of 3:6 ("saw...took") shows the rebellious nature of this act. The result of these unions was a warrior race known for its wickedness.

Come Close

NEEDING FAVOR: FINDING GOD'S GIFT

SCRIPTURE CONNECTION: GENESIS 6:5-9

Favor. It's something we pray for often. Favor in our jobs. Favor in our relationships. Favor in our personal endeavors. We read about the lives of women and men in the Bible such as Abel, Abraham, Noah, Hannah, and Jesus' mother, Mary, who all experienced the favor of God in one way or another. Whether it was for a season or a lifetime, the blessing of God's favor truly changed the lives of these individuals. God's favor still has the power to do so for us today.

There are quite a few mentions of God's favor (or "grace," depending on the translation) in the Bible. In a famous proverb, quoted multiple times in the New Testament, favor is attached to the character trait of humility (Proverbs 3:34; see James 4:6; 1 Peter 5:5). Could it be that our humility moves God to grant us favor? When we think of others who lost God's favor, such as Cain or King Saul, could a lack of humility have contributed?

Favor is a gift; we can't work ourselves into it. We accept and receive it by faith through our relationship with God. As we learn to love the Giver more than the gift, we will begin to see strands of his favor weaving throughout our lives.

REFLECT "For you bless the godly, O LORD; you surround them with your shield of love." PSALM 5:12

Lord, thank you for the gift of your gracious favor. May I walk humbly before you all the days of my life. Amen.

CONSIDER "Humility is the gateway into the grace and the favor of God." HAROLD WARNER

> God's favor is a gift; greater still is knowing the gift-Giver.

QUANTRILLA ARD, PhD, is a faith-based personal and spiritual development author, speaker, Bible teacher, and literary agent who believes in the power of collective strength, community, and fellowship.

GENESIS 6

⬥ 14

⁵The LORD observed the extent of human wickedness on the earth, and he saw that everything they thought or imagined was consistently and totally evil. ⁶So the LORD was sorry he had ever made them and put them on the earth. It broke his heart. ⁷And the LORD said, "I will wipe this human race I have created from the face of the earth. Yes, and I will destroy every living thing—all the people, the large animals, the small animals that scurry along the ground, and even the birds of the sky. I am sorry I ever made them." ⁸But Noah found favor with the LORD.

The Story of Noah

⁹This is the account of Noah and his family. Noah was a righteous man, the only blameless person living on earth at the time, and he walked in close fellowship with God. ¹⁰Noah was the father of three sons: Shem, Ham, and Japheth.

¹¹Now God saw that the earth had become corrupt and was filled with violence. ¹²God observed all this corruption in the world, for everyone on earth was corrupt. ¹³So God said to Noah, "I have decided to destroy all living creatures, for they have filled the earth with violence. Yes, I will wipe them all out along with the earth!

¹⁴"Build a large boat* from cypress wood* and waterproof it with tar, inside and out. Then construct decks and stalls throughout its interior. ¹⁵Make the boat 450 feet long, 75 feet wide, and 45 feet high.* ¹⁶Leave an 18-inch opening* below the roof all the way

6:14a Traditionally rendered *an ark.* 6:14b Or *gopher wood.* 6:15 Hebrew *300 cubits* [138 meters] *long, 50 cubits* [23 meters] *wide, and 30 cubits* [13.8 meters] *high.* 6:16 Hebrew *an opening of 1 cubit* [46 centimeters].

Insight — NOAH'S ARK

These illustrations depict what the ark might have looked like based on the descriptions we read in 6:14-16. Noah and his wife, and their sons and daughters-in-law, and all the creatures they brought on board survived the Flood in a boat like this.

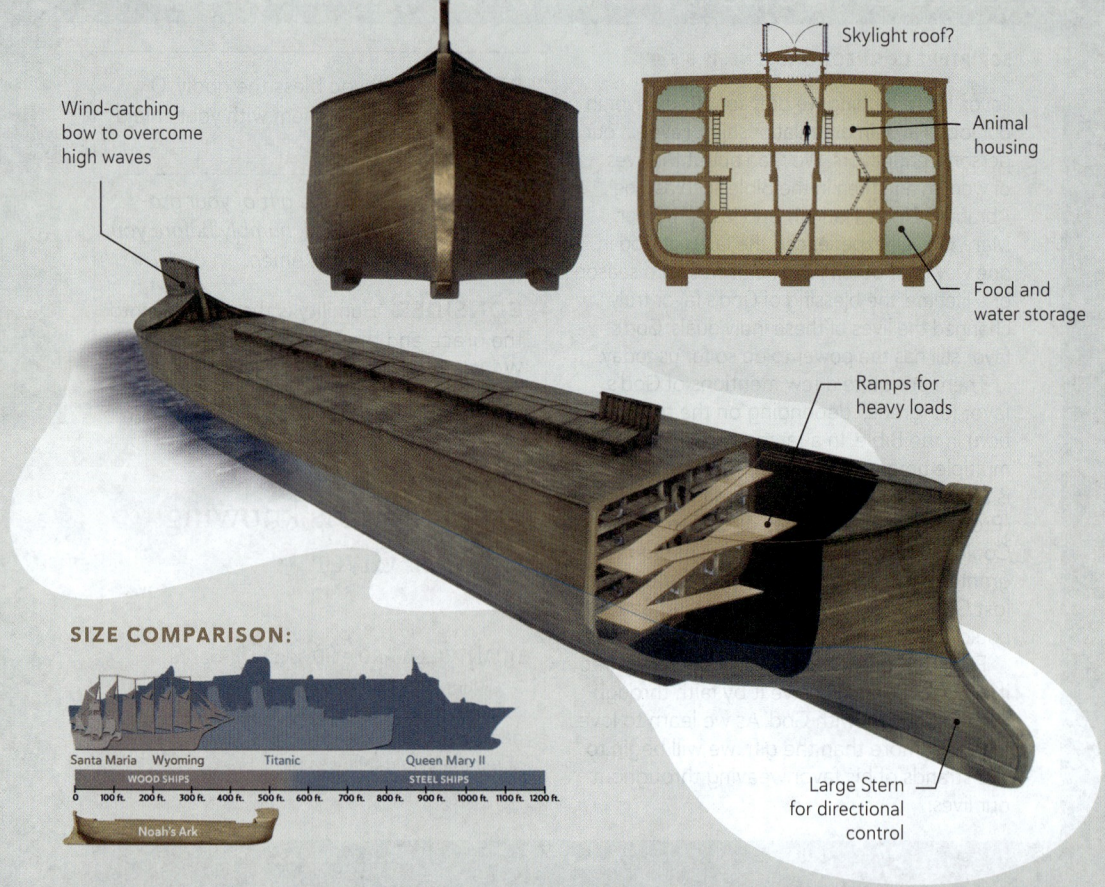

Wind-catching bow to overcome high waves

Skylight roof?

Animal housing

Food and water storage

Ramps for heavy loads

Large Stern for directional control

SIZE COMPARISON:
Santa Maria, Wyoming — WOOD SHIPS
Titanic, Queen Mary II — STEEL SHIPS
0, 100 ft., 200 ft., 300 ft., 400 ft., 500 ft., 600 ft., 700 ft., 800 ft., 900 ft., 1000 ft., 1100 ft., 1200 ft.
Noah's Ark

around the boat. Put the door on the side, and build three decks inside the boat—lower, middle, and upper.

¹⁷"Look! I am about to cover the earth with a flood that will destroy every living thing that breathes. Everything on earth will die. ¹⁸But I will confirm my covenant with you. So enter the boat—you and your wife and your sons and their wives. ¹⁹Bring a pair of every kind of animal—a male and a female—into the boat with you to keep them alive during the flood. ²⁰Pairs of every kind of bird, and every kind of animal, and every kind of small animal that scurries along the ground, will come to you to be kept alive. ²¹And be sure to take on board enough food for your family and for all the animals."

²²So Noah did everything exactly as God had commanded him.

The Flood Covers the Earth

7 When everything was ready, the LORD said to Noah, "Go into the boat with all your family, for among all the people of the earth, I can see that you alone are righteous. ²Take with you seven pairs—male and female—of each animal I have approved for eating and for sacrifice,* and take one pair of each of the others. ³Also take seven pairs of every kind of bird. There must be a male and a female in each pair to ensure that all life will survive on the earth after the flood. ⁴Seven days from now I will make the rains pour down on the earth. And it will rain for forty days and forty nights, until I have wiped from the earth all the living things I have created."

⁵So Noah did everything as the LORD commanded him.

⁶Noah was 600 years old when the flood covered the earth. ⁷He went on board the boat to escape the flood—he and his wife and his sons and their wives. ⁸With them were all the various kinds of animals—those approved for eating and for sacrifice and those that were not—along with all the birds and the small animals that scurry along the ground. ⁹They entered the boat in pairs, male and female, just as God had commanded Noah. ¹⁰After seven days, the waters of the flood came and covered the earth.

¹¹When Noah was 600 years old, on the seventeenth day of the second month, all the underground waters erupted from the earth, and the rain fell in mighty torrents from the sky. ¹²The rain continued to fall for forty days and forty nights.

¹³That very day Noah had gone into the boat with his wife and his sons—Shem, Ham, and Japheth—and their wives. ¹⁴With them in the boat were pairs of every kind of animal—domestic and wild, large and small—along with birds of every kind. ¹⁵Two by two they came into the boat, representing every living thing that breathes. ¹⁶A male and female of each kind entered, just as God had commanded Noah. Then the LORD closed the door behind them.

¹⁷For forty days the floodwaters grew deeper, covering the ground and lifting the boat high above the earth. ¹⁸As the waters rose higher and higher above the ground, the boat floated safely on the surface. ¹⁹Finally, the water covered even the highest mountains on the earth, ²⁰rising more than twenty-two feet* above the highest peaks. ²¹All the living things on earth died—birds, domestic animals, wild animals, small animals that scurry along the ground, and all the people. ²²Everything that breathed and lived on dry land died. ²³God wiped out every living thing on the earth—people, livestock, small animals that scurry along the ground, and the birds of the sky. All were destroyed. The only people who survived were Noah and those with him in the boat. ²⁴And the floodwaters covered the earth for 150 days.

The Flood Recedes

8 But God remembered Noah and all the wild animals and livestock with him in the boat. He sent a wind to blow across the earth, and the floodwaters began to recede. ²The underground waters stopped flowing, and the torrential rains from the sky were stopped. ³So the floodwaters gradually receded from the earth. After 150 days, ⁴exactly five months from the time the flood began,* the boat came to rest on the mountains of Ararat. ⁵Two and a half months later,* as the waters continued to go down, other mountain peaks became visible.

⁶After another forty days, Noah opened the window he had made in the boat ⁷and released a raven. The bird flew back and forth until the floodwaters on the earth had dried up. ⁸He also released a dove to see if the water had receded and it could find dry ground. ⁹But the dove could find no place to land because the water still covered the ground. So it returned to the boat, and Noah held out his hand and drew the dove back inside. ¹⁰After waiting another seven days, Noah released the dove again. ¹¹This time

---

7:2 Hebrew *of each clean animal;* similarly in 7:8.   **7:20** Hebrew *15 cubits* [6.9 meters].   **8:4** Hebrew *on the seventeenth day of the seventh month;* see 7:11.   **8:5** Hebrew *On the first day of the tenth month;* see 7:11 and note on 8:4.

6:11–7:24 Human wickedness had reached the point that God decided to start over with Noah, the only godly person alive. The Flood would return the world to its pre-created state—formless and empty, with water covering everything. Therefore, Noah and his family needed to preserve a pair of every animal to repopulate the earth after the Flood (see 8:17).

8:1 This verse is the center of a massive chiasm (or literary sandwich). What precedes this verse is a description of the building and boarding of the ark and the rising of the waters for 150 days. What follows is a description of the receding of the waters for 150 days and the disembarking of the animals. God's *remembering* Noah does not suggest that he forgot about him but marks the moment in which God took action to keep his promise.

the dove returned to him in the evening with a fresh olive leaf in its beak. Then Noah knew that the floodwaters were almost gone. [12]He waited another seven days and then released the dove again. This time it did not come back.

[13]Noah was now 601 years old. On the first day of the new year, ten and a half months after the flood began,* the floodwaters had almost dried up from the earth. Noah lifted back the covering of the boat and saw that the surface of the ground was drying. [14]Two more months went by,* and at last the earth was dry!

[15]Then God said to Noah, [16]"Leave the boat, all of you—you and your wife, and your sons and their wives. [17]Release all the animals—the birds, the livestock, and the small animals that scurry along the ground—so they can be fruitful and multiply throughout the earth."

[18]So Noah, his wife, and his sons and their wives left the boat. [19]And all of the large and small animals and birds came out of the boat, pair by pair.

[20]Then Noah built an altar to the LORD, and there he sacrificed as burnt offerings the animals and birds that had been approved for that purpose.* [21]And the LORD was pleased with the aroma of the sacrifice and said to himself, "I will never again curse the ground because of the human race, even though everything they think or imagine is bent toward evil from childhood. I will never again destroy all living things. [22]As long as the earth remains, there will be planting and harvest, cold and heat, summer and winter, day and night."

God Confirms His Covenant

9 Then God blessed Noah and his sons and told them, "Be fruitful and multiply. Fill the earth. [2]All the animals of the earth, all the birds of the sky, all the small animals that scurry along the ground, and all the fish in the sea will look on you with fear and terror. I have placed them in your power. [3]I have given them to you for food, just as I have given you grain and vegetables. [4]But you must never eat any meat that still has the lifeblood in it.

[5]"And I will require the blood of anyone who takes another person's life. If a wild animal kills a person, it must die. And anyone who murders a fellow human must die. [6]If anyone takes a human life, that person's life will also be taken by human hands. For God made human beings* in his own image. [7]Now be fruitful and multiply, and repopulate the earth."

[8]Then God told Noah and his sons, [9]"I hereby confirm my covenant with you and your descendants, [10]and with all the animals that were on the boat with you—the birds, the livestock, and all the wild animals—every living creature on earth. [11]Yes, I am confirming my covenant with you. Never again will floodwaters kill all living creatures; never again will a flood destroy the earth.

[12]Then God said, "I am giving you a sign of my covenant with you and with all living creatures, for all generations to come. [13]I have placed my rainbow in the clouds. It is the sign of my covenant with you and with all the earth. [14]When I send clouds over the earth, the rainbow will appear in the clouds, [15]and I will remember my covenant with you and with all living creatures. Never again will the floodwaters destroy all life. [16]When I see the rainbow in the clouds, I will remember the eternal covenant between God and every living creature on earth." [17]Then God said to Noah, "Yes, this rainbow is the sign of the covenant I am confirming with all the creatures on earth."

Noah's Sons

[18]The sons of Noah who came out of the boat with their father were Shem, Ham, and Japheth. (Ham is the father of Canaan.) [19]From these three sons of Noah came all the people who now populate the earth.

[20]After the flood, Noah began to cultivate the ground, and he planted a vineyard. [21]One day he drank some wine he had made, and he became drunk and lay naked inside his tent. [22]Ham, the father of Canaan, saw that his father was naked and went outside and told his brothers. [23]Then Shem and Japheth took a robe, held it over their shoulders, and backed into the tent to cover their father. As they did this, they looked the other way so they would not see him naked.

8:13 Hebrew *On the first day of the first month;* see 7:11. 8:14 Hebrew *The twenty-seventh day of the second month arrived;* see note on 8:13. 8:20 Hebrew *every clean animal and every clean bird.* 9:6 Or *man;* Hebrew reads *ha-adam.*

9:1-3 The blessing first given to Adam (1:28) was reissued to Noah, the "Adam" of the newly cleansed world in need of repopulation and cultural expansion. God introduced two modifications to the created order: Now animals would live in terror of humans, and humans were allowed to eat meat along with seed-bearing plants (see 1:29)—a change in diet related to the animals' terror.
9:5-6 Violence, including murder, was a major factor in bringing about God's judgment in the form of the Flood (4:8; 6:11, 13). At this new beginning for humans, God affirmed the sanctity of human life and established a system of retributive justice for the taking of human life. Being created in God's image gives humans a unique status and authority within creation. Since murder destroys a person made in God's image, a murderer incurred the ultimate penalty.
9:20-25 The significance of Ham's shameful behavior is not fully clear. He may have engaged sexually with his father or with his mother (this type of act is elsewhere referred to literally in the original language as "uncovering the nakedness of one's father," Leviticus 20:11). It is possible that he merely gazed upon his naked father and, rather than covering him and keeping the matter secret, dishonored him by mocking him to his brothers. The curse likely fell on Ham's son Canaan to emphasize the shameful father-son dynamic of Ham's sin.

²⁴When Noah woke up from his stupor, he learned what Ham, his youngest son, had done. ²⁵Then he cursed Canaan, the son of Ham:

"May Canaan be cursed!
    May he be the lowest of servants to his relatives."

²⁶Then Noah said,

"May the LORD, the God of Shem, be blessed,
    and may Canaan be his servant!
²⁷ May God expand the territory of Japheth!
    May Japheth share the prosperity of Shem,*
    and may Canaan be his servant."

²⁸Noah lived another 350 years after the great flood. ²⁹He lived 950 years, and then he died.

10 This is the account of the families of Shem, Ham, and Japheth, the three sons of Noah. Many children were born to them after the great flood.

Descendants of Japheth

²The descendants of Japheth were Gomer, Magog, Madai, Javan, Tubal, Meshech, and Tiras.
³The descendants of Gomer were Ashkenaz, Riphath, and Togarmah.
⁴The descendants of Javan were Elishah, Tarshish, Kittim, and Rodanim.* ⁵Their descendants became the seafaring peoples that spread out to various lands, each identified by its own language, clan, and national identity.

Descendants of Ham

⁶The descendants of Ham were Cush, Mizraim, Put, and Canaan.
⁷The descendants of Cush were Seba, Havilah, Sabtah, Raamah, and Sabteca. The descendants of Raamah were Sheba and Dedan.

⁸Cush was also the ancestor of Nimrod, who was the first heroic warrior on earth. ⁹Since he was the greatest hunter in the world,* his name became proverbial. People would say, "This man is like Nimrod, the greatest hunter in the world." ¹⁰He built his kingdom in the land of Babylonia,* with the cities of Babylon, Erech,

9:27 Hebrew *May he live in the tents of Shem.* 10:4 As in some Hebrew manuscripts and Greek version (see also 1 Chr 1:7); most Hebrew manuscripts read *Dodanim.* 10:9 Hebrew *a great hunter before the LORD;* also in 10:9b. 10:10 Hebrew *Shinar.*

10:1-32 The birth of many children after the Flood began to fulfill God's purposes for the renewed creation (9:1; see 1:26-28). This chapter, often called the Table of Nations, lists seventy nations descending from Noah's sons. The total of seventy names indicates completeness and symbolizes the totality of the world, which would later be blessed by the descendants of Abraham (12:3; 18:18). Women are not named because male heirs were the basis for genealogical records.

Perspective

Where are the women?

SCRIPTURE CONNECTION: GENESIS 10:1-32

Genesis 10 ranks among the most boring parts of the Bible. So many hard-to-pronounce names!

Are you bothered by how few women appear in these lists?

The ancient Israelites usually recorded only male heirs in their genealogies. A genealogy traced the transfer of wealth from one generation to another and identified tribal membership through fathers and sons. Without a complex chart, marriage alliances between clans were much more difficult to trace. Women were remembered through stories and songs, rather than through genealogies. And they took pride in the social standing of their fathers, husbands, and sons.

God revealed himself in ways that made sense to ancient cultures, and he engages with us in ways that make sense today. Our task is to read the Bible well in its ancient context, discern how it reveals God's character, and then ask how we can live out its principles in our contexts today.

VIEWPOINTS

HERS: How would an ancient Israelite woman have felt hearing her husband's name read aloud in a list such as this?
MINE: "I love finding women's names in Bible genealogies. It is rare, so when one does appear, it means she is notable in some way. I love to be a detective and find out why!"
YOURS: Can you imagine life as an ancient Israelite woman? Would you have been glad to stay in the shadows? Or would you have longed to play a bigger role in public life?

CARMEN JOY IMES, PhD, is an author, speaker, blogger, YouTuber, and serves as associate professor of Old Testament at Biola University in California.

Insight — NATIONS OF THE ANCIENT WORLD

The Flood survivors' descendants spread out after "the LORD scattered them" (11:1-9), and they became the nations of the ancient world. Over half the names listed in the genealogy in 10:1-32 are identifiable ancient peoples, and the areas where they lived are shown on this map.

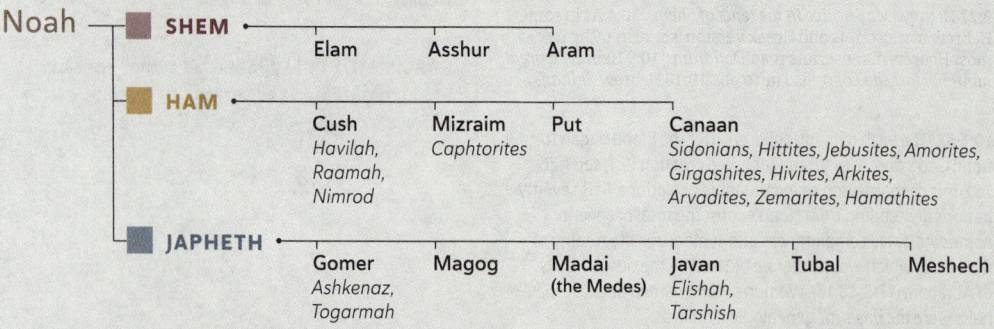

Noah
- **SHEM**: Elam, Asshur, Aram
- **HAM**:
  - Cush — Havilah, Raamah, Nimrod
  - Mizraim — Caphtorites
  - Put
  - Canaan — Sidonians, Hittites, Jebusites, Amorites, Girgashites, Hivites, Arkites, Arvadites, Zemarites, Hamathites
- **JAPHETH**:
  - Gomer — Ashkenaz, Togarmah
  - Magog
  - Madai (the Medes)
  - Javan — Elishah, Tarshish
  - Tubal
  - Meshech

Akkad, and Calneh. ¹¹From there he expanded his territory to Assyria,* building the cities of Nineveh, Rehoboth-ir, Calah, ¹²and Resen (the great city located between Nineveh and Calah). ¹³Mizraim was the ancestor of the Ludites, Anamites, Lehabites, Naphtuhites, ¹⁴Pathrusites, Casluhites, and the Caphtorites, from whom the Philistines came.*

¹⁵Canaan's oldest son was Sidon, the ancestor of the Sidonians. Canaan was also the ancestor of the Hittites,* ¹⁶Jebusites, Amorites, Girgashites, ¹⁷Hivites, Arkites, Sinites, ¹⁸Arvadites, Zemarites, and Hamathites. The Canaanite clans eventually spread out, ¹⁹and the territory of Canaan extended from Sidon in the north to Gerar and Gaza in the south, and east as far as Sodom, Gomorrah, Admah, and Zeboiim, near Lasha.

²⁰These were the descendants of Ham, identified by clan, language, territory, and national identity.

Descendants of Shem

²¹Sons were also born to Shem, the older brother of Japheth.* Shem was the ancestor of all the descendants of Eber.

²²The descendants of Shem were Elam, Asshur, Arphaxad, Lud, and Aram.

²³The descendants of Aram were Uz, Hul, Gether, and Mash.

²⁴Arphaxad was the father of Shelah,* and Shelah was the father of Eber.

²⁵Eber had two sons. The first was named Peleg (which means "division"), for during his lifetime the people of the world were divided into different language groups. His brother's name was Joktan.

²⁶Joktan was the ancestor of Almodad, Sheleph, Hazarmaveth, Jerah, ²⁷Hadoram, Uzal, Diklah, ²⁸Obal, Abimael, Sheba, ²⁹Ophir, Havilah, and Jobab. All these were descendants of Joktan. ³⁰The territory they occupied extended from Mesha all the way to Sephar in the eastern mountains.

³¹These were the descendants of Shem, identified by clan, language, territory, and national identity.

Conclusion

³²These are the clans that descended from Noah's sons, arranged by nation according to their lines of descent. All the nations of the earth descended from these clans after the great flood.

The Tower of Babel

11 At one time all the people of the world spoke the same language and used the same words. ²As the people migrated to the east, they found a plain in the land of Babylonia* and settled there.

³They began saying to each other, "Let's make bricks and harden them with fire." (In this region bricks were used instead of stone, and tar was used for mortar.) ⁴Then they said, "Come, let's build a great city for ourselves with a tower that reaches into the sky. This will make us famous and keep us from being scattered all over the world."

⁵But the LORD came down to look at the city and the tower the people were building. ⁶"Look!" he said. "The people are united, and they all speak the same language. After this, nothing they set out to do will be impossible for them! ⁷Come, let's go down and confuse the people with different languages. Then they won't be able to understand each other."

⁸In that way, the LORD scattered them all over the world, and they stopped building the city. ⁹That is why the city was called Babel,* because that is where the LORD confused the people with different languages. In this way he scattered them all over the world.

The Line of Descent from Shem to Abram

¹⁰This is the account of Shem's family.

Two years after the great flood, when Shem was 100 years old, he became the father of* Arphaxad. ¹¹After the birth of* Arphaxad, Shem lived another 500 years and had other sons and daughters.

¹²When Arphaxad was 35 years old, he became the father of Shelah. ¹³After the birth of Shelah, Arphaxad lived another 403 years and had other sons and daughters.*

10:11 Or *From that land Assyria went out.* **10:14** Hebrew *Casluhites, from whom the Philistines came, and Caphtorites.* Compare Jer 47:4; Amos 9:7. **10:15** Hebrew *ancestor of Heth.* **10:21** Or *Shem, whose older brother was Japheth.* **10:24** Greek version reads *Arphaxad was the father of Cainan, Cainan was the father of Shelah.* Compare Luke 3:36. **11:2** Hebrew *Shinar.* **11:9** Or *Babylon. Babel* sounds like a Hebrew term that means "confusion." **11:10** Or *the ancestor of;* also in 11:12, 14, 16, 18, 20, 22, 24. **11:11** Or *the birth of this ancestor of;* also in 11:13, 15, 17, 19, 21, 23, 25. **11:12-13** Greek version reads ¹²*When Arphaxad was 135 years old, he became the father of Cainan.* ¹³*After the birth of Cainan, Arphaxad lived another 430 years and had other sons and daughters, and then he died. When Cainan was 130 years old, he became the father of Shelah. After the birth of Shelah, Cainan lived another 330 years and had other sons and daughters, and then he died.* Compare Luke 3:35-36.

11:1-9 After the Flood, human civilization spread far and wide in fulfillment of God's purposes (9:1). Babel represented a vain attempt to avoid scattering. The tower was likely a ziggurat, a massive stepped tower built to support a staircase near a temple garden, likely intended to facilitate the descent of the gods to earth. Without divine instruction to build, the project represented a human attempt to dictate the terms of acceptable worship. The people's desire for fame and security apart from God prompted the Lord's response to confuse their building efforts.

GENESIS 11   ♦ 20

¹⁴When Shelah was 30 years old, he became the father of Eber. ¹⁵After the birth of Eber, Shelah lived another 403 years and had other sons and daughters.
¹⁶When Eber was 34 years old, he became the father of Peleg. ¹⁷After the birth of Peleg, Eber lived another 430 years and had other sons and daughters.
¹⁸When Peleg was 30 years old, he became the father of Reu. ¹⁹After the birth of Reu, Peleg lived another 209 years and had other sons and daughters.
²⁰When Reu was 32 years old, he became the father of Serug. ²¹After the birth of Serug, Reu lived another 207 years and had other sons and daughters.
²²When Serug was 30 years old, he became the father of Nahor. ²³After the birth of Nahor, Serug lived another 200 years and had other sons and daughters.
²⁴When Nahor was 29 years old, he became the father of Terah. ²⁵After the birth of Terah, Nahor lived another 119 years and had other sons and daughters.

Shalom IMAGE — MY STORY OF MY UNIQUE INFLUENCE

God's Call and Mine

SCRIPTURE CONNECTION: GENESIS 12:2-3

"What is my purpose?" I pleaded, scrambling down New Mexico's tallest mountain. A lightning storm above me, with no trees to protect me, I hurtled down the boulder field. For months, I'd asked God for my calling. Now, intensified by visions of a life cut short, I yelled it. Maybe you cry out for purpose too. As with Abram, God's calling comes:

- before we bless—Abram didn't earn God's blessing;
- to bless others—God empowered Abram to do good;
- to bless near and far—Abram gave life to family, nation, and ultimately, God's redemption plan.

Abram's calling fit within God's mission to reconcile his creation to himself, a mission God actively pursues throughout the Bible. God's purpose begins with God himself, not us; is empowered by him, not us; and comes through those he chooses, not by our choice alone.

As with Abram, God made his call clear for me, too. As I scuttled down, avoiding the lightning strikes, I sensed it. It came as though a whisper from God, "*I am your purpose.*"

"Ow," I yelped, as I caught a tree and hugged it, glad even for its rough bark that stopped my descent. Like the tree, this answer protected me from exposure to any lesser calling. My calling begins with, is empowered by, and is guided by God; no other source will do.

> Knowing my calling comes from God, not me, gives me confidence to press on.

IMAGINE

How might seeing God as your chief purpose guide you?

"In seminary, I learned to see the entire Bible reflecting God's mission to restore. Knowing my calling comes from God, not me, gives me confidence to live on purpose for a lifetime."

NAOMI CRAMER OVERTON, MBA, DIS, lives to realize beauty-filled visions that lift us to flourishing, with our families and beyond. Naomi has been CEO for Stonecroft and MOPS, director with Compassion International and World Vision, and General Editor for this Bible.

²⁶After Terah was 70 years old, he became the father of Abram, Nahor, and Haran.

The Family of Terah

²⁷This is the account of Terah's family. Terah was the father of Abram, Nahor, and Haran; and Haran was the father of Lot. ²⁸But Haran died in Ur of the Chaldeans, the land of his birth, while his father, Terah, was still living. ²⁹Meanwhile, Abram and Nahor both married. The name of Abram's wife was Sarai, and the name of Nahor's wife was Milcah. (Milcah and her sister Iscah were daughters of Nahor's brother Haran.) ³⁰But Sarai was unable to become pregnant and had no children.

³¹One day Terah took his son Abram, his daughter-in-law Sarai (his son Abram's wife), and his grandson Lot (his son Haran's child) and moved away from Ur of the Chaldeans. He was headed for the land of Canaan, but they stopped at Haran and settled there. ³²Terah lived for 205 years* and died while still in Haran.

The Call of Abram

12 The LORD had said to Abram, "Leave your native country, your relatives, and your father's family, and go to the land that I will show you. ²I will make you into a great nation. I will bless you and make you famous, and you will be a blessing to others. ³I will bless those who bless you and curse those who treat you with contempt. All the families on earth will be blessed through you."

⁴So Abram departed as the LORD had instructed, and Lot went with him. Abram was seventy-five years old when he left Haran. ⁵He took his wife, Sarai, his nephew Lot, and all his wealth—his livestock and all the people he had taken into his household at Haran—and headed for the land of Canaan. When they arrived in Canaan, ⁶Abram traveled through the land as far as Shechem. There he set up camp beside the oak of Moreh. At that time, the area was inhabited by Canaanites.

⁷Then the LORD appeared to Abram and said, "I will give this land to your descendants."* And Abram built an altar there and dedicated it to the LORD, who had appeared to him. ⁸After that, Abram traveled south and set up camp in the hill country, with Bethel to the west and Ai to the east. There he built another altar and dedicated it to the LORD, and he worshiped the LORD. ⁹Then Abram continued traveling south by stages toward the Negev.

Abram and Sarai in Egypt

¹⁰At that time a severe famine struck the land of Canaan, forcing Abram to go down to Egypt, where he lived as a foreigner. ¹¹As he was approaching the border of Egypt, Abram said to his wife, Sarai, "Look, you are a very beautiful woman. ¹²When the Egyptians see you, they will say, 'This is his wife. Let's kill him; then we can have her!' ¹³So please tell them you are my sister. Then they will spare my life and treat me well because of their interest in you."

¹⁴And sure enough, when Abram arrived in Egypt, everyone noticed Sarai's beauty. ¹⁵When the palace officials saw her, they sang her praises to Pharaoh, their king, and Sarai was taken into his palace. ¹⁶Then Pharaoh gave Abram many gifts because of her—sheep, goats, cattle, male and female donkeys, male and female servants, and camels.

¹⁷But the LORD sent terrible plagues upon Pharaoh and his household because of Sarai, Abram's wife. ¹⁸So Pharaoh summoned Abram and accused him sharply. "What have you done to me?" he demanded. "Why didn't you tell me she was your wife? ¹⁹Why did you say, 'She is my sister,' and allow me to take her as my wife? Now then, here is your wife. Take her and get out of here!" ²⁰Pharaoh ordered some of his men to escort them, and he sent Abram out of the country, along with his wife and all his possessions.

Abram and Lot Separate

13 So Abram left Egypt and traveled north into the Negev, along with his wife and Lot and all that they owned. ²(Abram was very rich in livestock, silver, and gold.) ³From the Negev, they continued traveling by stages toward Bethel, and they pitched their tents between Bethel and Ai, where they had camped before. ⁴This was the same place where

---

11:32 Some ancient versions read *145 years;* compare 11:26 and 12:4. **12:7** Hebrew *seed.*

11:30 Sarai, Rebekah, and Rachel all experienced infertility (25:21; 29:31). Sarai's infertility introduced a paradox between her experience and God's promise of many descendants (12:2). Frequently in the Old Testament, God demonstrated his sovereignty by miraculously giving children to women who had previously been unable to have children (Judges 13:3; 1 Samuel 1:2; 2:5; see also Psalm 113:9; Isaiah 54:1).

12:1-3 Before Abram could experience God's blessing, he had to step out in obedience by setting out on a journey of unknown length and destination. The exclusivity of God's covenant with Abram may seem troubling at first, but God blessed his family so that they could bless all the other families on earth. Abram's blessing was God's solution for the brokenness and violence of the post-Flood world (see Psalm 67).

12:10-20 Abram deceived Pharaoh regarding his wife's identity rather than trusting God's protection, putting both her and Pharaoh's household at risk (see 20:1-18; 26:1-11). Sarai was in fact his half sister (20:12), but Abram's deception resulted in their expulsion from Egypt.

13:1-18 God had asked Abram to leave his father's family (12:1), but he took his nephew Lot with him. Lot's company became problematic when the two households grew so large that the land could not support them both. Abram gave Lot first choice of land because he believed in God's promise. After they parted ways, God reaffirmed his plan to bless Abram (13:14-17).

GENESIS 14   ◆ 22

Insight: SARAI AND ABRAM'S TRAVELS

Abram, Sarai, their extended family, and their servants walked from Ur to Haran (600 miles), on to Canaan (400 miles), then down to Egypt (325 miles), and back to Canaan again. How many steps do you walk a day? Women worldwide walk 5,000 steps daily. If Sarai had done that, it would have taken her 660 days to complete this route.

5,000 steps per day • 660 days

Abram had built the altar, and there he worshiped the LORD again.

⁵Lot, who was traveling with Abram, had also become very wealthy with flocks of sheep and goats, herds of cattle, and many tents. ⁶But the land could not support both Abram and Lot with all their flocks and herds living so close together. ⁷So disputes broke out between the herdsmen of Abram and Lot. (At that time Canaanites and Perizzites were also living in the land.)

⁸Finally Abram said to Lot, "Let's not allow this conflict to come between us or our herdsmen. After all, we are close relatives! ⁹The whole countryside is open to you. Take your choice of any section of the land you want, and we will separate. If you want the land to the left, then I'll take the land on the right. If you prefer the land on the right, then I'll go to the left."

¹⁰Lot took a long look at the fertile plains of the Jordan Valley in the direction of Zoar. The whole area was well watered everywhere, like the garden of the LORD or the beautiful land of Egypt. (This was before the LORD destroyed Sodom and Gomorrah.) ¹¹Lot chose for himself the whole Jordan Valley to the east of them. He went there with his flocks and servants and parted company with his uncle Abram. ¹²So Abram settled in the land of Canaan, and Lot moved his tents to a place near Sodom and settled among the cities of the plain. ¹³But the people of this area were extremely wicked and constantly sinned against the LORD.

¹⁴After Lot had gone, the LORD said to Abram, "Look as far as you can see in every direction—north and south, east and west. ¹⁵I am giving all this land, as far as you can see, to you and your descendants* as a permanent possession. ¹⁶And I will give you so many descendants that, like the dust of the earth, they cannot be counted! ¹⁷Go and walk through the land in every direction, for I am giving it to you."

¹⁸So Abram moved his camp to Hebron and settled near the oak grove belonging to Mamre. There he built another altar to the LORD.

Abram Rescues Lot

14 About this time war broke out in the region. King Amraphel of Babylonia,* King Arioch of Ellasar, King Kedorlaomer of Elam, and King Tidal of Goiim ²fought against King Bera of Sodom, King Birsha of Gomorrah, King Shinab of Admah, King Shemeber of Zeboiim, and the king of Bela (also called Zoar).

³This second group of kings joined forces in Siddim Valley (that is, the valley of the Dead Sea*). ⁴For twelve years they had been subject to King Kedorlaomer, but in the thirteenth year they rebelled against him.

⁵One year later Kedorlaomer and his allies arrived and defeated the Rephaites at Ashteroth-karnaim, the Zuzites at Ham, the Emites at Shaveh-kiriathaim, ⁶and the Horites at Mount Seir, as far as El-paran at the edge of the wilderness. ⁷Then they turned back and came to En-mishpat (now called Kadesh) and conquered all the territory of the Amalekites, and also the Amorites living in Hazazon-tamar.

⁸Then the rebel kings of Sodom, Gomorrah, Admah, Zeboiim, and Bela (also called Zoar) prepared for battle in the valley of the Dead Sea.* ⁹They fought

13:15 Hebrew *seed;* also in 13:16. 14:1 Hebrew *Shinar;* also in 14:9. 14:3 Hebrew *Salt Sea.* 14:8 Hebrew *Siddim Valley* (see 14:3); also in 14:10.

against King Kedorlaomer of Elam, King Tidal of Goiim, King Amraphel of Babylonia, and King Arioch of Ellasar—four kings against five. ¹⁰As it happened, the valley of the Dead Sea was filled with tar pits. And as the army of the kings of Sodom and Gomorrah fled, some fell into the tar pits, while the rest escaped into the mountains. ¹¹The victorious invaders then plundered Sodom and Gomorrah and headed for home, taking with them all the spoils of war and the food supplies. ¹²They also captured Lot—Abram's nephew who lived in Sodom—and carried off everything he owned.

¹³But one of Lot's men escaped and reported everything to Abram the Hebrew, who was living near the oak grove belonging to Mamre the Amorite. Mamre and his relatives, Eshcol and Aner, were Abram's allies.

¹⁴When Abram heard that his nephew Lot had been captured, he mobilized the 318 trained men who had been born into his household. Then he pursued Kedorlaomer's army until he caught up with them at Dan. ¹⁵There he divided his men and attacked during the night. Kedorlaomer's army fled, but Abram chased them as far as Hobah, north of Damascus. ¹⁶Abram recovered all the goods that had been taken, and he brought back his nephew Lot with his possessions and all the women and other captives.

Melchizedek Blesses Abram

¹⁷After Abram returned from his victory over Kedorlaomer and all his allies, the king of Sodom went out to meet him in the valley of Shaveh (that is, the King's Valley).

¹⁸And Melchizedek, the king of Salem and a priest of God Most High,* brought Abram some bread and wine. ¹⁹Melchizedek blessed Abram with this blessing:

> "Blessed be Abram by God Most High,
>   Creator of heaven and earth.
> ²⁰ And blessed be God Most High,
>   who has defeated your enemies for you."

Then Abram gave Melchizedek a tenth of all the goods he had recovered.

²¹The king of Sodom said to Abram, "Give back my

14:18 Hebrew *El-Elyon;* also in 14:19, 20, 22.

14:11-16 Lot's unfortunate choice to live near Sodom resulted in trouble for himself and for Abram. Lot had chosen land that looked fruitful, but the violent and corrupt residents would ruin him (19:1-38).

14:18-20 The story of Melchizedek portrays the initial fulfillment of 12:1-3, where God declared that nations who blessed Abram would be blessed. Abram shared with Melchizedek the spoils of his victory. Melchizedek was a non-Israelite priest who feared God, pointing to the future expansion of the Kingdom of God among non-Israelites. The author of Hebrews saw justification for Christ's priesthood here. Like Melchizedek, Jesus was not from Israel's priestly line (see Hebrews 7).

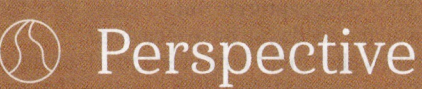

Perspective

God's ideal or our real?

SCRIPTURE CONNECTION: GENESIS 14:11-16

Is ancient Hebrew culture an ideal to emulate? Or is it incidental to the message?

In some cases, God gives instructions about how to live based on universal truths. For example, every human being is made in the image of God, so every human life is precious and worth protecting (9:6). But other times the Bible describes practices that do not easily transfer to our context today.

Abraham and Sarah lived as semi-nomadic tent dwellers who kept herds of animals. And in that day, the men would often fight battles and take women as plunder. But God is not asking us to move into tents, keep sheep, and carry swords. Does that mean these stories have nothing to teach us?

Ancient Hebrew culture does not provide a template for us to replicate. We are not called to re-create culture-specific elements in our own lives, and many times the characters are not models for emulation. But we can still learn a great deal about God through these stories, including the ways he shows himself to be faithful, even to flawed people—just like us.

VIEWPOINTS

HERS: *Sarah might shudder to think women would read her stories and think of her as a role model. She had her fair share of failures and likely felt she was often just muddling through.*

MINE: *"Seeing how God communicated to ancient cultures inspires me. God works in and through flawed people in less-than-ideal societies. That means he can work through me, too, even though I have a long way to go!"*

YOURS: *Can you think of aspects of our culture that are less than ideal? And can you see ways that God works in and through us anyway?*

CARMEN JOY IMES, PhD, is an author, speaker, blogger, YouTuber, and serves as associate professor of Old Testament at Biola University in California.

people who were captured. But you may keep for yourself all the goods you have recovered."

[22] Abram replied to the king of Sodom, "I solemnly swear to the LORD, God Most High, Creator of heaven and earth, [23] that I will not take so much as a single thread or sandal thong from what belongs to you. Otherwise you might say, 'I am the one who made Abram rich.' [24] I will accept only what my young warriors have already eaten, and I request that you give a fair share of the goods to my allies—Aner, Eshcol, and Mamre."

The LORD's Covenant Promise to Abram

15 Some time later, the LORD spoke to Abram in a vision and said to him, "Do not be afraid, Abram, for I will protect you, and your reward will be great."

[2] But Abram replied, "O Sovereign LORD, what good are all your blessings when I don't even have a son? Since you've given me no children, Eliezer of Damascus, a servant in my household, will inherit all my wealth. [3] You have given me no descendants of my own, so one of my servants will be my heir."

[4] Then the LORD said to him, "No, your servant will not be your heir, for you will have a son of your own who will be your heir." [5] Then the LORD took Abram outside and said to him, "Look up into the sky and count the stars if you can. That's how many descendants you will have!"

[6] And Abram believed the LORD, and the LORD counted him as righteous because of his faith.

[7] Then the LORD told him, "I am the LORD who brought you out of Ur of the Chaldeans to give you this land as your possession."

[8] But Abram replied, "O Sovereign LORD, how can I be sure that I will actually possess it?"

[9] The LORD told him, "Bring me a three-year-old heifer, a three-year-old female goat, a three-year-old ram, a turtledove, and a young pigeon." [10] So Abram presented all these to him and killed them. Then he cut each animal down the middle and laid the halves side by side; he did not, however, cut the birds in half. [11] Some vultures swooped down to eat the carcasses, but Abram chased them away.

[12] As the sun was going down, Abram fell into a deep sleep, and a terrifying darkness came down over him. [13] Then the LORD said to Abram, "You can be sure that your descendants will be strangers in a foreign land, where they will be oppressed as slaves for 400 years. [14] But I will punish the nation that enslaves them, and in the end they will come away with great wealth. [15] (As for you, you will die in peace and be buried at a ripe old age.) [16] After four generations your descendants will return here to this land, for the sins of the Amorites do not yet warrant their destruction."

[17] After the sun went down and darkness fell, Abram saw a smoking firepot and a flaming torch pass between the halves of the carcasses. [18] So the LORD made a covenant with Abram that day and said, "I have given this land to your descendants, all the way from the border of Egypt* to the great Euphrates River—[19] the land now occupied by the Kenites, Kenizzites, Kadmonites, [20] Hittites, Perizzites, Rephaites, [21] Amorites, Canaanites, Girgashites, and Jebusites."

The Birth of Ishmael

16 Now Sarai, Abram's wife, had not been able to bear children for him. But she had an Egyptian servant named Hagar. [2] So Sarai said to Abram, "The LORD has prevented me from having children. Go and sleep with my servant. Perhaps I can have children through her." And Abram agreed with Sarai's proposal. [3] So Sarai, Abram's wife, took Hagar the Egyptian servant and gave her to Abram as a wife. (This happened ten years after Abram had settled in the land of Canaan.)

[4] So Abram had sexual relations with Hagar, and she became pregnant. But when Hagar knew she was pregnant, she began to treat her mistress, Sarai, with contempt. [5] Then Sarai said to Abram, "This is all your fault! I put my servant into your arms, but now that she's pregnant she treats me with contempt. The LORD will show who's wrong—you or me!"

[6] Abram replied, "Look, she is your servant, so deal with her as you see fit." Then Sarai treated Hagar so harshly that she finally ran away.

15:18 Hebrew *the river of Egypt*, referring either to an eastern branch of the Nile River or to the Brook of Egypt in the Sinai (see Num 34:5).

15:1-6 Abram and Sarai's infertility was a source of consternation because it cast doubt on God's promise of many descendants. Abram freely expressed his doubts to God, and God reaffirmed the promise.

15:7-21 With a solemn ceremony, God made a binding covenant with Abram that guaranteed the fulfillment of his promises. Normally, in such a ceremony both parties would walk between the cut animals to symbolize the severity of the oath, staking their lives on their mutual commitment. However, Abram merely observed as a torch and firepot passed through the pieces, indicating God's unilateral commitment. The flame and smoke may have anticipated the pillars of fire and cloud that would lead Israel out of Egypt (Exodus 13:21-22).

16:1-3 Infertility is always painful, but in the case of Abram and Sarai, the lack of a child presented a theological crisis as God had promised Abram a son (15:1-6). Sarai resorted to the customary Mesopotamian strategy for dealing with childlessness by offering her servant to her husband as a surrogate. The child would be Abram's official heir.

16:4-6 After Hagar conceived, tension arose with Sarai. Hagar's air of superiority provoked mistreatment from Sarai. Ironically, Sarai's mistreatment of her Egyptian servant anticipated the Egyptians' mistreatment of Sarai's descendants (Exodus 1:11-12).

Hagar

IDENTITY — Honored by Names

"What's in a name? That which we call a rose by any other name would smell as sweet." Shakespeare penned these words spoken by Juliet, pondering the significance of names. For Hagar, being called by name and being allowed to name bring her honor.

Sarai was unable to get pregnant, despite God's promise, so she took matters into her own hands and arranged for Hagar, an enslaved Egyptian woman, to sleep with Abram. Hagar conceived, and her relationship with Sarai turned awful. Hagar was treated so harshly by Sarai that she decided to run away.

God went looking for Hagar and called her by name (16:8). Throughout the story, Abram and Sarai had never called Hagar by her name. But God knew her and her situation intimately. And they had a one-on-one conversation. Hagar, a Gentile who was considered property, enjoyed a powerful and tender exchange with the God of the universe.

When they had finished, Hagar gave God a name (16:13). She is the only one in Scripture to have this honor. She called him El-roi, which translates to "the God who sees me."

Hagar was seen and known by God and was allowed to know God right back. Through Hagar's story, God showed he values and honors women, even when others might not.

> When I feel invisible, I find hope in El-roi, the God who sees me and knows my name.

HAGAR'S STORY IS TOLD IN GENESIS 16; 21; SHE IS ALSO MENTIONED IN GALATIANS 4:21-31.

IDENTIFY

Have you ever felt overlooked or invisible?

What was that like?

Have you experienced God looking and calling for you?

What happened and how did you respond?

"When I feel invisible or overlooked, I find hope in El-roi, the God who sees me and knows my name and circumstances. He is near to you and me as we look to him."

VIVIAN MABUNI is a national speaker, author of *Open Hands, Willing Heart*, and podcast host of *Someday Is Here* for AAPI Christians, with over thirty years of ministry experience.

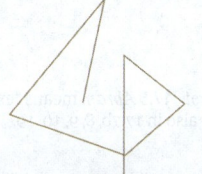

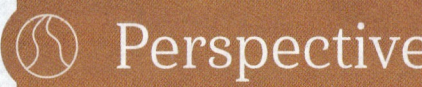

Perspective

Are concubines God's plan?

SCRIPTURE CONNECTION: GENESIS 16:1-10

Today, when we read about concubines, feelings of confusion or even disgust might tempt us to skip over these Scriptures. But each story of a marginalized woman in the Bible is another reminder that things are not the way they are supposed to be. No woman should be owned by someone else.

In ancient culture, concubines helped landowners build their households by increasing their offspring. The Old Testament doesn't explicitly condemn polygamy, but it repeatedly demonstrates its perils.

While some societies and individuals value women only as property, God elevates women to image-bearing status, marked by his love and reflecting his glory. Amid a worldly system that oppresses, God is at work to redeem, and his people can be a part of that redemption work.

VIEWPOINTS

HERS: *How do we see God care for Hagar, who was marginalized in this way?*

MINE: *"How can I trust that God sees me in circumstances where I am not valued?"*

YOURS: *When you feel unseen or devalued, how can you trust God to redeem those parts of your life?*

KAT ARMSTRONG, MA, is a Bible teacher, preacher, coach, and ministry leader. She cofounded the Polished Network and authored *No More Holding Back*, *The In-Between Place*, and the Storyline Bible Studies series.

⁷The angel of the LORD found Hagar beside a spring of water in the wilderness, along the road to Shur. ⁸The angel said to her, "Hagar, Sarai's servant, where have you come from, and where are you going?"

"I'm running away from my mistress, Sarai," she replied.

⁹The angel of the LORD said to her, "Return to your mistress, and submit to her authority." ¹⁰Then he added, "I will give you more descendants than you can count."

¹¹And the angel also said, "You are now pregnant and will give birth to a son. You are to name him Ishmael (which means 'God hears'), for the LORD has heard your cry of distress. ¹²This son of yours will be a wild man, as untamed as a wild donkey! He will raise his fist against everyone, and everyone will be against him. Yes, he will live in open hostility against all his relatives."

¹³Thereafter, Hagar used another name to refer to the LORD, who had spoken to her. She said, "You are the God who sees me."* She also said, "Have I truly seen the One who sees me?" ¹⁴So that well was named Beer-lahai-roi (which means "well of the Living One who sees me"). It can still be found between Kadesh and Bered.

¹⁵So Hagar gave Abram a son, and Abram named him Ishmael. ¹⁶Abram was eighty-six years old when Ishmael was born.

Abram Is Named Abraham

17 When Abram was ninety-nine years old, the LORD appeared to him and said, "I am El-Shaddai—'God Almighty.' Serve me faithfully and live a blameless life. ²I will make a covenant with you, by which I will guarantee to give you countless descendants."

³At this, Abram fell face down on the ground. Then God said to him, ⁴"This is my covenant with you: I will make you the father of a multitude of nations! ⁵What's more, I am changing your name. It will no longer be Abram. Instead, you will be called Abraham,* for you will be the father of many nations. ⁶I will make you extremely fruitful. Your descendants will become many nations, and kings will be among them!

⁷"I will confirm my covenant with you and your descendants* after you, from generation to generation. This is the everlasting covenant: I will always be your God and the God of your descendants after you. ⁸And I will give the entire land of Canaan, where you now live as a foreigner, to you and your descendants. It will be their possession forever, and I will be their God."

16:13 Hebrew *El-roi.* 17:5 *Abram* means "exalted father"; *Abraham* sounds like a Hebrew term that means "father of many." 17:7 Hebrew *seed;* also in 17:7b, 8, 9, 10, 19.

16:7-12 Hagar's distress did not go unnoticed. Even though her son would not be heir of God's covenant promises to Abram, God gave Ishmael promises of his own. God's instruction for Hagar to return to Sarai was not a universal call for submission to abuse. Later, God would allow Hagar to leave (21:8-21).

16:13 Hagar was the first person in the Bible to give God a name: "the God who sees me." Although she lacked power, wealth, and status in her household, she was not invisible to God. And although her son was not the heir of God's covenant promise, she was not outside God's care. God's promise to bless all nations through Abram's family would include the nations that descended from Ishmael.

The Mark of the Covenant

⁹Then God said to Abraham, "Your responsibility is to obey the terms of the covenant. You and all your descendants have this continual responsibility. ¹⁰This is the covenant that you and your descendants must keep: Each male among you must be circumcised. ¹¹You must cut off the flesh of your foreskin as a sign of the covenant between me and you. ¹²From generation to generation, every male child must be circumcised on the eighth day after his birth. This applies not only to members of your family but also to the servants born in your household and the foreign-born servants whom you have purchased. ¹³All must be circumcised. Your bodies will bear the mark of my everlasting covenant. ¹⁴Any male who fails to be circumcised will be cut off from the covenant family for breaking the covenant."

Sarai Is Named Sarah

¹⁵Then God said to Abraham, "Regarding Sarai, your wife—her name will no longer be Sarai. From now on her name will be Sarah.* ¹⁶And I will bless her and give you a son from her! Yes, I will bless her richly, and she will become the mother of many nations. Kings of nations will be among her descendants."

¹⁷Then Abraham bowed down to the ground, but he laughed to himself in disbelief. "How could I become a father at the age of 100?" he thought. "And how can Sarah have a baby when she is ninety years old?" ¹⁸So Abraham said to God, "May Ishmael live under your special blessing!"

¹⁹But God replied, "No—Sarah, your wife, will give birth to a son for you. You will name him Isaac,* and I will confirm my covenant with him and his descendants as an everlasting covenant. ²⁰As for Ishmael, I will bless him also, just as you have asked. I will make him extremely fruitful and multiply his descendants. He will become the father of twelve princes, and I will make him a great nation. ²¹But my covenant will be confirmed with Isaac, who will be born to you and Sarah about this time next year." ²²When God had finished speaking, he left Abraham.

²³On that very day Abraham took his son, Ishmael, and every male in his household, including those born there and those he had bought. Then he circumcised them, cutting off their foreskins, just as God had told him. ²⁴Abraham was ninety-nine years old when he was circumcised, ²⁵and Ishmael, his son, was thirteen. ²⁶Both Abraham and his son, Ishmael, were circumcised on that same day, ²⁷along with all the other men and boys of the household, whether they were born there or bought as servants. All were circumcised with him.

A Son Is Promised to Sarah

18 The LORD appeared again to Abraham near the oak grove belonging to Mamre. One day Abraham was sitting at the entrance to his tent during the hottest part of the day. ²He looked up and noticed three men standing nearby. When he saw them, he ran to meet them and welcomed them, bowing low to the ground.

³"My lord," he said, "if it pleases you, stop here for a while. ⁴Rest in the shade of this tree while water is brought to wash your feet. ⁵And since you've honored your servant with this visit, let me prepare some food to refresh you before you continue on your journey."

"All right," they said. "Do as you have said."

⁶So Abraham ran back to the tent and said to Sarah, "Hurry! Get three large measures* of your best flour, knead it into dough, and bake some bread." ⁷Then Abraham ran out to the herd and chose a tender calf and gave it to his servant, who quickly prepared it. ⁸When the food was ready, Abraham took some yogurt and milk and the roasted meat, and he served it to the men. As they ate, Abraham waited on them in the shade of the trees.

⁹"Where is Sarah, your wife?" the visitors asked.

"She's inside the tent," Abraham replied.

¹⁰Then one of them said, "I will return to you about

17:15 *Sarai* and *Sarah* both mean "princess"; the change in spelling may reflect the difference in dialect between Ur and Canaan. **17:19** *Isaac* means "he laughs." **18:6** Hebrew *3 seahs*, about half a bushel or 22 liters.

17:10-14 Male circumcision was the sign of membership in the covenant community. However, women were equally part of the covenant. They were the daughters, wives, and mothers of circumcised men and participated under their membership. The prohibition of intermarriage with uncircumcised peoples was not motivated by prejudice but was a means of protecting covenant continuity in Abraham's family. Foreigners who lived among the Israelites were also circumcised to show that they shared in the covenant.

17:15-16 God renamed Abram (Abraham) and Sarai (Sarah) to underscore his determination to bless their descendants, despite their unbelief and their highly dysfunctional family (see 16:1-16). Sarai and Sarah both mean "princess"; the change in spelling may reflect the difference in dialect between Ur and Canaan. The new name, fitting for one who would be the mother of kings, was a milestone in Sarah's calling and would serve as a constant reminder to her of God's promise.

18:5-8 Hospitality was a cardinal virtue in ancient culture. In an age before restaurants and grocery stores, travelers depended heavily upon the hospitality of people along their route. As the manager of a large household, Abraham coordinated the preparation of bread, meat, yogurt, and milk, and personally served his distinguished guests.

18:9-15 God had already promised that Sarah would bear a son (see 17:15-19). In that account, the narrator referred to God using his divine title, the Hebrew word *Elohim* ("God" in English translations). Here, Abraham experienced a physical visitation from a speaker who identified God by his covenant name, Yahweh ("LORD" in our English translations). Sarah's response to the promise mattered. Her incredulity prompted a poignant question: "Is anything too hard for the LORD?" (18:14).

this time next year, and your wife, Sarah, will have a son!"

Sarah was listening to this conversation from the tent. ¹¹Abraham and Sarah were both very old by this time, and Sarah was long past the age of having children. ¹²So she laughed silently to herself and said, "How could a worn-out woman like me enjoy such pleasure, especially when my master—my husband—is also so old?"

¹³Then the Lord said to Abraham, "Why did Sarah laugh? Why did she say, 'Can an old woman like me have a baby?' ¹⁴Is anything too hard for the Lord? I will return about this time next year, and Sarah will have a son."

¹⁵Sarah was afraid, so she denied it, saying, "I didn't laugh."

But the Lord said, "No, you did laugh."

Abraham Intercedes for Sodom

¹⁶Then the men got up from their meal and looked out toward Sodom. As they left, Abraham went with them to send them on their way.

¹⁷"Should I hide my plan from Abraham?" the Lord asked. ¹⁸"For Abraham will certainly become a great and mighty nation, and all the nations of the earth will be blessed through him. ¹⁹I have singled him out so that he will direct his sons and their families to keep the way of the Lord by doing what is right and just. Then I will do for Abraham all that I have promised."

²⁰So the Lord told Abraham, "I have heard a great outcry from Sodom and Gomorrah, because their sin is so flagrant. ²¹I am going down to see if their actions are as wicked as I have heard. If not, I want to know."

²²The other men turned and headed toward Sodom, but the Lord remained with Abraham. ²³Abraham approached him and said, "Will you sweep away both the righteous and the wicked? ²⁴Suppose you find fifty righteous people living there in the city—will you still sweep it away and not spare it for their sakes? ²⁵Surely you wouldn't do such a thing, destroying the righteous along with the wicked. Why, you would be treating the righteous and the wicked exactly the same! Surely you wouldn't do that! Should not the Judge of all the earth do what is right?"

²⁶And the Lord replied, "If I find fifty righteous people in Sodom, I will spare the entire city for their sake."

²⁷Then Abraham spoke again. "Since I have begun, let me speak further to my Lord, even though I am but dust and ashes. ²⁸Suppose there are only forty-five righteous people rather than fifty? Will you destroy the whole city for lack of five?"

And the Lord said, "I will not destroy it if I find forty-five righteous people there."

²⁹Then Abraham pressed his request further. "Suppose there are only forty?"

And the Lord replied, "I will not destroy it for the sake of the forty."

³⁰"Please don't be angry, my Lord," Abraham pleaded. "Let me speak—suppose only thirty righteous people are found?"

And the Lord replied, "I will not destroy it if I find thirty."

³¹Then Abraham said, "Since I have dared to speak to the Lord, let me continue—suppose there are only twenty?"

And the Lord replied, "Then I will not destroy it for the sake of the twenty."

³²Finally, Abraham said, "Lord, please don't be angry with me if I speak one more time. Suppose only ten are found there?"

And the Lord replied, "Then I will not destroy it for the sake of the ten."

³³When the Lord had finished his conversation with Abraham, he went on his way, and Abraham returned to his tent.

Sodom and Gomorrah Destroyed

19 That evening the two angels came to the entrance of the city of Sodom. Lot was sitting there, and when he saw them, he stood up to meet them. Then he welcomed them and bowed with his face to the ground. ²"My lords," he said, "come to my home to wash your feet, and be my guests for the night. You may then get up early in the morning and be on your way again."

"Oh no," they replied. "We'll just spend the night out here in the city square."

³But Lot insisted, so at last they went home with him. Lot prepared a feast for them, complete with fresh bread made without yeast, and they ate. ⁴But before they retired for the night, all the men of Sodom, young and old, came from all over the city and surrounded the house. ⁵They shouted to Lot, "Where are the men who came to spend the night with you? Bring them out to us so we can have sex with them!"

⁶So Lot stepped outside to talk to them, shutting the door behind him. ⁷"Please, my brothers," he begged, "don't do such a wicked thing. ⁸Look, I have two virgin daughters. Let me bring them out to you, and you can do with them as you wish. But please, leave these men alone, for they are my guests and are under my protection."

19:6-8 This story of Lot is deeply troubling. He offered his daughters to be raped, prioritizing the protection of his out-of-town guests. And his future sons-in-law were among those rioting outside (19:14)! Lot's willingness for his daughters to marry men who apparently were among the violent sex offenders, his disregard for his daughters' safety, and his hesitation to leave such a corrupt city (19:16) all demonstrate how depraved he had become. He may have been morally superior to his neighbors (2 Peter 2:7-8), but not by much. God's decision to destroy the city was thoroughly justified.

⁹"Stand back!" they shouted. "This fellow came to town as an outsider, and now he's acting like our judge! We'll treat you far worse than those other men!" And they lunged toward Lot to break down the door. ¹⁰But the two angels* reached out, pulled Lot into the house, and bolted the door. ¹¹Then they blinded all the men, young and old, who were at the door of the house, so they gave up trying to get inside.

¹²Meanwhile, the angels questioned Lot. "Do you have any other relatives here in the city?" they asked. "Get them out of this place—your sons-in-law, sons, daughters, or anyone else. ¹³For we are about to destroy this city completely. The outcry against this place is so great it has reached the LORD, and he has sent us to destroy it."

¹⁴So Lot rushed out to tell his daughters' fiancés, "Quick, get out of the city! The LORD is about to destroy it." But the young men thought he was only joking.

¹⁵At dawn the next morning the angels became insistent. "Hurry," they said to Lot. "Take your wife and your two daughters who are here. Get out right now, or you will be swept away in the destruction of the city!"

¹⁶When Lot still hesitated, the angels seized his hand and the hands of his wife and two daughters and rushed them to safety outside the city, for the LORD was merciful. ¹⁷When they were safely out of the city, one of the angels ordered, "Run for your lives! And don't look back or stop anywhere in the valley! Escape to the mountains, or you will be swept away!"

¹⁸"Oh no, my lord!" Lot begged. ¹⁹"You have been so gracious to me and saved my life, and you have shown such great kindness. But I cannot go to the mountains. Disaster would catch up to me there, and I would soon die. ²⁰See, there is a small village nearby. Please let me go there instead; don't you see how small it is? Then my life will be saved."

²¹"All right," the angel said, "I will grant your request. I will not destroy the little village. ²²But hurry! Escape to it, for I can do nothing until you arrive there." (This explains why that village was known as Zoar, which means "little place.")

²³Lot reached the village just as the sun was rising over the horizon. ²⁴Then the LORD rained down fire and burning sulfur from the sky on Sodom and Gomorrah. ²⁵He utterly destroyed them, along with the other cities and villages of the plain, wiping out all the people and every bit of vegetation. ²⁶But Lot's wife looked back as she was following behind him, and she turned into a pillar of salt.

19:10 Hebrew *men;* also in 19:12, 16.

19:26 Lot's wife did not simply glance over her shoulder. The verb translated "looked" here indicates prolonged, intense gazing—toward the world she loved (compare 15:5). Lot's wife was too attached to Sodom to accept God's mercy, so she was included in the judgment as she lingered in the valley.

Perspective

How could Lot do that?

SCRIPTURE CONNECTION: GENESIS 19:1-8

Some of us can instantly relate to how Lot's daughters surely felt about Lot's offer to the men of Sodom: disposable. We also have been compromised by people we trusted to love and protect us.

But God reaches for us in our peril. Lot, in his cowardice, is deemed by God as worthy to save. His daughters, reduced to sexual commodities, are deemed worthy to save. This makes us curious about God's love.

Jesus knows the feeling of being forsaken. And he showed that opposing realities can simultaneously be true: We can suffer intense rejection, deprivation, abandonment, devaluing, and crushing shame, while at the same time, we can celebrate a heavenly Father who loves us so unselfishly that he gave himself rather than giving us.

Lot offered to sacrifice his own daughters, perhaps to save himself. God sacrifices himself to save us.

VIEWPOINTS

HERS: *Based on their experiences with their earthly father, what might Lot's daughters have believed about themselves and God?*

MINE: *"As a young girl under my dad's protection, I knew I was safe. Loved. Treasured. Absent his protection, my world took a different spin. A godly father carries for us daughters a representation of God and a message of our worth."*

YOURS: *What ideas have you formed about yourself or of God based on experiences with your earthly father? In what ways might you challenge your negative beliefs as you reflect on your heavenly Father?*

MISTY ARTERBURN is an author and speaker, contributing to Bible projects, devotionals, and recovery materials for over twenty years. Wife and mom to five, Misty is the founder of Recovery Girls and the general editor of *The One Year Bible for Women.*

²⁷Abraham got up early that morning and hurried out to the place where he had stood in the LORD's presence. ²⁸He looked out across the plain toward Sodom and Gomorrah and watched as columns of smoke rose from the cities like smoke from a furnace.

²⁹But God had listened to Abraham's request and kept Lot safe, removing him from the disaster that engulfed the cities on the plain.

Lot and His Daughters

³⁰Afterward Lot left Zoar because he was afraid of the people there, and he went to live in a cave in the mountains with his two daughters. ³¹One day the older daughter said to her sister, "There are no men left anywhere in this entire area, so we can't get married like everyone else. And our father will soon be too old to have children. ³²Come, let's get him drunk with wine, and then we will have sex with him. That way we will preserve our family line through our father."

³³So that night they got him drunk with wine, and the older daughter went in and had intercourse with her father. He was unaware of her lying down or getting up again.

³⁴The next morning the older daughter said to her younger sister, "I had sex with our father last night. Let's get him drunk with wine again tonight, and you go in and have sex with him. That way we will preserve our family line through our father." ³⁵So that night they got him drunk with wine again, and the younger daughter went in and had intercourse with him. As before, he was unaware of her lying down or getting up again.

³⁶As a result, both of Lot's daughters became pregnant by their own father. ³⁷When the older daughter gave birth to a son, she named him Moab.* He became the ancestor of the nation now known as the Moabites. ³⁸When the younger daughter gave birth to a son, she named him Ben-ammi.* He became the ancestor of the nation now known as the Ammonites.

Abraham Deceives Abimelech

20 Abraham moved south to the Negev and lived for a while between Kadesh and Shur, and then he moved on to Gerar. While living there as a foreigner, ²Abraham introduced his wife, Sarah, by saying, "She is my sister." So King Abimelech of Gerar sent for Sarah and had her brought to him at his palace.

³But that night God came to Abimelech in a dream and told him, "You are a dead man, for that woman you have taken is already married!"

⁴But Abimelech had not slept with her yet, so he said, "Lord, will you destroy an innocent nation? ⁵Didn't Abraham tell me, 'She is my sister'? And she herself said, 'Yes, he is my brother.' I acted in complete innocence! My hands are clean."

⁶In the dream God responded, "Yes, I know you are innocent. That's why I kept you from sinning against me, and why I did not let you touch her. ⁷Now return the woman to her husband, and he will pray for you, for he is a prophet. Then you will live. But if you don't return her to him, you can be sure that you and all your people will die."

⁸Abimelech got up early the next morning and quickly called all his servants together. When he told them what had happened, his men were terrified. ⁹Then Abimelech called for Abraham. "What have you done to us?" he demanded. "What crime have I committed that deserves treatment like this, making me and my kingdom guilty of this great sin? No one should ever do what you have done! ¹⁰Whatever possessed you to do such a thing?"

¹¹Abraham replied, "I thought, 'This is a godless place. They will want my wife and will kill me to get her.' ¹²And she really is my sister, for we both have the same father, but different mothers. And I married her. ¹³When God called me to leave my father's home and to travel from place to place, I told her, 'Do me a favor. Wherever we go, tell the people that I am your brother.'"

¹⁴Then Abimelech took some of his sheep and goats, cattle, and male and female servants, and he presented them to Abraham. He also returned his wife, Sarah, to him. ¹⁵Then Abimelech said, "Look over my land and choose any place where you would like to live." ¹⁶And he said to Sarah, "Look, I am giving your 'brother' 1,000 pieces of silver* in the presence of all these witnesses. This is to compensate you for any wrong I may have done to you. This will settle any claim against me, and your reputation is cleared."

¹⁷Then Abraham prayed to God, and God healed Abimelech, his wife, and his female servants, so they

---

19:37 *Moab* sounds like a Hebrew term that means "from father." **19:38** *Ben-ammi* means "son of my kinsman." **20:16** Hebrew *1,000 [shekels] of silver,* about 25 pounds or 11.4 kilograms in weight.

19:30-35 Lot's daughters' plan to have sex with their drunk father showed that they, too, had been corrupted by Sodom's culture. They saw incest as the only way to carry on their family line. Ironically, their father had offered them to be raped (19:6-8), but they raped him instead. Their illicit unions produced the ancestors of the Moabites and Ammonites, perennial enemies of Israel (but see Deuteronomy 2:9, 19).

20:2 Abraham maintained his practice of introducing Sarah as his sister (see 12:13; 20:13), jeopardizing God's promise that Sarah would bear Abraham a son. His reasoning—"This is a godless place" (20:11)—was faulty. Abimelech responded immediately when God confronted him; his household was terrified of having offended a deity (20:3-10). Abimelech was angry that Abraham's deception had made him guilty of "this great sin" (20:9). Evidently, he knew taking another man's wife was wrong.

20:17-18 The barrenness of Abimelech's household suggests that some time had passed. The fact that infertility has been divine punishment for sin does not mean that it usually is. However, the story clearly conveys that God alone controls fertility.

Sarah

IDENTITY — Lies and Laughter

I can imagine Sarah being furious.

As she drew a king's attention for being beautiful, Abraham lied, "She is my sister."

"I'm your what?"

Sarah was marched off into the king's harem, even brought to the king himself.

Who we are is sometimes chosen for us. Amid the swirl of family, culture, and appearances, we can become someone we are most definitely not. And one day, as we sip our coffee, we realize that what we're doing is slowly sucking the life out of us. We wonder, "How did I get here?" Maybe someone else's fear—but most likely our own—has wrapped us in a bad-dream-of-a-life.

While Abraham got it wrong in this passage, Sarah herself got identity wrong a lot. Would she believe God was the one who could make her a mom, even though she was too old? Or would she laugh? Would she maintain faith that she would be the mother of many generations, or would she offer her servant to have a baby in her place? Would she be a "princess" (the meaning of the name Sarah) who cared for her subjects, or would she use her authority to harm her servant Hagar?

God intervened for Sarah. He spoke to the king in a dream, and the king scrambled to return her to Abraham, who fessed up. Sarah was restored to who she really was.

God knows our true identity, not just what others say about us or the ways we pigeonhole ourselves. As with Sarah, our identity, linked to his love, gives life.

> God loves the real you, not who others say you are. Your identity, trued to his love, gives life.

SARAH'S STORY IS TOLD IN GENESIS 11–23; SHE IS ALSO MENTIONED IN ISAIAH 51:2; ROMANS 4:19; 9:9; GALATIANS 4:21–31; HEBREWS 11:11; 1 PETER 3:6.

IDENTIFY

What words have you spoken, have others spoken, or has God spoken about who you are?

"Like Sarah, I once found myself living by others' lies. Turns out God made me for something that fits a lot better."

CARA DAY is a writer and illustrator. She has served with Stonecroft Ministries helping women live "extraordinary."

could have children. ¹⁸For the LORD had caused all the women to be infertile because of what happened with Abraham's wife, Sarah.

The Birth of Isaac

21 The LORD kept his word and did for Sarah exactly what he had promised. ²She became pregnant, and she gave birth to a son for Abraham in his old age. This happened at just the time God had said it would. ³And Abraham named their son Isaac. ⁴Eight days after Isaac was born, Abraham circumcised him as God had commanded. ⁵Abraham was 100 years old when Isaac was born.

⁶And Sarah declared, "God has brought me laughter.* All who hear about this will laugh with me. ⁷Who would have said to Abraham that Sarah would nurse a baby? Yet I have given Abraham a son in his old age!"

Hagar and Ishmael Are Sent Away

⁸When Isaac grew up and was about to be weaned, Abraham prepared a huge feast to celebrate the occasion. ⁹But Sarah saw Ishmael—the son of Abraham

21:6 The name *Isaac* means "he laughs."

21:1-2 Twenty-five years after God first promised Abraham a son (12:1-4), and one year after the angels visited Abraham and Sarah (18:1-15), Sarah gave birth. The intervening years had been filled with difficulty, and the wait was hard, but God kept his promise.

21:6 The name Isaac (*yitskhaq* in Hebrew) means "he laughs." Sarah's wordplay showed that the laughter of unbelief when the promise was given (18:12) had changed to the laughter of joy at its fulfillment. Sarah knew that everyone who had heard would laugh with her, rejoicing at the news. Hebrews 11:11 commends her faith in God's promise despite her struggle with unbelief.

Come Close

FEARFUL: GOD IS STRONGER STILL

SCRIPTURE CONNECTION: GENESIS 20:1-18

My dad has a letter from his sister, dated 1974. My favorite part is that it's in fancy, almost whimsical cursive. But she was a no-nonsense gal. She graduated college at a time when many women didn't go to college. And she was going to make sure my dad got an education too.

In many parts of the world today, women are not offered a full education. Even in Western culture, we are still gaining ground in elevating women's voices. In the ancient world, Sarah's voice would have been mostly unheard, while Abraham's voice would have rung influential and powerful.

> **My strongest place is trusting in the one true God.**

Sarah might have felt fearful and helpless as she was introduced to the pagan king Abimelech with the lie that she was Abraham's sister. But even as Abraham's fear held Sarah captive, God could free her still. God kept Abimelech from touching Sarah. And Sarah's faith could grow stronger as she witnessed God's deliverance.

There are a lot of strong women out there, and the ability to trust in God in the face of mistreatment is an important demonstration of strength.

REFLECT "That's why I kept you from sinning against me, and why I did not let you touch her." GENESIS 20:6

God, help me trust you when I feel helpless and voiceless. Make me strong, knowing you are a strong, trustworthy God. Amen.

CONSIDER "Man and woman are designed to rule together. Exclusion of women is the opposite of God's design. To exclude women is to exclude half of God's creation means of ruling the earth. This means that we must include and celebrate the influence and presence of women in all realms of life. Women should be sought after and encouraged, educated and equipped, taught, learned with and learned from, celebrated and needed as essential partners in the shared task" ELYSE FITZPATRICK AND ERIC SCHUMACHER, *Worthy: Celebrating the Value of Women*.

WHITNEY PUTNAM is the senior director of women's events and marketing at New Life Ministries. She is an overall joy-chaser and is often found dancing in her kitchen.

and her Egyptian servant Hagar—making fun of her son, Isaac.* ¹⁰So she turned to Abraham and demanded, "Get rid of that slave woman and her son. He is not going to share the inheritance with my son, Isaac. I won't have it!"

¹¹This upset Abraham very much because Ishmael was his son. ¹²But God told Abraham, "Do not be upset over the boy and your servant. Do whatever Sarah tells you, for Isaac is the son through whom your descendants will be counted. ¹³But I will also make a nation of the descendants of Hagar's son because he is your son, too."

¹⁴So Abraham got up early the next morning, prepared food and a container of water, and strapped them on Hagar's shoulders. Then he sent her away with their son, and she wandered aimlessly in the wilderness of Beersheba.

¹⁵When the water was gone, she put the boy in the shade of a bush. ¹⁶Then she went and sat down by herself about a hundred yards* away. "I don't want to watch the boy die," she said, as she burst into tears.

¹⁷But God heard the boy crying, and the angel of God called to Hagar from heaven, "Hagar, what's wrong? Do not be afraid! God has heard the boy crying as he lies there. ¹⁸Go to him and comfort him, for I will make a great nation from his descendants."

¹⁹Then God opened Hagar's eyes, and she saw a well full of water. She quickly filled her water container and gave the boy a drink.

²⁰And God was with the boy as he grew up in the wilderness. He became a skillful archer, ²¹and he settled in the wilderness of Paran. His mother arranged for him to marry a woman from the land of Egypt.

Abraham's Covenant with Abimelech

²²About this time, Abimelech came with Phicol, his army commander, to visit Abraham. "God is obviously with you, helping you in everything you do," Abimelech said. ²³"Swear to me in God's name that you will never deceive me, my children, or any of my descendants. I have been loyal to you, so now swear that you will be loyal to me and to this country where you are living as a foreigner."

²⁴Abraham replied, "Yes, I swear to it!" ²⁵Then Abraham complained to Abimelech about a well that Abimelech's servants had taken by force from Abraham's servants.

²⁶"This is the first I've heard of it," Abimelech answered. "I have no idea who is responsible. You have never complained about this before."

²⁷Abraham then gave some of his sheep, goats, and cattle to Abimelech, and they made a treaty. ²⁸But Abraham also took seven additional female lambs and set them off by themselves. ²⁹Abimelech asked, "Why have you set these seven apart from the others?"

³⁰Abraham replied, "Please accept these seven lambs to show your agreement that I dug this well." ³¹Then he named the place Beersheba (which means "well of the oath"), because that was where they had sworn the oath.

³²After making their covenant at Beersheba, Abimelech left with Phicol, the commander of his army, and they returned home to the land of the Philistines. ³³Then Abraham planted a tamarisk tree at Beersheba, and there he worshiped the LORD, the Eternal God.* ³⁴And Abraham lived as a foreigner in Philistine country for a long time.

Abraham's Faith Tested

22 Some time later, God tested Abraham's faith. "Abraham!" God called.

"Yes," he replied. "Here I am."

²"Take your son, your only son—yes, Isaac, whom you love so much—and go to the land of Moriah. Go and sacrifice him as a burnt offering on one of the mountains, which I will show you."

³The next morning Abraham got up early. He saddled his donkey and took two of his servants with him, along with his son, Isaac. Then he chopped wood for a fire for a burnt offering and set out for the place God had told him about. ⁴On the third day of their journey, Abraham looked up and saw the place in the distance. ⁵"Stay here with the donkey," Abraham told the servants. "The boy and I will travel a little farther. We will worship there, and then we will come right back."

⁶So Abraham placed the wood for the burnt offering on Isaac's shoulders, while he himself carried the fire and the knife. As the two of them walked on together, ⁷Isaac turned to Abraham and said, "Father?"

"Yes, my son?" Abraham replied.

"We have the fire and the wood," the boy said, "but where is the sheep for the burnt offering?"

21:9 As in Greek version and Latin Vulgate; Hebrew lacks *of her son, Isaac.* 21:16 Hebrew *a bowshot.* 21:33 Hebrew *El-Olam.*

21:9-10 Earlier, Sarah had mistreated Hagar to the point that Hagar had fled (16:6). When Hagar's son mistreated Isaac, Sarah demanded that "that slave woman and her son" leave. Sarah's initial lack of trust in God in giving Hagar to Abraham resulted in many years of exploitation and multigenerational rivalry.
21:14-21 Abraham gave Hagar meager resources when he sent her away, but God kept his promise to this Egyptian woman and her son. He heard their cries and provided for their needs, reiterating his plan to "make a great nation from his descendants" (see 16:10). Hagar later succeeded in finding Ishmael an Egyptian wife.
22:2 God's instructions to Abraham are troubling (see Perspective on page 34), but this story does not encourage child abuse. God's unique test of Abraham's faith related directly to the covenant promise about Isaac's descendants. Abraham's immediate and unquestioning obedience showed he trusted God to provide a substitute (22:3, 5, 8) or even raise Isaac from the dead (Hebrews 11:17-19).

Perspective

Where are the role models?

SCRIPTURE CONNECTION: GENESIS 22:1-19

If we open the Bible in search of role models, we soon run into trouble. Most Bible stories teach us about God's righteous character, but the humans in the stories are full of flaws. Their exploits are usually not a good example.

The Bible describes, rather than prescribes, their behavior. However, we take courage from the fact that God shows mercy to people who are flawed, just like us.

Passages like Genesis 22 are even more difficult. How can I trust a God who tells a father to kill his own son? What does this tell me about God's character?

Keep in mind that Abraham's situation is unique. And, as we see by the story's end, God never intended to put Isaac to death. He certainly does not ask us to sacrifice our children. In fact, there are numerous passages in the Bible that show God abhorring such practices. His instruction to Abraham was purely a test of trust. Would Abraham cling to the boy or entrust him to God?

VIEWPOINTS

HIS: *How did this experience change Abraham's view of God?*
MINE: *"Like Abraham, I am always in danger of clinging to what God has provided instead of clinging to God. Will I trust him when it looks like I may lose something dear to me?"*
YOURS: *Is there something that easily becomes more important to you than God? Does this passage help reorient your trust?*

CARMEN JOY IMES, PhD, is an author, speaker, blogger, YouTuber, and serves as associate professor of Old Testament at Biola University in California.

---

⁸"God will provide a sheep for the burnt offering, my son," Abraham answered. And they both walked on together. ⁹When they arrived at the place where God had told him to go, Abraham built an altar and arranged the wood on it. Then he tied his son, Isaac, and laid him on the altar on top of the wood. ¹⁰And Abraham picked up the knife to kill his son as a sacrifice. ¹¹At that moment the angel of the LORD called to him from heaven, "Abraham! Abraham!"

"Yes," Abraham replied. "Here I am!"

¹²"Don't lay a hand on the boy!" the angel said. "Do not hurt him in any way, for now I know that you truly fear God. You have not withheld from me even your son, your only son."

¹³Then Abraham looked up and saw a ram caught by its horns in a thicket. So he took the ram and sacrificed it as a burnt offering in place of his son. ¹⁴Abraham named the place Yahweh-Yireh (which means "the LORD will provide"). To this day, people still use that name as a proverb: "On the mountain of the LORD it will be provided."

¹⁵Then the angel of the LORD called again to Abraham from heaven. ¹⁶"This is what the LORD says: Because you have obeyed me and have not withheld even your son, your only son, I swear by my own name that ¹⁷I will certainly bless you. I will multiply your descendants* beyond number, like the stars in the sky and the sand on the seashore. Your descendants will conquer the cities of their enemies. ¹⁸And through your descendants all the nations of the earth will be blessed—all because you have obeyed me."

¹⁹Then they returned to the servants and traveled back to Beersheba, where Abraham continued to live.

²⁰Soon after this, Abraham heard that Milcah, his brother Nahor's wife, had borne Nahor eight sons. ²¹The oldest was named Uz, the next oldest was Buz, followed by Kemuel (the ancestor of the Arameans), ²²Kesed, Hazo, Pildash, Jidlaph, and Bethuel. ²³(Bethuel became the father of Rebekah.) In addition to these eight sons from Milcah, ²⁴Nahor had four other children from his concubine Reumah. Their names were Tebah, Gaham, Tahash, and Maacah.

The Burial of Sarah

23 When Sarah was 127 years old, ²she died at Kiriath-arba (now called Hebron) in the land of Canaan. There Abraham mourned and wept for her.

22:17 Hebrew *seed;* also in 22:17b, 18.

22:24 In some ancient cultures, concubines helped landowners increase their offspring and build larger households. As a member of the household, a concubine was assured continuous provision for her needs and the needs of her children, but her social status was not equal to a full wife. She was not available to marry another man or to be sold into another family's service (see Exodus 21:7-11). The Old Testament does not explicitly condemn polygamy, but Genesis repeatedly demonstrates its perils.

³Then, leaving her body, he said to the Hittite elders, ⁴"Here I am, a stranger and a foreigner among you. Please sell me a piece of land so I can give my wife a proper burial."

⁵The Hittites replied to Abraham, ⁶"Listen, my lord, you are an honored prince among us. Choose the finest of our tombs and bury her there. No one here will refuse to help you in this way."

⁷Then Abraham bowed low before the Hittites ⁸and said, "Since you are willing to help me in this way, be so kind as to ask Ephron son of Zohar ⁹to let me buy his cave at Machpelah, down at the end of his field. I will pay the full price in the presence of witnesses, so I will have a permanent burial place for my family."

¹⁰Ephron was sitting there among the others, and he answered Abraham as the others listened, speaking publicly before all the Hittite elders of the town. ¹¹"No, my lord," he said to Abraham, "please listen to me. I will give you the field and the cave. Here in the presence of my people, I give it to you. Go and bury your dead."

¹²Abraham again bowed low before the citizens of the land, ¹³and he replied to Ephron as everyone listened. "No, listen to me. I will buy it from you. Let me pay the full price for the field so I can bury my dead there."

¹⁴Ephron answered Abraham, ¹⁵"My lord, please listen to me. The land is worth 400 pieces* of silver, but what is that between friends? Go ahead and bury your dead."

¹⁶So Abraham agreed to Ephron's price and paid the amount he had suggested—400 pieces of silver, weighed according to the market standard. The Hittite elders witnessed the transaction.

¹⁷So Abraham bought the plot of land belonging to Ephron at Machpelah, near Mamre. This included the field itself, the cave that was in it, and all the surrounding trees. ¹⁸It was transferred to Abraham as his permanent possession in the presence of the Hittite elders at the city gate. ¹⁹Then Abraham buried his wife, Sarah, there in Canaan, in the cave of Machpelah, near Mamre (also called Hebron). ²⁰So the field and the cave were transferred from the Hittites to Abraham for use as a permanent burial place.

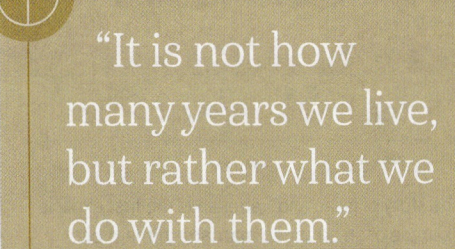

> "It is not how many years we live, but rather what we do with them."
>
> EVANGELINE CORY BOOTH
> (1865–1950) British theologian and Salvation Army general

A Wife for Isaac

24 Abraham was now a very old man, and the LORD had blessed him in every way. ²One day Abraham said to his oldest servant, the man in charge of his household, "Take an oath by putting your hand under my thigh. ³Swear by the LORD, the God of heaven and earth, that you will not allow my son to marry one of these local Canaanite women. ⁴Go instead to my homeland, to my relatives, and find a wife there for my son Isaac."

⁵The servant asked, "But what if I can't find a young woman who is willing to travel so far from home? Should I then take Isaac there to live among your relatives in the land you came from?"

⁶"No!" Abraham responded. "Be careful never to take my son there. ⁷For the LORD, the God of heaven, who took me from my father's house and my native land, solemnly promised to give this land to my descendants.* He will send his angel ahead of you, and he will see to it that you find a wife there for my son. ⁸If she is unwilling to come back with you, then you are free from this oath of mine. But under no circumstances are you to take my son there."

⁹So the servant took an oath by putting his hand under the thigh of his master, Abraham. He swore to follow Abraham's instructions. ¹⁰Then he loaded ten of Abraham's camels with all kinds of expensive gifts

---

23:15 Hebrew *400 shekels*, about 10 pounds or 4.6 kilograms in weight; also in 23:16. **24:7** Hebrew *seed;* also in 24:60.

23:1-4 God had promised Abraham land, numerous descendants through Sarah, and blessing for their family (12:1-3). However, until Sarah's death they owned no land. Abraham acquired a field and a cave to use as a family tomb. This transaction was the first sign that a permanent transition had taken place, as people normally buried dead relatives in their ancestral homeland (see 49:29-32; 50:24-25).

23:4-20 The negotiations between Abraham and the Hittites provide a fascinating window into ancient Mesopotamian culture. Although Ephron explicitly stated that he would "give" the land, Abraham took Ephron's casual mention of the value of the land as the price he expected to receive. The witness of community elders ensured that no one would later contest Abraham's ownership.

24:3-8 Abraham's unwillingness for Isaac to marry a Canaanite woman or to return to his father's homeland was rooted in God's covenant promises. Abraham sought to maintain faithfulness to God by avoiding intermarriage with uncircumcised Canaanites who would encourage them to worship other gods. He also insisted that Isaac remain in the land of Canaan in anticipation that it would be their land.

Perspective

Is the bride free to choose?

SCRIPTURE CONNECTION: GENESIS 24:1-67

The story of Isaac and Rebekah is the first explicit example of an arranged marriage in the Bible. Ironically, it's also the first mention of love between spouses. This juxtaposition of arranged marriage and love challenges those of us steeped in Western culture to ask how they coexist.

While coercion is bad, arrangements are not inherently bad. In fact, in many parts of the world today, there are flourishing arranged marriages.

Abraham was deeply invested in his son's (and his descendants') well-being. He entrusted his faithful servant with a most important mission: invite home a bride for Isaac.

When Rebekah appeared, she proved diligent in her work and generous in her spirit. She made two choices in this story—neither one by coercion. Her first choice was to eagerly serve Abraham's servant at the well. Then, when she was asked about her willingness to go with the servant, she made a second choice: "I will go."

Similarly, God entrusted Jesus with a most important mission to invite home a bride (a term used for believers, 2 Corinthians 11:2). God made the arrangements, and we freely choose. And find love.

VIEWPOINTS

HERS: *What choices were available to Rebekah?*

MINE: *"When pressed with demands, obligations, and afflictions, I may lose sight of my options and begin feeling trapped with no path for relief or joy. I often want to make 'external choices': change my environment or change other people. But I have learned that my most powerful choices rest within my own heart—the 'internal choices.' And the condition of my heart then affects everything else that I do."*

YOURS: *When faced with life's challenges, what external and internal choices are available for you? How might the condition of your heart affect your circumstances?*

MISTY ARTERBURN is an author and speaker, contributing to Bible projects, devotionals, and recovery materials for over twenty years. Wife and mom to five, Misty is the founder of Recovery Girls and the general editor of *The One Year Bible for Women*.

---

from his master, and he traveled to distant Aram-naharaim. There he went to the town where Abraham's brother Nahor had settled. ¹¹He made the camels kneel beside a well just outside the town. It was evening, and the women were coming out to draw water.

¹²"O Lord, God of my master, Abraham," he prayed. "Please give me success today, and show unfailing love to my master, Abraham. ¹³See, I am standing here beside this spring, and the young women of the town are coming out to draw water. ¹⁴This is my request. I will ask one of them, 'Please give me a drink from your jug.' If she says, 'Yes, have a drink, and I will water your camels, too!'—let her be the one you have selected as Isaac's wife. This is how I will know that you have shown unfailing love to my master."

¹⁵Before he had finished praying, he saw a young woman named Rebekah coming out with her water jug on her shoulder. She was the daughter of Bethuel, who was the son of Abraham's brother Nahor and his wife, Milcah. ¹⁶Rebekah was very beautiful and old enough to be married, but she was still a virgin. She went down to the spring, filled her jug, and came up again. ¹⁷Running over to her, the servant said, "Please give me a little drink of water from your jug."

¹⁸"Yes, my lord," she answered, "have a drink." And she quickly lowered her jug from her shoulder and gave him a drink. ¹⁹When she had given him a drink, she said, "I'll draw water for your camels, too, until they have had enough to drink." ²⁰So she quickly emptied her jug into the watering trough and ran back to the well to draw water for all his camels.

²¹The servant watched her in silence, wondering whether or not the Lord had given him success in his mission. ²²Then at last, when the camels had finished drinking, he took out a gold ring for her nose and two large gold bracelets* for her wrists.

²³"Whose daughter are you?" he asked. "And please tell me, would your father have any room to put us up for the night?"

²⁴"I am the daughter of Bethuel," she replied. "My grandparents are Nahor and Milcah. ²⁵Yes, we have plenty of straw and feed for the camels, and we have room for guests."

²⁶The man bowed low and worshiped the Lord. ²⁷"Praise the Lord, the God of my master, Abraham,"

24:22 Hebrew *a gold nose-ring weighing a beka* [0.2 ounces or 6 grams] *and two gold bracelets weighing 10* [shekels] [4 ounces or 114 grams].

24:11 This is the first of many similar events in the Bible (these are known as *type scenes*). Abraham's servant found a wife for Isaac at the well outside Abraham's hometown. Later, Jacob and Moses would each find a wife in the same way (Genesis 29:1-30; Exodus 2:15-22).

24:12-20 Rebekah, Abraham's great-niece, proved herself to be kind, generous, and capable, showing stellar hospitality to Abraham's servant. Ten thirsty camels could drink two hundred to three hundred gallons of water in one sitting, so a woman who would work that hard for a stranger was remarkable!

Rebekah

IDENTITY — More Than Her Circumstances

When she first entered the story, Rebekah seemed chosen. What were the chances? A man coming to town looking for a young woman who would offer him and his camels a drink, and there she was meeting that description perfectly. Then she gets whisked away to a life of comfort. It certainly looked like God's favor.

Then those problematic twins, Jacob and Esau, arrived, fighting before they were even born. Their brotherly rivalry was unmatched, and Rebekah got herself involved. She ended up deceiving her husband, Isaac, so that Jacob—her favorite—could become the family heir over his brother, Esau. They had their fair share of family issues.

At different points in her story, Rebekah might have labeled herself "blessed" or "cursed." But that dismisses how every part of her story was used for God's glory. God was present with Rebekah no matter the circumstances, the feelings, or the choices.

> God can use all of my story for his glory.

Like all of us, Rebekah is more than any single moment in her story. She could be identified at different moments as a sought-after bride, a conflicted mother, or a deceptive wife. Though each of these titles may ring true, more than anything she was known and used by God. This was true even amid her mistakes. As it turned out, Jesus was linked to Abraham's lineage through Jacob. Though God could have worked this out a million ways, he chose to make Rebekah's story part of Christ's story.

REBEKAH'S STORY IS TOLD IN GENESIS 24–27; SHE IS ALSO MENTIONED IN GENESIS 49:31 & ROMANS 9:10.

IDENTIFY

How can God redeem every part of your story?

"As with Rebekah, God can use my mistakes in creative ways for his purposes. My identity isn't tied up in what I do 'right' or 'wrong.' God sees me and can use all of my story for his glory."

ALEXANDRA KUYKENDALL is a cofounder of The Open Door Sisterhood and author of several books, including *Seeking Out Goodness: Finding the True and Beautiful All around You*.

Insight 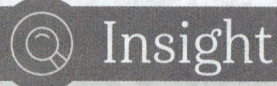 COULD YOU LIFT THAT?

Camels have been used to transport people and goods for thousands of years. Abraham's servant took ten camels with him on his journey to Haran to find a wife for Isaac. He and his camels met Rebekah at a well, a traditional place to find a wife in the Bible. He knew Rebekah was the one when she gave him a drink and then offered to water his camels, too. Rebekah was clearly a strong woman: Ten thirsty camels can drink around two hundred to three hundred gallons of water in one sitting.

10 CAMELS' WATER INTAKE = ~250 GALLONS OF WATER = ~2,085 POUNDS CARRIED

he said. "The LORD has shown unfailing love and faithfulness to my master, for he has led me straight to my master's relatives."

28 The young woman ran home to tell her family everything that had happened. 29 Now Rebekah had a brother named Laban, who ran out to meet the man at the spring. 30 He had seen the nose-ring and the bracelets on his sister's wrists, and had heard Rebekah tell what the man had said. So he rushed out to the spring, where the man was still standing beside his camels. 31 Laban said to him, "Come and stay with us, you who are blessed by the LORD! Why are you standing here outside the town when I have a room all ready for you and a place prepared for the camels?"

32 So the man went home with Laban, and Laban unloaded the camels, gave him straw for their bedding, fed them, and provided water for the man and the camel drivers to wash their feet. 33 Then food was served. But Abraham's servant said, "I don't want to eat until I have told you why I have come."

"All right," Laban said, "tell us."

34 "I am Abraham's servant," he explained. 35 "And the LORD has greatly blessed my master; he has become a wealthy man. The LORD has given him flocks of sheep and goats, herds of cattle, a fortune in silver and gold, and many male and female servants and camels and donkeys.

36 "When Sarah, my master's wife, was very old, she gave birth to my master's son, and my master has given him everything he owns. 37 And my master made me take an oath. He said, 'Do not allow my son to marry one of these local Canaanite women. 38 Go instead to my father's house, to my relatives, and find a wife there for my son.'

39 "But I said to my master, 'What if I can't find a young woman who is willing to go back with me?' 40 He responded, 'The LORD, in whose presence I have lived, will send his angel with you and will make your mission successful. Yes, you must find a wife for my son from among my relatives, from my father's family. 41 Then you will have fulfilled your obligation. But if you go to my relatives and they refuse to let her go with you, you will be free from my oath.'

42 "So today when I came to the spring, I prayed this prayer: 'O LORD, God of my master, Abraham, please give me success on this mission. 43 See, I am standing here beside this spring. This is my request. When a young woman comes to draw water, I will say to her, "Please give me a little drink of water from your jug." 44 If she says, "Yes, have a drink, and I will draw water for your camels, too," let her be the one you have selected to be the wife of my master's son.'

⁴⁵"Before I had finished praying in my heart, I saw Rebekah coming out with her water jug on her shoulder. She went down to the spring and drew water. So I said to her, 'Please give me a drink.' ⁴⁶She quickly lowered her jug from her shoulder and said, 'Yes, have a drink, and I will water your camels, too!' So I drank, and then she watered the camels.

⁴⁷"Then I asked, 'Whose daughter are you?' She replied, 'I am the daughter of Bethuel, and my grandparents are Nahor and Milcah.' So I put the ring on her nose, and the bracelets on her wrists.

⁴⁸"Then I bowed low and worshiped the LORD. I praised the LORD, the God of my master, Abraham, because he had led me straight to my master's niece to be his son's wife. ⁴⁹So tell me—will you or won't you show unfailing love and faithfulness to my master? Please tell me yes or no, and then I'll know what to do next."

⁵⁰Then Laban and Bethuel replied, "The LORD has obviously brought you here, so there is nothing we can say. ⁵¹Here is Rebekah; take her and go. Yes, let her be the wife of your master's son, as the LORD has directed."

⁵²When Abraham's servant heard their answer, he bowed down to the ground and worshiped the LORD. ⁵³Then he brought out silver and gold jewelry and clothing and presented them to Rebekah. He also gave expensive presents to her brother and mother. ⁵⁴Then they ate their meal, and the servant and the men with him stayed there overnight.

But early the next morning, Abraham's servant said, "Send me back to my master."

⁵⁵"But we want Rebekah to stay with us at least ten days," her brother and mother said. "Then she can go."

⁵⁶But he said, "Don't delay me. The LORD has made my mission successful; now send me back so I can return to my master."

⁵⁷"Well," they said, "we'll call Rebekah and ask her what she thinks." ⁵⁸So they called Rebekah. "Are you willing to go with this man?" they asked her.

And she replied, "Yes, I will go."

⁵⁹So they said good-bye to Rebekah and sent her away with Abraham's servant and his men. The woman who had been Rebekah's childhood nurse went along with her. ⁶⁰They gave her this blessing as she parted:

"Our sister, may you become
    the mother of many millions!
May your descendants be strong
    and conquer the cities of their enemies."

⁶¹Then Rebekah and her servant girls mounted the camels and followed the man. So Abraham's servant took Rebekah and went on his way.

⁶²Meanwhile, Isaac, whose home was in the Negev, had returned from Beer-lahai-roi. ⁶³One evening as he was walking and meditating in the fields, he looked up and saw the camels coming. ⁶⁴When Rebekah looked up and saw Isaac, she quickly dismounted from her camel. ⁶⁵"Who is that man walking through the fields to meet us?" she asked the servant.

And he replied, "It is my master." So Rebekah covered her face with her veil. ⁶⁶Then the servant told Isaac everything he had done.

⁶⁷And Isaac brought Rebekah into his mother Sarah's tent, and she became his wife. He loved her deeply, and she was a special comfort to him after the death of his mother.

The Death of Abraham

25 Abraham married another wife, whose name was Keturah. ²She gave birth to Zimran, Jokshan, Medan, Midian, Ishbak, and Shuah. ³Jokshan was the father of Sheba and Dedan. Dedan's descendants were the Asshurites, Letushites, and Leummites. ⁴Midian's sons were Ephah, Epher, Hanoch, Abida, and Eldaah. These were all descendants of Abraham through Keturah.

⁵Abraham gave everything he owned to his son Isaac. ⁶But before he died, he gave gifts to the sons of his concubines and sent them off to a land in the east, away from Isaac.

⁷Abraham lived for 175 years, ⁸and he died at a ripe old age, having lived a long and satisfying life. He breathed his last and joined his ancestors in death. ⁹His sons Isaac and Ishmael buried him in the cave of Machpelah, near Mamre, in the field of Ephron son of Zohar the Hittite. ¹⁰This was the field Abraham had purchased from the Hittites and where he had buried his wife Sarah. ¹¹After Abraham's death, God blessed his son Isaac, who settled near Beer-lahai-roi in the Negev.

24:51 In the ancient Near East, a woman's father normally bore responsibility for arranging her marriage. In this case, Rebekah's brother Laban also played a role, perhaps due to her father's advanced age. Given Abraham's obvious wealth and status as a close family relative, the servant quickly convinced them it was a good match. They did not consult her first, and she was not present for the negotiations the next morning (24:57), but she expressed willingness to go right away (24:58).
24:67 Not much is known about ancient marriage ceremonies. The negotiations between male relatives were likely the most complex part. Whether Isaac and Rebekah married immediately is not clear. What is clear is that arranged marriages did not necessarily lack affection. Isaac loved Rebekah deeply.
25:5-6 Abraham remarried after Sarah's death. The narrator has not called Keturah or Hagar concubines until this point, but clearly the status of their sons did not equal Isaac's. Abraham loved all his sons, so before he died, he gave each of them gifts. But to demonstrate and preserve Isaac's position as his heir, Abraham sent these other sons away, as he had previously sent away Ishmael (21:8-14).

A Good Name: Name Changes Reveal Purpose

SCRIPTURE CONNECTION: GENESIS 25:19-34; 32:22-32

In a powerful, public ceremony in India in 2011, two hundred young girls, whose parents had named them Nakusha (meaning "unwanted"), legally chose new names reflecting their new, positive identity.

What is the meaning of your name? Five name changes occur in Genesis. Eve, Abraham, Sarah, Jacob, and Joseph all experienced a name change, and each change reflected something of God's plan to redeem people. The name changes also signaled new self-images.

Eve was initially called *ishshah*, "the woman," the companion to *ish*, "the man." Adam recognized her as "bone from my bone, and flesh from my flesh" (2:23), an equal companion. But after the Fall, Adam renamed her Eve, "mother of all who live" (3:20), which could be viewed as narrowing her function to raising children. But God's purpose for her extended to his redemption plan; he promised that her offspring would overcome evil (3:15).

God's ideal, his plan, was thus not lost when sin entered the world, and the name changes of Abram, Sarai, and Jacob also look toward God's plan to restore humanity to himself.

Abram means "exalted father," but his new name, Abraham, means "father of many," that is, many nations (17:5). This was God's vision for Abraham and his offspring. And it was a seal of God's covenant relationship with Abraham. Sarai's name change doesn't result in a change in meaning, as both Sarai and Sarah mean "princess." But it did clearly include her in God's promise and further served as an expression of God's vision for this couple (see note on 17:15-16).

> God gives us good names for good purposes.

Jacob's name, "heel grabber," reflects his birth as the second-born twin who held on to his brother's heel (25:26). He later grabbed Esau's birthright and tricked Isaac into blessing him as the oldest son, which led to Jacob's having to flee. On Jacob's return to Canaan, he wrestled with a mysterious stranger and demanded a blessing from him. The stranger—evidently a messenger from God—gave him the new name Israel, which means "fighting with God" or "God fights" (32:22-32).

Joseph (meaning "may he add") was given a name change when he was promoted by Pharaoh to second-in-command in Egypt. The new name, Zaphenath-paneah ("God speaks and lives"), is never used of Joseph again. It was his Egyptian name, and while the name positioned Joseph to later help the Israelites, it didn't change his identity as a son of Jacob, belonging to the people of Israel.

These people are a part of our spiritual heritage. And their new names reflect God's good plans for them—and for all of us who are blessed through them.

IMAGINE

What does your name mean?

How might your name reflect how God wants to bless you and others?

"When I learned my name's meaning ('consecrated to God'), I saw God's call on my life from birth, as a pastor and later as a professor."

ELIZABETH GLANVILLE, PhD, is retired faculty from Fuller Theological Seminary, School of Mission and Theology. She is an international teacher on missions and leadership and chaplain for a local police department and her retirement community.

Ishmael's Descendants

¹²This is the account of the family of Ishmael, the son of Abraham through Hagar, Sarah's Egyptian servant. ¹³Here is a list, by their names and clans, of Ishmael's descendants: The oldest was Nebaioth, followed by Kedar, Adbeel, Mibsam, ¹⁴Mishma, Dumah, Massa, ¹⁵Hadad, Tema, Jetur, Naphish, and Kedemah. ¹⁶These twelve sons of Ishmael became the founders of twelve tribes named after them, listed according to the places they settled and camped. ¹⁷Ishmael lived for 137 years. Then he breathed his last and joined his ancestors in death. ¹⁸Ishmael's descendants occupied the region from Havilah to Shur, which is east of Egypt in the direction of Asshur. There they lived in open hostility toward all their relatives.*

The Births of Esau and Jacob

¹⁹This is the account of the family of Isaac, the son of Abraham. ²⁰When Isaac was forty years old, he married Rebekah, the daughter of Bethuel the Aramean from Paddan-aram and the sister of Laban the Aramean.

²¹Isaac pleaded with the LORD on behalf of his wife, because she was unable to have children. The LORD answered Isaac's prayer, and Rebekah became pregnant with twins. ²²But the two children struggled with each other in her womb. So she went to ask the LORD about it. "Why is this happening to me?" she asked.

²³And the LORD told her, "The sons in your womb will become two nations. From the very beginning, the two nations will be rivals. One nation will be stronger than the other; and your older son will serve your younger son."

²⁴And when the time came to give birth, Rebekah discovered that she did indeed have twins! ²⁵The first one was very red at birth and covered with thick hair like a fur coat. So they named him Esau.* ²⁶Then the other twin was born with his hand grasping Esau's heel. So they named him Jacob.* Isaac was sixty years old when the twins were born.

Esau Sells His Birthright

²⁷As the boys grew up, Esau became a skillful hunter. He was an outdoorsman, but Jacob had a quiet temperament, preferring to stay at home. ²⁸Isaac loved Esau because he enjoyed eating the wild game Esau brought home, but Rebekah loved Jacob.

²⁹One day when Jacob was cooking some stew, Esau arrived home from the wilderness exhausted and hungry. ³⁰Esau said to Jacob, "I'm starved! Give me some of that red stew!" (This is how Esau got his other name, Edom, which means "red.")

³¹"All right," Jacob replied, "but trade me your rights as the firstborn son."

³²"Look, I'm dying of starvation!" said Esau. "What good is my birthright to me now?"

³³But Jacob said, "First you must swear that your birthright is mine." So Esau swore an oath, thereby selling all his rights as the firstborn to his brother, Jacob.

³⁴Then Jacob gave Esau some bread and lentil stew. Esau ate the meal, then got up and left. He showed contempt for his rights as the firstborn.

Isaac Deceives Abimelech

26 A severe famine now struck the land, as had happened before in Abraham's time. So Isaac moved to Gerar, where Abimelech, king of the Philistines, lived.

²The LORD appeared to Isaac and said, "Do not go down to Egypt, but do as I tell you. ³Live here as a foreigner in this land, and I will be with you and bless you. I hereby confirm that I will give all these lands to you and your descendants,* just as I solemnly promised Abraham, your father. ⁴I will cause your descendants to become as numerous as the stars of the sky, and I will give them all these lands. And through your descendants all the nations of the earth will be blessed. ⁵I will do this because Abraham listened to me and obeyed all my requirements, commands, decrees, and instructions." ⁶So Isaac stayed in Gerar.

25:18 The meaning of the Hebrew is uncertain. **25:25** *Esau* sounds like a Hebrew term that means "hair." **25:26** *Jacob* sounds like the Hebrew words for "heel" and "deceiver." **26:3** Hebrew *seed;* also in 26:4, 24.

25:21 Like Sarah before her (16:1; 18:11) and Rachel after her (29:31; 30:1, 22-23), Rebekah struggled with infertility—in her case, for twenty years. Children continued the family line, helped protect the tribe, and provided crucial labor as survival depended upon the fruitfulness of crops and herds. Children also kept property within the family, cared for aging parents, and enacted the proper funeral rites. Infertility was therefore a crushing stigma for a woman and a source of anxiety for a man. Since it was understood that God could control fertility, infertility was viewed as a spiritual issue prompting fervent prayer.

25:22-23 Rebekah's twins frequently wrestled within her. She inquired of the Lord, seeking to understand why her children were not at peace. Although we are not told how the subsequent interaction took place, God clearly honored Rebekah's desire to know his will. God spoke to her, indicating that her sons would be rivals, with the older serving the younger. This may have fueled her special love for her younger son, Jacob (25:28).

25:31-33 The firstborn son had double the inheritance of his siblings, along with the responsibility to care for aging parents. Esau gave Jacob his esteemed status in exchange for a single bowl of stew, showing how shortsighted he was (see Hebrews 12:16).

26:2-6 God assured Isaac that he would inherit the covenant promises (see 12:1-3) because Abraham had faithfully listened to God and obeyed all his requirements, commands, decrees, and instructions. Moses used these same terms in Deuteronomy to describe God's covenant with Israel, implying that Abraham would have obeyed the stipulations of the Sinai covenant if he had known them.

⁷When the men who lived there asked Isaac about his wife, Rebekah, he said, "She is my sister." He was afraid to say, "She is my wife." He thought, "They will kill me to get her, because she is so beautiful." ⁸But some time later, Abimelech, king of the Philistines, looked out his window and saw Isaac caressing Rebekah.

⁹Immediately, Abimelech called for Isaac and exclaimed, "She is obviously your wife! Why did you say, 'She is my sister'?"

"Because I was afraid someone would kill me to get her from me," Isaac replied.

¹⁰"How could you do this to us?" Abimelech exclaimed. "One of my people might easily have taken your wife and slept with her, and you would have made us guilty of great sin."

¹¹Then Abimelech issued a public proclamation: "Anyone who touches this man or his wife will be put to death!"

Conflict over Water Rights

¹²When Isaac planted his crops that year, he harvested a hundred times more grain than he planted, for the LORD blessed him. ¹³He became a very rich man, and his wealth continued to grow. ¹⁴He acquired so many flocks of sheep and goats, herds of cattle, and servants that the Philistines became jealous of him. ¹⁵So the Philistines filled up all of Isaac's wells with dirt. These were the wells that had been dug by the servants of his father, Abraham.

¹⁶Finally, Abimelech ordered Isaac to leave the country. "Go somewhere else," he said, "for you have become too powerful for us."

¹⁷So Isaac moved away to the Gerar Valley, where he set up their tents and settled down. ¹⁸He reopened the wells his father had dug, which the Philistines had filled in after Abraham's death. Isaac also restored the names Abraham had given them.

¹⁹Isaac's servants also dug in the Gerar Valley and discovered a well of fresh water. ²⁰But then the shepherds from Gerar came and claimed the spring. "This is our water," they said, and they argued over it with Isaac's herdsmen. So Isaac named the well Esek (which means "argument"). ²¹Isaac's men then dug another well, but again there was a dispute over it. So Isaac named it Sitnah (which means "hostility"). ²²Abandoning that one, Isaac moved on and dug another well. This time there was no dispute over it, so Isaac named the place Rehoboth (which means "open space"), for he said, "At last the LORD has created enough space for us to prosper in this land."

²³From there Isaac moved to Beersheba, ²⁴where the LORD appeared to him on the night of his arrival. "I am the God of your father, Abraham," he said. "Do not be afraid, for I am with you and will bless you. I will multiply your descendants, and they will become a great nation. I will do this because of my promise to Abraham, my servant." ²⁵Then Isaac built an altar there and worshiped the LORD. He set up his camp at that place, and his servants dug another well.

Isaac's Covenant with Abimelech

²⁶One day King Abimelech came from Gerar with his adviser, Ahuzzath, and also Phicol, his army commander. ²⁷"Why have you come here?" Isaac asked. "You obviously hate me, since you kicked me off your land."

²⁸They replied, "We can plainly see that the LORD is with you. So we want to enter into a sworn treaty with you. Let's make a covenant. ²⁹Swear that you will not harm us, just as we have never troubled you. We have always treated you well, and we sent you away from us in peace. And now look how the LORD has blessed you!"

³⁰So Isaac prepared a covenant feast to celebrate the treaty, and they ate and drank together. ³¹Early the next morning, they each took a solemn oath not to interfere with each other. Then Isaac sent them home again, and they left him in peace.

³²That very day Isaac's servants came and told him about a new well they had dug. "We've found water!" they exclaimed. ³³So Isaac named the well Shibah (which means "oath"). And to this day the town that grew up there is called Beersheba (which means "well of the oath").

³⁴At the age of forty, Esau married two Hittite wives: Judith, the daughter of Beeri, and Basemath, the daughter of Elon. ³⁵But Esau's wives made life miserable for Isaac and Rebekah.

Jacob Steals Esau's Blessing

27 One day when Isaac was old and turning blind, he called for Esau, his older son, and said, "My son."

26:7-11 Isaac not only inherited the covenant from his father, but he also learned deception from him. He deceived the residents of Gerar into believing that his wife was his sister. (This Abimelech is probably not the same man as in Genesis 20. *Abimelech* means "my father is king," so it could have been a dynastic name or title.) As with Abraham, when Isaac jeopardized the covenant, God prevented disaster and preserved the marriage.

26:34-35 Disregarding the covenant faith of his grandfather Abraham, Esau married outside the extended family, causing tension with his parents. Intermarriage would likely lead Esau and his children to worship idols, rather than God. His marriages illustrate how unfit he was to lead the covenant people into God's blessings. His later marriage to a descendant of Ishmael further demonstrated that he did not revere the uniqueness of the covenant family (28:8-9).

27:1-46 Jacob, whose name means "heel grabber," learned deception from his mother, Rebekah. She conspired with Jacob to deceive his father, Isaac, now blind, to gain the blessing of the firstborn before he died. In this event, the entire family acted faithlessly: Isaac disregarded the prophecy from Rebekah's pregnancy (25:23), Esau ignored his agreement with Jacob (25:33), and Rebekah acted deviously, even tricking Isaac into sending Jacob away (27:46). Favoritism produces a toxic family dynamic.

WHAT THE BIBLE SAYS ABOUT Image

We Must Worship God—Not Other Images

"You must not make for yourself an idol of any kind or an image of anything in the heavens or on the earth or in the sea." **EXODUS 20:4**

I know the glorious day will come when each of you will throw away the gold idols and silver images your sinful hands have made. **ISAIAH 31:7**

To whom can you compare God? What image can you find to resemble him? **ISAIAH 40:18**

God Made Us in His Image

God said, "Let us make human beings in our image, to be like us. They will reign over the fish in the sea, the birds in the sky, the livestock, all the wild animals on the earth, and the small animals that scurry along the ground." So God created human beings in his own image. In the image of God he created them; male and female he created them. **GENESIS 1:26-27**

The Holy Spirit Shapes Our Image

The Lord is the Spirit, and wherever the Spirit of the Lord is, there is freedom. So all of us who have had that veil removed can see and reflect the glory of the Lord. And the Lord—who is the Spirit—makes us more and more like him as we are changed into his glorious image. **2 CORINTHIANS 3:17-18**

Jesus Shows Us God's True Image

Christ is the visible image of the invisible God. He existed before anything was created and is supreme over all creation, for through him God created everything in the heavenly realms and on earth. **COLOSSIANS 1:15-16**

"Yes, Father?" Esau replied.

²"I am an old man now," Isaac said, "and I don't know when I may die. ³Take your bow and a quiver full of arrows, and go out into the open country to hunt some wild game for me. ⁴Prepare my favorite dish, and bring it here for me to eat. Then I will pronounce the blessing that belongs to you, my firstborn son, before I die."

⁵But Rebekah overheard what Isaac had said to his son Esau. So when Esau left to hunt for the wild game, ⁶she said to her son Jacob, "Listen. I overheard your father say to Esau, ⁷'Bring me some wild game and prepare me a delicious meal. Then I will bless you in the LORD's presence before I die.' ⁸Now, my son, listen to me. Do exactly as I tell you. ⁹Go out to the flocks, and bring me two fine young goats. I'll use them to prepare your father's favorite dish. ¹⁰Then take the food to your father so he can eat it and bless you before he dies."

¹¹"But look," Jacob replied to Rebekah, "my brother, Esau, is a hairy man, and my skin is smooth. ¹²What if my father touches me? He'll see that I'm trying to trick him, and then he'll curse me instead of blessing me."

¹³But his mother replied, "Then let the curse fall on me, my son! Just do what I tell you. Go out and get the goats for me!"

¹⁴So Jacob went out and got the young goats for his mother. Rebekah took them and prepared a delicious meal, just the way Isaac liked it. ¹⁵Then she took Esau's favorite clothes, which were there in the house, and gave them to her younger son, Jacob. ¹⁶She covered his arms and the smooth part of his neck with the skin of the young goats. ¹⁷Then she gave Jacob the delicious meal, including freshly baked bread.

¹⁸So Jacob took the food to his father. "My father?" he said.

"Yes, my son," Isaac answered. "Who are you—Esau or Jacob?"

¹⁹Jacob replied, "It's Esau, your firstborn son. I've done as you told me. Here is the wild game. Now sit up and eat it so you can give me your blessing."

²⁰Isaac asked, "How did you find it so quickly, my son?"

"The LORD your God put it in my path!" Jacob replied.

²¹Then Isaac said to Jacob, "Come closer so I can touch you and make sure that you really are Esau." ²²So Jacob went closer to his father, and Isaac touched him. "The voice is Jacob's, but the hands are Esau's," Isaac said. ²³But he did not recognize Jacob, because Jacob's hands felt hairy just like Esau's. So Isaac prepared to bless Jacob. ²⁴"But are you really my son Esau?" he asked.

"Yes, I am," Jacob replied.

²⁵Then Isaac said, "Now, my son, bring me the wild game. Let me eat it, and then I will give you my blessing." So Jacob took the food to his father, and Isaac ate it. He also drank the wine that Jacob served him.

²⁶Then Isaac said to Jacob, "Please come a little closer and kiss me, my son."

²⁷So Jacob went over and kissed him. And when Isaac caught the smell of his clothes, he was finally convinced, and he blessed his son. He said, "Ah! The smell of my son is like the smell of the outdoors, which the LORD has blessed!

²⁸ "From the dew of heaven
    and the richness of the earth,
may God always give you abundant harvests of
    grain
    and bountiful new wine.
²⁹ May many nations become your servants,
    and may they bow down to you.
May you be the master over your brothers,
    and may your mother's sons bow down to you.
All who curse you will be cursed,
    and all who bless you will be blessed."

³⁰As soon as Isaac had finished blessing Jacob, and almost before Jacob had left his father, Esau returned from his hunt. ³¹Esau prepared a delicious meal and brought it to his father. Then he said, "Sit up, my father, and eat my wild game so you can give me your blessing."

³²But Isaac asked him, "Who are you?"

Esau replied, "It's your son, your firstborn son, Esau."

³³Isaac began to tremble uncontrollably and said, "Then who just served me wild game? I have already eaten it, and I blessed him just before you came. And yes, that blessing must stand!"

³⁴When Esau heard his father's words, he let out a loud and bitter cry. "Oh my father, what about me? Bless me, too!" he begged.

³⁵But Isaac said, "Your brother was here, and he tricked me. He has taken away your blessing."

³⁶Esau exclaimed, "No wonder his name is Jacob, for now he has cheated me twice.* First he took my rights as the firstborn, and now he has stolen my blessing. Oh, haven't you saved even one blessing for me?"

³⁷Isaac said to Esau, "I have made Jacob your master and have declared that all his brothers will be his servants. I have guaranteed him an abundance of grain and wine—what is left for me to give you, my son?"

³⁸Esau pleaded, "But do you have only one blessing? Oh my father, bless me, too!" Then Esau broke down and wept.

³⁹Finally, his father, Isaac, said to him,

"You will live away from the richness of the
    earth,
    and away from the dew of the heaven above.
⁴⁰ You will live by your sword,
    and you will serve your brother.
But when you decide to break free,
    you will shake his yoke from your neck."

27:36 *Jacob* sounds like the Hebrew words for "heel" and "deceiver."

Jacob Flees to Paddan-Aram

⁴¹From that time on, Esau hated Jacob because their father had given Jacob the blessing. And Esau began to scheme: "I will soon be mourning my father's death. Then I will kill my brother, Jacob."

⁴²But Rebekah heard about Esau's plans. So she sent for Jacob and told him, "Listen, Esau is consoling himself by plotting to kill you. ⁴³So listen carefully, my son. Get ready and flee to my brother, Laban, in Haran. ⁴⁴Stay there with him until your brother cools off. ⁴⁵When he calms down and forgets what you have done to him, I will send for you to come back. Why should I lose both of you in one day?"

⁴⁶Then Rebekah said to Isaac, "I'm sick and tired of these local Hittite women! I would rather die than see Jacob marry one of them."

28 So Isaac called for Jacob, blessed him, and said, "You must not marry any of these Canaanite women. ²Instead, go at once to Paddan-aram, to the house of your grandfather Bethuel, and marry one of your uncle Laban's daughters. ³May God Almighty* bless you and give you many children. And may your descendants multiply and become many nations! ⁴May God pass on to you and your descendants* the blessings he promised to Abraham. May you own this land where you are now living as a foreigner, for God gave this land to Abraham."

⁵So Isaac sent Jacob away, and he went to Paddan-aram to stay with his uncle Laban, his mother's brother, the son of Bethuel the Aramean.

⁶Esau knew that his father, Isaac, had blessed Jacob and sent him to Paddan-aram to find a wife, and that he had warned Jacob, "You must not marry a Canaanite woman." ⁷He also knew that Jacob had obeyed his parents and gone to Paddan-aram. ⁸It was now very clear to Esau that his father did not like the local Canaanite women. ⁹So Esau visited his uncle Ishmael's family and married one of Ishmael's daughters, in addition to the wives he already had. His new wife's name was Mahalath. She was the sister of Nebaioth and the daughter of Ishmael, Abraham's son.

Jacob's Dream at Bethel

¹⁰Meanwhile, Jacob left Beersheba and traveled toward Haran. ¹¹At sundown he arrived at a good place to set up camp and stopped there for the night. Jacob found a stone to rest his head against and lay down to sleep. ¹²As he slept, he dreamed of a stairway that reached from the earth up to heaven. And he saw the angels of God going up and down the stairway.

¹³At the top of the stairway stood the LORD, and he said, "I am the LORD, the God of your grandfather Abraham, and the God of your father, Isaac. The ground you are lying on belongs to you. I am giving it to you and your descendants. ¹⁴Your descendants will be as numerous as the dust of the earth! They will spread out in all directions—to the west and the east, to the north and the south. And all the families of the earth will be blessed through you and your descendants. ¹⁵What's more, I am with you, and I will protect you wherever you go. One day I will bring you back to this land. I will not leave you until I have finished giving you everything I have promised you."

¹⁶Then Jacob awoke from his sleep and said, "Surely the LORD is in this place, and I wasn't even aware of it!" ¹⁷But he was also afraid and said, "What an awesome place this is! It is none other than the house of God, the very gateway to heaven!"

¹⁸The next morning Jacob got up very early. He took the stone he had rested his head against, and he set it upright as a memorial pillar. Then he poured olive oil over it. ¹⁹He named that place Bethel (which means "house of God"), although it was previously called Luz.

²⁰Then Jacob made this vow: "If God will indeed be with me and protect me on this journey, and if he will provide me with food and clothing, ²¹and if I return safely to my father's home, then the LORD will certainly be my God. ²²And this memorial pillar I have set up will become a place for worshiping God, and I will present to God a tenth of everything he gives me."

Jacob Arrives at Paddan-Aram

29 Then Jacob hurried on, finally arriving in the land of the east. ²He saw a well in the distance. Three flocks of sheep and goats lay in an open field beside it, waiting to be watered. But a heavy stone covered the mouth of the well.

³It was the custom there to wait for all the flocks to arrive before removing the stone and watering the animals. Afterward the stone would be placed back over

---

28:3 Hebrew *El-Shaddai*. 28:4 Hebrew *seed*; also in 28:13, 14.

28:10-19 Although Isaac had already given the blessing to Jacob, God's appearance to Jacob in a dream confirmed that God would honor his covenant with Jacob and his descendants. Jacob's dream revealed a stairway, probably reminding readers of a ziggurat, a structure meant to facilitate travel for spiritual beings between heaven and earth (see note on 11:1-9).
28:20-22 Jacob revealed his lack of trust by giving God multiple conditions. Only if God protected and provided for him by allowing him to return safely would he worship the Lord, Yahweh, as his God. Jacob kept his bargain many years later (33:20).
29:1-14 For the second time, a descendant of Abraham found a wife through a meeting at a well (see 24:1-21). Laban rushed out to meet Jacob, as he did when Abraham's servant had arrived, perhaps expecting gold and jewelry (24:29-30). But Jacob, fleeing his brother, had come empty-handed. Jacob would have to work to pay the bride-price.

the mouth of the well. ⁴Jacob went over to the shepherds and asked, "Where are you from, my friends?"

"We are from Haran," they answered.

⁵"Do you know a man there named Laban, the grandson of Nahor?" he asked.

"Yes, we do," they replied.

⁶"Is he doing well?" Jacob asked.

"Yes, he's well," they answered. "Look, here comes his daughter Rachel with the flock now."

⁷Jacob said, "Look, it's still broad daylight—too early to round up the animals. Why don't you water the sheep and goats so they can get back out to pasture?"

⁸"We can't water the animals until all the flocks have arrived," they replied. "Then the shepherds move the stone from the mouth of the well, and we water all the sheep and goats."

⁹Jacob was still talking with them when Rachel arrived with her father's flock, for she was a shepherd. ¹⁰And because Rachel was his cousin—the daughter of Laban, his mother's brother—and because the sheep and goats belonged to his uncle Laban, Jacob went over to the well and moved the stone from its mouth and watered his uncle's flock. ¹¹Then Jacob kissed Rachel, and he wept aloud. ¹²He explained to Rachel that he was her cousin on her father's side—the son of her aunt Rebekah. So Rachel quickly ran and told her father, Laban.

¹³As soon as Laban heard that his nephew Jacob had arrived, he ran out to meet him. He embraced and kissed him and brought him home. When Jacob had told him his story, ¹⁴Laban exclaimed, "You really are my own flesh and blood!"

Jacob Marries Leah and Rachel

After Jacob had stayed with Laban for about a month, ¹⁵Laban said to him, "You shouldn't work for me without pay just because we are relatives. Tell me how much your wages should be."

¹⁶Now Laban had two daughters. The older daughter was named Leah, and the younger one was Rachel. ¹⁷There was no sparkle in Leah's eyes,* but Rachel had a beautiful figure and a lovely face. ¹⁸Since Jacob was in love with Rachel, he told her father, "I'll work for you for seven years if you'll give me Rachel, your younger daughter, as my wife."

¹⁹"Agreed!" Laban replied. "I'd rather give her to you than to anyone else. Stay and work with me." ²⁰So Jacob worked seven years to pay for Rachel. But his love for her was so strong that it seemed to him but a few days.

²¹Finally, the time came for him to marry her. "I have fulfilled my agreement," Jacob said to Laban. "Now give me my wife so I can sleep with her."

²²So Laban invited everyone in the neighborhood and prepared a wedding feast. ²³But that night, when it was dark, Laban took Leah to Jacob, and he slept with her. ²⁴(Laban had given Leah a servant, Zilpah, to be her maid.)

²⁵But when Jacob woke up in the morning—it was Leah! "What have you done to me?" Jacob raged at Laban. "I worked seven years for Rachel! Why have you tricked me?"

²⁶"It's not our custom here to marry off a younger daughter ahead of the firstborn," Laban replied. ²⁷"But wait until the bridal week is over; then we'll give you Rachel, too—provided you promise to work another seven years for me."

²⁸So Jacob agreed to work seven more years. A week after Jacob had married Leah, Laban gave him Rachel, too. ²⁹(Laban gave Rachel a servant, Bilhah, to be her maid.) ³⁰So Jacob slept with Rachel, too, and he loved her much more than Leah. He then stayed and worked for Laban the additional seven years.

Jacob's Many Children

³¹When the LORD saw that Leah was unloved, he enabled her to have children, but Rachel could not conceive. ³²So Leah became pregnant and gave birth to a son. She named him Reuben,* for she said, "The LORD has noticed my misery, and now my husband will love me."

³³She soon became pregnant again and gave birth to another son. She named him Simeon,* for she said, "The LORD heard that I was unloved and has given me another son."

³⁴Then she became pregnant a third time and gave birth to another son. He was named Levi,* for she said, "Surely this time my husband will feel affection for me, since I have given him three sons!"

³⁵Once again Leah became pregnant and gave birth to another son. She named him Judah,* for she said, "Now I will praise the LORD!" And then she stopped having children.

29:17 Or *Leah had dull eyes,* or *Leah had soft eyes.* The meaning of the Hebrew is uncertain. **29:32** *Reuben* means "Look, a son!" It also sounds like the Hebrew for "He has seen my misery." **29:33** *Simeon* probably means "one who hears." **29:34** *Levi* sounds like a Hebrew term that means "being attached" or "feeling affection for." **29:35** *Judah* is related to the Hebrew term for "praise."

29:15-20 A woman being given in marriage was not a commodity to be bought and sold. The so-called bride-price ensured the seriousness of the suitor and his long-term commitment to the bride's family. Seven years of service was a high bride-price in the ancient world, but Rachel was beautiful, and Jacob was in love with her. The father of the bride would normally provide her with a dowry as well to ensure her security.

29:21-30 Laban took advantage of Jacob's desire to marry Rachel. Jacob and his mother had deceived his father and brother to gain the blessing; now his mother's brother deceived him. Laban's words in 29:26 are ironic. Jacob, the younger son, had pretended to be his older brother to gain the blessing (27:1-40). Now Leah, the older sister, pretended to be the younger sister to get a husband. God allowed the deceiver to have a dose of his own deception, giving Jacob a chance to change.

30

When Rachel saw that she wasn't having any children for Jacob, she became jealous of her sister. She pleaded with Jacob, "Give me children, or I'll die!"

²Then Jacob became furious with Rachel. "Am I God?" he asked. "He's the one who has kept you from having children!"

³Then Rachel told him, "Take my maid, Bilhah, and sleep with her. She will bear children for me,* and through her I can have a family, too." ⁴So Rachel gave her servant, Bilhah, to Jacob as a wife, and he slept with her. ⁵Bilhah became pregnant and presented him with a son. ⁶Rachel named him Dan,* for she said, "God has vindicated me! He has heard my request and given me a son." ⁷Then Bilhah became pregnant again and gave Jacob a second son. ⁸Rachel named him Naphtali,* for she said, "I have struggled hard with my sister, and I'm winning!"

⁹Meanwhile, Leah realized that she wasn't getting pregnant anymore, so she took her servant, Zilpah, and gave her to Jacob as a wife. ¹⁰Soon Zilpah presented him with a son. ¹¹Leah named him Gad,* for she said, "How fortunate I am!" ¹²Then Zilpah gave Jacob a second son. ¹³And Leah named him Asher,* for she said, "What joy is mine! Now the other women will celebrate with me."

¹⁴One day during the wheat harvest, Reuben found some mandrakes growing in a field and brought

30:3 Hebrew *bear children on my knees.* 30:6 *Dan* means "he judged" or "he vindicated." 30:8 *Naphtali* means "my struggle." 30:11 *Gad* means "good fortune." 30:13 *Asher* means "happy."

30:1-13 In ancient Mesopotamia, it was devastating for a woman not to have children, and Rachel understandably felt wronged by her infertility. She resorted to a culturally acceptable solution for infertility in ancient times—she gave her servant to Jacob as a concubine. Rachel's decision to have children through her servant, and Jacob's compliance, recalls Sarai's use of Hagar (16:1-4). The resulting frenzy to bear children reads like an arms race, with each side stockpiling weapons (in this case, sons) to outmaneuver the other.

30:14-16 Ancient Mesopotamian people considered mandrakes an aphrodisiac and aid to conception. Rachel thought the mandrakes would help her get pregnant, so she offered to trade sleeping with Jacob for a night in exchange for the plant. Leah ended up pregnant rather than Rachel. Rachel's desperation to get pregnant clouded her judgment and distracted her from trusting God to intervene.

Insight: ISRAEL'S FAMILY TREE

From the time of Abraham, rivalry and competition were rife within the family, which might explain the legacy of contention among the tribes of Israel later. Hagar had contempt for Sarah (16:4-5), but Sarah felt threatened by Hagar's son, Ishmael (21:10). Rebekah and Isaac encouraged the rivalry foretold about Jacob and Esau (25:22-26, 28). The rivalry between sisters Rachel and Leah explains much of the later rivalry among their sons (see 37:1-36), and then between the tribes. But God had compassion on Leah, who was unloved, by enabling her to bear sons for Jacob. Despite Jacob's preference for Rachel and her children, Judah's kingly tribe and Levi's priestly line came through Leah.

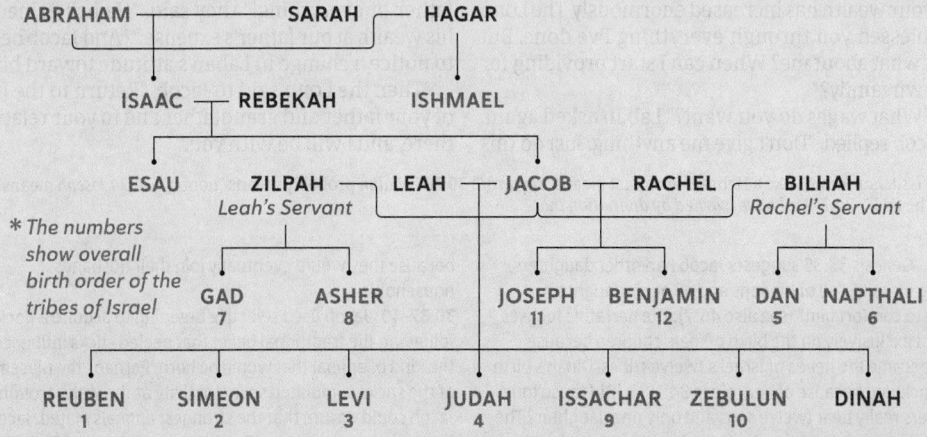

*The numbers show overall birth order of the tribes of Israel

them to his mother, Leah. Rachel begged Leah, "Please give me some of your son's mandrakes."

[15]But Leah angrily replied, "Wasn't it enough that you stole my husband? Now will you steal my son's mandrakes, too?"

Rachel answered, "I will let Jacob sleep with you tonight if you give me some of the mandrakes."

[16]So that evening, as Jacob was coming home from the fields, Leah went out to meet him. "You must come and sleep with me tonight!" she said. "I have paid for you with some mandrakes that my son found." So that night he slept with Leah. [17]And God answered Leah's prayers. She became pregnant again and gave birth to a fifth son for Jacob. [18]She named him Issachar,* for she said, "God has rewarded me for giving my servant to my husband as a wife." [19]Then Leah became pregnant again and gave birth to a sixth son for Jacob. [20]She named him Zebulun,* for she said, "God has given me a good reward. Now my husband will treat me with respect, for I have given him six sons." [21]Later she gave birth to a daughter and named her Dinah.

[22]Then God remembered Rachel's plight and answered her prayers by enabling her to have children. [23]She became pregnant and gave birth to a son. "God has removed my disgrace," she said. [24]And she named him Joseph,* for she said, "May the LORD add yet another son to my family."

Jacob's Wealth Increases

[25]Soon after Rachel had given birth to Joseph, Jacob said to Laban, "Please release me so I can go home to my own country. [26]Let me take my wives and children, for I have earned them by serving you, and let me be on my way. You certainly know how hard I have worked for you."

[27]"Please listen to me," Laban replied. "I have become wealthy, for* the LORD has blessed me because of you. [28]Tell me how much I owe you. Whatever it is, I'll pay it."

[29]Jacob replied, "You know how hard I've worked for you, and how your flocks and herds have grown under my care. [30]You had little indeed before I came, but your wealth has increased enormously. The LORD has blessed you through everything I've done. But now, what about me? When can I start providing for my own family?"

[31]"What wages do you want?" Laban asked again.

Jacob replied, "Don't give me anything. Just do this one thing, and I'll continue to tend and watch over your flocks. [32]Let me inspect your flocks today and remove all the sheep and goats that are speckled or spotted, along with all the black sheep. Give these to me as my wages. [33]In the future, when you check on the animals you have given me as my wages, you'll see that I have been honest. If you find in my flock any goats without speckles or spots, or any sheep that are not black, you will know that I have stolen them from you."

[34]"All right," Laban replied. "It will be as you say." [35]But that very day Laban went out and removed the male goats that were streaked and spotted, all the female goats that were speckled and spotted or had white patches, and all the black sheep. He placed them in the care of his own sons, [36]who took them a three-days' journey from where Jacob was. Meanwhile, Jacob stayed and cared for the rest of Laban's flock.

[37]Then Jacob took some fresh branches from poplar, almond, and plane trees and peeled off strips of bark, making white streaks on them. [38]Then he placed these peeled branches in the watering troughs where the flocks came to drink, for that was where they mated. [39]And when they mated in front of the white-streaked branches, they gave birth to young that were streaked, speckled, and spotted. [40]Jacob separated those lambs from Laban's flock. And at mating time he turned the flock to face Laban's animals that were streaked or black. This is how he built his own flock instead of increasing Laban's.

[41]Whenever the stronger females were ready to mate, Jacob would place the peeled branches in the watering troughs in front of them. Then they would mate in front of the branches. [42]But he didn't do this with the weaker ones, so the weaker lambs belonged to Laban, and the stronger ones were Jacob's. [43]As a result, Jacob became very wealthy, with large flocks of sheep and goats, female and male servants, and many camels and donkeys.

Jacob Flees from Laban

31 But Jacob soon learned that Laban's sons were grumbling about him. "Jacob has robbed our father of everything!" they said. "He has gained all his wealth at our father's expense." [2]And Jacob began to notice a change in Laban's attitude toward him.

[3]Then the LORD said to Jacob, "Return to the land of your father and grandfather and to your relatives there, and I will be with you."

30:18 *Issachar* sounds like a Hebrew term that means "reward." **30:20** *Zebulun* probably means "honor." **30:24** *Joseph* means "may he add." **30:27** Or *I have learned by divination that.*

30:21 Genesis 37:35 suggests Jacob had other daughters, saying literally, "all of his sons and all of his daughters arose to comfort him" (see also 46:7). The narrative focuses almost exclusively on the birth of male children because they became the heads of Israel's twelve tribes. Dinah's birth was included because of her role in 34:1-31. (Did those four mothers really bear twelve sons and only one daughter? The odds are against it.) Genealogies did not highlight daughters because they would eventually join their husbands' households.

30:37-40 Jacob used selective breeding to acquire a flock, following the traditional belief that peeled sticks influenced the kind of animal that would be born. Perhaps the placement of the sticks stimulated sexual activity at the water trough, so Jacob could ensure that the strongest animals mated. Jacob later acknowledged that God had prospered him (31:5-13).

Leah & Rachel

IDENTITY — Love Triangle Tragedy

A love triangle is never where you want to find sisters, yet that is exactly where we find Rachel and Leah. Leah, with "no sparkle in [her] eyes," and Rachel, with "a beautiful figure and a lovely face," both deeply desired the favor of Jacob, a cousin hired to work their father's fields who became husband to both sisters.

"Sleep with me!" Leah would cry to Jacob.

"Give me a son!" Rachel would plead.

What a juggling act Jacob had on his hands, and what discontent Rachel and Leah lugged around!

In that culture, the badge of bearing sons was like gold. It brought deep fulfillment to a woman's life and gave her a place in society. It's no wonder that Rachel envied Leah, who kept having one son after another. Rachel raged and found a way to her own "fulfillment" by giving an enslaved woman to Jacob to conceive a son for her. Leah then did the same. They were each determined to win, focused on gaining honor in their family and chasing satisfaction in what society deemed successful.

Although God listened to these women and granted their requests, finding happiness in proving ourselves isn't the lesson here. It's clear from the hungry hearts of Leah and Rachel that true fulfillment doesn't come from what the world considers success; it comes from being loved by, and loving, God. Whenever we're experiencing brokenness in our relationships, we can remember that God's love for us is deep, whole, and perfect.

> Only God satisfies the deep hunger of my heart.

LEAH'S AND RACHEL'S STORIES ARE TOLD IN GENESIS 29–35; THEY ARE ALSO MENTIONED IN RUTH 4:11.

IDENTIFY

What have you turned to for fulfillment?

Do you relate more to Leah or Rachel in this story? Why?

"All too quickly I can want to appear successful by the world's standards—whether it's the social-media-ready home, the well-mannered children, the A+ job, or the corner office. I like finding worth from the outside in. But my true worth comes from God."

WHITNEY PUTNAM is the senior director of women's events and marketing at New Life Ministries. She is an overall joy-chaser and is often found dancing in her kitchen.

⁴So Jacob called Rachel and Leah out to the field where he was watching his flock. ⁵He said to them, "I have noticed that your father's attitude toward me has changed. But the God of my father has been with me. ⁶You know how hard I have worked for your father, ⁷but he has cheated me, changing my wages ten times. But God has not allowed him to do me any harm. ⁸For if he said, 'The speckled animals will be your wages,' the whole flock began to produce speckled young. And when he changed his mind and said, 'The striped animals will be your wages,' then the whole flock produced striped young. ⁹In this way, God has taken your father's animals and given them to me.

¹⁰"One time during the mating season, I had a dream and saw that the male goats mating with the females were streaked, speckled, and spotted. ¹¹Then in my dream, the angel of God said to me, 'Jacob!' And I replied, 'Yes, here I am.'

¹²"The angel said, 'Look up, and you will see that only the streaked, speckled, and spotted males are mating with the females of your flock. For I have seen how Laban has treated you. ¹³I am the God who appeared to you at Bethel,* the place where you anointed the pillar of stone and made your vow to me. Now get ready and leave this country and return to the land of your birth.'"

¹⁴Rachel and Leah responded, "That's fine with us! We won't inherit any of our father's wealth anyway. ¹⁵He has reduced our rights to those of foreign women. And after he sold us, he wasted the money you paid him for us. ¹⁶All the wealth God has given you from our father legally belongs to us and our children. So go ahead and do whatever God has told you."

¹⁷So Jacob put his wives and children on camels, ¹⁸and he drove all his livestock in front of him. He packed all the belongings he had acquired in Paddan-aram and set out for the land of Canaan, where his father, Isaac, lived. ¹⁹At the time they left, Laban was some distance away, shearing his sheep. Rachel stole her father's household idols and took them with her. ²⁰Jacob outwitted Laban the Aramean, for they set out secretly and never told Laban they were leaving. ²¹So Jacob took all his possessions with him and crossed the Euphrates River,* heading for the hill country of Gilead.

Laban Pursues Jacob

²²Three days later, Laban was told that Jacob had fled. ²³So he gathered a group of his relatives and set out in hot pursuit. He caught up with Jacob seven days later in the hill country of Gilead. ²⁴But the previous night God had appeared to Laban the Aramean in a dream and told him, "I'm warning you—leave Jacob alone!"

²⁵Laban caught up with Jacob as he was camped in the hill country of Gilead, and he set up his camp not far from Jacob's. ²⁶"What do you mean by deceiving me like this?" Laban demanded. "How dare you drag my daughters away like prisoners of war? ²⁷Why did you slip away secretly? Why did you deceive me? And why didn't you say you wanted to leave? I would have given you a farewell feast, with singing and music, accompanied by tambourines and harps. ²⁸Why didn't you let me kiss my daughters and grandchildren and tell them good-bye? You have acted very foolishly! ²⁹I could destroy you, but the God of your father appeared to me last night and warned me, 'Leave Jacob alone!' ³⁰I can understand your feeling that you must go, and your intense longing for your father's home. But why have you stolen my gods?"

³¹"I rushed away because I was afraid," Jacob answered. "I thought you would take your daughters from me by force. ³²But as for your gods, see if you can find them, and let the person who has taken them die! And if you find anything else that belongs to you, identify it before all these relatives of ours, and I will give it back!" But Jacob did not know that Rachel had stolen the household idols.

³³Laban went first into Jacob's tent to search there, then into Leah's, and then the tents of the two servant wives—but he found nothing. Finally, he went into Rachel's tent. ³⁴But Rachel had taken the household idols and hidden them in her camel saddle, and now she was sitting on them. When Laban had thoroughly searched her tent without finding them, ³⁵she said to her father, "Please, sir, forgive me if I don't get up for you. I'm having my monthly period." So Laban continued his search, but he could not find the household idols.

³⁶Then Jacob became very angry, and he challenged Laban. "What's my crime?" he demanded. "What have I done wrong to make you chase after me as though I were a criminal? ³⁷You have rummaged through everything I own. Now show me what you found that belongs to you! Set it out here in front of us, before our relatives, for all to see. Let them judge between us!

³⁸"For twenty years I have been with you, caring for your flocks. In all that time your sheep and goats never miscarried. In all those years I never used a

---

31:13 As in Greek version and an Aramaic Targum; Hebrew reads *the God of Bethel.* 31:21 Hebrew *the river.*

31:19-20 Rachel may have wanted to regain some of the assets Laban had squandered. Possessing the idols may have constituted a claim to family inheritance, as later customs indicate. It is also probable that she worshiped idols since Jacob had not yet committed to the Lord, Yahweh, alone (see 28:20-22; 35:2-4). Laban apparently felt vulnerable without the idols because he chased Jacob's company and drew attention to them in his accusations.

31:30-35 Rachel used her monthly period as an excuse not to stand when her father entered. Although we have no indication that Rachel was actually menstruating, her bleeding would have defiled the gods. Laban scarcely would have suspected she would profane the idols. Whether or not she was menstruating, she successfully deceived her deceitful father.

single ram of yours for food. ³⁹If any were attacked and killed by wild animals, I never showed you the carcass and asked you to reduce the count of your flock. No, I took the loss myself! You made me pay for every stolen animal, whether it was taken in broad daylight or in the dark of night.

⁴⁰"I worked for you through the scorching heat of the day and through cold and sleepless nights. ⁴¹Yes, for twenty years I slaved in your house! I worked for fourteen years earning your two daughters, and then six more years for your flock. And you changed my wages ten times! ⁴²In fact, if the God of my father had not been on my side—the God of Abraham and the fearsome God of Isaac*—you would have sent me away empty-handed. But God has seen your abuse and my hard work. That is why he appeared to you last night and rebuked you!"

Jacob's Treaty with Laban

⁴³Then Laban replied to Jacob, "These women are my daughters, these children are my grandchildren, and these flocks are my flocks—in fact, everything you see is mine. But what can I do now about my daughters and their children? ⁴⁴So come, let's make a covenant, you and I, and it will be a witness to our commitment."

⁴⁵So Jacob took a stone and set it up as a monument. ⁴⁶Then he told his family members, "Gather some stones." So they gathered stones and piled them in a heap. Then Jacob and Laban sat down beside the pile of stones to eat a covenant meal. ⁴⁷To commemorate the event, Laban called the place Jegar-sahadutha (which means "witness pile" in Aramaic), and Jacob called it Galeed (which means "witness pile" in Hebrew).

⁴⁸Then Laban declared, "This pile of stones will stand as a witness to remind us of the covenant we have made today." This explains why it was called Galeed—"Witness Pile." ⁴⁹But it was also called Mizpah (which means "watchtower"), for Laban said, "May the LORD keep watch between us to make sure that we keep this covenant when we are out of each other's sight. ⁵⁰If you mistreat my daughters or if you marry other wives, God will see it even if no one else does. He is a witness to this covenant between us.

⁵¹"See this pile of stones," Laban continued, "and see this monument I have set between us. ⁵²They stand between us as witnesses of our vows. I will never pass this pile of stones to harm you, and you must never pass these stones or this monument to harm me. ⁵³I call on the God of our ancestors—the God of your grandfather Abraham and the God of my grandfather Nahor—to serve as a judge between us."

So Jacob took an oath before the fearsome God of his father, Isaac,* to respect the boundary line. ⁵⁴Then Jacob offered a sacrifice to God there on the mountain and invited everyone to a covenant feast. After they had eaten, they spent the night on the mountain.

⁵⁵*Laban got up early the next morning, and he kissed his grandchildren and his daughters and blessed them. Then he left and returned home.

32

¹*As Jacob started on his way again, angels of God came to meet him. ²When Jacob saw them, he exclaimed, "This is God's camp!" So he named the place Mahanaim.*

Jacob Sends Gifts to Esau

³Then Jacob sent messengers ahead to his brother, Esau, who was living in the region of Seir in the land of Edom. ⁴He told them, "Give this message to my master Esau: 'Humble greetings from your servant Jacob. Until now I have been living with Uncle Laban, ⁵and now I own cattle, donkeys, flocks of sheep and goats, and many servants, both men and women. I have sent these messengers to inform my lord of my coming, hoping that you will be friendly to me.'"

⁶After delivering the message, the messengers returned to Jacob and reported, "We met your brother, Esau, and he is already on his way to meet you—with an army of 400 men!" ⁷Jacob was terrified at the news. He divided his household, along with the flocks and herds and camels, into two groups. ⁸He thought, "If Esau meets one group and attacks it, perhaps the other group can escape."

⁹Then Jacob prayed, "O God of my grandfather Abraham, and God of my father, Isaac—O LORD, you told me, 'Return to your own land and to your relatives.' And you promised me, 'I will treat you kindly.' ¹⁰I am not worthy of all the unfailing love and faithfulness you have shown to me, your servant. When I left home and crossed the Jordan River, I owned nothing except a walking stick. Now my household fills two large camps! ¹¹O LORD, please rescue me from the hand of my brother, Esau. I am afraid that he is coming to attack me, along with my wives and children. ¹²But you promised me, 'I will surely treat you kindly, and I will multiply your descendants until they become as numerous as the sands along the seashore—too many to count.'"

¹³Jacob stayed where he was for the night. Then he selected these gifts from his possessions to present to his brother, Esau: ¹⁴200 female goats, 20 male goats, 200 ewes, 20 rams, ¹⁵30 female camels with their young, 40 cows, 10 bulls, 20 female donkeys,

---

31:42 Or *and the Fear of Isaac.* **31:53** Or *the Fear of his father, Isaac.* **31:55** Verse 31:55 is numbered 32:1 in Hebrew text.
32:1 Verses 32:1-32 are numbered 32:2-33 in Hebrew text. **32:2** *Mahanaim* means "two camps."

32:1-32 God had revealed himself to Jacob as he left Canaan (28:10-22). Upon his return, Jacob saw angels and wrestled with a mysterious stranger at night. The stranger changed his name from Jacob ("heel grabber") to Israel ("fights with God" or "God fights"), indicating a divine encounter. Throughout his life, Jacob had seized God's blessing. This wrestling match symbolized his whole life. Jacob's prayer in 32:9-12 finally acknowledged his own weakness and need for God's protection.

and 10 male donkeys. ¹⁶He divided these animals into herds and assigned each to different servants. Then he told his servants, "Go ahead of me with the animals, but keep some distance between the herds."

¹⁷He gave these instructions to the men leading the first group: "When my brother, Esau, meets you, he will ask, 'Whose servants are you? Where are you going? Who owns these animals?' ¹⁸You must reply, 'They belong to your servant Jacob, but they are a gift for his master Esau. Look, he is coming right behind us.'"

¹⁹Jacob gave the same instructions to the second and third herdsmen and to all who followed behind the herds: "You must say the same thing to Esau when you meet him. ²⁰And be sure to say, 'Look, your servant Jacob is right behind us.'"

Jacob thought, "I will try to appease him by sending gifts ahead of me. When I see him in person, perhaps he will be friendly to me." ²¹So the gifts were sent on ahead, while Jacob himself spent that night in the camp.

Jacob Wrestles with God

²²During the night Jacob got up and took his two wives, his two servant wives, and his eleven sons and crossed the Jabbok River with them. ²³After taking them to the other side, he sent over all his possessions.

²⁴This left Jacob all alone in the camp, and a man came and wrestled with him until the dawn began to break. ²⁵When the man saw that he would not win the match, he touched Jacob's hip and wrenched it out of its socket. ²⁶Then the man said, "Let me go, for the dawn is breaking!"

But Jacob said, "I will not let you go unless you bless me."

²⁷"What is your name?" the man asked.

He replied, "Jacob."

²⁸"Your name will no longer be Jacob," the man told him. "From now on you will be called Israel,* because you have fought with God and with men and have won."

²⁹"Please tell me your name," Jacob said.

"Why do you want to know my name?" the man replied. Then he blessed Jacob there.

³⁰Jacob named the place Peniel (which means "face of God"), for he said, "I have seen God face to face, yet my life has been spared." ³¹The sun was rising as Jacob left Peniel,* and he was limping because of the injury to his hip. ³²(Even today the people of Israel don't eat the tendon near the hip socket because of what happened that night when the man strained the tendon of Jacob's hip.)

Jacob and Esau Make Peace

33 Then Jacob looked up and saw Esau coming with his 400 men. So he divided the children among Leah, Rachel, and his two servant wives. ²He put the servant wives and their children at the front, Leah and her children next, and Rachel and Joseph last. ³Then Jacob went on ahead. As he approached his brother, he bowed to the ground seven times before him. ⁴Then Esau ran to meet him and embraced him, threw his arms around his neck, and kissed him. And they both wept.

⁵Then Esau looked at the women and children and asked, "Who are these people with you?"

"These are the children God has graciously given to me, your servant," Jacob replied. ⁶Then the servant wives came forward with their children and bowed before him. ⁷Next came Leah with her children, and they bowed before him. Finally, Joseph and Rachel came forward and bowed before him.

⁸"And what were all the flocks and herds I met as I came?" Esau asked.

Jacob replied, "They are a gift, my lord, to ensure your friendship."

⁹"My brother, I have plenty," Esau answered. "Keep what you have for yourself."

¹⁰But Jacob insisted, "No, if I have found favor with you, please accept this gift from me. And what a relief to see your friendly smile. It is like seeing the face of God! ¹¹Please take this gift I have brought you, for God has been very gracious to me. I have more than enough." And because Jacob insisted, Esau finally accepted the gift.

¹²"Well," Esau said, "let's be going. I will lead the way."

¹³But Jacob replied, "You can see, my lord, that some of the children are very young, and the flocks and herds have their young, too. If they are driven too hard, even for one day, all the animals could die. ¹⁴Please, my lord, go ahead of your servant. We will follow slowly, at a pace that is comfortable for the livestock and the children. I will meet you at Seir."

¹⁵"All right," Esau said, "but at least let me assign some of my men to guide and protect you."

Jacob responded, "That's not necessary. It's enough that you've received me warmly, my lord!"

¹⁶So Esau turned around and started back to Seir that same day. ¹⁷Jacob, on the other hand, traveled on to Succoth. There he built himself a house and

---

32:28 *Jacob* sounds like the Hebrew words for "heel" and "deceiver." *Israel* means "God fights." **32:31** Hebrew *Penuel*, a variant spelling of Peniel.

33:1-4 At first Jacob seems to be prioritizing his own safety over that of his wives and children by sending them ahead. However, as indicated in 33:3, he went ahead of all of them to meet Esau. His encounter with the mysterious stranger and the blessing he received gave him the courage to face his fear. He had dreaded this encounter for the entire journey, but Esau forgave him.

Insight — FAMILY TRAVELS THROUGH CANAAN

Jacob, Rachel and Leah, their servants, and their children journeyed across, around, and back through Canaan multiple times during their lifetimes. This map shows the routes they may have taken based on Genesis 32–38.

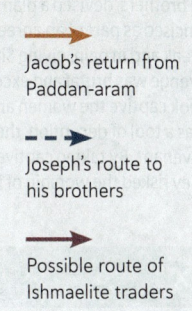

Jacob's return from Paddan-aram

Joseph's route to his brothers

Possible route of Ishmaelite traders

made shelters for his livestock. That is why the place was named Succoth (which means "shelters"). ¹⁸Later, having traveled all the way from Paddan-aram, Jacob arrived safely at the town of Shechem, in the land of Canaan. There he set up camp outside the town. ¹⁹Jacob bought the plot of land where he camped from the family of Hamor, the father of Shechem, for 100 pieces of silver.* ²⁰And there he built an altar and named it El-Elohe-Israel.*

Revenge against Shechem

34 One day Dinah, the daughter of Jacob and Leah, went to visit some of the young women who lived in the area. ²But when the local prince, Shechem son of Hamor the Hivite, saw Dinah, he seized her and raped her. ³But then he fell in love with her, and he tried to win her affection with tender words. ⁴He said to his father, Hamor, "Get me this young girl. I want to marry her."

⁵Soon Jacob heard that Shechem had defiled his daughter, Dinah. But since his sons were out in the fields herding his livestock, he said nothing until they returned. ⁶Hamor, Shechem's father, came to discuss the matter with Jacob. ⁷Meanwhile, Jacob's sons had come in from the field as soon as they heard what had happened. They were shocked and furious that their sister had been raped. Shechem had done a disgraceful thing against Jacob's family,* something that should never be done.

33:19 Hebrew *100 kesitahs;* the value or weight of the kesitah is no longer known.   33:20 *El-Elohe-Israel* means "God, the God of Israel."   34:7 Hebrew *a disgraceful thing in Israel.*

33:18-20 Jacob, like Abraham, built an altar to God at Shechem (see 12:6-7) and purchased land from local residents (23:1-20). Jacob's return to the land God promised to Abraham initiated the beginning of the next stage of covenant fulfillment.

34:1-31 The narrative includes few tales of Jacob's sons in Canaan. This tragic story is important because it illustrates the depravity of the Canaanites and explains the animosity between Jacob's sons and their neighbors. It also characterizes Levi and Simeon as violent (see 49:5-7) and Jacob as passive in his old age.

34:1-2 If Dinah's visit to the local women was unwise, the narrator does not suggest it, and she is not faulted for what she wore or what she said. The blame falls squarely on Shechem for violating Dinah. "Consent" in those days was primarily given by the men whose job it was to protect the women of their family, and Shechem had not sought Jacob's permission to wed. Instead, like Adam and Eve in the Garden of Eden, Shechem saw what he wanted and seized it—in this case, Dinah.

⁸Hamor tried to speak with Jacob and his sons. "My son Shechem is truly in love with your daughter," he said. "Please let him marry her. ⁹In fact, let's arrange other marriages, too. You give us your daughters for our sons, and we will give you our daughters for your sons. ¹⁰And you may live among us; the land is open to you! Settle here and trade with us. And feel free to buy property in the area."

¹¹Then Shechem himself spoke to Dinah's father and brothers. "Please be kind to me, and let me marry her," he begged. "I will give you whatever you ask. ¹²No matter what dowry or gift you demand, I will gladly pay it—just give me the girl as my wife."

¹³But since Shechem had defiled their sister, Dinah, Jacob's sons responded deceitfully to Shechem and his father, Hamor. ¹⁴They said to them, "We couldn't possibly allow this, because you're not circumcised. It would be a disgrace for our sister to marry a man like you! ¹⁵But here is a solution. If every man among you will be circumcised like we are, ¹⁶then we will give you our daughters, and we'll take your daughters for ourselves. We will live among you and become one people. ¹⁷But if you don't agree to be circumcised, we will take her and be on our way."

¹⁸Hamor and his son Shechem agreed to their proposal. ¹⁹Shechem wasted no time in acting on this request, for he wanted Jacob's daughter desperately. Shechem was a highly respected member of his family, ²⁰and he went with his father, Hamor, to present this proposal to the leaders at the town gate.

34:8-12 After sexually violating Dinah, Shechem kept her (34:26) while trying to get permission to marry her. His father, Hamor, saw intermarriage as a means to gain control of Jacob's wealth (34:10, 23), but God had promised to give Jacob the land (28:13-15). Intermarriage with the Canaanites would have jeopardized the integrity of the covenant family (24:1-8; 28:1-4).

34:13-31 Without waiting for their father to respond, Simeon and Levi, Dinah's full brothers, devised a plan to get revenge. Having been circumcised as part of an agreement, the men of Shechem were weak and in pain, giving Simeon and Levi the advantage. Their revenge was brutal and excessive. They killed every man and took captive the women and children. By using circumcision as a tool of deception, they showed disdain for the sign of the covenant. By taking captive Canaanites into their community, they risked the worship of idols.

Come Close

VIOLATED: THE REAL "FIX"

SCRIPTURE CONNECTION: GENESIS 34:1-4

The Bible does not mention anyone talking to Dinah about what had happened or how she felt. Was she hurt, afraid, ashamed, angry, or blaming herself? How did she feel as she saw the destruction that followed? Did she feel more shame, pain, or fear?

I know these feelings, the raw emotions of a rape survivor. My father didn't know how to react and did nothing—just like Jacob. My siblings were angry and wanted to remedy the situation—just like Dinah's brothers. People wanted to fix things so they could move on but looked past me, busying themselves with action. I needed peace in my soul to calm the rage, uncertainty, shame, hurt, and fear.

The night after, feeling so completely alone in a room full of people, John 14:27 hovered around my raging thoughts—peace, *not* as the world gives; *not* fixing, but peace.

I felt a hand on my heart, a palpable blanket of peace—covering, warm, quiet, unexplainable, undefinable, life-affirming.

REFLECT "I am leaving you with a gift—peace of mind and heart. And the peace I give is a gift the world cannot give." JOHN 14:27

Jesus, help me to trust you to give me what I really need—your peace. Amen.

CONSIDER "Whenever his hand is laid upon you, it gives inexpressible peace and comfort, and the sense that 'underneath are the everlasting arms' (Deuteronomy 33:27), full of support, provision, comfort, and strength" OSWALD CHAMBERS, *My Utmost for His Highest*.

Jesus gives you peace unlike anything this world has to offer.

ELISABETH SELZER ROGERS, MDiv, MA, PhD, is a passionate believer and follower of Christ, bringing his love to the secular world through mentoring, coaching, and modeling his unconditional love.

²¹"These men are our friends," they said. "Let's invite them to live here among us and trade freely. Look, the land is large enough to hold them. We can take their daughters as wives and let them marry ours. ²²But they will consider staying here and becoming one people with us only if all of our men are circumcised, just as they are. ²³But if we do this, all their livestock and possessions will eventually be ours. Come, let's agree to their terms and let them settle here among us."

²⁴So all the men in the town council agreed with Hamor and Shechem, and every male in the town was circumcised. ²⁵But three days later, when their wounds were still sore, two of Jacob's sons, Simeon and Levi, who were Dinah's full brothers, took their swords and entered the town without opposition. Then they slaughtered every male there, ²⁶including Hamor and his son Shechem. They killed them with their swords, then took Dinah from Shechem's house and returned to their camp.

²⁷Meanwhile, the rest of Jacob's sons arrived. Finding the men slaughtered, they plundered the town because their sister had been defiled there. ²⁸They seized all the flocks and herds and donkeys—everything they could lay their hands on, both inside the town and outside in the fields. ²⁹They looted all their wealth and plundered their houses. They also took all their little children and wives and led them away as captives.

³⁰Afterward Jacob said to Simeon and Levi, "You have ruined me! You've made me stink among all the people of this land—among all the Canaanites and Perizzites. We are so few that they will join forces and crush us. I will be ruined, and my entire household will be wiped out!"

³¹"But why should we let him treat our sister like a prostitute?" they retorted angrily.

Jacob's Return to Bethel

35 Then God said to Jacob, "Get ready and move to Bethel and settle there. Build an altar there to the God who appeared to you when you fled from your brother, Esau."

²So Jacob told everyone in his household, "Get rid of all your pagan idols, purify yourselves, and put on clean clothing. ³We are now going to Bethel, where I will build an altar to the God who answered my prayers when I was in distress. He has been with me wherever I have gone."

⁴So they gave Jacob all their pagan idols and earrings, and he buried them under the great tree near Shechem. ⁵As they set out, a terror from God spread over the people in all the towns of that area, so no one attacked Jacob's family.

⁶Eventually, Jacob and his household arrived at Luz (also called Bethel) in Canaan. ⁷Jacob built an altar there and named the place El-bethel (which means "God of Bethel"), because God had appeared to him there when he was fleeing from his brother, Esau.

⁸Soon after this, Rebekah's old nurse, Deborah, died. She was buried beneath the oak tree in the valley below Bethel. Ever since, the tree has been called Allon-bacuth (which means "oak of weeping").

⁹Now that Jacob had returned from Paddan-aram, God appeared to him again at Bethel. God blessed him, ¹⁰saying, "Your name is Jacob, but you will not be called Jacob any longer. From now on your name will be Israel."* So God renamed him Israel.

¹¹Then God said, "I am El-Shaddai—'God Almighty.' Be fruitful and multiply. You will become a great nation, even many nations. Kings will be among your descendants! ¹²And I will give you the land I once gave to Abraham and Isaac. Yes, I will give it to you and your descendants after you." ¹³Then God went up from the place where he had spoken to Jacob.

¹⁴Jacob set up a stone pillar to mark the place where God had spoken to him. Then he poured wine over it as an offering to God and anointed the pillar with olive oil. ¹⁵And Jacob named the place Bethel (which means "house of God"), because God had spoken to him there.

The Deaths of Rachel and Isaac

¹⁶Leaving Bethel, Jacob and his clan moved on toward Ephrath. But Rachel went into labor while they were still some distance away. Her labor pains were intense. ¹⁷After a very hard delivery, the midwife finally exclaimed, "Don't be afraid—you have another son!" ¹⁸Rachel was about to die, but with her last breath she named the baby Ben-oni (which means "son of my sorrow"). The baby's father, however, called him Benjamin (which means "son of my right hand"). ¹⁹So Rachel died and was buried on the way to Ephrath (that is, Bethlehem). ²⁰Jacob set up a stone monument over Rachel's grave, and it can be seen there to this day.

²¹Then Jacob* traveled on and camped beyond

35:10 *Jacob* sounds like the Hebrew words for "heel" and "deceiver." *Israel* means "God fights."   **35:21** Hebrew *Israel;* also in 35:22a. The names "Jacob" and "Israel" are often interchanged throughout the Old Testament, referring sometimes to the individual patriarch and sometimes to the nation.

35:1-15 Jacob had not committed himself exclusively to the God of Abraham until now. (Note his conditional worship in 28:20-22.) Here he vowed wholehearted devotion to God, requiring his family to destroy their idols. In response, God reiterated the creation blessing ("be fruitful and multiply," see 1:28) and his promise of fame and land.

35:16-20 Benjamin's birth completed the family, but Rachel died in childbirth. Rachel found the name "son of my sorrow" appropriate, but Jacob changed it to "son of my right hand." Jacob thus turned the day of sorrow into a day of hope. The tribe of Benjamin later inherited the land where Rachel was buried (see Joshua 18:21-28).

Migdal-eder. ²²While he was living there, Reuben had intercourse with Bilhah, his father's concubine, and Jacob soon heard about it.

These are the names of the twelve sons of Jacob:

²³The sons of Leah were Reuben (Jacob's oldest son), Simeon, Levi, Judah, Issachar, and Zebulun.
²⁴The sons of Rachel were Joseph and Benjamin.
²⁵The sons of Bilhah, Rachel's servant, were Dan and Naphtali.
²⁶The sons of Zilpah, Leah's servant, were Gad and Asher.

These are the names of the sons who were born to Jacob at Paddan-aram.

²⁷So Jacob returned to his father, Isaac, in Mamre, which is near Kiriath-arba (now called Hebron), where Abraham and Isaac had both lived as foreigners. ²⁸Isaac lived for 180 years. ²⁹Then he breathed his last and died at a ripe old age, joining his ancestors in death. And his sons, Esau and Jacob, buried him.

Descendants of Esau

36 This is the account of the descendants of Esau (also known as Edom). ²Esau married two young women from Canaan: Adah, the daughter of Elon the Hittite; and Oholibamah, the daughter of Anah and granddaughter of Zibeon the Hivite. ³He also married his cousin Basemath, who was the daughter of Ishmael and the sister of Nebaioth. ⁴Adah gave birth to a son named Eliphaz for Esau. Basemath gave birth to a son named Reuel. ⁵Oholibamah gave birth to sons named Jeush, Jalam, and Korah. All these sons were born to Esau in the land of Canaan.

⁶Esau took his wives, his children, and his entire household, along with his livestock and cattle—all the wealth he had acquired in the land of Canaan—and moved away from his brother, Jacob. ⁷There was not enough land to support them both because of all the livestock and possessions they had acquired. ⁸So Esau (also known as Edom) settled in the hill country of Seir.

⁹This is the account of Esau's descendants, the Edomites, who lived in the hill country of Seir.

¹⁰These are the names of Esau's sons: Eliphaz, the son of Esau's wife Adah; and Reuel, the son of Esau's wife Basemath.
¹¹The descendants of Eliphaz were Teman, Omar, Zepho, Gatam, and Kenaz. ¹²Timna, the concubine of Esau's son Eliphaz, gave birth to a son named Amalek. These are the descendants of Esau's wife Adah.
¹³The descendants of Reuel were Nahath, Zerah, Shammah, and Mizzah. These are the descendants of Esau's wife Basemath.
¹⁴Esau also had sons through Oholibamah, the daughter of Anah and granddaughter of Zibeon. Their names were Jeush, Jalam, and Korah.

¹⁵These are the descendants of Esau who became the leaders of various clans:

The descendants of Esau's oldest son, Eliphaz, became the leaders of the clans of Teman, Omar, Zepho, Kenaz, ¹⁶Korah, Gatam, and Amalek. These are the clan leaders in the land of Edom who descended from Eliphaz. All these were descendants of Esau's wife Adah.
¹⁷The descendants of Esau's son Reuel became the leaders of the clans of Nahath, Zerah, Shammah, and Mizzah. These are the clan leaders in the land of Edom who descended from Reuel. All these were descendants of Esau's wife Basemath.
¹⁸The descendants of Esau and his wife Oholibamah became the leaders of the clans of Jeush, Jalam, and Korah. These are the clan leaders who descended from Esau's wife Oholibamah, the daughter of Anah.

¹⁹These are the clans descended from Esau (also known as Edom), identified by their clan leaders.

Original Peoples of Edom

²⁰These are the names of the tribes that descended from Seir the Horite. They lived in the land of Edom: Lotan, Shobal, Zibeon, Anah, ²¹Dishon, Ezer, and Dishan. These were the Horite clan leaders, the descendants of Seir, who lived in the land of Edom.

²²The descendants of Lotan were Hori and Hemam. Lotan's sister was named Timna.
²³The descendants of Shobal were Alvan, Manahath, Ebal, Shepho, and Onam.
²⁴The descendants of Zibeon were Aiah and Anah. (This is the Anah who discovered the hot springs in the wilderness while he was grazing his father's donkeys.)
²⁵The descendants of Anah were his son, Dishon, and his daughter, Oholibamah.
²⁶The descendants of Dishon* were Hemdan, Eshban, Ithran, and Keran.

36:26 Hebrew *Dishan*, a variant spelling of Dishon; compare 36:21, 28.

35:22 The sexual exploitation of women was frighteningly common in ancient times, as it is today. Reuben had sex with Bilhah, thus defiling his father's marriage bed. Perhaps Reuben, as the oldest son, was trying to replace his father as head of the clan (see 2 Samuel 16:15-22), but by this action he lost his birthright (see Genesis 49:3-4).
35:23-26 The sons of Jacob appear in the order in which their mothers were intimate with Jacob. The result is a chiasm (literary sandwich), with Rachel's favored children in the center—Leah, Rachel, Bilhah, Zilpah. The last sentence is a generalization—Benjamin was born after they left Paddan-aram (35:16-18).
36:1-43 The careful record of Esau's line shows God's continuing concern for those who were not part of the covenant family. It reminds us of God's purpose to bless all nations through Abraham and Sarah's family.

²⁷The descendants of Ezer were Bilhan, Zaavan, and Akan.
²⁸The descendants of Dishan were Uz and Aran.
²⁹So these were the leaders of the Horite clans: Lotan, Shobal, Zibeon, Anah, ³⁰Dishon, Ezer, and Dishan. The Horite clans are named after their clan leaders, who lived in the land of Seir.

Rulers of Edom

³¹These are the kings who ruled in the land of Edom before any king ruled over the Israelites*:

³²Bela son of Beor, who ruled in Edom from his city of Dinhabah.
³³When Bela died, Jobab son of Zerah from Bozrah became king in his place.
³⁴When Jobab died, Husham from the land of the Temanites became king in his place.
³⁵When Husham died, Hadad son of Bedad became king in his place and ruled from the city of Avith. He was the one who defeated the Midianites in the land of Moab.
³⁶When Hadad died, Samlah from the city of Masrekah became king in his place.
³⁷When Samlah died, Shaul from the city of Rehoboth-on-the-River became king in his place.
³⁸When Shaul died, Baal-hanan son of Acbor became king in his place.
³⁹When Baal-hanan son of Acbor died, Hadad* became king in his place and ruled from the city of Pau. His wife was Mehetabel, the daughter of Matred and granddaughter of Me-zahab.

⁴⁰These are the names of the leaders of the clans descended from Esau, who lived in the places named for them: Timna, Alvah, Jetheth, ⁴¹Oholibamah, Elah, Pinon, ⁴²Kenaz, Teman, Mibzar, ⁴³Magdiel, and Iram. These are the leaders of the clans of Edom, listed according to their settlements in the land they occupied. They all descended from Esau, the ancestor of the Edomites.

Joseph's Dreams

37 So Jacob settled again in the land of Canaan, where his father had lived as a foreigner. ²This is the account of Jacob and his family. When Joseph was seventeen years old, he often tended his father's flocks. He worked for his half brothers, the sons of his father's wives Bilhah and Zilpah. But Joseph reported to his father some of the bad things his brothers were doing.

³Jacob* loved Joseph more than any of his other children because Joseph had been born to him in his old age. So one day Jacob had a special gift made for Joseph—a beautiful robe.* ⁴But his brothers hated Joseph because their father loved him more than the rest of them. They couldn't say a kind word to him.

⁵One night Joseph had a dream, and when he told his brothers about it, they hated him more than ever. ⁶"Listen to this dream," he said. ⁷"We were out in the field, tying up bundles of grain. Suddenly my bundle stood up, and your bundles all gathered around and bowed low before mine!"

⁸His brothers responded, "So you think you will be our king, do you? Do you actually think you will reign over us?" And they hated him all the more because of his dreams and the way he talked about them.

⁹Soon Joseph had another dream, and again he told his brothers about it. "Listen, I have had another dream," he said. "The sun, moon, and eleven stars bowed low before me!"

¹⁰This time he told the dream to his father as well as to his brothers, but his father scolded him. "What kind of dream is that?" he asked. "Will your mother and I and your brothers actually come and bow to the ground before you?" ¹¹But while his brothers were jealous of Joseph, his father wondered what the dreams meant.

¹²Soon after this, Joseph's brothers went to pasture their father's flocks at Shechem. ¹³When they had been gone for some time, Jacob said to Joseph, "Your brothers are pasturing the sheep at Shechem. Get ready, and I will send you to them."

"I'm ready to go," Joseph replied.

¹⁴"Go and see how your brothers and the flocks are getting along," Jacob said. "Then come back and bring me a report." So Jacob sent him on his way, and Joseph traveled to Shechem from their home in the valley of Hebron.

¹⁵When he arrived there, a man from the area noticed him wandering around the countryside. "What are you looking for?" he asked.

¹⁶"I'm looking for my brothers," Joseph replied. "Do you know where they are pasturing their sheep?"

¹⁷"Yes," the man told him. "They have moved on from here, but I heard them say, 'Let's go on to Dothan.'" So Joseph followed his brothers to Dothan and found them there.

36:31 Or *before an Israelite king ruled over them.* 36:39 As in some Hebrew manuscripts, Samaritan Pentateuch, and Syriac version (see also 1 Chr 1:50); most Hebrew manuscripts read *Hadar.* 37:3a Hebrew *Israel;* also in 37:13. See note on 35:21. 37:3b Traditionally rendered *a coat of many colors.* The exact meaning of the Hebrew is uncertain.

37:1–50:26 The Joseph saga is an important episode in the history of God's covenant people. Historians consider it one of the oldest novellas in the world, with brilliant character development and gripping dialogue. Joseph exhibited wisdom, faithfulness, and trust in God despite great suffering. God rewarded him with wealth, honor, and a family of his own. His wisdom ensured survival for both the Egyptians and his extended family during a severe famine.

37:4 Jacob's favoritism toward Joseph inflamed his other sons' hatred. Just as Isaac's and Rebekah's favoritism separated their family, Jacob's favoritism would separate him from his son Joseph.

> "Anybody who has survived [her] childhood has enough information about life to last … the rest of [her] days."
>
> FLANNERY O'CONNOR
> (1925–1964) American novelist and Christian

Joseph Sold into Slavery

¹⁸When Joseph's brothers saw him coming, they recognized him in the distance. As he approached, they made plans to kill him. ¹⁹"Here comes the dreamer!" they said. ²⁰"Come on, let's kill him and throw him into one of these cisterns. We can tell our father, 'A wild animal has eaten him.' Then we'll see what becomes of his dreams!"

²¹But when Reuben heard of their scheme, he came to Joseph's rescue. "Let's not kill him," he said. ²²"Why should we shed any blood? Let's just throw him into this empty cistern here in the wilderness. Then he'll die without our laying a hand on him." Reuben was secretly planning to rescue Joseph and return him to his father.

²³So when Joseph arrived, his brothers ripped off the beautiful robe he was wearing. ²⁴Then they grabbed him and threw him into the cistern. Now the cistern was empty; there was no water in it. ²⁵Then, just as they were sitting down to eat, they looked up and saw a caravan of camels in the distance coming toward them. It was a group of Ishmaelite traders taking a load of gum, balm, and aromatic resin from Gilead down to Egypt.

²⁶Judah said to his brothers, "What will we gain by killing our brother? We'd have to cover up the crime.* ²⁷Instead of hurting him, let's sell him to those Ishmaelite traders. After all, he is our brother—our own flesh and blood!" And his brothers agreed. ²⁸So when the Ishmaelites, who were Midianite traders, came by, Joseph's brothers pulled him out of the cistern and sold him to them for twenty pieces* of silver. And the traders took him to Egypt.

²⁹Some time later, Reuben returned to get Joseph out of the cistern. When he discovered that Joseph was missing, he tore his clothes in grief. ³⁰Then he went back to his brothers and lamented, "The boy is gone! What will I do now?"

³¹Then the brothers killed a young goat and dipped Joseph's robe in its blood. ³²They sent the beautiful robe to their father with this message: "Look at what we found. Doesn't this robe belong to your son?"

³³Their father recognized it immediately. "Yes," he said, "it is my son's robe. A wild animal must have eaten him. Joseph has clearly been torn to pieces!" ³⁴Then Jacob tore his clothes and dressed himself in burlap. He mourned deeply for his son for a long time. ³⁵His family all tried to comfort him, but he refused to be comforted. "I will go to my grave* mourning for my son," he would say, and then he would weep.

³⁶Meanwhile, the Midianite traders* arrived in Egypt, where they sold Joseph to Potiphar, an officer of Pharaoh, the king of Egypt. Potiphar was captain of the palace guard.

Judah and Tamar

38 About this time, Judah left home and moved to Adullam, where he stayed with a man named Hirah. ²There he saw a Canaanite woman, the daughter of Shua, and he married her. When he slept with her, ³she became pregnant and gave birth to a son, and he named the boy Er. ⁴Then she became pregnant again and gave birth to another son, and she named him Onan. ⁵And when she gave birth to a third son, she named him Shelah. At the time of Shelah's birth, they were living at Kezib.

⁶In the course of time, Judah arranged for his firstborn son, Er, to marry a young woman named Tamar. ⁷But Er was a wicked man in the Lord's sight, so the Lord took his life. ⁸Then Judah said to Er's brother Onan, "Go and marry Tamar, as our law requires of the brother of a man who has died. You must produce an heir for your brother."

37:26 Hebrew *cover his blood*. **37:28** Hebrew *20 [shekels]*, about 8 ounces or 228 grams in weight. **37:35** Hebrew *go down to Sheol*. **37:36** Hebrew *the Medanites*. The relationship between the Midianites and Medanites is unclear; compare 37:28. See also 25:2.

37:25 The Ishmaelite traders carried spices to Egypt for embalming. From Jacob's perspective, his son had already died. Ironically, Genesis ends with Joseph embalmed in a coffin in Egypt (50:26), but his sojourn there gave life. Through it, God preserved Joseph's life and the lives of his brothers and their families.
38:1-30 This story may seem like a random interruption to the Joseph saga, but it provides a crucial piece of the story—Judah's character transformation. It had been Judah's idea to sell his brother Joseph into slavery, a move to profit from his disappearance (37:26-27). His claim to care about his brother in 37:27 rings hollow. However, by the end of the saga, Judah had offered himself to be enslaved in place of his brother Benjamin (44:30-34).
38:8-10 This custom is known as levirate marriage (from the

⁹But Onan was not willing to have a child who would not be his own heir. So whenever he had intercourse with his brother's wife, he spilled the semen on the ground. This prevented her from having a child who would belong to his brother. ¹⁰But the LORD considered it evil for Onan to deny a child to his dead brother. So the LORD took Onan's life, too.

¹¹Then Judah said to Tamar, his daughter-in-law, "Go back to your parents' home and remain a widow until my son Shelah is old enough to marry you." (But Judah didn't really intend to do this because he was afraid Shelah would also die, like his two brothers.) So Tamar went back to live in her father's home.

Latin *levir*, "husband's brother"). If a man died childless, his brother or nearest relative was to marry his widow to produce a child to carry on the family name of the deceased and inherit his property (see Deuteronomy 25:5-10). The practice also provided a secure home for the childless widow. Onan demonstrated selfishness by using Tamar for sex while ensuring she would not get pregnant. God refused to tolerate this abuse.

38:11 Judah promised to give Tamar to his third son, Shelah, when he was ready to marry, but by sending her to her family, he proved unwilling to provide for her.

No Perfect Family

SCRIPTURE CONNECTION: GENESIS 38:1-30

If you're worried your family disqualifies you from serving God's purposes, you don't have to look far in the Bible to see families just as raw and flawed as yours. Families made of real people with real issues give hope that God doesn't just use the put-together and polished to move his purposes forward. He uses all of us just as we are.

Here are three things I've learned from families in Genesis that help me live my purpose with my own family:

- Conflicts don't have to define families. Abram told Lot, "Let's not allow this conflict to come between us or our herdsmen. After all, we are close relatives!" (13:8). With intentional conversation we can put differences aside.
- God fills in when I can't meet my children's needs. Hagar thought she was leaving her son to die, but she discovered otherwise. "God heard the boy crying, and the angel of God called to Hagar from heaven, . . . 'Go to him and comfort him, for I will make a great nation from his descendants'" (21:17-18).
- Honoring one another gains rewards—and truth comes out. After deception on the part of both Judah and his daughter-in-law, Tamar, Judah said, "She is more righteous than I am" (38:26). Family relationships help to highlight our true character.

> There are no perfect families. Only real ones. Loved ones.

My family, like Bible families, is made up of imperfect people. We fail each other, but that doesn't disqualify us from God's plan. If he can use the real problems of these real families, he can use me in mine.

IMAGINE

What do you observe about families and conflict in your experiences?

How can your family's pain points bring God glory?

"Every family has pain that God can use to further his purposes in the world. We might not see it yet, but he can redeem any family drama."

ALEXANDRA KUYKENDALL is a cofounder of The Open Door Sisterhood and author of several books, including *Seeking Out Goodness: Finding the True and Beautiful All around You*.

¹²Some years later Judah's wife died. After the time of mourning was over, Judah and his friend Hirah the Adullamite went up to Timnah to supervise the shearing of his sheep. ¹³Someone told Tamar, "Look, your father-in-law is going up to Timnah to shear his sheep."

¹⁴Tamar was aware that Shelah had grown up, but no arrangements had been made for her to come and marry him. So she changed out of her widow's clothing and covered herself with a veil to disguise herself. Then she sat beside the road at the entrance to the village of Enaim, which is on the road to Timnah. ¹⁵Judah noticed her and thought she was a prostitute, since she had covered her face. ¹⁶So he stopped and propositioned her. "Let me have sex with you," he said, not realizing that she was his own daughter-in-law.

"How much will you pay to have sex with me?" Tamar asked.

¹⁷"I'll send you a young goat from my flock," Judah promised.

"But what will you give me to guarantee that you will send the goat?" she asked.

¹⁸"What kind of guarantee do you want?" he replied.

She answered, "Leave me your identification seal and its cord and the walking stick you are carrying." So Judah gave them to her. Then he had intercourse with her, and she became pregnant. ¹⁹Afterward she went back home, took off her veil, and put on her widow's clothing as usual.

²⁰Later Judah asked his friend Hirah the Adullamite to take the young goat to the woman and to pick up the things he had given her as his guarantee. But Hirah couldn't find her. ²¹So he asked the men who lived there, "Where can I find the shrine prostitute who was sitting beside the road at the entrance to Enaim?"

"We've never had a shrine prostitute here," they replied.

²²So Hirah returned to Judah and told him, "I couldn't find her anywhere, and the men of the village claim they've never had a shrine prostitute there."

²³"Then let her keep the things I gave her," Judah said. "I sent the young goat as we agreed, but you couldn't find her. We'd be the laughingstock of the village if we went back again to look for her."

²⁴About three months later, Judah was told, "Tamar, your daughter-in-law, has acted like a prostitute. And now, because of this, she's pregnant."

"Bring her out, and let her be burned!" Judah demanded.

²⁵But as they were taking her out to kill her, she sent this message to her father-in-law: "The man who owns these things made me pregnant. Look closely. Whose seal and cord and walking stick are these?"

²⁶Judah recognized them immediately and said, "She is more righteous than I am, because I didn't arrange for her to marry my son Shelah." And Judah never slept with Tamar again.

²⁷When the time came for Tamar to give birth, it was discovered that she was carrying twins. ²⁸While she was in labor, one of the babies reached out his hand. The midwife grabbed it and tied a scarlet string around the child's wrist, announcing, "This one came out first." ²⁹But then he pulled back his hand, and out came his brother! "What!" the midwife exclaimed. "How did you break out first?" So he was named Perez.* ³⁰Then the baby with the scarlet string on his wrist was born, and he was named Zerah.*

Joseph in Potiphar's House

39 When Joseph was taken to Egypt by the Ishmaelite traders, he was purchased by Potiphar, an Egyptian officer. Potiphar was captain of the guard for Pharaoh, the king of Egypt.

²The LORD was with Joseph, so he succeeded in everything he did as he served in the home of his Egyptian master. ³Potiphar noticed this and realized that the LORD was with Joseph, giving him success in everything he did. ⁴This pleased Potiphar, so he soon made Joseph his personal attendant. He put him in charge of his entire household and everything he owned. ⁵From the day Joseph was put in charge of his master's household and property, the LORD began to bless Potiphar's household for Joseph's sake. All his household affairs ran smoothly, and his crops and livestock flourished. ⁶So Potiphar gave Joseph complete administrative responsibility over everything he owned. With Joseph there, he didn't worry about a thing—except what kind of food to eat!

Joseph was a very handsome and well-built young

38:29 *Perez* means "breaking out." 38:30 *Zerah* means "scarlet" or "brightness."

38:12-24 When Tamar saw that Judah had not kept his promise or fulfilled his responsibility as the closest male relative to marry her himself, she took matters into her own hands. She disguised herself and propositioned him, not out of lust or revenge, but out of duty to carry on his family line (see Judah's response in 38:26). Her plan worked, and she became pregnant with twins. The purpose of the story is not to hold up Tamar's actions as a model but to highlight Judah's hypocrisy. He would pay for what he thought was a prostitute but condemn Tamar for prostitution, all the while failing to provide for her.

38:25-26 Tamar became the great(times five)-grandmother of Boaz, who was the great-grandfather of King David (see Ruth 4:18-22). Her action led to the preservation of the tribe through which Israel's kings would come. At the story's climax, Tamar identified Judah as the father of her children. Rather than dismiss her charges, Judah acknowledged his wrongdoing. In the end, we see how this incident transformed his character. God can do remarkable things with those who acknowledge their sin and repent.

39:6-18 Back-to-back with the story of Judah and Tamar is another tale of power and sex. However, this time the woman had suffered no legal wrong. Potiphar's wife, unfaithful to her husband and mastered by lust, used constant pressure and physical force to try to seduce Joseph. When she failed, she lied to destroy his reputation.

Tamar

IDENTITY — Rewarded Anyway

Tamar remembers...

Sometimes it's hard to know what is right. But I believe God works for our good, like banks that direct a rushing river.

My first husband, Er, was an evil man. When he died, the law said that his next brother, Onan, was to give me an heir. He refused to fulfill that responsibility. But God saw him and caused Onan to die, too.

I thought I could rely on my father-in-law, Judah. He promised me his last son, though I would have to wait for him to come of age. It was all a lie.

When I saw an opportunity to make things right, I took it. I held Judah accountable to conceive an heir. I felt I had no other options. Judah had all the power, and I had none. So, I tricked him into obedience.

Judah realized what he did was even worse. He called me "more righteous" (38:26). More important than Judah's praise, God rewarded my desire to follow him. In time, my name would appear in the Messiah's family tree (Matthew 1:3).

Some say my action also changed Judah's heart. He acknowledged that he had failed to provide for a vulnerable woman in his family. He changed from the Judah who had sold one brother (Joseph) into slavery, to the Judah who risked his life to protect another brother (Benjamin). God redeemed not just one family, but all.

God created a way that brings life. Like banks of a rushing river, his Kingdom current rushes forward. Responding in faith, even imperfectly, can lead to reward.

TAMAR'S STORY IS TOLD IN GENESIS 38.

> Responding to God in faith, even imperfectly, can lead to reward.

IDENTIFY

How does Tamar's story encourage us to respond in faith, even if we aren't sure how?

> "Watching others break rules to protect themselves is disheartening. I know, though, that God's ways are like the banks of a river. They keep back the flood of sin and push his Kingdom forward in a strong current of accountability and responsibility."

CARA DAY is a writer and illustrator. She has served with Stonecroft Ministries helping women live "extraordinary."

man, ⁷and Potiphar's wife soon began to look at him lustfully. "Come and sleep with me," she demanded.

⁸But Joseph refused. "Look," he told her, "my master trusts me with everything in his entire household. ⁹No one here has more authority than I do. He has held back nothing from me except you, because you are his wife. How could I do such a wicked thing? It would be a great sin against God."

¹⁰She kept putting pressure on Joseph day after day, but he refused to sleep with her, and he kept out of her way as much as possible. ¹¹One day, however, no one else was around when he went in to do his work. ¹²She came and grabbed him by his cloak, demanding, "Come on, sleep with me!" Joseph tore himself away, but he left his cloak in her hand as he ran from the house.

¹³When she saw that she was holding his cloak and he had fled, ¹⁴she called out to her servants. Soon all the men came running. "Look!" she said. "My husband has brought this Hebrew slave here to make fools of us! He came into my room to rape me, but I screamed. ¹⁵When he heard me scream, he ran outside and got away, but he left his cloak behind with me."

¹⁶She kept the cloak with her until her husband came home. ¹⁷Then she told him her story. "That Hebrew slave you've brought into our house tried to come in and fool around with me," she said. ¹⁸"But when I screamed, he ran outside, leaving his cloak with me!"

Joseph Put in Prison

¹⁹Potiphar was furious when he heard his wife's story about how Joseph had treated her. ²⁰So he took Joseph and threw him into the prison where the

---

Come Close

LUST: NOTICE WHEN YOU NOTICE

SCRIPTURE CONNECTION: GENESIS 39:1-20

Our church service was beginning. I was about twelve years old. An older gentleman entered with three very handsome young men. My friend could not help herself.

"Ooooh," she said loudly. We laughed about it for weeks.

I'm betting Potiphar's wife murmured something to a handmaiden when Joseph entered her home. According to 39:6, "Joseph was a very handsome and well-built young man." She noticed. We notice. But noticing is not where it stopped. She "soon began to look at him lustfully" (39:7).

It always starts with noticing. The eyes, the smile, the build, the laugh, the kindness, or the instant connection. Something is noticed. This should be our first warning.

Joseph was in Potiphar's home for quite some time. That meant Potiphar's wife had time for second looks, innocent-seeming interactions, and excuses to catch him alone. Each moment was likely replayed in her mind.

The noticing became lusting.

Lust is a hungry monster that demands more. "One more look," it whispers. "Surely you have a reason to talk to him," it suggests. It will not stop until it has you crossing the line it wants you to. And across that line is always the ruin of someone's life.

Joseph got thrown into jail. Marriages fester. Families erode.

We will notice. It is what we do next that matters.

REFLECT "Potiphar's wife soon began to look at him lustfully." GENESIS 39:7

Lord, when I "notice," please help me, like Joseph, take immediate action to notice you noticing and flee from temptation. Amen.

CONSIDER "When something is awakened in us by another man ... we do have a choice in that moment. We choose to accept the awakening as an invitation to go find that with *our* man.... Or to pray, if we are single, that this sort of man ... will come to us from God's hand" STASI AND JOHN ELDREDGE, *Captivating*.

> Notice when you notice. It's what you do next that matters.

CARA DAY is a writer and illustrator. She has served with Stonecroft Ministries helping women live "extraordinary."

king's prisoners were held, and there he remained. ²¹But the LORD was with Joseph in the prison and showed him his faithful love. And the LORD made Joseph a favorite with the prison warden. ²²Before long, the warden put Joseph in charge of all the other prisoners and over everything that happened in the prison. ²³The warden had no more worries, because Joseph took care of everything. The LORD was with him and caused everything he did to succeed.

Joseph Interprets Two Dreams

40 Some time later, Pharaoh's chief cup-bearer and chief baker offended their royal master. ²Pharaoh became angry with these two officials, ³and he put them in the prison where Joseph was, in the palace of the captain of the guard. ⁴They remained in prison for quite some time, and the captain of the guard assigned them to Joseph, who looked after them.

⁵While they were in prison, Pharaoh's cup-bearer and baker each had a dream one night, and each dream had its own meaning. ⁶When Joseph saw them the next morning, he noticed that they both looked upset. ⁷"Why do you look so worried today?" he asked them.

⁸And they replied, "We both had dreams last night, but no one can tell us what they mean."

"Interpreting dreams is God's business," Joseph replied. "Go ahead and tell me your dreams."

⁹So the chief cup-bearer told Joseph his dream first. "In my dream," he said, "I saw a grapevine in front of me. ¹⁰The vine had three branches that began to bud and blossom, and soon it produced clusters of ripe grapes. ¹¹I was holding Pharaoh's wine cup in my hand, so I took a cluster of grapes and squeezed the juice into the cup. Then I placed the cup in Pharaoh's hand."

¹²"This is what the dream means," Joseph said. "The three branches represent three days. ¹³Within three days Pharaoh will lift you up and restore you to your position as his chief cup-bearer. ¹⁴And please remember me and do me a favor when things go well for you. Mention me to Pharaoh, so he might let me out of this place. ¹⁵For I was kidnapped from my homeland, the land of the Hebrews, and now I'm here in prison, but I did nothing to deserve it."

¹⁶When the chief baker saw that Joseph had given the first dream such a positive interpretation, he said to Joseph, "I had a dream, too. In my dream there were three baskets of white pastries stacked on my head. ¹⁷The top basket contained all kinds of pastries for Pharaoh, but the birds came and ate them from the basket on my head."

¹⁸"This is what the dream means," Joseph told him. "The three baskets also represent three days. ¹⁹Three days from now Pharaoh will lift you up and impale your body on a pole. Then birds will come and peck away at your flesh."

²⁰Pharaoh's birthday came three days later, and he prepared a banquet for all his officials and staff. He summoned* his chief cup-bearer and chief baker to join the other officials. ²¹He then restored the chief cup-bearer to his former position, so he could again hand Pharaoh his cup. ²²But Pharaoh impaled the chief baker, just as Joseph had predicted when he interpreted his dream. ²³Pharaoh's chief cup-bearer, however, forgot all about Joseph, never giving him another thought.

Pharaoh's Dreams

41 Two full years later, Pharaoh dreamed that he was standing on the bank of the Nile River. ²In his dream he saw seven fat, healthy cows come up out of the river and begin grazing in the marsh grass. ³Then he saw seven more cows come up behind them from the Nile, but these were scrawny and thin. These cows stood beside the fat cows on the riverbank. ⁴Then the scrawny, thin cows ate the seven healthy, fat cows! At this point in the dream, Pharaoh woke up.

⁵But he fell asleep again and had a second dream. This time he saw seven heads of grain, plump and beautiful, growing on a single stalk. ⁶Then seven more heads of grain appeared, but these were shriveled and withered by the east wind. ⁷And these thin heads swallowed up the seven plump, well-formed heads! Then Pharaoh woke up again and realized it was a dream.

⁸The next morning Pharaoh was very disturbed by the dreams. So he called for all the magicians and wise men of Egypt. When Pharaoh told them his dreams, not one of them could tell him what they meant.

⁹Finally, the king's chief cup-bearer spoke up. "Today I have been reminded of my failure," he told Pharaoh. ¹⁰"Some time ago, you were angry with the chief baker and me, and you imprisoned us in the palace of the captain of the guard. ¹¹One night the chief baker and I each had a dream, and each dream had its own meaning. ¹²There was a young Hebrew man

40:20 Hebrew *He lifted up the head of.*

39:19-23 In spite of false accusations resulting in Joseph's imprisonment, God was with Joseph and made him prosper. The warden soon noticed his administrative skills and put him in charge. As in Potiphar's household, Joseph excelled in his work because he was diligent, skilled, and trustworthy.

40:1-22 Joseph did not lose faith in God's promises. Joseph's own dreams had not been fulfilled (37:5-11), but his readiness to interpret others' dreams (40:8) shows that he had not abandoned hope in divine revelation.

40:23–41:32 The cupbearer forgot Joseph (40:23), but God did not. Soon Pharaoh asked Joseph to interpret a dream. By honoring God as the one who could help Pharaoh understand his dreams, Joseph encouraged Pharaoh to trust God (41:16).

with us in the prison who was a slave of the captain of the guard. We told him our dreams, and he told us what each of our dreams meant. [13]And everything happened just as he had predicted. I was restored to my position as cup-bearer, and the chief baker was executed and impaled on a pole."

[14]Pharaoh sent for Joseph at once, and he was quickly brought from the prison. After he shaved and changed his clothes, he went in and stood before Pharaoh. [15]Then Pharaoh said to Joseph, "I had a dream last night, and no one here can tell me what it means. But I have heard that when you hear about a dream you can interpret it."

[16]"It is beyond my power to do this," Joseph replied. "But God can tell you what it means and set you at ease."

[17]So Pharaoh told Joseph his dream. "In my dream," he said, "I was standing on the bank of the Nile River, [18]and I saw seven fat, healthy cows come up out of the river and begin grazing in the marsh grass. [19]But then I saw seven sick-looking cows, scrawny and thin, come up after them. I've never seen such sorry-looking animals in all the land of Egypt. [20]These thin, scrawny cows ate the seven fat cows. [21]But afterward you wouldn't have known it, for they were still as thin and scrawny as before! Then I woke up.

[22]"In my dream I also saw seven heads of grain, full and beautiful, growing on a single stalk. [23]Then seven more heads of grain appeared, but these were blighted, shriveled, and withered by the east wind. [24]And the shriveled heads swallowed the seven healthy heads. I told these dreams to the magicians, but no one could tell me what they mean."

[25]Joseph responded, "Both of Pharaoh's dreams mean the same thing. God is telling Pharaoh in advance what he is about to do. [26]The seven healthy cows and the seven healthy heads of grain both represent seven years of prosperity. [27]The seven thin, scrawny cows that came up later and the seven thin heads of grain, withered by the east wind, represent seven years of famine.

[28]"This will happen just as I have described it, for God has revealed to Pharaoh in advance what he is about to do. [29]The next seven years will be a period of great prosperity throughout the land of Egypt. [30]But afterward there will be seven years of famine so great that all the prosperity will be forgotten in Egypt. Famine will destroy the land. [31]This famine will be so severe that even the memory of the good years will be erased. [32]As for having two similar dreams, it means that these events have been decreed by God, and he will soon make them happen.

[33]"Therefore, Pharaoh should find an intelligent and wise man and put him in charge of the entire land of Egypt. [34]Then Pharaoh should appoint supervisors over the land and let them collect one-fifth of all the crops during the seven good years. [35]Have them gather all the food produced in the good years that are just ahead and bring it to Pharaoh's storehouses. Store it away, and guard it so there will be food in the cities. [36]That way there will be enough to eat when the seven years of famine come to the land of Egypt. Otherwise this famine will destroy the land."

Joseph Made Ruler of Egypt

[37]Joseph's suggestions were well received by Pharaoh and his officials. [38]So Pharaoh asked his officials, "Can we find anyone else like this man so obviously filled with the spirit of God?" [39]Then Pharaoh said to Joseph, "Since God has revealed the meaning of the dreams to you, clearly no one else is as intelligent or wise as you are. [40]You will be in charge of my court, and all my people will take orders from you. Only I, sitting on my throne, will have a rank higher than yours."

[41]Pharaoh said to Joseph, "I hereby put you in charge of the entire land of Egypt." [42]Then Pharaoh removed his signet ring from his hand and placed it on Joseph's finger. He dressed him in fine linen clothing and hung a gold chain around his neck. [43]Then he had Joseph ride in the chariot reserved for his second-in-command. And wherever Joseph went, the command was shouted, "Kneel down!" So Pharaoh put Joseph in charge of all Egypt. [44]And Pharaoh said to him, "I am Pharaoh, but no one will lift a hand or foot in the entire land of Egypt without your approval."

[45]Then Pharaoh gave Joseph a new Egyptian name, Zaphenath-paneah.* He also gave him a wife, whose name was Asenath. She was the daughter of Potiphera, the priest of On.* So Joseph took charge of the entire land of Egypt. [46]He was thirty years old when he began serving in the court of Pharaoh, the king of Egypt. And when Joseph left Pharaoh's presence, he inspected the entire land of Egypt.

[47]As predicted, for seven years the land produced bumper crops. [48]During those years, Joseph gathered all the crops grown in Egypt and stored the grain from the surrounding fields in the cities. [49]He piled up huge amounts of grain like sand on the seashore. Finally, he stopped keeping records because there was too much to measure.

[50]During this time, before the first of the famine years, two sons were born to Joseph and his wife, Asenath, the daughter of Potiphera, the priest of On. [51]Joseph named his older son Manasseh,* for he

---

41:45a *Zaphenath-paneah* probably means "God speaks and lives." **41:45b** Greek version reads *of Heliopolis;* also in 41:50.
41:51 *Manasseh* sounds like a Hebrew term that means "causing to forget."

41:33-49 Joseph's wisdom in managing national resources during a famine blessed not just Egypt but also surrounding nations. During Joseph's tenure, God's promise to bless all nations through Abraham's descendants began to be fulfilled (12:1-3). The mention of grain "like sand on the seashore" (41:49) evokes God's promise to Abraham (22:17).

said, "God has made me forget all my troubles and everyone in my father's family." ⁵²Joseph named his second son Ephraim,* for he said, "God has made me fruitful in this land of my grief."

⁵³At last the seven years of bumper crops throughout the land of Egypt came to an end. ⁵⁴Then the seven years of famine began, just as Joseph had predicted. The famine also struck all the surrounding countries, but throughout Egypt there was plenty of food. ⁵⁵Eventually, however, the famine spread throughout the land of Egypt as well. And when the people cried out to Pharaoh for food, he told them, "Go to Joseph, and do whatever he tells you." ⁵⁶So with severe famine everywhere, Joseph opened up the storehouses and distributed grain to the Egyptians, for the famine was severe throughout the land of Egypt. ⁵⁷And people from all around came to Egypt to buy grain from Joseph because the famine was severe throughout the world.

Joseph's Brothers Go to Egypt

42 When Jacob heard that grain was available in Egypt, he said to his sons, "Why are you standing around looking at one another? ²I have heard there is grain in Egypt. Go down there, and buy enough grain to keep us alive. Otherwise we'll die."

³So Joseph's ten older brothers went down to Egypt to buy grain. ⁴But Jacob wouldn't let Joseph's younger brother, Benjamin, go with them, for fear some harm might come to him. ⁵So Jacob's* sons arrived in Egypt along with others to buy food, for the famine was in Canaan as well.

⁶Since Joseph was governor of all Egypt and in charge of selling grain to all the people, it was to him that his brothers came. When they arrived, they bowed before him with their faces to the ground. ⁷Joseph recognized his brothers instantly, but he pretended to be a stranger and spoke harshly to them. "Where are you from?" he demanded.

"From the land of Canaan," they replied. "We have come to buy food."

⁸Although Joseph recognized his brothers, they didn't recognize him. ⁹And he remembered the dreams he'd had about them many years before. He said to them, "You are spies! You have come to see how vulnerable our land has become."

¹⁰"No, my lord!" they exclaimed. "Your servants have simply come to buy food. ¹¹We are all brothers—members of the same family. We are honest men, sir! We are not spies!"

¹²"Yes, you are!" Joseph insisted. "You have come to see how vulnerable our land has become."

¹³"Sir," they said, "there are actually twelve of us. We, your servants, are all brothers, sons of a man living in the land of Canaan. Our youngest brother is back there with our father right now, and one of our brothers is no longer with us."

¹⁴But Joseph insisted, "As I said, you are spies! ¹⁵This is how I will test your story. I swear by the life of Pharaoh that you will never leave Egypt unless your youngest brother comes here! ¹⁶One of you must go and get your brother. I'll keep the rest of you here in prison. Then we'll find out whether or not your story is true. By the life of Pharaoh, if it turns out that you don't have a younger brother, then I'll know you are spies."

¹⁷So Joseph put them all in prison for three days. ¹⁸On the third day Joseph said to them, "I am a God-fearing man. If you do as I say, you will live. ¹⁹If you really are honest men, choose one of your brothers to remain in prison. The rest of you may go home with grain for your starving families. ²⁰But you must bring your youngest brother back to me. This will prove that you are telling the truth, and you will not die." To this they agreed.

²¹Speaking among themselves, they said, "Clearly we are being punished because of what we did to Joseph long ago. We saw his anguish when he pleaded for his life, but we wouldn't listen. That's why we're in this trouble."

²²"Didn't I tell you not to sin against the boy?" Reuben asked. "But you wouldn't listen. And now we have to answer for his blood!"

²³Of course, they didn't know that Joseph understood them, for he had been speaking to them through an interpreter. ²⁴Now he turned away from them and began to weep. When he regained his composure, he spoke to them again. Then he chose Simeon from among them and had him tied up right before their eyes.

²⁵Joseph then ordered his servants to fill the men's sacks with grain, but he also gave secret instructions to return each brother's payment at the top of his

---

41:52 *Ephraim* sounds like a Hebrew term that means "fruitful." 42:5 Hebrew *Israel's*. See note on 35:21.

41:50-52 Joseph enjoyed immense success in Egypt, but his sons' names hint at his sorrow. When he named his son Ephraim, he called Egypt the "land of my grief" (41:52). Ironically, by naming his son Manasseh and declaring "God has made me forget all my troubles and everyone in my father's family," he indicated that he had not forgotten at all. He wanted to forget, but his deepest longing was to be reconciled. His strong emotional reaction to his brothers later in the story made this clear (42:24; 43:30; 45:1-15).
42:6-9 Joseph's brothers bowed to him, which fulfilled the dreams he had experienced as a boy (37:5-11). He proceeded to test them to discern whether their hearts had changed since selling him into slavery. The brothers had considered Joseph a spy for their father and had treated him roughly (37:2, 14, 18-28). Joseph put them in a similar situation to see how they would respond.
42:21-28 Since Joseph spoke to his brothers through a translator, he could listen to them discuss their predicament. They clearly regretted how they had treated Joseph. However, Joseph wanted to see more than regret. He wanted evidence of transformation. By requiring them to return with Benjamin, their father's other favorite son, he would see if the brothers had overcome their tendency to be jealous.

WHAT THE BIBLE SAYS ABOUT Work

We Work and Rest Following God's Rhythms

God blessed the seventh day and declared it holy, because it was the day when he rested from all his work of creation. **GENESIS 2:3**

You have six days each week for your ordinary work, but the seventh day must be a Sabbath day of complete rest, a holy day dedicated to the Lord. **EXODUS 35:2**

For all who have entered into God's rest have rested from their labors, just as God did after creating the world. **HEBREWS 4:10**

We Work for the Real Boss

Work willingly at whatever you do, as though you were working for the Lord rather than for people. Remember that the Lord will give you an inheritance as your reward, and that the Master you are serving is Christ. **COLOSSIANS 3:23-24**

Work Justly

Do not make your hired workers wait until the next day to receive their pay. **LEVITICUS 19:13**

As workers who tend a fig tree are allowed to eat the fruit, so workers who protect their employer's interests will be rewarded. **PROVERBS 27:18**

Work willingly at whatever you do ...

She is energetic and strong

Get Skilled

You have expert goldsmiths and silversmiths and workers of bronze and iron. Now begin the work, and may the LORD be with you!
1 CHRONICLES 22:16

Do you see any truly competent workers? They will serve kings rather than working for ordinary people.
PROVERBS 22:29

Our First "Job Description"

God blessed them and said, "Be fruitful and multiply. Fill the earth and govern it. Reign over the fish in the sea, the birds in the sky, and all the animals that scurry along the ground."
GENESIS 1:28

The LORD God placed the man in the Garden of Eden to tend and watch over it. **GENESIS 2:15**

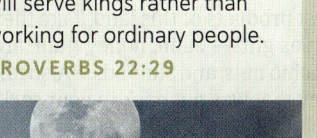

A Prayer for Our Work

May the Lord our God show us his approval and make our efforts successful. Yes, make our efforts successful!
PSALM 90:17

Work Hard

Lazy people are soon poor; hard workers get rich.
PROVERBS 10:4

A little extra sleep, a little more slumber, a little folding of the hands to rest—then poverty will pounce on you like a bandit; scarcity will attack you like an armed robber.
PROVERBS 24:33-34

She is energetic and strong, a hard worker. **PROVERBS 31:17**

How We Work Matters More Than Where We Work

Work willingly at whatever you do, as though you were working for the Lord rather than for people. Remember that the Lord will give you an inheritance as your reward, and that the Master you are serving is Christ. **COLOSSIANS 3:23-24**

Make it your goal to live a quiet life, minding your own business and working with your hands, just as we instructed you before. Then people who are not believers will respect the way you live, and you will not need to depend on others.
1 THESSALONIANS 4:11-12

sack. He also gave them supplies for their journey home. ²⁶So the brothers loaded their donkeys with the grain and headed for home.

²⁷But when they stopped for the night and one of them opened his sack to get grain for his donkey, he found his money in the top of his sack. ²⁸"Look!" he exclaimed to his brothers. "My money has been returned; it's here in my sack!" Then their hearts sank. Trembling, they said to each other, "What has God done to us?"

²⁹When the brothers came to their father, Jacob, in the land of Canaan, they told him everything that had happened to them. ³⁰"The man who is governor of the land spoke very harshly to us," they told him. "He accused us of being spies scouting the land. ³¹But we said, 'We are honest men, not spies. ³²We are twelve brothers, sons of one father. One brother is no longer with us, and the youngest is at home with our father in the land of Canaan.'

³³"Then the man who is governor of the land told us, 'This is how I will find out if you are honest men. Leave one of your brothers here with me, and take grain for your starving families and go on home. ³⁴But you must bring your youngest brother back to me. Then I will know you are honest men and not spies. Then I will give you back your brother, and you may trade freely in the land.'"

³⁵As they emptied out their sacks, there in each man's sack was the bag of money he had paid for the grain! The brothers and their father were terrified when they saw the bags of money. ³⁶Jacob exclaimed, "You are robbing me of my children! Joseph is gone! Simeon is gone! And now you want to take Benjamin, too. Everything is going against me!"

³⁷Then Reuben said to his father, "You may kill my two sons if I don't bring Benjamin back to you. I'll be responsible for him, and I promise to bring him back."

³⁸But Jacob replied, "My son will not go down with you. His brother Joseph is dead, and he is all I have left. If anything should happen to him on your journey, you would send this grieving, white-haired man to his grave.*"

The Brothers Return to Egypt

43 But the famine continued to ravage the land of Canaan. ²When the grain they had brought from Egypt was almost gone, Jacob said to his sons, "Go back and buy us a little more food."

³But Judah said, "The man was serious when he warned us, 'You won't see my face again unless your brother is with you.' ⁴If you send Benjamin with us, we will go down and buy more food. ⁵But if you don't let Benjamin go, we won't go either. Remember, the man said, 'You won't see my face again unless your brother is with you.'"

⁶"Why were you so cruel to me?" Jacob* moaned. "Why did you tell him you had another brother?"

⁷"The man kept asking us questions about our family," they replied. "He asked, 'Is your father still alive? Do you have another brother?' So we answered his questions. How could we know he would say, 'Bring your brother down here'?"

⁸Judah said to his father, "Send the boy with me, and we will be on our way. Otherwise we will all die of starvation—and not only we, but you and our little ones. ⁹I personally guarantee his safety. You may hold me responsible if I don't bring him back to you. Then let me bear the blame forever. ¹⁰If we hadn't wasted all this time, we could have gone and returned twice by now."

¹¹So their father, Jacob, finally said to them, "If it can't be avoided, then at least do this. Pack your bags with the best products of this land. Take them down to the man as gifts—balm, honey, gum, aromatic resin, pistachio nuts, and almonds. ¹²Also take double the money that was put back in your sacks, as it was probably someone's mistake. ¹³Then take your brother, and go back to the man. ¹⁴May God Almighty* give you mercy as you go before the man, so that he will release Simeon and let Benjamin return. But if I must lose my children, so be it."

¹⁵So the men packed Jacob's gifts and double the money and headed off with Benjamin. They finally arrived in Egypt and presented themselves to Joseph. ¹⁶When Joseph saw Benjamin with them, he said to the manager of his household, "These men will eat with me this noon. Take them inside the palace. Then go slaughter an animal, and prepare a big feast." ¹⁷So the man did as Joseph told him and took them into Joseph's palace.

¹⁸The brothers were terrified when they saw that they were being taken into Joseph's house. "It's because of the money someone put in our sacks last time we were here," they said. "He plans to pretend that we stole it. Then he will seize us, make us slaves, and take our donkeys."

42:38 Hebrew *to Sheol*.   43:6 Hebrew *Israel*; also in 43:11. See note on 35:21.   43:14 Hebrew *El-Shaddai*.

42:36-38 Jacob made it clear that losing Benjamin would be more than he could bear. Reuben was the first to take responsibility for Benjamin, though he offered his sons' lives rather than his own. His bargain exhibits a rather twisted logic that reminds us of Lot (19:8).

43:9 Judah demonstrated his change of heart by offering to take personal responsibility for Benjamin. He already knew what it felt like to carry the guilt for a lost brother. His offer was serious.

43:15—45:28 The brothers were terrified that they would be accused of stealing money, but Joseph and his household manager treated them kindly. Their relief turned to terror when Joseph's silver cup was found in Benjamin's sack. Joseph was testing them to see whether they would sacrifice themselves to prevent Benjamin's enslavement. Judah immediately stepped forward and offered himself instead of Benjamin, proving he had truly changed. Joseph revealed his identity, forgave his brothers, and invited them to move to Egypt to survive the famine.

A Feast at Joseph's Palace

¹⁹The brothers approached the manager of Joseph's household and spoke to him at the entrance to the palace. ²⁰"Sir," they said, "we came to Egypt once before to buy food. ²¹But as we were returning home, we stopped for the night and opened our sacks. Then we discovered that each man's money—the exact amount paid—was in the top of his sack! Here it is; we have brought it back with us. ²²We also have additional money to buy more food. We have no idea who put our money in our sacks."

²³"Relax. Don't be afraid," the household manager told them. "Your God, the God of your father, must have put this treasure into your sacks. I know I received your payment." Then he released Simeon and brought him out to them.

²⁴The manager then led the men into Joseph's palace. He gave them water to wash their feet and provided food for their donkeys. ²⁵They were told they would be eating there, so they prepared their gifts for Joseph's arrival at noon.

²⁶When Joseph came home, they gave him the gifts they had brought him, then bowed low to the ground before him. ²⁷After greeting them, he asked, "How is your father, the old man you spoke about? Is he still alive?"

²⁸"Yes," they replied. "Our father, your servant, is alive and well." And they bowed low again.

²⁹Then Joseph looked at his brother Benjamin, the son of his own mother. "Is this your youngest brother, the one you told me about?" Joseph asked. "May God be gracious to you, my son." ³⁰Then Joseph hurried from the room because he was overcome with emotion for his brother. He went into his private room, where he broke down and wept. ³¹After washing his face, he came back out, keeping himself under control. Then he ordered, "Bring out the food!"

³²The waiters served Joseph at his own table, and his brothers were served at a separate table. The Egyptians who ate with Joseph sat at their own table, because Egyptians despise Hebrews and refuse to eat with them. ³³Joseph told each of his brothers where to sit, and to their amazement, he seated them according to age, from oldest to youngest. ³⁴And Joseph filled their plates with food from his own table, giving Benjamin five times as much as he gave the others. So they feasted and drank freely with him.

Joseph's Silver Cup

44 When his brothers were ready to leave, Joseph gave these instructions to his palace manager: "Fill each of their sacks with as much grain as they can carry, and put each man's money back into his sack. ²Then put my personal silver cup at the top of the youngest brother's sack, along with the money for his grain." So the manager did as Joseph instructed him.

³The brothers were up at dawn and were sent on their journey with their loaded donkeys. ⁴But when they had gone only a short distance and were barely out of the city, Joseph said to his palace manager, "Chase after them and stop them. When you catch up with them, ask them, 'Why have you repaid my kindness with such evil? ⁵Why have you stolen my master's silver cup,* which he uses to predict the future? What a wicked thing you have done!'"

⁶When the palace manager caught up with the men, he spoke to them as he had been instructed.

⁷"What are you talking about?" the brothers responded. "We are your servants and would never do such a thing! ⁸Didn't we return the money we found in our sacks? We brought it back all the way from the land of Canaan. Why would we steal silver or gold from your master's house? ⁹If you find his cup with any one of us, let that man die. And all the rest of us, my lord, will be your slaves."

¹⁰"That's fair," the man replied. "But only the one who stole the cup will be my slave. The rest of you may go free."

¹¹They all quickly took their sacks from the backs of their donkeys and opened them. ¹²The palace manager searched the brothers' sacks, from the oldest to the youngest. And the cup was found in Benjamin's sack! ¹³When the brothers saw this, they tore their clothing in despair. Then they loaded their donkeys again and returned to the city.

¹⁴Joseph was still in his palace when Judah and his brothers arrived, and they fell to the ground before him. ¹⁵"What have you done?" Joseph demanded. "Don't you know that a man like me can predict the future?"

¹⁶Judah answered, "Oh, my lord, what can we say to you? How can we explain this? How can we prove our innocence? God is punishing us for our sins. My lord, we have all returned to be your slaves—all of us, not just our brother who had your cup in his sack."

¹⁷"No," Joseph said. "I would never do such a thing! Only the man who stole the cup will be my slave. The rest of you may go back to your father in peace."

Judah Speaks for His Brothers

¹⁸Then Judah stepped forward and said, "Please, my lord, let your servant say just one word to you. Please, do not be angry with me, even though you are as powerful as Pharaoh himself.

¹⁹"My lord, previously you asked us, your servants, 'Do you have a father or a brother?' ²⁰And we responded, 'Yes, my lord, we have a father who is an old man, and his youngest son is a child of his old age. His full brother is dead, and he alone is left of his mother's children, and his father loves him very much.'

²¹"And you said to us, 'Bring him here so I can see him with my own eyes.' ²²But we said to you, 'My lord, the boy cannot leave his father, for his father would

---

44:5 As in Greek version; Hebrew lacks this phrase.

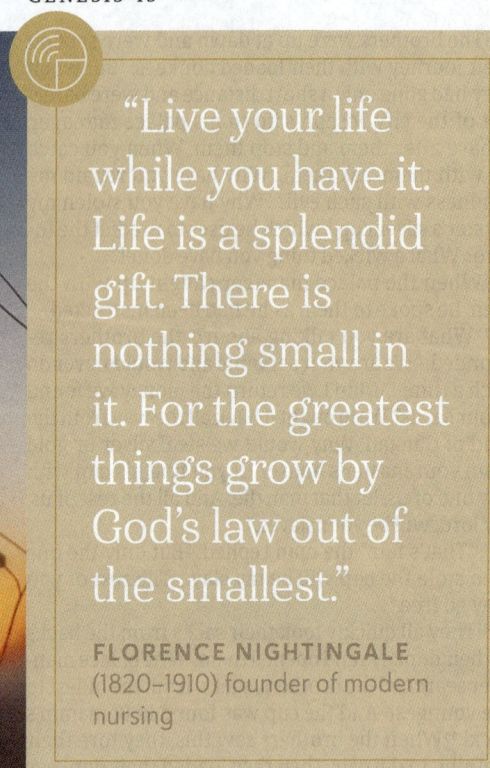

> "Live your life while you have it. Life is a splendid gift. There is nothing small in it. For the greatest things grow by God's law out of the smallest."
>
> **FLORENCE NIGHTINGALE**
> (1820–1910) founder of modern nursing

die.' ²³But you told us, 'Unless your youngest brother comes with you, you will never see my face again.'

²⁴"So we returned to your servant, our father, and told him what you had said. ²⁵Later, when he said, 'Go back again and buy us more food,' ²⁶we replied, 'We can't go unless you let our youngest brother go with us. We'll never get to see the man's face unless our youngest brother is with us.'

²⁷"Then my father said to us, 'As you know, my wife had two sons, ²⁸and one of them went away and never returned. Doubtless he was torn to pieces by some wild animal. I have never seen him since. ²⁹Now if you take his brother away from me, and any harm comes to him, you will send this grieving, white-haired man to his grave.'*

³⁰"And now, my lord, I cannot go back to my father without the boy. Our father's life is bound up in the boy's life. ³¹If he sees that the boy is not with us, our father will die. We, your servants, will indeed be responsible for sending that grieving, white-haired man to his grave. ³²My lord, I guaranteed to my father that I would take care of the boy. I told him, 'If I don't bring him back to you, I will bear the blame forever.'

³³"So please, my lord, let me stay here as a slave instead of the boy, and let the boy return with his brothers. ³⁴For how can I return to my father if the boy is not with me? I couldn't bear to see the anguish this would cause my father!"

Joseph Reveals His Identity

45 Joseph could stand it no longer. There were many people in the room, and he said to his attendants, "Out, all of you!" So he was alone with his brothers when he told them who he was. ²Then he broke down and wept. He wept so loudly the Egyptians could hear him, and word of it quickly carried to Pharaoh's palace.

³"I am Joseph!" he said to his brothers. "Is my father still alive?" But his brothers were speechless! They were stunned to realize that Joseph was standing there in front of them. ⁴"Please, come closer," he said to them. So they came closer. And he said again, "I am Joseph, your brother, whom you sold into slavery in Egypt. ⁵But don't be upset, and don't be angry with yourselves for selling me to this place. It was God who sent me here ahead of you to preserve your lives. ⁶This famine that has ravaged the land for two years will last five more years, and there will be neither plowing nor harvesting. ⁷God has sent me ahead of you to keep you and your families alive and to preserve many survivors.* ⁸So it was God who sent me here, not you! And he is the one who made me an adviser* to Pharaoh—the manager of his entire palace and the governor of all Egypt.

⁹"Now hurry back to my father and tell him, 'This is what your son Joseph says: God has made me master over all the land of Egypt. So come down to me immediately! ¹⁰You can live in the region of Goshen, where you can be near me with all your children and grandchildren, your flocks and herds, and everything you own. ¹¹I will take care of you there, for there are still five years of famine ahead of us. Otherwise you, your household, and all your animals will starve.'"

¹²Then Joseph added, "Look! You can see for yourselves, and so can my brother Benjamin, that I really am Joseph! ¹³Go tell my father of my honored position here in Egypt. Describe for him everything you have seen, and then bring my father here quickly." ¹⁴Weeping with joy, he embraced Benjamin, and Benjamin did the same. ¹⁵Then Joseph kissed each of his brothers and wept over them, and after that they began talking freely with him.

Pharaoh Invites Jacob to Egypt

¹⁶The news soon reached Pharaoh's palace: "Joseph's brothers have arrived!" Pharaoh and his officials were all delighted to hear this.

¹⁷Pharaoh said to Joseph, "Tell your brothers, 'This is what you must do: Load your pack animals, and hurry back to the land of Canaan. ¹⁸Then get your father and all of your families, and return here to

---

44:29 Hebrew *to Sheol;* also in 44:31. 45:7 Or *and to save you with an extraordinary rescue.* The meaning of the Hebrew is uncertain. 45:8 Hebrew *a father.*

me. I will give you the very best land in Egypt, and you will eat from the best that the land produces.'"

¹⁹Then Pharaoh said to Joseph, "Tell your brothers, 'Take wagons from the land of Egypt to carry your little children and your wives, and bring your father here. ²⁰Don't worry about your personal belongings, for the best of all the land of Egypt is yours.'"

²¹So the sons of Jacob* did as they were told. Joseph provided them with wagons, as Pharaoh had commanded, and he gave them supplies for the journey. ²²And he gave each of them new clothes—but to Benjamin he gave five changes of clothes and 300 pieces* of silver. ²³He also sent his father ten male donkeys loaded with the finest products of Egypt, and ten female donkeys loaded with grain and bread and other supplies he would need on his journey.

²⁴So Joseph sent his brothers off, and as they left, he called after them, "Don't quarrel about all this along the way!" ²⁵And they left Egypt and returned to their father, Jacob, in the land of Canaan.

²⁶"Joseph is still alive!" they told him. "And he is governor of all the land of Egypt!" Jacob was stunned at the news—he couldn't believe it. ²⁷But when they repeated to Jacob everything Joseph had told them, and when he saw the wagons Joseph had sent to carry him, their father's spirits revived.

²⁸Then Jacob exclaimed, "It must be true! My son Joseph is alive! I must go and see him before I die."

Jacob's Journey to Egypt

46 So Jacob* set out for Egypt with all his possessions. And when he came to Beersheba, he offered sacrifices to the God of his father, Isaac. ²During the night God spoke to him in a vision. "Jacob! Jacob!" he called.

"Here I am," Jacob replied.

³"I am God,* the God of your father," the voice said. "Do not be afraid to go down to Egypt, for there I will make your family into a great nation. ⁴I will go with you down to Egypt, and I will bring you back again. You will die in Egypt, but Joseph will be with you to close your eyes."

⁵So Jacob left Beersheba, and his sons took him to Egypt. They carried him and their little ones and their wives in the wagons Pharaoh had provided for them. ⁶They also took all their livestock and all the personal belongings they had acquired in the land of Canaan. So Jacob and his entire family went to Egypt—⁷sons and grandsons, daughters and granddaughters—all his descendants.

⁸These are the names of the descendants of Israel—the sons of Jacob—who went to Egypt:

Reuben was Jacob's oldest son. ⁹The sons of Reuben were Hanoch, Pallu, Hezron, and Carmi.
¹⁰The sons of Simeon were Jemuel, Jamin, Ohad, Jakin, Zohar, and Shaul. (Shaul's mother was a Canaanite woman.)
¹¹The sons of Levi were Gershon, Kohath, and Merari.
¹²The sons of Judah were Er, Onan, Shelah, Perez, and Zerah (though Er and Onan had died in the land of Canaan). The sons of Perez were Hezron and Hamul.
¹³The sons of Issachar were Tola, Puah,* Jashub,* and Shimron.
¹⁴The sons of Zebulun were Sered, Elon, and Jahleel.
¹⁵These were the sons of Leah and Jacob who were born in Paddan-aram, in addition to their daughter, Dinah. The number of Jacob's descendants (male and female) through Leah was thirty-three.

¹⁶The sons of Gad were Zephon,* Haggi, Shuni, Ezbon, Eri, Arodi, and Areli.
¹⁷The sons of Asher were Imnah, Ishvah, Ishvi, and Beriah. Their sister was Serah. Beriah's sons were Heber and Malkiel.
¹⁸These were the sons of Zilpah, the servant given to Leah by her father, Laban. The number of Jacob's descendants through Zilpah was sixteen.

¹⁹The sons of Jacob's wife Rachel were Joseph and Benjamin.
²⁰Joseph's sons, born in the land of Egypt, were Manasseh and Ephraim. Their mother was Asenath, daughter of Potiphera, the priest of On.*
²¹Benjamin's sons were Bela, Beker, Ashbel, Gera, Naaman, Ehi, Rosh, Muppim, Huppim, and Ard.
²²These were the sons of Rachel and Jacob. The number of Jacob's descendants through Rachel was fourteen.

²³The son of Dan was Hushim.
²⁴The sons of Naphtali were Jahzeel, Guni, Jezer, and Shillem.
²⁵These were the sons of Bilhah, the servant given to Rachel by her father, Laban. The number of Jacob's descendants through Bilhah was seven.

²⁶The total number of Jacob's direct descendants who went with him to Egypt, not counting his sons' wives, was sixty-six. ²⁷In addition, Joseph had two sons* who were born in Egypt. So altogether, there were seventy* members of Jacob's family in the land of Egypt.

45:21 Hebrew *Israel;* also in 45:28. See note on 35:21.   45:22 Hebrew *300 [shekels],* about 7.5 pounds or 3.4 kilograms in weight.   46:1 Hebrew *Israel;* also in 46:29, 30. See note on 35:21.   46:3 Hebrew *I am El.*   46:13a As in Syriac version and Samaritan Pentateuch (see also 1 Chr 7:1); Hebrew reads *Puvah.*   46:13b As in some Greek manuscripts and Samaritan Pentateuch (see also Num 26:24; 1 Chr 7:1); Hebrew reads *Iob.*   46:16 As in Greek version and Samaritan Pentateuch (see also Num 26:15); Hebrew reads *Ziphion.*   46:20 Greek version reads *of Heliopolis.*   46:27a Greek version reads *nine sons,* probably including Joseph's grandsons through Ephraim and Manasseh (see 1 Chr 7:14-20).   46:27b Greek version reads *seventy-five;* see note on Exod 1:5.

46:1-4 God promised to go with Jacob to Egypt, blessing his journey and bringing his descendants back to Canaan. A little over two hundred years earlier, Abraham had gone to Egypt during a famine in Canaan, and God had protected him there (12:10-20). In Scripture, Egypt was often God's source of provision for his people.

Insight: MOTHERS AND FATHERS OF FAITH

The Bible often looks back to its beginnings—mentioning the God of Abraham, Isaac, and Jacob (see, for example, Genesis 31:42; Exodus 2:24; 6:8; Deuteronomy 6:10; 2 Kings 13:23). This same God is also the God of Sarah, Hagar, Rebekah, Leah, and Rachel. What do we see about God's way of interacting with these ancestors of faith?

	MOTHERS AND GOD'S CHARACTER		FATHERS AND GOD'S CHARACTER
Eve	Formed her in God's image 1:27 Brought her to her husband 2:22 Enabled her to have children 4:1, 25 Safeguarded her son's (Cain's) life 4:15	Adam	Formed him in God's image 1:27 Provided the "just right" companion 2:18
Sarah	Made her beautiful 12:14 Blessed her with a son, made her a mother of many nations 17:15-16 Fulfilled covenant via her son 17:21 Visited her, spoke honestly to her ("you did laugh"), enabled her to have children 18:9-15 Kept his promises to her 21:1	Abraham	Called him to a new land and vocation; blessed him to be a blessing 12:1-3 Made a covenant with him 17:4 Made him father of nations and kings 17:5-6 Gave him land 12:7; 13:15-18; 17:8 Fulfilled covenant through Isaac 17:19
Hagar	Found by God 16:7 Allowed to give a name to God 16:13 Made her a mother of nations 21:13 Heard her son's cries 21:17 Revealed how to save her son's life 21:19		
Rebekah	Was brought to her husband by God 24:15 Was made lovely 24:16 Loved deeply by her husband 24:67 Was shown God's will for her children 25:22-23	Isaac	Confirmed covenant through him 17:19 Showed him unfailing love by selecting Rebekah 24:14 Answered his prayer for Rebekah to conceive 25:21
Leah	Not lovely or loved by her husband, but God took care of her 29:17, 31 Eventually praised God 29:35 Bore a son (Judah) whose direct line led to the Messiah Matthew 1:2-16 A mother of Israel Ruth 4:11	Jacob	Was given land, descendants, and God's presence 28:13-15 Led him to his wives 29:9-12, 22-30 Guided him home 31:3 Reconciled him to his brother, Esau 33:3-4 Renamed him Israel 35:10
Rachel	Lovely figure and face 29:17 Beloved by her husband 29:30 Conceived with God's help 30:22 Stole idols and lied, but God still made her a mother of Israel 31:34-35; Ruth 4:11 Birthed Joseph, who rescued Israel 35:24; 45:4-11 Last son honored as "son of (Jacob's) right hand" 35:18 Husband memorialized her grave 35:20		

Jacob's Family Arrives in Goshen

28 As they neared their destination, Jacob sent Judah ahead to meet Joseph and get directions to the region of Goshen. And when they finally arrived there, 29 Joseph prepared his chariot and traveled to Goshen to meet his father, Jacob. When Joseph arrived, he embraced his father and wept, holding him for a long time. 30 Finally, Jacob said to Joseph, "Now I am ready to die, since I have seen your face again and know you are still alive."

31 And Joseph said to his brothers and to his father's entire family, "I will go to Pharaoh and tell him, 'My brothers and my father's entire family have come to me from the land of Canaan. 32 These men are shepherds, and they raise livestock. They have brought with them their flocks and herds and everything they own.'

33 Then he said, "When Pharaoh calls for you and asks you about your occupation, 34 you must tell him, 'We, your servants, have raised livestock all our lives, as our ancestors have always done.' When you tell him this, he will let you live here in the region of Goshen, for the Egyptians despise shepherds."

Jacob Blesses Pharaoh

47 Then Joseph went to see Pharaoh and told him, "My father and my brothers have arrived from the land of Canaan. They have come with all their flocks and herds and possessions, and they are now in the region of Goshen."

2 Joseph took five of his brothers with him and presented them to Pharaoh. 3 And Pharaoh asked the brothers, "What is your occupation?"

They replied, "We, your servants, are shepherds, just like our ancestors. 4 We have come to live here in Egypt for a while, for there is no pasture for our flocks in Canaan. The famine is very severe there. So please, we request permission to live in the region of Goshen."

5 Then Pharaoh said to Joseph, "Now that your father and brothers have joined you here, 6 choose any place in the entire land of Egypt for them to live. Give them the best land of Egypt. Let them live in the region of Goshen. And if any of them have special skills, put them in charge of my livestock, too."

7 Then Joseph brought in his father, Jacob, and presented him to Pharaoh. And Jacob blessed Pharaoh.

8 "How old are you?" Pharaoh asked him.

9 Jacob replied, "I have traveled this earth for 130 hard years. But my life has been short compared to the lives of my ancestors." 10 Then Jacob blessed Pharaoh again before leaving his court.

11 So Joseph assigned the best land of Egypt—the region of Rameses—to his father and his brothers, and he settled them there, just as Pharaoh had commanded. 12 And Joseph provided food for his father and his brothers in amounts appropriate to the number of their dependents, including the smallest children.

Joseph's Leadership in the Famine

13 Meanwhile, the famine became so severe that all the food was used up, and people were starving throughout the lands of Egypt and Canaan. 14 By selling grain to the people, Joseph eventually collected all the money in Egypt and Canaan, and he put the money in Pharaoh's treasury. 15 When the people of Egypt and Canaan ran out of money, all the Egyptians came to Joseph. "Our money is gone!" they cried. "But please give us food, or we will die before your very eyes!"

16 Joseph replied, "Since your money is gone, bring me your livestock. I will give you food in exchange for your livestock." 17 So they brought their livestock to Joseph in exchange for food. In exchange for their horses, flocks of sheep and goats, herds of cattle, and donkeys, Joseph provided them with food for another year.

18 But that year ended, and the next year they came again and said, "We cannot hide the truth from you, my lord. Our money is gone, and all our livestock and cattle are yours. We have nothing left to give but our bodies and our land. 19 Why should we die before your very eyes? Buy us and our land in exchange for food; we offer our land and ourselves as slaves for Pharaoh. Just give us grain so we may live and not die, and so the land does not become empty and desolate."

20 So Joseph bought all the land of Egypt for Pharaoh. All the Egyptians sold him their fields because the famine was so severe, and soon all the land belonged to Pharaoh. 21 As for the people, he made them all slaves,* from one end of Egypt to the other. 22 The only land he did not buy was the land belonging to the priests. They received an allotment of food directly from Pharaoh, so they didn't need to sell their land.

23 Then Joseph said to the people, "Look, today I have bought you and your land for Pharaoh. I will provide you with seed so you can plant the fields. 24 Then when you harvest it, one-fifth of your crop will belong to Pharaoh. You may keep the remaining four-fifths as seed for your fields and as food for you, your households, and your little ones."

25 "You have saved our lives!" they exclaimed. "May it please you, my lord, to let us be Pharaoh's servants." 26 Joseph then issued a decree still in effect in the land of Egypt, that Pharaoh should receive one-fifth of all the crops grown on his land. Only the land belonging to the priests was not given to Pharaoh.

47:21 As in Greek version and Samaritan Pentateuch; Hebrew reads *he moved them all into the towns.*

47:10 Jacob blessed Pharaoh, though Pharaoh clearly had more power and wealth. Joseph had saved Pharaoh and all of Egypt from the devastating effects of a seven-year famine. This blessing was evidence that God's promise to Abraham was already being fulfilled—Abraham's descendants were indeed blessed to be a blessing to others (12:1-3).

²⁷Meanwhile, the people of Israel settled in the region of Goshen in Egypt. There they acquired property, and they were fruitful, and their population grew rapidly. ²⁸Jacob lived for seventeen years after his arrival in Egypt, so he lived 147 years in all.

²⁹As the time of his death drew near, Jacob* called for his son Joseph and said to him, "Please do me this favor. Put your hand under my thigh and swear that you will treat me with unfailing love by honoring this last request: Do not bury me in Egypt. ³⁰When I die, please take my body out of Egypt and bury me with my ancestors."

So Joseph promised, "I will do as you ask."

³¹"Swear that you will do it," Jacob insisted. So Joseph gave his oath, and Jacob bowed humbly at the head of his bed.*

Jacob Blesses Manasseh and Ephraim

48 One day not long after this, word came to Joseph, "Your father is failing rapidly." So Joseph went to visit his father, and he took with him his two sons, Manasseh and Ephraim.

²When Joseph arrived, Jacob was told, "Your son Joseph has come to see you." So Jacob* gathered his strength and sat up in his bed.

³Jacob said to Joseph, "God Almighty* appeared to me at Luz in the land of Canaan and blessed me. ⁴He said to me, 'I will make you fruitful, and I will multiply your descendants. I will make you a multitude of nations. And I will give this land of Canaan to your descendants* after you as an everlasting possession.'

⁵"Now I am claiming as my own sons these two boys of yours, Ephraim and Manasseh, who were born here in the land of Egypt before I arrived. They will be my sons, just as Reuben and Simeon are. ⁶But any children born to you in the future will be your own, and they will inherit land within the territories of their brothers Ephraim and Manasseh.

⁷"Long ago, as I was returning from Paddan-aram,* Rachel died in the land of Canaan. We were still on the way, some distance from Ephrath (that is, Bethlehem). So with great sorrow I buried her there beside the road to Ephrath."

⁸Then Jacob looked over at the two boys. "Are these your sons?" he asked.

⁹"Yes," Joseph told him, "these are the sons God has given me here in Egypt."

And Jacob said, "Bring them closer to me, so I can bless them."

¹⁰Jacob was half blind because of his age and could hardly see. So Joseph brought the boys close to him, and Jacob kissed and embraced them. ¹¹Then Jacob said to Joseph, "I never thought I would see your face again, but now God has let me see your children, too!"

¹²Joseph moved the boys, who were at their grandfather's knees, and he bowed with his face to the ground. ¹³Then he positioned the boys in front of Jacob. With his right hand he directed Ephraim toward Jacob's left hand, and with his left hand he put Manasseh at Jacob's right hand. ¹⁴But Jacob crossed his arms as he reached out to lay his hands on the boys' heads. He put his right hand on the head of Ephraim, though he was the younger boy, and his left hand on the head of Manasseh, though he was the firstborn. ¹⁵Then he blessed Joseph and said,

"May the God before whom my grandfather Abraham
and my father, Isaac, walked—
the God who has been my shepherd
all my life, to this very day,
¹⁶ the Angel who has redeemed me from all harm—
may he bless these boys.
May they preserve my name
and the names of Abraham and Isaac.
And may their descendants multiply greatly
throughout the earth."

¹⁷But Joseph was upset when he saw that his father placed his right hand on Ephraim's head. So Joseph lifted it to move it from Ephraim's head to Manasseh's head. ¹⁸"No, my father," he said. "This one is the firstborn. Put your right hand on his head."

¹⁹But his father refused. "I know, my son; I know," he replied. "Manasseh will also become a great people, but his younger brother will become even greater. And his descendants will become a multitude of nations."

²⁰So Jacob blessed the boys that day with this blessing: "The people of Israel will use your names when they give a blessing. They will say, 'May God make you as prosperous as Ephraim and Manasseh.'" In this way, Jacob put Ephraim ahead of Manasseh.

²¹Then Jacob said to Joseph, "Look, I am about to die, but God will be with you and will take you back to Canaan, the land of your ancestors. ²²And beyond

---

47:29 Hebrew *Israel;* also in 47:31b. See note on 35:21.   47:31 Greek version reads *and Israel bowed in worship as he leaned on his staff.* Compare Heb 11:21.   48:2 Hebrew *Israel;* also in 48:8, 10, 11, 13, 14, 21. See note on 35:21.   48:3 Hebrew *El-Shaddai.*   48:4 Hebrew *seed;* also in 48:19.   48:7 Hebrew *Paddan,* referring to Paddan-aram; compare Gen 35:9.

47:27-31 The Israelites increased in number in Egypt in fulfillment of the creation blessing (1:26-28). However, Jacob insisted that Joseph not bury him in Egypt. Jacob chose God's promises over Egypt's provision, knowing he belonged with his ancestors in Canaan, the land God promised him.

48:1-6 Jacob blessed Joseph by elevating his two sons as coheirs with their uncles—the tribes of Manasseh and Ephraim would receive land along with the other tribes. This doubled the size of Joseph's share of the inheritance, effectively treating Joseph as the firstborn. Ephraim and Manasseh became large and powerful tribes.

48:8-22 The right hand was for the head of the firstborn, but Jacob deliberately gave that position to the younger son, Ephraim. Four consecutive generations followed that pattern: Isaac over Ishmael, Jacob over Esau, Joseph over Reuben, and Ephraim over Manasseh. God refused to be limited by cultural convention.

what I have given your brothers, I am giving you an extra portion of the land* that I took from the Amorites with my sword and bow."

Jacob's Last Words to His Sons

49 Then Jacob called together all his sons and said, "Gather around me, and I will tell you what will happen to each of you in the days to come.

² "Come and listen, you sons of Jacob;
    listen to Israel, your father.

³ "Reuben, you are my firstborn, my strength,
    the child of my vigorous youth.
You are first in rank and first in power.
⁴ But you are as unruly as a flood,
    and you will be first no longer.
For you went to bed with my wife;
    you defiled my marriage couch.

⁵ "Simeon and Levi are two of a kind;
    their weapons are instruments of violence.
⁶ May I never join in their meetings;
    may I never be a party to their plans.
For in their anger they murdered men,
    and they crippled oxen just for sport.
⁷ A curse on their anger, for it is fierce;
    a curse on their wrath, for it is cruel.
I will scatter them among the descendants of Jacob;
    I will disperse them throughout Israel.

⁸ "Judah, your brothers will praise you.
    You will grasp your enemies by the neck.
    All your relatives will bow before you.
⁹ Judah, my son, is a young lion
    that has finished eating its prey.
Like a lion he crouches and lies down;
    like a lioness—who dares to rouse him?
¹⁰ The scepter will not depart from Judah,
    nor the ruler's staff from his descendants,*
until the coming of the one to whom it belongs,*
    the one whom all nations will honor.
¹¹ He ties his foal to a grapevine,
    the colt of his donkey to a choice vine.
He washes his clothes in wine,
    his robes in the blood of grapes.
¹² His eyes are darker than wine,
    and his teeth are whiter than milk.

¹³ "Zebulun will settle by the seashore
    and will be a harbor for ships;
    his borders will extend to Sidon.

¹⁴ "Issachar is a sturdy donkey,
    resting between two saddlepacks.*
¹⁵ When he sees how good the countryside is
    and how pleasant the land,
he will bend his shoulder to the load
    and submit himself to hard labor.

¹⁶ "Dan will govern his people,
    like any other tribe in Israel.
¹⁷ Dan will be a snake beside the road,
    a poisonous viper along the path
that bites the horse's hooves
    so its rider is thrown off.
¹⁸ I trust in you for salvation, O LORD!

¹⁹ "Gad will be attacked by marauding bands,
    but he will attack them when they retreat.

²⁰ "Asher will dine on rich foods
    and produce food fit for kings.

²¹ "Naphtali is a doe set free
    that bears beautiful fawns.

²² "Joseph is the foal of a wild donkey,
    the foal of a wild donkey at a spring—
    one of the wild donkeys on the ridge.*
²³ Archers attacked him savagely;
    they shot at him and harassed him.
²⁴ But his bow remained taut,
    and his arms were strengthened
by the hands of the Mighty One of Jacob,
    by the Shepherd, the Rock of Israel.
²⁵ May the God of your father help you;
    may the Almighty bless you
with the blessings of the heavens above,
    and blessings of the watery depths below,
    and blessings of the breasts and womb.
²⁶ May my fatherly blessings on you
    surpass the blessings of my ancestors,*
    reaching to the heights of the eternal hills.
May these blessings rest on the head of Joseph,
    who is a prince among his brothers.

²⁷ "Benjamin is a ravenous wolf,
    devouring his enemies in the morning
    and dividing his plunder in the evening."

²⁸These are the twelve tribes of Israel, and this is what their father said as he told his sons good-bye. He blessed each one with an appropriate message.

48:22 Or *an extra ridge of land*. The meaning of the Hebrew is uncertain.   **49:10a** Hebrew *from between his feet*.   **49:10b** Or *until tribute is brought to him and the peoples obey*; traditionally rendered *until Shiloh comes*.   **49:14** Or *sheepfolds*, or *hearths*.   **49:22** Or *Joseph is a fruitful tree, / a fruitful tree beside a spring. / His branches reach over the wall*. The meaning of the Hebrew is uncertain.   **49:26** Or *of the ancient mountains*.

49:1-28 God's blessings in Genesis contrasted sharply with those of pagan religions, which sought fortune and fertility through magic. Pagan cultic observances at shrines were performed to induce deities to act on behalf of the worshipers. By contrast, in Genesis, all life, fertility, and blessing came by God's decree. Jacob deliberately crafted prophetic oracles regarding the future settlement of Canaan. All the tribes would enter the land, but they would not participate equally. Their inheritance would partly reflect their degree of exemplary behavior.

GENESIS 50

Jacob's Death and Burial

²⁹Then Jacob instructed them, "Soon I will die and join my ancestors. Bury me with my father and grandfather in the cave in the field of Ephron the Hittite. ³⁰This is the cave in the field of Machpelah, near Mamre in Canaan, that Abraham bought from Ephron the Hittite as a permanent burial site. ³¹There Abraham and his wife Sarah are buried. There Isaac and his wife, Rebekah, are buried. And there I buried Leah. ³²It is the plot of land and the cave that my grandfather Abraham bought from the Hittites."

³³When Jacob had finished this charge to his sons, he drew his feet into the bed, breathed his last, and joined his ancestors in death.

50 Joseph threw himself on his father and wept over him and kissed him. ²Then Joseph told the physicians who served him to embalm his father's body; so Jacob* was embalmed. ³The embalming process took the usual forty days. And the Egyptians mourned his death for seventy days.

⁴When the period of mourning was over, Joseph approached Pharaoh's advisers and said, "Please do me this favor and speak to Pharaoh on my behalf. ⁵Tell him that my father made me swear an oath. He said to me, 'Listen, I am about to die. Take my body back to the land of Canaan, and bury me in the tomb I prepared for myself.' So please allow me to go and bury my father. After his burial, I will return without delay."

⁶Pharaoh agreed to Joseph's request. "Go and bury your father, as he made you promise," he said. ⁷So Joseph went up to bury his father. He was accompanied by all of Pharaoh's officials, all the senior members of Pharaoh's household, and all the senior officers of Egypt. ⁸Joseph also took his entire household and his brothers and their households. But they left their little children and flocks and herds in the land of Goshen. ⁹A great number of chariots and charioteers accompanied Joseph.

¹⁰When they arrived at the threshing floor of Atad, near the Jordan River, they held a very great and solemn memorial service, with a seven-day period of mourning for Joseph's father. ¹¹The local residents, the Canaanites, watched them mourning at the threshing floor of Atad. Then they renamed that place (which is near the Jordan) Abel-mizraim,* for they said, "This is a place of deep mourning for these Egyptians."

¹²So Jacob's sons did as he had commanded them. ¹³They carried his body to the land of Canaan and buried him in the cave in the field of Machpelah, near Mamre. This is the cave that Abraham had bought as a permanent burial site from Ephron the Hittite.

Joseph Reassures His Brothers

¹⁴After burying Jacob, Joseph returned to Egypt with his brothers and all who had accompanied him to his father's burial. ¹⁵But now that their father was dead, Joseph's brothers became fearful. "Now Joseph will show his anger and pay us back for all the wrong we did to him," they said.

¹⁶So they sent this message to Joseph: "Before your father died, he instructed us ¹⁷to say to you: 'Please forgive your brothers for the great wrong they did to you—for their sin in treating you so cruelly.' So we, the servants of the God of your father, beg you to forgive our sin." When Joseph received the message, he broke down and wept. ¹⁸Then his brothers came and threw themselves down before Joseph. "Look, we are your slaves!" they said.

¹⁹But Joseph replied, "Don't be afraid of me. Am I God, that I can punish you? ²⁰You intended to harm me, but God intended it all for good. He brought me to this position so I could save the lives of many people. ²¹No, don't be afraid. I will continue to take care of you and your children." So he reassured them by speaking kindly to them.

The Death of Joseph

²²So Joseph and his brothers and their families continued to live in Egypt. Joseph lived to the age of 110. ²³He lived to see three generations of descendants of his son Ephraim, and he lived to see the birth of the children of Manasseh's son Makir, whom he claimed as his own.*

²⁴"Soon I will die," Joseph told his brothers, "but God will surely come to help you and lead you out of this land of Egypt. He will bring you back to the land he solemnly promised to give to Abraham, to Isaac, and to Jacob."

²⁵Then Joseph made the sons of Israel swear an oath, and he said, "When God comes to help you and lead you back, you must take my bones with you." ²⁶So Joseph died at the age of 110. The Egyptians embalmed him, and his body was placed in a coffin in Egypt

---

50:2 Hebrew *Israel.* See note on 35:21. **50:11** *Abel-mizraim* means "mourning of the Egyptians." **50:23** Hebrew *who were born on Joseph's knees.*

50:1-13 Jacob's burial in Machpelah signified that Joseph and his brothers still believed God's promise to give them their true home, Canaan, though they lived in Egypt. Sarah was buried there (23:19), marking Abraham's first possession of land in Canaan. Others buried at the cave of Machpelah near Hebron were Abraham, Isaac, Rebekah, and Leah (49:30-31).

50:22-26 Joseph had succeeded in Egypt and lived a long life, but he insisted on being buried in Canaan. The book ends with Joseph's coffin in Egypt but points ahead to the day when Abraham's descendants would return to Canaan, the land God promised them. Joseph was eventually buried in Shechem (Joshua 24:32). We tend to think of death as the tragic end of life, but ancient people were satisfied knowing their families would carry on.

IMAGE — MY STORY WITH COMMUNITY, WORKPLACE & CHURCH

Work Is More Than a Four-Letter Word

SCRIPTURE CONNECTION: GENESIS 50:14-21

A mentor once encouraged me that, from God's perspective, work is a four-letter word: *GIFT*. Work is God's gift to us, and when we bring our gifts to the work he assigns, we enter a divinely directed realm of service.

Joseph's life was marked by his devotion to God and the faithful stewardship of assignments he was given. He brought his gifts to his work, and God used Joseph in his plan to save the children of Israel. Joseph's example inspires my view of work, as I labor alongside leaders of more than twelve hundred faith-based nonprofits. Here is what I see in Joseph that I want more of in me:

> The gift of work and our gifts at work have the power to transform!

- Confidence—Joseph knew God was with him (39:2).
- Conviction—Joseph quickly discerned situations and resisted temptation (39:12).
- Consistency—Joseph focused on the task at hand, ready to put his gifts to work (40:8).
- Compassion—Joseph resisted bitterness and chose forgiveness and mercy (50:20-21).

The gift of our work and our gifts at work have the power to transform us and advance God's greater purpose.

IMAGINE

If Joseph were your mentor, what lessons from his life might help you?

How would you put his story to work for you today?

"While Joseph was given big dreams, he trusted God and focused on the task at hand. I give thanks that God still gives us big dreams and the gift of pursuing them through everyday faithfulness."

TAMI HEIM is president and CEO of Christian Leadership Alliance and serves on many nonprofit boards. She and her husband lead mission teams to Haiti to love and disciple orphans.

Exodus

WHAT DO WE LEARN ABOUT GOD'S MISSION AND OURS?
God's presence and laws enable the people of Israel to fulfill God's mission.

WHO WROTE IT? Exodus is anonymous, but Jewish and Christian traditions attribute it to Moses (see 24:4).

WHEN DID IT HAPPEN? Either in the 1400s or 1200s BC, hundreds of years after the final events of Genesis.

HOW IS IT ORGANIZED?

- 1–2: God begins his rescue through Shiphrah and Puah, Moses' Mother and Miriam, and Pharaoh's daughter
- 3–15: God rescues his people from slavery in Egypt
- 16–18: God provides for his people's needs in the wilderness
- 19–24: God gives his people instructions for living
- 32: The people rebel against God
- 33–34: God speaks to Moses again
- 35–40: Building the Tabernacle

FEATURE HIGHLIGHTS

+ Five Women Who Made a Difference: Delivering and Raising Moses (81)
+ Why So Long? (82)
+ Failure Not Enough or Not Willing (85)
+ The Lord Himself Leads Us (99)

Words to Remember are highlighted throughout this book

HOW LONG DOES IT TAKE TO READ?

2:30

| :30 | 1:00 | 1:30 | 2:00 | 2:30 | 3:00 | 3:30 |

BC Timeline

BC	Event
1805	JOSEPH DIES
c. 1800–1446	ISRAELITES ENSLAVED IN EGYPT
1533	MIRIAM BORN TO AMRAM AND JOCHEBED
1529	AARON, BROTHER TO MIRIAM AND MOSES, BORN
1526	JOCHEBED GIVES BIRTH TO MOSES — Five women save Moses' life (Shiphrah, Puah, Jochebed, Miriam, and Pharaoh's daughter)
1486	MOSES FLEES TO MIDIAN, MARRIES ZIPPORAH — Zipporah saves Moses' life by circumcising their son
1446	EXODUS FROM EGYPT — Miriam leads the women in dancing, worship, celebration of God's victory
1445	TEN COMMANDMENTS GIVEN — Miriam and Aaron oppose Moses — Moses pleads for God to heal Miriam
1406	ISRAEL ENTERS CANAAN
1375	JUDGES (INCLUDING DEBORAH, GIDEON, AND SAMSON) BEGIN TO RULE
1050	KINGDOM UNITED UNDER SAUL

The Israelites in Egypt

1 These are the names of the sons of Israel (that is, Jacob) who moved to Egypt with their father, each with his family: ²Reuben, Simeon, Levi, Judah, ³Issachar, Zebulun, Benjamin, ⁴Dan, Naphtali, Gad, and Asher. ⁵In all, Jacob had seventy* descendants in Egypt, including Joseph, who was already there.

⁶In time, Joseph and all of his brothers died, ending that entire generation. ⁷But their descendants, the Israelites, had many children and grandchildren. In fact, they multiplied so greatly that they became extremely powerful and filled the land.

⁸Eventually, a new king came to power in Egypt who knew nothing about Joseph or what he had done. ⁹He said to his people, "Look, the people of Israel now outnumber us and are stronger than we are. ¹⁰We must make a plan to keep them from growing even more. If we don't, and if war breaks out, they will join our enemies and fight against us. Then they will escape from the country.*"

¹¹So the Egyptians made the Israelites their slaves. They appointed brutal slave drivers over them, hoping to wear them down with crushing labor. They forced them to build the cities of Pithom and Rameses as supply centers for the king. ¹²But the more the Egyptians oppressed them, the more the Israelites multiplied and spread, and the more alarmed the Egyptians became. ¹³So the Egyptians worked the people of Israel without mercy. ¹⁴They made their lives bitter, forcing them to mix mortar and make bricks and do all the work in the fields. They were ruthless in all their demands.

¹⁵Then Pharaoh, the king of Egypt, gave this order to the Hebrew midwives, Shiphrah and Puah: ¹⁶"When you help the Hebrew women as they give birth, watch as they deliver.* If the baby is a boy, kill him; if it is a girl, let her live." ¹⁷But because the midwives feared God, they refused to obey the king's orders. They allowed the boys to live, too.

¹⁸So the king of Egypt called for the midwives. "Why have you done this?" he demanded. "Why have you allowed the boys to live?"

¹⁹"The Hebrew women are not like the Egyptian women," the midwives replied. "They are more vigorous and have their babies so quickly that we cannot get there in time."

²⁰So God was good to the midwives, and the Israelites continued to multiply, growing more and more powerful. ²¹And because the midwives feared God, he gave them families of their own.

²²Then Pharaoh gave this order to all his people: "Throw every newborn Hebrew boy into the Nile River. But you may let the girls live."

The Birth of Moses

2 About this time, a man and woman from the tribe of Levi got married. ²The woman became pregnant and gave birth to a son. She saw that he was a special baby and kept him hidden for three months. ³But when she could no longer hide him, she got a basket made of papyrus reeds and waterproofed it with tar and pitch. She put the baby in the basket and laid it among the reeds along the bank of the Nile River. ⁴The baby's sister then stood at a distance, watching to see what would happen to him.

⁵Soon Pharaoh's daughter came down to bathe in the river, and her attendants walked along the riverbank. When the princess saw the basket among the reeds, she sent her maid to get it for her. ⁶When the princess opened it, she saw the baby. The little boy was crying, and she felt sorry for him. "This must be one of the Hebrew children," she said.

⁷Then the baby's sister approached the princess. "Should I go and find one of the Hebrew women to nurse the baby for you?" she asked.

⁸"Yes, do!" the princess replied. So the girl went and called the baby's mother.

⁹"Take this baby and nurse him for me," the princess told the baby's mother. "I will pay you for your help." So the woman took her baby home and nursed him.

¹⁰Later, when the boy was older, his mother brought him back to Pharaoh's daughter, who adopted him as her own son. The princess named him Moses,* for she explained, "I lifted him out of the water."

Moses Escapes to Midian

¹¹Many years later, when Moses had grown up, he went out to visit his own people, the Hebrews, and he saw how hard they were forced to work. During his visit, he saw an Egyptian beating one of his fellow Hebrews. ¹²After looking in all directions to make

---

1:5 Dead Sea Scrolls and Greek version read *seventy-five;* see notes on Gen 46:27. **1:10** Or *will take the country.* **1:16** Hebrew *look upon the two stones;* perhaps the reference is to a birthstool. **2:10** *Moses* sounds like a Hebrew term that means "to lift out."

1:15-22 Pharaoh was unaware of the history regarding Jacob's descendants and viewed them as a threat rather than a blessing. His method of controlling them toem ensure a robust labor force for his building projects was counterproductive. Killing the boys would mean fewer enslaved men. He let the girls live, underestimating their strength. Women undermined Pharaoh at every turn in this story, mostly because they feared God rather than him. The midwives, Moses' mom and sister, and even Pharaoh's daughter defied his edict.

2:1-9 The baby's mom saw that he was "special" (literally, "good"), echoing God's assessment of his creative work in Genesis (1:4, 10, 12, 18, 25, 31). All babies are good because each one is made in God's image (Genesis 1:26-28). Pharaoh's murderous policy contradicted God's creation blessing to produce offspring and fill the earth. These women conspired together at great danger to themselves to rescue a baby boy under a death sentence. The key players in this narrative remain nameless as if to protect their identity.

2:10 The princess named the baby Moses, which in Egyptian means "son of" and in Hebrew means "one who draws out." She memorialized his questionable origin (son of who?) as well as her audacity—rather than throwing him into the Nile as her father had commanded, she drew him out of it. Moses himself would draw the Hebrews out through the sea and into freedom.

Five Women Who Made a Difference

IDENTITY

Delivering and Raising Moses

Can we make a difference in difficult situations? Yes! When we creatively invest our faith, abilities, and resources, God can do great things through us. Take these examples:

- *Two Midwives: Shiphrah and Puah.* Pharaoh felt threatened by the escalating population of Hebrews in Egypt. Unable to contain them through slavery, he directed these two midwives to kill all newborn Hebrew boys. But they let the boys live and told Pharaoh that the mothers were giving birth and hiding the babies before they arrived (Exodus 1:15-21).
- *Moses' Mother: Jochebed.* Three months after giving birth to her third child, a boy, Jochebed couldn't hide him any longer and developed a plan. She reinforced a papyrus basket and set her baby afloat in the Nile (Exodus 2:1-3).
- *Pharaoh's Daughter.* While heading to bathe in the Nile, she discovered the crying baby in a basket and felt sorry for him. She rescued the baby and later adopted him (Exodus 2:5-10).
- *Moses' Sister: Miriam.* Jochebed stationed her firstborn along the bank to watch the basket. When Pharaoh's daughter discovered the baby, Miriam offered to find a nurse. Pharaoh's daughter agreed and even paid Jochebed to do it. Mother, sister, and baby were reunited until Moses joined Pharaoh's household, positioning him to become the rescuer of the Hebrew people (Exodus 2:4, 7-10).

These five women creatively invested themselves in difficult situations and great good resulted.

THESE FIVE WOMEN'S STORIES ARE TOLD IN EXODUS 1–2.

> When we invest ourselves in creative obedience, God can do great things through us.

IDENTIFY

How many lives might those midwives have saved?

How does Jochebed's instinct to save her son reflect God's heart to save his people?

While Pharaoh's daughter likely didn't know Israel's God, how might God have been working behind the scenes?

Could Miriam have possibly imagined serving at her brother's side, helping to lead Israel out of slavery?

> "It's easy to hang back, thinking our actions won't matter. But they do! Even what may seem small, unnoticed, frivolous, or frowned upon by others, when done in love for God, can change a life forever."

ELISA MORGAN, MDiv, speaks, writes, and cohosts podcasts for Our Daily Bread Ministries. For twenty years, she served as president of MOPS International, now as president emerita. Her motto is "Living really ... Really living."

Perspective

Why so long?

SCRIPTURE CONNECTION: EXODUS 2:23-25

If God cared about the Israelites, why did he let them be enslaved? And why did he wait so long to intervene?

God doesn't always reveal the reasons for his timing. But this passage shows that even though the wait was long, God had not forgotten his promise to bless the descendants of Abraham (see Genesis 12:1-3).

Egypt had provided refuge for the Israelites during a major famine, and Joseph had helped Egypt create a system to ensure survival. However, a later pharaoh exploited the Israelites to help himself. God's delay during their slavery in Egypt gave ample time for the oppressors to change their ways. It also allowed a broader demonstration of his power when he did free the Israelites.

The brokenness we experience drives us to cry out to God, too. Our earnest prayers cultivate trust that God will someday make all things new. And when he does, our only response will be to give him glory.

VIEWPOINTS

THEIRS: Did the Israelites wonder if God has forgotten his promises?
MINE: "Reconciliation and healing can seem so far away. When it feels like the world around me falls apart, will I trust God's promise to restore all things?"
YOURS: Does it seem like God is absent? Let this passage remind you: God has not forgotten you.

CARMEN JOY IMES, PhD, is an author, speaker, blogger, YouTuber, and serves as associate professor of Old Testament at Biola University in California.

---

people again, he saw two Hebrew men fighting. "Why are you beating up your friend?" Moses said to the one who had started the fight.

¹⁴The man replied, "Who appointed you to be our prince and judge? Are you going to kill me as you killed that Egyptian yesterday?"

Then Moses was afraid, thinking, "Everyone knows what I did." ¹⁵And sure enough, Pharaoh heard what had happened, and he tried to kill Moses. But Moses fled from Pharaoh and went to live in the land of Midian.

When Moses arrived in Midian, he sat down beside a well. ¹⁶Now the priest of Midian had seven daughters who came as usual to draw water and fill the water troughs for their father's flocks. ¹⁷But some other shepherds came and chased them away. So Moses jumped up and rescued the girls from the shepherds. Then he drew water for their flocks.

¹⁸When the girls returned to Reuel, their father, he asked, "Why are you back so soon today?"

¹⁹"An Egyptian rescued us from the shepherds," they answered. "And then he drew water for us and watered our flocks."

²⁰"Then where is he?" their father asked. "Why did you leave him there? Invite him to come and eat with us."

²¹Moses accepted the invitation, and he settled there with him. In time, Reuel gave Moses his daughter Zipporah to be his wife. ²²Later she gave birth to a son, and Moses named him Gershom,* for he explained, "I have been a foreigner in a foreign land."

²³Years passed, and the king of Egypt died. But the Israelites continued to groan under their burden of slavery. They cried out for help, and their cry rose up to God. ²⁴God heard their groaning, and he remembered his covenant promise to Abraham, Isaac, and Jacob. ²⁵He looked down on the people of Israel and knew it was time to act.*

Moses and the Burning Bush

3 One day Moses was tending the flock of his father-in-law, Jethro,* the priest of Midian. He led the flock far into the wilderness and came to Sinai,* the mountain of God. ²There the angel of the LORD appeared to him in a blazing fire from the middle of a bush. Moses stared in amazement. Though the bush was engulfed in flames, it didn't burn up. ³"This is amazing," Moses said to himself. "Why isn't that bush burning up? I must go see it."

⁴When the LORD saw Moses coming to take a closer look, God called to him from the middle of the bush, "Moses! Moses!"

"Here I am!" Moses replied.

⁵"Do not come any closer," the LORD warned. "Take off your sandals, for you are standing on holy ground. ⁶I am

---

sure no one was watching, Moses killed the Egyptian and hid the body in the sand.

¹³The next day, when Moses went out to visit his

2:22 *Gershom* sounds like a Hebrew term that means "a foreigner there." 2:25 Or *and acknowledged his obligation to help them.* 3:1a Moses' father-in-law went by two names, Jethro and Reuel. 3:1b Hebrew *Horeb*, another name for Sinai.

2:11-22 Moses seemed to share both his birth mother's and his adoptive mother's concern for justice. He acted to avenge the beating of a Hebrew man (2:11-12) and the bullying of Midianite women (2:17). However, his passionate burst in Egypt was no match for systemic injustice. He needed the Lord's calling and empowerment to rescue the Israelites from slavery.

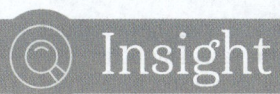

Insight: THE RELUCTANT LEADER

When God appeared to Moses in a burning bush and told him to lead the Israelites out of slavery in Egypt, Moses tried everything he could to avoid God's calling (3:1–4:17). Moses' excuses might sound familiar to you if you've ever wanted to avoid your calling. God responds to Moses point by point, answering his excuses with reassurance and provision.

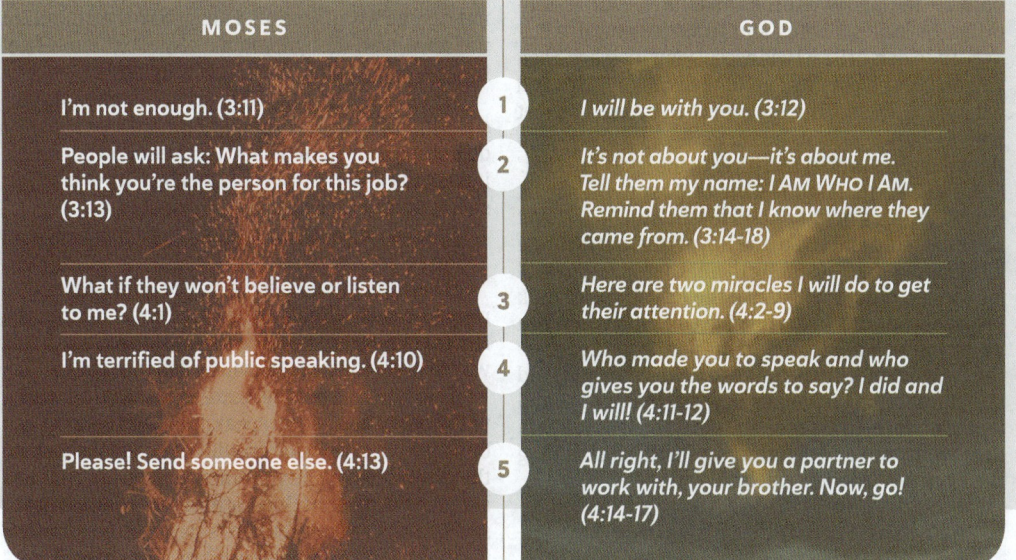

MOSES		GOD
I'm not enough. (3:11)	1	I will be with you. (3:12)
People will ask: What makes you think you're the person for this job? (3:13)	2	It's not about you—it's about me. Tell them my name: I AM WHO I AM. Remind them that I know where they came from. (3:14-18)
What if they won't believe or listen to me? (4:1)	3	Here are two miracles I will do to get their attention. (4:2-9)
I'm terrified of public speaking. (4:10)	4	Who made you to speak and who gives you the words to say? I did and I will! (4:11-12)
Please! Send someone else. (4:13)	5	All right, I'll give you a partner to work with, your brother. Now, go! (4:14-17)

the God of your father*—the God of Abraham, the God of Isaac, and the God of Jacob." When Moses heard this, he covered his face because he was afraid to look at God.

⁷Then the LORD told him, "I have certainly seen the oppression of my people in Egypt. I have heard their cries of distress because of their harsh slave drivers. Yes, I am aware of their suffering. ⁸So I have come down to rescue them from the power of the Egyptians and lead them out of Egypt into their own fertile and spacious land. It is a land flowing with milk and honey—the land where the Canaanites, Hittites, Amorites, Perizzites, Hivites, and Jebusites now live. ⁹Look! The cry of the people of Israel has reached me, and I have seen how harshly the Egyptians abuse them. ¹⁰Now go, for I am sending you to Pharaoh. You must lead my people Israel out of Egypt."

¹¹But Moses protested to God, "Who am I to appear before Pharaoh? Who am I to lead the people of Israel out of Egypt?"

¹²God answered, "I will be with you. And this is your sign that I am the one who has sent you: When you have brought the people out of Egypt, you will worship God at this very mountain."

¹³But Moses protested, "If I go to the people of Israel and tell them, 'The God of your ancestors has sent me to you,' they will ask me, 'What is his name?' Then what should I tell them?"

¹⁴God replied to Moses, "I AM WHO I AM.* Say this to the people of Israel: I AM has sent me to you." ¹⁵God also said to Moses, "Say this to the people of Israel: Yahweh,* the God of your ancestors—the God of Abraham, the God of Isaac, and the God of Jacob—has sent me to you.

3:6 Greek version reads *your fathers.* **3:14** Or *I WILL BE WHAT I WILL BE.* **3:15** *Yahweh* (also in 3:16) is a transliteration of the proper name YHWH that is sometimes rendered "Jehovah"; in this translation it is usually rendered "the LORD" (note the use of small capitals).

3:6 Who was Moses? Born of a Hebrew woman, raised by an Egyptian, he fled to the east and married a Midianite. So where did he belong? The name of his firstborn, Gershom, means "a foreigner there." Moses didn't feel at home anywhere. Here at the mountain, the Lord simultaneously revealed his own identity as well as Moses': "I am the God of your father." Which father? Hebrew? Egyptian? Midianite? "The God of Abraham." Moses found his true place with God's covenant people.

3:14-16 God graciously revealed his intimate name, Yahweh, to Moses, inviting him to be on a first-name basis. Yahweh is usually rendered "the LORD" (in all capital letters) in English. In Hebrew, Yahweh's name sounds like the statement "He is" or "He will be." God's name identifies him but does not limit him. He is The One Who Is, and the Israelites would discover the fullness of his character as he demonstrated it on their behalf.

This is my eternal name,
my name to remember for all generations.

¹⁶"Now go and call together all the elders of Israel. Tell them, 'Yahweh, the God of your ancestors—the God of Abraham, Isaac, and Jacob—has appeared to me. He told me, "I have been watching closely, and I see how the Egyptians are treating you. ¹⁷I have promised to rescue you from your oppression in Egypt. I will lead you to a land flowing with milk and honey—the land where the Canaanites, Hittites, Amorites, Perizzites, Hivites, and Jebusites now live."'

¹⁸"The elders of Israel will accept your message. Then you and the elders must go to the king of Egypt and tell him, 'The LORD, the God of the Hebrews, has met with us. So please let us take a three-day journey into the wilderness to offer sacrifices to the LORD, our God.'

¹⁹"But I know that the king of Egypt will not let you go unless a mighty hand forces him.* ²⁰So I will raise my hand and strike the Egyptians, performing all kinds of miracles among them. Then at last he will let you go. ²¹And I will cause the Egyptians to look favorably on you. They will give you gifts when you go so you will not leave empty-handed. ²²Every Israelite woman will ask for articles of silver and gold and fine clothing from her Egyptian neighbors and from the foreign women in their houses. You will dress your sons and daughters with these, stripping the Egyptians of their wealth."

Signs of the LORD's Power

4 But Moses protested again, "What if they won't believe me or listen to me? What if they say, 'The LORD never appeared to you'?"

²Then the LORD asked him, "What is that in your hand?"

"A shepherd's staff," Moses replied.

³"Throw it down on the ground," the LORD told him. So Moses threw down the staff, and it turned into a snake! Moses jumped back.

⁴Then the LORD told him, "Reach out and grab its tail." So Moses reached out and grabbed it, and it turned back into a shepherd's staff in his hand.

⁵"Perform this sign," the LORD told him. "Then they will believe that the LORD, the God of their ancestors—the God of Abraham, the God of Isaac, and the God of Jacob—really has appeared to you."

⁶Then the LORD said to Moses, "Now put your hand inside your cloak." So Moses put his hand inside his cloak, and when he took it out again, his hand was white as snow with a severe skin disease.* ⁷"Now put your hand back into your cloak," the LORD said. So Moses put his hand back in, and when he took it out again, it was as healthy as the rest of his body.

⁸The LORD said to Moses, "If they do not believe you and are not convinced by the first miraculous sign, they will be convinced by the second sign. ⁹And if they don't believe you or listen to you even after these two signs, then take some water from the Nile River and pour it out on the dry ground. When you do, the water from the Nile will turn to blood on the ground."

¹⁰But Moses pleaded with the LORD, "O Lord, I'm not very good with words. I never have been, and I'm not now, even though you have spoken to me. I get tongue-tied, and my words get tangled."

¹¹Then the LORD asked Moses, "Who makes a person's mouth? Who decides whether people speak or do not speak, hear or do not hear, see or do not see? Is it not I, the LORD? ¹²Now go! I will be with you as you speak, and I will instruct you in what to say."

¹³But Moses again pleaded, "Lord, please! Send anyone else."

¹⁴Then the LORD became angry with Moses. "All right," he said. "What about your brother, Aaron the Levite? I know he speaks well. And look! He is on his way to meet you now. He will be delighted to see you. ¹⁵Talk to him, and put the words in his mouth. I will be with both of you as you speak, and I will instruct you both in what to do. ¹⁶Aaron will be your spokesman to the people. He will be your mouthpiece, and you will stand in the place of God for him, telling him what to say. ¹⁷And take your shepherd's staff with you, and use it to perform the miraculous signs I have shown you."

Moses Returns to Egypt

¹⁸So Moses went back home to Jethro, his father-in-law. "Please let me return to my relatives in Egypt," Moses said. "I don't even know if they are still alive."

"Go in peace," Jethro replied.

¹⁹Before Moses left Midian, the LORD said to him, "Return to Egypt, for all those who wanted to kill you have died."

²⁰So Moses took his wife and sons, put them on a donkey, and headed back to the land of Egypt. In his hand he carried the staff of God.

²¹And the LORD told Moses, "When you arrive back in Egypt, go to Pharaoh and perform all the miracles I have empowered you to do. But I will harden his heart so he will refuse to let the people go. ²²Then you will tell him, 'This is what the LORD says: Israel is my firstborn son. ²³I commanded you, "Let my son go, so he can worship me." But since you have refused, I will now kill your firstborn son!'"

3:19 As in Greek and Latin versions; Hebrew reads *will not let you go, not by a mighty hand.* 4:6 Or *with leprosy.* The Hebrew word used here can describe various skin diseases.

3:22 Pharaoh had not worried about the Hebrew women, but a Hebrew woman gave birth to and raised the deliverer of God's people. Women would freely carry away the wealth of Egypt, and no one would object. Just as Pharaoh's daughter paid Moses' mother to nurse him, the Egyptians would give generously toward the Hebrews as they left Egypt. Perhaps the Egyptians desired to make reparations for years of exploitation at Pharaoh's hands (see 11:2-3).

[24] On the way to Egypt, at a place where Moses and his family had stopped for the night, the LORD confronted him and was about to kill him. [25] But Moses' wife, Zipporah, took a flint knife and circumcised her son. She touched his feet* with the foreskin and said, "Now you are a bridegroom of blood to me." [26] (When she said "a bridegroom of blood," she was referring to the circumcision.) After that, the LORD left him alone.

[27] Now the LORD had said to Aaron, "Go out into the wilderness to meet Moses." So Aaron went and met Moses at the mountain of God, and he embraced him. [28] Moses then told Aaron everything the LORD had commanded him to say. And he told him about the miraculous signs the LORD had commanded him to perform.

[29] Then Moses and Aaron returned to Egypt and called all the elders of Israel together. [30] Aaron told them everything the LORD had told Moses, and Moses performed the miraculous signs as they watched. [31] Then the people of Israel were convinced that the LORD had sent Moses and Aaron. When they heard that the LORD was concerned about them and had seen their misery, they bowed down and worshiped.

4:25 The Hebrew word for "feet" may refer here to the male sex organ.

4:24-26 This story may seem strange, but it underscores how essential it was for Moses to obey God. Male circumcision was the only command given to Abraham (Genesis 17:10) and was the sign of God's covenant with him. Moses could not lead the covenant people without complying himself. As in Exodus 1–2, a woman saved Moses from death. In Hebrew, Zipporah sounds like Shiphrah, the midwife's name in 1:15. These rescue stories frame Moses' call narrative in Exodus 3–4.

Come Close

FAILURE: NOT ENOUGH OR NOT WILLING?

SCRIPTURE CONNECTION: EXODUS 3:1–4:17

I know failure. I know trying hard, throwing myself in, and coming up short. As a result of such experiences, I longed for a simple, quiet life with low-key plans. That was before I knew how far God would go for me.

Moses knew failure too. Raised in a royal household, expectations were heaped upon his head, but a murder changed everything. Self-banishment seemed appropriate. In the wilderness, he would spend his days quietly. He'd watch after sheep. That would give him a lot of alone time to think about failure.

Then God appeared inside a burning bush and offered Moses a new job. I do not blame Moses one bit for trying five times to change God's mind. Sheep might be smelly and stupid, but they don't judge.

"Who am I?" Moses asked.

God's answer to that question isn't about Moses: It's about God. God gave his name, a miracle staff, multiple signs, the promise of riches, and someone to speak on Moses' behalf if he should get tongue-tied. And even when Moses' reluctance angered God, God didn't retaliate. Instead, he provided.

And that is what I am learning about God. His provision clears the path. God's call is bigger than our deficits. His call flows from his love, and he does the amazing when we finally say yes.

REFLECT "For everything comes from him and exists by his power and is intended for his glory." ROMANS 11:36

Lord, may I remember that what you invite me to do is by you and through you and for you. Amen.

CONSIDER "No one can hurt us if we don't do anything. We can't be rejected if we never attempt to blossom. *We won't have regrets*, we tell ourselves. But ... every woman longs to dream ... to move beyond coping and surviving." BONNIE GRAY, *Whispers of Rest*

When God calls, he provides, clearing the path for my "yes."

CARA DAY is a writer and illustrator. She has served with Stonecroft Ministries helping women live "extraordinary."

Moses and Aaron Speak to Pharaoh

5 After this presentation to Israel's leaders, Moses and Aaron went and spoke to Pharaoh. They told him, "This is what the Lord, the God of Israel, says: Let my people go so they may hold a festival in my honor in the wilderness."

²"Is that so?" retorted Pharaoh. "And who is the Lord? Why should I listen to him and let Israel go? I don't know the Lord, and I will not let Israel go."

³But Aaron and Moses persisted. "The God of the Hebrews has met with us," they declared. "So let us take a three-day journey into the wilderness so we can offer sacrifices to the Lord our God. If we don't, he will kill us with a plague or with the sword."

⁴Pharaoh replied, "Moses and Aaron, why are you distracting the people from their tasks? Get back to work! ⁵Look, there are many of your people in the land, and you are stopping them from their work."

Making Bricks without Straw

⁶That same day Pharaoh sent this order to the Egyptian slave drivers and the Israelite foremen: ⁷"Do not supply any more straw for making bricks. Make the people get it themselves! ⁸But still require them to make the same number of bricks as before. Don't reduce the quota. They are lazy. That's why they are crying out, 'Let us go and offer sacrifices to our God.' ⁹Load them down with more work. Make them sweat! That will teach them to listen to lies!"

¹⁰So the slave drivers and foremen went out and told the people: "This is what Pharaoh says: I will not provide any more straw for you. ¹¹Go and get it yourselves. Find it wherever you can. But you must produce just as many bricks as before!" ¹²So the people scattered throughout the land of Egypt in search of stubble to use as straw.

¹³Meanwhile, the Egyptian slave drivers continued to push hard. "Meet your daily quota of bricks, just as you did when we provided you with straw!" they demanded. ¹⁴Then they whipped the Israelite foremen they had put in charge of the work crews. "Why haven't you met your quotas either yesterday or today?" they demanded.

¹⁵So the Israelite foremen went to Pharaoh and pleaded with him. "Please don't treat your servants like this," they begged. ¹⁶"We are given no straw, but the slave drivers still demand, 'Make bricks!' We are being beaten, but it isn't our fault! Your own people are to blame!"

¹⁷But Pharaoh shouted, "You're just lazy! Lazy! That's why you're saying, 'Let us go and offer sacrifices to the Lord.' ¹⁸Now get back to work! No straw will be given to you, but you must still produce the full quota of bricks."

¹⁹The Israelite foremen could see that they were in serious trouble when they were told, "You must not reduce the number of bricks you make each day." ²⁰As they left Pharaoh's court, they confronted Moses and Aaron, who were waiting outside for them. ²¹The foremen said to them, "May the Lord judge and punish you for making us stink before Pharaoh and his officials. You have put a sword into their hands, an excuse to kill us!"

²²Then Moses went back to the Lord and protested, "Why have you brought all this trouble on your own people, Lord? Why did you send me? ²³Ever since I came to Pharaoh as your spokesman, he has been even more brutal to your people. And you have done nothing to rescue them!"

Promises of Deliverance

6 Then the Lord told Moses, "Now you will see what I will do to Pharaoh. When he feels the force of my strong hand, he will let the people go. In fact, he will force them to leave his land!"

²And God said to Moses, "I am Yahweh—'the Lord.'* ³I appeared to Abraham, to Isaac, and to Jacob as El-Shaddai—'God Almighty'*—but I did not reveal my name, Yahweh, to them. ⁴And I reaffirmed my covenant with them. Under its terms, I promised to give them the land of Canaan, where they were living as foreigners. ⁵You can be sure that I have heard the groans of the people of Israel, who are now slaves to the Egyptians. And I am well aware of my covenant with them.

⁶"Therefore, say to the people of Israel: 'I am the Lord. I will free you from your oppression and will rescue you from your slavery in Egypt. I will redeem you with a powerful arm and great acts of judgment. ⁷I will claim you as my own people, and I will be your God. Then you will know that I am the Lord your God who has freed you from your oppression in Egypt. ⁸I will bring you into the land I swore to give to Abraham, Isaac, and Jacob. I will give it to you as your very own possession. I am the Lord!'"

⁹So Moses told the people of Israel what the Lord had said, but they refused to listen anymore. They had become too discouraged by the brutality of their slavery.

6:2 *Yahweh* is a transliteration of the proper name *YHWH* that is sometimes rendered "Jehovah"; in this translation it is usually rendered "the Lord" (note the use of small capitals). 6:3 *El-Shaddai*, which means "God Almighty," is the name for God used in Gen 17:1; 28:3; 35:11; 43:14; 48:3.

5:1-2 The stated purpose for Israel's release was worship. The symmetry is clear: The people who served Pharaoh asked for time off to serve Yahweh. Pharaoh refused even this reasonable request, revealing his extreme greed. He claimed not to know who Yahweh was, but through the plagues, God would reveal himself.

6:1-13 God renewed his promises to his people. The declaration of rescue brought the real question to the surface, the question Pharaoh articulated earlier: Who is the Lord (5:2)? As much as the Israelites needed rescue from bondage, their greater need was to know the Lord. The climax of God's renewed promises was "you will know that I am the Lord your God" (6:7).

¹⁰Then the LORD said to Moses, ¹¹"Go back to Pharaoh, the king of Egypt, and tell him to let the people of Israel leave his country."

¹²"But LORD!" Moses objected. "My own people won't listen to me anymore. How can I expect Pharaoh to listen? I'm such a clumsy speaker!*"

¹³But the LORD spoke to Moses and Aaron and gave them orders for the Israelites and for Pharaoh, the king of Egypt. The LORD commanded Moses and Aaron to lead the people of Israel out of Egypt.

The Ancestors of Moses and Aaron

¹⁴These are the ancestors of some of the clans of Israel:

The sons of Reuben, Israel's oldest son, were Hanoch, Pallu, Hezron, and Carmi. Their descendants became the clans of Reuben.

¹⁵The sons of Simeon were Jemuel, Jamin, Ohad, Jakin, Zohar, and Shaul. (Shaul's mother was a Canaanite woman.) Their descendants became the clans of Simeon.

¹⁶These are the descendants of Levi, as listed in their family records: The sons of Levi were Gershon, Kohath, and Merari. (Levi lived to be 137 years old.)

¹⁷The descendants of Gershon included Libni and Shimei, each of whom became the ancestor of a clan.

¹⁸The descendants of Kohath included Amram, Izhar, Hebron, and Uzziel. (Kohath lived to be 133 years old.)

¹⁹The descendants of Merari included Mahli and Mushi.

These are the clans of the Levites, as listed in their family records.

²⁰Amram married his father's sister Jochebed, and she gave birth to his sons, Aaron and Moses. (Amram lived to be 137 years old.)

²¹The sons of Izhar were Korah, Nepheg, and Zicri. ²²The sons of Uzziel were Mishael, Elzaphan, and Sithri.

²³Aaron married Elisheba, the daughter of Amminadab and sister of Nahshon, and she gave birth to his sons, Nadab, Abihu, Eleazar, and Ithamar.

²⁴The sons of Korah were Assir, Elkanah, and Abiasaph. Their descendants became the clans of Korah.

²⁵Eleazar son of Aaron married one of the daughters of Putiel, and she gave birth to his son, Phinehas.

These are the ancestors of the Levite families, listed according to their clans.

²⁶The Aaron and Moses named in this list are the same ones to whom the LORD said, "Lead the people of Israel out of the land of Egypt like an army." ²⁷It was Moses and Aaron who spoke to Pharaoh, the king of Egypt, about leading the people of Israel out of Egypt.

²⁸When the LORD spoke to Moses in the land of Egypt, ²⁹he said to him, "I am the LORD! Tell Pharaoh, the king of Egypt, everything I am telling you." ³⁰But Moses argued with the LORD, saying, "I can't do it! I'm such a clumsy speaker! Why should Pharaoh listen to me?"

Aaron's Staff Becomes a Serpent

7 Then the LORD said to Moses, "Pay close attention to this. I will make you seem like God to Pharaoh, and your brother, Aaron, will be your prophet. ²Tell Aaron everything I command you, and Aaron must command Pharaoh to let the people of Israel leave his country. ³But I will make Pharaoh's heart stubborn so I can multiply my miraculous signs and wonders in the land of Egypt. ⁴Even then Pharaoh will refuse to listen to you. So I will bring down my fist on Egypt. Then I will rescue my forces—my people, the Israelites—from the land of Egypt with great acts of judgment. ⁵When I raise my powerful hand and bring out the Israelites, the Egyptians will know that I am the LORD."

⁶So Moses and Aaron did just as the LORD had commanded them. ⁷Moses was eighty years old, and Aaron was eighty-three when they made their demands to Pharaoh.

6:12 Hebrew *I have uncircumcised lips;* also in 6:30.

6:14-30 This genealogical interruption identifies how Moses and Aaron fit among Israel's families. It shows that God was continuing what he had done for their ancestors. The book of Exodus's recurring emphasis on Yahweh as the God of their ancestors comes explicitly (3:6 onward) and implicitly (1:1 onward). What God was about to do was not an unrelated action by some new god who devalued powerless older gods (a typical theme in ancient pagan literature). Unlike pagan gods, who aimed at personal power and fought among themselves, the true God has always had a single, overarching purpose for his creation to find fulfillment in proper relationship to him. Although God carries out that purpose in ever-expanding displays of creativity, the new activities always align with what he has already revealed of himself. Moses and Aaron did not suddenly appear out of the unknown. Rather, they belonged to those same people who God first revealed himself to. They belonged to the same people who God would soon show himself to even more grandly. The genealogies of Jesus have a similar purpose (Matthew 1:1-16; Luke 3:23-38).

7:3 God announced several times that he would harden Pharaoh's heart (4:21; 9:12; 10:1). Here he gave an exact reason: Pharaoh's stubbornness would demonstrate God's miraculous power. God's hardening of Pharaoh's heart did not override Pharaoh's own will. Pharaoh hardened his own heart many times (7:13, 22; 8:15, 32; 9:35). God gave him ample opportunity to respond in repentance, but Pharaoh persistently refused, so God confirmed Pharaoh's rebellious decision.

7:14–11:10 Each plague was an act of *uncreation*. The

⁸Then the LORD said to Moses and Aaron, ⁹"Pharaoh will demand, 'Show me a miracle.' When he does this, say to Aaron, 'Take your staff and throw it down in front of Pharaoh, and it will become a serpent.*'"

¹⁰So Moses and Aaron went to Pharaoh and did what the LORD had commanded them. Aaron threw down his staff before Pharaoh and his officials, and it became a serpent! ¹¹Then Pharaoh called in his own wise men and sorcerers, and these Egyptian magicians did the same thing with their magic. ¹²They threw down their staffs, which also became serpents! But then Aaron's staff swallowed up their staffs. ¹³Pharaoh's heart, however, remained hard. He still refused to listen, just as the LORD had predicted.

A Plague of Blood

¹⁴Then the LORD said to Moses, "Pharaoh's heart is stubborn,* and he still refuses to let the people go. ¹⁵So go to Pharaoh in the morning as he goes down to the river. Stand on the bank of the Nile and meet him there. Be sure to take along the staff that turned into a snake. ¹⁶Then announce to him, 'The LORD, the God of the Hebrews, has sent me to tell you, "Let my people go, so they can worship me in the wilderness." Until now, you have refused to listen to him. ¹⁷So this is what the LORD says: "I will show you that I am the LORD." Look! I will strike the water of the Nile with this staff in my hand, and the river will turn to blood. ¹⁸The fish in it will die, and the river will stink. The Egyptians will not be able to drink any water from the Nile.'"

¹⁹Then the LORD said to Moses: "Tell Aaron, 'Take your staff and raise your hand over the waters of Egypt—all its rivers, canals, ponds, and all the reservoirs. Turn all the water to blood. Everywhere in Egypt the water will turn to blood, even the water stored in wooden bowls and stone pots.'"

²⁰So Moses and Aaron did just as the LORD commanded them. As Pharaoh and all of his officials watched, Aaron raised his staff and struck the water of the Nile. Suddenly, the whole river turned to blood! ²¹The fish in the river died, and the water became so foul that the Egyptians couldn't drink it. There was blood everywhere throughout the land of Egypt. ²²But again the magicians of Egypt used their magic, and they, too, turned water into blood. So Pharaoh's heart remained hard. He refused to listen to Moses and Aaron, just as the LORD had predicted. ²³Pharaoh returned to his palace and put the whole thing out of his mind. ²⁴Then all the Egyptians dug along the riverbank to find drinking water, for they couldn't drink the water from the Nile.

²⁵Seven days passed from the time the LORD struck the Nile.

A Plague of Frogs

8 ¹*Then the LORD said to Moses, "Go back to Pharaoh and announce to him, 'This is what the LORD says: Let my people go, so they can worship me. ²If you refuse to let them go, I will send a plague of frogs across your entire land. ³The Nile River will swarm with frogs. They will come up out of the river and into your palace, even into your bedroom and onto your bed! They will enter the houses of your officials and your people. They will even jump into your ovens and your kneading bowls. ⁴Frogs will jump on you, your people, and all your officials.'"

⁵*Then the LORD said to Moses, "Tell Aaron, 'Raise the staff in your hand over all the rivers, canals, and ponds of Egypt, and bring up frogs over all the land.'" ⁶So Aaron raised his hand over the waters of Egypt, and frogs came up and covered the whole land! ⁷But the magicians were able to do the same thing with their magic. They, too, caused frogs to come up on the land of Egypt.

⁸Then Pharaoh summoned Moses and Aaron and begged, "Plead with the LORD to take the frogs away from me and my people. I will let your people go, so they can offer sacrifices to the LORD."

⁹"You set the time!" Moses replied. "Tell me when you want me to pray for you, your officials, and your people. Then you and your houses will be rid of the frogs. They will remain only in the Nile River."

¹⁰"Do it tomorrow," Pharaoh said.

"All right," Moses replied, "it will be as you have said. Then you will know that there is no one like the LORD our God. ¹¹The frogs will leave you and your houses, your officials, and your people. They will remain only in the Nile River."

¹²So Moses and Aaron left Pharaoh's palace, and Moses cried out to the LORD about the frogs he had inflicted on Pharaoh. ¹³And the LORD did just what Moses had predicted. The frogs in the houses, the courtyards, and the fields all died. ¹⁴The Egyptians piled them into great heaps, and a terrible stench filled the land. ¹⁵But when Pharaoh saw that relief had come, he became stubborn.* He refused to listen to Moses and Aaron, just as the LORD had predicted.

7:9 Hebrew *tannin*, which elsewhere refers to a sea monster. Greek version translates it "dragon." **7:14** Hebrew *heavy*. **8:1** Verses 8:1-4 are numbered 7:26-29 in Hebrew text. **8:5** Verses 8:5-32 are numbered 8:1-28 in Hebrew text. **8:15** Hebrew *made his heart heavy*; also in 8:32.

---

destructive policies of the pharaohs (killing infants and working enslaved people ruthlessly) opposed God's creation design by bringing death and bondage, rather than human flourishing. God responded by bringing disorder to Egypt: Water became undrinkable, frogs ran amok, gnats and flies filled the air, livestock died, people broke out in boils, hail destroyed crops, locusts ate what remained, and daytime turned into darkness. Eventually, the firstborn children of Egypt died.

8:25 Pharaoh attempted to bargain with God. He wanted to obey partially while still retaining control. James says people who divide loyalty between God and the world "[are] as unsettled as a wave of the sea that is blown and tossed by the wind" (James 1:6). Similarly,

Insight: TEN PLAGUES AGAINST TEN FALSE GODS

When God rescued his people from Egypt after many years of slavery there, he displayed his power over Egypt's gods through a series of plagues (7:14–11:10). Each plague can be understood as a direct challenge to a specific Egyptian deity.

Plague	Egyptian Deity
1. blood	Hapi — god of the Nile, bringer of fertility
2. frogs	Heqet — frog-headed goddess of fruitfulness
3. gnats	Geb — god of the earth, from which the gnats came
4. flies	Khepri — beetle-headed god of the morning sun
5. cattle	Hathor — cow-headed goddess of motherhood & childbirth
6. boils	Sekhmet — goddess of healing
7. hail	Nut — goddess of the sky
8. locusts	Shu — god of the wind
9. darkness	Ra — sun god, king of the gods, father of mankind
10. firstborn	Bes — protector of households

A Plague of Gnats

¹⁶So the LORD said to Moses, "Tell Aaron, 'Raise your staff and strike the ground. The dust will turn into swarms of gnats throughout the land of Egypt.'" ¹⁷So Moses and Aaron did just as the LORD had commanded them. When Aaron raised his hand and struck the ground with his staff, gnats infested the entire land, covering the Egyptians and their animals. All the dust in the land of Egypt turned into gnats. ¹⁸Pharaoh's magicians tried to do the same thing with their secret arts, but this time they failed. And the gnats covered everyone, people and animals alike.

¹⁹"This is the finger of God!" the magicians exclaimed to Pharaoh. But Pharaoh's heart remained hard. He wouldn't listen to them, just as the LORD had predicted.

A Plague of Flies

²⁰Then the LORD told Moses, "Get up early in the morning and stand in Pharaoh's way as he goes down to the river. Say to him, 'This is what the LORD says: Let my people go, so they can worship me. ²¹If you refuse, then I will send swarms of flies on you, your officials, your people, and all the houses. The Egyptian homes will be filled with flies, and the ground will be covered with them. ²²But this time I will spare the region of Goshen, where my people live. No flies will be found there. Then you will know that I am the LORD and that I am present even in the heart of your land. ²³I will make a clear distinction between* my people and your people. This miraculous sign will happen tomorrow.'"

²⁴And the LORD did just as he had said. A thick swarm of flies filled Pharaoh's palace and the houses of his officials. The whole land of Egypt was thrown into chaos by the flies.

²⁵Pharaoh called for Moses and Aaron. "All right! Go ahead and offer sacrifices to your God," he said. "But do it here in this land."

²⁶But Moses replied, "That wouldn't be right. The Egyptians detest the sacrifices that we offer to the LORD our God. Look, if we offer our sacrifices here

---

8:23 As in Greek and Latin versions; Hebrew reads *I will set redemption between*.

Jesus explains that anyone who divides their commitment works against God (Matthew 12:22-30).

8:26-27 Moses pointed out the impossibility of Pharaoh's request by noting the Egyptians' own prejudice. The Egyptians thought the Hebrew people were beneath them (see Genesis 43:32). The Hebrews asked to leave Egypt to worship God (see Exodus 5:1; 7:16; 8:1, 20). God's purpose for the Exodus was to lead his people into a proper relationship with him. The first step was to free them from Pharaoh's oppressive rule and the Egyptians' prejudice.

where the Egyptians can see us, they will stone us. ²⁷We must take a three-day trip into the wilderness to offer sacrifices to the LORD our God, just as he has commanded us."

²⁸"All right, go ahead," Pharaoh replied. "I will let you go into the wilderness to offer sacrifices to the LORD your God. But don't go too far away. Now hurry and pray for me."

²⁹Moses answered, "As soon as I leave you, I will pray to the LORD, and tomorrow the swarms of flies will disappear from you and your officials and all your people. But I am warning you, Pharaoh, don't lie to us again and refuse to let the people go to sacrifice to the LORD."

³⁰So Moses left Pharaoh's palace and pleaded with the LORD to remove all the flies. ³¹And the LORD did as Moses asked and caused the swarms of flies to disappear from Pharaoh, his officials, and his people. Not a single fly remained. ³²But Pharaoh again became stubborn and refused to let the people go.

A Plague against Livestock

9 "Go back to Pharaoh," the LORD commanded Moses. "Tell him, 'This is what the LORD, the God of the Hebrews, says: Let my people go, so they can worship me. ²If you continue to hold them and refuse to let them go, ³the hand of the LORD will strike all your livestock—your horses, donkeys, camels, cattle, sheep, and goats—with a deadly plague. ⁴But the LORD will again make a distinction between the livestock of the Israelites and that of the Egyptians. Not a single one of Israel's animals will die! ⁵The LORD has already set the time for the plague to begin. He has declared that he will strike the land tomorrow.'"

⁶And the LORD did just as he had said. The next morning all the livestock of the Egyptians died, but the Israelites didn't lose a single animal. ⁷Pharaoh sent his officials to investigate, and they discovered that the Israelites had not lost a single animal! But even so, Pharaoh's heart remained stubborn,* and he still refused to let the people go.

A Plague of Festering Boils

⁸Then the LORD said to Moses and Aaron, "Take handfuls of soot from a brick kiln, and have Moses toss it into the air while Pharaoh watches. ⁹The ashes will spread like fine dust over the whole land of Egypt, causing festering boils to break out on people and animals throughout the land."

¹⁰So they took soot from a brick kiln and went and stood before Pharaoh. As Pharaoh watched, Moses threw the soot into the air, and boils broke out on people and animals alike. ¹¹Even the magicians were unable to stand before Moses, because the boils had broken out on them and all the Egyptians. ¹²But the LORD hardened Pharaoh's heart, and just as the LORD had predicted to Moses, Pharaoh refused to listen.

A Plague of Hail

¹³Then the LORD said to Moses, "Get up early in the morning and stand before Pharaoh. Tell him, 'This is what the LORD, the God of the Hebrews, says: Let my people go, so they can worship me. ¹⁴If you don't, I will send more plagues on you* and your officials and your people. Then you will know that there is no one like me in all the earth. ¹⁵By now I could have lifted my hand and struck you and your people with a plague to wipe you off the face of the earth. ¹⁶But I have spared you for a purpose—to show you my power* and to spread my fame throughout the earth. ¹⁷But you still lord it over my people and refuse to let them go. ¹⁸So tomorrow at this time I will send a hailstorm more devastating than any in all the history of Egypt. ¹⁹Quick! Order your livestock and servants to come in from the fields to find shelter. Any person or animal left outside will die when the hail falls.'"

²⁰Some of Pharaoh's officials were afraid because of what the LORD had said. They quickly brought their servants and livestock in from the fields. ²¹But those who paid no attention to the word of the LORD left theirs out in the open.

²²Then the LORD said to Moses, "Lift your hand toward the sky so hail may fall on the people, the livestock, and all the plants throughout the land of Egypt."

²³So Moses lifted his staff toward the sky, and the LORD sent thunder and hail, and lightning flashed toward the earth. The LORD sent a tremendous hailstorm against all the land of Egypt. ²⁴Never in all the history of Egypt had there been a storm like that, with such devastating hail and continuous lightning. ²⁵It left all of Egypt in ruins. The hail struck down everything in the open field—people, animals, and plants alike. Even the trees were destroyed. ²⁶The only place without hail was the region of Goshen, where the people of Israel lived.

²⁷Then Pharaoh quickly summoned Moses and Aaron. "This time I have sinned," he confessed. "The LORD is the righteous one, and my people and I are wrong. ²⁸Please beg the LORD to end this terrifying thunder and hail. We've had enough. I will let you go; you don't need to stay any longer."

9:7 Hebrew *heavy.* 9:14 Hebrew *on your heart.* 9:16 Greek version reads *to display my power in you;* compare Rom 9:17.

9:14-17 God explained the plagues' purpose: to reveal (especially to Pharaoh) that "there is no one like me in all the earth" (9:14; see also Isaiah 46:9; Jeremiah 10:6-7). Thus, God did not destroy Pharaoh and Egypt in a single blow, as he could have done. Instead, God spared them (Exodus 9:16), allowing them to submit to his power, repent of their sins, and let the Israelites leave Egypt. But Pharaoh refused to humble himself and stop playing lord over the Lord's people (9:17).

29"All right," Moses replied. "As soon as I leave the city, I will lift my hands and pray to the LORD. Then the thunder and hail will stop, and you will know that the earth belongs to the LORD. 30But I know that you and your officials still do not fear the LORD God."

31(All the flax and barley were ruined by the hail, because the barley had formed heads and the flax was budding. 32But the wheat and the emmer wheat were spared, because they had not yet sprouted from the ground.)

33So Moses left Pharaoh's court and went out of the city. When he lifted his hands to the LORD, the thunder and hail stopped, and the downpour ceased. 34But when Pharaoh saw that the rain, hail, and thunder had stopped, he and his officials sinned again, and Pharaoh again became stubborn.* 35Because his heart was hard, Pharaoh refused to let the people leave, just as the LORD had predicted through Moses.

A Plague of Locusts

10 Then the LORD said to Moses, "Return to Pharaoh and make your demands again. I have made him and his officials stubborn* so I can display my miraculous signs among them. 2I've also done it so you can tell your children and grandchildren about how I made a mockery of the Egyptians and about the signs I displayed among them—and so you will know that I am the LORD."

3So Moses and Aaron went to Pharaoh and said, "This is what the LORD, the God of the Hebrews, says: How long will you refuse to submit to me? Let my people go, so they can worship me. 4If you refuse, watch out! For tomorrow I will bring a swarm of locusts on your country. 5They will cover the land so that you won't be able to see the ground. They will devour what little is left of your crops after the hailstorm, including all the trees growing in the fields. 6They will overrun your palaces and the homes of your officials and all the houses in Egypt. Never in the history of Egypt have your ancestors seen a plague like this one!" And with that, Moses turned and left Pharaoh.

7Pharaoh's officials now came to Pharaoh and appealed to him. "How long will you let this man hold us hostage? Let the men go to worship the LORD their God! Don't you realize that Egypt lies in ruins?"

8So Moses and Aaron were brought back to Pharaoh. "All right," he told them, "go and worship the LORD your God. But who exactly will be going with you?"

9Moses replied, "We will all go—young and old, our sons and daughters, and our flocks and herds. We must all join together in celebrating a festival to the LORD."

10Pharaoh retorted, "The LORD will certainly need to be with you if I let you take your little ones! I can see through your evil plan. 11Never! Only the men may go and worship the LORD, since that is what you requested." And Pharaoh threw them out of the palace.

12Then the LORD said to Moses, "Raise your hand over the land of Egypt to bring on the locusts. Let them cover the land and devour every plant that survived the hailstorm."

13So Moses raised his staff over Egypt, and the LORD caused an east wind to blow over the land all that day and through the night. When morning arrived, the east wind had brought the locusts. 14And the locusts swarmed over the whole land of Egypt, settling in dense swarms from one end of the country to the other. It was the worst locust plague in Egyptian history, and there has never been another one like it. 15For the locusts covered the whole country and darkened the land. They devoured every plant in the fields and all the fruit on the trees that had survived the hailstorm. Not a single leaf was left on the trees and plants throughout the land of Egypt.

16Pharaoh quickly summoned Moses and Aaron. "I have sinned against the LORD your God and against you," he confessed. 17"Forgive my sin, just this once, and plead with the LORD your God to take away this death from me."

18So Moses left Pharaoh's court and pleaded with the LORD. 19The LORD responded by shifting the wind, and the strong west wind blew the locusts into the Red Sea.* Not a single locust remained in all the land of Egypt. 20But the LORD hardened Pharaoh's heart again, so he refused to let the people go.

A Plague of Darkness

21Then the LORD said to Moses, "Lift your hand toward heaven, and the land of Egypt will be covered with a darkness so thick you can feel it." 22So Moses lifted his hand to the sky, and a deep darkness covered the entire land of Egypt for three days. 23During all that time the people could not see each other, and no one moved. But there was light as usual where the people of Israel lived.

24Finally, Pharaoh called for Moses. "Go and worship the LORD," he said. "But leave your flocks and herds here. You may even take your little ones with you."

25"No," Moses said, "you must provide us with animals for sacrifices and burnt offerings to the LORD our God. 26All our livestock must go with us, too; not a hoof can be left behind. We must choose our

---

9:34 Hebrew *made his heart heavy.* 10:1 Hebrew *have made his heart and his officials' hearts heavy.* 10:19 Hebrew *sea of reeds.*

9:29 There is no one like the Lord in all the earth (9:14), and all "the earth belongs to the LORD." This was the plagues' inescapable message, though the Egyptians had difficulty accepting it.
10:16-17 Pharaoh's recognition of his sin grew deeper the more he experienced God's judgment. He admitted that his pride and refusal to keep his word were sins. He recognized that sin cannot be ignored but requires God's forgiveness. But unfortunately, his correct theological understanding did not change his heart.

sacrifices for the LORD our God from among these animals. And we won't know how we are to worship the LORD until we get there."

²⁷But the LORD hardened Pharaoh's heart once more, and he would not let them go. ²⁸"Get out of here!" Pharaoh shouted at Moses. "I'm warning you. Never come back to see me again! The day you see my face, you will die!"

²⁹"Very well," Moses replied. "I will never see your face again."

Death for Egypt's Firstborn

11 Then the LORD said to Moses, "I will strike Pharaoh and the land of Egypt with one more blow. After that, Pharaoh will let you leave this country. In fact, he will be so eager to get rid of you that he will force you all to leave. ²Tell all the Israelite men and women to ask their Egyptian neighbors for articles of silver and gold." ³(Now the LORD had caused the Egyptians to look favorably on the people of Israel. And Moses was considered a very great man in the land of Egypt, respected by Pharaoh's officials and the Egyptian people alike.)

⁴Moses had announced to Pharaoh, "This is what the LORD says: At midnight tonight I will pass through the heart of Egypt. ⁵All the firstborn sons will die in every family in Egypt, from the oldest son of Pharaoh, who sits on his throne, to the oldest son of his lowliest servant girl who grinds the flour. Even the firstborn of all the livestock will die. ⁶Then a loud wail will rise throughout the land of Egypt, a wail like no one has heard before or will ever hear again. ⁷But among the Israelites it will be so peaceful that not even a dog will bark. Then you will know that the LORD makes a distinction between the Egyptians and the Israelites. ⁸All the officials of Egypt will run to me and fall to the ground before me. 'Please leave!' they will beg. 'Hurry! And take all your followers with you.' Only then will I go!" Then, burning with anger, Moses left Pharaoh.

⁹Now the LORD had told Moses earlier, "Pharaoh will not listen to you, but then I will do even more mighty miracles in the land of Egypt." ¹⁰Moses and Aaron performed these miracles in Pharaoh's presence, but the LORD hardened Pharaoh's heart, and he wouldn't let the Israelites leave the country.

The First Passover

12 While the Israelites were still in the land of Egypt, the LORD gave the following instructions to Moses and Aaron: ²"From now on, this month will be the first month of the year for you. ³Announce to the whole community of Israel that on the tenth day of this month each family must choose a lamb or a young goat for a sacrifice, one animal for each household. ⁴If a family is too small to eat a whole animal, let them share with another family in the neighborhood. Divide the animal according to the size of each family and how much they can eat. ⁵The animal you select must be a one-year-old male, either a sheep or a goat, with no defects.

⁶"Take special care of this chosen animal until the evening of the fourteenth day of this first month. Then the whole assembly of the community of Israel must slaughter their lamb or young goat at twilight. ⁷They are to take some of the blood and smear it on the sides and top of the doorframes of the houses where they eat the animal. ⁸That same night they must roast the meat over a fire and eat it along with bitter salad greens and bread made without yeast. ⁹Do not eat any of the meat raw or boiled in water. The whole animal—including the head, legs, and internal organs—must be roasted over a fire. ¹⁰Do not leave any of it until the next morning. Burn whatever is not eaten before morning.

¹¹"These are your instructions for eating this meal: Be fully dressed,* wear your sandals, and carry your walking stick in your hand. Eat the meal with urgency, for this is the LORD's Passover. ¹²On that night I will pass through the land of Egypt and strike down every firstborn son and firstborn male animal in the land of Egypt. I will execute judgment against all the gods of Egypt, for I am the LORD! ¹³But the blood on your doorposts will serve as a sign, marking the houses where you are staying. When I see the blood, I will pass over you. This plague of death will not touch you when I strike the land of Egypt.

¹⁴"This is a day to remember. Each year, from generation to generation, you must celebrate it as a special festival to the LORD. This is a law for all time. ¹⁵For seven days the bread you eat must be made without yeast. On the first day of the festival,

---

12:11 Hebrew *Bind up your loins.*

10:27-29 Pharaoh seemed to realize that he had reached a point of no return. If he would not submit—the only appropriate response to what he had learned from the plagues—then he must kill the messenger. This reasoning resembles what the Gospels say about the religious leaders' plot to kill Jesus. They refused to learn from Jesus' life and ministry appropriately, so they arranged to kill him (see John 11:45-53).
11:4-8 After months of stubborn resistance to the Lord's demands, Pharaoh brought a terrible consequence on his people. A previous pharaoh had demanded the death of Hebrew boys; now, Egyptian sons would die. In 4:22-23, God called Israel his firstborn son and stated that because Pharaoh refused to let Israel worship Yahweh, he would kill Pharaoh's firstborn son. Meanwhile, the Hebrew firstborn sons would be under God's protection as long as they showed allegiance to him through the Passover ritual.
12:1 This chapter of ritual instructions may feel like an odd interruption to an otherwise gripping story, but it serves an important function. The yearly Passover celebration would ensure that every generation would own the Exodus from Egypt as their story. The sounds, smells, and tastes of Passover made the Exodus come alive again every year.

remove every trace of yeast from your homes. Anyone who eats bread made with yeast during the seven days of the festival will be cut off from the community of Israel. ¹⁶On the first day of the festival and again on the seventh day, all the people must observe an official day for holy assembly. No work of any kind may be done on these days except in the preparation of food.

¹⁷"Celebrate this Festival of Unleavened Bread, for it will remind you that I brought your forces out of the land of Egypt on this very day. This festival will be a permanent law for you; celebrate this day from generation to generation. ¹⁸The bread you eat must be made without yeast from the evening of the fourteenth day of the first month until the evening of the twenty-first day of that month. ¹⁹During those seven days, there

Insight: ISRAEL'S CALENDAR OF FESTIVALS

Ancient Israel marked the beginning of each month at the new moon, which occurs on average every 29.5 days. Twelve lunar cycles results in a 354-day calendar, which is 11 days shorter than the solar year. The Israelites also celebrated several annual festivals. This regular cycle of celebrations helped the people of Israel remember what God had done for them in the past and how he would provide for them as they journeyed to a new land.

ANNUAL FESTIVALS

Passover
Leviticus 23:5

Unleavened Bread
Leviticus 23:6-8

First Harvest
Leviticus 23:9-14

Later Passover
Numbers 9:4-12

Harvest
Leviticus 23:15-22

Trumpets
Leviticus 23:23-25

Day of Atonement
Leviticus 23:26-32

Shelters
Leviticus 23:33-43

Dedication
John 10:22

Purim
Esther 9:1-32

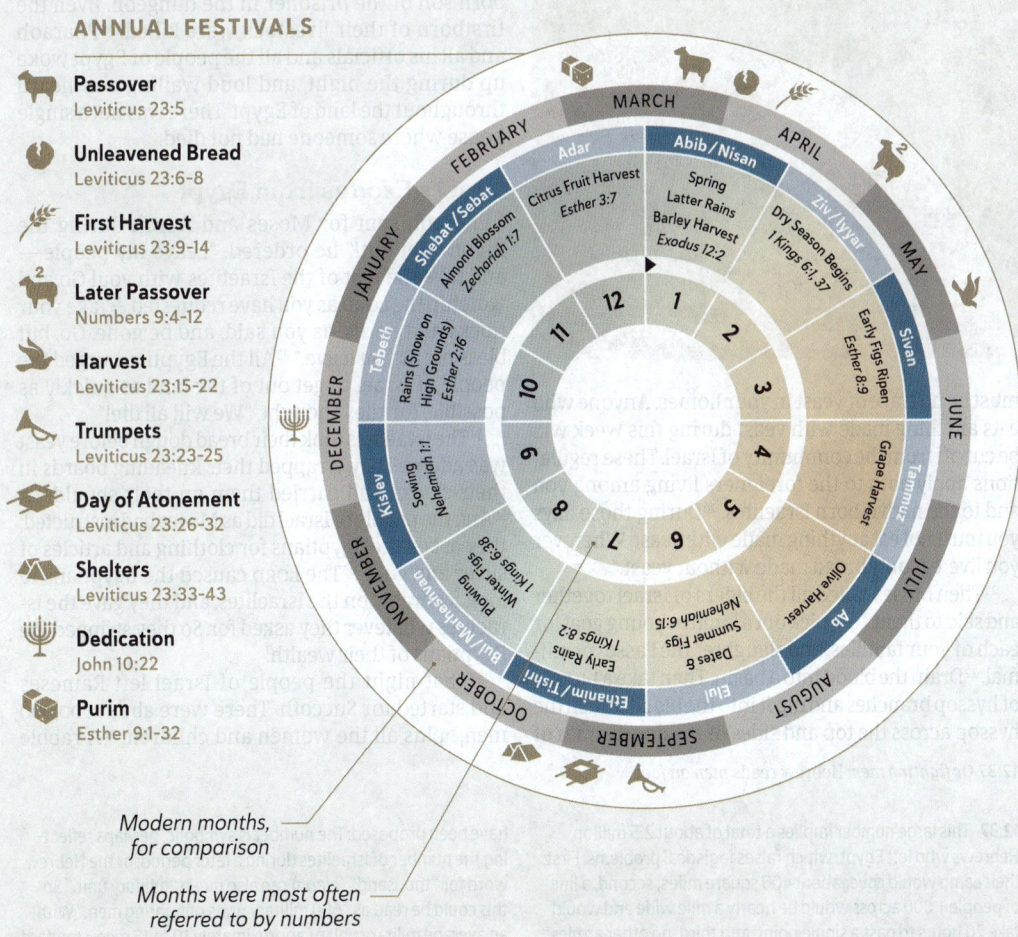

Modern months, for comparison

Months were most often referred to by numbers

> "When I left the house of bondage, … I went to the Lord and asked Him to give me a new name. And the Lord gave me Sojourner, because I was to travel up and down the land, showing the people their sins, and being a sign unto them. Afterwards I told the Lord I wanted another name, … and the Lord gave me Truth, because I was to declare the truth to the people."
>
> **SOJOURNER TRUTH**
> (1797–1883) evangelist, abolitionist, and women's rights activist

must be no trace of yeast in your homes. Anyone who eats anything made with yeast during this week will be cut off from the community of Israel. These regulations apply both to the foreigners living among you and to the native-born Israelites. ²⁰During those days you must not eat anything made with yeast. Wherever you live, eat only bread made without yeast."

²¹Then Moses called all the elders of Israel together and said to them, "Go, pick out a lamb or young goat for each of your families, and slaughter the Passover animal. ²²Drain the blood into a basin. Then take a bundle of hyssop branches and dip it into the blood. Brush the hyssop across the top and sides of the doorframes of your houses. And no one may go out through the door until morning. ²³For the LORD will pass through the land to strike down the Egyptians. But when he sees the blood on the top and sides of the doorframe, the LORD will pass over your home. He will not permit his death angel to enter your house and strike you down.

²⁴"Remember, these instructions are a permanent law that you and your descendants must observe forever. ²⁵When you enter the land the LORD has promised to give you, you will continue to observe this ceremony. ²⁶Then your children will ask, 'What does this ceremony mean?' ²⁷And you will reply, 'It is the Passover sacrifice to the LORD, for he passed over the houses of the Israelites in Egypt. And though he struck the Egyptians, he spared our families.'" When Moses had finished speaking, all the people bowed down to the ground and worshiped.

²⁸So the people of Israel did just as the LORD had commanded through Moses and Aaron. ²⁹And that night at midnight, the LORD struck down all the firstborn sons in the land of Egypt, from the firstborn son of Pharaoh, who sat on his throne, to the firstborn son of the prisoner in the dungeon. Even the firstborn of their livestock were killed. ³⁰Pharaoh and all his officials and all the people of Egypt woke up during the night, and loud wailing was heard throughout the land of Egypt. There was not a single house where someone had not died.

Israel's Exodus from Egypt

³¹Pharaoh sent for Moses and Aaron during the night. "Get out!" he ordered. "Leave my people—and take the rest of the Israelites with you! Go and worship the LORD as you have requested. ³²Take your flocks and herds, as you said, and be gone. Go, but bless me as you leave." ³³All the Egyptians urged the people of Israel to get out of the land as quickly as possible, for they thought, "We will all die!"

³⁴The Israelites took their bread dough before yeast was added. They wrapped their kneading boards in their cloaks and carried them on their shoulders. ³⁵And the people of Israel did as Moses had instructed; they asked the Egyptians for clothing and articles of silver and gold. ³⁶The LORD caused the Egyptians to look favorably on the Israelites, and they gave the Israelites whatever they asked for. So they stripped the Egyptians of their wealth!

³⁷That night the people of Israel left Rameses and started for Succoth. There were about 600,000 men,* plus all the women and children. ³⁸A rabble

12:37 Or *fighting men;* Hebrew reads *men on foot.*

12:37 This large number implies a total of about 2.5 million Hebrews who left Egypt, which raises logistical problems: First, their camp would cover about 400 square miles; second, a line of people 1,000 across would be nearly a mile wide and would take 20 hours to pass a single point; and third, no other armies were so large at that time. As a result, two viable alternatives have been proposed: The number is symbolic, perhaps reflecting the number of Israelites during a later period; or the Hebrew word for "thousand" (*eleph*) can also mean "military unit." So this could be read as "600 military units of fighting men." With an average military unit of approximately 10 to 15 men, standard for that time, the total population would be closer to 22,000.

of non-Israelites went with them, along with great flocks and herds of livestock. ³⁹For bread they baked flat cakes from the dough without yeast they had brought from Egypt. It was made without yeast because the people were driven out of Egypt in such a hurry that they had no time to prepare the bread or other food.

⁴⁰The people of Israel had lived in Egypt* for 430 years. ⁴¹In fact, it was on the last day of the 430th year that all the LORD's forces left the land. ⁴²On this night the LORD kept his promise to bring his people out of the land of Egypt. So this night belongs to him, and it must be commemorated every year by all the Israelites, from generation to generation.

Instructions for the Passover

⁴³Then the LORD said to Moses and Aaron, "These are the instructions for the festival of Passover. No outsiders are allowed to eat the Passover meal. ⁴⁴But any slave who has been purchased may eat it if he has been circumcised. ⁴⁵Temporary residents and hired servants may not eat it. ⁴⁶Each Passover lamb must be eaten in one house. Do not carry any of its meat outside, and do not break any of its bones. ⁴⁷The whole community of Israel must celebrate this Passover festival.

⁴⁸"If there are foreigners living among you who want to celebrate the LORD's Passover, let all their males be circumcised. Only then may they celebrate the Passover with you like any native-born Israelite. But no uncircumcised male may ever eat the Passover meal. ⁴⁹This instruction applies to everyone, whether a native-born Israelite or a foreigner living among you."

⁵⁰So all the people of Israel followed all the LORD's commands to Moses and Aaron. ⁵¹On that very day the LORD brought the people of Israel out of the land of Egypt like an army.

Dedication of the Firstborn

13 Then the LORD said to Moses, ²"Dedicate to me every firstborn among the Israelites. The first offspring to be born, of both humans and animals, belongs to me."

³So Moses said to the people, "This is a day to remember forever—the day you left Egypt, the place of your slavery. Today the LORD has brought you out by the power of his mighty hand. (Remember, eat no food containing yeast.) ⁴On this day in early spring, in the month of Abib,* you have been set free. ⁵You must celebrate this event in this month each year after the LORD brings you into the land of the Canaanites, Hittites, Amorites, Hivites, and Jebusites. (He swore to your ancestors that he would give you this land—a land flowing with milk and honey.) ⁶For seven days the bread you eat must be made without yeast. Then on the seventh day, celebrate a feast to the LORD. ⁷Eat bread without yeast during those seven days. In fact, there must be no yeast bread or any yeast at all found within the borders of your land during this time.

⁸"On the seventh day you must explain to your children, 'I am celebrating what the LORD did for me when I left Egypt.' ⁹This annual festival will be a visible sign to you, like a mark branded on your hand or your forehead. Let it remind you always to recite this teaching of the LORD: 'With a strong hand, the LORD rescued you from Egypt.'* ¹⁰So observe the decree of this festival at the appointed time each year.

¹¹"This is what you must do when the LORD fulfills the promise he swore to you and to your ancestors. When he gives you the land where the Canaanites now live, ¹²you must present all firstborn sons and firstborn male animals to the LORD, for they belong to him. ¹³A firstborn donkey may be bought back from the LORD by presenting a lamb or young goat in its place. But if you do not buy it back, you must break its neck. However, you must buy back every firstborn son.

¹⁴"And in the future, your children will ask you, 'What does all this mean?' Then you will tell them, 'With the power of his mighty hand, the LORD brought us out of Egypt, the place of our slavery. ¹⁵Pharaoh stubbornly refused to let us go, so the LORD killed all the firstborn males throughout the land of Egypt, both people and animals. That is why I now sacrifice all the firstborn males to the LORD—except that the firstborn sons are always bought back.' ¹⁶This ceremony will be like a mark branded on your hand or your forehead. It is a reminder that the power of the LORD's mighty hand brought us out of Egypt."

Israel's Wilderness Detour

¹⁷When Pharaoh finally let the people go, God did not lead them along the main road that runs through Philistine territory, even though that was the shortest route to the Promised Land. God said, "If the people are faced with a battle, they might change

---

12:40 Samaritan Pentateuch reads *in Canaan and Egypt;* Greek version reads *in Egypt and Canaan.* **13:4** Hebrew *On this day in the month of Abib.* This first month of the ancient Hebrew lunar calendar usually occurs within the months of March and April. **13:9** Or *Let it remind you always to keep the instructions of the LORD on the tip of your tongue, because with a strong hand, the LORD rescued you from Egypt.*

12:48 For the Israelites, male circumcision was a sign of covenant membership. While only men were circumcised, women were included in the covenant through their connection to circumcised men—their fathers, husbands, and sons. Foreigners were welcome to join the Israelite community by adopting this practice.

13:12 Selecting firstborn sons to belong to the Lord probably reflects Pharaoh's attempts to target Hebrew boys (1:16, 22). God set up a perpetual reminder that the Israelites were *his* people, rather than Pharaoh's.

their minds and return to Egypt." ¹⁸So God led them in a roundabout way through the wilderness toward the Red Sea.* Thus the Israelites left Egypt like an army ready for battle.*

¹⁹Moses took the bones of Joseph with him, for Joseph had made the sons of Israel swear to do this. He said, "God will certainly come to help you. When he does, you must take my bones with you from this place."

²⁰The Israelites left Succoth and camped at Etham on the edge of the wilderness. ²¹The LORD went ahead of them. He guided them during the day with a pillar of cloud, and he provided light at night with a pillar of fire. This allowed them to travel by day or by night. ²²And the LORD did not remove the pillar of cloud or pillar of fire from its place in front of the people.

14

Then the LORD gave these instructions to Moses: ²"Order the Israelites to turn back and camp by Pi-hahiroth between Migdol and the sea. Camp there along the shore, across from Baal-zephon. ³Then Pharaoh will think, 'The Israelites are confused. They are trapped in the wilderness!' ⁴And once again I will harden Pharaoh's heart, and he will chase after you.* I have planned this in order to display my glory through Pharaoh and his whole army. After this the Egyptians will know that I am the LORD!" So the Israelites camped there as they were told.

The Egyptians Pursue Israel

⁵When word reached the king of Egypt that the Israelites had fled, Pharaoh and his officials changed their minds. "What have we done, letting all those Israelite slaves get away?" they asked. ⁶So Pharaoh harnessed his chariot and called up his troops. ⁷He took with him 600 of Egypt's best chariots, along with the rest of the chariots of Egypt, each with its commander. ⁸The LORD hardened the heart of Pharaoh, the king of Egypt, so he chased after the people of Israel, who had left with fists raised in defiance. ⁹The Egyptians chased after them with all the forces in Pharaoh's army—all his horses and chariots, his charioteers, and his troops. The Egyptians caught up with the people of Israel as they were camped beside the shore near Pi-hahiroth, across from Baal-zephon.

¹⁰As Pharaoh approached, the people of Israel looked up and panicked when they saw the Egyptians overtaking them. They cried out to the LORD, ¹¹and they said to Moses, "Why did you bring us out here to die in the wilderness? Weren't there enough graves for us in Egypt? What have you done to us? Why did you make us leave Egypt? ¹²Didn't we tell you this would happen while we were still in Egypt? We said, 'Leave us alone! Let us be slaves to the Egyptians. It's better to be a slave in Egypt than a corpse in the wilderness!'"

¹³But Moses told the people, "Don't be afraid. Just stand still and watch the LORD rescue you today. The Egyptians you see today will never be seen again. ¹⁴The LORD himself will fight for you. Just stay calm."

Escape through the Red Sea

¹⁵Then the LORD said to Moses, "Why are you crying out to me? Tell the people to get moving! ¹⁶Pick up your staff and raise your hand over the sea. Divide the water so the Israelites can walk through the middle of the sea on dry ground. ¹⁷And I will harden the hearts of the Egyptians, and they will charge in after the Israelites. My great glory will be displayed through Pharaoh and his troops, his chariots, and his charioteers. ¹⁸When my glory is displayed through them, all Egypt will see my glory and know that I am the LORD!"

¹⁹Then the angel of God, who had been leading the people of Israel, moved to the rear of the camp. The pillar of cloud also moved from the front and stood behind them. ²⁰The cloud settled between the Egyptian and Israelite camps. As darkness fell, the cloud turned to fire, lighting up the night. But the Egyptians and Israelites did not approach each other all night.

²¹Then Moses raised his hand over the sea, and the LORD opened up a path through the water with a strong east wind. The wind blew all that night, turning the seabed into dry land. ²²So the people of Israel walked through the middle of the sea on dry ground, with walls of water on each side!

²³Then the Egyptians—all of Pharaoh's horses, chariots, and charioteers—chased them into the middle of the sea. ²⁴But just before dawn the LORD looked down on the Egyptian army from the pillar

---

13:18a Hebrew *sea of reeds.*   **13:18b** Greek version reads *left Egypt in the fifth generation.*   **14:4** Hebrew *after them.*

13:21-22 God graciously led his people with a cloud they could see day and night. This had a practical benefit since travel by night would be advantageous in a hot desert. The cloud also visibly demonstrated Yahweh's presence with them—a striking testimony to surrounding nations (see Joshua 2:8-11). God's people usually experience his guidance less dramatically—for example, through the Spirit convicting us of sin or giving us peace.

14:10-12 This complaint is the first time we see the sad refrain that the Israelites will repeat for the next forty years, as they wander in the wilderness. Instead of believing that God, who demonstrated his power so overwhelmingly, could now save them, the Israelites turned on their rescuer. The cry of the unsurrendered heart is always "Give me the security of slavery rather than the risk of faith!"

14:22 As with the plagues, naturalistic explanations for this event fall short. A strong, steady wind blowing across a shallow, contained body of water can change its depth dramatically. But it does not produce "dry ground, with walls of water on each side." The Lord can intervene and do with nature as he wishes.

of fire and cloud, and he threw their forces into total confusion. ²⁵He twisted* their chariot wheels, making their chariots difficult to drive. "Let's get out of here—away from these Israelites!" the Egyptians shouted. "The LORD is fighting for them against Egypt!"

²⁶When all the Israelites had reached the other side, the LORD said to Moses, "Raise your hand over the sea again. Then the waters will rush back and cover the Egyptians and their chariots and charioteers." ²⁷So as the sun began to rise, Moses raised his hand over the sea, and the water rushed back into its usual place. The Egyptians tried to escape, but the LORD swept them into the sea. ²⁸Then the waters returned and covered all the chariots and charioteers—the entire army of Pharaoh. Of all the Egyptians who had chased the Israelites into the sea, not a single one survived.

²⁹But the people of Israel had walked through the middle of the sea on dry ground, as the water stood up like a wall on both sides. ³⁰That is how the LORD rescued Israel from the hand of the Egyptians that day. And the Israelites saw the bodies of the Egyptians washed up on the seashore. ³¹When the people of Israel saw the mighty power that the LORD had unleashed against the Egyptians, they were filled with awe before him. They put their faith in the LORD and in his servant Moses.

A Song of Deliverance

15 Then Moses and the people of Israel sang this song to the LORD:

"I will sing to the LORD,
　for he has triumphed gloriously;

14:25 As in Greek version, Samaritan Pentateuch, and Syriac version; Hebrew reads *He removed.*

---

⑧ Come Close — OPPRESSED: CONFRONTING FEAR

SCRIPTURE CONNECTION: EXODUS 14:5-31

The overarching theme in all of God's signs is very clear to those of us who have been delivered from oppression: Do not be afraid. See, fear is the currency of oppression. To confront oppression is to confront fear.

I always understood that fear was a driving force in how power oppresses. Fear is what keeps people quiet when wrong things happen. Fear is what allows people to keep bowing under pressure. Fear is instilled in oppressed people to get them to submit to the oppression. It's how so many oppressors can govern and oppress people who outnumber them. The Israelites were afraid of Pharaoh, and that fear kept them under his control. I knew that. What I didn't know—and this information would change the way I think of oppression forever—is that Pharaoh was afraid of the Israelites.

Make no mistake. Both the oppressed and the oppressor are participating in the same fear. If you participate in fear, you will either oppress or you will be oppressed. Give it some thought and study. Every despot, every oppressive leader in the world, was terrified. . . . Terrified leaders oppress terrified people.

Is it any wonder that whenever God encounters his people, he leads with, "Do not be afraid"? He says this 365 times in the Bible—like we need to be reminded every day.

REFLECT "When the people of Israel saw the mighty power that the LORD had unleashed . . . [t]hey put their faith in the LORD and in his servant Moses." EXODUS 14:31

Lord, when I feel oppressed, help me look and point to you for courage. Amen.

CONSIDER "God's signs are not for themselves; they serve a purpose—have you listened to them lately?" DANIELLE STRICKLAND, *The Ultimate Exodus*

> Courageous people uplift those who feel oppressed by looking and pointing to God.

DANIELLE STRICKLAND • Content taken from *The Ultimate Exodus* by Danielle Strickland. Copyright © 2017 by The Salvation Army. Used by permission of NavPress, represented by Tyndale House Publishers. All rights reserved.

he has hurled both horse and rider
  into the sea.
² The Lord is my strength and my song;
  he has given me victory.
This is my God, and I will praise him—
  my father's God, and I will exalt him!
³ The Lord is a warrior;
  Yahweh* is his name!
⁴ Pharaoh's chariots and army
  he has hurled into the sea.
The finest of Pharaoh's officers
  are drowned in the Red Sea.*
⁵ The deep waters gushed over them;
  they sank to the bottom like a stone.
⁶ "Your right hand, O Lord,
  is glorious in power.
Your right hand, O Lord,
  smashes the enemy.
⁷ In the greatness of your majesty,
  you overthrow those who rise against you.
You unleash your blazing fury;
  it consumes them like straw.
⁸ At the blast of your breath,
  the waters piled up!
The surging waters stood straight like a wall;
  in the heart of the sea the deep waters became hard.
⁹ "The enemy boasted, 'I will chase them
  and catch up with them.
I will plunder them
  and consume them.
I will flash my sword;
  my powerful hand will destroy them.'
¹⁰ But you blew with your breath,
  and the sea covered them.
They sank like lead
  in the mighty waters.
¹¹ "Who is like you among the gods, O Lord—
  glorious in holiness,
awesome in splendor,
  performing great wonders?
¹² You raised your right hand,
  and the earth swallowed our enemies.
¹³ "With your unfailing love you lead
  the people you have redeemed.
In your might, you guide them
  to your sacred home.
¹⁴ The peoples hear and tremble;
  anguish grips those who live in Philistia.
¹⁵ The leaders of Edom are terrified;
  the nobles of Moab tremble.
All who live in Canaan melt away;
¹⁶ terror and dread fall upon them.
The power of your arm
  makes them lifeless as stone
until your people pass by, O Lord,
  until the people you purchased pass by.
¹⁷ You will bring them in and plant them on your own mountain—
  the place, O Lord, reserved for your own dwelling,
  the sanctuary, O Lord, that your hands have established.
¹⁸ The Lord will reign forever and ever!"

¹⁹When Pharaoh's horses, chariots, and charioteers rushed into the sea, the Lord brought the water crashing down on them. But the people of Israel had walked through the middle of the sea on dry ground! ²⁰Then Miriam the prophet, Aaron's sister, took a tambourine and led all the women as they played their tambourines and danced. ²¹And Miriam sang this song:

"Sing to the Lord,
  for he has triumphed gloriously;
he has hurled both horse and rider
  into the sea."

Bitter Water at Marah

²²Then Moses led the people of Israel away from the Red Sea, and they moved out into the desert of Shur. They traveled in this desert for three days without finding any water. ²³When they came to the oasis of Marah, the water was too bitter to drink. So they called the place Marah (which means "bitter").

²⁴Then the people complained and turned against Moses. "What are we going to drink?" they demanded. ²⁵So Moses cried out to the Lord for help, and the Lord showed him a piece of wood. Moses threw it into the water, and this made the water good to drink.

It was there at Marah that the Lord set before them the following decree as a standard to test their faithfulness to him. ²⁶He said, "If you will listen carefully to the voice of the Lord your God and do what is right in his sight, obeying his commands and keeping all his decrees, then I will not make you suffer any of the diseases I sent on the Egyptians; for I am the Lord who heals you."

15:3 *Yahweh* is a transliteration of the proper name *YHWH* that is sometimes rendered "Jehovah"; in this translation it is usually rendered "the Lord" (note the use of small capitals).   15:4 Hebrew *sea of reeds;* also in 15:22.

15:20-21 Miriam led the women in celebration of the Lord's victory over the Egyptian army. She is referred to as a prophet, making her the first in a long line of female prophets and teachers in the Bible, including Deborah (Judges 4:4), Hannah (1 Samuel 2:1-10), Huldah (2 Kings 22:14), Elizabeth (Luke 1:39-45), Mary (Luke 1:46-55), Anna (Luke 2:36), Priscilla (Acts 18:26), Philip's daughters (Acts 21:8-9), and Phoebe (Romans 16:1). Paul's restrictions on women's public ministry (see, for example, 1 Corinthians 14:34-35) seem to relate to problems particular to that context; Paul elsewhere permitted women to pray and prophesy in public (1 Corinthians 11:4-5).

²⁷After leaving Marah, the Israelites traveled on to the oasis of Elim, where they found twelve springs and seventy palm trees. They camped there beside the water.

Manna and Quail from Heaven

16 Then the whole community of Israel set out from Elim and journeyed into the wilderness of Sin,* between Elim and Mount Sinai. They arrived there on the fifteenth day of the second month, one month after leaving the land of Egypt.* ²There, too, the whole community of Israel complained about Moses and Aaron.

³"If only the LORD had killed us back in Egypt," they moaned. "There we sat around pots filled with meat and ate all the bread we wanted. But now you have brought us into this wilderness to starve us all to death."

16:1a The geographical name *Sin* is related to *Sinai* and should not be confused with the English word *sin*. **16:1b** The Exodus had occurred on the fifteenth day of the first month (see Num 33:3).

Koinonia

IMAGE — MY STORY WITH COMMUNITY, WORKPLACE & CHURCH

The Lord Himself Leads Us

SCRIPTURE CONNECTION:
EXODUS 14:1-31; 15:13; 16:12; 23:20-23; 29:42-46

I often think that if I'd witnessed God parting the Red Sea, it would be easier to trust him. And yet those who did witness it (and many other miracles) seem to have had short memories and a nearly immediate distrust of the Lord's leading. Amazingly, God didn't give up on them! Instead, he promised to lead them into a land of milk and honey. And all along the way, he longed for them to know him—the Lord their God.

When God has led me to try to turn around difficult situations, I've complained. I've wondered if God led me "out of Egypt" only to leave me "stranded in the wilderness." In those moments of wondering, I've forgotten who God is and why he leads us. Thankfully, God hasn't forgotten me. He also hasn't given up on his purpose to release the whole world from bondage to sin. He may even be leading me to play some small part in that grand plan.

The people's journey from Egypt to Israel reminds us how God faithfully loves us: He leads us from bondage to freedom. He hears our cries. And he keeps leading us to the Promised Land.

> The Lord leads us out of bondage and into his promises.

IMAGINE

How can you remember those times when God has led you and delivered you?

Where is he leading you now?

"Every time God leads me out of Egypt to wander in the wilderness, I may forget his bigger plan for the world. Thankfully, he has not. I can rest in knowing that all his plans unfold just as he intends, with the people he means to include, even me."

KATHERINE LEARY ALSDORF founded and directed Redeemer Church's Center for Faith & Work. She co-authored *Every Good Endeavor: Connecting Your Work to God's Work* with Timothy Keller.

EXODUS 16 ♦ 100

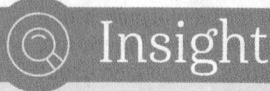

IF YOU COULD BRING JUST ONE FOOD ON A TRIP...

God provided for the people's nutritional needs miraculously while they were traveling from Egypt to Canaan with manna, quail, and water (Exodus 16–17). Why was manna the perfect food for the Israelites' journey to the Promised Land? How does it compare to what we eat today?

Manna Compared to Recent Snacking Trends*

Food for the Journey to the Promised Land

✓ **LESS SUGAR**
Manna tasted like honey but was healthy. 16:31

✓ **HIGH PROTEIN**
Custom made by the Creator for his creation's needs 16:15

✓ **FUNCTIONAL NUTRITION**
Manna provided energy, focus, and calm. Knowing God would feed them daily must have felt pretty peaceful! 16:35

✓ **FRESH**
Manna, made daily! 16:4

✓ **BITE-SIZED**
Manna was a similar color to a coriander seed and was "a flaky substance as fine as frost," so it potentially appeared as small wafers just perfect for packing and eating on the go. 16:14, 31

*Source: Glanbia Nutritionals

⁴Then the LORD said to Moses, "Look, I'm going to rain down food from heaven for you. Each day the people can go out and pick up as much food as they need for that day. I will test them in this to see whether or not they will follow my instructions. ⁵On the sixth day they will gather food, and when they prepare it, there will be twice as much as usual."

⁶So Moses and Aaron said to all the people of Israel, "By evening you will realize it was the LORD who brought you out of the land of Egypt. ⁷In the morning you will see the glory of the LORD, because he has heard your complaints, which are against him, not against us. What have we done that you should complain about us?" ⁸Then Moses added, "The LORD will give you meat to eat in the evening and bread to satisfy you in the morning, for he has heard all your complaints against him. What have we done? Yes, your complaints are against the LORD, not against us."

⁹Then Moses said to Aaron, "Announce this to the entire community of Israel: 'Present yourselves before the LORD, for he has heard your complaining.'" ¹⁰And as Aaron spoke to the whole community of Israel, they looked out toward the wilderness. There they could see the awesome glory of the LORD in the cloud.

¹¹Then the LORD said to Moses, ¹²"I have heard the Israelites' complaints. Now tell them, 'In the evening you will have meat to eat, and in the morning you will have all the bread you want. Then you will know that I am the LORD your God.'"

¹³That evening vast numbers of quail flew in and covered the camp. And the next morning the area around the camp was wet with dew. ¹⁴When the dew evaporated, a flaky substance as fine as frost blanketed the ground. ¹⁵The Israelites were puzzled when they saw it. "What is it?" they asked each other. They had no idea what it was.

16:4-5 These are the Lord's instructions for gathering the food he would provide in the wilderness. He gave enough for each day, with a double amount on the sixth day so that the people would not have to gather any on the Sabbath (see 16:21-30). The Israelites thus observed the Sabbath even before it was commanded (see 20:8-11). We instinctively resist a lifestyle in which we need to depend on God each day to supply our needs. We wish to have supplies in advance so that we can feel independent. God was training the people for a life of faith (see Matthew 6:11).

16:15 The Hebrew phrase *man hu* (which means "What is it?") became the name of the miraculous food "manna" (see 16:31). For forty years, the people ate *what is it?* Jesus referred to himself as the "true bread from heaven" that gives life. In this way, Jesus embodied this manna-miracle (John 6:32-35, 48, 51, 58).

Zipporah

⊙ IDENTITY — A Surprising Marriage

Zipporah remembers...

I met the man of my dreams—strong and handsome. He rescued me and my sisters from the shepherds who kept us from using a well. Then Father invited him to stay with us and arranged for me to be his wife. Life was looking good.

But then Moses' God appeared in a burning bush, and Moses said he had to go back to Egypt to save his people. What was that all about? Heading to Egypt wasn't part of my dream.

On the journey, I had to save Moses from God's anger. My husband hadn't circumcised our son, even though God had commanded Abraham and his descendants to do so. I took immediate action, and when God accepted the offering, we continued to Egypt.

Later, we went into the wilderness with all of Moses' people. After a while, Moses sent me and our two sons back to my father. Maybe Moses was too busy. Maybe he wanted to protect me. Maybe he was trying to leave me. I don't know.

But my father later brought me back to Moses. He helped Moses lighten his huge workload, and I stayed, but, wow, it was a hard life. It certainly wasn't my dream.

ZIPPORAH'S STORY IS TOLD IN EXODUS 2:15-22; 4:20-26; 18:1-8.

> Life is a journey of unexpected turns, but God's faithfulness helps us navigate it.

IDENTIFY

Have you ever found yourself in a place you never expected?

How did God meet you there?

> "When I married my husband, our dream was to work with college students at a Christian student organization. That never happened. God made sense of my wandering path in my fifties, calling me to start a career teaching at a seminary, working with students in a totally different capacity. While not what I planned, I am amazed and fulfilled."

ELIZABETH GLANVILLE, PhD, is retired faculty from Fuller Theological Seminary, School of Mission and Theology. She is an international teacher on missions and leadership and chaplain for a local police department and her retirement community.

men were always available to solve the people's common disputes. They brought the major cases to Moses, but they took care of the smaller matters themselves.

27 Soon after this, Moses said good-bye to his father-in-law, who returned to his own land.

The LORD Reveals Himself at Sinai

19 Exactly two months after the Israelites left Egypt,* they arrived in the wilderness of Sinai. 2 After breaking camp at Rephidim, they came to the wilderness of Sinai and set up camp there at the base of Mount Sinai.

3 Then Moses climbed the mountain to appear before God. The LORD called to him from the mountain and said, "Give these instructions to the family of Jacob; announce it to the descendants of Israel: 4 'You have seen what I did to the Egyptians. You know how I carried you on eagles' wings and brought you to myself. 5 Now if you will obey me and keep my covenant, you will be my own special treasure from among all the peoples on earth; for all the earth belongs to me. 6 And you will be my kingdom of priests, my holy nation.' This is the message you must give to the people of Israel."

7 So Moses returned from the mountain and called together the elders of the people and told them everything the LORD had commanded him. 8 And all the people responded together, "We will do everything the LORD has commanded." So Moses brought the people's answer back to the LORD.

9 Then the LORD said to Moses, "I will come to you in a thick cloud, Moses, so the people themselves can hear me when I speak with you. Then they will always trust you."

Moses told the LORD what the people had said. 10 Then the LORD told Moses, "Go down and prepare the people for my arrival. Consecrate them today and tomorrow, and have them wash their clothing. 11 Be sure they are ready on the third day, for on that day the LORD will come down on Mount Sinai as all the people watch. 12 Mark off a boundary all around the mountain. Warn the people, 'Be careful! Do not go up on the mountain or even touch its boundaries. Anyone who touches the mountain will certainly be put to death. 13 No hand may touch the person or animal that crosses the boundary; instead, stone them or shoot them with arrows. They must be put to death.' However, when the ram's horn sounds a long blast, then the people may go up on the mountain.*"

14 So Moses went down to the people. He consecrated them for worship, and they washed their clothes. 15 He told them, "Get ready for the third day, and until then abstain from having sexual intercourse."

16 On the morning of the third day, thunder roared and lightning flashed, and a dense cloud came down on the mountain. There was a long, loud blast from a ram's horn, and all the people trembled. 17 Moses led them out from the camp to meet with God, and they stood at the foot of the mountain. 18 All of Mount Sinai was covered with smoke because the LORD had descended on it in the form of fire. The smoke billowed into the sky like smoke from a brick kiln, and the whole mountain shook violently. 19 As the blast of the ram's horn grew louder and louder, Moses spoke, and God thundered his reply. 20 The LORD came down on the top of Mount Sinai and called Moses to the top of the mountain. So Moses climbed the mountain.

21 Then the LORD told Moses, "Go back down and warn the people not to break through the boundaries to see the LORD, or they will die. 22 Even the priests who regularly come near to the LORD must purify themselves so that the LORD does not break out and destroy them."

23 "But LORD," Moses protested, "the people cannot come up to Mount Sinai. You already warned us. You told me, 'Mark off a boundary all around the mountain to set it apart as holy.'"

24 But the LORD said, "Go down and bring Aaron back up with you. In the meantime, do not let the priests or the people break through to approach the LORD, or he will break out and destroy them."

25 So Moses went down to the people and told them what the LORD had said.

Ten Commandments for the Covenant Community

20 Then God gave the people all these instructions*:

2 "I am the LORD your God, who rescued you from the land of Egypt, the place of your slavery.

19:1 Hebrew *In the third month after the Israelites left Egypt, on the very day,* i.e., two lunar months to the day after leaving Egypt. Compare Num 33:3. 19:13 Or *up to the mountain.* 20:1 Hebrew *all these words.*

19:4-6 God had rescued the Israelites from serving Pharaoh, and now they were to serve him. At this crucial juncture in the Lord's relationship with Israel, he defined their new role. To be God's "own special treasure" indicated their appointment as Yahweh's preferred treaty partner. As a "kingdom of priests" and "holy nation," the Israelites' obedience to the terms of the covenant would set them apart for Yahweh's service.

19:7-8 The Israelites willingly signed on to their new role as the Lord's representatives. God did not impose the laws in Exodus 20–24 against their will. They agreed to God's reasonable instructions for a well-ordered society (see also 24:3). While the laws do not represent the ultimate ideal for society, they help regulate life in a fallen world.

19:10-15 The people received commands that would prepare them to receive God's covenant. They were to wash their clothing because God is pure. They were to prepare a boundary all around the mountain and be careful not to cross it because God is holy. They were to abstain from sex because that would ensure ritual purity. Things that are natural and right under ordinary circumstances were to be set aside for the extraordinary purpose of meeting God.

³"You must not have any other god but me.
⁴"You must not make for yourself an idol of any kind or an image of anything in the heavens or on the earth or in the sea. ⁵You must not bow down to them or worship them, for I, the LORD your God, am a jealous God who will not tolerate your affection for any other gods. I lay the sins of the parents upon their children; the entire family is affected—even children in the third and fourth generations of those who reject me. ⁶But I lavish unfailing love for a thousand generations on those* who love me and obey my commands.
⁷"You must not misuse the name of the LORD your God. The LORD will not let you go unpunished if you misuse his name.
⁸"Remember to observe the Sabbath day by keeping it holy. ⁹You have six days each week for your ordinary work, ¹⁰but the seventh day is a Sabbath day of rest dedicated to the LORD your God. On that day no one in your household may do any work. This includes you, your sons and daughters, your male and female servants, your livestock, and any foreigners living among you. ¹¹For in six days the LORD made the heavens, the earth, the sea, and everything in them; but on the seventh day he rested. That is why the LORD blessed the Sabbath day and set it apart as holy.
¹²"Honor your father and mother. Then you will live a long, full life in the land the LORD your God is giving you.
¹³"You must not murder.
¹⁴"You must not commit adultery.
¹⁵"You must not steal.
¹⁶"You must not testify falsely against your neighbor.
¹⁷"You must not covet your neighbor's house. You must not covet your neighbor's wife, male or female servant, ox or donkey, or anything else that belongs to your neighbor."

20:6 Hebrew *for thousands of those.*

20:1-17 The Ten Commandments outlined God's expectations for the covenant community. The Lord underscored his role as the one who rescued them from slavery (20:2). In response, they were to be a people who looked out for their neighbors and protected each other's right to rest, honor, life, property, reputation, and exclusive marriage. They were also to be a people who worshiped Yahweh exclusively and recognized that they belonged to him. The commands were addressed to male heads of households who were to use their power to protect, rather than exploit, the vulnerable.
20:5-6 "In the third and fourth generations . . . for a thousand generations": It is vital to keep both sides of this equation together. God does not punish children for their parents' sins. Rather, he says that our sins affect future generations. He graciously restricts sins' effects to three or four generations while extending obedience's effects to a thousand generations (literally "for thousands"; see also Exodus 34:6-7; Deuteronomy 7:9).

Perspective

Are women property or partners?

SCRIPTURE CONNECTION: EXODUS 20:17

Some aspects of biblical law sound jarring to our modern ears. It seems reasonable to prevent men from desiring someone else's wife, but why do wives appear in a list of what "belongs to your neighbor"? Were women considered property?

Not exactly. In ancient Israel, women lived under the protection and authority of their fathers and husbands. A wedding did include a wealth exchange (a bride price and a dowry). However, the money did not indicate a "sale." Instead, it ensured the marriage's stability and extended the family's support for the new union.

Perhaps Moses anticipated how this command could be misconstrued. In Deuteronomy 5:21, where he repeats God's instructions for the next generation, Moses rearranges the list. This time, he mentions the wife first, separate from the list of possessions.

VIEWPOINTS

HERS: *The Israelite wife found security in a marriage where she and her husband partnered in fulfilling God's commands with their families' support.*
MINE: *"When my husband and I married, my parents paid for the ceremony, while my mother-in-law provided the rehearsal dinner. Both families invested in our future."*
YOURS: *What is your attitude toward marriage? Do you see it as the partnering of two families?*

CARMEN JOY IMES, PhD, is an author, speaker, blogger, YouTuber, and serves as associate professor of Old Testament at Biola University in California.

EXODUS 21 ❖ 106

¹⁸When the people heard the thunder and the loud blast of the ram's horn, and when they saw the flashes of lightning and the smoke billowing from the mountain, they stood at a distance, trembling with fear.

¹⁹And they said to Moses, "You speak to us, and we will listen. But don't let God speak directly to us, or we will die!"

²⁰"Don't be afraid," Moses answered them, "for God has come in this way to test you, and so that your fear of him will keep you from sinning!"

²¹As the people stood in the distance, Moses approached the dark cloud where God was.

Proper Use of Altars

²²And the LORD said to Moses, "Say this to the people of Israel: You saw for yourselves that I spoke to you from heaven. ²³Remember, you must not make any idols of silver or gold to rival me.

²⁴"Build for me an altar made of earth, and offer your sacrifices to me—your burnt offerings and peace offerings, your sheep and goats, and your cattle. Build my altar wherever I cause my name to be remembered, and I will come to you and bless you. ²⁵If you use stones to build my altar, use only natural, uncut stones. Do not shape the stones with a tool, for that would make the altar unfit for holy use. ²⁶And do not approach my altar by going up steps. If you do, someone might look up under your clothing and see your nakedness."

Fair Treatment of Slaves

21 "These are the regulations you must present to Israel.

²"If you buy a Hebrew slave, he may serve for no more than six years. Set him free in the seventh year, and he will owe you nothing for his freedom. ³If he was single when he became your slave, he shall leave single. But if he was married before he became a slave, then his wife must be freed with him.

⁴"If his master gave him a wife while he was a slave and they had sons or daughters, then only the man will be free in the seventh year, but his wife and children will still belong to his master. ⁵But the slave may declare, 'I love my master, my wife, and my children. I don't want to go free.' ⁶If he does this, his master must present him before God.* Then his master must take him to the door or doorpost and publicly pierce his ear with an awl. After that, the slave will serve his master for life.

⁷"When a man sells his daughter as a slave, she will not be freed at the end of six years as the men are. ⁸If she does not satisfy her owner, he must allow her to be bought back again. But he is not allowed to sell her to foreigners, since he is the one who broke the contract with her. ⁹But if the slave's owner arranges for her to marry his son, he may no longer treat her as a slave but as a daughter.

¹⁰"If a man who has married a slave wife takes another wife for himself, he must not neglect the rights of the first wife to food, clothing, and sexual intimacy. ¹¹If he fails in any of these three obligations, she may leave as a free woman without making any payment.

Cases of Personal Injury

¹²"Anyone who assaults and kills another person must be put to death. ¹³But if it was simply an accident permitted by God, I will appoint a place of refuge where the slayer can run for safety. ¹⁴However, if someone deliberately kills another person, then the slayer must be dragged even from my altar and be put to death.

¹⁵"Anyone who strikes father or mother must be put to death.

¹⁶"Kidnappers must be put to death, whether they are caught in possession of their victims or have already sold them as slaves.

¹⁷"Anyone who dishonors* father or mother must be put to death.

¹⁸"Now suppose two men quarrel, and one hits the other with a stone or fist, and the injured person does not die but is confined to bed. ¹⁹If he is later able to walk outside again, even with a crutch, the assailant will not be punished but must compensate his victim for lost wages and provide for his full recovery.

21:6 Or *before the judges.* 21:17 Greek version reads *Anyone who speaks disrespectfully of.* Compare Matt 15:4; Mark 7:10.

20:26 God carefully protected against indecent exposure in worship to set the Israelites apart from other nations. Sex was an integral part of many Canaanite rituals because they associated fertility with the favor of certain gods. By prohibiting nakedness in the Tabernacle, Yahweh blessed the people with children and crops without compromising the exclusive sexual commitment between husband and wife. The fact that all of Israel's priests were fully clothed men distinguished them from other nations, who employed female cult prostitutes and priestesses to promote fertility (see also 28:42-43).

21:2-6 To prevent exploitation in Israel, God strictly regulated slavery. Obedience to the entire law would protect Israel's indentured servants from mistreatment, such as they had experienced in Egypt. Men could hire themselves out as indentured servants for a limited time. They might do so to avoid starvation or pay a debt incurred by theft. They retained the rights to marry and go free after they paid their debt. If they preferred serving the man who had purchased them, they could volunteer to serve for life.

21:7-11 The roles of an enslaved woman often included marriage. As with nearly all ancient marriages, the father made the arrangements. Her new home was to be permanent to prevent exploitation. If the man married her, he could not sell her if she displeased him or if he took another wife. If he arranged for her to marry his son instead, she was not available to the father as a sexual partner. These regulations were intended to preserve her dignity and rights.

²⁰"If a man beats his male or female slave with a club and the slave dies as a result, the owner must be punished. ²¹But if the slave recovers within a day or two, then the owner shall not be punished, since the slave is his property.

²²"Now suppose two men are fighting, and in the process they accidentally strike a pregnant woman so she gives birth prematurely.* If no further injury results, the man who struck the woman must pay the amount of compensation the woman's husband demands and the judges approve. ²³But if there is further injury, the punishment must match the injury: a life for a life, ²⁴an eye for an eye, a tooth for a tooth, a hand for a hand, a foot for a foot, ²⁵a burn for a burn, a wound for a wound, a bruise for a bruise.

²⁶"If a man hits his male or female slave in the eye and the eye is blinded, he must let the slave go free to compensate for the eye. ²⁷And if a man knocks out the tooth of his male or female slave, he must let the slave go free to compensate for the tooth.

²⁸"If an ox* gores a man or woman to death, the ox must be stoned, and its flesh may not be eaten. In such a case, however, the owner will not be held liable. ²⁹But suppose the ox had a reputation for goring, and the owner had been informed but failed to keep it under control. If the ox then kills someone, it must be stoned, and the owner must also be put to death. ³⁰However, the dead person's relatives may accept payment to compensate for the loss of life. The owner of the ox may redeem his life by paying whatever is demanded.

21:22 Or *so she has a miscarriage;* Hebrew reads *so her children come out.* 21:28 Or *bull,* or *cow;* also in 21:29-36.

21:20-21 In ancient Israelite culture, corporal punishment was considered acceptable. The Hebrew phrase translated here as "the slave is his property" reads literally, "he is his silver." Unlike 21:19, where an assailant had to compensate the victim for lost wages during the recovery period, in this case, it was the enslaver's loss if the enslaved person had to take time off work to recover from injuries the enslaver had inflicted. It was in his best interest to treat enslaved people well. Both enslaved women and men were considered fully human. Therefore, someone who killed an enslaved person was subject to the death penalty.
21:22-25 It appears that if a fight caused a child's premature birth and the child died (that is, there was further injury), the penalty for murder was to be enacted (a life for a life). The law of retaliation called for a penalty that matched the victim's injury. This law also served to limit the punishment, so that it did not exceed the original damage.
21:26-32 An enslaver did not have the right to injure an enslaved person's body. Permanent injury resulted in freedom, effectively canceling the enslaved person's debt. The life of an enslaved person—male or female—was valued just as highly as a free person's life. An animal who killed an enslaved person must die, and payment was made to the enslaver for the lost labor. This payment was equivalent to the unpaid debt as the slavery in view here was an indentured servitude.

Perspective

Does God condone slavery?

SCRIPTURE CONNECTION: EXODUS 21:1-11

God clearly opposed the Israelites' enslavement in Egypt. After all, he freed them. Why, then, would he allow the Israelites to keep enslaved people?

Israel's laws did not represent an ideal, just as our laws often fall short. They often aimed to minimize the effects of living in a broken world.

Slavery among the Israelites was generally the result of extreme poverty. Rather than starving to death, a person could willingly serve a benefactor to pay a debt. As we see in this passage, enslaved men and women had different parameters because when the women married, they entered the household of their enslaver. Even so, there were certain protections for the women as well (21:7-11). Many of the Israelite laws guarded against the exploitation of enslaved people and other vulnerable people (see, for example, 20:10; 21:16; 22:21-27).

Despite how this played out in Israel's legal system, slavery is not God's design. Every person —regardless of gender, ethnicity, or financial status—is an image-bearer of God, and he does not condone slavery in the past or the present.

VIEWPOINTS

HERS: *Marriage, even if it meant slavery, was one way to escape extreme poverty.*
MINE: *"I cannot imagine someone choosing a husband for me, but in many cultures, arranged marriages are the norm. A father was to look after his daughter's best interests."*
YOURS: *How has God provided for you when you had no good options?*

CARMEN JOY IMES, PhD, is an author, speaker, blogger, YouTuber, and serves as associate professor of Old Testament at Biola University in California.

³¹"The same regulation applies if the ox gores a boy or a girl. ³²But if the ox gores a slave, either male or female, the animal's owner must pay the slave's owner thirty silver coins,* and the ox must be stoned.

³³"Suppose someone digs or uncovers a pit and fails to cover it, and then an ox or a donkey falls into it. ³⁴The owner of the pit must pay full compensation to the owner of the animal, but then he gets to keep the dead animal.

³⁵"If someone's ox injures a neighbor's ox and the injured ox dies, then the two owners must sell the live ox and divide the price equally between them. They must also divide the dead animal. ³⁶But if the ox had a reputation for goring, yet its owner failed to keep it under control, he must pay full compensation—a live ox for the dead one—but he may keep the dead ox.

Protection of Property

22 ¹*"If someone steals an ox* or sheep and then kills or sells it, the thief must pay back five oxen for each ox stolen, and four sheep for each sheep stolen.

²*"If a thief is caught in the act of breaking into a house and is struck and killed in the process, the person who killed the thief is not guilty of murder. ³But if it happens in daylight, the one who killed the thief is guilty of murder.

"A thief who is caught must pay in full for everything he stole. If he cannot pay, he must be sold as a slave to pay for his theft. ⁴If someone steals an ox or a donkey or a sheep and it is found in the thief's possession, then the thief must pay double the value of the stolen animal.

⁵"If an animal is grazing in a field or vineyard and the owner lets it stray into someone else's field to graze, then the animal's owner must pay compensation from the best of his own grain or grapes.

⁶"If you are burning thornbushes and the fire gets out of control and spreads into another person's field, destroying the sheaves or the uncut grain or the whole crop, the one who started the fire must pay for the lost crop.

⁷"Suppose someone leaves money or goods with a neighbor for safekeeping, and they are stolen from the neighbor's house. If the thief is caught, the compensation is double the value of what was stolen.

⁸But if the thief is not caught, the neighbor must appear before God,* who will determine if he stole the property.

⁹"Suppose there is a dispute between two people who both claim to own a particular ox, donkey, sheep, article of clothing, or any lost property. Both parties must come before God, and the person whom God declares* guilty must pay double compensation to the other.

¹⁰"Now suppose someone leaves a donkey, ox, sheep, or any other animal with a neighbor for safekeeping, but it dies or is injured or is taken away, and no one sees what happened. ¹¹The neighbor must then take an oath in the presence of the LORD. If the LORD confirms that the neighbor did not steal the property, the owner must accept the verdict, and no payment will be required. ¹²But if the animal was indeed stolen, the guilty person must pay compensation to the owner. ¹³If it was torn to pieces by a wild animal, the remains of the carcass must be shown as evidence, and no compensation will be required.

¹⁴"If someone borrows an animal from a neighbor and it is injured or dies when the owner is absent, the person who borrowed it must pay full compensation. ¹⁵But if the owner was present, no compensation is required. And no compensation is required if the animal was rented, for this loss is covered by the rental fee.

Social Responsibility

¹⁶"If a man seduces a virgin who is not engaged to anyone and has sex with her, he must pay the customary bride price and marry her. ¹⁷But if her father refuses to let him marry her, the man must still pay him an amount equal to the bride price of a virgin.

¹⁸"You must not allow a sorceress to live.

¹⁹"Anyone who has sexual relations with an animal must certainly be put to death.

²⁰"Anyone who sacrifices to any god other than the LORD must be destroyed.*

²¹"You must not mistreat or oppress foreigners in any way. Remember, you yourselves were once foreigners in the land of Egypt.

²²"You must not exploit a widow or an orphan. ²³If you exploit them in any way and they cry out to me, then I will certainly hear their cry. ²⁴My anger will blaze against you, and I will kill you with the sword.

21:32 Hebrew *30 shekels of silver,* about 12 ounces or 342 grams in weight. **22:1a** Verse 22:1 is numbered 21:37 in Hebrew text. **22:1b** Or *bull,* or *cow;* also in 22:4, 9, 10. **22:2** Verses 22:2-31 are numbered 22:1-30 in Hebrew text. **22:8** Or *before the judges.* **22:9** Or *before the judges,* and the person whom the judges declare. **22:20** The Hebrew term used here refers to the complete consecration of things or people to the LORD, either by destroying them or by giving them as an offering.

22:16-17 This passage seems shocking—require a woman to marry the first man she slept with? However, the law was designed to underscore the seriousness of sex: Any man who seduced a woman had to be prepared to marry her. God did not tolerate sex outside of marriage. A woman's father could refuse the marriage if it were not in his daughter's best interests, but since the woman would likely never marry, the man had to pay the bride price to support her.

22:22-24 God takes seriously the care of vulnerable members of society. Exploitation incurs God's anger, and the penalty for taking advantage of the vulnerable was death.

Then your wives will be widows and your children fatherless.

²⁵"If you lend money to any of my people who are in need, do not charge interest as a money lender would. ²⁶If you take your neighbor's cloak as security for a loan, you must return it before sunset. ²⁷This coat may be the only blanket your neighbor has. How can a person sleep without it? If you do not return it and your neighbor cries out to me for help, then I will hear, for I am merciful.

²⁸"You must not dishonor God or curse any of your rulers.

²⁹"You must not hold anything back when you give me offerings from your crops and your wine.

"You must give me your firstborn sons.

³⁰"You must also give me the firstborn of your cattle, sheep, and goats. But leave the newborn animal with its mother for seven days; then give it to me on the eighth day.

³¹"You must be my holy people. Therefore, do not eat any animal that has been torn up and killed by wild animals. Throw it to the dogs.

A Call for Justice

23 "You must not pass along false rumors. You must not cooperate with evil people by lying on the witness stand.

²"You must not follow the crowd in doing wrong. When you are called to testify in a dispute, do not be swayed by the crowd to twist justice. ³And do not slant your testimony in favor of a person just because that person is poor.

⁴"If you come upon your enemy's ox or donkey that has strayed away, take it back to its owner. ⁵If you see that the donkey of someone who hates you has collapsed under its load, do not walk by. Instead, stop and help.

⁶"In a lawsuit, you must not deny justice to the poor.

⁷"Be sure never to charge anyone falsely with evil. Never sentence an innocent or blameless person to death, for I never declare a guilty person to be innocent.

⁸"Take no bribes, for a bribe makes you ignore something that you clearly see. A bribe makes even a righteous person twist the truth.

⁹"You must not oppress foreigners. You know what it's like to be a foreigner, for you yourselves were once foreigners in the land of Egypt.

¹⁰"Plant and harvest your crops for six years, ¹¹but let the land be renewed and lie uncultivated during the seventh year. Then let the poor among you harvest whatever grows on its own. Leave the rest for wild animals to eat. The same applies to your vineyards and olive groves.

¹²"You have six days each week for your ordinary work, but on the seventh day you must stop working. This gives your ox and your donkey a chance to rest. It also allows your slaves and the foreigners living among you to be refreshed.

¹³"Pay close attention to all my instructions. You must not call on the name of any other gods. Do not even speak their names.

Three Annual Festivals

¹⁴"Each year you must celebrate three festivals in my honor. ¹⁵First, celebrate the Festival of Unleavened Bread. For seven days the bread you eat must be made without yeast, just as I commanded you. Celebrate this festival annually at the appointed time in early spring, in the month of Abib,* for that is the anniversary of your departure from Egypt. No one may appear before me without an offering.

¹⁶"Second, celebrate the Festival of Harvest,* when you bring me the first crops of your harvest.

"Finally, celebrate the Festival of the Final Harvest* at the end of the harvest season, when you have harvested all the crops from your fields. ¹⁷At these three times each year, every man in Israel must appear before the Sovereign, the LORD.

¹⁸"You must not offer the blood of my sacrificial offerings together with any baked goods containing yeast. And do not leave the fat from the festival offerings until the next morning.

¹⁹"As you harvest your crops, bring the very best of the first harvest to the house of the LORD your God.

"You must not cook a young goat in its mother's milk.

A Promise of the LORD's Presence

²⁰"See, I am sending an angel before you to protect you on your journey and lead you safely to the place I have prepared for you. ²¹Pay close attention to him, and obey his instructions. Do not rebel against him, for he is my representative, and he will not forgive your rebellion. ²²But if you are careful to obey him, following all my instructions,

---

23:15 Hebrew *appointed time in the month of Abib*. This first month of the ancient Hebrew lunar calendar usually occurs within the months of March and April. **23:16a** Or *Festival of Weeks*. This was later called the Festival of Pentecost (see Acts 2:1). It is celebrated today as Shavuot (or Shabuoth). **23:16b** Or *Festival of Ingathering*. This was later called the Festival of Shelters or Festival of Tabernacles (see Lev 23:33-36). It is celebrated today as Sukkot (or Succoth).

23:14-17 Israel's festivals were an essential part of their community life because they reinforced God's role as their rescuer and provider. If they stopped celebrating what God had done on their behalf, they would lose sight of their identity as God's people. Only men were required to attend the celebrations, but women were also welcome. Between menstruation, pregnancy, childbirth, and caring for children, travel was much more difficult for women. God graciously allowed them to stay home from the festivals.

then I will be an enemy to your enemies, and I will oppose those who oppose you. ²³For my angel will go before you and bring you into the land of the Amorites, Hittites, Perizzites, Canaanites, Hivites, and Jebusites, so you may live there. And I will destroy them completely. ²⁴You must not worship the gods of these nations or serve them in any way or imitate their evil practices. Instead, you must utterly destroy them and smash their sacred pillars.

²⁵"You must serve only the LORD your God. If you do, I* will bless you with food and water, and I will protect you from illness. ²⁶There will be no miscarriages or infertility in your land, and I will give you long, full lives.

²⁷"I will send my terror ahead of you and create panic among all the people whose lands you invade. I will make all your enemies turn and run. ²⁸I will send terror* ahead of you to drive out the Hivites, Canaanites, and Hittites. ²⁹But I will not drive them out in a single year, because the land would become desolate and the wild animals would multiply and threaten you. ³⁰I will drive them out a little at a time until your population has increased enough to take possession of the land. ³¹And I will fix your boundaries from the Red Sea to the Mediterranean Sea,* and from the eastern wilderness to the Euphrates River.* I will hand over to you the people now living in the land, and you will drive them out ahead of you.

³²"Make no treaties with them or their gods. ³³They must not live in your land, or they will cause you to sin against me. If you serve their gods, you will be caught in the trap of idolatry."

Israel Accepts the LORD's Covenant

24 Then the LORD instructed Moses: "Come up here to me, and bring along Aaron, Nadab, Abihu, and seventy of Israel's elders. All of you must worship from a distance. ²Only Moses is allowed to come near to the LORD. The others must not come near, and none of the other people are allowed to climb up the mountain with him."

³Then Moses went down to the people and repeated all the instructions and regulations the LORD had given him. All the people answered with one voice, "We will do everything the LORD has commanded."

⁴Then Moses carefully wrote down all the LORD's instructions. Early the next morning Moses got up and built an altar at the foot of the mountain. He also set up twelve pillars, one for each of the twelve tribes of Israel. ⁵Then he sent some of the young Israelite men to present burnt offerings and to sacrifice bulls as peace offerings to the LORD. ⁶Moses drained half the blood from these animals into basins. The other half he splattered against the altar.

⁷Then he took the Book of the Covenant and read it aloud to the people. Again they all responded, "We will do everything the LORD has commanded. We will obey."

⁸Then Moses took the blood from the basins and splattered it over the people, declaring, "Look, this blood confirms the covenant the LORD has made with you in giving you these instructions."

⁹Then Moses, Aaron, Nadab, Abihu, and the seventy elders of Israel climbed up the mountain. ¹⁰There they saw the God of Israel. Under his feet there seemed to be a surface of brilliant blue lapis lazuli, as clear as the sky itself. ¹¹And though these nobles of Israel gazed upon God, he did not destroy them. In fact, they ate a covenant meal, eating and drinking in his presence!

¹²Then the LORD said to Moses, "Come up to me on the mountain. Stay there, and I will give you the tablets of stone on which I have inscribed the instructions and commands so you can teach the people." ¹³So Moses and his assistant Joshua set out, and Moses climbed up the mountain of God.

¹⁴Moses told the elders, "Stay here and wait for us until we come back. Aaron and Hur are here with you. If anyone has a dispute while I am gone, consult with them."

¹⁵Then Moses climbed up the mountain, and the cloud covered it. ¹⁶And the glory of the LORD settled down on Mount Sinai, and the cloud covered it for six days. On the seventh day the LORD called to Moses from inside the cloud. ¹⁷To the Israelites at the foot of the mountain, the glory of the LORD appeared at the summit like a consuming fire. ¹⁸Then Moses disappeared into the cloud as he climbed higher up the mountain. He remained on the mountain forty days and forty nights.

23:25 As in Greek and Latin versions; Hebrew reads *he*. **23:28** Often rendered *the hornet*. The meaning of the Hebrew is uncertain. **23:31a** Hebrew *from the sea of reeds to the sea of the Philistines*. **23:31b** Hebrew *from the wilderness to the river*.

23:25-26 Pagan rituals attempted to manipulate the forces of fertility and reproduction. God promised to provide these gifts if the people would faithfully carry out the terms of their covenant with him. In our broken world, we all experience illness. And many—including those in the community of faith—experience hunger or infertility. While this suffering is not God's ideal, he promises to work out his purposes in the end.

24:8 The splattered blood was significant. For the Israelites, blood symbolized ritual purity, enabling them to be in God's presence. The only other place mentioning splattered blood is the ceremony ordaining Aaron and his sons as priests in Leviticus 8. The splattered blood in Exodus 24 inaugurated God's covenant with Israel, in which they served as a kingdom of priests (19:6). Christians are referred to as royal priests (1 Peter 2:9) because of Christ's sprinkled blood (Hebrews 12:24).

Offerings for the Tabernacle

25 The LORD said to Moses, ²"Tell the people of Israel to bring me their sacred offerings. Accept the contributions from all whose hearts are moved to offer them. ³Here is a list of sacred offerings you may accept from them:

gold, silver, and bronze;
⁴ blue, purple, and scarlet thread;
fine linen and goat hair for cloth;
⁵ tanned ram skins and fine goatskin leather; acacia wood;
⁶ olive oil for the lamps;
spices for the anointing oil and the fragrant incense;
⁷ onyx stones, and other gemstones to be set in the ephod and the priest's chestpiece.

⁸"Have the people of Israel build me a holy sanctuary so I can live among them. ⁹You must build this Tabernacle and its furnishings exactly according to the pattern I will show you.

Plans for the Ark of the Covenant

¹⁰"Have the people make an Ark of acacia wood—a sacred chest 45 inches long, 27 inches wide, and 27 inches high.* ¹¹Overlay it inside and outside with pure gold, and run a molding of gold all around it. ¹²Cast four gold rings and attach them to its four feet, two rings on each side. ¹³Make poles from acacia wood, and overlay them with gold. ¹⁴Insert the poles into the rings at the sides of the Ark to carry it. ¹⁵These carrying poles must stay inside the rings; never remove them. ¹⁶When the Ark is finished, place inside it the stone tablets inscribed with the terms of the covenant,* which I will give to you.

¹⁷"Then make the Ark's cover—the place of atonement—from pure gold. It must be 45 inches long and 27 inches wide.* ¹⁸Then make two cherubim from hammered gold, and place them on the two ends of the atonement cover. ¹⁹Mold the cherubim on each end of the atonement cover, making it all of one piece of gold. ²⁰The cherubim will face each other and look down on the atonement cover. With their wings spread above it, they will protect it. ²¹Place inside the Ark the stone tablets inscribed with the terms of the covenant, which I will give to you. Then put the atonement cover on top of the Ark. ²²I will meet with you there and talk to you from above the atonement cover between the gold cherubim that hover over the Ark of the Covenant.* From there I will give you my commands for the people of Israel.

Plans for the Table

²³"Then make a table of acacia wood, 36 inches long, 18 inches wide, and 27 inches high.* ²⁴Overlay it with pure gold and run a gold molding around the edge. ²⁵Decorate it with a 3-inch border* all around, and run a gold molding along the border. ²⁶Make four gold rings for the table and attach them at the four corners next to the four legs. ²⁷Attach the rings near the border to hold the poles that are used to carry the table. ²⁸Make these poles from acacia wood, and overlay them with gold. ²⁹Make special containers of pure gold for the table—bowls, ladles, pitchers, and jars—to be used in pouring out liquid offerings. ³⁰Place the Bread of the Presence on the table to remain before me at all times.

Plans for the Lampstand

³¹"Make a lampstand of pure, hammered gold. Make the entire lampstand and its decorations of one piece—the base, center stem, lamp cups, buds, and petals. ³²Make it with six branches going out from the center stem, three on each side. ³³Each of the six branches will have three lamp cups shaped like almond blossoms, complete with buds and petals. ³⁴Craft the center stem of the lampstand with four lamp cups shaped like almond blossoms, complete with buds and petals. ³⁵There will also be an almond bud beneath each pair of branches where the six branches extend from the center stem. ³⁶The almond buds and branches must all be of one piece with the center stem, and they must be hammered from pure gold. ³⁷Then make the seven lamps for the lampstand, and set them so they reflect their light forward. ³⁸The lamp snuffers and trays must also be made of pure gold. ³⁹You will need 75 pounds* of pure gold for the lampstand and its accessories.

⁴⁰"Be sure that you make everything according to the pattern I have shown you here on the mountain.

25:10 Hebrew *2.5 cubits* [115 centimeters] *long, 1.5 cubits* [69 centimeters] *wide, and 1.5 cubits high.* **25:16** Hebrew *Place inside the Ark the Testimony;* similarly in 25:21. The Hebrew word for "testimony" refers to the terms of the LORD's covenant with Israel as written on stone tablets, and also to the covenant itself. **25:17** Hebrew *2.5 cubits* [115 centimeters] *long and 1.5 cubits* [69 centimeters] *wide.* **25:22** Or *Ark of the Testimony.* **25:23** Hebrew *2 cubits* [92 centimeters] *long, 1 cubit* [46 centimeters] *wide, and 1.5 cubits* [69 centimeters] *high.* **25:25** Hebrew *a border of a handbreadth* [8 centimeters]. **25:39** Hebrew *1 talent* [34 kilograms].

25:1–27:21 The Lord gave Moses detailed instructions for building a Tabernacle so that God could live among his people. The Tabernacle safeguarded God's holiness so that it was not dangerous for the people. God offered these blueprints before Israel's sin with the gold calf (Exodus 32), indicating that he already knew they would need a way to be cleansed and forgiven. Precise compliance with the plans was essential, which is why Exodus 35–38 gives a detailed record of the fulfillment of the task.

Plans for the Tabernacle

26 "Make the Tabernacle from ten curtains of finely woven linen. Decorate the curtains with blue, purple, and scarlet thread and with skillfully embroidered cherubim. ²These ten curtains must all be exactly the same size—42 feet long and 6 feet wide.* ³Join five of these curtains together to make one long curtain, then join the other five into a second long curtain. ⁴Put loops of blue yarn along the edge of the last curtain in each set. ⁵The fifty loops along the edge of one curtain are to match the fifty loops along the edge of the other curtain. ⁶Then make fifty gold clasps and fasten the long curtains together with the clasps. In this way, the Tabernacle will be made of one continuous piece.

⁷"Make eleven curtains of goat-hair cloth to serve as a tent covering for the Tabernacle. ⁸These eleven curtains must all be exactly the same size—45 feet long and 6 feet wide.* ⁹Join five of these curtains together to make one long curtain, and join the other six into a second long curtain. Allow 3 feet of material from the second set of curtains to hang over the front* of the sacred tent. ¹⁰Make fifty loops for one edge of each large curtain. ¹¹Then make fifty bronze clasps, and fasten the loops of the long curtains with the clasps. In this way, the tent covering will be made of one continuous piece. ¹²The remaining 3 feet* of this tent covering will be left to hang over the back of the Tabernacle. ¹³Allow 18 inches* of remaining material to hang down over each side, so the Tabernacle is completely covered. ¹⁴Complete the tent covering with a protective layer of tanned ram skins and a layer of fine goatskin leather.

¹⁵"For the framework of the Tabernacle, construct frames of acacia wood. ¹⁶Each frame must be 15 feet high and 27 inches wide,* ¹⁷with two pegs under each frame. Make all the frames identical. ¹⁸Make twenty of these frames to support the curtains on the south side of the Tabernacle. ¹⁹Also make forty silver bases—two bases under each frame, with the pegs fitting securely into the bases. ²⁰For the north side of the Tabernacle, make another twenty frames, ²¹with their forty silver bases, two bases under each frame. ²²Make six frames for the rear—the west side of the Tabernacle—²³along with two additional frames to reinforce the rear corners of the Tabernacle. ²⁴These corner frames will be matched at the bottom and firmly attached at the top with a single ring, forming a single corner unit. Make both of these corner units the same way. ²⁵So there will be eight frames at the rear of the Tabernacle, set in sixteen silver bases—two bases under each frame.

²⁶"Make crossbars of acacia wood to link the frames, five crossbars for the north side of the Tabernacle ²⁷and five for the south side. Also make five crossbars for the rear of the Tabernacle, which will face west. ²⁸The middle crossbar, attached halfway up the frames, will run all the way from one end of the Tabernacle to the other. ²⁹Overlay the frames with gold, and make gold rings to hold the crossbars. Overlay the crossbars with gold as well.

³⁰"Set up this Tabernacle according to the pattern you were shown on the mountain.

³¹"For the inside of the Tabernacle, make a special curtain of finely woven linen. Decorate it with blue, purple, and scarlet thread and with skillfully embroidered cherubim. ³²Hang this curtain on gold hooks attached to four posts of acacia wood. Overlay the posts with gold, and set them in four silver bases. ³³Hang the inner curtain from clasps, and put the Ark of the Covenant* in the room behind it. This curtain will separate the Holy Place from the Most Holy Place.

³⁴"Then put the Ark's cover—the place of atonement—on top of the Ark of the Covenant inside the Most Holy Place. ³⁵Place the table outside the inner curtain on the north side of the Tabernacle, and place the lampstand across the room on the south side.

³⁶"Make another curtain for the entrance to the sacred tent. Make it of finely woven linen and embroider it with exquisite designs, using blue, purple, and scarlet thread. ³⁷Craft five posts from acacia wood. Overlay them with gold, and hang the curtain from them with gold hooks. Cast five bronze bases for the posts.

26:2 Hebrew *28 cubits* [12.9 meters] *long and 4 cubits* [1.8 meters] *wide.* 26:8 Hebrew *30 cubits* [13.8 meters] *long and 4 cubits* [1.8 meters] *wide.* 26:9 Hebrew *Double over the sixth sheet at the front.* 26:12 Hebrew *The half sheet that is left over.* 26:13 Hebrew *1 cubit* [46 centimeters]. 26:16 Hebrew *10 cubits* [4.6 meters] *high and 1.5 cubits* [69 centimeters] *wide.* 26:33 Or *Ark of the Testimony;* also in 26:34.

26:1-37 The Tabernacle itself (as distinct from the surrounding courtyard) was not large. It was approximately 15 feet wide by 45 feet long. The supporting framework consisted of forty-eight vertical frames, 15 feet high by 27 inches wide (26:16). The frames were acacia wood overlaid with gold (26:15, 29) and locked together with horizontal crossbars to form a three-sided rectangle with an open end (26:26-28). Two large linen curtains (each composed of five smaller ones) then linked together and draped across the top of this framework. The span was long enough to hang down on the sides and rear (26:1-6), covering the walls and the roof. Over the linen draped a curtain of goat-hair cloth, constructed in the same way. It was 3 feet wider and 6 feet longer than the linen curtain (26:7-13), so it hung down farther than the linen curtain on all sides. Over these two curtains lay two protective coverings, one of tanned ram skins and the other of fine goatskin leather (26:14). Another beautifully embroidered curtain, hanging crosswise on four posts of acacia wood, divided the enclosed space in two. The two spaces were the Holy Place and the Most Holy Place (26:31-33).

26:33 The Most Holy Place was the Lord's earthly dwelling. It contained the Ark of the Covenant, from which the Lord would give his commands for the people of Israel (25:22). The Most Holy Place was approximately 15 feet wide, 15 feet deep, and 15 feet high.

Plans for the Altar of Burnt Offering

27 "Using acacia wood, construct a square altar 7½ feet wide, 7½ feet long, and 4½ feet high.* ²Make horns for each of its four corners so that the horns and altar are all one piece. Overlay the altar with bronze. ³Make ash buckets, shovels, basins, meat forks, and firepans, all of bronze. ⁴Make a bronze grating for it, and attach four bronze rings at its four corners. ⁵Install the grating halfway down the side of the altar, under the ledge. ⁶For carrying the altar, make poles from acacia wood, and overlay them with bronze. ⁷Insert the poles through the rings on the two sides of the altar. ⁸The altar must be hollow, made from planks. Build it just as you were shown on the mountain.

Plans for the Courtyard

⁹"Then make the courtyard for the Tabernacle, enclosed with curtains made of finely woven linen. On the south side, make the curtains 150 feet long.* ¹⁰They will be held up by twenty posts set securely in twenty bronze bases. Hang the curtains with silver hooks and rings. ¹¹Make the curtains the same on the north side—150 feet of curtains held up by twenty posts set securely in bronze bases. Hang the curtains with silver hooks and rings. ¹²The curtains

27:1 Hebrew *5 cubits* [2.3 meters] *wide, 5 cubits long, a square, and 3 cubits* [1.4 meters] *high.*   27:9 Hebrew *100 cubits* [46 meters]; also in 27:11.

27:1-19 These plans move outward from the center of the Tabernacle, from the altar of burnt offering to the courtyard. As with the sanctuary, the plans for the courtyard furnishings appear (27:1-8) before the plans for the courtyard itself (27:9-19).

Insight — THE TABERNACLE

Exodus 36–40 describes the construction of the Tabernacle and its accessories. The Tabernacle was the mobile sanctuary of God's presence with his people and the place where Israel made sacrifices and offerings in worship of the Lord.

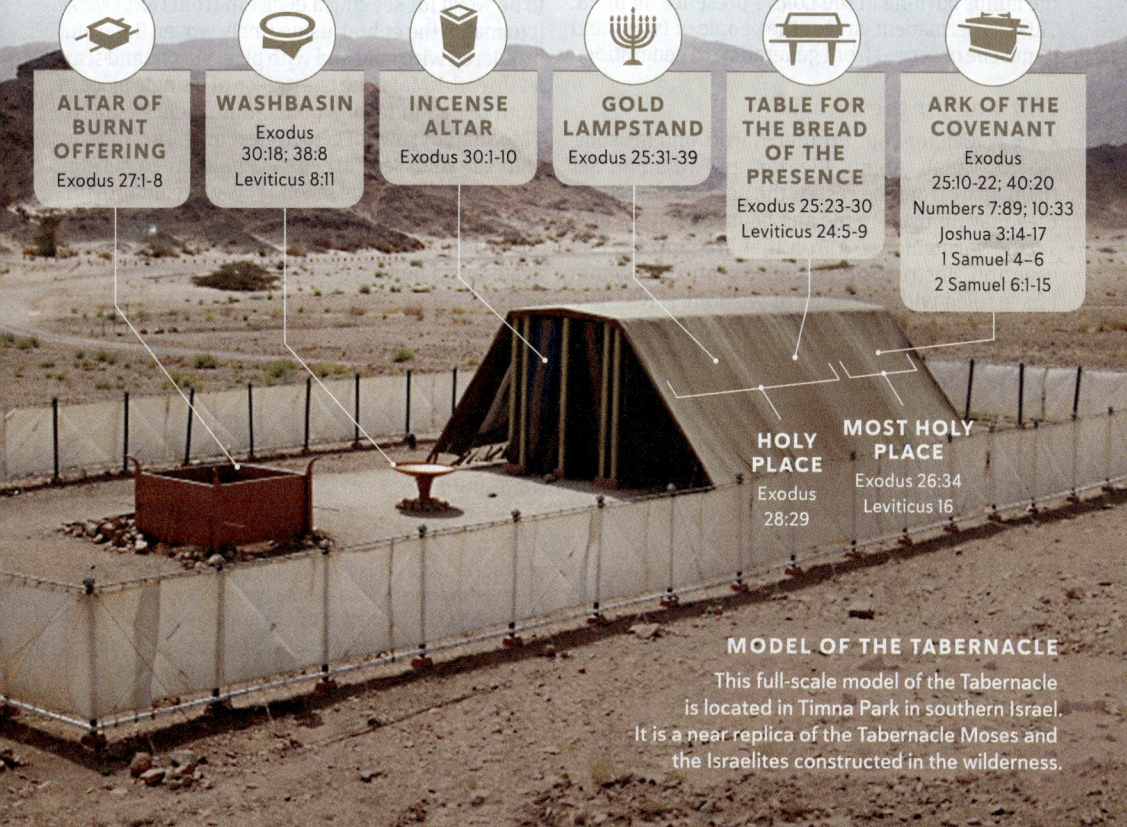

ALTAR OF BURNT OFFERING
Exodus 27:1-8

WASHBASIN
Exodus 30:18; 38:8
Leviticus 8:11

INCENSE ALTAR
Exodus 30:1-10

GOLD LAMPSTAND
Exodus 25:31-39

TABLE FOR THE BREAD OF THE PRESENCE
Exodus 25:23-30
Leviticus 24:5-9

ARK OF THE COVENANT
Exodus 25:10-22; 40:20
Numbers 7:89; 10:33
Joshua 3:14-17
1 Samuel 4–6
2 Samuel 6:1-15

HOLY PLACE
Exodus 28:29

MOST HOLY PLACE
Exodus 26:34
Leviticus 16

MODEL OF THE TABERNACLE
This full-scale model of the Tabernacle is located in Timna Park in southern Israel. It is a near replica of the Tabernacle Moses and the Israelites constructed in the wilderness.

on the west end of the courtyard will be 75 feet long,* supported by ten posts set into ten bases. ¹³The east end of the courtyard, the front, will also be 75 feet long. ¹⁴The courtyard entrance will be on the east end, flanked by two curtains. The curtain on the right side will be 22½ feet long,* supported by three posts set into three bases. ¹⁵The curtain on the left side will also be 22½ feet long, supported by three posts set into three bases.

¹⁶"For the entrance to the courtyard, make a curtain that is 30 feet long.* Make it from finely woven linen, and decorate it with beautiful embroidery in blue, purple, and scarlet thread. Support it with four posts, each securely set in its own base. ¹⁷All the posts around the courtyard must have silver rings and hooks and bronze bases. ¹⁸So the entire courtyard will be 150 feet long and 75 feet wide, with curtain walls 7½ feet high,* made from finely woven linen. The bases for the posts will be made of bronze.

¹⁹"All the articles used in the rituals of the Tabernacle, including all the tent pegs used to support the Tabernacle and the courtyard curtains, must be made of bronze.

Light for the Tabernacle

²⁰"Command the people of Israel to bring you pure oil of pressed olives for the light, to keep the lamps burning continually. ²¹The lampstand will stand in the Tabernacle, in front of the inner curtain that shields the Ark of the Covenant.* Aaron and his sons must keep the lamps burning in the LORD's presence all night. This is a permanent law for the people of Israel, and it must be observed from generation to generation.

Clothing for the Priests

28 "Call for your brother, Aaron, and his sons, Nadab, Abihu, Eleazar, and Ithamar. Set them apart from the rest of the people of Israel so they may minister to me and be my priests. ²Make sacred garments for Aaron that are glorious and beautiful. ³Instruct all the skilled craftsmen whom I have filled with the spirit of wisdom. Have them make garments for Aaron that will distinguish him as a priest set apart for my service. ⁴These are the garments they are to make: a chestpiece, an ephod, a robe, a patterned tunic, a turban, and a sash. They are to make these sacred garments for your brother, Aaron, and his sons to wear when they serve me as priests. ⁵So give them fine linen cloth, gold thread, and blue, purple, and scarlet thread.

Design of the Ephod

⁶"The craftsmen must make the ephod of finely woven linen and skillfully embroider it with gold and with blue, purple, and scarlet thread. ⁷It will consist of two pieces, front and back, joined at the shoulders with two shoulder-pieces. ⁸The decorative sash will be made of the same materials: finely woven linen embroidered with gold and with blue, purple, and scarlet thread.

⁹"Take two onyx stones, and engrave on them the names of the tribes of Israel. ¹⁰Six names will be on each stone, arranged in the order of the births of the original sons of Israel. ¹¹Engrave these names on the two stones in the same way a jeweler engraves a seal. Then mount the stones in settings of gold filigree. ¹²Fasten the two stones on the shoulder-pieces of the ephod as a reminder that Aaron represents the people of Israel. Aaron will carry these names on his shoulders as a constant reminder whenever he goes before the LORD. ¹³Make the settings of gold filigree, ¹⁴then braid two cords of pure gold and attach them to the filigree settings on the shoulders of the ephod.

Design of the Chestpiece

¹⁵"Then, with great skill and care, make a chestpiece to be worn for seeking a decision from God.* Make it to match the ephod, using finely woven linen embroidered with gold and with blue, purple, and scarlet thread. ¹⁶Make the chestpiece of a single piece of cloth folded to form a pouch nine inches* square. ¹⁷Mount four rows of gemstones* on it. The first row will contain a red carnelian, a pale-green peridot, and an emerald. ¹⁸The second row will contain a turquoise, a blue lapis lazuli, and a white moonstone. ¹⁹The third row will contain an orange jacinth, an agate, and a purple amethyst. ²⁰The fourth row will contain a blue-green beryl, an onyx, and a green jasper. All these stones will be set in gold filigree. ²¹Each stone will represent one of the twelve sons of Israel, and the name of that tribe will be engraved on it like a seal.

27:12 Hebrew *50 cubits* [23 meters]; also in 27:13. **27:14** Hebrew *15 cubits* [6.9 meters]; also in 27:15. **27:16** Hebrew *20 cubits* [9.2 meters]. **27:18** Hebrew *100 cubits* [46 meters] *long and 50 by 50* [23 meters] *wide and 5 cubits* [2.3 meters] *high*. **27:21** Hebrew *in the Tent of Meeting, outside the inner curtain that is in front of the Testimony*. See note on 25:16. **28:15** Hebrew *a chestpiece for decision*. **28:16** Hebrew *1 span* [23 centimeters]. **28:17** The identification of some of these gemstones is uncertain.

27:20–30:38 Following the structural designs for the Tabernacle comes instructions for the people and elements involved in service. Included are priestly functions (27:20-21; 29:38-46), clothing (28:1-43), dedication ceremonies (29:1-37), furnishings (30:1-10, 17-21), and supplies (30:11-16, 22-38).
28:1–29:46 The high priest was the best-dressed Israelite. The twelve gemstones on his chest symbolized his representative role, indicating that all twelve tribes would have a permanent share in his ministry. The gold medallion on his forehead bearing Yahweh's name showed the priest's status as Yahweh's representative. Later, the entire nation was called "a holy people, who belong to the LORD your God" (Deuteronomy 7:6). This phrase echoed the high priest's medallion to reinforce the people's priestly status (Exodus 19:6). The high priest was a visual model of the vocation of the entire nation.

²²"To attach the chestpiece to the ephod, make braided cords of pure gold thread. ²³Then make two gold rings and attach them to the top corners of the chestpiece. ²⁴Tie the two gold cords to the two rings on the chestpiece. ²⁵Tie the other ends of the cords to the gold settings on the shoulder-pieces of the ephod. ²⁶Then make two more gold rings and attach them to the inside edges of the chestpiece next to the ephod. ²⁷And make two more gold rings and attach them to the front of the ephod, below the shoulder-pieces, just above the knot where the decorative sash is fastened to the ephod. ²⁸Then attach the bottom rings of the chestpiece to the rings on the ephod with blue cords. This will hold the chestpiece securely to the ephod above the decorative sash.

²⁹"In this way, Aaron will carry the names of the tribes of Israel on the sacred chestpiece* over his heart when he goes into the Holy Place. This will be a continual reminder that he represents the people when he comes before the LORD. ³⁰Insert the Urim and Thummim into the sacred chestpiece so they will be carried over Aaron's heart when he goes into the LORD's presence. In this way, Aaron will always carry over his heart the objects used to determine the LORD's will for his people whenever he goes in before the LORD.

Additional Clothing for the Priests

³¹"Make the robe that is worn with the ephod from a single piece of blue cloth, ³²with an opening for Aaron's head in the middle of it. Reinforce the opening with a woven collar* so it will not tear. ³³Make pomegranates out of blue, purple, and scarlet yarn, and attach them to the hem of the robe, with gold bells between them. ³⁴The gold bells and pomegranates are to alternate all around the hem. ³⁵Aaron will wear this robe whenever he ministers before the LORD, and the bells will tinkle as he goes in and out of the LORD's presence in the Holy Place. If he wears it, he will not die.

³⁶"Next make a medallion of pure gold, and engrave it like a seal with these words: HOLY TO THE LORD. ³⁷Attach the medallion with a blue cord to the front of Aaron's turban, where it must remain. ³⁸Aaron must wear it on his forehead so he may take on himself any guilt of the people of Israel when they consecrate their sacred offerings. He must always wear it on his forehead so the LORD will accept the people.

³⁹"Weave Aaron's patterned tunic from fine linen cloth. Fashion the turban from this linen as well. Also make a sash, and decorate it with colorful embroidery.

⁴⁰"For Aaron's sons, make tunics, sashes, and special head coverings that are glorious and beautiful. ⁴¹Clothe your brother, Aaron, and his sons with these garments, and then anoint and ordain them. Consecrate them so they can serve as my priests. ⁴²Also make linen undergarments for them, to be worn next to their bodies, reaching from their hips to their thighs. ⁴³These must be worn whenever Aaron and his sons enter the Tabernacle* or approach the altar in the Holy Place to perform their priestly duties. Then they will not incur guilt and die. This is a permanent law for Aaron and all his descendants after him.

Dedication of the Priests

29 "This is the ceremony you must follow when you consecrate Aaron and his sons to serve me as priests: Take a young bull and two rams with no defects. ²Then, using choice wheat flour and no yeast, make loaves of bread, thin cakes mixed with olive oil, and wafers spread with oil. ³Place them all in a single basket, and present them at the entrance of the Tabernacle, along with the young bull and the two rams.

⁴"Present Aaron and his sons at the entrance of the Tabernacle,* and wash them with water. ⁵Dress Aaron in his priestly garments—the tunic, the robe worn with the ephod, the ephod itself, and the chestpiece. Then wrap the decorative sash of the ephod around him. ⁶Place the turban on his head, and fasten the sacred medallion to the turban. ⁷Then anoint him by pouring the anointing oil over his head. ⁸Next present his sons, and dress them in their tunics. ⁹Wrap the sashes around the waists of Aaron and his sons, and put their special head coverings on them. Then the right to the priesthood will be theirs by law forever. In this way, you will ordain Aaron and his sons.

¹⁰"Bring the young bull to the entrance of the Tabernacle, where Aaron and his sons will lay their hands on its head. ¹¹Then slaughter the bull in the LORD's presence at the entrance of the Tabernacle. ¹²Put some of its blood on the horns of the altar with your finger, and pour out the rest at the base of the altar. ¹³Take all the fat around the internal organs,

---

28:29 Hebrew *the chestpiece for decision;* also in 28:30. See 28:15. **28:32** The meaning of the Hebrew is uncertain.
28:43 Hebrew *Tent of Meeting.* **29:4** Hebrew *Tent of Meeting;* also in 29:10, 11, 30, 32, 42, 44.

29:1-37 Moses consecrated (or sanctified, set apart as sacred) Aaron and his sons to serve the Lord. This emphasis on making the priests holy appears throughout the ceremonies (29:4-9, 21, 28, 29, 34, 36, 37). The priests were set apart not merely to serve but to serve a God whose nature is utterly different from that of fallen, sinful humans. Leviticus 8–9 reports how the people carried out these instructions.
29:10-34 Consecrating Aaron into priesthood involved a sin offering (29:10-14), a burnt offering (29:15-18), and an ordination offering (29:19-28). The same patterns are expanded to the regular offerings of the people (see 29:38-46; Leviticus 1–7). In all three offerings, "Aaron and his sons will lay their hands on [the] head" of the sacrificial animals (Exodus 29:10, 15, 19). All three indicate that sin is a matter of life and death and that only death can remove it. Because blood represents life, it is prominent in these ceremonies (29:12, 16, 20, 21).

the long lobe of the liver, and the two kidneys and the fat around them, and burn it all on the altar. ¹⁴Then take the rest of the bull, including its hide, meat, and dung, and burn it outside the camp as a sin offering.

¹⁵"Next Aaron and his sons must lay their hands on the head of one of the rams. ¹⁶Then slaughter the ram, and splatter its blood against all sides of the altar. ¹⁷Cut the ram into pieces, and wash off the internal organs and the legs. Set them alongside the head and the other pieces of the body, ¹⁸then burn the entire animal on the altar. This is a burnt offering to the LORD; it is a pleasing aroma, a special gift presented to the LORD.

¹⁹"Now take the other ram, and have Aaron and his sons lay their hands on its head. ²⁰Then slaughter it, and apply some of its blood to the right earlobes of Aaron and his sons. Also put it on the thumbs of their right hands and the big toes of their right feet. Splatter the rest of the blood against all sides of the altar. ²¹Then take some of the blood from the altar and some of the anointing oil, and sprinkle it on Aaron and his sons and on their garments. In this way, they and their garments will be set apart as holy.

²²"Since this is the ram for the ordination of Aaron and his sons, take the fat of the ram, including the fat of the broad tail, the fat around the internal organs, the long lobe of the liver, and the two kidneys and the fat around them, along with the right thigh. ²³Then take one round loaf of bread, one thin cake mixed with olive oil, and one wafer from the basket of bread without yeast that was placed in the LORD's presence. ²⁴Put all these in the hands of Aaron and his sons to be lifted up as a special offering to the LORD. ²⁵Afterward take the various breads from their hands, and burn them on the altar along with the burnt offering. It is a pleasing aroma to the LORD, a special gift for him. ²⁶Then take the breast of Aaron's ordination ram, and lift it up in the LORD's presence as a special offering to him. Then keep it as your own portion.

²⁷"Set aside the portions of the ordination ram that belong to Aaron and his sons. This includes the breast and the thigh that were lifted up before the LORD as a special offering. ²⁸In the future, whenever the people of Israel lift up a peace offering, a portion of it must be set aside for Aaron and his descendants. This is their permanent right, and it is a sacred offering from the Israelites to the LORD.

²⁹"Aaron's sacred garments must be preserved for his descendants who succeed him, and they will wear them when they are anointed and ordained. ³⁰The descendant who succeeds him as high priest will wear these clothes for seven days as he ministers in the Tabernacle and the Holy Place.

³¹"Take the ram used in the ordination ceremony, and boil its meat in a sacred place. ³²Then Aaron and his sons will eat this meat, along with the bread in the basket, at the Tabernacle entrance. ³³They alone may eat the meat and bread used for their purification* in the ordination ceremony. No one else may eat them, for these things are set apart and holy. ³⁴If any of the ordination meat or bread remains until the morning, it must be burned. It may not be eaten, for it is holy.

³⁵"This is how you will ordain Aaron and his sons to their offices, just as I have commanded you. The ordination ceremony will go on for seven days. ³⁶Each day you must sacrifice a young bull as a sin offering to purify them, making them right with the LORD.* Afterward, cleanse the altar by purifying it*; make it holy by anointing it with oil. ³⁷Purify the altar, and consecrate it every day for seven days. After that, the altar will be absolutely holy, and whatever touches it will become holy.

³⁸"These are the sacrifices you are to offer regularly on the altar. Each day, offer two lambs that are a year old, ³⁹one in the morning and the other in the evening. ⁴⁰With one of them, offer two quarts of choice flour mixed with one quart of pure oil of pressed olives; also, offer one quart of wine* as a liquid offering. ⁴¹Offer the other lamb in the evening, along with the same offerings of flour and wine as in the morning. It will be a pleasing aroma, a special gift presented to the LORD.

⁴²"These burnt offerings are to be made each day from generation to generation. Offer them in the LORD's presence at the Tabernacle entrance; there I will meet with you and speak with you. ⁴³I will meet the people of Israel there, in the place made holy by my glorious presence. ⁴⁴Yes, I will consecrate the Tabernacle and the altar, and I will consecrate Aaron and his sons to serve me as priests. ⁴⁵Then I will live among the people of Israel and be their God, ⁴⁶and they will know that I am the LORD their God. I am the one who brought them out of the land of Egypt so that I could live among them. I am the LORD their God.

Plans for the Incense Altar

30 "Then make another altar of acacia wood for burning incense. ²Make it 18 inches square and 36 inches high,* with horns at the corners carved from the same piece of wood as the altar itself. ³Overlay the top, sides, and horns of the altar with pure gold, and run a gold molding around the entire altar. ⁴Make two gold rings, and attach them on opposite sides of the altar below the gold molding to hold the carrying poles. ⁵Make the poles of acacia wood and overlay them with gold. ⁶Place the incense altar just outside the inner curtain that shields the Ark of the Covenant,* in front of the Ark's cover—the place of atonement—that covers the tablets

---

29:33 Or *their atonement*. 29:36a Or *to make atonement*. 29:36b Or *by making atonement for it;* similarly in 29:37. 29:40 Hebrew ¹⁄₁₀ [of an ephah] [2.2 liters] of choice flour . . . ¼ of a hin [1 liter] of pure oil . . . ¼ of a hin of wine. 30:2 Hebrew *1 cubit* [46 centimeters] long and 1 cubit wide, a square, and 2 cubits [92 centimeters] high. 30:6a Or *Ark of the Testimony;* also in 30:26.

> The LORD himself will fight for you. Just stay calm.
>
> — EXODUS 14:14

inscribed with the terms of the covenant.* I will meet with you there.

⁷"Every morning when Aaron maintains the lamps, he must burn fragrant incense on the altar. ⁸And each evening when he lights the lamps, he must again burn incense in the LORD's presence. This must be done from generation to generation. ⁹Do not offer any unholy incense on this altar, or any burnt offerings, grain offerings, or liquid offerings.

¹⁰"Once a year Aaron must purify* the altar by smearing its horns with blood from the offering made to purify the people from their sin. This will be a regular, annual event from generation to generation, for this is the LORD's most holy altar."

Money for the Tabernacle

¹¹Then the LORD said to Moses, ¹²"Whenever you take a census of the people of Israel, each man who is counted must pay a ransom for himself to the LORD. Then no plague will strike the people as you count them. ¹³Each person who is counted must give a small piece of silver as a sacred offering to the LORD. (This payment is half a shekel,* based on the sanctuary shekel, which equals twenty gerahs.) ¹⁴All who have reached their twentieth birthday must give this sacred offering to the LORD. ¹⁵When this offering is given to the LORD to purify your lives, making you right with him,* the rich must not give more than the specified amount, and the poor must not give less. ¹⁶Receive this ransom money from the Israelites, and use it for the care of the Tabernacle.* It will bring the Israelites to the LORD's attention, and it will purify your lives."

Plans for the Washbasin

¹⁷Then the LORD said to Moses, ¹⁸"Make a bronze washbasin with a bronze stand. Place it between the Tabernacle and the altar, and fill it with water. ¹⁹Aaron and his sons will wash their hands and feet there. ²⁰They must wash with water whenever they go into the Tabernacle to appear before the LORD and when they approach the altar to burn up their special gifts to the LORD—or they will die! ²¹They must always wash their hands and feet, or they will die. This is a permanent law for Aaron and his descendants, to be observed from generation to generation."

The Anointing Oil

²²Then the LORD said to Moses, ²³"Collect choice spices—12½ pounds of pure myrrh, 6¼ pounds of fragrant cinnamon, 6¼ pounds of fragrant calamus,* ²⁴and 12½ pounds of cassia*—as measured by the weight of the sanctuary shekel. Also get one gallon of olive oil.* ²⁵Like a skilled incense maker, blend these ingredients to make a holy anointing oil. ²⁶Use this sacred oil to anoint the Tabernacle, the Ark of the Covenant, ²⁷the table and all its utensils, the lampstand and all its accessories, the incense altar, ²⁸the altar of burnt offering and all its utensils, and the washbasin with its stand. ²⁹Consecrate them to make them absolutely holy. After this, whatever touches them will also become holy.

³⁰"Anoint Aaron and his sons also, consecrating them to serve me as priests. ³¹And say to the people of Israel, 'This holy anointing oil is reserved for me from generation to generation. ³²It must never be used to anoint anyone else, and you must never make any blend like it for yourselves. It is holy, and you must treat it as holy. ³³Anyone who makes a blend like it or anoints someone other than a priest will be cut off from the community.'"

The Incense

³⁴Then the LORD said to Moses, "Gather fragrant spices—resin droplets, mollusk shell, and galbanum—and mix these fragrant spices with pure frankincense, weighed out in equal amounts. ³⁵Using the usual techniques of the incense maker, blend the spices together and sprinkle them with salt to produce a pure and holy incense. ³⁶Grind some of the mixture into a very fine powder and put it in front of the Ark of the Covenant,* where I will meet with you in the Tabernacle. You must treat this incense as most holy. ³⁷Never use this formula to make this incense for yourselves. It is reserved for the LORD, and you must treat it as holy. ³⁸Anyone who makes incense like this for personal use will be cut off from the community."

Craftsmen: Bezalel and Oholiab

31 Then the LORD said to Moses, ²"Look, I have specifically chosen Bezalel son of Uri, grandson of Hur, of the tribe of Judah. ³I have filled him with the Spirit of God, giving him great wisdom, ability, and

---

30:6b Hebrew *that covers the Testimony;* see note on 25:16. 30:10 Or *make atonement for;* also in 30:10b. 30:13 Or *0.2 ounces* [6 grams]. 30:15 Or *to make atonement for your lives;* similarly in 30:16. 30:16 Hebrew *Tent of Meeting;* also in 30:18, 20, 26, 36. 30:23 Hebrew *500 [shekels]* [5.7 kilograms] *of pure myrrh, 250 [shekels]* [2.9 kilograms] *of fragrant cinnamon, 250 [shekels] of fragrant calamus.* 30:24a Hebrew *500 [shekels]* [5.7 kilograms] *of cassia.* 30:24b Hebrew *1 hin* [3.8 liters] *of olive oil.* 30:36 Hebrew *in front of the Testimony;* see note on 25:16.

30:22-38 These recipes were designed for the Tabernacle's anointing oil and incense, and the people could not use them for other purposes. The worship of God was to be set apart from daily life. Even its aroma was distinct! Anyone who treated worship lightly was a danger to the community, so they had to be cut off from the community. (For a sobering example of this, see Leviticus 10:1-3, where Aaron's sons try a different recipe in the Tabernacle.)

31:1-11 The construction of the Tabernacle required trained craftspeople. Bezalel and Oholiab led the project, and the Spirit of God gave them special inspiration (31:3), but generous and skilled men and women assisted them in their work (see also 35:10-24). God is honored by people who use their creative gifts for his service.

expertise in all kinds of crafts. ⁴He is a master craftsman, expert in working with gold, silver, and bronze. ⁵He is skilled in engraving and mounting gemstones and in carving wood. He is a master at every craft!

⁶"And I have personally appointed Oholiab son of Ahisamach, of the tribe of Dan, to be his assistant. Moreover, I have given special skill to all the gifted craftsmen so they can make all the things I have commanded you to make:

- ⁷ the Tabernacle;*
  the Ark of the Covenant;*
  the Ark's cover—the place of atonement;
  all the furnishings of the Tabernacle;
- ⁸ the table and its utensils;
  the pure gold lampstand with all its accessories;
  the incense altar;
- ⁹ the altar of burnt offering with all its utensils;
  the washbasin with its stand;
- ¹⁰ the beautifully stitched garments—the
    sacred garments for Aaron the priest, and
    the garments for his sons to wear as they minister as priests;
- ¹¹ the anointing oil;
  the fragrant incense for the Holy Place.

The craftsmen must make everything as I have commanded you."

Instructions for the Sabbath

¹²The LORD then gave these instructions to Moses: ¹³"Tell the people of Israel: 'Be careful to keep my Sabbath day, for the Sabbath is a sign of the covenant between me and you from generation to generation. It is given so you may know that I am the LORD, who makes you holy. ¹⁴You must keep the Sabbath day, for it is a holy day for you. Anyone who desecrates it must be put to death; anyone who works on that day will be cut off from the community. ¹⁵You have six days each week for your ordinary work, but the seventh day must be a Sabbath day of complete rest, a holy day dedicated to the LORD. Anyone who works on the Sabbath must be put to death. ¹⁶The people of Israel must keep the Sabbath day by observing it from generation to generation. This is a covenant obligation for all time. ¹⁷It is a permanent sign of my covenant with the people of Israel. For in six days the LORD made heaven and earth, but on the seventh day he stopped working and was refreshed.'"

¹⁸When the LORD finished speaking with Moses on Mount Sinai, he gave him the two stone tablets inscribed with the terms of the covenant,* written by the finger of God.

The Gold Calf

32 When the people saw how long it was taking Moses to come back down the mountain, they gathered around Aaron. "Come on," they said, "make us some gods who can lead us. We don't know what happened to this fellow Moses, who brought us here from the land of Egypt."

²So Aaron said, "Take the gold rings from the ears of your wives and sons and daughters, and bring them to me."

³All the people took the gold rings from their ears and brought them to Aaron. ⁴Then Aaron took the gold, melted it down, and molded it into the shape of a calf. When the people saw it, they exclaimed, "O Israel, these are the gods who brought you out of the land of Egypt!"

⁵Aaron saw how excited the people were, so he built an altar in front of the calf. Then he announced, "Tomorrow will be a festival to the LORD!"

⁶The people got up early the next morning to sacrifice burnt offerings and peace offerings. After this, they celebrated with feasting and drinking, and they indulged in pagan revelry.

⁷The LORD told Moses, "Quick! Go down the mountain! Your people whom you brought from the land of Egypt have corrupted themselves. ⁸How quickly they have turned away from the way I commanded them to live! They have melted down gold and made a calf, and they have bowed down and sacrificed to it. They are saying, 'These are your gods, O Israel, who brought you out of the land of Egypt.'"

⁹Then the LORD said, "I have seen how stubborn and rebellious these people are. ¹⁰Now leave me alone so my fierce anger can blaze against them, and I will destroy them. Then I will make you, Moses, into a great nation."

¹¹But Moses tried to pacify the LORD his God. "O LORD!" he said. "Why are you so angry with your own people whom you brought from the land of Egypt with such great power and such a strong hand? ¹²Why let the Egyptians say, 'Their God rescued them with the evil intention of slaughtering them in the mountains and wiping them from the face of the earth'? Turn away from your fierce anger. Change your mind about this terrible disaster you have threatened against your people! ¹³Remember your servants Abraham, Isaac, and Jacob.* You bound yourself with an oath to them, saying, 'I will make your descendants as numerous as the stars of heaven. And I will give them all of this land that I have promised to your descendants, and they will possess it forever.'"

31:7a Hebrew *the Tent of Meeting.* **31:7b** Hebrew *the Ark of the Testimony.* **31:18** Hebrew *the two tablets of the Testimony;* see note on 25:16. **32:13** Hebrew *Israel.* The names "Jacob" and "Israel" are often interchanged throughout the Old Testament, referring sometimes to the individual patriarch and sometimes to the nation.

32:11-14 Moses interceded on Israel's behalf, persuading God that his promise to Abraham should result in protection rather than judgment. God was within his rights to punish the people for their rebellion. However, as this story illustrates, prayer is powerful. God invited Moses into his deliberations, entrusting him with his plans and responding to his request.

¹⁴So the LORD changed his mind about the terrible disaster he had threatened to bring on his people.

¹⁵Then Moses turned and went down the mountain. He held in his hands the two stone tablets inscribed with the terms of the covenant.* They were inscribed on both sides, front and back. ¹⁶These tablets were God's work; the words on them were written by God himself.

¹⁷When Joshua heard the boisterous noise of the people shouting below them, he exclaimed to Moses, "It sounds like war in the camp!"

¹⁸But Moses replied, "No, it's not a shout of victory nor the wailing of defeat. I hear the sound of a celebration."

¹⁹When they came near the camp, Moses saw the calf and the dancing, and he burned with anger. He threw the stone tablets to the ground, smashing them at the foot of the mountain. ²⁰He took the calf they had made and burned it. Then he ground it into powder, threw it into the water, and forced the people to drink it.

²¹Finally, he turned to Aaron and demanded, "What did these people do to you to make you bring such terrible sin upon them?"

²²"Don't get so upset, my lord," Aaron replied. "You yourself know how evil these people are. ²³They said to me, 'Make us gods who will lead us. We don't know what happened to this fellow Moses, who brought us here from the land of Egypt.' ²⁴So I told them, 'Whoever has gold jewelry, take it off.' When they brought it to me, I simply threw it into the fire—and out came this calf!"

²⁵Moses saw that Aaron had let the people get completely out of control, much to the amusement of their enemies.* ²⁶So he stood at the entrance to the camp and shouted, "All of you who are on the LORD's side, come here and join me." And all the Levites gathered around him.

²⁷Moses told them, "This is what the LORD, the God of Israel, says: Each of you, take your swords and go back and forth from one end of the camp to the other. Kill everyone—even your brothers, friends, and neighbors." ²⁸The Levites obeyed Moses' command, and about 3,000 people died that day.

²⁹Then Moses told the Levites, "Today you have ordained yourselves* for the service of the LORD, for you obeyed him even though it meant killing your own sons and brothers. Today you have earned a blessing."

Moses Intercedes for Israel

³⁰The next day Moses said to the people, "You have committed a terrible sin, but I will go back up to the LORD on the mountain. Perhaps I will be able to obtain forgiveness* for your sin."

³¹So Moses returned to the LORD and said, "Oh, what a terrible sin these people have committed. They have made gods of gold for themselves. ³²But now, if you will only forgive their sin—but if not, erase my name from the record you have written!"

³³But the LORD replied to Moses, "No, I will erase the name of everyone who has sinned against me. ³⁴Now go, lead the people to the place I told you about. Look! My angel will lead the way before you. And when I come to call the people to account, I will certainly hold them responsible for their sins."

³⁵Then the LORD sent a great plague upon the people because they had worshiped the calf Aaron had made.

33

The LORD said to Moses, "Get going, you and the people you brought up from the land of Egypt. Go up to the land I swore to give to Abraham, Isaac, and Jacob. I told them, 'I will give this land to your descendants.' ²And I will send an angel before you to drive out the Canaanites, Amorites, Hittites, Perizzites, Hivites, and Jebusites. ³Go up to this land that flows with milk and honey. But I will not travel among you, for you are a stubborn and rebellious people. If I did, I would surely destroy you along the way."

⁴When the people heard these stern words, they went into mourning and stopped wearing their jewelry and fine clothes. ⁵For the LORD had told Moses to tell them, "You are a stubborn and rebellious people. If I were to travel with you for even a moment, I would destroy you. Remove your jewelry and fine clothes while I decide what to do with you." ⁶So from the time they left Mount Sinai,* the Israelites wore no more jewelry or fine clothes.

⁷It was Moses' practice to take the Tent of Meeting* and set it up some distance from the camp. Everyone who wanted to make a request of the LORD would go to the Tent of Meeting outside the camp.

32:15 Hebrew *the two tablets of the Testimony;* see note on 25:15. **32:25** Or *out of control, and they mocked anyone who opposed them.* The meaning of the Hebrew is uncertain. **32:29** As in Greek and Latin versions; Hebrew reads *Today ordain yourselves.* **32:30** Or *to make atonement.* **33:6** Hebrew *Horeb,* another name for Sinai. **33:7** This "Tent of Meeting" is different from the Tabernacle described in chapters 26 and 36.

32:19-29 Moses' anger over the Israelites' rebellion mirrored God's (32:9-10). Although God had determined not to wipe out the entire nation, those responsible for this offense still suffered the death penalty. The Levites showed their commitment to worshiping Yahweh alone by carrying out God's judgment. Their loyalty to God was higher than their loyalty to family members.

33:1-23 Given the people's rebellious tendencies, God determined that he would not travel with them (33:3). This provoked great mourning (33:4), and Moses pled for God's presence to go with them, marking them as his people (33:15-16).

33:7 Before the Tabernacle existed, Moses would go outside the camp to meet with God. The Tabernacle would symbolize God's presence in the center of the Israelite community, where they would have reliable access to God. Previously, God showed up unpredictably at his initiative (for example, in Eden, in dreams, and on Mount Sinai). Now, in the Tabernacle, the Lord would make himself perpetually available to his people.

⁸Whenever Moses went out to the Tent of Meeting, all the people would get up and stand in the entrances of their own tents. They would all watch Moses until he disappeared inside. ⁹As he went into the tent, the pillar of cloud would come down and hover at its entrance while the LORD spoke with Moses. ¹⁰When the people saw the cloud standing at the entrance of the tent, they would stand and bow down in front of their own tents. ¹¹Inside the Tent of Meeting, the LORD would speak to Moses face to face, as one speaks to a friend. Afterward Moses would return to the camp, but the young man who assisted him, Joshua son of Nun, would remain behind in the Tent of Meeting.

Moses Sees the LORD's Glory

¹²One day Moses said to the LORD, "You have been telling me, 'Take these people up to the Promised Land.' But you haven't told me whom you will send with me. You have told me, 'I know you by name, and I look favorably on you.' ¹³If it is true that you look favorably on me, let me know your ways so I may understand you more fully and continue to enjoy your favor. And remember that this nation is your very own people."

¹⁴The LORD replied, "I will personally go with you, Moses, and I will give you rest—everything will be fine for you."

¹⁵Then Moses said, "If you don't personally go with us, don't make us leave this place. ¹⁶How will anyone know that you look favorably on me—on me and on your people—if you don't go with us? For your presence among us sets your people and me apart from all other people on the earth."

¹⁷The LORD replied to Moses, "I will indeed do what you have asked, for I look favorably on you, and I know you by name."

¹⁸Moses responded, "Then show me your glorious presence."

¹⁹The LORD replied, "I will make all my goodness pass before you, and I will call out my name, Yahweh,* before you. For I will show mercy to anyone I choose, and I will show compassion to anyone I choose. ²⁰But you may not look directly at my face, for no one may see me and live." ²¹The LORD continued, "Look, stand near me on this rock. ²²As my glorious presence passes by, I will hide you in the crevice of the rock and cover you with my hand until I have passed by. ²³Then I will remove my hand and let you see me from behind. But my face will not be seen."

A New Copy of the Covenant

34 Then the LORD told Moses, "Chisel out two stone tablets like the first ones. I will write on them the same words that were on the tablets you smashed. ²Be ready in the morning to climb up Mount Sinai and present yourself to me on the top of the mountain. ³No one else may come with you. In fact, no one is to appear anywhere on the mountain. Do not even let the flocks or herds graze near the mountain."

⁴So Moses chiseled out two tablets of stone like the first ones. Early in the morning he climbed Mount Sinai as the LORD had commanded him, and he carried the two stone tablets in his hands.

⁵Then the LORD came down in a cloud and stood there with him; and he called out his own name, Yahweh.* ⁶The LORD passed in front of Moses, calling out,

> "Yahweh!* The LORD!
> The God of compassion and mercy!
> I am slow to anger
> and filled with unfailing love and faithfulness.
> ⁷ I lavish unfailing love to a thousand
> generations.*
> I forgive iniquity, rebellion, and sin.
> But I do not excuse the guilty.
> I lay the sins of the parents upon their
> children and grandchildren;
> the entire family is affected—
> even children in the third and fourth
> generations."

⁸Moses immediately threw himself to the ground and worshiped. ⁹And he said, "O Lord, if it is true that I have found favor with you, then please travel with us. Yes, this is a stubborn and rebellious people, but please forgive our iniquity and our sins. Claim us as your own special possession."

¹⁰The LORD replied, "Listen, I am making a covenant with you in the presence of all your people. I will perform miracles that have never been performed anywhere in all the earth or in any nation. And all the people around you will see the power of the LORD—the awesome power I will display for you. ¹¹But listen carefully to everything I command you today. Then I will go ahead of you and drive out the Amorites, Canaanites, Hittites, Perizzites, Hivites, and Jebusites.

33:19 *Yahweh* is a transliteration of the proper name *YHWH* that is sometimes rendered "Jehovah"; in this translation it is usually rendered "the LORD" (note the use of small capitals). **34:5** *Yahweh* is a transliteration of the proper name *YHWH* that is sometimes rendered "Jehovah"; in this translation it is usually rendered "the LORD" (note the use of small capitals). **34:6** See note on 34:5. **34:7** Hebrew *for thousands.*

34:7 This passage describes God's actions in response to sin rather than his ideal for humanity. Our sins affect our descendants, but God restricts those natural effects to three or four generations (see also 20:5-6).

34:10-16 This covenant is not a different covenant than that described in Exodus 19–24. Here, God reiterated it to Moses to explain why he prohibited treaties with other nations. The prohibition of intermarriage with other ethnic groups in 34:16 served one purpose: to guard against worshiping other gods. Presumably, anyone who joined the Israelites (signified by male circumcision) and obeyed and worshiped Yahweh was exempt from this prohibition.

WHAT THE BIBLE SAYS ABOUT Extended Family

Speak Kindly

Never speak harshly to an older man, but appeal to him respectfully as you would to your own father. Talk to younger men as you would to your own brothers. Treat older women as you would your mother, and treat younger women with all purity as you would your own sisters. **1 TIMOTHY 5:1-2**

Honor Them

"I . . . know about everything you have done for your mother-in-law since the death of your husband. I have heard how you left your father and mother and your own land to live here among complete strangers. May the LORD, the God of Israel, under whose wings you have come to take refuge, reward you fully for what you have done." **RUTH 2:11-12**

Esther continued to keep her family background and nationality a secret. She was still following Mordecai's directions, just as she did when she lived in his home. **ESTHER 2:20**

Honor God First

"I have come to set a man against his father,
 a daughter against her mother,
and a daughter-in-law against her mother-in-law.
 Your enemies will be right in your own household!"
MATTHEW 10:35-36

Never speak harshly...

Listen to Them

"I will do everything you say," Ruth replied. So she went down to the threshing floor that night and followed the instructions of her mother-in-law. **RUTH 3:5-6**

"If you follow this advice, and if God commands you to do so, then you will be able to endure the pressures, and all these people will go home in peace." Moses listened to his father-in-law's advice and followed his suggestions. **EXODUS 18:23-24**

"Father will be divided against son
 and son against father;
mother against daughter
 and daughter against mother;
and mother-in-law against daughter-in-law
 and daughter-in-law against mother-in-law." **LUKE 12:53**

[12] "Be very careful never to make a treaty with the people who live in the land where you are going. If you do, you will follow their evil ways and be trapped. [13] Instead, you must break down their pagan altars, smash their sacred pillars, and cut down their Asherah poles. [14] You must worship no other gods, for the LORD, whose very name is Jealous, is a God who is jealous about his relationship with you.

[15] "You must not make a treaty of any kind with the people living in the land. They lust after their gods, offering sacrifices to them. They will invite you to join them in their sacrificial meals, and you will go with them. [16] Then you will accept their daughters, who sacrifice to other gods, as wives for your sons. And they will seduce your sons to commit adultery against me by worshiping other gods. [17] You must not make any gods of molten metal for yourselves.

[18] "You must celebrate the Festival of Unleavened Bread. For seven days the bread you eat must be made without yeast, just as I commanded you. Celebrate this festival annually at the appointed time in early spring, in the month of Abib,* for that is the anniversary of your departure from Egypt.

[19] "The firstborn of every animal belongs to me, including the firstborn males* from your herds of cattle and your flocks of sheep and goats. [20] A firstborn donkey may be bought back from the LORD by presenting a lamb or young goat in its place. But if you do not buy it back, you must break its neck. However, you must buy back every firstborn son.

"No one may appear before me without an offering.

[21] "You have six days each week for your ordinary work, but on the seventh day you must stop working, even during the seasons of plowing and harvest.

[22] "You must celebrate the Festival of Harvest* with the first crop of the wheat harvest, and celebrate the Festival of the Final Harvest* at the end of the harvest season. [23] Three times each year every man in Israel must appear before the Sovereign, the LORD, the God of Israel. [24] I will drive out the other nations ahead of you and expand your territory, so no one will covet and conquer your land while you appear before the LORD your God three times each year.

[25] "You must not offer the blood of my sacrificial offerings together with any baked goods containing yeast. And none of the meat of the Passover sacrifice may be kept over until the next morning.

[26] "As you harvest your crops, bring the very best of the first harvest to the house of the LORD your God.

"You must not cook a young goat in its mother's milk."

[27] Then the LORD said to Moses, "Write down all these instructions, for they represent the terms of the covenant I am making with you and with Israel."

[28] Moses remained there on the mountain with the LORD forty days and forty nights. In all that time he ate no bread and drank no water. And the LORD* wrote the terms of the covenant—the Ten Commandments*—on the stone tablets.

[29] When Moses came down Mount Sinai carrying the two stone tablets inscribed with the terms of the covenant,* he wasn't aware that his face had become radiant because he had spoken to the LORD. [30] So when Aaron and the people of Israel saw the radiance of Moses' face, they were afraid to come near him.

[31] But Moses called out to them and asked Aaron and all the leaders of the community to come over, and he talked with them. [32] Then all the people of Israel approached him, and Moses gave them all the instructions the LORD had given him on Mount Sinai. [33] When Moses finished speaking with them, he covered his face with a veil. [34] But whenever he went into the Tent of Meeting to speak with the LORD, he would remove the veil until he came out again. Then he would give the people whatever instructions the LORD had given him, [35] and the people of Israel would see the radiant glow of his face. So he would put the veil over his face until he returned to speak with the LORD.

Instructions for the Sabbath

35 Then Moses called together the whole community of Israel and told them, "These are the instructions the LORD has commanded you to follow. [2] You have six days each week for your ordinary work, but the seventh day must be a Sabbath day of complete rest, a holy day dedicated to the LORD. Anyone who works on that day must be put to death. [3] You must not even light a fire in any of your homes on the Sabbath."

Offerings for the Tabernacle

[4] Then Moses said to the whole community of Israel, "This is what the LORD has commanded: [5] Take a sacred offering for the LORD. Let those with generous hearts present the following gifts to the LORD:

34:18 Hebrew *appointed time in the month of Abib*. This first month of the ancient Hebrew lunar calendar usually occurs within the months of March and April.   34:19 As in Greek version; the meaning of the Hebrew word is uncertain.   34:22a Hebrew *Festival of Weeks;* compare 23:16. This was later called the Festival of Pentecost. It is celebrated today as Shavuot (or Shabuoth).   34:22b Or *Festival of Ingathering*. This was later called the Festival of Shelters or Festival of Tabernacles (see Lev 23:33-36). It is celebrated today as Sukkot (or Succoth).   34:28a Hebrew *he*.   34:28b Hebrew *the ten words*.   34:29 Hebrew *the two tablets of the Testimony;* see note on 25:16.

35:4–36:7 Unlike when Aaron created the gold calf and demanded one type of material (earrings), this passage invites people to bring various gifts (35:4-9). People gave as their "hearts were stirred" and "spirits were moved" (35:21). Perhaps because the variety of gifts meant that everyone could bring something, and the giving was voluntary, the people gave too much. Moses had to command them to stop (36:4-7).

gold, silver, and bronze; ⁶ blue, purple, and scarlet thread; fine linen and goat hair for cloth; ⁷ tanned ram skins and fine goatskin leather; acacia wood; ⁸ olive oil for the lamps; spices for the anointing oil and the fragrant incense; ⁹ onyx stones, and other gemstones to be set in the ephod and the priest's chestpiece.

¹⁰"Come, all of you who are gifted craftsmen. Construct everything that the LORD has commanded:

¹¹ the Tabernacle and its sacred tent, its covering, clasps, frames, crossbars, posts, and bases;
¹² the Ark and its carrying poles; the Ark's cover—the place of atonement; the inner curtain to shield the Ark;
¹³ the table, its carrying poles, and all its utensils; the Bread of the Presence;
¹⁴ for light, the lampstand, its accessories, the lamp cups, and the olive oil for lighting;
¹⁵ the incense altar and its carrying poles; the anointing oil and fragrant incense; the curtain for the entrance of the Tabernacle;
¹⁶ the altar of burnt offering; the bronze grating of the altar and its carrying poles and utensils; the washbasin with its stand;
¹⁷ the curtains for the walls of the courtyard; the posts and their bases; the curtain for the entrance to the courtyard;
¹⁸ the tent pegs of the Tabernacle and courtyard and their ropes;
¹⁹ the beautifully stitched garments for the priests to wear while ministering in the Holy Place— the sacred garments for Aaron the priest, and the garments for his sons to wear as they minister as priests."

²⁰So the whole community of Israel left Moses and returned to their tents. ²¹All whose hearts were stirred and whose spirits were moved came and brought their sacred offerings to the LORD. They brought all the materials needed for the Tabernacle,* for the performance of its rituals, and for the sacred garments. ²²Both men and women came, all whose hearts were willing. They brought to the LORD their offerings of gold—brooches, earrings, rings from their fingers, and necklaces. They presented gold objects of every kind as a special offering to the LORD. ²³All those who owned the following items willingly brought them: blue, purple, and scarlet thread; fine linen and goat hair for cloth; and tanned ram skins and fine goatskin leather. ²⁴And all who had silver and bronze objects gave them as a sacred offering to the LORD. And those who had acacia wood brought it for use in the project.

²⁵All the women who were skilled in sewing and spinning prepared blue, purple, and scarlet thread, and fine linen cloth. ²⁶All the women who were willing used their skills to spin the goat hair into yarn. ²⁷The leaders brought onyx stones and the special gemstones to be set in the ephod and the priest's chestpiece. ²⁸They also brought spices and olive oil for the light, the anointing oil, and the fragrant incense. ²⁹So the people of Israel—every man and woman who was eager to help in the work the LORD had given them through Moses—brought their gifts and gave them freely to the LORD.

³⁰Then Moses told the people of Israel, "The LORD has specifically chosen Bezalel son of Uri, grandson of Hur, of the tribe of Judah. ³¹The LORD has filled Bezalel with the Spirit of God, giving him great wisdom, ability, and expertise in all kinds of crafts. ³²He is a master craftsman, expert in working with gold, silver, and bronze. ³³He is skilled in engraving and mounting gemstones and in carving wood. He is a master at every craft. ³⁴And the LORD has given both him and Oholiab son of Ahisamach, of the tribe of Dan, the ability to teach their skills to others. ³⁵The LORD has given them special skills as engravers, designers, embroiderers in blue, purple, and scarlet thread on fine linen cloth, and weavers. They excel as craftsmen and as designers.

36

"The LORD has gifted Bezalel, Oholiab, and the other skilled craftsmen with wisdom and ability to perform any task involved in building the sanctuary. Let them construct and furnish the Tabernacle, just as the LORD has commanded."

²So Moses summoned Bezalel and Oholiab and all the others who were specially gifted by the LORD and were eager to get to work. ³Moses gave them the materials donated by the people of Israel as sacred offerings for the completion of the sanctuary. But the people continued to bring additional gifts each morning. ⁴Finally the craftsmen who were working on the sanctuary left their work. ⁵They went to Moses and reported, "The people have given more than enough materials to complete the job the LORD has commanded us to do!"

⁶So Moses gave the command, and this message was sent throughout the camp: "Men and women, don't prepare any more gifts for the sanctuary. We

---

35:21 Hebrew *Tent of Meeting*.

35:25-29 Both women and men participated in preparing the Tabernacle by using their skills and donating their finest possessions. These luxury items were likely those given to them by their neighbors as they left Egypt (12:35-36).

37:1-29 While the passage says Bezalel made the Ark, all the rest of the furnishings (37:1, 10, 17, 25) and the courtyard and its furnishings (38:1, 8, 9, 18), this likely means he was responsible. He probably directed other craftsmen and seamstresses.

have enough!" So the people stopped bringing their sacred offerings. ⁷Their contributions were more than enough to complete the whole project.

Building the Tabernacle

⁸The skilled craftsmen made ten curtains of finely woven linen for the Tabernacle. Then Bezalel* decorated the curtains with blue, purple, and scarlet thread and with skillfully embroidered cherubim. ⁹All ten curtains were exactly the same size—42 feet long and 6 feet wide.* ¹⁰Five of these curtains were joined together to make one long curtain, and the other five were joined to make a second long curtain. ¹¹He made fifty loops of blue yarn and put them along the edge of the last curtain in each set. ¹²The fifty loops along the edge of one curtain matched the fifty loops along the edge of the other curtain. ¹³Then he made fifty gold clasps and fastened the long curtains together with the clasps. In this way, the Tabernacle was made of one continuous piece.

¹⁴He made eleven curtains of goat-hair cloth to serve as a tent covering for the Tabernacle. ¹⁵These eleven curtains were all exactly the same size—45 feet long and 6 feet wide.* ¹⁶Bezalel joined five of these curtains together to make one long curtain, and the other six were joined to make a second long curtain. ¹⁷He made fifty loops for the edge of each large curtain. ¹⁸He also made fifty bronze clasps to fasten the long curtains together. In this way, the tent covering was made of one continuous piece. ¹⁹He completed the tent covering with a layer of tanned ram skins and a layer of fine goatskin leather.

²⁰For the framework of the Tabernacle, Bezalel constructed frames of acacia wood. ²¹Each frame was 15 feet high and 27 inches wide,* ²²with two pegs under each frame. All the frames were identical. ²³He made twenty of these frames to support the curtains on the south side of the Tabernacle. ²⁴He also made forty silver bases—two bases under each frame, with the pegs fitting securely into the bases. ²⁵For the north side of the Tabernacle, he made another twenty frames, ²⁶with their forty silver bases, two bases under each frame. ²⁷He made six frames for the rear—the west side of the Tabernacle—²⁸along with two additional frames to reinforce the rear corners of the Tabernacle. ²⁹These corner frames were matched at the bottom and firmly attached at the top with a single ring, forming a single corner unit. Both of these corner units were made the same way. ³⁰So there were eight frames at the rear of the Tabernacle, set in sixteen silver bases—two bases under each frame.

³¹Then he made crossbars of acacia wood to link the frames, five crossbars for the north side of the Tabernacle ³²and five for the south side. He also made five crossbars for the rear of the Tabernacle, which faced west. ³³He made the middle crossbar to attach halfway up the frames; it ran all the way from one end of the Tabernacle to the other. ³⁴He overlaid the frames with gold and made gold rings to hold the crossbars. Then he overlaid the crossbars with gold as well.

³⁵For the inside of the Tabernacle, Bezalel made a special curtain of finely woven linen. He decorated it with blue, purple, and scarlet thread and with skillfully embroidered cherubim. ³⁶For the curtain, he made four posts of acacia wood and four gold hooks. He overlaid the posts with gold and set them in four silver bases.

³⁷Then he made another curtain for the entrance to the sacred tent. He made it of finely woven linen and embroidered it with exquisite designs using blue, purple, and scarlet thread. ³⁸This curtain was hung on gold hooks attached to five posts. The posts with their decorated tops and hooks were overlaid with gold, and the five bases were cast from bronze.

Building the Ark of the Covenant

37 Next Bezalel made the Ark of acacia wood—a sacred chest 45 inches long, 27 inches wide, and 27 inches high.* ²He overlaid it inside and outside with pure gold, and he ran a molding of gold all around it. ³He cast four gold rings and attached them to its four feet, two rings on each side. ⁴Then he made poles from acacia wood and overlaid them with gold. ⁵He inserted the poles into the rings at the sides of the Ark to carry it.

⁶Then he made the Ark's cover—the place of atonement—from pure gold. It was 45 inches long and 27 inches wide.* ⁷He made two cherubim from hammered gold and placed them on the two ends of the atonement cover. ⁸He molded the cherubim on each end of the atonement cover, making it all of one piece of gold. ⁹The cherubim faced each other and looked down on the atonement cover. With their wings spread above it, they protected it.

Building the Table

¹⁰Then Bezalel* made the table of acacia wood, 36 inches long, 18 inches wide, and 27 inches high.* ¹¹He overlaid it with pure gold and ran a gold molding around the edge. ¹²He decorated it with a 3-inch border* all around, and he ran a gold molding along the border. ¹³Then he cast four gold rings for the table

---

36:8 Hebrew *he*; also in 36:16, 20, 35. See 37:1. **36:9** Hebrew *28 cubits* [12.9 meters] *long and 4 cubits* [1.8 meters] *wide*. **36:15** Hebrew *30 cubits* [13.8 meters] *long and 4 cubits* [1.8 meters] *wide*. **36:21** Hebrew *10 cubits* [4.6 meters] *high and 1.5 cubits* [69 centimeters] *wide*. **37:1** Hebrew *2.5 cubits* [115 centimeters] *long, 1.5 cubits* [69 centimeters] *wide, and 1.5 cubits high*. **37:6** Hebrew *2.5 cubits* [115 centimeters] *long and 1.5 cubits* [69 centimeters] *wide*. **37:10a** Hebrew *he*; also in 37:17, 25. **37:10b** Hebrew *2 cubits* [92 centimeters] *long, 1 cubit* [46 centimeters] *wide, and 1.5 cubits* [69 centimeters] *high*. **37:12** Hebrew *a border of a handbreadth* [8 centimeters].

and attached them at the four corners next to the four legs. ¹⁴The rings were attached near the border to hold the poles that were used to carry the table. ¹⁵He made these poles from acacia wood and overlaid them with gold. ¹⁶Then he made special containers of pure gold for the table—bowls, ladles, jars, and pitchers—to be used in pouring out liquid offerings.

Building the Lampstand

¹⁷Then Bezalel made the lampstand of pure, hammered gold. He made the entire lampstand and its decorations of one piece—the base, center stem, lamp cups, buds, and petals. ¹⁸The lampstand had six branches going out from the center stem, three on each side. ¹⁹Each of the six branches had three lamp cups shaped like almond blossoms, complete with buds and petals. ²⁰The center stem of the lampstand was crafted with four lamp cups shaped like almond blossoms, complete with buds and petals. ²¹There was an almond bud beneath each pair of branches where the six branches extended from the center stem, all made of one piece. ²²The almond buds and branches were all of one piece with the center stem, and they were hammered from pure gold.

²³He also made seven lamps for the lampstand, lamp snuffers, and trays, all of pure gold. ²⁴The entire lampstand, along with its accessories, was made from 75 pounds* of pure gold.

Building the Incense Altar

²⁵Then Bezalel made the incense altar of acacia wood. It was 18 inches square and 36 inches high,* with horns at the corners carved from the same piece of wood as the altar itself. ²⁶He overlaid the top, sides, and horns of the altar with pure gold, and he ran a gold molding around the entire altar. ²⁷He made two gold rings and attached them on opposite sides of the altar below the gold molding to hold the carrying poles. ²⁸He made the poles of acacia wood and overlaid them with gold.

²⁹Then he made the sacred anointing oil and the fragrant incense, using the techniques of a skilled incense maker.

Building the Altar of Burnt Offering

38 Next Bezalel* used acacia wood to construct the square altar of burnt offering. It was 7½ feet wide, 7½ feet long, and 4½ feet high.* ²He made horns for each of its four corners so that the horns and altar were all one piece. He overlaid the altar with bronze. ³Then he made all the altar utensils of bronze—the ash buckets, shovels, basins, meat forks, and firepans. ⁴Next he made a bronze grating and installed it halfway down the side of the altar, under the ledge. ⁵He cast four rings and attached them to the corners of the bronze grating to hold the carrying poles. ⁶He made the poles from acacia wood and overlaid them with bronze. ⁷He inserted the poles through the rings on the sides of the altar. The altar was hollow and was made from planks.

Building the Washbasin

⁸Bezalel made the bronze washbasin and its bronze stand from bronze mirrors donated by the women who served at the entrance of the Tabernacle.*

Building the Courtyard

⁹Then Bezalel made the courtyard, which was enclosed with curtains made of finely woven linen. On the south side the curtains were 150 feet long.* ¹⁰They were held up by twenty posts set securely in twenty bronze bases. He hung the curtains with silver hooks and rings. ¹¹He made a similar set of curtains for the north side—150 feet of curtains held up by twenty posts set securely in bronze bases. He hung the curtains with silver hooks and rings. ¹²The curtains on the west end of the courtyard were 75 feet long,* hung with silver hooks and rings and supported by ten posts set into ten bases. ¹³The east end, the front, was also 75 feet long.

¹⁴The courtyard entrance was on the east end, flanked by two curtains. The curtain on the right side was 22½ feet long* and was supported by three posts set into three bases. ¹⁵The curtain on the left side was also 22½ feet long and was supported by three posts set into three bases. ¹⁶All the curtains used in the courtyard were made of finely woven linen. ¹⁷Each post had a bronze base, and all the hooks and rings were silver. The tops of the posts of the courtyard were overlaid with silver, and the rings to hold up the curtains were made of silver.

¹⁸He made the curtain for the entrance to the courtyard of finely woven linen, and he decorated it with beautiful embroidery in blue, purple, and scarlet thread. It was 30 feet long, and its height was 7½ feet,* just like the curtains of the courtyard walls. ¹⁹It was supported by four posts, each set securely in its own bronze base. The tops of the posts were

---

37:24 Hebrew *1 talent* [34 kilograms]. **37:25** Hebrew *1 cubit* [46 centimeters] *long and 1 cubit wide, a square, and 2 cubits* [92 centimeters] *high*. **38:1a** Hebrew *he;* also in 38:8, 9. **38:1b** Hebrew *5 cubits* [2.3 meters] *wide, 5 cubits long, a square, and 3 cubits* [1.4 meters] *high*. **38:8** Hebrew *Tent of Meeting;* also in 38:30. **38:9** Hebrew *100 cubits* [46 meters]; also in 38:11. **38:12** Hebrew *50 cubits* [23 meters]; also in 38:13. **38:14** Hebrew *15 cubits* [6.9 meters]; also in 38:15. **38:18** Hebrew *20 cubits* [9.2 meters] *long and 5 cubits* [2.3 meters] *high*.

38:1-20 This section reports on building the courtyard (38:9-20) and its equipment, including the altar of burnt offering (38:1-7) and the washbasin (38:8).
38:21-29 The immense amount of metal in this inventory (more than a ton of gold, almost four tons of silver, and two-and-a-half tons of bronze) reflects the Egyptians' eagerness to send the Israelites away. They gave the Israelites anything they asked for their departure (see 12:35-36).

present it at the altar. ⁹The priest will take a representative portion of the grain offering and burn it on the altar. It is a special gift, a pleasing aroma to the LORD. ¹⁰The rest of the grain offering will then be given to Aaron and his sons as their food. This offering will be considered a most holy part of the special gifts presented to the LORD.

¹¹"Do not use yeast in preparing any of the grain offerings you present to the LORD, because no yeast or honey may be burned as a special gift presented to the LORD. ¹²You may add yeast and honey to an offering of the first crops of your harvest, but these must never be offered on the altar as a pleasing aroma to the LORD. ¹³Season all your grain offerings with salt to remind you of God's eternal covenant. Never forget to add salt to your grain offerings.

¹⁴"If you present a grain offering to the LORD from the first portion of your harvest, bring fresh grain that is coarsely ground and roasted on a fire. ¹⁵Put olive oil on this grain offering, and sprinkle it with frankincense. ¹⁶The priest will take a representative portion of the grain moistened with oil, together with all the frankincense, and burn it as a special gift presented to the LORD.

Procedures for the Peace Offering

3 "If you present an animal from the herd as a peace offering to the LORD, it may be a male or a female, but it must have no defects. ²Lay your hand on the animal's head, and slaughter it at the entrance of the Tabernacle.* Then Aaron's sons, the priests, will splatter its blood against all sides of the altar.

3:2 Hebrew *Tent of Meeting;* also in 3:8, 13.

Come Close   DISTANT: CALLED CLOSE

SCRIPTURE CONNECTION: LEVITICUS 1:4

Nothing brings comfort like being in God's presence. But during one season, I felt disconnected from God's closeness. It was a dull sensation. I knew God was still beside me, but it felt like I was constantly missing something. A tiredness of the soul seeped into my whole life.

At first, Leviticus may seem to be a book filled with confusing laws and intricate details about a time and culture that have nothing to do with our lives. How could ancient purification rituals help us draw closer to God? So I was shocked when the Holy Spirit used Leviticus 1:4 to open my eyes to see God's law and my season of distance in a fresh way.

This verse is about so much more than one detail of the ancient rituals; it is about a loving God calling his people into relationship. (In fact, the first words of this book, "The LORD called" [Leviticus 1:1], show how God reaches out to us *first*.) God was asking the Israelites to offer to him what was causing separation so he could remove the burden and guilt of sin and build a relationship.

I asked, *Am I ready to do what the altar represents—give everything to God?*

I wanted to skip the surrender part and do it myself. I was trying to make myself right, but I was leaving out the key part: letting God do it! I needed to ask, *Lord, what am I unwilling to sacrifice?* by saying, "Help me to freely surrender *all* to you."

Jesus made the ultimate sacrifice for our sins when he died on the cross, but so often we continue to try to purify ourselves. The Lord is saying, "Come close to me. Give me the offering of your burdens, timelines, to-do lists, anxieties, sins. Let's do this together."

> **REFLECT** "Lay your hand on the animal's head, and the LORD will accept its death in your place to purify you, making you right with him." LEVITICUS 1:4
>
> *Lord, what am I unwilling to sacrifice? Help me to freely surrender all to you. Amen.*
>
> **CONSIDER** "You must be willing to [eliminate] . . . every desire and affection not grounded in or directed toward God. But *you* don't eliminate it, God does." OSWALD CHAMBERS, *My Utmost for His Highest*

I wanted to skip surrender, but I was leaving out the key part: letting God do it!

EVIE POLSLEY, MS, loves stories of how God uses everyday people. A manager at Tyndale, her favorite roles are wife and mom.

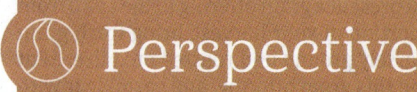

Perspective

What's up with all these sacrifices?

SCRIPTURE CONNECTION: LEVITICUS 1:1–7:38

At the end of Exodus, the visible presence of the Lord filled the Tabernacle. God's presence made it sacred, which meant it needed to be pure.

We can compare impurity and sacrifices to our modern understanding of bacteria and washing. We know that surgical areas need to be sterile, protecting the patient from harmful bacteria. Just as bacteria can't be allowed near a surgical patient, impurity can't come into God's presence.

Sacrifices were a means of cleansing those who wanted to be in the Lord's presence. Sometimes they needed cleansing because of sin. Other times they needed cleansing for different types of impurity, such as bodily emissions or skin diseases. These things weren't wrong or bad; they just weren't pure.

But some sacrifices weren't for cleansing sin or impurity. Instead, they were a way of saying thank you to God in worship. These offerings frequently included a meal shared with others.

Throughout the Bible, we see God making provision for his people to be pure so that we can be in his presence. In the Old Testament, God provided animal sacrifices. In the New Testament, God provided Jesus' death to purify us. In both eras, God invites his people to celebrate the sacrifice with one another and to delight in his presence.

VIEWPOINTS

THEIRS: *How can I enter the presence of a holy God?*

MINE: *"Jesus is the perfect sacrifice, making my relationship with God possible. Do I take that gift as seriously as I should? God is good, but he deserves reverence. I need to enter his presence with respect, awe, and gratitude."*

YOURS: *How might I demonstrate a recognition of God's holiness in my prayer, service, and worship?*

JENNIFER BROWN JONES, PhD, is an author, speaker, and instructor of Old Testament for Liberty University's PhD of Bible Exposition program. She loves helping others see how God speaks to them through the Bible today.

---

³The priest must present part of this peace offering as a special gift to the Lord. This includes all the fat around the internal organs, ⁴the two kidneys and the fat around them near the loins, and the long lobe of the liver. These must be removed with the kidneys, ⁵and Aaron's sons will burn them on top of the burnt offering on the wood burning on the altar. It is a special gift, a pleasing aroma to the Lord.

⁶"If you present an animal from the flock as a peace offering to the Lord, it may be a male or a female, but it must have no defects. ⁷If you present a sheep as your offering, bring it to the Lord, ⁸lay your hand on its head, and slaughter it in front of the Tabernacle. Aaron's sons will then splatter the sheep's blood against all sides of the altar. ⁹The priest must present the fat of this peace offering as a special gift to the Lord. This includes the fat of the broad tail cut off near the backbone, all the fat around the internal organs, ¹⁰the two kidneys and the fat around them near the loins, and the long lobe of the liver. These must be removed with the kidneys, ¹¹and the priest will burn them on the altar. It is a special gift of food presented to the Lord.

¹²"If you present a goat as your offering, bring it to the Lord, ¹³lay your hand on its head, and slaughter it in front of the Tabernacle. Aaron's sons will then splatter the goat's blood against all sides of the altar. ¹⁴The priest must present part of this offering as a special gift to the Lord. This includes all the fat around the internal organs, ¹⁵the two kidneys and the fat around them near the loins, and the long lobe of the liver. These must be removed with the kidneys, ¹⁶and the priest will burn them on the altar. It is a special gift of food, a pleasing aroma to the Lord. All the fat belongs to the Lord.

¹⁷"You must never eat any fat or blood. This is a permanent law for you, and it must be observed from generation to generation, wherever you live."

Procedures for the Sin Offering

4 Then the Lord said to Moses, ²"Give the following instructions to the people of Israel. This is how you are to deal with those who sin unintentionally by doing anything that violates one of the Lord's commands.

³"If the high priest* sins, bringing guilt upon the entire community, he must give a sin offering for the sin he has committed. He must present to the Lord a young bull with no defects. ⁴He must bring the bull to the Lord at the entrance of the Tabernacle,* lay

---

4:3 Hebrew *the anointed priest;* also in 4:5, 16.   **4:4** Hebrew *Tent of Meeting;* also in 4:5, 7, 14, 16, 18.

4:1–5:13 The sin offering may be better understood as a purification offering since it appears in contexts that involve both sin and ritual impurity. Merely offering a sacrifice did not suffice, though. The offeror also needed to repent or acknowledge impurity (5:5). The purification offering addressed unintentional violations rather than deliberate disobedience (Numbers 15:30-31).

his hand on the bull's head, and slaughter it before the Lord. ⁵The high priest will then take some of the bull's blood into the Tabernacle, ⁶dip his finger in the blood, and sprinkle it seven times before the Lord in front of the inner curtain of the sanctuary. ⁷The priest will then put some of the blood on the horns of the altar for fragrant incense that stands in the Lord's presence inside the Tabernacle. He will pour out the rest of the bull's blood at the base of the altar for burnt offerings at the entrance of the Tabernacle. ⁸Then the priest must remove all the fat of the bull to be offered as a sin offering. This includes all the fat around the internal organs, ⁹the two kidneys and the fat around them near the loins, and the long lobe of the liver. He must remove these along with the kidneys, ¹⁰just as he does with cattle offered as a peace offering, and burn them on the altar of burnt offerings. ¹¹But he must take whatever is left of the bull—its hide, meat, head, legs, internal organs, and dung—¹²and carry it away to a place outside the camp that is ceremonially clean, the place where the ashes are dumped. There, on the ash heap, he will burn it on a wood fire.

¹³"If the entire Israelite community sins by violating one of the Lord's commands, but the people don't realize it, they are still guilty. ¹⁴When they become aware of their sin, the people must bring a young bull as an offering for their sin and present it before the Tabernacle. ¹⁵The elders of the community must then lay their hands on the bull's head and slaughter it before the Lord. ¹⁶The high priest will then take some of the bull's blood into the Tabernacle, ¹⁷dip his finger in the blood, and sprinkle it seven times before the Lord in front of the inner curtain. ¹⁸He will then put some of the blood on the horns of the altar for fragrant incense that stands in the Lord's presence inside the Tabernacle. He will pour out the rest of the blood at the base of the altar for burnt offerings at the entrance of the Tabernacle. ¹⁹Then the priest must remove all the animal's fat and burn it on the altar, ²⁰just as he does with the bull offered as a sin offering for the high priest. Through this process, the priest will purify the people, making them right with the Lord,* and they will be forgiven. ²¹Then the priest must take what is left of the bull and carry it outside the camp and burn it there, just as is done with the sin offering for the high priest. This offering is for the sin of the entire congregation of Israel.

²²"If one of Israel's leaders sins by violating one of the commands of the Lord his God but doesn't realize it, he is still guilty. ²³When he becomes aware of his sin, he must bring as his offering a male goat with no defects. ²⁴He must lay his hand on the goat's head and slaughter it at the place where burnt offerings are slaughtered before the Lord. This is an offering for his sin. ²⁵Then the priest will dip his finger in the blood of the sin offering and put it on the horns of the altar for burnt offerings. He will pour out the rest of the blood at the base of the altar. ²⁶Then he must burn all the goat's fat on the altar, just as he does with the peace offering. Through this process, the priest will purify the leader from his sin, making him right with the Lord, and he will be forgiven.

²⁷"If any of the common people sin by violating one of the Lord's commands, but they don't realize it, they are still guilty. ²⁸When they become aware of their sin, they must bring as an offering for their sin a female goat with no defects. ²⁹They must lay a hand on the head of the sin offering and slaughter it at the place where burnt offerings are slaughtered. ³⁰Then the priest will dip his finger in the blood and put it on the horns of the altar for burnt offerings. He will pour out the rest of the blood at the base of the altar. ³¹Then he must remove all the goat's fat, just as he does with the fat of the peace offering. He will burn the fat on the altar, and it will be a pleasing aroma to the Lord. Through this process, the priest will purify the people, making them right with the Lord, and they will be forgiven.

³²"If the people bring a sheep as their sin offering, it must be a female with no defects. ³³They must lay a hand on the head of the sin offering and slaughter it at the place where burnt offerings are slaughtered. ³⁴Then the priest will dip his finger in the blood of the sin offering and put it on the horns of the altar for burnt offerings. He will pour out the rest of the blood at the base of the altar. ³⁵Then he must remove all the sheep's fat, just as he does with the fat of a sheep presented as a peace offering. He will burn the fat on the altar on top of the special gifts presented to the Lord. Through this process, the priest will purify the people from their sin, making them right with the Lord, and they will be forgiven.

Sins Requiring a Sin Offering

5 "If you are called to testify about something you have seen or that you know about, it is sinful to refuse to testify, and you will be punished for your sin.

²"Or suppose you unknowingly touch something that is ceremonially unclean, such as the carcass of an unclean animal. When you realize what you have done, you must admit your defilement and your guilt. This is true whether it is a wild animal, a domestic animal, or an animal that scurries along the ground.

³"Or suppose you unknowingly touch something that makes a person unclean. When you realize what you have done, you must admit your guilt.

⁴"Or suppose you make a foolish vow of any kind, whether its purpose is for good or for bad. When you realize its foolishness, you must admit your guilt.

⁵"When you become aware of your guilt in any of

4:20 Or *will make atonement for the people;* similarly in 4:26, 31, 35.

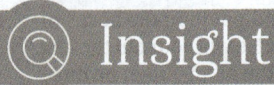

Insight: ISRAEL'S SACRIFICES

The book of Leviticus details instructions for sacrifices the people were to give to God. Some offered so God could forgive wrongdoing, or sin, while others simply honored and thanked God. All the sacrifices helped the Israelites live in God's presence. This chart describes each sacrifice in Leviticus 1–7.

OFFERING	DESCRIPTION	PURPOSE	EXAMPLES
BURNT OFFERING Leviticus 1:2-17; 6:8-13	*Atoning sacrifice* of a bull, ram, or male bird with no physical defect	To restore a person to closeness with God by forgiving wrongdoing, or sin.	Exodus 18:12; 29:38-42; 1 Chronicles 21:18–22:1; Job 42:8; Isaiah 1:11-20; Hebrews 10:1-18
GRAIN OFFERING Leviticus 2; 6:14-23; 7:9-10	*Non-atoning sacrifice* of grain, choice flour, or baked breads with olive oil, frankincense, and salt	To honor God with a worshipful gift	Nehemiah 10:33-39; 2 Corinthians 9:6-15
PEACE OFFERING Leviticus 3; 7:11-36; 22:21	*Non-atoning sacrifice* of any animal from the flock or herd, along with baked breads	To thank God through worship and sharing a meal with family and friends	Exodus 24:9-11; 1 Samuel 9:15-25; Acts 2:42; 1 Corinthians 11:17-34
SIN OFFERING Leviticus 4:1–5:13; 6:24-30; 16:3-22	*Atoning sacrifice* of animals with no physical defects. The required offering varied with the situation and station of the person receiving its benefits.	To seek forgiveness from God for unintentional sins of ritual impurity, neglect, or thoughtlessness	Numbers 15:22-31; Hebrews 10:26-31; 1 John 1:8-9
GUILT OFFERING Leviticus 5:14–6:7; 7:1-7	*Atoning sacrifice* of a ram or lamb with no physical defects	To pay for sins against God and the community	Matthew 5:23-24; Romans 6:12-23; 7:21–8:4

these ways, you must confess your sin. ⁶Then you must bring to the Lord as the penalty for your sin a female from the flock, either a sheep or a goat. This is a sin offering with which the priest will purify you from your sin, making you right with the Lord.*

⁷"But if you cannot afford to bring a sheep, you may bring to the Lord two turtledoves or two young pigeons as the penalty for your sin. One of the birds will be for a sin offering, and the other for a burnt offering. ⁸You must bring them to the priest, who will present the first bird as the sin offering. He will wring its neck but without severing its head from the body. ⁹Then he will sprinkle some of the blood of the sin offering against the sides of the altar, and the rest of the blood will be drained out at the base of the altar. This is an offering for sin. ¹⁰The priest will then prepare the second bird as a burnt offering, following all the procedures that have been prescribed. Through this process the priest will purify you from your sin, making you right with the Lord, and you will be forgiven.

¹¹"If you cannot afford to bring two turtledoves or two young pigeons, you may bring two quarts* of choice flour for your sin offering. Since it is an offering for sin, you must not moisten it with olive oil or put any frankincense on it. ¹²Take the flour to the priest, who will scoop out a handful as a representative portion. He will burn it on the altar on top of the special gifts presented to the Lord. It is an offering for sin. ¹³Through this process, the priest will purify those who are guilty of any of these sins, making them right with the Lord, and they will be forgiven. The rest of the flour will belong to the priest, just as with the grain offering."

5:6 Or *will make atonement for you for your sin;* similarly in 5:10, 13, 16, 18. **5:11** Hebrew ¹⁄₁₀ *of an ephah* [2.2 liters].

Procedures for the Guilt Offering

[14] Then the LORD said to Moses, [15] "If one of you commits a sin by unintentionally defiling the LORD's sacred property, you must bring a guilt offering to the LORD. The offering must be your own ram with no defects, or you may buy one of equal value with silver, as measured by the weight of the sanctuary shekel.* [16] You must make restitution for the sacred property you have harmed by paying for the loss, plus an additional 20 percent. When you give the payment to the priest, he will purify you with the ram sacrificed as a guilt offering, making you right with the LORD, and you will be forgiven.

[17] "Suppose you sin by violating one of the LORD's commands. Even if you are unaware of what you have done, you are guilty and will be punished for your sin. [18] For a guilt offering, you must bring to the priest your own ram with no defects, or you may buy one of equal value. Through this process the priest will purify you from your unintentional sin, making you right with the LORD, and you will be forgiven. [19] This is a guilt offering, for you have been guilty of an offense against the LORD."

Sins Requiring a Guilt Offering

6 [1]*Then the LORD said to Moses, [2] "Suppose one of you sins against your associate and is unfaithful to the LORD. Suppose you cheat in a deal involving a security deposit, or you steal or commit fraud, [3] or you find lost property and lie about it, or you lie while swearing to tell the truth, or you commit any other such sin. [4] If you have sinned in any of these ways, you are guilty. You must give back whatever you stole, or the money you took by extortion, or the security deposit, or the lost property you found, [5] or anything obtained by swearing falsely. You must make restitution by paying the full price plus an additional 20 percent to the person you have harmed. On the same day you must present a guilt offering. [6] As a guilt offering to the LORD, you must bring to the priest your own ram with no defects, or you may buy one of equal value. [7] Through this process, the priest will purify you before the LORD, making you right with him,* and you will be forgiven for any of these sins you have committed."

Further Instructions for the Burnt Offering

[8]*Then the LORD said to Moses, [9] "Give Aaron and his sons the following instructions regarding the burnt offering. The burnt offering must be left on top of the altar until the next morning, and the fire on the altar must be kept burning all night. [10] In the morning, after the priest on duty has put on his official linen clothing and linen undergarments, he must clean out the ashes of the burnt offering and put them beside the altar. [11] Then he must take off these garments, change back into his regular clothes, and carry the ashes outside the camp to a place that is ceremonially clean. [12] Meanwhile, the fire on the altar must be kept burning; it must never go out. Each morning the priest will add fresh wood to the fire and arrange the burnt offering on it. He will then burn the fat of the peace offerings on it. [13] Remember, the fire must be kept burning on the altar at all times. It must never go out.

Further Instructions for the Grain Offering

[14] "These are the instructions regarding the grain offering. Aaron's sons must present this offering to the LORD in front of the altar. [15] The priest on duty will take from the grain offering a handful of the choice flour moistened with olive oil, together with all the frankincense. He will burn this representative portion on the altar as a pleasing aroma to the LORD. [16] Aaron and his sons may eat the rest of the flour, but it must be baked without yeast and eaten in a sacred place within the courtyard of the Tabernacle.* [17] Remember, it must never be prepared with yeast. I have given it to the priests as their share of the special gifts presented to me. Like the sin offering and the guilt offering, it is most holy. [18] Any of Aaron's male descendants may eat from the special gifts presented to the LORD. This is their permanent right from generation to generation. Anyone or anything that touches these offerings will become holy."

Procedures for the Ordination Offering

[19] Then the LORD said to Moses, [20] "On the day Aaron and his sons are anointed, they must present to the

---

5:15 Each shekel was about 0.4 ounces or 11 grams in weight. **6:1** Verses 6:1-7 are numbered 5:20-26 in Hebrew text. **6:7** Or *will make atonement for you before the LORD*. **6:8** Verses 6:8-30 are numbered 6:1-23 in Hebrew text. **6:16** Hebrew *Tent of Meeting;* also in 6:26, 30.

5:14–6:7 The guilt offering covered wrongful actions involving sacred things. It also provided for sins against other people when the offender was unaware of the wrong. Finally, the guilt offering was used in situations where someone acted fraudulently or deceitfully toward another. In such cases, the offender needed to make restitution to the person they had harmed.
6:2-3 For those who follow God, there really is no such thing as a "secular" sin. All sin involves God, even sin directed against another person or group. In the sins requiring a guilt offering, God's forgiveness was needed and would be granted, but restitution to the injured individual had to be made first (6:4-7; see also Matthew 5:23-24). A guilt offering could free a person from punishment for unintentional offenses against *sacred* property (Leviticus 5:14-16), as well as accidental and intentional offenses against *secular* property could be forgiven.
6:5 The instructions for the guilt offering assumed that a person's conscience would induce voluntary repayment for damages. When restitution was voluntary, the surcharge for loss of use to the owner was always 20 percent. Penalties were more severe in other cases (see Exodus 22:1-15). There is a clear difference between voluntary confession and simply admitting sin after being caught.

LORD the standard grain offering of two quarts* of choice flour, half to be offered in the morning and half to be offered in the evening. ²¹It must be carefully mixed with olive oil and cooked on a griddle. Then slice* this grain offering and present it as a pleasing aroma to the LORD. ²²In each generation, the high priest* who succeeds Aaron must prepare this same offering. It belongs to the LORD and must be burned up completely. This is a permanent law. ²³All such grain offerings of a priest must be burned up entirely. None of it may be eaten."

Further Instructions for the Sin Offering

²⁴Then the LORD said to Moses, ²⁵"Give Aaron and his sons the following instructions regarding the sin offering. The animal given as an offering for sin is a most holy offering, and it must be slaughtered in the LORD's presence at the place where the burnt offerings are slaughtered. ²⁶The priest who offers the sacrifice as a sin offering must eat his portion in a sacred place within the courtyard of the Tabernacle. ²⁷Anyone or anything that touches the sacrificial meat will become holy. If any of the sacrificial blood spatters on a person's clothing, the soiled garment must be washed in a sacred place. ²⁸If a clay pot is used to boil the sacrificial meat, it must then be broken. If a bronze pot is used, it must be scoured and thoroughly rinsed with water. ²⁹Any male from a priest's family may eat from this offering; it is most holy. ³⁰But the offering for sin may not be eaten if its blood was brought into the Tabernacle as an offering for purification* in the Holy Place. It must be completely burned with fire.

Further Instructions for the Guilt Offering

7 "These are the instructions for the guilt offering. It is most holy. ²The animal sacrificed as a guilt offering must be slaughtered at the place where the burnt offerings are slaughtered, and its blood must be splattered against all sides of the altar. ³The priest will then offer all its fat on the altar, including the fat of the broad tail, the fat around the internal organs, ⁴the two kidneys and the fat around them near the loins, and the long lobe of the liver. These are to be removed with the kidneys, ⁵and the priests will burn them on the altar as a special gift presented to the LORD. This is the guilt offering. ⁶Any male from a priest's family may eat the meat. It must be eaten in a sacred place, for it is most holy.

⁷"The same instructions apply to both the guilt offering and the sin offering. Both belong to the priest who uses them to purify someone, making that person right with the LORD.* ⁸In the case of the burnt offering, the priest may keep the hide of the sacrificed animal. ⁹Any grain offering that has been baked in an oven, prepared in a pan, or cooked on a griddle belongs to the priest who presents it. ¹⁰All other grain offerings, whether made of dry flour or flour moistened with olive oil, are to be shared equally among all the priests, the descendants of Aaron.

Further Instructions for the Peace Offering

¹¹"These are the instructions regarding the different kinds of peace offerings that may be presented to the LORD. ¹²If you present your peace offering as an expression of thanksgiving, the usual animal sacrifice must be accompanied by various kinds of bread made without yeast—thin cakes mixed with olive oil, wafers spread with oil, and cakes made of choice flour mixed with olive oil. ¹³This peace offering of thanksgiving must also be accompanied by loaves of bread made with yeast. ¹⁴One of each kind of bread must be presented as a gift to the LORD. It will then belong to the priest who splatters the blood of the peace offering against the altar. ¹⁵The meat of the peace offering of thanksgiving must be eaten on the same day it is offered. None of it may be saved for the next morning.

¹⁶"If you bring an offering to fulfill a vow or as a voluntary offering, the meat must be eaten on the same day the sacrifice is offered, but whatever is left over may be eaten on the second day. ¹⁷Any meat left over until the third day must be completely burned up. ¹⁸If any of the meat from the peace offering is eaten on the third day, the person who presented it will not be accepted by the LORD. You will receive no credit for offering it. By then the meat will be contaminated; if you eat it, you will be punished for your sin.

¹⁹"Meat that touches anything ceremonially unclean may not be eaten; it must be completely burned up. The rest of the meat may be eaten, but only by people who are ceremonially clean. ²⁰If you are ceremonially unclean and you eat meat from a peace offering that was presented to the LORD, you will be cut off from the community. ²¹If you touch anything that is unclean (whether it is human defilement or an unclean animal or any other unclean, detestable thing) and then eat meat from a peace offering presented to the LORD, you will be cut off from the community."

The Forbidden Blood and Fat

²²Then the LORD said to Moses, ²³"Give the following instructions to the people of Israel. You must never eat fat, whether from cattle, sheep, or goats. ²⁴The fat of an animal found dead or torn to pieces by wild animals must never be eaten, though it may be used for any other purpose. ²⁵Anyone who eats fat from

---

6:20 Hebrew ¹⁄₁₀ of an ephah [2.2 liters]. 6:21 The meaning of this Hebrew term is uncertain. 6:22 Hebrew the anointed priest. 6:30 Or an offering to make atonement. 7:7 Or to make atonement.

an animal presented as a special gift to the LORD will be cut off from the community. ²⁶No matter where you live, you must never consume the blood of any bird or animal. ²⁷Anyone who consumes blood will be cut off from the community."

A Portion for the Priests

²⁸Then the LORD said to Moses, ²⁹"Give the following instructions to the people of Israel. When you present a peace offering to the LORD, bring part of it as a gift to the LORD. ³⁰Present it to the LORD with your own hands as a special gift to the LORD. Bring the fat of the animal, together with the breast, and lift up the breast as a special offering to the LORD. ³¹Then the priest will burn the fat on the altar, but the breast will belong to Aaron and his descendants. ³²Give the right thigh of your peace offering to the priest as a gift. ³³The right thigh must always be given to the priest who offers the blood and the fat of the peace offering. ³⁴For I have reserved the breast of the special offering and the right thigh of the sacred offering for the priests. It is the permanent right of Aaron and his descendants to share in the peace offerings brought by the people of Israel. ³⁵This is their rightful share. The special gifts presented to the LORD have been reserved for Aaron and his descendants from the time they were set apart to serve the LORD as priests. ³⁶On the day they were anointed, the LORD commanded the Israelites to give these portions to the priests as their permanent share from generation to generation."

³⁷These are the instructions for the burnt offering, the grain offering, the sin offering, and the guilt offering, as well as the ordination offering and the peace offering. ³⁸The LORD gave these instructions to Moses on Mount Sinai when he commanded the Israelites to present their offerings to the LORD in the wilderness of Sinai.

Ordination of the Priests

8 Then the LORD said to Moses, ²"Bring Aaron and his sons, along with their sacred garments, the anointing oil, the bull for the sin offering, the two rams, and the basket of bread made without yeast, ³and call the entire community of Israel together at the entrance of the Tabernacle.*"

⁴So Moses followed the LORD's instructions, and the whole community assembled at the Tabernacle entrance. ⁵Moses announced to them, "This is what the LORD has commanded us to do!" ⁶Then he presented Aaron and his sons and washed them with water. ⁷He put the official tunic on Aaron and tied the sash around his waist. He dressed him in the robe, placed the ephod on him, and attached the ephod securely with its decorative sash. ⁸Then Moses placed the chestpiece on Aaron and put the Urim and the Thummim inside it. ⁹He placed the turban on Aaron's head and attached the gold medallion—the badge of holiness—to the front of the turban, just as the LORD had commanded him.

¹⁰Then Moses took the anointing oil and anointed the Tabernacle and everything in it, making them holy. ¹¹He sprinkled the oil on the altar seven times, anointing it and all its utensils, as well as the washbasin and its stand, making them holy. ¹²Then he poured some of the anointing oil on Aaron's head, anointing him and making him holy for his work. ¹³Next Moses presented Aaron's sons. He clothed them in their tunics, tied their sashes around them, and put their special head coverings on them, just as the LORD had commanded him.

¹⁴Then Moses presented the bull for the sin offering. Aaron and his sons laid their hands on the bull's head, ¹⁵and Moses slaughtered it. Moses took some of the blood, and with his finger he put it on the four horns of the altar to purify it. He poured out the rest of the blood at the base of the altar. Through this process, he made the altar holy by purifying it.* ¹⁶Then Moses took all the fat around the internal organs, the long lobe of the liver, and the two kidneys and the fat around them, and he burned it all on the altar. ¹⁷He took the rest of the bull, including its hide, meat, and dung, and burned it on a fire outside the camp, just as the LORD had commanded him.

¹⁸Then Moses presented the ram for the burnt offering. Aaron and his sons laid their hands on the ram's head, ¹⁹and Moses slaughtered it. Then Moses took the ram's blood and splattered it against all sides of the altar. ²⁰Then he cut the ram into pieces, and he burned the head, some of its pieces, and the fat on the altar. ²¹After washing the internal organs and the legs with water, Moses burned the entire ram on the altar as a burnt offering. It was a pleasing aroma, a special gift presented to the LORD, just as the LORD had commanded him.

²²Then Moses presented the other ram, which was the ram of ordination. Aaron and his sons laid their hands on the ram's head, ²³and Moses slaughtered

---

8:3 Hebrew *Tent of Meeting;* also in 8:4, 31, 33, 35. **8:15** Or *by making atonement for it;* or *that offerings for purification might be made on it.*

7:28-36 While only men of a specific family lineage could be priests, all adult Israelites were invited and instructed to participate in worship. Women brought sacrifices, made vows, participated in sacred festivals, and shared in the food from the offerings.

8:1-36 In Exodus 28–29, the Lord gave Moses specific instructions for clothing and for ordaining Aaron and his sons as priests. In Exodus 39:1-31; 40:12-16; and Leviticus 8, the commands were carried out. Moses didn't just pass along the instructions verbally; he enacted the rituals to provide an example for the priests down to the last detail, "just as the LORD had commanded him" (8:9, 13, 17, 21, 29). Because the penalty for disobedience was death, God made sure the priests knew exactly what to do.

it. Then Moses took some of its blood and applied it to the lobe of Aaron's right ear, the thumb of his right hand, and the big toe of his right foot. ²⁴Next Moses presented Aaron's sons and applied some of the blood to the lobes of their right ears, the thumbs of their right hands, and the big toes of their right feet. He then splattered the rest of the blood against all sides of the altar.

²⁵Next Moses took the fat, including the fat of the broad tail, the fat around the internal organs, the long lobe of the liver, and the two kidneys and the fat around them, along with the right thigh. ²⁶On top of these he placed a thin cake of bread made without yeast, a cake of bread mixed with olive oil, and a wafer spread with olive oil. All these were taken from the basket of bread made without yeast that was placed in the Lord's presence. ²⁷He put all these in the hands of Aaron and his sons, and he lifted these gifts as a special offering to the Lord. ²⁸Moses then took all the offerings back from them and burned them on the altar on top of the burnt offering. This was the ordination offering. It was a pleasing aroma, a special gift presented to the Lord. ²⁹Then Moses took the breast and lifted it up as a special offering to the Lord. This was Moses' portion of the ram of ordination, just as the Lord had commanded him.

³⁰Next Moses took some of the anointing oil and some of the blood that was on the altar, and he sprinkled them on Aaron and his garments and on his sons and their garments. In this way, he made Aaron and his sons and their garments holy.

³¹Then Moses said to Aaron and his sons, "Boil the remaining meat of the offerings at the Tabernacle entrance, and eat it there, along with the bread that is in the basket of offerings for the ordination, just as I commanded when I said, 'Aaron and his sons will eat it.' ³²Any meat or bread that is left over must then be burned up. ³³You must not leave the Tabernacle entrance for seven days, for that is when the ordination ceremony will be completed. ³⁴Everything we have done today was commanded by the Lord in order to purify you, making you right with him.* ³⁵Now stay at the entrance of the Tabernacle day and night for seven days, and do everything the Lord requires. If you fail to do this, you will die, for this is what the Lord has commanded." ³⁶So Aaron and his sons did everything the Lord had commanded through Moses.

The Priests Begin Their Work

9 After the ordination ceremony, on the eighth day, Moses called together Aaron and his sons and the elders of Israel. ²He said to Aaron, "Take a young bull for a sin offering and a ram for a burnt offering, both without defects, and present them to the Lord. ³Then tell the Israelites, 'Take a male goat for a sin offering, and take a calf and a lamb, both a year old and without defects, for a burnt offering. ⁴Also take a bull* and a ram for a peace offering and flour moistened with olive oil for a grain offering. Present all these offerings to the Lord because the Lord will appear to you today.'"

⁵So the people presented all these things at the entrance of the Tabernacle,* just as Moses had commanded. Then the whole community came forward and stood before the Lord. ⁶And Moses said, "This is what the Lord has commanded you to do so that the glory of the Lord may appear to you."

⁷Then Moses said to Aaron, "Come to the altar and sacrifice your sin offering and your burnt offering to purify yourself and the people. Then present the offerings of the people to purify them, making them right with the Lord,* just as he has commanded."

⁸So Aaron went to the altar and slaughtered the calf as a sin offering for himself. ⁹His sons brought him the blood, and he dipped his finger in it and put it on the horns of the altar. He poured out the rest of the blood at the base of the altar. ¹⁰Then he burned on the altar the fat, the kidneys, and the long lobe of the liver from the sin offering, just as the Lord had commanded Moses. ¹¹The meat and the hide, however, he burned outside the camp.

¹²Next Aaron slaughtered the animal for the burnt offering. His sons brought him the blood, and he splattered it against all sides of the altar. ¹³Then they handed him each piece of the burnt offering, including the head, and he burned them on the altar. ¹⁴Then he washed the internal organs and the legs and burned them on the altar along with the rest of the burnt offering.

¹⁵Next Aaron presented the offerings of the people. He slaughtered the people's goat and presented it as

8:34 Or *to make atonement for you.* 9:4 Or *cow;* also in 9:18, 19. 9:5 Hebrew *Tent of Meeting;* also in 9:23. 9:7 Or *to make atonement for them.*

8:34 The details of the sacrifice rituals were symbolic and important in their own right. But most important, the priests were to obey God's commands. Complete obedience to God is a major theme in both the Old Testament and the New Testament: "Obedience is better than sacrifice" (1 Samuel 15:22).
9:2-4 These sacrifices—the sin and burnt offerings for the priests and the sin, burnt, peace, and grain offerings for the people—were offered at the beginning of the priests' ministry to make certain that all sin was atoned for and the covenant with God affirmed. Only the guilt offering was omitted.

9:6 Just as holiness describes God's person and nature, the "glory of the Lord" tangibly expresses his power and majesty (see Ezekiel 1:28; 10:4). God's glory was revealed on Mount Sinai (Exodus 24:16), at the dedication of the Tabernacle (Exodus 40:34-35), and in Solomon's Temple (1 Kings 8:11; 2 Chronicles 7:1). Yet it remained as vast as the heavens (Psalm 19:1). The New Testament speaks of God's glory being manifested by the Son and of Christ's glory as the image of God (2 Corinthians 4:4). Jesus was glorified in his death and resurrection (John 17:1-5).

an offering for their sin, just as he had first done with the offering for his own sin. ¹⁶Then he presented the burnt offering and sacrificed it in the prescribed way. ¹⁷He also presented the grain offering, burning a handful of the flour mixture on the altar, in addition to the regular burnt offering for the morning.

¹⁸Then Aaron slaughtered the bull and the ram for the people's peace offering. His sons brought him the blood, and he splattered it against all sides of the altar. ¹⁹Then he took the fat of the bull and the ram—the fat of the broad tail and from around the internal organs—along with the kidneys and the long lobes of the livers. ²⁰He placed these fat portions on top of the breasts of these animals and burned them on the altar. ²¹Aaron then lifted up the breasts and right thighs as a special offering to the LORD, just as Moses had commanded.

²²After that, Aaron raised his hands toward the people and blessed them. Then, after presenting the sin offering, the burnt offering, and the peace

Theos
IMAGE — MY STORY WITH GOD

God's Glory: An Invitation to Awe

SCRIPTURE CONNECTION: LEVITICUS 9:22-24

Have you ever seen something that took your breath away? Maybe it was a newborn baby. Or a double rainbow on the horizon. Such things arrest our attention, leading us to pause in awe.

These sights give us a faint glimpse of what the Bible calls the glory of the Lord. They are visible reminders that show the goodness, greatness, and grandeur of our invisible God. Seeing God's glory shows us what God is like. God is marked by absolute perfection. Pure goodness. True gentleness. Undistracted, undiluted, unconditional love.

We can also glimpse God's glory in simple things—the unprovoked kindness of a stranger, the effervescent joy of a child, the undeserved forgiveness of someone we wronged.

All of these glimpses remind me that God is real, powerful, active, creative, and purposeful. My perspective elevates, and my hope swells that God will also bring power, creativity, and purpose to my life. As I notice God's glory, my expectations and my courage lift. I, too, can choose goodness, gentleness, and unconditional love.

> God is marked by absolute perfection. Pure goodness. True gentleness. Undistracted, undiluted, unconditional love.

IMAGINE

What makes you pause in awe?

Whose life has shown you God?

"As we bring goodness, gentleness, and unconditional love into our relationships and world, we extend God's glory into the homes and workplaces where we live and lead. God worked through Moses to help his community experience God's glory; our lives can do the same."

MINDY CALIGUIRE is founder and president of Soul Care, dedicated to increasing soul health in the Body of Christ. Her books include *Discovering Soul Care* and *Spiritual Friendships*.

offering, he stepped down from the altar. ²³Then Moses and Aaron went into the Tabernacle, and when they came back out, they blessed the people again, and the glory of the LORD appeared to the whole community. ²⁴Fire blazed forth from the LORD's presence and consumed the burnt offering and the fat on the altar. When the people saw this, they shouted with joy and fell face down on the ground.

The Sin of Nadab and Abihu

10 Aaron's sons Nadab and Abihu put coals of fire in their incense burners and sprinkled incense over them. In this way, they disobeyed the LORD by burning before him the wrong kind of fire, different than he had commanded. ²So fire blazed forth from the LORD's presence and burned them up, and they died there before the LORD.

³Then Moses said to Aaron, "This is what the LORD meant when he said,

'I will display my holiness
through those who come near me.
I will display my glory
before all the people.'"

And Aaron was silent.

⁴Then Moses called for Mishael and Elzaphan, Aaron's cousins, the sons of Aaron's uncle Uzziel. He said to them, "Come forward and carry away the bodies of your relatives from in front of the sanctuary to a place outside the camp." ⁵So they came forward and picked them up by their garments and carried them out of the camp, just as Moses had commanded.

⁶Then Moses said to Aaron and his sons Eleazar and Ithamar, "Do not show grief by leaving your hair uncombed* or by tearing your clothes. If you do, you will die, and the LORD's anger will strike the whole community of Israel. However, the rest of the Israelites, your relatives, may mourn because of the LORD's fiery destruction of Nadab and Abihu. ⁷But you must not leave the entrance of the Tabernacle* or you will die, for you have been anointed with the LORD's anointing oil." So they did as Moses commanded.

Instructions for Priestly Conduct

⁸Then the LORD said to Aaron, ⁹"You and your descendants must never drink wine or any other alcoholic drink before going into the Tabernacle. If you do, you will die. This is a permanent law for you, and it must be observed from generation to generation. ¹⁰You must distinguish between what is sacred and what is common, between what is ceremonially unclean and what is clean. ¹¹And you must teach the Israelites all the decrees that the LORD has given them through Moses."

¹²Then Moses said to Aaron and his remaining sons, Eleazar and Ithamar, "Take what is left of the grain offering after a portion has been presented as a special gift to the LORD, and eat it beside the altar. Make sure it contains no yeast, for it is most holy. ¹³You must eat it in a sacred place, for it has been given to you and your descendants as your portion of the special gifts presented to the LORD. These are the commands I have been given. ¹⁴But the breast and thigh that were lifted up as a special offering may be eaten in any place that is ceremonially clean. These parts have been given to you and your descendants as your portion of the peace offerings presented by the people of Israel. ¹⁵You must lift up the thigh and breast as a special offering to the LORD, along with the fat of the special gifts. These parts will belong to you and your descendants as your permanent right, just as the LORD has commanded."

¹⁶Moses then asked them what had happened to the goat of the sin offering. When he discovered it had been burned up, he became very angry with Eleazar and Ithamar, Aaron's remaining sons. ¹⁷"Why didn't you eat the sin offering in the sacred area?" he demanded. "It is a holy offering! The LORD has given it to you to remove the guilt of the community and to purify the people, making them right with the LORD.* ¹⁸Since the animal's blood was not brought into the Holy Place, you should have eaten the meat in the sacred area as I ordered you."

¹⁹Then Aaron answered Moses, "Today my sons presented both their sin offering and their burnt offering to the LORD. And yet this tragedy has happened to me. If I had eaten the people's sin offering on such a tragic day as this, would the LORD have been pleased?" ²⁰And when Moses heard this, he was satisfied.

Ceremonially Clean and Unclean Animals

11 Then the LORD said to Moses and Aaron, ²"Give the following instructions to the people of Israel.

"Of all the land animals, these are the ones you may use for food. ³You may eat any animal that has completely split hooves and chews the cud. ⁴You may not,

---

10:6 Or *by uncovering your heads.* **10:7** Hebrew *Tent of Meeting;* also in 10:9. **10:17** Or *to make atonement for the people before the LORD.*

10:1-7 God is good, but being in his holy presence can be a dangerous thing. In fact, as the ancient Israelites discovered, it was a matter of life and death, and thus something to be taken very seriously. For failing to demonstrate reverence and obedience, Nadab and Abihu paid with their lives. Moses commanded the priests not to mourn, as mourning could have conveyed sympathy for or solidarity with family members who had blatantly disobeyed God's instructions.

11:1–15:33 These chapters detail the regulations pertaining to purity. The mixing of types of things was forbidden (see Deuteronomy 22:9-11) because it represented a violation of the normal created order. "Abnormal" creatures—such as fish without fins and scales, carnivores, crawling insects, and animals without split hooves—were not to cross boundaries with "normal" types and were unfit for food or offerings (see also Deuteronomy 14:1-21). The dietary, health, and sanitary laws were meant to distinguish Israel as a holy people from those of the surrounding nations (Leviticus 11:44-45).

Insight: HOLY, CLEAN, AND UNCLEAN

The practices establishing cleanness and uncleanness set Israel apart as God's chosen people and enabled them to live in the presence of a holy God. What is unclean is not necessarily sinful but represents a kind of unworthiness that cannot come into contact with what is holy. If it is cleansed, it acquires the potential for holiness and may be dedicated to God. Clean and unclean were not moral designations, and people and most objects would go through normal cycles of holy, clean, and unclean.

however, eat the following animals* that have split hooves or that chew the cud, but not both. The camel chews the cud but does not have split hooves, so it is ceremonially unclean for you. ⁵The hyrax* chews the cud but does not have split hooves, so it is unclean. ⁶The hare chews the cud but does not have split hooves, so it is unclean. ⁷The pig has evenly split hooves but does not chew the cud, so it is unclean. ⁸You may not eat the meat of these animals or even touch their carcasses. They are ceremonially unclean for you.

⁹"Of all the marine animals, these are ones you may use for food. You may eat anything from the water if it has both fins and scales, whether taken from salt water or from streams. ¹⁰But you must never eat animals from the sea or from rivers that do not have both fins and scales. They are detestable to you. This applies both to little creatures that live in shallow water and to all creatures that live in deep water. ¹¹They will always be detestable to you. You must never eat their meat or even touch their dead bodies. ¹²Any marine animal that does not have both fins and scales is detestable to you.

¹³"These are the birds that are detestable to you. You must never eat them: the griffon vulture, the bearded vulture, the black vulture, ¹⁴the kite, falcons of all kinds, ¹⁵ravens of all kinds, ¹⁶the eagle owl, the short-eared owl, the seagull, hawks of all kinds, ¹⁷the little owl, the cormorant, the great owl, ¹⁸the barn owl, the desert owl, the Egyptian vulture, ¹⁹the stork, herons of all kinds, the hoopoe, and the bat.

²⁰"You must not eat winged insects that walk along the ground; they are detestable to you. ²¹You may, however, eat winged insects that walk along the ground and have jointed legs so they can jump. ²²The insects you are permitted to eat include all kinds of locusts, bald locusts, crickets, and grasshoppers. ²³All other winged insects that walk along the ground are detestable to you.

11:4 The identification of some of the animals, birds, and insects in this chapter is uncertain. **11:5** Or *coney*, or *rock badger*.

11:2-8 Some scholars have suggested that unclean animals were to be avoided for reasons of public health, but the evidence does not support this. Horse meat, for example, is no less healthy than beef, yet it was considered unclean because the horse does not have a split hoof (see 11:2-3). The regulations existed because an unclean animal was unacceptable as an offering to God and, therefore, it was also unacceptable as food for God's people. Jesus proclaimed all foods clean (Mark 7:14-19; Acts 10:9-16).

Perspective

Why did having a baby make her unclean?

SCRIPTURE CONNECTION: LEVITICUS 12:1-8

Levitical laws addressed safety, protection, and quality of life. After a woman gave birth to a child, she was considered unclean (for a period of seven days for a son and fourteen days for a daughter) because of the bodily discharges of giving birth. She could not take part in religious activities until she completed her purification (a process that took forty days for a son and eighty days for a daughter).

From today's vantage point, this may seem excessive. But if we consider this purification period as a means of rest and protection for the mother and baby, we find God's wisdom and kindness for women woven into this ritual.

VIEWPOINTS

HERS: *Would an Israelite woman have viewed her season of purification as a blessing or setback? Why?*

MINE: *"When I read about purification here, I think of the 'forgotten ones'—postpartum mamas who must try to return to the tasks of life and do 'everything' during a vulnerable season. I advocate for women so they will not fall prey to postpartum depression and so their babies can thrive in their first year."*

YOURS: *How have you seen God's wisdom and kindness in a season of pause? Could he use that time to purify you? To protect you and give you rest?*

QUANTRILLA ARD, PhD, is a faith-based personal and spiritual development author, speaker, Bible teacher, and literary agent who believes in the power of collective strength, community, and fellowship.

---

24 "The following creatures will make you ceremonially unclean. If any of you touch their carcasses, you will be defiled until evening. 25 If you pick up their carcasses, you must wash your clothes, and you will remain defiled until evening.

26 "Any animal that has split hooves that are not evenly divided or that does not chew the cud is unclean for you. If you touch the carcass of such an animal, you will be defiled. 27 Of the animals that walk on all fours, those that have paws are unclean. If you touch the carcass of such an animal, you will be defiled until evening. 28 If you pick up its carcass, you must wash your clothes, and you will remain defiled until evening. These animals are unclean for you.

29 "Of the small animals that scurry along the ground, these are unclean for you: the mole rat, the rat, large lizards of all kinds, 30 the gecko, the monitor lizard, the common lizard, the sand lizard, and the chameleon. 31 All these small animals are unclean for you. If any of you touch the dead body of such an animal, you will be defiled until evening. 32 If such an animal dies and falls on something, that object will be unclean. This is true whether the object is made of wood, cloth, leather, or burlap. Whatever its use, you must dip it in water, and it will remain defiled until evening. After that, it will be ceremonially clean and may be used again.

33 "If such an animal falls into a clay pot, everything in the pot will be defiled, and the pot must be smashed. 34 If the water from such a container spills on any food, the food will be defiled. And any beverage in such a container will be defiled. 35 Any object on which the carcass of such an animal falls will be defiled. If it is an oven or hearth, it must be destroyed, for it is defiled, and you must treat it accordingly.

36 "However, if the carcass of such an animal falls into a spring or a cistern, the water will still be clean. But anyone who touches the carcass will be defiled. 37 If the carcass falls on seed grain to be planted in the field, the seed will still be considered clean. 38 But if the seed is wet when the carcass falls on it, the seed will be defiled.

39 "If an animal you are permitted to eat dies and you touch its carcass, you will be defiled until evening. 40 If you eat any of its meat or carry away its carcass, you must wash your clothes, and you will remain defiled until evening.

41 "All small animals that scurry along the ground are detestable, and you must never eat them. 42 This includes all animals that slither along on their bellies, as well as those with four legs and those with many feet. All such animals that scurry along the ground are detestable, and you must never eat them. 43 Do not defile yourselves by touching them. You must not make yourselves ceremonially unclean because of them. 44 For I am the LORD your God. You must consecrate yourselves and be holy, because I am holy. So do not defile yourselves with any of these small animals that scurry along the ground. 45 For I, the LORD, am the one who brought you up from the land of Egypt, that I might be your God. Therefore, you must be holy because I am holy.

46 "These are the instructions regarding land animals, birds, marine creatures, and animals that scurry along the ground. 47 By these instructions you will know what is unclean and clean, and which animals may be eaten and which may not be eaten."

Purification after Childbirth

12 The LORD said to Moses, ²"Give the following instructions to the people of Israel. If a woman becomes pregnant and gives birth to a son, she will be ceremonially unclean for seven days, just as she is unclean during her menstrual period. ³On the eighth day the boy's foreskin must be circumcised. ⁴After waiting thirty-three days, she will be purified from the bleeding of childbirth. During this time of purification, she must not touch anything that is set apart as holy. And she must not enter the sanctuary until her time of purification is over. ⁵If a woman gives birth to a daughter, she will be ceremonially unclean for two weeks, just as she is unclean during her menstrual period. After waiting sixty-six days, she will be purified from the bleeding of childbirth.

⁶"When the time of purification is completed for either a son or a daughter, the woman must bring a one-year-old lamb for a burnt offering and a young pigeon or turtledove for a purification offering. She must bring her offerings to the priest at the entrance of the Tabernacle.* ⁷The priest will then present them to the LORD to purify her.* Then she will be ceremonially clean again after her bleeding at childbirth. These are the instructions for a woman after the birth of a son or a daughter.

⁸"If a woman cannot afford to bring a lamb, she must bring two turtledoves or two young pigeons. One will be for the burnt offering and the other for the purification offering. The priest will sacrifice them to purify her, and she will be ceremonially clean."

Serious Skin Diseases

13 The LORD said to Moses and Aaron, ²"If anyone has a swelling or a rash or discolored skin that might develop into a serious skin disease,* that person must be brought to Aaron the priest or to one of his sons.* ³The priest will examine the affected area of the skin. If the hair in the affected area has turned white and the problem appears to be more than skin-deep, it is a serious skin disease, and the priest who examines it must pronounce the person ceremonially unclean.

⁴"But if the affected area of the skin is only a white discoloration and does not appear to be more than skin-deep, and if the hair on the spot has not turned white, the priest will quarantine the person for seven days. ⁵On the seventh day the priest will make another examination. If he finds the affected area has not changed and the problem has not spread on the skin, the priest will quarantine the person for seven more days. ⁶On the seventh day the priest will make another examination. If he finds the affected area has faded and has not spread, the priest will pronounce the person ceremonially clean. It was only a rash. The person's clothing must be washed, and the person will be ceremonially clean. ⁷But if the rash continues to spread after the person has been examined by the priest and has been pronounced clean, the infected person must return to be examined again. ⁸If the priest finds that the rash has spread, he must pronounce the person ceremonially unclean, for it is indeed a skin disease.

⁹"Anyone who develops a serious skin disease must go to the priest for an examination. ¹⁰If the priest finds a white swelling on the skin, and some hair on the spot has turned white, and there is an open sore in the affected area, ¹¹it is a chronic skin disease, and the priest must pronounce the person ceremonially unclean. In such cases the person need not be quarantined, for it is obvious that the skin is defiled by the disease.

¹²"Now suppose the disease has spread all over the person's skin, covering the body from head to foot. ¹³When the priest examines the infected person and finds that the disease covers the entire body, he will pronounce the person ceremonially clean. Since the skin has turned completely white, the person is clean. ¹⁴But if any open sores appear, the infected person will be pronounced ceremonially unclean. ¹⁵The priest must make this pronouncement as soon as he sees an open sore, since open sores indicate the presence of a skin disease. ¹⁶However, if the open sores heal and turn white like the rest of the skin, the person must return to the priest ¹⁷for another examination. If the affected areas have indeed turned white, the priest will then pronounce the person ceremonially clean by declaring, 'You are clean!'

¹⁸"If anyone has a boil on the skin that has started to heal, ¹⁹but a white swelling or a reddish white

---

12:6 Hebrew *Tent of Meeting.* **12:7** Or *to make atonement for her;* also in 12:8. **13:2a** Traditionally rendered *leprosy.* The Hebrew word used throughout this passage is used to describe various skin diseases. **13:2b** Or *one of his descendants.*

12:2-5 Various reasons have been proposed for the longer impurity period following a daughter's birth. One possibility is that, since the female infant carried the prospect of future menstrual bleeding, the mother was also thought to bear the daughter's potential for ritual uncleanness—thus necessitating the longer timeframe (see also Leviticus 15:25). Regardless, these special provisions are not meant to construe a value judgment. Women were a source of life and the continuation of God's holy people; all people bear the image of God (Genesis 1:26-27).

13:1–14:57 Concerning the regulations pertaining to infections, the principle of normal and abnormal comes into play again (see "Holy, Clean, and Unclean" on page 143). Whether in a person, clothing, or a building, infections are not normal: They indicate disease and death, the opposite of wholeness, and were therefore declared unclean.

13:2 Skin disorders that were potentially contagious, such as "swelling or a rash or discolored skin," required precautions to stop their spread. Until a disorder was healed, the person was considered unclean. The diseases described in this section (Leviticus 13:1-46) may range from something as simple as an allergic rash, ringworm, or eczema to something as serious as gangrene. In Old Testament times, skin conditions were diagnosed by observation. The priests not only had a religious function but they also served as physicians.

spot develops in its place, that person must go to the priest to be examined. ²⁰If the priest examines it and finds it to be more than skin-deep, and if the hair in the affected area has turned white, the priest must pronounce the person ceremonially unclean. The boil has become a serious skin disease. ²¹But if the priest finds no white hair on the affected area and the problem appears to be no more than skin-deep and has faded, the priest must quarantine the person for seven days. ²²If during that time the affected area spreads on the skin, the priest must pronounce the person ceremonially unclean, because it is a serious disease. ²³But if the area grows no larger and does not spread, it is merely the scar from the boil, and the priest will pronounce the person ceremonially clean.

²⁴"If anyone has suffered a burn on the skin and the burned area changes color, becoming either reddish white or shiny white, ²⁵the priest must examine it. If he finds that the hair in the affected area has turned white and the problem appears to be more than skin-deep, a skin disease has broken out in the burn. The priest must then pronounce the person ceremonially unclean, for it is clearly a serious skin disease. ²⁶But if the priest finds no white hair on the affected area and the problem appears to be no more than skin-deep and has faded, the priest must quarantine the infected person for seven days. ²⁷On the seventh day the priest must examine the person again. If the affected area has spread on the skin, the priest must pronounce that person ceremonially unclean, for it is clearly a serious skin disease. ²⁸But if the affected area has not changed or spread on the skin and has faded, it is simply a swelling from the burn. The priest will then pronounce the person ceremonially clean, for it is only the scar from the burn.

²⁹"If anyone, either a man or woman, has a sore on the head or chin, ³⁰the priest must examine it. If he finds it is more than skin-deep and has fine yellow hair on it, the priest must pronounce the person ceremonially unclean. It is a scabby sore of the head or chin. ³¹If the priest examines the scabby sore and finds that it is only skin-deep but there is no black hair on it, he must quarantine the person for seven days. ³²On the seventh day the priest must examine the sore again. If he finds that the scabby sore has not spread, and there is no yellow hair on it, and it appears to be only skin-deep, ³³the person must shave off all hair except the hair on the affected area. Then the priest must quarantine the person for another seven days. ³⁴On the seventh day he will examine the sore again. If it has not spread and appears to be no more than skin-deep, the priest will pronounce the person ceremonially clean. The person's clothing must be washed, and the person will be ceremonially clean. ³⁵But if the scabby sore begins to spread after the person is pronounced clean, ³⁶the priest must do another examination. If he finds that the sore has spread, the priest does not need to look for yellow hair. The infected person is ceremonially unclean. ³⁷But if the color of the scabby sore does not change and black hair has grown on it, it has healed. The priest will then pronounce the person ceremonially clean.

³⁸"If anyone, either a man or woman, has shiny white patches on the skin, ³⁹the priest must examine the affected area. If he finds that the shiny patches are only pale white, this is a harmless skin rash, and the person is ceremonially clean.

⁴⁰"If a man loses his hair and his head becomes bald, he is still ceremonially clean. ⁴¹And if he loses hair on his forehead, he simply has a bald forehead; he is still clean. ⁴²However, if a reddish white sore appears on the bald area on top of his head or on his forehead, this is a skin disease. ⁴³The priest must examine him, and if he finds swelling around the reddish white sore anywhere on the man's head and it looks like a skin disease, ⁴⁴the man is indeed infected with a skin disease and is unclean. The priest must pronounce him ceremonially unclean because of the sore on his head.

⁴⁵"Those who suffer from a serious skin disease must tear their clothing and leave their hair uncombed.* They must cover their mouth and call out, 'Unclean! Unclean!' ⁴⁶As long as the serious disease lasts, they will be ceremonially unclean. They must live in isolation in their place outside the camp.

Treatment of Contaminated Clothing

⁴⁷"Now suppose mildew* contaminates some woolen or linen clothing, ⁴⁸woolen or linen fabric, the hide of an animal, or anything made of leather. ⁴⁹If the contaminated area in the clothing, the animal hide, the fabric, or the leather article has turned greenish or reddish, it is contaminated with mildew and must be shown to the priest. ⁵⁰After examining the affected spot, the priest will put the article in quarantine for seven days. ⁵¹On the seventh day the priest must inspect it again. If the contaminated area has spread, the clothing or fabric or leather is clearly contaminated by a serious mildew and is ceremonially unclean. ⁵²The priest must burn the item— the clothing, the woolen or linen fabric, or piece of leather—for it has been contaminated by a serious mildew. It must be completely destroyed by fire.

⁵³"But if the priest examines it and finds that the contaminated area has not spread in the clothing, the fabric, or the leather, ⁵⁴the priest will order the object to be washed and then quarantined for seven more days. ⁵⁵Then the priest must examine the object again. If he finds that the contaminated area has not changed color after being washed, even if it did not spread, the object is defiled. It must be completely burned up, whether the contaminated spot* is on the inside or outside. ⁵⁶But if the priest

---

13:45 Or *and uncover their heads.* 13:47 Traditionally rendered *leprosy.* The Hebrew term used throughout this passage is the same term used for the various skin diseases described in 13:1-46. 13:55 The meaning of the Hebrew is uncertain.

examines it and finds that the contaminated area has faded after being washed, he must cut the spot from the clothing, the fabric, or the leather. ⁵⁷If the spot later reappears on the clothing, the fabric, or the leather article, the mildew is clearly spreading, and the contaminated object must be burned up. ⁵⁸But if the spot disappears from the clothing, the fabric, or the leather article after it has been washed, it must be washed again; then it will be ceremonially clean.

⁵⁹"These are the instructions for dealing with mildew that contaminates woolen or linen clothing or fabric or anything made of leather. This is how the priest will determine whether these items are ceremonially clean or unclean."

Cleansing from Skin Diseases

14 And the LORD said to Moses, ²"The following instructions are for those seeking ceremonial purification from a skin disease.* Those who have been healed must be brought to the priest, ³who will examine them at a place outside the camp. If the priest finds that someone has been healed of a serious skin disease, ⁴he will perform a purification ceremony, using two live birds that are ceremonially clean, a stick of cedar,* some scarlet yarn, and a hyssop branch. ⁵The priest will order that one bird be slaughtered over a clay pot filled with fresh water. ⁶He will take the live bird, the cedar stick, the scarlet yarn, and the hyssop branch, and dip them into the blood of the bird that was slaughtered over the fresh water. ⁷The priest will then sprinkle the blood of the dead bird seven times on the person being purified of the skin disease. When the priest has purified the person, he will release the live bird in the open field to fly away.

⁸"The persons being purified must then wash their clothes, shave off all their hair, and bathe themselves in water. Then they will be ceremonially clean and may return to the camp. However, they must remain outside their tents for seven days. ⁹On the seventh day they must again shave all the hair from their heads, including the hair of the beard and eyebrows. They must also wash their clothes and bathe themselves in water. Then they will be ceremonially clean.

¹⁰"On the eighth day each person being purified must bring two male lambs and a one-year-old female lamb, all with no defects, along with a grain offering of six quarts* of choice flour moistened with olive oil, and a cup* of olive oil. ¹¹Then the officiating priest will present that person for purification, along with the offerings, before the LORD at the entrance of the Tabernacle.* ¹²The priest will take one of the male lambs and the olive oil and present them as a guilt offering, lifting them up as a special offering before the LORD. ¹³He will then slaughter the male lamb in the sacred area where sin offerings and burnt offerings are slaughtered. As with the sin offering, the guilt offering belongs to the priest. It is a most holy offering. ¹⁴The priest will then take some of the blood of the guilt offering and apply it to the lobe of the right ear, the thumb of the right hand, and the big toe of the right foot of the person being purified.

¹⁵"Then the priest will pour some of the olive oil into the palm of his own left hand. ¹⁶He will dip his right finger into the oil in his palm and sprinkle some of it with his finger seven times before the LORD. ¹⁷The priest will then apply some of the oil in his palm over the blood from the guilt offering that is on the lobe of the right ear, the thumb of the right hand, and the big toe of the right foot of the person being purified. ¹⁸The priest will apply the oil remaining in his hand to the head of the person being purified. Through this process, the priest will purify* the person before the LORD.

¹⁹"Then the priest must present the sin offering to purify the person who was cured of the skin disease. After that, the priest will slaughter the burnt offering ²⁰and offer it on the altar along with the grain offering. Through this process, the priest will purify the person who was healed, and the person will be ceremonially clean.

²¹"But anyone who is too poor and cannot afford these offerings may bring one male lamb for a guilt offering, to be lifted up as a special offering for purification. The person must also bring two quarts* of choice flour moistened with olive oil for the grain offering and a cup of olive oil. ²²The offering must also include two turtledoves or two young pigeons, whichever the person can afford. One of the pair must be used for the sin offering and the other for a burnt offering. ²³On the eighth day of the purification ceremony, the person being purified must bring the offerings to the priest in the LORD's presence at the entrance of the Tabernacle. ²⁴The priest will take the lamb for the guilt offering, along with the olive oil, and lift them up as a special offering to the LORD. ²⁵Then the priest will slaughter the lamb for the guilt offering. He will take

---

14:2 Traditionally rendered *leprosy;* see note on 13:2a.   **14:4** Or *juniper;* also in 14:6, 49, 51.   **14:10a** Hebrew ³⁄₁₀ *of an ephah* [6.6 liters].   **14:10b** Hebrew *1 log* [0.3 liters]; also in 14:21.   **14:11** Hebrew *Tent of Meeting;* also in 14:23.   **14:18** Or *will make atonement for;* similarly in 14:19, 20, 21, 29, 31, 53.   **14:21** Hebrew ¹⁄₁₀ *of an ephah* [2.2 liters].

14:1-32 These verses, dealing with the purification of infected individuals, are best understood when read in conjunction with 13:1-46.

14:15-18 In the ancient world, olive oil was commonly used to aid healing (see Isaiah 1:6 where "soothing ointments" could alternately be translated "olive oil"; Luke 10:34). Its use here might symbolize the healing and cleansing of the infection, which allowed the person to return to the community. Perhaps it also represented restored union between God, the priest, and the worshiper.

some of its blood and apply it to the lobe of the right ear, the thumb of the right hand, and the big toe of the right foot of the person being purified. ²⁶"The priest will also pour some of the olive oil into the palm of his own left hand. ²⁷He will dip his right finger into the oil in his palm and sprinkle some of it seven times before the LORD. ²⁸The priest will then apply some of the oil in his palm over the blood from the guilt offering that is on the lobe of the right ear, the thumb of the right hand, and the big toe of the right foot of the person being purified. ²⁹The priest will apply the oil remaining in his hand to the head of the person being purified. Through this process, the priest will purify the person before the LORD.

³⁰"Then the priest will offer the two turtledoves or the two young pigeons, whichever the person can afford. ³¹One of them is for a sin offering and the other for a burnt offering, to be presented along with the grain offering. Through this process, the priest will purify the person before the LORD. ³²These are the instructions for purification for those who have recovered from a serious skin disease but who cannot afford to bring the offerings normally required for the ceremony of purification."

Treatment of Contaminated Houses

³³Then the LORD said to Moses and Aaron, ³⁴"When you arrive in Canaan, the land I am giving you as your own possession, I may contaminate some of the houses in your land with mildew.* ³⁵The owner of such a house must then go to the priest and say, 'It appears that my house has some kind of mildew.' ³⁶Before the priest goes in to inspect the house, he must have the house emptied so nothing inside will be pronounced ceremonially unclean. ³⁷Then the priest will go in and examine the mildew on the walls. If he finds greenish or reddish streaks and the contamination appears to go deeper than the wall's surface, ³⁸the priest will step outside the door and put the house in quarantine for seven days. ³⁹On the seventh day the priest must return for another inspection. If he finds that the mildew on the walls of the house has spread, ⁴⁰the priest must order that the stones from those areas be removed. The contaminated material will then be taken outside the town to an area designated as ceremonially unclean. ⁴¹Next the inside walls of the entire house must be scraped thoroughly and the scrapings dumped in the unclean place outside the town. ⁴²Other stones will be brought in to replace the ones that were removed, and the walls will be replastered.

⁴³"But if the mildew reappears after all the stones have been replaced and the house has been scraped and replastered, ⁴⁴the priest must return and inspect the house again. If he finds that the mildew has spread, the walls are clearly contaminated with a serious mildew, and the house is defiled. ⁴⁵It must be torn down, and all its stones, timbers, and plaster must be carried out of town to the place designated as ceremonially unclean. ⁴⁶Those who enter the house during the period of quarantine will be ceremonially unclean until evening, ⁴⁷and all who sleep or eat in the house must wash their clothing.

⁴⁸"But if the priest returns for his inspection and finds that the mildew has not reappeared in the house after the fresh plastering, he will pronounce it clean because the mildew is clearly gone. ⁴⁹To purify the house the priest must take two birds, a stick of cedar, some scarlet yarn, and a hyssop branch. ⁵⁰He will slaughter one of the birds over a clay pot filled with fresh water. ⁵¹He will take the cedar stick, the hyssop branch, the scarlet yarn, and the live bird, and dip them into the blood of the slaughtered bird and into the fresh water. Then he will sprinkle the house seven times. ⁵²When the priest has purified the house in exactly this way, ⁵³he will release the live bird in the open fields outside the town. Through this process, the priest will purify the house, and it will be ceremonially clean.

⁵⁴"These are the instructions for dealing with serious skin diseases,* including scabby sores; ⁵⁵and mildew,* whether on clothing or in a house; ⁵⁶and a swelling on the skin, a rash, or discolored skin. ⁵⁷This procedure will determine whether a person or object is ceremonially clean or unclean.

"These are the instructions regarding skin diseases and mildew."

Bodily Discharges

15 The LORD said to Moses and Aaron, ²"Give the following instructions to the people of Israel.

"Any man who has a bodily discharge is ceremonially unclean. ³This defilement is caused by his discharge, whether the discharge continues or stops. In either case the man is unclean. ⁴Any bed on which the man with the discharge lies and anything on which he sits will be ceremonially unclean. ⁵So if you touch the man's bed, you must wash your clothes and bathe yourself in water, and you will remain unclean until evening. ⁶If you sit where the man with the discharge has sat, you must wash your clothes and bathe yourself in water, and you will remain unclean until evening. ⁷If you touch the man with the discharge, you must wash your clothes and bathe yourself in water, and you will remain unclean until evening. ⁸If the man spits on you, you must wash your clothes and bathe yourself in water, and you will remain unclean until evening. ⁹Any saddle blanket on

---

14:34 Traditionally rendered *leprosy;* see note on 13:47. **14:54** Traditionally rendered *leprosy;* see note on 13:2a.
14:55 Traditionally rendered *leprosy;* see note on 13:47.

14:33-53 The contamination of buildings by rot or mildew made them unhealthy or even unsafe. These buildings were considered diseased and therefore not whole or clean (see "Holy, Clean, and Unclean" on page 143). The inspection and treatment process was similar to the one for mildew in clothing (13:47-59).

which the man rides will be ceremonially unclean. ¹⁰If you touch anything that was under the man, you will be unclean until evening. You must wash your clothes and bathe yourself in water, and you will remain unclean until evening. ¹¹If the man touches you without first rinsing his hands, you must wash your clothes and bathe yourself in water, and you will remain unclean until evening. ¹²Any clay pot the man touches must be broken, and any wooden utensil he touches must be rinsed with water.

¹³"When the man with the discharge is healed, he must count off seven days for the period of purification. Then he must wash his clothes and bathe himself in fresh water, and he will be ceremonially clean. ¹⁴On the eighth day he must get two turtledoves or two young pigeons and come before the LORD at the entrance of the Tabernacle* and give his offerings to the priest. ¹⁵The priest will offer one bird for a sin offering and the other for a burnt offering. Through this process, the priest will purify* the man before the LORD for his discharge.

¹⁶"Whenever a man has an emission of semen, he must bathe his entire body in water, and he will remain ceremonially unclean until the next evening.* ¹⁷Any clothing or leather with semen on it must be washed in water, and it will remain unclean until evening. ¹⁸After a man and a woman have sexual intercourse, they must each bathe in water, and they will remain unclean until the next evening.

¹⁹"Whenever a woman has her menstrual period, she will be ceremonially unclean for seven days. Anyone who touches her during that time will be unclean until evening. ²⁰Anything on which the woman lies or sits during the time of her period will be unclean. ²¹If any of you touch her bed, you must wash your clothes and bathe yourself in water, and you will remain unclean until evening. ²²If you touch any object she has sat on, you must wash your clothes and bathe yourself in water, and you will remain unclean until evening. ²³This includes her bed or any other object she has sat on; you will be unclean until evening if you touch it. ²⁴If a man has sexual intercourse with her and her blood touches him, her menstrual impurity will be transmitted to him. He will remain unclean for seven days, and any bed on which he lies will be unclean.

²⁵"If a woman has a flow of blood for many days that is unrelated to her menstrual period, or if the blood continues beyond the normal period, she is ceremonially unclean. As during her menstrual period, the woman will be unclean as long as the discharge continues. ²⁶Any bed she lies on and any object she sits on during that time will be unclean, just as during her normal menstrual period. ²⁷If any of you touch these things, you will be ceremonially unclean. You must wash your clothes and bathe yourself in water, and you will remain unclean until evening.

²⁸"When the woman's bleeding stops, she must count off seven days. Then she will be ceremonially clean. ²⁹On the eighth day she must bring two turtledoves or two young pigeons and present them to the priest at the entrance of the Tabernacle. ³⁰The priest will offer one for a sin offering and the other for a burnt offering. Through this process, the priest will purify her before the LORD for the ceremonial impurity caused by her bleeding.

³¹"This is how you will guard the people of Israel from ceremonial uncleanness. Otherwise they would die, for their impurity would defile my Tabernacle that stands among them. ³²These are the instructions for dealing with anyone who has a bodily discharge—a man who is unclean because of an emission of semen ³³or a woman during her menstrual period. It applies to any man or woman who has a bodily discharge, and to a man who has sexual intercourse with a woman who is ceremonially unclean."

The Day of Atonement

16 The LORD spoke to Moses after the death of Aaron's two sons, who died after they entered the LORD's presence and burned the wrong kind of fire before him. ²The LORD said to Moses, "Warn your brother, Aaron, not to enter the Most Holy Place behind the inner curtain whenever he chooses; if he does, he will die. For the Ark's cover—the place of atonement—is there, and I myself am present in the cloud above the atonement cover.

³"When Aaron enters the sanctuary area, he must follow these instructions fully. He must bring a young bull for a sin offering and a ram for a burnt offering. ⁴He must put on his linen tunic and the linen undergarments worn next to his body. He must tie the linen sash around his waist and put the linen turban on his head. These are sacred garments, so he must bathe himself in water before he puts them on.

15:14 Hebrew *Tent of Meeting;* also in 15:29.   15:15 Or *will make atonement for;* also in 15:30.   15:16 Hebrew *until evening;* also in 15:18.

15:19-30 Similar practices for handling impurity have appeared across many different cultures. For the ancient Israelites, periods of uncleanness—when a person was unable to touch something set apart as holy—could result from numerous scenarios. Such impurity often related to life and death—including the birth of a child or contact with a dead body. Blood represented life (Deuteronomy 12:23), a principle that probably informed the instructions here regarding menstruation. The types of offerings given after abnormal bleeding and childbirth were the same (Leviticus 12:6; 15:29). The so-called sin offering in 15:30 is better understood as a purification offering, as in 12:6; it was morally neutral.

16:1-34 The Israelite Day of Atonement (Yom Kippur) involved fasting, resting from work, and performing a sacrificial rite that cleansed both the sacred space and the people. This ritual ceremony provides the background for understanding Jesus' sacrificial death. Hebrews 9:11-28 describes Jesus as the ultimate high priest who entered the heavenly temple and made a one-time sacrifice of his own life, making all those who follow him right with God (see also 1 John 2:1-2).

⁵Aaron must take from the community of Israel two male goats for a sin offering and a ram for a burnt offering.

⁶"Aaron will present his own bull as a sin offering to purify himself and his family, making them right with the LORD.* ⁷Then he must take the two male goats and present them to the LORD at the entrance of the Tabernacle.* ⁸He is to cast sacred lots to determine which goat will be reserved as an offering to the LORD and which will carry the sins of the people to the wilderness of Azazel. ⁹Aaron will then present as a sin offering the goat chosen by lot for the LORD. ¹⁰The other goat, the scapegoat chosen by lot to be sent away, will be kept alive, standing before the LORD. When it is sent away to Azazel in the wilderness, the people will be purified and made right with the LORD.*

¹¹"Aaron will present his own bull as a sin offering to purify himself and his family, making them right with the LORD. After he has slaughtered the bull as a sin offering, ¹²he will fill an incense burner with burning coals from the altar that stands before the LORD. Then he will take two handfuls of fragrant powdered incense and will carry the burner and the incense behind the inner curtain. ¹³There in the LORD's presence he will put the incense on the burning coals so that a cloud of incense will rise over the Ark's cover—the place of atonement—that rests on the Ark of the Covenant.* If he follows these instructions, he will not die. ¹⁴Then he must take some of the blood of the bull, dip his finger in it, and sprinkle it on the east side of the atonement cover. He must sprinkle blood seven times with his finger in front of the atonement cover.

¹⁵"Then Aaron must slaughter the first goat as a sin offering for the people and carry its blood behind the inner curtain. There he will sprinkle the goat's blood over the atonement cover and in front of it, just as he did with the bull's blood. ¹⁶Through this process, he will purify* the Most Holy Place, and he will do the same for the entire Tabernacle, because of the defiling sin and rebellion of the Israelites. ¹⁷No one else is allowed inside the Tabernacle when Aaron enters it for the purification ceremony in the Most Holy Place. No one may enter until he comes out again after purifying himself, his family, and all the congregation of Israel, making them right with the LORD.

¹⁸"Then Aaron will come out to purify the altar that stands before the LORD. He will do this by taking some of the blood from the bull and the goat and putting it on each of the horns of the altar. ¹⁹Then he must sprinkle the blood with his finger seven times over the altar. In this way, he will cleanse it from Israel's defilement and make it holy.

²⁰"When Aaron has finished purifying the Most Holy Place and the Tabernacle and the altar, he must present the live goat. ²¹He will lay both of his hands on the goat's head and confess over it all the wickedness, rebellion, and sins of the people of Israel. In this way, he will transfer the people's sins to the head of the goat. Then a man specially chosen for the task will drive the goat into the wilderness. ²²As the goat goes into the wilderness, it will carry all the people's sins upon itself into a desolate land.

²³"When Aaron goes back into the Tabernacle, he must take off the linen garments he was wearing when he entered the Most Holy Place, and he must leave the garments there. ²⁴Then he must bathe himself with water in a sacred place, put on his regular garments, and go out to sacrifice a burnt offering for himself and a burnt offering for the people. Through this process, he will purify himself and the people, making them right with the LORD. ²⁵He must then burn all the fat of the sin offering on the altar.

²⁶"The man chosen to drive the scapegoat into the wilderness of Azazel must wash his clothes and bathe himself in water. Then he may return to the camp.

²⁷"The bull and the goat presented as sin offerings, whose blood Aaron takes into the Most Holy Place for the purification ceremony, will be carried outside the camp. The animals' hides, internal organs, and dung are all to be burned. ²⁸The man who burns them must wash his clothes and bathe himself in water before returning to the camp.

²⁹"On the tenth day of the appointed month in early autumn,* you must deny yourselves.* Neither native-born Israelites nor foreigners living among you may do any kind of work. This is a permanent law for you. ³⁰On that day offerings of purification will be made for you,* and you will be purified in the LORD's presence from all your sins. ³¹It will be a Sabbath day of complete rest for you, and you must deny yourselves. This is a permanent law for you. ³²In future generations, the purification* ceremony will be performed by the priest who has been anointed and ordained to serve as high priest in place of his ancestor Aaron. He will put on the holy linen garments ³³and purify the Most Holy Place, the Tabernacle, the

---

16:6 Or *to make atonement for himself and his family;* similarly in 16:11, 17b, 24, 34. **16:7** Hebrew *Tent of Meeting;* also in 16:16, 17, 20, 23, 33. **16:10** Or *wilderness, it will make atonement for the people.* **16:13** Hebrew *that is above the Testimony.* The Hebrew word for "testimony" refers to the terms of the LORD's covenant with Israel as written on stone tablets, which were kept in the Ark, and also to the covenant itself. **16:16** Or *make atonement for;* similarly in 16:17a, 18, 20, 27, 33. **16:29a** Hebrew *On the tenth day of the seventh month.* This day in the ancient Hebrew lunar calendar occurred in September or October. **16:29b** Or *must fast;* also in 16:31. **16:30** Or *atonement will be made for you, to purify you.* **16:32** Or *atonement.*

17:1–26:46 This section deals with how the community of Israel was to observe holiness. Holiness does not describe one attribute of God among many. Rather, it is the sum of all the attributes of his perfect person, nature, and character. His "glory" is the manifestation of these attributes (see 9:6). God's covenant with Israel meant that the people and the nation participated in God's holiness. This holiness depended on Israel's right relationship with God, which brought certain ethical and ritual expectations for Israel to uphold.

altar, the priests, and the entire congregation. ³⁴This is a permanent law for you, to purify the people of Israel from their sins, making them right with the LORD once each year."

Moses followed all these instructions exactly as the LORD had commanded him.

Prohibitions against Eating Blood

17 Then the LORD said to Moses, ²"Give the following instructions to Aaron and his sons and all the people of Israel. This is what the LORD has commanded.

³"If any native Israelite sacrifices a bull* or a lamb or a goat anywhere inside or outside the camp ⁴instead of bringing it to the entrance of the Tabernacle* to present it as an offering to the LORD, that person will be as guilty as a murderer.* Such a person has shed blood and will be cut off from the community. ⁵The purpose of this rule is to stop the Israelites from sacrificing animals in the open fields. It will ensure that they bring their sacrifices to the priest at the entrance of the Tabernacle, so he can present them to the LORD as peace offerings. ⁶Then the priest will be able to splatter the blood against the LORD's altar at the entrance of the Tabernacle, and he will burn the fat as a pleasing aroma to the LORD. ⁷The people must no longer be unfaithful to the LORD by offering sacrifices to the goat idols.* This is a permanent law for them, to be observed from generation to generation.

⁸"Give them this command as well. If any native Israelite or foreigner living among you offers a burnt offering or a sacrifice ⁹but does not bring it to the entrance of the Tabernacle to offer it to the LORD, that person will be cut off from the community.

¹⁰"And if any native Israelite or foreigner living among you eats or drinks blood in any form, I will turn against that person and cut him off from the community of your people, ¹¹for the life of the body is in its blood. I have given you the blood on the altar to purify you, making you right with the LORD.* It is the blood, given in exchange for a life, that makes purification possible. ¹²That is why I have said to the people of Israel, 'You must never eat or drink blood—neither you nor the foreigners living among you.'

¹³"And if any native Israelite or foreigner living among you goes hunting and kills an animal or bird that is approved for eating, he must drain its blood and cover it with earth. ¹⁴The life of every creature is in its blood. That is why I have said to the people of Israel, 'You must never eat or drink blood, for the life of any creature is in its blood.' So whoever consumes blood will be cut off from the community.

¹⁵"And if any native-born Israelites or foreigners eat the meat of an animal that died naturally or was torn up by wild animals, they must wash their clothes and bathe themselves in water. They will remain ceremonially unclean until evening, but then they will be clean. ¹⁶But if they do not wash their clothes and bathe themselves, they will be punished for their sin."

Forbidden Sexual Practices

18 Then the LORD said to Moses, ²"Give the following instructions to the people of Israel. I am the LORD your God. ³So do not act like the people in Egypt, where you used to live, or like the people of Canaan, where I am taking you. You must not imitate their way of life. ⁴You must obey all my regulations and be careful to obey my decrees, for I am the LORD your God. ⁵If you obey my decrees and my regulations, you will find life through them. I am the LORD.

⁶"You must never have sexual relations with a close relative, for I am the LORD.

⁷"Do not violate your father by having sexual relations with your mother. She is your mother; you must not have sexual relations with her.

⁸"Do not have sexual relations with any of your father's wives, for this would violate your father.

⁹"Do not have sexual relations with your sister or half sister, whether she is your father's daughter or your mother's daughter, whether she was born into your household or someone else's.

¹⁰"Do not have sexual relations with your granddaughter, whether she is your son's daughter or your daughter's daughter, for this would violate yourself.

¹¹"Do not have sexual relations with your stepsister, the daughter of any of your father's wives, for she is your sister.

¹²"Do not have sexual relations with your father's sister, for she is your father's close relative.

¹³"Do not have sexual relations with your mother's sister, for she is your mother's close relative.

¹⁴"Do not violate your uncle, your father's brother, by having sexual relations with his wife, for she is your aunt.

17:3 Or *cow.* 17:4a Hebrew *Tent of Meeting;* also in 17:5, 6, 9. 17:4b Hebrew *will be guilty of blood.* 17:7 Or *goat demons.* 17:11 Or *to make atonement for you.*

17:10-11 The people of Israel were forbidden to consume blood because it was symbolic of the life given by God and was reserved as God's portion of each animal offering. God had also designated the sacrificial blood as the means of atonement. In other words, God's grace permitted the life of the animal to be accepted in exchange for the life of the sinner. In the New Testament, the blood of Christ—representing his life freely given—has provided eternal redemption for those who follow him (Hebrews 9:12).

18:1-30; 20:1-27 Just as God gave serious attention to the ability to access the sacred space of the Tabernacle, he cares greatly about how people treat access to the human body, which in New Testament times is referred to as the temple of God's Spirit (1 Corinthians 6:18-20). Leviticus 18 identifies forbidden sexual practices, and Leviticus 20 outlines some of the penalties. The penalties—infertility, being cut off from the community, and death—show how seriously God takes sexual purity.

WHAT THE BIBLE SAYS ABOUT
Nourishing Our Bodies and Spirits

You satisfy the hunger and thirst of every living thing.

The Old Restriction Diet

"These are the instructions regarding land animals, birds, marine creatures, and animals that scurry along the ground. By these instructions you will know what is unclean and clean, and which animals may be eaten and which may not be eaten." LEVITICUS 11:46-47

"And if any native Israelite or foreigner living among you eats or drinks blood in any form, I will turn against that person and cut him off from the community of your people." LEVITICUS 17:10

Eat to Live

Do not carouse with drunkards
or feast with gluttons,
for they are on their way to
poverty,
and too much sleep clothes
them in rags.
PROVERBS 23:20-21

This is my body. . . .
Do this in remembrance of me.

Hunger for God

Yes, he humbled you by letting you go hungry and then feeding you with manna, a food previously unknown to you and your ancestors. He did it to teach you that people do not live by bread alone; rather, we live by every word that comes from the mouth of the LORD. **DEUTERONOMY 8:3**

God Feeds Us

The eyes of all look to you in hope;
    you give them their food as they need it.
When you open your hand,
    you satisfy the hunger and thirst of every living thing.
PSALM 145:15-16

On the night when he was betrayed, the Lord Jesus took some bread and gave thanks to God for it. Then he broke it in pieces and said, "This is my body, which is given for you. Do this in remembrance of me." In the same way, he took the cup of wine after supper, saying, "This cup is the new covenant between God and his people—an agreement confirmed with my blood. Do this in remembrance of me as often as you drink it." For every time you eat this bread and drink this cup, you are announcing the Lord's death until he comes again.
1 CORINTHIANS 11:23-26

The New Everything Diet

Then a voice said to [Peter], "Get up, Peter; kill and eat them."
"No, Lord," Peter declared. "I have never eaten anything that our Jewish laws have declared impure and unclean."
But the voice spoke again: "Do not call something unclean if God has made it clean."
ACTS 10:13-15

If I can thank God for the food and enjoy it, why should I be condemned for eating it? So whether you eat or drink, or whatever you do, do it all for the glory of God.
1 CORINTHIANS 10:30-31

¹⁵"Do not have sexual relations with your daughter-in-law; she is your son's wife, so you must not have sexual relations with her.

¹⁶"Do not have sexual relations with your brother's wife, for this would violate your brother.

¹⁷"Do not have sexual relations with both a woman and her daughter. And do not take* her granddaughter, whether her son's daughter or her daughter's daughter, and have sexual relations with her. They are close relatives, and this would be a wicked act.

¹⁸"While your wife is living, do not marry her sister and have sexual relations with her, for they would be rivals.

¹⁹"Do not have sexual relations with a woman during her period of menstrual impurity.

²⁰"Do not defile yourself by having sexual intercourse with your neighbor's wife.

²¹"Do not permit any of your children to be offered as a sacrifice to Molech, for you must not bring shame on the name of your God. I am the Lord.

²²"Do not practice homosexuality, having sex with another man as with a woman. It is a detestable sin.

²³"A man must not defile himself by having sex with an animal. And a woman must not offer herself to a male animal to have intercourse with it. This is a perverse act.

²⁴"Do not defile yourselves in any of these ways, for the people I am driving out before you have defiled themselves in all these ways. ²⁵Because the entire land has become defiled, I am punishing the people who live there. I will cause the land to vomit them out. ²⁶You must obey all my decrees and regulations. You must not commit any of these detestable sins. This applies both to native-born Israelites and to the foreigners living among you.

²⁷"All these detestable activities are practiced by the people of the land where I am taking you, and this is how the land has become defiled. ²⁸So do not defile the land and give it a reason to vomit you out, as it will vomit out the people who live there now. ²⁹Whoever commits any of these detestable sins will be cut off from the community of Israel. ³⁰So obey my instructions, and do not defile yourselves by committing any of these detestable practices that were committed by the people who lived in the land before you. I am the Lord your God."

Holiness in Personal Conduct

19 The Lord also said to Moses, ²"Give the following instructions to the entire community of Israel. You must be holy because I, the Lord your God, am holy.

³"Each of you must show great respect for your mother and father, and you must always observe my Sabbath days of rest. I am the Lord your God.

⁴"Do not put your trust in idols or make metal images of gods for yourselves. I am the Lord your God.

⁵"When you sacrifice a peace offering to the Lord, offer it properly so you* will be accepted by God. ⁶The sacrifice must be eaten on the same day you offer it or on the next day. Whatever is left over until the third day must be completely burned up. ⁷If any of the sacrifice is eaten on the third day, it will be contaminated, and I will not accept it. ⁸Anyone who eats it on the third day will be punished for defiling what is holy to the Lord and will be cut off from the community.

⁹"When you harvest the crops of your land, do not harvest the grain along the edges of your fields, and do not pick up what the harvesters drop. ¹⁰It is the same with your grape crop—do not strip every last bunch of grapes from the vines, and do not pick up the grapes that fall to the ground. Leave them for the poor and the foreigners living among you. I am the Lord your God.

¹¹"Do not steal.

"Do not deceive or cheat one another.

¹²"Do not bring shame on the name of your God by using it to swear falsely. I am the Lord.

¹³"Do not defraud or rob your neighbor.

"Do not make your hired workers wait until the next day to receive their pay.

¹⁴"Do not insult the deaf or cause the blind to stumble. You must fear your God; I am the Lord.

¹⁵"Do not twist justice in legal matters by favoring the poor or being partial to the rich and powerful. Always judge people fairly.

¹⁶"Do not spread slanderous gossip among your people.*

"Do not stand idly by when your neighbor's life is threatened. I am the Lord.

¹⁷"Do not nurse hatred in your heart for any of your relatives.* Confront people directly so you will not be held guilty for their sin.

¹⁸"Do not seek revenge or bear a grudge against a fellow Israelite, but love your neighbor as yourself. I am the Lord.

¹⁹"You must obey all my decrees.

"Do not mate two different kinds of animals. Do not plant your field with two different kinds of seed. Do not wear clothing woven from two different kinds of thread.

²⁰"If a man has sex with a slave girl whose freedom has never been purchased but who is committed to become another man's wife, he must pay full compensation to her master. But since she is not a

---

18:17 Or *do not marry.* 19:5 Or *it.* 19:16 Hebrew *Do not act as a merchant toward your own people.* 19:17 Hebrew *for your brother.*

19:1-37 Because God is holy, he calls his people to be holy. A life of holiness includes obedience to the Ten Commandments, five of which are repeated here. It also includes issues of justice and concern for inner thoughts. Here we find the statement, "Love your neighbor as yourself," which Jesus cites as one of the two most important commandments (Matthew 22:34-40). As we see from the statement's original context, this love involves actions and attitudes, not merely feelings or emotions. Likewise, holiness is not just some abstract concept; it has practical implications for everyday life.

free woman, neither the man nor the woman will be put to death. ²¹The man, however, must bring a ram as a guilt offering and present it to the LORD at the entrance of the Tabernacle.* ²²The priest will then purify him* before the LORD with the ram of the guilt offering, and the man's sin will be forgiven.

²³"When you enter the land and plant fruit trees, leave the fruit unharvested for the first three years and consider it forbidden.* Do not eat it. ²⁴In the fourth year the entire crop must be consecrated to the LORD as a celebration of praise. ²⁵Finally, in the fifth year you may eat the fruit. If you follow this pattern, your harvest will increase. I am the LORD your God.

²⁶"Do not eat meat that has not been drained of its blood.

"Do not practice fortune-telling or witchcraft. ²⁷"Do not trim off the hair on your temples or trim your beards.

²⁸"Do not cut your bodies for the dead, and do not mark your skin with tattoos. I am the LORD.

²⁹"Do not defile your daughter by making her a prostitute, or the land will be filled with prostitution and wickedness.

³⁰"Keep my Sabbath days of rest, and show reverence toward my sanctuary. I am the LORD.

³¹"Do not defile yourselves by turning to mediums or to those who consult the spirits of the dead. I am the LORD your God.

³²"Stand up in the presence of the elderly, and show respect for the aged. Fear your God. I am the LORD.

³³"Do not take advantage of foreigners who live among you in your land. ³⁴Treat them like native-born Israelites, and love them as you love yourself. Remember that you were once foreigners living in the land of Egypt. I am the LORD your God.

³⁵"Do not use dishonest standards when measuring length, weight, or volume. ³⁶Your scales and weights must be accurate. Your containers for measuring dry materials or liquids must be accurate.* I am the LORD your God who brought you out of the land of Egypt.

³⁷"You must be careful to keep all of my decrees and regulations by putting them into practice. I am the LORD."

Punishments for Disobedience

20 The LORD said to Moses, ²"Give the people of Israel these instructions, which apply both to native Israelites and to the foreigners living in Israel.

"If any of them offer their children as a sacrifice to Molech, they must be put to death. The people of the community must stone them to death. ³I myself will turn against them and cut them off from the community, because they have defiled my sanctuary and brought shame on my holy name by offering their children to Molech. ⁴And if the people of the community ignore those who offer their children to Molech and refuse to execute them, ⁵I myself will turn against them and their families and will cut them off from the community. This will happen to all who commit spiritual prostitution by worshiping Molech.

⁶"I will also turn against those who commit spiritual prostitution by putting their trust in mediums or in those who consult the spirits of the dead. I will cut them off from the community. ⁷So set yourselves apart to be holy, for I am the LORD your God. ⁸Keep all my decrees by putting them into practice, for I am the LORD who makes you holy.

⁹"Anyone who dishonors* father or mother must be put to death. Such a person is guilty of a capital offense.

¹⁰"If a man commits adultery with his neighbor's wife, both the man and the woman who have committed adultery must be put to death.

¹¹"If a man violates his father by having sex with one of his father's wives, both the man and the woman must be put to death, for they are guilty of a capital offense.

> "You are obliged to love your neighbor as yourself, and loving him, you ought to help him spiritually, with prayer, counseling him with words, and assisting him both spiritually and temporally, according to the need in which he may be, at least with your goodwill if you have nothing else."
>
> **CATHERINE OF SIENA**
> (1347–1380) spiritual writer, political influencer, and theologian

---

19:21 Hebrew *Tent of Meeting.* 19:22 Or *make atonement for him.* 19:23 Hebrew *consider it uncircumcised.* 19:36 Hebrew *Use an honest ephah* [a dry measure] *and an honest hin* [a liquid measure]. 20:9 Greek version reads *Anyone who speaks disrespectfully of.* Compare Matt 15:4; Mark 7:10.

¹²"If a man has sex with his daughter-in-law, both must be put to death. They have committed a perverse act and are guilty of a capital offense.

¹³"If a man practices homosexuality, having sex with another man as with a woman, both men have committed a detestable act. They must both be put to death, for they are guilty of a capital offense.

¹⁴"If a man marries both a woman and her mother, he has committed a wicked act. The man and both women must be burned to death to wipe out such wickedness from among you.

¹⁵"If a man has sex with an animal, he must be put to death, and the animal must be killed.

¹⁶"If a woman presents herself to a male animal to have intercourse with it, she and the animal must both be put to death. You must kill both, for they are guilty of a capital offense.

¹⁷"If a man marries his sister, the daughter of either his father or his mother, and they have sexual relations, it is a shameful disgrace. They must be publicly cut off from the community. Since the man has violated his sister, he will be punished for his sin.

¹⁸"If a man has sexual relations with a woman during her menstrual period, both of them must be cut off from the community, for together they have exposed the source of her blood flow.

¹⁹"Do not have sexual relations with your aunt, whether your mother's sister or your father's sister. This would dishonor a close relative. Both parties are guilty and will be punished for their sin.

²⁰"If a man has sex with his uncle's wife, he has violated his uncle. Both the man and woman will be punished for their sin, and they will die childless.

²¹"If a man marries his brother's wife, it is an act of impurity. He has violated his brother, and the guilty couple will remain childless.

²²"You must keep all my decrees and regulations by putting them into practice; otherwise the land to which I am bringing you as your new home will vomit you out. ²³Do not live according to the customs of the people I am driving out before you. It is because they do these shameful things that I detest them. ²⁴But I have promised you, 'You will possess their land because I will give it to you as your possession—a land flowing with milk and honey.' I am the LORD your God, who has set you apart from all other people.

²⁵"You must therefore make a distinction between ceremonially clean and unclean animals, and between clean and unclean birds. You must not defile yourselves by eating any unclean animal or bird or creature that scurries along the ground. I have identified them as being unclean for you. ²⁶You must be holy because I, the LORD, am holy. I have set you apart from all other people to be my very own.

²⁷"Men and women among you who act as mediums or who consult the spirits of the dead must be put to death by stoning. They are guilty of a capital offense."

Instructions for the Priests

21 The LORD said to Moses, "Give the following instructions to the priests, the descendants of Aaron.

"A priest must not make himself ceremonially unclean by touching the dead body of a relative. ²The only exceptions are his closest relatives—his mother or father, son or daughter, brother, ³or his virgin sister who depends on him because she has no husband. ⁴But a priest must not defile himself and make himself unclean for someone who is related to him only by marriage.

⁵"The priests must not shave their heads or trim their beards or cut their bodies. ⁶They must be set apart as holy to their God and must never bring shame on the name of God. They must be holy, for they are the ones who present the special gifts to the LORD, gifts of food for their God.

⁷"Priests may not marry a woman defiled by prostitution, and they may not marry a woman who is divorced from her husband, for the priests are set apart as holy to their God. ⁸You must treat them as holy because they offer up food to your God. You must consider them holy because I, the LORD, am holy, and I make you holy.

⁹"If a priest's daughter defiles herself by becoming a prostitute, she also defiles her father's holiness, and she must be burned to death.

¹⁰"The high priest has the highest rank of all the priests. The anointing oil has been poured on his head, and he has been ordained to wear the priestly garments. He must never leave his hair uncombed* or tear his clothing. ¹¹He must not defile himself by going near a dead body. He may not make himself ceremonially unclean even for his father or mother. ¹²He must not defile the sanctuary of his God by leaving it to attend to a dead person, for he has been made holy by the anointing oil of his God. I am the LORD.

¹³"The high priest may marry only a virgin. ¹⁴He may not marry a widow, a woman who is divorced,

---

21:10 Or *never uncover his head.*

20:22-26 God called his people to be different, to be set apart in devotion to him. This "separateness" played into many of the particular laws found in Leviticus, including the identification of clean and unclean animals and the related dietary laws the people were required to observe (Leviticus 11). Women who were responsible for food preparation would have played a key role in their family's obedience to such regulations. The barriers constructed by these dietary laws were removed by Christ (see Acts 10).

21:1–22:33 This section, which covers priestly regulations, is punctuated six times with the phrase "I am the LORD who makes . . . holy" (21:15, 23; 22:9, 16, 32; see also 21:8). The words reaffirm the necessary connection between the holiness of God and the holiness expected of the priesthood, and by extension, of all Israel (see 8:10; 11:44-45; 19:2). Priests are specifically addressed in 21:1–22:16, while both clergy and laypeople are included in 22:17-33. **21:10-15** The restrictions made on the common priests (21:1-8)

or a woman who has defiled herself by prostitution. She must be a virgin from his own clan, ¹⁵so that he will not dishonor his descendants among his clan, for I am the LORD who makes him holy."

¹⁶Then the LORD said to Moses, ¹⁷"Give the following instructions to Aaron: In all future generations, none of your descendants who has any defect will qualify to offer food to his God. ¹⁸No one who has a defect qualifies, whether he is blind, lame, disfigured, deformed, ¹⁹or has a broken foot or arm, ²⁰or is hunchbacked or dwarfed, or has a defective eye, or skin sores or scabs, or damaged testicles. ²¹No descendant of Aaron who has a defect may approach the altar to present special gifts to the LORD. Since he has a defect, he may not approach the altar to offer food to his God. ²²However, he may eat from the food offered to God, including the holy offerings and the most holy offerings. ²³Yet because of his physical defect, he may not enter the room behind the inner curtain or approach the altar, for this would defile my holy places. I am the LORD who makes them holy."

²⁴So Moses gave these instructions to Aaron and his sons and to all the Israelites.

22 The LORD said to Moses, ²"Tell Aaron and his sons to be very careful with the sacred gifts that the Israelites set apart for me, so they do not bring shame on my holy name. I am the LORD. ³Give them the following instructions.

"In all future generations, if any of your descendants is ceremonially unclean when he approaches the sacred offerings that the people of Israel consecrate to the LORD, he must be cut off from my presence. I am the LORD.

⁴"If any of Aaron's descendants has a skin disease* or any kind of discharge that makes him ceremonially unclean, he may not eat from the sacred offerings until he has been pronounced clean. He also becomes unclean by touching a corpse, or by having an emission of semen, ⁵or by touching a small animal that is unclean, or by touching someone who is ceremonially unclean for any reason. ⁶The man who is defiled in any of these ways will remain unclean until evening. He may not eat from the sacred offerings until he has bathed himself in water. ⁷When the sun goes down, he will be ceremonially clean again and may eat from the sacred offerings, for this is his food. ⁸He may not eat an animal that has died a natural death or has been torn apart by wild animals, for this would defile him. I am the LORD.

⁹"The priests must follow my instructions carefully. Otherwise they will be punished for their sin and will die for violating my instructions. I am the LORD who makes them holy.

¹⁰"No one outside a priest's family may eat the sacred offerings. Even guests and hired workers in a priest's home are not allowed to eat them. ¹¹However, if the priest buys a slave for himself, the slave may eat from the sacred offerings. And if his slaves have children, they also may share his food. ¹²If a priest's daughter marries someone outside the priestly family, she may no longer eat the sacred offerings. ¹³But if she becomes a widow or is divorced and has no children to support her, and she returns to live in her father's home as in her youth, she may eat her father's food again. Otherwise, no one outside a priest's family may eat the sacred offerings.

¹⁴"Any such person who eats the sacred offerings without realizing it must pay the priest for the amount eaten, plus an additional 20 percent. ¹⁵The priests must not let the Israelites defile the sacred offerings brought to the LORD ¹⁶by allowing unauthorized people to eat them. This would bring guilt upon them and require them to pay compensation. I am the LORD who makes them holy."

Worthy and Unworthy Offerings

¹⁷And the LORD said to Moses, ¹⁸"Give Aaron and his sons and all the Israelites these instructions, which apply both to native Israelites and to the foreigners living among you.

"If you present a gift as a burnt offering to the LORD, whether it is to fulfill a vow or is a voluntary offering, ¹⁹you* will be accepted only if your offering is a male animal with no defects. It may be a bull, a ram, or a male goat. ²⁰Do not present an animal with defects, because the LORD will not accept it on your behalf.

²¹"If you present a peace offering to the LORD from the herd or the flock, whether it is to fulfill a vow or is a voluntary offering, you must offer a perfect animal. It may have no defect of any kind. ²²You must not offer an animal that is blind, crippled, or injured, or that has a wart, a skin sore, or scabs. Such animals must never be offered on the altar as special gifts to the LORD. ²³If a bull* or lamb has a leg that is too

---

22:4 Traditionally rendered *leprosy;* see note on 13:2a.   22:19 Or *it.*   22:23 Or *cow.*

---

applied even more stringently to the high priest because he had to represent all Israel, including the other priests. The priest "must never leave his hair uncombed" (or another possible translation: "never uncover his head") or "tear his clothing" in mourning so that he would always be fit to minister. Although the common priest was permitted to marry a widow, the high priest was allowed to marry only a woman who was a virgin. This made certain that the future high priest and the common priests descended from that union would have an unquestioned lineage (21:15).

22:11 The only person outside the priest's family who could eat the priest's share was an enslaved person owned by the priest and any children born to that person. They would have no other food if this provision were denied them.
22:14-16 Similar to provisions for the guilt offering, a common person who accidentally ate the priestly portion had to repay 120 percent (see 5:14-16). However, the offering of a ram was not required in this case.

> "A prayerful heart and an obedient heart will learn, very slowly and not without sorrow, to stake everything on God Himself."
>
> **ELISABETH ELLIOT**
> (1926–2015) missionary, writer, and speaker

The Appointed Festivals

23 The LORD said to Moses, ²"Give the following instructions to the people of Israel. These are the LORD's appointed festivals, which you are to proclaim as official days for holy assembly.

³"You have six days each week for your ordinary work, but the seventh day is a Sabbath day of complete rest, an official day for holy assembly. It is the LORD's Sabbath day, and it must be observed wherever you live.

⁴"In addition to the Sabbath, these are the LORD's appointed festivals, the official days for holy assembly that are to be celebrated at their proper times each year.

Passover and the Festival of Unleavened Bread

⁵"The LORD's Passover begins at sundown on the fourteenth day of the first month.* ⁶On the next day, the fifteenth day of the month, you must begin celebrating the Festival of Unleavened Bread. This festival to the LORD continues for seven days, and during that time the bread you eat must be made without yeast. ⁷On the first day of the festival, all the people must stop their ordinary work and observe an official day for holy assembly. ⁸For seven days you must present special gifts to the LORD. On the seventh day the people must again stop all their ordinary work to observe an official day for holy assembly."

Celebration of First Harvest

⁹Then the LORD said to Moses, ¹⁰"Give the following instructions to the people of Israel. When you enter the land I am giving you and you harvest its first crops, bring the priest a bundle of grain from the first cutting of your grain harvest. ¹¹On the day after the Sabbath, the priest will lift it up before the LORD so it may be accepted on your behalf. ¹²On that same day you must sacrifice a one-year-old male lamb with no defects as a burnt offering to the LORD. ¹³With it you must present a grain offering consisting of four quarts* of choice flour moistened with olive oil. It will be a special gift, a pleasing aroma to the LORD. You must also offer one quart* of wine as a liquid offering. ¹⁴Do not eat any bread or roasted grain or fresh kernels on that day until you bring this offering to your God. This is a permanent law for you, and it must be observed from generation to generation wherever you live.

The Festival of Harvest

¹⁵"From the day after the Sabbath—the day you bring the bundle of grain to be lifted up as a special

long or too short, it may be offered as a voluntary offering, but it may not be offered to fulfill a vow. ²⁴If an animal has damaged testicles or is castrated, you may not offer it to the LORD. You must never do this in your own land, ²⁵and you must not accept such an animal from foreigners and then offer it as a sacrifice to your God. Such animals will not be accepted on your behalf, for they are mutilated or defective."

²⁶And the LORD said to Moses, ²⁷"When a calf or lamb or goat is born, it must be left with its mother for seven days. From the eighth day on, it will be acceptable as a special gift to the LORD. ²⁸But you must not slaughter a mother animal and her offspring on the same day, whether from the herd or the flock. ²⁹When you bring a thanksgiving offering to the LORD, sacrifice it properly so you will be accepted. ³⁰Eat the entire sacrificial animal on the day it is presented. Do not leave any of it until the next morning. I am the LORD.

³¹"You must faithfully keep all my commands by putting them into practice, for I am the LORD. ³²Do not bring shame on my holy name, for I will display my holiness among the people of Israel. I am the LORD who makes you holy. ³³It was I who rescued you from the land of Egypt, that I might be your God. I am the LORD."

23:5 This day in the ancient Hebrew lunar calendar occurred in late March, April, or early May. **23:13a** Hebrew ²⁄₁₀ *of an ephah* [4.4 liters]; also in 23:17. **23:13b** Hebrew ¼ *of a hin* [1 liter].

23:1–25:55 God designated sacred times for Israel to rest, worship, and celebrate, including the Sabbath, annual festivals, a Sabbath year, and the Year of Jubilee. The Sabbath year and the Year of Jubilee required great faith in the Lord's provision. For the Sabbath year, the people were not to sow any crops. They were to eat food that they had stored or that grew naturally. The Year of Jubilee leveled economic inequities, as all land was returned to its original owners and enslaved people were released.

MY STORY WITH COMMUNITY, WORKPLACE & CHURCH

Celebrating toward Our Destiny

SCRIPTURE CONNECTION: LEVITICUS 23:1-44

I sat in church, its musty scent lingering from all the days my siblings and I filled a back pew. The minister passed a basket with star-shaped pieces of paper, each bearing a word of hope.

I chose a star and, when I turned it over, I wondered if it chose me: *Celebrate*.

"Thou shalt celebrate." Surely, that's not one of God's commands. Or is it? God gave his people fifty-two Sabbaths and eighteen festival days. That's seventy days a year to rest, gather, give, feast, and rejoice. Why?

Is it about us—because we need it? Yes. *I* certainly need it. I struggle, working too many nights until 8:30 p.m. For the love of family, I work at working less and celebrating more.

But it's also more than that. These celebrations display God's good plan. And in his plan, we find our own. I like what John J. Parsons says about the annual festivals:

> God's eternal plan . . . is ingeniously revealed through the . . . Seven annual Feasts. . . . [T]he entire human race now exists between two of these feasts. . . . [Jesus] was crucified on Pesach [Passover], buried on Unleavened Bread, raised on First Fruits and sent the *Ruach Hakkodesh* [Holy Spirit] on Shavu'ot [Pentecost]. . . . [W]e have not yet seen the fulfillment of feast number five—Trumpets (John J. Parsons, "The Jewish Holidays—A Simplified Overview of the Feasts of the LORD," Hebrew for Christians website).

What we now celebrate in part, God will one day complete. This is previewed in Revelation 11:15: "Then the seventh angel blew his trumpet, and there were loud voices shouting in heaven: 'The world has now become the Kingdom of our Lord and of his Christ, and he will reign forever and ever.'"

Celebrating helps us focus on a Kingdom calendar—God's plan to guide our planner. As we celebrate with a view to our destiny, our calling for today comes into focus too.

> When we celebrate, we preview God's good plan.

IMAGINE

How does celebrating show us our part in God's bigger plan?

> "We plan, asking, 'What is the next way I can invest in my family, serve, or grow in my career?' As we celebrate God's big story and plan, our smaller plans shine."

NAOMI CRAMER OVERTON, MBA, DIS, lives to realize beauty-filled visions that lift us to flourishing, with our families and beyond. Naomi has been CEO for Stonecroft and MOPS, director with Compassion International and World Vision, and General Editor for this Bible.

offering—count off seven full weeks. ¹⁶Keep counting until the day after the seventh Sabbath, fifty days later. Then present an offering of new grain to the LORD. ¹⁷From wherever you live, bring two loaves of bread to be lifted up before the LORD as a special offering. Make these loaves from four quarts of choice flour, and bake them with yeast. They will be an offering to the LORD from the first of your crops. ¹⁸Along with the bread, present seven one-year-old male lambs with no defects, one young bull, and two rams as burnt offerings to the LORD. These burnt offerings, together with the grain offerings and liquid offerings, will be a special gift, a pleasing aroma to the LORD. ¹⁹Then you must offer one male goat as a sin offering and two one-year-old male lambs as a peace offering.

²⁰"The priest will lift up the two lambs as a special offering to the LORD, together with the loaves representing the first of your crops. These offerings, which are holy to the LORD, belong to the priests. ²¹That same day will be proclaimed an official day for holy assembly, a day on which you do no ordinary work. This is a permanent law for you, and it must be observed from generation to generation wherever you live.*

²²"When you harvest the crops of your land, do not harvest the grain along the edges of your fields, and do not pick up what the harvesters drop. Leave it for the poor and the foreigners living among you. I am the LORD your God."

The Festival of Trumpets

²³The LORD said to Moses, ²⁴"Give the following instructions to the people of Israel. On the first day of the appointed month in early autumn,* you are to observe a day of complete rest. It will be an official day for holy assembly, a day commemorated with loud blasts of a trumpet. ²⁵You must do no ordinary work on that day. Instead, you are to present special gifts to the LORD."

The Day of Atonement

²⁶Then the LORD said to Moses, ²⁷"Be careful to celebrate the Day of Atonement on the tenth day of that same month—nine days after the Festival of Trumpets.* You must observe it as an official day for holy assembly, a day to deny yourselves* and present special gifts to the LORD. ²⁸Do no work during that entire day because it is the Day of Atonement, when offerings of purification are made for you, making you right with* the LORD your God. ²⁹All who do not deny themselves that day will be cut off from God's people. ³⁰And I will destroy anyone among you who does any work on that day. ³¹You must not do any work at all! This is a permanent law for you, and it must be observed from generation to generation wherever you live. ³²This will be a Sabbath day of complete rest for you, and on that day you must deny yourselves. This day of rest will begin at sundown on the ninth day of the month and extend until sundown on the tenth day."

The Festival of Shelters

³³And the LORD said to Moses, ³⁴"Give the following instructions to the people of Israel. Begin celebrating the Festival of Shelters* on the fifteenth day of the appointed month—five days after the Day of Atonement.* This festival to the LORD will last for seven days. ³⁵On the first day of the festival you must proclaim an official day for holy assembly, when you do no ordinary work. ³⁶For seven days you must present special gifts to the LORD. The eighth day is another holy day on which you present your special gifts to the LORD. This will be a solemn occasion, and no ordinary work may be done that day.

³⁷("These are the LORD's appointed festivals. Celebrate them each year as official days for holy assembly by presenting special gifts to the LORD—burnt offerings, grain offerings, sacrifices, and liquid offerings—each on its proper day. ³⁸These festivals must be observed in addition to the LORD's regular Sabbath days, and the offerings are in addition to your personal gifts, the offerings you give to fulfill your vows, and the voluntary offerings you present to the LORD.)

³⁹"Remember that this seven-day festival to the LORD—the Festival of Shelters—begins on the fifteenth day of the appointed month,* after you have harvested all the produce of the land. The first day and the eighth day of the festival will be days of complete rest. ⁴⁰On the first day gather branches from magnificent trees*—palm fronds, boughs from leafy trees, and willows that grow by the streams. Then celebrate with joy before the LORD your God for seven days. ⁴¹You must observe this festival to the LORD for seven days every year. This is a permanent law for you, and it must be observed in the appointed month* from generation to generation. ⁴²For seven days you must live outside in little shelters. All native-born Israelites must live in shelters. ⁴³This will remind each new generation of Israelites that I made their ancestors live in shelters when I rescued them from the land of Egypt. I am the LORD your God."

⁴⁴So Moses gave the Israelites these instructions regarding the annual festivals of the LORD.

23:21 This celebration, called the Festival of Harvest or the Festival of Weeks, was later called the Festival of Pentecost (see Acts 2:1). It is celebrated today as Shavuot (or Shabuoth). **23:24** Hebrew *On the first day of the seventh month.* This day in the ancient Hebrew lunar calendar occurred in September or October. This festival is celebrated today as Rosh Hashanah, the Jewish new year. **23:27a** Hebrew *on the tenth day of the seventh month;* see 23:24 and the note there. This day in the ancient Hebrew lunar calendar occurred in September or October. It is celebrated today as Yom Kippur. **23:27b** Or *to fast;* similarly in 23:29, 32. **23:28** Or *when atonement is made for you before.* **23:34a** Or *Festival of Booths,* or *Festival of Tabernacles.* This was earlier called the Festival of the Final Harvest or Festival of Ingathering (see Exod 23:16b). It is celebrated today as Sukkot (or Succoth). **23:34b** Hebrew *on the fifteenth day of the seventh month;* see 23:27a and the note there. **23:39** Hebrew *on the fifteenth day of the seventh month.* **23:40** Or *gather fruit from majestic trees.* **23:41** Hebrew *the seventh month.*

Pure Oil and Holy Bread

24 The LORD said to Moses, ²"Command the people of Israel to bring you pure oil of pressed olives for the light, to keep the lamps burning continually. ³This is the lampstand that stands in the Tabernacle, in front of the inner curtain that shields the Ark of the Covenant.* Aaron must keep the lamps burning in the LORD's presence all night. This is a permanent law for you, and it must be observed from generation to generation. ⁴Aaron and the priests must tend the lamps on the pure gold lampstand continually in the LORD's presence.

⁵"You must bake twelve flat loaves of bread from choice flour, using four quarts* of flour for each loaf. ⁶Place the bread before the LORD on the pure gold table, and arrange the loaves in two stacks, with six loaves in each stack. ⁷Put some pure frankincense near each stack to serve as a representative offering, a special gift presented to the LORD. ⁸Every Sabbath day this bread must be laid out before the LORD as a gift from the Israelites; it is an ongoing expression of the eternal covenant. ⁹The loaves of bread will belong to Aaron and his descendants, who must eat them in a sacred place, for they are most holy. It is the permanent right of the priests to claim this portion of the special gifts presented to the LORD."

An Example of Just Punishment

¹⁰One day a man who had an Israelite mother and an Egyptian father came out of his tent and got into a fight with one of the Israelite men. ¹¹During the fight, this son of an Israelite woman blasphemed the Name of the LORD* with a curse. So the man was brought to Moses for judgment. His mother was Shelomith, the daughter of Dibri of the tribe of Dan. ¹²They kept the man in custody until the LORD's will in the matter should become clear to them.

¹³Then the LORD said to Moses, ¹⁴"Take the blasphemer outside the camp, and tell all those who heard the curse to lay their hands on his head. Then let the entire community stone him to death. ¹⁵Say to the people of Israel: Those who curse their God will be punished for their sin. ¹⁶Anyone who blasphemes the Name of the LORD must be stoned to death by the whole community of Israel. Any native-born Israelite or foreigner among you who blasphemes the Name of the LORD must be put to death.

¹⁷"Anyone who takes another person's life must be put to death.

¹⁸"Anyone who kills another person's animal must pay for it in full—a live animal for the animal that was killed.

¹⁹"Anyone who injures another person must be dealt with according to the injury inflicted—²⁰a fracture for a fracture, an eye for an eye, a tooth for a tooth. Whatever anyone does to injure another person must be paid back in kind.

²¹"Whoever kills an animal must pay for it in full, but whoever kills another person must be put to death.

²²"This same standard applies both to native-born Israelites and to the foreigners living among you. I am the LORD your God."

²³After Moses gave all these instructions to the Israelites, they took the blasphemer outside the camp and stoned him to death. The Israelites did just as the LORD had commanded Moses.

The Sabbath Year

25 While Moses was on Mount Sinai, the LORD said to him, ²"Give the following instructions to the people of Israel. When you have entered the land I am giving you, the land itself must observe a Sabbath rest before the LORD every seventh year. ³For six years you may plant your fields and prune your vineyards and harvest your crops, ⁴but during the seventh year the land must have a Sabbath year of complete rest. It is the LORD's Sabbath. Do not plant your fields or prune your vineyards during that year. ⁵And don't store away the crops that grow on their own or gather the grapes from your unpruned vines. The land must have a year of complete rest. ⁶But you may eat whatever the land produces on its own during its Sabbath. This applies to you, your male and female servants, your hired workers, and

---

24:3 Hebrew *in the Tent of Meeting, outside the inner curtain of the Testimony;* see note on 16:13. **24:5** Hebrew *2/10 of an ephah* [4.4 liters]. **24:11** Hebrew *the Name;* also in 24:16b.

24:19-20 The legal principle involved in "eye for an eye" is often called *lex talionis* ("law of retaliation"), which means that the penalty must fit the crime. When an injured party sought revenge on behalf of their family (see Numbers 35:19-21), excessive revenge naturally ensued instead of appropriate justice. This provoked even greater retaliation, resulting in a cycle of increasing violence. *Lex talionis* served to regulate the prosecution of crimes (see Leviticus 6:2-7; see also Exodus 21:24; Deuteronomy 19:21; Matthew 5:38-39).
24:22 Although foreigners who lived among the Israelites were not citizens, they were human beings just as entitled to equal justice under the law as the Israelites were. And they, too, were accountable to the laws of God just as the Israelites were (see 16:29, 31).

25:1-55 Just as seven days equaled a week ending in a Sabbath day, each seven years ended with a Sabbath year. Likewise, after seven Sabbath years (forty-nine years total) came a special year, the Year of Jubilee. Like so many holidays, these occasions were times of reflection on Israel's corporate identity and how they were shaped by their relationship with God. Because every Israelite, enslaved or free, had a part in God's Kingdom, those bound in servitude were freed in the Year of Jubilee (25:39-43). In order to curb economic hardship and foster well-being, land sales were limited to a maximum term of fifty years. The land was then to be returned to the original owner's family or clan. The land belonged to the Lord; the Israelites were merely tenants (25:23). It is unlikely, however, that these laws were observed much, since the best land fell into the hands of rich landowners (Isaiah 5:8-10; see also Amos 5:11).

the temporary residents who live with you. ⁷Your livestock and the wild animals in your land will also be allowed to eat what the land produces.

The Year of Jubilee

⁸"In addition, you must count off seven Sabbath years, seven sets of seven years, adding up to forty-nine years in all. ⁹Then on the Day of Atonement in the fiftieth year,* blow the ram's horn loud and long throughout the land. ¹⁰Set this year apart as holy, a time to proclaim freedom throughout the land for all who live there. It will be a jubilee year for you, when each of you may return to the land that belonged to your ancestors and return to your own clan. ¹¹This fiftieth year will be a jubilee for you. During that year you must not plant your fields or store away any of the crops that grow on their own, and don't gather the grapes from your unpruned vines. ¹²It will be a jubilee year for you, and you must keep it holy. But you may eat whatever the land produces on its own. ¹³In the Year of Jubilee each of you may return to the land that belonged to your ancestors.

¹⁴"When you make an agreement with your neighbor to buy or sell property, you must not take advantage of each other. ¹⁵When you buy land from your neighbor, the price you pay must be based on the number of years since the last jubilee. The seller must set the price by taking into account the number of years remaining until the next Year of Jubilee. ¹⁶The more years until the next jubilee, the higher the price; the fewer years, the lower the price. After all, the person selling the land is actually selling you a certain number of harvests. ¹⁷Show your fear of God by not taking advantage of each other. I am the Lord your God.

¹⁸"If you want to live securely in the land, follow my decrees and obey my regulations. ¹⁹Then the land will yield large crops, and you will eat your fill and live securely in it. ²⁰But you might ask, 'What will we eat during the seventh year, since we are not allowed to plant or harvest crops that year?' ²¹Be assured that I will send my blessing for you in the sixth year, so the land will produce a crop large enough for three years. ²²When you plant your fields in the eighth year, you will still be eating from the large crop of the sixth year. In fact, you will still be eating from that large crop when the new crop is harvested in the ninth year.

Redemption of Property

²³"The land must never be sold on a permanent basis, for the land belongs to me. You are only foreigners and tenant farmers working for me.

²⁴"With every purchase of land you must grant the seller the right to buy it back. ²⁵If one of your fellow Israelites falls into poverty and is forced to sell some family land, then a close relative should buy it back for him. ²⁶If there is no close relative to buy the land, but the person who sold it gets enough money to buy it back, ²⁷he then has the right to redeem it from the one who bought it. The price of the land will be discounted according to the number of years until the next Year of Jubilee. In this way the original owner can then return to the land. ²⁸But if the original owner cannot afford to buy back the land, it will remain with the new owner until the next Year of Jubilee. In the jubilee year, the land must be returned to the original owners so they can return to their family land.

²⁹"Anyone who sells a house inside a walled town has the right to buy it back for a full year after its sale. During that year, the seller retains the right to buy it back. ³⁰But if it is not bought back within a year, the sale of the house within the walled town cannot be reversed. It will become the permanent property of the buyer. It will not be returned to the original owner in the Year of Jubilee. ³¹But a house in a village—a settlement without fortified walls—will be treated like property in the countryside. Such a house may be bought back at any time, and it must be returned to the original owner in the Year of Jubilee.

³²"The Levites always have the right to buy back a house they have sold within the towns allotted to them. ³³And any property that is sold by the Levites—all houses within the Levitical towns—must be returned in the Year of Jubilee. After all, the houses in the towns reserved for the Levites are the only property they own in all Israel. ³⁴The open pastureland around the Levitical towns may never be sold. It is their permanent possession.

Redemption of the Poor and Enslaved

³⁵"If one of your fellow Israelites falls into poverty and cannot support himself, support him as you would a foreigner or a temporary resident and allow him to live with you. ³⁶Do not charge interest or make a profit at his expense. Instead, show your fear of God by letting him live with you as your relative. ³⁷Remember, do not charge interest on money you lend him or make a profit on food you sell him. ³⁸I am the Lord your God, who brought you out of the land of Egypt to give you the land of Canaan and to be your God.

³⁹"If one of your fellow Israelites falls into poverty and is forced to sell himself to you, do not treat him as a slave. ⁴⁰Treat him instead as a hired worker or

---

25:9 Hebrew *on the tenth day of the seventh month, on the Day of Atonement;* see 23:27a and the note there.

25:25 The Hebrew word translated "buy it back" (*gaal*) is often translated "redeem." It means "to restore something to its original or proper state of existence." The noun derived from this root (*goel*) indicates the close relative—family redeemer—who will restore what is out of order. The relative's duties were to redeem the property of their impoverished relative and keep it in the family (see Ruth 3:9; 4:1-4; Jeremiah 32:6-15); to seek out the murderer of a relative and bring the murderer to justice (Numbers 35:19-21); and to marry his brother's widow and father a male heir to inherit the estate of his dead relative (Deuteronomy 25:5-10; see Genesis 38:6-30; Ruth 4:9-10).

as a temporary resident who lives with you, and he will serve you only until the Year of Jubilee. ⁴¹At that time he and his children will no longer be obligated to you, and they will return to their clans and go back to the land originally allotted to their ancestors. ⁴²The people of Israel are my servants, whom I brought out of the land of Egypt, so they must never be sold as slaves. ⁴³Show your fear of God by not treating them harshly.

⁴⁴"However, you may purchase male and female slaves from among the nations around you. ⁴⁵You may also purchase the children of temporary residents who live among you, including those who have been born in your land. You may treat them as your property, ⁴⁶passing them on to your children as a permanent inheritance. You may treat them as slaves, but you must never treat your fellow Israelites this way.

⁴⁷"Suppose a foreigner or temporary resident becomes rich while living among you. If any of your fellow Israelites fall into poverty and are forced to sell themselves to such a foreigner or to a member of his family, ⁴⁸they still retain the right to be bought back, even after they have been purchased. They may be bought back by a brother, ⁴⁹an uncle, or a cousin. In fact, anyone from the extended family may buy them back. They may also redeem themselves if they have prospered. ⁵⁰They will negotiate the price of their freedom with the person who bought them. The price will be based on the number of years from the time they were sold until the next Year of Jubilee—whatever it would cost to hire a worker for that period of time. ⁵¹If many years still remain until the jubilee, they will repay the proper proportion of what they received when they sold themselves. ⁵²If only a few years remain until the Year of Jubilee, they will repay a small amount for their redemption. ⁵³The foreigner must treat them as workers hired on a yearly basis. You must not allow a foreigner to treat any of your fellow Israelites harshly. ⁵⁴If any Israelites have not been bought back by the time the Year of Jubilee arrives, they and their children must be set free at that time. ⁵⁵For the people of Israel belong to me. They are my servants, whom I brought out of the land of Egypt. I am the LORD your God.

Blessings for Obedience

26 "Do not make idols or set up carved images, or sacred pillars, or sculptured stones in your land so you may worship them. I am the LORD your God. ²You must keep my Sabbath days of rest and show reverence for my sanctuary. I am the LORD.

³"If you follow my decrees and are careful to obey my commands, ⁴I will send you the seasonal rains. The land will then yield its crops, and the trees of the field will produce their fruit. ⁵Your threshing season will overlap with the grape harvest, and your grape harvest will overlap with the season of planting grain. You will eat your fill and live securely in your own land.

⁶"I will give you peace in the land, and you will be able to sleep with no cause for fear. I will rid the land of wild animals and keep your enemies out of your land. ⁷In fact, you will chase down your enemies and slaughter them with your swords. ⁸Five of you will chase a hundred, and a hundred of you will chase ten thousand! All your enemies will fall beneath your sword.

⁹"I will look favorably upon you, making you fertile and multiplying your people. And I will fulfill my covenant with you. ¹⁰You will have such a surplus of crops that you will need to clear out the old grain to make room for the new harvest! ¹¹I will live among you, and I will not despise you. ¹²I will walk among you; I will be your God, and you will be my people. ¹³I am the LORD your God, who brought you out of the land of Egypt so you would no longer be their slaves. I broke the yoke of slavery from your neck so you can walk with your heads held high.

25:44-46 Enslaved people in Mesopotamia and Egypt were little more than chattel, with no protection or rights. Israelites were allowed to purchase non-Israelites, but they were to be treated well and not abused. Occasionally some enslaved people were even adopted into childless families (Genesis 15:2-4). Slavery continued into New Testament times, but the argument to end slavery was eventually made based on humanity's common origins in the Old Testament. Slavery stemmed from the Fall, when relationships based on power replaced those of fellowship and communication (see Genesis 3:16). The New Testament writers upheld the ideas of fellowship and communication by accepting the title "Christ's slave" or "servant" (Romans 1:1; Colossians 4:12; 2 Peter 1:1). In Paul's doctrine of the body of Christ (1 Corinthians 12:27; Ephesians 4:12), all followers of Jesus acquire a common identity (Galatians 3:28; Colossians 3:11; Philemon 1:16).

26:1 The people of Israel were not to make any idols or carved images to worship (see also Exodus 20:4-6). Creating an image to worship dishonors God by replacing the living God with something that is lifeless. Sometimes, God's people set up stones as memorials to various events (Genesis 28:18; Exodus 24:4), and some sculpture was clearly allowed in Israelite worship (see 1 Kings 7:25). However, any object that was set up for worship demonstrated the people's unfaithful hearts and alienated them from the true God. What does this have to do with us? Anything that stands above God in our hearts becomes an idol and disrupts our relationship with the loving Creator.

26:3-39 These blessings and curses reflect a key element of ancient Near Eastern treaties. In such a treaty, the suzerain king (that is, the more powerful king) promised to defend the vassal king and his state, while the vassal took an oath of loyalty to the suzerain. Blessings and curses in relation to the agreement followed, with the curses generally being lengthier, as is the case here. The treaties would typically call upon gods as witnesses and enforcers. In God's covenant with Israel, however, the Lord himself was one of the parties to the treaty. Since the Lord could swear by no one greater, he swore by himself (see also Genesis 22:16-17).

Punishments for Disobedience

¹⁴"However, if you do not listen to me or obey all these commands, ¹⁵and if you break my covenant by rejecting my decrees, treating my regulations with contempt, and refusing to obey my commands, ¹⁶I will punish you. I will bring sudden terrors upon you—wasting diseases and burning fevers that will cause your eyes to fail and your life to ebb away. You will plant your crops in vain because your enemies will eat them. ¹⁷I will turn against you, and you will be defeated by your enemies. Those who hate you will rule over you, and you will run even when no one is chasing you!

¹⁸"And if, in spite of all this, you still disobey me, I will punish you seven times over for your sins. ¹⁹I will break your proud spirit by making the skies as unyielding as iron and the earth as hard as bronze. ²⁰All your work will be for nothing, for your land will yield no crops, and your trees will bear no fruit.

²¹"If even then you remain hostile toward me and refuse to obey me, I will inflict disaster on you seven times over for your sins. ²²I will send wild animals that will rob you of your children and destroy your livestock. Your numbers will dwindle, and your roads will be deserted.

²³"And if you fail to learn the lesson and continue your hostility toward me, ²⁴then I myself will be hostile toward you. I will personally strike you with calamity seven times over for your sins. ²⁵I will send armies against you to carry out the curse of the covenant you have broken. When you run to your towns for safety, I will send a plague to destroy you there, and you will be handed over to your enemies. ²⁶I will destroy your food supply, so that ten women will need only one oven to bake bread for their families. They will ration your food by weight, and though you have food to eat, you will not be satisfied.

²⁷"If in spite of all this you still refuse to listen and still remain hostile toward me, ²⁸then I will give full vent to my hostility. I myself will punish you seven times over for your sins. ²⁹Then you will eat the flesh of your own sons and daughters. ³⁰I will destroy your pagan shrines and knock down your places of worship. I will leave your lifeless corpses piled on top of your lifeless idols,* and I will despise you. ³¹I will make your cities desolate and destroy your places of pagan worship. I will take no pleasure in your offerings that should be a pleasing aroma to me. ³²Yes, I myself will devastate your land, and your enemies who come to occupy it will be appalled at what they see. ³³I will scatter you among the nations and bring out my sword against you. Your land will become desolate, and your cities will lie in ruins. ³⁴Then at last the land will enjoy its neglected Sabbath years as it lies desolate while you are in exile in the land of your enemies. Then the land will finally rest and enjoy the Sabbaths it missed. ³⁵As long as the land lies in ruins, it will enjoy the rest you never allowed it to take every seventh year while you lived in it.

³⁶"And for those of you who survive, I will demoralize you in the land of your enemies. You will live in such fear that the sound of a leaf driven by the wind will send you fleeing. You will run as though fleeing from a sword, and you will fall even when no one pursues you. ³⁷Though no one is chasing you, you will stumble over each other as though fleeing from a sword. You will have no power to stand up against your enemies. ³⁸You will die among the foreign nations and be devoured in the land of your enemies. ³⁹Those of you who survive will waste away in your enemies' lands because of their sins and the sins of their ancestors.

⁴⁰"But at last my people will confess their sins and the sins of their ancestors for betraying me and being hostile toward me. ⁴¹When I have turned their hostility back on them and brought them to the land of their enemies, then at last their stubborn hearts will be humbled, and they will pay for their sins. ⁴²Then I will remember my covenant with Jacob and my covenant with Isaac and my covenant with Abraham, and I will remember the land. ⁴³For the land must be abandoned to enjoy its years of Sabbath rest as it lies deserted. At last the people will pay for their sins, for they have continually rejected my regulations and despised my decrees.

⁴⁴"But despite all this, I will not utterly reject or despise them while they are in exile in the land of their enemies. I will not cancel my covenant with them by wiping them out, for I am the LORD their God. ⁴⁵For their sakes I will remember my ancient covenant with their ancestors, whom I brought out of the land of Egypt in the sight of all the nations, that I might be their God. I am the LORD."

⁴⁶These are the decrees, regulations, and instructions that the LORD gave through Moses on Mount Sinai as evidence of the relationship between himself and the Israelites.

Redemption of Gifts Offered to the LORD

27 The LORD said to Moses, ²"Give the following instructions to the people of Israel. If anyone makes a special vow to dedicate someone to the LORD by paying the value of that person, ³here is the scale of values to be used. A man between the ages

---

26:30 The Hebrew term (literally *round things*) probably alludes to dung.

27:1-34 As a conclusion to the book, this chapter discusses various types of vows and ends with a provision for redeeming one's tithes. Under certain circumstances, such as an emergency, an individual might make a vow promising something to God, usually in exchange for God's answering their prayer (see Jonah 2:9). Once the prayer is answered, the individual might be tempted to discount the vow. Scripture requires that vows be made carefully (see Leviticus 5:4; Ecclesiastes 5:4-6) and then carried out. Jesus taught that oaths should not be commonly or carelessly made (Matthew 5:33-37; 23:16-22).

of twenty and sixty is valued at fifty shekels* of silver, as measured by the sanctuary shekel. ⁴A woman of that age is valued at thirty shekels* of silver. ⁵A boy between the ages of five and twenty is valued at twenty shekels of silver; a girl of that age is valued at ten shekels* of silver. ⁶A boy between the ages of one month and five years is valued at five shekels of silver; a girl of that age is valued at three shekels* of silver. ⁷A man older than sixty is valued at fifteen shekels of silver; a woman of that age is valued at ten shekels* of silver. ⁸If you desire to make such a vow but cannot afford to pay the required amount, take the person to the priest. He will determine the amount for you to pay based on what you can afford.

⁹"If your vow involves giving an animal that is acceptable as an offering to the LORD, any gift to the LORD will be considered holy. ¹⁰You may not exchange or substitute it for another animal—neither a good animal for a bad one nor a bad animal for a good one. But if you do exchange one animal for another, then both the original animal and its substitute will be considered holy. ¹¹If your vow involves an unclean animal—one that is not acceptable as an offering to the LORD—then you must bring the animal to the priest. ¹²He will assess its value, and his assessment will be final, whether high or low. ¹³If you want to buy back the animal, you must pay the value set by the priest, plus 20 percent.

¹⁴"If someone dedicates a house to the LORD, the priest will come to assess its value. The priest's assessment will be final, whether high or low. ¹⁵If the person who dedicated the house wants to buy it back, he must pay the value set by the priest, plus 20 percent. Then the house will again be his.

¹⁶"If someone dedicates to the LORD a piece of his family property, its value will be assessed according to the amount of seed required to plant it—fifty shekels of silver for a field planted with five bushels of barley seed.* ¹⁷If the field is dedicated to the LORD in the Year of Jubilee, then the entire assessment will apply. ¹⁸But if the field is dedicated after the Year of Jubilee, the priest will assess the land's value in proportion to the number of years left until the next Year of Jubilee. Its assessed value is reduced each year. ¹⁹If the person who dedicated the field wants to buy it back, he must pay the value set by the priest, plus 20 percent. Then the field will again be legally his. ²⁰But if he does not want to buy it back, and it is sold to someone else, the field can no longer be bought back. ²¹When the field is released in the Year of Jubilee, it will be holy, a field specially set apart* for the LORD. It will become the property of the priests.

²²"If someone dedicates to the LORD a field he has purchased but which is not part of his family property, ²³the priest will assess its value based on the number of years left until the next Year of Jubilee. On that day he must give the assessed value of the land as a sacred donation to the LORD. ²⁴In the Year of Jubilee the field must be returned to the person from whom he purchased it, the one who inherited it as family property. ²⁵(All the payments must be measured by the weight of the sanctuary shekel,* which equals twenty gerahs.)

²⁶"You may not dedicate a firstborn animal to the LORD, for the firstborn of your cattle, sheep, and goats already belong to him. ²⁷However, you may buy back the firstborn of a ceremonially unclean animal by paying the priest's assessment of its worth, plus 20 percent. If you do not buy it back, the priest will sell it at its assessed value.

²⁸"However, anything specially set apart for the LORD—whether a person, an animal, or family property—must never be sold or bought back. Anything devoted in this way has been set apart as holy, and it belongs to the LORD. ²⁹No person specially set apart for destruction may be bought back. Such a person must be put to death.

³⁰"One-tenth of the produce of the land, whether grain from the fields or fruit from the trees, belongs to the LORD and must be set apart to him as holy. ³¹If you want to buy back the LORD's tenth of the grain or fruit, you must pay its value, plus 20 percent. ³²Count off every tenth animal from your herds and flocks and set them apart for the LORD as holy. ³³You may not pick and choose between good and bad animals, and you may not substitute one for another. But if you do exchange one animal for another, then both the original animal and its substitute will be considered holy and cannot be bought back."

³⁴These are the commands that the LORD gave through Moses on Mount Sinai for the Israelites.

27:3 Or *20 ounces* [570 grams]. **27:4** Or *12 ounces* [342 grams]. **27:5** Or *A boy... 8 ounces* [228 grams] *of silver; a girl... 4 ounces* [114 grams]. **27:6** Or *A boy... 2 ounces* [57 grams] *of silver; a girl... 1.2 ounces* [34 grams]. **27:7** Or *A man... 6 ounces* [171 grams] *of silver; a woman... 4 ounces* [114 grams]. **27:16** Hebrew *50 shekels* [20 ounces or 570 grams] *of silver for a homer* [220 liters] *of barley seed.* **27:21** The Hebrew term used here refers to the complete consecration of things or people to the LORD, either by destroying them or by giving them as an offering; also in 27:28, 29. **27:25** Each shekel was about 0.4 ounces [11 grams] in weight.

27:3-7 This section reflects social rank in ancient Near Eastern cultures. An adult man of working age had the highest rank, followed by an adult woman of working age. A boy ranked higher than a girl, and both ranked higher than toddlers. Senior citizens, who were past prime working age, ranked comparably to boys and girls. The amount of fifty shekels would have represented about 20 ounces (570 grams) of silver, a significant amount. Comparisons with other literature of the time indicates that the biblical valuation is quite high and would have been out of reach for most people.

Numbers

WHAT DO WE LEARN ABOUT OUR MISSION AND GOD'S?
The road to God's best for us may not be short.

WHO WROTE IT? Numbers is anonymous, but Jewish and Christian traditions attribute it to Moses.

WHEN DID IT HAPPEN? In the 1400s or 1200s BC, from the time just prior to the Israelites' departure from Sinai through their forty-year journey in the wilderness

HOW IS IT ORGANIZED?

1–10: The Israelites organize for their journey

11–12: The people complain about the journey

13–14: The people refuse to enter the Promised Land

15–21: Laws about worship, more rebellion, Miriam and Aaron die

22–36: The Israelites prepare to enter the Promised Land and Balaam blesses them

FEATURE HIGHLIGHTS

+ Israel's Camp (169)
+ Miriam: Your Pain Is Building You (183)
+ Asking the Real Question (184)
+ Remembering: My Family Tassel (188)
+ Living Wholeheartedly (194)

Words to Remember are highlighted throughout this book

HOW LONG DOES IT TAKE TO READ?

2:30

:30 | 1:00 | 1:30 | 2:00 | 2:30 | 3:00 | 3:30

Timeline

BC	
1805	JOSEPH DIES
c. 1800 –1446	SLAVERY IN EGYPT
1446	EXODUS FROM EGYPT
1446 –1406	WILDERNESS WANDERINGS — *Miriam and Aaron complain about Moses' wife*
1445	TEN COMMANDMENTS GIVEN
1444	FIRST CENSUS
1443	FIRST SPY MISSION
1407	SECOND CENSUS; BALAAM PROPHESIES — *Daughters of Zelophehad speak out*
1406	MOSES, MIRIAM, AND AARON DIE; JOSHUA APPOINTED AS LEADER; ISRAELITES ENTER CANAAN
1375	JUDGES (INCLUDING DEBORAH, GIDEON, AND SAMSON) BEGIN TO RULE
1050	KINGDOM UNITED UNDER SAUL

NUMBERS 1

Registration of Israel's Troops

1 A year after Israel's departure from Egypt, the LORD spoke to Moses in the Tabernacle* in the wilderness of Sinai. On the first day of the second month* of that year he said, ²"From the whole community of Israel, record the names of all the warriors by their clans and families. List all the men ³twenty years old or older who are able to go to war. You and Aaron must register the troops, ⁴and you will be assisted by one family leader from each tribe.

⁵"These are the tribes and the names of the leaders who will assist you:

Tribe	Leader
Reuben	Elizur son of Shedeur
⁶ Simeon	Shelumiel son of Zurishaddai
⁷ Judah	Nahshon son of Amminadab
⁸ Issachar	Nethanel son of Zuar
⁹ Zebulun	Eliab son of Helon
¹⁰ Ephraim son of Joseph	Elishama son of Ammihud
Manasseh son of Joseph	Gamaliel son of Pedahzur
¹¹ Benjamin	Abidan son of Gideoni
¹² Dan	Ahiezer son of Ammishaddai
¹³ Asher	Pagiel son of Ocran
¹⁴ Gad	Eliasaph son of Deuel
¹⁵ Naphtali	Ahira son of Enan

¹⁶These are the chosen leaders of the community, the leaders of their ancestral tribes, the heads of the clans of Israel."

¹⁷So Moses and Aaron called together these chosen leaders, ¹⁸and they assembled the whole community of Israel on that very day.* All the people were registered according to their ancestry by their clans and families. The men of Israel who were twenty years old or older were listed one by one, ¹⁹just as the LORD had commanded Moses. So Moses recorded their names in the wilderness of Sinai.

²⁰⁻²¹This is the number of men twenty years old or older who were able to go to war, as their names were listed in the records of their clans and families*:

Tribe	Number
Reuben (Jacob's* oldest son)	46,500
²²⁻²³ Simeon	59,300
²⁴⁻²⁵ Gad	45,650
²⁶⁻²⁷ Judah	74,600
²⁸⁻²⁹ Issachar	54,400
³⁰⁻³¹ Zebulun	57,400
³²⁻³³ Ephraim son of Joseph	40,500
³⁴⁻³⁵ Manasseh son of Joseph	32,200
³⁶⁻³⁷ Benjamin	35,400
³⁸⁻³⁹ Dan	62,700
⁴⁰⁻⁴¹ Asher	41,500
⁴²⁻⁴³ Naphtali	53,400

⁴⁴These were the men registered by Moses and Aaron and the twelve leaders of Israel, all listed according to their ancestral descent. ⁴⁵They were registered by families—all the men of Israel who were twenty years old or older and able to go to war. ⁴⁶The total number was 603,550.

⁴⁷But this total did not include the Levites. ⁴⁸For the LORD had said to Moses, ⁴⁹"Do not include the tribe of Levi in the registration; do not count them with the rest of the Israelites. ⁵⁰Put the Levites in charge of the Tabernacle of the Covenant,* along with all its furnishings and equipment. They must carry the Tabernacle and all its furnishings as you travel, and they must take care of it and camp around it. ⁵¹Whenever it is time for the Tabernacle to move, the Levites will take it down. And when it is time to stop, they will set it up again. But any unauthorized person who goes too near the Tabernacle must be put to death. ⁵²Each tribe of Israel will camp in a designated area with its own family banner. ⁵³But the Levites will camp around the Tabernacle of the Covenant to protect the community of Israel from the LORD's anger. The Levites are responsible to stand guard around the Tabernacle."

⁵⁴So the Israelites did everything just as the LORD had commanded Moses.

Organization for Israel's Camp

2 Then the LORD gave these instructions to Moses and Aaron: ²"When the Israelites set up camp, each tribe will be assigned its own area. The tribal divisions will camp beneath their family banners on all four sides of the Tabernacle,* but at some distance from it.

³⁻⁴"The divisions of Judah, Issachar, and Zebulun are to camp toward the sunrise on the east side of the Tabernacle, beneath their family banners. These are the names of the tribes, their leaders, and the numbers of their registered troops:

1:1a Hebrew *the Tent of Meeting*.   1:1b This day in the ancient Hebrew lunar calendar occurred in April or May.   1:18 Hebrew *on the first day of the second month;* see 1:1.   1:20-21a In the Hebrew text, this sentence (*This is the number of men twenty years old or older who were able to go to war, as their names were listed in the records of their clans and families*) is repeated in 1:22, 24, 26, 28, 30, 32, 34, 36, 38, 40, 42.   1:20-21b Hebrew *Israel's*. The names "Jacob" and "Israel" are often interchanged throughout the Old Testament, referring sometimes to the individual patriarch and sometimes to the nation.   1:50 Or *Tabernacle of the Testimony;* also in 1:53.   2:2 Hebrew *the Tent of Meeting;* also in 2:17.

1:1–10:10 The Israelites prepared to leave for the Promised Land, and the Lord gave many instructions to Moses. The people were transitioning from slavery to nationhood.

1:2-16 In this effort to register Israel's men of military age, more information was gathered than in the previous registration (see Exodus 38:26). Hebrew culture was tribal, built around clans and families. The tribal leaders were readily identified and appear again as a group in Numbers 7. Moses and Aaron did not include Levi's tribe in this registration, since it had a special status in Israelite society (see 1:47-53; 26:57-62; Deuteronomy 18:5; 33:8-11).

NUMBERS 2

Tribe	Leader	Number
Judah	Nahshon son of Amminadab	74,600
5-6 Issachar	Nethanel son of Zuar	54,400
7-8 Zebulun	Eliab son of Helon	57,400

⁹So the total of all the troops on Judah's side of the camp is 186,400. These three tribes are to lead the way whenever the Israelites travel to a new campsite.

¹⁰⁻¹¹"The divisions of Reuben, Simeon, and Gad are to camp on the south side of the Tabernacle, beneath their family banners. These are the names of the tribes, their leaders, and the numbers of their registered troops:

2:1-34 Israel's camps were to be organized by tribal groupings. This arrangement may have reflected concerns for social status, access to water, and security for the Tabernacle, which represented the Lord's presence. The Egyptian army from approximately this same era camped in a similar defensive formation to protect the sacred objects that accompanied their field campaigns.
2:1-2 The Israelites' wilderness lives centered on the Tabernacle and God's presence among them. The people had continual reminders—both visual and audible—of the Lord's presence. Visually, God's presence appeared as a pillar of fire and a pillar of cloud. Audibly, the priests blew silver trumpets to call the community to assemble or to break camp (10:1-4). The physical setup of the camp tangibly represented their emphasis upon obedience and worship of God.

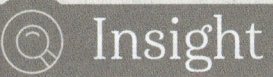

Insight — ISRAEL'S CAMP

Israel's military tribes camped in four groups, with the Tabernacle and the Levites in the center. Each of the four groups consisted of three tribes under the banner of that group's leading tribe—Judah on the east, Reuben on the south, Ephraim on the west, and Dan on the north. This arrangement ensured the protection of the priestly tribe of Levi and the Tabernacle and the Ark of the Covenant that were in their care.

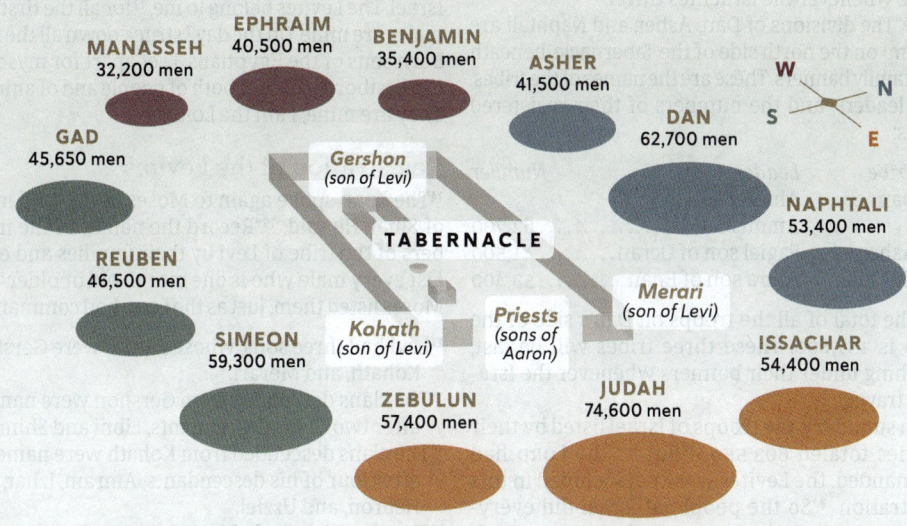

On the March

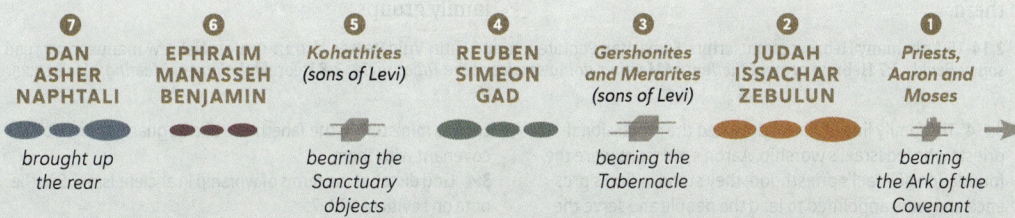

Tribe	Leader	Number
Reuben	Elizur son of Shedeur	46,500
12-13 Simeon	Shelumiel son of Zurishaddai	59,300
14-15 Gad	Eliasaph son of Deuel*	45,650

¹⁶So the total of all the troops on Reuben's side of the camp is 151,450. These three tribes will be second in line whenever the Israelites travel.

¹⁷"Then the Tabernacle, carried by the Levites, will set out from the middle of the camp. All the tribes are to travel in the same order that they camp, each in position under the appropriate family banner.

¹⁸⁻¹⁹"The divisions of Ephraim, Manasseh, and Benjamin are to camp on the west side of the Tabernacle, beneath their family banners. These are the names of the tribes, their leaders, and the numbers of their registered troops:

Tribe	Leader	Number
Ephraim	Elishama son of Ammihud	40,500
20-21 Manasseh	Gamaliel son of Pedahzur	32,200
22-23 Benjamin	Abidan son of Gideoni	35,400

²⁴So the total of all the troops on Ephraim's side of the camp is 108,100. These three tribes will be third in line whenever the Israelites travel.

²⁵⁻²⁶"The divisions of Dan, Asher, and Naphtali are to camp on the north side of the Tabernacle, beneath their family banners. These are the names of the tribes, their leaders, and the numbers of their registered troops:

Tribe	Leader	Number
Dan	Ahiezer son of Ammishaddai	62,700
27-28 Asher	Pagiel son of Ocran	41,500
29-30 Naphtali	Ahira son of Enan	53,400

³¹So the total of all the troops on Dan's side of the camp is 157,600. These three tribes will be last, marching under their banners whenever the Israelites travel."

³²In summary, the troops of Israel listed by their families totaled 603,550. ³³But as the LORD had commanded, the Levites were not included in this registration. ³⁴So the people of Israel did everything as the LORD had commanded Moses. Each clan and family set up camp and marched under their banners exactly as the LORD had instructed them.

Levites Appointed for Service

3 This is the family line of Aaron and Moses as it was recorded when the LORD spoke to Moses on Mount Sinai: ²The names of Aaron's sons were Nadab (the oldest), Abihu, Eleazar, and Ithamar. ³These sons of Aaron were anointed and ordained to minister as priests. ⁴But Nadab and Abihu died in the LORD's presence in the wilderness of Sinai when they burned before the LORD the wrong kind of fire, different than he had commanded. Since they had no sons, this left only Eleazar and Ithamar to serve as priests with their father, Aaron.

⁵Then the LORD said to Moses, ⁶"Call forward the tribe of Levi, and present them to Aaron the priest to serve as his assistants. ⁷They will serve Aaron and the whole community, performing their sacred duties in and around the Tabernacle.* ⁸They will also maintain all the furnishings of the sacred tent,* serving in the Tabernacle on behalf of all the Israelites. ⁹Assign the Levites to Aaron and his sons. They have been given from among all the people of Israel to serve as their assistants. ¹⁰Appoint Aaron and his sons to carry out the duties of the priesthood. But any unauthorized person who goes too near the sanctuary must be put to death."

¹¹And the LORD said to Moses, ¹²"Look, I have chosen the Levites from among the Israelites to serve as substitutes for all the firstborn sons of the people of Israel. The Levites belong to me, ¹³for all the firstborn males are mine. On the day I struck down all the firstborn sons of the Egyptians, I set apart for myself all the firstborn in Israel, both of people and of animals. They are mine; I am the LORD."

Registration of the Levites

¹⁴The LORD spoke again to Moses in the wilderness of Sinai. He said, ¹⁵"Record the names of the members of the tribe of Levi by their families and clans. List every male who is one month old or older." ¹⁶So Moses listed them, just as the LORD had commanded.

¹⁷Levi had three sons, whose names were Gershon, Kohath, and Merari.
¹⁸The clans descended from Gershon were named after two of his descendants, Libni and Shimei.
¹⁹The clans descended from Kohath were named after four of his descendants, Amram, Izhar, Hebron, and Uzziel.
²⁰The clans descended from Merari were named after two of his descendants, Mahli and Mushi. These were the Levite clans, listed according to their family groups.

2:14-15 As in many Hebrew manuscripts, Samaritan Pentateuch, and Latin Vulgate (see also 1:14); most Hebrew manuscripts read *son of Reuel.* 3:7 Hebrew *around the Tent of Meeting, doing service at the Tabernacle.* 3:8 Hebrew *the Tent of Meeting;* also in 3:25.

3:1-4 The family line of Aaron provided the professional priests who led Israel's worship. Aaron's four sons were the foundation of Israel's priesthood; they stood in God's presence and were appointed to lead the people and serve the Lord as ministers in the Tabernacle and as guardians of God's covenant with them.
3:4 God dictated the terms of worship in ancient Israel. See the note on Leviticus 10:1-7.

²¹The descendants of Gershon were composed of the clans descended from Libni and Shimei. ²²There were 7,500 males one month old or older among these Gershonite clans. ²³They were assigned the area to the west of the Tabernacle for their camp. ²⁴The leader of the Gershonite clans was Eliasaph son of Lael. ²⁵These two clans were responsible to care for the Tabernacle, including the sacred tent with its layers of coverings, the curtain at its entrance, ²⁶the curtains of the courtyard that surrounded the Tabernacle and altar, the curtain at the courtyard entrance, the ropes, and all the equipment related to their use.

²⁷The descendants of Kohath were composed of the clans descended from Amram, Izhar, Hebron, and Uzziel. ²⁸There were 8,600* males one month old or older among these Kohathite clans. They were responsible for the care of the sanctuary, ²⁹and they were assigned the area south of the Tabernacle for their camp. ³⁰The leader of the Kohathite clans was Elizaphan son of Uzziel. ³¹These four clans were responsible for the care of the Ark, the table, the lampstand, the altars, the various articles used in the sanctuary, the inner curtain, and all the equipment related to their use. ³²Eleazar, son of Aaron the priest, was the chief administrator over all the Levites, with special responsibility for the oversight of the sanctuary.

³³The descendants of Merari were composed of the clans descended from Mahli and Mushi. ³⁴There were 6,200 males one month old or older among these Merarite clans. ³⁵They were assigned the area north of the Tabernacle for their camp. The leader of the Merarite clans was Zuriel son of Abihail. ³⁶These two clans were responsible for the care of the frames supporting the Tabernacle, the crossbars, the pillars, the bases, and all the equipment related to their use. ³⁷They were also responsible for the posts of the courtyard and all their bases, pegs, and ropes.

³⁸The area in front of the Tabernacle, in the east toward the sunrise,* was reserved for the tents of Moses and of Aaron and his sons, who had the final responsibility for the sanctuary on behalf of the people of Israel. Anyone other than a priest or Levite who went too near the sanctuary was to be put to death.

³⁹When Moses and Aaron counted the Levite clans at the LORD's command, the total number was 22,000 males one month old or older.

Redeeming the Firstborn Sons

⁴⁰Then the LORD said to Moses, "Now count all the firstborn sons in Israel who are one month old or older, and make a list of their names. ⁴¹The Levites must be reserved for me as substitutes for the firstborn sons of Israel; I am the LORD. And the Levites' livestock must be reserved for me as substitutes for the firstborn livestock of the whole nation of Israel."

⁴²So Moses counted the firstborn sons of the people of Israel, just as the LORD had commanded. ⁴³The number of firstborn sons who were one month old or older was 22,273.

⁴⁴Then the LORD said to Moses, ⁴⁵"Take the Levites as substitutes for the firstborn sons of the people of Israel. And take the livestock of the Levites as substitutes for the firstborn livestock of the people of Israel. The Levites belong to me; I am the LORD. ⁴⁶There are 273 more firstborn sons of Israel than there are Levites. To redeem these extra firstborn sons, ⁴⁷collect five pieces of silver* for each of them (each piece weighing the same as the sanctuary shekel, which equals twenty gerahs). ⁴⁸Give the silver to Aaron and his sons as the redemption price for the extra firstborn sons."

⁴⁹So Moses collected the silver for redeeming the firstborn sons of Israel who exceeded the number of Levites. ⁵⁰He collected 1,365 pieces of silver* on behalf of these firstborn sons of Israel (each piece weighing the same as the sanctuary shekel). ⁵¹And Moses gave the silver for the redemption to Aaron and his sons, just as the LORD had commanded.

Duties of the Kohathite Clan

4 Then the LORD said to Moses and Aaron, ²"Record the names of the members of the clans and families of the Kohathite division of the tribe of Levi. ³List all the men between the ages of thirty and fifty who are eligible to serve in the Tabernacle.*

⁴"The duties of the Kohathites at the Tabernacle will relate to the most sacred objects. ⁵When the camp moves, Aaron and his sons must enter the Tabernacle first to take down the inner curtain and cover the Ark of the Covenant* with it. ⁶Then they must cover the inner curtain with fine goatskin leather and spread over that a single piece of blue cloth. Finally, they must put the carrying poles of the Ark in place.

⁷"Next they must spread a blue cloth over the table where the Bread of the Presence is displayed, and on the cloth they will place the bowls, ladles, jars, pitchers, and the special bread. ⁸They must spread a scarlet cloth over all of this, and finally a covering of fine goatskin leather on top of the scarlet cloth. Then they must insert the carrying poles into the table.

3:28 Some Greek manuscripts read *8,300;* see total in 3:39. 3:38 Hebrew *toward the sunrise, in front of the Tent of Meeting.*
3:47 Hebrew *5 shekels* [2 ounces or 57 grams]. 3:50 Hebrew *1,365* [*shekels*] *of silver* [34 pounds or 15.5 kilograms].
4:3 Hebrew *the Tent of Meeting;* also in 4:4, 15, 23, 25, 28, 30, 31, 33, 35, 37, 39, 41, 43, 47. 4:5 Or *Ark of the Testimony.*

4:1-49 Service isn't just about a person's abilities or what they like to do. These three Levite clans did the unheralded—but important—work of packing and carrying the Tabernacle and its furnishings. The individual assignments were given based simply on the family into which a person had been born. While God gives us gifts to serve his church (1 Corinthians 12), we must contribute wherever God calls us, which does not always align with where we feel most interested or gifted.

9"Next they must cover the lampstand with a blue cloth, along with its lamps, lamp snuffers, trays, and special jars of olive oil. 10Then they must cover the lampstand and its accessories with fine goatskin leather and place the bundle on a carrying frame.

11"Next they must spread a blue cloth over the gold incense altar and cover this cloth with fine goatskin leather. Then they must attach the carrying poles to the altar. 12They must take all the remaining furnishings of the sanctuary and wrap them in a blue cloth, cover them with fine goatskin leather, and place them on the carrying frame.

13"They must remove the ashes from the altar for sacrifices and cover the altar with a purple cloth. 14All the altar utensils—the firepans, meat forks, shovels, basins, and all the containers—must be placed on the cloth, and a covering of fine goatskin leather must be spread over them. Finally, they must put the carrying poles in place. 15The camp will be ready to move when Aaron and his sons have finished covering the sanctuary and all the sacred articles. The Kohathites will come and carry these things to the next destination. But they must not touch the sacred objects, or they will die. So these are the things from the Tabernacle that the Kohathites must carry.

16"Eleazar son of Aaron the priest will be responsible for the oil of the lampstand, the fragrant incense, the daily grain offering, and the anointing oil. In fact, Eleazar will be responsible for the entire Tabernacle and everything in it, including the sanctuary and its furnishings."

17Then the LORD said to Moses and Aaron, 18"Do not let the Kohathite clans be destroyed from among the Levites! 19This is what you must do so they will live and not die when they approach the most sacred objects. Aaron and his sons must always go in with them and assign a specific duty or load to each person. 20The Kohathites must never enter the sanctuary to look at the sacred objects for even a moment, or they will die."

Duties of the Gershonite Clan

21And the LORD said to Moses, 22"Record the names of the members of the clans and families of the Gershonite division of the tribe of Levi. 23List all the men between the ages of thirty and fifty who are eligible to serve in the Tabernacle.

24"These Gershonite clans will be responsible for general service and carrying loads. 25They must carry the curtains of the Tabernacle, the Tabernacle itself with its coverings, the outer covering of fine goatskin leather, and the curtain for the Tabernacle entrance. 26They are also to carry the curtains for the courtyard walls that surround the Tabernacle and altar, the curtain across the courtyard entrance, the ropes, and all the equipment related to their use. The Gershonites are responsible for all these items. 27Aaron and his sons will direct the Gershonites regarding all their duties, whether it involves moving the equipment or doing other work. They must assign the Gershonites responsibility for the loads they are to carry. 28So these are the duties assigned to the Gershonite clans at the Tabernacle. They will be directly responsible to Ithamar son of Aaron the priest.

Duties of the Merarite Clan

29"Now record the names of the members of the clans and families of the Merarite division of the tribe of Levi. 30List all the men between the ages of thirty and fifty who are eligible to serve in the Tabernacle.

31"Their only duty at the Tabernacle will be to carry loads. They will carry the frames of the Tabernacle, the crossbars, the posts, and the bases; 32also the posts for the courtyard walls with their bases, pegs, and ropes; and all the accessories and everything else related to their use. Assign the various loads to each man by name. 33So these are the duties of the Merarite clans at the Tabernacle. They are directly responsible to Ithamar son of Aaron the priest."

Summary of the Registration

34So Moses, Aaron, and the other leaders of the community listed the members of the Kohathite division by their clans and families. 35The list included all the men between thirty and fifty years of age who were eligible for service in the Tabernacle, 36and the total number came to 2,750. 37So this was the total of all those from the Kohathite clans who were eligible to serve at the Tabernacle. Moses and Aaron listed them, just as the LORD had commanded through Moses.

38The Gershonite division was also listed by its clans and families. 39The list included all the men between thirty and fifty years of age who were eligible for service in the Tabernacle, 40and the total number came to 2,630. 41So this was the total of all those from the Gershonite clans who were eligible to serve at the Tabernacle. Moses and Aaron listed them, just as the LORD had commanded.

42The Merarite division was also listed by its clans and families. 43The list included all the men between thirty and fifty years of age who were eligible for service in the Tabernacle, 44and the total number came to 3,200. 45So this was the total of all those from the Merarite clans who were eligible for service. Moses and Aaron listed them, just as the LORD had commanded through Moses.

46So Moses, Aaron, and the leaders of Israel listed all the Levites by their clans and families. 47All the men between thirty and fifty years of age who were eligible for service in the Tabernacle and for its transportation 48numbered 8,580. 49When their names were recorded, as the LORD had commanded through Moses, each man was assigned his task and told what to carry.

And so the registration was completed, just as the LORD had commanded Moses.

Purity in Israel's Camp

5 The LORD gave these instructions to Moses: ²"Command the people of Israel to remove from the camp anyone who has a skin disease* or a discharge, or who has become ceremonially unclean by touching a dead person. ³This command applies to men and women alike. Remove them so they will not defile the camp in which I live among them." ⁴So the Israelites did as the LORD had commanded Moses and removed such people from the camp.

⁵Then the LORD said to Moses, ⁶"Give the following instructions to the people of Israel: If any of the people—men or women—betray the LORD by doing wrong to another person, they are guilty. ⁷They must confess their sin and make full restitution for what they have done, adding an additional 20 percent and returning it to the person who was wronged. ⁸But if the person who was wronged is dead, and there are no near relatives to whom restitution can be made, the payment belongs to the LORD and must be given to the priest. Those who are guilty must also bring a ram as a sacrifice, and they will be purified and made right with the LORD.* ⁹All the sacred offerings that the Israelites bring to a priest will belong to him. ¹⁰Each priest may keep all the sacred donations that he receives."

Protecting Marital Faithfulness

¹¹And the LORD said to Moses, ¹²"Give the following instructions to the people of Israel.

"Suppose a man's wife goes astray, and she is unfaithful to her husband ¹³and has sex with another man, but neither her husband nor anyone else knows about it. She has defiled herself, even though there was no witness and she was not caught in the act. ¹⁴If her husband becomes jealous and is suspicious of his wife and needs to know whether or not she has defiled herself, ¹⁵the husband must bring his wife to the priest. He must also bring an offering of two quarts* of barley flour to be presented on her behalf. Do not mix it with olive oil or frankincense, for it is a jealousy offering—an offering to prove whether or not she is guilty.

¹⁶"The priest will then present her to stand trial before the LORD. ¹⁷He must take some holy water in a clay jar and pour into it dust he has taken from the Tabernacle floor. ¹⁸When the priest has presented the woman before the LORD, he must unbind her hair and place in her hands the offering of proof—the jealousy offering to determine whether her husband's suspicions are justified. The priest will stand before her, holding the jar of bitter water that brings a curse to those who are guilty. ¹⁹The priest will then put the woman under oath and say to her, 'If no other man has had sex with you, and you have not gone astray and defiled yourself while under your husband's authority, may you be immune from the effects of this bitter water that brings on the curse. ²⁰But if you have gone astray by being unfaithful to your husband, and have defiled yourself by having sex with another man—'

²¹"At this point the priest must put the woman under oath by saying, 'May the people know that the LORD's curse is upon you when he makes you infertile, causing your womb to shrivel* and your abdomen to swell. ²²Now may this water that brings the curse enter your body and cause your abdomen to swell and your womb to shrivel.*' And the woman will be required to say, 'Yes, let it be so.' ²³And the priest will write these curses on a piece of leather and wash them off into the bitter water. ²⁴He will make the woman drink the bitter water that brings on the curse. When the water enters her body, it will cause bitter suffering if she is guilty.

²⁵"The priest will take the jealousy offering from the woman's hand, lift it up before the LORD, and carry it to the altar. ²⁶He will take a handful of the flour as a token portion and burn it on the altar, and he will require the woman to drink the water. ²⁷If she has defiled herself by being unfaithful to her husband, the water that brings on the curse will cause bitter suffering. Her abdomen will swell and her womb will shrink,* and her name will become a curse among her people. ²⁸But if she has not defiled herself and is pure, then she will be unharmed and will still be able to have children.

²⁹"This is the ritual law for dealing with suspicion. If a woman goes astray and defiles herself while under her husband's authority, ³⁰or if a man becomes jealous and is suspicious that his wife has been unfaithful, the husband must present his wife before the LORD, and the priest will apply this entire ritual law to her. ³¹The husband will be innocent of any guilt in this matter, but his wife will be held accountable for her sin."

Nazirite Laws

6 Then the LORD said to Moses, ²"Give the following instructions to the people of Israel.

"If any of the people, either men or women, take

5:2 Traditionally rendered *leprosy.* The Hebrew word used here describes various skin diseases. **5:8** Or *bring a ram for atonement, which will make atonement for them.* **5:15** Hebrew *¹⁄₁₀ of an ephah* [2.2 liters]. **5:21** Hebrew *when he causes your thigh to waste away.* **5:22** Hebrew *and your thigh to waste away.* **5:27** Hebrew *and her thigh will waste away.*

5:11-31 This test offers the sole instance in Israelite law where God himself served as a person's judge. The practice protected the accused woman from judgment by her husband or by male priests. In the surrounding cultures, a woman's survival in such a "trial by ordeal" would have been miraculous. One test involved throwing the woman into a raging river. While the ordeal among the Israelites was undoubtedly terrifying, God provided a trial in which the woman could readily be proven innocent. A guilty finding would have been the miracle since the risk of drinking water and a little dirt would have been relatively minor.

May the LORD bless you and protect you.

NUMBERS 6:24

the special vow of a Nazirite, setting themselves apart to the LORD in a special way, ³they must give up wine and other alcoholic drinks. They must not use vinegar made from wine or from other alcoholic drinks, they must not drink fresh grape juice, and they must not eat grapes or raisins. ⁴As long as they are bound by their Nazirite vow, they are not allowed to eat or drink anything that comes from a grapevine—not even the grape seeds or skins.

⁵"They must never cut their hair throughout the time of their vow, for they are holy and set apart to the LORD. Until the time of their vow has been fulfilled, they must let their hair grow long. ⁶And they must not go near a dead body during the entire period of their vow to the LORD. ⁷Even if the dead person is their own father, mother, brother, or sister, they must not defile themselves, for the hair on their head is the symbol of their separation to God. ⁸This requirement applies as long as they are set apart to the LORD.

⁹"If someone falls dead beside them, the hair they have dedicated will be defiled. They must wait for seven days and then shave their heads. Then they will be cleansed from their defilement. ¹⁰On the eighth day they must bring two turtledoves or two young pigeons to the priest at the entrance of the Tabernacle.* ¹¹The priest will offer one of the birds for a sin offering and the other for a burnt offering. In this way, he will purify them* from the guilt they incurred through contact with the dead body. Then they must reaffirm their commitment and let their hair begin to grow again. ¹²The days of their vow that were completed before their defilement no longer count. They must rededicate themselves to the LORD as a Nazirite for the full term of their vow, and each must bring a one-year-old male lamb for a guilt offering.

¹³"This is the ritual law for Nazirites. At the conclusion of their time of separation as Nazirites, they must each go to the entrance of the Tabernacle ¹⁴and offer their sacrifices to the LORD: a one-year-old male lamb without defect for a burnt offering, a one-year-old female lamb without defect for a sin offering, a ram without defect for a peace offering, ¹⁵a basket of bread made without yeast—cakes of choice flour mixed with olive oil and wafers spread with olive oil—along with their prescribed grain offerings and liquid offerings. ¹⁶The priest will present these offerings before the LORD: first the sin offering and the burnt offering; ¹⁷then the ram for a peace offering, along with the basket of bread made without yeast. The priest must also present the prescribed grain offering and liquid offering to the LORD.

¹⁸"Then the Nazirites will shave their heads at the entrance of the Tabernacle. They will take the hair that had been dedicated and place it on the fire beneath the peace-offering sacrifice. ¹⁹After the Nazirite's head has been shaved, the priest will take for each of them the boiled shoulder of the ram, and he will take from the basket a cake and a wafer made without yeast. He will put them all into the Nazirite's hands. ²⁰Then the priest will lift them up as a special offering before the LORD. These are holy portions for the priest, along with the breast of the special offering and the thigh of the sacred offering that are lifted up before the LORD. After this ceremony the Nazirites may again drink wine.

²¹"This is the ritual law of the Nazirites, who vow to bring these offerings to the LORD. They may also bring additional offerings if they can afford it. And they must be careful to do whatever they vowed when they set themselves apart as Nazirites."

The Priestly Blessing

²²Then the LORD said to Moses, ²³"Tell Aaron and his sons to bless the people of Israel with this special blessing:

²⁴ 'May the LORD bless you
   and protect you.
²⁵ May the LORD smile on you
   and be gracious to you.
²⁶ May the LORD show you his favor
   and give you his peace.'

²⁷Whenever Aaron and his sons bless the people of Israel in my name, I myself will bless them."

Offerings of Dedication

7 On the day Moses set up the Tabernacle, he anointed it and set it apart as holy. He also anointed and set apart all its furnishings and the altar with its utensils. ²Then the leaders of Israel—the tribal leaders who had registered the troops—came and brought their offerings. ³Together they brought six large wagons and twelve oxen. There was a wagon for every two leaders and an ox for each leader. They presented these to the LORD in front of the Tabernacle.

6:10 Hebrew *the Tent of Meeting*; also in 6:13, 18. 6:11 Or *make atonement for them.*

6:22-27 The notion of being blessed in God's name (6:27) could be literally rendered, "[The priests] shall put my name on" the people. To bear the name of God meant that the people represented God to everyone around them. When they fell short, their behavior dishonored his name and did not demonstrate the reality of who God is. Christians also bear the name of God and are charged with representing him well to the world around us (1 Peter 4:14-16).

7:2-9 The same tribal leaders that assisted in the registration of Numbers 1:5-15 are found in 7:2-3. The non-Levitical tribes supplied the Gershonites and Merarites with the wagons and oxen needed to transport the heavy structural components of the Tabernacle and other items (see also 4:21-33). These vehicles and draft animals were the first offerings from the Hebrew tribes (7:2); in addition to these practical gifts, the tribal leaders also presented an abundant variety of choice offerings (7:10, 12-83).

⁴Then the LORD said to Moses, ⁵"Receive their gifts, and use these oxen and wagons for transporting the Tabernacle.* Distribute them among the Levites according to the work they have to do. ⁶So Moses took the wagons and oxen and presented them to the Levites. ⁷He gave two wagons and four oxen to the Gershonite division for their work, ⁸and he gave four wagons and eight oxen to the Merarite division for their work. All their work was done under the leadership of Ithamar son of Aaron the priest. ⁹But he gave none of the wagons or oxen to the Kohathite division, since they were required to carry the sacred objects of the Tabernacle on their shoulders.

¹⁰The leaders also presented dedication gifts for the altar at the time it was anointed. They each placed their gifts before the altar. ¹¹The LORD said to Moses, "Let one leader bring his gift each day for the dedication of the altar."

¹²On the first day Nahshon son of Amminadab, leader of the tribe of Judah, presented his offering.
¹³His offering consisted of a silver platter weighing 3¼ pounds and a silver basin weighing 1¾ pounds* (as measured by the weight of the sanctuary shekel). These were both filled with grain offerings of choice flour moistened with olive oil. ¹⁴He also brought a gold container weighing four ounces,* which was filled with incense. ¹⁵He brought a young bull, a ram, and a one-year-old male lamb for a burnt offering, ¹⁶and a male goat for a sin offering. ¹⁷For a peace offering he brought two bulls, five rams, five male goats, and five one-year-old male lambs. This was the offering brought by Nahshon son of Amminadab.

¹⁸On the second day Nethanel son of Zuar, leader of the tribe of Issachar, presented his offering.
¹⁹His offering consisted of a silver platter weighing 3¼ pounds and a silver basin weighing 1¾ pounds (as measured by the weight of the sanctuary shekel). These were both filled with grain offerings of choice flour moistened with olive oil. ²⁰He also brought a gold container weighing four ounces, which was filled with incense. ²¹He brought a young bull, a ram, and a one-year-old male lamb for a burnt offering, ²²and a male goat for a sin offering. ²³For a peace offering he brought two bulls, five rams, five male goats, and five one-year-old male lambs. This was the offering brought by Nethanel son of Zuar.

²⁴On the third day Eliab son of Helon, leader of the tribe of Zebulun, presented his offering.
²⁵His offering consisted of a silver platter weighing 3¼ pounds and a silver basin weighing 1¾ pounds (as measured by the weight of the sanctuary shekel). These were both filled with grain offerings of choice flour moistened with olive oil. ²⁶He also brought a gold container weighing four ounces, which was filled with incense. ²⁷He brought a young bull, a ram, and a one-year-old male lamb for a burnt offering, ²⁸and a male goat for a sin offering. ²⁹For a peace offering he brought two bulls, five rams, five male goats, and five one-year-old male lambs. This was the offering brought by Eliab son of Helon.

³⁰On the fourth day Elizur son of Shedeur, leader of the tribe of Reuben, presented his offering.
³¹His offering consisted of a silver platter weighing 3¼ pounds and a silver basin weighing 1¾ pounds (as measured by the weight of the sanctuary shekel). These were both filled with grain offerings of choice flour moistened with olive oil. ³²He also brought a gold container weighing four ounces, which was filled with incense. ³³He brought a young bull, a ram, and a one-year-old male lamb for a burnt offering, ³⁴and a male goat for a sin offering. ³⁵For a peace offering he brought two bulls, five rams, five male goats, and five one-year-old male lambs. This was the offering brought by Elizur son of Shedeur.

³⁶On the fifth day Shelumiel son of Zurishaddai, leader of the tribe of Simeon, presented his offering.
³⁷His offering consisted of a silver platter weighing 3¼ pounds and a silver basin weighing 1¾ pounds (as measured by the weight of the sanctuary shekel). These were both filled with grain offerings of choice flour moistened with olive oil. ³⁸He also brought a gold container weighing four ounces, which was filled with incense. ³⁹He brought a young bull, a ram, and a one-year-old male lamb for a burnt offering, ⁴⁰and a male goat for a sin offering. ⁴¹For a peace offering he brought two bulls, five rams, five male goats, and five one-year-old male lambs. This was the offering brought by Shelumiel son of Zurishaddai.

7:5 Hebrew *the Tent of Meeting;* also in 7:89. **7:13** Hebrew *silver platter weighing 130 [shekels]* [1.5 kilograms] *and a silver basin weighing 70 shekels* [800 grams]; also in 7:19, 25, 31, 37, 43, 49, 55, 61, 67, 73, 79, 85. **7:14** Hebrew *10 [shekels]* [114 grams]; also in 7:20, 26, 32, 38, 44, 50, 56, 62, 68, 74, 80, 86.

7:12-83 One by one, the tribal leaders brought their dedicatory gifts and offerings until the entire Hebrew confederation had participated. The repetitious pattern of describing each tribal gift emphasizes the communal nature of this ceremony; all tribes played a role in dedicating their place of worship to God. The detailed listing might reflect the meticulous record keeping of an archive or ledger. As noted in the record for each tribe, the silver vessels contained grain offerings, and the gold vessels held incense. Every tribe also brought animals as a burnt offering, a sin offering, and a peace offering, as specified in Leviticus.

⁴²On the sixth day Eliasaph son of Deuel, leader of the tribe of Gad, presented his offering.

⁴³His offering consisted of a silver platter weighing 3¼ pounds and a silver basin weighing 1¾ pounds (as measured by the weight of the sanctuary shekel). These were both filled with grain offerings of choice flour moistened with olive oil. ⁴⁴He also brought a gold container weighing four ounces, which was filled with incense. ⁴⁵He brought a young bull, a ram, and a one-year-old male lamb for a burnt offering, ⁴⁶and a male goat for a sin offering. ⁴⁷For a peace offering he brought two bulls, five rams, five male goats, and five one-year-old male lambs. This was the offering brought by Eliasaph son of Deuel.

⁴⁸On the seventh day Elishama son of Ammihud, leader of the tribe of Ephraim, presented his offering.

⁴⁹His offering consisted of a silver platter weighing 3¼ pounds and a silver basin weighing 1¾ pounds (as measured by the weight of the sanctuary shekel). These were both filled with grain offerings of choice flour moistened with olive oil. ⁵⁰He also brought a gold container weighing four ounces, which was filled with incense. ⁵¹He brought a young bull, a ram, and a one-year-old male lamb for a burnt offering, ⁵²and a male goat for a sin offering. ⁵³For a peace offering he brought two bulls, five rams, five male goats, and five one-year-old male lambs. This was the offering brought by Elishama son of Ammihud.

⁵⁴On the eighth day Gamaliel son of Pedahzur, leader of the tribe of Manasseh, presented his offering.

⁵⁵His offering consisted of a silver platter weighing 3¼ pounds and a silver basin weighing 1¾ pounds (as measured by the weight of the sanctuary shekel). These were both filled with grain offerings of choice flour moistened with olive oil. ⁵⁶He also brought a gold container weighing four ounces, which was filled with incense. ⁵⁷He brought a young bull, a ram, and a one-year-old male lamb for a burnt offering, ⁵⁸and a male goat for a sin offering. ⁵⁹For a peace offering he brought two bulls, five rams, five male goats, and five one-year-old male lambs. This was the offering brought by Gamaliel son of Pedahzur.

⁶⁰On the ninth day Abidan son of Gideoni, leader of the tribe of Benjamin, presented his offering.

⁶¹His offering consisted of a silver platter weighing 3¼ pounds and a silver basin weighing 1¾ pounds (as measured by the weight of the sanctuary shekel). These were both filled with grain offerings of choice flour moistened with olive oil. ⁶²He also brought a gold container weighing four ounces, which was filled with incense. ⁶³He brought a young bull, a ram, and a one-year-old male lamb for a burnt offering, ⁶⁴and a male goat for a sin offering. ⁶⁵For a peace offering he brought two bulls, five rams, five male goats, and five one-year-old male lambs. This was the offering brought by Abidan son of Gideoni.

⁶⁶On the tenth day Ahiezer son of Ammishaddai, leader of the tribe of Dan, presented his offering.

⁶⁷His offering consisted of a silver platter weighing 3¼ pounds and a silver basin weighing 1¾ pounds (as measured by the weight of the sanctuary shekel). These were both filled with grain offerings of choice flour moistened with olive oil. ⁶⁸He also brought a gold container weighing four ounces, which was filled with incense. ⁶⁹He brought a young bull, a ram, and a one-year-old male lamb for a burnt offering, ⁷⁰and a male goat for a sin offering. ⁷¹For a peace offering he brought two bulls, five rams, five male goats, and five one-year-old male lambs. This was the offering brought by Ahiezer son of Ammishaddai.

⁷²On the eleventh day Pagiel son of Ocran, leader of the tribe of Asher, presented his offering.

⁷³His offering consisted of a silver platter weighing 3¼ pounds and a silver basin weighing 1¾ pounds (as measured by the weight of the sanctuary shekel). These were both filled with grain offerings of choice flour moistened with olive oil. ⁷⁴He also brought a gold container weighing four ounces, which was filled with incense. ⁷⁵He brought a young bull, a ram, and a one-year-old male lamb for a burnt offering, ⁷⁶and a male goat for a sin offering. ⁷⁷For a peace offering he brought two bulls, five rams, five male goats, and five one-year-old male lambs. This was the offering brought by Pagiel son of Ocran.

⁷⁸On the twelfth day Ahira son of Enan, leader of the tribe of Naphtali, presented his offering.

⁷⁹His offering consisted of a silver platter weighing 3¼ pounds and a silver basin weighing 1¾ pounds (as measured by the weight of the sanctuary shekel). These were both filled with grain offerings of choice flour moistened with olive oil. ⁸⁰He also brought a gold container weighing four ounces, which was filled with incense. ⁸¹He brought a young bull, a ram, and a one-year-old male lamb for a burnt offering, ⁸²and a male goat for a sin offering. ⁸³For a peace offering he brought two bulls, five rams, five male goats, and five one-year-old male lambs. This was the offering brought by Ahira son of Enan.

⁸⁴So this was the dedication offering brought by the leaders of Israel at the time the altar was anointed: twelve silver platters, twelve silver basins, and twelve gold incense containers. ⁸⁵Each silver platter weighed 3¼ pounds, and each silver basin weighed 1¾ pounds. The total weight of the silver was 60 pounds* (as measured by the weight of the sanctuary shekel). ⁸⁶Each of the twelve gold containers that was filled with incense weighed four ounces (as measured by the weight of the sanctuary shekel). The total weight of the gold was three pounds.* ⁸⁷Twelve young bulls, twelve rams, and twelve one-year-old male lambs were donated for the burnt offerings, along with their prescribed grain offerings. Twelve male goats were brought for the sin offerings. ⁸⁸Twenty-four bulls, sixty rams, sixty male goats, and sixty one-year-old male lambs were donated for the peace offerings. This was the dedication offering for the altar after it was anointed.

⁸⁹Whenever Moses went into the Tabernacle to speak with the LORD, he heard the voice speaking to him from between the two cherubim above the Ark's cover—the place of atonement—that rests on the Ark of the Covenant.* The LORD spoke to him from there.

Preparing the Lamps

8 The LORD said to Moses, ²"Give Aaron the following instructions: When you set up the seven lamps in the lampstand, place them so their light shines forward in front of the lampstand." ³So Aaron did this. He set up the seven lamps so they reflected their light forward, just as the LORD had commanded Moses. ⁴The entire lampstand, from its base to its decorative blossoms, was made of beaten gold. It was built according to the exact design the LORD had shown Moses.

The Levites Dedicated

⁵Then the LORD said to Moses, ⁶"Now set the Levites apart from the rest of the people of Israel and make them ceremonially clean. ⁷Do this by sprinkling them with the water of purification, and have them shave their entire body and wash their clothing. Then they will be ceremonially clean. ⁸Have them bring a young bull and a grain offering of choice flour moistened with olive oil, along with a second young bull for a sin offering. ⁹Then assemble the whole community of Israel, and present the Levites at the entrance of the Tabernacle.* ¹⁰When you present the Levites before the LORD, the people of Israel must lay their hands on them. ¹¹Raising his hands, Aaron must then present the Levites to the LORD as a special offering from the people of Israel, thus dedicating them to the LORD's service.

¹²"Next the Levites will lay their hands on the heads of the young bulls. Present one as a sin offering and the other as a burnt offering to the LORD, to purify the Levites and make them right with the LORD.* ¹³Then have the Levites stand in front of Aaron and his sons, and raise your hands and present them as a special offering to the LORD. ¹⁴In this way, you will set the Levites apart from the rest of the people of Israel, and the Levites will belong to me. ¹⁵After this, they may go into the Tabernacle to do their work, because you have purified them and presented them as a special offering.

¹⁶"Of all the people of Israel, the Levites are reserved for me. I have claimed them for myself in place of all the firstborn sons of the Israelites; I have taken the Levites as their substitutes. ¹⁷For all the firstborn males among the people of Israel are mine, both of people and of animals. I set them apart for myself on the day I struck down all the firstborn sons of the Egyptians. ¹⁸Yes, I have claimed the Levites in place of all the firstborn sons of Israel. ¹⁹And of all the Israelites, I have assigned the Levites to Aaron and his sons. They will serve in the Tabernacle on behalf of the Israelites and make sacrifices to purify* the people so no plague will strike them when they approach the sanctuary."

²⁰So Moses, Aaron, and the whole community of Israel dedicated the Levites, carefully following all the LORD's instructions to Moses. ²¹The Levites purified themselves from sin and washed their clothes, and Aaron lifted them up and presented them to the LORD as a special offering. He then offered a sacrifice to purify them and make them right with the LORD.* ²²After that the Levites went into the Tabernacle to perform their duties, assisting Aaron and his sons. So they carried out all the commands that the LORD gave Moses concerning the Levites.

²³The LORD also instructed Moses, ²⁴"This is the rule the Levites must follow: They must begin serving in the Tabernacle at the age of twenty-five, ²⁵and they must retire at the age of fifty. ²⁶After retirement they may assist their fellow Levites by serving as guards at the Tabernacle, but they may not officiate in the service. This is how you must assign duties to the Levites."

7:85 Hebrew *2,400 [shekels]* [27.6 kilograms]. 7:86 Hebrew *120 [shekels]* [1.4 kilograms]. 7:89 Or *Ark of the Testimony.* 8:9 Hebrew *the Tent of Meeting;* also in 8:15, 19, 22, 24, 26. 8:12 Or *to make atonement for the Levites.* 8:19 Or *make atonement for.* 8:21 Or *then made atonement for them to purify them.*

8:12-22 The Levites needed to offer appropriate sacrifices in order to be purified before they could perform their duties in the Tabernacle (8:15, 22).

8:23-26 One version of the guidelines for the Levites' length of service is recorded here. Numbers 4:3 states that their Tabernacle service began at age thirty, but 8:24 gives the age as twenty-five. The discrepancy might reflect age requirements followed in different periods when the number of Levite men available for service varied, or those aged twenty-five to twenty-nine may have been considered unofficial workers or apprentices. Both passages establish the retirement age at fifty; retired Levites could serve the Tabernacle as guards (see Psalm 84:10).

The Second Passover

9 A year after Israel's departure from Egypt, the LORD spoke to Moses in the wilderness of Sinai. In the first month* of that year he said, ²"Tell the Israelites to celebrate the Passover at the prescribed time, ³at twilight on the fourteenth day of the first month.* Be sure to follow all my decrees and regulations concerning this celebration."

⁴So Moses told the people to celebrate the Passover ⁵in the wilderness of Sinai as twilight fell on the fourteenth day of the month. And they celebrated the festival there, just as the LORD had commanded Moses. ⁶But some of the men had been ceremonially defiled by touching a dead body, so they could not celebrate the Passover that day. They came to Moses and Aaron that day ⁷and said, "We have become ceremonially unclean by touching a dead body. But why should we be prevented from presenting the LORD's offering at the proper time with the rest of the Israelites?"

⁸Moses answered, "Wait here until I have received instructions for you from the LORD."

⁹This was the LORD's reply to Moses. ¹⁰"Give the following instructions to the people of Israel: If any of the people now or in future generations are ceremonially unclean at Passover time because of touching a dead body, or if they are on a journey and cannot be present at the ceremony, they may still celebrate the LORD's Passover. ¹¹They must offer the Passover sacrifice one month later, at twilight on the fourteenth day of the second month.* They must eat the Passover lamb at that time with bitter salad greens and bread made without yeast. ¹²They must not leave any of the lamb until the next morning, and they must not break any of its bones. They must follow all the normal regulations concerning the Passover.

¹³"But those who neglect to celebrate the Passover at the regular time, even though they are ceremonially clean and not away on a trip, will be cut off from the community of Israel. If they fail to present the LORD's offering at the proper time, they will suffer the consequences of their guilt. ¹⁴And if foreigners living among you want to celebrate the Passover to the LORD, they must follow these same decrees and regulations. The same laws apply both to native-born Israelites and to the foreigners living among you."

The Fiery Cloud

¹⁵On the day the Tabernacle was set up, the cloud covered it.* But from evening until morning the cloud over the Tabernacle looked like a pillar of fire. ¹⁶This was the regular pattern—at night the cloud that covered the Tabernacle had the appearance of fire. ¹⁷Whenever the cloud lifted from over the sacred tent, the people of Israel would break camp and follow it. And wherever the cloud settled, the people of Israel would set up camp. ¹⁸In this way, they traveled and camped at the LORD's command wherever he told them to go. Then they remained in their camp as long as the cloud stayed over the Tabernacle. ¹⁹If the cloud remained over the Tabernacle for a long time, the Israelites stayed and performed their duty to the LORD. ²⁰Sometimes the cloud would stay over the Tabernacle for only a few days, so the people would stay for only a few days, as the LORD commanded. Then at the LORD's command they would break camp and move on. ²¹Sometimes the cloud stayed only overnight and lifted the next morning. But day or night, when the cloud lifted, the people broke camp and moved on. ²²Whether the cloud stayed above the Tabernacle for two days, a month, or a year, the people of Israel stayed in camp and did not move on. But as soon as it lifted, they broke camp and moved on. ²³So they camped or traveled at the LORD's command, and they did whatever the LORD told them through Moses.

The Silver Trumpets

10 Now the LORD said to Moses, ²"Make two trumpets of hammered silver for calling the community to assemble and for signaling the breaking of camp. ³When both trumpets are blown, everyone must gather before you at the entrance of the Tabernacle.* ⁴But if only one trumpet is blown, then only the leaders—the heads of the clans of Israel—must present themselves to you.

⁵"When you sound the signal to move on, the tribes camped on the east side of the Tabernacle must break camp and move forward. ⁶When you sound the signal a second time, the tribes camped on the south will follow. You must sound short blasts as the signal for moving on. ⁷But when you call the people to an assembly, blow the trumpets with a different signal. ⁸Only the priests, Aaron's descendants, are allowed to blow the trumpets. This is a permanent law for you, to be observed from generation to generation.

9:1 The first month of the ancient Hebrew lunar calendar usually occurs within the months of March and April. **9:3** This day in the ancient Hebrew lunar calendar occurred in late March, April, or early May. **9:11** This day in the ancient Hebrew lunar calendar occurred in late April, May, or early June. **9:15** Hebrew *covered the Tabernacle, the Tent of the Testimony.* **10:3** Hebrew *Tent of Meeting.*

9:2-3 The Hebrews were told to celebrate the Passover at the prescribed time, on "the fourteenth day of the first month" (see Exodus 12:6). This day in the ancient Hebrew lunar calendar occurred in late March or in April. The Hebrew day begins at sundown, which is why the festival begins "at twilight." (See "Israel's Calendar of Festivals" on page 93.)

9:14 Foreigners who lived among the Hebrews and wanted to celebrate the Passover could do so by following the same laws, but circumcision was required for men who desired to eat the Passover meal (see also Exodus 12:48-49).

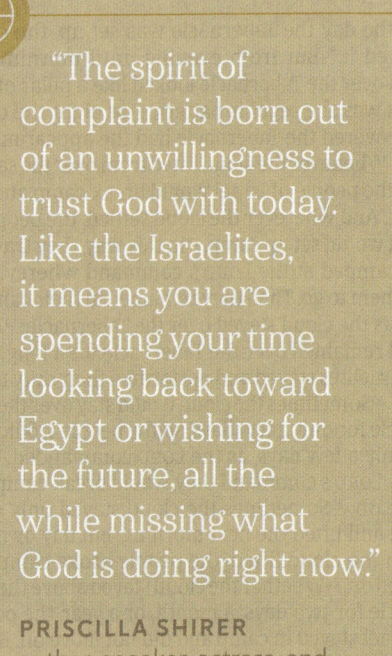

> "The spirit of complaint is born out of an unwillingness to trust God with today. Like the Israelites, it means you are spending your time looking back toward Egypt or wishing for the future, all the while missing what God is doing right now."
>
> **PRISCILLA SHIRER**
> author, speaker, actress, and evangelist

⁹"When you arrive in your own land and go to war against your enemies who attack you, sound the alarm with the trumpets. Then the Lord your God will remember you and rescue you from your enemies. ¹⁰Blow the trumpets in times of gladness, too, sounding them at your annual festivals and at the beginning of each month. And blow the trumpets over your burnt offerings and peace offerings. The trumpets will remind your God of his covenant with you. I am the Lord your God."

The Israelites Leave Sinai

¹¹In the second year after Israel's departure from Egypt—on the twentieth day of the second month*—the cloud lifted from the Tabernacle of the Covenant.* ¹²So the Israelites set out from the wilderness of Sinai and traveled on from place to place until the cloud stopped in the wilderness of Paran.

¹³When the people set out for the first time, following the instructions the Lord had given through Moses, ¹⁴Judah's troops led the way. They marched behind their banner, and their leader was Nahshon son of Amminadab. ¹⁵They were joined by the troops of the tribe of Issachar, led by Nethanel son of Zuar, ¹⁶and the troops of the tribe of Zebulun, led by Eliab son of Helon.

¹⁷Then the Tabernacle was taken down, and the Gershonite and Merarite divisions of the Levites were next in the line of march, carrying the Tabernacle with them. ¹⁸Reuben's troops went next, marching behind their banner. Their leader was Elizur son of Shedeur. ¹⁹They were joined by the troops of the tribe of Simeon, led by Shelumiel son of Zurishaddai, ²⁰and the troops of the tribe of Gad, led by Eliasaph son of Deuel.

²¹Next came the Kohathite division of the Levites, carrying the sacred objects from the Tabernacle. Before they arrived at the next camp, the Tabernacle would already be set up at its new location. ²²Ephraim's troops went next, marching behind their banner. Their leader was Elishama son of Ammihud. ²³They were joined by the troops of the tribe of Manasseh, led by Gamaliel son of Pedahzur, ²⁴and the troops of the tribe of Benjamin, led by Abidan son of Gideoni.

²⁵Dan's troops went last, marching behind their banner and serving as the rear guard for all the tribal camps. Their leader was Ahiezer son of Ammishaddai. ²⁶They were joined by the troops of the tribe of Asher, led by Pagiel son of Ocran, ²⁷and the troops of the tribe of Naphtali, led by Ahira son of Enan.

²⁸This was the order in which the Israelites marched, division by division.

²⁹One day Moses said to his brother-in-law, Hobab son of Reuel the Midianite, "We are on our way to the place the Lord promised us, for he said, 'I will give it to you.' Come with us and we will treat you well, for the Lord has promised wonderful blessings for Israel!"

³⁰But Hobab replied, "No, I will not go. I must return to my own land and family."

³¹"Please don't leave us," Moses pleaded. "You know the places in the wilderness where we should camp. Come, be our guide. ³²If you do, we'll share with you all the blessings the Lord gives us."

³³They marched for three days after leaving the mountain of the Lord, with the Ark of the Lord's Covenant moving ahead of them to show them where to stop and rest. ³⁴As they moved on each day, the cloud of the Lord hovered over them. ³⁵And whenever the Ark set out, Moses would shout, "Arise, O Lord, and let your enemies be scattered! Let them flee before you!" ³⁶And when the Ark was set down, he would say, "Return, O Lord, to the countless thousands of Israel!"

10:11a This day in the ancient Hebrew lunar calendar occurred in late April, May, or early June. 10:11b Or *Tabernacle of the Testimony.*

10:11-36 When the cloud of God's presence lifted from the Tabernacle, the Israelites packed up camp. While they didn't know where they were going, they followed God's specific instructions for packing (see Numbers 4) and traveled as God led them. Sometimes, we don't know where God is taking us. In those times, we can focus on our obedience in the small daily choices, trusting that we will see his plan in his time.

The People Complain to Moses

11 Soon the people began to complain about their hardship, and the LORD heard everything they said. Then the LORD's anger blazed against them, and he sent a fire to rage among them, and he destroyed some of the people in the outskirts of the camp. ²Then the people screamed to Moses for help, and when he prayed to the LORD, the fire stopped. ³After that, the area was known as Taberah (which means "the place of burning"), because fire from the LORD had burned among them there.

⁴Then the foreign rabble who were traveling with the Israelites began to crave the good things of Egypt. And the people of Israel also began to complain. "Oh, for some meat!" they exclaimed. ⁵"We remember the fish we used to eat for free in Egypt. And we had all the cucumbers, melons, leeks, onions, and garlic we wanted. ⁶But now our appetites are gone. All we ever see is this manna!"

⁷The manna looked like small coriander seeds, and it was pale yellow like gum resin. ⁸The people would go out and gather it from the ground. They made flour by grinding it with hand mills or pounding it in mortars. Then they boiled it in a pot and made it into flat cakes. These cakes tasted like pastries baked with olive oil. ⁹The manna came down on the camp with the dew during the night.

¹⁰Moses heard all the families standing in the doorways of their tents whining, and the LORD became extremely angry. Moses was also very aggravated. ¹¹And Moses said to the LORD, "Why are you treating me, your servant, so harshly? Have mercy on me! What did I do to deserve the burden of all these people? ¹²Did I give birth to them? Did I bring them into the world? Why did you tell me to carry them in my arms like a mother carries a nursing baby? How can I carry them to the land you swore to give their ancestors? ¹³Where am I supposed to get meat for all these people? They keep whining to me, saying, 'Give us meat to eat!' ¹⁴I can't carry all these people by myself! The load is far too heavy! ¹⁵If this is how you intend to treat me, just go ahead and kill me. Do me a favor and spare me this misery!"

Moses Chooses Seventy Leaders

¹⁶Then the LORD said to Moses, "Gather before me seventy men who are recognized as elders and leaders of Israel. Bring them to the Tabernacle* to stand there with you. ¹⁷I will come down and talk to you there. I will take some of the Spirit that is upon you, and I will put the Spirit upon them also. They will bear the burden of the people along with you, so you will not have to carry it alone.

¹⁸"And say to the people, 'Purify yourselves, for tomorrow you will have meat to eat. You were whining, and the LORD heard you when you cried, "Oh, for some meat! We were better off in Egypt!" Now the LORD will give you meat, and you will have to eat it. ¹⁹And it won't be for just a day or two, or for five or ten or even twenty. ²⁰You will eat it for a whole month until you gag and are sick of it. For you have rejected the LORD, who is here among you, and you have whined to him, saying, "Why did we ever leave Egypt?"'"

²¹But Moses responded to the LORD, "There are 600,000 foot soldiers here with me, and yet you say, 'I will give them meat for a whole month!' ²²Even if we butchered all our flocks and herds, would that satisfy them? Even if we caught all the fish in the sea, would that be enough?"

²³Then the LORD said to Moses, "Has my arm lost its power? Now you will see whether or not my word comes true!"

²⁴So Moses went out and reported the LORD's words to the people. He gathered the seventy elders and stationed them around the Tabernacle.* ²⁵And the LORD came down in the cloud and spoke to Moses. Then he gave the seventy elders the same Spirit that was upon Moses. And when the Spirit rested upon them, they prophesied. But this never happened again.

²⁶Two men, Eldad and Medad, had stayed behind in the camp. They were listed among the elders, but they had not gone out to the Tabernacle. Yet the Spirit rested upon them as well, so they prophesied there in the camp. ²⁷A young man ran and reported to Moses, "Eldad and Medad are prophesying in the camp!"

²⁸Joshua son of Nun, who had been Moses' assistant since his youth, protested, "Moses, my master, make them stop!"

²⁹But Moses replied, "Are you jealous for my sake? I wish that all the LORD's people were prophets and that the LORD would put his Spirit upon them all!" ³⁰Then Moses returned to the camp with the elders of Israel.

The LORD Sends Quail

³¹Now the LORD sent a wind that brought quail from the sea and let them fall all around the camp. For miles in every direction there were quail flying about three feet above the ground.* ³²So the

---

11:16 Hebrew *the Tent of Meeting.* 11:24 Hebrew *the tent;* also in 11:26. 11:31 Or *there were quail about 3 feet* [2 cubits or 92 centimeters] *deep on the ground.*

11:11-15 Moses' complaint is couched in the feminine imagery of a mother, indirectly pointing to God's role in giving birth to his people and nursing them. While we often focus on God as Father, here we see that God is not limited to roles traditionally associated with men. We see similar maternal imagery for God in Isaiah 49:15.
11:16-30 While this passage alludes specifically to male elders and prophets, the ability to prophesy in God's Spirit was not exclusive to men. (In the Bible, this has to do with telling truth from God, not necessarily telling future events.) God also spoke through female prophets, including Miriam (Exodus 15:20-21), Deborah (Judges 4–5), Huldah (2 Kings 22:14-20), and Anna (Luke 2:36-38). At Pentecost, God poured out his Spirit on both men and women, leading them to prophesy, just as he had promised (Acts 2; see Joel 2:28-29).

people went out and caught quail all that day and throughout the night and all the next day, too. No one gathered less than fifty bushels*! They spread the quail all around the camp to dry. ³³But while they were gorging themselves on the meat—while it was still in their mouths—the anger of the LORD blazed against the people, and he struck them with a severe plague. ³⁴So that place was called Kibroth-hattaavah (which means "graves of gluttony") because there they buried the people who had craved meat from Egypt. ³⁵From Kibroth-hattaavah the Israelites traveled to Hazeroth, where they stayed for some time.

The Complaints of Miriam and Aaron

12 While they were at Hazeroth, Miriam and Aaron criticized Moses because he had married a Cushite woman. ²They said, "Has the LORD spoken only through Moses? Hasn't he spoken through us, too?" But the LORD heard them. ³(Now Moses was very humble—more humble than any other person on earth.)

⁴So immediately the LORD called to Moses, Aaron, and Miriam and said, "Go out to the Tabernacle,* all three of you!" So the three of them went to the Tabernacle. ⁵Then the LORD descended in the pillar of cloud and stood at the entrance of the Tabernacle.* "Aaron and Miriam!" he called, and they stepped forward. ⁶And the LORD said to them, "Now listen to what I say:

"If there were prophets among you,
    I, the LORD, would reveal myself in visions.
    I would speak to them in dreams.
⁷ But not with my servant Moses.
    Of all my house, he is the one I trust.
⁸ I speak to him face to face,
    clearly, and not in riddles!
    He sees the LORD as he is.
So why were you not afraid
    to criticize my servant Moses?"

⁹The LORD was very angry with them, and he departed. ¹⁰As the cloud moved from above the Tabernacle, there stood Miriam, her skin as white as snow from leprosy.* When Aaron saw what had happened to her, ¹¹he cried out to Moses, "Oh, my master! Please don't punish us for this sin we have so foolishly committed. ¹²Don't let her be like a stillborn baby, already decayed at birth."

¹³So Moses cried out to the LORD, "O God, I beg you, please heal her!"

¹⁴But the LORD said to Moses, "If her father had done nothing more than spit in her face, wouldn't she be defiled for seven days? So keep her outside the camp for seven days, and after that she may be accepted back."

¹⁵So Miriam was kept outside the camp for seven days, and the people waited until she was brought back before they traveled again. ¹⁶Then they left Hazeroth and camped in the wilderness of Paran.

Twelve Scouts Explore Canaan

13 The LORD now said to Moses, ²"Send out men to explore the land of Canaan, the land I am giving to the Israelites. Send one leader from each of the twelve ancestral tribes." ³So Moses did as the LORD commanded him. He sent out twelve men, all tribal leaders of Israel, from their camp in the wilderness of Paran. ⁴These were the tribes and the names of their leaders:

Tribe	Leader
Reuben	Shammua son of Zaccur
⁵ Simeon	Shaphat son of Hori
⁶ Judah	Caleb son of Jephunneh
⁷ Issachar	Igal son of Joseph
⁸ Ephraim	Hoshea son of Nun
⁹ Benjamin	Palti son of Raphu
¹⁰ Zebulun	Gaddiel son of Sodi
¹¹ Manasseh son of Joseph	Gaddi son of Susi
¹² Dan	Ammiel son of Gemalli
¹³ Asher	Sethur son of Michael
¹⁴ Naphtali	Nahbi son of Vophsi
¹⁵ Gad	Geuel son of Maki

¹⁶These are the names of the men Moses sent out to explore the land. (Moses called Hoshea son of Nun by the name Joshua.)

¹⁷Moses gave the men these instructions as he sent them out to explore the land: "Go north through the Negev into the hill country. ¹⁸See what the land

---

11:32 Hebrew *10 homers* [2.2 kiloliters]. **12:4** Hebrew *the Tent of Meeting*. **12:5** Hebrew *the tent;* also in 12:10. **12:10** Or *with a skin disease*. The Hebrew word used here can describe various skin diseases.

12:1 Some suggest that "Cushite woman" referred to Zipporah, as there was a region near Midian called Cushan. Others think that Moses had taken a second wife. If Moses did take a second wife and Zipporah remained alive, two potential explanations arise: Polygamy was permitted both legally and culturally, so Moses was able to marry an additional wife, or Moses had divorced Zipporah (a possible interpretation of Exodus 18:2). Both possibilities present a less than ideal scenario and suggest we need to be careful about idealizing any human leader, even one chosen by God who met with him face to face. (For more on this passage, see "Asking the Real Question" on page 184.)

12:2-15 As it turns out, Miriam and Aaron's true complaint was tied to personal jealousy about Moses' unique status (12:2). The reason why only Miriam received the punishment of a skin disease remains unclear. It may be that she instigated the incident since her name is listed first in 12:1. Additionally, while Miriam and Aaron both make the complaint in 12:2, the Hebrew in 12:1 points to a single female speaker. As such, it is possible that Miriam alone voiced the complaint, and that Aaron simply stood with her. In this case, the initial complaint led to the punishment. (For more on this passage, see "Asking the Real Question" on page 184.)

Miriam

IDENTITY — Your Pain Is Building You

Frustration, fear, anxiety, pride, jealousy. Whatever brought Miriam to that place of complaint, it needed correcting. God allowed Miriam's actions to have consequences she would feel. Pain is often our greatest teacher, and sometimes God, out of great love, will allow pain.

I have felt the pain of job loss, financial strain, the loss of a child, and the sting of divorce. And sometimes I have had to dwell in the consequences of my decisions, asking God for relief that seemed long in coming.

We often think pain and love can't dwell together. We often assume that a life of faith must be without pain to testify to God's goodness.

Yet, your pain is building you.

God, out of great love, knowing what you want to be and what he has for you, is walking you through this pain. He is building your character, your heart, and your faith.

You're in pain, and God loves you. You're in pain, and God loves you! *You're in pain, and God loves you!* One does not cancel out the other.

Pain is not absent from a believer's life. It is there, it is real, and it is often the foundation of faith. When pain has done its work in our souls, relief comes, and—like Miriam—we can heal stronger and wiser.

> Today's pain is tomorrow's wisdom.

MIRIAM'S STORY IS TOLD IN EXODUS 2:1-10; 15:20-21; NUMBERS 12:1-15; 20:1;
SHE IS ALSO MENTIONED IN DEUTERONOMY 24:9; 1 CHRONICLES 6:3; MICAH 6:4.

IDENTIFY

How is pain building you?

How can you leverage your time as you wait for deliverance from the pain?

"Even in my deepest pain I have experienced God's love and faithfulness. I know that with him my tears are never wasted."

LISA D. EDMONDS is mother of two daughters, a Stonecroft Ministries speaker and speaker trainer, worship leader, and constituent care director for The Dr. James Dobson Family Institute.

is like, and find out whether the people living there are strong or weak, few or many. ¹⁹See what kind of land they live in. Is it good or bad? Do their towns have walls, or are they unprotected like open camps? ²⁰Is the soil fertile or poor? Are there many trees? Do your best to bring back samples of the crops you see." (It happened to be the season for harvesting the first ripe grapes.)

²¹So they went up and explored the land from the wilderness of Zin as far as Rehob, near Lebo-hamath. ²²Going north, they passed through the Negev and arrived at Hebron, where Ahiman, Sheshai, and Talmai—all descendants of Anak—lived. (The ancient town of Hebron was founded seven years before the Egyptian city of Zoan.) ²³When they came to the valley of Eshcol, they cut down a branch with

Koinonia

IMAGE — MY STORY WITH COMMUNITY, WORKPLACE & CHURCH

Asking the Real Question

SCRIPTURE CONNECTION: NUMBERS 12:1-16

What? Why was only Miriam, a prophet, punished? While the Hebrew suggests that Miriam was the instigator (see note on 12:2-15), it's easy to focus on the fact that Aaron wasn't punished. What's even harder to embrace is that when God gives us influence, we will be held responsible for how we use it.

Miriam and Aaron's complaint had two parts. They started by complaining about Moses' Cushite wife. But 12:2 reveals the true issue: They wanted more influence. God had spoken through them, too!

God addressed both parts. First, he described his unique relationship with Moses. God then focused on Miriam and Aaron's initial attack. He asked why they were not afraid to criticize Moses (12:8).

> We risk God's discipline when we criticize or create division.

So what was wrong with Miriam's attack on Moses' Cushite wife? If Moses' wife here was not Zipporah but a different wife, God's law didn't prohibit taking a second wife, nor did it forbid remarrying after a divorce. The marriage itself wasn't the problem, nor was marrying a Cushite. God did forbid intermarriage with the Canaanite peoples of the Promised Land. However, God did not forbid his people from marrying Cushites.

Since the marriage was permissible, is it possible that Miriam's use of "Cushite" was racially charged? A Cushite would have had darker skin. God punished Miriam by turning her brown skin "white as snow" (12:10). Whether or not the criticism was intended that way, Miriam and Aaron's complaint held the potential to divide God's people.

The real question for us is, what can we learn? In reaching for more influence, Miriam and Aaron judged what God had not. God's response was swift and uncompromising. Creating division, including along racial lines, is not acceptable to God. Nor is criticizing others to gain more influence.

IMAGINE

How has God called you to a role of influence?

How can you encourage others' influence?

How can you bring racial reconciliation and avoid promoting racial division?

"Father, guard me from creating division or reaching for things beyond your call."

JENNIFER BROWN JONES, PhD, is an author, speaker, and instructor of Old Testament for Liberty University's PhD of Bible Exposition program. She loves helping others see how God speaks to them through the Bible today.

a single cluster of grapes so large that it took two of them to carry it on a pole between them! They also brought back samples of the pomegranates and figs. ²⁴That place was called the valley of Eshcol (which means "cluster"), because of the cluster of grapes the Israelite men cut there.

The Scouting Report

²⁵After exploring the land for forty days, the men returned ²⁶to Moses, Aaron, and the whole community of Israel at Kadesh in the wilderness of Paran. They reported to the whole community what they had seen and showed them the fruit they had taken from the land. ²⁷This was their report to Moses: "We entered the land you sent us to explore, and it is indeed a bountiful country—a land flowing with milk and honey. Here is the kind of fruit it produces. ²⁸But the people living there are powerful, and their towns are large and fortified. We even saw giants there, the descendants of Anak! ²⁹The Amalekites live in the Negev, and the Hittites, Jebusites, and Amorites live in the hill country. The Canaanites live along the coast of the Mediterranean Sea* and along the Jordan Valley."

³⁰But Caleb tried to quiet the people as they stood before Moses. "Let's go at once to take the land," he said. "We can certainly conquer it!"

³¹But the other men who had explored the land with him disagreed. "We can't go up against them! They are stronger than we are!" ³²So they spread this bad report about the land among the Israelites: "The land we traveled through and explored will devour anyone who goes to live there. All the people we saw were huge. ³³We even saw giants* there, the descendants of Anak. Next to them we felt like grasshoppers, and that's what they thought, too!"

The People Rebel

14 Then the whole community began weeping aloud, and they cried all night. ²Their voices rose in a great chorus of protest against Moses and Aaron. "If only we had died in Egypt, or even here in the wilderness!" they complained. ³"Why is the LORD taking us to this country only to have us die in battle? Our wives and our little ones will be carried off as plunder! Wouldn't it be better for us to return to Egypt?" ⁴Then they plotted among themselves, "Let's choose a new leader and go back to Egypt!"

⁵Then Moses and Aaron fell face down on the ground before the whole community of Israel. ⁶Two of the men who had explored the land, Joshua son of Nun and Caleb son of Jephunneh, tore their clothing. ⁷They said to all the people of Israel, "The land we traveled through and explored is a wonderful land! ⁸And if the LORD is pleased with us, he will bring us safely into that land and give it to us. It is a rich land flowing with milk and honey. ⁹Do not rebel against the LORD, and don't be afraid of the people of the land. They are only helpless prey to us! They have no protection, but the LORD is with us! Don't be afraid of them!"

¹⁰But the whole community began to talk about stoning Joshua and Caleb. Then the glorious presence of the LORD appeared to all the Israelites at the Tabernacle.* ¹¹And the LORD said to Moses, "How long will these people treat me with contempt? Will they

---

13:29 Hebrew *the sea*. 13:33 Hebrew *nephilim*. 14:10 Hebrew *the Tent of Meeting*.

13:25–14:25 The scouts agreed about the facts but differed in their interpretations: Ten feared the land's inhabitants, but two trusted the Lord. Caleb and Joshua feared rebelling against God more than they feared the enemy. Unfortunately, the Israelites were persuaded by the negative report, and fear spread rapidly, sparking plots of rebellion and murder that were only stopped by God's visible appearance in their midst. While God forgave the people, they still had to live with the consequences of their rebellion.

Insight — OPINION POLL

QUESTION: Should Israel conquer the land of Canaan?

SAMPLING: Twelve spies who've been there for reconnaissance

When is following the majority a wrong move?

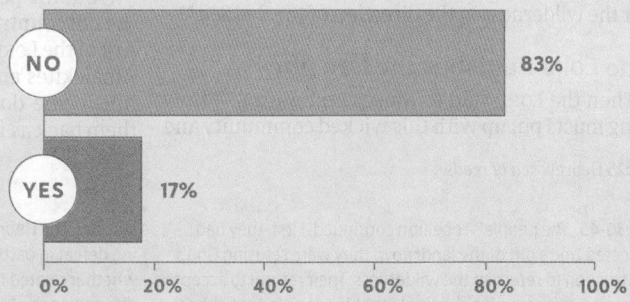

NO — 83%
YES — 17%

never believe me, even after all the miraculous signs I have done among them? ¹²I will disown them and destroy them with a plague. Then I will make you into a nation greater and mightier than they are!"

Moses Intercedes for the People

¹³But Moses objected. "What will the Egyptians think when they hear about it?" he asked the LORD. "They know full well the power you displayed in rescuing your people from Egypt. ¹⁴Now if you destroy them, the Egyptians will send a report to the inhabitants of this land, who have already heard that you live among your people. They know, LORD, that you have appeared to your people face to face and that your pillar of cloud hovers over them. They know that you go before them in the pillar of cloud by day and the pillar of fire by night. ¹⁵Now if you slaughter all these people with a single blow, the nations that have heard of your fame will say, ¹⁶'The LORD was not able to bring them into the land he swore to give them, so he killed them in the wilderness.'

¹⁷"Please, Lord, prove that your power is as great as you have claimed. For you said, ¹⁸'The LORD is slow to anger and filled with unfailing love, forgiving every kind of sin and rebellion. But he does not excuse the guilty. He lays the sins of the parents upon their children; the entire family is affected—even children in the third and fourth generations.' ¹⁹In keeping with your magnificent, unfailing love, please pardon the sins of this people, just as you have forgiven them ever since they left Egypt."

²⁰Then the LORD said, "I will pardon them as you have requested. ²¹But as surely as I live, and as surely as the earth is filled with the LORD's glory, ²²not one of these people will ever enter that land. They have all seen my glorious presence and the miraculous signs I performed both in Egypt and in the wilderness, but again and again they have tested me by refusing to listen to my voice. ²³They will never even see the land I swore to give their ancestors. None of those who have treated me with contempt will ever see it. ²⁴But my servant Caleb has a different attitude than the others have. He has remained loyal to me, so I will bring him into the land he explored. His descendants will possess their full share of that land. ²⁵Now turn around, and don't go on toward the land where the Amalekites and Canaanites live. Tomorrow you must set out for the wilderness in the direction of the Red Sea.*"

The LORD Punishes the Israelites

²⁶Then the LORD said to Moses and Aaron, ²⁷"How long must I put up with this wicked community and its complaints about me? Yes, I have heard the complaints the Israelites are making against me. ²⁸Now tell them this: 'As surely as I live, declares the LORD, I will do to you the very things I heard you say. ²⁹You will all drop dead in this wilderness! Because you complained against me, every one of you who is twenty years old or older and was included in the registration will die. ³⁰You will not enter and occupy the land I swore to give you. The only exceptions will be Caleb son of Jephunneh and Joshua son of Nun.

³¹"'You said your children would be carried off as plunder. Well, I will bring them safely into the land, and they will enjoy what you have despised. ³²But as for you, you will drop dead in this wilderness. ³³And your children will be like shepherds, wandering in the wilderness for forty years. In this way, they will pay for your faithlessness, until the last of you lies dead in the wilderness.

³⁴"'Because your men explored the land for forty days, you must wander in the wilderness for forty years—a year for each day, suffering the consequences of your sins. Then you will discover what it is like to have me for an enemy.' ³⁵I, the LORD, have spoken! I will certainly do these things to every member of the community who has conspired against me. They will be destroyed here in this wilderness, and here they will die!"

³⁶The ten men Moses had sent to explore the land—the ones who incited rebellion against the LORD with their bad report—³⁷were struck dead with a plague before the LORD. ³⁸Of the twelve who had explored the land, only Joshua and Caleb remained alive.

³⁹When Moses reported the LORD's words to all the Israelites, the people were filled with grief. ⁴⁰Then they got up early the next morning and went to the top of the range of hills. "Let's go," they said. "We realize that we have sinned, but now we are ready to enter the land the LORD has promised us."

⁴¹But Moses said, "Why are you now disobeying the LORD's orders to return to the wilderness? It won't work. ⁴²Do not go up into the land now. You will only be crushed by your enemies because the LORD is not with you. ⁴³When you face the Amalekites and Canaanites in battle, you will be slaughtered. The LORD will abandon you because you have abandoned the LORD."

⁴⁴But the people defiantly pushed ahead toward the hill country, even though neither Moses nor the Ark of the LORD's Covenant left the camp. ⁴⁵Then the Amalekites and the Canaanites who lived in those hills came down and attacked them and chased them back as far as Hormah.

14:25 Hebrew *sea of reeds*.

14:36-45 The people's rebellion continued. First, they had rejected God's gift of the land; now, they were refusing God's instruction to return to the wilderness. Their refusal to accept the consequences of their initial rebellion resulted in further disaster. The Hebrew wording of 14:45 points to a resounding defeat in battle. We must follow God's instructions, whether related to a promise of blessing or to a rebuke for disobedience.

Laws concerning Offerings

15 Then the LORD told Moses, ²"Give the following instructions to the people of Israel.

"When you finally settle in the land I am giving you, ³you will offer special gifts as a pleasing aroma to the LORD. These gifts may take the form of a burnt offering, a sacrifice to fulfill a vow, a voluntary offering, or an offering at any of your annual festivals, and they may be taken from your herds of cattle or your flocks of sheep and goats. ⁴When you present these offerings, you must also give the LORD a grain offering of two quarts* of choice flour mixed with one quart* of olive oil. ⁵For each lamb offered as a burnt offering or a special sacrifice, you must also present one quart of wine as a liquid offering.

⁶"If the sacrifice is a ram, give a grain offering of four quarts* of choice flour mixed with a third of a gallon* of olive oil, ⁷and give a third of a gallon of wine as a liquid offering. This will be a pleasing aroma to the LORD.

⁸"When you present a young bull as a burnt offering or as a sacrifice to fulfill a vow or as a peace offering to the LORD, ⁹you must also give a grain offering of six quarts* of choice flour mixed with two quarts* of olive oil, ¹⁰and give two quarts of wine as a liquid offering. This will be a special gift, a pleasing aroma to the LORD.

¹¹"Each sacrifice of a bull, ram, lamb, or young goat should be prepared in this way. ¹²Follow these instructions with each offering you present. ¹³All of you native-born Israelites must follow these instructions when you offer a special gift as a pleasing aroma to the LORD. ¹⁴And if any foreigners visit you or live among you and want to present a special gift as a pleasing aroma to the LORD, they must follow these same procedures. ¹⁵Native-born Israelites and foreigners are equal before the LORD and are subject to the same decrees. This is a permanent law for you, to be observed from generation to generation. ¹⁶The same instructions and regulations will apply both to you and to the foreigners living among you."

¹⁷Then the LORD said to Moses, ¹⁸"Give the following instructions to the people of Israel.

"When you arrive in the land where I am taking you, ¹⁹and you eat the crops that grow there, you must set some aside as a sacred offering to the LORD. ²⁰Present a cake from the first of the flour you grind, and set it aside as a sacred offering, as you do with the first grain from the threshing floor. ²¹Throughout the generations to come, you are to present a sacred offering to the LORD each year from the first of your ground flour.

²²"But suppose you unintentionally fail to carry out all these commands that the LORD has given you through Moses. ²³And suppose your descendants in the future fail to do everything the LORD has commanded through Moses. ²⁴If the mistake was made unintentionally, and the community was unaware of it, the whole community must present a young bull for a burnt offering as a pleasing aroma to the LORD. It must be offered along with its prescribed grain offering and liquid offering and with one male goat for a sin offering. ²⁵With it the priest will purify the whole community of Israel, making them right with the LORD,* and they will be forgiven. For it was an unintentional sin, and they have corrected it with their offerings to the LORD—the special gift and the sin offering. ²⁶The whole community of Israel will be forgiven, including the foreigners living among you, for all the people were involved in the sin.

²⁷"If one individual commits an unintentional sin, the guilty person must bring a one-year-old female goat for a sin offering. ²⁸The priest will sacrifice it to purify* the guilty person before the LORD, and that person will be forgiven. ²⁹These same instructions apply both to native-born Israelites and to the foreigners living among you.

³⁰"But those who brazenly violate the LORD's will, whether native-born Israelites or foreigners, have blasphemed the LORD, and they must be cut off from the community. ³¹Since they have treated the LORD's word with contempt and deliberately disobeyed his command, they must be completely cut off and suffer the punishment for their guilt."

Penalty for Breaking the Sabbath

³²One day while the people of Israel were in the wilderness, they discovered a man gathering wood on the Sabbath day. ³³The people who found him doing this took him before Moses, Aaron, and the rest of the community. ³⁴They held him in custody because they did not know what to do with him. ³⁵Then the LORD said to Moses, "The man must be put to death! The whole community must stone him outside the camp." ³⁶So the whole community took the man outside the camp and stoned him to death, just as the LORD had commanded Moses.

15:4a Hebrew ¹⁄₁₀ of an ephah [2.2 liters].   15:4b Hebrew ¼ of a hin [1 liter]; also in 15:5.   15:6a Hebrew ²⁄₁₀ of an ephah [4.4 liters].   15:6b Hebrew ⅓ of a hin [1.3 liters]; also in 15:7.   15:9a Hebrew ³⁄₁₀ of an ephah [6.6 liters].   15:9b Hebrew ½ of a hin [2 liters]; also in 15:10.   15:25 Or *will make atonement for the whole community of Israel.*   15:28 Or *to make atonement for.*

15:1-41 Numbers 1–14 took place in a relatively short period of time, but Numbers 15 describes the beginning of a long period—the bulk of the forty years in the wilderness. Relatively little is known about this time, though there are references to events that took place during the wilderness wanderings (for example, Deuteronomy 8:2-6; 29:5-6; Joshua 5:4-8; Ezekiel 20:10-26; Amos 5:25-26; Acts 7:42-43). During this period, Moses continued to deliver laws and guidelines to govern Israelite society, especially for that day when survivors of the wilderness would finally enter the Promised Land. This chapter deals with three categories of legal matters. Presented in the middle of stories about a stubborn and disobedient Israel, Numbers 15 raises hope that God was not finished with them yet and that the Promised Land still awaited Israel's descendants.

Tassels on Clothing

³⁷Then the LORD said to Moses, ³⁸"Give the following instructions to the people of Israel: Throughout the generations to come you must make tassels for the hems of your clothing and attach them with a blue cord. ³⁹When you see the tassels, you will remember and obey all the commands of the LORD instead of following your own desires and defiling yourselves, as you are prone to do. ⁴⁰The tassels will help you remember that you must obey all my commands and be holy to your God. ⁴¹I am the LORD your God who brought you out of the land of Egypt that I might be your God. I am the LORD your God!"

Korah's Rebellion

16 One day Korah son of Izhar, a descendant of Kohath son of Levi, conspired with Dathan and Abiram, the sons of Eliab, and On son of Peleth, from the tribe of Reuben. ²They incited a rebellion against Moses, along with 250 other leaders of the community, all prominent members of the assembly. ³They united against Moses and Aaron and said, "You have gone too far! The whole community of Israel has been set apart by the LORD, and he is with all of us. What right do you have to act as though you are greater than the rest of the LORD's people?"

⁴When Moses heard what they were saying, he

15:37-41 Had the Hebrews remembered their special relationship with the Lord, they might have avoided the problems reported in the book of Numbers. The tassels were to remind Israel of their covenant bond with a holy God who had redeemed them from slavery. In keeping with the call to covenant relationship, God expected them to observe the law (see Deuteronomy 6:6-9; Matthew 9:20; 14:36; 23:5). The color blue signified royalty and reflected God's holiness.

Come Close — REMEMBERING: MY FAMILY TASSEL

SCRIPTURE CONNECTION: NUMBERS 15:37-41

When I was growing up, I remember my grandmother Sophia would wake up at 4:00 a.m. every day to pray for each of her children and grandchildren by name. I have also watched my grandmother's prayer habit be passed on to the next generation. My mother, Gertrude, prays the same.

Unfortunately, as I grew older, I forgot our family traditions. I was lonely, hurt, and disappointed because I had abandoned the God of my ancestors and his Son, Jesus, whom my family would call to daily. But one day the Holy Spirit prompted me to return through a song titled "Crossroads" by Zimbabwean Christian pastor and gospel musician Prince Mafukidze. As I listened to the lyrics asking God to carry us through, I fell on my knees and remembered my grandmother's prayers.

I may not have a physical tassel, but my grandmother's prayers and that song have been intangible tassels that remind me of the commands set before us and of how Jesus created me with a clear purpose. We all have a tassel today that dwells with us, and it is Jesus himself, who breathes his commands and orders our steps.

Now, I have drawn my family tree in a study Bible. I hope to hand this Bible down to future generations. When I do, it will serve as a physical reminder for generations to come of God's faithfulness, like a family tassel. May my family seek God daily and trust God completely.

REFLECT "'For I know the plans I have for you,' says the LORD. 'They are plans for good and not for disaster, to give you a future and a hope.'" JEREMIAH 29:11

Dear Lord, you created me with a clear purpose. Thank you for the Holy Spirit, who prompts us to return when we stray. May we seek you daily and trust you completely. Amen.

CONSIDER "[A tassel] is a small way to express your commitment to the God of Israel. It's a special symbol to remind yourself and the rest of the world to whom you belong." DAVID WILBER

> Our tassel today dwells with us: Jesus himself breathes his commands and orders our steps.

ADELAIDE MANYARA MUCHETU shares true life experiences with many women and believes in relational evangelism. Discipleship is her mantra with exhortation being her greatest strength.

fell face down on the ground. ⁵Then he said to Korah and his followers, "Tomorrow morning the LORD will show us who belongs to him* and who is holy. The LORD will allow only those whom he selects to enter his own presence. ⁶Korah, you and all your followers must prepare your incense burners. ⁷Light fires in them tomorrow, and burn incense before the LORD. Then we will see whom the LORD chooses as his holy one. You Levites are the ones who have gone too far!"

⁸Then Moses spoke again to Korah: "Now listen, you Levites! ⁹Does it seem insignificant to you that the God of Israel has chosen you from among all the community of Israel to be near him so you can serve in the LORD's Tabernacle and stand before the people to minister to them? ¹⁰Korah, he has already given this special ministry to you and your fellow Levites. Are you now demanding the priesthood as well? ¹¹The LORD is the one you and your followers are really revolting against! For who is Aaron that you are complaining about him?"

¹²Then Moses summoned Dathan and Abiram, the sons of Eliab, but they replied, "We refuse to come before you! ¹³Isn't it enough that you brought us out of Egypt, a land flowing with milk and honey, to kill us here in this wilderness, and that you now treat us like your subjects? ¹⁴What's more, you haven't brought us into another land flowing with milk and honey. You haven't given us a new homeland with fields and vineyards. Are you trying to fool these men?* We will not come."

¹⁵Then Moses became very angry and said to the LORD, "Do not accept their grain offerings! I have not taken so much as a donkey from them, and I have never hurt a single one of them." ¹⁶And Moses said to Korah, "You and all your followers must come here tomorrow and present yourselves before the LORD. Aaron will also be here. ¹⁷You and each of your 250 followers must prepare an incense burner and put incense on it, so you can all present them before the LORD. Aaron will also bring his incense burner."

¹⁸So each of these men prepared an incense burner, lit the fire, and placed incense on it. Then they all stood at the entrance of the Tabernacle* with Moses and Aaron. ¹⁹Meanwhile, Korah had stirred up the entire community against Moses and Aaron, and they all gathered at the Tabernacle entrance. Then the glorious presence of the LORD appeared to the whole community, ²⁰and the LORD said to Moses and Aaron, ²¹"Get away from all these people so that I may instantly destroy them!"

²²But Moses and Aaron fell face down on the ground. "O God," they pleaded, "you are the God who gives breath to all creatures. Must you be angry with all the people when only one man sins?"

²³And the LORD said to Moses, ²⁴"Then tell all the people to get away from the tents of Korah, Dathan, and Abiram."

²⁵So Moses got up and rushed over to the tents of Dathan and Abiram, followed by the elders of Israel. ²⁶"Quick!" he told the people. "Get away from the tents of these wicked men, and don't touch anything that belongs to them. If you do, you will be destroyed for their sins." ²⁷So all the people stood back from the tents of Korah, Dathan, and Abiram. Then Dathan and Abiram came out and stood at the entrances of their tents, together with their wives and children and little ones.

²⁸And Moses said, "This is how you will know that the LORD has sent me to do all these things that I have done—for I have not done them on my own. ²⁹If these men die a natural death, or if nothing unusual happens, then the LORD has not sent me. ³⁰But if the LORD does something entirely new and the ground opens its mouth and swallows them and all their belongings, and they go down alive into the grave,* then you will know that these men have shown contempt for the LORD."

³¹He had hardly finished speaking the words when the ground suddenly split open beneath them. ³²The earth opened its mouth and swallowed the men, along with their households and all their followers who were standing with them, and everything they owned. ³³So they went down alive into the grave, along with all their belongings. The earth closed over them, and they all vanished from among the people of Israel. ³⁴All the people around them fled when they heard their screams. "The earth will swallow us, too!" they cried. ³⁵Then fire blazed forth from the LORD and burned up the 250 men who were offering incense.

³⁶*And the LORD said to Moses, ³⁷"Tell Eleazar son of Aaron the priest to pull all the incense burners from the fire, for they are holy. Also tell him to scatter the burning coals. ³⁸Take the incense burners of these men who have sinned at the cost of their lives, and hammer the metal into a thin sheet to overlay

---

16:5 Greek version reads *God has visited and knows those who are his.* Compare 2 Tim 2:19. **16:14** Hebrew *Are you trying to put out the eyes of these men?* **16:18** Hebrew *the Tent of Meeting;* also in 16:19, 42, 43, 50. **16:30** Hebrew *into Sheol;* also in 16:33. **16:36** Verses 16:36-50 are numbered 17:1-15 in Hebrew text.

16:8-11 In churches today, the congregation often selects the leadership, but God himself designated who would serve in which capacity in the Tabernacle. As such, Korah's rebellion was a rebellion against God himself (16:11). God did sometimes send prophets to confront those in power for their failures and abuses, but the Lord did not tolerate rebellion against his chosen leaders for the purpose of increasing one's own power.

16:20-24, 44-45 Twice in this chapter, Moses and Aaron prayed on behalf of the people with the result that the Lord changed course. God is not a raging tyrant who only with great difficulty can be persuaded to back down. Rather, he is much more inclined to be merciful than to insist on vengeance. So he invites those who are near him, like Moses and Aaron, to offer faithful intercession and give him an occasion for his mercy.

the altar. Since these burners were used in the LORD's presence, they have become holy. Let them serve as a warning to the people of Israel."

³⁹So Eleazar the priest collected the 250 bronze incense burners that had been used by the men who died in the fire, and the bronze was hammered into a thin sheet to overlay the altar. ⁴⁰This would warn the Israelites that no unauthorized person—no one who was not a descendant of Aaron—should ever enter the LORD's presence to burn incense. If anyone did, the same thing would happen to him as happened to Korah and his followers. So the LORD's instructions to Moses were carried out.

⁴¹But the very next morning the whole community of Israel began muttering again against Moses and Aaron, saying, "You have killed the LORD's people!" ⁴²As the community gathered to protest against Moses and Aaron, they turned toward the Tabernacle and saw that the cloud had covered it, and the glorious presence of the LORD appeared.

⁴³Moses and Aaron came and stood in front of the Tabernacle, ⁴⁴and the LORD said to Moses, ⁴⁵"Get away from all these people so that I can instantly destroy them!" But Moses and Aaron fell face down on the ground.

⁴⁶And Moses said to Aaron, "Quick, take an incense burner and place burning coals on it from the altar. Lay incense on it, and carry it out among the people to purify them and make them right with the LORD.* The LORD's anger is blazing against them—the plague has already begun."

⁴⁷Aaron did as Moses told him and ran out among the people. The plague had already begun to strike down the people, but Aaron burned the incense and purified* the people. ⁴⁸He stood between the dead and the living, and the plague stopped. ⁴⁹But 14,700 people died in that plague, in addition to those who had died in the affair involving Korah. ⁵⁰Then because the plague had stopped, Aaron returned to Moses at the entrance of the Tabernacle.

The Budding of Aaron's Staff

17 ¹*Then the LORD said to Moses, ²"Tell the people of Israel to bring you twelve wooden staffs, one from each leader of Israel's ancestral tribes, and inscribe each leader's name on his staff. ³Inscribe Aaron's name on the staff of the tribe of Levi, for there must be one staff for the leader of each ancestral tribe. ⁴Place these staffs in the Tabernacle in front of the Ark containing the tablets of the Covenant,* where I meet with you. ⁵Buds will sprout on the staff belonging to the man I choose. Then I will finally put an end to the people's murmuring and complaining against you."

⁶So Moses gave the instructions to the people of Israel, and each of the twelve tribal leaders, including Aaron, brought Moses a staff. ⁷Moses placed the staffs in the LORD's presence in the Tabernacle of the Covenant.* ⁸When he went into the Tabernacle of the Covenant the next day, he found that Aaron's staff, representing the tribe of Levi, had sprouted, budded, blossomed, and produced ripe almonds!

⁹When Moses brought all the staffs out from the LORD's presence, he showed them to the people. Each man claimed his own staff. ¹⁰And the LORD said to Moses: "Place Aaron's staff permanently before the Ark of the Covenant* to serve as a warning to rebels. This should put an end to their complaints against me and prevent any further deaths." ¹¹So Moses did as the LORD commanded him.

¹²Then the people of Israel said to Moses, "Look, we are doomed! We are dead! We are ruined! ¹³Everyone who even comes close to the Tabernacle of the LORD dies. Are we all doomed to die?"

Duties of Priests and Levites

18 Then the LORD said to Aaron: "You, your sons, and your relatives from the tribe of Levi will be held responsible for any offenses related to the sanctuary. But you and your sons alone will be held responsible for violations connected with the priesthood.

²"Bring your relatives of the tribe of Levi—your ancestral tribe—to assist you and your sons as you perform the sacred duties in front of the Tabernacle of the Covenant.* ³But as the Levites go about all their assigned duties at the Tabernacle, they must be careful not to go near any of the sacred objects or the altar. If they do, both you and they will die. ⁴The Levites must join you in fulfilling their responsibilities for the care and maintenance of the Tabernacle,* but no unauthorized person may assist you.

⁵"You yourselves must perform the sacred duties inside the sanctuary and at the altar. If you follow these instructions, the LORD's anger will never again blaze against the people of Israel. ⁶I myself have

---

16:46 Or *to make atonement for them.* **16:47** Or *and made atonement for.* **17:1** Verses 17:1-13 are numbered 17:16-28 in Hebrew text. **17:4** Hebrew *in the Tent of Meeting before the Testimony.* The Hebrew word for "testimony" refers to the terms of the LORD's covenant with Israel as written on stone tablets, which were kept in the Ark, and also to the covenant itself. **17:7** Or *Tabernacle of the Testimony;* also in 17:8. **17:10** Hebrew *before the Testimony;* see note on 17:4. **18:2** Or *Tabernacle of the Testimony.* **18:4** Hebrew *the Tent of Meeting;* also in 18:6, 21, 22, 23, 31.

17:1-13 Following the death of thousands in Korah's rebellion (16:46-50) and the reaffirmation of the priestly role of Aaron and his family (17:1-10), the people responded with terror. They recognized that the Lord and his Tabernacle were holy, and as such, his sanctuary was a dangerous place for those not qualified to enter it. Worship would happen on God's terms.

18:1-32 The instructions given here arose from the need demonstrated in 17:1-13 for clear boundaries between the people and the priests and Levites. The distinctive privileges of the Levites were matched by significant responsibilities. One very important aspect of their work was to safeguard the Tabernacle from unauthorized entry (16:1-50).

chosen your fellow Levites from among the Israelites to be your special assistants. They are a gift to you, dedicated to the LORD for service in the Tabernacle. ⁷But you and your sons, the priests, must personally handle all the priestly rituals associated with the altar and with everything behind the inner curtain. I am giving you the priesthood as your special privilege of service. Any unauthorized person who comes too near the sanctuary will be put to death."

Support for the Priests and Levites

⁸The LORD gave these further instructions to Aaron: "I myself have put you in charge of all the holy offerings that are brought to me by the people of Israel. I have given all these consecrated offerings to you and your sons as your permanent share. ⁹You are allotted the portion of the most holy offerings that is not burned on the fire. This portion of all the most holy offerings—including the grain offerings, sin

18:5-7 Only the priests (Aaron and his descendants) could perform sacred duties inside the sanctuary proper or approach the altar, a sacred space that deserved special reverence. Only the high priest could serve in the Most Holy Place. The Levites were to serve only in the courtyard, away from the altar, except when it was time to assemble or disassemble the Tabernacle (4:1-20).

Insight — ISRAEL IN THE WILDERNESS

When Israel left slavery in Egypt, "God did not lead them along the main road that runs through Philistine territory" (Exodus 13:17). Instead, they traveled deep into the wilderness of Sinai, where they met with God for a year (Exodus 19—Numbers 9) before setting out toward the Promised Land of Canaan (Numbers 11). Eventually, forty years after leaving Egypt, Israel arrived at Acacia Grove in Moab (22:1; 25:1), where Moses gave them final instructions (the book of Deuteronomy) before he died.

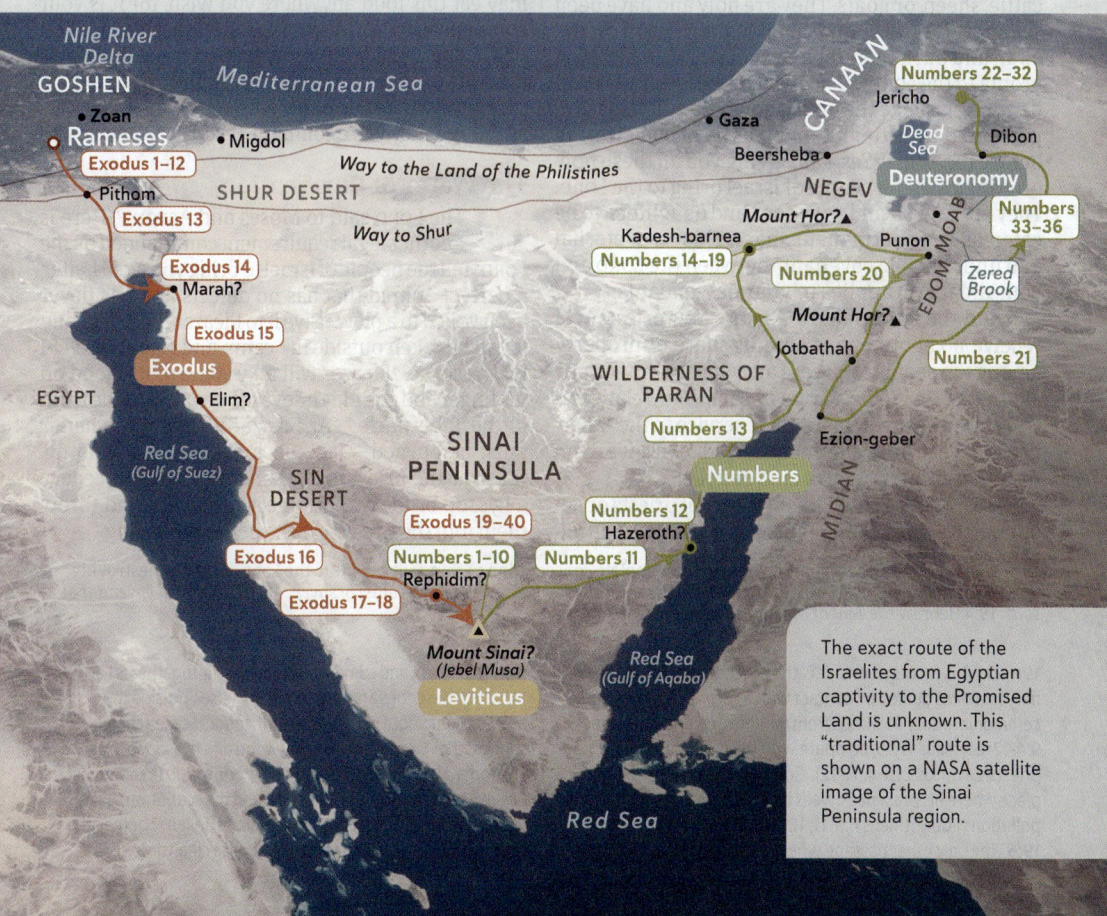

The exact route of the Israelites from Egyptian captivity to the Promised Land is unknown. This "traditional" route is shown on a NASA satellite image of the Sinai Peninsula region.

offerings, and guilt offerings—will be most holy, and it belongs to you and your sons. ¹⁰You must eat it as a most holy offering. All the males may eat of it, and you must treat it as most holy.

¹¹"All the sacred offerings and special offerings presented to me when the Israelites lift them up before the altar also belong to you. I have given them to you and to your sons and daughters as your permanent share. Any member of your family who is ceremonially clean may eat of these offerings.

¹²"I also give you the harvest gifts brought by the people as offerings to the LORD—the best of the olive oil, new wine, and grain. ¹³All the first crops of their land that the people present to the LORD belong to you. Any member of your family who is ceremonially clean may eat this food.

¹⁴"Everything in Israel that is specially set apart for the LORD* also belongs to you.

¹⁵"The firstborn of every mother, whether human or animal, that is offered to the LORD will be yours. But you must always redeem your firstborn sons and the firstborn of ceremonially unclean animals. ¹⁶Redeem them when they are one month old. The redemption price is five pieces of silver* (as measured by the weight of the sanctuary shekel, which equals twenty gerahs).

¹⁷"However, you may not redeem the firstborn of cattle, sheep, or goats. They are holy and have been set apart for the LORD. Sprinkle their blood on the altar, and burn their fat as a special gift, a pleasing aroma to the LORD. ¹⁸The meat of these animals will be yours, just like the breast and right thigh that are presented by lifting them up as a special offering before the altar. ¹⁹Yes, I am giving you all these holy offerings that the people of Israel bring to the LORD. They are for you and your sons and daughters, to be eaten as your permanent share. This is an eternal and unbreakable covenant* between the LORD and you, and it also applies to your descendants."

²⁰And the LORD said to Aaron, "You priests will receive no allotment of land or share of property among the people of Israel. I am your share and your allotment. ²¹As for the tribe of Levi, your relatives, I will compensate them for their service in the Tabernacle. Instead of an allotment of land, I will give them the tithes from the entire land of Israel.

²²"From now on, no Israelites except priests or Levites may approach the Tabernacle. If they come too near, they will be judged guilty and will die. ²³Only the Levites may serve at the Tabernacle, and they will be held responsible for any offenses against it. This is a permanent law for you, to be observed from generation to generation. The Levites will receive no allotment of land among the Israelites, ²⁴because I have given them the Israelites' tithes, which have been presented as sacred offerings to the LORD. This will be the Levites' share. That is why I said they would receive no allotment of land among the Israelites."

²⁵The LORD also told Moses, ²⁶"Give these instructions to the Levites: When you receive from the people of Israel the tithes I have assigned as your allotment, give a tenth of the tithes you receive—a tithe of the tithe—to the LORD as a sacred offering. ²⁷The LORD will consider this offering to be your harvest offering, as though it were the first grain from your own threshing floor or wine from your own winepress. ²⁸You must present one-tenth of the tithe received from the Israelites as a sacred offering to the LORD. This is the LORD's sacred portion, and you must present it to Aaron the priest. ²⁹Be sure to give to the LORD the best portions of the gifts given to you.

³⁰"Also, give these instructions to the Levites: When you present the best part as your offering, it will be considered as though it came from your own threshing floor or winepress. ³¹You Levites and your families may eat this food anywhere you wish, for it is your compensation for serving in the Tabernacle. ³²You will not be considered guilty for accepting the LORD's tithes if you give the best portion to the priests. But be careful not to treat the holy gifts of the people of Israel as though they were common. If you do, you will die."

The Water of Purification

19 The LORD said to Moses and Aaron, ²"Here is another legal requirement commanded by the LORD: Tell the people of Israel to bring you a red heifer, a perfect animal that has no defects and has never been yoked to a plow. ³Give it to Eleazar the priest, and it will be taken outside the camp and slaughtered in his presence. ⁴Eleazar will take some of its blood on his finger and sprinkle it seven times toward the front of the Tabernacle.* ⁵As Eleazar watches, the heifer must be burned—its hide, meat, blood, and dung. ⁶Eleazar the priest must then take a stick of cedar,* a hyssop branch, and some scarlet yarn and throw them into the fire where the heifer is burning.

18:14 The Hebrew term used here refers to the complete consecration of things or people to the LORD, either by destroying them or by giving them as an offering. 18:16 Hebrew 5 shekels [2 ounces or 57 grams] of silver. 18:19 Hebrew a covenant of salt. 19:4 Hebrew the Tent of Meeting. 19:6 Or juniper.

19:1-22 This account considers the procedure by which ordinary Israelites defiled by contact with a corpse could regain ceremonial purity and keep from defiling the Tabernacle (see 9:4-12; Leviticus 17:15; compare with the procedures regarding priests, Leviticus 21:1-4, 11-12). God's holiness requires that the place where his presence dwells be kept pure and set apart from pollution (1 Corinthians 6:9-11, 18-20).
19:6 The only other passage where a stick of cedar (or juniper), a hyssop branch, and some scarlet yarn occur together is Leviticus 14, which describes another ceremony (also "outside the camp") that brought about ceremonial purification. Some scholars suggest that Eleazar added cedarwood and hyssop to produce an aroma. Hyssop is associated with purification (Exodus 12:22; Psalm 51:7; see also Hebrews 9:19), and the scarlet yarn, like the red heifer, probably symbolized blood. Taken together, the cedarwood, hyssop, and scarlet symbolize cleansing.

⁷"Then the priest must wash his clothes and bathe himself in water. Afterward he may return to the camp, though he will remain ceremonially unclean until evening. ⁸The man who burns the animal must also wash his clothes and bathe himself in water, and he, too, will remain unclean until evening. ⁹Then someone who is ceremonially clean will gather up the ashes of the heifer and deposit them in a purified place outside the camp. They will be kept there for the community of Israel to use in the water for the purification ceremony. This ceremony is performed for the removal of sin. ¹⁰The man who gathers up the ashes of the heifer must also wash his clothes, and he will remain ceremonially unclean until evening. This is a permanent law for the people of Israel and any foreigners who live among them.

¹¹"All those who touch a dead human body will be ceremonially unclean for seven days. ¹²They must purify themselves on the third and seventh days with the water of purification; then they will be purified. But if they do not do this on the third and seventh days, they will continue to be unclean even after the seventh day. ¹³All those who touch a dead body and do not purify themselves in the proper way defile the LORD's Tabernacle, and they will be cut off from the community of Israel. Since the water of purification was not sprinkled on them, their defilement continues.

¹⁴"This is the ritual law that applies when someone dies inside a tent: All those who enter that tent and those who were inside when the death occurred will be ceremonially unclean for seven days. ¹⁵Any open container in the tent that was not covered with a lid is also defiled. ¹⁶And if someone in an open field touches the corpse of someone who was killed with a sword or who died a natural death, or if someone touches a human bone or a grave, that person will be defiled for seven days.

¹⁷"To remove the defilement, put some of the ashes from the burnt purification offering in a jar, and pour fresh water over them. ¹⁸Then someone who is ceremonially clean must take a hyssop branch and dip it into the water. That person must sprinkle the water on the tent, on all the furnishings in the tent, and on the people who were in the tent; also on the person who touched a human bone, or touched someone who was killed or who died naturally, or touched a grave. ¹⁹On the third and seventh days the person who is ceremonially clean must sprinkle the water on those who are defiled. Then on the seventh day the people being cleansed must wash their clothes and bathe themselves, and that evening they will be cleansed of their defilement.

²⁰"But those who become defiled and do not purify themselves will be cut off from the community, for they have defiled the sanctuary of the LORD. Since the water of purification has not been sprinkled on them, they remain defiled. ²¹This is a permanent law for the people. Those who sprinkle the water of purification must afterward wash their clothes, and anyone who then touches the water used for purification will remain defiled until evening. ²²Anything and anyone that a defiled person touches will be ceremonially unclean until evening."

Moses Strikes the Rock

20 In the first month of the year,* the whole community of Israel arrived in the wilderness of Zin and camped at Kadesh. While they were there, Miriam died and was buried.

²There was no water for the people to drink at that place, so they rebelled against Moses and Aaron. ³The people blamed Moses and said, "If only we had died in the LORD's presence with our brothers! ⁴Why have you brought the congregation of the LORD's people into this wilderness to die, along with all our livestock? ⁵Why did you make us leave Egypt and bring us here to this terrible place? This land has no grain, no figs, no grapes, no pomegranates, and no water to drink!"

⁶Moses and Aaron turned away from the people and went to the entrance of the Tabernacle,* where they fell face down on the ground. Then the glorious presence of the LORD appeared to them, ⁷and the LORD said to Moses, ⁸"You and Aaron must take the staff and assemble the entire community. As the people watch, speak to the rock over there, and it will pour out its water. You will provide enough water from the rock to satisfy the whole community and their livestock."

⁹So Moses did as he was told. He took the staff from the place where it was kept before the LORD. ¹⁰Then he and Aaron summoned the people to come and gather at the rock. "Listen, you rebels!" he shouted. "Must we bring you water from this rock?" ¹¹Then

---

20:1 The first month of the ancient Hebrew lunar calendar usually occurs within the months of March and April. The number of years since leaving Egypt is not specified. 20:6 Hebrew *the Tent of Meeting*.

20:1 The description of Miriam's death is much briefer than the descriptions for her brothers Aaron (20:22-29) and Moses (Deuteronomy 34:1-8). However, the fact that she is mentioned at all in a patriarchal context points to her importance within the community. Scripture doesn't point to Israel as an ideal culture to be emulated. Rather, God reveals himself to his people within their particular time and place. Yet even amid the patriarchal society of ancient Israel, God made specific provisions to protect those who lacked power (see, for example, Exodus 22:21-27; Deuteronomy 15:1-18).

20:9-12 God described Moses and Aaron's actions not only as disobedience but as rebellion (Numbers 20:24; 27:14). The Lord expected his chosen leaders to demonstrate his holiness (20:12). Whether our actions are intentional or unintentional (perhaps driven by emotion or done in ignorance), we need to consider how our seemingly minor disobedience might misrepresent God. Misrepresenting God's nature and holiness amounts to rebellion against God's instructions.

WHAT THE BIBLE SAYS ABOUT

Living Wholeheartedly

Living Wholeheartedly in God's Promised Land

[Caleb said,] "Moses solemnly promised me, 'The land of Canaan on which you were just walking will be your grant of land and that of your descendants forever, because you wholeheartedly followed the LORD my God.'" ... Hebron still belongs to the descendants of Caleb son of Jephunneh the Kenizzite because he wholeheartedly followed the LORD. **JOSHUA 14:9, 14**

"So go back home to the land that Moses, the servant of the LORD, gave you.... But be very careful to obey all the commands and the instructions that Moses gave to you. Love the LORD your God, walk in all his ways, obey his commands, hold firmly to him, and serve him with all your heart and all your soul." **JOSHUA 22:4-5**

"I [the LORD] will find joy doing good for them and will faithfully and wholeheartedly replant them in this land." **JEREMIAH 32:41**

Fear the LORD and serve him wholeheartedly.... Serve the LORD alone.

live peacefully with each other

Leaders Especially Must Be Wholehearted

[David prayed,] "O LORD,... Give my son Solomon the wholehearted desire to obey all your commands, laws, and decrees." **1 CHRONICLES 29:18-19**

Amaziah did what was pleasing in the LORD's sight, but not wholeheartedly. **2 CHRONICLES 25:2**

In all that he did... Hezekiah sought his God wholeheartedly. As a result, he was very successful. **2 CHRONICLES 31:21**

"Remember, O LORD, how I [Hezekiah] have always been faithful to you and have served you single-mindedly, always doing what pleases you." **ISAIAH 38:3**

We Draw Close to God through Wholehearted Commitment

"The LORD your God will change your heart and the hearts of all your descendants, so that you will love him with all your heart and soul and so you may live!" **DEUTERONOMY 30:6**

[The LORD says,] "Fear the LORD and serve him wholeheartedly. Put away forever the idols your ancestors worshiped when they lived beyond the Euphrates River and in Egypt. Serve the LORD alone." **JOSHUA 24:14**

"If you look for me [the LORD] wholeheartedly, you will find me." **JEREMIAH 29:13**

Thank God! Once you were slaves of sin, but now you wholeheartedly obey this teaching we have given you. **ROMANS 6:17**

Wholehearted Living Helps Us Relate Well to Others

Make me [Paul] truly happy by agreeing wholeheartedly with each other, loving one another, and working together with one mind and purpose. **PHILIPPIANS 2:2**

Show them great respect and wholehearted love because of their work. And live peacefully with each other. **1 THESSALONIANS 5:13**

You were cleansed from your sins when you obeyed the truth, so now you must show sincere love to each other as brothers and sisters. Love each other deeply with all your heart. **1 PETER 1:22**

Moses raised his hand and struck the rock twice with the staff, and water gushed out. So the entire community and their livestock drank their fill.

¹²But the LORD said to Moses and Aaron, "Because you did not trust me enough to demonstrate my holiness to the people of Israel, you will not lead them into the land I am giving them!" ¹³This place was known as the waters of Meribah (which means "arguing") because there the people of Israel argued with the LORD, and there he demonstrated his holiness among them.

Edom Refuses Israel Passage

¹⁴While Moses was at Kadesh, he sent ambassadors to the king of Edom with this message:

> "This is what your relatives, the people of Israel, say: You know all the hardships we have been through. ¹⁵Our ancestors went down to Egypt, and we lived there a long time, and we and our ancestors were brutally mistreated by the Egyptians. ¹⁶But when we cried out to the LORD, he heard us and sent an angel who brought us out of Egypt. Now we are camped at Kadesh, a town on the border of your land. ¹⁷Please let us travel through your land. We will be careful not to go through your fields and vineyards. We won't even drink water from your wells. We will stay on the king's road and never leave it until we have passed through your territory."

¹⁸But the king of Edom said, "Stay out of my land, or I will meet you with an army!"

¹⁹The Israelites answered, "We will stay on the main road. If our livestock drink your water, we will pay for it. Just let us pass through your country. That's all we ask."

²⁰But the king of Edom replied, "Stay out! You may not pass through our land." With that he mobilized his army and marched out against them with an imposing force. ²¹Because Edom refused to allow Israel to pass through their country, Israel was forced to turn around.

The Death of Aaron

²²The whole community of Israel left Kadesh and arrived at Mount Hor. ²³There, on the border of the land of Edom, the LORD said to Moses and Aaron, ²⁴"The time has come for Aaron to join his ancestors in death. He will not enter the land I am giving the people of Israel, because the two of you rebelled against my instructions concerning the water at Meribah. ²⁵Now take Aaron and his son Eleazar up Mount Hor. ²⁶There you will remove Aaron's priestly garments and put them on Eleazar, his son. Aaron will die there and join his ancestors."

²⁷So Moses did as the LORD commanded. The three of them went up Mount Hor together as the whole community watched. ²⁸At the summit, Moses removed the priestly garments from Aaron and put them on Eleazar, Aaron's son. Then Aaron died there on top of the mountain, and Moses and Eleazar went back down. ²⁹When the people realized that Aaron had died, all Israel mourned for him thirty days.

Victory over the Canaanites

21 The Canaanite king of Arad, who lived in the Negev, heard that the Israelites were approaching on the road through Atharim. So he attacked the Israelites and took some of them as prisoners. ²Then the people of Israel made this vow to the LORD: "If you will hand these people over to us, we will completely destroy* all their towns." ³The LORD heard the Israelites' request and gave them victory over the Canaanites. The Israelites completely destroyed them and their towns, and the place has been called Hormah* ever since.

The Bronze Snake

⁴Then the people of Israel set out from Mount Hor, taking the road to the Red Sea* to go around the land of Edom. But the people grew impatient with the long journey, ⁵and they began to speak against God and Moses. "Why have you brought us out of Egypt to die here in the wilderness?" they complained. "There is nothing to eat here and nothing to drink. And we hate this horrible manna!"

⁶So the LORD sent poisonous snakes among the people, and many were bitten and died. ⁷Then the people came to Moses and cried out, "We have sinned by speaking against the LORD and against you. Pray that the LORD will take away the snakes." So Moses prayed for the people.

⁸Then the LORD told him, "Make a replica of a poisonous snake and attach it to a pole. All who are bitten will live if they simply look at it!" ⁹So Moses made

---

21:2 The Hebrew term used here refers to the complete consecration of things or people to the LORD, either by destroying them or by giving them as an offering; also in 21:3. 21:3 *Hormah* means "destruction." 21:4 Hebrew *sea of reeds*.

21:1–22:1 In the march toward the Promised Land, Israel moved from Mount Hor (21:4) to the plains of Moab (22:1). The account of Israel's march is punctuated by the book's emphasis on the Lord's patient plan to lead Israel into Canaan despite their frailties. Although the general direction of travel is clear, the exact route taken by the Hebrews remains unknown. Many of the places are hard to identify, and the archaeological evidence from some sites does not fit the time frame usually associated with the wilderness period. Defining a precise wilderness itinerary still suffers from significant geographical and historical uncertainties.

21:2-3 The Hebrew term translated here as "completely destroy" (*kharam*) refers to the complete consecration of things or people to the Lord, either by destroying them or by giving them as an offering. Israel was instructed to completely destroy their enemies and their enemies' property (see Leviticus 27:28-29; Deuteronomy 7:2; 20:17; Joshua 6:1–7:26; 10:1–11:23). This battle reflects a play on words between *kharam* and *khormah* (Numbers 21:3, which means "destruction"; see also Joshua 12:14; Judges 1:16-17). It marks a turning point in Israel's interaction with the Canaanites, who remained a formidable enemy throughout the period of the conquest.

a snake out of bronze and attached it to a pole. Then anyone who was bitten by a snake could look at the bronze snake and be healed!

Israel's Journey to Moab

[10] The Israelites traveled next to Oboth and camped there. [11] Then they went on to Iye-abarim, in the wilderness on the eastern border of Moab. [12] From there they traveled to the valley of Zered Brook and set up camp. [13] Then they moved out and camped on the far side of the Arnon River, in the wilderness adjacent to the territory of the Amorites. The Arnon is the boundary line between the Moabites and the Amorites. [14] For this reason The Book of the Wars of the LORD speaks of "the town of Waheb in the area of Suphah, and the ravines of the Arnon River, [15] and the ravines that extend as far as the settlement of Ar on the border of Moab."

[16] From there the Israelites traveled to Beer,* which is the well where the LORD said to Moses, "Assemble the people, and I will give them water." [17] There the Israelites sang this song:

"Spring up, O well!
  Yes, sing its praises!
[18] Sing of this well,
  which princes dug,
  which great leaders hollowed out
   with their scepters and staffs."

Then the Israelites left the wilderness and proceeded on through Mattanah, [19] Nahaliel, and Bamoth. [20] After that they went to the valley in Moab where Pisgah Peak overlooks the wasteland.*

Victory over Sihon and Og

[21] The Israelites sent ambassadors to King Sihon of the Amorites with this message:

[22] "Let us travel through your land. We will be careful not to go through your fields and vineyards. We won't even drink water from your wells. We will stay on the king's road until we have passed through your territory."

[23] But King Sihon refused to let them cross his territory. Instead, he mobilized his entire army and attacked Israel in the wilderness, engaging them in battle at Jahaz. [24] But the Israelites slaughtered them with their swords and occupied their land from the Arnon River to the Jabbok River. They went only as far as the Ammonite border because the boundary of the Ammonites was fortified.* [25] So Israel captured all the towns of the Amorites and settled in them, including the city of Heshbon and its surrounding villages. [26] Heshbon had been the capital of King Sihon of the Amorites. He had defeated a former Moabite king and seized all his land as far as the Arnon River. [27] Therefore, the ancient poets wrote this about him:

"Come to Heshbon and let it be rebuilt!
  Let the city of Sihon be restored.
[28] A fire flamed forth from Heshbon,
  a blaze from the city of Sihon.
It burned the city of Ar in Moab;
  it destroyed the rulers of the Arnon heights.
[29] What sorrow awaits you, O people of Moab!
  You are finished, O worshipers of Chemosh!
Chemosh has left his sons as refugees,
  his daughters as captives of Sihon, the
    Amorite king.
[30] We have utterly destroyed them,
  from Heshbon to Dibon.
We have completely wiped them out
  as far away as Nophah and Medeba.*"

[31] So the people of Israel occupied the territory of the Amorites. [32] After Moses sent men to explore the Jazer area, they captured all the towns in the region and drove out the Amorites who lived there. [33] Then they turned and marched up the road to Bashan, but King Og of Bashan and all his people attacked them at Edrei. [34] The LORD said to Moses, "Do not be afraid of him, for I have handed him over to you, along with all his people and his land. Do the same to him as you did to King Sihon of the Amorites, who ruled in Heshbon." [35] And Israel killed King Og, his sons, and all his subjects; not a single survivor remained. Then Israel occupied their land.

Balak Sends for Balaam

22 Then the people of Israel traveled to the plains of Moab and camped east of the Jordan River, across from Jericho. [2] Balak son of Zippor, the Moabite king, had seen everything the Israelites did to the Amorites. [3] And when the people of Moab saw how many Israelites there were, they were terrified. [4] The king of Moab said to the elders of Midian, "This mob will devour everything in sight, like an ox devours grass in the field!"

So Balak, king of Moab, [5] sent messengers to call Balaam son of Beor, who was living in his native land of Pethor* near the Euphrates River.* His message said:

21:16 *Beer* means "well." 21:20 Or *overlooks Jeshimon.* 21:24 Or *because the terrain of the Ammonite frontier was rugged;* Hebrew reads *because the boundary of the Ammonites was strong.* 21:30 Or *until fire spread to Medeba.* The meaning of the Hebrew is uncertain. 22:5a Or *who was at Pethor in the land of the Amavites.* 22:5b Hebrew *the river.*

22:2–24:25 The narrative of Balak and Balaam describes a pivotal moment in Israel's history and contains humor, drama, and profound theological insights. The Lord's will must be accomplished—nothing could thwart his plan for Israel.

"Look, a vast horde of people has arrived from Egypt. They cover the face of the earth and are threatening me. ⁶Please come and curse these people for me because they are too powerful for me. Then perhaps I will be able to conquer them and drive them from the land. I know that blessings fall on any people you bless, and curses fall on people you curse."

⁷Balak's messengers, who were elders of Moab and Midian, set out with money to pay Balaam to place a curse upon Israel.* They went to Balaam and delivered Balak's message to him. ⁸"Stay here overnight," Balaam said. "In the morning I will tell you whatever the LORD directs me to say." So the officials from Moab stayed there with Balaam.

⁹That night God came to Balaam and asked him, "Who are these men visiting you?"

¹⁰Balaam said to God, "Balak son of Zippor, king of Moab, has sent me this message: ¹¹'Look, a vast horde of people has arrived from Egypt, and they cover the face of the earth. Come and curse these people for me. Then perhaps I will be able to stand up to them and drive them from the land.'"

¹²But God told Balaam, "Do not go with them. You are not to curse these people, for they have been blessed!"

¹³The next morning Balaam got up and told Balak's officials, "Go on home! The LORD will not let me go with you."

¹⁴So the Moabite officials returned to King Balak and reported, "Balaam refused to come with us." ¹⁵Then Balak tried again. This time he sent a larger number of even more distinguished officials than those he had sent the first time. ¹⁶They went to Balaam and delivered this message to him:

"This is what Balak son of Zippor says: Please don't let anything stop you from coming to help me. ¹⁷I will pay you very well and do whatever you tell me. Just come and curse these people for me!"

¹⁸But Balaam responded to Balak's messengers, "Even if Balak were to give me his palace filled with silver and gold, I would be powerless to do anything against the will of the LORD my God. ¹⁹But stay here one more night, and I will see if the LORD has anything else to say to me."

²⁰That night God came to Balaam and told him, "Since these men have come for you, get up and go with them. But do only what I tell you to do."

Balaam and His Donkey

²¹So the next morning Balaam got up, saddled his donkey, and started off with the Moabite officials. ²²But God was angry that Balaam was going, so he sent the angel of the LORD to stand in the road to block his way. As Balaam and two servants were riding along, ²³Balaam's donkey saw the angel of the LORD standing in the road with a drawn sword in his hand. The donkey bolted off the road into a field, but Balaam beat it and turned it back onto the road. ²⁴Then the angel of the LORD stood at a place where the road narrowed between two vineyard walls. ²⁵When the donkey saw the angel of the LORD, it tried to squeeze by and crushed Balaam's foot against the wall. So Balaam beat the donkey again. ²⁶Then the angel of the LORD moved farther down the road and stood in a place too narrow for the donkey to get by at all. ²⁷This time when the donkey saw the angel, it lay down under Balaam. In a fit of rage Balaam beat the animal again with his staff.

²⁸Then the LORD gave the donkey the ability to speak. "What have I done to you that deserves your beating me three times?" it asked Balaam.

²⁹"You have made me look like a fool!" Balaam shouted. "If I had a sword with me, I would kill you!"

³⁰"But I am the same donkey you have ridden all your life," the donkey answered. "Have I ever done anything like this before?"

"No," Balaam admitted.

³¹Then the LORD opened Balaam's eyes, and he saw the angel of the LORD standing in the roadway with a drawn sword in his hand. Balaam bowed his head and fell face down on the ground before him.

³²"Why did you beat your donkey those three times?" the angel of the LORD demanded. "Look, I have come to block your way because you are stubbornly resisting me. ³³Three times the donkey saw me and shied away; otherwise, I would certainly have killed you by now and spared the donkey."

³⁴Then Balaam confessed to the angel of the LORD, "I have sinned. I didn't realize you were standing in the road to block my way. I will return home if you are against my going."

³⁵But the angel of the LORD told Balaam, "Go with these men, but say only what I tell you to say." So Balaam went on with Balak's officials. ³⁶When King Balak heard that Balaam was on the way, he went out to meet him at a Moabite town on the Arnon River at the farthest border of his land.

22:7 Hebrew *set out with the money of divination in their hand.*

22:5-6 Balaam was a pagan religious specialist (called a *diviner*) from northwest Mesopotamia. Like other ancient peoples, Moab and Midian believed that the spoken word—in the form of a blessing or curse—was powerful when uttered by a skilled diviner. Members of this trained profession claimed to possess special powers to learn about and manipulate the future course of events (see Deuteronomy 18:14; 1 Samuel 6:2; 2 Kings 21:6; Isaiah 44:25; Daniel 2:1-12, 27-28; Micah 5:12; Zechariah 10:2). Israel's enemies appealed to Balaam to pronounce curses upon the Hebrews, for they believed that such spoken words would be effective against them. Ancient armies pronounced such curses on their enemies before they entered battle. Belief in the power of the spoken word was common in ancient Israel even when not linked with divination (for example, Genesis 27:1-40; Deuteronomy 27:15-26; 1 Samuel 14:24-28; see also Matthew 21:18-22).

37"Didn't I send you an urgent invitation? Why didn't you come right away?" Balak asked Balaam. "Didn't you believe me when I said I would reward you richly?"

38Balaam replied, "Look, now I have come, but I have no power to say whatever I want. I will speak only the message that God puts in my mouth." 39Then Balaam accompanied Balak to Kiriath-huzoth, 40where the king sacrificed cattle and sheep. He sent portions of the meat to Balaam and the officials who were with him. 41The next morning Balak took Balaam up to Bamoth-baal. From there he could see some of the people of Israel spread out below him.

Balaam Blesses Israel

23 Then Balaam said to King Balak, "Build me seven altars here, and prepare seven young bulls and seven rams for me to sacrifice." 2Balak followed his instructions, and the two of them sacrificed a young bull and a ram on each altar.

3Then Balaam said to Balak, "Stand here by your burnt offerings, and I will go to see if the LORD will respond to me. Then I will tell you whatever he reveals to me." So Balaam went alone to the top of a bare hill, 4and God met him there. Balaam said to him, "I have prepared seven altars and have sacrificed a young bull and a ram on each altar."

5The LORD gave Balaam a message for King Balak. Then he said, "Go back to Balak and give him my message."

6So Balaam returned and found the king standing beside his burnt offerings with all the officials of Moab. 7This was the message Balaam delivered:

"Balak summoned me to come from Aram;
    the king of Moab brought me from the
        eastern hills.
'Come,' he said, 'curse Jacob for me!
    Come and announce Israel's doom.'
8 But how can I curse those
    whom God has not cursed?
How can I condemn those
    whom the LORD has not condemned?
9 I see them from the cliff tops;
    I watch them from the hills.
I see a people who live by themselves,
    set apart from other nations.
10 Who can count Jacob's descendants, as
        numerous as dust?
    Who can count even a fourth of Israel's people?
Let me die like the righteous;
    let my life end like theirs."

11Then King Balak demanded of Balaam, "What have you done to me? I brought you to curse my enemies. Instead, you have blessed them!"

12But Balaam replied, "I will speak only the message that the LORD puts in my mouth."

Balaam's Second Message

13Then King Balak told him, "Come with me to another place. There you will see another part of the nation of Israel, but not all of them. Curse at least that many!" 14So Balak took Balaam to the plateau of Zophim on Pisgah Peak. He built seven altars there and offered a young bull and a ram on each altar.

15Then Balaam said to the king, "Stand here by your burnt offerings while I go over there to meet the LORD."

16And the LORD met Balaam and gave him a message. Then he said, "Go back to Balak and give him my message."

17So Balaam returned and found the king standing beside his burnt offerings with all the officials of Moab. "What did the LORD say?" Balak asked eagerly.

18This was the message Balaam delivered:

"Rise up, Balak, and listen!
    Hear me, son of Zippor.
19 God is not a man, so he does not lie.
    He is not human, so he does not change his
        mind.
Has he ever spoken and failed to act?
    Has he ever promised and not carried it
        through?
20 Listen, I received a command to bless;
    God has blessed, and I cannot reverse it!
21 No misfortune is in his plan for Jacob;
    no trouble is in store for Israel.
For the LORD their God is with them;
    he has been proclaimed their king.
22 God brought them out of Egypt;
    for them he is as strong as a wild ox.
23 No curse can touch Jacob;
    no magic has any power against Israel.
For now it will be said of Jacob,
    'What wonders God has done for Israel!'
24 These people rise up like a lioness,
    like a majestic lion rousing itself.
They refuse to rest
    until they have feasted on prey,
    drinking the blood of the slaughtered!"

25Then Balak said to Balaam, "Fine, but if you won't curse them, at least don't bless them!"

26But Balaam replied to Balak, "Didn't I tell you that I can do only what the LORD tells me?"

23:1-30 Curses changed reality negatively for the cursed party, while blessings had the opposite effect. At times, foreign diviners like Balaam received revelation through ancient divinatory practices; at other times, they sought to manipulate the spirits or gods they worshiped. While Israel did not allow such practices (Deuteronomy 18:10-11), God used Balaam, who was hired by Balak to curse the Israelites, to bless his people. God made it clear that he could not be manipulated and that his favor for Israel was nonnegotiable.

Balaam's Third Message

²⁷Then King Balak said to Balaam, "Come, I will take you to one more place. Perhaps it will please God to let you curse them from there."

²⁸So Balak took Balaam to the top of Mount Peor, overlooking the wasteland.* ²⁹Balaam again told Balak, "Build me seven altars, and prepare seven young bulls and seven rams for me to sacrifice." ³⁰So Balak did as Balaam ordered and offered a young bull and a ram on each altar.

24

By now Balaam realized that the LORD was determined to bless Israel, so he did not resort to divination as before. Instead, he turned and looked out toward the wilderness, ²where he saw the people of Israel camped, tribe by tribe. Then the Spirit of God came upon him, ³and this is the message he delivered:

"This is the message of Balaam son of Beor,
 the message of the man whose eyes see clearly,
⁴ the message of one who hears the words of God,
 who sees a vision from the Almighty,
 who bows down with eyes wide open:
⁵ How beautiful are your tents, O Jacob;
 how lovely are your homes, O Israel!
⁶ They spread before me like palm groves,*
 like gardens by the riverside.
 They are like tall trees planted by the LORD,
 like cedars beside the waters.
⁷ Water will flow from their buckets;
 their offspring have all they need.
 Their king will be greater than Agag;
 their kingdom will be exalted.
⁸ God brought them out of Egypt;
 for them he is as strong as a wild ox.
 He devours all the nations that oppose him,
 breaking their bones in pieces,
 shooting them with arrows.
⁹ Like a lion, Israel crouches and lies down;
 like a lioness, who dares to arouse her?
 Blessed is everyone who blesses you, O Israel,
 and cursed is everyone who curses you."

¹⁰King Balak flew into a rage against Balaam. He angrily clapped his hands and shouted, "I called you to curse my enemies! Instead, you have blessed them three times. ¹¹Now get out of here! Go back home! I promised to reward you richly, but the LORD has kept you from your reward."

¹²Balaam told Balak, "Don't you remember what I told your messengers? I said, ¹³'Even if Balak were to give me his palace filled with silver and gold, I would be powerless to do anything against the will of the LORD.' I told you that I could say only what the LORD says! ¹⁴Now I am returning to my own people. But first let me tell you what the Israelites will do to your people in the future."

Balaam's Final Messages

¹⁵This is the message Balaam delivered:

"This is the message of Balaam son of Beor,
 the message of the man whose eyes see clearly,
¹⁶ the message of one who hears the words of God,
 who has knowledge from the Most High,
 who sees a vision from the Almighty,
 who bows down with eyes wide open:
¹⁷ I see him, but not here and now.
 I perceive him, but far in the distant future.
 A star will rise from Jacob;
 a scepter will emerge from Israel.
 It will crush the heads of Moab's people,
 cracking the skulls* of the people of Sheth.
¹⁸ Edom will be taken over,
 and Seir, its enemy, will be conquered,
 while Israel marches on in triumph.
¹⁹ A ruler will rise in Jacob
 who will destroy the survivors of Ir."

²⁰Then Balaam looked over toward the people of Amalek and delivered this message:

"Amalek was the greatest of nations,
 but its destiny is destruction!"

²¹Then he looked over toward the Kenites and delivered this message:

"Your home is secure;
 your nest is set in the rocks.
²² But the Kenites will be destroyed
 when Assyria* takes you captive."

²³Balaam concluded his messages by saying:

"Alas, who can survive
 unless God has willed it?
²⁴ Ships will come from the coasts of Cyprus*;
 they will oppress Assyria and afflict Eber,
 but they, too, will be utterly destroyed."

²⁵Then Balaam left and returned home, and Balak also went on his way.

23:28 Or *overlooking Jeshimon.* 24:6 Or *like a majestic valley.* 24:17 As in Samaritan Pentateuch; the meaning of the Hebrew word is uncertain. 24:22 Hebrew *Asshur;* also in 24:24. 24:24 Hebrew *Kittim.*

24:1-2 Unlike previously (23:3, 15), Balaam did not resort to divination this time. He already knew that curses and magic could not harm Israel (23:23), so he quit looking for them. Instead, Balaam was directly inspired by the Spirit of God. **24:7-9** God's blessing would enable the Israelites to overcome their enemies (see 24:15-24). The Amalekites, a desert people, were traditional enemies of the Hebrews (see Exodus 17:8-16; Numbers 14:45), and it is likely that Agag was the traditional designation for their king. (Agag was also the name of an Amalekite king later defeated by Saul; 1 Samuel 15:7-9, 32-33.) God had brought Israel out of Egypt, and fought on their behalf, like a warrior and like a wild animal (ox and lion; Numbers 24:8-9).

Moab Seduces Israel

25 While the Israelites were camped at Acacia Grove,* some of the men defiled themselves by having* sexual relations with local Moabite women. ²These women invited them to attend sacrifices to their gods, so the Israelites feasted with them and worshiped the gods of Moab. ³In this way, Israel joined in the worship of Baal of Peor, causing the LORD's anger to blaze against his people.

⁴The LORD issued the following command to Moses: "Seize all the ringleaders and execute them before the LORD in broad daylight, so his fierce anger will turn away from the people of Israel."

⁵So Moses ordered Israel's judges, "Each of you must put to death the men under your authority who have joined in worshiping Baal of Peor."

⁶Just then one of the Israelite men brought a Midianite woman into his tent, right before the eyes of Moses and all the people, as everyone was weeping at the entrance of the Tabernacle.* ⁷When Phinehas son of Eleazar and grandson of Aaron the priest saw this, he jumped up and left the assembly. He took a spear ⁸and rushed after the man into his tent. Phinehas thrust the spear all the way through the man's body and into the woman's stomach. So the plague against the Israelites was stopped, ⁹but not before 24,000 people had died.

¹⁰Then the LORD said to Moses, ¹¹"Phinehas son of Eleazar and grandson of Aaron the priest has turned my anger away from the Israelites by being as zealous among them as I was. So I stopped destroying all Israel as I had intended to do in my zealous anger. ¹²Now tell him that I am making my special covenant of peace with him. ¹³In this covenant, I give him and his descendants a permanent right to the priesthood, for in his zeal for me, his God, he purified the people of Israel, making them right with me.*"

¹⁴The Israelite man killed with the Midianite woman was named Zimri son of Salu, the leader of a family from the tribe of Simeon. ¹⁵The woman's name was Cozbi; she was the daughter of Zur, the leader of a Midianite clan.

¹⁶Then the LORD said to Moses, ¹⁷"Attack the Midianites and destroy them, ¹⁸because they assaulted you with deceit and tricked you into worshiping Baal of Peor, and because of Cozbi, the daughter of a Midianite leader, who was killed at the time of the plague because of what happened at Peor."

The Second Registration of Israel's Troops

26 After the plague had ended,* the LORD said to Moses and to Eleazar son of Aaron the priest, ²"From the whole community of Israel, record the names of all the warriors by their families. List all the men twenty years old or older who are able to go to war."

³So there on the plains of Moab beside the Jordan River, across from Jericho, Moses and Eleazar the priest issued these instructions to the leaders of Israel: ⁴"List all the men of Israel twenty years old and older, just as the LORD commanded Moses."

This is the record of all the descendants of Israel who came out of Egypt.

The Tribe of Reuben

⁵These were the clans descended from the sons of Reuben, Jacob's* oldest son:

    The Hanochite clan, named after their ancestor Hanoch.
    The Palluite clan, named after their ancestor Pallu.
⁶   The Hezronite clan, named after their ancestor Hezron.
    The Carmite clan, named after their ancestor Carmi.

⁷These were the clans of Reuben. Their registered troops numbered 43,730.

⁸Pallu was the ancestor of Eliab, ⁹and Eliab was the father of Nemuel, Dathan, and Abiram. This Dathan and Abiram are the same community leaders who conspired with Korah against Moses and Aaron, rebelling against the LORD. ¹⁰But the earth opened up its mouth and swallowed them with Korah, and fire devoured 250 of their followers. This served as a warning to the entire nation of Israel. ¹¹However, the sons of Korah did not die that day.

The Tribe of Simeon

¹²These were the clans descended from the sons of Simeon:

25:1a Hebrew *Shittim.*   25:1b As in Greek version; Hebrew reads *some of the men began having.*   25:6 Hebrew *the Tent of Meeting.*   25:13 Or *he made atonement for the people of Israel.*   26:1 The initial phrase in verse 26:1 is numbered 25:19 in Hebrew text.   26:5 Hebrew *Israel's;* see note on 1:20-21b.

25:1-18 Balaam advised the women of Moab and Midian to seduce the Israelite men into sexual immorality and worshiping foreign gods (see 31:15-17). The men's disobedience resulted in a plague. The offense recorded here provides the reason for the commands that prohibited intermarriage (see Exodus 34:16; Deuteronomy 7:3-4; see also 1 Kings 11). While the Moabite and Midianite women may have been the instigators of disobedience, God held the Israelites responsible for their part. Zimri and Cozbi, both identified by name and family, may have been the most blatant offenders.

26:1-65 After nearly forty years, Israel again registered their men of military age (see Numbers 1–4) as they camped in the plains of Moab, across from Jericho. The overall population had changed only slightly, with 603,550 in the first registration and 601,730 in the second. This nearly complete replacement of population (26:63-65) showed that the Lord was faithful to Israel in spite of their repeated acts of rebellion.

Koinonia
IMAGE
MY STORY WITH COMMUNITY, WORKPLACE & CHURCH

Purity Is Public

SCRIPTURE CONNECTION: NUMBERS 25:1-18

At a youth meeting, the leader spoke to our energetic crowd of 150 high schoolers. The topic? Great sex.

Were we rowdy? No. Every eye was glued to the speaker, every ear opened.

I was fifteen years old. Like many, I was under the impression that sex by God's design entailed a longer list of don'ts than of dos. This suspicion seems confirmed when reading passages like Leviticus 18.

But when reading a story about sexual sin like in Numbers 25, we may begin to understand why God takes such matters so seriously. God's detailed don'ts were designed to protect, preserve, and provide for his people. Obedience to his sexual standards comes with the promise of life (Leviticus 18:5)! And this is still true today.

For years as a ministry leader, I have facilitated women's recovery groups for sexual and relational wellness. What I have found is that most often, our sexual missteps and resulting messes are caused by not heeding God's don'ts and forging ahead with our own dos. We likely feared missing out and thus simply did what we felt like doing. To our own detriment, a trade was made—God's blessing for ruin.

> Sexual wellness is available for us today as we walk with God.

The God who instructed the Israelites to safeguard purity, life, and favor for the whole nation is the same God we worship today. We can only imagine what our communities would be like if each of us surrendered to the practice of individual purity. Secure and connected with God and each other, together we could elevate our nation to new heights.

IMAGINE

If you could change any aspect of your sexual history or current behavior, what would it be?

How do you think such a change might affect your trajectory?

"When revisiting past sexual wounds or poor choices, I sometimes experience pain and regret. Today, I choose a deliberate path of recovery. Healing comes by walking with God and then ripples outward as I influence my community."

MISTY ARTERBURN is an author and speaker, contributing to Bible projects, devotionals, and recovery materials for over twenty years. Wife and mom to five, Misty is the founder of Recovery Girls and the general editor of *The One Year Bible for Women*.

The Jemuelite clan, named after their ancestor Jemuel.*
The Jaminite clan, named after their ancestor Jamin.
The Jakinite clan, named after their ancestor Jakin.
13 The Zoharite clan, named after their ancestor Zohar.*
The Shaulite clan, named after their ancestor Shaul.

14 These were the clans of Simeon. Their registered troops numbered 22,200.

The Tribe of Gad

15 These were the clans descended from the sons of Gad:
The Zephonite clan, named after their ancestor Zephon.
The Haggite clan, named after their ancestor Haggi.
The Shunite clan, named after their ancestor Shuni.
16 The Oznite clan, named after their ancestor Ozni.
The Erite clan, named after their ancestor Eri.
17 The Arodite clan, named after their ancestor Arodi.*
The Arelite clan, named after their ancestor Areli.

18 These were the clans of Gad. Their registered troops numbered 40,500.

The Tribe of Judah

19 Judah had two sons, Er and Onan, who had died in the land of Canaan. 20 These were the clans descended from Judah's surviving sons:
The Shelanite clan, named after their ancestor Shelah.
The Perezite clan, named after their ancestor Perez.
The Zerahite clan, named after their ancestor Zerah.

21 These were the subclans descended from the Perezites:
The Hezronites, named after their ancestor Hezron.
The Hamulites, named after their ancestor Hamul.

22 These were the clans of Judah. Their registered troops numbered 76,500.

The Tribe of Issachar

23 These were the clans descended from the sons of Issachar:
The Tolaite clan, named after their ancestor Tola.
The Puite clan, named after their ancestor Puah.*
24 The Jashubite clan, named after their ancestor Jashub.
The Shimronite clan, named after their ancestor Shimron.

25 These were the clans of Issachar. Their registered troops numbered 64,300.

The Tribe of Zebulun

26 These were the clans descended from the sons of Zebulun:
The Seredite clan, named after their ancestor Sered.
The Elonite clan, named after their ancestor Elon.
The Jahleelite clan, named after their ancestor Jahleel.

27 These were the clans of Zebulun. Their registered troops numbered 60,500.

The Tribe of Manasseh

28 Two clans were descended from Joseph through Manasseh and Ephraim.

29 These were the clans descended from Manasseh:
The Makirite clan, named after their ancestor Makir.
The Gileadite clan, named after their ancestor Gilead, Makir's son.

30 These were the subclans descended from the Gileadites:
The Iezerites, named after their ancestor Iezer.
The Helekites, named after their ancestor Helek.
31 The Asrielites, named after their ancestor Asriel.
The Shechemites, named after their ancestor Shechem.
32 The Shemidaites, named after their ancestor Shemida.
The Hepherites, named after their ancestor Hepher.
33 (One of Hepher's descendants, Zelophehad, had no sons, but his daughters' names were Mahlah, Noah, Hoglah, Milcah, and Tirzah.)

34 These were the clans of Manasseh. Their registered troops numbered 52,700.

26:12 As in Syriac version (see also Gen 46:10; Exod 6:15); Hebrew reads *Nemuelite . . . Nemuel.* **26:13** As in parallel texts at Gen 46:10 and Exod 6:15; Hebrew reads *Zerahite . . . Zerah.* **26:17** As in Samaritan Pentateuch and Greek and Syriac versions (see also Gen 46:16); Hebrew reads *Arod.* **26:23** As in Samaritan Pentateuch, Greek and Syriac versions, and Latin Vulgate (see also 1 Chr 7:1); Hebrew reads *The Punite clan, named after its ancestor Puvah.*

26:33 The daughters of Zelophehad initiated important legal reform (see 27:1-11; 36:1-12). See also "Daughters of Zelophehad" on page 207.

The Tribe of Ephraim

³⁵These were the clans descended from the sons of Ephraim:
The Shuthelahite clan, named after their ancestor Shuthelah.
The Bekerite clan, named after their ancestor Beker.
The Tahanite clan, named after their ancestor Tahan.

³⁶This was the subclan descended from the Shuthelahites:
The Eranites, named after their ancestor Eran.

³⁷These were the clans of Ephraim. Their registered troops numbered 32,500.

These clans of Manasseh and Ephraim were all descendants of Joseph.

The Tribe of Benjamin

³⁸These were the clans descended from the sons of Benjamin:
The Belaite clan, named after their ancestor Bela.
The Ashbelite clan, named after their ancestor Ashbel.
The Ahiramite clan, named after their ancestor Ahiram.
³⁹ The Shuphamite clan, named after their ancestor Shupham.*
The Huphamite clan, named after their ancestor Hupham.

⁴⁰These were the subclans descended from the Belaites:
The Ardites, named after their ancestor Ard.*
The Naamites, named after their ancestor Naaman.

⁴¹These were the clans of Benjamin. Their registered troops numbered 45,600.

The Tribe of Dan

⁴²These were the clans descended from the sons of Dan:
The Shuhamite clan, named after their ancestor Shuham.

⁴³These were the Shuhamite clans of Dan. Their registered troops numbered 64,400.

The Tribe of Asher

⁴⁴These were the clans descended from the sons of Asher:
The Imnite clan, named after their ancestor Imnah.
The Ishvite clan, named after their ancestor Ishvi.
The Beriite clan, named after their ancestor Beriah.

⁴⁵These were the subclans descended from the Beriites:
The Heberites, named after their ancestor Heber.
The Malkielites, named after their ancestor Malkiel.

⁴⁶Asher also had a daughter named Serah.

⁴⁷These were the clans of Asher. Their registered troops numbered 53,400.

The Tribe of Naphtali

⁴⁸These were the clans descended from the sons of Naphtali:
The Jahzeelite clan, named after their ancestor Jahzeel.
The Gunite clan, named after their ancestor Guni.
⁴⁹ The Jezerite clan, named after their ancestor Jezer.
The Shillemite clan, named after their ancestor Shillem.

⁵⁰These were the clans of Naphtali. Their registered troops numbered 45,400.

Results of the Registration

⁵¹In summary, the registered troops of all Israel numbered 601,730.

⁵²Then the LORD said to Moses, ⁵³"Divide the land among the tribes, and distribute the grants of land in proportion to the tribes' populations, as indicated by the number of names on the list. ⁵⁴Give the larger tribes more land and the smaller tribes less land, each group receiving a grant in proportion to the size of its population. ⁵⁵But you must assign the land by lot, and give land to each ancestral tribe according to the number of names on the list. ⁵⁶Each grant of land must be assigned by lot among the larger and smaller tribal groups."

The Tribe of Levi

⁵⁷This is the record of the Levites who were counted according to their clans:
The Gershonite clan, named after their ancestor Gershon.
The Kohathite clan, named after their ancestor Kohath.
The Merarite clan, named after their ancestor Merari.

⁵⁸The Libnites, the Hebronites, the Mahlites, the Mushites, and the Korahites were all subclans of the Levites.

Now Kohath was the ancestor of Amram, ⁵⁹and Amram's wife was named Jochebed. She also was a descendant of Levi, born among the Levites in the land of Egypt. Amram and Jochebed became the parents of

---

26:39 As in some Hebrew manuscripts, Samaritan Pentateuch, Greek and Syriac versions, and Latin Vulgate; most Hebrew manuscripts read *Shephupham*. 26:40 As in Samaritan Pentateuch, some Greek manuscripts, and Latin Vulgate; Hebrew lacks *named after their ancestor Ard*.

Aaron, Moses, and their sister, Miriam. ⁶⁰To Aaron were born Nadab, Abihu, Eleazar, and Ithamar. ⁶¹But Nadab and Abihu died when they burned before the LORD the wrong kind of fire, different than he had commanded.

⁶²The men from the Levite clans who were one month old or older numbered 23,000. But the Levites were not included in the registration of the rest of the people of Israel because they were not given an allotment of land when it was divided among the Israelites.

⁶³So these are the results of the registration of the people of Israel as conducted by Moses and Eleazar the priest on the plains of Moab beside the Jordan River, across from Jericho. ⁶⁴Not one person on this list had been among those listed in the previous registration taken by Moses and Aaron in the wilderness of Sinai. ⁶⁵For the LORD had said of them, "They will all die in the wilderness." Not one of them survived except Caleb son of Jephunneh and Joshua son of Nun.

The Daughters of Zelophehad

27 One day a petition was presented by the daughters of Zelophehad—Mahlah, Noah, Hoglah, Milcah, and Tirzah. Their father, Zelophehad, was a descendant of Hepher son of Gilead, son of Makir, son of Manasseh, son of Joseph. ²These women stood before Moses, Eleazar the priest, the tribal leaders, and the entire community at the entrance of the Tabernacle.* ³"Our father died in the wilderness," they said. "He was not among Korah's followers, who rebelled against the LORD; he died because of his own sin. But he had no sons. ⁴Why should the name of our father disappear from his clan just because he had no sons? Give us property along with the rest of our relatives."

⁵So Moses brought their case before the LORD. ⁶And the LORD replied to Moses, ⁷"The claim of the daughters of Zelophehad is legitimate. You must give them a grant of land along with their father's relatives. Assign them the property that would have been given to their father.

⁸"And give the following instructions to the people of Israel: If a man dies and has no son, then give his inheritance to his daughters. ⁹And if he has no daughter either, transfer his inheritance to his brothers. ¹⁰If he has no brothers, give his inheritance to his father's brothers. ¹¹But if his father has no brothers, give his inheritance to the nearest relative in his clan. This is a legal requirement for the people of Israel, just as the LORD commanded Moses."

Joshua Chosen to Lead Israel

¹²One day the LORD said to Moses, "Climb one of the mountains east of the river,* and look out over the land I have given the people of Israel. ¹³After you have seen it, you will die like your brother, Aaron, ¹⁴for you both rebelled against my instructions in the wilderness of Zin. When the people of Israel rebelled, you failed to demonstrate my holiness to them at the waters." (These are the waters of Meribah at Kadesh* in the wilderness of Zin.)

¹⁵Then Moses said to the LORD, ¹⁶"O LORD, you are the God who gives breath to all creatures. Please appoint a new man as leader for the community. ¹⁷Give them someone who will guide them wherever they go and will lead them into battle, so the community of the LORD will not be like sheep without a shepherd."

¹⁸The LORD replied, "Take Joshua son of Nun, who has the Spirit in him, and lay your hands on him. ¹⁹Present him to Eleazar the priest before the whole community, and publicly commission him to lead the people. ²⁰Transfer some of your authority to him so the whole community of Israel will obey him. ²¹When direction from the LORD is needed, Joshua will stand before Eleazar the priest, who will use the Urim—one of the sacred lots cast before the LORD—to determine his will. This is how Joshua and the rest of the community of Israel will determine everything they should do."

²²So Moses did as the LORD commanded. He presented Joshua to Eleazar the priest and the whole community. ²³Moses laid his hands on him and commissioned him to lead the people, just as the LORD had commanded through Moses.

The Daily Offerings

28 The LORD said to Moses, ²"Give these instructions to the people of Israel: The offerings you present as special gifts are a pleasing aroma to me; they are my food. See to it that they are brought at the appointed times and offered according to my instructions.

³"Say to the people: This is the special gift you must present to the LORD as your daily burnt offering. You must offer two one-year-old male lambs with no

---

27:2 Hebrew *the Tent of Meeting.* **27:12** Or *the mountains of Abarim.* **27:14** Hebrew *waters of Meribath-kadesh.*

27:1-11 The daughters' request was not solely about land inheritance but also about preserving the family name (27:4). While other ancient Near Eastern cultures allowed female inheritance, Israel did not. These women boldly came before their community and leaders, confronting the law's insufficiency and seeking redress. The Lord himself affirmed their claim, allowing them to receive their father's inheritance if they married within their tribe (36:1-12).

28:1–29:40 These two chapters contain information about Israel's ritual calendar, including a list of required daily, weekly, and monthly offerings and a list of annual religious events (see also "Israel's Calendar of Festivals" on page 93). Thus, Israel was instructed to worship God "properly and in order" (1 Corinthians 14:40). The annual cycle of sacrifices involved a tremendous investment of animals, grain, oil, and wine. Israel marked these special days by stopping their normal work, a kind of sacrifice that recognized the importance of these holy days. This annual cycle included seven different occasions for worship, all of which recalled Israel's relationship with the Lord. Each worship event included a different combination of burnt, grain, liquid, and sin offerings (see "Israel's Sacrifices" on page 136).

defects. ⁴Sacrifice one lamb in the morning and the other in the evening. ⁵With each lamb you must offer a grain offering of two quarts* of choice flour mixed with one quart* of pure oil of pressed olives. ⁶This is the regular burnt offering instituted at Mount Sinai as a special gift, a pleasing aroma to the LORD. ⁷Along with it you must present the proper liquid offering of one quart of alcoholic drink with each lamb, poured out in the Holy Place as an offering to the LORD. ⁸Offer the second lamb in the evening with the same grain offering and liquid offering. It, too, is a special gift, a pleasing aroma to the LORD.

The Sabbath Offerings

⁹"On the Sabbath day, sacrifice two one-year-old male lambs with no defects. They must be accompanied by a grain offering of four quarts* of choice flour moistened with olive oil, and a liquid offering. ¹⁰This is the burnt offering to be presented each Sabbath day, in addition to the regular burnt offering and its accompanying liquid offering.

The Monthly Offerings

¹¹"On the first day of each month, present an extra burnt offering to the LORD of two young bulls, one ram, and seven one-year-old male lambs, all with no defects. ¹²These must be accompanied by grain offerings of choice flour moistened with olive oil—six quarts* with each bull, four quarts with the ram, ¹³and two quarts with each lamb. This burnt offering will be a special gift, a pleasing aroma to the LORD. ¹⁴You must also present a liquid offering with each sacrifice: two quarts* of wine for each bull, a third of a gallon* for the ram, and one quart* for each lamb. Present this monthly burnt offering on the first day of each month throughout the year.

¹⁵"On the first day of each month, you must also offer one male goat for a sin offering to the LORD. This is in addition to the regular burnt offering and its accompanying liquid offering.

Offerings for the Passover

¹⁶"On the fourteenth day of the first month,* you must celebrate the LORD's Passover. ¹⁷On the following day—the fifteenth day of the month—a joyous, seven-day festival will begin, but no bread made with yeast may be eaten. ¹⁸The first day of the festival will be an official day for holy assembly, and no ordinary work may be done on that day. ¹⁹As a special gift you must present a burnt offering to the LORD—two young bulls, one ram, and seven one-year-old male lambs, all with no defects. ²⁰These will be accompanied by grain offerings of choice flour moistened with olive oil—six quarts with each bull, four quarts with the ram, ²¹and two quarts with each of the seven lambs. ²²You must also offer a male goat as a sin offering to purify yourselves and make yourselves right with the LORD.* ²³Present these offerings in addition to your regular morning burnt offering. ²⁴On each of the seven days of the festival, this is how you must prepare the food offering that is presented as a special gift, a pleasing aroma to the LORD. These will be offered in addition to the regular burnt offerings and liquid offerings. ²⁵The seventh day of the festival will be another official day for holy assembly, and no ordinary work may be done on that day.

Offerings for the Festival of Harvest

²⁶"At the Festival of Harvest,* when you present the first of your new grain to the LORD, you must call an official day for holy assembly, and you may do no ordinary work on that day. ²⁷Present a special burnt offering on that day as a pleasing aroma to the LORD. It will consist of two young bulls, one ram, and seven one-year-old male lambs. ²⁸These will be accompanied by grain offerings of choice flour moistened with olive oil—six quarts with each bull, four quarts with the ram, ²⁹and two quarts with each of the seven lambs. ³⁰Also, offer one male goat to purify yourselves and make yourselves right with the LORD. ³¹Prepare these special burnt offerings, along with their liquid offerings, in addition to the regular burnt offering and its accompanying grain offering. Be sure that all the animals you sacrifice have no defects.

Offerings for the Festival of Trumpets

29 "Celebrate the Festival of Trumpets each year on the first day of the appointed month in early autumn.* You must call an official day for holy assembly, and you may do no ordinary work. ²On that day you must present a burnt offering as

---

28:5a Hebrew ¹/₁₀ of an ephah [2.2 liters]; also in 28:13, 21, 29. **28:5b** Hebrew ¼ of a hin [1 liter]; also in 28:7. **28:9** Hebrew ²/₁₀ of an ephah [4.4 liters]; also in 28:12, 20, 28. **28:12** Hebrew ³/₁₀ of an ephah [6.6 liters]; also in 28:20, 28. **28:14a** Hebrew ½ of a hin [2 liters]. **28:14b** Hebrew ⅓ of a hin [1.3 liters]. **28:14c** Hebrew ¼ of a hin [1 liter]. **28:16** This day in the ancient Hebrew lunar calendar occurred in late March, April, or early May. **28:22** Or *to make atonement for yourselves;* also in 28:30. **28:26** Hebrew *Festival of Weeks.* This was later called the Festival of Pentecost (see Acts 2:1). It is celebrated today as Shavuot (or Shabuoth). **29:1** Hebrew *the first day of the seventh month.* This day in the ancient Hebrew lunar calendar occurred in September or October. This festival is celebrated today as Rosh Hashanah, the Jewish new year.

28:16-25 The Passover, followed by the Festival of Unleavened Bread, was the first of seven great annual festivals; it was held in early spring (sometime in late March to early May). The Passover required no public sacrifices—it was a family occasion celebrated at home (see also 9:1-5; Exodus 12:1–13:10; Leviticus 23:5-8; Deuteronomy 16:1-8). This festival played a special role in the background of the Last Supper (see Matthew 26:17-19, 26-28; Mark 14:12; John 11:55; 12:1; 13:1; 18:28, 39; 19:14, 31; see also 1 Corinthians 5:7). **29:1** "The first day of the appointed month in early autumn" in the ancient Hebrew lunar calendar occurred in September or October. This festival is celebrated today as Rosh Hashanah, the Jewish new year.

Daughters of Zelophehad

IDENTITY | Be Bold to Behold

Zelophehad's five daughters overcame tradition to seek legal rights to their father's inheritance. They knew and understood the law, making their appeal with wisdom. Moses brought the issue before God, and God ruled in favor of the daughters' request.

When entering the Promised Land, the daughters claimed their promised inheritance (Joshua 17:1-4). They followed God's ways, they knew that he is faithful, and they received what God gave.

As daughters of God, we inherit God's promises too. God has already ruled in our favor; through Christ, all God's promises are "Yes" and "Amen" (2 Corinthians 1:20). God is not sexist—in Christ, there is neither male nor female (Galatians 3:26-29). And God is not stingy. He gives security, worth, value, acceptance, forgiveness, joy, peace, favor, significance, purpose, and hope, just to name a few things (see Ephesians 1:3-11). His answer to us is indeed "Yes!"

> God holds out our inheritance, but we must claim it.

However, like the daughters of Zelophehad, we must wisely claim God's gifts. He promises, but we must believe to receive. We must step up to step into our inheritance.

ZELOPHEHAD'S DAUGHTERS' STORY IS TOLD IN NUMBERS 27:1-11; 36:1-12; JOSHUA 17:1-4.

IDENTIFY

For what promises do you need to be bold to behold?

How will you step up to step into your inheritance as a daughter of the King?

> "So often other voices try to define and confine me. Tradition, culture, legalism, humanism, even well-meaning family and friends. Freedom came when I surrendered to the truth: The only thing that is always true about me is what God says about me! And he says I am chosen, wanted, anointed, appointed, forgiven, accepted, and called. Let God alone define and refine you."

JULIE WRIGHT is author of *Redeeming Eve: When a Woman Lives Loved* and founder of Live Loved Ministry. Her passion is for women to embrace God's love and cultivate an authentic relationship with Jesus.

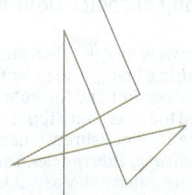

a pleasing aroma to the LORD. It will consist of one young bull, one ram, and seven one-year-old male lambs, all with no defects. ³These must be accompanied by grain offerings of choice flour moistened with olive oil—six quarts* with the bull, four quarts* with the ram, ⁴and two quarts* with each of the seven lambs. ⁵In addition, you must sacrifice a male goat as a sin offering to purify yourselves and make yourselves right with the LORD.* ⁶These special sacrifices are in addition to your regular monthly and daily burnt offerings, and they must be given with their prescribed grain offerings and liquid offerings. These offerings are given as a special gift to the LORD, a pleasing aroma to him.

Offerings for the Day of Atonement

⁷"Ten days later, on the tenth day of the same month,* you must call another holy assembly. On that day, the Day of Atonement, the people must go without food and must do no ordinary work. ⁸You must present a burnt offering as a pleasing aroma to the LORD. It will consist of one young bull, one ram, and seven one-year-old male lambs, all with no defects. ⁹These offerings must be accompanied by the prescribed grain offerings of choice flour moistened with olive oil—six quarts of choice flour with the bull, four quarts of choice flour with the ram, ¹⁰and two quarts of choice flour with each of the seven lambs. ¹¹You must also sacrifice one male goat for a sin offering. This is in addition to the sin offering of atonement and the regular daily burnt offering with its grain offering, and their accompanying liquid offerings.

Offerings for the Festival of Shelters

¹²"Five days later, on the fifteenth day of the same month,* you must call another holy assembly of all the people, and you may do no ordinary work on that day. It is the beginning of the Festival of Shelters,* a seven-day festival to the LORD. ¹³On the first day of the festival, you must present a burnt offering as a special gift, a pleasing aroma to the LORD. It will consist of thirteen young bulls, two rams, and fourteen one-year-old male lambs, all with no defects. ¹⁴Each of these offerings must be accompanied by a grain offering of choice flour moistened with olive oil—six quarts for each of the thirteen bulls, four quarts for each of the two rams, ¹⁵and two quarts for each of the fourteen lambs. ¹⁶You must also sacrifice a male goat as a sin offering, in addition to the regular burnt offering with its accompanying grain offering and liquid offering.

¹⁷"On the second day of this seven-day festival, sacrifice twelve young bulls, two rams, and fourteen one-year-old male lambs, all with no defects. ¹⁸Each of these offerings of bulls, rams, and lambs must be accompanied by its prescribed grain offering and liquid offering. ¹⁹You must also sacrifice a male goat as a sin offering, in addition to the regular burnt offering with its accompanying grain offering and liquid offering.

²⁰"On the third day of the festival, sacrifice eleven young bulls, two rams, and fourteen one-year-old male lambs, all with no defects. ²¹Each of these offerings of bulls, rams, and lambs must be accompanied by its prescribed grain offering and liquid offering. ²²You must also sacrifice a male goat as a sin offering, in addition to the regular burnt offering with its accompanying grain offering and liquid offering.

²³"On the fourth day of the festival, sacrifice ten young bulls, two rams, and fourteen one-year-old male lambs, all with no defects. ²⁴Each of these offerings of bulls, rams, and lambs must be accompanied by its prescribed grain offering and liquid offering. ²⁵You must also sacrifice a male goat as a sin offering, in addition to the regular burnt offering with its accompanying grain offering and liquid offering.

²⁶"On the fifth day of the festival, sacrifice nine young bulls, two rams, and fourteen one-year-old male lambs, all with no defects. ²⁷Each of these offerings of bulls, rams, and lambs must be accompanied by its prescribed grain offering and liquid offering. ²⁸You must also sacrifice a male goat as a sin offering, in addition to the regular burnt offering with its accompanying grain offering and liquid offering.

²⁹"On the sixth day of the festival, sacrifice eight young bulls, two rams, and fourteen one-year-old male lambs, all with no defects. ³⁰Each of these offerings of bulls, rams, and lambs must be accompanied

---

29:3a Hebrew ³/₁₀ of an ephah [6.6 liters]; also in 29:9, 14. **29:3b** Hebrew ²/₁₀ of an ephah [4.4 liters]; also in 29:9, 14. **29:4** Hebrew ¹/₁₀ of an ephah [2.2 liters]; also in 29:10, 15. **29:5** Or to make atonement for yourselves. **29:7** Hebrew On the tenth day of the seventh month; see 29:1 and the note there. This day in the ancient Hebrew lunar calendar occurred in September or October. It is celebrated today as Yom Kippur. **29:12a** Hebrew On the fifteenth day of the seventh month; see 29:1, 7 and the notes there. This day in the ancient Hebrew lunar calendar occurred in late September, October, or early November. **29:12b** Or Festival of Booths, or Festival of Tabernacles. This was earlier called the Festival of the Final Harvest or Festival of Ingathering (see Exod 23:16b). It is celebrated today as Sukkot (or Succoth).

29:7-11 The Day of Atonement was a solemn occasion, a day of fasting (see also Leviticus 16; 23:26-32; Romans 3:23-25; Hebrews 9:7-12, 23-28).
29:12-38 The Festival of Shelters began on the fifteenth day of the seventh month. It was an eight-day harvest celebration (Numbers 29:12, 35; Exodus 34:22) that required an enormous number of offerings. This harvest festival was an especially joyous occasion and a time for thanksgiving (see Nehemiah 8:13-18). The shelters also reminded the Israelites of dwelling in tents during their wilderness sojourn (see also Leviticus 23:33-43; 1 Kings 8:1-2).

by its prescribed grain offering and liquid offering. ³¹You must also sacrifice a male goat as a sin offering, in addition to the regular burnt offering with its accompanying grain offering and liquid offering.

³²"On the seventh day of the festival, sacrifice seven young bulls, two rams, and fourteen one-year-old male lambs, all with no defects. ³³Each of these offerings of bulls, rams, and lambs must be accompanied by its prescribed grain offering and liquid offering. ³⁴You must also sacrifice one male goat as a sin offering, in addition to the regular burnt offering with its accompanying grain offering and liquid offering.

³⁵"On the eighth day of the festival, proclaim another holy day. You must do no ordinary work on that day. ³⁶You must present a burnt offering as a special gift, a pleasing aroma to the LORD. It will consist of one young bull, one ram, and seven one-year-old male lambs, all with no defects. ³⁷Each of these offerings must be accompanied by its prescribed grain offering and liquid offering. ³⁸You must also sacrifice one male goat as a sin offering, in addition to the regular burnt offering with its accompanying grain offering and liquid offering.

³⁹"You must present these offerings to the LORD at your annual festivals. These are in addition to the sacrifices and offerings you present in connection with vows, or as voluntary offerings, burnt offerings, grain offerings, liquid offerings, or peace offerings."

⁴⁰*So Moses gave all of these instructions to the people of Israel as the LORD had commanded him.

Laws concerning Vows

30 ¹*Then Moses summoned the leaders of the tribes of Israel and told them, "This is what the LORD has commanded: ²A man who makes a vow to the LORD or makes a pledge under oath must never break it. He must do exactly what he said he would do.

³"If a young woman makes a vow to the LORD or a pledge under oath while she is still living at her father's home, ⁴and her father hears of the vow or pledge and does not object to it, then all her vows and pledges will stand. ⁵But if her father refuses to let her fulfill the vow or pledge on the day he hears of it, then all her vows and pledges will become invalid. The LORD will forgive her because her father would not let her fulfill them.

⁶"Now suppose a young woman makes a vow or binds herself with an impulsive pledge and later marries. ⁷If her husband learns of her vow or pledge and does not object on the day he hears of it, her vows and pledges will stand. ⁸But if her husband refuses to accept her vow or impulsive pledge on the day he hears of it, he nullifies her commitments, and the LORD will forgive her. ⁹If, however, a woman is a widow or is divorced, she must fulfill all her vows and pledges.

¹⁰"But suppose a woman is married and living in her husband's home when she makes a vow or binds herself with a pledge. ¹¹If her husband hears of it and does not object to it, her vow or pledge will stand. ¹²But if her husband refuses to accept it on the day he hears of it, her vow or pledge will be nullified, and the LORD will forgive her. ¹³So her husband may either confirm or nullify any vows or pledges she makes to deny herself. ¹⁴But if he does not object on the day he hears of it, then he is agreeing to all her vows and pledges. ¹⁵If he waits more than a day and then tries to nullify a vow or pledge, he will be punished for her guilt."

¹⁶These are the regulations the LORD gave Moses concerning relationships between a man and his wife, and between a father and a young daughter who still lives at home.

Conquest of the Midianites

31 Then the LORD said to Moses, ²"On behalf of the people of Israel, take revenge on the Midianites for leading them into idolatry. After that, you will die and join your ancestors."

³So Moses said to the people, "Choose some men, and arm them to fight the LORD's war of revenge against Midian. ⁴From each tribe of Israel, send 1,000 men into battle." ⁵So they chose 1,000 men from each tribe of Israel, a total of 12,000 men armed for battle. ⁶Then Moses sent them out, 1,000 men from each tribe, and Phinehas son of Eleazar the priest led them into battle. They carried along the holy objects

---

29:40 Verse 29:40 is numbered 30:1 in Hebrew text.   **30:1** Verses 30:1-16 are numbered 30:2-17 in Hebrew text.

30:3-15 Vows could include many things, such as monetary payment, sexual abstinence, or fasting. Given the fact that independent women were required to fulfill their vows (Numbers 30:9), the issue here is not whether God accepted women's vows in general. Instead, the provision allowing a father or husband to nullify a vow reflects the culture. Since patriarchs bore legal and economic responsibility for their extended families, this provision safeguarded their ability to ensure the family's stability.

31:1-2 The Lord ordered Moses to lead Israel in a war of retaliation against the Midianites, who had joined the Moabites in leading the Hebrews into idolatry (Numbers 25). The Midianites were a tribal people who inhabited the arid and semiarid regions south and east of Palestine and east of the Jordan River; they were counted among the "people of the east" (Judges 6:3, 33; 7:12). They lived in camps or settlements and were famous for their knowledge of desert transportation (see Genesis 37:28, 36; Isaiah 60:6). While they were descended from Abraham (Genesis 25:1-2) and had been friendly toward Moses (Exodus 2:15–3:1; see Numbers 10:29), the elders of Midian had joined Balak in hiring Balaam to curse Israel (22:4, 7), whose presence threatened the peoples of Transjordan (the region east of the Jordan).

of the sanctuary and the trumpets for sounding the charge. ⁷They attacked Midian as the LORD had commanded Moses, and they killed all the men. ⁸All five of the Midianite kings—Evi, Rekem, Zur, Hur, and Reba—died in the battle. They also killed Balaam son of Beor with the sword.

⁹Then the Israelite army captured the Midianite women and children and seized their cattle and flocks and all their wealth as plunder. ¹⁰They burned all the towns and villages where the Midianites had lived. ¹¹After they had gathered the plunder and captives, both people and animals, ¹²they brought them all to Moses and Eleazar the priest, and to the whole community of Israel, which was camped on the plains of Moab beside the Jordan River, across from Jericho. ¹³Moses, Eleazar the priest, and all the leaders of the community went to meet them outside the camp. ¹⁴But Moses was furious with all the generals and captains* who had returned from the battle.

¹⁵"Why have you let all the women live?" he demanded. ¹⁶"These are the very ones who followed Balaam's advice and caused the people of Israel to rebel against the LORD at Mount Peor. They are the ones who caused the plague to strike the LORD's people. ¹⁷So kill all the boys and all the women who have had intercourse with a man. ¹⁸Only the young girls who are virgins may live; you may keep them for yourselves. ¹⁹And all of you who have killed anyone or touched a dead body must stay outside the camp for seven days. You must purify yourselves and your captives on the third and seventh days. ²⁰Purify all your clothing, too, and everything made of leather, goat hair, or wood."

²¹Then Eleazar the priest said to the men who were in the battle, "The LORD has given Moses this legal requirement: ²²Anything made of gold, silver, bronze, iron, tin, or lead—²³that is, all metals that do not burn—must be passed through fire in order to be made ceremonially pure. These metal objects must then be further purified with the water of purification. But everything that burns must be purified by the water alone. ²⁴On the seventh day you must wash your clothes and be purified. Then you may return to the camp."

Division of the Plunder

²⁵And the LORD said to Moses, ²⁶"You and Eleazar the priest and the family leaders of each tribe are to make a list of all the plunder taken in the battle, including the people and animals. ²⁷Then divide the plunder into two parts, and give half to the men who fought the battle and half to the rest of the people. ²⁸From the army's portion, first give the LORD his share of the plunder—one of every 500 of the prisoners and of the cattle, donkeys, sheep, and goats. ²⁹Give this share of the army's half to Eleazar the priest as an offering to the LORD. ³⁰From the half that belongs to the people of Israel, take one of every fifty of the prisoners and of the cattle, donkeys, sheep, goats, and other animals. Give this share to the Levites, who are in charge of maintaining the LORD's Tabernacle." ³¹So Moses and Eleazar the priest did as the LORD commanded Moses.

³²The plunder remaining from everything the fighting men had taken totaled 675,000 sheep and goats, ³³72,000 cattle, ³⁴61,000 donkeys, ³⁵and 32,000 virgin girls.

³⁶Half of the plunder was given to the fighting men. It totaled 337,500 sheep and goats, ³⁷of which 675 were the LORD's share; ³⁸36,000 cattle, of which 72 were the LORD's share; ³⁹30,500 donkeys, of which 61 were the LORD's share; ⁴⁰and 16,000 virgin girls, of whom 32 were the LORD's share. ⁴¹Moses gave all the LORD's share to Eleazar the priest, just as the LORD had directed him.

⁴²Half of the plunder belonged to the people of Israel, and Moses separated it from the half belonging to the fighting men. ⁴³It totaled 337,500 sheep and goats, ⁴⁴36,000 cattle, ⁴⁵30,500 donkeys, ⁴⁶and 16,000 virgin girls. ⁴⁷From the half-share given to the people, Moses took one of every fifty prisoners and animals and gave them to the Levites, who maintained the LORD's Tabernacle. All this was done as the LORD had commanded Moses.

⁴⁸Then all the generals and captains came to Moses ⁴⁹and said, "We, your servants, have accounted for all the men who went out to battle under our command; not one of us is missing! ⁵⁰So we are presenting the items of gold we captured as an offering to the LORD from our share of the plunder—armbands, bracelets, rings, earrings, and necklaces. This will purify our lives before the LORD and make us right with him.*"

⁵¹So Moses and Eleazar the priest received the gold from all the military commanders—all kinds of jewelry and crafted objects. ⁵²In all, the gold that the generals and captains presented as a gift to the LORD weighed about 420 pounds.* ⁵³All the fighting men had taken some of the plunder for themselves. ⁵⁴So Moses and Eleazar the priest accepted the gifts from the generals and captains and brought the gold to the Tabernacle* as a reminder to the LORD that the people of Israel belong to him.

31:14 Hebrew *the commanders of thousands, and the commanders of hundreds;* also in 31:48, 52, 54. **31:50** Or *will make atonement for our lives before the LORD.* **31:52** Hebrew *16,750 shekels* [191 kilograms]. **31:54** Hebrew *the Tent of Meeting.*

31:14-18 The Israelite men who had chosen to worship Baal of Peor and have sex with local Midianite women had already been executed. Now the Midianite women, too, would be put to death, and only the women who were virgins—and so had not been part of the scheme to lead Israel to rebel—were spared.

32:1-5 From the time that Israel occupied the central part of the area east of the Jordan (during the military encounters described in 21:1-35) Israel had been preparing to invade Canaan. At a moment when the Hebrews needed to safeguard their unity, two tribes asked to settle east of the Jordan River.

The Tribes East of the Jordan

32 The tribes of Reuben and Gad owned vast numbers of livestock. So when they saw that the lands of Jazer and Gilead were ideally suited for their flocks and herds, ²they came to Moses, Eleazar the priest, and the other leaders of the community. They said, ³"Notice the towns of Ataroth, Dibon, Jazer, Nimrah, Heshbon, Elealeh, Sibmah,* Nebo, and Beon. ⁴The LORD has conquered this whole area for the community of Israel, and it is ideally suited for all our livestock. ⁵If we have found favor with you, please let us have this land as our property instead of giving us land across the Jordan River."

⁶"Do you intend to stay here while your brothers go across and do all the fighting?" Moses asked the men of Gad and Reuben. ⁷"Why do you want to discourage the rest of the people of Israel from going across to the land the LORD has given them? ⁸Your ancestors did the same thing when I sent them from Kadesh-barnea to explore the land. ⁹After they went up to the valley of Eshcol and explored the land, they discouraged the people of Israel from entering the land the LORD was giving them. ¹⁰Then the LORD was very angry with them, and he vowed, ¹¹'Of all those I rescued from Egypt, no one who is twenty years old or older will ever see the land I swore to give to Abraham, Isaac, and Jacob, for they have not obeyed me wholeheartedly. ¹²The only exceptions are Caleb son of Jephunneh the Kenizzite and Joshua son of Nun, for they have wholeheartedly followed the LORD.'

¹³"The LORD was angry with Israel and made them wander in the wilderness for forty years until the entire generation that sinned in the LORD's sight had died. ¹⁴But here you are, a brood of sinners, doing exactly the same thing! You are making the LORD even angrier with Israel. ¹⁵If you turn away from him like this and he abandons them again in the wilderness, you will be responsible for destroying this entire nation!"

¹⁶But they approached Moses and said, "We simply want to build pens for our livestock and fortified towns for our wives and children. ¹⁷Then we will arm ourselves and lead our fellow Israelites into battle until we have brought them safely to their land. Meanwhile, our families will stay in the fortified towns we build here, so they will be safe from any attacks by the local people. ¹⁸We will not return to our homes until all the people of Israel have received their portions of land. ¹⁹But we do not claim any of the land on the other side of the Jordan. We would rather live here on the east side and accept this as our grant of land."

²⁰Then Moses said, "If you keep your word and arm yourselves for the LORD's battles, ²¹and if your troops cross the Jordan and keep fighting until the LORD has driven out his enemies, ²²then you may return when the LORD has conquered the land. You will have fulfilled your duty to the LORD and to the rest of the people of Israel. And the land on the east side of the Jordan will be your property from the LORD. ²³But if you fail to keep your word, then you will have sinned against the LORD, and you may be sure that your sin will find you out. ²⁴Go ahead and build towns for your families and pens for your flocks, but do everything you have promised."

²⁵Then the men of Gad and Reuben replied, "We, your servants, will follow your instructions exactly. ²⁶Our children, wives, flocks, and cattle will stay here in the towns of Gilead. ²⁷But all who are able to bear arms will cross over to fight for the LORD, just as you have said."

²⁸So Moses gave orders to Eleazar the priest, Joshua son of Nun, and the leaders of the clans of Israel. ²⁹He said, "The men of Gad and Reuben who are armed for battle must cross the Jordan with you to fight for the LORD. If they do, give them the land of Gilead as their property when the land is conquered. ³⁰But if they refuse to arm themselves and cross over with you, then they must accept land with the rest of you in the land of Canaan."

³¹The tribes of Gad and Reuben said again, "We are your servants, and we will do as the LORD has commanded! ³²We will cross the Jordan into Canaan fully armed to fight for the LORD, but our property will be here on this side of the Jordan."

³³So Moses assigned land to the tribes of Gad, Reuben, and half the tribe of Manasseh son of Joseph. He gave them the territory of King Sihon of the Amorites and the land of King Og of Bashan—the whole land with its cities and surrounding lands.

³⁴The descendants of Gad built the towns of Dibon, Ataroth, Aroer, ³⁵Atroth-shophan, Jazer, Jogbehah, ³⁶Beth-nimrah, and Beth-haran. These were all fortified towns with pens for their flocks.

³⁷The descendants of Reuben built the towns of Heshbon, Elealeh, Kiriathaim, ³⁸Nebo, Baal-meon, and Sibmah. They changed the names of some of the towns they conquered and rebuilt.

³⁹Then the descendants of Makir of the tribe of Manasseh went to Gilead and conquered it, and they drove out the Amorites living there. ⁴⁰So Moses gave Gilead to the Makirites, descendants of Manasseh, and they settled there. ⁴¹The people of Jair, another clan of the tribe of Manasseh, captured many of the

---

32:3 As in Samaritan Pentateuch and Greek version (see also 32:38); Hebrew reads *Sebam*.

32:12 Caleb is identified as a Kenizzite, a descendant of Esau (see Genesis 36:10-11). Apparently Caleb was not a native Israelite, but a convert who was so thoroughly integrated into the life and faith of Israel that he was called upon to represent the tribe of Judah when the twelve scouts were sent out to survey the Promised Land (Numbers 13:6).

towns in Gilead and changed the name of that region to the Towns of Jair.* ⁴²Meanwhile, a man named Nobah captured the town of Kenath and its surrounding villages, and he renamed that area Nobah after himself.

Remembering Israel's Journey

33 This is the route the Israelites followed as they marched out of Egypt under the leadership of Moses and Aaron. ²At the LORD's direction, Moses kept a written record of their progress. These are the stages of their march, identified by the different places where they stopped along the way.

³They set out from the city of Rameses in early spring—on the fifteenth day of the first month*—on the morning after the first Passover celebration. The people of Israel left defiantly, in full view of all the Egyptians. ⁴Meanwhile, the Egyptians were burying all their firstborn sons, whom the LORD had killed the night before. The LORD had defeated the gods of Egypt that night with great acts of judgment!

⁵After leaving Rameses, the Israelites set up camp at Succoth.
⁶Then they left Succoth and camped at Etham on the edge of the wilderness.
⁷They left Etham and turned back toward Pi-hahiroth, opposite Baal-zephon, and camped near Migdol.
⁸They left Pi-hahiroth* and crossed the Red Sea* into the wilderness beyond. Then they traveled for three days into the Etham wilderness and camped at Marah.
⁹They left Marah and camped at Elim, where there were twelve springs of water and seventy palm trees.
¹⁰They left Elim and camped beside the Red Sea.*
¹¹They left the Red Sea and camped in the wilderness of Sin.*
¹²They left the wilderness of Sin and camped at Dophkah.
¹³They left Dophkah and camped at Alush.
¹⁴They left Alush and camped at Rephidim, where there was no water for the people to drink.
¹⁵They left Rephidim and camped in the wilderness of Sinai.
¹⁶They left the wilderness of Sinai and camped at Kibroth-hattaavah.
¹⁷They left Kibroth-hattaavah and camped at Hazeroth.
¹⁸They left Hazeroth and camped at Rithmah.
¹⁹They left Rithmah and camped at Rimmon-perez.
²⁰They left Rimmon-perez and camped at Libnah.
²¹They left Libnah and camped at Rissah.
²²They left Rissah and camped at Kehelathah.
²³They left Kehelathah and camped at Mount Shepher.
²⁴They left Mount Shepher and camped at Haradah.
²⁵They left Haradah and camped at Makheloth.
²⁶They left Makheloth and camped at Tahath.
²⁷They left Tahath and camped at Terah.
²⁸They left Terah and camped at Mithcah.
²⁹They left Mithcah and camped at Hashmonah.
³⁰They left Hashmonah and camped at Moseroth.
³¹They left Moseroth and camped at Bene-jaakan.
³²They left Bene-jaakan and camped at Hor-haggidgad.
³³They left Hor-haggidgad and camped at Jotbathah.
³⁴They left Jotbathah and camped at Abronah.
³⁵They left Abronah and camped at Ezion-geber.
³⁶They left Ezion-geber and camped at Kadesh in the wilderness of Zin.
³⁷They left Kadesh and camped at Mount Hor, at the border of Edom. ³⁸While they were at the foot of Mount Hor, Aaron the priest was directed by the LORD to go up the mountain, and there he died. This happened in midsummer, on the first day of the fifth month* of the fortieth year after Israel's departure from Egypt. ³⁹Aaron was 123 years old when he died there on Mount Hor.
⁴⁰At that time the Canaanite king of Arad, who

32:41 Hebrew *Havvoth-jair.* **33:3** This day in the ancient Hebrew lunar calendar occurred in late March, April, or early May. **33:8a** As in many Hebrew manuscripts, Samaritan Pentateuch, and Latin Vulgate (see also 33:7); most Hebrew manuscripts read *left from in front of Hahiroth.* **33:8b** Hebrew *the sea.* **33:10** Hebrew *sea of reeds;* also in 33:11. **33:11** The geographical name *Sin* is related to *Sinai* and should not be confused with the English word *sin.* **33:38** This day in the ancient Hebrew lunar calendar occurred in July or August.

33:1-56 This review of the entire wilderness period contains the longest integrated list of place-names in the Old Testament, from Israel's departure from Egypt (33:3; see Exodus 12:37) until their arrival in the plains of Moab, opposite Jericho (Numbers 33:49; see also 22:1). The forty-two way stations on this itinerary represent far more than a geographical journey; more importantly, they recall Israel's forty-year spiritual pilgrimage. In their travels between Rameses in Egypt (33:3) and Acacia on the plains of Moab (33:49), Israel finally became the people who could invade the land of Canaan and claim the promises God made to Abraham.

33:1-56 This itinerary does not provide enough data to plot an accurate, specific route. Most of the places cannot be identified with certainty; many of the sites appear nowhere else in the Hebrew Bible, and there are not enough clues to pinpoint their locations precisely. Furthermore, this list is partial or selective, omitting some of the place-names mentioned earlier in the journey. See "Israel in the Wilderness" on page 191.

lived in the Negev in the land of Canaan, heard that the people of Israel were approaching his land. ⁴¹Meanwhile, the Israelites left Mount Hor and camped at Zalmonah. ⁴²Then they left Zalmonah and camped at Punon. ⁴³They left Punon and camped at Oboth. ⁴⁴They left Oboth and camped at Iye-abarim on the border of Moab. ⁴⁵They left Iye-abarim* and camped at Dibon-gad. ⁴⁶They left Dibon-gad and camped at Almon-diblathaim. ⁴⁷They left Almon-diblathaim and camped in the mountains east of the river,* near Mount Nebo. ⁴⁸They left the mountains east of the river and camped on the plains of Moab beside the Jordan River, across from Jericho. ⁴⁹Along the Jordan River they camped from Beth-jeshimoth as far as the meadows of Acacia* on the plains of Moab.

⁵⁰While they were camped near the Jordan River on the plains of Moab opposite Jericho, the LORD said to Moses, ⁵¹"Give the following instructions to the people of Israel: When you cross the Jordan River into the land of Canaan, ⁵²you must drive out all the people living there. You must destroy all their carved and molten images and demolish all their pagan shrines. ⁵³Take possession of the land and settle in it, because I have given it to you to occupy. ⁵⁴You must distribute the land among the clans by sacred lot and in proportion to their size. A larger portion of land will be allotted to each of the larger clans, and a smaller portion will be allotted to each of the smaller clans. The decision of the sacred lot is final. In this way, the portions of land will be divided among your ancestral tribes. ⁵⁵But if you fail to drive out the people who live in the land, those who remain will be like splinters in your eyes and thorns in your sides. They will harass you in the land where you live. ⁵⁶And I will do to you what I had planned to do to them."

Boundaries of the Land

34 Then the LORD said to Moses, ²"Give these instructions to the Israelites: When you come into the land of Canaan, which I am giving you as your special possession, these will be the boundaries. ³The southern portion of your country will extend from the wilderness of Zin, along the edge of Edom. The southern boundary will begin on the east at the Dead Sea.* ⁴It will then run south past Scorpion Pass* in the direction of Zin. Its southernmost point will be Kadesh-barnea, from which it will go to Hazar-addar, and on to Azmon. ⁵From Azmon the boundary will turn toward the Brook of Egypt and end at the Mediterranean Sea.*

⁶"Your western boundary will be the coastline of the Mediterranean Sea.

⁷"Your northern boundary will begin at the Mediterranean Sea and run east to Mount Hor, ⁸then to Lebo-hamath, and on through Zedad ⁹and Ziphron to Hazar-enan. This will be your northern boundary.

¹⁰"The eastern boundary will start at Hazar-enan and run south to Shepham, ¹¹then down to Riblah on the east side of Ain. From there the boundary will run down along the eastern edge of the Sea of Galilee,* ¹²and then along the Jordan River to the Dead Sea. These are the boundaries of your land."

¹³Then Moses told the Israelites, "This territory is the homeland you are to divide among yourselves by sacred lot. The LORD has commanded that the land be divided among the nine and a half remaining tribes. ¹⁴The families of the tribes of Reuben, Gad, and half the tribe of Manasseh have already received their grants of land ¹⁵on the east side of the Jordan River, across from Jericho toward the sunrise."

Leaders to Divide the Land

¹⁶And the LORD said to Moses, ¹⁷"Eleazar the priest and Joshua son of Nun are the men designated to divide the grants of land among the people. ¹⁸Enlist one leader from each tribe to help them with the task. ¹⁹These are the tribes and the names of the leaders:

33:45 As in 33:44; Hebrew reads *Iyim*, another name for Iye-abarim. **33:47** Or *the mountains of Abarim;* also in 33:48. **33:49** Hebrew *as far as Abel-shittim*. **34:3** Hebrew *Salt Sea;* also in 34:12. **34:4** Or *the ascent of Akrabbim*. **34:5** Hebrew *the sea;* also in 34:6, 7. **34:11** Hebrew *Sea of Kinnereth*.

33:55-56 Israel failed to carry out God's instructions (33:51-53) and suffered the consequences predicted here (see Judges 1:1–2:5; 2:11–3:6). Israel's enemies in the period of the Judges were like splinters and thorns, harassing them militarily and spiritually.
34:1-29 God determined the borders of the land of Canaan, which Israel was to settle according to the guidelines in 26:52-56. Ever since the call of Abraham (Genesis 12:1-7), the Promised Land of Canaan had stood at the heart of the Old Testament story. Though an entire generation of Hebrews died in the wilderness because they refused to believe the report of the faithful spies (Numbers 13:25-33), God had reaffirmed his promise of land (33:53). Here, God reviewed the plan and identified the boundaries of the Promised Land in an idealized form (see also Joshua 13–19; Ezekiel 47–48). Old Testament Israel did not possess the exact extent of the territory described here (though it came close in the days of David and Solomon; for example, see 2 Samuel 24:1-9), but these borders describe the province of Canaan as generally defined by Egyptian texts dating 1500–1200 BC (the period of the Hebrew invasion). The region actually occupied by Israel changed from time to time.
34:19-28 Caleb son of Jephunneh is the only tribal leader who appears elsewhere in Numbers (13:6, 30; 14:6-38). Nearly all of the older generation had already died during the wilderness period (26:63-65), but the two faithful spies were still leading their people.

Tribe	Leader
Judah	Caleb son of Jephunneh
[20] Simeon	Shemuel son of Ammihud
[21] Benjamin	Elidad son of Kislon
[22] Dan	Bukki son of Jogli
[23] Manasseh son of Joseph	Hanniel son of Ephod
[24] Ephraim son of Joseph	Kemuel son of Shiphtan
[25] Zebulun	Elizaphan son of Parnach
[26] Issachar	Paltiel son of Azzan
[27] Asher	Ahihud son of Shelomi
[28] Naphtali	Pedahel son of Ammihud

[29] These are the men the LORD has appointed to divide the grants of land in Canaan among the Israelites."

Towns for the Levites

35 While Israel was camped beside the Jordan on the plains of Moab across from Jericho, the LORD said to Moses, [2] "Command the people of Israel to give to the Levites from their property certain towns to live in, along with the surrounding pasturelands. [3] These towns will be for the Levites to live in, and the surrounding lands will provide pasture for their cattle, flocks, and other livestock. [4] The pastureland assigned to the Levites around these towns will extend 1,500 feet* from the town walls in every direction. [5] Measure off 3,000 feet* outside the town walls in every direction—east, south, west, north—with the town at the center. This area will serve as the larger pastureland for the towns.

[6] "Six of the towns you give the Levites will be cities of refuge, where a person who has accidentally killed someone can flee for safety. In addition, give them forty-two other towns. [7] In all, forty-eight towns with the surrounding pastureland will be given to the Levites. [8] These towns will come from the property of the people of Israel. The larger tribes will give more towns to the Levites, while the smaller tribes will give fewer. Each tribe will give property in proportion to the size of its land."

35:4 Hebrew *1,000 cubits* [460 meters]. 35:5 Hebrew *2,000 cubits* [920 meters].

Cities of Refuge

[9] The LORD said to Moses, [10] "Give the following instructions to the people of Israel.

"When you cross the Jordan into the land of Canaan, [11] designate cities of refuge to which people can flee if they have killed someone accidentally. [12] These cities will be places of protection from a dead person's relatives who want to avenge the death. The slayer must not be put to death before being tried by the community. [13] Designate six cities of refuge for yourselves, [14] three on the east side of the Jordan River and three on the west in the land of Canaan. [15] These cities are for the protection of Israelites, foreigners living among you, and traveling merchants. Anyone who accidentally kills someone may flee there for safety.

[16] "But if someone strikes and kills another person with a piece of iron, it is murder, and the murderer must be executed. [17] Or if someone with a stone in his hand strikes and kills another person, it is murder, and the murderer must be put to death. [18] Or if someone strikes and kills another person with a wooden object, it is murder, and the murderer must be put to death. [19] The victim's nearest relative is responsible for putting the murderer to death. When they meet, the avenger must put the murderer to death. [20] So if someone hates another person and waits in ambush, then pushes him or throws something at him and he dies, it is murder. [21] Or if someone hates another person and hits him with a fist and he dies, it is murder. In such cases, the avenger must put the murderer to death when they meet.

[22] "But suppose someone pushes another person without having shown previous hostility, or throws something that unintentionally hits another person, [23] or accidentally drops a huge stone on someone, though they were not enemies, and the person dies. [24] If this should happen, the community must follow these regulations in making a judgment between the slayer and the avenger, the victim's nearest relative: [25] The community must protect the slayer from the avenger and must escort the slayer back to live in the

---

35:1-34 The tribe of Levi received no territory, but they were allotted forty-eight towns dispersed among the territories of Israel's other tribes (see Joshua 21; see also Leviticus 25:32-34; 1 Chronicles 13:2; 2 Chronicles 11:14). Just as the Levites had lived in the center of the Israelite camp during the wilderness period (see Numbers 2:17), in the Promised Land they were to live among the other tribes and have influence among them (see Deuteronomy 33:9-10; 2 Chronicles 17:7-9; 19:8-11; 35:3). The cities and their surrounding pastureland were not a "homeland" (see Numbers 18:23; 26:62), but only a tiny fraction of the Canaanite territory dispersed among the other tribes.
35:6-34 Six of the Levites' towns had a special purpose as cities of refuge, places "where a person who has accidentally killed someone can flee for safety." This unusual institution illustrates the humanitarian aspect of Hebrew law (see also Deuteronomy 4:41-43; 19:1-13; Joshua 20:1-9). These six Levitical towns provided a safe haven in cases of accidental or involuntary manslaughter (see Exodus 21:12-14). Just as the forty-eight Levite towns were widely distributed across Israel's territories, the six cities of refuge were dispersed so they would be widely accessible (see Joshua 20:7-8). These designated settlements supplemented the role of the altar as a temporary place of asylum (for example, 1 Kings 1:50-53; 2:28-34; see also Exodus 21:14). Other ancient peoples provided special places of asylum or refuge, often at the altar (see Exodus 21:12-14; 1 Kings 2:28-34), but only ancient Israel established whole settlements as places of sanctuary, reflecting a special interest in social justice.

city of refuge to which he fled. There he must remain until the death of the high priest, who was anointed with the sacred oil.

²⁶"But if the slayer ever leaves the limits of the city of refuge, ²⁷and the avenger finds him outside the city and kills him, it will not be considered murder. ²⁸The slayer should have stayed inside the city of refuge until the death of the high priest. But after the death of the high priest, the slayer may return to his own property. ²⁹These are legal requirements for you to observe from generation to generation, wherever you may live.

³⁰"All murderers must be put to death, but only if evidence is presented by more than one witness. No one may be put to death on the testimony of only one witness. ³¹Also, you must never accept a ransom payment for the life of someone judged guilty of murder and subject to execution; murderers must always be put to death. ³²And never accept a ransom payment from someone who has fled to a city of refuge, allowing a slayer to return to his property before the death of the high priest. ³³This will ensure that the land where you live will not be polluted, for murder pollutes the land. And no sacrifice except the execution of the murderer can purify the land from murder.* ³⁴You must not defile the land where you live, for I live there myself. I am the LORD, who lives among the people of Israel."

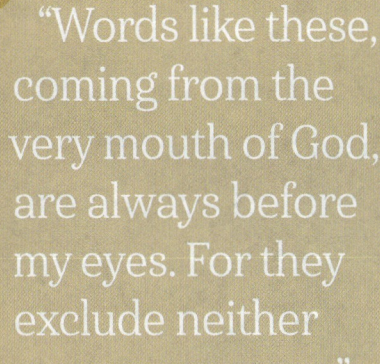

> "Words like these, coming from the very mouth of God, are always before my eyes. For they exclude neither woman nor man."
>
> ARGULA VON GRUMBACH
> (1492–1554) church reformer, mother, and writer

Women Who Inherit Property

36 Then the heads of the clans of Gilead—descendants of Makir, son of Manasseh, son of Joseph—came to Moses and the family leaders of Israel with a petition. ²They said, "Sir, the LORD instructed you to divide the land by sacred lot among the people of Israel. You were told by the LORD to give the grant of land owned by our brother Zelophehad to his daughters. ³But if they marry men from another tribe, their grants of land will go with them to the tribe into which they marry. In this way, the total area of our tribal land will be reduced. ⁴Then when the Year of Jubilee comes, their portion of land will be added to that of the new tribe, causing it to be lost forever to our ancestral tribe."

⁵So Moses gave the Israelites this command from the LORD: "The claim of the men of the tribe of Joseph is legitimate. ⁶This is what the LORD commands concerning the daughters of Zelophehad: Let them marry anyone they like, as long as it is within their own ancestral tribe. ⁷None of the territorial land may pass from tribe to tribe, for all the land given to each tribe must remain within the tribe to which it was first allotted. ⁸The daughters throughout the tribes of Israel who are in line to inherit property must marry within their tribe, so that all the Israelites will keep their ancestral property. ⁹No grant of land may pass from one tribe to another; each tribe of Israel must keep its allotted portion of land."

¹⁰The daughters of Zelophehad did as the LORD commanded Moses. ¹¹Mahlah, Tirzah, Hoglah, Milcah, and Noah all married cousins on their father's side. ¹²They married into the clans of Manasseh son of Joseph. Thus, their inheritance of land remained within their ancestral tribe.

¹³These are the commands and regulations that the LORD gave to the people of Israel through Moses while they were camped on the plains of Moab beside the Jordan River, across from Jericho.

35:33 Or *can make atonement for murder.*

36:1-4 Women who inherited land might marry men from another tribe; their land would then be lost by their ancestral tribe and transferred to their husband's tribe. The Year of Jubilee (see Leviticus 25:8-55) normally provided the means for land to return to its original owner, but it pertained only to land that was sold, not to land acquired through marriage.

36:10-12 As they had been instructed, Zelophehad's five daughters all married cousins on their father's side, keeping their father's allotment within his clan (36:5-9). Marriage to a first cousin was acceptable in ancient Hebrew society as well as in other ancient Near Eastern cultures. See 1 Chronicles 23:22 for another example. (See Leviticus 18, 20 for forbidden sexual practices.)

Deuteronomy

WHAT DO WE LEARN ABOUT GOD'S MISSION AND OURS?
On your way to a great future, don't forget the past.

WHO WROTE IT? Deuteronomy is anonymous, but Jewish and Christian traditions attribute it to Moses.

WHEN DID IT HAPPEN? In the early 1400s BC, Moses delivered these addresses right before the Israelites entered the Promised Land.

HOW IS IT ORGANIZED?

- **1–4:** Address 1—A history lesson and encouragement to obey
- **5–26:** Address 2—Ten Commandments and a call to love and obedience
- **27–30:** Address 3—Covenant blessings, curses, and commitment
- **31–34:** Moses commissions Joshua and says farewell

FEATURE HIGHLIGHTS

+ Trust: Just Go! (219)
+ Promises and Our Purpose (225)
+ The Cities of Refuge (237)
+ Vulnerable Women: Redefining Strong (239)
+ Do We Follow God When the Rules Seem Wrong? (240)

Words to Remember are highlighted throughout this book

HOW LONG DOES IT TAKE TO READ?

| :30 | 1:00 | 1:30 | 2:00 | 2:30 | 3:00 | 3:30 |

Timeline (BC)

- **1805** — JOSEPH DIES
- **c. 1800–1446** — SLAVERY IN EGYPT
- **1446** — EXODUS FROM EGYPT
- **1446–1406** — WILDERNESS WANDERINGS
  Daughters of Zelophehad petition for property rights
- **1406** — MOSES' DEATH; ISRAELITES ENTER CANAAN
- **1406–1050** — ISRAELITES TAKE POSSESSION OF THE LAND OF CANAAN
  Women taken captive, treated according to Deuteronomy 21:10-14
- **1375** — JUDGES (INCLUDING DEBORAH, GIDEON, AND SAMSON) BEGIN TO RULE
- **1050** — KINGDOM UNITED UNDER SAUL

DEUTERONOMY 1

Introduction to Moses' First Address

1 These are the words that Moses spoke to all the people of Israel while they were in the wilderness east of the Jordan River. They were camped in the Jordan Valley* near Suph, between Paran on one side and Tophel, Laban, Hazeroth, and Di-zahab on the other.

²Normally it takes only eleven days to travel from Mount Sinai* to Kadesh-barnea, going by way of Mount Seir. ³But forty years after the Israelites left Egypt, on the first day of the eleventh month,* Moses addressed the people of Israel, telling them everything the LORD had commanded him to say. ⁴This took place after he had defeated King Sihon of the Amorites, who ruled in Heshbon, and at Edrei had defeated King Og of Bashan, who ruled in Ashtaroth.

⁵While the Israelites were in the land of Moab east of the Jordan River, Moses carefully explained the LORD's instructions as follows.

The Command to Leave Sinai

⁶"When we were at Mount Sinai, the LORD our God said to us, 'You have stayed at this mountain long enough. ⁷It is time to break camp and move on. Go to the hill country of the Amorites and to all the neighboring regions—the Jordan Valley, the hill country, the western foothills,* the Negev, and the coastal plain. Go to the land of the Canaanites and to Lebanon, and all the way to the great Euphrates River. ⁸Look, I am giving all this land to you! Go in and occupy it, for it is the land the LORD swore to give to your ancestors Abraham, Isaac, and Jacob, and to all their descendants.'"

Moses Appoints Leaders from Each Tribe

⁹Moses continued, "At that time I told you, 'You are too great a burden for me to carry all by myself. ¹⁰The LORD your God has increased your population, making you as numerous as the stars! ¹¹And may the LORD, the God of your ancestors, multiply you a thousand times more and bless you as he promised! ¹²But you are such a heavy load to carry! How can I deal with all your problems and bickering? ¹³Choose some well-respected men from each tribe who are known for their wisdom and understanding, and I will appoint them as your leaders.'

¹⁴"Then you responded, 'Your plan is a good one.' ¹⁵So I took the wise and respected men you had selected from your tribes and appointed them to serve as judges and officials over you. Some were responsible for a thousand people, some for a hundred, some for fifty, and some for ten.

¹⁶"At that time I instructed the judges, 'You must hear the cases of your fellow Israelites and the foreigners living among you. Be perfectly fair in your decisions ¹⁷and impartial in your judgments. Hear the cases of those who are poor as well as those who are rich. Don't be afraid of anyone's anger, for the decision you make is God's decision. Bring me any cases that are too difficult for you, and I will handle them.'

¹⁸"At that time I gave you instructions about everything you were to do.

Scouts Explore the Land

¹⁹"Then, just as the LORD our God commanded us, we left Mount Sinai and traveled through the great and terrifying wilderness, as you yourselves remember, and headed toward the hill country of the Amorites. When we arrived at Kadesh-barnea, ²⁰I said to you, 'You have now reached the hill country of the Amorites that the LORD our God is giving us. ²¹Look! He has placed the land in front of you. Go and occupy it as the LORD, the God of your ancestors, has promised you. Don't be afraid! Don't be discouraged!'

²²"But you all came to me and said, 'First, let's send out scouts to explore the land for us. They will advise us on the best route to take and which towns we should enter.'

²³"This seemed like a good idea to me, so I chose twelve scouts, one from each of your tribes. ²⁴They headed for the hill country and came to the valley of Eshcol and explored it. ²⁵They picked some of its fruit and brought it back to us. And they reported, 'The land the LORD our God has given us is indeed a good land.'

Israel's Rebellion against the LORD

²⁶"But you rebelled against the command of the LORD your God and refused to go in. ²⁷You complained in your tents and said, 'The LORD must hate us. That's why he has brought us here from Egypt—to hand us

---

1:1 Hebrew *the Arabah;* also in 1:7. **1:2** Hebrew *Horeb,* another name for Sinai; also in 1:6, 19. **1:3** Hebrew *In the fortieth year, on the first day of the eleventh month.* This day in the ancient Hebrew lunar calendar occurred in January or February. **1:7** Hebrew *the Shephelah.*

1:6–3:29 The contents of Deuteronomy bear a striking resemblance to ancient suzerain-vassal treaties. These treaties often included a historical prologue describing the relationship history between the parties. This section highlights both God's faithfulness and the people's unfaithfulness during the wilderness wanderings after they left Sinai.
1:6 Deuteronomy frequently refers to God by his proper name, YHWH (Yahweh), which is rendered in English translations as LORD (in capital letters). While some debate the precise meaning of the name, it is often used in association with God's work both in creation and in history. The repeated references to "the LORD our God" and "the LORD your God" in Deuteronomy point to Israel's relationship with the God who both creates and sustains.
1:26-43 The generation that had rebelled against God and refused to enter the Promised Land had died in the wilderness. However, Moses here describes his current audience as

over to the Amorites to be slaughtered. ²⁸Where can we go? Our brothers have demoralized us with their report. They tell us, "The people of the land are taller and more powerful than we are, and their towns are large, with walls rising high into the sky! We even saw giants there—the descendants of Anak!"'

²⁹"But I said to you, 'Don't be shocked or afraid of them! ³⁰The LORD your God is going ahead of you. He will fight for you, just as you saw him do in Egypt. ³¹And you saw how the LORD your God cared for you all along the way as you traveled through the wilderness, just as a father cares for his child. Now he has brought you to this place.'

³²"But even after all he did, you refused to trust the LORD your God, ³³who goes before you looking for the best places to camp, guiding you with a pillar of fire by night and a pillar of cloud by day.

³⁴"When the LORD heard your complaining, he became very angry. So he solemnly swore, ³⁵'Not one of you from this wicked generation will live to see the good land I swore to give your ancestors, ³⁶except Caleb son of Jephunneh. He will see this land because he has followed the LORD completely. I will give to him and his descendants some of the very land he explored during his scouting mission.'

participants in the events at Kadesh-barnea recorded in Numbers 14. This tendency to collapse the two generations' identities appears throughout this history, suggesting that Moses wanted those who were preparing to enter the Promised Land to always hold close the Exodus generation's infidelity so they wouldn't repeat the same mistakes.

Come Close TRUST: JUST GO!

SCRIPTURE CONNECTION: DEUTERONOMY 1:1-5

What is *your* Promised Land? What act of obedience is needed for you to get there?

At the beginning of Deuteronomy, God's people stood on the threshold of their long-awaited Promised Land. This transition mattered greatly, not only for them but also for many generations of God's people to come. God's grand purposes were unfolding in real time, with very real people facing very real decisions about whether to step forward.

Can you see this dimension of present and future at work in your life? What decisions are you facing that will require courage, risk, and faith? And how might those decisions change both your own life and the lives of future generations?

Sometimes it's only in hindsight that we realize the significance of a courageous step. At other times, we stand at a very clear transition point, and we must act.

How does God meet us in such times? He reminds us that he is the Lord our God. He reminds us that he has acted in our personal history and has protected us, rescued us, and provided for us.

God can be trusted, and when he invites us into the next step, he understands the temptations of fear and discouragement that we're likely to face. And yet, he calls us forward.

Take time to recount the ways God has guided, protected, provided, or moved in your past. Then ask God about the decisions you face. What is he inviting you to do? Name your fears and any discouragement and then move forward.

REFLECT "Don't be afraid! Don't be discouraged!" DEUTERONOMY 1:21

Oh great God, thank you for your invitation into what is next for me. Thank you for the reminders of what you have done in the past. I am willing and ready to trust you. I will choose courage and act. Amen.

CONSIDER "It wasn't me, it was the Lord. I always told him, 'I trust to you. I don't know where to go or what to do, but I expect you to lead me,' and he always did." HARRIET TUBMAN

> God has protected and rescued and provided. I can trust him for the next step.

MINDY CALIGUIRE is founder and president of Soul Care, dedicated to increasing soul health in the Body of Christ. Her books include *Discovering Soul Care* and *Spiritual Friendships*.

³⁷"And the LORD was also angry with me because of you. He said to me, 'Moses, not even you will enter the Promised Land! ³⁸Instead, your assistant, Joshua son of Nun, will lead the people into the land. Encourage him, for he will lead Israel as they take possession of it. ³⁹I will give the land to your little ones—your innocent children. You were afraid they would be captured, but they will be the ones who occupy it. ⁴⁰As for you, turn around now and go on back through the wilderness toward the Red Sea.*'

⁴¹"Then you confessed, 'We have sinned against the LORD! We will go into the land and fight for it, as the LORD our God has commanded us.' So your men strapped on their weapons, thinking it would be easy to attack the hill country.

⁴²"But the LORD told me to tell you, 'Do not attack, for I am not with you. If you go ahead on your own, you will be crushed by your enemies.'

⁴³"This is what I told you, but you would not listen. Instead, you again rebelled against the LORD's command and arrogantly went into the hill country to fight. ⁴⁴But the Amorites who lived there came out against you like a swarm of bees. They chased and battered you all the way from Seir to Hormah. ⁴⁵Then you returned and wept before the LORD, but he refused to listen. ⁴⁶So you stayed there at Kadesh for a long time.

Remembering Israel's Wanderings

2 "Then we turned around and headed back across the wilderness toward the Red Sea,* just as the LORD had instructed me, and we wandered around in the region of Mount Seir for a long time.

²"Then at last the LORD said to me, ³'You have been wandering around in this hill country long enough; turn to the north. ⁴Give these orders to the people: "You will pass through the country belonging to your relatives the Edomites, the descendants of Esau, who live in Seir. The Edomites will feel threatened, so be careful. ⁵Do not bother them, for I have given them all the hill country around Mount Seir as their property, and I will not give you even one square foot of their land. ⁶If you need food to eat or water to drink, pay them for it. ⁷For the LORD your God has blessed you in everything you have done. He has watched your every step through this great wilderness. During these forty years, the LORD your God has been with you, and you have lacked nothing."'

⁸"So we bypassed the territory of our relatives, the descendants of Esau, who live in Seir. We avoided the road through the Arabah Valley that comes up from Elath and Ezion-geber.

"Then as we turned north along the desert route through Moab, ⁹the LORD warned us, 'Do not bother the Moabites, the descendants of Lot, or start a war with them. I have given them Ar as their property, and I will not give you any of their land.'"

¹⁰(A race of giants called the Emites had once lived in the area of Ar. They were as strong and numerous and tall as the Anakites, another race of giants. ¹¹Both the Emites and the Anakites are also known as the Rephaites, though the Moabites call them Emites. ¹²In earlier times the Horites had lived in Seir, but they were driven out and displaced by the descendants of Esau, just as Israel drove out the people of Canaan when the LORD gave Israel their land.)

¹³Moses continued, "Then the LORD said to us, 'Get moving. Cross the Zered Brook.' So we crossed the brook.

¹⁴"Thirty-eight years passed from the time we first left Kadesh-barnea until we finally crossed the Zered Brook! By then, all the men old enough to fight in battle had died in the wilderness, as the LORD had vowed would happen. ¹⁵The LORD struck them down until they had all been eliminated from the community.

¹⁶"When all the men of fighting age had died, ¹⁷the LORD said to me, ¹⁸'Today you will cross the border of Moab at Ar ¹⁹and enter the land of the Ammonites, the descendants of Lot. But do not bother them or start a war with them. I have given the land of Ammon to them as their property, and I will not give you any of their land.'"

1:40 Hebrew *sea of reeds.* 2:1 Hebrew *sea of reeds.*

1:37 Numbers 20:1-13 indicates that God barred Moses from entering the land because he did not demonstrate God's holiness at Meribah. But here, Moses blames the people. In one sense, his assertion is true: If the people had trusted God and entered the Promised Land following the scouts' report, the Meribah incident never would have happened. However, the Lord held Moses personally responsible for his own failure.
2:5 God's gift of a promised land was not limited to Israel. He also distributed lands to Edom, Moab (2:9), Ammon (2:19), and the Caphtorites (2:22-23). Although God had chosen Israel as a special nation (1:31; see also 7:6; 14:2; Exodus 19:5), he is also the God of all nations and has a place and purpose for each (Deuteronomy 32:8; Acts 17:26)—even for those that do not recognize his sovereignty (Romans 1:16-23).
2:9 Following the destruction of Sodom, Gomorrah, and the other cities of the plain, Lot (Abraham's nephew and Isaac's cousin) and his two unmarried daughters sheltered in a cave east of the Dead Sea (see Genesis 19:30-38), where Lot's daughters got their father drunk and raped him. Their descendants became the nations of Moab and Ammon. Because of their kinship with Israel, the Moabites were to be left undisturbed. David's great-grandmother Ruth descended from Moab (Ruth 1:4), and David sent his own family to the land of Moab for protection when he was pursued by Saul (1 Samuel 22:3-4). Ar was probably the capital of Moab.
2:19 Like the Moabites, the Ammonites were descendants of Lot and his younger daughter (see note on 2:9). Throughout most of their history, the Ammonites lived south and east of the Jabbok River. The nation's capital was Rabbath Ammon (modern Amman, Jordan). David arranged for Bathsheba's husband, Uriah, to be murdered in the siege of this city (2 Samuel 11:1, 14-21).

²⁰(That area was once considered the land of the Rephaites, who had lived there, though the Ammonites call them Zamzummites. ²¹They were also as strong and numerous and tall as the Anakites. But the LORD destroyed them so the Ammonites could occupy their land. ²²He had done the same for the descendants of Esau who lived in Seir, for he destroyed the Horites so they could settle there in their place. The descendants of Esau live there to this day. ²³A similar thing happened when the Caphtorites from Crete* invaded and destroyed the Avvites, who had lived in villages in the area of Gaza.)

²⁴Moses continued, "Then the LORD said, 'Now get moving! Cross the Arnon Gorge. Look, I will hand over to you Sihon the Amorite, king of Heshbon, and I will give you his land. Attack him and begin to occupy the land. ²⁵Beginning today I will make people throughout the earth terrified because of you. When they hear reports about you, they will tremble with dread and fear.'"

Victory over Sihon of Heshbon

²⁶Moses continued, "From the wilderness of Kedemoth I sent ambassadors to King Sihon of Heshbon with this proposal of peace:

²⁷'Let us travel through your land. We will stay on the main road and won't turn off into the fields on either side. ²⁸Sell us food to eat and water to drink, and we will pay for it. All we want is permission to pass through your land. ²⁹The descendants of Esau who live in Seir allowed us to go through their country, and so did the Moabites, who live in Ar. Let us pass through until we cross the Jordan into the land the LORD our God is giving us.'

³⁰"But King Sihon of Heshbon refused to allow us to pass through, because the LORD your God made Sihon stubborn and defiant so he could help you defeat him, as he has now done.

³¹"Then the LORD said to me, 'Look, I have begun to hand King Sihon and his land over to you. Begin now to conquer and occupy his land.'

³²"Then King Sihon declared war on us and mobilized his forces at Jahaz. ³³But the LORD our God handed him over to us, and we crushed him, his sons, and all his people. ³⁴We conquered all his towns and completely destroyed* everyone—men, women, and children. Not a single person was spared. ³⁵We took all the livestock as plunder for ourselves, along with anything of value from the towns we ransacked.

³⁶"The LORD our God also helped us conquer Aroer on the edge of the Arnon Gorge, and the town in the gorge, and the whole area as far as Gilead. No town had walls too strong for us. ³⁷However, we avoided the land of the Ammonites all along the Jabbok River and the towns in the hill country—all the places the LORD our God had commanded us to leave alone.

Victory over Og of Bashan

3 "Next we turned and headed for the land of Bashan, where King Og and his entire army attacked us at Edrei. ²But the LORD told me, 'Do not be afraid of him, for I have given you victory over Og and his entire army, and I will give you all his land. Treat him just as you treated King Sihon of the Amorites, who ruled in Heshbon.'

³"So the LORD our God handed King Og and all his people over to us, and we killed them all. Not a single person survived. ⁴We conquered all sixty of his towns—the entire Argob region in his kingdom of Bashan. Not a single town escaped our conquest. ⁵These towns were all fortified with high walls and barred gates. We also took many unwalled villages at the same time. ⁶We completely destroyed* the kingdom of Bashan, just as we had destroyed King Sihon of Heshbon. We destroyed all the people in every town we conquered—men, women, and children alike. ⁷But we kept all the livestock for ourselves and took plunder from all the towns.

⁸"So we took the land of the two Amorite kings east of the Jordan River—all the way from the Arnon Gorge to Mount Hermon. ⁹(Mount Hermon is called Sirion by the Sidonians, and the Amorites call it Senir.) ¹⁰We had now conquered all the cities on the plateau and all Gilead and Bashan, as far as the towns of Salecah and Edrei, which were part of Og's kingdom in Bashan. ¹¹(King Og of Bashan was the last survivor of the giant Rephaites. His bed was made of iron and was more than thirteen feet long and six feet wide.* It can still be seen in the Ammonite city of Rabbah.)

Land Division East of the Jordan

¹²"When we took possession of this land, I gave to the tribes of Reuben and Gad the territory beyond Aroer along the Arnon Gorge, plus half of the hill country of Gilead with its towns. ¹³Then I gave the rest of Gilead and all of Bashan—Og's former kingdom—to the half-tribe of Manasseh. (This entire Argob region of Bashan used to be known as the land of the Rephaites. ¹⁴Jair, a leader from the tribe of Manasseh, conquered the whole Argob region in Bashan, all the way to the border of the Geshurites and Maacathites. Jair renamed this region after himself, calling it the Towns of Jair,* as it is still known today.) ¹⁵I gave Gilead to the clan of Makir. ¹⁶But I also gave part of Gilead to the tribes of Reuben and Gad. The area I gave them extended from the middle of the Arnon Gorge

---

2:23 Hebrew *from Caphtor.* 2:34 The Hebrew term used here refers to the complete consecration of things or people to the LORD, either by destroying them or by giving them as an offering. 3:6 The Hebrew term used here refers to the complete consecration of things or people to the LORD, either by destroying them or by giving them as an offering; also in 3:6b. 3:11 Hebrew *9 cubits* [4.1 meters] *long and 4 cubits* [1.8 meters] *wide.* 3:14 Hebrew *Havvoth-jair.*

in the south to the Jabbok River on the Ammonite frontier. ¹⁷They also received the Jordan Valley, all the way from the Sea of Galilee down to the Dead Sea,* with the Jordan River serving as the western boundary. To the east were the slopes of Pisgah.

¹⁸At that time I gave this command to the tribes that would live east of the Jordan: 'Although the LORD your God has given you this land as your property, all your fighting men must cross the Jordan ahead of your Israelite relatives, armed and ready to assist them. ¹⁹Your wives, children, and numerous livestock, however, may stay behind in the towns I have given you. ²⁰When the LORD has given security to the rest of the Israelites, as he has to you, and when they occupy the land the LORD your God is giving them across the Jordan River, then you may all return here to the land I have given you.'

Moses Forbidden to Enter the Land

²¹"At that time I gave Joshua this charge: 'You have seen for yourself everything the LORD your God has done to these two kings. He will do the same to all the kingdoms on the west side of the Jordan. ²²Do not be afraid of the nations there, for the LORD your God will fight for you.'

²³"At that time I pleaded with the LORD and said, ²⁴'O Sovereign LORD, you have only begun to show your greatness and the strength of your hand to me, your servant. Is there any god in heaven or on earth who can perform such great and mighty deeds as you do? ²⁵Please let me cross the Jordan to see the wonderful land on the other side, the beautiful hill country and the Lebanon mountains.'

²⁶"But the LORD was angry with me because of you, and he would not listen to me. 'That's enough!' he declared. 'Speak of it no more. ²⁷But go up to Pisgah Peak, and look over the land in every direction. Take a good look, but you may not cross the Jordan River. ²⁸Instead, commission Joshua and encourage and strengthen him, for he will lead the people across the Jordan. He will give them all the land you now see before you as their possession.' ²⁹So we stayed in the valley near Beth-peor.

Moses Urges Israel to Obey

4 "And now, Israel, listen carefully to these decrees and regulations that I am about to teach you. Obey them so that you may live, so you may enter and occupy the land that the LORD, the God of your ancestors, is giving you. ²Do not add to or subtract from these commands I am giving you. Just obey the commands of the LORD your God that I am giving you.

³"You saw for yourself what the LORD did to you at Baal-peor. There the LORD your God destroyed everyone who had worshiped Baal, the god of Peor. ⁴But all of you who were faithful to the LORD your God are still alive today—every one of you.

⁵"Look, I now teach you these decrees and regulations just as the LORD my God commanded me, so that you may obey them in the land you are about to enter and occupy. ⁶Obey them completely, and you will display your wisdom and intelligence among the surrounding nations. When they hear all these decrees, they will exclaim, 'How wise and prudent are the people of this great nation!' ⁷For what great nation has a god as near to them as the LORD our God is near to us whenever we call on him? ⁸And what great nation has decrees and regulations as righteous and fair as this body of instructions that I am giving you today?

⁹"But watch out! Be careful never to forget what you yourself have seen. Do not let these memories escape from your mind as long as you live! And be sure to pass them on to your children and grandchildren. ¹⁰Never forget the day when you stood before the LORD your God at Mount Sinai,* where he told me, 'Summon the people before me, and I will personally instruct them. Then they will learn to fear me as long as they live, and they will teach their children to fear me also.'

¹¹"You came near and stood at the foot of the mountain, while flames from the mountain shot into the sky. The mountain was shrouded in black clouds and deep darkness. ¹²And the LORD spoke to you from the heart of the fire. You heard the sound of his words but didn't see his form; there was only a voice. ¹³He proclaimed his covenant—the Ten Commandments*—which he commanded you to keep, and which he wrote on two stone tablets. ¹⁴It was at that time that the LORD commanded me to teach you his decrees and regulations so you would obey them in the land you are about to enter and occupy.

A Warning against Idolatry

¹⁵"But be very careful! You did not see the LORD's form on the day he spoke to you from the heart of the fire at Mount Sinai. ¹⁶So do not corrupt yourselves by making an idol in any form—whether of

---

3:17 Hebrew *from Kinnereth to the Sea of the Arabah, the Salt Sea.*   **4:10** Hebrew *Horeb,* another name for Sinai; also in 4:15.
4:13 Hebrew *the ten words.*

3:24 Moses acknowledged the Lord's sovereignty and incomparability. God's strong hand brought Israel out of Egypt. And God not only delivered his people from slavery, but he also revealed his will to them. Moses' question in this verse is rhetorical, comparing the Lord to the so-called gods. (See also 33:26-29, where Moses proclaimed the uniqueness of God, who serves as a protector and refuge to his people.)

4:13 Covenant is a crucial concept in the Old Testament. A covenant was a legal arrangement involving two or more parties who entered into an agreement with mutually binding obligations. The covenant at Sinai (Exodus 19–24) codified the relationship between the Lord and Israel. In Deuteronomy, Moses reiterated, interpreted, and expanded this covenant for the new generation that was about to enter the Promised Land.

a man or a woman, ¹⁷an animal on the ground, a bird in the sky, ¹⁸a small animal that scurries along the ground, or a fish in the deepest sea. ¹⁹And when you look up into the sky and see the sun, moon, and stars—all the forces of heaven—don't be seduced into worshiping them. The LORD your God gave them to all the peoples of the earth. ²⁰Remember that the LORD rescued you from the iron-smelting furnace of Egypt in order to make you his very own people and his special possession, which is what you are today.

²¹"But the LORD was angry with me because of you. He vowed that I would not cross the Jordan River into the good land the LORD your God is giving you as your special possession. ²²You will cross the Jordan to occupy the land, but I will not. Instead, I will die here on the east side of the river. ²³So be careful not to break the covenant the LORD your God has made with you. Do not make idols of any shape or form, for the LORD your God has forbidden this. ²⁴The LORD your God is a devouring fire; he is a jealous God.

²⁵"In the future, when you have children and grandchildren and have lived in the land a long time, do not corrupt yourselves by making idols of any kind. This is evil in the sight of the LORD your God and will arouse his anger.

²⁶"Today I call on heaven and earth as witnesses against you. If you break my covenant, you will quickly disappear from the land you are crossing the Jordan to occupy. You will live there only a short time; then you will be utterly destroyed. ²⁷For the LORD will scatter you among the nations, where only a few of you will survive. ²⁸There, in a foreign land, you will worship idols made from wood and stone—gods that neither see nor hear nor eat nor smell. ²⁹But from there you will search again for the LORD your God. And if you search for him with all your heart and soul, you will find him.

³⁰"In the distant future, when you are suffering all these things, you will finally return to the LORD your God and listen to what he tells you. ³¹For the LORD your God is a merciful God; he will not abandon you or destroy you or forget the solemn covenant he made with your ancestors.

There Is Only One God

³²"Now search all of history, from the time God created people on the earth until now, and search from one end of the heavens to the other. Has anything as great as this ever been seen or heard before? ³³Has any nation ever heard the voice of God* speaking from fire—as you did—and survived? ³⁴Has any other god dared to take a nation for himself out of another nation by means of trials, miraculous signs, wonders, war, a strong hand, a powerful arm, and terrifying acts? Yet that is what the LORD your God did for you in Egypt, right before your eyes.

³⁵"He showed you these things so you would know that the LORD is God and there is no other. ³⁶He let you hear his voice from heaven so he could instruct you. He let you see his great fire here on earth so he could speak to you from it. ³⁷Because he loved your ancestors, he chose to bless their descendants, and he personally brought you out of Egypt with a great display of power. ³⁸He drove out nations far greater than you, so he could bring you in and give you their land as your special possession, as it is today.

³⁹"So remember this and keep it firmly in mind: The LORD is God both in heaven and on earth, and there is no other. ⁴⁰If you obey all the decrees and commands I am giving you today, all will be well with you and your children. I am giving you these instructions so you will enjoy a long life in the land the LORD your God is giving you for all time."

Eastern Cities of Refuge

⁴¹Then Moses set apart three cities of refuge east of the Jordan River. ⁴²Anyone who killed another person unintentionally, without previous hostility, could flee there to live in safety. ⁴³These were the cities: Bezer on the wilderness plateau for the tribe of Reuben; Ramoth in Gilead for the tribe of Gad; Golan in Bashan for the tribe of Manasseh.

Introduction to Moses' Second Address

⁴⁴This is the body of instruction that Moses presented to the Israelites. ⁴⁵These are the laws, decrees, and regulations that Moses gave to the people of Israel when they left Egypt, ⁴⁶and as they camped in the valley near Beth-peor east of the Jordan River. (This land was formerly occupied by the Amorites under King Sihon, who ruled from Heshbon. But Moses and the Israelites destroyed him and his people when they came up from Egypt. ⁴⁷Israel took possession of his land and that of King Og of Bashan—the two Amorite kings east of the Jordan. ⁴⁸So Israel conquered the entire area from Aroer at the edge of the Arnon Gorge all the way to Mount Sirion,* also called Mount Hermon. ⁴⁹And they conquered the eastern bank of the Jordan River as far south as the Dead Sea,* below the slopes of Pisgah.)

4:33 Or *voice of a god.* **4:48** As in Syriac version (see also 3:9); Hebrew reads *Mount Sion.* **4:49** Hebrew *took the Arabah on the east side of the Jordan as far as the sea of the Arabah.*

4:29 In the ancient world, the heart was often considered to be the location of a person's thoughts and intentions, while the soul was frequently considered the seat of passions and desires. Together, heart and soul could essentially refer to the entirety of a person's being, including emotions, desires, thoughts, and intentions. In 4:29, the Lord tells his people that when they seek him in repentance with the whole of their being, they will find him.

Ten Commandments for the Covenant Community

5 Moses called all the people of Israel together and said, "Listen carefully, Israel. Hear the decrees and regulations I am giving you today, so you may learn them and obey them!

² "The LORD our God made a covenant with us at Mount Sinai.* ³ The LORD did not make this covenant with our ancestors, but with all of us who are alive today. ⁴ At the mountain the LORD spoke to you face to face from the heart of the fire. ⁵ I stood as an intermediary between you and the LORD, for you were afraid of the fire and did not want to approach the mountain. He spoke to me, and I passed his words on to you. This is what he said:

⁶ "I am the LORD your God, who rescued you from the land of Egypt, the place of your slavery.

⁷ "You must not have any other god but me.

⁸ "You must not make for yourself an idol of any kind, or an image of anything in the heavens or on the earth or in the sea. ⁹ You must not bow down to them or worship them, for I, the LORD your God, am a jealous God who will not tolerate your affection for any other gods. I lay the sins of the parents upon their children; the entire family is affected—even children in the third and fourth generations of those who reject me. ¹⁰ But I lavish unfailing love for a thousand generations on those* who love me and obey my commands.

¹¹ "You must not misuse the name of the LORD your God. The LORD will not let you go unpunished if you misuse his name.

¹² "Observe the Sabbath day by keeping it holy, as the LORD your God has commanded you. ¹³ You have six days each week for your ordinary work, ¹⁴ but the seventh day is a Sabbath day of rest dedicated to the LORD your God. On that day no one in your household may do any work. This includes you, your sons and daughters, your male and female servants, your oxen and donkeys and other livestock, and any foreigners living among you. All your male and female servants must rest as you do. ¹⁵ Remember that you were once slaves in Egypt, but the LORD your God brought you out with his strong hand and powerful arm. That is why the LORD your God has commanded you to rest on the Sabbath day.

¹⁶ "Honor your father and mother, as the LORD your God commanded you. Then you will live a long, full life in the land the LORD your God is giving you.

¹⁷ "You must not murder.

¹⁸ "You must not commit adultery.

¹⁹ "You must not steal.

²⁰ "You must not testify falsely against your neighbor.

²¹ "You must not covet your neighbor's wife. You must not covet your neighbor's house or land, male or female servant, ox or donkey, or anything else that belongs to your neighbor.

²² "The LORD spoke these words to all of you assembled there at the foot of the mountain. He spoke with a loud voice from the heart of the fire, surrounded by clouds and deep darkness. This was all he said at that time, and he wrote his words on two stone tablets and gave them to me.

²³ "But when you heard the voice from the heart of the darkness, while the mountain was blazing with fire, all your tribal leaders and elders came to me. ²⁴ They said, 'Look, the LORD our God has shown us his glory and greatness, and we have heard his voice from the heart of the fire. Today we have seen that God can speak to us humans, and yet we live! ²⁵ But now, why should we risk death again? If the LORD our God speaks to us again, we will certainly die and be consumed by this awesome fire. ²⁶ Can any living thing hear the voice of the living God from the heart of the fire as we did and yet survive? ²⁷ Go yourself and listen to what the LORD our God says. Then come and tell us everything he tells you, and we will listen and obey.'

²⁸ "The LORD heard the request you made to me. And he said, 'I have heard what the people said to you, and they are right. ²⁹ Oh, that they would always have hearts like this, that they might fear me and obey all my commands! If they did, they and their descendants would prosper forever. ³⁰ Go and tell them, "Return to your tents." ³¹ But you stand here with me so I can give you all my commands, decrees, and regulations. You must teach them to the people so they can obey them in the land I am giving them as their possession.'"

³² So Moses told the people, "You must be careful to obey all the commands of the LORD your God, following his instructions in every detail. ³³ Stay on the path that the LORD your God has commanded you to follow. Then you will live long and prosperous lives in the land you are about to enter and occupy.

5:2 Hebrew *Horeb*, another name for Sinai.   **5:10** Hebrew *for thousands of those*.

5:6-21 Some have compared the Ten Commandments to a "bill of rights" that protects the rights of others by reminding the hearer that God is Lord over both the great and lowly. These instructions are presumably addressed to male heads of households (the Hebrew masculine "your" is used throughout). They can be viewed as guarding against a patriarch's potential abuses of power—with its specific mentions of vulnerable people (women, enslaved people, and foreigners). While Deuteronomy 5 mostly reiterates the wording of Exodus 20, a difference appears regarding Sabbath observance in that it is specifically tied to God's deliverance of his people from slavery in Egypt.

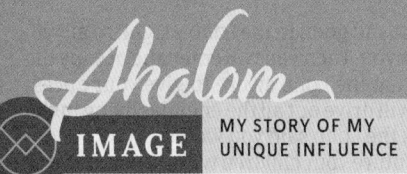

Promises and Our Purpose: Our Covenant-Keeping God

SCRIPTURE CONNECTION: DEUTERONOMY 5:1-33

Have you ever cried out to God in a crisis, "Where are you? What are you doing? I feel abandoned?" And then heard God say, "Believe my promises. I am in charge. Trust me."

A covenant is a promise between two people or, as is often the case in the Bible, between God and people. Most covenants essentially say, "If you keep your part, I will keep my part." But often God's covenants have no conditions. He is the initiator, promise keeper, and fulfiller of the covenant.

For example, he made a covenant with Noah to never again destroy humanity, even though he knew humanity would continue to fall short (Genesis 8:20-22). His covenant with Abraham starts with, "I will bless you ... and you will be a blessing to others" (12:1-2). Only later does he reaffirm the promise through the sign of circumcision and a son by Sarah.

However, God's covenant given through Moses had conditions. God gave the Ten Commandments (see also Exodus 20:1-17), along with numerous other laws, to govern Israel. The blessings would come only as Israel kept their side of the agreement (see Deuteronomy 28:1-14). When they failed, they had a way of reconciling with God—offering sacrifices. But if they did not seek to make things right with God, the covenant would be broken and disaster would result (see 28:15-68).

> God always keeps his promises; I can trust his love.

In his foresight, God knew that we in our human frailty could never keep our part of the covenant. The Israelites' failure set the stage for Jesus to keep the promises we could not. As the perfect sacrifice, Jesus covered our failures once and for all. He fulfilled our part of the deal—and God's part too.

God has now called us to take part in a new covenant (2 Corinthians 3:4-6). Our role is to confess our wrongdoings and turn back to God's ways (Romans 10:9-13). He always faithfully does his part—forgives (1 John 1:9). Then, we are set on a trajectory of following God, who always keeps his promises.

IMAGINE

Knowing that God promises to bless you (and others through you), how do you see your purpose?

"When I was forty-eight years old, God spoke, 'I have called you to be a leader, not just the wife of a leader. It's time to get back in the saddle.' I responded, 'What in the world do you mean by that?' Over the next ten years, one step at a time, I finished two degrees. Hearing God's promise allowed me to find a new level of fulfillment in a new career."

ELIZABETH GLANVILLE, PhD, is retired faculty from Fuller Theological Seminary, School of Mission and Theology. She is an international teacher on missions and leadership and chaplain for a local police department and her retirement community.

DEUTERONOMY 6

A Call for Wholehearted Commitment

6 "These are the commands, decrees, and regulations that the LORD your God commanded me to teach you. You must obey them in the land you are about to enter and occupy, ²and you and your children and grandchildren must fear the LORD your God as long as you live. If you obey all his decrees and commands, you will enjoy a long life. ³Listen closely, Israel, and be careful to obey. Then all will go well with you, and you will have many children in the land flowing with milk and honey, just as the LORD, the God of your ancestors, promised you.

⁴"Listen, O Israel! The LORD is our God, the LORD alone.* ⁵And you must love the LORD your God with all your heart, all your soul, and all your strength. ⁶And you must commit yourselves wholeheartedly to these commands that I am giving you today. ⁷Repeat them again and again to your children. Talk about them when you are at home and when you are on the road, when you are going to bed and when you are getting up. ⁸Tie them to your hands and wear them on your forehead as reminders. ⁹Write them on the doorposts of your house and on your gates.

¹⁰"The LORD your God will soon bring you into the land he swore to give you when he made a vow to your ancestors Abraham, Isaac, and Jacob. It is a land with large, prosperous cities that you did not build. ¹¹The houses will be richly stocked with goods you did not produce. You will draw water from cisterns you did not dig, and you will eat from vineyards and olive trees you did not plant. When you have eaten your fill in this land, ¹²be careful not to forget the LORD, who rescued you from slavery in the land of Egypt. ¹³You must fear the LORD your God and serve him. When you take an oath, you must use only his name.

¹⁴"You must not worship any of the gods of neighboring nations, ¹⁵for the LORD your God, who lives among you, is a jealous God. His anger will flare up against you, and he will wipe you from the face of the earth. ¹⁶You must not test the LORD your God as you did when you complained at Massah. ¹⁷You must diligently obey the commands of the LORD your God—all the laws and decrees he has given you. ¹⁸Do what is right and good in the LORD's sight, so all will go well with you. Then you will enter and occupy the good land that the LORD swore to give your ancestors. ¹⁹You will drive out all the enemies living in the land, just as the LORD said you would.

²⁰"In the future your children will ask you, 'What is the meaning of these laws, decrees, and regulations that the LORD our God has commanded us to obey?' ²¹"Then you must tell them, 'We were Pharaoh's slaves in Egypt, but the LORD brought us out of Egypt with his strong hand. ²²The LORD did miraculous signs and wonders before our eyes, dealing terrifying blows against Egypt and Pharaoh and all his people. ²³He brought us out of Egypt so he could give us this land he had sworn to give our ancestors. ²⁴And the LORD our God commanded us to obey all these decrees and to fear him so he can continue to bless us and preserve our lives, as he has done to this day. ²⁵For we will be counted as righteous when we obey all the commands the LORD our God has given us.'

The Privilege of Holiness

7 "When the LORD your God brings you into the land you are about to enter and occupy, he will clear away many nations ahead of you: the Hittites, Girgashites, Amorites, Canaanites, Perizzites, Hivites, and Jebusites. These seven nations are greater and more numerous than you. ²When the LORD your God hands these nations over to you and you conquer them, you must completely destroy* them. Make no treaties with them and show them no mercy. ³You must not intermarry with them. Do not let your daughters and sons marry their sons and daughters, ⁴for they will lead your children away from me to worship other gods. Then the anger of the LORD will burn against you, and he will quickly destroy you. ⁵This is what you must do. You must break down their pagan altars and shatter their sacred pillars. Cut down their Asherah poles and burn their idols. ⁶For you are a holy people, who belong to the LORD your God. Of all the people on earth, the LORD your God has chosen you to be his own special treasure.

⁷"The LORD did not set his heart on you and choose

6:4 Or *The LORD our God is one LORD;* or *The LORD our God, the LORD is one;* or *The LORD is our God, the LORD is one.* **7:2** The Hebrew term used here refers to the complete consecration of things or people to the LORD, either by destroying them or by giving them as an offering; also in 7:26.

6:4-5 The Shema (meaning "listen") is the fundamental statement of Israel's faith. Jesus described these verses as the greatest of the commandments (Matthew 22:34-39; Mark 12:28-31; Luke 10:25-28), a sentiment shared by ancient and modern Judaism. The rabbi Hillel (first century BC) spoke of the Shema as the central theological idea of the Hebrew Bible (the Old Testament), calling the rest mere commentary.

6:8 The Lord's commandments (6:6) were to be as interwoven into the hearts and minds of children as though they were tied to them. Eventually, this figurative phrase in Judaism was practiced literally by wrapping the forearm with cords representing the Torah. "Wear them" is a figure of speech that was represented literally in later Judaism by a small box containing a few brief Torah texts. The box and its contents (Hebrew *tefillin*; Greek *phylactery*) were reminders of the need to teach and obey the covenant (see also 11:18; Matthew 23:5).

7:3-4 The command against intermarriage was not about ethnic purity. It was fundamentally about safeguarding the Israelites' fidelity to the Lord. The Israelites had already experienced—with disastrous consequences—how sexual relationships could lead to worshiping other gods (Numbers 25). Later on, as the book of Judges records, intermarriage continued to plague the Israelites, leading them into idolatry and oppression by foreign powers (see Judges 3:5-6). Being God's holy people means guarding our commitment to him.

you because you were more numerous than other nations, for you were the smallest of all nations! ⁸Rather, it was simply that the LORD loves you, and he was keeping the oath he had sworn to your ancestors. That is why the LORD rescued you with such a strong hand from your slavery and from the oppressive hand of Pharaoh, king of Egypt. ⁹Understand, therefore, that the LORD your God is indeed God. He is the faithful God who keeps his covenant for a thousand generations and lavishes his unfailing love on those who love him and obey his commands. ¹⁰But he does not hesitate to punish and destroy those who reject him. ¹¹Therefore, you must obey all these commands, decrees, and regulations I am giving you today.

¹²"If you listen to these regulations and faithfully obey them, the LORD your God will keep his covenant of unfailing love with you, as he promised with an oath to your ancestors. ¹³He will love you and bless you, and he will give you many children. He will give fertility to your land and your animals. When you arrive in the land he swore to give your ancestors, you will have large harvests of grain, new wine, and olive oil, and great herds of cattle, sheep, and goats. ¹⁴You will be blessed above all the nations of the earth. None of your men or women will be childless, and all your livestock will bear young. ¹⁵And the LORD will protect you from all sickness. He will not let you suffer from the terrible diseases you knew in Egypt, but he will inflict them on all your enemies!

¹⁶"You must destroy all the nations the LORD your God hands over to you. Show them no mercy, and do not worship their gods, or they will trap you. ¹⁷Perhaps you will think to yourselves, 'How can we ever conquer these nations that are so much more powerful than we are?' ¹⁸But don't be afraid of them! Just remember what the LORD your God did to Pharaoh and to all the land of Egypt. ¹⁹Remember the great terrors the LORD your God sent against them. You saw it all with your own eyes! And remember the miraculous signs and wonders, and the strong hand and powerful arm with which he brought you out of Egypt. The LORD your God will use this same power against all the people you fear. ²⁰And then the LORD your God will send terror* to drive out the few survivors still hiding from you!

²¹"No, do not be afraid of those nations, for the LORD your God is among you, and he is a great and awesome God. ²²The LORD your God will drive those nations out ahead of you little by little. You will not clear them away all at once, otherwise the wild animals would multiply too quickly for you. ²³But the LORD your God will hand them over to you. He will throw them into complete confusion until they are destroyed. ²⁴He will put their kings in your power, and you will erase their names from the face of the earth. No one will be able to stand against you, and you will destroy them all.

²⁵"You must burn their idols in fire, and you must not covet the silver or gold that covers them. You must not take it or it will become a trap to you, for it is detestable to the LORD your God. ²⁶Do not bring any detestable objects into your home, for then you will be destroyed, just like them. You must utterly detest such things, for they are set apart for destruction.

A Call to Remember and Obey

8 "Be careful to obey all the commands I am giving you today. Then you will live and multiply, and you will enter and occupy the land the LORD swore to give your ancestors. ²Remember how the LORD your God led you through the wilderness for these forty years, humbling you and testing you to prove your character, and to find out whether or not you would obey his commands. ³Yes, he humbled you by letting you go hungry and then feeding you with manna, a food previously unknown to you and your ancestors. He did it to teach you that people do not live by bread alone; rather, we live by every word that comes from the mouth of the LORD. ⁴For all these forty years your clothes didn't wear out, and your feet didn't blister or swell. ⁵Think about it: Just as a parent disciplines a child, the LORD your God disciplines you for your own good.

⁶"So obey the commands of the LORD your God by walking in his ways and fearing him. ⁷For the LORD your God is bringing you into a good land of flowing streams and pools of water, with fountains and springs that gush out in the valleys and hills. ⁸It is a land of wheat and barley; of grapevines, fig trees, and pomegranates; of olive oil and honey. ⁹It is a land where food is plentiful and nothing is lacking. It is a land where iron is as common as stone, and copper is abundant in the hills. ¹⁰When you have eaten your fill, be sure to praise the LORD your God for the good land he has given you.

¹¹"But that is the time to be careful! Beware that in your plenty you do not forget the LORD your God and disobey his commands, regulations, and decrees that I am giving you today. ¹²For when you have become full and prosperous and have built fine homes to live in, ¹³and when your flocks and herds have become very large and your silver and gold have multiplied along with everything else, be careful! ¹⁴Do not become proud at that time and forget the LORD

7:20 Often rendered *the hornet*. The meaning of the Hebrew is uncertain.

8:1-20 Deuteronomy 8 highlights the importance of remembering. Moses told the people to remember both God's provision and his testing in the wilderness (8:2-5, 14-16). As they settled in the land, the people were not to forget the Lord and disobey his commands (8:11-13). It was important for them to recognize that any prosperity they experienced would be because of God's oath to their ancestors (8:18). Failure to remember would lead to idolatry (worshiping other things in place of God) and destruction (8:19-20).

your God, who rescued you from slavery in the land of Egypt. ¹⁵Do not forget that he led you through the great and terrifying wilderness with its poisonous snakes and scorpions, where it was so hot and dry. He gave you water from the rock! ¹⁶He fed you with manna in the wilderness, a food unknown to your ancestors. He did this to humble you and test you for your own good. ¹⁷He did all this so you would never say to yourself, 'I have achieved this wealth with my own strength and energy.' ¹⁸Remember the LORD your God. He is the one who gives you power to be successful, in order to fulfill the covenant he confirmed to your ancestors with an oath.

¹⁹"But I assure you of this: If you ever forget the LORD your God and follow other gods, worshiping and bowing down to them, you will certainly be destroyed. ²⁰Just as the LORD has destroyed other nations in your path, you also will be destroyed if you refuse to obey the LORD your God.

Victory by God's Grace

9 "Listen, O Israel! Today you are about to cross the Jordan River to take over the land belonging to nations much greater and more powerful than you. They live in cities with walls that reach to the sky! ²The people are strong and tall—descendants of the famous Anakite giants. You've heard the saying, 'Who can stand up to the Anakites?' ³But recognize today that the LORD your God is the one who will cross over ahead of you like a devouring fire to destroy them. He will subdue them so that you will quickly conquer them and drive them out, just as the LORD has promised.

⁴"After the LORD your God has done this for you, don't say in your hearts, 'The LORD has given us this land because we are such good people!' No, it is because of the wickedness of the other nations that he is pushing them out of your way. ⁵It is not because you are so good or have such integrity that you are about to occupy their land. The LORD your God will drive these nations out ahead of you only because of their wickedness, and to fulfill the oath he swore to your ancestors Abraham, Isaac, and Jacob. ⁶You must recognize that the LORD your God is not giving you this good land because you are good, for you are not—you are a stubborn people.

Remembering the Gold Calf

⁷"Remember and never forget how angry you made the LORD your God out in the wilderness. From the day you left Egypt until now, you have been constantly rebelling against him. ⁸Even at Mount Sinai* you made the LORD so angry he was ready to destroy you. ⁹This happened when I was on the mountain receiving the tablets of stone inscribed with the words of the covenant that the LORD had made with you. I was there for forty days and forty nights, and all that time I ate no food and drank no water. ¹⁰The LORD gave me the two tablets on which God had written with his own finger all the words he had spoken to you from the heart of the fire when you were assembled at the mountain.

¹¹"At the end of the forty days and nights, the LORD handed me the two stone tablets inscribed with the words of the covenant. ¹²Then the LORD said to me, 'Get up! Go down immediately, for the people you brought out of Egypt have corrupted themselves. How quickly they have turned away from the way I commanded them to live! They have melted gold and made an idol for themselves!'

¹³"The LORD also said to me, 'I have seen how stubborn and rebellious these people are. ¹⁴Leave me alone so I may destroy them and erase their name from under heaven. Then I will make a mighty nation of your descendants, a nation larger and more powerful than they are.'

¹⁵"So while the mountain was blazing with fire I turned and came down, holding in my hands the two stone tablets inscribed with the terms of the covenant. ¹⁶There below me I could see that you had sinned against the LORD your God. You had melted gold and made a calf idol for yourselves. How quickly you had turned away from the path the LORD had commanded you to follow! ¹⁷So I took the stone tablets and threw them to the ground, smashing them before your eyes.

¹⁸"Then, as before, I threw myself down before the LORD for forty days and nights. I ate no bread and drank no water because of the great sin you had committed by doing what the LORD hated, provoking him to anger. ¹⁹I feared that the furious anger of the LORD, which turned him against you, would drive him to destroy you. But again he listened to me. ²⁰The LORD was so angry with Aaron that he wanted to destroy him, too. But I prayed for Aaron, and the LORD spared him. ²¹I took your sin—the calf you had made—and I melted it down in the fire and ground it into fine dust. Then I threw the dust into the stream that flows down the mountain.

²²"You also made the LORD angry at Taberah,* Massah,* and Kibroth-hattaavah.* ²³And at Kadesh-

---

9:8 Hebrew *Horeb,* another name for Sinai.   **9:22a** *Taberah* means "place of burning." See Num 11:1-3.   **9:22b** *Massah* means "place of testing." See Exod 17:1-7.   **9:22c** *Kibroth-hattaavah* means "graves of gluttony." See Num 11:31-34.

9:6 "Stubborn" (literally "stiff-necked") describes a draft animal that is unwilling to bend its neck to the yoke (Exodus 32:9; 33:3, 5; Isaiah 48:4). Sadly, Israel was not just occasionally stubborn; stubbornness was the nation's characteristic behavior and attitude.
9:16 The gold calf idol Israel made at Sinai (Exodus 32) was probably modeled after cow-like deities of Egypt, such as the bull god Apis and the cow goddess Hathor, both associated with fertility. When the Israelites entered Canaan, they would be confronted with the fertility gods of the Canaanite cults. They would be tempted to rely upon these false gods, rather than the one true God, as the source of their blessings (see Deuteronomy 8:18-20).

barnea the LORD sent you out with this command: 'Go up and take over the land I have given you.' But you rebelled against the command of the LORD your God and refused to put your trust in him or obey him. ²⁴Yes, you have been rebelling against the LORD as long as I have known you.

²⁵"That is why I threw myself down before the LORD for forty days and nights—for the LORD said he would destroy you. ²⁶I prayed to the LORD and said, 'O Sovereign LORD, do not destroy them. They are your own people. They are your special possession, whom you redeemed from Egypt by your mighty power and your strong hand. ²⁷Please overlook the stubbornness and the awful sin of these people, and remember instead your servants Abraham, Isaac, and Jacob. ²⁸If you destroy these people, the Egyptians will say, "The Israelites died because the LORD wasn't able to bring them to the land he had promised to give them." Or they might say, "He destroyed them because he hated them; he deliberately took them into the wilderness to slaughter them." ²⁹But they are your people and your special possession, whom you brought out of Egypt by your great strength and powerful arm.'

A New Copy of the Covenant

10 "At that time the LORD said to me, 'Chisel out two stone tablets like the first ones. Also make a wooden Ark—a sacred chest to store them in. Come up to me on the mountain, ²and I will write on the tablets the same words that were on the ones you smashed. Then place the tablets in the Ark.'

³"So I made an Ark of acacia wood and cut two stone tablets like the first two. Then I went up the mountain with the tablets in my hand. ⁴Once again the LORD wrote the Ten Commandments* on the tablets and gave them to me. They were the same words the LORD had spoken to you from the heart of the fire on the day you were assembled at the foot of the mountain. ⁵Then I turned and came down the mountain and placed the tablets in the Ark of the Covenant, which I had made, just as the LORD commanded me. And the tablets are still there in the Ark."

⁶(The people of Israel set out from the wells of the people of Jaakan* and traveled to Moserah, where Aaron died and was buried. His son Eleazar ministered as high priest in his place. ⁷Then they journeyed to Gudgodah, and from there to Jotbathah, a land with many brooks and streams. ⁸At that time the LORD set apart the tribe of Levi to carry the Ark of the LORD's Covenant, and to stand before the LORD as his ministers, and to pronounce blessings in his name. These are their duties to this day. ⁹That is why the Levites have no share of property or possession of land among the other Israelite tribes. The LORD himself is their special possession, as the LORD your God told them.)

¹⁰"As for me, I stayed on the mountain in the LORD's presence for forty days and nights, as I had done the first time. And once again the LORD listened to my pleas and agreed not to destroy you. ¹¹Then the LORD said to me, 'Get up and resume the journey, and lead the people to the land I swore to give to their ancestors, so they may take possession of it.'

A Call to Love and Obedience

¹²"And now, Israel, what does the LORD your God require of you? He requires only that you fear the LORD your God, and live in a way that pleases him, and love him and serve him with all your heart and soul. ¹³And you must always obey the LORD's commands and decrees that I am giving you today for your own good.

¹⁴"Look, the highest heavens and the earth and everything in it all belong to the LORD your God. ¹⁵Yet the LORD chose your ancestors as the objects of his love. And he chose you, their descendants, above all other nations, as is evident today. ¹⁶Therefore, change your hearts* and stop being stubborn.

¹⁷"For the LORD your God is the God of gods and Lord of lords. He is the great God, the mighty and awesome God, who shows no partiality and cannot be bribed. ¹⁸He ensures that orphans and widows receive justice. He shows love to the foreigners living among you and gives them food and clothing. ¹⁹So you, too, must show love to foreigners, for you yourselves were once foreigners in the land of Egypt. ²⁰You must fear the LORD your God and worship him and cling to him. Your oaths must be in his name alone. ²¹He alone is your God, the only one who is worthy of your praise, the one who has done these mighty miracles that you have seen with your own eyes. ²²When your ancestors went down into Egypt, there were only seventy of them. But now the LORD your God has made you as numerous as the stars in the sky!

11 "You must love the LORD your God and always obey his requirements, decrees, regulations, and commands. ²Keep in mind that I am not talking now to your children, who have never experienced

---

10:4 Hebrew *the ten words.* **10:6** Or *set out from Beeroth of Bene-jaakan.* **10:16** Hebrew *circumcise the foreskin of your hearts.*

10:3 Acacia wood is from a durable desert tree that is probably the species *Acacia raddiana*. It is the only variety that grows large enough in the Negev to produce timber for building.
10:12–11:32 Moses appends this list of curses and blessings to the covenant stipulations (see 5:1–11:32). It is similar to those that follow the ratification of the covenant (27:11–28:68).
10:17 The phrase "God of gods" does not affirm the existence of other gods; rather, it affirms God's absolute sovereignty over all powers in heaven and earth. The Hebrew *'elohim,* translated "gods," can also refer to angels or other powerful beings (see Ps 82:1).
10:17 God "shows no partiality." He is not impressed with people who hold power and influence and therefore offers them no privileged consideration (see 1:17).

the discipline of the Lord your God or seen his greatness and his strong hand and powerful arm. ³They didn't see the miraculous signs and wonders he performed in Egypt against Pharaoh and all his land. ⁴They didn't see what the Lord did to the armies of Egypt and to their horses and chariots—how he drowned them in the Red Sea* as they were chasing you. He destroyed them, and they have not recovered to this very day!

⁵"Your children didn't see how the Lord cared for you in the wilderness until you arrived here. ⁶They didn't see what he did to Dathan and Abiram (the sons of Eliab, a descendant of Reuben) when the earth opened its mouth in the Israelite camp and swallowed them, along with their households and tents and every living thing that belonged to them. ⁷But you have seen the Lord perform all these mighty deeds with your own eyes!

The Blessings of Obedience

⁸"Therefore, be careful to obey every command I am giving you today, so you may have strength to go in and take over the land you are about to enter. ⁹If you obey, you will enjoy a long life in the land the Lord swore to give to your ancestors and to you, their descendants—a land flowing with milk and honey! ¹⁰For the land you are about to enter and take over is not like the land of Egypt from which you came, where you planted your seed and made irrigation ditches with your foot as in a vegetable garden. ¹¹Rather, the land you will soon take over is a land of hills and valleys with plenty of rain—¹²a land that the Lord your God cares for. He watches over it through each season of the year!

¹³"If you carefully obey the commands I am giving you today, and if you love the Lord your God and serve him with all your heart and soul, ¹⁴then he will send the rains in their proper seasons—the early and late rains—so you can bring in your harvests of grain, new wine, and olive oil. ¹⁵He will give you lush pastureland for your livestock, and you yourselves will have all you want to eat.

¹⁶"But be careful. Don't let your heart be deceived so that you turn away from the Lord and serve and worship other gods. ¹⁷If you do, the Lord's anger will burn against you. He will shut up the sky and hold back the rain, and the ground will fail to produce its harvests. Then you will quickly die in that good land the Lord is giving you.

¹⁸"So commit yourselves wholeheartedly to these words of mine. Tie them to your hands and wear them on your forehead as reminders. ¹⁹Teach them to your children. Talk about them when you are at home and when you are on the road, when you are going to bed and when you are getting up. ²⁰Write them on the doorposts of your house and on your gates, ²¹so that as long as the sky remains above the earth, you and your children may flourish in the land the Lord swore to give your ancestors.

²²"Be careful to obey all these commands I am giving you. Show love to the Lord your God by walking in his ways and holding tightly to him. ²³Then the Lord will drive out all the nations ahead of you, though they are much greater and stronger than you, and you will take over their land. ²⁴Wherever you set foot, that land will be yours. Your frontiers will stretch from the wilderness in the south to Lebanon in the north, and from the Euphrates River in the east to the Mediterranean Sea in the west.* ²⁵No one will be able to stand against you, for the Lord your God will cause the people to fear and dread you, as he promised, wherever you go in the whole land.

²⁶"Look, today I am giving you the choice between a blessing and a curse! ²⁷You will be blessed if you obey the commands of the Lord your God that I am giving you today. ²⁸But you will be cursed if you reject the commands of the Lord your God and turn away from him and worship gods you have not known before.

²⁹"When the Lord your God brings you into the land and helps you take possession of it, you must pronounce the blessing at Mount Gerizim and the curse at Mount Ebal. ³⁰(These two mountains are west of the Jordan River in the land of the Canaanites who live in the Jordan Valley,* near the town of Gilgal, not far from the oaks of Moreh.) ³¹For you are about to cross the Jordan River to take over the land the Lord your God is giving you. When you take that land and are living in it, ³²you must be careful to obey all the decrees and regulations I am giving you today.

The Lord's Chosen Place for Worship

12 "These are the decrees and regulations you must be careful to obey when you live in the land that the Lord, the God of your ancestors, is giving you. You must obey them as long as you live.

²"When you drive out the nations that live there, you must destroy all the places where they worship

---

11:4 Hebrew *sea of reeds*. **11:24** Hebrew *to the western sea*. **11:30** Hebrew *the Arabah*.

11:4 The common translation "Red Sea" (literally *sea of reeds*) comes from the Greek translation of the Old Testament. It was called the "Sea of Reeds" because of the marshy plants that grew along its shores.
11:6 In God's administration of the chosen people, he established levels of authority and command that were not to be transgressed. Because the Lord had appointed Moses and Aaron as leaders, the rebellion of Dathan and Abiram against Moses was the same as rebellion against God's sovereign rule (see Numbers 16:1-40).
12:1–26:15 After Moses laid out the principles of the covenant (5:1–11:32), he moved to the application of these principles in everyday life. Passages in this section expand on the Ten Commandments and cover some of the contingencies that inevitably arise in the complexity of human relationships.

their gods—high on the mountains, up on the hills, and under every green tree. ³Break down their altars and smash their sacred pillars. Burn their Asherah poles and cut down their carved idols. Completely erase the names of their gods!

⁴"Do not worship the Lord your God in the way these pagan peoples worship their gods. ⁵Rather, you must seek the Lord your God at the place of worship he himself will choose from among all the tribes—the place where his name will be honored. ⁶There you will bring your burnt offerings, your sacrifices, your tithes, your sacred offerings, your offerings to fulfill a vow, your voluntary offerings, and your offerings of the firstborn animals of your herds and flocks. ⁷There you and your families will feast in the presence of the Lord your God, and you will rejoice in all you have accomplished because the Lord your God has blessed you.

⁸"Your pattern of worship will change. Today all of you are doing as you please, ⁹because you have not yet arrived at the place of rest, the land the Lord your God is giving you as your special possession. ¹⁰But you will soon cross the Jordan River and live in the land the Lord your God is giving you. When he gives you rest from all your enemies and you're living safely in the land, ¹¹you must bring everything I command you—your burnt offerings, your sacrifices, your tithes, your sacred offerings, and your offerings to fulfill a vow—to the designated place of worship, the place the Lord your God chooses for his name to be honored.

¹²"You must celebrate there in the presence of the Lord your God with your sons and daughters and all your servants. And remember to include the Levites who live in your towns, for they will receive no allotment of land among you. ¹³Be careful not to sacrifice your burnt offerings just anywhere you like. ¹⁴You may do so only at the place the Lord will choose within one of your tribal territories. There you must offer your burnt offerings and do everything I command you.

¹⁵"But you may butcher your animals and eat their meat in any town whenever you want. You may freely eat the animals with which the Lord your God blesses you. All of you, whether ceremonially clean or unclean, may eat that meat, just as you now eat gazelle and deer. ¹⁶But you must not consume the blood. You must pour it out on the ground like water.

¹⁷"But you may not eat your offerings in your hometown—neither the tithe of your grain and new wine and olive oil, nor the firstborn of your flocks and herds, nor any offering to fulfill a vow, nor your voluntary offerings, nor your sacred offerings. ¹⁸You must eat these in the presence of the Lord your God at the place he will choose. Eat them there with your children, your servants, and the Levites who live in your towns, celebrating in the presence of the Lord your God in all you do. ¹⁹And be very careful never to neglect the Levites as long as you live in your land.

²⁰"When the Lord your God expands your territory as he has promised, and you have the urge to eat meat, you may freely eat meat whenever you want. ²¹It might happen that the designated place of worship—the place the Lord your God chooses for his name to be honored—is a long way from your home. If so, you may butcher any of the cattle, sheep, or goats the Lord has given you, and you may freely eat the meat in your hometown, as I have commanded you. ²²Anyone, whether ceremonially clean or unclean, may eat that meat, just as you do now with gazelle and deer. ²³But never consume the blood, for the blood is the life, and you must not consume the lifeblood with the meat. ²⁴Instead, pour out the blood on the ground like water. ²⁵Do not consume the blood, so that all may go well with you and your children after you, because you will be doing what pleases the Lord.

²⁶"Take your sacred gifts and your offerings given to fulfill a vow to the place the Lord chooses. ²⁷You must offer the meat and blood of your burnt offerings on the altar of the Lord your God. The blood of your other sacrifices must be poured out on the altar of the Lord your God, but you may eat the meat. ²⁸Be careful to obey all my commands, so that all will go well with you and your children after you, because you will be doing what is good and pleasing to the Lord your God.

> "Every day I worship my God almighty. I know of no other God besides him."
>
> CRISPINA
> (died 304) noblewoman and martyr

12:6 All of the offerings listed here are expressions of thanksgiving, fellowship, and loyalty to the Lord. In covenant relationships, the vassal offered tribute to the king as a sign of submission and a promise of dependability.

²⁹"When the Lord your God goes ahead of you and destroys the nations and you drive them out and live in their land, ³⁰do not fall into the trap of following their customs and worshiping their gods. Do not inquire about their gods, saying, 'How do these nations worship their gods? I want to follow their example.' ³¹You must not worship the Lord your God the way the other nations worship their gods, for they perform for their gods every detestable act that the Lord hates. They even burn their sons and daughters as sacrifices to their gods.

³²*"So be careful to obey all the commands I give you. You must not add anything to them or subtract anything from them."

A Warning against Idolatry

13 ¹*"Suppose there are prophets among you or those who dream dreams about the future, and they promise you signs or miracles, ²and the predicted signs or miracles occur. If they then say, 'Come, let us worship other gods'—gods you have not known before—³do not listen to them. The Lord your God is testing you to see if you truly love him with all your heart and soul. ⁴Serve only the Lord your God and fear him alone. Obey his commands, listen to his voice, and cling to him. ⁵The false prophets or visionaries who try to lead you astray must be put to death, for they encourage rebellion against the Lord your God, who redeemed you from slavery and brought you out of the land of Egypt. Since they try to lead you astray from the way the Lord your God commanded you to live, you must put them to death. In this way you will purge the evil from among you.

⁶"Suppose someone secretly entices you—even your brother, your son or daughter, your beloved wife, or your closest friend—and says, 'Let us go worship other gods'—gods that neither you nor your ancestors have known. ⁷They might suggest that you worship the gods of peoples who live nearby or who come from the ends of the earth. ⁸But do not give in or listen. Have no pity, and do not spare or protect them. ⁹You must put them to death! Strike the first blow yourself, and then all the people must join in. ¹⁰Stone the guilty ones to death because they have tried to draw you away from the Lord your God, who rescued you from the land of Egypt, the place of slavery. ¹¹Then all Israel will hear about it and be afraid, and no one will act so wickedly again.

¹²"When you begin living in the towns the Lord your God is giving you, you may hear ¹³that scoundrels among you are leading their fellow citizens astray by saying, 'Let us go worship other gods'—gods you have not known before. ¹⁴In such cases, you must examine the facts carefully. If you find that the report is true and such a detestable act has been committed among you, ¹⁵you must attack that town and completely destroy* all its inhabitants, as well as all the livestock. ¹⁶Then you must pile all the plunder in the middle of the open square and burn it. Burn the entire town as a burnt offering to the Lord your God. That town must remain a ruin forever; it may never be rebuilt. ¹⁷Keep none of the plunder that has been set apart for destruction. Then the Lord will turn from his fierce anger and be merciful to you. He will have compassion on you and make you a large nation, just as he swore to your ancestors.

¹⁸"The Lord your God will be merciful only if you listen to his voice and keep all his commands that I am giving you today, doing what pleases him.

Ceremonially Clean and Unclean Animals

14 ¹"Since you are the people of the Lord your God, never cut yourselves or shave the hair above your foreheads in mourning for the dead. ²You have been set apart as holy to the Lord your God, and he has chosen you from all the nations of the earth to be his own special treasure.

³"You must not eat any detestable animals that are ceremonially unclean. ⁴These are the animals* you may eat: the ox, the sheep, the goat, ⁵the deer, the gazelle, the roe deer, the wild goat, the addax, the antelope, and the mountain sheep.

⁶"You may eat any animal that has completely split hooves and chews the cud, ⁷but if the animal doesn't have both, it may not be eaten. So you may not eat the camel, the hare, or the hyrax.* They chew the cud but do not have split hooves, so they are ceremonially unclean for you. ⁸And you may not eat the pig. It has split hooves but does not chew the cud, so it is ceremonially unclean for you. You may not eat the meat of these animals or even touch their carcasses.

⁹"Of all the marine animals, you may eat whatever has both fins and scales. ¹⁰You may not, however, eat marine animals that do not have both fins and scales. They are ceremonially unclean for you.

12:32 Verse 12:32 is numbered 13:1 in Hebrew text. **13:1** Verses 13:1-18 are numbered 13:2-19 in Hebrew text. **13:15** The Hebrew term used here refers to the complete consecration of things or people to the Lord, either by destroying them or by giving them as an offering; similarly in 13:17. **14:4** The identification of some of the animals and birds listed in this chapter is uncertain. **14:7** Or *coney*, or *rock badger*.

13:6-11 Tempting others to practice idolatry was forbidden. God did not exempt family or close friends, either male or female, from this prohibition. Since Moses addressed the command to Israelite patriarchs, he specifically mentioned a wife rather than a husband; but given the crime's severity, a wife was also likely responsible to address her spouse's violation of this command.

14:1-2 The rites described in 14:1 relate to ancient Near Eastern cults of the dead and mourning rituals. God called the Israelites to be distinct even in how they mourned their dead. God had chosen them as his special possession and called them to reflect his character to the nations around them (Exodus 19:5-6).

¹¹"You may eat any bird that is ceremonially clean. ¹²These are the birds you may not eat: the griffon vulture, the bearded vulture, the black vulture, ¹³the kite, the falcon, buzzards of all kinds, ¹⁴ravens of all kinds, ¹⁵the eagle owl, the short-eared owl, the seagull, hawks of all kinds, ¹⁶the little owl, the great owl, the barn owl, ¹⁷the desert owl, the Egyptian vulture, the cormorant, ¹⁸the stork, herons of all kinds, the hoopoe, and the bat.

¹⁹"All winged insects that walk along the ground are ceremonially unclean for you and may not be eaten. ²⁰But you may eat any winged bird or insect that is ceremonially clean.

²¹"You must not eat anything that has died a natural death. You may give it to a foreigner living in your town, or you may sell it to a stranger. But do not eat it yourselves, for you are set apart as holy to the LORD your God.

"You must not cook a young goat in its mother's milk.

The Giving of Tithes

²²"You must set aside a tithe of your crops—one-tenth of all the crops you harvest each year. ²³Bring this tithe to the designated place of worship—the place the LORD your God chooses for his name to be honored—and eat it there in his presence. This applies to your tithes of grain, new wine, olive oil, and the firstborn males of your flocks and herds. Doing this will teach you always to fear the LORD your God.

²⁴"Now when the LORD your God blesses you with a good harvest, the place of worship he chooses for his name to be honored might be too far for you to bring the tithe. ²⁵If so, you may sell the tithe portion of your crops and herds, put the money in a pouch, and go to the place the LORD your God has chosen. ²⁶When you arrive, you may use the money to buy any kind of food you want—cattle, sheep, goats, wine, or other alcoholic drink. Then feast there in the presence of the LORD your God and celebrate with your household. ²⁷And do not neglect the Levites in your town, for they will receive no allotment of land among you.

²⁸"At the end of every third year, bring the entire tithe of that year's harvest and store it in the nearest town. ²⁹Give it to the Levites, who will receive no allotment of land among you, as well as to the foreigners living among you, the orphans, and the widows in your towns, so they can eat and be satisfied. Then the LORD your God will bless you in all your work.

Release for Debtors

15 "At the end of every seventh year you must cancel the debts of everyone who owes you money. ²This is how it must be done. Everyone must cancel the loans they have made to their fellow Israelites. They must not demand payment from their neighbors or relatives, for the LORD's time of release has arrived. ³This release from debt, however, applies only to your fellow Israelites—not to the foreigners living among you.

⁴"There should be no poor among you, for the LORD your God will greatly bless you in the land he is giving you as a special possession. ⁵You will receive this blessing if you are careful to obey all the commands of the LORD your God that I am giving you today. ⁶The LORD your God will bless you as he has promised. You will lend money to many nations but will never need to borrow. You will rule many nations, but they will not rule over you.

⁷"But if there are any poor Israelites in your towns when you arrive in the land the LORD your God is giving you, do not be hard-hearted or tightfisted toward them. ⁸Instead, be generous and lend them whatever they need. ⁹Do not be mean-spirited and refuse someone a loan because the year for canceling debts is close at hand. If you refuse to make the loan and the needy person cries out to the LORD, you will be considered guilty of sin. ¹⁰Give generously to the poor, not grudgingly, for the LORD your God will bless you in everything you do. ¹¹There will always be some in the land who are poor. That is why I am commanding you to share freely with the poor and with other Israelites in need.

Release for Hebrew Slaves

¹²"If a fellow Hebrew sells himself or herself to be your servant* and serves you for six years, in the seventh year you must set that servant free.

¹³"When you release a male servant, do not send him away empty-handed. ¹⁴Give him a generous farewell gift from your flock, your threshing floor, and your winepress. Share with him some of the bounty with which the LORD your God has blessed you. ¹⁵Remember that you were once slaves in the land of Egypt and the LORD your God redeemed you! That is why I am giving you this command.

¹⁶"But suppose your servant says, 'I will not leave you,' because he loves you and your family, and he has done well with you. ¹⁷In that case, take an awl and push it through his earlobe into the door. After that, he will be your servant for life. And do the same for your female servants.

15:12 Or *If a Hebrew man or woman is sold to you.*

15:1-18 The Law included the regulation of borrowing and lending so that the poor could survive deprivation. It provided restrictions to encourage the rich to help meet the needs of the poor without exploiting them.

15:11 The reality that there "will always be some . . . who are poor" in a fallen world is no excuse for indifference to their plight. Instead, it should emphasize the need for the rich to contribute to the well-being of the poor: "That is why I am commanding you to share freely" (see also Matthew 26:6-13).

¹⁸"You must not consider it a hardship when you release your servants. Remember that for six years they have given you services worth double the wages of hired workers, and the LORD your God will bless you in all you do.

Sacrificing Firstborn Male Animals

¹⁹"You must set aside for the LORD your God all the firstborn males from your flocks and herds. Do not use the firstborn of your herds to work your fields, and do not shear the firstborn of your flocks. ²⁰Instead, you and your family must eat these animals in the presence of the LORD your God each year at the place he chooses. ²¹But if this firstborn animal has any defect, such as lameness or blindness, or if anything else is wrong with it, you must not sacrifice it to the LORD your God. ²²Instead, use it for food for your family in your hometown. Anyone, whether ceremonially clean or unclean, may eat it, just as anyone may eat a gazelle or deer. ²³But you must not consume the blood. You must pour it out on the ground like water.

Passover and the Festival of Unleavened Bread

16 "In honor of the LORD your God, celebrate the Passover each year in the early spring, in the month of Abib,* for that was the month in which the LORD your God brought you out of Egypt by night. ²Your Passover sacrifice may be from either the flock or the herd, and it must be sacrificed to the LORD your God at the designated place of worship—the place he chooses for his name to be honored. ³Eat it with bread made without yeast. For seven days the bread you eat must be made without yeast, as when you escaped from Egypt in such a hurry. Eat this bread—the bread of suffering—so that as long as you live you will remember the day you departed from Egypt. ⁴Let no yeast be found in any house throughout your land for those seven days. And when you sacrifice the Passover lamb on the evening of the first day, do not let any of the meat remain until the next morning.

⁵"You may not sacrifice the Passover in just any of the towns that the LORD your God is giving you. ⁶You must offer it only at the designated place of worship—the place the LORD your God chooses for his name to be honored. Sacrifice it there in the evening as the sun goes down on the anniversary of your exodus from Egypt. ⁷Roast the lamb and eat it in the place the LORD your God chooses. Then you may go back to your tents the next morning. ⁸For the next six days you may not eat any bread made with yeast. On the seventh day proclaim another holy day in honor of the LORD your God, and no work may be done on that day.

The Festival of Harvest

⁹"Count off seven weeks from when you first begin to cut the grain at the time of harvest. ¹⁰Then celebrate the Festival of Harvest* to honor the LORD your God. Bring him a voluntary offering in proportion to the blessings you have received from him. ¹¹This is a time to celebrate before the LORD your God at the designated place of worship he will choose for his name to be honored. Celebrate with your sons and daughters, your male and female servants, the Levites from your towns, and the foreigners, orphans, and widows who live among you. ¹²Remember that you were once slaves in Egypt, so be careful to obey all these decrees.

The Festival of Shelters

¹³"You must observe the Festival of Shelters* for seven days at the end of the harvest season, after the grain has been threshed and the grapes have been pressed. ¹⁴This festival will be a happy time of celebrating with your sons and daughters, your male and female servants, and the Levites, foreigners, orphans, and widows from your towns. ¹⁵For seven days you must celebrate this festival to honor the LORD your God at the place he chooses, for it is he who blesses you with bountiful harvests and gives you success in all your work. This festival will be a time of great joy for all.

¹⁶"Each year every man in Israel must celebrate these three festivals: the Festival of Unleavened Bread, the Festival of Harvest, and the Festival of

---

16:1 Hebrew *Observe the month of Abib, and keep the Passover unto the LORD your God.* Abib, the first month of the ancient Hebrew lunar calendar, usually occurs within the months of March and April.   **16:10** Hebrew *Festival of Weeks;* also in 16:16. This was later called the Festival of Pentecost (see Acts 2:1). It is celebrated today as Shavuot (or Shabuoth).   **16:13** Or *Festival of Booths,* or *Festival of Tabernacles;* also in 16:16. This was earlier called the Festival of the Final Harvest or Festival of Ingathering (see Exod 23:16b). It is celebrated today as Sukkot (or Succoth).

16:1-22 Celebration permeates Deuteronomy 16. While the men were required to participate in the three great pilgrimage festivals (16:16), the entire community (including women, children, and enslaved people) was invited to participate (16:11, 14). The Passover with the associated Festival of Unleavened Bread commemorated God's deliverance of his people from slavery in Egypt. The Festival of Harvest (Pentecost) was a time of thanksgiving for the annual grain crop. The Festival of Shelters celebrated God's provision for his people in the wilderness and the year's final harvest. Remembering and celebrating are essential to worship.

16:11, 14 These passages explicitly include foreigners, orphans, and widows in the annual pilgrimage festivals. These individuals lived on society's outskirts and lacked a patriarchal figure responsible for their welfare. Deuteronomy repeatedly highlights the Israelite obligation not to ignore the marginalized but rather to make provision for them and include them within the community. As God's church, we are called to reflect his loving concern for those at risk in our own communities.

Shelters. On each of these occasions, all men must appear before the Lord your God at the place he chooses, but they must not appear before the Lord without a gift for him. ¹⁷All must give as they are able, according to the blessings given to them by the Lord your God.

Justice for the People

¹⁸"Appoint judges and officials for yourselves from each of your tribes in all the towns the Lord your God is giving you. They must judge the people fairly. ¹⁹You must never twist justice or show partiality. Never accept a bribe, for bribes blind the eyes of the wise and corrupt the decisions of the godly. ²⁰Let true justice prevail, so you may live and occupy the land that the Lord your God is giving you.

²¹"You must never set up a wooden Asherah pole beside the altar you build for the Lord your God. ²²And never set up sacred pillars for worship, for the Lord your God hates them.

17 "Never sacrifice sick or defective cattle, sheep, or goats to the Lord your God, for he detests such gifts.

²"When you begin living in the towns the Lord your God is giving you, a man or woman among you might do evil in the sight of the Lord your God and violate the covenant. ³For instance, they might serve other gods or worship the sun, the moon, or any of the stars—the forces of heaven—which I have strictly forbidden. ⁴When you hear about it, investigate the matter thoroughly. If it is true that this detestable thing has been done in Israel, ⁵then the man or woman who has committed such an evil act must be taken to the gates of the town and stoned to death. ⁶But never put a person to death on the testimony of only one witness. There must always be two or three witnesses. ⁷The witnesses must throw the first stones, and then all the people may join in. In this way, you will purge the evil from among you.

⁸"Suppose a case arises in a local court that is too hard for you to decide—for instance, whether someone is guilty of murder or only of manslaughter, or a difficult lawsuit, or a case involving different kinds of assault. Take such legal cases to the place the Lord your God will choose, ⁹and present them to the Levitical priests or the judge on duty at that time. They will hear the case and declare the verdict. ¹⁰You must carry out the verdict they announce and the sentence they prescribe at the place the Lord chooses. You must do exactly what they say. ¹¹After they have interpreted the law and declared their verdict, the sentence they impose must be fully executed; do not modify it in any way. ¹²Anyone arrogant enough to reject the verdict of the judge or of the priest who represents the Lord your God must die. In this way you will purge the evil from Israel. ¹³Then everyone else will hear about it and be afraid to act so arrogantly.

Guidelines for a King

¹⁴"You are about to enter the land the Lord your God is giving you. When you take it over and settle there, you may think, 'We should select a king to rule over us like the other nations around us.' ¹⁵If this happens, be sure to select as king the man the Lord your God chooses. You must appoint a fellow Israelite; he may not be a foreigner.

¹⁶"The king must not build up a large stable of horses for himself or send his people to Egypt to buy horses, for the Lord has told you, 'You must never return to Egypt.' ¹⁷The king must not take many wives for himself, because they will turn his heart away from the Lord. And he must not accumulate large amounts of wealth in silver and gold for himself.

¹⁸"When he sits on the throne as king, he must copy for himself this body of instruction on a scroll in the presence of the Levitical priests. ¹⁹He must always keep that copy with him and read it daily as long as he lives. That way he will learn to fear the Lord his God by obeying all the terms of these instructions and decrees. ²⁰This regular reading will prevent him from becoming proud and acting as if he is above his fellow citizens. It will also prevent him from turning away from these commands in the smallest way. And it will ensure that he and his descendants will reign for many generations in Israel.

Gifts for the Priests and Levites

18 "Remember that the Levitical priests—that is, the whole of the tribe of Levi—will receive no allotment of land among the other tribes in Israel. Instead, the priests and Levites will eat from the special gifts given to the Lord, for that is their share. ²They will have no land of their own among the Israelites. The Lord himself is their special possession, just as he promised them.

³"These are the parts the priests may claim as their share from the cattle, sheep, and goats that the people bring as offerings: the shoulder, the cheeks, and the stomach. ⁴You must also give to the priests the first share of the grain, the new wine, the olive oil, and the wool at shearing time. ⁵For the Lord your God chose the tribe of Levi out of all your tribes to minister in the Lord's name forever.

17:3 The "forces of heaven" are visible objects such as the sun, moon, and stars, as well as invisible beings such as angels. Worship of anyone or anything created by God is a clear violation of the second commandment (see 5:8-9).

17:17 Polygamy is neither prohibited nor sanctioned here. This guideline was meant to moderate and regulate the practice. In the ancient world, kings married many wives to cement political alliances with other kingdoms, showing trust in human power rather than God's provision. David (2 Samuel 5:13; 12:11) and Solomon (1 Kings 11:3-4) both ignored this warning to their own great harm and that of the nation. The amassing of wealth was another sign of dependence on human resources.

⁶"Suppose a Levite chooses to move from his town in Israel, wherever he is living, to the place the LORD chooses for worship. ⁷He may minister there in the name of the LORD his God, just like all his fellow Levites who are serving the LORD there. ⁸He may eat his share of the sacrifices and offerings, even if he also receives support from his family.

A Call to Holy Living

⁹"When you enter the land the LORD your God is giving you, be very careful not to imitate the detestable customs of the nations living there. ¹⁰For example, never sacrifice your son or daughter as a burnt offering.* And do not let your people practice fortune-telling, or use sorcery, or interpret omens, or engage in witchcraft, ¹¹or cast spells, or function as mediums or psychics, or call forth the spirits of the dead. ¹²Anyone who does these things is detestable to the LORD. It is because the other nations have done these detestable things that the LORD your God will drive them out ahead of you. ¹³But you must be blameless before the LORD your God. ¹⁴The nations you are about to displace consult sorcerers and fortune-tellers, but the LORD your God forbids you to do such things."

True and False Prophets

¹⁵Moses continued, "The LORD your God will raise up for you a prophet like me from among your fellow Israelites. You must listen to him. ¹⁶For this is what you yourselves requested of the LORD your God when you were assembled at Mount Sinai.* You said, 'Don't let us hear the voice of the LORD our God anymore or see this blazing fire, for we will die.'

¹⁷"Then the LORD said to me, 'What they have said is right. ¹⁸I will raise up a prophet like you from among their fellow Israelites. I will put my words in his mouth, and he will tell the people everything I command him. ¹⁹I will personally deal with anyone who will not listen to the messages the prophet proclaims on my behalf. ²⁰But any prophet who falsely claims to speak in my name or who speaks in the name of another god must die.'

²¹"But you may wonder, 'How will we know whether or not a prophecy is from the LORD?' ²²If the prophet speaks in the LORD's name but his prediction does not happen or come true, you will know that the LORD did not give that message. That prophet has spoken without my authority and need not be feared.

Cities of Refuge

19 "When the LORD your God destroys the nations whose land he is giving you, you will take over their land and settle in their towns and homes. ²Then you must set apart three cities of refuge in the land the LORD your God is giving you. ³Survey the territory,* and divide the land the LORD your God is giving you into three districts, with one of these cities in each district. Then anyone who has killed someone can flee to one of the cities of refuge for safety.

⁴"If someone kills another person unintentionally, without previous hostility, the slayer may flee to any of these cities to live in safety. ⁵For example, suppose someone goes into the forest with a neighbor to cut wood. And suppose one of them swings an ax to chop down a tree, and the ax head flies off the handle, killing the other person. In such cases, the slayer may flee to one of the cities of refuge to live in safety.

⁶"If the distance to the nearest city of refuge is too far, an enraged avenger might be able to chase down and kill the person who caused the death. Then the slayer would die unfairly, since he had never shown hostility toward the person who died. ⁷That is why I am commanding you to set aside three cities of refuge.

⁸"And if the LORD your God enlarges your territory, as he swore to your ancestors, and gives you all the land he promised them, ⁹you must designate three additional cities of refuge. (He will give you

---

18:10 Or *never make your son or daughter pass through the fire.* 18:16 Hebrew *Horeb,* another name for Sinai. 19:3 Or *Keep the roads in good repair.*

18:10 Some Canaanite religions included child sacrifice to appease their gods. Israel was strictly warned never to engage in this practice (Leviticus 18:21; 20:2-5). When they did, it aroused God's judgment (2 Kings 17:16-17; 21:6; Ezekiel 23:37).
18:10 Throughout the ancient Near East, diviners were considered experts at reading and interpreting omens. Divination was commonly done through extispicy, the examination of livers, kidneys, and other internal organs of various sacrificed animals. Sorcerers conjured up the spirits of the dead. Divining cups were often used to interpret omens (see Genesis 44:5). Drops of oil would be placed in containers of water, and the spread of the oil communicated some message to the expert. A parallel would be reading tea leaves. The practice of witchcraft included performing unusual acts or signs (Exodus 7:11) to mislead people (Malachi 3:5).
18:15 "A prophet like me" would be beyond the ordinary because Moses was without peer among the prophets (see Deuteronomy 34:10-11). This prophet would be "from among your fellow Israelites" (it could also be translated "from among your brothers"), and Israel was required to listen to him (18:19). The prophets of Old Testament Israel would partially fulfill the function of God's spokesperson to whom Israel must listen. Later, Judaism looked for this prophet as a major messianic figure (see John 1:21; 6:14; 7:40); the New Testament identifies Jesus as this prophet (Acts 3:18-26).
19:1-13 Cities of refuge (19:2) were strategically located throughout the land so those accused of homicide could find protective sanctuary until their cases came to trial (see 4:41; Numbers 35:6-29).
19:9 If Israel proved faithful to the covenant (19:8), God would grant the nation even more territory, so much so that three additional cities of refuge would be needed. Sadly, this need never arose because of Israel's disobedience to the Lord.

Insight: THE CITIES OF REFUGE

The cities of refuge were selected as safe havens to protect people from revenge. An avenger had the legal right to put the killer to death (Numbers 35:19; see Genesis 9:6). If a person caused someone's death accidentally, the slayer fled to a city of refuge to find temporary safety while awaiting trial (Numbers 35:22-28). The six cities of refuge dotted the Hebrew territory so that any Israelite could seek and reach asylum.

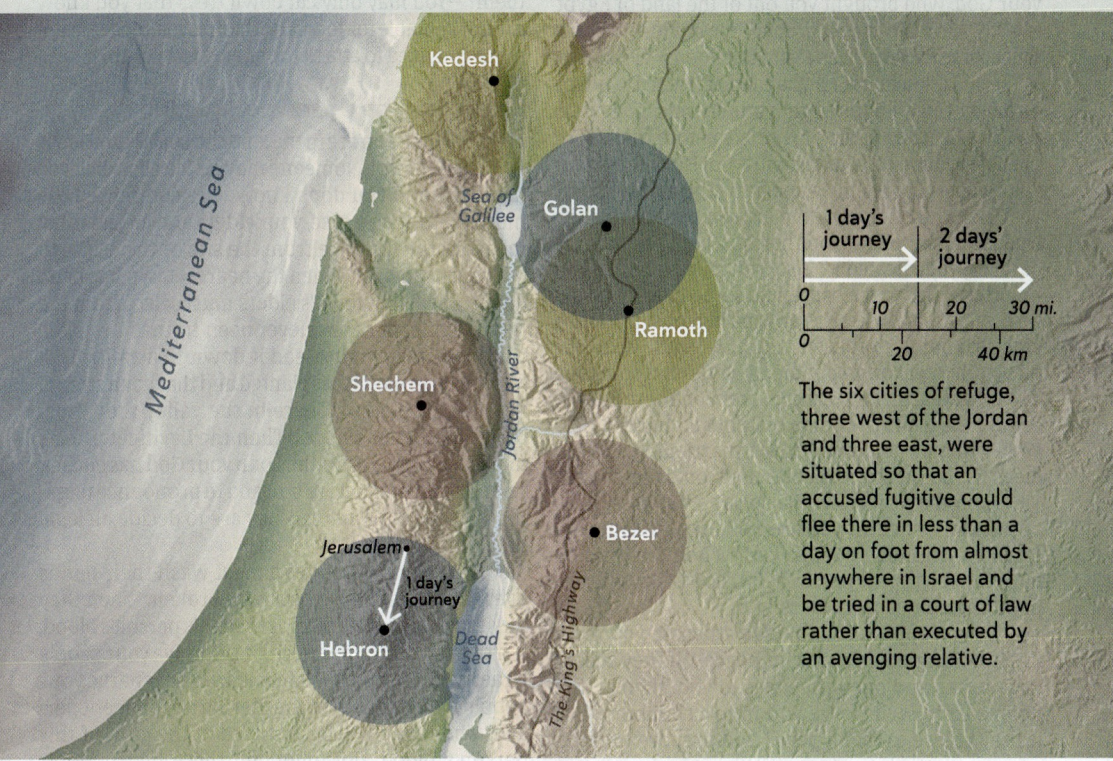

The six cities of refuge, three west of the Jordan and three east, were situated so that an accused fugitive could flee there in less than a day on foot from almost anywhere in Israel and be tried in a court of law rather than executed by an avenging relative.

this land if you are careful to obey all the commands I have given you—if you always love the LORD your God and walk in his ways.) ¹⁰That way you will prevent the death of innocent people in the land the LORD your God is giving you as your special possession. You will not be held responsible for the death of innocent people.

¹¹"But suppose someone is hostile toward a neighbor and deliberately ambushes and murders him and then flees to one of the cities of refuge. ¹²In that case, the elders of the murderer's hometown must send agents to the city of refuge to bring him back and hand him over to the dead person's avenger to be put to death. ¹³Do not feel sorry for that murderer! Purge from Israel the guilt of murdering innocent people; then all will go well with you.

Concern for Justice

¹⁴"When you arrive in the land the LORD your God is giving you as your special possession, you must never steal anyone's land by moving the boundary markers your ancestors set up to mark their property.

¹⁵"You must not convict anyone of a crime on the testimony of only one witness. The facts of the case must be established by the testimony of two or three witnesses.

¹⁶"If a malicious witness comes forward and accuses someone of a crime, ¹⁷then both the accuser and accused must appear before the LORD by coming to the priests and judges in office at that time. ¹⁸The judges must investigate the case thoroughly. If the accuser has brought false charges against his fellow Israelite, ¹⁹you must impose on the accuser

the sentence he intended for the other person. In this way, you will purge such evil from among you. ²⁰Then the rest of the people will hear about it and be afraid to do such an evil thing. ²¹You must show no pity for the guilty! Your rule should be life for life, eye for eye, tooth for tooth, hand for hand, foot for foot.

Regulations concerning War

20 "When you go out to fight your enemies and you face horses and chariots and an army greater than your own, do not be afraid. The LORD your God, who brought you out of the land of Egypt, is with you! ²When you prepare for battle, the priest must come forward to speak to the troops. ³He will say to them, 'Listen to me, all you men of Israel! Do not be afraid as you go out to fight your enemies today! Do not lose heart or panic or tremble before them. ⁴For the LORD your God is going with you! He will fight for you against your enemies, and he will give you victory!'

⁵"Then the officers of the army must address the troops and say, 'Has anyone here just built a new house but not yet dedicated it? If so, you may go home! You might be killed in the battle, and someone else would dedicate your house. ⁶Has anyone here just planted a vineyard but not yet eaten any of its fruit? If so, you may go home! You might die in battle, and someone else would eat the first fruit. ⁷Has anyone here just become engaged to a woman but not yet married her? Well, you may go home and get married! You might die in the battle, and someone else would marry her.'

⁸"Then the officers will also say, 'Is anyone here afraid or worried? If you are, you may go home before you frighten anyone else.' ⁹When the officers have finished speaking to their troops, they will appoint the unit commanders.

¹⁰"As you approach a town to attack it, you must first offer its people terms for peace. ¹¹If they accept your terms and open the gates to you, then all the people inside will serve you in forced labor. ¹²But if they refuse to make peace and prepare to fight, you must attack the town. ¹³When the LORD your God hands the town over to you, use your swords to kill every man in the town. ¹⁴But you may keep for yourselves all the women, children, livestock, and other plunder. You may enjoy the plunder from your enemies that the LORD your God has given you.

¹⁵"But these instructions apply only to distant towns, not to the towns of the nations in the land you will enter. ¹⁶In those towns that the LORD your God is giving you as a special possession, destroy every living thing. ¹⁷You must completely destroy* the Hittites, Amorites, Canaanites, Perizzites, Hivites, and Jebusites, just as the LORD your God has commanded you. ¹⁸This will prevent the people of the land from teaching you to imitate their detestable customs in the worship of their gods, which would cause you to sin deeply against the LORD your God.

¹⁹"When you are attacking a town and the war drags on, you must not cut down the trees with your axes. You may eat the fruit, but do not cut down the trees. Are the trees your enemies, that you should attack them? ²⁰You may only cut down trees that you know are not valuable for food. Use them to make the equipment you need to attack the enemy town until it falls.

Cleansing for Unsolved Murder

21 "When you are in the land the LORD your God is giving you, someone may be found murdered in a field, and you don't know who committed the murder. ²In such a case, your elders and judges must measure the distance from the site of the crime to the nearby towns. ³When the nearest town has been determined, that town's elders must select from the herd a heifer that has never been trained or yoked to a plow. ⁴They must lead it down to a valley that has not been plowed or planted and that has a stream running through it. There in the valley they must break the heifer's neck. ⁵Then the Levitical priests must step forward, for the LORD your God has chosen them to minister before him and to pronounce blessings in the LORD's name. They are to decide all legal and criminal cases.

⁶"The elders of the town must wash their hands over the heifer whose neck was broken. ⁷Then they must say, 'Our hands did not shed this person's blood, nor did we see it happen. ⁸O LORD, forgive your people Israel whom you have redeemed. Do not charge your people with the guilt of murdering an innocent person.' Then they will be absolved of the guilt of this person's blood. ⁹By following these instructions, you will do what is right in the LORD's sight and will cleanse the guilt of murder from your community.

Marriage to a Captive Woman

¹⁰"Suppose you go out to war against your enemies and the LORD your God hands them over to you, and you take some of them as captives. ¹¹And suppose you see among the captives a beautiful woman, and you are attracted to her and want to marry her. ¹²If this

---

20:17 The Hebrew term used here refers to the complete consecration of things or people to the LORD, either by destroying them or by giving them as an offering.

20:7 Babylonian texts included a similar provision. If the man in this situation died in battle, he would be deprived of offspring to carry on his name, which was a great tragedy in ancient Israel.
21:10-14 God provided the opportunity for a soldier to marry a female war captive. The acts of shaving hair, cutting nails, and changing clothes represented her transition to a new identity and status. Any woman would need to grieve the loss of her family and community; in this specific case, the woman was given a month to mourn. This time would also ensure that any children from the woman would be the soldier's. The law also protected her from later being divorced and enslaved.

Vulnerable Women

⊙ IDENTITY | Redefining Strong

Stripped—there is no other description for this unnamed woman. Taken for her beauty, her parents were likely dead, she was far from home, her clothing had been replaced, her nails had been cut, and her head had been shaved.

Scripture tells numerous stories of women who are taken in war, rejected by husbands, or left as widows. Perhaps we have felt pain similar to what these women experienced, even if the circumstances differed. Few today would share the scope of tragedy described in Deuteronomy 21:10-14, but many of us may relate to certain aspects of her loss. And we have all probably felt defined at times by our circumstances or our appearance, or by who loves us and why.

Whether you are a wife, a mom, or a CEO, none of those situations or relationships belonged to you at birth. Yet it can be so easy to define yourself by such things. Maybe you won the genetic lottery and find value in terms of worldly beauty.

> I am secure because I am God's.

But what if, one day, you find yourself without the relationships, place, job, or physical attributes that you now have? It is very likely that, at some point, we all will find ourselves without the thing that we think makes us who we are. That prospect sounds terrifying, but it points us to a problem: We often look for our identity in the people around us. And outside sources were never intended to define our inner strength.

You are a child of God, created in his image. You are loved and valued because you are his. Nothing can remove your status as his child, just as nothing could remove God's promised love and protection for his people, Israel (Hosea 11; see Romans 8:15-17, 31-39).

Mentally remove the outward things you think protect you or give you worth. Can you see yourself as strong? Valuable? Secure? God does.

THE PLIGHT OF CAPTIVE WOMEN IN ANCIENT TIMES IS DESCRIBED IN DEUTERONOMY 21:10-14.

IDENTIFY

Can you be fully exposed *and* fully secure?

In what areas of your life do you struggle to feel strong?

> *"I've known everything from abuse to homelessness to late-term miscarriages. Each was a stripping of its own. Yet I've learned that every experience, good or bad, will bear fruit in our lives for our sake and for the sake of the Kingdom."*

LISA D. EDMONDS is mother of two daughters, a Stonecroft Ministries speaker and speaker trainer, worship leader, and constituent care director for The Dr. James Dobson Family Institute.

Perspective

How do we follow God when the rules seem wrong?

SCRIPTURE CONNECTION: DEUTERONOMY 22:13-30

For a woman pursuing a relationship with God, these passages on adultery, virginity, rape, and consequence are some of the Bible's hardest. How could these laws that sound terrible to us be good for God's people? We seek answers, sometimes wondering whether to follow the God of this Bible.

Ancient Israelites built their society on honor, creating harsh consequences to deter behavior that threatened the stability of the whole community. To our modern-day understanding, the laws read as oppressive of women because we structure our society differently. We don't require proof of virginity to protect a family's honor. However, some Israelite practices, such as providing for a woman wrongly accused, protected women more than the laws of other similar ancient societies.

Scholars debate whether these rules show us more about humans' designs for living honorably or God's. Either way, when any society relies upon never-ending rules, we miss the spirit of God.

In studying these passages today, we recognize what *didn't* work. We see how these prescriptions proved our societal need for a savior. Only one death sentence could purge evil from among us; that sentence came at the Cross. The Messiah's death fulfilled the Law and gave life to women and men equally, allowing us to follow God's ways by experiencing God's heart.

VIEWPOINTS

HERS: *What type of strength was required of our Israelite sisters? How might we honor their fortitude?*
MINE: *"As an empowered woman today, I can seek God and his Spirit directly for wisdom to discern questionable religious and social practices."*
YOURS: *What is God's heart for you today, apart from societal prescriptions for your behavior?*

MISTY ARTERBURN is an author and speaker, contributing to Bible projects, devotionals, and recovery materials for over twenty years. Wife and mom to five, Misty is the founder of Recovery Girls and the general editor of *The One Year Bible for Women*.

happens, you may take her to your home, where she must shave her head, cut her nails, ¹³and change the clothes she was wearing when she was captured. She will stay in your home, but let her mourn for her father and mother for a full month. Then you may marry her, and you will be her husband and she will be your wife. ¹⁴But if you marry her and she does not please you, you must let her go free. You may not sell her or treat her as a slave, for you have humiliated her.

Rights of the Firstborn

¹⁵"Suppose a man has two wives, but he loves one and not the other, and both have given him sons. And suppose the firstborn son is the son of the wife he does not love. ¹⁶When the man divides his inheritance, he may not give the larger inheritance to his younger son, the son of the wife he loves, as if he were the firstborn son. ¹⁷He must recognize the rights of his oldest son, the son of the wife he does not love, by giving him a double portion. He is the first son of his father's virility, and the rights of the firstborn belong to him.

Dealing with a Rebellious Son

¹⁸"Suppose a man has a stubborn and rebellious son who will not obey his father or mother, even though they discipline him. ¹⁹In such a case, the father and mother must take the son to the elders as they hold court at the town gate. ²⁰The parents must say to the elders, 'This son of ours is stubborn and rebellious and refuses to obey. He is a glutton and a drunkard.' ²¹Then all the men of his town must stone him to death. In this way, you will purge this evil from among you, and all Israel will hear about it and be afraid.

Various Regulations

²²"If someone has committed a crime worthy of death and is executed and hung on a tree,* ²³the body must not remain hanging from the tree overnight. You must bury the body that same day, for anyone who is hung* is cursed in the sight of God. In this way, you will prevent the defilement of the land the LORD your God is giving you as your special possession.

22 "If you see your neighbor's ox or sheep or goat wandering away, don't ignore your responsibility.* Take it back to its owner. ²If its owner does not live nearby or you don't know who the owner is, take it to your place and keep it until the owner comes looking for it. Then you must return it. ³Do the same if you find your neighbor's donkey, clothing, or anything else your neighbor loses. Don't ignore your responsibility.

⁴"If you see that your neighbor's donkey or ox has collapsed on the road, do not look the other way. Go and help your neighbor get it back on its feet!

21:22 Or *impaled on a pole*; similarly in 21:23. 21:23 Greek version reads *for everyone who is hung on a tree.* Compare Gal 3:13. 22:1 Hebrew *don't hide yourself*; similarly in 22:3.

⁵"A woman must not put on men's clothing, and a man must not wear women's clothing. Anyone who does this is detestable in the sight of the LORD your God.

⁶"If you happen to find a bird's nest in a tree or on the ground, and there are young ones or eggs in it with the mother sitting in the nest, do not take the mother with the young. ⁷You may take the young, but let the mother go, so that you may prosper and enjoy a long life.

⁸"When you build a new house, you must build a railing around the edge of its flat roof. That way you will not be considered guilty of murder if someone falls from the roof.

⁹"You must not plant any other crop between the rows of your vineyard. If you do, you are forbidden to use either the grapes from the vineyard or the other crop.

¹⁰"You must not plow with an ox and a donkey harnessed together.

¹¹"You must not wear clothing made of wool and linen woven together.

¹²"You must put four tassels on the hem of the cloak with which you cover yourself—on the front, back, and sides.

Regulations for Sexual Purity

¹³"Suppose a man marries a woman, but after sleeping with her, he turns against her ¹⁴and publicly accuses her of shameful conduct, saying, 'When I married this woman, I discovered she was not a virgin.' ¹⁵Then the woman's father and mother must bring the proof of her virginity to the elders as they hold court at the town gate. ¹⁶Her father must say to them, 'I gave my daughter to this man to be his wife, and now he has turned against her. ¹⁷He has accused her of shameful conduct, saying, "I discovered that your daughter was not a virgin." But here is the proof of my daughter's virginity.' Then they must spread her bed sheet before the elders. ¹⁸The elders must then take the man and punish him. ¹⁹They must also fine him 100 pieces of silver,* which he must pay to the woman's father because he publicly accused a virgin of Israel of shameful conduct. The woman will then remain the man's wife, and he may never divorce her.

²⁰"But suppose the man's accusations are true, and he can show that she was not a virgin. ²¹The woman must be taken to the door of her father's home, and there the men of the town must stone her to death, for she has committed a disgraceful crime in Israel by being promiscuous while living in her parents' home. In this way, you will purge this evil from among you.

²²"If a man is discovered committing adultery, both he and the woman must die. In this way, you will purge Israel of such evil.

²³"Suppose a man meets a young woman, a virgin who is engaged to be married, and he has sexual intercourse with her. If this happens within a town, ²⁴you must take both of them to the gates of that town and stone them to death. The woman is guilty because she did not scream for help. The man must die because he violated another man's wife. In this way, you will purge this evil from among you.

²⁵"But if the man meets the engaged woman out in the country, and he rapes her, then only the man must die. ²⁶Do nothing to the young woman; she has committed no crime worthy of death. She is as innocent as a murder victim. ²⁷Since the man raped her out in the country, it must be assumed that she screamed, but there was no one to rescue her.

²⁸"Suppose a man has intercourse with a young woman who is a virgin but is not engaged to be married. If they are discovered, ²⁹he must pay her father fifty pieces of silver.* Then he must marry the young woman because he violated her, and he may never divorce her as long as he lives.

³⁰*"A man must not marry his father's former wife, for this would violate his father.

Regulations concerning Worship

23 ¹*"If a man's testicles are crushed or his penis is cut off, he may not be admitted to the assembly of the LORD.

²"If a person is illegitimate by birth, neither he nor his descendants for ten generations may be admitted to the assembly of the LORD.

22:19 Hebrew *100 [shekels] of silver*, about 2.5 pounds or 1.1 kilograms in weight. **22:29** Hebrew *50 [shekels] of silver*, about 1.25 pounds or 570 grams in weight. **22:30** Verse 22:30 is numbered 23:1 in Hebrew text. **23:1** Verses 23:1-25 are numbered 23:2-26 in Hebrew text.

22:5 To the ancient Israelites, the opposite of creation order was chaos, so the blurring of clearly delineated differences could pose a threat to God's designed order (see also 22:9-11). While this prohibition's precise meaning is often debated, the focus appears to be less on attire and more on maintaining gender roles. Blurring those identities may have been viewed as threatening creation order or bringing shame, as in the practice of some ancient powers to force captive men to wear women's attire and do work typically assigned to women.

22:13-21 The focus of this law was on protecting a woman from abusive behavior. Such slander was likely an attempt by the man to divorce her and get back what he had paid to marry the woman. Upon proof of the husband's duplicity, however, the shame would fall upon him. He would be flogged, would have to pay additional money, and would be unable to ever divorce her. However, if the wife's virginity could not be established, she would be stoned at her father's home, echoing the punishment of a rebellious son (21:18-21). The community saw both the daughter and the son in these situations as a threat because a society that was so based on kinship required family stability and communal trust. Behavior was not private; it was public.

23:1 Emasculation, associated with certain pagan rituals and customs, was abhorrent to the Lord (but see what the Lord intended for the future: Isaiah 56:3-4).

³"No Ammonite or Moabite or any of their descendants for ten generations may be admitted to the assembly of the LORD. ⁴These nations did not welcome you with food and water when you came out of Egypt. Instead, they hired Balaam son of Beor from Pethor in distant Aram-naharaim to curse you. ⁵But the LORD your God refused to listen to Balaam. He turned the intended curse into a blessing because the LORD your God loves you. ⁶As long as you live, you must never promote the welfare and prosperity of the Ammonites or Moabites.

⁷"Do not detest the Edomites or the Egyptians, because the Edomites are your relatives and you lived as foreigners among the Egyptians. ⁸The third generation of Edomites and Egyptians may enter the assembly of the LORD.

Miscellaneous Regulations

⁹"When you go to war against your enemies, be sure to stay away from anything that is impure.

¹⁰"Any man who becomes ceremonially defiled because of a nocturnal emission must leave the camp and stay away all day. ¹¹Toward evening he must bathe himself, and at sunset he may return to the camp.

¹²"You must have a designated area outside the camp where you can go to relieve yourself. ¹³Each of you must have a spade as part of your equipment. Whenever you relieve yourself, dig a hole with the spade and cover the excrement. ¹⁴The camp must be holy, for the LORD your God moves around in your camp to protect you and to defeat your enemies. He must not see any shameful thing among you, or he will turn away from you.

¹⁵"If slaves should escape from their masters and take refuge with you, you must not hand them over to their masters. ¹⁶Let them live among you in any town they choose, and do not oppress them.

¹⁷"No Israelite, whether man or woman, may become a temple prostitute. ¹⁸When you are bringing an offering to fulfill a vow, you must not bring to the house of the LORD your God any offering from the earnings of a prostitute, whether a man* or a woman, for both are detestable to the LORD your God.

¹⁹"Do not charge interest on the loans you make to a fellow Israelite, whether you loan money, or food, or anything else. ²⁰You may charge interest to foreigners, but you may not charge interest to Israelites, so that the LORD your God may bless you in everything you do in the land you are about to enter and occupy.

²¹"When you make a vow to the LORD your God, be prompt in fulfilling whatever you promised him. For the LORD your God demands that you promptly fulfill all your vows, or you will be guilty of sin. ²²However, it is not a sin to refrain from making a vow. ²³But once you have voluntarily made a vow, be careful to fulfill your promise to the LORD your God.

²⁴"When you enter your neighbor's vineyard, you may eat your fill of grapes, but you must not carry any away in a basket. ²⁵And when you enter your neighbor's field of grain, you may pluck the heads of grain with your hand, but you must not harvest it with a sickle.

24

"Suppose a man marries a woman but she does not please him. Having discovered something wrong with her, he writes a document of divorce, hands it to her, and sends her away from his house. ²When she leaves his house, she is free to marry another man. ³But if the second husband also turns against her, writes a document of divorce, hands it to her, and sends her away, or if he dies, ⁴the first husband may not marry her again, for she has been defiled. That would be detestable to the LORD. You must not bring guilt upon the land the LORD your God is giving you as a special possession.

⁵"A newly married man must not be drafted into the army or be given any other official responsibilities. He must be free to spend one year at home, bringing happiness to the wife he has married.

⁶"It is wrong to take a set of millstones, or even just the upper millstone, as security for a loan, for the owner uses it to make a living.

⁷"If anyone kidnaps a fellow Israelite and treats him as a slave or sells him, the kidnapper must die. In this way, you will purge the evil from among you.

⁸"In all cases involving serious skin diseases,* be careful to follow the instructions of the Levitical priests; obey all the commands I have given them. ⁹Remember what the LORD your God did to Miriam as you were coming from Egypt.

¹⁰"If you lend anything to your neighbor, do not enter his house to pick up the item he is giving as security. ¹¹You must wait outside while he goes in and brings it out to you. ¹²If your neighbor is poor and gives you his cloak as security for a loan, do not keep the cloak overnight. ¹³Return the cloak to its owner by sunset so he can stay warm through the night and bless you, and the LORD your God will count you as righteous.

23:18 Hebrew *a dog.* 24:8 Traditionally rendered *leprosy.* The Hebrew word used here can describe various skin diseases.

23:7 The Edomites were descendants of Jacob's brother, Esau (see 2:8).
23:17 A temple prostitute was commonly a part of Canaanite religious rituals, so they were forbidden in Israel.
24:1-4 These statements describe a situation in which a woman hadn't "pleased" her husband because of "something wrong with her." The nature of this "something wrong," or "shameful thing," is unknown, but it may refer to her behavior or perhaps a physical problem preventing intercourse. Regardless, the principles here do not seem designed to provide grounds for permissible divorce. Instead, they address something that was actually happening in the community (see Matthew 19:7-9). In such a case, God prohibited the first husband from remarrying the woman later, although the reason is unclear.

14"Never take advantage of poor and destitute laborers, whether they are fellow Israelites or foreigners living in your towns. 15You must pay them their wages each day before sunset because they are poor and are counting on it. If you don't, they might cry out to the LORD against you, and it would be counted against you as sin.

16"Parents must not be put to death for the sins of their children, nor children for the sins of their parents. Those deserving to die must be put to death for their own crimes.

17"True justice must be given to foreigners living among you and to orphans, and you must never accept a widow's garment as security for her debt. 18Always remember that you were slaves in Egypt and that the LORD your God redeemed you from your slavery. That is why I have given you this command.

19"When you are harvesting your crops and forget to bring in a bundle of grain from your field, don't go back to get it. Leave it for the foreigners, orphans, and widows. Then the LORD your God will bless you in all you do. 20When you beat the olives from your olive trees, don't go over the boughs twice. Leave the remaining olives for the foreigners, orphans, and widows. 21When you gather the grapes in your vineyard, don't glean the vines after they are picked. Leave the remaining grapes for the foreigners, orphans, and widows. 22Remember that you were slaves in the land of Egypt. That is why I am giving you this command.

25 "Suppose two people take a dispute to court, and the judges declare that one is right and the other is wrong. 2If the person in the wrong is sentenced to be flogged, the judge must command him to lie down and be beaten in his presence with the number of lashes appropriate to the crime. 3But never give more than forty lashes; more than forty lashes would publicly humiliate your neighbor.

4"You must not muzzle an ox to keep it from eating as it treads out the grain.

5"If two brothers are living together on the same property and one of them dies without a son, his widow may not be married to anyone from outside the family. Instead, her husband's brother should marry her and have intercourse with her to fulfill the duties of a brother-in-law. 6The first son she bears to him will be considered the son of the dead brother, so that his name will not be forgotten in Israel.

7"But if the man refuses to marry his brother's widow, she must go to the town gate and say to the elders assembled there, 'My husband's brother refuses to preserve his brother's name in Israel—he refuses to fulfill the duties of a brother-in-law by marrying me.' 8The elders of the town will then summon him and talk with him. If he still refuses and says, 'I don't want to marry her,' 9the widow must walk over to him in the presence of the elders, pull his sandal from his foot, and spit in his face. Then she must declare, 'This is what happens to a man who refuses to provide his brother with children.' 10Ever afterward in Israel his family will be referred to as 'the family of the man whose sandal was pulled off'!

11"If two Israelite men get into a fight and the wife of one tries to rescue her husband by grabbing the testicles of the other man, 12you must cut off her hand. Show her no pity.

13"You must use accurate scales when you weigh out merchandise, 14and you must use full and honest measures. 15Yes, always use honest weights and measures, so that you may enjoy a long life in the land the LORD your God is giving you. 16All who cheat with dishonest weights and measures are detestable to the LORD your God.

17"Never forget what the Amalekites did to you as you came from Egypt. 18They attacked you when you were exhausted and weary, and they struck down those who were straggling behind. They had no fear of God. 19Therefore, when the LORD your God has given you rest from all your enemies in the land he is giving you as a special possession, you must destroy the Amalekites and erase their memory from under heaven. Never forget this!

Harvest Offerings and Tithes

26 "When you enter the land the LORD your God is giving you as a special possession and you have conquered it and settled there, 2put some of the first produce from each crop you harvest into a basket and bring it to the designated place of worship—the place the LORD your God chooses for his name to be honored. 3Go to the priest in charge at that time and say to him, 'With this gift I acknowledge to the LORD your God that I have entered the land he swore to our ancestors he would give us.' 4The priest will then take the basket from your hand and set it before the altar of the LORD your God.

5"You must then say in the presence of the LORD your God, 'My ancestor Jacob was a wandering Aramean who went to live as a foreigner in Egypt. His family arrived few in number, but in Egypt they became a large and mighty nation. 6When the Egyptians oppressed and humiliated us by making us

---

25:5-10 The practice described here (known as levirate marriage) accomplished two things: It provided an heir for the deceased man and protection for his widow. In ancient Israel, a woman's identity and well-being were tied to the men in her life: her father, her husband, and her son(s). The men were responsible for the physical protection and economic security of the women in their household. Genesis 38 and the book of Ruth illustrate this practice.

26:5 Jacob's mother (Rebekah) was an Aramean (Genesis 24:10; 25:20, 26), and Jacob also lived in Aram for many years (Genesis 31:41-42). His lifestyle was seminomadic, hence "wandering." Jacob and his family totaled only seventy when they went to Egypt (see Genesis 46:27; Exodus 1:5).

"Listen...!
The LORD
is our
God, the LORD
alone."

DEUTERONOMY
6:4

their slaves, ⁷we cried out to the Lord, the God of our ancestors. He heard our cries and saw our hardship, toil, and oppression. ⁸So the Lord brought us out of Egypt with a strong hand and powerful arm, with overwhelming terror, and with miraculous signs and wonders. ⁹He brought us to this place and gave us this land flowing with milk and honey! ¹⁰And now, O Lord, I have brought you the first portion of the harvest you have given me from the ground.' Then place the produce before the Lord your God, and bow to the ground in worship before him. ¹¹Afterward you may go and celebrate because of all the good things the Lord your God has given to you and your household. Remember to include the Levites and the foreigners living among you in the celebration.

¹²"Every third year you must offer a special tithe of your crops. In this year of the special tithe you must give your tithes to the Levites, foreigners, orphans, and widows, so that they will have enough to eat in your towns. ¹³Then you must declare in the presence of the Lord your God, 'I have taken the sacred gift from my house and have given it to the Levites, foreigners, orphans, and widows, just as you commanded me. I have not violated or forgotten any of your commands. ¹⁴I have not eaten any of it while in mourning; I have not handled it while I was ceremonially unclean; and I have not offered any of it to the dead. I have obeyed the Lord my God and have done everything you commanded me. ¹⁵Now look down from your holy dwelling place in heaven and bless your people Israel and the land you swore to our ancestors to give us—a land flowing with milk and honey.'

A Call to Obey the Lord's Commands

¹⁶"Today the Lord your God has commanded you to obey all these decrees and regulations. So be careful to obey them wholeheartedly. ¹⁷You have declared today that the Lord is your God. And you have promised to walk in his ways, and to obey his decrees, commands, and regulations, and to do everything he tells you. ¹⁸The Lord has declared today that you are his people, his own special treasure, just as he promised, and that you must obey all his commands. ¹⁹And if you do, he will set you high above all the other nations he has made. Then you will receive praise, honor, and renown. You will be a nation that is holy to the Lord your God, just as he promised."

The Altar on Mount Ebal

27 Then Moses and the leaders of Israel gave this charge to the people: "Obey all these commands that I am giving you today. ²When you cross the Jordan River and enter the land the Lord your God is giving you, set up some large stones and coat them with plaster. ³Write this whole body of instruction on them when you cross the river to enter the land the Lord your God is giving you—a land flowing with milk and honey, just as the Lord, the God of your ancestors, promised you. ⁴When you cross the Jordan, set up these stones at Mount Ebal and coat them with plaster, as I am commanding you today.

⁵"Then build an altar there to the Lord your God, using natural, uncut stones. You must not shape the stones with an iron tool. ⁶Build the altar of uncut stones, and use it to offer burnt offerings to the Lord your God. ⁷Also sacrifice peace offerings on it, and celebrate by feasting there before the Lord your God. ⁸You must clearly write all these instructions on the stones coated with plaster."

⁹Then Moses and the Levitical priests addressed all Israel as follows: "O Israel, be quiet and listen! Today you have become the people of the Lord your God. ¹⁰So you must obey the Lord your God by keeping all these commands and decrees that I am giving you today."

Curses from Mount Ebal

¹¹That same day Moses also gave this charge to the people: ¹²"When you cross the Jordan River, the tribes of Simeon, Levi, Judah, Issachar, Joseph, and Benjamin must stand on Mount Gerizim to proclaim a blessing over the people. ¹³And the tribes of Reuben, Gad, Asher, Zebulun, Dan, and Naphtali must stand on Mount Ebal to proclaim a curse.

¹⁴"Then the Levites will shout to all the people of Israel:

¹⁵'Cursed is anyone who carves or casts an idol and secretly sets it up. These idols, the work of craftsmen, are detestable to the Lord.'
 And all the people will reply, 'Amen.'

¹⁶'Cursed is anyone who dishonors father or mother.'
 And all the people will reply, 'Amen.'

26:16-19 Having laid out the great covenant principles (5:1–11:32) and clarified their application (12:1–26:15), Moses urged the people to obey the covenant with all their hearts. The Lord had called them into a special relationship, a privilege that required obedience to the covenant prescriptions. The result of this submission was holiness, a state that reflected God's character and that would flow naturally from unbroken fellowship with him.
27:9-10 Relationship precedes obedience. Throughout the Bible, obedience to God's commands is not a precondition for a relationship with God, but rather is the expression of that relationship. Israel's obedience would allow them to fulfill their mission to be a "kingdom of priests," showing the nations who God was (Exodus 19:5-6). The apostle Paul expressed concern for those who "depend on the law to make them right with God" (Galatians 3:10), but even in Old Testament times, the law was never intended to earn a relationship with God. Instead, it was a grateful response for the Lord's deliverance.
27:11-26 Four of the twelve curses forbid engaging in certain sexual behaviors. Three of these banned a man from intercourse with women in his extended family. This protected women from a predatory man who was supposed to be a source of protection in that culture. All four sexual taboos addressed behavior that could easily remain secret, indicating that people are accountable to God even in so-called private behavior.

17 'Cursed is anyone who steals property from a neighbor by moving a boundary marker.'
And all the people will reply, 'Amen.'

18 'Cursed is anyone who leads a blind person astray on the road.'
And all the people will reply, 'Amen.'

19 'Cursed is anyone who denies justice to foreigners, orphans, or widows.'
And all the people will reply, 'Amen.'

20 'Cursed is anyone who has sexual intercourse with one of his father's wives, for he has violated his father.'
And all the people will reply, 'Amen.'

21 'Cursed is anyone who has sexual intercourse with an animal.'
And all the people will reply, 'Amen.'

22 'Cursed is anyone who has sexual intercourse with his sister, whether she is the daughter of his father or his mother.'
And all the people will reply, 'Amen.'

23 'Cursed is anyone who has sexual intercourse with his mother-in-law.'
And all the people will reply, 'Amen.'

24 'Cursed is anyone who attacks a neighbor in secret.'
And all the people will reply, 'Amen.'

25 'Cursed is anyone who accepts payment to kill an innocent person.'
And all the people will reply, 'Amen.'

26 'Cursed is anyone who does not affirm and obey the terms of these instructions.'
And all the people will reply, 'Amen.'

Blessings for Obedience

28 "If you fully obey the Lord your God and carefully keep all his commands that I am giving you today, the Lord your God will set you high above all the nations of the world. 2 You will experience all these blessings if you obey the Lord your God:

3 Your towns and your fields
will be blessed.
4 Your children and your crops
will be blessed.
The offspring of your herds and flocks
will be blessed.
5 Your fruit baskets and breadboards
will be blessed.
6 Wherever you go and whatever you do,
you will be blessed.

7 "The Lord will conquer your enemies when they attack you. They will attack you from one direction, but they will scatter from you in seven!

8 "The Lord will guarantee a blessing on everything you do and will fill your storehouses with grain. The Lord your God will bless you in the land he is giving you.

9 "If you obey the commands of the Lord your God and walk in his ways, the Lord will establish you as his holy people as he swore he would do. 10 Then all the nations of the world will see that you are a people claimed by the Lord, and they will stand in awe of you.

11 "The Lord will give you prosperity in the land he swore to your ancestors to give you, blessing you with many children, numerous livestock, and abundant crops. 12 The Lord will send rain at the proper time from his rich treasury in the heavens and will bless all the work you do. You will lend to many nations, but you will never need to borrow from them. 13 If you listen to these commands of the Lord your God that I am giving you today, and if you carefully obey them, the Lord will make you the head and not the tail, and you will always be on top and never at the bottom. 14 You must not turn away from any of the commands I am giving you today, nor follow after other gods and worship them.

Curses for Disobedience

15 "But if you refuse to listen to the Lord your God and do not obey all the commands and decrees I am giving you today, all these curses will come and overwhelm you:

16 Your towns and your fields
will be cursed.
17 Your fruit baskets and breadboards
will be cursed.
18 Your children and your crops
will be cursed.
The offspring of your herds and flocks
will be cursed.
19 Wherever you go and whatever you do,
you will be cursed.

20 "The Lord himself will send on you curses, confusion, and frustration in everything you do, until at last

---

28:9-10 The blessings for obedience not only provided security from the surrounding nations, but also material provision in a culture where meeting everyday needs was often hard. Beyond these benefits, though, obedience enabled Israel to fulfill its call to be God's "holy nation" and show the other nations what the Lord was like (Exodus 19:5-6). In other words, while obedience resulted in blessing, the blessing wasn't solely for Israel's benefit.

28:15-20 This section of Deuteronomy raises the question of how a loving God could send curses on people. It might be better to ask, however, how people who have experienced God's deliverance can fail to express love for him and fairly represent him to the world. The curses are consequences, and God gave his people every opportunity to avoid those consequences. Even amid these daunting curses, God displayed his desire for the people to return to him.

you are completely destroyed for doing evil and abandoning me. ²¹The LORD will afflict you with diseases until none of you are left in the land you are about to enter and occupy. ²²The LORD will strike you with wasting diseases, fever, and inflammation, with scorching heat and drought, and with blight and mildew. These disasters will pursue you until you die. ²³The skies above will be as unyielding as bronze, and the earth beneath will be as hard as iron. ²⁴The LORD will change the rain that falls on your land into powder, and dust will pour down from the sky until you are destroyed.

²⁵"The LORD will cause you to be defeated by your enemies. You will attack your enemies from one direction, but you will scatter from them in seven! You will be an object of horror to all the kingdoms of the earth. ²⁶Your corpses will be food for all the scavenging birds and wild animals, and no one will be there to chase them away.

²⁷"The LORD will afflict you with the boils of Egypt and with tumors, scurvy, and the itch, from which you cannot be cured. ²⁸The LORD will strike you with madness, blindness, and panic. ²⁹You will grope around in broad daylight like a blind person groping in the darkness, but you will not find your way. You will be oppressed and robbed continually, and no one will come to save you.

³⁰"You will be engaged to a woman, but another man will sleep with her. You will build a house, but someone else will live in it. You will plant a vineyard, but you will never enjoy its fruit. ³¹Your ox will be butchered before your eyes, but you will not eat a single bite of the meat. Your donkey will be taken from you, never to be returned. Your sheep and goats will be given to your enemies, and no one will be there to help you. ³²You will watch as your sons and daughters are taken away as slaves. Your heart will break for them, but you won't be able to help them. ³³A foreign nation you have never heard about will eat the crops you worked so hard to grow. You will suffer under constant oppression and harsh treatment. ³⁴You will go mad because of all the tragedy you see around you. ³⁵The LORD will cover your knees and legs with incurable boils. In fact, you will be covered from head to foot.

³⁶"The LORD will exile you and your king to a nation unknown to you and your ancestors. There in exile you will worship gods of wood and stone! ³⁷You will become an object of horror, ridicule, and mockery among all the nations to which the LORD sends you.

³⁸"You will plant much but harvest little, for locusts will eat your crops. ³⁹You will plant vineyards and care for them, but you will not drink the wine or eat the grapes, for worms will destroy the vines. ⁴⁰You will grow olive trees throughout your land, but you will never use the olive oil, for the fruit will drop before it ripens. ⁴¹You will have sons and daughters, but you will lose them, for they will be led away into captivity. ⁴²Swarms of insects will destroy your trees and crops.

⁴³"The foreigners living among you will become stronger and stronger, while you become weaker and weaker. ⁴⁴They will lend money to you, but you will not lend to them. They will be the head, and you will be the tail!

⁴⁵"If you refuse to listen to the LORD your God and to obey the commands and decrees he has given you, all these curses will pursue and overtake you until you are destroyed. ⁴⁶These horrors will serve as a sign and warning among you and your descendants forever. ⁴⁷If you do not serve the LORD your God with joy and enthusiasm for the abundant benefits you have received, ⁴⁸you will serve your enemies whom the LORD will send against you. You will be left hungry, thirsty, naked, and lacking in everything. The LORD will put an iron yoke on your neck, oppressing you harshly until he has destroyed you.

⁴⁹"The LORD will bring a distant nation against you from the end of the earth, and it will swoop down on you like a vulture. It is a nation whose language you do not understand, ⁵⁰a fierce and heartless nation that shows no respect for the old and no pity for the young. ⁵¹Its armies will devour your livestock and crops, and you will be destroyed. They will leave you no grain, new wine, olive oil, calves, or lambs, and you will starve to death. ⁵²They will attack your cities until all the fortified walls in your land—the walls you trusted to protect you—are knocked down. They will attack all the towns in the land the LORD your God has given you.

⁵³"The siege and terrible distress of the enemy's attack will be so severe that you will eat the flesh of your own sons and daughters, whom the LORD your God has given you. ⁵⁴The most tenderhearted man among you will have no compassion for his own brother, his beloved wife, and his surviving children. ⁵⁵He will refuse to share with them the flesh he is devouring—the flesh of one of his own children—because he has nothing else to eat during the siege and terrible distress that your enemy will inflict on all your towns. ⁵⁶The most tender and delicate woman among you—so delicate she would not so much as touch the ground with her foot—will be selfish toward the husband she loves and toward her own son or daughter. ⁵⁷She will hide from them the afterbirth and the new baby she has borne, so that she herself can secretly eat them. She will have nothing else to eat during the siege and terrible distress that your enemy will inflict on all your towns.

⁵⁸"If you refuse to obey all the words of instruction that are written in this book, and if you do not fear the glorious and awesome name of the LORD your God, ⁵⁹then the LORD will overwhelm you and your children with indescribable plagues. These plagues will be intense and without relief, making you miserable and unbearably sick. ⁶⁰He will afflict you with all the diseases of Egypt that you feared so much, and you will have no relief. ⁶¹The LORD will afflict you with every sickness and plague there is, even those

not mentioned in this Book of Instruction, until you are destroyed. ⁶²Though you become as numerous as the stars in the sky, few of you will be left because you would not listen to the LORD your God.

⁶³"Just as the LORD has found great pleasure in causing you to prosper and multiply, the LORD will find pleasure in destroying you. You will be torn from the land you are about to enter and occupy. ⁶⁴For the LORD will scatter you among all the nations from one end of the earth to the other. There you will worship foreign gods that neither you nor your ancestors have known, gods made of wood and stone! ⁶⁵There among those nations you will find no peace or place to rest. And the LORD will cause your heart to tremble, your eyesight to fail, and your soul to despair. ⁶⁶Your life will constantly hang in the balance. You will live night and day in fear, unsure if you will survive. ⁶⁷In the morning you will say, 'If only it were night!' And in the evening you will say, 'If only it were morning!' For you will be terrified by the awful horrors you see around you. ⁶⁸Then the LORD will send you back to Egypt in ships, to a destination I promised you would never see again. There you will offer to sell yourselves to your enemies as slaves, but no one will buy you."

29
¹*These are the terms of the covenant the LORD commanded Moses to make with the Israelites while they were in the land of Moab, in addition to the covenant he had made with them at Mount Sinai.*

Moses Reviews the Covenant

²*Moses summoned all the Israelites and said to them, "You have seen with your own eyes everything the LORD did in the land of Egypt to Pharaoh and to all his servants and to his whole country—³all the great tests of strength, the miraculous signs, and the amazing wonders. ⁴But to this day the LORD has not given you minds that understand, nor eyes that see, nor ears that hear! ⁵For forty years I led you through the wilderness, yet your clothes and sandals did not wear out. ⁶You ate no bread and drank no wine or other alcoholic drink, but he provided for you so you would know that he is the LORD your God.

⁷"When we came here, King Sihon of Heshbon and King Og of Bashan came out to fight against us, but we defeated them. ⁸We took their land and gave it to the tribes of Reuben and Gad and to the half-tribe of Manasseh as their grant of land.

⁹"Therefore, obey the terms of this covenant so that you will prosper in everything you do. ¹⁰All of you—tribal leaders, elders, officers, all the men of Israel—are standing today in the presence of the LORD your God. ¹¹Your little ones and your wives are with you, as well as the foreigners living among you who chop your wood and carry your water. ¹²You are standing here today to enter into the covenant of the LORD your God. The LORD is making this covenant, including the curses. ¹³By entering into the covenant today, he will establish you as his people and confirm that he is your God, just as he promised you and as he swore to your ancestors Abraham, Isaac, and Jacob.

¹⁴"But you are not the only ones with whom I am making this covenant with its curses. ¹⁵I am making this covenant both with you who stand here today in the presence of the LORD our God, and also with the future generations who are not standing here today.

¹⁶"You remember how we lived in the land of Egypt and how we traveled through the lands of enemy nations as we left. ¹⁷You have seen their detestable practices and their idols* made of wood, stone, silver, and gold. ¹⁸I am making this covenant with you so that no one among you—no man, woman, clan, or tribe—will turn away from the LORD our God to worship these gods of other nations, and so that no root among you bears bitter and poisonous fruit.

¹⁹"Those who hear the warnings of this curse should not congratulate themselves, thinking, 'I am safe, even though I am following the desires of my own stubborn heart.' This would lead to utter ruin! ²⁰The LORD will never pardon such people. Instead his anger and jealousy will burn against them. All the curses written in this book will come down on them, and the LORD will erase their names from under heaven. ²¹The LORD will separate them from all the tribes of Israel, to pour out on them all the curses of the covenant recorded in this Book of Instruction.

²²"Then the generations to come, both your own descendants and the foreigners who come from distant lands, will see the devastation of the land and the diseases the LORD inflicts on it. ²³They will exclaim, 'The whole land is devastated by sulfur and salt. It is a wasteland with nothing planted and nothing growing, not even a blade of grass. It is like the cities of Sodom and Gomorrah, Admah and Zeboiim, which the LORD destroyed in his intense anger.'

29:1a Verse 29:1 is numbered 28:69 in Hebrew text. **29:1b** Hebrew *Horeb*, another name for Sinai. **29:2** Verses 29:2-29 are numbered 29:1-28 in Hebrew text. **29:17** The Hebrew term (literally *round things*) probably alludes to dung.

29:2–30:20 Anticipating his death, Moses composed a farewell address, briefly reviewing Israel's history since the Exodus. He charged the nation to pledge their fidelity to the Lord. This section of Deuteronomy makes it clear that grace is not just a New Testament doctrine: It undergirds every aspect of Israel's relationship with the Lord.

29:15 The covenant made with Moses' generation was also for generations yet to be born. Abraham's descendants of the future would have the privileges of the covenant, but they would also need to obey it personally to enjoy its blessings (see 4:9).

24 "And all the surrounding nations will ask, 'Why has the LORD done this to this land? Why was he so angry?'

25 "And the answer will be, 'This happened because the people of the land abandoned the covenant that the LORD, the God of their ancestors, made with them when he brought them out of the land of Egypt. 26 Instead, they turned away to serve and worship gods they had not known before, gods that were not from the LORD. 27 That is why the LORD's anger has burned against this land, bringing down on it every curse recorded in this book. 28 In great anger and fury the LORD uprooted his people from their land and banished them to another land, where they still live today!'

29 "The LORD our God has secrets known to no one. We are not accountable for them, but we and our

Oikos Image — My Story with Family & Friends

Family Flourishing: I Want You to Love Jesus for the Rest of Your Life

SCRIPTURE CONNECTION: DEUTERONOMY 30:1-10

My eight-year-old grandson and I had a "Samuel and Eli" moment. He asked, "Lovie [my grandmother name], have you ever heard God talk to you? Like, have you ever heard his voice?"

I thought a moment and said, "No, not exactly. Have you?"

"The other night," he said, his eyes shining. "When everyone else was asleep, I felt a hand on my shoulder."

"Were you afraid?" I asked, knowing I might have been scared. (Now I admit, I wonder if he might have been dreaming.)

"No! I was really, really happy!"

"Well, what did God say to you?"

"God said, 'I want you to love Jesus for the rest of your life.'"

My heart leapt! I can't say for sure that my grandson literally heard God's voice, but I do think these are words God wants us to hear. And why was I, a grandmother, hearing these words from my grandchild? Maybe it's because I believe God wants to raise a generation of resilient disciples. A generation who will bend and flex but not break under the weight of an increasingly secular culture. A generation who will love Jesus for the rest of their lives. May my grandson and the children we love so dearly be a part of that generation of resilient disciples. And may they indeed love Jesus for the rest of their lives.

> God wants you to love Jesus for the rest of your life.

IMAGINE

The Bible repeatedly shows a pathway to family flourishing: Trust, obey, and love God with all your hearts. How can we put those steps into practice as a pathway for our families?

Do the children you love know why you are loving Jesus for the rest of your life?

"God may have given me this special moment with my grandson, but I believe he longs to hear these words from every follower of Jesus. The children and youth of our families and communities can witness our love for Jesus as the beginning of their own journey."

VALERIE BELL is an author of several books on children, including *RESILIENT: Child Discipleship and the Fearless Future of the Church*. Valerie serves as Awana's CEO emerita and 2050 vision caster.

children are accountable forever for all that he has revealed to us, so that we may obey all the terms of these instructions.

A Call to Return to the LORD

30 "In the future, when you experience all these blessings and curses I have listed for you, and when you are living among the nations to which the LORD your God has exiled you, take to heart all these instructions. ²If at that time you and your children return to the LORD your God, and if you obey with all your heart and all your soul all the commands I have given you today, ³then the LORD your God will restore your fortunes. He will have mercy on you and gather you back from all the nations where he has scattered you. ⁴Even though you are banished to the ends of the earth,* the LORD your God will gather you from there and bring you back again. ⁵The LORD your God will return you to the land that belonged to your ancestors, and you will possess that land again. Then he will make you even more prosperous and numerous than your ancestors!

⁶"The LORD your God will change your heart* and the hearts of all your descendants, so that you will love him with all your heart and soul and so you may live! ⁷The LORD your God will inflict all these curses on your enemies and on those who hate and persecute you. ⁸Then you will again obey the LORD and keep all his commands that I am giving you today.

⁹"The LORD your God will then make you successful in everything you do. He will give you many children and numerous livestock, and he will cause your fields to produce abundant harvests, for the LORD will again delight in being good to you as he was to your ancestors. ¹⁰The LORD your God will delight in you if you obey his voice and keep the commands and decrees written in this Book of Instruction, and if you turn to the LORD your God with all your heart and soul.

The Choice of Life or Death

¹¹"This command I am giving you today is not too difficult for you, and it is not beyond your reach. ¹²It is not kept in heaven, so distant that you must ask, 'Who will go up to heaven and bring it down so we can hear it and obey?' ¹³It is not kept beyond the sea, so far away that you must ask, 'Who will cross the sea to bring it to us so we can hear it and obey?' ¹⁴No, the message is very close at hand; it is on your lips and in your heart so that you can obey it.

¹⁵"Now listen! Today I am giving you a choice between life and death, between prosperity and disaster. ¹⁶For I command you this day to love the LORD your God and to keep his commands, decrees, and regulations by walking in his ways. If you do this, you will live and multiply, and the LORD your God will bless you and the land you are about to enter and occupy.

¹⁷"But if your heart turns away and you refuse to listen, and if you are drawn away to serve and worship other gods, ¹⁸then I warn you now that you will certainly be destroyed. You will not live a long, good life in the land you are crossing the Jordan to occupy.

¹⁹"Today I have given you the choice between life and death, between blessings and curses. Now I call on heaven and earth to witness the choice you make. Oh, that you would choose life, so that you and your descendants might live! ²⁰You can make this choice by loving the LORD your God, obeying him, and committing yourself firmly to him. This* is the key to your life. And if you love and obey the LORD, you will live long in the land the LORD swore to give your ancestors Abraham, Isaac, and Jacob."

Joshua Becomes Israel's Leader

31 When Moses had finished giving these instructions* to all the people of Israel, ²he said, "I am now 120 years old, and I am no longer able to lead you. The LORD has told me, 'You will not cross the Jordan River.' ³But the LORD your God himself will cross over ahead of you. He will destroy the nations living there, and you will take possession of their land. Joshua will lead you across the river, just as the LORD promised.

⁴"The LORD will destroy the nations living in the land, just as he destroyed Sihon and Og, the kings of the Amorites. ⁵The LORD will hand over to you the people who live there, and you must deal with them as I have commanded you. ⁶So be strong and courageous! Do not be afraid and do not panic before them. For the LORD your God will personally go ahead of you. He will neither fail you nor abandon you."

30:4 Hebrew *of the heavens.* **30:6** Hebrew *circumcise your heart.* **30:20** Or *He.* **31:1** As in Dead Sea Scrolls and Greek version; Masoretic Text reads *Moses went and spoke.*

30:11-20 Adherence to the covenant terms that Moses had outlined would give life; disobedience would surely bring death. Life and death refer to physical, mortal life in the land—of individuals and of the community of Israel.

30:20 In its most meaningful sense, "This is the key to your life" means that life consists of absolute commitment to the Lord. By following God and living in his ways, we can experience the abundance of life as God intended (John 10:10).

31:9-13 Despite Deuteronomy's tendency to address men, especially heads of households, the book explicitly includes women, children, and foreigners in the covenant renewal (see 29:11) and in the reading of the Book of Instruction (31:12). This reading ensured that each generation passed on to the next generation their history with God and God's covenant teachings. Women undoubtedly played an essential role in passing along this knowledge to their children.

[7] Then Moses called for Joshua, and as all Israel watched, he said to him, "Be strong and courageous! For you will lead these people into the land that the LORD swore to their ancestors he would give them. You are the one who will divide it among them as their grants of land. [8] Do not be afraid or discouraged, for the LORD will personally go ahead of you. He will be with you; he will neither fail you nor abandon you."

Public Reading of the Book of Instruction

[9] So Moses wrote this entire body of instruction in a book and gave it to the priests, who carried the Ark of the LORD's Covenant, and to the elders of Israel. [10] Then Moses gave them this command: "At the end of every seventh year, the Year of Release, during the Festival of Shelters, [11] you must read this Book of Instruction to all the people of Israel when they assemble before the LORD your God at the place he chooses. [12] Call them all together—men, women, children, and the foreigners living in your towns—so they may hear this Book of Instruction and learn to fear the LORD your God and carefully obey all the terms of these instructions. [13] Do this so that your children who have not known these instructions will hear them and will learn to fear the LORD your God. Do this as long as you live in the land you are crossing the Jordan to occupy."

Israel's Disobedience Predicted

[14] Then the LORD said to Moses, "The time has come for you to die. Call Joshua and present yourselves at the Tabernacle,* so that I may commission him there." So Moses and Joshua went and presented themselves at the Tabernacle. [15] And the LORD appeared to them in a pillar of cloud that stood at the entrance to the sacred tent.

[16] The LORD said to Moses, "You are about to die and join your ancestors. After you are gone, these people will begin to worship foreign gods, the gods of the land where they are going. They will abandon me and break my covenant that I have made with them. [17] Then my anger will blaze forth against them. I will abandon them, hiding my face from them, and they will be devoured. Terrible trouble will come down on them, and on that day they will say, 'These disasters have come down on us because God is no longer among us!' [18] At that time I will hide my face from them on account of all the evil they commit by worshiping other gods.

[19] "So write down the words of this song, and teach it to the people of Israel. Help them learn it, so it may serve as a witness for me against them. [20] For I will bring them into the land I swore to give their ancestors—a land flowing with milk and honey. There they will become prosperous, eat all the food they want, and become fat. But they will begin to worship other gods; they will despise me and break my covenant. [21] And when great disasters come down on them, this song will stand as evidence against them, for it will never be forgotten by their descendants. I know the intentions of these people, even now before they have entered the land I swore to give them."

[22] So that very day Moses wrote down the words of the song and taught it to the Israelites.

[23] Then the LORD commissioned Joshua son of Nun with these words: "Be strong and courageous, for you must bring the people of Israel into the land I swore to give them. I will be with you."

[24] When Moses had finished writing this entire body of instruction in a book, [25] he gave this command to the Levites who carried the Ark of the LORD's Covenant: [26] "Take this Book of Instruction and place it beside the Ark of the Covenant of the LORD your God, so it may remain there as a witness against the people of Israel. [27] For I know how rebellious and stubborn you are. Even now, while I am still alive and am here with you, you have rebelled against the LORD. How much more rebellious will you be after my death!

[28] "Now summon all the elders and officials of your tribes, so that I can speak to them directly and call

---

> "We are not rich, not great, but we are happy. Getting our daily bread direct from the loving hands of our heavenly Father,... depending altogether on our Father God, we have nothing to fear from anybody, nothing to lose, and nothing to regret. The Lord is our inexhaustible treasure."
>
> **PANDITA RAMABAI**
> (1858–1922) educator and social activist

31:14 Hebrew *Tent of Meeting*; also in 31:14b.

heaven and earth to witness against them. ²⁹I know that after my death you will become utterly corrupt and will turn from the way I have commanded you to follow. In the days to come, disaster will come down on you, for you will do what is evil in the LORD's sight, making him very angry with your actions."

The Song of Moses

³⁰So Moses recited this entire song publicly to the assembly of Israel:

32 "Listen, O heavens, and I will speak!
  Hear, O earth, the words that I say!
² Let my teaching fall on you like rain;
  let my speech settle like dew.
Let my words fall like rain on tender grass,
  like gentle showers on young plants.
³ I will proclaim the name of the LORD;
  how glorious is our God!
⁴ He is the Rock; his deeds are perfect.
  Everything he does is just and fair.
He is a faithful God who does no wrong;
  how just and upright he is!

⁵ "But they have acted corruptly toward him;
  when they act so perversely,
  are they really his children?*
  They are a deceitful and twisted generation.
⁶ Is this the way you repay the LORD,
  you foolish and senseless people?
Isn't he your Father who created you?
  Has he not made you and established you?
⁷ Remember the days of long ago;
  think about the generations past.
Ask your father, and he will inform you.
  Inquire of your elders, and they will tell you.
⁸ When the Most High assigned lands to the nations,
  when he divided up the human race,
he established the boundaries of the peoples
  according to the number in his heavenly court.*

⁹ "For the people of Israel belong to the LORD;
  Jacob is his special possession.
¹⁰ He found them in a desert land,
  in an empty, howling wasteland.
He surrounded them and watched over them;
  he guarded them as he would guard his own eyes.*
¹¹ Like an eagle that rouses her chicks
  and hovers over her young,
so he spread his wings to take them up
  and carried them safely on his pinions.
¹² The LORD alone guided them;
  they followed no foreign gods.
¹³ He let them ride over the highlands
  and feast on the crops of the fields.
He nourished them with honey from the rock
  and olive oil from the stony ground.
¹⁴ He fed them yogurt from the herd
  and milk from the flock,
  together with the fat of lambs.
He gave them choice rams from Bashan, and goats,
  together with the choicest wheat.
You drank the finest wine,
  made from the juice of grapes.

¹⁵ "But Israel* soon became fat and unruly;
  the people grew heavy, plump, and stuffed!
Then they abandoned the God who had made them;
  they made light of the Rock of their salvation.
¹⁶ They stirred up his jealousy by worshiping foreign gods;
  they provoked his fury with detestable deeds.
¹⁷ They offered sacrifices to demons, which are not God,
  to gods they had not known before,
  to new gods only recently arrived,
  to gods their ancestors had never feared.
¹⁸ You neglected the Rock who had fathered you;
  you forgot the God who had given you birth.

¹⁹ "The LORD saw this and drew back,
  provoked to anger by his own sons and daughters.
²⁰ He said, 'I will abandon them;
  then see what becomes of them.
For they are a twisted generation,
  children without integrity.
²¹ They have roused my jealousy by worshiping things that are not God;
  they have provoked my anger with their useless idols.
Now I will rouse their jealousy through people who are not even a people;
  I will provoke their anger through the foolish Gentiles.
²² For my anger blazes forth like fire
  and burns to the depths of the grave.*

32:5 The meaning of the Hebrew is uncertain. **32:8** As in Dead Sea Scrolls, which read *the number of the sons of God,* and Greek version, which reads *the number of the angels of God;* Masoretic Text reads *the number of the sons of Israel.* **32:10** Hebrew *as the pupil of his eye.* **32:15** Hebrew *Jeshurun,* a term of endearment for Israel. **32:22** Hebrew *of Sheol.*

32:1-43 Knowing his people would turn to other gods, the Lord gave Israel a song to memorize. When they turned away, this song would remind them of God's deliverance and faithfulness and of their covenant obligations (31:19-21). In the ancient Near East, losing to a foreign power suggested that one's deity could not or would not protect its people. By contrast, this song told the people that God himself would be the reason for their defeat and subjugation (32:19-25). However, Israel's enemies would also face God's judgment (32:36-43).

It devours the earth and all its crops
  and ignites the foundations of the
    mountains.
²³ I will heap disasters upon them
  and shoot them down with my arrows.
²⁴ I will weaken them with famine,
  burning fever, and deadly disease.
I will send the fangs of wild beasts
  and poisonous snakes that glide in
    the dust.
²⁵ Outside, the sword will bring death,
  and inside, terror will strike
both young men and young women,
  both infants and the aged.
²⁶ I would have annihilated them,
  wiping out even the memory of them.
²⁷ But I feared the taunt of Israel's enemy,
  who might misunderstand and say,
"Our own power has triumphed!
  The LORD had nothing to do with this!"

²⁸ "But Israel is a senseless nation;
  the people are foolish, without
    understanding.
²⁹ Oh, that they were wise and could
    understand this!
  Oh, that they might know their fate!
³⁰ How could one person chase a thousand of
    them,
  and two people put ten thousand to flight,
unless their Rock had sold them,
  unless the LORD had given them up?
³¹ But the rock of our enemies is not like our
    Rock,
  as even they recognize.*
³² Their vine grows from the vine of Sodom,
  from the vineyards of Gomorrah.
Their grapes are poison,
  and their clusters are bitter.
³³ Their wine is the venom of serpents,
  the deadly poison of cobras.

³⁴ "The LORD says, 'Am I not storing up these things,
  sealing them away in my treasury?
³⁵ I will take revenge; I will pay them back.
  In due time their feet will slip.
Their day of disaster will arrive,
  and their destiny will overtake them.'

³⁶ "Indeed, the LORD will give justice to his people,
  and he will change his mind about* his
    servants,
when he sees their strength is gone
  and no one is left, slave or free.
³⁷ Then he will ask, 'Where are their gods,
  the rocks they fled to for refuge?

³⁸ Where now are those gods,
  who ate the fat of their sacrifices
  and drank the wine of their offerings?
Let those gods arise and help you!
  Let them provide you with shelter!
³⁹ Look now; I myself am he!
  There is no other god but me!
I am the one who kills and gives life;
  I am the one who wounds and heals;
  no one can be rescued from my powerful
    hand!
⁴⁰ Now I raise my hand to heaven
  and declare, "As surely as I live,
⁴¹ when I sharpen my flashing sword
  and begin to carry out justice,
I will take revenge on my enemies
  and repay those who reject me.
⁴² I will make my arrows drunk with blood,
  and my sword will devour flesh—
the blood of the slaughtered and the captives,
  and the heads of the enemy leaders."'

⁴³ "Rejoice with him, you heavens,
  and let all of God's angels worship him.*
Rejoice with his people, you Gentiles,
  and let all the angels be strengthened in him.*
For he will avenge the blood of his children*;
  he will take revenge against his enemies.
He will repay those who hate him*
  and cleanse his people's land."

⁴⁴So Moses came with Joshua* son of Nun and recited all the words of this song to the people.

⁴⁵When Moses had finished reciting all these words to the people of Israel, ⁴⁶he added: "Take to heart all the words of warning I have given you today. Pass them on as a command to your children so they will obey every word of these instructions. ⁴⁷These instructions are not empty words—they are your life! By obeying them you will enjoy a long life in the land you will occupy when you cross the Jordan River."

Moses' Death Foretold

⁴⁸That same day the LORD said to Moses, ⁴⁹"Go to Moab, to the mountains east of the river,* and climb Mount Nebo, which is across from Jericho. Look out across the land of Canaan, the land I am giving to the people of Israel as their own special possession. ⁵⁰Then you will die there on the mountain. You will join your ancestors, just as Aaron, your brother, died on Mount Hor and joined his ancestors. ⁵¹For both of you betrayed me with the Israelites at the waters of Meribah at Kadesh* in the wilderness of Zin. You failed to demonstrate my holiness to the people of

---

32:31 The meaning of the Hebrew is uncertain. Greek version reads *our enemies are fools.* **32:36** Or *will take revenge for.* **32:43a** As in Dead Sea Scrolls and Greek version; Masoretic Text lacks the first two lines. Compare Heb 1:6. **32:43b** As in Greek version; Hebrew text lacks this sentence. Compare Rom 15:10. **32:43c** As in Dead Sea Scrolls and Greek version; Masoretic Text reads *his servants.* **32:43d** As in Dead Sea Scrolls and Greek version; Masoretic Text lacks this line. **32:44** Hebrew *Hoshea,* a variant name for Joshua. **32:49** Hebrew *the mountains of Abarim.* **32:51** Hebrew *waters of Meribath-kadesh.*

Israel there. ⁵²So you will see the land from a distance, but you may not enter the land I am giving to the people of Israel."

Moses Blesses the People

33 This is the blessing that Moses, the man of God, gave to the people of Israel before his death:

² "The LORD came from Mount Sinai
and dawned upon us* from Mount Seir;
he shone forth from Mount Paran
and came from Meribah-kadesh
with flaming fire at his right hand.*
³ Indeed, he loves his people;*
all his holy ones are in his hands.
They follow in his steps
and accept his teaching.
⁴ Moses gave us the LORD's instruction,
the special possession of the people of Israel.*
⁵ The LORD became king in Israel*—
when the leaders of the people assembled,
when the tribes of Israel gathered as one."

⁶Moses said this about the tribe of Reuben:*

"Let the tribe of Reuben live and not die out,
though they are few in number."

⁷Moses said this about the tribe of Judah:

"O LORD, hear the cry of Judah
and bring them together as a people.
Give them strength to defend their cause;
help them against their enemies!"

⁸Moses said this about the tribe of Levi:

"O LORD, you have given your Thummim and Urim—the sacred lots—
to your faithful servants the Levites.*
You put them to the test at Massah
and struggled with them at the waters of Meribah.
⁹ The Levites obeyed your word
and guarded your covenant.
They were more loyal to you
than to their own parents.
They ignored their relatives
and did not acknowledge their own children.
¹⁰ They teach your regulations to Jacob;
they give your instructions to Israel.
They present incense before you
and offer whole burnt offerings on the altar.
¹¹ Bless the ministry of the Levites, O LORD,
and accept all the work of their hands.
Hit their enemies where it hurts the most;
strike down their foes so they never rise again."

¹²Moses said this about the tribe of Benjamin:

"The people of Benjamin are loved by the LORD
and live in safety beside him.
He surrounds them continuously
and preserves them from every harm."

¹³Moses said this about the tribes of Joseph:

"May their land be blessed by the LORD
with the precious gift of dew from the heavens
and water from beneath the earth;
¹⁴ with the rich fruit that grows in the sun,
and the rich harvest produced each month;
¹⁵ with the finest crops of the ancient mountains,
and the abundance from the everlasting hills;
¹⁶ with the best gifts of the earth and its bounty,
and the favor of the one who appeared in the burning bush.
May these blessings rest on Joseph's head,
crowning the brow of the prince among his brothers.
¹⁷ Joseph has the majesty of a young bull;
he has the horns of a wild ox.
He will gore distant nations,
even to the ends of the earth.
This is my blessing for the multitudes of Ephraim
and the thousands of Manasseh."

¹⁸Moses said this about the tribes of Zebulun and Issachar*:

"May the people of Zebulun prosper in their travels.
May the people of Issachar prosper at home in their tents.
¹⁹ They summon the people to the mountain
to offer proper sacrifices there.

33:2a As in Greek and Syriac versions; Hebrew reads *upon them*. **33:2b** Or *came from myriads of holy ones, from the south, from his mountain slopes*. The meaning of the Hebrew is uncertain. **33:3** As in Greek version; Hebrew reads *Indeed, lover of the peoples*. **33:4** Hebrew *of Jacob*. The names "Jacob" and "Israel" are often interchanged throughout the Old Testament, referring sometimes to the individual patriarch and sometimes to the nation. **33:5** Hebrew *in Jeshurun*, a term of endearment for Israel. **33:6** Hebrew lacks *Moses said this about the tribe of Reuben*. **33:8** As in Greek version; Hebrew lacks *the Levites*. **33:18** Hebrew lacks *and Issachar*.

33:3 In covenant contexts, *to love* is frequently synonymous with *to choose*. The Lord does indeed love his people, but here it means that he chooses them as his special possession (4:20). The phrase "in his hands" figuratively conveys the security that Israel ("his holy ones") had in the Lord. Following the Lord requires adopting his lifestyle and going where he goes. "His teaching" refers particularly and pertinently to the Torah, the first five books of the Old Testament, in all its fullness.
33:5 "Israel" here (Hebrew *Jeshurun*) is a term of endearment for Israel showing God's great love for his people. The noun is derived from a verb meaning "to be upright" (see 32:15).

They benefit from the riches of the sea
and the hidden treasures in the sand."

²⁰Moses said this about the tribe of Gad:

"Blessed is the one who enlarges Gad's territory!
Gad is poised there like a lion
to tear off an arm or a head.
²¹ The people of Gad took the best land for
themselves;
a leader's share was assigned to them.
When the leaders of the people were assembled,
they carried out the LORD's justice
and obeyed his regulations for Israel."

²²Moses said this about the tribe of Dan:

"Dan is a lion's cub,
leaping out from Bashan."

²³Moses said this about the tribe of Naphtali:

"O Naphtali, you are rich in favor
and full of the LORD's blessings;
may you possess the west and the south."

²⁴Moses said this about the tribe of Asher:

"May Asher be blessed above other sons;
may he be esteemed by his brothers;
may he bathe his feet in olive oil.
²⁵ May the bolts of your gates be of iron and
bronze;
may you be secure all your days."

²⁶ "There is no one like the God of Israel.*
He rides across the heavens to help you,
across the skies in majestic splendor.
²⁷ The eternal God is your refuge,
and his everlasting arms are under you.
He drives out the enemy before you;
he cries out, 'Destroy them!'
²⁸ So Israel will live in safety,
prosperous Jacob in security,
in a land of grain and new wine,
while the heavens drop down dew.

²⁹ How blessed you are, O Israel!
Who else is like you, a people saved by the
LORD?
He is your protecting shield
and your triumphant sword!
Your enemies will cringe before you,
and you will stomp on their backs!"

The Death of Moses

34 Then Moses went up to Mount Nebo from the plains of Moab and climbed Pisgah Peak, which is across from Jericho. And the LORD showed him the whole land, from Gilead as far as Dan; ²all the land of Naphtali; the land of Ephraim and Manasseh; all the land of Judah, extending to the Mediterranean Sea*; ³the Negev; the Jordan Valley with Jericho—the city of palms—as far as Zoar. ⁴Then the LORD said to Moses, "This is the land I promised on oath to Abraham, Isaac, and Jacob when I said, 'I will give it to your descendants.' I have now allowed you to see it with your own eyes, but you will not enter the land."

⁵So Moses, the servant of the LORD, died there in the land of Moab, just as the LORD had said. ⁶The LORD buried him* in a valley near Beth-peor in Moab, but to this day no one knows the exact place. ⁷Moses was 120 years old when he died, yet his eyesight was clear, and he was as strong as ever. ⁸The people of Israel mourned for Moses on the plains of Moab for thirty days, until the customary period of mourning was over.

⁹Now Joshua son of Nun was full of the spirit of wisdom, for Moses had laid his hands on him. So the people of Israel obeyed him, doing just as the LORD had commanded Moses.

¹⁰There has never been another prophet in Israel like Moses, whom the LORD knew face to face. ¹¹The LORD sent him to perform all the miraculous signs and wonders in the land of Egypt against Pharaoh, and all his servants, and his entire land. ¹²With mighty power, Moses performed terrifying acts in the sight of all Israel.

33:26 Hebrew *of Jeshurun*, a term of endearment for Israel. 34:2 Hebrew *the western sea*. 34:6 Hebrew *He buried him*; Samaritan Pentateuch and some Greek manuscripts read *They buried him*.

34:10 While others briefly encountered the Lord, Moses' relationship with God was unique. Of all the people in the Old Testament, only Moses repeatedly went into God's presence to talk with him "face to face."

Joshua

WHAT DO WE LEARN ABOUT GOD'S MISSION AND OURS?
God is with us, so let's be brave.

WHO WROTE IT? Joshua, according to Jewish and Christian traditions, and it was likely completed by Israelite scribes after Joshua died.

WHEN DID IT HAPPEN? In the 1300s or 1200s BC, after the people of Israel had wandered in the wilderness and Moses had died.

HOW IS IT ORGANIZED?

- 1: Joshua becomes the leader
- 2: Rahab helps the spies in Jericho
- 3–5: The Israelites enter Canaan, the Promised Land
- 6: Israel conquers Jericho
- 7–12: God gives Israel the victory over the land
- 13–22: The people distribute the land
- 23–24: Joshua gives final instructions and dies

FEATURE HIGHLIGHTS

- Influence Where (and from Who) You Are (259)
- Companioned for Courage (261)
- Rahab: All I Can (265)
- Conquest of Canaan (268)
- Courage (276)
- Our Role: Courage to Serve (286)

Words to Remember are highlighted throughout this book

HOW LONG DOES IT TAKE TO READ?

	1:30					
:30	1:00	1:30	2:00	2:30	3:00	3:30

Timeline

BC

- 1446 — EXODUS FROM EGYPT
- 1406 — JOSHUA BEGINS TO LEAD; ISRAELITES ENTER CANAAN; RAHAB HELPS THE ISRAELITES CONQUER JERICHO
- 1375 — JUDGES (INCLUDING DEBORAH, GIDEON, AND SAMSON) BEGIN TO RULE ISRAEL
- 1050 — KINGDOM OF ISRAEL UNITES UNDER SAUL
- 1010 — DAVID BECOMES KING

The Lord's Charge to Joshua

1 After the death of Moses the Lord's servant, the Lord spoke to Joshua son of Nun, Moses' assistant. He said, ²"Moses my servant is dead. Therefore, the time has come for you to lead these people, the Israelites, across the Jordan River into the land I am giving them. ³I promise you what I promised Moses: 'Wherever you set foot, you will be on land I have given you—⁴from the Negev wilderness in the south to the Lebanon mountains in the north, from the Euphrates River in the east to the Mediterranean Sea* in the west, including all the land of the Hittites.' ⁵No one will be able to stand against you as long as you live. For I will be with you as I was with Moses. I will not fail you or abandon you.

⁶"Be strong and courageous, for you are the one who will lead these people to possess all the land I swore to their ancestors I would give them. ⁷Be strong and very courageous. Be careful to obey all the instructions Moses gave you. Do not deviate from them, turning either to the right or to the left. Then you will be successful in everything you do. ⁸Study this Book of Instruction continually. Meditate on it day and night so you will be sure to obey everything written in it. Only then will you prosper and succeed in all you do. ⁹This is my command—be strong and courageous! Do not be afraid or discouraged. For the Lord your God is with you wherever you go."

Joshua's Charge to the Israelites

¹⁰Joshua then commanded the officers of Israel, ¹¹"Go through the camp and tell the people to get their provisions ready. In three days you will cross the Jordan River and take possession of the land the Lord your God is giving you."

¹²Then Joshua called together the tribes of Reuben, Gad, and the half-tribe of Manasseh. He told them, ¹³"Remember what Moses, the servant of the Lord, commanded you: 'The Lord your God is giving you a place of rest. He has given you this land.' ¹⁴Your wives, children, and livestock may remain here in the land Moses assigned to you on the east side of the Jordan River. But your strong warriors, fully armed, must lead the other tribes across the Jordan to help them conquer their territory. Stay with them ¹⁵until the Lord gives them rest, as he has given you rest, and until they, too, possess the land the Lord your God is giving them. Only then may you return and settle here on the east side of the Jordan River in the land that Moses, the servant of the Lord, assigned to you."

¹⁶They answered Joshua, "We will do whatever you command us, and we will go wherever you send us. ¹⁷We will obey you just as we obeyed Moses. And may the Lord your God be with you as he was with Moses. ¹⁸Anyone who rebels against your orders and does not obey your words and everything you command will be put to death. So be strong and courageous!"

Rahab Protects the Spies

2 Then Joshua secretly sent out two spies from the Israelite camp at Acacia Grove.* He instructed them, "Scout out the land on the other side of the Jordan River, especially around Jericho." So the two men set out and came to the house of a prostitute named Rahab and stayed there that night.

²But someone told the king of Jericho, "Some Israelites have come here tonight to spy out the land." ³So the king of Jericho sent orders to Rahab: "Bring out the men who have come into your house, for they have come here to spy out the whole land."

⁴Rahab had hidden the two men, but she replied, "Yes, the men were here earlier, but I didn't know where they were from. ⁵They left the town at dusk, as the gates were about to close. I don't know where they went. If you hurry, you can probably catch up with them." ⁶(Actually, she had taken them up to the roof and hidden them beneath bundles of flax she had laid out.) ⁷So the king's men went looking for the spies along the road leading to the shallow crossings of the Jordan River. And as soon as the king's men had left, the gate of Jericho was shut.

1:4 Hebrew *the Great Sea.* 2:1 Hebrew *Shittim.*

1:1-5 After Moses' death, God passed the baton of leadership to Joshua. God promised his abiding presence with Joshua, just like he had been with Moses. God promised to give his people the land of Canaan as an inheritance. After all, the whole earth belongs to God and he determines boundaries (Exodus 19:5; Leviticus 25:23). The land of Canaan symbolized the space, sphere, realm, and opportunity for Israel to live and practice their faith in God. It is in this land they were to worship God and experience God's reign, provision, and protection.
1:6-9 Three times and for three reasons God instructed Joshua to be strong and courageous: to lead the people in taking possession of the land God had promised to their ancestors; to obey God's law and instructions; to trust in God's promised presence. All three required boldness to fight against any discouraging circumstances and external pressure from others.

1:12-18 God wanted all the people of Israel to work together to possess the land. The two-and-a-half tribes (the tribes of Gad, Reuben, and half the tribe of Manasseh) had claimed the river's east side (Numbers 32:1-41). Now, these tribes were reminded of their promise to help their fellow Israelites gain possession of the remaining land.
2:1-24; 6:22-25 Rahab had heard about how God supernaturally led Israel to cross the Red Sea on dry ground and to destroy the two Amorite kings, Sihon and Og. She decided to abandon her idols and to confess allegiance to the God of Israel. She hid the Israelite spies and negotiated protection and rescue for her own family. Rahab was a prostitute, a non-Israelite, and a worshiper of pagan gods; she even committed treason against her people. But she wanted her family to worship the God of Israel.

Shalom IMAGE — MY STORY OF MY UNIQUE INFLUENCE

Influence Where (and from Who) You Are

SCRIPTURE CONNECTION: JOSHUA 2:1-24

Even when we know we are healed and whole in God, we may find ourselves focusing on the brokenness in our past. I know I have felt that way, and I wonder if Rahab did too. God took her from shattered to *shalom* (the Hebrew word for God's peace, wholeness, and restoration).

Rahab, along with everyone in Canaan, had heard rumors of Yahweh and his miracles for Israel (2:9-10). I wonder if Rahab whispered a prayer, "God, if you are real, if the stories I've heard are true, make me want to want what you want." Deciding to act on what she knew of God, she was able to look past the lies she could have believed about herself. Lies like "You're shameful! You couldn't possibly be good enough to help these men who have a God like that!" But Rahab also knew that she was well-positioned to courageously offer the spies a plan.

When God designs each of us, he imprints gifts, abilities, traits, experiences, and positions in a combination unlike that of any other person. When we use these gifts to satisfy ourselves, we find darkness. But when we share them, our unique imprint radiates the light that comes from our Creator God. Identities are restored. Relationships are renewed. Futures are reclaimed. Shame turns to shalom.

> God took Rahab from shame to shalom.

Shalom engulfed Rahab's life as she acted in faith to help the Israelite spies, and God saw Rahab's heart, not her reputation. God beautified her name, her identity, her household, and her legacy.

As we surrender in faith, God can use both our broken and bold places to let down a scarlet rope of hope to a waiting world.

IMAGINE

How might you invite God to use you right where and as you are?

> "Like Rahab, I am both broken and bold; she and I both look like misfits for Kingdom work. Yet, when I pray, 'God help me want to want what you want,' he takes my bold and broken places and repurposes all for good in ways I never imagined."

SUZY SHEPHERD is the founder of SHINE, creator of Stonecroft's Where Love Lives outreach experience, and mom to a blended tribe of nine. She finds great joy in creating experiences for people to know God's love.

⁸Before the spies went to sleep that night, Rahab went up on the roof to talk with them. ⁹"I know the Lord has given you this land," she told them. "We are all afraid of you. Everyone in the land is living in terror. ¹⁰For we have heard how the Lord made a dry path for you through the Red Sea* when you left Egypt. And we know what you did to Sihon and Og, the two Amorite kings east of the Jordan River, whose people you completely destroyed.* ¹¹No wonder our hearts have melted in fear! No one has the courage to fight after hearing such things. For the Lord your God is the supreme God of the heavens above and the earth below.

¹²"Now swear to me by the Lord that you will be kind to me and my family since I have helped you. Give me some guarantee that ¹³when Jericho is conquered, you will let me live, along with my father and mother, my brothers and sisters, and all their families."

¹⁴"We offer our own lives as a guarantee for your safety," the men agreed. "If you don't betray us, we will keep our promise and be kind to you when the Lord gives us the land."

¹⁵Then, since Rahab's house was built into the town wall, she let them down by a rope through the window. ¹⁶"Escape to the hill country," she told them. "Hide there for three days from the men searching for you. Then, when they have returned, you can go on your way."

¹⁷Before they left, the men told her, "We will be bound by the oath we have taken only if you follow these instructions. ¹⁸When we come into the land, you must leave this scarlet rope hanging from the window through which you let us down. And all your family members—your father, mother, brothers, and all your relatives—must be here inside the house. ¹⁹If they go out into the street and are killed, it will not be our fault. But if anyone lays a hand on people inside this house, we will accept the responsibility for their death. ²⁰If you betray us, however, we are not bound by this oath in any way."

²¹"I accept your terms," she replied. And she sent them on their way, leaving the scarlet rope hanging from the window.

²²The spies went up into the hill country and stayed there three days. The men who were chasing them searched everywhere along the road, but they finally returned without success. ²³Then the two spies came down from the hill country, crossed the Jordan River, and reported to Joshua all that had happened to them. ²⁴"The Lord has given us the whole land," they said, "for all the people in the land are terrified of us."

The Israelites Cross the Jordan

3 Early the next morning Joshua and all the Israelites left Acacia Grove* and arrived at the banks of the Jordan River, where they camped before crossing. ²Three days later the Israelite officers went through the camp, ³giving these instructions to the people: "When you see the Levitical priests carrying the Ark of the Covenant of the Lord your God, move out from your positions and follow them. ⁴Since you have never traveled this way before, they will guide you. Stay about half a mile* behind them, keeping a clear distance between you and the Ark. Make sure you don't come any closer."

⁵Then Joshua told the people, "Purify yourselves, for tomorrow the Lord will do great wonders among you."

⁶In the morning Joshua said to the priests, "Lift up the Ark of the Covenant and lead the people across the river." And so they started out and went ahead of the people.

⁷The Lord told Joshua, "Today I will begin to make you a great leader in the eyes of all the Israelites. They will know that I am with you, just as I was with Moses. ⁸Give this command to the priests who carry the Ark of the Covenant: 'When you reach the banks of the Jordan River, take a few steps into the river and stop there.'"

⁹So Joshua told the Israelites, "Come and listen to what the Lord your God says. ¹⁰Today you will know that the living God is among you. He will surely drive out the Canaanites, Hittites, Hivites, Perizzites, Girgashites, Amorites, and Jebusites ahead of you. ¹¹Look, the Ark of the Covenant, which belongs to the Lord of the whole earth, will lead you across the Jordan River! ¹²Now choose twelve men from the tribes of Israel, one from each tribe. ¹³The priests will carry the Ark of the Lord, the Lord of all the earth. As soon as their feet touch the water, the flow of water will be cut off upstream, and the river will stand up like a wall."

¹⁴So the people left their camp to cross the Jordan, and the priests who were carrying the Ark of the Covenant went ahead of them. ¹⁵It was the harvest season, and the Jordan was overflowing its banks. But as soon as the feet of the priests who were carrying the

---

2:10a Hebrew *sea of reeds*. **2:10b** The Hebrew term used here refers to the complete consecration of things or people to the Lord, either by destroying them or by giving them as an offering. **3:1** Hebrew *Shittim*. **3:4** Hebrew *about 2,000 cubits* [920 meters].

3:1-17 The Jordan River crossing echoes the Red Sea crossing as God's supernatural and sacred endeavor. Joshua instructed the Israelites to make themselves pure and holy by avoiding unclean activities so that they would be prepared for coming into the Lord's presence (see also Exodus 19:9-15). Ahead of the troops, the priests carried the Ark of the Covenant, representing God's holy presence. Successfully crossing the Jordan showed the Israelites that just as God had been with Moses before, he was also with Joshua. It affirmed Joshua's leadership.

IMAGE — MY STORY OF MY UNIQUE INFLUENCE

Companioned for Courage

SCRIPTURE CONNECTION: JOSHUA 3:1–5:15

I've climbed thirty mountains over thirteen thousand feet high. But in heavy snow one day, I lost the path. I had to choose: shimmy down a slippery two-thousand-foot slope or scramble up a sheer rock face, five hundred feet to the summit?

Even when we've trained and followed expert climbers, life can terrify. And, like Joshua, we find courage from the one who guides us.

Joshua had been mentored by Moses for decades. He'd seen Moses climb Mount Sinai to meet with God. He'd seen Moses stand on a mountain above the battles. He'd seen God, through Moses, win.

But Joshua couldn't conclude, "Well, I'll just lead like Moses." When Moses held up a staff, Joshua brandished a weapon. While Moses met with God, Joshua was spying out the land. How would Joshua uniquely lead?

In my research, I studied how impactful women and men led fearLESSly. Like them we can:

- Trust God's Love is Enough—Joshua believed God was with him.
- Surrender—Joshua released fear, grabbing onto "Be strong and courageous."
- Step—After Joshua stepped into the Jordan River, it dried up. God parted waters for Moses, too. Just as God led Moses, God would lead Joshua. God will lead us, as we take that first step.

When we face a fearful choice, as I did, as Joshua did, we ask, "Am I enough?" The Bible's answer is clear: no. But God is. And God companions us for courage. We lead fearLESSly, hearing his "I am with you." And we step up.

> Courage is our calling because God is calling.

IMAGINE

What do you need to live fearLESSly? To believe God's Love is Enough? To Surrender? Do you need to Step?

"The antidote to fear is not courage; it is love. And God's love, God himself, goes with us."

NAOMI CRAMER OVERTON, MBA, DIS, lives to realize beauty-filled visions that lift us to flourishing, with our families and beyond. Naomi has been CEO for Stonecroft and MOPS, director with Compassion International and World Vision, and General Editor for this Bible.

Ark touched the water at the river's edge, ¹⁶the water above that point began backing up a great distance away at a town called Adam, which is near Zarethan. And the water below that point flowed on to the Dead Sea* until the riverbed was dry. Then all the people crossed over near the town of Jericho.

¹⁷Meanwhile, the priests who were carrying the Ark of the LORD's Covenant stood on dry ground in the middle of the riverbed as the people passed by. They waited there until the whole nation of Israel had crossed the Jordan on dry ground.

Memorials to the Jordan Crossing

4 When all the people had crossed the Jordan, the LORD said to Joshua, ²"Now choose twelve men, one from each tribe. ³Tell them, 'Take twelve stones from the very place where the priests are standing in the middle of the Jordan. Carry them out and pile them up at the place where you will camp tonight.'"

⁴So Joshua called together the twelve men he had chosen—one from each of the tribes of Israel. ⁵He told them, "Go into the middle of the Jordan, in front of the Ark of the LORD your God. Each of you must pick up one stone and carry it out on your shoulder—twelve stones in all, one for each of the twelve tribes of Israel. ⁶We will use these stones to build a memorial. In the future your children will ask you, 'What do these stones mean?' ⁷Then you can tell them, 'They remind us that the Jordan River stopped flowing when the Ark of the LORD's Covenant went across.' These stones will stand as a memorial among the people of Israel forever."

⁸So the men did as Joshua had commanded them. They took twelve stones from the middle of the Jordan River, one for each tribe, just as the LORD had told Joshua. They carried them to the place where they camped for the night and constructed the memorial there.

⁹Joshua also set up another pile of twelve stones in the middle of the Jordan, at the place where the priests who carried the Ark of the Covenant were standing. And they are there to this day.

¹⁰The priests who were carrying the Ark stood in the middle of the river until all of the LORD's commands that Moses had given to Joshua were carried out. Meanwhile, the people hurried across the riverbed. ¹¹And when everyone was safely on the other side, the priests crossed over with the Ark of the LORD as the people watched.

¹²The armed warriors from the tribes of Reuben, Gad, and the half-tribe of Manasseh led the Israelites across the Jordan, just as Moses had directed. ¹³These armed men—about 40,000 strong—were ready for battle, and the LORD was with them as they crossed over to the plains of Jericho.

¹⁴That day the LORD made Joshua a great leader in the eyes of all the Israelites, and for the rest of his life they revered him as much as they had revered Moses.

¹⁵The LORD had said to Joshua, ¹⁶"Command the priests carrying the Ark of the Covenant* to come up out of the riverbed." ¹⁷So Joshua gave the command. ¹⁸As soon as the priests carrying the Ark of the LORD's Covenant came up out of the riverbed and their feet were on high ground, the water of the Jordan returned and overflowed its banks as before.

¹⁹The people crossed the Jordan on the tenth day of the first month.* Then they camped at Gilgal, just east of Jericho. ²⁰It was there at Gilgal that Joshua piled up the twelve stones taken from the Jordan River.

²¹Then Joshua said to the Israelites, "In the future your children will ask, 'What do these stones mean?' ²²Then you can tell them, 'This is where the Israelites crossed the Jordan on dry ground.' ²³For the LORD your God dried up the river right before your eyes, and he kept it dry until you were all across, just as he did at the Red Sea* when he dried it up until we had all crossed over. ²⁴He did this so all the nations of the earth might know that the LORD's hand is powerful, and so you might fear the LORD your God forever."

5 When all the Amorite kings west of the Jordan and all the Canaanite kings who lived along the Mediterranean coast* heard how the LORD had dried up the Jordan River so the people of Israel could cross, they lost heart and were paralyzed with fear because of them.

Israel Reestablishes Covenant Ceremonies

²At that time the LORD told Joshua, "Make flint knives and circumcise this second generation of Israelites.*" ³So Joshua made flint knives and

---

3:16 Hebrew *the sea of the Arabah, the Salt Sea.* **4:16** Hebrew *Ark of the Testimony.* **4:19** This day in the ancient Hebrew lunar calendar occurred in late March, April, or early May. **4:23** Hebrew *sea of reeds.* **5:1** Hebrew *along the sea.* **5:2** Or *circumcise the Israelites a second time.*

4:1-24 God has foresight. He wanted the Israelites to remember and retell his marvelous works to their succeeding generations. So, he commanded them to build a memorial of their crossing the Jordan on dry ground using twelve stones taken from the middle of the river. The memorial stones were not meant for boasting nor nostalgia; they were to become a story retold to the next generation of Israelites to fear and obey God. **5:2-9** Although circumcision is physically painful, for the Israelites, it signifies the treaty, or covenant, between God and the people of Israel through Abraham. Circumcision set the Israelites apart from other nations, especially those living near them, identifying them as God's people. Joshua circumcised all the adult male Israelites to reaffirm their commitment to God's covenant. Gilgal (which means "to roll") is the name of the place where these circumcisions were performed. This name symbolizes their identity as enslaved people and foreigners rolling away.

circumcised the entire male population of Israel at Gibeath-haaraloth.*

⁴Joshua had to circumcise them because all the men who were old enough to fight in battle when they left Egypt had died in the wilderness. ⁵Those who left Egypt had all been circumcised, but none of those born after the Exodus, during the years in the wilderness, had been circumcised. ⁶The Israelites had traveled in the wilderness for forty years until all the men who were old enough to fight in battle when they left Egypt had died. For they had disobeyed the LORD, and the LORD vowed he would not let them enter the land he had sworn to give us—a land flowing with milk and honey. ⁷So Joshua circumcised their sons—those who had grown up to take their fathers' places—for they had not been circumcised on the way to the Promised Land. ⁸After all the males had been circumcised, they rested in the camp until they were healed.

⁹Then the LORD said to Joshua, "Today I have rolled away the shame of your slavery in Egypt." So that place has been called Gilgal* to this day.

¹⁰While the Israelites were camped at Gilgal on the plains of Jericho, they celebrated Passover on the evening of the fourteenth day of the first month.* ¹¹The very next day they began to eat unleavened bread and roasted grain harvested from the land. ¹²No manna appeared on the day they first ate from the crops of the land, and it was never seen again. So from that time on the Israelites ate from the crops of Canaan.

The LORD's Commander Confronts Joshua

¹³When Joshua was near the town of Jericho, he looked up and saw a man standing in front of him with sword in hand. Joshua went up to him and demanded, "Are you friend or foe?"

¹⁴"Neither one," he replied. "I am the commander of the LORD's army."

At this, Joshua fell with his face to the ground in reverence. "I am at your command," Joshua said. "What do you want your servant to do?"

¹⁵The commander of the LORD's army replied, "Take off your sandals, for the place where you are standing is holy." And Joshua did as he was told.

The Fall of Jericho

6 Now the gates of Jericho were tightly shut because the people were afraid of the Israelites. No one was allowed to go out or in. ²But the LORD said to Joshua, "I have given you Jericho, its king, and all its strong warriors. ³You and your fighting men should march around the town once a day for six days. ⁴Seven priests will walk ahead of the Ark, each carrying a ram's horn. On the seventh day you are to march around the town seven times, with the priests blowing the horns. ⁵When you hear the priests give one long blast on the rams' horns, have all the people shout as loud as they can. Then the walls of the town will collapse, and the people can charge straight into the town."

⁶So Joshua called together the priests and said, "Take up the Ark of the LORD's Covenant, and assign seven priests to walk in front of it, each carrying a ram's horn." ⁷Then he gave orders to the people: "March around the town, and the armed men will lead the way in front of the Ark of the LORD."

⁸After Joshua spoke to the people, the seven priests with the rams' horns started marching in the presence of the LORD, blowing the horns as they marched. And the Ark of the LORD's Covenant followed behind them. ⁹Some of the armed men marched in front of the priests with the horns and some behind the Ark, with the priests continually blowing the horns. ¹⁰"Do not shout; do not even talk," Joshua commanded. "Not a single word from any of you until I tell you to shout. Then shout!" ¹¹So the Ark of the LORD was carried around the town once that day, and then everyone returned to spend the night in the camp.

¹²Joshua got up early the next morning, and the priests again carried the Ark of the LORD. ¹³The seven

---

5:3 *Gibeath-haaraloth* means "hill of foreskins." **5:9** *Gilgal* sounds like the Hebrew word *galal*, meaning "to roll." **5:10** This day in the ancient Hebrew lunar calendar occurred in late March, April, or early May.

5:10-12 Passover is a ritual celebration to remember how God saved the people of Israel from enslavement in Egypt. We are a forgetful people. We can remember how God saved us from our sins and bondage by regularly taking the Lord's Supper, a Christian practice bringing to mind the Lord's saving work, similar to the Passover feast.

5:13-15 Joshua had a supernatural encounter with the commander of the Lord's army. This divine appearance sanctified the place. Joshua took off his shoes and fell facedown to show reverence to God's representative. This divine appearance shows that the real enemy was not flesh and blood but the spiritual beings Canaanites worshiped. The Canaanites could find salvation and join God's people if they pledged fidelity to the Lord, like Rahab and her family. The Israelites were merely foot soldiers under God's command.

6:1-21 The fall of Jericho is an important historical event in Israel's faith development. Although Jericho's fall led to the death of many people, military strength did not accomplish it. Instead, God used an unusual way of capturing the city. God instructed the people to march around Jericho once each day for seven days, with the priests carrying trumpets of ram's horns in front of the Ark and the armed men before and behind them. This display likely appeared strange at the time, and it would to us now too. But once again, this shows that God's ways are always higher than human ways. God's ways make what seems impossible become possible.

priests with the rams' horns marched in front of the Ark of the Lord, blowing their horns. Again the armed men marched both in front of the priests with the horns and behind the Ark of the Lord. All this time the priests were blowing their horns. ¹⁴On the second day they again marched around the town once and returned to the camp. They followed this pattern for six days.

¹⁵On the seventh day the Israelites got up at dawn and marched around the town as they had done before. But this time they went around the town seven times. ¹⁶The seventh time around, as the priests sounded the long blast on their horns, Joshua commanded the people, "Shout! For the Lord has given you the town! ¹⁷Jericho and everything in it must be completely destroyed* as an offering to the Lord. Only Rahab the prostitute and the others in her house will be spared, for she protected our spies.

¹⁸"Do not take any of the things set apart for destruction, or you yourselves will be completely destroyed, and you will bring trouble on the camp of Israel. ¹⁹Everything made from silver, gold, bronze, or iron is sacred to the Lord and must be brought into his treasury."

²⁰When the people heard the sound of the rams' horns, they shouted as loud as they could. Suddenly, the walls of Jericho collapsed, and the Israelites charged straight into the town and captured it. ²¹They completely destroyed everything in it with their swords—men and women, young and old, cattle, sheep, goats, and donkeys.

²²Meanwhile, Joshua said to the two spies, "Keep your promise. Go to the prostitute's house and bring her out, along with all her family."

²³The men who had been spies went in and brought out Rahab, her father, mother, brothers, and all the other relatives who were with her. They moved her whole family to a safe place near the camp of Israel.

²⁴Then the Israelites burned the town and everything in it. Only the things made from silver, gold, bronze, or iron were kept for the treasury of the Lord's house. ²⁵So Joshua spared Rahab the prostitute and her relatives who were with her in the house, because she had hidden the spies Joshua sent to Jericho. And she lives among the Israelites to this day.

²⁶At that time Joshua invoked this curse:

"May the curse of the Lord fall on anyone
    who tries to rebuild the town of Jericho.
At the cost of his firstborn son,
    he will lay its foundation.
At the cost of his youngest son,
    he will set up its gates."

²⁷So the Lord was with Joshua, and his reputation spread throughout the land.

Ai Defeats the Israelites

7 But Israel violated the instructions about the things set apart for the Lord.* A man named Achan had stolen some of these dedicated things, so the Lord was very angry with the Israelites. Achan was the son of Carmi, a descendant of Zimri* son of Zerah, of the tribe of Judah.

²Joshua sent some of his men from Jericho to spy out the town of Ai, east of Bethel, near Beth-aven. ³When they returned, they told Joshua, "There's no need for all of us to go up there; it won't take more than two or three thousand men to attack Ai. Since there are so few of them, don't make all our people struggle to go up there."

⁴So approximately 3,000 warriors were sent, but they were soundly defeated. The men of Ai ⁵chased the Israelites from the town gate as far as the quarries,* and they killed about thirty-six who were retreating down the slope. The Israelites were paralyzed with fear at this turn of events, and their courage melted away.

⁶Joshua and the elders of Israel tore their clothing in dismay, threw dust on their heads, and bowed face down to the ground before the Ark of the Lord until evening. ⁷Then Joshua cried out, "Oh, Sovereign Lord, why did you bring us across the Jordan River if you are going to let the Amorites kill us? If only we had been content to stay on the other side! ⁸Lord, what can I say now that Israel has fled from its enemies? ⁹For when the Canaanites and all the other people living in the land hear about it, they will surround us and wipe our name off the face of

---

6:17 The Hebrew term used here refers to the complete consecration of things or people to the Lord, either by destroying them or by giving them as an offering; similarly in 6:18, 21. **7:1a** The Hebrew term used here refers to the complete consecration of things or people to the Lord, either by destroying them or by giving them as an offering; similarly in 7:11, 12, 13, 15. **7:1b** As in parallel text at 1 Chr 2:6; Hebrew reads *Zabdi*. Also in 7:17, 18. **7:5** Or *as far as Shebarim*.

7:1 This verse summarizes Achan's acts and fate. The "things set apart for the Lord" in this context are objects (Deuteronomy 7:26) and people to be destroyed (Joshua 7:11-13) in taking possession of the land. (Leviticus 27:21, 28-29 deals with property or people specifically set apart to the Lord as *holy*.) The Lord had declared that the people living in the land and their possessions must be destroyed because they belonged to other gods (Numbers 33:50-56). As such, Achan should have brought these valuables into the Lord's treasury (Joshua 6:24). Unfortunately, Achan stole some, lied about it, and hid it.

7:6-9 Joshua and the elders mourned the Israelites' death and defeat from their battle with Ai. By this time, the Canaanites had already heard of God's fame in leading the Israelites in crossing the Red Sea and Jordan River. Joshua saw this defeat as bringing humiliation to the Lord's name.

Rahab

IDENTITY — All I Can

Rahab remembers . . .

I have done all I can. I hid the Hebrew spies and protected their escape. I don't know how this will end, but I have hope their God will prove strong.

The Israelites have been marching around our city for days, blowing horns. Today is the seventh day of their marching. How is walking going to lead to victory?

This last blow of horns and their shouting make my heart thump in my chest. The walls are shaking and shuddering all around me. I put my hands over my ears as the walls of mighty Jericho fall.

We hear the screams of the people as the Israelites destroy the city and everyone in it. I see the uncertainty in the eyes of my family. They're looking to me.

The knock at the door is followed by two familiar faces: the spies. We get up quickly. Though I am a prostitute and a foreigner to them, these men, and their God, cared enough to rescue me. And I know the Lord God is with us.

We step over bodies and rubble as they lead us to their camp. Safety. I am leaving this life to follow the supreme God of heaven and earth.

They light Jericho on fire, and as I watch it burn, I praise this God of heaven and earth. The old goes up in flames, and I gain a new life. The Lord God has done this.

I did all I could. God did the rest.

> When you see no way out, God can show you a good way forward.

RAHAB'S STORY IS TOLD IN JOSHUA 2:1-24; 6:17-25;
SHE IS ALSO MENTIONED IN MATTHEW 1:5; HEBREWS 11:31; JAMES 2:25.

IDENTIFY

What no-way-out situation do you need to trust God with?

> "My choices led me to a life that would tear me apart, as Rahab probably knew prostitution would. I wanted out but could not see the way. Just like Rahab, I chose to believe the God of heaven and earth. I obeyed his instructions, though they made no sense, and he delivered me into a new life."

CARA DAY is a writer and illustrator. She has served with Stonecroft Ministries helping women live "extraordinary."

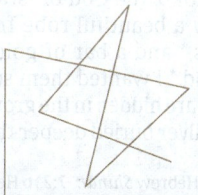

the earth. And then what will happen to the honor of your great name?"

¹⁰But the LORD said to Joshua, "Get up! Why are you lying on your face like this? ¹¹Israel has sinned and broken my covenant! They have stolen some of the things that I commanded must be set apart for me. And they have not only stolen them but have lied about it and hidden the things among their own belongings. ¹²That is why the Israelites are running from their enemies in defeat. For now Israel itself has been set apart for destruction. I will not remain with you any longer unless you destroy the things among you that were set apart for destruction.

¹³"Get up! Command the people to purify themselves in preparation for tomorrow. For this is what the LORD, the God of Israel, says: Hidden among you, O Israel, are things set apart for the LORD. You will never defeat your enemies until you remove these things from among you.

¹⁴"In the morning you must present yourselves by tribes, and the LORD will point out the tribe to which the guilty man belongs. That tribe must come forward with its clans, and the LORD will point out the guilty clan. That clan will then come forward, and the LORD will point out the guilty family. Finally, each member of the guilty family must come forward one by one. ¹⁵The one who has stolen what was set apart for destruction will himself be burned with fire, along with everything he has, for he has broken the covenant of the LORD and has done a horrible thing in Israel."

Achan's Sin

¹⁶Early the next morning Joshua brought the tribes of Israel before the LORD, and the tribe of Judah was singled out. ¹⁷Then the clans of Judah came forward, and the clan of Zerah was singled out. Then the families of Zerah came forward, and the family of Zimri was singled out. ¹⁸Every member of Zimri's family was brought forward person by person, and Achan was singled out.

¹⁹Then Joshua said to Achan, "My son, give glory to the LORD, the God of Israel, by telling the truth. Make your confession and tell me what you have done. Don't hide it from me."

²⁰Achan replied, "It is true! I have sinned against the LORD, the God of Israel. ²¹Among the plunder I saw a beautiful robe from Babylon,* 200 silver coins,* and a bar of gold weighing more than a pound.* I wanted them so much that I took them. They are hidden in the ground beneath my tent, with the silver buried deeper than the rest."

²²So Joshua sent some men to make a search. They ran to the tent and found the stolen goods hidden there, just as Achan had said, with the silver buried beneath the rest. ²³They took the things from the tent and brought them to Joshua and all the Israelites. Then they laid them on the ground in the presence of the LORD.

²⁴Then Joshua and all the Israelites took Achan, the silver, the robe, the bar of gold, his sons, daughters, cattle, donkeys, sheep, goats, tent, and everything he had, and they brought them to the valley of Achor. ²⁵Then Joshua said to Achan, "Why have you brought trouble on us? The LORD will now bring trouble on you." And all the Israelites stoned Achan and his family and burned their bodies. ²⁶They piled a great heap of stones over Achan, which remains to this day. That is why the place has been called the Valley of Trouble* ever since. So the LORD was no longer angry.

The Israelites Defeat Ai

8 Then the LORD said to Joshua, "Do not be afraid or discouraged. Take all your fighting men and attack Ai, for I have given you the king of Ai, his people, his town, and his land. ²You will destroy them as you destroyed Jericho and its king. But this time you may keep the plunder and the livestock for yourselves. Set an ambush behind the town."

³So Joshua and all the fighting men set out to attack Ai. Joshua chose 30,000 of his best warriors and sent them out at night ⁴with these orders: "Hide in ambush close behind the town and be ready for action. ⁵When our main army attacks, the men of Ai will come out to fight as they did before, and we will run away from them. ⁶We will let them chase us until we have drawn them away from the town. For they will say, 'The Israelites are running away from us as they did before.' Then, while we are running from them, ⁷you will jump up from your ambush and take possession of the town, for the LORD your God will give it to you. ⁸Set the town on fire, as the LORD has commanded. You have your orders."

⁹So they left and went to the place of ambush between Bethel and the west side of Ai. But Joshua remained among the people in the camp that night. ¹⁰Early the next morning Joshua roused his men and started toward Ai, accompanied by the elders of Israel. ¹¹All the fighting men who were with Joshua marched in front of the town and camped on the north side of Ai, with a valley between them and the town. ¹²That night Joshua sent about 5,000 men to lie in ambush between Bethel and Ai, on the west side of

---

7:21a Hebrew *Shinar.* 7:21b Hebrew *200 shekels of silver,* about 5 pounds or 2.3 kilograms in weight. 7:21c Hebrew *50 shekels,* about 20 ounces or 570 grams in weight. 7:26 Hebrew *valley of Achor.*

8:1-29 One present failure does not determine future failures. After the disappointing defeat at Ai, the Lord encouraged Joshua to continue to possess Ai's land. This time God guaranteed they would win, and this time they could take the plunder for their personal use.

the town. ¹³So they stationed the main army north of the town and the ambush west of the town. Joshua himself spent that night in the valley.

¹⁴When the king of Ai saw the Israelites across the valley, he and all his army hurried out early in the morning and attacked the Israelites at a place overlooking the Jordan Valley.* But he didn't realize there was an ambush behind the town. ¹⁵Joshua and the Israelite army fled toward the wilderness as though they were badly beaten. ¹⁶Then all the men in the town were called out to chase after them. In this way, they were lured away from the town. ¹⁷There was not a man left in Ai or Bethel* who did not chase after the Israelites, and the town was left wide open.

¹⁸Then the LORD said to Joshua, "Point the spear in your hand toward Ai, for I will hand the town over to you." Joshua did as he was commanded. ¹⁹As soon as Joshua gave this signal, all the men in ambush jumped up from their position and poured into the town. They quickly captured it and set it on fire.

²⁰When the men of Ai looked behind them, smoke from the town was filling the sky, and they had nowhere to go. For the Israelites who had fled in the direction of the wilderness now turned on their pursuers. ²¹When Joshua and all the other Israelites saw that the ambush had succeeded and that smoke was rising from the town, they turned and attacked the men of Ai. ²²Meanwhile, the Israelites who were inside the town came out and attacked the enemy from the rear. So the men of Ai were caught in the middle, with Israelite fighters on both sides. Israel attacked them, and not a single person survived or escaped. ²³Only the king of Ai was taken alive and brought to Joshua.

²⁴When the Israelite army finished chasing and killing all the men of Ai in the open fields, they went back and finished off everyone inside. ²⁵So the entire population of Ai, including men and women, was wiped out that day—12,000 in all. ²⁶For Joshua kept holding out his spear until everyone who had lived in Ai was completely destroyed.* ²⁷Only the livestock and the treasures of the town were not destroyed, for the Israelites kept these as plunder for themselves, as the LORD had commanded Joshua. ²⁸So Joshua burned the town of Ai,* and it became a permanent mound of ruins, desolate to this very day.

²⁹Joshua impaled the king of Ai on a sharpened pole and left him there until evening. At sunset the Israelites took down the body, as Joshua commanded, and threw it in front of the town gate. They piled a great heap of stones over him that can still be seen today.

The LORD's Covenant Renewed

³⁰Then Joshua built an altar to the LORD, the God of Israel, on Mount Ebal. ³¹He followed the commands that Moses the LORD's servant had written in the Book of Instruction: "Make me an altar from stones that are uncut and have not been shaped with iron tools."* Then on the altar they presented burnt offerings and peace offerings to the LORD. ³²And as the Israelites watched, Joshua copied onto the stones of the altar* the instructions Moses had given them.

³³Then all the Israelites—foreigners and native-born alike—along with the elders, officers, and judges, were divided into two groups. One group stood in front of Mount Gerizim, the other in front of Mount Ebal. Each group faced the other, and between them stood the Levitical priests carrying the Ark of the LORD's Covenant. This was all done according to the commands that Moses, the servant of the LORD, had previously given for blessing the people of Israel.

³⁴Joshua then read to them all the blessings and curses Moses had written in the Book of Instruction. ³⁵Every word of every command that Moses had ever given was read to the entire assembly of Israel, including the women and children and the foreigners who lived among them.

The Gibeonites Deceive Israel

9 Now all the kings west of the Jordan River heard about what had happened. These were the kings of the Hittites, Amorites, Canaanites, Perizzites, Hivites, and Jebusites, who lived in the hill country, in the western foothills,* and along the coast of the Mediterranean Sea* as far north as the Lebanon mountains. ²These kings combined their armies to fight as one against Joshua and the Israelites.

³But when the people of Gibeon heard what Joshua had done to Jericho and Ai, ⁴they resorted to deception to save themselves. They sent ambassadors to Joshua, loading their donkeys with weathered saddlebags and old, patched wineskins. ⁵They put on worn-out, patched sandals and ragged clothes. And the bread they took with them was dry and moldy. ⁶When they arrived at the camp of Israel

---

8:14 Hebrew *the Arabah.* **8:17** Some manuscripts lack *or Bethel.* **8:26** The Hebrew term used here refers to the complete consecration of things or people to the LORD, either by destroying them or by giving them as an offering. **8:28** *Ai* means "ruin." **8:31** Exod 20:25; Deut 27:5-6. **8:32** Hebrew *onto the stones.* **9:1a** Hebrew *the Shephelah.* **9:1b** Hebrew *the Great Sea.*

9:1-6 When the kings of the west side of the Jordan heard about Jericho's and Ai's destruction, they banded together to fight the Israelites. However, the Gibeonites used deception to avoid a physical battle with the Israelites and to save their lives. They wanted to make a peace treaty with the Israelites.

JOSHUA 9

at Gilgal, they told Joshua and the men of Israel, "We have come from a distant land to ask you to make a peace treaty with us."

⁷The Israelites replied to these Hivites, "How do we know you don't live nearby? For if you do, we cannot make a treaty with you."

⁸They replied, "We are your servants."

"But who are you?" Joshua demanded. "Where do you come from?"

⁹They answered, "Your servants have come from a very distant country. We have heard of the might of the LORD your God and of all he did in Egypt. ¹⁰We have also heard what he did to the two Amorite kings east of the Jordan River—King Sihon of Heshbon and King Og of Bashan (who lived in Ashtaroth). ¹¹So our elders and all our people instructed us, 'Take supplies for a long journey. Go meet with the people of Israel and tell them, "We are your servants; please make a treaty with us."'

¹²"This bread was hot from the ovens when we left our homes. But now, as you can see, it is dry and moldy. ¹³These wineskins were new when we filled them, but now they are old and split open. And our clothing and sandals are worn out from our very long journey."

¹⁴So the Israelites examined their food, but they did not consult the LORD. ¹⁵Then Joshua made a peace treaty with them and guaranteed their safety, and the leaders of the community ratified their agreement with a binding oath.

¹⁶Three days after making the treaty, they learned that these people actually lived nearby! ¹⁷The Israelites set out at once to investigate and reached their towns in three days. The names of these towns were Gibeon, Kephirah, Beeroth, and Kiriath-jearim. ¹⁸But the Israelites did not attack the towns, for the Israelite leaders had made a vow to them in the name of the LORD, the God of Israel.

9:9-15 Joshua and the Israelites fell for the Gibeonites' deception because they accepted at face value the condition of the bread, the wineskins, and the Gibeonites' gear. They should have asked the Lord first. Making a peace treaty with the Gibeonites meant they violated God's instructions (Deuteronomy 7:2). When we are making life decisions, acting impulsively can lead to regret. There is wisdom in deliberating and seeking God (compare to Nehemiah 2:1-5).

Insight — CONQUEST OF CANAAN

Sometimes when God pledges something good, that promised future may require us to work for it, together. Before the people of Israel could live in the land that God had promised them, they first had to conquer the people who were living there. This involved four battles:

1. The fall of Jericho (Joshua 6)
2. Achan's disobedience and Ai's fall (Joshua 7–8)
3. Gibeon's deceit and the fall of the southern kings (Joshua 9–10)
4. The fall of the northern kings (Joshua 11)

- → Israelites' movements
- → Opponents' movements
- ▲ Israelites' base camp
- ✸ Israelites' conquests

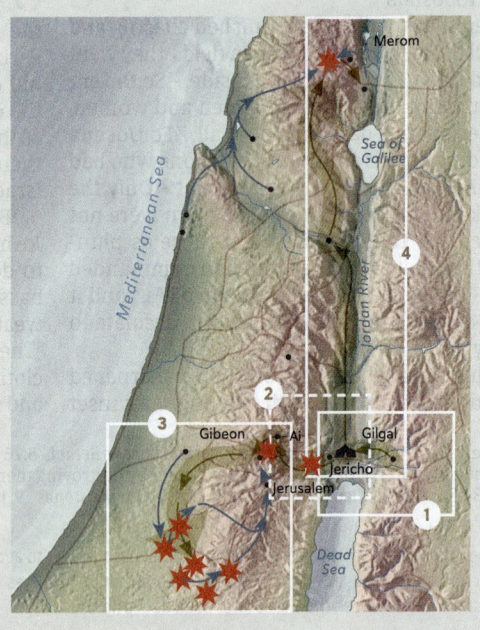

The people of Israel grumbled against their leaders because of the treaty. ¹⁹But the leaders replied, "Since we have sworn an oath in the presence of the LORD, the God of Israel, we cannot touch them. ²⁰This is what we must do. We must let them live, for divine anger would come upon us if we broke our oath. ²¹Let them live." So they made them woodcutters and water carriers for the entire community, as the Israelite leaders directed.

²²Joshua called together the Gibeonites and said, "Why did you lie to us? Why did you say that you live in a distant land when you live right here among us? ²³May you be cursed! From now on you will always be servants who cut wood and carry water for the house of my God."

²⁴They replied, "We did it because we—your servants—were clearly told that the LORD your God commanded his servant Moses to give you this entire land and to destroy all the people living in it. So we feared greatly for our lives because of you. That is why we have done this. ²⁵Now we are at your mercy—do to us whatever you think is right."

²⁶So Joshua did not allow the people of Israel to kill them. ²⁷But that day he made the Gibeonites the woodcutters and water carriers for the community of Israel and for the altar of the LORD—wherever the LORD would choose to build it. And that is what they do to this day.

Israel Defeats the Southern Armies

10 Adoni-zedek, king of Jerusalem, heard that Joshua had captured and completely destroyed* Ai and killed its king, just as he had destroyed the town of Jericho and killed its king. He also learned that the Gibeonites had made peace with Israel and were now their allies. ²He and his people became very afraid when they heard all this because Gibeon was a large town—as large as the royal cities and larger than Ai. And the Gibeonite men were strong warriors.

³So King Adoni-zedek of Jerusalem sent messengers to several other kings: Hoham of Hebron, Piram of Jarmuth, Japhia of Lachish, and Debir of Eglon. ⁴"Come and help me destroy Gibeon," he urged them, "for they have made peace with Joshua and the people of Israel." ⁵So these five Amorite kings combined their armies for a united attack. They moved all their troops into place and attacked Gibeon.

⁶The men of Gibeon quickly sent messengers to Joshua at his camp in Gilgal. "Don't abandon your servants now!" they pleaded. "Come at once! Save us! Help us! For all the Amorite kings who live in the hill country have joined forces to attack us."

⁷So Joshua and his entire army, including his best warriors, left Gilgal and set out for Gibeon. ⁸"Do not be afraid of them," the LORD said to Joshua, "for I have given you victory over them. Not a single one of them will be able to stand up to you."

⁹Joshua traveled all night from Gilgal and took the Amorite armies by surprise. ¹⁰The LORD threw them into a panic, and the Israelites slaughtered great numbers of them at Gibeon. Then the Israelites chased the enemy along the road to Beth-horon, killing them all along the way to Azekah and Makkedah. ¹¹As the Amorites retreated down the road from Beth-horon, the LORD destroyed them with a terrible hailstorm from heaven that continued until they reached Azekah. The hail killed more of the enemy than the Israelites killed with the sword.

¹²On the day the LORD gave the Israelites victory over the Amorites, Joshua prayed to the LORD in front of all the people of Israel. He said,

"Let the sun stand still over Gibeon,
and the moon over the valley of Aijalon."

¹³So the sun stood still and the moon stayed in place until the nation of Israel had defeated its enemies.

Is this event not recorded in The Book of Jashar*? The sun stayed in the middle of the sky, and it did not set as on a normal day.* ¹⁴There has never been a day like this one before or since, when the LORD answered such a prayer. Surely the LORD fought for Israel that day!

¹⁵Then Joshua and the Israelite army returned to their camp at Gilgal.

Joshua Kills the Five Southern Kings

¹⁶During the battle the five kings escaped and hid in a cave at Makkedah. ¹⁷When Joshua heard that they had been found, ¹⁸he issued this command: "Cover the opening of the cave with large rocks, and place guards at the entrance to keep the kings inside. ¹⁹The rest of you continue chasing the enemy and cut them down from the rear. Don't give them a chance to get back to their towns, for the LORD your God has given you victory over them."

²⁰So Joshua and the Israelite army continued the slaughter and completely crushed the enemy. They totally wiped out the five armies except for a

---

10:1 The Hebrew term used here refers to the complete consecration of things or people to the LORD, either by destroying them or by giving them as an offering; also in 10:28, 35, 37, 39, 40. **10:13a** Or *The Book of the Upright.* **10:13b** Or *did not set for about a whole day.*

10:5-11 Despite the regrettable treaty, God made the Israelites fulfill their obligation to the Gibeonites and fight against the Amorite kings. God threw the Amorites into a panic, and he used natural means—a hailstorm—to destroy them. How God brought the Israelites victory further proves that it's by God's power alone that the people took possession of the land. Their strength was minimal in comparison to God's.

tiny remnant that managed to reach their fortified towns. ²¹Then the Israelites returned safely to Joshua in the camp at Makkedah. After that, no one dared to speak even a word against Israel.

²²Then Joshua said, "Remove the rocks covering the opening of the cave, and bring the five kings to me." ²³So they brought the five kings out of the cave—the kings of Jerusalem, Hebron, Jarmuth, Lachish, and Eglon. ²⁴When they brought them out, Joshua told the commanders of his army, "Come and put your feet on the kings' necks." And they did as they were told.

²⁵"Don't ever be afraid or discouraged," Joshua told his men. "Be strong and courageous, for the LORD is going to do this to all of your enemies." ²⁶Then Joshua killed each of the five kings and impaled them on five sharpened poles, where they hung until evening.

²⁷As the sun was going down, Joshua gave instructions for the bodies of the kings to be taken down from the poles and thrown into the cave where they had been hiding. Then they covered the opening of the cave with a pile of large rocks, which remains to this very day.

Israel Destroys the Southern Towns

²⁸That same day Joshua captured and destroyed the town of Makkedah. He killed everyone in it, including the king, leaving no survivors. He destroyed them all, and he killed the king of Makkedah as he had killed the king of Jericho. ²⁹Then Joshua and the Israelites went to Libnah and attacked it. ³⁰There, too, the LORD gave them the town and its king. He killed everyone in it, leaving no survivors. Then Joshua killed the king of Libnah as he had killed the king of Jericho.

³¹From Libnah, Joshua and the Israelites went to Lachish and attacked it. ³²Here again, the LORD gave them Lachish. Joshua took it on the second day and killed everyone in it, just as he had done at Libnah. ³³During the attack on Lachish, King Horam of Gezer arrived with his army to help defend the town. But Joshua's men killed him and his army, leaving no survivors.

³⁴Then Joshua and the Israelite army went on to Eglon and attacked it. ³⁵They captured it that day and killed everyone in it. He completely destroyed everyone, just as he had done at Lachish. ³⁶From Eglon, Joshua and the Israelite army went up to Hebron and attacked it. ³⁷They captured the town and killed everyone in it, including its king, leaving no survivors. They did the same thing to all of its surrounding villages. And just as he had done at Eglon, he completely destroyed the entire population.

³⁸Then Joshua and the Israelites turned back and attacked Debir. ³⁹He captured the town, its king, and all of its surrounding villages. He completely destroyed everyone in it, leaving no survivors. He did to Debir and its king just what he had done to Hebron and to Libnah and its king.

⁴⁰So Joshua conquered the whole region—the kings and people of the hill country, the Negev, the western foothills,* and the mountain slopes. He completely destroyed everyone in the land, leaving no survivors, just as the LORD, the God of Israel, had commanded. ⁴¹Joshua slaughtered them from Kadesh-barnea to Gaza and from the region around the town of Goshen up to Gibeon. ⁴²Joshua conquered all these kings and their land in a single campaign, for the LORD, the God of Israel, was fighting for his people.

⁴³Then Joshua and the Israelite army returned to their camp at Gilgal.

Israel Defeats the Northern Armies

11 When King Jabin of Hazor heard what had happened, he sent messages to the following kings: King Jobab of Madon; the king of Shimron; the king of Acshaph; ²all the kings of the northern hill country; the kings in the Jordan Valley south of Galilee*; the kings in the Galilean foothills*; the kings of Naphoth-dor on the west; ³the kings of Canaan, both east and west; the kings of the Amorites, the Hittites, the Perizzites, the Jebusites in the hill country, and the Hivites in the towns on the slopes of Mount Hermon in the land of Mizpah.

⁴All these kings came out to fight. Their combined armies formed a vast horde. And with all their horses and chariots, they covered the landscape like the sand on the seashore. ⁵The kings joined forces and established their camp around the water near Merom to fight against Israel.

⁶Then the LORD said to Joshua, "Do not be afraid of them. By this time tomorrow I will hand all of them over to Israel as dead men. Then you must cripple their horses and burn their chariots."

⁷So Joshua and all his fighting men traveled to

10:40 Hebrew *the Shephelah.* **11:2a** Hebrew *in the Arabah south of Kinnereth.* **11:2b** Hebrew *the Shephelah;* also in 11:16.

11:1-16 Through the more detailed accounts of Joshua's campaign in southern Canaan (6:1–10:43), the narrator firmly established that the Israelites needed God's help to succeed. What had been true in the southern campaign would also be true in the northern campaign (11:1-23), so the details were unnecessary.

11:1-3 Hazor lay along the international trade route and was by far the largest and most important inland city of Canaan (see 11:10). Virtually all of northern Canaan joined the coalition of King Jabin against Israel. This region stretched from the Mediterranean Sea in the west to the desert in the east and from Phoenicia's borders in the north to the hill country and the Jordan Valley in the south. The term *Jebusites* typically refers to the people of Jerusalem (formerly Jebus) and towns under its control. Perhaps men from Jebus were mercenaries to Jabin. *Mizpah* means "watchtower" or "lookout." Several places had this name; this one was the vast region of the lower slopes of Mount Hermon, the highest peak of the Promised Land.

the water near Merom and attacked suddenly. ⁸And the LORD gave them victory over their enemies. The Israelites chased them as far as Greater Sidon and Misrephoth-maim, and eastward into the valley of Mizpah, until not one enemy warrior was left alive. ⁹Then Joshua crippled the horses and burned all the chariots, as the LORD had instructed.

¹⁰Joshua then turned back and captured Hazor and killed its king. (Hazor had at one time been the capital of all these kingdoms.) ¹¹The Israelites completely destroyed* every living thing in the city, leaving no survivors. Not a single person was spared. And then Joshua burned the city.

¹²Joshua slaughtered all the other kings and their people, completely destroying them, just as Moses, the servant of the LORD, had commanded. ¹³But the Israelites did not burn any of the towns built on mounds except Hazor, which Joshua burned. ¹⁴And the Israelites took all the plunder and livestock of the ravaged towns for themselves. But they killed all the people, leaving no survivors. ¹⁵As the LORD had commanded his servant Moses, so Moses commanded Joshua. And Joshua did as he was told, carefully obeying all the commands that the LORD had given to Moses.

¹⁶So Joshua conquered the entire region—the hill country, the entire Negev, the whole area around the town of Goshen, the western foothills, the Jordan Valley,* the mountains of Israel, and the Galilean foothills. ¹⁷The Israelite territory now extended all the way from Mount Halak, which leads up to Seir in the south, as far north as Baal-gad at the foot of Mount Hermon in the valley of Lebanon. Joshua killed all the kings of those territories, ¹⁸waging war for a long time to accomplish this. ¹⁹No one in this region made peace with the Israelites except the Hivites of Gibeon. All the others were defeated. ²⁰For the LORD hardened their hearts and caused them to fight the Israelites. So they were completely destroyed without mercy, as the LORD had commanded Moses.

²¹During this period Joshua destroyed all the descendants of Anak, who lived in the hill country of Hebron, Debir, Anab, and the entire hill country of Judah and Israel. He killed them all and completely destroyed their towns. ²²None of the descendants of Anak were left in all the land of Israel, though some still remained in Gaza, Gath, and Ashdod.

²³So Joshua took control of the entire land, just as the LORD had instructed Moses. He gave it to the people of Israel as their special possession, dividing the land among the tribes. So the land finally had rest from war.

Kings Defeated East of the Jordan

12 These are the kings east of the Jordan River who had been killed by the Israelites and whose land was taken. Their territory extended from the Arnon Gorge to Mount Hermon and included all the land east of the Jordan Valley.*

²King Sihon of the Amorites, who lived in Heshbon, was defeated. His kingdom included Aroer, on the edge of the Arnon Gorge, and extended from the middle of the Arnon Gorge to the Jabbok River, which serves as a border for the Ammonites. This territory included the southern half of the territory of Gilead. ³Sihon also controlled the Jordan Valley and regions to the east—from as far north as the Sea of Galilee to as far south as the Dead Sea,* including the road to Beth-jeshimoth and southward to the slopes of Pisgah.

⁴King Og of Bashan, the last of the Rephaites, lived at Ashtaroth and Edrei. ⁵He ruled a territory stretching from Mount Hermon to Salecah in the north and to all of Bashan in the east, and westward to the borders of the kingdoms of Geshur and Maacah. This territory included the northern half of Gilead, as far as the boundary of King Sihon of Heshbon.

⁶Moses, the servant of the LORD, and the Israelites had destroyed the people of King Sihon and King Og. And Moses gave their land as a possession to the tribes of Reuben, Gad, and the half-tribe of Manasseh.

Kings Defeated West of the Jordan

⁷The following is a list of the kings that Joshua and the Israelite armies defeated on the west side of the Jordan, from Baal-gad in the valley of Lebanon to Mount Halak, which leads up to Seir. (Joshua gave this land to the tribes of Israel as their possession, ⁸including the hill country, the western foothills,* the Jordan Valley, the mountain slopes, the Judean wilderness, and the Negev. The people who lived in this region were the Hittites, the Amorites, the

---

11:11 The Hebrew term used here refers to the complete consecration of things or people to the LORD, either by destroying them or by giving them as an offering; also in 11:12, 20, 21. **11:16** Hebrew *the Shephelah, the Arabah.* **12:1** Hebrew *the Arabah;* also in 12:3, 8. **12:3** Hebrew *from the Sea of Kinnereth to the Sea of the Arabah, which is the Salt Sea.* **12:8** Hebrew *the Shephelah.*

11:11 Archaeological excavations confirm that fire destroyed parts of Hazor in the Late Bronze Age.

12:1-24 This chapter summarizes Israel's conquests on both sides of the Jordan and transitions to Joshua's distribution of the land of Canaan among the tribes of Israel (13:1–21:45).

12:7-24 Joshua and the Israelite armies faithfully carried out the tasks God gave them. This summary showcases their successes, providing proper recognition for their faithfulness. God gave the Israelites their promised inheritance while bringing about the long-delayed judgment of the Canaanites. This roster of defeated kings, identified by their city-states, provides evidence of God's accomplished purposes. The list of kings that Israel defeated symbolizes God's mighty acts for his people and exalts his own great name.

"Be strong and courageous! ...For the LORD your God is with you."

JOSHUA 1:9

Canaanites, the Perizzites, the Hivites, and the Jebusites.) These are the kings Israel defeated:

⁹ The king of Jericho
The king of Ai, near Bethel
¹⁰ The king of Jerusalem
The king of Hebron
¹¹ The king of Jarmuth
The king of Lachish
¹² The king of Eglon
The king of Gezer
¹³ The king of Debir
The king of Geder
¹⁴ The king of Hormah
The king of Arad
¹⁵ The king of Libnah
The king of Adullam
¹⁶ The king of Makkedah
The king of Bethel
¹⁷ The king of Tappuah
The king of Hepher
¹⁸ The king of Aphek
The king of Lasharon
¹⁹ The king of Madon
The king of Hazor
²⁰ The king of Shimron-meron
The king of Acshaph
²¹ The king of Taanach
The king of Megiddo
²² The king of Kedesh
The king of Jokneam in Carmel
²³ The king of Dor in the town of Naphoth-dor*
The king of Goyim in Gilgal*
²⁴ The king of Tirzah.

In all, thirty-one kings were defeated.

The Land Yet to Be Conquered

13 When Joshua was an old man, the Lord said to him, "You are growing old, and much land remains to be conquered. ²This is the territory that remains: all the regions of the Philistines and the Geshurites, ³and the larger territory of the Canaanites, extending from the stream of Shihor on the border of Egypt, northward to the boundary of Ekron. It includes the territory of the five Philistine rulers of Gaza, Ashdod, Ashkelon, Gath, and Ekron. The land of the Avvites ⁴in the south also remains to be conquered. In the north, the following area has not yet been conquered: all the land of the Canaanites, including Mearah (which belongs to the Sidonians), stretching northward to Aphek on the border of the Amorites; ⁵the land of the Gebalites and all of the Lebanon mountain area to the east, from Baal-gad below Mount Hermon to Lebo-hamath; ⁶and all the hill country from Lebanon to Misrephoth-maim, including all the land of the Sidonians.

"I myself will drive these people out of the land ahead of the Israelites. So be sure to give this land to Israel as a special possession, just as I have commanded you. ⁷Include all this territory as Israel's possession when you divide this land among the nine tribes and the half-tribe of Manasseh."

The Land Divided East of the Jordan

⁸Half the tribe of Manasseh and the tribes of Reuben and Gad had already received their grants of land on the east side of the Jordan, for Moses, the servant of the Lord, had previously assigned this land to them.

⁹Their territory extended from Aroer on the edge of the Arnon Gorge (including the town in the middle of the gorge) to the plain beyond Medeba, as far as Dibon. ¹⁰It also included all the towns of King Sihon of the Amorites, who had reigned in Heshbon, and extended as far as the borders of Ammon. ¹¹It included Gilead, the territory of the kingdoms of Geshur and Maacah, all of Mount Hermon, all of Bashan as far as Salecah, ¹²and all the territory of King Og of Bashan, who had reigned in Ashtaroth and Edrei. King Og was the last of the Rephaites, for Moses had attacked them and driven them out. ¹³But the Israelites failed to drive out the people of Geshur and Maacah, so they continue to live among the Israelites to this day.

An Allotment for the Tribe of Levi

¹⁴Moses did not assign any allotment of land to the tribe of Levi. Instead, as the Lord had promised them, their allotment came from the offerings burned on the altar to the Lord, the God of Israel.

The Land Given to the Tribe of Reuben

¹⁵Moses had assigned the following area to the clans of the tribe of Reuben.

¹⁶Their territory extended from Aroer on the edge of the Arnon Gorge (including the town in the middle of the gorge) to the plain beyond Medeba. ¹⁷It included Heshbon and the other towns on the plain—Dibon, Bamoth-baal, Beth-baal-meon, ¹⁸Jahaz, Kedemoth, Mephaath, ¹⁹Kiriathaim, Sibmah, Zereth-shahar on the

---

12:23a Hebrew *Naphath-dor*, a variant spelling of Naphoth-dor. **12:23b** Greek version reads *Goyim in Galilee*.

13:14 The tribe of Levi did not take possession of any land inheritance. They did not till the land, but worked in the Tabernacle and acted as mediators between God and his people. God provided for their physical needs through the offerings and sacrifices offered by the other tribes. Thus, God was their inheritance. (See also 13:33; 14:3-4; 18:7; 21:41.)

hill above the valley, ²⁰Beth-peor, the slopes of Pisgah, and Beth-jeshimoth.

²¹The land of Reuben also included all the towns of the plain and the entire kingdom of Sihon. Sihon was the Amorite king who had reigned in Heshbon and was killed by Moses along with the leaders of Midian—Evi, Rekem, Zur, Hur, and Reba—princes living in the region who were allied with Sihon. ²²The Israelites had also killed Balaam son of Beor, who used magic to tell the future. ²³The Jordan River marked the western boundary for the tribe of Reuben. The towns and their surrounding villages in this area were given as a homeland to the clans of the tribe of Reuben.

The Land Given to the Tribe of Gad

²⁴Moses had assigned the following area to the clans of the tribe of Gad.

²⁵Their territory included Jazer, all the towns of Gilead, and half of the land of Ammon, as far as the town of Aroer just west of* Rabbah. ²⁶It extended from Heshbon to Ramath-mizpeh and Betonim, and from Mahanaim to the territory of Lo-debar.* ²⁷In the valley were Beth-haram, Beth-nimrah, Succoth, Zaphon, and the rest of the kingdom of King Sihon of Heshbon. The western boundary ran along the Jordan River, extended as far north as the tip of the Sea of Galilee,* and then turned eastward. ²⁸The towns and their surrounding villages in this area were given as a homeland to the clans of the tribe of Gad.

The Land Given to the Half-Tribe of Manasseh

²⁹Moses had assigned the following area to the clans of the half-tribe of Manasseh.

³⁰Their territory extended from Mahanaim, including all of Bashan, all the former kingdom of King Og, and the sixty towns of Jair in Bashan. ³¹It also included half of Gilead and King Og's royal cities of Ashtaroth and Edrei. All this was given to the clans of the descendants of Makir, who was Manasseh's son.

³²These are the allotments Moses had made while he was on the plains of Moab, across the Jordan River, east of Jericho. ³³But Moses gave no allotment of land to the tribe of Levi, for the LORD, the God of Israel, had promised that he himself would be their allotment.

The Land Divided West of the Jordan

14 The remaining tribes of Israel received land in Canaan as allotted by Eleazar the priest, Joshua son of Nun, and the tribal leaders. ²These nine and a half tribes received their grants of land by means of sacred lots, in accordance with the LORD's command through Moses. ³Moses had already given a grant of land to the two and a half tribes on the east side of the Jordan River, but he had given the Levites no such allotment. ⁴The descendants of Joseph had become two separate tribes—Manasseh and Ephraim. And the Levites were given no land at all, only towns to live in with surrounding pasturelands for their livestock and all their possessions. ⁵So the land was distributed in strict accordance with the LORD's commands to Moses.

Caleb Requests His Land

⁶A delegation from the tribe of Judah, led by Caleb son of Jephunneh the Kenizzite, came to Joshua at Gilgal. Caleb said to Joshua, "Remember what the LORD said to Moses, the man of God, about you and me when we were at Kadesh-barnea. ⁷I was forty years old when Moses, the servant of the LORD, sent me from Kadesh-barnea to explore the land of Canaan. I returned and gave an honest report, ⁸but my brothers who went with me frightened the people from entering the Promised Land. For my part, I wholeheartedly followed the LORD my God. ⁹So that day Moses solemnly promised me, 'The land of Canaan on which you were just walking will be your grant of land and that of your descendants forever, because you wholeheartedly followed the LORD my God.'

¹⁰"Now, as you can see, the LORD has kept me alive and well as he promised for all these forty-five years since Moses made this promise—even while Israel wandered in the wilderness. Today I am eighty-five years old. ¹¹I am as strong now as I was when Moses sent me on that journey, and I can still travel and fight as well as I could then. ¹²So give me the hill country that the LORD promised me. You will remember that as scouts we found the descendants of Anak

---

13:25 Hebrew *in front of.* **13:26** Hebrew *Li-debir,* apparently a variant spelling of Lo-debar (compare 2 Sam 9:4; 17:27; Amos 6:13). **13:27** Hebrew *Sea of Kinnereth.*

14:1–19:51 The allotment of land given to the tribes on the west side of the Jordan describes what God intended for each tribe to possess. This section begins with the land assigned to Caleb (14:6-15) and ends with that assigned to Joshua (19:49-51). Only Caleb and Joshua had expressed faith in God that Israel could conquer the land (Numbers 13:30; 14:6-9).

14:4 Joseph, the elder son of Jacob's favorite wife, Rachel, received a double portion of land through Manasseh and Ephraim, his sons. Because the Levites did not receive a separate tribal territory (13:14), the total number of tribes with land remained at twelve.

living there in great, walled towns. But if the LORD is with me, I will drive them out of the land, just as the LORD said."

¹³So Joshua blessed Caleb son of Jephunneh and gave Hebron to him as his portion of land. ¹⁴Hebron still belongs to the descendants of Caleb son of Jephunneh the Kenizzite because he wholeheartedly followed the LORD, the God of Israel. ¹⁵(Previously Hebron had been called Kiriath-arba. It had been named after Arba, a great hero of the descendants of Anak.)

And the land had rest from war.

The Land Given to the Tribe of Judah

15 The allotment for the clans of the tribe of Judah reached southward to the border of Edom, as far south as the wilderness of Zin.

²The southern boundary began at the south bay of the Dead Sea,* ³ran south of Scorpion Pass* into the wilderness of Zin, and then went south of Kadesh-barnea to Hezron. Then it went up to Addar, where it turned toward Karka. ⁴From there it passed to Azmon until it finally reached the Brook of Egypt, which it followed to the Mediterranean Sea.* This was their* southern boundary.

⁵The eastern boundary extended along the Dead Sea to the mouth of the Jordan River.

The northern boundary began at the bay where the Jordan River empties into the Dead Sea, ⁶went up from there to Beth-hoglah, then proceeded north of Beth-arabah to the Stone of Bohan. (Bohan was Reuben's son.) ⁷From that point it went through the valley of Achor to Debir, turning north toward Gilgal, which is across from the slopes of Adummim on the south side of the valley. From there the boundary extended to the springs at En-shemesh and on to En-rogel. ⁸The boundary then passed through the valley of Ben-Hinnom, along the southern slopes of the Jebusites, where the city of Jerusalem is located. Then it went west to the top of the mountain above the valley of Hinnom, and on up to the northern end of the valley of Rephaim. ⁹From there the boundary extended from the top of the mountain to the spring at the waters of Nephtoah,* and from there to the towns on Mount Ephron. Then it turned toward Baalah (that is, Kiriath-jearim). ¹⁰The boundary circled west of Baalah to Mount Seir, passed along to the town of Kesalon on the northern slope of Mount Jearim, and went down to Beth-shemesh and on to Timnah. ¹¹The boundary then proceeded to the slope of the hill north of Ekron, where it turned toward Shikkeron and Mount Baalah. It passed Jabneel and ended at the Mediterranean Sea.

¹²The western boundary was the shoreline of the Mediterranean Sea.*

These are the boundaries for the clans of the tribe of Judah.

The Land Given to Caleb

¹³The LORD commanded Joshua to assign some of Judah's territory to Caleb son of Jephunneh. So Caleb was given the town of Kiriath-arba (that is, Hebron), which had been named after Anak's ancestor. ¹⁴Caleb drove out the three groups of Anakites—the descendants of Sheshai, Ahiman, and Talmai, the sons of Anak.

¹⁵From there he went to fight against the people living in the town of Debir (formerly called Kiriath-sepher). ¹⁶Caleb said, "I will give my daughter Acsah in marriage to the one who attacks and captures Kiriath-sepher." ¹⁷Othniel, the son of Caleb's brother Kenaz, was the one who conquered it, so Acsah became Othniel's wife.

¹⁸When Acsah married Othniel, she urged him* to ask her father for a field. As she got down off her donkey, Caleb asked her, "What's the matter?"

¹⁹She said, "Give me another gift. You have already given me land in the Negev; now please give me springs of water, too." So Caleb gave her the upper and lower springs.

The Towns Allotted to Judah

²⁰This was the homeland allocated to the clans of the tribe of Judah.

²¹The towns of Judah situated along the borders of Edom in the extreme south were Kabzeel, Eder, Jagur, ²²Kinah, Dimonah, Adadah, ²³Kedesh, Hazor, Ithnan, ²⁴Ziph, Telem, Bealoth, ²⁵Hazor-hadattah, Kerioth-hezron (that is, Hazor), ²⁶Amam, Shema, Moladah, ²⁷Hazar-gaddah,

---

15:2 Hebrew *the Salt Sea;* also in 15:5. **15:3** Hebrew *Akrabbim.* **15:4a** Hebrew *the sea;* also in 15:11. **15:4b** Hebrew *your.* **15:9** Or *the spring at Me-nephtoah.* **15:12** Hebrew *the Great Sea;* also in 15:47. **15:18** Some Greek manuscripts read *he urged her.*

15:1-63 The land that the tribe of Judah received is described in greater detail than that of the other tribes. His elder brothers' failures (Genesis 34:1-31; 35:22) put Judah in line to receive the mantle of leadership. Thus, the tribe of Judah received a central geographical position among the tribes, guaranteeing its leadership in the nation (Genesis 49:8-12; Deuteronomy 33:7).

15:18-19 No water source existed for the town Othniel conquered in the semi-arid Negev ("dry land"), the southernmost of Judah's districts. The upper and lower springs were close together but too far from Debir to belong to it naturally, so Acsah asked her father, Caleb, for the water rights.

WHAT THE BIBLE SAYS ABOUT Courage

God Wants Us to Be Courageous

"Be strong and courageous! Do not be afraid and do not panic before them. For the LORD your God will personally go ahead of you. He will neither fail you nor abandon you." **DEUTERONOMY 31:6**

"As for you, be strong and courageous, for your work will be rewarded." **2 CHRONICLES 15:7**

Be brave and courageous

Having hope will give you courage.

Focusing on God—Not on People and Problems—Gives Courage

Be strong and courageous,
 all you who put your hope in the LORD!
PSALM 31:24

Fearing people is a dangerous trap,
 but trusting the LORD means safety.
PROVERBS 29:25

Wait patiently for the LORD.
 Be brave and courageous.
 Yes, wait patiently for the LORD.
PSALM 27:14

Dear children, remain in fellowship with Christ so that when he returns, you will be full of courage and not shrink back from him in shame. **1 JOHN 2:28**

God Gives Us Courage

"Having hope will give you courage.
 You will be protected and will rest in safety."
JOB 11:18

I prayed to the LORD, and he answered me.
 He freed me from all my fears.
PSALM 34:4

They were all terrified when they saw him. But Jesus spoke to them at once. "Don't be afraid," he said. "Take courage! I am here!" **MARK 6:50**

Take courage! For I believe God. It will be just as he said. **ACTS 27:25**

Heshmon, Beth-pelet, ²⁸Hazar-shual, Beersheba, Biziothiah, ²⁹Baalah, Iim, Ezem, ³⁰Eltolad, Kesil, Hormah, ³¹Ziklag, Madmannah, Sansannah, ³²Lebaoth, Shilhim, Ain, and Rimmon—twenty-nine towns with their surrounding villages.

³³The following towns situated in the western foothills* were also given to Judah: Eshtaol, Zorah, Ashnah, ³⁴Zanoah, En-gannim, Tappuah, Enam, ³⁵Jarmuth, Adullam, Socoh, Azekah, ³⁶Shaaraim, Adithaim, Gederah, and Gederothaim—fourteen towns with their surrounding villages.

³⁷Also included were Zenan, Hadashah, Migdal-gad, ³⁸Dilean, Mizpeh, Joktheel, ³⁹Lachish, Bozkath, Eglon, ⁴⁰Cabbon, Lahmam, Kitlish, ⁴¹Gederoth, Beth-dagon, Naamah, and Makkedah—sixteen towns with their surrounding villages.

⁴²Besides these, there were Libnah, Ether, Ashan, ⁴³Iphtah, Ashnah, Nezib, ⁴⁴Keilah, Aczib, and Mareshah—nine towns with their surrounding villages.

⁴⁵The territory of the tribe of Judah also included Ekron and its surrounding settlements and villages. ⁴⁶From Ekron the boundary extended west and included the towns near Ashdod with their surrounding villages. ⁴⁷It also included Ashdod with its surrounding settlements and villages and Gaza with its settlements and villages, as far as the Brook of Egypt and along the coast of the Mediterranean Sea.

⁴⁸Judah also received the following towns in the hill country: Shamir, Jattir, Socoh, ⁴⁹Dannah, Kiriath-sannah (that is, Debir), ⁵⁰Anab, Eshtemoh, Anim, ⁵¹Goshen, Holon, and Giloh—eleven towns with their surrounding villages.

⁵²Also included were the towns of Arab, Dumah, Eshan, ⁵³Janim, Beth-tappuah, Aphekah, ⁵⁴Humtah, Kiriath-arba (that is, Hebron), and Zior—nine towns with their surrounding villages.

⁵⁵Besides these, there were Maon, Carmel, Ziph, Juttah, ⁵⁶Jezreel, Jokdeam, Zanoah, ⁵⁷Kain, Gibeah, and Timnah—ten towns with their surrounding villages.

⁵⁸In addition, there were Halhul, Beth-zur, Gedor, ⁵⁹Maarath, Beth-anoth, and Eltekon—six towns with their surrounding villages.

⁶⁰There were also Kiriath-baal (that is, Kiriath-jearim) and Rabbah—two towns with their surrounding villages.

⁶¹In the wilderness there were the towns of Beth-arabah, Middin, Secacah, ⁶²Nibshan, the City of Salt, and En-gedi—six towns with their surrounding villages.

⁶³But the tribe of Judah could not drive out the Jebusites, who lived in the city of Jerusalem, so the Jebusites live there among the people of Judah to this day.

The Land Given to Ephraim and West Manasseh

16 The allotment for the descendants of Joseph extended from the Jordan River near Jericho, east of the springs of Jericho, through the wilderness and into the hill country of Bethel. ²From Bethel (that is, Luz)* it ran over to Ataroth in the territory of the Arkites. ³Then it descended westward to the territory of the Japhletites as far as Lower Beth-horon, then to Gezer and over to the Mediterranean Sea.*

⁴This was the homeland allocated to the families of Joseph's sons, Manasseh and Ephraim.

The Land Given to Ephraim

⁵The following territory was given to the clans of the tribe of Ephraim.

The boundary of their homeland began at Ataroth-addar in the east. From there it ran to Upper Beth-horon, ⁶then on to the Mediterranean Sea. From Micmethath on the north, the boundary curved eastward past Taanath-shiloh to the east of Janoah. ⁷From Janoah it turned southward to Ataroth and Naarah, touched Jericho, and ended at the Jordan River. ⁸From Tappuah the boundary extended westward, following the Kanah Ravine to the Mediterranean Sea. This is the homeland allocated to the clans of the tribe of Ephraim.

⁹In addition, some towns with their surrounding villages in the territory allocated to the half-tribe of Manasseh were set aside for the tribe of Ephraim. ¹⁰They did not drive the Canaanites out of Gezer, however, so the people of Gezer live as slaves among the people of Ephraim to this day.

15:33 Hebrew *the Shephelah.* **16:2** As in Greek version (also see 18:13); Hebrew reads *From Bethel to Luz.* **16:3** Hebrew *the sea;* also in 16:6, 8.

15:63 Even though Jerusalem was assigned to the tribe of Benjamin (18:28), it was not conquered in Joshua's day. The Jebusites' continued presence caused trouble (Judges 1:21). Jerusalem remained in Canaanite hands until King David's day. **16:1–17:18** Joseph had two sons, Manasseh and Ephraim (Genesis 41:50-52). Half of Manasseh's descendants had received their inheritance east of the Jordan River. The tribe of Ephraim and the rest of the tribe of Manasseh now received their allotments. This brought the allotments to twelve and fulfilled the blessing Jacob had pronounced upon Joseph (Genesis 49:22-26). Like Judah in the south, Joseph's tribes exercised leadership from their central position in the north.

The Land Given to West Manasseh

17 The next allotment of land was given to the half-tribe of Manasseh, the descendants of Joseph's older son. Makir, the firstborn son of Manasseh, was the father of Gilead. Because his descendants were experienced soldiers, the regions of Gilead and Bashan on the east side of the Jordan had already been given to them. ²So the allotment on the west side of the Jordan was for the remaining families within the clans of the tribe of Manasseh: Abiezer, Helek, Asriel, Shechem, Hepher, and Shemida. These clans represent the male descendants of Manasseh son of Joseph.

³However, Zelophehad, a descendant of Hepher son of Gilead, son of Makir, son of Manasseh, had no sons. He had only daughters, whose names were Mahlah, Noah, Hoglah, Milcah, and Tirzah. ⁴These women came to Eleazar the priest, Joshua son of Nun, and the Israelite leaders and said, "The LORD commanded Moses to give us a grant of land along with the men of our tribe."

So Joshua gave them a grant of land along with their uncles, as the LORD had commanded. ⁵As a result, Manasseh's total allocation came to ten parcels of land, in addition to the land of Gilead and Bashan across the Jordan River, ⁶because the female descendants of Manasseh received a grant of land along with the male descendants. (The land of Gilead was given to the rest of the male descendants of Manasseh.)

⁷The boundary of the tribe of Manasseh extended from the border of Asher to Micmethath, near Shechem. Then the boundary went south from Micmethath to the settlement near the spring of Tappuah. ⁸The land surrounding Tappuah belonged to Manasseh, but the town of Tappuah itself, on the border of Manasseh's territory, belonged to the tribe of Ephraim. ⁹From the spring of Tappuah, the boundary of Manasseh followed the Kanah Ravine to the Mediterranean Sea.* Several towns south of the ravine were inside Manasseh's territory, but they actually belonged to the tribe of Ephraim. ¹⁰In general, however, the land south of the ravine belonged to Ephraim, and the land north of the ravine belonged to Manasseh. Manasseh's boundary ran along the northern side of the ravine and ended at the Mediterranean Sea. North of Manasseh was the territory of Asher, and to the east was the territory of Issachar.

¹¹The following towns within the territory of Issachar and Asher, however, were given to Manasseh: Beth-shan,* Ibleam, Dor (that is, Naphoth-dor),* Endor, Taanach, and Megiddo, each with their surrounding settlements.

¹²But the descendants of Manasseh were unable to occupy these towns because the Canaanites were determined to stay in that region. ¹³Later, however, when the Israelites became strong enough, they forced the Canaanites to work as slaves. But they did not drive them out of the land.

¹⁴The descendants of Joseph came to Joshua and asked, "Why have you given us only one portion of land as our homeland when the LORD has blessed us with so many people?"

¹⁵Joshua replied, "If there are so many of you, and if the hill country of Ephraim is not large enough for you, clear out land for yourselves in the forest where the Perizzites and Rephaites live."

¹⁶The descendants of Joseph responded, "It's true that the hill country is not large enough for us. But all the Canaanites in the lowlands have iron chariots, both those in Beth-shan and its surrounding settlements and those in the valley of Jezreel. They are too strong for us."

¹⁷Then Joshua said to the tribes of Ephraim and Manasseh, the descendants of Joseph, "Since you are so large and strong, you will be given more than one portion. ¹⁸The forests of the hill country will be yours as well. Clear as much of the land as you wish, and take possession of its farthest corners. And you will drive out the Canaanites from the valleys, too, even though they are strong and have iron chariots."

The Allotments of the Remaining Land

18 Now that the land was under Israelite control, the entire community of Israel gathered at Shiloh and set up the Tabernacle.* ²But there remained seven tribes who had not yet been allotted their grants of land.

³Then Joshua asked them, "How long are you going to wait before taking possession of the remaining land the LORD, the God of your ancestors, has given to you? ⁴Select three men from each tribe, and I will send them out to explore the land and map it out. They will then return to me with a written report of their proposed divisions of their new homeland. ⁵Let them divide the land into seven sections, excluding Judah's territory in the south and Joseph's

---

17:9 Hebrew *the sea;* also in 17:10.   17:11a Hebrew *Beth-shean,* a variant spelling of Beth-shan; also in 17:16.   17:11b The meaning of the Hebrew here is uncertain.   18:1 Hebrew *Tent of Meeting.*

17:14-18 Joshua was pleased with the request for more land. Despite the threat of iron chariots, he emboldened the two tribes to claim the neighboring spaces. God often expands our influence if we hold on to our faith in him.

18:1-10 Joshua identified the negligence of these seven tribes of Israel in capturing the remaining land. They were perhaps weary and afraid of the Canaanites, but Joshua did not tolerate their disregard for what God had commanded them. He gave them specific instructions on what to do. Procrastinating in doing God's work can hint at a lack of faith.

territory in the north. ⁶And when you record the seven divisions of the land and bring them to me, I will cast sacred lots in the presence of the Lord our God to assign land to each tribe.

⁷"The Levites, however, will not receive any allotment of land. Their role as priests of the Lord is their allotment. And the tribes of Gad, Reuben, and the half-tribe of Manasseh won't receive any more land, for they have already received their grant of land, which Moses, the servant of the Lord, gave them on the east side of the Jordan River."

⁸As the men started on their way to map out the land, Joshua commanded them, "Go and explore the land and write a description of it. Then return to me, and I will assign the land to the tribes by casting sacred lots here in the presence of the Lord at Shiloh." ⁹The men did as they were told and mapped the entire territory into seven sections, listing the towns in each section. They made a written record and then returned to Joshua in the camp at Shiloh. ¹⁰And there at Shiloh, Joshua cast sacred lots in the presence of the Lord to determine which tribe should have each section.

The Land Given to Benjamin

¹¹The first allotment of land went to the clans of the tribe of Benjamin. It lay between the territory assigned to the tribes of Judah and Joseph.

¹²The northern boundary of Benjamin's land began at the Jordan River, went north of the slope of Jericho, then west through the hill country and the wilderness of Beth-aven. ¹³From there the boundary went south to Luz (that is, Bethel) and proceeded down to Ataroth-addar on the hill that lies south of Lower Beth-horon.

¹⁴The boundary then made a turn and swung south along the western edge of the hill facing Beth-horon, ending at the village of Kiriath-baal (that is, Kiriath-jearim), a town belonging to the tribe of Judah. This was the western boundary.

¹⁵The southern boundary began at the outskirts of Kiriath-jearim. From that western point it ran* to the spring at the waters of Nephtoah,* ¹⁶and down to the base of the mountain beside the valley of Ben-Hinnom, at the northern end of the valley of Rephaim. From there it went down the valley of Hinnom, crossing south of the slope where the Jebusites lived, and continued down to En-rogel. ¹⁷From En-rogel the boundary proceeded in a northerly direction and came to En-shemesh and on to Geliloth (which is across from the slopes of Adummim). Then it went down to the Stone of Bohan. (Bohan was Reuben's son.) ¹⁸From there it passed along the north side of the slope overlooking the Jordan Valley.* The border then went down into the valley, ¹⁹ran past the north slope of Beth-hoglah, and ended at the north bay of the Dead Sea,* which is the southern end of the Jordan River. This was the southern boundary.

²⁰The eastern boundary was the Jordan River.

These were the boundaries of the homeland allocated to the clans of the tribe of Benjamin.

The Towns Given to Benjamin

²¹These were the towns given to the clans of the tribe of Benjamin.

Jericho, Beth-hoglah, Emek-keziz, ²²Beth-arabah, Zemaraim, Bethel, ²³Avvim, Parah, Ophrah, ²⁴Kephar-ammoni, Ophni, and Geba—twelve towns with their surrounding villages. ²⁵Also Gibeon, Ramah, Beeroth, ²⁶Mizpah, Kephirah, Mozah, ²⁷Rekem, Irpeel, Taralah, ²⁸Zela, Haeleph, the Jebusite town (that is, Jerusalem), Gibeah, and Kiriath-jearim*—fourteen towns with their surrounding villages.

This was the homeland allocated to the clans of the tribe of Benjamin.

The Land Given to Simeon

19 The second allotment of land went to the clans of the tribe of Simeon. Their homeland was surrounded by Judah's territory.

²Simeon's homeland included Beersheba, Sheba, Moladah, ³Hazar-shual, Balah, Ezem, ⁴Eltolad, Bethul, Hormah, ⁵Ziklag, Beth-marcaboth, Hazar-susah, ⁶Beth-lebaoth, and Sharuhen—thirteen towns with their surrounding villages. ⁷It also included Ain, Rimmon, Ether, and Ashan—four towns with their villages, ⁸including all the surrounding villages as far south as Baalath-beer (also known as Ramah of the Negev).

This was the homeland allocated to the clans of the tribe of Simeon. ⁹Their allocation of land came from part of what had been given to Judah because Judah's territory was too large for them. So the tribe of Simeon received an allocation within the territory of Judah.

18:15a Or *From there it went to Mozah.* The meaning of the Hebrew is uncertain.   18:15b Or *the spring at Me-nephtoah.*   18:18 Hebrew *overlooking the Arabah,* or *overlooking Beth-arabah.*   18:19 Hebrew *Salt Sea.*   18:28 As in Greek version; Hebrew reads *Kiriath.*

19:1-9 Simeon, Jacob and Leah's second son, was older than Judah. However, he had forfeited a leading role because of his violent actions against Shechem (Genesis 34:25-26). His descendants' inheritance reflected this; their land was carved out of Judah's territory on the southern periphery of the Negev. This arid land stood far from any centers of influence and power.

The Land Given to Zebulun

¹⁰The third allotment of land went to the clans of the tribe of Zebulun.

The boundary of Zebulun's homeland started at Sarid. ¹¹From there it went west, going past Maralah, touching Dabbesheth, and proceeding to the brook east of Jokneam. ¹²In the other direction, the boundary went east from Sarid to the border of Kisloth-tabor, and from there to Daberath and up to Japhia. ¹³Then it continued east to Gath-hepher, Eth-kazin, and Rimmon and turned toward Neah. ¹⁴The northern boundary of Zebulun passed Hannathon and ended at the valley of Iphtah-el. ¹⁵The towns in these areas included Kattath, Nahalal, Shimron, Idalah, and Bethlehem—twelve towns with their surrounding villages.

¹⁶The homeland allocated to the clans of the tribe of Zebulun included these towns and their surrounding villages.

The Land Given to Issachar

¹⁷The fourth allotment of land went to the clans of the tribe of Issachar.

¹⁸Its boundaries included the following towns: Jezreel, Kesulloth, Shunem, ¹⁹Hapharaim, Shion, Anaharath, ²⁰Rabbith, Kishion, Ebez, ²¹Remeth, En-gannim, En-haddah, and Beth-pazzez. ²²The boundary also touched Tabor, Shahazumah, and Beth-shemesh, ending at the Jordan River—sixteen towns with their surrounding villages.

²³The homeland allocated to the clans of the tribe of Issachar included these towns and their surrounding villages.

The Land Given to Asher

²⁴The fifth allotment of land went to the clans of the tribe of Asher.

²⁵Its boundaries included these towns: Helkath, Hali, Beten, Acshaph, ²⁶Allammelech, Amad, and Mishal. The boundary on the west touched Carmel and Shihor-libnath, ²⁷then it turned east toward Beth-dagon, and ran as far as Zebulun in the valley of Iphtah-el, going north to Beth-emek and Neiel. It then continued north to Cabul, ²⁸Abdon,* Rehob, Hammon, Kanah, and as far as Greater Sidon. ²⁹Then the boundary turned toward Ramah and the fortress of Tyre, where it turned toward Hosah and came to the Mediterranean Sea.* The territory also included Mehebel, Aczib, ³⁰Ummah, Aphek, and Rehob—twenty-two towns with their surrounding villages.

³¹The homeland allocated to the clans of the tribe of Asher included these towns and their surrounding villages.

The Land Given to Naphtali

³²The sixth allotment of land went to the clans of the tribe of Naphtali.

³³Its boundary ran from Heleph, from the oak at Zaanannim, and extended across to Adami-nekeb, Jabneel, and as far as Lakkum, ending at the Jordan River. ³⁴The western boundary ran past Aznoth-tabor, then to Hukkok, and touched the border of Zebulun in the south, the border of Asher on the west, and the Jordan River* on the east. ³⁵The fortified towns included in this territory were Ziddim, Zer, Hammath, Rakkath, Kinnereth, ³⁶Adamah, Ramah, Hazor, ³⁷Kedesh, Edrei, En-hazor, ³⁸Yiron, Migdal-el, Horem, Beth-anath, and Beth-shemesh—nineteen towns with their surrounding villages.

³⁹The homeland allocated to the clans of the tribe of Naphtali included these towns and their surrounding villages.

The Land Given to Dan

⁴⁰The seventh allotment of land went to the clans of the tribe of Dan.

⁴¹The land allocated as their homeland included the following towns: Zorah, Eshtaol, Ir-shemesh, ⁴²Shaalabbin, Aijalon, Ithlah, ⁴³Elon, Timnah, Ekron, ⁴⁴Eltekeh, Gibbethon, Baalath, ⁴⁵Jehud, Bene-berak, Gath-rimmon,

> "I fear nothing for God is with me!"
>
> **JOAN OF ARC**
> (1412–1431) military leader and martyr

19:28 As in some Hebrew manuscripts (see also 21:30); most Hebrew manuscripts read *Ebron.* 19:29 Hebrew *the sea.*
19:34 Hebrew *and Judah at the Jordan River.*

19:10-48 The five small remaining tribes received land on the edges of the Israelite territory and had little national influence.

⁴⁶Me-jarkon, Rakkon, and the territory across from Joppa.

⁴⁷But the tribe of Dan had trouble taking possession of their land,* so they attacked the town of Laish.* They captured it, slaughtered its people, and settled there. They renamed the town Dan after their ancestor.

⁴⁸The homeland allocated to the clans of the tribe of Dan included these towns and their surrounding villages.

The Land Given to Joshua

⁴⁹After all the land was divided among the tribes, the Israelites gave a piece of land to Joshua as his allocation. ⁵⁰For the LORD had said he could have any town he wanted. He chose Timnath-serah in the hill country of Ephraim. He rebuilt the town and lived there.

⁵¹These are the territories that Eleazar the priest, Joshua son of Nun, and the tribal leaders allocated as grants of land to the tribes of Israel by casting sacred lots in the presence of the LORD at the entrance of the Tabernacle* at Shiloh. So the division of the land was completed.

The Cities of Refuge

20 The LORD said to Joshua, ²"Now tell the Israelites to designate the cities of refuge, as I instructed Moses. ³Anyone who kills another person accidentally and unintentionally can run to one of these cities; they will be places of refuge from relatives seeking revenge for the person who was killed.

⁴"Upon reaching one of these cities, the one who caused the death will appear before the elders at the city gate and present his case. They must allow him to enter the city and give him a place to live among them. ⁵If the relatives of the victim come to avenge the killing, the leaders must not release the slayer to them, for he killed the other person unintentionally and without previous hostility. ⁶But the slayer must stay in that city and be tried by the local assembly, which will render a judgment. And he must continue to live in that city until the death of the high priest who was in office at the time of the accident. After that, he is free to return to his own home in the town from which he fled."

⁷The following cities were designated as cities of refuge: Kedesh of Galilee, in the hill country of Naphtali; Shechem, in the hill country of Ephraim; and Kiriath-arba (that is, Hebron), in the hill country of Judah. ⁸On the east side of the Jordan River, across from Jericho, the following cities were designated: Bezer, in the wilderness plain of the tribe of Reuben; Ramoth in Gilead, in the territory of the tribe of Gad; and Golan in Bashan, in the land of the tribe of Manasseh. ⁹These cities were set apart for all the Israelites as well as the foreigners living among them. Anyone who accidentally killed another person could take refuge in one of these cities. In this way, they could escape being killed in revenge prior to standing trial before the local assembly.

The Towns Given to the Levites

21 Then the leaders of the tribe of Levi came to consult with Eleazar the priest, Joshua son of Nun, and the leaders of the other tribes of Israel. ²They came to them at Shiloh in the land of Canaan and said, "The LORD commanded Moses to give us towns to live in and pasturelands for our livestock." ³So by the command of the LORD the people of Israel gave the Levites the following towns and pasturelands out of their own grants of land.

⁴The descendants of Aaron, who were members of the Kohathite clan within the tribe of Levi, were allotted thirteen towns that were originally assigned to the tribes of Judah, Simeon, and Benjamin. ⁵The other families of the Kohathite clan were allotted ten towns from the tribes of Ephraim, Dan, and the half-tribe of Manasseh.

⁶The clan of Gershon was allotted thirteen towns from the tribes of Issachar, Asher, Naphtali, and the half-tribe of Manasseh in Bashan.

⁷The clan of Merari was allotted twelve towns from the tribes of Reuben, Gad, and Zebulun.

⁸So the Israelites obeyed the LORD's command to Moses and assigned these towns and pasturelands to the Levites by casting sacred lots.

⁹The Israelites gave the following towns from the tribes of Judah and Simeon ¹⁰to the descendants of Aaron, who were members of the Kohathite clan within the tribe of Levi, since the sacred lot fell to them first: ¹¹Kiriath-arba (that is, Hebron), in the hill country of Judah, along with its surrounding pasturelands. (Arba was an ancestor of Anak.) ¹²But the open fields beyond the town and the surrounding villages were given to Caleb son of Jephunneh as his possession.

19:47a Or *had trouble holding on to their land*. **19:47b** Hebrew *Leshem*, a variant spelling of Laish. **19:51** Hebrew *Tent of Meeting*.

20:1-6 When God judges us, he looks not only at our external actions, but also into our hearts and motives. God specified how to protect from personal revenge those who had killed someone accidentally and unintentionally. The cities of refuge were safe havens for manslaughter offenders but not for murderers (see also Numbers 35:6-34).

20:9 The treatment of foreigners in Israel was a significant advance in human relations. Resident aliens received every justice offered to native Israelites (see Exodus 22:21; Leviticus 19:33-34; 24:22; Numbers 15:15-16).

21:1-8 The towns given to the tribe of Levi were determined by Israel's leaders casting lots.

[13] The following towns with their pasturelands were given to the descendants of Aaron the priest: Hebron (a city of refuge for those who accidentally killed someone), Libnah, [14] Jattir, Eshtemoa, [15] Holon, Debir, [16] Ain, Juttah, and Beth-shemesh—nine towns from these two tribes.

[17] From the tribe of Benjamin the priests were given the following towns with their pasturelands: Gibeon, Geba, [18] Anathoth, and Almon—four towns. [19] So in all, thirteen towns with their pasturelands were given to the priests, the descendants of Aaron.

[20] The rest of the Kohathite clan from the tribe of Levi was allotted the following towns and pasturelands from the tribe of Ephraim: [21] Shechem in the hill country of Ephraim (a city of refuge for those who accidentally killed someone), Gezer, [22] Kibzaim, and Beth-horon—four towns.

[23] The following towns and pasturelands were allotted to the priests from the tribe of Dan: Eltekeh, Gibbethon, [24] Aijalon, and Gath-rimmon—four towns.

[25] The half-tribe of Manasseh allotted the following towns with their pasturelands to the priests: Taanach and Gath-rimmon—two towns. [26] So in all, ten towns with their pasturelands were given to the rest of the Kohathite clan.

[27] The descendants of Gershon, another clan within the tribe of Levi, received the following towns with their pasturelands from the half-tribe of Manasseh: Golan in Bashan (a city of refuge for those who accidentally killed someone) and Beeshterah—two towns.

[28] From the tribe of Issachar they received the following towns with their pasturelands: Kishion, Daberath, [29] Jarmuth, and En-gannim—four towns.

[30] From the tribe of Asher they received the following towns with their pasturelands: Mishal, Abdon, [31] Helkath, and Rehob—four towns.

[32] From the tribe of Naphtali they received the following towns with their pasturelands: Kedesh in Galilee (a city of refuge for those who accidentally killed someone), Hammoth-dor, and Kartan—three towns. [33] So in all, thirteen towns with their pasturelands were allotted to the clan of Gershon.

[34] The rest of the Levites—the Merari clan—were given the following towns with their pasturelands from the tribe of Zebulun: Jokneam, Kartah, [35] Dimnah, and Nahalal—four towns.

[36] From the tribe of Reuben they received the following towns with their pasturelands: Bezer, Jahaz,* [37] Kedemoth, and Mephaath—four towns.

[38] From the tribe of Gad they received the following towns with their pasturelands: Ramoth in Gilead (a city of refuge for those who accidentally killed someone), Mahanaim, [39] Heshbon, and Jazer—four towns. [40] So in all, twelve towns were allotted to the clan of Merari.

[41] The total number of towns and pasturelands within Israelite territory given to the Levites came to forty-eight. [42] Every one of these towns had pasturelands surrounding it.

[43] So the LORD gave to Israel all the land he had sworn to give their ancestors, and they took possession of it and settled there. [44] And the LORD gave them rest on every side, just as he had solemnly promised their ancestors. None of their enemies could stand against them, for the LORD helped them conquer all their enemies. [45] Not a single one of all the good promises the LORD had given to the family of Israel was left unfulfilled; everything he had spoken came true.

The Eastern Tribes Return Home

22 Then Joshua called together the tribes of Reuben, Gad, and the half-tribe of Manasseh. [2] He told them, "You have done as Moses, the servant of the LORD, commanded you, and you have obeyed every order I have given you. [3] During all this time you have not deserted the other tribes. You have been careful to obey the commands of the LORD your God right up to the present day. [4] And now the LORD your God has given the other tribes rest, as he promised them. So go back home to the land that Moses, the servant of the LORD, gave you as your possession on the east side of the Jordan River. [5] But be very careful to obey all the commands and the instructions that Moses gave to you. Love the LORD your God, walk in all his ways, obey his commands, hold firmly to him, and serve him with all your heart and all your soul." [6] So Joshua blessed them and sent them away, and they went home.

[7] Moses had given the land of Bashan, east of the Jordan River, to the half-tribe of Manasseh. (The other half of the tribe was given land west of the Jordan.) As Joshua sent them away and blessed them, [8] he said to them, "Go back to your homes with the great wealth you have taken from your enemies—the vast herds of livestock, the silver, gold, bronze, and iron, and the large supply of clothing. Share the plunder with your relatives."

[9] So the men of Reuben, Gad, and the half-tribe of Manasseh left the rest of Israel at Shiloh in the land of Canaan. They started the journey back to their own land of Gilead, the territory that belonged to them according to the LORD's command through Moses.

21:36 Hebrew *Jahzah*, a variant spelling of Jahaz.

21:45 God had made Israel many good promises, and not one had failed. He kept his promise to give Israel possession of the land and save them from their surrounding enemies.

The Eastern Tribes Build an Altar

¹⁰But while they were still in Canaan, and when they came to a place called Geliloth* near the Jordan River, the men of Reuben, Gad, and the half-tribe of Manasseh stopped to build a large and imposing altar.

¹¹The rest of Israel heard that the people of Reuben, Gad, and the half-tribe of Manasseh had built an altar at Geliloth at the edge of the land of Canaan, on the west side of the Jordan River. ¹²So the whole community of Israel gathered at Shiloh and prepared to go to war against them. ¹³First, however, they sent a delegation led by Phinehas son of Eleazar, the priest, to talk with the tribes of Reuben, Gad, and the half-tribe of Manasseh. ¹⁴In this delegation were ten leaders of Israel, one from each of the ten tribes, and each the head of his family within the clans of Israel.

¹⁵When they arrived in the land of Gilead, they said to the tribes of Reuben, Gad, and the half-tribe of Manasseh, ¹⁶"The whole community of the LORD demands to know why you are betraying the God of Israel. How could you turn away from the LORD and build an altar for yourselves in rebellion against him? ¹⁷Was our sin at Peor not enough? To this day we are not fully cleansed of it, even after the plague that struck the entire community of the LORD. ¹⁸And yet today you are turning away from following the LORD. If you rebel against the LORD today, he will be angry with all of us tomorrow.

¹⁹"If you need the altar because the land you possess is defiled, then join us in the LORD's land, where the Tabernacle of the LORD is situated, and share our land with us. But do not rebel against the LORD or against us by building an altar other than the one true altar of the LORD our God. ²⁰Didn't divine anger fall on the entire community of Israel when Achan, a member of the clan of Zerah, sinned by stealing the things set apart for the LORD*? He was not the only one who died because of his sin."

²¹Then the people of Reuben, Gad, and the half-tribe of Manasseh answered the heads of the clans of Israel: ²²"The LORD, the Mighty One, is God! The LORD, the Mighty One, is God! He knows the truth, and may Israel know it, too! We have not built the altar in treacherous rebellion against the LORD. If we have done so, do not spare our lives this day. ²³If we have built an altar for ourselves to turn away from the LORD or to offer burnt offerings or grain offerings or peace offerings, may the LORD himself punish us.

²⁴"The truth is, we have built this altar because we fear that in the future your descendants will say to ours, 'What right do you have to worship the LORD, the God of Israel? ²⁵The LORD has placed the Jordan River as a barrier between our people and you people of Reuben and Gad. You have no claim to the LORD.' So your descendants may prevent our descendants from worshiping the LORD.

²⁶"So we decided to build the altar, not for burnt offerings or sacrifices, ²⁷but as a memorial. It will remind our descendants and your descendants that we, too, have the right to worship the LORD at his sanctuary with our burnt offerings, sacrifices, and peace offerings. Then your descendants will not be able to say to ours, 'You have no claim to the LORD.'

²⁸"If they say this, our descendants can reply, 'Look at this copy of the LORD's altar that our ancestors made. It is not for burnt offerings or sacrifices; it is a reminder of the relationship both of us have with the LORD.' ²⁹Far be it from us to rebel against the LORD or turn away from him by building our own altar for burnt offerings, grain offerings, or sacrifices. Only the altar of the LORD our God that stands in front of the Tabernacle may be used for that purpose."

³⁰When Phinehas the priest and the leaders of the community—the heads of the clans of Israel—heard this from the tribes of Reuben, Gad, and the half-tribe of Manasseh, they were satisfied. ³¹Phinehas son of Eleazar, the priest, replied to them, "Today we know the LORD is among us because you have not committed this treachery against the LORD as we thought. Instead, you have rescued Israel from being destroyed by the hand of the LORD."

³²Then Phinehas son of Eleazar, the priest, and the other leaders left the tribes of Reuben and Gad in Gilead and returned to the land of Canaan to tell the Israelites what had happened. ³³And all the Israelites were satisfied and praised God and spoke no more of war against Reuben and Gad.

³⁴The people of Reuben and Gad named the altar "Witness,"* for they said, "It is a witness between us and them that the LORD is our God, too."

22:10 Or *to the circle of stones;* similarly in 22:11. **22:20** The Hebrew term used here refers to the complete consecration of things or people to the LORD, either by destroying them or by giving them as an offering. **22:34** Some manuscripts lack this word.

22:10-20 The direct and hard-hitting statements and questions of the delegation made sure that God's wrath would not come upon the nation because of rebellion like Achan's (7:1-15) or the episode at Peor (Numbers 25).

22:19 Being defiled, or unclean, was not necessarily the result of rebellion or a moral lapse (see "Holy, Clean, and Unclean" on page 143). However, it did prevent people from participating in regular worship activities, including offering sacrifices. If the eastern tribes had defiled the land itself, the Israelites could not offer sacrifices to the Lord within it. This concern provides evidence that the eastern tribes had built their altar on the western bank of the Jordan (22:11). The land west of the Jordan was considered the Lord's land. The delegation from the western tribes made a very generous offer, inviting the eastern tribes to share their land. This demonstrated their commitment to national unity in faithfulness to God.

Joshua's Final Words to Israel

23 The years passed, and the LORD had given the people of Israel rest from all their enemies. Joshua, who was now very old, ²called together all the elders, leaders, judges, and officers of Israel. He said to them, "I am now a very old man. ³You have seen everything the LORD your God has done for you during my lifetime. The LORD your God has fought for you against your enemies. ⁴I have allotted to you as your homeland all the land of the nations yet unconquered, as well as the land of those we have already conquered—from the Jordan River to the Mediterranean Sea* in the west. ⁵This land will be yours, for the LORD your God will himself drive out all the people living there now. You will take possession of their land, just as the LORD your God promised you.

⁶"So be very careful to follow everything Moses wrote in the Book of Instruction. Do not deviate from it, turning either to the right or to the left. ⁷Make sure you do not associate with the other people still remaining in the land. Do not even mention the names of their gods, much less swear by them or serve them or worship them. ⁸Rather, cling tightly to the LORD your God as you have done until now.

⁹"For the LORD has driven out great and powerful nations for you, and no one has yet been able to defeat you. ¹⁰Each one of you will put to flight a thousand of the enemy, for the LORD your God fights for you, just as he has promised. ¹¹So be very careful to love the LORD your God.

¹²"But if you turn away from him and cling to the customs of the survivors of these nations remaining among you, and if you intermarry with them, ¹³then know for certain that the LORD your God will no longer drive them out of your land. Instead, they will be a snare and a trap to you, a whip for your backs and thorny brambles in your eyes, and you will vanish from this good land the LORD your God has given you.

¹⁴"Soon I will die, going the way of everything on earth. Deep in your hearts you know that every promise of the LORD your God has come true. Not a single one has failed! ¹⁵But as surely as the LORD your God has given you the good things he promised, he will also bring disaster on you if you disobey him. He will completely destroy you from this good land he has given you. ¹⁶If you break the covenant of the LORD your God by worshiping and serving other gods, his anger will burn against you, and you will quickly vanish from the good land he has given you."

The LORD's Covenant Renewed

24 Then Joshua summoned all the tribes of Israel to Shechem, including their elders, leaders, judges, and officers. So they came and presented themselves to God.

²Joshua said to the people, "This is what the LORD, the God of Israel, says: Long ago your ancestors, including Terah, the father of Abraham and Nahor, lived beyond the Euphrates River,* and they worshiped other gods. ³But I took your ancestor Abraham from the land beyond the Euphrates and led him into the land of Canaan. I gave him many descendants through his son Isaac. ⁴To Isaac I gave Jacob and Esau. To Esau I gave the mountains of Seir, while Jacob and his children went down into Egypt.

⁵"Then I sent Moses and Aaron, and I brought terrible plagues on Egypt; and afterward I brought you out as a free people. ⁶But when your ancestors arrived at the Red Sea,* the Egyptians chased after you with chariots and charioteers. ⁷When your ancestors cried out to the LORD, I put darkness between you and the Egyptians. I brought the sea crashing down on the Egyptians, drowning them. With your very own eyes you saw what I did. Then you lived in the wilderness for many years.

⁸"Finally, I brought you into the land of the Amorites on the east side of the Jordan. They fought against you, but I destroyed them before you. I gave you victory over them, and you took possession of their land. ⁹Then Balak son of Zippor, king of Moab, started a war against Israel. He summoned Balaam son of Beor to curse you, ¹⁰but I would not listen to him. Instead, I made Balaam bless you, and so I rescued you from Balak.

¹¹"When you crossed the Jordan River and came to Jericho, the men of Jericho fought against you, as did the Amorites, the Perizzites, the Canaanites, the Hittites, the Girgashites, the Hivites, and the Jebusites. But I gave you victory over them. ¹²And I sent terror* ahead of you to drive out the two kings of the Amorites. It was not your swords or bows that brought you victory. ¹³I gave you land you had

---

23:4 Hebrew *the Great Sea.* 24:2 Hebrew *the river;* also in 24:3, 14, 15. 24:6 Hebrew *sea of reeds.* 24:12 Often rendered *the hornet.* The meaning of the Hebrew is uncertain.

23:1-16 Joshua knew that he was going to die soon. He gave no new policies to the leaders of Israel but reminded them of God's faithfulness and urged them to obey God's law. Joshua wanted them to continue living by God's commands. It was not about himself, but about God's plan for Israel.

24:1-27 In both form and content, this covenant statement resembled an ancient Near Eastern suzerain-vassal treaty, a legal agreement made between two parties where one is dominant (the suzerain) and the other subordinate (the vassal). This covenant begins with a preamble of Israel's origins (24:2). It continues with a historical account of the suzerain's (God's) gracious acts on behalf of the people (24:3-13), followed by a list of stipulations (24:14-15) and curses and blessings (24:19-20). It then notes where the text should remain for periodic reading and renewal (implied, 24:26). The passage records the people's response (24:16-18) and lists witnesses to the covenant (24:22, 27).

not worked on, and I gave you towns you did not build—the towns where you are now living. I gave you vineyards and olive groves for food, though you did not plant them.

¹⁴"So fear the Lord and serve him wholeheartedly. Put away forever the idols your ancestors worshiped when they lived beyond the Euphrates River and in Egypt. Serve the Lord alone. ¹⁵But if you refuse to serve the Lord, then choose today whom you will serve. Would you prefer the gods your ancestors served beyond the Euphrates? Or will it be the gods of the Amorites in whose land you now live? But as for me and my family, we will serve the Lord."

¹⁶The people replied, "We would never abandon the Lord and serve other gods. ¹⁷For the Lord our God is the one who rescued us and our ancestors from slavery in the land of Egypt. He performed mighty miracles before our very eyes. As we traveled through the wilderness among our enemies, he preserved us. ¹⁸It was the Lord who drove out the Amorites and the other nations living here in the land. So we, too, will serve the Lord, for he alone is our God."

¹⁹Then Joshua warned the people, "You are not able to serve the Lord, for he is a holy and jealous God. He will not forgive your rebellion and your sins. ²⁰If you abandon the Lord and serve other gods, he will turn against you and destroy you, even though he has been so good to you."

²¹But the people answered Joshua, "No, we will serve the Lord!"

²²"You are a witness to your own decision," Joshua said. "You have chosen to serve the Lord."

"Yes," they replied, "we are witnesses to what we have said.

Come Close

OUR ROLE: COURAGE TO SERVE

SCRIPTURE CONNECTION: JOSHUA 24:1-28

We see in Joshua 24 a pattern: *remember* God's covenant and how he is fulfilling it, *decide* if you want to serve God, and *commit to serve* only God wholeheartedly. But how do we find the courage to serve God?

What is God's standard of evaluation for you and me in our given roles? Success? Perfection? . . .

Faithfulness is God's standard! As His servants, we are not required to be perfect or successful—simply faithful. We have been given a trust. We have been entrusted with many things: our natural gifts, our spiritual gifts, our financial resources. Our assigned role is also a trust. In His love, He has given each of us the gift of singleness or the gift of marriage or the gift of widowhood. In His sovereignty, He has said it is in this role we can best glorify Him.

Will you trust Him that your assigned cup and portion come from His loving hand? Will you choose to use your role as a place to serve others? Will you pray this prayer?

Holy Father, You know the joys, the heartaches of my role. I confess that I have fought against what You have given. Grant me the courage to be a servant. Oh, God, I long to be faithful to You. I accept my assigned role as a gift. Teach me to "cease striving and know that You are God."

REFLECT "Each one of you will put to flight a thousand of the enemy, for the Lord your God fights for you, just as he has promised. So be very careful to love the Lord your God." JOSHUA 23:10-11

Dear Lord, when I have roles that overwhelm me, thank you for reminding me that you are the one who fights for me. Thank you that you ask not that I become perfect, but that I take great care to love you. Amen.

CONSIDER "God didn't call me to be successful, he called me to be faithful." MOTHER TERESA

God, grant me the courage to serve.

LINDA DILLOW • Content taken from *Calm My Anxious Heart* by Linda Dillow. Copyright © 2007, 2020 by Linda Dillow and Copyright © 2020 by Paniym Group, Inc. Used by permission of NavPress, represented by Tyndale House Publishers. All rights reserved.

²³"All right then," Joshua said, "destroy the idols among you, and turn your hearts to the LORD, the God of Israel."

²⁴The people said to Joshua, "We will serve the LORD our God. We will obey him alone."

²⁵So Joshua made a covenant with the people that day at Shechem, committing them to follow the decrees and regulations of the LORD. ²⁶Joshua recorded these things in the Book of God's Instructions. As a reminder of their agreement, he took a huge stone and rolled it beneath the terebinth tree beside the Tabernacle of the LORD.

²⁷Joshua said to all the people, "This stone has heard everything the LORD said to us. It will be a witness to testify against you if you go back on your word to God."

²⁸Then Joshua sent all the people away to their own homelands.

Leaders Buried in the Promised Land

²⁹After this, Joshua son of Nun, the servant of the LORD, died at the age of 110. ³⁰They buried him in the land he had been allocated, at Timnath-serah in the hill country of Ephraim, north of Mount Gaash.

³¹The people of Israel served the LORD throughout the lifetime of Joshua and of the elders who outlived him—those who had personally experienced all that the LORD had done for Israel.

³²The bones of Joseph, which the Israelites had brought along with them when they left Egypt, were buried at Shechem, in the plot of land Jacob had bought from the sons of Hamor for 100 pieces of silver.* This land was located in the territory allotted to the descendants of Joseph.

³³Eleazar son of Aaron also died. He was buried in the hill country of Ephraim, in the town of Gibeah, which had been given to his son Phinehas.

24:32 Hebrew *100 kesitahs;* the value or weight of the kesitah is no longer known.

24:26 The Book of God's Instructions was a scroll containing the writings of Moses. It was probably carried to Shiloh and stored with other documents of national importance. The "huge stone" was likely a *stela,* a standing stone monument. Joshua might have had a memorial inscription chiseled into it.

24:31 Joshua's legacy was so strong that Israel remained faithful to God even "throughout the lifetime . . . of the elders who outlived him."

Judges

WHAT DO WE LEARN ABOUT GOD'S MISSION AND OURS?
God forgives us as we return to his ways.

WHO WROTE IT? Judges is anonymous, but tradition attributes it to Samuel.

WHEN DID IT HAPPEN? In the 1300s or 1200s BC to around 1050 BC, beginning a generation after the people of Israel had settled in the Promised Land and spanning roughly two hundred years.

HOW IS IT ORGANIZED?

- **1–2:** The pattern—disobedience, defeat, deliverance
- **3:** Othniel, Ehud, and Shamgar judge
- **4–5:** Deborah, Barak, and Jael defeat Sisera
- **6–9:** Gideon and Abimelech judge
- **10–12:** A quick succession of several judges
- **13–16:** Samson judges Israel, meets Delilah
- **17–21:** More examples of spiritual corruption

FEATURE HIGHLIGHTS

+ *Leading by Words and Deeds (294)*
+ *How Can a Woman's Faithfulness Lead to Victory? (296)*
+ *Deborah: Leading by Singing (297)*
+ *Hiding: Step Away from the Small (300)*
+ *A Guilty or Clean Conscience (306)*

Words to Remember are highlighted throughout this book

HOW LONG DOES IT TAKE TO READ?

1:30 (out of :30 | 1:00 | 1:30 | 2:00 | 2:30 | 3:00 | 3:30)

Timeline

BC	Event
1446	EXODUS FROM EGYPT
1406	ISRAELITES ENTER CANAAN; RAHAB HELPS THEM TO CONQUER JERICHO
1375	JUDGES BEGIN TO RULE
1367–1327	OTHNIEL JUDGES ISRAEL
1309–1229	EHUD JUDGES ISRAEL
1209–1169	DEBORAH JUDGES ISRAEL; JAEL KILLS SISERA
1162–1122	GIDEON JUDGES ISRAEL
c. 1100	RUTH AND NAOMI MOVE TO BETHLEHEM; RUTH MARRIES BOAZ
1105	HANNAH GIVES BIRTH TO SAMUEL
1075	SAMSON, SON OF MANOAH AND HIS WIFE, BECOMES JUDGE
1055	SAMSON DIES, AFTER DELILAH BETRAYS HIM TO THE PHILISTINES
1050	KINGDOM OF ISRAEL UNITES UNDER SAUL
1010	DAVID BECOMES KING

Judah and Simeon Conquer the Land

1 After the death of Joshua, the Israelites asked the LORD, "Which tribe should go first to attack the Canaanites?"

²The LORD answered, "Judah, for I have given them victory over the land."

³The men of Judah said to their relatives from the tribe of Simeon, "Join with us to fight against the Canaanites living in the territory allotted to us. Then we will help you conquer your territory." So the men of Simeon went with Judah.

⁴When the men of Judah attacked, the LORD gave them victory over the Canaanites and Perizzites, and they killed 10,000 enemy warriors at the town of Bezek. ⁵While at Bezek they encountered King Adoni-bezek and fought against him, and the Canaanites and Perizzites were defeated. ⁶Adoni-bezek escaped, but the Israelites soon captured him and cut off his thumbs and big toes.

⁷Adoni-bezek said, "I once had seventy kings with their thumbs and big toes cut off, eating scraps from under my table. Now God has paid me back for what I did to them." They took him to Jerusalem, and he died there.

⁸The men of Judah attacked Jerusalem and captured it, killing all its people and setting the city on fire. ⁹Then they went down to fight the Canaanites living in the hill country, the Negev, and the western foothills.* ¹⁰Judah marched against the Canaanites in Hebron (formerly called Kiriath-arba), defeating the forces of Sheshai, Ahiman, and Talmai.

¹¹From there they went to fight against the people living in the town of Debir (formerly called Kiriath-sepher). ¹²Caleb said, "I will give my daughter Acsah in marriage to the one who attacks and captures Kiriath-sepher." ¹³Othniel, the son of Caleb's younger brother, Kenaz, was the one who conquered it, so Acsah became Othniel's wife.

¹⁴When Acsah married Othniel, she urged him* to ask her father for a field. As she got down off her donkey, Caleb asked her, "What's the matter?"

¹⁵She said, "Let me have another gift. You have already given me land in the Negev; now please give me springs of water, too." So Caleb gave her the upper and lower springs.

¹⁶When the tribe of Judah left Jericho—the city of palms—the Kenites, who were descendants of Moses' father-in-law, traveled with them into the wilderness of Judah. They settled among the people there, near the town of Arad in the Negev.

¹⁷Then Judah joined with Simeon to fight against the Canaanites living in Zephath, and they completely destroyed* the town. So the town was named Hormah.* ¹⁸In addition, Judah captured the towns of Gaza, Ashkelon, and Ekron, along with their surrounding territories.

Israel Fails to Conquer the Land

¹⁹The LORD was with the people of Judah, and they took possession of the hill country. But they failed to drive out the people living in the plains, who had iron chariots. ²⁰The town of Hebron was given to Caleb as Moses had promised. And Caleb drove out the people living there, who were descendants of the three sons of Anak.

²¹The tribe of Benjamin, however, failed to drive out the Jebusites, who were living in Jerusalem. So to this day the Jebusites live in Jerusalem among the people of Benjamin.

²²The descendants of Joseph attacked the town of Bethel, and the LORD was with them. ²³They sent men to scout out Bethel (formerly known as Luz). ²⁴They confronted a man coming out of the town and said to him, "Show us a way into the town, and we will have mercy on you." ²⁵So he showed them a way in, and they killed everyone in the town except that man and his family. ²⁶Later the man moved to the land of the Hittites, where he built a town. He named it Luz, which is its name to this day.

²⁷The tribe of Manasseh failed to drive out the people living in Beth-shan,* Taanach, Dor, Ibleam, Megiddo, and all their surrounding settlements, because the Canaanites were determined to stay

---

1:9 Hebrew *the Shephelah.* **1:14** Greek version and Latin Vulgate read *he urged her.* **1:17a** The Hebrew term used here refers to the complete consecration of things or people to the LORD, either by destroying them or by giving them as an offering. **1:17b** *Hormah* means "destruction." **1:27** Hebrew *Beth-shean,* a variant spelling of Beth-shan.

1:12-13 Was Acsah a trophy wife? She was given as a prize to the man who won territory for her father. While this is how readers from the global West might interpret this story, other cultures might have a different point of view and could shed new light on it. In South Asia, for example, arranged marriages are traditionally the norm, with daughters brought up to understand that her family will choose wisely and, often, with her consent. Indian epic poems and folk tales frequently feature princesses whose hand must be won by some heroic act. Acsah may have considered it an honor to marry so valiant a warrior as Othniel. We are not sure whether Othniel was a cousin or uncle, but marrying the latter is also common in Indian communities, though strictly from the maternal line.

1:14-15 In ancient Israel, property passed to male descendants. Women had to make a special appeal for inheritance and only in cases where there were no male heirs (Numbers 27:1-11). Acsah seems to have received property from her father as dowry. It is extraordinary that she requested additional land, especially land with the precious resource of springs of water. Just as unusual is how readily her father granted her request. Something to watch for in Judges is the gradual deterioration of Israelite society. This downward slide can be measured by the stories of the treatment of women. At the beginning of the book, Acsah dismounts from a donkey to receive life-giving wells. Toward the book's end, another woman would be loaded onto a donkey, and at the end of the journey be hacked into pieces (Judges 19:1-30).

in that region. ²⁸When the Israelites grew stronger, they forced the Canaanites to work as slaves, but they never did drive them completely out of the land.

²⁹The tribe of Ephraim failed to drive out the Canaanites living in Gezer, so the Canaanites continued to live there among them.

³⁰The tribe of Zebulun failed to drive out the residents of Kitron and Nahalol, so the Canaanites continued to live among them. But the Canaanites were forced to work as slaves for the people of Zebulun.

³¹The tribe of Asher failed to drive out the residents of Acco, Sidon, Ahlab, Aczib, Helbah, Aphik, and Rehob. ³²Instead, the people of Asher moved in among the Canaanites, who controlled the land, for they failed to drive them out.

³³Likewise, the tribe of Naphtali failed to drive out the residents of Beth-shemesh and Beth-anath. Instead, they moved in among the Canaanites, who controlled the land. Nevertheless, the people of Beth-shemesh and Beth-anath were forced to work as slaves for the people of Naphtali.

³⁴As for the tribe of Dan, the Amorites forced them back into the hill country and would not let them come down into the plains. ³⁵The Amorites were determined to stay in Mount Heres, Aijalon, and Shaalbim, but when the descendants of Joseph became stronger, they forced the Amorites to work as slaves. ³⁶The boundary of the Amorites ran from Scorpion Pass* to Sela and continued upward from there.

The LORD's Messenger Comes to Bokim

2 The angel of the LORD went up from Gilgal to Bokim and said to the Israelites, "I brought you out of Egypt into this land that I swore to give your ancestors, and I said I would never break my covenant with you. ²For your part, you were not to make any covenants with the people living in this land; instead, you were to destroy their altars. But you disobeyed my command. Why did you do this? ³So now I declare that I will no longer drive out the people living in your land. They will be thorns in your sides,* and their gods will be a constant temptation to you."

⁴When the angel of the LORD finished speaking to all the Israelites, the people wept loudly. ⁵So they called the place Bokim (which means "weeping"), and they offered sacrifices there to the LORD.

The Death of Joshua

⁶After Joshua sent the people away, each of the tribes left to take possession of the land allotted to them. ⁷And the Israelites served the LORD throughout the lifetime of Joshua and the leaders who outlived him—those who had seen all the great things the LORD had done for Israel.

⁸Joshua son of Nun, the servant of the LORD, died at the age of 110. ⁹They buried him in the land he had been allocated, at Timnath-serah* in the hill country of Ephraim, north of Mount Gaash.

Israel Disobeys the LORD

¹⁰After that generation died, another generation grew up who did not acknowledge the LORD or remember the mighty things he had done for Israel.

¹¹The Israelites did evil in the LORD's sight and served the images of Baal. ¹²They abandoned the LORD, the God of their ancestors, who had brought them out of Egypt. They went after other gods, worshiping the gods of the people around them. And they angered the LORD. ¹³They abandoned the LORD to serve Baal and the images of Ashtoreth. ¹⁴This made the LORD burn with anger against Israel, so he handed them over to raiders who stole their possessions. He turned them over to their enemies all around, and they were no longer able to resist them. ¹⁵Every time Israel went out to battle, the LORD fought against them, causing them to be defeated, just as he had warned. And the people were in great distress.

The LORD Rescues His People

¹⁶Then the LORD raised up judges to rescue the Israelites from their attackers. ¹⁷Yet Israel did not listen to the judges but prostituted themselves by worshiping other gods. How quickly they turned away from the path of their ancestors, who had walked in obedience to the LORD's commands.

¹⁸Whenever the LORD raised up a judge over Israel, he was with that judge and rescued the people from their enemies throughout the judge's lifetime. For the LORD took pity on his people, who were burdened by oppression and suffering. ¹⁹But when the judge died, the people returned to their corrupt ways, behaving worse than those who had lived before them. They went after other gods, serving and worshiping them. And they refused to give up their evil practices and stubborn ways.

1:36 Hebrew *Akrabbim*. 2:3 Hebrew *They will be in your sides*; compare Num 33:55. 2:9 As in parallel text at Josh 24:30; Hebrew reads *Timnath-heres*, a variant spelling of Timnath-serah.

2:10-19 Joshua was dead, the new generation had not experienced God's saving power, and the Canaanites continued to live in the land. What resulted was a cycle of rebellion and partial restoration. This section introduces that cycle, which the body of the book exemplifies.

2:15 God was not simply absent; he was actively involved in Israel's defeat, and the outcome of the battle belonged to the Lord (see 2 Chronicles 20:15).

JUDGES 3

²⁰So the LORD burned with anger against Israel. He said, "Because these people have violated my covenant, which I made with their ancestors, and have ignored my commands, ²¹I will no longer drive out the nations that Joshua left unconquered when he died. ²²I did this to test Israel—to see whether or not they would follow the ways of the LORD as their ancestors did." ²³That is why the LORD left those nations in place. He did not quickly drive them out or allow Joshua to conquer them all.

The Nations Left in Canaan

3 These are the nations that the LORD left in the land to test those Israelites who had not experienced the wars of Canaan. ²He did this to teach warfare to generations of Israelites who had no experience in battle. ³These are the nations: the Philistines (those living under the five Philistine rulers), all the Canaanites, the Sidonians, and the Hivites living in the mountains of Lebanon from Mount Baal-hermon

2:20-23 The remaining Canaanites and their religion would become a source of temptation to the Israelites, offering an alternative to faithfully following the Lord and his covenant ways. This was known and even planned by God (see 3:4). God does not deliberately set his people up to sin (James 1:12-15). Temptations abound, but the choice to obey God or yield to temptation rests with those who claim to know him. Israel had a duty to possess the land fully, but God, not humankind, determines victory or failure.

3:1-4 The ongoing presence of the Philistines and Canaanites in the land had an instructional purpose. Skills in warfare were necessary for survival in the ancient world. God allowed the ongoing presence of enemies, but they would become his provision for Israel's training and well-being.

Insight — THE CYCLE OF JUDGES

The book of Judges follows a clear pattern: The Israelites rebel against God's covenant, so God gives them over to their enemies. Then, the Israelites turn from their wicked ways and ask the Lord for help. God sends a leader (*judge*) to help the people. And the cycle repeats. We have an ages-old pattern of drawing close to God and then falling away. This explains why we need a savior, a Messiah, to make us right with God. We cannot consistently be "good enough" for God on our own (Titus 3:4-7).

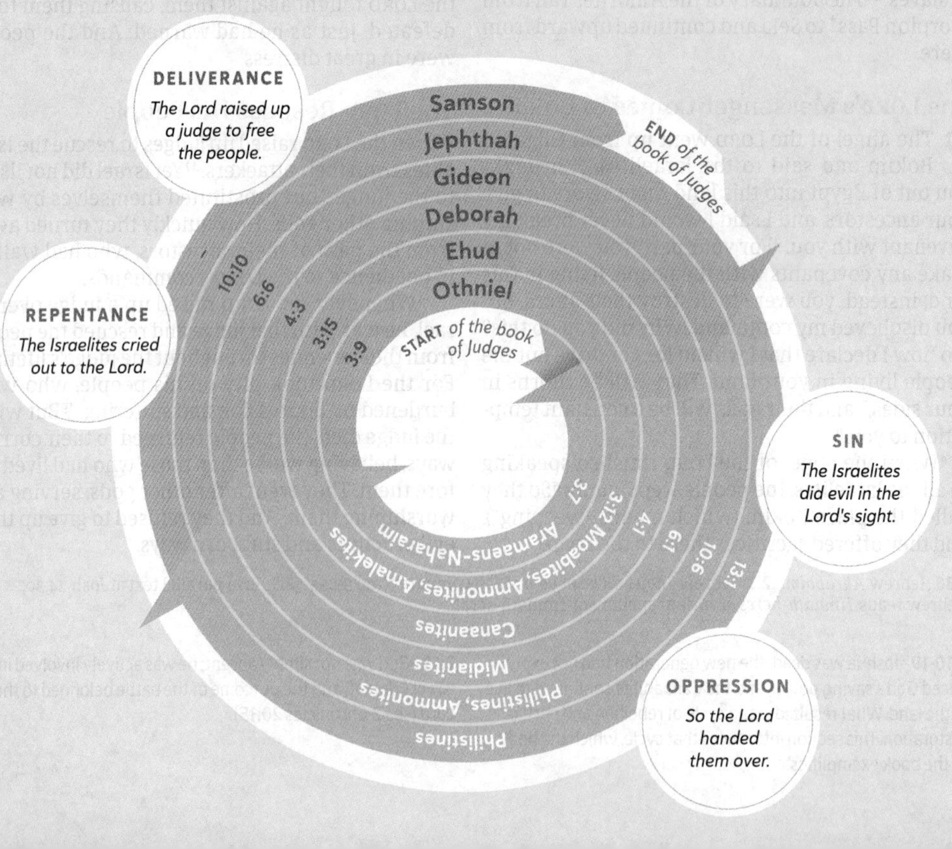

DELIVERANCE
The Lord raised up a judge to free the people.

REPENTANCE
The Israelites cried out to the Lord.

SIN
The Israelites did evil in the Lord's sight.

OPPRESSION
So the Lord handed them over.

END of the book of Judges:
Samson
Jephthah
Gideon
Deborah
Ehud
Othniel
START of the book of Judges

10:10, 6:6, 4:3, 3:15, 3:9

3:7, 3:12 Moabites, 4:1 Aramens-Naharaim, 6:1 Ammonites, Amalekites, 10:6 Canaanites, 13:1 Midianites, Philistines, Ammonites, Philistines

to Lebo-hamath. ⁴These people were left to test the Israelites—to see whether they would obey the commands the LORD had given to their ancestors through Moses.

⁵So the people of Israel lived among the Canaanites, Hittites, Amorites, Perizzites, Hivites, and Jebusites, ⁶and they intermarried with them. Israelite sons married their daughters, and Israelite daughters were given in marriage to their sons. And the Israelites served their gods.

Othniel Becomes Israel's Judge

⁷The Israelites did evil in the LORD's sight. They forgot about the LORD their God, and they served the images of Baal and the Asherah poles. ⁸Then the LORD burned with anger against Israel, and he turned them over to King Cushan-rishathaim of Aram-naharaim.* And the Israelites served Cushan-rishathaim for eight years.

⁹But when the people of Israel cried out to the LORD for help, the LORD raised up a rescuer to save them. His name was Othniel, the son of Caleb's younger brother, Kenaz. ¹⁰The Spirit of the LORD came upon him, and he became Israel's judge. He went to war against King Cushan-rishathaim of Aram, and the LORD gave Othniel victory over him. ¹¹So there was peace in the land for forty years. Then Othniel son of Kenaz died.

Ehud Becomes Israel's Judge

¹²Once again the Israelites did evil in the LORD's sight, and the LORD gave King Eglon of Moab control over Israel because of their evil. ¹³Eglon enlisted the Ammonites and Amalekites as allies, and then he went out and defeated Israel, taking possession of Jericho, the city of palms. ¹⁴And the Israelites served Eglon of Moab for eighteen years.

¹⁵But when the people of Israel cried out to the LORD for help, the LORD again raised up a rescuer to save them. His name was Ehud son of Gera, a left-handed man of the tribe of Benjamin. The Israelites sent Ehud to deliver their tribute money to King Eglon of Moab. ¹⁶So Ehud made a double-edged dagger that was about a foot* long, and he strapped it to his right thigh, keeping it hidden under his clothing. ¹⁷He brought the tribute money to Eglon, who was very fat.

¹⁸After delivering the payment, Ehud started home with those who had helped carry the tribute. ¹⁹But when Ehud reached the stone idols near Gilgal, he turned back. He came to Eglon and said, "I have a secret message for you."

So the king commanded his servants, "Be quiet!" and he sent them all out of the room.

²⁰Ehud walked over to Eglon, who was sitting alone in a cool upstairs room. And Ehud said, "I have a message from God for you!" As King Eglon rose from his seat, ²¹Ehud reached with his left hand, pulled out the dagger strapped to his right thigh, and plunged it into the king's belly. ²²The dagger went so deep that the handle disappeared beneath the king's fat. So Ehud did not pull out the dagger, and the king's bowels emptied.* ²³Then Ehud closed and locked the doors of the room and escaped down the latrine.*

²⁴After Ehud was gone, the king's servants returned and found the doors to the upstairs room locked. They thought he might be using the latrine in the room, ²⁵so they waited. But when the king didn't come out after a long delay, they became concerned and got a key. And when they opened the doors, they found their master dead on the floor.

²⁶While the servants were waiting, Ehud escaped, passing the stone idols on his way to Seirah. ²⁷When he arrived in the hill country of Ephraim, Ehud sounded a call to arms. Then he led a band of Israelites down from the hills.

²⁸"Follow me," he said, "for the LORD has given you victory over Moab your enemy." So they followed him. And the Israelites took control of the shallow crossings of the Jordan River across from Moab, preventing anyone from crossing.

²⁹They attacked the Moabites and killed about 10,000 of their strongest and most able-bodied warriors. Not one of them escaped. ³⁰So Moab was conquered by Israel that day, and there was peace in the land for eighty years.

Shamgar Becomes Israel's Judge

³¹After Ehud, Shamgar son of Anath rescued Israel. He once killed 600 Philistines with an ox goad.

Deborah Becomes Israel's Judge

4 After Ehud's death, the Israelites again did evil in the LORD's sight. ²So the LORD turned them over to King Jabin of Hazor, a Canaanite king. The commander of his army was Sisera, who lived in Harosheth-haggoyim. ³Sisera, who had 900 iron chariots, ruthlessly oppressed the Israelites for twenty years. Then the people of Israel cried out to the LORD for help.

3:8 *Aram-naharaim* means "Aram of the two rivers," thought to have been located between the Euphrates and Balih Rivers in northwestern Mesopotamia. **3:16** Hebrew *gomed,* the length of which is uncertain. **3:22** Or *and it came out behind.* **3:23** Or *and went out through the porch;* the meaning of the Hebrew is uncertain.

3:19-21 The message had to be secret to ensure that Ehud would be left alone with the king; it had to be from God to guarantee that the ploy would work. Eglon probably stood up because he expected some message from the Lord, which was exactly what he received.

IMAGE — MY STORY OF MY UNIQUE INFLUENCE

Leading by Words and Deeds

SCRIPTURE CONNECTION: JUDGES 4:1–5:31

Like all good leaders, Deborah learned how to lead others by first leading herself. She spoke wisdom into her home and family, which positioned her for leadership in her community. Deborah served as a counselor, a judge, and ultimately as a deliverer over all Israel.

One of the ways Deborah led was by judging Israel, and she held authority in a time when it was rare for a woman to lead, especially in a military context. This uncommon political leadership is echoed by Shirley Chisholm, the first African-American Congresswoman, who is quoted as having said, "Tremendous amounts of talent are being lost to our just society because that talent wears a skirt." Deborah led faithfully. As she sat under a palm tree day by day, people brought issues large and small for her to settle.

We often lead by our words, followed by our deeds. Our mouths speak life over ourselves, our families, our vocations, and our futures. We can identify with Deborah in her leadership and follow her example.

Deborah's journey shows us that leading involves:

- *Choosing leaders*—Deborah called Barak, delivered God's message to him, and commanded him to go to war.
- *Delegating*—She gave Barak a clear battle plan.
- *Equipping*—When Barak refused to go to battle without her, Deborah accompanied him.

> Deborah learned to lead others by first leading herself.

Through Deborah's song in Judges 5, we learn firsthand the details of her leadership as she praised God for victory. Deborah was a wise leader, and her leadership of words and deeds brought Israel victory over their enemy.

IMAGINE

How did Deborah learn to lead herself first?

How do you see God's invitation to leadership?

What do your words and deeds say about your leadership?

"Ever since I was a child, others followed my words and deeds. Like Deborah, leadership was a part of my destiny."

VIRGINIA WARD, MA, DMin, serves as the Dean of the Boston Campus for Gordon-Conwell Theological Seminary. She is a wife, a mother, and an associate pastor at Abundant Life Church in Cambridge, MA.

⁴Deborah, the wife of Lappidoth, was a prophet who was judging Israel at that time. ⁵She would sit under the Palm of Deborah, between Ramah and Bethel in the hill country of Ephraim, and the Israelites would go to her for judgment. ⁶One day she sent for Barak son of Abinoam, who lived in Kedesh in the land of Naphtali. She said to him, "This is what the LORD, the God of Israel, commands you: Call out 10,000 warriors from the tribes of Naphtali and Zebulun at Mount Tabor. ⁷And I will call out Sisera, commander of Jabin's army, along with his chariots and warriors, to the Kishon River. There I will give you victory over him."

⁸Barak told her, "I will go, but only if you go with me."

⁹"Very well," she replied, "I will go with you. But you will receive no honor in this venture, for the LORD's victory over Sisera will be at the hands of a woman." So Deborah went with Barak to Kedesh. ¹⁰At Kedesh, Barak called together the tribes of Zebulun and Naphtali, and 10,000 warriors went up with him. Deborah also went with him.

¹¹Now Heber the Kenite, a descendant of Moses' brother-in-law* Hobab, had moved away from the other members of his tribe and pitched his tent by the oak of Zaanannim near Kedesh.

¹²When Sisera was told that Barak son of Abinoam had gone up to Mount Tabor, ¹³he called for all 900 of his iron chariots and all of his warriors, and they marched from Harosheth-haggoyim to the Kishon River.

¹⁴Then Deborah said to Barak, "Get ready! This is the day the LORD will give you victory over Sisera, for the LORD is marching ahead of you." So Barak led his 10,000 warriors down the slopes of Mount Tabor into battle. ¹⁵When Barak attacked, the LORD threw Sisera and all his chariots and warriors into a panic. Sisera leaped down from his chariot and escaped on foot. ¹⁶Then Barak chased the chariots and the enemy army all the way to Harosheth-haggoyim, killing all of Sisera's warriors. Not a single one was left alive.

¹⁷Meanwhile, Sisera ran to the tent of Jael, the wife of Heber the Kenite, because Heber's family was on friendly terms with King Jabin of Hazor. ¹⁸Jael went out to meet Sisera and said to him, "Come into my tent, sir. Come in. Don't be afraid." So he went into her tent, and she covered him with a blanket.

¹⁹"Please give me some water," he said. "I'm thirsty." So she gave him some milk from a leather bag and covered him again.

²⁰"Stand at the door of the tent," he told her. "If anybody comes and asks you if there is anyone here, say no."

²¹But when Sisera fell asleep from exhaustion, Jael quietly crept up to him with a hammer and tent peg in her hand. Then she drove the tent peg through his temple and into the ground, and so he died.

²²When Barak came looking for Sisera, Jael went out to meet him. She said, "Come, and I will show you the man you are looking for." So he followed her into the tent and found Sisera lying there dead, with the tent peg through his temple.

4:11 Or *father-in-law.*

4:4-5 *Lappidoth* means "torches." It may have been a personal name, the name of Deborah's husband. If so, the Hebrew descriptor "woman of Lappidoth" would mean "wife of Lappidoth," as is translated in the NLT. A more interesting possibility is that the Hebrew phrase could simply be describing Deborah as a "fiery woman"! She was a prophet and an arbitrator of justice. She was the highest court in the country, superseding the local courts governed by town elders. She may have been identified not by her husband, but for burning bright for truth!

4:6 As a prophet, Deborah performed the role of commissioning Barak. Interestingly, she was to Barak what the angel of the Lord would be to Gideon in the next story. While her name means "bee," his is initially much more promising for a military leader—Barak means "lightning."

4:8-9 While we can understand this to mean that Barak was honoring Deborah in his request, Deborah did not seem to approve. The norm was male leadership on the battlefield, and she saw Barak as reluctant to take on God's commission. He would take on leadership only if Deborah, a female prophet, stood by his side, providing the validation he needed before the people. Barak was no thunderbolt. On the contrary, Deborah saw him as a reluctant commander. For this, he would forfeit the honor of gaining the prize in this war—the head of the enemy commander—to a woman.

4:18-19 Jael going out to meet Sisera is an ironic twist on the ancient Israelite custom that women would go out to welcome a hero returning from battle (1 Samuel 18:6). But here is a defeated soldier fleeing for his life. The narrative conveys this by making Jael the one who acts and Sisera the one acted upon. She went out, met him, welcomed him, and seemed to grant him asylum in her home. The reader cannot miss the sarcasm in an ironsmith's wife (the Kenites were metalworkers) encouraging a commander not to be afraid! Even the words he spoke to Jael show his dependency on her: She must satisfy his thirst and save his life. Jael was in control of the situation from start to finish.

4:20 Most of the Old Testament was written in Hebrew, and like many languages, Hebrew words can have gender embedded in them. When Sisera directed Jael to "stand," his command was grammatically masculine, even though he was addressing a woman. Here was a man used to commanding other men, slipping into default language. As it happened, Jael would switch into a role unanticipated for a woman. She would slaughter him as mercilessly as the Israelite men pursuing him would have done.

4:21 Considering her family's traditional profession as smiths (they were the descendants of Tubal-cain; see Genesis 4:22), we understand how Jael had access to the implements she chose as her weapons. Also, we understand why she wielded them with such ease. Jael needed no more than a metal nail to fell a man who was the commander of nine hundred iron chariots. The story begins with Israel lamenting their lack of metallurgy expertise. Their deliverer comes from a family specializing in metalwork. What's more, a Kenite woman became the solution to a national crisis. Jael gave the Israelites a lesson in "where there's a will, there's a way"!

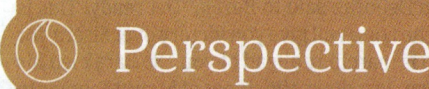
Perspective

How can a woman's faithfulness lead to victory?

SCRIPTURE CONNECTION: JUDGES 4:9, 17-22; 5:24-27

"You're going to be beaten by a woman" might sound more like an immature taunt than a prophetic message to a military general.

Deborah, the prophet and judge, was not taunting the general. She was relaying the sober message to Barak that God's victory over the opposing general, Sisera, would not come through Barak's military prowess. It would come at the hands of a woman (4:9). Jael was that woman.

When the Canaanite troops started losing, Sisera ran to Jael for protection. But she upheld the Israelite war mission and God's command to Barak. In her bravery and strength, she fulfilled Deborah's prophecy and administered the final blow.

In the ancient world, military battles and fighting were a man's domain, so for women to have victory here brought dishonor to Barak and Sisera. But God raised up Jael, and Deborah, as women, to have influence. Being a judge in Israel made Deborah a judicial and military leader over God's people. Barak failed to obey God's command, but Deborah and Jael didn't waver in their obedience. God gave these women an incredible victory because of their faithfulness.

VIEWPOINTS

HERS: *Did Jael expect she would be a critical warrior in the history of Israel? How did her ordinary circumstances empower her for victory?*

MINE: *"All too often, I underestimate the importance of my routine circumstances. God is on a mission, and I am a critical warrior in the history of his kingdom. Today, my battle is to meet deadlines at work and equip my daughter for algebra."*

YOURS: *In preparing for battle, whether physical, mental, or spiritual, how do you grow strong for your tasks? Where is your battleground today?*

MISTY ARTERBURN is an author and speaker, contributing to Bible projects, devotionals, and recovery materials for over twenty years. Wife and mom to five, Misty is the founder of Recovery Girls and the general editor of *The One Year Bible for Women*.

---

²³So on that day Israel saw God defeat Jabin, the Canaanite king. ²⁴And from that time on Israel became stronger and stronger against King Jabin until they finally destroyed him.

The Song of Deborah

5 On that day Deborah and Barak son of Abinoam sang this song:

² "Israel's leaders took charge,
  and the people gladly followed.
Praise the LORD!

³ "Listen, you kings!
  Pay attention, you mighty rulers!
For I will sing to the LORD.
  I will make music to the LORD, the God of Israel.

⁴ "LORD, when you set out from Seir
  and marched across the fields of Edom,
the earth trembled,
  and the cloudy skies poured down rain.
⁵ The mountains quaked in the presence of the LORD,
  the God of Mount Sinai—
in the presence of the LORD,
  the God of Israel.

⁶ "In the days of Shamgar son of Anath,
  and in the days of Jael,
people avoided the main roads,
  and travelers stayed on winding pathways.
⁷ There were few people left in the villages of Israel*—
  until Deborah arose as a mother for Israel.
⁸ When Israel chose new gods,
  war erupted at the city gates.
Yet not a shield or spear could be seen
  among forty thousand warriors in Israel!
⁹ My heart is with the commanders of Israel,
  with those who volunteered for war.
Praise the LORD!

¹⁰ "Consider this, you who ride on fine donkeys,
  you who sit on fancy saddle blankets,
  and you who walk along the road.
¹¹ Listen to the village musicians*
  gathered at the watering holes.
They recount the righteous victories of the LORD
  and the victories of his villagers in Israel.
Then the people of the LORD
  marched down to the city gates.

¹² "Wake up, Deborah, wake up!
  Wake up, wake up, and sing a song!
Arise, Barak!
  Lead your captives away, son of Abinoam!

5:7 The meaning of the Hebrew is uncertain. 5:11 The meaning of the Hebrew is uncertain.

Deborah

IDENTITY · Leading by Singing

Deborah remembers…

When victory was secured and we returned from battle, Barak and I were exuberant! I wanted everyone to remember what had happened, so we sang this song about it.

It was God who won! We were frightened, scattered people, but God chose me to speak on his behalf and lead. I did what I could as God's prophet and judge, but circumstances kept the people from seeing the Lord's might. Then God marched ahead of Barak with trembling earth and torrential rain. Our enemy fell into chaos, and Sisera ran off like a frightened child!

We were not ready for war, but God was. Even as my people worshiped idols and hid from enemies, God prepared to deliver us from King Jabin.

I am proud of Barak and my people for following my instructions and marching into battle obediently. May their faith be renewed from what they witnessed, and may our song remind them that God is great.

Lord, may you bring justice against oppressors! But may those who love you rise like the sun in all its power!

With precision, God orchestrated the battle, the assassination, and the victory. All we did was obey. I must sing of your wondrous deeds!

DEBORAH'S STORY IS TOLD IN JUDGES 4–5.

> When an unexpected victory frees me, I will sing, write, draw, paint, or dance a song of praise to God.

IDENTIFY

What victories has God given to us?

How can we commemorate his work creatively?

"I have lived buried beneath the anxiety of my circumstances, unable to act with courage. Yet God gave me victory, showing his love and care for me. I look back in my journals, my songs of praise to God. I see God's faithfulness in my frozen fearfulness. I have learned to 'sing' victory-memories of all he does."

CARA DAY is a writer and illustrator. She has served with Stonecroft Ministries helping women live "extraordinary."

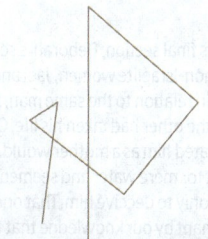

JUDGES 5

¹³ "Down from Tabor marched the few against the nobles.
 The people of the LORD marched down against mighty warriors.
¹⁴ They came down from Ephraim—
 a land that once belonged to the Amalekites;
 they followed you, Benjamin, with your troops.
 From Makir the commanders marched down;
 from Zebulun came those who carry a commander's staff.
¹⁵ The princes of Issachar were with Deborah and Barak.
 They followed Barak, rushing into the valley.
 But in the tribe of Reuben
 there was great indecision.*
¹⁶ Why did you sit at home among the sheepfolds—
 to hear the shepherds whistle for their flocks?
 Yes, in the tribe of Reuben
 there was great indecision.
¹⁷ Gilead remained east of the Jordan.
 And why did Dan stay home?
 Asher sat unmoved at the seashore,
 remaining in his harbors.
¹⁸ But Zebulun risked his life,
 as did Naphtali, on the heights of the battlefield.

¹⁹ "The kings of Canaan came and fought,
 at Taanach near Megiddo's springs,
 but they carried off no silver treasures.
²⁰ The stars fought from heaven.
 The stars in their orbits fought against Sisera.
²¹ The Kishon River swept them away—
 that ancient torrent, the Kishon.
 March on with courage, my soul!
²² Then the horses' hooves hammered the ground,
 the galloping, galloping of Sisera's mighty steeds.
²³ 'Let the people of Meroz be cursed,' said the angel of the LORD.
 'Let them be utterly cursed,
 because they did not come to help the LORD—
 to help the LORD against the mighty warriors.'

²⁴ "Most blessed among women is Jael,
 the wife of Heber the Kenite.
 May she be blessed above all women who live in tents.
²⁵ Sisera asked for water,
 and she gave him milk.
 In a bowl fit for nobles,
 she brought him yogurt.
²⁶ Then with her left hand she reached for a tent peg,
 and with her right hand for the workman's hammer.
 She struck Sisera with the hammer, crushing his head.
 With a shattering blow, she pierced his temples.
²⁷ He sank, he fell,
 he lay still at her feet.
 And where he sank,
 there he died.

²⁸ "From the window Sisera's mother looked out.
 Through the window she watched for his return, saying,
 'Why is his chariot so long in coming?
 Why don't we hear the sound of chariot wheels?'
²⁹ "Her wise women answer,
 and she repeats these words to herself:
³⁰ 'They must be dividing the captured plunder—
 with a woman or two for every man.
 There will be colorful robes for Sisera,
 and colorful, embroidered robes for me.
 Yes, the plunder will include
 colorful robes embroidered on both sides.'

³¹ "LORD, may all your enemies die like Sisera!
 But may those who love you rise like the sun in all its power!"

Then there was peace in the land for forty years.

5:15 As in some Hebrew manuscripts and Syriac version, which read *searchings of heart;* Masoretic Text reads *resolve of heart.*

5:24-30 In its final section, Deborah's song devotes two full sections to two non-Israelite women, Jael and Sisera's mother, portraying both in relation to the same man, Sisera. One had given birth to him; the other had taken his life. One was his mother; the other had treated him as a mother would. She brought him milk at his request for mere water and seemed to risk herself to safeguard him—only to deceive him. That one was waiting for him is made poignant by our knowledge that the other had assassinated him. Both waited for him as women awaited a warrior returning from war (see the note on 4:18-19). One waited at the doorway of her tent and the other at her palace window. Each held a self-serving intent. One looked for the spoil of war; to the other, he became the spoil of war. The mother expected Sisera to be raping a captive woman or two (contrast Deuteronomy 21:10-14). Meanwhile, Jael inflicted a symbolic reverse rape on Sisera by violently penetrating his body with a tent peg. The woman or two that Sisera might have engaged with turned out to be not his victims but the victors—Deborah and Jael. In stark audible contrast, the chatter of women idly waiting stands against the deadly sound of a tent peg that struck, crushed, shattered, and pierced Sisera's head. The contrasts throw into relief the part played by Deborah and even more so by Jael in bringing about Israel's victory. Who would have expected that a Kenite ironsmith's wife would get such pride of place in an Israelite victory hymn! But she does because she was resourceful, had courage, and risked all in the service of Israel's God.

Gideon Becomes Israel's Judge

6 The Israelites did evil in the LORD's sight. So the LORD handed them over to the Midianites for seven years. ²The Midianites were so cruel that the Israelites made hiding places for themselves in the mountains, caves, and strongholds. ³Whenever the Israelites planted their crops, marauders from Midian, Amalek, and the people of the east would attack Israel, ⁴camping in the land and destroying crops as far away as Gaza. They left the Israelites with nothing to eat, taking all the sheep, goats, cattle, and donkeys. ⁵These enemy hordes, coming with their livestock and tents, were as thick as locusts; they arrived on droves of camels too numerous to count. And they stayed until the land was stripped bare. ⁶So Israel was reduced to starvation by the Midianites. Then the Israelites cried out to the LORD for help.

⁷When they cried out to the LORD because of Midian, ⁸the LORD sent a prophet to the Israelites. He said, "This is what the LORD, the God of Israel, says: I brought you up out of slavery in Egypt. ⁹I rescued you from the Egyptians and from all who oppressed you. I drove out your enemies and gave you their land. ¹⁰I told you, 'I am the LORD your God. You must not worship the gods of the Amorites, in whose land you now live.' But you have not listened to me."

¹¹Then the angel of the LORD came and sat beneath the great tree at Ophrah, which belonged to Joash of the clan of Abiezer. Gideon son of Joash was threshing wheat at the bottom of a winepress to hide the grain from the Midianites. ¹²The angel of the LORD appeared to him and said, "Mighty hero, the LORD is with you!"

¹³"Sir," Gideon replied, "if the LORD is with us, why has all this happened to us? And where are all the miracles our ancestors told us about? Didn't they say, 'The LORD brought us up out of Egypt'? But now the LORD has abandoned us and handed us over to the Midianites."

¹⁴Then the LORD turned to him and said, "Go with the strength you have, and rescue Israel from the Midianites. I am sending you!"

¹⁵"But Lord," Gideon replied, "how can I rescue Israel? My clan is the weakest in the whole tribe of Manasseh, and I am the least in my entire family!"

¹⁶The LORD said to him, "I will be with you. And you will destroy the Midianites as if you were fighting against one man."

¹⁷Gideon replied, "If you are truly going to help me, show me a sign to prove that it is really the LORD speaking to me. ¹⁸Don't go away until I come back and bring my offering to you."

He answered, "I will stay here until you return."

¹⁹Gideon hurried home. He cooked a young goat, and with a basket* of flour he baked some bread without yeast. Then, carrying the meat in a basket and the broth in a pot, he brought them out and presented them to the angel, who was under the great tree.

²⁰The angel of God said to him, "Place the meat and the unleavened bread on this rock, and pour the broth over it." And Gideon did as he was told. ²¹Then the angel of the LORD touched the meat and bread with the tip of the staff in his hand, and fire flamed up from the rock and consumed all he had brought. And the angel of the LORD disappeared.

²²When Gideon realized that it was the angel of the LORD, he cried out, "Oh, Sovereign LORD, I'm doomed! I have seen the angel of the LORD face to face!"

²³"It is all right," the LORD replied. "Do not be afraid. You will not die." ²⁴And Gideon built an altar to the LORD there and named it Yahweh-Shalom (which means "the LORD is peace"). The altar remains in Ophrah in the land of the clan of Abiezer to this day.

²⁵That night the LORD said to Gideon, "Take the second bull from your father's herd, the one that is seven years old. Pull down your father's altar to Baal, and cut down the Asherah pole standing beside it. ²⁶Then build an altar to the LORD your God here on this hilltop sanctuary, laying the stones carefully. Sacrifice the bull as a burnt offering on the altar, using as fuel the wood of the Asherah pole you cut down."

²⁷So Gideon took ten of his servants and did as the LORD had commanded. But he did it at night because he was afraid of the other members of his father's household and the people of the town.

²⁸Early the next morning, as the people of the town began to stir, someone discovered that the altar of Baal had been broken down and that the Asherah pole beside it had been cut down. In their place a new altar had been built, and on it were the remains of the bull that had been sacrificed. ²⁹The people said to each other, "Who did this?" And after asking around and making a careful search, they learned that it was Gideon, the son of Joash.

³⁰"Bring out your son," the men of the town demanded of Joash. "He must die for destroying the altar of Baal and for cutting down the Asherah pole."

6:19 Hebrew *an ephah* [20 quarts or 22 liters].

6:1-6 After forty years of peace, religious syncretism had brought about political instability, and marauding nomads had reduced the Israelites to living as fugitives. The Midianites were once thought to have been a purely nomadic tribe centered in northwest Arabia, but they are now known to have built cities and for a time to have dominated much of the Arabian peninsula and southern Transjordan (the area east of the Jordan). They are joined here by Amalekites (who earlier were part of a Moabite coalition) and the mysterious people of the east (see 1 Kings 4:30; Ezekiel 25:4, 10). The pattern of attack was seasonal but devastating.
6:25 In Canaanite worship, Baal was a storm god, while Asherah the fertility goddess was often represented as a sacred tree.

JUDGES 6

³¹But Joash shouted to the mob that confronted him, "Why are you defending Baal? Will you argue his case? Whoever pleads his case will be put to death by morning! If Baal truly is a god, let him defend himself and destroy the one who broke down his altar!" ³²From then on Gideon was called Jerubbaal, which means "Let Baal defend himself," because he broke down Baal's altar.

Gideon Asks for a Sign

³³Soon afterward the armies of Midian, Amalek, and the people of the east formed an alliance against Israel and crossed the Jordan, camping in the valley of Jezreel. ³⁴Then the Spirit of the LORD clothed Gideon with power. He blew a ram's horn as a call to arms, and the men of the clan of Abiezer came to him. ³⁵He also sent messengers throughout Manasseh, Asher, Zebulun, and Naphtali, summoning their warriors, and all of them responded.

³⁶Then Gideon said to God, "If you are truly going to use me to rescue Israel as you promised, ³⁷prove it to me in this way. I will put a wool fleece on the threshing floor tonight. If the fleece is wet with dew in the morning but the ground is dry, then I will know that you are going to help me rescue Israel as you promised." ³⁸And that is just what happened. When

---

6:31 The first person to follow Gideon's inspired act of leadership and abandon Baal for the Lord was Gideon's father, Joash. He was, ironically, the keeper of the Baal shrine.

7:2 The Lord does not require a large force to save his people (see 1 Samuel 14:6). A large number might even have hindered success because the element of surprise was crucial to the Lord's battle plan. Gideon was to pare down the army to maintain godly humility, not for reasons of military strategy.

Come Close
HIDING: STEP AWAY FROM THE SMALL

SCRIPTURE CONNECTION: JUDGES 6:11-24

The bills bigger than your paycheck. The diagnosis scarier than you thought. The fear larger than your faith. I think all of us have had a "no-way moment" when we pull the covers over our heads and spend just a few more moments hiding from the hardship.

Gideon hid in a winepress. The enemy was real. He feared he and his people would come to ruin.

Have you hidden in the safety of the small?

I have, as God woos me to roles that feel ridiculously large. Like Gideon, even when I step away from the shadows, I find more challenge than comfort. As I edge into the light, I find both God's presence and not enough of myself.

God asked Gideon to shrink the army, smaller and smaller (7:2-7). The point became clear: Trust God, not your strategy. Trust God, not your strength. Trust God. Oh, and by the way, you are not enough.

The beauty of having no way out is God is all you have. He is our way out of "no way." While we hide under those covers, avoiding the gathering or fantasizing about quitting, he uses the strength we have, even when it feels small to us.

Trust that God excels in sending us. Look back at how he came through; he plans to come through again.

REFLECT "Then the LORD turned to him and said, 'Go with the strength you have, and rescue Israel from the Midianites. I am sending you!'" JUDGES 6:14

All-powerful God, may I be okay with the fact that the strength I have is in "no way" enough. Give me the strength to go anyway because you send me. Amen.

CONSIDER "Start where you are. Use what you have. Do what you can."
ARTHUR ASHE

God is our way out of "no way."

NAOMI CRAMER OVERTON, MBA, DIS, lives to realize beauty-filled visions that lift us to flourishing, with our families and beyond. Naomi has been CEO for Stonecroft and MOPS, director with Compassion International and World Vision, and General Editor for this Bible.

Gideon got up early the next morning, he squeezed the fleece and wrung out a whole bowlful of water. ³⁹Then Gideon said to God, "Please don't be angry with me, but let me make one more request. Let me use the fleece for one more test. This time let the fleece remain dry while the ground around it is wet with dew." ⁴⁰So that night God did as Gideon asked. The fleece was dry in the morning, but the ground was covered with dew.

Gideon Defeats the Midianites

7 So Jerub-baal (that is, Gideon) and his army got up early and went as far as the spring of Harod. The armies of Midian were camped north of them in the valley near the hill of Moreh. ²The LORD said to Gideon, "You have too many warriors with you. If I let all of you fight the Midianites, the Israelites will boast to me that they saved themselves by their own strength. ³Therefore, tell the people, 'Whoever is timid or afraid may leave this mountain* and go home.'" So 22,000 of them went home, leaving only 10,000 who were willing to fight.

⁴But the LORD told Gideon, "There are still too many! Bring them down to the spring, and I will test them to determine who will go with you and who will not." ⁵When Gideon took his warriors down to the water, the LORD told him, "Divide the men into two groups. In one group put all those who cup water in their hands and lap it up with their tongues like dogs. In the other group put all those who kneel down and drink with their mouths in the stream." ⁶Only 300 of the men drank from their hands. All the others got down on their knees and drank with their mouths in the stream.

⁷The LORD told Gideon, "With these 300 men I will rescue you and give you victory over the Midianites. Send all the others home." ⁸So Gideon collected the provisions and rams' horns of the other warriors and sent them home. But he kept the 300 men with him.

The Midianite camp was in the valley just below Gideon. ⁹That night the LORD said, "Get up! Go down into the Midianite camp, for I have given you victory over them! ¹⁰But if you are afraid to attack, go down to the camp with your servant Purah. ¹¹Listen to what the Midianites are saying, and you will be greatly encouraged. Then you will be eager to attack."

So Gideon took Purah and went down to the edge of the enemy camp. ¹²The armies of Midian, Amalek, and the people of the east had settled in the valley like a swarm of locusts. Their camels were like grains of sand on the seashore—too many to count! ¹³Gideon crept up just as a man was telling his companion about a dream. The man said, "I had this dream, and in my dream a loaf of barley bread came tumbling down into the Midianite camp. It hit a tent, turned it over, and knocked it flat!"

¹⁴His companion answered, "Your dream can mean only one thing—God has given Gideon son of Joash, the Israelite, victory over Midian and all its allies!"

¹⁵When Gideon heard the dream and its interpretation, he bowed in worship before the LORD.* Then he returned to the Israelite camp and shouted, "Get up! For the LORD has given you victory over the Midianite hordes!" ¹⁶He divided the 300 men into three groups and gave each man a ram's horn and a clay jar with a torch in it.

¹⁷Then he said to them, "Keep your eyes on me. When I come to the edge of the camp, do just as I do. ¹⁸As soon as I and those with me blow the rams' horns, blow your horns, too, all around the entire camp, and shout, 'For the LORD and for Gideon!'"

¹⁹It was just after midnight,* after the changing of the guard, when Gideon and the 100 men with him reached the edge of the Midianite camp. Suddenly, they blew the rams' horns and broke their clay jars. ²⁰Then all three groups blew their horns and broke their jars. They held the blazing torches in their left hands and the horns in their right hands, and they all shouted, "A sword for the LORD and for Gideon!"

²¹Each man stood at his position around the camp and watched as all the Midianites rushed around in a panic, shouting as they ran to escape. ²²When the 300 Israelites blew their rams' horns, the LORD caused the warriors in the camp to fight against each other with their swords. Those who were not killed fled to places as far away as Beth-shittah near Zererah and to the border of Abel-meholah near Tabbath.

²³Then Gideon sent for the warriors of Naphtali, Asher, and Manasseh, who joined in chasing the army of Midian. ²⁴Gideon also sent messengers throughout the hill country of Ephraim, saying, "Come down to attack the Midianites. Cut them off at the shallow crossings of the Jordan River at Beth-barah."

So all the men of Ephraim did as they were told. ²⁵They captured Oreb and Zeeb, the two Midianite commanders, killing Oreb at the rock of Oreb, and Zeeb at the winepress of Zeeb. And they continued to chase the Midianites. Afterward the Israelites brought the heads of Oreb and Zeeb to Gideon, who was by the Jordan River.

7:3 Hebrew *may leave Mount Gilead.* The identity of Mount Gilead is uncertain in this context. It is perhaps used here as another name for Mount Gilboa. 7:15 As in Greek version; Hebrew reads *he bowed.* 7:19 Hebrew *at the beginning of the second watch.*

7:21 The warriors stood in place while God fought the battle (see Exodus 14:13; 1 Samuel 12:16; Revelation 19:11-16). The Midianites' camels (Judges 6:5) might have contributed to the panic. Camels usually provided a military advantage, but they would have been a liability in this situation: Like horses, camels can become spooked.

> "A woman is a warrior too.... Sometime before the sorrows of life did their best to kill it in us, most young women wanted to be a part of something grand, something important."
>
> **STASI ELDREDGE**
> minister, writer, and speaker

Gideon Kills Zebah and Zalmunna

8 Then the people of Ephraim asked Gideon, "Why have you treated us this way? Why didn't you send for us when you first went out to fight the Midianites?" And they argued heatedly with Gideon.

² But Gideon replied, "What have I accomplished compared to you? Aren't even the leftover grapes of Ephraim's harvest better than the entire crop of my little clan of Abiezer? ³ God gave you victory over Oreb and Zeeb, the commanders of the Midianite army. What have I accomplished compared to that?" When the men of Ephraim heard Gideon's answer, their anger subsided.

⁴ Gideon then crossed the Jordan River with his 300 men, and though exhausted, they continued to chase the enemy. ⁵ When they reached Succoth, Gideon asked the leaders of the town, "Please give my warriors some food. They are very tired. I am chasing Zebah and Zalmunna, the kings of Midian."

⁶ But the officials of Succoth replied, "Catch Zebah and Zalmunna first, and then we will feed your army."

⁷ So Gideon said, "After the LORD gives me victory over Zebah and Zalmunna, I will return and tear your flesh with the thorns and briers from the wilderness."

⁸ From there Gideon went up to Peniel* and again asked for food, but he got the same answer. ⁹ So he said to the people of Peniel, "After I return in victory, I will tear down this tower."

¹⁰ By this time Zebah and Zalmunna were in Karkor with about 15,000 warriors—all that remained of the allied armies of the east, for 120,000 had already been killed. ¹¹ Gideon circled around by the caravan route east of Nobah and Jogbehah, taking the Midianite army by surprise. ¹² Zebah and Zalmunna, the two Midianite kings, fled, but Gideon chased them down and captured all their warriors.

¹³ After this, Gideon returned from the battle by way of Heres Pass. ¹⁴ There he captured a young man from Succoth and demanded that he write down the names of all the seventy-seven officials and elders in the town. ¹⁵ Gideon then returned to Succoth and said to the leaders, "Here are Zebah and Zalmunna. When we were here before, you taunted me, saying, 'Catch Zebah and Zalmunna first, and then we will feed your exhausted army.'" ¹⁶ Then Gideon took the elders of the town and taught them a lesson, punishing them with thorns and briers from the wilderness. ¹⁷ He also tore down the tower of Peniel and killed all the men in the town.

¹⁸ Then Gideon asked Zebah and Zalmunna, "The men you killed at Tabor—what were they like?"

"Like you," they replied. "They all had the look of a king's son."

¹⁹ "They were my brothers, the sons of my own mother!" Gideon exclaimed. "As surely as the LORD lives, I wouldn't kill you if you hadn't killed them." ²⁰ Turning to Jether, his oldest son, he said, "Kill them!" But Jether did not draw his sword, for he was only a boy and was afraid.

²¹ Then Zebah and Zalmunna said to Gideon, "Be a man! Kill us yourself!" So Gideon killed them both and took the royal ornaments from the necks of their camels.

8:8 Hebrew *Penuel*, a variant spelling of Peniel; also in 8:9, 17.

8:1-3 Ephraim, the dominant tribe of the north-central hill country, produced only a minor judge, Tola (10:1). The Ephraimites resented their omission from the battle, if only because they had hoped for a share of the booty. Nevertheless, when summoned, they did the job at hand. Gideon gave a gracious and humble answer, which turned away Ephraim's anger (see Proverbs 15:1; contrast Jephthah, Judges 12:1-4). Gideon's and Ephraim's victories over Oreb and Zeeb and their armies became the stuff of legend (see Psalm 83:11-12; Isaiah 10:26).

8:13-17 The return journey was probably a straight course (through the unknown Heres Pass) rather than the circular approach needed for the earlier ambush. That a typical young man from Succoth could write down the names is evidence that the newly developed alphabetic writing system had taken root in Israel. Gideon's practice of retribution and execution was the norm in his time. But his reputation as the Lord's servant was better served by his skillful diplomacy (8:1-3) than by vindictive punishment.

Gideon's Sacred Ephod

²²Then the Israelites said to Gideon, "Be our ruler! You and your son and your grandson will be our rulers, for you have rescued us from Midian."

²³But Gideon replied, "I will not rule over you, nor will my son. The LORD will rule over you! ²⁴However, I do have one request—that each of you give me an earring from the plunder you collected from your fallen enemies." (The enemies, being Ishmaelites, all wore gold earrings.)

²⁵"Gladly!" they replied. They spread out a cloak, and each one threw in a gold earring he had gathered from the plunder. ²⁶The weight of the gold earrings was forty-three pounds,* not including the royal ornaments and pendants, the purple clothing worn by the kings of Midian, or the chains around the necks of their camels.

²⁷Gideon made a sacred ephod from the gold and put it in Ophrah, his hometown. But soon all the Israelites prostituted themselves by worshiping it, and it became a trap for Gideon and his family.

²⁸That is the story of how the people of Israel defeated Midian, which never recovered. Throughout the rest of Gideon's lifetime—about forty years—there was peace in the land.

²⁹Then Gideon* son of Joash returned home. ³⁰He had seventy sons born to him, for he had many wives. ³¹He also had a concubine in Shechem, who gave birth to a son, whom he named Abimelech. ³²Gideon died when he was very old, and he was buried in the grave of his father, Joash, at Ophrah in the land of the clan of Abiezer.

³³As soon as Gideon died, the Israelites prostituted themselves by worshiping the images of Baal, making Baal-berith their god. ³⁴They forgot the LORD their God, who had rescued them from all their enemies surrounding them. ³⁵Nor did they show any loyalty to the family of Jerub-baal (that is, Gideon), despite all the good he had done for Israel.

Abimelech Rules over Shechem

9 One day Gideon's* son Abimelech went to Shechem to visit his uncles—his mother's brothers. He said to them and to the rest of his mother's family, ²"Ask the leading citizens of Shechem whether they want to be ruled by all seventy of Gideon's sons or by one man. And remember that I am your own flesh and blood!"

³So Abimelech's uncles gave his message to all the citizens of Shechem on his behalf. And after listening to this proposal, the people of Shechem decided in favor of Abimelech because he was their relative. ⁴They gave him seventy silver coins from the temple of Baal-berith, which he used to hire some reckless troublemakers who agreed to follow him. ⁵He went to his father's home at Ophrah, and there, on one stone, they killed all seventy of his half brothers, the sons of Gideon.* But the youngest brother, Jotham, escaped and hid.

⁶Then all the leading citizens of Shechem and Beth-millo called a meeting under the oak beside the pillar* at Shechem and made Abimelech their king.

Jotham's Parable

⁷When Jotham heard about this, he climbed to the top of Mount Gerizim and shouted,

"Listen to me, citizens of Shechem!
   Listen to me if you want God to listen to you!
⁸ Once upon a time the trees decided to choose a king.
   First they said to the olive tree,
      'Be our king!'
⁹ But the olive tree refused, saying,
   'Should I quit producing the olive oil
      that blesses both God and people,
   just to wave back and forth over the trees?'
¹⁰ "Then they said to the fig tree,
      'You be our king!'
¹¹ But the fig tree also refused, saying,
   'Should I quit producing my sweet fruit
      just to wave back and forth over the trees?'
¹² "Then they said to the grapevine,
      'You be our king!'
¹³ But the grapevine also refused, saying,
   'Should I quit producing the wine
      that cheers both God and people,
   just to wave back and forth over the trees?'
¹⁴ "Then all the trees finally turned to the thornbush and said,
      'Come, you be our king!'
¹⁵ And the thornbush replied to the trees,
   'If you truly want to make me your king,
      come and take shelter in my shade.
   If not, let fire come out from me
      and devour the cedars of Lebanon.'"

¹⁶Jotham continued, "Now make sure you have acted honorably and in good faith by making Abimelech your king, and that you have done right by Gideon and all of his descendants. Have you treated him with the honor he deserves for all he

---

8:26 Hebrew *1,700 [shekels]* [19.4 kilograms]. **8:29** Hebrew *Jerub-baal;* see 6:32. **9:1** Hebrew *Jerub-baal's* (see 6:32); also in 9:2, 24. **9:5** Hebrew *Jerub-baal* (see 6:32); also in 9:16, 19, 28, 57. **9:6** The meaning of the Hebrew is uncertain.

8:27-32 God had given Gideon spiritual blessings and leadership to defeat the Midianites. Although there was no peace, it seems that the rest of Gideon's life was tarnished by a worldly outlook and a decline in God's presence.

accomplished? ¹⁷For he fought for you and risked his life when he rescued you from the Midianites. ¹⁸But today you have revolted against my father and his descendants, killing his seventy sons on one stone. And you have chosen his slave woman's son, Abimelech, to be your king just because he is your relative.

¹⁹"If you have acted honorably and in good faith toward Gideon and his descendants today, then may you find joy in Abimelech, and may he find joy in you. ²⁰But if you have not acted in good faith, then may fire come out from Abimelech and devour the leading citizens of Shechem and Beth-millo; and may fire come out from the citizens of Shechem and Beth-millo and devour Abimelech!"

²¹Then Jotham escaped and lived in Beer because he was afraid of his brother Abimelech.

Shechem Rebels against Abimelech

²²After Abimelech had ruled over Israel for three years, ²³God sent a spirit that stirred up trouble between Abimelech and the leading citizens of Shechem, and they revolted. ²⁴God was punishing Abimelech for murdering Gideon's seventy sons, and the citizens of Shechem for supporting him in this treachery of murdering his brothers. ²⁵The citizens of Shechem set an ambush for Abimelech on the hilltops and robbed everyone who passed that way. But someone warned Abimelech about their plot.

²⁶One day Gaal son of Ebed moved to Shechem with his brothers and gained the confidence of the leading citizens of Shechem. ²⁷During the annual harvest festival at Shechem, held in the temple of the local god, the wine flowed freely, and everyone began cursing Abimelech. ²⁸"Who is Abimelech?" Gaal shouted. "He's not a true son of Shechem,* so why should we be his servants? He's merely the son of Gideon, and this Zebul is merely his deputy. Serve the true sons of Hamor, the founder of Shechem. Why should we serve Abimelech? ²⁹If I were in charge here, I would get rid of Abimelech. I would say* to him, 'Get some soldiers, and come out and fight!'"

³⁰But when Zebul, the leader of the city, heard what Gaal was saying, he was furious. ³¹He sent messengers to Abimelech in Arumah,* telling him, "Gaal son of Ebed and his brothers have come to live in Shechem, and now they are inciting the city to rebel against you. ³²Come by night with an army and hide out in the fields. ³³In the morning, as soon as it is daylight, attack the city. When Gaal and those who are with him come out against you, you can do with them as you wish."

³⁴So Abimelech and all his men went by night and split into four groups, stationing themselves around Shechem. ³⁵Gaal was standing at the city gates when Abimelech and his army came out of hiding. ³⁶When Gaal saw them, he said to Zebul, "Look, there are people coming down from the hilltops!"

Zebul replied, "It's just the shadows on the hills that look like men."

³⁷But again Gaal said, "No, people are coming down from the hills.* And another group is coming down the road past the Diviners' Oak.*"

³⁸Then Zebul turned on him and asked, "Now where is that big mouth of yours? Wasn't it you that said, 'Who is Abimelech, and why should we be his servants?' The men you mocked are right outside the city! Go out and fight them!"

³⁹So Gaal led the leading citizens of Shechem into battle against Abimelech. ⁴⁰But Abimelech chased him, and many of Shechem's men were wounded and fell along the road as they retreated to the city gate. ⁴¹Abimelech returned to Arumah, and Zebul drove Gaal and his brothers out of Shechem.

⁴²The next day the people of Shechem went out into the fields to battle. When Abimelech heard about it, ⁴³he divided his men into three groups and set an ambush in the fields. When Abimelech saw the people coming out of the city, he and his men jumped up from their hiding places and attacked them. ⁴⁴Abimelech and his group stormed the city gate to keep the men of Shechem from getting back in, while Abimelech's other two groups cut them down in the fields. ⁴⁵The battle went on all day before Abimelech finally captured the city. He killed the people, leveled the city, and scattered salt all over the ground.

⁴⁶When the leading citizens who lived in the tower of Shechem heard what had happened, they ran and hid in the temple of Baal-berith.* ⁴⁷Someone reported to Abimelech that the citizens had gathered in the temple, ⁴⁸so he led his forces to Mount Zalmon. He took an ax and chopped some branches from a tree, then put them on his shoulder. "Quick, do as I have done!" he told his men. ⁴⁹So each of them cut down some branches, following Abimelech's example. They piled the branches against the walls of the temple and set them on fire. So all the people who had lived in the tower of Shechem died—about 1,000 men and women.

⁵⁰Then Abimelech attacked the town of Thebez and captured it. ⁵¹But there was a strong tower inside the town, and all the men and women—the entire population—fled to it. They barricaded themselves in and climbed up to the roof of the tower. ⁵²Abimelech followed them to attack the tower. But as he prepared to set fire to the entrance, ⁵³a woman on the roof dropped a millstone that landed on Abimelech's head and crushed his skull.

9:28 Hebrew *Who is Shechem?* 9:29 As in Greek version; Hebrew reads *And he said.* 9:31 Or *in secret;* Hebrew reads *in Tormah;* compare 9:41. 9:37a Or *the center of the land.* 9:37b Hebrew *Elon-meonenim.* 9:46 Hebrew *El-berith,* another name for Baal-berith; compare 9:4.

⁵⁴He quickly said to his young armor bearer, "Draw your sword and kill me! Don't let it be said that a woman killed Abimelech!" So the young man ran him through with his sword, and he died. ⁵⁵When Abimelech's men saw that he was dead, they disbanded and returned to their homes.

⁵⁶In this way, God punished Abimelech for the evil he had done against his father by murdering his seventy brothers. ⁵⁷God also punished the men of Shechem for all their evil. So the curse of Jotham son of Gideon was fulfilled.

Tola Becomes Israel's Judge

10 After Abimelech died, Tola son of Puah, son of Dodo, was the next person to rescue Israel. He was from the tribe of Issachar but lived in the town of Shamir in the hill country of Ephraim. ²He judged Israel for twenty-three years. When he died, he was buried in Shamir.

Jair Becomes Israel's Judge

³After Tola died, Jair from Gilead judged Israel for twenty-two years. ⁴His thirty sons rode around on thirty donkeys, and they owned thirty towns in the land of Gilead, which are still called the Towns of Jair.* ⁵When Jair died, he was buried in Kamon.

The Ammonites Oppress Israel

⁶Again the Israelites did evil in the LORD's sight. They served the images of Baal and Ashtoreth, and the gods of Aram, Sidon, Moab, Ammon, and Philistia. They abandoned the LORD and no longer served him at all. ⁷So the LORD burned with anger against Israel, and he turned them over to the Philistines and the Ammonites, ⁸who began to oppress them that year. For eighteen years they oppressed all the Israelites east of the Jordan River in the land of the Amorites (that is, in Gilead). ⁹The Ammonites also crossed to the west side of the Jordan and attacked Judah, Benjamin, and Ephraim.

The Israelites were in great distress. ¹⁰Finally, they cried out to the LORD for help, saying, "We have sinned against you because we have abandoned you as our God and have served the images of Baal."

¹¹The LORD replied, "Did I not rescue you from the Egyptians, the Amorites, the Ammonites, the Philistines, ¹²the Sidonians, the Amalekites, and the Maonites? When they oppressed you, you cried out to me for help, and I rescued you. ¹³Yet you have abandoned me and served other gods. So I will not rescue you anymore. ¹⁴Go and cry out to the gods you have chosen! Let them rescue you in your hour of distress!"

¹⁵But the Israelites pleaded with the LORD and said, "We have sinned. Punish us as you see fit, only rescue us today from our enemies." ¹⁶Then the Israelites put aside their foreign gods and served the LORD. And he was grieved by their misery.

¹⁷At that time the armies of Ammon had gathered for war and were camped in Gilead, and the people of Israel assembled and camped at Mizpah. ¹⁸The leaders of Gilead said to each other, "Whoever attacks the Ammonites first will become ruler over all the people of Gilead."

Jephthah Becomes Israel's Judge

11 Now Jephthah of Gilead was a great warrior. He was the son of Gilead, but his mother was a prostitute. ²Gilead's wife also had several sons, and when these half brothers grew up, they chased Jephthah off the land. "You will not get any of our father's inheritance," they said, "for you are the son of a prostitute." ³So Jephthah fled from his brothers and lived in the land of Tob. Soon he had a band of worthless rebels following him.

⁴At about this time, the Ammonites began their war against Israel. ⁵When the Ammonites attacked, the elders of Gilead sent for Jephthah in the land of Tob. ⁶The elders said, "Come and be our commander! Help us fight the Ammonites!"

⁷But Jephthah said to them, "Aren't you the ones who hated me and drove me from my father's house? Why do you come to me now when you're in trouble?"

10:4 Hebrew *Havvoth-jair*.

9:53-54 In the ancient world, war was a man's business. Women entered battle only when men defaulted, as in Deborah's case accompanying Barak (Judges 4), or in an emergency. This case is the latter. To die at the hands of a woman was therefore considered shameful for a man. This explains Abimelech's response. He would rather die by suicide than have his name posthumously "sullied" by the report that a woman had killed him. Ironically, he did not save his reputation.

10:6-16 The Lord responded to his people's total apostasy by allowing crushing oppression (10:8). As usual, Israel "cried out to the LORD for help" (10:10) only after experiencing great distress (10:9). Usually, Israel's cry led to divine intervention. However, God's decision to leave them to their chosen gods marks a shift in the cycle described in 2:10-19. Only when "the Israelites put aside their foreign gods and served the LORD" did he again act to redeem them (10:17–11:33).

10:18 The leaders of Gilead, in their desperation for leadership, did not consult the Lord (see 1:1; 20:18) but said that whoever stepped up to lead would become ruler over Gilead.

11:1-3 Multiple wives and concubines were not unusual in the family of a wealthy man. The sons born to concubines would have inheritance rights, like the sons born to Jacob through Bilhah and Zilpah, the maids of his wives (Genesis 30:1-24). However, a son born to a prostitute, even if raised in his father's home, could not hope for part of the family property.

WHAT THE BIBLE SAYS ABOUT

A Guilty or Clean Conscience

Only God Can Free Us from Our Guilt

God saved you by his grace when you believed. And you can't take credit for this; it is a gift from God. Salvation is not a reward for the good things we have done, so none of us can boast about it. **EPHESIANS 2:8-9**

Ignoring Guilt Doesn't Work

Remember, it is sin to know what you ought to do and then not do it. **JAMES 4:17**

"But those who still reject me are like the restless sea,
    which is never still
    but continually churns up mud and dirt.
There is no peace for the wicked,"
    says my God.
ISAIAH 57:20-21

Our Wrongdoing Makes Us Guilty

For everyone has sinned; we all fall short of God's glorious standard. **ROMANS 3:23**

My guilt overwhelms me—
    it is a burden too heavy to bear.
PSALM 38:4

All of us, like sheep, have
    strayed away.
    We have left God's paths
    to follow our own.
Yet the LORD laid on him
    the sins of us all.
ISAIAH 53:6

GUILTY?

CLEAN

God Shows Us How to Live with a Clean Conscience

Even Gentiles, who do not have God's written law, show that they know his law when they instinctively obey it, even without having heard it. They demonstrate that God's law is written in their hearts, for their own conscience and thoughts either accuse them or tell them they are doing right. **ROMANS 2:14-15**

"If he finds it, I tell you the truth, he will rejoice over it more than over the ninety-nine that didn't wander away! In the same way, it is not my heavenly Father's will that even one of these little ones should perish." **MATTHEW 18:13-14**

Jesus Makes Us Clean

If we claim we have no sin, we are only fooling ourselves and not living in the truth. But if we confess our sins to him, he is faithful and just to forgive us our sins and to cleanse us from all wickedness. **1 JOHN 1:8-9**

God showed his great love for us by sending Christ to die for us while we were still sinners. **ROMANS 5:8**

Christ suffered for our sins once for all time. He never sinned, but he died for sinners to bring you safely home to God. **1 PETER 3:18**

Believing Leads to Life

"I tell you the truth, those who listen to my message and believe in God who sent me have eternal life. They will never be condemned for their sins, but they have already passed from death into life." **JOHN 5:24**

To all who believed him and accepted him, he gave the right to become children of God. **JOHN 1:12**

...from death into life

⁸"Because we need you," the elders replied. "If you lead us in battle against the Ammonites, we will make you ruler over all the people of Gilead."

⁹Jephthah said to the elders, "Let me get this straight. If I come with you and if the LORD gives me victory over the Ammonites, will you really make me ruler over all the people?"

¹⁰"The LORD is our witness," the elders replied. "We promise to do whatever you say."

¹¹So Jephthah went with the elders of Gilead, and the people made him their ruler and commander of the army. At Mizpah, in the presence of the LORD, Jephthah repeated what he had said to the elders.

¹²Then Jephthah sent messengers to the king of Ammon, asking, "Why have you come out to fight against my land?"

¹³The king of Ammon answered Jephthah's messengers, "When the Israelites came out of Egypt, they stole my land from the Arnon River to the Jabbok River and all the way to the Jordan. Now then, give back the land peaceably."

¹⁴Jephthah sent this message back to the Ammonite king:

¹⁵"This is what Jephthah says: Israel did not steal any land from Moab or Ammon. ¹⁶When the people of Israel arrived at Kadesh on their journey from Egypt after crossing the Red Sea,* ¹⁷they sent messengers to the king of Edom asking for permission to pass through his land. But their request was denied. Then they asked the king of Moab for similar permission, but he wouldn't let them pass through either. So the people of Israel stayed in Kadesh.

¹⁸"Finally, they went around Edom and Moab through the wilderness. They traveled along Moab's eastern border and camped on the other side of the Arnon River. But they never once crossed the Arnon River into Moab, for the Arnon was the border of Moab.

¹⁹"Then Israel sent messengers to King Sihon of the Amorites, who ruled from Heshbon, asking for permission to cross through his land to get to their destination. ²⁰But King Sihon didn't trust Israel to pass through his land. Instead, he mobilized his army at Jahaz and attacked them. ²¹But the LORD, the God of Israel, gave his people victory over King Sihon. So Israel took control of all the land of the Amorites, who lived in that region, ²²from the Arnon River to the Jabbok River, and from the eastern wilderness to the Jordan.

²³"So you see, it was the LORD, the God of Israel, who took away the land from the Amorites and gave it to Israel. Why, then, should we give it back to you? ²⁴You keep whatever your god Chemosh gives you, and we will keep whatever the LORD our God gives us. ²⁵Are you any better than Balak son of Zippor, king of Moab? Did he try to make a case against Israel for disputed land? Did he go to war against them?

²⁶"Israel has been living here for 300 years, inhabiting Heshbon and its surrounding settlements, all the way to Aroer and its settlements, and in all the towns along the Arnon River. Why have you made no effort to recover it before now? ²⁷Therefore, I have not sinned against you. Rather, you have wronged me by attacking me. Let the LORD, who is judge, decide today which of us is right—Israel or Ammon."

²⁸But the king of Ammon paid no attention to Jephthah's message.

Jephthah's Vow

²⁹At that time the Spirit of the LORD came upon Jephthah, and he went throughout the land of Gilead and Manasseh, including Mizpah in Gilead, and from there he led an army against the Ammonites. ³⁰And Jephthah made a vow to the LORD. He said, "If you give me victory over the Ammonites, ³¹I will give to the LORD whatever comes out of my house to meet me when I return in triumph. I will sacrifice it as a burnt offering."

³²So Jephthah led his army against the Ammonites, and the LORD gave him victory. ³³He crushed the Ammonites, devastating about twenty towns from Aroer to an area near Minnith and as far away as Abel-keramim. In this way Israel defeated the Ammonites.

³⁴When Jephthah returned home to Mizpah, his daughter came out to meet him, playing on a tambourine and dancing for joy. She was his one and only child; he had no other sons or daughters. ³⁵When he saw her, he tore his clothes in anguish.

11:16 Hebrew *sea of reeds.*

11:34-40 In the Old Testament, the term "burnt offering" invariably refers to non-human sacrifice (11:31). The Old Testament is uncompromising on its prohibition of human sacrifices: for example, Leviticus 18:21; 2 Chronicles 33:6; Jeremiah 32:35; Ezekiel 16:20-21. Against this, Jephthah promised to offer not *whatever* but *whoever* would come out the door of his house to meet him when he returned victorious from the battle (the Hebrew in Judges 11:31 allows both senses, and the NLT uses "whatever"). Animals cannot recognize a returning victor, but people can. In ancient Israel, the tradition was that women went out to celebrate their returning heroes (5:28-30; Exodus 15:19-21; 1 Samuel 18:6-9). It would seem that Jephthah was so acclimated to the Canaanite customs around him, which did practice human sacrifice, that he deliberately bartered the life of a member of his household to assure himself the victory (see 2 Kings 3:27). The incident drives home the point that God does not always intervene to prevent "collateral damage" from our wrongdoing. Innocent people can get badly hurt or even die because of our sinful actions.

"Oh, my daughter!" he cried out. "You have completely destroyed me! You've brought disaster on me! For I have made a vow to the LORD, and I cannot take it back."

36 And she said, "Father, if you have made a vow to the LORD, you must do to me what you have vowed, for the LORD has given you a great victory over your enemies, the Ammonites. 37 But first let me do this one thing: Let me go up and roam in the hills and weep with my friends for two months, because I will die a virgin."

38 "You may go," Jephthah said. And he sent her away for two months. She and her friends went into the hills and wept because she would never have children. 39 When she returned home, her father kept the vow he had made, and she died a virgin.

So it has become a custom in Israel 40 for young Israelite women to go away for four days each year to lament the fate of Jephthah's daughter.

Ephraim Fights with Jephthah

12 Then the people of Ephraim mobilized an army and crossed over the Jordan River to Zaphon. They sent this message to Jephthah: "Why didn't you call for us to help you fight against the Ammonites? We are going to burn down your house with you in it!"

2 Jephthah replied, "I summoned you at the beginning of the dispute, but you refused to come! You failed to help us in our struggle against Ammon. 3 So when I realized you weren't coming, I risked my life and went to battle without you, and the LORD gave me victory over the Ammonites. So why have you now come to fight me?"

4 The people of Ephraim responded, "You men of Gilead are nothing more than fugitives from Ephraim and Manasseh." So Jephthah gathered all the men of Gilead and attacked the men of Ephraim and defeated them.

5 Jephthah captured the shallow crossings of the Jordan River, and whenever a fugitive from Ephraim tried to go back across, the men of Gilead would challenge him. "Are you a member of the tribe of Ephraim?" they would ask. If the man said, "No, I'm not," 6 they would tell him to say "Shibboleth." If he was from Ephraim, he would say "Sibboleth," because people from Ephraim cannot pronounce the word correctly. Then they would take him and kill him at the shallow crossings of the Jordan. In all, 42,000 Ephraimites were killed at that time.

7 Jephthah judged Israel for six years. When he died, he was buried in one of the towns of Gilead.

Ibzan Becomes Israel's Judge

8 After Jephthah died, Ibzan from Bethlehem judged Israel. 9 He had thirty sons and thirty daughters. He sent his daughters to marry men outside his clan, and he brought in thirty young women from outside his clan to marry his sons. Ibzan judged Israel for seven years. 10 When he died, he was buried at Bethlehem.

Elon Becomes Israel's Judge

11 After Ibzan died, Elon from the tribe of Zebulun judged Israel for ten years. 12 When he died, he was buried at Aijalon in Zebulun.

Abdon Becomes Israel's Judge

13 After Elon died, Abdon son of Hillel, from Pirathon, judged Israel. 14 He had forty sons and thirty grandsons, who rode on seventy donkeys. He judged Israel for eight years. 15 When he died, he was buried at Pirathon in Ephraim, in the hill country of the Amalekites.

The Birth of Samson

13 Again the Israelites did evil in the LORD's sight, so the LORD handed them over to the Philistines, who oppressed them for forty years.

2 In those days a man named Manoah from the tribe of Dan lived in the town of Zorah. His wife was unable to become pregnant, and they had no children. 3 The angel of the LORD appeared to Manoah's wife and said, "Even though you have been unable to have children, you will soon become pregnant and give birth to a son. 4 So be careful; you must not drink wine or any other alcoholic drink nor eat any forbidden food.* 5 You will become pregnant and give birth to a son, and his hair must never be cut. For he will be dedicated to God as a Nazirite from birth. He will begin to rescue Israel from the Philistines."

6 The woman ran and told her husband, "A man of God appeared to me! He looked like one of God's angels, terrifying to see. I didn't ask where he was from, and he didn't tell me his name. 7 But he told me, 'You will become pregnant and give birth to a son. You must not drink wine or any other alcoholic drink nor eat any forbidden food. For your son will be dedicated to God as a Nazirite from the moment of his birth until the day of his death.'"

8 Then Manoah prayed to the LORD, saying, "Lord, please let the man of God come back to us again and give us more instructions about this son who is to be born."

13:4 Hebrew *any unclean thing;* also in 13:7, 14.

12:4 It is unclear why the people of Ephraim were taunting the men of Gilead. Perhaps they resented or looked down on the Israelites who lived east of the Jordan River.
12:7 Like all the judges after Gideon, Jephthah's years as judge were short. Despite his limitations, Jephthah was buried honorably, reflecting that he had been an inspired and successful warrior (11:29).

⁹God answered Manoah's prayer, and the angel of God appeared once again to his wife as she was sitting in the field. But her husband, Manoah, was not with her. ¹⁰So she quickly ran and told her husband, "The man who appeared to me the other day is here again!"

¹¹Manoah ran back with his wife and asked, "Are you the man who spoke to my wife the other day?"

"Yes," he replied, "I am."

¹²So Manoah asked him, "When your words come true, what kind of rules should govern the boy's life and work?"

¹³The angel of the LORD replied, "Be sure your wife follows the instructions I gave her. ¹⁴She must not eat grapes or raisins, drink wine or any other alcoholic drink, or eat any forbidden food."

¹⁵Then Manoah said to the angel of the LORD, "Please stay here until we can prepare a young goat for you to eat."

¹⁶"I will stay," the angel of the LORD replied, "but I will not eat anything. However, you may prepare a burnt offering as a sacrifice to the LORD." (Manoah didn't realize it was the angel of the LORD.)

¹⁷Then Manoah asked the angel of the LORD, "What is your name? For when all this comes true, we want to honor you."

¹⁸"Why do you ask my name?" the angel of the LORD replied. "It is too wonderful for you to understand."

¹⁹Then Manoah took a young goat and a grain offering and offered it on a rock as a sacrifice to the LORD. And as Manoah and his wife watched, the LORD did an amazing thing. ²⁰As the flames from the altar shot up toward the sky, the angel of the LORD ascended in the fire. When Manoah and his wife saw this, they fell with their faces to the ground.

²¹The angel did not appear again to Manoah and his wife. Manoah finally realized it was the angel of the LORD, ²²and he said to his wife, "We will certainly die, for we have seen God!"

²³But his wife said, "If the LORD were going to kill us, he wouldn't have accepted our burnt offering and grain offering. He wouldn't have appeared to us and told us this wonderful thing and done these miracles."

²⁴When her son was born, she named him Samson. And the LORD blessed him as he grew up. ²⁵And the Spirit of the LORD began to stir him while he lived in Mahaneh-dan, which is located between the towns of Zorah and Eshtaol.

Samson's Riddle

14 One day when Samson was in Timnah, one of the Philistine women caught his eye. ²When he returned home, he told his father and mother, "A young Philistine woman in Timnah caught my eye. I want to marry her. Get her for me."

³His father and mother objected. "Isn't there even one woman in our tribe or among all the Israelites you could marry?" they asked. "Why must you go to the pagan Philistines to find a wife?"

But Samson told his father, "Get her for me! She looks good to me." ⁴His father and mother didn't realize the LORD was at work in this, creating an opportunity to work against the Philistines, who ruled over Israel at that time.

⁵As Samson and his parents were going down to Timnah, a young lion suddenly attacked Samson near the vineyards of Timnah. ⁶At that moment the Spirit of the LORD came powerfully upon him, and he ripped the lion's jaws apart with his bare hands. He did it as easily as if it were a young goat. But he didn't tell his father or mother about it. ⁷When Samson arrived in Timnah, he talked with the woman and was very pleased with her.

⁸Later, when he returned to Timnah for the wedding, he turned off the path to look at the carcass of the lion. And he found that a swarm of bees had made some honey in the carcass. ⁹He scooped some of the honey into his hands and ate it along the way. He also gave some to his father and mother, and they ate it. But he didn't tell them he had taken the honey from the carcass of the lion.

¹⁰As his father was making final arrangements for the marriage, Samson threw a party at Timnah, as was the custom for elite young men. ¹¹When the bride's parents* saw him, they selected thirty young men from the town to be his companions.

14:11 Hebrew *they*.

13:9-17 In this patriarchal culture, the angel's reappearance to the woman was a deliberate slight to the man. The text reveals its anti-Manoah bias by showcasing his foolishness and her wisdom and favor with God. A careful reading of the conversation reveals that Manoah rebuffed the angel at every turn (13:11-17). He learned not a single detail more than what his wife had already told him. Instead, he was twice pointedly referred back to what his wife had received as instructions.

13:24 When the baby was finally born, Manoah's wife named him, which is an act that the Old Testament shows mothers doing as much as or more than fathers (for example, see Genesis 25:25-26; 29:31–30:24). Samson, unfortunately, would not take after his mother, but rather after his unperceptive father. And though a devout woman gave birth to him, Samson would allow a devious one to bring about his death.

14:1-7 Today, arranged marriages often look something like Samson's to the Philistine woman from Timnah, blending the individual element with the communal. A person may find a marriage partner or choose from recommendations made by the family. The potential groom and his family go to "see" the potential bride in her maternal home, just as Samson and his parents did. If both individuals and families agree with the match, the families negotiate the wedding's terms and conditions. Traditionally, the wedding occurs at the bride's place. In this passage, we see Samson begin to act for his own benefit, rather than God's, yet the Lord used Samson's bad choices to bring the Israelites deliverance from their enemies.

Wife of Manoah

IDENTITY: An Unnamed Wise Woman

The woman's namelessness might, at first glance, suggest she doesn't matter. But, as we read more closely, we see three ways God honored Manoah's wife:

- First, the woman's childlessness (13:2) echoes the infertility of Israel's matriarchs: Sarah, Rebekah, and Rachel (Genesis 11:30; 25:21; 29:31). This association elevated her status in the eyes of God.
- Second, she is given instructions on how to raise the miracle child (Judges 13:3-5). Such instructions to a woman were unusual in a patriarchal society.
- Most significantly, the wife outstrips Manoah in wisdom. Manoah's wife only needed to see the mysterious being's appearance to recognize an angel (13:6). Manoah, by comparison, only realized this later.

While Manoah blundered, his wife honored God's messenger. She believed the angel. When the couple grasped that they had seen God, her response was as enlightened as his was dim (13:21-23). Why would they die when the divine purpose was for her to give birth?

> God honors wise women.

The entire episode showcases the woman. It opens with divine favor and closes with her naming the wonder child (13:24). This unnamed woman joins the other capable women featured in the book of Judges, like Deborah and Jael. God honored Manoah's wife, and she trusted his message. We gain favor, too, as we trust God's words.

MANOAH'S WIFE'S STORY IS TOLD IN JUDGES 13.

IDENTIFY

How has God spoken to you? What did he say?

What do you need to do to respond to God's call on your life with wisdom?

"We ourselves feel that what we are doing is just a drop in the ocean. But the ocean would be less because of that missing drop." Mother Teresa

HAVILAH DHARAMRAJ, PhD, serves at South Asia Institute of Advanced Christian Studies, Bangalore, India. Her research interests include biblical narrative and comparative literature. She encourages her students to retrieve traditional storytelling methods for ministry.

¹²Samson said to them, "Let me tell you a riddle. If you solve my riddle during these seven days of the celebration, I will give you thirty fine linen robes and thirty sets of festive clothing. ¹³But if you can't solve it, then you must give me thirty fine linen robes and thirty sets of festive clothing."

"All right," they agreed, "let's hear your riddle." ¹⁴So he said:

"Out of the one who eats came something to eat;
out of the strong came something sweet."

Three days later they were still trying to figure it out. ¹⁵On the fourth* day they said to Samson's wife, "Entice your husband to explain the riddle for us, or we will burn down your father's house with you in it. Did you invite us to this party just to make us poor?" ¹⁶So Samson's wife came to him in tears and said, "You don't love me; you hate me! You have given my people a riddle, but you haven't told me the answer."

"I haven't even given the answer to my father or mother," he replied. "Why should I tell you?" ¹⁷So she cried whenever she was with him and kept it up for the rest of the celebration. At last, on the seventh day he told her the answer because she was tormenting him with her nagging. Then she explained the riddle to the young men.

¹⁸So before sunset of the seventh day, the men of the town came to Samson with their answer:

"What is sweeter than honey?
What is stronger than a lion?"

Samson replied, "If you hadn't plowed with my heifer, you wouldn't have solved my riddle!"

¹⁹Then the Spirit of the LORD came powerfully upon him. He went down to the town of Ashkelon, killed thirty men, took their belongings, and gave their clothing to the men who had solved his riddle. But Samson was furious about what had happened, and he went back home to live with his father and mother. ²⁰So his wife was given in marriage to the man who had been Samson's best man at the wedding.

Samson's Vengeance on the Philistines

15 Later on, during the wheat harvest, Samson took a young goat as a present to his wife. He said, "I'm going into my wife's room to sleep with her," but her father wouldn't let him in.

²"I truly thought you must hate her," her father explained, "so I gave her in marriage to your best man. But look, her younger sister is even more beautiful than she is. Marry her instead."

³Samson said, "This time I cannot be blamed for everything I am going to do to you Philistines." ⁴Then he went out and caught 300 foxes. He tied their tails together in pairs, and he fastened a torch to each pair of tails. ⁵Then he lit the torches and let the foxes run through the grain fields of the Philistines. He burned all their grain to the ground, including the sheaves and the uncut grain. He also destroyed their vineyards and olive groves.

⁶"Who did this?" the Philistines demanded.

"Samson," was the reply, "because his father-in-law from Timnah gave Samson's wife to be married to his best man." So the Philistines went and got the woman and her father and burned them to death.

⁷"Because you did this," Samson vowed, "I won't rest until I take my revenge on you!" ⁸So he attacked the Philistines with great fury and killed many of them. Then he went to live in a cave in the rock of Etam.

⁹The Philistines retaliated by setting up camp in Judah and spreading out near the town of Lehi. ¹⁰The men of Judah asked the Philistines, "Why are you attacking us?"

The Philistines replied, "We've come to capture Samson. We've come to pay him back for what he did to us."

14:15 As in Greek version; Hebrew reads *seventh*.

14:16 In ancient Israel, a man's family priorities started with his parents, which is why Samson responded to his new wife's question with what may feel like rudeness to us. The wife was further down the list, perhaps even after significant male relatives such as uncles and brothers. This is still true in traditional families in some parts of the world, especially joint families in which several generations live together. In such situations, the saying "blood is thicker than water" works against the wife, who is perceived as an outsider.
14:17 Weddings that lasted several days were common in ancient Israel. Since relatives and friends would travel some distance, and since the hosts usually invited the whole community, it made sense to celebrate for several days.
14:20 This appears to be a case of a deserted bride. Other than virgin daughters still living in their parental home, single women such as widows and divorcees were vulnerable because they had no male guardian. A deserted bride occupied that no-man's-land between her father's house and her husband's home. Once the couple had sex, any prospects of a second marriage were dim. The father, in this case, acted in his daughter's best interests to protect her. He must have been relieved that one of the wedding party would marry her.
15:1 Some Near Eastern matrilineal communities, both ancient and present-day, keep the custom of the *sadiqa* marriage where there is no permanent cohabitation for husband and wife. Instead, the wife continues to live in her home, with her husband visiting her occasionally, bringing gifts. This may explain why Samson returned to his wife's home, assuming she had remained available to him, and is upset to find that she was not.
15:2 In traditional arranged marriages, the daughter would grow up conditioned to marry the man her male family members would choose for her. This explains how the father offered his younger daughter to Samson with no thought of consulting her. Usually, the male relatives considered the girl's best interests, but this father acted quickly to save himself from Samson's wrath.

¹¹So 3,000 men of Judah went down to get Samson at the cave in the rock of Etam. They said to Samson, "Don't you realize the Philistines rule over us? What are you doing to us?"

But Samson replied, "I only did to them what they did to me."

¹²But the men of Judah told him, "We have come to tie you up and hand you over to the Philistines."

"All right," Samson said. "But promise that you won't kill me yourselves."

¹³"We will only tie you up and hand you over to the Philistines," they replied. "We won't kill you." So they tied him up with two new ropes and brought him up from the rock.

¹⁴As Samson arrived at Lehi, the Philistines came shouting in triumph. But the Spirit of the LORD came powerfully upon Samson, and he snapped the ropes on his arms as if they were burnt strands of flax, and they fell from his wrists. ¹⁵Then he found the jawbone of a recently killed donkey. He picked it up and killed 1,000 Philistines with it. ¹⁶Then Samson said,

"With the jawbone of a donkey,
    I've piled them in heaps!
With the jawbone of a donkey,
    I've killed a thousand men!"

¹⁷When he finished his boasting, he threw away the jawbone; and the place was named Jawbone Hill.*

¹⁸Samson was now very thirsty, and he cried out to the LORD, "You have accomplished this great victory by the strength of your servant. Must I now die of thirst and fall into the hands of these pagans?" ¹⁹So God caused water to gush out of a hollow in the ground at Lehi, and Samson was revived as he drank. Then he named that place "The Spring of the One Who Cried Out,"* and it is still in Lehi to this day.

²⁰Samson judged Israel for twenty years during the period when the Philistines dominated the land.

Samson Carries Away Gaza's Gates

16 One day Samson went to the Philistine town of Gaza and spent the night with a prostitute. ²Word soon spread* that Samson was there, so the men of Gaza gathered together and waited all night at the town gates. They kept quiet during the night, saying to themselves, "When the light of morning comes, we will kill him."

³But Samson stayed in bed only until midnight. Then he got up, took hold of the doors of the town gate, including the two posts, and lifted them up, bar and all. He put them on his shoulders and carried them all the way to the top of the hill across from Hebron.

Samson and Delilah

⁴Some time later Samson fell in love with a woman named Delilah, who lived in the valley of Sorek. ⁵The rulers of the Philistines went to her and said, "Entice Samson to tell you what makes him so strong and how he can be overpowered and tied up securely. Then each of us will give you 1,100 pieces* of silver."

⁶So Delilah said to Samson, "Please tell me what makes you so strong and what it would take to tie you up securely."

⁷Samson replied, "If I were tied up with seven new bowstrings that have not yet been dried, I would become as weak as anyone else."

⁸So the Philistine rulers brought Delilah seven new bowstrings, and she tied Samson up with them. ⁹She had hidden some men in one of the inner rooms of her house, and she cried out, "Samson! The Philistines have come to capture you!" But Samson snapped the bowstrings as a piece of string snaps when it is burned by a fire. So the secret of his strength was not discovered.

¹⁰Afterward Delilah said to him, "You've been making fun of me and telling me lies! Now please tell me how you can be tied up securely."

¹¹Samson replied, "If I were tied up with brand-new ropes that had never been used, I would become as weak as anyone else."

¹²So Delilah took new ropes and tied him up with them. The men were hiding in the inner room as before, and again Delilah cried out, "Samson! The Philistines have come to capture you!" But again Samson snapped the ropes from his arms as if they were thread.

¹³Then Delilah said, "You've been making fun of me and telling me lies! Now tell me how you can be tied up securely."

Samson replied, "If you were to weave the seven braids of my hair into the fabric on your loom and tighten it with the loom shuttle, I would become as weak as anyone else."

So while he slept, Delilah wove the seven braids of his hair into the fabric. ¹⁴Then she tightened it with the loom shuttle.* Again she cried out, "Samson! The Philistines have come to capture you!" But Samson woke up, pulled back the loom shuttle, and yanked his hair away from the loom and the fabric.

15:17 Hebrew *Ramath-lehi*.   15:19 Hebrew *En-hakkore*.   16:2 As in Greek and Syriac versions and Latin Vulgate; Hebrew lacks *Word soon spread*.   16:5 Hebrew *1,100 [shekels]*, about 28 pounds or 12.5 kilograms in weight.   16:13-14 As in Greek version and Latin Vulgate; Hebrew lacks *I would become as weak as anyone else. / So while he slept, Delilah wove the seven braids of his hair into the fabric.* ¹⁴*Then she tightened it with the loom shuttle.*

16:4-22 Samson's dissipation and defeat by Delilah, who tempted him to sin, shows the depths of Samson's foolish and reckless behavior.

16:5-6 The desire for silver rather than self-preservation (see 14:15) seems to have motivated Delilah; she apparently did not reciprocate Samson's love.

JUDGES 16

¹⁵Then Delilah pouted, "How can you tell me, 'I love you,' when you don't share your secrets with me? You've made fun of me three times now, and you still haven't told me what makes you so strong!" ¹⁶She tormented him with her nagging day after day until he was sick to death of it.

¹⁷Finally, Samson shared his secret with her. "My hair has never been cut," he confessed, "for I was dedicated to God as a Nazirite from birth. If my head were shaved, my strength would leave me, and I would become as weak as anyone else."

¹⁸Delilah realized he had finally told her the truth, so she sent for the Philistine rulers. "Come back one more time," she said, "for he has finally told me his secret." So the Philistine rulers returned with the money in their hands. ¹⁹Delilah lulled Samson to sleep with his head in her lap, and then she called in a man to shave off the seven locks of his hair. In this way she began to bring him down,* and his strength left him.

²⁰Then she cried out, "Samson! The Philistines have come to capture you!"

When he woke up, he thought, "I will do as before and shake myself free." But he didn't realize the LORD had left him.

²¹So the Philistines captured him and gouged out his eyes. They took him to Gaza, where he was bound with bronze chains and forced to grind grain in the prison.

²²But before long, his hair began to grow back.

16:19 Or *she began to torment him.* Greek version reads *He began to grow weak.*

16:22 There was no certainty that the Lord would revive Samson's strength when his hair began to grow back. There was only the hope that the Lord's earlier promise—that he would begin to rescue Israel through this strange and now broken hero (13:5)—still stood.

Come Close

USED OR USER: FIND FREEDOM TO CHOOSE

SCRIPTURE CONNECTION: JUDGES 16:4-22

When reading Samson and Delilah's story, we often focus on Samson's tendency to repeatedly make poor choices. While this is true, we also need to consider Delilah's choices: Greed may have motivated her to intentionally defeat Samson. He used her to meet his physical needs, and she used him to gain a payday. And in a time when women were regarded as less than men, she could also make a name for herself. The Philistines capitalized on Samson's affection and made her an offer she could have refused—but didn't.

Would we view this story differently if Delilah hadn't been a willing participant? If the Philistines and Samson had used her without her consent? Probably so. However, Delilah had a choice to do what was right, just like Samson. Are there times you feel like you must choose based on your circumstances, rather than on what's right? How can we decide to upend patterns of destruction, even if we are the victims of someone else's poor choices? One way is by coming to know God's purpose for our lives.

Samson knew his purpose from birth yet still chose his own way, short-circuiting the influence he could have had. May we take Samson and Delilah as examples of what not to do. May we choose what is right in God's eyes; may we move toward our purpose, not away.

REFLECT "But if you refuse to serve the LORD, then choose today whom you will serve." JOSHUA 24:15

Lord, you are so kind to us. You created us with the power to choose. Please help us to choose the good that leads to you. And Lord, when we get stuck in our circumstances, grant us discernment and wisdom to see beyond them. Thank you in advance. In Jesus' name, amen.

CONSIDER "Choices are the hinges of destiny." EDWIN MARKHAM

Patterns of destruction change as we find God's purpose.

QUANTRILLA ARD, PhD, is a faith-based personal and spiritual development author, speaker, Bible teacher, and literary agent who believes in the power of collective strength, community, and fellowship.

Samson's Final Victory

[23] The Philistine rulers held a great festival, offering sacrifices and praising their god, Dagon. They said, "Our god has given us victory over our enemy Samson!"

[24] When the people saw him, they praised their god, saying, "Our god has delivered our enemy to us! The one who killed so many of us is now in our power!"

[25] Half drunk by now, the people demanded, "Bring out Samson so he can amuse us!" So he was brought from the prison to amuse them, and they had him stand between the pillars supporting the roof.

[26] Samson said to the young servant who was leading him by the hand, "Place my hands against the pillars that hold up the temple. I want to rest against them." [27] Now the temple was completely filled with people. All the Philistine rulers were there, and there were about 3,000 men and women on the roof who were watching as Samson amused them.

[28] Then Samson prayed to the LORD, "Sovereign LORD, remember me again. O God, please strengthen me just one more time. With one blow let me pay back the Philistines for the loss of my two eyes." [29] Then Samson put his hands on the two center pillars that held up the temple. Pushing against them with both hands, [30] he prayed, "Let me die with the Philistines." And the temple crashed down on the Philistine rulers and all the people. So he killed more people when he died than he had during his entire lifetime.

[31] Later his brothers and other relatives went down to get his body. They took him back home and buried him between Zorah and Eshtaol, where his father, Manoah, was buried. Samson had judged Israel for twenty years.

Micah's Idols

17 There was a man named Micah, who lived in the hill country of Ephraim. [2] One day he said to his mother, "I heard you place a curse on the person who stole 1,100 pieces* of silver from you. Well, I have the money. I was the one who took it."

"The LORD bless you for admitting it," his mother replied. [3] He returned the money to her, and she said, "I now dedicate these silver coins to the LORD. In honor of my son, I will have an image carved and an idol cast."

[4] So when he returned the money to his mother, she took 200 silver coins and gave them to a silversmith, who made them into an image and an idol. And these were placed in Micah's house. [5] Micah set up a shrine for the idol, and he made a sacred ephod and some household idols. Then he installed one of his sons as his personal priest.

[6] In those days Israel had no king; all the people did whatever seemed right in their own eyes.

[7] One day a young Levite, who had been living in Bethlehem in Judah, arrived in that area. [8] He had left Bethlehem in search of another place to live, and as he traveled, he came to the hill country of Ephraim. He happened to stop at Micah's house as he was traveling through. [9] "Where are you from?" Micah asked him.

He replied, "I am a Levite from Bethlehem in Judah, and I am looking for a place to live."

[10] "Stay here with me," Micah said, "and you can be a father and priest to me. I will give you ten pieces of silver* a year, plus a change of clothes and your food." [11] The Levite agreed to this, and the young man became like one of Micah's sons.

[12] So Micah installed the Levite as his personal priest, and he lived in Micah's house. [13] "I know the LORD will bless me now," Micah said, "because I have a Levite serving as my priest."

Idolatry in the Tribe of Dan

18 Now in those days Israel had no king. And the tribe of Dan was trying to find a place where they could settle, for they had not yet moved into the land assigned to them when the land was divided among the tribes of Israel. [2] So the men of Dan chose from their clans five capable warriors from the towns of Zorah and Eshtaol to scout out a land for them to settle in.

17:2 Hebrew *1,100 [shekels]*, about 28 pounds or 12.5 kilograms in weight. **17:10** Hebrew *10 [shekels] of silver*, about 4 ounces or 114 grams in weight.

17:1–21:25 These two epilogues (17:1–18:31 and 19:1–21:25) attest that unstructured leadership and mere lip service to God cannot endure. During the relentless march toward social disintegration and civil war, the refrain, "In those days Israel had no king," occurs four times. Additionally, "all the people did whatever seemed right in their own eyes" is added twice (17:6; 18:1; 19:1; 21:25). The era of inspired leadership spiraled downward and culminated in chaos. Something was clearly missing.

17:2-3 Micah's mother was indulgent and idolatrous, yet she invoked the Lord's name in both cursing and blessing. Words uttered in curses and blessings were understood to have power, particularly if the speaker had the authority to utter such pronouncements (see Genesis 27; Isaiah 55:11). Micah's mother was hoping that the blessing would effectively neutralize her earlier curse. The large number of pieces of silver was probably her life savings or dowry. Interestingly, Delilah was bribed with the same amount (Judges 16:5).

18:1-31 The migration of the Danites (see Joshua 19:40-48) is the story of that tribe's failure to obey God's covenant, and it demonstrates Israel's decline. What began as Micah's private sin (Judges 17:4-5) would become the wrongdoing of an entire tribe (18:30-31). What started as covenant failure (1:19-36) turned into social breakdown in the days of Jephthah and Samson (11:1–16:31). In the end, robbery and looting replaced law and order (18:27-28).

18:2 Scouts were selected from the area where the Spirit of the Lord had begun to stir Samson (13:25). The mention of the two towns is a grim reminder that what began with Samson had not been completed, either by his own tribe (Dan) or by their powerful neighbor (Judah). Rather than fighting the Lord's battles, these capable warriors used treachery, bullied their fellow Israelites (18:24-25), and attacked a defenseless city (18:27; see Genesis 49:17).

When these warriors arrived in the hill country of Ephraim, they came to Micah's house and spent the night there. ³While at Micah's house, they recognized the young Levite's accent, so they went over and asked him, "Who brought you here, and what are you doing in this place? Why are you here?" ⁴He told them about his agreement with Micah and that he had been hired as Micah's personal priest.

⁵Then they said, "Ask God whether or not our journey will be successful."

⁶"Go in peace," the priest replied. "For the LORD is watching over your journey."

⁷So the five men went on to the town of Laish, where they noticed the people living carefree lives, like the Sidonians; they were peaceful and secure.* The people were also wealthy because their land was very fertile. And they lived a great distance from Sidon and had no allies nearby.

⁸When the men returned to Zorah and Eshtaol, their relatives asked them, "What did you find?"

⁹The men replied, "Come on, let's attack them! We have seen the land, and it is very good. What are you waiting for? Don't hesitate to go and take possession of it. ¹⁰When you get there, you will find the people living carefree lives. God has given us a spacious and fertile land, lacking in nothing!"

¹¹So 600 men from the tribe of Dan, armed with weapons of war, set out from Zorah and Eshtaol. ¹²They camped at a place west of Kiriath-jearim in Judah, which is called Mahaneh-dan* to this day. ¹³Then they went on from there into the hill country of Ephraim and came to the house of Micah.

¹⁴The five men who had scouted out the land around Laish explained to the others, "These buildings contain a sacred ephod, as well as some household idols, a carved image, and a cast idol. What do you think you should do?" ¹⁵Then the five men turned off the road and went over to Micah's house, where the young Levite lived, and greeted him kindly. ¹⁶As the 600 armed warriors from the tribe of Dan stood at the entrance of the gate, ¹⁷the five scouts entered the shrine and removed the carved image, the sacred ephod, the household idols, and the cast idol. Meanwhile, the priest was standing at the gate with the 600 armed warriors.

¹⁸When the priest saw the men carrying all the sacred objects out of Micah's shrine, he said, "What are you doing?"

¹⁹"Be quiet and come with us," they said. "Be a father and priest to all of us. Isn't it better to be a priest for an entire tribe and clan of Israel than for the household of just one man?"

²⁰The young priest was quite happy to go with them, so he took along the sacred ephod, the household idols, and the carved image. ²¹They turned and started on their way again, placing their children, livestock, and possessions in front of them.

²²When the people from the tribe of Dan were quite a distance from Micah's house, the people who lived near Micah came chasing after them. ²³They were shouting as they caught up with them. The men of Dan turned around and said to Micah, "What's the matter? Why have you called these men together and chased after us like this?"

²⁴"What do you mean, 'What's the matter?'" Micah replied. "You've taken away all the gods I have made, and my priest, and I have nothing left!"

²⁵The men of Dan said, "Watch what you say! There are some short-tempered men around here who might get angry and kill you and your family." ²⁶So the men of Dan continued on their way. When Micah saw that there were too many of them for him to attack, he turned around and went home.

²⁷Then, with Micah's idols and his priest, the men of Dan came to the town of Laish, whose people were peaceful and secure. They attacked with swords and burned the town to the ground. ²⁸There was no one to rescue the people, for they lived a great distance from Sidon and had no allies nearby. This happened in the valley near Beth-rehob.

Then the people of the tribe of Dan rebuilt the town and lived there. ²⁹They renamed the town Dan after their ancestor, Israel's son, but it had originally been called Laish.

³⁰Then they set up the carved image, and they appointed Jonathan son of Gershom, son of Moses,* as their priest. This family continued as priests for the tribe of Dan until the Exile. ³¹So Micah's carved image was worshiped by the tribe of Dan as long as the Tabernacle of God remained at Shiloh.

The Levite and His Concubine

19 Now in those days Israel had no king. There was a man from the tribe of Levi living in a remote area of the hill country of Ephraim. One day he brought home a woman from Bethlehem in Judah to be his concubine. ²But she became angry with him* and returned to her father's home in Bethlehem.

After about four months, ³her husband set out for Bethlehem to speak personally to her and persuade her to come back. He took with him a servant and a pair of donkeys. When he arrived at* her father's house, her father saw him and welcomed him. ⁴Her father urged him to stay awhile, so he stayed three days, eating, drinking, and sleeping there.

⁵On the fourth day the man was up early, ready to leave, but the woman's father said to his son-in-law, "Have something to eat before you go." ⁶So the two men sat down together and had something to eat and drink. Then the woman's father said, "Please stay another night and enjoy yourself." ⁷The man got up to leave, but his father-in-law kept urging him to stay, so he finally gave in and stayed the night.

18:7 The meaning of the Hebrew is uncertain. **18:12** *Mahaneh-dan* means "the camp of Dan." **18:30** As in an ancient Hebrew tradition, some Greek manuscripts, and Latin Vulgate; Masoretic Text reads *son of Manasseh.* **19:2** Or *she was unfaithful to him.* **19:3** As in Greek version; Hebrew reads *When she brought him to.*

⁸On the morning of the fifth day he was up early again, ready to leave, and again the woman's father said, "Have something to eat; then you can leave later this afternoon." So they had another day of feasting. ⁹Later, as the man and his concubine and servant were preparing to leave, his father-in-law said, "Look, it's almost evening. Stay the night and enjoy yourself. Tomorrow you can get up early and be on your way."

¹⁰But this time the man was determined to leave. So he took his two saddled donkeys and his concubine and headed in the direction of Jebus (that is, Jerusalem). ¹¹It was late in the day when they neared Jebus, and the man's servant said to him, "Let's stop at this Jebusite town and spend the night there."

¹²"No," his master said, "we can't stay in this foreign town where there are no Israelites. Instead, we will go on to Gibeah. ¹³Come on, let's try to get as far as Gibeah or Ramah, and we'll spend the night in one of those towns." ¹⁴So they went on. The sun was setting as they came to Gibeah, a town in the land of Benjamin, ¹⁵so they stopped there to spend the night. They rested in the town square, but no one took them in for the night.

¹⁶That evening an old man came home from his work in the fields. He was from the hill country of Ephraim, but he was living in Gibeah, where the people were from the tribe of Benjamin. ¹⁷When he saw the travelers sitting in the town square, he asked them where they were from and where they were going.

¹⁸"We have been in Bethlehem in Judah," the man replied. "We are on our way to a remote area in the hill country of Ephraim, which is my home. I traveled to Bethlehem, and now I'm returning home.* But no one has taken us in for the night, ¹⁹even though we have everything we need. We have straw and feed for our donkeys and plenty of bread and wine for ourselves."

²⁰"You are welcome to stay with me," the old man said. "I will give you anything you might need. But whatever you do, don't spend the night in the square." ²¹So he took them home with him and fed the donkeys. After they washed their feet, they ate and drank together.

²²While they were enjoying themselves, a crowd of troublemakers from the town surrounded the house. They began beating at the door and shouting to the old man, "Bring out the man who is staying with you so we can have sex with him."

²³The old man stepped outside to talk to them. "No, my brothers, don't do such an evil thing. For this man is a guest in my house, and such a thing would be shameful. ²⁴Here, take my virgin daughter and this man's concubine. I will bring them out to you, and you can abuse them and do whatever you like. But don't do such a shameful thing to this man."

²⁵But they wouldn't listen to him. So the Levite took hold of his concubine and pushed her out the door. The men of the town abused her all night, taking turns raping her until morning. Finally, at dawn they let her go. ²⁶At daybreak the woman returned to the house where her husband was staying. She collapsed at the door of the house and lay there until it was light.

²⁷When her husband opened the door to leave, there lay his concubine with her hands on the threshold. ²⁸He said, "Get up! Let's go!" But there was no answer.* So he put her body on his donkey and took her home.

²⁹When he got home, he took a knife and cut his concubine's body into twelve pieces. Then he sent one piece to each tribe throughout all the territory of Israel.

19:18 As in Greek version (see also 19:29); Hebrew reads *now I'm going to the Tabernacle of the* LORD. 19:28 Greek version adds *for she was dead.*

19:24 The older man's speech parallels that of Lot in Genesis 19:7-8. In both, the host's obligation to protect his male guests should have covered the women in the house. The hosts tragically perverted Israel's laws that shielded women under the same privileges as men (see Exodus 20:17; Leviticus 25:6; Deuteronomy 5:14, 21; 15:17). Gibeah's morality was no better than Sodom and Gomorrah, proverbial for their wickedness. So, the host thought it would be "shameful" were the Levite to be raped but thought nothing of using the women to shield male honor.
19:25 The negotiations seemed to be going nowhere. The older man sensed that if he didn't act quickly, his guest the Levite was going to end up gang raped. To save himself, the Levite performed the first action that would result in his concubine's rape and death. By seizing her and pushing her out the door, he forced her to take his place as a rape victim. The Levite was as culpable as the men of Gibeah.
19:26-27 Even in her extreme condition, and in a strange city, the concubine was able to make her way back to the house. This suggests that the nightlong gang rape occurred where the Levite—the man responsible for her safety—could see and hear. How poignant that she collapsed at the threshold of the house, her hands outstretched for help but finding none from the men who had sacrificed her for their own protection and honor. The brokenness of our world means that vulnerable people are treated with violence and injustice. This sinful state of the world grieves the Lord, but we can fight for justice, trusting that one day he will bring justice and heal the broken (Revelation 21:4).
19:28-29 The narrator does not say when exactly the concubine died. Was it on the threshold? Was it on the long trip back home? Was it at the hands of the Levite? And why did the Levite, whose hands were adept at dismembering sacrificial animals, employ his skill so perversely? If the concubine was still breathing when he took a knife to her, he murdered her. If she was already dead, he desecrated her body. The Levite's ghastly action was to avenge himself for the dishonorable treatment he had received in Gibeah. He was thinking only about himself, not his concubine. Considering the terrible outcome of his selfishness, we understand why Jesus teaches us to "do to others whatever you would like them to do to you" (Matthew 7:12).

Perspective

How should we respond to violence against women?

SCRIPTURE CONNECTION: JUDGES 19:1–21:25

The horrifying events of Judges 19 disturb and surprise us, and we might want to rush past them in our Bible reading and study. This story may remind us of how some Christians stay silent about abuse, sexual assault, and violence. Nearly half of all women will experience sexual violence in their lifetimes, and we cannot stay silent. The Bible is also fraught with this content, just as are our world and at times the church, and we must bear witness to this violence and confront it.

Just because these events are recorded in Scripture does not mean God approves of them. These chapters expose the human tendency to take what isn't ours and deem other people as disposable.

The woman in this story was betrayed by her fellow Israelites at every turn. This story's chronological position toward the end of Judges shows how far the people had strayed from the Lord to do "whatever seemed right in their own eyes" (21:25). But this woman was an image-bearer of God, and so are all people no matter what kind of abuse they have endured.

These are all issues of *inhospitality*, of not welcoming others and treating them with dignity. Those who bore witness asked what we also must: "What are we going to do? Who's going to speak up?" (19:30).

VIEWPOINTS

HERS: *What might these women have felt about themselves, their supposed protectors, and God?*
MINE: *"At times, I have stayed silent, and this passage condemns that. But there is hope: Jesus embodies hospitality. Jesus takes on human form, welcomes, identifies with, and dies for the 'other,' for us. Jesus empowers us to respond."*
YOURS: *What keeps you from receiving Christ's hospitality? How can you offer his hospitality to protect the vulnerable?*

ALEXIANA FRY, MDiv, PhD, is a devoted academic in the Hebrew Bible. She is a professor, wife, and pug mom who is working on her first book post-dissertation.

---

30 Everyone who saw it said, "Such a horrible crime has not been committed in all the time since Israel left Egypt. Think about it! What are we going to do? Who's going to speak up?"

Israel's War with Benjamin

20 Then all the Israelites were united as one man, from Dan in the north to Beersheba in the south, including those from across the Jordan in the land of Gilead. The entire community assembled in the presence of the Lord at Mizpah. ²The leaders of all the people and all the tribes of Israel—400,000 warriors armed with swords—took their positions in the assembly of the people of God. ³(Word soon reached the land of Benjamin that the other tribes had gone up to Mizpah.) The Israelites then asked how this terrible crime had happened.

⁴The Levite, the husband of the woman who had been murdered, said, "My concubine and I came to spend the night in Gibeah, a town that belongs to the people of Benjamin. ⁵That night some of the leading citizens of Gibeah surrounded the house, planning to kill me, and they raped my concubine until she was dead. ⁶So I cut her body into twelve pieces and sent the pieces throughout the territory assigned to Israel, for these men have committed a terrible and shameful crime. ⁷Now then, all of you—the entire community of Israel—must decide here and now what should be done about this!"

⁸And all the people rose to their feet in unison and declared, "None of us will return home! No, not even one of us! ⁹Instead, this is what we will do to Gibeah; we will draw lots to decide who will attack it. ¹⁰One-tenth of the men* from each tribe will be chosen to supply the warriors with food, and the rest of us will take revenge on Gibeah* of Benjamin for this shameful thing they have done in Israel." ¹¹So all the Israelites were completely united, and they gathered together to attack the town.

¹²The Israelites sent messengers to the tribe of Benjamin, saying, "What a terrible thing has been done among you! ¹³Give up those evil men, those troublemakers from Gibeah, so we can execute them and purge Israel of this evil."

But the people of Benjamin would not listen. ¹⁴Instead, they came from their towns and gathered at Gibeah to fight the Israelites. ¹⁵In all, 26,000 of their

---

20:10a Hebrew *10 men from every hundred, 100 men from every thousand, and 1,000 men from every 10,000.*
20:10b Hebrew *Geba,* in this case a variant spelling of Gibeah; also in 20:33.

20:12-13 Israel recognized corporate responsibility. The leading citizens of Gibeah were guilty (20:5), and all of Gibeah had become an accessory to their crimes by failing to discipline them. The tribe of Benjamin, in turn, had a responsibility to bring Gibeah to justice; failing that, they all shared the guilt. Had Israel not done something about Benjamin's sin, the guilt would have extended to the entire nation.

warriors armed with swords arrived in Gibeah to join the 700 elite troops who lived there. [16]Among Benjamin's elite troops, 700 were left-handed, and each of them could sling a rock and hit a target within a hairsbreadth without missing. [17]Israel had 400,000 experienced soldiers armed with swords, not counting Benjamin's warriors.

[18]Before the battle the Israelites went to Bethel and asked God, "Which tribe should go first to attack the people of Benjamin?"

The LORD answered, "Judah is to go first."

[19]So the Israelites left early the next morning and camped near Gibeah. [20]Then they advanced toward Gibeah to attack the men of Benjamin. [21]But Benjamin's warriors, who were defending the town, came out and killed 22,000 Israelites on the battlefield that day.

[22]But the Israelites encouraged each other and took their positions again at the same place they had fought the previous day. [23]For they had gone up to Bethel and wept in the presence of the LORD until evening. They had asked the LORD, "Should we fight against our relatives from Benjamin again?"

And the LORD had said, "Go out and fight against them."

[24]So the next day they went out again to fight against the men of Benjamin, [25]but the men of Benjamin killed another 18,000 Israelites, all of whom were experienced with the sword.

[26]Then all the Israelites went up to Bethel and wept in the presence of the LORD and fasted until evening. They also brought burnt offerings and peace offerings to the LORD. [27]The Israelites went up seeking direction from the LORD. (In those days the Ark of the Covenant of God was in Bethel, [28]and Phinehas son of Eleazar and grandson of Aaron was the priest.) The Israelites asked the LORD, "Should we fight against our relatives from Benjamin again, or should we stop?"

The LORD said, "Go! Tomorrow I will hand them over to you."

[29]So the Israelites set an ambush all around Gibeah. [30]They went out on the third day and took their positions at the same place as before. [31]When the men of Benjamin came out to attack, they were drawn away from the town. And as they had done before, they began to kill the Israelites. About thirty Israelites died in the open fields and along the roads, one leading to Bethel and the other leading back to Gibeah.

[32]Then the warriors of Benjamin shouted, "We're defeating them as we did before!" But the Israelites had planned in advance to run away so that the men of Benjamin would chase them along the roads and be drawn away from the town.

[33]When the main group of Israelite warriors reached Baal-tamar, they turned and took up their positions. Meanwhile, the Israelites hiding in ambush to the west* of Gibeah jumped up to fight. [34]There were 10,000 elite Israelite troops who advanced against Gibeah. The fighting was so heavy that Benjamin didn't realize the impending disaster. [35]So the LORD helped Israel defeat Benjamin, and that day the Israelites killed 25,100 of Benjamin's warriors, all of whom were experienced swordsmen. [36]Then the men of Benjamin saw that they were beaten.

The Israelites had retreated from Benjamin's warriors in order to give those hiding in ambush more room to maneuver against Gibeah. [37]Then those who were hiding rushed in from all sides and killed everyone in the town. [38]They had arranged to send up a large cloud of smoke from the town as a signal. [39]When the Israelites saw the smoke, they turned and attacked Benjamin's warriors.

By that time Benjamin's warriors had killed about thirty Israelites, and they shouted, "We're defeating them as we did in the first battle!" [40]But when the warriors of Benjamin looked behind them and saw the smoke rising into the sky from every part of the town, [41]the men of Israel turned and attacked. At this point the men of Benjamin became terrified, because they realized disaster was close at hand. [42]So they turned around and fled before the Israelites toward the wilderness. But they couldn't escape the battle, and the people who came out of the nearby towns were also killed.* [43]The Israelites surrounded the men of Benjamin and chased them relentlessly, finally overtaking them east of Gibeah.* [44]That day 18,000 of Benjamin's strongest warriors died in battle. [45]The survivors fled into the wilderness toward the rock of Rimmon, but Israel killed 5,000 of them along the road. They continued the chase until they had killed another 2,000 near Gidom.

[46]So that day the tribe of Benjamin lost 25,000 strong warriors armed with swords, [47]leaving only 600 men who escaped to the rock of Rimmon, where they lived for four months. [48]And the Israelites returned and slaughtered every living thing in all the towns—the people, the livestock, and everything they found. They also burned down all the towns they came to.

20:33 As in Greek and Syriac versions and Latin Vulgate; Hebrew reads *hiding in the open space.* 20:42 Or *battle, for the people from the nearby towns also came out and killed them.* 20:43 The meaning of the Hebrew is uncertain.

20:19-21 The three battles took place around the guilty city. Despite superior numbers and asking the Lord for guidance, the Israelite troops faced a sound defeat the first day.
20:36-45 This section gives a second account of the battle.

Israel Provides Wives for Benjamin

21 The Israelites had vowed at Mizpah, "We will never give our daughters in marriage to a man from the tribe of Benjamin." ²Now the people went to Bethel and sat in the presence of God until evening, weeping loudly and bitterly. ³"O LORD, God of Israel," they cried out, "why has this happened in Israel? Now one of our tribes is missing from Israel!"

⁴Early the next morning the people built an altar and presented their burnt offerings and peace offerings on it. ⁵Then they said, "Who among the tribes of Israel did not join us at Mizpah when we held our assembly in the presence of the LORD?" At that time they had taken a solemn oath in the LORD's presence, vowing that anyone who refused to come would be put to death.

⁶The Israelites felt sorry for their brother Benjamin and said, "Today one of the tribes of Israel has been cut off. ⁷How can we find wives for the few who remain, since we have sworn by the LORD not to give them our daughters in marriage?"

⁸So they asked, "Who among the tribes of Israel did not join us at Mizpah when we assembled in the presence of the LORD?" And they discovered that no one from Jabesh-gilead had attended the assembly. ⁹For after they counted all the people, no one from Jabesh-gilead was present.

¹⁰So the assembly sent 12,000 of their best warriors to Jabesh-gilead with orders to kill everyone there, including women and children. ¹¹"This is what you are to do," they said. "Completely destroy* all the males and every woman who is not a virgin." ¹²Among the residents of Jabesh-gilead they found 400 young virgins who had never slept with a man, and they brought them to the camp at Shiloh in the land of Canaan.

¹³The Israelite assembly sent a peace delegation to the remaining people of Benjamin who were living at the rock of Rimmon. ¹⁴Then the men of Benjamin returned to their homes, and the 400 women of Jabesh-gilead who had been spared were given to them as wives. But there were not enough women for all of them.

¹⁵The people felt sorry for Benjamin because the LORD had made this gap among the tribes of Israel. ¹⁶So the elders of the assembly asked, "How can we find wives for the few who remain, since the women of the tribe of Benjamin are dead? ¹⁷There must be heirs for the survivors so that an entire tribe of Israel is not wiped out. ¹⁸But we cannot give them our own daughters in marriage because we have sworn with a solemn oath that anyone who does this will fall under God's curse."

¹⁹Then they thought of the annual festival of the LORD held in Shiloh, south of Lebonah and north of Bethel, along the east side of the road that goes from Bethel to Shechem. ²⁰They told the men of Benjamin who still needed wives, "Go and hide in the vineyards. ²¹When you see the young women of Shiloh come out for their dances, rush out from the vineyards, and each of you can take one of them home to the land of Benjamin to be your wife! ²²And when their fathers and brothers come to us in protest, we will tell them, 'Please be sympathetic. Let them have your daughters, for we didn't find wives for all of them when we destroyed Jabesh-gilead. And you are not guilty of breaking the vow since you did not actually give your daughters to them in marriage.'"

²³So the men of Benjamin did as they were told. Each man caught one of the women as she danced in the celebration and carried her off to be his wife. They returned to their own land, and they rebuilt their towns and lived in them.

²⁴Then the people of Israel departed by tribes and families, and they returned to their own homes.

²⁵In those days Israel had no king; all the people did whatever seemed right in their own eyes.

21:11 The Hebrew term used here refers to the complete consecration of things or people to the LORD, either by destroying them or by giving them as an offering.

21:12-14 Deuteronomy 21:10-14 explains the process Israelite soldiers were to follow when they captured women while at war. Israelite soldiers were forbidden by the law from practicing the same war customs as other ancient Near Eastern peoples, who raped conquered women on the battlefield and sold them into slavery. But these four hundred young Israelite women were treated with far less dignity and compassion than was prescribed for Israelites taking foreign women in battle. The attack on their clan was purely to capture them and then forcibly marry them off. In a book where the narrator tracks Israelite society's health by how Israel treats women, this incident signals that Israel had hit rock bottom.

21:23-25 The rape of the concubine spiraled out into civil war, multiplying atrocities against women. Four hundred women were taken captive in war, and another two hundred were kidnapped in broad daylight while celebrating an annual festival in the town of Shiloh, where the Tabernacle was. All six hundred were forced into marriage. These acts substantiate the closing refrain of Judges: "All the people did whatever seemed right in their own eyes" (21:25). This contrasts starkly with the exhortation to do what is "good and pleasing to the LORD your God" (Deuteronomy 12:28).

Ruth

WHAT DO WE LEARN ABOUT GOD'S MISSION AND OURS?
Our faithful God honors our faithfulness.

WHO WROTE IT? We don't know, but it was potentially written by someone who lived after David became king, since he's named in the closing.

WHEN DID IT HAPPEN? Sometime between 1300 and 1100 BC, when judges, not kings, led the nation.

HOW IS IT ORGANIZED?

1: Naomi's and Ruth's husbands die; they return to Israel

2: Ruth and Boaz meet

3: Naomi helps Ruth

4: Boaz marries Ruth

FEATURE HIGHLIGHTS

+ *Grief: Finding Blessing in Community (324)*
+ *Presence As Love (326)*
+ *How Does God Show He Values Immigrants? (327)*
+ *Ruth: Nothing to Everything (329)*

Words to Remember are highlighted throughout this book

HOW LONG DOES IT TAKE TO READ?

:15 | :30 | 1:00 | 1:30 | 2:00 | 2:30 | 3:00 | 3:30

Timeline

BC

- **1446** — EXODUS FROM EGYPT
- **1406** — ISRAELITES ENTER CANAAN
- **1375** — JUDGES (INCLUDING DEBORAH, GIDEON, AND SAMSON) BEGIN TO RULE ISRAEL
- **c. 1100** — RUTH'S AND NAOMI'S HUSBANDS DIE; BOAZ "REDEEMS" THEIR FAMILY; RUTH JOINS THE MESSIAH'S LINEAGE BY GIVING BIRTH TO OBED
- **1010** — DAVID BECOMES KING

Elimelech Moves His Family to Moab

1 In the days when the judges ruled in Israel, a severe famine came upon the land. So a man from Bethlehem in Judah left his home and went to live in the country of Moab, taking his wife and two sons with him. ²The man's name was Elimelech, and his wife was Naomi. Their two sons were Mahlon and Kilion. They were Ephrathites from Bethlehem in the land of Judah. And when they reached Moab, they settled there.

³Then Elimelech died, and Naomi was left with her two sons. ⁴The two sons married Moabite women. One married a woman named Orpah, and the other a woman named Ruth. But about ten years later, ⁵both Mahlon and Kilion died. This left Naomi alone, without her two sons or her husband.

Naomi and Ruth Return

⁶Then Naomi heard in Moab that the Lord had blessed his people in Judah by giving them good crops again. So Naomi and her daughters-in-law got ready to leave Moab to return to her homeland. ⁷With her two daughters-in-law she set out from the place where she had been living, and they took the road that would lead them back to Judah.

⁸But on the way, Naomi said to her two daughters-in-law, "Go back to your mothers' homes. And may the Lord reward you for your kindness to your husbands and to me. ⁹May the Lord bless you with the security of another marriage." Then she kissed them good-bye, and they all broke down and wept.

¹⁰"No," they said. "We want to go with you to your people."

1:1-6 The book of Ruth uses irony throughout, as well as themes of reversal. The two sons were named Mahlon, which means "sickly," and Kilion, which means "failing." Their names preview what would happen to them. The town of Bethlehem translates from the Hebrew as "house of bread." Yet the family had to leave it due to famine—or lack of bread. Even Moab, where they fled to find plenty, became the place of death and barrenness. Nothing seemed to work out, yet it was in this place of helplessness that the story begins. If you are feeling helpless right now, it is not the end of your story.

Come Close — GRIEF: FINDING BLESSING IN COMMUNITY

SCRIPTURE CONNECTION: RUTH 1:1-22

Losing loved ones can make deciding what to do next hard. Sometimes we worry we will make the wrong choice.

Here we meet three women who were grieving. Each chose differently, yet each found comfort for her grief in community.

At first, Naomi urged her daughters-in-law to leave her alone and go back to their people. Orpah sensibly decided to return home to Moab, just as Naomi urged. Ruth refused, opting to stay by Naomi's side and move to a new town, Naomi's hometown of Bethlehem.

In one of the most passionate speeches in the Bible, Ruth pledged to stay by Naomi's side (1:16-17). Ruth revealed God's love to Naomi in a very tangible way. Because of Ruth's choice, both women stayed together and drew near to Naomi's God and family.

Ruth and Naomi moved to Bethlehem and began a new life together. Although Naomi was bitter at first (1:20), Ruth's decision led to blessings by the story's end. Neither woman had expected to find blessings, but God honored their faithfulness to one another by bringing them even greater community and a new family (4:14-15).

Living life together while grieving is not easy. Nevertheless, choosing community creates amazing opportunities.

REFLECT "So the two of them continued on their journey." RUTH 1:19

Lord, help us journey together in both bitterness and blessing. Amen.

CONSIDER "You will never be in control of your life circumstances, but you can relax and trust in [God's] control.... [God is] always doing something new.... Be on the lookout for all that [God has] prepared for you!" SARAH YOUNG, *Jesus Calling*

> Grief can whisper "go it alone," but we find blessing together.

JENNIFER M. MATHENY, PhD, is associate professor of Old Testament at Nazarene Theological Seminary, Missouri, and director of the Wynkoop Center for Women in Leadership. She enjoys speaking engagements and research.

¹¹But Naomi replied, "Why should you go on with me? Can I still give birth to other sons who could grow up to be your husbands? ¹²No, my daughters, return to your parents' homes, for I am too old to marry again. And even if it were possible, and I were to get married tonight and bear sons, then what? ¹³Would you wait for them to grow up and refuse to marry someone else? No, of course not, my daughters! Things are far more bitter for me than for you, because the LORD himself has raised his fist against me."

¹⁴And again they wept together, and Orpah kissed her mother-in-law good-bye. But Ruth clung tightly to Naomi. ¹⁵"Look," Naomi said to her, "your sister-in-law has gone back to her people and to her gods. You should do the same."

¹⁶But Ruth replied, "Don't ask me to leave you and turn back. Wherever you go, I will go; wherever you live, I will live. Your people will be my people, and your God will be my God. ¹⁷Wherever you die, I will die, and there I will be buried. May the LORD punish me severely if I allow anything but death to separate us!" ¹⁸When Naomi saw that Ruth was determined to go with her, she said nothing more.

¹⁹So the two of them continued on their journey. When they came to Bethlehem, the entire town was excited by their arrival. "Is it really Naomi?" the women asked.

²⁰"Don't call me Naomi," she responded. "Instead, call me Mara,* for the Almighty has made life very bitter for me. ²¹I went away full, but the LORD has brought me home empty. Why call me Naomi when the LORD has caused me to suffer* and the Almighty has sent such tragedy upon me?"

²²So Naomi returned from Moab, accompanied by her daughter-in-law Ruth, the young Moabite woman. They arrived in Bethlehem in late spring, at the beginning of the barley harvest.

Ruth Works in Boaz's Field

2 Now there was a wealthy and influential man in Bethlehem named Boaz, who was a relative of Naomi's husband, Elimelech.

²One day Ruth the Moabite said to Naomi, "Let me go out into the harvest fields to pick up the stalks of grain left behind by anyone who is kind enough to let me do it."

Naomi replied, "All right, my daughter, go ahead." ³So Ruth went out to gather grain behind the harvesters. And as it happened, she found herself working in a field that belonged to Boaz, the relative of her father-in-law, Elimelech.

⁴While she was there, Boaz arrived from Bethlehem and greeted the harvesters. "The LORD be with you!" he said.

"The LORD bless you!" the harvesters replied.

⁵Then Boaz asked his foreman, "Who is that young woman over there? Who does she belong to?"

⁶And the foreman replied, "She is the young woman from Moab who came back with Naomi. ⁷She asked me this morning if she could gather grain behind the harvesters. She has been hard at work ever since, except for a few minutes' rest in the shelter."

⁸Boaz went over and said to Ruth, "Listen, my daughter. Stay right here with us when you gather grain; don't go to any other fields. Stay right behind the young women working in my field. ⁹See which part of the field they are harvesting, and then follow them. I have warned the young men not to treat you roughly. And when you are thirsty, help yourself to the water they have drawn from the well."

¹⁰Ruth fell at his feet and thanked him warmly. "What have I done to deserve such kindness?" she asked. "I am only a foreigner."

¹¹"Yes, I know," Boaz replied. "But I also know about everything you have done for your mother-in-law since the death of your husband. I have heard how you left your father and mother and your own land to live here among complete strangers. ¹²May the LORD, the God of Israel, under whose wings you have come to take refuge, reward you fully for what you have done."

¹³"I hope I continue to please you, sir," she replied. "You have comforted me by speaking so kindly to me, even though I am not one of your workers."

¹⁴At mealtime Boaz called to her, "Come over here, and help yourself to some food. You can dip your bread in the sour wine." So she sat with his harvesters, and Boaz gave her some roasted grain to eat. She ate all she wanted and still had some left over.

¹⁵When Ruth went back to work again, Boaz ordered his young men, "Let her gather grain right among the sheaves without stopping her. ¹⁶And pull out some heads of barley from the bundles and drop them on purpose for her. Let her pick them up, and don't give her a hard time!"

1:20 *Naomi* means "pleasant"; *Mara* means "bitter". 1:21 Or *has testified against me.*

1:20 Naomi invokes the Lord's name by calling him the "Almighty," which translates the Hebrew word *Shaddai* and often describes God's power. But in this story, Naomi called upon the God of sufficiency, fruitfulness, enough-ness, as she considered her lack. In a maternal way, *Shaddai* may also mean "many breasted one," and so Naomi's words are a picture of crying out to her parent in hunger and thirst like a child at her mother's breast. Naomi's hope in God, her faith and belief in who God claims to be, made her situation even more heartbreaking. How does this change how you see others grieve and mourn?

2:14 When the author introduces food in the story, we see a reversal. This verse ends as Ruth eats "all she wanted and still had some left over." Compare this to how the book began. God as provider seems absent in the first chapter. Yet God heard Naomi's cries, using ordinary places and people to answer in abundance. Have you seen God use everyday, ordinary things to answer your prayers?

MY STORY WITH FAMILY & FRIENDS

Presence As Love

SCRIPTURE CONNECTION: RUTH 1:16-17; 3:1–4:12

Naomi and Ruth. A mother-in-law and daughter-in-law, widows both, bound by grief, desperation, and love. Together, they faced hard choices: stay in Moab and starve or become refugees and return to Judah in search of food. They chose Judah.

But even in difficulty, they held a great treasure: each other. Their presence in each other's lives was love.

Ruth's plea to Naomi is one of the greatest expressions of love ever spoken:

> Don't ask me to leave you and turn back. Wherever you go, I will go; wherever you live, I will live. Your people will be my people, and your God will be my God. Wherever you die, I will die, and there I will be buried. May the LORD punish me severely if I allow anything but death to separate us! (1:16-17)

And on that desperate night, when Ruth dressed to impress and followed Naomi's advice to wear perfume before she lay down at Boaz's feet to perform that risky act of submission and humble pleading, she did it as much for Naomi as for herself. Boaz was their best hope because he was one of their family redeemers (a near relative who could help when a family member experienced economic hardship) and he had already extended kindness and generosity to them (3:12-13; see also 2:8-12). And on that same desperate night, by saying yes, he became known for all time as much more than a farmer. He became a type, a preview of Jesus, rescuer of humanity, of us.

We women bear a natural empathy for one another. No wonder Ruth's words, words of love between two women in desperate need, illuminate God's love.

> **Our presence in each other's lives is love.**

IMAGINE

What woman gives you the gift of presence?

To whom could you offer "presence as love"?

> "This Scripture brings my mother-in-law, Kathryn Bell, to mind. After my mother's death, Kathryn became my close ally—encouraging…affirming…and sometimes even taking my side. Until her death, Kathryn was my loyal friend and the woman who first 'blessed' me with her presence and love."

VALERIE BELL is an author of several books on children, including *RESILIENT: Child Discipleship and the Fearless Future of the Church*. Valerie serves as Awana's CEO emerita and 2050 vision caster.

¹⁷So Ruth gathered barley there all day, and when she beat out the grain that evening, it filled an entire basket.* ¹⁸She carried it back into town and showed it to her mother-in-law. Ruth also gave her the roasted grain that was left over from her meal.

¹⁹"Where did you gather all this grain today?" Naomi asked. "Where did you work? May the LORD bless the one who helped you!"

So Ruth told her mother-in-law about the man in whose field she had worked. She said, "The man I worked with today is named Boaz."

²⁰"May the LORD bless him!" Naomi told her daughter-in-law. "He is showing his kindness to us as well as to your dead husband.* That man is one of our closest relatives, one of our family redeemers."

²¹Then Ruth* said, "What's more, Boaz even told me to come back and stay with his harvesters until the entire harvest is completed."

²²"Good!" Naomi exclaimed. "Do as he said, my daughter. Stay with his young women right through the whole harvest. You might be harassed in other fields, but you'll be safe with him."

²³So Ruth worked alongside the women in Boaz's fields and gathered grain with them until the end of the barley harvest. Then she continued working with them through the wheat harvest in early summer. And all the while she lived with her mother-in-law.

Ruth at the Threshing Floor

3 One day Naomi said to Ruth, "My daughter, it's time that I found a permanent home for you, so that you will be provided for. ²Boaz is a close relative of ours, and he's been very kind by letting you gather grain with his young women. Tonight he will be winnowing barley at the threshing floor. ³Now do as I tell you—take a bath and put on perfume and dress in your nicest clothes. Then go to the threshing floor, but don't let Boaz see you until he has finished eating and drinking. ⁴Be sure to notice where he lies down; then go and uncover his feet and lie down there. He will tell you what to do."

⁵"I will do everything you say," Ruth replied. ⁶So she went down to the threshing floor that night and followed the instructions of her mother-in-law.

⁷After Boaz had finished eating and drinking and was in good spirits, he lay down at the far end of the pile of grain and went to sleep. Then Ruth came

2:17 Hebrew *it was about an ephah* [20 quarts or 22 liters]. 2:20 Hebrew *to the living and to the dead.* 2:21 Hebrew *Ruth the Moabite.*

3:5 While selflessly moving forward to provide for Naomi, Ruth did not mindlessly submit but radically acted on behalf of both women's futures. Ruth's words are echoed in Luke 1:38, this time said by Mary, the mother of Jesus. As noted in Luke 3:32 and Matthew 1:5, Ruth belongs to Christ's lineage. We may never fully grasp what our bold faith, what saying yes, may bring.

Perspective

How does God show he values immigrants?

SCRIPTURE CONNECTION: RUTH 2:5-12; 3:7-13; 4:1-22

If there ever was an outsider, it was Ruth. Moving to Bethlehem was hard. Small town and new people!

Ruth was also an immigrant from a place that the Israelites distrusted. The Israelites hated Moab's people because of their past as enemies (Numbers 21–25). But God showed grace and care for Ruth and showed how he values people: No matter where we're from, God includes us in his work in the world.

Once settled, Ruth gleaned in the fields for work. According to the law of Moses, people who were poor or immigrants could pick up leftovers from the edges of harvested fields (Leviticus 19:9-10). They worked hard, providing for themselves.

One day, the field's owner came over to her to talk. Ruth considered herself a foreigner, an outsider; she expected to go unnoticed (Ruth 2:10). But Boaz used his power to encourage her (2:11-12).

Boaz did *not* call Ruth a "foreigner," though she was from Moab. Boaz heard about all she had done and sacrificed for Naomi, and instead called her a "virtuous woman" (3:11).

Boaz married Ruth (4:13). Now Ruth was no longer an outsider, and she became part of the line that led to King David and ultimately to Jesus. In Jesus' family, Ruth moved from outsider to insider. So do we.

VIEWPOINTS

HERS: *Ruth saw herself as different. The women of Bethlehem did too (4:15). How do you think Ruth might have described herself later in her story?*
MINE: *"Like Ruth, I have often felt like an outsider. Fortunately, people in my life remind me that I can trust what God sees in me, even if I do not yet see it in myself. I feel grateful for these voices in my story."*
YOURS: *How do you view yourself? How do you think God sees you?*

JENNIFER M. MATHENY, PhD, is associate professor of Old Testament at Nazarene Theological Seminary, Missouri, and director of the Wynkoop Center for Women in Leadership. She enjoys speaking engagements and research.

> "Faith is what makes life bearable, with all its tragedies and ambiguities and sudden, startling joys."
>
> MADELEINE L'ENGLE
> (1918–2007) novelist and poet

quietly, uncovered his feet, and lay down. ⁸Around midnight Boaz suddenly woke up and turned over. He was surprised to find a woman lying at his feet! ⁹"Who are you?" he asked.

"I am your servant Ruth," she replied. "Spread the corner of your covering over me, for you are my family redeemer."

¹⁰"The LORD bless you, my daughter!" Boaz exclaimed. "You are showing even more family loyalty now than you did before, for you have not gone after a younger man, whether rich or poor. ¹¹Now don't worry about a thing, my daughter. I will do what is necessary, for everyone in town knows you are a virtuous woman. ¹²But while it's true that I am one of your family redeemers, there is another man who is more closely related to you than I am. ¹³Stay here tonight, and in the morning I will talk to him. If he is willing to redeem you, very well. Let him marry you. But if he is not willing, then as surely as the LORD lives, I will redeem you myself! Now lie down here until morning."

¹⁴So Ruth lay at Boaz's feet until the morning, but she got up before it was light enough for people to recognize each other. For Boaz had said, "No one must know that a woman was here at the threshing floor." ¹⁵Then Boaz said to her, "Bring your cloak and spread it out." He measured six scoops* of barley into the cloak and placed it on her back. Then he* returned to the town.

¹⁶When Ruth went back to her mother-in-law, Naomi asked, "What happened, my daughter?"

Ruth told Naomi everything Boaz had done for her, ¹⁷and she added, "He gave me these six scoops of barley and said, 'Don't go back to your mother-in-law empty-handed.'"

¹⁸Then Naomi said to her, "Just be patient, my daughter, until we hear what happens. The man won't rest until he has settled things today."

Boaz Marries Ruth

4 Boaz went to the town gate and took a seat there. Just then the family redeemer he had mentioned came by, so Boaz called out to him, "Come over here and sit down, friend. I want to talk to you." So they sat down together. ²Then Boaz called ten leaders from the town and asked them to sit as witnesses. ³And Boaz said to the family redeemer, "You know Naomi, who came back from Moab. She is selling the land that belonged to our relative Elimelech. ⁴I thought I should speak to you about it so that you can redeem it if you wish. If you want the land, then buy it here in the presence of these witnesses. But if you don't want it, let me know right away, because I am next in line to redeem it after you."

The man replied, "All right, I'll redeem it."

⁵Then Boaz told him, "Of course, your purchase of the land from Naomi also requires that you marry Ruth, the Moabite widow. That way she can have children who will carry on her husband's name and keep the land in the family."

⁶"Then I can't redeem it," the family redeemer replied, "because this might endanger my own estate. You redeem the land; I cannot do it."

⁷Now in those days it was the custom in Israel for anyone transferring a right of purchase to remove his sandal and hand it to the other party. This publicly validated the transaction. ⁸So the other family redeemer drew off his sandal as he said to Boaz, "You buy the land."

3:15a Hebrew *six measures,* an unknown quantity. 3:15b Most Hebrew manuscripts read *he;* many Hebrew manuscripts, Syriac version, and Latin Vulgate read *she.*

3:17 Look back at 1:21. Now read 3:17 one more time. Although we already see how Boaz is an answer to prayer, Ruth brought forth what Naomi had prayed for, ensuring Naomi's hands were not empty anymore. God heard Naomi's words, her lament, her complaint. God still hears. While Naomi may have felt that God had utterly failed her, God provided for Naomi as he did for Job, reversing the situation and resurrecting in abundance.

4:6 At the very beginning of the book of Ruth, we also met a sensible, practical-minded character in Orpah. Both Orpah and the "other" family redeemer (4:1) were not wrong in their actions. But both Orpah and the other redeemer missed out. Some would call them wise, but the true wisdom embodied in the story would probably be called foolish to most. This story isn't just romantic or a simplified formula to follow for your best life now. This story swells with characters making sacrifices for one another. They display *khesed,* a Hebrew word that lacks a great one-word English translation, a word we call "love" but is better rendered "loving faithfulness," "steadfast love," or "unfailing love."

Ruth
IDENTITY | Nothing to Everything

Ruth remembers...

I didn't know whose field it was, only that I could gather food there. I had nothing to give but was given much.

I learned the owner's name, Boaz, and he asked me to stay in his fields and promised I would be safe. He treated me beyond what I expected or deserved. I was overwhelmed by his goodness to me. I fell at his feet.

His kindness continued as he said a blessing over me. He called me to share his meal: I, a foreigner, received good words and abundant gifts.

I felt seen and safe and provided for.

Naomi was excited when I brought her a bounty and told her about Boaz. I learned about the Hebrew family redeemer, a man who can honor a dead relative's name and family, like Naomi's husband and sons. Like me. She urged me to keep going back to Boaz's fields through the harvest.

Boaz, my family redeemer. So kind and generous. I hope that I will see him tomorrow.

> When I seem to have nothing, I will look to God, who has everything.

RUTH'S STORY IS TOLD IN THE BOOK OF RUTH; SHE IS ALSO MENTIONED IN MATTHEW 1:5.

IDENTIFY

Can you recall a time when God provided for you and you didn't feel deserving?

How did God's provision change you?

"I had little money to my name as a college student, and I hated to ask my parents, who already did so much for me. I remember being hungrier than ever before in my life. I ate a can of soup for lunch, but it didn't fill me. Then a friend invited me to dinner. Even though she didn't know my situation, it was a lifeline, like Boaz offered to Ruth. I learned that God sends others to provide as a way of loving us and advancing his good plans."

CARA DAY is a writer and illustrator. She has served with Stonecroft Ministries helping women live "extraordinary."

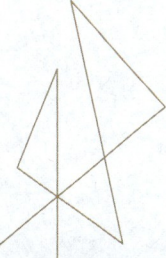

⁹Then Boaz said to the elders and to the crowd standing around, "You are witnesses that today I have bought from Naomi all the property of Elimelech, Kilion, and Mahlon. ¹⁰And with the land I have acquired Ruth, the Moabite widow of Mahlon, to be my wife. This way she can have a son to carry on the family name of her dead husband and to inherit the family property here in his hometown. You are all witnesses today."

¹¹Then the elders and all the people standing in the gate replied, "We are witnesses! May the LORD make this woman who is coming into your home like Rachel and Leah, from whom all the nation of Israel descended! May you prosper in Ephrathah and be famous in Bethlehem. ¹²And may the LORD give you descendants by this young woman who will be like those of our ancestor Perez, the son of Tamar and Judah."

The Descendants of Boaz

¹³So Boaz took Ruth into his home, and she became his wife. When he slept with her, the LORD enabled her to become pregnant, and she gave birth to a son. ¹⁴Then the women of the town said to Naomi, "Praise the LORD, who has now provided a redeemer for your family! May this child be famous in Israel. ¹⁵May he restore your youth and care for you in your old age. For he is the son of your daughter-in-law who loves you and has been better to you than seven sons!"

¹⁶Naomi took the baby and cuddled him to her breast. And she cared for him as if he were her own. ¹⁷The neighbor women said, "Now at last Naomi has a son again!" And they named him Obed. He became the father of Jesse and the grandfather of David.

¹⁸This is the genealogical record of their ancestor Perez:

Perez was the father of Hezron.
¹⁹ Hezron was the father of Ram.
Ram was the father of Amminadab.
²⁰ Amminadab was the father of Nahshon.
Nahshon was the father of Salmon.*
²¹ Salmon was the father of Boaz.
Boaz was the father of Obed.
²² Obed was the father of Jesse.
Jesse was the father of David.

4:20 As in some Greek manuscripts (see also 4:21); Hebrew reads *Salma*.

4:18-22 The book of Ruth ends with a genealogy of ten generations—from Perez, the son of Judah (Jacob's son), to David, grandson of Obed. Besides being one of the world's greatest stories, this tale concerns the family history of David, Israel's greatest king. This also means that Ruth and Boaz were the ancestors of an even greater king than David, who would come much later: Jesus, the Messiah.

"Your God will be my God."

RUTH 1:16

1 Samuel

WHAT DO WE LEARN ABOUT GOD'S MISSION AND OURS?
God wants us to love him wholeheartedly.

WHO WROTE IT? According to Jewish and Christian tradition, it is attributed to Samuel. Since his death is recorded in 25:1, it was probably written or finished by someone who had access to official historical records.

WHEN DID IT HAPPEN? Between 1100 and 1000 BC, beginning late in the period of the judges and continuing through the beginning of Israel's monarchy to the end of Saul's reign.

HOW IS IT ORGANIZED?

- **1–3:** The Lord gives Hannah a son; Samuel's ministry begins
- **4–7:** The Philistines capture and return the Ark of the Covenant; the Israelites subdue the Philistines during Samuel's lifetime
- **8–15:** The beginning of Saul's reign as Israel's first king and his failures
- **16:** Samuel anoints David king
- **17–20:** David's popularity grows, and so does Saul's jealousy
- **21–30:** David runs from Saul; Abigail shows great wisdom
- **31:** Saul's last battle

Words to Remember are highlighted throughout this book

HOW LONG DOES IT TAKE TO READ?
:30 | 1:00 | 1:30 | 2:00 | 2:30 | 3:00 | 3:30

Timeline

BC	
1105	HANNAH GIVES BIRTH TO SAMUEL
1075–1040	SAMUEL JUDGES ISRAEL
1080	SAUL IS BORN
1050	SAUL BECOMES KING
1040	DAVID IS BORN TO NITZEVET (THE NAME OF DAVID'S MOTHER, ACCORDING TO JEWISH TRADITION) AND JESSE
1025	SAMUEL ANOINTS DAVID; DAVID KILLS GOLIATH AND MARRIES MICHAL, SAUL'S DAUGHTER
1010	SAUL DIES; DAVID BECOMES JUDAH'S KING
1003	DAVID BECOMES KING OVER ALL ISRAEL
c. 997	DAVID TAKES BATHSHEBA, THEN KILLS HER HUSBAND, URIAH
c. 991	BATHSHEBA GIVES BIRTH TO SOLOMON
c. 980	DAVID TAKES A CENSUS
970	BATHSHEBA ADVOCATES FOR DAVID TO MAKE SOLOMON KING; SOLOMON BECOMES KING
930	THE KINGDOM DIVIDES

1 SAMUEL 1

Elkanah and His Family

1 There was a man named Elkanah who lived in Ramah in the region of Zuph* in the hill country of Ephraim. He was the son of Jeroham, son of Elihu, son of Tohu, son of Zuph, of Ephraim. ²Elkanah had two wives, Hannah and Peninnah. Peninnah had children, but Hannah did not.

³Each year Elkanah would travel to Shiloh to worship and sacrifice to the LORD of Heaven's Armies at the Tabernacle. The priests of the LORD at that time were the two sons of Eli—Hophni and Phinehas. ⁴On the days Elkanah presented his sacrifice, he would give portions of the meat to Peninnah and each of her children. ⁵And though he loved Hannah,

1:1 As in Greek version; Hebrew reads *in Ramathaim-zophim*; compare 1:19.

Persisting in Prayer

MY STORY WITH GOD

SCRIPTURE CONNECTION: 1 SAMUEL 1:1–2:11

Sometimes it's hard to keep praying when we're not sure anything is happening. Are we willing to keep praying for as long as it takes?

Hannah persistently prayed and—eventually—received her heart's desire. As a beloved wife of Elkanah, Hannah enjoyed her husband's favor. Still, she was childless, which—in her cultural context—caused despair. Peninnah, her husband's second wife, delivered children with little effort and cruelly mocked Hannah, inflicting even greater pain (1:1-8).

Year after year, Hannah accompanied Elkanah to worship, begging God for a child. One year her plea was so fervent that Eli, the priest who observed her, concluded she was drunk. Not so. She was simply lost in passionate prayer (1:9-16). Eli told Hannah that God had heard her prayer. Sure enough, months later, Hannah gave birth to a son she named Samuel, meaning "I asked the LORD for him" (1:20). Hannah used Samuel's name to proclaim to everyone how God answered her persistent prayers.

> Are you willing to pray for as long as it takes?

Why did God grant Hannah's request? The passage does not tell us exactly, but Samuel's name might give us a clue. We do see in Hannah a posture of ongoing asking. Hannah believed God listens, and year after year, she prayed for her heart's desire. She kept asking until she received God's response. Hannah was willing to pray for as long as it took.

IMAGINE

What is the prayer you are asking of God? How can you strengthen your resolve to keep praying?

Like Hannah, has God provided an answer in your life when you prayed for it persistently?

"Sometimes our prayers remain unanswered in our lifetimes, don't they? But when we continue to ask, we may see a response we'd otherwise miss. Prayer can take time and multiple askings. Are you willing to pray for as long as it takes?"

ELISA MORGAN, MDiv, speaks, writes, and cohosts podcasts for Our Daily Bread Ministries. For twenty years, she served as president of MOPS International, now as president emerita. Her motto is "Living really... Really living."

he would give her only one choice portion* because the LORD had given her no children. ⁶So Peninnah would taunt Hannah and make fun of her because the LORD had kept her from having children. ⁷Year after year it was the same—Peninnah would taunt Hannah as they went to the Tabernacle.* Each time, Hannah would be reduced to tears and would not even eat.

⁸"Why are you crying, Hannah?" Elkanah would ask. "Why aren't you eating? Why be downhearted just because you have no children? You have me—isn't that better than having ten sons?"

Hannah's Prayer for a Son

⁹Once after a sacrificial meal at Shiloh, Hannah got up and went to pray. Eli the priest was sitting at his customary place beside the entrance of the Tabernacle.* ¹⁰Hannah was in deep anguish, crying bitterly as she prayed to the LORD. ¹¹And she made this vow: "O LORD of Heaven's Armies, if you will look upon my sorrow and answer my prayer and give me a son, then I will give him back to you. He will be yours for his entire lifetime, and as a sign that he has been dedicated to the LORD, his hair will never be cut.*"

¹²As she was praying to the LORD, Eli watched her. ¹³Seeing her lips moving but hearing no sound, he thought she had been drinking. ¹⁴"Must you come here drunk?" he demanded. "Throw away your wine!"

¹⁵"Oh no, sir!" she replied. "I haven't been drinking wine or anything stronger. But I am very discouraged, and I was pouring out my heart to the LORD. ¹⁶Don't think I am a wicked woman! For I have been praying out of great anguish and sorrow."

¹⁷"In that case," Eli said, "go in peace! May the God of Israel grant the request you have asked of him."

¹⁸"Oh, thank you, sir!" she exclaimed. Then she went back and began to eat again, and she was no longer sad.

Samuel's Birth and Dedication

¹⁹The entire family got up early the next morning and went to worship the LORD once more. Then they returned home to Ramah. When Elkanah slept with Hannah, the LORD remembered her plea, ²⁰and in due time she gave birth to a son. She named him Samuel,* for she said, "I asked the LORD for him."

²¹The next year Elkanah and his family went on their annual trip to offer a sacrifice to the LORD and to keep his vow. ²²But Hannah did not go. She told her husband, "Wait until the boy is weaned. Then I will take him to the Tabernacle and leave him there with the LORD permanently.*"

²³"Whatever you think is best," Elkanah agreed. "Stay here for now, and may the LORD help you keep your promise.*" So she stayed home and nursed the boy until he was weaned.

²⁴When the child was weaned, Hannah took him to the Tabernacle in Shiloh. They brought along a three-year-old bull* for the sacrifice and a basket* of flour and some wine. ²⁵After sacrificing the bull, they brought the boy to Eli. ²⁶"Sir, do you remember me?" Hannah asked. "I am the very woman who stood here several years ago praying to the LORD. ²⁷I asked the LORD to give me this boy, and he has granted my request. ²⁸Now I am giving him to the LORD, and he will belong to the LORD his whole life." And they* worshiped the LORD there.

Hannah's Prayer of Praise

2 Then Hannah prayed:

"My heart rejoices in the LORD!
  The LORD has made me strong.*
Now I have an answer for my enemies;
  I rejoice because you rescued me.
² No one is holy like the LORD!
  There is no one besides you;
  there is no Rock like our God.

1:5 Or *And because he loved Hannah, he would give her a choice portion.* The meaning of the Hebrew is uncertain. **1:7** Hebrew *the house of the LORD;* also in 1:24. **1:9** Hebrew *the Temple of the LORD.* **1:11** Some manuscripts add *He will drink neither wine nor intoxicants.* **1:20** *Samuel* sounds like the Hebrew term for "asked of God" or "heard by God." **1:22** Some manuscripts add *I will offer him as a Nazirite for all time.* **1:23** As in Dead Sea Scrolls and Greek version; Masoretic Text reads *may the LORD keep his promise.* **1:24a** As in Dead Sea Scrolls, Greek and Syriac versions; Masoretic Text reads *three bulls.* **1:24b** Hebrew *and an ephah* [20 quarts or 22 liters]. **1:28** Hebrew *he.* **2:1** Hebrew *has exalted my horn.*

1:6-10 Notice the context of Hannah's story: The book of Ruth comes right before 1 Samuel, and Ruth and Naomi's story previews why Hannah felt so desolate about not having children. Like Naomi, Hannah could become kin-less. She would have no one to support her after her husband died, leaving her destitute.

1:11; 2:20-21 Hannah's vow dedicating her son to the Lord is beautiful, but it could hold a deeper meaning for Hannah's hopeful future. In Israel, people often gave the first portion of their harvest or dedicated their firstborn son to the Lord in hopes of receiving greater blessing (Exodus 13:2, 12-15; 23:16, 19; 34:19-20, 22, 26). By offering Samuel as a sort of first portion, Hannah may have hoped for more children in return. These motives may seem complex, yet God answered. Have you seen God answer, even when your motivations were a little messy?

2:1-10 Hannah's prayer echoes throughout the Israelite sisterhood; many women have offered up a battle song of victory or a declaration of praise in light of good circumstances (Exodus 15:20-21; Judges 5:1-31; 11:34; Luke 1:42-45, 46-55; 2:38). How might you join the sisterhood with your own song, celebrating how the Lord has moved in your life?

3 "Stop acting so proud and haughty!
   Don't speak with such arrogance!
For the LORD is a God who knows what you have done;
   he will judge your actions.
4 The bow of the mighty is now broken,
   and those who stumbled are now strong.
5 Those who were well fed are now starving,
   and those who were starving are now full.
The childless woman now has seven children,
   and the woman with many children wastes away.
6 The LORD gives both death and life;
   he brings some down to the grave* but raises others up.
7 The LORD makes some poor and others rich;
   he brings some down and lifts others up.
8 He lifts the poor from the dust
   and the needy from the garbage dump.
He sets them among princes,
   placing them in seats of honor.
For all the earth is the LORD's,
   and he has set the world in order.

9 "He will protect his faithful ones,
   but the wicked will disappear in darkness.
No one will succeed by strength alone.
10   Those who fight against the LORD will be shattered.
He thunders against them from heaven;
   the LORD judges throughout the earth.
He gives power to his king;
   he increases the strength* of his anointed one."

11 Then Elkanah returned home to Ramah without Samuel. And the boy served the LORD by assisting Eli the priest.

Eli's Wicked Sons

12 Now the sons of Eli were scoundrels who had no respect for the LORD 13 or for their duties as priests. Whenever anyone offered a sacrifice, Eli's sons would send over a servant with a three-pronged fork. While the meat of the sacrificed animal was still boiling, 14 the servant would stick the fork into the pot and demand that whatever it brought up be given to Eli's sons. All the Israelites who came to worship at Shiloh were treated this way. 15 Sometimes the servant would come even before the animal's fat had been burned on the altar. He would demand raw meat before it had been boiled so that it could be used for roasting.

16 The man offering the sacrifice might reply, "Take as much as you want, but the fat must be burned first." Then the servant would demand, "No, give it to me now, or I'll take it by force." 17 So the sin of these young men was very serious in the LORD's sight, for they treated the LORD's offerings with contempt.

18 But Samuel, though he was only a boy, served the LORD. He wore a linen garment like that of a priest.* 19 Each year his mother made a small coat for him and brought it to him when she came with her husband for the sacrifice. 20 Before they returned home, Eli would bless Elkanah and his wife and say, "May the LORD give you other children to take the place of this one she gave to the LORD.*" 21 And the LORD blessed Hannah, and she conceived and gave birth to three sons and two daughters. Meanwhile, Samuel grew up in the presence of the LORD.

22 Now Eli was very old, but he was aware of what his sons were doing to the people of Israel. He knew, for instance, that his sons were seducing the young women who assisted at the entrance of the Tabernacle.* 23 Eli said to them, "I have been hearing reports from all the people about the wicked things you are doing. Why do you keep sinning? 24 You must stop, my sons! The reports I hear among the LORD's people are not good. 25 If someone sins against another person, God* can mediate for the guilty party. But if someone sins against the LORD, who can intercede?" But Eli's sons wouldn't listen to their father, for the LORD was already planning to put them to death.

26 Meanwhile, the boy Samuel grew taller and grew in favor with the LORD and with the people.

A Warning for Eli's Family

27 One day a man of God came to Eli and gave him this message from the LORD: "I revealed myself* to your ancestors when they were Pharaoh's slaves in

2:6 Hebrew *to Sheol.* 2:10 Hebrew *he exalts the horn.* 2:18 Hebrew *He wore a linen ephod.* 2:20 As in Dead Sea Scrolls and Greek version; Masoretic Text reads *this one he requested of the LORD.* 2:22 Hebrew *Tent of Meeting.* Some manuscripts lack this entire sentence. 2:25 Or *the judges.* 2:27 As in Greek and Syriac versions; Hebrew reads *Did I reveal myself.*

2:3-10 Hannah's prayer encapsulates her own life's themes, including the poor relationship with Peninnah. Some of these are insights that the book's author wants you to be aware of in reading the rest of the story, which hint or foreshadow what God will do. Pay attention to how God will guard the steps of those who follow him, shatter those who oppose him, and lift the poor and give them places of honor.
2:12-17 First Samuel belongs to a group of books called the Former Prophets, which include Joshua, Judges, 1–2 Samuel, and 1–2 Kings. As a group, they tell the history of Israel from the time the people settled in the Promised Land after having been enslaved in Egypt to the time when they were exiled from the land by foreign conquerors. Starting from Judges (Judges 17–21), we see priests who acted quite wickedly. Eli's sons continued this pattern (see Leviticus 3:3-17 to understand the sons' offenses against God).
2:27-30 God's words to Eli and his sons can trouble us. Was God going back on the promise he had made to their ancestors? Notice the hereditary principle at work here, or what can be called "biological succession." We see this everywhere in the Bible and in world cultures through time, where the son is expected to learn from his father and eventually take over the work, wealth, and family responsibilities from him. This seemingly logical sequence gets upended regularly in this book, and for a good reason. God does not take wicked actions lightly, and he is in the business of turning things upside down to purge and purify.

Hannah

◎ IDENTITY **Empty to Overflow**

Hannah remembers…

Peninnah had children; I did not.

   Peninnah taunted me, wanting me to know she had first place. Though I knew my husband loved me, I still lacked in the one way I wanted to abound.

   Every year, I prayed to the Lord of Heaven's Armies that he would grant me children, my heart so sick with grief I could not eat. It upset my husband because he wanted so much to be enough for me.

   Then, one year, I was in deep anguish, crying bitterly to God. I even promised him I would give back whatever son he gave me. The high priest thought I was drunk, but I explained my sorrow. He blessed me and interceded on my behalf.

   When we returned home, the Lord remembered my plea. Later that year, I gave birth to Samuel, a name that means "I asked the LORD for him" (1:20).

   Peninnah wanted me to see my emptiness. My husband wanted me to see him. I wanted to see God answer my prayer. And God did.

HANNAH'S STORY IS TOLD IN 1 SAMUEL 1:1–2:21.

> Sometimes others want us to see their needs. Only, always, God sees us and our needs.

IDENTIFY

Where do you look for your deepest needs and longings to be met?

Are you looking to God alone?

> "I had been called to something I did not feel qualified for, but a friend reminded me that the call of God on our lives will always be stronger than what we think we lack. I took a step of faith based on what I knew about God and what he asked me to do. It filled me in a way that made it easy to pour it all back out on others, just like Hannah could give Samuel back to God for service."

CARA DAY is a writer and illustrator. She has served with Stonecroft Ministries helping women live "extraordinary."

1 SAMUEL 3

Egypt. ²⁸I chose your ancestor Aaron* from among all the tribes of Israel to be my priest, to offer sacrifices on my altar, to burn incense, and to wear the priestly vest* as he served me. And I assigned the sacrificial offerings to you priests. ²⁹So why do you scorn my sacrifices and offerings? Why do you give your sons more honor than you give me—for you and they have become fat from the best offerings of my people Israel!

³⁰"Therefore, the LORD, the God of Israel, says: I promised that your branch of the tribe of Levi* would always be my priests. But I will honor those who honor me, and I will despise those who think lightly of me. ³¹The time is coming when I will put an end to your family, so it will no longer serve as my priests. All the members of your family will die before their time. None will reach old age. ³²You will watch with envy as I pour out prosperity on the people of Israel. But no members of your family will ever live out their days. ³³The few not cut off from serving at my altar will survive, but only so their eyes can go blind and their hearts break, and their children will die a violent death.* ³⁴And to prove that what I have said will come true, I will cause your two sons, Hophni and Phinehas, to die on the same day!

³⁵"Then I will raise up a faithful priest who will serve me and do what I desire. I will establish his family, and they will be priests to my anointed kings forever. ³⁶Then all of your surviving family will bow before him, begging for money and food. 'Please,' they will say, 'give us jobs among the priests so we will have enough to eat.'"

The LORD Speaks to Samuel

3 Meanwhile, the boy Samuel served the LORD by assisting Eli. Now in those days messages from the LORD were very rare, and visions were quite uncommon.

²One night Eli, who was almost blind by now, had gone to bed. ³The lamp of God had not yet gone out, and Samuel was sleeping in the Tabernacle* near the Ark of God. ⁴Suddenly the LORD called out, "Samuel!"

"Yes?" Samuel replied. "What is it?" ⁵He got up and ran to Eli. "Here I am. Did you call me?"

"I didn't call you," Eli replied. "Go back to bed." So he did.

⁶Then the LORD called out again, "Samuel!"

Again Samuel got up and went to Eli. "Here I am. Did you call me?"

"I didn't call you, my son," Eli said. "Go back to bed."

⁷Samuel did not yet know the LORD because he had never had a message from the LORD before. ⁸So the LORD called a third time, and once more Samuel got up and went to Eli. "Here I am. Did you call me?"

Then Eli realized it was the LORD who was calling the boy. ⁹So he said to Samuel, "Go and lie down again, and if someone calls again, say, 'Speak, LORD, your servant is listening.'" So Samuel went back to bed.

¹⁰And the LORD came and called as before, "Samuel! Samuel!"

And Samuel replied, "Speak, your servant is listening."

¹¹Then the LORD said to Samuel, "I am about to do a shocking thing in Israel. ¹²I am going to carry out all my threats against Eli and his family, from beginning to end. ¹³I have warned him that judgment is coming upon his family forever, because his sons are blaspheming God* and he hasn't disciplined them. ¹⁴So I have vowed that the sins of Eli and his sons will never be forgiven by sacrifices or offerings."

Samuel Speaks for the LORD

¹⁵Samuel stayed in bed until morning, then got up and opened the doors of the Tabernacle* as usual. He was afraid to tell Eli what the LORD had said to him. ¹⁶But Eli called out to him, "Samuel, my son."

"Here I am," Samuel replied.

¹⁷"What did the LORD say to you? Tell me everything. And may God strike you and even kill you if you hide anything from me!" ¹⁸So Samuel told Eli everything; he didn't hold anything back. "It is the LORD's will," Eli replied. "Let him do what he thinks best."

¹⁹As Samuel grew up, the LORD was with him, and everything Samuel said proved to be reliable. ²⁰And all Israel, from Dan in the north to Beersheba in the south, knew that Samuel was confirmed as a prophet of the LORD. ²¹The LORD continued to appear at Shiloh and gave messages to Samuel there at the Tabernacle. ⁴:¹And Samuel's words went out to all the people of Israel.

The Philistines Capture the Ark

4 At that time Israel was at war with the Philistines. The Israelite army was camped near Ebenezer, and the Philistines were at Aphek. ²The Philistines attacked and defeated the army of Israel, killing 4,000

2:28a Hebrew *your father.* **2:28b** Hebrew *an ephod.* **2:30** Hebrew *that your house and your father's house.* **2:33** As in Dead Sea Scrolls and Greek version, which read *die by the sword;* Masoretic Text reads *die like mortals.* **3:3** Hebrew *the Temple of the LORD.* **3:13** As in Greek version; Hebrew reads *his sons have made themselves contemptible.* **3:15** Hebrew *the house of the LORD.*

3:1 God was not disclosing his will through prophets or priests, so the period was spiritually dark. However, that darkness was about to end when God communicated with Samuel (3:2–4:1).

3:14 Neither blood sacrifices nor offerings would be acceptable on behalf of Eli and his sons. The offerings of Leviticus 4–5 were for sins committed inadvertently or unintentionally, whereas the sins of Eli and his sons were deliberate and rebellious.

Insight: THE ARK OF THE COVENANT

The Ark reminded the people of God's presence, so having enemies capture it felt disheartening. The Ark was "the Ark of the LORD's Covenant" (Numbers 10:33; Deuteronomy 10:8; 31:9, 25-26). At various times, it contained the tablets (the Ten Commandments), a jar of manna, and Aaron's staff that had sprouted leaves and budded (Hebrews 9:4). The Ark reminded Israel of God's agreement with them and rested within the Most Holy Place, the innermost part of the Tabernacle and, eventually, the Temple. (Exodus 26–27; 2 Kings 6)

This image of the Ark reflects an understanding of the cherubim as human-like creatures with wings.

---

men. ³After the battle was over, the troops retreated to their camp, and the elders of Israel asked, "Why did the LORD allow us to be defeated by the Philistines?" Then they said, "Let's bring the Ark of the Covenant of the LORD from Shiloh. If we carry it into battle with us, it* will save us from our enemies."

⁴So they sent men to Shiloh to bring the Ark of the Covenant of the LORD of Heaven's Armies, who is enthroned between the cherubim. Hophni and Phinehas, the sons of Eli, were also there with the Ark of the Covenant of God. ⁵When all the Israelites saw the Ark of the Covenant of the LORD coming into the camp, their shout of joy was so loud it made the ground shake!

⁶"What's going on?" the Philistines asked. "What's all the shouting about in the Hebrew camp?" When they were told it was because the Ark of the LORD had arrived, ⁷they panicked. "The gods have* come into their camp!" they cried. "This is a disaster! We have never had to face anything like this before! ⁸Help! Who can save us from these mighty gods of Israel? They are the same gods who destroyed the Egyptians with plagues when Israel was in the wilderness. ⁹Fight as never before, Philistines! If you don't, we will become the Hebrews' slaves just as they have been ours! Stand up like men and fight!"

¹⁰So the Philistines fought desperately, and Israel was defeated again. The slaughter was great; 30,000 Israelite soldiers died that day. The survivors turned and fled to their tents. ¹¹The Ark of God was captured, and Hophni and Phinehas, the two sons of Eli, were killed.

The Death of Eli

¹²A man from the tribe of Benjamin ran from the battlefield and arrived at Shiloh later that same day. He had torn his clothes and put dust on his head to show his grief. ¹³Eli was waiting beside the road to hear the news of the battle, for his heart trembled for the safety of the Ark of God. When the messenger arrived and told what had happened, an outcry resounded throughout the town.

¹⁴"What is all the noise about?" Eli asked.

The messenger rushed over to Eli, ¹⁵who was ninety-eight years old and blind. ¹⁶He said to Eli, "I have just come from the battlefield—I was there this very day."

4:3 Or *he.* 4:7 Or *A god has.*

4:3 The Israelites were often defeated in war because of one individual's or the entire nation's wrongs (see Joshua 7). In this defeat, no one inquired whether sin was the cause. Apparently, no one had even asked the Lord if they should engage the Philistines in the first place (see 1 Chronicles 14:13-16). Instead, the Israelites treated the Ark, the most sacred symbol of the Lord's presence, as a charm to ward off misfortune. Carrying the Ark into battle was not necessarily wrong (see Joshua 6:2-21), but this act would not ensure God's blessing and victory.

4:11 The Philistines' capture of the Ark was devastating to the Israelites (4:12-22). The deaths of Hophni and Phinehas fulfilled the Lord's word to Eli (2:34). Although they are the only casualties named, they were not the only Israelites who had sinned (see 7:3-6).

"What happened, my son?" Eli demanded.

[17] "Israel has been defeated by the Philistines," the messenger replied. "The people have been slaughtered, and your two sons, Hophni and Phinehas, were also killed. And the Ark of God has been captured."

[18] When the messenger mentioned what had happened to the Ark of God, Eli fell backward from his seat beside the gate. He broke his neck and died, for he was old and overweight. He had been Israel's judge for forty years.

[19] Eli's daughter-in-law, the wife of Phinehas, was pregnant and near her time of delivery. When she heard that the Ark of God had been captured and that her father-in-law and husband were dead, she went into labor and gave birth. [20] She died in childbirth, but before she passed away the midwives tried to encourage her. "Don't be afraid," they said. "You have a baby boy!" But she did not answer or pay attention to them.

[21] She named the child Ichabod (which means "Where is the glory?"), for she said, "Israel's glory is gone." She named him this because the Ark of God had been captured and because her father-in-law and husband were dead. [22] Then she said, "The glory has departed from Israel, for the Ark of God has been captured."

The Ark in Philistia

5 After the Philistines captured the Ark of God, they took it from the battleground at Ebenezer to the town of Ashdod. [2] They carried the Ark of God into the temple of Dagon and placed it beside an idol of Dagon. [3] But when the citizens of Ashdod went to see it the next morning, Dagon had fallen with his face to the ground in front of the Ark of the LORD! So they took Dagon and put him in his place again. [4] But the next morning the same thing happened—Dagon had fallen face down before the Ark of the LORD again. This time his head and hands had broken off and were lying in the doorway. Only the trunk of his body was left intact. [5] That is why to this day neither the priests of Dagon nor anyone who enters the temple of Dagon in Ashdod will step on its threshold.

[6] Then the LORD's heavy hand struck the people of Ashdod and the nearby villages with a plague of tumors.* [7] When the people realized what was happening, they cried out, "We can't keep the Ark of the God of Israel here any longer! He is against us! We will all be destroyed along with Dagon, our god." [8] So they called together the rulers of the Philistine towns and asked, "What should we do with the Ark of the God of Israel?"

The rulers discussed it and replied, "Move it to the town of Gath." So they moved the Ark of the God of Israel to Gath. [9] But when the Ark arrived at Gath, the LORD's heavy hand fell on its men, young and old; he struck them with a plague of tumors, and there was a great panic.

[10] So they sent the Ark of God to the town of Ekron, but when the people of Ekron saw it coming they cried out, "They are bringing the Ark of the God of Israel here to kill us, too!" [11] The people summoned the Philistine rulers again and begged them, "Please send the Ark of the God of Israel back to its own country, or it* will kill us all." For the deadly plague from God had already begun, and great fear was sweeping across the town. [12] Those who didn't die were afflicted with tumors; and the cry from the town rose to heaven.

The Philistines Return the Ark

6 The Ark of the LORD remained in Philistine territory seven months in all. [2] Then the Philistines called in their priests and diviners and asked them, "What should we do about the Ark of the LORD? Tell us how to return it to its own country."

[3] "Send the Ark of the God of Israel back with a gift," they were told. "Send a guilt offering so the plague will stop. Then, if you are healed, you will know it was his hand that caused the plague."

[4] "What sort of guilt offering should we send?" they asked.

And they were told, "Since the plague has struck both you and your five rulers, make five gold tumors and five gold rats, just like those that have ravaged your land. [5] Make these things to show honor to the God of Israel. Perhaps then he will stop afflicting you, your gods, and your land. [6] Don't be stubborn and rebellious as Pharaoh and the Egyptians were. By the time God was finished with them, they were eager to let Israel go.

[7] "Now build a new cart, and find two cows that have just given birth to calves. Make sure the cows have never been yoked to a cart. Hitch the cows to the cart, but shut their calves away from them in a pen. [8] Put the Ark of the LORD on the cart, and beside it place a chest containing the gold rats and gold tumors you are sending as a guilt offering. Then let the cows go wherever they want. [9] If they cross the border of our land and go to Beth-shemesh, we will know it was the LORD who brought this great

---

5:6 Greek version and Latin Vulgate read *tumors; and rats appeared in their land, and death and destruction were throughout the city.* 5:11 Or *he.*

5:1-12 The Israelites probably felt that they had lost the war with the Philistines winning the battle. But often, in the story of God, what seems to have been a great defeat turns out to be the exact opposite. The idol of Dagon couldn't even remain standing in the presence of the Ark of God and eventually broke into pieces. Even when the Israelite army faltered, God was still more powerful than their enemies. Have you experienced what you thought was a great loss only for it to turn out to be better than you had ever hoped?

disaster upon us. If they don't, we will know it was not his hand that caused the plague. It came simply by chance."

¹⁰So these instructions were carried out. Two cows were hitched to the cart, and their newborn calves were shut up in a pen. ¹¹Then the Ark of the LORD and the chest containing the gold rats and gold tumors were placed on the cart. ¹²And sure enough, without veering off in other directions, the cows went straight along the road toward Beth-shemesh, lowing as they went. The Philistine rulers followed them as far as the border of Beth-shemesh.

¹³The people of Beth-shemesh were harvesting wheat in the valley, and when they saw the Ark, they were overjoyed! ¹⁴The cart came into the field of a man named Joshua and stopped beside a large rock. So the people broke up the wood of the cart for a fire and killed the cows and sacrificed them to the LORD as a burnt offering. ¹⁵Several men of the tribe of Levi lifted the Ark of the LORD and the chest containing the gold rats and gold tumors from the cart and placed them on the large rock. Many sacrifices and burnt offerings were offered to the LORD that day by the people of Beth-shemesh. ¹⁶The five Philistine rulers watched all this and then returned to Ekron that same day.

¹⁷The five gold tumors sent by the Philistines as a guilt offering to the LORD were gifts from the rulers of Ashdod, Gaza, Ashkelon, Gath, and Ekron. ¹⁸The five gold rats represented the five Philistine towns and their surrounding villages, which were controlled by the five rulers. The large rock* at Beth-shemesh, where they set the Ark of the LORD, still stands in the field of Joshua as a witness to what happened there.

The Ark Moved to Kiriath-Jearim

¹⁹But the LORD killed seventy men* from Beth-shemesh because they looked into the Ark of the LORD. And the people mourned greatly because of what the LORD had done. ²⁰"Who is able to stand in the presence of the LORD, this holy God?" they cried out. "Where can we send the Ark from here?"

²¹So they sent messengers to the people at Kiriath-jearim and told them, "The Philistines have returned the Ark of the LORD. Come here and get it!"

7 So the men of Kiriath-jearim came to get the Ark of the LORD. They took it to the hillside home of Abinadab and ordained Eleazar, his son, to be in charge of it. ²The Ark remained in Kiriath-jearim for a long time—twenty years in all. During that time all Israel mourned because it seemed the LORD had abandoned them.

Samuel Leads Israel to Victory

³Then Samuel said to all the people of Israel, "If you want to return to the LORD with all your hearts, get rid of your foreign gods and your images of Ashtoreth. Turn your hearts to the LORD and obey him alone; then he will rescue you from the Philistines." ⁴So the Israelites got rid of their images of Baal and Ashtoreth and worshiped only the LORD.

⁵Then Samuel told them, "Gather all of Israel to Mizpah, and I will pray to the LORD for you." ⁶So they gathered at Mizpah and, in a great ceremony, drew water from a well and poured it out before the LORD. They also went without food all day and confessed that they had sinned against the LORD. (It was at Mizpah that Samuel became Israel's judge.)

⁷When the Philistine rulers heard that Israel had gathered at Mizpah, they mobilized their army and advanced. The Israelites were badly frightened when they learned that the Philistines were approaching. ⁸"Don't stop pleading with the LORD our God to save us from the Philistines!" they begged Samuel. ⁹So Samuel took a young lamb and offered it to the LORD as a whole burnt offering. He pleaded with the LORD to help Israel, and the LORD answered him.

¹⁰Just as Samuel was sacrificing the burnt offering, the Philistines arrived to attack Israel. But the LORD spoke with a mighty voice of thunder from heaven that day, and the Philistines were thrown into such confusion that the Israelites defeated them. ¹¹The men of Israel chased them from Mizpah to a place below Beth-car, slaughtering them all along the way.

¹²Samuel then took a large stone and placed it between the towns of Mizpah and Jeshanah.* He named it Ebenezer (which means "the stone of help"), for he said, "Up to this point the LORD has helped us!"

¹³So the Philistines were subdued and didn't invade Israel again for some time. And throughout Samuel's lifetime, the LORD's powerful hand was

---

6:18 As in some Hebrew manuscripts and Greek version; most Hebrew manuscripts read *great meadow* or *Abel-haggedolah*.
6:19 As in a few Hebrew manuscripts; most Hebrew manuscripts read *70 men, 50,000 men.* Perhaps the text should be understood to read *the LORD killed 70 men and 50 oxen.* 7:12 As in Greek and Syriac versions; Hebrew reads *Shen*.

6:17-20 Any tendency to treat God as something to wield against others has negative consequences. Have you tried to fit God into a box, into someone you can control or use to justify your actions? Ironically, it was the Philistines who got it right: They gave a guilt offering. And it was the Israelites who got it wrong: They treated God's presence with disrespect. How can we, too, repent of our wrong actions and attitudes toward the Lord?
7:3 People cannot expect God's blessing unless they get rid of what is contrary to his will. Just so, the Israelites needed to rid themselves of idols (see Genesis 35:2; Joshua 24:14).

Ashtoreth (also called Asherah) was the Canaanite goddess of fertility associated with Baal (1 Samuel 7:4). Worship of Asherah had been an ongoing problem throughout Israel's history (for example, Deuteronomy 12:3; 1 Kings 16:33). The Israelites had started worshiping idols during the twenty years mentioned in 1 Samuel 7:2 and had done so ever since the forty years in the wilderness (8:8; Judges 6:25; Amos 5:25-26). Israel's devastating defeat by the Philistines was due not only to the sins of Eli's two sons but also to several generations of unfaithfulness to God.

"Don't be afraid. ...Make sure now that you worship the LORD with all your heart."

1 SAMUEL 12:20

raised against the Philistines. ¹⁴The Israelite villages near Ekron and Gath that the Philistines had captured were restored to Israel, along with the rest of the territory that the Philistines had taken. And there was peace between Israel and the Amorites in those days.

¹⁵Samuel continued as Israel's judge for the rest of his life. ¹⁶Each year he traveled around, setting up his court first at Bethel, then at Gilgal, and then at Mizpah. He judged the people of Israel at each of these places. ¹⁷Then he would return to his home at Ramah, and he would hear cases there, too. And Samuel built an altar to the LORD at Ramah.

Israel Requests a King

8 As Samuel grew old, he appointed his sons to be judges over Israel. ²Joel and Abijah, his oldest sons, held court in Beersheba. ³But they were not like their father, for they were greedy for money. They accepted bribes and perverted justice.

⁴Finally, all the elders of Israel met at Ramah to discuss the matter with Samuel. ⁵"Look," they told him, "you are now old, and your sons are not like you. Give us a king to judge us like all the other nations have."

⁶Samuel was displeased with their request and went to the LORD for guidance. ⁷"Do everything they say to you," the LORD replied, "for they are rejecting me, not you. They don't want me to be their king any longer. ⁸Ever since I brought them from Egypt they have continually abandoned me and followed other gods. And now they are giving you the same treatment. ⁹Do as they ask, but solemnly warn them about the way a king will reign over them."

Samuel Warns against a Kingdom

¹⁰So Samuel passed on the LORD's warning to the people who were asking him for a king. ¹¹"This is how a king will reign over you," Samuel said. "The king will draft your sons and assign them to his chariots and his charioteers, making them run before his chariots. ¹²Some will be generals and captains in his army,* some will be forced to plow in his fields and harvest his crops, and some will make his weapons and chariot equipment. ¹³The king will take your daughters from you and force them to cook and bake and make perfumes for him. ¹⁴He will take away the best of your fields and vineyards and olive groves and give them to his own officials. ¹⁵He will take a tenth of your grain and your grape harvest and distribute it among his officers and attendants. ¹⁶He will take your male and female slaves and demand the finest of your cattle* and donkeys for his own use. ¹⁷He will demand a tenth of your flocks, and you will be his slaves. ¹⁸When that day comes, you will beg for relief from this king you are demanding, but then the LORD will not help you."

¹⁹But the people refused to listen to Samuel's warning. "Even so, we still want a king," they said. ²⁰"We want to be like the nations around us. Our king will judge us and lead us into battle."

²¹So Samuel repeated to the LORD what the people had said, ²²and the LORD replied, "Do as they say, and give them a king." Then Samuel agreed and sent the people home.

Saul Meets Samuel

9 There was a wealthy, influential man named Kish from the tribe of Benjamin. He was the son of Abiel, son of Zeror, son of Becorath, son of Aphiah, of the tribe of Benjamin. ²His son Saul was the most handsome man in Israel—head and shoulders taller than anyone else in the land.

³One day Kish's donkeys strayed away, and he told Saul, "Take a servant with you, and go look for the donkeys." ⁴So Saul took one of the servants and traveled through the hill country of Ephraim, the land of Shalishah, the Shaalim area, and the entire land of Benjamin, but they couldn't find the donkeys anywhere.

⁵Finally, they entered the region of Zuph, and Saul said to his servant, "Let's go home. By now my father will be more worried about us than about the donkeys!"

⁶But the servant said, "I've just thought of something! There is a man of God who lives here in this town. He is held in high honor by all the people because everything he says comes true. Let's go find him. Perhaps he can tell us which way to go."

⁷"But we don't have anything to offer him," Saul replied. "Even our food is gone, and we don't have a thing to give him."

⁸"Well," the servant said, "I have one small silver piece.* We can at least offer it to the man of God and see what happens!" ⁹(In those days if people wanted a message from God, they would say, "Let's go and ask the seer," for prophets used to be called seers.)

¹⁰"All right," Saul agreed, "let's try it!" So they started into the town where the man of God lived.

8:12 Hebrew *commanders of thousands and commanders of fifties.* **8:16** As in Greek version; Hebrew reads *young men.* **9:8** Hebrew ¼ *shekel of silver,* about 0.1 ounces or 3 grams in weight.

7:15 Once Saul became king (1 Samuel 10), Samuel's role was more judicial than military.

8:19-20 The people of Israel were trying to establish themselves as a recognizable nation using other nations' criteria. In so doing, they compromised the standards that God had given them. Sometimes, while we are attempting to figure out who we are, we use the wrong criteria and compromise pieces of ourselves in the process.

9:2; 10:23 Saul was tall and handsome, and his appearance was striking and inspired loyalty among the people (compare with 16:12; 2 Samuel 14:25-26). But as 1 Samuel has made clear so far, things that outwardly impress can hide the whole story. Are there other character clues about Saul in the text that give some hints about his true nature? Has your bias blinded you before?

1 SAMUEL 10

¹¹As they were climbing the hill to the town, they met some young women coming out to draw water. So Saul and his servant asked, "Is the seer here today?"

¹²"Yes," they replied. "Stay right on this road. He is at the town gates. He has just arrived to take part in a public sacrifice up at the place of worship. ¹³Hurry and catch him before he goes up there to eat. The guests won't begin eating until he arrives to bless the food."

¹⁴So they entered the town, and as they passed through the gates, Samuel was coming out toward them to go up to the place of worship.

¹⁵Now the LORD had told Samuel the previous day, ¹⁶"About this time tomorrow I will send you a man from the land of Benjamin. Anoint him to be the leader of my people, Israel. He will rescue them from the Philistines, for I have looked down on my people in mercy and have heard their cry."

¹⁷When Samuel saw Saul, the LORD said, "That's the man I told you about! He will rule my people."

¹⁸Just then Saul approached Samuel at the gateway and asked, "Can you please tell me where the seer's house is?"

¹⁹"I am the seer!" Samuel replied. "Go up to the place of worship ahead of me. We will eat there together, and in the morning I'll tell you what you want to know and send you on your way. ²⁰And don't worry about those donkeys that were lost three days ago, for they have been found. And I am here to tell you that you and your family are the focus of all Israel's hopes."

²¹Saul replied, "But I'm only from the tribe of Benjamin, the smallest tribe in Israel, and my family is the least important of all the families of that tribe! Why are you talking like this to me?"

²²Then Samuel brought Saul and his servant into the hall and placed them at the head of the table, honoring them above the thirty special guests. ²³Samuel then instructed the cook to bring Saul the finest cut of meat, the piece that had been set aside for the guest of honor. ²⁴So the cook brought in the meat and placed it before Saul. "Go ahead and eat it," Samuel said. "I was saving it for you even before I invited these others!" So Saul ate with Samuel that day.

²⁵When they came down from the place of worship and returned to town, Samuel took Saul up to the roof of the house and prepared a bed for him there.* ²⁶At daybreak the next morning, Samuel called to Saul, "Get up! It's time you were on your way." So Saul got ready, and he and Samuel left the house together. ²⁷When they reached the edge of town, Samuel told Saul to send his servant on ahead. After the servant was gone, Samuel said, "Stay here, for I have received a special message for you from God."

Samuel Anoints Saul as King

10 Then Samuel took a flask of olive oil and poured it over Saul's head. He kissed Saul and said, "I am doing this because the LORD has appointed you to be the ruler over Israel, his special possession.* ²When you leave me today, you will see two men beside Rachel's tomb at Zelzah, on the border of Benjamin. They will tell you that the donkeys have been found and that your father has stopped worrying about them and is now worried about you. He is asking, 'Have you seen my son?'

³"When you get to the oak of Tabor, you will see three men coming toward you who are on their way to worship God at Bethel. One will be bringing three young goats, another will have three loaves of bread, and the third will be carrying a wineskin full of wine. ⁴They will greet you and offer you two of the loaves, which you are to accept.

⁵"When you arrive at Gibeah of God,* where the garrison of the Philistines is located, you will meet a band of prophets coming down from the place of worship. They will be playing a harp, a tambourine, a flute, and a lyre, and they will be prophesying. ⁶At that time the Spirit of the LORD will come powerfully upon you, and you will prophesy with them. You will be changed into a different person. ⁷After these signs take place, do what must be done, for God is with you. ⁸Then go down to Gilgal ahead of me. I will join you there to sacrifice burnt offerings and peace offerings. You must wait for seven days until I arrive and give you further instructions."

Samuel's Signs Are Fulfilled

⁹As Saul turned and started to leave, God gave him a new heart, and all Samuel's signs were fulfilled that day. ¹⁰When Saul and his servant arrived at Gibeah, they saw a group of prophets coming toward them. Then the Spirit of God came powerfully upon Saul, and he, too, began to prophesy. ¹¹When those who knew Saul heard about it, they exclaimed, "What? Is even Saul a prophet? How did the son of Kish become a prophet?"

¹²And one of those standing there said, "Can anyone become a prophet, no matter who his father is?"* So that is the origin of the saying "Is even Saul a prophet?"

¹³When Saul had finished prophesying, he went up to the place of worship. ¹⁴"Where have you been?" Saul's uncle asked him and his servant.

"We were looking for the donkeys," Saul replied, "but we couldn't find them. So we went to Samuel to ask him where they were."

9:25 As in Greek version; Hebrew reads *and talked with him there.* **10:1** Greek version reads *over Israel. And you will rule over the LORD's people and save them from their enemies around them. This will be the sign to you that the LORD has appointed you to be leader over his special possession.* **10:5** Hebrew *Gibeath-haelohim.* **10:12** Hebrew *said, "Who is their father?"*

10:2-6 These three "signs" were to convince a reluctant Saul (9:21) that he had been chosen to be king.

10:9 When God gave Saul "a new heart," God was giving Saul courage and strength, helping him overcome his hesitancy and enabling him to be king (10:6).

¹⁵"Oh? And what did he say?" his uncle asked.
¹⁶"He told us that the donkeys had already been found," Saul replied. But Saul didn't tell his uncle what Samuel said about the kingdom.

Saul Is Acclaimed King

¹⁷Later Samuel called all the people of Israel to meet before the LORD at Mizpah. ¹⁸And he said, "This is what the LORD, the God of Israel, has declared: I brought you from Egypt and rescued you from the Egyptians and from all of the nations that were oppressing you. ¹⁹But though I have rescued you from your misery and distress, you have rejected your God today and have said, 'No, we want a king instead!' Now, therefore, present yourselves before the LORD by tribes and clans."

²⁰So Samuel brought all the tribes of Israel before the LORD, and the tribe of Benjamin was chosen by lot. ²¹Then he brought each family of the tribe of Benjamin before the LORD, and the family of the Matrites was chosen. And finally Saul son of Kish was chosen from among them. But when they looked for him, he had disappeared! ²²So they asked the LORD, "Where is he?"

And the LORD replied, "He is hiding among the baggage." ²³So they found him and brought him out, and he stood head and shoulders above anyone else.

²⁴Then Samuel said to all the people, "This is the man the LORD has chosen as your king. No one in all Israel is like him!"

And all the people shouted, "Long live the king!"

²⁵Then Samuel told the people what the rights and duties of a king were. He wrote them down on a scroll and placed it before the LORD. Then Samuel sent the people home again.

²⁶When Saul returned to his home at Gibeah, a group of men whose hearts God had touched went with him. ²⁷But there were some scoundrels who complained, "How can this man save us?" And they scorned him and refused to bring him gifts. But Saul ignored them.

[Nahash, king of the Ammonites, had been grievously oppressing the people of Gad and Reuben who lived east of the Jordan River. He gouged out the right eye of each of the Israelites living there, and he didn't allow anyone to come and rescue them. In fact, of all the Israelites east of the Jordan, there wasn't a single one whose right eye Nahash had not gouged out. But there were 7,000 men who had escaped from the Ammonites, and they had settled in Jabesh-gilead.]*

Saul Defeats the Ammonites

11 About a month later,* King Nahash of Ammon led his army against the Israelite town of Jabesh-gilead. But all the citizens of Jabesh asked for peace. "Make a treaty with us, and we will be your servants," they pleaded.

²"All right," Nahash said, "but only on one condition. I will gouge out the right eye of every one of you as a disgrace to all Israel!"

³"Give us seven days to send messengers throughout Israel!" replied the elders of Jabesh. "If no one comes to save us, we will agree to your terms."

⁴When the messengers came to Gibeah of Saul and told the people about their plight, everyone broke into tears. ⁵Saul had been plowing a field with his oxen, and when he returned to town, he asked, "What's the matter? Why is everyone crying?" So they told him about the message from Jabesh.

⁶Then the Spirit of God came powerfully upon Saul, and he became very angry. ⁷He took two oxen and cut them into pieces and sent the messengers to carry them throughout Israel with this message: "This is what will happen to the oxen of anyone who refuses to follow Saul and Samuel into battle!" And the LORD made the people afraid of Saul's anger, and all of them came out together as one. ⁸When Saul mobilized them at Bezek, he found that there were 300,000 men from Israel and 30,000* men from Judah.

⁹So Saul sent the messengers back to Jabesh-gilead to say, "We will rescue you by noontime tomorrow!" There was great joy throughout the town when that message arrived!

¹⁰The men of Jabesh then told their enemies, "Tomorrow we will come out to you, and you can do to us whatever you wish." ¹¹But before dawn the next morning, Saul arrived, having divided his army into three detachments. He launched a surprise attack against the Ammonites and slaughtered them the whole morning. The remnant of their army was so badly scattered that no two of them were left together.

¹²Then the people exclaimed to Samuel, "Now where are those men who said, 'Why should Saul rule over us?' Bring them here, and we will kill them!"

¹³But Saul replied, "No one will be executed today, for today the LORD has rescued Israel!"

¹⁴Then Samuel said to the people, "Come, let us all go to Gilgal to renew the kingdom." ¹⁵So they all went to Gilgal, and in a solemn ceremony before the LORD they made Saul king. Then they offered peace offerings to the LORD, and Saul and all the Israelites were filled with joy.

10:27 This paragraph, which is not included in the Masoretic Text, is found in Dead Sea Scroll ⁴QSamᵃ. **11:1** As in Dead Sea Scroll ⁴QSamᵃ and Greek version; Masoretic Text lacks *About a month later*. **11:8** Dead Sea Scrolls and Greek version read *70,000*.

11:1-15 Saul's kingship was confirmed through a military victory, the very reason the people wanted a king (8:20).
11:15 The "solemn ceremony before the LORD" acknowledged Saul's sovereignty as king while affirming that the Lord was Israel's true King. Peace offerings often accompanied historic occasions that inaugurated important institutions (see Exodus 24:5; Leviticus 9:4, 18, 22; 1 Kings 8:63-64).

WHAT THE BIBLE SAYS ABOUT Prayer

Prayer Blesses Us!

Don't worry about anything; instead, pray about everything. Tell God what you need, and thank him for all he has done. Then you will experience God's peace, which exceeds anything we can understand. His peace will guard your hearts and minds as you live in Christ Jesus. **PHILIPPIANS 4:6-7**

Confess your sins to each other and pray for each other so that you may be healed. The earnest prayer of a righteous person has great power and produces wonderful results. **JAMES 5:16**

> Don't worry about anything; instead, pray about everything.

Pray Anytime

"May these words that I have prayed in the presence of the LORD be before him constantly, day and night, so that the LORD our God may give justice to me and to his people Israel, according to each day's needs." **1 KINGS 8:59**

I have not stopped thanking God for you. I pray for you constantly. **EPHESIANS 1:16**

God Helps Us Pray

"Your Father knows exactly what you need even before you ask him! Pray like this:

Our Father in heaven,
    may your name be kept holy.
May your Kingdom come soon.
May your will be done on earth,
    as it is in heaven.
Give us today the food we need,
and forgive us our sins,
    as we have forgiven those who
        sin against us.
And don't let us yield to
        temptation,
    but rescue us from the evil one."
MATTHEW 6:8-13

The Holy Spirit helps us in our weakness. For example, we don't know what God wants us to pray for. But the Holy Spirit prays for us with groanings that cannot be expressed in words.
ROMANS 8:26

Pray for God's Guidance

Search me, O God, and know my heart;
    test me and know my anxious thoughts.
Point out anything in me that offends you,
    and lead me along the path of everlasting life.
PSALM 139:23-24

If you need wisdom, ask our generous God, and he will give it to you. He will not rebuke you for asking. **JAMES 1:5**

Keep on seeking, and you will find.

Keep on Praying

"Keep on asking, and you will receive what you ask for. Keep on seeking, and you will find. Keep on knocking, and the door will be opened to you. For everyone who asks, receives. Everyone who seeks, finds. And to everyone who knocks, the door will be opened." **MATTHEW 7:7-8**

"If you remain in me and my words remain in you, you may ask for anything you want, and it will be granted!"
JOHN 15:7

Samuel's Farewell Address

12 Then Samuel addressed all Israel: "I have done as you asked and given you a king. ²Your king is now your leader. I stand here before you—an old, gray-haired man—and my sons serve you. I have served as your leader from the time I was a boy to this very day. ³Now testify against me in the presence of the LORD and before his anointed one. Whose ox or donkey have I stolen? Have I ever cheated any of you? Have I ever oppressed you? Have I ever taken a bribe and perverted justice? Tell me and I will make right whatever I have done wrong."

⁴"No," they replied, "you have never cheated or oppressed us, and you have never taken even a single bribe."

⁵"The LORD and his anointed one are my witnesses today," Samuel declared, "that my hands are clean."

"Yes, he is a witness," they replied.

⁶"It was the LORD who appointed Moses and Aaron," Samuel continued. "He brought your ancestors out of the land of Egypt. ⁷Now stand here quietly before the LORD as I remind you of all the great things the LORD has done for you and your ancestors. ⁸"When the Israelites were* in Egypt and cried out to the LORD, he sent Moses and Aaron to rescue them from Egypt and to bring them into this land. ⁹But the people soon forgot about the LORD their God, so he handed them over to Sisera, the commander of Hazor's army, and also to the Philistines and to the king of Moab, who fought against them.

¹⁰"Then they cried to the LORD again and confessed, 'We have sinned by turning away from the LORD and worshiping the images of Baal and Ashtoreth. But we will worship you and you alone if you will rescue us from our enemies.' ¹¹Then the LORD sent Gideon,* Bedan,* Jephthah, and Samuel* to save you, and you lived in safety.

¹²"But when you were afraid of Nahash, the king of Ammon, you came to me and said that you wanted a king to reign over you, even though the LORD your God was already your king. ¹³All right, here is the king you have chosen. You asked for him, and the LORD has granted your request.

¹⁴"Now if you fear and worship the LORD and listen to his voice, and if you do not rebel against the LORD's commands, then both you and your king will show that you recognize the LORD as your God. ¹⁵But if you rebel against the LORD's commands and refuse to listen to him, then his hand will be as heavy upon you as it was upon your ancestors.

¹⁶"Now stand here and see the great thing the LORD is about to do. ¹⁷You know that it does not rain at this time of the year during the wheat harvest. I will ask the LORD to send thunder and rain today. Then you will realize how wicked you have been in asking the LORD for a king!"

¹⁸So Samuel called to the LORD, and the LORD sent thunder and rain that day. And all the people were terrified of the LORD and of Samuel. ¹⁹"Pray to the LORD your God for us, or we will die!" they all said to Samuel. "For now we have added to our sins by asking for a king."

²⁰"Don't be afraid," Samuel reassured them. "You have certainly done wrong, but make sure now that you worship the LORD with all your heart, and don't turn your back on him. ²¹Don't go back to worshiping worthless idols that cannot help or rescue you—they are totally useless! ²²The LORD will not abandon his people, because that would dishonor his great name. For it has pleased the LORD to make you his very own people.

²³"As for me, I will certainly not sin against the LORD by ending my prayers for you. And I will continue to teach you what is good and right. ²⁴But be sure to fear the LORD and faithfully serve him. Think of all the wonderful things he has done for you. ²⁵But if you continue to sin, you and your king will be swept away."

Continued War with Philistia

13 Saul was thirty* years old when he became king, and he reigned for forty-two years.*

²Saul selected 3,000 special troops from the army of Israel and sent the rest of the men home. He took 2,000 of the chosen men with him to Micmash and the hill country of Bethel. The other 1,000 went with Saul's son Jonathan to Gibeah in the land of Benjamin.

³Soon after this, Jonathan attacked and defeated the garrison of Philistines at Geba. The news spread quickly among the Philistines. So Saul blew the ram's horn throughout the land, saying, "Hebrews, hear this! Rise up in revolt!" ⁴All Israel heard the news that Saul had destroyed the Philistine garrison at Geba and that the Philistines now hated the Israelites more than ever. So the entire Israelite army was summoned to join Saul at Gilgal.

⁵The Philistines mustered a mighty army of 3,000* chariots, 6,000 charioteers, and as many warriors as the grains of sand on the seashore! They camped at

---

12:8 Hebrew *When Jacob was.* The names "Jacob" and "Israel" are often interchanged throughout the Old Testament, referring sometimes to the individual patriarch and sometimes to the nation. **12:11a** Hebrew *Jerub-baal,* another name for Gideon; see Judg 6:32. **12:11b** Greek and Syriac versions read *Barak.* **12:11c** Greek and Syriac versions read *Samson.* **13:1a** As in a few Greek manuscripts; the number is missing in the Hebrew. **13:1b** Hebrew *reigned ... and two;* the number is incomplete in the Hebrew. Compare Acts 13:21. **13:5** As in Greek and Syriac versions; Hebrew reads *30,000.*

12:1-25 The reaffirmation of Saul's kingship at Gilgal (11:12-15) was the final step in his installation as king. The event was a fitting occasion for Samuel's farewell address as leader of Israel.

12:6-25 In 12:1-5, Samuel put himself on trial and was found innocent. Then, in 12:6-25, he put the nation on trial and found it guilty.

Micmash east of Beth-aven. ⁶The men of Israel saw what a tight spot they were in; and because they were hard pressed by the enemy, they tried to hide in caves, thickets, rocks, holes, and cisterns. ⁷Some of them crossed the Jordan River and escaped into the land of Gad and Gilead.

Saul's Disobedience and Samuel's Rebuke

Meanwhile, Saul stayed at Gilgal, and his men were trembling with fear. ⁸Saul waited there seven days for Samuel, as Samuel had instructed him earlier, but Samuel still didn't come. Saul realized that his troops were rapidly slipping away. ⁹So he demanded, "Bring me the burnt offering and the peace offerings!" And Saul sacrificed the burnt offering himself.

¹⁰Just as Saul was finishing with the burnt offering, Samuel arrived. Saul went out to meet and welcome him, ¹¹but Samuel said, "What is this you have done?"

Saul replied, "I saw my men scattering from me, and you didn't arrive when you said you would, and the Philistines are at Micmash ready for battle. ¹²So I said, 'The Philistines are ready to march against us at Gilgal, and I haven't even asked for the LORD's help!' So I felt compelled to offer the burnt offering myself before you came."

¹³"How foolish!" Samuel exclaimed. "You have not kept the command the LORD your God gave you. Had you kept it, the LORD would have established your kingdom over Israel forever. ¹⁴But now your kingdom must end, for the LORD has sought out a man after his own heart. The LORD has already appointed him to be the leader of his people, because you have not kept the LORD's command."

Israel's Military Disadvantage

¹⁵Samuel then left Gilgal and went on his way, but the rest of the troops went with Saul to meet the army. They went up from Gilgal to Gibeah in the land of Benjamin.* When Saul counted the men who were still with him, he found only 600 were left! ¹⁶Saul and Jonathan and the troops with them were staying at Geba in the land of Benjamin. The Philistines set up their camp at Micmash. ¹⁷Three raiding parties soon left the camp of the Philistines. One went north toward Ophrah in the land of Shual, ¹⁸another went west to Beth-horon, and the third moved toward the border above the valley of Zeboim near the wilderness.

¹⁹There were no blacksmiths in the land of Israel in those days. The Philistines wouldn't allow them for fear they would make swords and spears for the Hebrews. ²⁰So whenever the Israelites needed to sharpen their plowshares, picks, axes, or sickles,* they had to take them to a Philistine blacksmith. ²¹The charges were as follows: a quarter of an ounce* of silver for sharpening a plowshare or a pick, and an eighth of an ounce* for sharpening an ax or making the point of an ox goad. ²²So on the day of the battle none of the people of Israel had a sword or spear, except for Saul and Jonathan.

²³The pass at Micmash had meanwhile been secured by a contingent of the Philistine army.

Jonathan's Daring Plan

14 One day Jonathan said to his armor bearer, "Come on, let's go over to where the Philistines have their outpost." But Jonathan did not tell his father what he was doing.

²Meanwhile, Saul and his 600 men were camped on the outskirts of Gibeah, around the pomegranate tree* at Migron. ³Among Saul's men was Ahijah the priest, who was wearing the ephod, the priestly vest. Ahijah was the son of Ichabod's brother Ahitub, son of Phinehas, son of Eli, the priest of the LORD who had served at Shiloh.

No one realized that Jonathan had left the Israelite camp. ⁴To reach the Philistine outpost, Jonathan had to go down between two rocky cliffs that were called Bozez and Seneh. ⁵The cliff on the north was in front of Micmash, and the one on the south was in front of Geba. ⁶"Let's go across to the outpost of those pagans," Jonathan said to his armor bearer. "Perhaps the LORD will help us, for nothing can hinder the LORD. He can win a battle whether he has many warriors or only a few!"

⁷"Do what you think is best," the armor bearer replied. "I'm with you completely, whatever you decide."

⁸"All right, then," Jonathan told him. "We will cross over and let them see us. ⁹If they say to us, 'Stay where you are or we'll kill you,' then we will stop and not go up to them. ¹⁰But if they say, 'Come on up and fight,' then we will go up. That will be the LORD's sign that he will help us defeat them."

¹¹When the Philistines saw them coming, they shouted, "Look! The Hebrews are crawling out of their holes!" ¹²Then the men from the outpost shouted to Jonathan, "Come on up here, and we'll teach you a lesson!"

13:15 As in Greek version; Hebrew reads *Samuel then left Gilgal and went to Gibeah in the land of Benjamin.* **13:20** As in Greek version; Hebrew reads *or plowshares.* **13:21a** Hebrew *1 pim* [8 grams]. **13:21b** Hebrew *⅓ [of a shekel]* [4 grams]. **14:2** Or *around the rock of Rimmon;* compare Judg 20:45, 47; 21:13.

13:19-22 The Philistines had been keeping the Israelites unarmed by monopolizing the iron needed to make weapons. Iron technology had not existed long in Canaan; it might have been developed in the Aegean area, and metalworking skills were possibly introduced into Canaan through seafaring peoples, including the Philistines. This may hint at why the people hoped in a king with military prowess. Was Israel a truly independent nation? Had they really inherited this Promised Land? The battle was not even over, and it might explain why God felt rejected as they sought other help.

"Come on, climb right behind me," Jonathan said to his armor bearer, "for the LORD will help us defeat them!"

¹³So they climbed up using both hands and feet, and the Philistines fell before Jonathan, and his armor bearer killed those who came behind them. ¹⁴They killed some twenty men in all, and their bodies were scattered over about half an acre.*

¹⁵Suddenly, panic broke out in the Philistine army, both in the camp and in the field, including even the outposts and raiding parties. And just then an earthquake struck, and everyone was terrified.

Israel Defeats the Philistines

¹⁶Saul's lookouts in Gibeah of Benjamin saw a strange sight—the vast army of Philistines began to melt away in every direction.* ¹⁷"Call the roll and find out who's missing," Saul ordered. And when they checked, they found that Jonathan and his armor bearer were gone.

¹⁸Then Saul shouted to Ahijah, "Bring the ephod here!" For at that time Ahijah was wearing the ephod in front of the Israelites.* ¹⁹But while Saul was talking to the priest, the confusion in the Philistine camp grew louder and louder. So Saul said to the priest, "Never mind; let's get going!"*

²⁰Then Saul and all his men rushed out to the battle and found the Philistines killing each other. There was terrible confusion everywhere. ²¹Even the Hebrews who had previously gone over to the Philistine army revolted and joined in with Saul, Jonathan, and the rest of the Israelites. ²²Likewise, the men of Israel who were hiding in the hill country of Ephraim joined the chase when they saw the Philistines running away. ²³So the LORD saved Israel that day, and the battle continued to rage even beyond Beth-aven.

Saul's Foolish Oath

²⁴Now the men of Israel were pressed to exhaustion that day, because Saul had placed them under an oath, saying, "Let a curse fall on anyone who eats before evening—before I have full revenge on my enemies." So no one ate anything all day, ²⁵even though they had all found honeycomb on the ground in the forest. ²⁶They didn't dare touch the honey because they all feared the oath they had taken.

²⁷But Jonathan had not heard his father's command, and he dipped the end of his stick into a piece of honeycomb and ate the honey. After he had eaten it, he felt refreshed.* ²⁸But one of the men saw him and said, "Your father made the army take a strict oath that anyone who eats food today will be cursed. That is why everyone is weary and faint."

²⁹"My father has made trouble for us all!" Jonathan exclaimed. "A command like that only hurts us. See how refreshed I am now that I have eaten this little bit of honey. ³⁰If the men had been allowed to eat freely from the food they found among our enemies, think how many more Philistines we could have killed!"

³¹They chased and killed the Philistines all day from Micmash to Aijalon, growing more and more faint. ³²That evening they rushed for the battle plunder and butchered the sheep, goats, cattle, and calves, but they ate them without draining the blood. ³³Someone reported to Saul, "Look, the men are sinning against the LORD by eating meat that still has blood in it."

"That is very wrong," Saul said. "Find a large stone and roll it over here. ³⁴Then go out among the troops and tell them, 'Bring the cattle, sheep, and goats here to me. Kill them here, and drain the blood before you eat them. Do not sin against the LORD by eating meat with the blood still in it.'"

So that night all the troops brought their animals and slaughtered them there. ³⁵Then Saul built an altar to the LORD; it was the first of the altars he built to the LORD.

³⁶Then Saul said, "Let's chase the Philistines all night and plunder them until sunrise. Let's destroy every last one of them."

His men replied, "We'll do whatever you think is best."

But the priest said, "Let's ask God first."

³⁷So Saul asked God, "Should we go after the Philistines? Will you help us defeat them?" But God made no reply that day.

³⁸Then Saul said to the leaders, "Something's wrong! I want all my army commanders to come here. We must find out what sin was committed today. ³⁹I vow by the name of the LORD who rescued Israel that the sinner will surely die, even if it is my own son Jonathan!" But no one would tell him what the trouble was.

⁴⁰Then Saul said, "Jonathan and I will stand over here, and all of you stand over there."

And the people responded to Saul, "Whatever you think is best."

⁴¹Then Saul prayed, "O LORD, God of Israel, please show us who is guilty and who is innocent.*" Then they cast sacred lots, and Jonathan and Saul were

---

14:14 Hebrew *half a yoke;* a "yoke" was the amount of land plowed by a pair of yoked oxen in one day. **14:16** As in Greek version; Hebrew reads *they went and there.* **14:18** As in some Greek manuscripts; Hebrew reads *"Bring the Ark of God." For at that time the Ark of God was with the Israelites.* **14:19** Hebrew *Withdraw your hand.* **14:27** Or *his eyes brightened;* similarly in 14:29. **14:41** Greek version adds *If the fault is with me or my son Jonathan, respond with Urim; but if the men of Israel are at fault, respond with Thummim.*

14:24, 39 Saul's vows here sound like Jephthah's vow in Judges 11, but Saul's vows are even more problematic. Saul now knew that Jonathan could die and still he made the second vow (14:39). As Saul's son, Jonathan was the successor to the throne and could have seemed like a current threat. Was Saul speaking this vow in ignorance or intentionally? Was Saul attempting to keep the kingship at any cost, trying to control the situation he has already lost (13:8-9, 13-14)?

chosen as the guilty ones, and the people were declared innocent.

⁴²Then Saul said, "Now cast lots again and choose between me and Jonathan." And Jonathan was shown to be the guilty one.

⁴³"Tell me what you have done," Saul demanded of Jonathan.

"I tasted a little honey," Jonathan admitted. "It was only a little bit on the end of my stick. Does that deserve death?"

⁴⁴"Yes, Jonathan," Saul said, "you must die! May God strike me and even kill me if you do not die for this."

⁴⁵But the people broke in and said to Saul, "Jonathan has won this great victory for Israel. Should he die? Far from it! As surely as the LORD lives, not one hair on his head will be touched, for God helped him do a great deed today." So the people rescued Jonathan, and he was not put to death.

⁴⁶Then Saul called back the army from chasing the Philistines, and the Philistines returned home.

Saul's Military Successes

⁴⁷Now when Saul had secured his grasp on Israel's throne, he fought against his enemies in every direction—against Moab, Ammon, Edom, the kings of Zobah, and the Philistines. And wherever he turned, he was victorious.* ⁴⁸He performed great deeds and conquered the Amalekites, saving Israel from all those who had plundered them.

⁴⁹Saul's sons included Jonathan, Ishbosheth,* and Malkishua. He also had two daughters: Merab, who was older, and Michal. ⁵⁰Saul's wife was Ahinoam, the daughter of Ahimaaz. The commander of Saul's army was Abner, the son of Saul's uncle Ner. ⁵¹Saul's father, Kish, and Abner's father, Ner, were both sons of Abiel.

⁵²The Israelites fought constantly with the Philistines throughout Saul's lifetime. So whenever Saul observed a young man who was brave and strong, he drafted him into his army.

Saul Defeats the Amalekites

15 One day Samuel said to Saul, "It was the LORD who told me to anoint you as king of his people, Israel. Now listen to this message from the LORD! ²This is what the LORD of Heaven's Armies has declared: I have decided to settle accounts with the nation of Amalek for opposing Israel when they came from Egypt. ³Now go and completely destroy* the entire Amalekite nation—men, women, children, babies, cattle, sheep, goats, camels, and donkeys."

⁴So Saul mobilized his army at Telaim. There were 200,000 soldiers from Israel and 10,000 men from Judah. ⁵Then Saul and his army went to a town of the Amalekites and lay in wait in the valley. ⁶Saul sent this warning to the Kenites: "Move away from where the Amalekites live, or you will die with them. For you showed kindness to all the people of Israel when they came up from Egypt." So the Kenites packed up and left.

⁷Then Saul slaughtered the Amalekites from Havilah all the way to Shur, east of Egypt. ⁸He captured Agag, the Amalekite king, but completely destroyed everyone else. ⁹Saul and his men spared Agag's life and kept the best of the sheep and goats, the cattle, the fat calves, and the lambs—everything, in fact, that appealed to them. They destroyed only what was worthless or of poor quality.

The LORD Rejects Saul

¹⁰Then the LORD said to Samuel, ¹¹"I am sorry that I ever made Saul king, for he has not been loyal to me and has refused to obey my command." Samuel was so deeply moved when he heard this that he cried out to the LORD all night.

¹²Early the next morning Samuel went to find Saul. Someone told him, "Saul went to the town of Carmel to set up a monument to himself; then he went on to Gilgal."

¹³When Samuel finally found him, Saul greeted him cheerfully. "May the LORD bless you," he said. "I have carried out the LORD's command!"

¹⁴"Then what is all the bleating of sheep and goats and the lowing of cattle I hear?" Samuel demanded.

¹⁵"It's true that the army spared the best of the sheep, goats, and cattle," Saul admitted. "But they are going to sacrifice them to the LORD your God. We have destroyed everything else."

¹⁶Then Samuel said to Saul, "Stop! Listen to what the LORD told me last night!"

"What did he tell you?" Saul asked.

¹⁷And Samuel told him, "Although you may think little of yourself, are you not the leader of the tribes

---

14:47 As in Greek version; Hebrew reads *he acted wickedly*. **14:49** Hebrew *Ishvi*, a variant name for Ishbosheth; also known as Esh-baal. **15:3** The Hebrew term used here refers to the complete consecration of things or people to the LORD, either by destroying them or by giving them as an offering; also in 15:8, 9, 15, 18, 20, 21.

14:45-47 Fortunately, the people came to Jonathan's rescue. Aware of God's blessing on the real hero of the day, the people were wiser than their king. They made the *third* oath in this section, invoking the name of Yahweh and opposing Saul. They intervened and mediated when Saul wouldn't. Thankfully, God heard this vow and honored it, but Saul's vows are the only oaths in the whole Old Testament made in Yahweh's name yet not fulfilled. Not only this, but God had refused to talk to Saul earlier as well (14:37). We can be thankful that God knows our hearts and not just what comes out of our mouths (16:7). Still, we can and should speak the truth (Matthew 5:33-37).

15:13 Saul apparently thought his actions were justified (15:15), even though he had failed to follow God's words exactly (15:3). Samuel, however, cut through Saul's pretense (15:17-19) and carried out God's command himself (15:32-33).

of Israel? The LORD has anointed you king of Israel. ¹⁸And the LORD sent you on a mission and told you, 'Go and completely destroy the sinners, the Amalekites, until they are all dead.' ¹⁹Why haven't you obeyed the LORD? Why did you rush for the plunder and do what was evil in the LORD's sight?"

²⁰"But I did obey the LORD," Saul insisted. "I carried out the mission he gave me. I brought back King Agag, but I destroyed everyone else. ²¹Then my troops brought in the best of the sheep, goats, cattle, and plunder to sacrifice to the LORD your God in Gilgal."

²²But Samuel replied,

"What is more pleasing to the LORD:
   your burnt offerings and sacrifices
   or your obedience to his voice?
Listen! Obedience is better than sacrifice,
   and submission is better than offering the fat
      of rams.
²³ Rebellion is as sinful as witchcraft,
   and stubbornness as bad as worshiping idols.
So because you have rejected the command of
      the LORD,
   he has rejected you as king."

Saul Pleads for Forgiveness

²⁴Then Saul admitted to Samuel, "Yes, I have sinned. I have disobeyed your instructions and the LORD's command, for I was afraid of the people and did what they demanded. ²⁵But now, please forgive my sin and come back with me so that I may worship the LORD."

²⁶But Samuel replied, "I will not go back with you! Since you have rejected the LORD's command, he has rejected you as king of Israel."

²⁷As Samuel turned to go, Saul tried to hold him back and tore the hem of his robe. ²⁸And Samuel said to him, "The LORD has torn the kingdom of Israel from you today and has given it to someone else— one who is better than you. ²⁹And he who is the Glory of Israel will not lie, nor will he change his mind, for he is not human that he should change his mind!"

³⁰Then Saul pleaded again, "I know I have sinned. But please, at least honor me before the elders of my people and before Israel by coming back with me so that I may worship the LORD your God." ³¹So Samuel finally agreed and went back with him, and Saul worshiped the LORD.

Samuel Executes King Agag

³²Then Samuel said, "Bring King Agag to me." Agag arrived full of hope, for he thought, "Surely the worst is over, and I have been spared!"* ³³But Samuel said, "As your sword has killed the sons of many mothers, now your mother will be childless." And Samuel cut Agag to pieces before the LORD at Gilgal.

³⁴Then Samuel went home to Ramah, and Saul returned to his house at Gibeah of Saul. ³⁵Samuel never went to meet with Saul again, but he mourned constantly for him. And the LORD was sorry he had ever made Saul king of Israel.

Samuel Anoints David as King

16 Now the LORD said to Samuel, "You have mourned long enough for Saul. I have rejected him as king of Israel, so fill your flask with olive oil and go to Bethlehem. Find a man named Jesse who lives there, for I have selected one of his sons to be my king."

²But Samuel asked, "How can I do that? If Saul hears about it, he will kill me."

"Take a heifer with you," the LORD replied, "and say that you have come to make a sacrifice to the LORD. ³Invite Jesse to the sacrifice, and I will show you which of his sons to anoint for me."

⁴So Samuel did as the LORD instructed. When he arrived at Bethlehem, the elders of the town came trembling to meet him. "What's wrong?" they asked. "Do you come in peace?"

⁵"Yes," Samuel replied. "I have come to sacrifice to the LORD. Purify yourselves and come with me to the sacrifice." Then Samuel performed the purification rite for Jesse and his sons and invited them to the sacrifice, too.

⁶When they arrived, Samuel took one look at Eliab and thought, "Surely this is the LORD's anointed!"

⁷But the LORD said to Samuel, "Don't judge by his appearance or height, for I have rejected him. The LORD doesn't see things the way you see them. People judge by outward appearance, but the LORD looks at the heart."

15:32 Dead Sea Scrolls and Greek version read *Agag arrived hesitantly, for he thought, "Surely this is the bitterness of death."*

15:22 God values obedience much more than ritual (see Psalm 40:6; Hosea 6:6; Matthew 12:7).

15:23 Rebellion and stubbornness, sins of the heart, are as bad as the sinful practices of idolatrous pagans. Saul committed both of these sins. Scripture also condemns witchcraft (see Deuteronomy 18:10), and Saul would later consult a medium (1 Samuel 28:3-25).

16:1-23 David was Saul's replacement. There are a few striking similarities between the two: Samuel anointed both, and neither was pursuing the position. Both were unlikely candidates (Saul was from the smallest tribe; David was the youngest son). Both were impressive in appearance (9:2; 16:12). And the Spirit came mightily on them as each was anointed king (10:10; 11:6; 16:13). The key difference was that David was "a man after [God's] own heart" (13:14; see also 16:7), while Saul was not.

16:6-7 Eliab impressed Samuel with his appearance and height, just like Saul had (see 9:2; 10:23). But God had a different person in mind to be Israel's king. As Samuel was reminded here, God can see past outward appearances to what is in our hearts. God can give a new heart (10:9), touch hearts (10:26), and peer into the motivations of the heart (Psalm 139:1). God sees what people cannot see—a person's true character.

⁸Then Jesse told his son Abinadab to step forward and walk in front of Samuel. But Samuel said, "This is not the one the LORD has chosen." ⁹Next Jesse summoned Shimea,* but Samuel said, "Neither is this the one the LORD has chosen." ¹⁰In the same way all seven of Jesse's sons were presented to Samuel. But Samuel said to Jesse, "The LORD has not chosen any of these." ¹¹Then Samuel asked, "Are these all the sons you have?"

"There is still the youngest," Jesse replied. "But he's out in the fields watching the sheep and goats."

"Send for him at once," Samuel said. "We will not sit down to eat until he arrives."

¹²So Jesse sent for him. He was dark and handsome, with beautiful eyes.

And the LORD said, "This is the one; anoint him."

¹³So as David stood there among his brothers, Samuel took the flask of olive oil he had brought and anointed David with the oil. And the Spirit of the LORD came powerfully upon David from that day on. Then Samuel returned to Ramah.

David Serves in Saul's Court

¹⁴Now the Spirit of the LORD had left Saul, and the LORD sent a tormenting spirit* that filled him with depression and fear.

¹⁵Some of Saul's servants said to him, "A tormenting spirit from God is troubling you. ¹⁶Let us find a good musician to play the harp whenever the tormenting spirit troubles you. He will play soothing music, and you will soon be well again."

¹⁷"All right," Saul said. "Find me someone who plays well, and bring him here."

¹⁸One of the servants said to Saul, "One of Jesse's sons from Bethlehem is a talented harp player. Not only that—he is a brave warrior, a man of war, and has good judgment. He is also a fine-looking young man, and the LORD is with him."

¹⁹So Saul sent messengers to Jesse to say, "Send me your son David, the shepherd." ²⁰Jesse responded by sending David to Saul, along with a young goat, a donkey loaded with bread, and a wineskin full of wine.

²¹So David went to Saul and began serving him. Saul loved David very much, and David became his armor bearer.

²²Then Saul sent word to Jesse asking, "Please let David remain in my service, for I am very pleased with him."

²³And whenever the tormenting spirit from God troubled Saul, David would play the harp. Then Saul would feel better, and the tormenting spirit would go away.

Goliath Challenges the Israelites

17 The Philistines now mustered their army for battle and camped between Socoh in Judah and Azekah at Ephes-dammim. ²Saul countered by gathering his Israelite troops near the valley of Elah. ³So the Philistines and Israelites faced each other on opposite hills, with the valley between them.

⁴Then Goliath, a Philistine champion from Gath, came out of the Philistine ranks to face the forces of Israel. He was over nine feet* tall! ⁵He wore a bronze helmet, and his bronze coat of mail weighed 125 pounds.* ⁶He also wore bronze leg armor, and he carried a bronze javelin on his shoulder. ⁷The shaft of his spear was as heavy and thick as a weaver's beam, tipped with an iron spearhead that weighed 15 pounds.* His armor bearer walked ahead of him carrying a shield.

⁸Goliath stood and shouted a taunt across to the Israelites. "Why are you all coming out to fight?" he called. "I am the Philistine champion, but you are only the servants of Saul. Choose one man to come down here and fight me! ⁹If he kills me, then we will be your slaves. But if I kill him, you will be our slaves! ¹⁰I defy the armies of Israel today! Send me a man who will fight me!" ¹¹When Saul and the Israelites heard this, they were terrified and deeply shaken.

Jesse Sends David to Saul's Camp

¹²Now David was the son of a man named Jesse, an Ephrathite from Bethlehem in the land of Judah. Jesse was an old man at that time, and he had eight sons. ¹³Jesse's three oldest sons—Eliab, Abinadab, and Shimea*—had already joined Saul's army to fight the Philistines. ¹⁴David was the youngest son. David's three oldest brothers stayed with Saul's army, ¹⁵but David went back and forth so he could help his father with the sheep in Bethlehem.

¹⁶For forty days, every morning and evening, the Philistine champion strutted in front of the Israelite army.

¹⁷One day Jesse said to David, "Take this basket* of roasted grain and these ten loaves of bread, and carry them quickly to your brothers. ¹⁸And give these ten cuts of cheese to their captain. See how your brothers are getting along, and bring back a report on how they are doing.*" ¹⁹David's brothers were with Saul and the Israelite army at the valley of Elah, fighting against the Philistines.

²⁰So David left the sheep with another shepherd and set out early the next morning with the gifts, as Jesse had directed him. He arrived at the camp just as the Israelite army was leaving for the battlefield with shouts and battle cries. ²¹Soon the Israelite and Philistine forces stood facing each other, army

---

16:9 Hebrew *Shammah,* a variant spelling of Shimea; compare 1 Chr 2:13; 20:7.   **16:14** Or *an evil spirit;* also in 16:15, 16, 23.   **17:4** Hebrew *6 cubits and 1 span* [which totals about 9.75 feet or 3 meters]; Dead Sea Scrolls and Greek version read *4 cubits and 1 span* [which totals about 6.75 feet or 2 meters].   **17:5** Hebrew *5,000 shekels* [57 kilograms].   **17:7** Hebrew *600 shekels* [6.8 kilograms].   **17:13** Hebrew *Shammah,* a variant spelling of Shimea; compare 1 Chr 2:13; 20:7.   **17:17** Hebrew *ephah* [20 quarts or 22 liters].   **17:18** Hebrew *and take their pledge.*

against army. ²²David left his things with the keeper of supplies and hurried out to the ranks to greet his brothers. ²³As he was talking with them, Goliath, the Philistine champion from Gath, came out from the Philistine ranks. Then David heard him shout his usual taunt to the army of Israel.

²⁴As soon as the Israelite army saw him, they began to run away in fright. ²⁵"Have you seen the giant?" the men asked. "He comes out each day to defy Israel. The king has offered a huge reward to anyone who kills him. He will give that man one of his daughters for a wife, and the man's entire family will be exempted from paying taxes!"

²⁶David asked the soldiers standing nearby, "What will a man get for killing this Philistine and ending his defiance of Israel? Who is this pagan Philistine anyway, that he is allowed to defy the armies of the living God?"

²⁷And these men gave David the same reply. They said, "Yes, that is the reward for killing him."

²⁸But when David's oldest brother, Eliab, heard David talking to the men, he was angry. "What are you doing around here anyway?" he demanded. "What about those few sheep you're supposed to be taking care of? I know about your pride and deceit. You just want to see the battle!"

²⁹"What have I done now?" David replied. "I was only asking a question!" ³⁰He walked over to some others and asked them the same thing and received the same answer. ³¹Then David's question was reported to King Saul, and the king sent for him.

David Kills Goliath

³²"Don't worry about this Philistine," David told Saul. "I'll go fight him!"

³³"Don't be ridiculous!" Saul replied. "There's no way you can fight this Philistine and possibly win! You're only a boy, and he's been a man of war since his youth."

³⁴But David persisted. "I have been taking care of my father's sheep and goats," he said. "When a lion or a bear comes to steal a lamb from the flock, ³⁵I go after it with a club and rescue the lamb from its mouth. If the animal turns on me, I catch it by the jaw and club it to death. ³⁶I have done this to both lions and bears, and I'll do it to this pagan Philistine, too, for he has defied the armies of the living God! ³⁷The LORD who rescued me from the claws of the lion and the bear will rescue me from this Philistine!"

Saul finally consented. "All right, go ahead," he said. "And may the LORD be with you!"

17:52 As in some Greek manuscripts; Hebrew reads *a valley*.

³⁸Then Saul gave David his own armor—a bronze helmet and a coat of mail. ³⁹David put it on, strapped the sword over it, and took a step or two to see what it was like, for he had never worn such things before.

"I can't go in these," he protested to Saul. "I'm not used to them." So David took them off again. ⁴⁰He picked up five smooth stones from a stream and put them into his shepherd's bag. Then, armed only with his shepherd's staff and sling, he started across the valley to fight the Philistine.

⁴¹Goliath walked out toward David with his shield bearer ahead of him, ⁴²sneering in contempt at this ruddy-faced boy. ⁴³"Am I a dog," he roared at David, "that you come at me with a stick?" And he cursed David by the names of his gods. ⁴⁴"Come over here, and I'll give your flesh to the birds and wild animals!" Goliath yelled.

⁴⁵David replied to the Philistine, "You come to me with sword, spear, and javelin, but I come to you in the name of the LORD of Heaven's Armies—the God of the armies of Israel, whom you have defied. ⁴⁶Today the LORD will conquer you, and I will kill you and cut off your head. And then I will give the dead bodies of your men to the birds and wild animals, and the whole world will know that there is a God in Israel! ⁴⁷And everyone assembled here will know that the LORD rescues his people, but not with sword and spear. This is the LORD's battle, and he will give you to us!"

⁴⁸As Goliath moved closer to attack, David quickly ran out to meet him. ⁴⁹Reaching into his shepherd's bag and taking out a stone, he hurled it with his sling and hit the Philistine in the forehead. The stone sank in, and Goliath stumbled and fell face down on the ground.

⁵⁰So David triumphed over the Philistine with only a sling and a stone, for he had no sword. ⁵¹Then David ran over and pulled Goliath's sword from its sheath. David used it to kill him and cut off his head.

Israel Routs the Philistines

When the Philistines saw that their champion was dead, they turned and ran. ⁵²Then the men of Israel and Judah gave a great shout of triumph and rushed after the Philistines, chasing them as far as Gath* and the gates of Ekron. The bodies of the dead and wounded Philistines were strewn all along the road from Shaaraim, as far as Gath and Ekron. ⁵³Then the Israelite army returned and plundered the deserted Philistine camp. ⁵⁴(David took the Philistine's head to Jerusalem, but he stored the man's armor in his own tent.)

⁵⁵As Saul watched David go out to fight the Philistine, he asked Abner, the commander of his army, "Abner, whose son is this young man?"

17:48-52 A sling was a leather pouch attached to two leather straps. When the sling containing a stone was whirled rapidly, one of the straps could be released, sending the stone toward its target. As a shepherd, David probably had become deadly accurate with a sling, but warriors used the sling as well (Judges 20:16). We might read this as a classic underdog tale. Still, in ancient warfare, the advantage of the sling bearer's agility against an opponent weighed down by heavy armor made sense. Some saw David's actions as foolish (1 Samuel 17:33), but they showed wisdom, and God exalted David.

"I really don't know," Abner declared. ⁵⁶"Well, find out who he is!" the king told him. ⁵⁷As soon as David returned from killing Goliath, Abner brought him to Saul with the Philistine's head still in his hand. ⁵⁸"Tell me about your father, young man," Saul said.

And David replied, "His name is Jesse, and we live in Bethlehem."

Saul Becomes Jealous of David

18 After David had finished talking with Saul, he met Jonathan, the king's son. There was an immediate bond between them, for Jonathan loved David. ²From that day on Saul kept David with him and wouldn't let him return home. ³And Jonathan made a solemn pact with David, because he loved him as he loved himself. ⁴Jonathan sealed the pact by taking off his robe and giving it to David, together with his tunic, sword, bow, and belt.

⁵Whatever Saul asked David to do, David did it successfully. So Saul made him a commander over the men of war, an appointment that was welcomed by the people and Saul's officers alike.

⁶When the victorious Israelite army was returning home after David had killed the Philistine, women from all the towns of Israel came out to meet King Saul. They sang and danced for joy with tambourines and cymbals.* ⁷This was their song:

"Saul has killed his thousands,
   and David his ten thousands!"

18:6 The type of instrument represented by the word *cymbals* is uncertain.

Come Close — COMPETING: CELEBRATING OUR TEAM

SCRIPTURE CONNECTION: 1 SAMUEL 17:1–20:42

There she is again on your social media. *She's so pretty*, you think. *It looks like her children obey her*, you continue as you look around your kitchen, dishes strewn across countertops.

I have a tendency to compare my messy life to everyone else's picture-perfect ones. It only takes a slip of a finger. One scroll sends my mind reeling, not in high praise of my friends' lives but in a lower view of my own.

Cut to a new scene. Saul and David fight a common enemy, but David rises to stardom. Women sing in the streets, "Saul has killed his thousands, and David his ten thousands!" (18:7).

Saul seethes.

"They credit David with ten thousands," he says, "and me with only thousands." And from that time on, Saul keeps a close eye on David. In our day, Saul would follow David's social media posts.

It is Saul's thoughts that sent him spiraling. Thoughts of competing with David over celebrating his victory.

Meanwhile, another man bridges the two men he loves and models the right response to David's success. Jonathan, son of Saul and friend to David, could have envied David's newfound celebrity status and fought for his own. Instead, he celebrated rather than competing. Jonathan knew he and his friend were on the same team.

As daughters of God, we can choose celebration over competition, joy over judgment. We can choose capturing, not coddling, jealous thoughts. We are, after all, on the same team, public image and all.

REFLECT "This made Saul very angry. 'What's this?' he said. 'They credit David with ten thousands and me with only thousands. Next they'll be making him their king!'" 1 SAMUEL 18:8

Lord, help me see that I am on the same team as my sisters. Help me celebrate, not compete. Amen.

CONSIDER "If love often comes from a place of safety, then judgment often comes from a place of fear." LISA WHITTLE, *Jesus Over Everything*

> As daughters of God, we can choose celebration over competition, joy over judgment.

WHITNEY PUTNAM is the senior director of women's events and marketing at New Life Ministries. She is an overall joy-chaser and is often found dancing in her kitchen.

⁸This made Saul very angry. "What's this?" he said. "They credit David with ten thousands and me with only thousands. Next they'll be making him their king!" ⁹So from that time on Saul kept a jealous eye on David.

¹⁰The very next day a tormenting spirit* from God overwhelmed Saul, and he began to rave in his house like a madman. David was playing the harp, as he did each day. But Saul had a spear in his hand, ¹¹and he suddenly hurled it at David, intending to pin him to the wall. But David escaped him twice.

¹²Saul was then afraid of David, for the LORD was with David and had turned away from Saul. ¹³Finally, Saul sent him away and appointed him commander over 1,000 men, and David faithfully led his troops into battle.

¹⁴David continued to succeed in everything he did, for the LORD was with him. ¹⁵When Saul recognized this, he became even more afraid of him. ¹⁶But all Israel and Judah loved David because he was so successful at leading his troops into battle.

David Marries Saul's Daughter

¹⁷One day Saul said to David, "I am ready to give you my older daughter, Merab, as your wife. But first you must prove yourself to be a real warrior by fighting the LORD's battles." For Saul thought, "I'll send him out against the Philistines and let them kill him rather than doing it myself."

¹⁸"Who am I, and what is my family in Israel that I should be the king's son-in-law?" David exclaimed. "My father's family is nothing!" ¹⁹So* when the time came for Saul to give his daughter Merab in marriage to David, he gave her instead to Adriel, a man from Meholah.

²⁰In the meantime, Saul's daughter Michal had fallen in love with David, and Saul was delighted when he heard about it. ²¹"Here's another chance to see him killed by the Philistines!" Saul said to himself. But to David he said, "Today you have a second chance to become my son-in-law!"

²²Then Saul told his men to say to David, "The king really likes you, and so do we. Why don't you accept the king's offer and become his son-in-law?"

²³When Saul's men said these things to David, he replied, "How can a poor man from a humble family afford the bride price for the daughter of a king?"

²⁴When Saul's men reported this back to the king, ²⁵he told them, "Tell David that all I want for the bride price is 100 Philistine foreskins! Vengeance on my enemies is all I really want." But what Saul had in mind was that David would be killed in the fight.

²⁶David was delighted to accept the offer. Before the time limit expired, ²⁷he and his men went out and killed 200 Philistines. Then David fulfilled the king's requirement by presenting all their foreskins to him. So Saul gave his daughter Michal to David to be his wife.

²⁸When Saul realized that the LORD was with David and how much his daughter Michal loved him, ²⁹Saul became even more afraid of him, and he remained David's enemy for the rest of his life.

³⁰Every time the commanders of the Philistines attacked, David was more successful against them than all the rest of Saul's officers. So David's name became very famous.

Saul Tries to Kill David

19 Saul now urged his servants and his son Jonathan to assassinate David. But Jonathan, because of his strong affection for David, ²told him what his father was planning. "Tomorrow morning," he warned him, "you must find a hiding place out in the fields. ³I'll ask my father to go out there with me, and I'll talk to him about you. Then I'll tell you everything I can find out."

⁴The next morning Jonathan spoke with his father about David, saying many good things about him. "The king must not sin against his servant David," Jonathan said. "He's never done anything to harm you. He has always helped you in any way he could. ⁵Have you forgotten about the time he risked his life to kill the Philistine giant and how the LORD brought a great victory to all Israel as a result? You were certainly happy about it then. Why should you murder an innocent man like David? There is no reason for it at all!"

⁶So Saul listened to Jonathan and vowed, "As surely as the LORD lives, David will not be killed."

⁷Afterward Jonathan called David and told him what had happened. Then he brought David to Saul, and David served in the court as before.

⁸War broke out again after that, and David led his troops against the Philistines. He attacked them with such fury that they all ran away.

18:10 Or *an evil spirit.* **18:19** Or *But.*

18:20-30 Saul had promised his daughter to anyone who could slay Goliath (17:25; compare with Joshua 15:16; Judges 1:12), but he tacked on additional risks for David (see also 1 Samuel 18:21, 25). Political marriages happened often. Sometimes, as we know from folktales, they work as traps for men and women alike. Saul had devious plans in mind when offering Merab and Michal, as he continued his attempt to hold on to being king. Lack of control over a situation or fear that something may be taken away from us can lead us to make choices we regret.

19:6 Violating a vow was a serious offense against God (see Numbers 30:2; Deuteronomy 23:21-23; Ecclesiastes 5:4-5). But Saul soon disregarded his promise and again sought to kill David (1 Samuel 19:9–20:3).

19:1-18 Siblings Jonathan (19:1-7) and Michal (19:11-18) saved David from their father and undermined their father's plans to eliminate him. Thus, Saul's royal family members played a significant role in David's rise, though David did not usurp Saul's throne.

⁹But one day when Saul was sitting at home, with spear in hand, the tormenting spirit* from the LORD suddenly came upon him again. As David played his harp, ¹⁰Saul hurled his spear at David. But David dodged out of the way, and leaving the spear stuck in the wall, he fled and escaped into the night.

Michal Saves David's Life

¹¹Then Saul sent troops to watch David's house. They were told to kill David when he came out the next morning. But Michal, David's wife, warned him, "If you don't escape tonight, you will be dead by morning." ¹²So she helped him climb out through a window, and he fled and escaped. ¹³Then she took an idol* and put it in his bed, covered it with blankets, and put a cushion of goat's hair at its head.

¹⁴When the troops came to arrest David, she told them he was sick and couldn't get out of bed.

¹⁵But Saul sent the troops back to get David. He ordered, "Bring him to me in his bed so I can kill him!" ¹⁶But when they came to carry David out, they discovered that it was only an idol in the bed with a cushion of goat's hair at its head.

¹⁷"Why have you betrayed me like this and let my enemy escape?" Saul demanded of Michal.

"I had to," Michal replied. "He threatened to kill me if I didn't help him."

¹⁸So David escaped and went to Ramah to see Samuel, and he told him all that Saul had done to him. Then Samuel took David with him to live at Naioth. ¹⁹When the report reached Saul that David was at Naioth in Ramah, ²⁰he sent troops to capture him. But when they arrived and saw Samuel leading a group of prophets who were prophesying, the Spirit of God came upon Saul's men, and they also began to prophesy. ²¹When Saul heard what had happened, he sent other troops, but they, too, prophesied! The same thing happened a third time. ²²Finally, Saul himself went to Ramah and arrived at the great well in Secu. "Where are Samuel and David?" he demanded.

"They are at Naioth in Ramah," someone told him.

²³But on the way to Naioth in Ramah the Spirit of God came even upon Saul, and he, too, began to prophesy all the way to Naioth! ²⁴He tore off his clothes and lay naked on the ground all day and all night, prophesying in the presence of Samuel. The people who were watching exclaimed, "What? Is even Saul a prophet?"

Jonathan Helps David

20 David now fled from Naioth in Ramah and found Jonathan. "What have I done?" he exclaimed. "What is my crime? How have I offended your father that he is so determined to kill me?"

²"That's not true!" Jonathan protested. "You're not going to die. He always tells me everything he's going to do, even the little things. I know my father wouldn't hide something like this from me. It just isn't so!"

³Then David took an oath before Jonathan and said, "Your father knows perfectly well about our friendship, so he has said to himself, 'I won't tell Jonathan—why should I hurt him?' But I swear to you that I am only a step away from death! I swear it by the LORD and by your own soul!"

⁴"Tell me what I can do to help you," Jonathan exclaimed.

⁵David replied, "Tomorrow we celebrate the new moon festival. I've always eaten with the king on this occasion, but tomorrow I'll hide in the field and stay there until the evening of the third day. ⁶If your father asks where I am, tell him I asked permission to go home to Bethlehem for an annual family sacrifice. ⁷If he says, 'Fine!' you will know all is well. But if he is angry and loses his temper, you will know he is determined to kill me. ⁸Show me this loyalty as my sworn friend—for we made a solemn pact before the LORD—or kill me yourself if I have sinned against your father. But please don't betray me to him!"

⁹"Never!" Jonathan exclaimed. "You know that if I had the slightest notion my father was planning to kill you, I would tell you at once."

¹⁰Then David asked, "How will I know whether or not your father is angry?"

¹¹"Come out to the field with me," Jonathan replied. And they went out there together. ¹²Then Jonathan told David, "I promise by the LORD, the God of Israel, that by this time tomorrow, or the next day at the latest, I will talk to my father and let you know at once how he feels about you. If he speaks favorably about you, I will let you know. ¹³But if he is angry and wants you killed, may the LORD strike me and even kill me if I don't warn you so you can escape and live. May the LORD be with you as he used to be with my father. ¹⁴And may you treat me with the faithful love of the LORD as long as I live. But if I die, ¹⁵treat my family with this faithful love, even when the LORD destroys all your enemies from the face of the earth."

19:9 Or *evil spirit.* 19:13 Hebrew *teraphim;* also in 19:16.

19:13 *Teraphim* were household idols (see Genesis 31:30; Judges 17:5; 2 Kings 23:24). An idol's presence in David and Michal's home might show the pervasive influence of idol worship among the Israelites. Perhaps the idol belonged to Michal, but it appears David did not object to its presence. (Compare this to Rachel's theft of her father's household idols in Genesis 31:19.)
20:8 The Hebrew word translated here as "loyalty" (Hebrew *khesed*) means faithfulness between covenant partners (see also 18:3; 20:16).
20:14-16 It was reasonable for Jonathan to be concerned that David might kill Saul's descendants who could claim the throne. After all, Jonathan was the biological heir to Saul's throne. Jonathan was reminding David to keep his commitment. Later, Saul made a similar request of David (24:21).

¹⁶So Jonathan made a solemn pact with David,* saying, "May the LORD destroy all your enemies!" ¹⁷And Jonathan made David reaffirm his vow of friendship again, for Jonathan loved David as he loved himself.

¹⁸Then Jonathan said, "Tomorrow we celebrate the new moon festival. You will be missed when your place at the table is empty. ¹⁹The day after tomorrow, toward evening, go to the place where you hid before, and wait there by the stone pile.* ²⁰I will come out and shoot three arrows to the side of the stone pile as though I were shooting at a target. ²¹Then I will send a boy to bring the arrows back. If you hear me tell him, 'They're on this side,' then you will know, as surely as the LORD lives, that all is well, and there is no trouble. ²²But if I tell him, 'Go farther—the arrows are still ahead of you,' then it will mean that you must leave immediately, for the LORD is sending you away. ²³And may the LORD make us keep our promises to each other, for he has witnessed them."

²⁴So David hid himself in the field, and when the new moon festival began, the king sat down to eat. ²⁵He sat at his usual place against the wall, with Jonathan sitting opposite him* and Abner beside him. But David's place was empty. ²⁶Saul didn't say anything about it that day, for he said to himself, "Something must have made David ceremonially unclean." ²⁷But when David's place was empty again the next day, Saul asked Jonathan, "Why hasn't the son of Jesse been here for the meal either yesterday or today?"

²⁸Jonathan replied, "David earnestly asked me if he could go to Bethlehem. ²⁹He said, 'Please let me go, for we are having a family sacrifice. My brother demanded that I be there. So please let me get away to see my brothers.' That's why he isn't here at the king's table."

³⁰Saul boiled with rage at Jonathan. "You stupid son of a whore!"* he swore at him. "Do you think I don't know that you want him to be king in your place, shaming yourself and your mother? ³¹As long as that son of Jesse is alive, you'll never be king. Now go and get him so I can kill him!"

³²"But why should he be put to death?" Jonathan asked his father. "What has he done?" ³³Then Saul hurled his spear at Jonathan, intending to kill him. So at last Jonathan realized that his father was really determined to kill David.

³⁴Jonathan left the table in fierce anger and refused to eat on that second day of the festival, for he was crushed by his father's shameful behavior toward David.

³⁵The next morning, as agreed, Jonathan went out into the field and took a young boy with him to gather his arrows. ³⁶"Start running," he told the boy, "so you can find the arrows as I shoot them." So the boy ran, and Jonathan shot an arrow beyond him. ³⁷When the boy had almost reached the arrow, Jonathan shouted, "The arrow is still ahead of you. ³⁸Hurry, hurry, don't wait." So the boy quickly gathered up the arrows and ran back to his master. ³⁹He, of course, suspected nothing; only Jonathan and David understood the signal. ⁴⁰Then Jonathan gave his bow and arrows to the boy and told him to take them back to town.

⁴¹As soon as the boy was gone, David came out from where he had been hiding near the stone pile.* Then David bowed three times to Jonathan with his face to the ground. Both of them were in tears as they embraced each other and said good-bye, especially David.

⁴²At last Jonathan said to David, "Go in peace, for we have sworn loyalty to each other in the LORD's name. The LORD is the witness of a bond between us and our children forever." Then David left, and Jonathan returned to the town.*

David Runs from Saul

21 ¹*David went to the town of Nob to see Ahimelech the priest. Ahimelech trembled when he saw him. "Why are you alone?" he asked. "Why is no one with you?"

²"The king has sent me on a private matter," David said. "He told me not to tell anyone why I am here. I have told my men where to meet me later. ³Now, what is there to eat? Give me five loaves of bread or anything else you have."

⁴"We don't have any regular bread," the priest replied. "But there is the holy bread, which you can have if your young men have not slept with any women recently."

⁵"Don't worry," David replied. "I never allow my men to be with women when we are on a campaign. And since they stay clean even on ordinary trips, how much more on this one!"

⁶Since there was no other food available, the priest gave him the holy bread—the Bread of the Presence that was placed before the LORD in the Tabernacle. It had just been replaced that day with fresh bread.

20:16 Hebrew *with the house of David.* **20:19** Hebrew *the stone Ezel.* The meaning of the Hebrew is uncertain. **20:25** As in Greek version; Hebrew reads *with Jonathan standing.* **20:30** Hebrew *You son of a perverse and rebellious woman.* **20:41** As in Greek version; Hebrew reads *near the south edge.* **20:42** This sentence is numbered 21:1 in Hebrew text. **21:1** Verses 21:1-15 are numbered 21:2-16 in Hebrew text.

20:41 Jonathan had the higher social rank, so David's homage was fitting. For the first time, the author shows that the emotion between these two men was mutual (see 18:1, 3-4; 20:17).

21:1-15 David lied to conceal his outlaw status and to dispel Abimelech's worries. We can easily demonize Saul, but we cannot turn aside from the morally wrong things that David also did. Even the people God selects for important tasks may fail at times, but God will still hold them accountable for their sins. This passage reminds us that the complexity of both good and evil dwells in our own lives too.

21:11 David's reputation as a greater warrior than King Saul (see 18:7) had grown to the point where foreigners began referring to him as Israel's king.

Insight — DAVID ON THE RUN

David faithfully served Saul, but Saul responded with murderous jealousy. So, David fled from Saul's court at Gibeah. David spent years on the run, living in the wilderness, in caves, and among the Philistines. Saul continued to hunt David down; on a couple of occasions, David could have killed Saul, but he refused to harm the Lord's anointed (24:6-10; 26:9-11). During this time, David's entourage grew as those displeased with Saul's reign joined him. Eventually, Saul died in battle, and David's kingdom began.

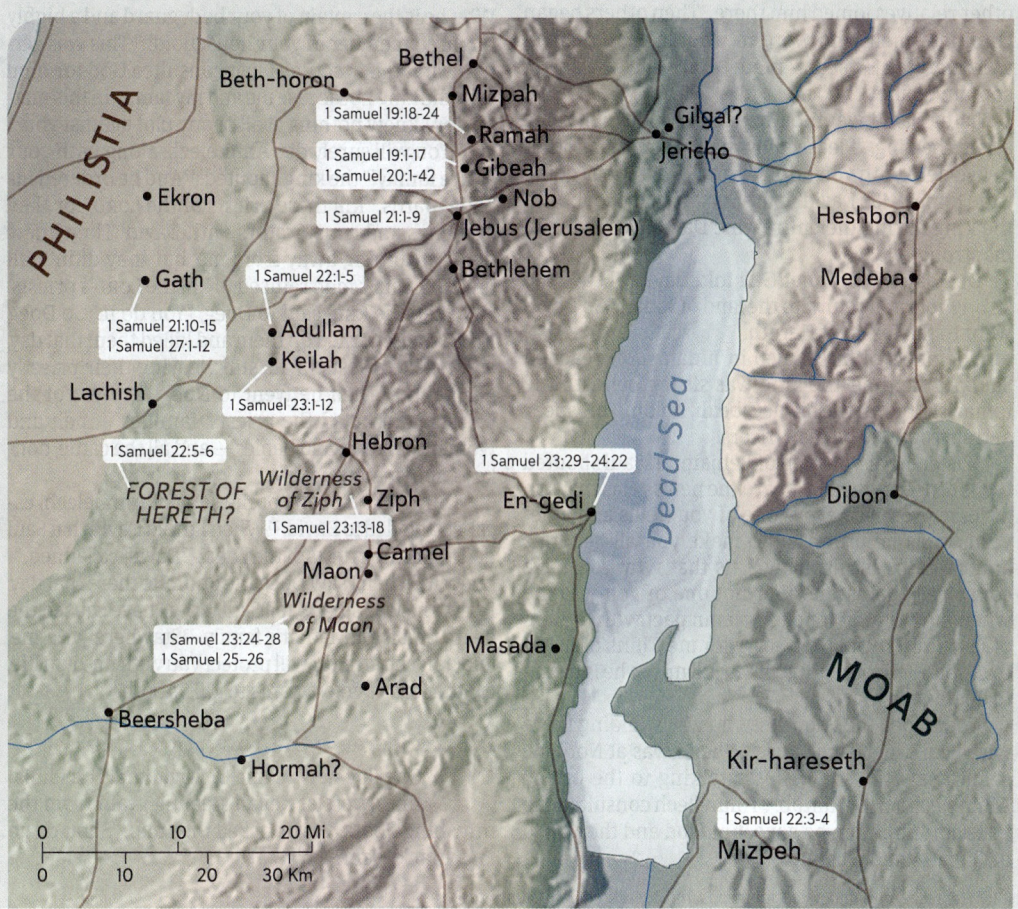

7 Now Doeg the Edomite, Saul's chief herdsman, was there that day, having been detained before the LORD.*

8 David asked Ahimelech, "Do you have a spear or sword? The king's business was so urgent that I didn't even have time to grab a weapon!"

9 "I only have the sword of Goliath the Philistine, whom you killed in the valley of Elah," the priest replied. "It is wrapped in a cloth behind the ephod. Take that if you want it, for there is nothing else here."

21:7 The meaning of the Hebrew is uncertain.

"There is nothing like it!" David replied. "Give it to me!"

10 So David escaped from Saul and went to King Achish of Gath. 11 But the officers of Achish were unhappy about his being there. "Isn't this David, the king of the land?" they asked. "Isn't he the one the people honor with dances, singing,

'Saul has killed his thousands,
    and David his ten thousands'?"

¹²David heard these comments and was very afraid of what King Achish of Gath might do to him. ¹³So he pretended to be insane, scratching on doors and drooling down his beard.

¹⁴Finally, King Achish said to his men, "Must you bring me a madman? ¹⁵We already have enough of them around here! Why should I let someone like this be my guest?"

David at the Cave of Adullam

22 So David left Gath and escaped to the cave of Adullam. Soon his brothers and all his other relatives joined him there. ²Then others began coming—men who were in trouble or in debt or who were just discontented—until David was the captain of about 400 men.

³Later David went to Mizpeh in Moab, where he asked the king, "Please allow my father and mother to live here with you until I know what God is going to do for me." ⁴So David's parents stayed in Moab with the king during the entire time David was living in his stronghold.

⁵One day the prophet Gad told David, "Leave the stronghold and return to the land of Judah." So David went to the forest of Hereth.

⁶The news of his arrival in Judah soon reached Saul. At the time, the king was sitting beneath the tamarisk tree on the hill at Gibeah, holding his spear and surrounded by his officers.

⁷"Listen here, you men of Benjamin!" Saul shouted to his officers when he heard the news. "Has that son of Jesse promised every one of you fields and vineyards? Has he promised to make you all generals and captains in his army?* ⁸Is that why you have conspired against me? For not one of you told me when my own son made a solemn pact with the son of Jesse. You're not even sorry for me. Think of it! My own son—encouraging him to kill me, as he is trying to do this very day!"

⁹Then Doeg the Edomite, who was standing there with Saul's men, spoke up. "When I was at Nob," he said, "I saw the son of Jesse talking to the priest, Ahimelech son of Ahitub. ¹⁰Ahimelech consulted the LORD for him. Then he gave him food and the sword of Goliath the Philistine."

The Slaughter of the Priests

¹¹King Saul immediately sent for Ahimelech and all his family, who served as priests at Nob. ¹²When they arrived, Saul shouted at him, "Listen to me, you son of Ahitub!"

"What is it, my king?" Ahimelech asked.

¹³"Why have you and the son of Jesse conspired against me?" Saul demanded. "Why did you give him food and a sword? Why have you consulted God for him? Why have you encouraged him to kill me, as he is trying to do this very day?"

¹⁴"But sir," Ahimelech replied, "is anyone among all your servants as faithful as David, your son-in-law? Why, he is the captain of your bodyguard and a highly honored member of your household! ¹⁵This was certainly not the first time I had consulted God for him! May the king not accuse me and my family in this matter, for I knew nothing at all of any plot against you."

¹⁶"You will surely die, Ahimelech, along with your entire family!" the king shouted. ¹⁷And he ordered his bodyguards, "Kill these priests of the LORD, for they are allies and conspirators with David! They knew he was running away from me, but they didn't tell me!" But Saul's men refused to kill the LORD's priests.

¹⁸Then the king said to Doeg, "You do it." So Doeg the Edomite turned on them and killed them that day, eighty-five priests in all, still wearing their priestly garments. ¹⁹Then he went to Nob, the town of the priests, and killed the priests' families—men and women, children and babies—and all the cattle, donkeys, sheep, and goats.

²⁰Only Abiathar, one of the sons of Ahimelech, escaped and fled to David. ²¹When he told David that Saul had killed the priests of the LORD, ²²David exclaimed, "I knew it! When I saw Doeg the Edomite there that day, I knew he was sure to tell Saul. Now I have caused the death of all your father's family. ²³Stay here with me, and don't be afraid. I will protect you with my own life, for the same person wants to kill us both."

David Protects the Town of Keilah

23 One day news came to David that the Philistines were at Keilah stealing grain from the threshing floors. ²David asked the LORD, "Should I go and attack them?"

22:7 Hebrew *commanders of thousands and commanders of hundreds?*

22:1-23 Saul's character becomes evident here. Unable to exact revenge on David himself, Saul slaughtered those he believed to be guilty of giving aid and comfort to David.

22:2 By attracting such down-and-out people ("men who were in trouble or in debt or who were just discontented"), David foreshadowed Jesus. Jesus also drew the hurting, the burdened, and the outcast (Matthew 11:25-30).

22:3-4 Mizpeh in Moab lay east of the Dead Sea and the Jordan River—not an easy trip from Adullam, especially if the four hundred men (22:2) accompanied David. David's parents may have stayed in Moab due to their family connections there.

Jesse's grandmother was Ruth, a Moabite (Ruth 4:13-22). Scripture mentions David's mother only one other time in Scripture (see Psalm 86:16: "son of your servant," which could also mean "son of your female servant," meaning the psalmist's mother). While the Bible never mentions her name, Jewish tradition suggests her name was Nitzevet.

22:18 As a non-Israelite, Doeg had no concern for the sanctity of God-anointed priests. He knew he was executing innocent men. This evil man partially fulfilled the prophecy about the condemned priestly line of Eli (2:27-34; see 1 Kings 2:27). This incident illustrates how unstable Saul had become. Not even those holding a sacred office were safe.

"Yes, go and save Keilah," the LORD told him. ³But David's men said, "We're afraid even here in Judah. We certainly don't want to go to Keilah to fight the whole Philistine army!"

⁴So David asked the LORD again, and again the LORD replied, "Go down to Keilah, for I will help you conquer the Philistines."

⁵So David and his men went to Keilah. They slaughtered the Philistines and took all their livestock and rescued the people of Keilah. ⁶Now when Abiathar son of Ahimelech fled to David at Keilah, he brought the ephod with him.

⁷Saul soon learned that David was at Keilah. "Good!" he exclaimed. "We've got him now! God has handed him over to me, for he has trapped himself in a walled town!" ⁸So Saul mobilized his entire army to march to Keilah and besiege David and his men.

⁹But David learned of Saul's plan and told Abiathar the priest to bring the ephod and ask the LORD what he should do. ¹⁰Then David prayed, "O LORD, God of Israel, I have heard that Saul is planning to come and destroy Keilah because I am here. ¹¹Will the leaders of Keilah betray me to him?* And will Saul actually come as I have heard? O LORD, God of Israel, please tell me."

And the LORD said, "He will come."

¹²Again David asked, "Will the leaders of Keilah betray me and my men to Saul?"

And the LORD replied, "Yes, they will betray you."

David Hides in the Wilderness

¹³So David and his men—about 600 of them now—left Keilah and began roaming the countryside. Word soon reached Saul that David had escaped, so he didn't go to Keilah after all. ¹⁴David now stayed in the strongholds of the wilderness and in the hill country of Ziph. Saul hunted him day after day, but God didn't let Saul find him.

¹⁵One day near Horesh, David received the news that Saul was on the way to Ziph to search for him and kill him. ¹⁶Jonathan went to find David and encouraged him to stay strong in his faith in God. ¹⁷"Don't be afraid," Jonathan reassured him. "My father will never find you! You are going to be the king of Israel, and I will be next to you, as my father, Saul, is well aware." ¹⁸So the two of them renewed their solemn pact before the LORD. Then Jonathan returned home, while David stayed at Horesh.

¹⁹But now the men of Ziph went to Saul in Gibeah and betrayed David to him. "We know where David is hiding," they said. "He is in the strongholds of Horesh on the hill of Hakilah, which is in the southern part of Jeshimon. ²⁰Come down whenever you're ready, O king, and we will catch him and hand him over to you!"

²¹"The LORD bless you," Saul said. "At last someone is concerned about me! ²²Go and check again to be sure of where he is staying and who has seen him there, for I know that he is very crafty. ²³Discover his hiding places, and come back when you are sure. Then I'll go with you. And if he is in the area at all, I'll track him down, even if I have to search every hiding place in Judah!" ²⁴So the men of Ziph returned home ahead of Saul.

Meanwhile, David and his men had moved into the wilderness of Maon in the Arabah Valley south of Jeshimon. ²⁵When David heard that Saul and his men were searching for him, he went even farther into the wilderness to the great rock, and he remained there in the wilderness of Maon. But Saul kept after him in the wilderness.

²⁶Saul and David were now on opposite sides of a mountain. Just as Saul and his men began to close in on David and his men, ²⁷an urgent message reached Saul that the Philistines were raiding Israel again. ²⁸So Saul quit chasing David and returned to fight the Philistines. Ever since that time, the place where David was camped has been called the Rock of Escape.* ²⁹*David then went to live in the strongholds of En-gedi.

David Spares Saul's Life

24 ¹*After Saul returned from fighting the Philistines, he was told that David had gone into the wilderness of En-gedi. ²So Saul chose 3,000 elite troops from all Israel and went to search for David and his men near the rocks of the wild goats.

³At the place where the road passes some sheepfolds, Saul went into a cave to relieve himself. But as it happened, David and his men were hiding farther back in that very cave!

⁴"Now's your opportunity!" David's men whispered to him. "Today the LORD is telling you, 'I will certainly put your enemy into your power, to do with as you wish.'" So David crept forward and cut off a piece of the hem of Saul's robe.

⁵But then David's conscience began bothering him because he had cut Saul's robe. ⁶He said to his men, "The LORD forbid that I should do this to my lord the king. I shouldn't attack the LORD's anointed one, for the LORD himself has chosen him." ⁷So David restrained his men and did not let them kill Saul.

23:11 Some manuscripts lack the first sentence of 23:11. **23:28** Hebrew *Sela-hammahlekoth*. **23:29** Verse 23:29 is numbered 24:1 in Hebrew text. **24:1** Verses 24:1-22 are numbered 24:2-23 in Hebrew text.

23:1-29 Thanks to informants, Saul was able to stay on David's trail. But David also had informants, allowing him to keep one step ahead of Saul (23:1, 9, 15, 25). However, David's chief advantage was access to divine guidance and resources (23:2, 4, 12), which Saul lacked.

23:20 Both Keilah (23:12) and Ziph (23:14; Psalm 54 title) were in Judah, but neither gave David sanctuary, even though he was a native of Judah. Thus, David's ascension to power was not the result of his own tribe's loyalty but because of God's will.

After Saul had left the cave and gone on his way, ⁸David came out and shouted after him, "My lord the king!" And when Saul looked around, David bowed low before him.

⁹Then he shouted to Saul, "Why do you listen to the people who say I am trying to harm you? ¹⁰This very day you can see with your own eyes it isn't true. For the LORD placed you at my mercy back there in the cave. Some of my men told me to kill you, but I spared you. For I said, 'I will never harm the king—he is the LORD's anointed one.' ¹¹Look, my father, at what I have in my hand. It is a piece of the hem of your robe! I cut it off, but I didn't kill you. This proves that I am not trying to harm you and that I have not sinned against you, even though you have been hunting for me to kill me.

¹²"May the LORD judge between us. Perhaps the LORD will punish you for what you are trying to do to me, but I will never harm you. ¹³As that old proverb says, 'From evil people come evil deeds.' So you can be sure I will never harm you. ¹⁴Who is the king of Israel trying to catch anyway? Should he spend his time chasing one who is as worthless as a dead dog or a single flea? ¹⁵May the LORD therefore judge which of us is right and punish the guilty one. He is my advocate, and he will rescue me from your power!"

¹⁶When David had finished speaking, Saul called back, "Is that really you, my son David?" Then he began to cry. ¹⁷And he said to David, "You are a better man than I am, for you have repaid me good for evil. ¹⁸Yes, you have been amazingly kind to me today, for when the LORD put me in a place where you could have killed me, you didn't do it. ¹⁹Who else would let his enemy get away when he had him in his power? May the LORD reward you well for the kindness you have shown me today. ²⁰And now I realize that you are surely going to be king, and that the kingdom of Israel will flourish under your rule. ²¹Now swear to me by the LORD that when that happens you will not kill my family and destroy my line of descendants!"

²²So David promised this to Saul with an oath. Then Saul went home, but David and his men went back to their stronghold.

The Death of Samuel

25 Now Samuel died, and all Israel gathered for his funeral. They buried him at his house in Ramah.

Nabal Angers David

Then David moved down to the wilderness of Maon.* ²There was a wealthy man from Maon who owned property near the town of Carmel. He had 3,000 sheep and 1,000 goats, and it was sheep-shearing time. ³This man's name was Nabal, and his wife, Abigail, was a sensible and beautiful woman. But Nabal, a descendant of Caleb, was crude and mean in all his dealings.

⁴When David heard that Nabal was shearing his sheep, ⁵he sent ten of his young men to Carmel with this message for Nabal: ⁶"Peace and prosperity to you, your family, and everything you own! ⁷I am told that it is sheep-shearing time. While your shepherds stayed among us near Carmel, we never harmed them, and nothing was ever stolen from them. ⁸Ask your own men, and they will tell you this is true. So would you be kind to us, since we have come at a time of celebration? Please share any provisions you might have on hand with us and with your friend David." ⁹David's young men gave this message to Nabal in David's name, and they waited for a reply.

¹⁰"Who is this fellow David?" Nabal sneered to the young men. "Who does this son of Jesse think he is? There are lots of servants these days who run away from their masters. ¹¹Should I take my bread and my water and my meat that I've slaughtered for my shearers and give it to a band of outlaws who come from who knows where?"

¹²So David's young men returned and told him what Nabal had said. ¹³"Get your swords!" was David's reply as he strapped on his own. Then 400 men started off with David, and 200 remained behind to guard their equipment.

¹⁴Meanwhile, one of Nabal's servants went to Abigail and told her, "David sent messengers from the wilderness to greet our master, but he screamed insults at them. ¹⁵These men have been very good to us, and we never suffered any harm from them. Nothing was stolen from us the whole time they were with us. ¹⁶In fact, day and night they were like a wall of protection to us and the sheep. ¹⁷You need to know this and figure out what to do, for there is going to be trouble for our master and his whole family. He's so ill-tempered that no one can even talk to him!"

¹⁸Abigail wasted no time. She quickly gathered 200 loaves of bread, two wineskins full of wine, five sheep that had been slaughtered, nearly a bushel* of roasted grain, 100 clusters of raisins, and 200 fig

---

25:1 As in Greek version (see also 25:2); Hebrew reads *Paran*. 25:18 Hebrew *5 seahs* [36.5 liters].

24:12 There was no human authority to judge between Saul and David, so they needed the Lord to decide (see Genesis 16:5; 31:53; Exodus 5:21; Judges 11:27). David rested in God's will rather than trying to force God's hand.
24:20 This was Saul's first open admission of the truth that David would one day be king (see Jonathan's admission at 23:17).
25:1-44 This episode about Nabal falls between two accounts—of Saul pursuing David and of David sparing Saul's life. This chapter may seem oddly out of place, sandwiched between the never-ending Saul-versus-David escapades. Yet Nabal's story matters, as Nabal mirrors Saul himself. David had not killed Nabal's herds or shepherds; in fact, David and his men had protected Israel from the Philistines. David showed restraint twice due to Abigail's wisdom. Both Nabal and Saul were committed to preserving themselves. Do we see these tendencies in ourselves?

MY STORY WITH FAMILY & FRIENDS

A Wise Wife

SCRIPTURE CONNECTION: 1 SAMUEL 25:1-44

Not all women marry good men. Abigail reminds such women that they're not the first to find themselves in a less-than-ideal marriage.

Abigail's life also encourages us all, regardless of who we marry (or don't), to find our difference-making moment. She shows us that God's mission may be possible *because* of our challenging circumstances and relationships, rather than despite them. Let's consider four lessons this ancient woman of God teaches:

- "One of Nabal's servants" (25:14) went to Abigail for help. Likely, Abigail had a track record for acting wisely when her husband, Nabal, did not. She must have made conscious choices not to succumb to his poor influences. She couldn't fix her mean and foolish husband. She could have chosen to do nothing. But she didn't.
- She used her resources for good. Food and wine were within her reach and became her tools for effective reconciliation.
- When Abigail went to David, she asked forgiveness for any offense she had caused, even though she was not the offender. She took responsibility for the family mistake. She cared more about making things right than about seeming blameless.
- Abigail acknowledged the unfortunate truth about her husband's character and amended his wrongdoing with her own actions. She did not accept or ignore her husband's foolhardy response. She acted against his wishes, when necessary, to prevent harm to others.

> We might live our mission *because* of our challenges, not despite them.

IMAGINE

How might you reframe your challenges to prepare for your difference-making moment or mission?

How does Abigail's example of honoring God's chosen leader help you decide who to honor most?

"To understand submission to God's mission, I look at the whole Bible. Scripture recognizes and celebrates various women of God, like Abigail and her ancient contemporaries Deborah (Judges 4–5) and Huldah (2 Kings 22)."

DONNA LEE LAMOTHE, MA, is executive director and founder of inSPIRE Channels at RSVP Ministries. She teaches and guides all to find wholeness through faith in Jesus.

cakes. She packed them on donkeys ¹⁹and said to her servants, "Go on ahead. I will follow you shortly." But she didn't tell her husband Nabal what she was doing.

²⁰As she was riding her donkey into a mountain ravine, she saw David and his men coming toward her. ²¹David had just been saying, "A lot of good it did to help this fellow. We protected his flocks in the wilderness, and nothing he owned was lost or stolen. But he has repaid me evil for good. ²²May God strike me and kill me* if even one man of his household is still alive tomorrow morning!"

Abigail Intercedes for Nabal

²³When Abigail saw David, she quickly got off her donkey and bowed low before him. ²⁴She fell at his feet and said, "I accept all blame in this matter, my lord. Please listen to what I have to say. ²⁵I know Nabal is a wicked and ill-tempered man; please don't pay any attention to him. He is a fool, just as his name suggests.* But I never even saw the young men you sent.

²⁶"Now, my lord, as surely as the LORD lives and you yourself live, since the LORD has kept you from murdering and taking vengeance into your own hands, let all your enemies and those who try to harm you be as cursed as Nabal is. ²⁷And here is a present that I, your servant, have brought to you and your young men. ²⁸Please forgive me if I have offended you in any way. The LORD will surely reward you with a lasting dynasty, for you are fighting the LORD's battles. And you have not done wrong throughout your entire life.

²⁹"Even when you are chased by those who seek to kill you, your life is safe in the care of the LORD your God, secure in his treasure pouch! But the lives of your enemies will disappear like stones shot from a sling! ³⁰When the LORD has done all he promised and has made you leader of Israel, ³¹don't let this be a blemish on your record. Then your conscience won't have to bear the staggering burden of needless bloodshed and vengeance. And when the LORD has done these great things for you, please remember me, your servant!"

³²David replied to Abigail, "Praise the LORD, the God of Israel, who has sent you to meet me today! ³³Thank God for your good sense! Bless you for keeping me from murder and from carrying out vengeance with my own hands. ³⁴For I swear by the LORD, the God of Israel, who has kept me from hurting you, that if you had not hurried out to meet me, not one of Nabal's men would still be alive tomorrow morning." ³⁵Then David accepted her present and told her, "Return home in peace. I have heard what you said. We will not kill your husband."

³⁶When Abigail arrived home, she found that Nabal was throwing a big party and was celebrating like a king. He was very drunk, so she didn't tell him anything about her meeting with David until dawn the next day. ³⁷In the morning when Nabal was sober, his wife told him what had happened. As a result he had a stroke,* and he lay paralyzed on his bed like a stone. ³⁸About ten days later, the LORD struck him, and he died.

David Marries Abigail

³⁹When David heard that Nabal was dead, he said, "Praise the LORD, who has avenged the insult I received from Nabal and has kept me from doing it myself. Nabal has received the punishment for his sin." Then David sent messengers to Abigail to ask her to become his wife.

⁴⁰When the messengers arrived at Carmel, they told Abigail, "David has sent us to take you back to marry him."

⁴¹She bowed low to the ground and responded, "I, your servant, would be happy to marry David. I would even be willing to become a slave, washing the feet of his servants!" ⁴²Quickly getting ready, she took along five of her servant girls as attendants, mounted her donkey, and went with David's messengers. And so she became his wife. ⁴³David also married Ahinoam from Jezreel, making both of them his wives. ⁴⁴Saul, meanwhile, had given his daughter Michal, David's wife, to a man from Gallim named Palti son of Laish.

David Spares Saul Again

26 Now some men from Ziph came to Saul at Gibeah to tell him, "David is hiding on the hill of Hakilah, which overlooks Jeshimon."

²So Saul took 3,000 of Israel's elite troops and went to hunt him down in the wilderness of Ziph. ³Saul camped along the road beside the hill of Hakilah, near Jeshimon, where David was hiding. When David learned that Saul had come after him into the wilderness, ⁴he sent out spies to verify the report of Saul's arrival.

⁵David slipped over to Saul's camp one night to look around. Saul and Abner son of Ner, the commander of his army, were sleeping inside a ring formed by the slumbering warriors. ⁶"Who will volunteer to go in there with me?" David asked Ahimelech the Hittite and Abishai son of Zeruiah, Joab's brother.

25:22 As in Greek version; Hebrew reads *May God strike and kill the enemies of David.* 25:25 The name *Nabal* means "fool." 25:37 Hebrew *his heart failed him.*

26:1-25 This was the last time Saul and David were together. The Ziphites told Saul for the second time where David was hiding (see 23:19-20), and David spared Saul's life a second time as he did in the cave at En-gedi (see 24:1-22).

26:3 Saul pursued David again, despite his earlier remorse (24:17-21). Saul had become incapable of acting rationally or speaking truthfully.

"I'll go with you," Abishai replied. ⁷So David and Abishai went right into Saul's camp and found him asleep, with his spear stuck in the ground beside his head. Abner and the soldiers were lying asleep around him.

⁸"God has surely handed your enemy over to you this time!" Abishai whispered to David. "Let me pin him to the ground with one thrust of the spear; I won't need to strike twice!"

⁹"No!" David said. "Don't kill him. For who can remain innocent after attacking the LORD's anointed one? ¹⁰Surely the LORD will strike Saul down someday, or he will die of old age or in battle. ¹¹The LORD forbid that I should kill the one he has anointed! But take his spear and that jug of water beside his head, and then let's get out of here!"

¹²So David took the spear and jug of water that were near Saul's head. Then he and Abishai got away without anyone seeing them or even waking up, because the LORD had put Saul's men into a deep sleep.

¹³David climbed the hill opposite the camp until he was at a safe distance. ¹⁴Then he shouted down to the soldiers and to Abner son of Ner, "Wake up, Abner!"

"Who is it?" Abner demanded.

¹⁵"Well, Abner, you're a great man, aren't you?" David taunted. "Where in all Israel is there anyone as mighty? So why haven't you guarded your master the king when someone came to kill him? ¹⁶This isn't good at all! I swear by the LORD that you and your men deserve to die, because you failed to protect your master, the LORD's anointed! Look around! Where are the king's spear and the jug of water that were beside his head?"

¹⁷Saul recognized David's voice and called out, "Is that you, my son David?"

And David replied, "Yes, my lord the king. ¹⁸Why are you chasing me? What have I done? What is my crime? ¹⁹But now let my lord the king listen to his servant. If the LORD has stirred you up against me, then let him accept my offering. But if this is simply a human scheme, then may those involved be cursed by the LORD. For they have driven me from my home, so I can no longer live among the LORD's people, and they have said, 'Go, worship pagan gods.' ²⁰Must I die on foreign soil, far from the presence of the LORD? Why has the king of Israel come out to search for a single flea? Why does he hunt me down like a partridge on the mountains?"

²¹Then Saul confessed, "I have sinned. Come back home, my son, and I will no longer try to harm you, for you valued my life today. I have been a fool and very, very wrong."

²²"Here is your spear, O king," David replied. "Let one of your young men come over and get it. ²³The LORD gives his own reward for doing good and for being loyal, and I refused to kill you even when the LORD placed you in my power, for you are the LORD's anointed one. ²⁴Now may the LORD value my life, even as I have valued yours today. May he rescue me from all my troubles."

²⁵And Saul said to David, "Blessings on you, my son David. You will do many heroic deeds, and you will surely succeed." Then David went away, and Saul returned home.

David among the Philistines

27 But David kept thinking to himself, "Someday Saul is going to get me. The best thing I can do is escape to the Philistines. Then Saul will stop hunting for me in Israelite territory, and I will finally be safe."

²So David took his 600 men and went over and joined Achish son of Maoch, the king of Gath. ³David and his men and their families settled there with Achish at Gath. David brought his two wives along with him—Ahinoam from Jezreel and Abigail, Nabal's widow from Carmel. ⁴Word soon reached Saul that David had fled to Gath, so he stopped hunting for him.

⁵One day David said to Achish, "If it is all right with you, we would rather live in one of the country towns instead of here in the royal city."

⁶So Achish gave him the town of Ziklag (which still belongs to the kings of Judah to this day), ⁷and they lived there among the Philistines for a year and four months.

> "We must have courage—determination—to go on with the task of becoming free—not only for ourselves, but for the nation and the world—cooperate with each other. Have faith in God and ourselves."
>
> **ROSA PARKS**
> (1913–2005) civil rights activist and leader, seamstress

27:1-12 David fled to the Philistines to get away from Saul for good. Rather than killing him, David chose the dangerous life of a fugitive.

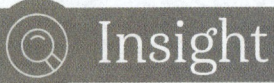

Insight: SAUL'S JOURNEY AWAY FROM GOD

Saul's trajectory away from his mission and from God's favor shows us how living outside God's plan is a series of deliberate choices. The Lord chose Saul as Israel's first king, but Saul lacked confidence in himself and the Lord. At first, Saul was moving toward God and his mission, but Saul's early disobedience set him on a path of destruction and alienation from God.

We can make choices that lead us toward God, too. And, as we move toward who God has made us to be, we bless others, and we and live out our unique influence in this world.

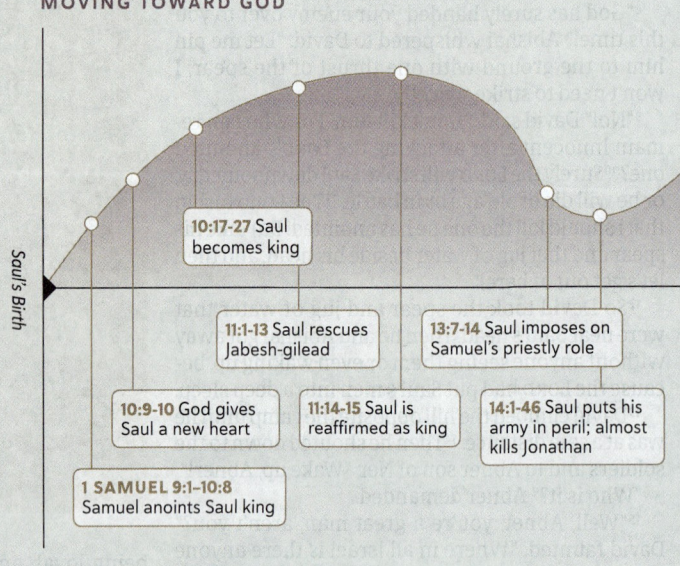

MOVING TOWARD GOD / MOVING AWAY FROM GOD

- Saul's Birth
- 1 SAMUEL 9:1–10:8 Samuel anoints Saul king
- 10:9-10 God gives Saul a new heart
- 10:17-27 Saul becomes king
- 11:1-13 Saul rescues Jabesh-gilead
- 11:14-15 Saul is reaffirmed as king
- 13:7-14 Saul imposes on Samuel's priestly role
- 14:1-46 Saul puts his army in peril; almost kills Jonathan

---

⁸David and his men spent their time raiding the Geshurites, the Girzites, and the Amalekites—people who had lived near Shur, toward the land of Egypt, since ancient times. ⁹David did not leave one person alive in the villages he attacked. He took the sheep, goats, cattle, donkeys, camels, and clothing before returning home to see King Achish.

¹⁰"Where did you make your raid today?" Achish would ask.

And David would reply, "Against the south of Judah, the Jerahmeelites, and the Kenites."

¹¹No one was left alive to come to Gath and tell where he had really been. This happened again and again while he was living among the Philistines. ¹²Achish believed David and thought to himself, "By now the people of Israel must hate him bitterly. Now he will have to stay here and serve me forever!"

Saul Consults a Medium

28 About that time the Philistines mustered their armies for another war with Israel. King Achish told David, "You and your men will be expected to join me in battle."

²"Very well!" David agreed. "Now you will see for yourself what we can do."

Then Achish told David, "I will make you my personal bodyguard for life."

³Meanwhile, Samuel had died, and all Israel had mourned for him. He was buried in Ramah, his hometown. And Saul had banned from the land of Israel all mediums and those who consult the spirits of the dead.

⁴The Philistines set up their camp at Shunem, and Saul gathered all the army of Israel and camped at Gilboa. ⁵When Saul saw the vast Philistine army, he became frantic with fear. ⁶He asked the LORD what he should do, but the LORD refused to answer him, either by dreams or by sacred lots* or by the prophets. ⁷Saul then said to his advisers, "Find a woman who is a medium, so I can go and ask her what to do."

His advisers replied, "There is a medium at Endor."

⁸So Saul disguised himself by wearing ordinary clothing instead of his royal robes. Then he went to

28:6 Hebrew *by Urim.*

27:10 David misled Achish by claiming his attacks were against his people of Judah and two other related groups. The text does not commend David for lying to the foreign king, but neither does it condemn him.

28:7 The woman at Endor reminds us that there were still people among the Israelites who believed differently. Wider cultural practices still occurred. Yet even when people practice what God says to avoid, he finds a way to speak.

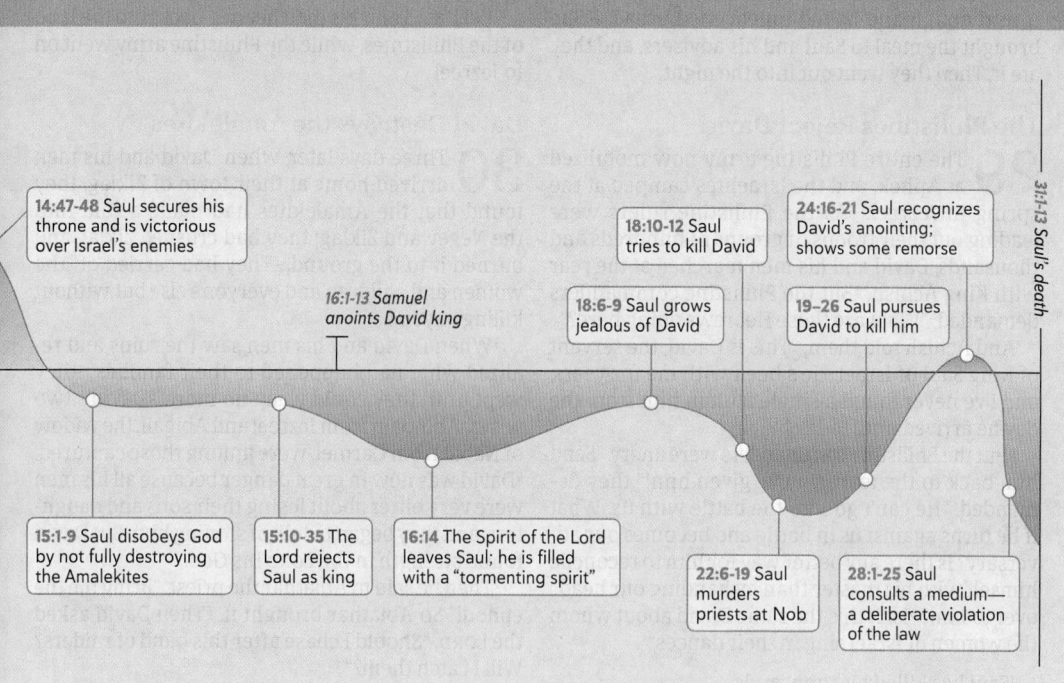

the woman's home at night, accompanied by two of his men.

"I have to talk to a man who has died," he said. "Will you call up his spirit for me?"

⁹"Are you trying to get me killed?" the woman demanded. "You know that Saul has outlawed all the mediums and all who consult the spirits of the dead. Why are you setting a trap for me?"

¹⁰But Saul took an oath in the name of the LORD and promised, "As surely as the LORD lives, nothing bad will happen to you for doing this."

¹¹Finally, the woman said, "Well, whose spirit do you want me to call up?"

"Call up Samuel," Saul replied.

¹²When the woman saw Samuel, she screamed, "You've deceived me! You are Saul!"

¹³"Don't be afraid!" the king told her. "What do you see?"

"I see a god* coming up out of the earth," she said.

¹⁴"What does he look like?" Saul asked.

"He is an old man wrapped in a robe," she replied. Saul realized it was Samuel, and he fell to the ground before him.

¹⁵"Why have you disturbed me by calling me back?" Samuel asked Saul.

"Because I am in deep trouble," Saul replied. "The Philistines are at war with me, and God has left me and won't reply by prophets or dreams. So I have called for you to tell me what to do."

¹⁶But Samuel replied, "Why ask me, since the LORD has left you and has become your enemy? ¹⁷The LORD has done just as he said he would. He has torn the kingdom from you and given it to your rival, David. ¹⁸The LORD has done this to you today because you refused to carry out his fierce anger against the Amalekites. ¹⁹What's more, the LORD will hand you and the army of Israel over to the Philistines tomorrow, and you and your sons will be here with me. The LORD will bring down the entire army of Israel in defeat."

²⁰Saul fell full length on the ground, paralyzed with fright because of Samuel's words. He was also faint with hunger, for he had eaten nothing all day and all night.

²¹When the woman saw how distraught he was, she said, "Sir, I obeyed your command at the risk of my life. ²²Now do what I say, and let me give you a little something to eat so you can regain your strength for the trip back."

²³But Saul refused to eat anything. Then his advisers joined the woman in urging him to eat, so he finally yielded and got up from the ground and sat on the couch.

28:13 Or *gods*.

²⁴The woman had been fattening a calf, so she hurried out and killed it. She took some flour, kneaded it into dough and baked unleavened bread. ²⁵She brought the meal to Saul and his advisers, and they ate it. Then they went out into the night.

The Philistines Reject David

29 The entire Philistine army now mobilized at Aphek, and the Israelites camped at the spring in Jezreel. ²As the Philistine rulers were leading out their troops in groups of hundreds and thousands, David and his men marched at the rear with King Achish. ³But the Philistine commanders demanded, "What are these Hebrews doing here?"

And Achish told them, "This is David, the servant of King Saul of Israel. He's been with me for years, and I've never found a single fault in him from the day he arrived until today."

⁴But the Philistine commanders were angry. "Send him back to the town you've given him!" they demanded. "He can't go into the battle with us. What if he turns against us in battle and becomes our adversary? Is there any better way for him to reconcile himself with his master than by handing our heads over to him? ⁵Isn't this the same David about whom the women of Israel sing in their dances,

'Saul has killed his thousands,
  and David his ten thousands'?"

⁶So Achish finally summoned David and said to him, "I swear by the LORD that you have been a trustworthy ally. I think you should go with me into battle, for I've never found a single flaw in you from the day you arrived until today. But the other Philistine rulers won't hear of it. ⁷Please don't upset them, but go back quietly."

⁸"What have I done to deserve this treatment?" David demanded. "What have you ever found in your servant, that I can't go and fight the enemies of my lord the king?"

⁹But Achish insisted, "As far as I'm concerned, you're as perfect as an angel of God. But the Philistine commanders are afraid to have you with them in the battle. ¹⁰Now get up early in the morning, and leave with your men as soon as it gets light."

¹¹So David and his men headed back into the land of the Philistines, while the Philistine army went on to Jezreel.

David Destroys the Amalekites

30 Three days later, when David and his men arrived home at their town of Ziklag, they found that the Amalekites had made a raid into the Negev and Ziklag; they had crushed Ziklag and burned it to the ground. ²They had carried off the women and children and everyone else but without killing anyone.

³When David and his men saw the ruins and realized what had happened to their families, ⁴they wept until they could weep no more. ⁵David's two wives, Ahinoam from Jezreel and Abigail, the widow of Nabal from Carmel, were among those captured. ⁶David was now in great danger because all his men were very bitter about losing their sons and daughters, and they began to talk of stoning him. But David found strength in the LORD his God.

⁷Then he said to Abiathar the priest, "Bring me the ephod!" So Abiathar brought it. ⁸Then David asked the LORD, "Should I chase after this band of raiders? Will I catch them?"

And the LORD told him, "Yes, go after them. You will surely recover everything that was taken from you!"

⁹So David and his 600 men set out, and they came to the brook Besor. ¹⁰But 200 of the men were too exhausted to cross the brook, so David continued the pursuit with 400 men.

¹¹Along the way they found an Egyptian man in a field and brought him to David. They gave him some bread to eat and water to drink. ¹²They also gave him part of a fig cake and two clusters of raisins, for he hadn't had anything to eat or drink for three days and nights. Before long his strength returned.

¹³"To whom do you belong, and where do you come from?" David asked him.

"I am an Egyptian—the slave of an Amalekite," he

28:24-25 The meal that the medium shared with Saul was a major undertaking, a model of hospitality (see also Genesis 18:5-7). It echoes the fine meal Samuel had shared with Saul before anointing Saul as king (1 Samuel 9:22-24). That meal with God's prophet marked the beginning of Saul's kingship, and this meal with a condemned medium came shortly before his death. The Hebrew verb translated here as "killed" is the same verb used for sacrifice when slaughtering. The text then has us wrestle with this woman at Endor: She was performing a priestly function like Samuel, but her actions were ambiguous. She practiced a forbidden craft, yet she showed excellent hospitality and care. Distinguishing good from bad can sometimes feel complicated; not everything appears clear (see further discussion at the note on 21:1-15).

29:1-11 Divine providence spared David from fighting against his own people.

29:6 Achish used the unique name of Israel's God to prove his own sincerity. He swore that David was "a trustworthy ally," but this assertion was not wholly true, though Achish did not realize it (27:8-12).

30:2 There were no fighting men left in Ziklag to protect the women and children at risk of attack from their enemies. The Amalekites had a reputation for preying on the weak and vulnerable (see Deuteronomy 25:17-18). The Amalekites were not compassionate by not killing their captives; women and children were more useful alive than dead.

30:10 David's men had traveled for three days (30:1) and were now in hot pursuit of the Amalekites without having rested. David did not upbraid them or drive them on mercilessly (see 30:21-25).

replied. "My master abandoned me three days ago because I was sick. ¹⁴We were on our way back from raiding the Kerethites in the Negev, the territory of Judah, and the land of Caleb, and we had just burned Ziklag."

¹⁵"Will you lead me to this band of raiders?" David asked.

The young man replied, "If you take an oath in God's name that you will not kill me or give me back to my master, then I will guide you to them."

¹⁶So he led David to them, and they found the Amalekites spread out across the fields, eating and drinking and dancing with joy because of the vast amount of plunder they had taken from the Philistines and the land of Judah. ¹⁷David and his men rushed in among them and slaughtered them throughout that night and the entire next day until evening. None of the Amalekites escaped except 400 young men who fled on camels. ¹⁸David got back everything the Amalekites had taken, and he rescued his two wives. ¹⁹Nothing was missing: small or great, son or daughter, nor anything else that had been taken. David brought everything back. ²⁰He also recovered all the flocks and herds, and his men drove them ahead of the other livestock. "This plunder belongs to David!" they said.

²¹Then David returned to the brook Besor and met up with the 200 men who had been left behind because they were too exhausted to go with him. They went out to meet David and his men, and David greeted them joyfully. ²²But some evil troublemakers among David's men said, "They didn't go with us, so they can't have any of the plunder we recovered. Give them their wives and children, and tell them to be gone."

²³But David said, "No, my brothers! Don't be selfish with what the LORD has given us. He has kept us safe and helped us defeat the band of raiders that attacked us. ²⁴Who will listen when you talk like this? We share and share alike—those who go to battle and those who guard the equipment." ²⁵From then on David made this a decree and regulation for Israel, and it is still followed today.

²⁶When he arrived at Ziklag, David sent part of the plunder to the elders of Judah, who were his friends. "Here is a present for you, taken from the LORD's enemies," he said.

²⁷The gifts were sent to the people of the following towns David had visited: Bethel, Ramoth-negev, Jattir, ²⁸Aroer, Siphmoth, Eshtemoa, ²⁹Racal,* the towns of the Jerahmeelites, the towns of the Kenites, ³⁰Hormah, Bor-ashan, Athach, ³¹Hebron, and all the other places David and his men had visited.

The Death of Saul

31 Now the Philistines attacked Israel, and the men of Israel fled before them. Many were slaughtered on the slopes of Mount Gilboa. ²The Philistines closed in on Saul and his sons, and they killed three of his sons—Jonathan, Abinadab, and Malkishua. ³The fighting grew very fierce around Saul, and the Philistine archers caught up with him and wounded him severely.

⁴Saul groaned to his armor bearer, "Take your sword and kill me before these pagan Philistines come to run me through and taunt and torture me."

But his armor bearer was afraid and would not do it. So Saul took his own sword and fell on it. ⁵When his armor bearer realized that Saul was dead, he fell on his own sword and died beside the king. ⁶So Saul, his three sons, his armor bearer, and his troops all died together that same day.

⁷When the Israelites on the other side of the Jezreel Valley and beyond the Jordan saw that the Israelite army had fled and that Saul and his sons were dead, they abandoned their towns and fled. So the Philistines moved in and occupied their towns.

⁸The next day, when the Philistines went out to strip the dead, they found the bodies of Saul and his three sons on Mount Gilboa. ⁹So they cut off Saul's head and stripped off his armor. Then they proclaimed the good news of Saul's death in their pagan temple and to the people throughout the land of Philistia. ¹⁰They placed his armor in the temple of the Ashtoreths, and they fastened his body to the wall of the city of Beth-shan.

¹¹But when the people of Jabesh-gilead heard what the Philistines had done to Saul, ¹²all their mighty warriors traveled through the night to Beth-shan and took the bodies of Saul and his sons down from the wall. They brought them to Jabesh, where they burned the bodies. ¹³Then they took their bones and buried them beneath the tamarisk tree at Jabesh, and they fasted for seven days.

30:29 Greek version reads *Carmel*.

30:26 David extended his generosity to influential people throughout his tribal area, possibly to secure their support.
31:1-6 This book ends as Samuel had predicted (28:19), with the tragic death of Saul and three of his sons. Genesis, Deuteronomy, and Joshua end with a main character's death (Joseph, Moses, and Joshua), keeping this book aligned with the other stories in Israel's history. Even when a poor example like Saul dies, we see grieving for loss of life, as all people reflect God's image.

2 Samuel

WHAT DO WE LEARN ABOUT GOD'S MISSION AND OURS?
Only God is our perfect leader.

WHO WROTE IT? We don't know for sure, but it was probably a court official or someone who had access to official historical records.

WHEN DID IT HAPPEN? Around 1010–970 BC, from just after Saul's death through most of David's reign.

HOW IS IT ORGANIZED?

- **1:** David mourns Saul's and Jonathan's deaths
- **2–4:** David becomes Judah's king
- **5–10:** David consolidates his rule over all Israel
- **11–12:** David sins against Bathsheba and Uriah
- **13–20:** Absalom's rebellion, civil war
- **21–24:** David's reign and highlights

FEATURE HIGHLIGHTS

+ *Michal: A Pawn to Play (375)*
+ *David's Wives and Their Children (376)*
+ *Influence and Leadership (382)*
+ *What Leads Us Down the Path Toward Harm? (389)*
+ *Unfairness: Finding God Near (390)*
+ *Bitterness and Healing (394)*

Words to Remember are highlighted throughout this book

HOW LONG DOES IT TAKE TO READ?

	1:30					
:30	1:00	1:30	2:00	2:30	3:00	3:30

Timeline

BC	
1375	JUDGES (INCLUDING DEBORAH, GIDEON, AND SAMSON) BEGIN TO RULE
1050	SAUL BECOMES KING
1025	SAMUEL ANOINTS DAVID, DAVID SLAYS GOLIATH AND MARRIES SAUL'S DAUGHTER, MICHAL
1010	SAUL DIES; DAVID BECOMES JUDAH'S KING
1003	DAVID BECOMES KING OVER ALL ISRAEL
c. 997	DAVID TAKES BATHSHEBA, THEN KILLS HER HUSBAND, URIAH
c. 991	BATHSHEBA GIVES BIRTH TO SOLOMON
c. 980	DAVID TAKES A CENSUS
970	BATHSHEBA ADVOCATES FOR DAVID TO MAKE SOLOMON KING; DAVID DIES; SOLOMON BECOMES KING
930	THE KINGDOM DIVIDES

David Learns of Saul's Death

1 After the death of Saul, David returned from his victory over the Amalekites and spent two days in Ziklag. ²On the third day a man arrived from Saul's army camp. He had torn his clothes and put dirt on his head to show that he was in mourning. He fell to the ground before David in deep respect.

³"Where have you come from?" David asked.

"I escaped from the Israelite camp," the man replied.

⁴"What happened?" David demanded. "Tell me how the battle went."

The man replied, "Our entire army fled from the battle. Many of the men are dead, and Saul and his son Jonathan are also dead."

⁵"How do you know Saul and Jonathan are dead?" David demanded of the young man.

⁶The man answered, "I happened to be on Mount Gilboa, and there was Saul leaning on his spear with the enemy chariots and charioteers closing in on him. ⁷When he turned and saw me, he cried out for me to come to him. 'How can I help?' I asked him.

⁸"He responded, 'Who are you?'

"'I am an Amalekite,' I told him.

⁹"Then he begged me, 'Come over here and put me out of my misery, for I am in terrible pain and want to die.'

¹⁰"So I killed him," the Amalekite told David, "for I knew he couldn't live. Then I took his crown and his armband, and I have brought them here to you, my lord."

¹¹David and his men tore their clothes in sorrow when they heard the news. ¹²They mourned and wept and fasted all day for Saul and his son Jonathan, and for the LORD's army and the nation of Israel, because they had died by the sword that day.

¹³Then David said to the young man who had brought the news, "Where are you from?"

And he replied, "I am a foreigner, an Amalekite, who lives in your land."

¹⁴"Why were you not afraid to kill the LORD's anointed one?" David asked.

¹⁵Then David said to one of his men, "Kill him!" So the man thrust his sword into the Amalekite and killed him. ¹⁶"You have condemned yourself," David said, "for you yourself confessed that you killed the LORD's anointed one."

David's Song for Saul and Jonathan

¹⁷Then David composed a funeral song for Saul and Jonathan, ¹⁸and he commanded that it be taught to the people of Judah. It is known as the Song of the Bow, and it is recorded in The Book of Jashar.*

¹⁹ Your pride and joy, O Israel, lies dead on the hills!
   Oh, how the mighty heroes have fallen!
²⁰ Don't announce the news in Gath,
     don't proclaim it in the streets of Ashkelon,
   or the daughters of the Philistines will rejoice
     and the pagans will laugh in triumph.
²¹ O mountains of Gilboa,
     let there be no dew or rain upon you,
     nor fruitful fields producing offerings of grain.*
   For there the shield of the mighty heroes was defiled;
     the shield of Saul will no longer be anointed with oil.
²² The bow of Jonathan was powerful,
     and the sword of Saul did its mighty work.
   They shed the blood of their enemies
     and pierced the bodies of mighty heroes.
²³ How beloved and gracious were Saul and Jonathan!
   They were together in life and in death.
   They were swifter than eagles,
     stronger than lions.
²⁴ O women of Israel, weep for Saul,
     for he dressed you in luxurious scarlet clothing,
     in garments decorated with gold.
²⁵ Oh, how the mighty heroes have fallen in battle!
   Jonathan lies dead on the hills.
²⁶ How I weep for you, my brother Jonathan!
     Oh, how much I loved you!
   And your love for me was deep,
     deeper than the love of women!
²⁷ Oh, how the mighty heroes have fallen!
     Stripped of their weapons, they lie dead.

1:18 Or *The Book of the Upright.* **1:21** The meaning of the Hebrew is uncertain.

1:1-27 The forty years of Saul's reign came to a painful end. The Philistines inflicted a crushing blow on Saul's people, killing his sons and dismembering Saul's body after his suicide (1 Samuel 31). On the heels of these tragedies, David's career as leader came into focus.
1:23 Saul and Jonathan's relationship was strained, especially by how Saul treated David (see 1 Samuel 20:30-34). Nevertheless, Jonathan fought and died alongside his father while defending Israel against the Philistines.
1:26 Jonathan's loyalty to and friendship with David involved personal risk and sacrifice. The depth of this relationship was unmatched in David's experience: Both he and Jonathan approached each other as equals and were committed to not getting in the way of what God had planned. It's unsurprising, then, that the closeness of this friendship surpassed the love in David's marriages, many of which seem to resemble business transactions more than loving partnerships. While the wording may sound to modern ears like it's describing a same-sex relationship, the phrase denotes a deep and significant friendship that is highlighted three times in 1 Samuel (18:1, 3; 20:17).

David Anointed King of Judah

2 After this, David asked the LORD, "Should I move back to one of the towns of Judah?"

"Yes," the LORD replied.

Then David asked, "Which town should I go to?"

"To Hebron," the LORD answered.

²David's two wives were Ahinoam from Jezreel and Abigail, the widow of Nabal from Carmel. So David and his wives ³and his men and their families all moved to Judah, and they settled in the villages near Hebron. ⁴Then the men of Judah came to David and anointed him king over the people of Judah.

When David heard that the men of Jabesh-gilead had buried Saul, ⁵he sent them this message: "May the LORD bless you for being so loyal to your master Saul and giving him a decent burial. ⁶May the LORD be loyal to you in return and reward you with his unfailing love! And I, too, will reward you for what you have done. ⁷Now that Saul is dead, I ask you to be my strong and loyal subjects like the people of Judah, who have anointed me as their new king."

Ishbosheth Proclaimed King of Israel

⁸But Abner son of Ner, the commander of Saul's army, had already gone to Mahanaim with Saul's son Ishbosheth.* ⁹There he proclaimed Ishbosheth king over Gilead, Jezreel, Ephraim, Benjamin, the land of the Ashurites, and all the rest of Israel.

¹⁰Ishbosheth, Saul's son, was forty years old when he became king, and he ruled from Mahanaim for two years. Meanwhile, the people of Judah remained loyal to David. ¹¹David made Hebron his capital, and he ruled as king of Judah for seven and a half years.

War between Israel and Judah

¹²One day Abner led Ishbosheth's troops from Mahanaim to Gibeon. ¹³About the same time, Joab son of Zeruiah led David's troops out and met them at the pool of Gibeon. The two groups sat down there, facing each other from opposite sides of the pool.

¹⁴Then Abner suggested to Joab, "Let's have a few of our warriors fight hand to hand here in front of us."

"All right," Joab agreed. ¹⁵So twelve men were chosen to fight from each side—twelve men of Benjamin representing Ishbosheth son of Saul, and twelve representing David. ¹⁶Each one grabbed his opponent by the hair and thrust his sword into the other's side so that all of them died. So this place at Gibeon has been known ever since as the Field of Swords.*

¹⁷A fierce battle followed that day, and Abner and the men of Israel were defeated by the forces of David.

The Death of Asahel

¹⁸Joab, Abishai, and Asahel—the three sons of Zeruiah—were among David's forces that day. Asahel could run like a gazelle, ¹⁹and he began chasing Abner. He pursued him relentlessly, not stopping for anything. ²⁰When Abner looked back and saw him coming, he called out, "Is that you, Asahel?"

"Yes, it is," he replied.

²¹"Go fight someone else!" Abner warned. "Take on one of the younger men, and strip him of his weapons." But Asahel kept right on chasing Abner.

²²Again Abner shouted to him, "Get away from here! I don't want to kill you. How could I ever face your brother Joab again?"

²³But Asahel refused to turn back, so Abner thrust the butt end of his spear through Asahel's stomach, and the spear came out through his back. He stumbled to the ground and died there. And everyone who came by that spot stopped and stood still when they saw Asahel lying there.

²⁴When Joab and Abishai found out what had happened, they set out after Abner. The sun was just going down as they arrived at the hill of Ammah near Giah, along the road to the wilderness of Gibeon. ²⁵Abner's troops from the tribe of Benjamin regrouped there at the top of the hill to take a stand.

²⁶Abner shouted down to Joab, "Must we always be killing each other? Don't you realize that bitterness is the only result? When will you call off your men from chasing their Israelite brothers?"

²⁷Then Joab said, "God only knows what would have happened if you hadn't spoken, for we would have chased you all night if necessary." ²⁸So Joab blew the ram's horn, and his men stopped chasing the troops of Israel.

²⁹All that night Abner and his men retreated through the Jordan Valley.* They crossed the Jordan River, traveling all through the morning,* and didn't stop until they arrived at Mahanaim.

³⁰Meanwhile, Joab and his men also returned home. When Joab counted his casualties, he discovered that only 19 men were missing in addition to Asahel. ³¹But 360 of Abner's men had been killed, all from the tribe of Benjamin. ³²Joab and his men took Asahel's body to Bethlehem and buried him there in his father's tomb. Then they traveled all night and reached Hebron at daybreak.

2:8 *Ishbosheth* is another name for Esh-baal. **2:16** Hebrew *Helkath-hazzurim*. **2:29a** Hebrew *the Arabah*. **2:29b** Or *continued on through the Bithron*. The meaning of the Hebrew is uncertain.

2:8-11 Israel was divided, with two different men as the potential king. Saul and David's feuding continued through Saul's remaining sons and allies. Can you imagine what David might have felt as he mourned his closest friend, Jonathan, and did not yet see God's promise come to fruition?

2:26 Realizing that civil wars can go on generation after generation, Abner wisely negotiated a truce. Abner spoke words of wisdom. If we read the books of 1 and 2 Samuel together, they show us why peacemaking matters. God blesses those who work for peace (Matthew 5:9).

3 That was the beginning of a long war between those who were loyal to Saul and those loyal to David. As time passed David became stronger and stronger, while Saul's dynasty became weaker and weaker.

David's Sons Born in Hebron

²These are the sons who were born to David in Hebron:

The oldest was Amnon, whose mother was Ahinoam from Jezreel.
³ The second was Daniel,* whose mother was Abigail, the widow of Nabal from Carmel.
The third was Absalom, whose mother was Maacah, the daughter of Talmai, king of Geshur.
⁴ The fourth was Adonijah, whose mother was Haggith.
The fifth was Shephatiah, whose mother was Abital.
⁵ The sixth was Ithream, whose mother was Eglah, David's wife.

These sons were all born to David in Hebron.

Abner Joins Forces with David

⁶As the war between the house of Saul and the house of David went on, Abner became a powerful leader among those loyal to Saul. ⁷One day Ishbosheth,* Saul's son, accused Abner of sleeping with one of his father's concubines, a woman named Rizpah, daughter of Aiah.

⁸Abner was furious. "Am I some Judean dog to be kicked around like this?" he shouted. "After all I have done for your father, Saul, and his family and friends by not handing you over to David, is this my reward—that you find fault with me about this woman? ⁹May God strike me and even kill me if I don't do everything I can to help David get what the LORD has promised him! ¹⁰I'm going to take Saul's kingdom and give it to David. I will establish the throne of David over Israel as well as Judah, all the way from Dan in the north to Beersheba in the south." ¹¹Ishbosheth didn't dare say another word because he was afraid of what Abner might do.

¹²Then Abner sent messengers to David, saying, "Doesn't the entire land belong to you? Make a solemn pact with me, and I will help turn over all of Israel to you."

¹³"All right," David replied, "but I will not negotiate with you unless you bring back my wife Michal, Saul's daughter, when you come."

¹⁴David then sent this message to Ishbosheth, Saul's son: "Give me back my wife Michal, for I bought her with the lives* of 100 Philistines."

¹⁵So Ishbosheth took Michal away from her husband, Palti* son of Laish. ¹⁶Palti followed along behind her as far as Bahurim, weeping as he went. Then Abner told him, "Go back home!" So Palti returned.

¹⁷Meanwhile, Abner had consulted with the elders of Israel. "For some time now," he told them, "you have wanted to make David your king. ¹⁸Now is the time! For the LORD has said, 'I have chosen David to save my people Israel from the hands of the Philistines and from all their other enemies.'" ¹⁹Abner also spoke with the men of Benjamin. Then he went to Hebron to tell David that all the people of Israel and Benjamin had agreed to support him.

²⁰When Abner and twenty of his men came to Hebron, David entertained them with a great feast. ²¹Then Abner said to David, "Let me go and call an assembly of all Israel to support my lord the king. They will make a covenant with you to make you their king, and you will rule over everything your heart desires." So David sent Abner safely on his way.

Joab Murders Abner

²²But just after David had sent Abner away in safety, Joab and some of David's troops returned from a raid, bringing much plunder with them. ²³When Joab arrived, he was told that Abner had just been there visiting the king and had been sent away in safety.

²⁴Joab rushed to the king and demanded, "What have you done? What do you mean by letting Abner get away? ²⁵You know perfectly well that he came to spy on you and find out everything you're doing!"

²⁶Joab then left David and sent messengers to catch up with Abner, asking him to return. They found him at the well of Sirah and brought him back, though David knew nothing about it. ²⁷When Abner arrived back at Hebron, Joab took him aside at the gateway as if to speak with him privately. But then he stabbed Abner in the stomach and killed him in revenge for killing his brother Asahel.

²⁸When David heard about it, he declared, "I vow by the LORD that I and my kingdom are forever

---

3:3 As in parallel text at 1 Chr 3:1 (see also Greek version, which reads *Daluia*, and possible support by Dead Sea Scrolls); Hebrew reads *Kileab*. **3:7** *Ishbosheth* is another name for Esh-baal. **3:14** Hebrew *the foreskins*. **3:15** As in 1 Sam 25:44; Hebrew reads *Paltiel*, a variant spelling of Palti.

3:1-39 The house of David increased while Saul's house dwindled. The crucial occasion came when Abner, the real political power in Saul's camp, chose and influenced relatives to switch allegiance to David.
3:21 The narrator emphasized that "David sent Abner safely on his way" as a friend and an ally (restated in 3:22-23). David was at peace with Abner and was not involved in the renowned military leader's murder (see 3:28-29). Despite the murder of Abner (3:27), the northern tribes eventually did make a covenant agreement with David to make him their king, just as Abner had promised (5:1-3).

Michal

IDENTITY — A Pawn to Play

Falling in love with a future king is the dream of many little girls. It's what fairy tales are made of!

Except in this historical account, Michal became a pawn in a political chess match between powerful men. It started when King Saul, Michal's father, gave Michal to David as a battle reward.

As time passed, Saul grew jealous and tried to kill David. Michal helped her husband escape and even lied for him. We don't know why, but Saul then gave Michal to Palti to be his wife. Years later, after Saul died, David forcibly reclaimed Michal. Upset about losing his wife, Palti followed the procession in tears until he was forced to turn back. This act seems to have destroyed any love for David that remained in Michal's heart. The next time we see her, she was feeling disgust for David as he danced before the Lord.

Did being a pawn for powerful men dim Michal's view of her worth? Some would see David and Saul's actions and conclude they thought about their own agendas more than Michal's heart. Perhaps Michal believed these powerful men rather than putting her trust in God.

Even when we are abused, discarded, and manipulated, we can root our value in God. God knew how men had used Michal. He understood her hurt intimately. Even still, God loved her immensely. Even when our lives look nothing like what our little-girl selves dreamed about, God loves us, too.

> God understands your hurt and hears the questions that linger.

MICHAL'S STORY IS TOLD IN 1 SAMUEL 18:20–19:18; 25:44; 2 SAMUEL 3:12-16; 6:16-23.

IDENTIFY

Have injustices committed against you damaged how you feel about your worth? Ask God to help you understand your immeasurable value and heal you from these lies.

Do you know you reflect God's image? To learn more about how we reflect God's image, see "Being God's Image—Finding Our Human Identity and Vocation" (page 5).

> "God knows intimately the hurt I've experienced, and he loves me immensely. I can rest in that truth!"

MELISSA HOUDMANN is the cofounder of GotQuestions Ministries, a website dedicated to answering Bible questions. She also wrote Stonecroft Ministries' *Why Believe* study.

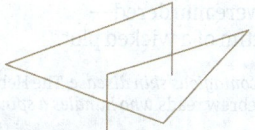

Insight: DAVID'S WIVES AND THEIR CHILDREN

By the end of his reign, David (like other kings of his time) had acquired numerous wives, who had many children. Several women who married David play prominent roles in the Bible's story. Michal was the daughter of Saul and David's first wife (read more about Michal on page 375). Abigail rescued her first husband and their household from David's wrath and married him after her husband had died (read more about Abigail on page 363). Bathsheba became David's wife after he got her pregnant and murdered her first husband, Uriah; she became the mother of the next king, Solomon (read more about Bathsheba on page 386).

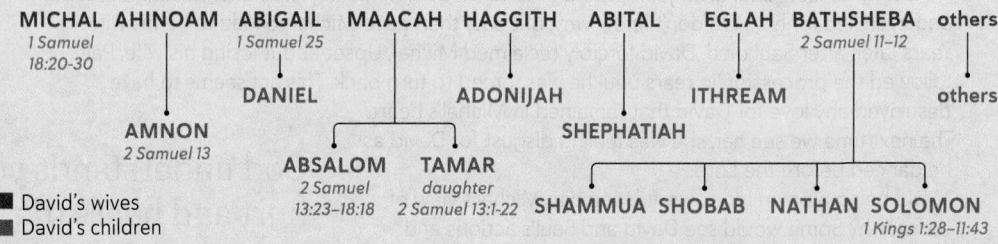

■ David's wives
■ David's children

---

innocent of this crime against Abner son of Ner. ²⁹Joab and his family are the guilty ones. May the family of Joab be cursed in every generation with a man who has open sores or leprosy* or who walks on crutches* or dies by the sword or begs for food!"

³⁰So Joab and his brother Abishai killed Abner because Abner had killed their brother Asahel at the battle of Gibeon.

David Mourns Abner's Death

³¹Then David said to Joab and all those who were with him, "Tear your clothes and put on burlap. Mourn for Abner." And King David himself walked behind the procession to the grave. ³²They buried Abner in Hebron, and the king and all the people wept at his graveside. ³³Then the king sang this funeral song for Abner:

"Should Abner have died as fools die?
³⁴ Your hands were not bound;
  your feet were not chained.
No, you were murdered—
  the victim of a wicked plot."

All the people wept again for Abner. ³⁵David had refused to eat anything on the day of the funeral, and now everyone begged him to eat. But David had made a vow, saying, "May God strike me and even kill me if I eat anything before sundown."

³⁶This pleased the people very much. In fact, everything the king did pleased them! ³⁷So everyone in Judah and all Israel understood that David was not responsible for Abner's murder.

³⁸Then King David said to his officials, "Don't you realize that a great commander has fallen today in Israel? ³⁹And even though I am the anointed king, these two sons of Zeruiah—Joab and Abishai—are too strong for me to control. So may the LORD repay these evil men for their evil deeds."

The Murder of Ishbosheth

4 When Ishbosheth,* Saul's son, heard about Abner's death at Hebron, he lost all courage, and all Israel became paralyzed with fear. ²Now there were two brothers, Baanah and Recab, who were captains of Ishbosheth's raiding parties. They were sons of Rimmon, a member of the tribe of Benjamin

---

3:29a Or *or a contagious skin disease.* The Hebrew word used here can describe various skin diseases. 3:29b Or *who is effeminate;* Hebrew reads *who handles a spindle.* 4:1 *Ishbosheth* is another name for Esh-baal.

3:29 The Hebrew word translated here as "leprosy" can describe various skin diseases. While it is a possible translation, the term here probably refers to a broader range of skin inflammations. This curse effectively alienated Joab from David, and from this point on, they had only a professional relationship. David's deathbed order to Solomon to get rid of Joab (1 Kings 2:5-6) and Solomon's pardoning David in Abner's death (1 Kings 2:31-33) show that David's mourning over Abner was genuine.

who lived in Beeroth. The town of Beeroth is now part of Benjamin's territory ³because the original people of Beeroth fled to Gittaim, where they still live as foreigners.

⁴(Saul's son Jonathan had a son named Mephibosheth,* who was crippled as a child. He was five years old when the report came from Jezreel that Saul and Jonathan had been killed in battle. When the child's nurse heard the news, she picked him up and fled. But as she hurried away, she dropped him, and he became crippled.)

⁵One day Recab and Baanah, the sons of Rimmon from Beeroth, went to Ishbosheth's house around noon as he was taking his midday rest. ⁶The doorkeeper, who had been sifting wheat, became drowsy and fell asleep. So Recab and Baanah slipped past her.* ⁷They went into the house and found Ishbosheth sleeping on his bed. They struck and killed him and cut off his head. Then, taking his head with them, they fled across the Jordan Valley* through the night. ⁸When they arrived at Hebron, they presented Ishbosheth's head to David. "Look!" they exclaimed to the king. "Here is the head of Ishbosheth, the son of your enemy Saul who tried to kill you. Today the LORD has given my lord the king revenge on Saul and his entire family!"

⁹But David said to Recab and Baanah, "The LORD, who saves me from all my enemies, is my witness. ¹⁰Someone once told me, 'Saul is dead,' thinking he was bringing me good news. But I seized him and killed him at Ziklag. That's the reward I gave him for his news! ¹¹How much more should I reward evil men who have killed an innocent man in his own house and on his own bed? Shouldn't I hold you responsible for his blood and rid the earth of you?"

¹²So David ordered his young men to kill them, and they did. They cut off their hands and feet and hung their bodies beside the pool in Hebron. Then they took Ishbosheth's head and buried it in Abner's tomb in Hebron.

David Becomes King of All Israel

5 Then all the tribes of Israel went to David at Hebron and told him, "We are your own flesh and blood. ²In the past,* when Saul was our king, you were the one who really led the forces of Israel. And the LORD told you, 'You will be the shepherd of my people Israel. You will be Israel's leader.'"

³So there at Hebron, King David made a covenant before the LORD with all the elders of Israel. And they anointed him king of Israel.

⁴David was thirty years old when he began to reign, and he reigned forty years in all. ⁵He had reigned over Judah from Hebron for seven years and six months, and from Jerusalem he reigned over all Israel and Judah for thirty-three years.

David Captures Jerusalem

⁶David then led his men to Jerusalem to fight against the Jebusites, the original inhabitants of the land who were living there. The Jebusites taunted David, saying, "You'll never get in here! Even the blind and lame could keep you out!" For the Jebusites thought they were safe. ⁷But David captured the fortress of Zion, which is now called the City of David.

⁸On the day of the attack, David said to his troops, "I hate those 'lame' and 'blind' Jebusites.* Whoever attacks them should strike by going into the city through the water tunnel.*" That is the origin of the saying, "The blind and the lame may not enter the house."*

⁹So David made the fortress his home, and he called it the City of David. He extended the city, starting at the supporting terraces* and working inward. ¹⁰And David became more and more powerful, because the LORD God of Heaven's Armies was with him.

¹¹Then King Hiram of Tyre sent messengers to David, along with cedar timber and carpenters and stonemasons, and they built David a palace. ¹²And David realized that the LORD had confirmed him as king over Israel and had blessed his kingdom for the sake of his people Israel.

¹³After moving from Hebron to Jerusalem, David married more concubines and wives, and they had more sons and daughters. ¹⁴These are the names of David's sons who were born in Jerusalem: Shammua, Shobab, Nathan, Solomon, ¹⁵Ibhar, Elishua, Nepheg, Japhia, ¹⁶Elishama, Eliada, and Eliphelet.

4:4 *Mephibosheth* is another name for Merib-baal.   **4:6** As in Greek version; Hebrew reads *So they went into the house pretending to fetch wheat, but they stabbed him in the stomach. Then Recab and Baanah escaped.*   **4:7** Hebrew *the Arabah.*   **5:2** Or *For some time.*   **5:8a** Or *Those 'lame' and 'blind' Jebusites hate me.*   **5:8b** Or *with scaling hooks.* The meaning of the Hebrew is uncertain.   **5:8c** The meaning of this saying is uncertain.   **5:9** Hebrew *the millo.* The meaning of the Hebrew is uncertain.

4:9-12 Does this story sound familiar? It's almost identical to how 2 Samuel begins with David receiving the news of Saul's death (1:11-16). Both times, the characters thought they were delivering great news to David of his supposed enemy's death. Both times, David responded with mourning and by putting the messenger to death. This response seems odd and severe. In what ways does it complicate how we think David viewed his enemies? What might that mean for us and our enemies?

5:3 King David made a covenant that demanded the people's loyalty yet allowed them to maintain a sense of tribal privilege and individual dignity. It served as a constitution, containing stipulations obligating both the king and the people. While Samuel had already anointed David (1 Samuel 16:13), this public ceremony demonstrated that the people accepted David as king.

Insight   JERUSALEM: THE CITY OF DAVID

The people of Israel considered Jerusalem a holy city because God chose to live among his people there (2 Chronicles 6:34-35). Jerusalem existed as early as four hundred years before David. It was never fully captured during the conquest and the period of the judges (Joshua 15:63; Judges 1:8, 21), and peaceful relations appeared to develop between the autonomous Jebusite people and the surrounding Israelites (Judges 19:10-12). Under David, Jerusalem became Israel's spiritual and political capital. The city was fortified and on a hill, which made it extremely difficult to attack.

Jerusalem in the time of David
was a small fortress city, well-situated in the Judean hills. After reigning over Judah for seven years in Hebron, David captured the city of Jerusalem from its Jebusite inhabitants and made it the capital of the united kingdom.

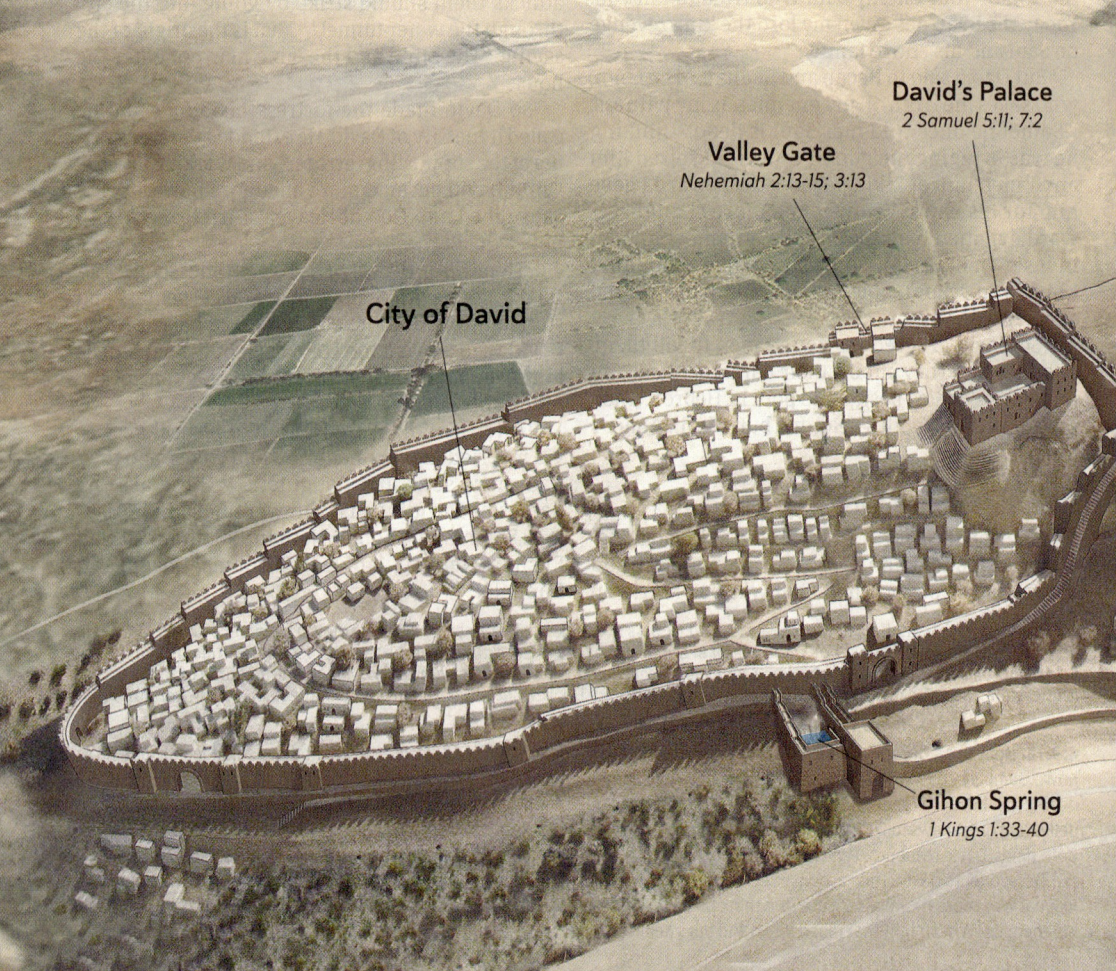

David's Palace
2 Samuel 5:11; 7:2

Valley Gate
Nehemiah 2:13-15; 3:13

City of David

Gihon Spring
1 Kings 1:33-40

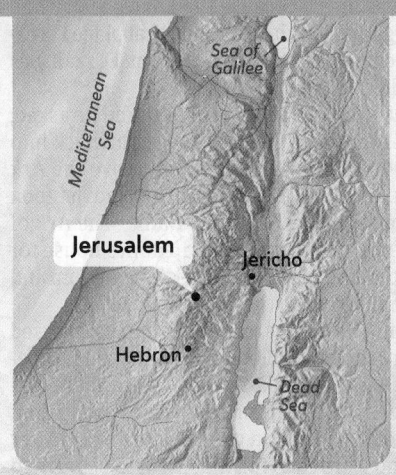

The rock at the top of the mount is where the Most Holy Place would be located in the Temple (1 Kings 6:16).

Araunah's Threshing Floor
The threshing floor on the top of Mount Zion was owned by a Jebusite named Araunah. David purchased the site and dedicated it for the Temple after sacrificing to the Lord there (1 Chronicles 21:1–22:1; 2 Chronicles 3:1-2).

Mount Zion/ Mount Moriah

Central Valley

David's Escape
When David had to leave Jerusalem during Absalom's rebellion, he and his men traveled east across the Kidron Valley toward the Jordan River (2 Samuel 15:13-23).

Kidron Valley

David Conquers the Philistines

[17] When the Philistines heard that David had been anointed king of Israel, they mobilized all their forces to capture him. But David was told they were coming, so he went into the stronghold. [18] The Philistines arrived and spread out across the valley of Rephaim. [19] So David asked the LORD, "Should I go out to fight the Philistines? Will you hand them over to me?"

The LORD replied to David, "Yes, go ahead. I will certainly hand them over to you."

[20] So David went to Baal-perazim and defeated the Philistines there. "The LORD did it!" David exclaimed. "He burst through my enemies like a raging flood!" So he named that place Baal-perazim (which means "the Lord who bursts through"). [21] The Philistines had abandoned their idols there, so David and his men confiscated them.

[22] But after a while the Philistines returned and again spread out across the valley of Rephaim. [23] And again David asked the LORD what to do. "Do not attack them straight on," the LORD replied. "Instead, circle around behind and attack them near the poplar* trees. [24] When you hear a sound like marching feet in the tops of the poplar trees, be on the alert! That will be the signal that the LORD is moving ahead of you to strike down the Philistine army." [25] So David did what the LORD commanded, and he struck down the Philistines all the way from Gibeon* to Gezer.

Moving the Ark to Jerusalem

6 Then David again gathered all the elite troops in Israel, 30,000 in all. [2] He led them to Baalah of Judah* to bring back the Ark of God, which bears the name of the LORD of Heaven's Armies,* who is enthroned between the cherubim. [3] They placed the Ark of God on a new cart and brought it from Abinadab's house, which was on a hill. Uzzah and Ahio, Abinadab's sons, were guiding the cart [4] that carried the Ark of God.* Ahio walked in front of the Ark. [5] David and all the people of Israel were celebrating before the LORD, singing songs* and playing all kinds of musical instruments—lyres, harps, tambourines, castanets, and cymbals.

[6] But when they arrived at the threshing floor of Nacon, the oxen stumbled, and Uzzah reached out his hand and steadied the Ark of God. [7] Then the LORD's anger was aroused against Uzzah, and God struck him dead because of this.* So Uzzah died right there beside the Ark of God.

[8] David was angry because the LORD's anger had burst out against Uzzah. He named that place Perez-uzzah (which means "to burst out against Uzzah"), as it is still called today.

[9] David was now afraid of the LORD, and he asked, "How can I ever bring the Ark of the LORD back into my care?" [10] So David decided not to move the Ark of the LORD into the City of David. Instead, he took it to the house of Obed-edom of Gath. [11] The Ark of the LORD remained there in Obed-edom's house for three months, and the LORD blessed Obed-edom and his entire household.

[12] Then King David was told, "The LORD has blessed Obed-edom's household and everything he has because of the Ark of God." So David went there and brought the Ark of God from the house of Obed-edom to the City of David with a great celebration. [13] After the men who were carrying the Ark of the LORD had gone six steps, David sacrificed a bull and a fattened calf. [14] And David danced before the LORD with all his might, wearing a priestly garment.* [15] So David and all the people of Israel brought up the Ark of the LORD with shouts of joy and the blowing of rams' horns.

Michal's Contempt for David

[16] But as the Ark of the LORD entered the City of David, Michal, the daughter of Saul, looked down from her window. When she saw King David leaping and dancing before the LORD, she was filled with contempt for him.

[17] They brought the Ark of the LORD and set it in its place inside the special tent David had prepared for it. And David sacrificed burnt offerings and peace offerings to the LORD. [18] When he had finished his sacrifices, David blessed the people in the name of the LORD of Heaven's Armies. [19] Then he gave to every Israelite man and woman in the crowd a loaf of bread, a cake of dates,* and a cake of raisins. Then all the people returned to their homes.

[20] When David returned home to bless his own family, Michal, the daughter of Saul, came out to meet him. She said in disgust, "How distinguished the king of Israel looked today, shamelessly exposing himself to the servant girls like any vulgar person might do!"

5:23 Or *aspen*, or *balsam*; also in 5:24. The exact identification of this tree is uncertain. **5:25** As in Greek version (see also 1 Chr 14:16); Hebrew reads *Geba*. **6:2a** Hebrew *Baale of Judah*, another name for Kiriath-jearim; compare 1 Chr 13:6. **6:2b** Or *the Ark of God where the Name is proclaimed—the name of the LORD of Heaven's Armies*. **6:4** As in Dead Sea Scrolls and some Greek manuscripts; Masoretic Text reads *⁴and they brought it from Abinadab's house, which was on a hill, with the Ark of God*. **6:5** As in Dead Sea Scrolls and Greek version (see also 1 Chr 13:8); Masoretic Text reads *before the LORD with all manner of cypress wood*. **6:7** As in Dead Sea Scrolls; Masoretic Text reads *because of his irreverence*. **6:14** Hebrew *a linen ephod*. **6:19** Or *a portion of meat*. The meaning of the Hebrew is uncertain.

5:17-25 David's life has been portrayed thus far in 2 Samuel with a repeated pattern: In Hebron, he was crowned king over Judah (2:3-4), won a battle (2:12-17), became stronger (3:1), and started a large family (3:2-5). Now he was crowned king over all Israel (5:3-4), became stronger (5:10), expanded his family (5:13-14), and won a battle (5:17-25). This parallel structure draws attention to both of David's coronations with signs of divine blessing and prosperity.

²¹David retorted to Michal, "I was dancing before the LORD, who chose me above your father and all his family! He appointed me as the leader of Israel, the people of the LORD, so I celebrate before the LORD. ²²Yes, and I am willing to look even more foolish than this, even to be humiliated in my own eyes! But those servant girls you mentioned will indeed think I am distinguished!" ²³So Michal, the daughter of Saul, remained childless throughout her entire life.

The LORD's Covenant Promise to David

7 When King David was settled in his palace and the LORD had given him rest from all the surrounding enemies, ²the king summoned Nathan the prophet. "Look," David said, "I am living in a beautiful cedar palace,* but the Ark of God is out there in a tent!"

³Nathan replied to the king, "Go ahead and do whatever you have in mind, for the LORD is with you."

⁴But that same night the LORD said to Nathan,

⁵"Go and tell my servant David, 'This is what the LORD has declared: Are you the one to build a house for me to live in? ⁶I have never lived in a house, from the day I brought the Israelites out of Egypt until this very day. I have always moved from one place to another with a tent and a Tabernacle as my dwelling. ⁷Yet no matter where I have gone with the Israelites, I have never once complained to Israel's tribal leaders, the shepherds of my people Israel. I have never asked them, "Why haven't you built me a beautiful cedar house?"'

⁸"Now go and say to my servant David, 'This is what the LORD of Heaven's Armies has declared: I took you from tending sheep in the pasture and selected you to be the leader of my people Israel. ⁹I have been with you wherever you have gone, and I have destroyed all your enemies before your eyes. Now I will make your name as famous as anyone who has ever lived on the earth! ¹⁰And I will provide a homeland for my people Israel, planting them in a secure place where they will never be disturbed. Evil nations won't oppress them as they've done in the past, ¹¹starting from the time I appointed judges to rule my people Israel. And I will give you rest from all your enemies.

"'Furthermore, the LORD declares that he will make a house for you—a dynasty of kings! ¹²For when you die and are buried with your ancestors, I will raise up one of your descendants, your own offspring, and I will make his kingdom strong. ¹³He is the one who will build a house—a temple—for my name. And I will secure his royal throne forever. ¹⁴I will be his father, and he will be my son. If he sins, I will correct and discipline him with the rod, like any father would do. ¹⁵But my favor will not be taken from him as I took it from Saul, whom I removed from your sight. ¹⁶Your house and your kingdom will continue before me* for all time, and your throne will be secure forever.'"

¹⁷So Nathan went back to David and told him everything the LORD had said in this vision.

David's Prayer of Thanks

¹⁸Then King David went in and sat before the LORD and prayed,

"Who am I, O Sovereign LORD, and what is my family, that you have brought me this far? ¹⁹And now, Sovereign LORD, in addition to everything else, you speak of giving your servant a lasting dynasty! Do you deal with everyone this way, O Sovereign LORD?*

²⁰"What more can I say to you? You know what your servant is really like, Sovereign LORD. ²¹Because of your promise and according to your will, you have done all these great things and have made them known to your servant.

²²"How great you are, O Sovereign LORD! There is no one like you. We have never even heard of another God like you! ²³What other nation on earth is like your people Israel? What other nation, O God, have you redeemed from slavery to be your own people? You made a great name for yourself when you redeemed your people from

---

7:2 Hebrew *a house of cedar.* 7:16 As in Greek version and some Hebrew manuscripts; Masoretic Text reads *before you.*
7:19 Or *This is your instruction for all humanity, O Sovereign LORD.*

6:21-23 Michal was taken away from David by Saul himself, therefore annulling their marriage (1 Samuel 25:44). As part of uniting Israel under his leadership, David negotiated to have her taken from her current husband and brought back to him (2 Samuel 3:12-16). But the love that Michal had once had for David seemed to be no more. Consider the newfound position Michal would find herself in—childless. In the ancient world, and in certain cultures today, those who don't have children won't have descendants to remember them, and thus won't have "eternal life." Michal would go from having everything to a future of potential poverty and dishonor. Can you see this through Michal's eyes as time went by? Have you ever lost everything or given up what you valued most? Sometimes we don't know that God is all we need until God is all we have (Matthew 19:27; Mark 10:28; Romans 8:32).

7:8-17 Instead of David's building God a house, God promised to build David a house, a permanent dynasty from David's descendants.

7:18-24 David responded to the words from the Lord reported by Nathan with a prayer of thanksgiving. David began with a posture of humility and a proclamation of who he knew God to be. Sometimes, when we pray, it feels as if we don't have the words. David's model here can be a helpful start, not only in thanksgiving but also in reminding us of who it is we follow.

WHAT THE BIBLE SAYS ABOUT

Influence and Leadership

You are the light of the world.

Jesus Is Our Ultimate Leader

"I have given you an example to follow. Do as I have done to you." **JOHN 13:15**

For God called you to do good, even if it means suffering, just as Christ suffered for you. He is your example, and you must follow in his steps. **1 PETER 2:21**

He is your example, and you must follow in his steps.

We All Have Influence

"You are the light of the world—like a city on a hilltop that cannot be hidden. No one lights a lamp and then puts it under a basket. Instead, a lamp is placed on a stand, where it gives light to everyone in the house. In the same way, let your good deeds shine out for all to see, so that everyone will praise your heavenly Father." MATTHEW 5:14-16

Don't let anyone think less of you because you are young. Be an example to all believers in what you say, in the way you live, in your love, your faith, and your purity. 1 TIMOTHY 4:12

We Lead with Love

Live a life filled with love, following the example of Christ. He loved us and offered himself as a sacrifice for us, a pleasing aroma to God. EPHESIANS 5:2

Do everything without complaining and arguing, so that no one can criticize you. Live clean, innocent lives as children of God, shining like bright lights in a world full of crooked and perverse people. PHILIPPIANS 2:14-15

Be careful to live properly among your unbelieving neighbors. Then even if they accuse you of doing wrong, they will see your honorable behavior, and they will give honor to God when he judges the world. 1 PETER 2:12

Our Influence Ripples

God had mercy on me so that Christ Jesus could use me as a prime example of his great patience with even the worst sinners. Then others will realize that they, too, can believe in him and receive eternal life. 1 TIMOTHY 1:16

God can point to us in all future ages as examples of the incredible wealth of his grace and kindness toward us, as shown in all he has done for us who are united with Christ Jesus. EPHESIANS 2:7

Egypt. You performed awesome miracles and drove out the nations and gods that stood in their way.* ²⁴You made Israel your very own people forever, and you, O LORD, became their God.

²⁵"And now, O LORD God, I am your servant; do as you have promised concerning me and my family. Confirm it as a promise that will last forever. ²⁶And may your name be honored forever so that everyone will say, 'The LORD of Heaven's Armies is God over Israel!' And may the house of your servant David continue before you forever.

²⁷"O LORD of Heaven's Armies, God of Israel, I have been bold enough to pray this prayer to you because you have revealed all this to your servant, saying, 'I will build a house for you—a dynasty of kings!' ²⁸For you are God, O Sovereign LORD. Your words are truth, and you have promised these good things to your servant. ²⁹And now, may it please you to bless the house of your servant, so that it may continue forever before you. For you have spoken, and when you grant a blessing to your servant, O Sovereign LORD, it is an eternal blessing!"

David's Military Victories

8 After this, David defeated and subdued the Philistines by conquering Gath, their largest town.* ²David also conquered the land of Moab. He made the people lie down on the ground in a row, and he measured them off in groups with a length of rope. He measured off two groups to be executed for every one group to be spared. The Moabites who were spared became David's subjects and paid him tribute money.

³David also destroyed the forces of Hadadezer son of Rehob, king of Zobah, when Hadadezer marched out to strengthen his control along the Euphrates River. ⁴David captured 1,000 chariots, 7,000 charioteers,* and 20,000 foot soldiers. He crippled all the chariot horses except enough for 100 chariots.

⁵When Arameans from Damascus arrived to help King Hadadezer, David killed 22,000 of them. ⁶Then he placed several army garrisons in Damascus, the Aramean capital, and the Arameans became David's subjects and paid him tribute money. So the LORD made David victorious wherever he went.

⁷David brought the gold shields of Hadadezer's officers to Jerusalem, ⁸along with a large amount of bronze from Hadadezer's towns of Tebah* and Berothai.

⁹When King Toi of Hamath heard that David had destroyed the entire army of Hadadezer, ¹⁰he sent his son Joram to congratulate King David for his successful campaign. Hadadezer and Toi had been enemies and were often at war. Joram presented David with many gifts of silver, gold, and bronze.

¹¹King David dedicated all these gifts to the LORD, as he did with the silver and gold from the other nations he had defeated—¹²from Edom,* Moab, Ammon, Philistia, and Amalek—and from Hadadezer son of Rehob, king of Zobah.

¹³So David became even more famous when he returned from destroying 18,000 Edomites* in the Valley of Salt. ¹⁴He placed army garrisons throughout Edom, and all the Edomites became David's subjects. In fact, the LORD made David victorious wherever he went.

¹⁵So David reigned over all Israel and did what was just and right for all his people. ¹⁶Joab son of Zeruiah was commander of the army. Jehoshaphat son of Ahilud was the royal historian. ¹⁷Zadok son of Ahitub and Ahimelech son of Abiathar were the priests. Seraiah was the court secretary. ¹⁸Benaiah son of Jehoiada was captain of the king's bodyguard.* And David's sons served as priestly leaders.*

David's Kindness to Mephibosheth

9 One day David asked, "Is anyone in Saul's family still alive—anyone to whom I can show kindness for Jonathan's sake?" ²He summoned a man named Ziba, who had been one of Saul's servants. "Are you Ziba?" the king asked.

"Yes sir, I am," Ziba replied.

7:23 As in Greek version (see also 1 Chr 17:21); Hebrew reads *You made a name for yourself and awesome miracles for your land in the sight of your people, whom you redeemed from Egypt, the nations and their gods.* **8:1** Hebrew *by conquering Metheg-ammah,* a name that means "the bridle," possibly referring to the size of the town or the tribute money taken from it. Compare 1 Chr 18:1. **8:4** As in Dead Sea Scrolls and Greek version (see also 1 Chr 18:4); Masoretic Text reads *captured 1,700 charioteers.* **8:8** As in some Greek manuscripts (see also 1 Chr 18:8); Hebrew reads *Betah.* **8:12** As in a few Hebrew manuscripts and Greek and Syriac versions (see also 8:14; 1 Chr 18:11); most Hebrew manuscripts read *Aram.* **8:13** As in a few Hebrew manuscripts and Greek and Syriac versions (see also 8:14; 1 Chr 18:12); most Hebrew manuscripts read *Arameans.* **8:18a** Hebrew *of the Kerethites and Pelethites.* **8:18b** Hebrew *David's sons were priests;* compare parallel text at 1 Chr 18:17.

8:1-18 The expansion of David's kingdom through military victories (8:1-14) and the establishment of his royal administration (8:15-18) fulfilled God's promise of a famous name (7:9; see 8:13). **8:18** David was from the tribe of Judah and was not a Levite, so it is strange that his sons are named as priests here. Alongside the traditional priesthood, David might have inaugurated a religious class tied explicitly to his dynasty, probably to serve the royal court. This is a warning sign for us too. God is the one who appoints priests, which makes David's action at odds with Deuteronomy 18:5. If we read 1 and 2 Samuel as one whole book, we remember how wickedly the sons of both Eli and Samuel acted as priests. Just because you may find yourself in a position of authority does not mean you can bend the rules. **9:1-13** David showed mercy to Mephibosheth, Jonathan's son who had a physical disability. The incident is sandwiched between David's victories in battle (8:1-18; 10:1-19), indicating that David also had concern for individuals and a compassionate heart.

³The king then asked him, "Is anyone still alive from Saul's family? If so, I want to show God's kindness to them."

Ziba replied, "Yes, one of Jonathan's sons is still alive. He is crippled in both feet."

⁴"Where is he?" the king asked.

"In Lo-debar," Ziba told him, "at the home of Makir son of Ammiel."

⁵So David sent for him and brought him from Makir's home. ⁶His name was Mephibosheth*; he was Jonathan's son and Saul's grandson. When he came to David, he bowed low to the ground in deep respect. David said, "Greetings, Mephibosheth."

Mephibosheth replied, "I am your servant."

⁷"Don't be afraid!" David said. "I intend to show kindness to you because of my promise to your father, Jonathan. I will give you all the property that once belonged to your grandfather Saul, and you will eat here with me at the king's table!"

⁸Mephibosheth bowed respectfully and exclaimed, "Who is your servant, that you should show such kindness to a dead dog like me?"

⁹Then the king summoned Saul's servant Ziba and said, "I have given your master's grandson everything that belonged to Saul and his family. ¹⁰You and your sons and servants are to farm the land for him to produce food for your master's household.* But Mephibosheth, your master's grandson, will eat here at my table." (Ziba had fifteen sons and twenty servants.)

¹¹Ziba replied, "Yes, my lord the king; I am your servant, and I will do all that you have commanded." And from that time on, Mephibosheth ate regularly at David's table,* like one of the king's own sons.

¹²Mephibosheth had a young son named Mica. From then on, all the members of Ziba's household were Mephibosheth's servants. ¹³And Mephibosheth, who was crippled in both feet, lived in Jerusalem and ate regularly at the king's table.

David Defeats the Ammonites

10 Some time after this, King Nahash* of the Ammonites died, and his son Hanun became king. ²David said, "I am going to show loyalty to Hanun just as his father, Nahash, was always loyal to me." So David sent ambassadors to express sympathy to Hanun about his father's death.

But when David's ambassadors arrived in the land of Ammon, ³the Ammonite commanders said to Hanun, their master, "Do you really think these men are coming here to honor your father? No! David has sent them to spy out the city so they can come in and conquer it!"

⁴So Hanun seized David's ambassadors and shaved off half of each man's beard, cut off their robes at the buttocks, and sent them back to David in shame.

⁵When David heard what had happened, he sent messengers to tell the men, "Stay at Jericho until your beards grow out, and then come back." For they felt deep shame because of their appearance.

⁶When the people of Ammon realized how seriously they had angered David, they sent and hired 20,000 Aramean foot soldiers from the lands of Beth-rehob and Zobah, 1,000 from the king of Maacah, and 12,000 from the land of Tob. ⁷When David heard about this, he sent Joab and all his warriors to fight them. ⁸The Ammonite troops came out and drew up their battle lines at the entrance of the city gate, while the Arameans from Zobah and Rehob and the men from Tob and Maacah positioned themselves to fight in the open fields.

⁹When Joab saw that he would have to fight on both the front and the rear, he chose some of Israel's elite troops and placed them under his personal command to fight the Arameans in the fields. ¹⁰He left the rest of the army under the command of his brother Abishai, who was to attack the Ammonites. ¹¹"If the Arameans are too strong for me, then come over and help me," Joab told his brother. "And if the Ammonites are too strong for you, I will come and help you. ¹²Be courageous! Let us fight bravely for our people and the cities of our God. May the LORD's will be done."

¹³When Joab and his troops attacked, the Arameans began to run away. ¹⁴And when the Ammonites saw the Arameans running, they ran from Abishai and retreated into the city. After the battle was over, Joab returned to Jerusalem.

¹⁵The Arameans now realized that they were no match for Israel. So when they regrouped, ¹⁶they were joined by additional Aramean troops summoned by Hadadezer from the other side of the Euphrates River.* These troops arrived at Helam under the command of Shobach, the commander of Hadadezer's forces.

¹⁷When David heard what was happening, he mobilized all Israel, crossed the Jordan River, and led the army to Helam. The Arameans positioned themselves in battle formation and fought against David. ¹⁸But again the Arameans fled from the Israelites. This time David's forces killed 700 charioteers and 40,000 foot soldiers,* including Shobach, the commander of their army. ¹⁹When all the kings allied with Hadadezer saw that they had been defeated by Israel, they surrendered to Israel and became their subjects. After that, the Arameans were afraid to help the Ammonites.

9:6 *Mephibosheth* is another name for Merib-baal. **9:10** As in Greek version; Hebrew reads *your master's grandson.* **9:11** As in Greek version; Hebrew reads *my table.* **10:1** As in parallel text at 1 Chr 19:1; Hebrew reads *the king.* **10:16** Hebrew *the river.* **10:18** As in some Greek manuscripts (see also 1 Chr 19:18); Hebrew reads *charioteers.*

10:17-19 Turn back to reread 2:26. While we know these are wise words, thousands of people died, and this action brought only a temporary façade of peace. Israel wanted to be like other nations (1 Samuel 8:19-20). Now, the other nations were either afraid or were holding bitterness and resentment against Israel. Remember: just because something is in the Bible does not mean that God condones that attitude or action.

David and Bathsheba

11 In the spring of the year,* when kings normally go out to war, David sent Joab and the Israelite army to fight the Ammonites. They destroyed the Ammonite army and laid siege to the city of Rabbah. However, David stayed behind in Jerusalem.

²Late one afternoon, after his midday rest, David got out of bed and was walking on the roof of the palace. As he looked out over the city, he noticed a woman of unusual beauty taking a bath. ³He sent someone to find out who she was, and he was told, "She is Bathsheba, the daughter of Eliam and the wife of Uriah the Hittite." ⁴Then David sent messengers to get her; and when she came to the palace, he slept with her. She had just completed the purification rites after having her menstrual period. Then she returned home. ⁵Later, when Bathsheba discovered that she was pregnant, she sent David a message, saying, "I'm pregnant."

⁶Then David sent word to Joab: "Send me Uriah the Hittite." So Joab sent him to David. ⁷When Uriah arrived, David asked him how Joab and the army were getting along and how the war was progressing. ⁸Then he told Uriah, "Go on home and relax.*" David even sent a gift to Uriah after he had left the palace. ⁹But Uriah didn't go home. He slept that night at the palace entrance with the king's palace guard.

¹⁰When David heard that Uriah had not gone home, he summoned him and asked, "What's the matter? Why didn't you go home last night after being away for so long?"

¹¹Uriah replied, "The Ark and the armies of Israel and Judah are living in tents,* and Joab and my master's men are camping in the open fields. How could I go home to wine and dine and sleep with my wife? I swear that I would never do such a thing."

¹²"Well, stay here today," David told him, "and tomorrow you may return to the army." So Uriah stayed in Jerusalem that day and the next. ¹³Then David invited him to dinner and got him drunk. But even then he couldn't get Uriah to go home to his wife. Again he slept at the palace entrance with the king's palace guard.

David Arranges for Uriah's Death

¹⁴So the next morning David wrote a letter to Joab and gave it to Uriah to deliver. ¹⁵The letter instructed Joab, "Station Uriah on the front lines where the battle is fiercest. Then pull back so that he will be killed." ¹⁶So Joab assigned Uriah to a spot close to the city wall where he knew the enemy's strongest men were fighting. ¹⁷And when the enemy soldiers came out of the city to fight, Uriah the Hittite was killed along with several other Israelite soldiers.

¹⁸Then Joab sent a battle report to David. ¹⁹He told his messenger, "Report all the news of the battle to the king. ²⁰But he might get angry and ask, 'Why did the troops go so close to the city? Didn't they know there would be shooting from the walls? ²¹Wasn't Abimelech son of Gideon* killed at Thebez by a woman who threw a millstone down on him from the wall? Why would you get so close to the wall?' Then tell him, 'Uriah the Hittite was killed, too.'"

²²So the messenger went to Jerusalem and gave a complete report to David. ²³"The enemy came out against us in the open fields," he said. "And as we chased them back to the city gate, ²⁴the archers on the wall shot arrows at us. Some of the king's men were killed, including Uriah the Hittite."

²⁵"Well, tell Joab not to be discouraged," David said. "The sword devours this one today and that one tomorrow! Fight harder next time, and conquer the city!"

²⁶When Uriah's wife heard that her husband was dead, she mourned for him. ²⁷When the period of mourning was over, David sent for her and brought her to the palace, and she became one of his wives. Then she gave birth to a son. But the LORD was displeased with what David had done.

11:1 Hebrew *At the turn of the year.* The first day of the year in the ancient Hebrew lunar calendar occurred in March or April. **11:8** Hebrew *and wash your feet,* an expression that may also have a connotation of ritualistic washing. **11:11** Or *at Succoth.* **11:21** Hebrew *son of Jerub-besheth.* Jerub-besheth is a variation on the name Jerub-baal, which is another name for Gideon; see Judg 6:32.

11:1-27 The turning point for the sorrowful parts of David's history begins here. In these times, women had limited choices when powerful men wanted to have sex with them. They could agree, refuse and face harsh reprisals like death or imprisonment, or refuse and be raped anyway. This passage should be read as sexual abuse of power or rape, rather than seduction or mutual consent. This is especially true given the power imbalance between a king and his subject, and as we see in the rest of 2 Samuel, the consequences of David's actions affect his family and the whole of Israel. Sexual exploitation, unfortunately, is still the story of many women and girls today.
11:2-5 Bathsheba would have been bathing to clean herself after menstruating. She was following rituals she needed to obey, being faithful to the law of Moses. The text says only that she was purifying herself, not that she was seeking David's attention. Given the power difference between a king and his subjects, we can conclude that Bathsheba had no real choice in the matter. To have attempted refusal presumably would have resulted in dire consequences such as rape or death. Notice where God is in this passage: David does not consult God in these horrifying actions. The passage does not condone using power to satisfy ourselves.
11:27 While some have suggested that David and Bathsheba had a genuine relationship because they eventually were married, the law of Moses suggests otherwise. Deuteronomy 22:28-29 indicates that any man who exploited or raped a woman should be held responsible for this innocent victim's lifelong care. This prevented Bathsheba from going to the margins as a widow with a fatherless child; it required David to provide for her. It is okay to feel conflicted about these texts. Bring these concerns to God, who hears and knows. Nowhere in Scripture does God condone rape.

Nathan Rebukes David

12 So the LORD sent Nathan the prophet to tell David this story: "There were two men in a certain town. One was rich, and one was poor. ²The rich man owned a great many sheep and cattle. ³The poor man owned nothing but one little lamb he had bought. He raised that little lamb, and it grew up with his children. It ate from the man's own plate and drank from his cup. He cuddled it in his arms like a baby daughter. ⁴One day a guest arrived at the home of the rich man. But instead of killing an animal from his own flock or herd, he took the poor man's lamb and killed it and prepared it for his guest."

⁵David was furious. "As surely as the LORD lives," he vowed, "any man who would do such a thing

12:1 The Lord sent Nathan to David at least nine months after he took Bathsheba and murdered Uriah. Nathan's story is a rare Old Testament instance of a parable (see also Judges 9:8-15). Such stories can effectively communicate truth (see, for example, Matthew 13). David was rich: in his royal treasuries, his number of wives, and God's promises for his descendants. Uriah, by contrast, was poor: He had one home, one wife, and no children.

Insight — GOD HAS A BETTER PLAN

We all have plans for our lives, or at least a vision for how they might go, and the women of the Bible were no different. Bathsheba's life plan, her plan A, was probably to continue living a quiet life, worshiping God, raising a family, and working alongside her husband, Uriah. She didn't plan to be taken from her husband or for him to be killed. She certainly didn't plan to become King David's wife. What came next was plan B.

So how did God reward her as she lived plan B? Not only did she have a son who would become king of Israel, God blessed her by making her an ancestor of the Savior of the world, Jesus (see Matthew 1:6). Bathsheba is not the only woman who trusted God while living plan B and was blessed.

PERSON	PLAN A	PLAN B's BLESSING
Bathsheba 2 Samuel 11:1–12:25; 1 Kings 1:11-31	She lives with her husband, Uriah, and raises a family with him.	She marries a king, mothers the next king, and joins the family line of the Savior, Jesus.
Abigail 1 Samuel 25:1-42	She stays with Nabal and keeps trying to correct his mistakes.	She is freed from her "crude and mean" (1 Samuel 25:3) husband and marries the king.
Ruth Ruth 1–4	She lives with her first husband and family in her homeland.	She joins Jesus' family line (Matthew 1:5).
Rahab Joshua 2:1-24; 6:17, 22-23	She runs her inn and minds her own business.	She rescues the Israelite spies and is rescued in return. She joins the Messiah's family line (Matthew 1:5).
Sarah Genesis 11:29–23:20	She marries Abraham and stays in her city for the rest of her life.	She sees God do a miracle in helping her conceive and becomes the mother of nations.
You	How have you seen this in your own life? What was your plan A?	How can you embrace God's plan B for blessing?

deserves to die! ⁶He must repay four lambs to the poor man for the one he stole and for having no pity."

⁷Then Nathan said to David, "You are that man! The LORD, the God of Israel, says: I anointed you king of Israel and saved you from the power of Saul. ⁸I gave you your master's house and his wives and the kingdoms of Israel and Judah. And if that had not been enough, I would have given you much, much more. ⁹Why, then, have you despised the word of the LORD and done this horrible deed? For you have murdered Uriah the Hittite with the sword of the Ammonites and stolen his wife. ¹⁰From this time on, your family will live by the sword because you have despised me by taking Uriah's wife to be your own.

¹¹"This is what the LORD says: Because of what you have done, I will cause your own household to rebel against you. I will give your wives to another man before your very eyes, and he will go to bed with them in public view. ¹²You did it secretly, but I will make this happen to you openly in the sight of all Israel."

David Confesses His Guilt

¹³Then David confessed to Nathan, "I have sinned against the LORD."

Nathan replied, "Yes, but the LORD has forgiven you, and you won't die for this sin. ¹⁴Nevertheless, because you have shown utter contempt for the word of the LORD* by doing this, your child will die."

¹⁵After Nathan returned to his home, the LORD sent a deadly illness to the child of David and Uriah's wife. ¹⁶David begged God to spare the child. He went without food and lay all night on the bare ground. ¹⁷The elders of his household pleaded with him to get up and eat with them, but he refused.

¹⁸Then on the seventh day the child died. David's advisers were afraid to tell him. "He wouldn't listen to reason while the child was ill," they said. "What drastic thing will he do when we tell him the child is dead?"

¹⁹When David saw them whispering, he realized what had happened. "Is the child dead?" he asked.

"Yes," they replied, "he is dead."

²⁰Then David got up from the ground, washed himself, put on lotions,* and changed his clothes. He went to the Tabernacle and worshiped the LORD. After that, he returned to the palace and was served food and ate.

²¹His advisers were amazed. "We don't understand you," they told him. "While the child was still living, you wept and refused to eat. But now that the child is dead, you have stopped your mourning and are eating again."

²²David replied, "I fasted and wept while the child was alive, for I said, 'Perhaps the LORD will be gracious to me and let the child live.' ²³But why should I fast when he is dead? Can I bring him back again? I will go to him one day, but he cannot return to me."

²⁴Then David comforted Bathsheba, his wife, and slept with her. She became pregnant and gave birth to a son, and David* named him Solomon. The LORD loved the child ²⁵and sent word through Nathan the prophet that they should name him Jedidiah (which means "beloved of the LORD"), as the LORD had commanded.*

David Captures Rabbah

²⁶Meanwhile, Joab was fighting against Rabbah, the capital of Ammon, and he captured the royal fortifications.* ²⁷Joab sent messengers to tell David, "I have fought against Rabbah and captured its water supply.* ²⁸Now bring the rest of the army and capture the city. Otherwise, I will capture it and get credit for the victory."

²⁹So David gathered the rest of the army and went to Rabbah, and he fought against it and captured it. ³⁰David removed the crown from the king's head,* and it was placed on his own head. The crown was made of gold and set with gems, and it weighed seventy-five pounds.* David took a vast amount of plunder from the city. ³¹He also made slaves of the people of Rabbah and forced them to labor with* saws, iron picks, and iron axes, and to work in the brick kilns.* That is how he dealt with the people of all the Ammonite towns. Then David and all the army returned to Jerusalem.

The Rape of Tamar

13 Now David's son Absalom had a beautiful sister named Tamar. And Amnon, her half brother, fell desperately in love with her. ²Amnon became so obsessed with Tamar that he became ill. She was a virgin, and Amnon thought he could never have her.

³But Amnon had a very crafty friend—his cousin Jonadab. He was the son of David's brother Shimea.* ⁴One day Jonadab said to Amnon, "What's the trouble? Why should the son of a king look so dejected morning after morning?"

So Amnon told him, "I am in love with Tamar, my brother Absalom's sister."

⁵"Well," Jonadab said, "I'll tell you what to do. Go back to bed and pretend you are ill. When your father comes to see you, ask him to let Tamar come and prepare some

---

12:14 As in Dead Sea Scrolls; Masoretic Text reads *the enemies of the LORD*. **12:20** Hebrew *anointed himself*. **12:24** Hebrew *he;* an alternate Hebrew reading and some Hebrew manuscripts read *she*. **12:25** As in Greek version; Hebrew reads *because of the LORD*. **12:26** Or *the royal city*. **12:27** Or *captured the city of water*. **12:30a** Or *from the head of Milcom* (as in Greek version). Milcom, also called Molech, was the god of the Ammonites. **12:30b** Hebrew *1 talent [34 kilograms]*. **12:31a** Hebrew *He also brought out the people [of Rabbah] and put them under*. **12:31b** Hebrew *and he made them pass through the brick kilns*. **13:3** Hebrew *Shimeah* (also in 13:32), a variant spelling of Shimea; compare 1 Chr 2:13.

12:23 His son's death forced David to face his mortality. But he also showed his confidence in the afterlife.
12:30 David had, in effect, become the Ammonites' king. Instructions against taking such wealth during a conquest (Deuteronomy 7:25-26) show how dangerous David's actions were. Such wealth might seduce the king's heart away from God.

food for you. Tell him you'll feel better if she prepares it as you watch and feeds you with her own hands."

⁶So Amnon lay down and pretended to be sick. And when the king came to see him, Amnon asked him, "Please let my sister Tamar come and cook my favorite dish* as I watch. Then I can eat it from her own hands." ⁷So David agreed and sent Tamar to Amnon's house to prepare some food for him.

⁸When Tamar arrived at Amnon's house, she went to the place where he was lying down so he could watch her mix some dough. Then she baked his favorite dish for him. ⁹But when she set the serving tray before him, he refused to eat. "Everyone get out of here," Amnon told his servants. So they all left.

¹⁰Then he said to Tamar, "Now bring the food into my bedroom and feed it to me here." So Tamar took his favorite dish to him. ¹¹But as she was feeding him, he grabbed her and demanded, "Come to bed with me, my darling sister."

¹²"No, my brother!" she cried. "Don't be foolish! Don't do this to me! Such wicked things aren't done in Israel. ¹³Where could I go in my shame? And you would be called one of the greatest fools in Israel. Please, just speak to the king about it, and he will let you marry me."

¹⁴But Amnon wouldn't listen to her, and since he was stronger than she was, he raped her. ¹⁵Then suddenly Amnon's love turned to hate, and he hated her even more than he had loved her. "Get out of here!" he snarled at her.

¹⁶"No, no!" Tamar cried. "Sending me away now is worse than what you've already done to me."

But Amnon wouldn't listen to her. ¹⁷He shouted for his servant and demanded, "Throw this woman out, and lock the door behind her!"

¹⁸So the servant put her out and locked the door behind her. She was wearing a long, beautiful robe,* as was the custom in those days for the king's virgin daughters. ¹⁹But now Tamar tore her robe and put ashes on her head. And then, with her face in her hands, she went away crying.

²⁰Her brother Absalom saw her and asked, "Is it true that Amnon has been with you? Well, my sister, keep quiet for now, since he's your brother. Don't you worry about it." So Tamar lived as a desolate woman in her brother Absalom's house.

²¹When King David heard what had happened, he was very angry.* ²²And though Absalom never spoke to Amnon about this, he hated Amnon deeply because of what he had done to his sister.

13:6 Or *a couple of cakes*; also in 13:8, 10.   13:18 Or *a robe with sleeves*, or *an ornamented robe*. The meaning of the Hebrew is uncertain.   13:21 Dead Sea Scrolls and Greek version add *But he did not punish his son Amnon, because he loved him, for he was his firstborn.*

Perspective

What leads us down the path toward harm?

SCRIPTURE CONNECTION: 2 SAMUEL 13:1-22

Most of us do not wake up one day and suddenly commit heinous acts of evil. No, most often, our ability to harm others increases with practice, over time.

Born with demanding survival instincts, we arrive self-focused but not instinctively intent on harming others. As we grow, if our obsession with self goes unchallenged, we may inch our way into an appetite that destroys. We observe this with Amnon.

What progression led to the incestuous rape of his half sister, Tamar? Where was the first sign of trouble in this appalling event? Sexual attraction toward Tamar turned into an *obsession* mislabeled as love. Obsession led to secrecy, enlisting a crafty friend. Plotting and lies led to duplicity, then demands. Then heinous acts of evil.

As we examine our daily actions, are we progressing toward evil or toward love? Love empowers, uplifts; love does not cause harm.

VIEWPOINTS

HERS: As Amnon spewed anger and hatred upon her, what twisted messages did Tamar endure, further adding to her suffering?
MINE: "It is a wise practice to frequently pray and consider, 'Where have I been self-serving today? Have my actions harmed others, even in smaller ways? How may I instead reach for humility, amend my wrongdoing, and move in true love today?'"
YOURS: For harms done to you and harms you've done to others, how might you invite God to heal today?

MISTY ARTERBURN is an author and speaker, contributing to Bible projects, devotionals, and recovery materials for over twenty years. Wife and mom to five, Misty is the founder of Recovery Girls and the general editor of *The One Year Bible for Women.*

13:21-29 This whole passage uses relational language, reminding us that even the people closest to us, in our families, can harm us. The fact that David does not seek justice for his daughter and overlooks Amnon's sin does not mean that God would do the same. May we weep alongside our sisters in pain and seek righteous justice wherever abuse occurs.

Absalom's Revenge on Amnon

²³Two years later, when Absalom's sheep were being sheared at Baal-hazor near Ephraim, Absalom invited all the king's sons to come to a feast. ²⁴He went to the king and said, "My sheep-shearers are now at work. Would the king and his servants please come to celebrate the occasion with me?"

²⁵The king replied, "No, my son. If we all came, we would be too much of a burden on you." Absalom pressed him, but the king would not come, though he gave Absalom his blessing.

²⁶"Well, then," Absalom said, "if you can't come, how about sending my brother Amnon with us?"

"Why Amnon?" the king asked. ²⁷But Absalom kept on pressing the king until he finally agreed to let all his sons attend, including Amnon. So Absalom prepared a feast fit for a king.*

²⁸Absalom told his men, "Wait until Amnon gets drunk; then at my signal, kill him! Don't be afraid. I'm the one who has given the command. Take courage and do it!" ²⁹So at Absalom's signal they murdered Amnon. Then the other sons of the king jumped on their mules and fled.

³⁰As they were on the way back to Jerusalem, this report reached David: "Absalom has killed all the king's sons; not one is left alive!" ³¹The king got up,

13:27 As in Greek and Latin versions (compare also Dead Sea Scrolls); the Hebrew text lacks this sentence.

Come Close
UNFAIRNESS: FINDING GOD NEAR

SCRIPTURE CONNECTION: 2 SAMUEL 6:16-23; 13:1-20

How many times do we get our stomach in knots when we feel unfairness's heavy hand? How many times do we wince, knowing *we* are unfair?

Reading the stories of two childless women, Michal and Tamar, we can guess their pain. Being a mother was one of the culture's most prized roles. The reasons for being childless? Michal selfishly criticized; Tamar, victimized, could not remarry.

My heart aches for Tamar—the violence and injustice committed against her were reprehensible! And I cannot condemn Michal. Her punishment was so severe for one judgmental moment. I know I am not innocent of judging. So how do we find what's fair? Here's a little of what the Bible says about God's fairness [emphasis added]:

"His government and its peace will never end. He will rule with *fairness and justice* from the throne of his ancestor David for all eternity" (Isaiah 9:7).

"This faith was given to you because of the *justice and fairness* of Jesus Christ, our God and Savior" (2 Peter 1:1).

The "justice and fairness of Jesus Christ," a descendant of King David, amends the pain we inflict and the pain we bear. We can be forgiven, forgive others, and draw closer to God. He knows our hearts, our pain; he knows us and he stays.

When life is unfair—or we are unfair—Jesus forgives, Jesus loves, and Jesus is there.

REFLECT "This faith was given to you because of the justice and fairness of Jesus Christ, our God and Savior." 2 PETER 1:1

Jesus, help me trust when you say "I know and I am here" to soothe me when the world is unfair. Please help me acknowledge when you say "I know, I am here" when I have been unfair and need your grace. Amen.

CONSIDER "We rarely think of the air we breathe, yet it is in us and around us all the time. In similar fashion, the presence of God penetrates us, is all around us, is always embracing us." THOMAS KEATING, *Open Mind, Open Heart: The Contemplative Dimension of the Gospel*

> When life is unfair, or we are unfair, Jesus' forgiving, faithful love is there.

ELISABETH SELZER ROGERS, MDiv, MA, PhD, is a passionate believer and follower of Christ, bringing his love to the secular world through mentoring, coaching, and modeling his unconditional love.

tore his robe, and threw himself on the ground. His advisers also tore their clothes in horror and sorrow.

³²But just then Jonadab, the son of David's brother Shimea, arrived and said, "No, don't believe that all the king's sons have been killed! It was only Amnon! Absalom has been plotting this ever since Amnon raped his sister Tamar. ³³No, my lord the king, your sons aren't all dead! It was only Amnon." ³⁴Meanwhile Absalom escaped.

Then the watchman on the Jerusalem wall saw a great crowd coming down the hill on the road from the west. He ran to tell the king, "I see a crowd of people coming from the Horonaim road along the side of the hill."*

³⁵"Look!" Jonadab told the king. "There they are now! The king's sons are coming, just as I said."

³⁶They soon arrived, weeping and sobbing, and the king and all his servants wept bitterly with them. ³⁷And David mourned many days for his son Amnon.

Absalom fled to his grandfather, Talmai son of Ammihud, the king of Geshur. ³⁸He stayed there in Geshur for three years. ³⁹And King David,* now reconciled to Amnon's death, longed to be reunited with his son Absalom.*

Joab Arranges for Absalom's Return

14 Joab realized how much the king longed to see Absalom. ²So he sent for a woman from Tekoa who had a reputation for great wisdom. He said to her, "Pretend you are in mourning; wear mourning clothes and don't put on lotions.* Act like a woman who has been mourning for the dead for a long time. ³Then go to the king and tell him the story I am about to tell you." Then Joab told her what to say.

⁴When the woman from Tekoa approached* the king, she bowed with her face to the ground in deep respect and cried out, "O king! Help me!"

⁵"What's the trouble?" the king asked.

"Alas, I am a widow!" she replied. "My husband is dead. ⁶My two sons had a fight out in the field. And since no one was there to stop it, one of them was killed. ⁷Now the rest of the family is demanding, 'Let us have your son. We will execute him for murdering his brother. He doesn't deserve to inherit his family's property.' They want to extinguish the only coal I have left, and my husband's name and family will disappear from the face of the earth."

⁸"Leave it to me," the king told her. "Go home, and I'll see to it that no one touches him."

⁹"Oh, thank you, my lord the king," the woman from Tekoa replied. "If you are criticized for helping me, let the blame fall on me and on my father's house, and let the king and his throne be innocent."

¹⁰"If anyone objects," the king said, "bring him to me. I can assure you he will never harm you again!"

¹¹Then she said, "Please swear to me by the LORD your God that you won't let anyone take vengeance against my son. I want no more bloodshed."

"As surely as the LORD lives," he replied, "not a hair on your son's head will be disturbed!"

¹²"Please allow me to ask one more thing of my lord the king," she said.

"Go ahead and speak," he responded.

¹³She replied, "Why don't you do as much for the people of God as you have promised to do for me? You have convicted yourself in making this decision, because you have refused to bring home your own banished son. ¹⁴All of us must die eventually. Our lives are like water spilled out on the ground, which cannot be gathered up again. But God does not just sweep life away; instead, he devises ways to bring us back when we have been separated from him.

¹⁵"I have come to plead with my lord the king because people have threatened me. I said to myself, 'Perhaps the king will listen to me ¹⁶and rescue us from those who would cut us off from the inheritance* God has given us. ¹⁷Yes, my lord the king will give us peace of mind again.' I know that you are like an angel of God in discerning good from evil. May the LORD your God be with you."

¹⁸"I must know one thing," the king replied, "and tell me the truth."

"Yes, my lord the king," she responded.

¹⁹"Did Joab put you up to this?"

And the woman replied, "My lord the king, how can I deny it? Nobody can hide anything from you. Yes, Joab sent me and told me what to say. ²⁰He did it to place the matter before you in a different light. But you are as wise as an angel of God, and you understand everything that happens among us!"

²¹So the king sent for Joab and told him, "All right, go and bring back the young man Absalom."

²²Joab bowed with his face to the ground in deep respect and said, "At last I know that I have gained your approval, my lord the king, for you have granted me this request!"

²³Then Joab went to Geshur and brought Absalom back to Jerusalem. ²⁴But the king gave this order: "Absalom may go to his own house, but he must never come into my presence." So Absalom did not see the king.

Absalom Reconciled to David

²⁵Now Absalom was praised as the most handsome man in all Israel. He was flawless from head to foot. ²⁶He cut his hair only once a year, and then only because it was so heavy. When he weighed it out, it came to five pounds!* ²⁷He had three sons and one daughter. His daughter's name was Tamar, and she was very beautiful.

13:34 As in Greek version; Hebrew lacks this sentence. **13:39a** Dead Sea Scrolls and Greek version read *And the spirit of the king.* **13:39b** Or *no longer felt a need to go out after Absalom.* **14:2** Hebrew *don't anoint yourself with oil.* **14:4** As in many Hebrew manuscripts and Greek and Syriac versions; Masoretic Text reads *spoke to.* **14:16** Or *the property;* or *the people.* **14:26** Hebrew *200 shekels* [2.3 kilograms] *by the royal standard.*

²⁸Absalom lived in Jerusalem for two years, but he never got to see the king. ²⁹Then Absalom sent for Joab to ask him to intercede for him, but Joab refused to come. Absalom sent for him a second time, but again Joab refused to come. ³⁰So Absalom said to his servants, "Go and set fire to Joab's barley field, the field next to mine." So they set his field on fire, as Absalom had commanded.

³¹Then Joab came to Absalom at his house and demanded, "Why did your servants set my field on fire?"

³²And Absalom replied, "Because I wanted you to ask the king why he brought me back from Geshur if he didn't intend to see me. I might as well have stayed there. Let me see the king; if he finds me guilty of anything, then let him kill me."

³³So Joab told the king what Absalom had said. Then at last David summoned Absalom, who came and bowed low before the king, and the king kissed him.

Absalom's Rebellion

15 After this, Absalom bought a chariot and horses, and he hired fifty bodyguards to run ahead of him. ²He got up early every morning and went out to the gate of the city. When people brought a case to the king for judgment, Absalom would ask where in Israel they were from, and they would tell him their tribe. ³Then Absalom would say, "You've really got a strong case here! It's too bad the king doesn't have anyone to hear it. ⁴I wish I were the judge. Then everyone could bring their cases to me for judgment, and I would give them justice!"

⁵When people tried to bow before him, Absalom wouldn't let them. Instead, he took them by the hand and kissed them. ⁶Absalom did this with everyone who came to the king for judgment, and so he stole the hearts of all the people of Israel.

⁷After four years,* Absalom said to the king, "Let me go to Hebron to offer a sacrifice to the LORD and fulfill a vow I made to him. ⁸For while your servant was at Geshur in Aram, I promised to sacrifice to the LORD in Hebron* if he would bring me back to Jerusalem."

⁹"All right," the king told him. "Go and fulfill your vow."

So Absalom went to Hebron. ¹⁰But while he was there, he sent secret messengers to all the tribes of Israel to stir up a rebellion against the king. "As soon as you hear the ram's horn," his message read, "you are to say, 'Absalom has been crowned king in Hebron.'" ¹¹He took 200 men from Jerusalem with him as guests, but they knew nothing of his intentions. ¹²While Absalom was offering the sacrifices, he sent for Ahithophel, one of David's counselors who lived in Giloh. Soon many others also joined Absalom, and the conspiracy gained momentum.

David Escapes from Jerusalem

¹³A messenger soon arrived in Jerusalem to tell David, "All Israel has joined Absalom in a conspiracy against you!"

¹⁴"Then we must flee at once, or it will be too late!" David urged his men. "Hurry! If we get out of the city before Absalom arrives, both we and the city of Jerusalem will be spared from disaster."

¹⁵"We are with you," his advisers replied. "Do what you think is best."

¹⁶So the king and all his household set out at once. He left no one behind except ten of his concubines to look after the palace. ¹⁷The king and all his people set out on foot, pausing at the last house ¹⁸to let all the king's men move past to lead the way. There were 600 men from Gath who had come with David, along with the king's bodyguard.*

¹⁹Then the king turned and said to Ittai, a leader of the men from Gath, "Why are you coming with us? Go on back to King Absalom, for you are a guest in Israel, a foreigner in exile. ²⁰You arrived only recently, and should I force you today to wander with us? I don't even know where we will go. Go on back and take your kinsmen with you, and may the LORD show you his unfailing love and faithfulness.*"

²¹But Ittai said to the king, "I vow by the LORD and by your own life that I will go wherever my lord the king goes, no matter what happens—whether it means life or death."

²²David replied, "All right, come with us." So Ittai and all his men and their families went along.

²³Everyone cried loudly as the king and his followers passed by. They crossed the Kidron Valley and then went out toward the wilderness.

²⁴Zadok and all the Levites also came along, carrying the Ark of the Covenant of God. They set down the Ark of God, and Abiathar offered sacrifices* until everyone had passed out of the city.

²⁵Then the king instructed Zadok to take the Ark of God back into the city. "If the LORD sees fit," David said, "he will bring me back to see the Ark and the Tabernacle* again. ²⁶But if he is through with me, then let him do what seems best to him."

²⁷The king also told Zadok the priest, "Look,* here is my plan. You and Abiathar* should return quietly to the city with your son Ahimaaz and Abiathar's son Jonathan. ²⁸I will stop at the shallows of the Jordan

---

15:7 As in Greek and Syriac versions; Hebrew reads *forty years*. **15:8** As in some Greek manuscripts; Hebrew lacks *in Hebron*. **15:18** Hebrew *the Kerethites and Pelethites*. **15:20** As in Greek version; Hebrew reads *and may unfailing love and faithfulness go with you*. **15:24** Or *Abiathar went up*. **15:25** Hebrew *and his dwelling place*. **15:27a** As in Greek version; Hebrew reads *Are you a seer?* or *Do you see?* **15:27b** Hebrew lacks *and Abiathar;* compare 15:29.

15:19-22 Ittai was a Philistine from Gath, which may surprise us. Here was Ittai, received into the fold, in a text where the people generally attempted to get rid of the Philistines. As we read the Bible, we can pay attention to "unexpected" people who join what God is doing. What does the appearance of such people tell us about the heart of God and our understanding of him?

Tamar

Reliving or Living?

Tamar remembers...

His request for his favorite food didn't bother me, and I was just concerned that he was ill. How could I have known what he really wanted?

I review that day again and again in my mind. What warning signs did I miss? Should I have said no to Amnon's request to cook? I retrace my steps along every choice that would have kept me from his clutches.

I relive the never-ending loop of my naivete and desolation. I'm bound up in his wrongdoing, his moment of his pleasure, his hot anger.

But reliving it does not change one thing. No matter how I try to rewrite my story, I will always have the history of his hands on me.

My father, King David, has said that God's love never fails, that we can cry out to God in our distress. My father never stopped crying out to God, as he waited fifteen years for a promised throne. But, because he refuses to discipline my rapist, his son, my father fails me now in *my* desolation.

It is hard to see God's unfailing love in my distress. I cannot see my future, but I, too, will take each step of faith I can and keep looking to God.

> God pulls us from our pain by his promises.

TAMAR'S STORY IS TOLD IN 2 SAMUEL 13:1-22.

IDENTIFY

Are you stuck in a time loop of regret or grief? Have you asked God to pull you out of it and help you look toward the future?

Tamar's memory of David's distress refers to instances recorded in some of his psalms (for example, Psalm 18). Which psalm helps you look up and forward instead of back and down?

"The things that happen to us by someone else's hand can wreck us for life. The trauma can keep us looking at the past, threatening to erase our future. Though I have replayed moments, days, and decisions, I refuse to live looking over my shoulder—it won't stop the pain. I choose to look up and forward to God, who leads me to wide-open, hopeful spaces."

CARA DAY is a writer and illustrator. She has served with Stonecroft Ministries helping women live "extraordinary."

WHAT THE BIBLE SAYS ABOUT
Bitterness and Healing

Bitterness Hurts Us

Each heart knows its own bitterness,
  and no one else can fully share its joy.
PROVERBS 14:10

I envied the proud
  when I saw them prosper despite their wickedness....
Then I realized that my heart was bitter,
  and I was all torn up inside.
PSALM 73:3, 21

Surely resentment destroys the fool,
  and jealousy kills the simple.
JOB 5:2

Healing Comes from God and Others

Look after each other so that none of you fails to receive the grace of God. Watch out that no poisonous root of bitterness grows up to trouble you, corrupting many.
HEBREWS 12:15

"Repent of your wickedness and pray to the Lord. Perhaps he will forgive your evil thoughts, for I can see that you are full of bitter jealousy and are held captive by sin."
ACTS 8:22-23

Get rid of all bitterness, rage, anger, harsh words, and slander, as well as all types of evil behavior. Instead, be kind to each other, tenderhearted, forgiving one another, just as God through Christ has forgiven you.
EPHESIANS 4:31-32

...Instead, be kind to each other...

River* and wait there for a report from you." ²⁹So Zadok and Abiathar took the Ark of God back to the city and stayed there.

³⁰David walked up the road to the Mount of Olives, weeping as he went. His head was covered and his feet were bare as a sign of mourning. And the people who were with him covered their heads and wept as they climbed the hill. ³¹When someone told David that his adviser Ahithophel was now backing Absalom, David prayed, "O LORD, let Ahithophel give Absalom foolish advice!"

³²When David reached the summit of the Mount of Olives where people worshiped God, Hushai the Arkite was waiting there for him. Hushai had torn his clothing and put dirt on his head as a sign of mourning. ³³But David told him, "If you go with me, you will only be a burden. ³⁴Return to Jerusalem and tell Absalom, 'I will now be your adviser, O king, just as I was your father's adviser in the past.' Then you can frustrate and counter Ahithophel's advice. ³⁵Zadok and Abiathar, the priests, will be there. Tell them about the plans being made in the king's palace, ³⁶and they will send their sons Ahimaaz and Jonathan to tell me what is going on."

³⁷So David's friend Hushai returned to Jerusalem, getting there just as Absalom arrived.

David and Ziba

16 When David had gone a little beyond the summit of the Mount of Olives, Ziba, the servant of Mephibosheth,* was waiting there for him. He had two donkeys loaded with 200 loaves of bread, 100 clusters of raisins, 100 bunches of summer fruit, and a wineskin full of wine.

²"What are these for?" the king asked Ziba.

Ziba replied, "The donkeys are for the king's people to ride on, and the bread and summer fruit are for the young men to eat. The wine is for those who become exhausted in the wilderness."

³"And where is Mephibosheth, Saul's grandson?" the king asked him.

"He stayed in Jerusalem," Ziba replied. "He said, 'Today I will get back the kingdom of my grandfather Saul.'"

⁴"In that case," the king told Ziba, "I give you everything Mephibosheth owns."

"I bow before you," Ziba replied. "May I always be pleasing to you, my lord the king."

Shimei Curses David

⁵As King David came to Bahurim, a man came out of the village cursing them. It was Shimei son of Gera, from the same clan as Saul's family. ⁶He threw stones at the king and the king's officers and all the mighty warriors who surrounded him. ⁷"Get out of here, you murderer, you scoundrel!" he shouted at David.

⁸"The LORD is paying you back for all the bloodshed in Saul's clan. You stole his throne, and now the LORD has given it to your son Absalom. At last you will taste some of your own medicine, for you are a murderer!"

⁹"Why should this dead dog curse my lord the king?" Abishai son of Zeruiah demanded. "Let me go over and cut off his head!"

¹⁰"No!" the king said. "Who asked your opinion, you sons of Zeruiah! If the LORD has told him to curse me, who are you to stop him?"

¹¹Then David said to Abishai and to all his servants, "My own son is trying to kill me. Doesn't this relative of Saul* have even more reason to do so? Leave him alone and let him curse, for the LORD has told him to do it. ¹²And perhaps the LORD will see that I am being wronged* and will bless me because of these curses today." ¹³So David and his men continued down the road, and Shimei kept pace with them on a nearby hillside, cursing and throwing stones and dirt at David.

¹⁴The king and all who were with him grew weary along the way, so they rested when they reached the Jordan River.*

Ahithophel Advises Absalom

¹⁵Meanwhile, Absalom and all the army of Israel arrived at Jerusalem, accompanied by Ahithophel. ¹⁶When David's friend Hushai the Arkite arrived, he went immediately to see Absalom. "Long live the king!" he exclaimed. "Long live the king!"

¹⁷"Is this the way you treat your friend David?" Absalom asked him. "Why aren't you with him?"

¹⁸"I'm here because I belong to the man who is chosen by the LORD and by all the men of Israel," Hushai replied. ¹⁹"And anyway, why shouldn't I serve you? Just as I was your father's adviser, now I will be your adviser!"

²⁰Then Absalom turned to Ahithophel and asked him, "What should I do next?"

²¹Ahithophel told him, "Go and sleep with your father's concubines, for he has left them here to look after the palace. Then all Israel will know that you have insulted your father beyond hope of reconciliation, and they will throw their support to you." ²²So they set up a tent on the palace roof where everyone could see it, and Absalom went in and had sex with his father's concubines.

²³Absalom followed Ahithophel's advice, just as David had done. For every word Ahithophel spoke seemed as wise as though it had come directly from the mouth of God.

17 Now Ahithophel urged Absalom, "Let me choose 12,000 men to start out after David tonight. ²I will catch up with him while he is weary and discouraged. He and his troops will panic, and everyone will run away. Then I will kill only the king,

---

15:28 Hebrew *at the crossing points of the wilderness.* **16:1** *Mephibosheth* is another name for Merib-baal. **16:11** Hebrew *this Benjaminite.* **16:12** As in Greek and Syriac versions; Hebrew reads *see my iniquity.* **16:14** As in Greek version (see also 17:16); Hebrew reads *when they reached their destination.*

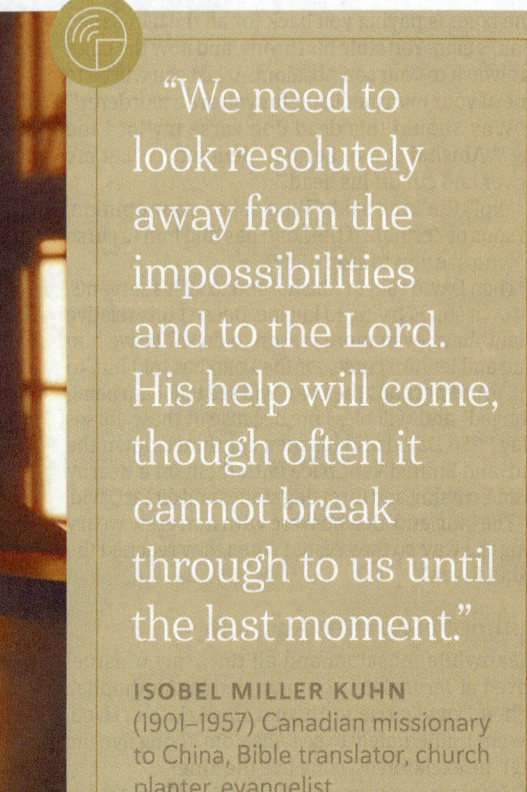

> "We need to look resolutely away from the impossibilities and to the Lord. His help will come, though often it cannot break through to us until the last moment."
>
> ISOBEL MILLER KUHN
> (1901–1957) Canadian missionary to China, Bible translator, church planter, evangelist

the word will spread that Absalom's men are being slaughtered. ¹⁰Then even the bravest soldiers, though they have the heart of a lion, will be paralyzed with fear. For all Israel knows what a mighty warrior your father is and how courageous his men are.

¹¹"I recommend that you mobilize the entire army of Israel, bringing them from as far away as Dan in the north and Beersheba in the south. That way you will have an army as numerous as the sand on the seashore. And I advise that you personally lead the troops. ¹²When we find David, we'll fall on him like dew that falls on the ground. Then neither he nor any of his men will be left alive. ¹³And if David were to escape into some town, you will have all Israel there at your command. Then we can take ropes and drag the walls of the town into the nearest valley until every stone is torn down."

¹⁴Then Absalom and all the men of Israel said, "Hushai's advice is better than Ahithophel's." For the LORD had determined to defeat the counsel of Ahithophel, which really was the better plan, so that he could bring disaster on Absalom!

Hushai Warns David to Escape

¹⁵Hushai told Zadok and Abiathar, the priests, what Ahithophel had said to Absalom and the elders of Israel and what he himself had advised instead. ¹⁶"Quick!" he told them. "Find David and urge him not to stay at the shallows of the Jordan River* tonight. He must go across at once into the wilderness beyond. Otherwise he will die and his entire army with him."

¹⁷Jonathan and Ahimaaz had been staying at En-rogel so as not to be seen entering and leaving the city. Arrangements had been made for a servant girl to bring them the message they were to take to King David. ¹⁸But a boy spotted them at En-rogel, and he told Absalom about it. So they quickly escaped to Bahurim, where a man hid them down inside a well in his courtyard. ¹⁹The man's wife put a cloth over the top of the well and scattered grain on it to dry in the sun; so no one suspected they were there.

²⁰When Absalom's men arrived, they asked her, "Have you seen Ahimaaz and Jonathan?"

The woman replied, "They were here, but they crossed over the brook." Absalom's men looked for them without success and returned to Jerusalem.

²¹Then the two men crawled out of the well and hurried on to King David. "Quick!" they told him, "cross the Jordan tonight!" And they told him how Ahithophel had advised that he be captured and killed. ²²So David and all the people with him went across the Jordan River during the night, and they were all on the other bank before dawn.

²³When Ahithophel realized that his advice had not been followed, he saddled his donkey, went to

³and I will bring all the people back to you as a bride returns to her husband. After all, it is only one man's life that you seek.* Then you will be at peace with all the people." ⁴This plan seemed good to Absalom and to all the elders of Israel.

Hushai Counters Ahithophel's Advice

⁵But then Absalom said, "Bring in Hushai the Arkite. Let's see what he thinks about this." ⁶When Hushai arrived, Absalom told him what Ahithophel had said. Then he asked, "What is your opinion? Should we follow Ahithophel's advice? If not, what do you suggest?"

⁷"Well," Hushai replied to Absalom, "this time Ahithophel has made a mistake. ⁸You know your father and his men; they are mighty warriors. Right now they are as enraged as a mother bear who has been robbed of her cubs. And remember that your father is an experienced man of war. He won't be spending the night among the troops. ⁹He has probably already hidden in some pit or cave. And when he comes out and attacks and a few of your men fall, there will be panic among your troops, and

---

17:3 As in Greek version; Hebrew reads *like the return of all is the man whom you seek.* 17:16 Hebrew *at the crossing points of the wilderness.*

his hometown, set his affairs in order, and hanged himself. He died there and was buried in the family tomb.

24David soon arrived at Mahanaim. By now, Absalom had mobilized the entire army of Israel and was leading his troops across the Jordan River. 25Absalom had appointed Amasa as commander of his army, replacing Joab, who had been commander under David. (Amasa was Joab's cousin. His father was Jether,* an Ishmaelite.* His mother, Abigail daughter of Nahash, was the sister of Joab's mother, Zeruiah.) 26Absalom and the Israelite army set up camp in the land of Gilead.

27When David arrived at Mahanaim, he was warmly greeted by Shobi son of Nahash, who came from Rabbah of the Ammonites, and by Makir son of Ammiel from Lo-debar, and by Barzillai of Gilead from Rogelim. 28They brought sleeping mats, cooking pots, serving bowls, wheat and barley, flour and roasted grain, beans, lentils, 29honey, butter, sheep, goats, and cheese for David and those who were with him. For they said, "You must all be very hungry and tired and thirsty after your long march through the wilderness."

Absalom's Defeat and Death

18 David now mustered the men who were with him and appointed generals and captains* to lead them. 2He sent the troops out in three groups, placing one group under Joab, one under Joab's brother Abishai son of Zeruiah, and one under Ittai, the man from Gath. The king told his troops, "I am going out with you."

3But his men objected strongly. "You must not go," they urged. "If we have to turn and run—and even if half of us die—it will make no difference to Absalom's troops; they will be looking only for you. You are worth 10,000 of us,* and it is better that you stay here in the town and send help if we need it."

4"If you think that's the best plan, I'll do it," the king answered. So he stood alongside the gate of the town as all the troops marched out in groups of hundreds and of thousands.

5And the king gave this command to Joab, Abishai, and Ittai: "For my sake, deal gently with young Absalom." And all the troops heard the king give this order to his commanders.

6So the battle began in the forest of Ephraim, 7and the Israelite troops were beaten back by David's men. There was a great slaughter that day, and 20,000 men laid down their lives. 8The battle raged all across the countryside, and more men died because of the forest than were killed by the sword.

9During the battle, Absalom happened to come upon some of David's men. He tried to escape on his mule, but as he rode beneath the thick branches of a great tree, his hair* got caught in the tree. His mule kept going and left him dangling in the air. 10One of David's men saw what had happened and told Joab, "I saw Absalom dangling from a great tree."

11"What?" Joab demanded. "You saw him there and didn't kill him? I would have rewarded you with ten pieces of silver* and a hero's belt!"

12"I would not kill the king's son for even a thousand pieces of silver,*" the man replied to Joab. "We all heard the king say to you and Abishai and Ittai, 'For my sake, please spare young Absalom.' 13And if I had betrayed the king by killing his son—and the king would certainly find out who did it—you yourself would be the first to abandon me."

14"Enough of this nonsense," Joab said. Then he took three daggers and plunged them into Absalom's heart as he dangled, still alive, in the great tree. 15Ten of Joab's young armor bearers then surrounded Absalom and killed him.

16Then Joab blew the ram's horn, and his men returned from chasing the army of Israel. 17They threw Absalom's body into a deep pit in the forest and piled a great heap of stones over it. And all Israel fled to their homes.

18During his lifetime, Absalom had built a monument to himself in the King's Valley, for he said, "I have no son to carry on my name." He named the monument after himself, and it is known as Absalom's Monument to this day.

David Mourns Absalom's Death

19Then Zadok's son Ahimaaz said, "Let me run to the king with the good news that the LORD has rescued him from his enemies."

20"No," Joab told him, "it wouldn't be good news to the king that his son is dead. You can be my messenger another time, but not today."

21Then Joab said to a man from Ethiopia,* "Go tell the king what you have seen." The man bowed and ran off.

22But Ahimaaz continued to plead with Joab, "Whatever happens, please let me go, too."

"Why should you go, my son?" Joab replied. "There will be no reward for your news."

23"Yes, but let me go anyway," he begged.

Joab finally said, "All right, go ahead." So Ahimaaz took the less demanding route by way of the plain and ran to Mahanaim ahead of the Ethiopian.

24While David was sitting between the inner and outer gates of the town, the watchman climbed to

---

17:25a Hebrew *Ithra*, a variant spelling of *Jether*. **17:25b** As in some Greek manuscripts (see also 1 Chr 2:17); Hebrew reads *an Israelite*. **18:1** Hebrew *appointed commanders of thousands and commanders of hundreds*. **18:3** As in two Hebrew manuscripts and some Greek and Latin manuscripts; most Hebrew manuscripts read *Now there are 10,000 like us*. **18:9** Hebrew *his head*. **18:11** Hebrew *10 [shekels] of silver*, about 4 ounces or 114 grams in weight. **18:12** Hebrew *1,000 [shekels] of silver*, about 25 pounds or 11.4 kilograms in weight. **18:21** Hebrew *from Cush*; similarly in 18:23, 31, 32.

the roof of the gateway by the wall. As he looked, he saw a lone man running toward them. ²⁵He shouted the news down to David, and the king replied, "If he is alone, he has news."

As the messenger came closer, ²⁶the watchman saw another man running toward them. He shouted down, "Here comes another one!"

The king replied, "He also will have news."

²⁷"The first man runs like Ahimaaz son of Zadok," the watchman said.

"He is a good man and comes with good news," the king replied.

²⁸Then Ahimaaz cried out to the king, "Everything is all right!" He bowed before the king with his face to the ground and said, "Praise to the LORD your God, who has handed over the rebels who dared to stand against my lord the king."

²⁹"What about young Absalom?" the king demanded. "Is he all right?"

Ahimaaz replied, "When Joab told me to come, there was a lot of commotion. But I didn't know what was happening."

³⁰"Wait here," the king told him. So Ahimaaz stepped aside.

³¹Then the man from Ethiopia arrived and said, "I have good news for my lord the king. Today the LORD has rescued you from all those who rebelled against you."

³²"What about young Absalom?" the king demanded. "Is he all right?"

And the Ethiopian replied, "May all of your enemies, my lord the king, both now and in the future, share the fate of that young man!"

³³*The king was overcome with emotion. He went up to the room over the gateway and burst into tears. And as he went, he cried, "O my son Absalom! My son, my son Absalom! If only I had died instead of you! O Absalom, my son, my son."

Joab Rebukes the King

19 ¹*Word soon reached Joab that the king was weeping and mourning for Absalom. ²As all the people heard of the king's deep grief for his son, the joy of that day's victory was turned into deep sadness. ³They crept back into the town that day as though they were ashamed and had deserted in battle. ⁴The king covered his face with his hands and kept on crying, "O my son Absalom! O Absalom, my son, my son!"

⁵Then Joab went to the king's room and said to him, "We saved your life today and the lives of your sons, your daughters, and your wives and concubines. Yet you act like this, making us feel ashamed of ourselves. ⁶You seem to love those who hate you and hate those who love you. You have made it clear today that your commanders and troops mean nothing to you. It seems that if Absalom had lived and all of us had died, you would be pleased. ⁷Now go out there and congratulate your troops, for I swear by the LORD that if you don't go out, not a single one of them will remain here tonight. Then you will be worse off than ever before."

⁸So the king went out and took his seat at the town gate, and as the news spread throughout the town that he was there, everyone went to him.

Meanwhile, the Israelites who had supported Absalom fled to their homes. ⁹And throughout all the tribes of Israel there was much discussion and argument going on. The people were saying, "The king rescued us from our enemies and saved us from the Philistines, but Absalom chased him out of the country. ¹⁰Now Absalom, whom we anointed to rule over us, is dead. Why not ask David to come back and be our king again?"

¹¹Then King David sent Zadok and Abiathar, the priests, to say to the elders of Judah, "Why are you the last ones to welcome back the king into his palace? For I have heard that all Israel is ready. ¹²You are my relatives, my own tribe, my own flesh and blood! So why are you the last ones to welcome back the king?" ¹³And David told them to tell Amasa, "Since you are my own flesh and blood, like Joab, may God strike me and even kill me if I do not appoint you as commander of my army in his place."

¹⁴Then Amasa* convinced all the men of Judah, and they responded unanimously. They sent word to the king, "Return to us, and bring back all who are with you."

David's Return to Jerusalem

¹⁵So the king started back to Jerusalem. And when he arrived at the Jordan River, the people of Judah came to Gilgal to meet him and escort him across the river. ¹⁶Shimei son of Gera, the man from Bahurim in Benjamin, hurried across with the men of Judah to welcome King David. ¹⁷A thousand other men from the tribe of Benjamin were with him, including Ziba, the chief servant of the house of Saul, and Ziba's fifteen sons and twenty servants. They rushed down to the Jordan to meet the king. ¹⁸They crossed the shallows

---

18:33 Verse 18:33 is numbered 19:1 in Hebrew text. **19:1** Verses 19:1-43 are numbered 19:2-44 in Hebrew text. **19:14** Or *David;* Hebrew reads *he.*

18:33 David's private family life powerfully affected his public life because of his position. His past wrongdoings included abuse of power, sexual exploitation, and murder, and he did not seek justice when his son raped his own daughter. David's private-life issues haunted the nation under his leadership. While David did repent for what he had done to Bathsheba and her husband, the consequences still followed him. Showing repentance is crucial to having a right relationship with God and others. As we consider what it means to influence or lead, what might we need to repent of in our private and public lives?

of the Jordan to bring the king's household across the river, helping him in every way they could.

David's Mercy to Shimei

As the king was about to cross the river, Shimei fell down before him. [19] "My lord the king, please forgive me," he pleaded. "Forget the terrible thing your servant did when you left Jerusalem. May the king put it out of his mind. [20] I know how much I sinned. That is why I have come here today, the very first person in all Israel* to greet my lord the king."

[21] Then Abishai son of Zeruiah said, "Shimei should die, for he cursed the LORD's anointed king!"

[22] "Who asked your opinion, you sons of Zeruiah!" David exclaimed. "Why have you become my adversary* today? This is not a day for execution, for today I am once again the king of Israel!" [23] Then, turning to Shimei, David vowed, "Your life will be spared."

David's Kindness to Mephibosheth

[24] Now Mephibosheth,* Saul's grandson, came down from Jerusalem to meet the king. He had not cared for his feet, trimmed his beard, or washed his clothes since the day the king left Jerusalem. [25] "Why didn't you come with me, Mephibosheth?" the king asked him.

[26] Mephibosheth replied, "My lord the king, my servant Ziba deceived me. I told him, 'Saddle my donkey* so I can go with the king.' For as you know I am crippled. [27] Ziba has slandered me by saying that I refused to come. But I know that my lord the king is like an angel of God, so do what you think is best. [28] All my relatives and I could expect only death from you, my lord, but instead you have honored me by allowing me to eat at your own table! What more can I ask?"

[29] "You've said enough," David replied. "I've decided that you and Ziba will divide your land equally between you."

[30] "Give him all of it," Mephibosheth said. "I am content just to have you safely back again, my lord the king!"

David's Kindness to Barzillai

[31] Barzillai of Gilead had come down from Rogelim to escort the king across the Jordan. [32] He was very old—eighty years of age—and very wealthy. He was the one who had provided food for the king during his stay in Mahanaim. [33] "Come across with me and live in Jerusalem," the king said to Barzillai. "I will take care of you there."

[34] "No," he replied, "I am far too old to go with the king to Jerusalem. [35] I am eighty years old today, and I can no longer enjoy anything. Food and wine are no longer tasty, and I cannot hear the singers as they sing. I would only be a burden to my lord the king. [36] Just to go across the Jordan River with the king is all the honor I need! [37] Then let me return again to die in my own town, where my father and mother are buried. But here is your servant, my son Kimham. Let him go with my lord the king and receive whatever you want to give him."

[38] "Good," the king agreed. "Kimham will go with me, and I will help him in any way you would like. And I will do for you anything you want." [39] So all the people crossed the Jordan with the king. After David had blessed Barzillai and kissed him, Barzillai returned to his own home.

[40] The king then crossed over to Gilgal, taking Kimham with him. All the troops of Judah and half the troops of Israel escorted the king on his way.

An Argument over the King

[41] But all the men of Israel complained to the king, "The men of Judah stole the king and didn't give us the honor of helping take you, your household, and all your men across the Jordan."

[42] The men of Judah replied, "The king is one of our own kinsmen. Why should this make you angry? We haven't eaten any of the king's food or received any special favors!"

[43] "But there are ten tribes in Israel," the others replied. "So we have ten times as much right to the king as you do. What right do you have to treat us with such contempt? Weren't we the first to speak of bringing him back to be our king again?" The argument continued back and forth, and the men of Judah spoke even more harshly than the men of Israel.

The Revolt of Sheba

20 There happened to be a troublemaker there named Sheba son of Bicri, a man from the tribe of Benjamin. Sheba blew a ram's horn and began to chant:

"Down with the dynasty of David!
 We have no interest in the son of Jesse.
Come on, you men of Israel,
 back to your homes!"

[2] So all the men of Israel deserted David and followed Sheba son of Bicri. But the men of Judah stayed with their king and escorted him from the Jordan River to Jerusalem.

[3] When David came to his palace in Jerusalem, he took the ten concubines he had left to look after the palace and placed them in seclusion. Their needs were provided for, but he no longer slept with them. So each of them lived like a widow until she died.

[4] Then the king told Amasa, "Mobilize the army of Judah within three days, and report back at that time." [5] So Amasa went out to notify Judah, but it took him longer than the time he had been given.

[6] Then David said to Abishai, "Sheba son of Bicri is

19:20 Hebrew *in the house of Joseph.* **19:22** Or *my prosecutor.* **19:24** *Mephibosheth* is another name for Merib-baal. **19:26** As in Greek, Syriac, and Latin versions; Hebrew reads *I will saddle a donkey for myself.*

going to hurt us more than Absalom did. Quick, take my troops and chase after him before he gets into a fortified town where we can't reach him."

[7] So Abishai and Joab,* together with the king's bodyguard* and all the mighty warriors, set out from Jerusalem to go after Sheba. [8] As they arrived at the great stone in Gibeon, Amasa met them. Joab was wearing his military tunic with a dagger strapped to his belt. As he stepped forward to greet Amasa, he slipped the dagger from its sheath.*

[9] "How are you, my cousin?" Joab said and took him by the beard with his right hand as though to kiss him. [10] Amasa didn't notice the dagger in his left hand, and Joab stabbed him in the stomach with it so that his insides gushed out onto the ground. Joab did not need to strike again, and Amasa soon died. Joab and his brother Abishai left him lying there and continued after Sheba.

[11] One of Joab's young men shouted to Amasa's troops, "If you are for Joab and David, come and follow Joab." [12] But Amasa lay in his blood in the middle of the road, and Joab's man saw that everyone was stopping to stare at him. So he pulled him off the road into a field and threw a cloak over him. [13] With Amasa's body out of the way, everyone went on with Joab to capture Sheba son of Bicri.

[14] Meanwhile, Sheba traveled through all the tribes of Israel and eventually came to the town of Abel-beth-maacah. All the members of his own clan, the Bicrites,* assembled for battle and followed him into the town. [15] When Joab's forces arrived, they attacked Abel-beth-maacah. They built a siege ramp against the town's fortifications and began battering down the wall. [16] But a wise woman in the town called out to Joab, "Listen to me, Joab. Come over here so I can talk to you." [17] As he approached, the woman asked, "Are you Joab?"

"I am," he replied.

So she said, "Listen carefully to your servant."

"I'm listening," he said.

[18] Then she continued, "There used to be a saying, 'If you want to settle an argument, ask advice at the town of Abel.' [19] I am one who is peace loving and faithful in Israel. But you are destroying an important town in Israel.* Why do you want to devour what belongs to the LORD?"

[20] And Joab replied, "Believe me, I don't want to devour or destroy your town! [21] That's not my purpose. All I want is a man named Sheba son of Bicri from the hill country of Ephraim, who has revolted against King David. If you hand over this one man to me, I will leave the town in peace."

"All right," the woman replied, "we will throw his head over the wall to you." [22] Then the woman went to all the people with her wise advice, and they cut off Sheba's head and threw it out to Joab. So he blew the ram's horn and called his troops back from the attack. They all returned to their homes, and Joab returned to the king at Jerusalem.

[23] Now Joab was the commander of the army of Israel. Benaiah son of Jehoiada was captain of the king's bodyguard. [24] Adoniram* was in charge of forced labor. Jehoshaphat son of Ahilud was the royal historian. [25] Sheva was the court secretary. Zadok and Abiathar were the priests. [26] And Ira, a descendant of Jair, was David's personal priest.

David Avenges the Gibeonites

21 There was a famine during David's reign that lasted for three years, so David asked the LORD about it. And the LORD said, "The famine has come because Saul and his family are guilty of murdering the Gibeonites."

[2] So the king summoned the Gibeonites. They were not part of Israel but were all that was left of the nation of the Amorites. The people of Israel had sworn not to kill them, but Saul, in his zeal for Israel and Judah, had tried to wipe them out. [3] David asked them, "What can I do for you? How can I make amends so that you will bless the LORD's people again?"

[4] "Well, money can't settle this matter between us and the family of Saul," the Gibeonites replied. "Neither can we demand the life of anyone in Israel."

"What can I do then?" David asked. "Just tell me and I will do it for you."

[5] Then they replied, "It was Saul who planned to destroy us, to keep us from having any place at all in the territory of Israel. [6] So let seven of Saul's sons be handed over to us, and we will execute them before the LORD at Gibeon, on the mountain of the LORD.*"

"All right," the king said, "I will do it." [7] The king spared Jonathan's son Mephibosheth,* who was Saul's grandson, because of the oath David and Jonathan had sworn before the LORD. [8] But he gave them Saul's two sons Armoni and Mephibosheth, whose mother was Rizpah daughter of Aiah. He also gave them the five sons of Saul's daughter Merab,* the wife of Adriel son of Barzillai from Meholah. [9] The men of Gibeon executed them on the mountain

---

20:7a Hebrew *So Joab's men.* **20:7b** Hebrew *the Kerethites and Pelethites*; also in 20:23. **20:8** Hebrew *As he stepped forward, it fell out.* **20:14** As in Greek and Latin versions; Hebrew reads *All the Berites.* **20:19** Hebrew *a town that is a mother in Israel.* **20:24** As in Greek version (see also 1 Kgs 4:6; 5:14); Hebrew reads *Adoram.* **21:6** As in Greek version (see also 21:9); Hebrew reads *at Gibeah of Saul, the chosen of the LORD.* **21:7** *Mephibosheth* is another name for Merib-baal. **21:8** As in a few Hebrew and Greek manuscripts and Syriac version (see also 1 Sam 18:19); most Hebrew manuscripts read *Michal.*

20:16-22 We've met two wise women, one in Tekoa (14:1-24) and this woman in Abel-beth-maacah. Both had authority people knew and recognized. They used their quick thinking and speech to help those around them. Do you have wise women like this in your own life? What have you learned from wise women you know?

before the Lord. So all seven of them died together at the beginning of the barley harvest.

¹⁰Then Rizpah daughter of Aiah, the mother of two of the men, spread burlap on a rock and stayed there the entire harvest season. She prevented the scavenger birds from tearing at their bodies during the day and stopped wild animals from eating them at night. ¹¹When David learned what Rizpah, Saul's concubine, had done, ¹²he went to the people of Jabesh-gilead and retrieved the bones of Saul and his son Jonathan. (When the Philistines had killed Saul and Jonathan on Mount Gilboa, the people of Jabesh-gilead stole their bodies from the public square of Beth-shan, where the Philistines had hung them.) ¹³So David obtained the bones of Saul and Jonathan, as well as the bones of the men the Gibeonites had executed.

¹⁴Then the king ordered that they bury the bones in the tomb of Kish, Saul's father, at the town of Zela in the land of Benjamin. After that, God ended the famine in the land.

Battles against Philistine Giants

¹⁵Once again the Philistines were at war with Israel. And when David and his men were in the thick of battle, David became weak and exhausted. ¹⁶Ishbi-benob was a descendant of the giants*; his bronze spearhead weighed more than seven pounds,* and he was armed with a new sword. He had cornered David and was about to kill him. ¹⁷But Abishai son of Zeruiah came to David's rescue and killed the Philistine. Then David's men declared, "You are not going out to battle with us again! Why risk snuffing out the light of Israel?"

¹⁸After this, there was another battle against the Philistines at Gob. As they fought, Sibbecai from Hushah killed Saph, another descendant of the giants. ¹⁹During another battle at Gob, Elhanan son of Jair* from Bethlehem killed the brother of Goliath of Gath.* The handle of his spear was as thick as a weaver's beam!

²⁰In another battle with the Philistines at Gath, they encountered a huge man* with six fingers on each hand and six toes on each foot, twenty-four in all, who was also a descendant of the giants. ²¹But when he defied and taunted Israel, he was killed by Jonathan, the son of David's brother Shimea.*

²²These four Philistines were descendants of the giants of Gath, but David and his warriors killed them.

David's Song of Praise

22 David sang this song to the Lord on the day the Lord rescued him from all his enemies and from Saul. ²He sang:

"The Lord is my rock, my fortress, and my
    savior;
³   my God is my rock, in whom I find protection.
He is my shield, the power that saves me,
    and my place of safety.
He is my refuge, my savior,
    the one who saves me from violence.
⁴ I called on the Lord, who is worthy of praise,
    and he saved me from my enemies.

⁵ "The waves of death overwhelmed me;
    floods of destruction swept over me.
⁶ The grave* wrapped its ropes around me;
    death laid a trap in my path.
⁷ But in my distress I cried out to the Lord;
    yes, I cried to my God for help.
He heard me from his sanctuary;
    my cry reached his ears.

⁸ "Then the earth quaked and trembled.
    The foundations of the heavens shook;
    they quaked because of his anger.
⁹ Smoke poured from his nostrils;
    fierce flames leaped from his mouth.
    Glowing coals blazed forth from him.
¹⁰ He opened the heavens and came down;
    dark storm clouds were beneath his feet.
¹¹ Mounted on a mighty angelic being,* he flew,
    soaring* on the wings of the wind.
¹² He shrouded himself in darkness,
    veiling his approach with dense rain clouds.
¹³ A great brightness shone around him,
    and burning coals* blazed forth.
¹⁴ The Lord thundered from heaven;
    the voice of the Most High resounded.
¹⁵ He shot arrows and scattered his enemies;
    his lightning flashed, and they were confused.
¹⁶ Then at the command of the Lord,
    at the blast of his breath,
the bottom of the sea could be seen,
    and the foundations of the earth were laid bare.

¹⁷ "He reached down from heaven and rescued me;
    he drew me out of deep waters.
¹⁸ He rescued me from my powerful enemies,
    from those who hated me and were too
        strong for me.

21:16a Or *a descendant of the Rapha;* also in 21:18, 20, 22. **21:16b** Hebrew *300 [shekels]* [3.4 kilograms]. **21:19a** As in parallel text at 1 Chr 20:5; Hebrew reads *son of Jaare-oregim.* **21:19b** As in parallel text at 1 Chr 20:5; Hebrew reads *killed Goliath of Gath.* **21:20** As in parallel text at 1 Chr 20:6; Hebrew reads *a Midianite.* **21:21** As in parallel text at 1 Chr 20:7; Hebrew reads *Shimei,* a variant spelling of Shimea. **22:6** Hebrew *Sheol.* **22:11a** Hebrew *a cherub.* **22:11b** As in some Hebrew manuscripts (see also Ps 18:10); other Hebrew manuscripts read *appearing.* **22:13** Or *and lightning bolts.*

22:1 This verse lets us know when this may have been written and sung to the Lord. What's interesting about the timing is that David expresses both grief and thanksgiving simultaneously, indicating the potential that he may have sung this song around the same time that he sang 1:19-27. God can handle the messiness of our emotions and feelings.

"All the LORD's promises prove true."

2 SAMUEL 22:31

¹⁹ They attacked me at a moment when I was in distress,
　but the LORD supported me.
²⁰ He led me to a place of safety;
　he rescued me because he delights in me.
²¹ The LORD rewarded me for doing right;
　he restored me because of my innocence.
²² For I have kept the ways of the LORD;
　I have not turned from my God to follow evil.
²³ I have followed all his regulations;
　I have never abandoned his decrees.
²⁴ I am blameless before God;
　I have kept myself from sin.
²⁵ The LORD rewarded me for doing right.
　He has seen my innocence.
²⁶ "To the faithful you show yourself faithful;
　to those with integrity you show integrity.
²⁷ To the pure you show yourself pure,
　but to the crooked you show yourself shrewd.
²⁸ You rescue the humble,
　but your eyes watch the proud and humiliate them.
²⁹ O LORD, you are my lamp.
　The LORD lights up my darkness.
³⁰ In your strength I can crush an army;
　with my God I can scale any wall.
³¹ "God's way is perfect.
　All the LORD's promises prove true.
　He is a shield for all who look to him for protection.
³² For who is God except the LORD?
　Who but our God is a solid rock?
³³ God is my strong fortress,
　and he makes my way perfect.
³⁴ He makes me as surefooted as a deer,
　enabling me to stand on mountain heights.
³⁵ He trains my hands for battle;
　he strengthens my arm to draw a bronze bow.
³⁶ You have given me your shield of victory;
　your help* has made me great.
³⁷ You have made a wide path for my feet
　to keep them from slipping.
³⁸ "I chased my enemies and destroyed them;
　I did not stop until they were conquered.
³⁹ I consumed them;
　I struck them down so they did not get up;
　they fell beneath my feet.
⁴⁰ You have armed me with strength for the battle;
　you have subdued my enemies under my feet.
⁴¹ You placed my foot on their necks.
　I have destroyed all who hated me.
⁴² They looked for help, but no one came to their rescue.
　They even cried to the LORD, but he refused to answer.
⁴³ I ground them as fine as the dust of the earth;
　I trampled them* in the gutter like dirt.
⁴⁴ "You gave me victory over my accusers.
　You preserved me as the ruler over nations;
　people I don't even know now serve me.
⁴⁵ Foreign nations cringe before me;
　as soon as they hear of me, they submit.
⁴⁶ They all lose their courage
　and come trembling* from their strongholds.
⁴⁷ "The LORD lives! Praise to my Rock!
　May God, the Rock of my salvation, be exalted!
⁴⁸ He is the God who pays back those who harm me;
　he brings down the nations under me
⁴⁹ 　and delivers me from my enemies.
　You hold me safe beyond the reach of my enemies;
　you save me from violent opponents.
⁵⁰ For this, O LORD, I will praise you among the nations;
　I will sing praises to your name.
⁵¹ You give great victories to your king;
　you show unfailing love to your anointed,
　to David and all his descendants forever."

David's Last Words

23 These are the last words of David:

"David, the son of Jesse, speaks—
　David, the man who was raised up so high,
　David, the man anointed by the God of Jacob,
　David, the sweet psalmist of Israel.*

² "The Spirit of the LORD speaks through me;
　his words are upon my tongue.
³ The God of Israel spoke.
　The Rock of Israel said to me:
'The one who rules righteously,
　who rules in the fear of God,
⁴ is like the light of morning at sunrise,
　like a morning without clouds,
like the gleaming of the sun
　on new grass after rain.'

⁵ "Is it not my family God has chosen?
　Yes, he has made an everlasting covenant with me.
His agreement is arranged and guaranteed in every detail.
　He will ensure my safety and success.
⁶ But the godless are like thorns to be thrown away,
　for they tear the hand that touches them.
⁷ One must use iron tools to chop them down;
　they will be totally consumed by fire."

22:36 As in Dead Sea Scrolls; Masoretic Text reads *your answering.* **22:43** As in Dead Sea Scrolls (see also Ps 18:42); Masoretic Text reads *I crushed and trampled them.* **22:46** As in parallel text at Ps 18:45; Hebrew reads *come girding themselves.* **23:1** Or *the favorite subject of the songs of Israel;* or *the favorite of the Strong One of Israel.*

David's Mightiest Warriors

⁸These are the names of David's mightiest warriors. The first was Jashobeam the Hacmonite,* who was leader of the Three*—the three mightiest warriors among David's men. He once used his spear to kill 800 enemy warriors in a single battle.*

⁹Next in rank among the Three was Eleazar son of Dodai, a descendant of Ahoah. Once Eleazar and David stood together against the Philistines when the entire Israelite army had fled. ¹⁰He killed Philistines until his hand was too tired to lift his sword, and the LORD gave him a great victory that day. The rest of the army did not return until it was time to collect the plunder!

¹¹Next in rank was Shammah son of Agee from Harar. One time the Philistines gathered at Lehi and attacked the Israelites in a field full of lentils. The Israelite army fled, ¹²but Shammah* held his ground in the middle of the field and beat back the Philistines. So the LORD brought about a great victory.

¹³Once during the harvest, when David was at the cave of Adullam, the Philistine army was camped in the valley of Rephaim. The Three (who were among the Thirty—an elite group among David's fighting men) went down to meet him there. ¹⁴David was staying in the stronghold at the time, and a Philistine detachment had occupied the town of Bethlehem.

¹⁵David remarked longingly to his men, "Oh, how I would love some of that good water from the well by the gate in Bethlehem." ¹⁶So the Three broke through the Philistine lines, drew some water from the well by the gate in Bethlehem, and brought it back to David. But he refused to drink it. Instead, he poured it out as an offering to the LORD. ¹⁷"The LORD forbid that I should drink this!" he exclaimed. "This water is as precious as the blood of these men* who risked their lives to bring it to me." So David did not drink it. These are examples of the exploits of the Three.

David's Thirty Mighty Men

¹⁸Abishai son of Zeruiah, the brother of Joab, was the leader of the Thirty.* He once used his spear to kill 300 enemy warriors in a single battle. It was by such feats that he became as famous as the Three. ¹⁹Abishai was the most famous of the Thirty* and was their commander, though he was not one of the Three.

²⁰There was also Benaiah son of Jehoiada, a valiant warrior* from Kabzeel. He did many heroic deeds, which included killing two champions* of Moab. Another time, on a snowy day, he chased a lion down into a pit and killed it. ²¹Once, armed only with a club, he killed an imposing Egyptian warrior who was armed with a spear. Benaiah wrenched the spear from the Egyptian's hand and killed him with it. ²²Deeds like these made Benaiah as famous as the Three mightiest warriors. ²³He was more honored than the other members of the Thirty, though he was not one of the Three. And David made him captain of his bodyguard.

²⁴Other members of the Thirty included:

Asahel, Joab's brother;
Elhanan son of Dodo from Bethlehem;
²⁵ Shammah from Harod;
Elika from Harod;
²⁶ Helez from Pelon*;
Ira son of Ikkesh from Tekoa;
²⁷ Abiezer from Anathoth;
Sibbecai* from Hushah;
²⁸ Zalmon from Ahoah;
Maharai from Netophah;
²⁹ Heled* son of Baanah from Netophah;
Ithai* son of Ribai from Gibeah (in the land of Benjamin);
³⁰ Benaiah from Pirathon;
Hurai* from Nahale-gaash*;
³¹ Abi-albon from Arabah;
Azmaveth from Bahurim;
³² Eliahba from Shaalbon;
the sons of Jashen;
Jonathan ³³son of Shagee* from Harar;
Ahiam son of Sharar from Harar;
³⁴ Eliphelet son of Ahasbai from Maacah;
Eliam son of Ahithophel from Giloh;
³⁵ Hezro from Carmel;
Paarai from Arba;
³⁶ Igal son of Nathan from Zobah;
Bani from Gad;
³⁷ Zelek from Ammon;
Naharai from Beeroth, the armor bearer of Joab son of Zeruiah;
³⁸ Ira from Jattir;
Gareb from Jattir;
³⁹ Uriah the Hittite.

There were thirty-seven in all.

23:8a As in parallel text at 1 Chr 11:11; Hebrew reads *Josheb-basshebeth the Tahkemonite*. 23:8b As in Greek and Latin versions (see also 1 Chr 11:11); the meaning of the Hebrew is uncertain. 23:8c As in some Greek manuscripts (see also 1 Chr 11:11); the meaning of the Hebrew is uncertain, though it might be rendered *the Three. It was Adino the Eznite who killed 800 men at one time*. 23:12 Hebrew *he*. 23:17 Hebrew *Shall I drink the blood of these men?* 23:18 As in a few Hebrew manuscripts and Syriac version; most Hebrew manuscripts read *the Three*. 23:19 As in Syriac version; Hebrew reads *the Three*. 23:20a Or *son of Jehoiada, son of Ish-hai*. 23:20b Hebrew *two of Ariel*. 23:26 As in parallel text at 1 Chr 11:27 (see also 1 Chr 27:10); Hebrew reads *from Palti*. 23:27 As in some Greek manuscripts (see also 1 Chr 11:29); Hebrew reads *Mebunnai*. 23:29a As in some Hebrew manuscripts (see also 1 Chr 11:30); most Hebrew manuscripts read *Heleb*. 23:29b As in parallel text at 1 Chr 11:31; Hebrew reads *Ittai*. 23:30a As in some Greek manuscripts (see also 1 Chr 11:32); Hebrew reads *Hiddai*. 23:30b Or *from the ravines of Gaash*. 23:33 As in parallel text at 1 Chr 11:34; Hebrew reads *Jonathan, Shammah;* some Greek manuscripts read *Jonathan son of Shammah*.

David Takes a Census

24 Once again the anger of the LORD burned against Israel, and he caused David to harm them by taking a census. "Go and count the people of Israel and Judah," the LORD told him.

²So the king said to Joab and the commanders* of the army, "Take a census of all the tribes of Israel—from Dan in the north to Beersheba in the south—so I may know how many people there are."

³But Joab replied to the king, "May the LORD your God let you live to see a hundred times as many people as there are now! But why, my lord the king, do you want to do this?"

⁴But the king insisted that they take the census, so Joab and the commanders of the army went out to count the people of Israel. ⁵First they crossed the Jordan and camped at Aroer, south of the town in the valley, in the direction of Gad. Then they went on to Jazer, ⁶then to Gilead in the land of Tahtim-hodshi* and to Dan-jaan and around to Sidon. ⁷Then they came to the fortress of Tyre, and all the towns of the Hivites and Canaanites. Finally, they went south to Judah* as far as Beersheba.

⁸Having gone through the entire land for nine months and twenty days, they returned to Jerusalem. ⁹Joab reported the number of people to the king. There were 800,000 capable warriors in Israel who could handle a sword, and 500,000 in Judah.

Judgment for David's Sin

¹⁰But after he had taken the census, David's conscience began to bother him. And he said to the LORD, "I have sinned greatly by taking this census. Please forgive my guilt, LORD, for doing this foolish thing."

¹¹The next morning the word of the LORD came to the prophet Gad, who was David's seer. This was the message: ¹²"Go and say to David, 'This is what the LORD says: I will give you three choices. Choose one of these punishments, and I will inflict it on you.'"

¹³So Gad came to David and asked him, "Will you choose three* years of famine throughout your land, three months of fleeing from your enemies, or three days of severe plague throughout your land? Think this over and decide what answer I should give the LORD who sent me."

¹⁴"I'm in a desperate situation!" David replied to Gad. "But let us fall into the hands of the LORD, for his mercy is great. Do not let me fall into human hands."

¹⁵So the LORD sent a plague upon Israel that morning, and it lasted for three days.* A total of 70,000 people died throughout the nation, from Dan in the north to Beersheba in the south. ¹⁶But as the angel was preparing to destroy Jerusalem, the LORD relented and said to the death angel, "Stop! That is enough!" At that moment the angel of the LORD was by the threshing floor of Araunah the Jebusite.

¹⁷When David saw the angel, he said to the LORD, "I am the one who has sinned and done wrong! But these people are as innocent as sheep—what have they done? Let your anger fall against me and my family."

David Builds an Altar

¹⁸That day Gad came to David and said to him, "Go up and build an altar to the LORD on the threshing floor of Araunah the Jebusite."

¹⁹So David went up to do what the LORD had commanded him. ²⁰When Araunah saw the king and his men coming toward him, he came and bowed before the king with his face to the ground. ²¹"Why have you come, my lord the king?" Araunah asked.

David replied, "I have come to buy your threshing floor and to build an altar to the LORD there, so that he will stop the plague."

²²"Take it, my lord the king, and use it as you wish," Araunah said to David. "Here are oxen for the burnt offering, and you can use the threshing boards and ox yokes for wood to build a fire on the altar. ²³I will give it all to you, Your Majesty, and may the LORD your God accept your sacrifice."

²⁴But the king replied to Araunah, "No, I insist on buying it, for I will not present burnt offerings to the LORD my God that have cost me nothing." So David paid him fifty pieces of silver* for the threshing floor and the oxen.

²⁵David built an altar there to the LORD and sacrificed burnt offerings and peace offerings. And the LORD answered his prayer for the land, and the plague on Israel was stopped.

24:2 As in Greek version (see also 24:4 and 1 Chr 21:2); Hebrew reads *Joab the commander*. **24:6** Greek version reads *to Gilead and to Kadesh in the land of the Hittites*. **24:7** Or *they went to the Negev of Judah*. **24:13** As in Greek version (see also 1 Chr 21:12); Hebrew reads *seven*. **24:15** Hebrew *for the designated time*. **24:24** Hebrew *50 shekels of silver*, about 20 ounces or 570 grams in weight.

24:11-25 The last four chapters share an assortment of stories and poems from David's reign that complicate our picture of David even further. We see beautiful songs of God alongside David's selfishness and sin. What do we do with this man who God described as "a man after his own heart" (1 Samuel 13:14) and who, paradoxically, acted wickedly? What do we do with ourselves, as we, too, do both? We take heart in knowing that despite all we can stack up against David, he was still a man after God's own heart. Restoration is possible, and this is good news.

1 Kings

WHAT DO WE LEARN ABOUT GOD'S MISSION AND OURS?
If we don't listen to God, we'll wish we had.

WHO WROTE IT? Anonymous, but probably a court official or someone who had access to official historical records.

WHEN DID IT HAPPEN? Between 970 and 850 BC, during Solomon's reign, the events surrounding Israel's division, and the early kings of the two kingdoms.

HOW IS IT ORGANIZED?

1–3: Solomon becomes king after David's death

4–10: Solomon builds his wealth and the Temple

11: Solomon's decline and death

12: The kingdom splits between Judah (David's descendants) and the rest of Israel

13–16: The early divided kingdom

17–21: Elijah contests Ahab and Jezebel's evil rule

22: Ahab dies; Jehoshaphat rules Judah

FEATURE HIGHLIGHTS

+ *Solomon's Wealth (420)*
+ *Satisfaction: One Turn Away (423)*
+ *The Widow at Zarephath: When It's Hard to Trust (431)*
+ *Have I Allowed Evil to Influence My Choices? (436)*

Words to Remember are highlighted throughout this book

HOW LONG DOES IT TAKE TO READ?

| :30 | 1:00 | 1:30 | **2:00** | 2:30 | 3:00 | 3:30 |

Timeline (BC)

BC	Event
1010	DAVID BECOMES KING
970	SOLOMON, BATHSHEBA'S SON, BECOMES KING
959	THE TEMPLE IS COMPLETED
930	THE KINGDOM DIVIDES
926	SHISHAK INVADES JERUSALEM
910	ASA, MAACAH'S GRANDSON, BECOMES JUDAH'S KING
875–848	ELIJAH'S MINISTRY
874	AHAB BECOMES ISRAEL'S KING, MARRIES JEZEBEL
872	JEHOSHAPHAT, AZUBAH'S SON, BECOMES JUDAH'S KING
857	BEN-HADAD ATTACKS SAMARIA
853	AHAB DIES IN BATTLE

David in His Old Age

1 King David was now very old, and no matter how many blankets covered him, he could not keep warm. ²So his advisers told him, "Let us find a young virgin to wait on you and look after you, my lord. She will lie in your arms and keep you warm."

³So they searched throughout the land of Israel for a beautiful girl, and they found Abishag from Shunem and brought her to the king. ⁴The girl was very beautiful, and she looked after the king and took care of him. But the king had no sexual relations with her.

Adonijah Claims the Throne

⁵About that time David's son Adonijah, whose mother was Haggith, began boasting, "I will make myself king." So he provided himself with chariots and charioteers and recruited fifty men to run in front of him. ⁶Now his father, King David, had never disciplined him at any time, even by asking, "Why are you doing that?" Adonijah had been born next after Absalom, and he was very handsome.

⁷Adonijah took Joab son of Zeruiah and Abiathar the priest into his confidence, and they agreed to help him become king. ⁸But Zadok the priest, Benaiah son of Jehoiada, Nathan the prophet, Shimei, Rei, and David's personal bodyguard refused to support Adonijah.

⁹Adonijah went to the Stone of Zoheleth* near the spring of En-rogel, where he sacrificed sheep, cattle, and fattened calves. He invited all his brothers—the other sons of King David—and all the royal officials of Judah. ¹⁰But he did not invite Nathan the prophet or Benaiah or the king's bodyguard or his brother Solomon.

¹¹Then Nathan went to Bathsheba, Solomon's mother, and asked her, "Haven't you heard that Haggith's son, Adonijah, has made himself king, and our lord David doesn't even know about it? ¹²If you want to save your own life and the life of your son Solomon, follow my advice. ¹³Go at once to King David and say to him, 'My lord the king, didn't you make a vow and say to me, "Your son Solomon will surely be the next king and will sit on my throne"? Why then has Adonijah become king?' ¹⁴And while you are still talking with him, I will come and confirm everything you have said."

¹⁵So Bathsheba went into the king's bedroom. (He was very old now, and Abishag was taking care of him.) ¹⁶Bathsheba bowed down before the king.

"What can I do for you?" he asked her.

¹⁷She replied, "My lord, you made a vow before the LORD your God when you said to me, 'Your son Solomon will surely be the next king and will sit on my throne.' ¹⁸But instead, Adonijah has made himself king, and my lord the king does not even know about it. ¹⁹He has sacrificed many cattle, fattened calves, and sheep, and he has invited all the king's sons to attend the celebration. He also invited Abiathar the priest and Joab, the commander of the army. But he did not invite your servant Solomon. ²⁰And

---

1:9 Or *to the Serpent's Stone;* Greek version supports reading *Zoheleth* as a proper name.

1:1–22:53 Similar to Ezra—Nehemiah and 1–2 Samuel, 1–2 Kings was originally one volume and later divided into two. Reading these books together will help us see how the entire story flows more clearly.

1:1-4 Abishag was from Shunem, a town in Galilee near Nazareth that was connected to Saul's family. Abishag's presence helped unite the two rival regions, Judah and the northern tribes. David struggled to "keep warm." This indicates more than bodily warmth and signals to the reader that David was aging and could not have sexual relations. In ancient royal courts, bringing in women was often a way to form political alliances. So Abishag's presence was twofold: to comfort David as he was dying and to act as a symbol of good relations between the northern tribes and David's monarchy. The fact that Abishag is named in the story indicates her important role.

1:5 Haggith is listed as one of David's wives at Hebron (2 Samuel 3:2-5).

1:6 David led God's people as king and he was a powerful warrior and leader. As a father, he was passive, which harmed many in his family, and, ultimately, harmed the nation of Israel. David missed moments when he should have defended some of his children, like Tamar, and disciplined others, like Amnon (2 Samuel 13:1-39). His passivity wreaked havoc on his children's relationships with himself and one another. It is important to remain active and present in our relationships, even when we struggle ourselves.

1:7-10 Adonijah was aware of the possibility that he could be in line to be king and abruptly declared, "I will make myself king" (1:5). In a ceremony that he hosted, critical figures in the royal court were missing, including Nathan the prophet and Adonijah's brother Solomon. This was an intentional guest list meant to exclude anyone who would support Solomon as the rightful next king. Adonijah acts prematurely, conspiring to take the throne, and invites only his supporters.

1:11 Nathan was a prophet to the king (see 2 Samuel 12:1-31). In many ancient societies, kings were often associated with gods and occasionally even considered gods. These "semidivine kings" usually served in a religious capacity as a high-ranking—if not the highest-ranking—priest or seer. While the surrounding nations consolidated spiritual authority and political power in the office of king, Israel kept the roles distinct. True prophets spoke God's words, and kings listened to them, often heeding their advice and changing their course of action. The prophets reminded Israel's kings that they were responsible to God for their actions. It is vital to have friends, mentors, or others in our lives who will speak the truth, even when it is hard to hear.

1:11 Bathsheba was David's wife and held influence in the royal court. See more of her story in 2 Samuel 11:1–12:31. She experienced loss and difficulty, and through no fault of her own led a life marked with pain and grief. As in our lives, God works through the messiness.

1:14-21 Bathsheba initiated an audience with David after hearing about Adonijah's conspiracy to become king. She respectfully entered his presence and reminded David of his oath to make their son Solomon king. Bathsheba revealed her inner strength and boldness by acting on behalf of her son.

now, my lord the king, all Israel is waiting for you to announce who will become king after you. ²¹If you do not act, my son Solomon and I will be treated as criminals as soon as my lord the king has died."

²²While she was still speaking with the king, Nathan the prophet arrived. ²³The king's officials told him, "Nathan the prophet is here to see you."

Nathan went in and bowed before the king with his face to the ground. ²⁴Nathan asked, "My lord the king, have you decided that Adonijah will be the next king and that he will sit on your throne? ²⁵Today he has sacrificed many cattle, fattened calves, and sheep, and he has invited all the king's sons to attend the celebration. He also invited the commanders of the army and Abiathar the priest. They are feasting and drinking with him and shouting, 'Long live King Adonijah!' ²⁶But he did not invite me or Zadok the priest or Benaiah or your servant Solomon. ²⁷Has my lord the king really done this without letting any of his officials know who should be the next king?"

David Makes Solomon King

²⁸King David responded, "Call Bathsheba!" So she came back in and stood before the king. ²⁹And the king repeated his vow: "As surely as the LORD lives, who has rescued me from every danger, ³⁰your son Solomon will be the next king and will sit on my throne this very day, just as I vowed to you before the LORD, the God of Israel."

³¹Then Bathsheba bowed down with her face to the ground before the king and exclaimed, "May my lord King David live forever!"

³²Then King David ordered, "Call Zadok the priest, Nathan the prophet, and Benaiah son of Jehoiada." When they came into the king's presence, ³³the king said to them, "Take Solomon and my officials down to Gihon Spring. Solomon is to ride on my own mule. ³⁴There Zadok the priest and Nathan the prophet are to anoint him king over Israel. Blow the ram's horn and shout, 'Long live King Solomon!' ³⁵Then escort him back here, and he will sit on my throne. He will succeed me as king, for I have appointed him to be ruler over Israel and Judah."

³⁶"Amen!" Benaiah son of Jehoiada replied. "May the LORD, the God of my lord the king, decree that it happen. ³⁷And may the LORD be with Solomon as he has been with you, my lord the king, and may he make Solomon's reign even greater than yours!"

³⁸So Zadok the priest, Nathan the prophet, Benaiah son of Jehoiada, and the king's bodyguard* took Solomon down to Gihon Spring, with Solomon riding on King David's own mule. ³⁹There Zadok the priest took the flask of olive oil from the sacred tent and anointed Solomon with the oil. Then they sounded the ram's horn and all the people shouted, "Long live King Solomon!" ⁴⁰And all the people followed Solomon into Jerusalem, playing flutes and shouting for joy. The celebration was so joyous and noisy that the earth shook with the sound.

⁴¹Adonijah and his guests heard the celebrating and shouting just as they were finishing their banquet. When Joab heard the sound of the ram's horn, he asked, "What's going on? Why is the city in such an uproar?"

⁴²And while he was still speaking, Jonathan son of Abiathar the priest arrived. "Come in," Adonijah said to him, "for you are a good man. You must have good news."

⁴³"Not at all!" Jonathan replied. "Our lord King David has just declared Solomon king! ⁴⁴The king sent him down to Gihon Spring with Zadok the priest, Nathan the prophet, and Benaiah son of Jehoiada, protected by the king's bodyguard. They had him ride on the king's own mule, ⁴⁵and Zadok and Nathan have anointed him at Gihon Spring as the new king. They have just returned, and the whole city is celebrating and rejoicing. That's what all the noise is about. ⁴⁶What's more, Solomon is now sitting on the royal throne as king. ⁴⁷And all the royal officials have gone to King David and congratulated him, saying, 'May your God make Solomon's fame even greater than your own, and may Solomon's reign be even greater than yours!' Then the king bowed his head in worship as he lay in his bed, ⁴⁸and he said, 'Praise the LORD, the God of Israel, who today has chosen a successor to sit on my throne while I am still alive to see it.'"

⁴⁹Then all of Adonijah's guests jumped up in panic from the banquet table and quickly scattered. ⁵⁰Adonijah was afraid of Solomon, so he rushed to the

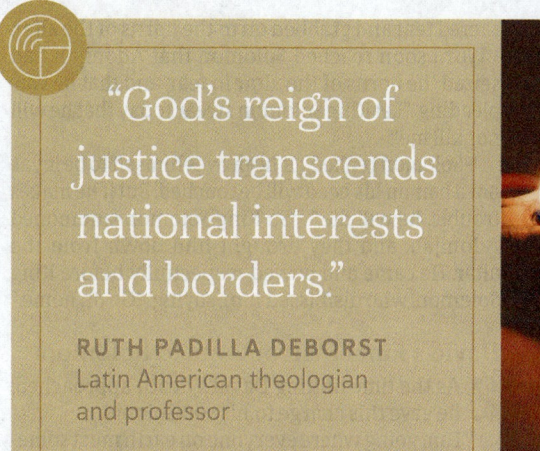

> "God's reign of justice transcends national interests and borders."
>
> RUTH PADILLA DEBORST
> Latin American theologian and professor

1:38 Hebrew *the Kerethites and Pelethites;* also in 1:44.

1:28-30 David reassured Bathsheba that Solomon would be the next king by repeating his earlier vow before the Lord God (see 1:17).

sacred tent and grabbed on to the horns of the altar. ⁵¹Word soon reached Solomon that Adonijah had seized the horns of the altar in fear, and that he was pleading, "Let King Solomon swear today that he will not kill me!"

⁵²Solomon replied, "If he proves himself to be loyal, not a hair on his head will be touched. But if he makes trouble, he will die." ⁵³So King Solomon summoned Adonijah, and they brought him down from the altar. He came and bowed respectfully before King Solomon, who dismissed him, saying, "Go on home."

David's Final Instructions to Solomon

2 As the time of King David's death approached, he gave this charge to his son Solomon:

²"I am going where everyone on earth must someday go. Take courage and be a man. ³Observe the requirements of the Lord your God, and follow all his ways. Keep the decrees, commands, regulations, and laws written in the Law of Moses so that you will be successful in all you do and wherever you go. ⁴If you do this, then the Lord will keep the promise he made to me. He told me, 'If your descendants live as they should and follow me faithfully with all their heart and soul, one of them will always sit on the throne of Israel.'

⁵"And there is something else. You know what Joab son of Zeruiah did to me when he murdered my two army commanders, Abner son of Ner and Amasa son of Jether. He pretended that it was an act of war, but it was done in a time of peace,* staining his belt and sandals with innocent blood.* ⁶Do with him what you think best, but don't let him grow old and go to his grave in peace.*

⁷"Be kind to the sons of Barzillai of Gilead. Make them permanent guests at your table, for they took care of me when I fled from your brother Absalom.

⁸"And remember Shimei son of Gera, the man from Bahurim in Benjamin. He cursed me with a terrible curse as I was fleeing to Mahanaim. When he came down to meet me at the Jordan River, I swore by the Lord that I would not kill him. ⁹But that oath does not make him innocent. You are a wise man, and you will know how to arrange a bloody death for him.*"

¹⁰Then David died and was buried with his ancestors in the City of David. ¹¹David had reigned over Israel for forty years, seven of them in Hebron and thirty-three in Jerusalem. ¹²Solomon became king and sat on the throne of David his father, and his kingdom was firmly established.

Solomon Establishes His Rule

¹³One day Adonijah, whose mother was Haggith, came to see Bathsheba, Solomon's mother. "Have you come with peaceful intentions?" she asked him.

"Yes," he said, "I come in peace. ¹⁴In fact, I have a favor to ask of you."

"What is it?" she asked.

¹⁵He replied, "As you know, the kingdom was rightfully mine; all Israel wanted me to be the next king. But the tables were turned, and the kingdom went to my brother instead; for that is the way the Lord wanted it. ¹⁶So now I have just one favor to ask of you. Please don't turn me down."

"What is it?" she asked.

¹⁷He replied, "Speak to King Solomon on my behalf, for I know he will do anything you request. Ask him to let me marry Abishag, the girl from Shunem."

¹⁸"All right," Bathsheba replied. "I will speak to the king for you."

¹⁹So Bathsheba went to King Solomon to speak on Adonijah's behalf. The king rose from his throne to meet her, and he bowed down before her. When he sat down on his throne again, the king ordered that a throne be brought for his mother, and she sat at his right hand.

²⁰"I have one small request to make of you," she said. "I hope you won't turn me down."

"What is it, my mother?" he asked. "You know I won't refuse you."

²¹"Then let your brother Adonijah marry Abishag, the girl from Shunem," she replied.

²²"How can you possibly ask me to give Abishag to Adonijah?" King Solomon demanded. "You might as well ask me to give him the kingdom! You know that he is my older brother, and that he has Abiathar the priest and Joab son of Zeruiah on his side."

²³Then King Solomon made a vow before the Lord: "May God strike me and even kill me if Adonijah has not sealed his fate with this request. ²⁴The Lord has confirmed me and placed me on the throne of my father, David; he has established my dynasty as he promised. So as surely as the Lord lives, Adonijah will die this very day!" ²⁵So King Solomon ordered Benaiah son of Jehoiada to execute him, and Adonijah was put to death.

²⁶Then the king said to Abiathar the priest, "Go back to your home in Anathoth. You deserve to die, but I will not kill you now, because you carried the Ark of the Sovereign Lord for David my father and you shared all his hardships." ²⁷So Solomon deposed

---

2:5a Or *He murdered them during a time of peace as revenge for deaths they had caused in time of war.* **2:5b** As in some Greek and Old Latin manuscripts; Hebrew reads *with the blood of war.* **2:6** Hebrew *don't let his white head go down to Sheol in peace.* **2:9** Hebrew *how to bring his white head down to Sheol in blood.*

2:13-22 Adonijah's request to acquire Abishag as a wife was politically motivated because any aggressive act toward the king's harem would be understood as an affront to the king. Since Abishag had been a companion of King David, Adonijah's marriage to her would signal his political power to the people and would challenge Solomon as David's chosen heir to the throne. Solomon saw right through this scheme and acted swiftly.

Abiathar from his position as priest of the LORD, thereby fulfilling the prophecy the LORD had given at Shiloh concerning the descendants of Eli.

²⁸Joab had not joined Absalom's earlier rebellion, but he had joined Adonijah's rebellion. So when Joab heard about Adonijah's death, he ran to the sacred tent of the LORD and grabbed on to the horns of the altar. ²⁹When this was reported to King Solomon, he sent Benaiah son of Jehoiada to execute him.

³⁰Benaiah went to the sacred tent of the LORD and said to Joab, "The king orders you to come out!"

But Joab answered, "No, I will die here."

So Benaiah returned to the king and told him what Joab had said.

³¹"Do as he said," the king replied. "Kill him there beside the altar and bury him. This will remove the guilt of Joab's senseless murders from me and from my father's family. ³²The LORD will repay him* for the murders of two men who were more righteous and better than he. For my father knew nothing about the deaths of Abner son of Ner, commander of the army of Israel, and of Amasa son of Jether, commander of the army of Judah. ³³May their blood be on Joab and his descendants forever, and may the LORD grant peace forever to David, his descendants, his dynasty, and his throne."

³⁴So Benaiah son of Jehoiada returned to the sacred tent and killed Joab, and he was buried at his home in the wilderness. ³⁵Then the king appointed Benaiah to command the army in place of Joab, and he installed Zadok the priest to take the place of Abiathar.

³⁶The king then sent for Shimei and told him, "Build a house here in Jerusalem and live there. But don't step outside the city to go anywhere else. ³⁷On the day you so much as cross the Kidron Valley, you will surely die; and your blood will be on your own head."

³⁸Shimei replied, "Your sentence is fair; I will do whatever my lord the king commands." So Shimei lived in Jerusalem for a long time.

³⁹But three years later two of Shimei's slaves ran away to King Achish son of Maacah of Gath. When Shimei learned where they were, ⁴⁰he saddled his donkey and went to Gath to search for them. When he found them, he brought them back to Jerusalem.

⁴¹Solomon heard that Shimei had left Jerusalem and had gone to Gath and returned. ⁴²So the king sent for Shimei and demanded, "Didn't I make you swear by the LORD and warn you not to go anywhere else or you would surely die? And you replied, 'The sentence is fair; I will do as you say.' ⁴³Then why haven't you kept your oath to the LORD and obeyed my command?"

⁴⁴The king also said to Shimei, "You certainly remember all the wicked things you did to my father, David. May the LORD now bring that evil on your own head. ⁴⁵But may I, King Solomon, receive the LORD's blessings, and may one of David's descendants always sit on this throne in the presence of the LORD." ⁴⁶Then, at the king's command, Benaiah son of Jehoiada took Shimei outside and killed him.

So the kingdom was now firmly in Solomon's grip.

Solomon Asks for Wisdom

3 Solomon made an alliance with Pharaoh, the king of Egypt, and married one of his daughters. He brought her to live in the City of David until he could finish building his palace and the Temple of the LORD and the wall around the city. ²At that time the people of Israel sacrificed their offerings at local places of worship, for a temple honoring the name of the LORD had not yet been built.

³Solomon loved the LORD and followed all the decrees of his father, David, except that Solomon, too, offered sacrifices and burned incense at the local places of worship. ⁴The most important of these places of worship was at Gibeon, so the king went there and sacrificed 1,000 burnt offerings. ⁵That night the LORD appeared to Solomon in a dream, and God said, "What do you want? Ask, and I will give it to you!"

⁶Solomon replied, "You showed great and faithful love to your servant my father, David, because he was honest and true and faithful to you. And you have continued to show this great and faithful love to him today by giving him a son to sit on his throne.

⁷"Now, O LORD my God, you have made me king instead of my father, David, but I am like a little child who doesn't know his way around. ⁸And here I am in the midst of your own chosen people, a nation so great and numerous they cannot be counted! ⁹Give me an understanding heart so that I can govern your people well and know the difference between right and wrong. For who by himself is able to govern this great people of yours?"

¹⁰The Lord was pleased that Solomon had asked for wisdom. ¹¹So God replied, "Because you have asked for wisdom in governing my people with justice and have not asked for a long life or wealth or the death of your enemies— ¹²I will give you what you asked for! I will give you a wise and understanding heart such as no one else has had or ever will have! ¹³And I will also give you what you did not ask for—riches and fame! No other king in all the world will be compared to you for the rest of your life! ¹⁴And if you follow me and obey my decrees and my commands as your father, David, did, I will give you a long life."

2:32 Hebrew *will return his blood on his own head*.

3:5-15 During Solomon's dream, God said, "Ask, and I will give it to you!" Solomon asked for wisdom, and this pleased God. Solomon's answer revealed his heart for God at the beginning of his time as king. If you were asked this question by God, how might you respond?

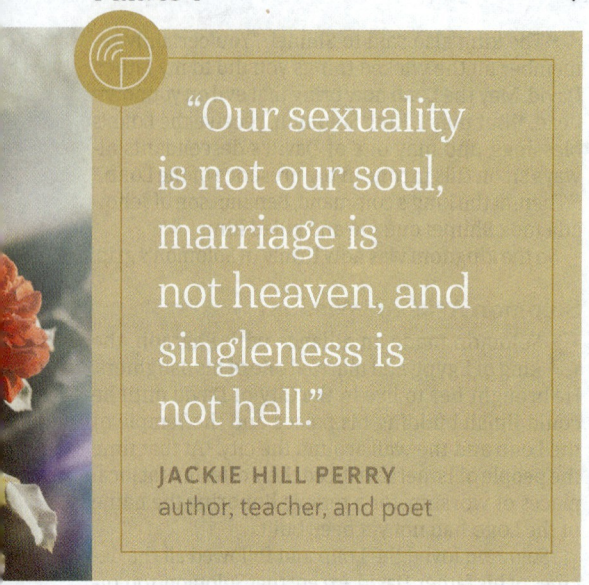

> "Our sexuality is not our soul, marriage is not heaven, and singleness is not hell."
>
> **JACKIE HILL PERRY**
> author, teacher, and poet

Solomon Judges Wisely

¹⁵Then Solomon woke up and realized it had been a dream. He returned to Jerusalem and stood before the Ark of the Lord's Covenant, where he sacrificed burnt offerings and peace offerings. Then he invited all his officials to a great banquet.

¹⁶Some time later two prostitutes came to the king to have an argument settled. ¹⁷"Please, my lord," one of them began, "this woman and I live in the same house. I gave birth to a baby while she was with me in the house. ¹⁸Three days later this woman also had a baby. We were alone; there were only two of us in the house.

¹⁹"But her baby died during the night when she rolled over on it. ²⁰Then she got up in the night and took my son from beside me while I was asleep. She laid her dead child in my arms and took mine to sleep beside her. ²¹And in the morning when I tried to nurse my son, he was dead! But when I looked more closely in the morning light, I saw that it wasn't my son at all."

²²Then the other woman interrupted, "It certainly was your son, and the living child is mine."

"No," the first woman said, "the living child is mine, and the dead one is yours." And so they argued back and forth before the king.

²³Then the king said, "Let's get the facts straight. Both of you claim the living child is yours, and each says that the dead one belongs to the other. ²⁴All right, bring me a sword." So a sword was brought to the king.

²⁵Then he said, "Cut the living child in two, and give half to one woman and half to the other!"

²⁶Then the woman who was the real mother of the living child, and who loved him very much, cried out, "Oh no, my lord! Give her the child—please do not kill him!"

But the other woman said, "All right, he will be neither yours nor mine; divide him between us!"

²⁷Then the king said, "Do not kill the child, but give him to the woman who wants him to live, for she is his mother!"

²⁸When all Israel heard the king's decision, the people were in awe of the king, for they saw the wisdom God had given him for rendering justice.

Solomon's Officials and Governors

4 King Solomon now ruled over all Israel, ²and these were his high officials:

Azariah son of Zadok was the priest.
³ Elihoreph and Ahijah, the sons of Shisha, were court secretaries.
Jehoshaphat son of Ahilud was the royal historian.
⁴ Benaiah son of Jehoiada was commander of the army.
Zadok and Abiathar were priests.
⁵ Azariah son of Nathan was in charge of the district governors.
Zabud son of Nathan, a priest, was a trusted adviser to the king.
⁶ Ahishar was manager of the palace property.
Adoniram son of Abda was in charge of forced labor.

⁷Solomon also had twelve district governors who were over all Israel. They were responsible for providing food for the king's household. Each of them arranged provisions for one month of the year. ⁸These are the names of the twelve governors:

Ben-hur, in the hill country of Ephraim.
⁹ Ben-deker, in Makaz, Shaalbim, Beth-shemesh, and Elon-bethhanan.
¹⁰ Ben-hesed, in Arubboth, including Socoh and all the land of Hepher.
¹¹ Ben-abinadab, in all of Naphoth-dor.* (He was married to Taphath, one of Solomon's daughters.)
¹² Baana son of Ahilud, in Taanach and Megiddo, all of Beth-shan* near Zarethan below Jezreel, and all the territory from Beth-shan to Abel-meholah and over to Jokmeam.

4:11 Hebrew *Naphath-dor,* a variant spelling of Naphoth-dor.   4:12 Hebrew *Beth-shean,* a variant spelling of Beth-shan; also in 4:12b.

3:16-28 This famous story reveals the incredible depth of Solomon's wisdom. He found a solution to the women's disagreement that quickly pinpointed the true mother. This story also shows us that, in those days, common people were allowed in the king's presence for judicial matters. Imagine going before a president, a prime minister, or another national leader with this type of problem!

¹³ Ben-geber, in Ramoth-gilead, including the Towns of Jair (named for Jair of the tribe of Manasseh*) in Gilead, and in the Argob region of Bashan, including sixty large fortified towns with bronze bars on their gates.
¹⁴ Ahinadab son of Iddo, in Mahanaim.
¹⁵ Ahimaaz, in Naphtali. (He was married to Basemath, another of Solomon's daughters.)
¹⁶ Baana son of Hushai, in Asher and in Aloth.
¹⁷ Jehoshaphat son of Paruah, in Issachar.
¹⁸ Shimei son of Ela, in Benjamin.
¹⁹ Geber son of Uri, in the land of Gilead,* including the territories of King Sihon of the Amorites and King Og of Bashan.
There was also one governor over the land of Judah.*

Solomon's Prosperity and Wisdom

²⁰The people of Judah and Israel were as numerous as the sand on the seashore. They were very contented, with plenty to eat and drink. ²¹*Solomon ruled over all the kingdoms from the Euphrates River* in the north to the land of the Philistines and the border of Egypt in the south. The conquered peoples of those lands sent tribute money to Solomon and continued to serve him throughout his lifetime.

²²The daily food requirements for Solomon's palace were 150 bushels of choice flour and 300 bushels of meal*; ²³also 10 oxen from the fattening pens, 20 pasture-fed cattle, 100 sheep or goats, as well as deer, gazelles, roe deer, and choice poultry.*

²⁴Solomon's dominion extended over all the kingdoms west of the Euphrates River, from Tiphsah to Gaza. And there was peace on all his borders. ²⁵During the lifetime of Solomon, all of Judah and Israel lived in peace and safety. And from Dan in the north to Beersheba in the south, each family had its own home and garden.*

²⁶Solomon had 4,000* stalls for his chariot horses, and he had 12,000 horses.*

²⁷The district governors faithfully provided food for King Solomon and his court; each made sure nothing was lacking during the month assigned to him. ²⁸They also brought the necessary barley and straw for the royal horses in the stables.

²⁹God gave Solomon very great wisdom and understanding, and knowledge as vast as the sands of the seashore. ³⁰In fact, his wisdom exceeded that of all the wise men of the East and the wise men of Egypt. ³¹He was wiser than anyone else, including Ethan the Ezrahite and the sons of Mahol—Heman, Calcol, and Darda. His fame spread throughout all the surrounding nations. ³²He composed some 3,000 proverbs and wrote 1,005 songs. ³³He could speak with authority about all kinds of plants, from the great cedar of Lebanon to the tiny hyssop that grows from cracks in a wall. He could also speak about animals, birds, small creatures, and fish. ³⁴And kings from every nation sent their ambassadors to listen to the wisdom of Solomon.

Preparations for Building the Temple

5 ¹*King Hiram of Tyre had always been a loyal friend of David. When Hiram learned that David's son Solomon was the new king of Israel, he sent ambassadors to congratulate him.

²Then Solomon sent this message back to Hiram:

³"You know that my father, David, was not able to build a Temple to honor the name of the LORD his God because of the many wars waged against him by surrounding nations. He could not build until the LORD gave him victory over all his enemies. ⁴But now the LORD my God has given me peace on every side; I have no enemies, and all is well. ⁵So I am planning to build a Temple to honor the name of the LORD my God, just as he had instructed my father, David. For the LORD told him, 'Your son, whom I will place on your throne, will build the Temple to honor my name.'

⁶"Therefore, please command that cedars from Lebanon be cut for me. Let my men work alongside yours, and I will pay your men whatever wages you ask. As you know, there is no one among us who can cut timber like you Sidonians!"

4:13 Hebrew *Jair son of Manasseh;* compare 1 Chr 2:22. **4:19a** Greek version reads *of Gad;* compare 4:13. **4:19b** As in some Greek manuscripts; Hebrew lacks *of Judah.* The meaning of the Hebrew is uncertain. **4:21a** Verses 4:21-34 are numbered 5:1-14 in Hebrew text. **4:21b** Hebrew *the river;* also in 4:24. **4:22** Hebrew *30 cors* [6.6 kiloliters] *of choice flour and 60 cors* [13.2 kiloliters] *of meal.* **4:23** Or *and fattened geese.* **4:25** Hebrew *each family lived under its own grapevine and under its own fig tree.* **4:26a** As in some Greek manuscripts (see also 2 Chr 9:25); Hebrew reads *40,000.* **4:26b** Or *12,000 charioteers.* **5:1** Verses 5:1-18 are numbered 5:15-32 in Hebrew text.

4:20-21 God's promise to Abraham (Genesis 15:18-21; 17:8; 22:17) found historical fulfillment in his blessing of Solomon. The surrounding lands conquered by David and Solomon remained loyal to Solomon. They "sent tribute money . . . and continued to serve him throughout" his long reign. We can trust God to keep his promises, even those we have yet to see fulfilled.

4:32-34 Solomon's wisdom wasn't only for making good decisions in his court. Solomon is credited with writing and compiling the book of Proverbs, and he composed Psalms 72 and 127. His knowledge of plants and animals reflected his careful observation of nature (see Proverbs 6:6-8). Solomon's wisdom and literary skills are reflected in the Song of Songs and Ecclesiastes. It's no wonder that many, including a queen (1 Kings 10:1-9; see Matthew 12:42), sought Solomon's wisdom.

5:2-6 Solomon responded to Hiram by sending word through Hiram's ambassadors that he intended to "build a Temple to honor the name of the LORD," following his father's desire and securing provisions for its construction (2 Samuel 7:1-3; 1 Chronicles 17:1-15; 22:14-19; 28:9-12).

⁷When Hiram received Solomon's message, he was very pleased and said, "Praise the LORD today for giving David a wise son to be king of the great nation of Israel." ⁸Then he sent this reply to Solomon:

"I have received your message, and I will supply all the cedar and cypress timber you need. ⁹My servants will bring the logs from the Lebanon mountains to the Mediterranean Sea* and make them into rafts and float them along the coast to whatever place you choose. Then we will break the rafts apart so you can carry the logs away. You can pay me by supplying me with food for my household."

¹⁰So Hiram supplied as much cedar and cypress timber as Solomon desired. ¹¹In return, Solomon sent him an annual payment of 100,000 bushels* of wheat for his household and 110,000 gallons* of pure olive oil. ¹²So the LORD gave wisdom to Solomon, just as he had promised. And Hiram and Solomon made a formal alliance of peace.

¹³Then King Solomon conscripted a labor force of 30,000 men from all Israel. ¹⁴He sent them to Lebanon in shifts, 10,000 every month, so that each man would be one month in Lebanon and two months at home. Adoniram was in charge of this labor force. ¹⁵Solomon also had 70,000 common laborers, 80,000 quarry workers in the hill country, ¹⁶and 3,600* foremen to supervise the work. ¹⁷At the king's command, they quarried large blocks of high-quality stone and shaped them to make the foundation of the Temple. ¹⁸Men from the city of Gebal helped Solomon's and Hiram's builders prepare the timber and stone for the Temple.

Solomon Builds the Temple

6 It was in midspring, in the month of Ziv,* during the fourth year of Solomon's reign, that he began to construct the Temple of the LORD. This was 480 years after the people of Israel were rescued from their slavery in the land of Egypt.

²The Temple that King Solomon built for the LORD was 90 feet long, 30 feet wide, and 45 feet high.* ³The entry room at the front of the Temple was 30 feet* wide, running across the entire width of the Temple. It projected outward 15 feet* from the front of the Temple. ⁴Solomon also made narrow recessed windows throughout the Temple.

⁵He built a complex of rooms against the outer walls of the Temple, all the way around the sides and rear of the building. ⁶The complex was three stories high, the bottom floor being 7½ feet wide, the second floor 9 feet wide, and the top floor 10½ feet wide.* The rooms were connected to the walls of the Temple by beams resting on ledges built out from the wall. So the beams were not inserted into the walls themselves.

⁷The stones used in the construction of the Temple were finished at the quarry, so there was no sound of hammer, ax, or any other iron tool at the building site.

⁸The entrance to the bottom floor* was on the south side of the Temple. There were winding stairs going up to the second floor, and another flight of stairs between the second and third floors. ⁹After completing the Temple structure, Solomon put in a ceiling made of cedar beams and planks. ¹⁰As already stated, he built a complex of rooms along the sides of the building, attached to the Temple walls by cedar timbers. Each story of the complex was 7½ feet* high.

¹¹Then the LORD gave this message to Solomon: ¹²"Concerning this Temple you are building, if you keep all my decrees and regulations and obey all my commands, I will fulfill through you the promise I made to your father, David. ¹³I will live among the Israelites and will never abandon my people Israel."

The Temple's Interior

¹⁴So Solomon finished building the Temple. ¹⁵The entire inside, from floor to ceiling, was paneled with wood. He paneled the walls and ceilings with cedar, and he used planks of cypress for the floors. ¹⁶He partitioned off an inner sanctuary—the Most Holy Place—at the far end of the Temple. It was 30 feet deep and was paneled with cedar from floor to ceiling. ¹⁷The main room of the Temple, outside the Most Holy Place, was 60 feet* long. ¹⁸Cedar paneling completely covered the stone walls throughout the

---

5:9 Hebrew *the sea.* **5:11a** Hebrew *20,000 cors* [4,400 kiloliters]. **5:11b** As in Greek version, which reads *20,000 baths* [420 kiloliters] (see also 2 Chr 2:10); Hebrew reads *20 cors,* about 1,000 gallons or 4.4 kiloliters in volume. **5:16** As in some Greek manuscripts (see also 2 Chr 2:2, 18); Hebrew reads *3,300.* **6:1** Hebrew *It was in the month of Ziv, which is the second month.* This month of the ancient Hebrew lunar calendar usually occurs within the months of April and May. **6:2** Hebrew *60 cubits* [27.6 meters] *long, 20 cubits* [9.2 meters] *wide, and 30 cubits* [13.8 meters] *high.* **6:3a** Hebrew *20 cubits* [9.2 meters]; also in 6:16, 20. **6:3b** Hebrew *10 cubits* [4.6 meters]. **6:6** Hebrew *the bottom floor being 5 cubits* [2.3 meters] *wide, the second floor 6 cubits* [2.8 meters] *wide, and the top floor 7 cubits* [3.2 meters] *wide.* **6:8** As in Greek version; Hebrew reads *middle floor.* **6:10** Hebrew *5 cubits* [2.3 meters]. **6:17** Hebrew *40 cubits* [18.4 meters].

6:1–8:66 The construction of the Temple and the palace was a high point in Solomon's reign. The Temple was even more beautiful and ornate than the palace. Signifying the Lord's presence, the Temple was the place where Israelites would worship, sacrifice, and pray to God. Even with the Ark of the Covenant coming to this beautiful Temple, Solomon's prayer of dedication reveals his awareness that God cannot be contained on this earth. Solomon prayed, "But will God really live on earth? Why, even the highest heavens cannot contain you. How much less this Temple I have built!" (8:27). Jesus has promised that God's very presence, the Holy Spirit, is with us and in us today. God's Spirit guides and directs us, reminding us that we are loved and never alone (John 14:15-17).

Temple, and the paneling was decorated with carvings of gourds and open flowers.

¹⁹He prepared the inner sanctuary at the far end of the Temple, where the Ark of the LORD's Covenant would be placed. ²⁰This inner sanctuary was 30 feet long, 30 feet wide, and 30 feet high. He overlaid the inside with solid gold. He also overlaid the altar made of cedar.* ²¹Then Solomon overlaid the rest of the Temple's interior with solid gold, and he made gold chains to protect the entrance* to the Most Holy Place. ²²So he finished overlaying the entire Temple with gold, including the altar that belonged to the Most Holy Place.

²³He made two cherubim of wild olive* wood, each 15 feet* tall, and placed them in the inner sanctuary. ²⁴The wingspan of each of the cherubim was 15 feet, each wing being 7½ feet* long. ²⁵The two cherubim were identical in shape and size; ²⁶each was 15 feet tall. ²⁷He placed them side by side in the inner sanctuary of the Temple. Their outspread wings reached from wall to wall, while their inner wings touched at the center of the room. ²⁸He overlaid the two cherubim with gold.

²⁹He decorated all the walls of the inner sanctuary and the main room with carvings of cherubim, palm trees, and open flowers. ³⁰He overlaid the floor in both rooms with gold.

³¹For the entrance to the inner sanctuary, he made double doors of wild olive wood with five-sided doorposts.* ³²These double doors were decorated with carvings of cherubim, palm trees, and open flowers. The doors, including the decorations of cherubim and palm trees, were overlaid with gold.

³³Then he made four-sided doorposts of wild olive wood for the entrance to the Temple. ³⁴There were two folding doors of cypress wood, and each door was hinged to fold back upon itself. ³⁵These doors were decorated with carvings of cherubim, palm trees, and open flowers—all overlaid evenly with gold.

³⁶The walls of the inner courtyard were built so that there was one layer of cedar beams between every three layers of finished stone.

³⁷The foundation of the LORD's Temple was laid in midspring, in the month of Ziv,* during the fourth year of Solomon's reign. ³⁸The entire building was completed in every detail by midautumn, in the month of Bul,* during the eleventh year of his reign. So it took seven years to build the Temple.

Solomon Builds His Palace

7 Solomon also built a palace for himself, and it took him thirteen years to complete the construction.

²One of Solomon's buildings was called the Palace of the Forest of Lebanon. It was 150 feet long, 75 feet wide, and 45 feet high.* There were four rows of cedar pillars, and great cedar beams rested on the pillars. ³The hall had a cedar roof. Above the beams on the pillars were forty-five side rooms,* arranged in three tiers of fifteen each. ⁴On each end of the long hall were three rows of windows facing each other. ⁵All the doorways and doorposts* had rectangular frames and were arranged in sets of three, facing each other.

⁶Solomon also built the Hall of Pillars, which was 75 feet long and 45 feet wide.* There was a porch in front, along with a canopy supported by pillars.

⁷Solomon also built the throne room, known as the Hall of Justice, where he sat to hear legal matters. It was paneled with cedar from floor to ceiling.* ⁸Solomon's living quarters surrounded a courtyard behind this hall, and they were constructed the same way. He also built similar living quarters for Pharaoh's daughter, whom he had married.

⁹From foundation to eaves, all these buildings were built from huge blocks of high-quality stone, cut with saws and trimmed to exact measure on all sides. ¹⁰Some of the huge foundation stones were 15 feet long, and some were 12 feet* long. ¹¹The blocks of high-quality stone used in the walls were also cut to measure, and cedar beams were also used. ¹²The walls of the great courtyard were built so that there was one layer of cedar beams between every three layers of finished stone, just like the walls of the inner courtyard of the LORD's Temple with its entry room.

6:20 Or *overlaid the altar with cedar*. The meaning of the Hebrew is uncertain. **6:21** Or *to draw curtains across*. The meaning of the Hebrew is uncertain. **6:23a** Or *pine;* Hebrew reads *oil tree;* also in 6:31, 33. **6:23b** Hebrew *10 cubits* [4.6 meters]; also in 6:24, 26. **6:24** Hebrew *5 cubits* [2.3 meters]. **6:31** The meaning of the Hebrew is uncertain. **6:37** Hebrew *was laid in the month of Ziv*. This month of the ancient Hebrew lunar calendar usually occurs within the months of April and May. **6:38** Hebrew *by the month of Bul, which is the eighth month*. This month of the ancient Hebrew lunar calendar usually occurs within the months of October and November. **7:2** Hebrew *100 cubits* [46 meters] *long, 50 cubits* [23 meters] *wide, and 30 cubits* [13.8 meters] *high*. **7:3** Or *45 rafters,* or *45 beams,* or *45 pillars*. The architectural details in 7:2-6 can be interpreted in many different ways. **7:5** Greek version reads *windows*. **7:6** Hebrew *50 cubits* [23 meters] *long and 30 cubits* [13.8 meters] *wide*. **7:7** As in Syriac version and Latin Vulgate; Hebrew reads *from floor to floor*. **7:10** Hebrew *10 cubits* [4.6 meters] . . . *8 cubits* [3.7 meters].

7:1-12 Before describing the Temple's furnishings, the writer mentions the construction of Solomon's palace complex. The multiple buildings within this complex took nearly twice as long to build (thirteen years) as the Temple (seven years, 6:38). The entire building project took twenty years (9:10). Although construction details are brief, archaeological discovery of two of Solomon's buildings provides an idea of how this palace might have looked. Despite its grandeur, Solomon's palace is not the author's focus; his interest is in the Temple, God's dwelling place.
7:9-11 As with the Temple, the stones for Solomon's palace complex were "high-quality stone, cut . . . and trimmed to exact" specifications. Similar stonework has been found at Megiddo, another ancient Israelite city. Cedar beams between the walls provided better protection against earthquakes.

Furnishings for the Temple

¹³King Solomon then asked for a man named Huram* to come from Tyre. ¹⁴He was half Israelite, since his mother was a widow from the tribe of Naphtali, and his father had been a craftsman in bronze from Tyre. Huram was extremely skillful and talented in any work in bronze, and he came to do all the metal work for King Solomon.

¹⁵Huram cast two bronze pillars, each 27 feet tall and 18 feet in circumference.* ¹⁶For the tops of the pillars he cast bronze capitals, each 7½ feet* tall. ¹⁷Each capital was decorated with seven sets of latticework and interwoven chains. ¹⁸He also encircled the latticework with two rows of pomegranates to decorate the capitals over the pillars. ¹⁹The capitals on the columns inside the entry room were shaped like water lilies, and they were six feet* tall. ²⁰The capitals on the two pillars had 200 pomegranates in two rows around them, beside the rounded surface next to the latticework. ²¹Huram set the pillars at the entrance of the Temple, one toward the south and one toward the north. He named the one on the south Jakin, and the one on the north Boaz.* ²²The capitals on the pillars were shaped like water lilies. And so the work on the pillars was finished.

²³Then Huram cast a great round basin, 15 feet across from rim to rim, called the Sea. It was 7½ feet deep and about 45 feet in circumference.* ²⁴It was encircled just below its rim by two rows of decorative gourds. There were about six gourds per foot* all the way around, and they were cast as part of the basin.

²⁵The Sea was placed on a base of twelve bronze oxen,* all facing outward. Three faced north, three faced west, three faced south, and three faced east, and the Sea rested on them. ²⁶The walls of the Sea were about three inches* thick, and its rim flared out like a cup and resembled a water lily blossom. It could hold about 11,000 gallons* of water.

²⁷Huram also made ten bronze water carts, each 6 feet long, 6 feet wide, and 4½ feet tall.* ²⁸They were constructed with side panels braced with crossbars. ²⁹Both the panels and the crossbars were decorated with carved lions, oxen, and cherubim. Above and below the lions and oxen were wreath decorations. ³⁰Each of these carts had four bronze wheels and bronze axles. There were supporting posts for the bronze basins at the corners of the carts; these supports were decorated on each side with carvings of wreaths. ³¹The top of each cart had a rounded frame for the basin. It projected 1½ feet* above the cart's top like a round pedestal, and its opening was 2¼ feet* across; it was decorated on the outside with carvings of wreaths. The panels of the carts were square, not round. ³²Under the panels were four wheels that were connected to axles that had been cast as one unit with the cart. The wheels were 2¼ feet in diameter ³³and were similar to chariot wheels. The axles, spokes, rims, and hubs were all cast from molten bronze.

³⁴There were handles at each of the four corners of the carts, and these, too, were cast as one unit with the cart. ³⁵Around the top of each cart was a rim nine inches wide.* The corner supports and side panels were cast as one unit with the cart. ³⁶Carvings of cherubim, lions, and palm trees decorated the panels and corner supports wherever there was room, and there were wreaths all around. ³⁷All ten water carts were the same size and were made alike, for each was cast from the same mold.

³⁸Huram also made ten smaller bronze basins, one for each cart. Each basin was six feet across and could hold 220 gallons* of water. ³⁹He set five water carts on the south side of the Temple and five on the north side. The great bronze basin called the Sea was placed near the southeast corner of the Temple. ⁴⁰He also made the necessary washbasins, shovels, and bowls.

So at last Huram completed everything King Solomon had assigned him to make for the Temple of the LORD:

⁴¹ the two pillars;
the two bowl-shaped capitals on top of the pillars;
the two networks of interwoven chains that decorated the capitals;
⁴² the 400 pomegranates that hung from the chains on the capitals (two rows of pomegranates for each of the chain networks that decorated the capitals on top of the pillars);
⁴³ the ten water carts holding the ten basins;
⁴⁴ the Sea and the twelve oxen under it;
⁴⁵ the ash buckets, the shovels, and the bowls.

Huram made all these things of burnished bronze for the Temple of the LORD, just as King Solomon had directed. ⁴⁶The king had them cast in clay molds in the Jordan Valley between Succoth and Zarethan. ⁴⁷Solomon did not weigh all these things because there were so many; the weight of the bronze could not be measured.

7:13 Hebrew *Hiram* (also in 7:40, 45); compare 2 Chr 2:13. This is not the same person mentioned in 5:1. **7:15** Hebrew *18 cubits* [8.3 meters] *tall and 12 cubits* [5.5 meters] *in circumference.* **7:16** Hebrew *5 cubits* [2.3 meters]. **7:19** Hebrew *4 cubits* [1.8 meters]; also in 7:38. **7:21** *Jakin* probably means "he establishes"; *Boaz* probably means "in him is strength." **7:23** Hebrew *10 cubits* [4.6 meters] *across. . . . 5 cubits* [2.3 meters] *deep and 30 cubits* [13.8 meters] *in circumference.* **7:24** Or *20 gourds per meter;* Hebrew reads *10 per cubit.* **7:25** Hebrew *12 oxen;* compare 2 Kgs 16:17, which specifies *bronze oxen.* **7:26a** Hebrew *a handbreadth* [8 centimeters]. **7:26b** Hebrew *2,000 baths* [42 kiloliters]. **7:27** Hebrew *4 cubits* [1.8 meters] *long, 4 cubits wide, and 3 cubits* [1.4 meters] *high.* **7:31a** Hebrew *a cubit* [46 centimeters]. **7:31b** Hebrew *1½ cubits* [69 centimeters]; also in 7:32. **7:35** Hebrew *half a cubit wide* [23 centimeters]. **7:38** Hebrew *40 baths* [840 liters].

⁴⁸Solomon also made all the furnishings of the Temple of the LORD:

the gold altar;
the gold table for the Bread of the Presence;
⁴⁹ the lampstands of solid gold, five on the south and five on the north, in front of the Most Holy Place;
the flower decorations, lamps, and tongs—all of gold;
⁵⁰ the small bowls, lamp snuffers, bowls, ladles, and incense burners—all of solid gold;
the doors for the entrances to the Most Holy Place and the main room of the Temple, with their fronts overlaid with gold.

⁵¹So King Solomon finished all his work on the Temple of the LORD. Then he brought all the gifts his father, David, had dedicated—the silver, the gold, and the various articles—and he stored them in the treasuries of the LORD's Temple.

The Ark Brought to the Temple

8 Solomon then summoned to Jerusalem the elders of Israel and all the heads of the tribes—the leaders of the ancestral families of the Israelites. They were to bring the Ark of the LORD's Covenant to the Temple from its location in the City of David, also known as Zion. ²So all the men of Israel assembled before King Solomon at the annual Festival of Shelters, which is held in early autumn in the month of Ethanim.*

³When all the elders of Israel arrived, the priests picked up the Ark. ⁴The priests and Levites brought up the Ark of the LORD along with the special tent* and all the sacred items that had been in it. ⁵There, before the Ark, King Solomon and the entire community of Israel sacrificed so many sheep, goats, and cattle that no one could keep count!

⁶Then the priests carried the Ark of the LORD's Covenant into the inner sanctuary of the Temple—the Most Holy Place—and placed it beneath the wings of the cherubim. ⁷The cherubim spread their wings over the Ark, forming a canopy over the Ark and its carrying poles. ⁸These poles were so long that their ends could be seen from the Holy Place, which is in front of the Most Holy Place, but not from the outside. They are still there to this day. ⁹Nothing was in the Ark except the two stone tablets that Moses had placed in it at Mount Sinai,* where the LORD made a covenant with the people of Israel when they left the land of Egypt.

¹⁰When the priests came out of the Holy Place, a thick cloud filled the Temple of the LORD. ¹¹The priests could not continue their service because of the cloud, for the glorious presence of the LORD filled the Temple of the LORD.

Solomon Praises the LORD

¹²Then Solomon prayed, "O LORD, you have said that you would live in a thick cloud of darkness. ¹³Now I have built a glorious Temple for you, a place where you can live forever!*"

¹⁴Then the king turned around to the entire community of Israel standing before him and gave this blessing: ¹⁵"Praise the LORD, the God of Israel, who has kept the promise he made to my father, David. For he told my father, ¹⁶'From the day I brought my people Israel out of Egypt, I have never chosen a city among any of the tribes of Israel as the place where a Temple should be built to honor my name. But I have chosen David to be king over my people Israel.'"

¹⁷Then Solomon said, "My father, David, wanted to build this Temple to honor the name of the LORD, the God of Israel. ¹⁸But the LORD told him, 'You wanted to build the Temple to honor my name. Your intention is good, ¹⁹but you are not the one to do it. One of your own sons will build the Temple to honor me.'

²⁰"And now the LORD has fulfilled the promise he made, for I have become king in my father's place, and now I sit on the throne of Israel, just as the LORD promised. I have built this Temple to honor the name of the LORD, the God of Israel. ²¹And I have prepared a place there for the Ark, which contains the covenant that the LORD made with our ancestors when he brought them out of Egypt."

8:2 Hebrew *at the festival in the month Ethanim, which is the seventh month.* The Festival of Shelters began on the fifteenth day of the seventh month of the ancient Hebrew lunar calendar. This day occurred in late September, October, or early November. **8:4** Hebrew *the Tent of Meeting*; i.e., the tent mentioned in 2 Sam 6:17 and 1 Chr 16:1. **8:9** Hebrew *at Horeb,* another name for Sinai. **8:13** Some Greek texts add the line *Is this not written in the Book of Jashar?*

8:1-66 Solomon's building activities climaxed with the Ark's move to the newly erected Temple. The king offered both prayer (8:22-53) and words of praise and blessing (8:56-61) to dedicate the Temple for the Lord's service. After the dedication, the assembled gathering enjoyed the great Festival of Shelters. The focus of the account is on Solomon praising God and blessing the people (8:12-61).
8:10-11 As the priests came out of the Holy Place, they were greeted with music praising the Lord (2 Chronicles 5:11-14). Previously, the glorious presence of the Lord had filled the Tabernacle (Exodus 40:34-35). Now it filled the Temple to show that God was again dwelling among his people. Ezekiel recorded its later departure from the Temple (Ezekiel 10:18-19; 11:22-23), to return at a blessed future time (Ezekiel 43:1-5). In the New Testament, John wrote that God dwells among his people through his son, Jesus Christ (John 1:14). Paul affirmed that Christ now dwells in each believer (Colossians 1:27) as a foretaste of a future when "God's home is . . . among his people" (Revelation 21:3).

Solomon's Prayer of Dedication

²²Then Solomon stood before the altar of the LORD in front of the entire community of Israel. He lifted his hands toward heaven, ²³and he prayed,

"O LORD, God of Israel, there is no God like you in all of heaven above or on the earth below. You keep your covenant and show unfailing love to all who walk before you in wholehearted devotion. ²⁴You have kept your promise to your servant David, my father. You made that promise with your own mouth, and with your own hands you have fulfilled it today.

²⁵"And now, O LORD, God of Israel, carry out the additional promise you made to your servant David, my father. For you said to him, 'If your descendants guard their behavior and faithfully follow me as you have done, one of them will always sit on the throne of Israel.' ²⁶Now, O God of Israel, fulfill this promise to your servant David, my father.

²⁷"But will God really live on earth? Why, even the highest heavens cannot contain you. How much less this Temple I have built! ²⁸Nevertheless, listen to my prayer and my plea, O LORD my God. Hear the cry and the prayer that your servant is making to you today. ²⁹May you watch over this Temple night and day, this place where you have said, 'My name will be there.' May you always hear the prayers I make toward this place. ³⁰May you hear the humble and earnest requests from me and your people Israel when we pray toward this place. Yes, hear us from heaven where you live, and when you hear, forgive.

³¹"If someone wrongs another person and is required to take an oath of innocence in front of your altar in this Temple, ³²then hear from heaven and judge between your servants—the accuser and the accused. Punish the guilty as they deserve. Acquit the innocent because of their innocence.

³³"If your people Israel are defeated by their enemies because they have sinned against you, and if they turn to you and acknowledge your name and pray to you here in this Temple, ³⁴then hear from heaven and forgive the sin of your people Israel and return them to this land you gave their ancestors.

³⁵"If the skies are shut up and there is no rain because your people have sinned against you, and if they pray toward this Temple and acknowledge your name and turn from their sins because you have punished them, ³⁶then hear from heaven and forgive the sins of your servants, your people Israel. Teach them to follow the right path, and send rain on your land that you have given to your people as their special possession.

³⁷"If there is a famine in the land or a plague or crop disease or attacks of locusts or caterpillars, or if your people's enemies are in the land besieging their towns—whatever disaster or disease there is—³⁸and if your people Israel pray about their troubles, raising their hands toward this Temple, ³⁹then hear from heaven where you live, and forgive. Give your people what their actions deserve, for you alone know each human heart. ⁴⁰Then they will fear you as long as they live in the land you gave to our ancestors.

⁴¹"In the future, foreigners who do not belong to your people Israel will hear of you. They will come from distant lands because of your name, ⁴²for they will hear of your great name and your strong hand and your powerful arm. And when they pray toward this Temple, ⁴³then hear from heaven where you live, and grant what they ask of you. In this way, all the people of the earth will come to know and fear you, just as your own people Israel do. They, too, will know that this Temple I have built honors your name.

⁴⁴"If your people go out where you send them to fight their enemies, and if they pray to the LORD by turning toward this city you have chosen and toward this Temple I have built to honor your name, ⁴⁵then hear their prayers from heaven and uphold their cause.

⁴⁶"If they sin against you—and who has never sinned?—you might become angry with them and let their enemies conquer them and take them captive to their land far away or near. ⁴⁷But in that land of exile, they might turn to you in repentance and pray, 'We have sinned, done evil, and acted wickedly.' ⁴⁸If they turn to you with their whole heart and soul in the land of their enemies and pray toward the land you gave to their ancestors—toward this city you have chosen, and toward this Temple I have built to honor your name—⁴⁹then hear their prayers and their petition from heaven where you live, and uphold their cause. ⁵⁰Forgive your people who have sinned against you. Forgive all the offenses they have committed against you. Make their captors merciful to them, ⁵¹for they are your people—your special possession—whom you brought out of the iron-smelting furnace of Egypt.

⁵²"May your eyes be open to my requests and to the requests of your people Israel. May you hear and answer them whenever they cry out to you. ⁵³For when you brought our ancestors out of Egypt, O Sovereign LORD, you told your servant Moses that you had set Israel apart from all the nations of the earth to be your own special possession."

The Dedication of the Temple

⁵⁴When Solomon finished making these prayers and petitions to the LORD, he stood up in front of the altar of the LORD, where he had been kneeling with his hands raised toward heaven. ⁵⁵He stood and in a loud voice blessed the entire congregation of Israel:

⁵⁶"Praise the LORD who has given rest to his people Israel, just as he promised. Not one word has failed of all the wonderful promises he gave through his servant Moses. ⁵⁷May the LORD our God be with us as he was with our ancestors; may he never leave us or abandon us. ⁵⁸May he give us the desire to do his will in everything and to obey all the commands, decrees, and regulations that he gave our ancestors. ⁵⁹And may these words that I have prayed in the presence of the LORD be before him constantly, day and night, so that the LORD our God may give justice to me and to his people Israel, according to each day's needs. ⁶⁰Then people all over the earth will know that the LORD alone is God and there is no other. ⁶¹And may you be completely faithful to the LORD our God. May you always obey his decrees and commands, just as you are doing today."

⁶²Then the king and all Israel with him offered sacrifices to the LORD. ⁶³Solomon offered to the LORD a peace offering of 22,000 cattle and 120,000 sheep and goats. And so the king and all the people of Israel dedicated the Temple of the LORD.

⁶⁴That same day the king consecrated the central area of the courtyard in front of the LORD's Temple. He offered burnt offerings, grain offerings, and the fat of peace offerings there, because the bronze altar in the LORD's presence was too small to hold all the burnt offerings, grain offerings, and the fat of the peace offerings.

⁶⁵Then Solomon and all Israel celebrated the Festival of Shelters* in the presence of the LORD our God. A large congregation had gathered from as far away as Lebo-hamath in the north and the Brook of Egypt in the south. The celebration went on for fourteen days in all—seven days for the dedication of the altar and seven days for the Festival of Shelters.* ⁶⁶After the festival was over,* Solomon sent the people home. They blessed the king and went to their homes joyful and glad because the LORD had been good to his servant David and to his people Israel.

The LORD's Response to Solomon

9 So Solomon finished building the Temple of the LORD, as well as the royal palace. He completed everything he had planned to do. ²Then the LORD appeared to Solomon a second time, as he had done before at Gibeon. ³The LORD said to him,

"I have heard your prayer and your petition. I have set this Temple apart to be holy—this place you have built where my name will be honored forever. I will always watch over it, for it is dear to my heart.

⁴"As for you, if you will follow me with integrity and godliness, as David your father did, obeying all my commands, decrees, and regulations, ⁵then I will establish the throne of your dynasty over Israel forever. For I made this promise to your father, David: 'One of your descendants will always sit on the throne of Israel.'

⁶"But if you or your descendants abandon me and disobey the commands and decrees I have given you, and if you serve and worship other gods, ⁷then I will uproot Israel from this land that I have given them. I will reject this Temple that I have made holy to honor my name. I will make Israel an object of mockery and ridicule among the nations. ⁸And though this Temple is impressive now, all who pass by will be appalled and will gasp in horror. They will ask, 'Why did the LORD do such terrible things to this land and to this Temple?'

⁹"And the answer will be, 'Because his people abandoned the LORD their God, who brought their ancestors out of Egypt, and they worshiped other gods instead and bowed down to them. That is why the LORD has brought all these disasters on them.'"

Solomon's Agreement with Hiram

¹⁰It took Solomon twenty years to build the LORD's Temple and his own royal palace. At the end of that time, ¹¹he gave twenty towns in the land of Galilee to King Hiram of Tyre. (Hiram had previously provided all the cedar and cypress timber and gold that Solomon had requested.) ¹²But when Hiram came from Tyre to see the towns Solomon had given him, he was not at all pleased with them. ¹³"What kind of towns are these, my brother?" he asked. So Hiram called that area Cabul (which means "worthless"), as it is still known today. ¹⁴Nevertheless, Hiram paid* Solomon 9,000 pounds* of gold.

Solomon's Many Achievements

¹⁵This is the account of the forced labor that King Solomon conscripted to build the LORD's Temple, the royal palace, the supporting terraces,* the wall of Jerusalem, and the cities of Hazor, Megiddo, and

---

8:65a Hebrew *the festival;* see note on 8:2. **8:65b** Hebrew *seven days and seven days, fourteen days;* compare parallel text at 2 Chr 7:8-10. **8:66** Hebrew *On the eighth day,* probably referring to the day following the seven-day Festival of Shelters; compare parallel text at 2 Chr 7:9-10. **9:14a** Or *For Hiram had paid.* **9:14b** Hebrew *120 talents* [4,000 kilograms]. **9:15** Hebrew *the millo;* also in 9:24. The meaning of the Hebrew is uncertain.

9:2 The Lord had previously appeared to Solomon when granting his desire for wisdom (3:3-15). The author of 2 Chronicles provides additional details of God's blessings or judgments, depending on the faithfulness of Solomon and Israel (2 Chronicles 7:11-22).

9:3-9 The Lord answered Solomon's prayer by reviewing the conditions of the covenant. Obedience would bring prosperity and the Lord's blessing. Disobedience could mean utter disaster, including destruction of the city and Temple, and deportation of God's people (see Deuteronomy 28:36-37, 63-68). Although God's covenant was permanent, receiving its blessings depended upon faithfulness to its terms (Psalm 89:24-37).

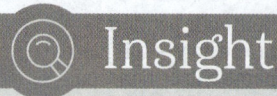

Insight: SOLOMON'S WEALTH

Wealth is a blessing that requires great maturity and wisdom to be handled well without destroying the owner. Solomon may have been one of the wealthiest people who ever lived. Here's a look at his diverse portfolio. Even with all this, Solomon considered wealth meaningless (Ecclesiastes 5:8-20). Instead, Solomon's wealth and wisdom pointed others, such as the Queen of Sheba, to God's glory (1 Kings 10:1-9; see "Queen of Sheba" on page 529).

MILITARY
1,400 chariots
4,000 stalls for chariot horses
12,000 horses

WEALTH
25 tons of gold annually from all tributes
16 tons of gold from Ophir
9,000 pounds of gold from Sheba

KINGDOM
45,000 square miles

DAILY FOOD REQUIREMENTS FOR THE PALACE
300 bushels of meal
150 bushels of choice flour
100 sheep or goats
20 pasture-fed cattle
10 oxen
Deer, gazelle, roe deer, choice poultry

LABOR
3,600 foremen
30,000 Israelite men conscripted in shifts
70,000 common laborers
80,000 quarry laborers

Gezer. ¹⁶(Pharaoh, the king of Egypt, had attacked and captured Gezer, killing the Canaanite population and burning it down. He gave the city to his daughter as a wedding gift when she married Solomon. ¹⁷So Solomon rebuilt the city of Gezer.) He also built up the towns of Lower Beth-horon, ¹⁸Baalath, and Tamar* in the wilderness within his land. ¹⁹He built towns as supply centers and constructed towns where his chariots and horses* could be stationed. He built everything he desired in Jerusalem and Lebanon and throughout his entire realm.

²⁰There were still some people living in the land who were not Israelites, including Amorites, Hittites, Perizzites, Hivites, and Jebusites. ²¹These were descendants of the nations whom the people of Israel had not completely destroyed.* So Solomon conscripted them as slaves, and they serve as forced laborers to this day. ²²But Solomon did not conscript any of the Israelites for forced labor. Instead, he assigned them to serve as fighting men, government officials, officers and captains in his army, commanders of his chariots, and charioteers. ²³Solomon appointed 550 of them to supervise the people working on his various projects.

²⁴Solomon moved his wife, Pharaoh's daughter, from the City of David to the new palace he had built for her. Then he constructed the supporting terraces.

²⁵Three times each year Solomon presented burnt offerings and peace offerings on the altar he had built for the Lord. He also burned incense to the Lord. And so he finished the work of building the Temple.

9:18 An alternate reading in the Masoretic Text reads *Tadmor.* 9:19 Or *and charioteers.* 9:21 The Hebrew term used here refers to the complete consecration of things or people to the Lord, either by destroying them or by giving them as an offering.

9:24 The new palace Solomon built for Pharaoh's daughter was separate from Solomon's own residence because his palace was deemed holy, "for the Ark of the Lord has been there" (2 Chronicles 8:11). The place where the Ark resided was considered sacred, since it embodied God's presence and made its surroundings holy (see Exodus 25:22; see also 2 Samuel 6:7; 1 Chronicles 15:11-13).

9:25 Solomon presented offerings at the national festivals of Unleavened Bread, Harvest (or Pentecost or Weeks) and Shelters (Deuteronomy 16:16).

²⁶King Solomon also built a fleet of ships at Eziongeber, a port near Elath* in the land of Edom, along the shore of the Red Sea.* ²⁷Hiram sent experienced crews of sailors to sail the ships with Solomon's men. ²⁸They sailed to Ophir and brought back to Solomon some sixteen tons* of gold.

Visit of the Queen of Sheba

10 When the queen of Sheba heard of Solomon's fame, which brought honor to the name of the LORD,* she came to test him with hard questions. ²She arrived in Jerusalem with a large group of attendants and a great caravan of camels loaded with spices, large quantities of gold, and precious jewels. When she met with Solomon, she talked with him about everything she had on her mind. ³Solomon had answers for all her questions; nothing was too hard for the king to explain to her. ⁴When the queen of Sheba realized how very wise Solomon was, and when she saw the palace he had built, ⁵she was overwhelmed. She was also amazed at the food on his tables, the organization of his officials and their splendid clothing, the cupbearers, and the burnt offerings Solomon made at the Temple of the LORD.

⁶She exclaimed to the king, "Everything I heard in my country about your achievements* and wisdom is true! ⁷I didn't believe what was said until I arrived here and saw it with my own eyes. In fact, I had not heard the half of it! Your wisdom and prosperity are far beyond what I was told. ⁸How happy your people* must be! What a privilege for your officials to stand here day after day, listening to your wisdom! ⁹Praise the LORD your God, who delights in you and has placed you on the throne of Israel. Because of the LORD's eternal love for Israel, he has made you king so you can rule with justice and righteousness."

¹⁰Then she gave the king a gift of 9,000 pounds* of gold, great quantities of spices, and precious jewels. Never again were so many spices brought in as those the queen of Sheba gave to King Solomon.

¹¹(In addition, Hiram's ships brought gold from Ophir, and they also brought rich cargoes of red sandalwood* and precious jewels. ¹²The king used the sandalwood to make railings for the Temple of the LORD and the royal palace, and to construct lyres and harps for the musicians. Never before or since has there been such a supply of sandalwood.)

¹³King Solomon gave the queen of Sheba whatever she asked for, besides all the customary gifts he had so generously given. Then she and all her attendants returned to their own land.

Solomon's Wealth and Splendor

¹⁴Each year Solomon received about 25 tons* of gold. ¹⁵This did not include the additional revenue he received from merchants and traders, all the kings of Arabia, and the governors of the land.

¹⁶King Solomon made 200 large shields of hammered gold, each weighing more than fifteen pounds.* ¹⁷He also made 300 smaller shields of hammered gold, each weighing nearly four pounds.* The king placed these shields in the Palace of the Forest of Lebanon.

¹⁸Then the king made a huge throne, decorated with ivory and overlaid with fine gold. ¹⁹The throne had six steps and a rounded back. There were armrests on both sides of the seat, and the figure of a lion stood on each side of the throne. ²⁰There were also twelve other lions, one standing on each end of the six steps. No other throne in all the world could be compared with it!

²¹All of King Solomon's drinking cups were solid gold, as were all the utensils in the Palace of the Forest of Lebanon. They were not made of silver, for silver was considered worthless in Solomon's day!

²²The king had a fleet of trading ships of Tarshish that sailed with Hiram's fleet. Once every three years the ships returned, loaded with gold, silver, ivory, apes, and peacocks.*

²³So King Solomon became richer and wiser than any other king on earth. ²⁴People from every nation came to consult him and to hear the wisdom God had given him. ²⁵Year after year everyone who visited brought him gifts of silver and gold, clothing, weapons, spices, horses, and mules.

²⁶Solomon built up a huge force of chariots and horses.* He had 1,400 chariots and 12,000 horses. He stationed some of them in the chariot cities and some near him in Jerusalem. ²⁷The king made silver as plentiful in Jerusalem as stone. And valuable cedar

---

9:26a As in Greek version (see also 2 Kgs 14:22; 16:6); Hebrew reads *Eloth*, a variant spelling of Elath. **9:26b** Hebrew *sea of reeds*. **9:28** Hebrew *420 talents* [14 metric tons]. **10:1** Or *which was due to the name of the LORD*. The meaning of the Hebrew is uncertain. **10:6** Hebrew *your words*. **10:8** Greek and Syriac versions and Latin Vulgate read *your wives*. **10:10** Hebrew *120 talents* [4,000 kilograms]. **10:11** Hebrew *almug wood*; also in 10:12. **10:14** Hebrew *666 talents* [23 metric tons]. **10:16** Hebrew *600 [shekels] of gold* [6.8 kilograms]. **10:17** Hebrew *3 minas* [1.8 kilograms]. **10:22** Or *and baboons*. **10:26** Or *charioteers*; also in 10:26b.

10:1-13 The queen of Sheba visited to test the accuracy of accounts concerning Solomon's wisdom (10:1, 3, 6-7). She may also have sought commercial partnership (10:2, 10, 13). All of Solomon's accomplishments resulted from his God-given wisdom, as the queen of Sheba testifies in the central speech of the narrative (10:6-9).
10:3-5 The queen was satisfied with Solomon's wisdom. He answered all her questions well, and she was overwhelmed by the applied wisdom in his building activities, well-organized administration and staff, and commitment to God. Jesus commended the queen's search for truth while condemning the Pharisees and teachers of religious law who failed to recognize him—the one who was greater than Solomon (Matthew 12:42).

timber was as common as the sycamore-fig trees that grow in the foothills of Judah.* ²⁸Solomon's horses were imported from Egypt* and from Cilicia*; the king's traders acquired them from Cilicia at the standard price. ²⁹At that time chariots from Egypt could be purchased for 600 pieces of silver,* and horses for 150 pieces of silver.* They were then exported to the kings of the Hittites and the kings of Aram.

Solomon's Many Wives

11 Now King Solomon loved many foreign women. Besides Pharaoh's daughter, he married women from Moab, Ammon, Edom, Sidon, and from among the Hittites. ²The LORD had clearly instructed the people of Israel, "You must not marry them, because they will turn your hearts to their gods." Yet Solomon insisted on loving them anyway. ³He had 700 wives of royal birth and 300 concubines. And in fact, they did turn his heart away from the LORD.

⁴In Solomon's old age, they turned his heart to worship other gods instead of being completely faithful to the LORD his God, as his father, David, had been. ⁵Solomon worshiped Ashtoreth, the goddess of the Sidonians, and Molech,* the detestable god of the Ammonites. ⁶In this way, Solomon did what was evil in the LORD's sight; he refused to follow the LORD completely, as his father, David, had done.

⁷On the Mount of Olives, east of Jerusalem,* he even built a pagan shrine for Chemosh, the detestable god of Moab, and another for Molech, the detestable god of the Ammonites. ⁸Solomon built such shrines for all his foreign wives to use for burning incense and sacrificing to their gods.

⁹The LORD was very angry with Solomon, for his heart had turned away from the LORD, the God of Israel, who had appeared to him twice. ¹⁰He had warned Solomon specifically about worshiping other gods, but Solomon did not listen to the LORD's command. ¹¹So now the LORD said to him, "Since you have not kept my covenant and have disobeyed my decrees, I will surely tear the kingdom away from you and give it to one of your servants. ¹²But for the sake of your father, David, I will not do this while you are still alive. I will take the kingdom away from your son. ¹³And even so, I will not take away the entire kingdom; I will let him be king of one tribe, for the sake of my servant David and for the sake of Jerusalem, my chosen city."

Solomon's Adversaries

¹⁴Then the LORD raised up Hadad the Edomite, a member of Edom's royal family, to be Solomon's adversary. ¹⁵Years before, David had defeated Edom. Joab, his army commander, had stayed to bury some of the Israelite soldiers who had died in battle. While there, they killed every male in Edom. ¹⁶Joab and the army of Israel had stayed there for six months, killing them.

¹⁷But Hadad and a few of his father's royal officials escaped and headed for Egypt. (Hadad was just a boy at the time.) ¹⁸They set out from Midian and went to Paran, where others joined them. Then they traveled to Egypt and went to Pharaoh, who gave them a home, food, and some land. ¹⁹Pharaoh grew very fond of Hadad, and he gave him his wife's sister in marriage—the sister of Queen Tahpenes. ²⁰She bore him a son named Genubath. Tahpenes raised him* in Pharaoh's palace among Pharaoh's own sons.

²¹When the news reached Hadad in Egypt that David and his commander Joab were both dead, he said to Pharaoh, "Let me return to my own country."

²²"Why?" Pharaoh asked him. "What do you lack here that makes you want to go home?"

"Nothing," he replied. "But even so, please let me return home."

²³God also raised up Rezon son of Eliada as Solomon's adversary. Rezon had fled from his master, King Hadadezer of Zobah, ²⁴and had become the leader of a gang of rebels. After David conquered Hadadezer, Rezon and his men fled to Damascus, where he became king. ²⁵Rezon was Israel's bitter adversary for the rest of Solomon's reign, and he made trouble, just as Hadad did. Rezon hated Israel intensely and continued to reign in Aram.

Jeroboam Rebels against Solomon

²⁶Another rebel leader was Jeroboam son of Nebat, one of Solomon's own officials. He came from the town of Zeredah in Ephraim, and his mother was Zeruah, a widow.

²⁷This is the story behind his rebellion. Solomon was rebuilding the supporting terraces* and

---

10:27 Hebrew *the Shephelah.* **10:28a** Possibly *Muzur*, a district near Cilicia; also in 10:29. **10:28b** Hebrew *Kue*, probably another name for Cilicia. **10:29a** Hebrew *600 [shekels] of silver*, about 15 pounds or 6.8 kilograms in weight. **10:29b** Hebrew *150 [shekels]*, about 3.8 pounds or 1.7 kilograms in weight. **11:5** Hebrew *Milcom*, a variant spelling of Molech; also in 11:33. **11:7** Hebrew *On the mountain east of Jerusalem.* **11:20** As in Greek version; Hebrew reads *weaned him.* **11:27** Hebrew *the millo.* The meaning of the Hebrew is uncertain.

11:1-3 Despite his God-given wisdom, Solomon blatantly violated the law of Moses with his many wives and accumulation of excessive wealth (see Exodus 34:12-17; Deuteronomy 7:3-4; 17:17). Taking wives to form foreign alliances compromised Solomon's spiritual commitment, as predicted, and turned "his heart away from the LORD." The spiritual and political consequences for his people were disastrous (see 1 Kings 11:4-13; 12:4, 16; 2 Kings 17:5-23; 25:1-23).

11:4-8 After David had committed grievous sin, he genuinely repented when rebuked by God's prophet (2 Samuel 11:1–12:23; Psalm 51:1-4). However, Solomon failed to heed God's warnings (1 Kings 3:14; 6:12-13; 9:4-9) or to learn from Israel's past; instead, he reproduced their sins.

repairing the walls of the city of his father, David. ²⁸Jeroboam was a very capable young man, and when Solomon saw how industrious he was, he put him in charge of the labor force from the tribes of Ephraim and Manasseh, the descendants of Joseph.

²⁹One day as Jeroboam was leaving Jerusalem, the prophet Ahijah from Shiloh met him along the way. Ahijah was wearing a new cloak. The two of them were alone in a field, ³⁰and Ahijah took hold of the new cloak he was wearing and tore it into twelve pieces. ³¹Then he said to Jeroboam, "Take ten of these pieces, for this is what the LORD, the God of Israel, says: 'I am about to tear the kingdom from the hand of Solomon, and I will give ten of the tribes to you! ³²But I will leave him one tribe for the sake of my servant David and for the sake of Jerusalem, which I have chosen out of all the tribes of Israel. ³³For Solomon has* abandoned me and worshiped Ashtoreth, the goddess of the Sidonians; Chemosh, the god of Moab; and Molech, the god of the Ammonites. He has not followed my ways and done what is pleasing in my sight. He has not obeyed my decrees and regulations as David his father did.

³⁴"'But I will not take the entire kingdom from Solomon at this time. For the sake of my servant David, the one whom I chose and who obeyed my commands and decrees, I will keep Solomon as leader for the rest of his life. ³⁵But I will take the kingdom away from his son and give ten of the tribes to you. ³⁶His son will have one tribe so that the descendants

11:33 As in Greek, Syriac, and Latin Vulgate; Hebrew reads *For they have.*

Come Close

SATISFACTION: ONE TURN AWAY

SCRIPTURE CONNECTION: 1 KINGS 11:1-13

"One in a million"—any bride would be delighted to be described and esteemed by her groom in this way. To be recognized, respected, and regarded for her uniqueness and loved for all she is would fill her heart with joy and satisfaction.

"One *among* millions" is more how I felt in 1995 when the Internet debuted in our house and brought the world to my doorstep. When a bride must compete for her husband's attention over a multitude of seductive others from within her own home, she has been relegated.

A wife or concubine of "wise" King Solomon would know the struggle. She would be literally "one of a thousand" surrounding him, competing for his attention and relegated to the group.

Just as we don't appreciate being one among many, neither does God (Deuteronomy 10:12). When Solomon followed his heart for women—and likely also the political power his marriages to foreign wives afforded—his heart turned to idols. How is it that one so capable of love as Solomon (described in the Song of Songs) could become so deceived, trading in wisdom for folly? Even he was not immune to mortal lusts in his search for satisfaction, and those misdirected desires led Solomon to worship other gods and betray the Lord.

Wisdom alone will not prevent our missteps. A mere heart-turn from God is all it takes to start down a wayward path. Thankfully, another mere heart-turn is all it takes to redirect toward satisfaction in him, our *one* true God.

> **REFLECT** "The LORD was very angry with Solomon, for his heart had turned away from the LORD, the God of Israel."
> 1 KINGS 11:9
>
> *Lord, may I do what it takes today to keep my heart turned toward you. Amen.*
>
> **CONSIDER** "By making time for God's engagement with us, we are changed, transformed, redeemed." JO SAXTON, *The Dream of You*

If I'm feeling wayward today, a mere heart-turn toward God will lead me back.

MISTY ARTERBURN is an author and speaker, contributing to Bible projects, devotionals, and recovery materials for over twenty years. Wife and mom to five, Misty is the founder of Recovery Girls and the general editor of *The One Year Bible for Women*.

of David my servant will continue to reign, shining like a lamp in Jerusalem, the city I have chosen to be the place for my name. ³⁷And I will place you on the throne of Israel, and you will rule over all that your heart desires. ³⁸If you listen to what I tell you and follow my ways and do whatever I consider to be right, and if you obey my decrees and commands, as my servant David did, then I will always be with you. I will establish an enduring dynasty for you as I did for David, and I will give Israel to you. ³⁹Because of Solomon's sin I will punish the descendants of David—though not forever.'"

⁴⁰Solomon tried to kill Jeroboam, but he fled to King Shishak of Egypt and stayed there until Solomon died.

Summary of Solomon's Reign

⁴¹The rest of the events in Solomon's reign, including all his deeds and his wisdom, are recorded in The Book of the Acts of Solomon. ⁴²Solomon ruled in Jerusalem over all Israel for forty years. ⁴³When he died, he was buried in the City of David, named for his father. Then his son Rehoboam became the next king.

The Northern Tribes Revolt

12 Rehoboam went to Shechem, where all Israel had gathered to make him king. ²When Jeroboam son of Nebat heard of this, he returned from Egypt,* for he had fled to Egypt to escape from King Solomon. ³The leaders of Israel summoned him, and Jeroboam and the whole assembly of Israel went to speak with Rehoboam. ⁴"Your father was a hard master," they said. "Lighten the harsh labor demands and heavy taxes that your father imposed on us. Then we will be your loyal subjects."

⁵Rehoboam replied, "Give me three days to think this over. Then come back for my answer." So the people went away.

⁶Then King Rehoboam discussed the matter with the older men who had counseled his father, Solomon. "What is your advice?" he asked. "How should I answer these people?"

⁷The older counselors replied, "If you are willing to be a servant to these people today and give them a favorable answer, they will always be your loyal subjects."

⁸But Rehoboam rejected the advice of the older men and instead asked the opinion of the young men who had grown up with him and were now his advisers. ⁹"What is your advice?" he asked them. "How should I answer these people who want me to lighten the burdens imposed by my father?"

¹⁰The young men replied, "This is what you should tell those complainers who want a lighter burden: 'My little finger is thicker than my father's waist! ¹¹Yes, my father laid heavy burdens on you, but I'm going to make them even heavier! My father beat you with whips, but I will beat you with scorpions!'"

¹²Three days later Jeroboam and all the people returned to hear Rehoboam's decision, just as the king had ordered. ¹³But Rehoboam spoke harshly to the people, for he rejected the advice of the older counselors ¹⁴and followed the counsel of his younger advisers. He told the people, "My father laid heavy burdens on you, but I'm going to make them even heavier! My father beat you with whips, but I will beat you with scorpions!"

¹⁵So the king paid no attention to the people. This turn of events was the will of the LORD, for it fulfilled the LORD's message to Jeroboam son of Nebat through the prophet Ahijah from Shiloh.

¹⁶When all Israel realized that the king had refused to listen to them, they responded,

"Down with the dynasty of David!
We have no interest in the son of Jesse.
Back to your homes, O Israel!
Look out for your own house, O David!"

So the people of Israel returned home. ¹⁷But Rehoboam continued to rule over the Israelites who lived in the towns of Judah.

¹⁸King Rehoboam sent Adoniram,* who was in charge of forced labor, to restore order, but the people of Israel stoned him to death. When this news reached King Rehoboam, he quickly jumped into his chariot and fled to Jerusalem. ¹⁹And to this day the northern tribes of Israel have refused to be ruled by a descendant of David.

²⁰When the people of Israel learned of Jeroboam's return from Egypt, they called an assembly and made him king over all Israel. So only the tribe of Judah remained loyal to the family of David.

12:2 As in Greek version and Latin Vulgate (see also 2 Chr 10:2); Hebrew reads *he lived in Egypt.* **12:18** As in some Greek manuscripts and Syriac version (see also 4:6; 5:14); Hebrew reads *Adoram.*

11:39 David's descendant Jesus would later inherit his rightful throne, as God had promised David (2 Samuel 7:13, 16-19; Psalm 89:35-37), Abraham (Genesis 17:1-8; Luke 1:67-79), and Judah (Genesis 49:10). Jesus has established a new covenant with God's people and he will reign forever (Jeremiah 31:31-36; Ezekiel 37:22-28; 2 Corinthians 3:6).

12:1 Shechem, located in the heart of territory belonging to the northern tribes, had been a strategic site and religious center since the pre-Israelite occupation of Canaan (Genesis 12:6-7; 33:18-20), and it became important in Israel as a Levitical city and a city of refuge (Joshua 20:7; 21:20-22; 24:1). Rehoboam knew that if he wanted to be king over a united kingdom, he would need the approval and support of the politically and religiously strong northern tribes. Shechem later became the provisional capital of the northern kingdom (1 Kings 12:25). Rehoboam reigned from 931 to 913 BC.

Shemaiah's Prophecy

²¹When Rehoboam arrived at Jerusalem, he mobilized the men of Judah and the tribe of Benjamin—180,000 select troops—to fight against the men of Israel and to restore the kingdom to himself.

²²But God said to Shemaiah, the man of God, ²³"Say to Rehoboam son of Solomon, king of Judah, and to all the people of Judah and Benjamin, and to the rest of the people, ²⁴'This is what the LORD says: Do not fight against your relatives, the Israelites. Go back home, for what has happened is my doing!'" So they obeyed the message of the LORD and went home, as the LORD had commanded.

Jeroboam Makes Gold Calves

²⁵Jeroboam then built up the city of Shechem in the hill country of Ephraim, and it became his capital. Later he went and built up the town of Peniel.*

²⁶Jeroboam thought to himself, "Unless I am careful, the kingdom will return to the dynasty of David. ²⁷When these people go to Jerusalem to offer sacrifices at the Temple of the LORD, they will again give their allegiance to King Rehoboam of Judah. They will kill me and make him their king instead."

²⁸So on the advice of his counselors, the king made two gold calves. He said to the people,* "It is too much trouble for you to worship in Jerusalem. Look, Israel, these are the gods who brought you out of Egypt!" ²⁹He placed these calf idols in Bethel and in Dan—at either end of his kingdom. ³⁰But this became a great sin, for the people worshiped the idols, traveling as far north as Dan to worship the one there.

³¹Jeroboam also erected buildings at the pagan shrines and ordained priests from the common people—those who were not from the priestly tribe of Levi. ³²And Jeroboam instituted a religious festival in Bethel, held on the fifteenth day of the eighth month,* in imitation of the annual Festival of Shelters in Judah. There at Bethel he himself offered sacrifices to the calves he had made, and he appointed priests for the pagan shrines he had made. ³³So on the fifteenth day of the eighth month, a day that he himself had designated, Jeroboam offered sacrifices on the altar at Bethel. He instituted a religious festival for Israel, and he went up to the altar to burn incense.

A Prophet Denounces Jeroboam

13 At the LORD's command, a man of God from Judah went to Bethel, arriving there just as Jeroboam was approaching the altar to burn incense. ²Then at the LORD's command, he shouted, "O altar, altar! This is what the LORD says: A child named Josiah will be born into the dynasty of David. On you he will sacrifice the priests from the pagan shrines who come here to burn incense, and human bones will be burned on you." ³That same day the man of God gave a sign to prove his message. He said, "The LORD has promised to give this sign: This altar will split apart, and its ashes will be poured out on the ground."

⁴When King Jeroboam heard the man of God speaking against the altar at Bethel, he pointed at him and shouted, "Seize that man!" But instantly the king's hand became paralyzed in that position, and he couldn't pull it back. ⁵At the same time a wide crack appeared in the altar, and the ashes poured out, just as the man of God had predicted in his message from the LORD.

⁶The king cried out to the man of God, "Please ask the LORD your God to restore my hand again!" So the man of God prayed to the LORD, and the king's hand was restored and he could move it again.

⁷Then the king said to the man of God, "Come to the palace with me and have something to eat, and I will give you a gift."

⁸But the man of God said to the king, "Even if you gave me half of everything you own, I would not go with you. I would not eat or drink anything in this place. ⁹For the LORD gave me this command: 'You must not eat or drink anything while you are there, and do not return to Judah by the same way you came.'" ¹⁰So he left Bethel and went home another way.

¹¹As it happened, there was an old prophet living in Bethel, and his sons* came home and told him what the man of God had done in Bethel that day. They also told their father what the man had said to the king. ¹²The old prophet asked them, "Which way did he go?" So they showed their father* which road the man of God had taken. ¹³"Quick, saddle the donkey," the old man said. So they saddled the donkey for him, and he mounted it.

¹⁴Then he rode after the man of God and found him sitting under a great tree. The old prophet asked him, "Are you the man of God who came from Judah?"

"Yes, I am," he replied.

¹⁵Then he said to the man of God, "Come home with me and eat some food."

¹⁶"No, I cannot," he replied. "I am not allowed to eat or drink anything here in this place. ¹⁷For the LORD

12:25 Hebrew *Penuel*, a variant spelling of Peniel. **12:28** Hebrew *to them*. **12:32** This day of the ancient Hebrew lunar calendar occurred in late October or early November, exactly one month after the annual Festival of Shelters in Judah (see Lev 23:34).
13:11 As in Greek version; Hebrew reads *son*. **13:12** As in Greek version; Hebrew reads *They had seen*.

13:1-10 The account of the unnamed man of God who denounced Jeroboam's false altar at Bethel emphasizes the authority of God's word. Like Isaiah's prophecy of Cyrus's coming (Isaiah 44:28; 45:1) and Micah's prophecy about Bethlehem as the Messiah's birthplace (Micah 5:2), this prophecy gave a distinctive proper name associated with an event long before it happened (2 Kings 23:12-20). Such prophecies give assurance of God's power and authority.

gave me this command: 'You must not eat or drink anything while you are there, and do not return to Judah by the same way you came.'"

¹⁸But the old prophet answered, "I am a prophet, too, just as you are. And an angel gave me this command from the LORD: 'Bring him home with you so he can have something to eat and drink.'" But the old man was lying to him. ¹⁹So they went back together, and the man of God ate and drank at the prophet's home.

²⁰Then while they were sitting at the table, a command from the LORD came to the old prophet. ²¹He cried out to the man of God from Judah, "This is what the LORD says: You have defied the word of the LORD and have disobeyed the command the LORD your God gave you. ²²You came back to this place and ate and drank where he told you not to eat or drink. Because of this, your body will not be buried in the grave of your ancestors."

²³After the man of God had finished eating and drinking, the old prophet saddled his own donkey for him, ²⁴and the man of God started off again. But as he was traveling along, a lion came out and killed him. His body lay there on the road, with the donkey and the lion standing beside it. ²⁵People who passed by saw the body lying in the road and the lion standing beside it, and they went and reported it in Bethel, where the old prophet lived.

²⁶When the prophet heard the report, he said, "It is the man of God who disobeyed the LORD's command. The LORD has fulfilled his word by causing the lion to attack and kill him."

²⁷Then the prophet said to his sons, "Saddle a donkey for me." So they saddled a donkey, ²⁸and he went out and found the body lying in the road. The donkey and lion were still standing there beside it, for the lion had not eaten the body nor attacked the donkey. ²⁹So the prophet laid the body of the man of God on the donkey and took it back to the town to mourn over him and bury him. ³⁰He laid the body in his own grave, crying out in grief, "Oh, my brother!"

³¹Afterward the prophet said to his sons, "When I die, bury me in the grave where the man of God is buried. Lay my bones beside his bones. ³²For the message the LORD told him to proclaim against the altar in Bethel and against the pagan shrines in the towns of Samaria will certainly come true."

³³But even after this, Jeroboam did not turn from his evil ways. He continued to choose priests from the common people. He appointed anyone who wanted to become a priest for the pagan shrines. ³⁴This became a great sin and resulted in the utter destruction of Jeroboam's dynasty from the face of the earth.

Ahijah's Prophecy against Jeroboam

14 At that time Jeroboam's son Abijah became very sick. ²So Jeroboam told his wife, "Disguise yourself so that no one will recognize you as my wife. Then go to the prophet Ahijah at Shiloh—the man who told me I would become king. ³Take him a gift of ten loaves of bread, some cakes, and a jar of honey, and ask him what will happen to the boy."

⁴So Jeroboam's wife went to Ahijah's home at Shiloh. He was an old man now and could no longer see. ⁵But the LORD had told Ahijah, "Jeroboam's wife will come here, pretending to be someone else. She will ask you about her son, for he is very sick. Give her the answer I give you."

⁶So when Ahijah heard her footsteps at the door, he called out, "Come in, wife of Jeroboam! Why are you pretending to be someone else?" Then he told her, "I have bad news for you. ⁷Give your husband, Jeroboam, this message from the LORD, the God of Israel: 'I promoted you from the ranks of the common people and made you ruler over my people Israel. ⁸I ripped the kingdom away from the family of David and gave it to you. But you have not been like my servant David, who obeyed my commands and followed me with all his heart and always did whatever I wanted. ⁹You have done more evil than all who lived before you. You have made other gods for yourself and have made me furious with your gold calves. And since you have turned your back on me, ¹⁰I will bring disaster on your dynasty and will destroy every one of your male descendants, slave and free alike, anywhere in Israel. I will burn up your royal dynasty as one burns up trash until it is all gone. ¹¹The members of Jeroboam's family who die in the city will be eaten by dogs, and those who die in the field will be eaten by vultures. I, the LORD, have spoken.'"

¹²Then Ahijah said to Jeroboam's wife, "Go on home, and when you enter the city, the child will die. ¹³All Israel will mourn for him and bury him. He is the only member of your family who will have a proper burial, for this child is the only good thing that the LORD, the God of Israel, sees in the entire family of Jeroboam.

¹⁴"In addition, the LORD will raise up a king over Israel who will destroy the family of Jeroboam. This

---

14:5 The name of Jeroboam's wife is not recorded, and she does not speak. However, she is a crucial figure in hearing the prophet Ahijah's prophecy of Jeroboam's downfall. God is often at work through people we may never know, but they play a valuable part in God's purposes.

14:15 Asherah was thought to be the consort of Baal, the elder god of ancient Canaan. Asherah worship included fertility rites at sacred trees or poles; it became a chronic sin for God's people (15:13; 16:33; 18:19; see Deuteronomy 16:21; Judges 3:7). In today's culture, what are ways we are tempted to rely on something other than God to have "the good life"?

will happen today, even now! ¹⁵Then the LORD will shake Israel like a reed whipped about in a stream. He will uproot the people of Israel from this good land that he gave their ancestors and will scatter them beyond the Euphrates River,* for they have angered the LORD with the Asherah poles they have set up for worship. ¹⁶He will abandon Israel because Jeroboam sinned and made Israel sin along with him."

¹⁷So Jeroboam's wife returned to Tirzah, and the child died just as she walked through the door of her home. ¹⁸And all Israel buried him and mourned for him, as the LORD had promised through the prophet Ahijah.

¹⁹The rest of the events in Jeroboam's reign, including all his wars and how he ruled, are recorded in The Book of the History of the Kings of Israel. ²⁰Jeroboam reigned in Israel twenty-two years. When Jeroboam died, his son Nadab became the next king.

Rehoboam Rules in Judah

²¹Meanwhile, Rehoboam son of Solomon was king in Judah. He was forty-one years old when he became king, and he reigned seventeen years in Jerusalem, the city the LORD had chosen from among all the tribes of Israel as the place to honor his name. Rehoboam's mother was Naamah, an Ammonite woman.

²²During Rehoboam's reign, the people of Judah did what was evil in the LORD's sight, provoking his anger with their sin, for it was even worse than that of their ancestors. ²³For they also built for themselves pagan shrines and set up sacred pillars and Asherah poles on every high hill and under every green tree. ²⁴There were even male and female shrine prostitutes throughout the land. The people imitated the detestable practices of the pagan nations the LORD had driven from the land ahead of the Israelites.

²⁵In the fifth year of King Rehoboam's reign, King Shishak of Egypt came up and attacked Jerusalem. ²⁶He ransacked the treasuries of the LORD's Temple and the royal palace; he stole everything, including all the gold shields Solomon had made. ²⁷King Rehoboam later replaced them with bronze shields as substitutes, and he entrusted them to the care of the commanders of the guard who protected the entrance to the royal palace. ²⁸Whenever the king went to the Temple of the LORD, the guards would also take the shields and then return them to the guardroom.

²⁹The rest of the events in Rehoboam's reign and everything he did are recorded in The Book of the History of the Kings of Judah. ³⁰There was constant war between Rehoboam and Jeroboam. ³¹When Rehoboam died, he was buried among his ancestors in the City of David. His mother was Naamah, an Ammonite woman. Then his son Abijam* became the next king.

Abijam Rules in Judah

15 Abijam* began to rule over Judah in the eighteenth year of Jeroboam's reign in Israel. ²He reigned in Jerusalem three years. His mother was Maacah, the granddaughter of Absalom.*

³He committed the same sins as his father before him, and he was not faithful to the LORD his God, as his ancestor David had been. ⁴But for David's sake, the LORD his God allowed his descendants to continue ruling, shining like a lamp, and he gave Abijam a son to rule after him in Jerusalem. ⁵For David had done what was pleasing in the LORD's sight and had obeyed the LORD's commands throughout his life, except in the affair concerning Uriah the Hittite.

⁶There was war between Abijam and Jeroboam* throughout Abijam's reign. ⁷The rest of the events in Abijam's reign and everything he did are recorded in The Book of the History of the Kings of Judah. There was constant war between Abijam and Jeroboam. ⁸When Abijam died, he was buried in the City of David. Then his son Asa became the next king.

Asa Rules in Judah

⁹Asa began to rule over Judah in the twentieth year of Jeroboam's reign in Israel. ¹⁰He reigned in Jerusalem forty-one years. His grandmother* was Maacah, the granddaughter of Absalom.

¹¹Asa did what was pleasing in the LORD's sight, as his ancestor David had done. ¹²He banished the male and female shrine prostitutes from the land and got rid of all the idols* his ancestors had made. ¹³He even deposed his grandmother Maacah from her position as queen mother because she had made an obscene Asherah pole. He cut down her obscene pole and burned it in the Kidron Valley. ¹⁴Although the pagan shrines were not removed, Asa's heart remained completely faithful to the LORD throughout his life. ¹⁵He brought into the Temple of the LORD the silver and gold and the various items that he and his father had dedicated.

¹⁶There was constant war between King Asa of Judah and King Baasha of Israel. ¹⁷King Baasha of Israel invaded Judah and fortified Ramah in order to prevent anyone from entering or leaving King Asa's territory in Judah.

14:15 Hebrew *the river.* 14:31 Also known as *Abijah.* 15:1 Also known as *Abijah.* 15:2 Hebrew *Abishalom* (also in 15:10), a variant spelling of Absalom; compare 2 Chr 11:20. 15:6 As in a few Hebrew and Greek manuscripts; most Hebrew manuscripts read *between Rehoboam and Jeroboam.* 15:10 Or *The queen mother;* Hebrew reads *His mother* (also in 15:13); compare 15:2. 15:12 The Hebrew term (literally *round things*) probably alludes to dung.

¹⁸Asa responded by removing all the silver and gold that was left in the treasuries of the Temple of the LORD and the royal palace. He sent it with some of his officials to Ben-hadad son of Tabrimmon, son of Hezion, the king of Aram, who was ruling in Damascus, along with this message:

¹⁹"Let there be a treaty* between you and me like the one between your father and my father. See, I am sending you a gift of silver and gold. Break your treaty with King Baasha of Israel so that he will leave me alone."

²⁰Ben-hadad agreed to King Asa's request and sent the commanders of his army to attack the towns of Israel. They conquered the towns of Ijon, Dan, Abel-beth-maacah, and all Kinnereth, and all the land of Naphtali. ²¹As soon as Baasha of Israel heard what was happening, he abandoned his project of fortifying Ramah and withdrew to Tirzah. ²²Then King Asa sent an order throughout Judah, requiring that everyone, without exception, help to carry away the building stones and timbers that Baasha had been using to fortify Ramah. Asa used these materials to fortify the town of Geba in Benjamin and the town of Mizpah.

²³The rest of the events in Asa's reign—the extent of his power, everything he did, and the names of the cities he built—are recorded in The Book of the History of the Kings of Judah. In his old age his feet became diseased. ²⁴When Asa died, he was buried with his ancestors in the City of David.

Then Jehoshaphat, Asa's son, became the next king.

Nadab Rules in Israel

²⁵Nadab son of Jeroboam began to rule over Israel in the second year of King Asa's reign in Judah. He reigned in Israel two years. ²⁶But he did what was evil in the LORD's sight and followed the example of his father, continuing the sins that Jeroboam had led Israel to commit.

²⁷Then Baasha son of Ahijah, from the tribe of Issachar, plotted against Nadab and assassinated him while he and the Israelite army were laying siege to the Philistine town of Gibbethon. ²⁸Baasha killed Nadab in the third year of King Asa's reign in Judah, and he became the next king of Israel.

²⁹He immediately slaughtered all the descendants of King Jeroboam, so that not one of the royal family was left, just as the LORD had promised concerning Jeroboam by the prophet Ahijah from Shiloh. ³⁰This was done because Jeroboam had provoked the anger of the LORD, the God of Israel, by the sins he had committed and the sins he had led Israel to commit.

³¹The rest of the events in Nadab's reign and everything he did are recorded in The Book of the History of the Kings of Israel.

Baasha Rules in Israel

³²There was constant war between King Asa of Judah and King Baasha of Israel. ³³Baasha son of Ahijah began to rule over all Israel in the third year of King Asa's reign in Judah. Baasha reigned in Tirzah twenty-four years. ³⁴But he did what was evil in the LORD's sight and followed the example of Jeroboam, continuing the sins that Jeroboam had led Israel to commit.

16 This message from the LORD was delivered to King Baasha by the prophet Jehu son of Hanani: ²"I lifted you out of the dust to make you ruler of my people Israel, but you have followed the evil example of Jeroboam. You have provoked my anger by causing my people Israel to sin. ³So now I will destroy you and your family, just as I destroyed the descendants of Jeroboam son of Nebat. ⁴The members of Baasha's family who die in the city will be eaten by dogs, and those who die in the field will be eaten by vultures."

⁵The rest of the events in Baasha's reign and the extent of his power are recorded in The Book of the History of the Kings of Israel. ⁶When Baasha died, he was buried in Tirzah. Then his son Elah became the next king.

⁷The message from the LORD against Baasha and his family came through the prophet Jehu son of Hanani. It was delivered because Baasha had done what was evil in the LORD's sight (just as the family of Jeroboam had done), and also because Baasha had destroyed the family of Jeroboam. The LORD's anger was provoked by Baasha's sins.

Elah Rules in Israel

⁸Elah son of Baasha began to rule over Israel in the twenty-sixth year of King Asa's reign in Judah. He reigned in the city of Tirzah for two years.

⁹Then Zimri, who commanded half of the royal chariots, made plans to kill him. One day in Tirzah, Elah was getting drunk at the home of Arza, the supervisor of the palace. ¹⁰Zimri walked in and struck him down and killed him. This happened in the twenty-seventh year of King Asa's reign in Judah. Then Zimri became the next king.

¹¹Zimri immediately killed the entire royal family of Baasha, leaving him not even a single male child. He even destroyed distant relatives and friends. ¹²So Zimri destroyed the dynasty of Baasha as the LORD had promised through the prophet Jehu. ¹³This happened because of all the sins Baasha and his son Elah had committed, and because of the sins they led Israel to commit. They provoked the anger of the LORD, the God of Israel, with their worthless idols.

¹⁴The rest of the events in Elah's reign and everything he did are recorded in The Book of the History of the Kings of Israel.

15:19 As in Greek version; Hebrew reads *There is a treaty.*

Zimri Rules in Israel

¹⁵Zimri began to rule over Israel in the twenty-seventh year of King Asa's reign in Judah, but his reign in Tirzah lasted only seven days. The army of Israel was then attacking the Philistine town of Gibbethon. ¹⁶When they heard that Zimri had committed treason and had assassinated the king, that very day they chose Omri, commander of the army, as the new king of Israel. ¹⁷So Omri led the entire army of Israel up from Gibbethon to attack Tirzah, Israel's capital. ¹⁸When Zimri saw that the city had been taken, he went into the citadel of the palace and burned it down over himself and died in the flames. ¹⁹For he, too, had done what was evil in the LORD's sight. He followed the example of Jeroboam in all the sins he had committed and led Israel to commit.

²⁰The rest of the events in Zimri's reign and his conspiracy are recorded in The Book of the History of the Kings of Israel.

Omri Rules in Israel

²¹But now the people of Israel were split into two factions. Half the people tried to make Tibni son of Ginath their king, while the other half supported Omri. ²²But Omri's supporters defeated the supporters of Tibni. So Tibni was killed, and Omri became the next king.

²³Omri began to rule over Israel in the thirty-first year of King Asa's reign in Judah. He reigned twelve years in all, six of them in Tirzah. ²⁴Then Omri bought the hill now known as Samaria from its owner, Shemer, for 150 pounds of silver.* He built a city on it and called the city Samaria in honor of Shemer.

²⁵But Omri did what was evil in the LORD's sight, even more than any of the kings before him. ²⁶He followed the example of Jeroboam son of Nebat in all the sins he had committed and led Israel to commit. The people provoked the anger of the LORD, the God of Israel, with their worthless idols.

²⁷The rest of the events in Omri's reign, the extent of his power, and everything he did are recorded in The Book of the History of the Kings of Israel. ²⁸When Omri died, he was buried in Samaria. Then his son Ahab became the next king.

Ahab Rules in Israel

²⁹Ahab son of Omri began to rule over Israel in the thirty-eighth year of King Asa's reign in Judah. He reigned in Samaria twenty-two years. ³⁰But Ahab son of Omri did what was evil in the LORD's sight, even more than any of the kings before him. ³¹And as though it were not enough to follow the sinful example of Jeroboam, he married Jezebel, the daughter of King Ethbaal of the Sidonians, and he began to bow down in worship of Baal. ³²First Ahab built a temple and an altar for Baal in Samaria. ³³Then he set up an Asherah pole. He did more to provoke the anger of the LORD, the God of Israel, than any of the other kings of Israel before him.

³⁴It was during his reign that Hiel, a man from Bethel, rebuilt Jericho. When he laid its foundations, it cost him the life of his oldest son, Abiram. And when he completed it and set up its gates, it cost him the life of his youngest son, Segub.* This all happened according to the message from the LORD concerning Jericho spoken by Joshua son of Nun.

Elijah Fed by Ravens

17 Now Elijah, who was from Tishbe in Gilead, told King Ahab, "As surely as the LORD, the God of Israel, lives—the God I serve—there will be no dew or rain during the next few years until I give the word!"

²Then the LORD said to Elijah, ³"Go to the east and hide by Kerith Brook, near where it enters the Jordan River. ⁴Drink from the brook and eat what the ravens bring you, for I have commanded them to bring you food."

⁵So Elijah did as the LORD told him and camped beside Kerith Brook, east of the Jordan. ⁶The ravens brought him bread and meat each morning and evening, and he drank from the brook. ⁷But after a while the brook dried up, for there was no rainfall anywhere in the land.

The Widow at Zarephath

⁸Then the LORD said to Elijah, ⁹"Go and live in the village of Zarephath, near the city of Sidon. I have instructed a widow there to feed you."

¹⁰So he went to Zarephath. As he arrived at the gates of the village, he saw a widow gathering sticks,

---

16:24 Hebrew *for 2 talents* [68 kilograms] *of silver.* **16:34** An ancient Hebrew scribal tradition reads *He killed his oldest son when he laid its foundations, and he killed his youngest son when he set up its gates.*

16:29-33 Ahab, a descendant of evil King Omri (16:21-28), did not desire wisdom like Solomon, and he ruled oppressively. He married Jezebel, a Phoenician princess, as a political alliance. Together, they were a treacherous couple, leading Israel astray to worship other gods such as the Canaanite deity Baal.

17:1 Elijah was a prophet from Gilead to the northern kingdom during the reigns of the third-dynasty kings Ahab (874–853 BC) and Ahaziah (853–852 BC) and into that of Joram (852–841 BC). He was bold in speaking truth to powerful people, especially to King Ahab and Queen Jezebel. Elijah withheld the dew and rain as a direct affront to Baal, who supposedly controlled these natural forces. The dryness lasted until God led Elijah to give the word for rain, and initiated the contest with Baal that would climax on Mount Carmel (18:1-40).

17:2-7 Kerith Brook provided a haven for Elijah during the divinely instituted drought (see 17:1). The supply of food and water assured Elijah of God's protection. When Elijah's source of water dried up, a change of location was needed.

and he asked her, "Would you please bring me a little water in a cup?" ¹¹As she was going to get it, he called to her, "Bring me a bite of bread, too."

¹²But she said, "I swear by the Lord your God that I don't have a single piece of bread in the house. And I have only a handful of flour left in the jar and a little cooking oil in the bottom of the jug. I was just gathering a few sticks to cook this last meal, and then my son and I will die."

¹³But Elijah said to her, "Don't be afraid! Go ahead and do just what you've said, but make a little bread for me first. Then use what's left to prepare a meal for yourself and your son. ¹⁴For this is what the Lord, the God of Israel, says: There will always be flour and olive oil left in your containers until the time when the Lord sends rain and the crops grow again!"

¹⁵So she did as Elijah said, and she and Elijah and her family continued to eat for many days. ¹⁶There was always enough flour and olive oil left in the containers, just as the Lord had promised through Elijah.

¹⁷Some time later the woman's son became sick. He grew worse and worse, and finally he died. ¹⁸Then she said to Elijah, "O man of God, what have you done to me? Have you come here to point out my sins and kill my son?"

¹⁹But Elijah replied, "Give me your son." And he took the child's body from her arms, carried him up the stairs to the room where he was staying, and laid the body on his bed. ²⁰Then Elijah cried out to the Lord, "O Lord my God, why have you brought tragedy to this widow who has opened her home to me, causing her son to die?"

²¹And he stretched himself out over the child three times and cried out to the Lord, "O Lord my God, please let this child's life return to him." ²²The Lord heard Elijah's prayer, and the life of the child returned, and he revived! ²³Then Elijah brought him down from the upper room and gave him to his mother. "Look!" he said. "Your son is alive!"

²⁴Then the woman told Elijah, "Now I know for sure that you are a man of God, and that the Lord truly speaks through you."

The Contest on Mount Carmel

18 Later on, in the third year of the drought, the Lord said to Elijah, "Go and present yourself to King Ahab. Tell him that I will soon send rain!" ²So Elijah went to appear before Ahab.

Meanwhile, the famine had become very severe in Samaria. ³So Ahab summoned Obadiah, who was in charge of the palace. (Obadiah was a devoted follower of the Lord. ⁴Once when Jezebel had tried to kill all the Lord's prophets, Obadiah had hidden 100 of them in two caves. He put fifty prophets in each cave and supplied them with food and water.) ⁵Ahab said to Obadiah, "We must check every spring and valley in the land to see if we can find enough grass to save at least some of my horses and mules." ⁶So they divided the land between them. Ahab went one way by himself, and Obadiah went another way by himself.

⁷As Obadiah was walking along, he suddenly saw Elijah coming toward him. Obadiah recognized him at once and bowed low to the ground before him. "Is it really you, my lord Elijah?" he asked.

⁸"Yes, it is," Elijah replied. "Now go and tell your master, 'Elijah is here.'"

⁹"Oh, sir," Obadiah protested, "what harm have I done to you that you are sending me to my death at the hands of Ahab? ¹⁰For I swear by the Lord your God that the king has searched every nation and kingdom on earth from end to end to find you. And each time he was told, 'Elijah isn't here,' King Ahab forced the king of that nation to swear to the truth of his claim. ¹¹And now you say, 'Go and tell your master, "Elijah is here."' ¹²But as soon as I leave you, the Spirit of the Lord will carry you away to who knows where. When Ahab comes and cannot find you, he will kill me. Yet I have been a true servant of the Lord all my life. ¹³Has no one told you, my lord, about the time when Jezebel was trying to kill the Lord's prophets? I hid 100 of them in two caves and supplied them with food and water. ¹⁴And now you say, 'Go and tell your master, "Elijah is here."' Sir, if I do that, Ahab will certainly kill me."

¹⁵But Elijah said, "I swear by the Lord Almighty, in whose presence I stand, that I will present myself to Ahab this very day."

¹⁶So Obadiah went to tell Ahab that Elijah had come, and Ahab went out to meet Elijah. ¹⁷When Ahab saw him, he exclaimed, "So, is it really you, you troublemaker of Israel?"

¹⁸"I have made no trouble for Israel," Elijah replied. "You and your family are the troublemakers, for you have refused to obey the commands of the Lord and have worshiped the images of Baal

---

17:13-16 God sent Elijah to a widow in Zarephath, which was located in Phoenician territory and outside Ahab's jurisdiction. Ironically, God provided Elijah a place of refuge in Jezebel's homeland, which was associated with worship of Baal. This widow had a son and owned very little, but she shared it with Elijah at his request. God multiplied what she shared and took care of all of them throughout the drought.

17:17-24 The widow's son became gravely ill. The Phoenician belief system equated hardship as judgment by the gods. Her son's illness, in her understanding, meant the gods were punishing her. Elijah boldly stepped into this moment and prayed to the God of Israel. God answered Elijah's cry for help and healed the boy. The widow responded, "Now I know for sure that you are a man of God, and that the Lord truly speaks through you" (17:24). God cared about this woman and her son.

The Widow at Zarephath

IDENTITY

When It's Hard to Trust

She was a desperate woman, down to her last bit of flour and water, the last meal for her and her starving son. *Where was God?* He told her he was right there with her, and she should feed this stranger. Even though she'd heard from God, she doubted. When Elijah showed up, all she could think about was what little they had.

But she chose to trust anyway. She chose to put her fears of "not enough" aside and believe that God would provide for her needs if she obeyed. It worked out—there was lots of food for her and her son. When the unimaginable happened—her son's death—her doubt came back with a vengeance.

How could she be so stupid to trust this man, Elijah? To trust God? Was she angry? Perhaps even embarrassed that she had believed that God would have good for her?

Yet she chose to trust again, and God came through again when he brought her son back to life. In the widow's story, we see a cycle of doubt, God's provision, and trust. Many of us work through this cycle multiple times in a lifetime (or even in a single day).

It turned out that her doubts and fears did not define her. Rather, her meager faith and obedience to trust anyway showed that she trusted God even when trust was hard. The widow's real circumstances, from hunger to health, mattered to God, and he showed her with his provision that she mattered to him. God keeps his promises even when we doubt.

> God keeps his promises even when we doubt.

THE WIDOW OF ZAREPHATH'S STORY IS TOLD IN 1 KINGS 17:8-24; SHE IS ALSO MENTIONED IN LUKE 4:26.

IDENTIFY

What causes you to doubt God's goodness or his provision? How has he provided for you in desperate circumstances?

"Like the widow at Zarephath I've felt scared that there wouldn't be enough. My doubts don't define me. God provides regardless of my feelings."

ALEXANDRA KUYKENDALL is a cofounder of The Open Door Sisterhood and author of several books, including *Seeking Out Goodness: Finding the True and Beautiful All around You*.

instead. ¹⁹Now summon all Israel to join me at Mount Carmel, along with the 450 prophets of Baal and the 400 prophets of Asherah who are supported by Jezebel.*"

²⁰So Ahab summoned all the people of Israel and the prophets to Mount Carmel. ²¹Then Elijah stood in front of them and said, "How much longer will you waver, hobbling between two opinions? If the LORD is God, follow him! But if Baal is God, then follow him!" But the people were completely silent.

²²Then Elijah said to them, "I am the only prophet of the LORD who is left, but Baal has 450 prophets. ²³Now bring two bulls. The prophets of Baal may choose whichever one they wish and cut it into pieces and lay it on the wood of their altar, but without setting fire to it. I will prepare the other bull and lay it on the wood on the altar, but not set fire to it. ²⁴Then call on the name of your god, and I will call on the name of the LORD. The god who answers by setting fire to the wood is the true God!" And all the people agreed.

²⁵Then Elijah said to the prophets of Baal, "You go first, for there are many of you. Choose one of the bulls, and prepare it and call on the name of your god. But do not set fire to the wood."

18:19 Hebrew *who eat at Jezebel's table.*

18:19-20 Mount Carmel is a ridge dividing the coastal plains of Palestine. The mountain was significant in the Canaanite religion, although an altar to the Lord had also been built there and now sat derelict (18:30). As a sacred site for worshiping Baal, this location should have given the prophets of Baal a distinct advantage when facing off against Elijah.

Come Close — FACE OFF

SCRIPTURE CONNECTION: 1 KINGS 18:1-40

With silent anticipation, the people watched Elijah face off with the prophets of Baal. Hundreds of prophets confidently (and pointlessly) counted on their false god to come through. The stakes were high.

Most days, my own choices are not so extreme. I don't know about you, but I tend to gloss over this passage, congratulating myself on the lack of a gold statue in my living room. Today's idolatry seems a lot more sly and slippery, but we face the same challenge: "How much longer will you waver, hobbling between two opinions? If the LORD is God, follow him! But if Baal is God, then follow him!" (1 Kings 18:21).

Often our idols manifest between the good and the better. We long for something deeply fulfilling, and we think, *Maybe one more episode, a few more minutes of social media, or a little more money for the latest trend.* Lately, I notice my own idolatry when I depend on something or someone else while I hear God quietly wooing me to turn to him.

We have two possible "opinions" (or actions) to choose between: follow God or follow idols. Which way do we choose?

Like he did for Elijah, God gives us strength to choose his best with courage and confidence. We're invited to seek at the Source, letting go of the false gods who can never truly satisfy. Then we can receive our Father's abundant love, peace, provision, satisfaction and joy—what our hearts long for.

REFLECT "If the LORD is God, follow him!" 1 KINGS 18:21

God, help me look to you to fulfill my deepest longings, trusting that by turning away from idols, I'll grow closer to you. You give us strength to choose what's best with courage and confidence. Amen.

CONSIDER "We are . . . fooling about with drink and sex and ambition when infinite joy is offered us, like an ignorant child who . . . cannot imagine what is meant by the offer of a holiday at the sea. We are far too easily pleased."
C. S. LEWIS, *The Weight of Glory*

> God's ways give us strength to choose the best with courage and confidence.

MARGARET FITZWATER, MS, MBA, is a Navigator and life and leadership coach. Her passion is helping others live and lead from the Word to thrive in their lives and ministries.

²⁶So they prepared one of the bulls and placed it on the altar. Then they called on the name of Baal from morning until noontime, shouting, "O Baal, answer us!" But there was no reply of any kind. Then they danced, hobbling around the altar they had made.

²⁷About noontime Elijah began mocking them. "You'll have to shout louder," he scoffed, "for surely he is a god! Perhaps he is daydreaming, or is relieving himself.* Or maybe he is away on a trip, or is asleep and needs to be wakened!" ²⁸So they shouted louder, and following their normal custom, they cut themselves with knives and swords until the blood gushed out. ²⁹They raved all afternoon until the time of the evening sacrifice, but still there was no sound, no reply, no response.

³⁰Then Elijah called to the people, "Come over here!" They all crowded around him as he repaired the altar of the Lord that had been torn down. ³¹He took twelve stones, one to represent each of the tribes of Israel,* ³²and he used the stones to rebuild the altar in the name of the Lord. Then he dug a trench around the altar large enough to hold about three gallons.* ³³He piled wood on the altar, cut the bull into pieces, and laid the pieces on the wood.*

Then he said, "Fill four large jars with water, and pour the water over the offering and the wood."

³⁴After they had done this, he said, "Do the same thing again!" And when they were finished, he said, "Now do it a third time!" So they did as he said, ³⁵and the water ran around the altar and even filled the trench.

³⁶At the usual time for offering the evening sacrifice, Elijah the prophet walked up to the altar and prayed, "O Lord, God of Abraham, Isaac, and Jacob,* prove today that you are God in Israel and that I am your servant. Prove that I have done all this at your command. ³⁷O Lord, answer me! Answer me so these people will know that you, O Lord, are God and that you have brought them back to yourself."

³⁸Immediately the fire of the Lord flashed down from heaven and burned up the young bull, the wood, the stones, and the dust. It even licked up all the water in the trench! ³⁹And when all the people saw it, they fell face down on the ground and cried out, "The Lord—he is God! Yes, the Lord is God!"

⁴⁰Then Elijah commanded, "Seize all the prophets of Baal. Don't let a single one escape!" So the people seized them all, and Elijah took them down to the Kishon Valley and killed them there.

Elijah Prays for Rain

⁴¹Then Elijah said to Ahab, "Go get something to eat and drink, for I hear a mighty rainstorm coming!"

⁴²So Ahab went to eat and drink. But Elijah climbed to the top of Mount Carmel and bowed low to the ground and prayed with his face between his knees.

⁴³Then he said to his servant, "Go and look out toward the sea."

The servant went and looked, then returned to Elijah and said, "I didn't see anything."

Seven times Elijah told him to go and look. ⁴⁴Finally the seventh time, his servant told him, "I saw a little cloud about the size of a man's hand rising from the sea."

Then Elijah shouted, "Hurry to Ahab and tell him, 'Climb into your chariot and go back home. If you don't hurry, the rain will stop you!'"

⁴⁵And soon the sky was black with clouds. A heavy wind brought a terrific rainstorm, and Ahab left quickly for Jezreel. ⁴⁶Then the Lord gave special strength to Elijah. He tucked his cloak into his belt* and ran ahead of Ahab's chariot all the way to the entrance of Jezreel.

Elijah Flees to Sinai

19 When Ahab got home, he told Jezebel everything Elijah had done, including the way he had killed all the prophets of Baal. ²So Jezebel sent this message to Elijah: "May the gods strike me and even kill me if by this time tomorrow I have not killed you just as you killed them."

³Elijah was afraid and fled for his life. He went to Beersheba, a town in Judah, and he left his servant there. ⁴Then he went on alone into the wilderness, traveling all day. He sat down under a solitary broom tree and prayed that he might die. "I have had enough, Lord," he said. "Take my life, for I am no better than my ancestors who have already died."

⁵Then he lay down and slept under the broom tree. But as he was sleeping, an angel touched him and

---

18:27 Or *is busy somewhere else*, or *is engaged in business*. **18:31** Hebrew *each of the tribes of the sons of Jacob to whom the Lord had said, "Your name will be Israel."* **18:32** Hebrew *2 seahs* [14.6 liters] *of seed*. **18:33** Verse 18:34 in the Hebrew text begins here. **18:36** Hebrew *and Israel*. The names "Jacob" and "Israel" are often interchanged throughout the Old Testament, referring sometimes to the individual patriarch and sometimes to the nation. **18:46** Hebrew *He bound up his loins*.

18:28-29 The prophets of Baal engaged in pain-inducing behavior that was common in ancient religions, but their efforts produced no response. There is only one true God, and he had specifically forbidden self-mutilation (Deuteronomy 14:1). Calling out to any other god was doomed to failure (Isaiah 45:22).

18:37 The call-and-answer motif appears frequently in the Old Testament, often depicting the petitioner's intimate relationship with the Lord (Job 14:15; Psalms 4:1; 91:15; 102:2; Isaiah 65:24; Jeremiah 33:3).

18:38-45 Whether by lightning strike or supernatural means, the Lord sent fire to consume everything, including all the water in the trench. This was convincing proof that "the Lord is God." The continuing story demonstrates conclusively that the Lord—not the storm god Baal, whose titles included "Lord of Rain"—controls storms, rain, and all weather.

told him, "Get up and eat!" ⁶He looked around and there beside his head was some bread baked on hot stones and a jar of water! So he ate and drank and lay down again.

⁷Then the angel of the LORD came again and touched him and said, "Get up and eat some more, or the journey ahead will be too much for you."

⁸So he got up and ate and drank, and the food gave him enough strength to travel forty days and forty nights to Mount Sinai,* the mountain of God. ⁹There he came to a cave, where he spent the night.

The LORD Speaks to Elijah

But the LORD said to him, "What are you doing here, Elijah?"

¹⁰Elijah replied, "I have zealously served the LORD God Almighty. But the people of Israel have broken their covenant with you, torn down your altars, and killed every one of your prophets. I am the only one left, and now they are trying to kill me, too."

¹¹"Go out and stand before me on the mountain," the LORD told him. And as Elijah stood there, the LORD passed by, and a mighty windstorm hit the mountain. It was such a terrible blast that the rocks were torn loose, but the LORD was not in the wind. After the wind there was an earthquake, but the LORD was not in the earthquake. ¹²And after the earthquake there was a fire, but the LORD was not in the fire. And after the fire there was the sound of a gentle whisper. ¹³When Elijah heard it, he wrapped his face in his cloak and went out and stood at the entrance of the cave.

And a voice said, "What are you doing here, Elijah?"

¹⁴He replied again, "I have zealously served the LORD God Almighty. But the people of Israel have broken their covenant with you, torn down your altars, and killed every one of your prophets. I am the only one left, and now they are trying to kill me, too."

¹⁵Then the LORD told him, "Go back the same way you came, and travel to the wilderness of Damascus. When you arrive there, anoint Hazael to be king of Aram. ¹⁶Then anoint Jehu grandson of Nimshi* to be king of Israel, and anoint Elisha son of Shaphat from the town of Abel-meholah to replace you as my prophet. ¹⁷Anyone who escapes from Hazael will be killed by Jehu, and those who escape Jehu will be killed by Elisha! ¹⁸Yet I will preserve 7,000 others in Israel who have never bowed down to Baal or kissed him!"

The Call of Elisha

¹⁹So Elijah went and found Elisha son of Shaphat plowing a field. There were twelve teams of oxen in the field, and Elisha was plowing with the twelfth team. Elijah went over to him and threw his cloak across his shoulders and then walked away. ²⁰Elisha left the oxen standing there, ran after Elijah, and said to him, "First let me go and kiss my father and mother good-bye, and then I will go with you!"

Elijah replied, "Go on back, but think about what I have done to you."

²¹So Elisha returned to his oxen and slaughtered them. He used the wood from the plow to build a fire to roast their flesh. He passed around the meat to the townspeople, and they all ate. Then he went with Elijah as his assistant.

Ben-Hadad Attacks Samaria

20 About that time King Ben-hadad of Aram mobilized his army, supported by the chariots and horses of thirty-two allied kings. They went to besiege Samaria, the capital of Israel, and launched attacks against it. ²Ben-hadad sent messengers into the city to relay this message to King Ahab of Israel: "This is what Ben-hadad says: ³'Your silver and gold are mine, and so are your wives and the best of your children!'"

⁴"All right, my lord the king," Israel's king replied. "All that I have is yours!"

⁵Soon Ben-hadad's messengers returned again and said, "This is what Ben-hadad says: 'I have already demanded that you give me your silver, gold, wives, and children. ⁶But about this time tomorrow I will send my officials to search your palace and the homes of your officials. They will take away everything you consider valuable!'"

⁷Then Ahab summoned all the elders of the land and said to them, "Look how this man is stirring up trouble! I already agreed with his demand that I give him my wives and children and silver and gold."

⁸"Don't give in to any more demands," all the elders and the people advised.

⁹So Ahab told the messengers from Ben-hadad, "Say this to my lord the king: 'I will give you everything you asked for the first time, but I cannot accept this last demand of yours.'" So the messengers returned to Ben-hadad with that response.

¹⁰Then Ben-hadad sent this message to Ahab: "May the gods strike me and even kill me if there

---

19:8 Hebrew *to Horeb*, another name for Sinai. **19:16** Hebrew *descendant of Nimshi;* compare 2 Kgs 9:2, 14.

19:9-10 Some interpreters have suggested that Elijah came to the very place where God had appeared to Moses (Exodus 33:21-23). The Lord asked him, "What are you doing here, Elijah?" This question may have a double implication: Why had Elijah come, and did he understand the significance of the spot where he stood? Elijah replied to the former part of the question. Elijah had boldly announced that he was alone in his stand for the Lord (1 Kings 18:22); here, that feeling had turned to self-pity. **19:19-21** The anointing of Elisha is a conclusion to the Lord's charge to Elijah. The two other anointings that God assigned to Elijah (19:15-16) were carried out or delegated by Elisha instead (2 Kings 8:7-15; 9:1-10).

remains enough dust from Samaria to provide even a handful for each of my soldiers."

¹¹The king of Israel sent back this answer: "A warrior putting on his sword for battle should not boast like a warrior who has already won."

¹²Ahab's reply reached Ben-hadad and the other kings as they were drinking in their tents.* "Prepare to attack!" Ben-hadad commanded his officers. So they prepared to attack the city.

Ahab's Victory over Ben-Hadad

¹³Then a certain prophet came to see King Ahab of Israel and told him, "This is what the LORD says: Do you see all these enemy forces? Today I will hand them all over to you. Then you will know that I am the LORD."

¹⁴Ahab asked, "How will he do it?"

And the prophet replied, "This is what the LORD says: The troops of the provincial commanders will do it."

"Should we attack first?" Ahab asked.

"Yes," the prophet answered.

¹⁵So Ahab mustered the troops of the 232 provincial commanders. Then he called out the rest of the army of Israel, some 7,000 men. ¹⁶About noontime, as Ben-hadad and the thirty-two allied kings were still in their tents drinking themselves into a stupor, ¹⁷the troops of the provincial commanders marched out of the city as the first contingent.

As they approached, Ben-hadad's scouts reported to him, "Some troops are coming from Samaria."

¹⁸"Take them alive," Ben-hadad commanded, "whether they have come for peace or for war."

¹⁹But Ahab's provincial commanders and the entire army had now come out to fight. ²⁰Each Israelite soldier killed his Aramean opponent, and suddenly the entire Aramean army panicked and fled. The Israelites chased them, but King Ben-hadad and a few of his charioteers escaped on horses. ²¹However, the king of Israel destroyed the other horses and chariots and slaughtered the Arameans.

²²Afterward the prophet said to King Ahab, "Get ready for another attack. Begin making plans now, for the king of Aram will come back next spring.*"

Ben-Hadad's Second Attack

²³After their defeat, Ben-hadad's officers said to him, "The Israelite gods are gods of the hills; that is why they won. But we can beat them easily on the plains. ²⁴Only this time replace the kings with field commanders! ²⁵Recruit another army like the one you lost. Give us the same number of horses, chariots, and men, and we will fight against them on the plains. There's no doubt that we will beat them." So King Ben-hadad did as they suggested.

²⁶The following spring he called up the Aramean army and marched out against Israel, this time at Aphek. ²⁷Israel then mustered its army, set up supply lines, and marched out for battle. But the Israelite army looked like two little flocks of goats in comparison to the vast Aramean forces that filled the countryside!

²⁸Then the man of God went to the king of Israel and said, "This is what the LORD says: The Arameans have said, 'The LORD is a god of the hills and not of the plains.' So I will defeat this vast army for you. Then you will know that I am the LORD."

²⁹The two armies camped opposite each other for seven days, and on the seventh day the battle began. The Israelites killed 100,000 Aramean foot soldiers in one day. ³⁰The rest fled into the town of Aphek, but the wall fell on them and killed another 27,000. Ben-hadad fled into the town and hid in a secret room.

³¹Ben-hadad's officers said to him, "Sir, we have heard that the kings of Israel are merciful. So let's humble ourselves by wearing burlap around our waists and putting ropes on our heads, and surrender to the king of Israel. Then perhaps he will let you live."

³²So they put on burlap and ropes, and they went to the king of Israel and begged, "Your servant Ben-hadad says, 'Please let me live!'"

The king of Israel responded, "Is he still alive? He is my brother!"

³³The men took this as a good sign and quickly picked up on his words. "Yes," they said, "your brother Ben-hadad!"

"Go and get him," the king of Israel told them. And when Ben-hadad arrived, Ahab invited him up into his chariot.

³⁴Ben-hadad told him, "I will give back the towns my father took from your father, and you may establish places of trade in Damascus, as my father did in Samaria."

Then Ahab said, "I will release you under these conditions." So they made a new treaty, and Ben-hadad was set free.

A Prophet Condemns Ahab

³⁵Meanwhile, the LORD instructed one of the group of prophets to say to another man, "Hit me!" But the man refused to hit the prophet. ³⁶Then the prophet told him, "Because you have not obeyed the voice of the LORD, a lion will kill you as soon as you leave me." And when he had gone, a lion did attack and kill him.

³⁷Then the prophet turned to another man and said, "Hit me!" So he struck the prophet and wounded him.

³⁸The prophet placed a bandage over his eyes to disguise himself and then waited beside the road for the king. ³⁹As the king passed by, the prophet called out to him, "Sir, I was in the thick of battle, and suddenly a man brought me a prisoner. He said, 'Guard

---

20:12 Or *in Succoth;* also in 20:16.   20:22 Hebrew *at the turn of the year;* similarly in 20:26. The first day of the year in the ancient Hebrew lunar calendar occurred in March or April.

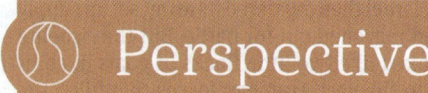

Perspective

Have I allowed evil to influence my choices?

SCRIPTURE CONNECTION: 1 KINGS 21:1-29

Most of us can identify people in our lives who have had the greatest impact. Their methods inspired or challenged us positively or led us into trouble. Whether or not we recognize it, we do the same for others. We send ripple after ripple into the world by what we say, what we do, and what we intend.

No woman in the Bible is identified more for her destructive influence than Jezebel (21:25). Scripture reveals that her husband, Ahab, did much evil in the Lord's sight, and his marriage to Jezebel was a grave error and a deliberate breaking of God's command against marrying foreign wives (Deuteronomy 7:3-4; 1 Kings 11:2).

As the queen of Israel, Jezebel was a force to be reckoned with, using her power for evil. Many people followed her in idolatry, bloodshed, and eventually their own destruction. Others resisted and paid the price with their lives.

This is not to say that Jezebel was entirely corrupt, but she was entirely human. Raised in a society that worshiped Baal, she embraced this evil influence and then chose to perpetuate it (16:31). She was a woman wrestling through her life and making her own choices, like you and me. But Jezebel chose evil. What will we choose?

VIEWPOINTS

HERS: *What types of evil done to Jezebel may have fueled her drive to send evil forward?*
MINE: *"I am entirely responsible for my own life choices, no matter how I was raised, and I can choose to follow God. I was influenced by evil at a young age, and each day I decide what to do with that, as I have also been influenced by love."*
YOURS: *What would it take for you to challenge the influence of evils done to you? What will your influence in the world be?*

MISTY ARTERBURN is an author and speaker, contributing to Bible projects, devotionals, and recovery materials for over twenty years. Wife and mom to five, Misty is the founder of Recovery Girls and the general editor of *The One Year Bible for Women*.

---

this man; if for any reason he gets away, you will either die or pay a fine of seventy-five pounds* of silver!' ⁴⁰But while I was busy doing something else, the prisoner disappeared!"

"Well, it's your own fault," the king replied. "You have brought the judgment on yourself."

⁴¹Then the prophet quickly pulled the bandage from his eyes, and the king of Israel recognized him as one of the prophets. ⁴²The prophet said to him, "This is what the Lord says: Because you have spared the man I said must be destroyed,* now you must die in his place, and your people will die instead of his people." ⁴³So the king of Israel went home to Samaria angry and sullen.

Naboth's Vineyard

21 Now there was a man named Naboth, from Jezreel, who owned a vineyard in Jezreel beside the palace of King Ahab of Samaria. ²One day Ahab said to Naboth, "Since your vineyard is so convenient to my palace, I would like to buy it to use as a vegetable garden. I will give you a better vineyard in exchange, or if you prefer, I will pay you for it."

³But Naboth replied, "The Lord forbid that I should give you the inheritance that was passed down by my ancestors."

⁴So Ahab went home angry and sullen because of Naboth's answer. The king went to bed with his face to the wall and refused to eat!

⁵"What's the matter?" his wife Jezebel asked him. "What's made you so upset that you're not eating?"

⁶"I asked Naboth to sell me his vineyard or trade it, but he refused!" Ahab told her.

⁷"Are you the king of Israel or not?" Jezebel demanded. "Get up and eat something, and don't worry about it. I'll get you Naboth's vineyard!"

⁸So she wrote letters in Ahab's name, sealed them with his seal, and sent them to the elders and other leaders of the town where Naboth lived. ⁹In her letters she commanded: "Call the citizens together for a time of fasting, and give Naboth a place of honor.

20:39 Hebrew *1 talent* [34 kilograms]. **20:42** The Hebrew term used here refers to the complete consecration of things or people to the Lord, either by destroying them or by giving them as an offering.

21:2-3 Naboth's vineyard was part of his family land and family inheritance. Land linked the people of Israel to their identity as God's people, and it was important for land to remain within the family (Leviticus 25:23-34; Numbers 36:7-9). Sometimes a family would sell their land if they could not afford to keep it. Once they could redeem the land, it was important to do so (for example, Ruth 4:1-12). Under Israelite law, the king could not seize land (1 Samuel 8:11-17).

21:7-26 King Ahab wanted Naboth's vineyard and requested to buy it. Naboth refused, so Jezebel devised an evil plan involving false charges, deceit, and murder. Her influence over Ahab was powerful. Jezebel would meet a violent end to her life, just as Elijah had prophesied (21:23; 2 Kings 9:30-37).

¹⁰And then seat two scoundrels across from him who will accuse him of cursing God and the king. Then take him out and stone him to death."

¹¹So the elders and other town leaders followed the instructions Jezebel had written in the letters. ¹²They called for a fast and put Naboth at a prominent place before the people. ¹³Then the two scoundrels came and sat down across from him. And they accused Naboth before all the people, saying, "He cursed God and the king." So he was dragged outside the town and stoned to death. ¹⁴The town leaders then sent word to Jezebel, "Naboth has been stoned to death."

¹⁵When Jezebel heard the news, she said to Ahab, "You know the vineyard Naboth wouldn't sell you? Well, you can have it now! He's dead!" ¹⁶So Ahab immediately went down to the vineyard of Naboth to claim it.

¹⁷But the LORD said to Elijah,* ¹⁸"Go down to meet King Ahab of Israel, who rules in Samaria. He will be at Naboth's vineyard in Jezreel, claiming it for himself. ¹⁹Give him this message: 'This is what the LORD says: Wasn't it enough that you killed Naboth? Must you rob him, too? Because you have done this, dogs will lick your blood at the very place where they licked the blood of Naboth!'"

²⁰"So, my enemy, you have found me!" Ahab exclaimed to Elijah.

"Yes," Elijah answered, "I have come because you have sold yourself to what is evil in the LORD's sight. ²¹So now the LORD says,* 'I will bring disaster on you and consume you. I will destroy every one of your male descendants, slave and free alike, anywhere in Israel! ²²I am going to destroy your family as I did the family of Jeroboam son of Nebat and the family of Baasha son of Ahijah, for you have made me very angry and have led Israel into sin.'

²³"And regarding Jezebel, the LORD says, 'Dogs will eat Jezebel's body at the plot of land in Jezreel.*'

²⁴"The members of Ahab's family who die in the city will be eaten by dogs, and those who die in the field will be eaten by vultures."

²⁵(No one else so completely sold himself to what was evil in the LORD's sight as Ahab did under the influence of his wife Jezebel. ²⁶His worst outrage was worshiping idols* just as the Amorites had done—the people whom the LORD had driven out from the land ahead of the Israelites.)

²⁷But when Ahab heard this message, he tore his clothing, dressed in burlap, and fasted. He even slept in burlap and went about in deep mourning.

²⁸Then another message from the LORD came to Elijah: ²⁹"Do you see how Ahab has humbled himself before me? Because he has done this, I will not do what I promised during his lifetime. It will happen to his sons; I will destroy his dynasty."

Jehoshaphat and Ahab

22 For three years there was no war between Aram and Israel. ²Then during the third year, King Jehoshaphat of Judah went to visit King Ahab of Israel. ³During the visit, the king of Israel said to his officials, "Do you realize that the town of Ramoth-gilead belongs to us? And yet we've done nothing to recapture it from the king of Aram!"

⁴Then he turned to Jehoshaphat and asked, "Will you join me in battle to recover Ramoth-gilead?"

Jehoshaphat replied to the king of Israel, "Why, of course! You and I are as one. My troops are your troops, and my horses are your horses." ⁵Then Jehoshaphat added, "But first let's find out what the LORD says."

⁶So the king of Israel summoned the prophets, about 400 of them, and asked them, "Should I go to war against Ramoth-gilead, or should I hold back?"

They all replied, "Yes, go right ahead! The Lord will give the king victory."

⁷But Jehoshaphat asked, "Is there not also a prophet of the LORD here? We should ask him the same question."

⁸The king of Israel replied to Jehoshaphat, "There is one more man who could consult the LORD for us, but I hate him. He never prophesies anything but trouble for me! His name is Micaiah son of Imlah."

Jehoshaphat replied, "That's not the way a king should talk! Let's hear what he has to say."

21:17 Hebrew *Elijah the Tishbite;* also in 21:28.   **21:21** As in Greek version; Hebrew lacks *So now the LORD says.*   **21:23** As in several Hebrew manuscripts, Syriac, and Latin Vulgate (see also 2 Kgs 9:26, 36); most Hebrew manuscripts read *at the city wall.*   **21:26** The Hebrew term (literally *round things*) probably alludes to dung.

21:27-29 Ahab was a complex character. Although justly condemned for his evil actions, here he repented when the Lord's prophet brought rebuke (21:20-29). Because of Ahab's repentance, the Lord sent Elijah to postpone the sentence against Ahab and instead impose it on his equally wicked sons (2 Kings 1:17; 9:24-26; 10:1-11).

22:2-4 Jehoshaphat and Ahab were in-laws by the marriage of Ahab's daughter Athaliah to Jehoshaphat's son Jehoram (2 Kings 8:16-24). However cordial Jehoshaphat may have intended his visit to be, he quickly became involved in Ahab's plan to occupy Ramoth-gilead. The Assyrian menace prevented Ahab from taking control of this key area that dominated the eastern end of the Plain of Jezreel. Now it needed to be taken by force, and Jehoshaphat placed his troops and horses at Ahab's disposal.

22:5-9 In accordance with ancient Near Eastern custom, Jehoshaphat requested that the two kings determine the will of the Lord before going into battle. Examples of this custom are common in Aramean, Moabite, and Assyrian inscriptions as well as in the Old Testament (1 Samuel 23:2-4; 2 Samuel 5:19-25). Despite Ahab's misgivings, Jehoshaphat insisted on summoning Micaiah, a genuine prophet of the Lord. However, Micaiah promised only that he would faithfully deliver the Lord's word (see Numbers 22:38; 24:13).

⁹So the king of Israel called one of his officials and said, "Quick! Bring Micaiah son of Imlah."

Micaiah Prophesies against Ahab

¹⁰King Ahab of Israel and King Jehoshaphat of Judah, dressed in their royal robes, were sitting on thrones at the threshing floor near the gate of Samaria. All of Ahab's prophets were prophesying there in front of them. ¹¹One of them, Zedekiah son of Kenaanah, made some iron horns and proclaimed, "This is what the LORD says: With these horns you will gore the Arameans to death!"

¹²All the other prophets agreed. "Yes," they said, "go up to Ramoth-gilead and be victorious, for the LORD will give the king victory!"

¹³Meanwhile, the messenger who went to get Micaiah said to him, "Look, all the prophets are promising victory for the king. Be sure that you agree with them and promise success."

¹⁴But Micaiah replied, "As surely as the LORD lives, I will say only what the LORD tells me to say."

¹⁵When Micaiah arrived before the king, Ahab asked him, "Micaiah, should we go to war against Ramoth-gilead, or should we hold back?"

Micaiah replied sarcastically, "Yes, go up and be victorious, for the LORD will give the king victory!"

¹⁶But the king replied sharply, "How many times must I demand that you speak only the truth to me when you speak for the LORD?"

¹⁷Then Micaiah told him, "In a vision I saw all Israel scattered on the mountains, like sheep without a shepherd. And the LORD said, 'Their master has been killed.* Send them home in peace.'"

¹⁸"Didn't I tell you?" the king of Israel exclaimed to Jehoshaphat. "He never prophesies anything but trouble for me."

¹⁹Then Micaiah continued, "Listen to what the LORD says! I saw the LORD sitting on his throne with all the armies of heaven around him, on his right and on his left. ²⁰And the LORD said, 'Who can entice Ahab to go into battle against Ramoth-gilead so he can be killed?'

"There were many suggestions, ²¹and finally a spirit approached the LORD and said, 'I can do it!'

²²"'How will you do this?' the LORD asked.

"And the spirit replied, 'I will go out and inspire all of Ahab's prophets to speak lies.'

"'You will succeed,' said the LORD. 'Go ahead and do it.'

²³"So you see, the LORD has put a lying spirit in the mouths of all your prophets. For the LORD has pronounced your doom."

²⁴Then Zedekiah son of Kenaanah walked up to Micaiah and slapped him across the face. "Since when did the Spirit of the LORD leave me to speak to you?" he demanded.

²⁵And Micaiah replied, "You will find out soon enough when you are trying to hide in some secret room!"

²⁶"Arrest him!" the king of Israel ordered. "Take him back to Amon, the governor of the city, and to my son Joash. ²⁷Give them this order from the king: 'Put this man in prison, and feed him nothing but bread and water until I return safely from the battle!'"

²⁸But Micaiah replied, "If you return safely, it will mean that the LORD has not spoken through me!" Then he added to those standing around, "Everyone mark my words!"

The Death of Ahab

²⁹So King Ahab of Israel and King Jehoshaphat of Judah led their armies against Ramoth-gilead. ³⁰The king of Israel said to Jehoshaphat, "As we go into battle, I will disguise myself so no one will recognize me, but you wear your royal robes." So the king of Israel disguised himself, and they went into battle.

³¹Meanwhile, the king of Aram had issued these orders to his thirty-two chariot commanders: "Attack only the king of Israel. Don't bother with anyone else!" ³²So when the Aramean chariot commanders saw Jehoshaphat in his royal robes, they went after him. "There is the king of Israel!" they shouted. But when Jehoshaphat called out, ³³the chariot commanders realized he was not the king of Israel, and they stopped chasing him.

³⁴An Aramean soldier, however, randomly shot an arrow at the Israelite troops and hit the king of Israel between the joints of his armor. "Turn the horses* and get me out of here!" Ahab groaned to the driver of his chariot. "I'm badly wounded!"

³⁵The battle raged all that day, and the king remained propped up in his chariot facing the Arameans. The blood from his wound ran down to the floor of his chariot, and as evening arrived he died. ³⁶Just as the sun was setting, the cry ran through his troops: "We're done for! Run for your lives!"

³⁷So the king died, and his body was taken to Samaria and buried there. ³⁸Then his chariot was washed beside the pool of Samaria, and dogs came and licked his blood at the place where the prostitutes bathed,* just as the LORD had promised.

³⁹The rest of the events in Ahab's reign and everything he did, including the story of the ivory palace and the towns he built, are recorded in The Book of the History of the Kings of Israel. ⁴⁰So Ahab died, and his son Ahaziah became the next king.

Jehoshaphat Rules in Judah

⁴¹Jehoshaphat son of Asa began to rule over Judah in the fourth year of King Ahab's reign in Israel. ⁴²Jehoshaphat was thirty-five years old when he became

---

22:17 Hebrew *These people have no master.* 22:34 Hebrew *Turn your hand.* 22:38 Or *his blood, and the prostitutes bathed [in it];* or *his blood, and they washed his armor.*

king, and he reigned in Jerusalem twenty-five years. His mother was Azubah, the daughter of Shilhi.

⁴³Jehoshaphat was a good king, following the example of his father, Asa. He did what was pleasing in the LORD's sight. *During his reign, however, he failed to remove all the pagan shrines, and the people still offered sacrifices and burned incense there. ⁴⁴Jehoshaphat also made peace with the king of Israel.

⁴⁵The rest of the events in Jehoshaphat's reign, the extent of his power, and the wars he waged are recorded in The Book of the History of the Kings of Judah. ⁴⁶He banished from the land the rest of the male and female shrine prostitutes, who still continued their practices from the days of his father, Asa.

⁴⁷(There was no king in Edom at that time, only a deputy.)

⁴⁸Jehoshaphat also built a fleet of trading ships* to sail to Ophir for gold. But the ships never set sail, for they met with disaster in their home port of Ezion-geber. ⁴⁹At one time Ahaziah son of Ahab had proposed to Jehoshaphat, "Let my men sail with your men in the ships." But Jehoshaphat refused the request.

⁵⁰When Jehoshaphat died, he was buried with his ancestors in the City of David. Then his son Jehoram became the next king.

Ahaziah Rules in Israel

⁵¹Ahaziah son of Ahab began to rule over Israel in the seventeenth year of King Jehoshaphat's reign in Judah. He reigned in Samaria two years. ⁵²But he did what was evil in the LORD's sight, following the example of his father and mother and the example of Jeroboam son of Nebat, who had led Israel to sin. ⁵³He served Baal and worshiped him, provoking the anger of the LORD, the God of Israel, just as his father had done.

22:43 Verses 22:43b-53 are numbered 22:44-54 in Hebrew text. **22:48** Hebrew *fleet of ships of Tarshish.*

22:48-49 Jehoshaphat built this fleet of trading ships (literally "fleet of ships of Tarshish") in alliance with Ahaziah (see 2 Chronicles 20:35-37). Like Solomon, the two kings planned to send a fleet to Ophir in search of gold (1 Kings 9:27-28; 10:11). The venture was ill-fated; to fulfill a prophetic warning (2 Chronicles 20:37), the Lord destroyed the fleet before it left port. Jehoshaphat wisely did not become entangled with Ahaziah a second time.

2 Kings

WHAT DO WE LEARN ABOUT GOD'S MISSION AND OURS?
We become like what we worship.

WHO WROTE IT? Anonymous, but probably a court official or someone who had access to official historical records.

WHEN DID IT HAPPEN? Between 850 and 586 BC, during the latter time of Israel's divided kingdom.

HOW IS IT ORGANIZED?

- 1–8: The end of Elijah's ministry; Elisha's ministry begins
- 9–16: The divided kingdom continues to decline
- 17: The fall of Israel, the northern kingdom
- 18–25: The last era of Judah, the southern kingdom, and its fall

FEATURE HIGHLIGHTS

- *Twice the Power* (444)
- *Our Call to the Vulnerable* (446)
- *The Enslaved Girl in Naaman's Household: Small Acts Change Everything* (449)
- *The Woman from Shunem: Dare to Desire* (453)
- *What Makes One Woman Choose Evil and Another Good?* (457)
- *A Family Blessing* (470)
- *The Power of Owning Our Place and Part* (472)

Words to Remember are highlighted throughout this book

HOW LONG DOES IT TAKE TO READ?

2:00

| :30 | 1:00 | 1:30 | 2:00 | 2:30 | 3:00 | 3:30 |

Timeline (BC)

- **930** — THE KINGDOM DIVIDES
- **848** — ELISHA'S MINISTRY BEGINS
  - The woman from Shunem hosts Elisha
  - The enslaved girl points Naaman to healing
- **841** — JEHU BECOMES ISRAEL'S KING
- **841** — QUEEN ATHALIAH KILLS MOST OF JUDAH'S HEIRS; JEHOSHEBA RESCUES JOASH
- **835** — JOASH, ZIBIAH'S SON, BECOMES JUDAH'S KING
- **793** — JEROBOAM II BECOMES ISRAEL'S KING
- **753** — HOSEA'S MINISTRY BEGINS
- **740** — ISAIAH'S MINISTRY BEGINS
- **722** — ISRAEL (NORTHERN KINGDOM) FALLS
- **715** — HEZEKIAH, ABIJAH'S SON, BECOMES JUDAH'S KING
- **640** — JOSIAH, JEDIDAH'S SON, BECOMES JUDAH'S KING
- **627** — JEREMIAH'S MINISTRY BEGINS
- **622** — HULDAH COUNSELS KING JOSIAH ON THE LAW
- **605** — FIRST DEPORTATION FROM JUDAH—DANIEL TAKEN
- **597** — SECOND DEPORTATION FROM JUDAH—EZEKIEL TAKEN
- **586** — JUDAH (SOUTHERN KINGDOM) FALLS; TEMPLE DESTROYED

2 KINGS 1

Elijah Confronts King Ahaziah

1 After King Ahab's death, the land of Moab rebelled against Israel.

²One day Israel's new king, Ahaziah, fell through the latticework of an upper room at his palace in Samaria and was seriously injured. So he sent messengers to the temple of Baal-zebub, the god of Ekron, to ask whether he would recover.

³But the angel of the Lord told Elijah, who was from Tishbe, "Go and confront the messengers of the king of Samaria and ask them, 'Is there no God in Israel? Why are you going to Baal-zebub, the god of Ekron, to ask whether the king will recover? ⁴Now, therefore, this is what the Lord says: You will never leave the bed you are lying on; you will surely die.'" So Elijah went to deliver the message.

⁵When the messengers returned to the king, he asked them, "Why have you returned so soon?"

⁶They replied, "A man came up to us and told us to go back to the king and give him this message. 'This is what the Lord says: Is there no God in Israel? Why are you sending men to Baal-zebub, the god of Ekron, to ask whether you will recover? Therefore, because you have done this, you will never leave the bed you are lying on; you will surely die.'"

⁷"What sort of man was he?" the king demanded. "What did he look like?"

⁸They replied, "He was a hairy man,* and he wore a leather belt around his waist."

"Elijah from Tishbe!" the king exclaimed.

⁹Then he sent an army captain with fifty soldiers to arrest him. They found him sitting on top of a hill. The captain said to him, "Man of God, the king has commanded you to come down with us."

¹⁰But Elijah replied to the captain, "If I am a man of God, let fire come down from heaven and destroy you and your fifty men!" Then fire fell from heaven and killed them all.

¹¹So the king sent another captain with fifty men. The captain said to him, "Man of God, the king demands that you come down at once."

¹²Elijah replied, "If I am a man of God, let fire come down from heaven and destroy you and your fifty men!" And again the fire of God fell from heaven and killed them all.

¹³Once more the king sent a third captain with fifty men. But this time the captain went up the hill and fell to his knees before Elijah. He pleaded with him, "O man of God, please spare my life and the lives of these, your fifty servants. ¹⁴See how the fire from heaven came down and destroyed the first two groups. But now please spare my life!"

¹⁵Then the angel of the Lord said to Elijah, "Go down with him, and don't be afraid of him." So Elijah got up and went with him to the king.

¹⁶And Elijah said to the king, "This is what the Lord says: Why did you send messengers to Baal-zebub, the god of Ekron, to ask whether you will recover? Is there no God in Israel to answer your question? Therefore, because you have done this, you will never leave the bed you are lying on; you will surely die."

¹⁷So Ahaziah died, just as the Lord had promised through Elijah. Since Ahaziah did not have a son to succeed him, his brother Joram* became the next king. This took place in the second year of the reign of Jehoram son of Jehoshaphat, king of Judah.

¹⁸The rest of the events in Ahaziah's reign and everything he did are recorded in The Book of the History of the Kings of Israel.

Elijah Taken into Heaven

2 When the Lord was about to take Elijah up to heaven in a whirlwind, Elijah and Elisha were traveling from Gilgal. ²And Elijah said to Elisha, "Stay here, for the Lord has told me to go to Bethel."

But Elisha replied, "As surely as the Lord lives and you yourself live, I will never leave you!" So they went down together to Bethel.

³The group of prophets from Bethel came to Elisha and asked him, "Did you know that the Lord is going to take your master away from you today?"

"Of course I know," Elisha answered. "But be quiet about it."

⁴Then Elijah said to Elisha, "Stay here, for the Lord has told me to go to Jericho."

But Elisha replied again, "As surely as the Lord lives and you yourself live, I will never leave you." So they went on together to Jericho.

⁵Then the group of prophets from Jericho came to Elisha and asked him, "Did you know that the Lord is going to take your master away from you today?"

1:8 Or *He was wearing clothing made of hair.* **1:17** Hebrew *Jehoram,* a variant spelling of Joram.

1:1 In ancient manuscripts, 1 and 2 Kings were originally one book, so it's best to read them together. At the beginning of 2 Kings, Israel's story continues as a kingdom split into two: the northern kingdom of Israel and the southern kingdom of Judah. This once united and powerful kingdom struggled to live obediently under God's rule. God sent prophets such as Elijah, Elisha, and Isaiah to remind Israel and Judah to be faithful to the covenant.

1:3-17 Elijah, who had previously confronted Ahaziah's father, Ahab, had a twofold message for the king: a condemnation for failure to acknowledge that Yahweh, not Baal, is God (see 1 Kings 18:16-18), and a pronouncement of the king's certain death (see 1 Kings 21:17-24). Hearing Elijah's message, the king first decided to have him arrested. Two army captains in Ahaziah's armies and the soldiers who accompanied them were destroyed by the Lord. In contrast to the first two officers, the third commander pleaded for mercy before Elijah and God. It's not clear whether Ahaziah would have recovered from his fall, but the king's clear disdain for the Lord and his messenger, Elijah, sealed his fate.

"Of course I know," Elisha answered. "But be quiet about it."

⁶Then Elijah said to Elisha, "Stay here, for the LORD has told me to go to the Jordan River."

But again Elisha replied, "As surely as the LORD lives and you yourself live, I will never leave you." So they went on together.

⁷Fifty men from the group of prophets also went and watched from a distance as Elijah and Elisha stopped beside the Jordan River. ⁸Then Elijah folded his cloak together and struck the water with it. The river divided, and the two of them went across on dry ground!

⁹When they came to the other side, Elijah said to Elisha, "Tell me what I can do for you before I am taken away."

And Elisha replied, "Please let me inherit a double share of your spirit and become your successor."

¹⁰"You have asked a difficult thing," Elijah replied. "If you see me when I am taken from you, then you will get your request. But if not, then you won't."

¹¹As they were walking along and talking, suddenly a chariot of fire appeared, drawn by horses of fire. It drove between the two men, separating them, and Elijah was carried by a whirlwind into heaven. ¹²Elisha saw it and cried out, "My father! My father! I see the chariots and charioteers of Israel!" And as they disappeared from sight, Elisha tore his clothes in distress.

¹³Elisha picked up Elijah's cloak, which had fallen when he was taken up. Then Elisha returned to the bank of the Jordan River. ¹⁴He struck the water with Elijah's cloak and cried out, "Where is the LORD, the God of Elijah?" Then the river divided, and Elisha went across.

¹⁵When the group of prophets from Jericho saw from a distance what happened, they exclaimed, "Elijah's spirit rests upon Elisha!" And they went to meet him and bowed to the ground before him. ¹⁶"Sir," they said, "just say the word and fifty of our strongest men will search the wilderness for your master. Perhaps the Spirit of the LORD has left him on some mountain or in some valley."

"No," Elisha said, "don't send them." ¹⁷But they kept urging him until they shamed him into agreeing, and he finally said, "All right, send them." So fifty men searched for three days but did not find Elijah. ¹⁸Elisha was still at Jericho when they returned. "Didn't I tell you not to go?" he asked.

Elisha's First Miracles

¹⁹One day the leaders of the town of Jericho visited Elisha. "We have a problem, my lord," they told him. "This town is located in pleasant surroundings, as you can see. But the water is bad, and the land is unproductive."

²⁰Elisha said, "Bring me a new bowl with salt in it." So they brought it to him. ²¹Then he went out to the spring that supplied the town with water and threw the salt into it. And he said, "This is what the LORD says: I have purified this water. It will no longer cause death or infertility.*" ²²And the water has remained pure ever since, just as Elisha said.

²³Elisha left Jericho and went up to Bethel. As he was walking along the road, a group of boys from the town began mocking and making fun of him. "Go away, baldy!" they chanted. "Go away, baldy!" ²⁴Elisha turned around and looked at them, and he cursed them in the name of the LORD. Then two bears came out of the woods and mauled forty-two of them. ²⁵From there Elisha went to Mount Carmel and finally returned to Samaria.

War between Israel and Moab

3 Ahab's son Joram* began to rule over Israel in the eighteenth year of King Jehoshaphat's reign in Judah. He reigned in Samaria twelve years. ²He did what was evil in the LORD's sight, but not to the same extent as his father and mother. He at least tore down the sacred pillar of Baal that his father had set up. ³Nevertheless, he continued in the sins that Jeroboam son of Nebat had committed and led the people of Israel to commit.

⁴King Mesha of Moab was a sheep breeder. He used to pay the king of Israel an annual tribute of 100,000 lambs and the wool of 100,000 rams. ⁵But after Ahab's death, the king of Moab rebelled against the king of Israel. ⁶So King Joram promptly mustered the army of Israel and marched from Samaria. ⁷On the way, he sent this message to King Jehoshaphat of Judah: "The king of Moab has rebelled against me. Will you join me in battle against him?"

And Jehoshaphat replied, "Why, of course! You and I are as one. My troops are your troops, and my horses are your horses." ⁸Then Jehoshaphat asked, "What route will we take?"

"We will attack from the wilderness of Edom," Joram replied.

2:21 Or *or make the land unproductive;* Hebrew reads *or barrenness.* **3:1** Hebrew *Jehoram,* a variant spelling of Joram; also in 3:6.

2:9-12 Elisha requested a double portion of Elijah's spirit. This request for a "double share" resembles the firstborn son's inheritance rights (Deuteronomy 21:17). Elijah acknowledged that this was an unusual and difficult request, as only the Lord had the power to provide this. Elijah said that it would be granted if Elisha saw him taken up into heaven. Elisha did witness this incredible moment when Elijah ascended to heaven in a whirlwind. As Elijah's successor, Elisha was a legitimate heir to this prophetic role.

2:12-14 Elisha revealed his deep sorrow by tearing his clothes. This was a demonstration of grief. Later in the story, King Josiah would tear his clothes and weep because of Judah's unfaithfulness (22:19). Grief was expressed in very physical ways in ancient cultures, as shown in the Bible. We learn how expressing grief helps us identify what we value, such as the people and things that matter to us.

Insight — TWICE THE POWER

As the fiery Elijah prepared to leave this world, his mild-mannered assistant, Elisha, asked him for "a double share" of his spirit (2 Kings 2:9). Surprisingly, Elisha's request was granted. How might we dare to ask God to use us greatly?

ELIJAH'S MIRACLES

1. Called for a three-year drought 1 Kings 17:1
2. Multiplied a widow's food supply 1 Kings 17:15-16
3. Raised the widow's son back to life
   1 Kings 17:19-24
4. Called down heavenly fire at Mount Carmel
   1 Kings 18:36-38
5. Unleashed a rainstorm to end the drought
   1 Kings 18:41-46
6. Correctly predicted King Ahab's demise
   1 Kings 21:17-24
7. Called down fire on King Ahaziah's first set of soldiers 2 Kings 1:10
8. Called down fire on King Ahaziah's second set of soldiers 2 Kings 1:11-12
9. Divided the Jordan River 2 Kings 2:8

ELISHA'S MIRACLES

1. Divided the Jordan River 2 Kings 2:13-14
2. Purified a town's water supply 2 Kings 2:20-22
3. Called down instant judgment on disrespectful boys 2 Kings 2:23-24
4. Provided enough water to satisfy three thirsty armies 2 Kings 3:9-20
5. Multiplied a widow's oil supply to keep her from bankruptcy 2 Kings 4:3-7
6. Correctly predicted a pregnancy 2 Kings 4:15-17
7. Raised a boy back to life 2 Kings 4:32-37
8. Stopped an epidemic of food poisoning
   2 Kings 4:40-41
9. Multiplied food to feed 100 men 2 Kings 4:43-44
10. Healed an Aramean general of a skin disease
    2 Kings 5:10-14
11. Exposed his servant's secret greed and judged him
    2 Kings 5:26-27
12. Made an ax head float 2 Kings 6:6
13. Struck Aramean invaders with blindness
    2 Kings 6:18
14. Correctly predicted a hit man's arrival
    2 Kings 6:32-33
15. Correctly predicted the lifting of Samaria's siege-related famine, as well as a doubter's ugly demise
    2 Kings 7:1-2
16. Correctly predicted King Ben-hadad's death and Hazael's political rise 2 Kings 8:10-15
17. Correctly predicted Jehu leading a regime change
    2 Kings 9:1-3
18. Correctly predicted King Jehoash's military successes against Aram 2 Kings 13:14-19
19. Triggered a dead man's resuscitation when the body came in contact with his bones
    2 Kings 13:20-21

⁹The king of Edom and his troops joined them, and all three armies traveled along a roundabout route through the wilderness for seven days. But there was no water for the men or their animals.

¹⁰"What should we do?" the king of Israel cried out. "The LORD has brought the three of us here to let the king of Moab defeat us."

¹¹But King Jehoshaphat of Judah asked, "Is there no prophet of the LORD with us? If there is, we can ask the LORD what to do through him."

One of King Joram's officers replied, "Elisha son of Shaphat is here. He used to be Elijah's personal assistant.*"

¹²Jehoshaphat said, "Yes, the LORD speaks through him." So the king of Israel, King Jehoshaphat of Judah, and the king of Edom went to consult with Elisha.

¹³"Why are you coming to me?"* Elisha asked the king of Israel. "Go to the pagan prophets of your father and mother!"

But King Joram of Israel said, "No! For it was the LORD who called us three kings here—only to be defeated by the king of Moab!"

¹⁴Elisha replied, "As surely as the LORD Almighty lives, whom I serve, I wouldn't even bother with you except for my respect for King Jehoshaphat of Judah. ¹⁵Now bring me someone who can play the harp."

While the harp was being played, the power* of the LORD came upon Elisha, ¹⁶and he said, "This is what the LORD says: This dry valley will be filled with pools of water! ¹⁷You will see neither wind nor rain, says the LORD, but this valley will be filled with water. You will have plenty for yourselves and your cattle and other animals. ¹⁸But this is only a simple thing for the LORD, for he will make you victorious over the army of Moab! ¹⁹You will conquer the best of their towns, even the fortified ones. You will cut down all their good trees, stop up all their springs, and ruin all their good land with stones."

²⁰The next day at about the time when the morning sacrifice was offered, water suddenly appeared! It was flowing from the direction of Edom, and soon there was water everywhere.

²¹Meanwhile, when the people of Moab heard about the three armies marching against them, they mobilized every man who was old enough to strap on a sword, and they stationed themselves along their border. ²²But when they got up the next morning, the sun was shining across the water, making it appear red to the Moabites—like blood. ²³"It's blood!" the Moabites exclaimed. "The three armies must have attacked and killed each other! Let's go, men of Moab, and collect the plunder!"

²⁴But when the Moabites arrived at the Israelite camp, the army of Israel rushed out and attacked them until they turned and ran. The army of Israel chased them into the land of Moab, destroying everything as they went.* ²⁵They destroyed the towns, covered their good land with stones, stopped up all the springs, and cut down all the good trees. Finally, only Kir-hareseth and its stone walls were left, but men with slings surrounded and attacked it.

²⁶When the king of Moab saw that he was losing the battle, he led 700 of his swordsmen in a desperate attempt to break through the enemy lines near the king of Edom, but they failed. ²⁷Then the king of Moab took his oldest son, who would have been the next king, and sacrificed him as a burnt offering on the wall. So there was great anger against Israel,* and the Israelites withdrew and returned to their own land.

Elisha Helps a Poor Widow

4 One day the widow of a member of the group of prophets came to Elisha and cried out, "My husband who served you is dead, and you know how he feared the LORD. But now a creditor has come, threatening to take my two sons as slaves."

²"What can I do to help you?" Elisha asked. "Tell me, what do you have in the house?"

"Nothing at all, except a flask of olive oil," she replied.

³And Elisha said, "Borrow as many empty jars as you can from your friends and neighbors. ⁴Then go into your house with your sons and shut the door behind you. Pour olive oil from your flask into the jars, setting each one aside when it is filled."

⁵So she did as she was told. Her sons kept bringing jars to her, and she filled one after another. ⁶Soon every container was full to the brim!

"Bring me another jar," she said to one of her sons.

"There aren't any more!" he told her. And then the olive oil stopped flowing.

⁷When she told the man of God what had happened, he said to her, "Now sell the olive oil and pay your debts, and you and your sons can live on what is left over."

Elisha and the Woman from Shunem

⁸One day Elisha went to the town of Shunem. A wealthy woman lived there, and she urged him to come to her

---

3:11 Hebrew *He used to pour water on the hands of Elijah.* 3:13 Hebrew *What is there in common between you and me?* 3:15 Hebrew *the hand.* 3:24 The meaning of the Hebrew is uncertain. 3:27 Or *So Israel's anger was great.* The meaning of the Hebrew is uncertain.

4:1-7 This Israelite widow was in desperate need and asked Elisha for help. She was worried about her sons being enslaved, as she was destitute. During this time, debts could be paid through debt-slavery (Exodus 21:1-11; Deuteronomy 15:1-18). Elisha helped this woman in need, and this story reveals the heart of God, who cares for the vulnerable, the poor, and the oppressed. (See Deuteronomy 10:18; 24:17, 22; 26:12-13; 27:19; Jeremiah 7:6; 22:3.)

home for a meal. After that, whenever he passed that way, he would stop there for something to eat.

⁹She said to her husband, "I am sure this man who stops in from time to time is a holy man of God. ¹⁰Let's build a small room for him on the roof and furnish it with a bed, a table, a chair, and a lamp. Then he will have a place to stay whenever he comes by."

¹¹One day Elisha returned to Shunem, and he went up to this upper room to rest. ¹²He said to his servant Gehazi, "Tell the woman from Shunem I want to speak to her." When she appeared, ¹³Elisha said to Gehazi, "Tell her, 'We appreciate the kind concern you have shown us. What can we do for you? Can we put in a good word for you to the king or to the commander of the army?'"

"No," she replied, "my family takes good care of me."

¹⁴Later Elisha asked Gehazi, "What can we do for her?"

Gehazi replied, "She doesn't have a son, and her husband is an old man."

¹⁵"Call her back again," Elisha told him. When the woman returned, Elisha said to her as she stood in the doorway, ¹⁶"Next year at this time you will be holding a son in your arms!"

"No, my lord!" she cried. "O man of God, don't deceive me and get my hopes up like that."

¹⁷But sure enough, the woman soon became pregnant. And at that time the following year she had a son, just as Elisha had said.

4:11-17 Elisha was thankful for the woman from Shunem's hospitality. The Hebrew could also be translated "great woman." She was wealthy and respected. Elisha discovered from Gehazi that she did not have a son and her husband was old. She had probably given up hope that she would have children, as had Sarah (Genesis 18:12-13). Elisha told her that she would have a son. To her delight, this prophetic word came true. With God, all things are possible!

Koinonia

IMAGE — MY STORY WITH COMMUNITY, WORKPLACE & CHURCH

Our Call to the Vulnerable

SCRIPTURE CONNECTION: 2 KINGS 4:1-7

"What can I do to help you?" It's a question we are asked regularly, but how often do we ask the question?

A widow in crisis whose sons are about to be enslaved turns to Elisha for help. He asks what she has to offer. The widow explains she has only a small jar of olive oil; however, it comes with big faith. Elisha tells her to gather as many jars as possible.

God is about to take what appears to be worthless and turn it into a miracle.

As she begins pouring, the oil flows until all the jars fill. She sells the oil to pay the debts in full and keep her sons free.

God patiently waits for us to want him and his help. He will fill every need we have when we bring those needs to him. And when we see someone in need who is vulnerable, we can be the one God uses to meet that need, like he used Elisha.

> **God patiently waits for us to want him.**

IMAGINE

How has God used you to help someone in a crisis?

Do you tend to lead those in need to God or leave them in need?

"Like the widow, I have learned that when I see what I do have, not what I don't have, God can use me."

ROBIN REESE is a volunteer leader with Stonecroft Ministries. She and her husband, Terry, love to travel, enjoy the company of their son and two corgis, and live life to the fullest!

¹⁸One day when her child was older, he went out to help his father, who was working with the harvesters. ¹⁹Suddenly he cried out, "My head hurts! My head hurts!"

His father said to one of the servants, "Carry him home to his mother."

²⁰So the servant took him home, and his mother held him on her lap. But around noontime he died. ²¹She carried him up and laid him on the bed of the man of God, then shut the door and left him there. ²²She sent a message to her husband: "Send one of the servants and a donkey so that I can hurry to the man of God and come right back."

²³"Why go today?" he asked. "It is neither a new moon festival nor a Sabbath."

But she said, "It will be all right."

²⁴So she saddled the donkey and said to the servant, "Hurry! Don't slow down unless I tell you to."

²⁵As she approached the man of God at Mount Carmel, Elisha saw her in the distance. He said to Gehazi, "Look, the woman from Shunem is coming. ²⁶Run out to meet her and ask her, 'Is everything all right with you, your husband, and your child?'"

"Yes," the woman told Gehazi, "everything is fine."

²⁷But when she came to the man of God at the mountain, she fell to the ground before him and caught hold of his feet. Gehazi began to push her away, but the man of God said, "Leave her alone. She is deeply troubled, but the LORD has not told me what it is."

²⁸Then she said, "Did I ask you for a son, my lord? And didn't I say, 'Don't deceive me and get my hopes up'?"

²⁹Then Elisha said to Gehazi, "Get ready to travel*; take my staff and go! Don't talk to anyone along the way. Go quickly and lay the staff on the child's face."

³⁰But the boy's mother said, "As surely as the LORD lives and you yourself live, I won't go home unless you go with me." So Elisha returned with her.

³¹Gehazi hurried on ahead and laid the staff on the child's face, but nothing happened. There was no sign of life. He returned to meet Elisha and told him, "The child is still dead."

³²When Elisha arrived, the child was indeed dead, lying there on the prophet's bed. ³³He went in alone and shut the door behind him and prayed to the LORD. ³⁴Then he lay down on the child's body, placing his mouth on the child's mouth, his eyes on the child's eyes, and his hands on the child's hands. And as he stretched out on him, the child's body began to grow warm again! ³⁵Elisha got up, walked back and forth across the room once, and then stretched himself out again on the child. This time the boy sneezed seven times and opened his eyes!

³⁶Then Elisha summoned Gehazi. "Call the child's mother!" he said. And when she came in, Elisha said, "Here, take your son!" ³⁷She fell at his feet and bowed before him, overwhelmed with gratitude. Then she took her son in her arms and carried him downstairs.

Miracles during a Famine

³⁸Elisha now returned to Gilgal, and there was a famine in the land. One day as the group of prophets was seated before him, he said to his servant, "Put a large pot on the fire, and make some stew for the rest of the group."

³⁹One of the young men went out into the field to gather herbs and came back with a pocketful of wild gourds. He shredded them and put them into the pot without realizing they were poisonous. ⁴⁰Some of the stew was served to the men. But after they had eaten a bite or two they cried out, "Man of God, there's poison in this stew!" So they would not eat it.

⁴¹Elisha said, "Bring me some flour." Then he threw it into the pot and said, "Now it's all right; go ahead and eat." And then it did not harm them.

⁴²One day a man from Baal-shalishah brought the man of God a sack of fresh grain and twenty loaves of barley bread made from the first grain of his harvest. Elisha said, "Give it to the people so they can eat."

⁴³"What?" his servant exclaimed. "Feed a hundred people with only this?"

But Elisha repeated, "Give it to the people so they can eat, for this is what the LORD says: Everyone will eat, and there will even be some left over!" ⁴⁴And when they gave it to the people, there was plenty for all and some left over, just as the LORD had promised.

The Healing of Naaman

5 The king of Aram had great admiration for Naaman, the commander of his army, because through him the LORD had given Aram great victories. But though Naaman was a mighty warrior, he suffered from leprosy.*

4:29 Hebrew *Bind up your loins.* **5:1** Or *from a contagious skin disease.* The Hebrew word used here and throughout this passage can describe various skin diseases.

4:18-36 The woman from Shunem's miracle child fell ill and died in her arms, possibly from heatstroke or an aneurysm. Despite the horrific tragedy she was experiencing, this incredible woman had the presence of mind to find Elisha and refused to leave without him. Elisha responded to this woman's request through prayer and action. In this exchange, the Lord's healing power was shown through Elisha, whose response to crisis was prayer. This is a powerful reminder that we are not alone when a crisis comes into our lives and we can always turn to God in prayer.

5:1 Naaman was an army commander of Aram. Even though Aram was Israel's enemy, the text describes Naaman as a "mighty warrior" (or another possible translation, "great man"). Naaman was a well-respected person, but he also had a skin disease. Most Bible translations call this *leprosy*, though it was most likely another ailment, such as psoriasis or eczema. A wide range of skin conditions could infect someone. Some could be cured while others could not (Leviticus 13).

²At this time Aramean raiders had invaded the land of Israel, and among their captives was a young girl who had been given to Naaman's wife as a maid. ³One day the girl said to her mistress, "I wish my master would go to see the prophet in Samaria. He would heal him of his leprosy."

⁴So Naaman told the king what the young girl from Israel had said. ⁵"Go and visit the prophet," the king of Aram told him. "I will send a letter of introduction for you to take to the king of Israel." So Naaman started out, carrying as gifts 750 pounds of silver, 150 pounds of gold,* and ten sets of clothing. ⁶The letter to the king of Israel said: "With this letter I present my servant Naaman. I want you to heal him of his leprosy."

⁷When the king of Israel read the letter, he tore his clothes in dismay and said, "Am I God, that I can give life and take it away? Why is this man asking me to heal someone with leprosy? I can see that he's just trying to pick a fight with me."

⁸But when Elisha, the man of God, heard that the king of Israel had torn his clothes in dismay, he sent this message to him: "Why are you so upset? Send Naaman to me, and he will learn that there is a true prophet here in Israel."

⁹So Naaman went with his horses and chariots and waited at the door of Elisha's house. ¹⁰But Elisha sent a messenger out to him with this message: "Go and wash yourself seven times in the Jordan River. Then your skin will be restored, and you will be healed of your leprosy."

¹¹But Naaman became angry and stalked away. "I thought he would certainly come out to meet me!" he said. "I expected him to wave his hand over the leprosy and call on the name of the LORD his God and heal me! ¹²Aren't the rivers of Damascus, the Abana and the Pharpar, better than any of the rivers of Israel? Why shouldn't I wash in them and be healed?" So Naaman turned and went away in a rage.

¹³But his officers tried to reason with him and said, "Sir,* if the prophet had told you to do something very difficult, wouldn't you have done it? So you should certainly obey him when he says simply, 'Go and wash and be cured!'" ¹⁴So Naaman went down to the Jordan River and dipped himself seven times, as the man of God had instructed him. And his skin became as healthy as the skin of a young child, and he was healed!

¹⁵Then Naaman and his entire party went back to find the man of God. They stood before him, and Naaman said, "Now I know that there is no God in all the world except in Israel. So please accept a gift from your servant."

¹⁶But Elisha replied, "As surely as the LORD lives, whom I serve, I will not accept any gifts." And though Naaman urged him to take the gift, Elisha refused.

¹⁷Then Naaman said, "All right, but please allow me to load two of my mules with earth from this place, and I will take it back home with me. From now on I will never again offer burnt offerings or sacrifices to any other god except the LORD. ¹⁸However, may the LORD pardon me in this one thing: When my master the king goes into the temple of the god Rimmon to worship there and leans on my arm, may the LORD pardon me when I bow, too."

¹⁹"Go in peace," Elisha said. So Naaman started home again.

The Greed of Gehazi

²⁰But Gehazi, the servant of Elisha, the man of God, said to himself, "My master should not have let this Aramean get away without accepting any of his gifts. As surely as the LORD lives, I will chase after him and get something from him." ²¹So Gehazi set off after Naaman.

When Naaman saw Gehazi running after him, he climbed down from his chariot and went to meet him. "Is everything all right?" Naaman asked.

²²"Yes," Gehazi said, "but my master has sent me to tell you that two young prophets from the hill country of Ephraim have just arrived. He would like 75 pounds* of silver and two sets of clothing to give to them."

²³"By all means, take twice as much* silver," Naaman insisted. He gave him two sets of clothing, tied up the money in two bags, and sent two of his servants to carry the gifts for Gehazi. ²⁴But when they arrived at the citadel,* Gehazi took the gifts from the servants and sent the men back. Then he went and hid the gifts inside the house.

²⁵When he went in to his master, Elisha asked him, "Where have you been, Gehazi?"

"I haven't been anywhere," he replied.

²⁶But Elisha asked him, "Don't you realize that I was there in spirit when Naaman stepped down from his chariot to meet you? Is this the time to receive money and clothing, olive groves and vineyards, sheep and cattle, and male and female servants? ²⁷Because you have done this, you and your

---

5:5 Hebrew *10 talents* [340 kilograms] *of silver, 6,000 [shekels]* [68 kilograms] *of gold.* **5:13** Hebrew *My father.* **5:22** Hebrew *1 talent* [34 kilograms]. **5:23** Hebrew *take 2 talents* [150 pounds or 68 kilograms]. **5:24** Hebrew *the Ophel.*

5:2-4 This young Israelite girl had been taken captive by armed bandits from Aram. While serving Naaman's wife, she learned about Naaman's condition. She told them about the Lord's healing power through the prophet Elisha. This was a bold move from this captive young woman! Her desire to help those who had wronged her reveals a life of courage and kindness. Because she spoke up, Naaman would experience God's healing power. God's healing of Naaman shows how God cares for all people, even those who are outside Israel. We can see how God was working out his plan to save the whole world through Israel in moments like these long before Jesus' full revelation.

The Enslaved Girl IN NAAMAN'S HOUSEHOLD

IDENTITY

Small Acts Change Everything

She was an enslaved girl, captured by Syrians who invaded her country. Now she served the commander's wife. The commander, a powerful man, had leprosy, and while it would have been easy to hate him for what he had done to her people and to her, this young woman felt compassion for him.

She knew a secret: She knew that Elisha, the prophet of the Lord God Almighty, could heal the commander. But should she tell the commander? Would he listen to her?

This young, enslaved girl boldly told Naaman's wife, who then told Naaman, who followed her advice to visit Elisha. The commander returned home a fully healed person.

This young girl dared to offer God's healing to the enemy army commander. By this small act of compassion, she changed this powerful leader, bringing him to faith in the God of Israel.

We don't even know her name, but we remember her compassion, her trust in God. And her lasting impact.

THE ENSLAVED GIRL'S STORY IS TOLD IN 2 KINGS 5:1-19.

> Even small acts of love change everything.

IDENTIFY

Has the Lord ever challenged you to pray for your "enemy," someone who has wronged you in some way? How did you respond?

Are there people you disagree with that you may need to reach out to with compassion?

How do you respond when you feel you don't have any power, position, or voice to make a change?

"When I took on a new leadership role at work, I became aware of inter-departmental tensions that directly affected my ability to function. Rather than being angry at those who seemed to be the roadblock, I learned to listen deeply. I kept asking questions until we found common ground. Together we found solutions that worked for all."

ELIZABETH GLANVILLE, PhD, is retired faculty from Fuller Theological Seminary, School of Mission and Theology. She is an international teacher on missions and leadership and chaplain for a local police department and her retirement community.

descendants will suffer from Naaman's leprosy forever." When Gehazi left the room, he was covered with leprosy; his skin was white as snow.

The Floating Ax Head

6 One day the group of prophets came to Elisha and told him, "As you can see, this place where we meet with you is too small. ²Let's go down to the Jordan River, where there are plenty of logs. There we can build a new place for us to meet."

"All right," he told them, "go ahead."

³"Please come with us," someone suggested.

"I will," he said. ⁴So he went with them.

When they arrived at the Jordan, they began cutting down trees. ⁵But as one of them was cutting a tree, his ax head fell into the river. "Oh, sir!" he cried. "It was a borrowed ax!"

⁶"Where did it fall?" the man of God asked. When he showed him the place, Elisha cut a stick and threw it into the water at that spot. Then the ax head floated to the surface. ⁷"Grab it," Elisha said. And the man reached out and grabbed it.

Elisha Traps the Arameans

⁸When the king of Aram was at war with Israel, he would confer with his officers and say, "We will mobilize our forces at such and such a place."

⁹But immediately Elisha, the man of God, would warn the king of Israel, "Do not go near that place, for the Arameans are planning to mobilize their troops there." ¹⁰So the king of Israel would send word to the place indicated by the man of God. Time and again Elisha warned the king, so that he would be on the alert there.

¹¹The king of Aram became very upset over this. He called his officers together and demanded, "Which of you is the traitor? Who has been informing the king of Israel of my plans?"

¹²"It's not us, my lord the king," one of the officers replied. "Elisha, the prophet in Israel, tells the king of Israel even the words you speak in the privacy of your bedroom!"

¹³"Go and find out where he is," the king commanded, "so I can send troops to seize him."

And the report came back: "Elisha is at Dothan." ¹⁴So one night the king of Aram sent a great army with many chariots and horses to surround the city.

¹⁵When the servant of the man of God got up early the next morning and went outside, there were troops, horses, and chariots everywhere. "Oh, sir, what will we do now?" the young man cried to Elisha.

¹⁶"Don't be afraid!" Elisha told him. "For there are more on our side than on theirs!" ¹⁷Then Elisha prayed, "O LORD, open his eyes and let him see!" The LORD opened the young man's eyes, and when he looked up, he saw that the hillside around Elisha was filled with horses and chariots of fire.

¹⁸As the Aramean army advanced toward him, Elisha prayed, "O LORD, please make them blind." So the LORD struck them with blindness as Elisha had asked.

¹⁹Then Elisha went out and told them, "You have come the wrong way! This isn't the right city! Follow me, and I will take you to the man you are looking for." And he led them to the city of Samaria.

²⁰As soon as they had entered Samaria, Elisha prayed, "O LORD, now open their eyes and let them see." So the LORD opened their eyes, and they discovered that they were in the middle of Samaria.

²¹When the king of Israel saw them, he shouted to Elisha, "My father, should I kill them? Should I kill them?"

²²"Of course not!" Elisha replied. "Do we kill prisoners of war? Give them food and drink and send them home again to their master."

²³So the king made a great feast for them and then sent them home to their master. After that, the Aramean raiders stayed away from the land of Israel.

Ben-Hadad Besieges Samaria

²⁴Some time later, however, King Ben-hadad of Aram mustered his entire army and besieged Samaria. ²⁵As a result, there was a great famine in the city. The siege lasted so long that a donkey's head sold for eighty pieces of silver, and a cup of dove's dung sold for five pieces* of silver.

²⁶One day as the king of Israel was walking along the wall of the city, a woman called to him, "Please help me, my lord the king!"

²⁷He answered, "If the LORD doesn't help you, what can I do? I have neither food from the threshing floor nor wine from the press to give you." ²⁸But then the king asked, "What is the matter?"

She replied, "This woman said to me: 'Come on, let's eat your son today, then we will eat my son tomorrow.' ²⁹So we cooked my son and ate him. Then the next day I said to her, 'Kill your son so we can eat him,' but she has hidden her son."

³⁰When the king heard this, he tore his clothes in despair. And as the king walked along the wall, the people could see that he was wearing burlap under his robe next to his skin. ³¹"May God strike me and even kill me if I don't separate Elisha's head from his shoulders this very day," the king vowed.

³²Elisha was sitting in his house with the elders of Israel when the king sent a messenger to summon him. But before the messenger arrived, Elisha said to the elders, "A murderer has sent a man to cut off my head. When he arrives, shut the door and keep him out. We will soon hear his master's steps following him."

6:25 Hebrew *sold for 80 [shekels]* [2 pounds or 0.9 kilograms] *of silver, and ¼ of a cab* [0.3 liters] *of dove's dung sold for 5 [shekels]* [2 ounces or 57 grams]. *Dove's dung* may be a variety of wild vegetable.

33 While Elisha was still saying this, the messenger arrived. And the king* said, "All this misery is from the LORD! Why should I wait for the LORD any longer?"

7 Elisha replied, "Listen to this message from the LORD! This is what the LORD says: By this time tomorrow in the markets of Samaria, six quarts of choice flour will cost only one piece of silver,* and twelve quarts of barley grain will cost only one piece of silver.*"

2 The officer assisting the king said to the man of God, "That couldn't happen even if the LORD opened the windows of heaven!"

But Elisha replied, "You will see it happen with your own eyes, but you won't be able to eat any of it!"

Outcasts Visit the Enemy Camp

3 Now there were four men with leprosy* sitting at the entrance of the city gates. "Why should we sit here waiting to die?" they asked each other. 4 "We will starve if we stay here, but with the famine in the city, we will starve if we go back there. So we might as well go out and surrender to the Aramean army. If they let us live, so much the better. But if they kill us, we would have died anyway."

5 So at twilight they set out for the camp of the Arameans. But when they came to the edge of the camp, no one was there! 6 For the Lord had caused the Aramean army to hear the clatter of speeding chariots and the galloping of horses and the sounds of a great army approaching. "The king of Israel has hired the Hittites and Egyptians* to attack us!" they cried to one another. 7 So they panicked and ran into the night, abandoning their tents, horses, donkeys, and everything else, as they fled for their lives.

8 When the men with leprosy arrived at the edge of the camp, they went into one tent after another, eating and drinking wine; and they carried off silver and gold and clothing and hid it. 9 Finally, they said to each other, "This is not right. This is a day of good news, and we aren't sharing it with anyone! If we wait until morning, some calamity will certainly fall upon us. Come on, let's go back and tell the people at the palace."

10 So they went back to the city and told the gatekeepers what had happened. "We went out to the Aramean camp," they said, "and no one was there! The horses and donkeys were tethered and the tents were all in order, but there wasn't a single person around!" 11 Then the gatekeepers shouted the news to the people in the palace.

Israel Plunders the Camp

12 The king got out of bed in the middle of the night and told his officers, "I know what has happened. The Arameans know we are starving, so they have left their camp and have hidden in the fields. They are expecting us to leave the city, and then they will take us alive and capture the city."

13 One of his officers replied, "We had better send out scouts to check into this. Let them take five of the remaining horses. If something happens to them, it will be no worse than if they stay here and die with the rest of us."

14 So two chariots with horses were prepared, and the king sent scouts to see what had happened to the Aramean army. 15 They went all the way to the Jordan River, following a trail of clothing and equipment that the Arameans had thrown away in their mad rush to escape. The scouts returned and told the king about it. 16 Then the people of Samaria rushed out and plundered the Aramean camp. So it was true that six quarts of choice flour were sold that day for one piece of silver, and twelve quarts of barley grain were sold for one piece of silver, just as the LORD had promised. 17 The king appointed his officer to control the traffic at the gate, but he was knocked down and trampled to death as the people rushed out.

So everything happened exactly as the man of God had predicted when the king came to his house. 18 The man of God had said to the king, "By this time tomorrow in the markets of Samaria, six quarts of choice flour will cost one piece of silver, and twelve quarts of barley grain will cost one piece of silver."

19 The king's officer had replied, "That couldn't happen even if the LORD opened the windows of heaven!" And the man of God had said, "You will see it happen with your own eyes, but you won't be able to eat any of it!" 20 And so it was, for the people trampled him to death at the gate!

The Woman from Shunem Returns Home

8 Elisha had told the woman whose son he had brought back to life, "Take your family and move to some other place, for the LORD has called for a famine on Israel that will last for seven years." 2 So the woman did as the man of God instructed. She took her family and settled in the land of the Philistines for seven years.

3 After the famine ended she returned from the land of the Philistines, and she went to see the king about getting back her house and land. 4 As she came in, the king was talking with Gehazi, the servant of the man of God. The king had just said, "Tell me some stories about the great things Elisha has done." 5 And Gehazi was telling the king about the time Elisha had brought a boy back to life. At that very moment, the mother of the boy walked in to make her appeal to the king about her house and land.

6:33 Hebrew *he*. 7:1a Hebrew *1 seah* [7.3 liters] *of choice flour will cost 1 shekel* [0.4 ounces or 11 grams]; also in 7:16, 18.
7:1b Hebrew *2 seahs* [14.6 liters] *of barley grain will cost 1 shekel* [0.4 ounces or 11 grams]; also in 7:16, 18. 7:3 Or *with a contagious skin disease*. The Hebrew word used here and throughout this passage can describe various skin diseases.
7:6 Possibly *and the people of Muzur*, a district near Cilicia.

"Look, my lord the king!" Gehazi exclaimed. "Here is the woman now, and this is her son—the very one Elisha brought back to life!"

⁶"Is this true?" the king asked her. And she told him the story. So he directed one of his officials to see that everything she had lost was restored to her, including the value of any crops that had been harvested during her absence.

Hazael Murders Ben-Hadad

⁷Elisha went to Damascus, the capital of Aram, where King Ben-hadad lay sick. When someone told the king that the man of God had come, ⁸the king said to Hazael, "Take a gift to the man of God. Then tell him to ask the LORD, 'Will I recover from this illness?'"

⁹So Hazael loaded down forty camels with the finest products of Damascus as a gift for Elisha. He went to him and said, "Your servant Ben-hadad, the king of Aram, has sent me to ask, 'Will I recover from this illness?'"

¹⁰And Elisha replied, "Go and tell him, 'You will surely recover.' But actually the LORD has shown me that he will surely die!" ¹¹Elisha stared at Hazael* with a fixed gaze until Hazael became uneasy.* Then the man of God started weeping.

¹²"What's the matter, my lord?" Hazael asked him.

Elisha replied, "I know the terrible things you will do to the people of Israel. You will burn their fortified cities, kill their young men with the sword, dash their little children to the ground, and rip open their pregnant women!"

¹³Hazael responded, "How could a nobody like me* ever accomplish such great things?"

Elisha answered, "The LORD has shown me that you are going to be the king of Aram."

¹⁴When Hazael left Elisha and went back, the king asked him, "What did Elisha tell you?"

And Hazael replied, "He told me that you will surely recover."

¹⁵But the next day Hazael took a blanket, soaked it in water, and held it over the king's face until he died. Then Hazael became the next king of Aram.

Jehoram Rules in Judah

¹⁶Jehoram son of King Jehoshaphat of Judah began to rule over Judah in the fifth year of the reign of Joram son of Ahab, king of Israel. ¹⁷Jehoram was thirty-two years old when he became king, and he reigned in Jerusalem eight years. ¹⁸But Jehoram followed the example of the kings of Israel and was as wicked as King Ahab, for he had married one of Ahab's daughters. So Jehoram did what was evil in the LORD's sight. ¹⁹But the LORD did not want to destroy Judah, for he had promised his servant David that his descendants would continue to rule, shining like a lamp forever.

²⁰During Jehoram's reign, the Edomites revolted against Judah and crowned their own king. ²¹So Jehoram* went with all his chariots to attack the town of Zair.* The Edomites surrounded him and his chariot commanders, but he went out at night and attacked them* under cover of darkness. But Jehoram's army deserted him and fled to their homes. ²²So Edom has been independent from Judah to this day. The town of Libnah also revolted about that same time.

²³The rest of the events in Jehoram's reign and everything he did are recorded in The Book of the History of the Kings of Judah. ²⁴When Jehoram died, he was buried with his ancestors in the City of David. Then his son Ahaziah became the next king.

Ahaziah Rules in Judah

²⁵Ahaziah son of Jehoram began to rule over Judah in the twelfth year of the reign of Joram son of Ahab, king of Israel.

²⁶Ahaziah was twenty-two years old when he became king, and he reigned in Jerusalem one year. His mother was Athaliah, a granddaughter of King Omri of Israel. ²⁷Ahaziah followed the evil example of King Ahab's family. He did what was evil in the LORD's sight, just as Ahab's family had done, for he was related by marriage to the family of Ahab.

²⁸Ahaziah joined Joram son of Ahab in his war against King Hazael of Aram at Ramoth-gilead. When the Arameans wounded King Joram in the battle, ²⁹he returned to Jezreel to recover from the wounds he had received at Ramoth.* Because Joram was wounded, King Ahaziah of Judah went to Jezreel to visit him.

Jehu Anointed King of Israel

9 Meanwhile, Elisha the prophet had summoned a member of the group of prophets. "Get ready to travel,"* he told him, "and take this flask of olive oil with you. Go to Ramoth-gilead, ²and find Jehu son of Jehoshaphat, son of Nimshi. Call him into a private room away from his friends, ³and pour the oil over his head. Say to him, 'This is what the LORD says: I anoint you to be the king over Israel.' Then open the door and run for your life!"

8:11a Hebrew *He stared at him.* **8:11b** The meaning of the Hebrew is uncertain. **8:13** Hebrew *a dog.* **8:21a** Hebrew *Joram,* a variant spelling of Jehoram; also in 8:23, 24. **8:21b** Greek version reads *Seir.* **8:21c** Or *he went out and escaped.* The meaning of the Hebrew is uncertain. **8:29** Hebrew *Ramah,* a variant spelling of Ramoth. **9:1** Hebrew *Bind up your loins.*

8:26-27 Ahaziah was only twenty-two years old when he began his short reign as king of Judah. His mother was Athaliah, who was a descendant of Omri and daughter of Ahab. Through her, Ahaziah was related to two of Israel's most evil kings. Overall, Judah had kings who perpetuated less evil than Israel, but Ahaziah followed the example of his family and did not follow the Lord.

The Woman from Shunem

IDENTITY

Dare to Desire

"Please! Join us for a meal," she urged, knowing a good meal is always appreciated. He accepted, which led to many more meals and even a place to stay. She was a wealthy woman, and so she provided for Elisha out of her abundance. She didn't need him to return the favor.

When in gratitude, Elisha told the woman from Shunem she'd soon have a child, the hidden, anguished cry of her heart unveiled: "No! Don't get my hopes up!" Being a mother was the one identity she longed for, the one she'd been denied.

Sometimes life doesn't rise to our expectations. We think we've come to terms with it until something stirs up the ashes of our hope. Then how do we respond? Embrace possibility—or stay within the safety of what we can control?

Later, when faced with the unthinkable loss of her cherished son, her identity as a mother, and her family's hope for the future, she did not quietly acquiesce. Ignoring the facts, she ran straight to Elisha, through whom God had proven himself to be bigger than facts. As her identity in God had grown, so had her confidence that God would keep his word. Possibility is worth embracing!

Still, God wasn't through; he also provided out of abundance. As this brave woman walked through each day, God prepared her for each tomorrow, putting in place everything she'd need. He does the same for us—and where we end up will always be a story worth telling.

> When we put our identity in God, we become more.

THE WOMAN FROM SHUNEM'S STORY IS TOLD IN 2 KINGS 4:8-37; 8:1-6.

IDENTIFY

Is there an identity you've longed for that remains elusive, or one you've lost and long to regain?

How might God be drawing you toward rekindled hope?

"I've been there—afraid to get my hopes up, preferring to stay in my safety zone. Crushing disappointment left me unsure of who I was, afraid to trust God and embrace possibility. But when I grabbed his hand and followed, he opened doors I'd never imagined."

JANICE MAYO MATHERS is author of multiple books and Bible studies, including *Every Season: Embracing a Forever Kind of Purpose* (Stonecroft) and *Mothers-in-Law vs. Daughters-in-Law: Let There Be Peace*. She helps women see adverse circumstances as godly challenges.

⁴So the young prophet did as he was told and went to Ramoth-gilead. ⁵When he arrived there, he found Jehu sitting around with the other army officers. "I have a message for you, Commander," he said.

"For which one of us?" Jehu asked.

"For you, Commander," he replied.

⁶So Jehu left the others and went into the house. Then the young prophet poured the oil over Jehu's head and said, "This is what the LORD, the God of Israel, says: I anoint you king over the LORD's people, Israel. ⁷You are to destroy the family of Ahab, your master. In this way, I will avenge the murder of my prophets and all the LORD's servants who were killed by Jezebel. ⁸The entire family of Ahab must be wiped out. I will destroy every one of his male descendants, slave and free alike, anywhere in Israel. ⁹I will destroy the family of Ahab as I destroyed the families of Jeroboam son of Nebat and of Baasha son of Ahijah. ¹⁰Dogs will eat Ahab's wife Jezebel at the plot of land in Jezreel, and no one will bury her." Then the young prophet opened the door and ran.

¹¹Jehu went back to his fellow officers, and one of them asked him, "What did that madman want? Is everything all right?"

"You know how a man like that babbles on," Jehu replied.

¹²"You're hiding something," they said. "Tell us."

So Jehu told them, "He said to me, 'This is what the LORD says: I have anointed you to be king over Israel.'"

¹³Then they quickly spread out their cloaks on the bare steps and blew the ram's horn, shouting, "Jehu is king!"

Jehu Kills Joram and Ahaziah

¹⁴So Jehu son of Jehoshaphat, son of Nimshi, led a conspiracy against King Joram. (Now Joram had been with the army at Ramoth-gilead, defending Israel against the forces of King Hazael of Aram. ¹⁵But King Joram* was wounded in the fighting and returned to Jezreel to recover from his wounds.) So Jehu told the men with him, "If you want me to be king, don't let anyone leave town and go to Jezreel to report what we have done."

¹⁶Then Jehu got into a chariot and rode to Jezreel to find King Joram, who was lying there wounded. King Ahaziah of Judah was there, too, for he had gone to visit him. ¹⁷The watchman on the tower of Jezreel saw Jehu and his company approaching, so he shouted to Joram, "I see a company of troops coming!"

"Send out a rider to ask if they are coming in peace," King Joram ordered.

¹⁸So a horseman went out to meet Jehu and said, "The king wants to know if you are coming in peace."

Jehu replied, "What do you know about peace? Fall in behind me!"

The watchman called out to the king, "The messenger has met them, but he's not returning."

¹⁹So the king sent out a second horseman. He rode up to them and said, "The king wants to know if you come in peace."

Again Jehu answered, "What do you know about peace? Fall in behind me!"

²⁰The watchman exclaimed, "The messenger has met them, but he isn't returning either! It must be Jehu son of Nimshi, for he's driving like a madman."

²¹"Quick! Get my chariot ready!" King Joram commanded.

Then King Joram of Israel and King Ahaziah of Judah rode out in their chariots to meet Jehu. They met him at the plot of land that had belonged to Naboth of Jezreel. ²²King Joram demanded, "Do you come in peace, Jehu?"

Jehu replied, "How can there be peace as long as the idolatry and witchcraft of your mother, Jezebel, are all around us?"

²³Then King Joram turned the horses around* and fled, shouting to King Ahaziah, "Treason, Ahaziah!" ²⁴But Jehu drew his bow and shot Joram between the shoulders. The arrow pierced his heart, and he sank down dead in his chariot.

²⁵Jehu said to Bidkar, his officer, "Throw him into the plot of land that belonged to Naboth of Jezreel. Do you remember when you and I were riding along behind his father, Ahab? The LORD pronounced this message against him: ²⁶'I solemnly swear that I will repay him here on this plot of land, says the LORD, for the murder of Naboth and his sons that I saw yesterday.' So throw him out on Naboth's property, just as the LORD said."

²⁷When King Ahaziah of Judah saw what was happening, he fled along the road to Beth-haggan. Jehu rode after him, shouting, "Shoot him, too!" So they shot Ahaziah* in his chariot at the Ascent of Gur, near Ibleam. He was able to go on as far as Megiddo, but he died there. ²⁸His servants took him by chariot to Jerusalem, where they buried him with his ancestors in the City of David. ²⁹Ahaziah had become king over Judah in the eleventh year of the reign of Joram son of Ahab.

The Death of Jezebel

³⁰When Jezebel, the queen mother, heard that Jehu had come to Jezreel, she painted her eyelids and fixed her hair and sat at a window. ³¹When Jehu entered the gate of the palace, she shouted at him, "Have you come in peace, you murderer? You're just like Zimri, who murdered his master!"*

9:15 Hebrew *Jehoram*, a variant spelling of Joram; also in 9:17, 21, 22, 23, 24. **9:23** Hebrew *turned his hands.* **9:27** As in Greek and Syriac versions; Hebrew lacks *So they shot Ahaziah.* **9:31** See 1 Kgs 16:9-10, where Zimri killed his master, King Elah.

9:30-37 Jezebel was cruel and ruthless, murdering the Lord's prophets and people (1 Kings 18:1–19:2; 21:1-14). But wealth and power did not save her from a terrible fate. After her death, all that remained of her body were her skull, feet, and hands. There was nothing left of her to bury. Her fate was one of disgrace because of her open disdain for the Lord, his prophets, and his law.

³²Jehu looked up and saw her at the window and shouted, "Who is on my side?" And two or three eunuchs looked out at him. ³³"Throw her down!" Jehu yelled. So they threw her out the window, and her blood spattered against the wall and on the horses. And Jehu trampled her body under his horses' hooves.

³⁴Then Jehu went into the palace and ate and drank. Afterward he said, "Someone go and bury this cursed woman, for she is the daughter of a king." ³⁵But when they went out to bury her, they found only her skull, her feet, and her hands.

³⁶When they returned and told Jehu, he stated, "This fulfills the message from the LORD, which he spoke through his servant Elijah from Tishbe: 'At the plot of land in Jezreel, dogs will eat Jezebel's body. ³⁷Her remains will be scattered like dung on the plot of land in Jezreel, so that no one will be able to recognize her.'"

Jehu Kills Ahab's Family

10 Ahab had seventy sons living in the city of Samaria. So Jehu wrote letters and sent them to Samaria, to the elders and officials of the city,* and to the guardians of King Ahab's sons. He said, ²"The king's sons are with you, and you have at your disposal chariots, horses, a fortified city, and weapons. As soon as you receive this letter, ³select the best qualified of your master's sons to be your king, and prepare to fight for Ahab's dynasty."

⁴But they were paralyzed with fear and said, "We've seen that two kings couldn't stand against this man! What can we do?"

⁵So the palace and city administrators, together with the elders and the guardians of the king's sons, sent this message to Jehu: "We are your servants and will do anything you tell us. We will not make anyone king; do whatever you think is best."

⁶Jehu responded with a second letter: "If you are on my side and are going to obey me, bring the heads of your master's sons to me at Jezreel by this time tomorrow." Now the seventy sons of the king were being cared for by the leaders of Samaria, where they had been raised since childhood. ⁷When the letter arrived, the leaders killed all seventy of the king's sons. They placed their heads in baskets and presented them to Jehu at Jezreel.

⁸A messenger went to Jehu and said, "They have brought the heads of the king's sons."

So Jehu ordered, "Pile them in two heaps at the entrance of the city gate, and leave them there until morning."

⁹In the morning he went out and spoke to the crowd that had gathered around them. "You are not to blame," he told them. "I am the one who conspired against my master and killed him. But who killed all these? ¹⁰You can be sure that the message of the LORD that was spoken concerning Ahab's family will not fail. The LORD declared through his servant Elijah that this would happen." ¹¹Then Jehu killed all who were left of Ahab's relatives living in Jezreel and all his important officials, his personal friends, and his priests. So Ahab was left without a single survivor.

¹²Then Jehu set out for Samaria. Along the way, while he was at Beth-eked of the Shepherds, ¹³he met some relatives of King Ahaziah of Judah. "Who are you?" he asked them.

And they replied, "We are relatives of King Ahaziah. We are going to visit the sons of King Ahab and the sons of the queen mother."

¹⁴"Take them alive!" Jehu shouted to his men. And they captured all forty-two of them and killed them at the well of Beth-eked. None of them escaped.

¹⁵When Jehu left there, he met Jehonadab son of Recab, who was coming to meet him. After they had greeted each other, Jehu said to him, "Are you as loyal to me as I am to you?"

"Yes, I am," Jehonadab replied.

"If you are," Jehu said, "then give me your hand." So Jehonadab put out his hand, and Jehu helped him into the chariot. ¹⁶Then Jehu said, "Now come with me, and see how devoted I am to the LORD." So Jehonadab rode along with him.

¹⁷When Jehu arrived in Samaria, he killed everyone who was left there from Ahab's family, just as the LORD had promised through Elijah.

Jehu Kills the Priests of Baal

¹⁸Then Jehu called a meeting of all the people of the city and said to them, "Ahab's worship of Baal was nothing compared to the way I will worship him! ¹⁹Therefore, summon all the prophets and worshipers of Baal, and call together all his priests. See to it that every one of them comes, for I am going to offer a great sacrifice to Baal. Anyone who fails to come will be put to death." But Jehu's cunning plan was to destroy all the worshipers of Baal.

²⁰Then Jehu ordered, "Prepare a solemn assembly to worship Baal!" So they did. ²¹He sent messengers throughout all Israel summoning those who worshiped Baal. They all came—not a single one remained behind—and they filled the temple of Baal from one end to the other. ²²And Jehu instructed the keeper of the wardrobe, "Be sure that every worshiper of Baal wears one of these robes." So robes were given to them.

²³Then Jehu went into the temple of Baal with Jehonadab son of Recab. Jehu said to the worshipers of Baal, "Make sure no one who worships the LORD is here—only those who worship Baal." ²⁴So they were all inside the temple to offer sacrifices and burnt offerings. Now Jehu had stationed eighty of his men outside the building and had warned them, "If you let anyone escape, you will pay for it with your own life."

10:1 As in some Greek manuscripts and Latin Vulgate (see also 10:6); Hebrew reads *of Jezreel*.

²⁵As soon as Jehu had finished sacrificing the burnt offering, he commanded his guards and officers, "Go in and kill all of them. Don't let a single one escape!" So they killed them all with their swords, and the guards and officers dragged their bodies outside.* Then Jehu's men went into the innermost fortress* of the temple of Baal. ²⁶They dragged out the sacred pillar* used in the worship of Baal and burned it. ²⁷They smashed the sacred pillar and wrecked the temple of Baal, converting it into a public toilet, as it remains to this day.

²⁸In this way, Jehu destroyed every trace of Baal worship from Israel. ²⁹He did not, however, destroy the gold calves at Bethel and Dan, with which Jeroboam son of Nebat had caused Israel to sin.

³⁰Nonetheless the LORD said to Jehu, "You have done well in following my instructions to destroy the family of Ahab. Therefore, your descendants will be kings of Israel down to the fourth generation." ³¹But Jehu did not obey the Law of the LORD, the God of Israel, with all his heart. He refused to turn from the sins that Jeroboam had led Israel to commit.

The Death of Jehu

³²At about that time the LORD began to cut down the size of Israel's territory. King Hazael conquered several sections of the country ³³east of the Jordan River, including all of Gilead, Gad, Reuben, and Manasseh. He conquered the area from the town of Aroer by the Arnon Gorge to as far north as Gilead and Bashan.

³⁴The rest of the events in Jehu's reign—everything he did and all his achievements—are recorded in The Book of the History of the Kings of Israel.

³⁵When Jehu died, he was buried in Samaria. Then his son Jehoahaz became the next king. ³⁶In all, Jehu reigned over Israel from Samaria for twenty-eight years.

Queen Athaliah Rules in Judah

11 When Athaliah, the mother of King Ahaziah of Judah, learned that her son was dead, she began to destroy the rest of the royal family. ²But Ahaziah's sister Jehosheba, the daughter of King Jehoram,* took Ahaziah's infant son, Joash, and stole him away from among the rest of the king's children, who were about to be killed. She put Joash and his nurse in a bedroom, and they hid him from Athaliah, so the child was not murdered. ³Joash remained hidden in the Temple of the LORD for six years while Athaliah ruled over the land.

Revolt against Athaliah

⁴In the seventh year of Athaliah's reign, Jehoiada the priest summoned the commanders, the Carite mercenaries, and the palace guards to come to the Temple of the LORD. He made a solemn pact with them and made them swear an oath of loyalty there in the LORD's Temple; then he showed them the king's son.

⁵Jehoiada told them, "This is what you must do. A third of you who are on duty on the Sabbath are to guard the royal palace itself. ⁶Another third of you are to stand guard at the Sur Gate. And the final third must stand guard behind the palace guard. These three groups will all guard the palace. ⁷The other two units who are off duty on the Sabbath must stand guard for the king at the LORD's Temple. ⁸Form a bodyguard around the king and keep your weapons in hand. Kill anyone who tries to break through. Stay with the king wherever he goes."

⁹So the commanders did everything as Jehoiada the priest ordered. The commanders took charge of the men reporting for duty that Sabbath, as well as those who were going off duty. They brought them all to Jehoiada the priest, ¹⁰and he supplied them with the spears and small shields that had once belonged to King David and were stored in the Temple of the LORD. ¹¹The palace guards stationed themselves around the king, with their weapons ready. They formed a line from the south side of the Temple around to the north side and all around the altar.

¹²Then Jehoiada brought out Joash, the king's son, placed the crown on his head, and presented him with a copy of God's laws.* They anointed him and proclaimed him king, and everyone clapped their hands and shouted, "Long live the king!"

The Death of Athaliah

¹³When Athaliah heard the noise made by the palace guards and the people, she hurried to the LORD's Temple to see what was happening. ¹⁴When

---

10:25a Or *and they left their bodies lying there;* or *and they threw them out into the outermost court.* **10:25b** Hebrew *city.* **10:26** As in Greek and Syriac versions and Latin Vulgate; Hebrew reads *sacred pillars.* **11:2** Hebrew *Joram,* a variant spelling of Jehoram. **11:12** Or *a copy of the covenant.*

11:1 Athaliah seized power after her son's death and sought to destroy the royal family. She would reign over Judah for six years. Because she was from the line of Omri, her rule was not legitimate. The text never calls her a queen and does not summarize her reign, as it does for the authorized rulers (see 10:34-36; 12:19-21). She was a ruthless ruler.

11:2-21 To protect Joash, son of Ahaziah, Jehosheba carried him away because the royal princes were about to be killed. She took Joash to the Temple for safety. There, he was hidden for six years and raised by his wet nurse. Jehoida the priest initiated the plan to place Joash on the throne and overthrow Athaliah. Joash was in the line of David and the rightful heir to the throne. Even though she is unnamed and only briefly mentioned, the wet nurse took care of this child, risking her life in secrecy for six years. This brief notation of this woman is a reminder that God notices our sacrifices and sees us, even when we or our deeds are hidden from the world's view.

she arrived, she saw the newly crowned king standing in his place of authority by the pillar, as was the custom at times of coronation. The commanders and trumpeters were surrounding him, and people from all over the land were rejoicing and blowing trumpets. When Athaliah saw all this, she tore her clothes in despair and shouted, "Treason! Treason!"

¹⁵Then Jehoiada the priest ordered the commanders who were in charge of the troops, "Take her to the soldiers in front of the Temple,* and kill anyone who tries to rescue her." For the priest had said, "She must not be killed in the Temple of the LORD." ¹⁶So they seized her and led her out to the gate where horses enter the palace grounds, and she was killed there.

Jehoiada's Religious Reforms

¹⁷Then Jehoiada made a covenant between the LORD and the king and the people that they would be the LORD's people. He also made a covenant between the king and the people. ¹⁸And all the people of the land went over to the temple of Baal and tore it down. They demolished the altars and smashed the idols to pieces, and they killed Mattan the priest of Baal in front of the altars.

Jehoiada the priest stationed guards at the Temple of the LORD. ¹⁹Then the commanders, the Carite mercenaries, the palace guards, and all the people of the land escorted the king from the Temple of the LORD. They went through the gate of the guards and into the palace, and the king took his seat on the royal throne. ²⁰So all the people of the land rejoiced, and the city was peaceful because Athaliah had been killed at the king's palace.

²¹*Joash* was seven years old when he became king.

Joash Repairs the Temple

12 ¹*Joash* began to rule over Judah in the seventh year of King Jehu's reign in Israel. He reigned in Jerusalem forty years. His mother was Zibiah from Beersheba. ²All his life Joash did what was pleasing in the LORD's sight because Jehoiada the priest instructed him. ³Yet even so, he did not

---

11:15 Or *Bring her out from between the ranks;* or *Take her out of the Temple precincts.* The meaning of the Hebrew is uncertain. 11:21a Verse 11:21 is numbered 12:1 in Hebrew text. 11:21b Hebrew *Jehoash,* a variant spelling of Joash. 12:1a Verses 12:1-21 are numbered 12:2-22 in Hebrew text. 12:1b Hebrew *Jehoash,* a variant spelling of Joash; also in 12:2, 4, 6, 7, 18.

12:1-3 Joash is commended for living obediently for God and doing what was "pleasing" in God's sight. The priest Jehoiada, and Joash's mother, Zibiah, were instrumental in his ability to rule wisely at such a young age. Wise counselors matter, especially for those leading in places of power. During his reign, Joash collected money and began the vital task of repairing the Temple.

Perspective

What makes one woman choose evil and another good?

SCRIPTURE CONNECTION: 2 KINGS 11:1-3

Scripture records a tale of two women—one a killer, the other a rescuer. Juxtaposed forever in history, the two alternately confound or inspire us.

Descended from Baal worshipers, Athaliah was King Ahab's daughter who went on to marry the king of Judah. During her time as queen and then as queen mother, she used her influence for evil. After her son's death, Athaliah brutally consolidated power, killing her own grandchildren so she could rule. Although she was the only woman to rule Judah, Athaliah left the wrong kind of legacy, a legacy of evil and one of destruction.

Enter Jehosheba. In contrast to the wicked queen, Jehosheba heroically undermined Athaliah's plans. The rightful heir to the throne and future ancestor of Jesus, our rightful King, was saved, and Jehosheba's bravery restored David's line to the throne of Judah.

A woman with evil intentions may succeed for a time on earth, but she cannot fully thwart God's will for his people. A woman who chooses what is right can rely on God's power to succeed. Whether we choose good or evil is often motivated by our attitude toward and relationship with God.

VIEWPOINTS

HERS: *What moved Jehosheba to risk her life and oppose the rule of evil?*
MINE: "There are times I feel uncertain I have what it takes to rise in a critical moment. And then I remember that God will empower me, just as he does in the smaller battles that seem too big for me today."
YOURS: *Do you face a battle against oppression? What strategy could you employ today?*

MISTY ARTERBURN is an author and speaker, contributing to Bible projects, devotionals, and recovery materials for over twenty years. Wife and mom to five, Misty is the founder of Recovery Girls and the general editor of *The One Year Bible for Women.*

destroy the pagan shrines, and the people still offered sacrifices and burned incense there.

⁴One day King Joash said to the priests, "Collect all the money brought as a sacred offering to the LORD's Temple, whether it is a regular assessment, a payment of vows, or a voluntary gift. ⁵Let the priests take some of that money to pay for whatever repairs are needed at the Temple."

⁶But by the twenty-third year of Joash's reign, the priests still had not repaired the Temple. ⁷So King Joash called for Jehoiada and the other priests and asked them, "Why haven't you repaired the Temple? Don't use any more money for your own needs. From now on, it must all be spent on Temple repairs." ⁸So the priests agreed not to accept any more money from the people, and they also agreed to let others take responsibility for repairing the Temple.

⁹Then Jehoiada the priest bored a hole in the lid of a large chest and set it on the right-hand side of the altar at the entrance of the Temple of the LORD. The priests guarding the entrance put all of the people's contributions into the chest. ¹⁰Whenever the chest became full, the court secretary and the high priest counted the money that had been brought to the LORD's Temple and put it into bags. ¹¹Then they gave the money to the construction supervisors, who used it to pay the people working on the LORD's Temple—the carpenters, the builders, ¹²the masons, and the stonecutters. They also used the money to buy the timber and the finished stone needed for repairing the LORD's Temple, and they paid any other expenses related to the Temple's restoration.

¹³The money brought to the Temple was not used for making silver bowls, lamp snuffers, basins, trumpets, or other articles of gold or silver for the Temple of the LORD. ¹⁴It was paid to the workmen, who used it for the Temple repairs. ¹⁵No accounting of this money was required from the construction supervisors, because they were honest and trustworthy men. ¹⁶However, the money that was contributed for guilt offerings and sin offerings was not brought into the LORD's Temple. It was given to the priests for their own use.

The End of Joash's Reign

¹⁷About this time King Hazael of Aram went to war against Gath and captured it. Then he turned to attack Jerusalem. ¹⁸King Joash collected all the sacred objects that Jehoshaphat, Jehoram, and Ahaziah, the previous kings of Judah, had dedicated, along with what he himself had dedicated. He sent them all to Hazael, along with all the gold in the treasuries of the LORD's Temple and the royal palace. So Hazael called off his attack on Jerusalem.

¹⁹The rest of the events in Joash's reign and everything he did are recorded in The Book of the History of the Kings of Judah.

²⁰Joash's officers plotted against him and assassinated him at Beth-millo on the road to Silla. ²¹The assassins were Jozacar* son of Shimeath and Jehozabad son of Shomer—both trusted advisers. Joash was buried with his ancestors in the City of David. Then his son Amaziah became the next king.

Jehoahaz Rules in Israel

13 Jehoahaz son of Jehu began to rule over Israel in the twenty-third year of King Joash's reign in Judah. He reigned in Samaria seventeen years. ²But he did what was evil in the LORD's sight. He followed the example of Jeroboam son of Nebat, continuing the sins that Jeroboam had led Israel to commit. ³So the LORD was very angry with Israel, and he allowed King Hazael of Aram and his son Ben-hadad to defeat them repeatedly.

⁴Then Jehoahaz prayed for the LORD's help, and the LORD heard his prayer, for he could see how severely the king of Aram was oppressing Israel. ⁵So the LORD provided someone to rescue the Israelites from the tyranny of the Arameans. Then Israel lived in safety again as they had in former days.

⁶But they continued to sin, following the evil example of Jeroboam. They also allowed the Asherah pole in Samaria to remain standing. ⁷Finally, Jehoahaz's army was reduced to 50 charioteers, 10 chariots, and 10,000 foot soldiers. The king of Aram had killed the others, trampling them like dust under his feet.

⁸The rest of the events in Jehoahaz's reign—everything he did and the extent of his power—are recorded in The Book of the History of the Kings of Israel. ⁹When Jehoahaz died, he was buried in Samaria. Then his son Jehoash* became the next king.

Jehoash Rules in Israel

¹⁰Jehoash son of Jehoahaz began to rule over Israel in the thirty-seventh year of King Joash's reign in Judah. He reigned in Samaria sixteen years. ¹¹But he did what was evil in the LORD's sight. He refused to turn from the sins that Jeroboam son of Nebat had led Israel to commit.

¹²The rest of the events in Jehoash's reign and everything he did, including the extent of his power and his war with King Amaziah of Judah, are recorded in The Book of the History of the Kings of

---

12:21 As in Greek and Syriac versions; Hebrew reads *Jozabad*. **13:9** Hebrew *Joash*, a variant spelling of Jehoash; also in 13:10, 12, 13, 14, 25.

13:6 Despite God's rescue, Israel continued to sin, eventually resulting in the fall of the northern kingdom (17:21-23; see 1 Kings 14:15-16). This Asherah pole (a Canaanite fertility symbol put up by Ahab, 1 Kings 16:32-33) had apparently been spared in Jehu's purge of Baal worship (2 Kings 10:26-29).

Israel. ¹³When Jehoash died, he was buried in Samaria with the kings of Israel. Then his son Jeroboam II became the next king.

Elisha's Final Prophecy

¹⁴When Elisha was in his last illness, King Jehoash of Israel visited him and wept over him. "My father! My father! I see the chariots and charioteers of Israel!" he cried.

¹⁵Elisha told him, "Get a bow and some arrows." And the king did as he was told. ¹⁶Elisha told him, "Put your hand on the bow," and Elisha laid his own hands on the king's hands.

¹⁷Then he commanded, "Open that eastern window," and he opened it. Then he said, "Shoot!" So he shot an arrow. Elisha proclaimed, "This is the LORD's arrow, an arrow of victory over Aram, for you will completely conquer the Arameans at Aphek."

¹⁸Then he said, "Now pick up the other arrows and strike them against the ground." So the king picked them up and struck the ground three times. ¹⁹But the man of God was angry with him. "You should have struck the ground five or six times!" he exclaimed. "Then you would have beaten Aram until it was entirely destroyed. Now you will be victorious only three times."

²⁰Then Elisha died and was buried.

Groups of Moabite raiders used to invade the land each spring. ²¹Once when some Israelites were burying a man, they spied a band of these raiders. So they hastily threw the corpse into the tomb of Elisha and fled. But as soon as the body touched Elisha's bones, the dead man revived and jumped to his feet!

²²King Hazael of Aram had oppressed Israel during the entire reign of King Jehoahaz. ²³But the LORD was gracious and merciful to the people of Israel, and they were not totally destroyed. He pitied them because of his covenant with Abraham, Isaac, and Jacob. And to this day he still has not completely destroyed them or banished them from his presence.

²⁴King Hazael of Aram died, and his son Ben-hadad became the next king. ²⁵Then Jehoash son of Jehoahaz recaptured from Ben-hadad son of Hazael the towns that had been taken from Jehoash's father, Jehoahaz. Jehoash defeated Ben-hadad on three occasions, and he recovered the Israelite towns.

Amaziah Rules in Judah

14 Amaziah son of Joash began to rule over Judah in the second year of the reign of King Jehoash* of Israel. ²Amaziah was twenty-five years old when he became king, and he reigned in Jerusalem twenty-nine years. His mother was Jehoaddin from Jerusalem. ³Amaziah did what was pleasing in the LORD's sight, but not like his ancestor David. Instead, he followed the example of his father, Joash. ⁴Amaziah did not destroy the pagan shrines, and the people still offered sacrifices and burned incense there.

⁵When Amaziah was well established as king, he executed the officials who had assassinated his father. ⁶However, he did not kill the children of the assassins, for he obeyed the command of the LORD as written by Moses in the Book of the Law: "Parents must not be put to death for the sins of their children, nor children for the sins of their parents. Those deserving to die must be put to death for their own crimes."*

⁷Amaziah also killed 10,000 Edomites in the Valley of Salt. He also conquered Sela and changed its name to Joktheel, as it is called to this day.

⁸One day Amaziah sent messengers with this challenge to Israel's king Jehoash, the son of Jehoahaz and grandson of Jehu: "Come and meet me in battle!"*

⁹But King Jehoash of Israel replied to King Amaziah of Judah with this story: "Out in the Lebanon mountains, a thistle sent a message to a mighty cedar tree: 'Give your daughter in marriage to my son.' But just then a wild animal of Lebanon came by and stepped on the thistle, crushing it!

¹⁰"You have indeed defeated Edom, and you are proud of it. But be content with your victory and stay at home! Why stir up trouble that will only bring disaster on you and the people of Judah?"

¹¹But Amaziah refused to listen, so King Jehoash of Israel mobilized his army against King Amaziah of Judah. The two armies drew up their battle lines at Beth-shemesh in Judah. ¹²Judah was routed by the army of Israel, and its army scattered and fled for home. ¹³King Jehoash of Israel captured Judah's king, Amaziah son of Joash and grandson of Ahaziah, at Beth-shemesh. Then he marched to Jerusalem, where he demolished 600 feet* of Jerusalem's wall, from the Ephraim Gate to the Corner Gate. ¹⁴He carried off all the gold and silver and all the articles from the Temple of the LORD. He also seized

---

14:1 Hebrew *Joash*, a variant spelling of Jehoash; also in 14:13, 23, 27. **14:6** Deut 24:16. **14:8** Hebrew *Come, let us look one another in the face.* **14:13** Hebrew *400 cubits* [180 meters].

13:23 Despite Israel's continued infidelity, God remained faithful to his covenant with Abraham (Genesis 12:1-3; 13:15-17; 15:18-21; 17:6-8). By listing Abraham, Isaac, and Jacob, the writer emphasizes Israel's spiritual identity with the Lord and the people's possession of the Land of Promise (see Genesis 50:24; Exodus 3:6, 15-16; 6:3, 6-8; Deuteronomy 6:10; 9:5; 34:4).

14:3-4 While Amaziah's basic spiritual evaluation was satisfactory, he did not serve the Lord wholeheartedly (2 Chronicles 25:2) as his ancestor David had. David continued to be the spiritual standard for evaluating the kings of Judah (2 Kings 16:2; 18:3; see 1 Kings 15:5, 11). Judah's tolerance for long-established pagan shrines remained a stumbling block (2 Kings 12:3; see 1 Kings 14:23; 15:14; 22:43).

14:13-14 The extensive demolition of Jerusalem's wall and the thorough looting of the city testify to Jehoash's overwhelming victory. Carrying off Temple and palace treasures and taking hostages are often noted in the annals of victorious Assyrian kings. (See also 12:17-18; 18:13-15; 24:13-14; 25:8-21; 1 Kings 14:25-26.)

the treasures from the royal palace, along with hostages, and then returned to Samaria.

¹⁵The rest of the events in Jehoash's reign and everything he did, including the extent of his power and his war with King Amaziah of Judah, are recorded in The Book of the History of the Kings of Israel. ¹⁶When Jehoash died, he was buried in Samaria with the kings of Israel. And his son Jeroboam II became the next king.

¹⁷King Amaziah of Judah lived for fifteen years after the death of King Jehoash of Israel. ¹⁸The rest of the events in Amaziah's reign are recorded in The Book of the History of the Kings of Judah.

¹⁹There was a conspiracy against Amaziah's life in Jerusalem, and he fled to Lachish. But his enemies sent assassins after him, and they killed him there. ²⁰They brought his body back to Jerusalem on a horse, and he was buried with his ancestors in the City of David.

²¹All the people of Judah had crowned Amaziah's sixteen-year-old son, Uzziah,* as king in place of his father, Amaziah. ²²After his father's death, Uzziah rebuilt the town of Elath and restored it to Judah.

Jeroboam II Rules in Israel

²³Jeroboam II, the son of Jehoash, began to rule over Israel in the fifteenth year of King Amaziah's reign in Judah. He reigned in Samaria forty-one years. ²⁴He did what was evil in the LORD's sight. He refused to turn from the sins that Jeroboam son of Nebat had led Israel to commit. ²⁵Jeroboam II recovered the territories of Israel between Lebo-hamath and the Dead Sea,* just as the LORD, the God of Israel, had promised through Jonah son of Amittai, the prophet from Gath-hepher.

²⁶For the LORD saw the bitter suffering of everyone in Israel, and that there was no one in Israel, slave or free, to help them. ²⁷And because the LORD had not said he would blot out the name of Israel completely, he used Jeroboam II, the son of Jehoash, to save them.

²⁸The rest of the events in the reign of Jeroboam II and everything he did—including the extent of his power, his wars, and how he recovered for Israel both Damascus and Hamath, which had belonged to Judah*—are recorded in The Book of the History of the Kings of Israel. ²⁹When Jeroboam II died, he was buried in Samaria* with the kings of Israel. Then his son Zechariah became the next king.

Uzziah Rules in Judah

15 Uzziah* son of Amaziah began to rule over Judah in the twenty-seventh year of the reign of King Jeroboam II of Israel. ²He was sixteen years old when he became king, and he reigned in Jerusalem fifty-two years. His mother was Jecoliah from Jerusalem.

³He did what was pleasing in the LORD's sight, just as his father, Amaziah, had done. ⁴But he did not destroy the pagan shrines, and the people still offered sacrifices and burned incense there. ⁵The LORD struck the king with leprosy,* which lasted until the day he died. He lived in isolation in a separate house. The king's son Jotham was put in charge of the royal palace, and he governed the people of the land.

⁶The rest of the events in Uzziah's reign and everything he did are recorded in The Book of the History of the Kings of Judah. ⁷When Uzziah died, he was buried with his ancestors in the City of David. And his son Jotham became the next king.

Zechariah Rules in Israel

⁸Zechariah son of Jeroboam II began to rule over Israel in the thirty-eighth year of King Uzziah's reign in Judah. He reigned in Samaria six months. ⁹Zechariah did what was evil in the LORD's sight, as his ancestors had done. He refused to turn from the sins that Jeroboam son of Nebat had led Israel to commit. ¹⁰Then Shallum son of Jabesh conspired against Zechariah, assassinated him in public,* and became the next king.

¹¹The rest of the events in Zechariah's reign are recorded in The Book of the History of the Kings of Israel. ¹²So the LORD's message to Jehu came true: "Your descendants will be kings of Israel down to the fourth generation."

Shallum Rules in Israel

¹³Shallum son of Jabesh began to rule over Israel in the thirty-ninth year of King Uzziah's reign in Judah. Shallum reigned in Samaria only one month. ¹⁴Then Menahem son of Gadi went to Samaria from Tirzah and assassinated him, and he became the next king.

¹⁵The rest of the events in Shallum's reign, including his conspiracy, are recorded in The Book of the History of the Kings of Israel.

Menahem Rules in Israel

¹⁶At that time Menahem destroyed the town of Tappuah* and all the surrounding countryside as far as Tirzah, because its citizens refused to surrender

---

14:21 Hebrew *Azariah,* a variant spelling of Uzziah. **14:25** Hebrew *the sea of the Arabah.* **14:28** Or *to Yaudi.* The meaning of the Hebrew is uncertain. **14:29** As in some Greek manuscripts; Hebrew lacks *he was buried in Samaria.* **15:1** Hebrew *Azariah,* a variant spelling of Uzziah; also in 15:6, 7, 8, 17, 23, 27. **15:5** Or *with a contagious skin disease.* The Hebrew word used here and throughout this passage can describe various skin diseases. **15:10** Or *at Ibleam.* **15:16** As in some Greek manuscripts; Hebrew reads *Tiphsah.*

15:1-3 The name Uzziah means "Yahweh is my strength." Uzziah's fifty-two-year reign (792–740 BC) reflects changed conditions in the early 700s BC. Assyria was in decline and relations between Israel and Judah were peaceful. Uzziah's spiritual convictions earned God's blessings so that Judah enjoyed its greatest prosperity since the days of Solomon (2 Chronicles 26:9-10).

15:4 Despite his good spiritual commendation, Uzziah continued to allow worship at the pagan shrines (see also 14:4).

the town. He killed the entire population and ripped open the pregnant women.

¹⁷Menahem son of Gadi began to rule over Israel in the thirty-ninth year of King Uzziah's reign in Judah. He reigned in Samaria ten years. ¹⁸But Menahem did what was evil in the LORD's sight. During his entire reign, he refused to turn from the sins that Jeroboam son of Nebat had led Israel to commit.

¹⁹Then King Tiglath-pileser* of Assyria invaded the land. But Menahem paid him thirty-seven tons* of silver to gain his support in tightening his grip on royal power. ²⁰Menahem extorted the money from the rich of Israel, demanding that each of them pay fifty pieces* of silver to the king of Assyria. So the king of Assyria turned from attacking Israel and did not stay in the land.

²¹The rest of the events in Menahem's reign and everything he did are recorded in The Book of the History of the Kings of Israel. ²²When Menahem died, his son Pekahiah became the next king.

Pekahiah Rules in Israel

²³Pekahiah son of Menahem began to rule over Israel in the fiftieth year of King Uzziah's reign in Judah. He reigned in Samaria two years. ²⁴But Pekahiah did what was evil in the LORD's sight. He refused to turn from the sins that Jeroboam son of Nebat had led Israel to commit.

²⁵Then Pekah son of Remaliah, the commander of Pekahiah's army, conspired against him. With fifty men from Gilead, Pekah assassinated the king, along with Argob and Arieh, in the citadel of the palace at Samaria. And Pekah reigned in his place.

²⁶The rest of the events in Pekahiah's reign and everything he did are recorded in The Book of the History of the Kings of Israel.

Pekah Rules in Israel

²⁷Pekah son of Remaliah began to rule over Israel in the fifty-second year of King Uzziah's reign in Judah. He reigned in Samaria twenty years. ²⁸But Pekah did what was evil in the LORD's sight. He refused to turn from the sins that Jeroboam son of Nebat had led Israel to commit.

²⁹During Pekah's reign, King Tiglath-pileser of Assyria attacked Israel again, and he captured the towns of Ijon, Abel-beth-maacah, Janoah, Kedesh, and Hazor. He also conquered the regions of Gilead, Galilee, and all of Naphtali, and he took the people to Assyria as captives. ³⁰Then Hoshea son of Elah conspired against Pekah and assassinated him. He began to rule over Israel in the twentieth year of Jotham son of Uzziah.

³¹The rest of the events in Pekah's reign and everything he did are recorded in The Book of the History of the Kings of Israel.

Jotham Rules in Judah

³²Jotham son of Uzziah began to rule over Judah in the second year of King Pekah's reign in Israel. ³³He was twenty-five years old when he became king, and he reigned in Jerusalem sixteen years. His mother was Jerusha, the daughter of Zadok.

³⁴Jotham did what was pleasing in the LORD's sight. He did everything his father, Uzziah, had done. ³⁵But he did not destroy the pagan shrines, and the people still offered sacrifices and burned incense there. He rebuilt the upper gate of the Temple of the LORD.

³⁶The rest of the events in Jotham's reign and everything he did are recorded in The Book of the History of the Kings of Judah. ³⁷In those days the LORD began to send King Rezin of Aram and King Pekah of Israel to attack Judah. ³⁸When Jotham died, he was buried with his ancestors in the City of David. And his son Ahaz became the next king.

Ahaz Rules in Judah

16 Ahaz son of Jotham began to rule over Judah in the seventeenth year of King Pekah's reign in Israel. ²Ahaz was twenty years old when he became king, and he reigned in Jerusalem sixteen years. He did not do what was pleasing in the sight of the LORD his God, as his ancestor David had done. ³Instead, he followed the example of the kings of Israel, even sacrificing his own son in the fire.* In this way, he followed the detestable practices of the pagan nations the LORD had driven from the land ahead of the Israelites. ⁴He offered sacrifices and burned incense at the pagan shrines and on the hills and under every green tree.

⁵Then King Rezin of Aram and King Pekah of Israel came up to attack Jerusalem. They besieged Ahaz but could not conquer him. ⁶At that time the king of Edom* recovered the town of Elath for Edom.* He drove out the people of Judah and sent Edomites* to live there, as they do to this day.

15:19a Hebrew *Pul*, another name for Tiglath-pileser. **15:19b** Hebrew *1,000 talents* [34 metric tons]. **15:20** Hebrew *50 shekels* [20 ounces or 570 grams]. **16:3** Or *even making his son pass through the fire.* **16:6a** As in Latin Vulgate; Hebrew reads *Rezin king of Aram.* **16:6b** As in Latin Vulgate; Hebrew reads *Aram.* **16:6c** As in Greek version, Latin Vulgate, and an alternate reading of the Masoretic Text; the other alternate reads *Arameans.*

16:5-6 The alliance between the kings of Aram and Israel was intended to free the area of Assyrian dominance under Tiglath-pileser III (15:29-30; Isaiah 9:1). The attack against Judah may have occurred to force Judah into the alliance or to replace the Judean king with one of their own choosing (Isaiah 7:3-6). The result was captivity and widespread death for the people of Judah (2 Chronicles 28:5-15). Judah also suffered further attacks by the Edomites and Philistines (2 Chronicles 28:17-18). All of this was God's will due to Ahaz's detestable spiritual practices, which led to great sin among the people of Judah (2 Chronicles 28:5, 19).

⁷King Ahaz sent messengers to King Tiglath-pileser of Assyria with this message: "I am your servant and your vassal.* Come up and rescue me from the attacking armies of Aram and Israel." ⁸Then Ahaz took the silver and gold from the Temple of the LORD and the palace treasury and sent it as a payment to the Assyrian king. ⁹So the king of Assyria attacked the Aramean capital of Damascus and led its population away as captives, resettling them in Kir. He also killed King Rezin.

¹⁰King Ahaz then went to Damascus to meet with King Tiglath-pileser of Assyria. While he was there, he took special note of the altar. Then he sent a model of the altar to Uriah the priest, along with its design in full detail. ¹¹Uriah followed the king's instructions and built an altar just like it, and it was ready before the king returned from Damascus. ¹²When the king returned, he inspected the altar and made offerings on it. ¹³He presented a burnt offering and a grain offering, he poured out a liquid offering, and he sprinkled the blood of peace offerings on the altar.

¹⁴Then King Ahaz removed the old bronze altar from its place in front of the LORD's Temple, between the entrance and the new altar, and placed it on the north side of the new altar. ¹⁵He told Uriah the priest, "Use the new altar* for the morning sacrifices of burnt offering, the evening grain offering, the king's burnt offering and grain offering, and the burnt offerings of all the people, as well as their grain offerings and liquid offerings. Sprinkle the blood from all the burnt offerings and sacrifices on the new altar. The bronze altar will be for my personal use only." ¹⁶Uriah the priest did just as King Ahaz commanded him.

¹⁷Then the king removed the side panels and basins from the portable water carts. He also removed the great bronze basin called the Sea from the backs of the bronze oxen and placed it on the stone pavement. ¹⁸In deference to the king of Assyria, he also removed the canopy that had been constructed inside the palace for use on the Sabbath day,* as well as the king's outer entrance to the Temple of the LORD.

¹⁹The rest of the events in Ahaz's reign and everything he did are recorded in The Book of the History of the Kings of Judah. ²⁰When Ahaz died, he was buried with his ancestors in the City of David. Then his son Hezekiah became the next king.

Hoshea Rules in Israel

17 Hoshea son of Elah began to rule over Israel in the twelfth year of King Ahaz's reign in Judah. He reigned in Samaria nine years. ²He did what was evil in the LORD's sight, but not to the same extent as the kings of Israel who ruled before him.

³King Shalmaneser of Assyria attacked King Hoshea, so Hoshea was forced to pay heavy tribute to Assyria. ⁴But Hoshea stopped paying the annual tribute and conspired against the king of Assyria by asking King So of Egypt* to help him shake free of Assyria's power. When the king of Assyria discovered this treachery, he seized Hoshea and put him in prison.

Samaria Falls to Assyria

⁵Then the king of Assyria invaded the entire land, and for three years he besieged the city of Samaria. ⁶Finally, in the ninth year of King Hoshea's reign, Samaria fell, and the people of Israel were exiled to Assyria. They were settled in colonies in Halah, along the banks of the Habor River in Gozan, and in the cities of the Medes.

⁷This disaster came upon the people of Israel because they worshiped other gods. They sinned against the LORD their God, who had brought them safely out of Egypt and had rescued them from the power of Pharaoh, the king of Egypt. ⁸They had followed the practices of the pagan nations the LORD had driven from the land ahead of them, as well as the practices the kings of Israel had introduced. ⁹The people of Israel had also secretly done many things that were not pleasing to the LORD their God. They built pagan shrines for themselves in all their towns, from the smallest outpost to the largest walled city. ¹⁰They set up sacred pillars and Asherah poles at the top of every hill and under every green tree. ¹¹They offered sacrifices on all the hilltops, just like the nations the LORD had driven from the land ahead of them. So the people of Israel had done many evil things, arousing the LORD's anger. ¹²Yes, they worshiped idols,* despite the LORD's specific and repeated warnings.

¹³Again and again the LORD had sent his prophets and seers to warn both Israel and Judah: "Turn from all your evil ways. Obey my commands and decrees—the entire law that I commanded your ancestors to obey, and that I gave you through my servants the prophets."

¹⁴But the Israelites would not listen. They were as stubborn as their ancestors who had refused to believe

---

16:7 Hebrew *your son.* **16:15** Hebrew *the great altar.* **16:18** The meaning of the Hebrew is uncertain. **17:4** Or *by asking the king of Egypt at Sais.* **17:12** The Hebrew term (literally *round things*) probably alludes to dung.

16:10-19 In further rejection of the Lord, Ahaz removed the Temple utensils "and broke them into pieces" (2 Chronicles 28:24). He then closed the Temple and discontinued services there, instead promoting paganism throughout the land (2 Chronicles 28:25; 29:7). In redirecting Judah's worship so completely, Ahaz's rejection of God, his law, and worship in the Temple resembled Jeroboam's (see 2 Kings 3:3; 13:2; 16:2-4; 17:21; 1 Kings 12:25-33; 16:26; 22:52).

17:1 Hoshea's reign began in 732 BC and is listed as beginning in "the twentieth year of Jotham" (15:30) and in the twelfth year of King Ahaz's reign in Judah. Ahaz apparently co-reigned with Jotham from about 743 BC, when he was twelve years old, but Ahaz's official years as king were calculated from 731 BC (16:2).

in the LORD their God. ¹⁵They rejected his decrees and the covenant he had made with their ancestors, and they despised all his warnings. They worshiped worthless idols, so they became worthless themselves. They followed the example of the nations around them, disobeying the LORD's command not to imitate them.

¹⁶They rejected all the commands of the LORD their God and made two calves from metal. They set up an Asherah pole and worshiped Baal and all the forces of heaven. ¹⁷They even sacrificed their own sons and daughters in the fire.* They consulted fortune-tellers and practiced sorcery and sold themselves to evil, arousing the LORD's anger.

¹⁸Because the LORD was very angry with Israel, he swept them away from his presence. Only the tribe of Judah remained in the land. ¹⁹But even the people of Judah refused to obey the commands of the LORD their God, for they followed the evil practices that Israel had introduced. ²⁰The LORD rejected all the descendants of Israel. He punished them by handing them over to their attackers until he had banished Israel from his presence.

²¹For when the LORD* tore Israel away from the kingdom of David, they chose Jeroboam son of Nebat as their king. But Jeroboam drew Israel away from following the LORD and made them commit a great sin. ²²And the people of Israel persisted in all the evil ways of Jeroboam. They did not turn from these sins ²³until the LORD finally swept them away from his presence, just as all his prophets had warned. So Israel was exiled from their land to Assyria, where they remain to this day.

Foreigners Settle in Israel

²⁴The king of Assyria transported groups of people from Babylon, Cuthah, Avva, Hamath, and Sepharvaim and resettled them in the towns of Samaria, replacing the people of Israel. They took possession of Samaria and lived in its towns. ²⁵But since these foreign settlers did not worship the LORD when they first arrived, the LORD sent lions among them, which killed some of them.

²⁶So a message was sent to the king of Assyria: "The people you have sent to live in the towns of Samaria do not know the religious customs of the God of the land. He has sent lions among them to destroy them because they have not worshiped him correctly."

> "I now see that the error of my religious life has been a desire for signs and wonders. Like Naaman, I have wanted some great thing, unwilling to rely unwaveringly on the still small voice of the Spirit, speaking through the naked Word."
>
> **PHOEBE PALMER**
> (1807–1874) evangelist and temperance activist

²⁷The king of Assyria then commanded, "Send one of the exiled priests back to Samaria. Let him live there and teach the new residents the religious customs of the God of the land." ²⁸So one of the priests who had been exiled from Samaria returned to Bethel and taught the new residents how to worship the LORD.

²⁹But these various groups of foreigners also continued to worship their own gods. In town after town where they lived, they placed their idols at the pagan shrines that the people of Samaria had built. ³⁰Those from Babylon worshiped idols of their god Succoth-benoth. Those from Cuthah worshiped their god Nergal. And those from Hamath worshiped Ashima. ³¹The Avvites worshiped their gods Nibhaz and Tartak. And the people from Sepharvaim even burned their own children as sacrifices to their gods Adrammelech and Anammelech.

17:17 Or *They even made their sons and daughters pass through the fire.* 17:21 Hebrew *he;* compare 1 Kgs 11:31-32.

17:23 Israel was removed from its place of prominence and exiled, just as the prophets had warned. The people refused to be faithful to God alone, to stop their evil deeds, and to take care of the oppressed, orphan, foreigner, and widow (Jeremiah 7:5-7). Even while they were in exile, God did not forget them. God continually worked to draw them back. Even when Israel was not faithful, God continued to be faithful. In our lives, God is faithful to us, even when we struggle to be faithful.

17:26-31 Religious belief in the ancient Near East held that the peace and success of a land was strongly identified with its god and the rites associated with his worship. "One of the priests . . . returned to Bethel" (17:28), though his instruction in how to worship the Lord was doubtless influenced by the religion of Jeroboam I and mixed with paganism. The non-Israelites also continued to worship their own gods and simply added the worship of Israel's God to their existing pantheons. Although most of the false gods mentioned here are unknown, Nergal was the Mesopotamian name for the Elamite god of war, pestilence, and the underworld, and Nibhaz and Tartak may also have been Elamite deities. The names of other gods may have been altered by Jewish scribes.

[32] These new residents worshiped the LORD, but they also appointed from among themselves all sorts of people as priests to offer sacrifices at their places of worship. [33] And though they worshiped the LORD, they continued to follow their own gods according to the religious customs of the nations from which they came. [34] And this is still going on today. They continue to follow their former practices instead of truly worshiping the LORD and obeying the decrees, regulations, instructions, and commands he gave the descendants of Jacob, whose name he changed to Israel.

[35] For the LORD had made a covenant with the descendants of Jacob and commanded them: "Do not worship any other gods or bow before them or serve them or offer sacrifices to them. [36] But worship only the LORD, who brought you out of Egypt with great strength and a powerful arm. Bow down to him alone, and offer sacrifices only to him. [37] Be careful at all times to obey the decrees, regulations, instructions, and commands that he wrote for you. You must not worship other gods. [38] Do not forget the covenant I made with you, and do not worship other gods. [39] You must worship only the LORD your God. He is the one who will rescue you from all your enemies."

[40] But the people would not listen and continued to follow their former practices. [41] So while these new residents worshiped the LORD, they also worshiped their idols. And to this day their descendants do the same.

Hezekiah Rules in Judah

18 Hezekiah son of Ahaz began to rule over Judah in the third year of King Hoshea's reign in Israel. [2] He was twenty-five years old when he became king, and he reigned in Jerusalem twenty-nine years. His mother was Abijah,* the daughter of Zechariah. [3] He did what was pleasing in the LORD's sight, just as his ancestor David had done. [4] He removed the pagan shrines, smashed the sacred pillars, and cut down the Asherah poles. He broke up the bronze serpent that Moses had made, because the people of Israel had been offering sacrifices to it. The bronze serpent was called Nehushtan.*

[5] Hezekiah trusted in the LORD, the God of Israel. There was no one like him among all the kings of Judah, either before or after his time. [6] He remained faithful to the LORD in everything, and he carefully obeyed all the commands the LORD had given Moses. [7] So the LORD was with him, and Hezekiah was successful in everything he did. He revolted against the king of Assyria and refused to pay him tribute. [8] He also conquered the Philistines as far distant as Gaza and its territory, from their smallest outpost to their largest walled city.

[9] During the fourth year of Hezekiah's reign, which was the seventh year of King Hoshea's reign in Israel, King Shalmaneser of Assyria attacked the city of Samaria and began a siege against it. [10] Three years later, during the sixth year of King Hezekiah's reign and the ninth year of King Hoshea's reign in Israel, Samaria fell. [11] At that time the king of Assyria exiled the Israelites to Assyria and placed them in colonies in Halah, along the banks of the Habor River in Gozan, and in the cities of the Medes. [12] For they refused to listen to the LORD their God and obey him. Instead, they violated his covenant—all the laws that Moses the LORD's servant had commanded them to obey.

Assyria Invades Judah

[13] In the fourteenth year of King Hezekiah's reign,* King Sennacherib of Assyria came to attack the fortified towns of Judah and conquered them. [14] King Hezekiah sent this message to the king of Assyria at Lachish: "I have done wrong. I will pay whatever tribute money you demand if you will only withdraw." The king of Assyria then demanded a settlement of more than eleven tons of silver and one ton of gold.* [15] To gather this amount, King Hezekiah used all the silver stored in the Temple of the LORD and in the palace treasury. [16] Hezekiah even stripped the gold from the doors of the LORD's Temple and from the doorposts he had overlaid with gold, and he gave it all to the Assyrian king.

[17] Nevertheless, the king of Assyria sent his commander in chief, his field commander, and his chief of staff* from Lachish with a huge army to confront King Hezekiah in Jerusalem. The Assyrians took up a position beside the aqueduct that feeds water into the upper pool, near the road leading to the field where cloth is washed.* [18] They summoned King Hezekiah, but the king sent these officials to meet with them: Eliakim son of Hilkiah, the palace administrator; Shebna the court secretary; and Joah son of Asaph, the royal historian.

18:2 As in parallel text at 2 Chr 29:1; Hebrew reads *Abi*, a variant spelling of Abijah. **18:4** *Nehushtan* sounds like the Hebrew terms that mean "snake," "bronze," and "unclean thing." **18:13** The fourteenth year of Hezekiah's reign was 701 B.C. **18:14** Hebrew *300 talents* [10 metric tons] *of silver and 30 talents* [1 metric ton] *of gold.* **18:17a** Or *the rabshakeh;* also in 18:19, 26, 27, 28, 37. **18:17b** Or *bleached.*

18:1-5 "Hezekiah trusted in the LORD, the God of Israel. There was no one like him among all the kings of Judah, either before or after his time" (18:5). Like his ancestor David, King Hezekiah chose to follow God and not follow the ways of his father, King Ahaz. This story provides a great example of children not repeating the bad decisions of their parents. We don't have to follow our parents and repeat their mistakes either.

18:13 The fourteenth year of Hezekiah's reign was 701 BC. The annals of King Sennacherib of Assyria describe this invasion during his third military campaign. He advanced swiftly down the Mediterranean coast through the Phoenician cities and into Philistine territory, then turned inland.

Sennacherib Threatens Jerusalem

[19] Then the Assyrian king's chief of staff told them to give this message to Hezekiah:

> "This is what the great king of Assyria says: What are you trusting in that makes you so confident? [20] Do you think that mere words can substitute for military skill and strength? Who are you counting on, that you have rebelled against me? [21] On Egypt? If you lean on Egypt, it will be like a reed that splinters beneath your weight and pierces your hand. Pharaoh, the king of Egypt, is completely unreliable!
>
> [22] "But perhaps you will say to me, 'We are trusting in the Lord our God!' But isn't he the one who was insulted by Hezekiah? Didn't Hezekiah tear down his shrines and altars and make everyone in Judah and Jerusalem worship only at the altar here in Jerusalem?
>
> [23] "I'll tell you what! Strike a bargain with my master, the king of Assyria. I will give you 2,000 horses if you can find that many men to ride on them! [24] With your tiny army, how can you think of challenging even the weakest contingent of my master's troops, even with the help of Egypt's chariots and charioteers? [25] What's more, do you think we have invaded your land without the Lord's direction? The Lord himself told us, 'Attack this land and destroy it!'"

[26] Then Eliakim son of Hilkiah, Shebna, and Joah said to the Assyrian chief of staff, "Please speak to us in Aramaic, for we understand it well. Don't speak in Hebrew,* for the people on the wall will hear."

[27] But Sennacherib's chief of staff replied, "Do you think my master sent this message only to you and your master? He wants all the people to hear it, for when we put this city under siege, they will suffer along with you. They will be so hungry and thirsty that they will eat their own dung and drink their own urine."

[28] Then the chief of staff stood and shouted in Hebrew to the people on the wall, "Listen to this message from the great king of Assyria! [29] This is what the king says: Don't let Hezekiah deceive you. He will never be able to rescue you from my power. [30] Don't let him fool you into trusting in the Lord by saying, 'The Lord will surely rescue us. This city will never fall into the hands of the Assyrian king!'

[31] "Don't listen to Hezekiah! These are the terms the king of Assyria is offering: Make peace with me—open the gates and come out. Then each of you can continue eating from your own grapevine and fig tree and drinking from your own well. [32] Then I will arrange to take you to another land like this one—a land of grain and new wine, bread and vineyards, olive groves and honey. Choose life instead of death!

"Don't listen to Hezekiah when he tries to mislead you by saying, 'The Lord will rescue us!' [33] Have the gods of any other nations ever saved their people from the king of Assyria? [34] What happened to the gods of Hamath and Arpad? And what about the gods of Sepharvaim, Hena, and Ivvah? Did any god rescue Samaria from my power? [35] What god of any nation has ever been able to save its people from my power? So what makes you think that the Lord can rescue Jerusalem from me?"

[36] But the people were silent and did not utter a word because Hezekiah had commanded them, "Do not answer him."

[37] Then Eliakim son of Hilkiah, the palace administrator; Shebna the court secretary; and Joah son of Asaph, the royal historian, went back to Hezekiah. They tore their clothes in despair, and they went in to see the king and told him what the Assyrian chief of staff had said.

Hezekiah Seeks the Lord's Help

19 When King Hezekiah heard their report, he tore his clothes and put on burlap and went into the Temple of the Lord. [2] And he sent Eliakim the palace administrator, Shebna the court secretary, and the leading priests, all dressed in burlap, to the prophet Isaiah son of Amoz. [3] They told him, "This is what King Hezekiah says: Today is a day of trouble, insults, and disgrace. It is like when a child is ready to be born, but the mother has no strength to deliver the baby. [4] But perhaps the Lord your God has heard the Assyrian chief of staff,* sent by the king to defy the living God, and will punish him for his words. Oh, pray for those of us who are left!"

18:26 Hebrew *in the dialect of Judah;* also in 18:28.   19:4 Or *the rabshakeh;* also in 19:8.

18:19-22 In earlier days, the term *great king* was reserved for the kings of the leading military powers, but it had become a standard epithet for Assyrian kings. The Assyrian officer asserted that the citizens of Jerusalem, faced with Assyria's overwhelming military superiority, would be foolish to trust in Hezekiah's words. Similarly, soliciting help from Egypt would be foolish. Finally, the chief of staff argued that trust in the Lord would also be misplaced. Perhaps the officer hoped to gain the loyalty of citizens who worshiped at the shrines and altars that Hezekiah had destroyed.

18:26 Hezekiah's representatives wanted the Assyrian delegation to speak in Aramaic, the language of diplomacy, so that the people who were listening would not understand and become discouraged or frightened.

19:1-7 King Hezekiah sent his officials to the prophet Isaiah for wise counsel. Hezekiah knew he needed God's help and could not lead alone.

19:4 Hezekiah was not denying his own relationship to the Lord by referring to him as "your God"; rather, he was acknowledging God's special call upon Isaiah.

⁵After King Hezekiah's officials delivered the king's message to Isaiah, ⁶the prophet replied, "Say to your master, 'This is what the LORD says: Do not be disturbed by this blasphemous speech against me from the Assyrian king's messengers. ⁷Listen! I myself will move against him,* and the king will receive a message that he is needed at home. So he will return to his land, where I will have him killed with a sword.'"

⁸Meanwhile, the Assyrian chief of staff left Jerusalem and went to consult the king of Assyria, who had left Lachish and was attacking Libnah.

⁹Soon afterward King Sennacherib received word that King Tirhakah of Ethiopia* was leading an army to fight against him. Before leaving to meet the attack, he sent messengers back to Hezekiah in Jerusalem with this message:

¹⁰"This message is for King Hezekiah of Judah. Don't let your God, in whom you trust, deceive you with promises that Jerusalem will not be captured by the king of Assyria. ¹¹You know perfectly well what the kings of Assyria have done wherever they have gone. They have completely destroyed everyone who stood in their way! Why should you be any different? ¹²Have the gods of other nations rescued them—such nations as Gozan, Haran, Rezeph, and the people of Eden who were in Tel-assar? My predecessors destroyed them all! ¹³What happened to the king of Hamath and the king of Arpad? What happened to the kings of Sepharvaim, Hena, and Ivvah?"

¹⁴After Hezekiah received the letter from the messengers and read it, he went up to the LORD's Temple and spread it out before the LORD. ¹⁵And Hezekiah prayed this prayer before the LORD: "O LORD, God of Israel, you are enthroned between the mighty cherubim! You alone are God of all the kingdoms of the earth. You alone created the heavens and the earth. ¹⁶Bend down, O LORD, and listen! Open your eyes, O LORD, and see! Listen to Sennacherib's words of defiance against the living God.

¹⁷"It is true, LORD, that the kings of Assyria have destroyed all these nations. ¹⁸And they have thrown the gods of these nations into the fire and burned them. But of course the Assyrians could destroy them! They were not gods at all—only idols of wood and stone shaped by human hands. ¹⁹Now, O LORD our God, rescue us from his power; then all the kingdoms of the earth will know that you alone, O LORD, are God."

Isaiah Predicts Judah's Deliverance

²⁰Then Isaiah son of Amoz sent this message to Hezekiah: "This is what the LORD, the God of Israel, says: I have heard your prayer about King Sennacherib of Assyria. ²¹And the LORD has spoken this word against him:

"The virgin daughter of Zion
  despises you and laughs at you.
The daughter of Jerusalem
  shakes her head in derision as you flee.

²² "Whom have you been defying and ridiculing?
  Against whom did you raise your voice?
At whom did you look with such haughty eyes?
  It was the Holy One of Israel!
²³ By your messengers you have defied the Lord.
  You have said, 'With my many chariots
I have conquered the highest mountains—
  yes, the remotest peaks of Lebanon.
I have cut down its tallest cedars
  and its finest cypress trees.
I have reached its farthest corners
  and explored its deepest forests.
²⁴ I have dug wells in many foreign lands
  and refreshed myself with their water.
With the sole of my foot
  I stopped up all the rivers of Egypt!'

²⁵ "But have you not heard?
  I decided this long ago.
Long ago I planned it,
  and now I am making it happen.
I planned for you to crush fortified cities
  into heaps of rubble.
²⁶ That is why their people have so little power
  and are so frightened and confused.
They are as weak as grass,
  as easily trampled as tender green shoots.
They are like grass sprouting on a housetop,
  scorched before it can grow lush and tall.

²⁷ "But I know you well—
  where you stay
and when you come and go.
  I know the way you have raged against me.
²⁸ And because of your raging against me
  and your arrogance, which I have heard for myself,
I will put my hook in your nose
  and my bit in your mouth.
I will make you return
  by the same road on which you came."

²⁹Then Isaiah said to Hezekiah, "Here is the proof that what I say is true:

"This year you will eat only what grows up by itself,
  and next year you will eat what springs up from that.
But in the third year you will plant crops and harvest them;
  you will tend vineyards and eat their fruit.
³⁰ And you who are left in Judah,
  who have escaped the ravages of the siege,
will put roots down in your own soil
  and will grow up and flourish.

19:7 Hebrew *I will put a spirit in him.* 19:9 Hebrew *of Cush.*

³¹ For a remnant of my people will spread out from Jerusalem,
> a group of survivors from Mount Zion.
> The passionate commitment of the LORD of Heaven's Armies*
> will make this happen!

³²"And this is what the LORD says about the king of Assyria:

> "His armies will not enter Jerusalem.
> They will not even shoot an arrow at it.
> They will not march outside its gates with their shields
> nor build banks of earth against its walls.
> ³³ The king will return to his own country
> by the same road on which he came.
> He will not enter this city,
> says the LORD.
> ³⁴ For my own honor and for the sake of my servant David,
> I will defend this city and protect it."

³⁵ That night the angel of the LORD went out to the Assyrian camp and killed 185,000 Assyrian soldiers. When the surviving Assyrians* woke up the next morning, they found corpses everywhere. ³⁶ Then King Sennacherib of Assyria broke camp and returned to his own land. He went home to his capital of Nineveh and stayed there.

³⁷ One day while he was worshiping in the temple of his god Nisroch, his sons* Adrammelech and Sharezer killed him with their swords. They then escaped to the land of Ararat, and another son, Esarhaddon, became the next king of Assyria.

Hezekiah's Sickness and Recovery

20 About that time Hezekiah became deathly ill, and the prophet Isaiah son of Amoz went to visit him. He gave the king this message: "This is what the LORD says: Set your affairs in order, for you are going to die. You will not recover from this illness."

²When Hezekiah heard this, he turned his face to the wall and prayed to the LORD, ³"Remember, O LORD, how I have always been faithful to you and have served you single-mindedly, always doing what pleases you." Then he broke down and wept bitterly.

⁴But before Isaiah had left the middle courtyard,* this message came to him from the LORD: ⁵"Go back to Hezekiah, the leader of my people. Tell him, 'This is what the LORD, the God of your ancestor David, says: I have heard your prayer and seen your tears. I will heal you, and three days from now you will get out of bed and go to the Temple of the LORD. ⁶I will add fifteen years to your life, and I will rescue you and this city from the king of Assyria. I will defend this city for my own honor and for the sake of my servant David.'"

⁷Then Isaiah said, "Make an ointment from figs." So Hezekiah's servants spread the ointment over the boil, and Hezekiah recovered!

⁸Meanwhile, Hezekiah had said to Isaiah, "What sign will the LORD give to prove that he will heal me and that I will go to the Temple of the LORD three days from now?"

⁹Isaiah replied, "This is the sign from the LORD to prove that he will do as he promised. Would you like the shadow on the sundial to go forward ten steps or backward ten steps?*"

¹⁰"The shadow always moves forward," Hezekiah replied, "so that would be easy. Make it go ten steps backward instead." ¹¹So Isaiah the prophet asked the LORD to do this, and he caused the shadow to move ten steps backward on the sundial* of Ahaz!

Envoys from Babylon

¹²Soon after this, Merodach-baladan* son of Baladan, king of Babylon, sent Hezekiah his best wishes and a gift, for he had heard that Hezekiah had been

---

19:31 As in Greek and Syriac versions, Latin Vulgate, and an alternate reading of the Masoretic Text (see also Isa 37:32); the other alternate reads *the LORD*. **19:35** Hebrew *When they*. **19:37** As in Greek version and an alternate reading of the Masoretic Text (see also Isa 37:38); the other alternate reading lacks *his sons*. **20:4** As in Greek version and an alternate reading in the Masoretic Text; the other alternate reads *the middle of the city*. **20:9** Or *The shadow on the sundial has gone forward ten steps; do you want it to go backward ten steps?* **20:11** Hebrew *the steps*. **20:12** As in some Hebrew manuscripts and Greek and Syriac versions (see also Isa 39:1); Masoretic Text reads *Berodach-baladan*.

19:31 The theme of the remnant, or remainder, occurs frequently in the Old Testament. God's preservation of his people often serves as a promise of his care for them in the distant future (see Isaiah 4:2-6; 9:1-7; Zephaniah 3:8-20; Revelation 7:1-12). God's people can be assured of their survival, for the Lord is committed to accomplishing his plans.
19:32-34 Sennacherib's armies did not enter Jerusalem but returned home. In Sennacherib's own account, he gave details of capturing and despoiling forty-six cities of Judah. He made no mention of the capture of Jerusalem but recorded only that he shut up Hezekiah "in Jerusalem . . . like a bird in a cage." In light of Sennacherib's blasphemies and arrogance against God (18:25, 28-30; 19:10-13, 21, 27-28)—and for the sake of the Lord's servant David, who God had made his covenant promise to (2 Samuel 7:8-16) and whose faith Hezekiah had emulated (2 Kings 18:1-3), the Lord would defend Jerusalem (see 20:6). The Lord decisively demonstrated that he alone is God and that he is faithful to his people who trust in him.
20:1-19 This general time reference indicates that the order of events is thematic rather than chronological. The episode concerning Merodach-baladan (20:12-19), whom Sennacherib had driven from Babylon before 701 BC, happened earlier than the events of 2 Kings 18–19 but after Hezekiah's illness (20:12).
20:1 Since Isaiah was already active in Hezekiah's reign before Sennacherib moved to take Jerusalem, he was readily available to the king during that emergency (19:2). He carried the Lord's message that Hezekiah would die. Hezekiah's illness was terminal.

very sick. ¹³Hezekiah received the Babylonian envoys and showed them everything in his treasure-houses—the silver, the gold, the spices, and the aromatic oils. He also took them to see his armory and showed them everything in his royal treasuries! There was nothing in his palace or kingdom that Hezekiah did not show them.

¹⁴Then Isaiah the prophet went to King Hezekiah and asked him, "What did those men want? Where were they from?"

Hezekiah replied, "They came from the distant land of Babylon."

¹⁵"What did they see in your palace?" Isaiah asked.

"They saw everything," Hezekiah replied. "I showed them everything I own—all my royal treasuries."

¹⁶Then Isaiah said to Hezekiah, "Listen to this message from the LORD: ¹⁷The time is coming when everything in your palace—all the treasures stored up by your ancestors until now—will be carried off to Babylon. Nothing will be left, says the LORD. ¹⁸Some of your very own sons will be taken away into exile. They will become eunuchs who will serve in the palace of Babylon's king."

¹⁹Then Hezekiah said to Isaiah, "This message you have given me from the LORD is good." For the king was thinking, "At least there will be peace and security during my lifetime."

²⁰The rest of the events in Hezekiah's reign, including the extent of his power and how he built a pool and dug a tunnel* to bring water into the city, are recorded in The Book of the History of the Kings of Judah. ²¹Hezekiah died, and his son Manasseh became the next king.

Manasseh Rules in Judah

21 Manasseh was twelve years old when he became king, and he reigned in Jerusalem fifty-five years. His mother was Hephzibah. ²He did what was evil in the LORD's sight, following the detestable practices of the pagan nations that the LORD had driven from the land ahead of the Israelites. ³He rebuilt the pagan shrines his father, Hezekiah, had destroyed. He constructed altars for Baal and set up an Asherah pole, just as King Ahab of Israel had done. He also bowed before all the powers of the heavens and worshiped them.

⁴He built pagan altars in the Temple of the LORD, the place where the LORD had said, "My name will remain in Jerusalem forever." ⁵He built these altars for all the powers of the heavens in both courtyards of the LORD's Temple. ⁶Manasseh also sacrificed his own son in the fire.* He practiced sorcery and divination, and he consulted with mediums and psychics. He did much that was evil in the LORD's sight, arousing his anger.

⁷Manasseh even made a carved image of Asherah and set it up in the Temple, the very place where the LORD had told David and his son Solomon: "My name will be honored forever in this Temple and in Jerusalem—the city I have chosen from among all the tribes of Israel. ⁸If the Israelites will be careful to obey my commands—all the laws my servant Moses gave them—I will not send them into exile from this land that I gave their ancestors." ⁹But the people refused to listen, and Manasseh led them to do even more evil than the pagan nations that the LORD had destroyed when the people of Israel entered the land.

¹⁰Then the LORD said through his servants the prophets: ¹¹"King Manasseh of Judah has done many detestable things. He is even more wicked than the Amorites, who lived in this land before Israel. He has caused the people of Judah to sin with his idols.* ¹²So this is what the LORD, the God of Israel, says: I will bring such disaster on Jerusalem and Judah that the ears of those who hear about it will tingle with horror. ¹³I will judge Jerusalem by the same standard I used for Samaria and the same measure* I used for the family of Ahab. I will wipe away the people of Jerusalem as one wipes a dish and turns it upside down. ¹⁴Then I will reject even the remnant of my own people who are left, and I will hand them over as plunder for their enemies. ¹⁵For they have done great evil in my sight and have angered me ever since their ancestors came out of Egypt."

¹⁶Manasseh also murdered many innocent people until Jerusalem was filled from one end to the other with innocent blood. This was in addition to the sin that he caused the people of Judah to commit, leading them to do evil in the LORD's sight.

¹⁷The rest of the events in Manasseh's reign and everything he did, including the sins he committed, are recorded in The Book of the History of the Kings of Judah. ¹⁸When Manasseh died, he was buried in the palace garden, the garden of Uzza. Then his son Amon became the next king.

Amon Rules in Judah

¹⁹Amon was twenty-two years old when he became king, and he reigned in Jerusalem two years. His mother was Meshullemeth, the daughter of Haruz

---

20:20 Hebrew *watercourse*. **21:6** Or *also made his son pass through the fire*. **21:11** The Hebrew term (literally *round things*) probably alludes to dung; also in 21:21. **21:13** Hebrew *the same plumb line I used for Samaria and the same plumb bob*.

21:1-2 Manasseh's long reign (697–642 BC) certainly cannot be attributed to his faithfulness to the Lord but to the Lord's continued honoring of his covenant promises (see also 8:19; 19:34; 20:6; 2 Samuel 7:11-16). External conditions were largely stable. Though the Assyrian kings Esarhaddon (680–669 BC) and Ashurbanipal (668–626 BC) conducted a number of military campaigns, none was directed against Judah until later in Manasseh's reign, probably around 650–648 BC (see 2 Chronicles 33:10-13). Ashurbanipal's attention was more on building projects, religious pursuits, and the arts, including a great library. Manasseh was the most wicked of Judah's kings; discussion of his reign focuses on his evil religious practices (2 Chronicles 33:1-20).

from Jotbah. ²⁰He did what was evil in the LORD's sight, just as his father, Manasseh, had done. ²¹He followed the example of his father, worshiping the same idols his father had worshiped. ²²He abandoned the LORD, the God of his ancestors, and he refused to follow the LORD's ways.

²³Then Amon's own officials conspired against him and assassinated him in his palace. ²⁴But the people of the land killed all those who had conspired against King Amon, and they made his son Josiah the next king.

²⁵The rest of the events in Amon's reign and what he did are recorded in The Book of the History of the Kings of Judah. ²⁶He was buried in his tomb in the garden of Uzza. Then his son Josiah became the next king.

Josiah Rules in Judah

22 Josiah was eight years old when he became king, and he reigned in Jerusalem thirty-one years. His mother was Jedidah, the daughter of Adaiah from Bozkath. ²He did what was pleasing in the LORD's sight and followed the example of his ancestor David. He did not turn away from doing what was right.

³In the eighteenth year of his reign, King Josiah sent Shaphan son of Azaliah and grandson of Meshullam, the court secretary, to the Temple of the LORD. He told him, ⁴"Go to Hilkiah the high priest and have him count the money the gatekeepers have collected from the people at the LORD's Temple. ⁵Entrust this money to the men assigned to supervise the restoration of the LORD's Temple. Then they can use it to pay workers to repair the Temple. ⁶They will need to hire carpenters, builders, and masons. Also have them buy the timber and the finished stone needed to repair the Temple. ⁷But don't require the construction supervisors to keep account of the money they receive, for they are honest and trustworthy men."

Hilkiah Discovers God's Law

⁸Hilkiah the high priest said to Shaphan the court secretary, "I have found the Book of the Law in the LORD's Temple!" Then Hilkiah gave the scroll to Shaphan, and he read it.

⁹Shaphan went to the king and reported, "Your officials have turned over the money collected at the Temple of the LORD to the workers and supervisors at the Temple." ¹⁰Shaphan also told the king, "Hilkiah the priest has given me a scroll." So Shaphan read it to the king.

¹¹When the king heard what was written in the Book of the Law, he tore his clothes in despair. ¹²Then he gave these orders to Hilkiah the priest, Ahikam son of Shaphan, Acbor son of Micaiah, Shaphan the court secretary, and Asaiah the king's personal adviser: ¹³"Go to the Temple and speak to the LORD for me and for the people and for all Judah. Inquire about the words written in this scroll that has been found. For the LORD's great anger is burning against us because our ancestors have not obeyed the words in this scroll. We have not been doing everything it says we must do."

¹⁴So Hilkiah the priest, Ahikam, Acbor, Shaphan, and Asaiah went to the New Quarter* of Jerusalem to consult with the prophet Huldah. She was the wife of Shallum son of Tikvah, son of Harhas, the keeper of the Temple wardrobe.

¹⁵She said to them, "The LORD, the God of Israel, has spoken! Go back and tell the man who sent you, ¹⁶'This is what the LORD says: I am going to bring disaster on this city* and its people. All the words written in the scroll that the king of Judah has read will come true. ¹⁷For my people have abandoned me and offered sacrifices to pagan gods, and I am very angry with them for everything they have done. My anger will burn against this place, and it will not be quenched.'

¹⁸"But go to the king of Judah who sent you to seek the LORD and tell him: 'This is what the LORD, the God of Israel, says concerning the message you have just heard: ¹⁹You were sorry and humbled yourself before the LORD when you heard what I said against this city and its people—that this land would be cursed and become desolate. You tore your clothing in despair and wept before me in repentance. And I have indeed heard you, says the LORD. ²⁰So I will not send the promised disaster until after you have died and been buried in peace. You will not see the disaster I am going to bring on this city.'"

So they took her message back to the king.

Josiah's Religious Reforms

23 Then the king summoned all the elders of Judah and Jerusalem. ²And the king went up to the Temple of the LORD with all the people of Judah and Jerusalem, along with the priests and the prophets—all the people from the least to the greatest. There the king read to them the entire Book of the Covenant that had been found in the LORD's

---

22:14 Or *the Second Quarter*, a newer section of Jerusalem. Hebrew reads *the Mishneh*. 22:16 Hebrew *this place*; also in 22:19, 20.

22:11 Josiah was so moved by the reading the Book of the Law that he tore his clothes and wept. This outburst of emotion was a sign of mourning and repentance. Josiah deeply desired for everyone to follow God's instructions.

22:14 Huldah is one of the four named women prophets in the Old Testament. She was a trusted prophet from a priestly family and was part of King Josiah's reform. She spoke with authority, using the prophetic saying, "This is what the LORD says" (22:15-18). Huldah announced words of judgment on Judah and some words of comfort for King Josiah (22:20).

23:1-2 In the spirit of the instructions of Deuteronomy (Deuteronomy 31:10-13) and like Joshua before him (Joshua 8:30-35), Josiah "summoned all the elders" to hear the reading of the entire Book of the Covenant.

Temple. ³The king took his place of authority beside the pillar and renewed the covenant in the LORD's presence. He pledged to obey the LORD by keeping all his commands, laws, and decrees with all his heart and soul. In this way, he confirmed all the terms of the covenant that were written in the scroll, and all the people pledged themselves to the covenant.

⁴Then the king instructed Hilkiah the high priest and the priests of the second rank and the Temple gatekeepers to remove from the LORD's Temple all the articles that were used to worship Baal, Asherah, and all the powers of the heavens. The king had all these things burned outside Jerusalem on the terraces of the Kidron Valley, and he carried the ashes away to Bethel. ⁵He did away with the idolatrous priests, who had been appointed by the previous kings of Judah, for they had offered sacrifices at the pagan shrines throughout Judah and even in the vicinity of Jerusalem. They had also offered sacrifices to Baal, and to the sun, the moon, the constellations, and to all the powers of the heavens. ⁶The king removed the Asherah pole from the LORD's Temple and took it outside Jerusalem to the Kidron Valley, where he burned it. Then he ground the ashes of the pole to dust and threw the dust over the graves of the people. ⁷He also tore down the living quarters of the male and female shrine prostitutes that were inside the Temple of the LORD, where the women wove coverings for the Asherah pole.

Oikos IMAGE — MY STORY WITH FAMILY & FRIENDS

A Family Blessing

SCRIPTURE CONNECTION: 2 KINGS 22:1-2

Josiah was a good king—at last! But he didn't raise himself. His mother, Jedidah, had good examples to offer, as a daughter of a God-honoring man and his wife. How might we, too, guide the next generations?

I gave my seven-year-old grandson a Bible with tooled leather covers. It was beautiful but had impossibly small print for my grandmother-eyes. I saw him reading it and offered, "You know, Lovie [my grandma-name] could get you a kid Bible with lots of pictures and fun things for children. Would you like that?"

"Oh no, Lovie! This is the Holy Bible, and you gave it to me."

A pair of old Bibles sits nearby as I write. The black leather was my mother's, and she gave me the blue leather on my sixteenth birthday. She wrote a telling dedication, "Therefore, beloved ... be diligent. (2 Peter 3:14)"—a clue that she had felt a certain teenage girl needed to buckle down.

> Live your faith for the next generation to follow.

I cherish these Bibles, my mother's particularly. Yes, she gave some verses the neon highlighter treatment. Even if I cannot decode the meaning of its highlighted colors, I can easily guess what each verse meant to her. What's more, she lived a faith legacy for her children, grandchildren, and now my grandchildren. It is the Holy Bible, and she gave it to all who follow her trail of faith.

My grandson got it right. He just never met the woman who really gave it to him—my mother.

IMAGINE

What generational blessing can you provide to point young people to God?

Who provided a legacy that you can follow?

> *"My mother not only underlined the Bible, she lived it."*

VALERIE BELL is an author of several books on children, including *RESILIENT: Child Discipleship and the Fearless Future of the Church*. Valerie serves as Awana's CEO emerita and 2050 vision caster.

⁸Josiah brought to Jerusalem all the priests who were living in other towns of Judah. He also defiled the pagan shrines, where they had offered sacrifices—all the way from Geba to Beersheba. He destroyed the shrines at the entrance to the gate of Joshua, the governor of Jerusalem. This gate was located to the left of the city gate as one enters the city. ⁹The priests who had served at the pagan shrines were not allowed to serve at* the LORD's altar in Jerusalem, but they were allowed to eat unleavened bread with the other priests.

¹⁰Then the king defiled the altar of Topheth in the valley of Ben-Hinnom, so no one could ever again use it to sacrifice a son or daughter in the fire* as an offering to Molech. ¹¹He removed from the entrance of the LORD's Temple the horse statues that the former kings of Judah had dedicated to the sun. They were near the quarters of Nathan-melech the eunuch, an officer of the court.* The king also burned the chariots dedicated to the sun.

¹²Josiah tore down the altars that the kings of Judah had built on the palace roof above the upper room of Ahaz. The king destroyed the altars that Manasseh had built in the two courtyards of the LORD's Temple. He smashed them to bits* and scattered the pieces in the Kidron Valley. ¹³The king also desecrated the pagan shrines east of Jerusalem, to the south of the Mount of Corruption, where King Solomon of Israel had built shrines for Ashtoreth, the detestable goddess of the Sidonians; and for Chemosh, the detestable god of the Moabites; and for Molech,* the vile god of the Ammonites. ¹⁴He smashed the sacred pillars and cut down the Asherah poles. Then he desecrated these places by scattering human bones over them.

¹⁵The king also tore down the altar at Bethel—the pagan shrine that Jeroboam son of Nebat had made when he caused Israel to sin. He burned down the shrine and ground it to dust, and he burned the Asherah pole. ¹⁶Then Josiah turned around and noticed several tombs in the side of the hill. He ordered that the bones be brought out, and he burned them on the altar at Bethel to desecrate it. (This happened just as the LORD had promised through the man of God when Jeroboam stood beside the altar at the festival.)

Then Josiah turned and looked up at the tomb of the man of God* who had predicted these things. ¹⁷"What is that monument over there?" Josiah asked.

And the people of the town told him, "It is the tomb of the man of God who came from Judah and predicted the very things that you have just done to the altar at Bethel!"

¹⁸Josiah replied, "Leave it alone. Don't disturb his bones." So they did not burn his bones or those of the old prophet from Samaria.

¹⁹Then Josiah demolished all the buildings at the pagan shrines in the towns of Samaria, just as he had done at Bethel. They had been built by the various kings of Israel and had made the LORD* very angry. ²⁰He executed the priests of the pagan shrines on their own altars, and he burned human bones on the altars to desecrate them. Finally, he returned to Jerusalem.

Josiah Celebrates Passover

²¹King Josiah then issued this order to all the people: "You must celebrate the Passover to the LORD your God, as required in this Book of the Covenant." ²²There had not been a Passover celebration like that since the time when the judges ruled in Israel, nor throughout all the years of the kings of Israel and Judah. ²³But in the eighteenth year of King Josiah's reign, this Passover was celebrated to the LORD in Jerusalem.

²⁴Josiah also got rid of the mediums and psychics, the household gods, the idols,* and every other kind of detestable practice, both in Jerusalem and throughout the land of Judah. He did this in obedience to the laws written in the scroll that Hilkiah the priest had found in the LORD's Temple. ²⁵Never before had there been a king like Josiah, who turned to the LORD with all his heart and soul and strength, obeying all the laws of Moses. And there has never been a king like him since.

23:9 Hebrew *did not come up to.* **23:10** Or *to make a son or daughter pass through the fire.* **23:11** The meaning of the Hebrew is uncertain. **23:12** Or *He quickly removed them.* **23:13** Hebrew *Milcom,* a variant spelling of Molech. **23:16** As in Greek version; Hebrew lacks *when Jeroboam stood beside the altar at the festival. Then Josiah turned and looked up at the tomb of the man of God.* **23:19** As in Greek and Syriac versions and Latin Vulgate; Hebrew lacks *the LORD.* **23:24** The Hebrew term (literally *round things*) probably alludes to dung.

23:10 Topheth was a precinct in the valley of Ben-Hinnom, which lay southwest of the city of David and led into the Kidron Valley. The detestable rite of child sacrifice had occurred there (Jeremiah 7:31-32). Molech has been identified with a number of deities (see 1 Kings 11:5, 7, 33) and with a sacrifice offered to Baal (Jeremiah 19:5-6; 32:35).

23:11 The horse is frequently depicted in sun worship in the ancient Near East. The Assyrian sun god Shamash and other deities were depicted riding across the sky on horses or in horse-drawn chariots. Archaeological evidence suggests that a solar cult existed in Israel as early as the 800s BC. The cult's popularity likely increased during the reigns of Manasseh and Amon, when it was sponsored by the crown (21:3-5, 21-22). Despite his reforms, shortly after Josiah's death Ezekiel denounced the sun worshipers again for performing their rituals within the inner court of the Temple (Ezekiel 8:16).

23:21-23 Josiah ordered all the people to celebrate the Passover, as instructed in the Book of the Covenant. The first Passover was recorded in Exodus and was first celebrated by Israelite families in Egypt, on the eve of redemption, when Moses led Israel out of slavery under Pharaoh. The people were to celebrate Passover every year, to remember all God had done for them. This Passover celebration ordered by Josiah was special because it took place in Jerusalem, at the central place of worship (Deuteronomy 16:1-8).

²⁶Even so, the LORD was very angry with Judah because of all the wicked things Manasseh had done to provoke him. ²⁷For the LORD said, "I will also banish Judah from my presence just as I have banished Israel. And I will reject my chosen city of Jerusalem and the Temple where my name was to be honored."

²⁸The rest of the events in Josiah's reign and all his deeds are recorded in The Book of the History of the Kings of Judah.

²⁹While Josiah was king, Pharaoh Neco, king of Egypt, went to the Euphrates River to help the king of Assyria. King Josiah and his army marched out to fight him,* but King Neco* killed him when they met at Megiddo. ³⁰Josiah's officers took his body back in a chariot from Megiddo to Jerusalem and buried him in his own tomb. Then the people of the land anointed Josiah's son Jehoahaz and made him the next king.

Jehoahaz Rules in Judah

³¹Jehoahaz was twenty-three years old when he became king, and he reigned in Jerusalem three months. His mother was Hamutal, the daughter of Jeremiah from Libnah. ³²He did what was evil in the LORD's sight, just as his ancestors had done.

³³Pharaoh Neco put Jehoahaz in prison at Riblah in the land of Hamath to prevent him from ruling* in Jerusalem. He also demanded that Judah pay 7,500 pounds of silver and 75 pounds of gold* as tribute.

23:29a Or *Josiah went out to meet him.* 23:29b Hebrew *he.* 23:33a The meaning of the Hebrew is uncertain. 23:33b Hebrew *100 talents [3,400 kilograms] of silver and 1 talent [34 kilograms] of gold.*

Insight — THE POWER OF OWNING OUR PLACE AND PART

Whether these people were leading in reforming worship in Israel, rebuilding Jerusalem's wall, or rescuing the Jewish people, all showed the power of working wherever God put them to do good. We can serve God precisely where we are, even if we'd rather not be there. Look at these examples, then consider your own.

PERSON	POSITION	DOING THEIR PART
Josiah *1 Kings 13:1-5; 2 Kings 21:23-24, 26; 22:1–23:30; see especially 23:25*	Eight-year-old child who was probably not ready to be king as soon as he was forced to	• Read God's Word to the people • Reformed worship and brought back important religious celebration
Nehemiah *Book of Nehemiah, see especially 1:11*	Cupbearer to the king, a trusted court official who could have taken it easy	• Prayed and let God lead him in working for the people's benefit • Led returning exiles in rebuilding the protective wall around Jerusalem
Esther *Book of Esther, see especially 2:8; 4:14-16*	Orphaned girl, taken to join the king's harem, likely against her will	• Agreed with her uncle that she might be queen "for just such a time as this"(Esther 4:14) • Asked others to join her, prayed and fasted, advocated for her people • Risked her life to save her people
Daniel *Book of Daniel, see especially 1:18-21; 6:1-4*	Teenager whose world was brutally upended when taken captive by a foreign empire	• Handled his responsibilities with discretion and wisdom • Became invaluable to the kings he served • Represented himself and his faith well
You *What are important verses or callings on your life that lead you to do good where you are?*	Where are you that you wish you weren't?	What good could you do, right where you are?

Jehoiakim Rules in Judah

³⁴Pharaoh Neco then installed Eliakim, another of Josiah's sons, to reign in place of his father, and he changed Eliakim's name to Jehoiakim. Jehoahaz was taken to Egypt as a prisoner, where he died.

³⁵In order to get the silver and gold demanded as tribute by Pharaoh Neco, Jehoiakim collected a tax from the people of Judah, requiring them to pay in proportion to their wealth.

³⁶Jehoiakim was twenty-five years old when he became king, and he reigned in Jerusalem eleven years. His mother was Zebidah, the daughter of Pedaiah from Rumah. ³⁷He did what was evil in the LORD's sight, just as his ancestors had done.

24 During Jehoiakim's reign, King Nebuchadnezzar of Babylon invaded the land of Judah. Jehoiakim surrendered and paid him tribute for three years but then rebelled. ²Then the LORD sent bands of Babylonian,* Aramean, Moabite, and Ammonite raiders against Judah to destroy it, just as the LORD had promised through his prophets. ³These disasters happened to Judah because of the LORD's command. He had decided to banish Judah from his presence because of the many sins of Manasseh, ⁴who had filled Jerusalem with innocent blood. The LORD would not forgive this.

⁵The rest of the events in Jehoiakim's reign and all his deeds are recorded in The Book of the History of the Kings of Judah. ⁶When Jehoiakim died, his son Jehoiachin became the next king.

⁷The king of Egypt did not venture out of his country after that, for the king of Babylon captured the entire area formerly claimed by Egypt—from the Brook of Egypt to the Euphrates River.

Jehoiachin Rules in Judah

⁸Jehoiachin was eighteen years old when he became king, and he reigned in Jerusalem three months. His mother was Nehushta, the daughter of Elnathan from Jerusalem. ⁹Jehoiachin did what was evil in the LORD's sight, just as his father had done.

¹⁰During Jehoiachin's reign, the officers of King Nebuchadnezzar of Babylon came up against Jerusalem and besieged it. ¹¹Nebuchadnezzar himself arrived at the city during the siege. ¹²Then King Jehoiachin, along with the queen mother, his advisers, his commanders, and his officials, surrendered to the Babylonians.

In the eighth year of Nebuchadnezzar's reign, he took Jehoiachin prisoner. ¹³As the LORD had said beforehand, Nebuchadnezzar carried away all the treasures from the LORD's Temple and the royal palace. He stripped away* all the gold objects that King Solomon of Israel had placed in the Temple. ¹⁴King Nebuchadnezzar took all of Jerusalem captive, including all the commanders and the best of the soldiers, craftsmen, and artisans—10,000 in all. Only the poorest people were left in the land.

¹⁵Nebuchadnezzar led King Jehoiachin away as a captive to Babylon, along with the queen mother, his wives and officials, and all Jerusalem's elite. ¹⁶He also exiled 7,000 of the best troops and 1,000 craftsmen and artisans, all of whom were strong and fit for war. ¹⁷Then the king of Babylon installed Mattaniah, Jehoiachin's* uncle, as the next king, and he changed Mattaniah's name to Zedekiah.

Zedekiah Rules in Judah

¹⁸Zedekiah was twenty-one years old when he became king, and he reigned in Jerusalem eleven years. His mother was Hamutal, the daughter of Jeremiah from Libnah. ¹⁹But Zedekiah did what was evil in the LORD's sight, just as Jehoiakim had done. ²⁰These things happened because of the LORD's anger against the people of Jerusalem and Judah, until he finally banished them from his presence and sent them into exile.

24:2 Or *Chaldean.* 24:13 Or *He cut apart.* 24:17 Hebrew *his.*

24:1 In 605 BC, Nebuchadnezzar commanded forces that defeated the remaining Assyrian army and an Egyptian contingent at Carchemish (see Jeremiah 46:2). While he campaigned in the west, his father died, and Nebuchadnezzar returned home to assume the throne as Nebuchadnezzar II (605–562 BC). When he rejoined his troops, they easily moved down the Mediterranean coast. Sometime during this campaign, he invaded the land of Judah and took spoils of war and many captives to Babylon, including Daniel and his three friends (Daniel 1:1-7). Jehoiakim was made a vassal to Nebuchadnezzar and paid him tribute for three years. When Pharaoh Neco defeated the Babylonians at the Egyptian border in 601 BC, Jehoiakim rebelled, seizing the opportunity to gain his independence.

24:14-16 In addition to Jehoiachin, the prophet Ezekiel was also taken into captivity (Ezekiel 1:1). Throughout the book of Ezekiel, events in Ezekiel's life are dated in terms of the years since Jehoiachin had been taken captive. The 10,000 taken captive by Nebuchadnezzar likely includes 7,000 troops, 1,000 craftsmen and artisans, and a number of administrative officials and leading citizens of Jerusalem. In any case, 10,000 is probably a rounded figure (see also Jeremiah 52:28).

24:18-20 Zedekiah's reign of eleven years in Jerusalem (597–586 BC) mirrored Jehoiakim's evil reign (23:36-37). The Lord was judging Jerusalem and Judah for their sins (see 17:19; 20:16-17; 21:12-15; 22:15-20; 23:26-27). Zedekiah's rebellion may have coincided with an anti-Babylonian alliance spearheaded by Pharaoh Apries of Egypt. When Apries became king of Egypt in about 589 BC, he cherished hopes of recovering Egypt's past glory. Zedekiah appears to have placed his confidence in him (see Ezekiel 17:15-18). Nevertheless, like earlier kings (2 Kings 17:4; 24:1-3), Zedekiah learned that Egypt would be of little help (see 18:20-21; Jeremiah 37:3-10; Ezekiel 29:6-7).

> "If I had a choice, I would still choose to remain blind … for when I die, the first face I will ever see will be the face of my blessed Saviour."
>
> FANNY CROSBY
> (1820–1915) hymn lyricist and poet

⁵But the Babylonian* troops chased the king and overtook him on the plains of Jericho, for his men had all deserted him and scattered. ⁶They captured the king and took him to the king of Babylon at Riblah, where they pronounced judgment upon Zedekiah. ⁷They made Zedekiah watch as they slaughtered his sons. Then they gouged out Zedekiah's eyes, bound him in bronze chains, and led him away to Babylon.

The Temple Destroyed

⁸On August 14 of that year,* which was the nineteenth year of King Nebuchadnezzar's reign, Nebuzaradan, the captain of the guard and an official of the Babylonian king, arrived in Jerusalem. ⁹He burned down the Temple of the Lord, the royal palace, and all the houses of Jerusalem. He destroyed all the important buildings* in the city. ¹⁰Then he supervised the entire Babylonian army as they tore down the walls of Jerusalem on every side. ¹¹Then Nebuzaradan, the captain of the guard, took as exiles the rest of the people who remained in the city, the defectors who had declared their allegiance to the king of Babylon, and the rest of the population. ¹²But the captain of the guard allowed some of the poorest people to stay behind to care for the vineyards and fields.

¹³The Babylonians broke up the bronze pillars in front of the Lord's Temple, the bronze water carts, and the great bronze basin called the Sea, and they carried all the bronze away to Babylon. ¹⁴They also took all the ash buckets, shovels, lamp snuffers, ladles, and all the other bronze articles used for making sacrifices at the Temple. ¹⁵The captain of the guard also took the incense burners and basins, and all the other articles made of pure gold or silver.

¹⁶The weight of the bronze from the two pillars, the Sea, and the water carts was too great to be measured. These things had been made for the Lord's Temple in the days of Solomon. ¹⁷Each of the pillars was 27 feet* tall. The bronze capital on top of each pillar was 7½ feet* high and was decorated with a network of bronze pomegranates all the way around.

¹⁸Nebuzaradan, the captain of the guard, took with him as prisoners Seraiah the high priest, Zephaniah the priest of the second rank, and the three

The Fall of Jerusalem

Zedekiah rebelled against the king of Babylon.

25 So on January 15,* during the ninth year of Zedekiah's reign, King Nebuchadnezzar of Babylon led his entire army against Jerusalem. They surrounded the city and built siege ramps against its walls. ²Jerusalem was kept under siege until the eleventh year of King Zedekiah's reign.

³By July 18 in the eleventh year of Zedekiah's reign,* the famine in the city had become very severe, and the last of the food was entirely gone. ⁴Then a section of the city wall was broken down. Since the city was surrounded by the Babylonians,* the soldiers waited for nightfall and escaped* through the gate between the two walls behind the king's garden. Then they headed toward the Jordan Valley.*

25:1 Hebrew *on the tenth day of the tenth month*, of the ancient Hebrew lunar calendar. A number of events in 2 Kings can be cross-checked with dates in surviving Babylonian records and related accurately to our modern calendar. This day was January 15, 588 B.C. **25:3** Hebrew *By the ninth day of the [fourth] month* [in the eleventh year of Zedekiah's reign] (compare Jer 39:2; 52:6 and the notes there). This day was July 18, 586 B.C.; also see note on 25:1. **25:4a** Or *the Chaldeans;* also in 25:13, 25, 26. **25:4b** As in Greek version (see also Jer 39:4; 52:7); Hebrew lacks *escaped*. **25:4c** Hebrew *the Arabah*. **25:5** Or *Chaldean;* also in 25:10, 24. **25:8** Hebrew *On the seventh day of the fifth month*, of the ancient Hebrew lunar calendar. This day was August 14, 586 B.C.; also see note on 25:1. **25:9** Or *destroyed the houses of all the important people*. **25:17a** Hebrew *18 cubits* [8.3 meters]. **25:17b** As in parallel texts at 1 Kgs 7:16, 2 Chr 3:15, and Jer 52:22, all of which read *5 cubits* [2.3 meters]; Hebrew reads *3 cubits*, which is 4.5 feet or 1.4 meters.

25:11-12, 18-20 The Babylonians took the majority of the population into exile, even some who willingly defected (Jeremiah 39:9; 52:15). Because the poorest people were unlikely to cause trouble, they were left behind to work the vineyards and fields. Instead of deporting key citizens and officials as in the Babylonian invasion of 597 BC (2 Kings 24:14), Nebuchadnezzar had these leaders put to death. Even religious leaders were executed. Although Seraiah the high priest was killed, his son Jehozadak was sent into exile (1 Chronicles 6:14-15). Thus, the priestly line continued even in captivity and later returned to Jerusalem beginning in 538 BC (Ezra 1:1–2:39).

chief gatekeepers. ¹⁹And from among the people still hiding in the city, he took an officer who had been in charge of the Judean army; five of the king's personal advisers; the army commander's chief secretary, who was in charge of recruitment; and sixty other citizens. ²⁰Nebuzaradan, the captain of the guard, took them all to the king of Babylon at Riblah. ²¹And there at Riblah, in the land of Hamath, the king of Babylon had them all put to death. So the people of Judah were sent into exile from their land.

Gedaliah Governs in Judah

²²Then King Nebuchadnezzar appointed Gedaliah son of Ahikam and grandson of Shaphan as governor over the people he had left in Judah. ²³When all the army commanders and their men learned that the king of Babylon had appointed Gedaliah as governor, they went to see him at Mizpah. These included Ishmael son of Nethaniah, Johanan son of Kareah, Seraiah son of Tanhumeth the Netophathite, Jezaniah* son of the Maacathite, and all their men. ²⁴Gedaliah vowed to them that the Babylonian officials meant them no harm. "Don't be afraid of them. Live in the land and serve the king of Babylon, and all will go well for you," he promised.

²⁵But in midautumn of that year,* Ishmael son of Nethaniah and grandson of Elishama, who was a member of the royal family, went to Mizpah with ten men and killed Gedaliah. He also killed all the Judeans and Babylonians who were with him at Mizpah. ²⁶Then all the people of Judah, from the least to the greatest, as well as the army commanders, fled in panic to Egypt, for they were afraid of what the Babylonians would do to them.

Hope for Israel's Royal Line

²⁷In the thirty-seventh year of the exile of King Jehoiachin of Judah, Evil-merodach ascended to the Babylonian throne. He was kind to* Jehoiachin and released him* from prison on April 2 of that year.* ²⁸He spoke kindly to Jehoiachin and gave him a higher place than all the other exiled kings in Babylon. ²⁹He supplied Jehoiachin with new clothes to replace his prison garb and allowed him to dine in the king's presence for the rest of his life. ³⁰So the king gave him a regular food allowance as long as he lived.

25:23 As in parallel text at Jer 40:8; Hebrew reads *Jaazaniah*, a variant spelling of Jezaniah.   25:25 Hebrew *in the seventh month*, of the ancient Hebrew lunar calendar. This month occurred within the months of October and November 586 B.C.; also see note on 25:1.   25:27a Hebrew *He raised the head of*.   25:27b As in some Hebrew manuscripts and Greek and Syriac versions (see also Jer 52:31); Masoretic Text lacks *released him*.   25:27c Hebrew *on the twenty-seventh day of the twelfth month*, of the ancient Hebrew lunar calendar. This day was April 2, 561 B.C.; also see note on 25:1.

25:21 Like the northern kingdom before them (17:5-17), Judah was exiled as punishment for their unfaithfulness to the covenant God made with them. A remnant later returned to the Promised Land in 538 BC (2 Chronicles 36:22-23; Ezra 1:1–2:70; see also 2 Chronicles 36:15-21; Jeremiah 25:11; 29:10; Daniel 9:2).
25:23-24 Because Gedaliah came from a family experienced in civic affairs, his governorship was initially well accepted (see also Jeremiah 40:1-12). A seal impression recovered from Lachish confirms Gedaliah's importance as the "manager of the palace property" (see 1 Kings 4:6). In addition to the army commanders, the prophet Jeremiah also went to Mizpah to support Gedaliah (Jeremiah 40:6). This Mizpah was a border town in Benjamin; it had been prominent in Israelite history as a place of religious assembly (1 Samuel 7:5-6). The men listed here held important posts. Ishmael was from a prominent family of royal lineage (2 Kings 25:25; Jeremiah 36:12). Johanan served Gedaliah faithfully (Jeremiah 40:13-16). The name Jezaniah (as in parallel text at Jeremiah 40:8; Hebrew reads *Jaazaniah*, a variant spelling of *Jezaniah*) occurs on materials recovered from excavations at Tell en-Nasbeh.
25:25 Gedaliah had been warned that Ishmael was plotting to assassinate him but was unconvinced (Jeremiah 40:13-16); his trust cost him his life. Ishmael also killed many Judeans and Babylonians, fled with many captives, and escaped to Ammon (Jeremiah 41:4-15).
25:27-30 Evil-merodach (known historically as Amel-marduk, which means "man of Marduk") succeeded Nebuchadnezzar II at his death and reigned a short time (561–560 BC). Babylonian annals give details of the rations Jehoiachin received in prison. The narrator's mention of Jehoiachin living in gracious circumstances is perhaps intended to provide hope that God would preserve and restore a repentant people to their land (see 1 Kings 8:46-53; Isaiah 35:8-10; 51:11; Jeremiah 29:10-14; Zephaniah 3:20).

1 Chronicles

WHAT DO WE LEARN ABOUT GOD'S MISSION AND OURS?
A godly person has great impact.

WHO WROTE IT? Likely Ezra, or someone writing after the Exile.

WHEN DID IT HAPPEN? Between 1010 and 970 BC, retelling the story of Israel's monarchy beginning with David.

HOW IS IT ORGANIZED?

- 1–9: List of descendants of the people of Israel
- 10–21: David rules in Israel
- 22–29: David prepares for the Temple to be built by Solomon

FEATURE HIGHLIGHTS
+ *Our Bodies* (480)
+ *Jerusalem through Time* (496)
+ *The Praise Factor* (499)
+ *My Plans: God's Perfect One* (501)
+ *Succession: Everyone Is an Interim* (505)

Words to Remember are highlighted throughout this book

HOW LONG DOES IT TAKE TO READ?

| :30 | 1:00 | 1:30 | 2:00 | 2:30 | 3:00 | 3:30 |

BC | Timeline

BC	Event
1050	SAUL BECOMES KING
1010	SAUL DIES; DAVID BECOMES KING OF JUDAH
1003	DAVID BECOMES KING OVER ALL ISRAEL
1000	DAVID CAPTURES JERUSALEM
997(?)	DAVID CAPTURES RABBAH
980(?)	DAVID'S CENSUS
970	SOLOMON, BATHSHEBA'S SON, BECOMES KING
930	THE KINGDOM DIVIDES

1 CHRONICLES 1

From Adam to Noah's Sons

1 The descendants of Adam were Seth, Enosh, ²Kenan, Mahalalel, Jared, ³Enoch, Methuselah, Lamech, ⁴and Noah.
The sons of Noah were* Shem, Ham, and Japheth.

Descendants of Japheth

⁵The descendants of Japheth were Gomer, Magog, Madai, Javan, Tubal, Meshech, and Tiras.
⁶The descendants of Gomer were Ashkenaz, Riphath,* and Togarmah.
⁷The descendants of Javan were Elishah, Tarshish, Kittim, and Rodanim.

Descendants of Ham

⁸The descendants of Ham were Cush, Mizraim,* Put, and Canaan.
⁹The descendants of Cush were Seba, Havilah, Sabtah, Raamah, and Sabteca. The descendants of Raamah were Sheba and Dedan. ¹⁰Cush was also the ancestor of Nimrod, who was the first heroic warrior on earth.
¹¹Mizraim was the ancestor of the Ludites, Anamites, Lehabites, Naphtuhites, ¹²Pathrusites, Casluhites, and the Caphtorites, from whom the Philistines came.*
¹³Canaan's oldest son was Sidon, the ancestor of the Sidonians. Canaan was also the ancestor of the Hittites,* ¹⁴Jebusites, Amorites, Girgashites, ¹⁵Hivites, Arkites, Sinites, ¹⁶Arvadites, Zemarites, and Hamathites.

Descendants of Shem

¹⁷The descendants of Shem were Elam, Asshur, Arphaxad, Lud, and Aram.
The descendants of Aram were* Uz, Hul, Gether, and Mash.*
¹⁸Arphaxad was the father of Shelah.
Shelah was the father of Eber.
¹⁹Eber had two sons. The first was named Peleg (which means "division"), for during his lifetime the people of the world were divided into different language groups. His brother's name was Joktan.
²⁰Joktan was the ancestor of Almodad, Sheleph, Hazarmaveth, Jerah, ²¹Hadoram, Uzal, Diklah, ²²Obal,* Abimael, Sheba, ²³Ophir, Havilah, and Jobab. All these were descendants of Joktan.
²⁴So this is the family line descended from Shem: Arphaxad, Shelah,* ²⁵Eber, Peleg, Reu, ²⁶Serug, Nahor, Terah, ²⁷and Abram, later known as Abraham.

Descendants of Abraham

²⁸The sons of Abraham were Isaac and Ishmael.
²⁹These are their genealogical records:
The sons of Ishmael were Nebaioth (the oldest), Kedar, Adbeel, Mibsam, ³⁰Mishma, Dumah, Massa, Hadad, Tema, ³¹Jetur, Naphish, and Kedemah. These were the sons of Ishmael.

³²The sons of Keturah, Abraham's concubine, were Zimran, Jokshan, Medan, Midian, Ishbak, and Shuah.
The sons of Jokshan were Sheba and Dedan.
³³The sons of Midian were Ephah, Epher, Hanoch, Abida, and Eldaah.
All these were descendants of Abraham through his concubine Keturah.

Descendants of Isaac

³⁴Abraham was the father of Isaac. The sons of Isaac were Esau and Israel.*

Descendants of Esau

³⁵The sons of Esau were Eliphaz, Reuel, Jeush, Jalam, and Korah.

1:4 As in Greek version (see also Gen 5:3-32); Hebrew lacks *The sons of Noah were.* **1:6** As in some Hebrew manuscripts and Greek version (see also Gen 10:3); most Hebrew manuscripts read *Diphath.* **1:8** Or *Egypt;* also in 1:11. **1:12** Hebrew *Casluhites, from whom the Philistines came, Caphtorites.* See Jer 47:4; Amos 9:7. **1:13** Hebrew *ancestor of Heth.* **1:17a** As in one Hebrew manuscript and some Greek manuscripts (see also Gen 10:23); most Hebrew manuscripts lack *The descendants of Aram were.* **1:17b** As in parallel text at Gen 10:23; Hebrew reads *and Meshech.* **1:22** As in some Hebrew manuscripts and Syriac version (see also Gen 10:28); most Hebrew manuscripts read *Ebal.* **1:24** Some Greek manuscripts read *Arphaxad, Cainan, Shelah.* See notes on Gen 10:24; 11:12-13. **1:34** *Israel* is the name that God gave to Jacob.

1:1–2:2 The chronicler begins by showing Israel's place among the nations, tracing their descent from Adam to Jacob, using genealogies also found in Genesis 5:3-32; 10:2-31; 11:10-26; 35:23-26; 36:10-19. Originally one unit, 1 and 2 Chronicles were later divided due to length. The Chronicles were compiled after Babylon had conquered Judah. After this devastation, it was essential to keep track of the list of descendants. These genealogies functioned for social, official, and religious purposes, not to prove hierarchy or status.
1:27 God changed Abram's name to Abraham in Genesis (Genesis 17:4-5). Abraham means "father of multitudes." In this story, the name of Abraham's wife Sarai changed to Sarah. God gave the reason for these name changes: to remind Abraham and Sarah that through them would come a great nation. Through this couple, all people on the earth would be blessed (Genesis 12:2-3). Looking at the list of descendants in 1 Chronicles, we begin to see more than mere names but lives testifying to God's faithfulness.
1:28 Ishmael and Isaac descended from Abraham, Sarah, and Hagar. The stories of their births are in Genesis 16:1-16; 21:1-21.
1:34 In a divine encounter, God changed Jacob's name to Israel (Genesis 32:22-32). Jacob was previously known as a deceiver, which is what his name means. Even though he faced difficult moments while growing up, God chose to work with Jacob through his mistakes, giving him purpose and a new identity (Genesis 32:28). Through Israel (Jacob), his wives (Leah and Rachel), and his concubines (Bilhah and Zilpah) came twelve sons. These sons became the nation of Israel.

³⁶The descendants of Eliphaz were Teman, Omar, Zepho,* Gatam, Kenaz, and Amalek, who was born to Timna.*
³⁷The descendants of Reuel were Nahath, Zerah, Shammah, and Mizzah.

Original Peoples of Edom

³⁸The descendants of Seir were Lotan, Shobal, Zibeon, Anah, Dishon, Ezer, and Dishan.
³⁹The descendants of Lotan were Hori and Hemam.* Lotan's sister was named Timna.
⁴⁰The descendants of Shobal were Alvan,* Manahath, Ebal, Shepho,* and Onam.
The descendants of Zibeon were Aiah and Anah.
⁴¹The son of Anah was Dishon.
The descendants of Dishon were Hemdan,* Eshban, Ithran, and Keran.
⁴²The descendants of Ezer were Bilhan, Zaavan, and Akan.*
The descendants of Dishan* were Uz and Aran.

Rulers of Edom

⁴³These are the kings who ruled in the land of Edom before any king ruled over the Israelites*:

Bela son of Beor, who ruled from his city of Dinhabah.
⁴⁴When Bela died, Jobab son of Zerah from Bozrah became king in his place.
⁴⁵When Jobab died, Husham from the land of the Temanites became king in his place.
⁴⁶When Husham died, Hadad son of Bedad became king in his place and ruled from the city of Avith. He was the one who destroyed the Midianite army in the land of Moab.
⁴⁷When Hadad died, Samlah from the city of Masrekah became king in his place.
⁴⁸When Samlah died, Shaul from the city of Rehoboth-on-the-River became king in his place.
⁴⁹When Shaul died, Baal-hanan son of Acbor became king in his place.
⁵⁰When Baal-hanan died, Hadad became king in his place and ruled from the city of Pau.* His wife was Mehetabel, the daughter of Matred and granddaughter of Me-zahab. ⁵¹Then Hadad died.

The clan leaders of Edom were Timna, Alvah,* Jetheth, ⁵²Oholibamah, Elah, Pinon, ⁵³Kenaz, Teman, Mibzar, ⁵⁴Magdiel, and Iram. These are the clan leaders of Edom.

Descendants of Israel

2 The sons of Israel* were Reuben, Simeon, Levi, Judah, Issachar, Zebulun, ²Dan, Joseph, Benjamin, Naphtali, Gad, and Asher.

Descendants of Judah

³Judah had three sons from Bathshua, a Canaanite woman. Their names were Er, Onan, and Shelah. But the LORD saw that the oldest son, Er, was a wicked man, so he killed him. ⁴Later Judah had twin sons from Tamar, his widowed daughter-in-law. Their names were Perez and Zerah. So Judah had five sons in all.
⁵The sons of Perez were Hezron and Hamul.
⁶The sons of Zerah were Zimri, Ethan, Heman, Calcol, and Darda*—five in all.
⁷The son of Carmi (a descendant of Zimri) was Achan,* who brought disaster on Israel by taking plunder that had been set apart for the LORD.*
⁸The son of Ethan was Azariah.

From Judah's Grandson Hezron to David

⁹The sons of Hezron were Jerahmeel, Ram, and Caleb.*
¹⁰ Ram was the father of Amminadab. Amminadab was the father of Nahshon, a leader of Judah.
¹¹ Nahshon was the father of Salmon.* Salmon was the father of Boaz.

1:36a As in many Hebrew manuscripts and a few Greek manuscripts (see also Gen 36:11); most Hebrew manuscripts read *Zephi*. **1:36b** As in some Greek manuscripts (see also Gen 36:12); Hebrew reads *Kenaz, Timna, and Amalek*. **1:39** As in parallel text at Gen 36:22; Hebrew reads *and Homam*. **1:40a** As in many Hebrew manuscripts and a few Greek manuscripts (see also Gen 36:23); most Hebrew manuscripts read *Alian*. **1:40b** As in some Hebrew manuscripts (see also Gen 36:23); most Hebrew manuscripts read *Shephi*. **1:41** As in many Hebrew manuscripts and some Greek manuscripts (see also Gen 36:26); most Hebrew manuscripts read *Hamran*. **1:42a** As in many Hebrew and Greek manuscripts (see also Gen 36:27); most Hebrew manuscripts read *Jaakan*. **1:42b** Hebrew *Dishon*; compare 1:38 and parallel text at Gen 36:28. **1:43** Or *before an Israelite king ruled over them*. **1:50** As in many Hebrew manuscripts, some Greek manuscripts, Syriac version, and Latin Vulgate (see also Gen 36:39); most Hebrew manuscripts read *Pai*. **1:51** As in an alternate reading of the Masoretic Text (see also Gen 36:40); the other alternate reads *Aliah*. **2:1** *Israel* is the name that God gave to Jacob. **2:6** As in many Hebrew manuscripts, some Greek manuscripts, and Syriac version (see also 1 Kgs 4:31); Hebrew reads *Dara*. **2:7a** Hebrew *Achar;* compare Josh 7:1. *Achar* means "disaster." **2:7b** The Hebrew term used here refers to the complete consecration of things or people to the LORD, either by destroying them or by giving them as an offering. **2:9** Hebrew *Kelubai*, a variant spelling of Caleb; compare 2:18. **2:11** As in Greek version (see also Ruth 4:20); Hebrew reads *Salma*.

2:3–9:1 These genealogies might focus on an individual and their line or even skip some people because the chronicler is focusing primarily on Judah, Levi, and Benjamin. Keeping track of Israel's identity and connection to Judah's kingdom—and in particular to David—mattered during the Exile so that when they returned to the land, they could reestablish their kingdom. Remembering who we are and God's purpose and promise can be difficult when we become displaced or devastated through loss. Even in hard circumstances, these lists remind God's people that we are part of a great story that includes all humanity, going back to Adam (1:1).

WHAT THE BIBLE SAYS ABOUT **Our Bodies**

Jesus' Body Unites Us with God and Each Other

Let us go right into the presence of God with sincere hearts fully trusting him. For our guilty consciences have been sprinkled with Christ's blood to make us clean, and our bodies have been washed with pure water. **HEBREWS 10:22**

Under the old system, the high priest brought the blood of animals into the Holy Place as a sacrifice for sin, and the bodies of the animals were burned outside the camp. So also Jesus suffered and died outside the city gates to make his people holy by means of his own blood. **HEBREWS 13:11-12**

The human body has many parts, but the many parts make up one whole body. So it is with the body of Christ. Some of us are Jews, some are Gentiles, some are slaves, and some are free. But we have all been baptized into one body by one Spirit, and we all share the same Spirit. **1 CORINTHIANS 12:12-13**

Our bodies are buried in brokenness, but they will be raised in glory.

With my whole being,...

We Will Receive New Bodies

For we know that when this earthly tent we live in is taken down (that is, when we die and leave this earthly body), we will have a house in heaven, an eternal body made for us by God himself and not by human hands. We grow weary in our present bodies, and we long to put on our heavenly bodies like new clothing. For we will put on heavenly bodies; we will not be spirits without bodies. **2 CORINTHIANS 5:1-3**

Our bodies are buried in brokenness, but they will be raised in glory. They are buried in weakness, but they will be raised in strength. **1 CORINTHIANS 15:43**

[Jesus] will take our weak mortal bodies and change them into glorious bodies like his own, using the same power with which he will bring everything under his control.
PHILIPPIANS 3:21

While we live in these earthly bodies, we groan and sigh, but it's not that we want to die and get rid of these bodies that clothe us. Rather, we want to put on our new bodies so that these dying bodies will be swallowed up by life.
2 CORINTHIANS 5:4

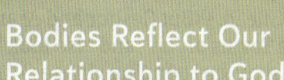

Bodies Reflect Our Relationship to God

"All must be circumcised. Your bodies will bear the mark of my everlasting covenant." **GENESIS 17:13**

I long, yes, I faint with longing
  to enter the courts of the
  LORD.
With my whole being, body
  and soul,
  I will shout joyfully to the
  living God.
PSALM 84:2

"The priests must not shave their heads or trim their beards or cut their bodies."
LEVITICUS 21:5

12 Boaz was the father of Obed. Obed was the father of Jesse.
13 Jesse's first son was Eliab, his second was Abinadab, his third was Shimea, 14his fourth was Nethanel, his fifth was Raddai, 15his sixth was Ozem, and his seventh was David.
16 Their sisters were named Zeruiah and Abigail. Zeruiah had three sons named Abishai, Joab, and Asahel. 17Abigail married a man named Jether, an Ishmaelite, and they had a son named Amasa.

Other Descendants of Hezron

18 Hezron's son Caleb had sons from his wife Azubah and from Jerioth.* Her sons were named Jesher, Shobab, and Ardon. 19After Azubah died, Caleb married Ephrathah,* and they had a son named Hur. 20Hur was the father of Uri. Uri was the father of Bezalel.
21 When Hezron was sixty years old, he married Gilead's sister, the daughter of Makir. They had a son named Segub. 22Segub was the father of Jair, who ruled twenty-three towns in the land of Gilead. 23(But Geshur and Aram captured the Towns of Jair* and also took Kenath and its sixty surrounding villages.) All these were descendants of Makir, the father of Gilead.
24 Soon after Hezron died in the town of Caleb-ephrathah, his wife Abijah gave birth to a son named Ashhur (the father of* Tekoa).

Descendants of Hezron's Son Jerahmeel

25 The sons of Jerahmeel, the oldest son of Hezron, were Ram (the firstborn), Bunah, Oren, Ozem, and Ahijah. 26Jerahmeel had a second wife named Atarah. She was the mother of Onam.
27 The sons of Ram, the oldest son of Jerahmeel, were Maaz, Jamin, and Eker.
28 The sons of Onam were Shammai and Jada. The sons of Shammai were Nadab and Abishur.
29 The sons of Abishur and his wife Abihail were Ahban and Molid.
30 The sons of Nadab were Seled and Appaim. Seled died without children, 31but Appaim had a son named Ishi. The son of Ishi was Sheshan. Sheshan had a descendant named Ahlai.
32 The sons of Jada, Shammai's brother, were Jether and Jonathan. Jether died without children, 33but Jonathan had two sons named Peleth and Zaza. These were all descendants of Jerahmeel.

34 Sheshan had no sons, though he did have daughters. He also had an Egyptian servant named Jarha. 35Sheshan gave one of his daughters to be the wife of Jarha, and they had a son named Attai.
36 Attai was the father of Nathan. Nathan was the father of Zabad.
37 Zabad was the father of Ephlal. Ephlal was the father of Obed.
38 Obed was the father of Jehu. Jehu was the father of Azariah.
39 Azariah was the father of Helez. Helez was the father of Eleasah.
40 Eleasah was the father of Sismai. Sismai was the father of Shallum.
41 Shallum was the father of Jekamiah. Jekamiah was the father of Elishama.

Descendants of Hezron's Son Caleb

42 The descendants of Caleb, the brother of Jerahmeel, included Mesha (the firstborn), who became the father of Ziph. Caleb's descendants also included the sons of Mareshah, the father of Hebron.*
43 The sons of Hebron were Korah, Tappuah, Rekem, and Shema. 44Shema was the father of Raham. Raham was the father of Jorkeam. Rekem was the father of Shammai. 45The son of Shammai was Maon. Maon was the father of Beth-zur.
46 Caleb's concubine Ephah gave birth to Haran, Moza, and Gazez. Haran was the father of Gazez.
47 The sons of Jahdai were Regem, Jotham, Geshan, Pelet, Ephah, and Shaaph.
48 Another of Caleb's concubines, Maacah, gave birth to Sheber and Tirhanah. 49She also gave birth to Shaaph (the father of Madmannah) and Sheva (the father of Macbenah and Gibea). Caleb also had a daughter named Acsah.
50 These were all descendants of Caleb.

Descendants of Caleb's Son Hur

The sons of Hur, the oldest son of Caleb's wife Ephrathah, were Shobal (the founder of Kiriath-jearim), 51Salma (the founder of Bethlehem), and Hareph (the founder of Beth-gader).
52 The descendants of Shobal (the founder of Kiriath-jearim) were Haroeh, half the Manahathites, 53and the families of Kiriath-jearim—the Ithrites, Puthites, Shumathites, and Mishraites, from whom came the people of Zorah and Eshtaol.

2:18 Or *Caleb had a daughter named Jerioth from his wife, Azubah*. The meaning of the Hebrew is uncertain. **2:19** Hebrew *Ephrath*, a variant spelling of Ephrathah; compare 2:50 and 4:4. **2:23** Or *captured Havvoth-jair*. **2:24** Or *the founder of*; also in 2:42, 45, 49. **2:42** Or *who founded Hebron*. The meaning of the Hebrew is uncertain.

2:12 Boaz was the husband of Ruth, and their story is described in the book of Ruth. From the lineage of Ruth and Boaz came David (Ruth 4:22) and eventually Jesus (Matthew 1:5, 16). Each name in these lists represents a story. These stories, like ours, have high points and low points. God continues to work through mistakes and tragedies. The story of Boaz and Ruth reminds us of God's faithfulness. What stories do you remember, as you consider the names in your family?

54 The descendants of Salma were the people of Bethlehem, the Netophathites, Atroth-beth-joab, the other half of the Manahathites, the Zorites, 55 and the families of scribes living at Jabez—the Tirathites, Shimeathites, and Sucathites. All these were Kenites who descended from Hammath, the father of the family of Recab.*

Descendants of David

3 These are the sons of David who were born in Hebron:

The oldest was Amnon, whose mother was Ahinoam from Jezreel.
The second was Daniel, whose mother was Abigail from Carmel.
2 The third was Absalom, whose mother was Maacah, the daughter of Talmai, king of Geshur.
The fourth was Adonijah, whose mother was Haggith.
3 The fifth was Shephatiah, whose mother was Abital.
The sixth was Ithream, whose mother was Eglah, David's wife.

4 These six sons were born to David in Hebron, where he reigned seven and a half years.

Then David reigned another thirty-three years in Jerusalem. 5 The sons born to David in Jerusalem included Shammua,* Shobab, Nathan, and Solomon. Their mother was Bathsheba,* the daughter of Ammiel. 6 David also had nine other sons: Ibhar, Elishua,* Elpelet,* 7 Nogah, Nepheg, Japhia, 8 Elishama, Eliada, and Eliphelet.

9 These were the sons of David, not including his sons born to his concubines. Their sister was named Tamar.

Descendants of Solomon

10 The descendants of Solomon were Rehoboam, Abijah, Asa, Jehoshaphat, 11 Jehoram,* Ahaziah, Joash, 12 Amaziah, Uzziah,* Jotham, 13 Ahaz, Hezekiah, Manasseh, 14 Amon, and Josiah.
15 The sons of Josiah were Johanan (the oldest), Jehoiakim (the second), Zedekiah (the third), and Jehoahaz* (the fourth).
16 The successors of Jehoiakim were his son Jehoiachin and his brother Zedekiah.*

Descendants of Jehoiachin

17 The sons of Jehoiachin,* who was taken prisoner by the Babylonians, were Shealtiel, 18 Malkiram, Pedaiah, Shenazzar, Jekamiah, Hoshama, and Nedabiah.

19 The sons of Pedaiah were Zerubbabel and Shimei.

The sons of Zerubbabel were Meshullam and Hananiah. (Their sister was Shelomith.) 20 His five other sons were Hashubah, Ohel, Berekiah, Hasadiah, and Jushab-hesed.
21 The sons of Hananiah were Pelatiah and Jeshaiah. Jeshaiah's son was Rephaiah. Rephaiah's son was Arnan. Arnan's son was Obadiah. Obadiah's son was Shecaniah.
22 The descendants of Shecaniah were Shemaiah and his sons, Hattush, Igal, Bariah, Neariah, and Shaphat—six in all.
23 The sons of Neariah were Elioenai, Hizkiah, and Azrikam—three in all.
24 The sons of Elioenai were Hodaviah, Eliashib, Pelaiah, Akkub, Johanan, Delaiah, and Anani—seven in all.

Other Descendants of Judah

4 The descendants of Judah were Perez, Hezron, Carmi, Hur, and Shobal.
2 Shobal's son Reaiah was the father of Jahath. Jahath was the father of Ahumai and Lahad. These were the families of the Zorathites.
3 The descendants of* Etam were Jezreel, Ishma, Idbash, their sister Hazzelelponi, 4 Penuel (the father of* Gedor), and Ezer (the father of Hushah). These were the descendants of Hur (the firstborn of Ephrathah), the ancestor of Bethlehem.
5 Ashhur (the father of Tekoa) had two wives, named Helah and Naarah. 6 Naarah gave birth to Ahuzzam, Hepher, Temeni, and Haahashtari. 7 Helah gave birth to Zereth, Izhar,* Ethnan,

---

2:55 Or *the founder of Beth-recab.* 3:5a As in Syriac version (see also 14:4; 2 Sam 5:14); Hebrew reads *Shimea.* 3:5b Hebrew *Bathshua,* a variant spelling of Bathsheba. 3:6a As in some Hebrew and Greek manuscripts (see also 14:5-7 and 2 Sam 5:15); most Hebrew manuscripts read *Elishama.* 3:6b Hebrew *Eliphelet;* compare parallel text at 14:5-7. 3:11 Hebrew *Joram,* a variant spelling of Jehoram. 3:12 Hebrew *Azariah,* a variant spelling of Uzziah. 3:15 Hebrew *Shallum,* another name for Jehoahaz. 3:16 Hebrew *The sons of Jehoiakim were his son Jeconiah* [a variant spelling of Jehoiachin] *and his son Zedekiah.* 3:17 Hebrew *Jeconiah,* a variant spelling of Jehoiachin. 4:3 As in Greek version; Hebrew reads *father of.* The meaning of the Hebrew is uncertain. 4:4 Or *the founder of;* also in 4:5, 12, 14, 17, 18, and perhaps other instances where the text reads *the father of.* 4:7 As in an alternate reading in the Masoretic Text (see also Latin Vulgate); the other alternate and the Greek version read *Zohar.*

3:1 Abigail intervened in David's life at a crucial moment, during his difficult time in the wilderness. She eventually married David. Her story is found in 1 Samuel 25.
3:5 Bathsheba was married to David, and their son Solomon became king after his father. Solomon also built the Temple in Jerusalem (1 Kings 5–7). Bathsheba's story is in 2 Samuel 11–12 and 1 Kings 1.

3:9 Tamar was David's daughter. Even though difficult things happened in her life, Tamar was still valued by God and was important in God's story. Both the good things and the hard things that happen in our lives matter to God. We find Tamar's story in 2 Samuel 13.

⁸and Koz, who became the ancestor of Anub, Zobebah, and all the families of Aharhel son of Harum.

⁹There was a man named Jabez who was more honorable than any of his brothers. His mother named him Jabez* because his birth had been so painful. ¹⁰He was the one who prayed to the God of Israel, "Oh, that you would bless me and expand my territory! Please be with me in all that I do, and keep me from all trouble and pain!" And God granted him his request.

¹¹Kelub (the brother of Shuhah) was the father of Mehir. Mehir was the father of Eshton. ¹²Eshton was the father of Beth-rapha, Paseah, and Tehinnah. Tehinnah was the father of Ir-nahash. These were the descendants of Recah.

¹³The sons of Kenaz were Othniel and Seraiah. Othniel's sons were Hathath and Meonothai.* ¹⁴Meonothai was the father of Ophrah. Seraiah was the father of Joab, the founder of the Valley of Craftsmen,* so called because they were craftsmen.

¹⁵The sons of Caleb son of Jephunneh were Iru, Elah, and Naam. The son of Elah was Kenaz.

¹⁶The sons of Jehallelel were Ziph, Ziphah, Tiria, and Asarel.

¹⁷The sons of Ezrah were Jether, Mered, Epher, and Jalon. One of Mered's wives became* the mother of Miriam, Shammai, and Ishbah (the father of Eshtemoa). ¹⁸He married a woman from Judah, who became the mother of Jered (the father of Gedor), Heber (the father of Soco), and Jekuthiel (the father of Zanoah). Mered also married Bithia, a daughter of Pharaoh, and she bore him children.

¹⁹Hodiah's wife was the sister of Naham. One of her sons was the father of Keilah the Garmite, and another was the father of Eshtemoa the Maacathite.

²⁰The sons of Shimon were Amnon, Rinnah, Ben-hanan, and Tilon.
The descendants of Ishi were Zoheth and Ben-zoheth.

Descendants of Judah's Son Shelah

²¹Shelah was one of Judah's sons. The descendants of Shelah were Er (the father of Lecah); Laadah (the father of Mareshah); the families of linen workers at Beth-ashbea; ²²Jokim; the men of Cozeba; and Joash and Saraph, who ruled over Moab and Jashubi-lehem. These names all come from ancient records. ²³They were the pottery makers who lived in Netaim and Gederah. They lived there and worked for the king.

Descendants of Simeon

²⁴The sons of Simeon were Jemuel,* Jamin, Jarib, Zohar,* and Shaul.

²⁵The descendants of Shaul were Shallum, Mibsam, and Mishma.

²⁶The descendants of Mishma were Hammuel, Zaccur, and Shimei.

²⁷Shimei had sixteen sons and six daughters, but none of his brothers had large families. So Simeon's tribe never grew as large as the tribe of Judah.

²⁸They lived in Beersheba, Moladah, Hazar-shual, ²⁹Bilhah, Ezem, Tolad, ³⁰Bethuel, Hormah, Ziklag, ³¹Beth-marcaboth, Hazar-susim, Beth-biri, and Shaaraim. These towns were under their control until the time of King David. ³²Their descendants also lived in Etam, Ain, Rimmon, Token, and Ashan—five towns ³³and their surrounding villages as far away as Baalath.* This was their territory, and these names are listed in their genealogical records.

³⁴Other descendants of Simeon included Meshobab, Jamlech, Joshah son of Amaziah, ³⁵Joel, Jehu son of Joshibiah, son of Seraiah, son of Asiel, ³⁶Elioenai, Jaakobah, Jeshohaiah, Asaiah, Adiel, Jesimiel, Benaiah, ³⁷and Ziza son of Shiphi, son of Allon, son of Jedaiah, son of Shimri, son of Shemaiah.

³⁸These were the names of some of the leaders of Simeon's wealthy clans. Their families grew, ³⁹and they traveled to the region of Gerar,* in the east part of the valley, seeking pastureland for their flocks. ⁴⁰They found lush pastures there, and the land was spacious, quiet, and peaceful.

Some of Ham's descendants had been living in that region. ⁴¹But during the reign of King Hezekiah of Judah, these leaders of Simeon invaded the region and completely destroyed* the homes of the descendants of Ham and of the Meunites. No trace of

---

4:9 *Jabez* sounds like a Hebrew word meaning "distress" or "pain."   **4:13** As in some Greek manuscripts and Latin Vulgate; Hebrew lacks *and Meonothai*.   **4:14** Or *Joab, the father of Ge-harashim*.   **4:17** Or *Jether's wife became;* Hebrew reads *She became*.   **4:24a** As in Syriac version (see also Gen 46:10; Exod 6:15); Hebrew reads *Nemuel*.   **4:24b** As in parallel texts at Gen 46:10 and Exod 6:15; Hebrew reads *Zerah*.   **4:33** As in some Greek manuscripts (see also Josh 19:8); Hebrew reads *Baal*.   **4:39** As in Greek version; Hebrew reads *Gedor*.   **4:41** The Hebrew term used here refers to the complete consecration of things or people to the Lord, either by destroying them or by giving them as an offering.

4:9-10 This brief story of Jabez is the first narrative attached to a name in Chronicles. His mother named him, exclaiming that he was birthed in pain. The Hebrew root *abats* forms the name of Jabez, and his name is a wordplay with the Hebrew term for pain, *atsab*. Though born from pain, Jabez grew into a man of honor and a man of prayer, who directed his request to the "God of Israel" (4:10). This is the first time the phrase "God of Israel" appears in Chronicles. The use of this name for God reveals hope in Israel's God, even during the time of Israel's displacement and Exile.

them remains today. They killed everyone who lived there and took the land for themselves, because they wanted its good pastureland for their flocks. ⁴²Five hundred of these invaders from the tribe of Simeon went to Mount Seir, led by Pelatiah, Neariah, Rephaiah, and Uzziel—all sons of Ishi. ⁴³They destroyed the few Amalekites who had survived, and they have lived there ever since.

Descendants of Reuben

5 The oldest son of Israel* was Reuben. But since he dishonored his father by sleeping with one of his father's concubines, his birthright was given to the sons of his brother Joseph. For this reason, Reuben is not listed in the genealogical records as the firstborn son. ²The descendants of Judah became the most powerful tribe and provided a ruler for the nation,* but the birthright belonged to Joseph.

³The sons of Reuben, the oldest son of Israel, were Hanoch, Pallu, Hezron, and Carmi.

⁴The descendants of Joel were Shemaiah, Gog, Shimei, ⁵Micah, Reaiah, Baal, ⁶and Beerah. Beerah was the leader of the Reubenites when they were taken into captivity by King Tiglath-pileser* of Assyria. ⁷Beerah's* relatives are listed in their genealogical records by their clans: Jeiel (the leader), Zechariah, ⁸and Bela son of Azaz, son of Shema, son of Joel. The Reubenites lived in the area that stretches from Aroer to Nebo and Baal-meon. ⁹And since they had so many livestock in the land of Gilead, they spread east toward the edge of the desert that stretches to the Euphrates River.

¹⁰During the reign of Saul, the Reubenites defeated the Hagrites in battle. Then they moved into the Hagrite settlements all along the eastern edge of Gilead.

Descendants of Gad

¹¹Next to the Reubenites, the descendants of Gad lived in the land of Bashan as far east as Salecah. ¹²Joel was the leader in the land of Bashan, and Shapham was second-in-command, followed by Janai and Shaphat.

¹³Their relatives, the leaders of seven other clans, were Michael, Meshullam, Sheba, Jorai, Jacan, Zia, and Eber. ¹⁴These were all descendants of Abihail son of Huri, son of Jaroah, son of Gilead, son of Michael, son of Jeshishai, son of Jahdo, son of Buz. ¹⁵Ahi son of Abdiel, son of Guni, was the leader of their clans.

¹⁶The Gadites lived in the land of Gilead, in Bashan and its villages, and throughout all the pasturelands of Sharon. ¹⁷All of these were listed in the genealogical records during the days of King Jotham of Judah and King Jeroboam of Israel.

The Tribes East of the Jordan

¹⁸There were 44,760 capable warriors in the armies of Reuben, Gad, and the half-tribe of Manasseh. They were all skilled in combat and armed with shields, swords, and bows. ¹⁹They waged war against the Hagrites, the Jeturites, the Naphishites, and the Nodabites. ²⁰They cried out to God during the battle, and he answered their prayer because they trusted in him. So the Hagrites and all their allies were defeated. ²¹The plunder taken from the Hagrites included 50,000 camels, 250,000 sheep and goats, 2,000 donkeys, and 100,000 captives. ²²Many of the Hagrites were killed in the battle because God was fighting against them. The people of Reuben, Gad, and Manasseh lived in their land until they were taken into exile.

²³The half-tribe of Manasseh was very large and spread through the land from Bashan to Baal-hermon, Senir, and Mount Hermon. ²⁴These were the leaders of their clans: Epher,* Ishi, Eliel, Azriel, Jeremiah, Hodaviah, and Jahdiel. These men had a great reputation as mighty warriors and leaders of their clans.

²⁵But these tribes were unfaithful to the God of their ancestors. They worshiped the gods of the nations that God had destroyed. ²⁶So the God of Israel caused King Pul of Assyria (also known as Tiglath-pileser) to invade the land and take away the people of Reuben, Gad, and the half-tribe of Manasseh as captives. The Assyrians exiled them to Halah, Habor, Hara, and the Gozan River, where they remain to this day.

The Priestly Line

6 ¹*The sons of Levi were Gershon, Kohath, and Merari.
²The descendants of Kohath included Amram, Izhar, Hebron, and Uzziel.

5:1 *Israel* is the name that God gave to Jacob.   **5:2** Or *and from Judah came a prince.*   **5:6** Hebrew *Tilgath-pilneser*, a variant spelling of Tiglath-pileser; also in 5:26.   **5:7** Hebrew *His.*   **5:24** As in Greek version and Latin Vulgate; Hebrew reads *and Epher.*   **6:1** Verses 6:1-15 are numbered 5:27-41 in Hebrew text.

5:1-2 Although Reuben was the oldest son of Israel (Jacob), he did not receive his birthright because he had sex with his father's concubine (Genesis 35:22). Jacob transferred this right to his son Joseph by giving Joseph's sons, Ephraim and Manasseh, full membership among the tribes (Genesis 48:5). This gave Joseph a double portion of the birthright that traditionally belonged to the firstborn and would have gone to Reuben (Deuteronomy 21:15-17). As Jacob saw in advance, Judah surpassed his brothers and became the ruling tribe's forefather (Genesis 49:8-10). However, Reuben's name still comes first (1 Chronicles 2:1).

6:1-48 This section gives the genealogies of the three most significant groups of the tribe of Levi: the high priests (6:1-15), the three Levite clans (6:16-30), and the musicians (6:31-47).

³The children of Amram were Aaron, Moses, and Miriam.

The sons of Aaron were Nadab, Abihu, Eleazar, and Ithamar.

4 Eleazar was the father of Phinehas.
Phinehas was the father of Abishua.
5 Abishua was the father of Bukki.
Bukki was the father of Uzzi.
6 Uzzi was the father of Zerahiah.
Zerahiah was the father of Meraioth.
7 Meraioth was the father of Amariah.
Amariah was the father of Ahitub.
8 Ahitub was the father of Zadok.
Zadok was the father of Ahimaaz.
9 Ahimaaz was the father of Azariah.
Azariah was the father of Johanan.
10 Johanan was the father of Azariah, the high priest at the Temple* built by Solomon in Jerusalem.
11 Azariah was the father of Amariah.
Amariah was the father of Ahitub.
12 Ahitub was the father of Zadok.
Zadok was the father of Shallum.
13 Shallum was the father of Hilkiah.
Hilkiah was the father of Azariah.
14 Azariah was the father of Seraiah.
Seraiah was the father of Jehozadak, ¹⁵who went into exile when the LORD sent the people of Judah and Jerusalem into captivity under Nebuchadnezzar.

The Levite Clans

¹⁶*The sons of Levi were Gershon,* Kohath, and Merari.
¹⁷The descendants of Gershon included Libni and Shimei.
¹⁸The descendants of Kohath included Amram, Izhar, Hebron, and Uzziel.
¹⁹The descendants of Merari included Mahli and Mushi.

The following were the Levite clans, listed according to their ancestral descent:

²⁰The descendants of Gershon included Libni, Jahath, Zimmah, ²¹Joah, Iddo, Zerah, and Jeatherai.
²²The descendants of Kohath included Amminadab, Korah, Assir, ²³Elkanah, Abiasaph,* Assir, ²⁴Tahath, Uriel, Uzziah, and Shaul.
²⁵The descendants of Elkanah included Amasai, Ahimoth, ²⁶Elkanah, Zophai, Nahath, ²⁷Eliab, Jeroham, Elkanah, and Samuel.*

²⁸The sons of Samuel were Joel* (the older) and Abijah (the second).
²⁹The descendants of Merari included Mahli, Libni, Shimei, Uzzah, ³⁰Shimea, Haggiah, and Asaiah.

The Temple Musicians

³¹David assigned the following men to lead the music at the house of the LORD after the Ark was placed there. ³²They ministered with music at the Tabernacle* until Solomon built the Temple of the LORD in Jerusalem. They carried out their work, following all the regulations handed down to them. ³³These are the men who served, along with their sons:

Heman the musician was from the clan of Kohath. His genealogy was traced back through Joel, Samuel, ³⁴Elkanah, Jeroham, Eliel, Toah, ³⁵Zuph, Elkanah, Mahath, Amasai, ³⁶Elkanah, Joel, Azariah, Zephaniah, ³⁷Tahath, Assir, Abiasaph, Korah, ³⁸Izhar, Kohath, Levi, and Israel.*
³⁹Heman's first assistant was Asaph from the clan of Gershon.* Asaph's genealogy was traced back through Berekiah, Shimea, ⁴⁰Michael, Baaseiah, Malkijah, ⁴¹Ethni, Zerah, Adaiah, ⁴²Ethan, Zimmah, Shimei, ⁴³Jahath, Gershon, and Levi.
⁴⁴Heman's second assistant was Ethan from the clan of Merari. Ethan's genealogy was traced back through Kishi, Abdi, Malluch, ⁴⁵Hashabiah, Amaziah, Hilkiah, ⁴⁶Amzi, Bani, Shemer, ⁴⁷Mahli, Mushi, Merari, and Levi.

⁴⁸Their fellow Levites were appointed to various other tasks in the Tabernacle, the house of God.

Aaron's Descendants

⁴⁹Only Aaron and his descendants served as priests. They presented the offerings on the altar of burnt offering and the altar of incense, and they performed all the other duties related to the Most Holy Place. They made atonement for Israel by doing everything that Moses, the servant of God, had commanded them.

⁵⁰The descendants of Aaron were Eleazar, Phinehas, Abishua, ⁵¹Bukki, Uzzi, Zerahiah, ⁵²Meraioth, Amariah, Ahitub, ⁵³Zadok, and Ahimaaz.

Territory for the Levites

⁵⁴This is a record of the towns and territory assigned by means of sacred lots to the descendants of Aaron, who were from the clan of Kohath. ⁵⁵This

---

6:10 Hebrew *the house.* 6:16a Verses 6:16-81 are numbered 6:1-66 in Hebrew text. 6:16b Hebrew *Gershom,* a variant spelling of Gershon (see 6:1); also in 6:17, 20, 43, 62, 71. 6:23 Hebrew *Ebiasaph,* a variant spelling of Abiasaph (also in 6:37); compare parallel text at Exod 6:24. 6:27 As in some Greek manuscripts (see also 6:33-34); Hebrew lacks *and Samuel.* 6:28 As in some Greek manuscripts and the Syriac version (see also 6:33 and 1 Sam 8:2); Hebrew lacks *Joel.* 6:32 Hebrew *the Tabernacle, the Tent of Meeting.* 6:38 *Israel* is the name that God gave to Jacob. 6:39 Hebrew lacks *from the clan of Gershon;* see 6:43.

6:3 Miriam was the sister of Moses and Aaron (Exodus 2:1-8; 15:20-21; Numbers 12:1-15). Miriam is one of the four named women prophets in the Old Testament, along with Deborah (Judges 4–5), Huldah (2 Kings 22:14-20; 2 Chronicles 34:22-28), and Noadiah (Nehemiah 6:14).

territory included Hebron and its surrounding pasturelands in Judah, ⁵⁶but the fields and outlying areas belonging to the city were given to Caleb son of Jephunneh. ⁵⁷So the descendants of Aaron were given the following towns, each with its pasturelands: Hebron (a city of refuge),* Libnah, Jattir, Eshtemoa, ⁵⁸Holon,* Debir, ⁵⁹Ain,* Juttah,* and Beth-shemesh. ⁶⁰And from the territory of Benjamin they were given Gibeon,* Geba, Alemeth, and Anathoth, each with its pasturelands. So thirteen towns were given to the descendants of Aaron. ⁶¹The remaining descendants of Kohath received ten towns from the territory of the half-tribe of Manasseh by means of sacred lots.

⁶²The descendants of Gershon received by sacred lots thirteen towns from the territories of Issachar, Asher, Naphtali, and from the Bashan area of Manasseh, east of the Jordan.

⁶³The descendants of Merari received by sacred lots twelve towns from the territories of Reuben, Gad, and Zebulun.

⁶⁴So the people of Israel assigned all these towns and pasturelands to the Levites. ⁶⁵The towns in the territories of Judah, Simeon, and Benjamin, mentioned above, were assigned to them by means of sacred lots.

⁶⁶The descendants of Kohath were given the following towns from the territory of Ephraim, each with its pasturelands: ⁶⁷Shechem (a city of refuge in the hill country of Ephraim),* Gezer, ⁶⁸Jokmeam, Beth-horon, ⁶⁹Aijalon, and Gath-rimmon. ⁷⁰The remaining descendants of Kohath were assigned the towns of Aner and Bileam from the territory of the half-tribe of Manasseh, each with its pasturelands.

⁷¹The descendants of Gershon received the towns of Golan (in Bashan) and Ashtaroth from the territory of the half-tribe of Manasseh, each with its pasturelands. ⁷²From the territory of Issachar, they were given Kedesh, Daberath, ⁷³Ramoth, and Anem, each with its pasturelands. ⁷⁴From the territory of Asher, they received Mashal, Abdon, ⁷⁵Hukok, and Rehob, each with its pasturelands. ⁷⁶From the territory of Naphtali, they were given Kedesh in Galilee, Hammon, and Kiriathaim, each with its pasturelands.

⁷⁷The remaining descendants of Merari received the towns of Jokneam, Kartah,* Rimmon,* and Tabor from the territory of Zebulun, each with its pasturelands. ⁷⁸From the territory of Reuben, east of the Jordan River opposite Jericho, they received Bezer (a desert town), Jahaz,* ⁷⁹Kedemoth, and Mephaath, each with its pasturelands. ⁸⁰And from the territory of Gad, they received Ramoth in Gilead, Mahanaim, ⁸¹Heshbon, and Jazer, each with its pasturelands.

Descendants of Issachar

7 The four sons of Issachar were Tola, Puah, Jashub, and Shimron.
²The sons of Tola were Uzzi, Rephaiah, Jeriel, Jahmai, Ibsam, and Shemuel. Each of them was the leader of an ancestral clan. At the time of King David, the total number of mighty warriors listed in the records of these clans was 22,600.
³The son of Uzzi was Izrahiah. The sons of Izrahiah were Michael, Obadiah, Joel, and Isshiah. These five became the leaders of clans. ⁴All of them had many wives and many sons, so the total number of men available for military service among their descendants was 36,000.
⁵The total number of mighty warriors from all the clans of the tribe of Issachar was 87,000. All of them were listed in their genealogical records.

Descendants of Benjamin

⁶Three of Benjamin's sons were Bela, Beker, and Jediael.
⁷The five sons of Bela were Ezbon, Uzzi, Uzziel, Jerimoth, and Iri. Each of them was the leader of an ancestral clan. The total number of mighty warriors from these clans was 22,034, as listed in their genealogical records.
⁸The sons of Beker were Zemirah, Joash, Eliezer, Elioenai, Omri, Jeremoth, Abijah, Anathoth, and Alemeth. ⁹Each of them was the leader of an ancestral clan. The total number of mighty warriors and leaders from these clans was 20,200, as listed in their genealogical records.
¹⁰The son of Jediael was Bilhan. The sons of Bilhan were Jeush, Benjamin, Ehud, Kenaanah, Zethan, Tarshish, and Ahishahar. ¹¹Each of them was the leader of an ancestral clan. From these clans the total number of mighty warriors ready for war was 17,200.
¹²The sons of Ir were Shuppim and Huppim. Hushim was the son of Aher.

Descendants of Naphtali

¹³The sons of Naphtali were Jahzeel,* Guni, Jezer, and Shillem.* They were all descendants of Jacob's concubine Bilhah.

6:57 As in parallel text at Josh 21:13; Hebrew reads *were given the cities of refuge: Hebron, and the following towns, each with its pasturelands*. **6:58** As in parallel text at Josh 21:15; Masoretic Text reads *Hilez;* other manuscripts read *Hilen*. **6:59a** As in parallel text at Josh 21:16; Hebrew reads *Ashan*. **6:59b** As in Syriac version (see also Josh 21:16); Hebrew lacks *Juttah*. **6:60** As in parallel text at Josh 21:17; Hebrew lacks *Gibeon*. **6:66-67** As in parallel text at Josh 21:21; Hebrew text reads *were given the cities of refuge: Shechem in the hill country of Ephraim, and the following towns, each with its pasturelands*. **6:77a** As in Greek version (see also Josh 21:34); Hebrew lacks *Jokneam, Kartah*. **6:77b** As in Greek version (see also Josh 19:13); Hebrew reads *Rimmono*. **6:78** Hebrew *Jahzah,* a variant spelling of Jahaz. **7:13a** As in parallel text at Gen 46:24; Hebrew reads *Jahziel,* a variant spelling of Jahzeel. **7:13b** As in some Hebrew and Greek manuscripts (see also Gen 46:24; Num 26:49); most Hebrew manuscripts read *Shallum*.

> "Bless me and expand my territory! Please be with me in all that I do…"
>
> — 1 CHRONICLES 4:10

Descendants of Manasseh

¹⁴The descendants of Manasseh through his Aramean concubine included Asriel. She also bore Makir, the father of Gilead. ¹⁵Makir found wives for* Huppim and Shuppim. Makir had a sister named Maacah. One of his descendants was Zelophehad, who had only daughters.

¹⁶Makir's wife, Maacah, gave birth to a son whom she named Peresh. His brother's name was Sheresh. The sons of Peresh were Ulam and Rakem. ¹⁷The son of Ulam was Bedan. All these were considered Gileadites, descendants of Makir son of Manasseh.

¹⁸Makir's sister Hammoleketh gave birth to Ishhod, Abiezer, and Mahlah.

¹⁹The sons of Shemida were Ahian, Shechem, Likhi, and Aniam.

Descendants of Ephraim

²⁰The descendants of Ephraim were Shuthelah, Bered, Tahath, Eleadah, Tahath, ²¹Zabad, Shuthelah, Ezer, and Elead. These two were killed trying to steal livestock from the local farmers near Gath. ²²Their father, Ephraim, mourned for them a long time, and his relatives came to comfort him. ²³Afterward Ephraim slept with his wife, and she became pregnant and gave birth to a son. Ephraim named him Beriah* because of the tragedy his family had suffered. ²⁴He had a daughter named Sheerah. She built the towns of Lower and Upper Beth-horon and Uzzen-sheerah.

²⁵The descendants of Ephraim included Rephah, Resheph, Telah, Tahan, ²⁶Ladan, Ammihud, Elishama, ²⁷Nun, and Joshua.

²⁸The descendants of Ephraim lived in the territory that included Bethel and its surrounding towns to the south, Naaran to the east, Gezer and its villages to the west, and Shechem and its surrounding villages to the north as far as Ayyah and its towns. ²⁹Along the border of Manasseh were the towns of Beth-shan,* Taanach, Megiddo, Dor, and their surrounding villages. The descendants of Joseph son of Israel* lived in these towns.

Descendants of Asher

³⁰The sons of Asher were Imnah, Ishvah, Ishvi, and Beriah. They had a sister named Serah. ³¹The sons of Beriah were Heber and Malkiel (the father of Birzaith).

³²The sons of Heber were Japhlet, Shomer, and Hotham. They had a sister named Shua.

³³The sons of Japhlet were Pasach, Bimhal, and Ashvath.

³⁴The sons of Shomer were Ahi,* Rohgah, Hubbah, and Aram.

³⁵The sons of his brother Helem* were Zophah, Imna, Shelesh, and Amal.

³⁶The sons of Zophah were Suah, Harnepher, Shual, Beri, Imrah, ³⁷Bezer, Hod, Shamma, Shilshah, Ithran,* and Beera.

³⁸The sons of Jether were Jephunneh, Pispah, and Ara.

³⁹The sons of Ulla were Arah, Hanniel, and Rizia.

⁴⁰Each of these descendants of Asher was the head of an ancestral clan. They were all select men—mighty warriors and outstanding leaders. The total number of men available for military service was 26,000, as listed in their genealogical records.

Descendants of Benjamin

8 Benjamin's first son was Bela, the second was Ashbel, the third was Aharah, ²the fourth was Nohah, and the fifth was Rapha.

³The sons of Bela were Addar, Gera, Abihud,* ⁴Abishua, Naaman, Ahoah, ⁵Gera, Shephuphan, and Huram.

⁶The sons of Ehud, leaders of the clans living at Geba, were exiled to Manahath. ⁷Ehud's sons were Naaman, Ahijah, and Gera. Gera, who led them into exile, was the father of Uzza and Ahihud.*

⁸After Shaharaim divorced his wives Hushim and Baara, he had children in the land of Moab. ⁹His wife Hodesh gave birth to Jobab, Zibia, Mesha, Malcam, ¹⁰Jeuz, Sakia, and Mirmah. These sons all became the leaders of clans.

¹¹Shaharaim's wife Hushim had already given birth to Abitub and Elpaal. ¹²The sons of Elpaal were Eber, Misham, Shemed (who built the towns of Ono and Lod and their nearby villages), ¹³Beriah, and Shema. They were the leaders of the clans living in Aijalon, and they drove out the inhabitants of Gath.

¹⁴Ahio, Shashak, Jeremoth, ¹⁵Zebadiah, Arad, Eder, ¹⁶Michael, Ishpah, and Joha were the sons of Beriah.

7:15 Or *Makir took a wife from*. The meaning of the Hebrew is uncertain. **7:23** *Beriah* sounds like a Hebrew term meaning "tragedy" or "misfortune." **7:29a** Hebrew *Beth-shean*, a variant spelling of Beth-shan. **7:29b** *Israel* is the name that God gave to Jacob. **7:34** Or *The sons of Shomer, his brother, were*. **7:35** Possibly another name for *Hotham;* compare 7:32. **7:37** Possibly another name for *Jether;* compare 7:38. **8:3** Possibly *Gera the father of Ehud;* compare 8:6. **8:7** Or *Gera, that is Heglam, was the father of Uzza and Ahihud.*

7:15 Manasseh was the ancestor of Zelophehad, a man who had only daughters. Their story is found in Numbers 27:1-11 and reveals insight into women's rights to inherit property and God's care for his people.

¹⁷Zebadiah, Meshullam, Hizki, Heber, ¹⁸Ishmerai, Izliah, and Jobab were the sons of Elpaal.
¹⁹Jakim, Zicri, Zabdi, ²⁰Elienai, Zillethai, Eliel, ²¹Adaiah, Beraiah, and Shimrath were the sons of Shimei.
²²Ishpan, Eber, Eliel, ²³Abdon, Zicri, Hanan, ²⁴Hananiah, Elam, Anthothijah, ²⁵Iphdeiah, and Penuel were the sons of Shashak.
²⁶Shamsherai, Shehariah, Athaliah, ²⁷Jaareshiah, Elijah, and Zicri were the sons of Jeroham.
²⁸These were the leaders of the ancestral clans; they were listed in their genealogical records, and they all lived in Jerusalem.

The Family of Saul

²⁹Jeiel* (the father of* Gibeon) lived in the town of Gibeon. His wife's name was Maacah, ³⁰and his oldest son was named Abdon. Jeiel's other sons were Zur, Kish, Baal, Ner,* Nadab, ³¹Gedor, Ahio, Zechariah,* ³²and Mikloth, who was the father of Shimeam.* All these families lived near each other in Jerusalem.

³³ Ner was the father of Kish.
Kish was the father of Saul.
Saul was the father of Jonathan, Malkishua, Abinadab, and Esh-baal.

³⁴ Jonathan was the father of Merib-baal.
Merib-baal was the father of Micah.

³⁵ Micah was the father of Pithon, Melech, Tahrea,* and Ahaz.

³⁶ Ahaz was the father of Jadah.*
Jadah was the father of Alemeth, Azmaveth, and Zimri.
Zimri was the father of Moza.

³⁷ Moza was the father of Binea.
Binea was the father of Rephaiah.*
Rephaiah was the father of Eleasah.
Eleasah was the father of Azel.

³⁸Azel had six sons: Azrikam, Bokeru, Ishmael, Sheariah, Obadiah, and Hanan. These were the sons of Azel.

³⁹Azel's brother Eshek had three sons: the first was Ulam, the second was Jeush, and the third was Eliphelet. ⁴⁰Ulam's sons were all mighty warriors and expert archers. They had many sons and grandsons—150 in all.

All these were descendants of Benjamin.

9 So all Israel was listed in the genealogical records in The Book of the Kings of Israel.

The Returning Exiles

The people of Judah were exiled to Babylon because they were unfaithful to the LORD. ²The first of the exiles to return to their property in their former towns were priests, Levites, Temple servants, and other Israelites. ³Some of the people from the tribes of Judah, Benjamin, Ephraim, and Manasseh came and settled in Jerusalem.

⁴One family that returned was that of Uthai son of Ammihud, son of Omri, son of Imri, son of Bani, a descendant of Perez son of Judah.
⁵Others returned from the Shilonite clan, including Asaiah (the oldest) and his sons.
⁶From the Zerahite clan, Jeuel returned with his relatives.
In all, 690 families from the tribe of Judah returned.

⁷From the tribe of Benjamin came Sallu son of Meshullam, son of Hodaviah, son of Hassenuah; ⁸Ibneiah son of Jeroham; Elah son of Uzzi, son of Micri; and Meshullam son of Shephatiah, son of Reuel, son of Ibnijah.
⁹These men were all leaders of clans, and they were listed in their genealogical records. In all, 956 families from the tribe of Benjamin returned.

The Returning Priests

¹⁰Among the priests who returned were Jedaiah, Jehoiarib, Jakin, ¹¹Azariah son of Hilkiah, son of Meshullam, son of Zadok, son of Meraioth, son of Ahitub. Azariah was the chief officer of the house of God.

8:29a As in some Greek manuscripts (see also 9:35); Hebrew lacks *Jeiel*. 8:29b Or *the founder of*. 8:30 As in some Greek manuscripts (see also 9:36); Hebrew lacks *Ner*. 8:31 As in parallel text at 9:37; Hebrew reads *Zeker*, a variant spelling of Zechariah. 8:32 As in parallel text at 9:38; Hebrew reads *Shimeah*, a variant spelling of Shimeam. 8:35 As in parallel text at 9:41; Hebrew reads *Tarea*, a variant spelling of Tahrea. 8:36 As in parallel text at 9:42; Hebrew reads *Jehoaddah*, a variant spelling of Jadah. 8:37 As in parallel text at 9:43; Hebrew reads *Raphah*, a variant spelling of Rephaiah.

8:33-40 The chronicler includes Saul's genealogy, starting two generations before Saul. Thus, Saul is connected with his larger tribal history and with a noble heritage. Who is in your family history, or in a family history that you admire, who might inspire you to live into the influence that God gives you?

9:1-34 The chronicler shows how people and institutions who returned from the Exile had continuity with the past. The Levites and the priests are prominent in this summary of Israel, expressing the chronicler's view that they were central to the organization of the nation. They were crucial to Israel's function and success as a nation where God was the King. Drawing upon the records of ancient times as far back as Moses and David (9:14-22), the chronicler describes each group's homeland and rank.

9:1 The statement that "all Israel was listed in the genealogical records" reveals the crux of the chronicler's thought: that all Israel was represented by the community of Judah at the time, which had continuity with Israel's past. The people of Judah were exiled for unfaithfulness, as the other tribes had been (5:25-26; 6:15; see 2 Chronicles 36:20-21).

9:1 *The Book of the Kings of Israel* is a source document that the authors of both Kings and Chronicles used but has now been lost.

¹²Other returning priests were Adaiah son of Jeroham, son of Pashhur, son of Malkijah, and Maasai son of Adiel, son of Jahzerah, son of Meshullam, son of Meshillemith, son of Immer. ¹³In all, 1,760 priests returned. They were heads of clans and very able men. They were responsible for ministering at the house of God.

The Returning Levites

¹⁴The Levites who returned were Shemaiah son of Hasshub, son of Azrikam, son of Hashabiah, a descendant of Merari; ¹⁵Bakbakkar; Heresh; Galal; Mattaniah son of Mica, son of Zicri, son of Asaph; ¹⁶Obadiah son of Shemaiah, son of Galal, son of Jeduthun; and Berekiah son of Asa, son of Elkanah, who lived in the area of Netophah.

¹⁷The gatekeepers who returned were Shallum, Akkub, Talmon, Ahiman, and their relatives. Shallum was the chief gatekeeper. ¹⁸Prior to this time, they were responsible for the King's Gate on the east side. These men served as gatekeepers for the camps of the Levites. ¹⁹Shallum was the son of Kore, a descendant of Abiasaph,* from the clan of Korah. He and his relatives, the Korahites, were responsible for guarding the entrance to the sanctuary, just as their ancestors had guarded the Tabernacle in the camp of the LORD.

²⁰Phinehas son of Eleazar had been in charge of the gatekeepers in earlier times, and the LORD had been with him. ²¹And later Zechariah son of Meshelemiah was responsible for guarding the entrance to the Tabernacle.*

²²In all, there were 212 gatekeepers in those days, and they were listed according to the genealogies in their villages. David and Samuel the seer had appointed their ancestors because they were reliable men. ²³These gatekeepers and their descendants, by their divisions, were responsible for guarding the entrance to the house of the LORD when that house was a tent. ²⁴The gatekeepers were stationed on all four sides—east, west, north, and south. ²⁵Their relatives in the villages came regularly to share their duties for seven-day periods.

²⁶The four chief gatekeepers, all Levites, were trusted officials, for they were responsible for the rooms and treasuries at the house of God. ²⁷They would spend the night around the house of God, since it was their duty to guard it and to open the gates every morning.

²⁸Some of the gatekeepers were assigned to care for the various articles used in worship. They checked them in and out to avoid any loss. ²⁹Others were responsible for the furnishings, the items in the sanctuary, and the supplies, such as choice flour, wine, olive oil, frankincense, and spices. ³⁰But it was the priests who blended the spices. ³¹Mattithiah, a Levite and the oldest son of Shallum the Korahite, was entrusted with baking the bread used in the offerings. ³²And some members of the clan of Kohath were in charge of preparing the bread to be set on the table each Sabbath day.

³³The musicians, all prominent Levites, lived at the Temple. They were exempt from other responsibilities since they were on duty at all hours. ³⁴All these men lived in Jerusalem. They were the heads of Levite families and were listed as prominent leaders in their genealogical records.

King Saul's Family Tree

³⁵Jeiel (the father of* Gibeon) lived in the town of Gibeon. His wife's name was Maacah, ³⁶and his oldest son was named Abdon. Jeiel's other sons were Zur, Kish, Baal, Ner, Nadab, ³⁷Gedor, Ahio, Zechariah, and Mikloth. ³⁸Mikloth was the father of Shimeam. All these families lived near each other in Jerusalem.

³⁹ Ner was the father of Kish.
Kish was the father of Saul.
Saul was the father of Jonathan, Malkishua, Abinadab, and Esh-baal.
⁴⁰ Jonathan was the father of Merib-baal.
Merib-baal was the father of Micah.
⁴¹ The sons of Micah were Pithon, Melech, Tahrea, and Ahaz.*
⁴² Ahaz was the father of Jadah.*
Jadah was the father of Alemeth, Azmaveth, and Zimri.
Zimri was the father of Moza.
⁴³ Moza was the father of Binea.
Binea's son was Rephaiah.
Rephaiah's son was Eleasah.
Eleasah's son was Azel.
⁴⁴Azel had six sons, whose names were Azrikam, Bokeru, Ishmael, Sheariah, Obadiah, and Hanan. These were the sons of Azel.

The Death of King Saul

10 Now the Philistines attacked Israel, and the men of Israel fled before them. Many were slaughtered on the slopes of Mount Gilboa. ²The Philistines closed in on Saul and his sons, and they killed three of his sons—Jonathan, Abinadab, and Malkishua. ³The fighting grew very fierce around Saul, and the Philistine archers caught up with him and wounded him.

⁴Saul groaned to his armor bearer, "Take your sword and kill me before these pagan Philistines come to taunt and torture me."

9:19 Hebrew *Ebiasaph*, a variant spelling of Abiasaph; compare Exod 6:24. 9:21 Hebrew *Tent of Meeting*. 9:35 Or *the founder of*. 9:41 As in Syriac version and Latin Vulgate (see also 8:35); Hebrew lacks *and Ahaz*. 9:42 As in some Hebrew manuscripts and Greek version (see also 8:36); Hebrew reads *Jarah*.

But his armor bearer was afraid and would not do it. So Saul took his own sword and fell on it. ⁵When his armor bearer realized that Saul was dead, he fell on his own sword and died. ⁶So Saul and his three sons died there together, bringing his dynasty to an end.

⁷When all the Israelites in the Jezreel Valley saw that their army had fled and that Saul and his sons were dead, they abandoned their towns and fled. So the Philistines moved in and occupied their towns.

⁸The next day, when the Philistines went out to strip the dead, they found the bodies of Saul and his sons on Mount Gilboa. ⁹So they stripped off Saul's armor and cut off his head. Then they proclaimed the good news of Saul's death before their idols and to the people throughout the land of Philistia. ¹⁰They placed his armor in the temple of their gods, and they fastened his head to the temple of Dagon.

¹¹But when everyone in Jabesh-gilead heard about everything the Philistines had done to Saul, ¹²all their mighty warriors brought the bodies of Saul and his sons back to Jabesh. Then they buried their bones beneath the great tree at Jabesh, and they fasted for seven days.

¹³So Saul died because he was unfaithful to the LORD. He failed to obey the LORD's command, and he even consulted a medium ¹⁴instead of asking the LORD for guidance. So the LORD killed him and turned the kingdom over to David son of Jesse.

David Becomes King of All Israel

11 Then all Israel gathered before David at Hebron and told him, "We are your own flesh and blood. ²In the past,* even when Saul was king, you were the one who really led the forces of Israel. And the LORD your God told you, 'You will be the shepherd of my people Israel. You will be the leader of my people Israel.'"

³So there at Hebron, David made a covenant before the LORD with all the elders of Israel. And they anointed him king of Israel, just as the LORD had promised through Samuel.

David Captures Jerusalem

⁴Then David and all Israel went to Jerusalem (or Jebus, as it used to be called), where the Jebusites, the original inhabitants of the land, were living. ⁵The people of Jebus taunted David, saying, "You'll never get in here!" But David captured the fortress of Zion, which is now called the City of David.

⁶David had said to his troops, "Whoever is first to attack the Jebusites will become the commander of my armies!" And Joab, the son of David's sister Zeruiah, was first to attack, so he became the commander of David's armies.

⁷David made the fortress his home, and that is why it is called the City of David. ⁸He extended the city from the supporting terraces* to the surrounding area, while Joab rebuilt the rest of Jerusalem. ⁹And David became more and more powerful, because the LORD of Heaven's Armies was with him.

David's Mightiest Warriors

¹⁰These are the leaders of David's mighty warriors. Together with all Israel, they decided to make David their king, just as the LORD had promised concerning Israel.

¹¹Here is the record of David's mightiest warriors: The first was Jashobeam the Hacmonite, who was leader of the Three—the mightiest warriors among David's men.* He once used his spear to kill 300 enemy warriors in a single battle.

¹²Next in rank among the Three was Eleazar son of Dodai,* a descendant of Ahoah. ¹³He was with David when the Philistines gathered for battle at Pasdammim and attacked the Israelites in a field full of barley. The Israelite army fled, ¹⁴but Eleazar and David* held their ground in the middle of the field and beat back the Philistines. So the LORD saved them by giving them a great victory.

¹⁵Once when David was at the rock near the cave of Adullam, the Philistine army was camped in the valley of Rephaim. The Three (who were among the Thirty—an elite group among David's fighting men) went down to meet him there. ¹⁶David was staying in the stronghold at the time, and a Philistine detachment had occupied the town of Bethlehem.

¹⁷David remarked longingly to his men, "Oh, how I would love some of that good water from the well by the gate in Bethlehem." ¹⁸So the Three broke through the Philistine lines, drew some water from the well by the gate in Bethlehem, and brought it back to David. But David refused to drink it. Instead, he poured it out as an offering to the LORD. ¹⁹"God forbid that I should drink this!" he exclaimed. "This

---

11:2 Or *For some time.* **11:8** Hebrew *the millo.* The meaning of the Hebrew is uncertain. **11:11** As in some Greek manuscripts (see also 2 Sam 23:8); Hebrew reads *leader of the Thirty,* or *leader of the captains.* **11:12** As in parallel text at 2 Sam 23:9 (see also 1 Chr 27:4); Hebrew reads *Dodo,* a variant spelling of Dodai. **11:14** Hebrew *they.*

10:6-14 The chronicler does not mention Saul's armor bearer or the rest of his troops that also died that day (see 1 Samuel 31:6), emphasizing God's action in removing Saul and replacing him with David.
11:10 David's kingship was God's choice, not David's self-promotion or the people's trying to circumvent God's will (see 11:3; 1 Samuel 16:11-13).
11:10-47 This account of David's mighty warriors demonstrates that David had the support of Israel's best and bravest men, as well as the support of all Israel (see also 2 Samuel 23:8-39).

water is as precious as the blood of these men* who risked their lives to bring it to me." So David did not drink it. These are examples of the exploits of the Three.

David's Thirty Mighty Men

²⁰Abishai, the brother of Joab, was the leader of the Thirty.* He once used his spear to kill 300 enemy warriors in a single battle. It was by such feats that he became as famous as the Three. ²¹Abishai was the most famous of the Thirty and was their commander, though he was not one of the Three.

²²There was also Benaiah son of Jehoiada, a valiant warrior from Kabzeel. He did many heroic deeds, which included killing two champions* of Moab. Another time, on a snowy day, he chased a lion down into a pit and killed it. ²³Once, armed only with a club, he killed an Egyptian warrior who was 7½ feet* tall and who was armed with a spear as thick as a weaver's beam. Benaiah wrenched the spear from the Egyptian's hand and killed him with it. ²⁴Deeds like these made Benaiah as famous as the three mightiest warriors. ²⁵He was more honored than the other members of the Thirty, though he was not one of the Three. And David made him captain of his bodyguard.

²⁶David's mighty warriors also included:

Asahel, Joab's brother;
Elhanan son of Dodo from Bethlehem;
²⁷ Shammah from Harod;*
Helez from Pelon;
²⁸ Ira son of Ikkesh from Tekoa;
Abiezer from Anathoth;
²⁹ Sibbecai from Hushah;
Zalmon* from Ahoah;
³⁰ Maharai from Netophah;
Heled son of Baanah from Netophah;
³¹ Ithai son of Ribai from Gibeah (in the land of Benjamin);
Benaiah from Pirathon;
³² Hurai from near Nahale-gaash*;
Abi-albon* from Arabah;
³³ Azmaveth from Bahurim*;
Eliahba from Shaalbon;
³⁴ the sons of Jashen* from Gizon;
Jonathan son of Shagee from Harar;
³⁵ Ahiam son of Sharar* from Harar;
Eliphal son of Ur;
³⁶ Hepher from Mekerah;
Ahijah from Pelon;
³⁷ Hezro from Carmel;
Paarai* son of Ezbai;
³⁸ Joel, the brother of Nathan;
Mibhar son of Hagri;
³⁹ Zelek from Ammon;
Naharai from Beeroth, the armor bearer of Joab son of Zeruiah;
⁴⁰ Ira from Jattir;
Gareb from Jattir;
⁴¹ Uriah the Hittite;
Zabad son of Ahlai;
⁴² Adina son of Shiza, the Reubenite leader who had thirty men with him;
⁴³ Hanan son of Maacah;
Joshaphat from Mithna;
⁴⁴ Uzzia from Ashtaroth;
Shama and Jeiel, the sons of Hotham, from Aroer;
⁴⁵ Jediael son of Shimri;
Joha, his brother, from Tiz;
⁴⁶ Eliel from Mahavah;
Jeribai and Joshaviah, the sons of Elnaam;
Ithmah from Moab;
⁴⁷ Eliel and Obed;
Jaasiel from Zobah.*

Warriors Join David's Army

12 The following men joined David at Ziklag while he was hiding from Saul son of Kish. They were among the warriors who fought beside David in battle. ²All of them were expert archers, and they could shoot arrows or sling stones with their left hand as well as their right. They were all relatives of Saul from the tribe of Benjamin. ³Their leader was Ahiezer son of Shemaah from Gibeah; his brother Joash was second-in-command. These were the other warriors:

Jeziel and Pelet, sons of Azmaveth;
Beracah;
Jehu from Anathoth;
⁴ Ishmaiah from Gibeon, a famous warrior and leader among the Thirty;

11:19 Hebrew *Shall I drink the lifeblood of these men?* **11:20** As in Syriac version; Hebrew reads *the Three*; also in 11:21. **11:22** Or *two sons of Ariel.* **11:23** Hebrew *5 cubits* [2.3 meters]. **11:27** As in parallel text at 2 Sam 23:25; Hebrew reads *Shammoth from Haror.* **11:29** As in parallel text at 2 Sam 23:28; Hebrew reads *Ilai.* **11:32a** Or *from the ravines of Gaash.* **11:32b** As in parallel text at 2 Sam 23:31; Hebrew reads *Abiel.* **11:33** As in parallel text at 2 Sam 23:31; Hebrew reads *Baharum.* **11:34** As in parallel text at 2 Sam 23:32; Hebrew reads *sons of Hashem.* **11:35** As in parallel text at 2 Sam 23:33; Hebrew reads *son of Sacar.* **11:37** As in parallel text at 2 Sam 23:35; Hebrew reads *Naarai.* **11:47** Or *the Mezobaite.*

12:1-22 Support for making David king did not begin with Saul's demise. While Saul was still king and David was a fugitive, warriors went to David and eventually became a vast camp of various tribes, representing all Israel. Even relatives of Saul supported David as king (12:2). Of course, David was prudent about such deserters (12:17), making sure they were not traitors who would betray him to Saul. Before David's anointing took place, the people's will reflected God's will that David should become king.

*Jeremiah, Jahaziel, Johanan, and Jozabad from Gederah;
5 Eluzai, Jerimoth, Bealiah, Shemariah, and Shephatiah from Haruph;
6 Elkanah, Isshiah, Azarel, Joezer, and Jashobeam, who were Korahites;
7 Joelah and Zebadiah, sons of Jeroham from Gedor.

8 Some brave and experienced warriors from the tribe of Gad also defected to David while he was at the stronghold in the wilderness. They were expert with both shield and spear, as fierce as lions and as swift as deer on the mountains.

9 Ezer was their leader.
Obadiah was second.
Eliab was third.
10 Mishmannah was fourth.
Jeremiah was fifth.
11 Attai was sixth.
Eliel was seventh.
12 Johanan was eighth.
Elzabad was ninth.
13 Jeremiah was tenth.
Macbannai was eleventh.

14 These warriors from Gad were army commanders. The weakest among them could take on a hundred regular troops, and the strongest could take on a thousand! 15 These were the men who crossed the Jordan River during its seasonal flooding at the beginning of the year and drove out all the people living in the lowlands on both the east and west banks.

16 Others from Benjamin and Judah came to David at the stronghold. 17 David went out to meet them and said, "If you have come in peace to help me, we are friends. But if you have come to betray me to my enemies when I am innocent, then may the God of our ancestors see it and punish you."

18 Then the Spirit came upon Amasai, the leader of the Thirty, and he said,

"We are yours, David!
We are on your side, son of Jesse.
Peace and prosperity be with you,
and success to all who help you,
for your God is the one who helps you."

So David let them join him, and he made them officers over his troops.

19 Some men from Manasseh defected from the Israelite army and joined David when he set out with the Philistines to fight against Saul. But as it turned out, the Philistine rulers refused to let David and his men go with them. After much discussion, they sent them back, for they said, "It will cost us our heads if David switches loyalties to Saul and turns against us."

20 Here is a list of the men from Manasseh who defected to David as he was returning to Ziklag: Adnah, Jozabad, Jediael, Michael, Jozabad, Elihu, and Zillethai. Each commanded 1,000 troops from the tribe of Manasseh. 21 They helped David chase down bands of raiders, for they were all brave and able warriors who became commanders in his army. 22 Day after day more men joined David until he had a great army, like the army of God.

23 These are the numbers of armed warriors who joined David at Hebron. They were all eager to see David become king instead of Saul, just as the LORD had promised.

24 From the tribe of Judah, there were 6,800 warriors armed with shields and spears.
25 From the tribe of Simeon, there were 7,100 brave warriors.
26 From the tribe of Levi, there were 4,600 warriors. 27 This included Jehoiada, leader of the family of Aaron, who had 3,700 under his command. 28 This also included Zadok, a brave young warrior, with 22 members of his family who were all officers.
29 From the tribe of Benjamin, Saul's relatives, there were 3,000 warriors. Most of the men from Benjamin had remained loyal to Saul until this time.
30 From the tribe of Ephraim, there were 20,800 brave warriors, each highly respected in his own clan.
31 From the half-tribe of Manasseh west of the Jordan, 18,000 men were designated by name to help David become king.
32 From the tribe of Issachar, there were 200 leaders of the tribe with their relatives. All these men understood the signs of the times and knew the best course for Israel to take.
33 From the tribe of Zebulun, there were 50,000 skilled warriors. They were fully armed and prepared for battle and completely loyal to David.
34 From the tribe of Naphtali, there were 1,000 officers and 37,000 warriors armed with shields and spears.
35 From the tribe of Dan, there were 28,600 warriors, all prepared for battle.
36 From the tribe of Asher, there were 40,000 trained warriors, all prepared for battle.
37 From the east side of the Jordan River—where the tribes of Reuben and Gad and the half-tribe of Manasseh lived—there were 120,000 troops armed with every kind of weapon.

38 All these men came in battle array to Hebron with the single purpose of making David the king over all Israel. In fact, everyone in Israel agreed that David should be their king. 39 They feasted and drank with David for three days, for preparations had been made by their relatives for their arrival. 40 And people

---

12:4 Verses 12:4b-40 are numbered 12:5-41 in Hebrew text.

from as far away as Issachar, Zebulun, and Naphtali brought food on donkeys, camels, mules, and oxen. Vast supplies of flour, fig cakes, clusters of raisins, wine, olive oil, cattle, sheep, and goats were brought to the celebration. There was great joy throughout the land of Israel.

David Attempts to Move the Ark

13 David consulted with all his officials, including the generals and captains of his army.* ²Then he addressed the entire assembly of Israel as follows: "If you approve and if it is the will of the LORD our God, let us send messages to all the Israelites throughout the land, including the priests and Levites in their towns and pasturelands. Let us invite them to come and join us. ³It is time to bring back the Ark of our God, for we neglected it during the reign of Saul."

⁴The whole assembly agreed to this, for the people could see it was the right thing to do. ⁵So David summoned all Israel, from the Shihor Brook of Egypt in the south all the way to the town of Lebo-hamath in the north, to join in bringing the Ark of God from Kiriath-jearim. ⁶Then David and all Israel went to Baalah of Judah (also called Kiriath-jearim) to bring back the Ark of God, which bears the name* of the LORD who is enthroned between the cherubim. ⁷They placed the Ark of God on a new cart and brought it from Abinadab's house. Uzzah and Ahio were guiding the cart. ⁸David and all Israel were celebrating before God with all their might, singing songs and playing all kinds of musical instruments—lyres, harps, tambourines, cymbals, and trumpets.

⁹But when they arrived at the threshing floor of Nacon,* the oxen stumbled, and Uzzah reached out his hand to steady the Ark. ¹⁰Then the LORD's anger was aroused against Uzzah, and he struck him dead because he had laid his hand on the Ark. So Uzzah died there in the presence of God.

¹¹David was angry because the LORD's anger had burst out against Uzzah. He named that place Perez-uzzah (which means "to burst out against Uzzah"), as it is still called today.

¹²David was now afraid of God, and he asked, "How can I ever bring the Ark of God back into my care?" ¹³So David did not move the Ark into the City of David. Instead, he took it to the house of Obed-edom of Gath. ¹⁴The Ark of God remained there in Obed-edom's house for three months, and the LORD blessed the household of Obed-edom and everything he owned.

David's Palace and Family

14 Then King Hiram of Tyre sent messengers to David, along with cedar timber, and stonemasons and carpenters to build him a palace. ²And David realized that the LORD had confirmed him as king over Israel and had greatly blessed his kingdom for the sake of his people Israel.

³Then David married more wives in Jerusalem, and they had more sons and daughters. ⁴These are the names of David's sons who were born in Jerusalem: Shammua, Shobab, Nathan, Solomon, ⁵Ibhar, Elishua, Elpelet, ⁶Nogah, Nepheg, Japhia, ⁷Elishama, Eliada,* and Eliphelet.

David Conquers the Philistines

⁸When the Philistines heard that David had been anointed king over all Israel, they mobilized all their forces to capture him. But David was told they were coming, so he marched out to meet them. ⁹The Philistines arrived and made a raid in the valley of Rephaim. ¹⁰So David asked God, "Should I go out to fight the Philistines? Will you hand them over to me?"

The LORD replied, "Yes, go ahead. I will hand them over to you."

¹¹So David and his troops went up to Baal-perazim and defeated the Philistines there. "God did it!" David exclaimed. "He used me to burst through my enemies like a raging flood!" So they named that place Baal-perazim (which means "the Lord who bursts through"). ¹²The Philistines had abandoned their gods there, so David gave orders to burn them.

¹³But after a while the Philistines returned and raided the valley again. ¹⁴And once again David asked God what to do. "Do not attack them straight on," God replied. "Instead, circle around behind and attack them near the poplar* trees. ¹⁵When you hear a sound like marching feet in the tops of the poplar trees, go out and attack! That will be the signal that God is moving ahead of you to strike

---

13:1 Hebrew *the commanders of thousands and of hundreds.* 13:6 Or *the Ark of God, where the Name is proclaimed—the name.* 13:9 As in parallel text at 2 Sam 6:6; Hebrew reads *Kidon.* 14:7 Hebrew *Beeliada,* a variant spelling of Eliada; compare 3:8 and parallel text at 2 Sam 5:16. 14:14 Or *aspen,* or *balsam;* also in 14:15. The exact identification of this tree is uncertain.

13:9-11 With Uzzah's death, Israel's celebration abruptly turned to sorrow. Touching the Ark, even well-meaningly, resulted in death because its holiness had been violated (see 15:13).
13:12 David's response to Uzzah's death might have been an expression of his own inadequacy to bring the Ark to Jerusalem.

14:1-7 Even though the Ark was not in Jerusalem (13:1-14), God blessed David's palace, his children, and his conquest of the Philistines. God's blessing did not depend on the Ark's presence. These blessings eventually encouraged David to carry out his original plan to bring the Ark into Jerusalem (15:1-29). Has an awareness of your blessings ever encouraged you to trust God more and try hard things?

Insight 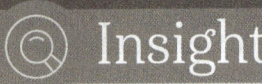 JERUSALEM THROUGH TIME

Jerusalem—God's chosen city for his Kingdom and his Temple—has grown through time, mainly because of various leaders' building projects. David brought the Ark of the Covenant to Jerusalem and established the city as the center of Israel's worship (1 Chronicles 13–16). David also purchased the site (2 Samuel 24:18-25) where Solomon would eventually build the Temple (1 Kings 5–7; 2 Chronicles 2–7)—the location where God had rescued Abraham from sacrificing Isaac (Genesis 22). Jerusalem and the Temple were destroyed during the Exile, but Zerubbabel, Ezra, and Nehemiah led the returning Jewish exiles in rebuilding both. Later, under the Roman Empire, Herod would undertake Jerusalem's building and beautifying projects.

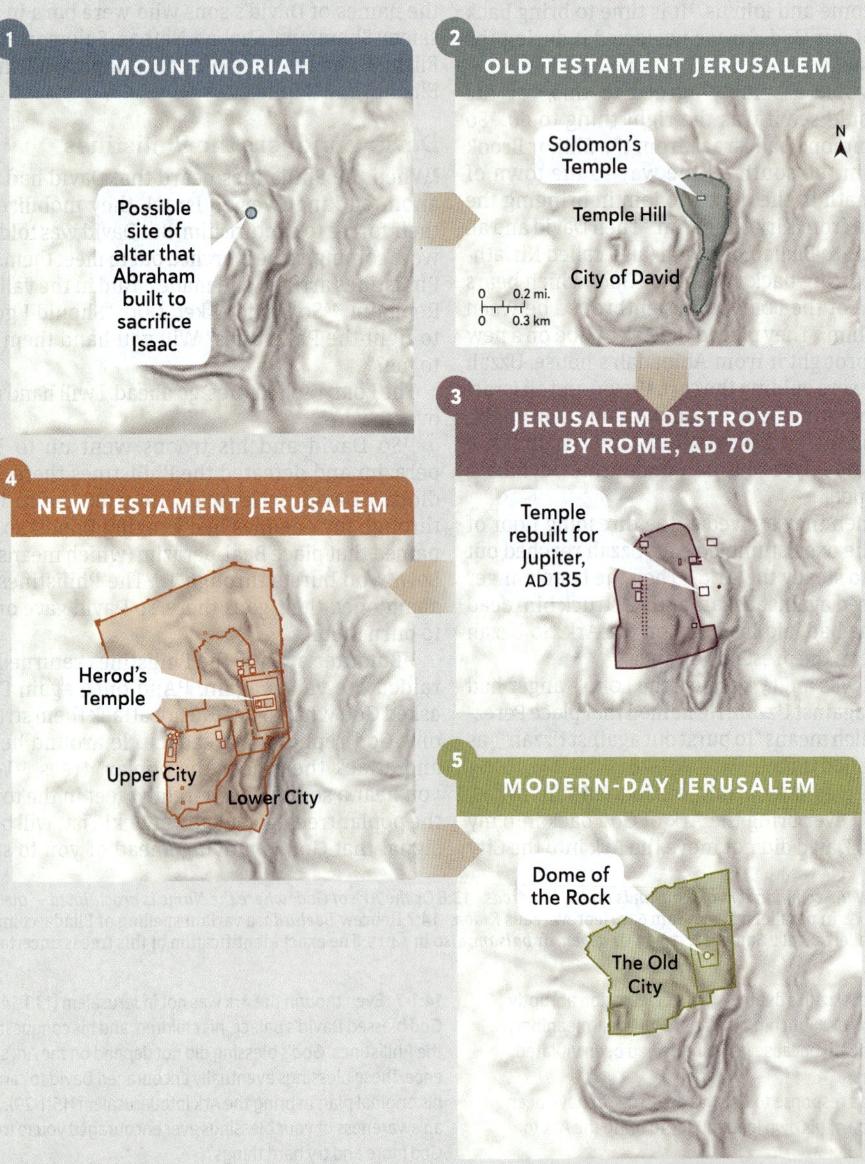

1. MOUNT MORIAH
Possible site of altar that Abraham built to sacrifice Isaac

2. OLD TESTAMENT JERUSALEM
Solomon's Temple
Temple Hill
City of David

3. JERUSALEM DESTROYED BY ROME, AD 70
Temple rebuilt for Jupiter, AD 135

4. NEW TESTAMENT JERUSALEM
Herod's Temple
Upper City
Lower City

5. MODERN-DAY JERUSALEM
Dome of the Rock
The Old City

down the Philistine army." ¹⁶So David did what God commanded, and they struck down the Philistine army all the way from Gibeon to Gezer.

¹⁷So David's fame spread everywhere, and the LORD caused all the nations to fear David.

Preparing to Move the Ark

15 David now built several buildings for himself in the City of David. He also prepared a place for the Ark of God and set up a special tent for it. ²Then he commanded, "No one except the Levites may carry the Ark of God. The LORD has chosen them to carry the Ark of the LORD and to serve him forever."

³Then David summoned all Israel to Jerusalem to bring the Ark of the LORD to the place he had prepared for it. ⁴This is the number of the descendants of Aaron (the priests) and the Levites who were called together:

⁵From the clan of Kohath, 120, with Uriel as their leader.
⁶From the clan of Merari, 220, with Asaiah as their leader.
⁷From the clan of Gershon,* 130, with Joel as their leader.
⁸From the descendants of Elizaphan, 200, with Shemaiah as their leader.
⁹From the descendants of Hebron, 80, with Eliel as their leader.
¹⁰From the descendants of Uzziel, 112, with Amminadab as their leader.

¹¹Then David summoned the priests, Zadok and Abiathar, and these Levite leaders: Uriel, Asaiah, Joel, Shemaiah, Eliel, and Amminadab. ¹²He said to them, "You are the leaders of the Levite families. You must purify yourselves and all your fellow Levites, so you can bring the Ark of the LORD, the God of Israel, to the place I have prepared for it. ¹³Because you Levites did not carry the Ark the first time, the anger of the LORD our God burst out against us. We failed to ask God how to move it properly." ¹⁴So the priests and the Levites purified themselves in order to bring the Ark of the LORD, the God of Israel, to Jerusalem. ¹⁵Then the Levites carried the Ark of God on their shoulders with its carrying poles, just as the LORD had instructed Moses.

¹⁶David also ordered the Levite leaders to appoint a choir of Levites who were singers and musicians to sing joyful songs to the accompaniment of harps, lyres, and cymbals. ¹⁷So the Levites appointed Heman son of Joel along with his fellow Levites: Asaph son of Berekiah, and Ethan son of Kushaiah from the clan of Merari. ¹⁸The following men were chosen as their assistants: Zechariah, Jaaziel,* Shemiramoth, Jehiel, Unni, Eliab, Benaiah, Maaseiah, Mattithiah, Eliphelehu, Mikneiah, and the gatekeepers—Obed-edom and Jeiel.

¹⁹The musicians Heman, Asaph, and Ethan were chosen to sound the bronze cymbals. ²⁰Zechariah, Aziel, Shemiramoth, Jehiel, Unni, Eliab, Maaseiah, and Benaiah were chosen to play the harps.* ²¹Mattithiah, Eliphelehu, Mikneiah, Obed-edom, Jeiel, and Azaziah were chosen to play the lyres.* ²²Kenaniah, the head Levite, was chosen as the choir leader because of his skill.

²³Berekiah and Elkanah were chosen to guard* the Ark. ²⁴Shebaniah, Joshaphat, Nethanel, Amasai, Zechariah, Benaiah, and Eliezer—all of whom were priests—were chosen to blow the trumpets as they marched in front of the Ark of God. Obed-edom and Jehiah were chosen to guard the Ark.

Moving the Ark to Jerusalem

²⁵Then David and the elders of Israel and the generals of the army* went to the house of Obed-edom to bring the Ark of the LORD's Covenant up to Jerusalem with a great celebration. ²⁶And because God was clearly helping the Levites as they carried the Ark of the LORD's Covenant, they sacrificed seven bulls and seven rams.

²⁷David was dressed in a robe of fine linen, as were all the Levites who carried the Ark, and also the singers, and Kenaniah the choir leader. David was also wearing a priestly garment.* ²⁸So all Israel brought up the Ark of the LORD's Covenant with shouts of joy, the blowing of rams' horns and trumpets, the crashing of cymbals, and loud playing on harps and lyres.

²⁹But as the Ark of the LORD's Covenant entered the City of David, Michal, the daughter of Saul, looked down from her window. When she saw King David skipping about and laughing with joy, she was filled with contempt for him.

15:7 Hebrew *Gershom*, a variant spelling of Gershon. **15:18** As in several Hebrew manuscripts and Greek version (see also parallel lists in 15:20; 16:5); Masoretic Text reads *Zechariah ben Jaaziel*. **15:20** Hebrew adds *according to Alamoth*, which is probably a musical term. The meaning of the Hebrew is uncertain. **15:21** Hebrew adds *according to the Sheminith*, which is probably a musical term. The meaning of the Hebrew is uncertain. **15:23** Hebrew *chosen as gatekeepers for*; also in 15:24. **15:25** Hebrew *the commanders of thousands*. **15:27** Hebrew *a linen ephod*.

15:1-3 The first attempt to bring the Ark to Jerusalem (13:1-14) failed because of improper procedure (see 15:13). This time, David prepared a place for the Ark in Jerusalem and organized Levites to carry the Ark because this was their responsibility (Deuteronomy 10:8; 18:5). The special tent that David prepared for the Ark was not the Tabernacle, which was located at Gibeon at the time (see 1 Chronicles 16:39; 21:29).

15:29 Michal's disgust stands in stark contrast with the jubilant celebration going on in the streets below. It's possible that her attitude mirrored her father's disregard for the Lord, or perhaps this occasion was colored by her resentment for David—the man she had once loved and defended, only for him to abandon her at court and later break up her marriage to Palti.

16 They brought the Ark of God and placed it inside the special tent David had prepared for it. And they presented burnt offerings and peace offerings to God. ²When he had finished his sacrifices, David blessed the people in the name of the Lord. ³Then he gave to every man and woman in all Israel a loaf of bread, a cake of dates,* and a cake of raisins.

⁴David appointed the following Levites to lead the people in worship before the Ark of the Lord—to invoke his blessings, to give thanks, and to praise the Lord, the God of Israel. ⁵Asaph, the leader of this group, sounded the cymbals. Second to him was Zechariah, followed by Jeiel, Shemiramoth, Jehiel, Mattithiah, Eliab, Benaiah, Obed-edom, and Jeiel. They played the harps and lyres. ⁶The priests, Benaiah and Jahaziel, played the trumpets regularly before the Ark of God's Covenant.

David's Song of Praise

⁷On that day David gave to Asaph and his fellow Levites this song of thanksgiving to the Lord:

⁸ Give thanks to the Lord and proclaim his greatness.
 Let the whole world know what he has done.
⁹ Sing to him; yes, sing his praises.
 Tell everyone about his wonderful deeds.
¹⁰ Exult in his holy name;
 rejoice, you who worship the Lord.
¹¹ Search for the Lord and for his strength;
 continually seek him.
¹² Remember the wonders he has performed,
 his miracles, and the rulings he has given,
¹³ you children of his servant Israel,
 you descendants of Jacob, his chosen ones.

¹⁴ He is the Lord our God.
 His justice is seen throughout the land.
¹⁵ Remember his covenant forever—
 the commitment he made to a thousand generations.
¹⁶ This is the covenant he made with Abraham
 and the oath he swore to Isaac.
¹⁷ He confirmed it to Jacob as a decree,
 and to the people of Israel as a never-ending covenant:
¹⁸ "I will give you the land of Canaan
 as your special possession."

¹⁹ He said this when you were few in number,
 a tiny group of strangers in Canaan.
²⁰ They wandered from nation to nation,
 from one kingdom to another.
²¹ Yet he did not let anyone oppress them.
 He warned kings on their behalf:
²² "Do not touch my chosen people,
 and do not hurt my prophets."

²³ Let the whole earth sing to the Lord!
 Each day proclaim the good news that he saves.
²⁴ Publish his glorious deeds among the nations.
 Tell everyone about the amazing things he does.
²⁵ Great is the Lord! He is most worthy of praise!
 He is to be feared above all gods.
²⁶ The gods of other nations are mere idols,
 but the Lord made the heavens!
²⁷ Honor and majesty surround him;
 strength and joy fill his dwelling.

²⁸ O nations of the world, recognize the Lord,
 recognize that the Lord is glorious and strong.
²⁹ Give to the Lord the glory he deserves!
 Bring your offering and come into his presence.
 Worship the Lord in all his holy splendor.
³⁰ Let all the earth tremble before him.
 The world stands firm and cannot be shaken.
³¹ Let the heavens be glad, and the earth rejoice!
 Tell all the nations, "The Lord reigns!"
³² Let the sea and everything in it shout his praise!
 Let the fields and their crops burst out with joy!
³³ Let the trees of the forest sing for joy before the Lord,
 for he is coming to judge the earth.

³⁴ Give thanks to the Lord, for he is good!
 His faithful love endures forever.
³⁵ Cry out, "Save us, O God of our salvation!
 Gather and rescue us from among the nations,
 so we can thank your holy name
 and rejoice and praise you."

³⁶ Praise the Lord, the God of Israel,
 who lives from everlasting to everlasting!

And all the people shouted "Amen!" and praised the Lord.

Worship at Jerusalem and Gibeon

³⁷David arranged for Asaph and his fellow Levites to serve regularly before the Ark of the Lord's Covenant, doing whatever needed to be done each day. ³⁸This group included Obed-edom (son of Jeduthun), Hosah, and sixty-eight other Levites as gatekeepers.

16:3 Or *a portion of meat.* The meaning of the Hebrew is uncertain.

16:11 David celebrated and worshiped God before the Ark of the Covenant. David recalled all God had done and encouraged the worshipers to seek the face of God. The metaphor "face of God," translated here as "continually seek him," is used in several places in the Old Testament where it can be translated several ways (Genesis 32:30; Numbers 6:24-26; Psalms 11:7; 27:8; 44:3; 80:3; 105:4; 2 Chronicles 7:14). Seeking God's face means a life-changing encounter. Seeking the face of God signifies presence, blessing, favor, protection, and discovering God's glory. Like David, we can seek God's face through worship and prayer.

MY STORY WITH GOD

The Praise Factor

SCRIPTURE CONNECTION: 1 CHRONICLES 16:7-36; 17:16-27; 29:10-20

We often think of *praise* as music in a church service and with good reason. These terms are closely related. King David was a masterful musician who gave us songs of praise, thanks, and even laments. David danced before God, calling out for trumpets, cymbals, harps, and voice. He led his people, and then many subsequent generations of worshipers, in praising the Lord.

David did not limit his praise to music, however. First Chronicles conveys that David praised God through generous, joyous, and wholehearted giving to build God's dwelling place on earth. Alongside giving, song, and dance, David declared the Lord's glory to all who would listen, read, and recite. David's heartfelt prayer in 29:11 so captures the essence of praise that we repeat versions of it today. We sing and speak words close to this in the traditional language of the Lord's Prayer: "For thine is the kingdom, and the power, and the glory, forever."

This humble Hebrew king's legacy teaches us that praise

- is timeless and eternal,
- expresses our emotions tangibly, and
- ascribes rightful honor to the King of kings, the Almighty God.

> My practice of praise will leave a spiritual legacy.

IMAGINE

How can your life express joyful praise?

How might being a woman of habitual praise impact your spiritual influence, your eternal imprint?

"I have, at times, wondered if we should limit our public praise. When we are in doubt, despair, or freshly emerging from challenges or sin, is it somehow wrong, hypocritical, or disingenuous to praise God? A broken yet sincere worshiper, King David calls out, no! As 1 Chronicles 16:29 says, 'Give to the LORD the glory he deserves!'"

DONNA LEE LAMOTHE, MA, is executive director and founder of inSPIRE Channels at RSVP Ministries. She teaches and guides all to find wholeness through faith in Jesus.

³⁹Meanwhile, David stationed Zadok the priest and his fellow priests at the Tabernacle of the LORD at the place of worship in Gibeon, where they continued to minister before the LORD. ⁴⁰They sacrificed the regular burnt offerings to the LORD each morning and evening on the altar set aside for that purpose, obeying everything written in the Law of the LORD, as he had commanded Israel. ⁴¹David also appointed Heman, Jeduthun, and the others chosen by name to give thanks to the LORD, for "his faithful love endures forever." ⁴²They used their trumpets, cymbals, and other instruments to accompany their songs of praise to God.* And the sons of Jeduthun were appointed as gatekeepers.

⁴³Then all the people returned to their homes, and David turned and went home to bless his own family.

The LORD's Covenant Promise to David

17 When David was settled in his palace, he summoned Nathan the prophet. "Look," David said, "I am living in a beautiful cedar palace,* but the Ark of the LORD's Covenant is out there under a tent!"

²Nathan replied to David, "Do whatever you have in mind, for God is with you."

³But that same night God said to Nathan,

⁴"Go and tell my servant David, 'This is what the LORD has declared: You are not the one to build a house for me to live in. ⁵I have never lived in a house, from the day I brought the Israelites out of Egypt until this very day. My home has always been a tent, moving from one place to another in a Tabernacle. ⁶Yet no matter where I have gone with the Israelites, I have never once complained to Israel's leaders, the shepherds of my people. I have never asked them, "Why haven't you built me a beautiful cedar house?"'

⁷"Now go and say to my servant David, 'This is what the LORD of Heaven's Armies has declared: I took you from tending sheep in the pasture and selected you to be the leader of my people Israel. ⁸I have been with you wherever you have gone, and I have destroyed all your enemies before your eyes. Now I will make your name as famous as anyone who has ever lived on the earth! ⁹And I will provide a homeland for my people Israel, planting them in a secure place where they will never be disturbed. Evil nations won't oppress them as they've done in the past, ¹⁰starting from the time I appointed judges to rule my people Israel. And I will defeat all your enemies.

"'Furthermore, I declare that the LORD will build a house for you—a dynasty of kings! ¹¹For when you die and join your ancestors, I will raise up one of your descendants, one of your sons, and I will make his kingdom strong. ¹²He is the one who will build a house—a temple—for me. And I will secure his throne forever. ¹³I will be his father, and he will be my son. I will never take my favor from him as I took it from the one who ruled before you. ¹⁴I will confirm him as king over my house and my kingdom for all time, and his throne will be secure forever.'"

¹⁵So Nathan went back to David and told him everything the LORD had said in this vision.

David's Prayer of Thanks

¹⁶Then King David went in and sat before the LORD and prayed,

"Who am I, O LORD God, and what is my family, that you have brought me this far? ¹⁷And now, O God, in addition to everything else, you speak of giving your servant a lasting dynasty! You speak as though I were someone very great,* O LORD God!

¹⁸"What more can I say to you about the way you have honored me? You know what your servant is really like. ¹⁹For the sake of your servant, O LORD, and according to your will, you have done all these great things and have made them known.

²⁰"O LORD, there is no one like you. We have never even heard of another God like you! ²¹What other nation on earth is like your people Israel? What other nation, O God, have you redeemed from slavery to be your own people? You made a great name for yourself when you redeemed your people from Egypt. You performed awesome miracles and drove out the nations that stood in their way. ²²You chose Israel to be your very own people forever, and you, O LORD, became their God.

²³"And now, O LORD, I am your servant; do as you have promised concerning me and my family. May it be a promise that will last forever. ²⁴And may your name be established and honored forever so that everyone will say, 'The LORD of Heaven's Armies, the God of Israel, is Israel's God!' And may the house of your servant David continue before you forever.

²⁵"O my God, I have been bold enough to pray to you because you have revealed to your

---

16:42 Or *to accompany the sacred music;* or *to accompany singing to God.* **17:1** Hebrew *a house of cedar.* **17:17** The meaning of the Hebrew is uncertain.

17:10-20 David wanted to build the house for God—the Temple. God planned to build a house for David through descendants, rather than a physical structure. God chose Solomon, David's son, to construct the Temple instead of allowing David to build it. David responded with a humble heart, even though he must have felt disappointed. David's response reveals that he trusted God, even when God said no.

servant that you will build a house for him—a dynasty of kings! ²⁶For you are God, O LORD. And you have promised these good things to your servant. ²⁷And now, it has pleased you to bless the house of your servant, so that it will continue forever before you. For when you grant a blessing, O LORD, it is an eternal blessing!"

David's Military Victories

18 After this, David defeated and subdued the Philistines by conquering Gath and its surrounding towns. ²David also conquered the land of Moab, and the Moabites who were spared became David's subjects and paid him tribute money.

³David also destroyed the forces of Hadadezer, king of Zobah, as far as Hamath,* when Hadadezer

18:3 The meaning of the Hebrew is uncertain.

18:1 The Philistines posed a constant threat to David's kingdom. They remained entrenched in their coastal settlements; although David conquered Gath and its surrounding towns, a Philistine king remained in Gath at the end of David's reign (1 Kings 2:39).

Come Close — MY PLANS: GOD'S PERFECT ONE

SCRIPTURE CONNECTION: 1 CHRONICLES 17:1-27

After decades of life and leadership, it's dangerously easy for me to organize God-sized plans. Through the test of time, I've grown confident in my competencies.

When I add that I daily desire to know, love, and serve God, one might reason this is a winning formula for the *best plans possible*. How can you go wrong when proven competence meets God-centered intentions? Right?

Not so much. Not so much for me. Not so much for David.

I know I am on the road to woe when I ask God to *bless my plans*. Often the hardest thing to surrender is my belief about what will work best.

I imagine Nathan wasn't looking forward to bringing God's no to David, especially after giving the king a verbal high five, declaring, "Do whatever you have in mind, for God is with you" (17:2). But God lovingly brought David into the best plan, and David wholeheartedly received it. As he prayed, David

- recognized God's abundant favor and grace,
- acknowledged God's authority over all, and
- praised God for faithfulness to his chosen people, Israel.

The greatest outcomes occur when we enter a holy dependence on God, when we, like David, surrender our best plans to embrace God's perfect one.

REFLECT "'For I know the plans I have for you,' says the LORD. 'They are plans for good and not for disaster, to give you a future and a hope.'" JEREMIAH 29:11

Father, when I seek and call upon you, you listen and respond. Thank you for faithfully guiding me to your perfect plan. Amen.

CONSIDER "Prayer lays hold of God's plan and becomes the link between his will and its accomplishment on earth.... Amazing things happen, and we are given the privilege of being the channels of the Holy Spirit's prayer." ELISABETH ELLIOT, *Keep a Quiet Heart*

Today I surrender my best plans to embrace God's perfect one.

TAMI HEIM is president and CEO of Christian Leadership Alliance and serves on many nonprofit boards. She and her husband lead mission teams to Haiti to love and disciple orphans.

marched out to strengthen his control along the Euphrates River. ⁴David captured 1,000 chariots, 7,000 charioteers, and 20,000 foot soldiers. He crippled all the chariot horses except enough for 100 chariots.

⁵When Arameans from Damascus arrived to help King Hadadezer, David killed 22,000 of them. ⁶Then he placed several army garrisons* in Damascus, the Aramean capital, and the Arameans became David's subjects and paid him tribute money. So the LORD made David victorious wherever he went.

⁷David brought the gold shields of Hadadezer's officers to Jerusalem, ⁸along with a large amount of bronze from Hadadezer's towns of Tebah* and Cun. Later Solomon melted the bronze and molded it into the great bronze basin called the Sea, the pillars, and the various bronze articles used at the Temple.

⁹When King Toi* of Hamath heard that David had destroyed the entire army of King Hadadezer of Zobah, ¹⁰he sent his son Joram* to congratulate King David for his successful campaign. Hadadezer and Toi had been enemies and were often at war. Joram presented David with many gifts of gold, silver, and bronze.

¹¹King David dedicated all these gifts to the LORD, along with the silver and gold he had taken from the other nations—from Edom, Moab, Ammon, Philistia, and Amalek.

¹²Abishai son of Zeruiah destroyed 18,000 Edomites in the Valley of Salt. ¹³He placed army garrisons in Edom, and all the Edomites became David's subjects. In fact, the LORD made David victorious wherever he went.

¹⁴So David reigned over all Israel and did what was just and right for all his people. ¹⁵Joab son of Zeruiah was commander of the army. Jehoshaphat son of Ahilud was the royal historian. ¹⁶Zadok son of Ahitub and Ahimelech* son of Abiathar were the priests. Seraiah* was the court secretary. ¹⁷Benaiah son of Jehoiada was captain of the king's bodyguard.* And David's sons served as the king's chief assistants.

David Defeats the Ammonites

19 Some time after this, King Nahash of the Ammonites died, and his son Hanun* became king. ²David said, "I am going to show loyalty to Hanun because his father, Nahash, was always loyal to me." So David sent messengers to express sympathy to Hanun about his father's death.

But when David's ambassadors arrived in the land of Ammon, ³the Ammonite commanders said to Hanun, "Do you really think these men are coming here to honor your father? No! David has sent them to spy out the land so they can come in and conquer it!" ⁴So Hanun seized David's ambassadors and shaved them, cut off their robes at the buttocks, and sent them back to David in shame.

⁵When David heard what had happened to the men, he sent messengers to tell them, "Stay at Jericho until your beards grow out, and then come back." For they felt deep shame because of their appearance.

⁶When the people of Ammon realized how seriously they had angered David, Hanun and the Ammonites sent 75,000 pounds* of silver to hire chariots and charioteers from Aram-naharaim, Aram-maacah, and Zobah. ⁷They also hired 32,000 chariots and secured the support of the king of Maacah and his army. These forces camped at Medeba, where they were joined by the Ammonite troops that Hanun had recruited from his own towns. ⁸When David heard about this, he sent Joab and all his warriors to fight them. ⁹The Ammonite troops came out and drew up their battle lines at the entrance of the city, while the other kings positioned themselves to fight in the open fields.

¹⁰When Joab saw that he would have to fight on both the front and the rear, he chose some of Israel's elite troops and placed them under his personal command to fight the Arameans in the fields. ¹¹He left the rest of the army under the command of his brother Abishai, who was to attack the Ammonites. ¹²"If the Arameans are too strong for me, then come over and help me," Joab told his brother. "And if the Ammonites are too strong for you, I will help you. ¹³Be courageous! Let us fight bravely for our people and the cities of our God. May the LORD's will be done."

¹⁴When Joab and his troops attacked, the Arameans began to run away. ¹⁵And when the Ammonites saw the Arameans running, they also ran from Abishai and retreated into the city. Then Joab returned to Jerusalem.

¹⁶The Arameans now realized that they were no match for Israel, so they sent messengers and summoned additional Aramean troops from the other side of the Euphrates River.* These troops were under the command of Shobach,* the commander of Hadadezer's forces.

18:6 As in Greek version and Latin Vulgate (see also 2 Sam 8:6); Hebrew lacks *several army garrisons*. **18:8** Hebrew reads *Tibhath*, a variant spelling of Tebah; compare parallel text at 2 Sam 8:8. **18:9** As in parallel text at 2 Sam 8:9; Hebrew reads *Tou*; also in 18:10. **18:10** As in parallel text at 2 Sam 8:10; Hebrew reads *Hadoram*, a variant spelling of Joram. **18:16a** As in some Hebrew manuscripts, Syriac version, and Latin Vulgate (see also 2 Sam 8:17); most Hebrew manuscripts read *Abimelech*. **18:16b** As in parallel text at 2 Sam 8:17; Hebrew reads *Shavsha*. **18:17** Hebrew *of the Kerethites and Pelethites*. **19:1** As in parallel text at 2 Sam 10:1; Hebrew lacks *Hanun*. **19:6** Hebrew *1,000 talents* [34,000 kilograms]. **19:16a** Hebrew *the river*. **19:16b** As in parallel text at 2 Sam 10:16; Hebrew reads *Shophach*; also in 19:18.

19:1-7 The new Ammonite ruler, Hanun, took exception to Israel's presence so close to his nation. The Ammonites hired Aramean armies from the north, and these combined forces assembled at Medeba to challenge David's control of Moab's plateau.

¹⁷When David heard what was happening, he mobilized all Israel, crossed the Jordan River, and positioned his troops in battle formation. Then David engaged the Arameans in battle, and they fought against him. ¹⁸But again the Arameans fled from the Israelites. This time David's forces killed 7,000 charioteers and 40,000 foot soldiers, including Shobach, the commander of their army. ¹⁹When Hadadezer's allies saw that they had been defeated by Israel, they surrendered to David and became his subjects. After that, the Arameans were no longer willing to help the Ammonites.

David Captures Rabbah

20 In the spring of the year,* when kings normally go out to war, Joab led the Israelite army in successful attacks against the land of the Ammonites. In the process he laid siege to the city of Rabbah, attacking and destroying it. However, David stayed behind in Jerusalem.

²Then David went to Rabbah and removed the crown from the king's head,* and it was placed on his own head. The crown was made of gold and set with gems, and he found that it weighed seventy-five pounds.* David took a vast amount of plunder from the city. ³He also made slaves of the people of Rabbah and forced them to labor with saws, iron picks, and iron axes.* That is how David dealt with the people of all the Ammonite towns. Then David and all the army returned to Jerusalem.

Battles against Philistine Giants

⁴After this, war broke out with the Philistines at Gezer. As they fought, Sibbecai from Hushah killed Saph,* a descendant of the giants,* and so the Philistines were subdued.

⁵During another battle with the Philistines, Elhanan son of Jair killed Lahmi, the brother of Goliath of Gath. The handle of Lahmi's spear was as thick as a weaver's beam!

⁶In another battle with the Philistines at Gath, they encountered a huge man with six fingers on each hand and six toes on each foot, twenty-four in all, who was also a descendant of the giants. ⁷But when he defied and taunted Israel, he was killed by Jonathan, the son of David's brother Shimea.

⁸These Philistines were descendants of the giants of Gath, but David and his warriors killed them.

David Takes a Census

21 Satan rose up against Israel and caused David to take a census of the people of Israel. ²So David said to Joab and the commanders of the army, "Take a census of all the people of Israel—from Beersheba in the south to Dan in the north—and bring me a report so I may know how many there are."

³But Joab replied, "May the LORD increase the number of his people a hundred times over! But why, my lord the king, do you want to do this? Are they not all your servants? Why must you cause Israel to sin?"

⁴But the king insisted that they take the census, so Joab traveled throughout all Israel to count the people. Then he returned to Jerusalem ⁵and reported the number of people to David. There were 1,100,000 warriors in all Israel who could handle a sword, and 470,000 in Judah. ⁶But Joab did not include the tribes of Levi and Benjamin in the census because he was so distressed at what the king had made him do.

Judgment for David's Sin

⁷God was very displeased with the census, and he punished Israel for it. ⁸Then David said to God, "I have sinned greatly by taking this census. Please forgive my guilt for doing this foolish thing."

⁹Then the LORD spoke to Gad, David's seer. This was the message: ¹⁰"Go and say to David, 'This is what the LORD says: I will give you three choices. Choose one of these punishments, and I will inflict it on you.'"

¹¹So Gad came to David and said, "These are the choices the LORD has given you. ¹²You may choose three years of famine, three months of destruction by the sword of your enemies, or three days of severe plague as the angel of the LORD brings devastation throughout the land of Israel. Decide what answer I should give the LORD who sent me."

¹³"I'm in a desperate situation!" David replied to Gad. "But let me fall into the hands of the LORD, for his mercy is very great. Do not let me fall into human hands."

¹⁴So the LORD sent a plague upon Israel, and 70,000 people died as a result. ¹⁵And God sent an angel to

---

20:1 Hebrew *At the turn of the year*. The first day of the year in the ancient Hebrew lunar calendar occurred in March or April. **20:2a** Or *from the head of Milcom* (as in Greek version and Latin Vulgate). Milcom, also called Molech, was the god of the Ammonites. **20:2b** Hebrew *1 talent* [34 kilograms]. **20:3** As in parallel text at 2 Sam 12:31; Hebrew reads *and cut them with saws, iron picks, and saws*. **20:4a** As in parallel text at 2 Sam 21:18; Hebrew reads *Sippai*. **20:4b** Hebrew *descendant of the Rephaites*; also in 20:6, 8.

20:1-3 This war against the Ammonites was the backdrop to David's rape of Bathsheba and devising the murder of her husband, Uriah (2 Samuel 11:2–12:25).

21:1-8 The Hebrew term *satan* means "adversary" and does not refer to a proper noun or a personal name. Here, this is not a specific name for Satan, also called the devil, as described in the New Testament (Matthew 4:1; Revelation 12:9). This unnamed adversary tempted David, and David gave in. Rather than trusting that God would be enough to fight the battle, David decided to count the potential fighting men. When David realized he had sinned, he immediately repented and asked forgiveness. David's response shows how we can turn back to God after we sin. God is quick to forgive because he loves us and wants us to learn how to live faithful and obedient lives.

destroy Jerusalem. But just as the angel was preparing to destroy it, the LORD relented and said to the death angel, "Stop! That is enough!" At that moment the angel of the LORD was standing by the threshing floor of Araunah* the Jebusite.

¹⁶David looked up and saw the angel of the LORD standing between heaven and earth with his sword drawn, reaching out over Jerusalem. So David and the leaders of Israel put on burlap to show their deep distress and fell face down on the ground. ¹⁷And David said to God, "I am the one who called for the census! I am the one who has sinned and done wrong! But these people are as innocent as sheep—what have they done? O LORD my God, let your anger fall against me and my family, but do not destroy your people."

David Builds an Altar

¹⁸Then the angel of the LORD told Gad to instruct David to go up and build an altar to the LORD on the threshing floor of Araunah the Jebusite. ¹⁹So David went up to do what the LORD had commanded him through Gad. ²⁰Araunah, who was busy threshing wheat at the time, turned and saw the angel there. His four sons, who were with him, ran away and hid. ²¹When Araunah saw David approaching, he left his threshing floor and bowed before David with his face to the ground.

²²David said to Araunah, "Let me buy this threshing floor from you at its full price. Then I will build an altar to the LORD there, so that he will stop the plague."

²³"Take it, my lord the king, and use it as you wish," Araunah said to David. "I will give the oxen for the burnt offerings, and the threshing boards for wood to build a fire on the altar, and the wheat for the grain offering. I will give it all to you."

²⁴But King David replied to Araunah, "No, I insist on buying it for the full price. I will not take what is yours and give it to the LORD. I will not present burnt offerings that have cost me nothing!" ²⁵So David gave Araunah 600 pieces of gold* in payment for the threshing floor.

²⁶David built an altar there to the LORD and sacrificed burnt offerings and peace offerings. And when David prayed, the LORD answered him by sending fire from heaven to burn up the offering on the altar. ²⁷Then the LORD spoke to the angel, who put the sword back into its sheath.

²⁸When David saw that the LORD had answered his prayer, he offered sacrifices there at Araunah's threshing floor. ²⁹At that time the Tabernacle of the LORD and the altar of burnt offering that Moses had made in the wilderness were located at the place of worship in Gibeon. ³⁰But David was not able to go there to inquire of God, because he was terrified by the drawn sword of the angel of the LORD.

22

Then David said, "This will be the location for the Temple of the LORD God and the place of the altar for Israel's burnt offerings!"

Preparations for the Temple

²So David gave orders to call together the foreigners living in Israel, and he assigned them the task of preparing finished stone for building the Temple of God. ³David provided large amounts of iron for the nails that would be needed for the doors in the gates and for the clamps, and he gave more bronze than could be weighed. ⁴He also provided innumerable cedar logs, for the men of Tyre and Sidon had brought vast amounts of cedar to David.

⁵David said, "My son Solomon is still young and inexperienced. And since the Temple to be built for the LORD must be a magnificent structure, famous and glorious throughout the world, I will begin making preparations for it now." So David collected vast amounts of building materials before his death.

⁶Then David sent for his son Solomon and instructed him to build a Temple for the LORD, the God of Israel. ⁷"My son, I wanted to build a Temple to honor the name of the LORD my God," David told him. ⁸"But the LORD said to me, 'You have killed many men in the battles you have fought. And since you have shed so much blood in my sight, you will not be the one to build a Temple to honor my name. ⁹But you will have a son who will be a man of peace. I will give him peace with his enemies in all the surrounding lands. His name will be Solomon,* and I will give peace and quiet to Israel during his reign. ¹⁰He is the one who will build a Temple to honor my name. He will be my son, and I will be his father. And I will secure the throne of his kingdom over Israel forever.'

¹¹"Now, my son, may the LORD be with you and give you success as you follow his directions in building the Temple of the LORD your God. ¹²And may the LORD give you wisdom and understanding, that you

---

21:15 As in parallel text at 2 Sam 24:16; Hebrew reads *Ornan*, another name for Araunah; also in 21:18-28. 21:25 Hebrew *600 shekels of gold*, about 15 pounds or 6.8 kilograms in weight. 22:9 *Solomon* sounds like and is probably derived from the Hebrew word for "peace."

22:5 While Solomon was "young and inexperienced" (see also 29:1; 1 Kings 3:7), David showed his wisdom and skill in preparing for building the Temple. David also designed the Temple (1 Chronicles 28:11-12). Later, God gave Solomon the wisdom needed to build the Temple and govern well (see 2 Chronicles 1:7-12). Like David, we are not called to do everything (1 Chronicles 22:8) but to do what God directs, and sometimes that means we prepare the way for a successor or the next generation. No matter whether we are young or old, how might we invest in someone else for the future?

MY STORY WITH COMMUNITY, WORKPLACE & CHURCH

Succession: Everyone Is an Interim

SCRIPTURE CONNECTION: 1 CHRONICLES 22–29

One of my mentors once told me that all of us are "interims," meaning we only serve in a particular role for a limited time. As I reflected, I found a new perspective on my purpose and position in God's eternal plan. Each of us serves, leads, works, and nurtures for a season and a reason. And being mindful of our interim status keeps us looking for those who will carry the work forward when our season completes.

King David's life provides an excellent example of an interim. He reached leadership's pinnacle and raised others, positioning their unique gifts for God's Kingdom work. David had a clear desire to build a house to honor the Lord. He engaged the whole community in the process, collecting the best items by utilizing all his networks.

David lived to obey God, even when it meant yielding his desires. He accepted God's words about not being the one to build the Temple and positioned his son, the next generation, to do what David wanted to do. Unlike Saul, who feared being replaced and chased David, David prepared his successor by:

- inviting others to the table,
- supplying resources, and
- sharing knowledge of how to do the work.

> We serve, lead, work, and nurture for a season and a reason.

An interim proves vital, preparing everyone for what comes next. David's willingness to serve his successor promoted a secure future for his household, Israel's children, the land, and the surrounding kingdoms. Everybody is an interim: We serve, lead, work, and nurture for a season and a reason.

IMAGINE

In what areas or relationships is God inviting you to serve as an interim?

How might you prepare your heart and mind for succession?

"Knowing everybody is an interim helps me fulfill my mission and equip others to do the same."

VIRGINIA WARD, MA, DMin, serves as the Dean of the Boston Campus for Gordon-Conwell Theological Seminary. She is a wife, a mother, and an associate pastor at Abundant Life Church in Cambridge, MA.

may obey the Law of the LORD your God as you rule over Israel. ¹³For you will be successful if you carefully obey the decrees and regulations that the LORD gave to Israel through Moses. Be strong and courageous; do not be afraid or lose heart!

¹⁴"I have worked hard to provide materials for building the Temple of the LORD—nearly 4,000 tons of gold, 40,000 tons of silver,* and so much iron and bronze that it cannot be weighed. I have also gathered timber and stone for the walls, though you may need to add more. ¹⁵You have a large number of skilled stonemasons and carpenters and craftsmen of every kind. ¹⁶You have expert goldsmiths and silversmiths and workers of bronze and iron. Now begin the work, and may the LORD be with you!"

¹⁷Then David ordered all the leaders of Israel to assist Solomon in this project. ¹⁸"The LORD your God is with you," he declared. "He has given you peace with the surrounding nations. He has handed them over to me, and they are now subject to the LORD and his people. ¹⁹Now seek the LORD your God with all your heart and soul. Build the sanctuary of the LORD God so that you can bring the Ark of the LORD's Covenant and the holy vessels of God into the Temple built to honor the LORD's name."

Duties of the Levites

23 When David was an old man, he appointed his son Solomon to be king over Israel. ²David summoned all the leaders of Israel, together with the priests and Levites. ³All the Levites who were thirty years old or older were counted, and the total came to 38,000. ⁴Then David said, "From all the Levites, 24,000 will supervise the work at the Temple of the LORD. Another 6,000 will serve as officials and judges. ⁵Another 4,000 will work as gatekeepers, and 4,000 will praise the LORD with the musical instruments I have made." ⁶Then David divided the Levites into divisions named after the clans descended from the three sons of Levi—Gershon, Kohath, and Merari.

The Gershonites

⁷The Gershonite family units were defined by their lines of descent from Libni* and Shimei, the sons of Gershon. ⁸Three of the descendants of Libni were Jehiel (the family leader), Zetham, and Joel. ⁹These were the leaders of the family of Libni.

Three of the descendants of Shimei were Shelomoth, Haziel, and Haran. ¹⁰Four other descendants of Shimei were Jahath, Ziza,* Jeush, and Beriah. ¹¹Jahath was the family leader, and Ziza was next. Jeush and Beriah were counted as a single family because neither had many sons.

The Kohathites

¹²Four of the descendants of Kohath were Amram, Izhar, Hebron, and Uzziel. ¹³The sons of Amram were Aaron and Moses. Aaron and his descendants were set apart to dedicate the most holy things, to offer sacrifices in the LORD's presence, to serve the LORD, and to pronounce blessings in his name forever.

¹⁴As for Moses, the man of God, his sons were included with the tribe of Levi. ¹⁵The sons of Moses were Gershom and Eliezer. ¹⁶The descendants of Gershom included Shebuel, the family leader. ¹⁷Eliezer had only one son, Rehabiah, the family leader. Rehabiah had numerous descendants.

¹⁸The descendants of Izhar included Shelomith, the family leader.

¹⁹The descendants of Hebron included Jeriah (the family leader), Amariah (the second), Jahaziel (the third), and Jekameam (the fourth).

²⁰The descendants of Uzziel included Micah (the family leader) and Isshiah (the second).

The Merarites

²¹The descendants of Merari included Mahli and Mushi.

The sons of Mahli were Eleazar and Kish. ²²Eleazar died with no sons, only daughters. His daughters married their cousins, the sons of Kish.

²³Three of the descendants of Mushi were Mahli, Eder, and Jerimoth.

²⁴These were the descendants of Levi by clans, the leaders of their family groups, registered carefully by name. Each had to be twenty years old or older to qualify for service in the house of the LORD. ²⁵For David said, "The LORD, the God of Israel, has given us peace, and he will always live in Jerusalem. ²⁶Now the Levites will no longer need to carry the Tabernacle and its furnishings from place to place." ²⁷In accordance with David's final instructions, all the Levites twenty years old or older were registered for service.

22:14 Hebrew *100,000 talents* [3,400 metric tons] *of gold, 1,000,000 talents* [34,000 metric tons] *of silver.* 23:7 Hebrew *Ladan* (also in 23:8, 9), a variant spelling of Libni; compare 6:17. 23:10 As in Greek version and Latin Vulgate (see also 23:11); Hebrew reads *Zina.*

23:3-5 The Levites are recorded according to their roles rather than their families.
23:6-23 "David divided the Levites into divisions" according to their ancestral families. The number of available priests far exceeded the requirements for a single Temple. The divisions provided a necessary time-sharing mechanism that enabled all the priests and Levites to serve in the Temple periodically (see Luke 1:5, 8).
23:28-32 "The work of the Levites was to assist the priests," which they accomplished in various ways: maintaining the Temple, setting out the sacred bread and other offerings, singing, and helping the priests with the sacrifices.

[28] The work of the Levites was to assist the priests, the descendants of Aaron, as they served at the house of the Lord. They also took care of the courtyards and side rooms, helped perform the ceremonies of purification, and served in many other ways in the house of God. [29] They were in charge of the sacred bread that was set out on the table, the choice flour for the grain offerings, the wafers made without yeast, the cakes cooked in olive oil, and the other mixed breads. They were also responsible to check all the weights and measures. [30] And each morning and evening they stood before the Lord to sing songs of thanks and praise to him. [31] They assisted with the burnt offerings that were presented to the Lord on Sabbath days, at new moon celebrations, and at all the appointed festivals. The required number of Levites served in the Lord's presence at all times, following all the procedures they had been given.

[32] And so, under the supervision of the priests, the Levites watched over the Tabernacle and the Temple* and faithfully carried out their duties of service at the house of the Lord.

Duties of the Priests

24 This is how Aaron's descendants, the priests, were divided into groups for service. The sons of Aaron were Nadab, Abihu, Eleazar, and Ithamar. [2] But Nadab and Abihu died before their father, and they had no sons. So only Eleazar and Ithamar were left to carry on as priests.

[3] With the help of Zadok, who was a descendant of Eleazar, and of Ahimelech, who was a descendant of Ithamar, David divided Aaron's descendants into groups according to their various duties. [4] Eleazar's descendants were divided into sixteen groups and Ithamar's into eight, for there were more family leaders among the descendants of Eleazar.

[5] All tasks were assigned to the various groups by means of sacred lots so that no preference would be shown, for there were many qualified officials serving God in the sanctuary from among the descendants of both Eleazar and Ithamar. [6] Shemaiah son of Nethanel, a Levite, acted as secretary and wrote down the names and assignments in the presence of the king, the officials, Zadok the priest, Ahimelech son of Abiathar, and the family leaders of the priests and Levites. The descendants of Eleazar and Ithamar took turns casting lots.

[7] The first lot fell to Jehoiarib.
The second lot fell to Jedaiah.
[8] The third lot fell to Harim.
The fourth lot fell to Seorim.
[9] The fifth lot fell to Malkijah.
The sixth lot fell to Mijamin.
[10] The seventh lot fell to Hakkoz.
The eighth lot fell to Abijah.
[11] The ninth lot fell to Jeshua.
The tenth lot fell to Shecaniah.
[12] The eleventh lot fell to Eliashib.
The twelfth lot fell to Jakim.
[13] The thirteenth lot fell to Huppah.
The fourteenth lot fell to Jeshebeab.
[14] The fifteenth lot fell to Bilgah.
The sixteenth lot fell to Immer.
[15] The seventeenth lot fell to Hezir.
The eighteenth lot fell to Happizzez.
[16] The nineteenth lot fell to Pethahiah.
The twentieth lot fell to Jehezkel.
[17] The twenty-first lot fell to Jakin.
The twenty-second lot fell to Gamul.
[18] The twenty-third lot fell to Delaiah.
The twenty-fourth lot fell to Maaziah.

[19] Each group carried out its appointed duties in the house of the Lord according to the procedures established by their ancestor Aaron in obedience to the commands of the Lord, the God of Israel.

Family Leaders among the Levites

[20] These were the other family leaders descended from Levi:

From the descendants of Amram, the leader was Shebuel.*
From the descendants of Shebuel, the leader was Jehdeiah.
[21] From the descendants of Rehabiah, the leader was Isshiah.
[22] From the descendants of Izhar, the leader was Shelomith.*
From the descendants of Shelomith, the leader was Jahath.
[23] From the descendants of Hebron, Jeriah was the leader,* Amariah was second, Jahaziel was third, and Jekameam was fourth.
[24] From the descendants of Uzziel, the leader was Micah.
From the descendants of Micah, the leader was Shamir, [25] along with Isshiah, the brother of Micah.
From the descendants of Isshiah, the leader was Zechariah.
[26] From the descendants of Merari, the leaders were Mahli and Mushi.

23:32 Hebrew *the Tent of Meeting and the sanctuary.* **24:20** Hebrew *Shubael* (also in 24:20b), a variant spelling of Shebuel; compare 23:16 and 26:24. **24:22** Hebrew *Shelomoth* (also in 24:22b), a variant spelling of Shelomith; compare 23:18. **24:23** Hebrew *From the descendants of Jeriah;* compare 23:19.

24:1-2 The organization of the priests into their divisions for service began with Aaron's sons Eleazar and Ithamar; all of Israel's priests were descended from these two men.

24:3-6 Zadok and Ahimelech were the leaders of the two families of priests during David's time (see 6:8; 18:16; 2 Samuel 8:17).

From the descendants of Jaaziah, the leader was Beno.
27 From the descendants of Merari through Jaaziah, the leaders were Beno, Shoham, Zaccur, and Ibri.
28 From the descendants of Mahli, the leader was Eleazar, though he had no sons.
29 From the descendants of Kish, the leader was Jerahmeel.
30 From the descendants of Mushi, the leaders were Mahli, Eder, and Jerimoth.

These were the descendants of Levi in their various families. 31Like the descendants of Aaron, they were assigned to their duties by means of sacred lots, without regard to age or rank. Lots were drawn in the presence of King David, Zadok, Ahimelech, and the family leaders of the priests and the Levites.

Duties of the Musicians

25 David and the army commanders then appointed men from the families of Asaph, Heman, and Jeduthun to proclaim God's messages to the accompaniment of lyres, harps, and cymbals. Here is a list of their names and their work:

2From the sons of Asaph, there were Zaccur, Joseph, Nethaniah, and Asarelah. They worked under the direction of their father, Asaph, who proclaimed God's messages by the king's orders.
3From the sons of Jeduthun, there were Gedaliah, Zeri, Jeshaiah, Shimei,* Hashabiah, and Mattithiah, six in all. They worked under the direction of their father, Jeduthun, who proclaimed God's messages to the accompaniment of the lyre, offering thanks and praise to the LORD.
4From the sons of Heman, there were Bukkiah, Mattaniah, Uzziel, Shubael,* Jerimoth, Hananiah, Hanani, Eliathah, Giddalti, Romamti-ezer, Joshbekashah, Mallothi, Hothir, and Mahazioth.
5All these were the sons of Heman, the king's seer, for God had honored him with fourteen sons and three daughters.

6All these men were under the direction of their fathers as they made music at the house of the LORD. Their responsibilities included the playing of cymbals, harps, and lyres at the house of God. Asaph, Jeduthun, and Heman reported directly to the king.
7They and their families were all trained in making music before the LORD, and each of them—288 in all—was an accomplished musician. 8The musicians were appointed to their term of service by means of sacred lots, without regard to whether they were young or old, teacher or student.

9 The first lot fell to Joseph of the Asaph clan and twelve of his sons and relatives.*
The second lot fell to Gedaliah and twelve of his sons and relatives.
10 The third lot fell to Zaccur and twelve of his sons and relatives.
11 The fourth lot fell to Zeri* and twelve of his sons and relatives.
12 The fifth lot fell to Nethaniah and twelve of his sons and relatives.
13 The sixth lot fell to Bukkiah and twelve of his sons and relatives.
14 The seventh lot fell to Asarelah* and twelve of his sons and relatives.
15 The eighth lot fell to Jeshaiah and twelve of his sons and relatives.
16 The ninth lot fell to Mattaniah and twelve of his sons and relatives.
17 The tenth lot fell to Shimei and twelve of his sons and relatives.
18 The eleventh lot fell to Uzziel* and twelve of his sons and relatives.
19 The twelfth lot fell to Hashabiah and twelve of his sons and relatives.
20 The thirteenth lot fell to Shubael and twelve of his sons and relatives.
21 The fourteenth lot fell to Mattithiah and twelve of his sons and relatives.
22 The fifteenth lot fell to Jerimoth* and twelve of his sons and relatives.
23 The sixteenth lot fell to Hananiah and twelve of his sons and relatives.
24 The seventeenth lot fell to Joshbekashah* and twelve of his sons and relatives.
25 The eighteenth lot fell to Hanani and twelve of his sons and relatives.
26 The nineteenth lot fell to Mallothi and twelve of his sons and relatives.
27 The twentieth lot fell to Eliathah and twelve of his sons and relatives.
28 The twenty-first lot fell to Hothir and twelve of his sons and relatives.
29 The twenty-second lot fell to Giddalti and twelve of his sons and relatives.

25:3 As in one Hebrew manuscript and some Greek manuscripts (see also 25:17); most Hebrew manuscripts lack *Shimei*. 25:4 Hebrew *Shebuel,* a variant spelling of Shubael; compare 25:20. 25:9 As in Greek version; Hebrew lacks *and twelve of his sons and relatives.* 25:11 Hebrew *Izri,* a variant spelling of Zeri; compare 25:3. 25:14 Hebrew *Jesarelah,* a variant spelling of Asarelah; compare 25:2. 25:18 Hebrew *Azarel,* a variant spelling of Uzziel; compare 25:4. 25:22 Hebrew *Jeremoth,* a variant spelling of Jerimoth; compare 25:4. 25:24 Hebrew *Joshbekasha,* a variant spelling of Joshbekashah; compare 25:4.

25:1-7 The musicians who served at the time of King David are listed according to their membership in the families of Asaph, Heman, and Jeduthun.

30 The twenty-third lot fell to Mahazioth and twelve of his sons and relatives.
31 The twenty-fourth lot fell to Romamti-ezer and twelve of his sons and relatives.

Duties of the Gatekeepers

26 These are the divisions of the gatekeepers:

From the Korahites, there was Meshelemiah son of Kore, of the family of Abiasaph.* ²The sons of Meshelemiah were Zechariah (the oldest), Jediael (the second), Zebadiah (the third), Jathniel (the fourth), ³Elam (the fifth), Jehohanan (the sixth), and Eliehoenai (the seventh). ⁴The sons of Obed-edom, also gatekeepers, were Shemaiah (the oldest), Jehozabad (the second), Joah (the third), Sacar (the fourth), Nethanel (the fifth), ⁵Ammiel (the sixth), Issachar (the seventh), and Peullethai (the eighth). God had richly blessed Obed-edom.

⁶Obed-edom's son Shemaiah had sons with great ability who earned positions of great authority in the clan. ⁷Their names were Othni, Rephael, Obed, and Elzabad. Their relatives, Elihu and Semakiah, were also very capable men.

⁸All of these descendants of Obed-edom, including their sons and grandsons—sixty-two of them in all—were very capable men, well qualified for their work.

⁹Meshelemiah's eighteen sons and relatives were also very capable men.

¹⁰Hosah, of the Merari clan, appointed Shimri as the leader among his sons, though he was not the oldest. ¹¹His other sons included Hilkiah (the second), Tebaliah (the third), and Zechariah (the fourth). Hosah's sons and relatives, who served as gatekeepers, numbered thirteen in all.

¹²These divisions of the gatekeepers were named for their family leaders, and like the other Levites, they served at the house of the LORD. ¹³They were assigned by families for guard duty at the various gates, without regard to age or training, for it was all decided by means of sacred lots.

¹⁴The responsibility for the east gate went to Meshelemiah* and his group. The north gate was assigned to his son Zechariah, a man of unusual wisdom. ¹⁵The south gate went to Obed-edom, and his sons were put in charge of the storehouse. ¹⁶Shuppim and Hosah were assigned the west gate and the gateway leading up to the Temple.* Guard duties were divided evenly. ¹⁷Six Levites were assigned each day to the east gate, four to the north gate, four to the south gate, and two pairs at the storehouse. ¹⁸Six were assigned each day to the west gate, four to the gateway leading up to the Temple, and two to the courtyard.*

¹⁹These were the divisions of the gatekeepers from the clans of Korah and Merari.

Treasurers and Other Officials

²⁰Other Levites, led by Ahijah, were in charge of the treasuries of the house of God and the treasuries of the gifts dedicated to the LORD. ²¹From the family of Libni* in the clan of Gershon, Jehiel* was the leader. ²²The sons of Jehiel, Zetham and his brother Joel, were in charge of the treasuries of the house of the LORD.

²³These are the leaders that descended from Amram, Izhar, Hebron, and Uzziel:

²⁴From the clan of Amram, Shebuel was a descendant of Gershom son of Moses. He was the chief officer of the treasuries. ²⁵His relatives through Eliezer were Rehabiah, Jeshaiah, Joram, Zicri, and Shelomoth.

²⁶Shelomoth and his relatives were in charge of the treasuries containing the gifts that King David, the family leaders, and the generals and captains* and other officers of the army had dedicated to the LORD. ²⁷These men dedicated some of the plunder they had gained in battle to maintain the house of the LORD. ²⁸Shelomoth* and his relatives also cared for the gifts dedicated to the LORD by Samuel the seer, Saul son of Kish, Abner son of Ner, and Joab son of Zeruiah. All the other dedicated gifts were in their care, too.

²⁹From the clan of Izhar came Kenaniah. He and his sons were given administrative responsibilities* over Israel as officials and judges.

³⁰From the clan of Hebron came Hashabiah. He and his relatives—1,700 capable men—were put in charge of the Israelite lands west of the Jordan

---

26:1 As in Greek version (see also Exod 6:24); Hebrew reads *Asaph*. 26:14 Hebrew *Shelemiah*, a variant spelling of Meshelemiah; compare 26:2. 26:16 Or *the gate of Shalleketh on the upper road* (also in 26:18). The meaning of the Hebrew is uncertain. 26:18 Or *the colonnade*. The meaning of the Hebrew is uncertain. 26:21a Hebrew *Ladan*, a variant spelling of Libni; compare 6:17. 26:21b Hebrew *Jehieli* (also in 26:22), a variant spelling of Jehiel; compare 23:8. 26:26 Hebrew *the commanders of thousands and of hundreds*. 26:28 Hebrew *Shelomith*, a variant spelling of Shelomoth. 26:29 Or *were given outside work;* or *were given work away from the Temple area.*

26:20-32 In preparation for Solomon's succession to the throne, David appointed these officials as part of his comprehensive organization of the Levitical orders at the end of his reign. The officers included treasurers, administrators, and judges who were part of the political structure.

26:20-28 The Levites were in charge of the Lord's treasuries and property (see 2 Chronicles 24:11; 31:12). Some spoils of war were always dedicated to God (1 Chronicles 26:26-28).

River. They were responsible for all matters related to the things of the LORD and the service of the king in that area.

31 Also from the clan of Hebron came Jeriah,* who was the leader of the Hebronites according to the genealogical records. (In the fortieth year of David's reign, a search was made in the records, and capable men from the clan of Hebron were found at Jazer in the land of Gilead.) 32 There were 2,700 capable men among the relatives of Jeriah. King David sent them to the east side of the Jordan River and put them in charge of the tribes of Reuben and Gad and the half-tribe of Manasseh. They were responsible for all matters related to God and to the king.

Military Commanders and Divisions

27 This is the list of Israelite generals and captains,* and their officers, who served the king by supervising the army divisions that were on duty each month of the year. Each division served for one month and had 24,000 troops.

2 Jashobeam son of Zabdiel was commander of the first division of 24,000 troops, which was on duty during the first month. 3 He was a descendant of Perez and was in charge of all the army officers for the first month.

4 Dodai, a descendant of Ahoah, was commander of the second division of 24,000 troops, which was on duty during the second month. Mikloth was his chief officer.

5 Benaiah son of Jehoiada the priest was commander of the third division of 24,000 troops, which was on duty during the third month. 6 This was the Benaiah who commanded David's elite military group known as the Thirty. His son Ammizabad was his chief officer.

7 Asahel, the brother of Joab, was commander of the fourth division of 24,000 troops, which was on duty during the fourth month. Asahel was succeeded by his son Zebadiah.

8 Shammah* the Izrahite was commander of the fifth division of 24,000 troops, which was on duty during the fifth month.

9 Ira son of Ikkesh from Tekoa was commander of the sixth division of 24,000 troops, which was on duty during the sixth month.

10 Helez, a descendant of Ephraim from Pelon, was commander of the seventh division of 24,000 troops, which was on duty during the seventh month.

11 Sibbecai, a descendant of Zerah from Hushah, was commander of the eighth division of 24,000 troops, which was on duty during the eighth month.

12 Abiezer from Anathoth in the territory of Benjamin was commander of the ninth division of 24,000 troops, which was on duty during the ninth month.

13 Maharai, a descendant of Zerah from Netophah, was commander of the tenth division of 24,000 troops, which was on duty during the tenth month.

14 Benaiah from Pirathon in Ephraim was commander of the eleventh division of 24,000 troops, which was on duty during the eleventh month.

15 Heled,* a descendant of Othniel from Netophah, was commander of the twelfth division of 24,000 troops, which was on duty during the twelfth month.

Leaders of the Tribes

16 The following were the tribes of Israel and their leaders:

Tribe	Leader
Reuben	Eliezer son of Zicri
Simeon	Shephatiah son of Maacah
17 Levi	Hashabiah son of Kemuel
Aaron (the priests)	Zadok
18 Judah	Elihu (a brother of David)
Issachar	Omri son of Michael
19 Zebulun	Ishmaiah son of Obadiah
Naphtali	Jeremoth son of Azriel
20 Ephraim	Hoshea son of Azaziah
Manasseh (west)	Joel son of Pedaiah
21 Manasseh in Gilead (east)	Iddo son of Zechariah
Benjamin	Jaasiel son of Abner
22 Dan	Azarel son of Jeroham

These were the leaders of the tribes of Israel.

23 When David took his census, he did not count those who were younger than twenty years of age, because the LORD had promised to make the Israelites as numerous as the stars in heaven. 24 Joab son of Zeruiah began the census but never finished it because* the anger of God fell on Israel. The total number was never recorded in King David's official records.

26:31 Hebrew *Jerijah,* a variant spelling of Jeriah; compare 23:19.   27:1 Hebrew *commanders of thousands and of hundreds.*   27:8 Hebrew *Shamhuth,* a variant spelling of Shammah; compare 11:27 and 2 Sam 23:25.   27:15 Hebrew *Heldai,* a variant spelling of Heled; compare 11:30 and 2 Sam 23:29.   27:24 Or *never finished it, and yet.*

27:16-22 The order of the tribes roughly follows Numbers 1:5-15: the six sons of Leah, the two sons of Rachel (the "tribe" of Joseph comprising Ephraim and Manasseh, then Benjamin), and the two sons of Bilhah (Dan and Naphtali). Changes from the order of that list are that Naphtali is transferred to his geographical location next to Zebulun, and the tribe of Levi is inserted at the position of Levi's birth order, with the family of Aaron (the priests) listed separately. Absent from this list are the two sons of Zilpah (Gad and Asher).

Officials of David's Kingdom

²⁵Azmaveth son of Adiel was in charge of the palace treasuries.

Jonathan son of Uzziah was in charge of the regional treasuries throughout the towns, villages, and fortresses of Israel.

²⁶Ezri son of Kelub was in charge of the field workers who farmed the king's lands.

²⁷Shimei from Ramah was in charge of the king's vineyards.

Zabdi from Shepham was responsible for the grapes and the supplies of wine.

²⁸Baal-hanan from Geder was in charge of the king's olive groves and sycamore-fig trees in the foothills of Judah.*

Joash was responsible for the supplies of olive oil.

²⁹Shitrai from Sharon was in charge of the cattle on the Sharon Plain.

Shaphat son of Adlai was responsible for the cattle in the valleys.

³⁰Obil the Ishmaelite was in charge of the camels.

Jehdeiah from Meronoth was in charge of the donkeys.

³¹Jaziz the Hagrite was in charge of the king's flocks of sheep and goats.

All these officials were overseers of King David's property.

³²Jonathan, David's uncle, was a wise counselor to the king, a man of great insight, and a scribe. Jehiel the Hacmonite was responsible for teaching the king's sons. ³³Ahithophel was the royal adviser. Hushai the Arkite was the king's friend. ³⁴Ahithophel was succeeded by Jehoiada son of Benaiah and by Abiathar. Joab was commander of the king's army.

David's Instructions to Solomon

28 David summoned all the officials of Israel to Jerusalem—the leaders of the tribes, the commanders of the army divisions, the other generals and captains,* the overseers of the royal property and livestock, the palace officials, the mighty men, and all the other brave warriors in the kingdom. ²David rose to his feet and said: "My brothers and my people! It was my desire to build a Temple where the Ark of the LORD's Covenant, God's footstool, could rest permanently. I made the necessary preparations for building it, ³but God said to me, 'You must not build a Temple to honor my name, for you are a warrior and have shed much blood.'

⁴"Yet the LORD, the God of Israel, has chosen me from among all my father's family to be king over Israel forever. For he has chosen the tribe of Judah to rule, and from among the families of Judah he chose my father's family. And from among my father's sons the LORD was pleased to make me king over all Israel. ⁵And from among my sons—for the LORD has given me many—he chose Solomon to succeed me on the throne of Israel and to rule over the LORD's kingdom. ⁶He said to me, 'Your son Solomon will build my Temple and its courtyards, for I have chosen him as my son, and I will be his father. ⁷And if he continues to obey my commands and regulations as he does now, I will make his kingdom last forever.'

⁸"So now, with God as our witness, and in the sight of all Israel—the LORD's assembly—I give you this charge. Be careful to obey all the commands of the LORD your God, so that you may continue to possess this good land and leave it to your children as a permanent inheritance.

⁹"And Solomon, my son, learn to know the God of your ancestors intimately. Worship and serve him with your whole heart and a willing mind. For the LORD sees every heart and knows every plan and thought. If you seek him, you will find him. But if you forsake him, he will reject you forever. ¹⁰So take this seriously. The LORD has chosen you to build a Temple as his sanctuary. Be strong, and do the work."

¹¹Then David gave Solomon the plans for the Temple and its surroundings, including the entry room, the storerooms, the upstairs rooms, the

---

27:28 Hebrew *the Shephelah.* 28:1 Hebrew *the commanders of thousands and commanders of hundreds.*

27:25-31 Ancient kings, including David, acquired large amounts of property for themselves, despite God's warning against this kind of behavior for Israel's kings (Deuteronomy 17:16-17). This list records various aspects of David's estate, including storehouses in Jerusalem and the provinces, property used for agricultural purposes, and various types of livestock.
28:2-10 The account of David's first discourse includes a message addressed to his people (28:2-8) and a message to Solomon (28:9-10). The main focus of the address is David's desire for Solomon to build a Temple. In addition, David addressed two other important themes: God's selection of Solomon and the people's obligation to keep God's commandments.
28:2 David described the Temple as a place where the "Ark of the LORD's Covenant... could rest." The term "rest" describes the conquest of the land and the establishment of peace (for example, Deuteronomy 12:9). In the wilderness, the Ark rested at the end of battle (Numbers 10:35-36). When David brought the Ark to Jerusalem, the Ark's "rest" became permanent, as David expressed in a psalm of worship: "Arise, O LORD, and enter your resting place, along with the Ark, the symbol of your power" (Psalm 132:8). God had chosen Mount Zion as his resting place.
28:9-10 David's message to Solomon did not stress the privileges of being chosen as king but emphasized the responsibilities of assuming the throne. The primary obligation was to seek the Lord, to worship and serve him. The Lord also required an unflinching resolve to build the Temple sanctuary.
28:11-21 God gave David the actual plans for the Temple through divine inspiration (28:19). On other occasions God also provided plans for the Tabernacle in the wilderness (Exodus 25:9) and for the future Temple of Ezekiel (Ezekiel 40:4).

inner rooms, and the inner sanctuary—which was the place of atonement. ¹²David also gave Solomon all the plans he had in mind* for the courtyards of the LORD's Temple, the outside rooms, the treasuries, and the rooms for the gifts dedicated to the LORD. ¹³The king also gave Solomon the instructions concerning the work of the various divisions of priests and Levites in the Temple of the LORD. And he gave specifications for the items in the Temple that were to be used for worship.

¹⁴David gave instructions regarding how much gold and silver should be used to make the items needed for service. ¹⁵He told Solomon the amount of gold needed for the gold lampstands and lamps, and the amount of silver for the silver lampstands and lamps, depending on how each would be used. ¹⁶He designated the amount of gold for the table on which the Bread of the Presence would be placed and the amount of silver for other tables.

¹⁷David also designated the amount of gold for the solid gold meat hooks used to handle the sacrificial meat and for the basins, pitchers, and dishes, as well as the amount of silver for every dish. ¹⁸He designated the amount of refined gold for the altar of incense. Finally, he gave him a plan for the LORD's "chariot"—the gold cherubim* whose wings were stretched out over the Ark of the LORD's Covenant. ¹⁹"Every part of this plan," David told Solomon, "was given to me in writing from the hand of the LORD.*"

²⁰Then David continued, "Be strong and courageous, and do the work. Don't be afraid or discouraged, for the LORD God, my God, is with you. He will not fail you or forsake you. He will see to it that all the work related to the Temple of the LORD is finished correctly. ²¹The various divisions of priests and Levites will serve in the Temple of God. Others with skills of every kind will volunteer, and the officials and the entire nation are at your command."

Gifts for Building the Temple

29 Then King David turned to the entire assembly and said, "My son Solomon, whom God has clearly chosen as the next king of Israel, is still young and inexperienced. The work ahead of him is enormous, for the Temple he will build is not for mere mortals—it is for the LORD God himself! ²Using every resource at my command, I have gathered as much as I could for building the Temple of my God. Now there is enough gold, silver, bronze, iron, and wood, as well as great quantities of onyx, other precious stones, costly jewels, and all kinds of fine stone and marble.

³"And now, because of my devotion to the Temple of my God, I am giving all of my own private treasures of gold and silver to help in the construction. This is in addition to the building materials I have already collected for his holy Temple. ⁴I am donating more than 112 tons of gold* from Ophir and 262 tons of refined silver* to be used for overlaying the walls of the buildings ⁵and for the other gold and silver work to be done by the craftsmen. Now then, who will follow my example and give offerings to the LORD today?"

⁶Then the family leaders, the leaders of the tribes of Israel, the generals and captains of the army,* and the king's administrative officers all gave willingly. ⁷For the construction of the Temple of God, they gave about 188 tons of gold,* 10,000 gold coins,* 375 tons of silver,* 675 tons of bronze,* and 3,750 tons of iron.* ⁸They also contributed numerous precious stones, which were deposited in the treasury of the house of the LORD under the care of Jehiel, a descendant of Gershon. ⁹The people rejoiced over the offerings, for they had given freely and wholeheartedly to the LORD, and King David was filled with joy.

David's Prayer of Praise

¹⁰Then David praised the LORD in the presence of the whole assembly:

28:12 Or *the plans of the spirit that was with him.* **28:18** Hebrew *for the gold cherub chariot.* **28:19** Or *was written under the direction of the LORD.* **29:4a** Hebrew *3,000 talents* [102 metric tons] *of gold.* **29:4b** Hebrew *7,000 talents* [238 metric tons] *of silver.* **29:6** Hebrew *the commanders of thousands and commanders of hundreds.* **29:7a** Hebrew *5,000 talents* [170 metric tons] *of gold.* **29:7b** Hebrew *10,000 darics* [a Persian coin] *of gold,* about 185 pounds or 84 kilograms in weight. **29:7c** Hebrew *10,000 talents* [340 metric tons] *of silver.* **29:7d** Hebrew *18,000 talents* [612 metric tons] *of bronze.* **29:7e** Hebrew *100,000 talents* [3,400 metric tons] *of iron.*

28:14-18 This list of vessels legitimized each object in the Temple by specifically recounting what God had communicated about them through David.

28:18 The cherubim were a celestial composite of various creatures, and depictions of similar hybrid beasts appear in ancient Near Eastern art and architecture. Almost always depicted in pairs, the Assyrian equivalent guarded the entrances of buildings and cities, and the Phoenician winged sphinxes were carved in relief on votive thrones. In God's throne room (the Most Holy Place of Israel's sanctuary), cherubim flanked the Ark of the Covenant (see Exodus 25:18-22; 2 Samuel 6:2; Psalm 99:1; compare Ezekiel 10).

29:1-9 David persuaded the assembly of Israel's leaders (28:1) to offer gifts to the Lord for the Temple. David's own generous gift provided an example of the amounts leaders should consider. The Chronicler emphasized that the heavy expense of building the Temple was not shouldered by Solomon alone. Solomon added to the contributions made by David and the leaders of Israel (see 22:14).

29:10-19 David's prayer of praise concluded his addresses at Solomon's coronation. The prayer extols God's power and the glory of his kingdom, and it served to dedicate the offerings given for building the Temple. The prayer is composed of three parts: the doxology (29:10b-13), the presentation and dedication of the offerings (29:14-17), and the petition (29:18-19).

"O LORD, the God of our ancestor Israel,* may you be praised forever and ever! ¹¹Yours, O LORD, is the greatness, the power, the glory, the victory, and the majesty. Everything in the heavens and on earth is yours, O LORD, and this is your kingdom. We adore you as the one who is over all things. ¹²Wealth and honor come from you alone, for you rule over everything. Power and might are in your hand, and at your discretion people are made great and given strength.

¹³"O our God, we thank you and praise your glorious name! ¹⁴But who am I, and who are my people, that we could give anything to you? Everything we have has come from you, and we give you only what you first gave us! ¹⁵We are here for only a moment, visitors and strangers in the land as our ancestors were before us. Our days on earth are like a passing shadow, gone so soon without a trace.

¹⁶"O LORD our God, even this material we have gathered to build a Temple to honor your holy name comes from you! It all belongs to you! ¹⁷I know, my God, that you examine our hearts and rejoice when you find integrity there. You know I have done all this with good motives, and I have watched your people offer their gifts willingly and joyously.

¹⁸"O LORD, the God of our ancestors Abraham, Isaac, and Israel, make your people always want to obey you. See to it that their love for you never changes. ¹⁹Give my son Solomon the wholehearted desire to obey all your commands, laws, and decrees, and to do everything necessary to build this Temple, for which I have made these preparations."

²⁰Then David said to the whole assembly, "Give praise to the LORD your God!" And the entire assembly praised the LORD, the God of their ancestors, and they bowed low and knelt before the LORD and the king.

Solomon Named as King

²¹The next day they brought 1,000 bulls, 1,000 rams, and 1,000 male lambs as burnt offerings to the LORD. They also brought liquid offerings and many other sacrifices on behalf of all Israel. ²²They feasted and drank in the LORD's presence with great joy that day.

And again they crowned David's son Solomon as their new king. They anointed him before the LORD as their leader, and they anointed Zadok as priest. ²³So Solomon took the throne of the LORD in place of his father, David, and he succeeded in everything, and all Israel obeyed him. ²⁴All the officials, the warriors, and the sons of King David pledged their loyalty to King Solomon. ²⁵And the LORD exalted Solomon in the sight of all Israel, and he gave Solomon greater royal splendor than any king in Israel before him.

Summary of David's Reign

²⁶So David son of Jesse reigned over all Israel. ²⁷He reigned over Israel for forty years, seven of them in Hebron and thirty-three in Jerusalem. ²⁸He died at a ripe old age, having enjoyed long life, wealth, and honor. Then his son Solomon ruled in his place.

²⁹All the events of King David's reign, from beginning to end, are written in The Record of Samuel the Seer, The Record of Nathan the Prophet, and The Record of Gad the Seer. ³⁰These accounts include the mighty deeds of his reign and everything that happened to him and to Israel and to all the surrounding kingdoms.

29:10 *Israel* is the name that God gave to Jacob.

29:18-19 David did not ask God to grant power, victory, or riches, or for the establishment of Solomon's kingdom. Instead, he asked God to make the people of Israel, and Solomon in particular, "always want to obey" the Lord. Gaining this kind of desire is a gift from the Lord; success and prosperity are secondary.

29:21-25 Sacrifices followed the speeches and prayers at Solomon's coronation. Solomon and Zadok were anointed, and Solomon succeeded to the throne. Zadok was not beginning his priestly role but was being dedicated to serve in the Temple itself. (The descendants of Zadok are mentioned in Ezekiel 40:46; 43:19; 44:15; 48:11.)

29:29 The sources used for the chronicles of David's reign are associated with three prophets, named in the order in which they appear in 1 Chronicles: Samuel (11:3), Nathan (17:1-27), and Gad (21:9). The chronicler had access to various sources in addition to the books of Samuel and Kings (see also 1 Kings 11:41-43; 14:19-20, 29-31).

2 Chronicles

WHAT DO WE LEARN ABOUT GOD'S MISSION AND OURS?
Relying on the Lord makes us a good influence.

WHO WROTE IT? Likely Ezra, or someone who wrote during Ezra's time.

WHEN DID IT HAPPEN? Between 970 and 586 BC, from Solomon's reign until Jerusalem's defeat by Babylon.

HOW IS IT ORGANIZED?

1–9: Solomon's reign

10–12: The kingdom splits during Rehoboam's reign

13–31: The ups and downs of the kingdom of Judah

32–36: The descent to the Exile

FEATURE HIGHLIGHTS
+ Giving (518)
+ Solomon's Temple (522)
+ Queen of Sheba: A Foreign Queen Who Worshiped God (529)
+ Wholehearted: Covered (546)
+ Huldah: A Prophet of Courage and Boldness (553)

Words to Remember are highlighted throughout this book

HOW LONG DOES IT TAKE TO READ?

| :30 | 1:00 | 1:30 | 2:00 | 2:30 | 3:00 | 3:30 |

(2:00)

Timeline

BC	Event
970	SOLOMON, BATHSHEBA'S SON, BECOMES KING
959	THE TEMPLE IS COMPLETED — Queen of Sheba visits Solomon
930	THE KINGDOM DIVIDES
910	ASA, MAACAH'S GRANDSON, BECOMES JUDAH'S KING
872	JEHOSHAPHAT, AZUBAH'S SON, BECOMES JUDAH'S KING
853	AHAB IS KILLED IN BATTLE
841	ATHALIAH SEIZES THE THRONE; JEHOSHEBA HIDES JOASH
792	UZZIAH, JECOLIAH'S SON, BECOMES JUDAH'S KING
722	ISRAEL (NORTHERN KINGDOM) FALLS
715	HEZEKIAH, ABIJAH'S SON, BECOMES JUDAH'S KING
701	SENNACHERIB TAUNTS HEZEKIAH
640	JOSIAH, JEDIDAH'S SON, BECOMES JUDAH'S KING
622	THE BOOK OF THE LAW FOUND; JOSIAH SENDS FOR HULDAH'S COUNSEL
586	JUDAH (SOUTHERN KINGDOM) FALLS
538	CYRUS'S DECREE ALLOWS THE EXILES TO RETURN

Solomon Asks for Wisdom

1 Solomon son of David took firm control of his kingdom, for the LORD his God was with him and made him very powerful.

²Solomon called together all the leaders of Israel—the generals and captains of the army,* the judges, and all the political and clan leaders. ³Then he led the entire assembly to the place of worship in Gibeon, for God's Tabernacle* was located there. (This was the Tabernacle that Moses, the LORD's servant, had made in the wilderness.)

⁴David had already moved the Ark of God from Kiriath-jearim to the tent he had prepared for it in Jerusalem. ⁵But the bronze altar made by Bezalel son of Uri and grandson of Hur was there* at Gibeon in front of the Tabernacle of the LORD. So Solomon and the people gathered in front of it to consult the LORD.* ⁶There in front of the Tabernacle, Solomon went up to the bronze altar in the LORD's presence and sacrificed 1,000 burnt offerings on it.

⁷That night God appeared to Solomon and said, "What do you want? Ask, and I will give it to you!"

⁸Solomon replied to God, "You showed great and faithful love to David, my father, and now you have made me king in his place. ⁹O LORD God, please continue to keep your promise to David my father, for you have made me king over a people as numerous as the dust of the earth! ¹⁰Give me the wisdom and knowledge to lead them properly,* for who could possibly govern this great people of yours?"

¹¹God said to Solomon, "Because your greatest desire is to help your people, and you did not ask for wealth, riches, fame, or even the death of your enemies or a long life, but rather you asked for wisdom and knowledge to properly govern my people—¹²I will certainly give you the wisdom and knowledge you requested. But I will also give you wealth, riches, and fame such as no other king has had before you or will ever have in the future!"

¹³Then Solomon returned to Jerusalem from the Tabernacle at the place of worship in Gibeon, and he reigned over Israel.

¹⁴Solomon built up a huge force of chariots and horses.* He had 1,400 chariots and 12,000 horses. He stationed some of them in the chariot cities and some near him in Jerusalem. ¹⁵The king made silver and gold as plentiful in Jerusalem as stone. And valuable cedar timber was as common as the sycamore-fig trees that grow in the foothills of Judah.* ¹⁶Solomon's horses were imported from Egypt* and from Cilicia*; the king's traders acquired them from Cilicia at the standard price. ¹⁷At that time chariots from Egypt could be purchased for 600 pieces of silver,* and horses for 150 pieces of silver.* They were then exported to the kings of the Hittites and the kings of Aram.

Preparations for Building the Temple

2 ¹*Solomon decided to build a Temple to honor the name of the LORD, and also a royal palace for himself. ²*He enlisted a force of 70,000 laborers, 80,000 men to quarry stone in the hill country, and 3,600 foremen.

³Solomon also sent this message to King Hiram* at Tyre:

"Send me cedar logs as you did for my father, David, when he was building his palace. ⁴I am about to build a Temple to honor the name of the LORD my God. It will be a place set apart to burn fragrant incense before him, to display the special sacrificial bread, and to sacrifice burnt offerings each morning and evening, on the Sabbaths, at new moon celebrations, and at the other appointed festivals of the LORD our God. He has commanded Israel to do these things forever.

⁵"This must be a magnificent Temple because our God is greater than all other gods. ⁶But who can really build him a worthy home? Not even

---

1:2 Hebrew *the commanders of thousands and of hundreds.* **1:3** Hebrew *Tent of Meeting;* also in 1:6, 13. **1:5a** As in Greek version and Latin Vulgate, and some Hebrew manuscripts; Masoretic Text reads *he placed.* **1:5b** Hebrew *to consult him.* **1:10** Hebrew *to go out and come in before this people.* **1:14** Or *charioteers;* also in 1:14b. **1:15** Hebrew *the Shephelah.* **1:16a** Possibly *Muzur,* a district near Cilicia; also in 1:17. **1:16b** Hebrew *Kue,* probably another name for Cilicia. **1:17a** Hebrew *600 [shekels] of silver,* about 15 pounds or 6.8 kilograms in weight. **1:17b** Hebrew *150 [shekels],* about 3.8 pounds or 1.7 kilograms in weight. **2:1** Verse 2:1 is numbered 1:18 in Hebrew text. **2:2** Verses 2:2-18 are numbered 2:1-17 in Hebrew text. **2:3** Hebrew *Huram,* a variant spelling of Hiram; also in 2:11.

1:1 This book opens with a focus on Solomon, the son of David. Peace and rest for the kingdom characterize the first nine chapters, detailing the transition from King David to King Solomon.

1:7-12 God appeared to Solomon at night in a dream. This moment is also recorded in 1 Kings 3:1-15. In this vision, God asked Solomon what he desired. Solomon provided an example of someone who hoped to use his power to benefit others. Solomon asked for wisdom to rule God's people well. Solomon's seeking understanding pleased God, and God granted him not only wisdom but also wealth and honor. James 1:5 states, "If you need wisdom, ask our generous God, and he will give it to you. He will not rebuke you for asking." Is there a situation in your life where you need wisdom? All you need to do is ask God for it!

2:1 God chose Solomon to build the Temple, not his father David, who yearned to do this job (2 Samuel 7). David was still part of the process, assisting in planning and gathering materials. Sometimes, we cannot do everything we desire, but we can always take our part in God's plan. Identifying and doing what is ours requires trust in God and others. Each of us is part of a larger story. We can think of our part as an interim, which is for a season. David and Solomon were chosen for a specific task in a specific season (see "Succession: Everyone Is an Interim," page 505).

2:5-6 The greatness of the Temple and the greatness of God were not of the same order, since "not even the highest heavens can contain" God.

the highest heavens can contain him! So who am I to consider building a Temple for him, except as a place to burn sacrifices to him?

⁷"So send me a master craftsman who can work with gold, silver, bronze, and iron, as well as with purple, scarlet, and blue cloth. He must be a skilled engraver who can work with the craftsmen of Judah and Jerusalem who were selected by my father, David.

⁸"Also send me cedar, cypress, and red sandalwood* logs from Lebanon, for I know that your men are without equal at cutting timber in Lebanon. I will send my men to help them. ⁹An immense amount of timber will be needed, for the Temple I am going to build will be very large and magnificent. ¹⁰In payment for your woodcutters, I will send 100,000 bushels of crushed wheat, 100,000 bushels of barley,* 110,000 gallons of wine, and 110,000 gallons of olive oil.*"

¹¹King Hiram sent this letter of reply to Solomon:

"It is because the LORD loves his people that he has made you their king! ¹²Praise the LORD, the God of Israel, who made the heavens and the earth! He has given King David a wise son, gifted with skill and understanding, who will build a Temple for the LORD and a royal palace for himself.

¹³"I am sending you a master craftsman named Huram-abi, who is extremely talented. ¹⁴His mother is from the tribe of Dan in Israel, and his father is from Tyre. He is skillful at making things from gold, silver, bronze, and iron, and he also works with stone and wood. He can work with purple, blue, and scarlet cloth and fine linen. He is also an engraver and can follow any design given to him. He will work with your craftsmen and those appointed by my lord David, your father.

¹⁵"Send along the wheat, barley, olive oil, and wine that my lord has mentioned. ¹⁶We will cut whatever timber you need from the Lebanon mountains and will float the logs in rafts down the coast of the Mediterranean Sea* to Joppa. From there you can transport the logs up to Jerusalem."

¹⁷Solomon took a census of all foreigners in the land of Israel, like the census his father had taken, and he counted 153,600. ¹⁸He assigned 70,000 of them as common laborers, 80,000 as quarry workers in the hill country, and 3,600 as foremen.

Solomon Builds the Temple

3 So Solomon began to build the Temple of the LORD in Jerusalem on Mount Moriah, where the LORD had appeared to David, his father. The Temple was built on the threshing floor of Araunah* the Jebusite, the site that David had selected. ²The construction began in midspring,* during the fourth year of Solomon's reign.

³These are the dimensions Solomon used for the foundation of the Temple of God (using the old standard of measurement).* It was 90 feet long and 30 feet wide.* ⁴The entry room at the front of the Temple was 30 feet* wide, running across the entire width of the Temple, and 30 feet* high. He overlaid the inside with pure gold.

⁵He paneled the main room of the Temple with cypress wood, overlaid it with fine gold, and decorated it with carvings of palm trees and chains. ⁶He decorated the walls of the Temple with beautiful jewels and with gold from the land of Parvaim. ⁷He overlaid the beams, thresholds, walls, and doors throughout the Temple with gold, and he carved figures of cherubim on the walls.

⁸He made the Most Holy Place 30 feet wide, corresponding to the width of the Temple, and 30 feet deep. He overlaid its interior with 23 tons* of fine gold.

2:8 Or *juniper*; Hebrew reads *algum*, perhaps a variant spelling of *almug*; compare 9:10-11 and parallel text at 1 Kgs 10:11-12. **2:10a** Hebrew *20,000 cors* [4,400 kiloliters] *of crushed wheat, 20,000 cors of barley*. **2:10b** Hebrew *20,000 baths* [420 kiloliters] *of wine, and 20,000 baths of olive oil*. **2:16** Hebrew *the sea*. **3:1** Hebrew reads *Ornan*, a variant spelling of *Araunah*; compare 2 Sam 24:16. **3:2** Hebrew *on the second [day] of the second month*. This day of the ancient Hebrew lunar calendar occurred in April or May. **3:3a** The "old standard of measurement" was a cubit equal to 18 inches [46 centimeters]. The new standard was a cubit of approximately 21 inches [53 centimeters]. **3:3b** Hebrew *60 cubits* [27.6 meters] *long and 20 cubits* [9.2 meters] *wide*. **3:4a** Hebrew *20 cubits* [9.2 meters]; also in 3:8, 11, 13. **3:4b** As in some Greek and Syriac manuscripts, which read *20 cubits* [9.2 meters]; Hebrew reads *120 [cubits]*, which is 180 feet or 55 meters. **3:8** Hebrew *600 talents* [20.4 metric tons].

2:8 The cedar logs used for building the Temple are from *Cedrus libani* ("cedar of Lebanon"), a tree renowned for its beauty, impressive height (sometimes reaching one hundred feet), and fragrant wood. Kings from Egypt, Phoenicia, Assyria, Babylon, Persia, and Greece used cedar timber from Lebanon for building temples and palaces. Red sandalwood was used to make supports for the Temple (possibly pillars or balustrades) as well as musical instruments (see 1 Kings 10:11). Often mentioned in ancient writings, the exact identity of this hard, reddish-brown wood is uncertain.

3:1 The Temple was constructed in Jerusalem on Mount Moriah. David purchased this land from Araunah the Jebusite (1 Chronicles 21:18-30). This Temple site held deep theological significance in Israel's history. In Genesis, this is the place where Abraham brought Isaac, and God provided a ram to sacrifice in Isaac's place (Genesis 22). Abraham called that place "the LORD will provide" (Genesis 22:14). The chronicler connects God's presence to this important place held in Israel's memory.

3:8 A special area was constructed at the extreme interior of the hall known as the Most Holy Place (the divine throne room). It might have been a sacred throne space within the long hall, or it might have been a secondary room within the main hall. The dimensions of the Most Holy Place were equally thirty feet in all directions. It might have rested on an elevated platform, as did some of the shrines in other temples, and a space might have existed between the room and the roof. The Most Holy Place was prepared as a resting place for the Ark, which contained the terms of the covenant.

WHAT THE BIBLE SAYS ABOUT Giving

God Wants Us to Use Our Money to Help Others

Tell them to use their money to do good. They should be rich in good works and generous to those in need, always being ready to share with others. **1 TIMOTHY 6:18**

The generous will prosper

Generous People Flourish

They share freely and give generously to those in need.
 Their good deeds will be remembered forever.
 They will have influence and honor.
PSALM 112:9

The generous will prosper;
 those who refresh others will themselves be
 refreshed.
PROVERBS 11:25

If you help the poor, you are lending to the LORD—
 and he will repay you!
PROVERBS 19:17

Honor the LORD with your wealth...

A Cheerful Attitude Is Contagious

When we take your gifts to those who need them, they will thank God. **2 CORINTHIANS 9:11**

Give God the Best, Not Leftovers

Honor the LORD with your wealth
and with the best part of everything you produce. **PROVERBS 3:9**

How We Give Shows What We Feel About God

If someone has enough money to live well and sees a brother or sister in need but shows no compassion—how can God's love be in that person? **1 JOHN 3:17**

Those who oppress the poor insult their Maker,
but helping the poor honors him. **PROVERBS 14:31**

Attitude Matters

"Watch out! Don't do your good deeds publicly, to be admired by others, for you will lose the reward from your Father in heaven. When you give to someone in need, don't do as the hypocrites do—blowing trumpets in the synagogues and streets to call attention to their acts of charity! I tell you the truth, they have received all the reward they will ever get. But when you give to someone in need, don't let your left hand know what your right hand is doing. Give your gifts in private, and your Father, who sees everything, will reward you." **MATTHEW 6:1-4**

You must each decide in your heart how much to give. And don't give reluctantly or in response to pressure. "For God loves a person who gives cheerfully." And God will generously provide all you need. Then you will always have everything you need and plenty left over to share with others. **2 CORINTHIANS 9:7-8**

Whatever you give is acceptable if you give it eagerly. And give according to what you have, not what you don't have. Of course, I don't mean your giving should make life easy for others and hard for yourselves. I only mean that there should be some equality. **2 CORINTHIANS 8:12-13**

⁹The gold nails that were used weighed 20 ounces* each. He also overlaid the walls of the upper rooms with gold.

¹⁰He made two figures shaped like cherubim, overlaid them with gold, and placed them in the Most Holy Place. ¹¹The total wingspan of the two cherubim standing side by side was 30 feet. One wing of the first figure was 7½ feet* long, and it touched the Temple wall. The other wing, also 7½ feet long, touched one of the wings of the second figure. ¹²In the same way, the second figure had one wing 7½ feet long that touched the opposite wall. The other wing, also 7½ feet long, touched the wing of the first figure. ¹³So the wingspan of the two cherubim side by side was 30 feet. They stood on their feet and faced out toward the main room of the Temple.

¹⁴Across the entrance of the Most Holy Place he hung a curtain made of fine linen, decorated with blue, purple, and scarlet thread and embroidered with figures of cherubim.

¹⁵For the front of the Temple, he made two pillars that were 27 feet* tall, each topped by a capital extending upward another 7½ feet. ¹⁶He made a network of interwoven chains* and used them to decorate the tops of the pillars. He also made 100 decorative pomegranates and attached them to the chains. ¹⁷Then he set up the two pillars at the entrance of the Temple, one to the south of the entrance and the other to the north. He named the one on the south Jakin, and the one on the north Boaz.*

Furnishings for the Temple

4 Solomon* also made a bronze altar 30 feet long, 30 feet wide, and 15 feet high.* ²Then he cast a great round basin, 15 feet across from rim to rim, called the Sea. It was 7½ feet deep and about 45 feet in circumference.* ³It was encircled just below its rim by two rows of figures that resembled oxen. There were about six oxen per foot* all the way around, and they were cast as part of the basin.

⁴The Sea was placed on a base of twelve bronze oxen, all facing outward. Three faced north, three faced west, three faced south, and three faced east, and the Sea rested on them. ⁵The walls of the Sea were about three inches* thick, and its rim flared out like a cup and resembled a water lily blossom. It could hold about 16,500 gallons* of water.

⁶He also made ten smaller basins for washing the utensils for the burnt offerings. He set five on the south side and five on the north. But the priests washed themselves in the Sea.

⁷He then cast ten gold lampstands according to the specifications that had been given, and he put them in the Temple. Five were placed against the south wall, and five were placed against the north wall.

⁸He also built ten tables and placed them in the Temple, five along the south wall and five along the north wall. Then he molded 100 gold basins.

⁹He then built a courtyard for the priests, and also the large outer courtyard. He made doors for the courtyard entrances and overlaid them with bronze. ¹⁰The great bronze basin called the Sea was placed near the southeast corner of the Temple.

¹¹Huram-abi also made the necessary washbasins, shovels, and bowls.

So at last Huram-abi completed everything King Solomon had assigned him to make for the Temple of God:

¹² the two pillars;
 the two bowl-shaped capitals on top of the pillars;
 the two networks of interwoven chains that decorated the capitals;
¹³ the 400 pomegranates that hung from the chains on the capitals (two rows of pomegranates for each of the chain networks that decorated the capitals on top of the pillars);
¹⁴ the water carts holding the basins;
¹⁵ the Sea and the twelve oxen under it;
¹⁶ the ash buckets, the shovels, the meat hooks, and all the related articles.

3:9 Hebrew *50 shekels* [570 grams]. **3:11** Hebrew *5 cubits* [2.3 meters]; also in 3:11b, 12, 15. **3:15** As in Syriac version (see also 1 Kgs 7:15; 2 Kgs 25:17; Jer 52:21), which reads *18 cubits* [8.3 meters]; Hebrew reads *35 cubits*, which is 52.5 feet or 16.5 meters. **3:16** Hebrew *He made chains in the inner sanctuary*. The meaning of the Hebrew is uncertain. **3:17** *Jakin* probably means "he establishes"; *Boaz* probably means "in him is strength." **4:1a** Or *Huram-abi*; Hebrew reads *He*. **4:1b** Hebrew *20 cubits* [9.2 meters] *long, 20 cubits wide, and 10 cubits* [4.6 meters] *high*. **4:2** Hebrew *10 cubits* [4.6 meters] *across . . . 5 cubits* [2.3 meters] *deep and 30 cubits* [13.8 meters] *in circumference*. **4:3** Or *20 oxen per meter;* Hebrew reads *10 per cubit*. **4:5a** Hebrew *a handbreadth* [8 centimeters]. **4:5b** Hebrew *3,000 baths* [63 kiloliters].

3:10-13 The "figures shaped like cherubim" were made of costly wild olive wood and were covered with gold. Cherubim were composite creatures, and depictions of similar hybrid beasts appear in ancient Near Eastern art and architecture. Phoenician votive thrones have been found with winged sphinxes carved on each side, their wings serving as armrests and rising up to form the seat back. The cherubim of Solomon's Temple were distinct because they were not designed to adorn a human throne. Instead, they flanked the Ark, their outstretched wings touching in the middle and extending to the walls of the Most Holy Place.

4:2-5 The Temple, God's house, depicted the Garden of Eden (see Isaiah 51:3). The massive washbasin that rested on the backs of the twelve bronze oxen may have represented either cosmic waters that existed before creation or the waters of life that flowed from the Garden of Eden. God subdued the waters of chaos (Genesis 1:2) so that they would provide life-giving nourishment for plant, animal, and human life (see Revelation 21:1, where the sea is removed forever).

Huram-abi made all these things of burnished bronze for the Temple of the LORD, just as King Solomon had directed. ¹⁷The king had them cast in clay molds in the Jordan Valley between Succoth and Zarethan.* ¹⁸Solomon used such great quantities of bronze that its weight could not be determined.

¹⁹Solomon also made all the furnishings for the Temple of God:

the gold altar;
the tables for the Bread of the Presence;
²⁰ the lampstands and their lamps of solid gold, to burn in front of the Most Holy Place as prescribed;
²¹ the flower decorations, lamps, and tongs—all of the purest gold;
²² the lamp snuffers, bowls, ladles, and incense burners—all of solid gold;
the doors for the entrances to the Most Holy Place and the main room of the Temple, overlaid with gold.

5 So Solomon finished all his work on the Temple of the LORD. Then he brought all the gifts his father, David, had dedicated—the silver, the gold, and the various articles—and he stored them in the treasuries of the Temple of God.

The Ark Brought to the Temple

²Solomon then summoned to Jerusalem the elders of Israel and all the heads of tribes—the leaders of the ancestral families of Israel. They were to bring the Ark of the LORD's Covenant to the Temple from its location in the City of David, also known as Zion. ³So all the men of Israel assembled before the king at the annual Festival of Shelters, which is held in early autumn.*

⁴When all the elders of Israel arrived, the Levites picked up the Ark. ⁵The priests and Levites brought up the Ark along with the special tent* and all the sacred items that had been in it. ⁶There, before the Ark, King Solomon and the entire community of Israel sacrificed so many sheep, goats, and cattle that no one could keep count!

⁷Then the priests carried the Ark of the LORD's Covenant into the inner sanctuary of the Temple—the Most Holy Place—and placed it beneath the wings of the cherubim. ⁸The cherubim spread their wings over the Ark, forming a canopy over the Ark and its carrying poles. ⁹These poles were so long that their ends could be seen from the Holy Place,* which is in front of the Most Holy Place, but not from the outside. They are still there to this day. ¹⁰Nothing was in the Ark except the two stone tablets that Moses had placed in it at Mount Sinai,* where the LORD made a covenant with the people of Israel when they left Egypt.

¹¹Then the priests left the Holy Place. All the priests who were present had purified themselves, whether or not they were on duty that day. ¹²And the Levites who were musicians—Asaph, Heman, Jeduthun, and all their sons and brothers—were dressed in fine linen robes and stood at the east side of the altar playing cymbals, lyres, and harps. They were joined by 120 priests who were playing trumpets. ¹³The trumpeters and singers performed together in unison to praise and give thanks to the LORD. Accompanied by trumpets, cymbals, and other instruments, they raised their voices and praised the LORD with these words:

"He is good!
His faithful love endures forever!"

At that moment a thick cloud filled the Temple of the LORD. ¹⁴The priests could not continue their service because of the cloud, for the glorious presence of the LORD filled the Temple of God.

Solomon Praises the LORD

6 Then Solomon prayed, "O LORD, you have said that you would live in a thick cloud of darkness. ²Now I have built a glorious Temple for you, a place where you can live forever!"

³Then the king turned around to the entire community of Israel standing before him and gave this blessing: ⁴"Praise the LORD, the God of Israel, who has kept the promise he made to my father, David. For he told my father, ⁵'From the day I brought my people out of the land of Egypt, I have never chosen a city among any of the tribes of Israel as the place where a Temple should be built to honor my name.

4:17 As in parallel text at 1 Kgs 7:46; Hebrew reads *Zeredah*. 5:3 Hebrew *at the festival that is in the seventh month*. The Festival of Shelters began on the fifteenth day of the seventh month of the ancient Hebrew lunar calendar. This day occurred in late September, October, or early November. 5:5 Hebrew *the Tent of Meeting*; i.e., the tent mentioned in 2 Sam 6:17 and 1 Chr 16:1. 5:9 As in some Hebrew manuscripts and Greek version (see also 1 Kgs 8:8); Masoretic Text reads *from the Ark*. 5:10 Hebrew *Horeb*, another name for Sinai.

5:3 The Temple dedication took place during the annual Festival of Shelters, in early autumn. This occurred in late September, October, or early November and required a pilgrimage to the central place of worship (Deuteronomy 16:13-15). The timing marked the end of Israel's harvest, allowing landowners to leave for a week without concern for their fields or crops.

5:11-14 The writer describes the Temple dedication in detail. When the priests exited, the musicians raised their song, and the cloud of the "glorious presence of the LORD filled the Temple." Can you imagine what that might have been like? When have you experienced God's presence with you, or wondered if you had? In the New Testament, believers in God's Son can have the Lord's presence, also known as the Holy Spirit, living not in a building but in their very being (Acts 2:33; Romans 8:15; 2 Timothy 1:14).

Insight SOLOMON'S TEMPLE

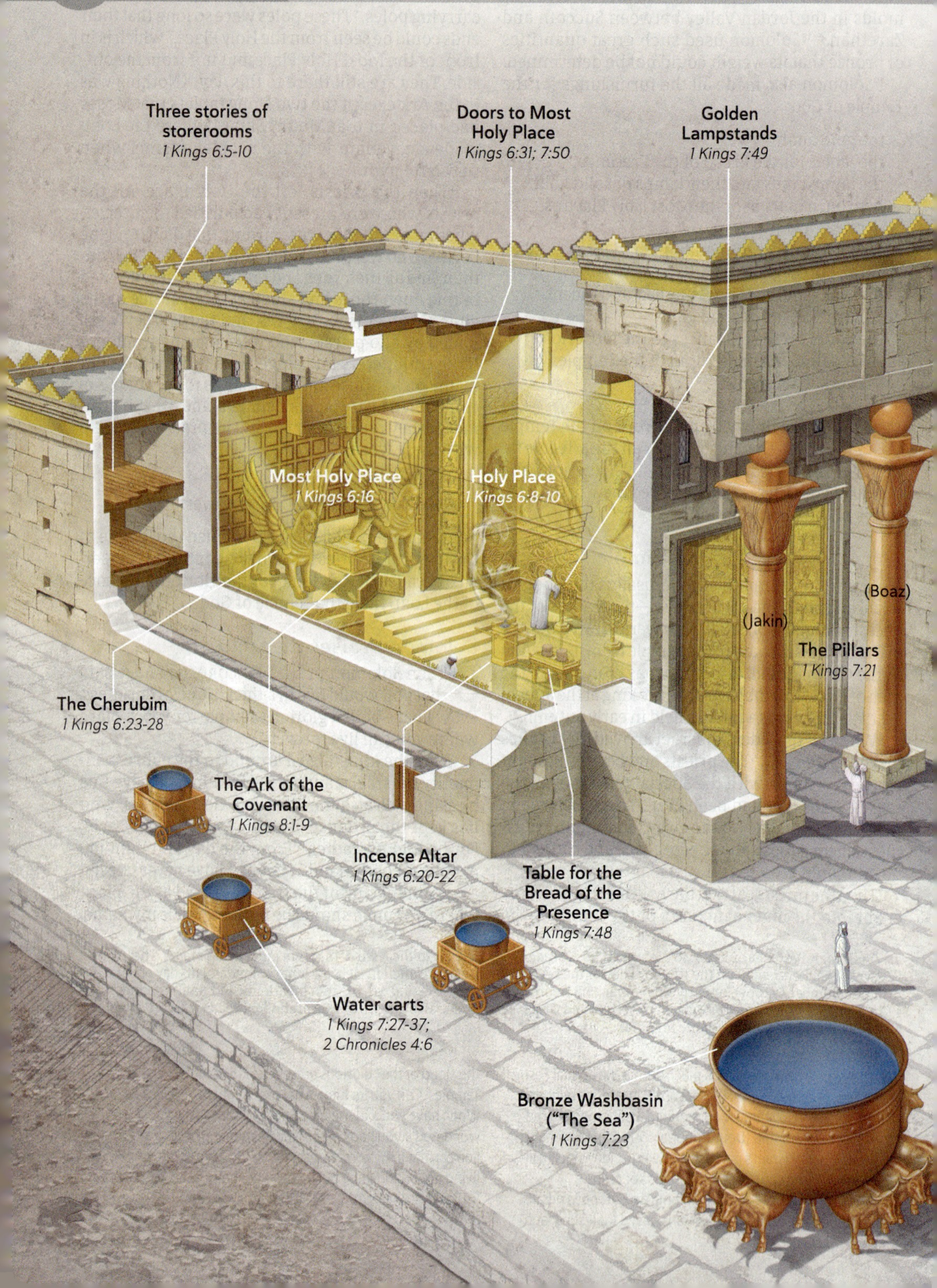

Three stories of storerooms
1 Kings 6:5-10

Doors to Most Holy Place
1 Kings 6:31; 7:50

Golden Lampstands
1 Kings 7:49

Most Holy Place
1 Kings 6:16

Holy Place
1 Kings 6:8-10

(Jakin)

(Boaz)

The Pillars
1 Kings 7:21

The Cherubim
1 Kings 6:23-28

The Ark of the Covenant
1 Kings 8:1-9

Incense Altar
1 Kings 6:20-22

Table for the Bread of the Presence
1 Kings 7:48

Water carts
1 Kings 7:27-37;
2 Chronicles 4:6

Bronze Washbasin ("The Sea")
1 Kings 7:23

It took Solomon seven years to build the Temple in Jerusalem, beginning in the fourth year of his reign (967 BC; 1 Kings 6:1–9:1 and 2 Chronicles 3:1–5:14). The Temple, laid out like the Tabernacle before it, stood until Jerusalem was destroyed in 586 BC. The Temple was large—90 feet long, 30 feet wide, and 45 feet high, with an entrance 30 feet wide and 15 feet deep (see 1 Kings 6:2-10). It employed the era's most sophisticated building techniques, and no expense was spared in construction, ornamentation, or equipment. Even so, Solomon readily confessed that the Temple could not adequately house the eternal God (1 Kings 8:27).

Altar of Burnt Offering
1 Kings 9:25; 1 Chronicles 22:1;
2 Chronicles 7:7; 8:12

Nor have I chosen a king to lead my people Israel. ⁶But now I have chosen Jerusalem as the place for my name to be honored, and I have chosen David to be king over my people Israel.'"

⁷Then Solomon said, "My father, David, wanted to build this Temple to honor the name of the Lord, the God of Israel. ⁸But the Lord told him, 'You wanted to build the Temple to honor my name. Your intention is good, ⁹but you are not the one to do it. One of your own sons will build the Temple to honor me.'

¹⁰"And now the Lord has fulfilled the promise he made, for I have become king in my father's place, and now I sit on the throne of Israel, just as the Lord promised. I have built this Temple to honor the name of the Lord, the God of Israel. ¹¹There I have placed the Ark, which contains the covenant that the Lord made with the people of Israel."

Solomon's Prayer of Dedication

¹²Then Solomon stood before the altar of the Lord in front of the entire community of Israel, and he lifted his hands in prayer. ¹³Now Solomon had made a bronze platform 7½ feet long, 7½ feet wide, and 4½ feet high* and had placed it at the center of the Temple's outer courtyard. He stood on the platform, and then he knelt in front of the entire community of Israel and lifted his hands toward heaven. ¹⁴He prayed,

> "O Lord, God of Israel, there is no God like you in all of heaven and earth. You keep your covenant and show unfailing love to all who walk before you in wholehearted devotion. ¹⁵You have kept your promise to your servant David, my father. You made that promise with your own mouth, and with your own hands you have fulfilled it today.
>
> ¹⁶"And now, O Lord, God of Israel, carry out the additional promise you made to your servant David, my father. For you said to him, 'If your descendants guard their behavior and faithfully follow my Law as you have done, one of them will always sit on the throne of Israel.' ¹⁷Now, O Lord, God of Israel, fulfill this promise to your servant David.
>
> ¹⁸"But will God really live on earth among people? Why, even the highest heavens cannot contain you. How much less this Temple I have built! ¹⁹Nevertheless, listen to my prayer and my plea, O Lord my God. Hear the cry and the prayer that your servant is making to you. ²⁰May you watch over this Temple day and night, this place where you have said you would put your name. May you always hear the prayers I make toward this place. ²¹May you hear the humble and earnest requests from me and your people Israel when we pray toward this place. Yes, hear us from heaven where you live, and when you hear, forgive.
>
> ²²"If someone wrongs another person and is required to take an oath of innocence in front of your altar at this Temple, ²³then hear from heaven and judge between your servants—the accuser and the accused. Pay back the guilty as they deserve. Acquit the innocent because of their innocence.
>
> ²⁴"If your people Israel are defeated by their enemies because they have sinned against you, and if they turn back and acknowledge your name and pray to you here in this Temple, ²⁵then hear from heaven and forgive the sin of your people Israel and return them to this land you gave to them and to their ancestors.
>
> ²⁶"If the skies are shut up and there is no rain because your people have sinned against you, and if they pray toward this Temple and acknowledge your name and turn from their sins because you have punished them, ²⁷then hear from heaven and forgive the sins of your servants, your people Israel. Teach them to follow the right path, and send rain on your land that you have given to your people as their special possession.
>
> ²⁸"If there is a famine in the land or a plague or crop disease or attacks of locusts or caterpillars, or if your people's enemies are in the land besieging their towns—whatever disaster or disease there is—²⁹and if your people Israel pray about their troubles or sorrow, raising their hands toward this Temple, ³⁰then hear from heaven where you live, and forgive. Give your people what their actions deserve, for you alone know each human heart. ³¹Then they will fear you and walk in your ways as long as they live in the land you gave to our ancestors.

6:13 Hebrew *5 cubits* [2.3 meters] *long, 5 cubits wide, and 3 cubits* [1.4 meters] *high*.

6:14-42 Solomon's prayer of dedication for the Temple included seven petitions: justice and forgiveness (6:22-23); forgiveness after defeat (6:24-25); forgiveness and guidance after drought, (6:26-27); forgiveness after famine and pestilence (6:28-31); foreigners who seek God to be heard (6:32-33); upholding the cause during war (6:34-35); exile leading to repentance bringing forgiveness (6:36-39). Solomon called on God to remember his great love for them, the love promised to David.

6:26 In ancient times, people believed that natural disasters directly resulted from displeasing a deity. The book of Job is a helpful example of this ancient mindset and its downfalls: Job was a righteous man yet still suffered. In the New Testament, Jesus is the perfect human, sinless, and yet he suffered.

³²"In the future, foreigners who do not belong to your people Israel will hear of you. They will come from distant lands when they hear of your great name and your strong hand and your powerful arm. And when they pray toward this Temple, ³³then hear from heaven where you live, and grant what they ask of you. In this way, all the people of the earth will come to know and fear you, just as your own people Israel do. They, too, will know that this Temple I have built honors your name.

³⁴"If your people go out where you send them to fight their enemies, and if they pray to you by turning toward this city you have chosen and toward this Temple I have built to honor your name, ³⁵then hear their prayers from heaven and uphold their cause.

³⁶"If they sin against you—and who has never sinned?—you might become angry with them and let their enemies conquer them and take them captive to a foreign land far away or near. ³⁷But in that land of exile, they might turn to you in repentance and pray, 'We have sinned, done evil, and acted wickedly.' ³⁸If they turn to you with their whole heart and soul in the land of their captivity and pray toward the land you gave to their ancestors—toward this city you have chosen, and toward this Temple I have built to honor your name—³⁹then hear their prayers and their petitions from heaven where you live, and uphold their cause. Forgive your people who have sinned against you.

⁴⁰"O my God, may your eyes be open and your ears attentive to all the prayers made to you in this place.

⁴¹ "And now arise, O Lord God, and enter your resting place,
along with the Ark, the symbol of your power.
May your priests, O Lord God, be clothed with salvation;
may your loyal servants rejoice in your goodness.
⁴² O Lord God, do not reject the king you have anointed.
Remember your unfailing love for your servant David."

The Dedication of the Temple

7 When Solomon finished praying, fire flashed down from heaven and burned up the burnt offerings and sacrifices, and the glorious presence of the Lord filled the Temple. ²The priests could not enter the Temple of the Lord because the glorious presence of the Lord filled it. ³When all the people of Israel saw the fire coming down and the glorious presence of the Lord filling the Temple, they fell face down on the ground and worshiped and praised the Lord, saying,

"He is good!
His faithful love endures forever!"

⁴Then the king and all the people offered sacrifices to the Lord. ⁵King Solomon offered a sacrifice of 22,000 cattle and 120,000 sheep and goats. And so the king and all the people dedicated the Temple of God. ⁶The priests took their assigned positions, and so did the Levites who were singing, "His faithful love endures forever!" They accompanied the singing with music from the instruments King David had made for praising the Lord. Across from the Levites, the priests blew the trumpets, while all Israel stood.

⁷Solomon then consecrated the central area of the courtyard in front of the Lord's Temple. He offered burnt offerings and the fat of peace offerings there, because the bronze altar he had built could not hold all the burnt offerings, grain offerings, and sacrificial fat.

⁸For the next seven days Solomon and all Israel celebrated the Festival of Shelters.* A large congregation had gathered from as far away as Lebo-hamath in the north and the Brook of Egypt in the south. ⁹On the eighth day they had a closing ceremony, for they had celebrated the dedication of the altar for seven days and the Festival of Shelters for seven days. ¹⁰Then at the end of the celebration,* Solomon sent the people home. They were all joyful and glad because the Lord had been so good to David and to Solomon and to his people Israel.

The Lord's Response to Solomon

¹¹So Solomon finished the Temple of the Lord, as well as the royal palace. He completed everything he had planned to do in the construction of the Temple and the palace. ¹²Then one night the Lord appeared to Solomon and said,

---

7:8 Hebrew *the festival* (also in 7:9); see note on 5:3. **7:10** Hebrew *Then on the twenty-third day of the seventh month*. This day of the ancient Hebrew lunar calendar occurred in October or early November.

6:41-42 Solomon's prayer concludes with a paraphrased portion of a psalm (Psalm 132:8-10). This prayer was the final part of transferring the Ark to its place in the Temple. Prayers with psalms had also accompanied David's transfer of the Ark to Jerusalem (1 Chronicles 16:7-36). Solomon's use of a psalm recalls the time when the Ark was first brought to its proper place. God is called to arise, not to war (see Numbers 10:35), but to his resting place in the Temple.
6:42 In harmony with the opening of the prayer (6:15-17), Solomon asks God to remember his "unfailing love for . . . David"; this refers to the covenant promise that God made to David (1 Chronicles 17:4-14; see Isaiah 55:3).

"I have heard your prayer and have chosen this Temple as the place for making sacrifices. ¹³At times I might shut up the heavens so that no rain falls, or command grasshoppers to devour your crops, or send plagues among you. ¹⁴Then if my people who are called by my name will humble themselves and pray and seek my face and turn from their wicked ways, I will hear from heaven and will forgive their sins and restore their land. ¹⁵My eyes will be open and my ears attentive to every prayer made in this place. ¹⁶For I have chosen this Temple and set it apart to be holy—a place where my name will be honored forever. I will always watch over it, for it is dear to my heart.

¹⁷"As for you, if you faithfully follow me as David your father did, obeying all my commands, decrees, and regulations, ¹⁸then I will establish the throne of your dynasty. For I made this covenant with your father, David, when I said, 'One of your descendants will always rule over Israel.'

¹⁹"But if you or your descendants abandon me and disobey the decrees and commands I have given you, and if you serve and worship other gods, ²⁰then I will uproot the people from this land that I have given them. I will reject this Temple that I have made holy to honor my name. I will make it an object of mockery and ridicule among the nations. ²¹And though this Temple is impressive now, all who pass by will be appalled. They will ask, 'Why did the LORD do such terrible things to this land and to this Temple?'

²²"And the answer will be, 'Because his people abandoned the LORD, the God of their ancestors, who brought them out of Egypt, and they worshiped other gods instead and bowed down to them. That is why he has brought all these disasters on them.'"

Solomon's Many Achievements

8 It took Solomon twenty years to build the LORD's Temple and his own royal palace. At the end of that time, ²Solomon turned his attention to rebuilding the towns that King Hiram* had given him, and he settled Israelites in them.

³Solomon also fought against the town of Hamath-zobah and conquered it. ⁴He rebuilt Tadmor in the wilderness and built towns in the region of Hamath as supply centers. ⁵He fortified the towns of Upper Beth-horon and Lower Beth-horon, rebuilding their walls and installing barred gates. ⁶He also rebuilt Baalath and other supply centers and constructed towns where his chariots and horses* could be stationed. He built everything he desired in Jerusalem and Lebanon and throughout his entire realm.

⁷There were still some people living in the land who were not Israelites, including the Hittites, Amorites, Perizzites, Hivites, and Jebusites. ⁸These were descendants of the nations whom the people of Israel had not destroyed. So Solomon conscripted them for his labor force, and they serve as forced laborers to this day. ⁹But Solomon did not conscript any of the Israelites for his labor force. Instead, he assigned them to serve as fighting men, officers in his army, commanders of his chariots, and charioteers. ¹⁰King Solomon appointed 250 of them to supervise the people.

¹¹Solomon moved his wife, Pharaoh's daughter, from the City of David to the new palace he had built for her. He said, "My wife must not live in King David's palace, for the Ark of the LORD has been there, and it is holy ground."

¹²Then Solomon presented burnt offerings to the LORD on the altar he had built for him in front of the entry room of the Temple. ¹³He offered the sacrifices for the Sabbaths, the new moon festivals, and the three annual festivals—the Passover celebration, the Festival of Harvest,* and the Festival of Shelters—as Moses had commanded.

8:2 Hebrew *Huram*, a variant spelling of Hiram; also in 8:18. **8:6** Or *and charioteers*. **8:13** Or *Festival of Weeks*.

7:13-15 Solomon's prayer contains a few of the best-known verses in Chronicles and lays out God's plan for Israel. Note that 7:14 expresses the author's understanding of how God works with his people, Israel: Each person experiences the consequences for obedience or disobedience within their own lifetime. Hezekiah provides a prominent example of this principle operating in the lives of the kings of Judah. When Hezekiah began to restore worship at the Temple, he summoned the people to attend the festival in Jerusalem (30:1-9). The priests and the Levites blessed the people who came, and the Lord healed the people (2 Chronicles 29–30). Failure to repent of our sins will result in judgment. But there is no situation beyond the reach of redemption for those willing to humble themselves before God.
7:17-18 God declared to Solomon that God's kingdom would last forever. Where 1 Kings 9:5 states that one of his descendants would always be on Israel's throne, the writer of Chronicles says, "One of your descendants will always rule over Israel." Since there was no throne in Israel during the chronicler's time, this statement previews the reign of the Messiah (see Micah 5:2)
8:11 Solomon's marriage to the pharaoh's daughter was a political alliance, and the text is not clear why Solomon thought she could not dwell in the palace that had once contained the Ark, but he built a separate palace for her. Marriage to non-Israelite women had been forbidden not out of racial discrimination but because it could lead to worshiping other gods (Deuteronomy 7.3-4). Solomon married many women from cultures that worshiped other gods, and as he aged, his wives turned his heart to worship their gods (1 Kings 11:1-4). The Bible paints a complex portrait that includes non-Israelite women's importance to the Bible's story. In many critical moments, these women rescued Israel's people and contributed to God's plan to bless the world. Pharaoh's daughter adopted Moses, Zipporah saved Moses (Exodus), Rahab protected the Israelite spies (Joshua), and Ruth preserved Naomi's family (Ruth).

¹⁴In assigning the priests to their duties, Solomon followed the regulations of his father, David. He also assigned the Levites to lead the people in praise and to assist the priests in their daily duties. And he assigned the gatekeepers to their gates by their divisions, following the commands of David, the man of God. ¹⁵Solomon did not deviate in any way from David's commands concerning the priests and Levites and the treasuries.

¹⁶So Solomon made sure that all the work related to building the Temple of the LORD was carried out, from the day its foundation was laid to the day of its completion.

¹⁷Later Solomon went to Ezion-geber and Elath,* ports along the shore of the Red Sea* in the land of Edom. ¹⁸Hiram sent him ships commanded by his own officers and manned by experienced crews of sailors. These ships sailed to Ophir with Solomon's men and brought back to Solomon almost seventeen tons* of gold.

Visit of the Queen of Sheba

9 When the queen of Sheba heard of Solomon's fame, she came to Jerusalem to test him with hard questions. She arrived with a large group of attendants and a great caravan of camels loaded with spices, large quantities of gold, and precious jewels. When she met with Solomon, she talked with him about everything she had on her mind. ²Solomon had answers for all her questions; nothing was too hard for him to explain to her. ³When the queen of Sheba realized how wise Solomon was, and when she saw the palace he had built, ⁴she was overwhelmed. She was also amazed at the food on his tables, the organization of his officials and their splendid clothing, the cup-bearers and their robes, and the burnt offerings* Solomon made at the Temple of the LORD.

⁵She exclaimed to the king, "Everything I heard in my country about your achievements* and wisdom is true! ⁶I didn't believe what was said until I arrived here and saw it with my own eyes. In fact, I had not heard the half of your great wisdom! It is far beyond what I was told. ⁷How happy your people must be! What a privilege for your officials to stand here day after day, listening to your wisdom! ⁸Praise the LORD your God, who delights in you and has placed you on the throne as king to rule for him. Because God loves Israel and desires this kingdom to last forever, he has made you king over them so you can rule with justice and righteousness."

⁹Then she gave the king a gift of 9,000 pounds* of gold, great quantities of spices, and precious jewels. Never before had there been spices as fine as those the queen of Sheba gave to King Solomon.

¹⁰(In addition, the crews of Hiram and Solomon brought gold from Ophir, and they also brought red sandalwood* and precious jewels. ¹¹The king used the sandalwood to make steps* for the Temple of the LORD and the royal palace, and to construct lyres and harps for the musicians. Never before had such beautiful things been seen in Judah.)

¹²King Solomon gave the queen of Sheba whatever she asked for—gifts of greater value than the gifts she had given him. Then she and all her attendants returned to their own land.

Solomon's Wealth and Splendor

¹³Each year Solomon received about 25 tons* of gold. ¹⁴This did not include the additional revenue he received from merchants and traders. All the kings of Arabia and the governors of the provinces also brought gold and silver to Solomon.

¹⁵King Solomon made 200 large shields of hammered gold, each weighing more than 15 pounds.* ¹⁶He also made 300 smaller shields of hammered gold, each weighing more than 7½ pounds.* The king placed these shields in the Palace of the Forest of Lebanon.

¹⁷Then the king made a huge throne, decorated with ivory and overlaid with pure gold. ¹⁸The throne had six steps, with a footstool of gold. There were armrests on both sides of the seat, and the figure of a lion stood on each side of the throne. ¹⁹There were also twelve other lions, one standing on each end of the six steps. No other throne in all the world could be compared with it!

²⁰All of King Solomon's drinking cups were solid gold, as were all the utensils in the Palace of the Forest of Lebanon. They were not made of silver, for silver was considered worthless in Solomon's day!

²¹The king had a fleet of trading ships of Tarshish manned by the sailors sent by Hiram.* Once every three years the ships returned, loaded with gold, silver, ivory, apes, and peacocks.*

8:17a As in Greek version (see also 2 Kgs 14:22; 16:6); Hebrew reads *Eloth*, a variant spelling of Elath. **8:17b** As in parallel text at 1 Kgs 9:26; Hebrew reads *the sea*. **8:18** Hebrew *450 talents* [15.3 metric tons]. **9:4** As in Greek and Syriac versions (see also 1 Kgs 10:5); Hebrew reads *and the ascent*. **9:5** Hebrew *your words*. **9:9** Hebrew *120 talents* [4,000 kilograms]. **9:10** Hebrew *algum wood* (also in 9:11); perhaps a variant spelling of *almug*. Compare parallel text at 1 Kgs 10:11-12. **9:11** Or *gateways*. The meaning of the Hebrew is uncertain. **9:13** Hebrew *666 talents* [23 metric tons]. **9:15** Hebrew *600 [shekels] of hammered gold* [6.8 kilograms]. **9:16** Hebrew *300 [shekels] of gold* [3.4 kilograms]. **9:21a** Hebrew *Huram*, a variant spelling of Hiram. **9:21b** Or *and baboons*.

9:1-8 Solomon's wisdom was famous. The queen of Sheba was a powerful, influential woman who wanted to "test him with hard questions" (9:1). Seeing was believing for this queen! She was so impressed that she praised Solomon's God and offered him generous gifts. In return, Solomon gave the queen of Sheba even more precious gifts. Sometimes, what God is doing is hard to believe because it is beyond the scope of what we previously have experienced. It helps to go see the amazing things God is doing, just like the queen of Sheba did. Doing so can strengthen our faith in God.

22So King Solomon became richer and wiser than any other king on earth. 23Kings from every nation came to consult him and to hear the wisdom God had given him. 24Year after year everyone who visited brought him gifts of silver and gold, clothing, weapons, spices, horses, and mules.

25Solomon had 4,000 stalls for his horses and chariots, and he had 12,000 horses.* He stationed some of them in the chariot cities, and some near him in Jerusalem. 26He ruled over all the kings from the Euphrates River* in the north to the land of the Philistines and the border of Egypt in the south. 27The king made silver as plentiful in Jerusalem as stone. And valuable cedar timber was as common as the sycamore-fig trees that grow in the foothills of Judah.* 28Solomon's horses were imported from Egypt* and many other countries.

Summary of Solomon's Reign

29The rest of the events of Solomon's reign, from beginning to end, are recorded in The Record of Nathan the Prophet, and The Prophecy of Ahijah from Shiloh, and also in The Visions of Iddo the Seer, concerning Jeroboam son of Nebat. 30Solomon ruled in Jerusalem over all Israel for forty years. 31When he died, he was buried in the City of David, named for his father. Then his son Rehoboam became the next king.

The Northern Tribes Revolt

10 Rehoboam went to Shechem, where all Israel had gathered to make him king. 2When Jeroboam son of Nebat heard of this, he returned from Egypt, for he had fled to Egypt to escape from King Solomon. 3The leaders of Israel summoned him, and Jeroboam and all Israel went to speak with Rehoboam. 4"Your father was a hard master," they said. "Lighten the harsh labor demands and heavy taxes that your father imposed on us. Then we will be your loyal subjects."

5Rehoboam replied, "Come back in three days for my answer." So the people went away.

6Then King Rehoboam discussed the matter with the older men who had counseled his father, Solomon. "What is your advice?" he asked. "How should I answer these people?"

7The older counselors replied, "If you are good to these people and do your best to please them and give them a favorable answer, they will always be your loyal subjects."

8But Rehoboam rejected the advice of the older men and instead asked the opinion of the young men who had grown up with him and were now his advisers. 9"What is your advice?" he asked them. "How should I answer these people who want me to lighten the burdens imposed by my father?"

10The young men replied, "This is what you should tell those complainers who want a lighter burden: 'My little finger is thicker than my father's waist! 11Yes, my father laid heavy burdens on you, but I'm going to make them even heavier! My father beat you with whips, but I will beat you with scorpions!'"

12Three days later Jeroboam and all the people returned to hear Rehoboam's decision, just as the king had ordered. 13But Rehoboam spoke harshly to them, for he rejected the advice of the older counselors 14and followed the counsel of his younger advisers. He told the people, "My father laid* heavy burdens on you, but I'm going to make them even heavier! My father beat you with whips, but I will beat you with scorpions!"

15So the king paid no attention to the people. This turn of events was the will of God, for it fulfilled the LORD's message to Jeroboam son of Nebat through the prophet Ahijah from Shiloh.

16When all Israel realized* that the king had refused to listen to them, they responded,

"Down with the dynasty of David!
We have no interest in the son of Jesse.
Back to your homes, O Israel!
Look out for your own house, O David!"

So all the people of Israel returned home. 17But Rehoboam continued to rule over the Israelites who lived in the towns of Judah.

18King Rehoboam sent Adoniram,* who was in charge of forced labor, to restore order, but the people of Israel stoned him to death. When this news reached King Rehoboam, he quickly jumped into his chariot and fled to Jerusalem. 19And to this day the northern tribes of Israel have refused to be ruled by a descendant of David.

9:25 Or *12,000 charioteers.* 9:26 Hebrew *the river.* 9:27 Hebrew *the Shephelah.* 9:28 Possibly *Muzur,* a district near Cilicia. 10:14 As in Greek version and many Hebrew manuscripts (see also 1 Kgs 12:14); Masoretic Text reads *I will lay.* 10:16 As in Syriac version, Latin Vulgate, and many Hebrew manuscripts (see also 1 Kgs 12:16); Masoretic Text lacks *realized.* 10:18 Hebrew *Hadoram,* a variant spelling of Adoniram; compare 1 Kgs 4:6; 5:14; 12:18.

10:1-19 The kingdom that had united under David and Solomon split into two under the leadership of Jeroboam and Rehoboam. Jeroboam led ten tribes in the north to form the kingdom of Israel. Judah and Benjamin followed Rehoboam and remained in the south, forming the kingdom of Judah.

10:7-11 Rehoboam rejected the wise advice of the experienced counselors and consulted with the inexperienced people he had known growing up. These younger advisers (who may have wanted to tell their king what he wanted to hear) encouraged Rehoboam to lead oppressively. Rehoboam had moments of obeying the Lord but ultimately was remembered as an evil king because "he did not seek the LORD with all his heart" (12:14). Seeking advice from wise people who may not tell us what we want to hear can help us do good.

Queen of Sheba

IDENTITY — A Foreign Queen Who Worshiped God

Can someone who does not follow God see God's hand at work? Can someone who does not believe in God spot his work in someone who believes?

The queen of Sheba did. She made an extensive journey from ancient Sheba (modern-day Yemen) to meet someone she had heard much about—King Solomon. She traveled about 1,400 miles, a long and arduous journey for the queen, her entourage, and the many gifts they brought for Solomon.

She aimed to question this king and see for herself if the stories were accurate. She found that King Solomon could answer every hard question she asked, and she was overwhelmed (9:2-4).

She saw the king's wisdom, as well as the splendor of his palace, his table, his officials, his servants, and his clothing. All were even greater than told. So, she blessed him and delighted in paying tribute to him—and his God (9:7-8).

God reaches out to people in many ways, and one way is through the lives of his followers. Solomon's wisdom and the grandeur of his kingdom pointed the queen of Sheba to the God who provides all our blessings. And God can draw people to himself through our lives, too, if we are available to him.

> Even when we think no one's looking, others watch God working in our lives.

THE QUEEN OF SHEBA'S STORY IS TOLD IN 1 KINGS 10:1-13; 2 CHRONICLES 9:1-12.

IDENTIFY

Even though we are not kings, how can the world see God through us? Consider John 17:20, 23.

How can we draw others to God with wisdom?

"As a chaplain for the local police department, my witness is through my presence. I am not supposed to preach or share the gospel unless asked, so I speak through my life. Amazing opportunities come from being consistently present, praying for officers, and showing interest and concern."

ELIZABETH GLANVILLE, PhD, is retired faculty from Fuller Theological Seminary, School of Mission and Theology. She is an international teacher on missions and leadership and chaplain for a local police department and her retirement community.

Shemaiah's Prophecy

11 When Rehoboam arrived at Jerusalem, he mobilized the men of Judah and Benjamin—180,000 select troops—to fight against Israel and to restore the kingdom to himself.

²But the LORD said to Shemaiah, the man of God, ³"Say to Rehoboam son of Solomon, king of Judah, and to all the Israelites in Judah and Benjamin: ⁴'This is what the LORD says: Do not fight against your relatives. Go back home, for what has happened is my doing!'" So they obeyed the message of the LORD and did not fight against Jeroboam.

Rehoboam Fortifies Judah

⁵Rehoboam remained in Jerusalem and fortified various towns for the defense of Judah. ⁶He built up Bethlehem, Etam, Tekoa, ⁷Beth-zur, Soco, Adullam, ⁸Gath, Mareshah, Ziph, ⁹Adoraim, Lachish, Azekah, ¹⁰Zorah, Aijalon, and Hebron. These became the fortified towns of Judah and Benjamin. ¹¹Rehoboam strengthened their defenses and stationed commanders in them, and he stored supplies of food, olive oil, and wine. ¹²He also put shields and spears in these towns as a further safety measure. So only Judah and Benjamin remained under his control.

¹³But all the priests and Levites living among the northern tribes of Israel sided with Rehoboam. ¹⁴The Levites even abandoned their pasturelands and property and moved to Judah and Jerusalem, because Jeroboam and his sons would not allow them to serve the LORD as priests. ¹⁵Jeroboam appointed his own priests to serve at the pagan shrines, where they worshiped the goat and calf idols he had made. ¹⁶From all the tribes of Israel, those who sincerely wanted to worship the LORD, the God of Israel, followed the Levites to Jerusalem, where they could offer sacrifices to the LORD, the God of their ancestors. ¹⁷This strengthened the kingdom of Judah, and for three years they supported Rehoboam son of Solomon, for during those years they faithfully followed in the footsteps of David and Solomon.

Rehoboam's Family

¹⁸Rehoboam married his cousin Mahalath, the daughter of David's son Jerimoth and of Abihail, the daughter of Eliab son of Jesse. ¹⁹Mahalath had three sons—Jeush, Shemariah, and Zaham.

²⁰Later Rehoboam married another cousin, Maacah, the granddaughter of Absalom. Maacah gave birth to Abijah, Attai, Ziza, and Shelomith. ²¹Rehoboam loved Maacah more than any of his other wives and concubines. In all, he had eighteen wives and sixty concubines, and they gave birth to twenty-eight sons and sixty daughters.

²²Rehoboam appointed Maacah's son Abijah as leader among the princes, making it clear that he would be the next king. ²³Rehoboam also wisely gave responsibilities to his other sons and stationed some of them in the fortified towns throughout the land of Judah and Benjamin. He provided them with generous provisions, and he found many wives for them.

Egypt Invades Judah

12 But when Rehoboam was firmly established and strong, he abandoned the Law of the LORD, and all Israel followed him in this sin. ²Because they were unfaithful to the LORD, King Shishak of Egypt came up and attacked Jerusalem in the fifth year of King Rehoboam's reign. ³He came with 1,200 chariots, 60,000 horses,* and a countless army of foot soldiers, including Libyans, Sukkites, and Ethiopians.* ⁴Shishak conquered Judah's fortified towns and then advanced to attack Jerusalem.

⁵The prophet Shemaiah then met with Rehoboam and Judah's leaders, who had all fled to Jerusalem because of Shishak. Shemaiah told them, "This is what the LORD says: You have abandoned me, so I am abandoning you to Shishak."

⁶Then the leaders of Israel and the king humbled themselves and said, "The LORD is right in doing this to us!"

⁷When the LORD saw their change of heart, he gave this message to Shemaiah: "Since the people have humbled themselves, I will not completely destroy them and will soon give them some relief. I will not use Shishak to pour out my anger on Jerusalem. ⁸But they will become his subjects, so they will know the difference between serving me and serving earthly rulers."

⁹So King Shishak of Egypt came up and attacked Jerusalem. He ransacked the treasuries of the LORD's Temple and the royal palace; he stole everything, including all the gold shields Solomon had made. ¹⁰King Rehoboam later replaced them with bronze shields as substitutes, and he entrusted them to the care of the commanders of the guard who protected the entrance to the royal palace. ¹¹Whenever

---

12:3a Or *charioteers*, or *horsemen*. 12:3b Hebrew *and Cushites*.

11:5-23 The Lord's blessing on Rehoboam shows in his building activities, the faithful priests, the people defecting from the north to the south, and his large family. It is so easy to see where life is hard and miss where God has made our work and relationships go well. Consider pausing right now and asking God to show you the ways your life reflects his good gifts.
12:1-2 The book of 1 Kings (1 Kings 14) states no theological reason for Egypt's invasion, but the author of 2 Chronicles does: The Egyptians attacked Jerusalem because Rehoboam had abandoned the covenant and rebelled against the Lord.
12:6-7 Shemaiah's speech expresses the elements required in Solomon's prayer at the Temple's dedication (7:14). "The leaders of Israel...humbled themselves," and the wrath of judgment on Jerusalem was lessened.

the king went to the Temple of the LORD, the guards would also take the shields and then return them to the guardroom. ¹²Because Rehoboam humbled himself, the LORD's anger was turned away, and he did not destroy him completely. There were still some good things in the land of Judah.

Summary of Rehoboam's Reign

¹³King Rehoboam firmly established himself in Jerusalem and continued to rule. He was forty-one years old when he became king, and he reigned seventeen years in Jerusalem, the city the LORD had chosen from among all the tribes of Israel as the place to honor his name. Rehoboam's mother was Naamah, a woman from Ammon. ¹⁴But he was an evil king, for he did not seek the LORD with all his heart.

¹⁵The rest of the events of Rehoboam's reign, from beginning to end, are recorded in The Record of Shemaiah the Prophet and The Record of Iddo the Seer, which are part of the genealogical record. Rehoboam and Jeroboam were continually at war with each other. ¹⁶When Rehoboam died, he was buried in the City of David. Then his son Abijah became the next king.

Abijah's War with Jeroboam

13 Abijah began to rule over Judah in the eighteenth year of Jeroboam's reign in Israel. ²He reigned in Jerusalem three years. His mother was Maacah,* the daughter of Uriel from Gibeah.

Then war broke out between Abijah and Jeroboam. ³Judah, led by King Abijah, fielded 400,000 select warriors, while Jeroboam mustered 800,000 select troops from Israel.

⁴When the army of Judah arrived in the hill country of Ephraim, Abijah stood on Mount Zemaraim and shouted to Jeroboam and all Israel: "Listen to me! ⁵Don't you realize that the LORD, the God of Israel, made a lasting covenant* with David, giving him and his descendants the throne of Israel forever? ⁶Yet Jeroboam son of Nebat, a mere servant of David's son Solomon, rebelled against his master. ⁷Then a whole gang of scoundrels joined him, defying Solomon's son Rehoboam when he was young and inexperienced and could not stand up to them.

⁸"Do you really think you can stand against the kingdom of the LORD that is led by the descendants of David? You may have a vast army, and you have those gold calves that Jeroboam made as your gods. ⁹But you have chased away the priests of the LORD (the descendants of Aaron) and the Levites, and you have appointed your own priests, just like the pagan nations. You let anyone become a priest these days! Whoever comes to be dedicated with a young bull and seven rams can become a priest of these so-called gods of yours!

¹⁰"But as for us, the LORD is our God, and we have not abandoned him. Only the descendants of Aaron serve the LORD as priests, and the Levites alone may help them in their work. ¹¹They present burnt offerings and fragrant incense to the LORD every morning and evening. They place the Bread of the Presence on the holy table, and they light the gold lampstand every evening. We are following the instructions of the LORD our God, but you have abandoned him. ¹²So you see, God is with us. He is our leader. His priests blow their trumpets and lead us into battle against you. O people of Israel, do not fight against the LORD, the God of your ancestors, for you will not succeed!"

¹³Meanwhile, Jeroboam had secretly sent part of his army around behind the men of Judah to ambush them. ¹⁴When Judah realized that they were being attacked from the front and the rear, they cried out to the LORD for help. Then the priests blew the trumpets, ¹⁵and the men of Judah began to shout. At the sound of their battle cry, God defeated Jeroboam and all Israel and routed them before Abijah and the army of Judah.

¹⁶The Israelite army fled from Judah, and God handed them over to Judah in defeat. ¹⁷Abijah and his army inflicted heavy losses on them; 500,000 of Israel's select troops were killed that day. ¹⁸So Judah defeated Israel on that occasion because they trusted in the LORD, the God of their ancestors. ¹⁹Abijah and his army pursued Jeroboam's troops and captured some of his towns, including Bethel, Jeshanah, and Ephron, along with their surrounding villages.

²⁰So Jeroboam of Israel never regained his power during Abijah's lifetime, and finally the LORD struck him down and he died. ²¹Meanwhile, Abijah of Judah grew more and more powerful. He married fourteen wives and had twenty-two sons and sixteen daughters.

²²The rest of the events of Abijah's reign, including his words and deeds, are recorded in The Commentary of Iddo the Prophet.

Early Years of Asa's Reign

14 ¹*When Abijah died, he was buried in the City of David. Then his son Asa became the next king. There was peace in the land for ten years. ²*Asa did what was pleasing and good in the sight of the

---

13:2 As in most Greek manuscripts and Syriac version (see also 2 Chr 11:20-21; 1 Kgs 15:2); Hebrew reads *Micaiah*, a variant spelling of Maacah. **13:5** Hebrew *a covenant of salt*. **14:1** Verse 14:1 is numbered 13:23 in Hebrew text. **14:2** Verses 14:2-15 are numbered 14:1-14 in Hebrew text.

13:13-19 God's people turning to him and his helping them, even after the kingdom had been disrupted, provided hope for the original readers facing a similar situation. How might we turn to God today, even if something has fallen apart in our lives in the past?

LORD his God. ³He removed the foreign altars and the pagan shrines. He smashed the sacred pillars and cut down the Asherah poles. ⁴He commanded the people of Judah to seek the LORD, the God of their ancestors, and to obey his law and his commands. ⁵Asa also removed the pagan shrines, as well as the incense altars from every one of Judah's towns. So Asa's kingdom enjoyed a period of peace. ⁶During those peaceful years, he was able to build up the fortified towns throughout Judah. No one tried to make war against him at this time, for the LORD was giving him rest from his enemies.

⁷Asa told the people of Judah, "Let us build towns and fortify them with walls, towers, gates, and bars. The land is still ours because we sought the LORD our God, and he has given us peace on every side." So they went ahead with these projects and brought them to completion.

⁸King Asa had an army of 300,000 warriors from the tribe of Judah, armed with large shields and spears. He also had an army of 280,000 warriors from the tribe of Benjamin, armed with small shields and bows. Both armies were composed of well-trained fighting men.

⁹Once an Ethiopian* named Zerah attacked Judah with an army of 1,000,000 men* and 300 chariots. They advanced to the town of Mareshah, ¹⁰so Asa deployed his armies for battle in the valley north of Mareshah.* ¹¹Then Asa cried out to the LORD his God, "O LORD, no one but you can help the powerless against the mighty! Help us, O LORD our God, for we trust in you alone. It is in your name that we have come against this vast horde. O LORD, you are our God; do not let mere men prevail against you!"

¹²So the LORD defeated the Ethiopians* in the presence of Asa and the army of Judah, and the enemy fled. ¹³Asa and his army pursued them as far as Gerar, and so many Ethiopians fell that they were unable to rally. They were destroyed by the LORD and his army, and the army of Judah carried off a vast amount of plunder.

¹⁴While they were at Gerar, they attacked all the towns in that area, and terror from the LORD came upon the people there. As a result, a vast amount of plunder was taken from these towns, too. ¹⁵They also attacked the camps of herdsmen and captured many sheep, goats, and camels before finally returning to Jerusalem.

Asa's Religious Reforms

15 Then the Spirit of God came upon Azariah son of Oded, ²and he went out to meet King Asa as he was returning from the battle. "Listen to me, Asa!" he shouted. "Listen, all you people of Judah and Benjamin! The LORD will stay with you as long as you stay with him! Whenever you seek him, you will find him. But if you abandon him, he will abandon you. ³For a long time Israel was without the true God, without a priest to teach them, and without the Law to instruct them. ⁴But whenever they were in trouble and turned to the LORD, the God of Israel, and sought him out, they found him.

⁵"During those dark times, it was not safe to travel. Problems troubled the people of every land. ⁶Nation fought against nation, and city against city, for God was troubling them with every kind of problem. ⁷But as for you, be strong and courageous, for your work will be rewarded."

⁸When Asa heard this message from Azariah the prophet,* he took courage and removed all the detestable idols from the land of Judah and Benjamin and in the towns he had captured in the hill country of Ephraim. And he repaired the altar of the LORD, which stood in front of the entry room of the LORD's Temple.

⁹Then Asa called together all the people of Judah and Benjamin, along with the people of Ephraim, Manasseh, and Simeon who had settled among them. For many from Israel had moved to Judah during Asa's reign when they saw that the LORD his God was with him. ¹⁰The people gathered at Jerusalem in late spring,* during the fifteenth year of Asa's reign.

¹¹On that day they sacrificed to the LORD 700 cattle and 7,000 sheep and goats from the plunder they had taken in the battle. ¹²Then they entered into a covenant to seek the LORD, the God of their ancestors, with all their heart and soul. ¹³They agreed that anyone who refused to seek the LORD, the God of Israel, would be put to death—whether young or old, man or woman. ¹⁴They shouted out their oath of loyalty to the LORD with trumpets blaring and rams' horns sounding. ¹⁵All in Judah were happy about this covenant, for they had entered into it with all their heart. They earnestly sought after God, and they found him. And the LORD gave them rest from their enemies on every side.

¹⁶King Asa even deposed his grandmother* Maacah from her position as queen mother because she

---

14:9a Hebrew *a Cushite.* **14:9b** Or *an army of thousands and thousands;* Hebrew reads *an army of a thousand thousands.* **14:10** As in Greek version; Hebrew reads *valley of Zephathah near Mareshah.* **14:12** Hebrew *Cushites;* also in 14:13. **15:8** As in Syriac version and Latin Vulgate (see also 15:1); Hebrew reads *from Oded the prophet.* **15:10** Hebrew *in the third month.* This month of the ancient Hebrew lunar calendar usually occurs within the months of May and June. **15:16** Hebrew *his mother.*

14:4 The phrase "seek the LORD" is the writer's formula for restoration, and one can consider Asa's reign in terms of how he did, or did not, seek God (see 15:2, 12-13; 16:12). When we consider leaders today in a similar manner, how might we note and pray for which ones seek God's best and seek God over other things?

15:16 The queen mother was the most influential lady in Judah, usually holding the title as long as she lived. Throughout Chronicles, the author notes the names of the kings' mothers. When she died, the title passed to the mother of the heir apparent. There is no indication that the queen mother held official duties, but she wielded considerable influence.

had made an obscene Asherah pole. He cut down her obscene pole, broke it up, and burned it in the Kidron Valley. ¹⁷Although the pagan shrines were not removed from Israel, Asa's heart remained completely faithful throughout his life. ¹⁸He brought into the Temple of God the silver and gold and the various items that he and his father had dedicated.

¹⁹So there was no more war until the thirty-fifth year of Asa's reign.

Final Years of Asa's Reign

16 In the thirty-sixth year of Asa's reign, King Baasha of Israel invaded Judah and fortified Ramah in order to prevent anyone from entering or leaving King Asa's territory in Judah.

²Asa responded by removing the silver and gold from the treasuries of the Temple of the LORD and the royal palace. He sent it to King Ben-hadad of Aram, who was ruling in Damascus, along with this message:

³"Let there be a treaty* between you and me like the one between your father and my father. See, I am sending you silver and gold. Break your treaty with King Baasha of Israel so that he will leave me alone."

⁴Ben-hadad agreed to King Asa's request and sent the commanders of his army to attack the towns of Israel. They conquered the towns of Ijon, Dan, Abel-beth-maacah,* and all the store cities in Naphtali. ⁵As soon as Baasha of Israel heard what was happening, he abandoned his project of fortifying Ramah and stopped all work on it. ⁶Then King Asa called out all the men of Judah to carry away the building stones and timbers that Baasha had been using to fortify Ramah. Asa used these materials to fortify the towns of Geba and Mizpah.

⁷At that time Hanani the seer came to King Asa and told him, "Because you have put your trust in the king of Aram instead of in the LORD your God, you missed your chance to destroy the army of the king of Aram. ⁸Don't you remember what happened to the Ethiopians* and Libyans and their vast army, with all of their chariots and charioteers?* At that time you relied on the LORD, and he handed them over to you. ⁹The eyes of the LORD search the whole earth in order to strengthen those whose hearts are fully committed to him. What a fool you have been! From now on you will be at war."

¹⁰Asa became so angry with Hanani for saying this that he threw him into prison and put him in stocks. At that time Asa also began to oppress some of his people.

Summary of Asa's Reign

¹¹The rest of the events of Asa's reign, from beginning to end, are recorded in The Book of the Kings of Judah and Israel. ¹²In the thirty-ninth year of his reign, Asa developed a serious foot disease. Yet even with the severity of his disease, he did not seek the LORD's help but turned only to his physicians. ¹³So he died in the forty-first year of his reign. ¹⁴He was buried in the tomb he had carved out for himself in the City of David. He was laid on a bed perfumed with sweet spices and fragrant ointments, and the people built a huge funeral fire in his honor.

Jehoshaphat Rules in Judah

17 Then Jehoshaphat, Asa's son, became the next king. He strengthened Judah to stand against any attack from Israel. ²He stationed troops in all the fortified towns of Judah, and he assigned additional garrisons to the land of Judah and to the towns of Ephraim that his father, Asa, had captured.

³The LORD was with Jehoshaphat because he followed the example of his father's early years* and did not worship the images of Baal. ⁴He sought his father's God and obeyed his commands instead of following the evil practices of the kingdom of Israel. ⁵So the LORD established Jehoshaphat's control over the kingdom of Judah. All the people of Judah brought gifts to Jehoshaphat, so he became very wealthy and highly esteemed. ⁶He was deeply committed to* the ways of the LORD. He removed the pagan shrines and Asherah poles from Judah.

⁷In the third year of his reign Jehoshaphat sent his officials to teach in all the towns of Judah. These officials included Ben-hail, Obadiah, Zechariah, Nethanel, and Micaiah. ⁸He sent Levites along with them, including Shemaiah, Nethaniah, Zebadiah, Asahel,

---

16:3 As in Greek version; Hebrew reads *There is a treaty.* 16:4 As in parallel text at 1 Kgs 15:20; Hebrew reads *Abel-maim,* another name for Abel-beth-maacah. 16:8a Hebrew *Cushites.* 16:8b Or *and horsemen?* 17:3 Some Hebrew manuscripts read *the example of his father, David.* 17:6 Hebrew *His heart was courageous in.*

16:1-10 Asa provides a sad example of the human tendency to rely on our own resources (see Proverbs 11:7; Isaiah 31:1; Jeremiah 17:5-6) and to get mad when corrected. Even those who experience God's power often make the same mistake (2 Chronicles 16:8). The Bible uplifts a better way—of relying on God and welcoming God's guidance (see Psalms 33:18; 37:7; Isaiah 50:10; Jeremiah 17:7-8; Acts 13:43). Life is a long lesson in trusting God, and not our personal ambitions.

17:1–21:1 Jehoshaphat succeeded his father, Asa, becoming Judah's fourth king (872–848 BC). Like Hezekiah and Josiah after him, Jehoshaphat trusted God throughout his life and worked to remove most forms of idol worship from Israel (2 Chronicles 17:6). He also insisted on hearing from a true prophet of the Lord before going to battle. In one of the most stirring Old Testament descriptions on the eve of war, Jehoshaphat preached to the army and the people of Judah before entering the battle. As a result, God caused the armies from Ammon, Moab, and their allies to turn against each other (20:1-30). Jehoshaphat died when he was about sixty years old and was buried in Jerusalem.

Shemiramoth, Jehonathan, Adonijah, Tobijah, and Tob-adonijah. He also sent out the priests Elishama and Jehoram. ⁹They took copies of the Book of the Law of the Lord and traveled around through all the towns of Judah, teaching the people.

¹⁰Then the fear of the Lord fell over all the surrounding kingdoms so that none of them wanted to declare war on Jehoshaphat. ¹¹Some of the Philistines brought him gifts and silver as tribute, and the Arabs brought 7,700 rams and 7,700 male goats.

¹²So Jehoshaphat became more and more powerful and built fortresses and storage cities throughout Judah. ¹³He stored numerous supplies in Judah's towns and stationed an army of seasoned troops at Jerusalem. ¹⁴His army was enrolled according to ancestral clans.

From Judah there were 300,000 troops organized in units of 1,000, under the command of Adnah. ¹⁵Next in command was Jehohanan, who commanded 280,000 troops. ¹⁶Next was Amasiah son of Zicri, who volunteered for the Lord's service, with 200,000 troops under his command.

¹⁷From Benjamin there were 200,000 troops equipped with bows and shields. They were under the command of Eliada, a veteran soldier. ¹⁸Next in command was Jehozabad, who commanded 180,000 armed men.

¹⁹These were the troops stationed in Jerusalem to serve the king, besides those Jehoshaphat stationed in the fortified towns throughout Judah.

Jehoshaphat and Ahab

18 Jehoshaphat enjoyed great riches and high esteem, and he made an alliance with Ahab of Israel by having his son marry Ahab's daughter. ²A few years later he went to Samaria to visit Ahab, who prepared a great banquet for him and his officials. They butchered great numbers of sheep, goats, and cattle for the feast. Then Ahab enticed Jehoshaphat to join forces with him to recover Ramoth-gilead.

³"Will you go with me to Ramoth-gilead?" King Ahab of Israel asked King Jehoshaphat of Judah.

Jehoshaphat replied, "Why, of course! You and I are as one, and my troops are your troops. We will certainly join you in battle." ⁴Then Jehoshaphat added, "But first let's find out what the Lord says."

⁵So the king of Israel summoned the prophets, 400 of them, and asked them, "Should we go to war against Ramoth-gilead, or should I hold back?"

They all replied, "Yes, go right ahead! God will give the king victory."

⁶But Jehoshaphat asked, "Is there not also a prophet of the Lord here? We should ask him the same question."

⁷The king of Israel replied to Jehoshaphat, "There is one more man who could consult the Lord for us, but I hate him. He never prophesies anything but trouble for me! His name is Micaiah son of Imlah."

Jehoshaphat replied, "That's not the way a king should talk! Let's hear what he has to say."

⁸So the king of Israel called one of his officials and said, "Quick! Bring Micaiah son of Imlah."

Micaiah Prophesies against Ahab

⁹King Ahab of Israel and King Jehoshaphat of Judah, dressed in their royal robes, were sitting on thrones at the threshing floor near the gate of Samaria. All of Ahab's prophets were prophesying there in front of them. ¹⁰One of them, Zedekiah son of Kenaanah, made some iron horns and proclaimed, "This is what the Lord says: With these horns you will gore the Arameans to death!"

¹¹All the other prophets agreed. "Yes," they said, "go up to Ramoth-gilead and be victorious, for the Lord will give the king victory!"

¹²Meanwhile, the messenger who went to get Micaiah said to him, "Look, all the prophets are promising victory for the king. Be sure that you agree with them and promise success."

¹³But Micaiah replied, "As surely as the Lord lives, I will say only what my God says."

¹⁴When Micaiah arrived before the king, Ahab asked him, "Micaiah, should we go to war against Ramoth-gilead, or should I hold back?"

Micaiah replied sarcastically, "Yes, go up and be victorious, for you will have victory over them!"

¹⁵But the king replied sharply, "How many times must I demand that you speak only the truth to me when you speak for the Lord?"

¹⁶Then Micaiah told him, "In a vision I saw all Israel scattered on the mountains, like sheep without a shepherd. And the Lord said, 'Their master has been killed.* Send them home in peace.'"

¹⁷"Didn't I tell you?" the king of Israel exclaimed to Jehoshaphat. "He never prophesies anything but trouble for me."

¹⁸Then Micaiah continued, "Listen to what the Lord says! I saw the Lord sitting on his throne with all the armies of heaven around him, on his right and on his left. ¹⁹And the Lord said, 'Who can entice King Ahab of Israel to go into battle against Ramoth-gilead so he can be killed?'

"There were many suggestions, ²⁰and finally a spirit approached the Lord and said, 'I can do it!'

"'How will you do this?' the Lord asked.

²¹"And the spirit replied, 'I will go out and inspire all of Ahab's prophets to speak lies.'

"'You will succeed,' said the Lord. 'Go ahead and do it.'

²²"So you see, the Lord has put a lying spirit in the mouths of your prophets. For the Lord has pronounced your doom."

²³Then Zedekiah son of Kenaanah walked up to

18:16 Hebrew *These people have no master.*

Micaiah and slapped him across the face. "Since when did the Spirit of the LORD leave me to speak to you?" he demanded.

²⁴And Micaiah replied, "You will find out soon enough when you are trying to hide in some secret room!"

²⁵"Arrest him!" the king of Israel ordered. "Take him back to Amon, the governor of the city, and to my son Joash. ²⁶Give them this order from the king: 'Put this man in prison, and feed him nothing but bread and water until I return safely from the battle!'"

²⁷But Micaiah replied, "If you return safely, it will mean that the LORD has not spoken through me!" Then he added to those standing around, "Everyone mark my words!"

The Death of Ahab

²⁸So King Ahab of Israel and King Jehoshaphat of Judah led their armies against Ramoth-gilead. ²⁹The king of Israel said to Jehoshaphat, "As we go into battle, I will disguise myself so no one will recognize me, but you wear your royal robes." So the king of Israel disguised himself, and they went into battle.

³⁰Meanwhile, the king of Aram had issued these orders to his chariot commanders: "Attack only the king of Israel! Don't bother with anyone else." ³¹So when the Aramean chariot commanders saw Jehoshaphat in his royal robes, they went after him. "There is the king of Israel!" they shouted. But Jehoshaphat called out, and the LORD saved him. God helped him by turning the attackers away from him. ³²As soon as the chariot commanders realized he was not the king of Israel, they stopped chasing him.

³³An Aramean soldier, however, randomly shot an arrow at the Israelite troops and hit the king of Israel between the joints of his armor. "Turn the horses* and get me out of here!" Ahab groaned to the driver of the chariot. "I'm badly wounded!"

³⁴The battle raged all that day, and the king of Israel propped himself up in his chariot facing the Arameans. In the evening, just as the sun was setting, he died.

Jehoshaphat Appoints Judges

19 When King Jehoshaphat of Judah arrived safely home in Jerusalem, ²Jehu son of Hanani the seer went out to meet him. "Why should you help the wicked and love those who hate the LORD?" he asked the king. "Because of what you have done, the LORD is very angry with you. ³Even so, there is some good in you, for you have removed the Asherah poles throughout the land, and you have committed yourself to seeking God."

⁴Jehoshaphat lived in Jerusalem, but he went out among the people, traveling from Beersheba to the hill country of Ephraim, encouraging the people to return to the LORD, the God of their ancestors. ⁵He appointed judges throughout the nation in all the fortified towns, ⁶and he said to them, "Always think carefully before pronouncing judgment. Remember that you do not judge to please people but to please the LORD. He will be with you when you render the verdict in each case. ⁷Fear the LORD and judge with integrity, for the LORD our God does not tolerate perverted justice, partiality, or the taking of bribes."

⁸In Jerusalem, Jehoshaphat appointed some of the Levites and priests and clan leaders in Israel to serve as judges* for cases involving the LORD's regulations and for civil disputes. ⁹These were his instructions to them: "You must always act in the fear of the LORD, with faithfulness and an undivided heart. ¹⁰Whenever a case comes to you from fellow citizens in an outlying town, whether a murder case or some other violation of God's laws, commands, decrees, or regulations, you must warn them not to sin against the LORD, so that he will not be angry with you and them. Do this and you will not be guilty.

¹¹"Amariah the high priest will have final say in all cases involving the LORD. Zebadiah son of Ishmael, a leader from the tribe of Judah, will have final say in all civil cases. The Levites will assist you in making sure that justice is served. Take courage as you fulfill your duties, and may the LORD be with those who do what is right."

War with Surrounding Nations

20 After this, the armies of the Moabites, Ammonites, and some of the Meunites* declared war on Jehoshaphat. ²Messengers came and told Jehoshaphat, "A vast army from Edom* is marching against you from beyond the Dead Sea.* They are already at Hazazon-tamar." (This was another name for En-gedi.)

³Jehoshaphat was terrified by this news and begged the LORD for guidance. He also ordered everyone in Judah to begin fasting. ⁴So people from all the towns of Judah came to Jerusalem to seek the LORD's help.

⁵Jehoshaphat stood before the community of Judah and Jerusalem in front of the new courtyard at the Temple of the LORD. ⁶He prayed, "O LORD, God of our ancestors, you alone are the God who is in heaven. You are ruler of all the kingdoms of the earth. You are powerful and mighty; no one can stand against you! ⁷O our God, did you not drive out those who lived in this land when your people Israel arrived? And did you not give this

---

18:33 Hebrew *Turn your hand.* 19:8 As in Greek version; the meaning of the Hebrew is uncertain. 20:1 As in some Greek manuscripts (see also 26:7); Hebrew repeats *Ammonites.* 20:2a As in one Hebrew manuscript; most Hebrew manuscripts and ancient versions read *Aram.* 20:2b Hebrew *the sea.*

> "The women did what they were told to do. They didn't ask questions or take the task any further. I asked questions; I wanted to know why. They got used to me asking questions and being the only woman there."
>
> **KATHERINE JOHNSON**
> (1918–2020) NASA mathematician and trailblazer for racial equality

land forever to the descendants of your friend Abraham? ⁸Your people settled here and built this Temple to honor your name. ⁹They said, 'Whenever we are faced with any calamity such as war,* plague, or famine, we can come to stand in your presence before this Temple where your name is honored. We can cry out to you to save us, and you will hear us and rescue us.'

¹⁰"And now see what the armies of Ammon, Moab, and Mount Seir are doing. You would not let our ancestors invade those nations when Israel left Egypt, so they went around them and did not destroy them. ¹¹Now see how they reward us! For they have come to throw us out of your land, which you gave us as an inheritance. ¹²O our God, won't you stop them? We are powerless against this mighty army that is about to attack us. We do not know what to do, but we are looking to you for help."

¹³As all the men of Judah stood before the Lord with their little ones, wives, and children, ¹⁴the Spirit of the Lord came upon one of the men standing there. His name was Jahaziel son of Zechariah, son of Benaiah, son of Jeiel, son of Mattaniah, a Levite who was a descendant of Asaph.

¹⁵He said, "Listen, all you people of Judah and Jerusalem! Listen, King Jehoshaphat! This is what the Lord says: Do not be afraid! Don't be discouraged by this mighty army, for the battle is not yours, but God's. ¹⁶Tomorrow, march out against them. You will find them coming up through the ascent of Ziz at the end of the valley that opens into the wilderness of Jeruel. ¹⁷But you will not even need to fight. Take your positions; then stand still and watch the Lord's victory. He is with you, O people of Judah and Jerusalem. Do not be afraid or discouraged. Go out against them tomorrow, for the Lord is with you!"

¹⁸Then King Jehoshaphat bowed low with his face to the ground. And all the people of Judah and Jerusalem did the same, worshiping the Lord. ¹⁹Then the Levites from the clans of Kohath and Korah stood to praise the Lord, the God of Israel, with a very loud shout.

²⁰Early the next morning the army of Judah went out into the wilderness of Tekoa. On the way Jehoshaphat stopped and said, "Listen to me, all you people of Judah and Jerusalem! Believe in the Lord your God, and you will be able to stand firm. Believe in his prophets, and you will succeed."

²¹After consulting the people, the king appointed singers to walk ahead of the army, singing to the Lord and praising him for his holy splendor. This is what they sang:

"Give thanks to the Lord;
    his faithful love endures forever!"

²²At the very moment they began to sing and give praise, the Lord caused the armies of Ammon, Moab, and Mount Seir to start fighting among themselves. ²³The armies of Moab and Ammon turned against their allies from Mount Seir and killed every one of them. After they had destroyed the army of Seir, they began attacking each other. ²⁴So when the army of Judah arrived at the lookout point in the wilderness, all they saw were dead bodies lying on the ground as far as they could see. Not a single one of the enemy had escaped.

²⁵King Jehoshaphat and his men went out to gather the plunder. They found vast amounts of equipment, clothing,* and other valuables—more than they could carry. There was so much plunder that it took them three days just to collect it all! ²⁶On the fourth day they gathered in the Valley of Blessing,* which got its name that day because the people

---

20:9 Or *sword of judgment;* or *sword, judgment.* 20:25 As in some Hebrew manuscripts and Latin Vulgate; most Hebrew manuscripts read *corpses.* 20:26 Hebrew *valley of Beracah.*

praised and thanked the LORD there. It is still called the Valley of Blessing today.

²⁷Then all the men returned to Jerusalem, with Jehoshaphat leading them, overjoyed that the LORD had given them victory over their enemies. ²⁸They marched into Jerusalem to the music of harps, lyres, and trumpets, and they proceeded to the Temple of the LORD.

²⁹When all the surrounding kingdoms heard that the LORD himself had fought against the enemies of Israel, the fear of God came over them. ³⁰So Jehoshaphat's kingdom was at peace, for his God had given him rest on every side.

Summary of Jehoshaphat's Reign

³¹So Jehoshaphat ruled over the land of Judah. He was thirty-five years old when he became king, and he reigned in Jerusalem twenty-five years. His mother was Azubah, the daughter of Shilhi.

³²Jehoshaphat was a good king, following the ways of his father, Asa. He did what was pleasing in the LORD's sight. ³³During his reign, however, he failed to remove all the pagan shrines, and the people never fully committed themselves to follow the God of their ancestors.

³⁴The rest of the events of Jehoshaphat's reign, from beginning to end, are recorded in The Record of Jehu Son of Hanani, which is included in The Book of the Kings of Israel.

³⁵Some time later King Jehoshaphat of Judah made an alliance with King Ahaziah of Israel, who was very wicked.* ³⁶Together they built a fleet of trading ships* at the port of Ezion-geber. ³⁷Then Eliezer son of Dodavahu from Mareshah prophesied against Jehoshaphat. He said, "Because you have allied yourself with King Ahaziah, the LORD will destroy your work." So the ships met with disaster and never put out to sea.*

Jehoram Rules in Judah

21 When Jehoshaphat died, he was buried with his ancestors in the City of David. Then his son Jehoram became the next king.

²Jehoram's brothers—the other sons of Jehoshaphat—were Azariah, Jehiel, Zechariah, Azariahu, Michael, and Shephatiah; all these were the sons of Jehoshaphat king of Judah.* ³Their father had given each of them valuable gifts of silver, gold, and costly items, and also some of Judah's fortified towns. However, he designated Jehoram as the next king because he was the oldest. ⁴But when Jehoram had become solidly established as king, he killed all his brothers and some of the other leaders of Judah.

⁵Jehoram was thirty-two years old when he became king, and he reigned in Jerusalem eight years. ⁶But Jehoram followed the example of the kings of Israel and was as wicked as King Ahab, for he had married one of Ahab's daughters. So Jehoram did what was evil in the LORD's sight. ⁷But the LORD did not want to destroy David's dynasty, for he had made a covenant with David and promised that his descendants would continue to rule, shining like a lamp forever.

⁸During Jehoram's reign, the Edomites revolted against Judah and crowned their own king. ⁹So Jehoram went out with his full army and all his chariots. The Edomites surrounded him and his chariot commanders, but he went out at night and attacked them* under cover of darkness. ¹⁰Even so, Edom has been independent from Judah to this day. The town of Libnah also revolted about that same time. All this happened because Jehoram had abandoned the LORD, the God of his ancestors. ¹¹He had built pagan shrines in the hill country of Judah and had led the people of Jerusalem and Judah to give themselves to pagan gods and to go astray.

¹²Then Elijah the prophet wrote Jehoram this letter:

"This is what the LORD, the God of your ancestor David, says: You have not followed the good example of your father, Jehoshaphat, or your grandfather King Asa of Judah. ¹³Instead, you have been as evil as the kings of Israel. You have led the people of Jerusalem and Judah to worship idols, just as King Ahab did in Israel. And you have even killed your own brothers, men who were better than you. ¹⁴So now the LORD is about to strike you, your people, your children, your wives, and all that is yours with a heavy blow. ¹⁵You yourself will suffer with a severe intestinal disease that will get worse each day until your bowels come out."

¹⁶Then the LORD stirred up the Philistines and the Arabs, who lived near the Ethiopians,* to attack Jehoram. ¹⁷They marched against Judah, broke down

---

20:35 Or *who made him do what was wicked.* **20:36** Hebrew *fleet of ships that could go to Tarshish.* **20:37** Hebrew *never set sail for Tarshish.* **21:2** Masoretic Text reads *of Israel;* also in 21:4. The author of Chronicles sees Judah as representative of the true Israel. (Some Hebrew manuscripts, Greek and Syriac versions, and Latin Vulgate read *of Judah.*) **21:9** Or *he went out and escaped.* The meaning of the Hebrew is uncertain. **21:16** Hebrew *the Cushites.*

21:5-7 In this evaluation of Jehoram's reign, the author of Chronicles indicates that Jehoram was unfaithful to the Lord. Even so, hope remained. The Lord had made a covenant promise to David and his descendants that David's line would continue (2 Samuel 7:8-16). This promise was fulfilled ultimately through Jesus, David's descendant, who reigns forever.

21:6-11 Jehoram's reign exhibited violence, oppression, and the worship of false gods. He was married to Athaliah, the daughter of Ahab. After Jehoram died, Ahaziah became king and followed in his father's wrongdoing. After Ahaziah's death, Athaliah usurped the throne and led with cruelty and violence.

its defenses, and carried away everything of value in the royal palace, including the king's sons and his wives. Only his youngest son, Ahaziah,* was spared.

¹⁸After all this, the LORD struck Jehoram with an incurable intestinal disease. ¹⁹The disease grew worse and worse, and at the end of two years it caused his bowels to come out, and he died in agony. His people did not build a great funeral fire to honor him as they had done for his ancestors.

²⁰Jehoram was thirty-two years old when he became king, and he reigned in Jerusalem eight years. No one was sorry when he died. They buried him in the City of David, but not in the royal cemetery.

Ahaziah Rules in Judah

22 Then the people of Jerusalem made Ahaziah, Jehoram's youngest son, their next king, since the marauding bands who came with the Arabs* had killed all the older sons. So Ahaziah son of Jehoram reigned as king of Judah.

²Ahaziah was twenty-two* years old when he became king, and he reigned in Jerusalem one year. His mother was Athaliah, a granddaughter of King Omri. ³Ahaziah also followed the evil example of King Ahab's family, for his mother encouraged him in doing wrong. ⁴He did what was evil in the LORD's sight, just as Ahab's family had done. They even became his advisers after the death of his father, and they led him to ruin.

⁵Following their evil advice, Ahaziah joined Joram,* the son of King Ahab of Israel, in his war against King Hazael of Aram at Ramoth-gilead. When the Arameans* wounded Joram in the battle, ⁶he returned to Jezreel to recover from the wounds he had received at Ramoth.* Because Joram was wounded, King Ahaziah* of Judah went to Jezreel to visit him.

⁷But God had decided that this visit would be Ahaziah's downfall. While he was there, Ahaziah went out with Joram to meet Jehu grandson of Nimshi,* whom the LORD had appointed to destroy the dynasty of Ahab.

⁸While Jehu was executing judgment against the family of Ahab, he happened to meet some of Judah's officials and Ahaziah's relatives* who were traveling with Ahaziah. So Jehu killed them all. ⁹Then Jehu's men searched for Ahaziah, and they found him hiding in the city of Samaria. They brought him to Jehu, who killed him. Ahaziah was given a decent burial because the people said, "He was the grandson of Jehoshaphat—a man who sought the LORD with all his heart." But none of the surviving members of Ahaziah's family was capable of ruling the kingdom.

Queen Athaliah Rules in Judah

¹⁰When Athaliah, the mother of King Ahaziah of Judah, learned that her son was dead, she began to destroy the rest of Judah's royal family. ¹¹But Ahaziah's sister Jehosheba,* the daughter of King Jehoram, took Ahaziah's infant son, Joash, and stole him away from among the rest of the king's children, who were about to be killed. She put Joash and his nurse in a bedroom. In this way, Jehosheba, wife of Jehoiada the priest and sister of Ahaziah, hid the child so that Athaliah could not murder him. ¹²Joash remained hidden in the Temple of God for six years while Athaliah ruled over the land.

Revolt against Athaliah

23 In the seventh year of Athaliah's reign, Jehoiada the priest decided to act. He summoned his courage and made a pact with five army commanders: Azariah son of Jeroham, Ishmael son of Jehohanan, Azariah son of Obed, Maaseiah son of Adaiah, and Elishaphat son of Zicri. ²These men traveled secretly throughout Judah and summoned the Levites and clan leaders in all the towns to come to Jerusalem. ³They all gathered at the Temple of God, where they made a solemn pact with Joash, the young king.

Jehoiada said to them, "Here is the king's son! The time has come for him to reign! The LORD has promised that a descendant of David will be our king. ⁴This is what you must do. When you priests and Levites come on duty on the Sabbath, a third of you will serve as gatekeepers. ⁵Another third will go over to the royal palace, and the final third will be at the Foundation Gate. Everyone else should stay in the courtyards of the LORD's Temple. ⁶Remember, only the priests and Levites on duty may enter the Temple of the LORD, for they are set apart as holy. The rest of the people must obey the LORD's instructions and stay outside. ⁷You Levites, form a bodyguard around the king and keep your weapons in hand. Kill anyone who tries to enter the Temple. Stay with the king wherever he goes."

⁸So the Levites and all the people of Judah did everything as Jehoiada the priest ordered. The commanders took charge of the men reporting for duty that Sabbath, as well as those who were going off duty. Jehoiada the priest did not let anyone go home after their shift ended. ⁹Then Jehoiada supplied the commanders with the spears and the large and small shields that had once belonged to King David and were stored in the Temple of God. ¹⁰He stationed all the people around the king, with their weapons ready.

21:17 Hebrew *Jehoahaz*, a variant spelling of Ahaziah; compare 22:1. **22:1** Or *marauding bands of Arabs*. **22:2** As in some Greek manuscripts and Syriac version (see also 2 Kgs 8:26); Hebrew reads *forty-two*. **22:5a** Hebrew *Jehoram*, a variant spelling of Joram; also in 22:6, 7. **22:5b** As in two Hebrew manuscripts and Latin Vulgate (see also 2 Kgs 8:28); Masoretic Text reads *the archers*. **22:6a** Hebrew *Ramah*, a variant spelling of Ramoth. **22:6b** As in some Hebrew manuscripts, Greek and Syriac versions, and Latin Vulgate (see also 2 Kgs 8:29); most Hebrew manuscripts read *Azariah*. **22:7** Hebrew *descendant of Nimshi*; compare 2 Kgs 9:2, 14. **22:8** As in Greek version (see also 2 Kgs 10:13); Hebrew reads *and sons of the brothers of Ahaziah*. **22:11** As in parallel text at 2 Kgs 11:2; Hebrew lacks *Ahaziah's sister* and reads *Jehoshabeath* [a variant spelling of Jehosheba].

They formed a line from the south side of the Temple around to the north side and all around the altar.

¹¹Then Jehoiada and his sons brought out Joash, the king's son, placed the crown on his head, and presented him with a copy of God's laws.* They anointed him and proclaimed him king, and everyone shouted, "Long live the king!"

The Death of Athaliah

¹²When Athaliah heard the noise of the people running and the shouts of praise to the king, she hurried to the LORD's Temple to see what was happening. ¹³When she arrived, she saw the newly crowned king standing in his place of authority by the pillar at the Temple entrance. The commanders and trumpeters were surrounding him, and people from all over the land were rejoicing and blowing trumpets. Singers with musical instruments were leading the people in a great celebration. When Athaliah saw all this, she tore her clothes in despair and shouted, "Treason! Treason!"

¹⁴Then Jehoiada the priest ordered the commanders who were in charge of the troops, "Take her to the soldiers in front of the Temple,* and kill anyone who tries to rescue her." For the priest had said, "She must not be killed in the Temple of the LORD." ¹⁵So they seized her and led her out to the entrance of the Horse Gate on the palace grounds, and they killed her there.

Jehoiada's Religious Reforms

¹⁶Then Jehoiada made a covenant between himself and the king and the people that they would be the LORD's people. ¹⁷And all the people went over to the temple of Baal and tore it down. They demolished the altars and smashed the idols, and they killed Mattan the priest of Baal in front of the altars.

¹⁸Jehoiada now put the priests and Levites in charge of the Temple of the LORD, following all the directions given by David. He also commanded them to present burnt offerings to the LORD, as prescribed by the Law of Moses, and to sing and rejoice as David had instructed. ¹⁹He also stationed gatekeepers at the gates of the LORD's Temple to keep out those who for any reason were ceremonially unclean.

²⁰Then the commanders, nobles, rulers, and all the people of the land escorted the king from the Temple of the LORD. They went through the upper gate and into the palace, and they seated the king on the royal throne. ²¹So all the people of the land rejoiced, and the city was peaceful because Athaliah had been killed.

Joash Repairs the Temple

24 Joash was seven years old when he became king, and he reigned in Jerusalem forty years. His mother was Zibiah from Beersheba. ²Joash did what was pleasing in the LORD's sight throughout the lifetime of Jehoiada the priest. ³Jehoiada chose two wives for Joash, and he had sons and daughters.

⁴At one point Joash decided to repair and restore the Temple of the LORD. ⁵He summoned the priests and Levites and gave them these instructions: "Go to all the towns of Judah and collect the required annual offerings, so that we can repair the Temple of your God. Do not delay!" But the Levites did not act immediately.

⁶So the king called for Jehoiada the high priest and asked him, "Why haven't you demanded that the Levites go out and collect the Temple taxes from the towns of Judah and from Jerusalem? Moses, the servant of the LORD, levied this tax on the community of Israel in order to maintain the Tabernacle of the Covenant.*"

⁷Over the years the followers of wicked Athaliah had broken into the Temple of God, and they had used all the dedicated things from the Temple of the LORD to worship the images of Baal.

⁸So now the king ordered a chest to be made and set outside the gate leading to the Temple of the LORD. ⁹Then a proclamation was sent throughout Judah and Jerusalem, telling the people to bring to the LORD the tax that Moses, the servant of God, had required of the Israelites in the wilderness. ¹⁰This pleased all the leaders and the people, and they gladly brought their money and filled the chest with it.

¹¹Whenever the chest became full, the Levites would carry it to the king's officials. Then the court secretary and an officer of the high priest would come and empty the chest and take it back to the Temple again. This went on day after day, and a large amount of money was collected. ¹²The king and Jehoiada gave the money to the construction supervisors, who hired masons and carpenters to restore the Temple of the LORD. They also hired metalworkers, who made articles of iron and bronze for the LORD's Temple.

¹³The men in charge of the renovation worked hard and made steady progress. They restored the Temple of God according to its original design and strengthened it. ¹⁴When all the repairs were finished, they brought the remaining money to the king and Jehoiada. It was used to make various articles for the Temple of the LORD—articles for worship services and for burnt offerings, including ladles and other articles made of gold and silver. And the

---

23:11 Or *a copy of the covenant.* 23:14 Or *Bring her out from between the ranks;* or *Take her out of the Temple precincts.* The meaning of the Hebrew is uncertain. 24:6 Hebrew *Tent of the Testimony.*

24:12-14 The book of 2 Kings indicates that the funds collected for repairing the Temple were used only for wages and repair (2 Kings 12:13-14); 2 Chronicles further explains that the funds were used for Temple artifacts only after the repairs were completed.

burnt offerings were sacrificed continually in the Temple of the LORD during the lifetime of Jehoiada the priest. ¹⁵Jehoiada lived to a very old age, finally dying at 130. ¹⁶He was buried among the kings in the City of David, because he had done so much good in Israel for God and his Temple.

Jehoiada's Reforms Reversed

¹⁷But after Jehoiada's death, the leaders of Judah came and bowed before King Joash and persuaded him to listen to their advice. ¹⁸They decided to abandon the Temple of the LORD, the God of their ancestors, and they worshiped Asherah poles and idols instead! Because of this sin, divine anger fell on Judah and Jerusalem. ¹⁹Yet the LORD sent prophets to bring them back to him. The prophets warned them, but still the people would not listen.

²⁰Then the Spirit of God came upon Zechariah son of Jehoiada the priest. He stood before the people and said, "This is what God says: Why do you disobey the LORD's commands and keep yourselves from prospering? You have abandoned the LORD, and now he has abandoned you!"

²¹Then the leaders plotted to kill Zechariah, and King Joash ordered that they stone him to death in the courtyard of the LORD's Temple. ²²That was how King Joash repaid Jehoiada for his loyalty—by killing his son. Zechariah's last words as he died were, "May the LORD see what they are doing and avenge my death!"

The End of Joash's Reign

²³In the spring of the year* the Aramean army marched against Joash. They invaded Judah and Jerusalem and killed all the leaders of the nation. Then they sent all the plunder back to their king in Damascus. ²⁴Although the Arameans attacked with only a small army, the LORD helped them conquer the much larger army of Judah. The people of Judah had abandoned the LORD, the God of their ancestors, so judgment was carried out against Joash.

²⁵The Arameans withdrew, leaving Joash severely wounded. But his own officials plotted to kill him for murdering the son* of Jehoiada the priest. They assassinated him as he lay in bed. Then he was buried in the City of David, but not in the royal cemetery. ²⁶The assassins were Jozacar,* the son of an Ammonite woman named Shimeath, and Jehozabad, the son of a Moabite woman named Shomer.*

²⁷The account of the sons of Joash, the prophecies about him, and the record of his restoration of the Temple of God are written in The Commentary on the Book of the Kings. His son Amaziah became the next king.

Amaziah Rules in Judah

25 Amaziah was twenty-five years old when he became king, and he reigned in Jerusalem twenty-nine years. His mother was Jehoaddin* from Jerusalem. ²Amaziah did what was pleasing in the LORD's sight, but not wholeheartedly.

³When Amaziah was well established as king, he executed the officials who had assassinated his father. ⁴However, he did not kill the children of the assassins, for he obeyed the command of the LORD as written by Moses in the Book of the Law: "Parents must not be put to death for the sins of their children, nor children for the sins of their parents. Those deserving to die must be put to death for their own crimes."*

⁵Then Amaziah organized the army, assigning generals and captains* for all Judah and Benjamin. He took a census and found that he had an army of 300,000 select troops, twenty years old and older, all trained in the use of spear and shield. ⁶He also paid about 7,500 pounds* of silver to hire 100,000 experienced fighting men from Israel.

⁷But a man of God came to him and said, "Your Majesty, do not hire troops from Israel, for the LORD is not with Israel. He will not help those people of Ephraim! ⁸If you let them go with your troops into battle, you will be defeated by the enemy no matter how well you fight. God will overthrow you, for he has the power to help you or to trip you up."

24:23 Hebrew *At the turn of the year.* The first day of the year in the ancient Hebrew lunar calendar occurred in March or April. 24:25 As in Greek version and Latin Vulgate; Hebrew reads *sons.* 24:26a As in parallel text at 2 Kgs 12:21; Hebrew reads *Zabad.* 24:26b As in parallel text at 2 Kgs 12:21; Hebrew reads *Shimrith,* a variant spelling of Shomer. 25:1 As in parallel text at 2 Kgs 14:2; Hebrew reads *Jehoaddan,* a variant spelling of Jehoaddin. 25:4 Deut 24:16. 25:5 Hebrew *commanders of thousands and commanders of hundreds.* 25:6 Hebrew *100 talents* [3,400 kilograms].

24:20-22 Jehoiada had scrupulously preserved the courtyard of the Lord's Temple from bloodshed and the dynasty of David from extinction. Yet ironically after Jehoiada's death, Zechariah his son was murdered in the very place and by the very king, Joash, who was protected during the coup. Jesus made reference to this murder when he was criticizing the religious leaders (Matthew 23:35; Luke 11:51). Zechariah's prayer for vengeance was similar to those that King David himself had prayed against the injustices done to him by Saul (Psalms 5:10; 7:9; 9:19-20; 28:4; 56:7; 139:19).
24:25-26 Jehoiada had received a royal burial (24:15-16), but Joash was buried in disgrace.

24:27 *The Commentary on the Book of the Kings* that the chronicler used as a source is no longer available to us.
25:6 Amaziah's force of 300,000 was smaller than Asa's (580,000) or Jehoshaphat's (1,160,000) had been; this might explain Amaziah's desire to hire additional troops from Israel (the northern kingdom).
25:7-8 The phrase "a man of God" was a way to refer to a prophet (as in Deuteronomy 33:1; 1 Samuel 2:27; 9:6-10; 1 Kings 13:1-31). The kingdom of Israel was politically foreign and spiritually rebellious. Relying on Israel's troops for military strength would bring spiritual compromise and God's opposition.

⁹Amaziah asked the man of God, "But what about all that silver I paid to hire the army of Israel?"

The man of God replied, "The LORD is able to give you much more than this!" ¹⁰So Amaziah discharged the hired troops and sent them back to Ephraim. This made them very angry with Judah, and they returned home in a great rage.

¹¹Then Amaziah summoned his courage and led his army to the Valley of Salt, where they killed 10,000 Edomite troops from Seir. ¹²They captured another 10,000 and took them to the top of a cliff and threw them off, dashing them to pieces on the rocks below.

¹³Meanwhile, the hired troops that Amaziah had sent home raided several of the towns of Judah between Samaria and Beth-horon. They killed 3,000 people and carried off great quantities of plunder.

¹⁴When King Amaziah returned from slaughtering the Edomites, he brought with him idols taken from the people of Seir. He set them up as his own gods, bowed down in front of them, and offered sacrifices to them! ¹⁵This made the LORD very angry, and he sent a prophet to ask, "Why do you turn to gods who could not even save their own people from you?"

¹⁶But the king interrupted him and said, "Since when have I made you the king's counselor? Be quiet now before I have you killed!"

So the prophet stopped with this warning: "I know that God has determined to destroy you because you have done this and have refused to accept my counsel."

¹⁷After consulting with his advisers, King Amaziah of Judah sent this challenge to Israel's king Jehoash,* the son of Jehoahaz and grandson of Jehu: "Come and meet me in battle!"*

¹⁸But King Jehoash of Israel replied to King Amaziah of Judah with this story: "Out in the Lebanon mountains, a thistle sent a message to a mighty cedar tree: 'Give your daughter in marriage to my son.' But just then a wild animal of Lebanon came by and stepped on the thistle, crushing it!

¹⁹"You are saying, 'I have defeated Edom,' and you are very proud of it. But my advice is to stay at home. Why stir up trouble that will only bring disaster on you and the people of Judah?"

²⁰But Amaziah refused to listen, for God was determined to destroy him for turning to the gods of Edom. ²¹So King Jehoash of Israel mobilized his army against King Amaziah of Judah. The two armies drew up their battle lines at Beth-shemesh in Judah. ²²Judah was routed by the army of Israel, and its army scattered and fled for home. ²³King Jehoash of Israel captured Judah's king, Amaziah son of Joash and grandson of Ahaziah, at Beth-shemesh. Then he brought him to Jerusalem, where he demolished 600 feet* of Jerusalem's wall, from the Ephraim Gate to the Corner Gate. ²⁴He carried off all the gold and silver and all the articles from the Temple of God that had been in the care of Obed-edom. He also seized the treasures of the royal palace, along with hostages, and then returned to Samaria.

²⁵King Amaziah of Judah lived for fifteen years after the death of King Jehoash of Israel. ²⁶The rest of the events in Amaziah's reign, from beginning to end, are recorded in The Book of the Kings of Judah and Israel.

²⁷After Amaziah turned away from the LORD, there was a conspiracy against his life in Jerusalem, and he fled to Lachish. But his enemies sent assassins after him, and they killed him there. ²⁸They brought his body back on a horse, and he was buried with his ancestors in the City of David.*

Uzziah Rules in Judah

26 All the people of Judah had crowned Amaziah's sixteen-year-old son, Uzziah, as king in place of his father. ²After his father's death, Uzziah rebuilt the town of Elath* and restored it to Judah.

³Uzziah was sixteen years old when he became king, and he reigned in Jerusalem fifty-two years. His mother was Jecoliah from Jerusalem. ⁴He did what was pleasing in the LORD's sight, just as his father, Amaziah, had done. ⁵Uzziah sought God during the days of Zechariah, who taught him to fear God.* And as long as the king sought guidance from the LORD, God gave him success.

25:17a Hebrew *Joash*, a variant spelling of Jehoash; also in 25:18, 21, 23, 25.   25:17b Hebrew *Come, let us look one another in the face.*   25:23 Hebrew *400 cubits* [180 meters].   25:28 As in some Hebrew manuscripts and other ancient versions (see also 2 Kgs 14:20); most Hebrew manuscripts read *the city of Judah.*   26:2 As in Greek version (see also 2 Kgs 14:22; 16:6); Hebrew reads *Eloth*, a variant spelling of Elath.   26:5 As in Syriac and Greek versions; Hebrew reads *who instructed him in divine visions.*

25:11 The Valley of Salt was a perennial battlefield south of the Dead Sea. David had also fought with the Edomites there (2 Samuel 8:13; see Psalm 60). Ahaziah did not capture the port at Elath along the shore of the Red Sea (26:2); his conquest was limited to northern Edom.

25:20 Amaziah's pride was manifested in his failure to seek God. While he seriously overestimated his military capability after defeating Edom, his decision to go to war against Israel's king Jehoash was actually the result of trusting other gods and of ignoring God's judgment that followed (see 18:9-34; 2 Thessalonians 2:11).

25:21 Beth-shemesh protected the entrance to the Sorek Valley and Jerusalem's access to the coast. Jehoash might have been seeking to cut off Jerusalem's access to trade, or he might have been trying to increase his own access.

26:1-5 The chronicler gave Uzziah a double introduction (26:1-2, 3-5), quoting two passages found in Kings (2 Kings 14:21-22; 15:2-3). The fifty-two years of Uzziah's reign (792–740 BC) included a long co-regency with his father, Amaziah (from 792 to 767 BC), and a co-regency with his son Jotham (from 750 to 740 BC).

⁶Uzziah declared war on the Philistines and broke down the walls of Gath, Jabneh, and Ashdod. Then he built new towns in the Ashdod area and in other parts of Philistia. ⁷God helped him in his wars against the Philistines, his battles with the Arabs of Gur,* and his wars with the Meunites. ⁸The Meunites* paid annual tribute to him, and his fame spread even to Egypt, for he had become very powerful.

⁹Uzziah built fortified towers in Jerusalem at the Corner Gate, at the Valley Gate, and at the angle in the wall. ¹⁰He also constructed forts in the wilderness and dug many water cisterns, because he kept great herds of livestock in the foothills of Judah* and on the plains. He was also a man who loved the soil. He had many workers who cared for his farms and vineyards, both on the hillsides and in the fertile valleys.

¹¹Uzziah had an army of well-trained warriors, ready to march into battle, unit by unit. This army had been mustered and organized by Jeiel, the secretary of the army, and his assistant, Maaseiah. They were under the direction of Hananiah, one of the king's officials. ¹²These regiments of mighty warriors were commanded by 2,600 clan leaders. ¹³The army consisted of 307,500 men, all elite troops. They were prepared to assist the king against any enemy.

¹⁴Uzziah provided the entire army with shields, spears, helmets, coats of mail, bows, and sling stones. ¹⁵And he built structures on the walls of Jerusalem, designed by experts to protect those who shot arrows and hurled large stones* from the towers and the corners of the wall. His fame spread far and wide, for the LORD gave him marvelous help, and he became very powerful.

Uzziah's Sin and Punishment

¹⁶But when he had become powerful, he also became proud, which led to his downfall. He sinned against the LORD his God by entering the sanctuary of the LORD's Temple and personally burning incense on the incense altar. ¹⁷Azariah the high priest went in after him with eighty other priests of the LORD, all brave men. ¹⁸They confronted King Uzziah and said, "It is not for you, Uzziah, to burn incense to the LORD. That is the work of the priests alone, the descendants of Aaron who are set apart for this work. Get out of the sanctuary, for you have sinned. The LORD God will not honor you for this!"

¹⁹Uzziah, who was holding an incense burner, became furious. But as he was standing there raging at the priests before the incense altar in the LORD's Temple, leprosy* suddenly broke out on his forehead. ²⁰When Azariah the high priest and all the other priests saw the leprosy, they rushed him out. And the king himself was eager to get out because the LORD had struck him. ²¹So King Uzziah had leprosy until the day he died. He lived in isolation in a separate house, for he was excluded from the Temple of the LORD. His son Jotham was put in charge of the royal palace, and he governed the people of the land.

²²The rest of the events of Uzziah's reign, from beginning to end, are recorded by the prophet Isaiah son of Amoz. ²³When Uzziah died, he was buried with his ancestors; his grave was in a nearby burial field belonging to the kings, for the people said, "He had leprosy." And his son Jotham became the next king.

Jotham Rules in Judah

27 Jotham was twenty-five years old when he became king, and he reigned in Jerusalem sixteen years. His mother was Jerusha, the daughter of Zadok.

²Jotham did what was pleasing in the LORD's sight. He did everything his father, Uzziah, had done, except that Jotham did not sin by entering the Temple of the LORD. But the people continued in their corrupt ways.

26:7 As in Greek version; Hebrew reads *Gur-baal.* 26:8 As in Greek version; Hebrew reads *Ammonites.* Compare 26:7. 26:10 Hebrew *the Shephelah.* 26:15 Or *to shoot arrows and hurl large stones.* 26:19 Or *a contagious skin disease.* The Hebrew word used here and throughout this passage can describe various skin diseases.

26:6-8 These verses summarize Uzziah's international achievements. His conquests were to the west, south, and southeast, but not to the north, where Jeroboam II's kingdom was powerful (2 Kings 14:23-29). Uzziah's strategy, with God's guidance (2 Chronicles 26:7), was to achieve control over the coastal highway and then build towns in the conquered territory.

26:9-10 Uzziah repaired damage done to Jerusalem's walls by Jehoash in his campaign against Amaziah; Uzziah might also have repaired damage from the famous earthquake during his time (Amos 1:1; Zechariah 14:5). Towers and cisterns from excavations in Qumran, Gibeah, Beersheba, and other sites date to this period. Uzziah was a patron of agriculture, a vital industry for an independent society.

26:11-14 Uzziah's large and well-equipped army enabled him to expand and defend his territory. His name has been found on a fragmentary text of Tiglath-pileser III of Assyria, identifying Uzziah as head of a coalition.

26:16-21 Uzziah's leprosy was a judgment on the covenant violation of his burning incense within the Temple, an activity reserved exclusively for priests (Exodus 30:7-9; Numbers 16). "Leprosy" could also simply indicate a contagious skin disease. The Hebrew word used here and throughout this passage can describe various skin diseases. The leprosy forced King Uzziah to spend the end of his life in quarantine in a separate house (literally *a free house*). The significance of this term is not known. It is often interpreted to mean that he was free from the duties of the monarchy. In Ugaritic texts, it seems to be a euphemism for a place of total confinement.

³Jotham rebuilt the upper gate of the Temple of the LORD. He also did extensive rebuilding on the wall at the hill of Ophel. ⁴He built towns in the hill country of Judah and constructed fortresses and towers in the wooded areas. ⁵Jotham went to war against the Ammonites and conquered them. Over the next three years he received from them an annual tribute of 7,500 pounds* of silver, 50,000 bushels of wheat, and 50,000 bushels of barley.*

⁶King Jotham became powerful because he was careful to live in obedience to the LORD his God.

⁷The rest of the events of Jotham's reign, including all his wars and other activities, are recorded in The Book of the Kings of Israel and Judah. ⁸He was twenty-five years old when he became king, and he reigned in Jerusalem sixteen years. ⁹When Jotham died, he was buried in the City of David. And his son Ahaz became the next king.

Ahaz Rules in Judah

28 Ahaz was twenty years old when he became king, and he reigned in Jerusalem sixteen years. He did not do what was pleasing in the sight of the LORD, as his ancestor David had done. ²Instead, he followed the example of the kings of Israel. He cast metal images for the worship of Baal. ³He offered sacrifices in the valley of Ben-Hinnom, even sacrificing his own sons in the fire.* In this way, he followed the detestable practices of the pagan nations the LORD had driven from the land ahead of the Israelites. ⁴He offered sacrifices and burned incense at the pagan shrines and on the hills and under every green tree.

⁵Because of all this, the LORD his God allowed the king of Aram to defeat Ahaz and to exile large numbers of his people to Damascus. The armies of the king of Israel also defeated Ahaz and inflicted many casualties on his army. ⁶In a single day Pekah son of Remaliah, Israel's king, killed 120,000 of Judah's troops, all of them experienced warriors, because they had abandoned the LORD, the God of their ancestors. ⁷Then Zicri, a warrior from Ephraim, killed Maaseiah, the king's son; Azrikam, the king's palace commander; and Elkanah, the king's second-in-command. ⁸The armies of Israel captured 200,000 women and children from Judah and seized tremendous amounts of plunder, which they took back to Samaria.

⁹But a prophet of the LORD named Oded was there in Samaria when the army of Israel returned home. He went out to meet them and said, "The LORD, the God of your ancestors, was angry with Judah and let you defeat them. But you have gone too far, killing them without mercy, and all heaven is disturbed. ¹⁰And now you are planning to make slaves of these people from Judah and Jerusalem. What about your own sins against the LORD your God? ¹¹Listen to me and return these prisoners you have taken, for they are your own relatives. Watch out, because now the LORD's fierce anger has been turned against you!"

¹²Then some of the leaders of Israel*—Azariah son of Jehohanan, Berekiah son of Meshillemoth, Jehizkiah son of Shallum, and Amasa son of Hadlai—agreed with this and confronted the men returning from battle. ¹³"You must not bring the prisoners here!" they declared. "We cannot afford to add to our sins and guilt. Our guilt is already great, and the LORD's fierce anger is already turned against Israel."

¹⁴So the warriors released the prisoners and handed over the plunder in the sight of the leaders and all the people. ¹⁵Then the four men just mentioned by name came forward and distributed clothes from the plunder to the prisoners who were naked. They provided clothing and sandals to wear, gave them enough food and drink, and dressed their wounds with olive oil. They put those who were weak on donkeys and took all the prisoners back to their own people in Jericho, the city of palms. Then they returned to Samaria.

Ahaz Closes the Temple

¹⁶At that time King Ahaz of Judah asked the king of Assyria for help. ¹⁷The armies of Edom had again invaded Judah and taken captives. ¹⁸And the Philistines had raided towns located in the foothills of Judah* and in the Negev of Judah. They had already captured and occupied Beth-shemesh, Aijalon, Gederoth, Soco with its villages, Timnah with its

---

27:5a Hebrew *100 talents* [3,400 kilograms]. 27:5b Hebrew *10,000 cors* [2,200 kiloliters] *of wheat, and 10,000 cors of barley.*
28:3 Or *even making his sons pass through the fire.* 28:12 Hebrew *Ephraim,* referring to the northern kingdom of Israel.
28:18 Hebrew *the Shephelah.*

27:1 After a co-regency of eleven years with his father, Uzziah (750–740 BC), Jotham became king in his own right and reigned five more years (740–735 BC). This represents the sixteen years mentioned in the text. Jotham lived at least four more years, for we read that Hoshea came to power in the northern kingdom "in the twentieth year of Jotham son of Uzziah" (2 Kings 15:30). But Jotham's son, Ahaz, had already begun a co-regency with Jotham (see note on 2 Kings 17:1). After Jotham's sixteen official years, Ahaz began to rule in his father's stead. However, Ahaz presumably had his official accession ceremony following his father's death in 732 BC, so the author of 2 Chronicles reckons Ahaz's official time of rule starting in 731 BC (see 2 Chronicles 28:1).
27:3-4 Jotham's rebuilding endeavors were like those of his father; he continued the work of restoration begun by Uzziah. He also constructed fortresses and towers in the forests, providing a network of lookouts and highway defenses within the kingdom and on the frontier.
28:17-18 The Edomites and the Philistines were natural enemies of Judah. The towns captured by these armies were all along the Aijalon, Sorek, and Elah valleys in the buffer zone of the foothills of Judah (Hebrew *the Shephelah*) or the Negev.

villages, and Gimzo with its villages. ¹⁹The Lord was humbling Judah because of King Ahaz of Judah,* for he had encouraged his people to sin and had been utterly unfaithful to the Lord.

²⁰So when King Tiglath-pileser* of Assyria arrived, he attacked Ahaz instead of helping him. ²¹Ahaz took valuable items from the Lord's Temple, the royal palace, and from the homes of his officials and gave them to the king of Assyria as tribute. But this did not help him.

²²Even during this time of trouble, King Ahaz continued to reject the Lord. ²³He offered sacrifices to the gods of Damascus who had defeated him, for he said, "Since these gods helped the kings of Aram, they will help me, too, if I sacrifice to them." But instead, they led to his ruin and the ruin of all Judah.

²⁴The king took the various articles from the Temple of God and broke them into pieces. He shut the doors of the Lord's Temple so that no one could worship there, and he set up altars to pagan gods in every corner of Jerusalem. ²⁵He made pagan shrines in all the towns of Judah for offering sacrifices to other gods. In this way, he aroused the anger of the Lord, the God of his ancestors.

²⁶The rest of the events of Ahaz's reign and everything he did, from beginning to end, are recorded in The Book of the Kings of Judah and Israel. ²⁷When Ahaz died, he was buried in Jerusalem but not in the royal cemetery of the kings of Judah. Then his son Hezekiah became the next king.

Hezekiah Rules in Judah

29 Hezekiah was twenty-five years old when he became the king of Judah, and he reigned in Jerusalem twenty-nine years. His mother was Abijah, the daughter of Zechariah. ²He did what was pleasing in the Lord's sight, just as his ancestor David had done.

Hezekiah Reopens the Temple

³In the very first month of the first year of his reign, Hezekiah reopened the doors of the Temple of the Lord and repaired them. ⁴He summoned the priests and Levites to meet him at the courtyard east of the Temple. ⁵He said to them, "Listen to me, you Levites! Purify yourselves, and purify the Temple of the Lord, the God of your ancestors. Remove all the defiled things from the sanctuary. ⁶Our ancestors were unfaithful and did what was evil in the sight of the Lord our God. They abandoned the Lord and his dwelling place; they turned their backs on him. ⁷They also shut the doors to the Temple's entry room, and they snuffed out the lamps. They stopped burning incense and presenting burnt offerings at the sanctuary of the God of Israel.

⁸"That is why the Lord's anger has fallen upon Judah and Jerusalem. He has made them an object of dread, horror, and ridicule, as you can see with your own eyes. ⁹Because of this, our fathers have been killed in battle, and our sons and daughters and wives have been captured. ¹⁰But now I will make a covenant with the Lord, the God of Israel, so that his fierce anger will turn away from us. ¹¹My sons, do not neglect your duties any longer! The Lord has chosen you to stand in his presence, to minister to him, and to lead the people in worship and present offerings to him."

¹²Then these Levites got right to work:

From the clan of Kohath: Mahath son of Amasai and Joel son of Azariah.

From the clan of Merari: Kish son of Abdi and Azariah son of Jehallelel.

From the clan of Gershon: Joah son of Zimmah and Eden son of Joah.

¹³ From the family of Elizaphan: Shimri and Jeiel.
From the family of Asaph: Zechariah and Mattaniah.

¹⁴ From the family of Heman: Jehiel and Shimei.
From the family of Jeduthun: Shemaiah and Uzziel.

¹⁵These men called together their fellow Levites, and they all purified themselves. Then they began to cleanse the Temple of the Lord, just as the king had commanded. They were careful to follow all the Lord's instructions in their work. ¹⁶The priests went into the sanctuary of the Temple of the Lord to

---

28:19 Masoretic Text reads *of Israel;* also in 28:23, 27. The author of Chronicles sees Judah as representative of the true Israel. (Some Hebrew manuscripts and Greek version read *of Judah.*) **28:20** Hebrew *Tilgath-pilneser,* a variant spelling of Tiglath-pileser.

28:24-25 Judah reached its spiritual rock bottom—a condition similar to exile—under King Ahaz.
28:26 Samaria, the capital of the northern kingdom of Israel, fell to Assyria in 722 BC, during the twenty-first year of Ahaz's reign in Judah (2 Kings 17:1-6). The chronicler, whose emphasis was on the southern kingdom, did not even mention this event.
29:3-4 Hezekiah's first act as king was to repair the doors of the Temple (29:3). The verb used (*vayekhazzeqem,* "he made them strong") is a deliberate pun on the name of King Hezekiah (*yekhizqiyyahu,* "Yah makes strong"). This action provided a setting for the king's speech to the priests and Levites (29:5-11).

29:5-11 Hezekiah's speech used vocabulary typical of that used by prophets before the Exile to describe the failure of the nation. As in the days of the separation under Rehoboam (12:1; compare to 13:10), the people had been unfaithful and then abandoned the Lord.
29:12-36 To begin the process of sanctifying the Temple, these Levites began with their own sanctification. First, "they all purified themselves," probably by bringing offerings (29:15; see 30:15); "then they began to cleanse the Temple." Two separate acts were required to restore the Temple: purification (the removal of pollution, 29:15-17) and sanctification (the rededication of the Temple for holy worship, 29:20-36).

cleanse it, and they took out to the Temple courtyard all the defiled things they found. From there the Levites carted it all out to the Kidron Valley.

¹⁷They began the work in early spring, on the first day of the new year,* and in eight days they had reached the entry room of the LORD's Temple. Then they purified the Temple of the LORD itself, which took another eight days. So the entire task was completed in sixteen days.

The Temple Rededication

¹⁸Then the Levites went to King Hezekiah and gave him this report: "We have cleansed the entire Temple of the LORD, the altar of burnt offering with all its utensils, and the table of the Bread of the Presence with all its utensils. ¹⁹We have also recovered all the items discarded by King Ahaz when he was unfaithful and closed the Temple. They are now in front of the altar of the LORD, purified and ready for use."

²⁰Early the next morning King Hezekiah gathered the city officials and went to the Temple of the LORD. ²¹They brought seven bulls, seven rams, and seven male lambs as a burnt offering, together with seven male goats as a sin offering for the kingdom, for the Temple, and for Judah. The king commanded the priests, who were descendants of Aaron, to sacrifice the animals on the altar of the LORD.

²²So they killed the bulls, and the priests took the blood and sprinkled it on the altar. Next they killed the rams and sprinkled their blood on the altar. And finally, they did the same with the male lambs. ²³The male goats for the sin offering were then brought before the king and the assembly of people, who laid their hands on them. ²⁴The priests then killed the goats as a sin offering and sprinkled their blood on the altar to make atonement for the sins of all Israel. The king had specifically commanded that this burnt offering and sin offering should be made for all Israel.

²⁵King Hezekiah then stationed the Levites at the Temple of the LORD with cymbals, lyres, and harps. He obeyed all the commands that the LORD had given to King David through Gad, the king's seer, and the prophet Nathan. ²⁶The Levites then took their positions around the Temple with the instruments of David, and the priests took their positions with the trumpets.

²⁷Then Hezekiah ordered that the burnt offering be placed on the altar. As the burnt offering was presented, songs of praise to the LORD were begun, accompanied by the trumpets and other instruments of David, the former king of Israel. ²⁸The entire assembly worshiped the LORD as the singers sang and the trumpets blew, until all the burnt offerings were finished. ²⁹Then the king and everyone with him bowed down in worship. ³⁰King Hezekiah and the officials ordered the Levites to praise the LORD with the psalms written by David and by Asaph the seer. So they offered joyous praise and bowed down in worship.

³¹Then Hezekiah declared, "Now that you have consecrated yourselves to the LORD, bring your sacrifices and thanksgiving offerings to the Temple of the LORD." So the people brought their sacrifices and thanksgiving offerings, and all whose hearts were willing brought burnt offerings, too. ³²The people brought to the LORD 70 bulls, 100 rams, and 200 male lambs for burnt offerings. ³³They also brought 600 cattle and 3,000 sheep and goats as sacred offerings.

³⁴But there were too few priests to prepare all the burnt offerings. So their relatives the Levites helped them until the work was finished and more priests had been purified, for the Levites had been more conscientious about purifying themselves than the priests had been. ³⁵There was an abundance of burnt offerings, along with the usual liquid offerings, and a great deal of fat from the many peace offerings.

So the Temple of the LORD was restored to service. ³⁶And Hezekiah and all the people rejoiced because of what God had done for the people, for everything had been accomplished so quickly.

Preparations for Passover

30 King Hezekiah now sent word to all Israel and Judah, and he wrote letters of invitation to the people of Ephraim and Manasseh. He asked everyone to come to the Temple of the LORD at Jerusalem to celebrate the Passover of the LORD, the God of Israel. ²The king, his officials, and all the community of Jerusalem decided to celebrate Passover a month later than usual.* ³They were unable to celebrate it at the prescribed time because not enough priests could be purified by then, and the people had not yet assembled at Jerusalem.

⁴This plan for keeping the Passover seemed right to the king and all the people. ⁵So they sent a proclamation throughout all Israel, from Beersheba in the south to Dan in the north, inviting everyone to come to Jerusalem to celebrate the Passover of the LORD, the God of Israel. The people had not been celebrating it in great numbers as required in the Law.

29:17 Hebrew *on the first day of the first month.* This day in the ancient Hebrew lunar calendar occurred in March or early April, 715 B.C. **30:2** Hebrew *in the second month.* Passover was normally observed in the first month (of the ancient Hebrew lunar calendar).

29:21 The bulls, rams, and lambs were for the burnt offering, and the male goats were for the sin offering (see Leviticus 1; 4:1–5:13).

⁶At the king's command, runners were sent throughout Israel and Judah. They carried letters that said:

"O people of Israel, return to the Lord, the God of Abraham, Isaac, and Israel,* so that he will return to the few of us who have survived the conquest of the Assyrian kings. ⁷Do not be like your ancestors and relatives who abandoned the Lord, the God of their ancestors, and became an object of derision, as you yourselves can see. ⁸Do not be stubborn, as they were, but submit yourselves to the Lord. Come to his Temple, which he has set apart as holy forever. Worship the Lord your God so that his fierce anger will turn away from you.

⁹"For if you return to the Lord, your relatives and your children will be treated mercifully by their captors, and they will be able to return to this land. For the Lord your God is gracious and merciful. If you return to him, he will not continue to turn his face from you."

Celebration of Passover

¹⁰The runners went from town to town throughout Ephraim and Manasseh and as far as the territory of Zebulun. But most of the people just laughed at the runners and made fun of them. ¹¹However, some people from Asher, Manasseh, and Zebulun humbled themselves and went to Jerusalem.

30:6 *Israel* is the name that God gave to Jacob.

Come Close — WHOLEHEARTED: COVERED

SCRIPTURE CONNECTION: 2 CHRONICLES 29–32

When we find it difficult to do the right thing or when we observe others doing the wrong thing, it is easier to stay silent or hide. But a wholehearted leader seeks God to work through the failures.

King Hezekiah went in the opposite direction of his father, who was a wicked king (28:1-2). Hezekiah sought God *wholeheartedly* (31:21). These chapters show why we need leaders with full hearts.

Even when he made a misstep, Hezekiah humbled himself before God (32:25-26). When others made mistakes, he humbled himself and asked God to accept the people; they were seeking the Lord, even though they hadn't followed all the rules correctly (30:18-20).

Hezekiah followed what Jesus later called the most important commands: love God and love neighbor (Mark 12:29-31). These require actions. Hezekiah wholeheartedly covered others' faults in seeking God for forgiveness on their behalf (2 Chronicles 30:17-20). Jesus wholeheartedly died so we might wholeheartedly live (John 10:10).

As a leader, I, too, must seek the Lord in prayer, fill my heart, and call the people I care for to return to God wholeheartedly. Hezekiah's passion for cleansing Temple idolatry and drawing others to God inspires me to press on (2 Chronicles 29:31-36; 31:1).

We remember and find comfort today: Those who seek God are covered in compassion, *wholeheartedly*.

REFLECT "The Lord listened to Hezekiah's prayer and healed the people."
2 CHRONICLES 30:20

Some people use breath prayer in their own spiritual walk. Why not try? As you inhale, pray—The Lord hears and acts for me today. *Then as you* exhale, pray—May my lips shout God's praise! Amen.

CONSIDER "I don't have to figure my present circumstances out.... All I have to do is trust. So,... I sit quietly in His presence and simply say, 'God, I want Your truth to be the loudest voice in my life. Correct me. Comfort me. Come closer still. And I will trust.'" LYSA TERKEURST, *Uninvited: Living Loved When You Feel Less Than, Left Out, and Lonely*

> Those who seek God are covered, *wholeheartedly*.

ALEXIANA FRY, MDiv, PhD, is a devoted academic in the Hebrew Bible. She is a professor, wife, and pug mom who is working on her first book post-dissertation.

¹²At the same time, God's hand was on the people in the land of Judah, giving them all one heart to obey the orders of the king and his officials, who were following the word of the LORD. ¹³So a huge crowd assembled at Jerusalem in midspring* to celebrate the Festival of Unleavened Bread. ¹⁴They set to work and removed the pagan altars from Jerusalem. They took away all the incense altars and threw them into the Kidron Valley.

¹⁵On the fourteenth day of the second month, one month later than usual,* the people slaughtered the Passover lamb. This shamed the priests and Levites, so they purified themselves and brought burnt offerings to the Temple of the LORD. ¹⁶Then they took their places at the Temple as prescribed in the Law of Moses, the man of God. The Levites brought the sacrificial blood to the priests, who then sprinkled it on the altar.

¹⁷Since many of the people had not purified themselves, the Levites had to slaughter their Passover lamb for them, to set them apart for the LORD. ¹⁸Most of those who came from Ephraim, Manasseh, Issachar, and Zebulun had not purified themselves. But King Hezekiah prayed for them, and they were allowed to eat the Passover meal anyway, even though this was contrary to the requirements of the Law. For Hezekiah said, "May the LORD, who is good, pardon those ¹⁹who decide to follow the LORD, the God of their ancestors, even though they are not properly cleansed for the ceremony." ²⁰And the LORD listened to Hezekiah's prayer and healed the people.

²¹So the people of Israel who were present in Jerusalem joyously celebrated the Festival of Unleavened Bread for seven days. Each day the Levites and priests sang to the LORD, accompanied by loud instruments.* ²²Hezekiah encouraged all the Levites regarding the skill they displayed as they served the LORD. The celebration continued for seven days. Peace offerings were sacrificed, and the people gave thanks to the LORD, the God of their ancestors.

²³The entire assembly then decided to continue the festival another seven days, so they celebrated joyfully for another week. ²⁴King Hezekiah gave the people 1,000 bulls and 7,000 sheep and goats for offerings, and the officials donated 1,000 bulls and 10,000 sheep and goats. Meanwhile, many more priests purified themselves.

²⁵The entire assembly of Judah rejoiced, including the priests, the Levites, all who came from the land of Israel, the foreigners who came to the festival, and all those who lived in Judah. ²⁶There was great joy in the city, for Jerusalem had not seen a celebration like this one since the days of Solomon, King David's son. ²⁷Then the priests and Levites stood and blessed the people, and God heard their prayer from his holy dwelling in heaven.

Hezekiah's Religious Reforms

31 When the festival ended, the Israelites who attended went to all the towns of Judah, Benjamin, Ephraim, and Manasseh, and they smashed all the sacred pillars, cut down the Asherah poles, and removed the pagan shrines and altars. After this, the Israelites returned to their own towns and homes.

²Hezekiah then organized the priests and Levites into divisions to offer the burnt offerings and peace offerings, and to worship and give thanks and praise to the LORD at the gates of the Temple. ³The king also made a personal contribution of animals for the daily morning and evening burnt offerings, the weekly Sabbath festivals, the monthly new moon festivals, and the annual festivals as prescribed in the Law of the LORD. ⁴In addition, he required the people in Jerusalem to bring a portion of their goods to the priests and Levites, so they could devote themselves fully to the Law of the LORD.

⁵When the people of Israel heard these requirements, they responded generously by bringing the first share of their grain, new wine, olive oil, honey, and all the produce of their fields. They brought a large quantity—a tithe of all they produced. ⁶The people who had moved to Judah from Israel, and the people of Judah themselves, brought in the

---

30:13 Hebrew *in the second month*. The second month of the ancient Hebrew lunar calendar usually occurs within the months of April and May. 30:15 Hebrew *On the fourteenth day of the second month*. Passover normally began on the fourteenth day of the first month (see Lev 23:5). 30:21 Or *sang to the LORD with all their strength*.

30:11-20 The Passover was an important commemoration of the Exodus. Exodus 12:1–13:10 records the first Passover, when the people were under the oppressive Egyptian pharaoh and before Moses led Israel from slavery to freedom. Passover was a remembrance festival, highlighting the Lord's mighty saving acts and rooting the Israelite exiles into their history, identity, and story. Hezekiah improperly held the Passover celebration, not preparing correctly before partaking. Some people from the tribes of Ephraim, Manasseh, Issachar, and Zebulun ate the lamb without first purifying themselves. Hezekiah was a good leader, and when he realized this, he prayed for them. The Lord heard Hezekiah and healed them.
31:1 Following the purification and rededication of the Temple, the city of Jerusalem, and the people, Hezekiah initiated the third stage of his reform, purifying the entire land of pagan objects of worship, not only in Judah, but also in the territories of the north.
31:3-10 Provisions for the Temple came from both the king and his subjects. Judah united in its support of the Temple, and the response was far greater than anticipated or required.
31:6 The tithes of the animals that "piled . . . up in great heaps" might refer to the proceeds from the sale of animals rather than the animals themselves. The law permitted the people to exchange the yield of the field for money (Deuteronomy 14:24-26) and to consume the meat at their homes (Deuteronomy 12:15).

tithes of their cattle, sheep, and goats and a tithe of the things that had been dedicated to the LORD their God, and they piled them up in great heaps. ⁷They began piling them up in late spring, and the heaps continued to grow until early autumn.* ⁸When Hezekiah and his officials came and saw these huge piles, they thanked the LORD and his people Israel!

⁹"Where did all this come from?" Hezekiah asked the priests and Levites.

¹⁰And Azariah the high priest, from the family of Zadok, replied, "Since the people began bringing their gifts to the LORD's Temple, we have had enough to eat and plenty to spare. The LORD has blessed his people, and all this is left over."

¹¹Hezekiah ordered that storerooms be prepared in the Temple of the LORD. When this was done, ¹²the people faithfully brought all the gifts, tithes, and other items dedicated for use in the Temple. Conaniah the Levite was put in charge, assisted by his brother Shimei. ¹³The supervisors under them were Jehiel, Azaziah, Nahath, Asahel, Jerimoth, Jozabad, Eliel, Ismakiah, Mahath, and Benaiah. These appointments were made by King Hezekiah and Azariah, the chief official in the Temple of God.

¹⁴Kore son of Imnah the Levite, who was the gatekeeper at the East Gate, was put in charge of distributing the voluntary offerings given to God, the gifts, and the things that had been dedicated to the LORD. ¹⁵His faithful assistants were Eden, Miniamin, Jeshua, Shemaiah, Amariah, and Shecaniah. They distributed the gifts among the families of priests in their towns by their divisions, dividing the gifts fairly among old and young alike. ¹⁶They distributed the gifts to all males three years old or older, regardless of their place in the genealogical records. The distribution went to all who would come to the LORD's Temple to perform their daily duties according to their divisions. ¹⁷They distributed gifts to the priests who were listed by their families in the genealogical records, and to the Levites twenty years old or older who were listed according to their jobs and their divisions. ¹⁸Food allotments were also given to the families of all those listed in the genealogical records, including their little babies, wives, sons, and daughters. For they had all been faithful in purifying themselves.

¹⁹As for the priests, the descendants of Aaron, who were living in the open villages around the towns, men were appointed by name to distribute portions to every male among the priests and to all the Levites listed in the genealogical records.

²⁰In this way, King Hezekiah handled the distribution throughout all Judah, doing what was pleasing and good in the sight of the LORD his God. ²¹In all that he did in the service of the Temple of God and in his efforts to follow God's laws and commands, Hezekiah sought his God wholeheartedly. As a result, he was very successful.

Assyria Invades Judah

32 After Hezekiah had faithfully carried out this work, King Sennacherib of Assyria invaded Judah. He laid siege to the fortified towns, giving orders for his army to break through their walls. ²When Hezekiah realized that Sennacherib also intended to attack Jerusalem, ³he consulted with his officials and military advisers, and they decided to stop the flow of the springs outside the city. ⁴They organized a huge work crew to stop the flow of the springs, cutting off the brook that ran through the fields. For they said, "Why should the kings of Assyria come here and find plenty of water?"

⁵Then Hezekiah worked hard at repairing all the broken sections of the wall, erecting towers, and constructing a second wall outside the first. He also reinforced the supporting terraces* in the City of David and manufactured large numbers of weapons and shields. ⁶He appointed military officers over the people and assembled them before him in the square at the city gate. Then Hezekiah encouraged them by saying: ⁷"Be strong and courageous! Don't be afraid or discouraged because of the king of Assyria or his mighty army, for there is a power far greater on our side! ⁸He may have a great army, but they are merely men. We have the LORD our God to help us and to fight our battles for us!" Hezekiah's words greatly encouraged the people.

Sennacherib Threatens Jerusalem

⁹While King Sennacherib of Assyria was still besieging the town of Lachish, he sent his officers to Jerusalem with this message for Hezekiah and all the people in the city:

¹⁰"This is what King Sennacherib of Assyria says: What are you trusting in that makes you think you can survive my siege of Jerusalem? ¹¹Hezekiah has said, 'The LORD our God will rescue us from the king of Assyria.' Surely Hezekiah is misleading you, sentencing you to death by famine and thirst! ¹²Don't you realize that Hezekiah is the very person who destroyed all the LORD's shrines and altars? He commanded Judah and Jerusalem to worship only at the altar at the Temple and to offer sacrifices on it alone.

¹³"Surely you must realize what I and the other kings of Assyria before me have done to all the people of the earth! Were any of the gods

---

31:7 Hebrew *in the third month . . . until the seventh month.* The third month of the ancient Hebrew lunar calendar usually occurs within the months of May and June; the seventh month usually occurs within September and October. **32:5** Hebrew *the millo.* The meaning of the Hebrew is uncertain.

of those nations able to rescue their people from my power? [14]Which of their gods was able to rescue its people from the destructive power of my predecessors? What makes you think your God can rescue you from me? [15]Don't let Hezekiah deceive you! Don't let him fool you like this! I say it again—no god of any nation or kingdom has ever yet been able to rescue his people from me or my ancestors. How much less will your God rescue you from my power!"

[16]And Sennacherib's officers further mocked the LORD God and his servant Hezekiah, heaping insult upon insult. [17]The king also sent letters scorning the LORD, the God of Israel. He wrote, "Just as the gods of all the other nations failed to rescue their people from my power, so the God of Hezekiah will also fail." [18]The Assyrian officials who brought the letters shouted this in Hebrew* to the people gathered on the walls of the city, trying to terrify them so it would be easier to capture the city. [19]These officers talked about the God of Jerusalem as though he were one of the pagan gods, made by human hands.

[20]Then King Hezekiah and the prophet Isaiah son of Amoz cried out in prayer to God in heaven. [21]And the LORD sent an angel who destroyed the Assyrian army with all its commanders and officers. So Sennacherib was forced to return home in disgrace to his own land. And when he entered the temple of his god, some of his own sons killed him there with a sword.

[22]That is how the LORD rescued Hezekiah and the people of Jerusalem from King Sennacherib of Assyria and from all the others who threatened them. So there was peace throughout the land. [23]From then on King Hezekiah became highly respected among all the surrounding nations, and many gifts for the LORD arrived at Jerusalem, with valuable presents for King Hezekiah, too.

Hezekiah's Sickness and Recovery

[24]About that time Hezekiah became deathly ill. He prayed to the LORD, who healed him and gave him a miraculous sign. [25]But Hezekiah did not respond appropriately to the kindness shown him, and he became proud. So the LORD's anger came against him and against Judah and Jerusalem. [26]Then Hezekiah humbled himself and repented of his pride, as did the people of Jerusalem. So the LORD's anger did not fall on them during Hezekiah's lifetime.

[27]Hezekiah was very wealthy and highly honored. He built special treasury buildings for his silver, gold, precious stones, and spices, and for his shields and other valuable items. [28]He also constructed many storehouses for his grain, new wine, and olive oil; and he made many stalls for his cattle and pens for his flocks of sheep and goats. [29]He built many towns and acquired vast flocks and herds, for God had given him great wealth. [30]He blocked up the upper spring of Gihon and brought the water down through a tunnel to the west side of the City of David. And so he succeeded in everything he did.

[31]However, when ambassadors arrived from Babylon to ask about the remarkable events that had taken place in the land, God withdrew from Hezekiah in order to test him and to see what was really in his heart.

Summary of Hezekiah's Reign

[32]The rest of the events in Hezekiah's reign and his acts of devotion are recorded in The Vision of the Prophet Isaiah Son of Amoz, which is included in The Book of the Kings of Judah and Israel. [33]When Hezekiah died, he was buried in the upper area of the royal cemetery, and all Judah and Jerusalem honored him at his death. And his son Manasseh became the next king.

Manasseh Rules in Judah

33 Manasseh was twelve years old when he became king, and he reigned in Jerusalem fifty-five years. [2]He did what was evil in the LORD's sight, following the detestable practices of the pagan nations that the LORD had driven from the land ahead of the Israelites. [3]He rebuilt the pagan shrines his father, Hezekiah, had broken down. He constructed altars for the images of Baal and set up Asherah poles. He also bowed before all the powers of the heavens and worshiped them.

[4]He built pagan altars in the Temple of the LORD, the place where the LORD had said, "My name will remain in Jerusalem forever." [5]He built these altars for all the powers of the heavens in both courtyards of the LORD's Temple. [6]Manasseh also sacrificed his own sons in the fire* in the valley of Ben-Hinnom.

32:18 Hebrew *in the dialect of Judah.* 33:6 Or *also made his sons pass through the fire.*

32:31 The chronicler writes that Hezekiah faced testing. Testing reveals a person's character in the same way a mirror reflects a face. God's testing is meant to strengthen a person, not to trick them into failing. Hezekiah's testing proved that, when he did falter, he quickly turned back to God. David is another person who failed tests at times but promptly repented and turned back to God (2 Samuel 12). If you find that you have struggled at times, you are not alone. The people in the Bible were not perfect. After failing and messing up, many turned back to God. Their lives reveal that they continued to do extraordinary things for God, even after failure! And so might we as we return to God.

33:1-20 Manasseh ruled fifty-five years (697–642 BC), longer than any other king in Judah. The years of his reign included a co-regency with his father, Hezekiah, from 697 to 686 BC. Such a long reign was usually a sign of blessing, even though Manasseh "did what was evil in the LORD's sight" (2 Chronicles 33:2) So, the chronicler tells of his humiliation, repentance, and restoration of worship in Judah.

He practiced sorcery, divination, and witchcraft, and he consulted with mediums and psychics. He did much that was evil in the LORD's sight, arousing his anger.

⁷Manasseh even took a carved idol he had made and set it up in God's Temple, the very place where God had told David and his son Solomon: "My name will be honored forever in this Temple and in Jerusalem—the city I have chosen from among all the tribes of Israel. ⁸If the Israelites will be careful to obey my commands—all the laws, decrees, and regulations given through Moses—I will not send them into exile from this land that I set aside for your ancestors." ⁹But Manasseh led the people of Judah and Jerusalem to do even more evil than the pagan nations that the LORD had destroyed when the people of Israel entered the land.

¹⁰The LORD spoke to Manasseh and his people, but they ignored all his warnings. ¹¹So the LORD sent the commanders of the Assyrian armies, and they took Manasseh prisoner. They put a ring through his nose, bound him in bronze chains, and led him away to Babylon. ¹²But while in deep distress, Manasseh sought the LORD his God and sincerely humbled himself before the God of his ancestors. ¹³And when he prayed, the LORD listened to him and was moved by his request. So the LORD brought Manasseh back to Jerusalem and to his kingdom. Then Manasseh finally realized that the LORD alone is God!

¹⁴After this Manasseh rebuilt the outer wall of the City of David, from west of the Gihon Spring in the Kidron Valley to the Fish Gate, and continuing around the hill of Ophel. He built the wall very high. And he stationed his military officers in all of the fortified towns of Judah. ¹⁵Manasseh also removed the foreign gods and the idol from the LORD's Temple. He tore down all the altars he had built on the hill where the Temple stood and all the altars that were in Jerusalem, and he dumped them outside the city. ¹⁶Then he restored the altar of the LORD and sacrificed peace offerings and thanksgiving offerings on it. He also encouraged the people of Judah to worship the LORD, the God of Israel. ¹⁷However, the people still sacrificed at the pagan shrines, though only to the LORD their God.

¹⁸The rest of the events of Manasseh's reign, his prayer to God, and the words the seers spoke to him in the name of the LORD, the God of Israel, are recorded in The Book of the Kings of Israel. ¹⁹Manasseh's prayer, the account of the way God answered him, and an account of all his sins and unfaithfulness are recorded in The Record of the Seers.* It includes a list of the locations where he built pagan shrines and set up Asherah poles and idols before he humbled himself and repented. ²⁰When Manasseh died, he was buried in his palace. Then his son Amon became the next king.

Amon Rules in Judah

²¹Amon was twenty-two years old when he became king, and he reigned in Jerusalem two years. ²²He did what was evil in the LORD's sight, just as his father, Manasseh, had done. He worshiped and sacrificed to all the idols his father had made. ²³But unlike his father, he did not humble himself before the LORD. Instead, Amon sinned even more.

²⁴Then Amon's own officials conspired against him and assassinated him in his palace. ²⁵But the people of the land killed all those who had conspired against King Amon, and they made his son Josiah the next king.

Josiah Rules in Judah

34 Josiah was eight years old when he became king, and he reigned in Jerusalem thirty-one years. ²He did what was pleasing in the LORD's sight and followed the example of his ancestor David. He did not turn away from doing what was right.

³During the eighth year of his reign, while he was still young, Josiah began to seek the God of his ancestor David. Then in the twelfth year he began to purify Judah and Jerusalem, destroying all the pagan shrines, the Asherah poles, and the carved idols and cast images. ⁴He ordered that the altars of Baal be demolished and that the incense altars which stood above them be broken down. He also made sure that the Asherah poles, the carved idols, and the cast images were smashed and scattered over the graves of those who had sacrificed to them. ⁵He burned the bones of the pagan priests on their own altars, and so he purified Judah and Jerusalem.

⁶He did the same thing in the towns of Manasseh, Ephraim, and Simeon, even as far as Naphtali, and in the regions* all around them. ⁷He destroyed the pagan altars and the Asherah poles, and he crushed the idols into dust. He cut down all the incense altars

---

33:19 Or *The Record of Hozai.* 34:6 As in Syriac version; Hebrew reads *in their temples,* or *in their ruins.* The meaning of the Hebrew is uncertain.

33:12 Manasseh's response followed the requirements of Solomon's prayer at the dedication of the Temple (7:14).
33:12-17 The book of 2 Kings does not mention Manasseh's repentance, telling only of the promise of judgment resulting from his wicked deeds (see 2 Kings 21:10-16). Second Chronicles tells the good things he did after he repented, following his father Hezekiah's example. However, Manasseh's actions were unable to turn the hearts of the people back to the Lord or to avert God's judgment on Judah (2 Chronicles 33:17).
33:13 Manasseh's experience was a microcosm of what the nation would experience: exile and bondage brought on by abandoning God, then repentance and returning to the Lord.

throughout the land of Israel. Finally, he returned to Jerusalem.

⁸In the eighteenth year of his reign, after he had purified the land and the Temple, Josiah appointed Shaphan son of Azaliah, Maaseiah the governor of Jerusalem, and Joah son of Joahaz, the royal historian, to repair the Temple of the LORD his God. ⁹They gave Hilkiah the high priest the money that had been collected by the Levites who served as gatekeepers at the Temple of God. The gifts were brought by people from Manasseh, Ephraim, and from all the remnant of Israel, as well as from all Judah, Benjamin, and the people of Jerusalem.

¹⁰He entrusted the money to the men assigned to supervise the restoration of the LORD's Temple. Then they paid the workers who did the repairs and renovation of the Temple. ¹¹They hired carpenters and builders, who purchased finished stone for the walls and timber for the rafters and beams. They restored what earlier kings of Judah had allowed to fall into ruin.

¹²The workers served faithfully under the leadership of Jahath and Obadiah, Levites of the Merarite clan, and Zechariah and Meshullam, Levites of the Kohathite clan. Other Levites, all of whom were skilled musicians, ¹³were put in charge of the laborers of the various trades. Still others assisted as secretaries, officials, and gatekeepers.

Hilkiah Discovers God's Law

¹⁴While they were bringing out the money collected at the LORD's Temple, Hilkiah the priest found the Book of the Law of the LORD that was written by Moses. ¹⁵Hilkiah said to Shaphan the court secretary, "I have found the Book of the Law in the LORD's Temple!" Then Hilkiah gave the scroll to Shaphan.

¹⁶Shaphan took the scroll to the king and reported, "Your officials are doing everything they were assigned to do. ¹⁷The money that was collected at the Temple of the LORD has been turned over to the supervisors and workmen." ¹⁸Shaphan also told the king, "Hilkiah the priest has given me a scroll." So Shaphan read it to the king.

¹⁹When the king heard what was written in the Law, he tore his clothes in despair. ²⁰Then he gave these orders to Hilkiah, Ahikam son of Shaphan, Acbor son of Micaiah,* Shaphan the court secretary, and Asaiah the king's personal adviser: ²¹"Go to the Temple and speak to the LORD for me and for all the remnant of Israel and Judah. Inquire about the words written in the scroll that has been found. For the LORD's great anger has been poured out on us because our ancestors have not obeyed the word of the LORD. We have not been doing everything this scroll says we must do."

²²So Hilkiah and the other men went to the New Quarter* of Jerusalem to consult with the prophet Huldah. She was the wife of Shallum son of Tikvah, son of Harhas,* the keeper of the Temple wardrobe.

²³She said to them, "The LORD, the God of Israel, has spoken! Go back and tell the man who sent you, ²⁴'This is what the LORD says: I am going to bring disaster on this city* and its people. All the curses written in the scroll that was read to the king of Judah will come true. ²⁵For my people have abandoned me and offered sacrifices to pagan gods, and I am very angry with them for everything they have done. My anger will be poured out on this place, and it will not be quenched.'

²⁶"But go to the king of Judah who sent you to seek the LORD and tell him: 'This is what the LORD, the God of Israel, says concerning the message you have just heard: ²⁷You were sorry and humbled yourself before God when you heard his words against this city and its people. You humbled yourself and tore your clothing in despair and wept before me in repentance. And I have indeed heard you, says the LORD. ²⁸So I will not send the promised disaster until after you have died and been buried in peace. You yourself will not see the disaster I am going to bring on this city and its people.'"

So they took her message back to the king.

Josiah's Religious Reforms

²⁹Then the king summoned all the elders of Judah and Jerusalem. ³⁰And the king went up to the Temple of the LORD with all the people of Judah and Jerusalem, along with the priests and the Levites—all

---

34:20 As in parallel text at 2 Kgs 22:12; Hebrew reads *Abdon son of Micah*. 34:22a Or *the Second Quarter*, a newer section of Jerusalem. Hebrew reads *the Mishneh*. 34:22b As in parallel text at 2 Kgs 22:14; Hebrew reads *son of Tokhath, son of Hasrah*. 34:24 Hebrew *this place*; also in 34:27, 28.

34:22 Huldah is one of the four named Old Testament prophets who were women (Miriam, Deborah, and Noadiah). Huldah was respected and trusted; when a priest discovered the Book of the Law in the Temple, King Josiah's officials sought her out. She proclaimed a message from God, encouraging King Josiah and the people. Part of her message was difficult, but it was honest. A prophet's role was to remind people about their promise to be faithful to God and to each other. We see examples of God engaging women in the role of prophet in the Bible and beyond (Miriam in Exodus 15:20-21; Deborah in Judges 4–5; Noadiah in Nehemiah 6:14). The Bible clearly shows that God uses women be a voice for him (Joel 2:28-29; Acts 2:17-18).

34:30-33 King Josiah publicly read from the Book of the Covenant discovered in the Temple. This book probably contained all or part of Deuteronomy or possibly the entire Pentateuch (the term for the first five books of the Old Testament). In this moment, Josiah rededicated the people and renewed the covenant with the Lord. He encouraged everyone to love and obey the Lord. This covenant renewal ceremony was followed by the removal of all the idols of false worship. Josiah's reforms and the public reading of this book reminded everyone of their identity as the people of God. Just so, reading God's Word can wonderfully renew our relationship with God.

the people from the greatest to the least. There the king read to them the entire Book of the Covenant that had been found in the LORD's Temple. ³¹The king took his place of authority beside the pillar and renewed the covenant in the LORD's presence. He pledged to obey the LORD by keeping all his commands, laws, and decrees with all his heart and soul. He promised to obey all the terms of the covenant that were written in the scroll. ³²And he required everyone in Jerusalem and the people of Benjamin to make a similar pledge. The people of Jerusalem did so, renewing their covenant with God, the God of their ancestors.

³³So Josiah removed all detestable idols from the entire land of Israel and required everyone to worship the LORD their God. And throughout the rest of his lifetime, they did not turn away from the LORD, the God of their ancestors.

Josiah Celebrates Passover

35 Then Josiah announced that the Passover of the LORD would be celebrated in Jerusalem, and so the Passover lamb was slaughtered on the fourteenth day of the first month.* ²Josiah also assigned the priests to their duties and encouraged them in their work at the Temple of the LORD. ³He issued this order to the Levites, who were to teach all Israel and who had been set apart to serve the LORD: "Put the holy Ark in the Temple that was built by Solomon son of David, the king of Israel. You no longer need to carry it back and forth on your shoulders. Now spend your time serving the LORD your God and his people Israel. ⁴Report for duty according to the family divisions of your ancestors, following the directions of King David of Israel and the directions of his son Solomon.

⁵"Then stand in the sanctuary at the place appointed for your family division and help the families assigned to you as they bring their offerings to the Temple. ⁶Slaughter the Passover lambs, purify yourselves, and prepare to help those who come. Follow all the directions that the LORD gave through Moses."

⁷Then Josiah provided 30,000 lambs and young goats for the people's Passover offerings, along with 3,000 cattle, all from the king's own flocks and herds. ⁸The king's officials also made willing contributions to the people, priests, and Levites. Hilkiah, Zechariah, and Jehiel, the administrators of God's Temple, gave the priests 2,600 lambs and young goats and 300 cattle as Passover offerings. ⁹The Levite leaders—Conaniah and his brothers Shemaiah and Nethanel, as well as Hashabiah, Jeiel, and Jozabad—gave 5,000 lambs and young goats and 500 cattle to the Levites for their Passover offerings.

¹⁰When everything was ready for the Passover celebration, the priests and the Levites took their places, organized by their divisions, as the king had commanded. ¹¹The Levites then slaughtered the Passover lambs and presented the blood to the priests, who sprinkled the blood on the altar while the Levites prepared the animals. ¹²They divided the burnt offerings among the people by their family groups, so they could offer them to the LORD as prescribed in the Book of Moses. They did the same with the cattle. ¹³Then they roasted the Passover lambs as prescribed; and they boiled the holy offerings in pots, kettles, and pans, and brought them out quickly so the people could eat them.

¹⁴Afterward the Levites prepared Passover offerings for themselves and for the priests—the descendants of Aaron—because the priests had been busy from morning till night offering the burnt offerings and the fat portions. The Levites took responsibility for all these preparations.

¹⁵The musicians, descendants of Asaph, were in their assigned places, following the commands that had been given by David, Asaph, Heman, and Jeduthun, the king's seer. The gatekeepers guarded the gates and did not need to leave their posts of duty, for their Passover offerings were prepared for them by their fellow Levites.

¹⁶The entire ceremony for the LORD's Passover was completed that day. All the burnt offerings were sacrificed on the altar of the LORD, as King Josiah had commanded. ¹⁷All the Israelites present in Jerusalem celebrated Passover and the Festival of Unleavened Bread for seven days. ¹⁸Never since the time of the prophet Samuel had there been such a Passover. None of the kings of Israel had ever kept a Passover as Josiah did, involving all the priests and Levites, all the people of Jerusalem, and people from all over Judah and Israel. ¹⁹This Passover was celebrated in the eighteenth year of Josiah's reign.

Josiah Dies in Battle

²⁰After Josiah had finished restoring the Temple, King Neco of Egypt led his army up from Egypt to do battle at Carchemish on the Euphrates River, and Josiah and his army marched out to fight him.* ²¹But King Neco sent messengers to Josiah with this message:

"What do you want with me, king of Judah? I have no quarrel with you today! I am on my way to fight another nation, and God has told me to hurry! Do not interfere with God, who is with me, or he will destroy you."

²²But Josiah refused to listen to Neco, to whom God had indeed spoken, and he would not turn back. Instead, he disguised himself and led his army into battle on the plain of Megiddo. ²³But the

---

35:1 This day in the ancient Hebrew lunar calendar was April 5, 622 B.C. **35:20** Or *Josiah went out to meet him.*

Huldah

IDENTITY — A Prophet of Courage and Boldness

When King Josiah needed a word from the Lord, the king's messengers sought out the prophet Huldah. Perhaps they visited her instead of the other well-known prophets in Jerusalem because they thought, "She'll give the king a good word. We don't think the prophets Isaiah or Jeremiah will do that. They just speak words of judgment."

But Huldah was not fooled. She knew her God and she knew the trouble the nation had invited. She knew that they had denied God and lost their way.

The message she delivered from the Lord was that the kingdom was being judged and disaster would come. However, God would spare Josiah's life, and judgment would wait until after his death.

Huldah said nothing of the reforms Josiah had made and would continue to make. The reforms were all good, but most important to God was Josiah's humility: Josiah worked to make things right after he heard the reading of the Law in the Temple.

> She stayed true to God's voice.

While Huldah's message probably wasn't what the king's men hoped to hear, she stayed true to God's voice. She spoke with clarity and boldness, addressing the heart of the matter.

Huldah is the only named female prophet from this period of Judah's history. She sets an example of one who spoke God's truth over satisfying the expectations of others.

HULDAH'S STORY IS TOLD IN 2 KINGS 22:8-20; 2 CHRONICLES 34:14-28.

IDENTIFY

Is your audience the "audience of One," the Lord God of Heaven?

How might God be challenging your tendency to be a people pleaser? Can you be bold to speak what others may not expect you to say?

"As a chaplain in several different contexts, I feel constantly challenged to speak the truth in love with sensitivity and boldness. It is not always easy, but it is God's challenge to me. Like Huldah, I aim to speak God's words over mine."

ELIZABETH GLANVILLE, PhD, is retired faculty from Fuller Theological Seminary, School of Mission and Theology. She is an international teacher on missions and leadership and chaplain for a local police department and her retirement community.

enemy archers hit King Josiah with their arrows and wounded him. He cried out to his men, "Take me from the battle, for I am badly wounded!"

²⁴So they lifted Josiah out of his chariot and placed him in another chariot. Then they brought him back to Jerusalem, where he died. He was buried there in the royal cemetery. And all Judah and Jerusalem mourned for him. ²⁵The prophet Jeremiah composed funeral songs for Josiah, and to this day choirs still sing these sad songs about his death. These songs of sorrow have become a tradition and are recorded in The Book of Laments.

²⁶The rest of the events of Josiah's reign and his acts of devotion (carried out according to what was written in the Law of the LORD), ²⁷from beginning to end—all are recorded in The Book of the Kings of Israel and Judah.

Jehoahaz Rules in Judah

36 Then the people of the land took Josiah's son Jehoahaz and made him the next king in Jerusalem.

²Jehoahaz* was twenty-three years old when he became king, and he reigned in Jerusalem three months.

³Then he was deposed by the king of Egypt, who demanded that Judah pay 7,500 pounds of silver and 75 pounds of gold* as tribute.

Jehoiakim Rules in Judah

⁴The king of Egypt then installed Eliakim, the brother of Jehoahaz, as the next king of Judah and Jerusalem, and he changed Eliakim's name to Jehoiakim. Then Neco took Jehoahaz to Egypt as a prisoner.

⁵Jehoiakim was twenty-five years old when he became king, and he reigned in Jerusalem eleven years. He did what was evil in the sight of the LORD his God.

⁶Then King Nebuchadnezzar of Babylon came to Jerusalem and captured it, and he bound Jehoiakim in bronze chains and led him away to Babylon. ⁷Nebuchadnezzar also took some of the treasures from the Temple of the LORD, and he placed them in his palace* in Babylon.

⁸The rest of the events in Jehoiakim's reign, including all the evil things he did and everything found against him, are recorded in The Book of the Kings of Israel and Judah. Then his son Jehoiachin became the next king.

Jehoiachin Rules in Judah

⁹Jehoiachin was eighteen* years old when he became king, and he reigned in Jerusalem three months and ten days. Jehoiachin did what was evil in the LORD's sight.

¹⁰In the spring of the year* King Nebuchadnezzar took Jehoiachin to Babylon. Many treasures from the Temple of the LORD were also taken to Babylon at that time. And Nebuchadnezzar installed Jehoiachin's uncle,* Zedekiah, as the next king in Judah and Jerusalem.

Zedekiah Rules in Judah

¹¹Zedekiah was twenty-one years old when he became king, and he reigned in Jerusalem eleven years. ¹²But Zedekiah did what was evil in the sight of the LORD his God, and he refused to humble himself when the prophet Jeremiah spoke to him directly from the LORD. ¹³He also rebelled against King Nebuchadnezzar, even though he had taken an oath of loyalty in God's name. Zedekiah was a hard and stubborn man, refusing to turn to the LORD, the God of Israel.

¹⁴Likewise, all the leaders of the priests and the people became more and more unfaithful. They followed all the pagan practices of the surrounding nations, desecrating the Temple of the LORD that had been consecrated in Jerusalem.

¹⁵The LORD, the God of their ancestors, repeatedly sent his prophets to warn them, for he had compassion on his people and his Temple. ¹⁶But the people mocked these messengers of God and despised their words. They scoffed at the prophets until the LORD's anger could no longer be restrained and nothing could be done.

The Fall of Jerusalem

¹⁷So the LORD brought the king of Babylon against them. The Babylonians* killed Judah's young men, even chasing after them into the Temple. They had no pity on the people, killing both young men and young women, the old and the infirm. God handed all of them over to Nebuchadnezzar. ¹⁸The king took home to Babylon all the articles, large and small, used in the Temple of God, and the treasures from both the LORD's Temple and from the palace of the king and his officials. ¹⁹Then his army burned the Temple of God, tore down the walls of Jerusalem, burned all the palaces, and completely destroyed everything of value.* ²⁰The few who survived were taken as exiles

---

36:2 Hebrew *Joahaz*, a variant spelling of Jehoahaz; also in 36:4.   **36:3** Hebrew *100 talents* [3,400 kilograms] *of silver and 1 talent* [34 kilograms] *of gold*.   **36:7** Or *temple*.   **36:9** As in one Hebrew manuscript, some Greek manuscripts, and Syriac version (see also 2 Kgs 24:8); most Hebrew manuscripts read *eight*.   **36:10a** Hebrew *At the turn of the year*. The first day of this year in the ancient Hebrew lunar calendar was April 13, 597 B.C.   **36:10b** As in parallel text at 2 Kgs 24:17; Hebrew reads *brother*, or *relative*.   **36:17** Or *Chaldeans*.   **36:19** Or *destroyed all the valuable articles from the Temple*.

36:13 The vassal oath imposed on him was probably similar to those known from Assyrian treaties, sworn in the name of the vassal's god.   **36:19** The Temple was destroyed in August 586 BC (see 2 Kings 25:8-9; Jeremiah 52:12-13).

to Babylon, and they became servants to the king and his sons until the kingdom of Persia came to power.

²¹So the message of the LORD spoken through Jeremiah was fulfilled. The land finally enjoyed its Sabbath rest, lying desolate until the seventy years were fulfilled, just as the prophet had said.

Cyrus Allows the Exiles to Return

²²In the first year of King Cyrus of Persia,* the LORD fulfilled the prophecy he had given through Jeremiah.* He stirred the heart of Cyrus to put this proclamation in writing and to send it throughout his kingdom:

²³"This is what King Cyrus of Persia says:

"The LORD, the God of heaven, has given me all the kingdoms of the earth. He has appointed me to build him a Temple at Jerusalem, which is in Judah. Any of you who are his people may go there for this task. And may the LORD your God be with you!"

36:22a The first year of Cyrus's reign over Babylon was 538 B.C. 36:22b See Jer 25:11-12; 29:10.

36:22-23 Second Chronicles ends with a decree from Cyrus, the king of Persia. At the time of this decree, the Temple had been destroyed by the Babylonian Empire, which in turn had been conquered by King Cyrus and had been absorbed into the Persian Empire. Yet, even with kingdoms rising and falling and a foreign king ruling, the Lord was at work. The new world superpower, the Persian Empire, was marked by unprecedented religious tolerance, and Cyrus's decree allowed people to worship their own gods. The book of Ezra details how the Jews lived out Cyrus's decree, with the exiles returning to Judah to rebuild the Temple.

Ezra

WHAT DO WE LEARN ABOUT GOD'S MISSION AND OURS?
Time reading and studying God's Word and praying is time well spent.

WHO WROTE IT? Likely Ezra, or someone who wrote during Ezra's time.

WHEN DID IT HAPPEN? Between 538 and 450 BC, during the Jewish people's return from exile.

HOW IS IT ORGANIZED?

- 1–2: Cyrus authorizes the first exiles to return and rebuild the Temple
- 3: Temple worship revives
- 4–6: Temple rebuilding completed
- 7–8: Ezra goes to Jerusalem and teaches God's law
- 9–10: Ezra reforms marriage practices

FEATURE HIGHLIGHTS

+ *How Do I Live My Faith at Work?* (559)
+ *What the Bible Says about Faithfulness* (562)
+ *Surprising Influence* (567)
+ *What's the Cost of Ignoring God?* (570)

Words to Remember are highlighted throughout this book

HOW LONG DOES IT TAKE TO READ?

:40						
:30	1:00	1:30	2:00	2:30	3:00	3:30

BC Timeline

BC	Event
586	JERUSALEM IS DESTROYED; EXILES ARE TAKEN TO BABYLON
538	FIRST EXILES RETURN TO JERUSALEM
536	TEMPLE RECONSTRUCTION BEGINS
530	TEMPLE WORK IS HALTED
520	TEMPLE WORK IS RESUMED; HAGGAI AND ZECHARIAH DELIVER MESSAGES FROM THE LORD
515	TEMPLE IS COMPLETED
486	XERXES (AHASUERUS) BECOMES PERSIA'S KING
c. 483	VASHTI IS DEPOSED
479	ESTHER BECOMES QUEEN
474	HAMAN PLOTS TO DESTROY THE JEWS
473	FIRST FESTIVAL OF PURIM IS CELEBRATED
465	ARTAXERXES BECOMES PERSIA'S KING
458	EZRA TRAVELS TO JERUSALEM
445	ARTAXERXES, WITH HIS QUEEN SEATED BY HIM, APPROVES NEHEMIAH'S RETURN TO JERUSALEM
445	NEHEMIAH TRAVELS TO JERUSALEM TO REBUILD THE WALL

Cyrus Allows the Exiles to Return

1 In the first year of King Cyrus of Persia,* the LORD fulfilled the prophecy he had given through Jeremiah.* He stirred the heart of Cyrus to put this proclamation in writing and to send it throughout his kingdom:

² "This is what King Cyrus of Persia says:

"The LORD, the God of heaven, has given me all the kingdoms of the earth. He has appointed me to build him a Temple at Jerusalem, which is in Judah. ³ Any of you who are his people may go to Jerusalem in Judah to rebuild this Temple of the LORD, the God of Israel, who lives in Jerusalem. And may your God be with you! ⁴ Wherever this Jewish remnant is found, let their neighbors contribute toward their expenses by giving them silver and gold, supplies for the journey, and livestock, as well as a voluntary offering for the Temple of God in Jerusalem."

⁵ Then God stirred the hearts of the priests and Levites and the leaders of the tribes of Judah and Benjamin to go to Jerusalem to rebuild the Temple of the LORD. ⁶ And all their neighbors assisted by giving them articles of silver and gold, supplies for the journey, and livestock. They gave them many valuable gifts in addition to all the voluntary offerings.

⁷ King Cyrus himself brought out the articles that King Nebuchadnezzar had taken from the LORD's Temple in Jerusalem and had placed in the temple of his own gods. ⁸ Cyrus directed Mithredath, the treasurer of Persia, to count these items and present them to Sheshbazzar, the leader of the exiles returning to Judah.* ⁹ This is a list of the items that were returned:

gold basins	30
silver basins	1,000
silver incense burners*	29
¹⁰ gold bowls	30
silver bowls	410
other items	1,000

¹¹ In all, there were 5,400 articles of gold and silver. Sheshbazzar brought all of these along when the exiles went from Babylon to Jerusalem.

Exiles Who Returned with Zerubbabel

2 Here is the list of the Jewish exiles of the provinces who returned from their captivity. King Nebuchadnezzar had deported them to Babylon, but now they returned to Jerusalem and the other towns in Judah where they originally lived. ² Their leaders were Zerubbabel, Jeshua, Nehemiah, Seraiah, Reelaiah, Mordecai, Bilshan, Mispar, Bigvai, Rehum, and Baanah.

This is the number of the men of Israel who returned from exile:

³ The family of Parosh	2,172
⁴ The family of Shephatiah	372
⁵ The family of Arah	775
⁶ The family of Pahath-moab (descendants of Jeshua and Joab)	2,812
⁷ The family of Elam	1,254
⁸ The family of Zattu	945
⁹ The family of Zaccai	760
¹⁰ The family of Bani	642
¹¹ The family of Bebai	623
¹² The family of Azgad	1,222
¹³ The family of Adonikam	666
¹⁴ The family of Bigvai	2,056
¹⁵ The family of Adin	454
¹⁶ The family of Ater (descendants of Hezekiah)	98

1:1a The first year of Cyrus's reign over Babylon was 538 B.C. **1:1b** See Jer 25:11-12; 29:10. **1:8** Hebrew *Sheshbazzar, the prince of Judah*. **1:9** The meaning of this Hebrew word is uncertain.

1:1 According to ancient manuscripts, the books of Ezra and Nehemiah were originally written on one scroll. Reading these books together helps us understand how the Israelites in exile answered the questions, "Who are we, and who is God?" This is the story of a people rebuilding their lives and society after loss. The memoirs and ministry of Ezra and Nehemiah interweave, and remembering that these two books go together helps us see the whole story. King Artaxerxes tasked Ezra, a priest and scribe, to perform administrative duties in Jerusalem, in the province of Judah (7:21-26). These duties included rebuilding the Temple.
1:1 The time period for the book of Ezra begins in 538 BC, almost fifty years after the Babylonians had conquered Jerusalem. Many Jewish people had been forcibly deported to Babylon and were living in exile, while others were allowed to remain in Judah. The story of Daniel is an example of being taken into exile; Esther and Mordecai are stories of Jewish people living under the rule of other nations. In Ezra's book, King Cyrus allowed the exiles to return home but remain under Persia's rule to strengthen support politically and geographically.
1:2 Although Cyrus practiced Zoroastrianism, the edict mentioned here speaks of "the LORD, the God of heaven." This proclamation, written in Hebrew, presents Cyrus as a servant of the Jewish God, and likely sought to legitimize his rule while cultivating goodwill among his new subjects. A similar royal inscription, written in Babylonian, frames Cyrus as the champion of the Babylonian god Marduk. Similarly, the words here reflect that God had appointed him to build him a Temple at Jerusalem (see Isaiah 44:28; 45:1, 13). Cyrus might have learned of such prophecies from Daniel, who served in his court as a high government official (Daniel 6:28). God had long planned to raise up Cyrus and restore worship in Jerusalem (Isaiah 44:28; 45:1, 13; 48:14-15).
1:7 Many articles from the Lord's Temple were taken by the Babylonians when the people were exiled (see 2 Chronicles 36:7; Daniel 1:2). By putting these items in his pagan temple, Nebuchadnezzar had attempted to show his god's power over the God of Israel. However, God had promised to return all the items (see Jeremiah 27:16-22). The items from the Temple were holy utensils, acceptable to God for worship and very valuable to the returning worshipers.

17 The family of Bezai 323
18 The family of Jorah 112
19 The family of Hashum 223
20 The family of Gibbar.................................. 95
21 The people of Bethlehem 123
22 The people of Netophah.......................... 56
23 The people of Anathoth 128
24 The people of Beth-azmaveth* 42
25 The people of Kiriath-jearim,* Kephirah,
     and Beeroth 743
26 The people of Ramah and Geba 621
27 The people of Micmash........................... 122
28 The people of Bethel and Ai 223
29 The citizens of Nebo 52
30 The citizens of Magbish 156
31 The citizens of West Elam* 1,254
32 The citizens of Harim............................. 320
33 The citizens of Lod, Hadid, and Ono 725
34 The citizens of Jericho........................... 345
35 The citizens of Senaah........................ 3,630

36 These are the priests who returned from exile:
     The family of Jedaiah (through the line of
     Jeshua) 973
37 The family of Immer............................ 1,052
38 The family of Pashhur 1,247
39 The family of Harim 1,017

40 These are the Levites who returned from exile:
     The families of Jeshua and Kadmiel
     (descendants of Hodaviah) 74
41 The singers of the family of Asaph 128
42 The gatekeepers of the families of Shallum, Ater,
     Talmon, Akkub, Hatita, and Shobai 139

43 The descendants of the following Temple servants
returned from exile:
     Ziha, Hasupha, Tabbaoth,
44   Keros, Siaha, Padon,
45   Lebanah, Hagabah, Akkub,
46   Hagab, Shalmai,* Hanan,
47   Giddel, Gahar, Reaiah,
48   Rezin, Nekoda, Gazzam,
49   Uzza, Paseah, Besai,
50   Asnah, Meunim, Nephusim,
51   Bakbuk, Hakupha, Harhur,
52   Bazluth, Mehida, Harsha,
53   Barkos, Sisera, Temah,
54   Neziah, and Hatipha.

55 The descendants of the servants of King Solomon
returned from exile:
     Sotai, Hassophereth, Peruda,
56   Jaalah, Darkon, Giddel,
57   Shephatiah, Hattil, Pokereth-hazzebaim, and Ami.

58 In all, the Temple servants and the descendants of
Solomon's servants numbered 392.

Perspective

How do I live my faith at work?

SCRIPTURE CONNECTION: EZRA 1:1-6

Most of the nearly eight billion people on this planet do not work at a place where faith is a high priority. They work hard manual labor or with high academic prowess or somewhere in the middle with priorities like money, deadlines, and rules. Sometimes living in a way that pleases God can lead to a reprimand.

The Israelites faced the task of rebuilding God's sacred Temple while serving someone who did not believe in the God of Israel. In the workplace, we may face this same unsteady ground when how we live what we believe conflicts with or offends the people who control our employment.

Ezra led the returning Jews to rebuild God's Temple with faith that kept their eyes on God's authority rather than on other people's. Yet, they still obeyed the rules of the land.

VIEWPOINTS

THEIRS: *When God asks us to build something for his glory, we can trust he will see it through, even if the work is hard and unpopular.*
MINE: *"I can trust God to clear the path for his plans while I also honor the appropriate bounds of human authority."*
YOURS: *When your workplace feels hostile to your faith, ask God to show you how to honor him and those who lead you.*

CARA DAY is a writer and illustrator. She has served with Stonecroft Ministries helping women live "extraordinary."

2:24 As in parallel text at Neh 7:28; Hebrew reads *Azmaveth*. **2:25** As in some Hebrew manuscripts and Greek version (see also Neh 7:29); Hebrew reads *Kiriath-arim*. **2:31** Or *of the other Elam*. **2:46** As in an alternate reading of the Masoretic Text (see also Neh 7:48); the other alternate reads *Shamlai*.

⁵⁹Another group returned at this time from the towns of Tel-melah, Tel-harsha, Kerub, Addan, and Immer. However, they could not prove that they or their families were descendants of Israel. ⁶⁰This group included the families of Delaiah, Tobiah, and Nekoda—a total of 652 people.

⁶¹Three families of priests—Hobaiah, Hakkoz, and Barzillai—also returned. (This Barzillai had married a woman who was a descendant of Barzillai of Gilead, and he had taken her family name.) ⁶²They searched for their names in the genealogical records, but they were not found, so they were disqualified from serving as priests. ⁶³The governor told them not to eat the priests' share of food from the sacrifices until a priest could consult the LORD about the matter by using the Urim and Thummim—the sacred lots.

⁶⁴So a total of 42,360 people returned to Judah, ⁶⁵in addition to 7,337 servants and 200 singers, both men and women. ⁶⁶They took with them 736 horses, 245 mules, ⁶⁷435 camels, and 6,720 donkeys.

⁶⁸When they arrived at the Temple of the LORD in Jerusalem, some of the family leaders made voluntary offerings toward the rebuilding of God's Temple on its original site, ⁶⁹and each leader gave as much as he could. The total of their gifts came to 61,000 gold coins,* 6,250 pounds* of silver, and 100 robes for the priests.

⁷⁰So the priests, the Levites, the singers, the gatekeepers, the Temple servants, and some of the common people settled in villages near Jerusalem. The rest of the people returned to their own towns throughout Israel.

The Altar Is Rebuilt

3 In early autumn,* when the Israelites had settled in their towns, all the people assembled in Jerusalem with a unified purpose. ²Then Jeshua son of Jehozadak* joined his fellow priests and Zerubbabel son of Shealtiel with his family in rebuilding the altar of the God of Israel. They wanted to sacrifice burnt offerings on it, as instructed in the Law of Moses, the man of God. ³Even though the people were afraid of the local residents, they rebuilt the altar at its old site. Then they began to sacrifice burnt offerings on the altar to the LORD each morning and evening.

⁴They celebrated the Festival of Shelters as prescribed in the Law, sacrificing the number of burnt offerings specified for each day of the festival. ⁵They also offered the regular burnt offerings and the offerings required for the new moon celebrations and the annual festivals as prescribed by the LORD. The people also gave voluntary offerings to the LORD. ⁶Fifteen days before the Festival of Shelters began,* the priests had begun to sacrifice burnt offerings to the LORD. This was even before they had started to lay the foundation of the LORD's Temple.

The People Begin to Rebuild the Temple

⁷Then the people hired masons and carpenters and bought cedar logs from the people of Tyre and Sidon, paying them with food, wine, and olive oil. The logs were brought down from the Lebanon mountains and floated along the coast of the Mediterranean Sea* to Joppa, for King Cyrus had given permission for this.

⁸The construction of the Temple of God began in midspring,* during the second year after they arrived in Jerusalem. The work force was made up of everyone who had returned from exile, including Zerubbabel son of Shealtiel, Jeshua son of Jehozadak and his fellow priests, and all the Levites. The Levites who were twenty years old or older were put in charge of rebuilding the LORD's Temple. ⁹The workers at the Temple of God were supervised by Jeshua with his sons and relatives, and Kadmiel and his sons, all descendants of Hodaviah.* They were helped in this task by the Levites of the family of Henadad.

2:69a Hebrew *61,000 darics of gold,* about 1,100 pounds or 500 kilograms in weight. **2:69b** Hebrew *5,000 minas* [3,000 kilograms]. **3:1** Hebrew *In the seventh month.* The year is not specified, so it may have been during Cyrus's first year (538 B.C.) or second year (537 B.C.). The seventh month of the ancient Hebrew lunar calendar occurred within the months of September/October 538 B.C. and October/November 537 B.C. **3:2** Hebrew *Jozadak,* a variant spelling of Jehozadak; also in 3:8. **3:6** Hebrew *On the first day of the seventh month.* This day in the ancient Hebrew lunar calendar occurred in September or October. The Festival of Shelters began on the fifteenth day of the seventh month. **3:7** Hebrew *the sea.* **3:8** Hebrew *in the second month.* This month in the ancient Hebrew lunar calendar occurred within the months of April and May 536 B.C. **3:9** Hebrew *sons of Judah* (i.e., *bene Yehudah*). *Bene* might also be read here as the proper name Binnui; *Yehudah* is probably another name for Hodaviah. Compare 2:40; Neh 7:43; 1 Esdras 5:58.

2:59-63 Establishing a family heritage, especially back to Abraham, helped the Jewish people prove and maintain a shared identity and community belonging when they were returning from exile. But just like those who were not able to prove a Hebrew family heritage, we may sometimes feel disqualified. Even so, we can make valuable contributions to God's mission, as did Rahab and Ruth.

2:63 The Urim and Thummim were stones, probably dark and light, that enabled the high priest to ascertain yes or no answers from the Lord. The high priest carried them in his breast pocket, over his heart (Exodus 28:30), which symbolized the seat of emotions, decisions, and will. Although Scripture does not physically describe the Urim and Thummim, using them may have been similar to throwing dice with a divinely-controlled outcome.

2:68-69 As when the Tabernacle was built (Exodus 25:2-7; 35:4-9) and the Temple was renovated (2 Kings 12:1-16), the people gave voluntary offerings to finance this effort. These funds supplemented the money and goods provided by Darius (Ezra 6:8-9) and gifts from the Jewish people who stayed in Babylon. These people gave as much as they could based on their resources.

3:1-13 Women were vital participants in community religious life, even though they are not always visible in the narrative. Here "all the people" help construct the altar (3:1). Everyone— women, men, and children—rejoiced and celebrated with the Temple rebuilding. And everyone participated in religious festivals such as the Festival of Shelters and Passover (6:19).

[10]When the builders completed the foundation of the LORD's Temple, the priests put on their robes and took their places to blow their trumpets. And the Levites, descendants of Asaph, clashed their cymbals to praise the LORD, just as King David had prescribed. [11]With praise and thanks, they sang this song to the LORD:

"He is so good!
His faithful love for Israel endures forever!"

Then all the people gave a great shout, praising the LORD because the foundation of the LORD's Temple had been laid.

[12]But many of the older priests, Levites, and other leaders who had seen the first Temple wept aloud when they saw the new Temple's foundation. The others, however, were shouting for joy. [13]The joyful shouting and weeping mingled together in a loud noise that could be heard far in the distance.

Enemies Oppose the Rebuilding

4 The enemies of Judah and Benjamin heard that the exiles were rebuilding a Temple to the LORD, the God of Israel. [2]So they approached Zerubbabel and the other leaders and said, "Let us build with you, for we worship your God just as you do. We have sacrificed to him ever since King Esarhaddon of Assyria brought us here."

[3]But Zerubbabel, Jeshua, and the other leaders of Israel replied, "You may have no part in this work. We alone will build the Temple for the LORD, the God of Israel, just as King Cyrus of Persia commanded us."

[4]Then the local residents tried to discourage and frighten the people of Judah to keep them from their work. [5]They bribed agents to work against them and to frustrate their plans. This went on during the entire reign of King Cyrus of Persia and lasted until King Darius of Persia took the throne.*

Later Opposition under Xerxes and Artaxerxes

[6]Years later when Xerxes* began his reign, the enemies of Judah wrote a letter of accusation against the people of Judah and Jerusalem.

[7]Even later, during the reign of King Artaxerxes of Persia,* the enemies of Judah, led by Bishlam, Mithredath, and Tabeel, sent a letter to Artaxerxes in the Aramaic language, and it was translated for the king.

[8]*Rehum the governor and Shimshai the court secretary wrote the letter, telling King Artaxerxes about the situation in Jerusalem. [9]They greeted the king for all their colleagues—the judges and local leaders, the people of Tarpel, the Persians, the Babylonians, and the people of Erech and Susa (that is, Elam). [10]They also sent greetings from the rest of the people whom the great and noble Ashurbanipal* had deported and relocated in Samaria and throughout the neighboring lands of the province west of the Euphrates River.* [11]This is a copy of their letter:

"To King Artaxerxes, from your loyal subjects in the province west of the Euphrates River.

[12]"The king should know that the Jews who came here to Jerusalem from Babylon are rebuilding this rebellious and evil city. They have already laid the foundation and will soon finish its walls. [13]And the king should know that if this city is rebuilt and its walls are completed, it will be much to your disadvantage, for the Jews will then refuse to pay their tribute, customs, and tolls to you.

[14]"Since we are your loyal subjects* and do not want to see the king dishonored in this way, we have sent the king this information. [15]We suggest that a search be made in your ancestors' records, where you will discover what a rebellious city this has been in the past. In fact, it was destroyed because of its long and troublesome history of revolt against the kings and countries who controlled it. [16]We declare to the king that if this city is rebuilt and its walls are completed, the province west of the Euphrates River will be lost to you."

[17]Then King Artaxerxes sent this reply:

"To Rehum the governor, Shimshai the court secretary, and their colleagues living in Samaria and throughout the province west of the Euphrates River. Greetings.

[18]"The letter you sent has been translated and read to me. [19]I ordered a search of the records and have found that Jerusalem has indeed been a hotbed of insurrection against many kings.

4:5 Darius reigned 521–486 B.C. 4:6 Hebrew *Ahasuerus*, another name for Xerxes. He reigned 486–465 B.C. 4:7 Artaxerxes reigned 465–424 B.C. 4:8 The original text of 4:8–6:18 is in Aramaic. 4:10a Aramaic *Osnappar*, another name for Ashurbanipal. 4:10b Aramaic *the province beyond the river*; also in 4:11, 16, 17, 20. 4:14 Aramaic *Since we eat the salt of the palace*.

4:2 King Esarhaddon of Assyria (680–669 BC) had deported the people of Israel to foreign lands and had relocated other conquered peoples to the land of Israel during the reign of King Manasseh in Judah. These foreigners had learned about the Lord when they entered the land of Israel but had also continued to worship their own gods (2 Kings 17:27-34, 40-41).
4:6 In Hebrew, *Ahasuerus* is how Xerxes' name is spelled. He ruled the Persian Empire from 486 BC to 465 BC and was Esther's husband.
4:10 Ashurbanipal was the last king of the Neo-Assyrian Empire, ruling from 669 BC to 630 BC. A collection of over 30,000 clay tablets were discovered in the ruins of the capital. Perhaps the most famous discovery in this so-called library is the set of fragments containing parts of the *Epic of Gilgamesh*. These archaeological discoveries give us a glimpse into the life and times of people who lived at the same time as the Israelites during the Old Testament. It reveals the importance of keeping records and remembering important stories.

WHAT THE BIBLE SAYS ABOUT Faithfulness

God Rewards Faithfulness

For if we are faithful to the end, trusting God just as firmly as when we first believed, we will share in all that belongs to Christ. **HEBREWS 3:14**

Just as you accepted Christ Jesus as your Lord, you must continue to follow him. Let your roots grow down into him, and let your lives be built on him. Then your faith will grow strong in the truth you were taught, and you will overflow with thankfulness. **COLOSSIANS 2:6-7**

God Is Faithful

Your unfailing love, O Lord, is as vast as the heavens;
   your faithfulness reaches beyond the clouds.
PSALM 36:5

Great is his faithfulness;
   his mercies begin afresh each morning.
LAMENTATIONS 3:23

The Word became human and made his home among us. He was full of unfailing love and faithfulness. And we have seen his glory, the glory of the Father's one and only Son. **JOHN 1:14**

Great is his faithfulness...

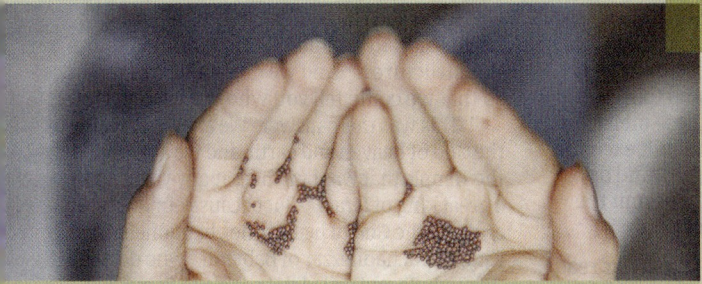

Hold on to Faith

Dear brothers and sisters, when troubles of any kind come your way, consider it an opportunity for great joy. For you know that when your faith is tested, your endurance has a chance to grow. **JAMES 1:2-3**

These trials will show that your faith is genuine. It is being tested as fire tests and purifies gold—though your faith is far more precious than mere gold. So when your faith remains strong through many trials, it will bring you much praise and glory and honor on the day when Jesus Christ is revealed to the whole world. **1 PETER 1:7**

Therefore, since we are surrounded by such a huge crowd of witnesses to the life of faith, let us strip off every weight that slows us down, especially the sin that so easily trips us up. And let us run with endurance the race God has set before us. We do this by keeping our eyes on Jesus, the champion who initiates and perfects our faith. **HEBREWS 12:1-2**

It's Good to Talk about God's Faithfulness

It is good to proclaim your unfailing love in the morning,
your faithfulness in the evening.
PSALM 92:2

I will sing of the LORD's unfailing love forever!
Young and old will hear of your faithfulness.
PSALM 89:1

Let us hold tightly without wavering to the hope we affirm.

Faithfulness Brings Flourishing

Let's not get tired of doing what is good. At just the right time we will reap a harvest of blessing if we don't give up. **GALATIANS 6:9**

I am certain that God, who began the good work within you, will continue his work until it is finally finished on the day when Christ Jesus returns. **PHILIPPIANS 1:6**

Let us hold tightly without wavering to the hope we affirm, for God can be trusted to keep his promise. **HEBREWS 10:23**

In fact, rebellion and revolt are normal there! ²⁰Powerful kings have ruled over Jerusalem and the entire province west of the Euphrates River, receiving tribute, customs, and tolls. ²¹Therefore, issue orders to have these men stop their work. That city must not be rebuilt except at my express command. ²²Be diligent, and don't neglect this matter, for we must not permit the situation to harm the king's interests."

²³When this letter from King Artaxerxes was read to Rehum, Shimshai, and their colleagues, they hurried to Jerusalem. Then, with a show of strength, they forced the Jews to stop building.

The Rebuilding Resumes

²⁴So the work on the Temple of God in Jerusalem had stopped, and it remained at a standstill until the second year of the reign of King Darius of Persia.*

5 At that time the prophets Haggai and Zechariah son of Iddo prophesied to the Jews in Judah and Jerusalem. They prophesied in the name of the God of Israel who was over them. ²Zerubbabel son of Shealtiel and Jeshua son of Jehozadak* responded by starting again to rebuild the Temple of God in Jerusalem. And the prophets of God were with them and helped them.

³But Tattenai, governor of the province west of the Euphrates River,* and Shethar-bozenai and their colleagues soon arrived in Jerusalem and asked, "Who gave you permission to rebuild this Temple and restore this structure?" ⁴They also asked for* the names of all the men working on the Temple. ⁵But because their God was watching over them, the leaders of the Jews were not prevented from building until a report was sent to Darius and he returned his decision.

Tattenai's Letter to King Darius

⁶This is a copy of the letter that Tattenai the governor, Shethar-bozenai, and the other officials of the province west of the Euphrates River sent to King Darius:

⁷"To King Darius. Greetings.

⁸"The king should know that we went to the construction site of the Temple of the great God in the province of Judah. It is being rebuilt with specially prepared stones, and timber is being laid in its walls. The work is going forward with great energy and success.

⁹"We asked the leaders, 'Who gave you permission to rebuild this Temple and restore this structure?' ¹⁰And we demanded their names so that we could tell you who the leaders were.

¹¹"This was their answer: 'We are the servants of the God of heaven and earth, and we are rebuilding the Temple that was built here many years ago by a great king of Israel. ¹²But because our ancestors angered the God of heaven, he abandoned them to King Nebuchadnezzar of Babylon,* who destroyed this Temple and exiled the people to Babylonia. ¹³However, King Cyrus of Babylon,* during the first year of his reign, issued a decree that the Temple of God should be rebuilt. ¹⁴King Cyrus returned the gold and silver cups that Nebuchadnezzar had taken from the Temple of God in Jerusalem and had placed in the temple of Babylon. These cups were taken from that temple and presented to a man named Sheshbazzar, whom King Cyrus appointed as governor of Judah. ¹⁵The king instructed him to return the cups to their place in Jerusalem and to rebuild the Temple of God there on its original site. ¹⁶So this Sheshbazzar came and laid the foundations of the Temple of God in Jerusalem. The people have been working on it ever since, though it is not yet completed.'

¹⁷"Therefore, if it pleases the king, we request that a search be made in the royal archives of Babylon to discover whether King Cyrus ever issued a decree to rebuild God's Temple in Jerusalem. And then let the king send us his decision in this matter."

Darius Approves the Rebuilding

6 So King Darius issued orders that a search be made in the Babylonian archives, which were stored in the treasury. ²But it was at the fortress at Ecbatana in the province of Media that a scroll was found. This is what it said:

"Memorandum:

³"In the first year of King Cyrus's reign, a decree was sent out concerning the Temple of God at Jerusalem.

"Let the Temple be rebuilt on the site where Jews used to offer their sacrifices, using the original foundations. Its height will be ninety feet, and its width will be ninety feet.* ⁴Every

---

4:24 The second year of Darius's reign was 520 B.C. The narrative started in 4:1-5 is resumed at verse 24. **5:2** Aramaic *Jozadak*, a variant spelling of Jehozadak. **5:3** Aramaic *the province beyond the river;* also in 5:6. **5:4** As in one Hebrew manuscript and Greek and Syriac versions; Masoretic Text reads *Then we told them.* **5:12** Aramaic *Nebuchadnezzar the Chaldean.* **5:13** King Cyrus of Persia is here identified as the king of Babylon because Persia had conquered the Babylonian Empire. **6:3** Aramaic *Its height will be 60 cubits* [27.6 meters], *and its width will be 60 cubits.* It is commonly held that this verse should be emended to read: "Its height will be 30 cubits [45 feet or 13.8 meters], its length will be 60 cubits [90 feet or 27.6 meters], and its width will be 20 cubits [30 feet or 9.2 meters]"; compare 1 Kgs 6:2. The emendation regarding the width is supported by the Syriac version.

5:1 Haggai first prophesied on August 29, 520 BC (Haggai 1:1). Zechariah began prophesying about two months later (Zechariah 1:1). The books of Haggai and Zechariah record their messages.

three layers of specially prepared stones will be topped by a layer of timber. All expenses will be paid by the royal treasury. ⁵Furthermore, the gold and silver cups, which were taken to Babylon by Nebuchadnezzar from the Temple of God in Jerusalem, must be returned to Jerusalem and put back where they belong. Let them be taken back to the Temple of God."

⁶So King Darius sent this message:

"Now therefore, Tattenai, governor of the province west of the Euphrates River,* and Shethar-bozenai, and your colleagues and other officials west of the Euphrates River—stay away from there! ⁷Do not disturb the construction of the Temple of God. Let it be rebuilt on its original site, and do not hinder the governor of Judah and the elders of the Jews in their work.

⁸"Moreover, I hereby decree that you are to help these elders of the Jews as they rebuild this Temple of God. You must pay the full construction costs, without delay, from my taxes collected in the province west of the Euphrates River so that the work will not be interrupted.

⁹"Give the priests in Jerusalem whatever is needed in the way of young bulls, rams, and male lambs for the burnt offerings presented to the God of heaven. And without fail, provide them with as much wheat, salt, wine, and olive oil as they need each day. ¹⁰Then they will be able to offer acceptable sacrifices to the God of heaven and pray for the welfare of the king and his sons.

¹¹"Those who violate this decree in any way will have a beam pulled from their house. Then they will be lifted up and impaled on it, and their house will be reduced to a pile of rubble.* ¹²May the God who has chosen the city of Jerusalem as the place to honor his name destroy any king or nation that violates this command and destroys this Temple.

"I, Darius, have issued this decree. Let it be obeyed with all diligence."

The Temple's Dedication

¹³Tattenai, governor of the province west of the Euphrates River, and Shethar-bozenai and their colleagues complied at once with the command of King Darius. ¹⁴So the Jewish elders continued their work, and they were greatly encouraged by the preaching of the prophets Haggai and Zechariah son of Iddo.

> "Help me, Lord, to remember that religion is not to be confined to the church... nor exercised only in prayer and meditation, but that everywhere I am in Thy Presence."
>
> **SUSANNA WESLEY**
> (1669–1742) faithful Christian, known as the mother of Methodism

The Temple was finally finished, as had been commanded by the God of Israel and decreed by Cyrus, Darius, and Artaxerxes, the kings of Persia. ¹⁵The Temple was completed on March 12,* during the sixth year of King Darius's reign.

¹⁶The Temple of God was then dedicated with great joy by the people of Israel, the priests, the Levites, and the rest of the people who had returned from exile. ¹⁷During the dedication ceremony for the Temple of God, 100 young bulls, 200 rams, and 400 male lambs were sacrificed. And 12 male goats were presented as a sin offering for the twelve tribes of Israel. ¹⁸Then the priests and Levites were divided into their various divisions to serve at the Temple of God in Jerusalem, as prescribed in the Book of Moses.

Celebration of Passover

¹⁹On April 21* the returned exiles celebrated Passover. ²⁰The priests and Levites had purified themselves and were ceremonially clean. So they slaughtered the Passover lamb for all the returned exiles, for their fellow priests, and for themselves. ²¹The Passover meal was eaten by the people of Israel who had returned from exile and by the others in the land who had turned from their corrupt practices to

---

6:6 Aramaic *the province beyond the river;* also in 6:6b, 8, 13. **6:11** Aramaic *a dunghill.* **6:15** Aramaic *on the third day of the month Adar,* of the ancient Hebrew lunar calendar. A number of events in Ezra can be cross-checked with dates in surviving Persian records and related accurately to our modern calendar. This day was March 12, 515 B.C. **6:19** Hebrew *On the fourteenth day of the first month,* of the ancient Hebrew lunar calendar. This day was April 21, 515 B.C.; also see note on 6:15.

6:19 The people celebrated the first Passover before Moses led Israel from slavery under the oppressive Egyptian pharaoh to freedom (Exodus 12:1–13:10). Passover was a festival of remembrance, highlighting the mighty saving acts of the Lord and deeply connecting the exiles in Ezra with their history, identity, and story. Setting aside time to remember important moments in our lives strengthens our faith as we recall God's mighty work in our histories. God was with us in the past and will go with us into our future.

worship the Lord, the God of Israel. ²²Then they celebrated the Festival of Unleavened Bread for seven days. There was great joy throughout the land because the Lord had caused the king of Assyria* to be favorable to them, so that he helped them to rebuild the Temple of God, the God of Israel.

Ezra Arrives in Jerusalem

7 Many years later, during the reign of King Artaxerxes of Persia,* there was a man named Ezra. He was the son* of Seraiah, son of Azariah, son of Hilkiah, ²son of Shallum, son of Zadok, son of Ahitub, ³son of Amariah, son of Azariah, son* of Meraioth, ⁴son of Zerahiah, son of Uzzi, son of Bukki, ⁵son of Abishua, son of Phinehas, son of Eleazar, son of Aaron the high priest.* ⁶This Ezra was a scribe who was well versed in the Law of Moses, which the Lord, the God of Israel, had given to the people of Israel. He came up to Jerusalem from Babylon, and the king gave him everything he asked for, because the gracious hand of the Lord his God was on him. ⁷Some of the people of Israel, as well as some of the priests, Levites, singers, gatekeepers, and Temple servants, traveled up to Jerusalem with him in the seventh year of King Artaxerxes' reign.

⁸Ezra arrived in Jerusalem in August* of that year. ⁹He had arranged to leave Babylon on April 8, the first day of the new year,* and he arrived at Jerusalem on August 4,* for the gracious hand of his God was on him. ¹⁰This was because Ezra had determined to study and obey the Law of the Lord and to teach those decrees and regulations to the people of Israel.

Artaxerxes' Letter to Ezra

¹¹King Artaxerxes had given a copy of the following letter to Ezra, the priest and scribe who studied and taught the commands and decrees of the Lord to Israel:

> ¹²*"From Artaxerxes, the king of kings, to Ezra the priest, the teacher of the law of the God of heaven. Greetings.
>
> ¹³"I decree that any of the people of Israel in my kingdom, including the priests and Levites, may volunteer to return to Jerusalem with you. ¹⁴I and my council of seven hereby instruct you to conduct an inquiry into the situation in Judah and Jerusalem, based on your God's law, which is in your hand. ¹⁵We also commission you to take with you silver and gold, which we are freely presenting as an offering to the God of Israel who lives in Jerusalem.
>
> ¹⁶"Furthermore, you are to take any silver and gold that you may obtain from the province of Babylon, as well as the voluntary offerings of the people and the priests that are presented for the Temple of their God in Jerusalem. ¹⁷These donations are to be used specifically for the purchase of bulls, rams, male lambs, and the appropriate grain offerings and liquid offerings, all of which will be offered on the altar of the Temple of your God in Jerusalem. ¹⁸Any silver and gold that is left over may be used in whatever way you and your colleagues feel is the will of your God.
>
> ¹⁹"But as for the cups we are entrusting to you for the service of the Temple of your God, deliver them all to the God of Jerusalem. ²⁰If you need anything else for your God's Temple or for any similar needs, you may take it from the royal treasury.
>
> ²¹"I, Artaxerxes the king, hereby send this decree to all the treasurers in the province west of the Euphrates River*: 'You are to give Ezra, the priest and teacher of the law of the God of heaven, whatever he requests of you. ²²You are to give him up to 7,500 pounds* of silver, 500 bushels* of wheat, 550 gallons of wine, 550 gallons of olive oil,* and an unlimited supply of salt. ²³Be careful to provide whatever the God of heaven demands for his Temple, for why should we risk bringing God's anger against the realm of the king and his sons? ²⁴I also decree that no priest, Levite, singer, gatekeeper, Temple servant, or other worker in this Temple of God will be required to pay tribute, customs, or tolls of any kind.'

6:22 King Darius of Persia is here identified as the king of Assyria because Persia had conquered the Babylonian Empire, which included the earlier Assyrian Empire. **7:1a** Artaxerxes reigned 465–424 B.C. **7:1b** Or *descendant*; see 1 Chr 6:14. **7:3** Or *descendant*; see 1 Chr 6:6-10. **7:5** Or *the first priest*. **7:8** Hebrew *in the fifth month*. This month in the ancient Hebrew lunar calendar occurred within the months of August and September 458 B.C. **7:9a** Hebrew *on the first day of the first month*, of the ancient Hebrew lunar calendar. This day was April 8, 458 B.C.; also see note on 6:15. **7:9b** Hebrew *on the first day of the fifth month*, of the ancient Hebrew lunar calendar. This day was August 4, 458 B.C.; also see note on 6:15. **7:12** The original text of 7:12-26 is in Aramaic. **7:21** Aramaic *the province beyond the river*; also in 7:25. **7:22a** Aramaic *100 talents* [3,400 kilograms]. **7:22b** Aramaic *100 cors* [22 kiloliters]. **7:22c** Aramaic *100 baths* [2.1 kiloliters] *of wine, 100 baths of olive oil*.

7:1 Many years later, Ezra arrived in Jerusalem in 458 BC, about fifty-seven years after the dedication of the second Temple. Ezra had been recording events that occurred before his time, but now he began to record his own history. His father, Seraiah, had been the high priest under Zedekiah and had been executed by Nebuchadnezzar in 586 BC (2 Kings 25:18-21).

7:11-26 In this letter, King Artaxerxes granted Ezra the power and responsibility to evaluate the situation in Jerusalem (7:14), present freewill offerings to God (7:15-20), obtain supplies and finances from local authorities (7:21-24), and institute judicial reforms (7:25-26).

7:23 "The God of heaven" is the title the Jewish people used for the Lord (5:11-12) and that Cyrus had used (1:2). As part of the Persian Empire's policy of religious tolerance, respect was shown for each region's god or gods, and this is reflected in the wording of official documents. Artaxerxes here encourages that no expense be spared in providing the worship that "the God of Jerusalem" (7:19) required.

25 "And you, Ezra, are to use the wisdom your God has given you to appoint magistrates and judges who know your God's laws to govern all the people in the province west of the Euphrates River. Teach the law to anyone who does not know it. 26 Anyone who refuses to obey the law of your God and the law of the king will be punished immediately, either by death, banishment, confiscation of goods, or imprisonment."

7:25-26 Ezra was to teach God's laws and govern the area occupied by the Jewish people in accordance with God's laws and the law of the king—here, Persian civil law.

Koinonia

IMAGE — MY STORY WITH COMMUNITY, WORKPLACE & CHURCH

Surprising Influence

SCRIPTURE CONNECTION: EZRA 7:1-28

Influence is the capacity to affect someone's character, development, or behavior. In this passage, we see how one woman's influence may have gone further than she could have imagined.

A group of Jews was preparing to travel to Jerusalem, with Ezra leading them. God used an unlikely figure to make this journey possible—Artaxerxes, king of the Persian Empire. Artaxerxes authorized and financed the trip, and despite not being Jewish, he seems to have known God's powerful ways.

Artaxerxes was a son of King Xerxes, the husband of Queen Esther. Although Artaxerxes was the son of another of Xerxes's royal wives, Esther may have influenced him.

> When we live for God, our influence reaches further than we imagine.

Why did King Artaxerxes support the Jews? The Bible says that Artaxerxes gave Ezra what he needed because "the gracious hand of the LORD his God was" on Ezra (7:6). The rulers of the Persian Empire recognized the political importance of religious tolerance, and Artaxerxes may have been motivated to keep the peace in his empire by respecting the God of the Jews (7:23). We cannot know with certainty, but perhaps he also witnessed firsthand the miraculous ways God saved the Jews of Susa. Or maybe Queen Esther or her cousin Mordecai told him what God had done.

Did Queen Esther know this little boy would grow up to support her Jewish people in remarkable ways? Esther's courage in stepping forward may have influenced events further than she probably imagined: She may have impacted the rebuilding of Jerusalem's Temple and walls.

We all want the best for the people around us. Are you sharing God's love with those around you and recounting the powerful ways God has worked in your life?

Your influence goes further than you think.

IMAGINE

Where or how is God asking you to step forward as an influencer?

What opportunities can you take to tell of God's mighty power in your life?

"I don't always understand my influence, like Esther may not have. I ask God to help me be faithful, and I hope to guide future generations to love and serve Jesus."

MELISSA HOUDMANN is the cofounder of GotQuestions Ministries, a website dedicated to answering Bible questions. She also wrote Stonecroft Ministries' *Why Believe* study.

Ezra Praises the LORD

27 Praise the LORD, the God of our ancestors, who made the king want to beautify the Temple of the LORD in Jerusalem! 28 And praise him for demonstrating such unfailing love to me by honoring me before the king, his council, and all his mighty nobles! I felt encouraged because the gracious hand of the LORD my God was on me. And I gathered some of the leaders of Israel to return with me to Jerusalem.

Exiles Who Returned with Ezra

8 Here is a list of the family leaders and the genealogies of those who came with me from Babylon during the reign of King Artaxerxes:

2 From the family of Phinehas: Gershom.
From the family of Ithamar: Daniel.
From the family of David: Hattush, 3 a descendant of Shecaniah.
From the family of Parosh: Zechariah and 150 other men were registered.
4 From the family of Pahath-moab: Eliehoenai son of Zerahiah and 200 other men.
5 From the family of Zattu*: Shecaniah son of Jahaziel and 300 other men.
6 From the family of Adin: Ebed son of Jonathan and 50 other men.
7 From the family of Elam: Jeshaiah son of Athaliah and 70 other men.
8 From the family of Shephatiah: Zebadiah son of Michael and 80 other men.
9 From the family of Joab: Obadiah son of Jehiel and 218 other men.
10 From the family of Bani*: Shelomith son of Josiphiah and 160 other men.
11 From the family of Bebai: Zechariah son of Bebai and 28 other men.
12 From the family of Azgad: Johanan son of Hakkatan and 110 other men.
13 From the family of Adonikam, who came later*: Eliphelet, Jeuel, Shemaiah, and 60 other men.
14 From the family of Bigvai: Uthai, Zaccur,* and 70 other men.

Ezra's Journey to Jerusalem

15 I assembled the exiles at the Ahava Canal, and we camped there for three days while I went over the lists of the people and the priests who had arrived. I found that not one Levite had volunteered to come along. 16 So I sent for Eliezer, Ariel, Shemaiah, Elnathan, Jarib, Elnathan, Nathan, Zechariah, and Meshullam, who were leaders of the people. I also sent for Joiarib and Elnathan, who were men of discernment. 17 I sent them to Iddo, the leader of the Levites at Casiphia, to ask him and his relatives and the Temple servants to send us ministers for the Temple of God at Jerusalem.

18 Since the gracious hand of our God was on us, they sent us a man named Sherebiah, along with eighteen of his sons and brothers. He was a very astute man and a descendant of Mahli, who was a descendant of Levi son of Israel.* 19 They also sent Hashabiah, together with Jeshaiah from the descendants of Merari, and twenty of his sons and brothers, 20 and 220 Temple servants. The Temple servants were assistants to the Levites—a group of Temple workers first instituted by King David and his officials. They were all listed by name.

21 And there by the Ahava Canal, I gave orders for all of us to fast and humble ourselves before our God. We prayed that he would give us a safe journey and protect us, our children, and our goods as we traveled. 22 For I was ashamed to ask the king for soldiers and horsemen* to accompany us and protect us from enemies along the way. After all, we had told the king, "Our God's hand of protection is on all who worship him, but his fierce anger rages against those who abandon him." 23 So we fasted and earnestly prayed that our God would take care of us, and he heard our prayer.

24 I appointed twelve leaders of the priests—Sherebiah, Hashabiah, and ten other priests—25 to be in charge of transporting the silver, the gold, the gold bowls, and the other items that the king, his council, his officials, and all the people of Israel had presented for the Temple of God. 26 I weighed the treasure as I gave it to them and found the totals to be as follows:

24 tons* of silver,
7,500 pounds* of silver articles,
7,500 pounds of gold,
27 20 gold bowls, equal in value to 1,000 gold coins,*
2 fine articles of polished bronze, as precious as gold.

28 And I said to these priests, "You and these treasures have been set apart as holy to the LORD. This silver and gold is a voluntary offering to the LORD, the God of our ancestors. 29 Guard these treasures well until you present them to the leading priests, the Levites, and the leaders of Israel, who will weigh them at the storerooms of the LORD's Temple in Jerusalem." 30 So the priests and the Levites accepted the task of transporting these treasures of silver and gold to the Temple of our God in Jerusalem.

8:5 As in some Greek manuscripts (see also 1 Esdras 8:32); Hebrew lacks *Zattu.* 8:10 As in some Greek manuscripts (see also 1 Esdras 8:36); Hebrew lacks *Bani.* 8:13 Or *who were the last of his family.* 8:14 As in Greek and Syriac versions and an alternate reading of the Masoretic Text; the other alternate reads *Zabbud.* 8:18 *Israel* is the name that God gave to Jacob. 8:22 Or *charioteers.* 8:26a Hebrew *650 talents* [22 metric tons]. 8:26b Hebrew *100 talents* [3,400 kilograms]; also in 8:26c. 8:27 Hebrew *1,000 darics,* about 19 pounds or 8.6 kilograms in weight.

[31] We broke camp at the Ahava Canal on April 19* and started off to Jerusalem. And the gracious hand of our God protected us and saved us from enemies and bandits along the way. [32] So we arrived safely in Jerusalem, where we rested for three days.

[33] On the fourth day after our arrival, the silver, gold, and other valuables were weighed at the Temple of our God and entrusted to Meremoth son of Uriah the priest and to Eleazar son of Phinehas, along with Jozabad son of Jeshua and Noadiah son of Binnui—both of whom were Levites. [34] Everything was accounted for by number and weight, and the total weight was officially recorded.

[35] Then the exiles who had come out of captivity sacrificed burnt offerings to the God of Israel. They presented twelve bulls for all the people of Israel, as well as ninety-six rams and seventy-seven male lambs. They also offered twelve male goats as a sin offering. All this was given as a burnt offering to the LORD. [36] The king's decrees were delivered to his highest officers and the governors of the province west of the Euphrates River,* who then cooperated by supporting the people and the Temple of God.

Ezra's Prayer concerning Intermarriage

9 When these things had been done, the Jewish leaders came to me and said, "Many of the people of Israel, and even some of the priests and Levites, have not kept themselves separate from the other peoples living in the land. They have taken up the detestable practices of the Canaanites, Hittites, Perizzites, Jebusites, Ammonites, Moabites, Egyptians, and Amorites. [2] For the men of Israel have married women from these people and have taken them as wives for their sons. So the holy race has become polluted by these mixed marriages. Worse yet, the leaders and officials have led the way in this outrage."

[3] When I heard this, I tore my cloak and my shirt, pulled hair from my head and beard, and sat down utterly shocked. [4] Then all who trembled at the words of the God of Israel came and sat with me because of this outrage committed by the returned exiles. And I sat there utterly appalled until the time of the evening sacrifice.

[5] At the time of the sacrifice, I stood up from where I had sat in mourning with my clothes torn. I fell to my knees and lifted my hands to the LORD my God. [6] I prayed,

"O my God, I am utterly ashamed; I blush to lift up my face to you. For our sins are piled higher than our heads, and our guilt has reached to the heavens. [7] From the days of our ancestors until now, we have been steeped in sin. That is why we and our kings and our priests have been at the mercy of the pagan kings of the land. We have been killed, captured, robbed, and disgraced, just as we are today.

[8] "But now we have been given a brief moment of grace, for the LORD our God has allowed a few of us to survive as a remnant. He has given us security in this holy place. Our God has brightened our eyes and granted us some relief from our slavery. [9] For we were slaves, but in his unfailing love our God did not abandon us in our slavery. Instead, he caused the kings of Persia to treat us favorably. He revived us so we could rebuild the Temple of our God and repair its ruins. He has given us a protective wall in Judah and Jerusalem.

[10] "And now, O our God, what can we say after all of this? For once again we have abandoned your commands! [11] Your servants the prophets warned us when they said, 'The land you are entering to possess is totally defiled by the detestable practices of the people living there. From one end to the other, the land is filled with corruption. [12] Don't let your daughters marry their sons! Don't take their daughters as wives for your sons. Don't ever promote the peace and prosperity of those nations. If you follow these instructions, you will be strong and will enjoy the good things the land produces, and you will leave this prosperity to your children forever.'

[13] "Now we are being punished because of our wickedness and our great guilt. But we have actually been punished far less than we deserve, for you, our God, have allowed some of us to survive as a remnant. [14] But even so, we are again breaking your commands and intermarrying with people who do these detestable things. Won't your anger be enough to destroy us, so that even this little remnant no longer survives? [15] O LORD, God of Israel, you are just. We come before you in our guilt as nothing but an escaped remnant, though in such a condition none of us can stand in your presence."

8:31 Hebrew *on the twelfth day of the first month,* of the ancient Hebrew lunar calendar. This day was April 19, 458 B.C.; also see note on 6:15.   **8:36** Hebrew *the province beyond the river.*

9:1–10:15 After returning to Jerusalem, Ezra gathered the people to discuss the marriages of those who had married non-Jewish women. With religious identity concerns in mind, Ezra radically demanded that these men immediately divorce their foreign wives. The requirement for marrying within the Jewish community was not racially motivated: Instead, they did not want to be influenced to worship other gods (Deuteronomy 7:1-6). In our lives, sometimes we cut people off so that we can more fully commit to the Lord. At times, this separation proves wise and helpful; at other times, this separation harms and is unnecessary. In Ezra, not everyone agreed with the drastic decision to send the non-Jewish women and children away. Jonathan, Jahzeiah, Meshullam, and Shabbethai opposed Ezra (see Ezra 10:15).

Perspective

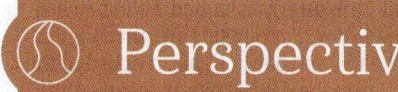

What's the cost of ignoring God?

SCRIPTURE CONNECTION: EZRA 9–10

After the Jews' return to Jerusalem, Ezra learned that the people had intermarried, in direct contradiction of God's instruction, and had adopted other gods. Ezra was grieved, tore his clothes, and pulled hair from his head.

As Ezra was praying, a large group of Israelites came to repent. They proposed to divorce these spouses and abandon false gods. Ezra agreed, and they united in dealing with their sin. They recognized God's holiness and made this heart-wrenching decision.

Did the foreign women and children suffer because of this sinful situation? Undoubtedly, yes. Sin always has victims, and there were broken hearts all around.

How is this fair? When God told Israel to be holy, he instructed them not to marry people from other nations because intermarriage would lead the people into worshiping their spouses' false gods (Deuteronomy 7:1-6). As his special people, the Jews were to worship the one true God so the world would know they belonged to the Lord alone. God's warning against intermarriage was not about race but about holiness.

VIEWPOINTS

HERS: *These women likely left with provisions and returned to their fathers' homes. Some may have gained a new start, a chance to reintegrate into their family's society.*
MINE: *"Like Ezra, I want to look within my heart and ask the Holy Spirit to show me the depth and seriousness of my sin. Lord, help me be holy."*
YOURS: *How can we stay alert to sin's seriousness so we do not dishonor God and harm people?*

MELISSA HOUDMANN is the cofounder of GotQuestions Ministries, a website dedicated to answering Bible questions. She also wrote Stonecroft Ministries' *Why Believe* study.

The People Confess Their Sin

10 While Ezra prayed and made this confession, weeping and lying face down on the ground in front of the Temple of God, a very large crowd of people from Israel—men, women, and children—gathered and wept bitterly with him. ²Then Shecaniah son of Jehiel, a descendant of Elam, said to Ezra, "We have been unfaithful to our God, for we have married these pagan women of the land. But in spite of this there is hope for Israel. ³Let us now make a covenant with our God to divorce our pagan wives and to send them away with their children. We will follow the advice given by you and by the others who respect the commands of our God. Let it be done according to the Law of God. ⁴Get up, for it is your duty to tell us how to proceed in setting things straight. We are behind you, so be strong and take action."

⁵So Ezra stood up and demanded that the leaders of the priests and the Levites and all the people of Israel swear that they would do as Shecaniah had said. And they all swore a solemn oath. ⁶Then Ezra left the front of the Temple of God and went to the room of Jehohanan son of Eliashib. He spent the night* there without eating or drinking anything. He was still in mourning because of the unfaithfulness of the returned exiles.

⁷Then a proclamation was made throughout Judah and Jerusalem that all the exiles should come to Jerusalem. ⁸Those who failed to come within three days would, if the leaders and elders so decided, forfeit all their property and be expelled from the assembly of the exiles.

⁹Within three days, all the people of Judah and Benjamin had gathered in Jerusalem. This took place on December 19,* and all the people were sitting in the square before the Temple of God. They were trembling both because of the seriousness of the matter and because it was raining. ¹⁰Then Ezra the priest stood and said to them: "You have committed a terrible sin. By marrying pagan women, you have increased Israel's guilt. ¹¹So now confess your sin to the LORD, the God of your ancestors, and do what he demands. Separate yourselves from the people of the land and from these pagan women."

¹²Then the whole assembly raised their voices and answered, "Yes, you are right; we must do as you say!" ¹³Then they added, "This isn't something

10:6 As in parallel text at 1 Esdras 9:2; Hebrew reads *He went*.
10:9 Hebrew *on the twentieth day of the ninth month*, of the ancient Hebrew lunar calendar. This day was December 19, 458 B.C.; also see note on 6:15.

10:1-14 The trauma of recent exile shaped how religious decisions were made about who belonged and who did not belong. Important issues centered on their shared identity. When we look at the Bible as a whole, by contrast, we see how God loves all people. God brings people in from the outside, such as Tamar (Genesis 38), Zipporah (Exodus 4:24-26), Rahab (Joshua 2), and Ruth (Ruth 1). These women were not only brought into the community but helped advance God's good purposes during critical times.

that can be done in a day or two, for many of us are involved in this extremely sinful affair. And this is the rainy season, so we cannot stay out here much longer. ¹⁴Let our leaders act on behalf of us all. Let everyone who has a pagan wife come at a scheduled time, accompanied by the leaders and judges of his city, so that the fierce anger of our God concerning this affair may be turned away from us."

¹⁵Only Jonathan son of Asahel and Jahzeiah son of Tikvah opposed this course of action, and they were supported by Meshullam and Shabbethai the Levite.

¹⁶So this was the plan they followed. Ezra selected leaders to represent their families, designating each of the representatives by name. On December 29,* the leaders sat down to investigate the matter. ¹⁷By March 27, the first day of the new year,* they had finished dealing with all the men who had married pagan wives.

Those Guilty of Intermarriage

¹⁸These are the priests who had married pagan wives:
From the family of Jeshua son of Jehozadak* and his brothers: Maaseiah, Eliezer, Jarib, and Gedaliah. ¹⁹They vowed to divorce their wives, and they each acknowledged their guilt by offering a ram as a guilt offering.
²⁰From the family of Immer: Hanani and Zebadiah.
²¹From the family of Harim: Maaseiah, Elijah, Shemaiah, Jehiel, and Uzziah.
²²From the family of Pashhur: Elioenai, Maaseiah, Ishmael, Nethanel, Jozabad, and Elasah.
²³These are the Levites who were guilty: Jozabad, Shimei, Kelaiah (also called Kelita), Pethahiah, Judah, and Eliezer.
²⁴This is the singer who was guilty: Eliashib.
These are the gatekeepers who were guilty: Shallum, Telem, and Uri.

²⁵These are the other people of Israel who were guilty:
From the family of Parosh: Ramiah, Izziah, Malkijah, Mijamin, Eleazar, Hashabiah,* and Benaiah.
²⁶From the family of Elam: Mattaniah, Zechariah, Jehiel, Abdi, Jeremoth, and Elijah.
²⁷From the family of Zattu: Elioenai, Eliashib, Mattaniah, Jeremoth, Zabad, and Aziza.
²⁸From the family of Bebai: Jehohanan, Hananiah, Zabbai, and Athlai.
²⁹From the family of Bani: Meshullam, Malluch, Adaiah, Jashub, Sheal, and Jeremoth.
³⁰From the family of Pahath-moab: Adna, Kelal, Benaiah, Maaseiah, Mattaniah, Bezalel, Binnui, and Manasseh.
³¹From the family of Harim: Eliezer, Ishijah, Malkijah, Shemaiah, Shimeon, ³²Benjamin, Malluch, and Shemariah.
³³From the family of Hashum: Mattenai, Mattattah, Zabad, Eliphelet, Jeremai, Manasseh, and Shimei.
³⁴From the family of Bani: Maadai, Amram, Uel, ³⁵Benaiah, Bedeiah, Keluhi, ³⁶Vaniah, Meremoth, Eliashib, ³⁷Mattaniah, Mattenai, and Jaasu.
³⁸From the family of Binnui*: Shimei, ³⁹Shelemiah, Nathan, Adaiah, ⁴⁰Macnadebai, Shashai, Sharai, ⁴¹Azarel, Shelemiah, Shemariah, ⁴²Shallum, Amariah, and Joseph.
⁴³From the family of Nebo: Jeiel, Mattithiah, Zabad, Zebina, Jaddai, Joel, and Benaiah.

⁴⁴Each of these men had a pagan wife, and some even had children by these wives.*

10:16 Hebrew *On the first day of the tenth month*, of the ancient Hebrew lunar calendar. This day was December 29, 458 B.C.; also see note on 6:15. **10:17** Hebrew *By the first day of the first month*, of the ancient Hebrew lunar calendar. This day was March 27, 457 B.C.; also see note on 6:15. **10:18** Hebrew *Jozadak*, a variant spelling of Jehozadak. **10:25** As in parallel text at 1 Esdras 9:26; Hebrew reads *Malkijah*. **10:37-38** As in Greek version; Hebrew reads *Jaasu, ³⁸Bani, Binnui*. **10:44** Or *and they sent them away with their children*. The meaning of the Hebrew is uncertain.

10:15 Not everyone agreed with the drastic decision to send the non-Jewish women and children away. Questions after any loss revolve around "Who are we?"; "How did this happen?"; and "What can we do to keep this from happening again?" Ezra chose to draw strict boundaries around those who belonged to the community. Part of the reason for these boundaries was to address the spiritual concern that those not from the community could lead Israel to worship foreign gods, ultimately leading them away from the Lord as had happened so many times in Israel's history. This fear centered on spiritual concerns, not prohibitions against interracial intermarriage. Jonathan, Jahzeiah, Meshullam, and Shabbethai opposed Ezra's decision.

10:44 Ezra is a book that details the hard work of rebuilding and repairing. After the Babylonians destroyed the Temple, they took the devastated people captive and exiled them. With freedom now before them, God's people committed themselves fully to the Lord. They prepared themselves for the taxing physical and spiritual work of rebuilding and repairing. Today, God offers us a way to be restored from hardship and devastation, and be renewed, making us a temple where he dwells (1 Peter 2:5). God invites us to join him in rebuilding and repairing the world. Our lives continue to be rebuilt with new beginnings through relationship with God and one another.

"later he donned a devout air, for many of us are involved in this entire ruined situation. And there is a heavy season so we cannot stay out here much longer. Let our leaders act on behalf of us all. Let everyone in our cities who has come here as secluded... the villages of the... and concern...

"These are the gatekeepers who were guilty: Shallum, Telem, and Uri.

"These are the other people of Israel who were guilty:

"From the family of Parosh: Ramiah, Izziah, Malchijah, Mijamin, Eleazar, Hashabiah, and Benaiah.

"From the family of Elam: Mattaniah, Zechariah, Jehiel, Abdi, Jeremoth, and Elijah.

"From the family of Zattu: Elioenai, Eliashib, Mattaniah, Jeremoth, Zabad, and Aziza.

"From the family of Bebai: Jehohanan, Hananiah, Zabbai, and Athlai.

"From the family of Bani: Meshullam, Malluch, Adaiah, Jashub, Sheal, and Jeremoth.

"From the family of Pahath-moab: Adna, Kelal, Benaiah, Maaseiah, Mattaniah, Bezalel, Binnui, and Manasseh.

"From the family of Harim: Eliezer, Ishijah, Malkijah, Shemaiah, Shimeon, Benjamin, Malluch, and Shemariah.

"From the family of Hashum: Mattenai, Mattattah, Zabad, Eliphelet, Jeremai, Manasseh, and Shimei.

"From the family of Bani: Maadai, Amram, Uel, Benaiah, Bediah, Keluhi, Vaniah, Meremoth,

Nehemiah

WHAT DO WE LEARN ABOUT GOD'S MISSION AND OURS?
God rebuilds when our hearts belong to him.

WHO WROTE IT? Probably an official historian who used Ezra's and Nehemiah's memoirs and records.

WHEN DID IT HAPPEN? Between 445 and 430 BC, during the Jewish people's return from exile.

HOW IS IT ORGANIZED?

- **1:** Nehemiah's proposal and the king's approval
- **2:** Nehemiah travels to Jerusalem, inspects the wall, and encounters opposition
- **3–6:** The people work on rebuilding the wall
- **7:** Nehemiah takes an account of the people
- **8–10:** Ezra leads the people's recommitment to God's law
- **11–12:** Leaders are assigned to resettle in Jerusalem and the wall is dedicated
- **13:** Nehemiah returns to Jerusalem and confronts the neglect of God's law

FEATURE HIGHLIGHTS

+ *Pray-paring for Our Purpose (575)*
+ *How Do We Lead When We Lack Power? (580)*
+ *Disrepair: Persist (590)*

Words to Remember are highlighted throughout this book

HOW LONG DOES IT TAKE TO READ?

| :30 | :50 1:00 | 1:30 | 2:00 | 2:30 | 3:00 | 3:30 |

Timeline (BC)

BC	Event
586	JERUSALEM IS DESTROYED; EXILES ARE TAKEN TO BABYLON
538	FIRST EXILES RETURN TO JERUSALEM
515	TEMPLE IS COMPLETED
486	XERXES (AHASUERUS) BECOMES PERSIA'S KING
c. 483	VASHTI IS DEPOSED
479	ESTHER BECOMES QUEEN
474	HAMAN PLOTS TO DESTROY THE JEWS
473	FIRST FESTIVAL OF PURIM IS CELEBRATED
465	ARTAXERXES BECOMES PERSIA'S KING
458	EZRA TRAVELS TO JERUSALEM
445	ARTAXERXES, WITH HIS QUEEN SEATED BY HIM, APPROVES NEHEMIAH'S RETURN TO JUDAH; JERUSALEM'S WALL IS REBUILT
433	NEHEMIAH RETURNS TO PERSIA
432	NEHEMIAH GOES BACK TO JERUSALEM
430	MALACHI BEGINS HIS MINISTRY

ized to care for the city's physical and spiritual protection.
NEHEMIAH 1

1 These are the memoirs of Nehemiah son of Hacaliah.

Nehemiah's Concern for Jerusalem

In late autumn, in the month of Kislev, in the twentieth year of King Artaxerxes' reign,* I was at the fortress of Susa. ²Hanani, one of my brothers, came to visit me with some other men who had just arrived from Judah. I asked them about the Jews who had returned there from captivity and about how things were going in Jerusalem.

³They said to me, "Things are not going well for those who returned to the province of Judah. They are in great trouble and disgrace. The wall of Jerusalem has been torn down, and the gates have been destroyed by fire."

⁴When I heard this, I sat down and wept. In fact, for days I mourned, fasted, and prayed to the God of heaven. ⁵Then I said,

"O Lord, God of heaven, the great and awesome God who keeps his covenant of unfailing love with those who love him and obey his commands, ⁶listen to my prayer! Look down and see me praying night and day for your people Israel. I confess that we have sinned against you. Yes, even my own family and I have sinned! ⁷We have sinned terribly by not obeying the commands, decrees, and regulations that you gave us through your servant Moses.

⁸"Please remember what you told your servant Moses: 'If you are unfaithful to me, I will scatter you among the nations. ⁹But if you return to me and obey my commands and live by them, then even if you are exiled to the ends of the earth,* I will bring you back to the place I have chosen for my name to be honored.'

¹⁰"The people you rescued by your great power and strong hand are your servants. ¹¹O Lord, please hear my prayer! Listen to the prayers of those of us who delight in honoring you. Please grant me success today by making the king favorable to me.* Put it into his heart to be kind to me."

In those days I was the king's cup-bearer.

Nehemiah Goes to Jerusalem

2 Early the following spring, in the month of Nisan,* during the twentieth year of King Artaxerxes' reign, I was serving the king his wine. I had never before appeared sad in his presence. ²So the king asked me, "Why are you looking so sad? You don't look sick to me. You must be deeply troubled."

Then I was terrified, ³but I replied, "Long live the king! How can I not be sad? For the city where my ancestors are buried is in ruins, and the gates have been destroyed by fire."

⁴The king asked, "Well, how can I help you?"

With a prayer to the God of heaven, ⁵I replied, "If it please the king, and if you are pleased with me, your servant, send me to Judah to rebuild the city where my ancestors are buried."

⁶The king, with the queen sitting beside him, asked, "How long will you be gone? When will you return?" After I told him how long I would be gone, the king agreed to my request.

1:1 Hebrew *In the month of Kislev of the twentieth year.* A number of dates in the book of Nehemiah can be cross-checked with dates in surviving Persian records and related accurately to our modern calendar. This month of the ancient Hebrew lunar calendar occurred within the months of November and December 446 B.C. The *twentieth year* probably refers to the reign of King Artaxerxes I; compare 2:1; 5:14.   **1:9** Hebrew *of the heavens.*   **1:11** Hebrew *today in the sight of this man.*   **2:1** Hebrew *In the month of Nisan.* This month of the ancient Hebrew lunar calendar occurred within the months of April and May 445 B.C.

1:1-4 Nehemiah led the third wave of the Israelites' return to Jerusalem in 445 BC. Zerubbabel led the first group (538 BC), and Ezra the second (458 BC). While Ezra's group had worked to repair the Temple, Nehemiah focused on rebuilding the city walls. He was distressed to see Jerusalem vulnerable and organized groups to care for the city's physical and spiritual protection.

1:2-4 Jerusalem held special meaning for the Jews. It was the capital of Judah and represented the Jewish people's religious and national identity. Nehemiah felt deeply connected to this city, even though he had spent most of his life in exile in Babylon. Nehemiah used his position and influence to assist in rebuilding the broken walls. Have you ever noticed that sometimes we can't stop thinking about an area in the world or even a city or people group? That pull on our hearts may be God's invitation to partner in prayer and sometimes even to join in the work of restoration and reconciliation.

1:4-11 Nehemiah's prayer flowed from deep sorrow. In his sadness, Nehemiah allowed his emotions to flow by weeping, fasting, confessing, and praying. Nehemiah recalled God as the keeper of his "covenant of unfailing love" (1:5). The Hebrew word for "unfailing love" is *khesed*, meaning "faithful love." God was faithful during Nehemiah's time and is still faithful today. The book of Nehemiah demonstrates the power of prayer in these verses, which serves as a model for us when we see others are in trouble. Rather than becoming overwhelmed or numbing our concern, we can pray.

1:11 Nehemiah was a cupbearer to King Artaxerxes. As cupbearer, Nehemiah was entrusted with filling the king's cup and protecting the king's wine to ensure it was not poisoned. Every day was spent in the presence of the king. Every day, Nehemiah had to be focused and alert to prevent the king from being harmed. Who is someone you serve? How might you take that relationship to prayer so you consistently look out for their good? Serving faithfully not only honors God (Deuteronomy 6:4-7) but—as in Nehemiah's story—can position you to gain favor that allows you to make a difference.

2:1-3 A servant was not to let their personal life interfere with their responsibilities, and a sad appearance might raise the king's suspicions that Nehemiah was aware of a plot. If the king doubted Nehemiah in any way, he could lose his position or his life. Nehemiah affirmed his loyalty with the customary "long live the king!" (see also Daniel 2:4), yet he did not deny his sadness.

⁷I also said to the king, "If it please the king, let me have letters addressed to the governors of the province west of the Euphrates River,* instructing them to let me travel safely through their territories on my way to Judah. ⁸And please give me a letter addressed to Asaph, the manager of the king's forest, instructing him to give me timber. I will need it to make beams for the gates of the Temple fortress, for the city walls, and for a house for myself." And the king granted these requests, because the gracious hand of God was on me.

⁹When I came to the governors of the province west of the Euphrates River, I delivered the king's

2:7 Hebrew *the province beyond the river;* also in 2:9.

2:9 Because Nehemiah was a government official, he had an armed escort of officers and horsemen for his trip to Jerusalem (see Ezra 8:22).

Theos IMAGE — MY STORY WITH GOD: Pray-paring for Our Purpose

SCRIPTURE CONNECTION: NEHEMIAH 1:1–2:9

I have always been a "doer," ready to jump in. So Nehemiah's commitment to pray before responding challenges me. Building the walls took only fifty-two days (6:15), but Nehemiah spent four months—Kislev to Nisan (1:1; 2:1)—in intense prayer and planning. He spent another three months gathering materials and traveling to Jerusalem. That is seven months of prayer and preparation for a project that took less than two months! I can imagine him crying out to God:

> I've spent the last four months weeping, repenting, and praying over the destruction of the holy city, Jerusalem. My heart breaks for my people. God, you've heard my cries. Now, you have given me a strategy. Give me favor before the king; I've never shown my sorrow in his presence. Let him see me now and ask. (My paraphrase of Ezra 1:5-11.)

> **Prayer and strategizing before the Lord digs the foundation for profitable service.**

King Artaxerxes did notice and ask (2:1-4). He saw Nehemiah's distress and trusted his cupbearer. So Nehemiah prayed again—a quick prayer (2:4)—before detailing the need and strategy to rebuild the walls.

With the king's approval and help (2:5-8), Nehemiah gathered a team, collected materials, and completed the reconstruction project (2:7-9). The walls went up quickly, yes, but the foundation of prayer was laid first: deeply and slowly.

IMAGINE

When we sense an urgency to act for the Lord, do we stop and pray about it first?

When the Lord puts something on our hearts, what is our first response?

> *"I am learning to slow down for those essential prayer times and listen to God's still small voice."*

ELIZABETH GLANVILLE, PhD, is retired faculty from Fuller Theological Seminary, School of Mission and Theology. She is an international teacher on missions and leadership and chaplain for a local police department and her retirement community.

> "People should not say that this or that is not worth learning, giving as their reason that it will not be put to use. They can no more know what information they will need in the future than they will know the weather two hundred years from today."
>
> **CLARA BARTON**
> (1821–1912) nurse, founder of the American Red Cross

letters to them. The king, I should add, had sent along army officers and horsemen* to protect me. [10] But when Sanballat the Horonite and Tobiah the Ammonite official heard of my arrival, they were very displeased that someone had come to help the people of Israel.

Nehemiah Inspects Jerusalem's Wall

[11] So I arrived in Jerusalem. Three days later, [12] I slipped out during the night, taking only a few others with me. I had not told anyone about the plans God had put in my heart for Jerusalem. We took no pack animals with us except the donkey I was riding. [13] After dark I went out through the Valley Gate, past the Jackal's Well,* and over to the Dung Gate to inspect the broken walls and burned gates. [14] Then I went to the Fountain Gate and to the King's Pool, but my donkey couldn't get through the rubble. [15] So, though it was still dark, I went up the Kidron Valley* instead, inspecting the wall before I turned back and entered again at the Valley Gate.

[16] The city officials did not know I had been out there or what I was doing, for I had not yet said anything to anyone about my plans. I had not yet spoken to the Jewish leaders—the priests, the nobles, the officials, or anyone else in the administration. [17] But now I said to them, "You know very well what trouble we are in. Jerusalem lies in ruins, and its gates have been destroyed by fire. Let us rebuild the wall of Jerusalem and end this disgrace!" [18] Then I told them about how the gracious hand of God had been on me, and about my conversation with the king.

They replied at once, "Yes, let's rebuild the wall!" So they began the good work.

[19] But when Sanballat, Tobiah, and Geshem the Arab heard of our plan, they scoffed contemptuously. "What are you doing? Are you rebelling against the king?" they asked.

[20] I replied, "The God of heaven will help us succeed. We, his servants, will start rebuilding this wall. But you have no share, legal right, or historic claim in Jerusalem."

Rebuilding the Wall of Jerusalem

3 Then Eliashib the high priest and the other priests started to rebuild at the Sheep Gate. They dedicated it and set up its doors, building the wall as far as the Tower of the Hundred, which they dedicated, and the Tower of Hananel. [2] People from the town of Jericho worked next to them, and beyond them was Zaccur son of Imri.

[3] The Fish Gate was built by the sons of Hassenaah. They laid the beams, set up its doors, and installed its bolts and bars. [4] Meremoth son of Uriah and grandson of Hakkoz repaired the next section of wall. Beside him were Meshullam son of Berekiah and grandson of Meshezabel, and then Zadok son of Baana. [5] Next were the people from Tekoa, though their leaders refused to work with the construction supervisors.

[6] The Old City Gate* was repaired by Joiada son of Paseah and Meshullam son of Besodeiah. They laid the beams, set up its doors, and installed its bolts and bars. [7] Next to them were Melatiah from Gibeon, Jadon from Meronoth, people from Gibeon, and people from Mizpah, the headquarters of the governor of the province west of the Euphrates River.* [8] Next was Uzziel son of Harhaiah, a goldsmith by trade, who also worked on the wall. Beyond him was

2:9 Or *charioteers.* **2:13** Or *Serpent's Well.* **2:15** Hebrew *the valley.* **3:6** Or *The Mishneh Gate,* or *The Jeshanah Gate.* **3:7** Hebrew *the province beyond the river.*

2:13 Jackal's Well (or Serpent's Well) might have been En-rogel, a water source located about 400 yards south of the city, or the pool of Siloam, which was filled by water flowing through Hezekiah's meandering, serpentine tunnel. The Dung Gate (called the "Gate of Broken Pots" in Jeremiah 19:2) at the southern end of the western wall (see Nehemiah 3:13) led to the Hinnom Valley, where city inhabitants threw their garbage.
2:14 The King's Pool was either the pool of Siloam or another pool southeast of the city; both were created from the overflow of the Gihon Spring (see 2 Kings 20:20).
3:7 Gibeon and Mizpah were about six miles north of Jerusalem.

Hananiah, a manufacturer of perfumes. They left out a section of Jerusalem as they built the Broad Wall.*

⁹Rephaiah son of Hur, the leader of half the district of Jerusalem, was next to them on the wall. ¹⁰Next Jedaiah son of Harumaph repaired the wall across from his own house, and next to him was Hattush son of Hashabneiah. ¹¹Then came Malkijah son of Harim and Hasshub son of Pahath-moab, who repaired another section of the wall and the Tower of the Ovens. ¹²Shallum son of Hallohesh and his daughters repaired the next section. He was the leader of the other half of the district of Jerusalem.

¹³The Valley Gate was repaired by the people from Zanoah, led by Hanun. They set up its doors and installed its bolts and bars. They also repaired the 1,500 feet* of wall to the Dung Gate.

¹⁴The Dung Gate was repaired by Malkijah son of Recab, the leader of the Beth-hakkerem district. He rebuilt it, set up its doors, and installed its bolts and bars.

¹⁵The Fountain Gate was repaired by Shallum* son of Col-hozeh, the leader of the Mizpah district. He rebuilt it, roofed it, set up its doors, and installed its bolts and bars. Then he repaired the wall of the pool of Siloam* near the king's garden, and he rebuilt the wall as far as the stairs that descend from the City of David. ¹⁶Next to him was Nehemiah son of Azbuk, the leader of half the district of Beth-zur. He rebuilt the wall from a place across from the tombs of David's family as far as the water reservoir and the House of the Warriors.

¹⁷Next to him, repairs were made by a group of Levites working under the supervision of Rehum son of Bani. Then came Hashabiah, the leader of half the district of Keilah, who supervised the building of the wall on behalf of his own district. ¹⁸Next down the line were his countrymen led by Binnui* son of Henadad, the leader of the other half of the district of Keilah.

¹⁹Next to them, Ezer son of Jeshua, the leader of Mizpah, repaired another section of wall across from the ascent to the armory near the angle in the wall. ²⁰Next to him was Baruch son of Zabbai, who zealously repaired an additional section from the angle to the door of the house of Eliashib the high priest. ²¹Meremoth son of Uriah and grandson of Hakkoz rebuilt another section of the wall extending from the door of Eliashib's house to the end of the house.

²²The next repairs were made by the priests from the surrounding region. ²³After them, Benjamin and Hasshub repaired the section across from their house, and Azariah son of Maaseiah and grandson of Ananiah repaired the section across from his house. ²⁴Next was Binnui son of Henadad, who rebuilt another section of the wall from Azariah's house to the angle and the corner. ²⁵Palal son of Uzai carried on the work from a point opposite the angle and the tower that projects up from the king's upper house beside the court of the guard. Next to him were Pedaiah son of Parosh, ²⁶with the Temple servants living on the hill of Ophel, who repaired the wall as far as a point across from the Water Gate to the east and the projecting tower. ²⁷Then came the people of Tekoa, who repaired another section across from the great projecting tower and over to the wall of Ophel.

²⁸Above the Horse Gate, the priests repaired the wall. Each one repaired the section immediately across from his own house. ²⁹Next Zadok son of Immer also rebuilt the wall across from his own house, and beyond him was Shemaiah son of Shecaniah, the gatekeeper of the East Gate. ³⁰Next Hananiah son of Shelemiah and Hanun, the sixth son of Zalaph, repaired another section, while Meshullam son of Berekiah rebuilt the wall across from where he lived. ³¹Malkijah, one of the goldsmiths, repaired the wall as far as the housing for the Temple servants and merchants, across from the Inspection Gate. Then he continued as far as the upper room at the corner. ³²The other goldsmiths and merchants repaired the wall from that corner to the Sheep Gate.

Enemies Oppose the Rebuilding

4 ¹*Sanballat was very angry when he learned that we were rebuilding the wall. He flew into a rage and mocked the Jews, ²saying in front of his friends and the Samarian army officers, "What does this bunch of poor, feeble Jews think they're doing? Do they think they can build the wall in a single day by just offering a few sacrifices?* Do they actually think they can make something of stones from a rubbish heap—and charred ones at that?"

³Tobiah the Ammonite, who was standing beside him, remarked, "That stone wall would collapse if even a fox walked along the top of it!"

⁴Then I prayed, "Hear us, our God, for we are being mocked. May their scoffing fall back on their own

---

3:8 Or *They fortified Jerusalem up to the Broad Wall.* **3:13** Hebrew *1,000 cubits* [460 meters]. **3:15a** As in Syriac version; Hebrew reads *Shallun.* **3:15b** Hebrew *pool of Shelah,* another name for the pool of Siloam. **3:18** As in a few Hebrew manuscripts, some Greek manuscripts, and Syriac version (see also 3:24; 10:9); most Hebrew manuscripts read *Bavvai.* **4:1** Verses 4:1-6 are numbered 3:33-38 in Hebrew text. **4:2** The meaning of the Hebrew is uncertain.

3:11 The Tower of the Ovens on the western wall of the city might have been a place to bake bread or to burnish pottery (Jeremiah 19:1-2).

3:12 Shallum's daughters participated in repairing the walls. While the mention of women participating in rebuilding the walls is notable, we also have records from ancient Athens where the entire population, including women and children, were called upon to help rebuild the wall. We don't often see women specifically mentioned in this type of circumstance in the Bible, but we must remember that women were participating in the daily work of society.

Insight — STRONG HEADWINDS

The books of Ezra and Nehemiah describe how the returning Jewish exiles faced many obstacles as they attempted to rebuild their homeland. If it wasn't one thing, it was another.

Ezra

3:3	Returning exiles feel nervous	"The people were afraid of the local residents"
3:12	Elders make comparisons	"Many of the older priests, Levites, and other leaders who had seen the first Temple wept aloud when they saw the new Temple's foundation."
4:2	Neighbors try to help	"Let us build with you, for we worship your God."
4:4-5	Local residents intimidate	"The local residents tried to discourage and frighten the people of Judah to keep them from their work. They bribed agents to work against them."
4:12	The governor complains	"The king should know that the Jews who came here … are rebuilding this rebellious and evil city."
4:21-22	The king is persuaded	"Therefore, issue orders to have these men stop their work. That city must not be rebuilt except at my express command. Be diligent, and don't neglect this matter, for we must not permit the situation to harm the king's interests."
5:3	Another governor questions	"Who gave you permission to rebuild this Temple?"
9:2	Returning exiles establish ungodly homes	"The men of Israel have married women from these people and have taken them as wives for their sons. So the holy race has become polluted by these mixed marriages."

Nehemiah

Reference	Event	Quote
3:5	Some leaders won't get their hands dirty	[In a list of work crews:] "Next were the people from Tekoa, though their leaders refused to work with the construction supervisors."
4:2-3	Enemies make disparaging comments	"What does this bunch of poor, feeble Jews think they're doing?" … "That stone wall would collapse if even a fox walked along the top of it!"
4:10	The team becomes exhausted	"The people of Judah began to complain, 'The workers are getting tired, and there is so much rubble to be moved.'"
5:1	Internal dissension grows	"Some of the men and their wives raised a cry of protest against their fellow Jews."
6:6-7	Rumors spread	"There is a rumor among the surrounding nations, and Geshem tells me it is true, that you and the Jews are planning to rebel…. I suggest that you come and talk it over with me."
13:7-8	A priest welcomes the enemy	"When I arrived back in Jerusalem, I learned about Eliashib's evil deed in providing Tobiah with a room in the courtyards of the Temple of God. I became very upset."
13:15	The Sabbath is ignored	"I saw men of Judah treading out their winepresses on the Sabbath. They were also bringing in grain … to sell on the Sabbath."
13:23	Ungodly marriages are made	"I realized that some of the men of Judah had married women from Ashdod, Ammon, and Moab."

heads, and may they themselves become captives in a foreign land! ⁵Do not ignore their guilt. Do not blot out their sins, for they have provoked you to anger here in front of* the builders."

⁶At last the wall was completed to half its height around the entire city, for the people had worked with enthusiasm.

⁷*But when Sanballat and Tobiah and the Arabs, Ammonites, and Ashdodites heard that the work was going ahead and that the gaps in the wall of Jerusalem were being repaired, they were furious. ⁸They all made plans to come and fight against Jerusalem and throw us into confusion. ⁹But we prayed to our God and guarded the city day and night to protect ourselves.

¹⁰Then the people of Judah began to complain, "The workers are getting tired, and there is so much rubble to be moved. We will never be able to build the wall by ourselves."

¹¹Meanwhile, our enemies were saying, "Before they know what's happening, we will swoop down on them and kill them and end their work."

¹²The Jews who lived near the enemy came and told us again and again, "They will come from all directions and attack us!"* ¹³So I placed armed guards behind the lowest parts of the wall in the exposed areas. I stationed the people to stand guard by families, armed with swords, spears, and bows.

¹⁴Then as I looked over the situation, I called together the nobles and the rest of the people and said to them, "Don't be afraid of the enemy! Remember the Lord, who is great and glorious, and fight for your brothers, your sons, your daughters, your wives, and your homes!"

¹⁵When our enemies heard that we knew of their plans and that God had frustrated them, we all returned to our work on the wall. ¹⁶But from then on, only half my men worked while the other half stood guard with spears, shields, bows, and coats of mail. The leaders stationed themselves behind the people of Judah ¹⁷who were building the wall. The laborers carried on their work with one hand supporting their load and one hand holding a weapon. ¹⁸All the builders had a sword belted to their side. The trumpeter stayed with me to sound the alarm.

¹⁹Then I explained to the nobles and officials and all the people, "The work is very spread out, and we are widely separated from each other along the wall. ²⁰When you hear the blast of the trumpet, rush to wherever it is sounding. Then our God will fight for us!"

²¹We worked early and late, from sunrise to sunset. And half the men were always on guard. ²²I also told everyone living outside the walls to stay in Jerusalem. That way they and their servants could help with guard duty at night and work during the day. ²³During this time, none of us—not I, nor my relatives, nor my servants, nor the guards who were with me—ever took off our clothes. We carried our weapons with us at all times, even when we went for water.*

Nehemiah Defends the Oppressed

5 About this time some of the men and their wives raised a cry of protest against their fellow Jews. ²They were saying, "We have such large families. We need more food to survive."

³Others said, "We have mortgaged our fields, vineyards, and homes to get food during the famine."

⁴And others said, "We have had to borrow money on our fields and vineyards to pay our taxes. ⁵We belong to the same family as those who are wealthy, and our children are just like theirs. Yet we must sell our children into slavery just to get enough money to live. We have already sold some of our daughters, and we are helpless to do anything about it, for our fields and vineyards are already mortgaged to others."

⁶When I heard their complaints, I was very angry. ⁷After thinking it over, I spoke out against these nobles and officials. I told them, "You are hurting your own relatives by charging interest when they borrow money!" Then I called a public meeting to deal with the problem.

⁸At the meeting I said to them, "We are doing all we can to redeem our Jewish relatives who have had to sell themselves to pagan foreigners, but you are selling them back into slavery again. How often must we redeem them?" And they had nothing to say in their defense.

⁹Then I pressed further, "What you are doing is not right! Should you not walk in the fear of our God in order to avoid being mocked by enemy nations? ¹⁰I myself, as well as my brothers and my workers, have been lending the people money and grain, but now let us stop this business of charging interest. ¹¹You must restore their fields, vineyards, olive groves, and homes to them this very day. And repay the interest you charged when you lent them money, grain, new wine, and olive oil."

¹²They replied, "We will give back everything and demand nothing more from the people. We will do as you say." Then I called the priests and made the nobles and officials swear to do what they had promised.

¹³I shook out the folds of my robe and said, "If you fail to keep your promise, may God shake you like this from your homes and from your property!"

The whole assembly responded, "Amen," and they praised the Lord. And the people did as they had promised.

¹⁴For the entire twelve years that I was governor of Judah—from the twentieth year to the thirty-second year of the reign of King Artaxerxes*—neither I nor

---

4:5 Or *for they have thrown insults in the face of.* **4:7** Verses 4:7-23 are numbered 4:1-17 in Hebrew text. **4:12** The meaning of the Hebrew is uncertain. **4:23** Or *Each carried his weapon in his right hand.* Hebrew reads *Each his weapon the water.* The meaning of the Hebrew is uncertain. **5:14** That is, 445–433 B.C.

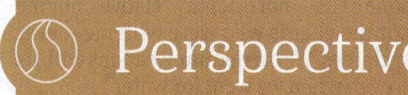

Perspective

How do we lead when we lack power?

SCRIPTURE CONNECTION:
NEHEMIAH 2:1-8; ESTHER 5:1-8

We may often think, "Oh, if I had that powerful position, I could do great things for God." But the Bible shows that God sometimes calls us to lead, even when we lack official power.

Nehemiah was cupbearer, a trusted and influential but not authoritative position. Esther was a queen, but as a royal wife, she had no inherent power over the empire's issues. Nehemiah knew the dangers of appearing sad before the king: He could lose his job or his life. Esther knew the dangers too: Her predecessor Vashti was banished because she disobeyed the king (Esther 1:10-22).

Both received word about their people's plight. Both turned to the Lord in prayer, and then both took appropriate action. Nehemiah asked for support, supplies, and a sabbatical; he returned to Jerusalem and rebuilt the walls. Esther acted within the expected protocol, offering the king two banquets.

God intervened for both, though they "led from below." And their actions salvaged God's people.

VIEWPOINTS

THEIRS: Esther: "I had no political power, but I took a risk and did what I could—provide a banquet for the king and make a request." Nehemiah: "I could be killed with the king's snap of a finger, but I prayed to God and sought the king's support."
MINE: "As a new program director, I needed to bring reconciliation to hostile groups. Without a powerful position, I had to ask questions and find suggestions that ultimately led to solutions."
YOURS: Was there a time when you felt compelled to bring change but lacked leadership power? How did you navigate that? What did you learn?

ELIZABETH GLANVILLE, PhD, is retired faculty from Fuller Theological Seminary, School of Mission and Theology. She is an international teacher on missions and leadership and chaplain for a local police department and her retirement community.

my officials drew on our official food allowance. ¹⁵The former governors, in contrast, had laid heavy burdens on the people, demanding a daily ration of food and wine, besides forty pieces* of silver. Even their assistants took advantage of the people. But because I feared God, I did not act that way.

¹⁶I also devoted myself to working on the wall and refused to acquire any land. And I required all my servants to spend time working on the wall. ¹⁷I asked for nothing, even though I regularly fed 150 Jewish officials at my table, besides all the visitors from other lands! ¹⁸The provisions I paid for each day included one ox, six choice sheep or goats, and a large number of poultry. And every ten days we needed a large supply of all kinds of wine. Yet I refused to claim the governor's food allowance because the people already carried a heavy burden.

¹⁹Remember, O my God, all that I have done for these people, and bless me for it.

Continued Opposition to Rebuilding

6 Sanballat, Tobiah, Geshem the Arab, and the rest of our enemies found out that I had finished rebuilding the wall and that no gaps remained—though we had not yet set up the doors in the gates. ²So Sanballat and Geshem sent a message asking me to meet them at one of the villages* in the plain of Ono.

But I realized they were plotting to harm me, ³so I replied by sending this message to them: "I am engaged in a great work, so I can't come. Why should I stop working to come and meet with you?"

⁴Four times they sent the same message, and each time I gave the same reply. ⁵The fifth time, Sanballat's servant came with an open letter in his hand, ⁶and this is what it said:

> "There is a rumor among the surrounding nations, and Geshem* tells me it is true, that you and the Jews are planning to rebel and that is why you are building the wall. According to his reports, you plan to be their king. ⁷He also reports that you have appointed prophets in Jerusalem to proclaim about you, 'Look! There is a king in Judah!'
>
> "You can be very sure that this report will get back to the king, so I suggest that you come and talk it over with me."

⁸I replied, "There is no truth in any part of your story. You are making up the whole thing."

⁹They were just trying to intimidate us, imagining that they could discourage us and stop the work. So I continued the work with even greater determination.*

5:15 Hebrew *40 shekels* [1 pound or 456 grams]. **6:2** As in Greek version; Hebrew reads *at Kephirim*. **6:6** Hebrew *Gashmu,* a variant spelling of Geshem. **6:9** As in Greek version; Hebrew reads *But now to strengthen my hands.*

¹⁰Later I went to visit Shemaiah son of Delaiah and grandson of Mehetabel, who was confined to his home. He said, "Let us meet together inside the Temple of God and bolt the doors shut. Your enemies are coming to kill you tonight."

¹¹But I replied, "Should someone in my position run from danger? Should someone in my position enter the Temple to save his life? No, I won't do it!" ¹²I realized that God had not spoken to him, but that he had uttered this prophecy against me because Tobiah and Sanballat had hired him. ¹³They were hoping to intimidate me and make me sin. Then they would be able to accuse and discredit me.

¹⁴Remember, O my God, all the evil things that Tobiah and Sanballat have done. And remember Noadiah the prophet and all the prophets like her who have tried to intimidate me.

The Builders Complete the Wall

¹⁵So on October 2* the wall was finished—just fifty-two days after we had begun. ¹⁶When our enemies and the surrounding nations heard about it, they were frightened and humiliated. They realized this work had been done with the help of our God.

¹⁷During those fifty-two days, many letters went back and forth between Tobiah and the nobles of Judah. ¹⁸For many in Judah had sworn allegiance to him because his father-in-law was Shecaniah son of Arah, and his son Jehohanan was married to the daughter of Meshullam son of Berekiah. ¹⁹They kept telling me about Tobiah's good deeds, and then they told him everything I said. And Tobiah kept sending threatening letters to intimidate me.

7 After the wall was finished and I had set up the doors in the gates, the gatekeepers, singers, and Levites were appointed. ²I gave the responsibility of governing Jerusalem to my brother Hanani, along with Hananiah, the commander of the fortress, for he was a faithful man who feared God more than most. ³I said to them, "Do not leave the gates open during the hottest part of the day.* And even while the gatekeepers are on duty, have them shut and bar the doors. Appoint the residents of Jerusalem to act as guards, everyone on a regular watch. Some will serve at sentry posts and some in front of their own homes."

Nehemiah Registers the People

⁴At that time the city was large and spacious, but the population was small, and none of the houses had been rebuilt. ⁵So my God gave me the idea to call together all the nobles and leaders of the city, along with the ordinary citizens, for registration. I had found the genealogical record of those who had first returned to Judah. This is what was written there:

⁶Here is the list of the Jewish exiles of the provinces who returned from their captivity. King Nebuchadnezzar had deported them to Babylon, but now they returned to Jerusalem and the other towns in Judah where they originally lived. ⁷Their leaders were Zerubbabel, Jeshua, Nehemiah, Seraiah,* Reelaiah,* Nahamani, Mordecai, Bilshan, Mispar,* Bigvai, Rehum,* and Baanah.

This is the number of the men of Israel who returned from exile:

⁸ The family of Parosh 2,172
⁹ The family of Shephatiah................... 372
¹⁰ The family of Arah........................... 652
¹¹ The family of Pahath-moab
 (descendants of Jeshua and Joab) 2,818
¹² The family of Elam 1,254
¹³ The family of Zattu 845
¹⁴ The family of Zaccai 760
¹⁵ The family of Bani*.......................... 648
¹⁶ The family of Bebai 628
¹⁷ The family of Azgad 2,322
¹⁸ The family of Adonikam 667
¹⁹ The family of Bigvai 2,067
²⁰ The family of Adin........................... 655
²¹ The family of Ater
 (descendants of Hezekiah)................ 98
²² The family of Hashum....................... 328
²³ The family of Bezai 324
²⁴ The family of Jorah*....................... 112
²⁵ The family of Gibbar*......................... 95
²⁶ The people of Bethlehem and Netophah...188

6:15 Hebrew *on the twenty-fifth day of the month Elul*, of the ancient Hebrew lunar calendar. This day was October 2, 445 B.C.; also see note on 1:1. **7:3** Or *Keep the gates of Jerusalem closed until the sun is hot.* **7:7a** As in parallel text at Ezra 2:2; Hebrew reads *Azariah*. **7:7b** As in parallel text at Ezra 2:2; Hebrew reads *Raamiah*. **7:7c** As in parallel text at Ezra 2:2; Hebrew reads *Mispereth*. **7:7d** As in parallel text at Ezra 2:2; Hebrew reads *Nehum*. **7:15** As in parallel text at Ezra 2:10; Hebrew reads *Binnui*. **7:24** As in parallel text at Ezra 2:18; Hebrew reads *Hariph*. **7:25** As in parallel text at Ezra 2:20; Hebrew reads *Gibeon*.

6:14 Noadiah was a prophet who was a woman and most likely led the prophets who opposed Nehemiah, probably opposing his rebuilding the walls. It is also possible that this group of prophets disagreed on other issues, such as Nehemiah's decree to send away the foreign wives and children. It is clear from Nehemiah's prayer that this group of prophets was trying to threaten him and he viewed them as false prophets.
7:1 The actual dedication of the wall is reported in 12:27-43. The Levites usually assisted with caring for the Temple area, including guarding its gates.
7:3 The gatekeepers were apparently supposed to close the gates during the time in the afternoon when people were resting and not prepared to defend the city from attack. Elsewhere, similar language refers to the portion of the day when the sun is the hottest and people retreat inside (Genesis 18:1; 2 Samuel 4:5).

²⁷ The people of Anathoth 128
²⁸ The people of Beth-azmaveth 42
²⁹ The people of Kiriath-jearim, Kephirah,
    and Beeroth.............................. 743
³⁰ The people of Ramah and Geba 621
³¹ The people of Micmash 122
³² The people of Bethel and Ai 123
³³ The people of West Nebo* 52
³⁴ The citizens of West Elam* 1,254
³⁵ The citizens of Harim..................... 320
³⁶ The citizens of Jericho.................... 345
³⁷ The citizens of Lod, Hadid, and Ono 721
³⁸ The citizens of Senaah.................. 3,930

³⁹These are the priests who returned from exile:
    The family of Jedaiah (through the line of
      Jeshua).................................973
⁴⁰ The family of Immer..................... 1,052
⁴¹ The family of Pashhur 1,247
⁴² The family of Harim 1,017

⁴³These are the Levites who returned from exile:
    The families of Jeshua and Kadmiel
      (descendants of Hodaviah*) 74
⁴⁴ The singers of the family of Asaph......... 148
⁴⁵ The gatekeepers of the families of Shallum,
    Ater, Talmon, Akkub, Hatita, and Shobai 138

⁴⁶The descendants of the following Temple
servants returned from exile:
    Ziha, Hasupha, Tabbaoth,
⁴⁷ Keros, Siaha,* Padon,
⁴⁸ Lebanah, Hagabah, Shalmai,
⁴⁹ Hanan, Giddel, Gahar,
⁵⁰ Reaiah, Rezin, Nekoda,
⁵¹ Gazzam, Uzza, Paseah,
⁵² Besai, Meunim, Nephusim,*
⁵³ Bakbuk, Hakupha, Harhur,
⁵⁴ Bazluth,* Mehida, Harsha,
⁵⁵ Barkos, Sisera, Temah,
⁵⁶ Neziah, and Hatipha.

⁵⁷The descendants of these servants of King
Solomon returned from exile:
    Sotai, Hassophereth, Peruda,*
⁵⁸ Jaalah,* Darkon, Giddel,
⁵⁹ Shephatiah, Hattil, Pokereth-hazzebaim, and
    Ami.*

⁶⁰In all, the Temple servants and the descendants of Solomon's servants numbered 392.

⁶¹Another group returned at this time from the towns of Tel-melah, Tel-harsha, Kerub, Addan,* and Immer. However, they could not prove that they or their families were descendants of Israel. ⁶²This group included the families of Delaiah, Tobiah, and Nekoda—a total of 642 people.

⁶³Three families of priests—Hobaiah, Hakkoz, and Barzillai—also returned. (This Barzillai had married a woman who was a descendant of Barzillai of Gilead, and he had taken her family name.) ⁶⁴They searched for their names in the genealogical records, but they were not found, so they were disqualified from serving as priests. ⁶⁵The governor told them not to eat the priests' share of food from the sacrifices until a priest could consult the LORD about the matter by using the Urim and Thummim—the sacred lots.

⁶⁶So a total of 42,360 people returned to Judah, ⁶⁷in addition to 7,337 servants and 245 singers, both men and women. ⁶⁸They took with them 736 horses, 245 mules,* ⁶⁹435 camels, and 6,720 donkeys.

⁷⁰Some of the family leaders gave gifts for the work. The governor gave to the treasury 1,000 gold coins,* 50 gold basins, and 530 robes for the priests. ⁷¹The other leaders gave to the treasury a total of 20,000 gold coins* and some 2,750 pounds* of silver for the work. ⁷²The rest of the people gave 20,000 gold coins, about 2,500 pounds* of silver, and 67 robes for the priests.

⁷³So the priests, the Levites, the gatekeepers, the singers, the Temple servants, and some of the common people settled near Jerusalem. The rest of the people returned to their own towns throughout Israel.

Ezra Reads the Law

8 In October,* when the Israelites had settled in their towns, ⁸:¹all the people assembled with a unified purpose at the square just inside the Water Gate. They asked Ezra the scribe to bring out the Book of the Law of Moses, which the LORD had given for Israel to obey.

7:33 Or *of the other Nebo.* **7:34** Or *of the other Elam.* **7:43** As in parallel text at Ezra 2:40; Hebrew reads *Hodevah.* **7:47** As in parallel text at Ezra 2:44; Hebrew reads *Sia.* **7:52** As in parallel text at Ezra 2:50; Hebrew reads *Nephushesim.* **7:54** As in parallel text at Ezra 2:52; Hebrew reads *Bazlith.* **7:57** As in parallel text at Ezra 2:55; Hebrew reads *Sotai, Sophereth, Perida.* **7:58** As in parallel text at Ezra 2:56; Hebrew reads *Jaala.* **7:59** As in parallel text at Ezra 2:57; Hebrew reads *Amon.* **7:61** As in parallel text at Ezra 2:59; Hebrew reads *Addon.* **7:68** As in some Hebrew manuscripts (see also Ezra 2:66); most Hebrew manuscripts lack this verse. Verses 7:69-73 are numbered 7:68-72 in Hebrew text. **7:70** Hebrew *1,000 darics of gold,* about 19 pounds or 8.6 kilograms in weight. **7:71a** Hebrew *20,000 darics of gold,* about 375 pounds or 170 kilograms in weight; also in 7:72. **7:71b** Hebrew *2,200 minas* [1,300 kilograms]. **7:72** Hebrew *2,000 minas* [1,200 kilograms]. **7:73** Hebrew *In the seventh month.* This month of the ancient Hebrew lunar calendar occurred within the months of October and November 445 B.C.

8:1-12 The public reading of the Book of the Law of Moses involved everyone: men, women, and children. The people gathered to listen and to celebrate. Hearing the words of the Lord prompted the people to weep. Their hearts were ready to receive instruction. When God's Word is read and studied, it often prompts us to respond from within. Similarly, how might we put ourselves in situations where we hear God's Word read aloud? And how can we create times when we read it with or to others as well?

²So on October 8* Ezra the priest brought the Book of the Law before the assembly, which included the men and women and all the children old enough to understand. ³He faced the square just inside the Water Gate from early morning until noon and read aloud to everyone who could understand. All the people listened closely to the Book of the Law.

⁴Ezra the scribe stood on a high wooden platform that had been made for the occasion. To his right stood Mattithiah, Shema, Anaiah, Uriah, Hilkiah, and Maaseiah. To his left stood Pedaiah, Mishael, Malkijah, Hashum, Hashbaddanah, Zechariah, and Meshullam. ⁵Ezra stood on the platform in full view of all the people. When they saw him open the book, they all rose to their feet.

⁶Then Ezra praised the LORD, the great God, and all the people chanted, "Amen! Amen!" as they lifted their hands. Then they bowed down and worshiped the LORD with their faces to the ground.

⁷The Levites—Jeshua, Bani, Sherebiah, Jamin, Akkub, Shabbethai, Hodiah, Maaseiah, Kelita, Azariah, Jozabad, Hanan, and Pelaiah—then instructed the people in the Law while everyone remained in their places. ⁸They read from the Book of the Law of God and clearly explained the meaning of what was being read, helping the people understand each passage.

⁹Then Nehemiah the governor, Ezra the priest and scribe, and the Levites who were interpreting for the people said to them, "Don't mourn or weep on such a day as this! For today is a sacred day before the LORD your God." For the people had all been weeping as they listened to the words of the Law.

¹⁰And Nehemiah* continued, "Go and celebrate with a feast of rich foods and sweet drinks, and share gifts of food with people who have nothing prepared. This is a sacred day before our Lord. Don't be dejected and sad, for the joy of the LORD is your strength!"

¹¹And the Levites, too, quieted the people, telling them, "Hush! Don't weep! For this is a sacred day." ¹²So the people went away to eat and drink at a festive meal, to share gifts of food, and to celebrate with great joy because they had heard God's words and understood them.

The Festival of Shelters

¹³On October 9* the family leaders of all the people, together with the priests and Levites, met with Ezra the scribe to go over the Law in greater detail. ¹⁴As they studied the Law, they discovered that the LORD had commanded through Moses that the Israelites should live in shelters during the festival to be held that month.* ¹⁵He had said that a proclamation should be made throughout their towns and in Jerusalem, telling the people to go to the hills to get branches from olive, wild olive,* myrtle, palm, and other leafy trees. They were to use these branches to make shelters in which they would live during the festival, as prescribed in the Law.

¹⁶So the people went out and cut branches and used them to build shelters on the roofs of their houses, in their courtyards, in the courtyards of God's Temple, or in the squares just inside the Water Gate and the Ephraim Gate. ¹⁷So everyone who had returned from captivity lived in these shelters during the festival, and they were all filled with great joy! The Israelites had not celebrated like this since the days of Joshua* son of Nun.

¹⁸Ezra read from the Book of the Law of God on each of the seven days of the festival. Then on the eighth day they held a solemn assembly, as was required by law.

The People Confess Their Sins

9 On October 31* the people assembled again, and this time they fasted and dressed in burlap and sprinkled dust on their heads. ²Those of Israelite descent separated themselves from all foreigners as they confessed their own sins and the sins of their ancestors. ³They remained standing in place for three hours* while the Book of the Law of the LORD their God was read aloud to them. Then for three more hours they confessed their sins and worshiped the LORD their God. ⁴The Levites—Jeshua, Bani, Kadmiel, Shebaniah, Bunni, Sherebiah, Bani, and Kenani—stood on the stairway of the Levites and cried out to the LORD their God with loud voices.

8:2 Hebrew *on the first day of the seventh month,* of the ancient Hebrew lunar calendar. This day was October 8, 445 B.C.; also see note on 1:1. 8:10 Hebrew *he.* 8:13 Hebrew *On the second day,* of the seventh month of the ancient Hebrew lunar calendar. This day was October 9, 445 B.C.; also see notes on 1:1 and 8:2. 8:14 Hebrew *in the seventh month.* This month of the ancient Hebrew lunar calendar usually occurs within the months of September and October. See Lev 23:39-43. 8:15 Or *pine;* Hebrew reads *oil tree.* 8:17 Hebrew *Jeshua,* a variant spelling of Joshua. 9:1 Hebrew *On the twenty-fourth day of that same month,* the seventh month of the ancient Hebrew lunar calendar. This day was October 31, 445 B.C.; also see notes on 1:1 and 8:2. 9:3 Hebrew *for a quarter of a day.*

8:14-17 The Festival of Shelters was a seven-day festival that involved living outdoors, almost like the community camping together. The people were to celebrate this festival every year, remembering how the Lord had rescued Israel from Egypt and how they had spent their time in the wilderness, living in tents (Leviticus 23:43). In the Jewish way of thinking, remembering through festivals involves mental recall and physical participation, such as constructing the family's shelter together and moving their cooking, clothes, and selves to another spot for a week. Celebrating is a powerful way to remember how God has been with his people and rescued them. How has God been with you in critical moments in your story? Are there places or seasons that you want to remember and could celebrate in some tangible way?

WHAT THE BIBLE SAYS ABOUT

Falling Short and Favor

Falling Short Doesn't Get the Final Word

We are sure [that we will live again] because Christ was raised from the dead, and he will never die again. Death no longer has any power over him. When he died, he died once to break the power of sin. But now that he lives, he lives for the glory of God. So you also should consider yourselves to be dead to the power of sin and alive to God through Christ Jesus. **ROMANS 6:9-11**

God Turns Falling Short to Favor

Even though we were dead because of our sins, he gave us life when he raised Christ from the dead. (It is only by God's grace that you have been saved!) **EPHESIANS 2:5**

God saved us and called us to live a holy life. He did this, not because we deserved it, but because that was his plan from before the beginning of time—to show us his grace through Christ Jesus. **2 TIMOTHY 1:9**

God our Savior... saved us, not because of the righteous things we had done, but because of his mercy. He washed away our sins, giving us a new birth and new life through the Holy Spirit. **TITUS 3:4-5**

Whatever I am now, it is all because God poured out his special favor on me—and not without results. **1 CORINTHIANS 15:10**

> God saved us and called us to live a holy life.

We've All Fallen Short

Not a single person on earth is always good and never sins. **ECCLESIASTES 7:20**

No one is truly wise;
  no one is seeking God. **ROMANS 3:11**

⁵Then the leaders of the Levites—Jeshua, Kadmiel, Bani, Hashabneiah, Sherebiah, Hodiah, Shebaniah, and Pethahiah—called out to the people: "Stand up and praise the LORD your God, for he lives from everlasting to everlasting!" Then they prayed:

"May your glorious name be praised! May it be exalted above all blessing and praise!

⁶"You alone are the LORD. You made the skies and the heavens and all the stars. You made the earth and the seas and everything in them. You preserve them all, and the angels of heaven worship you.

⁷"You are the LORD God, who chose Abram and brought him from Ur of the Chaldeans and renamed him Abraham. ⁸When he had proved himself faithful, you made a covenant with him to give him and his descendants the land of the Canaanites, Hittites, Amorites, Perizzites, Jebusites, and Girgashites. And you have done what you promised, for you are always true to your word.

⁹"You saw the misery of our ancestors in Egypt, and you heard their cries from beside the Red Sea.* ¹⁰You displayed miraculous signs and wonders against Pharaoh, his officials, and all his people, for you knew how arrogantly they were treating our ancestors. You have a glorious reputation that has never been forgotten. ¹¹You divided the sea for your people so they could walk through on dry land! And then you hurled their enemies into the depths of the sea. They sank like stones beneath the mighty waters. ¹²You led our ancestors by a pillar of cloud during the day and a pillar of fire at night so that they could find their way.

¹³"You came down at Mount Sinai and spoke to them from heaven. You gave them regulations and instructions that were just, and decrees and commands that were good. ¹⁴You instructed them concerning your holy Sabbath. And you commanded them, through Moses your servant, to obey all your commands, decrees, and instructions.

¹⁵"You gave them bread from heaven when they were hungry and water from the rock when they were thirsty. You commanded them to go and take possession of the land you had sworn to give them.

¹⁶"But our ancestors were proud and stubborn, and they paid no attention to your commands. ¹⁷They refused to obey and did not remember the miracles you had done for them. Instead, they became stubborn and appointed a leader to take them back to their slavery in Egypt.* But you are a God of forgiveness, gracious and merciful, slow to become angry, and rich in unfailing love. You did not abandon them, ¹⁸even when they made an idol shaped like a calf and said, 'This is your god who brought you out of Egypt!' They committed terrible blasphemies.

¹⁹"But in your great mercy you did not abandon them to die in the wilderness. The pillar of cloud still led them forward by day, and the pillar of fire showed them the way through the night. ²⁰You sent your good Spirit to instruct them, and you did not stop giving them manna from heaven or water for their thirst. ²¹For forty years you sustained them in the wilderness, and they lacked nothing. Their clothes did not wear out, and their feet did not swell!

²²"Then you helped our ancestors conquer kingdoms and nations, and you placed your people in every corner of the land.* They took over the land of King Sihon of Heshbon and the land of King Og of Bashan. ²³You made their descendants as numerous as the stars in the sky and brought them into the land you had promised to their ancestors.

²⁴"They went in and took possession of the land. You subdued whole nations before them. Even the Canaanites, who inhabited the land, were powerless! Your people could deal with these nations and their kings as they pleased. ²⁵Our ancestors captured fortified cities and fertile land. They took over houses full of good things, with cisterns already dug and vineyards and olive groves and fruit trees in abundance. So they ate until they were full and grew fat and enjoyed themselves in all your blessings.

²⁶"But despite all this, they were disobedient and rebelled against you. They turned their backs on your Law, they killed your prophets who warned them to return to you, and they committed terrible blasphemies. ²⁷So you handed them over to their enemies, who made them suffer. But in their time of trouble they cried to you, and you heard them from heaven. In your great mercy, you sent them liberators who rescued them from their enemies.

9:9 Hebrew *sea of reeds*. **9:17** As in Greek version; Hebrew reads *in their rebellion*. **9:22** The meaning of the Hebrew is uncertain.

9:9 God had paid attention to his people's misery under foreign domination (Exodus 2:23-25; 3:7; 14:10-14), which was analogous to their present situation (Nehemiah 9:32-37).
9:12-21 This prayer reminded the people of God's miraculous direction of Israel in the wilderness (Exodus 13:21-22), his personal appearance at Mount Sinai to reveal his covenant laws through Moses (see Exodus 19–20), and his faithfulness in providing bread and water (see Exodus 16:4; 17:1-6). Despite all of that, Israel's ancestors had been proud and stubborn and refused to obey (see Exodus 32; Numbers 14:4). Yet in his grace, God remained faithful and compassionate (see Exodus 34:6) and provided his Spirit to direct and teach them (see Exodus 33:2; Numbers 11:17).

28"But as soon as they were at peace, your people again committed evil in your sight, and once more you let their enemies conquer them. Yet whenever your people turned and cried to you again for help, you listened once more from heaven. In your wonderful mercy, you rescued them many times!

29"You warned them to return to your Law, but they became proud and obstinate and disobeyed your commands. They did not follow your regulations, by which people will find life if only they obey. They stubbornly turned their backs on you and refused to listen. 30In your love, you were patient with them for many years. You sent your Spirit, who warned them through the prophets. But still they wouldn't listen! So once again you allowed the peoples of the land to conquer them. 31But in your great mercy, you did not destroy them completely or abandon them forever. What a gracious and merciful God you are!

32"And now, our God, the great and mighty and awesome God, who keeps his covenant of unfailing love, do not let all the hardships we have suffered seem insignificant to you. Great trouble has come upon us and upon our kings and leaders and priests and prophets and ancestors—all of your people—from the days when the kings of Assyria first triumphed over us until now. 33Every time you punished us you were being just. We have sinned greatly, and you gave us only what we deserved. 34Our kings, leaders, priests, and ancestors did not obey your Law or listen to the warnings in your commands and laws. 35Even while they had their own kingdom, they did not serve you, though you showered your goodness on them. You gave them a large, fertile land, but they refused to turn from their wickedness.

36"So now today we are slaves in the land of plenty that you gave our ancestors for their enjoyment! We are slaves here in this good land. 37The lush produce of this land piles up in the hands of the kings whom you have set over us because of our sins. They have power over us and our livestock. We serve them at their pleasure, and we are in great misery."

The People Agree to Obey

38*The people responded, "In view of all this,* we are making a solemn promise and putting it in writing. On this sealed document are the names of our leaders and Levites and priests."

10 1*The document was ratified and sealed with the following names:

The governor:
  Nehemiah son of Hacaliah, and also Zedekiah.

2The following priests:
  Seraiah, Azariah, Jeremiah, 3Pashhur, Amariah, Malkijah, 4Hattush, Shebaniah, Malluch, 5Harim, Meremoth, Obadiah, 6Daniel, Ginnethon, Baruch, 7Meshullam, Abijah, Mijamin, 8Maaziah, Bilgai, and Shemaiah. These were the priests.
9The following Levites:
  Jeshua son of Azaniah, Binnui from the family of Henadad, Kadmiel, 10and their fellow Levites: Shebaniah, Hodiah, Kelita, Pelaiah, Hanan, 11Mica, Rehob, Hashabiah, 12Zaccur, Sherebiah, Shebaniah, 13Hodiah, Bani, and Beninu.
14The following leaders:
  Parosh, Pahath-moab, Elam, Zattu, Bani, 15Bunni, Azgad, Bebai, 16Adonijah, Bigvai, Adin, 17Ater, Hezekiah, Azzur, 18Hodiah, Hashum, Bezai, 19Hariph, Anathoth, Nebai, 20Magpiash, Meshullam, Hezir, 21Meshezabel, Zadok, Jaddua, 22Pelatiah, Hanan, Anaiah, 23Hoshea, Hananiah, Hasshub, 24Hallohesh, Pilha, Shobek, 25Rehum, Hashabnah, Maaseiah, 26Ahiah, Hanan, Anan, 27Malluch, Harim, and Baanah.

The Vow of the People

28Then the rest of the people—the priests, Levites, gatekeepers, singers, Temple servants, and all who had separated themselves from the pagan people of the land in order to obey the Law of God, together with their wives, sons, daughters, and all who were old enough to understand—29joined their leaders and bound themselves with an oath. They swore a curse on themselves if they failed to obey the Law of God as issued by his servant Moses. They solemnly promised to carefully follow all the commands, regulations, and decrees of the LORD our Lord:

> 30"We promise not to let our daughters marry the pagan people of the land, and not to let our sons marry their daughters.
>
> 31"We also promise that if the people of the land should bring any merchandise or grain to be sold on the Sabbath or on any other holy day, we will refuse to buy it. Every seventh year we will let our land rest, and we will cancel all debts owed to us.
>
> 32"In addition, we promise to obey the command to pay the annual Temple tax of one-eighth of an ounce of silver* for the care of the Temple of our God. 33This will provide for the Bread of the Presence; for the regular grain offerings and burnt offerings; for the offerings on the Sabbaths, the new moon celebrations, and the annual festivals; for the holy offerings; and for the sin offerings to make atonement for Israel. It will provide for everything necessary for the work of the Temple of our God.
>
> 34"We have cast sacred lots to determine when—at regular times each year—the families

---

9:38a Verse 9:38 is numbered 10:1 in Hebrew text.   9:38b Or *In spite of all this.*   10:1 Verses 10:1-39 are numbered 10:2-40 in Hebrew text.   10:32 Hebrew *tax of ⅓ of a shekel* [4 grams].

of the priests, Levites, and the common people should bring wood to God's Temple to be burned on the altar of the LORD our God, as is written in the Law.

35 "We promise to bring the first part of every harvest to the LORD's Temple year after year—whether it be a crop from the soil or from our fruit trees. 36 We agree to give God our oldest sons and the firstborn of all our herds and flocks, as prescribed in the Law. We will present them to the priests who minister in the Temple of our God. 37 We will store the produce in the storerooms of the Temple of our God. We will bring the best of our flour and other grain offerings, the best of our fruit, and the best of our new wine and olive oil. And we promise to bring to the Levites a tenth of everything our land produces, for it is the Levites who collect the tithes in all our rural towns.

38 "A priest—a descendant of Aaron—will be with the Levites as they receive these tithes. And a tenth of all that is collected as tithes will be delivered by the Levites to the Temple of our God and placed in the storerooms. 39 The people and the Levites must bring these offerings of grain, new wine, and olive oil to the storerooms and place them in the sacred containers near the ministering priests, the gatekeepers, and the singers.

"We promise together not to neglect the Temple of our God."

The People Occupy Jerusalem

11 The leaders of the people were living in Jerusalem, the holy city. A tenth of the people from the other towns of Judah and Benjamin were chosen by sacred lots to live there, too, while the rest stayed where they were. 2 And the people commended everyone who volunteered to resettle in Jerusalem.

3 Here is a list of the names of the provincial officials who came to live in Jerusalem. (Most of the people, priests, Levites, Temple servants, and descendants of Solomon's servants continued to live in their own homes in the various towns of Judah, 4 but some of the people from Judah and Benjamin resettled in Jerusalem.)

From the tribe of Judah:
Athaiah son of Uzziah, son of Zechariah, son of Amariah, son of Shephatiah, son of Mahalalel, of the family of Perez. 5 Also Maaseiah son of Baruch, son of Col-hozeh, son of Hazaiah, son of Adaiah, son of Joiarib, son of Zechariah, of the family of Shelah.* 6 There were 468 descendants of Perez who lived in Jerusalem—all outstanding men.

7 From the tribe of Benjamin:
Sallu son of Meshullam, son of Joed, son of Pedaiah, son of Kolaiah, son of Maaseiah, son of Ithiel, son of Jeshaiah. 8 After him were Gabbai and Sallai and a total of 928 relatives. 9 Their chief officer was Joel son of Zicri, who was assisted by Judah son of Hassenuah, second-in-command over the city.

10 From the priests:
Jedaiah son of Joiarib; Jakin; 11 and Seraiah son of Hilkiah, son of Meshullam, son of Zadok, son of Meraioth, son of Ahitub, the supervisor of the Temple of God. 12 Also 822 of their associates, who worked at the Temple. Also Adaiah son of Jeroham, son of Pelaliah, son of Amzi, son of Zechariah, son of Pashhur, son of Malkijah, 13 along with 242 of his associates, who were heads of their families. Also Amashsai son of Azarel, son of Ahzai, son of Meshillemoth, son of Immer, 14 and 128 of his* outstanding associates. Their chief officer was Zabdiel son of Haggedolim.

15 From the Levites:
Shemaiah son of Hasshub, son of Azrikam, son of Hashabiah, son of Bunni. 16 Also Shabbethai and Jozabad, who were in charge of the work outside the Temple of God. 17 Also Mattaniah son of Mica, son of Zabdi, a descendant of Asaph, who led in thanksgiving and prayer. Also Bakbukiah, who was Mattaniah's assistant, and Abda son of Shammua, son of Galal, son of Jeduthun. 18 In all, there were 284 Levites in the holy city.

19 From the gatekeepers:
Akkub, Talmon, and 172 of their associates, who guarded the gates.

20 The other priests, Levites, and the rest of the Israelites lived wherever their family inheritance was located in any of the towns of Judah. 21 The Temple servants, however, whose leaders were Ziha and Gishpa, all lived on the hill of Ophel.

22 The chief officer of the Levites in Jerusalem was Uzzi son of Bani, son of Hashabiah, son of Mattaniah, son of Mica, a descendant of Asaph, whose family served as singers at God's Temple. 23 Their daily responsibilities were carried out according to the terms of a royal command.

24 Pethahiah son of Meshezabel, a descendant of Zerah son of Judah, was the royal adviser in all matters of public administration.

25 As for the surrounding villages with their open fields, some of the people of Judah lived in Kiriath-arba with its settlements, Dibon with its settlements, and Jekabzeel with its villages. 26 They also lived in Jeshua, Moladah, Beth-pelet, 27 Hazar-shual, Beer-sheba with its settlements, 28 Ziklag, and Meconah with its settlements. 29 They also lived in En-rimmon, Zorah, Jarmuth, 30 Zanoah, and Adullam with their surrounding villages. They also lived in Lachish with

---

11:5 Hebrew *son of the Shilonite*. 11:14 As in Greek version; Hebrew reads *their*.

its nearby fields and Azekah with its surrounding villages. So the people of Judah were living all the way from Beersheba in the south to the valley of Hinnom.

31 Some of the people of Benjamin lived at Geba, Micmash, Aija, and Bethel with its settlements. 32 They also lived in Anathoth, Nob, Ananiah, 33 Hazor, Ramah, Gittaim, 34 Hadid, Zeboim, Neballat, 35 Lod, Ono, and the Valley of Craftsmen.* 36 Some of the Levites who lived in Judah were sent to live with the tribe of Benjamin.

A History of the Priests and Levites

12 Here is the list of the priests and Levites who returned with Zerubbabel son of Shealtiel and Jeshua the high priest:

Seraiah, Jeremiah, Ezra,
2 Amariah, Malluch, Hattush,
3 Shecaniah, Harim,* Meremoth,
4 Iddo, Ginnethon,* Abijah,
5 Miniamin, Moadiah,* Bilgah,
6 Shemaiah, Joiarib, Jedaiah,
7 Sallu, Amok, Hilkiah, and Jedaiah.

These were the leaders of the priests and their associates in the days of Jeshua.

8 The Levites who returned with them were Jeshua, Binnui, Kadmiel, Sherebiah, Judah, and Mattaniah, who with his associates was in charge of the songs of thanksgiving. 9 Their associates, Bakbukiah and Unni, stood opposite them during the service.

10 Jeshua the high priest was the father of Joiakim.
Joiakim was the father of Eliashib.
Eliashib was the father of Joiada.
11 Joiada was the father of Johanan.*
Johanan was the father of Jaddua.

12 Now when Joiakim was high priest, the family leaders of the priests were as follows:

Meraiah was leader of the family of Seraiah.
Hananiah was leader of the family of Jeremiah.
13 Meshullam was leader of the family of Ezra.
Jehohanan was leader of the family of Amariah.
14 Jonathan was leader of the family of Malluch.*
Joseph was leader of the family of Shecaniah.*
15 Adna was leader of the family of Harim.
Helkai was leader of the family of Meremoth.*
16 Zechariah was leader of the family of Iddo.
Meshullam was leader of the family of Ginnethon.
17 Zicri was leader of the family of Abijah.
There was also a* leader of the family of Miniamin.
Piltai was leader of the family of Moadiah.
18 Shammua was leader of the family of Bilgah.
Jehonathan was leader of the family of Shemaiah.
19 Mattenai was leader of the family of Joiarib.
Uzzi was leader of the family of Jedaiah.
20 Kallai was leader of the family of Sallu.*
Eber was leader of the family of Amok.
21 Hashabiah was leader of the family of Hilkiah.
Nethanel was leader of the family of Jedaiah.

22 A record of the Levite families was kept during the years when Eliashib, Joiada, Johanan, and Jaddua served as high priest. Another record of the priests was kept during the reign of Darius the Persian.* 23 A record of the heads of the Levite families was kept in The Book of History down to the days of Johanan, the grandson* of Eliashib.

24 These were the family leaders of the Levites: Hashabiah, Sherebiah, Jeshua, Binnui,* Kadmiel, and other associates, who stood opposite them during the ceremonies of praise and thanksgiving, one section responding to the other, as commanded by David, the man of God. 25 This included Mattaniah, Bakbukiah, and Obadiah.

Meshullam, Talmon, and Akkub were the gatekeepers in charge of the storerooms at the gates. 26 These all served in the days of Joiakim son of Jeshua, son of Jehozadak,* and in the days of Nehemiah the governor and of Ezra the priest and scribe.

Dedication of Jerusalem's Wall

27 For the dedication of the new wall of Jerusalem, the Levites throughout the land were asked to come to Jerusalem to assist in the ceremonies. They were to take part in the joyous occasion with their songs of

---

11:35 Or *and Ge-harashim.* **12:3** Hebrew *Rehum;* compare 7:42; 12:15; Ezra 2:39. **12:4** As in some Hebrew manuscripts and Latin Vulgate (see also 12:16); most Hebrew manuscripts read *Ginnethoi.* **12:5** Hebrew *Mijamin, Maadiah;* compare 12:17. **12:11** Hebrew *Jonathan;* compare 12:22. **12:14a** As in Greek version (see also 10:4; 12:2); Hebrew reads *Malluchi.* **12:14b** As in many Hebrew manuscripts, some Greek manuscripts, and Syriac version (see also 12:3); most Hebrew manuscripts read *Shebaniah.* **12:15** As in some Greek manuscripts (see also 12:3); Hebrew reads *Meraioth.* **12:17** Hebrew lacks the name of this family leader. **12:20** Hebrew *Sallai;* compare 12:7. **12:22** *Darius the Persian* is probably Darius II, who reigned 423–404 B.C., or possibly Darius III, who reigned 336–331 B.C. **12:23** Hebrew *descendant;* compare 12:10-11. **12:24** Hebrew *son of* (i.e., *ben*), which should probably be read here as the proper name Binnui; compare Ezra 3:9 and the note there. **12:26** Hebrew *Jozadak,* a variant spelling of Jehozadak.

12:1-9 Only those who could prove their priestly lineage could serve at the Temple, so it was important to maintain an accurate genealogical record of these families (see Ezra 2:36-63).

12:10-11 Joiakim probably served in the early years of Ezra's service. Eliashib and Joiada served during Nehemiah's time (3:1; 13:4, 28). An Aramaic papyrus document from a Jewish colony that settled in Elephantine, Egypt (about 410 BC), and Josephus (*The Antiquities of the Jews,* book 11, chapter 5, paragraph 4, AD 93) both mention Johanan serving after Nehemiah's time.

thanksgiving and with the music of cymbals, harps, and lyres. ²⁸The singers were brought together from the region around Jerusalem and from the villages of the Netophathites. ²⁹They also came from Beth-gilgal and the rural areas near Geba and Azmaveth, for the singers had built their own settlements around Jerusalem. ³⁰The priests and Levites first purified themselves; then they purified the people, the gates, and the wall.

³¹I led the leaders of Judah to the top of the wall and organized two large choirs to give thanks. One of the choirs proceeded southward* along the top of the wall to the Dung Gate. ³²Hoshaiah and half the leaders of Judah followed them, ³³along with Azariah, Ezra, Meshullam, ³⁴Judah, Benjamin, Shemaiah, and Jeremiah. ³⁵Then came some priests who played trumpets, including Zechariah son of Jonathan, son of Shemaiah, son of Mattaniah, son of Micaiah, son of Zaccur, a descendant of Asaph. ³⁶And Zechariah's colleagues were Shemaiah, Azarel, Milalai, Gilalai, Maai, Nethanel, Judah, and Hanani. They used the musical instruments prescribed by David, the man of God. Ezra the scribe led this procession. ³⁷At the Fountain Gate they went straight up the steps on the ascent of the city wall toward the City of David. They passed the house of David and then proceeded to the Water Gate on the east.

³⁸The second choir giving thanks went northward* around the other way to meet them. I followed them, together with the other half of the people, along the top of the wall past the Tower of the Ovens to the Broad Wall, ³⁹then past the Ephraim Gate to the Old City Gate,* past the Fish Gate and the Tower of Hananel, and on to the Tower of the Hundred. Then we continued on to the Sheep Gate and stopped at the Guard Gate.

⁴⁰The two choirs that were giving thanks then proceeded to the Temple of God, where they took their places. So did I, together with the group of leaders who were with me. ⁴¹We went together with the trumpet-playing priests—Eliakim, Maaseiah, Miniamin, Micaiah, Elioenai, Zechariah, and Hananiah—⁴²and the singers—Maaseiah, Shemaiah, Eleazar, Uzzi, Jehohanan, Malkijah, Elam, and Ezer. They played and sang loudly under the direction of Jezrahiah the choir director.

⁴³Many sacrifices were offered on that joyous day, for God had given the people cause for great joy. The women and children also participated in the celebration, and the joy of the people of Jerusalem could be heard far away.

Provisions for Temple Worship

⁴⁴On that day men were appointed to be in charge of the storerooms for the offerings, the first part of the harvest, and the tithes. They were responsible to collect from the fields outside the towns the portions required by the Law for the priests and Levites. For all the people of Judah took joy in the priests and Levites and their work. ⁴⁵They performed the service of their God and the service of purification, as commanded by David and his son Solomon, and so did the singers and the gatekeepers. ⁴⁶The custom of having choir directors to lead the choirs in hymns of praise and thanksgiving to God began long ago in the days of David and Asaph. ⁴⁷So now, in the days of Zerubbabel and of Nehemiah, all Israel brought a daily supply of food for the singers, the gatekeepers, and the Levites. The Levites, in turn, gave a portion of what they received to the priests, the descendants of Aaron.

Nehemiah's Various Reforms

13 On that same day, as the Book of Moses was being read to the people, the passage was found that said no Ammonite or Moabite should ever be permitted to enter the assembly of God.* ²For they had not provided the Israelites with food and water in the wilderness. Instead, they hired Balaam to curse them, though our God turned the curse into a blessing. ³When this passage of the Law was read, all those of foreign descent were immediately excluded from the assembly.

⁴Before this had happened, Eliashib the priest, who had been appointed as supervisor of the storerooms of the Temple of our God and who was also a relative of Tobiah, ⁵had converted a large storage room and placed it at Tobiah's disposal. The room had previously been used for storing the grain offerings, the frankincense, various articles for the Temple, and the tithes of grain, new wine, and olive oil (which were prescribed for the Levites, the singers, and the gatekeepers), as well as the offerings for the priests.

⁶I was not in Jerusalem at that time, for I had returned to King Artaxerxes of Babylon in the thirty-second year of his reign,* though I later asked his permission to return. ⁷When I arrived back in Jerusalem, I learned about Eliashib's evil deed in providing Tobiah with a room in the courtyards of the Temple of God. ⁸I became very upset and threw all of Tobiah's belongings out of the room. ⁹Then I demanded that the rooms be purified, and I brought back the articles for God's Temple, the grain offerings, and the frankincense.

¹⁰I also discovered that the Levites had not been given their prescribed portions of food, so they and the singers who were to conduct the worship services had all returned to work their fields. ¹¹I immediately confronted the leaders and demanded, "Why has the Temple of God been neglected?" Then I called all the Levites back again and restored them to their

---

12:31 Hebrew *to the right.* **12:38** Hebrew *to the left.* **12:39** Or *the Mishneh Gate,* or *the Jeshanah Gate.* **13:1** See Deut 23:3-6. **13:6** King Artaxerxes of Persia is here identified as the king of Babylon because Persia had conquered the Babylonian Empire. The thirty-second year of Artaxerxes was 433 B.C.

proper duties. ¹²And once more all the people of Judah began bringing their tithes of grain, new wine, and olive oil to the Temple storerooms.

¹³I assigned supervisors for the storerooms: Shelemiah the priest, Zadok the scribe, and Pedaiah, one of the Levites. And I appointed Hanan son of Zaccur and grandson of Mattaniah as their assistant. These men had an excellent reputation, and it was their job to make honest distributions to their fellow Levites.

¹⁴Remember this good deed, O my God, and do not forget all that I have faithfully done for the Temple of my God and its services.

¹⁵In those days I saw men of Judah treading out their winepresses on the Sabbath. They were also bringing in grain, loading it on donkeys, and bringing their wine, grapes, figs, and all sorts of produce to Jerusalem to sell on the Sabbath. So I rebuked them for selling their produce on that day. ¹⁶Some men from Tyre, who lived in Jerusalem, were bringing in fish and all kinds of merchandise. They were selling it on the Sabbath to the people of Judah—and in Jerusalem at that!

¹⁷So I confronted the nobles of Judah. "Why are you profaning the Sabbath in this evil way?" I asked. ¹⁸"Wasn't it just this sort of thing that your ancestors did that caused our God to bring all this trouble upon us and our city? Now you are bringing even more wrath upon Israel by permitting the Sabbath to be desecrated in this way!"

¹⁹Then I commanded that the gates of Jerusalem should be shut as darkness fell every Friday

13:17 The Sabbath rest was a day celebrated and honored every week, given by God as a *gift* (Genesis 2:2-3). This day of rest began on Friday at sunset until sunset on Saturday. Everyone was to rest on this day, even the working animals. Nehemiah enforced Sabbath-keeping by directing that the gates be shut to traders so that everyone might choose worship over work.

⑧ Come Close — DISREPAIR: PERSIST

SCRIPTURE CONNECTION: NEHEMIAH 13:1-31

Nehemiah left Jerusalem for a time. After all his effort to equip the Israelites, after all his sacrifices to rebuild the wall, he returned to a people in disrepair.

There are times when our best efforts fall apart—our relationships, our career, our health, the laundry! Even when we persist in obeying God, the road can feel long.

When Nehemiah could have felt down, he rose. How did he persist in doing what he knew was right?

- He took bold, direct action.
- He asked for help and delegated.
- He reminded the Israelites of the past.

Like Nehemiah, we can act boldly, we can ask for help, and we can remember that God is faithful.

Creating lasting good isn't something we can think or feel our way into. It rises from bold action. We must stand and say, "Let's go!" time and time again.

The book of Nehemiah closes with the words, "Remember this in my favor, O my God." (13:31). Persistence solidifies faith. And it's through action—God's activity to bring wholeness and our actively doing good (Ephesians 2:8-10)—that God restores.

REFLECT "Remember this in my favor, O my God." NEHEMIAH 13:31

God, when my work dismantles, may I faithfully respond. Amen.

CONSIDER "Your perseverance does count. Others are watching the way you handle trials, and they are being enriched by your response. Besides, when you get to heaven, you will see the immense value your sacrifices of service have accomplished in the lives of others. So, don't give up. Do not throw in the towel. Friend, today, keep persevering." JONI EARECKSON TADA, "Perseverance Matters," Joni and Friends Ministry podcast

Creating lasting good rises from bold action.

JENNIFER KELLER, MA Min, is a pastor at a multisite church in Central Indiana and has self-published three Bible studies. She is a devoted Christ-follower, wife, and mom of four.

evening,* not to be opened until the Sabbath ended. I sent some of my own servants to guard the gates so that no merchandise could be brought in on the Sabbath day. ²⁰The merchants and tradesmen with a variety of wares camped outside Jerusalem once or twice. ²¹But I spoke sharply to them and said, "What are you doing out here, camping around the wall? If you do this again, I will arrest you!" And that was the last time they came on the Sabbath. ²²Then I commanded the Levites to purify themselves and to guard the gates in order to preserve the holiness of the Sabbath.

> Remember this good deed also, O my God! Have compassion on me according to your great and unfailing love.

²³About the same time I realized that some of the men of Judah had married women from Ashdod, Ammon, and Moab. ²⁴Furthermore, half their children spoke the language of Ashdod or of some other people and could not speak the language of Judah at all. ²⁵So I confronted them and called down curses on them. I beat some of them and pulled out their hair. I made them swear in the name of God that they would not let their children intermarry with the pagan people of the land.

²⁶"Wasn't this exactly what led King Solomon of Israel into sin?" I demanded. "There was no king from any nation who could compare to him, and God loved him and made him king over all Israel. But even he was led into sin by his foreign wives. ²⁷How could you even think of committing this sinful deed and acting unfaithfully toward God by marrying foreign women?"

²⁸One of the sons of Joiada son of Eliashib the high priest had married a daughter of Sanballat the Horonite, so I banished him from my presence.

> ²⁹Remember them, O my God, for they have defiled the priesthood and the solemn vows of the priests and Levites.

³⁰So I purged out everything foreign and assigned tasks to the priests and Levites, making certain that each knew his work. ³¹I also made sure that the supply of wood for the altar and the first portions of the harvest were brought at the proper times.

> Remember this in my favor, O my God.

13:19 Hebrew *on the day before the Sabbath.*

13:23-26 Nehemiah was overcome with frustration at the influence of the foreign women from Ashdod, Ammon, and Moab, who were married to men from Judah. These regions were close to Judah. Like Ezra, Nehemiah wants the Jewish people to remember their identity after having been exiles. He responded by warning the people of King Solomon's mistake in marrying foreign women. These foreign women had led Solomon to worship other gods, affecting the entire kingdom. Yet, there are significant differences between these exiles and Solomon living in a palace. Nehemiah responded out of a strong desire for the people to remain faithful yet neglected to note the differences between Solomon's example and life in exile. Some view Nehemiah's (and Ezra's) response to send the wives away as the correct one. Others view their responses as an overreaction to traumatized people attempting to rebuild their lives and identities.

13:27 Nehemiah's strong reaction reflects a desire to be faithful to God. It is a reminder that those in the Bible are human and sometimes do not necessarily act virtuously (examples include Jephthah [Judges 11]; Samson [Judges 14]; and the Levite [Judges 19–20]). Ezra responded similarly and was challenged by several in the community. (See the notes on Ezra 9:1–10:15; 10:1-14; 10:15.) It is encouraging to know that God faithfully fulfills his promise to bless the world even through imperfect people. God never gives up on us.

Esther

WHAT DO WE LEARN ABOUT GOD'S MISSION AND OURS?
God can use our obedience, right where we are, for great impact.

WHO WROTE IT? Anonymous, likely a Jew living in Persia in the fifth century BC.

WHEN DID IT HAPPEN? Around 480 BC, after the Exile, when some Jews had gone back to Jerusalem while others remained in Persia.

HOW IS IT ORGANIZED?

1: King Xerxes rejects Queen Vashti

2: Esther becomes queen

3: Haman plots to wipe out the Jews

4–8: Esther and Mordecai save their people

9: Jews celebrate the Festival of Purim

10: Mordecai is honored; he and Esther work for the good of their people

FEATURE HIGHLIGHTS

+ *What Is a Woman's Worth?* (595)
+ *Esther: Opportunity through Others* (597)
+ *Esther: Victor or Victim?* (598)

Words to Remember are highlighted throughout this book

HOW LONG DOES IT TAKE TO READ?

:30						
:30	1:00	1:30	2:00	2:30	3:00	3:30

BC | Timeline

BC	
586	JERUSALEM IS DESTROYED; EXILES ARE TAKEN TO BABYLON
538	FIRST EXILES RETURN TO JERUSALEM
515	TEMPLE RECONSTRUCTION IS COMPLETED
486	XERXES (AHASUERUS) BECOMES PERSIA'S KING
c. 483	VASHTI IS DEPOSED
479	ESTHER BECOMES QUEEN
474	HAMAN PLOTS TO DESTROY THE JEWS
473	FIRST FESTIVAL OF PURIM IS CELEBRATED

The King's Banquet

1 These events happened in the days of King Xerxes,* who reigned over 127 provinces stretching from India to Ethiopia.* ²At that time Xerxes ruled his empire from his royal throne at the fortress of Susa. ³In the third year of his reign, he gave a banquet for all his nobles and officials. He invited all the military officers of Persia and Media as well as the princes and nobles of the provinces. ⁴The celebration lasted 180 days—a tremendous display of the opulent wealth of his empire and the pomp and splendor of his majesty.

⁵When it was all over, the king gave a banquet for all the people, from the greatest to the least, who were in the fortress of Susa. It lasted for seven days and was held in the courtyard of the palace garden. ⁶The courtyard was beautifully decorated with white cotton curtains and blue hangings, which were fastened with white linen cords and purple ribbons to silver rings embedded in marble pillars. Gold and silver couches stood on a mosaic pavement of porphyry, marble, mother-of-pearl, and other costly stones.

⁷Drinks were served in gold goblets of many designs, and there was an abundance of royal wine, reflecting the king's generosity. ⁸By edict of the king, no limits were placed on the drinking, for the king had instructed all his palace officials to serve each man as much as he wanted.

⁹At the same time, Queen Vashti gave a banquet for the women in the royal palace of King Xerxes.

Queen Vashti Deposed

¹⁰On the seventh day of the feast, when King Xerxes was in high spirits because of the wine, he told the seven eunuchs who attended him—Mehuman, Biztha, Harbona, Bigtha, Abagtha, Zethar, and Carcas—¹¹to bring Queen Vashti to him with the royal crown on her head. He wanted the nobles and all the other men to gaze on her beauty, for she was a very beautiful woman. ¹²But when they conveyed the king's order to Queen Vashti, she refused to come. This made the king furious, and he burned with anger.

¹³He immediately consulted with his wise advisers, who knew all the Persian laws and customs, for he always asked their advice. ¹⁴The names of these men were Carshena, Shethar, Admatha, Tarshish, Meres, Marsena, and Memucan—seven nobles of Persia and Media. They met with the king regularly and held the highest positions in the empire.

¹⁵"What must be done to Queen Vashti?" the king demanded. "What penalty does the law provide for a queen who refuses to obey the king's orders, properly sent through his eunuchs?"

¹⁶Memucan answered the king and his nobles, "Queen Vashti has wronged not only the king but also every noble and citizen throughout your empire. ¹⁷Women everywhere will begin to despise their husbands when they learn that Queen Vashti has refused to appear before the king. ¹⁸Before this day is out, the wives of all the king's nobles throughout Persia and Media will hear what the queen did and will start treating their husbands the same way. There will be no end to their contempt and anger.

¹⁹"So if it please the king, we suggest that you issue a written decree, a law of the Persians and Medes that cannot be revoked. It should order that Queen Vashti be forever banished from the presence of King Xerxes, and that the king should choose another queen more worthy than she. ²⁰When this decree is published throughout the king's vast empire, husbands everywhere, whatever their rank, will receive proper respect from their wives!"

²¹The king and his nobles thought this made good sense, so he followed Memucan's counsel. ²²He sent

---

1:1a Hebrew *Ahasuerus*, another name for Xerxes; also throughout the book of Esther. Xerxes reigned 486–465 B.C.
1:1b Hebrew *to Cush*.

1:1 The opening phrase, "These events happened in the days of…," marks the story's literary period and political background. These opening words resemble the book of Ruth. Esther and Ruth share important connections as the only two Bible books named after women. Both books also begin outside the land of Israel.

1:1-22 Three extravagant parties happen in the opening scenes, revealing King Xerxes's lavish lifestyle. The term used to describe the party, *mishteh*, along with the various goblets (1:7), indicates that the party involved excessive drinking. This is the same type of party that Samson hosted in Judges 14. Here, the king hosted the first party (1:1-4), which lasted 180 days. The guest list details individuals with rank, such as governors, officials, and people with administrative positions in the Persian Empire. The second party (1:5-22) lasted seven days and included people of varying importance, from "the greatest to the least" (1:5). Queen Vashti hosted a third party for the women (1:9).

1:10-19 At the party's end, on the seventh day (1:10), the king commanded that Vashti leave her role as host for the women's party and appear before him in her crown. This was possibly a request for her to parade unclothed, in which case she would have been treated as an object before the guests. The king sent seven eunuchs to retrieve her. Vashti refused, and the king consulted with seven advisers. The number seven is symbolic, communicating completeness and wholeness. The sense of completeness through the number seven reveals irony, as Vashti refused to complete the request. Though she did not speak, her actions sent a strong message. As a result, the king removed Vashti from her position as queen.

1:22 The king's adviser Memucan issued an oppressive decree because of Vashti's non-consent. Ironically, the decree enforced husbands' rulership over their wives, already the broad custom in the ancient Near East that the original audience of this story would have had in mind. This decree threatened legal prosecution, an example of the abuse of power. This decree was extreme and shame-based, and for maximum impact, it was copied in the local language of each province of the Persian Empire.

letters to all parts of the empire, to each province in its own script and language, proclaiming that every man should be the ruler of his own home and should say whatever he pleases.*

Esther Becomes Queen

2 But after Xerxes' anger had subsided, he began thinking about Vashti and what she had done and the decree he had made. ²So his personal attendants suggested, "Let us search the empire to find beautiful young virgins for the king. ³Let the king appoint agents in each province to bring these beautiful young women into the royal harem at the fortress of Susa. Hegai, the king's eunuch in charge of the harem, will see that they are all given beauty treatments. ⁴After that, the young woman who most pleases the king will be made queen instead of Vashti." This advice was very appealing to the king, so he put the plan into effect.

⁵At that time there was a Jewish man in the fortress of Susa whose name was Mordecai son of Jair. He was from the tribe of Benjamin and was a descendant of Kish and Shimei. ⁶His family* had been among those who, with King Jehoiachin* of Judah, had been exiled from Jerusalem to Babylon by King Nebuchadnezzar. ⁷This man had a very beautiful and lovely young cousin, Hadassah, who was also called Esther. When her father and mother died, Mordecai adopted her into his family and raised her as his own daughter.

⁸As a result of the king's decree, Esther, along with many other young women, was brought to the king's harem at the fortress of Susa and placed in Hegai's care. ⁹Hegai was very impressed with Esther and treated her kindly. He quickly ordered a special menu for her and provided her with beauty treatments. He also assigned her seven maids specially chosen from the king's palace, and he moved her and her maids into the best place in the harem.

¹⁰Esther had not told anyone of her nationality and family background, because Mordecai had directed her not to do so. ¹¹Every day Mordecai

1:22 Or *and should speak in the language of his own people.* 2:6a Hebrew *He.* 2:6b Hebrew *Jeconiah,* a variant spelling of Jehoiachin.

2:7-8 Esther had already experienced significant losses as an orphan and a refugee. After Esther's cousin Mordecai adopted her, she was forced away from her family a second time, because of the king's edict to "bring these beautiful young women into the royal harem at the fortress of Susa" (2:3).

2:10 Mordecai instructed Esther to keep her Jewish identity hidden. She headed into an unknown environment where her identity could put her at a disadvantage. In our day, we often want to be known and reveal who we are with boldness, even if it creates divisions. In Esther's day, it proved wise to wait, especially in a potentially hostile political environment.

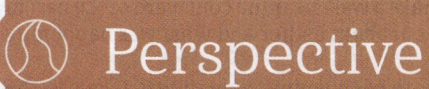

Perspective

What is a woman's worth?

SCRIPTURE CONNECTION: ESTHER 1:10-22

Have you ever felt like you had no choices? Maybe you've felt like God was silent, and no matter what decision you made, your fate was sealed?

Facing a similar no-win situation, Vashti decided to reject the oppressive system where she found herself. In turn, she was rejected.

Some scholars believe the drunken party led to the king demanding Vashti appear naked, wearing only her crown. Despite her position as a royal wife, Vashti would be reduced to the sum of her body parts.

But the God she may not have even known knew her and had a plan that included her. Regardless of the reason, her act of defiance made it possible for God's salvation of his people through Esther. God wastes no part of our story. He uses it all for his glory.

VIEWPOINTS

HERS: *How do you think Vashti viewed her worth before the king's request? Do you think her view changed afterward?*
MINE: *"Self-worth isn't something we gain at birth. It's something we experience through relationships with others (family, friends, authority figures, etc.). I struggled with my worth for a long time, and if Vashti had doubts about refusing the king's request, I would not have faulted her. I am so grateful to have her story in God's Word to know that it's okay to know your worth as a woman."*
YOURS: *What struggles have you had with self-worth? How does Vashti's story encourage you?*

QUANTRILLA ARD, PhD, is a faith-based personal and spiritual development author, speaker, Bible teacher, and literary agent who believes in the power of collective strength, community, and fellowship.

would take a walk near the courtyard of the harem to find out about Esther and what was happening to her.

¹²Before each young woman was taken to the king's bed, she was given the prescribed twelve months of beauty treatments—six months with oil of myrrh, followed by six months with special perfumes and ointments. ¹³When it was time for her to go to the king's palace, she was given her choice of whatever clothing or jewelry she wanted to take from the harem. ¹⁴That evening she was taken to the king's private rooms, and the next morning she was brought to the second harem,* where the king's wives lived. There she would be under the care of Shaashgaz, the king's eunuch in charge of the concubines. She would never go to the king again unless he had especially enjoyed her and requested her by name.

¹⁵Esther was the daughter of Abihail, who was Mordecai's uncle. (Mordecai had adopted his younger cousin Esther.) When it was Esther's turn to go to the king, she accepted the advice of Hegai, the eunuch in charge of the harem. She asked for nothing except what he suggested, and she was admired by everyone who saw her.

¹⁶Esther was taken to King Xerxes at the royal palace in early winter* of the seventh year of his reign. ¹⁷And the king loved Esther more than any of the other young women. He was so delighted with her that he set the royal crown on her head and declared her queen instead of Vashti. ¹⁸To celebrate the occasion, he gave a great banquet in Esther's honor for all his nobles and officials, declaring a public holiday for the provinces and giving generous gifts to everyone.

¹⁹Even after all the young women had been transferred to the second harem* and Mordecai had become a palace official,* ²⁰Esther continued to keep her family background and nationality a secret. She was still following Mordecai's directions, just as she did when she lived in his home.

Mordecai's Loyalty to the King

²¹One day as Mordecai was on duty at the king's gate, two of the king's eunuchs, Bigthana* and Teresh—who were guards at the door of the king's private quarters—became angry at King Xerxes and plotted to assassinate him. ²²But Mordecai heard about the plot and gave the information to Queen Esther. She then told the king about it and gave Mordecai credit for the report. ²³When an investigation was made and Mordecai's story was found to be true, the two men were impaled on a sharpened pole. This was all recorded in *The Book of the History of King Xerxes' Reign.*

Haman's Plot against the Jews

3 Some time later King Xerxes promoted Haman son of Hammedatha the Agagite over all the other nobles, making him the most powerful official in the empire. ²All the king's officials would bow down before Haman to show him respect whenever he passed by, for so the king had commanded. But Mordecai refused to bow down or show him respect.

³Then the palace officials at the king's gate asked Mordecai, "Why are you disobeying the king's command?" ⁴They spoke to him day after day, but still he refused to comply with the order. So they spoke to Haman about this to see if he would tolerate Mordecai's conduct, since Mordecai had told them he was a Jew.

⁵When Haman saw that Mordecai would not bow down or show him respect, he was filled with rage. ⁶He had learned of Mordecai's nationality,

---

2:14 Or *to another part of the harem.* 2:16 Hebrew *in the tenth month, the month of Tebeth.* A number of dates in the book of Esther can be cross-checked with dates in surviving Persian records and related accurately to our modern calendar. This month of the ancient Hebrew lunar calendar occurred within the months of December 479 B.C. and January 478 B.C. 2:19a The meaning of the Hebrew is uncertain. 2:19b Hebrew *and Mordecai was sitting in the gate of the king.* 2:21 Hebrew *Bigthan;* compare 6:2.

2:15 Esther was "admired by everyone who saw her." The Hebrew term for this is *hen,* which means embodied "grace" or "favor." *Hen* indicates more than outward beauty and communicates the quality of her identity as a woman. Esther embodied grace.

2:23 Although the phrase "impaled on a sharpened pole" has historically been translated "hanged on a gallows," impalement was a method of execution for rebels and enemies of the state in the Persian Empire. Inscriptions from the time period relate that Xerxes's father, Darius I, impaled rebels by the dozen while putting down a Babylonian revolt. In some cases, criminals may have been executed first and then displayed on a stake, as with the execution of Haman's sons (9:5-14). Mordecai was not rewarded for his role in exposing this assassination plot until much later (6:1-14).

While various records of Xerxes's reign have been found, the particular book mentioned has not.

3:2-5 Mordecai's and Haman's families had a long history of hostility. Mordecai the Jew was a Benjamite (2:5), and Haman was a descendant of the Amalekites (3:1). This hostility shows up in several Old Testament passages (Exodus 17:16; Deuteronomy 25:17-19; 1 Samuel 14–15). The story of the battle between Saul and the Amalekites highlights that Saul rescued Israel from the Amalekites, the ones who plundered Israel (1 Samuel 14:48). Later in Esther's story, the writer notes that the Jews would not take revenge in the same way. They would defend themselves but would not plunder their oppressors (Esther 9:10, 15). Israel's decision not to return evil for evil may relate to the idea that it is up to God to take revenge, not us (Deuteronomy 32:35). What might we need to trust God to handle?

Esther

IDENTITY: Opportunity through Others

"What am I doing here?" she may have wondered. "I don't belong to these people. I'm a Jew, but my cousin, my guardian, told me not to tell anyone. Can I become the queen? Or will I end up being tossed away like everyone else after one night with the king? There are so many other beautiful women. Do I even have a chance?... I need help, someone to guide me."

While the name of God never appears in the book of Esther, we see his hand at work behind the scenes in providing connections and the timing of significant events. Thus, it is no accident that the eunuch in charge of all these young women, Hegai, took a special interest in Esther. He took care of her to see that she had all the best beauty treatments, food, and maids.

When her time came to go with the king, Esther naturally sought Hegai's advice. His advice made the difference and enabled her to win the favor of the king, who then had her crowned his queen.

> God often guides us to rely on others to open doors of opportunity

ESTHER'S STORY IS TOLD IN THE BOOK OF ESTHER.

IDENTIFY

Have you had people in your life who opened doors of opportunity?

Who has encouraged you to take daring steps that led to your growth?

"I started a new career in academia because someone went to the Dean and said I was the person he needed for that position. As with Esther, that conversation led to a position of influence. I became director of the doctoral programs and began a whole new career in my fifties."

ELIZABETH GLANVILLE, PhD, is retired faculty from Fuller Theological Seminary, School of Mission and Theology. She is an international teacher on missions and leadership and chaplain for a local police department and her retirement community.

MY STORY WITH GOD

Esther: Victor or Victim?

SCRIPTURE CONNECTION: ESTHER 4:1-17

"Oooh, I want to be Miss America!" I said as I jumped up from the shaggy rug to touch the TV. I was awed by the pageant—with the gowns, the glitter, the graceful glides, and the women who vowed to create "world peace."

"What?" my older sister objected. "No, you don't. That pageant victimizes women." She spoke with heading-for-Stanford-eighteen-year-old knowing. At age seven, all I saw was pretty—the shoes, the stage, the shiny.

So it was with Esther. When I first met her, I thought, "Wow, to be the most beautiful in the land!"

And then I spied the behind-the-curtain ugliness of her victimization:

- parents who died
- a king who tore her from home for his own pleasure, and
- a night of proving herself in the bedroom. At best, she would marry the king who had impulsively banished his last wife; at worst, she would emerge a concubine living in the harem unless the king remembered her by name.

Throughout history, we see victimization from human power. Sometimes people, like King Xerxes, want sex with every beautiful woman in the country, not considering how this demeans their dignity. Other people, like Haman, hunger for more power and will destroy anyone who stands in their way.

> God's love gives us victories.

Is it any wonder that Esther understandably hesitated from another victimization when she learned that her husband planned to kill the Jews? Could she even hear, "Who knows if perhaps you were made queen for just such a time as this?" (4:14).

Like Esther, we may be tempted to hide in victimhood, not daring to hope for victory.

We might forget Esther became queen despite being orphaned, abducted, and violated. God was with Esther in childhood, providing Mordecai. God was with Esther in the harem, granting the eunuch's favor. God would be with Esther as she went to the king unbidden. Trusting God, she breathed: "If I must die, I must die" (4:16).

God's love gives us victories so that we can give victory to others. God does not condone women being used for others' gain, but he is not vanquished by it. Our backstage ugliness becomes the onstage crown. Enrobed in God's love, we victoriously do change the world.

IMAGINE

What allowed Esther to make her unique imprint?

How has God designed you to bless others?

> "Like Esther, I have faced both hardship and honor. And, like her, I can use both to serve God."

NAOMI CRAMER OVERTON, MBA, DIS, lives to realize beauty-filled visions that lift us to flourishing, with our families and beyond. Naomi has been CEO for Stonecroft and MOPS, director with Compassion International and World Vision, and General Editor for this Bible.

so he decided it was not enough to lay hands on Mordecai alone. Instead, he looked for a way to destroy all the Jews throughout the entire empire of Xerxes.

⁷So in the month of April,* during the twelfth year of King Xerxes' reign, lots were cast in Haman's presence (the lots were called *purim*) to determine the best day and month to take action. And the day selected was March 7, nearly a year later.*

⁸Then Haman approached King Xerxes and said, "There is a certain race of people scattered through all the provinces of your empire who keep themselves separate from everyone else. Their laws are different from those of any other people, and they refuse to obey the laws of the king. So it is not in the king's interest to let them live. ⁹If it please the king, issue a decree that they be destroyed, and I will give 10,000 large sacks* of silver to the government administrators to be deposited in the royal treasury."

¹⁰The king agreed, confirming his decision by removing his signet ring from his finger and giving it to Haman son of Hammedatha the Agagite, the enemy of the Jews. ¹¹The king said, "The money and the people are both yours to do with as you see fit."

¹²So on April 17* the king's secretaries were summoned, and a decree was written exactly as Haman dictated. It was sent to the king's highest officers, the governors of the respective provinces, and the nobles of each province in their own scripts and languages. The decree was written in the name of King Xerxes and sealed with the king's signet ring. ¹³Dispatches were sent by swift messengers into all the provinces of the empire, giving the order that all Jews—young and old, including women and children—must be killed, slaughtered, and annihilated on a single day. This was scheduled to happen on March 7 of the next year.* The property of the Jews would be given to those who killed them.

¹⁴A copy of this decree was to be issued as law in every province and proclaimed to all peoples, so that they would be ready to do their duty on the appointed day. ¹⁵At the king's command, the decree went out by swift messengers, and it was also proclaimed in the fortress of Susa. Then the king and Haman sat down to drink, but the city of Susa fell into confusion.

Mordecai Requests Esther's Help

4 When Mordecai learned about all that had been done, he tore his clothes, put on burlap and ashes, and went out into the city, crying with a loud and bitter wail. ²He went as far as the gate of the palace, for no one was allowed to enter the palace gate while wearing clothes of mourning. ³And as news of the king's decree reached all the provinces, there was great mourning among the Jews. They fasted, wept, and wailed, and many people lay in burlap and ashes.

⁴When Queen Esther's maids and eunuchs came and told her about Mordecai, she was deeply distressed. She sent clothing to him to replace the burlap, but he refused it. ⁵Then Esther sent for Hathach, one of the king's eunuchs who had been appointed as her attendant. She ordered him to go to Mordecai and find out what was troubling him and why he was in mourning. ⁶So Hathach went out to Mordecai in the square in front of the palace gate.

⁷Mordecai told him the whole story, including the exact amount of money Haman had promised to pay into the royal treasury for the destruction of the Jews. ⁸Mordecai gave Hathach a copy of the decree issued in Susa that called for the death of all Jews. He asked Hathach to show it to Esther and explain the situation to her. He also asked Hathach to direct her to go to the king to beg for mercy and plead for her people. ⁹So Hathach returned to Esther with Mordecai's message.

¹⁰Then Esther told Hathach to go back and relay this message to Mordecai: ¹¹"All the king's officials and even the people in the provinces know that anyone who appears before the king in his inner court without being invited is doomed to die unless the king holds out his gold scepter. And the king has not called for me to come to him for thirty days." ¹²So Hathach* gave Esther's message to Mordecai.

¹³Mordecai sent this reply to Esther: "Don't think for a moment that because you're in the palace you will escape when all other Jews are killed. ¹⁴If you keep quiet at a time like this, deliverance and relief for the Jews will arise from some other place, but you and your relatives will die. Who knows if perhaps you were made queen for just such a time as this?"

¹⁵Then Esther sent this reply to Mordecai: ¹⁶"Go and gather together all the Jews of Susa and fast for

---

3:7a Hebrew *in the first month, the month of Nisan*. This month of the ancient Hebrew lunar calendar occurred within the months of April and May 474 B.C.; also see note on 2:16. **3:7b** As in 3:13, which reads *the thirteenth day of the twelfth month, the month of Adar*; Hebrew reads *in the twelfth month*, of the ancient Hebrew lunar calendar. The date selected was March 7, 473 B.C.; also see note on 2:16. **3:9** Hebrew *10,000 talents*, about 375 tons or 340 metric tons in weight. **3:12** Hebrew *On the thirteenth day of the first month*, of the ancient Hebrew lunar calendar. This day was April 17, 474 B.C.; also see note on 2:16. **3:13** Hebrew *on the thirteenth day of the twelfth month, the month of Adar*, of the ancient Hebrew lunar calendar. The date selected was March 7, 473 B.C.; also see note on 2:16. **4:12** As in Greek version; Hebrew reads *they*.

4:15-17 Esther responded to Mordecai's report with a plea to fast. Fasting is intentionally abstaining from food for spiritual purposes. The Jews living in Susa and Esther's palace attendants joined her in her fast. Throughout the Bible, fasting is a vital time of prayer that acknowledges something is wrong and that God's help is needed (Exodus 34:28; Deuteronomy 9:9; Ezra 8:21-23; Daniel 9:3).

me. Do not eat or drink for three days, night or day. My maids and I will do the same. And then, though it is against the law, I will go in to see the king. If I must die, I must die." ¹⁷So Mordecai went away and did everything as Esther had ordered him.

Esther's Request to the King

5 On the third day of the fast, Esther put on her royal robes and entered the inner court of the palace, just across from the king's hall. The king was sitting on his royal throne, facing the entrance. ²When he saw Queen Esther standing there in the inner court, he welcomed her and held out the gold scepter to her. So Esther approached and touched the end of the scepter.

³Then the king asked her, "What do you want, Queen Esther? What is your request? I will give it to you, even if it is half the kingdom!"

⁴And Esther replied, "If it please the king, let the king and Haman come today to a banquet I have prepared for the king."

⁵The king turned to his attendants and said, "Tell Haman to come quickly to a banquet, as Esther has requested." So the king and Haman went to Esther's banquet.

⁶And while they were drinking wine, the king said to Esther, "Now tell me what you really want. What is your request? I will give it to you, even if it is half the kingdom!"

⁷Esther replied, "This is my request and deepest wish. ⁸If I have found favor with the king, and if it pleases the king to grant my request and do what I ask, please come with Haman tomorrow to the banquet I will prepare for you. Then I will explain what this is all about."

Haman's Plan to Kill Mordecai

⁹Haman was a happy man as he left the banquet! But when he saw Mordecai sitting at the palace gate, not standing up or trembling nervously before him, Haman became furious. ¹⁰However, he restrained himself and went on home.

Then Haman gathered together his friends and Zeresh, his wife, ¹¹and boasted to them about his great wealth and his many children. He bragged about the honors the king had given him and how he had been promoted over all the other nobles and officials.

¹²Then Haman added, "And that's not all! Queen Esther invited only me and the king himself to the banquet she prepared for us. And she has invited me to dine with her and the king again tomorrow!" ¹³Then he added, "But this is all worth nothing as long as I see Mordecai the Jew just sitting there at the palace gate."

¹⁴So Haman's wife, Zeresh, and all his friends suggested, "Set up a sharpened pole that stands seventy-five feet* tall, and in the morning ask the king to impale Mordecai on it. When this is done, you can go on your merry way to the banquet with the king." This pleased Haman, and he ordered the pole set up.

The King Honors Mordecai

6 That night the king had trouble sleeping, so he ordered an attendant to bring the book of the history of his reign so it could be read to him. ²In those records he discovered an account of how Mordecai had exposed the plot of Bigthana and Teresh, two of the eunuchs who guarded the door to the king's private quarters. They had plotted to assassinate King Xerxes.

³"What reward or recognition did we ever give Mordecai for this?" the king asked.

His attendants replied, "Nothing has been done for him."

⁴"Who is that in the outer court?" the king inquired. As it happened, Haman had just arrived in the outer court of the palace to ask the king to impale Mordecai on the pole he had prepared.

⁵So the attendants replied to the king, "Haman is out in the court."

"Bring him in," the king ordered. ⁶So Haman came in, and the king said, "What should I do to honor a man who truly pleases me?"

Haman thought to himself, "Whom would the king wish to honor more than me?" ⁷So he replied, "If the king wishes to honor someone, ⁸he should bring out one of the king's own royal robes, as well as a horse that the king himself has ridden—one with a royal emblem on its head. ⁹Let the robes and the horse be handed over to one of the king's most noble officials. And let him see that the man whom the king wishes to honor is dressed in the king's robes and led through the city square on the king's horse. Have the official shout as they go, 'This is what the king does for someone he wishes to honor!'"

5:14 Hebrew *50 cubits* [23 meters].

5:14 Seventy-five feet (in Hebrew, fifty cubits) would be unusually high, and the number may be hyperbole for effect or may reflect a stake on a raised platform for public viewing. Haman clearly wanted to make an example of Mordecai.

6:1 God was working to protect Esther and Mordecai by keeping the king awake at night and listening to an attendant reading the history of his reign. Ancient kings had royal records kept of their time as king.

"Who knows if perhaps you were made… for just such a time as this?"

ESTHER 4:14

ESTHER 7

¹⁰"Excellent!" the king said to Haman. "Quick! Take the robes and my horse, and do just as you have said for Mordecai the Jew, who sits at the gate of the palace. Leave out nothing you have suggested!"

¹¹So Haman took the robes and put them on Mordecai, placed him on the king's own horse, and led him through the city square, shouting, "This is what the king does for someone he wishes to honor!" ¹²Afterward Mordecai returned to the palace gate, but Haman hurried home dejected and completely humiliated.

¹³When Haman told his wife, Zeresh, and all his friends what had happened, his wise advisers and his wife said, "Since Mordecai—this man who has humiliated you—is of Jewish birth, you will never succeed in your plans against him. It will be fatal to continue opposing him."

¹⁴While they were still talking, the king's eunuchs arrived and quickly took Haman to the banquet Esther had prepared.

The King Executes Haman

7 So the king and Haman went to Queen Esther's banquet. ²On this second occasion, while they were drinking wine, the king again said to Esther, "Tell me what you want, Queen Esther. What is your request? I will give it to you, even if it is half the kingdom!"

³Queen Esther replied, "If I have found favor with the king, and if it pleases the king to grant my request, I ask that my life and the lives of my people will be spared. ⁴For my people and I have been sold to those who would kill, slaughter, and annihilate us. If we had merely been sold as slaves, I could remain quiet, for that would be too trivial a matter to warrant disturbing the king."

⁵"Who would do such a thing?" King Xerxes demanded. "Who would be so presumptuous as to touch you?"

⁶Esther replied, "This wicked Haman is our adversary and our enemy." Haman grew pale with fright before the king and queen. ⁷Then the king jumped to his feet in a rage and went out into the palace garden.

Haman, however, stayed behind to plead for his life with Queen Esther, for he knew that the king intended to kill him. ⁸In despair he fell on the couch where Queen Esther was reclining, just as the king was returning from the palace garden.

The king exclaimed, "Will he even assault the queen right here in the palace, before my very eyes?" And as soon as the king spoke, his attendants covered Haman's face, signaling his doom.

⁹Then Harbona, one of the king's eunuchs, said, "Haman has set up a sharpened pole that stands seventy-five feet* tall in his own courtyard. He intended to use it to impale Mordecai, the man who saved the king from assassination."

"Then impale Haman on it!" the king ordered. ¹⁰So they impaled Haman on the pole he had set up for Mordecai, and the king's anger subsided.

A Decree to Help the Jews

8 On that same day King Xerxes gave the property of Haman, the enemy of the Jews, to Queen Esther. Then Mordecai was brought before the king, for Esther had told the king how they were related. ²The king took off his signet ring—which he had taken back from Haman—and gave it to Mordecai. And Esther appointed Mordecai to be in charge of Haman's property.

³Then Esther went again before the king, falling down at his feet and begging him with tears to stop

---

7:9 Hebrew *50 cubits* [23 meters].

6:10-12 Haman sought honor and prestige through plots and selfish motives. By contrast, Mordecai lived an honorable life, even when no one was watching. Motives do matter and, in this scene, Mordecai gained recognition for his faithful service. In a twist of irony, Haman, seeking honor, would be humiliated.

7:3-4 The statement that someone wanted to kill the queen and her family must have surprised and shocked the king. Esther carefully referred to the huge price Haman had paid the king to approve the decree (3:8-11). She also used the exact terminology of Haman's decree when she said that its purpose was to kill, slaughter, and annihilate (see 3:13). Esther humbly justified her request as due to the severity of the attack on her and her people.

7:6-7 Esther finally identified Haman as the enemy. With this surprising and aggressive accusation by the queen and the evident rage of the king, Haman's doom suddenly became apparent.

7:8 To touch a royal wife, much less be on the same couch with her, was a huge breach of etiquette in the royal court. Haman would have known this, and it's possible, given the loose and draped nature of Persian court dress, that he slipped or lost his balance. Another, less likely, explanation is that he intentionally threw himself down to beg for mercy. The king saw this unfold, and his exaggerated rhetorical question assigned to Haman the worst possible motives.

7:9 Harbona, one of the king's seven eunuchs (1:10), was apparently no friend of Haman and was already aware of Haman's plot. This great reversal of fortunes demonstrates the guiding hand of God. Regarding impalement, see the note on 2:23.

8:1 Just as Haman had promised the wealth of the Jews to those who would kill them (3:13), Xerxes gave the property of Haman, the enemy of the Jews, to Queen Esther.

8:2 The signet ring that Haman had used to seal the decree to destroy the Jewish people (3:10) was now given to the Jewish person he had most wanted to destroy.

the evil plot devised by Haman the Agagite against the Jews. ⁴Again the king held out the gold scepter to Esther. So she rose and stood before him.

⁵Esther said, "If it please the king, and if I have found favor with him, and if he thinks it is right, and if I am pleasing to him, let there be a decree that reverses the orders of Haman son of Hammedatha the Agagite, who ordered that Jews throughout all the king's provinces should be destroyed. ⁶For how can I endure to see my people and my family slaughtered and destroyed?"

⁷Then King Xerxes said to Queen Esther and Mordecai the Jew, "I have given Esther the property of Haman, and he has been impaled on a pole because he tried to destroy the Jews. ⁸Now go ahead and send a message to the Jews in the king's name, telling them whatever you want, and seal it with the king's signet ring. But remember that whatever has already been written in the king's name and sealed with his signet ring can never be revoked."

⁹So on June 25* the king's secretaries were summoned, and a decree was written exactly as Mordecai dictated. It was sent to the Jews and to the highest officers, the governors, and the nobles of all the 127 provinces stretching from India to Ethiopia.* The decree was written in the scripts and languages of all the peoples of the empire, including that of the Jews. ¹⁰The decree was written in the name of King Xerxes and sealed with the king's signet ring. Mordecai sent the dispatches by swift messengers, who rode fast horses especially bred for the king's service.

¹¹The king's decree gave the Jews in every city authority to unite to defend their lives. They were allowed to kill, slaughter, and annihilate anyone of any nationality or province who might attack them or their children and wives, and to take the property of their enemies. ¹²The day chosen for this event throughout all the provinces of King Xerxes was March 7 of the next year.*

¹³A copy of this decree was to be issued as law in every province and proclaimed to all peoples, so that the Jews would be ready to take revenge on their enemies on the appointed day. ¹⁴So urged on by the king's command, the messengers rode out swiftly on fast horses bred for the king's service. The same decree was also proclaimed in the fortress of Susa.

¹⁵Then Mordecai left the king's presence, wearing the royal robe of blue and white, the great crown of gold, and an outer cloak of fine linen and purple. And the people of Susa celebrated the new decree. ¹⁶The Jews were filled with joy and gladness and were honored everywhere. ¹⁷In every province and city, wherever the king's decree arrived, the Jews rejoiced and had a great celebration and declared a public festival and holiday. And many of the people of the land became Jews themselves, for they feared what the Jews might do to them.

> "Never forget that in a life of intense prayer, God becomes your defense in all the virtues. When needed, the mighty Lord will come to your defense, fully armed."
>
> **THEODORA OF ALEXANDRIA** (fourth century AD) desert mother

The Victory of the Jews

9 So on March 7* the two decrees of the king were put into effect. On that day, the enemies of the Jews had hoped to overpower them, but quite the opposite happened. It was the Jews who overpowered their enemies. ²The Jews gathered in their cities throughout all the king's provinces to attack anyone who tried to harm them. But no one could make a stand against them, for everyone was afraid of them. ³And all the nobles of the provinces, the highest officers, the governors, and the royal officials helped the Jews for fear of Mordecai. ⁴For

---

8:9a Hebrew *on the twenty-third day of the third month, the month of Sivan,* of the ancient Hebrew lunar calendar. This day was June 25, 474 B.C.; also see note on 2:16.   **8:9b** Hebrew *to Cush.*   **8:12** Hebrew *the thirteenth day of the twelfth month, the month of Adar,* of the ancient Hebrew lunar calendar. The date selected was March 7, 473 B.C.; also see note on 2:16.
9:1 Hebrew *on the thirteenth day of the twelfth month, the month of Adar,* of the ancient Hebrew lunar calendar. This day was March 7, 473 B.C.; also see note on 2:16.

Mordecai had been promoted in the king's palace, and his fame spread throughout all the provinces as he became more and more powerful.

⁵So the Jews went ahead on the appointed day and struck down their enemies with the sword. They killed and annihilated their enemies and did as they pleased with those who hated them. ⁶In the fortress of Susa itself, the Jews killed 500 men. ⁷They also killed Parshandatha, Dalphon, Aspatha, ⁸Poratha, Adalia, Aridatha, ⁹Parmashta, Arisai, Aridai, and Vaizatha—¹⁰the ten sons of Haman son of Hammedatha, the enemy of the Jews. But they did not take any plunder.

¹¹That very day, when the king was informed of the number of people killed in the fortress of Susa, ¹²he called for Queen Esther. He said, "The Jews have killed 500 men in the fortress of Susa alone, as well as Haman's ten sons. If they have done that here, what has happened in the rest of the provinces? But now, what more do you want? It will be granted to you; tell me and I will do it."

¹³Esther responded, "If it please the king, give the Jews in Susa permission to do again tomorrow as they have done today, and let the bodies of Haman's ten sons be impaled on a pole."

¹⁴So the king agreed, and the decree was announced in Susa. And they impaled the bodies of Haman's ten sons. ¹⁵Then the Jews at Susa gathered together on March 8* and killed 300 more men, and again they took no plunder.

¹⁶Meanwhile, the other Jews throughout the king's provinces had gathered together to defend their lives. They gained relief from all their enemies, killing 75,000 of those who hated them. But they did not take any plunder. ¹⁷This was done throughout the provinces on March 7, and on March 8 they rested,* celebrating their victory with a day of feasting and gladness. ¹⁸(The Jews at Susa killed their enemies on March 7 and again on March 8, then rested on March 9,* making that their day of feasting and gladness.) ¹⁹So to this day, rural Jews living in remote villages celebrate an annual festival and holiday on the appointed day in late winter,* when they rejoice and send gifts of food to each other.

The Festival of Purim

²⁰Mordecai recorded these events and sent letters to the Jews near and far, throughout all the provinces of King Xerxes, ²¹calling on them to celebrate an annual festival on these two days.* ²²He told them to celebrate these days with feasting and gladness and by giving gifts of food to each other and presents to the poor. This would commemorate a time when the Jews gained relief from their enemies, when their sorrow was turned into gladness and their mourning into joy.

²³So the Jews accepted Mordecai's proposal and adopted this annual custom. ²⁴Haman son of Hammedatha the Agagite, the enemy of the Jews, had plotted to crush and destroy them on the date determined by casting lots (the lots were called *purim*). ²⁵But when Esther came before the king, he issued a decree causing Haman's evil plot to backfire, and Haman and his sons were impaled on a sharpened pole. ²⁶That is why this celebration is called Purim, because it is the ancient word for casting lots.

So because of Mordecai's letter and because of what they had experienced, ²⁷the Jews throughout the realm agreed to inaugurate this tradition and to pass it on to their descendants and to all who became Jews. They declared they would never fail to celebrate these two prescribed days at the appointed time each year. ²⁸These days would be remembered and kept from generation to generation and celebrated by every family throughout the provinces and cities of the empire. This Festival of Purim would never cease to be celebrated among the Jews, nor would the memory of what happened ever die out among their descendants.

²⁹Then Queen Esther, the daughter of Abihail, along with Mordecai the Jew, wrote another letter putting the queen's full authority behind Mordecai's letter to establish the Festival of Purim. ³⁰Letters wishing peace and security were sent to the Jews throughout the 127 provinces of the empire of Xerxes. ³¹These letters established the Festival of Purim—an annual celebration of these days at the appointed time, decreed by both Mordecai the Jew and Queen Esther. (The people decided to observe this festival, just as they had decided for

---

9:15 Hebrew *the fourteenth day of the month of Adar,* of the ancient Hebrew lunar calendar. This day was March 8, 473 B.C.; also see note on 2:16. **9:17** Hebrew *on the thirteenth day of the month of Adar, and on the fourteenth day they rested.* These days were March 7 and 8, 473 B.C.; also see note on 2:16. **9:18** Hebrew *killed their enemies on the thirteenth day and the fourteenth day, and then rested on the fifteenth day,* of the Hebrew month of Adar. **9:19** Hebrew *on the fourteenth day of the month of Adar.* This day of the ancient Hebrew lunar calendar occurs in February or March. **9:21** Hebrew *on the fourteenth and fifteenth days of Adar,* of the ancient Hebrew lunar calendar.

9:19 The annual festival and holiday of Purim celebrates God's blessing of peace from the Jews' enemies (see Deuteronomy 25:19; Joshua 21:44; 1 Samuel 7:11-14). The narrator reports that the festival was celebrated "to this day." Now, more than 2,400 years later, it is still celebrated annually by Jewish people. The first Purim was celebrated on the fourteenth and fifteenth days of the month of Adar. In the ancient Hebrew lunar calendar, these days occur in the modern months of February or March, when Purim is still celebrated. The exchange of gifts of food demonstrates the unity of the people and their care for one another, and helps spread an atmosphere of joy.

themselves and their descendants to establish the times of fasting and mourning.) ³²So the command of Esther confirmed the practices of Purim, and it was all written down in the records.

The Greatness of Xerxes and Mordecai

10 King Xerxes imposed a tribute throughout his empire, even to the distant coastlands. ²His great achievements and the full account of the greatness of Mordecai, whom the king had promoted, are recorded in *The Book of the History of the Kings of Media and Persia*. ³Mordecai the Jew became the prime minister, with authority next to that of King Xerxes himself. He was very great among the Jews, who held him in high esteem, because he continued to work for the good of his people and to speak up for the welfare of all their descendants.

10:3 One of the striking characteristics of Esther's story is God's absence. As in the Song of Songs, God is not mentioned by name. Even though the book of Esther does not overtly reveal God, he is at work through individuals' brave responses, such as fasting, weeping, and wailing (4:3), and Esther's determination to go to the king (4:16). Esther and Mordecai lived out faithfulness to God in a dark season, and God saved an entire nation from annihilation.

Job

WHAT DO WE LEARN ABOUT GOD'S MISSION AND OURS?
When life falls apart, we can trust God's wisdom and know he stays with us.

WHO WROTE IT? The book is anonymous; the author was likely part of a class of wisdom teachers in Israel.

WHEN DID IT HAPPEN? Perhaps around the 1100s BC or before, but it's not known with certainty. Some think during the time of the judges; others say much earlier, during the time of Abraham, Isaac, and Jacob.

HOW IS IT ORGANIZED?

- **1:** Satan asks God's permission to test Job; Job loses everything but does not sin
- **2:** Job loses his health; Job's wife encourages him to curse God
- **3–31:** Job's friends, Eliphaz, Bildad, and Zophar, talk with him about suffering and God's justice
- **32–37:** Elihu rebukes Job and his friends
- **38–42:** God speaks, then restores Job and his family

Words to Remember are highlighted throughout this book

FEATURE HIGHLIGHTS
+ *What Can God See That We Can't?* (610)
+ *Job's Wife: Grieving to Perceiving* (611)
+ *Dissatisfied: Open-Handed* (612)
+ *Numbering Job's Losses* (615)
+ *Relying on God's Wisdom* (620)
+ *How to Grieve with Others* (623)
+ *Desperate Words but Solid Identity* (626)
+ *Reflecting God's Love in Relationships* (635)
+ *Did Anyone Get It Right?* (637)
+ *Do We Get What We Deserve?* (640)
+ *Pained? Pursue* (643)
+ *Job's Daughters: What's in a Name* (645)

HOW LONG DOES IT TAKE TO READ?

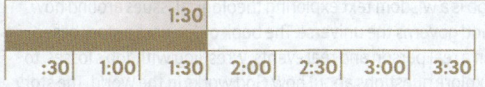

Prologue

1 There once was a man named Job who lived in the land of Uz. He was blameless—a man of complete integrity. He feared God and stayed away from evil. ²He had seven sons and three daughters. ³He owned 7,000 sheep, 3,000 camels, 500 teams of oxen, and 500 female donkeys. He also had many servants. He was, in fact, the richest person in that entire area.

⁴Job's sons would take turns preparing feasts in their homes, and they would also invite their three sisters to celebrate with them. ⁵When these celebrations ended—sometimes after several days—Job would purify his children. He would get up early in the morning and offer a burnt offering for each of them. For Job said to himself, "Perhaps my children have sinned and have cursed God in their hearts." This was Job's regular practice.

Job's First Test

⁶One day the members of the heavenly court* came to present themselves before the Lord, and the Accuser, Satan,* came with them. ⁷"Where have you come from?" the Lord asked Satan.

Satan answered the Lord, "I have been patrolling the earth, watching everything that's going on."

⁸Then the Lord asked Satan, "Have you noticed my servant Job? He is the finest man in all the earth. He is blameless—a man of complete integrity. He fears God and stays away from evil."

⁹Satan replied to the Lord, "Yes, but Job has good reason to fear God. ¹⁰You have always put a wall of protection around him and his home and his property. You have made him prosper in everything he does. Look how rich he is! ¹¹But reach out and take away everything he has, and he will surely curse you to your face!"

¹²"All right, you may test him," the Lord said to Satan. "Do whatever you want with everything he possesses, but don't harm him physically." So Satan left the Lord's presence.

¹³One day when Job's sons and daughters were feasting at the oldest brother's house, ¹⁴a messenger arrived at Job's home with this news: "Your oxen were plowing, with the donkeys feeding beside them, ¹⁵when the Sabeans raided us. They stole all the animals and killed all the farmhands. I am the only one who escaped to tell you."

¹⁶While he was still speaking, another messenger arrived with this news: "The fire of God has fallen from heaven and burned up your sheep and all the shepherds. I am the only one who escaped to tell you."

1:6a Hebrew *the sons of God.* **1:6b** Hebrew *and the satan;* similarly throughout this chapter.

1:1–2:13 Job opens by describing a scene in the "heavenly court" (1:6). In the ancient world, those who worshiped multiple deities believed that their gods and goddesses met in a heavenly council (or court) to discuss governing the universe. The Old Testament reflects a similar understanding of the divine world. However, Yahweh, Israel's god, reigns supreme among angels and other kinds of divine beings rather than merely being the most powerful deity. The discussion in the heavenly court confirms Job's integrity for the book's audience, although Job and his friends are never told about the discussions. Their lack of knowledge allows for a test of whether Job simply acted blamelessly out of concern for his own best interests or whether he actually feared God. (See note on 1:9-11.)

1:1 Uz's location is debated, but it was outside what would later become Israel. It was either in Edom to the south or in Aram to the north. The text describes Job as "blameless." The Hebrew word (*tam*) does not suggest that Job was sinless and perfect. Rather, it means he was a person of character and integrity, perhaps based on human standards of the time. The description of him as "a man of complete integrity" indicates that he was also someone who lived according to God's ways.

1:2-3 Job possessed great wealth and an ideal family (seven sons and three daughters), based on other ancient literature from the region.

1:5 Ritual washing and changing clothes were common ways for individuals to purify themselves before offering a sacrifice (Genesis 35:2; Exodus 19:10, 14). The common time for prayer or making personal sacrifices was "early in the morning" (see Genesis 22:3; Psalm 5:3; Mark 1:35). Job sacrificed burnt offerings like this because he was concerned that his children, while celebrating together, might have "cursed God in their hearts," which was a capital crime (Leviticus 24:10-16; 1 Kings 21:9-13; see Job 1:11; 2:5, 9). Job understood that having a sinful attitude in one's heart constitutes sin (Jeremiah 17:9-10; Mark 7:21-23). Job acted as a priest for his family, similar to how the Levites would act for all Israelites.

1:6 "Satan" reflects the traditional translation of the Hebrew term used here (literally, *the satan*), but the Hebrew word includes a definite article, so it is not a name. Instead of referring to this member of the heavenly court by name, "the satan" refers to a title or a legal role within the court. The title "the accuser" reflects this sense but carries a negative connotation that may not have been originally intended. A more neutral rendering might be "the challenger."

1:9-11 Satan, the accuser/challenger, questioned whether Job feared God genuinely. What he proposed depends on the "retribution principle," the theory that righteous people prosper and wicked suffer. In other words, if you're a good person, good things will come to you; if you're a bad person, then bad things will come back to you. Ancient Israelites assumed this was how the world worked; further, God's justice required that God keep to this principle, too. But if Job received benefits for fearing God, were his initial motives pure? Did he truly fear God, or was he simply acting in his own best interests? The accuser was challenging the impact of God's ways of rewarding the just.

1:12; 2:6 The idea that God allows harm to prove a point raises serious theological concerns. Some suggest that the book of Job is a wisdom text exploring theological issues around how God governs the universe. The book of Job uses a story based on a real person and real events, wrestling with Job's losses, to explore questions about how God works in the world. The story invites us to trust God's wisdom when there are no answers.

¹⁷While he was still speaking, a third messenger arrived with this news: "Three bands of Chaldean raiders have stolen your camels and killed your servants. I am the only one who escaped to tell you."

¹⁸While he was still speaking, another messenger arrived with this news: "Your sons and daughters were feasting in their oldest brother's home. ¹⁹Suddenly, a powerful wind swept in from the wilderness and hit the house on all sides. The house collapsed, and all your children are dead. I am the only one who escaped to tell you."

²⁰Job stood up and tore his robe in grief. Then he shaved his head and fell to the ground to worship. ²¹He said,

"I came naked from my mother's womb,
    and I will be naked when I leave.
The LORD gave me what I had,
    and the LORD has taken it away.
Praise the name of the LORD!"

²²In all of this, Job did not sin by blaming God.

Job's Second Test

2 One day the members of the heavenly court* came again to present themselves before the LORD, and the Accuser, Satan,* came with them. ²"Where have you come from?" the LORD asked Satan.

Satan answered the LORD, "I have been patrolling the earth, watching everything that's going on."

³Then the LORD asked Satan, "Have you noticed my servant Job? He is the finest man in all the earth. He is blameless—a man of complete integrity. He fears God and stays away from evil. And he has maintained his integrity, even though you urged me to harm him without cause."

⁴Satan replied to the LORD, "Skin for skin! A man will give up everything he has to save his life. ⁵But reach out and take away his health, and he will surely curse you to your face!"

⁶"All right, do with him as you please," the LORD said to Satan. "But spare his life." ⁷So Satan left the LORD's presence, and he struck Job with terrible boils from head to foot.

⁸Job scraped his skin with a piece of broken pottery as he sat among the ashes. ⁹His wife said to him, "Are you still trying to maintain your integrity? Curse God and die."

¹⁰But Job replied, "You talk like a foolish woman. Should we accept only good things from the hand of God and never anything bad?" So in all this, Job said nothing wrong.

Job's Three Friends Share His Anguish

¹¹When three of Job's friends heard of the tragedy he had suffered, they got together and traveled from their homes to comfort and console him. Their names were Eliphaz the Temanite, Bildad the Shuhite, and Zophar the Naamathite. ¹²When they saw Job from a distance, they scarcely recognized him. Wailing loudly, they tore their robes and threw dust into the air over their heads to show their grief. ¹³Then they sat on the ground with him for seven

---

2:1a Hebrew *the sons of God.* 2:1b Hebrew *and the satan;* similarly throughout this chapter.

1:20 Satan, the accuser/challenger, expected Job to curse God to his face defiantly (1:11). After Job lost all his children and possessions, he instead blessed God. He fell in worship and proclaimed, "Praise the name of the LORD!"

2:9-10 While Job responded harshly to his wife, her comment foreshadowed Job's own speech: He did not take her advice to "curse God and die," but he would curse the day of his birth and long for death (3:3-26). Her words also raise a central issue in the book: How can Job bless God and still maintain his integrity if he believes God has not acted justly?

2:9 Job's wife first summarized the essence of Job's temptation by echoing God's words (2:3); Job was trying to maintain his integrity. In her frustration and anguish, however, she then counseled Job to curse God and thus unknowingly fulfill the accuser's/challenger's ("Satan's") prediction (1:11; 2:5).

2:10 By saying "nothing wrong," Job controlled his tongue, an essential behavior in Wisdom Literature (Proverbs 13:3; 21:23; see James 3:2). This comment has greater relevance, though. The phrase "said nothing wrong" could more literally be translated as "did not sin with his lips." Thus, we see that not only did Job wisely control his speech but he also did not sin against God. When we speak truth in painful circumstances, we can consider how to honor God in what we say and how we say it.

2:11 It might have taken several months for Job's friends to hear of his afflictions (see 7:3). The text implies that Job's friends were Edomites, a people who were famous for their wisdom (see Jeremiah 49:7; Obadiah 1:8). Eliphaz the Temanite was probably a descendant of Esau's grandson Teman (Genesis 36:10-11, 15), and his land was located in Edom (Ezekiel 25:13; Amos 1:11-12). Bildad the Shuhite's name may indicate that he was from Edom, like Bilhan, a descendant of Esau (Genesis 36:27; 1 Chronicles 1:42) and like Bedad, father of the Edomite king Hadad (Genesis 36:35; 1 Chronicles 1:46). No place named Shuah is known, but Abraham's son Shuah was sent to "a land in the east" (Genesis 25:1-2, 6; 1 Chronicles 1:32). The Greek Old Testament lists Zophar (instead of Zepho) as one of Esau's grandsons (Genesis 36:11, 15; 1 Chronicles 1:36). A Naamathite might reside in a town named Naamah, but no such location is known. Two OT women are named Naamah, but neither is a likely relative of Zophar (Genesis 4:22; 1 Kings 14:21).

2:12-13 The language describing Job's friends' actions in 2:12 parallels the language used in Exodus 9:8-10 where Moses throws ashes and the plague of boils breaks out in Egypt. It suggests that this act was not just part of an ancient mourning ritual (Joshua 7:6; Lamentations 2:10; Ezekiel 27:30). Instead, throwing dust into the air was the friends' symbolic way of asking God to afflict them with the same suffering and sores from which their friend Job suffered. Before they condemned Job with their speech, they were willing to share his pain. When we hear of someone's pain, it's easy to minimize it or give them our easy answers. Before we verbally respond, how can we first enter their suffering with them?

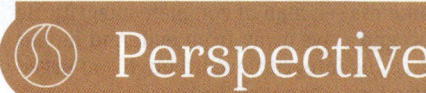

Perspective

What can God see that we can't?

SCRIPTURE CONNECTION: JOB 1:6-12; 2:1-7

The book of Job offers a rare glimpse of God's heavenly council, where God deliberates with angels on how to rule. This scene is troubling.

As readers, we learn why Job will suffer, but Job does not. Like all of us, his earthly experience lacks a backstage pass.

The book opens with an emphasis on Job's good character ("He was blameless—a man of complete integrity," 1:1). Job is not sinless, but his practice is to carefully address any sin, known or unknown, by offering the sacrifices God required (1:5). Job knows his suffering is undeserved, so he questions whether God is just. But his friends assume that Job must have sinned terribly. None of them can comprehend the reason for Job's devastation.

But we can. We know that God bragged about Job to the heavenly court (1:8; 2:3). We know that the adversary—"the Accuser, Satan" (1:6)—thought Job's righteousness was motivated by what he could gain (1:9-11; 2:4-5). Convinced of Job's integrity, God invited the adversary to conduct a costly test (1:12; 2:6). Job suffered not because of his failure but because of his virtue.

We are not in a position to know why *we* suffer. Like Job, we sit under stage lights with everyone's eyes on us, and we can't see backstage. This book invites us to trust God's wisdom, even when we don't understand his ways.

VIEWPOINTS

HIS: Job questioned God's justice because he could not see the whole story.
MINE: "When my life comes unglued, I want answers, but God offers himself."
YOURS: Is it freeing to realize you don't need to figure out the reason for life's hardships? Simply trust the One who sees it all.

CARMEN JOY IMES, PhD, is an author, speaker, blogger, YouTuber, and serves as associate professor of Old Testament at Biola University in California.

days and nights. No one said a word to Job, for they saw that his suffering was too great for words.

Job's First Speech

3 At last Job spoke, and he cursed the day of his birth. ²He said:

³ "Let the day of my birth be erased,
   and the night I was conceived.
⁴ Let that day be turned to darkness.
   Let it be lost even to God on high,
   and let no light shine on it.
⁵ Let the darkness and utter gloom claim that day for its own.
   Let a black cloud overshadow it,
   and let the darkness terrify it.
⁶ Let that night be blotted off the calendar,
   never again to be counted among the days of the year,
   never again to appear among the months.
⁷ Let that night be childless.
   Let it have no joy.
⁸ Let those who are experts at cursing—
   whose cursing could rouse Leviathan*—
   curse that day.
⁹ Let its morning stars remain dark.
   Let it hope for light, but in vain;
   may it never see the morning light.
¹⁰ Curse that day for failing to shut my mother's womb,
   for letting me be born to see all this trouble.

¹¹ "Why wasn't I born dead?
   Why didn't I die as I came from the womb?
¹² Why was I laid on my mother's lap?
   Why did she nurse me at her breasts?
¹³ Had I died at birth, I would now be at peace.
   I would be asleep and at rest.

3:8 The identification of Leviathan is disputed, ranging from an earthly creature to a mythical sea monster in ancient literature.

3:1–27:23 This second section includes a poetic dialogue between Job and his friends. It represents some of the Bible's most sophisticated poetry. The section opens with Job's lament and then moves to three cycles of speeches. In each cycle, Job responds to his friends' speeches.
3:1-26 Up to this point, Job has responded piously, but when Job curses the very day of his birth, we might ask why he has been called "patient." The idea of the "patience of Job" comes from the King James Version's translation of James 5:11. The NLT is more accurate: "You know about Job, a man of great endurance." Job's endurance was not always pretty or patient, but his faith did endure. Despite his pain, anger, and questions, he kept seeking God. When we face the greatest hardships of our lives, such as caring for aging parents or a child with special needs, being in a relationship that feels like it's failing, or struggling to make ends meet, we need not pressure ourselves to be someone else's idea of perfect. Rather, as we continue to seek God, as Job did, we can honor God in our long-lasting suffering.

Job's Wife

IDENTITY — Grieving to Perceiving

Job's wife remembers...

Those were my children, too! All my children died in that collapsed house.

That was my family and livelihood. Gone in one day. So, I told my husband to curse God.

Before you judge me, before you decide I was wrong to say what I did, think about how you would feel if it happened to you.

Even one loss is enough to undo the faithful. Try losing your entire family and worldly goods. I was in pain and shock. So when my husband, all I had left, was struck with illness, I had no reserves for that.

I had descended to a place of grief that no trite phrase or pat answer was going to fix. I was honest about how I felt. I said the thing that most people are unwilling to say when the pain is a wave you can be crushed under.

My husband's friends tried to explain it away and point fingers. Their ranting did nothing to solve the problem. My words may have been few, but I didn't try to fix our pain by fixing him.

So, what am I learning, now that God is restoring my husband and our lives (Job 42:10-16)? Grief is different for every human being. Don't try to solve someone else's pain. And don't judge them for it either. Only God understands, and he remains good.

JOB'S WIFE'S STORY IS TOLD IN THE BOOK OF JOB.

> Only God understands our pain fully, and he remains good through it all.

IDENTIFY

What do you do when you feel crushed by sadness?

Has there been a time when you experienced loss and grief? How did you respond to other people and to God?

"I have been grieving and have found others' solutions to be uninformed. What I most often need is someone to sit with me quietly, in the pain, without a formula for my grief. When we're hurting, we can say things we do not mean. Having others judge us is not helpful."

CARA DAY is a writer and illustrator. She has served with Stonecroft Ministries helping women live "extraordinary."

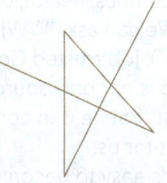

14 I would rest with the world's kings and prime ministers,
  whose great buildings now lie in ruins.
15 I would rest with princes, rich in gold,
  whose palaces were filled with silver.
16 Why wasn't I buried like a stillborn child,
  like a baby who never lives to see the light?
17 For in death the wicked cause no trouble,
  and the weary are at rest.
18 Even captives are at ease in death,
  with no guards to curse them.
19 Rich and poor are both there,
  and the slave is free from his master.
20 "Oh, why give light to those in misery,
  and life to those who are bitter?
21 They long for death, and it won't come.
  They search for death more eagerly than for hidden treasure.
22 They're filled with joy when they finally die,
  and rejoice when they find the grave.
23 Why is life given to those with no future,
  those God has surrounded with difficulties?
24 I cannot eat for sighing;
  my groans pour out like water.
25 What I always feared has happened to me.
  What I dreaded has come true.
26 I have no peace, no quietness.
  I have no rest; only trouble comes."

3:14 The dead were thought to continue their identities and social status after death, so Job expected to be among "the world's kings and prime ministers" once he died.

Come Close

DISSATISFIED: OPEN-HANDED

SCRIPTURE CONNECTION: JOB 1:20-22

When I worked in a corporate environment, my mindset was focused on this world. I thought about what I would and could buy, obtain, and possess—all material things. The question in my mind was usually, *What can I buy next?* I was all about the labels.

Job was not all about the labels and he had abundance. When everything was taken away, he still gave all glory to God (see 1:21). The New Testament also teaches us to hold our material possessions loosely and learn contentment by trusting God. In a letter, Paul reminds Timothy of Job's attitude toward wealth: "Yet true godliness with contentment is itself great wealth. After all, we brought nothing with us . . . and we can't take anything with us when we leave it" (1 Timothy 6:6-7).

Just like Job, something has probably been taken away from you on this earth, maybe loved ones, health, or material things.

We can ask, "WWJD?" ("What would Job do?"). Job trusted God as his only source. God is our only source as well, and we can trust that he is in control and knows what's best for us.

It's easy to become too attached to what we have in this world, so Job reminds us that we came in with nothing and will leave with nothing. We can trust God for abundance that endures.

REFLECT "I came naked from my mother's womb, and I will be naked when I leave. The LORD gave me what I had, and the LORD has taken it away. Praise the name of the LORD!" JOB 1:21

God, please help me to trust you in all you do and praise your name. Amen.

CONSIDER "It's important to not give up on God when life appears to have given up on you. . . . [S]ometimes, you have to trust God when you don't see the benefits, the blessings, and all the frills of the faith." TONY EVANS

> When life is hard, we can trust God as our only source.

RACHEL LINDSAY McCANTS is an author, speaker, and founder of R. Lindsay Unlimited, which encourages, inspires, and challenges ladies to raise their self-worth and standards and to walk in God's will, in Jesus' name.

Eliphaz's First Response to Job

4 Then Eliphaz the Temanite replied to Job:

² "Will you be patient and let me say a word?
  For who could keep from speaking out?

³ "In the past you have encouraged many people;
  you have strengthened those who were weak.
⁴ Your words have supported those who were falling;
  you encouraged those with shaky knees.
⁵ But now when trouble strikes, you lose heart.
  You are terrified when it touches you.
⁶ Doesn't your reverence for God give you confidence?
  Doesn't your life of integrity give you hope?

⁷ "Stop and think! Do the innocent die?
  When have the upright been destroyed?
⁸ My experience shows that those who plant trouble
  and cultivate evil will harvest the same.
⁹ A breath from God destroys them.
  They vanish in a blast of his anger.
¹⁰ The lion roars and the wildcat snarls,
  but the teeth of strong lions will be broken.
¹¹ The fierce lion will starve for lack of prey,
  and the cubs of the lioness will be scattered.

¹² "This truth was given to me in secret,
  as though whispered in my ear.
¹³ It came to me in a disturbing vision at night,
  when people are in a deep sleep.
¹⁴ Fear gripped me,
  and my bones trembled.
¹⁵ A spirit* swept past my face,
  and my hair stood on end.*
¹⁶ The spirit stopped, but I couldn't see its shape.
  There was a form before my eyes.
  In the silence I heard a voice say,
¹⁷ 'Can a mortal be innocent before God?
  Can anyone be pure before the Creator?'

¹⁸ "If God does not trust his own angels
  and has charged his messengers with foolishness,
¹⁹ how much less will he trust people made of clay!
  They are made of dust, crushed as easily as a moth.
²⁰ They are alive in the morning but dead by evening,
  gone forever without a trace.
²¹ Their tent-cords are pulled and the tent collapses,
  and they die in ignorance.

Eliphaz's Response Continues

5 "Cry for help, but will anyone answer you?
  Which of the angels* will help you?
² Surely resentment destroys the fool,
  and jealousy kills the simple.
³ I have seen that fools may be successful for the moment,
  but then comes sudden disaster.
⁴ Their children are abandoned far from help;
  they are crushed in court with no one to defend them.
⁵ The hungry devour their harvest,
  even when it is guarded by brambles.*
  The thirsty pant after their wealth.*
⁶ But evil does not spring from the soil,
  and trouble does not sprout from the earth.
⁷ People are born for trouble
  as readily as sparks fly up from a fire.

⁸ "If I were you, I would go to God
  and present my case to him.

4:15a Or *wind;* also in 4:16. **4:15b** Or *its wind sent shivers up my spine.* **5:1** Hebrew *the holy ones.* **5:5a** The meaning of the Hebrew for this phrase is uncertain. **5:5b** As in Greek and Syriac versions; Hebrew reads *A snare snatches their wealth.*

4:1–14:22 This section includes the first of the three rounds of speeches (4:1–27:23) by Job and his friends. In this first round, Job's friends encourage him to seek God so that he can again enjoy prosperity.
4:6-9 These verses reflect the retribution principle: righteous people prosper, and wicked people suffer (see study note on 1:9-11). Eliphaz based his belief on his own experience (4:8); however, we might wonder about his "experience." To what extent did Eliphaz assume that someone was good or bad because they had good or bad circumstances? To what extent did he see actual righteous behaviors rewarded and wicked ones punished? How can we avoid judging someone as "good" or "bad" based on what has happened to them and not on what they have done?
4:17 As the characters in the book repeatedly acknowledge, no one is truly innocent or pure (see 9:2; 15:14; 25:4; 35:7) because all have done wrong or been corrupted by sin (Psalm 14:3; 53:3; Romans 3:10-11). Eliphaz used these terms to mean that human beings are sinful creatures and God is the sinless Creator. Job and God used them to mean that Job had faithfully carried out the duties inherent in his relationship with God (for example, Job 1:8; 2:3). Job and Eliphaz never agreed on the meaning of these terms.
5:8-16 Eliphaz framed his advice to Job by praising God, making observations about him that ring true. God does send rain (5:10), but sometimes God withholds rain (Job 12:15; 1 Kings 17:1). We also know that Job was blameless, while Eliphaz implied Job was suffering because he was guilty of something. In Job, then, we must be careful to interpret individual statements in context. As Wisdom Literature, the book includes a dialogue where people disagree with one another. We cannot take a verse out of context and say it is "true" without considering whether it is true within the context of the book and the wider context of the Bible. We also need to recognize that, as Wisdom Literature, its sayings are generally, but not always, true.
5:8 To "go to God" meant lodging a formal appeal with God for assistance, counsel, or vindication, sometimes by way of repentance (Amos 5:4, 6) and possibly through prophecy (Genesis 25:22; 1 Samuel 9:9; 1 Kings 22:8). Job wanted to present his case to God (Job 13:3, 15, 18; 23:3-8), and later he attempted to do so (29:1–31:40).

⁹ He does great things too marvelous to understand.
  He performs countless miracles.
¹⁰ He gives rain for the earth
  and water for the fields.
¹¹ He gives prosperity to the poor
  and protects those who suffer.
¹² He frustrates the plans of schemers
  so the work of their hands will not succeed.
¹³ He traps the wise in their own cleverness
  so their cunning schemes are thwarted.
¹⁴ They find it is dark in the daytime,
  and they grope at noon as if it were night.
¹⁵ He rescues the poor from the cutting words of the strong,
  and rescues them from the clutches of the powerful.
¹⁶ And so at last the poor have hope,
  and the snapping jaws of the wicked are shut.
¹⁷ "But consider the joy of those corrected by God!
  Do not despise the discipline of the Almighty when you sin.
¹⁸ For though he wounds, he also bandages.
  He strikes, but his hands also heal.
¹⁹ From six disasters he will rescue you;
  even in the seventh, he will keep you from evil.
²⁰ He will save you from death in time of famine,
  from the power of the sword in time of war.
²¹ You will be safe from slander
  and have no fear when destruction comes.
²² You will laugh at destruction and famine;
  wild animals will not terrify you.
²³ You will be at peace with the stones of the field,
  and its wild animals will be at peace with you.
²⁴ You will know that your home is safe.
  When you survey your possessions, nothing will be missing.
²⁵ You will have many children;
  your descendants will be as plentiful as grass!
²⁶ You will go to the grave at a ripe old age,
  like a sheaf of grain harvested at the proper time!
²⁷ "We have studied life and found all this to be true.
  Listen to my counsel, and apply it to yourself."

Job's Second Speech: A Response to Eliphaz

6 Then Job spoke again:

² "If my misery could be weighed
  and my troubles be put on the scales,
³ they would outweigh all the sands of the sea.
  That is why I spoke impulsively.
⁴ For the Almighty has struck me down with his arrows.
  Their poison infects my spirit.
  God's terrors are lined up against me.
⁵ Don't I have a right to complain?
  Don't wild donkeys bray when they find no grass,
  and oxen bellow when they have no food?
⁶ Don't people complain about unsalted food?
  Does anyone want the tasteless white of an egg?*
⁷ My appetite disappears when I look at it;
  I gag at the thought of eating it!
⁸ "Oh, that I might have my request,
  that God would grant my desire.
⁹ I wish he would crush me.
  I wish he would reach out his hand and kill me.
¹⁰ At least I can take comfort in this:
  Despite the pain,
  I have not denied the words of the Holy One.
¹¹ But I don't have the strength to endure.
  I have nothing to live for.
¹² Do I have the strength of a stone?
  Is my body made of bronze?
¹³ No, I am utterly helpless,
  without any chance of success.

¹⁴ "One should be kind to a fainting friend,
  but you accuse me without any fear of the Almighty.*
¹⁵ My brothers, you have proved as unreliable as a seasonal brook
  that overflows its banks in the spring
¹⁶ when it is swollen with ice and melting snow.
¹⁷ But when the hot weather arrives, the water disappears.
  The brook vanishes in the heat.
¹⁸ The caravans turn aside to be refreshed,
  but there is nothing to drink, so they die.
¹⁹ The caravans from Tema search for this water;
  the travelers from Sheba hope to find it.
²⁰ They count on it but are disappointed.
  When they arrive, their hopes are dashed.
²¹ You, too, have given no help.
  You have seen my calamity, and you are afraid.
²² But why? Have I ever asked you for a gift?
  Have I begged for anything of yours for myself?

6:6 Or *the tasteless juice of the mallow plant?* 6:14 Or *friend, / or he might lose his fear of the Almighty.*

6:1–7:21 Job's response attacks his counselors (6:1-30) and challenges God (7:6-21). He excuses his passionate words by referencing the depths of his misery (6:2-3; 7:11). Job says that Eliphaz has failed to offer comfort or sympathy as a friend, having chosen instead to haggle over stale theological principles.

6:21 Job's comment raises a question for us: When we walk through suffering with a friend, are our words driven by the fear that something similar could happen to us? Are we willing to sit quietly with them, pray for them, and offer tangible help? Or are we more like Job's friends, offering platitudes that do more harm than good?

Insight: NUMBERING JOB'S LOSSES

When we experience loss, we may find ourselves detailing a list of what is missing, perhaps as part of grieving or maybe for the insurance company. We may tally these lost things in our minds, hoping we will see them restored someday.

Job lost everyone that he loved, everything that he and his family had worked for, and his excellent health (Job 1:1–2:10). In the face of such immense loss and suffering, even his wife questioned him and God.

SABEAN RAIDERS
1,000 oxen and 500 female donkeys captured and all farmhands killed

FIREBALL FROM THE SKY
7,000 sheep and all their herders incinerated

CHALDEAN RAIDERS
3,000 camels stolen and their handlers killed

TORNADO
Seven sons and three daughters killed when house collapsed

BOILS FROM HEAD TO TOE
Loss of health

What unwanted events have stolen or destroyed relationships, possessions or positions, or well-being that you valued? This chart includes possible examples and questions to help you reflect on your experiences with loss and how those have impacted your understanding of God.

YOUR LIFE EVENT	YOUR LOSS	NEW VIEW OF GOD
Cutbacks at work	Losing the community I interacted with every day, my sense of security, and even maybe my identity.	I found I could trust God to provide (Psalm 34; Matthew 6:25-34).
My spouse, my friend, or my adult child pulling away	Finding comfort in being a family and in the closeness of people who know me best.	I found freedom in realizing that God lets his creation walk away from him, too. And yet, he pursues them in love. While the absence daily breaks my heart, I learned to pray and know God takes care of those I love, even when I cannot (Luke 15:11-32).
What life event brought you grief and pain?	What did you lose?	How did your losses lead you to experience God differently?

²³ Have I asked you to rescue me from my enemies,
    or to save me from ruthless people?
²⁴ Teach me, and I will keep quiet.
    Show me what I have done wrong.
²⁵ Honest words can be painful,
    but what do your criticisms amount to?
²⁶ Do you think your words are convincing
    when you disregard my cry of desperation?
²⁷ You would even send an orphan into slavery*
    or sell a friend.
²⁸ Look at me!
    Would I lie to your face?
²⁹ Stop assuming my guilt,
    for I have done no wrong.
³⁰ Do you think I am lying?
    Don't I know the difference between right and wrong?

7 "Is not all human life a struggle?
    Our lives are like that of a hired hand,
² like a worker who longs for the shade,
    like a servant waiting to be paid.
³ I, too, have been assigned months of futility,
    long and weary nights of misery.
⁴ Lying in bed, I think, 'When will it be morning?'
    But the night drags on, and I toss till dawn.
⁵ My body is covered with maggots and scabs.
    My skin breaks open, oozing with pus.

Job Cries Out to God

⁶ "My days fly faster than a weaver's shuttle.
    They end without hope.
⁷ O God, remember that my life is but a breath,
    and I will never again feel happiness.
⁸ You see me now, but not for long.
    You will look for me, but I will be gone.
⁹ Just as a cloud dissipates and vanishes,
    those who die* will not come back.
¹⁰ They are gone forever from their home—
    never to be seen again.

¹¹ "I cannot keep from speaking.
    I must express my anguish.
    My bitter soul must complain.
¹² Am I a sea monster or a dragon
    that you must place me under guard?
¹³ I think, 'My bed will comfort me,
    and sleep will ease my misery,'
¹⁴ but then you shatter me with dreams
    and terrify me with visions.
¹⁵ I would rather be strangled—
    rather die than suffer like this.
¹⁶ I hate my life and don't want to go on living.
    Oh, leave me alone for my few remaining days.

¹⁷ "What are people, that you should make so much of us,
    that you should think of us so often?
¹⁸ For you examine us every morning
    and test us every moment.
¹⁹ Why won't you leave me alone,
    at least long enough for me to swallow!
²⁰ If I have sinned, what have I done to you,
    O watcher of all humanity?
    Why make me your target?
    Am I a burden to you?*
²¹ Why not just forgive my sin
    and take away my guilt?
    For soon I will lie down in the dust and die.
    When you look for me, I will be gone."

Bildad's First Response to Job

8 Then Bildad the Shuhite replied to Job:

² "How long will you go on like this?
    You sound like a blustering wind.
³ Does God twist justice?
    Does the Almighty twist what is right?
⁴ Your children must have sinned against him,
    so their punishment was well deserved.
⁵ But if you pray to God
    and seek the favor of the Almighty,
⁶ and if you are pure and live with integrity,
    he will surely rise up and restore your happy home.
⁷ And though you started with little,
    you will end with much.

⁸ "Just ask the previous generation.
    Pay attention to the experience of our ancestors.
⁹ For we were born but yesterday and know nothing.
    Our days on earth are as fleeting as a shadow.

6:27 Hebrew *even gamble over an orphan.* **7:9** Hebrew *who go down to Sheol.* **7:20** As in Greek version; Hebrew reads *target, so that I am a burden to myself.*

7:3 Job's ordeal might already have gone on for months. The Hebrew term (*amal*) that runs throughout Job is translated as "misery," or "miserable" (3:20; 7:3; 11:16; 16:2; 20:22), or as "trouble" (3:10; 4:8; 5:6, 7; 15:35).
7:9 This is the first explicit mention of Sheol, the ancient Israelite place of the dead, in Job. It is described as a place of rest from earthly pressures and distinctions (3:13-19); a dark dwelling place (10:21-22; 17:13); deep in the earth (11:8); and covered in dust (17:16). In the Old Testament, it was the destiny of all the living (30:23) from which no one could return (10:21; see Genesis 37:35; 2 Samuel 22:6).

8:1 Like Eliphaz, Bildad the Shuhite (see 2:11) believed that Job's sufferings were God's retribution (8:3-6, 13; see 4:7-8; 5:2-3). This counselor revered the wisdom of the past (8:8-10; see 4:7) and addressed Job with a mixture of instruction (8:3-6, 8-10; see 5:9-16) and encouragement (8:5-7, 20-22; see 4:6; 5:19-26). His point was that Job should quit blustering. He advised Job to repent and allow God's justice to bring about restoration (8:1-7). However, if Job were to take this advice, then Satan (the accuser/challenger) would be proven right: Job's actions would be driven by self-interest (see study note on 1:9-11).

10 But those who came before us will teach you.
   They will teach you the wisdom of old.
11 "Can papyrus reeds grow tall without a marsh?
   Can marsh grass flourish without water?
12 While they are still flowering, not ready to be cut,
   they begin to wither more quickly than grass.
13 The same happens to all who forget God.
   The hopes of the godless evaporate.
14 Their confidence hangs by a thread.
   They are leaning on a spider's web.
15 They cling to their home for security, but it won't last.
   They try to hold it tight, but it will not endure.
16 The godless seem like a lush plant growing in the sunshine,
   its branches spreading across the garden.
17 Its roots grow down through a pile of stones;
   it takes hold on a bed of rocks.
18 But when it is uprooted,
   it's as though it never existed!
19 That's the end of its life,
   and others spring up from the earth to replace it.
20 "But look, God will not reject a person of integrity,
   nor will he lend a hand to the wicked.
21 He will once again fill your mouth with laughter
   and your lips with shouts of joy.
22 Those who hate you will be clothed with shame,
   and the home of the wicked will be destroyed."

Job's Third Speech: A Response to Bildad

9 Then Job spoke again:

2 "Yes, I know all this is true in principle.
   But how can a person be declared innocent in God's sight?
3 If someone wanted to take God to court,*
   would it be possible to answer him even once in a thousand times?
4 For God is so wise and so mighty.
   Who has ever challenged him successfully?
5 "Without warning, he moves the mountains,
   overturning them in his anger.
6 He shakes the earth from its place,
   and its foundations tremble.
7 If he commands it, the sun won't rise
   and the stars won't shine.
8 He alone has spread out the heavens
   and marches on the waves of the sea.
9 He made all the stars—the Bear and Orion,
   the Pleiades and the constellations of the southern sky.
10 He does great things too marvelous to understand.
   He performs countless miracles.
11 "Yet when he comes near, I cannot see him.
   When he moves by, I do not see him go.
12 If he snatches someone in death, who can stop him?
   Who dares to ask, 'What are you doing?'
13 And God does not restrain his anger.
   Even the monsters of the sea* are crushed beneath his feet.
14 "So who am I, that I should try to answer God
   or even reason with him?
15 Even if I were right, I would have no defense.
   I could only plead for mercy.
16 And even if I summoned him and he responded,
   I'm not sure he would listen to me.
17 For he attacks me with a storm
   and repeatedly wounds me without cause.
18 He will not let me catch my breath,
   but fills me instead with bitter sorrows.
19 If it's a question of strength, he's the strong one.
   If it's a matter of justice, who dares to summon him* to court?
20 Though I am innocent, my own mouth would pronounce me guilty.
   Though I am blameless, it* would prove me wicked.
21 "I am innocent,
   but it makes no difference to me—
   I despise my life.
22 Innocent or wicked, it is all the same to God.
   That's why I say, 'He destroys both the blameless and the wicked.'
23 When a plague* sweeps through,
   he laughs at the death of the innocent.
24 The whole earth is in the hands of the wicked,
   and God blinds the eyes of the judges.
   If he's not the one who does it, who is?
25 "My life passes more swiftly than a runner.
   It flees away without a glimpse of happiness.
26 It disappears like a swift papyrus boat,
   like an eagle swooping down on its prey.
27 If I decided to forget my complaints,
   to put away my sad face and be cheerful,

9:3 Or *If God wanted to take someone to court.* 9:13 Hebrew *the helpers of Rahab,* the name of a mythical sea monster that represents chaos in ancient literature. 9:19 As in Greek version; Hebrew reads *me.* 9:20 Or *he.* 9:23 Or *disaster.*

9:1-35 Job responded to Bildad by describing God's cosmic and judicial power. His speech sounds like a complicated legal case, with a summons and response (9:3, 14-16, 19, 32), the possibility of self-incrimination (9:20), an arbiter (9:33-34), an accusatory question (9:12), a legal sentence (9:22), and a declaration of guilt (9:28-29).

28 I would still dread all the pain,
   for I know you will not find me innocent,
      O God.
29 Whatever happens, I will be found guilty.
   So what's the use of trying?
30 Even if I were to wash myself with soap
   and clean my hands with lye,
31 you would plunge me into a muddy ditch,
   and my own filthy clothing would hate me.
32 "God is not a mortal like me,
   so I cannot argue with him or take him to trial.
33 If only there were a mediator between us,
   someone who could bring us together.
34 The mediator could make God stop beating me,
   and I would no longer live in terror of his punishment.
35 Then I could speak to him without fear,
   but I cannot do that in my own strength.

Job Frames His Plea to God

10 "I am disgusted with my life.
   Let me complain freely.
   My bitter soul must complain.
2 I will say to God, 'Don't simply condemn me—
   tell me the charge you are bringing against me.
3 What do you gain by oppressing me?
   Why do you reject me, the work of your own hands,
   while smiling on the schemes of the wicked?
4 Are your eyes like those of a human?
   Do you see things only as people see them?
5 Is your lifetime only as long as ours?
   Is your life so short
6 that you must quickly probe for my guilt
   and search for my sin?
7 Although you know I am not guilty,
   no one can rescue me from your hands.
8 "'You formed me with your hands; you made me,
   yet now you completely destroy me.
9 Remember that you made me from dust—
   will you turn me back to dust so soon?
10 You guided my conception
   and formed me in the womb.*
11 You clothed me with skin and flesh,
   and you knit my bones and sinews together.
12 You gave me life and showed me your unfailing love.
   My life was preserved by your care.
13 "'Yet your real motive—
   your true intent—

14 was to watch me, and if I sinned,
   you would not forgive my guilt.
15 If I am guilty, too bad for me;
   and even if I'm innocent, I can't hold my head high,
   because I am filled with shame and misery.
16 And if I hold my head high, you hunt me like a lion
   and display your awesome power against me.
17 Again and again you witness against me.
   You pour out your growing anger on me
   and bring fresh armies against me.
18 "'Why, then, did you deliver me from my mother's womb?
   Why didn't you let me die at birth?
19 It would be as though I had never existed,
   going directly from the womb to the grave.
20 I have only a few days left, so leave me alone,
   that I may have a moment of comfort
21 before I leave—never to return—
   for the land of darkness and utter gloom.
22 It is a land as dark as midnight,
   a land of gloom and confusion,
   where even the light is dark as midnight.'"

Zophar's First Response to Job

11 Then Zophar the Naamathite replied to Job:

2 "Shouldn't someone answer this torrent of words?
   Is a person proved innocent just by a lot of talking?
3 Should I remain silent while you babble on?
   When you mock God, shouldn't someone make you ashamed?
4 You claim, 'My beliefs are pure,'
   and 'I am clean in the sight of God.'
5 If only God would speak;
   if only he would tell you what he thinks!
6 If only he would tell you the secrets of wisdom,
   for true wisdom is not a simple matter.
   Listen! God is doubtless punishing you
   far less than you deserve!

7 "Can you solve the mysteries of God?
   Can you discover everything about the Almighty?
8 Such knowledge is higher than the heavens—
   and who are you?
   It is deeper than the underworld*—
   what do you know?
9 It is broader than the earth
   and wider than the sea.

10:10 Hebrew *You poured me out like milk / and curdled me like cheese.*   11:8 Hebrew *than Sheol.*

10:8-11 A succession of images describes God's role in creating Job. First, Job says, "You formed me with your hands . . . you made me from dust." This was how a potter made a vessel, and although the potter has undeniable authority over the clay (Isaiah 45:9; Jeremiah 18:5-12; Romans 9:20-25), Job was questioning God. That humans are made from clay or dust is a common motif in Job and represents the temporary nature of life (Job 4:19; 7:9-10, 21; 14:1-2, 10; see Genesis 3:19).

¹⁰ If God comes and puts a person in prison
  or calls the court to order, who can stop him?
¹¹ For he knows those who are false,
  and he takes note of all their sins.
¹² An empty-headed person won't become wise
  any more than a wild donkey can bear a
    human child.*

¹³ "If only you would prepare your heart
    and lift up your hands to him in prayer!
¹⁴ Get rid of your sins,
    and leave all iniquity behind you.
¹⁵ Then your face will brighten with innocence.
    You will be strong and free of fear.
¹⁶ You will forget your misery;
    it will be like water flowing away.
¹⁷ Your life will be brighter than the noonday.
    Even darkness will be as bright as morning.
¹⁸ Having hope will give you courage.
    You will be protected and will rest in safety.
¹⁹ You will lie down unafraid,
    and many will look to you for help.
²⁰ But the wicked will be blinded.
    They will have no escape.
    Their only hope is death."

Job's Fourth Speech: A Response to Zophar

12 Then Job spoke again:

² "You people really know everything, don't you?
    And when you die, wisdom will die with you!
³ Well, I know a few things myself—
    and you're no better than I am.
    Who doesn't know these things you've been
      saying?
⁴ Yet my friends laugh at me,
    for I call on God and expect an answer.
  I am a just and blameless man,
    yet they laugh at me.
⁵ People who are at ease mock those in trouble.
    They give a push to people who are stumbling.
⁶ But robbers are left in peace,
    and those who provoke God live in safety—
    though God keeps them in his power.*

⁷ "Just ask the animals, and they will teach you.
    Ask the birds of the sky, and they will tell you.
⁸ Speak to the earth, and it will instruct you.
    Let the fish in the sea speak to you.

⁹ For they all know
    that my disaster* has come from the hand of
    the LORD.
¹⁰ For the life of every living thing is in his hand,
    and the breath of every human being.
¹¹ The ear tests the words it hears
    just as the mouth distinguishes between foods.
¹² Wisdom belongs to the aged,
    and understanding to the old.

¹³ "But true wisdom and power are found in God;
    counsel and understanding are his.
¹⁴ What he destroys cannot be rebuilt.
    When he puts someone in prison, there is no
      escape.
¹⁵ If he holds back the rain, the earth becomes a
      desert.
    If he releases the waters, they flood the earth.
¹⁶ Yes, strength and wisdom are his;
    deceivers and deceived are both in his power.
¹⁷ He leads counselors away, stripped of good
      judgment;
    wise judges become fools.
¹⁸ He removes the royal robe of kings.
    They are led away with ropes around their
      waist.
¹⁹ He leads priests away, stripped of status;
    he overthrows those with long years in
      power.
²⁰ He silences the trusted adviser
    and removes the insight of the elders.
²¹ He pours disgrace upon princes
    and disarms the strong.

²² "He uncovers mysteries hidden in darkness;
    he brings light to the deepest gloom.
²³ He builds up nations, and he destroys them.
    He expands nations, and he abandons them.
²⁴ He strips kings of understanding
    and leaves them wandering in a pathless
      wasteland.
²⁵ They grope in the darkness without a light.
    He makes them stagger like drunkards.

Job Wants to Argue His Case with God

13 "Look, I have seen all this with my own eyes
    and heard it with my own ears, and now I
    understand.
² I know as much as you do.
    You are no better than I am.

11:12 Or *than a wild male donkey can bear a tame colt.* **12:6** Or *safety—those who try to manipulate God.* The meaning of the Hebrew is uncertain. **12:9** Hebrew *that this.*

11:13-14 Zophar laid out three conditions for restoration (Job 11:15): First, "prepare your heart" in an inward act that is not just a ritual; then, "lift up your hands" in a symbolic gesture of prayer, appeal (Exodus 9:29; Proverbs 1:24; Isaiah 1:15; see Hebrews 11:6; James 5:16), or surrender; and finally, "leave all iniquity," not only by sacrifice and remorse but by quitting the sin (James 4:8).

12:17 The NLT includes "of good judgment" for clarity. In this image, God metaphorically strips leaders of their abilities. It could also refer to being stripped of the symbols of office or to becoming naked captives (12:18-19).

Insight 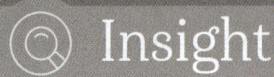 RELYING ON GOD'S WISDOM

In the midst of his great suffering, Job discussed his experience with his three friends—Eliphaz, Bildad, and Zophar—and a younger man, Elihu. Job's friends believed that God's justice meant good things happen to good people, and bad things happen to bad people. Job defended his innocence, but the other men defended what most people believed about how God rewards or punishes. Job resisted their advice and demanded to hear from God. The conversation threads summarize what each person had to say.

While some cringe at Job's story because it reminds us how we could lose everything, it also offers hope: God is still with us no matter what we lose. No matter what bad advice we get from well-meaning people, we can call out to God, and he answers.

ACT 1 (JOB 3–14)

JOB: I wish I were never born.

ELIPHAZ: You must have done something wrong to deserve this suffering. Let God discipline you.

JOB: Stop assuming my guilt, for I have done no wrong. Is not all human life a struggle?

BILDAD: You must have sinned, and so you deserved your punishment. That is the way it works!

JOB: True wisdom and power are found in God. I want to argue my case before God himself.

ZOPHAR: Is a person proven innocent just by a lot of talking? Get rid of your sins.

ACT 2 (JOB 15–21)

ELIPHAZ: Wisdom tells us that people suffer because they are wicked.

JOB: You all are terrible comforters. I have done no wrong, and you should be encouraging me.

BILDAD: Bad things happen to bad people.

JOB: God has wronged me, but I will be vindicated.

ZOPHAR: The wicked only prosper for a short time.

JOB: You're wrong—the wicked do have lifelong success.

ACT 3 (JOB 22–26)

ELIPHAZ: There's no limit to your sins, Job. You must have done something terrible that you can't remember.

JOB: Where is God? I can't find him.

BILDAD: God is so great. Can anyone be innocent before him? (No.)

JOB: You are so unhelpful to me, and you seem not to comprehend God's greatness.

ACT 4 (JOB 27–37)

JOB: My conscience is clear. I have lived a life of blessing and riches, yet now no one defends me in my pain. Let God answer me.

ELIHU: Job, you're wrong, and your friends are weak! You are an arrogant liar! God's justice is greater than we can understand, but you have still sinned greatly.

ACT 5 (JOB 38–42)

GOD: How can you question my wisdom in governing the world? Where were you when I laid the earth's foundations?

JOB: I have nothing more to say.

GOD: Will you discredit my justice and condemn me just to prove that you are right? Look at all I have created. Everything under heaven is mine.

JOB: I take back everything I said, and I sit in dust and ashes to show my repentance.

³ As for me, I would speak directly to the Almighty.
  I want to argue my case with God himself.
⁴ As for you, you smear me with lies.
  As physicians, you are worthless quacks.
⁵ If only you could be silent!
  That's the wisest thing you could do.
⁶ Listen to my charge;
  pay attention to my arguments.

⁷ "Are you defending God with lies?
  Do you make your dishonest arguments for his sake?
⁸ Will you slant your testimony in his favor?
  Will you argue God's case for him?
⁹ What will happen when he finds out what you are doing?
  Can you fool him as easily as you fool people?
¹⁰ No, you will be in trouble with him
  if you secretly slant your testimony in his favor.
¹¹ Doesn't his majesty terrify you?
  Doesn't your fear of him overwhelm you?
¹² Your platitudes are as valuable as ashes.
  Your defense is as fragile as a clay pot.

¹³ "Be silent now and leave me alone.
  Let me speak, and I will face the consequences.
¹⁴ Why should I put myself in mortal danger*
  and take my life in my own hands?
¹⁵ God might kill me, but I have no other hope.*
  I am going to argue my case with him.
¹⁶ But this is what will save me—I am not godless.
  If I were, I could not stand before him.

¹⁷ "Listen closely to what I am about to say.
  Hear me out.
¹⁸ I have prepared my case;
  I will be proved innocent.
¹⁹ Who can argue with me over this?
  And if you prove me wrong, I will remain silent and die.

Job Asks How He Has Sinned

²⁰ "O God, grant me these two things,
  and then I will be able to face you.
²¹ Remove your heavy hand from me,
  and don't terrify me with your awesome presence.
²² Now summon me, and I will answer!
  Or let me speak to you, and you reply.
²³ Tell me, what have I done wrong?
  Show me my rebellion and my sin.
²⁴ Why do you turn away from me?
  Why do you treat me as your enemy?
²⁵ Would you terrify a leaf blown by the wind?
  Would you chase dry straw?

²⁶ "You write bitter accusations against me
  and bring up all the sins of my youth.
²⁷ You put my feet in the stocks.
  You examine all my paths.
  You trace all my footprints.
²⁸ I waste away like rotting wood,
  like a moth-eaten coat.

14 "How frail is humanity!
  How short is life, how full of trouble!
² We blossom like a flower and then wither.
  Like a passing shadow, we quickly disappear.
³ Must you keep an eye on such a frail creature
  and demand an accounting from me?
⁴ Who can bring purity out of an impure person?
  No one!
⁵ You have decided the length of our lives.
  You know how many months we will live,
  and we are not given a minute longer.
⁶ So leave us alone and let us rest!
  We are like hired hands, so let us finish our work in peace.

⁷ "Even a tree has more hope!
  If it is cut down, it will sprout again
  and grow new branches.
⁸ Though its roots have grown old in the earth
  and its stump decays,
⁹ at the scent of water it will bud
  and sprout again like a new seedling.

¹⁰ "But when people die, their strength is gone.
  They breathe their last, and then where are they?
¹¹ As water evaporates from a lake
  and a river disappears in drought,
¹² people are laid to rest and do not rise again.
  Until the heavens are no more, they will not wake up
  nor be roused from their sleep.

13:14 Hebrew *Why should I take my flesh in my teeth.* **13:15** An alternate reading in the Masoretic Text reads *God might kill me, but I hope in him.*

13:15 The Hebrew phrase rendered, "but I have no other hope," proves difficult to translate. "But" is an English addition that tries to help the reader make sense of the text's logic. The word translated "hope" can also mean "wait." In this context, it may be the better choice to translate: "God might kill me; I will not wait. I am going to argue my case with him." Job would continue seeking an audience with God, no matter the consequences. Sometimes we think that being a person of faith means not airing our grievances with God. The Bible, however, shows the opposite—that God can handle and even welcomes our taking our woes to him.
13:22-23 Job wanted God to "summon" him, and then Job would "answer" in his own defense; or Job would "speak to" God, and then God would "reply" to substantiate the charges against Job. Since God did not take the first option, Job initiated the second one (13:23). Eventually, God did summon Job (38:1-3; 40:1-2), but Job was unable to reply (40:3-5).

¹³ "I wish you would hide me in the grave*
    and forget me there until your anger has passed.
    But mark your calendar to think of me again!
¹⁴ Can the dead live again?
    If so, this would give me hope through all my
        years of struggle,
    and I would eagerly await the release of death.
¹⁵ You would call and I would answer,
    and you would yearn for me, your handiwork.
¹⁶ For then you would guard my steps,
    instead of watching for my sins.
¹⁷ My sins would be sealed in a pouch,
    and you would cover my guilt.

¹⁸ "But instead, as mountains fall and crumble
    and as rocks fall from a cliff,
¹⁹ as water wears away the stones
    and floods wash away the soil,
    so you destroy people's hope.
²⁰ You always overpower them, and they pass from
        the scene.
    You disfigure them in death and send them
        away.
²¹ They never know if their children grow up in honor
    or sink to insignificance.
²² They suffer painfully;
    their life is full of trouble."

Eliphaz's Second Response to Job

15 Then Eliphaz the Temanite replied:

² "A wise man wouldn't answer with such empty
        talk!
    You are nothing but a windbag.
³ The wise don't engage in empty chatter.
    What good are such words?
⁴ Have you no fear of God,
    no reverence for him?
⁵ Your sins are telling your mouth what to say.
    Your words are based on clever deception.
⁶ Your own mouth condemns you, not I.
    Your own lips testify against you.

⁷ "Were you the first person ever born?
    Were you born before the hills were made?
⁸ Were you listening at God's secret council?
    Do you have a monopoly on wisdom?
⁹ What do you know that we don't?
    What do you understand that we do not?
¹⁰ On our side are aged, gray-haired men
    much older than your father!

¹¹ "Is God's comfort too little for you?
    Is his gentle word not enough?
¹² What has taken away your reason?
    What has weakened your vision,*
¹³ that you turn against God
    and say all these evil things?
¹⁴ Can any mortal be pure?
    Can anyone born of a woman be just?
¹⁵ Look, God does not even trust the angels.*
    Even the heavens are not absolutely pure in
        his sight.
¹⁶ How much less pure is a corrupt and sinful person
    with a thirst for wickedness!

¹⁷ "If you will listen, I will show you.
    I will answer you from my own experience.
¹⁸ And it is confirmed by the reports of wise men
    who have heard the same thing from their
        fathers—
¹⁹ from those to whom the land was given
    long before any foreigners arrived.

²⁰ "The wicked writhe in pain throughout their lives.
    Years of trouble are stored up for the ruthless.
²¹ The sound of terror rings in their ears,
    and even on good days they fear the attack of
        the destroyer.
²² They dare not go out into the darkness
    for fear they will be murdered.
²³ They wander around, saying, 'Where can I find
        bread?'*
    They know their day of destruction is near.
²⁴ That dark day terrifies them.
    They live in distress and anguish,
    like a king preparing for battle.

14:13 Hebrew *in Sheol.* **15:12** Or *Why do your eyes flash with anger;* Hebrew reads *Why do your eyes blink.* **15:15** Hebrew *the holy ones.* **15:23** Greek version reads *He is appointed to be food for a vulture.*

14:18-22 While Job's friends painted a rosy picture of restoration if only Job would repent (5:24-26; 8:21-22; 11:13-19), Job did not believe in such hope. He was not motivated by a restoration of his wealth or family. He wanted vindication (13:18-22).
14:22 Job no longer saw Sheol (the place of the dead) as a haven (3:13-19; 14:13-17). The Old Testament sometimes depicts the dead as being without feeling or remembrance (Psalm 88:12; Ecclesiastes 9:5; but note Isaiah 50:11; 66:24). The doctrine that the dead can "suffer painfully" is clearer in the New Testament (Luke 16:23, 28; Revelation 14:11).
15:1–21:34 In this second round of speeches, Job's friends focus on the fate of the wicked and imply that Job's condition shows he has sinned.

15:4-6; 22:4-11 Eliphaz found Job guilty. In his second speech, Eliphaz condemned Job because of his words, believing only the wicked would speak as Job had spoken. In his third speech, Eliphaz went further, listing several possible sins and suggesting that Job had gotten what he deserved. When we are in an argument that goes on, it's typical for both sides to "polarize," to feel their opinions more strongly. As women who want to speak truth, how might we create pauses, and seek counsel so we hear God's opinion, and listen to others' as well, rather than making our own arguments more pointed?
15:20-35 The wicked also suffer everything that happened to Job (see 1:16-19)—attacks by marauders (15:21), loss of possessions (15:29), crumbled houses (15:28), and scorching heat and fire (15:30, 34).

25 For they shake their fists at God,
    defying the Almighty.
26 Holding their strong shields,
    they defiantly charge against him.
27 "These wicked people are heavy and prosperous;
    their waists bulge with fat.
28 But their cities will be ruined.
    They will live in abandoned houses
    that are ready to tumble down.
29 Their riches will not last,
    and their wealth will not endure.
    Their possessions will no longer spread
    across the horizon.

MY STORY WITH GOD — How to Grieve with Others

SCRIPTURE CONNECTION: JOB 4–26

Have you ever been misunderstood in your grief?

Job's friends made unhelpful comments as he was suffering horribly. When this righteous man lost everything dear to him—children, fortune, home, and health—his friends said hurtful things in his time of grief.

They came up with reasons for his troubles: Maybe he "refused water for the thirsty and food for the hungry" (22:7) or "sent widows away empty-handed" (22:9), they said. They even accused him of doing evil (4:7-8; 8:20; 11:13-15; 22:5) and abandoning God (8:13; 15:4; 20:4-5).

His friends mixed some of God's truths with some lies. Though their intentions may have been to help, their words harmed.

Job had done nothing to deserve his suffering, and God did not appreciate Job's friends distorting his character. In the end, God rebuked them: "I am angry with you and your two friends, for you have not spoken accurately about me, as my servant Job has" (42:7).

Genuine compassion for a person in pain chooses not to project our formulas onto their suffering. Instead, we comfort our friends by sitting with them in their grief and loss (2:11-13) and praying with them to the One who hears their cries.

> Naming our grief means getting honest with God—and allowing others to be honest, too.

IMAGINE

Job rightly directed his grief toward God. What is something you may be grieving over that you could offer to God?

How can you incorporate a prayer of lament into your prayer time each day?

How might you support another person in prayer as they grieve?

"The Bible expresses honest emotion: Job and Jeremiah cursed being born (Job 3:1; Jeremiah 20:14). These are the kinds of dark feelings I'd never processed. My past felt too painful. But grieving requires going with God—backward to process our pain and forward in the present, with today's pain."

ESTHER FLEECE ALLEN is an international speaker and bestselling author of *No More Faking Fine: Ending the Pretending* and *Your New Name: Saying Goodbye to the Labels That Limit.*

30 "They will not escape the darkness.
   The burning sun will wither their shoots,
   and the breath of God will destroy them.
31 Let them no longer fool themselves by trusting in empty riches,
   for emptiness will be their only reward.
32 They will be cut down in the prime of life;
   their branches will never again be green.
33 They will be like a vine whose grapes are harvested too early,
   like an olive tree that loses its blossoms before the fruit can form.
34 For the godless are barren.
   Their homes, enriched through bribery, will burn.
35 They conceive trouble and give birth to evil.
   Their womb produces deceit."

Job's Fifth Speech: A Response to Eliphaz

16 Then Job spoke again:

2 "I have heard all this before.
   What miserable comforters you are!
3 Won't you ever stop blowing hot air?
   What makes you keep on talking?
4 I could say the same things if you were in my place.
   I could spout off criticism and shake my head at you.
5 But if it were me, I would encourage you.
   I would try to take away your grief.
6 Instead, I suffer if I defend myself,
   and I suffer no less if I refuse to speak.

7 "O God, you have ground me down
   and devastated my family.
8 As if to prove I have sinned, you've reduced me to skin and bones.
   My gaunt flesh testifies against me.
9 God hates me and angrily tears me apart.
   He snaps his teeth at me
   and pierces me with his eyes.
10 People jeer and laugh at me.
    They slap my cheek in contempt.
    A mob gathers against me.
11 God has handed me over to sinners.
    He has tossed me into the hands of the wicked.
12 "I was living quietly until he shattered me.
    He took me by the neck and broke me in pieces.
    Then he set me up as his target,
13 and now his archers surround me.
    His arrows pierce me without mercy.
    The ground is wet with my blood.*
14 Again and again he smashes against me,
    charging at me like a warrior.
15 I wear burlap to show my grief.
    My pride lies in the dust.
16 My eyes are red with weeping;
    dark shadows circle my eyes.
17 Yet I have done no wrong,
    and my prayer is pure.

18 "O earth, do not conceal my blood.
    Let it cry out on my behalf.
19 Even now my witness is in heaven.
    My advocate is there on high.
20 My friends scorn me,
    but I pour out my tears to God.
21 I need someone to mediate between God and me,
    as a person mediates between friends.
22 For soon I must go down that road
    from which I will never return.

Job Continues to Defend His Innocence

17 "My spirit is crushed,
    and my life is nearly snuffed out.
    The grave is ready to receive me.
2 I am surrounded by mockers.
    I watch how bitterly they taunt me.

3 "You must defend my innocence, O God,
    since no one else will stand up for me.
4 You have closed their minds to understanding,
    but do not let them triumph.
5 They betray their friends for their own advantage,
    so let their children faint with hunger.

6 "God has made a mockery of me among the people;
    they spit in my face.
7 My eyes are swollen with weeping,
    and I am but a shadow of my former self.
8 The virtuous are horrified when they see me.
    The innocent rise up against the ungodly.

16:13 Hebrew *my gall.*

16:7-14 Job saw God as the one attacking him. He viewed God acting as a "warrior" (Job 16:14; see Exodus 15:3; Psalm 24:8) who did not defend him or offer him salvation (contrast with Jeremiah 20:11; Zephaniah 3:17). While we know that Satan as the accuser/challenger was directly responsible for Job's suffering, God allowed it and could be seen as indirectly responsible. With respect to this theological issue, see the study note on Job 1:12; 2:6.
16:15 Since Job insisted on his innocence, his wearing burlap (literally "I sewed on burlap") was a sign of mourning, not penitence. Perhaps it was attached to indicate that he would never remove it because he could never be consoled (Genesis 37:34-35). Job's words, "My pride lies in the dust," which could also be translated "I have buried my horn in the dust." A horn symbolized dignity and power (1 Samuel 2:1; Psalms 75:4-5; 89:17, 24; 92:10; 112:9; 148:14); cutting it off inflicted degrading humiliation (Psalm 75:10; Jeremiah 48:25; Zechariah 1:21).

⁹ The righteous keep moving forward,
   and those with clean hands become stronger
      and stronger.
¹⁰ "As for all of you, come back with a better
      argument,
   though I still won't find a wise man among you.
¹¹ My days are over.
   My hopes have disappeared.
   My heart's desires are broken.
¹² These men say that night is day;
   they claim that the darkness is light.
¹³ What if I go to the grave*
   and make my bed in darkness?
¹⁴ What if I call the grave my father,
   and the maggot my mother or my sister?
¹⁵ Where then is my hope?
   Can anyone find it?
¹⁶ No, my hope will go down with me to the grave.
   We will rest together in the dust!"

Bildad's Second Response to Job

18 Then Bildad the Shuhite replied:

² "How long before you stop talking?
   Speak sense if you want us to answer!
³ Do you think we are mere animals?
   Do you think we are stupid?
⁴ You may tear out your hair in anger,
   but will that destroy the earth?
   Will it make the rocks tremble?

⁵ "Surely the light of the wicked will be snuffed out.
   The sparks of their fire will not glow.
⁶ The light in their tent will grow dark.
   The lamp hanging above them will be
      quenched.
⁷ The confident stride of the wicked will be
      shortened.
   Their own schemes will be their downfall.
⁸ The wicked walk into a net.
   They fall into a pit.
⁹ A trap grabs them by the heel.
   A snare holds them tight.
¹⁰ A noose lies hidden on the ground.
   A rope is stretched across their path.

¹¹ "Terrors surround the wicked
   and trouble them at every step.
¹² Hunger depletes their strength,
   and calamity waits for them to stumble.
¹³ Disease eats their skin;
   death devours their limbs.
¹⁴ They are torn from the security of their homes
   and are brought down to the king of terrors.
¹⁵ The homes of the wicked will burn down;
   burning sulfur rains on their houses.
¹⁶ Their roots will dry up,
   and their branches will wither.
¹⁷ All memory of their existence will fade from the
      earth;
   no one will remember their names.
¹⁸ They will be thrust from light into darkness,
   driven from the world.
¹⁹ They will have neither children nor
      grandchildren,
   nor any survivor in the place where they
      lived.
²⁰ People in the west are appalled at their fate;
   people in the east are horrified.
²¹ They will say, 'This was the home of a wicked
      person,
   the place of one who rejected God.'"

Job's Sixth Speech:
A Response to Bildad

19 Then Job spoke again:

² "How long will you torture me?
   How long will you try to crush me with your
      words?
³ You have already insulted me ten times.
   You should be ashamed of treating me so
      badly.
⁴ Even if I have sinned,
   that is my concern, not yours.
⁵ You think you're better than I am,
   using my humiliation as evidence of my sin.
⁶ But it is God who has wronged me,
   capturing me in his net.*

⁷ "I cry out, 'Help!' but no one answers me.
   I protest, but there is no justice.
⁸ God has blocked my way so I cannot move.
   He has plunged my path into darkness.
⁹ He has stripped me of my honor
   and removed the crown from my head.
¹⁰ He has demolished me on every side, and I am
      finished.
   He has uprooted my hope like a fallen tree.
¹¹ His fury burns against me;
   he counts me as an enemy.
¹² His troops advance.
   They build up roads to attack me.
   They camp all around my tent.

17:13 Hebrew *to Sheol*; also in 17:16.   19:6 Or *for I am like a city under siege.*

17:13 The realm of the dead was visualized as a house (30:23; Psalm 49:11; Ecclesiastes 12:5).

18:11-13 Bildad applies the retribution principle (18:8-10) to Job, as do Eliphaz (15:21-23) and Zophar (20:25). See study note on 1:9-11.

JOB 19 • 626

13 "My relatives stay far away,
    and my friends have turned against me.
14 My family is gone,
    and my close friends have forgotten me.
15 My servants and maids consider me a stranger.
    I am like a foreigner to them.
16 When I call my servant, he doesn't come;
    I have to plead with him!
17 My breath is repulsive to my wife.
    I am rejected by my own family.
18 Even young children despise me.
    When I stand to speak, they turn their backs on me.
19 My close friends detest me.
    Those I loved have turned against me.
20 I have been reduced to skin and bones
    and have escaped death by the skin of my teeth.

21 "Have mercy on me, my friends, have mercy,
    for the hand of God has struck me.
22 Must you also persecute me, like God does?
    Haven't you chewed me up enough?

Koinonia

IMAGE — MY STORY WITH COMMUNITY, WORKPLACE & CHURCH

Desperate Words but Solid Identity

SCRIPTURE CONNECTION: JOB 2:8-10; 19:17; 31:10

In one day, Job and his wife lost everything. All they owned and even their children—instantly taken. And then, Job developed sores all over his body.

Job's wife, as she saw their absolute loss, must have felt that God had turned against them. What else could these horrifying events mean? This was her breaking point. In anger and anguish, fearful of the future, she lashed out at Job, the only person left even to hear her.

I wonder how she felt after she said those reckless things. Did she feel justified? Satisfied? Horrified? I wonder if she was characterized by this type of outburst. Or if these were desperate words in a desperate moment.

I've done that. When I found out about my husband's affair, I screamed my feelings about God to our pastor. My world had crumbled, and I was shouting whatever came to mind. Unfiltered.

My pastor didn't judge me. He knew my words came from my hopelessness, my loss.

In the same way, Job understood his wife's words were rash and didn't judge her character. Later, Job told his so-called friends that criticizing what desperate people say isn't helpful (6:25-26). God didn't condemn Job's wife either. He knew how deep her grief was. In the end the Lord gave her and Job more children and more wealth than before (42:10-17).

> Our desperate words are not who we are.

IMAGINE

How can you relate to Job's wife?

The desperate words we utter in our pain are not necessarily who we are. How has God reinforced your true identity as his beloved child as he draws near to you in trials?

> "I have shouted words in desperation that do not reflect my identity but show my hopelessness. God knows my pain, tenderly meets me, and shows me the loss I see now is not my story's end."

VANEETHA RENDALL RISNER is the author of *Walking Through Fire*. She and her family live in North Carolina, where she writes and speaks about how God meets us in suffering.

²³ "Oh, that my words could be recorded.
   Oh, that they could be inscribed on a monument,
²⁴ carved with an iron chisel and filled with lead,
   engraved forever in the rock.
²⁵ "But as for me, I know that my Redeemer lives,
   and he will stand upon the earth at last.
²⁶ And after my body has decayed,
   yet in my body I will see God!*
²⁷ I will see him for myself.
   Yes, I will see him with my own eyes.
   I am overwhelmed at the thought!
²⁸ "How dare you go on persecuting me,
   saying, 'It's his own fault'?
²⁹ You should fear punishment yourselves,
   for your attitude deserves punishment.
   Then you will know that there is indeed a judgment."

Zophar's Second Response to Job

20 Then Zophar the Naamathite replied:

² "I must reply
   because I am greatly disturbed.
³ I've had to endure your insults,
   but now my spirit prompts me to reply.
⁴ "Don't you realize that from the beginning of time,
   ever since people were first placed on the earth,
⁵ the triumph of the wicked has been short lived
   and the joy of the godless has been only temporary?
⁶ Though the pride of the godless reaches to the heavens
   and their heads touch the clouds,
⁷ yet they will vanish forever,
   thrown away like their own dung.
   Those who knew them will ask,
   'Where are they?'
⁸ They will fade like a dream and not be found.
   They will vanish like a vision in the night.
⁹ Those who once saw them will see them no more.
   Their families will never see them again.
¹⁰ Their children will beg from the poor,
   for they must give back their stolen riches.
¹¹ Though they are young,
   their bones will lie in the dust.
¹² "They enjoyed the sweet taste of wickedness,
   letting it melt under their tongue.
¹³ They savored it,
   holding it long in their mouths.
¹⁴ But suddenly the food in their bellies turns sour,
   a poisonous venom in their stomach.
¹⁵ They will vomit the wealth they swallowed.
   God won't let them keep it down.
¹⁶ They will suck the poison of cobras.
   The viper will kill them.
¹⁷ They will never again enjoy streams of olive oil
   or rivers of milk and honey.
¹⁸ They will give back everything they worked for.
   Their wealth will bring them no joy.
¹⁹ For they oppressed the poor and left them destitute.
   They foreclosed on their homes.
²⁰ They were always greedy and never satisfied.
   Nothing remains of all the things they dreamed about.
²¹ Nothing is left after they finish gorging themselves.
   Therefore, their prosperity will not endure.
²² "In the midst of plenty, they will run into trouble
   and be overcome by misery.
²³ May God give them a bellyful of trouble.
   May God rain down his anger upon them.
²⁴ When they try to escape an iron weapon,
   a bronze-tipped arrow will pierce them.
²⁵ The arrow is pulled from their back,
   and the arrowhead glistens with blood.*
   The terrors of death are upon them.
²⁶ Their treasures will be thrown into deepest darkness.
   A wildfire will devour their goods,
   consuming all they have left.
²⁷ The heavens will reveal their guilt,
   and the earth will testify against them.
²⁸ A flood will sweep away their house.
   God's anger will descend on them in torrents.
²⁹ This is the reward that God gives the wicked.
   It is the inheritance decreed by God."

19:26 Or *without my body I will see God.* The meaning of the Hebrew is uncertain. 20:25 Hebrew *with gall.*

19:25 The Hebrew "redeemer" (*goel*) was a legal role. This person could buy back lost property, avenge murder, rescue someone from slavery caused by debt, or marry a brother's widow. Job's redeemer would argue his legal case against God. While Jesus is a redeemer, he fulfills a different role than the one Job envisioned. Jesus does not argue for us that we have been unjustly treated as Job's redeemer would. Jesus takes our sin and just punishment upon himself, rescuing us from eternal death. **19:26** Some understand this verse to refer to resurrection, although such references are generally considered rare in the Old Testament. Since the word translated "body" usually means "skin" and "decayed" can mean "destroyed," Job is likely referring to his skin. Job's skin had been afflicted with boils and scraped away (2:7-8). The idea of seeing God refers to being restored to or refreshed by God's favor (Exodus 24:11; Psalms 11:7; 17:15; 27:4; 63:2). **19:29** Given the commands against bearing false witness (Exodus 20:16; 23:1; Deuteronomy 5:20; see Job 13:7-11), Job warned his friends that they should fear God's judgment. They did eventually face his judgment, but they also received mercy (42:7-8). **20:25** Although the words "of death" are not in the Hebrew, they are implied because "the arrowhead glistens with blood," indicating a deadly hit on a vital organ (Job 6:4; 16:13; Psalm 7:12).

Job's Seventh Speech: A Response to Zophar

21 Then Job spoke again:

2 "Listen closely to what I am saying.
   That's one consolation you can give me.
3 Bear with me, and let me speak.
   After I have spoken, you may resume mocking me.

4 "My complaint is with God, not with people.
   I have good reason to be so impatient.
5 Look at me and be stunned.
   Put your hand over your mouth in shock.
6 When I think about what I am saying, I shudder.
   My body trembles.

7 "Why do the wicked prosper,
   growing old and powerful?
8 They live to see their children grow up and settle down,
   and they enjoy their grandchildren.
9 Their homes are safe from every fear,
   and God does not punish them.
10 Their bulls never fail to breed.
    Their cows bear calves and never miscarry.
11 They let their children frisk about like lambs.
    Their little ones skip and dance.
12 They sing with tambourine and harp.
    They celebrate to the sound of the flute.
13 They spend their days in prosperity,
    then go down to the grave* in peace.
14 And yet they say to God, 'Go away.
    We want no part of you and your ways.
15 Who is the Almighty, and why should we obey him?
    What good will it do us to pray?'
16 (They think their prosperity is of their own doing,
    but I will have nothing to do with that kind of thinking.)

17 "Yet the light of the wicked never seems to be extinguished.
    Do they ever have trouble?
    Does God distribute sorrows to them in anger?
18 Are they driven before the wind like straw?
    Are they carried away by the storm like chaff?
    Not at all!
19 "'Well,' you say, 'at least God will punish their children!'
    But I say he should punish the ones who sin,
    so that they understand his judgment.
20 Let them see their destruction with their own eyes.
    Let them drink deeply of the anger of the Almighty.
21 For they will not care what happens to their family
    after they are dead.

22 "But who can teach a lesson to God,
    since he judges even the most powerful?
23 One person dies in prosperity,
    completely comfortable and secure,
24 the picture of good health,
    vigorous and fit.
25 Another person dies in bitter poverty,
    never having tasted the good life.
26 But both are buried in the same dust,
    both eaten by the same maggots.

27 "Look, I know what you're thinking.
    I know the schemes you plot against me.
28 You will tell me of rich and wicked people
    whose houses have vanished because of their sins.
29 But ask those who have been around,
    and they will tell you the truth.
30 Evil people are spared in times of calamity
    and are allowed to escape disaster.
31 No one criticizes them openly
    or pays them back for what they have done.
32 When they are carried to the grave,
    an honor guard keeps watch at their tomb.
33 A great funeral procession goes to the cemetery.
    Many pay their respects as the body is laid to rest,
    and the earth gives sweet repose.

34 "How can your empty clichés comfort me?
    All your explanations are lies!"

Eliphaz's Third Response to Job

22 Then Eliphaz the Temanite replied:

2 "Can a person do anything to help God?
   Can even a wise person be helpful to him?
3 Is it any advantage to the Almighty if you are righteous?
   Would it be any gain to him if you were perfect?
4 Is it because you're so pious that he accuses you
   and brings judgment against you?
5 No, it's because of your wickedness!
   There's no limit to your sins.

21:13 Hebrew *to Sheol.*

21:8 Despite what Eliphaz (5:4), Bildad (18:19), and Zophar (20:10) said, Job noted that the wicked enjoy children and grandchildren, which should be the reward of the righteous (Proverbs 17:6) but apparently not in his case (Job 1:18-19; but see 42:13-16).

22:1–26:14 In this third round of speeches, Job's friends explicitly accuse Job of being among the wicked and sharing their fate.

⁶ "For example, you must have lent money to your friend
and demanded clothing as security.
Yes, you stripped him to the bone.
⁷ You must have refused water for the thirsty
and food for the hungry.
⁸ You probably think the land belongs to the powerful
and only the privileged have a right to it!
⁹ You must have sent widows away empty-handed
and crushed the hopes of orphans.
¹⁰ That is why you are surrounded by traps
and tremble from sudden fears.
¹¹ That is why you cannot see in the darkness,
and waves of water cover you.

¹² "God is so great—higher than the heavens,
higher than the farthest stars.
¹³ But you reply, 'That's why God can't see what I am doing!
How can he judge through the thick darkness?
¹⁴ For thick clouds swirl about him, and he cannot see us.
He is way up there, walking on the vault of heaven.'

¹⁵ "Will you continue on the old paths
where evil people have walked?
¹⁶ They were snatched away in the prime of life,
the foundations of their lives washed away.
¹⁷ For they said to God, 'Leave us alone!
What can the Almighty do to us?'
¹⁸ Yet he was the one who filled their homes with good things,
so I will have nothing to do with that kind of thinking.

¹⁹ "The righteous will be happy to see the wicked destroyed,
and the innocent will laugh in contempt.
²⁰ They will say, 'See how our enemies have been destroyed.
The last of them have been consumed in the fire.'

²¹ "Submit to God, and you will have peace;
then things will go well for you.
²² Listen to his instructions,
and store them in your heart.
²³ If you return to the Almighty, you will be restored—
so clean up your life.
²⁴ If you give up your lust for money
and throw your precious gold into the river,
²⁵ the Almighty himself will be your treasure.
He will be your precious silver!

²⁶ "Then you will take delight in the Almighty
and look up to God.
²⁷ You will pray to him, and he will hear you,
and you will fulfill your vows to him.
²⁸ You will succeed in whatever you choose to do,
and light will shine on the road ahead of you.
²⁹ If people are in trouble and you say, 'Help them,'
God will save them.
³⁰ Even sinners will be rescued;
they will be rescued because your hands are pure."

Job's Eighth Speech: A Response to Eliphaz

23 Then Job spoke again:

² "My complaint today is still a bitter one,
and I try hard not to groan aloud.
³ If only I knew where to find God,
I would go to his court.
⁴ I would lay out my case
and present my arguments.
⁵ Then I would listen to his reply
and understand what he says to me.
⁶ Would he use his great power to argue with me?
No, he would give me a fair hearing.
⁷ Honest people can reason with him,
so I would be forever acquitted by my judge.
⁸ I go east, but he is not there.
I go west, but I cannot find him.
⁹ I do not see him in the north, for he is hidden.
I look to the south, but he is concealed.

¹⁰ "But he knows where I am going.
And when he tests me, I will come out as pure as gold.
¹¹ For I have stayed on God's paths;
I have followed his ways and not turned aside.
¹² I have not departed from his commands,
but have treasured his words more than daily food.
¹³ But once he has made his decision, who can change his mind?
Whatever he wants to do, he does.

22:23 Bildad (8:5-6) and Zophar (11:13-14) had already urged Job to "return to the Almighty," and now Eliphaz does so as well. However, if Job "returns" by admitting guilt, he will have proven the accuser/challenger (Satan) right (see study note on 1:9-11) and forfeited his integrity.

22:27 Ironically, Job will pray, God will hear, and Eliphaz will reap the benefits (42:8). Vows were often inspired by repentance and forgiveness (Hosea 14:2; Jonah 1:16; 2:9) and when seeking divine intervention (Judges 11:29-40; 1 Samuel 1:1-28; Psalms 22:25; 61:5, 8; 116:14, 18). Vows are binding (Numbers 30:2; Deuteronomy 23:23; Ecclesiastes 5:4-6).

23:6-7 Earlier, Job had believed that God was too strong for him to summon (9:19), so he had requested a mediator (9:33-34) and asked God not to terrify him (13:21). Here he expressed more hope that God would grant him "a fair hearing." Job did not want to be pardoned as a guilty man but to be declared innocent (13:18; see Psalms 17:2-3; 26:1-3).

14 So he will do to me whatever he has planned.
   He controls my destiny.
15 No wonder I am so terrified in his presence.
   When I think of it, terror grips me.
16 God has made me sick at heart;
   the Almighty has terrified me.
17 Darkness is all around me;
   thick, impenetrable darkness is everywhere.

Job Asks Why the Wicked Are Not Punished

24 "Why doesn't the Almighty bring the wicked to judgment?
   Why must the godly wait for him in vain?
2 Evil people steal land by moving the boundary markers.
   They steal livestock and put them in their own pastures.
3 They take the orphan's donkey
   and demand the widow's ox as security for a loan.
4 The poor are pushed off the path;
   the needy must hide together for safety.
5 Like wild donkeys in the wilderness,
   the poor must spend all their time looking for food,
   searching even in the desert for food for their children.
6 They harvest a field they do not own,
   and they glean in the vineyards of the wicked.
7 All night they lie naked in the cold,
   without clothing or covering.
8 They are soaked by mountain showers,
   and they huddle against the rocks for want of a home.
9 "The wicked snatch a widow's child from her breast,
   taking the baby as security for a loan.
10 The poor must go about naked, without any clothing.
   They harvest food for others while they themselves are starving.
11 They press out olive oil without being allowed to taste it,
   and they tread in the winepress as they suffer from thirst.
12 The groans of the dying rise from the city,
   and the wounded cry for help,
   yet God ignores their moaning.
13 "Wicked people rebel against the light.
   They refuse to acknowledge its ways
   or stay in its paths.
14 The murderer rises in the early dawn
   to kill the poor and needy;
   at night he is a thief.
15 The adulterer waits for the twilight,
   saying, 'No one will see me then.'
   He hides his face so no one will know him.
16 Thieves break into houses at night
   and sleep in the daytime.
   They are not acquainted with the light.
17 The black night is their morning.
   They ally themselves with the terrors of the darkness.
18 "But they disappear like foam down a river.
   Everything they own is cursed,
   and they are afraid to enter their own vineyards.
19 The grave* consumes sinners
   just as drought and heat consume snow.
20 Their own mothers will forget them.
   Maggots will find them sweet to eat.
   No one will remember them.
   Wicked people are broken like a tree in the storm.
21 They cheat the woman who has no son to help her.
   They refuse to help the needy widow.
22 "God, in his power, drags away the rich.
   They may rise high, but they have no assurance of life.
23 They may be allowed to live in security,
   but God is always watching them.
24 And though they are great now,
   in a moment they will be gone like all others,
   cut off like heads of grain.
25 Can anyone claim otherwise?
   Who can prove me wrong?"

24:19 Hebrew *Sheol*.

24:2-17 While Job's friends believed that good people receive good and evil people receive evil, Job's personal experience raised questions about whether that belief was valid. In these verses, Job described how the poor and most vulnerable in society were exploited and harmed by the wicked. His own experience of suffering without cause had helped him to see that suffering people's circumstances are not necessarily related to their behavior. Have you ever noticed that some people who have suffered significantly are more compassionate? We can ask God to use our suffering to help us respond in love, not judgment.

24:10-11 The phrase "without being allowed to taste it" is not in the original text but is implied by the parallel with "starving" and "suffer from thirst." To force workers to "tread in the winepress as they suffer from thirst" violates the principle of letting workers enjoy some of the produce they are harvesting (see Deuteronomy 25:4; 2 Timothy 2:6).

24:18-24 These sentiments appear to oppose Job's observations, so some scholars suggest that they were the words of Bildad or Zophar. However, Job might have been pronouncing curses on the wicked, sarcastically quoting his friends' views, or saying that the fate of the wicked presented by Eliphaz (5:2-7; 15:17-25), Bildad (8:8-19; 18:5-21), and Zophar (20:4-29) also overtakes the righteous (21:23-26).

Bildad's Third Response to Job

25 Then Bildad the Shuhite replied:

2 "God is powerful and dreadful.
    He enforces peace in the heavens.
3 Who is able to count his heavenly army?
    Doesn't his light shine on all the earth?
4 How can a mortal be innocent before God?
    Can anyone born of a woman be pure?
5 God is more glorious than the moon;
    he shines brighter than the stars.
6 In comparison, people are maggots;
    we mortals are mere worms."

Job's Ninth Speech: A Response to Bildad

26 Then Job spoke again:

2 "How you have helped the powerless!
    How you have saved the weak!
3 How you have enlightened my stupidity!
    What wise advice you have offered!
4 Where have you gotten all these wise sayings?
    Whose spirit speaks through you?

5 "The dead tremble—
    those who live beneath the waters.
6 The underworld* is naked in God's presence.
    The place of destruction* is uncovered.
7 God stretches the northern sky over empty space
    and hangs the earth on nothing.
8 He wraps the rain in his thick clouds,
    and the clouds don't burst with the weight.
9 He covers the face of the moon,*
    shrouding it with his clouds.
10 He created the horizon when he separated the waters;
    he set the boundary between day and night.
11 The foundations of heaven tremble;
    they shudder at his rebuke.
12 By his power the sea grew calm.
    By his skill he crushed the great sea monster.*
13 His Spirit made the heavens beautiful,
    and his power pierced the gliding serpent.
14 These are just the beginning of all that he does,
    merely a whisper of his power.
    Who, then, can comprehend the thunder of his power?"

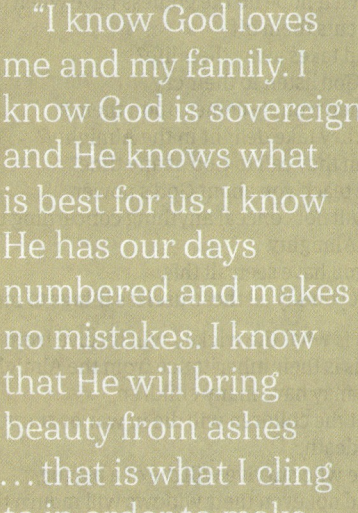

"I know God loves me and my family. I know God is sovereign and He knows what is best for us. I know He has our days numbered and makes no mistakes. I know that He will bring beauty from ashes ... that is what I cling to in order to make it through another twenty-four hours."

MARY BETH CHAPMAN
author, speaker, and president of Show Hope

Job's Final Speech

27 Job continued speaking:

2 "I vow by the living God, who has taken away my rights,
    by the Almighty who has embittered my soul—
3 As long as I live,
    while I have breath from God,
4 my lips will speak no evil,
    and my tongue will speak no lies.
5 I will never concede that you are right;
    I will defend my integrity until I die.
6 I will maintain my innocence without wavering.
    My conscience is clear for as long as I live.

26:6a Hebrew *Sheol*. 26:6b Hebrew *Abaddon*. 26:9 Or *covers his throne*. 26:12 Hebrew *Rahab*, the name of a mythical sea monster that represents chaos in ancient literature.

26:5-6 "The underworld" (Hebrew *Sheol*), the home of all the dead, was located "beneath the waters" of the sea. "The place of destruction" (Hebrew *Abaddon*) existed specifically for those who do evil.

26:7 The Hebrew translated here as "northern" is a figure of speech that originally referred to Mount Zaphon, a sacred mountain at the northern end of Canaan where the storm god Baal was believed to reside. (See also note on 37:22.) Here the NLT understands it to refer to the "sky," stretched out "over empty space" (see Genesis 1:6-8; Psalm 104:2-3; Isaiah 40:22-23).

27:1-6 Satan, the accuser/challenger, was proven wrong (1:9-11). Job had maintained his integrity despite all that he suffered and despite his friends' advice. While he believed that his pain had come from God, he refused to "repent." Instead, he questioned the idea that "bad things happen to bad people" and maintained his innocence.

⁷ "May my enemy be punished like the wicked,
   my adversary like those who do evil.
⁸ For what hope do the godless have when God cuts them off
   and takes away their life?
⁹ Will God listen to their cry
   when trouble comes upon them?
¹⁰ Can they take delight in the Almighty?
   Can they call to God at any time?
¹¹ I will teach you about God's power.
   I will not conceal anything concerning the Almighty.
¹² But you have seen all this,
   yet you say all these useless things to me.

¹³ "This is what the wicked will receive from God;
   this is their inheritance from the Almighty.
¹⁴ They may have many children,
   but the children will die in war or starve to death.
¹⁵ Those who survive will die of a plague,
   and not even their widows will mourn them.

¹⁶ "Evil people may have piles of money
   and may store away mounds of clothing.
¹⁷ But the righteous will wear that clothing,
   and the innocent will divide that money.
¹⁸ The wicked build houses as fragile as a spider's web,*
   as flimsy as a shelter made of branches.
¹⁹ The wicked go to bed rich
   but wake to find that all their wealth is gone.
²⁰ Terror overwhelms them like a flood,
   and they are blown away in the storms of the night.
²¹ The east wind carries them away, and they are gone.
   It sweeps them away.
²² It whirls down on them without mercy.
   They struggle to flee from its power.
²³ But everyone jeers at them
   and mocks them.

Job Speaks of Wisdom and Understanding

28 "People know where to mine silver
   and how to refine gold.
² They know where to dig iron from the earth
   and how to smelt copper from rock.
³ They know how to shine light in the darkness
   and explore the farthest regions of the earth
   as they search in the dark for ore.
⁴ They sink a mine shaft into the earth
   far from where anyone lives.
   They descend on ropes, swinging back and forth.
⁵ Food is grown on the earth above,
   but down below, the earth is melted as by fire.
⁶ Here the rocks contain precious lapis lazuli,
   and the dust contains gold.
⁷ These are treasures no bird of prey can see,
   no falcon's eye observe.
⁸ No wild animal has walked upon these treasures;
   no lion has ever set his paw there.
⁹ People know how to tear apart flinty rocks
   and overturn the roots of mountains.
¹⁰ They cut tunnels in the rocks
   and uncover precious stones.
¹¹ They dam up the trickling streams
   and bring to light the hidden treasures.

¹² "But do people know where to find wisdom?
   Where can they find understanding?
¹³ No one knows where to find it,*
   for it is not found among the living.
¹⁴ 'It is not here,' says the ocean.
   'Nor is it here,' says the sea.
¹⁵ It cannot be bought with gold.
   It cannot be purchased with silver.
¹⁶ It's worth more than all the gold of Ophir,
   greater than precious onyx or lapis lazuli.
¹⁷ Wisdom is more valuable than gold and crystal.
   It cannot be purchased with jewels mounted in fine gold.
¹⁸ Coral and jasper are worthless in trying to get it.
   The price of wisdom is far above rubies.
¹⁹ Precious peridot from Ethiopia* cannot be exchanged for it.
   It's worth more than the purest gold.

²⁰ "But do people know where to find wisdom?
   Where can they find understanding?
²¹ It is hidden from the eyes of all humanity.
   Even the sharp-eyed birds in the sky cannot discover it.
²² Destruction* and Death say,
   'We've heard only rumors of where wisdom can be found.'

27:18 As in Greek and Syriac versions (see also 8:14); Hebrew reads *a moth.* **28:13** As in Greek version; Hebrew reads *knows its value.* **28:19** Hebrew *from Cush.* **28:22** Hebrew *Abaddon.*

27:9-23 Some interpreters see a new speech here and ascribe it to Zophar because otherwise Zophar has no speech in this cycle (see also note on 28:1-28).
28:1-28 This section is a self-contained speech. No speaker is listed, so it could be a continuation of the preceding words (either Job's or Zophar's; see note on 27:9-23). However, some consider this a poetic interlude by the narrator of Job that sums up the argument to this point, emphasizes the failure of human wisdom, and lays the foundation for the Lord's speeches (38:1–41:34).
28:23-27 When God "looks throughout the whole earth" (28:24), he sees his own wisdom expressed in his creation. God later showcased his wisdom for Job when he took him on a stellar and planetary tour (38:1–41:34).

²³ "God alone understands the way to wisdom;
  he knows where it can be found,
²⁴ for he looks throughout the whole earth
  and sees everything under the heavens.
²⁵ He decided how hard the winds should blow
  and how much rain should fall.
²⁶ He made the laws for the rain
  and laid out a path for the lightning.
²⁷ Then he saw wisdom and evaluated it.
  He set it in place and examined it thoroughly.
²⁸ And this is what he says to all humanity:
  'The fear of the Lord is true wisdom;
  to forsake evil is real understanding.'"

Job Speaks of His Former Blessings

29 Job continued speaking:

² "I long for the years gone by
  when God took care of me,
³ when he lit up the way before me
  and I walked safely through the darkness.
⁴ When I was in my prime,
  God's friendship was felt in my home.
⁵ The Almighty was still with me,
  and my children were around me.
⁶ My steps were awash in cream,
  and the rocks gushed olive oil for me.
⁷ "Those were the days when I went to the city gate
  and took my place among the honored leaders.
⁸ The young stepped aside when they saw me,
  and even the aged rose in respect at my coming.
⁹ The princes stood in silence
  and put their hands over their mouths.
¹⁰ The highest officials of the city stood quietly,
  holding their tongues in respect.
¹¹ "All who heard me praised me.
  All who saw me spoke well of me.
¹² For I assisted the poor in their need
  and the orphans who required help.
¹³ I helped those without hope, and they blessed me.
  And I caused the widows' hearts to sing for joy.
¹⁴ Everything I did was honest.
  Righteousness covered me like a robe,
  and I wore justice like a turban.

¹⁵ I served as eyes for the blind
  and feet for the lame.
¹⁶ I was a father to the poor
  and assisted strangers who needed help.
¹⁷ I broke the jaws of godless oppressors
  and plucked their victims from their teeth.
¹⁸ "I thought, 'Surely I will die surrounded by my family
  after a long, good life.*
¹⁹ For I am like a tree whose roots reach the water,
  whose branches are refreshed with the dew.
²⁰ New honors are constantly bestowed on me,
  and my strength is continually renewed.'
²¹ "Everyone listened to my advice.
  They were silent as they waited for me to speak.
²² And after I spoke, they had nothing to add,
  for my counsel satisfied them.
²³ They longed for me to speak as people long for rain.
  They drank my words like a refreshing spring rain.
²⁴ When they were discouraged, I smiled at them.
  My look of approval was precious to them.
²⁵ Like a chief, I told them what to do.
  I lived like a king among his troops
  and comforted those who mourned.

Job Speaks of His Anguish

30 "But now I am mocked by people younger than I,
  by young men whose fathers are not worthy
  to run with my sheepdogs.
² A lot of good they are to me—
  those worn-out wretches!
³ They are gaunt from poverty and hunger.
  They claw the dry ground in desolate wastelands.
⁴ They pluck wild greens from among the bushes
  and eat from the roots of broom trees.
⁵ They are driven from human society,
  and people shout at them as if they were thieves.
⁶ So now they live in frightening ravines,
  in caves and among the rocks.

29:18 Hebrew *after I have counted my days like sand.*

28:28 While Proverbs 1:7 also speaks of the fear of God, this verse has two differences: First, in Job, the phrase "fear of the Lord" (*Adonai*) refers to a master who has authority; in Proverbs the "fear of the Lord" (*Yahweh*) uses God's personal name. Second, Job's fear "is true wisdom"; the fear in Proverbs is only the "foundation of true knowledge." In Job 28:28, we see that wisdom consists of reverential awe (fear) of God. Wisdom also shuns what God, as our authority, considers evil.

29:1–31:40 Job contrasts his former happiness, honor, and wealth (29:1-25) with his loss of social dignity and divine favor (30:1-31). He concludes his speech with wide-ranging oaths of innocence (31:1-40).

29:5-17 Job longed for his days at the center of his family and social world. He had been surrounded first by his children (29:5); then by the men of his community, who fell silent at his entrance (29:7-11), and finally by the marginalized whom he had helped (29:12-17). When we suffer losses, often what we miss most is feeling a sense of belonging. We can reach out to others who have faced rejection, knowing that our simple friendship can help in their healing.

⁷ They sound like animals howling among the bushes,
 huddled together beneath the nettles.
⁸ They are nameless fools,
 outcasts from society.

⁹ "And now they mock me with vulgar songs!
 They taunt me!
¹⁰ They despise me and won't come near me,
 except to spit in my face.
¹¹ For God has cut my bowstring.
 He has humbled me,
 so they have thrown off all restraint.
¹² These outcasts oppose me to my face.
 They send me sprawling
 and lay traps in my path.
¹³ They block my road
 and do everything they can to destroy me.
 They know I have no one to help me.
¹⁴ They come at me from all directions.
 They jump on me when I am down.
¹⁵ I live in terror now.
 My honor has blown away in the wind,
 and my prosperity has vanished like a cloud.

¹⁶ "And now my life seeps away.
 Depression haunts my days.
¹⁷ At night my bones are filled with pain,
 which gnaws at me relentlessly.
¹⁸ With a strong hand, God grabs my shirt.*
 He grips me by the collar of my coat.
¹⁹ He has thrown me into the mud.
 I'm nothing more than dust and ashes.

²⁰ "I cry to you, O God, but you don't answer.
 I stand before you, but you don't even look.
²¹ You have become cruel toward me.
 You use your power to persecute me.
²² You throw me into the whirlwind
 and destroy me in the storm.
²³ And I know you are sending me to my death—
 the destination of all who live.

²⁴ "Surely no one would turn against the needy
 when they cry for help in their trouble.
²⁵ Did I not weep for those in trouble?
 Was I not deeply grieved for the needy?
²⁶ So I looked for good, but evil came instead.
 I waited for the light, but darkness fell.
²⁷ My heart is troubled and restless.
 Days of suffering torment me.
²⁸ I walk in gloom, without sunlight.
 I stand in the public square and cry for help.
²⁹ Instead, I am considered a brother to jackals
 and a companion to owls.
³⁰ My skin has turned dark,
 and my bones burn with fever.
³¹ My harp plays sad music,
 and my flute accompanies those who weep.

Job's Final Protest of Innocence

31 "I made a covenant with my eyes
 not to look with lust at a young woman.
² For what has God above chosen for us?
 What is our inheritance from the Almighty on high?
³ Isn't it calamity for the wicked
 and misfortune for those who do evil?
⁴ Doesn't he see everything I do
 and every step I take?

⁵ "Have I lied to anyone
 or deceived anyone?
⁶ Let God weigh me on the scales of justice,
 for he knows my integrity.
⁷ If I have strayed from his pathway,
 or if my heart has lusted for what my eyes have seen,
 or if I am guilty of any other sin,
⁸ then let someone else eat the crops I have planted.
 Let all that I have planted be uprooted.

⁹ "If my heart has been seduced by a woman,
 or if I have lusted for my neighbor's wife,
¹⁰ then let my wife serve* another man;
 let other men sleep with her.
¹¹ For lust is a shameful sin,
 a crime that should be punished.
¹² It is a fire that burns all the way to hell.*
 It would wipe out everything I own.

30:18 As in Greek version; Hebrew reads *hand, my garment is disfigured.* 31:10 Hebrew *grind for.* 31:12 Hebrew *to Abaddon.*

30:12-14 The series of images presented here is drawn from a military advance against a fortified city. Job had already used this image for God's attack on him (19:10-12). The Hebrew word translated as "traps" might refer to siege ramps raised against a city's walls.

30:29 In ancient Israelite culture, jackals and owls were traditionally associated with the wasteland or wilderness (Isaiah 13:21-22; 34:13), where social outcasts would have roamed (Job 30:3, 7-8). In his loss and suffering, Job feared exile to those same places rather than regaining his rightful place at the center of his family and community (see study note on 29:5-17). However, God's eventual response (38:1–41:34) would lack Job's focus on human communities. God delights in these wild places. While we may yearn for community, God can use what feels like times of isolation to show us more of who he is.

31:1-40 In a strong assertion of his innocence, Job called down curses on himself if he were found guilty of the accusations made against him. Such curses were believed to be effective: If they did not happen, Job would be silently vindicated. Except for his mention of idolatry (31:26-27), Job addressed his faithfulness to God in terms of the second half of the Ten Commandments (Exodus 20:13-17; Deuteronomy 5:17-21), summarized by the command to "love your neighbor as yourself" (Leviticus 19:18; Romans 13:9).

¹³ "If I have been unfair to my male or female servants
  when they brought their complaints to me,
¹⁴ how could I face God?
  What could I say when he questioned me?
¹⁵ For God created both me and my servants.
  He created us both in the womb.

¹⁶ "Have I refused to help the poor,
  or crushed the hopes of widows?
¹⁷ Have I been stingy with my food
  and refused to share it with orphans?
¹⁸ No, from childhood I have cared for orphans like a father,
  and all my life I have cared for widows.
¹⁹ Whenever I saw the homeless without clothes
  and the needy with nothing to wear,
²⁰ did they not praise me
  for providing wool clothing to keep them warm?
²¹ "If I raised my hand against an orphan,
  knowing the judges would take my side,
²² then let my shoulder be wrenched out of place!
  Let my arm be torn from its socket!

Reflecting God's Love in Relationships

SCRIPTURE CONNECTION: JOB 31:1-40

Like most people, my family is one of my most important relationships. I am not alone. According to a Barna Group research study, Americans say their most important relationship is not God but their family. Ironically, our human relationships reflect how we relate to God, which is what Job 31 teaches us. Job lists a myriad of possibilities for his sinning against the people he encountered, and thus sinning against God.

Job was "a man of complete integrity" (1:1), so he wasn't guilty of these interpersonal wrongdoings. But what made Job righteous? It was because he understood the righteous God. Job lived a virtuous life as the fruit of his reverence for God.

We see this principle in Scripture broadly, in Job, and in the life and ministry of Jesus. Christ Jesus honored his Father's desire to bring us, his wayward children, close. He acted on his love for the Father and us, particularly by dying in our place for our wrongdoing. Jesus taught that loving God above all things and others as ourselves is God's will (Matthew 22:37-39; Mark 12:30-31). To love others well, we must first love God. Jesus' conduct—and Job's, to a great extent—testifies to God's own integrity.

Certainly, valuing our relationships aligns with God's will. But to establish healthy and fruitful relationships with the people we love, a strong relationship with God comes first.

> **Fruitful relationships come from a strong relationship with God.**

IMAGINE

According to Job 31, how do we see Job's reverence for God in his relationships?

Considering Job's and Jesus' lives, how can we show what's important to God in how we love others?

"Being intentional about loving my family is not always easy. During challenging moments, I remember that we love because he loved us first (1 John 4:19)."

MILLIE SERRANO is a faithful follower of Jesus Christ devoted to supporting women in their pursuit of growing a biblical, strong, and fruitful relationship with God through his Son, Jesus.

²³ That would be better than facing God's judgment.
  For if the majesty of God opposes me, what hope is there?
²⁴ "Have I put my trust in money
  or felt secure because of my gold?
²⁵ Have I gloated about my wealth
  and all that I own?
²⁶ "Have I looked at the sun shining in the skies,
  or the moon walking down its silver pathway,
²⁷ and been secretly enticed in my heart
  to throw kisses at them in worship?
²⁸ If so, I should be punished by the judges,
  for it would mean I had denied the God of heaven.
²⁹ "Have I ever rejoiced when disaster struck my enemies,
  or become excited when harm came their way?
³⁰ No, I have never sinned by cursing anyone
  or by asking for revenge.
³¹ "My servants have never said,
  'He let others go hungry.'
³² I have never turned away a stranger
  but have opened my doors to everyone.
³³ "Have I tried to hide my sins like other people do,
  concealing my guilt in my heart?
³⁴ Have I feared the crowd
  or the contempt of the masses,
  so that I kept quiet and stayed indoors?
³⁵ "If only someone would listen to me!
  Look, I will sign my name to my defense.
  Let the Almighty answer me.
  Let my accuser write out the charges against me.
³⁶ I would face the accusation proudly.
  I would wear it like a crown.
³⁷ For I would tell him exactly what I have done.
  I would come before him like a prince.
³⁸ "If my land accuses me
  and all its furrows cry out together,
³⁹ or if I have stolen its crops
  or murdered its owners,
⁴⁰ then let thistles grow on that land instead of wheat,
  and weeds instead of barley."

Job's words are ended.

Elihu Responds to Job's Friends

32 Job's three friends refused to reply further to him because he kept insisting on his innocence.

²Then Elihu son of Barakel the Buzite, of the clan of Ram, became angry. He was angry because Job refused to admit that he had sinned and that God was right in punishing him. ³He was also angry with Job's three friends, for they made God* appear to be wrong by their inability to answer Job's arguments. ⁴Elihu had waited for the others to speak to Job because they were older than he. ⁵But when he saw that they had no further reply, he spoke out angrily. ⁶Elihu son of Barakel the Buzite said,

"I am young and you are old,
  so I held back from telling you what I think.
⁷ I thought, 'Those who are older should speak,
  for wisdom comes with age.'
⁸ But there is a spirit* within people,
  the breath of the Almighty within them,
  that makes them intelligent.
⁹ Sometimes the elders are not wise.
  Sometimes the aged do not understand justice.
¹⁰ So listen to me,
  and let me tell you what I think.

¹¹ "I have waited all this time,
  listening very carefully to your arguments,
  listening to you grope for words.
¹² I have listened,
  but not one of you has refuted Job
  or answered his arguments.
¹³ And don't tell me, 'He is too wise for us.
  Only God can convince him.'
¹⁴ If Job had been arguing with me,
  I would not answer with your kind of logic!
¹⁵ You sit there baffled,
  with nothing more to say.
¹⁶ Should I continue to wait, now that you are silent?
  Must I also remain silent?
¹⁷ No, I will say my piece.
  I will speak my mind.
¹⁸ For I am full of pent-up words,
  and the spirit within me urges me on.
¹⁹ I am like a cask of wine without a vent,
  like a new wineskin ready to burst!
²⁰ I must speak to find relief,
  so let me give my answers.

32:3 As in ancient Hebrew scribal tradition; the Masoretic Text reads *Job*. 32:8 Or *Spirit*; also in 32:18.

32:1–37:24 Having completed three cycles of speeches between Job and his three friends, we now hear from a new voice. Elihu has not been previously introduced, but he is a young man who has listened to everything the others have said. **32:18-20** The length of Elihu's speech (32:1–37:24) demonstrates that he truly was "full of pent-up words." Elihu probably thought "the spirit within [him]" was prophetic urgency (32:8, 19-20; Psalm 39:3), but the reader might find him full of *wind* (both "spirit" and "wind" are possible translations of the same Hebrew word, *ruakh*, depending on the context). Like Zophar (Job 20:2), Elihu spoke "to find relief" (32:20).

²¹ I won't play favorites
   or try to flatter anyone.
²² For if I tried flattery,
   my Creator would soon destroy me.

Elihu Presents His Case against Job

33 ¹"Listen to my words, Job;
   pay attention to what I have to say.
² Now that I have begun to speak,
   let me continue.
³ I speak with all sincerity;
   I speak the truth.
⁴ For the Spirit of God has made me,
   and the breath of the Almighty gives me life.
⁵ Answer me, if you can;
   make your case and take your stand.
⁶ Look, you and I both belong to God.
   I, too, was formed from clay.
⁷ So you don't need to be afraid of me.
   I won't come down hard on you.

⁸ "You have spoken in my hearing,
   and I have heard your very words.
⁹ You said, 'I am pure; I am without sin;
   I am innocent; I have no guilt.
¹⁰ God is picking a quarrel with me,
   and he considers me his enemy.
¹¹ He puts my feet in the stocks
   and watches my every move.'

¹² "But you are wrong, and I will show you why.
   For God is greater than any human being.
¹³ So why are you bringing a charge against him?
   Why say he does not respond to people's complaints?
¹⁴ For God speaks again and again,
   though people do not recognize it.
¹⁵ He speaks in dreams, in visions of the night,
   when deep sleep falls on people
   as they lie in their beds.
¹⁶ He whispers in their ears
   and terrifies them with warnings.
¹⁷ He makes them turn from doing wrong;
   he keeps them from pride.
¹⁸ He protects them from the grave,
   from crossing over the river of death.
¹⁹ Or God disciplines people with pain on their sickbeds,
   with ceaseless aching in their bones.
²⁰ They lose their appetite
   for even the most delicious food.
²¹ Their flesh wastes away,
   and their bones stick out.
²² They are at death's door;
   the angels of death wait for them.

²³ "But if an angel from heaven appears—
   a special messenger to intercede for a person
   and declare that he is upright—
²⁴ he will be gracious and say,
   'Rescue him from the grave,
   for I have found a ransom for his life.'
²⁵ Then his body will become as healthy as a child's,
   firm and youthful again.
²⁶ When he prays to God,
   he will be accepted.

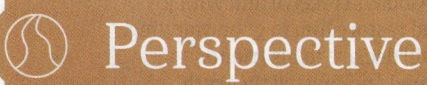

Perspective

Did anyone get it right?

SCRIPTURE CONNECTION: JOB 32–37

We like to characterize people as "good guys" or "bad guys," but most are more complex. Take Elihu, for example. This book's opening and closing do not mention him. Job does not answer him. God does not condemn him.

Try as I might, I cannot decide whether Elihu is a good example or a bad one. He rightly condemns Job's friends for their wild imaginations. His effort to defend God against Job's accusations seems admirable, except that God speaks for himself (38:1–42:8).

At times Elihu sounds humble, at other times, arrogant. Perhaps he is purposely ambiguous, forcing us to think more deeply. The timing of his words—after the friends and before God—makes us ask if there is any meaningful speech in the face of suffering.

VIEWPOINTS

HIS: *Elihu appoints himself as God's spokesperson, putting Job and his friends in their places.*
MINE: *"Suffering cries for answers, but sometimes silence is the greatest gift we can offer."*
YOURS: *How do you know whether it's time to speak up or to be silent?*

CARMEN JOY IMES, PhD, is an author, speaker, blogger, YouTuber, and serves as associate professor of Old Testament at Biola University in California.

33:14-22 Elihu believed that God communicates with people in two ways: through dreams or visions and through suffering. Unlike Eliphaz, Bildad, and Zophar, Elihu suggested that Job's suffering was not a punishment for misdeeds. Instead, it was instructional and designed to preserve his life.

And God will receive him with joy
and restore him to good standing.
²⁷ He will declare to his friends,
'I sinned and twisted the truth,
but it was not worth it.*
²⁸ God rescued me from the grave,
and now my life is filled with light.'

²⁹ "Yes, God does these things
again and again for people.
³⁰ He rescues them from the grave
so they may enjoy the light of life.
³¹ Mark this well, Job. Listen to me,
for I have more to say.
³² But if you have anything to say, go ahead.
Speak, for I am anxious to see you justified.
³³ But if not, then listen to me.
Keep silent and I will teach you wisdom!"

Elihu Accuses Job of Arrogance

34 Then Elihu said:

² "Listen to me, you wise men.
Pay attention, you who have knowledge.
³ Job said, 'The ear tests the words it hears
just as the mouth distinguishes between foods.'
⁴ So let us discern for ourselves what is right;
let us learn together what is good.
⁵ For Job also said, 'I am innocent,
but God has taken away my rights.
⁶ I am innocent, but they call me a liar.
My suffering is incurable, though I have not sinned.'

⁷ "Tell me, has there ever been a man like Job,
with his thirst for irreverent talk?
⁸ He chooses evil people as companions.
He spends his time with wicked men.
⁹ He has even said, 'Why waste time
trying to please God?'

¹⁰ "Listen to you who have understanding.
Everyone knows that God doesn't sin!
The Almighty can do no wrong.
¹¹ He repays people according to their deeds.
He treats people as they deserve.
¹² Truly, God will not do wrong.
The Almighty will not twist justice.
¹³ Did someone else put the world in his care?
Who set the whole world in place?
¹⁴ If God were to take back his spirit
and withdraw his breath,
¹⁵ all life would cease,
and humanity would turn again to dust.

¹⁶ "Now listen to me if you are wise.
Pay attention to what I say.
¹⁷ Could God govern if he hated justice?
Are you going to condemn the almighty judge?
¹⁸ For he says to kings, 'You are wicked,'
and to nobles, 'You are unjust.'
¹⁹ He doesn't care how great a person may be,
and he pays no more attention to the rich than to the poor.
He made them all.
²⁰ In a moment they die.
In the middle of the night they pass away;
the mighty are removed without human hand.

²¹ "For God watches how people live;
he sees everything they do.
²² No darkness is thick enough
to hide the wicked from his eyes.
²³ We don't set the time
when we will come before God in judgment.
²⁴ He brings the mighty to ruin without asking anyone,
and he sets up others in their place.
²⁵ He knows what they do,
and in the night he overturns and destroys them.
²⁶ He strikes them down because they are wicked,
doing it openly for all to see.
²⁷ For they turned away from following him.
They have no respect for any of his ways.
²⁸ They cause the poor to cry out, catching God's attention.
He hears the cries of the needy.
²⁹ But if he chooses to remain quiet,
who can criticize him?
When he hides his face, no one can find him,
whether an individual or a nation.
³⁰ He prevents the godless from ruling
so they cannot be a snare to the people.

³¹ "Why don't people say to God, 'I have sinned,
but I will sin no more'?
³² Or 'I don't know what evil I have done—tell me.
If I have done wrong, I will stop at once'?
³³ "Must God tailor his justice to your demands?
But you have rejected him!
The choice is yours, not mine.
Go ahead, share your wisdom with us.

33:27 Greek version reads *but he* [God] *did not punish me as my sin deserved.*

34:17 The implied answer was that God could *not* "govern if he hated justice" (see Romans 3:4-7; 7:7, 13; 9:14; Galatians 2:17, 6:14). God also asked if Job was "going to condemn the almighty judge" (see also Job 40:8).

34 After all, bright people will tell me,
and wise people will hear me say,
35 'Job speaks out of ignorance;
his words lack insight.'
36 Job, you deserve the maximum penalty
for the wicked way you have talked.
37 For you have added rebellion to your sin;
you show no respect,
and you speak many angry words against God."

Elihu Reminds Job of God's Justice

35 Then Elihu said:

2 "Do you think it is right for you to claim,
'I am righteous before God'?
3 For you also ask, 'What's in it for me?
What's the use of living a righteous life?'

4 "I will answer you
and all your friends, too.
5 Look up into the sky,
and see the clouds high above you.
6 If you sin, how does that affect God?
Even if you sin again and again,
what effect will it have on him?
7 If you are good, is this some great gift to him?
What could you possibly give him?
8 No, your sins affect only people like yourself,
and your good deeds also affect only humans.

9 "People cry out when they are oppressed.
They groan beneath the power of the mighty.
10 Yet they don't ask, 'Where is God my Creator,
the one who gives songs in the night?
11 Where is the one who makes us smarter than
the animals
and wiser than the birds of the sky?'
12 And when they cry out, God does not answer
because of their pride.
13 But it is wrong to say God doesn't listen,
to say the Almighty isn't concerned.
14 You say you can't see him,
but he will bring justice if you will only wait.*
15 You say he does not respond to sinners with
anger
and is not greatly concerned about
wickedness.*
16 But you are talking nonsense, Job.
You have spoken like a fool."

36 Elihu continued speaking:

2 "Let me go on, and I will show you the truth.
For I have not finished defending God!
3 I will present profound arguments
for the righteousness of my Creator.
4 I am telling you nothing but the truth,
for I am a man of great knowledge.

5 "God is mighty, but he does not despise anyone!
He is mighty in both power and
understanding.
6 He does not let the wicked live
but gives justice to the afflicted.
7 He never takes his eyes off the innocent,
but he sets them on thrones with kings
and exalts them forever.
8 If they are bound in chains
and caught up in a web of trouble,
9 he shows them the reason.
He shows them their sins of pride.
10 He gets their attention
and commands that they turn from evil.

11 "If they listen and obey God,
they will be blessed with prosperity
throughout their lives.
All their years will be pleasant.
12 But if they refuse to listen to him,
they will cross over the river of death,
dying from lack of understanding.
13 For the godless are full of resentment.
Even when he punishes them,
they refuse to cry out to him for help.
14 They die when they are young,
after wasting their lives in immoral living.
15 But by means of their suffering, he rescues those
who suffer.
For he gets their attention through adversity.

16 "God is leading you away from danger, Job,
to a place free from distress.
He is setting your table with the best food.
17 But you are obsessed with whether the godless
will be judged.
Don't worry, judgment and justice will be
upheld.
18 But watch out, or you may be seduced by
wealth.*
Don't let yourself be bribed into sin.

35:13-14 These verses can also be translated as follows: *13Indeed, God doesn't listen to their empty plea; / the Almighty is not concerned. / 14How much less will he listen when you say you don't see him, / and that your case is before him and you're waiting for justice.* 35:15 As in Greek and Latin versions; the meaning of this Hebrew word is uncertain. 36:18 Or *But don't let your anger lead you to mockery.*

35:8-13 According to Elihu, Job could approach God either by praying for relief or seeking God as his wise creator. Elihu observed that God does not answer prideful prayers. By implication, Job should seek to know God himself rather than only seeking relief or vindication.

36:7 Elihu believed the biblical principle that God "never takes his eyes off the innocent" (see 2 Chronicles 16:9; Psalms 33:18; 34:15; 1 Peter 3:12) should have comforted Job. But he does not address Job's perspective that God's attention is hostile rather than loving (Job 7:17-21).

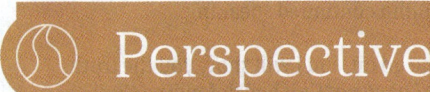

Perspective

Do we get what we deserve?

SCRIPTURE CONNECTION: JOB 32–37

The ancient "retribution principle" means that those who do good receive rewards, and those who do bad get punished. It describes how Job's friends would have understood justice; everything was all black and white.

Therefore, Job's situation was a conundrum. How can someone who claims innocence suffer? Perhaps this is why Job's three friends tried to assign guilt. They sought to fit Job's situation and God's actions into their simplistic system.

Elihu's speech offers a different perspective. Perhaps God is more intricate than our black and white view of justice. If God is truly God, his ways and wisdom are beyond us: "Look, God is greater than we can understand" (36:26).

Perhaps we, too, peer through a "retribution principle" lens when we would do better to perceive God as both loving and just, even though we can't fully understand how it all works.

VIEWPOINTS

HIS: His friends thought they had God figured out. Job had not and so could only keep wrestling with God. How did Job and his three friends view God differently?

MINE: "Like Job, when I am confused by God's ways, I often judge God by his action and inaction. While I can bring my questions to God, as Job did, I also need to remember that his ways are higher. Even when it doesn't make sense, I can trust God because he is a loving God who created and rules over all things."

YOURS: How might you be judging God on your terms? How might you trust God because he is loving and just?

MAY YOUNG, MDiv, PhD, is an associate professor of biblical studies at Taylor University, with a passion for discipleship, teaching, and writing.

---

19 Could all your wealth*
or all your mighty efforts
keep you from distress?
20 Do not long for the cover of night,
for that is when people will be destroyed.*
21 Be on guard! Turn back from evil,
for God sent this suffering
to keep you from a life of evil.

Elihu Reminds Job of God's Power

22 "Look, God is all-powerful.
Who is a teacher like him?
23 No one can tell him what to do,
or say to him, 'You have done wrong.'
24 Instead, glorify his mighty works,
singing songs of praise.
25 Everyone has seen these things,
though only from a distance.

26 "Look, God is greater than we can understand.
His years cannot be counted.
27 He draws up the water vapor
and then distills it into rain.
28 The rain pours down from the clouds,
and everyone benefits.
29 Who can understand the spreading of the clouds
and the thunder that rolls forth from heaven?
30 See how he spreads the lightning around him
and how it lights up the depths of the sea.
31 By these mighty acts he nourishes* the people,
giving them food in abundance.
32 He fills his hands with lightning bolts
and hurls each at its target.
33 The thunder announces his presence;
the storm announces his indignant anger.*

37 "My heart pounds as I think of this.
It trembles within me.
2 Listen carefully to the thunder of God's voice
as it rolls from his mouth.
3 It rolls across the heavens,
and his lightning flashes in every direction.
4 Then comes the roaring of the thunder—
the tremendous voice of his majesty.
He does not restrain it when he speaks.
5 God's voice is glorious in the thunder.
We can't even imagine the greatness of his power.

6 "He directs the snow to fall on the earth
and tells the rain to pour down.
7 Then everyone stops working
so they can watch his power.
8 The wild animals take cover
and stay inside their dens.

36:19 Or *Could all your cries for help.* **36:16-20** The meaning of the Hebrew in this passage is uncertain. **36:31** Or *he governs.* **36:33** Or *even the cattle know when a storm is coming.* The meaning of the Hebrew is uncertain.

⁹ The stormy wind comes from its chamber,
and the driving winds bring the cold.
¹⁰ God's breath sends the ice,
freezing wide expanses of water.
¹¹ He loads the clouds with moisture,
and they flash with his lightning.
¹² The clouds churn about at his direction.
They do whatever he commands throughout the earth.
¹³ He makes these things happen either to punish people
or to show his unfailing love.
¹⁴ "Pay attention to this, Job.
Stop and consider the wonderful miracles of God!
¹⁵ Do you know how God controls the storm
and causes the lightning to flash from his clouds?
¹⁶ Do you understand how he moves the clouds
with wonderful perfection and skill?
¹⁷ When you are sweltering in your clothes
and the south wind dies down and everything is still,
¹⁸ he makes the skies reflect the heat like a bronze mirror.
Can you do that?
¹⁹ "So teach the rest of us what to say to God.
We are too ignorant to make our own arguments.
²⁰ Should God be notified that I want to speak?
Can people even speak when they are confused?*
²¹ We cannot look at the sun,
for it shines brightly in the sky
when the wind clears away the clouds.
²² So also, golden splendor comes from the mountain of God.*
He is clothed in dazzling splendor.
²³ We cannot imagine the power of the Almighty;
but even though he is just and righteous,
he does not destroy us.
²⁴ No wonder people everywhere fear him.
All who are wise show him reverence.*"

The Lord Challenges Job

38 Then the Lord answered Job from the whirlwind:

² "Who is this that questions my wisdom
with such ignorant words?
³ Brace yourself like a man,
because I have some questions for you,
and you must answer them.

⁴ "Where were you when I laid the foundations of the earth?
Tell me, if you know so much.
⁵ Who determined its dimensions
and stretched out the surveying line?
⁶ What supports its foundations,
and who laid its cornerstone
⁷ as the morning stars sang together
and all the angels* shouted for joy?

⁸ "Who kept the sea inside its boundaries
as it burst from the womb,
⁹ and as I clothed it with clouds
and wrapped it in thick darkness?
¹⁰ For I locked it behind barred gates,
limiting its shores.
¹¹ I said, 'This far and no farther will you come.
Here your proud waves must stop!'

¹² "Have you ever commanded the morning to appear
and caused the dawn to rise in the east?
¹³ Have you made daylight spread to the ends of the earth,
to bring an end to the night's wickedness?
¹⁴ As the light approaches,
the earth takes shape like clay pressed beneath a seal;
it is robed in brilliant colors.*
¹⁵ The light disturbs the wicked
and stops the arm that is raised in violence.

¹⁶ "Have you explored the springs from which the seas come?
Have you explored their depths?
¹⁷ Do you know where the gates of death are located?
Have you seen the gates of utter gloom?

37:20 Or *speak without being swallowed up?* 37:22 Or *from the north;* or *from the abode.* 37:24 As in Greek version; Hebrew reads *He is not impressed by the wise.* 38:7 Hebrew *the sons of God.* 38:14 Or *its features stand out like folds in a robe.*

37:22 The literature of Ugarit, an influential port city in the Bronze Age, describes Mount Zaphon as the mountain home of the storm god Baal. Because the mountain was situated north of Ugarit, the word *Zaphon* entered common usage referring to the direction north, and this figure of speech appears elsewhere in the Old Testament (see text notes for Psalm 48:2 and Isaiah 14:13). Here it is translated "the mountain of God" and metaphorically refers to God's lofty home in the heavens.
38:1–40:5 God finally appeared, reframing the issues. While Job and his friends had focused on justice and the retribution principle (see note on 1:9-11), God pointed Job to the real issue: God's wisdom. Using an extended series of rhetorical questions, God first focused on his work in creation itself (38:4-21) before turning to his ongoing providence in maintaining that creation (38:22–39:30). While highlighting Job's limitations, the questions were not meant to humiliate him. Instead, they sought to create in Job a sense of awe at the greatness of God.
38:1-3 God challenged Job from out of the whirlwind. The Old Testament commonly associates storms with God's presence (2 Kings 2:1, 11; Ezekiel 1:4; Nahum 1:3). Job finally had an audience with God (13:22-23).

¹⁸ Do you realize the extent of the earth?
  Tell me about it if you know!
¹⁹ "Where does light come from,
  and where does darkness go?
²⁰ Can you take each to its home?
  Do you know how to get there?
²¹ But of course you know all this!
  For you were born before it was all created,
  and you are so very experienced!
²² "Have you visited the storehouses of the snow
  or seen the storehouses of hail?
²³ (I have reserved them as weapons for the time of trouble,
  for the day of battle and war.)
²⁴ Where is the path to the source of light?
  Where is the home of the east wind?
²⁵ "Who created a channel for the torrents of rain?
  Who laid out the path for the lightning?
²⁶ Who makes the rain fall on barren land,
  in a desert where no one lives?
²⁷ Who sends rain to satisfy the parched ground
  and make the tender grass spring up?
²⁸ "Does the rain have a father?
  Who gives birth to the dew?
²⁹ Who is the mother of the ice?
  Who gives birth to the frost from the heavens?
³⁰ For the water turns to ice as hard as rock,
  and the surface of the water freezes.
³¹ "Can you direct the movement of the stars—
  binding the cluster of the Pleiades
  or loosening the cords of Orion?
³² Can you direct the constellations through the seasons
  or guide the Bear with her cubs across the heavens?
³³ Do you know the laws of the universe?
  Can you use them to regulate the earth?
³⁴ "Can you shout to the clouds
  and make it rain?
³⁵ Can you make lightning appear
  and cause it to strike as you direct?
³⁶ Who gives intuition to the heart
  and instinct to the mind?

³⁷ Who is wise enough to count all the clouds?
  Who can tilt the water jars of heaven
³⁸ when the parched ground is dry
  and the soil has hardened into clods?
³⁹ "Can you stalk prey for a lioness
  and satisfy the young lions' appetites
⁴⁰ as they lie in their dens
  or crouch in the thicket?
⁴¹ Who provides food for the ravens
  when their young cry out to God
  and wander about in hunger?

The Lord's Challenge Continues

39 "Do you know when the wild goats give birth?
  Have you watched as deer are born in the wild?
² Do you know how many months they carry their young?
  Are you aware of the time of their delivery?
³ They crouch down to give birth to their young
  and deliver their offspring.
⁴ Their young grow up in the open fields,
  then leave home and never return.
⁵ "Who gives the wild donkey its freedom?
  Who untied its ropes?
⁶ I have placed it in the wilderness;
  its home is the wasteland.
⁷ It hates the noise of the city
  and has no driver to shout at it.
⁸ The mountains are its pastureland,
  where it searches for every blade of grass.
⁹ "Will the wild ox consent to being tamed?
  Will it spend the night in your stall?
¹⁰ Can you hitch a wild ox to a plow?
  Will it plow a field for you?
¹¹ Given its strength, can you trust it?
  Can you leave and trust the ox to do your work?
¹² Can you rely on it to bring home your grain
  and deliver it to your threshing floor?
¹³ "The ostrich flaps her wings grandly,
  but they are no match for the feathers of the stork.

38:36 The Hebrew words rendered *heart* and *mind* here can also be translated "ibis" and "rooster," respectively. The ibis was associated with Thoth, the Egyptian god of wisdom, and before their extinction in Egypt, their migration pattern coincided with the annual flooding of the Nile River, the most important seasonal event in ancient Egypt. Israel's rabbis thought the rooster could forecast rain or that its crow distinguished day from night. With this line of thinking, the idea would then be "Who taught the ibis when the Nile floods and the rooster when it rains?" (See also Psalm 51:6; Proverbs 2:6; James 1:5, 17.)

39:13-18 In the ancient Near East, the ostrich had a reputation as a bird that God had deprived of wisdom. The ostrich is a symbol of neglect for her young (Lamentations 4:3) because she "lays her eggs on top of the earth"; she appears to leave her eggs to die when a predator approaches them (although she is probably attempting to lure the predator away from the nest); and she lays her eggs with several other hens in one nest, so most of the eggs are not her own. Based on general observation, the ostrich seems foolish, but even though she has her limitations (or we lack full understanding of her ways), God made her faster than "the swiftest horse with its rider." God, in his wisdom, still created her with her own skills and advantages.

14 She lays her eggs on top of the earth,
    letting them be warmed in the dust.
15 She doesn't worry that a foot might crush them
    or a wild animal might destroy them.
16 She is harsh toward her young,
    as if they were not her own.
    She doesn't care if they die.
17 For God has deprived her of wisdom.
    He has given her no understanding.
18 But whenever she jumps up to run,
    she passes the swiftest horse with its rider.
19 "Have you given the horse its strength
    or clothed its neck with a flowing mane?
20 Did you give it the ability to leap like a locust?
    Its majestic snorting is terrifying!
21 It paws the earth and rejoices in its strength
    when it charges out to battle.
22 It laughs at fear and is unafraid.
    It does not run from the sword.
23 The arrows rattle against it,
    and the spear and javelin flash.
24 It paws the ground fiercely
    and rushes forward into battle when the
        ram's horn blows.
25 It snorts at the sound of the horn.
    It senses the battle in the distance.
    It quivers at the captain's commands and the
        noise of battle.
26 "Is it your wisdom that makes the hawk soar
    and spread its wings toward the south?
27 Is it at your command that the eagle rises
    to the heights to make its nest?
28 It lives on the cliffs,
    making its home on a distant, rocky crag.

Come Close — PAINED? PURSUE

SCRIPTURE CONNECTION: JOB 38–41

God doesn't seem thrilled with Job's questions—and we may wonder if God wants us to check our brains at the doorway of our faith, to numb and push down our pain. But there's a way to read this differently.

God doesn't reprimand Job for querying but for criticizing: "You are God's critic, but do you have the answers?" (40:2). Elsewhere, God commands us to love him with all our minds (Matthew 22:37; Mark 12:30; Luke 10:27). So, we pursue God in our pain by understanding the Bible, which invites us to ask, and yet honor the one we're asking.

We also pursue God by asking wise people our questions. I queried scholar May Young, who has spent decades studying the Bible, "How was God just and loving to Job?" She said,

> God's love shows through his willingness to interact with Job and that God did not withdraw his presence. Regarding justice, . . . God vindicated Job before his friends, and what he lost was restored.

However, this book is not ultimately about God's justice or his love. God's justice is beyond our understanding—that's why God never answers Job directly but only raises more questions that Job cannot answer.

By pursuing God with our questions, we refuse to shove down our wonderings. By pursuing, we can glimpse a glorious God full of wisdom. And a glorious God can hold us, our sincere questions, and our very life.

REFLECT "Jesus replied, 'You must love the LORD your God with all your heart, all your soul, and all your mind.'" MATTHEW 22:37

God, thank you for inviting me to love you with the brain you gave me. And thank you even more that I can trust your glory and your heart more than any answer. Amen.

CONSIDER "Faith sees the invisible, believes the unbelievable, and receives the impossible." CORRIE TEN BOOM

We grasp God's loving justice only as we glimpse God's glory.

NAOMI CRAMER OVERTON, MBA, DIS, lives to realize beauty-filled visions that lift us to flourishing, with our families and beyond. Naomi has been CEO for Stonecroft and MOPS, director with Compassion International and World Vision, and General Editor for this Bible.

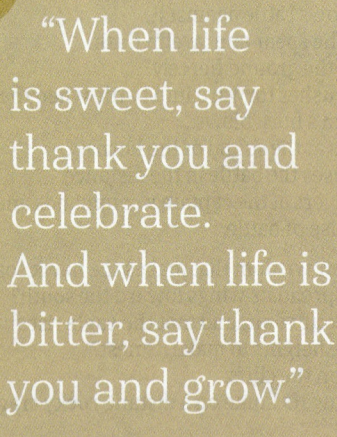

> "When life is sweet, say thank you and celebrate. And when life is bitter, say thank you and grow."
>
> SHAUNA NIEQUIST
> bestselling author, wife, and mother

²⁹ From there it hunts its prey,
  keeping watch with piercing eyes.
³⁰ Its young gulp down blood.
  Where there's a carcass, there you'll find it."

40

Then the LORD said to Job,

² "Do you still want to argue with the Almighty? You are God's critic, but do you have the answers?"

Job Responds to the LORD

³ Then Job replied to the LORD,

⁴ "I am nothing—how could I ever find the answers?
  I will cover my mouth with my hand.
⁵ I have said too much already.
  I have nothing more to say."

The LORD Challenges Job Again

⁶ Then the LORD answered Job from the whirlwind:

⁷ "Brace yourself like a man,
  because I have some questions for you,
  and you must answer them.
⁸ "Will you discredit my justice
  and condemn me just to prove you are right?
⁹ Are you as strong as God?
  Can you thunder with a voice like his?
¹⁰ All right, put on your glory and splendor,
  your honor and majesty.
¹¹ Give vent to your anger.
  Let it overflow against the proud.
¹² Humiliate the proud with a glance;
  walk on the wicked where they stand.
¹³ Bury them in the dust.
  Imprison them in the world of the dead.
¹⁴ Then even I would praise you,
  for your own strength would save you.

¹⁵ "Take a look at Behemoth,*
  which I made, just as I made you.
  It eats grass like an ox.
¹⁶ See its powerful loins
  and the muscles of its belly.
¹⁷ Its tail is as strong as a cedar.
  The sinews of its thighs are knit tightly together.
¹⁸ Its bones are tubes of bronze.
  Its limbs are bars of iron.
¹⁹ It is a prime example of God's handiwork,
  and only its Creator can threaten it.
²⁰ The mountains offer it their best food,
  where all the wild animals play.
²¹ It lies under the lotus plants,*
  hidden by the reeds in the marsh.
²² The lotus plants give it shade
  among the willows beside the stream.
²³ It is not disturbed by the raging river,
  not concerned when the swelling Jordan rushes around it.
²⁴ No one can catch it off guard
  or put a ring in its nose and lead it away.

40:15 The identification of Behemoth is disputed, ranging from an earthly creature to a mythical sea monster in ancient literature. 40:21 Or *bramble bushes*; also in 40:22.

40:3-5 Job's brief and humble response does not acknowledge guilt, but it does admit his insignificance (40:4). He had previously thought that he could approach God like a prince (31:37) or even cross-examine him (13:22-23).
40:4 Job was not yet repenting from sin (see 42:6). Like Abraham, he recognized his unworthiness before God (Genesis 18:27). Job had asked his comforters to cover their mouths to acknowledge shock (Job 21:5); here he does so himself in reaction to his own rash words.

40:15-24 Following a list of various animals (39:1-30), God describes Behemoth and Leviathan (41:1-34) as creatures that humans cannot tame. Job couldn't tame the wild donkey or ox (39:5-12), let alone Behemoth and Leviathan, but God created them and could control them, and Job had to acknowledge that he couldn't (41:2). Although no one knows for certain, Behemoth seems to have been a real creature: God says that he made it, just as he made Job, and describes it as an herbivore. Behemoth is usually identified as a hippopotamus, because it is a huge, powerful, grass-eating animal that lies in the river among the lotus plants and reeds.

Job's Daughters

IDENTITY — What's in a Name

What's the significance of your name? Potentially, a lot! Someone likely chose your name for a reason. Sometimes we are given a family name, sometimes a name they just liked, or a name God whispered to them, meant for you.

Job's family provides a good example of giving meaningful names. Though he had seven sons and three daughters, the passage only mentions the daughters' names! This stands out in a time and a culture that valued sons most.

The women's names are significant. Jemimah means "warm or affectionate" or "dove"; Keziah means "cassia," a bark-like cinnamon with a fragrant aroma; and Keren-happuch means "horn of antimony," a valuable metal used as eye makeup in the ancient world.

Their names alone suggest that their father valued these young women. And, more surprisingly, he wrote them into his will, when only sons typically inherited anything.

Names matter in the Bible, and they say something important about the person. God often changed names or named people to signify their Kingdom value and calling. For example, the angel announced Jesus' name at conception (Luke 1:31), and Jesus renamed Simon to Peter, "rock" (Matthew 16:18), and many others.

Name meanings are still powerful and can make a statement about our identity. In October 2011, over two hundred young girls participated in a ceremony in India to change their names from Nakusha (meaning "unwanted" and given to them at birth) to a name each chose that signified value. This life-changing event gave them hope for the future.

No matter what others have named you, God gives all his children new names, filled with meaning, and an inheritance with Jesus (Galatians 4:1-7; Revelation 2:17).

> Names can shape how we see ourselves and others, but only God can show us our true identities.

THE STORY OF JOB'S DAUGHTERS IS TOLD IN JOB 42:13-15.

IDENTIFY

What does your name mean? Why did someone choose it?

What valuable qualities do you believe God and others might see—and name—in you?

"My given name is Elizabeth because it is a family name from both parents' sides. But later in life, I learned its meaning: "consecrated to God." My name has confirmed all that God has called me to be and do and it constantly reminds me of his hand on my life."

ELIZABETH GLANVILLE, PhD, is retired faculty from Fuller Theological Seminary, School of Mission and Theology. She is an international teacher on missions and leadership and chaplain for a local police department and her retirement community.

The LORD's Challenge Continues

41 ¹*"Can you catch Leviathan* with a hook
or put a noose around its jaw?
² Can you tie it with a rope through the nose
or pierce its jaw with a spike?
³ Will it beg you for mercy
or implore you for pity?
⁴ Will it agree to work for you,
to be your slave for life?
⁵ Can you make it a pet like a bird,
or give it to your little girls to play with?
⁶ Will merchants try to buy it
to sell it in their shops?
⁷ Will its hide be hurt by spears
or its head by a harpoon?
⁸ If you lay a hand on it,
you will certainly remember the battle that follows.
You won't try that again!
⁹*No, it is useless to try to capture it.
The hunter who attempts it will be knocked down.
¹⁰ And since no one dares to disturb it,
who then can stand up to me?
¹¹ Who has given me anything that I need to pay back?
Everything under heaven is mine.

¹² "I want to emphasize Leviathan's limbs
and its enormous strength and graceful form.
¹³ Who can strip off its hide,
and who can penetrate its double layer of armor?*
¹⁴ Who could pry open its jaws?
For its teeth are terrible!
¹⁵ The scales on its back are like* rows of shields
tightly sealed together.
¹⁶ They are so close together
that no air can get between them.
¹⁷ Each scale sticks tight to the next.
They interlock and cannot be penetrated.
¹⁸ "When it sneezes, it flashes light!
Its eyes are like the red of dawn.
¹⁹ Lightning leaps from its mouth;
flames of fire flash out.
²⁰ Smoke streams from its nostrils
like steam from a pot heated over burning rushes.
²¹ Its breath would kindle coals,
for flames shoot from its mouth.

²² "The tremendous strength in Leviathan's neck
strikes terror wherever it goes.
²³ Its flesh is hard and firm
and cannot be penetrated.
²⁴ Its heart is hard as rock,
hard as a millstone.
²⁵ When it rises, the mighty are afraid,
gripped by terror.
²⁶ No sword can stop it,
no spear, dart, or javelin.
²⁷ Iron is nothing but straw to that creature,
and bronze is like rotten wood.
²⁸ Arrows cannot make it flee.
Stones shot from a sling are like bits of grass.
²⁹ Clubs are like a blade of grass,
and it laughs at the swish of javelins.
³⁰ Its belly is covered with scales as sharp as glass.
It plows up the ground as it drags through the mud.

³¹ "Leviathan makes the water boil with its commotion.
It stirs the depths like a pot of ointment.
³² The water glistens in its wake,
making the sea look white.
³³ Nothing on earth is its equal,
no other creature so fearless.
³⁴ Of all the creatures, it is the proudest.
It is the king of beasts."

Job Responds to the LORD

42 Then Job replied to the LORD:

² "I know that you can do anything,
and no one can stop you.
³ You asked, 'Who is this that questions my wisdom with such ignorance?'
It is I—and I was talking about things I knew nothing about,
things far too wonderful for me.

41:1a Verses 41:1-8 are numbered 40:25-32 in Hebrew text. **41:1b** The identification of Leviathan is disputed, ranging from an earthly creature to a mythical sea monster in ancient literature. **41:9** Verses 41:9-34 are numbered 41:1-26 in Hebrew text. **41:13** As in Greek version; Hebrew reads *its bridle?* **41:15** As in some Greek manuscripts and Latin Vulgate; Hebrew reads *Its pride is in its.*

41:1-34 Leviathan has been identified as everything from an observable animal to a mythical creature, but one thing is clear: Where the Behemoth was peaceful, Leviathan was menacing. Most commentators who suggest Leviathan was a real animal identify it with the crocodile, which would fit the description of powerful jaws, an armored hide, and the ability to churn water when attacking. On the other hand, Leviathan is described as fire-breathing, a swift and coiling serpent (Isaiah 27:1). The phrasing in Isaiah 27:1 is strikingly similar to several lines of ancient Ugaritic literature that detail Lotan, the seven-headed sea serpent with which the storm god must contend. Adversarial sea serpents appear in ancient Near Eastern mythology, where they represent chaos and must be subdued by an powerful deity. These themes are echoed in the Bible, where an unruly sea monster serves as an image for chaos and wickedness, and whose head the Lord ultimately crushes (Psalm 74:14; Isaiah 27:1; see also Job 9:13 text note; 26:12; Psalm 89:9-10; Isaiah 30:7; 51:9).

4 You said, 'Listen and I will speak!
   I have some questions for you,
   and you must answer them.'
5 I had only heard about you before,
   but now I have seen you with my own eyes.
6 I take back everything I said,
   and I sit in dust and ashes to show my
      repentance."

Conclusion: The LORD Blesses Job

7 After the LORD had finished speaking to Job, he said to Eliphaz the Temanite: "I am angry with you and your two friends, for you have not spoken accurately about me, as my servant Job has. 8 So take seven bulls and seven rams and go to my servant Job and offer a burnt offering for yourselves. My servant Job will pray for you, and I will accept his prayer on your behalf. I will not treat you as you deserve, for you have not spoken accurately about me, as my servant Job has." 9 So Eliphaz the Temanite, Bildad the Shuhite, and Zophar the Naamathite did as the LORD commanded them, and the LORD accepted Job's prayer.

10 When Job prayed for his friends, the LORD restored his fortunes. In fact, the LORD gave him twice as much as before! 11 Then all his brothers, sisters, and former friends came and feasted with him in his home. And they consoled him and comforted him because of all the trials the LORD had brought against him. And each of them brought him a gift of money* and a gold ring.

12 So the LORD blessed Job in the second half of his life even more than in the beginning. For now he had 14,000 sheep, 6,000 camels, 1,000 teams of oxen, and 1,000 female donkeys. 13 He also gave Job seven more sons and three more daughters. 14 He named his first daughter Jemimah, the second Keziah, and the third Keren-happuch. 15 In all the land no women were as lovely as the daughters of Job. And their father put them into his will along with their brothers.

16 Job lived 140 years after that, living to see four generations of his children and grandchildren. 17 Then he died, an old man who had lived a long, full life.

42:11 Hebrew *a kesitah*; the value or weight of the kesitah is no longer known.

42:1-6 Something fundamental had changed for Job because of his encounter with God. While Job had been immersed in his suffering, God had taken him through time, back to the universe's beginning. Further, while Job focused on his human losses—material, physical, and social—God highlighted his love for the untamed creatures found in the wilderness, the place Job feared. In his divine tour of the universe, Job not only experienced awe at God's greatness and wisdom, his understanding of the world was also reframed (see study note on 29:5-17).

42:5 Up to this point, Job had not seen God (see 23:8); now, like Isaiah, he had been in God's presence and was overwhelmed by God's holiness (Isaiah 6:1). His complaints and demands had arisen out of his rational knowledge of God; his awe and subsequent repentance came from his personal encounter with the Lord he worshiped.

42:7-8 The translation "you have not spoken accurately *about me*, as my servant Job has" (emphasis added) raises questions. Not all Job's speech about God had been accurate (see 30:18-23). However, the Hebrew can also be translated as "you have not rightly spoken *to me*, as my servant Job has." This latter rendering may fit better, especially since Job was the only person to speak *to* God; the friends only spoke *about* God and his ways. Like Job, we can speak to God, carrying our concerns to him. Unlike Job, though, we have an even greater revelation of what God is like. In Hebrews 4:14-16 we are reminded that God became human, just like us, so he "understands our weaknesses." Because of the work of Jesus, we can boldly approach God's throne with our needs and "will find grace to help us when we need it most."

42:14 The beautiful names of Job's new daughters spoke of Job's renewed and pleasant fortunes. *Jemimah* means "soft-voiced turtledove" (see Song of Songs 2:14). *Keziah* means "cassia" or "cinnamon flower" (see Psalm 45:8). *Keren-happuch* means "horn of antimony," which refers to a valuable metal used for cosmetics.

42:15 Daughters normally inherited only when there were no male heirs (Numbers 27, 36). Perhaps Job's unusual action reflected a new perspective after he had felt what it was like to be marginalized in his community. He could not change his culture, but he could change his own choices. (See note on Job 24:2-17.)

Psalms

WHAT DO WE LEARN ABOUT GOD'S MISSION AND OURS?
God desires and deserves our true selves and our full range of emotions.

WHO WROTE IT? King David wrote many of the psalms, or songs, with other songwriters (mostly anonymous) contributing too. Since the psalms were written to be used in worship, Levitical or priestly poets and musicians wrote many of them.

WHEN DID IT HAPPEN? These songs were written over almost one thousand years, starting with the earliest one around 1400 BC and the latest around 500 BC. Most psalms came from the time when Israel's kingdom was united.

HOW IS IT ORGANIZED? There are no themed sections, exactly, but the Psalms divide into five collections:

Book 1: Psalms 1–41
Book 2: Psalms 42–72
Book 3: Psalms 73–89
Book 4: Psalms 90–106
Book 5: Psalms 107–150

Words to Remember are highlighted throughout this book

FEATURE HIGHLIGHTS
- *The Discipline of Delight* (651)
- *Jesus in the Psalms* (652)
- *Kinds of Psalms* (656)
- *What Is My Purpose?* (660)
- *The Good Shepherd: Assurance of Light* (667)
- *Cruddy Mood? Cry Out* (669)
- *Pursuing God's Justice* (676)
- *Mountains and God* (680)
- *Caught: Come Clean* (686)
- *Our Feelings* (690)
- *God's Word Invites Women to Use Our Voices* (696)
- *Tell Me a Story* (704)
- *The Music of the Psalms* (709)
- *Anger* (721)
- *It's Good to Remember* (728)
- *Women of the Word* (734)
- *Women Wanderers: Where to Find Help* (737)
- *Faithful Lover: Finding Strength to Overcome* (743)
- *False Image: True Worth* (744)
- *How Can I Be More Comfortable in My Own Skin?* (746)

HOW LONG DOES IT TAKE TO READ? 3:30

BOOK ONE (PSALMS 1–41)

Psalm 1

¹ Oh, the joys of those who do not
follow the advice of the wicked,
or stand around with sinners,
or join in with mockers.
² But they delight in the law of the LORD,
meditating on it day and night.
³ They are like trees planted along the riverbank,
bearing fruit each season.
Their leaves never wither,
and they prosper in all they do.

⁴ But not the wicked!
They are like worthless chaff, scattered by the wind.
⁵ They will be condemned at the time of judgment.
Sinners will have no place among the godly.
⁶ For the LORD watches over the path of the godly,
but the path of the wicked leads to destruction.

Psalm 2

¹ Why are the nations so angry?
Why do they waste their time with futile plans?
² The kings of the earth prepare for battle;
the rulers plot together
against the LORD
and against his anointed one.
³ "Let us break their chains," they cry,
"and free ourselves from slavery to God."

⁴ But the one who rules in heaven laughs.
The Lord scoffs at them.
⁵ Then in anger he rebukes them,
terrifying them with his fierce fury.
⁶ For the Lord declares, "I have placed my chosen king on the throne
in Jerusalem,* on my holy mountain."

⁷ The king proclaims the LORD's decree:
"The LORD said to me, 'You are my son.*
Today I have become your Father.*
⁸ Only ask, and I will give you the nations as your inheritance,
the whole earth as your possession.
⁹ You will break* them with an iron rod
and smash them like clay pots.'"

¹⁰ Now then, you kings, act wisely!
Be warned, you rulers of the earth!
¹¹ Serve the LORD with reverent fear,
and rejoice with trembling.
¹² Submit to God's royal son,* or he will become angry,
and you will be destroyed in the midst of all your activities—
for his anger flares up in an instant.
But what joy for all who take refuge in him!

Psalm 3

A psalm of David, regarding the time David fled from his son Absalom.

¹ O LORD, I have so many enemies;
so many are against me.

2:6 Hebrew *on Zion.* **2:7a** Or *Son;* also in 2:12. **2:7b** Or *Today I reveal you as my son.* **2:9** Greek version reads *rule.* Compare Rev 2:27. **2:12** The meaning of the Hebrew is uncertain.

Book One (Psalms 1–41) Book One reveals God's purpose in the world, God's order in creation, and the significance of wisdom. It issues an invitation to dwell on the mountain of the Lord and gives insights into the psalm writers' lives and struggles.
Psalms 1–2 The first two psalms are an introduction to the entire Psalter. Psalm 1 introduces the Lord's instruction in wisdom, while Psalm 2 introduces God's rule over a rebellious, sinful world. Together, these psalms invite people to leave the way of folly that leads to destruction and to enter the way of God that leads to wisdom and salvation. The New Testament affirms that God will rule the nations through Jesus Christ, his appointed agent (Hebrews 1:5; Revelation 12:5; 19:15).
1:1 The Hebrew term for "the joys" (*ashrey*) is used twenty-six times in Psalms. Some translate it as "blessed," but a different term (*barak*) is used in specific contexts of blessing (Psalm 5:12; 45:2; 107:38). It could also be translated translate it as "happy" or "fortunate." The Greek synonym of "the joys" (*makarios*) is found in the beatitudes of Jesus' Sermon on the Mount (Matthew 5:3-10; Luke 6:20-23).
1:1 The godly do not permit themselves to live under the influence of sinners. Those who do not fear the Lord are wicked (Psalm 36:1); they are the enemies of those who love God, those who do right, and the poor and oppressed (see 10:2-13; 37:14). The wicked might appear pious (50:16) and sometimes enjoy temporary prosperity (37:35), but sorrow and destruction await them when their deeds catch up with them (9:16). Mockers hate the Lord, scorn his wisdom, and insult anyone who attempts to correct them (Proverbs 9:7-8). They seek only the "wisdom" that justifies their actions. These brash people have little regard for the Lord, his plans, or his children (see Psalms 86:14; 119:51, 69, 78, 85, 122).
1:2 To "delight in the law of the LORD" sounds strange to us. However, "instruction" better reflects the meaning of the Hebrew word *torah* than "law," which is how the word is usually translated. The joyful, happy, or fortunate person (see first study note on 1:1) continually meditates on God's instructions. This meditation leads to a life centered on God's teachings, resulting in an abundant life.
Psalm 2 This royal psalm pertains to the Lord's appointment of a king descended from David. It celebrates the mission of all the kings in David's line, and it introduces the hope of an ideal ruler who will accomplish the Lord's goal of bringing all nations into submission (Psalm 2:11) or to destruction (2:9). The New Testament identifies Jesus as this descendant (see Acts 13:33; 1 Corinthians 15:25-27; Hebrews 1:5; 5:5; Revelation 19:15).
2:7 People in ancient Israel considered the king to be the son of the nation's deity, with "today" likely referring to the king's coronation. The references to Jesus as the Son of God in the New Testament differ from the ancient Israelite understanding. These passages focus not only on Jesus' human lineage from David but also on his identity as an eternal member of the Godhead (John 1:1; Acts 13:33; Hebrews 1:5; 5:5).

² So many are saying,
"God will never rescue him!" *Interlude**

³ But you, O LORD, are a shield around me;
you are my glory, the one who holds my head high.

⁴ I cried out to the LORD,
and he answered me from his holy mountain. *Interlude*

⁵ I lay down and slept,
yet I woke up in safety,

3:2 Hebrew *Selah*. The meaning of this word is uncertain, though it is probably a musical or literary term. It is rendered *Interlude* throughout the Psalms.

Psalm 3 This psalm laments a sad episode in David's life (see 2 Samuel 15–18) and helps readers keep the promises of Psalm 2 in perspective. When beset by enemies, we can take our circumstances to the Lord. When we remember our past experiences of his faithfulness, we can move from complaint to confident trust in his goodness and expect God to rescue us.

3:3 In this context, *glory* relates to what makes a person influential in the community. A person's reputation was not rooted in achievements but rather in the identity of the God who would defend and restore us.

MY STORY WITH GOD

The Discipline of Delight

SCRIPTURE CONNECTION: PSALM 1:1-6

Whose voice do you listen to? I admit, sometimes I hear my inner critic saying "I can't" or "I'm not good enough."

Psalm 1 says that if we listen to wrongdoers' advice, we will head toward destruction. That is also true if we entertain negative self-talk. But when we make a habit of delighting in what God says, we flourish.

We become like healthy trees firmly planted by water, as the psalmist says (1:3). Jesus also mentions this water in John 7:38: "Anyone who believes in me may come and drink! For the Scriptures declare, 'Rivers of living water will flow from his heart.'" This living water represents God's Holy Spirit (John 7:39), who speaks Jesus' life-giving words into all we do (John 14:26).

God loves it when we listen to him; he wants us to come not out of duty but with delight. And he lavishly delights in us (Psalm 37:23; 149:4; Ephesians 1:3-8).

When we delight in God's words, we step into a stream where abundance flows, where no storm uproots, and where God himself speaks life.

> When we make a habit of delighting in what God says, we flourish.

IMAGINE

What one thing can you do today to develop the discipline of delighting in God's words?

What blessings remind you of how God delights in you?

"Tuning my ears to God's voice and delighting in what he says allows me to embrace his destiny for me. God silences my negative thoughts about how I am not enough."

GABRIELA MAGAÑA BANKS, PhD, is an author, teacher, and certified HeartSync inner healing prayer minister who facilitates freedom. Biblical principles and powerful moves of the Holy Spirit are her passion.

for the LORD was watching over me.
⁶ I am not afraid of ten thousand enemies
   who surround me on every side.

⁷ Arise, O LORD!
   Rescue me, my God!
Slap all my enemies in the face!
   Shatter the teeth of the wicked!

⁸ Victory comes from you, O LORD.
   May you bless your people.   *Interlude*

Psalm 4
For the choir director: A psalm of David, to be accompanied by stringed instruments.

¹ Answer me when I call to you,
   O God who declares me innocent.
Free me from my troubles.
   Have mercy on me and hear my prayer.

² How long will you people ruin my reputation?
   How long will you make groundless accusations?
   How long will you continue your lies?   *Interlude*

³ You can be sure of this:
   The LORD set apart the godly for himself.
   The LORD will answer when I call to him.

⁴ Don't sin by letting anger control you.
   Think about it overnight and remain silent.   *Interlude*

⁵ Offer sacrifices in the right spirit,
   and trust the LORD.

Psalm 4 This individual lament includes a prayer for rescue (4:1), a rebuke of the psalm writer's enemy (4:2-3), an encouragement to the godly (4:4-5), and an expression of confidence (4:6-8).

Insight: JESUS IN THE PSALMS

The New Testament authors strongly connect Jesus with the Psalms. Jesus completes David's dynasty and offers the hope that all people can have an intimate, everlasting relationship with God. Jesus is the Messiah, the Anointed One, chosen by God to rescue all creation from sin and death. One reason Christians believe that Jesus is God's promised Restorer is that Jesus' life and death and return to life (resurrection) fulfilled Old Testament expectations for the Messiah that long pre-dated Jesus' birth.

Title of the Messiah	Reference in the Psalms	Applied to Jesus
Messiah (Anointed One)	2:2	Matthew 16:16; Acts 4:23-30
Son of God	2:7, 12	Matthew 3:17; 17:5; Acts 13:33; Romans 1:4; Hebrews 1:5; 5:5
Sovereign King	8:4-6	1 Corinthians 15:27; Hebrews 2:8
Suffering Servant	22:1-31	Matthew 27:35, 46; Mark 15:34; John 19:24
Faithful Servant	40:6-8; 69:1-36	John 2:17; Romans 15:3; Hebrews 10:7
Victorious King	68:18	Ephesians 4:8
Exalted Lord	110:1	Matthew 22:41-45; Acts 2:32-36; Hebrews 1:10-13
Royal High Priest	110:4	Hebrews 5:6; 7:17, 21
Precious Stone	118:22	Matthew 21:42; Mark 12:10-11; Luke 20:17; Acts 4:11; 1 Peter 2:7
Blessed King	118:26	Matthew 21:9; 23:39; Mark 11:9-10; Luke 13:35; 19:38; John 12:13; 1 Corinthians 15:25-27

⁶ Many people say, "Who will show us better times?"
  Let your face smile on us, LORD.
⁷ You have given me greater joy
  than those who have abundant harvests of
    grain and new wine.
⁸ In peace I will lie down and sleep,
  for you alone, O LORD, will keep me safe.

Psalm 5
For the choir director: A psalm of David, to be accompanied by the flute.

¹ O LORD, hear me as I pray;
  pay attention to my groaning.
² Listen to my cry for help, my King and my God,
  for I pray to no one but you.
³ Listen to my voice in the morning, LORD.
  Each morning I bring my requests to you and
    wait expectantly.
⁴ O God, you take no pleasure in wickedness;
  you cannot tolerate the sins of the wicked.
⁵ Therefore, the proud may not stand in your
    presence,
  for you hate all who do evil.
⁶ You will destroy those who tell lies.
  The LORD detests murderers and deceivers.
⁷ Because of your unfailing love, I can enter your
    house;
  I will worship at your Temple with deepest awe.
⁸ Lead me in the right path, O LORD,
  or my enemies will conquer me.
  Make your way plain for me to follow.
⁹ My enemies cannot speak a truthful word.
  Their deepest desire is to destroy others.
  Their talk is foul, like the stench from an open
    grave.
  Their tongues are filled with flattery.*
¹⁰ O God, declare them guilty.
  Let them be caught in their own traps.
  Drive them away because of their many sins,
  for they have rebelled against you.

¹¹ But let all who take refuge in you rejoice;
  let them sing joyful praises forever.
  Spread your protection over them,
  that all who love your name may be filled with joy.
¹² For you bless the godly, O LORD;
  you surround them with your shield of love.

Psalm 6
*For the choir director: A psalm of David, to be accompanied by an eight-stringed instrument.**

¹ O LORD, don't rebuke me in your anger
  or discipline me in your rage.
² Have compassion on me, LORD, for I am weak.
  Heal me, LORD, for my bones are in agony.
³ I am sick at heart.
  How long, O LORD, until you restore me?
⁴ Return, O LORD, and rescue me.
  Save me because of your unfailing love.
⁵ For the dead do not remember you.
  Who can praise you from the grave?*
⁶ I am worn out from sobbing.
  All night I flood my bed with weeping,
  drenching it with my tears.
⁷ My vision is blurred by grief;
  my eyes are worn out because of all my enemies.
⁸ Go away, all you who do evil,
  for the LORD has heard my weeping.
⁹ The LORD has heard my plea;
  the LORD will answer my prayer.
¹⁰ May all my enemies be disgraced and terrified.
  May they suddenly turn back in shame.

Psalm 7
A psalm of David, which he sang to the LORD concerning Cush of the tribe of Benjamin.*

¹ I come to you for protection, O LORD my God.
  Save me from my persecutors—rescue me!
² If you don't, they will maul me like a lion,
  tearing me to pieces with no one to rescue me.

5:9 Greek version reads *with lies.* Compare Rom 3:13.   6:TITLE Hebrew *with stringed instruments; according to the sheminith.*   6:5 Hebrew *from Sheol?*   7:TITLE Hebrew *A shiggaion,* probably indicating a musical setting for the psalm.

4:6 The psalmist seeks God's favor and peace (Numbers 6:25-26), which can transform darkness into light (see Psalm 27:1). Confident trust in the Lord is an antidote to anger, resentment, jealousy, and materialism.
Psalm 5 This morning prayer (5:3) expresses unwavering confidence in the Lord's help and protection. The psalmist asks for and awaits God's response (5:1-3). He describes the schemes of the wicked in detail but does not get lost in his circumstances. The psalmist also knows that the wicked cannot coexist with God (5:4-6, 9; see 1:5). He keeps returning to the Lord (5:7-8, 10; see 5:1-3), and then he prays for the godly community (5:10-12; see 3:8).
5:7 God promises his "unfailing love"—his covenant goodness and faithfulness—to his people (see 25:6; 69:16; Lamentations 3:32). The godly long to come into God's presence with reverence and awe (see Hebrews 12:28).

Psalm 6 This psalm includes an individual prayer or complaint. Some believe the psalm writer initially sought deliverance from persecution by his enemies (6:7b–10), while others believe he sought healing from disease (6:5—7a). Either is possible, but it may also be that the psalm originally functioned as a formulaic prayer to use in various situations. Since ancient poetry was composed to be used and reused, the original setting is less important than the idea that we can use it as a model for praying in our own difficulties.
6:5 In the Old Testament, Sheol ("the grave") is the place of the dead. It is not necessarily associated with punishment. The idea that deities could not be praised from the realm of the dead is also found in ancient Near Eastern compositions.
Psalm 7 This prayer for help includes an opening plea for rescue (7:1-2), an oath of innocence (7:3-5), an appeal to God's justice (7:6-9), a confession of trust (7:10-16), and a vow to praise God (7:17).

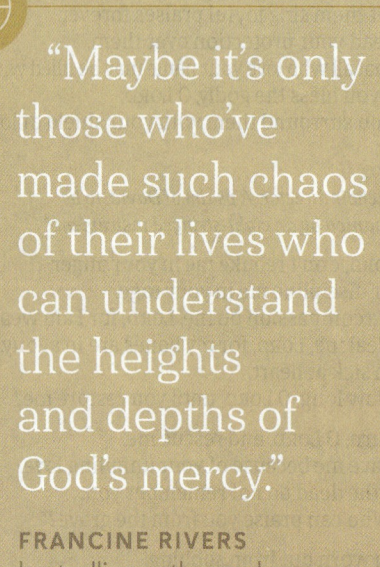

> "Maybe it's only those who've made such chaos of their lives who can understand the heights and depths of God's mercy."
>
> **FRANCINE RIVERS**
> bestselling author and award-winning novelist

³ O Lord my God, if I have done wrong
  or am guilty of injustice,
⁴ if I have betrayed a friend
  or plundered my enemy without cause,
⁵ then let my enemies capture me.
  Let them trample me into the ground
  and drag my honor in the dust.   *Interlude*

⁶ Arise, O Lord, in anger!
  Stand up against the fury of my enemies!
  Wake up, my God, and bring justice!
⁷ Gather the nations before you.
  Rule over them from on high.
⁸   The Lord judges the nations.
  Declare me righteous, O Lord,
  for I am innocent, O Most High!
⁹ End the evil of those who are wicked,
  and defend the righteous.

For you look deep within the mind and heart,
  O righteous God.
¹⁰ God is my shield,
  saving those whose hearts are true and right.
¹¹ God is an honest judge.
  He is angry with the wicked every day.
¹² If a person does not repent,
  God* will sharpen his sword;
  he will bend and string his bow.
¹³ He will prepare his deadly weapons
  and shoot his flaming arrows.
¹⁴ The wicked conceive evil;
  they are pregnant with trouble
  and give birth to lies.
¹⁵ They dig a deep pit to trap others,
  then fall into it themselves.
¹⁶ The trouble they make for others backfires on
    them.
  The violence they plan falls on their own heads.
¹⁷ I will thank the Lord because he is just;
  I will sing praise to the name of the Lord Most
    High.

Psalm 8

For the choir director: A psalm of David, to be accompanied by a stringed instrument.

¹ O Lord, our Lord, your majestic name fills the
    earth!
  Your glory is higher than the heavens.
² You have taught children and infants
  to tell of your strength,*
silencing your enemies
  and all who oppose you.

³ When I look at the night sky and see the work of
    your fingers—
  the moon and the stars you set in place—
⁴ what are mere mortals that you should think
    about them,
  human beings that you should care for them?*
⁵ Yet you made them only a little lower than God*
  and crowned them* with glory and honor.
⁶ You gave them charge of everything you made,
  putting all things under their authority—

7:12 Hebrew *he.*   **8:TITLE** Hebrew *according to the gittith.*   **8:2** Greek version reads *to give you praise.* Compare Matt 21:16.   **8:4** Hebrew *what is man that you should think of him, / the son of man that you should care for him?*   **8:5a** Or *Yet you made them only a little lower than the angels;* Hebrew reads *Yet you made him* [i.e., *man*] *a little lower than Elohim.*   **8:5b** Hebrew *him* [i.e., *man*]; similarly in 8:6.

7:17 The laments in Psalms 3–7 usually move from lament to praise, as does the book of Psalms as a whole. "Most High" is an ancient designation for God that expresses the Lord's exalted status (Genesis 14:19) as the ruler and protector of the godly. God is just and reliable, so his order prevails in this world.
Psalm 8 The psalmist celebrates God's creation and the dignity of humanity in the first hymn of the Psalter, the first psalm that is all praise.
8:5 The Hebrew word *elohim* can refer to God as in the NLT or to subordinate divine beings. Here, the Greek translation of the Old Testament translates it as angels. Humans bear God's image; the Lord has created humans with dignity and charged them to rule (Genesis 1:26-27). Our value comes from our origin as God's creation and the vocation that he has given us. Hebrews 2:6-8 applies these words to Jesus, the ideal human who fully realized God's purposes.

⁷ the flocks and the herds
   and all the wild animals,
⁸ the birds in the sky, the fish in the sea,
   and everything that swims the ocean currents.
⁹ O Lord, our Lord, your majestic name fills the earth!

Psalm 9

For the choir director: A psalm of David, to be sung to the tune "Death of the Son."

¹ I will praise you, Lord, with all my heart;
   I will tell of all the marvelous things you have done.
² I will be filled with joy because of you.
   I will sing praises to your name, O Most High.
³ My enemies retreated;
   they staggered and died when you appeared.
⁴ For you have judged in my favor;
   from your throne you have judged with fairness.
⁵ You have rebuked the nations and destroyed the wicked;
   you have erased their names forever.
⁶ The enemy is finished, in endless ruins;
   the cities you uprooted are now forgotten.
⁷ But the Lord reigns forever,
   executing judgment from his throne.
⁸ He will judge the world with justice
   and rule the nations with fairness.
⁹ The Lord is a shelter for the oppressed,
   a refuge in times of trouble.
¹⁰ Those who know your name trust in you,
   for you, O Lord, do not abandon those who search for you.
¹¹ Sing praises to the Lord who reigns in Jerusalem.*
   Tell the world about his unforgettable deeds.
¹² For he who avenges murder cares for the helpless.
   He does not ignore the cries of those who suffer.
¹³ Lord, have mercy on me.
   See how my enemies torment me.
   Snatch me back from the jaws of death.
¹⁴ Save me so I can praise you publicly at Jerusalem's gates,
   so I can rejoice that you have rescued me.
¹⁵ The nations have fallen into the pit they dug for others.
   Their own feet have been caught in the trap they set.
¹⁶ The Lord is known for his justice.
   The wicked are trapped by their own deeds.
   *Quiet Interlude**
¹⁷ The wicked will go down to the grave.*
   This is the fate of all the nations who ignore God.
¹⁸ But the needy will not be ignored forever;
   the hopes of the poor will not always be crushed.
¹⁹ Arise, O Lord!
   Do not let mere mortals defy you!
   Judge the nations!
²⁰ Make them tremble in fear, O Lord.
   Let the nations know they are merely human.
   Interlude

Psalm 10

¹ O Lord, why do you stand so far away?
   Why do you hide when I am in trouble?
² The wicked arrogantly hunt down the poor.
   Let them be caught in the evil they plan for others.
³ For they brag about their evil desires;
   they praise the greedy and curse the Lord.
⁴ The wicked are too proud to seek God.
   They seem to think that God is dead.
⁵ Yet they succeed in everything they do.
   They do not see your punishment awaiting them.
   They sneer at all their enemies.
⁶ They think, "Nothing bad will ever happen to us!
   We will be free of trouble forever!"
⁷ Their mouths are full of cursing, lies, and threats.*
   Trouble and evil are on the tips of their tongues.

9:11 Hebrew *Zion;* also in 9:14.   9:16 Hebrew *Higgaion Selah.* The meaning of this phrase is uncertain.   9:17 Hebrew *to Sheol.*
10:7 Greek version reads *cursing and bitterness.* Compare Rom 3:14.

Psalms 9–10 This hymn celebrates the Lord's kingship and victory over evil. It might also serve as a response to the laments of Psalms 3–7. Some believe that Psalms 9 and 10 should be read together as one psalm in two parts because Psalm 9 includes a title and Psalm 10 does not; and although several letters are missing or inverted, the two psalms connect as an acrostic of the Hebrew alphabet (see note on Psalm 25; other such alphabetic acrostics are Psalms 25, 34, 37, 111–112, 119, 145). The ancient Greek and Latin translations treat Psalms 9 and 10 as one composition.
9:9 The Lord provides shelter in dangerous circumstances and refuge from powerful and oppressive people. The Psalter includes many similar images of the Lord, such as fortress (18:2; 31:2), refuge (59:16-17), rock (18:2; 42:9), strength (18:1), and tower of safety (144:2). Similar images occur frequently in the royal prayers (see 9:9; 18:30). Even oppressed, afflicted, and marginalized people (10:17; 74:21) can enjoy divine protection. The "in trouble" and "times of trouble" (10:1; 20:1) stand in contrast with appointed times when the Lord is openly implored to grant his favor upon the afflicted (69:13; 102:13; see 107:6).
Psalm 10 The lament of 9:13-20 continues in Psalm 10 (see note on Psalms 9–10), but the mood changes from confident assertion to anguished questioning. The psalm writer prays for rescue, believing that the Lord, as a just king, would take care of the needy.

Insight: KINDS OF PSALMS

The psalms express a wide range of emotions. Each psalm resonates with one or more main themes—for example, praise, thanksgiving, wisdom, justice, and lament. The grid below represents each psalm, grouping it by main theme. The sizes of each circle correspond to the psalm's length.

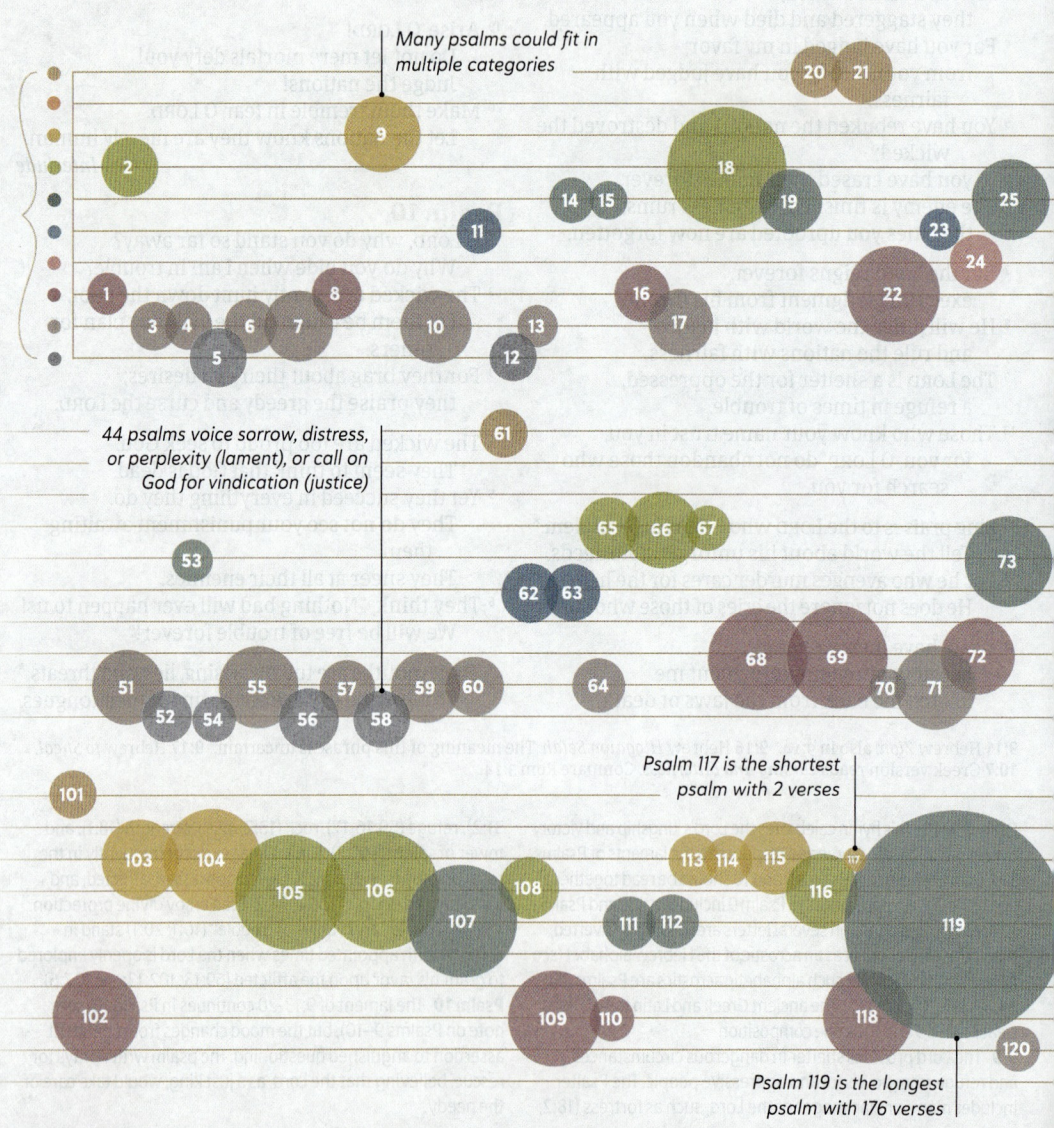

Many psalms could fit in multiple categories

44 psalms voice sorrow, distress, or perplexity (lament), or call on God for vindication (justice)

Psalm 117 is the shortest psalm with 2 verses

Psalm 119 is the longest psalm with 176 verses

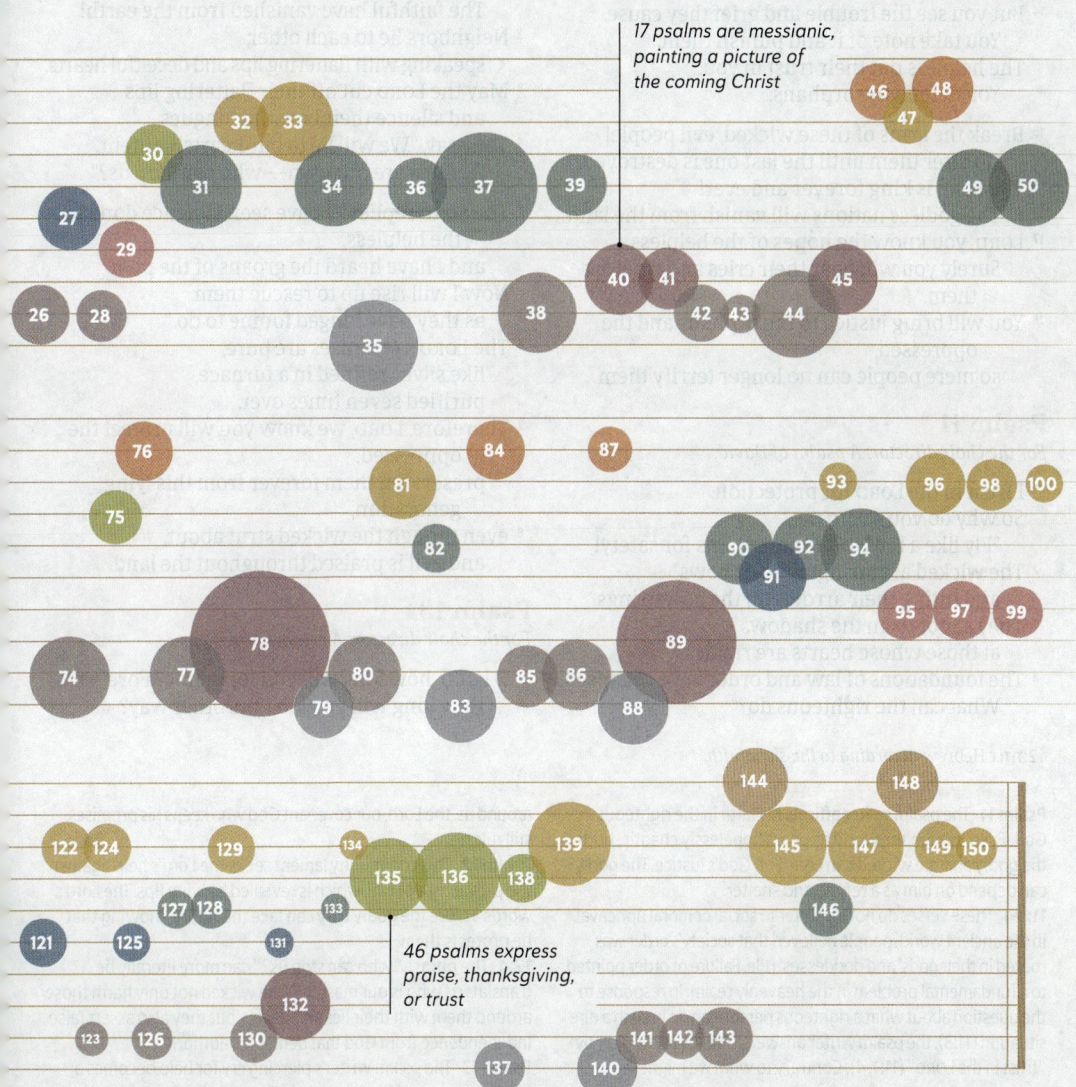

⁸ They lurk in ambush in the villages,
  waiting to murder innocent people.
  They are always searching for helpless victims.
⁹ Like lions crouched in hiding,
  they wait to pounce on the helpless.
  Like hunters they capture the helpless
  and drag them away in nets.
¹⁰ Their helpless victims are crushed;
  they fall beneath the strength of the wicked.
¹¹ The wicked think, "God isn't watching us!
  He has closed his eyes and won't even see what we do!"

¹² Arise, O LORD!
  Punish the wicked, O God!
  Do not ignore the helpless!
¹³ Why do the wicked get away with despising God?
  They think, "God will never call us to account."
¹⁴ But you see the trouble and grief they cause.
  You take note of it and punish them.
  The helpless put their trust in you.
  You defend the orphans.

¹⁵ Break the arms of these wicked, evil people!
  Go after them until the last one is destroyed.
¹⁶ The LORD is king forever and ever!
  The godless nations will vanish from the land.
¹⁷ LORD, you know the hopes of the helpless.
  Surely you will hear their cries and comfort them.
¹⁸ You will bring justice to the orphans and the oppressed,
  so mere people can no longer terrify them.

Psalm 11
For the choir director: A psalm of David.

¹ I trust in the LORD for protection.
  So why do you say to me,
  "Fly like a bird to the mountains for safety!
² The wicked are stringing their bows
  and fitting their arrows on the bowstrings.
  They shoot from the shadows
  at those whose hearts are right.
³ The foundations of law and order have collapsed.
  What can the righteous do?"

12:TITLE Hebrew *according to the sheminith.*

⁴ But the LORD is in his holy Temple;
  the LORD still rules from heaven.
  He watches everyone closely,
  examining every person on earth.
⁵ The LORD examines both the righteous and the wicked.
  He hates those who love violence.
⁶ He will rain down blazing coals and burning sulfur on the wicked,
  punishing them with scorching winds.
⁷ For the righteous LORD loves justice.
  The virtuous will see his face.

Psalm 12
For the choir director: A psalm of David, to be accompanied by an eight-stringed instrument.*

¹ Help, O LORD, for the godly are fast disappearing!
  The faithful have vanished from the earth!
² Neighbors lie to each other,
  speaking with flattering lips and deceitful hearts.
³ May the LORD cut off their flattering lips
  and silence their boastful tongues.
⁴ They say, "We will lie to our hearts' content.
  Our lips are our own—who can stop us?"

⁵ The LORD replies, "I have seen violence done to the helpless,
  and I have heard the groans of the poor.
  Now I will rise up to rescue them,
  as they have longed for me to do."
⁶ The LORD's promises are pure,
  like silver refined in a furnace,
  purified seven times over.

⁷ Therefore, LORD, we know you will protect the oppressed,
  preserving them forever from this lying generation,
⁸ even though the wicked strut about,
  and evil is praised throughout the land.

Psalm 13
For the choir director: A psalm of David.

¹ O LORD, how long will you forget me? Forever?
  How long will you look the other way?

Psalm 11 The psalm writer affirms his faith in the righteous God. Even though the world appears hopelessly chaotic, both the godly and the wicked can count on God's justice. The godly can depend on him as a refuge and shelter.
11:1-4 These verses do not just refer to social or moral upheaval. In the ancient world, people believed that society's order was rooted in their gods' and goddesses' rule. Failure of order pointed to a fundamental problem in the heavenly realm. In response to the question about what a righteous person can do in such a dire situation (11:3), the psalm writer answers, directly and indirectly: "trust in the LORD" (11:1, 4). Contrary to what we might see around us, the Lord, our covenant God who keeps his promises, still rules.
Psalm 12 This community lament seeks the Lord's help against the prevalence of evil, which is revealed by lying lips. The Lord's words assure the godly they can face the future knowing that he protects them.
12:4 The phrase "who can stop us?" can more literally be translated "who is our master?" The wicked not only harm those around them with their lies and deceit, but they also assert false independence from God that denies his authority.
Psalm 13 The psalm writer's piercing cry for help becomes a confident song of hope in a typical song of lament.

² How long must I struggle with anguish in my soul,
with sorrow in my heart every day?
How long will my enemy have the upper hand?

³ Turn and answer me, O LORD my God!
Restore the sparkle to my eyes, or I will die.
⁴ Don't let my enemies gloat, saying, "We have defeated him!"
Don't let them rejoice at my downfall.
⁵ But I trust in your unfailing love.
I will rejoice because you have rescued me.
⁶ I will sing to the LORD
because he is good to me.

Psalm 14
For the choir director: A psalm of David.

¹ Only fools say in their hearts,
"There is no God."
They are corrupt, and their actions are evil;
not one of them does good!

² The LORD looks down from heaven
on the entire human race;
he looks to see if anyone is truly wise,
if anyone seeks God.
³ But no, all have turned away;
all have become corrupt.*
No one does good,
not a single one!

⁴ Will those who do evil never learn?
They eat up my people like bread
and wouldn't think of praying to the LORD.
⁵ Terror will grip them,
for God is with those who obey him.
⁶ The wicked frustrate the plans of the oppressed,
but the LORD will protect his people.
⁷ Who will come from Mount Zion to rescue Israel?
When the LORD restores his people,
Jacob will shout with joy, and Israel will rejoice.

Psalm 15
A psalm of David.

¹ Who may worship in your sanctuary, LORD?
Who may enter your presence on your holy hill?
² Those who lead blameless lives and do what is right,
speaking the truth from sincere hearts.
³ Those who refuse to gossip
or harm their neighbors
or speak evil of their friends.
⁴ Those who despise flagrant sinners,
and honor the faithful followers of the LORD,
and keep their promises even when it hurts.
⁵ Those who lend money without charging interest,
and who cannot be bribed to lie about the innocent.
Such people will stand firm forever.

Psalm 16
A psalm of David.*

¹ Keep me safe, O God,
for I have come to you for refuge.

² I said to the LORD, "You are my Master!
Every good thing I have comes from you."
³ The godly people in the land
are my true heroes!
I take pleasure in them!
⁴ Troubles multiply for those who chase after other gods.
I will not take part in their sacrifices of blood
or even speak the names of their gods.

14:3 Greek version reads *have become useless*. Compare Rom 3:12. **16:TITLE** Hebrew *miktam*. This may be a literary or musical term.

13:2 A sense of anguish and sorrow closes off any perspective of hope (6:3). Unless the Lord answers the psalm writer's prayers (22:1), death seems inescapable, torturous, and slow (6:6; 32:3; 55:4; 61:2; 102:5; 116:3). The psalm writer hardly knows how to pray and is longing for God's redemption (25:17-18; 31:10; 38:8; 39:2).
Psalm 14 This wisdom psalm contains some characteristics of lament and prophecy. The ideals of Psalm 8 have run aground on the reality of foolish human attitudes and sinful actions. With the exception of 14:5-6 and the use of God's personal name instead of a more general reference "God," this psalm parallels Psalm 53.
14:1 An intelligent person can be a "fool." The issue is not the person's ability to reason, but rather their refusal to acknowledge God and live by his instructions (see Proverbs 1:7). Foolishness and wickedness are not merely internal; they show in the actions of those who believe they can live independently of the Lord.
14:7 The psalmist prays for the renewal of God's relationship with his people. "Jacob" is a synonym for Israel (see Genesis 35:9-10).
Psalm 15 The questions in this psalm invite readers to examine themselves and to look away from problems with the wicked. The question of who dwells in God's presence leads into a description of godly character qualities (see 24:3-6; Isaiah 33:14-16).
15:1 The space surrounding God's presence in his tent (the Tabernacle) and later in the Temple was sacred. Those who entered had to be ritually pure (see Leviticus 1–7, 12–15). This psalm teaches that our words, attitudes, and actions also matter. Coming into the presence of a holy God must be taken seriously.
Psalm 16 In this psalm of confidence, the poet moves quickly from a short petition (16:1), to expressions of passionate commitment to God and his people (16:2-6), to a conclusion of confident praise (16:7-11).
16:1 Taking refuge in God is a common metaphor in the Old Testament (see note on 9:9). Prayers such as this one model one way we can take refuge in God's strength, providence, and salvation.

MY STORY WITH GOD

God Declares Our Purpose

SCRIPTURE CONNECTION: PSALM 16:11

Have you ever tried to persevere in a difficult task without a clear purpose? It's unnerving, and discouragement always lurks about when we don't know where we're heading or why. Without purpose, our effort toward any finish line rests on our moment-by-moment feelings....

Who made me? Why am I here? What is my purpose? These are questions that each of us asks when everyday rhythms feel monotonous and insignificant—or when life's crossroads seem *too* significant, and we stretch to understand how we fit....

Our Father made us, saved us, and sanctifies us daily to glorify Him...

- as image-bearers (Genesis 1:27)
- as imitators of Christ (Ephesians 5:1-2)
- as ambassadors (2 Corinthians 5:20)
- as salt and light (Matthew 5:13-16)
- as doers of good works (Ephesians 2:10)
- as disciple makers (Matthew 28:19)

None of these positions of purpose can exist apart from God's provision to fulfill them. You and I have purpose today because He declares it. In the most mundane and the most magical seasons alike, our purpose does not change.

"What is the chief end of man?" asks the first question of the Westminster Shorter Catechism. And succinctly, it answers, *"... to glorify God and to enjoy him forever."*

To glorify Him by loving Him... to glorify Him *because we love Him*.

> What is the chief purpose of man—and woman? To glorify and enjoy God forever.

IMAGINE

What Scripture might you memorize, or post around your home and on your device, to remind you of your God-given purpose?

How might you discover how you, uniquely, shine God's goodness? Consider asking a trusted friend how your actions and words best glorify God.

"In working with hundreds of thousands of women in my years of ministry, the number one question asked is, 'What is my purpose?' What a confidence-booster to know that God answers, giving beautiful purpose that is not only about doing good but also about enjoying that God is good." Dr. Naomi Cramer Overton

RUTH CHOU SIMONS
Taken from: *GraceLaced*, Copyright © 2017 by Ruth Chou Simons. Published by Harvest House Publishers, Eugene, Oregon 97408. www.harvesthousepublishers.com

5 LORD, you alone are my inheritance, my cup of blessing.
   You guard all that is mine.
6 The land you have given me is a pleasant land.
   What a wonderful inheritance!
7 I will bless the LORD who guides me;
   even at night my heart instructs me.
8 I know the LORD is always with me.
   I will not be shaken, for he is right beside me.
9 No wonder my heart is glad, and I rejoice.*
   My body rests in safety.
10 For you will not leave my soul among the dead*
   or allow your holy one* to rot in the grave.
11 You will show me the way of life,
   granting me the joy of your presence
   and the pleasures of living with you forever.*

Psalm 17
A prayer of David.

1 O LORD, hear my plea for justice.
   Listen to my cry for help.
   Pay attention to my prayer,
   for it comes from honest lips.
2 Declare me innocent,
   for you see those who do right.
3 You have tested my thoughts and examined my heart in the night.
   You have scrutinized me and found nothing wrong.
   I am determined not to sin in what I say.
4 I have followed your commands,
   which keep me from following cruel and evil people.
5 My steps have stayed on your path;
   I have not wavered from following you.
6 I am praying to you because I know you will answer, O God.
   Bend down and listen as I pray.
7 Show me your unfailing love in wonderful ways.
   By your mighty power you rescue
   those who seek refuge from their enemies.
8 Guard me as you would guard your own eyes.*
   Hide me in the shadow of your wings.

9 Protect me from wicked people who attack me,
   from murderous enemies who surround me.
10 They are without pity.
   Listen to their boasting!
11 They track me down and surround me,
   watching for the chance to throw me to the ground.
12 They are like hungry lions, eager to tear me apart—
   like young lions hiding in ambush.
13 Arise, O LORD!
   Stand against them, and bring them to their knees!
   Rescue me from the wicked with your sword!
14 By the power of your hand, O LORD,
   destroy those who look to this world for their reward.
   But satisfy the hunger of your treasured ones.
   May their children have plenty,
   leaving an inheritance for their descendants.
15 Because I am righteous, I will see you.
   When I awake, I will see you face to face and be satisfied.

Psalm 18
For the choir director: A psalm of David, the servant of the LORD. He sang this song to the LORD on the day the LORD rescued him from all his enemies and from Saul. He sang:

1 I love you, LORD;
   you are my strength.
2 The LORD is my rock, my fortress, and my savior;
   my God is my rock, in whom I find protection.
   He is my shield, the power that saves me,
   and my place of safety.
3 I called on the LORD, who is worthy of praise,
   and he saved me from my enemies.
4 The ropes of death entangled me;
   floods of destruction swept over me.
5 The grave* wrapped its ropes around me;
   death laid a trap in my path.
6 But in my distress I cried out to the LORD;
   yes, I prayed to my God for help.
   He heard me from his sanctuary;
   my cry to him reached his ears.

16:9 Greek version reads *and my tongue shouts his praises.* Compare Acts 2:26. **16:10a** Hebrew *in Sheol.* **16:10b** Or *your Holy One.* **16:11** Greek version reads *You have shown me the way of life, / and you will fill me with the joy of your presence.* Compare Acts 2:28. **17:8** Hebrew *as the pupil of your eye.* **18:5** Hebrew *Sheol.*

16:10 The apostles applied this text to the resurrection of Jesus (Acts 2:25-33; 13:35).
Psalm 17 The psalmist pleads for God's protection and vindication, affirms his own integrity, and prays that the Lord will prevail against his fierce enemies.
17:15 The Israelites considered morning to be a time of deliverance (5:3; 30:5; 46:5; 130:6). The psalmist is confident that he will encounter God's presence then, evoking the memory of God's close relationship with Moses (Numbers 12:8). It also points to the priestly blessing (Numbers 6:24-26) in which God promises his favor by turning his face toward his people.
Psalm 18 This royal drama of divine rescue (also found with minor variations in 2 Samuel 22:1-51) encourages readers who are praying the laments and requests for rescue in Psalms 16 and 17. The psalmist describes the dramatic nature of God's rescue in three different ways (18:7-15, 16-19, 30-36). The psalm also extends hope that a future Son of David will be totally victorious over evil (18:43-50; see Psalm 2).

⁷ Then the earth quaked and trembled.
  The foundations of the mountains shook;
    they quaked because of his anger.
⁸ Smoke poured from his nostrils;
    fierce flames leaped from his mouth.
  Glowing coals blazed forth from him.
⁹ He opened the heavens and came down;
    dark storm clouds were beneath his feet.
¹⁰ Mounted on a mighty angelic being,* he flew,
    soaring on the wings of the wind.
¹¹ He shrouded himself in darkness,
    veiling his approach with dark rain clouds.
¹² Thick clouds shielded the brightness around him
    and rained down hail and burning coals.*
¹³ The Lord thundered from heaven;
    the voice of the Most High resounded
      amid the hail and burning coals.
¹⁴ He shot his arrows and scattered his enemies;
    great bolts of lightning flashed, and they were
      confused.
¹⁵ Then at your command, O Lord,
    at the blast of your breath,
  the bottom of the sea could be seen,
    and the foundations of the earth were laid
      bare.
¹⁶ He reached down from heaven and rescued me;
    he drew me out of deep waters.
¹⁷ He rescued me from my powerful enemies,
    from those who hated me and were too
      strong for me.
¹⁸ They attacked me at a moment when I was in
    distress,
  but the Lord supported me.
¹⁹ He led me to a place of safety;
    he rescued me because he delights in me.
²⁰ The Lord rewarded me for doing right;
    he restored me because of my innocence.
²¹ For I have kept the ways of the Lord;
    I have not turned from my God to follow evil.
²² I have followed all his regulations;
    I have never abandoned his decrees.
²³ I am blameless before God;
    I have kept myself from sin.
²⁴ The Lord rewarded me for doing right.
    He has seen my innocence.
²⁵ To the faithful you show yourself faithful;
    to those with integrity you show integrity.
²⁶ To the pure you show yourself pure,
    but to the crooked you show yourself shrewd.
²⁷ You rescue the humble,
    but you humiliate the proud.

²⁸ You light a lamp for me.
    The Lord, my God, lights up my darkness.
²⁹ In your strength I can crush an army;
    with my God I can scale any wall.
³⁰ God's way is perfect.
  All the Lord's promises prove true.
    He is a shield for all who look to him for
      protection.
³¹ For who is God except the Lord?
    Who but our God is a solid rock?
³² God arms me with strength,
    and he makes my way perfect.
³³ He makes me as surefooted as a deer,
    enabling me to stand on mountain heights.
³⁴ He trains my hands for battle;
    he strengthens my arm to draw a bronze bow.
³⁵ You have given me your shield of victory.
    Your right hand supports me;
    your help* has made me great.
³⁶ You have made a wide path for my feet
    to keep them from slipping.
³⁷ I chased my enemies and caught them;
    I did not stop until they were conquered.
³⁸ I struck them down so they could not get up;
    they fell beneath my feet.
³⁹ You have armed me with strength for the battle;
    you have subdued my enemies under my feet.
⁴⁰ You placed my foot on their necks.
    I have destroyed all who hated me.
⁴¹ They called for help, but no one came to their
    rescue.
  They even cried to the Lord, but he refused to
    answer.
⁴² I ground them as fine as dust in the wind.
    I swept them into the gutter like dirt.
⁴³ You gave me victory over my accusers.
    You appointed me ruler over nations;
    people I don't even know now serve me.
⁴⁴ As soon as they hear of me, they submit;
    foreign nations cringe before me.
⁴⁵ They all lose their courage
    and come trembling from their strongholds.
⁴⁶ The Lord lives! Praise to my Rock!
    May the God of my salvation be exalted!
⁴⁷ He is the God who pays back those who harm me;
    he subdues the nations under me
⁴⁸   and rescues me from my enemies.
  You hold me safe beyond the reach of my enemies;
    you save me from violent opponents.
⁴⁹ For this, O Lord, I will praise you among the nations;
    I will sing praises to your name.

18:10 Hebrew *a cherub.*   18:12 Or *and lightning bolts;* also in 18:13.   18:35 Hebrew *your humility;* compare 2 Sam 22:36.

18:20-24 The psalmist affirms that God rewards loyalty. He put his trust in the Lord (see 16:1) and committed himself to living with integrity (see 1, 15, 24; 19:12-14). The psalmist faithfully obeyed God's instructions (25:8-10), rejected the way of folly (see Psalms 1, 14), and chose the way of wisdom (1, 15). The blameless and sinless state claimed by the psalmist likely related to obedience to the teachings and instructions of the Bible's first five books, called the Torah (Genesis to Deuteronomy).

⁵⁰ You give great victories to your king;
 you show unfailing love to your anointed,
 to David and all his descendants forever.

Psalm 19
For the choir director: A psalm of David.

¹ The heavens proclaim the glory of God.
 The skies display his craftsmanship.
² Day after day they continue to speak;
 night after night they make him known.
³ They speak without a sound or word;
 their voice is never heard.*
⁴ Yet their message has gone throughout the earth,
 and their words to all the world.

 God has made a home in the heavens for the sun.
⁵ It bursts forth like a radiant bridegroom after his wedding.
 It rejoices like a great athlete eager to run the race.
⁶ The sun rises at one end of the heavens
 and follows its course to the other end.
 Nothing can hide from its heat.

⁷ The instructions of the LORD are perfect,
 reviving the soul.
 The decrees of the LORD are trustworthy,
 making wise the simple.
⁸ The commandments of the LORD are right,
 bringing joy to the heart.
 The commands of the LORD are clear,
 giving insight for living.
⁹ Reverence for the LORD is pure,
 lasting forever.
 The laws of the LORD are true;
 each one is fair.
¹⁰ They are more desirable than gold,
 even the finest gold.
 They are sweeter than honey,
 even honey dripping from the comb.
¹¹ They are a warning to your servant,
 a great reward for those who obey them.

¹² How can I know all the sins lurking in my heart?
 Cleanse me from these hidden faults.
¹³ Keep your servant from deliberate sins!
 Don't let them control me.
 Then I will be free of guilt
 and innocent of great sin.

¹⁴ May the words of my mouth
 and the meditation of my heart
 be pleasing to you,
 O LORD, my rock and my redeemer.

Psalm 20
For the choir director: A psalm of David.

¹ In times of trouble, may the LORD answer your cry.
 May the name of the God of Jacob keep you safe from all harm.
² May he send you help from his sanctuary
 and strengthen you from Jerusalem.*
³ May he remember all your gifts
 and look favorably on your burnt offerings.
  Interlude
⁴ May he grant your heart's desires
 and make all your plans succeed.
⁵ May we shout for joy when we hear of your victory
 and raise a victory banner in the name of our God.
 May the LORD answer all your prayers.

⁶ Now I know that the LORD rescues his anointed king.
 He will answer him from his holy heaven
 and rescue him by his great power.
⁷ Some nations boast of their chariots and horses,
 but we boast in the name of the LORD our God.
⁸ Those nations will fall down and collapse,
 but we will rise up and stand firm.

⁹ Give victory to our king, O LORD!
 Answer our cry for help.

Psalm 21
For the choir director: A psalm of David.

¹ How the king rejoices in your strength, O LORD!
 He shouts with joy because you give him victory.
² For you have given him his heart's desire;
 you have withheld nothing he requested.
  Interlude

³ You welcomed him back with success and prosperity.
 You placed a crown of finest gold on his head.
⁴ He asked you to preserve his life,
 and you granted his request.
 The days of his life stretch on forever.

19:3 Or *There is no speech or language where their voice is not heard.* 20:2 Hebrew *Zion.*

Psalm 19 God's wisdom is manifest in heaven (19:1-4), in nature (19:4-6), in his instruction (19:7-11), and in the life of the psalmist (19:12-14). Like Psalm 8, this hymn uses creation to motivate reflection. The psalm begins with creation as a source of wisdom, then moves to God's teachings and judgments as the perfect source of wisdom, and ends with the human need for redemption.
19:7-11 God's instructions to humans reveal his character and wisdom. God's instruction is precious and pleasant (119:103). It nourishes the person (Proverbs 16:24; 24:14) and is of more value than objects of human worth (Psalm 81:13-16). These instructions the psalmist describes are especially found in the first five books of the Bible (Genesis—Deuteronomy).
Psalm 20 This prayer for God's victory (20:1-5) leads to confidence in God's rescue of the king (20:6-8) and a communal request for God's deliverance (20:9).
Psalm 21 God's people thank him for giving victory to the king.

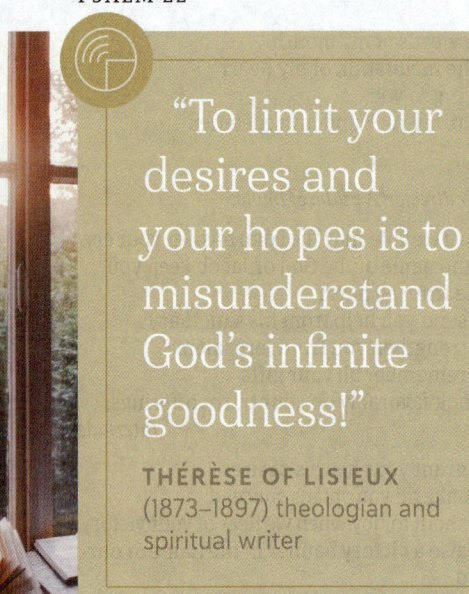

> "To limit your desires and your hopes is to misunderstand God's infinite goodness!"
>
> **THÉRÈSE OF LISIEUX**
> (1873–1897) theologian and spiritual writer

⁵ Your victory brings him great honor,
    and you have clothed him with splendor and majesty.
⁶ You have endowed him with eternal blessings
    and given him the joy of your presence.
⁷ For the king trusts in the LORD.
    The unfailing love of the Most High will keep him from stumbling.
⁸ You will capture all your enemies.
    Your strong right hand will seize all who hate you.
⁹ You will throw them in a flaming furnace
    when you appear.
    The LORD will consume them in his anger;
    fire will devour them.
¹⁰ You will wipe their children from the face of the earth;
    they will never have descendants.
¹¹ Although they plot against you,
    their evil schemes will never succeed.
¹² For they will turn and run
    when they see your arrows aimed at them.
¹³ Rise up, O LORD, in all your power.
    With music and singing we celebrate your mighty acts.

Psalm 22

For the choir director: A psalm of David, to be sung to the tune "Doe of the Dawn."

¹ My God, my God, why have you abandoned me?
    Why are you so far away when I groan for help?
² Every day I call to you, my God, but you do not answer.
    Every night I lift my voice, but I find no relief.

³ Yet you are holy,
    enthroned on the praises of Israel.
⁴ Our ancestors trusted in you,
    and you rescued them.
⁵ They cried out to you and were saved.
    They trusted in you and were never disgraced.

⁶ But I am a worm and not a man.
    I am scorned and despised by all!
⁷ Everyone who sees me mocks me.
    They sneer and shake their heads, saying,
⁸ "Is this the one who relies on the LORD?
    Then let the LORD save him!
    If the LORD loves him so much,
    let the LORD rescue him!"

⁹ Yet you brought me safely from my mother's womb
    and led me to trust you at my mother's breast.
¹⁰ I was thrust into your arms at my birth.
    You have been my God from the moment I was born.

¹¹ Do not stay so far from me,
    for trouble is near,
    and no one else can help me.
¹² My enemies surround me like a herd of bulls;
    fierce bulls of Bashan have hemmed me in!
¹³ Like lions they open their jaws against me,
    roaring and tearing into their prey.
¹⁴ My life is poured out like water,
    and all my bones are out of joint.
    My heart is like wax,
    melting within me.
¹⁵ My strength has dried up like sunbaked clay.
    My tongue sticks to the roof of my mouth.
    You have laid me in the dust and left me for dead.

21:8-12 These verses include an interpretive issue that repeatedly arises in the Psalms: voicing. Who is the "you" addressed in 21:8? Based on the preceding verses, the psalmist seems to address the Lord as the one who will defeat his enemies. However, the explicit mention of God's name in 21:9 suggests that the psalmist may have shifted to addressing the king. Since the king would likely be the instrument of the Lord's justice, the difference is a matter of emphasis: the Lord's defeat of his enemies or the Lord's empowerment of the king to do so.

Psalm 22 All previous laments pale in comparison with this outcry against the enemy and God's abandonment. The psalm contains two main sections: the lament (22:1-21) and praise for redemption (22:22-31), which leads naturally to Psalm 23. The apostles saw in this psalm an expression of the sufferings of Jesus Christ, who ultimately fulfilled the purpose of David's humiliation, rejection by people, and divine abandonment (Matthew 27:35, 39, 43, 46; Mark 15:34; John 19:23-24, 28; Hebrews 2:12).

16 My enemies surround me like a pack of dogs;
   an evil gang closes in on me.
   They have pierced* my hands and feet.
17 I can count all my bones.
   My enemies stare at me and gloat.
18 They divide my garments among themselves
   and throw dice* for my clothing.

19 O LORD, do not stay far away!
   You are my strength; come quickly to my aid!
20 Save me from the sword;
   spare my precious life from these dogs.
21 Snatch me from the lion's jaws
   and from the horns of these wild oxen.

22 I will proclaim your name to my brothers and sisters.*
   I will praise you among your assembled people.
23 Praise the LORD, all you who fear him!
   Honor him, all you descendants of Jacob!
   Show him reverence, all you descendants of Israel!
24 For he has not ignored or belittled the suffering of the needy.
   He has not turned his back on them,
   but has listened to their cries for help.

25 I will praise you in the great assembly.
   I will fulfill my vows in the presence of those who worship you.
26 The poor will eat and be satisfied.
   All who seek the LORD will praise him.
   Their hearts will rejoice with everlasting joy.
27 The whole earth will acknowledge the LORD and return to him.
   All the families of the nations will bow down before him.
28 For royal power belongs to the LORD.
   He rules all the nations.

29 Let the rich of the earth feast and worship.
   Bow before him, all who are mortal,
   all whose lives will end as dust.
30 Our children will also serve him.
   Future generations will hear about the wonders of the Lord.
31 His righteous acts will be told to those not yet born.
   They will hear about everything he has done.

Psalm 23
A psalm of David.

1 The LORD is my shepherd;
   I have all that I need.
2 He lets me rest in green meadows;
   he leads me beside peaceful streams.
3   He renews my strength.
   He guides me along right paths,
   bringing honor to his name.
4 Even when I walk
      through the darkest valley,*
   I will not be afraid,
      for you are close beside me.
   Your rod and your staff
      protect and comfort me.
5 You prepare a feast for me
      in the presence of my enemies.
   You honor me by anointing my head with oil.
   My cup overflows with blessings.
6 Surely your goodness and unfailing love will pursue me
   all the days of my life,
   and I will live in the house of the LORD forever.

Psalm 24
A psalm of David.

1 The earth is the LORD's, and everything in it.
   The world and all its people belong to him.
2 For he laid the earth's foundation on the seas
   and built it on the ocean depths.
3 Who may climb the mountain of the LORD?
   Who may stand in his holy place?
4 Only those whose hands and hearts are pure,
   who do not worship idols
   and never tell lies.
5 They will receive the LORD's blessing
   and have a right relationship with God their savior.

22:16 As in some Hebrew manuscripts and Greek and Syriac versions; most Hebrew manuscripts read *They are like a lion at.*
22:18 Hebrew *cast lots.*   22:22 Hebrew *my brothers.*   23:4 Or *the dark valley of death.*

22:16 The wild "pack of dogs" represents fierce and unscrupulous people. "They have pierced" reflects the text of some Hebrew manuscripts of this psalm as well as the Greek and Syriac translations; most Hebrew manuscripts read "like a lion." However, the meaning of this translation in the current context is unclear.
Psalm 23 This psalm of trust and confidence in the Lord has been a favorite of God's people for generations. It expresses assurance of God's presence amid adversity. It evokes images of the Good Shepherd (23:1-3; see Ezekiel 34:12; John 10:11) and of the messianic banquet (Psalm 23:5-6; see Isaiah 25:6; Revelation 19:9).

23:2 While we often picture lush green pastures, "green meadows" must be understood in Israel's geographical context. It may be that these meadows represent the ideal environment for a flock. Alternatively, the focus may instead be on the shepherd's provision of green grass in the middle of a harsh and dry landscape where adequate food may be hard to find. Either way, the Lord is the one who provides for his people's needs.
Psalm 24 The shepherd of Psalm 23, who is also the King of the whole world, takes possession of Zion, another name for Jerusalem and the mountain where it sits.

⁶ Such people may seek you
  and worship in your presence, O God of
    Jacob.*   *Interlude*

⁷ Open up, ancient gates!
  Open up, ancient doors,
    and let the King of glory enter.
⁸ Who is the King of glory?
  The LORD, strong and mighty;
    the LORD, invincible in battle.
⁹ Open up, ancient gates!
  Open up, ancient doors,
    and let the King of glory enter.
¹⁰ Who is the King of glory?
  The LORD of Heaven's Armies—
    he is the King of glory.   *Interlude*

Psalm 25*
A psalm of David.

¹ O LORD, I give my life to you.
²   I trust in you, my God!
  Do not let me be disgraced,
    or let my enemies rejoice in my defeat.
³ No one who trusts in you will ever be disgraced,
    but disgrace comes to those who try to
      deceive others.

⁴ Show me the right path, O LORD;
    point out the road for me to follow.
⁵ Lead me by your truth and teach me,
    for you are the God who saves me.
  All day long I put my hope in you.
⁶ Remember, O LORD, your compassion and
      unfailing love,
    which you have shown from long ages past.
⁷ Do not remember the rebellious sins of my youth.
  Remember me in the light of your unfailing
      love,
    for you are merciful, O LORD.

⁸ The LORD is good and does what is right;
    he shows the proper path to those who go astray.
⁹ He leads the humble in doing right,
    teaching them his way.

¹⁰ The LORD leads with unfailing love and
      faithfulness
    all who keep his covenant and obey his
      demands.
¹¹ For the honor of your name, O LORD,
    forgive my many, many sins.
¹² Who are those who fear the LORD?
  He will show them the path they should choose.
¹³ They will live in prosperity,
    and their children will inherit the land.
¹⁴ The LORD is a friend to those who fear him.
  He teaches them his covenant.
¹⁵ My eyes are always on the LORD,
    for he rescues me from the traps of my enemies.

¹⁶ Turn to me and have mercy,
    for I am alone and in deep distress.
¹⁷ My problems go from bad to worse.
  Oh, save me from them all!
¹⁸ Feel my pain and see my trouble.
  Forgive all my sins.
¹⁹ See how many enemies I have
    and how viciously they hate me!
²⁰ Protect me! Rescue my life from them!
  Do not let me be disgraced, for in you I take
      refuge.
²¹ May integrity and honesty protect me,
    for I put my hope in you.

²² O God, ransom Israel
    from all its troubles.

Psalm 26
A psalm of David.

¹ Declare me innocent, O LORD,
    for I have acted with integrity;
  I have trusted in the LORD without wavering.
² Put me on trial, LORD, and cross-examine me.
  Test my motives and my heart.
³ For I am always aware of your unfailing love,
    and I have lived according to your truth.
⁴ I do not spend time with liars
    or go along with hypocrites.

24:6 As in two Hebrew manuscripts and Greek and Syriac versions; most Hebrew manuscripts read *O Jacob*. **25** This psalm is a Hebrew acrostic poem; each verse begins with a successive letter of the Hebrew alphabet.

24:7-10 While the first part of the psalm focuses on people's entrance into the Lord's presence, this section focuses on the Lord's entry into the human realm, namely the Temple. The psalm likely describes a procession bringing the Ark of the Covenant into the Temple, which is represented by the gates and doors.
Psalm 25 This psalm is a Hebrew acrostic poem; each verse begins with a successive letter of the Hebrew alphabet. It includes instruction in wisdom and a community lament; it begins and ends with an affirmation of trust in the Lord (25:1-3, 15-22). The psalmist prays for guidance (25:4-7) and encourages the godly to practice a lifestyle of wisdom (25:12-14). In addition to the enemies who trouble him, the psalmist confesses his sins (25:7, 11, 18) as part of his anguish. Trust develops with understanding God's character: He is compassionate, faithful, and good (25:8-10).
25:5 Biblical hope does not mean wishing for an event to turn out favorably. Hope trusts the Lord's will and gives the courage to face disappointments (33:22; 130:5).
Psalm 26 In this individual lament, the psalmist prays for redemption based on the Lord's character and justice.
26:1-3 Compared to Paul's assertion that all have sinned (Romans 3:23), these verses can sound arrogant. However, Psalm 26:3 provides the key to understanding: The psalmist's deep awareness of God's "unfailing love" and "faithfulness" serves as a foundation for his prayer and confidence. "Faithfulness" is another way of translating the Hebrew *emet*, which the NLT renders "truth."

The Good Shepherd

IDENTITY — Assurance of Light

I came to this prayer time desperate. I'm a ministry leader and had learned that ministering from empty doesn't go well—for me or anyone else. I told God, "I refuse to lead from empty again! I need you to do something with this dry, drained me."

As I read Psalm 23, I asked, "How can you meet me in *my* dark valley, Good Shepherd?"

I found a painting that illuminated my next step, *Expectation* by Richard Oelze. With storm clouds and a thundering horizon, it shows women and men in neutral colors, with expressionless faces. Most of them are turned away, fixed on the threat in the distance. But one woman, close to the light, is turned, possibly with purpose. Undeterred, her lapel and hat each bear a blush-colored brooch. Her face almost seems to shine.

And Psalm 23's words in my Bible read newly to me: "Even though I walk through the valley of the shadow of death, I fear no evil, for You are with me; Your rod and Your staff, they comfort me" (23:4, NASB).

I glimpsed this: I am not in the valley of death. But the valley of the shadow of death. And I am not here forever. I am walking through.

A shadow means that somewhere, light shines. A shadow reminds me—like the woman in the painting—to walk on, in the light. And if it's too dark to see, then a shadow reminds me to stick close enough to feel the Good Shepherd's hand on my head, calming me.

There is a Good Shepherd who assures me of light, not dark. Who masterfully guides me through, and who is with me, even on a soul-dry day.

> We have a Good Shepherd even in our dark valleys.

THE GOOD SHEPHERD'S SONG IS PSALM 23.

IDENTIFY

Take a moment to search online for *Expectation* by Richard Oelze. Dwell on it: What do you notice about where most people are looking? What about the woman who is closest to the light?

As you consider your dark valleys, where do you see your Good Shepherd? How would you like to step forward now?

"Prayer, worship, Bible reading, and service... had prepared me to enter the valley of the shadow of death [with] my Good Shepherd. Even when the darkness... made that valley very dark indeed..., I was sustained... through practicing disciplines to follow him daily." Michelle Van Loon, "Daily (Eternal) Investments," *Today's Christian Woman*

NAOMI CRAMER OVERTON, MBA, DIS, lives to realize beauty-filled visions that lift us to flourishing, with our families and beyond. Naomi has been CEO for Stonecroft and MOPS, director with Compassion International and World Vision, and General Editor for this Bible.

⁵ I hate the gatherings of those who do evil,
and I refuse to join in with the wicked.
⁶ I wash my hands to declare my innocence.
I come to your altar, O Lord,
⁷ singing a song of thanksgiving
and telling of all your wonders.
⁸ I love your sanctuary, Lord,
the place where your glorious presence
dwells.

⁹ Don't let me suffer the fate of sinners.
Don't condemn me along with murderers.
¹⁰ Their hands are dirty with evil schemes,
and they constantly take bribes.
¹¹ But I am not like that; I live with integrity.
So redeem me and show me mercy.
¹² Now I stand on solid ground,
and I will publicly praise the Lord.

Psalm 27
A psalm of David.

¹ The Lord is my light and my salvation—
so why should I be afraid?
The Lord is my fortress, protecting me from
danger,
so why should I tremble?
² When evil people come to devour me,
when my enemies and foes attack me,
they will stumble and fall.
³ Though a mighty army surrounds me,
my heart will not be afraid.
Even if I am attacked,
I will remain confident.

⁴ The one thing I ask of the Lord—
the thing I seek most—
is to live in the house of the Lord all the days of
my life,
delighting in the Lord's perfections
and meditating in his Temple.
⁵ For he will conceal me there when troubles
come;
he will hide me in his sanctuary.
He will place me out of reach on a high rock.
⁶ Then I will hold my head high
above my enemies who surround me.
At his sanctuary I will offer sacrifices with
shouts of joy,
singing and praising the Lord with music.

⁷ Hear me as I pray, O Lord.
Be merciful and answer me!
⁸ My heart has heard you say, "Come and talk with
me."
And my heart responds, "Lord, I am coming."
⁹ Do not turn your back on me.
Do not reject your servant in anger.
You have always been my helper.
Don't leave me now; don't abandon me,
O God of my salvation!
¹⁰ Even if my father and mother abandon me,
the Lord will hold me close.

¹¹ Teach me how to live, O Lord.
Lead me along the right path,
for my enemies are waiting for me.
¹² Do not let me fall into their hands.
For they accuse me of things I've never done;
with every breath they threaten me with
violence.
¹³ Yet I am confident I will see the Lord's
goodness
while I am here in the land of the living.

¹⁴ Wait patiently for the Lord.
Be brave and courageous.
Yes, wait patiently for the Lord.

Psalm 28
A psalm of David.

¹ I pray to you, O Lord, my rock.
Do not turn a deaf ear to me.
For if you are silent,
I might as well give up and die.
² Listen to my prayer for mercy
as I cry out to you for help,
as I lift my hands toward your holy sanctuary.

³ Do not drag me away with the wicked—
with those who do evil—
those who speak friendly words to their
neighbors
while planning evil in their hearts.
⁴ Give them the punishment they so richly
deserve!
Measure it out in proportion to their
wickedness.
Pay them back for all their evil deeds!
Give them a taste of what they have done to
others.
⁵ They care nothing for what the Lord has done
or for what his hands have made.
So he will tear them down,
and they will never be rebuilt!

Psalm 27 This psalm mixes two genres—a psalm of confidence (27:1-6) and an individual lament (27:7-14)—held together by the theme of longing for the Lord's presence. The psalmist focuses on the Lord; his circumstances are secondary. The strength of the psalmist's faith is expressed in his openness to the Lord's instruction, timing, and priorities.
27:4-6 Because of his confidence in God (26:1-3), the psalmist can seek what is most important—the Lord's presence—rather than petitioning for deliverance. He trusts that in seeking God's presence, the Lord will provide the needed rescue.
Psalm 28 In this individual lament, the psalmist pleads for justice and mercy. He expresses confidence in the Lord's strength and faithfulness, and he intercedes for the Lord's people.

⁶ Praise the LORD!
　For he has heard my cry for mercy.
⁷ The LORD is my strength and shield.
　I trust him with all my heart.
　He helps me, and my heart is filled with joy.
　I burst out in songs of thanksgiving.

⁸ The LORD gives his people strength.
　He is a safe fortress for his anointed king.
⁹ Save your people!
　Bless Israel, your special possession.*

Lead them like a shepherd,
　and carry them in your arms forever.

Psalm 29
A psalm of David.

¹ Honor the LORD, you heavenly beings*;
　honor the LORD for his glory and strength.
² Honor the LORD for the glory of his name.
　Worship the LORD in the splendor of his holiness.

28:9 Hebrew *Bless your inheritance.* 29:1 Hebrew *you sons of God.*

28:6-8 Psalms of lament generally include two sections: a plea or prayer and praise. The psalmist's prayer is in 28:1-5. While 26:6-8 can be read as praise anticipating God's answer, there are two other possibilities: the psalmist has received a word of assurance from the Lord, perhaps through a priest; or time has passed since the initial prayer, and the psalmist is expressing praise for actual deliverance.

Psalm 29 This nature hymn in praise of the Creator declares that the Lord holds all power over nature.

Come Close — CRUDDY MOOD? CRY OUT

SCRIPTURE CONNECTION: PSALM 27

Have you ever stood on a ridge, enjoying the thrill of being on high, but knowing your soul felt like it belonged in the depths below?

I have, and that's why I love the Psalms. I love their permission—no, their invitation—to shun appearances of high places, of having it all together. Sometimes as a Christian woman and leader, I feel pressured never to have a wayward emotion. Nothing but calm, courageous, cheerful me, please.

I love how honest, admired psalm writers unearth their sunken places. I love how the God the psalms are written to brings us close, often through U-turns:

- *"Though a mighty army surrounds me . . ."* though life invites ongoing sacrifice; though I get labeled by age, supposed beliefs, and skin color; though leading is hard *". . . my heart will not be afraid"* (27:3).
- *"Even if I am attacked . . ."* by others hurting those I love, by hearing "that's not how we would do it;" by those saying that I am too much, or too little, *". . . I will remain confident"* (27:3).

I could read the Psalms merely as "attitude adjustments." But the prize, the psalmist writes, is allowing God to loosen the ties I let bind me and to pull me to where I hear my creator's heart beating. There, I lament, I let loose. I hear what he thinks and what he will do. I regain God-confidence anew.

REFLECT My heart has heard you say, "Come and talk with me." And my heart responds, "LORD, I am coming." PSALM 27:8

God, thank you for wanting my full range of emotions. Thank you for showing me your perspective, but—best of all—thank you for holding the real me really close.

CONSIDER "Faith is confidence in the kindness of God, no matter the confusion of circumstances." ANN VOSKAMP (Twitter, August 27, 2015)

Confidence is ours as we let loose and linger with our good God.

NAOMI CRAMER OVERTON, MBA, DIS, lives to realize beauty-filled visions that lift us to flourishing, with our families and beyond. Naomi has been CEO for Stonecroft and MOPS, director with Compassion International and World Vision, and General Editor for this Bible.

³ The voice of the LORD echoes above the sea.
  The God of glory thunders.
  The LORD thunders over the mighty sea.
⁴ The voice of the LORD is powerful;
  the voice of the LORD is majestic.
⁵ The voice of the LORD splits the mighty cedars;
  the LORD shatters the cedars of Lebanon.
⁶ He makes Lebanon's mountains skip like a calf;
  he makes Mount Hermon* leap like a young wild ox.
⁷ The voice of the LORD strikes
  with bolts of lightning.
⁸ The voice of the LORD makes the barren wilderness quake;
  the LORD shakes the wilderness of Kadesh.
⁹ The voice of the LORD twists mighty oaks*
  and strips the forests bare.
In his Temple everyone shouts, "Glory!"
¹⁰ The LORD rules over the floodwaters.
  The LORD reigns as king forever.
¹¹ The LORD gives his people strength.
  The LORD blesses them with peace.

Psalm 30

A psalm of David. A song for the dedication of the Temple.

¹ I will exalt you, LORD, for you rescued me.
  You refused to let my enemies triumph over me.
² O LORD my God, I cried to you for help,
  and you restored my health.
³ You brought me up from the grave,* O LORD.
  You kept me from falling into the pit of death.
⁴ Sing to the LORD, all you godly ones!
  Praise his holy name.
⁵ For his anger lasts only a moment,
  but his favor lasts a lifetime!
Weeping may last through the night,
  but joy comes with the morning.
⁶ When I was prosperous, I said,
  "Nothing can stop me now!"
⁷ Your favor, O LORD, made me as secure as a mountain.
  Then you turned away from me, and I was shattered.
⁸ I cried out to you, O LORD.
  I begged the Lord for mercy, saying,
⁹ "What will you gain if I die,
  if I sink into the grave?
Can my dust praise you?
  Can it tell of your faithfulness?
¹⁰ Hear me, LORD, and have mercy on me.
  Help me, O LORD."
¹¹ You have turned my mourning into joyful dancing.
  You have taken away my clothes of mourning
  and clothed me with joy,
¹² that I might sing praises to you and not be silent.
  O LORD my God, I will give you thanks forever!

Psalm 31

For the choir director: A psalm of David.

¹ O LORD, I have come to you for protection;
  don't let me be disgraced.
Save me, for you do what is right.
² Turn your ear to listen to me;
  rescue me quickly.
Be my rock of protection,
  a fortress where I will be safe.
³ You are my rock and my fortress.
  For the honor of your name, lead me out of this danger.
⁴ Pull me from the trap my enemies set for me,
  for I find protection in you alone.
⁵ I entrust my spirit into your hand.
  Rescue me, LORD, for you are a faithful God.
⁶ I hate those who worship worthless idols.
  I trust in the LORD.
⁷ I will be glad and rejoice in your unfailing love,
  for you have seen my troubles,
  and you care about the anguish of my soul.
⁸ You have not handed me over to my enemies
  but have set me in a safe place.
⁹ Have mercy on me, LORD, for I am in distress.
  Tears blur my eyes.
  My body and soul are withering away.
¹⁰ I am dying from grief;
  my years are shortened by sadness.
Sin has drained my strength;
  I am wasting away from within.
¹¹ I am scorned by all my enemies
  and despised by my neighbors—
  even my friends are afraid to come near me.

29:6 Hebrew *Sirion*, another name for Mount Hermon.   29:9 Or *causes the deer to writhe in labor.*   30:3 Hebrew *from Sheol.*

29:3-9 The seven references in this psalm to "the voice of the LORD" poetically echo the repeated thunder of a great storm. People in the ancient world often described a god's appearance (called a *theophany*) with such imagery. Here, the Lord's appearance sweeps across the land, focusing the audience's attention on his power and sovereignty, leading them to inevitable praise (29:9).

Psalm 30 This individual thanksgiving psalm opens in praise to the Lord for his salvation (30:1-3), then contrasts God's favor with his anger (30:4-7). It ends with a transformation from mourning to dancing (30:8-12).

Psalm 31 The psalmist encourages the godly to find refuge in the Lord and wait for his salvation. Despite having had a death-like experience, he testifies to the Lord's faithfulness. This psalm (31:5) foreshadows the suffering of Jesus (Luke 23:46).

When they see me on the street,
    they run the other way.
¹² I am ignored as if I were dead,
    as if I were a broken pot.
¹³ I have heard the many rumors about me,
    and I am surrounded by terror.
    My enemies conspire against me,
    plotting to take my life.
¹⁴ But I am trusting you, O Lord,
    saying, "You are my God!"
¹⁵ My future is in your hands.
    Rescue me from those who hunt me down relentlessly.
¹⁶ Let your favor shine on your servant.
    In your unfailing love, rescue me.
¹⁷ Don't let me be disgraced, O Lord,
    for I call out to you for help.
    Let the wicked be disgraced;
    let them lie silent in the grave.*
¹⁸ Silence their lying lips—
    those proud and arrogant lips that accuse the godly.
¹⁹ How great is the goodness
    you have stored up for those who fear you.
    You lavish it on those who come to you for protection,
    blessing them before the watching world.
²⁰ You hide them in the shelter of your presence,
    safe from those who conspire against them.
    You shelter them in your presence,
    far from accusing tongues.
²¹ Praise the Lord,
    for he has shown me the wonders of his unfailing love.
    He kept me safe when my city was under attack.
²² In panic I cried out,
    "I am cut off from the Lord!"
    But you heard my cry for mercy
    and answered my call for help.
²³ Love the Lord, all you godly ones!
    For the Lord protects those who are loyal to him,
    but he harshly punishes the arrogant.
²⁴ So be strong and courageous,
    all you who put your hope in the Lord!

Psalm 32

A psalm* of David.

¹ Oh, what joy for those
    whose disobedience is forgiven,
    whose sin is put out of sight!
² Yes, what joy for those
    whose record the Lord has cleared of guilt,*
    whose lives are lived in complete honesty!
³ When I refused to confess my sin,
    my body wasted away,
    and I groaned all day long.
⁴ Day and night your hand of discipline was heavy on me.
    My strength evaporated like water in the summer heat.   *Interlude*
⁵ Finally, I confessed all my sins to you
    and stopped trying to hide my guilt.
    I said to myself, "I will confess my rebellion to the Lord."
    And you forgave me! All my guilt is gone.   *Interlude*
⁶ Therefore, let all the godly pray to you while there is still time,
    that they may not drown in the floodwaters of judgment.
⁷ For you are my hiding place;
    you protect me from trouble.
    You surround me with songs of victory.   *Interlude*
⁸ The Lord says, "I will guide you along the best pathway for your life.
    I will advise you and watch over you.
⁹ Do not be like a senseless horse or mule
    that needs a bit and bridle to keep it under control."
¹⁰ Many sorrows come to the wicked,
    but unfailing love surrounds those who trust the Lord.
¹¹ So rejoice in the Lord and be glad, all you who obey him!
    Shout for joy, all you whose hearts are pure!

Psalm 33

¹ Let the godly sing for joy to the Lord;
    it is fitting for the pure to praise him.
² Praise the Lord with melodies on the lyre;
    make music for him on the ten-stringed harp.

31:17 Hebrew *in Sheol*.   32:title Hebrew *maskil*. This may be a literary or musical term.   32:2 Greek version reads *of sin*. Compare Rom 4:8.

Psalm 32 This wisdom psalm of confession and thanksgiving encourages and exhorts the godly to learn from the psalmist's experience of sin, denial, confession, and forgiveness. This psalm was one of the seven psalms of penitence used in the early church (also Psalms 6, 38, 51, 102, 130, 143).
32:1-2 "What joy" translates the Hebrew word *ashrey*, which can also be translated as "blessed," "happy," or "fortunate." See the first study note on Psalm 1:1.

Psalm 33 This hymn of creation (see also Psalms 8, 19, 104, 145) exhorts readers to praise God (33:1-3), to recognize the power of his word in creation (33:4-7), and to fear the Creator (33:8-11). It offers hope to forgiven sinners (see 32:1-7) that they can live a new life in the fear of the Lord and under divine protection.

³ Sing a new song of praise to him;
    play skillfully on the harp, and sing with joy.
⁴ For the word of the LORD holds true,
    and we can trust everything he does.
⁵ He loves whatever is just and good;
    the unfailing love of the LORD fills the earth.

⁶ The LORD merely spoke,
    and the heavens were created.
  He breathed the word,
    and all the stars were born.
⁷ He assigned the sea its boundaries
    and locked the oceans in vast reservoirs.
⁸ Let the whole world fear the LORD,
    and let everyone stand in awe of him.
⁹ For when he spoke, the world began!
    It appeared at his command.

¹⁰ The LORD frustrates the plans of the nations
    and thwarts all their schemes.
¹¹ But the LORD's plans stand firm forever;
    his intentions can never be shaken.

¹² What joy for the nation whose God is the LORD,
    whose people he has chosen as his
      inheritance.

¹³ The LORD looks down from heaven
    and sees the whole human race.
¹⁴ From his throne he observes
    all who live on the earth.
¹⁵ He made their hearts,
    so he understands everything they do.
¹⁶ The best-equipped army cannot save a king,
    nor is great strength enough to save a warrior.
¹⁷ Don't count on your warhorse to give you
      victory—
    for all its strength, it cannot save you.

¹⁸ But the LORD watches over those who fear him,
    those who rely on his unfailing love.
¹⁹ He rescues them from death
    and keeps them alive in times of famine.

²⁰ We put our hope in the LORD.
    He is our help and our shield.
²¹ In him our hearts rejoice,
    for we trust in his holy name.
²² Let your unfailing love surround us, LORD,
    for our hope is in you alone.

Psalm 34*

A psalm of David, regarding the time he pretended to be insane in front of Abimelech, who sent him away.

¹ I will praise the LORD at all times.
    I will constantly speak his praises.
² I will boast only in the LORD;
    let all who are helpless take heart.
³ Come, let us tell of the LORD's greatness;
    let us exalt his name together.

⁴ I prayed to the LORD, and he answered me.
    He freed me from all my fears.
⁵ Those who look to him for help will be radiant
      with joy;
    no shadow of shame will darken their faces.
⁶ In my desperation I prayed, and the LORD listened;
    he saved me from all my troubles.
⁷ For the angel of the LORD is a guard;
    he surrounds and defends all who fear him.

⁸ Taste and see that the LORD is good.
    Oh, the joys of those who take refuge in him!
⁹ Fear the LORD, you his godly people,
    for those who fear him will have all they need.
¹⁰ Even strong young lions sometimes go hungry,
    but those who trust in the LORD will lack no
      good thing.

¹¹ Come, my children, and listen to me,
    and I will teach you to fear the LORD.
¹² Does anyone want to live a life
    that is long and prosperous?
¹³ Then keep your tongue from speaking evil
    and your lips from telling lies!
¹⁴ Turn away from evil and do good.
    Search for peace, and work to maintain it.

¹⁵ The eyes of the LORD watch over those who do
      right;
    his ears are open to their cries for help.
¹⁶ But the LORD turns his face against those who do
      evil;
    he will erase their memory from the earth.
¹⁷ The LORD hears his people when they call to him
      for help.
    He rescues them from all their troubles.
¹⁸ The LORD is close to the brokenhearted;
    he rescues those whose spirits are crushed.

34 This psalm is a Hebrew acrostic poem; each verse begins with a successive letter of the Hebrew alphabet.

33:6 While those familiar with the Bible may take for granted the idea that God created the cosmos by his spoken word, the concept was unique in the ancient world. Israel's polytheistic neighbors often tied creation or bringing order to a war between different gods and goddesses. That the Lord simply spoke the cosmos into existence demonstrated his unique power beyond any other supposed deities.

33:8-11 Fear of the Lord begins with awe for God and for his powerful word. His word created everything and continues to order and sustain creation. He frustrates the plans of people who oppose his plans.

Psalm 34 This psalm is a Hebrew acrostic poem; each verse begins with a successive letter of the Hebrew alphabet. The acrostic is missing one letter (*vav*) and has an additional verse at the end (34:22). This wisdom psalm includes a thanksgiving hymn (34:1-7) that celebrates the Lord's care for and protection of godly sufferers. It also includes an invitation to wisdom (34:8-14) and examples of wisdom worked out in the Lord's care for the needy and the suffering of the wicked (34:15-22).

I am confident I will see the Lord's goodness.

PSALM 27:13

¹⁹ The righteous person faces many troubles,
  but the LORD comes to the rescue each time.
²⁰ For the LORD protects the bones of the righteous;
  not one of them is broken!
²¹ Calamity will surely destroy the wicked,
  and those who hate the righteous will be punished.
²² But the LORD will redeem those who serve him.
  No one who takes refuge in him will be condemned.

Psalm 35

A psalm of David.

¹ O LORD, oppose those who oppose me.
  Fight those who fight against me.
² Put on your armor, and take up your shield.
  Prepare for battle, and come to my aid.
³ Lift up your spear and javelin
  against those who pursue me.
 Let me hear you say,
  "I will give you victory!"
⁴ Bring shame and disgrace on those trying to kill me;
  turn them back and humiliate those who want to harm me.
⁵ Blow them away like chaff in the wind—
  a wind sent by the angel of the LORD.
⁶ Make their path dark and slippery,
  with the angel of the LORD pursuing them.
⁷ I did them no wrong, but they laid a trap for me.
  I did them no wrong, but they dug a pit to catch me.
⁸ So let sudden ruin come upon them!
  Let them be caught in the trap they set for me!
  Let them be destroyed in the pit they dug for me.
⁹ Then I will rejoice in the LORD.
  I will be glad because he rescues me.
¹⁰ With every bone in my body I will praise him:
  "LORD, who can compare with you?
 Who else rescues the helpless from the strong?
  Who else protects the helpless and poor from those who rob them?"
¹¹ Malicious witnesses testify against me.
  They accuse me of crimes I know nothing about.
¹² They repay me evil for good.
  I am sick with despair.
¹³ Yet when they were ill, I grieved for them.
  I denied myself by fasting for them,
  but my prayers returned unanswered.
¹⁴ I was sad, as though they were my friends or family,
  as if I were grieving for my own mother.
¹⁵ But they are glad now that I am in trouble;
  they gleefully join together against me.
 I am attacked by people I don't even know;
  they slander me constantly.
¹⁶ They mock me and call me names;
  they snarl at me.
¹⁷ How long, O Lord, will you look on and do nothing?
  Rescue me from their fierce attacks.
  Protect my life from these lions!
¹⁸ Then I will thank you in front of the great assembly.
  I will praise you before all the people.
¹⁹ Don't let my treacherous enemies rejoice over my defeat.
  Don't let those who hate me without cause gloat over my sorrow.
²⁰ They don't talk of peace;
  they plot against innocent people who mind their own business.
²¹ They shout, "Aha! Aha!
  With our own eyes we saw him do it!"
²² O LORD, you know all about this.
  Do not stay silent.
  Do not abandon me now, O Lord.
²³ Wake up! Rise to my defense!
  Take up my case, my God and my Lord.
²⁴ Declare me not guilty, O LORD my God, for you give justice.
  Don't let my enemies laugh about me in my troubles.
²⁵ Don't let them say, "Look, we got what we wanted!
  Now we will eat him alive!"
²⁶ May those who rejoice at my troubles
  be humiliated and disgraced.
 May those who triumph over me
  be covered with shame and dishonor.
²⁷ But give great joy to those who came to my defense.
  Let them continually say, "Great is the LORD,
  who delights in blessing his servant with peace!"
²⁸ Then I will proclaim your justice,
  and I will praise you all day long.

Psalm 35 In this lament, the Lord's troubled servant calls for God to see his circumstances and vindicate him.

35:4-8 Unexpectedly, the imagery shifts from military language to a call for the Lord to send his angel to intervene against the psalmist's opponent. The line "blow them away like chaff in the wind" (35:5) is reminiscent of 1:4-5, where the wicked are "scattered by the wind" and stand "condemned at the time of judgment." The "dark and slippery" path sought in 35:6 also echoes the imagery of the wicked's path leading to destruction in 1:6.

Psalm 36

For the choir director: A psalm of David, the servant of the Lord.

1 Sin whispers to the wicked, deep within their hearts.*
They have no fear of God at all.
2 In their blind conceit,
they cannot see how wicked they really are.
3 Everything they say is crooked and deceitful.
They refuse to act wisely or do good.
4 They lie awake at night, hatching sinful plots.
Their actions are never good.
They make no attempt to turn from evil.

5 Your unfailing love, O Lord, is as vast as the heavens;
your faithfulness reaches beyond the clouds.
6 Your righteousness is like the mighty mountains,
your justice like the ocean depths.
You care for people and animals alike, O Lord.
7 How precious is your unfailing love, O God!
All humanity finds shelter
in the shadow of your wings.
8 You feed them from the abundance of your own house,
letting them drink from your river of delights.
9 For you are the fountain of life,
the light by which we see.

10 Pour out your unfailing love on those who love you;
give justice to those with honest hearts.
11 Don't let the proud trample me
or the wicked push me around.
12 Look! Those who do evil have fallen!
They are thrown down, never to rise again.

Psalm 37*

A psalm of David.

1 Don't worry about the wicked
or envy those who do wrong.
2 For like grass, they soon fade away.
Like spring flowers, they soon wither.
3 Trust in the Lord and do good.
Then you will live safely in the land and prosper.
4 Take delight in the Lord,
and he will give you your heart's desires.
5 Commit everything you do to the Lord.
Trust him, and he will help you.
6 He will make your innocence radiate like the dawn,
and the justice of your cause will shine like the noonday sun.

7 Be still in the presence of the Lord,
and wait patiently for him to act.
Don't worry about evil people who prosper
or fret about their wicked schemes.

8 Stop being angry!
Turn from your rage!
Do not lose your temper—
it only leads to harm.
9 For the wicked will be destroyed,
but those who trust in the Lord will possess the land.

10 Soon the wicked will disappear.
Though you look for them, they will be gone.
11 The lowly will possess the land
and will live in peace and prosperity.

12 The wicked plot against the godly;
they snarl at them in defiance.
13 But the Lord just laughs,
for he sees their day of judgment coming.

14 The wicked draw their swords
and string their bows
to kill the poor and the oppressed,
to slaughter those who do right.
15 But their swords will stab their own hearts,
and their bows will be broken.

16 It is better to be godly and have little
than to be evil and rich.
17 For the strength of the wicked will be shattered,
but the Lord takes care of the godly.

18 Day by day the Lord takes care of the innocent,
and they will receive an inheritance that lasts forever.
19 They will not be disgraced in hard times;
even in famine they will have more than enough.

36:1 As in some Hebrew manuscripts and Syriac version, which read *in his heart*. Masoretic Text reads *in my heart*. 37 This psalm is a Hebrew acrostic poem; each stanza begins with a successive letter of the Hebrew alphabet.

Psalm 36 This psalm contrasts the character of the wicked with the character of Israel's faithful God, the Lord. While the wicked lack fear of the Lord (the foundation of a wise life), God is known by his "unfailing love" (36:5, 7, 10). In that love, he cares for all creation and will intervene to bring about justice in his world. The righteous will enjoy God's protection, but the wicked will perish.

Psalm 37 This instructional wisdom psalm is a Hebrew acrostic poem, with every second verse beginning with a successive letter of the Hebrew alphabet. It elaborates on a variety of questions: How should the godly respond to the reality of evil? When will the Lord bring justice? Why does he permit the wicked to destroy his created order? Psalm 37 offers clear responses that reduce these tensions with alternating contrasts between the godly and the wicked.

37:1-7 The wise respond to evil by trusting in the Lord. Trust includes four dimensions: renouncing irritability and envy (37:1-2), delighting in the Lord (37:3-4), submitting to the Lord (37:5-6), and practicing patience in hope (37:7).

20 But the wicked will die.
The LORD's enemies are like flowers in a field—
they will disappear like smoke.
21 The wicked borrow and never repay,
but the godly are generous givers.
22 Those the LORD blesses will possess the land,
but those he curses will die.
23 The LORD directs the steps of the godly.
He delights in every detail of their lives.
24 Though they stumble, they will never fall,
for the LORD holds them by the hand.
25 Once I was young, and now I am old.
Yet I have never seen the godly abandoned
or their children begging for bread.
26 The godly always give generous loans to others,
and their children are a blessing.
27 Turn from evil and do good,
and you will live in the land forever.
28 For the LORD loves justice,
and he will never abandon the godly.

He will keep them safe forever,
but the children of the wicked will die.

Pursuing God's Justice

SCRIPTURE CONNECTION: PSALM 37

Psalm 37 reminds me of Dr. Martin Luther King Jr.'s clear call for justice: "Darkness cannot drive out darkness: Only light can do that." Being aware of injustice is one thing, and seeking to root it out is another.

Actively pursuing God's justice doesn't come easily, but the psalm writer gives sound advice for how to do this:

1. *Trust* in the Lord. We are urged: "Don't worry" (37:1) but "trust ... and do good" (37:3). Injustice may overwhelm us, but we can press forward, knowing that God is in control.
2. *Hope* in the Lord. The psalm catalogs the activities of "the wicked" (37:10, 12, 14) and notes that a downfall follows each (37:11, 13, 15). The psalm instructs us to "Put [our] hope in the LORD" (37:34).
3. *Delight* in God. Keeping our focus on God as we pursue his justice aligns us: "Take delight in the LORD, and he will give you your heart's desires" (37:4), and "the LORD directs the steps of the godly" (37:23).
4. *Dwell* in the inheritance. The psalm writer draws attention to the land he promised his people, Israel, as the reward for his justice seekers (37:3, 9, 11, 22, 27, 29, 34). As we seek God's justice now, we can be confident in his victory to come (37:6, 37) and our inheritance in his Kingdom (Matthew 5:9-10).

> Trust, hope, delight, and dwell—to pursue God's justice.

IMAGINE

What injustices do you see around you? Consider injustice on multiples levels: personal, national, global.

How can you seek God's justice as you delight in the Lord?

"People have asked, 'Why would you want to work in politics? It's such a dark place!' But that's exactly why I want to be there—to bring more of God's light into darkness."

SARAH OVERTON, MA, is a researcher specializing in refugee and asylum policy. She has worked in the UK Parliament, public-policy think tanks, and at Lambeth Palace.

²⁹ The godly will possess the land
    and will live there forever.
³⁰ The godly offer good counsel;
    they teach right from wrong.
³¹ They have made God's law their own,
    so they will never slip from his path.
³² The wicked wait in ambush for the godly,
    looking for an excuse to kill them.
³³ But the LORD will not let the wicked succeed
    or let the godly be condemned when they are put on trial.
³⁴ Put your hope in the LORD.
    Travel steadily along his path.
    He will honor you by giving you the land.
    You will see the wicked destroyed.
³⁵ I have seen wicked and ruthless people
    flourishing like a tree in its native soil.
³⁶ But when I looked again, they were gone!
    Though I searched for them, I could not find them!
³⁷ Look at those who are honest and good,
    for a wonderful future awaits those who love peace.
³⁸ But the rebellious will be destroyed;
    they have no future.
³⁹ The LORD rescues the godly;
    he is their fortress in times of trouble.
⁴⁰ The LORD helps them,
    rescuing them from the wicked.
    He saves them,
    and they find shelter in him.

Psalm 38
A psalm of David, asking God to remember him.

¹ O LORD, don't rebuke me in your anger
    or discipline me in your rage!
² Your arrows have struck deep,
    and your blows are crushing me.
³ Because of your anger, my whole body is sick;
    my health is broken because of my sins.
⁴ My guilt overwhelms me—
    it is a burden too heavy to bear.
⁵ My wounds fester and stink
    because of my foolish sins.
⁶ I am bent over and racked with pain.
    All day long I walk around filled with grief.
⁷ A raging fever burns within me,
    and my health is broken.
⁸ I am exhausted and completely crushed.
    My groans come from an anguished heart.
⁹ You know what I long for, Lord;
    you hear my every sigh.
¹⁰ My heart beats wildly, my strength fails,
    and I am going blind.
¹¹ My loved ones and friends stay away, fearing my disease.
    Even my own family stands at a distance.
¹² Meanwhile, my enemies lay traps to kill me.
    Those who wish me harm make plans to ruin me.
    All day long they plan their treachery.
¹³ But I am deaf to all their threats.
    I am silent before them as one who cannot speak.
¹⁴ I choose to hear nothing,
    and I make no reply.
¹⁵ For I am waiting for you, O LORD.
    You must answer for me, O Lord my God.
¹⁶ I prayed, "Don't let my enemies gloat over me
    or rejoice at my downfall."
¹⁷ I am on the verge of collapse,
    facing constant pain.
¹⁸ But I confess my sins;
    I am deeply sorry for what I have done.
¹⁹ I have many aggressive enemies;
    they hate me without reason.
²⁰ They repay me evil for good
    and oppose me for pursuing good.
²¹ Do not abandon me, O LORD.
    Do not stand at a distance, my God.
²² Come quickly to help me,
    O Lord my savior.

Psalm 39
For Jeduthun, the choir director: A psalm of David.

¹ I said to myself, "I will watch what I do
    and not sin in what I say.
    I will hold my tongue
    when the ungodly are around me."
² But as I stood there in silence—
    not even speaking of good things—
    the turmoil within me grew worse.
³ The more I thought about it,
    the hotter I got,
    igniting a fire of words:

Psalm 38 Many consider this passage to be a prayer for physical healing. However, literary devices within this poetry make it possible to understand the suffering as a metaphor for the speaker's sin and need for repentance. This second interpretation matches the fact that this psalm traditionally is identified as one of the seven confessional psalms (Psalms 6, 32, 38, 51, 102, 130, 143). Within this context, the psalmist's sin rather than any physical ailment was what required the Lord's intervention.

38:3 Sin can lead to sickness and even death (1 Corinthians 11:30). Whether the psalmist actually felt physically ill or his sickness was a metaphor for spiritual or emotional turmoil, he knew that it came from God and threatened his life (see Psalms 32:3; 39:10).

Psalm 39 This prayer for rescue reflects the psalmist's discouragement, which comes from having a limited perspective on his situation.

⁴ "LORD, remind me how brief my time on earth
   will be.
      Remind me that my days are numbered—
         how fleeting my life is.
⁵ You have made my life no longer than the width
   of my hand.
      My entire lifetime is just a moment to you;
         at best, each of us is but a breath."

Interlude

⁶ We are merely moving shadows,
      and all our busy rushing ends in nothing.
   We heap up wealth,
      not knowing who will spend it.
⁷ And so, Lord, where do I put my hope?
      My only hope is in you.
⁸ Rescue me from my rebellion.
      Do not let fools mock me.
⁹ I am silent before you; I won't say a word,
      for my punishment is from you.
¹⁰ But please stop striking me!
      I am exhausted by the blows from your hand.
¹¹ When you discipline us for our sins,
      you consume like a moth what is precious to us.
   Each of us is but a breath.

Interlude

¹² Hear my prayer, O LORD!
      Listen to my cries for help!
      Don't ignore my tears.
   For I am your guest—
      a traveler passing through,
      as my ancestors were before me.
¹³ Leave me alone so I can smile again
      before I am gone and exist no more.

Psalm 40

For the choir director: A psalm of David.

¹ I waited patiently for the LORD to help me,
      and he turned to me and heard my cry.
² He lifted me out of the pit of despair,
      out of the mud and the mire.
   He set my feet on solid ground
      and steadied me as I walked along.
³ He has given me a new song to sing,
      a hymn of praise to our God.
   Many will see what he has done and be amazed.
      They will put their trust in the LORD.

⁴ Oh, the joys of those who trust the LORD,
      who have no confidence in the proud
         or in those who worship idols.
⁵ O LORD my God, you have performed many
   wonders for us.
      Your plans for us are too numerous to list.
         You have no equal.
   If I tried to recite all your wonderful deeds,
      I would never come to the end of them.

⁶ You take no delight in sacrifices or offerings.
      Now that you have made me listen, I finally
         understand*—
      you don't require burnt offerings or sin
         offerings.
⁷ Then I said, "Look, I have come.
      As is written about me in the Scriptures:
⁸ I take joy in doing your will, my God,
      for your instructions are written on my heart."

⁹ I have told all your people about your justice.
      I have not been afraid to speak out,
         as you, O LORD, well know.
¹⁰ I have not kept the good news of your justice
      hidden in my heart;
   I have talked about your faithfulness and
      saving power.
   I have told everyone in the great assembly
      of your unfailing love and faithfulness.

¹¹ LORD, don't hold back your tender mercies
      from me.
   Let your unfailing love and faithfulness
      always protect me.
¹² For troubles surround me—
      too many to count!
   My sins pile up so high
      I can't see my way out.
   They outnumber the hairs on my head.
      I have lost all courage.
¹³ Please, LORD, rescue me!
      Come quickly, LORD, and help me.
¹⁴ May those who try to destroy me
      be humiliated and put to shame.
   May those who take delight in my trouble
      be turned back in disgrace.
¹⁵ Let them be horrified by their shame,
      for they said, "Aha! We've got him now!"

40:6 Greek version reads *You have given me a body.* Compare Heb 10:5.

39:12 "Guest" translates the Hebrew term *ger*, which refers to someone who lacked a kinship tie to the community. It is often translated as "stranger" or "foreigner." This lack of ties in a society structured around family relationships placed a person at risk when they encountered hardships. The psalmist expresses social isolation but clings to their relationship with God.
Psalm 40 This psalm includes a thanksgiving song (40:1-10) followed by a plea for help (40:11-17). The thanksgiving song includes the reason for the offered thanks (40:1-5), an affirmation of commitment (40:6-8), and a public testimony of God's character (40:7-10). The plea concerns the psalmist's troubles because of his sins (40:11-12) and is followed by two prayers for vindication (40:13-15, 17).
40:6 While some interpret "you don't require burnt offerings or sin offerings" as a condemnation of Israel's sacrificial system, that very system was given to Israel by God (Leviticus 1, 4–6). Considering this context, the petitioner more likely had presented the sacrifices necessary for coming into God's presence. Those sacrifices, though, were not a ritual requirement for the speaker to make the petition for deliverance found in this psalm.

16 But may all who search for you
    be filled with joy and gladness in you.
  May those who love your salvation
    repeatedly shout, "The LORD is great!"
17 As for me, since I am poor and needy,
    let the Lord keep me in his thoughts.
  You are my helper and my savior.
    O my God, do not delay.

Psalm 41
For the choir director: A psalm of David.

1 Oh, the joys of those who are kind to the poor!
    The LORD rescues them when they are in
      trouble.
2 The LORD protects them
    and keeps them alive.
  He gives them prosperity in the land
    and rescues them from their enemies.
3 The LORD nurses them when they are sick
    and restores them to health.
4 "O LORD," I prayed, "have mercy on me.
    Heal me, for I have sinned against you."
5 But my enemies say nothing but evil about me.
    "How soon will he die and be forgotten?"
      they ask.
6 They visit me as if they were my friends,
    but all the while they gather gossip,
    and when they leave, they spread it
      everywhere.
7 All who hate me whisper about me,
    imagining the worst.
8 "He has some fatal disease," they say.
    "He will never get out of that bed!"
9 Even my best friend, the one I trusted
      completely,
    the one who shared my food, has turned
      against me.
10 LORD, have mercy on me.
    Make me well again, so I can pay them back!

11 I know you are pleased with me,
    for you have not let my enemies triumph
      over me.
12 You have preserved my life because I am
      innocent;
    you have brought me into your presence
      forever.
13 Praise the LORD, the God of Israel,
    who lives from everlasting to everlasting.
  Amen and amen!

BOOK TWO (PSALMS 42–72)

Psalm 42
For the choir director: A psalm* of the descendants of Korah.

1 As the deer longs for streams of water,
    so I long for you, O God.
2 I thirst for God, the living God.
    When can I go and stand before him?
3 Day and night I have only tears for food,
    while my enemies continually taunt me,
      saying,
    "Where is this God of yours?"

4 My heart is breaking
    as I remember how it used to be:
  I walked among the crowds of worshipers,
    leading a great procession to the house
      of God,
  singing for joy and giving thanks
    amid the sound of a great celebration!

5 Why am I discouraged?
    Why is my heart so sad?
  I will put my hope in God!
    I will praise him again—
      my Savior and 6my God!

  Now I am deeply discouraged,
    but I will remember you—

42:TITLE Hebrew *maskil*. This may be a literary or musical term.

Psalm 41 In this psalm, which opens with a teaching tone, the psalmist prays for healing (41:4, 10), laments his distress (41:5-9), and expresses confidence in the Lord's blessing (41:1-3, 11-12).

41:13 This doxology, or praise hymn, closes the first book of the Psalms (Psalms 1–41). Similar doxologies appear at the end of the other four books (see 72:18-19; 89:52; 106:48; 150:6). These doxologies suggest that while the genres and content of the individual psalms may vary, the book as a whole should be read as a book of praise.

Book Two (Psalms 42–72) Book Two includes psalms by many authors; eighteen psalms of David (Psalms 51–65, 68–70), eight psalms of the descendants of Korah (Psalms 42, 44–49), one psalm ascribed to Asaph (Psalm 50), one to Solomon (Psalm 72), and several with no author credited.

Psalms 42–43 These psalms, like Psalms 9 and 10, form a unit comprising a lament with a bittersweet refrain of hope (42:5, 11; 43:5). In many Hebrew manuscripts these psalms are considered as one, which leads the majority of interpreters to assume this was originally a unified work. The historical context is uncertain; these psalms might be the voice of God's people in exile, confessing their loyalty to God as he punishes them for their prevailing apostasy. The psalmist longs for such fellowship with God as he enjoyed in Jerusalem (42:4); his memories only make him more discouraged. As the psalmist cries out to God, he recalls God's love and faithfulness (42:8), which moves him to plead for vindication (43:1-4).

42:1-4 The psalmist's longing for God comes from being far away from the Temple as he remembers the past. The verb translated "longs" is found only here and in Joel 1:20 ("cry out"); in both cases it refers to extreme thirst in a waterless desert (see Psalms 63:1; 143:6; see also 84:2).

even from distant Mount Hermon, the source of
 the Jordan,
  from the land of Mount Mizar.
⁷ I hear the tumult of the raging seas
  as your waves and surging tides sweep over
   me.
⁸ But each day the LORD pours his unfailing love
  upon me,
 and through each night I sing his songs,
  praying to God who gives me life.
⁹ "O God my rock," I cry,
  "why have you forgotten me?
 Why must I wander around in grief,
  oppressed by my enemies?"
¹⁰ Their taunts break my bones.
  They scoff, "Where is this God of yours?"
¹¹ Why am I discouraged?
  Why is my heart so sad?
 I will put my hope in God!
  I will praise him again—
   my Savior and my God!

Psalm 43

¹ Declare me innocent, O God!
  Defend me against these ungodly people.
  Rescue me from these unjust liars.
² For you are God, my only safe haven.
  Why have you tossed me aside?
 Why must I wander around in grief,
  oppressed by my enemies?
³ Send out your light and your truth;
  let them guide me.
 Let them lead me to your holy mountain,
  to the place where you live.
⁴ There I will go to the altar of God,
  to God—the source of all my joy.
 I will praise you with my harp,
  O God, my God!
⁵ Why am I discouraged?
  Why is my heart so sad?
 I will put my hope in God!
  I will praise him again—
   my Savior and my God!

42:8 While this verse at first may seem out of place amid the psalmist's lament, it can call us to an intentional practice of remembrance: recalling God's character and past faithfulness. In light of these, we can sing praise and seek him in prayer.
43:5 This verse is repeated in 42:5, 11. This repetition is why many read Psalms 42–43 as one unit.

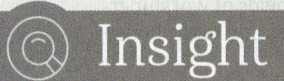

Insight — MOUNTAINS AND GOD

The Bible describes mountains as places of significance. They serve as spiritual meeting places (Exodus 19:3; Matthew 4:8; 17:1; 2 Peter 1:18) and uphold the current—and future—holy city of Jerusalem (Psalm 43:3; 48:1-2; 87:1; 99:9; Isaiah 11:9; Revelation 21:10).

One frequently mentioned mountain, Mount Hermon, stands at Israel's northern boundary (Deuteronomy 3:8; Joshua 11:17; 1 Chronicles 5:23), between Lebanon and Damascus. The mountain itself is about 13 miles long and rises to 9,232 feet. In biblical poetry, Mount Hermon signifies a faraway place (Psalm 42:6); it is praised for its stature, as a source of water (133:3), and for its wildlife (Song of Songs 4:8).

Psalm 44

For the choir director: A psalm* of the descendants of Korah.

1 O God, we have heard it with our own ears—
  our ancestors have told us
of all you did in their day,
  in days long ago:
2 You drove out the pagan nations by your power
  and gave all the land to our ancestors.
You crushed their enemies
  and set our ancestors free.
3 They did not conquer the land with their swords;
  it was not their own strong arm that gave them victory.
It was your right hand and strong arm
  and the blinding light from your face that helped them,
  for you loved them.

4 You are my King and my God.
  You command victories for Israel.*
5 Only by your power can we push back our enemies;
  only in your name can we trample our foes.
6 I do not trust in my bow;
  I do not count on my sword to save me.
7 You are the one who gives us victory over our enemies;
  you disgrace those who hate us.
8 O God, we give glory to you all day long
  and constantly praise your name.   *Interlude*

9 But now you have tossed us aside in dishonor.
  You no longer lead our armies to battle.
10 You make us retreat from our enemies
  and allow those who hate us to plunder our land.
11 You have butchered us like sheep
  and scattered us among the nations.
12 You sold your precious people for a pittance,
  making nothing on the sale.
13 You let our neighbors mock us.
  We are an object of scorn and derision to those around us.
14 You have made us the butt of their jokes;
  they shake their heads at us in scorn.

15 We can't escape the constant humiliation;
  shame is written across our faces.
16 All we hear are the taunts of our mockers.
  All we see are our vengeful enemies.

17 All this has happened though we have not forgotten you.
  We have not violated your covenant.
18 Our hearts have not deserted you.
  We have not strayed from your path.
19 Yet you have crushed us in the jackal's desert home.
  You have covered us with darkness and death.
20 If we had forgotten the name of our God
  or spread our hands in prayer to foreign gods,
21 God would surely have known it,
  for he knows the secrets of every heart.
22 But for your sake we are killed every day;
  we are being slaughtered like sheep.

23 Wake up, O Lord! Why do you sleep?
  Get up! Do not reject us forever.
24 Why do you look the other way?
  Why do you ignore our suffering and oppression?
25 We collapse in the dust,
  lying face down in the dirt.
26 Rise up! Help us!
  Ransom us because of your unfailing love.

Psalm 45

For the choir director: A love song to be sung to the tune "Lilies." A psalm* of the descendants of Korah.

1 Beautiful words stir my heart.
  I will recite a lovely poem about the king,
  for my tongue is like the pen of a skillful poet.

2 You are the most handsome of all.
  Gracious words stream from your lips.
  God himself has blessed you forever.
3 Put on your sword, O mighty warrior!
  You are so glorious, so majestic!
4 In your majesty, ride out to victory,
  defending truth, humility, and justice.
  Go forth to perform awe-inspiring deeds!
5 Your arrows are sharp, piercing your enemies' hearts.
  The nations fall beneath your feet.

44:TITLE Hebrew *maskil*. This may be a literary or musical term. 44:4 Hebrew *for Jacob*. The names "Jacob" and "Israel" are often interchanged throughout the Old Testament, referring sometimes to the individual patriarch and sometimes to the nation. 45:TITLE Hebrew *maskil*. This may be a literary or musical term.

Psalm 44 This communal lament continues the tone of the previous two psalms, including reflecting on an unspecified moment in Israel's history and calling on God for salvation. The voicing alternates between a leader and the people. They recite God's past acts of rescue (44:1-3), acknowledge God's power to save (44:4-8), describe their humiliation in exile (44:9-16), claim their innocence and lament the injustice of their current situation (44:17-22), and cry for vindication (44:23-26).

44:4 The names "Jacob" and "Israel" are often interchanged throughout the Old Testament, referring sometimes to the individual patriarch and sometimes to the nation.
Psalm 45 This psalm celebrates a royal wedding; it might have been sung on many occasions and not just at one wedding. As God's representative, the king carried the responsibility of dispensing justice and maintaining order in God's world (see Psalm 2).

⁶ Your throne, O God,* endures forever and ever.
  You rule with a scepter of justice.
⁷ You love justice and hate evil.
  Therefore God, your God, has anointed you,
    pouring out the oil of joy on you more than on
      anyone else.
⁸ Myrrh, aloes, and cassia perfume your robes.
  In ivory palaces the music of strings
    entertains you.
⁹ Kings' daughters are among your noble women.
  At your right side stands the queen,
    wearing jewelry of finest gold from Ophir!

¹⁰ Listen to me, O royal daughter; take to heart
     what I say.
   Forget your people and your family far away.
¹¹ For your royal husband delights in your beauty;
     honor him, for he is your lord.
¹² The princess of Tyre* will shower you with gifts.
     The wealthy will beg your favor.
¹³ The bride, a princess, looks glorious
     in her golden gown.
¹⁴ In her beautiful robes, she is led to the king,
     accompanied by her bridesmaids.
¹⁵ What a joyful and enthusiastic procession
     as they enter the king's palace!

¹⁶ Your sons will become kings like their father.
   You will make them rulers over many lands.
¹⁷ I will bring honor to your name in every generation.
   Therefore, the nations will praise you forever
     and ever.

Psalm 46
*For the choir director: A song of the descendants of Korah, to be sung by soprano voices.**

¹ God is our refuge and strength,
    always ready to help in times of trouble.
² So we will not fear when earthquakes come
    and the mountains crumble into the sea.
³ Let the oceans roar and foam.
    Let the mountains tremble as the waters
      surge!   *Interlude*

⁴ A river brings joy to the city of our God,
    the sacred home of the Most High.
⁵ God dwells in that city; it cannot be destroyed.
    From the very break of day, God will
      protect it.
⁶ The nations are in chaos,
    and their kingdoms crumble!
  God's voice thunders,
    and the earth melts!
⁷ The LORD of Heaven's Armies is here among us;
    the God of Israel* is our fortress.   *Interlude*

⁸ Come, see the glorious works of the LORD:
    See how he brings destruction upon the
      world.
⁹ He causes wars to end throughout the earth.
    He breaks the bow and snaps the spear;
      he burns the shields with fire.

¹⁰ "Be still, and know that I am God!
     I will be honored by every nation.
     I will be honored throughout the world."

¹¹ The LORD of Heaven's Armies is here among us;
     the God of Israel is our fortress.   *Interlude*

Psalm 47
For the choir director: A psalm of the descendants of Korah.

¹ Come, everyone! Clap your hands!
    Shout to God with joyful praise!
² For the LORD Most High is awesome.
    He is the great King of all the earth.
³ He subdues the nations before us,
    putting our enemies beneath our feet.
⁴ He chose the Promised Land as our inheritance,
    the proud possession of Jacob's descendants,
      whom he loves.   *Interlude*

⁵ God has ascended with a mighty shout.
    The LORD has ascended with trumpets blaring.
⁶ Sing praises to God, sing praises;
    sing praises to our King, sing praises!

45:6 Or *Your divine throne.* **45:12** Hebrew *The daughter of Tyre.* **46:TITLE** Hebrew *according to alamoth.* **46:7** Hebrew *of Jacob;* also in 46:11. See note on 44:4.

45:6-7 "Your throne" can also be translated as "your divine throne." As translated here, the people of Israel may have thought the king represented God since God had anointed him. As a divine representative, the king dispensed justice. The writer to the Hebrews applies these verses to Jesus as he argues that the Son is greater than the angels (Hebrews 1:8-9).
45:9 Marriages often sealed diplomatic connections between ancient kings, and the women traded in these transactions became part of the royal harem. The law of Moses banned this practice, but the kings of Israel did it anyway—not without consequences. The spiritual and political fallout for Israel was disastrous (see 1 Kings 11:4-13; 12:4, 16; 2 Kings 17:5-23; 25:1-23).
Psalm 46 This psalm of Zion celebrates God's special presence in Jerusalem (see also Psalms 48, 76, 87, 122), inviting confidence in the Lord because the citizens of Zion enjoy his protection.

46:5 In the ancient Near East, people believed that as long as the cult image of a deity remained in their temple, a city would be safe from attack. This belief is attested in ancient inscriptions and letters, and appears here and serves as the foundation for false assurance in Jeremiah's day (see Jeremiah 7:3-11). While the belief in God's presence was true, he was unwilling to stay in his Temple because of the people's sin. Ezekiel 10 records the departure of the Lord's glory before the fall of Jerusalem to the Babylonians in 586 BC.
Psalm 47 This psalm celebrates God's kingship over all the earth; it tells of God's victory in dealing with Israel and the nations. Both Israel (47:3-4) and the nations (47:9) participate in God's Kingdom.
47:5 Likely, the reference to God ascending described the Ark of the Covenant's return to the Temple after a military victory. First Chronicles 28:2 describes the Ark as the footstool of God's throne.

⁷ For God is the King over all the earth.
　　Praise him with a psalm.*
⁸ God reigns above the nations,
　　sitting on his holy throne.
⁹ The rulers of the world have gathered together
　　with the people of the God of Abraham.
　For all the kings of the earth belong to God.
　　He is highly honored everywhere.

Psalm 48

A song. A psalm of the descendants of Korah.

¹ How great is the LORD,
　　how deserving of praise,
　in the city of our God,
　　which sits on his holy mountain!
² It is high and magnificent;
　　the whole earth rejoices to see it!
　Mount Zion, the holy mountain,*
　　is the city of the great King!
³ God himself is in Jerusalem's towers,
　　revealing himself as its defender.
⁴ The kings of the earth joined forces
　　and advanced against the city.
⁵ But when they saw it, they were stunned;
　　they were terrified and ran away.
⁶ They were gripped with terror
　　and writhed in pain like a woman in labor.
⁷ You destroyed them like the mighty ships of Tarshish
　　shattered by a powerful east wind.
⁸ We had heard of the city's glory,
　　but now we have seen it ourselves—
　　the city of the LORD of Heaven's Armies.
　It is the city of our God;
　　he will make it safe forever.　　*Interlude*
⁹ O God, we meditate on your unfailing love
　　as we worship in your Temple.
¹⁰ As your name deserves, O God,
　　you will be praised to the ends of the earth.
　Your strong right hand is filled with victory.
¹¹ Let the people on Mount Zion rejoice.
　　Let all the towns of Judah be glad
　　because of your justice.
¹² Go, inspect the city of Jerusalem.*
　　Walk around and count the many towers.

> "My strength returns to me with my cup of coffee and the reading of the psalms."
>
> **DOROTHY DAY**
> (1897–1980) journalist and Christian activist

¹³ Take note of the fortified walls,
　　and tour all the citadels,
　that you may describe them
　　to future generations.
¹⁴ For that is what God is like.
　　He is our God forever and ever,
　　and he will guide us until we die.

Psalm 49

For the choir director: A psalm of the descendants of Korah.

¹ Listen to this, all you people!
　　Pay attention, everyone in the world!
² High and low,
　　rich and poor—listen!
³ For my words are wise,
　　and my thoughts are filled with insight.
⁴ I listen carefully to many proverbs
　　and solve riddles with inspiration from a harp.
⁵ Why should I fear when trouble comes,
　　when enemies surround me?
⁶ They trust in their wealth
　　and boast of great riches.

47:7 Hebrew *maskil*. This may be a literary or musical term.　48:2 Or *Mount Zion, in the far north*; Hebrew reads *Mount Zion, the heights of Zaphon*.　48:12 Hebrew *Zion*.

47:7 People from "all the earth" (see 96:1-3) will worship God. While many psalms focus on God's special relationship with Israel, here we see a glimpse of the universal reign of God that is described in the New Testament.
Psalm 48 This song of Zion (see also Psalms 46, 76, 87, 122) explicitly views Jerusalem (Zion) as the city of the great King where the godly find protection (48:1-3). God rules from Zion in faithfulness, righteousness, and justice, and he inspires his subjects with confidence and joy (48:9-11). They themselves have seen the glory of Zion, and they commit to tell the next generation about it (48:8, 12-14).
Psalm 49 In this wisdom psalm, a wise teacher warns against enemies, whom he portrays as living a rich lifestyle and caring only for themselves (49:5-9). They cannot keep anyone alive, least of all themselves, even in their memories (49:10-12). Like fattened animals, they are led to slaughter (49:14-20).

⁷ Yet they cannot redeem themselves from death*
  by paying a ransom to God.
⁸ Redemption does not come so easily,
  for no one can ever pay enough
⁹ to live forever
  and never see the grave.
¹⁰ Those who are wise must finally die,
  just like the foolish and senseless,
  leaving all their wealth behind.
¹¹ The grave* is their eternal home,
  where they will stay forever.
  They may name their estates after themselves,
¹² but their fame will not last.
  They will die, just like animals.
¹³ This is the fate of fools,
  though they are remembered as being wise.*
                                        Interlude
¹⁴ Like sheep, they are led to the grave,*
  where death will be their shepherd.
  In the morning the godly will rule over them.
  Their bodies will rot in the grave,
  far from their grand estates.
¹⁵ But as for me, God will redeem my life.
  He will snatch me from the power of the
    grave.   Interlude
¹⁶ So don't be dismayed when the wicked grow rich
  and their homes become ever more splendid.
¹⁷ For when they die, they take nothing with them.
  Their wealth will not follow them into the
    grave.
¹⁸ In this life they consider themselves fortunate
  and are applauded for their success.
¹⁹ But they will die like all before them
  and never again see the light of day.
²⁰ People who boast of their wealth don't
    understand;
  they will die, just like animals.

Psalm 50

A psalm of Asaph.

¹ The LORD, the Mighty One, is God,
  and he has spoken;
  he has summoned all humanity
  from where the sun rises to where it sets.
² From Mount Zion, the perfection of beauty,
  God shines in glorious radiance.
³ Our God approaches,
  and he is not silent.
  Fire devours everything in his way,
  and a great storm rages around him.
⁴ He calls on the heavens above and earth below
  to witness the judgment of his people.
⁵ "Bring my faithful people to me—
  those who made a covenant with me by
    giving sacrifices."
⁶ Then let the heavens proclaim his justice,
  for God himself will be the judge.   Interlude

⁷ "O my people, listen as I speak.
  Here are my charges against you, O Israel:
  I am God, your God!
⁸ I have no complaint about your sacrifices
  or the burnt offerings you constantly offer.
⁹ But I do not need the bulls from your barns
  or the goats from your pens.
¹⁰ For all the animals of the forest are mine,
  and I own the cattle on a thousand hills.
¹¹ I know every bird on the mountains,
  and all the animals of the field are mine.
¹² If I were hungry, I would not tell you,
  for all the world is mine and everything in it.
¹³ Do I eat the meat of bulls?
  Do I drink the blood of goats?
¹⁴ Make thankfulness your sacrifice to God,
  and keep the vows you made to the
    Most High.
¹⁵ Then call on me when you are in trouble,
  and I will rescue you,
  and you will give me glory."

¹⁶ But God says to the wicked:
  "Why bother reciting my decrees
  and pretending to obey my covenant?
¹⁷ For you refuse my discipline
  and treat my words like trash.
¹⁸ When you see thieves, you approve of them,
  and you spend your time with adulterers.
¹⁹ Your mouth is filled with wickedness,
  and your tongue is full of lies.
²⁰ You sit around and slander your brother—
  your own mother's son.
²¹ While you did all this, I remained silent,
  and you thought I didn't care.
  But now I will rebuke you,
  listing all my charges against you.

49:7 Some Hebrew manuscripts read *no one can redeem the life of another.* **49:11** As in Greek and Syriac versions; Hebrew reads *Their inward [thought].* **49:13** The meaning of the Hebrew is uncertain. **49:14** Hebrew *Sheol;* also in 49:14b, 15.

49:15 Bible interpreters debate how to understand this verse. While some describe it as the arrogant expectation of the rich (see 49:20), others believe it refers to life after death. This latter interpretation is likely, reflecting the psalmist's hope that life with God would extend eternally, such as the continuation of life that Enoch (Genesis 5:24) and Elijah (2 Kings 2:3, 5) received. **Psalm 50** God appears as judge to remind the godly and the ungodly in turn that outward performance of sacrifices and offerings and knowing the law are worthless without thankfulness, repentance, and justice.

50:8-14 These verses point to the true reason for bringing sacrifices and burnt offerings: They were an expression of obedient thanks to the people's covenant God. This reason contrasts with the surrounding nations' perspective that offerings provided necessary food for the gods in order to please or placate them.

22 Repent, all of you who forget me,
   or I will tear you apart,
   and no one will help you.
23 But giving thanks is a sacrifice that truly honors me.
   If you keep to my path,
   I will reveal to you the salvation of God."

Psalm 51

For the choir director: A psalm of David, regarding the time Nathan the prophet came to him after David had committed adultery with Bathsheba.

1 Have mercy on me, O God,
   because of your unfailing love.
   Because of your great compassion,
   blot out the stain of my sins.
2 Wash me clean from my guilt.
   Purify me from my sin.
3 For I recognize my rebellion;
   it haunts me day and night.
4 Against you, and you alone, have I sinned;
   I have done what is evil in your sight.
   You will be proved right in what you say,
   and your judgment against me is just.*
5 For I was born a sinner—
   yes, from the moment my mother conceived me.
6 But you desire honesty from the womb,*
   teaching me wisdom even there.
7 Purify me from my sins,* and I will be clean;
   wash me, and I will be whiter than snow.
8 Oh, give me back my joy again;
   you have broken me—
   now let me rejoice.
9 Don't keep looking at my sins.
   Remove the stain of my guilt.
10 Create in me a clean heart, O God.
   Renew a loyal spirit within me.
11 Do not banish me from your presence,
   and don't take your Holy Spirit* from me.
12 Restore to me the joy of your salvation,
   and make me willing to obey you.
13 Then I will teach your ways to rebels,
   and they will return to you.
14 Forgive me for shedding blood, O God who saves;
   then I will joyfully sing of your forgiveness.
15 Unseal my lips, O Lord,
   that my mouth may praise you.
16 You do not desire a sacrifice, or I would offer one.
   You do not want a burnt offering.
17 The sacrifice you desire is a broken spirit.
   You will not reject a broken and repentant heart, O God.
18 Look with favor on Zion and help her;
   rebuild the walls of Jerusalem.
19 Then you will be pleased with sacrifices offered in the right spirit—
   with burnt offerings and whole burnt offerings.
   Then bulls will again be sacrificed on your altar.

Psalm 52

For the choir director: A psalm of David, regarding the time Doeg the Edomite said to Saul, "David has gone to see Ahimelech."*

1 Why do you boast about your crimes, great warrior?
   Don't you realize God's justice continues forever?
2 All day long you plot destruction.
   Your tongue cuts like a sharp razor;
   you're an expert at telling lies.
3 You love evil more than good
   and lies more than truth.   *Interlude*
4 You love to destroy others with your words, you liar!
5 But God will strike you down once and for all.
   He will pull you from your home
   and uproot you from the land of the living.   *Interlude*

51:4 Greek version reads *and you will win your case in court.* Compare Rom 3:4. **51:6** Or *from the heart;* Hebrew reads *in the inward parts.* **51:7** Hebrew *Purify me with the hyssop branch.* **51:11** Or *your spirit of holiness.* **52:TITLE** Hebrew *maskil.* This may be a literary or musical term.

Psalm 51 This moving prayer for restoration asks for God's favor, mercy, forgiveness, and cleansing. Out of a broken spirit, David confesses and accepts responsibility for his sin (51:3-6), then petitions God to remove his guilt and renew him inwardly (51:7-12). He then recommits himself to a lifestyle of wisdom, joy, and a humble spirit in the service of God and others (51:13-17).
51:Title The Hebrew words here do not say David "committed adultery with Bathsheba," which could imply her consent. Rather, it describes David having "gone in to Bathsheba." The Hebrew focuses on David's guilt alone. Given the power difference between a king and his subjects, the cultural context and the Bible's wording support the idea that Bathsheba had no say. See study notes on 2 Samuel 11:1-27; 11:2-4; 11:27.
51:6 The Hebrew reads "in the inward parts." While it is rendered "from the womb" here, a better translation is "from the heart."
51:16 While some argue this verse reflects an overall rejection of the need for sacrifices, it may be that the sin was a "brazen violation" (Numbers 15:30) for which no sacrifice was possible. Notably, the Mosaic law did not provide any instructions for sacrifices that would cover the sins of rape or murder. Considering the title (the text introducing the psalm), which ties this psalm to David's sin against Bathsheba and her husband, it's likely that God had not provided a sacrifice to atone for this speaker's sin.
Psalm 52 Wicked people use words to destroy relationships and communities. They foolishly think that they can be heroes by their words (52:1-4), but their fate suddenly overtakes them (52:5-7). In contrast, the godly renew their commitment to the Lord (52:8-9) and find their future secure in him.

6 The righteous will see it and be amazed.
They will laugh and say,
7 "Look what happens to mighty warriors
who do not trust in God.
They trust their wealth instead
and grow more and more bold in their
wickedness."
8 But I am like an olive tree, thriving in the house
of God.
I will always trust in God's unfailing love.
9 I will praise you forever, O God,
for what you have done.
I will trust in your good name
in the presence of your faithful people.

Psalm 53
For the choir director: A meditation; a psalm* of David.

1 Only fools say in their hearts,
"There is no God."
They are corrupt, and their actions are evil;
not one of them does good!

2 God looks down from heaven
on the entire human race;
he looks to see if anyone is truly wise,
if anyone seeks God.

3 But no, all have turned away;
all have become corrupt.*
No one does good,
not a single one!

53:TITLE Hebrew *According to mahalath; a maskil.* These may be literary or musical terms. 53:3 Greek version reads *have become useless.* Compare Rom 3:12.

Psalm 53 This psalm parallels Psalm 14, except Psalm 53 does not use the divine name (LORD) and 53:5 and 14:5 differ in content.

Come Close

CAUGHT: COME CLEAN

SCRIPTURE CONNECTION: PSALM 51

After watching a science show, I wanted to see what would happen if I dripped red food coloring on a piece of paper. I was watching the red spread so intently that I didn't notice it dripping through the paper ... onto my bright pink bedroom carpet.

Nothing I did could lighten that crimson splotch. It could be seen by all, including my parents. For years, even after we moved out of that house, it sickened me to think of that stain.

We sometimes do that with our failures, too. The sharp pain of regret, the nausea of shame, and the unrelenting embarrassment linger longer than the consequences. These intense feelings keep us from knowing how to come clean.

David wasn't perfect, but he did unearth his sins before God. Notice that he never said, "Just tell me what to do to make this right!" Instead, he acknowledged that only God could wash away the red splotch of sin (51:7). David understood that he could never undo what he had done. What he could do was repent, ask God to wash him clean (51:2), and start to obey (51:12).

REFLECT "Create in me a clean heart, O God. Renew a loyal spirit within me." PSALM 51:10

Only you, Father, can clean me up when I've been caught. Don't let my feelings stop me from coming to you for the powerful cleaning that only you can do.

CONSIDER "She who turns back soonest is the most progressive. She who repents most makes the most progress—you always go farther traveling light. She who repents of seemingly little sins knows that all sins are great—and knows a greater God. Repentance is as much air to a Christ-follower as faith." ANN VOSKAMP, *The Greatest Gift*

God, only you can clean sin's splotches for good.

CARA DAY is a writer and illustrator. She has served with Stonecroft Ministries helping women live "extraordinary."

⁴ Will those who do evil never learn?
   They eat up my people like bread
   and wouldn't think of praying to God.
⁵ Terror will grip them,
   terror like they have never known before.
   God will scatter the bones of your enemies.
   You will put them to shame, for God has
     rejected them.
⁶ Who will come from Mount Zion to rescue
     Israel?
   When God restores his people,
   Jacob will shout with joy, and Israel will rejoice.

Psalm 54

For the choir director: A psalm* of David, regarding the time the Ziphites came and said to Saul, "We know where David is hiding." To be accompanied by stringed instruments.

¹ Come with great power, O God, and rescue me!
   Defend me with your might.
² Listen to my prayer, O God.
   Pay attention to my plea.
³ For strangers are attacking me;
   violent people are trying to kill me.
   They care nothing for God.   *Interlude*
⁴ But God is my helper.
   The Lord keeps me alive!
⁵ May the evil plans of my enemies be turned
     against them.
   Do as you promised and put an end to them.
⁶ I will sacrifice a voluntary offering to you;
   I will praise your name, O LORD,
     for it is good.
⁷ For you have rescued me from my troubles
   and helped me to triumph over my enemies.

Psalm 55

For the choir director: A psalm* of David, to be accompanied by stringed instruments.

¹ Listen to my prayer, O God.
   Do not ignore my cry for help!
² Please listen and answer me,
   for I am overwhelmed by my troubles.

³ My enemies shout at me,
   making loud and wicked threats.
   They bring trouble on me
   and angrily hunt me down.
⁴ My heart pounds in my chest.
   The terror of death assaults me.
⁵ Fear and trembling overwhelm me,
   and I can't stop shaking.
⁶ Oh, that I had wings like a dove;
   then I would fly away and rest!
⁷ I would fly far away
   to the quiet of the wilderness.   *Interlude*
⁸ How quickly I would escape—
   far from this wild storm of hatred.
⁹ Confuse them, Lord, and frustrate their plans,
   for I see violence and conflict in the city.
¹⁰ Its walls are patrolled day and night against
     invaders,
    but the real danger is wickedness within
     the city.
¹¹ Everything is falling apart;
    threats and cheating are rampant in the
     streets.
¹² It is not an enemy who taunts me—
    I could bear that.
    It is not my foes who so arrogantly insult me—
    I could have hidden from them.
¹³ Instead, it is you—my equal,
    my companion and close friend.
¹⁴ What good fellowship we once enjoyed
    as we walked together to the house of God.
¹⁵ Let death stalk my enemies;
    let the grave* swallow them alive,
    for evil makes its home within them.
¹⁶ But I will call on God,
    and the LORD will rescue me.
¹⁷ Morning, noon, and night
    I cry out in my distress,
    and the LORD hears my voice.
¹⁸ He ransoms me and keeps me safe
    from the battle waged against me,
    though many still oppose me.

54:TITLE Hebrew *maskil*. This may be a literary or musical term.   55:TITLE Hebrew *maskil*. This may be a literary or musical term.   55:15 Hebrew *let Sheol*.

Psalm 54 In this individual lament, occasioned by violent and godless people (54:3), the psalmist turns to God in prayer and maintains his focus on God's help (54:4). He prays for God to save him from evil and to judge his enemies (54:5, 7).

Psalm 55 The psalmist is overwhelmed with anguish, faced with adversaries and the betrayal of a former friend (55:12-14). He turns to the Lord in prayer and commits himself to the Lord for justice (55:22-23).

55:12-21 The focus shifts from a group of enemies to a single enemy who was once a friend; memories of that close relationship bring the psalm writer pain (see 31:11).

55:17 Anyone who has spent time with children knows the difference between "hearing" what we have said and "listening" to it. When that child "listens," they follow our instructions. In the ancient world, the idea of God hearing the psalmist's cry meant that God would act on it, not just that he heard the petition. We can take comfort in knowing that "the LORD hears" and responds to our prayers. He will act out of his faithful love. That doesn't mean he will give us what we ask for, but it does mean that he will act in a way that reflects his love and justice as he works in our lives and the world around us.

PSALM 56

¹⁹ God, who has ruled forever,
   will hear me and humble them. *Interlude*
For my enemies refuse to change their ways;
   they do not fear God.

²⁰ As for my companion, he betrayed his friends;
   he broke his promises.
²¹ His words are as smooth as butter,
   but in his heart is war.
His words are as soothing as lotion,
   but underneath are daggers!

²² Give your burdens to the LORD,
   and he will take care of you.
He will not permit the godly to slip and fall.

²³ But you, O God, will send the wicked
   down to the pit of destruction.
Murderers and liars will die young,
   but I am trusting you to save me.

Psalm 56

For the choir director: A psalm* of David, regarding the time the Philistines seized him in Gath. To be sung to the tune "Dove on Distant Oaks."

¹ O God, have mercy on me,
   for people are hounding me.
My foes attack me all day long.
² I am constantly hounded by those who slander me,
   and many are boldly attacking me.
³ But when I am afraid,
   I will put my trust in you.
⁴ I praise God for what he has promised.
   I trust in God, so why should I be afraid?
   What can mere mortals do to me?

⁵ They are always twisting what I say;
   they spend their days plotting to harm me.
⁶ They come together to spy on me—
   watching my every step, eager to kill me.
⁷ Don't let them get away with their wickedness;
   in your anger, O God, bring them down.

⁸ You keep track of all my sorrows.*
   You have collected all my tears in your bottle.
   You have recorded each one in your book.

⁹ My enemies will retreat when I call to you for help.
   This I know: God is on my side!
¹⁰ I praise God for what he has promised;
   yes, I praise the LORD for what he has promised.
¹¹ I trust in God, so why should I be afraid?
   What can mere mortals do to me?

¹² I will fulfill my vows to you, O God,
   and will offer a sacrifice of thanks for your help.
¹³ For you have rescued me from death;
   you have kept my feet from slipping.
So now I can walk in your presence, O God,
   in your life-giving light.

Psalm 57

For the choir director: A psalm* of David, regarding the time he fled from Saul and went into the cave. To be sung to the tune "Do Not Destroy!"

¹ Have mercy on me, O God, have mercy!
   I look to you for protection.
I will hide beneath the shadow of your wings
   until the danger passes by.
² I cry out to God Most High,*
   to God who will fulfill his purpose for me.
³ He will send help from heaven to rescue me,
   disgracing those who hound me. *Interlude*
My God will send forth his unfailing love and
   faithfulness.

⁴ I am surrounded by fierce lions
   who greedily devour human prey—
whose teeth pierce like spears and arrows,
   and whose tongues cut like swords.

⁵ Be exalted, O God, above the highest heavens!
   May your glory shine over all the earth.

⁶ My enemies have set a trap for me.
   I am weary from distress.
They have dug a deep pit in my path,
   but they themselves have fallen into it. *Interlude*

⁷ My heart is confident in you, O God;
   my heart is confident.
No wonder I can sing your praises!
⁸ Wake up, my heart!
Wake up, O lyre and harp!
   I will wake the dawn with my song.

⁹ I will thank you, Lord, among all the people.
   I will sing your praises among the nations.
¹⁰ For your unfailing love is as high as the heavens.
   Your faithfulness reaches to the clouds.

56:TITLE Hebrew *miktam*. This may be a literary or musical term. **56:8** Or *my wanderings*. **57:TITLE** Hebrew *miktam*. This may be a literary or musical term. **57:2** Hebrew *Elohim-Elyon*.

Psalm 56 This individual lament moves from petition to confidence two times (56:1-4, 5-13), focusing more on the psalmist's trust in God than on the problem.
Psalm 57 The psalmist's cry for mercy and protection quickly turns into an affirmation of trust and confidence in the Lord (57:1-4). When the wicked fall into their own traps (57:6), the psalmist will praise the Lord (57:7-10).

57:1 Ancient Near Eastern art and literature portrayed the gods as protecting individuals, particularly kings, under their wings, drawing on the image of a mother bird's protective wings. Alternatively, for the Israelites, the wings may refer to the extended wings of the cherubim found on the Ark of the Covenant and in the Temple (1 Kings 6:23-28). Either way, the shadow of God's wings is a place of protection from enemies and adversity (see Psalms 17:8; 36:7; 61:4; 63:7; 91:4).

¹¹ Be exalted, O God, above the highest heavens.
   May your glory shine over all the earth.

Psalm 58

For the choir director: A psalm* of David, to be sung to the tune "Do Not Destroy!"

¹ Justice—do you rulers* know the meaning of the word?
   Do you judge the people fairly?
² No! You plot injustice in your hearts.
   You spread violence throughout the land.
³ These wicked people are born sinners;
   even from birth they have lied and gone their own way.
⁴ They spit venom like deadly snakes;
   they are like cobras that refuse to listen,
⁵ ignoring the tunes of the snake charmers,
   no matter how skillfully they play.
⁶ Break off their fangs, O God!
   Smash the jaws of these lions, O Lord!
⁷ May they disappear like water into thirsty ground.
   Make their weapons useless in their hands.*
⁸ May they be like snails that dissolve into slime,
   like a stillborn child who will never see the sun.
⁹ God will sweep them away, both young and old,
   faster than a pot heats over burning thorns.
¹⁰ The godly will rejoice when they see injustice avenged.
   They will wash their feet in the blood of the wicked.
¹¹ Then at last everyone will say,
   "There truly is a reward for those who live for God;
   surely there is a God who judges justly here on earth."

Psalm 59

For the choir director: A psalm* of David, regarding the time Saul sent soldiers to watch David's house in order to kill him. To be sung to the tune "Do Not Destroy!"

¹ Rescue me from my enemies, O God.
   Protect me from those who have come to destroy me.
² Rescue me from these criminals;
   save me from these murderers.
³ They have set an ambush for me.
   Fierce enemies are out there waiting, Lord,
   though I have not sinned or offended them.
⁴ I have done nothing wrong,
   yet they prepare to attack me.
   Wake up! See what is happening and help me!
⁵ O Lord God of Heaven's Armies, the God of Israel,
   wake up and punish those hostile nations.
   Show no mercy to wicked traitors.
   Interlude
⁶ They come out at night,
   snarling like vicious dogs
   as they prowl the streets.
⁷ Listen to the filth that comes from their mouths;
   their words cut like swords.
   "After all, who can hear us?" they sneer.
⁸ But Lord, you laugh at them.
   You scoff at all the hostile nations.
⁹ You are my strength; I wait for you to rescue me,
   for you, O God, are my fortress.
¹⁰ In his unfailing love, my God will stand with me.
   He will let me look down in triumph on all my enemies.
¹¹ Don't kill them, for my people soon forget such lessons;
   stagger them with your power, and bring them to their knees,
   O Lord our shield.
¹² Because of the sinful things they say,
   because of the evil that is on their lips,
   let them be captured by their pride,
   their curses, and their lies.
¹³ Destroy them in your anger!
   Wipe them out completely!
   Then the whole world will know
   that God reigns in Israel.*
   Interlude
¹⁴ My enemies come out at night,
   snarling like vicious dogs
   as they prowl the streets.
¹⁵ They scavenge for food
   but go to sleep unsatisfied.*

58:title Hebrew *miktam*. This may be a literary or musical term. **58:1** Or *you gods*. **58:7** Or *Let them be trodden down and wither like grass. The meaning of the Hebrew is uncertain.* **59:title** Hebrew *miktam*. This may be a literary or musical term. **59:13** Hebrew *in Jacob.* See note on 44:4. **59:15** Or *and growl if they don't get enough.*

Psalm 58 The administration of justice is a mark of good government. God expects nothing less from his people. The psalmist condemns Israel's leaders for abusing their power, and he calls on the Lord to rain down his curses upon the wicked. The demonstration of divine justice will reassure the godly that God is just.

58:1 "Rulers" was a designation used for high officials and administrators of justice. Elsewhere, it might refer to angelic creatures (89:7) or to the gods of the nations (82:1; Daniel 11:36).

58:10 The image of bathing one's feet in the blood of their enemies is graphic and intensely disturbing. However, it is subdued compared to some imagery found in other surrounding cultures of that time. It is important to note that the blood resulted from God's just, avenging action rather than from vengeance taken by people. God's justice can always be trusted; our desire for vengeance can't.

Psalm 59 The psalmist laments the power of enemies who conspire with other nations.

59:11, 13 While these prayers seem contradictory, we need to focus on the motive. In 59:11, the psalmist wants his community to learn that sin and evil will be punished. In 59:13, the psalmist wants the nations to know that "God reigns in Israel."

WHAT THE BIBLE SAYS ABOUT Our Feelings

Let Our Feelings Inform—Not Control—Us

Guard your heart above all else,
 for it determines the course of your life.
PROVERBS 4:23

Avoiding a fight is a mark of honor;
 only fools insist on quarreling.
PROVERBS 20:3

Don't sin by letting anger control you.
 Think about it overnight and remain silent.
PSALM 4:4

Even if we feel guilty, God is greater than our feelings, and he knows everything. **1 JOHN 3:20**

Feelings Welcome

Then Jesus wept. **JOHN 11:35**

"Don't think I am a wicked woman! For I have been praying out of great anguish and sorrow." **1 SAMUEL 1:16**

A cheerful look brings joy to the heart;
 good news makes for good health.
PROVERBS 15:30

I will be glad and rejoice in your unfailing love,
 for you have seen my troubles,
 and you care about the anguish of my soul.
PSALM 31:7

Sorrow is better than laughter,
 for sadness has a refining influence on us.
ECCLESIASTES 7:3

Be happy with those who are happy, and weep with those who weep. **ROMANS 12:15**

And Moses told them, "It is the food the LORD has given you to eat. ¹⁶These are the LORD's instructions: Each household should gather as much as it needs. Pick up two quarts* for each person in your tent."

¹⁷So the people of Israel did as they were told. Some gathered a lot, some only a little. ¹⁸But when they measured it out,* everyone had just enough. Those who gathered a lot had nothing left over, and those who gathered only a little had enough. Each family had just what it needed.

¹⁹Then Moses told them, "Do not keep any of it until morning." ²⁰But some of them didn't listen and kept some of it until morning. But by then it was full of maggots and had a terrible smell. Moses was very angry with them.

²¹After this the people gathered the food morning by morning, each family according to its need. And as the sun became hot, the flakes they had not picked up melted and disappeared. ²²On the sixth day, they gathered twice as much as usual—four quarts* for each person instead of two. Then all the leaders of the community came and asked Moses for an explanation. ²³He told them, "This is what the LORD commanded: Tomorrow will be a day of complete rest, a holy Sabbath day set apart for the LORD. So bake or boil as much as you want today, and set aside what is left for tomorrow."

²⁴So they put some aside until morning, just as Moses had commanded. And in the morning the leftover food was wholesome and good, without maggots or odor. ²⁵Moses said, "Eat this food today, for today is a Sabbath day dedicated to the LORD. There will be no food on the ground today. ²⁶You may gather the food for six days, but the seventh day is the Sabbath. There will be no food on the ground that day."

²⁷Some of the people went out anyway on the seventh day, but they found no food. ²⁸The LORD asked Moses, "How long will these people refuse to obey my commands and instructions? ²⁹They must realize that the Sabbath is the LORD's gift to you. That is why he gives you a two-day supply on the sixth day, so there will be enough for two days. On the Sabbath day you must each stay in your place. Do not go out to pick up food on the seventh day." ³⁰So the people did not gather any food on the seventh day.

³¹The Israelites called the food manna.* It was white like coriander seed, and it tasted like honey wafers.

³²Then Moses said, "This is what the LORD has commanded: Fill a two-quart container with manna to preserve it for your descendants. Then later generations will be able to see the food I gave you in the wilderness when I set you free from Egypt."

³³Moses said to Aaron, "Get a jar and fill it with two quarts of manna. Then put it in a sacred place before the LORD to preserve it for all future generations." ³⁴Aaron did just as the LORD had commanded Moses. He eventually placed it in the Ark of the Covenant—in front of the stone tablets inscribed with the terms of the covenant.* ³⁵So the people of Israel ate manna for forty years until they arrived at the land where they would settle. They ate manna until they came to the border of the land of Canaan.

³⁶The container used to measure the manna was an omer, which was one-tenth of an ephah; it held about two quarts.*

Water from the Rock

17 At the LORD's command, the whole community of Israel left the wilderness of Sin* and moved from place to place. Eventually they camped at Rephidim, but there was no water there for the people to drink. ²So once more the people complained against Moses. "Give us water to drink!" they demanded.

"Quiet!" Moses replied. "Why are you complaining against me? And why are you testing the LORD?"

³But tormented by thirst, they continued to argue with Moses. "Why did you bring us out of Egypt? Are you trying to kill us, our children, and our livestock with thirst?"

⁴Then Moses cried out to the LORD, "What should I do with these people? They are ready to stone me!"

⁵The LORD said to Moses, "Walk out in front of the people. Take your staff, the one you used when you struck the water of the Nile, and call some of the elders of Israel to join you. ⁶I will stand before you on the rock at Mount Sinai.* Strike the rock, and water will come gushing out. Then the people will be able to drink." So Moses struck the rock as he was told, and water gushed out as the elders looked on.

⁷Moses named the place Massah (which means "test") and Meribah (which means "arguing") because the people of Israel argued with Moses and tested the LORD by saying, "Is the LORD here with us or not?"

Israel Defeats the Amalekites

⁸While the people of Israel were still at Rephidim, the warriors of Amalek attacked them. ⁹Moses commanded Joshua, "Choose some men to go out and fight the army of Amalek for us. Tomorrow, I will stand at the top of the hill, holding the staff of God in my hand."

¹⁰So Joshua did what Moses had commanded and fought the army of Amalek. Meanwhile, Moses,

---

16:16 Hebrew *1 omer* [2.2 liters]; also in 16:32, 33.   **16:18** Hebrew *measured it with an omer.*   **16:22** Hebrew *2 omers* [4.4 liters].   **16:31** *Manna* means "What is it?" See 16:15.   **16:34** Hebrew *He placed it in front of the Testimony;* see note on 25:16.   **16:36** Hebrew *An omer is one-tenth of an ephah.*   **17:1** The geographical name *Sin* is related to *Sinai* and should not be confused with the English word *sin.*   **17:6** Hebrew *Horeb,* another name for Sinai.

17:2 The people doubted that God stayed with or cared for them, and they demanded proof of his presence and care with a test (see 17:7). God invites a test based on faith ("I do believe, but help me overcome my unbelief," Mark 9:24). Still, he detests a test based on doubt (for example, *I don't believe, and I think God should prove himself to me,* as in John 6:30). A test based on doubt makes us the judge and God the defendant, which is the opposite of our rightful position.

Aaron, and Hur climbed to the top of a nearby hill. ¹¹As long as Moses held up the staff in his hand, the Israelites had the advantage. But whenever he dropped his hand, the Amalekites gained the advantage. ¹²Moses' arms soon became so tired he could no longer hold them up. So Aaron and Hur found a stone for him to sit on. Then they stood on each side of Moses, holding up his hands. So his hands held steady until sunset. ¹³As a result, Joshua overwhelmed the army of Amalek in battle.

¹⁴After the victory, the LORD instructed Moses, "Write this down on a scroll as a permanent reminder, and read it aloud to Joshua: I will erase the memory of Amalek from under heaven." ¹⁵Moses built an altar there and named it Yahweh-Nissi (which means "the LORD is my banner"). ¹⁶He said, "They have raised their fist against the LORD's throne, so now* the LORD will be at war with Amalek generation after generation."

Jethro's Visit to Moses

18 Moses' father-in-law, Jethro, the priest of Midian, heard about everything God had done for Moses and his people, the Israelites. He heard especially about how the LORD had rescued them from Egypt.

²Earlier, Moses had sent his wife, Zipporah, and his two sons back to Jethro, who had taken them in. ³(Moses' first son was named Gershom,* for Moses had said when the boy was born, "I have been a foreigner in a foreign land." ⁴His second son was named Eliezer,* for Moses had said, "The God of my ancestors was my helper; he rescued me from the sword of Pharaoh.") ⁵Jethro, Moses' father-in-law, now came to visit Moses in the wilderness. He brought Moses' wife and two sons with him, and they arrived while Moses and the people were camped near the mountain of God. ⁶Jethro had sent a message to Moses, saying, "I, Jethro, your father-in-law, am coming to see you with your wife and your two sons."

⁷So Moses went out to meet his father-in-law. He bowed low and kissed him. They asked about each other's welfare and then went into Moses' tent. ⁸Moses told his father-in-law everything the LORD had done to Pharaoh and Egypt on behalf of Israel. He also told about all the hardships they had experienced along the way and how the LORD had rescued his people from all their troubles. ⁹Jethro was delighted when he heard about all the good things the LORD had done for Israel as he rescued them from the hand of the Egyptians.

¹⁰"Praise the LORD," Jethro said, "for he has rescued you from the Egyptians and from Pharaoh. Yes, he has rescued Israel from the powerful hand of Egypt! ¹¹I know now that the LORD is greater than all other gods, because he rescued his people from the oppression of the proud Egyptians."

¹²Then Jethro, Moses' father-in-law, brought a burnt offering and sacrifices to God. Aaron and all the elders of Israel came out and joined him in a sacrificial meal in God's presence.

Jethro's Wise Advice

¹³The next day, Moses took his seat to hear the people's disputes against each other. They waited before him from morning till evening.

¹⁴When Moses' father-in-law saw all that Moses was doing for the people, he asked, "What are you really accomplishing here? Why are you trying to do all this alone while everyone stands around you from morning till evening?"

¹⁵Moses replied, "Because the people come to me to get a ruling from God. ¹⁶When a dispute arises, they come to me, and I am the one who settles the case between the quarreling parties. I inform the people of God's decrees and give them his instructions."

¹⁷"This is not good!" Moses' father-in-law exclaimed. ¹⁸"You're going to wear yourself out—and the people, too. This job is too heavy a burden for you to handle all by yourself. ¹⁹Now listen to me, and let me give you a word of advice, and may God be with you. You should continue to be the people's representative before God, bringing their disputes to him. ²⁰Teach them God's decrees, and give them his instructions. Show them how to conduct their lives. ²¹But select from all the people some capable, honest men who fear God and hate bribes. Appoint them as leaders over groups of one thousand, one hundred, fifty, and ten. ²²They should always be available to solve the people's common disputes, but have them bring the major cases to you. Let the leaders decide the smaller matters themselves. They will help you carry the load, making the task easier for you. ²³If you follow this advice, and if God commands you to do so, then you will be able to endure the pressures, and all these people will go home in peace."

²⁴Moses listened to his father-in-law's advice and followed his suggestions. ²⁵He chose capable men from all over Israel and appointed them as leaders over the people. He put them in charge of groups of one thousand, one hundred, fifty, and ten. ²⁶These

---

17:16 Or *Hands have been lifted up to the LORD's throne, and now foreigner there.* **18:4** *Eliezer* means "God is my helper." **18:3** *Gershom* sounds like a Hebrew term that means "a

---

17:9-13 This victory was God's gift, as the description here makes clear. The determining factor was God's blessing, as indicated by Moses' upraised hands. This principle appears again and again in the conquest of the land of Canaan. Without God's blessing, Israel could do nothing (see Numbers 14:42-45; Joshua 7:10-12). **18:2** Moses and Zipporah may have had irreconcilable differences resulting in divorce ("sent...back" could imply this). Or they may have lived separately for a time for the sake of the task God had given Moses to do. Numbers 12:1 refers to Moses' "Cushite" wife, which may have been intended as a sort of racial slur about Zipporah, or it could imply that Zipporah was no longer in the picture (had either died or was divorced).

Watch Out for Anger and Jealousy

The LORD accepted Abel and his gift, but he did not accept Cain and his gift. This made Cain very angry, and he looked dejected.... One day Cain suggested to his brother, "Let's go out into the fields." And while they were in the field, Cain attacked his brother, Abel, and killed him. GENESIS 4:4-5, 8

Saul had a spear in his hand, and he suddenly hurled it at David, intending to pin him to the wall. But David escaped him twice. Saul was then afraid of David, for the LORD was with David and had turned away from Saul. 1 SAMUEL 18:10-12

Anger is cruel, and wrath is like a flood,
　but jealousy is even more dangerous.
PROVERBS 27:4

Worship God with Emotion

Come, everyone! Clap your hands!
　Shout to God with joyful praise!
PSALM 47:1

With praise and thanks, they sang this song to the LORD:

"He is so good!
　His faithful love for Israel endures forever!"

Then all the people gave a great shout, praising the LORD because the foundation of the LORD's Temple had been laid.... The joyful shouting and weeping mingled together in a loud noise that could be heard far in the distance. EZRA 3:11, 13

Let us be glad and rejoice,
　and let us give honor to him.
REVELATION 19:7

Be happy with those who are happy, and weep with those who weep.

16 But as for me, I will sing about your power.
> Each morning I will sing with joy about your
> unfailing love.
> For you have been my refuge,
> a place of safety when I am in distress.

17 O my Strength, to you I sing praises,
> for you, O God, are my refuge,
> the God who shows me unfailing love.

Psalm 60

For the choir director: A psalm* of David useful for teaching, regarding the time David fought Aram-naharaim and Aram-zobah, and Joab returned and killed 12,000 Edomites in the Valley of Salt. To be sung to the tune "Lily of the Testimony."

1 You have rejected us, O God, and broken our
> defenses.
> You have been angry with us; now restore us
> to your favor.

2 You have shaken our land and split it open.
> Seal the cracks, for the land trembles.

3 You have been very hard on us,
> making us drink wine that sent us reeling.

4 But you have raised a banner for those who fear
> you—
> a rallying point in the face of attack.

Interlude

5 Now rescue your beloved people.
> Answer and save us by your power.

6 God has promised this by his holiness*:
> "I will divide up Shechem with joy.
> I will measure out the valley of Succoth.

7 Gilead is mine,
> and Manasseh, too.
> Ephraim, my helmet, will produce my warriors,
> and Judah, my scepter, will produce my kings.

8 But Moab, my washbasin, will become my
> servant,
> and I will wipe my feet on Edom
> and shout in triumph over Philistia."

9 Who will bring me into the fortified city?
> Who will bring me victory over Edom?

10 Have you rejected us, O God?
> Will you no longer march with our armies?

11 Oh, please help us against our enemies,
> for all human help is useless.

12 With God's help we will do mighty things,
> for he will trample down our foes.

Psalm 61

For the choir director: A psalm of David, to be accompanied by stringed instruments.

1 O God, listen to my cry!
> Hear my prayer!

2 From the ends of the earth,
> I cry to you for help
> when my heart is overwhelmed.
> Lead me to the towering rock of safety,

3 for you are my safe refuge,
> a fortress where my enemies cannot reach me.

4 Let me live forever in your sanctuary,
> safe beneath the shelter of your wings!

Interlude

5 For you have heard my vows, O God.
> You have given me an inheritance reserved
> for those who fear your name.

6 Add many years to the life of the king!
> May his years span the generations!

7 May he reign under God's protection forever.
> May your unfailing love and faithfulness
> watch over him.

8 Then I will sing praises to your name forever
> as I fulfill my vows each day.

Psalm 62

For Jeduthun, the choir director: A psalm of David.

1 I wait quietly before God,
> for my victory comes from him.

2 He alone is my rock and my salvation,
> my fortress where I will never be shaken.

3 So many enemies against one man—
> all of them trying to kill me.
> To them I'm just a broken-down wall
> or a tottering fence.

60:TITLE Hebrew *miktam*. This may be a literary or musical term. 60:6 Or *in his sanctuary.*

Psalm 60 The psalmist laments a national defeat and cries out to God for rescue.
60:6-8 These verses record God's promise. However, they also function as a reminder to God of that promise and a foundation for the psalmist's request.
Psalm 61 The lamenting psalmist petitions God to protect him and lead him into his presence (61:4-5), trusting in the character of God. He prays for God to extend and protect the king's rule and makes vows to praise God.
61:2 The "ends of the earth" can refer to faraway places. Or it may refer to the boundary between the worlds of the living and the dead, describing a near-death experience (Jonah 2:6). Either way, the psalmist's heart is "overwhelmed" or "faint."
61:5 The psalmist's vows might also be a part of ceremonial sacrifices (Psalm 66:13-15; 76:11; 116:14, 18). He praises and thanks God for his rescue. The "inheritance" refers to the promise of the land (see Psalm 60), the sacredness of the Temple, the joy of God's presence (119:111), or any similar reward (16:6; 37:9, 11, 18, 22, 29, 34; 127:3).
Psalm 62 This psalm expresses confidence in God. The psalmist rests in God despite his difficulties. Although his deceptive and powerful adversaries push hard against him, he remains undaunted. He encourages himself and his people to trust in God and to see their human adversaries from God's perspective, where they appear frail, fleeting, and deceptive (62:9).

⁴ They plan to topple me from my high position.
　　They delight in telling lies about me.
　They praise me to my face
　　but curse me in their hearts. *Interlude*

⁵ Let all that I am wait quietly before God,
　　for my hope is in him.
⁶ He alone is my rock and my salvation,
　　my fortress where I will not be shaken.
⁷ My victory and honor come from God alone.
　　He is my refuge, a rock where no enemy can reach me.
⁸ O my people, trust in him at all times.
　　Pour out your heart to him,
　　for God is our refuge. *Interlude*

⁹ Common people are as worthless as a puff of wind,
　　and the powerful are not what they appear to be.
　If you weigh them on the scales,
　　together they are lighter than a breath of air.
¹⁰ Don't make your living by extortion
　　or put your hope in stealing.
　And if your wealth increases,
　　don't make it the center of your life.
¹¹ God has spoken plainly,
　　and I have heard it many times:
　Power, O God, belongs to you;
¹²　unfailing love, O Lord, is yours.
　Surely you repay all people
　　according to what they have done.

Psalm 63
A psalm of David, regarding a time when David was in the wilderness of Judah.

¹ O God, you are my God;
　　I earnestly search for you.
　My soul thirsts for you;
　　my whole body longs for you
　in this parched and weary land
　　where there is no water.
² I have seen you in your sanctuary
　　and gazed upon your power and glory.
³ Your unfailing love is better than life itself;
　　how I praise you!
⁴ I will praise you as long as I live,
　　lifting up my hands to you in prayer.
⁵ You satisfy me more than the richest feast.
　　I will praise you with songs of joy.
⁶ I lie awake thinking of you,
　　meditating on you through the night.

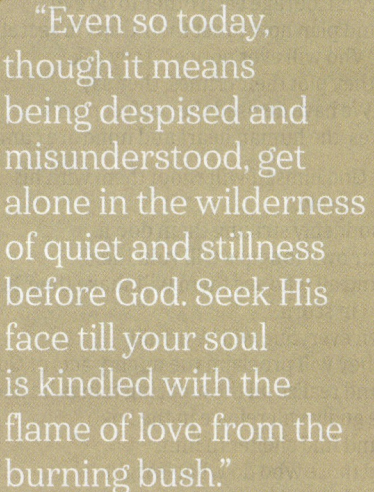

"Even so today, though it means being despised and misunderstood, get alone in the wilderness of quiet and stillness before God. Seek His face till your soul is kindled with the flame of love from the burning bush."

AIMEE SEMPLE MCPHERSON
(1890–1944) evangelist and founder of Foursquare Church

⁷ Because you are my helper,
　　I sing for joy in the shadow of your wings.
⁸ I cling to you;
　　your strong right hand holds me securely.
⁹ But those plotting to destroy me will come to ruin.
　　They will go down into the depths of the earth.
¹⁰ They will die by the sword
　　and become the food of jackals.
¹¹ But the king will rejoice in God.
　　All who swear to tell the truth will praise him,
　　while liars will be silenced.

Psalm 64
For the choir director: A psalm of David.

¹ O God, listen to my complaint.
　　Protect my life from my enemies' threats.
² Hide me from the plots of this evil mob,
　　from this gang of wrongdoers.
³ They sharpen their tongues like swords
　　and aim their bitter words like arrows.

62:9 The translations "common people" and "the powerful" reflect the meaning of similar expressions found in Babylonian and Egyptian texts. The underlying Hebrew language may have that meaning, but it may also simply be two different expressions for humans in general. Either way, the words point to humanity's frailty and transience compared to God.

Psalm 63 Focusing on confidence and thanksgiving, the king longs for God's presence so vividly that he eats, drinks, and sees God's goodness. Though worn out and harassed by the wicked, the king sees God, and this animates him with praise. God becomes his life (63:3), while the wicked perish (63:9).

Psalm 64 This lament seeks God's deliverance from the destructive plots and arrogant attitude of the wicked (64:1-6). The psalmist turns to God in prayer and takes heart in God's justice, because whatever the wicked do will be undone by the righteous judge. The godly will rejoice and grow in wisdom as they reflect on God's mighty acts.

⁴ They shoot from ambush at the innocent,
    attacking suddenly and fearlessly.
⁵ They encourage each other to do evil
    and plan how to set their traps in secret.
    "Who will ever notice?" they ask.
⁶ As they plot their crimes, they say,
    "We have devised the perfect plan!"
    Yes, the human heart and mind are cunning.

⁷ But God himself will shoot them with his
        arrows,
    suddenly striking them down.
⁸ Their own tongues will ruin them,
    and all who see them will shake their heads
        in scorn.
⁹ Then everyone will be afraid;
    they will proclaim the mighty acts of God
    and realize all the amazing things he does.
¹⁰ The godly will rejoice in the LORD
    and find shelter in him.
    And those who do what is right
        will praise him.

Psalm 65
For the choir director: A song. A psalm of David.

¹ What mighty praise, O God,
    belongs to you in Zion.
    We will fulfill our vows to you,
²   for you answer our prayers.
    All of us must come to you.
³ Though we are overwhelmed by our sins,
    you forgive them all.
⁴ What joy for those you choose to bring near,
    those who live in your holy courts.
    What festivities await us
        inside your holy Temple.

⁵ You faithfully answer our prayers with
        awesome deeds,
    O God our savior.
    You are the hope of everyone on earth,
    even those who sail on distant seas.
⁶ You formed the mountains by your power
    and armed yourself with mighty strength.
⁷ You quieted the raging oceans
    with their pounding waves
    and silenced the shouting of the nations.
⁸ Those who live at the ends of the earth
    stand in awe of your wonders.
    From where the sun rises to where it sets,
        you inspire shouts of joy.

⁹ You take care of the earth and water it,
    making it rich and fertile.
    The river of God has plenty of water;
    it provides a bountiful harvest of grain,
        for you have ordered it so.
¹⁰ You drench the plowed ground with rain,
    melting the clods and leveling the ridges.
    You soften the earth with showers
    and bless its abundant crops.
¹¹ You crown the year with a bountiful harvest;
    even the hard pathways overflow with
        abundance.
¹² The grasslands of the wilderness become a lush
        pasture,
    and the hillsides blossom with joy.
¹³ The meadows are clothed with flocks of sheep,
    and the valleys are carpeted with grain.
    They all shout and sing for joy!

Psalm 66
For the choir director: A song. A psalm.

¹ Shout joyful praises to God, all the earth!
²   Sing about the glory of his name!
    Tell the world how glorious he is.
³ Say to God, "How awesome are your deeds!
    Your enemies cringe before your mighty
        power.
⁴ Everything on earth will worship you;
    they will sing your praises,
    shouting your name in glorious songs."
                                                        Interlude

⁵ Come and see what our God has done,
    what awesome miracles he performs for
        people!
⁶ He made a dry path through the Red Sea,*
    and his people went across on foot.
    There we rejoiced in him.
⁷ For by his great power he rules forever.
    He watches every movement of the
        nations;
    let no rebel rise in defiance.   *Interlude*

⁸ Let the whole world bless our God
    and loudly sing his praises.
⁹ Our lives are in his hands,
    and he keeps our feet from stumbling.
¹⁰ You have tested us, O God;
    you have purified us like silver.
¹¹ You captured us in your net
    and laid the burden of slavery on our backs.
¹² Then you put a leader over us.*
    We went through fire and flood,
    but you brought us to a place of great
        abundance.

66:6 Hebrew *the sea.* 66:12 Or *You made people ride over our heads.*

Psalm 65 This psalm recounts the reasons why all people should praise and revere God for his almighty power and merciful care for his universe. It focuses on God's forgiveness (65:1-4), power (65:5-8), and provision in creation (65:9-13).

Psalm 66 This psalm opens with a communal thanksgiving hymn (66:1-12) and then transitions to an individual thanksgiving hymn (65:13-20). Both parts praise God for his redemption.

¹³ Now I come to your Temple with burnt offerings
  to fulfill the vows I made to you—
¹⁴ yes, the sacred vows that I made
  when I was in deep trouble.
¹⁵ That is why I am sacrificing burnt offerings to you—
  the best of my rams as a pleasing aroma,
  and a sacrifice of bulls and male goats.
          Interlude

¹⁶ Come and listen, all you who fear God,
  and I will tell you what he did for me.
¹⁷ For I cried out to him for help,
  praising him as I spoke.
¹⁸ If I had not confessed the sin in my heart,
  the Lord would not have listened.
¹⁹ But God did listen!
  He paid attention to my prayer.
²⁰ Praise God, who did not ignore my prayer
  or withdraw his unfailing love from me.

Psalm 67

For the choir director: A song. A psalm, to be accompanied by stringed instruments.

¹ May God be merciful and bless us.
  May his face smile with favor on us.
          Interlude

² May your ways be known throughout the earth,
  your saving power among people everywhere.
³ May the nations praise you, O God.
  Yes, may all the nations praise you.
⁴ Let the whole world sing for joy,
  because you govern the nations with justice
  and guide the people of the whole world.
          Interlude

⁵ May the nations praise you, O God.
  Yes, may all the nations praise you.
⁶ Then the earth will yield its harvests,
  and God, our God, will richly bless us.
⁷ Yes, God will bless us,
  and people all over the world will fear him.

68:4 Or *rides through the deserts.* **68:11** Or *a host of women.*

Psalm 68

For the choir director: A song. A psalm of David.

¹ Rise up, O God, and scatter your enemies.
  Let those who hate God run for their lives.
² Blow them away like smoke.
  Melt them like wax in a fire.
  Let the wicked perish in the presence of God.
³ But let the godly rejoice.
  Let them be glad in God's presence.
  Let them be filled with joy.
⁴ Sing praises to God and to his name!
  Sing loud praises to him who rides the clouds.*
  His name is the LORD—
  rejoice in his presence!

⁵ Father to the fatherless, defender of widows—
  this is God, whose dwelling is holy.
⁶ God places the lonely in families;
  he sets the prisoners free and gives them joy.
  But he makes the rebellious live in a sun-scorched land.

⁷ O God, when you led your people out from Egypt,
  when you marched through the dry wasteland,   *Interlude*
⁸ the earth trembled, and the heavens poured down rain
  before you, the God of Sinai,
  before God, the God of Israel.
⁹ You sent abundant rain, O God,
  to refresh the weary land.
¹⁰ There your people finally settled,
  and with a bountiful harvest, O God,
  you provided for your needy people.

¹¹ The Lord gives the word,
  and a great army* brings the good news.
¹² Enemy kings and their armies flee,
  while the women of Israel divide the plunder.
¹³ Even those who lived among the sheepfolds found treasures—
  doves with wings of silver
  and feathers of gold.

66:13 This verse includes an abrupt transition from a communal focus on God to an individual's offering in the Temple. (The NLT adds "now" to smooth the transition.) The shift in focus invites us to consider how the two sections relate and what the psalm can teach us about worshiping God. Here we see the complexity of our relationship with God. We encounter him as both individuals and in community. We see his acts in the universe and our own lives. This psalm teaches us to respond with praise and thanks to the wide variety of our experiences with God.
Psalm 67 In this prayer for God's blessing, the psalmist addresses the knowledge and worship of God among the nations (see 64:9; 65:8).
67:1-2 This prayer is based on the priestly blessing found in Numbers 6:24-26. God's goodness to Israel affects his reputation among the nations (see Psalm 96:1-3).

Psalm 68 This prayer for God's victorious rule traces God's march from Sinai to Zion (68:7, 16-18, 24). He rescued the nation of Israel from Egypt, guided it through the wilderness, brought it into the Promised Land, and established his Kingdom. He is a caring and victorious God, whose nature is unchanging. Therefore, the godly hope and rejoice in the prospect of God's universal dominion.
68:4 The phrase "him who rides the clouds" was an ancient descriptor of Baal, a Canaanite storm deity. The psalmist applies it to the Lord as the true "Rider of the Clouds" (see 68:33; 104:3) to reinforce that God wields power over the clouds and the rain. Another possible translation for this Hebrew phrase is "him who rides through the deserts."

Shalom IMAGE — MY STORY OF MY UNIQUE INFLUENCE

God's Word Invites Women to Use Our Voices

SCRIPTURE CONNECTION: PSALM 68

When I received an invitation to speak at a graduation ceremony for two women who specialized in the Old Testament, I felt led to speak on Psalm 68. This psalm recounts all the good that God had done for his people Israel, looks forward to the coming rule of God's Messiah, and makes clear that women play an integral role in this proclamation.

Psalm 68:11 uses the Hebrew term *mevasserot*, which can be translated as "a host of women brings the good news." Other possible translations include "women who proclaim [the word]" (NIV); "many, many women spread the good news" (NET); and "women who proclaim good news" (NASB).

Based on the Hebrew wording, I gave this message to my two friends: The psalmist tells us that God chooses women like you to proclaim the only message that can change the world—the good news of the Kingdom of God.

This message comes from the living God who places it in the hearts and minds of women who follow him. As a rule, the Hebrew word for "good news" (*basar*) indicates that the message is joyful, that the news is good, and that the good tidings are well received.

God chooses women as his mouthpiece to proclaim his message with boldness, courage, clarity, and simplicity. The women assigned to this task are numerous; we form "a host of women," "a great army."

Let us lend our voices to preach the gospel of the Kingdom. Let us join the army of women who spread God's good news to the world.

> Let us join the great army of women to bring the good news!

IMAGINE

Do you see yourself in this army of women who proclaim God's message of the Kingdom?

Are you letting life's obstacles stop you from being bold in your mission for God? If so, how can you overcome and press on when barriers appear on the road?

"There is much work that remains for us to do on this earth. Why not jump in with both feet, without fear, and speak forth the Word to those who need to hear from God?"

HÉLÈNE M. DALLAIRE, PhD, serves as Earl S. Kalland Professor of Old Testament and Semitic Languages at Denver Seminary. She is deeply involved in the Messianic movement, serving in worship, prayer, teaching, and preaching.

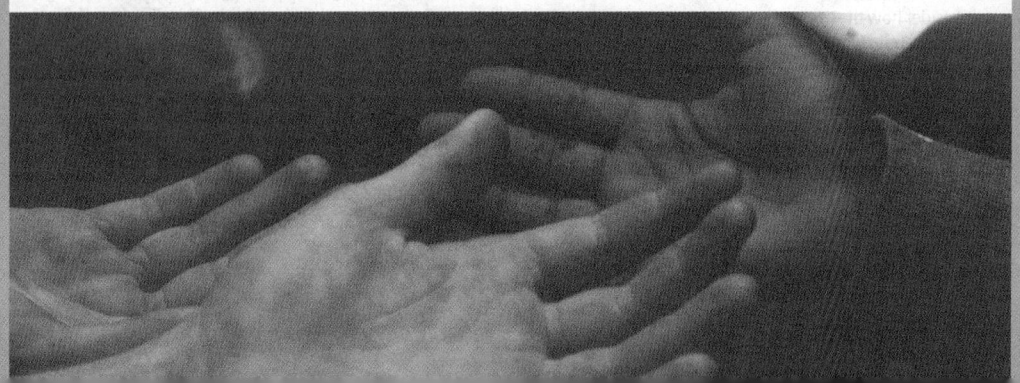

14 The Almighty scattered the enemy kings
   like a blowing snowstorm on Mount Zalmon.
15 The mountains of Bashan are majestic,
   with many peaks stretching high into the sky.
16 Why do you look with envy, O rugged mountains,
   at Mount Zion, where God has chosen to live,
   where the LORD himself will live forever?
17 Surrounded by unnumbered thousands of chariots,
   the Lord came from Mount Sinai into his sanctuary.
18 When you ascended to the heights,
   you led a crowd of captives.
   You received gifts from the people,
   even from those who rebelled against you.
   Now the LORD God will live among us there.
19 Praise the Lord; praise God our savior!
   For each day he carries us in his arms.
                                        Interlude
20 Our God is a God who saves!
   The Sovereign LORD rescues us from death.
21 But God will smash the heads of his enemies,
   crushing the skulls of those who love their guilty ways.
22 The Lord says, "I will bring my enemies down from Bashan;
   I will bring them up from the depths of the sea.
23 You, my people, will wash* your feet in their blood,
   and even your dogs will get their share!"
24 Your procession has come into view, O God—
   the procession of my God and King as he goes into the sanctuary.
25 Singers are in front, musicians behind;
   between them are young women playing tambourines.
26 Praise God, all you people of Israel;
   praise the LORD, the source of Israel's life.
27 Look, the little tribe of Benjamin leads the way.
   Then comes a great throng of rulers from Judah
   and all the rulers of Zebulun and Naphtali.
28 Summon your might, O God.*
   Display your power, O God, as you have in the past.
29 The kings of the earth are bringing tribute
   to your Temple in Jerusalem.
30 Rebuke these enemy nations—
   these wild animals lurking in the reeds,
   this herd of bulls among the weaker calves.
   Make them bring bars of silver in humble tribute.
   Scatter the nations that delight in war.
31 Let Egypt come with gifts of precious metals*;
   let Ethiopia* bring tribute to God.
32 Sing to God, you kingdoms of the earth.
   Sing praises to the Lord.   *Interlude*
33 Sing to the one who rides across the ancient heavens,
   his mighty voice thundering from the sky.
34 Tell everyone about God's power.
   His majesty shines down on Israel;
   his strength is mighty in the heavens.
35 God is awesome in his sanctuary.
   The God of Israel gives power and strength to his people.

Praise be to God!

Psalm 69

For the choir director: A psalm of David, to be sung to the tune "Lilies."

1 Save me, O God,
   for the floodwaters are up to my neck.
2 Deeper and deeper I sink into the mire;
   I can't find a foothold.
   I am in deep water,
   and the floods overwhelm me.
3 I am exhausted from crying for help;
   my throat is parched.
   My eyes are swollen with weeping,
   waiting for my God to help me.
4 Those who hate me without cause
   outnumber the hairs on my head.
   Many enemies try to destroy me with lies,
   demanding that I give back what I didn't steal.
5 O God, you know how foolish I am;
   my sins cannot be hidden from you.
6 Don't let those who trust in you be ashamed because of me,
   O Sovereign LORD of Heaven's Armies.
   Don't let me cause them to be humiliated,
   O God of Israel.
7 For I endure insults for your sake;
   humiliation is written all over my face.
8 Even my own brothers pretend they don't know me;
   they treat me like a stranger.

68:23 As in Greek and Syriac versions; Hebrew reads *shatter*. **68:28** As in some Hebrew manuscripts and Greek and Syriac versions; most Hebrew manuscripts read *Your God has commanded your strength.* **68:31a** Or *of rich cloth.* **68:31b** Hebrew *Cush.*

68:16 The idea that God would live on Mount Zion in Jerusalem can seem odd to readers who think of God as being in heaven or of the Holy Spirit as residing within his followers. In the Israelite worldview, the Temple was where the human and divine realms met. Thus, while God remained in the divine (or heavenly) realm, Israel could physically come into God's presence.

Psalm 69 In this individual lament, the psalmist expresses his vulnerability, humiliation, and overwhelming pain, asking God to vindicate him for the sake of the righteous.

9 Passion for your house has consumed me,
and the insults of those who insult you have
fallen on me.
10 When I weep and fast,
they scoff at me.
11 When I dress in burlap to show sorrow,
they make fun of me.
12 I am the favorite topic of town gossip,
and all the drunks sing about me.
13 But I keep praying to you, LORD,
hoping this time you will show me favor.
In your unfailing love, O God,
answer my prayer with your sure salvation.
14 Rescue me from the mud;
don't let me sink any deeper!
Save me from those who hate me,
and pull me from these deep waters.
15 Don't let the floods overwhelm me,
or the deep waters swallow me,
or the pit of death devour me.
16 Answer my prayers, O LORD,
for your unfailing love is wonderful.
Take care of me,
for your mercy is so plentiful.
17 Don't hide from your servant;
answer me quickly, for I am in deep trouble!
18 Come and redeem me;
free me from my enemies.
19 You know of my shame, scorn, and disgrace.
You see all that my enemies are doing.
20 Their insults have broken my heart,
and I am in despair.
If only one person would show some pity;
if only one would turn and comfort me.
21 But instead, they give me poison* for food;
they offer me sour wine for my thirst.
22 Let the bountiful table set before them become
a snare
and their prosperity become a trap.*
23 Let their eyes go blind so they cannot see,
and make their bodies shake continually.*
24 Pour out your fury on them;
consume them with your burning anger.
25 Let their homes become desolate
and their tents be deserted.
26 To the one you have punished, they add insult to
injury;
they add to the pain of those you have hurt.
27 Pile their sins up high,
and don't let them go free.
28 Erase their names from the Book of Life;
don't let them be counted among the righteous.
29 I am suffering and in pain.
Rescue me, O God, by your saving power.
30 Then I will praise God's name with singing,
and I will honor him with thanksgiving.
31 For this will please the LORD more than
sacrificing cattle,
more than presenting a bull with its horns
and hooves.
32 The humble will see their God at work and be
glad.
Let all who seek God's help be encouraged.
33 For the LORD hears the cries of the needy;
he does not despise his imprisoned people.
34 Praise him, O heaven and earth,
the seas and all that move in them.
35 For God will save Jerusalem*
and rebuild the towns of Judah.
His people will live there
and settle in their own land.
36 The descendants of those who obey him will
inherit the land,
and those who love him will live there in safety.

Psalm 70

For the choir director: A psalm of David, asking God to remember him.

1 Please, God, rescue me!
Come quickly, LORD, and help me.
2 May those who try to kill me
be humiliated and put to shame.
May those who take delight in my trouble
be turned back in disgrace.
3 Let them be horrified by their shame,
for they said, "Aha! We've got him now!"
4 But may all who search for you
be filled with joy and gladness in you.

69:21 Or *gall.* 69:22 Greek version reads *Let their bountiful table set before them become a snare, / a trap that makes them think all is well. / Let their blessings cause them to stumble, / and let them get what they deserve.* Compare Rom 11:9. 69:23 Greek version reads *and let their backs be bent forever.* Compare Rom 11:10. 69:35 Hebrew *Zion.*

69:34-36 While the psalm has focused primarily on the psalmist's multifaceted suffering, the transition here moves to a more cosmic focus. The psalmist calls on heaven, earth, the seas, and all their creatures, to praise God. This praise, though, is not thanking God for the psalmist's own deliverance. Instead, it is for the deliverance of Jerusalem and Judah. This shift resembles God's response to Job, where God focused beyond Job's individual pain. Here, the psalmist encourages us to bring our personal pain to our sovereign God and remember his wider perspective.
Psalm 70 This psalm, which is nearly identical to 40:13-17, contains an urgency (70:1, 5) that fits with the surrounding psalms (see 69:17; 71:12). The inclusion of similar material in two different psalms points to how people reused these songs in new and different contexts. The frequent lack of specific, individual circumstances invites us to pray these prayers again and again in our own lives, whether in praise or anguish.

May those who love your salvation
    repeatedly shout, "God is great!"
⁵ But as for me, I am poor and needy;
    please hurry to my aid, O God.
You are my helper and my savior;
    O LORD, do not delay.

Psalm 71

¹ O LORD, I have come to you for protection;
    don't let me be disgraced.
² Save me and rescue me,
    for you do what is right.
Turn your ear to listen to me,
    and set me free.
³ Be my rock of safety
    where I can always hide.
Give the order to save me,
    for you are my rock and my fortress.
⁴ My God, rescue me from the power of the
        wicked,
    from the clutches of cruel oppressors.
⁵ O Lord, you alone are my hope.
    I've trusted you, O LORD, from childhood.
⁶ Yes, you have been with me from birth;
    from my mother's womb you have cared for
        me.
    No wonder I am always praising you!
⁷ My life is an example to many,
    because you have been my strength and
        protection.
⁸ That is why I can never stop praising you;
    I declare your glory all day long.
⁹ And now, in my old age, don't set me aside.
    Don't abandon me when my strength is failing.
¹⁰ For my enemies are whispering against me.
    They are plotting together to kill me.
¹¹ They say, "God has abandoned him.
    Let's go and get him,
    for no one will help him now."
¹² O God, don't stay away.
    My God, please hurry to help me.
¹³ Bring disgrace and destruction on my accusers.
    Humiliate and shame those who want to
        harm me.
¹⁴ But I will keep on hoping for your help;
    I will praise you more and more.

71:15 Or *though I cannot count it.*

¹⁵ I will tell everyone about your righteousness.
    All day long I will proclaim your saving
        power,
    though I am not skilled with words.*
¹⁶ I will praise your mighty deeds, O Sovereign
        LORD.
    I will tell everyone that you alone are just.
¹⁷ O God, you have taught me from my earliest
        childhood,
    and I constantly tell others about the
        wonderful things you do.
¹⁸ Now that I am old and gray,
    do not abandon me, O God.
Let me proclaim your power to this new
        generation,
    your mighty miracles to all who come after me.
¹⁹ Your righteousness, O God, reaches to the
        highest heavens.
    You have done such wonderful things.
    Who can compare with you, O God?
²⁰ You have allowed me to suffer much hardship,
    but you will restore me to life again
    and lift me up from the depths of the earth.
²¹ You will restore me to even greater honor
    and comfort me once again.
²² Then I will praise you with music on the harp,
    because you are faithful to your promises,
        O my God.
I will sing praises to you with a lyre,
    O Holy One of Israel.
²³ I will shout for joy and sing your praises,
    for you have ransomed me.
²⁴ I will tell about your righteous deeds
    all day long,
    for everyone who tried to hurt me
    has been shamed and humiliated.

Psalm 72
A psalm of Solomon.

¹ Give your love of justice to the king, O God,
    and righteousness to the king's son.
² Help him judge your people in the right way;
    let the poor always be treated fairly.
³ May the mountains yield prosperity for all,
    and may the hills be fruitful.

Psalm 71 This untitled lament by an aging believer is more of a confession of confidence and hope than the cry of someone abandoned by God. The psalmist experienced God's power and protection in his youth (71:5-8) and now prays for rescue from the adversaries who stalk him in his old age (71:9-13). Even amid his peril, he continues to tell of God's past faithfulness and looks forward with hope to a time when he can testify to the next generation that God is faithful and righteous.
71:20 The psalmist hopes for the renewal of an abundant earthly life. This may have become part of the grounds for belief in the resurrection of the dead later in Jewish thinking.
Psalm 72 This royal psalm closes Book Two, with 72:18-20 functioning as an epilogue to all of Book Two. The psalmist reflects on the prospects of David's royal line and on Zion (see Psalms 46, 48). He prays that Israel's kings will be good and prosperous, extending the Lord's blessing on his people throughout the whole earth. The surpassing righteousness and dominion sought in this prayer foreshadow the coming of Jesus, the Son of David.

⁴ Help him to defend the poor,
   to rescue the children of the needy,
   and to crush their oppressors.
⁵ May they fear you* as long as the sun shines,
   as long as the moon remains in the sky.
   Yes, forever!

⁶ May the king's rule be refreshing like spring
      rain on freshly cut grass,
   like the showers that water the earth.
⁷ May all the godly flourish during his reign.
   May there be abundant prosperity until the
      moon is no more.
⁸ May he reign from sea to sea,
   and from the Euphrates River* to the ends of
      the earth.
⁹ Desert nomads will bow before him;
   his enemies will fall before him in the dust.
¹⁰ The western kings of Tarshish and other distant
      lands
   will bring him tribute.
The eastern kings of Sheba and Seba
   will bring him gifts.
¹¹ All kings will bow before him,
   and all nations will serve him.

¹² He will rescue the poor when they cry to him;
   he will help the oppressed, who have no one
      to defend them.
¹³ He feels pity for the weak and the needy,
   and he will rescue them.
¹⁴ He will redeem them from oppression and
      violence,
   for their lives are precious to him.

¹⁵ Long live the king!
   May the gold of Sheba be given to him.
   May the people always pray for him
   and bless him all day long.
¹⁶ May there be abundant grain throughout the land,
   flourishing even on the hilltops.
May the fruit trees flourish like the trees of
      Lebanon,
   and may the people thrive like grass in a field.
¹⁷ May the king's name endure forever;
   may it continue as long as the sun shines.
May all nations be blessed through him
   and bring him praise.

¹⁸ Praise the LORD God, the God of Israel,
   who alone does such wonderful things.
¹⁹ Praise his glorious name forever!
   Let the whole earth be filled with his glory.
   Amen and amen!

²⁰ (This ends the prayers of David son of Jesse.)

BOOK THREE (PSALMS 73–89)

Psalm 73
A psalm of Asaph.

¹ Truly God is good to Israel,
   to those whose hearts are pure.
² But as for me, I almost lost my footing.
   My feet were slipping, and I was almost gone.
³ For I envied the proud
   when I saw them prosper despite their
      wickedness.
⁴ They seem to live such painless lives;
   their bodies are so healthy and strong.
⁵ They don't have troubles like other people;
   they're not plagued with problems like
      everyone else.
⁶ They wear pride like a jeweled necklace
   and clothe themselves with cruelty.
⁷ These fat cats have everything
   their hearts could ever wish for!
⁸ They scoff and speak only evil;
   in their pride they seek to crush others.
⁹ They boast against the very heavens,
   and their words strut throughout the earth.

72:5 Greek version reads *May they endure.* **72:8** Hebrew *the river.*

72:4 We tend to think of being poor and needy in economic terms: lacking what we need to sustain life. While this idea is certainly present here, this language frequently relates to those marginalized or at risk and those oppressed by unjust practices more broadly. As God's representative, the king held responsibility for the people's well-being. He especially needed to tend to widows, orphans, and foreigners, who lacked a social safety net, and Christians today share this calling (James 1:27; 2:14-17).
Book Three (Psalms 73–89) Book Three begins with the problem of inequity in the world: The wicked enjoy prosperity while the righteous suffer. Psalm 73 also prepares readers to contemplate the collapse of David's dynasty, which forms the context for the end of Book Three (Psalm 89). Book Three consists of two collections: psalms by Asaph that focus on God restoring his people and judging his enemies (Psalms 73–83); and psalms by the "descendants of Korah," David, and Ethan the Ezrahite (Psalms 84–89).

Psalms 73–75 The apparent prosperity of the wicked (Psalm 73) and God's apparent rejection of his people (Psalm 74) raise questions about his justice. But God is sovereign over the whole world, and he determines the time for judgment (Psalm 75).
Psalm 73 This wisdom psalm examines the injustice of the wicked prospering. The psalmist affirms that God is good to the godly but his own experience has differed (73:2-12). Nearly overcome by his doubts (73:13-16), the psalmist meets the Lord in the sanctuary and gains a perspective that stretches beyond his life, renewing his confidence in God (73:17-26). His disturbing doubts stir a greater passion for truth. He knows that he can trust God and that God will rescue him (73:27-28).
73:Title Asaph was a Levitical singer appointed by David (1 Chronicles 6:39; 15:16-17); several of his descendants were also singers and instrumentalists. Many of the psalms of Asaph (Psalms 50, 73–83) were probably written by Asaph's descendants at a later time in Israel's history (for example, Psalm 74).

¹⁰ And so the people are dismayed and confused,
    drinking in all their words.
¹¹ "What does God know?" they ask.
    "Does the Most High even know what's
        happening?"
¹² Look at these wicked people—
    enjoying a life of ease while their riches
        multiply.

¹³ Did I keep my heart pure for nothing?
    Did I keep myself innocent for no reason?
¹⁴ I get nothing but trouble all day long;
    every morning brings me pain.

¹⁵ If I had really spoken this way to others,
    I would have been a traitor to your people.
¹⁶ So I tried to understand why the wicked prosper.
    But what a difficult task it is!
¹⁷ Then I went into your sanctuary, O God,
    and I finally understood the destiny of the
        wicked.
¹⁸ Truly, you put them on a slippery path
    and send them sliding over the cliff to
        destruction.
¹⁹ In an instant they are destroyed,
    completely swept away by terrors.
²⁰ When you arise, O Lord,
    you will laugh at their silly ideas
    as a person laughs at dreams in the morning.

²¹ Then I realized that my heart was bitter,
    and I was all torn up inside.
²² I was so foolish and ignorant—
    I must have seemed like a senseless animal
        to you.
²³ Yet I still belong to you;
    you hold my right hand.
²⁴ You guide me with your counsel,
    leading me to a glorious destiny.
²⁵ Whom have I in heaven but you?
    I desire you more than anything on earth.
²⁶ My health may fail, and my spirit may grow weak,
    but God remains the strength of my heart;
    he is mine forever.

²⁷ Those who desert him will perish,
    for you destroy those who abandon you.
²⁸ But as for me, how good it is to be near God!
    I have made the Sovereign LORD my shelter,
    and I will tell everyone about the wonderful
        things you do.

Psalm 74
A psalm* of Asaph.

¹ O God, why have you rejected us so long?
    Why is your anger so intense against the
        sheep of your own pasture?
² Remember that we are the people you chose
        long ago,
    the tribe you redeemed as your own special
        possession!
    And remember Jerusalem,* your home here
        on earth.
³ Walk through the awful ruins of the city;
    see how the enemy has destroyed your
        sanctuary.

⁴ There your enemies shouted their victorious
        battle cries;
    there they set up their battle standards.
⁵ They swung their axes
    like woodcutters in a forest.
⁶ With axes and picks,
    they smashed the carved paneling.
⁷ They burned your sanctuary to the ground.
    They defiled the place that bears your name.
⁸ Then they thought, "Let's destroy everything!"
    So they burned down all the places where God
        was worshiped.

⁹ We no longer see your miraculous signs.
    All the prophets are gone,
    and no one can tell us when it will end.
¹⁰ How long, O God, will you allow our enemies to
        insult you?
    Will you let them dishonor your name forever?
¹¹ Why do you hold back your strong right hand?
    Unleash your powerful fist and destroy them.

¹² You, O God, are my king from ages past,
    bringing salvation to the earth.
¹³ You split the sea by your strength
    and smashed the heads of the sea monsters.
¹⁴ You crushed the heads of Leviathan*
    and let the desert animals eat him.
¹⁵ You caused the springs and streams to gush forth,
    and you dried up rivers that never run dry.
¹⁶ Both day and night belong to you;
    you made the starlight* and the sun.
¹⁷ You set the boundaries of the earth,
    and you made both summer and winter.

74:TITLE Hebrew *maskil*. This may be a literary or musical term. 74:2 Hebrew *Mount Zion*. 74:14 The identification of Leviathan is disputed, ranging from an earthly creature to a mythical sea monster in ancient literature. 74:16 Or *moon*; Hebrew reads *light*.

73:13 The same Hebrew word (*akh*, "truly") opens 73:1, 13, 18, but here this word remains untranslated. This Hebrew word sometimes marks a statement that is uncontestable and true. But here it points to what *seems* true based on the psalmist's experiences and observations—that the effort to maintain purity and innocence was pointless. It is not saying that aiming to live in a pure way is pointless. At times, we, too, may feel that our efforts of honoring God do not pay off, at least not immediately. However, the psalmist—and we—sense a call to press on.
Psalm 74 The psalmist laments the destruction of the Temple in Jerusalem (586 BC) with vivid imagery, questions, fresh memories, and a direct appeal for the Lord to act (74:19-23).

¹⁸ See how these enemies insult you, LORD.
　A foolish nation has dishonored your name.
¹⁹ Don't let these wild beasts destroy your
　　turtledoves.
　Don't forget your suffering people forever.
²⁰ Remember your covenant promises,
　for the land is full of darkness and violence!
²¹ Don't let the downtrodden be humiliated again.
　Instead, let the poor and needy praise your
　　name.
²² Arise, O God, and defend your cause.
　Remember how these fools insult you all day
　　long.
²³ Don't overlook what your enemies have said
　or their growing uproar.

Psalm 75

For the choir director: A psalm of Asaph. A song to be sung to the tune "Do Not Destroy!"

¹ We thank you, O God!
　We give thanks because you are near.
　People everywhere tell of your wonderful
　　deeds.
² God says, "At the time I have planned,
　I will bring justice against the wicked.
³ When the earth quakes and its people live in
　　turmoil,
　I am the one who keeps its foundations firm.
　　　　　　　　　　　　　　　Interlude
⁴ "I warned the proud, 'Stop your boasting!'
　I told the wicked, 'Don't raise your fists!
⁵ Don't raise your fists in defiance at the heavens
　or speak with such arrogance.'"
⁶ For no one on earth—from east or west,
　or even from the wilderness—
　should raise a defiant fist.*
⁷ It is God alone who judges;
　he decides who will rise and who will fall.
⁸ For the LORD holds a cup in his hand
　that is full of foaming wine mixed with spices.
　He pours out the wine in judgment,
　and all the wicked must drink it,
　　draining it to the dregs.

⁹ But as for me, I will always proclaim what God
　　has done;
　I will sing praises to the God of Jacob.
¹⁰ For God says, "I will break the strength of
　　the wicked,
　but I will increase the power of the godly."

Psalm 76

For the choir director: A psalm of Asaph. A song to be accompanied by stringed instruments.

¹ God is honored in Judah;
　his name is great in Israel.
² Jerusalem* is where he lives;
　Mount Zion is his home.
³ There he has broken the fiery arrows of
　　the enemy,
　the shields and swords and weapons of war.
　　　　　　　　　　　　　　　Interlude
⁴ You are glorious and more majestic
　than the everlasting mountains.*
⁵ Our boldest enemies have been plundered.
　They lie before us in the sleep of death.
　No warrior could lift a hand against us.
⁶ At the blast of your breath, O God of Jacob,
　their horses and chariots lay still.
⁷ No wonder you are greatly feared!
　Who can stand before you when your anger
　　explodes?
⁸ From heaven you sentenced your enemies;
　the earth trembled and stood silent
　　before you.
⁹ You stand up to judge those who do evil,
　　O God,
　and to rescue the oppressed of the earth.
　　　　　　　　　　　　　　　Interlude
¹⁰ Human defiance only enhances your glory,
　for you use it as a weapon.*
¹¹ Make vows to the LORD your God, and keep
　　them.
　Let everyone bring tribute to the
　　Awesome One.
¹² For he breaks the pride of princes,
　and the kings of the earth fear him.

75:6 Hebrew *should lift.* 76:2 Hebrew *Salem,* another name for Jerusalem. 76:4 As in Greek version; Hebrew reads *than mountains filled with beasts of prey.* 76:10 The meaning of the Hebrew is uncertain.

Psalm 75 This hymn of thanksgiving includes two direct messages from God that provide assurance of his justice (75:2-3, 10). The Lord rebukes arrogant people who defy him, promising to forcibly humble them (75:4-8). Together, the community and the psalmist respond with thanksgiving for God's character (75:1, 9). **75:8** The portrayal of God's judgment as a cup or a cup of wine is found in the prophets (Isaiah 51:17; Jeremiah 25:15-17, 28; 49:12; 51:7; Ezekiel 23:31-33). The reference to "foaming wine mixed with spices" may allude to the fermentation process, which took time, eventually releasing gases that created foam. Spices could enhance the strength of the drink. Here, then, the image may suggest the strength and appropriate timing of God's judgment.
Psalm 76 This psalm appears to celebrate a victory, focusing on God as the divine warrior. The victory might have been recent, such as over the Assyrians (based on the Greek translation of the title; see also Isaiah 37); or the psalm might be recalling God's great acts of rescue in the past.
76:11 "Awesome One" could also be translated as "Fearsome One." Both renderings are appropriate. For those who have experienced deliverance, the focus would be on awe at God's power. For those whom he has routed, this fear could be terror as well.

Psalm 77

For Jeduthun, the choir director: A psalm of Asaph.

¹ I cry out to God; yes, I shout.
  Oh, that God would listen to me!
² When I was in deep trouble,
  I searched for the Lord.
  All night long I prayed, with hands lifted toward heaven,
  but my soul was not comforted.
³ I think of God, and I moan,
  overwhelmed with longing for his help.
          Interlude

⁴ You don't let me sleep.
  I am too distressed even to pray!
⁵ I think of the good old days,
  long since ended,
⁶ when my nights were filled with joyful songs.
  I search my soul and ponder the difference now.
⁷ Has the Lord rejected me forever?
  Will he never again be kind to me?
⁸ Is his unfailing love gone forever?
  Have his promises permanently failed?
⁹ Has God forgotten to be gracious?
  Has he slammed the door on his compassion?
          Interlude

¹⁰ And I said, "This is my fate;
  the Most High has turned his hand against me."
¹¹ But then I recall all you have done, O LORD;
  I remember your wonderful deeds of long ago.
¹² They are constantly in my thoughts.
  I cannot stop thinking about your mighty works.
¹³ O God, your ways are holy.
  Is there any god as mighty as you?
¹⁴ You are the God of great wonders!
  You demonstrate your awesome power among the nations.
¹⁵ By your strong arm, you redeemed your people,
  the descendants of Jacob and Joseph.
          Interlude

¹⁶ When the Red Sea* saw you, O God,
  its waters looked and trembled!
  The sea quaked to its very depths.
¹⁷ The clouds poured down rain;
  the thunder rumbled in the sky.
  Your arrows of lightning flashed.
¹⁸ Your thunder roared from the whirlwind;
  the lightning lit up the world!
  The earth trembled and shook.
¹⁹ Your road led through the sea,
  your pathway through the mighty waters—
  a pathway no one knew was there!
²⁰ You led your people along that road like a flock of sheep,
  with Moses and Aaron as their shepherds.

Psalm 78

A psalm of Asaph.*

¹ O my people, listen to my instructions.
  Open your ears to what I am saying,
² for I will speak to you in a parable.
  I will teach you hidden lessons from our past—
³ stories we have heard and known,
  stories our ancestors handed down to us.
⁴ We will not hide these truths from our children;
  we will tell the next generation
  about the glorious deeds of the LORD,
  about his power and his mighty wonders.
⁵ For he issued his laws to Jacob;
  he gave his instructions to Israel.
  He commanded our ancestors
  to teach them to their children,
⁶ so the next generation might know them—
  even the children not yet born—
  and they in turn will teach their own children.
⁷ So each generation should set its hope anew on God,
  not forgetting his glorious miracles
  and obeying his commands.
⁸ Then they will not be like their ancestors—
  stubborn, rebellious, and unfaithful,
  refusing to give their hearts to God.

⁹ The warriors of Ephraim, though armed with bows,
  turned their backs and fled on the day of battle.
¹⁰ They did not keep God's covenant
  and refused to live by his instructions.
¹¹ They forgot what he had done—
  the great wonders he had shown them,
¹² the miracles he did for their ancestors
  on the plain of Zoan in the land of Egypt.
¹³ For he divided the sea and led them through,
  making the water stand up like walls!
¹⁴ In the daytime he led them by a cloud,
  and all night by a pillar of fire.

77:16 Hebrew *the waters*. 78:TITLE Hebrew *maskil*. This may be a literary or musical term.

Psalm 77 The psalmist laments that God has turned away from him, even though he feels innocent. He reflects on his situation (77:3, 6, 12) and finds hope in remembering God's past deeds (77:11).

Psalm 78 This psalm reflects on God's people's past faithlessness and God's response to that faithlessness. It encourages those who follow him to hope in God based on his past miracles and to obey his instructions (78:7). Remembering our failures and God's faithfulness can strengthen us, too.

78:5-6 The telling of the story should motivate God's people to obey what he commanded (Deuteronomy 6:4-9).

15 He split open the rocks in the wilderness
    to give them water, as from a gushing spring.
16 He made streams pour from the rock,
    making the waters flow down like a river!
17 Yet they kept on sinning against him,
    rebelling against the Most High in the desert.
18 They stubbornly tested God in their hearts,
    demanding the foods they craved.
19 They even spoke against God himself, saying,
    "God can't give us food in the wilderness.
20 Yes, he can strike a rock so water gushes out,
    but he can't give his people bread and meat."
21 When the LORD heard them, he was furious.
    The fire of his wrath burned against Jacob.
    Yes, his anger rose against Israel,
22 for they did not believe God
    or trust him to care for them.
23 But he commanded the skies to open;
    he opened the doors of heaven.
24 He rained down manna for them to eat;
    he gave them bread from heaven.
25 They ate the food of angels!
    God gave them all they could hold.
26 He released the east wind in the heavens
    and guided the south wind by his mighty power.

Oikos IMAGE — MY STORY WITH FAMILY & FRIENDS

Tell Me a Story

SCRIPTURE CONNECTION: PSALM 78:1-11

"Tell me a story, Nana." My granddaughter loves stories. When she stays overnight, at bedtime we read a book and pray. Then she invariably asks for a story. This is my opportunity.

It's a perfect time to share stories of God's working in her great grandparents', grandparents', or her parents' lives. She listens with great intent.

Psalm 78 directs us to talk with the next generation about God's work in our families' lives. More than stories of ancestry, I call it our spiritual heritage. These stories not only look back but look ahead, giving our lives eternal significance.

Verbal storytelling is powerful. Jesus often used stories to help his followers understand his message. Likewise, our families' faith stories are gems that the psalmist says lead children and grandchildren to hope in God (78:7).

Telling our God-stories models authentic faith, helping children:

- understand that God is real and can be trusted,
- see that we know God, assuring them that they can too, and
- hear of a relationship with God that is for now, not just Bible times.

> Our families' faith stories lead children to hope in God.

IMAGINE

When might you ask those who have lived longer than you how they have seen God in their lives?

What can you do to capture and communicate these stories to the next generation?

"As a grandmother, I consciously look for opportunities to share my family's spiritual heritage with my grandchildren."

NANCY CHAMBERLIN SPROWLS is a devotional writer, mother, and grandmother. She encourages women to have a passion for God's Word and to leave a spiritual legacy for their families.

27 He rained down meat as thick as dust—
   birds as plentiful as the sand on the seashore!
28 He caused the birds to fall within their camp
   and all around their tents.
29 The people ate their fill.
   He gave them what they craved.
30 But before they satisfied their craving,
   while the meat was yet in their mouths,
31 the anger of God rose against them,
   and he killed their strongest men.
   He struck down the finest of Israel's young men.
32 But in spite of this, the people kept sinning.
   Despite his wonders, they refused to trust him.
33 So he ended their lives in failure,
   their years in terror.
34 When God began killing them,
   they finally sought him.
   They repented and took God seriously.
35 Then they remembered that God was their rock,
   that God Most High* was their redeemer.
36 But all they gave him was lip service;
   they lied to him with their tongues.
37 Their hearts were not loyal to him.
   They did not keep his covenant.
38 Yet he was merciful and forgave their sins
   and did not destroy them all.
   Many times he held back his anger
   and did not unleash his fury!
39 For he remembered that they were merely mortal,
   gone like a breath of wind that never returns.
40 Oh, how often they rebelled against him in the wilderness
   and grieved his heart in that dry wasteland.
41 Again and again they tested God's patience
   and provoked the Holy One of Israel.
42 They did not remember his power
   and how he rescued them from their enemies.
43 They did not remember his miraculous signs in Egypt,
   his wonders on the plain of Zoan.
44 For he turned their rivers into blood,
   so no one could drink from the streams.
45 He sent vast swarms of flies to consume them
   and hordes of frogs to ruin them.
46 He gave their crops to caterpillars;
   their harvest was consumed by locusts.
47 He destroyed their grapevines with hail
   and shattered their sycamore-figs with sleet.
48 He abandoned their cattle to the hail,
   their livestock to bolts of lightning.
49 He loosed on them his fierce anger—
   all his fury, rage, and hostility.
   He dispatched against them
   a band of destroying angels.
50 He turned his anger against them;
   he did not spare the Egyptians' lives
   but ravaged them with the plague.
51 He killed the oldest son in each Egyptian family,
   the flower of youth throughout the land of Egypt.*
52 But he led his own people like a flock of sheep,
   guiding them safely through the wilderness.
53 He kept them safe so they were not afraid;
   but the sea covered their enemies.
54 He brought them to the border of his holy land,
   to this land of hills he had won for them.
55 He drove out the nations before them;
   he gave them their inheritance by lot.
   He settled the tribes of Israel into their homes.
56 But they kept testing and rebelling against God Most High.
   They did not obey his laws.
57 They turned back and were as faithless as their parents.
   They were as undependable as a crooked bow.
58 They angered God by building shrines to other gods;
   they made him jealous with their idols.
59 When God heard them, he was very angry,
   and he completely rejected Israel.
60 Then he abandoned his dwelling at Shiloh,
   the Tabernacle where he had lived among the people.
61 He allowed the Ark of his might to be captured;
   he surrendered his glory into enemy hands.
62 He gave his people over to be butchered by the sword,
   because he was so angry with his own people—his special possession.
63 Their young men were killed by fire;
   their young women died before singing their wedding songs.
64 Their priests were slaughtered,
   and their widows could not mourn their deaths.
65 Then the Lord rose up as though waking from sleep,
   like a warrior aroused from a drunken stupor.
66 He routed his enemies
   and sent them to eternal shame.
67 But he rejected Joseph's descendants;
   he did not choose the tribe of Ephraim.
68 He chose instead the tribe of Judah,
   and Mount Zion, which he loved.
69 There he built his sanctuary as high as the heavens,
   as solid and enduring as the earth.
70 He chose his servant David,
   calling him from the sheep pens.
71 He took David from tending the ewes and lambs
   and made him the shepherd of Jacob's descendants—
   God's own people, Israel.
72 He cared for them with a true heart
   and led them with skillful hands.

78:35 Hebrew *El-Elyon.* **78:51** Hebrew *in the tents of Ham.*

Psalm 79

A psalm of Asaph.

1 O God, pagan nations have conquered your land,
   your special possession.
 They have defiled your holy Temple
   and made Jerusalem a heap of ruins.
2 They have left the bodies of your servants
   as food for the birds of heaven.
 The flesh of your godly ones
   has become food for the wild animals.
3 Blood has flowed like water all around Jerusalem;
   no one is left to bury the dead.
4 We are mocked by our neighbors,
   an object of scorn and derision to those
     around us.
5 O Lord, how long will you be angry with us?
     Forever?
 How long will your jealousy burn like fire?
6 Pour out your wrath on the nations that refuse
     to acknowledge you—
   on kingdoms that do not call upon your name.
7 For they have devoured your people Israel,*
   making the land a desolate wilderness.
8 Do not hold us guilty for the sins of our ancestors!
   Let your compassion quickly meet our needs,
   for we are on the brink of despair.
9 Help us, O God of our salvation!
   Help us for the glory of your name.
 Save us and forgive our sins
   for the honor of your name.
10 Why should pagan nations be allowed to scoff,
    asking, "Where is their God?"
 Show us your vengeance against the nations,
   for they have spilled the blood of your servants.
11 Listen to the moaning of the prisoners.
    Demonstrate your great power by saving
      those condemned to die.
12 O Lord, pay back our neighbors seven times
    for the scorn they have hurled at you.
13 Then we your people, the sheep of your pasture,
    will thank you forever and ever,
    praising your greatness from generation to
      generation.

Psalm 80

For the choir director: A psalm of Asaph, to be sung to the tune "Lilies of the Covenant."

1 Please listen, O Shepherd of Israel,
   you who lead Joseph's descendants like a
     flock.
 O God, enthroned above the cherubim,
   display your radiant glory
2   to Ephraim, Benjamin, and Manasseh.
 Show us your mighty power.
   Come to rescue us!
3 Turn us again to yourself, O God.
   Make your face shine down upon us.
   Only then will we be saved.
4 O Lord God of Heaven's Armies,
   how long will you be angry with our prayers?
5 You have fed us with sorrow
   and made us drink tears by the bucketful.
6 You have made us the scorn* of neighboring
     nations.
   Our enemies treat us as a joke.
7 Turn us again to yourself, O God of Heaven's
     Armies.
   Make your face shine down upon us.
   Only then will we be saved.
8 You brought us from Egypt like a grapevine;
   you drove away the pagan nations and
     transplanted us into your land.
9 You cleared the ground for us,
   and we took root and filled the land.
10 Our shade covered the mountains;
    our branches covered the mighty cedars.
11 We spread our branches west to the
      Mediterranean Sea;
    our shoots spread east to the Euphrates River.*
12 But now, why have you broken down our walls
    so that all who pass by may steal our fruit?
13 The wild boar from the forest devours it,
    and the wild animals feed on it.
14 Come back, we beg you, O God of Heaven's
      Armies.
    Look down from heaven and see our plight.
    Take care of this grapevine

79:7 Hebrew *devoured Jacob*. See note on 44:4.   80:6 As in Syriac version; Hebrew reads *the strife.*   80:11 Hebrew *west to the sea, . . . east to the river.*

Psalm 79 This lament describes Jerusalem's fall in 586 BC. Israel's continual rebellions described in Psalm 78 finally provoked God's wrath, resulting in the desolation of Jerusalem, the defilement of the Temple, and the disgraced bodies that littered the landscape. Psalm 79 appears to have initially been part of what the Israelites recited to seek forgiveness during their time in exile. Parts continued to be incorporated into Jewish prayers on the Ninth of Ab. This date commemorates the destruction of the Jerusalem temple and other disastrous events, including the destruction of the second Temple (70 AD), pogroms, and the Holocaust. Having shared ways to lament can unite us, help us affirm what is wrong, and lean on God to make the world right. Such times can reinvigorate us to join God in building his Kingdom.

Psalm 80 This psalm of lament might have originated with the remnant of the northern kingdom after its fall in 722 BC; if so, it may have undergone later revision. The people call on God as their Shepherd and as the God of Heaven's Armies in the hope that he will return to them and restore them. They remember the Exodus and their special relationship with the Lord and conclude with an expression of renewed commitment to him (80:18).

15 that you yourself have planted,
    this son you have raised for yourself.
16 For we are chopped up and burned by our enemies.
    May they perish at the sight of your frown.
17 Strengthen the man you love,
    the son of your choice.
18 Then we will never abandon you again.
    Revive us so we can call on your name once more.
19 Turn us again to yourself, O LORD God of Heaven's Armies.
    Make your face shine down upon us.
    Only then will we be saved.

Psalm 81

For the choir director: A psalm of Asaph, to be accompanied by a stringed instrument.*

1 Sing praises to God, our strength.
    Sing to the God of Jacob.
2 Sing! Beat the tambourine.
    Play the sweet lyre and the harp.
3 Blow the ram's horn at new moon,
    and again at full moon to call a festival!
4 For this is required by the decrees of Israel;
    it is a regulation of the God of Jacob.
5 He made it a law for Israel*
    when he attacked Egypt to set us free.

    I heard an unknown voice say,
6 "Now I will take the load from your shoulders;
    I will free your hands from their heavy tasks.
7 You cried to me in trouble, and I saved you;
    I answered out of the thundercloud
    and tested your faith when there was no water at Meribah. *Interlude*
8 "Listen to me, O my people, while I give you stern warnings.
    O Israel, if you would only listen to me!
9 You must never have a foreign god;
    you must not bow down before a false god.
10 For it was I, the LORD your God,
    who rescued you from the land of Egypt.
    Open your mouth wide, and I will fill it with good things.

11 "But no, my people wouldn't listen.
    Israel did not want me around.
12 So I let them follow their own stubborn desires,
    living according to their own ideas.
13 Oh, that my people would listen to me!
    Oh, that Israel would follow me, walking in my paths!
14 How quickly I would then subdue their enemies!
    How soon my hands would be upon their foes!
15 Those who hate the LORD would cringe before him;
    they would be doomed forever.
16 But I would feed you with the finest wheat.
    I would satisfy you with wild honey from the rock."

Psalm 82

A psalm of Asaph.

1 God presides over heaven's court;
    he pronounces judgment on the heavenly beings:
2 "How long will you hand down unjust decisions
    by favoring the wicked? *Interlude*
3 "Give justice to the poor and the orphan;
    uphold the rights of the oppressed and the destitute.
4 Rescue the poor and helpless;
    deliver them from the grasp of evil people.
5 But these oppressors know nothing;
    they are so ignorant!
    They wander about in darkness,
    while the whole world is shaken to the core.

81:TITLE Hebrew *according to the gittith.* **81:5** Hebrew *for Joseph.*

80:14-18 Israel is frequently depicted with vine imagery in the prophets (Isaiah 5:1-7; 27:2-6; Jeremiah 2:21; 12:10; Ezekiel 15:1-8; 19:10-14; Hosea 10:1). Given the plural pronouns in Psalm 80:14, 16, the reference to "this son" likely refers to the whole nation. The phrase "the man you love" may refer to the king as a representative of the nation or the nation itself. It can more literally be translated as "the man at your right hand." If it alludes to the nation, it could refer to Ephraim (whom Jacob blessed with his right hand and whose tribe is associated with the northern kingdom; see study note on 81:5). Or it may refer to Benjamin, whose name means "son of the right hand" and is associated with the southern kingdom. If the psalmist meant Ephraim or Benjamin, which the plural pronouns in 80:18 suggest, then these verses focus on a cry for God to deliver his chosen nation rather than to deliver a single person he loves.

Psalm 81 While Psalms 79 and 80 reflect the people's experience of devastation, Psalm 81 offers insight into God's perspective. Following an opening call to worship, God speaks (81:6-16), describing his historic acts for his people, their ungrateful and disobedient choices, and the consequences. He then calls them to return to him in obedience and indicates that he will deliver them from their enemies when they do.

81:5 The phrase translated here as "for Israel" literally says "for Joseph." This refers to Joseph's sons, Ephraim and Manasseh, and the tribes descended from them. These tribes are used here to refer to the entire nation of Israel.

Psalm 82 As in Psalm 81, Psalm 82 gives a divine view (see study note on Job 1:6). Today's concept of monotheism denies that other deities exist. By contrast, the Old Testament points to divine beings or "gods" who answered to Israel's God, perhaps angels or demons by modern understanding. In this psalm, God judges these divine beings for the injustices that they have allowed. These ideas also appear in Ephesians 6:10-18. Christians are called to "stand firm against all strategies of the devil," knowing that we are engaged in a spiritual battle.

⁶ I say, 'You are gods;
  you are all children of the Most High.
⁷ But you will die like mere mortals
  and fall like every other ruler.'"
⁸ Rise up, O God, and judge the earth,
  for all the nations belong to you.

Psalm 83
A song. A psalm of Asaph.

¹ O God, do not be silent!
  Do not be deaf.
  Do not be quiet, O God.
² Don't you hear the uproar of your enemies?
  Don't you see that your arrogant enemies are rising up?
³ They devise crafty schemes against your people;
  they conspire against your precious ones.
⁴ "Come," they say, "let us wipe out Israel as a nation.
  We will destroy the very memory of its existence."
⁵ Yes, this was their unanimous decision.
  They signed a treaty as allies against you—
⁶ these Edomites and Ishmaelites;
  Moabites and Hagrites;
⁷ Gebalites, Ammonites, and Amalekites;
  and people from Philistia and Tyre.
⁸ Assyria has joined them, too,
  and is allied with the descendants of Lot. *Interlude*

⁹ Do to them as you did to the Midianites
  and as you did to Sisera and Jabin at the Kishon River.
¹⁰ They were destroyed at Endor,
  and their decaying corpses fertilized the soil.
¹¹ Let their mighty nobles die as Oreb and Zeeb did.
  Let all their princes die like Zebah and Zalmunna,
¹² for they said, "Let us seize for our own use these pasturelands of God!"
¹³ O my God, scatter them like tumbleweed,
  like chaff before the wind!
¹⁴ As a fire burns a forest
  and as a flame sets mountains ablaze,
¹⁵ chase them with your fierce storm;
  terrify them with your tempest.
¹⁶ Utterly disgrace them
  until they submit to your name, O LORD.
¹⁷ Let them be ashamed and terrified forever.
  Let them die in disgrace.
¹⁸ Then they will learn that you alone are called the LORD,
  that you alone are the Most High,
  supreme over all the earth.

Psalm 84
For the choir director: A psalm of the descendants of Korah, to be accompanied by a stringed instrument.*

¹ How lovely is your dwelling place,
  O LORD of Heaven's Armies.
² I long, yes, I faint with longing
  to enter the courts of the LORD.
  With my whole being, body and soul,
  I will shout joyfully to the living God.
³ Even the sparrow finds a home,
  and the swallow builds her nest and raises her young
  at a place near your altar,
  O LORD of Heaven's Armies, my King and my God!
⁴ What joy for those who can live in your house,
  always singing your praises. *Interlude*

⁵ What joy for those whose strength comes from the LORD,
  who have set their minds on a pilgrimage to Jerusalem.
⁶ When they walk through the Valley of Weeping,*
  it will become a place of refreshing springs.
  The autumn rains will clothe it with blessings.
⁷ They will continue to grow stronger,
  and each of them will appear before God in Jerusalem.*
⁸ O LORD God of Heaven's Armies, hear my prayer.
  Listen, O God of Jacob. *Interlude*

⁹ O God, look with favor upon the king, our shield!
  Show favor to the one you have anointed.

84:TITLE Hebrew *according to the gittith.* **84:6** Or *Valley of Poplars;* Hebrew reads *valley of Baca.* **84:7** Hebrew *Zion.*

82:6-7 The "gods . . . like mere mortals" cannot escape the judgment common to human rulers. Jesus quoted from this passage in John 10:34.
Psalm 83 This community lament asks God for rescue and victory. The terse poetry suggests difficult times. A powerful coalition desires to destroy Israel (83:1-4) and allies itself against God (83:5-8). Recalling the fate of others who came against Israel (83:9-12), the psalmist prays that the same will happen to these enemies (83:13-16) so that God would receive honor among them (83:17-18). It is unclear whether this psalm arose out of a specific historical instance of opposition by these nations, or if it is a poetic collage of nations representing Israel's enemies.
83:6-7 The Edomites, descendants of Esau, were located to the southeast of Judah (see Genesis 25:30; 32:3; 36:1-8). Ishmaelites were desert-dwelling descendants of Hagar. Moabites and Ammonites descended from Lot; both were located to the east of Israel and Judah. The Hagrites were possibly located north of the Ammonites (1 Chronicles 5:10).
Psalm 84 This psalm is traditionally considered to be a song of celebration for use on a pilgrimage to Jerusalem (see 84:5). It focuses on the pilgrim's longing to worship in God's presence in the Temple. Some have explicitly tied this psalm to the Festival of Shelters in the autumn.
84:9 Both kings and priests were anointed to dedicate them for service (see 132:17; Exodus 28:41; 1 Samuel 9:16; 16:1-13; see also Isaiah 61:1; Acts 10:38).

¹⁰ A single day in your courts
    is better than a thousand anywhere else!
  I would rather be a gatekeeper in the house of
      my God
    than live the good life in the homes of the wicked.
¹¹ For the LORD God is our sun and our shield.
    He gives us grace and glory.
  The LORD will withhold no good thing
    from those who do what is right.
¹² O LORD of Heaven's Armies,
    what joy for those who trust in you.

85:1 Hebrew *of Jacob.* See note on 44:4.

Psalm 85
For the choir director: A psalm of the descendants of Korah.

¹ LORD, you poured out blessings on your land!
    You restored the fortunes of Israel.*
² You forgave the guilt of your people—
    yes, you covered all their sins.   *Interlude*
³ You held back your fury.
    You kept back your blazing anger.

⁴ Now restore us again, O God of our salvation.
    Put aside your anger against us once more.

Psalm 85 The psalmist leads the postexilic community in lament and prayer for full redemption. He ponders God's past rescue of Israel from exile (85:1-3), longs for greater evidence of God's goodness, and leads the community in prayer for full restoration (85:4-7). God responds with a message of peace (85:8-9), and the psalm concludes with a lyrical outburst at the grandeur of God's salvation (85:10-13).

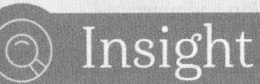

Insight — THE MUSIC OF THE PSALMS

The psalms on the page may look like regular poetry to us—we should also remember that these poetic prayers were Israel's worship songs. We no longer know what these songs sounded like or what specific beat or tempo the original psalm writer had in mind. But some psalms still have musical notations or instructions that indicate how these songs were to be played and sung. The Israelites sang these psalms to worship God, and we can still worship God with these psalms today. How does knowing that Psalms is a songbook help you feel free to sing, write, or speak about things close to your heart?

MUSICAL INSTRUCTIONS	PSALMS
Interlude *(Selah)*	3:2, 4, 8; etc. (cited 71 times in Psalms)
Accompanied by stringed instruments	4, 54, 55, 61, 67, 76
Accompanied by the flute	5
Accompanied by an eight-string instrument	6, 12
Accompanied by a stringed instrument	8, 81, 84
Accompanied by stringed instruments	4, 54, 55, 61, 67, 76
Sung to the tune "Death of the Son"	9
Sung to the tune "Doe of the Dawn"	22
Sung to the tune "Lilies"	45, 69
Sung by soprano voices *(alamoth)*	46
Sung to the tune "Dove on Distant Oaks"	56
Sung to the tune "Do Not Destroy!"	57–59, 75
Sung to the tune "Lily of the Testimony"	60
Sung to the tune "Lilies of the Covenant"	80
Sung to the tune "The Suffering of Affliction"	88

(All full-psalm listings refer to the inscriptions at the top of the psalm.)

5 Will you be angry with us always?
 Will you prolong your wrath to all generations?
6 Won't you revive us again,
 so your people can rejoice in you?
7 Show us your unfailing love, O LORD,
 and grant us your salvation.

8 I listen carefully to what God the LORD is saying,
 for he speaks peace to his faithful people.
 But let them not return to their foolish ways.
9 Surely his salvation is near to those who fear him,
 so our land will be filled with his glory.

10 Unfailing love and truth have met together.
 Righteousness and peace have kissed!
11 Truth springs up from the earth,
 and righteousness smiles down from heaven.
12 Yes, the LORD pours down his blessings.
 Our land will yield its bountiful harvest.
13 Righteousness goes as a herald before him,
 preparing the way for his steps.

Psalm 86
A prayer of David.

1 Bend down, O LORD, and hear my prayer;
 answer me, for I need your help.
2 Protect me, for I am devoted to you.
 Save me, for I serve you and trust you.
 You are my God.
3 Be merciful to me, O Lord,
 for I am calling on you constantly.
4 Give me happiness, O Lord,
 for I give myself to you.
5 O Lord, you are so good, so ready to forgive,
 so full of unfailing love for all who ask for your help.
6 Listen closely to my prayer, O LORD;
 hear my urgent cry.
7 I will call to you whenever I'm in trouble,
 and you will answer me.

8 No pagan god is like you, O Lord.
 None can do what you do!
9 All the nations you made
 will come and bow before you, Lord;
 they will praise your holy name.
10 For you are great and perform wonderful deeds.
 You alone are God.

11 Teach me your ways, O LORD,
 that I may live according to your truth!
 Grant me purity of heart,
 so that I may honor you.
12 With all my heart I will praise you, O Lord my God.
 I will give glory to your name forever,
13 for your love for me is very great.
 You have rescued me from the depths of death.*

14 O God, insolent people rise up against me;
 a violent gang is trying to kill me.
 You mean nothing to them.
15 But you, O Lord,
 are a God of compassion and mercy,
 slow to get angry
 and filled with unfailing love and faithfulness.
16 Look down and have mercy on me.
 Give your strength to your servant;
 save me, the son of your servant.
17 Send me a sign of your favor.
 Then those who hate me will be put to shame,
 for you, O LORD, help and comfort me.

Psalm 87
A song. A psalm of the descendants of Korah.

1 On the holy mountain
 stands the city founded by the LORD.
2 He loves the city of Jerusalem
 more than any other city in Israel.*
3 O city of God,
 what glorious things are said of you!

Interlude

4 I will count Egypt* and Babylon among those who know me—
 also Philistia and Tyre, and even distant Ethiopia.*
 They have all become citizens of Jerusalem!

86:13 Hebrew *of Sheol.* 87:2 Hebrew *He loves the gates of Zion more than all the dwellings of Jacob.* See note on 44:4.
87:4a Hebrew *Rahab,* the name of a mythical sea monster that represents chaos in ancient literature. The name is used here as a poetic name for Egypt. 87:4b Hebrew *Cush.*

85:10-11 These poetic words point to the knowledge that God's work of restoration displays his unfailing love and truth. "Truth" here can also be translated as "faithfulness" and describes God. This restoration will also be noteworthy for its social justice. In Deuteronomy 16:18-20, the words "fairly" and "true justice" can also be rendered as "righteous judgment," which God expects of his judges and officials. "Peace" or "well-being" results from the presence of this "justice" and "righteousness" (Isaiah 32:16-17).
85:10-13 In the glorious world of renewal and salvation, all the qualities of God's care—love, truth, righteousness, and peace—come together and transform the created order into something new (see Isaiah 32:15-20).

Psalm 86 This is the only psalm attributed to David in the third part of the book. It appears after the "prayers of David" officially end at 72:20. Some have observed that Psalm 86 creatively reuses parts of previous Davidic psalms, particularly Psalms 40–41, 69–71, and 72. By combining these texts with a focus on Sinai (as in Exodus 33–34), the psalmist provides a biblically grounded way for people who came after David to pray.
86:15 This verse builds on God's character as described in Exodus 34:6-7. God is "gracious and merciful" (Psalm 111:4), "slow to get angry" (103:8; 145:8), and filled with "unfailing love and faithfulness" (85:10; 143:1).
Psalm 87 This psalm envisions Jerusalem as the city of God where all the nations are citizens.

⁵ Regarding Jerusalem* it will be said,
  "Everyone enjoys the rights of citizenship
    there."
  And the Most High will personally bless this
    city.
⁶ When the Lord registers the nations, he will say,
  "They have all become citizens of Jerusalem."
                                                    Interlude

⁷ The people will play flutes* and sing,
  "The source of my life springs from
    Jerusalem!"

Psalm 88

For the choir director: A psalm of the descendants of Korah. A song to be sung to the tune "The Suffering of Affliction." A psalm* of Heman the Ezrahite.

¹ O Lord, God of my salvation,
  I cry out to you by day.
  I come to you at night.
² Now hear my prayer;
  listen to my cry.
³ For my life is full of troubles,
  and death* draws near.
⁴ I am as good as dead,
  like a strong man with no strength left.
⁵ They have left me among the dead,
  and I lie like a corpse in a grave.
  I am forgotten,
    cut off from your care.
⁶ You have thrown me into the lowest pit,
  into the darkest depths.
⁷ Your anger weighs me down;
  with wave after wave you have engulfed me.
                                                    Interlude

⁸ You have driven my friends away
  by making me repulsive to them.
  I am in a trap with no way of escape.
⁹ My eyes are blinded by my tears.
  Each day I beg for your help, O Lord;
  I lift my hands to you for mercy.
¹⁰ Are your wonderful deeds of any use to the dead?
  Do the dead rise up and praise you?
                                                    Interlude

¹¹ Can those in the grave declare your unfailing
    love?
  Can they proclaim your faithfulness in the
    place of destruction?*

¹² Can the darkness speak of your wonderful
    deeds?
  Can anyone in the land of forgetfulness talk
    about your righteousness?
¹³ O Lord, I cry out to you.
  I will keep on pleading day by day.
¹⁴ O Lord, why do you reject me?
  Why do you turn your face from me?
¹⁵ I have been sick and close to death since my
    youth.
  I stand helpless and desperate before your
    terrors.
¹⁶ Your fierce anger has overwhelmed me.
  Your terrors have paralyzed me.
¹⁷ They swirl around me like floodwaters all day
    long.
  They have engulfed me completely.
¹⁸ You have taken away my companions and loved
    ones.
  Darkness is my closest friend.

Psalm 89

A psalm* of Ethan the Ezrahite.

¹ I will sing of the Lord's unfailing love forever!
  Young and old will hear of your faithfulness.
² Your unfailing love will last forever.
  Your faithfulness is as enduring as the heavens.

³ The Lord said, "I have made a covenant with
    David, my chosen servant.
  I have sworn this oath to him:
⁴ 'I will establish your descendants as kings forever;
    they will sit on your throne from now until
    eternity.'"   *Interlude*

⁵ All heaven will praise your great wonders, Lord;
  myriads of angels will praise you for your
    faithfulness.
⁶ For who in all of heaven can compare with the
    Lord?
  What mightiest angel is anything like the Lord?
⁷ The highest angelic powers stand in awe of God.
  He is far more awesome than all who
    surround his throne.
⁸ O Lord God of Heaven's Armies!
  Where is there anyone as mighty as you,
    O Lord?
  You are entirely faithful.

87:5 Hebrew *Zion*.   87:7 Or *will dance*.   88:TITLE Hebrew *maskil*. This may be a literary or musical term.   88:3 Hebrew *Sheol*.
88:11 Hebrew *in Abaddon*?   89:TITLE Hebrew *maskil*. This may be a literary or musical term.

Psalm 88 Songs of lament usually include both a plea and praise; however, this one focuses solely on the psalmist's experience of suffering and cry for relief. Not only does he feel abandoned by God (88:5), but he blames God for his suffering (88:6-8, 16-18). In doing so, he resembles Job. While such accusations can seem sinful, their inclusion in Scripture, along with the book of Job as a whole, invites us to approach God with both honesty and reverence.

Psalm 89 While this psalm opens on a note of praise and a remembrance of the Davidic covenant, it then leads into the true purpose: to lament and cry for a restored relationship between the Lord and his people (89:38-51). Like Psalm 88, Psalm 89 closes without deliverance or restoration. Sometimes we add a positive word after any complaint to show our good attitude or strong faith. The Bible's pattern shows that it is okay to pour out feelings to God without needing an immediate fix.

9 You rule the oceans.
   You subdue their storm-tossed waves.
10 You crushed the great sea monster.*
   You scattered your enemies with your mighty arm.
11 The heavens are yours, and the earth is yours;
   everything in the world is yours—you created it all.
12 You created north and south.
   Mount Tabor and Mount Hermon praise your name.
13 Powerful is your arm!
   Strong is your hand!
   Your right hand is lifted high in glorious strength.
14 Righteousness and justice are the foundation of your throne.
   Unfailing love and truth walk before you as attendants.
15 Happy are those who hear the joyful call to worship,
   for they will walk in the light of your presence, LORD.
16 They rejoice all day long in your wonderful reputation.
   They exult in your righteousness.
17 You are their glorious strength.
   It pleases you to make us strong.
18 Yes, our protection comes from the LORD,
   and he, the Holy One of Israel, has given us our king.
19 Long ago you spoke in a vision to your faithful people.
   You said, "I have raised up a warrior.
   I have selected him from the common people to be king.
20 I have found my servant David.
   I have anointed him with my holy oil.
21 I will steady him with my hand;
   with my powerful arm I will make him strong.
22 His enemies will not defeat him,
   nor will the wicked overpower him.
23 I will beat down his adversaries before him
   and destroy those who hate him.
24 My faithfulness and unfailing love will be with him,
   and by my authority he will grow in power.
25 I will extend his rule over the sea,
   his dominion over the rivers.
26 And he will call out to me, 'You are my Father,
   my God, and the Rock of my salvation.'
27 I will make him my firstborn son,
   the mightiest king on earth.
28 I will love him and be kind to him forever;
   my covenant with him will never end.
29 I will preserve an heir for him;
   his throne will be as endless as the days of heaven.
30 But if his descendants forsake my instructions
   and fail to obey my regulations,
31 if they do not obey my decrees
   and fail to keep my commands,
32 then I will punish their sin with the rod,
   and their disobedience with beating.
33 But I will never stop loving him
   nor fail to keep my promise to him.
34 No, I will not break my covenant;
   I will not take back a single word I said.
35 I have sworn an oath to David,
   and in my holiness I cannot lie:
36 His dynasty will go on forever;
   his kingdom will endure as the sun.
37 It will be as eternal as the moon,
   my faithful witness in the sky!" *Interlude*
38 But now you have rejected him and cast him off.
   You are angry with your anointed king.
39 You have renounced your covenant with him;
   you have thrown his crown in the dust.
40 You have broken down the walls protecting him
   and ruined every fort defending him.
41 Everyone who comes along has robbed him,
   and he has become a joke to his neighbors.
42 You have strengthened his enemies
   and made them all rejoice.
43 You have made his sword useless
   and refused to help him in battle.
44 You have ended his splendor
   and overturned his throne.
45 You have made him old before his time
   and publicly disgraced him. *Interlude*
46 O LORD, how long will this go on?
   Will you hide yourself forever?
   How long will your anger burn like fire?
47 Remember how short my life is,
   how empty and futile this human existence!
48 No one can live forever; all will die.
   No one can escape the power of the grave.*
    Interlude
49 Lord, where is your unfailing love?
   You promised it to David with a faithful pledge.
50 Consider, Lord, how your servants are disgraced!
   I carry in my heart the insults of so many people.
51 Your enemies have mocked me, O LORD;
   they mock your anointed king wherever he goes.
52 Praise the LORD forever!
   Amen and amen!

89:10 Hebrew *Rahab*, the name of a mythical sea monster that represents chaos in ancient literature. 89:48 Hebrew *of Sheol*.

89:52 This doxology concludes Book Three (Psalms 73–89); it is not intended to be read as part of Psalm 89. It stands in stark contrast to the anguish and questioning of Psalm 89. See also the doxologies in 41:13; 106:48, the ends of Books One and Four.

BOOK FOUR (PSALMS 90–106)

Psalm 90

A prayer of Moses, the man of God.

1 Lord, through all the generations
   you have been our home!
2 Before the mountains were born,
   before you gave birth to the earth and the world,
   from beginning to end, you are God.

3 You turn people back to dust, saying,
   "Return to dust, you mortals!"
4 For you, a thousand years are as a passing day,
   as brief as a few night hours.
5 You sweep people away like dreams that disappear.
   They are like grass that springs up in the morning.
6 In the morning it blooms and flourishes,
   but by evening it is dry and withered.

7 We wither beneath your anger;
   we are overwhelmed by your fury.
8 You spread out our sins before you—
   our secret sins—and you see them all.
9 We live our lives beneath your wrath,
   ending our years with a groan.

10 Seventy years are given to us!
    Some even live to eighty.
   But even the best years are filled with pain and trouble;
    soon they disappear, and we fly away.
11 Who can comprehend the power of your anger?
    Your wrath is as awesome as the fear you deserve.
12 Teach us to realize the brevity of life,
    so that we may grow in wisdom.

13 O LORD, come back to us!
    How long will you delay?
    Take pity on your servants!
14 Satisfy us each morning with your unfailing love,
    so we may sing for joy to the end of our lives.
15 Give us gladness in proportion to our former misery!
    Replace the evil years with good.
16 Let us, your servants, see you work again;
    let our children see your glory.

> "Wide awake to the presence of God, I realized I had been so focused on asking why a good God allowed bad things to happen that I was missing out on the nearness of God all along. In becoming preoccupied with the *why*, I was missing the *Who*."
>
> **MARGARET FEINBERG**
> writer and Bible teacher

17 And may the Lord our God show us his approval
    and make our efforts successful.
    Yes, make our efforts successful!

Psalm 91

1 Those who live in the shelter of the Most High
    will find rest in the shadow of the Almighty.
2 This I declare about the LORD:
    He alone is my refuge, my place of safety;
    he is my God, and I trust him.
3 For he will rescue you from every trap
    and protect you from deadly disease.
4 He will cover you with his feathers.
    He will shelter you with his wings.
    His faithful promises are your armor and protection.

Book Four (Psalms 90–106) Book Four can be understood as a poetic response to the problem of the Exile and the apparent suspension of David's royal line (see Psalm 89). The response is that the Lord rules over the created order; his kingdom overcomes all chaos, anarchy, and confusion.

Psalm 90 This is the only psalm associated with Moses. Tying the opening psalm of Book Four to the man who led Israel out of Egypt's bondage may point Israel back to the teachings of the first five books of the Old Testament, or the Torah (Genesis to Deuteronomy). Alternatively, it may be the kind of prayer that Moses would have prayed for his subjugated people. Either way, the psalm recognizes that deliverance from suffering does not always come quickly but that God remains sovereign and faithful.

90:11-12 In the search for wisdom, no one can comprehend the Lord (see Isaiah 40:13). The appropriate human response to the Lord is godly fear (see Psalm 60:4). The Lord alone can teach humans to follow the path of wisdom (25:4-6).

Psalm 91 This psalm expresses confidence in God Almighty, who provides a shelter for those who take refuge in him. They receive redemption, life, and honor from the Lord, who loves and cares for those who seek him. It can be read as the praise that is often part of prayers of lament, in this case following the pain of Psalms 88–90.

⁵ Do not be afraid of the terrors of the night,
   nor the arrow that flies in the day.
⁶ Do not dread the disease that stalks in darkness,
   nor the disaster that strikes at midday.
⁷ Though a thousand fall at your side,
   though ten thousand are dying around you,
   these evils will not touch you.
⁸ Just open your eyes,
   and see how the wicked are punished.
⁹ If you make the LORD your refuge,
   if you make the Most High your shelter,
¹⁰ no evil will conquer you;
   no plague will come near your home.
¹¹ For he will order his angels
   to protect you wherever you go.
¹² They will hold you up with their hands
   so you won't even hurt your foot on a stone.
¹³ You will trample upon lions and cobras;
   you will crush fierce lions and serpents under your feet!
¹⁴ The LORD says, "I will rescue those who love me.
   I will protect those who trust in my name.
¹⁵ When they call on me, I will answer;
   I will be with them in trouble.
   I will rescue and honor them.
¹⁶ I will reward them with a long life
   and give them my salvation."

Psalm 92

A psalm. A song to be sung on the Sabbath Day.

¹ It is good to give thanks to the LORD,
   to sing praises to the Most High.
² It is good to proclaim your unfailing love in the morning,
   your faithfulness in the evening,
³ accompanied by a ten-stringed instrument,
   a harp,
   and the melody of a lyre.
⁴ You thrill me, LORD, with all you have done for me!
   I sing for joy because of what you have done.
⁵ O LORD, what great works you do!
   And how deep are your thoughts.
⁶ Only a simpleton would not know,
   and only a fool would not understand this:
⁷ Though the wicked sprout like weeds
   and evildoers flourish,
   they will be destroyed forever.
⁸ But you, O LORD, will be exalted forever.
⁹ Your enemies, LORD, will surely perish;
   all evildoers will be scattered.
¹⁰ But you have made me as strong as a wild ox.
   You have anointed me with the finest oil.
¹¹ My eyes have seen the downfall of my enemies;
   my ears have heard the defeat of my wicked opponents.
¹² But the godly will flourish like palm trees
   and grow strong like the cedars of Lebanon.
¹³ For they are transplanted to the LORD's own house.
   They flourish in the courts of our God.
¹⁴ Even in old age they will still produce fruit;
   they will remain vital and green.
¹⁵ They will declare, "The LORD is just!
   He is my rock!
   There is no evil in him!"

Psalm 93

¹ The LORD is king! He is robed in majesty.
   Indeed, the LORD is robed in majesty and armed with strength.
   The world stands firm
   and cannot be shaken.
² Your throne, O LORD, has stood from time immemorial.
   You yourself are from the everlasting past.
³ The floods have risen up, O LORD.
   The floods have roared like thunder;
   the floods have lifted their pounding waves.
⁴ But mightier than the violent raging of the seas,
   mightier than the breakers on the shore—
   the LORD above is mightier than these!
⁵ Your royal laws cannot be changed.
   Your reign, O LORD, is holy forever and ever.

91:14-16 God himself speaks, encouraging his followers with words promising protection and provision.

Psalm 92 Thanksgiving and praise open this psalm. The Lord—the Most High—is faithful and just in discerning between the godly and the wicked. The godly will enjoy a glorious, vigorous future, while the wicked will perish. The wise see and understand the Lord's works as they reveal his justice (92:6-7, 11, 15). The wicked, like weeds, are quickly destroyed (92:7-10).

92:1-15 Jewish tradition assigned one psalm to each day of the week: Sunday (Psalm 24), Monday (Psalm 48), Tuesday (Psalm 82), Wednesday (Psalm 94), Thursday (Psalm 81), Friday (Psalm 93), and the Sabbath (Psalm 92). This is the only psalm that indicates this use in its title. The Dead Sea Scrolls, a set of Jewish writings dating between 350 BC and AD 50 indicate that by the second century BC services were held on the Sabbath. Hymns such as this one may have been part of the worship.

Psalms 93–100 These psalms challenge the doubts created by the Exile (see Psalm 89) and answer the questions asked in 90:11, 13. The Lord has established a Kingdom (Psalm 93) that is characterized by the punishment of the wicked (Psalm 94), reverent obedience among his people (Psalm 95), justice for the poor (Psalm 96), celebration in Zion (Psalm 97), salvation for Israel (Psalm 98), holiness (Psalm 99), and praise (Psalm 100). Psalms 93–99 in particular celebrate the kingship of God.

Psalm 93 The everlasting Lord gloriously establishes his kingship (see also Psalms 47, 99–100).

Psalm 94

1 O LORD, the God of vengeance,
   O God of vengeance, let your glorious justice shine forth!
2 Arise, O Judge of the earth.
   Give the proud what they deserve.
3 How long, O LORD?
   How long will the wicked be allowed to gloat?
4 How long will they speak with arrogance?
   How long will these evil people boast?
5 They crush your people, LORD,
   hurting those you claim as your own.
6 They kill widows and foreigners
   and murder orphans.
7 "The LORD isn't looking," they say,
   "and besides, the God of Israel* doesn't care."

8 Think again, you fools!
   When will you finally catch on?
9 Is he deaf—the one who made your ears?
   Is he blind—the one who formed your eyes?
10 He punishes the nations—won't he also punish you?
    He knows everything—doesn't he also know what you are doing?
11 The LORD knows people's thoughts;
    he knows they are worthless!

12 Joyful are those you discipline, LORD,
    those you teach with your instructions.
13 You give them relief from troubled times
    until a pit is dug to capture the wicked.
14 The LORD will not reject his people;
    he will not abandon his special possession.
15 Judgment will again be founded on justice,
    and those with virtuous hearts will pursue it.

16 Who will protect me from the wicked?
    Who will stand up for me against evildoers?
17 Unless the LORD had helped me,
    I would soon have settled in the silence of the grave.
18 I cried out, "I am slipping!"
    but your unfailing love, O LORD, supported me.
19 When doubts filled my mind,
    your comfort gave me renewed hope and cheer.

20 Can unjust leaders claim that God is on their side—
    leaders whose decrees permit injustice?
21 They gang up against the righteous
    and condemn the innocent to death.
22 But the LORD is my fortress;
    my God is the mighty rock where I hide.
23 God will turn the sins of evil people back on them.
    He will destroy them for their sins.
    The LORD our God will destroy them.

Psalm 95

1 Come, let us sing to the LORD!
   Let us shout joyfully to the Rock of our salvation.
2 Let us come to him with thanksgiving.
   Let us sing psalms of praise to him.
3 For the LORD is a great God,
   a great King above all gods.
4 He holds in his hands the depths of the earth
   and the mightiest mountains.
5 The sea belongs to him, for he made it.
   His hands formed the dry land, too.

6 Come, let us worship and bow down.
   Let us kneel before the LORD our maker,
7 for he is our God.
   We are the people he watches over,
   the flock under his care.

If only you would listen to his voice today!
8 The LORD says, "Don't harden your hearts as Israel did at Meribah,
   as they did at Massah in the wilderness.
9 For there your ancestors tested and tried my patience,
   even though they saw everything I did.
10 For forty years I was angry with them, and I said,
   'They are a people whose hearts turn away from me.
   They refuse to do what I tell them.'
11 So in my anger I took an oath:
   'They will never enter my place of rest.'"

94:7 Hebrew *of Jacob*. See note on 44:4.

Psalm 94 This plea for the Lord's justice includes both communal and individual expressions of lament (94:1-7, 16-23). The psalmist not only gives voice to the pain and suffering caused by the wicked but also depicts the comfort and stability of the Lord's protection. He calls on the Lord to avenge the needy against the arrogant and foolish, rebukes such people for their folly (94:8-11), and pronounces a blessing on the wise (94:12-15). While not explicitly mentioning God's kingship, it is implicit in his roles as judge and vindicator.

Psalm 95 This call to worship urges the people to live lives of responsive obedience to the Lord. Such obedience would contrast with the wilderness generation, who hardened their hearts and refused to obey God. Their disobedience prevented them from entering God's rest in the Promised Land.

95:8 To "harden your hearts" means to be stubborn and resist the Lord's grace (see Numbers 20:2-13; see also Matthew 13:3-23; John 12:37-43; Ephesians 4:17-32; Hebrews 3:6-19; 4:6-11).

95:11 The generation of Israelites that wandered in the wilderness for forty years failed to enter the "place of rest" that Israel enjoyed after the conquest of the land (1 Kings 8:56; see Deuteronomy 12:9). The Lord promised them the land and gave it to them (Isaiah 28:12), but they did not obey him (Isaiah 28:1). The warning reminds every generation of the need to obey in faith. The rest that God provides includes peace, provision, and protection (Psalm 132:14-18). The author of Hebrews challenged a new generation to enter the rest provided by Jesus Christ (Hebrews 3:7–4:13).

Psalm 96

1 Sing a new song to the LORD!
  Let the whole earth sing to the LORD!
2 Sing to the LORD; praise his name.
  Each day proclaim the good news that he saves.
3 Publish his glorious deeds among the nations.
  Tell everyone about the amazing things he does.
4 Great is the LORD! He is most worthy of praise!
  He is to be feared above all gods.
5 The gods of other nations are mere idols,
  but the LORD made the heavens!
6 Honor and majesty surround him;
  strength and beauty fill his sanctuary.

7 O nations of the world, recognize the LORD;
  recognize that the LORD is glorious and strong.
8 Give to the LORD the glory he deserves!
  Bring your offering and come into his courts.
9 Worship the LORD in all his holy splendor.
  Let all the earth tremble before him.
10 Tell all the nations, "The LORD reigns!"
  The world stands firm and cannot be shaken.
  He will judge all peoples fairly.

11 Let the heavens be glad, and the earth rejoice!
  Let the sea and everything in it shout his praise!
12 Let the fields and their crops burst out with joy!
  Let the trees of the forest sing for joy
13 before the LORD, for he is coming!
  He is coming to judge the earth.
  He will judge the world with justice,
  and the nations with his truth.

Psalm 97

1 The LORD is king!
  Let the earth rejoice!
  Let the farthest coastlands be glad.
2 Dark clouds surround him.

97:8 Hebrew *Zion*.

  Righteousness and justice are the foundation
    of his throne.
3 Fire spreads ahead of him
  and burns up all his foes.
4 His lightning flashes out across the world.
  The earth sees and trembles.
5 The mountains melt like wax before the LORD,
  before the Lord of all the earth.
6 The heavens proclaim his righteousness;
  every nation sees his glory.
7 Those who worship idols are disgraced—
  all who brag about their worthless gods—
  for every god must bow to him.
8 Jerusalem* has heard and rejoiced,
  and all the towns of Judah are glad
  because of your justice, O LORD!
9 For you, O LORD, are supreme over all the earth;
  you are exalted far above all gods.

10 You who love the LORD, hate evil!
  He protects the lives of his godly people
  and rescues them from the power of the wicked.
11 Light shines on the godly,
  and joy on those whose hearts are right.
12 May all who are godly rejoice in the LORD
  and praise his holy name!

Psalm 98

A psalm.

1 Sing a new song to the LORD,
  for he has done wonderful deeds.
  His right hand has won a mighty victory;
  his holy arm has shown his saving power!
2 The LORD has announced his victory
  and has revealed his righteousness to every
    nation!
3 He has remembered his promise to love and be
    faithful to Israel.

Psalm 96 This psalm proclaims and praises the Lord's universal kingship (see Psalm 93) and prepares for the coming of the Lord to bring justice and righteousness into the world. The psalmist invites everyone to worship the Lord (96:1-3), the glorious Creator of all the earth (96:4-6), because worship is due to him alone (96:7-9). The universe joins in praise as the righteous Judge establishes a new order (96:10-13). This psalm (along with 105:1-15; 106:1, 47-48) is included in David's song of praise recorded in 1 Chronicles 16:1-43. **96:1** The psalm urges God's people to sing a "new song," but what is new? The broader context of the psalm offers hints. It appears within psalms celebrating God's kingship (Psalms 93–99), lamenting the exilic experience (Psalms 88–90), and teaching a history lesson (95:8-11). Here, then, understanding who they are and how humanity has lived in the past, God's people are called to worship him anew. They are called to remember the past but to refresh their worship of God as the true King worthy of their adoration and obedience.
Psalm 97 God is greatly exalted over the gods and over all the earth. Awe-inspiring phenomena accompany his coming. Even the created order is visibly affected and the wicked perish, but the people of Zion love his coming and rejoice.

97:2-5 These verses describe a theophany, which is an appearance of the Lord. Theophanies often involve storms, earthquakes, and fire (Psalms 18:8-16; 50:3; Exodus 19:16-20; 24:10, 16-17; Deuteronomy 5:4; 9:10, 15; Habakkuk 3:3-12). God also appears in the quiet after the storm (1 Kings 19:11-13) and as a human in the person of Jesus. However, his appearance in the storm points to his power and evokes awe, appropriate before entering his presence. Yes, God loves us. Yes, Jesus calls us friends (John 15:15). However, that does not mean that we should treat him casually. He remains the Lord and Creator of the universe, and we must honor him as such, preparing ourselves before we worship God. We might dedicate space in our homes and time on our calendars to purely enjoying God.
Psalm 98 This psalm celebrates the Lord's kingship. The Lord is Israel's true King, its champion and savior. His people sing a new song celebrating his victorious power and faithfulness to them. The Lord displays his righteous rule to all the nations throughout the earth, which will culminate in a worldwide kingdom of justice (98:2, 9). So all the earth is exhorted to worship and rejoice, because the Lord is coming (98:4-6).

The ends of the earth have seen the victory
  of our God.
⁴ Shout to the Lord, all the earth;
  break out in praise and sing for joy!
⁵ Sing your praise to the Lord with the harp,
  with the harp and melodious song,
⁶ with trumpets and the sound of the ram's horn.
  Make a joyful symphony before the Lord,
      the King!

⁷ Let the sea and everything in it shout his praise!
  Let the earth and all living things join in.
⁸ Let the rivers clap their hands in glee!
  Let the hills sing out their songs of joy
⁹ before the Lord,
  for he is coming to judge the earth.
  He will judge the world with justice,
  and the nations with fairness.

Psalm 99

¹ The Lord is king!
  Let the nations tremble!
  He sits on his throne between the cherubim.
  Let the whole earth quake!
² The Lord sits in majesty in Jerusalem,*
  exalted above all the nations.
³ Let them praise your great and awesome name.
  Your name is holy!
⁴ Mighty King, lover of justice,
  you have established fairness.
  You have acted with justice
  and righteousness throughout Israel.*
⁵ Exalt the Lord our God!
  Bow low before his feet, for he is holy!

⁶ Moses and Aaron were among his priests;
  Samuel also called on his name.
  They cried to the Lord for help,
  and he answered them.
⁷ He spoke to Israel from the pillar of cloud,
  and they followed the laws and decrees he
      gave them.

⁸ O Lord our God, you answered them.
  You were a forgiving God to them,
  but you punished them when they went wrong.

⁹ Exalt the Lord our God,
  and worship at his holy mountain in
      Jerusalem,
  for the Lord our God is holy!

Psalm 100

A psalm of thanksgiving.

¹ Shout with joy to the Lord, all the earth!
² Worship the Lord with gladness.
  Come before him, singing with joy.
³ Acknowledge that the Lord is God!
  He made us, and we are his.*
  We are his people, the sheep of his pasture.
⁴ Enter his gates with thanksgiving;
  go into his courts with praise.
  Give thanks to him and praise his name.
⁵ For the Lord is good.
  His unfailing love continues forever,
  and his faithfulness continues to each generation.

Psalm 101

A psalm of David.

¹ I will sing of your love and justice, Lord.
  I will praise you with songs.
² I will be careful to live a blameless life—
  when will you come to help me?
  I will lead a life of integrity
      in my own home.
³ I will refuse to look at
      anything vile and vulgar.
  I hate all who deal crookedly;
  I will have nothing to do with them.
⁴ I will reject perverse ideas
  and stay away from every evil.
⁵ I will not tolerate people who slander their
      neighbors.
  I will not endure conceit and pride.

99:2 Hebrew *Zion.* **99:4** Hebrew *Jacob.* See note on 44:4. **100:3** As in an alternate reading in the Masoretic Text; the other alternate and some ancient versions read *and not we ourselves.*

Psalm 99 The psalmist calls the nations to worship the Lord, the king of the earth who rules from Zion (see note on Psalm 93).
99:1 It is fitting to tremble and quake in response to the Lord's holiness (see 96:9 and the study note on 97:2-5). The "throne between the cherubim" refers to the cover of the Ark of the Covenant (Exodus 25:17-22).
99:6-8 The psalmist highlights God's responsiveness to three key figures from Israel's ancient past who sought his help. While God answered their prayers, they did not escape consequences when they fell short of God's instructions. We, too, must realize that God takes his commands seriously but consequences do not mean that God abandons us. Instead, he is disciplining us because he is a loving Father (Proverbs 3:12; Hebrews 12:6). So, too, when we see others facing consequences for their wrongdoing, we can stay in their lives and, rather than judging them, point them to God's desire to do the same.

Psalm 100 This psalm calls all nations to worship the Lord and acknowledge his goodness.
100:3 The Lord is the one who determines who his people are. God will guide and protect his people, who are "the sheep of his pasture" (see 23:1, 4).
Psalm 101 This hymn, which may originally have been associated with a king, expresses a commitment to live with integrity and to avoid evil.
101:2 The translation of the phrase "I will be careful to live a blameless life" is somewhat debated. The verb often means "to have understanding" or "to ponder." Here, the psalmist appears to commit himself to ponder on the "way of blamelessness" so he can live by it. To be "blameless" does not mean being sinless or perfect. Rather, it can refer to living with character and integrity (as in Job's case; see the study note on Job 1:1).

His unfailing love continues forever, and his faithfulness continues to each generation.

PSALM 100:5

⁶ I will search for faithful people
   to be my companions.
  Only those who are above reproach
   will be allowed to serve me.
⁷ I will not allow deceivers to serve in my house,
   and liars will not stay in my presence.
⁸ My daily task will be to ferret out the wicked
   and free the city of the LORD from their grip.

Psalm 102

A prayer of one overwhelmed with trouble, pouring out problems before the LORD.

¹ LORD, hear my prayer!
   Listen to my plea!
² Don't turn away from me
   in my time of distress.
  Bend down to listen,
   and answer me quickly when I call to you.
³ For my days disappear like smoke,
   and my bones burn like red-hot coals.
⁴ My heart is sick, withered like grass,
   and I have lost my appetite.
⁵ Because of my groaning,
   I am reduced to skin and bones.
⁶ I am like an owl in the desert,
   like a little owl in a far-off wilderness.
⁷ I lie awake,
   lonely as a solitary bird on the roof.
⁸ My enemies taunt me day after day.
   They mock and curse me.
⁹ I eat ashes for food.
   My tears run down into my drink
¹⁰ because of your anger and wrath.
   For you have picked me up and thrown me out.
¹¹ My life passes as swiftly as the evening shadows.
   I am withering away like grass.
¹² But you, O LORD, will sit on your throne forever.
   Your fame will endure to every generation.
¹³ You will arise and have mercy on Jerusalem*—
   and now is the time to pity her,
   now is the time you promised to help.
¹⁴ For your people love every stone in her walls
   and cherish even the dust in her streets.
¹⁵ Then the nations will tremble before the LORD.
   The kings of the earth will tremble before his glory.
¹⁶ For the LORD will rebuild Jerusalem.
   He will appear in his glory.

¹⁷ He will listen to the prayers of the destitute.
   He will not reject their pleas.
¹⁸ Let this be recorded for future generations,
   so that a people not yet born will praise the LORD.
¹⁹ Tell them the LORD looked down
   from his heavenly sanctuary.
  He looked down to earth from heaven
²⁰ to hear the groans of the prisoners,
   to release those condemned to die.
²¹ And so the LORD's fame will be celebrated in Zion,
   his praises in Jerusalem,
²² when multitudes gather together
   and kingdoms come to worship the LORD.
²³ He broke my strength in midlife,
   cutting short my days.
²⁴ But I cried to him, "O my God, who lives forever,
   don't take my life while I am so young!
²⁵ Long ago you laid the foundation of the earth
   and made the heavens with your hands.
²⁶ They will perish, but you remain forever;
   they will wear out like old clothing.
  You will change them like a garment
   and discard them.
²⁷ But you are always the same;
   you will live forever.
²⁸ The children of your people
   will live in security.
  Their children's children
   will thrive in your presence."

Psalm 103

A psalm of David.

¹ Let all that I am praise the LORD;
   with my whole heart, I will praise his holy name.
² Let all that I am praise the LORD;
   may I never forget the good things he does for me.
³ He forgives all my sins
   and heals all my diseases.
⁴ He redeems me from death
   and crowns me with love and tender mercies.
⁵ He fills my life with good things.
   My youth is renewed like the eagle's!
⁶ The LORD gives righteousness
   and justice to all who are treated unfairly.

102:13 Hebrew *Zion*; also in 102:16.

Psalm 102 This psalm expresses the prayer, complaint, and confidence of a suffering individual. It is unique within the Psalms in that its superscription, the words that appear above the poem, identifies when it should be prayed. This introductory remark highlights that the psalms are models for all time, for God's people to pray. It is not just a book of ancient prayers for ancient circumstances.

102:23-28 Although the psalmist suffers in the present, he bases his hope for the future on the Lord's past faithfulness.

Psalm 103 This hymn celebrates the Lord's perfection, compassion, forgiveness, and goodness, focusing particularly on God's unfailing love.

⁷ He revealed his character to Moses
   and his deeds to the people of Israel.
⁸ The LORD is compassionate and merciful,
   slow to get angry and filled with unfailing love.
⁹ He will not constantly accuse us,
   nor remain angry forever.
¹⁰ He does not punish us for all our sins;
   he does not deal harshly with us, as we deserve.
¹¹ For his unfailing love toward those who fear him
   is as great as the height of the heavens above the earth.
¹² He has removed our sins as far from us
   as the east is from the west.
¹³ The LORD is like a father to his children,
   tender and compassionate to those who fear him.
¹⁴ For he knows how weak we are;
   he remembers we are only dust.
¹⁵ Our days on earth are like grass;
   like wildflowers, we bloom and die.
¹⁶ The wind blows, and we are gone—
   as though we had never been here.
¹⁷ But the love of the LORD remains forever
   with those who fear him.
   His salvation extends to the children's children
¹⁸   of those who are faithful to his covenant,
   of those who obey his commandments!
¹⁹ The LORD has made the heavens his throne;
   from there he rules over everything.
²⁰ Praise the LORD, you angels,
   you mighty ones who carry out his plans,
   listening for each of his commands.
²¹ Yes, praise the LORD, you armies of angels
   who serve him and do his will!
²² Praise the LORD, everything he has created,
   everything in all his kingdom.

Let all that I am praise the LORD.

Psalm 104

¹ Let all that I am praise the LORD.

O LORD my God, how great you are!
You are robed with honor and majesty.
² You are dressed in a robe of light.
You stretch out the starry curtain of the heavens;
³ you lay out the rafters of your home in the rain clouds.
You make the clouds your chariot;
   you ride upon the wings of the wind.
⁴ The winds are your messengers;
   flames of fire are your servants.*
⁵ You placed the world on its foundation
   so it would never be moved.
⁶ You clothed the earth with floods of water,
   water that covered even the mountains.
⁷ At your command, the water fled;
   at the sound of your thunder, it hurried away.
⁸ Mountains rose and valleys sank
   to the levels you decreed.
⁹ Then you set a firm boundary for the seas,
   so they would never again cover the earth.
¹⁰ You make springs pour water into the ravines,
   so streams gush down from the mountains.
¹¹ They provide water for all the animals,
   and the wild donkeys quench their thirst.
¹² The birds nest beside the streams
   and sing among the branches of the trees.
¹³ You send rain on the mountains from your heavenly home,
   and you fill the earth with the fruit of your labor.
¹⁴ You cause grass to grow for the livestock
   and plants for people to use.
You allow them to produce food from the earth—
¹⁵   wine to make them glad,
olive oil to soothe their skin,
   and bread to give them strength.
¹⁶ The trees of the LORD are well cared for—
   the cedars of Lebanon that he planted.
¹⁷ There the birds make their nests,
   and the storks make their homes in the cypresses.
¹⁸ High in the mountains live the wild goats,
   and the rocks form a refuge for the hyraxes.*
¹⁹ You made the moon to mark the seasons,
   and the sun knows when to set.
²⁰ You send the darkness, and it becomes night,
   when all the forest animals prowl about.

104:4 Greek version reads *He sends his angels like the winds, / his servants like flames of fire.* Compare Heb 1:7. **104:18** Or *coneys*, or *rock badgers*.

103:7-8 God personally described his character to Moses in Exodus 34:6-7, which is repeated in Psalm 103:8. However, the word "character" (103:7) can more literally be translated "ways." Throughout Moses' life and Israel's history, God's people came to know him through his actions. Just as our words do not matter if our actions do not match, the same is true of God. However, Scripture tells of God's acts of unfailing love, mercy, compassion, and slowness to anger. His deeds reflect his character. One way to strengthen our faith, and others' faith, is to recount God's faithful actions in our lives.
Psalms 104–106 All these psalms close with the words "Praise the LORD" ("Hallelujah" in other translations), which spell out the two underlying Hebrew words *halelu-yah*. *Yah* is a short form of God's personal name; *halelu* is an imperative call to praise. While these words can be translated as "praise the LORD" (as they are above), the Hebrew words were also used in communal cries of praise. We see this in the Greek version of 150:6 and Revelation 19:4, which include the Hebrew words spelled with Greek letters.
Psalm 104 This creation hymn (see also Psalms 8, 33, 145) exalts God's goodness and majesty. The psalmist reflects on the present world, the original creation, and a future new creation. He sees both creations as marvelously and wisely made (see 139:14), as the work of the Lord's Spirit (104:30; Genesis 1:2; 2 Corinthians 3:6).

WHAT THE BIBLE SAYS ABOUT Anger

Hang Out with the Cool(-Headed) People

A gentle answer deflects anger,
　but harsh words make tempers flare.
A hot-tempered person starts fights;
　a cool-tempered person stops them.
PROVERBS 15:1, 18

Don't befriend angry people
　or associate with hot-tempered people,
or you will learn to be like them
　and endanger your soul.
PROVERBS 22:24-25

A fool is quick-tempered,
　but a wise person stays calm when insulted.
PROVERBS 12:16

Respond, Don't React

"Don't sin by letting anger control you." Don't let the sun go down while you are still angry, for anger gives a foothold to the devil. **EPHESIANS 4:26-27**

Sensible people control their temper;
　they earn respect by overlooking wrongs.
PROVERBS 19:11

Start from Your Heart

Understand this, my dear brothers and sisters: You must all be quick to listen, slow to speak, and slow to get angry. Human anger does not produce the righteousness God desires. So get rid of all the filth and evil in your lives, and humbly accept the word God has planted in your hearts, for it has the power to save your souls. **JAMES 1:19-21**

"So if you are presenting a sacrifice at the altar in the Temple and you suddenly remember that someone has something against you, leave your sacrifice there at the altar. Go and be reconciled to that person. Then come and offer your sacrifice to God." **MATTHEW 5:23-24**

Now is the time to get rid of anger, rage, malicious behavior, slander, and dirty language. Don't lie to each other, for you have stripped off your old sinful nature and all its wicked deeds. **COLOSSIANS 3:8-9**

21 Then the young lions roar for their prey,
   stalking the food provided by God.
22 At dawn they slink back
   into their dens to rest.
23 Then people go off to their work,
   where they labor until evening.

24 O Lord, what a variety of things you have made!
   In wisdom you have made them all.
   The earth is full of your creatures.
25 Here is the ocean, vast and wide,
   teeming with life of every kind,
   both large and small.
26 See the ships sailing along,
   and Leviathan,* which you made to play in the sea.

27 They all depend on you
   to give them food as they need it.
28 When you supply it, they gather it.
   You open your hand to feed them,
   and they are richly satisfied.
29 But if you turn away from them, they panic.
   When you take away their breath,
   they die and turn again to dust.
30 When you give them your breath,* life is created,
   and you renew the face of the earth.

31 May the glory of the Lord continue forever!
   The Lord takes pleasure in all he has made!
32 The earth trembles at his glance;
   the mountains smoke at his touch.

33 I will sing to the Lord as long as I live.
   I will praise my God to my last breath!
34 May all my thoughts be pleasing to him,
   for I rejoice in the Lord.
35 Let all sinners vanish from the face of the earth;
   let the wicked disappear forever.

Let all that I am praise the Lord.

Praise the Lord!

Psalm 105

1 Give thanks to the Lord and proclaim his greatness.
   Let the whole world know what he has done.
2 Sing to him; yes, sing his praises.
   Tell everyone about his wonderful deeds.
3 Exult in his holy name;
   rejoice, you who worship the Lord.
4 Search for the Lord and for his strength;
   continually seek him.
5 Remember the wonders he has performed,
   his miracles, and the rulings he has given,
6 you children of his servant Abraham,
   you descendants of Jacob, his chosen ones.

7 He is the Lord our God.
   His justice is seen throughout the land.
8 He always stands by his covenant—
   the commitment he made to a thousand generations.
9 This is the covenant he made with Abraham
   and the oath he swore to Isaac.
10 He confirmed it to Jacob as a decree,
   and to the people of Israel as a never-ending covenant:
11 "I will give you the land of Canaan
   as your special possession."

12 He said this when they were few in number,
   a tiny group of strangers in Canaan.
13 They wandered from nation to nation,
   from one kingdom to another.
14 Yet he did not let anyone oppress them.
   He warned kings on their behalf:
15 "Do not touch my chosen people,
   and do not hurt my prophets."

16 He called for a famine on the land of Canaan,
   cutting off its food supply.
17 Then he sent someone to Egypt ahead of them—
   Joseph, who was sold as a slave.
18 They bruised his feet with fetters
   and placed his neck in an iron collar.

104:26 The identification of Leviathan is disputed, ranging from an earthly creature to a mythical sea monster in ancient literature. 104:30 Or *When you send your Spirit.*

104:26 Commercial vessels and maritime trade routes enabled relatively distant ancient Near Eastern civilizations to more easily conduct business with one another (see Isaiah 2:16; 23:1, 3). Leviathan has been identified as everything from an observable animal to a mythical sea monster, but the psalmist likens this feared creature to the Lord's pet playing in the sea.
Psalms 105–106 These psalms offer us two views of the same relationship. Psalm 105 focuses on God's faithfulness. Psalm 106 pictures the people's unfaithfulness and rebellion (which God repeatedly responded to by delivering them). Perhaps we can ask God how he sees both our individual and shared relationships with him today.
Psalm 105 This hymn praises the Lord's faithfulness, focusing on his work in the lives of Abraham and his descendants in all their journeys—from Ur to Canaan (105:12), to Egypt (105:17, 23), through the wilderness (105:37, 41), and back to Canaan (105:44). All of this fulfilled the Lord's promise to Abraham (105:9, 42), which was the basis for Israel's very existence. Joseph, whose suffering was changed into glory, is a paradigm of encouragement for Israel (105:16-25). David's song of praise recorded in 1 Chronicles 16:1-43 includes Psalm 105: 1-15 (along with 96; 106:1, 47-48).
105:6-11 The story of Israel was based on the Lord's commitment to Abraham. Even when a question had arisen about the future of God's covenant with David (Psalm 89), God's covenant with Abraham stood, as does the spiritual bond between God and Israel, Abraham's descendants.

¹⁹ Until the time came to fulfill his dreams,*
   the LORD tested Joseph's character.
²⁰ Then Pharaoh sent for him and set him free;
   the ruler of the nation opened his prison door.
²¹ Joseph was put in charge of all the king's household;
   he became ruler over all the king's possessions.
²² He could instruct* the king's aides as he pleased
   and teach the king's advisers.
²³ Then Israel arrived in Egypt;
   Jacob lived as a foreigner in the land of Ham.
²⁴ And the LORD multiplied the people of Israel
   until they became too mighty for their enemies.
²⁵ Then he turned the Egyptians against the Israelites,
   and they plotted against the LORD's servants.
²⁶ But the LORD sent his servant Moses,
   along with Aaron, whom he had chosen.
²⁷ They performed miraculous signs among the Egyptians,
   and wonders in the land of Ham.
²⁸ The LORD blanketed Egypt in darkness,
   for they had defied* his commands to let his people go.
²⁹ He turned their water into blood,
   poisoning all the fish.
³⁰ Then frogs overran the land
   and even invaded the king's bedrooms.
³¹ When the LORD spoke, flies descended on the Egyptians,
   and gnats swarmed across Egypt.
³² He sent them hail instead of rain,
   and lightning flashed over the land.
³³ He ruined their grapevines and fig trees
   and shattered all the trees.
³⁴ He spoke, and hordes of locusts came—
   young locusts beyond number.
³⁵ They ate up everything green in the land,
   destroying all the crops in their fields.
³⁶ Then he killed the oldest son in each Egyptian home,
   the pride and joy of each family.
³⁷ The LORD brought his people out of Egypt,
   loaded with silver and gold;
   and not one among the tribes of Israel even stumbled.
³⁸ Egypt was glad when they were gone,
   for they feared them greatly.
³⁹ The LORD spread a cloud above them as a covering
   and gave them a great fire to light the darkness.
⁴⁰ They asked for meat, and he sent them quail;
   he satisfied their hunger with manna—bread from heaven.
⁴¹ He split open a rock, and water gushed out
   to form a river through the dry wasteland.
⁴² For he remembered his sacred promise
   to his servant Abraham.
⁴³ So he brought his people out of Egypt with joy,
   his chosen ones with rejoicing.
⁴⁴ He gave his people the lands of pagan nations,
   and they harvested crops that others had planted.
⁴⁵ All this happened so they would follow his decrees
   and obey his instructions.

Praise the LORD!

Psalm 106

¹ Praise the LORD!

Give thanks to the LORD, for he is good!
   His faithful love endures forever.
² Who can list the glorious miracles of the LORD?
   Who can ever praise him enough?
³ There is joy for those who deal justly with others
   and always do what is right.

⁴ Remember me, LORD, when you show favor to your people;
   come near and rescue me.
⁵ Let me share in the prosperity of your chosen ones.
   Let me rejoice in the joy of your people;
   let me praise you with those who are your heritage.

⁶ Like our ancestors, we have sinned.
   We have done wrong! We have acted wickedly!
⁷ Our ancestors in Egypt
   were not impressed by the LORD's miraculous deeds.

105:19 Hebrew *his word.* **105:22** As in Greek and Syriac versions; Hebrew reads *bind* or *imprison.* **105:28** As in Greek and Syriac versions; Hebrew reads *had not defied.*

Psalm 106 The Israelite community in exile confessed the Lord's goodness and justice and their own historic sinfulness. From the humble state of exile, they pleaded for redemption and restoration, asking to be gathered back from all the places the Lord had scattered them in his wrath. The psalm does not end in despair but with the memory of the Lord's former mercy and the hope that his mercy will be renewed (106:44-48). Israel failed, but the Lord is constant. David's song of praise recorded in 1 Chronicles 16:1-43 includes Psalm 106:1, 47-48 (along with Psalms 96; 105:1-15).
106:1 This refrain, "Praise the LORD!" (Hebrew *halelu-yah*), characterizes four small subgroups: Psalms 104–106, 111–113, 115–117, and 146–150. While it closes Psalms 104–106 (see study note), it also opens Psalm 106.

PSALM 106

They soon forgot his many acts of kindness
to them.
Instead, they rebelled against him at the
Red Sea.*

8 Even so, he saved them—
to defend the honor of his name
and to demonstrate his mighty power.
9 He commanded the Red Sea* to dry up.
He led Israel across the sea as if it were a
desert.
10 So he rescued them from their enemies
and redeemed them from their foes.
11 Then the water returned and covered their
enemies;
not one of them survived.
12 Then his people believed his promises.
Then they sang his praise.

13 Yet how quickly they forgot what he had done!
They wouldn't wait for his counsel!
14 In the wilderness their desires ran wild,
testing God's patience in that dry
wasteland.
15 So he gave them what they asked for,
but he sent a plague along with it.
16 The people in the camp were jealous of Moses
and envious of Aaron, the LORD's holy priest.
17 Because of this, the earth opened up;
it swallowed Dathan
and buried Abiram and the other rebels.
18 Fire fell upon their followers;
a flame consumed the wicked.

19 The people made a calf at Mount Sinai*;
they bowed before an image made of gold.
20 They traded their glorious God
for a statue of a grass-eating bull.
21 They forgot God, their savior,
who had done such great things in Egypt—
22 such wonderful things in the land of Ham,
such awesome deeds at the Red Sea.
23 So he declared he would destroy them.
But Moses, his chosen one, stepped between
the LORD and the people.
He begged him to turn from his anger and not
destroy them.

24 The people refused to enter the pleasant land,
for they wouldn't believe his promise to care
for them.
25 Instead, they grumbled in their tents
and refused to obey the LORD.
26 Therefore, he solemnly swore
that he would kill them in the wilderness,
27 that he would scatter their descendants* among
the nations,
exiling them to distant lands.

28 Then our ancestors joined in the worship of Baal
at Peor;
they even ate sacrifices offered to the dead!
29 They angered the LORD with all these things,
so a plague broke out among them.
30 But Phinehas had the courage to intervene,
and the plague was stopped.
31 So he has been regarded as a righteous man
ever since that time.

32 At Meribah, too, they angered the LORD,
causing Moses serious trouble.
33 They made Moses angry,*
and he spoke foolishly.

34 Israel failed to destroy the nations in the land,
as the LORD had commanded them.
35 Instead, they mingled among the pagans
and adopted their evil customs.
36 They worshiped their idols,
which led to their downfall.
37 They even sacrificed their sons
and their daughters to the demons.
38 They shed innocent blood,
the blood of their sons and daughters.
By sacrificing them to the idols of Canaan,
they polluted the land with murder.
39 They defiled themselves by their evil deeds,
and their love of idols was adultery in the
LORD's sight.

40 That is why the LORD's anger burned against his
people,
and he abhorred his own special possession.
41 He handed them over to pagan nations,
and they were ruled by those who hated
them.
42 Their enemies crushed them
and brought them under their cruel power.
43 Again and again he rescued them,
but they chose to rebel against him,
and they were finally destroyed by their sin.
44 Even so, he pitied them in their distress
and listened to their cries.
45 He remembered his covenant with them
and relented because of his unfailing love.
46 He even caused their captors
to treat them with kindness.

47 Save us, O LORD our God!
Gather us back from among the nations,
so we can thank your holy name
and rejoice and praise you.

48 Praise the LORD, the God of Israel,
who lives from everlasting to everlasting!
Let all the people say, "Amen!"

Praise the LORD.

106:7 Hebrew *at the sea, the sea of reeds.* **106:9** Hebrew *sea of reeds;* also in 106:22. **106:19** Hebrew *at Horeb,* another name for Sinai. **106:27** As in Syriac version; Hebrew reads *he would cause their descendants to fall.* **106:33** Hebrew *They embittered his spirit.*

BOOK FIVE (PSALMS 107–150)

Psalm 107

1 Give thanks to the LORD, for he is good!
   His faithful love endures forever.
2 Has the LORD redeemed you? Then speak out!
   Tell others he has redeemed you from your enemies.
3 For he has gathered the exiles from many lands,
   from east and west,
   from north and south.*

4 Some wandered in the wilderness,
   lost and homeless.
5 Hungry and thirsty,
   they nearly died.
6 "LORD, help!" they cried in their trouble,
   and he rescued them from their distress.
7 He led them straight to safety,
   to a city where they could live.
8 Let them praise the LORD for his great love
   and for the wonderful things he has done for them.
9 For he satisfies the thirsty
   and fills the hungry with good things.

10 Some sat in darkness and deepest gloom,
   imprisoned in iron chains of misery.
11 They rebelled against the words of God,
   scorning the counsel of the Most High.
12 That is why he broke them with hard labor;
   they fell, and no one was there to help them.
13 "LORD, help!" they cried in their trouble,
   and he saved them from their distress.
14 He led them from the darkness and deepest gloom;
   he snapped their chains.
15 Let them praise the LORD for his great love
   and for the wonderful things he has done for them.
16 For he broke down their prison gates of bronze;
   he cut apart their bars of iron.

17 Some were fools; they rebelled
   and suffered for their sins.
18 They couldn't stand the thought of food,
   and they were knocking on death's door.
19 "LORD, help!" they cried in their trouble,
   and he saved them from their distress.
20 He sent out his word and healed them,
   snatching them from the door of death.
21 Let them praise the LORD for his great love
   and for the wonderful things he has done for them.
22 Let them offer sacrifices of thanksgiving
   and sing joyfully about his glorious acts.

23 Some went off to sea in ships,
   plying the trade routes of the world.
24 They, too, observed the LORD's power in action,
   his impressive works on the deepest seas.
25 He spoke, and the winds rose,
   stirring up the waves.
26 Their ships were tossed to the heavens
   and plunged again to the depths;
   the sailors cringed in terror.
27 They reeled and staggered like drunkards
   and were at their wits' end.
28 "LORD, help!" they cried in their trouble,
   and he saved them from their distress.
29 He calmed the storm to a whisper
   and stilled the waves.
30 What a blessing was that stillness
   as he brought them safely into harbor!
31 Let them praise the LORD for his great love
   and for the wonderful things he has done for them.
32 Let them exalt him publicly before the congregation
   and before the leaders of the nation.

33 He changes rivers into deserts,
   and springs of water into dry, thirsty land.
34 He turns the fruitful land into salty wastelands,
   because of the wickedness of those who live there.
35 But he also turns deserts into pools of water,
   the dry land into springs of water.
36 He brings the hungry to settle there
   and to build their cities.
37 They sow their fields, plant their vineyards,
   and harvest their bumper crops.
38 How he blesses them!
   They raise large families there,
   and their herds of livestock increase.

107:3 Hebrew *and sea*.

Book Five (Psalms 107–150) This final book of the Psalter was shaped in the context of Israel's return from exile in Babylon. God's sovereign power and loving faithfulness to his covenant people were demonstrated as he restored and exalted them. The uncertainty in Book Four about the future of David's royal line (see 89:38) finds positive resolution in Book Five. The psalms of David occur in greater number in this final book than they do in Books Three and Four, and David is remembered for the covenant he received and for his devotion to the Lord (for example, Psalm 132). Thus, there remains the prospect of a coming King. Book Five also contains two early liturgical collections: the "Egyptian Hallel" (Psalms 113–118) and the "Songs of Ascents" or "Pilgrim Psalms" (Psalms 120–134). The Psalter then returns to its roots with a collection of David's psalms dominated by lament (Psalms 138–145), followed by a section of praise to conclude the whole book of Psalms (Psalms 146–150).

Psalm 107 This psalm is a communal hymn praising God as redeemer that includes four examples of God's deliverance. He delivers his people from wandering in the wilderness (107:4-9), from prison (107:10-16), illness (107:17-22), and a storm at sea (107:23-32). The psalm's opening praises God for his "faithful love" and redemption from exile (107:1-3). It includes God's response to his people's plea for restoration in 106:47.

107:3 People came from all nations where the people of Israel and Judah had been scattered.

⁹⁹ When they decrease in number and become impoverished
through oppression, trouble, and sorrow,
⁴⁰ the LORD pours contempt on their princes,
causing them to wander in trackless wastelands.
⁴¹ But he rescues the poor from trouble
and increases their families like flocks of sheep.
⁴² The godly will see these things and be glad,
while the wicked are struck silent.
⁴³ Those who are wise will take all this to heart;
they will see in our history the faithful love of the LORD.

Psalm 108

A song. A psalm of David.

¹ My heart is confident in you, O God;
no wonder I can sing your praises with all my heart!
² Wake up, lyre and harp!
I will wake the dawn with my song.
³ I will thank you, LORD, among all the people.
I will sing your praises among the nations.
⁴ For your unfailing love is higher than the heavens.
Your faithfulness reaches to the clouds.
⁵ Be exalted, O God, above the highest heavens.
May your glory shine over all the earth.
⁶ Now rescue your beloved people.
Answer and save us by your power.
⁷ God has promised this by his holiness*:
"I will divide up Shechem with joy.
I will measure out the valley of Succoth.
⁸ Gilead is mine,
and Manasseh, too.
Ephraim, my helmet, will produce my warriors,
and Judah, my scepter, will produce my kings.
⁹ But Moab, my washbasin, will become my servant,
and I will wipe my feet on Edom
and shout in triumph over Philistia."
¹⁰ Who will bring me into the fortified city?
Who will bring me victory over Edom?
¹¹ Have you rejected us, O God?
Will you no longer march with our armies?
¹² Oh, please help us against our enemies,
for all human help is useless.
¹³ With God's help we will do mighty things,
for he will trample down our foes.

Psalm 109

For the choir director: A psalm of David.

¹ O God, whom I praise,
don't stand silent and aloof
² while the wicked slander me
and tell lies about me.
³ They surround me with hateful words
and fight against me for no reason.
⁴ I love them, but they try to destroy me with accusations
even as I am praying for them!
⁵ They repay evil for good,
and hatred for my love.
⁶ They say,* "Get an evil person to turn against him.
Send an accuser to bring him to trial.
⁷ When his case comes up for judgment,
let him be pronounced guilty.
Count his prayers as sins.
⁸ Let his years be few;
let someone else take his position.
⁹ May his children become fatherless,
and his wife a widow.
¹⁰ May his children wander as beggars
and be driven from* their ruined homes.
¹¹ May creditors seize his entire estate,
and strangers take all he has earned.
¹² Let no one be kind to him;
let no one pity his fatherless children.
¹³ May all his offspring die.
May his family name be blotted out in the next generation.
¹⁴ May the LORD never forget the sins of his fathers;
may his mother's sins never be erased from the record.
¹⁵ May the LORD always remember these sins,
and may his name disappear from human memory.
¹⁶ For he refused all kindness to others;
he persecuted the poor and needy,
and he hounded the brokenhearted to death.

108:7 Or *in his sanctuary.* 109:6 Hebrew lacks *They say.* 109:10 As in Greek version; Hebrew reads *and seek.*

Psalm 108 This psalm combines two excerpts from David's other psalms (57:5, 7-11; 60:5-12). Minor changes have been made to the original compositions so that Psalms 108–110 of David are tied together. Psalm 108 includes a plea for God's military intervention, while Psalm 109 laments ongoing personal attacks. Both the military and personal attacks find their resolution in Psalm 110. In our lives, we find value in recording our experiences with God during hard times and good. Taking a moment to record our journeys from dark to light reminds us that God will be there next time, when we walk through difficulties, just as he has been in the past.

Psalm 109 The psalmist begins this lament with a general charge against his accusers: They do evil in return for good (109:1-5). At the end of the psalm, he turns to the Lord in prayer, asking for his protection (109:21-25) and vengeance (109:26-31).
109:6-19 The NLT translates these verses as the words of the psalmist's accusers, but the Hebrew lacks "They say," which makes it unclear who is speaking. Another possibility is that these verses are curses that the psalmist wishes God to send on his enemies. See the study note on 137:8-9.

¹⁷ He loved to curse others;
   now you curse him.
   He never blessed others;
   now don't you bless him.
¹⁸ Cursing is as natural to him as his clothing,
   or the water he drinks,
   or the rich food he eats.
¹⁹ Now may his curses return and cling to him like clothing;
   may they be tied around him like a belt."

²⁰ May those curses become the LORD's punishment
   for my accusers who speak evil of me.
²¹ But deal well with me, O Sovereign LORD,
   for the sake of your own reputation!
   Rescue me
   because you are so faithful and good.
²² For I am poor and needy,
   and my heart is full of pain.
²³ I am fading like a shadow at dusk;
   I am brushed off like a locust.
²⁴ My knees are weak from fasting,
   and I am skin and bones.
²⁵ I am a joke to people everywhere;
   when they see me, they shake their heads in scorn.

²⁶ Help me, O LORD my God!
   Save me because of your unfailing love.
²⁷ Let them see that this is your doing,
   that you yourself have done it, LORD.
²⁸ Then let them curse me if they like,
   but you will bless me!

When they attack me, they will be disgraced!
But I, your servant, will go right on rejoicing!
²⁹ May my accusers be clothed with disgrace;
   may their humiliation cover them like a cloak.
³⁰ But I will give repeated thanks to the LORD,
   praising him to everyone.
³¹ For he stands beside the needy,
   ready to save them from those who condemn them.

Psalm 110

A psalm of David.

¹ The LORD said to my Lord,*
   "Sit in the place of honor at my right hand
   until I humble your enemies,
   making them a footstool under your feet."

² The LORD will extend your powerful kingdom from Jerusalem*;
   you will rule over your enemies.
³ When you go to war,
   your people will serve you willingly.
   You are arrayed in holy garments,
   and your strength will be renewed each day
   like the morning dew.

⁴ The LORD has taken an oath and will not break his vow:
   "You are a priest forever in the order of Melchizedek."

⁵ The Lord stands at your right hand to protect you.
   He will strike down many kings when his anger erupts.

110:1 Or *my lord.* 110:2 Hebrew *Zion.*

109:21-25 Vulnerable and miserable, the psalmist appeals to his Lord for help. The accusations have killed his inner spirit and even his physical stamina. If his accusers have described him as oppressing the "poor and needy" (109:16; see study note on 109:6-19), the psalmist denies the accusation, describing himself as being the one who is actually "poor and needy" (109:22).
Psalm 110 This psalm reaffirms God's covenant with David and gives hope for the future (see 2 Samuel 7:8-16). Jesus and the apostles cite this psalm to explain Jesus' unique ministry and status as the Messiah (Matthew 22:43-45; Acts 2:32-36; Hebrews 1:13; 5:6; 7:15-17, 21).
110:1 The king of Israel had the great privilege of being considered the Lord's adopted son (Psalm 2; 1 Chronicles 22:10), but he fell (Psalm 89). This decree restores and heightens his position. "The LORD" reflects the Hebrew word *Yahweh,* the personal name of God (see Exodus 3:6-14; 6:2-8; 20:2). "My Lord" translates the Hebrew word *adoni,* which means "my master" or "my superior." The psalmist viewed God's king or messianic ruler as his superior. The New Testament frequently cites this psalm to validate Jesus' claim to be the Messiah (Matthew 22:44-45; Mark 12:36-37; Luke 20:42-44; Acts 2:34-35; Hebrews 1:13). The Lord's "right hand" represents his authority, strength, presence, and benefits. The Lord chose the descendant of David and raised him up to be close to him (Psalm 80:17). Jesus claimed this position for himself (Matthew 26:64; Mark 14:62; 16:19; Luke 22:69), and the apostles announced that Jesus, having ascended to heaven, sits at the right hand of the Father (Acts 2:33; 5:31; 7:55-56; Romans 8:34; Ephesians 1:20; Colossians 3:1; Hebrews 1:3; 8:1; 10:12; 12:2). Ancient Near Eastern kings were sometimes portrayed as placing their feet on the backs of their conquered enemies as on a footstool (see Hebrews 10:12-13).
110:4 The Lord had made an unbreakable oath and covenant, so his apparent rejection of David's dynasty (89:38) in the Exile had led to a crisis. The placement of Psalm 110 in Book Five reaffirms the future of the dynasty: David's descendant must conform to God's standard of integrity (Psalm 101). His ministry will be transformed as he serves under God's kingship (Psalms 93–100). The role of God's anointed (messianic) ruler expands beyond David's role. The priestly kingship of David and his descendants extended to serving as patrons of the Temple. David had the Ark brought to Jerusalem (2 Samuel 6:15) and arranged for the Temple service (1 Chronicles 6:31-48; 15:11-26; 16:4-42; 23:4-32; 25:1). Solomon supervised the Temple construction and furnishings (1 Kings 5:1–7:51). Even so, Israel's kingship was generally separate from its priesthood. In the messianic kingdom, the king would also minister as priest, as Melchizedek, king of Salem, had done (see Genesis 14:17-24). The New Testament develops the ministry of Jesus Christ as a fulfillment of this new order (see Hebrews 5:6-10; 6:20–7:25).

⁶ He will punish the nations
    and fill their lands with corpses;
    he will shatter heads over the whole earth.
⁷ But he himself will be refreshed from brooks
        along the way.
    He will be victorious.

Psalm 111*

¹ Praise the LORD!

I will thank the LORD with all my heart
    as I meet with his godly people.
² How amazing are the deeds of the LORD!
    All who delight in him should ponder them.
³ Everything he does reveals his glory and majesty.
    His righteousness never fails.
⁴ He causes us to remember his wonderful works.
    How gracious and merciful is our LORD!
⁵ He gives food to those who fear him;
    he always remembers his covenant.
⁶ He has shown his great power to his people
    by giving them the lands of other nations.
⁷ All he does is just and good,
    and all his commandments are trustworthy.
⁸ They are forever true,
    to be obeyed faithfully and with integrity.
⁹ He has paid a full ransom for his people.
    He has guaranteed his covenant with them
        forever.
    What a holy, awe-inspiring name he has!

---

111 This psalm is a Hebrew acrostic poem; after the introductory note of praise, each line begins with a successive letter of the Hebrew alphabet.

Psalms 111–117 The refrain "Praise the LORD!" (Hebrew *halelu-yah*; see study note on Psalms 104–106) characterizes this group of psalms. In the Greek translation of the Old Testament, the "praise the LORD" at the end of Psalm 113 is moved to the beginning of Psalm 114, which lacks the phrase in the Hebrew.

Come Close — WONDERING? RELEASE

SCRIPTURE CONNECTION: PSALMS 111–113

Did I do enough? you may wonder when dropping your kids off at school the first time, when they go to college or marry, or when someone you love struggles after you've invested in them.

We can't control the results of our efforts. But we can accept that we did our best. We must then leave the results to God.

I often carry a feeling of responsibility for those I nurture, disciple, and teach. When released from those duties, it's easy for me to try to bear the success or failure of my efforts rather than trusting God for the outcome.

"Dear daughter," I hear Jesus say throughout Psalms 111–113, "I simply asked you to reverence and obey me. When you do, I provide wisdom. You've done your job. Now trust me with the results."

God doesn't want us to micromanage the outcomes of our obedient acts. Instead, look at what he promises in Psalm 112:

- Those we mentor, disciple, and raise will be successful (by God's definition).
- An entire generation of godly people will be blessed through our efforts.
- Our good deeds will be remembered forever.
- We will have confidence, influence, and honor.

Friend, trust your obedient efforts to God. He will multiply them in ways you may never see until heaven.

> **REFLECT** "How joyful are those who fear the LORD.... An entire generation of godly people will be blessed." PSALM 112:1-2
>
> *Lord, bless a generation because of my obedience. Multiply the influence you've given me. Help me to trust in your faithfulness, not my limitations. Amen.*
>
> **CONSIDER** "God doesn't require us to succeed; he only requires that you try." MOTHER TERESA

Trust God with your obedience.

BRENDA L. YODER, MA, LMHC, is a licensed mental health counselor and school counselor whose passion is encouraging others when life doesn't fit the storybook image.

¹⁰ Fear of the LORD is the foundation of true wisdom.
All who obey his commandments will grow in wisdom.

Praise him forever!

Psalm 112*
¹ Praise the LORD!

How joyful are those who fear the LORD
and delight in obeying his commands.
² Their children will be successful everywhere;
an entire generation of godly people will be blessed.
³ They themselves will be wealthy,
and their good deeds will last forever.
⁴ Light shines in the darkness for the godly.
They are generous, compassionate, and righteous.
⁵ Good comes to those who lend money generously
and conduct their business fairly.
⁶ Such people will not be overcome by evil.
Those who are righteous will be long remembered.
⁷ They do not fear bad news;
they confidently trust the LORD to care for them.
⁸ They are confident and fearless
and can face their foes triumphantly.
⁹ They share freely and give generously to those in need.
Their good deeds will be remembered forever.
They will have influence and honor.
¹⁰ The wicked will see this and be infuriated.
They will grind their teeth in anger;
they will slink away, their hopes thwarted.

Psalm 113
¹ Praise the LORD!

Yes, give praise, O servants of the LORD.
Praise the name of the LORD!
² Blessed be the name of the LORD
now and forever.
³ Everywhere—from east to west—
praise the name of the LORD.
⁴ For the LORD is high above the nations;
his glory is higher than the heavens.

⁵ Who can be compared with the LORD our God,
who is enthroned on high?
⁶ He stoops to look down
on heaven and on earth.
⁷ He lifts the poor from the dust
and the needy from the garbage dump.
⁸ He sets them among princes,
even the princes of his own people!
⁹ He gives the childless woman a family,
making her a happy mother.

Praise the LORD!

Psalm 114
¹ When the Israelites escaped from Egypt—
when the family of Jacob left that foreign land—
² the land of Judah became God's sanctuary,
and Israel became his kingdom.

³ The Red Sea* saw them coming and hurried out of their way!
The water of the Jordan River turned away.
⁴ The mountains skipped like rams,
the hills like lambs!
⁵ What's wrong, Red Sea, that made you hurry out of their way?

---

112 This psalm is a Hebrew acrostic poem; after the introductory note of praise, each line begins with a successive letter of the Hebrew alphabet. **114:3** Hebrew *the sea;* also in 114:5.

Psalms 111–112 These two psalms are "twins," sharing a poetic structure (an acrostic) and key Hebrew terms, such as "fear," "delight," "righteousness" or "good deeds," "godly people," "just" or "fairly," "good," and "remember." Psalm 111 focuses on praising God and concludes that the "fear of the LORD is the foundation of true wisdom" (111:10). Psalm 112 then builds on the end of 111:10, describing the life of the person who fears the Lord. When we read a principle for how to live as followers of God, we also need to put that idea into action.

Psalm 111 This psalm is a Hebrew acrostic poem; after the introductory note of praise, each line begins with a successive letter of the Hebrew alphabet. This wisdom psalm contains many references to the works of the Lord that reveal his character. God is righteous, gracious, compassionate, faithful, just, trustworthy, upright, holy, and awe-inspiring (111:3, 4, 7, 8, 9). God's character gives hope in the covenant relationship (111:5). He rescued Israel from Egypt (111:9), gave them the land (111:6), and provides for his people (111:5). However, God demands that his people also live with righteousness and integrity.

Psalm 112 This psalm is a Hebrew acrostic poem; after the introductory note of praise, each line begins with a successive letter of the Hebrew alphabet. The psalm reiterates the themes of wisdom and the fear of the Lord (Psalm 111). The wise have reason to be happy (112:1-5) and vigorous (112:6-10).

Psalm 113 This hymn of praise exalts the greatness of the Lord's name and glory. God is greatly exalted and glorious over the heavens (113:4); he also stoops down to take care of the lowly and needy on earth (113:5-9).

Psalms 113–118 These psalms form what is known as the "Egyptian Hallel" (*hallel* means "praise") because Jews use the collection when celebrating Passover (Exodus 12). Psalms 113–114 are recited before the Passover meal and 115–118 afterward.

Psalm 114 This lyrical celebration of the Lord's power in nature recalls Israel's beginning as a nation at the Exodus (114:1-2) and upon their entry into the Promised Land (114:3-6). It promotes reverence for the God of Jacob (114:7-8).

What happened, Jordan River, that you
  turned away?
⁶ Why, mountains, did you skip like rams?
  Why, hills, like lambs?

⁷ Tremble, O earth, at the presence of the Lord,
  at the presence of the God of Jacob.
⁸ He turned the rock into a pool of water;
  yes, a spring of water flowed from solid rock.

Psalm 115

¹ Not to us, O LORD, not to us,
  but to your name goes all the glory
  for your unfailing love and faithfulness.
² Why let the nations say,
  "Where is their God?"
³ Our God is in the heavens,
  and he does as he wishes.
⁴ Their idols are merely things of silver and gold,
  shaped by human hands.
⁵ They have mouths but cannot speak,
  and eyes but cannot see.
⁶ They have ears but cannot hear,
  and noses but cannot smell.
⁷ They have hands but cannot feel,
  and feet but cannot walk,
  and throats but cannot make a sound.
⁸ And those who make idols are just like them,
  as are all who trust in them.

⁹ O Israel, trust the LORD!
  He is your helper and your shield.
¹⁰ O priests, descendants of Aaron, trust the LORD!
  He is your helper and your shield.
¹¹ All you who fear the LORD, trust the LORD!
  He is your helper and your shield.

¹² The LORD remembers us and will bless us.
  He will bless the people of Israel
  and bless the priests, the descendants of Aaron.
¹³ He will bless those who fear the LORD,
  both great and lowly.

¹⁴ May the LORD richly bless
  both you and your children.
¹⁵ May you be blessed by the LORD,
  who made heaven and earth.
¹⁶ The heavens belong to the LORD,
  but he has given the earth to all humanity.
¹⁷ The dead cannot sing praises to the LORD,
  for they have gone into the silence of the grave.
¹⁸ But we can praise the LORD
  both now and forever!

Praise the LORD!

Psalm 116

¹ I love the LORD because he hears my voice
  and my prayer for mercy.
² Because he bends down to listen,
  I will pray as long as I have breath!
³ Death wrapped its ropes around me;
  the terrors of the grave* overtook me.
  I saw only trouble and sorrow.
⁴ Then I called on the name of the LORD:
  "Please, LORD, save me!"
⁵ How kind the LORD is! How good he is!
  So merciful, this God of ours!
⁶ The LORD protects those of childlike faith;
  I was facing death, and he saved me.
⁷ Let my soul be at rest again,
  for the LORD has been good to me.
⁸ He has saved me from death,
  my eyes from tears,
  my feet from stumbling.
⁹ And so I walk in the LORD's presence
  as I live here on earth!
¹⁰ I believed in you, so I said,
  "I am deeply troubled, LORD."
¹¹ In my anxiety I cried out to you,
  "These people are all liars!"
¹² What can I offer the LORD
  for all he has done for me?
¹³ I will lift up the cup of salvation
  and praise the LORD's name for saving me.
¹⁴ I will keep my promises to the LORD
  in the presence of all his people.
¹⁵ The LORD cares deeply
  when his loved ones die.

116:3 Hebrew *of Sheol.*

Psalm 115 In this hymn of thanksgiving for God's blessings, the community ascribes all glory to the name of the Lord, who is the true source of hope and blessing. Meanwhile, those who trust in idols are greatly disappointed. The blessing of the Creator of heaven and earth extends to future generations (115:14) and specifically mentions the priesthood (115:12).

115:9-11 The Hebrew word translated "helper" (*ezer*) is the same word the Lord uses in Genesis 2:18: "It is not good for the man to be alone. I will make a helper [*ezer*] who is just right for him." The use of the term here to describe God himself as one whom people are to trust suggests that Eve's role should not be understood as subordinate to Adam's. By contrast, she joined her husband as a partner in the divinely-given vocation of ruling over God's creation (Genesis 1:26-28).

Psalm 116 This hymn of thanksgiving rejoices in God's character and in rescue from death (116:1-11). It gives an assurance of God's protection in life and reminds the godly that the Lord watches over them even at death. The psalmist commits to living as God's servant and resolves to honor him publicly (116:12-19).

16 O Lord, I am your servant;
yes, I am your servant, born into your
household;
you have freed me from my chains.
17 I will offer you a sacrifice of thanksgiving
and call on the name of the Lord.
18 I will fulfill my vows to the Lord
in the presence of all his people—
19 in the house of the Lord
in the heart of Jerusalem.

Praise the Lord!

Psalm 117

1 Praise the Lord, all you nations.
Praise him, all you people of the earth.
2 For his unfailing love for us is powerful;
the Lord's faithfulness endures forever.

Praise the Lord!

Psalm 118

1 Give thanks to the Lord, for he is good!
His faithful love endures forever.

2 Let all Israel repeat:
"His faithful love endures forever."
3 Let Aaron's descendants, the priests, repeat:
"His faithful love endures forever."
4 Let all who fear the Lord repeat:
"His faithful love endures forever."

5 In my distress I prayed to the Lord,
and the Lord answered me and set me free.
6 The Lord is for me, so I will have no fear.
What can mere people do to me?
7 Yes, the Lord is for me; he will help me.
I will look in triumph at those who hate me.
8 It is better to take refuge in the Lord
than to trust in people.
9 It is better to take refuge in the Lord
than to trust in princes.

10 Though hostile nations surrounded me,
I destroyed them all with the authority of the
Lord.
11 Yes, they surrounded and attacked me,
but I destroyed them all with the authority of
the Lord.
12 They swarmed around me like bees;
they blazed against me like a crackling fire.
But I destroyed them all with the authority of
the Lord.
13 My enemies did their best to kill me,
but the Lord rescued me.
14 The Lord is my strength and my song;
he has given me victory.
15 Songs of joy and victory are sung in the camp of
the godly.
The strong right arm of the Lord has done
glorious things!
16 The strong right arm of the Lord is raised in
triumph.
The strong right arm of the Lord has done
glorious things!
17 I will not die; instead, I will live
to tell what the Lord has done.
18 The Lord has punished me severely,
but he did not let me die.

19 Open for me the gates where the righteous enter,
and I will go in and thank the Lord.
20 These gates lead to the presence of the Lord,
and the godly enter there.
21 I thank you for answering my prayer
and giving me victory!

22 The stone that the builders rejected
has now become the cornerstone.
23 This is the Lord's doing,
and it is wonderful to see.
24 This is the day the Lord has made.
We will rejoice and be glad in it.

25 Please, Lord, please save us.
Please, Lord, please give us success.
26 Bless the one who comes in the name of the
Lord.
We bless you from the house of the Lord.
27 The Lord is God, shining upon us.
Take the sacrifice and bind it with cords on
the altar.
28 You are my God, and I will praise you!
You are my God, and I will exalt you!

29 Give thanks to the Lord, for he is good!
His faithful love endures forever.

116:16 Someone born into a master's household would be enslaved for life, without any hope of emancipation. Unexpectedly and without obligation, though, God has liberated the psalmist. In that freedom, the liberated person *chooses* to serve God, willingly sacrificing offerings, fulfilling vows, and worshiping God in his Temple.

Psalm 117 This psalm, the shortest in the Psalter, invites "all... people of the earth" to "praise the Lord" because of his "unfailing love" and enduring faithfulness.

Psalm 118 With an exultant testimony, the psalmist gives thanks for the Lord's goodness and encourages others to trust in his faithful love (118:1-4, 29). This psalm is widely used in the Christian tradition as part of the church's Easter celebrations. On Palm Sunday, 118:1-2, 19-29 is often read. On Easter itself, 118:1-2, 14-24 is often read. See study note on 118:26 for some of the psalms that the New Testament cites.

118:26 The "one who comes in the name of the Lord" brings the Lord's complete victory (see 118:10-12). During Jesus' triumphant entry into Jerusalem, the crowds called out various blessings, including phrases taken from this verse (Matthew 21:9; Mark 11:9; Luke 19:38; John 12:13). Jesus himself quoted this passage as he wept over Jerusalem (Matthew 23:39; Luke 13:35).

Psalm 119*

Aleph

1 Joyful are people of integrity,
   who follow the instructions of the Lord.
2 Joyful are those who obey his laws
   and search for him with all their hearts.
3 They do not compromise with evil,
   and they walk only in his paths.
4 You have charged us
   to keep your commandments carefully.
5 Oh, that my actions would consistently
   reflect your decrees!
6 Then I will not be ashamed
   when I compare my life with your commands.
7 As I learn your righteous regulations,
   I will thank you by living as I should!
8 I will obey your decrees.
   Please don't give up on me!

Beth

9 How can a young person stay pure?
   By obeying your word.
10 I have tried hard to find you—
    don't let me wander from your commands.
11 I have hidden your word in my heart,
    that I might not sin against you.
12 I praise you, O Lord;
    teach me your decrees.
13 I have recited aloud
    all the regulations you have given us.
14 I have rejoiced in your laws
    as much as in riches.
15 I will study your commandments
    and reflect on your ways.
16 I will delight in your decrees
    and not forget your word.

Gimel

17 Be good to your servant,
    that I may live and obey your word.
18 Open my eyes to see
    the wonderful truths in your instructions.
19 I am only a foreigner in the land.
    Don't hide your commands from me!
20 I am always overwhelmed
    with a desire for your regulations.
21 You rebuke the arrogant;
    those who wander from your commands
    are cursed.
22 Don't let them scorn and insult me,
    for I have obeyed your laws.
23 Even princes sit and speak against me,
    but I will meditate on your decrees.
24 Your laws please me;
    they give me wise advice.

Daleth

25 I lie in the dust;
    revive me by your word.
26 I told you my plans, and you answered.
    Now teach me your decrees.
27 Help me understand the meaning of your
    commandments,
    and I will meditate on your wonderful deeds.
28 I weep with sorrow;
    encourage me by your word.
29 Keep me from lying to myself;
    give me the privilege of knowing your
    instructions.
30 I have chosen to be faithful;
    I have determined to live by your regulations.
31 I cling to your laws.
    Lord, don't let me be put to shame!
32 I will pursue your commands,
    for you expand my understanding.

He

33 Teach me your decrees, O Lord;
    I will keep them to the end.
34 Give me understanding and I will obey your
    instructions;
    I will put them into practice with all my heart.
35 Make me walk along the path of your commands,
    for that is where my happiness is found.
36 Give me an eagerness for your laws
    rather than a love for money!
37 Turn my eyes from worthless things,
    and give me life through your word.*

---

119 This psalm is a Hebrew acrostic poem; there are twenty-two stanzas, one for each successive letter of the Hebrew alphabet. Each of the eight verses within each stanza begins with the Hebrew letter named in its heading. **119:37** Some manuscripts read *in your ways*.

Psalm 119 This psalm is a Hebrew acrostic poem with twenty-two stanzas, one for each successive letter of the Hebrew alphabet. Each of the eight verses within each stanza begins with the Hebrew letter named in its heading. Psalm 119 combines elements of wisdom, lament, praise, thanksgiving, and confession. The opening verses introduce keywords found throughout the psalm. "Instructions" (119:1) translates the same Hebrew word found in 1:2, which describes the joyful person as one who delights or meditates on God's laws. "Paths" (119:3) point to lives reflecting God's character (Exodus 34:6-7). "Word" (Psalm 119:9) refers to God's communication generally but can specifically mean the Ten Commandments or prophetic messages. The Hebrew word translated "commandments" (119:4) is unique to the Psalms. It may refer to specific provisions of the Mosaic covenant, particularly Exodus 21–23 and Deuteronomy 12–26. "Decrees" (Psalm 119:5), "commands" (119:6), and "regulations" (119:7) also all relate to Israel's covenant or agreement with God. Together, these words encourage love for and obedience to God's instructions. These words may have focused on how God taught the people in Genesis to Deuteronomy. However, passages such as 2 Timothy 3:14-17 remind us that all of God's instructions equip us for lives of faith.

38 Reassure me of your promise,
   made to those who fear you.
39 Help me abandon my shameful ways;
   for your regulations are good.
40 I long to obey your commandments!
   Renew my life with your goodness.

Waw

41 LORD, give me your unfailing love,
   the salvation that you promised me.
42 Then I can answer those who taunt me,
   for I trust in your word.
43 Do not snatch your word of truth from me,
   for your regulations are my only hope.
44 I will keep on obeying your instructions
   forever and ever.
45 I will walk in freedom,
   for I have devoted myself to your
     commandments.
46 I will speak to kings about your laws,
   and I will not be ashamed.
47 How I delight in your commands!
   How I love them!
48 I honor and love your commands.
   I meditate on your decrees.

Zayin

49 Remember your promise to me;
   it is my only hope.
50 Your promise revives me;
   it comforts me in all my troubles.
51 The proud hold me in utter contempt,
   but I do not turn away from your
     instructions.
52 I meditate on your age-old regulations;
   O LORD, they comfort me.
53 I become furious with the wicked,
   because they reject your instructions.
54 Your decrees have been the theme of my songs
   wherever I have lived.
55 I reflect at night on who you are, O LORD;
   therefore, I obey your instructions.
56 This is how I spend my life:
   obeying your commandments.

Heth

57 LORD, you are mine!
   I promise to obey your words!
58 With all my heart I want your blessings.
   Be merciful as you promised.
59 I pondered the direction of my life,
   and I turned to follow your laws.
60 I will hurry, without delay,
   to obey your commands.
61 Evil people try to drag me into sin,
   but I am firmly anchored to your
     instructions.
62 I rise at midnight to thank you
   for your just regulations.
63 I am a friend to anyone who fears you—
   anyone who obeys your commandments.
64 O LORD, your unfailing love fills the earth;
   teach me your decrees.

Teth

65 You have done many good things for me, LORD,
   just as you promised.
66 I believe in your commands;
   now teach me good judgment and knowledge.
67 I used to wander off until you disciplined me;
   but now I closely follow your word.
68 You are good and do only good;
   teach me your decrees.
69 Arrogant people smear me with lies,
   but in truth I obey your commandments with
     all my heart.
70 Their hearts are dull and stupid,
   but I delight in your instructions.
71 My suffering was good for me,
   for it taught me to pay attention to your decrees.
72 Your instructions are more valuable to me
   than millions in gold and silver.

Yodh

73 You made me; you created me.
   Now give me the sense to follow your
     commands.
74 May all who fear you find in me a cause for joy,
   for I have put my hope in your word.
75 I know, O LORD, that your regulations are fair;
   you disciplined me because I needed it.
76 Now let your unfailing love comfort me,
   just as you promised me, your servant.
77 Surround me with your tender mercies so I may
     live,
   for your instructions are my delight.
78 Bring disgrace upon the arrogant people who
     lied about me;
   meanwhile, I will concentrate on your
     commandments.
79 Let me be united with all who fear you,
   with those who know your laws.
80 May I be blameless in keeping your decrees;
   then I will never be ashamed.

Kaph

81 I am worn out waiting for your rescue,
   but I have put my hope in your word.
82 My eyes are straining to see your promises
     come true.
   When will you comfort me?
83 I am shriveled like a wineskin in the smoke,
   but I have not forgotten to obey your decrees.
84 How long must I wait?
   When will you punish those who persecute me?
85 These arrogant people who hate your
     instructions
   have dug deep pits to trap me.

⁸⁶ All your commands are trustworthy.
   Protect me from those who hunt me down
      without cause.
⁸⁷ They almost finished me off,
   but I refused to abandon your commandments.
⁸⁸ In your unfailing love, spare my life;
   then I can continue to obey your laws.

Lamedh

⁸⁹ Your eternal word, O Lord,
   stands firm in heaven.
⁹⁰ Your faithfulness extends to every generation,
   as enduring as the earth you created.
⁹¹ Your regulations remain true to this day,
   for everything serves your plans.
⁹² If your instructions hadn't sustained me with joy,
   I would have died in my misery.
⁹³ I will never forget your commandments,
   for by them you give me life.
⁹⁴ I am yours; rescue me!
   For I have worked hard at obeying your
      commandments.
⁹⁵ Though the wicked hide along the way to kill me,
   I will quietly keep my mind on your laws.
⁹⁶ Even perfection has its limits,
   but your commands have no limit.

Women of the Word

SCRIPTURE CONNECTION: PSALM 119:1-176

He became my enemy, this man I'd never met but who planned to advance his career by bringing down my husband's. It felt like being eaten alive, helpless before one more powerful, captured by hatred.

Jesus told us to "love your enemies! Pray for those who persecute you!" (Matthew 5:44). Not a command I wanted to read; not one I could ignore.

How? I prayed. *The same way you pray for your husband* came the immediate thought.

At first, my prayers were only words, only prayed in obedience. Gradually they grew heartfelt for this man, transformative for me. No longer hate-controlled, altered by God.

That's the potency of the Bible, this powerhouse of guidance from God to direct all our steps, this solution for everything necessary to live on purpose, in joy, with influence and significance. It harbors no danger of wrong advice. It whispers pure truth and timeless wisdom.

With God's Word as a plumb line for our choices, our priorities change. Uttered in prayer, it transforms our thoughts. Memorized, it shields from life's harms. Teachers, speakers, writers can get it wrong, but God's Word speaks right. The more we yield to God's Word, the more we reflect his character.

> The more consistently we yield to God's Word, the more consistently we reflect his character.

IMAGINE

What distracts you from turning to the Bible?

What circumstance could most benefit from acting on God's Word?

"Books and teachers can lend perspective, but I hear God most accurately in the words of my Bible."

JANICE MAYO MATHERS is author of multiple books and Bible studies, including *Every Season: Embracing a Forever Kind of Purpose* (Stonecroft) and *Mothers-in-Law vs. Daughters-in-Law: Let There Be Peace*. She helps women see adverse circumstances as godly challenges.

Mem

97 Oh, how I love your instructions!
 I think about them all day long.
98 Your commands make me wiser than my enemies,
 for they are my constant guide.
99 Yes, I have more insight than my teachers,
 for I am always thinking of your laws.
100 I am even wiser than my elders,
 for I have kept your commandments.
101 I have refused to walk on any evil path,
 so that I may remain obedient to your word.
102 I haven't turned away from your regulations,
 for you have taught me well.
103 How sweet your words taste to me;
 they are sweeter than honey.
104 Your commandments give me understanding;
 no wonder I hate every false way of life.

Nun

105 Your word is a lamp to guide my feet
 and a light for my path.
106 I've promised it once, and I'll promise it again:
 I will obey your righteous regulations.
107 I have suffered much, O LORD;
 restore my life again as you promised.
108 LORD, accept my offering of praise,
 and teach me your regulations.
109 My life constantly hangs in the balance,
 but I will not stop obeying your instructions.
110 The wicked have set their traps for me,
 but I will not turn from your commandments.
111 Your laws are my treasure;
 they are my heart's delight.
112 I am determined to keep your decrees
 to the very end.

Samekh

113 I hate those with divided loyalties,
 but I love your instructions.
114 You are my refuge and my shield;
 your word is my source of hope.
115 Get out of my life, you evil-minded people,
 for I intend to obey the commands of my God.
116 LORD, sustain me as you promised, that I may live!
 Do not let my hope be crushed.
117 Sustain me, and I will be rescued;
 then I will meditate continually on your decrees.
118 But you have rejected all who stray from your decrees.
 They are only fooling themselves.
119 You skim off the wicked of the earth like scum;
 no wonder I love to obey your laws!
120 I tremble in fear of you;
 I stand in awe of your regulations.

Ayin

121 Don't leave me to the mercy of my enemies,
 for I have done what is just and right.
122 Please guarantee a blessing for me.
 Don't let the arrogant oppress me!
123 My eyes strain to see your rescue,
 to see the truth of your promise fulfilled.
124 I am your servant; deal with me in unfailing love,
 and teach me your decrees.
125 Give discernment to me, your servant;
 then I will understand your laws.
126 LORD, it is time for you to act,
 for these evil people have violated your instructions.
127 Truly, I love your commands
 more than gold, even the finest gold.
128 Each of your commandments is right.
 That is why I hate every false way.

Pe

129 Your laws are wonderful.
 No wonder I obey them!
130 The teaching of your word gives light,
 so even the simple can understand.
131 I pant with expectation,
 longing for your commands.
132 Come and show me your mercy,
 as you do for all who love your name.
133 Guide my steps by your word,
 so I will not be overcome by evil.
134 Ransom me from the oppression of evil people;
 then I can obey your commandments.
135 Look upon me with love;
 teach me your decrees.
136 Rivers of tears gush from my eyes
 because people disobey your instructions.

Tsadhe

137 O LORD, you are righteous,
 and your regulations are fair.
138 Your laws are perfect
 and completely trustworthy.
139 I am overwhelmed with indignation,
 for my enemies have disregarded your words.
140 Your promises have been thoroughly tested;
 that is why I love them so much.
141 I am insignificant and despised,
 but I don't forget your commandments.
142 Your justice is eternal,
 and your instructions are perfectly true.
143 As pressure and stress bear down on me,
 I find joy in your commands.
144 Your laws are always right;
 help me to understand them so I may live.

Qoph

145 I pray with all my heart; answer me, LORD!
 I will obey your decrees.

¹⁴⁶ I cry out to you; rescue me,
 that I may obey your laws.
¹⁴⁷ I rise early, before the sun is up;
 I cry out for help and put my hope in your words.
¹⁴⁸ I stay awake through the night,
 thinking about your promise.
¹⁴⁹ In your faithful love, O LORD, hear my cry;
 let me be revived by following your regulations.
¹⁵⁰ Lawless people are coming to attack me;
 they live far from your instructions.
¹⁵¹ But you are near, O LORD,
 and all your commands are true.
¹⁵² I have known from my earliest days
 that your laws will last forever.

Resh

¹⁵³ Look upon my suffering and rescue me,
 for I have not forgotten your instructions.
¹⁵⁴ Argue my case; take my side!
 Protect my life as you promised.
¹⁵⁵ The wicked are far from rescue,
 for they do not bother with your decrees.
¹⁵⁶ LORD, how great is your mercy;
 let me be revived by following your regulations.
¹⁵⁷ Many persecute and trouble me,
 yet I have not swerved from your laws.
¹⁵⁸ Seeing these traitors makes me sick at heart,
 because they care nothing for your word.
¹⁵⁹ See how I love your commandments, LORD.
 Give back my life because of your unfailing love.
¹⁶⁰ The very essence of your words is truth;
 all your just regulations will stand forever.

Shin

¹⁶¹ Powerful people harass me without cause,
 but my heart trembles only at your word.
¹⁶² I rejoice in your word
 like one who discovers a great treasure.
¹⁶³ I hate and abhor all falsehood,
 but I love your instructions.
¹⁶⁴ I will praise you seven times a day
 because all your regulations are just.

¹⁶⁵ Those who love your instructions have great peace
 and do not stumble.
¹⁶⁶ I long for your rescue, LORD,
 so I have obeyed your commands.
¹⁶⁷ I have obeyed your laws,
 for I love them very much.
¹⁶⁸ Yes, I obey your commandments and laws
 because you know everything I do.

Taw

¹⁶⁹ O LORD, listen to my cry;
 give me the discerning mind you promised.
¹⁷⁰ Listen to my prayer;
 rescue me as you promised.
¹⁷¹ Let praise flow from my lips,
 for you have taught me your decrees.
¹⁷² Let my tongue sing about your word,
 for all your commands are right.
¹⁷³ Give me a helping hand,
 for I have chosen to follow your commandments.
¹⁷⁴ O LORD, I have longed for your rescue,
 and your instructions are my delight.
¹⁷⁵ Let me live so I can praise you,
 and may your regulations help me.
¹⁷⁶ I have wandered away like a lost sheep;
 come and find me,
 for I have not forgotten your commands.

Psalm 120

A song for pilgrims ascending to Jerusalem.

¹ I took my troubles to the LORD;
 I cried out to him, and he answered my prayer.
² Rescue me, O LORD, from liars
 and from all deceitful people.
³ O deceptive tongue, what will God do to you?
 How will he increase your punishment?
⁴ You will be pierced with sharp arrows
 and burned with glowing coals.

⁵ How I suffer in far-off Meshech.
 It pains me to live in distant Kedar.
⁶ I am tired of living
 among people who hate peace.
⁷ I search for peace;
 but when I speak of peace, they want war!

Psalms 120–134 These short songs were sung during pilgrims' journeys to Jerusalem for the national festivals three times per year (Deuteronomy 16:16). The title of these psalms includes the Hebrew word for stairs, which some take to mean "ascending to Jerusalem." These psalms (sometimes called the Songs of Ascents) take the reader on a pilgrimage to Jerusalem to praise God for his goodness to Israel throughout history.

Psalm 120 This short, individual lament expresses the psalmist's trust that the Lord will deal with deceptive evildoers. It also laments living as a stranger among hateful liars. The psalmist's picture of his life in a foreign land might have been a reality as he set out for Jerusalem, or it might depict his feelings and concerns as he begins his pilgrimage. Overwhelmed with injustice, he trusts God and looks forward to arriving in the Lord's presence.

120:5 Meshech was a Japhethite territory far to the north of Canaan. Kedar was an Ishmaelite territory in Arabia. Violent people lived in both locations. Meshech was the home of a famous slave trade (Ezekiel 27:13; see Exodus 21:16) and Kedar of renowned warriors (Isaiah 21:16-17). Since a person cannot be in opposite directions simultaneously, the reference here should be understood as a metaphorical reference to the threats, violence, and chaos around the psalmist.

Women Wanderers

IDENTITY — Where to Find Help

Growing up in Chile, I saw the Andes Mountains as a constant, visible reminder of God's strength. They were a reminder I needed.

As a child with a terrifying father, I longed for strong, protective arms to shield my physical body and my soul.

Some may see Psalm 121's mountains as massive obstacles to overcome. Others see them as God's mighty power.

Generations of women like you and me have found God along winding mountain roads, through pilgrimages such as those of Psalms 120–134. Women wanderers moving toward the Father's love.

So, where does your help come from? Are you on a long, fiery journey? Psalm 121 reminds us to fear not because God is here. Your heavenly Father "keeps you from all harm and watches over your life" (121:7). The psalm writer's faith grew by walking through hardship, finding the love-filled arms of God.

No matter what terrors we face, God's love is real. And with him, we never face the mountain alone.

THE SONGS OF ASCENTS, FOR WOMEN WANDERERS, ARE PSALMS 120–134.

> God's love is real. And with him, we never face the mountain alone.

IDENTIFY

What kind of journey are you on now? How can you move toward God?

"My heavenly Father has been a balm to my soul every day since I first discovered his love. He lets me joyously journey to share his love—through dangerous favelas in Brazil, on buses in Eastern Europe, in villages in Southeast Asia, and other places where his Spirit guides."

BELÉN PETERS is a mobilizer with Scatter Global. Since 2002, she has been mobilizing mission-minded Latinos to take their passion and profession to places where Christ is unknown.

Psalm 121

A song for pilgrims ascending to Jerusalem.

1 I look up to the mountains—
    does my help come from there?
2 My help comes from the LORD,
    who made heaven and earth!

3 He will not let you stumble;
    the one who watches over you will not slumber.
4 Indeed, he who watches over Israel
    never slumbers or sleeps.

5 The LORD himself watches over you!
    The LORD stands beside you as your protective shade.
6 The sun will not harm you by day,
    nor the moon at night.

7 The LORD keeps you from all harm
    and watches over your life.
8 The LORD keeps watch over you as you come and go,
    both now and forever.

Psalm 122

A song for pilgrims ascending to Jerusalem. A psalm of David.

1 I was glad when they said to me,
    "Let us go to the house of the LORD."
2 And now here we are,
    standing inside your gates, O Jerusalem.

3 Jerusalem is a well-built city;
    its seamless walls cannot be breached.
4 All the tribes of Israel—the LORD's people—
    make their pilgrimage here.
    They come to give thanks to the name of the LORD,
    as the law requires of Israel.
5 Here stand the thrones where judgment is given,
    the thrones of the dynasty of David.

6 Pray for peace in Jerusalem.
    May all who love this city prosper.
7 O Jerusalem, may there be peace within your walls
    and prosperity in your palaces.
8 For the sake of my family and friends, I will say,
    "May you have peace."
9 For the sake of the house of the LORD our God,
    I will seek what is best for you, O Jerusalem.

Psalm 123

A song for pilgrims ascending to Jerusalem.

1 I lift my eyes to you,
    O God, enthroned in heaven.
2 We keep looking to the LORD our God for his mercy,
    just as servants keep their eyes on their master,
    as a slave girl watches her mistress for the slightest signal.

3 Have mercy on us, LORD, have mercy,
    for we have had our fill of contempt.
4 We have had more than our fill of the scoffing of the proud
    and the contempt of the arrogant.

Psalm 124

A song for pilgrims ascending to Jerusalem. A psalm of David.

1 What if the LORD had not been on our side?
    Let all Israel repeat:
2 What if the LORD had not been on our side
    when people attacked us?
3 They would have swallowed us alive
    in their burning anger.
4 The waters would have engulfed us;
    a torrent would have overwhelmed us.
5 Yes, the raging waters of their fury
    would have overwhelmed our very lives.

6 Praise the LORD,
    who did not let their teeth tear us apart!
7 We escaped like a bird from a hunter's trap.
    The trap is broken, and we are free!
8 Our help is from the LORD,
    who made heaven and earth.

Psalm 125

A song for pilgrims ascending to Jerusalem.

1 Those who trust in the LORD are as secure as Mount Zion;
    they will not be defeated but will endure forever.

Psalm 121 This psalm expresses a pilgrim's hope and confidence in God in a world filled with potential threats and dangers.
121:1 Some believe that the psalmist was looking toward God's Temple on Mount Zion as a place of safety and deliverance. Others think the verse negates the usefulness of forbidden altars built on high places (2 Kings 23:1-20). Still, others see a threat, suggesting the speaker needs help because of the dangers lurking in the mountains on any journey. The reference's ambiguity allows the psalm to be meaningful in a variety of circumstances.
Psalm 122 This psalm is a "Song of Zion" celebrating Jerusalem, where pilgrims celebrated three annual feasts. Jerusalem's real value is in the Temple, where God lived among his people. Jerusalem is here idealized as the city of God, the city of David, and the city of faith. A group of people on a pilgrimage joyfully arrive in the city (122:1-2). The poet sings an ode to Jerusalem (122:3-5) and prays for the city's peace (122:6-9).
Psalm 123 This lament on the psalmist's lowly position expresses vivid trust in the Lord (123:1-2). The psalmist prays for God's favor on the community, as the reality of evil surrounds them (123:3-4). The poet looks beyond Jerusalem (Psalm 122) to God's throne in heaven.
Psalm 124 This song offers the answer to the complaint in Psalm 123. The pilgrims remembered and thanked God for his past deliverance and expressed their trust in him.
124:1-2 The negative rhetorical questions emphasize the positive idea that the Lord was indeed on their side.
Psalm 125 The psalmist expresses the community's confidence in the Lord's protection (125:1-2) and prays for peace (125:3-5).

² Just as the mountains surround Jerusalem,
　　so the LORD surrounds his people, both now
　　　and forever.
³ The wicked will not rule the land of the godly,
　　for then the godly might be tempted to do
　　　wrong.
⁴ O LORD, do good to those who are good,
　　whose hearts are in tune with you.
⁵ But banish those who turn to crooked ways,
　　O LORD.
　　Take them away with those who do evil.

　　May Israel have peace!

Psalm 126
A song for pilgrims ascending to Jerusalem.

¹ When the LORD brought back his exiles to
　　　Jerusalem,*
　　it was like a dream!
² We were filled with laughter,
　　and we sang for joy.
　　And the other nations said,
　　　"What amazing things the LORD has done
　　　　for them."
³ Yes, the LORD has done amazing things for us!
　　What joy!

⁴ Restore our fortunes, LORD,
　　as streams renew the desert.
⁵ Those who plant in tears
　　will harvest with shouts of joy.
⁶ They weep as they go to plant their seed,
　　but they sing as they return with the harvest.

Psalm 127
A song for pilgrims ascending to Jerusalem. A psalm of Solomon.

¹ Unless the LORD builds a house,
　　the work of the builders is wasted.
　　Unless the LORD protects a city,
　　　guarding it with sentries will do no good.
² It is useless for you to work so hard
　　from early morning until late at night,
　　anxiously working for food to eat;
　　for God gives rest to his loved ones.

³ Children are a gift from the LORD;
　　they are a reward from him.
⁴ Children born to a young man
　　are like arrows in a warrior's hands.
⁵ How joyful is the man whose quiver is full
　　　of them!
　　He will not be put to shame when he
　　　confronts his accusers at the city gates.

Psalm 128
A song for pilgrims ascending to Jerusalem.

¹ How joyful are those who fear the LORD—
　　all who follow his ways!
² You will enjoy the fruit of your labor.
　　How joyful and prosperous you will be!
³ Your wife will be like a fruitful grapevine,
　　flourishing within your home.
　　Your children will be like vigorous young
　　　olive trees
　　as they sit around your table.
⁴ That is the LORD's blessing
　　for those who fear him.

⁵ May the LORD continually bless you from Zion.
　　May you see Jerusalem prosper as long as
　　　you live.
⁶ May you live to enjoy your grandchildren.
　　May Israel have peace!

Psalm 129
A song for pilgrims ascending to Jerusalem.

¹ From my earliest youth my enemies have
　　　persecuted me.
　　Let all Israel repeat this:
² From my earliest youth my enemies have
　　　persecuted me,
　　but they have never defeated me.
³ My back is covered with cuts,
　　as if a farmer had plowed long furrows.

126:1 Hebrew *Zion.*

Psalm 126 This hymn celebrates Israel's return from exile (126:1-3). The psalmist prays for full restoration (126:4-6).
126:4-6 The prophets had spoken of the restoration as a time when the wilderness would change into the Garden of Eden (Isaiah 51:3; Ezekiel 47); the reality fell far short of paradise. Here the restoration community prays for full redemption (see Haggai 2:19). The seasonal rains filled the dry river beds (called *wadis*), and the land turned green again. The prayer looks for a similar transformation of Israel's fortunes, a fulfillment of the imagery of the "second Exodus" in Isaiah. The harvest represents God's full restoration.
Psalm 127 Blessing and protection come from God. Without his presence, there is no success (127:1-2). This is particularly true of children, who are God's gift (127:3-5). The relationship between God's building, protecting, and providing rest (127:1-2) and children as a gift (127:3) may not be obvious. It has led some to argue that the verses focusing on children were originally part of a separate composition. However, they tell us more about what may be meant by the "house" mentioned in 127:1.
Psalm 128 This wisdom psalm teaches that the godly, who fear the Lord, will know true happiness (128:1-2). The Lord is with them (see 127:1-2), building their home life (128:3-4) and blessing them across the generations (128:5-6).
128:3 Wisdom was often addressed specifically to sons (see study note on Proverbs 1:1-2). The type of psalm (wisdom) and male-dominated context influence this focus on the wife and children as a blessing to a man.
Psalm 129 The psalmist briefly reviews Israel's history of trouble (129:1-2) and redemption (129:3-4). He concludes with curses against the enemies and blessings on the godly (129:5-6).

⁴ But the LORD is good;
  he has cut me free from the ropes of the ungodly.
⁵ May all who hate Jerusalem*
  be turned back in shameful defeat.
⁶ May they be as useless as grass on a rooftop,
  turning yellow when only half grown,
⁷ ignored by the harvester,
  despised by the binder.
⁸ And may those who pass by
  refuse to give them this blessing:
  "The LORD bless you;
  we bless you in the LORD's name."

Psalm 130
A song for pilgrims ascending to Jerusalem.

¹ From the depths of despair, O LORD,
  I call for your help.
² Hear my cry, O Lord.
  Pay attention to my prayer.
³ LORD, if you kept a record of our sins,
  who, O Lord, could ever survive?
⁴ But you offer forgiveness,
  that we might learn to fear you.
⁵ I am counting on the LORD;
  yes, I am counting on him.
  I have put my hope in his word.
⁶ I long for the Lord
  more than sentries long for the dawn,
  yes, more than sentries long for the dawn.
⁷ O Israel, hope in the LORD;
  for with the LORD there is unfailing love.
  His redemption overflows.
⁸ He himself will redeem Israel
  from every kind of sin.

Psalm 131
A song for pilgrims ascending to Jerusalem. A psalm of David.

¹ LORD, my heart is not proud;
  my eyes are not haughty.
  I don't concern myself with matters too great
  or too awesome for me to grasp.
² Instead, I have calmed and quieted myself,
  like a weaned child who no longer cries for its
    mother's milk.
  Yes, like a weaned child is my soul within me.
³ O Israel, put your hope in the LORD—
  now and always.

Psalm 132
A song for pilgrims ascending to Jerusalem.

¹ LORD, remember David
  and all that he suffered.
² He made a solemn promise to the LORD.
  He vowed to the Mighty One of Israel,*
³ "I will not go home;
  I will not let myself rest.
⁴ I will not let my eyes sleep
  nor close my eyelids in slumber
⁵ until I find a place to build a house for the LORD,
  a sanctuary for the Mighty One of Israel."
⁶ We heard that the Ark was in Ephrathah;
  then we found it in the distant countryside
    of Jaar.
⁷ Let us go to the sanctuary of the LORD;
  let us worship at the footstool of his throne.
⁸ Arise, O LORD, and enter your resting place,
  along with the Ark, the symbol of your power.
⁹ May your priests be clothed in godliness;
  may your loyal servants sing for joy.
¹⁰ For the sake of your servant David,
  do not reject the king you have anointed.
¹¹ The LORD swore an oath to David
  with a promise he will never take back:
  "I will place one of your descendants
    on your throne.
¹² If your descendants obey the terms of my
    covenant
  and the laws that I teach them,
  then your royal line
    will continue forever and ever."

129:5 Hebrew *Zion.* **132:2** Hebrew *of Jacob;* also in 132:5. See note on 44:4.

Psalm 130 As a representative of the community, the psalmist cries for God's mercy (130:1-3) out of deep distress. He places his hope in the Lord (130:4-6), knowing that the Lord will rescue when and as he chooses. Based on this confidence, the psalmist invites Israel to wait for the Lord (130:7-8).

130:7-8 The concept of "redemption" and the associated verb "redeem" refer to buying someone's freedom from slavery. The Old Testament uses this metaphor for God delivering Israel from Egypt (see Exodus 6:6-8; Deuteronomy 7:8; 2 Samuel 7:23-24). The New Testament uses similar language to describe God's work in Jesus (Titus 2:14; Hebrews 9:12; 1 Peter 1:18). It is easy to use the word "redeem" casually, without identifying what enslaved us and how God freed us. Going deep with this word helps us own and tell others of our God-bought freedom (Ephesians 2:8-10; 2 Timothy 1:9; Titus 3:5,).

Psalm 131 Out of his contentment in the Lord, the psalmist invites Israel to rest in God (131:3).

131:2 God is revealed to us to as Father, Son, and Spirit. While Scripture affirms that God is both Father and Son, this reality does not limit God's character or roles to those traditionally associated with men. In 131:2, we see God compared to a nursing mother whose care brings comfort and satisfies her child's needs (see also Isaiah 1:2-4; 46:3-4).

Psalm 132 This psalm celebrates the Lord's faithfulness to David. When David wanted to bring the Ark into Jerusalem (132:1-5), the Lord granted the request and made Jerusalem his earthly home (132:6-10). The choice of Jerusalem marked God's election of David's line (132:11-13), of Zion (132:14-17), and of the priesthood (132:9, 16).

¹³ For the LORD has chosen Jerusalem*;
 he has desired it for his home.
¹⁴ "This is my resting place forever," he said.
 "I will live here, for this is the home I desired.
¹⁵ I will bless this city and make it prosperous;
 I will satisfy its poor with food.
¹⁶ I will clothe its priests with godliness;
 its faithful servants will sing for joy.
¹⁷ Here I will increase the power of David;
 my anointed one will be a light for my people.
¹⁸ I will clothe his enemies with shame,
 but he will be a glorious king."

Psalm 133

A song for pilgrims ascending to Jerusalem. A psalm of David.

¹ How wonderful and pleasant it is
 when brothers live together in harmony!
² For harmony is as precious as the anointing oil
 that was poured over Aaron's head,
 that ran down his beard
 and onto the border of his robe.
³ Harmony is as refreshing as the dew from Mount Hermon
 that falls on the mountains of Zion.
 And there the LORD has pronounced his blessing,
 even life everlasting.

Psalm 134

A song for pilgrims ascending to Jerusalem.

¹ Oh, praise the LORD, all you servants of the LORD,
 you who serve at night in the house of the LORD.
² Lift your hands toward the sanctuary,
 and praise the LORD.
³ May the LORD, who made heaven and earth,
 bless you from Jerusalem.*

Psalm 135

¹ Praise the LORD!

Praise the name of the LORD!
 Praise him, you who serve the LORD,
² you who serve in the house of the LORD,
 in the courts of the house of our God.

132:13 Hebrew *Zion.* 134:3 Hebrew *Zion.*

> "Hope is central to the faith journey. It is the bedrock of Christian life. It is how we all, in some way or another, discover God. It is how we all, in some way or another, continue to move forward in time when we feel we simply cannot."
>
> **GRACE JI-SUN KIM**
> professor of theology, minister, and writer

³ Praise the LORD, for the LORD is good;
 celebrate his lovely name with music.
⁴ For the LORD has chosen Jacob for himself,
 Israel for his own special treasure.
⁵ I know the greatness of the LORD—
 that our Lord is greater than any other god.
⁶ The LORD does whatever pleases him
 throughout all heaven and earth,
 and on the seas and in their depths.
⁷ He causes the clouds to rise over the whole earth.
 He sends the lightning with the rain
 and releases the wind from his storehouses.

Psalm 133 In this wisdom psalm (see Psalm 1), peaceful and harmonious relationships manifest the presence of God. "Brothers" may refer to biological brothers or it may refer to the wider community, in which case women would be included.
133:2 Since the mention of the high priest Aaron does not occur until the third line in the original Hebrew, this verse evokes two images: the anointing of an individual and the anointing of the high priest. Scented oil was used for hair and skin in the dry climate of the ancient Near East. It was poured on visitors' heads as a refreshing act of hospitality and welcome. Anointing oil was also used during Aaron's investiture as high priest (Leviticus 8:12). The oil's significance here is somewhat debated, but it may compare harmony to welcome and refreshment. Harmony may also connect to celebrating Israel's ability to approach God in worship due to the priest's consecration.
Psalm 134 In the last of the pilgrims' songs (Psalms 120–134), the travelers call the Temple workers to praise the Lord. In return, they will receive a much-anticipated blessing.
Psalm 135 God, the Creator and the Lord of history, "made heaven and earth" (134:3). He deserves praise because, unlike idols, he redeems his people.
135:4 The synonyms "Jacob" and "Israel" include all twelve tribes. The Lord cherishes his chosen people. They are his treasure out of all the kingdoms of the world (Exodus 19:5-6).

⁸ He destroyed the firstborn in each Egyptian home,
  both people and animals.
⁹ He performed miraculous signs and wonders in Egypt
  against Pharaoh and all his people.
¹⁰ He struck down great nations
  and slaughtered mighty kings—
¹¹ Sihon king of the Amorites,
  Og king of Bashan,
  and all the kings of Canaan.
¹² He gave their land as an inheritance,
  a special possession to his people Israel.

¹³ Your name, O LORD, endures forever;
  your fame, O LORD, is known to every generation.
¹⁴ For the LORD will give justice to his people
  and have compassion on his servants.

¹⁵ The idols of the nations are merely things of silver and gold,
  shaped by human hands.
¹⁶ They have mouths but cannot speak,
  and eyes but cannot see.
¹⁷ They have ears but cannot hear,
  and mouths but cannot breathe.
¹⁸ And those who make idols are just like them,
  as are all who trust in them.

¹⁹ O Israel, praise the LORD!
  O priests—descendants of Aaron—praise the LORD!
²⁰ O Levites, praise the LORD!
  All you who fear the LORD, praise the LORD!
²¹ The LORD be praised from Zion,
  for he lives here in Jerusalem.

  Praise the LORD!

Psalm 136

¹ Give thanks to the LORD, for he is good!
  His faithful love endures forever.
² Give thanks to the God of gods.
  His faithful love endures forever.
³ Give thanks to the Lord of lords.
  His faithful love endures forever.
⁴ Give thanks to him who alone does mighty miracles.
  His faithful love endures forever.
⁵ Give thanks to him who made the heavens so skillfully.
  His faithful love endures forever.
⁶ Give thanks to him who placed the earth among the waters.
  His faithful love endures forever.
⁷ Give thanks to him who made the heavenly lights—
  His faithful love endures forever.
⁸ the sun to rule the day,
  His faithful love endures forever.
⁹ and the moon and stars to rule the night.
  His faithful love endures forever.
¹⁰ Give thanks to him who killed the firstborn of Egypt.
  His faithful love endures forever.
¹¹ He brought Israel out of Egypt.
  His faithful love endures forever.
¹² He acted with a strong hand and powerful arm.
  His faithful love endures forever.
¹³ Give thanks to him who parted the Red Sea.*
  His faithful love endures forever.
¹⁴ He led Israel safely through,
  His faithful love endures forever.
¹⁵ but he hurled Pharaoh and his army into the Red Sea.
  His faithful love endures forever.
¹⁶ Give thanks to him who led his people through the wilderness.
  His faithful love endures forever.
¹⁷ Give thanks to him who struck down mighty kings.
  His faithful love endures forever.
¹⁸ He killed powerful kings—
  His faithful love endures forever.
¹⁹ Sihon king of the Amorites,
  His faithful love endures forever.
²⁰ and Og king of Bashan.
  His faithful love endures forever.
²¹ God gave the land of these kings as an inheritance—
  His faithful love endures forever.
²² a special possession to his servant Israel.
  His faithful love endures forever.
²³ He remembered us in our weakness.
  His faithful love endures forever.
²⁴ He saved us from our enemies.
  His faithful love endures forever.
²⁵ He gives food to every living thing.
  His faithful love endures forever.
²⁶ Give thanks to the God of heaven.
  His faithful love endures forever.

136:13 Hebrew *sea of reeds;* also in 136:15.

135:15-18 Israel was forbidden from making idols (Exodus 20:4, 23; Deuteronomy 4:15-19; 5:8). Before Mesopotamian cult statues could be placed in a temple, they underwent ritual ceremonies that were believed to bring them to life and purify them for contact with the divine. A surviving Babylonian account of this ceremony records that the idol could not smell, eat, or drink until it underwent this ritual. However, these verses deny that such a ceremony transformed the idol in any way.

Psalm 136 This psalm is known in Jewish tradition as the Great Hallel (or praise) psalm. It distinctively repeats the refrain "His faithful love endures forever" in every verse. The hymn is framed by a call to praise (136:1-3, 26). It proclaims the Lord as the Creator of all and the Redeemer of Israel, both in the distant (136:10-22) and in the recent past (136:23-24).

Faithful Lover

IDENTITY — Finding Strength to Overcome

When we look at the Psalms, we repeatedly see God described as a Faithful Lover. From our first breaths, we need safety and protection from our caregivers: *Will you faithfully love me?* As we grow, even if we feel secure in our parents' love, we may still encounter insincere love, "love" that uses us, that is fleeting, that betrays.

What is my foundation? What am I building my life upon? Is it my experience or skills? Is it my education or recognition?

Or is it my Faithful Lover's never-ending mercy and love?

What fuels my energy and passion? Is it people's approval and applause? Is it the number of followers or friends?

Or is it my Faithful Lover's delight in me, and love that is unconditional and eternal?

Let the Psalms encourage us to rest our identity in God as our Faithful Lover. Like the psalm writers, we may remember and recount the ways that God has shown us his trustworthiness throughout our lives. As our greatest caregiver, God is with us when we face challenges, so we can say with the psalmist,

> Give thanks to the LORD, for he is good!
> His faithful love endures forever. (136:1)

If we know that we are loved, we can have the strength to overcome life's dark moments. But if we know we are loved by God, whose faithfulness is higher than the mountains, we can always overcome, no matter what.

> Even if I am not faithful, God remains faithful. My Faithful Lover is my strong foundation for life.

FIFTY-SIX VERSES IN THE BOOK OF PSALMS MENTION GOD'S FAITHFUL LOVE; YOU CAN FIND THEM IN PSALMS 25, 36, 40, 57, 61, 86, 89, 92, 98, 100, 106, 107, 108, 115, 117, 118, 119, 136, 138.

IDENTIFY

How many times did God break through to meet you where you are even when you felt you deserved it the least?

"The glory of God's faithfulness is that no sin of ours has ever made him unfaithful." Charles Spurgeon

ANGELA TKACHENKO is an evangelist, worshiper, and leader of Steiger Ukraine mission. She is passionate to see this generation love the Bible.

Psalm 137

1 Beside the rivers of Babylon, we sat and wept
  as we thought of Jerusalem.*
2 We put away our harps,
  hanging them on the branches of poplar trees.
3 For our captors demanded a song from us.
  Our tormentors insisted on a joyful hymn:
  "Sing us one of those songs of Jerusalem!"
4 But how can we sing the songs of the LORD
  while in a pagan land?
5 If I forget you, O Jerusalem,
  let my right hand forget how to play the harp.
6 May my tongue stick to the roof of my mouth
  if I fail to remember you,
  if I don't make Jerusalem my greatest joy.

137:1 Hebrew *Zion*; also in 137:3.

Psalm 137 In response to the pain of exile (137:1-4), the psalmist resolves to remember Jerusalem even though the memories cause him pain (137:4-6). He concludes with an astounding imprecation, or prayer for vengeance (137:7-9).

137:2-4 Because the music of Jerusalem was tied to the joys of life in the Promised Land, the Exile removed any occasion for singing joyous songs. The Babylonians wanted the Judeans to sing and dance for them, but the exiles' grief made doing so either distasteful or impossible. The songs celebrating the Lord speak of his power and goodness, but his people were filled with doubts and questions. They hung their harps in trees, perhaps signifying the death of their joy under God's curse (Deuteronomy 21:23).

Come Close

FALSE IMAGE: TRUE WORTH

SCRIPTURE CONNECTION: PSALM 139:1-24

We live in a world that constantly tells us who we are and what is best for us. The world tells me how I must look and act and what I should own. If I don't, then I am valueless, insignificant. So, I have pointlessly struggled to obtain the world's acceptance—all to my harm. My name is Alice. I am a follower of Christ Jesus, and I am an American Black woman.

When I see violent acts against Black people, I see that some people hate me and those who look like me. I will never understand the depths of their hate, and many years ago, I gave up trying. It was God's enemy that truly began the lie that God's image-bearers are more than one race. A lie so pernicious that people could enslave, oppress, discriminate, and hate others based upon the supposed superiority of one skin color over another.

Psalm 139 tells me that I am "wonderfully complex" and that his workmanship is "marvelous" (139:14)—and this is true of you, too. I am proud to be a Black woman. I live with discrimination daily, but I have never let them—"the haters"—define me. Are you letting how others see you define you?

The truth is we are one human race. We believe that we can all trace our ancestry back to Adam and Eve, to God. One God. One race. We are all God's marvelous workmanship, and we can all live in that truth.

REFLECT "Thank you for making me so wonderfully complex! Your workmanship is marvelous—how well I know it."
PSALM 139:14

Lord, when I begin to doubt who I am, remind me that I am a daughter of the almighty God, lovingly and purposely made by him for his glory. Amen.

CONSIDER "Psalm 139 is not a psalm about me, fearfully and wonderfully made. It is a psalm about my Maker, fearful and wonderful. It is a psalm intended to inspire awe." JEN WILKIN

> One God. One race who bears his image. All are God's marvelous workmanship.

ALICE PATTERSON, JD, is an associate court attorney in New York who has a fondness for teaching the Old Testament. She encourages everyone to put down the world's lies and put on God's truth.

⁷ O LORD, remember what the Edomites did
    on the day the armies of Babylon captured
        Jerusalem.
  "Destroy it!" they yelled.
  "Level it to the ground!"
⁸ O Babylon, you will be destroyed.
    Happy is the one who pays you back
        for what you have done to us.
⁹ Happy is the one who takes your babies
    and smashes them against the rocks!

Psalm 138

A psalm of David.

¹ I give you thanks, O LORD, with all my heart;
    I will sing your praises before the gods.
² I bow before your holy Temple as I worship.
    I praise your name for your unfailing love and
        faithfulness;
  for your promises are backed
    by all the honor of your name.
³ As soon as I pray, you answer me;
    you encourage me by giving me strength.

⁴ Every king in all the earth will thank you, LORD,
    for all of them will hear your words.
⁵ Yes, they will sing about the LORD's ways,
    for the glory of the LORD is very great.
⁶ Though the LORD is great, he cares for the
        humble,
    but he keeps his distance from the proud.

⁷ Though I am surrounded by troubles,
    you will protect me from the anger of my
        enemies.
  You reach out your hand,
    and the power of your right hand saves me.
⁸ The LORD will work out his plans for my life—
    for your faithful love, O LORD, endures
        forever.
  Don't abandon me, for you made me.

139:8 Hebrew *to Sheol.*

Psalm 139

For the choir director: A psalm of David.

¹ O LORD, you have examined my heart
    and know everything about me.
² You know when I sit down or stand up.
    You know my thoughts even when I'm far away.
³ You see me when I travel
    and when I rest at home.
  You know everything I do.
⁴ You know what I am going to say
    even before I say it, LORD.
⁵ You go before me and follow me.
    You place your hand of blessing on my head.
⁶ Such knowledge is too wonderful for me,
    too great for me to understand!

⁷ I can never escape from your Spirit!
    I can never get away from your presence!
⁸ If I go up to heaven, you are there;
    if I go down to the grave,* you are there.
⁹ If I ride the wings of the morning,
    if I dwell by the farthest oceans,
¹⁰ even there your hand will guide me,
    and your strength will support me.
¹¹ I could ask the darkness to hide me
    and the light around me to become night—
¹² but even in darkness I cannot hide from you.
  To you the night shines as bright as day.
    Darkness and light are the same to you.

¹³ You made all the delicate, inner parts of my body
    and knit me together in my mother's womb.
¹⁴ Thank you for making me so wonderfully
        complex!
    Your workmanship is marvelous—how well
        I know it.
¹⁵ You watched me as I was being formed in utter
        seclusion,
    as I was woven together in the dark of the
        womb.

137:8-9 These verses contain disturbing imagery. While they are horrifying, we must remember that the people who uttered these words survived significant trauma and lived with utter despair. Their willingness to submit their rage and desire for vengeance to God rather than to act on it reveals a commitment to nonviolence. These people expressed their pain in all its vitriol, but they trusted God to handle it justly. So, too, when we feel enraged, we can come to God and remember that he can handle both our anger and the solution. He will always act in line with his perfect character and can be trusted to bring true justice in his time.

Psalms 138–145 These psalms comprise the final collection of psalms of David. It opens and closes with praise psalms (Psalms 138, 145).

Psalm 138 In this thanksgiving psalm, the Lord is presented as the God of gods. He rescued his people, and all nations will praise him. This song would have reminded its audience of their identity as God's beloved people. These people could trust him no matter their circumstances because of God's unfailing, faithful love (138:2, 8).

Psalm 139 The genre of Psalm 139 is debated. Some see it as a hymn, while others focus on its wisdom teachings or the petition in 139:19-24. While the genre is uncertain, the psalm could be considered a reflection on God, who knows everything about an individual (see study note on 139:7-11). That knowledge ultimately leads us to praise, awe, and bringing our requests to God.

139:7-12 Based on 139:10, these verses are often read with a sense of wonder and comfort at a God who never leaves us (Deuteronomy 31:6). However, we can also read Psalm 139:7-9 through the lenses of Jonah and Job. Jonah sought to flee the Lord but could not do so (Jonah 1:3, 9-10). Job, believing that God had become his enemy, desperately wanted to escape the Lord's attention (Job 16:7-14). The combination of God's concern to guide and support and an inability to escape God's Spirit creates a sense of reverence.

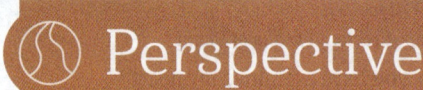

Perspective

How can I be more comfortable in my own skin?

SCRIPTURE CONNECTION: PSALM 139

It's one thing to read that we are "wonderfully complex" and that God's "workmanship is marvelous" (139:14), but it's another thing to feel it. Sometimes our complexity does not seem like a blessing, and we feel far short of marvelous!

Self-esteem and body image are complicated. Trauma can disrupt our sense of self and even make us wonder if God gave us the wrong body. But Psalm 139 says the Creator knew what he was doing.

We are broken. This world is broken. But God designed us to flourish, and he can help us as we pursue wholeness. The Psalms model an openness in prayer that can help to restore our true identities.

VIEWPOINTS

HIS: David learned to present all his thoughts to God, even the ugly ones (see 139:19-22), trusting that God would grow him through adversity.
MINE: "Family stresses took a toll on my body in college, and I developed a chronic health condition that lasted many months. I experienced firsthand how trauma impacts our health. The Psalms have played an important role in my healing journey."
YOURS: Do you struggle with body image, identity, or the physical effects of trauma? Alongside professional counseling, honest prayer can play a crucial role in becoming comfortable in your own skin.

CARMEN JOY IMES, PhD, is an author, speaker, blogger, YouTuber, and serves as associate professor of Old Testament at Biola University in California.

16 You saw me before I was born.
    Every day of my life was recorded in your book.
    Every moment was laid out
        before a single day had passed.
17 How precious are your thoughts about me,*
        O God.
    They cannot be numbered!
18 I can't even count them;
        they outnumber the grains of sand!
    And when I wake up,
        you are still with me!
19 O God, if only you would destroy the wicked!
        Get out of my life, you murderers!
20 They blaspheme you;
        your enemies misuse your name.
21 O Lord, shouldn't I hate those who hate you?
        Shouldn't I despise those who oppose you?
22 Yes, I hate them with total hatred,
        for your enemies are my enemies.
23 Search me, O God, and know my heart;
        test me and know my anxious thoughts.
24 Point out anything in me that offends you,
        and lead me along the path of everlasting life.

Psalm 140

For the choir director: A psalm of David.

1 O Lord, rescue me from evil people.
    Protect me from those who are violent,
2 those who plot evil in their hearts
    and stir up trouble all day long.
3 Their tongues sting like a snake;
    the venom of a viper drips from their lips.
                                            Interlude

4 O Lord, keep me out of the hands of the wicked.
    Protect me from those who are violent,
    for they are plotting against me.
5 The proud have set a trap to catch me;
    they have stretched out a net;
    they have placed traps all along the way.
                                            Interlude

6 I said to the Lord, "You are my God!"
    Listen, O Lord, to my cries for mercy!
7 O Sovereign Lord, the strong one who rescued me,
    you protected me on the day of battle.
8 Lord, do not let evil people have their way.
    Do not let their evil schemes succeed,
    or they will become proud.   *Interlude*

139:17 Or *How precious to me are your thoughts.*

139:17 God's investigation reveals his loving care for us. Fellowship with the Lord provides riches beyond description such that we cannot even begin to count them.
Psalm 140 In this individual lament, the psalmist artistically sketches God's enemies with all their evil intents. He prays for the Lord's protection and rescue with confidence in God's strength and justice. He foresees the evil as being judged by fire (140:9-11) and himself as being vindicated and dwelling in the Lord's presence (140:13).
140:7 The address "Sovereign Lord" comes from combining the name *Yahweh* with the title *Adonai* (Master). See also 68:20; 69:6; 71:16; 73:28; 109:21; 140:7; 141:8.

⁹ Let my enemies be destroyed
    by the very evil they have planned for me.
¹⁰ Let burning coals fall down on their heads.
    Let them be thrown into the fire
    or into watery pits from which they can't
        escape.
¹¹ Don't let liars prosper here in our land.
    Cause great disasters to fall on the violent.
¹² But I know the LORD will help those they
        persecute;
    he will give justice to the poor.
¹³ Surely righteous people are praising your name;
    the godly will live in your presence.

Psalm 141
A psalm of David.

¹ O LORD, I am calling to you. Please hurry!
    Listen when I cry to you for help!
² Accept my prayer as incense offered to you,
    and my upraised hands as an evening
        offering.
³ Take control of what I say, O LORD,
    and guard my lips.
⁴ Don't let me drift toward evil
    or take part in acts of wickedness.
    Don't let me share in the delicacies
    of those who do wrong.

⁵ Let the godly strike me!
    It will be a kindness!
    If they correct me, it is soothing medicine.
    Don't let me refuse it.

    But I pray constantly
    against the wicked and their deeds.
⁶ When their leaders are thrown down from a cliff,
    the wicked will listen to my words and find
        them true.
⁷ Like rocks brought up by a plow,
    the bones of the wicked will lie scattered
        without burial.*

⁸ I look to you for help, O Sovereign LORD.
    You are my refuge; don't let them kill me.
⁹ Keep me from the traps they have set for me,
    from the snares of those who do wrong.
¹⁰ Let the wicked fall into their own nets,
    but let me escape.

Psalm 142
A psalm of David, regarding his experience in the cave.
A prayer.*

¹ I cry out to the LORD;
    I plead for the LORD's mercy.
² I pour out my complaints before him
    and tell him all my troubles.
³ When I am overwhelmed,
    you alone know the way I should turn.
    Wherever I go,
    my enemies have set traps for me.
⁴ I look for someone to come and help me,
    but no one gives me a passing thought!
    No one will help me;
    no one cares a bit what happens to me.
⁵ Then I pray to you, O LORD.
    I say, "You are my place of refuge.
    You are all I really want in life.
⁶ Hear my cry,
    for I am very low.
    Rescue me from my persecutors,
    for they are too strong for me.
⁷ Bring me out of prison
    so I can thank you.
    The godly will crowd around me,
    for you are good to me."

Psalm 143
A psalm of David.

¹ Hear my prayer, O LORD;
    listen to my plea!
    Answer me because you are faithful and
        righteous.
² Don't put your servant on trial,
    for no one is innocent before you.
³ My enemy has chased me.
    He has knocked me to the ground
    and forces me to live in darkness like those in
        the grave.
⁴ I am losing all hope;
    I am paralyzed with fear.
⁵ I remember the days of old.
    I ponder all your great works
    and think about what you have done.
⁶ I lift my hands to you in prayer.
    I thirst for you as parched land thirsts for rain.
                                        Interlude

141:7 Hebrew *our bones will be scattered at the mouth of Sheol.* **142:TITLE** Hebrew *maskil.* This may be a literary or musical term.

Psalm 141 The psalmist prays for rescue and wisdom, and he envisions the end of evil. The principle of retribution (141:10) unifies the psalm.
Psalm 142 The psalmist faces severe persecution, so he cries to the Lord and knows that the Lord will rescue him.
142:6 The reference to being "low" may relate to emotions. But when we read this psalm alongside neighboring psalms, it may also refer to weakness, poverty, or oppression.

Psalm 143 In this lament, the psalmist feels overwhelmed by constant harassment from his foes, so he turns to the Lord's love, righteousness, and faithfulness. He remembers God's acts in the past and yearns for the renewal of the Lord's love. He opens himself to God's wisdom because he knows that instruction will lead to life.

⁷ Come quickly, Lord, and answer me,
  for my depression deepens.
Don't turn away from me,
  or I will die.
⁸ Let me hear of your unfailing love each morning,
  for I am trusting you.
Show me where to walk,
  for I give myself to you.
⁹ Rescue me from my enemies, Lord;
  I run to you to hide me.
¹⁰ Teach me to do your will,
  for you are my God.
May your gracious Spirit lead me forward
  on a firm footing.
¹¹ For the glory of your name, O Lord, preserve my life.
Because of your faithfulness, bring me out of this distress.
¹² In your unfailing love, silence all my enemies
  and destroy all my foes,
  for I am your servant.

Psalm 144
A psalm of David.

¹ Praise the Lord, who is my rock.
  He trains my hands for war
  and gives my fingers skill for battle.
² He is my loving ally and my fortress,
  my tower of safety, my rescuer.
He is my shield, and I take refuge in him.
  He makes the nations* submit to me.
³ O Lord, what are human beings that you should notice them,
  mere mortals that you should think about them?
⁴ For they are like a breath of air;
  their days are like a passing shadow.
⁵ Open the heavens, Lord, and come down.
  Touch the mountains so they billow smoke.
⁶ Hurl your lightning bolts and scatter your enemies!
  Shoot your arrows and confuse them!
⁷ Reach down from heaven and rescue me;
  rescue me from deep waters,
  from the power of my enemies.
⁸ Their mouths are full of lies;
  they swear to tell the truth, but they lie instead.
⁹ I will sing a new song to you, O God!
  I will sing your praises with a ten-stringed harp.
¹⁰ For you grant victory to kings!
  You rescued your servant David from the fatal sword.
¹¹ Save me!
  Rescue me from the power of my enemies.
Their mouths are full of lies;
  they swear to tell the truth, but they lie instead.
¹² May our sons flourish in their youth
  like well-nurtured plants.
May our daughters be like graceful pillars,
  carved to beautify a palace.
¹³ May our barns be filled
  with crops of every kind.
May the flocks in our fields multiply by the thousands,
  even tens of thousands,
¹⁴ and may our oxen be loaded down with produce.
May there be no enemy breaking through our walls,
  no going into captivity,
  no cries of alarm in our town squares.
¹⁵ Yes, joyful are those who live like this!
  Joyful indeed are those whose God is the Lord.

Psalm 145*
A psalm of praise of David.

¹ I will exalt you, my God and King,
  and praise your name forever and ever.
² I will praise you every day;
  yes, I will praise you forever.
³ Great is the Lord! He is most worthy of praise!
  No one can measure his greatness.

144:2 Some manuscripts read *my people.* 145 This psalm is a Hebrew acrostic poem; each verse (including 13b) begins with a successive letter of the Hebrew alphabet.

Psalm 144 This lament begins with an exclamation of praise for the Lord and then a reflection on the transitory nature of life (144:3-4). The psalmist prays for divine intervention and anticipates victory (144:5-11). A new song (144:9-10) and a prayer for rescue (144:11) open up the theme of the Lord's blessing through his provisions and protection (144:12-15).
144:3-4 The question *What are human beings?* in 8:4-6 elicits the answer that humans are mere mortals but are also glorious rulers. Here, though, the psalmist depicts humans as having a transitory existence (see 90:3, 7-10; 102:11; 109:23; 146:4).
144:12-14 Given the shift from an individual petition in 144:11 to plural language, 144:12-14 can be interpreted several ways. These lines can be understood as a prayer or a description of the community's experience or confident expectation.
Psalm 145 This psalm is a Hebrew acrostic poem; each verse (including the second line of 145:13) begins with a successive letter of the Hebrew alphabet. This hymn of praise is the last in this collection of David's psalms (138–145). Within Jewish tradition, Psalm 145 is to be recited three times each day, just like the *Shema* (Deuteronomy 6:4-5). One manuscript of the Dead Sea Scrolls includes the words "Blessed is the Lord and blessed is his name forever and ever" after each verse. This refrain suggests that the community may have used this psalm in their worship.

4 Let each generation tell its children of your
       mighty acts;
    let them proclaim your power.
5 I will meditate on your majestic, glorious
       splendor
    and your wonderful miracles.
6 Your awe-inspiring deeds will be on every
       tongue;
    I will proclaim your greatness.
7 Everyone will share the story of your wonderful
       goodness;
    they will sing with joy about your
       righteousness.

8 The LORD is merciful and compassionate,
    slow to get angry and filled with unfailing
       love.
9 The LORD is good to everyone.
    He showers compassion on all his creation.
10 All of your works will thank you, LORD,
    and your faithful followers will praise you.
11 They will speak of the glory of your kingdom;
    they will give examples of your power.
12 They will tell about your mighty deeds
    and about the majesty and glory of your
       reign.
13 For your kingdom is an everlasting kingdom.
    You rule throughout all generations.

   The LORD always keeps his promises;
    he is gracious in all he does.*
14 The LORD helps the fallen
    and lifts those bent beneath their loads.
15 The eyes of all look to you in hope;
    you give them their food as they need it.
16 When you open your hand,
    you satisfy the hunger and thirst of every
       living thing.
17 The LORD is righteous in everything he does;
    he is filled with kindness.
18 The LORD is close to all who call on him,
    yes, to all who call on him in truth.
19 He grants the desires of those who fear him;
    he hears their cries for help and rescues them.
20 The LORD protects all those who love him,
    but he destroys the wicked.
21 I will praise the LORD,
    and may everyone on earth bless his holy
       name
       forever and ever.

Psalm 146
1 Praise the LORD!

   Let all that I am praise the LORD.
2   I will praise the LORD as long as I live.
    I will sing praises to my God with my dying
       breath.

3 Don't put your confidence in powerful people;
    there is no help for you there.
4 When they breathe their last, they return to
       the earth,
    and all their plans die with them.
5 But joyful are those who have the God of Israel*
       as their helper,
    whose hope is in the LORD their God.
6 He made heaven and earth,
    the sea, and everything in them.
    He keeps every promise forever.
7 He gives justice to the oppressed
    and food to the hungry.
   The LORD frees the prisoners.
8   The LORD opens the eyes of the blind.
   The LORD lifts up those who are weighed down.
   The LORD loves the godly.
9 The LORD protects the foreigners among us.
    He cares for the orphans and widows,
    but he frustrates the plans of the wicked.

10 The LORD will reign forever.
    He will be your God, O Jerusalem,* throughout
       the generations.

   Praise the LORD!

Psalm 147
1 Praise the LORD!

   How good to sing praises to our God!
    How delightful and how fitting!
2 The LORD is rebuilding Jerusalem
    and bringing the exiles back to Israel.
3 He heals the brokenhearted
    and bandages their wounds.
4 He counts the stars
    and calls them all by name.
5 How great is our Lord! His power is absolute!
    His understanding is beyond
       comprehension!
6 The LORD supports the humble,
    but he brings the wicked down into the dust.
7 Sing out your thanks to the LORD;
    sing praises to our God with a harp.

145:13 As in Dead Sea Scrolls and Greek and Syriac versions; the Masoretic Text lacks the final two lines of this verse.
146:5 Hebrew *of Jacob*. See note on 44:4. 146:10 Hebrew *Zion*.

Psalms 146–150 The Psalter ends with five hallelujah psalms, so named because each begins and ends with "Praise the LORD!" (Hebrew *halelu-yah*).
Psalm 146 This psalm is a thanksgiving hymn that celebrates God's acts in creation and his ongoing care of the marginalized (146:5-9). Considering God's character and acts, his people can trust him rather than in powerful people (146:3-4). Today, when we face political unrest, believers in God can do the same.
Psalm 147 The psalmist calls for the Lord to be praised for restoring and blessing Zion, caring for the poor, displaying his power over nature, and revealing himself to his people.

> "Faith is not believing in my own unshakable belief. Faith is believing an unshakable God when everything in me trembles and quakes."
>
> **BETH MOORE**
> author, teacher, and writer

how swiftly his word flies!
¹⁶ He sends the snow like white wool;
 he scatters frost upon the ground like ashes.
¹⁷ He hurls the hail like stones.*
 Who can stand against his freezing cold?
¹⁸ Then, at his command, it all melts.
 He sends his winds, and the ice thaws.
¹⁹ He has revealed his words to Jacob,
 his decrees and regulations to Israel.
²⁰ He has not done this for any other nation;
 they do not know his regulations.

Praise the Lord!

Psalm 148

¹ Praise the Lord!

Praise the Lord from the heavens!
 Praise him from the skies!
² Praise him, all his angels!
 Praise him, all the armies of heaven!
³ Praise him, sun and moon!
 Praise him, all you twinkling stars!
⁴ Praise him, skies above!
 Praise him, vapors high above the clouds!
⁵ Let every created thing give praise to the Lord,
 for he issued his command, and they came into being.
⁶ He set them in place forever and ever.
 His decree will never be revoked.

⁷ Praise the Lord from the earth,
 you creatures of the ocean depths,
⁸ fire and hail, snow and clouds,*
 wind and weather that obey him,
⁹ mountains and all hills,
 fruit trees and all cedars,
¹⁰ wild animals and all livestock,
 small scurrying animals and birds,
¹¹ kings of the earth and all people,
 rulers and judges of the earth,
¹² young men and young women,
 old men and children.

¹³ Let them all praise the name of the Lord.
 For his name is very great;
 his glory towers over the earth and heaven!
¹⁴ He has made his people strong,

⁸ He covers the heavens with clouds,
 provides rain for the earth,
 and makes the grass grow in mountain pastures.
⁹ He gives food to the wild animals
 and feeds the young ravens when they cry.
¹⁰ He takes no pleasure in the strength of a horse
 or in human might.
¹¹ No, the Lord's delight is in those who fear him,
 those who put their hope in his unfailing love.

¹² Glorify the Lord, O Jerusalem!
 Praise your God, O Zion!
¹³ For he has strengthened the bars of your gates
 and blessed your children within your walls.
¹⁴ He sends peace across your nation
 and satisfies your hunger with the finest wheat.
¹⁵ He sends his orders to the world—

147:17 Hebrew *like bread crumbs.* **148:8** Or *mist,* or *smoke.*

147:19-20 When people in the ancient world encountered difficulties, they often believed that they had angered the gods. They did not necessarily know which deity they had offended or what they could do to make things right. But Israel was different because the Lord had revealed his will and what he expected by giving them instructions and laws. In the ancient context, that knowledge was an invaluable gift. So too, when we know what God desires, we find freedom from continually guessing. God has told us how we can walk closely with him. In his teaching, we find freedom from trying to please people, trying to earn a relationship with God, or misusing God's gifts meant to serve others.

Psalm 148 This psalm calls for the whole created order to praise the Lord, both in the heavens and on the earth.

148:8 Many ancient Near Eastern cultures believed that separate aspects of nature were controlled by different gods. The Lord, however, reigns sovereign over all natural phenomena; all the parts of creation are his servants, bringing praise to him through their obedience (77:17-18; 104:4; 135:7; 147:8, 15-18; Numbers 11:31).

honoring his faithful ones—
the people of Israel who are close to him.

Praise the LORD!

Psalm 149

¹ Praise the LORD!

Sing to the LORD a new song.
Sing his praises in the assembly of the faithful.

² O Israel, rejoice in your Maker.
O people of Jerusalem,* exult in your King.
³ Praise his name with dancing,
accompanied by tambourine and harp.
⁴ For the LORD delights in his people;
he crowns the humble with victory.
⁵ Let the faithful rejoice that he honors them.
Let them sing for joy as they lie on their beds.
⁶ Let the praises of God be in their mouths,
and a sharp sword in their hands—
⁷ to execute vengeance on the nations
and punishment on the peoples,
⁸ to bind their kings with shackles
and their leaders with iron chains,
⁹ to execute the judgment written against them.
This is the glorious privilege of his faithful ones.

Praise the LORD!

Psalm 150

¹ Praise the LORD!

Praise God in his sanctuary;
praise him in his mighty heaven!
² Praise him for his mighty works;
praise his unequaled greatness!
³ Praise him with a blast of the ram's horn;
praise him with the lyre and harp!
⁴ Praise him with the tambourine and dancing;
praise him with strings and flutes!
⁵ Praise him with a clash of cymbals;
praise him with loud clanging cymbals.
⁶ Let everything that breathes sing praises to the LORD!

Praise the LORD!

149:2 Hebrew *Zion*.

Psalm 149 This hymn of praise celebrates the Lord's victory. He is the Maker of Israel (149:1-2) and the victorious King who shares his glory with his faithful ones (149:3-9).
149:6-9 The military imagery interwoven through the praises of these five closing hymns seems jarring. Many interpreters see Psalm 149 as a twin to Psalm 2, which celebrates God's rule over all kings of the earth. In this context, vengeance (149:7) was part of a legal custom to restore justice when normal channels proved inadequate. These verses, then, point to the fulfillment of God's reign described in Psalm 2, which will include executing justice.
Psalm 150 Everything that breathes is commanded to praise the Lord as he deserves. The whole Psalter describes the greatness of the Lord, so this psalm is a fitting conclusion.

Proverbs

WHAT DO WE LEARN ABOUT GOD'S MISSION AND OURS?
We need—and can find—God's wisdom for life.

WHO WROTE IT? King Solomon and other wise people.

WHEN DID IT HAPPEN? Solomon wrote and recorded most of these wise sayings during his reign in the 900s BC, when Israel was united as one kingdom. Advisers and scribes during King Hezekiah's time added more sayings and likely put the book into its current form (25:1).

HOW IS IT ORGANIZED?

1–9:	Wisdom's way is the best way
10:1–22:16:	Solomon's proverbs
22:17–24:34:	Other wise sayings
25–29:	More sayings of Solomon
30:	Agur's sayings
31:	King Lemuel's sayings

Words to Remember are highlighted throughout this book

FEATURE HIGHLIGHTS
+ Wisdom Where? Here, Now (755)
+ Why the Warning about an "Immoral Woman"? (760)
+ Woman Wisdom: Call and I Will Answer (763)
+ Does Proverbs Say Men Are Wiser than Women? (764)
+ The Right Kind of Busy: Monkey or Monk? (768)
+ Watching Our Words (772)
+ Themes in Proverbs (775)
+ Wisdom (784)
+ Small Size, Big Wisdom (787)
+ An Excellent Woman: Qualities to Guide (789)

HOW LONG DOES IT TAKE TO READ?

| :30 | 1:00 | 1:15 | 1:30 | 2:00 | 2:30 | 3:00 | 3:30 |

The Purpose of Proverbs

1 These are the proverbs of Solomon, David's son, king of Israel.

² Their purpose is to teach people wisdom and discipline,
  to help them understand the insights of the wise.
³ Their purpose is to teach people to live disciplined and successful lives,
  to help them do what is right, just, and fair.
⁴ These proverbs will give insight to the simple,
  knowledge and discernment to the young.

⁵ Let the wise listen to these proverbs and become even wiser.
  Let those with understanding receive guidance
⁶ by exploring the meaning in these proverbs and parables,
  the words of the wise and their riddles.

⁷ Fear of the LORD is the foundation of true knowledge,
  but fools despise wisdom and discipline.

A Father's Exhortation: Acquire Wisdom

⁸ My child,* listen when your father corrects you.
  Don't neglect your mother's instruction.
⁹ What you learn from them will crown you with grace
  and be a chain of honor around your neck.

¹⁰ My child, if sinners entice you,
  turn your back on them!
¹¹ They may say, "Come and join us.
  Let's hide and kill someone!
  Just for fun, let's ambush the innocent!
¹² Let's swallow them alive, like the grave*;
  let's swallow them whole, like those who go down to the pit of death.
¹³ Think of the great things we'll get!
  We'll fill our houses with all the stuff we take.
¹⁴ Come, throw in your lot with us;
  we'll all share the loot."

¹⁵ My child, don't go along with them!
  Stay far away from their paths.
¹⁶ They rush to commit evil deeds.
  They hurry to commit murder.
¹⁷ If a bird sees a trap being set,
  it knows to stay away.
¹⁸ But these people set an ambush for themselves;
  they are trying to get themselves killed.
¹⁹ Such is the fate of all who are greedy for money;
  it robs them of life.

Wisdom Shouts in the Streets

²⁰ Wisdom shouts in the streets.
  She cries out in the public square.
²¹ She calls to the crowds along the main street,
  to those gathered in front of the city gate:
²² "How long, you simpletons,
  will you insist on being simpleminded?
  How long will you mockers relish your mocking?
  How long will you fools hate knowledge?
²³ Come and listen to my counsel.
  I'll share my heart with you
  and make you wise.

²⁴ "I called you so often, but you wouldn't come.
  I reached out to you, but you paid no attention.
²⁵ You ignored my advice
  and rejected the correction I offered.
²⁶ So I will laugh when you are in trouble!
  I will mock you when disaster overtakes you—
²⁷ when calamity overtakes you like a storm,
  when disaster engulfs you like a cyclone,
  and anguish and distress overwhelm you.

1:8 Hebrew *My son;* also in 1:10, 15. 1:12 Hebrew *like Sheol.*

1:1-2 These short sayings instruct us in wise living. Wisdom includes knowledge but goes further. Wisdom is also the ability to make ethical and moral choices that result in actions that honor God and benefit our communities. True wisdom involves the whole person, shaping our thoughts, beliefs, and behaviors. Wisdom may look different in various cultures since some circumstances will differ depending on where and when one lives. Proverbs frequently imparts wisdom to a "son" rather than a "child," reflecting Israel's culture, in which men predominantly led everything. (See study note on 1:8–9:18.)
1:3 Doing "what is right, just, and fair" characterizes the "disciplined and successful" life described here. The word translated "successful" can also mean "prudent," so it does not focus simply on one's career or financial achievements, which is how our contemporary culture often conceives of success. Instead, this "success" or "prudence" focuses on character qualities demonstrated in behaviors that honor God.
1:7 The "fear of the LORD" describes an attitude of reverence for the God who loves us and has made relating to him possible. This reverence results in a life that seeks to honor him in all our words, thoughts, and actions. Fear of the Lord overflows from our relationship with God rather than earning us a relationship with God.
1:8–9:18 Like other wisdom literature of the ancient Near East, much of Proverbs 1–9 is a father's—and occasionally, a mother's, (1:8; 6:20; 31:1)— instruction to a son. Because the son is being trained to follow in his father's profession, much of the teaching concerns the son's occupation. The NLT usually translates the term as *child* since the lessons are applicable to both sons and daughters.
1:8-19 The instructions in Proverbs focus on a person's choice between two ways: the way of wisdom or the path of folly. In this passage, we are warned about the dangers of following the path of folly.
1:22 While wisdom comes from fearing God, this verse describes three types of people who have chosen the other path. Simpletons have not hardened themselves against God's wisdom and are most open to correction (see 1:4). Fools have heard God's wisdom but resist it. Mockers not only resist wisdom but ridicule it.

28 "When they cry for help, I will not answer.
Though they anxiously search for me, they will not find me.
29 For they hated knowledge
and chose not to fear the LORD.
30 They rejected my advice
and paid no attention when I corrected them.
31 Therefore, they must eat the bitter fruit of living their own way,
choking on their own schemes.
32 For simpletons turn away from me—to death.
Fools are destroyed by their own complacency.

33 But all who listen to me will live in peace,
untroubled by fear of harm."

The Benefits of Wisdom

2 My child,* listen to what I say,
and treasure my commands.
2 Tune your ears to wisdom,
and concentrate on understanding.
3 Cry out for insight,
and ask for understanding.
4 Search for them as you would for silver;
seek them like hidden treasures.

2:1 Hebrew *My son.*

1:29-30 There is no middle ground in the language of Proverbs. One either loves and embraces Wisdom or hates and rejects her.

2:1-8 Wisdom results from listening to, seeking out, and living by sound instruction. While it flows from our fear of God, wisdom also leads to a deeper experiential understanding of God, to the "knowledge of God." This knowledge includes the way we think but ultimately shows in how we live.

Come Close — WISDOM WHERE? HERE, NOW

SCRIPTURE CONNECTION: PROVERBS 1:1-7

Wisdom. The word may conjure up images of fictional sages who spout truisms, like Yoda in *Star Wars.* Or it may seem like something only for women in their "golden years." But Proverbs, one of the Bible's wisdom books, addresses everyone's everyday.

We do not know how old the author, Solomon, was when he wrote many of these sayings. We do know that he was young when he asked God for the wisdom that inspired these timeless messages. God offered to give him anything he wanted, and a young Solomon asked for only one thing—wisdom (1 Kings 3:3-15).

I was a child when I heard Solomon's story using his "one wish" to ask for wisdom. So, I decided to do the same, every day, until I became wise. "Lord, give me wisdom," I prayed.

The process of asking for wisdom fueled my desire to know God's Word. My expectation and experience of discovering counsel for real life from the Bible increased.

As you ask God for wisdom, be prepared to find it in Scripture's living words you are reading right here, right now. Lean in, drink deeply. Wisdom lies so much closer than a sage from a far-off planet or our future selves, decades wiser.

REFLECT "Choose my instruction rather than silver, and knowledge rather than pure gold." PROVERBS 8:10

Lord, give me wisdom! Help me apply your instruction with my whole heart, in my circumstances, today. Amen.

CONSIDER "Lady Wisdom isn't wise because of random chance. She is wise because she intentionally chose the path of *wisdom.* She chose the path of God... of *life.* On the other hand, Madame Folly chose the path of foolishness and sin. She decides what is right and what is wrong, rather than looking to God's Word." KRISTEN CLARK, "Are You a Lady Wisdom or a Madame Folly?"

Expect to find wisdom in Scriptures' living words, right here, right now.

DONNA LEE LAMOTHE, MA, is executive director and founder of inSPIRE Channels at RSVP Ministries. She teaches and guides all to find wholeness through faith in Jesus.

⁵ Then you will understand what it means to fear the Lord,
and you will gain knowledge of God.
⁶ For the Lord grants wisdom!
From his mouth come knowledge and understanding.
⁷ He grants a treasure of common sense to the honest.
He is a shield to those who walk with integrity.
⁸ He guards the paths of the just
and protects those who are faithful to him.
⁹ Then you will understand what is right, just, and fair,
and you will find the right way to go.
¹⁰ For wisdom will enter your heart,
and knowledge will fill you with joy.
¹¹ Wise choices will watch over you.
Understanding will keep you safe.
¹² Wisdom will save you from evil people,
from those whose words are twisted.
¹³ These men turn from the right way
to walk down dark paths.
¹⁴ They take pleasure in doing wrong,
and they enjoy the twisted ways of evil.
¹⁵ Their actions are crooked,
and their ways are wrong.
¹⁶ Wisdom will save you from the immoral woman,
from the seductive words of the promiscuous woman.
¹⁷ She has abandoned her husband
and ignores the covenant she made before God.
¹⁸ Entering her house leads to death;
it is the road to the grave.*
¹⁹ The man who visits her is doomed.
He will never reach the paths of life.
²⁰ So follow the steps of the good,
and stay on the paths of the righteous.
²¹ For only the godly will live in the land,
and those with integrity will remain in it.
²² But the wicked will be removed from the land,
and the treacherous will be uprooted.

Trusting in the Lord

3 My child,* never forget the things I have taught you.
Store my commands in your heart.
² If you do this, you will live many years,
and your life will be satisfying.

³ Never let loyalty and kindness leave you!
Tie them around your neck as a reminder.
Write them deep within your heart.
⁴ Then you will find favor with both God and people,
and you will earn a good reputation.
⁵ Trust in the Lord with all your heart;
do not depend on your own understanding.
⁶ Seek his will in all you do,
and he will show you which path to take.
⁷ Don't be impressed with your own wisdom.
Instead, fear the Lord and turn away from evil.
⁸ Then you will have healing for your body
and strength for your bones.
⁹ Honor the Lord with your wealth
and with the best part of everything you produce.
¹⁰ Then he will fill your barns with grain,
and your vats will overflow with good wine.
¹¹ My child, don't reject the Lord's discipline,
and don't be upset when he corrects you.
¹² For the Lord corrects those he loves,
just as a father corrects a child in whom he delights.*
¹³ Joyful is the person who finds wisdom,
the one who gains understanding.
¹⁴ For wisdom is more profitable than silver,
and her wages are better than gold.
¹⁵ Wisdom is more precious than rubies;
nothing you desire can compare with her.
¹⁶ She offers you long life in her right hand,
and riches and honor in her left.
¹⁷ She will guide you down delightful paths;
all her ways are satisfying.
¹⁸ Wisdom is a tree of life to those who embrace her;
happy are those who hold her tightly.
¹⁹ By wisdom the Lord founded the earth;
by understanding he created the heavens.
²⁰ By his knowledge the deep fountains of the earth burst forth,
and the dew settles beneath the night sky.
²¹ My child, don't lose sight of common sense and discernment.
Hang on to them,
²² for they will refresh your soul.
They are like jewels on a necklace.

2:18 Hebrew *to the spirits of the dead.* **3:1** Hebrew *My son;* also in 3:11, 21. **3:12** Greek version reads *loves, / and he punishes those he accepts as his children.* Compare Heb 12:6.

2:6 "The Lord grants wisdom" to those who learn it from the Scriptures, which come "from his mouth" (2 Timothy 3:16; 2 Peter 1:20-21). It is impossible to become wise through observable experience alone.

*Seek his will
...and he
will show
you which path
to take.*

PROVERBS
3:6

²³ They keep you safe on your way,
and your feet will not stumble.
²⁴ You can go to bed without fear;
you will lie down and sleep soundly.
²⁵ You need not be afraid of sudden disaster
or the destruction that comes upon the wicked,
²⁶ for the LORD is your security.
He will keep your foot from being caught in a trap.

²⁷ Do not withhold good from those who deserve it
when it's in your power to help them.
²⁸ If you can help your neighbor now, don't say,
"Come back tomorrow, and then I'll help you."

²⁹ Don't plot harm against your neighbor,
for those who live nearby trust you.
³⁰ Don't pick a fight without reason,
when no one has done you harm.

³¹ Don't envy violent people
or copy their ways.
³² Such wicked people are detestable to the LORD,
but he offers his friendship to the godly.
³³ The LORD curses the house of the wicked,
but he blesses the home of the upright.
³⁴ The LORD mocks the mockers
but is gracious to the humble.*
³⁵ The wise inherit honor,
but fools are put to shame!

A Father's Wise Advice

4 My children,* listen when your father corrects you.
Pay attention and learn good judgment,
² for I am giving you good guidance.
Don't turn away from my instructions.
³ For I, too, was once my father's son,
tenderly loved as my mother's only child.

⁴ My father taught me,
"Take my words to heart.
Follow my commands, and you will live.
⁵ Get wisdom; develop good judgment.
Don't forget my words or turn away from them.
⁶ Don't turn your back on wisdom, for she will protect you.
Love her, and she will guard you.
⁷ Getting wisdom is the wisest thing you can do!
And whatever else you do, develop good judgment.
⁸ If you prize wisdom, she will make you great.
Embrace her, and she will honor you.
⁹ She will place a lovely wreath on your head;
she will present you with a beautiful crown."

¹⁰ My child,* listen to me and do as I say,
and you will have a long, good life.
¹¹ I will teach you wisdom's ways
and lead you in straight paths.
¹² When you walk, you won't be held back;
when you run, you won't stumble.
¹³ Take hold of my instructions; don't let them go.
Guard them, for they are the key to life.

¹⁴ Don't do as the wicked do,
and don't follow the path of evildoers.
¹⁵ Don't even think about it; don't go that way.
Turn away and keep moving.
¹⁶ For evil people can't sleep until they've done their evil deed for the day.
They can't rest until they've caused someone to stumble.
¹⁷ They eat the food of wickedness
and drink the wine of violence!

¹⁸ The way of the righteous is like the first gleam of dawn,
which shines ever brighter until the full light of day.
¹⁹ But the way of the wicked is like total darkness.
They have no idea what they are stumbling over.

²⁰ My child, pay attention to what I say.
Listen carefully to my words.
²¹ Don't lose sight of them.
Let them penetrate deep into your heart,
²² for they bring life to those who find them,
and healing to their whole body.

²³ Guard your heart above all else,
for it determines the course of your life.

²⁴ Avoid all perverse talk;
stay away from corrupt speech.

²⁵ Look straight ahead,
and fix your eyes on what lies before you.
²⁶ Mark out a straight path for your feet;
stay on the safe path.
²⁷ Don't get sidetracked;
keep your feet from following evil.

3:34 Greek version reads *The LORD opposes the proud / but gives grace to the humble.* Compare Jas 4:6; 1 Pet 5:5. **4:1** Hebrew *My sons.* **4:10** Hebrew *My son;* also in 4:20.

3:27-28 A wise person is a kind and helpful neighbor. Proverbs strongly emphasizes helping people who are financially needy (11:24; 28:27; 29:7, 14).

4:23 In the Old Testament, the heart represents the center of emotions, thinking, and reasoning (for example, Deuteronomy 4:29; Psalm 131:1). The heart is crucial in the battle between wisdom and foolishness, between righteousness and evil (see Matthew 5:8; 13:15; John 12:40; Romans 6:17).

4:24 Because a person's words originate in the heart, Proverbs teaches extensively about speech. One of the most basic lessons is to avoid "perverse" or "corrupt" speech, later defined as lies, slander, gossip, and rumor (6:12; 17:4; 18:8).

Avoid Immoral Women

5 My son, pay attention to my wisdom;
   listen carefully to my wise counsel.
² Then you will show discernment,
   and your lips will express what you've learned.
³ For the lips of an immoral woman are as sweet as honey,
   and her mouth is smoother than oil.
⁴ But in the end she is as bitter as poison,
   as dangerous as a double-edged sword.
⁵ Her feet go down to death;
   her steps lead straight to the grave.*
⁶ For she cares nothing about the path to life.
   She staggers down a crooked trail and doesn't realize it.

⁷ So now, my sons, listen to me.
   Never stray from what I am about to say:
⁸ Stay away from her!
   Don't go near the door of her house!
⁹ If you do, you will lose your honor
   and will lose to merciless people all you have achieved.
¹⁰ Strangers will consume your wealth,
   and someone else will enjoy the fruit of your labor.
¹¹ In the end you will groan in anguish
   when disease consumes your body.
¹² You will say, "How I hated discipline!
   If only I had not ignored all the warnings!
¹³ Oh, why didn't I listen to my teachers?
   Why didn't I pay attention to my instructors?
¹⁴ I have come to the brink of utter ruin,
   and now I must face public disgrace."

¹⁵ Drink water from your own well—
   share your love only with your wife.*
¹⁶ Why spill the water of your springs in the streets,
   having sex with just anyone?*
¹⁷ You should reserve it for yourselves.
   Never share it with strangers.
¹⁸ Let your wife be a fountain of blessing for you.
   Rejoice in the wife of your youth.
¹⁹ She is a loving deer, a graceful doe.
   Let her breasts satisfy you always.
   May you always be captivated by her love.

> "Marriage is not promised or preferred.... It's not the prize for faithfulness, nor the source. Jesus Christ is the prize. The Holy Spirit is the source. God is our Father, our husband, our friend."
>
> — RACHEL GILSON
> writer and speaker

²⁰ Why be captivated, my son, by an immoral woman,
   or fondle the breasts of a promiscuous woman?
²¹ For the LORD sees clearly what a man does,
   examining every path he takes.
²² An evil man is held captive by his own sins;
   they are ropes that catch and hold him.
²³ He will die for lack of self-control;
   he will be lost because of his great foolishness.

5:5 Hebrew *to Sheol.* **5:15** Hebrew *Drink water from your own cistern, / flowing water from your own well.* **5:16** Hebrew *Why spill your springs in the streets, / your streams in the city squares?*

5:15-18 To "drink...from your own well" (see also Song of Songs 4:12, 15) is to enjoy sex only within marriage. Rather than waste sex on a casual partner, this passage instructs us to cultivate a healthy sexual relationship with our spouses only. Because of the book's father-son narrative framework, Proverbs focuses on sexual ethics from a man's perspective, but these principles apply to women and our sexual choices, too (see the study note on Proverbs 1:8–9:18). Song of Songs 1:2-4 makes clear that a woman's sexuality is also important to God.

5:21-23 God holds each person responsible for their own choices. "The LORD sees" (5:21) can also be translated "before the eyes of the LORD." This reference can mean that not only does God see a person's actions, but a person's deeds actually take place in the Lord's presence. What seems hidden is fully known and will be judged. Our choices should be guided by the knowledge that God is near us at every moment. How might our words be kinder, our actions purer? How might we pause and consult God before reacting?

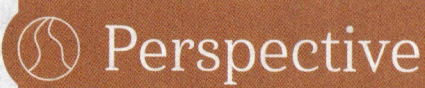

Perspective

Why the warning about an "immoral woman"?

**SCRIPTURE CONNECTION:
PROVERBS 5:1-23; 6:20–7:27**

King Solomon warns his sons about people living an immoral lifestyle, specifically portrayed here as an "immoral woman." This wording does not imply that only women behave immorally, nor does it assign blame for men's sexual wanderings to women. Solomon knew better (see 5:21-23 and his own sexual failings).

It's important to remember that Proverbs is framed as a discussion between a parent—usually a father but a mother's instruction is mentioned too (1:8; 6:20)—and a son already on the path to wisdom. The parent wants to keep his son on that path, and one of the biggest threats to that goal is sexual temptation, especially infidelity.

This ancient advice can still apply to us today. Do not allow excess sexual supply create in you unhealthy demand. We would be wise to heed this same caution as the internet brings temptation ever closer, and social media can keep illicit relationships more secret than ever. Temptation is all around us, but how we respond to it is our responsibility.

VIEWPOINTS

HERS: *The "immoral woman" seems to be in a sad and lonely place, seeking out strangers for sex. What may have happened to her and what choices might have been made that brought her to that place?*
MINE: *"Among the many reasons a woman may be looking for sex outside marriage, she may be trying to confirm self-worth or fill a void in her life.. The deeper aim of love, however, will never be met this way. Only God can complete us."*
YOURS: *How has sexual temptation affected your life? How can you incorporate the ancient wisdom of Proverbs as you continue on the path to wisdom?*

MISTY ARTERBURN is an author and speaker, contributing to Bible projects, devotionals, and recovery materials for over twenty years. Wife and mom to five, Misty is the founder of Recovery Girls and the general editor of *The One Year Bible for Women*.

Lessons for Daily Life

6 My child,* if you have put up security for a friend's debt
or agreed to guarantee the debt of a stranger—
² if you have trapped yourself by your agreement
and are caught by what you said—
³ follow my advice and save yourself,
for you have placed yourself at your friend's mercy.
Now swallow your pride;
go and beg to have your name erased.
⁴ Don't put it off; do it now!
Don't rest until you do.
⁵ Save yourself like a gazelle escaping from a hunter,
like a bird fleeing from a net.

⁶ Take a lesson from the ants, you lazybones.
Learn from their ways and become wise!
⁷ Though they have no prince
or governor or ruler to make them work,
⁸ they labor hard all summer,
gathering food for the winter.
⁹ But you, lazybones, how long will you sleep?
When will you wake up?
¹⁰ A little extra sleep, a little more slumber,
a little folding of the hands to rest—
¹¹ then poverty will pounce on you like a bandit;
scarcity will attack you like an armed robber.

¹² What are worthless and wicked people like?
They are constant liars,
¹³ signaling their deceit with a wink of the eye,
a nudge of the foot, or the wiggle of fingers.
¹⁴ Their perverted hearts plot evil,
and they constantly stir up trouble.
¹⁵ But they will be destroyed suddenly,
broken in an instant beyond all hope of healing.

¹⁶ There are six things the LORD hates—
no, seven things he detests:
¹⁷ haughty eyes,
a lying tongue,
hands that kill the innocent,
¹⁸ a heart that plots evil,
feet that race to do wrong,
¹⁹ a false witness who pours out lies,
a person who sows discord in a family.

²⁰ My son, obey your father's commands,
and don't neglect your mother's instruction.
²¹ Keep their words always in your heart.
Tie them around your neck.

6:1 Hebrew *My son*.

6:16-19 The first line gives a number followed by a second line that increases that number by one. This device (called *number parallelism*) introduces a list of items and often, as here, draws attention to the climactic final item (see also 30:15-23).

²² When you walk, their counsel will lead you.
   When you sleep, they will protect you.
   When you wake up, they will advise you.
²³ For their command is a lamp
   and their instruction a light;
   their corrective discipline
   is the way to life.
²⁴ It will keep you from the immoral woman,
   from the smooth tongue of a promiscuous
   woman.
²⁵ Don't lust for her beauty.
   Don't let her coy glances seduce you.
²⁶ For a prostitute will bring you to poverty,*
   but sleeping with another man's wife will cost
   you your life.
²⁷ Can a man scoop a flame into his lap
   and not have his clothes catch on fire?
²⁸ Can he walk on hot coals
   and not blister his feet?
²⁹ So it is with the man who sleeps with another
   man's wife.
   He who embraces her will not go unpunished.
³⁰ Excuses might be found for a thief
   who steals because he is starving.
³¹ But if he is caught, he must pay back seven times
   what he stole,
   even if he has to sell everything in his house.
³² But the man who commits adultery is an utter
   fool,
   for he destroys himself.
³³ He will be wounded and disgraced.
   His shame will never be erased.
³⁴ For the woman's jealous husband will be furious,
   and he will show no mercy when he takes
   revenge.
³⁵ He will accept no compensation,
   nor be satisfied with a payoff of any size.

Another Warning about Immoral Women

7 Follow my advice, my son;
   always treasure my commands.
² Obey my commands and live!
   Guard my instructions as you guard your
   own eyes.*
³ Tie them on your fingers as a reminder.
   Write them deep within your heart.
⁴ Love wisdom like a sister;
   make insight a beloved member of your family.
⁵ Let them protect you from an affair with an
   immoral woman,
   from listening to the flattery of a promiscuous
   woman.
⁶ While I was at the window of my house,
   looking through the curtain,
⁷ I saw some naive young men,
   and one in particular who lacked common
   sense.
⁸ He was crossing the street near the house of an
   immoral woman,
   strolling down the path by her house.
⁹ It was at twilight, in the evening,
   as deep darkness fell.
¹⁰ The woman approached him,
   seductively dressed and sly of heart.
¹¹ She was the brash, rebellious type,
   never content to stay at home.
¹² She is often in the streets and markets,
   soliciting at every corner.
¹³ She threw her arms around him and kissed him,
   and with a brazen look she said,
¹⁴ "I've just made my peace offerings
   and fulfilled my vows.
¹⁵ You're the one I was looking for!
   I came out to find you, and here you are!
¹⁶ My bed is spread with beautiful blankets,
   with colored sheets of Egyptian linen.
¹⁷ I've perfumed my bed
   with myrrh, aloes, and cinnamon.
¹⁸ Come, let's drink our fill of love until morning.
   Let's enjoy each other's caresses,
¹⁹ for my husband is not home.
   He's away on a long trip.
²⁰ He has taken a wallet full of money with him
   and won't return until later this month.*"
²¹ So she seduced him with her pretty speech
   and enticed him with her flattery.
²² He followed her at once,
   like an ox going to the slaughter.
   He was like a stag caught in a trap,*
²³ awaiting the arrow that would pierce its heart.
   He was like a bird flying into a snare,
   little knowing it would cost him his life.
²⁴ So listen to me, my sons,
   and pay attention to my words.
²⁵ Don't let your hearts stray away toward her.
   Don't wander down her wayward path.
²⁶ For she has been the ruin of many;
   many men have been her victims.
²⁷ Her house is the road to the grave.*
   Her bedroom is the den of death.

6:26 Hebrew *to a loaf of bread.*   **7:2** Hebrew *as the pupil of your eye.*   **7:20** Hebrew *until the moon is full.*   **7:22** As in Greek and Syriac versions; Hebrew reads *slaughter, as shackles are for the discipline of a fool.*   **7:27** Hebrew *to Sheol.*

7:24-27 The father reasserts the point of his lesson: While a night with an immoral person might look good and a relationship with them is enticing, the consequences can be serious. For the original audience, the law of Moses prescribed death to anyone who had sex outside of a heterosexual marriage (Leviticus 20:10-16). Sexual immorality tempts most people, but the Bible is clear that following only our instincts on what feels good or exciting sexually can lead to ruin.

Wisdom Calls for a Hearing

8 Listen as Wisdom calls out!
  Hear as understanding raises her voice!
² On the hilltop along the road,
  she takes her stand at the crossroads.
³ By the gates at the entrance to the town,
  on the road leading in, she cries aloud,
⁴ "I call to you, to all of you!
  I raise my voice to all people.
⁵ You simple people, use good judgment.
  You foolish people, show some understanding.
⁶ Listen to me! For I have important things to tell you.
  Everything I say is right,
⁷ for I speak the truth
  and detest every kind of deception.
⁸ My advice is wholesome.
  There is nothing devious or crooked in it.
⁹ My words are plain to anyone with understanding,
  clear to those with knowledge.
¹⁰ Choose my instruction rather than silver,
  and knowledge rather than pure gold.
¹¹ For wisdom is far more valuable than rubies.
  Nothing you desire can compare with it.

¹² "I, Wisdom, live together with good judgment.
  I know where to discover knowledge and discernment.
¹³ All who fear the LORD will hate evil.
  Therefore, I hate pride and arrogance, corruption and perverse speech.
¹⁴ Common sense and success belong to me.
  Insight and strength are mine.
¹⁵ Because of me, kings reign,
  and rulers make just decrees.
¹⁶ Rulers lead with my help,
  and nobles make righteous judgments.*
¹⁷ "I love all who love me.
  Those who search will surely find me.
¹⁸ I have riches and honor,
  as well as enduring wealth and justice.
¹⁹ My gifts are better than gold, even the purest gold,
  my wages better than sterling silver!
²⁰ I walk in righteousness,
  in paths of justice.
²¹ Those who love me inherit wealth.
  I will fill their treasuries.

²² "The LORD formed me from the beginning,
  before he created anything else.
²³ I was appointed in ages past,
  at the very first, before the earth began.
²⁴ I was born before the oceans were created,
  before the springs bubbled forth their waters.
²⁵ Before the mountains were formed,
  before the hills, I was born—
²⁶ before he had made the earth and fields
  and the first handfuls of soil.
²⁷ I was there when he established the heavens,
  when he drew the horizon on the oceans.
²⁸ I was there when he set the clouds above,
  when he established springs deep in the earth.
²⁹ I was there when he set the limits of the seas,
  so they would not spread beyond their boundaries.
  And when he marked off the earth's foundations,
³⁰   I was the architect at his side.
  I was his constant delight,
  rejoicing always in his presence.
³¹ And how happy I was with the world he created;
  how I rejoiced with the human family!

³² "And so, my children,* listen to me,
  for all who follow my ways are joyful.
³³ Listen to my instruction and be wise.
  Don't ignore it.
³⁴ Joyful are those who listen to me,
  watching for me daily at my gates,
  waiting for me outside my home!
³⁵ For whoever finds me finds life
  and receives favor from the LORD.
³⁶ But those who miss me injure themselves.
  All who hate me love death."

9 Wisdom has built her house;
  she has carved its seven columns.
² She has prepared a great banquet,
  mixed the wines, and set the table.
³ She has sent her servants to invite everyone to come.
  She calls out from the heights overlooking the city.

8:16 Some Hebrew manuscripts and Greek version read *and nobles are judges over the earth.*   **8:32** Hebrew *my sons.*

8:1–9:18 The first part of Proverbs culminates with the son encountering two women. Both invite the young man, and the reader with him, into an intimate relationship. The young man and the reader must decide between the woman called Wisdom, personifying the true wisdom of God (8:1–9:6), and the woman called Folly (9:13-18), representing the wisdom of the world (1 Corinthians 1:18–2:16). The choice between the two women thus represents the choice we have between the true God and false gods. **8:17-21** Proverbial sayings and teachings point to what is generally true. They do not make promises. While material wealth may result from wise behavior and choices, wisdom's intangible gifts are more greatly desired. **8:22-25** God's wisdom has always existed. His wisdom is here personified, but wisdom itself is not a person. Wisdom does not exist outside of God; wisdom is an expression of his character and nature. Unlike pagan gods, God needs no outside counselor to give him instructions (see Isaiah 40:13-14). Jesus is the apex of God's wisdom (see Colossians 1:15-17; 2:3).

Woman Wisdom

IDENTITY — Call and I Will Answer

Woman Wisdom calls...

I am not far off from anyone. I do not hide. I call to anyone with ears to hear.

Many will be tempted to think I am not needed. They will look at logic and history and make decisions in rooms without windows. They will think information is above my reach and can replace my voice.

My words are the bridge between the heart and the mind. Throughout history, humanity has valued one over the other in a pendulum of extremes. Neither alone can lead to sound decisions.

Then there are those who reject me altogether. I give a sure sign that points to bring good to others, but they cannot see past their own noses, their own selfish desires.

I am a promised resource to those who seek me. Why would you not ask and receive? Why would you move through life without my gift?

I amplify common sense. I embody truth. I bountifully supply knowledge.

When you are trapped in a circumstance full of rocks and hard places, you might be tempted to shove at them in frustration. I never see a dead end. I wait nearby with a feast of solutions, served upon platters of goodness, righteousness, knowledge, joy, and strength.

Will you call? I promise to answer.

WOMAN WISDOM'S SAYINGS ARE RECORDED IN PROVERBS 8–9.

> Go to Wisdom's table. Enjoy her abundant, available feast of knowledge, goodness, and joy.

IDENTIFY

What situation are you facing right now that needs wisdom?

What images in Proverbs 8 and 9 speak the loudest to your need for wisdom?

> "Have you ever uttered in frustration, 'I just want to know what to do!'? I have, many times. Then I learned how God wants to make wisdom abundantly available. I've learned to ask for wisdom over and over again, and then wait on his answer."

CARA DAY is a writer and illustrator. She has served with Stonecroft Ministries helping women live "extraordinary."

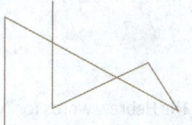

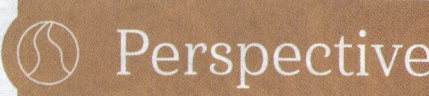

Perspective

Does Proverbs say men are wiser than women?

SCRIPTURE CONNECTION: PROVERBS 8–9

It can be off-putting how often Proverbs warns men about dangerous women. What gives? This book frames a father's advice to his son, who must learn to exercise wisdom in sexual relationships.

Wisdom and folly are grammatically feminine in Hebrew, so the book creatively personifies them as Woman Wisdom and Woman Folly. Proverbs 31 brings these imaginative metaphors to a satisfying conclusion: The young man chooses to marry Woman Wisdom.

As female readers, we must also read with imagination. Proverbs invites us to beware of *anyone* whose smooth talk might lead us into sin. When it comes to wisdom, neither gender corners the market.

VIEWPOINTS

HERS: In a male-dominated society, the depiction of Woman Wisdom in Proverbs showed women that their choices matter. They, too, have influence and can live wisely.

MINE: "Choosing who to marry was one of the weightiest decisions I've ever made. After twenty-two years, I can say with confidence that I found a 'Proverbs 31 Man' who exhibits wisdom."

YOURS: Which of Woman Wisdom's qualities do you most desire?

CARMEN JOY IMES, PhD, is an author, speaker, blogger, YouTuber, and serves as associate professor of Old Testament at Biola University in California.

---

⁴ "Come in with me," she urges the simple.
To those who lack good judgment, she says,
⁵ "Come, eat my food,
and drink the wine I have mixed.
⁶ Leave your simple ways behind, and begin to live;
learn to use good judgment."

⁷ Anyone who rebukes a mocker will get an insult in return.
Anyone who corrects the wicked will get hurt.
⁸ So don't bother correcting mockers;
they will only hate you.
But correct the wise,
and they will love you.
⁹ Instruct the wise,
and they will be even wiser.
Teach the righteous,
and they will learn even more.

¹⁰ Fear of the LORD is the foundation of wisdom.
Knowledge of the Holy One results in good judgment.
¹¹ Wisdom will multiply your days
and add years to your life.
¹² If you become wise, you will be the one to benefit.
If you scorn wisdom, you will be the one to suffer.

Folly Calls for a Hearing

¹³ The woman named Folly is brash.
She is ignorant and doesn't know it.
¹⁴ She sits in her doorway
on the heights overlooking the city.
¹⁵ She calls out to men going by
who are minding their own business.
¹⁶ "Come in with me," she urges the simple.
To those who lack good judgment, she says,
¹⁷ "Stolen water is refreshing;
food eaten in secret tastes the best!"
¹⁸ But little do they know that the dead are there.
Her guests are in the depths of the grave.*

The Proverbs of Solomon

10 The proverbs of Solomon:

A wise child* brings joy to a father;
a foolish child brings grief to a mother.

9:18 Hebrew *in Sheol*. 10:1 Hebrew *son*; also in 10:1b.

9:13-18 The Hebrew words for "wisdom" and "folly" are grammatically feminine, but this does not mean they are fundamental characteristics of women. The speaker makes folly and wisdom into characters, using the literary device of personification, which considers concepts or nonhuman objects as a person. The women's invitations in Proverbs 8–9 point to the choice each of us faces between two ways of life. (See study note on 1:8-19.)
9:14 "On the heights overlooking the city" was the traditional location for a temple. Woman Folly personifies the false gods and goddesses that competed for the affection and loyalty of God's people. Woman Folly just "sits in her doorway" and calls out, while Woman Wisdom industriously prepares and invites everyone (9:2-3).
9:16 Woman Folly's invitation opens the same way that Woman Wisdom's invitation does in 9:4: "'Come in with me,' she urges the simple." The right choice may not always be immediately obvious to us.

² Tainted wealth has no lasting value,
   but right living can save your life.

³ The LORD will not let the godly go hungry,
   but he refuses to satisfy the craving of the wicked.

⁴ Lazy people are soon poor;
   hard workers get rich.

⁵ A wise youth harvests in the summer,
   but one who sleeps during harvest is a disgrace.

⁶ The godly are showered with blessings;
   the words of the wicked conceal violent intentions.

⁷ We have happy memories of the godly,
   but the name of a wicked person rots away.

⁸ The wise are glad to be instructed,
   but babbling fools fall flat on their faces.

⁹ People with integrity walk safely,
   but those who follow crooked paths will be exposed.

¹⁰ People who wink at wrong cause trouble,
   but a bold reproof promotes peace.*

¹¹ The words of the godly are a life-giving fountain;
   the words of the wicked conceal violent intentions.

¹² Hatred stirs up quarrels,
   but love makes up for all offenses.

¹³ Wise words come from the lips of people with understanding,
   but those lacking sense will be beaten with a rod.

¹⁴ Wise people treasure knowledge,
   but the babbling of a fool invites disaster.

¹⁵ The wealth of the rich is their fortress;
   the poverty of the poor is their destruction.

¹⁶ The earnings of the godly enhance their lives,
   but evil people squander their money on sin.

¹⁷ People who accept discipline are on the pathway to life,
   but those who ignore correction will go astray.

¹⁸ Hiding hatred makes you a liar;
   slandering others makes you a fool.

¹⁹ Too much talk leads to sin.
   Be sensible and keep your mouth shut.

²⁰ The words of the godly are like sterling silver;
   the heart of a fool is worthless.

²¹ The words of the godly encourage many,
   but fools are destroyed by their lack of common sense.

²² The blessing of the LORD makes a person rich,
   and he adds no sorrow with it.

²³ Doing wrong is fun for a fool,
   but living wisely brings pleasure to the sensible.

²⁴ The fears of the wicked will be fulfilled;
   the hopes of the godly will be granted.

²⁵ When the storms of life come, the wicked are whirled away,
   but the godly have a lasting foundation.

²⁶ Lazy people irritate their employers,
   like vinegar to the teeth or smoke in the eyes.

²⁷ Fear of the LORD lengthens one's life,
   but the years of the wicked are cut short.

²⁸ The hopes of the godly result in happiness,
   but the expectations of the wicked come to nothing.

²⁹ The way of the LORD is a stronghold to those with integrity,
   but it destroys the wicked.

³⁰ The godly will never be disturbed,
   but the wicked will be removed from the land.

³¹ The mouth of the godly person gives wise advice,
   but the tongue that deceives will be cut off.

³² The lips of the godly speak helpful words,
   but the mouth of the wicked speaks perverse words.

10:10 As in Greek version; Hebrew reads *but babbling fools fall flat on their faces.*

10:1–22:16 This long section is called "the proverbs of Solomon," which consist mostly of brief bits of advice and observation. These sayings make heavy use of antithetical parallelism, where the second part of a saying negates or presents a contrast to the first part. This is used to contrast wisdom and righteousness with folly and wickedness. The arrangement of these proverbs appears to be essentially random, which also resembles Egyptian and Mesopotamian wisdom literature. Some proverbs are repeated (see 6:10-11 and 24:33-34; 14:12 and 16:25; 18:8 and 26:22; 19:24 and 26:15; 20:16 and 27:13; 21:9 and 25:24; 22:3 and 27:12). Sometimes a group of proverbs shares a similar theme (for example, 16:1-11).

10:1-5 The focus on the child/youth (literally "son") at the beginning and end of these verses has led some to read them as a brief collection to be read as a group instead of separately to determine their meaning. When reading them together we see that we find our true security in the Lord (10:3), while noting the importance of hard work (10:4) and right living (10:2).

10:3 This proverb can be misused if outward results are regarded as a measure of godliness. Job's three friends, for example, wrongly reasoned that Job must have sinned to earn his suffering (see Job 22:6-11).

11 ¹ The LORD detests the use of dishonest scales,
but he delights in accurate weights.

² Pride leads to disgrace,
but with humility comes wisdom.

³ Honesty guides good people;
dishonesty destroys treacherous people.

⁴ Riches won't help on the day of judgment,
but right living can save you from death.

⁵ The godly are directed by honesty;
the wicked fall beneath their load of sin.

⁶ The godliness of good people rescues them;
the ambition of treacherous people traps them.

⁷ When the wicked die, their hopes die with them,
for they rely on their own feeble strength.

⁸ The godly are rescued from trouble,
and it falls on the wicked instead.

⁹ With their words, the godless destroy their friends,
but knowledge will rescue the righteous.

¹⁰ The whole city celebrates when the godly succeed;
they shout for joy when the wicked die.

¹¹ Upright citizens are good for a city and make it prosper,
but the talk of the wicked tears it apart.

¹² It is foolish to belittle one's neighbor;
a sensible person keeps quiet.

¹³ A gossip goes around telling secrets,
but those who are trustworthy can keep a confidence.

¹⁴ Without wise leadership, a nation falls;
there is safety in having many advisers.

¹⁵ There's danger in putting up security for a stranger's debt;
it's safer not to guarantee another person's debt.

¹⁶ A gracious woman gains respect,
but ruthless men gain only wealth.

¹⁷ Your kindness will reward you,
but your cruelty will destroy you.

¹⁸ Evil people get rich for the moment,
but the reward of the godly will last.

¹⁹ Godly people find life;
evil people find death.

²⁰ The LORD detests people with crooked hearts,
but he delights in those with integrity.

²¹ Evil people will surely be punished,
but the children of the godly will go free.

²² A beautiful woman who lacks discretion
is like a gold ring in a pig's snout.

²³ The godly can look forward to a reward,
while the wicked can expect only judgment.

²⁴ Give freely and become more wealthy;
be stingy and lose everything.

²⁵ The generous will prosper;
those who refresh others will themselves be refreshed.

²⁶ People curse those who hoard their grain,
but they bless the one who sells in time of need.

²⁷ If you search for good, you will find favor;
but if you search for evil, it will find you!

²⁸ Trust in your money and down you go!
But the godly flourish like leaves in spring.

²⁹ Those who bring trouble on their families inherit the wind.
The fool will be a servant to the wise.

³⁰ The seeds of good deeds become a tree of life;
a wise person wins friends.*

³¹ If the righteous are rewarded here on earth,
what will happen to wicked sinners?*

12 To learn, you must love discipline;
it is stupid to hate correction.

² The LORD approves of those who are good,
but he condemns those who plan wickedness.

³ Wickedness never brings stability,
but the godly have deep roots.

⁴ A worthy wife is a crown for her husband,
but a disgraceful woman is like cancer in his bones.

⁵ The plans of the godly are just;
the advice of the wicked is treacherous.

⁶ The words of the wicked are like a murderous ambush,
but the words of the godly save lives.

⁷ The wicked die and disappear,
but the family of the godly stands firm.

11:30 Or *and those who win souls are wise.* **11:31** Greek version reads *If the righteous are barely saved, / what will happen to godless sinners?* Compare 1 Pet 4:18.

11:10 Our actions, whether godly or wicked, affect the whole city (see Ecclesiastes 8:9-13).
11:28 Proverbs usually portrays wealth as a good thing, but this verse teaches that how we think about and use finances matter. Trusting money is foolish, and refusing to help those in need is not righteous (11:26). The contrast with the godly who flourish implies that the one who trusts in money is heading for a fall. That person has not chosen wisdom.

⁸ A sensible person wins admiration,
  but a warped mind is despised.

⁹ Better to be an ordinary person with a servant
  than to be self-important but have no food.

¹⁰ The godly care for their animals,
  but the wicked are always cruel.

¹¹ A hard worker has plenty of food,
  but a person who chases fantasies has no sense.

¹² Thieves are jealous of each other's loot,
  but the godly are well rooted and bear their own fruit.

¹³ The wicked are trapped by their own words,
  but the godly escape such trouble.

¹⁴ Wise words bring many benefits,
  and hard work brings rewards.

¹⁵ Fools think their own way is right,
  but the wise listen to others.

¹⁶ A fool is quick-tempered,
  but a wise person stays calm when insulted.

¹⁷ An honest witness tells the truth;
  a false witness tells lies.

¹⁸ Some people make cutting remarks,
  but the words of the wise bring healing.

¹⁹ Truthful words stand the test of time,
  but lies are soon exposed.

²⁰ Deceit fills hearts that are plotting evil;
  joy fills hearts that are planning peace!

²¹ No harm comes to the godly,
  but the wicked have their fill of trouble.

²² The LORD detests lying lips,
  but he delights in those who tell the truth.

²³ The wise don't make a show of their knowledge,
  but fools broadcast their foolishness.

²⁴ Work hard and become a leader;
  be lazy and become a slave.

²⁵ Worry weighs a person down;
  an encouraging word cheers a person up.

²⁶ The godly give good advice to their friends;*
  the wicked lead them astray.

²⁷ Lazy people don't even cook the game they catch,
  but the diligent make use of everything they find.

²⁸ The way of the godly leads to life;
  that path does not lead to death.

13

¹ A wise child accepts a parent's discipline;*
  a mocker refuses to listen to correction.

² Wise words will win you a good meal,
  but treacherous people have an appetite for violence.

³ Those who control their tongue will have a long life;
  opening your mouth can ruin everything.

⁴ Lazy people want much but get little,
  but those who work hard will prosper.

⁵ The godly hate lies;
  the wicked cause shame and disgrace.

⁶ Godliness guards the path of the blameless,
  but the evil are misled by sin.

⁷ Some who are poor pretend to be rich;
  others who are rich pretend to be poor.

⁸ The rich can pay a ransom for their lives,
  but the poor won't even get threatened.

⁹ The life of the godly is full of light and joy,
  but the light of the wicked will be snuffed out.

¹⁰ Pride leads to conflict;
  those who take advice are wise.

¹¹ Wealth from get-rich-quick schemes quickly disappears;
  wealth from hard work grows over time.

¹² Hope deferred makes the heart sick,
  but a dream fulfilled is a tree of life.

¹³ People who despise advice are asking for trouble;
  those who respect a command will succeed.

¹⁴ The instruction of the wise is like a life-giving fountain;
  those who accept it avoid the snares of death.

¹⁵ A person with good sense is respected;
  a treacherous person is headed for destruction.*

¹⁶ Wise people think before they act;
  fools don't—and even brag about their foolishness.

12:26 Or *The godly are cautious in friendship;* or *The godly are freed from evil.* The meaning of the Hebrew is uncertain.
13:1 Hebrew *A wise son accepts his father's discipline.* 13:15 As in Greek version; Hebrew reads *the way of the treacherous is lasting.*

13:3 Sometimes, we do better to keep our thoughts to ourselves, but this isn't always easy. James 3:1-12 develops this idea, describing the power of our words, our difficulty controlling them, and the hypocrisy of human speech. Throughout the Bible, we see that what a person says and does not say matters. Our words should reflect our identity as God's image-bearers by honoring God and loving others.

IMAGE — MY STORY OF MY UNIQUE INFLUENCE

The Right Kind of Busy: Monkey or Monk?

SCRIPTURE CONNECTION: PROVERBS 10:4; 12:11; 13:4; 14:23; 19:2; 21:25

Have you ever seen that classic wind-up toy—the cute, vested monkey that plays cymbals after you wind up the key in its back? That monkey can serve as an image of the wrong kind of busy (Psalm 39:6; Ecclesiastes 2:22-23).

In Western culture, when we ask each other how we are, a common answer is "Busy." And, for many, "busy" equals "good." But what does God think of *busy*? Proverbs repeatedly warns against becoming lazy and shows we are wise to take care of our resources and work productively. But this isn't a blanket endorsement for busyness.

A seventeenth-century French monk, Brother Lawrence, learned to rest continually, amid all the mundane daily chores and religious duties by cultivating a robust prayer life: "It is necessary to take particular care to begin, if only for a moment, your exterior actions with this interior gaze [on God]." *The Practice of the Presence of God*, a collection of his teachings, demonstrates how to live the right kind of busy that Proverbs encourages.

So how can we abide by the counsel of Proverbs to not be lazy yet avoid being like a noisy monkey? The apostle Paul describes anything done without love as just "a clanging cymbal" (1 Corinthians 13:1). To be formed more in love and be wise like Solomon, we can have a constant conversation with God throughout the day. Praying can tell us what to do and when, calm us when we are anxious, and let us know when and how to stop.

We don't need to be actual monks. Through continual prayer, God quiets the monkeys.

> We don't need to be actual monks. Through continual prayer, God quiets the monkeys.

IMAGINE

How would you describe your level of busyness? Do you feel like a cymbal-banging monkey? Or have you learned how to find a healthy balance?

Many times, we begin a day with prayer, as if God is winding up our crank for the day. How might we try beginning each hour with a moment or two of prayer?

"As I learn to pray even more frequently, I learn to hear the constant voice of God's Spirit telling me what, and why, and when, and how."

SUSAN I. BUBBERS, MDiv, DMin, PhD, is the Dean of the Center for Anglican Theology in Orlando, FL. She is a professor, Anglican priest, spiritual director, and a Fellow of the Oxford Centre for Animal Ethics.

¹⁷ An unreliable messenger stumbles into trouble,
     but a reliable messenger brings healing.

¹⁸ If you ignore criticism, you will end in poverty
         and disgrace;
     if you accept correction, you will be honored.

¹⁹ It is pleasant to see dreams come true,
     but fools refuse to turn from evil to attain them.

²⁰ Walk with the wise and become wise;
     associate with fools and get in trouble.

²¹ Trouble chases sinners,
     while blessings reward the righteous.

²² Good people leave an inheritance to their
         grandchildren,
     but the sinner's wealth passes to the godly.

²³ A poor person's farm may produce much food,
     but injustice sweeps it all away.

²⁴ Those who spare the rod of discipline hate their
         children.
     Those who love their children care enough to
         discipline them.

²⁵ The godly eat to their hearts' content,
     but the belly of the wicked goes hungry.

14

A wise woman builds her home,
     but a foolish woman tears it down with
         her own hands.

² Those who follow the right path fear the LORD;
     those who take the wrong path despise him.

³ A fool's proud talk becomes a rod that beats him,
     but the words of the wise keep them safe.

⁴ Without oxen a stable stays clean,
     but you need a strong ox for a large harvest.

⁵ An honest witness does not lie;
     a false witness breathes lies.

⁶ A mocker seeks wisdom and never finds it,
     but knowledge comes easily to those with
         understanding.

⁷ Stay away from fools,
     for you won't find knowledge on their lips.

⁸ The prudent understand where they are going,
     but fools deceive themselves.

⁹ Fools make fun of guilt,
     but the godly acknowledge it and seek
         reconciliation.

¹⁰ Each heart knows its own bitterness,
     and no one else can fully share its joy.

¹¹ The house of the wicked will be destroyed,
     but the tent of the godly will flourish.

¹² There is a path before each person that seems right,
     but it ends in death.

¹³ Laughter can conceal a heavy heart,
     but when the laughter ends, the grief remains.

¹⁴ Backsliders get what they deserve;
     good people receive their reward.

¹⁵ Only simpletons believe everything they're told!
     The prudent carefully consider their steps.

¹⁶ The wise are cautious* and avoid danger;
     fools plunge ahead with reckless confidence.

¹⁷ Short-tempered people do foolish things,
     and schemers are hated.

¹⁸ Simpletons are clothed with foolishness,*
     but the prudent are crowned with knowledge.

¹⁹ Evil people will bow before good people;
     the wicked will bow at the gates of the godly.

²⁰ The poor are despised even by their neighbors,
     while the rich have many "friends."

²¹ It is a sin to belittle one's neighbor;
     blessed are those who help the poor.

²² If you plan to do evil, you will be lost;
     if you plan to do good, you will receive
         unfailing love and faithfulness.

²³ Work brings profit,
     but mere talk leads to poverty!

²⁴ Wealth is a crown for the wise;
     the effort of fools yields only foolishness.

²⁵ A truthful witness saves lives,
     but a false witness is a traitor.

14:16 Hebrew *The wise fear.* 14:18 Or *inherit foolishness.*

13:17 Oral messages were the primary form of communication in ancient Israel, so an unreliable messenger delivering the wrong message could incite all kinds of trouble.
13:23 Hard work does not always bring prosperity (compare this to 10:4-6; 12:11; 13:4) because injustice occurs in the world.
14:2 The path is a metaphor for life and conduct (see 2:13, 20; 3:6; 4:11; 6:23). For more on "the fear of the LORD," see 1:7.
14:12; 16:25 Humans are limited and fallible. At times we are led astray by our reasoning; at other times, we choose the wrong path because we focus on our desires. Sometimes, we cannot see the right choice because of our natural limitations. Whatever the cause, choosing the wrong path has serious consequences. While these verses simply offer the warning, the fear of the Lord that is the source of true knowledge (1:7) can guard our steps. When we fear and trust God, we live by faith in him rather than by what we can see (2 Corinthians 5:7).
14:24 This proverb states a general principle, even though fools sometimes have wealth (10:2; 11:18), and poverty is not always the result of foolishness (see 13:23; 16:8).

²⁶ Those who fear the LORD are secure;
   he will be a refuge for their children.

²⁷ Fear of the LORD is a life-giving fountain;
   it offers escape from the snares of death.

²⁸ A growing population is a king's glory;
   a prince without subjects has nothing.

²⁹ People with understanding control their anger;
   a hot temper shows great foolishness.

³⁰ A peaceful heart leads to a healthy body;
   jealousy is like cancer in the bones.

³¹ Those who oppress the poor insult their Maker,
   but helping the poor honors him.

³² The wicked are crushed by disaster,
   but the godly have a refuge when they die.

³³ Wisdom is enshrined in an understanding heart;
   wisdom is not* found among fools.

³⁴ Godliness makes a nation great,
   but sin is a disgrace to any people.

³⁵ A king rejoices in wise servants
   but is angry with those who disgrace him.

15

¹ A gentle answer deflects anger,
   but harsh words make tempers flare.

² The tongue of the wise makes knowledge appealing,
   but the mouth of a fool belches out foolishness.

³ The LORD is watching everywhere,
   keeping his eye on both the evil and the good.

⁴ Gentle words are a tree of life;
   a deceitful tongue crushes the spirit.

⁵ Only a fool despises a parent's* discipline;
   whoever learns from correction is wise.

⁶ There is treasure in the house of the godly,
   but the earnings of the wicked bring trouble.

⁷ The lips of the wise give good advice;
   the heart of a fool has none to give.

⁸ The LORD detests the sacrifice of the wicked,
   but he delights in the prayers of the upright.

⁹ The LORD detests the way of the wicked,
   but he loves those who pursue godliness.

¹⁰ Whoever abandons the right path will be severely disciplined;
   whoever hates correction will die.

¹¹ Even Death and Destruction* hold no secrets from the LORD.
   How much more does he know the human heart!

¹² Mockers hate to be corrected,
   so they stay away from the wise.

¹³ A glad heart makes a happy face;
   a broken heart crushes the spirit.

¹⁴ A wise person is hungry for knowledge,
   while the fool feeds on trash.

¹⁵ For the despondent, every day brings trouble;
   for the happy heart, life is a continual feast.

¹⁶ Better to have little, with fear for the LORD,
   than to have great treasure and inner turmoil.

¹⁷ A bowl of vegetables with someone you love
   is better than steak with someone you hate.

¹⁸ A hot-tempered person starts fights;
   a cool-tempered person stops them.

¹⁹ A lazy person's way is blocked with briers,
   but the path of the upright is an open highway.

²⁰ Sensible children bring joy to their father;
   foolish children despise their mother.

²¹ Foolishness brings joy to those with no sense;
   a sensible person stays on the right path.

²² Plans go wrong for lack of advice;
   many advisers bring success.

²³ Everyone enjoys a fitting reply;
   it is wonderful to say the right thing at the right time!

²⁴ The path of life leads upward for the wise;
   they leave the grave* behind.

²⁵ The LORD tears down the house of the proud,
   but he protects the property of widows.

²⁶ The LORD detests evil plans,
   but he delights in pure words.

²⁷ Greed brings grief to the whole family,
   but those who hate bribes will live.

²⁸ The heart of the godly thinks carefully before speaking;
   the mouth of the wicked overflows with evil words.

²⁹ The LORD is far from the wicked,
   but he hears the prayers of the righteous.

14:33 As in Greek and Syriac versions; Hebrew lacks *not*. **15:5** Hebrew *father's*. **15:11** Hebrew *Sheol and Abaddon*. **15:24** Hebrew *Sheol*.

15:25 The proud think that they are self-sufficient. Widows in the ancient Near East were just the opposite—completely vulnerable and without means of support or protection.

30 A cheerful look brings joy to the heart;
    good news makes for good health.
31 If you listen to constructive criticism,
    you will be at home among the wise.
32 If you reject discipline, you only harm yourself;
    but if you listen to correction, you grow in understanding.
33 Fear of the LORD teaches wisdom;
    humility precedes honor.

16

We can make our own plans,
    but the LORD gives the right answer.
2 People may be pure in their own eyes,
    but the LORD examines their motives.
3 Commit your actions to the LORD,
    and your plans will succeed.
4 The LORD has made everything for his own purposes,
    even the wicked for a day of disaster.
5 The LORD detests the proud;
    they will surely be punished.
6 Unfailing love and faithfulness make atonement for sin.
    By fearing the LORD, people avoid evil.
7 When people's lives please the LORD,
    even their enemies are at peace with them.
8 Better to have little, with godliness,
    than to be rich and dishonest.
9 We can make our plans,
    but the LORD determines our steps.
10 The king speaks with divine wisdom;
    he must never judge unfairly.
11 The LORD demands accurate scales and balances;
    he sets the standards for fairness.
12 A king detests wrongdoing,
    for his rule is built on justice.
13 The king is pleased with words from righteous lips;
    he loves those who speak honestly.
14 The anger of the king is a deadly threat;
    the wise will try to appease it.
15 When the king smiles, there is life;
    his favor refreshes like a spring rain.
16 How much better to get wisdom than gold,
    and good judgment than silver!

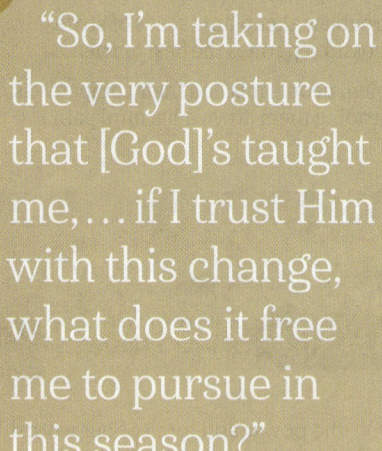

"So, I'm taking on the very posture that [God]'s taught me, ... if I trust Him with this change, what does it free me to pursue in this season?"

CHRISTY NOCKELS
worship leader and songwriter

17 The path of the virtuous leads away from evil;
    whoever follows that path is safe.
18 Pride goes before destruction,
    and haughtiness before a fall.
19 Better to live humbly with the poor
    than to share plunder with the proud.
20 Those who listen to instruction will prosper;
    those who trust the LORD will be joyful.
21 The wise are known for their understanding,
    and pleasant words are persuasive.
22 Discretion is a life-giving fountain to those who possess it,
    but discipline is wasted on fools.
23 From a wise mind comes wise speech;
    the words of the wise are persuasive.
24 Kind words are like honey—
    sweet to the soul and healthy for the body.
25 There is a path before each person that seems right,
    but it ends in death.
26 It is good for workers to have an appetite;
    an empty stomach drives them on.

16:6 God's unfailing love and faithfulness are foundational in his agreement and relationship (covenant) with Israel (see Exodus 15:13; 34:6-7; Numbers 14:18-19; Deuteronomy 7:9-11).

16:10-15 This series of sayings reflects on the king, who represents God's power on earth.

PROVERBS 16 ◆ 772

27 Scoundrels create trouble;
  their words are a destructive blaze.
28 A troublemaker plants seeds of strife;
  gossip separates the best of friends.
29 Violent people mislead their companions,
  leading them down a harmful path.
30 With narrowed eyes, people plot evil;
  with a smirk, they plan their mischief.
31 Gray hair is a crown of glory;
  it is gained by living a godly life.
32 Better to be patient than powerful;
  better to have self-control than to conquer a city.

Oikos IMAGE — MY STORY WITH FAMILY & FRIENDS

Watching Our Words

SCRIPTURE CONNECTION: PROVERBS 16:24

Oh, the power and force of our words! They can be a soothing balm or a sword that cuts painfully. They can either build others up or tear them down. This proverb calls us to stop and think before we speak and to choose our words wisely so that they will bring health rather than hurt. Just as honey is a life-producing substance, a universal medicine that brings health and energy to the body and sweetness to food, words of kindness are sweet gifts to their hearers. Kind words can bring healing to relationships; even when they are few, they can powerfully encourage others and infuse them with hope while soothing their fear and pain. Gracious words actually promote positive energy and health in their hearers so that they can do their best. Ask God to fill you with kind and nourishing words for all the people you encounter each day—especially those you live or work with who may strain your patience. It is when people are the most irritating and unlovable that they need kind, loving words the most.

> **Kind words are sweet gifts to their hearers.**

LORD, give me kind words—your words of life—with which to bless those around me. Since my words are born in my heart, sweeten my soul with your Spirit, and soften and expand my heart to hold your love for others. May my words be gifts of sweetness to those around me today.

IMAGINE

How might you stop next time you think a negative thought about yourself or others and speak a kind word in prayer instead?

Is there a time of day or week you can schedule to stop, think about the people in your life, and contact them with kind words?

"Cold words freeze people, and hot words scorch them, and bitter words make them bitter, and wrathful words make them wrathful. Kind words . . . soothe, quiet, and comfort the hearer."
— Blaise Pascal

CHERI FULLER • Content taken from *The One Year Praying Through the Bible* by Cheri Fuller. Copyright © 2003 by Cheri Fuller. Used by permission of Tyndale House Publishers. All rights reserved.

33 We may throw the dice,*
    but the LORD determines how they fall.

17

Better a dry crust eaten in peace
    than a house filled with feasting—and conflict.

2 A wise servant will rule over the master's disgraceful son
    and will share the inheritance of the master's children.

3 Fire tests the purity of silver and gold,
    but the LORD tests the heart.

4 Wrongdoers eagerly listen to gossip;
    liars pay close attention to slander.

5 Those who mock the poor insult their Maker;
    those who rejoice at the misfortune of others will be punished.

6 Grandchildren are the crowning glory of the aged;
    parents* are the pride of their children.

7 Eloquent words are not fitting for a fool;
    even less are lies fitting for a ruler.

8 A bribe is like a lucky charm;
    whoever gives one will prosper!

9 Love prospers when a fault is forgiven,
    but dwelling on it separates close friends.

10 A single rebuke does more for a person of understanding
    than a hundred lashes on the back of a fool.

11 Evil people are eager for rebellion,
    but they will be severely punished.

12 It is safer to meet a bear robbed of her cubs
    than to confront a fool caught in foolishness.

13 If you repay good with evil,
    evil will never leave your house.

14 Starting a quarrel is like opening a floodgate,
    so stop before a dispute breaks out.

15 Acquitting the guilty and condemning the innocent—
    both are detestable to the LORD.

16 It is senseless to pay to educate a fool,
    since he has no heart for learning.

17 A friend is always loyal,
    and a brother is born to help in time of need.

18 It's poor judgment to guarantee another person's debt
    or put up security for a friend.

19 Anyone who loves to quarrel loves sin;
    anyone who trusts in high walls invites disaster.

20 The crooked heart will not prosper;
    the lying tongue tumbles into trouble.

21 It is painful to be the parent of a fool;
    there is no joy for the father of a rebel.

22 A cheerful heart is good medicine,
    but a broken spirit saps a person's strength.

23 The wicked take secret bribes
    to pervert the course of justice.

24 Sensible people keep their eyes glued on wisdom,
    but a fool's eyes wander to the ends of the earth.

25 Foolish children* bring grief to their father
    and bitterness to the one who gave them birth.

26 It is wrong to punish the godly for being good
    or to flog leaders for being honest.

27 A truly wise person uses few words;
    a person with understanding is even-tempered.

28 Even fools are thought wise when they keep silent;
    with their mouths shut, they seem intelligent.

18

Unfriendly people care only about themselves;
    they lash out at common sense.

2 Fools have no interest in understanding;
    they only want to air their own opinions.

3 Doing wrong leads to disgrace,
    and scandalous behavior brings contempt.

4 Wise words are like deep waters;
    wisdom flows from the wise like a bubbling brook.

5 It is not right to acquit the guilty
    or deny justice to the innocent.

6 Fools' words get them into constant quarrels;
    they are asking for a beating.

7 The mouths of fools are their ruin;
    they trap themselves with their lips.

8 Rumors are dainty morsels
    that sink deep into one's heart.

9 A lazy person is as bad as
    someone who destroys things.

16:33 Hebrew *We may cast lots.* 17:6 Hebrew *fathers.* 17:25 Hebrew *A foolish son.*

17:4 Lies (6:16-19; 14:5, 25; 25:18), gossip (11:13; 18:8), and slander (10:18) distort reality for malicious purposes.

¹⁰ The name of the Lord is a strong fortress;
the godly run to him and are safe.

¹¹ The rich think of their wealth as a strong defense;
they imagine it to be a high wall of safety.

¹² Haughtiness goes before destruction;
humility precedes honor.

¹³ Spouting off before listening to the facts
is both shameful and foolish.

¹⁴ The human spirit can endure a sick body,
but who can bear a crushed spirit?

¹⁵ Intelligent people are always ready to learn.
Their ears are open for knowledge.

¹⁶ Giving a gift can open doors;
it gives access to important people!

¹⁷ The first to speak in court sounds right—
until the cross-examination begins.

¹⁸ Flipping a coin* can end arguments;
it settles disputes between powerful opponents.

¹⁹ An offended friend is harder to win back than a fortified city.
Arguments separate friends like a gate locked with bars.

²⁰ Wise words satisfy like a good meal;
the right words bring satisfaction.

²¹ The tongue can bring death or life;
those who love to talk will reap the consequences.

²² The man who finds a wife finds a treasure,
and he receives favor from the Lord.

²³ The poor plead for mercy;
the rich answer with insults.

²⁴ There are "friends" who destroy each other,
but a real friend sticks closer than a brother.

19

Better to be poor and honest
than to be dishonest and a fool.

² Enthusiasm without knowledge is no good;
haste makes mistakes.

³ People ruin their lives by their own foolishness
and then are angry at the Lord.

⁴ Wealth makes many "friends";
poverty drives them all away.

⁵ A false witness will not go unpunished,
nor will a liar escape.

⁶ Many seek favors from a ruler;
everyone is the friend of a person who gives gifts!

⁷ The relatives of the poor despise them;
how much more will their friends avoid them!
Though the poor plead with them,
their friends are gone.

⁸ To acquire wisdom is to love yourself;
people who cherish understanding will prosper.

⁹ A false witness will not go unpunished,
and a liar will be destroyed.

¹⁰ It isn't right for a fool to live in luxury
or for a slave to rule over princes!

¹¹ Sensible people control their temper;
they earn respect by overlooking wrongs.

¹² The king's anger is like a lion's roar,
but his favor is like dew on the grass.

¹³ A foolish child* is a calamity to a father;
a quarrelsome wife is as annoying as constant dripping.

¹⁴ Fathers can give their sons an inheritance of houses and wealth,
but only the Lord can give an understanding wife.

¹⁵ Lazy people sleep soundly,
but idleness leaves them hungry.

¹⁶ Keep the commandments and keep your life;
despising them leads to death.

¹⁷ If you help the poor, you are lending to the Lord—
and he will repay you!

¹⁸ Discipline your children while there is hope.
Otherwise you will ruin their lives.

¹⁹ Hot-tempered people must pay the penalty.
If you rescue them once, you will have to do it again.

18:18 Hebrew *Casting lots.* 19:13 Hebrew *son;* also in 19:27.

18:23 God will punish the powerful who disparage the poor; wise people care for the needy (11:24; 28:27; 29:7, 14).
19:13 Because of its context in the male-led ancient Israelite culture, Proverbs often focuses on the importance of family relationships from a man's perspective. A wife's character was important. A good wife was "a crown" (12:4), "a treasure" (18:22), and a gift from the Lord (19:14), but a "quarrelsome wife" could make life miserable (see also 27:15-16). Strife creates a toxic environment for everyone, though, not just for men. Both women and men can consider how we can promote peace within our homes, particularly with our speech. (See the study note on 13:3.)
19:16 Keeping God's commandments (which here is a reference to the law of Moses) protects one's life (see Deuteronomy 28:15-68).

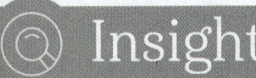

Insight: THEMES IN PROVERBS

The book of Proverbs teaches wisdom and addresses many of life's important topics. This diagram illustrates repeated themes in well-known proverbs, such as happiness, foolishness, working, and money.

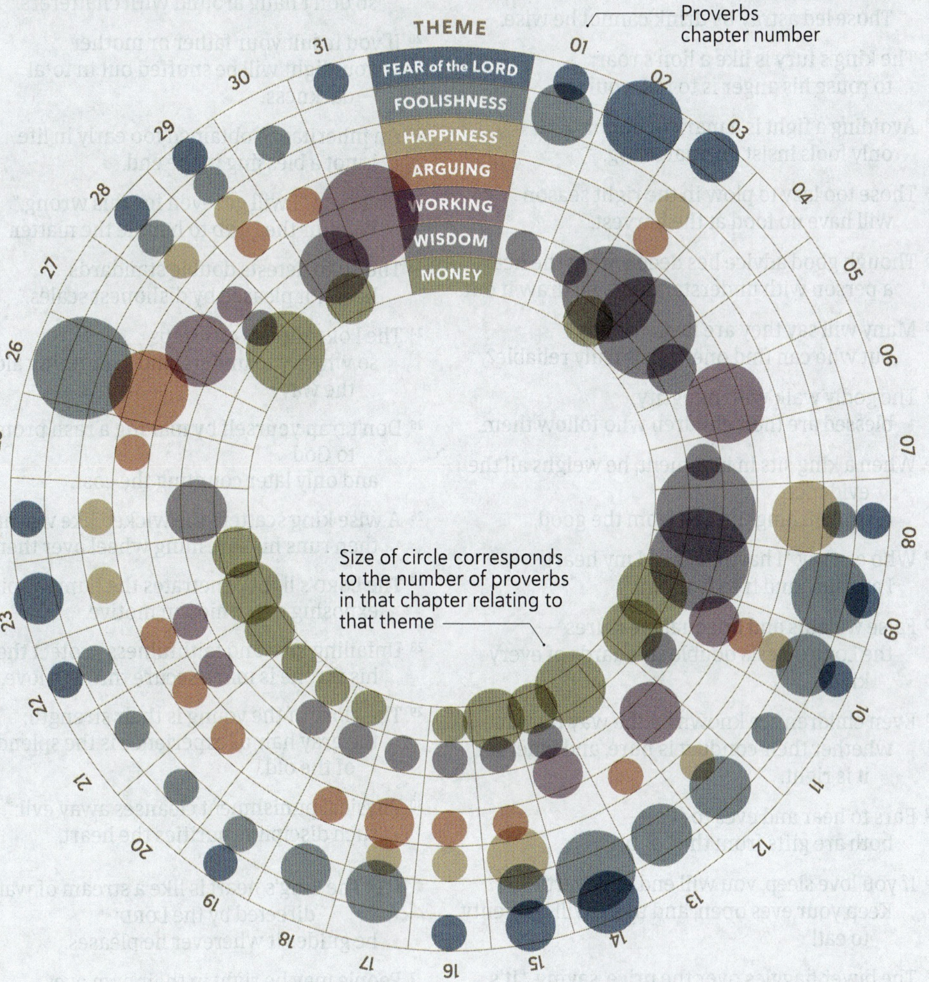

THEME: FEAR of the LORD, FOOLISHNESS, HAPPINESS, ARGUING, WORKING, WISDOM, MONEY

Proverbs chapter number (01–31)

Size of circle corresponds to the number of proverbs in that chapter relating to that theme

20 Get all the advice and instruction you can,
 so you will be wise the rest of your life.
21 You can make many plans,
 but the LORD's purpose will prevail.
22 Loyalty makes a person attractive.
 It is better to be poor than dishonest.
23 Fear of the LORD leads to life,
 bringing security and protection from harm.
24 Lazy people take food in their hand
 but don't even lift it to their mouth.
25 If you punish a mocker, the simpleminded will
 learn a lesson;
 if you correct the wise, they will be all the wiser.
26 Children who mistreat their father or chase
 away their mother
 are an embarrassment and a public disgrace.

²⁷ If you stop listening to instruction, my child,
you will turn your back on knowledge.

²⁸ A corrupt witness makes a mockery of justice;
the mouth of the wicked gulps down evil.

²⁹ Punishment is made for mockers,
and the backs of fools are made to be beaten.

20

Wine produces mockers; alcohol leads to brawls.
Those led astray by drink cannot be wise.

² The king's fury is like a lion's roar;
to rouse his anger is to risk your life.

³ Avoiding a fight is a mark of honor;
only fools insist on quarreling.

⁴ Those too lazy to plow in the right season
will have no food at the harvest.

⁵ Though good advice lies deep within the heart,
a person with understanding will draw it out.

⁶ Many will say they are loyal friends,
but who can find one who is truly reliable?

⁷ The godly walk with integrity;
blessed are their children who follow them.

⁸ When a king sits in judgment, he weighs all the evidence,
distinguishing the bad from the good.

⁹ Who can say, "I have cleansed my heart;
I am pure and free from sin"?

¹⁰ False weights and unequal measures*—
the LORD detests double standards of every kind.

¹¹ Even children are known by the way they act,
whether their conduct is pure, and whether it is right.

¹² Ears to hear and eyes to see—
both are gifts from the LORD.

¹³ If you love sleep, you will end in poverty.
Keep your eyes open, and there will be plenty to eat!

¹⁴ The buyer haggles over the price, saying, "It's worthless,"
then brags about getting a bargain!

¹⁵ Wise words are more valuable
than much gold and many rubies.

¹⁶ Get security from someone who guarantees a stranger's debt.
Get a deposit if he does it for foreigners.*

¹⁷ Stolen bread tastes sweet,
but it turns to gravel in the mouth.

¹⁸ Plans succeed through good counsel;
don't go to war without wise advice.

¹⁹ A gossip goes around telling secrets,
so don't hang around with chatterers.

²⁰ If you insult your father or mother,
your light will be snuffed out in total darkness.

²¹ An inheritance obtained too early in life
is not a blessing in the end.

²² Don't say, "I will get even for this wrong."
Wait for the LORD to handle the matter.

²³ The LORD detests double standards;
he is not pleased by dishonest scales.

²⁴ The LORD directs our steps,
so why try to understand everything along the way?

²⁵ Don't trap yourself by making a rash promise to God
and only later counting the cost.

²⁶ A wise king scatters the wicked like wheat,
then runs his threshing wheel over them.

²⁷ The LORD's light penetrates the human spirit,*
exposing every hidden motive.

²⁸ Unfailing love and faithfulness protect the king;
his throne is made secure through love.

²⁹ The glory of the young is their strength;
the gray hair of experience is the splendor of the old.

³⁰ Physical punishment cleanses away evil;*
such discipline purifies the heart.

21

The king's heart is like a stream of water directed by the LORD;
he guides it wherever he pleases.

² People may be right in their own eyes,
but the LORD examines their heart.

³ The LORD is more pleased when we do what is right and just
than when we offer him sacrifices.

20:10 Hebrew *A stone and a stone, an ephah and an ephah.* 20:16 An alternate reading in the Masoretic Text is *for a promiscuous woman.* 20:27 Or *The human spirit is the LORD's light.* 20:30 The meaning of the Hebrew is uncertain.

20:1 Too much alcohol clouds a person's judgment. The Old Testament is not against drinking alcohol in moderation (3:10; 9:5; Psalm 104:14-15), but it adamantly opposes excessive drinking (Proverbs 21:17; 23:29-35; 31:4-5).

21:3 God is not pleased with worship unless godly actions flow from a godly heart (see Psalm 40:6-8; Micah 6:6-8).

⁴ Haughty eyes, a proud heart,
  and evil actions are all sin.

⁵ Good planning and hard work lead to prosperity,
  but hasty shortcuts lead to poverty.

⁶ Wealth created by a lying tongue
  is a vanishing mist and a deadly trap.*

⁷ The violence of the wicked sweeps them away,
  because they refuse to do what is just.

⁸ The guilty walk a crooked path;
  the innocent travel a straight road.

⁹ It's better to live alone in the corner of an attic
  than with a quarrelsome wife in a lovely home.

¹⁰ Evil people desire evil;
  their neighbors get no mercy from them.

¹¹ If you punish a mocker, the simpleminded become wise;
  if you instruct the wise, they will be all the wiser.

¹² The Righteous One* knows what is going on in the homes of the wicked;
  he will bring disaster on them.

¹³ Those who shut their ears to the cries of the poor
  will be ignored in their own time of need.

¹⁴ A secret gift calms anger;
  a bribe under the table pacifies fury.

¹⁵ Justice is a joy to the godly,
  but it terrifies evildoers.

¹⁶ The person who strays from common sense
  will end up in the company of the dead.

¹⁷ Those who love pleasure become poor;
  those who love wine and luxury will never be rich.

¹⁸ The wicked are punished in place of the godly,
  and traitors in place of the honest.

¹⁹ It's better to live alone in the desert
  than with a quarrelsome, complaining wife.

²⁰ The wise have wealth and luxury,
  but fools spend whatever they get.

²¹ Whoever pursues righteousness and unfailing love
  will find life, righteousness, and honor.

²² The wise conquer the city of the strong
  and level the fortress in which they trust.

²³ Watch your tongue and keep your mouth shut,
  and you will stay out of trouble.

²⁴ Mockers are proud and haughty;
  they act with boundless arrogance.

²⁵ Despite their desires, the lazy will come to ruin,
  for their hands refuse to work.

²⁶ Some people are always greedy for more,
  but the godly love to give!

²⁷ The sacrifice of an evil person is detestable,
  especially when it is offered with wrong motives.

²⁸ A false witness will be cut off,
  but a credible witness will be allowed to speak.

²⁹ The wicked bluff their way through,
  but the virtuous think before they act.

³⁰ No human wisdom or understanding or plan
  can stand against the Lord.

³¹ The horse is prepared for the day of battle,
  but the victory belongs to the Lord.

22

Choose a good reputation over great riches;
being held in high esteem is better than silver or gold.

² The rich and poor have this in common:
  The Lord made them both.

³ A prudent person foresees danger and takes precautions.
  The simpleton goes blindly on and suffers the consequences.

⁴ True humility and fear of the Lord
  lead to riches, honor, and long life.

⁵ Corrupt people walk a thorny, treacherous road;
  whoever values life will avoid it.

⁶ Direct your children onto the right path,
  and when they are older, they will not leave it.

21:6 As in Greek version; Hebrew reads *mist for those who seek death.* 21:12 Or *The righteous man.*

21:9, 19 See study note on 19:13.
21:12 God sees what the wicked do in the privacy of their homes and will punish them for their sins. Alternatively, "the Righteous One" might refer to the insight of any righteous individual.
22:2 Remembering that "the Lord made them both" helps prevent the exploitation of the poor. Regardless of one's status or material circumstances, all people are made in God's image and deserve to be treated with dignity and love (Genesis 1:26-28).
22:6 For parents, teaching God's ways to their children is important, but we would do well to consider this verse within the wider book. In particular, Proverbs 1–9 focus on a child's need to listen to parental instruction and fear God. Ultimately, while what we teach our children has a long-term impact, children must choose their own paths. When we read this verse in the whole book's context, we cannot take it as a promise that if we teach our children correctly, they will follow God. If our children or our friends' children choose to turn away from God, we can pray for and love them, rather than second-guess failures. Judging does not honor the fact that each has the will to choose God or not.

7 Just as the rich rule the poor,
    so the borrower is servant to the lender.
8 Those who plant injustice will harvest disaster,
    and their reign of terror will come to an end.*
9 Blessed are those who are generous,
    because they feed the poor.
10 Throw out the mocker, and fighting goes, too.
    Quarrels and insults will disappear.
11 Whoever loves a pure heart and gracious speech
    will have the king as a friend.
12 The LORD preserves those with knowledge,
    but he ruins the plans of the treacherous.
13 The lazy person claims, "There's a lion out there!
    If I go outside, I might be killed!"
14 The mouth of an immoral woman is a dangerous trap;
    those who make the LORD angry will fall into it.
15 A youngster's heart is filled with foolishness,
    but physical discipline will drive it far away.
16 A person who gets ahead by oppressing the poor
    or by showering gifts on the rich will end in poverty.

Sayings of the Wise

17 Listen to the words of the wise;
    apply your heart to my instruction.
18 For it is good to keep these sayings in your heart
    and always ready on your lips.
19 I am teaching you today—yes, you—
    so you will trust in the LORD.
20 I have written thirty sayings* for you,
    filled with advice and knowledge.
21 In this way, you may know the truth
    and take an accurate report to those who sent you.
22 Don't rob the poor just because you can,
    or exploit the needy in court.
23 For the LORD is their defender.
    He will ruin anyone who ruins them.
24 Don't befriend angry people
    or associate with hot-tempered people,
25 or you will learn to be like them
    and endanger your soul.
26 Don't agree to guarantee another person's debt
    or put up security for someone else.
27 If you can't pay it,
    even your bed will be snatched from under you.
28 Don't cheat your neighbor by moving the ancient boundary markers
    set up by previous generations.
29 Do you see any truly competent workers?
    They will serve kings
    rather than working for ordinary people.

23

While dining with a ruler,
    pay attention to what is put before you.
2 If you are a big eater,
    put a knife to your throat;
3 don't desire all the delicacies,
    for he might be trying to trick you.
4 Don't wear yourself out trying to get rich.
    Be wise enough to know when to quit.
5 In the blink of an eye wealth disappears,
    for it will sprout wings
    and fly away like an eagle.
6 Don't eat with people who are stingy;
    don't desire their delicacies.
7 They are always thinking about how much it costs.*
    "Eat and drink," they say, but they don't mean it.
8 You will throw up what little you've eaten,
    and your compliments will be wasted.
9 Don't waste your breath on fools,
    for they will despise the wisest advice.
10 Don't cheat your neighbor by moving the ancient boundary markers;
    don't take the land of defenseless orphans.
11 For their Redeemer* is strong;
    he himself will bring their charges against you.
12 Commit yourself to instruction;
    listen carefully to words of knowledge.
13 Don't fail to discipline your children.
    The rod of punishment won't kill them.

22:8 The Greek version includes an additional proverb: *God blesses a man who gives cheerfully, / but his worthless deeds will come to an end.* Compare 2 Cor 9:7. **22:20** Or *excellent sayings;* the meaning of the Hebrew is uncertain. **23:7** The meaning of the Hebrew is uncertain. **23:11** Or *redeemer.* **23:14** Hebrew *from Sheol.*

22:17–24:22 This section is modeled after an Egyptian composition called the *Instruction of Amenemope*, suggesting that Israel's sages gleaned wisdom from other cultures. But that wisdom was not unquestioningly adopted. The sages reflected on it critically, seeking what might encourage a person to "trust in the LORD" (22:19) and to "know the truth" (22:21). Similarly, as we consume information, we should ask God to show us how to use what we learn to advance God's good plan.

23:10-11 The wise avoid unfair business practices and illegitimate gains (see 22:28), knowing that the Lord will judge wrongdoing. By capitalizing the word *Redeemer,* the NLT identifies him with God, although it is possible a human redeemer might be intended. **23:13-16** While 23:13-14 highlights discipline's role in shaping a child, including physical punishment, 23:15-16 points to the parent's love for that child. Proverbs does not encourage, excuse, or justify abuse in any way.

¹⁴ Physical discipline
   may well save them from death.*
¹⁵ My child,* if your heart is wise,
   my own heart will rejoice!
¹⁶ Everything in me will celebrate
   when you speak what is right.

¹⁷ Don't envy sinners,
   but always continue to fear the LORD.
¹⁸ You will be rewarded for this;
   your hope will not be disappointed.

¹⁹ My child, listen and be wise:
   Keep your heart on the right course.
²⁰ Do not carouse with drunkards
   or feast with gluttons,
²¹ for they are on their way to poverty,
   and too much sleep clothes them in rags.

²² Listen to your father, who gave you life,
   and don't despise your mother when she is old.
²³ Get the truth and never sell it;
   also get wisdom, discipline, and good judgment.
²⁴ The father of godly children has cause for joy.
   What a pleasure to have children who are wise.*
²⁵ So give your father and mother joy!
   May she who gave you birth be happy.

²⁶ O my son, give me your heart.
   May your eyes take delight in following my ways.
²⁷ A prostitute is a dangerous trap;
   a promiscuous woman is as dangerous as falling into a narrow well.
²⁸ She hides and waits like a robber,
   eager to make more men unfaithful.

²⁹ Who has anguish? Who has sorrow?
   Who is always fighting? Who is always complaining?
   Who has unnecessary bruises? Who has bloodshot eyes?
³⁰ It is the one who spends long hours in the taverns,
   trying out new drinks.
³¹ Don't gaze at the wine, seeing how red it is,
   how it sparkles in the cup, how smoothly it goes down.
³² For in the end it bites like a poisonous snake;
   it stings like a viper.
³³ You will see hallucinations,
   and you will say crazy things.
³⁴ You will stagger like a sailor tossed at sea,
   clinging to a swaying mast.

³⁵ And you will say, "They hit me, but I didn't feel it.
   I didn't even know it when they beat me up.
   When will I wake up
   so I can look for another drink?"

24

Don't envy evil people
   or desire their company.
² For their hearts plot violence,
   and their words always stir up trouble.

³ A house is built by wisdom
   and becomes strong through good sense.
⁴ Through knowledge its rooms are filled
   with all sorts of precious riches and valuables.

⁵ The wise are mightier than the strong,*
   and those with knowledge grow stronger and stronger.
⁶ So don't go to war without wise guidance;
   victory depends on having many advisers.

⁷ Wisdom is too lofty for fools.
   Among leaders at the city gate, they have nothing to say.

⁸ A person who plans evil
   will get a reputation as a troublemaker.
⁹ The schemes of a fool are sinful;
   everyone detests a mocker.

¹⁰ If you fail under pressure,
   your strength is too small.

¹¹ Rescue those who are unjustly sentenced to die;
   save them as they stagger to their death.
¹² Don't excuse yourself by saying, "Look, we didn't know."
   For God understands all hearts, and he sees you.
   He who guards your soul knows you knew.
   He will repay all people as their actions deserve.

¹³ My child,* eat honey, for it is good,
   and the honeycomb is sweet to the taste.
¹⁴ In the same way, wisdom is sweet to your soul.
   If you find it, you will have a bright future,
   and your hopes will not be cut short.

¹⁵ Don't wait in ambush at the home of the godly,
   and don't raid the house where the godly live.
¹⁶ The godly may trip seven times, but they will get up again.
   But one disaster is enough to overthrow the wicked.

¹⁷ Don't rejoice when your enemies fall;
   don't be happy when they stumble.
¹⁸ For the LORD will be displeased with you
   and will turn his anger away from them.

23:15 Hebrew *My son;* also in 23:19. 23:24 Hebrew *to have a wise son.* 24:5 As in Greek version; Hebrew reads *A wise man is strength.* 24:13 Hebrew *My son;* also in 24:21.

24:17-18 This saying foreshadows Jesus' call to love our enemies (Matthew 5:43-48).

A house is built by wisdom and... its rooms are filled with... precious riches.

PROVERBS
24:3-4

¹⁹ Don't fret because of evildoers;
 don't envy the wicked.
²⁰ For evil people have no future;
 the light of the wicked will be snuffed out.

²¹ My child, fear the LORD and the king.
 Don't associate with rebels,
²² for disaster will hit them suddenly.
 Who knows what punishment will come
 from the LORD and the king?

More Sayings of the Wise

²³ Here are some further sayings of the wise:

It is wrong to show favoritism when passing judgment.
²⁴ A judge who says to the wicked, "You are innocent,"
 will be cursed by many people and denounced by the nations.
²⁵ But it will go well for those who convict the guilty;
 rich blessings will be showered on them.

²⁶ An honest answer
 is like a kiss of friendship.

²⁷ Do your planning and prepare your fields
 before building your house.

²⁸ Don't testify against your neighbors without cause;
 don't lie about them.
²⁹ And don't say, "Now I can pay them back for what they've done to me!
 I'll get even with them!"

³⁰ I walked by the field of a lazy person,
 the vineyard of one with no common sense.
³¹ I saw that it was overgrown with nettles.
 It was covered with weeds,
 and its walls were broken down.
³² Then, as I looked and thought about it,
 I learned this lesson:
³³ A little extra sleep, a little more slumber,
 a little folding of the hands to rest—
³⁴ then poverty will pounce on you like a bandit;
 scarcity will attack you like an armed robber.

More Proverbs of Solomon

25 These are more proverbs of Solomon, collected by the advisers of King Hezekiah of Judah.

² It is God's privilege to conceal things
 and the king's privilege to discover them.

³ No one can comprehend the height of heaven,
 the depth of the earth,
 or all that goes on in the king's mind!

⁴ Remove the impurities from silver,
 and the sterling will be ready for the silversmith.
⁵ Remove the wicked from the king's court,
 and his reign will be made secure by justice.

⁶ Don't demand an audience with the king
 or push for a place among the great.
⁷ It's better to wait for an invitation to the head table
 than to be sent away in public disgrace.

Just because you've seen something,
⁸ don't be in a hurry to go to court.
For what will you do in the end
 if your neighbor deals you a shameful defeat?

⁹ When arguing with your neighbor,
 don't betray another person's secret.
¹⁰ Others may accuse you of gossip,
 and you will never regain your good reputation.

¹¹ Timely advice is lovely,
 like golden apples in a silver basket.

¹² To one who listens, valid criticism
 is like a gold earring or other gold jewelry.

¹³ Trustworthy messengers refresh like snow in summer.
 They revive the spirit of their employer.

¹⁴ A person who promises a gift but doesn't give it
 is like clouds and wind that bring no rain.

¹⁵ Patience can persuade a prince,
 and soft speech can break bones.

¹⁶ Do you like honey?
 Don't eat too much, or it will make you sick!

¹⁷ Don't visit your neighbors too often,
 or you will wear out your welcome.

¹⁸ Telling lies about others
 is as harmful as hitting them with an ax,
wounding them with a sword,
 or shooting them with a sharp arrow.

¹⁹ Putting confidence in an unreliable person in times of trouble
 is like chewing with a broken tooth or walking on a lame foot.

²⁰ Singing cheerful songs to a person with a heavy heart
 is like taking someone's coat in cold weather
 or pouring vinegar in a wound.*

25:20 As in Greek version; Hebrew reads *pouring vinegar on soda*.

25:2-3 This warning reminds young men entering service to the king that some things cannot be understood, including the king's sometimes mysterious reasoning (for example, 2 Samuel 11:14-25; 24:3).

²¹ If your enemies are hungry, give them food to eat.
   If they are thirsty, give them water to drink.
²² You will heap burning coals of shame on their heads,
   and the Lord will reward you.
²³ As surely as a north wind brings rain,
   so a gossiping tongue causes anger!
²⁴ It's better to live alone in the corner of an attic
   than with a quarrelsome wife in a lovely home.
²⁵ Good news from far away
   is like cold water to the thirsty.
²⁶ If the godly give in to the wicked,
   it's like polluting a fountain or muddying a spring.
²⁷ It's not good to eat too much honey,
   and it's not good to seek honors for yourself.
²⁸ A person without self-control
   is like a city with broken-down walls.

26

Honor is no more associated with fools
than snow with summer or rain with harvest.

² Like a fluttering sparrow or a darting swallow,
   an undeserved curse will not land on its intended victim.
³ Guide a horse with a whip, a donkey with a bridle,
   and a fool with a rod to his back!
⁴ Don't answer the foolish arguments of fools,
   or you will become as foolish as they are.
⁵ Be sure to answer the foolish arguments of fools,
   or they will become wise in their own estimation.
⁶ Trusting a fool to convey a message
   is like cutting off one's feet or drinking poison!
⁷ A proverb in the mouth of a fool
   is as useless as a paralyzed leg.
⁸ Honoring a fool
   is as foolish as tying a stone to a slingshot.
⁹ A proverb in the mouth of a fool
   is like a thorny branch brandished by a drunk.

¹⁰ An employer who hires a fool or a bystander
   is like an archer who shoots at random.
¹¹ As a dog returns to its vomit,
   so a fool repeats his foolishness.
¹² There is more hope for fools
   than for people who think they are wise.
¹³ The lazy person claims, "There's a lion on the road!
   Yes, I'm sure there's a lion out there!"
¹⁴ As a door swings back and forth on its hinges,
   so the lazy person turns over in bed.
¹⁵ Lazy people take food in their hand
   but don't even lift it to their mouth.
¹⁶ Lazy people consider themselves smarter
   than seven wise counselors.
¹⁷ Interfering in someone else's argument
   is as foolish as yanking a dog's ears.
¹⁸ Just as damaging
   as a madman shooting a deadly weapon
¹⁹ is someone who lies to a friend
   and then says, "I was only joking."
²⁰ Fire goes out without wood,
   and quarrels disappear when gossip stops.
²¹ A quarrelsome person starts fights
   as easily as hot embers light charcoal or fire lights wood.
²² Rumors are dainty morsels
   that sink deep into one's heart.
²³ Smooth* words may hide a wicked heart,
   just as a pretty glaze covers a clay pot.
²⁴ People may cover their hatred with pleasant words,
   but they're deceiving you.
²⁵ They pretend to be kind, but don't believe them.
   Their hearts are full of many evils.*
²⁶ While their hatred may be concealed by trickery,
   their wrongdoing will be exposed in public.
²⁷ If you set a trap for others,
   you will get caught in it yourself.
   If you roll a boulder down on others,
   it will crush you instead.
²⁸ A lying tongue hates its victims,
   and flattering words cause ruin.

26:23 As in Greek version; Hebrew reads *Burning*.   26:25 Hebrew *seven evils*.

25:24 For more on the "quarrelsome wife," see study note on 19:13.

26:2 Curses and blessings can have real effect (see Genesis 27:1-41; 48:8-9, 15-20; Numbers 6:23-27), but an undeserved curse has no effect.

26:4-5 These two verses' seemingly contradictory advice reflects the situational nature of many proverbial sayings. Both can be true but not at the same time. The wise person must consider people and circumstances in deciding how to respond to a foolish argument. Such discernment is crucial, however, since a proverb misapplied might actually cause harm (26:9).

27

Don't brag about tomorrow,
   since you don't know what the day will bring.

² Let someone else praise you, not your own mouth—
   a stranger, not your own lips.

³ A stone is heavy and sand is weighty,
   but the resentment caused by a fool is even heavier.

⁴ Anger is cruel, and wrath is like a flood,
   but jealousy is even more dangerous.

⁵ An open rebuke
   is better than hidden love!

⁶ Wounds from a sincere friend
   are better than many kisses from an enemy.

⁷ A person who is full refuses honey,
   but even bitter food tastes sweet to the hungry.

⁸ A person who strays from home
   is like a bird that strays from its nest.

⁹ The heartfelt counsel of a friend
   is as sweet as perfume and incense.

¹⁰ Never abandon a friend—
   either yours or your father's.
   When disaster strikes, you won't have to ask your brother for assistance.
   It's better to go to a neighbor than to a brother who lives far away.

¹¹ Be wise, my child,* and make my heart glad.
   Then I will be able to answer my critics.

¹² A prudent person foresees danger and takes precautions.
   The simpleton goes blindly on and suffers the consequences.

¹³ Get security from someone who guarantees a stranger's debt.
   Get a deposit if he does it for foreigners.*

¹⁴ A loud and cheerful greeting early in the morning
   will be taken as a curse!

¹⁵ A quarrelsome wife is as annoying
   as constant dripping on a rainy day.

¹⁶ Stopping her complaints is like trying to stop the wind
   or trying to hold something with greased hands.

¹⁷ As iron sharpens iron,
   so a friend sharpens a friend.

¹⁸ As workers who tend a fig tree are allowed to eat the fruit,
   so workers who protect their employer's interests will be rewarded.

¹⁹ As a face is reflected in water,
   so the heart reflects the real person.

²⁰ Just as Death and Destruction* are never satisfied,
   so human desire is never satisfied.

²¹ Fire tests the purity of silver and gold,
   but a person is tested by being praised.*

²² You cannot separate fools from their foolishness,
   even though you grind them like grain with mortar and pestle.

²³ Know the state of your flocks,
   and put your heart into caring for your herds,
²⁴ for riches don't last forever,
   and the crown might not be passed to the next generation.
²⁵ After the hay is harvested and the new crop appears
   and the mountain grasses are gathered in,
²⁶ your sheep will provide wool for clothing,
   and your goats will provide the price of a field.
²⁷ And you will have enough goats' milk for yourself,
   your family, and your servant girls.

28

The wicked run away when no one is chasing them,
   but the godly are as bold as lions.

² When there is moral rot within a nation, its government topples easily.
   But wise and knowledgeable leaders bring stability.

³ A poor person who oppresses the poor
   is like a pounding rain that destroys the crops.

⁴ To reject the law is to praise the wicked;
   to obey the law is to fight them.

⁵ Evil people don't understand justice,
   but those who follow the LORD understand completely.

⁶ Better to be poor and honest
   than to be dishonest and rich.

27:11 Hebrew *my son.* 27:13 As in Greek and Latin versions (see also 20:16); Hebrew reads *for a promiscuous woman.* 27:20 Hebrew *Sheol and Abaddon.* 27:21 Or *by flattery.*

27:2 The Hebrew word translated "praise" comes from the same root as "brag" in 27:1. Bragging (self-praise) is foolish. **27:15-16** For more on the "quarrelsome wife," see study note on 19:13.

27:20 In Hebrew, "Death and Destruction" are *Sheol* and *Abaddon. Sheol* was the abode of the dead; a synonym for Sheol, *Abaddon* adds the implication of punishment. "Human desire is never satisfied" by money, power, or pleasure.

WHAT THE BIBLE SAYS ABOUT Wisdom

> The fear of the Lord is true wisdom...

Wisdom Brings Good

To acquire wisdom is to love yourself;
   people who cherish understanding will prosper.
PROVERBS 19:8

Wisdom and money can get you almost anything,
   but only wisdom can save your life.
ECCLESIASTES 7:12

Human Wisdom Has Limits

I have always tried my best to let wisdom guide my thoughts and actions. I said to myself, "I am determined to be wise." But it didn't work. **ECCLESIASTES 7:23**

God in his wisdom saw to it that the world would never know him through human wisdom. **1 CORINTHIANS 1:21**

For the wisdom of this world is foolishness to God. **1 CORINTHIANS 3:19**

For jealousy and selfishness are not God's kind of wisdom.... But the wisdom from above is first of all pure. It is also peace loving, gentle at all times, and willing to yield to others. It is full of mercy and the fruit of good deeds. It shows no favoritism and is always sincere. **JAMES 3:15, 17**

We Need Wisdom for Godly Character and Influence

And may the LORD give you wisdom and understanding, that you may obey the Law of the LORD your God. **1 CHRONICLES 22:12**

The king speaks with divine wisdom;
    he must never judge unfairly.
PROVERBS 16:10

The next Sabbath [Jesus] began teaching in the synagogue, and many who heard him were amazed. They asked, "Where did he get all this wisdom?" **MARK 6:2**

Brothers, select seven men who are well respected and are full of the Spirit and wisdom. We will give them this responsibility. **ACTS 6:3**

True Wisdom Comes from God

I have filled him with the Spirit of God, giving him great wisdom. **EXODUS 31:3**

"God alone understands the way to wisdom;
    he knows where it can be found....
And this is what he says to all humanity:
    'The fear of the Lord is true wisdom.'"
JOB 28:23, 28

Fear of the LORD is the foundation of true wisdom.
    All who obey his commandments will grow in wisdom.
PSALM 111:10

If you need wisdom, ask our generous God, and he will give it to you. **JAMES 1:5**

Blessing and glory and wisdom... belong to our God forever and ever!
REVELATION 7:12

Wise Words Impart Wisdom

To discipline a child produces wisdom. **PROVERBS 29:15**

So we tell others about Christ... teaching everyone with all the wisdom God has given us. **COLOSSIANS 1:28**

You have been taught the holy Scriptures from childhood, and they have given you the wisdom to receive the salvation that comes by trusting in Christ Jesus. **2 TIMOTHY 3:15**

⁷ Young people who obey the law are wise;
   those with wild friends bring shame to their parents.*

⁸ Income from charging high interest rates
   will end up in the pocket of someone who is kind to the poor.

⁹ God detests the prayers
   of a person who ignores the law.

¹⁰ Those who lead good people along an evil path
   will fall into their own trap,
   but the honest will inherit good things.

¹¹ Rich people may think they are wise,
   but a poor person with discernment can see right through them.

¹² When the godly succeed, everyone is glad.
   When the wicked take charge, people go into hiding.

¹³ People who conceal their sins will not prosper,
   but if they confess and turn from them, they will receive mercy.

¹⁴ Blessed are those who fear to do wrong,*
   but the stubborn are headed for serious trouble.

¹⁵ A wicked ruler is as dangerous to the poor
   as a roaring lion or an attacking bear.

¹⁶ A ruler with no understanding will oppress his people,
   but one who hates corruption will have a long life.

¹⁷ A murderer's tormented conscience will drive him into the grave.
   Don't protect him!

¹⁸ The blameless will be rescued from harm,
   but the crooked will be suddenly destroyed.

¹⁹ A hard worker has plenty of food,
   but a person who chases fantasies ends up in poverty.

²⁰ The trustworthy person will get a rich reward,
   but a person who wants quick riches will get into trouble.

²¹ Showing partiality is never good,
   yet some will do wrong for a mere piece of bread.

²² Greedy people try to get rich quick
   but don't realize they're headed for poverty.

²³ In the end, people appreciate honest criticism
   far more than flattery.

²⁴ Anyone who steals from his father and mother
   and says, "What's wrong with that?"
   is no better than a murderer.

²⁵ Greed causes fighting;
   trusting the LORD leads to prosperity.

²⁶ Those who trust their own insight are foolish,
   but anyone who walks in wisdom is safe.

²⁷ Whoever gives to the poor will lack nothing,
   but those who close their eyes to poverty will be cursed.

²⁸ When the wicked take charge, people go into hiding.
   When the wicked meet disaster, the godly flourish.

29

Whoever stubbornly refuses to accept criticism
will suddenly be destroyed beyond recovery.

² When the godly are in authority, the people rejoice.
   But when the wicked are in power, they groan.

³ The man who loves wisdom brings joy to his father,
   but if he hangs around with prostitutes, his wealth is wasted.

⁴ A just king gives stability to his nation,
   but one who demands bribes destroys it.

⁵ To flatter friends
   is to lay a trap for their feet.

⁶ Evil people are trapped by sin,
   but the righteous escape, shouting for joy.

⁷ The godly care about the rights of the poor;
   the wicked don't care at all.

⁸ Mockers can get a whole town agitated,
   but the wise will calm anger.

⁹ If a wise person takes a fool to court,
   there will be ranting and ridicule but no satisfaction.

¹⁰ The bloodthirsty hate blameless people,
   but the upright seek to help them.*

¹¹ Fools vent their anger,
   but the wise quietly hold it back.

28:7 Hebrew *their father*. **28:14** Or *those who fear the LORD;* Hebrew reads *those who fear.* **29:10** Or *The bloodthirsty hate blameless people, / and they seek to kill the upright;* Hebrew reads *The bloodthirsty hate blameless people; / as for the upright, they seek their life.*

28:8 The law of Moses prohibited charging needy Israelites interest on loans (Exodus 22:25; Leviticus 25:36; Deuteronomy 23:19). The rich were instructed to lend generously to the poor (Proverbs 3:27-28; 11:24; 28:27; 29:7, 14).
28:9 The English use of the word "law" for the Hebrew word *torah* usually reflects the ancient Greek translation of the Old Testament (the Septuagint); "instruction" is a better translation. In this case, the instruction likely means the sayings that have been the focus of Proverbs. In effect, it says that if we refuse to listen to and live by wisdom, then God will not listen to our prayers.

¹² If a ruler pays attention to liars,
all his advisers will be wicked.

¹³ The poor and the oppressor have this in common—
the LORD gives sight to the eyes of both.

¹⁴ If a king judges the poor fairly,
his throne will last forever.

¹⁵ To discipline a child produces wisdom,
but a mother is disgraced by an undisciplined child.

¹⁶ When the wicked are in authority, sin flourishes,
but the godly will live to see their downfall.

¹⁷ Discipline your children, and they will give you peace of mind
and will make your heart glad.

¹⁸ When people do not accept divine guidance, they run wild.
But whoever obeys the law is joyful.

29:18 The wise "accept divine guidance" from God's instruction and receive blessing.

Shalom IMAGE
MY STORY OF MY UNIQUE INFLUENCE

Our Footprint, Our Legacy

SCRIPTURE CONNECTION: PROVERBS 30:24-31

Like many ancient literary texts, Proverbs 30 references the natural world for wisdom and illustration. But when we as modern readers look to nature, what we see happening to it can be troubling. How do we interact with the natural world?

When God instituted ancient Israel's laws, he embedded his expectations for how people were to relate to their environment. He prescribed sustainable agricultural practices and instructed the people to show respect for living creatures and ecosystems.

These instructions prioritized caring for creation over convenience or profit, and the people were to embrace this facet of living holy lives.

Although ancient Israel's laws were just that—laws for a certain nation in a certain time—in them we glimpse God's heart for his creation. Caring for the land and the life sustained by it was not an afterthought, and its importance continues today.

How we interact with our world and its resources—whether we use them judiciously and sustainably or overuse them shortsightedly or selfishly—matters. The choices we make and the attitudes we adopt affect not just us; they create a legacy we leave to future generations.

As we wrestle with competing demands on our time and resources, we remember the Israelites' sacred responsibility. God knew what he was doing when he mandated that his people live sustainably, and his intent echoes through time to us today.

> "The land belongs to me," God says, "and you are borrowing it."

IMAGINE

How can we, as God's representatives on earth, respect and work to protect the world he loves?

"Being intentional about environmental impact isn't easy, but our values ultimately inspire our actions."

AVA JAMES is an editor who advocates for living with compassion and respect.

¹⁹ Words alone will not discipline a servant;
   the words may be understood, but they are
      not heeded.

²⁰ There is more hope for a fool
   than for someone who speaks without
      thinking.

²¹ A servant pampered from childhood
   will become a rebel.

²² An angry person starts fights;
   a hot-tempered person commits all kinds
      of sin.

²³ Pride ends in humiliation,
   while humility brings honor.

²⁴ If you assist a thief, you only hurt yourself.
   You are sworn to tell the truth, but you dare
      not testify.

²⁵ Fearing people is a dangerous trap,
   but trusting the LORD means safety.

²⁶ Many seek the ruler's favor,
   but justice comes from the LORD.

²⁷ The righteous despise the unjust;
   the wicked despise the godly.

The Sayings of Agur

30 The sayings of Agur son of Jakeh contain this message.*

I am weary, O God;
   I am weary and worn out, O God.*
² I am too stupid to be human,
   and I lack common sense.
³ I have not mastered human wisdom,
   nor do I know the Holy One.
⁴ Who but God goes up to heaven and comes back
      down?
   Who holds the wind in his fists?
   Who wraps up the oceans in his cloak?
   Who has created the whole wide world?
   What is his name—and his son's name?
      Tell me if you know!
⁵ Every word of God proves true.
   He is a shield to all who come to him for
      protection.
⁶ Do not add to his words,
   or he may rebuke you and expose you as a liar.

⁷ O God, I beg two favors from you;
   let me have them before I die.
⁸ First, help me never to tell a lie.
   Second, give me neither poverty nor riches!
   Give me just enough to satisfy my needs.
⁹ For if I grow rich, I may deny you and say, "Who
      is the LORD?"
   And if I am too poor, I may steal and thus
      insult God's holy name.

¹⁰ Never slander a worker to the employer,
   or the person will curse you, and you will pay
      for it.

¹¹ Some people curse their father
   and do not thank their mother.
¹² They are pure in their own eyes,
   but they are filthy and unwashed.
¹³ They look proudly around,
   casting disdainful glances.
¹⁴ They have teeth like swords
   and fangs like knives.
   They devour the poor from the earth
   and the needy from among humanity.

¹⁵ The leech has two suckers
   that cry out, "More, more!"*

There are three things that are never satisfied—
   no, four that never say, "Enough!":
¹⁶ the grave,*
   the barren womb,
   the thirsty desert,
   the blazing fire.

¹⁷ The eye that mocks a father
   and despises a mother's instructions
   will be plucked out by ravens of the valley
   and eaten by vultures.

¹⁸ There are three things that amaze me—
   no, four things that I don't understand:
¹⁹ how an eagle glides through the sky,
   how a snake slithers on a rock,
   how a ship navigates the ocean,
   how a man loves a woman.

²⁰ An adulterous woman consumes a man,
   then wipes her mouth and says, "What's
      wrong with that?"

²¹ There are three things that make the earth
      tremble—
   no, four it cannot endure:

30:1a Or *son of Jakeh from Massa*; or *son of Jakeh, an oracle.* **30:1b** The Hebrew can also be translated *The man declares this to Ithiel, / to Ithiel and to Ucal.* **30:15** Hebrew *two daughters who cry out, "Give, give!"* **30:16** Hebrew *Sheol.*

30:1 This superscription probably refers to the whole of Proverbs 30. The Hebrew indicates that Agur's father, Jakeh, may have been from a place called Massa. Apart from this reference, Agur and Jakeh are unknown. If Massa was the home of Agur, then he was a non-Israelite (the tribe of Massa is known from Assyrian texts).

30:21-23 This proverb lists four injustices that "make the earth tremble" because they overturn the general order of how the world works. The phrase translated "who prospers" literally says "who is full of bread." In the ancient Near East as in much of the non-industrialized world today, having adequate food (bread) was a sign of prosperity.

An Excellent Woman

IDENTITY | Qualities to Guide

While reading Proverbs 31, many of you, like me, have probably cringed at what appear to be standards for women—and impossible ones at that. But we miss the point because the poem's original structure is lost to us in translation, and because we are not all wives. But each of us can find inspiration from this woman to live with God-honoring excellence.

Imagine an older man sitting down three thousand years ago to write something to honor his wife on some special occasion: Starting with the twenty-two letters of the Hebrew alphabet, he bases his writing on his mother's teachings (31:1). He creates twenty-two phrases that describe the woman he loves with a lot of flourish and perhaps a bit of exaggeration.

Keep in mind he wrote this in a society that expected all women to be wives, mothers, and in charge of their households. How might we apply a similar idea today? Perhaps we need a new acrostic to honor a WOMAN. She is:

Wise in business and at home,
Open to listen to others,
Mindful of those less fortunate,
Attentive to God's Spirit
Neighborly—a friend to all she meets.

This, too, is an ideal that none of us entirely fulfills. So, how do you be "a virtuous and capable" *you*? (31:10)

Try asking God how he sees you. Write an acrostic using the letters of your name. Using Scripture, pen how you are God's beloved image-bearer and steward of creation (Genesis 1:26-28), daughter of God and heir to the Kingdom (Romans 8:17), gifted and called to serve God (Philippians 3:12-13), and more!

The good news is that God knows you. He calls you by name. And his Word shows us all how to live as women "who fear the LORD" and "will be greatly praised" (31:30).

THE SAYINGS ABOUT AN EXCELLENT WOMAN ARE RECORDED IN PROVERBS 31:10-31.

> God knows you. He calls you by your name. He shows us all how to live.

IDENTIFY

How is God shaping you into a "virtuous and capable" person?

Does reflecting on how God sees you change how you view yourself?

*"Using my nickname, Betsy, I came up with an acrostic that describes me: She is a **B**lessing to others, **E**ncouraging and enthusiastic, a **T**eacher of many, a **S**ailor who loves adventure, and **Y**oung at heart. This encourages and challenges me to live as the woman God calls me to be."*

ELIZABETH GLANVILLE, PhD, is retired faculty from Fuller Theological Seminary, School of Mission and Theology. She is an international teacher on missions and leadership and chaplain for a local police department and her retirement community.

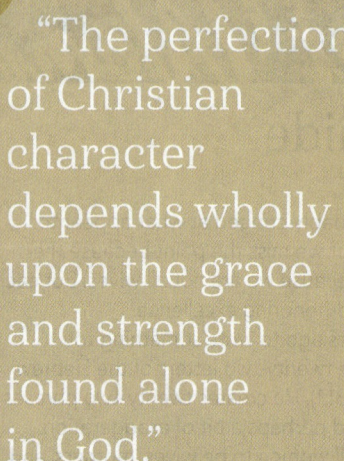

> "The perfection of Christian character depends wholly upon the grace and strength found alone in God."
>
> **ELLEN G. WHITE**
> (1827–1915) author and cofounder of the Seventh-Day Adventist Church

²² a slave who becomes a king,
  an overbearing fool who prospers,
²³   a bitter woman who finally gets a husband,
  a servant girl who supplants her mistress.

²⁴ There are four things on earth that are small but unusually wise:
²⁵ Ants—they aren't strong,
  but they store up food all summer.
²⁶ Hyraxes*—they aren't powerful,
  but they make their homes among the rocks.
²⁷ Locusts—they have no king,
  but they march in formation.
²⁸ Lizards—they are easy to catch,
  but they are found even in kings' palaces.

²⁹ There are three things that walk with stately stride—
  no, four that strut about:
³⁰ the lion, king of animals, who won't turn aside for anything,
³¹   the strutting rooster,
  the male goat,
  a king as he leads his army.

³² If you have been a fool by being proud or plotting evil,
  cover your mouth in shame.
³³ As the beating of cream yields butter
  and striking the nose causes bleeding,
  so stirring up anger causes quarrels.

The Sayings of King Lemuel

31 The sayings of King Lemuel contain this message,* which his mother taught him.
² O my son, O son of my womb,
  O son of my vows,
³ do not waste your strength on women,
  on those who ruin kings.

⁴ It is not for kings, O Lemuel, to guzzle wine.
  Rulers should not crave alcohol.
⁵ For if they drink, they may forget the law
  and not give justice to the oppressed.
⁶ Alcohol is for the dying,
  and wine for those in bitter distress.
⁷ Let them drink to forget their poverty
  and remember their troubles no more.

⁸ Speak up for those who cannot speak for themselves;
  ensure justice for those being crushed.
⁹ Yes, speak up for the poor and helpless,
  and see that they get justice.

A Wife of Noble Character

¹⁰ *Who can find a virtuous and capable wife?
  She is more precious than rubies.
¹¹ Her husband can trust her,
  and she will greatly enrich his life.
¹² She brings him good, not harm,
  all the days of her life.
¹³ She finds wool and flax
  and busily spins it.
¹⁴ She is like a merchant's ship,
  bringing her food from afar.

30:26 Or *Coneys*, or *Rock badgers*. 31:1 Or *of Lemuel, king of Massa;* or *of King Lemuel, an oracle.* 31:10 Verses 10-31 comprise a Hebrew acrostic poem; each verse begins with a successive letter of the Hebrew alphabet.

31:1-9 These verses record the wise instruction of the king's mother (see 1:8; 6:20; 30:17). While queen mothers played an influential role in the ancient world, no other culture includes a collection of her wise instruction. The inclusion of such a collection in a culture where men dominated society, even though voiced by a man, highlights a woman's ability to influence her children and that Israelite men saw women as sources of wisdom.

31:10-31 Some read this "virtuous and capable wife" as Woman Wisdom herself, while others see her as an ideal human wife. Rather than rejecting either perspective, looking at the poem at two levels helps understand it. Within the book of Proverbs as a whole, the son of Proverbs 1–9 has embraced and married Woman Wisdom, heeding his parents' instruction. Focusing on 31:10-31 as an independent unit, we see a human woman who embodies the ideals of wisdom in her labor and influence.

15 She gets up before dawn to prepare breakfast
    for her household
  and plan the day's work for her servant girls.
16 She goes to inspect a field and buys it;
  with her earnings she plants a vineyard.
17 She is energetic and strong,
  a hard worker.
18 She makes sure her dealings are profitable;
  her lamp burns late into the night.
19 Her hands are busy spinning thread,
  her fingers twisting fiber.
20 She extends a helping hand to the poor
  and opens her arms to the needy.
21 She has no fear of winter for her household,
  for everyone has warm* clothes.
22 She makes her own bedspreads.
  She dresses in fine linen and purple gowns.
23 Her husband is well known at the city gates,
  where he sits with the other civic leaders.
24 She makes belted linen garments
  and sashes to sell to the merchants.
25 She is clothed with strength and dignity,
  and she laughs without fear of the future.
26 When she speaks, her words are wise,
  and she gives instructions with kindness.
27 She carefully watches everything in her
    household
  and suffers nothing from laziness.
28 Her children stand and bless her.
  Her husband praises her:
29 "There are many virtuous and capable women in
    the world,
  but you surpass them all!"
30 Charm is deceptive, and beauty does not last;
  but a woman who fears the Lord will be
    greatly praised.
31 Reward her for all she has done.
  Let her deeds publicly declare her praise.

31:21 As in Greek and Latin versions; Hebrew reads *scarlet*.

31:10, 29 The Hebrew word translated "virtuous and capable" (*khayil*) can refer to strength or wealth and was used to describe soldiers. The traditional rendering "virtuous" comes from the Latin word *virtus*, which could refer to masculine excellence. The focus here is on the woman's strength and excellence. Some Hebrew manuscripts place Ruth immediately after Proverbs, suggesting some viewed her as an example of this "virtuous [*khayil*] woman" (Ruth 3:11).

Sometimes we as women aren't sure if God wants us to be strong. This passage showcases a woman's strength in various life roles—as wife, businesswoman, mother, caretaker of the poor, and more. Where God calls us, he desires to strengthen us for capable, virtuous, excellent work, loving him and serving those around us.

31:30-31 The book concludes where it began, by affirming the ultimate importance of the fear of the Lord (see 1:7).

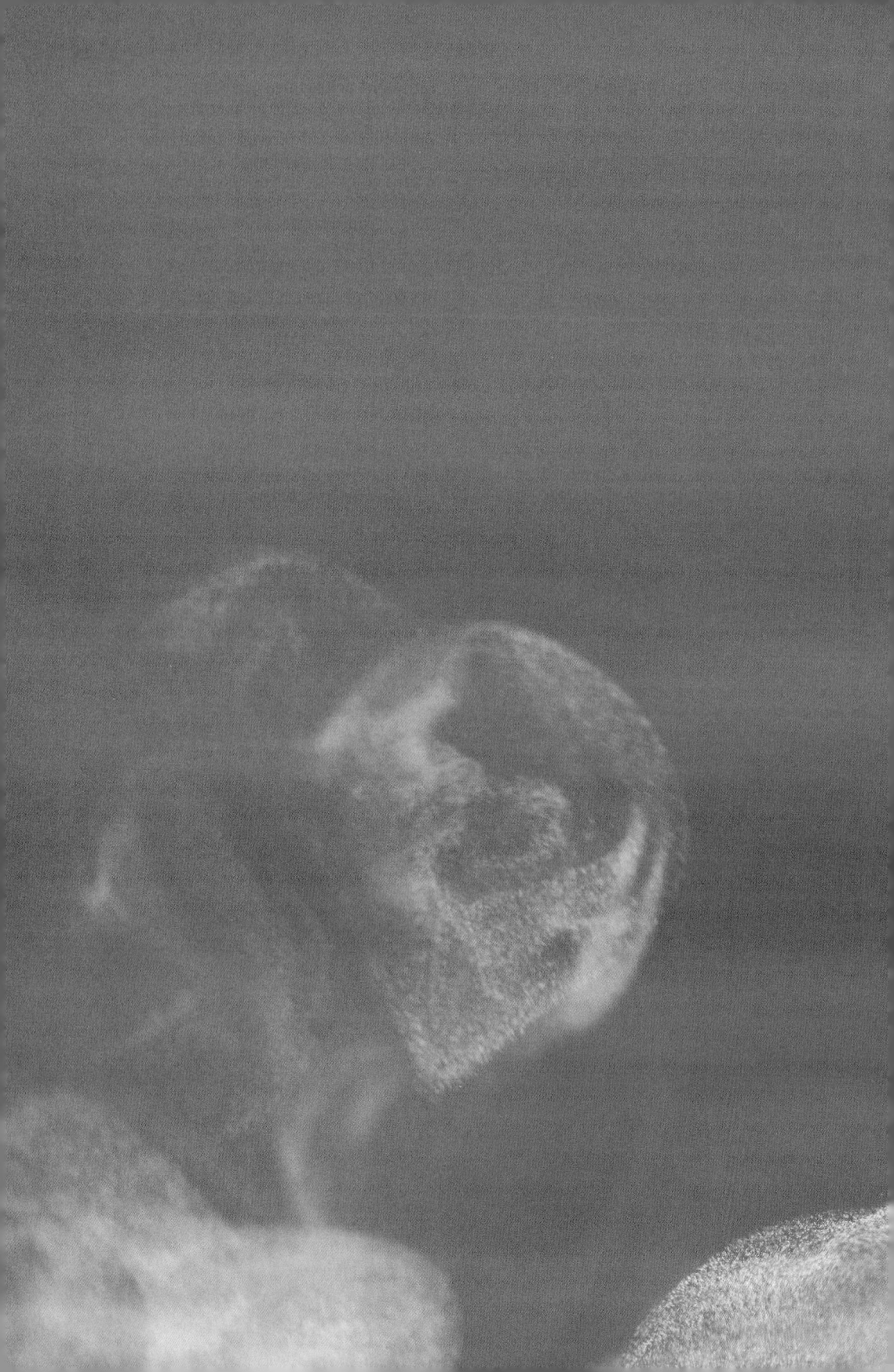

Ecclesiastes

WHAT DO WE LEARN ABOUT GOD'S MISSION AND OURS? Following God alone is our purpose, and nothing and no one else will satisfy our desires.

WHO WROTE IT? King Solomon, traditionally, but some suggest a later author since the book is technically anonymous (the author refers to himself as "the Teacher," 1:1).

WHEN DID IT HAPPEN? If Solomon wrote it, it would fit during his reign in the period of Israel's united kingdom (970–930 BC). It may have been written as early as 935 BC.

HOW IS IT ORGANIZED?

- 1:1-11: Life is meaningless apart from God
- 1:12–6:9: A search for life's meaning
- 6:10–12:7: Though life is meaningless, we can enjoy our days as a gift from God
- 12:8-14: The bottom line? Trust, enjoy, and obey God.

Words to Remember are highlighted throughout this book

FEATURE HIGHLIGHTS

- *Should We Try Everything to Know What's True? (795)*
- *A Good Companion: Ruth and Naomi, Paired for Life (799)*
- *Stressed? Savor (800)*
- *Enjoyment (802)*
- *The Fear We Need (806)*

HOW LONG DOES IT TAKE TO READ?

:30 | 1:00 | 1:30 | 2:00 | 2:30 | 3:00 | 3:30

ECCLESIASTES 1

1 These are the words of the Teacher,* King David's son, who ruled in Jerusalem.

Everything Is Meaningless

²"Everything is meaningless," says the Teacher, "completely meaningless!"

³What do people get for all their hard work under the sun? ⁴Generations come and generations go, but the earth never changes. ⁵The sun rises and the sun sets, then hurries around to rise again. ⁶The wind blows south, and then turns north. Around and around it goes, blowing in circles. ⁷Rivers run into the sea, but the sea is never full. Then the water returns again to the rivers and flows out again to the sea. ⁸Everything is wearisome beyond description. No matter how much we see, we are never satisfied. No matter how much we hear, we are not content.

⁹History merely repeats itself. It has all been done before. Nothing under the sun is truly new. ¹⁰Sometimes people say, "Here is something new!" But actually it is old; nothing is ever truly new. ¹¹We don't remember what happened in the past, and in future generations, no one will remember what we are doing now.

The Teacher Speaks: The Futility of Wisdom

¹²I, the Teacher, was king of Israel, and I lived in Jerusalem. ¹³I devoted myself to search for understanding and to explore by wisdom everything being done under heaven. I soon discovered that God has dealt a tragic existence to the human race. ¹⁴I observed everything going on under the sun, and really, it is all meaningless—like chasing the wind.

¹⁵ What is wrong cannot be made right.
   What is missing cannot be recovered.

¹⁶I said to myself, "Look, I am wiser than any of the kings who ruled in Jerusalem before me. I have greater wisdom and knowledge than any of them." ¹⁷So I set out to learn everything from wisdom to madness and folly. But I learned firsthand that pursuing all this is like chasing the wind.

¹⁸ The greater my wisdom, the greater my grief.
   To increase knowledge only increases sorrow.

The Futility of Pleasure

2 I said to myself, "Come on, let's try pleasure. Let's look for the 'good things' in life." But I found that this, too, was meaningless. ²So I said, "Laughter is silly. What good does it do to seek pleasure?" ³After much thought, I decided to cheer myself with wine. And while still seeking wisdom, I clutched at foolishness. In this way, I tried to experience the only happiness most people find during their brief life in this world.

⁴I also tried to find meaning by building huge homes for myself and by planting beautiful vineyards. ⁵I made gardens and parks, filling them with all kinds of fruit trees. ⁶I built reservoirs to collect the water to irrigate my many flourishing groves. ⁷I bought slaves, both men and women, and others were born into my household. I also owned large herds and flocks, more than any of the kings who had lived in Jerusalem before me. ⁸I collected great sums of silver and gold, the treasure of many kings and provinces. I hired wonderful singers, both men and women, and had many beautiful concubines. I had everything a man could desire!

⁹So I became greater than all who had lived in Jerusalem before me, and my wisdom never failed me. ¹⁰Anything I wanted, I would take. I denied myself no pleasure. I even found great pleasure in hard work, a reward for all my labors. ¹¹But as I looked at everything I had worked so hard to accomplish, it was all so meaningless—like chasing the wind. There was nothing really worthwhile anywhere.

The Wise and the Foolish

¹²So I decided to compare wisdom with foolishness and madness (for who can do this better than I, the king?*). ¹³I thought, "Wisdom is better than

---

1:1 Hebrew *Qoheleth*; this term is rendered "the Teacher" throughout this book.   **2:12** The meaning of the Hebrew is uncertain.

1:1 The title "Teacher" (Hebrew *Qoheleth*) comes from the Hebrew verb meaning "to assemble" or "to gather." *Qoheleth* is often called "the preacher" or "the teacher." Authorship has traditionally been attributed to Solomon because of the phrase "King David's son" in 1:1 and because of Solomon's association with Proverbs (Proverbs 1:1), even though Ecclesiastes does not directly mention Solomon. Due to certain Persian words and later Hebrew vocabulary that appears in Ecclesiastes, many scholars remain uncertain about who authored this book. These study notes refer to *Qoheleth* as "the Teacher."
1:2 Meaninglessness is a repeated theme throughout Ecclesiastes; the Hebrew term is *hevel*, which can be translated as "meaningless, breath, or vanity." The use of this key theme reminds us that all things in life, whether good or difficult, are not permanent. This includes work (1:14; 2:11), knowledge (1:17), power (4:16), greed (5:10), wealth (6:2), injustice (8:14), and pleasure (2:1)— "everything" (1:2; 11:8; 12:8).
2:3 The Teacher understands that trying to cheer himself with wine was foolishness, but he did it "while still seeking wisdom"—his attempt to understand how "to experience . . . happiness." This proved to be empty (2:11).
2:12-23 The Teacher next looks at the value of wisdom (2:12-17) and hard work (2:18-23). He determines that these, too, are ultimately "meaningless" (2:17) because the prospect of death overwhelms the benefits of these virtues.
2:12 The meaning of the Hebrew "who can do this better than I, the king?" is uncertain. The Teacher is possibly implying that no one after him will have any better perspective for comparing wisdom and folly because nothing new will be done under the sun (1:9-10).

foolishness, just as light is better than darkness. ¹⁴For the wise can see where they are going, but fools walk in the dark." Yet I saw that the wise and the foolish share the same fate. ¹⁵Both will die. So I said to myself, "Since I will end up the same as the fool, what's the value of all my wisdom? This is all so meaningless!" ¹⁶For the wise and the foolish both die. The wise will not be remembered any longer than the fool. In the days to come, both will be forgotten.

¹⁷So I came to hate life because everything done here under the sun is so troubling. Everything is meaningless—like chasing the wind.

The Futility of Work

¹⁸I came to hate all my hard work here on earth, for I must leave to others everything I have earned. ¹⁹And who can tell whether my successors will be wise or foolish? Yet they will control everything I have gained by my skill and hard work under the sun. How meaningless! ²⁰So I gave up in despair, questioning the value of all my hard work in this world.

²¹Some people work wisely with knowledge and skill, then must leave the fruit of their efforts to someone who hasn't worked for it. This, too, is meaningless, a great tragedy. ²²So what do people get in this life for all their hard work and anxiety? ²³Their days of labor are filled with pain and grief; even at night their minds cannot rest. It is all meaningless.

²⁴So I decided there is nothing better than to enjoy food and drink and to find satisfaction in work. Then I realized that these pleasures are from the hand of God. ²⁵For who can eat or enjoy anything apart from him?* ²⁶God gives wisdom, knowledge, and joy to those who please him. But if a sinner becomes wealthy, God takes the wealth away and gives it to those who please him. This, too, is meaningless—like chasing the wind.

A Time for Everything

3 For everything there is a season,
   a time for every activity under heaven.
² A time to be born and a time to die.
   A time to plant and a time to harvest.
³ A time to kill and a time to heal.
   A time to tear down and a time to build up.

2:25 As in Greek and Syriac versions; Hebrew reads *apart from me*.

2:13-14 Wisdom has value in navigating life successfully. It cannot, however, save one from the fate of death or provide meaning for our lives, ultimately (2:15-16). The Teacher emphasizes here that wisdom is good, but that it cannot be our reason for living, building his case for the meaningless of everything.

2:15-16 If both the wise and the foolish will die, what advantage is there in being wise? Those who follow us will not remember us or our accomplishments, so our efforts will come to nothing (see also 1:11; 9:13-16). Since the lives of both wise and foolish people are fleeting, the conclusion is that all is meaningless.

Perspective

Should we try everything to know what's true?

SCRIPTURE CONNECTION: ECCLESIASTES 1:2-18

Ecclesiastes is called "wisdom literature." Yet, so-called wise King Solomon (or, "the Teacher," 1:1) fills the text with what feels like anti-wisdom.

After all his searching for the meaning of life, he concludes that life is meaningless, futile (1:2; 2:17; 12:8). Like the breath that evaporates as it leaves my mouth on a chilly winter day, nothing lasts. The book gives wisdom about what *not* to do. We also learn what *is* good: to delight in what we have.

I think of Jesus coming to earth eating and drinking (Luke 7:29-35). This true wisest-King-of-all embraced life's simple pleasures and Ecclesiastes' conclusion to "fear God and obey his commands" (Ecclesiastes 12:13).

VIEWPOINTS

HIS: *Can you list what Solomon tried for satisfaction (see 1:12–2:26)? What have you tried?*

MINE: *"I was born and raised in the church, but I didn't want my parents' faith. I wanted my own. So, I went looking. While I wouldn't want anyone to learn the hard way, as Solomon and I did, my experience led me to nod my head in deep agreement with him. In practicing gratitude for life's simple pleasures, God met the author of Ecclesiastes, God meets me, and God will meet you too."*

YOURS: *What does it look like to rejoice in the small things today?*

ALEXIANA FRY, MDiv, PhD, is a devoted academic in the Hebrew Bible. She is a professor, wife, and pug mom who is working on her first book post-dissertation.

3:1-8 This passage is a well-known poem that you may have heard before in song lyrics or read publicly. There are twenty-eight contrary movements throughout this poem, each having a purpose, depending on the season of life. This poem is a reminder that life is *hevel*, a "breath." The Teacher reminds us to be thankful for the life that is given: "People should eat and drink and enjoy the fruits of their labor, for these are gifts from God" (3:13).

God has made everything beautiful for its own time.

ECCLESIASTES 3:11

⁴ A time to cry and a time to laugh.
  A time to grieve and a time to dance.
⁵ A time to scatter stones and a time to gather stones.
  A time to embrace and a time to turn away.
⁶ A time to search and a time to quit searching.
  A time to keep and a time to throw away.
⁷ A time to tear and a time to mend.
  A time to be quiet and a time to speak.
⁸ A time to love and a time to hate.
  A time for war and a time for peace.

⁹What do people really get for all their hard work? ¹⁰I have seen the burden God has placed on us all. ¹¹Yet God has made everything beautiful for its own time. He has planted eternity in the human heart, but even so, people cannot see the whole scope of God's work from beginning to end. ¹²So I concluded there is nothing better than to be happy and enjoy ourselves as long as we can. ¹³And people should eat and drink and enjoy the fruits of their labor, for these are gifts from God.

¹⁴And I know that whatever God does is final. Nothing can be added to it or taken from it. God's purpose is that people should fear him. ¹⁵What is happening now has happened before, and what will happen in the future has happened before, because God makes the same things happen over and over again.

The Injustices of Life

¹⁶I also noticed that under the sun there is evil in the courtroom. Yes, even the courts of law are corrupt! ¹⁷I said to myself, "In due season God will judge everyone, both good and bad, for all their deeds."

¹⁸I also thought about the human condition—how God proves to people that they are like animals. ¹⁹For people and animals share the same fate—both breathe* and both must die. So people have no real advantage over the animals. How meaningless! ²⁰Both go to the same place—they came from dust and they return to dust. ²¹For who can prove that the human spirit goes up and the spirit of animals goes down into the earth? ²²So I saw that there is nothing better for people than to be happy in their work. That is our lot in life. And no one can bring us back to see what happens after we die.

4 Again, I observed all the oppression that takes place under the sun. I saw the tears of the oppressed, with no one to comfort them. The oppressors have great power, and their victims are helpless. ²So I concluded that the dead are better off than the living. ³But most fortunate of all are those who are not yet born. For they have not seen all the evil that is done under the sun.

⁴Then I observed that most people are motivated to success because they envy their neighbors. But this, too, is meaningless—like chasing the wind.

⁵ "Fools fold their idle hands,
  leading them to ruin."

⁶And yet,

"Better to have one handful with quietness
  than two handfuls with hard work
  and chasing the wind."

The Advantages of Companionship

⁷I observed yet another example of something meaningless under the sun. ⁸This is the case of a man who is all alone, without a child or a brother, yet who works hard to gain as much wealth as he can. But then he asks himself, "Who am I working for? Why am I giving up so much pleasure now?" It is all so meaningless and depressing.

⁹Two people are better off than one, for they can help each other succeed. ¹⁰If one person falls, the other can reach out and help. But someone who falls alone is in real trouble. ¹¹Likewise, two people lying close together can keep each other warm. But how can one be warm alone? ¹²A person standing alone can be attacked and defeated, but two can stand back-to-back and conquer. Three are even better, for a triple-braided cord is not easily broken.

The Futility of Political Power

¹³It is better to be a poor but wise youth than an old and foolish king who refuses all advice. ¹⁴Such a youth could rise from poverty and succeed. He might even become king, though he has been in prison. ¹⁵But then everyone rushes to the side of yet another youth* who replaces him. ¹⁶Endless crowds stand around him,* but then another generation grows up and rejects him, too. So it is all meaningless—like chasing the wind.

Approaching God with Care

5 ¹*As you enter the house of God, keep your ears open and your mouth shut. It is evil to make mindless offerings to God. ²*Don't make rash promises, and don't be hasty in bringing matters before God. After all, God is in heaven, and you are here on earth. So let your words be few.

³Too much activity gives you restless dreams; too many words make you a fool.

3:19 Or *both have the same spirit.* **4:15** Hebrew *the second youth.* **4:16** Hebrew *There is no end to all the people, to all those who are before them.* **5:1** Verse 5:1 is numbered 4:17 in Hebrew text. **5:2** Verses 5:2-20 are numbered 5:1-19 in Hebrew text.

4:1-16 The Teacher acknowledges that those in power will sometimes use this power to abuse the oppressed. Later in this same passage, power and wealth are criticized when used foolishly (4:13-16). The passage reminds us to use these gifts from God, the gifts of power and wisdom, to help others when we can (4:9-12).

⁴When you make a promise to God, don't delay in following through, for God takes no pleasure in fools. Keep all the promises you make to him. ⁵It is better to say nothing than to make a promise and not keep it. ⁶Don't let your mouth make you sin. And don't defend yourself by telling the Temple messenger that the promise you made was a mistake. That would make God angry, and he might wipe out everything you have achieved.

⁷Talk is cheap, like daydreams and other useless activities. Fear God instead.

The Futility of Wealth

⁸Don't be surprised if you see a poor person being oppressed by the powerful and if justice is being miscarried throughout the land. For every official is under orders from higher up, and matters of justice get lost in red tape and bureaucracy. ⁹Even the king milks the land for his own profit!*

¹⁰Those who love money will never have enough. How meaningless to think that wealth brings true happiness! ¹¹The more you have, the more people come to help you spend it. So what good is wealth—except perhaps to watch it slip through your fingers!

¹²People who work hard sleep well, whether they eat little or much. But the rich seldom get a good night's sleep.

¹³There is another serious problem I have seen under the sun. Hoarding riches harms the saver. ¹⁴Money is put into risky investments that turn sour, and everything is lost. In the end, there is nothing left to pass on to one's children. ¹⁵We all come to the end of our lives as naked and empty-handed as on the day we were born. We can't take our riches with us.

¹⁶And this, too, is a very serious problem. People leave this world no better off than when they came. All their hard work is for nothing—like working for the wind. ¹⁷Throughout their lives, they live under a cloud—frustrated, discouraged, and angry.

¹⁸Even so, I have noticed one thing, at least, that is good. It is good for people to eat, drink, and enjoy their work under the sun during the short life God has given them, and to accept their lot in life. ¹⁹And it is a good thing to receive wealth from God and the good health to enjoy it. To enjoy your work and accept your lot in life—this is indeed a gift from God.

5:9 The meaning of the Hebrew in verses 8 and 9 is uncertain.

²⁰God keeps such people so busy enjoying life that they take no time to brood over the past.

6 There is another serious tragedy I have seen under the sun, and it weighs heavily on humanity. ²God gives some people great wealth and honor and everything they could ever want, but then he doesn't give them the chance to enjoy these things. They die, and someone else, even a stranger, ends up enjoying their wealth! This is meaningless—a sickening tragedy.

³A man might have a hundred children and live to be very old. But if he finds no satisfaction in life and doesn't even get a decent burial, it would have been better for him to be born dead. ⁴His birth would have been meaningless, and he would have ended in darkness. He wouldn't even have had a name, ⁵and he would never have seen the sun or known of its existence. Yet he would have had more peace than in growing up to be an unhappy man. ⁶He might live a thousand years twice over but still not find contentment. And since he must die like everyone else—well, what's the use?

⁷All people spend their lives scratching for food, but they never seem to have enough. ⁸So are wise people really better off than fools? Do poor people gain anything by being wise and knowing how to act in front of others?

⁹Enjoy what you have rather than desiring what you don't have. Just dreaming about nice things is meaningless—like chasing the wind.

The Future—Determined and Unknown

¹⁰Everything has already been decided. It was known long ago what each person would be. So there's no use arguing with God about your destiny.

¹¹The more words you speak, the less they mean. So what good are they?

¹²In the few days of our meaningless lives, who knows how our days can best be spent? Our lives are like a shadow. Who can tell what will happen on this earth after we are gone?

Wisdom for Life

7 A good reputation is more valuable than costly perfume.
And the day you die is better than the day you are born.

5:8-9 The meaning of the Hebrew here is uncertain. The NLT understands these verses to mean that bureaucracy brings oppression rather than justice, all the way up to the king (see also 1 Samuel 8:11-18). This should not be surprising, because that is how bureaucracies tend to function. Other Bible translations interpret the verses to mean that the king and his officials provide oversight to restrain injustice and oppression, rendering the passage like this: "For one official watches over another, and higher officials are over them. The land benefits from a king who cultivates the field." The former view is more in keeping with the realistic perspective of the Teacher.
5:16-20 The Teacher observes that enjoying the simple pleasures in life, like eating and drinking, and finding joy in what we do is good. Enjoying these things is a "gift from God."
6:1-6 This unfortunate man parable resembles 4:7-8 and 5:13-17. It is "a sickening tragedy" when someone succeeds but then cannot "enjoy these things." Such a person has missed out on the only available benefit of success.

A Good Companion

IDENTITY — Ruth and Naomi, Paired for Life

In life, we need companionship, and we need to be a companion to others.

Ecclesiastes 4:9-12 explains the qualities of a good companion and how two are better than one. It encourages me to expand my thinking about companionship. We read this and sometimes may wonder, "Do I have to be married for that to be true?" or "Do I have to have a significant other?" or "How does that apply to me if I'm all alone?" Is marriage the only form of companionship the Bible exalts? How can those who are single or lonely (not always the same thing!) still go through life paired with another?

I believe the wisdom that "two people are better off than one" also means being an excellent friend.

Naomi and Ruth are a good example of this wisdom in the Bible. After losing her husband and two sons, Naomi was distraught. She was distraught to the point that she wanted to change her identity, call herself Mara (which means "bitter"), and send her daughters-in-law away.

She must have felt so alone, isolated, and concerned because she had lost the crucial male protection and provision her culture required and because she could not provide for herself or her daughters-in-law.

But our identity is first and foremost in Christ, who is our perfect companion. Our first response is to him, then, and what he calls us to do, regardless of our marital status. Ruth knew Naomi's plight and her feelings, knew she needed a companion, and clung to her. Ruth chose to follow God and be a good companion to Naomi. We can fulfill our needs for companionship, and be a good companion, by following Christ's words—to love God with all we are and to love others as ourselves. Practically speaking, it may not look like Ruth's commitment. Being a good companion may start with noticing—today—who needs care and reaching out to them.

> Ruth knew Naomi's need for a companion and clung to her.

THE STORY OF A GOOD COMPANION IS TOLD IN ECCLESIASTES 4:9-12;
RUTH AND NAOMI'S STORY IS TOLD IN THE BOOK OF RUTH.

IDENTIFY

What does Ecclesiastes say are the benefits of companionship for us?

Are you in a season of life where you identify more with Ruth—you can reach out to be a companion—or Naomi—you need a companion alongside you? Has God called you to be a companion or blessed you with one?

"Because of my identity in Christ, I have a call to be a companion, and I, too, have needed a companion. God knows who we need and provides for us. Thank you, Jesus!"

RACHEL LINDSAY McCANTS is an author, speaker, and founder of R. Lindsay Unlimited, which encourages, inspires, and challenges ladies to raise their self-worth and standards and to walk in God's will, in Jesus' name.

ECCLESIASTES 7

2 Better to spend your time at funerals than at parties.
After all, everyone dies—
so the living should take this to heart.
3 Sorrow is better than laughter,
for sadness has a refining influence on us.
4 A wise person thinks a lot about death,
while a fool thinks only about having a good time.
5 Better to be criticized by a wise person
than to be praised by a fool.
6 A fool's laughter is quickly gone,
like thorns crackling in a fire.
This also is meaningless.
7 Extortion turns wise people into fools,
and bribes corrupt the heart.
8 Finishing is better than starting.
Patience is better than pride.
9 Control your temper,
for anger labels you a fool.
10 Don't long for "the good old days."
This is not wise.
11 Wisdom is even better when you have money.
Both are a benefit as you go through life.
12 Wisdom and money can get you almost anything,
but only wisdom can save your life.
13 Accept the way God does things,
for who can straighten what he has made crooked?
14 Enjoy prosperity while you can,
but when hard times strike, realize that both come from God.
Remember that nothing is certain in this life.

Come Close — STRESSED? SAVOR

SCRIPTURE CONNECTION: ECCLESIASTES 5:18-20

My commute drained me. The work pummeled me. The daily to-do list beat me over the head. If you over-prioritize work, it's easy to believe the lie that "If I just get *this* done, there will be a break coming soon." I believed this long enough for my health to deteriorate and my soul to cower in the corner.

Solomon tried it all, including being a workaholic (2:18-23). He saw that chasing after success, power, fame, and wealth were all meaningless (4:13-16; 5:8-17). His soul probably had cowered too. But he did learn, and his words reached me when my job was a shroud of joyless tasks.

"Even so," Solomon writes, "I have noticed one thing, at least, that is good" (5:18).

My ears pricked up at that. One thing? I could handle that. I could learn one thing from someone who had tried it all, because I was truly dying inside.

"It is good for people to eat, drink, and enjoy their work under the sun during the short life God has given them" (5:18).

I read in those words, "Sit down to a good meal. Sip on that cool beverage. Find one thing to enjoy about your work." I was challenged.

I started small. I put a chair on my porch in the evenings and enjoyed the sunset in complete silence.

Now, I find ways each day of enjoying what God has assigned. My chasing has turned to gratitude.

REFLECT "God keeps such people so busy enjoying life that they take no time to brood over the past." ECCLESIASTES 5:20

Lord, today I will make time to enjoy the life you have given me. Amen.

CONSIDER "Life moves pretty fast. If you don't stop and look around once in a while, you could miss it." *Ferris Bueller's Day Off*

> Today, I will make time to enjoy the life God has given me.

CARA DAY is a writer and illustrator. She has served with Stonecroft Ministries helping women live "extraordinary."

The Limits of Human Wisdom

¹⁵I have seen everything in this meaningless life, including the death of good young people and the long life of wicked people. ¹⁶So don't be too good or too wise! Why destroy yourself? ¹⁷On the other hand, don't be too wicked either. Don't be a fool! Why die before your time? ¹⁸Pay attention to these instructions, for anyone who fears God will avoid both extremes.*

¹⁹One wise person is stronger than ten leading citizens of a town!

²⁰Not a single person on earth is always good and never sins.

²¹Don't eavesdrop on others—you may hear your servant curse you. ²²For you know how often you yourself have cursed others.

²³I have always tried my best to let wisdom guide my thoughts and actions. I said to myself, "I am determined to be wise." But it didn't work. ²⁴Wisdom is always distant and difficult to find. ²⁵I searched everywhere, determined to find wisdom and to understand the reason for things. I was determined to prove to myself that wickedness is stupid and that foolishness is madness.

²⁶I discovered that a seductive woman* is a trap more bitter than death. Her passion is a snare, and her soft hands are chains. Those who are pleasing to God will escape her, but sinners will be caught in her snare.

²⁷"This is my conclusion," says the Teacher. "I discovered this after looking at the matter from every possible angle. ²⁸Though I have searched repeatedly, I have not found what I was looking for. Only one out of a thousand men is virtuous, but not one woman! ²⁹But I did find this: God created people to be virtuous, but they have each turned to follow their own downward path."

8

How wonderful to be wise,
   to analyze and interpret things.
Wisdom lights up a person's face,
   softening its harshness.

Obedience to the King

²Obey the king since you vowed to God that you would. ³Don't try to avoid doing your duty, and don't stand with those who plot evil, for the king can do whatever he wants. ⁴His command is backed by great power. No one can resist or question it. ⁵Those who obey him will not be punished. Those who are wise will find a time and a way to do what is right, ⁶for there is a time and a way for everything, even when a person is in trouble.

⁷Indeed, how can people avoid what they don't know is going to happen? ⁸None of us can hold back our spirit from departing. None of us has the power to prevent the day of our death. There is no escaping that obligation, that dark battle. And in the face of death, wickedness will certainly not rescue the wicked.

The Wicked and the Righteous

⁹I have thought deeply about all that goes on here under the sun, where people have the power to hurt each other. ¹⁰I have seen wicked people buried with honor. Yet they were the very ones who frequented the Temple and are now praised* in the same city where they committed their crimes! This, too, is meaningless. ¹¹When a crime is not punished quickly, people feel it is safe to do wrong. ¹²But even though a person sins a hundred times and still lives a long time, I know that those who fear God will be better off. ¹³The wicked will not prosper, for they do not fear God. Their days will never grow long like the evening shadows.

¹⁴And this is not all that is meaningless in our world. In this life, good people are often treated as though they were wicked, and wicked people are often treated as though they were good. This is so meaningless!

¹⁵So I recommend having fun, because there is nothing better for people in this world than to eat, drink, and enjoy life. That way they will experience

---

7:18 Or *will follow them both.* **7:26** Hebrew *a woman.* **8:10** As in some Hebrew manuscripts and Greek version; many Hebrew manuscripts read *and are forgotten.*

7:15-18 The Teacher reminds the reader to avoid extremes in pursuing anything, even wisdom. The key here is to "fear God" (for example, 3:14; 5:7; 8:12-13; 12:13), a phrase describing a person's reverent relationship with God. Fearing God means respecting God and standing in wonder and amazement at who God is, which has been revealed by what he has done. Proverbs 1:7 emphasizes that "Fear of the LORD is the foundation of true knowledge, but fools despise wisdom and discipline." Fearing God is the key to gaining wisdom. James 1:5 also reminds us that if we seek wisdom, all we need to do is ask God for it!
7:26 What is translated here in this verse as "a seductive woman" in the Hebrew is literally "a woman." The book of Proverbs personifies Woman Wisdom and Woman Folly, which helps us understand this negative reference in Ecclesiastes. Some scholars suggest that this verse does not refer to an immoral woman nor characterize women in general. Instead, this description of a "seductive woman" refers to choices, contrasting wise and unwise choices, as we see throughout Proverbs 1–9.
7:28 Interpretations of this woman have vacillated between Eve or a personal figure in the Teacher's life, such as his mother. This woman could also represent the Teacher's perception of all women or perhaps is used as a metaphor for the death of wisdom (wisdom is embodied as Woman Wisdom in Proverbs 1:1–9:18). In the context here, the personification of Woman Wisdom is a likely connection.
8:12-13 Injustice is momentary and does not upset God's plans for justice (3:16-17; 12:14). In reality, wickedness does not pay.
8:15 The Teacher's conclusion is familiar (2:24-25; 3:12-13, 22; 5:18-20; 6:9). In spite of tragedies and hard labor, we can enjoy life and be happy. In Hebrew, the word translated "having fun" means finding enjoyment in our daily activities, not pursuing pleasure or entertainment for its own sake.

WHAT THE BIBLE SAYS ABOUT Enjoyment

Some people may think of Ecclesiastes as the "bummer book," citing phrases like "everything is meaningless" (1:2; 2:17; 12:8). But Ecclesiastes mentions the word enjoy *more than any other book in the Bible! What can we learn about enjoying life, even as we—like the writer of Ecclesiastes—look at life full-on?*

For who can eat or enjoy anything apart from him?

God Gives Enjoyment

I decided there is nothing better than to enjoy food and drink and to find satisfaction in work. Then I realized that these pleasures are from the hand of God. For who can eat or enjoy anything apart from him? **ECCLESIASTES 2:24-25**

People should eat and drink and enjoy the fruits of their labor, for these are gifts from God. **ECCLESIASTES 3:13**

It is a good thing to receive wealth from God and the good health to enjoy it. To enjoy your work and accept your lot in life—this is indeed a gift from God. **ECCLESIASTES 5:19**

...for these are gifts from God

God Is Still God—In Good Times and Bad

Enjoy prosperity while you can, but when hard times strike, realize that both come from God. Remember that nothing is certain in this life. ECCLESIASTES 7:14

I recommend having fun, because there is nothing better for people in this world than to eat, drink, and enjoy life. That way they will experience some happiness along with all the hard work God gives them under the sun. ECCLESIASTES 8:15

Young people, it's wonderful to be young! Enjoy every minute of it. Do everything you want to do; take it all in. But remember that you must give an account to God for everything you do. ECCLESIASTES 11:9

Enjoying Is Wise!

I concluded there is nothing better than to be happy and enjoy ourselves as long as we can. ECCLESIASTES 3:12

I have noticed one thing, at least, that is good. It is good for people to eat, drink, and enjoy their work under the sun during the short life God has given them, and to accept their lot in life. . . . God keeps such people so busy enjoying life that they take no time to brood over the past. ECCLESIASTES 5:18, 20

God gives some people great wealth and honor and everything they could ever want, but then he doesn't give them the chance to enjoy these things. They die, and someone else, even a stranger, ends up enjoying their wealth! This is meaningless—a sickening tragedy. ECCLESIASTES 6:2

Enjoy what you have rather than desiring what you don't have. Just dreaming about nice things is meaningless—like chasing the wind. ECCLESIASTES 6:9

some happiness along with all the hard work God gives them under the sun.

¹⁶In my search for wisdom and in my observation of people's burdens here on earth, I discovered that there is ceaseless activity, day and night. ¹⁷I realized that no one can discover everything God is doing under the sun. Not even the wisest people discover everything, no matter what they claim.

Death Comes to All

9 This, too, I carefully explored: Even though the actions of godly and wise people are in God's hands, no one knows whether God will show them favor. ²The same destiny ultimately awaits everyone, whether righteous or wicked, good or bad,* ceremonially clean or unclean, religious or irreligious. Good people receive the same treatment as sinners, and people who make promises to God are treated like people who don't.

³It seems so wrong that everyone under the sun suffers the same fate. Already twisted by evil, people choose their own mad course, for they have no hope. There is nothing ahead but death anyway. ⁴There is hope only for the living. As they say, "It's better to be a live dog than a dead lion!"

⁵The living at least know they will die, but the dead know nothing. They have no further reward, nor are they remembered. ⁶Whatever they did in their lifetime—loving, hating, envying—is all long gone. They no longer play a part in anything here on earth. ⁷So go ahead. Eat your food with joy, and drink your wine with a happy heart, for God approves of this! ⁸Wear fine clothes, with a splash of cologne!

⁹Live happily with the woman you love through all the meaningless days of life that God has given you under the sun. The wife God gives you is your reward for all your earthly toil. ¹⁰Whatever you do, do well. For when you go to the grave,* there will be no work or planning or knowledge or wisdom.

¹¹I have observed something else under the sun. The fastest runner doesn't always win the race, and the strongest warrior doesn't always win the battle. The wise sometimes go hungry, and the skillful are not necessarily wealthy. And those who are educated don't always lead successful lives. It is all decided by chance, by being in the right place at the right time.

¹²People can never predict when hard times might come. Like fish in a net or birds in a trap, people are caught by sudden tragedy.

Thoughts on Wisdom and Folly

¹³Here is another bit of wisdom that has impressed me as I have watched the way our world works. ¹⁴There was a small town with only a few people, and a great king came with his army and besieged it. ¹⁵A poor, wise man knew how to save the town, and so it was rescued. But afterward no one thought to thank him. ¹⁶So even though wisdom is better than strength, those who are wise will be despised if they are poor. What they say will not be appreciated for long.

¹⁷ Better to hear the quiet words of a wise person
than the shouts of a foolish king.
¹⁸ Better to have wisdom than weapons of war,
but one sinner can destroy much that is good.

10 As dead flies cause even a bottle of perfume to stink,
so a little foolishness spoils great wisdom and honor.

² A wise person chooses the right road;
a fool takes the wrong one.
³ You can identify fools
just by the way they walk down the street!
⁴ If your boss is angry at you, don't quit!
A quiet spirit can overcome even great mistakes.

The Ironies of Life

⁵There is another evil I have seen under the sun. Kings and rulers make a grave mistake ⁶when they give great authority to foolish people and low positions to people of proven worth. ⁷I have even seen servants riding horseback like princes—and princes walking like servants!

⁸ When you dig a well,
you might fall in.
When you demolish an old wall,
you could be bitten by a snake.
⁹ When you work in a quarry,
stones might fall and crush you.
When you chop wood,
there is danger with each stroke of your ax.

¹⁰ Using a dull ax requires great strength,
so sharpen the blade.
That's the value of wisdom;
it helps you succeed.

9:2 As in Greek and Syriac versions and Latin Vulgate; Hebrew lacks *or bad.* **9:10** Hebrew *to Sheol.*

9:10 In the Old Testament, *Sheol* (or "the grave") is the abode of the dead. It is not necessarily associated with punishment, a perspective that gains more prominence in later Jewish thinking.
9:13-18 This poor man's particular wise action was effective in saving a whole town. Wisdom is better than power or strength (see 4:13; 7:19; 10:4), yet the worthy are not always honored, and even the wise are forgotten (see 2:16; 4:16).
10:5-7 The unjust and destructive delegation of authority to those incapable of using it wisely is a "grave mistake." Favoritism, nepotism, extortion, and bribery place unqualified people in powerful positions and should be avoided.
10:8-9 Every activity requires wisdom. Wisdom is evident in the safety precautions taken by those engaged in every profession, yet there is always a degree of risk in whatever we do.

¹¹ If a snake bites before you charm it,
what's the use of being a snake charmer?

¹² Wise words bring approval,
but fools are destroyed by their own words.

¹³ Fools base their thoughts on foolish assumptions,
so their conclusions will be wicked madness;
¹⁴ they chatter on and on.

No one really knows what is going to happen;
no one can predict the future.

¹⁵ Fools are so exhausted by a little work
that they can't even find their way home.

¹⁶ What sorrow for the land ruled by a servant,*
the land whose leaders feast in the morning.
¹⁷ Happy is the land whose king is a noble leader
and whose leaders feast at the proper time
to gain strength for their work, not to get drunk.

¹⁸ Laziness leads to a sagging roof;
idleness leads to a leaky house.

¹⁹ A party gives laughter,
wine gives happiness,
and money gives everything!

²⁰ Never make light of the king, even in your thoughts.
And don't make fun of the powerful, even in your own bedroom.
For a little bird might deliver your message
and tell them what you said.

The Uncertainties of Life

11 Send your grain across the seas,
and in time, profits will flow back to you.*
² But divide your investments among many places,*
for you do not know what risks might lie ahead.

³ When clouds are heavy, the rains come down.
Whether a tree falls north or south, it stays where it falls.

⁴ Farmers who wait for perfect weather never plant.
If they watch every cloud, they never harvest.

⁵ Just as you cannot understand the path of the wind or the mystery of a tiny baby growing in its mother's womb,* so you cannot understand the activity of God, who does all things.

⁶ Plant your seed in the morning and keep busy all afternoon, for you don't know if profit will come from one activity or another—or maybe both.

Advice for Young and Old

⁷ Light is sweet; how pleasant to see a new day dawning.

⁸ When people live to be very old, let them rejoice in every day of life. But let them also remember there will be many dark days. Everything still to come is meaningless.

⁹ Young people,* it's wonderful to be young! Enjoy every minute of it. Do everything you want to do; take it all in. But remember that you must give an account to God for everything you do. ¹⁰ So refuse to worry, and keep your body healthy. But remember that youth, with a whole life before you, is meaningless.

12 Don't let the excitement of youth cause you to forget your Creator. Honor him in your youth before you grow old and say, "Life is not pleasant anymore." ² Remember him before the light of the sun, moon, and stars is dim to your old eyes, and rain clouds continually darken your sky. ³ Remember him before your legs—the guards of your house—start to tremble; and before your shoulders—the strong men—stoop. Remember him before your teeth—your few remaining servants—stop grinding; and before your eyes—the women looking through the windows—see dimly.

⁴ Remember him before the door to life's opportunities is closed and the sound of work fades. Now you rise at the first chirping of the birds, but then all their sounds will grow faint.

⁵ Remember him before you become fearful of falling and worry about danger in the streets; before your hair turns white like an almond tree in bloom, and you drag along without energy like a dying grasshopper, and the caperberry no longer inspires sexual desire. Remember him before you near the grave, your everlasting home, when the mourners will weep at your funeral.

10:16 Or *a child*.   **11:1** Or *Give generously, / for your gifts will return to you later.* Hebrew reads *Throw your bread on the waters, / for after many days you will find it again.*   **11:2** Hebrew *among seven or even eight.*   **11:5** Some manuscripts read *Just as you cannot understand how breath comes to a tiny baby in its mother's womb.*   **11:9** Hebrew *Young man.*

10:15-20 The audience for the Teacher's speech might have been an assembly of government workers. How should one rule when power and wealth invite a lack of accountability?

11:2-10 The Teacher's repeated phrase translated here as "you do not know" and "you cannot understand" is heightened with the use of the feminine imagery of the womb (11:2, 5 [twice], 6). Mysteries surrounding conception, similar to so many mysteries in life, are knowable only by God. The Teacher encourages those who will listen not to "worry" (11:10) and to "enjoy" life while they are living (11:9)! Worrying takes away from our daily moments.

The Fear We Need

MY STORY WITH GOD

SCRIPTURE CONNECTION: ECCLESIASTES 12:13-14

When I was young, I remember being *so* excited when my dad pulled into the driveway after a long day at work. My brother and I would squeal and come running for hugs, burying our faces in his shirt and inhaling sawdust ... unless, of course, we had been naughty. Then "Daddy's home!" would be more ominous because of expected discipline.

Fear of God is similar. We fear God *because* we love him and want him to be pleased with us. Fear is an appropriate sense of awe at God's authority. We had no less "fear" of our dad on the days we ran to greet him. We just knew that he would be happy to see us.

Ecclesiastes paints a rather bleak picture of success. No matter how hard we work, life offers no guarantee.

The book's ending reminds us that even without earthly reward, God is still watching and weighing our deeds. It matters to God how we live.

> Fear is an appropriate sense of awe at God's authority. It matters to God how we live.

IMAGINE

Imagine that God showed up at your house. Would you run to meet him or cower in the closet? What does this say about the state of your heart?

What would it look like to cultivate a healthy fear of God?

> *"It's easy to fear the wrong things, such as how others see us and our work. Only God's assessment truly matters. How freeing to know that we work for an audience of one!"*

CARMEN JOY IMES, PhD, is an author, speaker, blogger, YouTuber, and serves as associate professor of Old Testament at Biola University in California.

⁶Yes, remember your Creator now while you are young, before the silver cord of life snaps and the golden bowl is broken. Don't wait until the water jar is smashed at the spring and the pulley is broken at the well. ⁷For then the dust will return to the earth, and the spirit will return to God who gave it.

Concluding Thoughts about the Teacher

⁸"Everything is meaningless," says the Teacher, "completely meaningless."

⁹Keep this in mind: The Teacher was considered wise, and he taught the people everything he knew. He listened carefully to many proverbs, studying and classifying them. ¹⁰The Teacher sought to find just the right words to express truths clearly.*

¹¹The words of the wise are like cattle prods—painful but helpful. Their collected sayings are like a nail-studded stick with which a shepherd* drives the sheep.

¹²But, my child,* let me give you some further advice: Be careful, for writing books is endless, and much study wears you out.

¹³That's the whole story. Here now is my final conclusion: Fear God and obey his commands, for this is everyone's duty. ¹⁴God will judge us for everything we do, including every secret thing, whether good or bad.

12:10 Or *sought to write what was upright and true.* 12:11 Or *one shepherd.* 12:12 Hebrew *my son.*

12:8-14 "Everything is meaningless," says the Teacher, "completely meaningless" (12:8). This main theme repeats as Ecclesiastes comes to a close. This word *hevel* ("meaningless") also means "a breath," "vanity," and "vapor," so this could also be translated as "Everything is a breath," emphasizing life's fleetingness. Therefore, the Teacher instructs all who will listen to "Fear God and obey his commands, for this is everyone's duty." The Teacher indicates that a person's meaning, purpose, and the enduring nature of our lives and work directly connect to our reverent and obedient relationship with God. God knows everything we do (12:14). How we choose to live matters, during the good times and the hard times, whether we are wealthy or poor, have status in this life or not. These final verses are an epilogue of wisdom, providing a dialogue between hopelessness and faith and the realities of life on earth.

Song of Songs

WHAT DO WE LEARN ABOUT GOD'S MISSION AND OURS?
God created us to long for and enjoy intimacy with another.

WHO WROTE IT? The book's first line suggests Solomon, but many interpreters believe this is a collection from several authors, as is Proverbs.

WHEN DID IT HAPPEN? Song of Songs was possibly written during the late 900s BC, during the period of Israel's united kingdom, or later.

HOW IS IT ORGANIZED?

1: The lovers' first meeting

2: Second meeting

3–4: Third meeting

5: Fourth meeting

6–7: Fifth meeting

8: Together at last

Words to Remember are highlighted throughout this book

FEATURE HIGHLIGHTS

+ *Sisters Who Help You Wait (812)*
+ *Sex (814)*
+ *Young Woman: Chosen and Cherished (817)*
+ *What Is God's Design for Sex? (818)*

HOW LONG DOES IT TAKE TO READ?

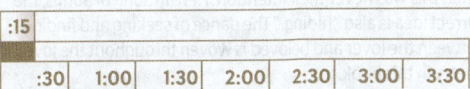

SONG OF SONGS 1

1 This is Solomon's song of songs, more wonderful than any other.

*Young Woman**

² Kiss me and kiss me again,
  for your love is sweeter than wine.
³ How pleasing is your fragrance;
  your name is like the spreading fragrance of scented oils.
  No wonder all the young women love you!
⁴ Take me with you; come, let's run!
  The king has brought me into his bedroom.

Young Women of Jerusalem

  How happy we are for you, O king.
  We praise your love even more than wine.

Young Woman

  How right they are to adore you.

⁵ I am dark but beautiful,
  O women of Jerusalem—
  dark as the tents of Kedar,
  dark as the curtains of Solomon's tents.
⁶ Don't stare at me because I am dark—
  the sun has darkened my skin.
  My brothers were angry with me;
  they forced me to care for their vineyards,
  so I couldn't care for myself—my own vineyard.

⁷ Tell me, my love, where are you leading your flock today?
  Where will you rest your sheep at noon?
  For why should I wander like a prostitute*
  among your friends and their flocks?

Young Man

⁸ If you don't know, O most beautiful woman,
  follow the trail of my flock,
  and graze your young goats by the shepherds' tents.
⁹ You are as exciting, my darling,
  as a mare among Pharaoh's stallions.
¹⁰ How lovely are your cheeks;
  your earrings set them afire!
  How lovely is your neck,
  enhanced by a string of jewels.
¹¹ We will make for you earrings of gold
  and beads of silver.

Young Woman

¹² The king is lying on his couch,
  enchanted by the fragrance of my perfume.
¹³ My lover is like a sachet of myrrh
  lying between my breasts.
¹⁴ He is like a bouquet of sweet henna blossoms
  from the vineyards of En-gedi.

Young Man

¹⁵ How beautiful you are, my darling,
  how beautiful!
  Your eyes are like doves.

1:1 The headings identifying the speakers are not in the original text, though the Hebrew usually gives clues by means of the gender of the person speaking. 1:7 Hebrew *like a veiled woman*.

1:1–8:14 Song of Songs is a collection of love poems. Egyptian love songs from the thirteenth through twelfth centuries BC provide a parallel to this type of ancient literature. As with Egyptian love poetry, Song of Songs includes different singing parts, which were likely added later to the text. In Song of Songs, there is a male singer, a female singer, and a chorus of voices (friends—the young women of Jerusalem).

1:1 The Hebrew title of this book, *Song of Songs*, is superlative, meaning this song is the greatest of all songs! Other superlatives in the Bible are "king of kings" (Ezekiel 26:7) and "Most Holy Place" (Exodus 26:33). This is a unique Bible book because it is a collection of love poems that describe longing and desire, hiding and seeking. They reveal intimacy through dialogue.

1:1 Traditionally, Solomon is thought to be the author because his name is in the 1:1 superscription, "Solomon's song of songs." Although the book mentions his name throughout (1:1; 3:7, 9, 11; 8:11, 12), the Hebrew text uses the third person. This can mean that the song is attributed to Solomon but may not have been written by him. This poem portrays an exclusive love relationship, while Solomon chose to have many wives and concubines.

1:5-6 The opening line here can also be translated as "dark and lovely" or "black and beautiful." The Septuagint (the Greek translation of the Old Testament) translates the Hebrew as "black and beautiful." In this context, the term "dark" does not refer only to her ethnicity but to her time working in the sun (1:6). The word for "dark" is used in other places to describe black hair (Leviticus 13:31) and black horses (Zechariah 6:2, 6). She is the only woman in the Old Testament who uses her own voice to describe herself. Her voice throughout Song of Songs reveals her to be a strong and confident woman. What a wonderful example for us, when we are prone to allow others' views to dictate how we should feel about ourselves. Throughout Song of Songs, this woman speaks for herself and celebrates her beauty!

1:7 The term translated here as "prostitute" is more literally "veil" in Hebrew and is not used very often in the Old Testament. Unfortunately, some interpretations mistake the term *veil* for "prostitute," but this is a false connection. According to the Middle Assyrian laws, prostitutes were not supposed to wear a veil, and one who did received painful penalties such as being beaten or having hot tar poured over her head. One biblical example that misleads some interpreters about prostitutes and veils is Tamar veiling herself in Genesis 38:15. Judah *thought* she was a prostitute, but the text does not state that she purposely dressed as one. The Hebrew for Judah's mistaken idea about Tamar is *khashav*, and it is a term that can mean "false assessment." The correct understanding of Tamar's veil is one of *hiding*. The Hebrew term for *veil* can be a cloak or robe, as also seen in 1 Samuel 28:14 (Samuel "wrapped in a robe"). As in these inaccurate interpretations, and for many women today, women can be mistaken by others as intending to be seen as sexual objects when this was never their intention. Here in Song of Songs, the correct idea is also "hiding." The dance of seeking and finding between the lover and beloved is woven throughout the love poetry in this book.

Young Woman

[16] You are so handsome, my love,
   pleasing beyond words!
   The soft grass is our bed;
[17] fragrant cedar branches are the beams of
   our house,
   and pleasant smelling firs are the rafters.

Young Woman

2 I am the spring crocus blooming on the
   Sharon Plain,*
   the lily of the valley.

Young Man

[2] Like a lily among thistles
   is my darling among young women.

Young Woman

[3] Like the finest apple tree in the orchard
   is my lover among other young men.
   I sit in his delightful shade
   and taste his delicious fruit.
[4] He escorts me to the banquet hall;
   it's obvious how much he loves me.
[5] Strengthen me with raisin cakes,
   refresh me with apples,
   for I am weak with love.
[6] His left arm is under my head,
   and his right arm embraces me.
[7] Promise me, O women of Jerusalem,
   by the gazelles and wild deer,
   not to awaken love until the time is right.*
[8] Ah, I hear my lover coming!
   He is leaping over the mountains,
   bounding over the hills.
[9] My lover is like a swift gazelle
   or a young stag.
   Look, there he is behind the wall,
   looking through the window,
   peering into the room.
[10] My lover said to me,
   "Rise up, my darling!
   Come away with me, my fair one!

[11] Look, the winter is past,
   and the rains are over and gone.
[12] The flowers are springing up,
   the season of singing birds* has come,
   and the cooing of turtledoves fills the air.
[13] The fig trees are forming young fruit,
   and the fragrant grapevines are blossoming.
   Rise up, my darling!
   Come away with me, my fair one!"

Young Man

[14] My dove is hiding behind the rocks,
   behind an outcrop on the cliff.
   Let me see your face;
   let me hear your voice.
   For your voice is pleasant,
   and your face is lovely.

Young Women of Jerusalem

[15] Catch all the foxes,
   those little foxes,
   before they ruin the vineyard of love,
   for the grapevines are blossoming!

Young Woman

[16] My lover is mine, and I am his.
   He browses among the lilies.
[17] Before the dawn breezes blow
   and the night shadows flee,
   return to me, my love, like a gazelle
   or a young stag on the rugged mountains.*

Young Woman

3 One night as I lay in bed, I yearned for my lover.
   I yearned for him, but he did not come.
[2] So I said to myself, "I will get up and roam the city,
   searching in all its streets and squares.
   I will search for the one I love."
   So I searched everywhere but did not find him.
[3] The watchmen stopped me as they made their
   rounds,
   and I asked, "Have you seen the one I love?"
[4] Then scarcely had I left them
   when I found my love!

2:1 Traditionally rendered *I am the rose of Sharon.* Sharon Plain is a region in the coastal plain of Palestine. **2:7** Or *not to awaken love until it is ready.* **2:12** Or *the season of pruning vines.* **2:17** Or *on the hills of Bether.*

2:1-2 "I am the spring crocus blooming on the Sharon Plain" is traditionally rendered "I am the rose of Sharon." Sharon Plain is a region in the coastal plain of Palestine. The Hebrew for "the lily of the valley" shows the woman's modesty and humility, as she claims to be but one flower among many in Sharon and in the expansive valleys of Israel. The man affirms her comparison to a lily but says that her beauty is far from common; she is "a lily among thistles." The Young Man refers to his beloved as "my darling": the Hebrew has the meaning of "companion." They are in love, and they are also friends.

2:7 This plea is obviously important to the Song of Songs; it is repeated in 3:5 and 8:4. A promise is requested. When a promise was made, witnesses were needed, and the wild animals were the only witnesses present. These graceful animals suggest a romantic pastoral setting. The phrase "not to awaken love until the time is right" could also be translated "not to awaken love until it is ready." As in 8:8-9, this promise shows the cultural value of virginity. The woman warns the women of Jerusalem to be cautious and not to hurry love.

3:4 The phrase referencing the young woman's "mother's house" is unusual in the Old Testament and appears in two other places: Ruth 1:8 and Genesis 24:28 (here, "home to . . . her family" in the NLT). For the woman to bring her lover to her mother's house is a bold move, characteristic of the woman throughout the poems. The use of the phrase "mother's house" reveals the stability of the maternal role and is symbolic of life, conception, identity, and nurturing support (for example, Song of Songs 6:9; 8:1). This phrase creates a strong sense of "home." This scene also displays a sense of humor in her boldness.

> I caught and held him tightly,
>   then I brought him to my mother's house,
>   into my mother's bed, where I had been
>   conceived.
> ⁵ Promise me, O women of Jerusalem,
>   by the gazelles and wild deer,
>   not to awaken love until the time is right.*

3:5 Or *not to awaken love until it is ready.*

Young Women of Jerusalem
> ⁶ Who is this sweeping in from the wilderness
>   like a cloud of smoke?
>   Who is it, fragrant with myrrh and frankincense
>   and every kind of spice?
> ⁷ Look, it is Solomon's carriage,
>   surrounded by sixty heroic men,
>   the best of Israel's soldiers.

Koinonia
IMAGE — MY STORY WITH COMMUNITY, WORKPLACE & CHURCH

Sisters Who Help You Wait
SCRIPTURE CONNECTION: SONG OF SONGS 2:7; 3:5; 8:4

Spiritual sisters can encourage us to be and stay in God's will. But our sisters in Christ can also encourage in ways that may unintentionally persuade us out of God's will.

Sisters in Christ pass their knowledge, success, and failures along to others. They make disciples of whatever they've done—whether good or not-so-good. As a result, sometimes we may get off track and go with our lustful feelings based on their experiences.

But the woman in Song of Songs sets a great example (2:7). Solomon's future bride shares her experience about saving sex for the right time, which shows us that:

- God gives us community so we can uplift each other to do the right thing.
- Sex is for the covenant (marriage) God created it for.

Have you had a friend help you stay pure and away from sexual immorality? Have you helped a friend do so?

This woman is a great example because she does wait for God's blessing of sex in marriage (3:11–5:3). And she was all the better for her obedience. The impeccable advice she gives provides wisdom for us to follow, too. Let's seek strong spiritual sisters who help us save sex for marriage and be spiritual sisters who do the same for others.

> Seek strong spiritual sisters who help you save sex for marriage.

IMAGINE

What has helped you or others save sex for marriage?

How have you seen women help their sisters abstain from sex before marriage?

"I am single as I write this and know the passion she felt in this passage. I thank God for the strength of my sisters in Christ that God has placed around me to keep me in his will."

RACHEL LINDSAY McCANTS is an author, speaker, and founder of R. Lindsay Unlimited, which encourages, inspires, and challenges ladies to raise their self-worth and standards and to walk in God's will, in Jesus' name.

8 They are all skilled swordsmen,
    experienced warriors.
  Each wears a sword on his thigh,
    ready to defend the king against an attack in the night.
9 King Solomon's carriage is built
    of wood imported from Lebanon.
10 Its posts are silver,
    its canopy gold;
    its cushions are purple.
  It was decorated with love
    by the young women of Jerusalem.

Young Woman
11 Come out to see King Solomon,
    young women of Jerusalem.*
  He wears the crown his mother gave him on his wedding day,
    his most joyous day.

Young Man
4 You are beautiful, my darling,
    beautiful beyond words.
  Your eyes are like doves
    behind your veil.
  Your hair falls in waves,
    like a flock of goats winding down the slopes of Gilead.
2 Your teeth are as white as sheep,
    recently shorn and freshly washed.
  Your smile is flawless,
    each tooth matched with its twin.*
3 Your lips are like scarlet ribbon;
    your mouth is inviting.
  Your cheeks are like rosy pomegranates
    behind your veil.
4 Your neck is as beautiful as the tower of David,
    jeweled with the shields of a thousand heroes.
5 Your breasts are like two fawns,
    twin fawns of a gazelle grazing among the lilies.
6 Before the dawn breezes blow
    and the night shadows flee,
  I will hurry to the mountain of myrrh
    and to the hill of frankincense.
7 You are altogether beautiful, my darling,
    beautiful in every way.

8 Come with me from Lebanon, my bride,
    come with me from Lebanon.
  Come down* from Mount Amana,
    from the peaks of Senir and Hermon,
    where the lions have their dens
    and leopards live among the hills.
9 You have captured my heart,
    my treasure,* my bride.
  You hold it hostage with one glance of your eyes,
    with a single jewel of your necklace.
10 Your love delights me,
    my treasure, my bride.
  Your love is better than wine,
    your perfume more fragrant than spices.
11 Your lips are as sweet as nectar, my bride.
    Honey and milk are under your tongue.
  Your clothes are scented
    like the cedars of Lebanon.

12 You are my private garden, my treasure, my bride,
    a secluded spring, a hidden fountain.
13 Your thighs shelter a paradise of pomegranates
    with rare spices—
    henna with nard,
14   nard and saffron,
    fragrant calamus and cinnamon,
  with all the trees of frankincense, myrrh, and aloes,
    and every other lovely spice.
15 You are a garden fountain,
    a well of fresh water
    streaming down from Lebanon's mountains.

Young Woman
16 Awake, north wind!
    Rise up, south wind!
  Blow on my garden
    and spread its fragrance all around.
  Come into your garden, my love;
    taste its finest fruits.

3:11 Hebrew *of Zion.* 4:2 Hebrew *Not one is missing; each has a twin.* 4:8 Or *Look down.* 4:9 Hebrew *my sister;* also in 4:10, 12.

3:6-11 Song of Songs could also be understood as describing a love triangle between the king, the king's concubine, and her true love, a common shepherd. According to this reading, Solomon's humility and generosity show in his attending this wedding of a woman who prefers a common shepherd's love over his. With Solomon in attendance, this ordinary wedding becomes a magnificent ceremony. If the Song is a collection of love poems, rather than a continuous narrative, then this poem describes what appears to be Solomon's wedding procession. People are amazed by the opulence of his carriage and the power represented by his entourage. The grandeur of the wedding displays the wealth of the king and the celebratory nature of a new marriage and all that it represents, which is an element many of our modern-day cultures still share.

4:1–5:1 The consummation of the marriage is described here. This poem is the first "descriptive poem" in the book (see also 5:10-16; 6:4-6; 7:2-8). Scholars commonly refer to these poems by the Arabic term *wasf* ("description") because these poems are similar in form to songs sung at modern Arabic weddings. These sensuous poems are preludes to sexual intimacy. In their descriptions of physical beauty, they often move—as this one does—from the head downward.
4:1 The man is about to consummate his love with the one who is his friend as well as his lover (see also 1:9; 4:7). He says that her hair is "like a flock of goats winding down the slopes of Gilead." Some Middle Eastern goats are very dark, almost black.

WHAT THE BIBLE SAYS ABOUT Sex

Our Sexual Desires Can Lead Us

King Solomon loved many foreign women.... The LORD had clearly instructed the people of Israel, "You must not marry them, because they will turn your hearts to their gods." Yet Solomon insisted on loving them anyway.... And in fact, they did turn his heart away from the LORD. **1 KINGS 11:1-3**

"But I say, anyone who even looks at a woman with lust has already committed adultery with her in his heart." **MATTHEW 5:28**

God Made Sex for Marriage

The husband should fulfill his wife's sexual needs, and the wife should fulfill her husband's needs.... Do not deprive each other of sexual relations, unless you both agree to refrain from sexual intimacy for a limited time so you can give yourselves more completely to prayer. Afterward, you should come together again so that Satan won't be able to tempt you because of your lack of self-control. **1 CORINTHIANS 7:3, 5**

Give honor to marriage ...

...and remain faithful to one another

Sex Is God's Good Idea

"This one is bone from my bone,
  and flesh from my flesh!
She will be called 'woman,'
  because she was taken from 'man.'"

This explains why a man leaves his father and mother and is joined to his wife, and the two are united into one. Now the man and his wife were both naked, but they felt no shame.
GENESIS 2:23-25

You say, "I am allowed to do anything"—but not everything is good for you.... You can't say that our bodies were made for sexual immorality. They were made for the Lord, and the Lord cares about our bodies.
1 CORINTHIANS 6:12-13

God Encourages Believers to Live in Sexual Purity

Run from sexual sin! No other sin so clearly affects the body as this one does. For sexual immorality is a sin against your own body. Don't you realize that your body is the temple of the Holy Spirit, who lives in you and was given to you by God? You do not belong to yourself, for God bought you with a high price. So you must honor God with your body. **1 CORINTHIANS 6:18-20**

Can a man scoop a flame into his lap
  and not have his clothes catch on fire?...

The man who commits adultery is an utter fool,
  for he destroys himself.
PROVERBS 6:27, 32

God's will is for you to be holy, so stay away from all sexual sin. Then each of you will control his own body and live in holiness and honor—not in lustful passion like the pagans who do not know God and his ways. **1 THESSALONIANS 4:3-5**

SONG OF SONGS 5

Young Man

5 ¹ I have entered my garden, my treasure,* my bride!
   I gather myrrh with my spices
and eat honeycomb with my honey.
   I drink wine with my milk.

Young Women of Jerusalem

Oh, lover and beloved, eat and drink!
   Yes, drink deeply of your love!

Young Woman

² I slept, but my heart was awake,
   when I heard my lover knocking and calling:
"Open to me, my treasure, my darling,
   my dove, my perfect one.
My head is drenched with dew,
   my hair with the dampness of the night."

³ But I responded,
"I have taken off my robe.
   Should I get dressed again?
I have washed my feet.
   Should I get them soiled?"

⁴ My lover tried to unlatch the door,
   and my heart thrilled within me.
⁵ I jumped up to open the door for my love,
   and my hands dripped with perfume.
My fingers dripped with lovely myrrh
   as I pulled back the bolt.
⁶ I opened to my lover,
   but he was gone!
   My heart sank.
I searched for him
   but could not find him anywhere.
I called to him,
   but there was no reply.
⁷ The night watchmen found me
   as they made their rounds.
They beat and bruised me
   and stripped off my veil,
   those watchmen on the walls.

⁸ Make this promise, O women of Jerusalem—
   If you find my lover,
   tell him I am weak with love.

Young Women of Jerusalem

⁹ Why is your lover better than all others,
   O woman of rare beauty?
What makes your lover so special
   that we must promise this?

Young Woman

¹⁰ My lover is dark and dazzling,
   better than ten thousand others!
¹¹ His head is finest gold,
   his wavy hair is black as a raven.
¹² His eyes sparkle like doves
   beside springs of water;
they are set like jewels
   washed in milk.
¹³ His cheeks are like gardens of spices
   giving off fragrance.
His lips are like lilies,
   perfumed with myrrh.
¹⁴ His arms are like rounded bars of gold,
   set with beryl.
His body is like bright ivory,
   glowing with lapis lazuli.
¹⁵ His legs are like marble pillars
   set in sockets of finest gold.
His posture is stately,
   like the noble cedars of Lebanon.
¹⁶ His mouth is sweetness itself;
   he is desirable in every way.
Such, O women of Jerusalem,
   is my lover, my friend.

Young Women of Jerusalem

6 ¹ Where has your lover gone,
   O woman of rare beauty?
Which way did he turn
   so we can help you find him?

Young Woman

² My lover has gone down to his garden,
   to his spice beds,
to browse in the gardens
   and gather the lilies.
³ I am my lover's, and my lover is mine.
   He browses among the lilies.

Young Man

⁴ You are beautiful, my darling,
   like the lovely city of Tirzah.
Yes, as beautiful as Jerusalem,
   as majestic as an army with billowing banners.
⁵ Turn your eyes away,
   for they overpower me.

5:1 Hebrew *my sister;* also in 5:2.

5:1 In entering "the garden," which is a reference to the woman's vagina, the man finds that there is no limit to what he can enjoy. The couple is ecstatic over finally unlocking the enjoyment of intercourse. The Young Women of Jerusalem encourage the couple to enjoy their sexual union to the fullest; there should be no guilt or shame in the physical and emotional pleasure between husband and wife.

5:2 This is an apt definition of a dream; she was physically asleep, but emotionally and psychologically awake. Opening doors was a metaphor for sexual activity in the ancient Near East (see also note on 8:9). By describing the man as knocking at the door and requesting entry, the poem suggests that the man is requesting sexual union. He awaits permission; he does not presume.

5:4-6 The man persists in his attempts to arouse the woman, and she eventually responds positively to his overtures. However, by the time she responds, he has given up or become otherwise occupied. This is a powerful poetic picture of the struggles of two lovers to be sexually intimate with each other.

5:7 The watchmen who were protectors in 3:3 now become demonized characters in her dream. What they do describes how she feels—pummeled and wounded. She feels that she has lost her dignity.

Young Woman

IDENTITY | Chosen and Cherished

We were created for love, to love with all our hearts and to be loved, cherished, and known. We desperately seek and search for a love that never fails, for a safe place for our fragile hearts, and for a deep connection that comes from being completely known.

Some of us might read about this beautiful bride and think, *Well, lucky her. But I'm not 'all that,' and I won't find that kind of love.* But many see Song of Songs pointing to another love—one available to all. This book, while telling us about one woman and one man, also points to a love relationship God has for each of us. It hints at how we can find our deepest desire to love and be loved by God's Son, Jesus.

In Song of Songs 3:2-4, the Young Woman searches for the lover of her soul. When she finally finds him, she holds him tightly, clinging to his love for her. In Matthew 10:39, Jesus invites us to similarly choose him rather than clinging to our lives.

The Young Woman's lover then comes for her in a carriage (Song of Songs 3:9), to carry her to a relationship prepared just for her. The carriage is made of splendid light-colored wood from Lebanon—the same wood used to build the Temple—befitting the luxury of his royal position. The posts are costly silver and the canopy incorruptible, pure gold, reflecting the value of their love (3:10). The cushions are purple, the color of the curtain to the Temple's Most Holy Place. This wedding celebrates their love relationship as royally set apart, decorated with love, delight, and passionate affection. For all who follow Jesus, we see a wedding feast as a repeating theme in the Bible (for example, Revelation 19:6-9).

The Young Man exudes a fragrant perfume of love that dispels any lingering, residual odors of rejection, neglect, or abandonment (Song of Songs 3:6). And, just so, Jesus cleanses our hearts, leaving only the sweet aroma of his acceptance, forgiveness, and redeeming love (Titus 3:5; Hebrews 10:22).

In this secret place with Jesus and in the safety of his unfailing love, all of us—not just one chosen Young Woman—can experience the love we were created for.

> In this secret place with Jesus and in the safety of his unfailing love, we can experience the love we were created for.

THE YOUNG WOMAN'S STORY IS TOLD IN SONG OF SONGS.

IDENTIFY

What does the splendor of the relationship described in Song of Songs show you about how God loves you?

"God—your bridegroom—is calling! He has prepared a special place for you to experience him as the lover of your soul. He wants you! He delights in you! He likes you! And he loves you! You are valuable, chosen, and cherished by God."

JULIE WRIGHT is author of *Redeeming Eve: When a Woman Lives Loved* and founder of Live Loved Ministry. Her passion is for women to embrace God's love and cultivate an authentic relationship with Jesus.

SONG OF SONGS 7

Your hair falls in waves,
  like a flock of goats winding down the slopes
    of Gilead.
⁶ Your teeth are as white as sheep
    that are freshly washed.
Your smile is flawless,
    each tooth matched with its twin.*
⁷ Your cheeks are like rosy pomegranates
    behind your veil.

⁸ Even among sixty queens
    and eighty concubines
    and countless young women,
⁹ I would still choose my dove, my perfect one—
    the favorite of her mother,
    dearly loved by the one who bore her.
The young women see her and praise her;
    even queens and royal concubines sing her
      praises:
¹⁰ "Who is this, arising like the dawn,
    as fair as the moon,
as bright as the sun,
    as majestic as an army with billowing
      banners?"

Young Woman
¹¹ I went down to the grove of walnut trees
    and out to the valley to see the new spring
      growth,
to see whether the grapevines had budded
    or the pomegranates were in bloom.
¹² Before I realized it,
    my strong desires had taken me to the chariot
      of a noble man.*

Young Women of Jerusalem
¹³ *Return, return to us, O maid of Shulam.
    Come back, come back, that we may see
      you again.

Young Man
Why do you stare at this young woman of Shulam,
    as she moves so gracefully between two lines
      of dancers?*

7
¹ *How beautiful are your sandaled feet,
    O queenly maiden.
Your rounded thighs are like jewels,
    the work of a skilled craftsman.
² Your navel is perfectly formed
    like a goblet filled with mixed wine.
Between your thighs lies a mound of wheat
    bordered with lilies.
³ Your breasts are like two fawns,
    twin fawns of a gazelle.

6:6 Hebrew *Not one is missing; each has a twin.* 6:12 Or *to the royal chariots of my people,* or *to the chariots of Amminadab.* The meaning of the Hebrew is uncertain. 6:13a Verse 6:13 is numbered 7:1 in Hebrew text. 6:13b Or *as you would at the movements of two armies?* or *as you would at the dance of Mahanaim?* The meaning of the Hebrew is uncertain. 7:1 Verses 7:1-13 are numbered 7:2-14 in Hebrew text.

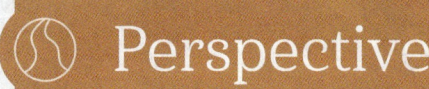
Perspective

What is God's design for sex?

SCRIPTURE CONNECTION: SONG OF SONGS 8:6-7

Every culture has varying ideas about sexual fulfillment. Is sex a taboo subject or widely regarded as a healthy expression of love? Is it strictly for reproduction or is it also for fun? Is it intended to control women or to empower and liberate our agency and desires?

Song of Songs portrays poetic and explicit love between newlyweds. Though it never mentions the Creator, his brilliant design is on full display between this young wife and her husband.

God has gifted women and men as uniquely sexual beings. Unlike other creatures who reproduce only as a function of instinct, God intended our experience to be whole and intimate, sacred and bonding, covenantal and even thrilling.

But what God originally designed can sadly be different from our experience in our broken world. Indulging in casual sex can cheapen the experience and create unintended emotional pain. Having a self-centered partner can leave us feeling unsatisfied, with our emotional and physical needs unmet. Avoiding natural, healthy discussions about sex can lead to undeserved shame and lasting trauma.

Like the Young Woman in these verses, we can acknowledge that God's design for sex is a healthy, fulfilling, intimate experience with a loving and attentive husband.

VIEWPOINTS

HERS: *As the Young Woman is embraced, we sense no hint of reservation. What is her level of trust with her husband?*
MINE: *"My greatest thrill in lovemaking derives not from risk but safety, knowing and being known in covenant and love."*
YOURS: *Most of us have suffered chasms between God's design and our life experiences. How might God be inviting you to begin bridging that gap?*

MISTY ARTERBURN is an author and speaker, contributing to Bible projects, devotionals, and recovery materials for over twenty years. Wife and mom to five, Misty is the founder of Recovery Girls and the general editor of *The One Year Bible for Women*.

⁴ Your neck is as beautiful as an ivory tower.
  Your eyes are like the sparkling pools in Heshbon
    by the gate of Bath-rabbim.
  Your nose is as fine as the tower of Lebanon
    overlooking Damascus.
⁵ Your head is as majestic as Mount Carmel,
    and the sheen of your hair radiates royalty.
  The king is held captive by its tresses.
⁶ Oh, how beautiful you are!
  How pleasing, my love, how full of delights!
⁷ You are slender like a palm tree,
    and your breasts are like its clusters of fruit.
⁸ I said, "I will climb the palm tree
    and take hold of its fruit."
  May your breasts be like grape clusters,
    and the fragrance of your breath like apples.
⁹ May your kisses be as exciting as the best wine—

Young Woman
  Yes, wine that goes down smoothly for my lover,
    flowing gently over lips and teeth.*
¹⁰ I am my lover's,
    and he claims me as his own.
¹¹ Come, my love, let us go out to the fields
    and spend the night among the wildflowers.*
¹² Let us get up early and go to the vineyards
    to see if the grapevines have budded,
  if the blossoms have opened,
    and if the pomegranates have bloomed.
  There I will give you my love.
¹³ There the mandrakes give off their fragrance,
    and the finest fruits are at our door,
  new delights as well as old,
    which I have saved for you, my lover.

Young Woman

8 Oh, I wish you were my brother,
    who nursed at my mother's breasts.
  Then I could kiss you no matter who was watching,
    and no one would criticize me.
² I would bring you to my childhood home,
    and there you would teach me.*
  I would give you spiced wine to drink,
    my sweet pomegranate wine.
³ Your left arm would be under my head,
    and your right arm would embrace me.
⁴ Promise me, O women of Jerusalem,
    not to awaken love until the time is right.*

Young Women of Jerusalem
⁵ Who is this sweeping in from the desert,
    leaning on her lover?

Young Woman
  I aroused you under the apple tree,
    where your mother gave you birth,
    where in great pain she delivered you.
⁶ Place me like a seal over your heart,
    like a seal on your arm.
  For love is as strong as death,
    its jealousy* as enduring as the grave.*
  Love flashes like fire,
    the brightest kind of flame.
⁷ Many waters cannot quench love,
    nor can rivers drown it.
  If a man tried to buy love
    with all his wealth,
    his offer would be utterly scorned.

The Young Woman's Brothers
⁸ We have a little sister
    too young to have breasts.
  What will we do for our sister
    if someone asks to marry her?
⁹ If she is a virgin, like a wall,
    we will protect her with a silver tower.
  But if she is promiscuous, like a swinging door,
    we will block her door with a cedar bar.

Young Woman
¹⁰ I was a virgin, like a wall;
    now my breasts are like towers.
  When my lover looks at me,
    he is delighted with what he sees.
¹¹ Solomon has a vineyard at Baal-hamon,
    which he leases out to tenant farmers.
  Each of them pays a thousand pieces of silver
    for harvesting its fruit.
¹² But my vineyard is mine to give,
    and Solomon need not pay a thousand pieces
      of silver.
  But I will give two hundred pieces
    to those who care for its vines.

Young Man
¹³ O my darling, lingering in the gardens,
    your companions are fortunate to hear your
      voice.
  Let me hear it, too!

Young Woman
¹⁴ Come away, my love! Be like a gazelle
    or a young stag on the mountains
      of spices.

7:9 As in Greek and Syriac versions and Latin Vulgate; Hebrew reads *over lips of sleepers*. 7:11 Or *in the villages*. 8:2 Or *there she will teach me*. 8:4 Or *not to awaken love until it is ready*. 8:6a Or *its passion*. 8:6b Hebrew *as Sheol*.

8:9 There appear to be two metaphorical meanings for the term *wall*: First, the prepubescent girl's chest is like a wall (see 8:10); or, second, until she is married, she should be abstinent, impenetrable like a wall. Towers were used as lookouts for protecting the city; a silver one would be more prominent and impregnable. If the woman is already a wall, having kept her virginity, her brothers will honor and reinforce her resolve. On the other hand, a "swinging door" indicates promiscuity, and if the woman has been promiscuous, the brothers will force her to restrain herself.

Isaiah

WHAT DO WE LEARN ABOUT GOD'S MISSION AND OURS?
God won't overlook our wrongs, but he longs to forgive and restore.

WHO WROTE IT? Isaiah, son of Amoz, prophet to Judah.

WHEN DID IT HAPPEN? During the time of Israel's divided kingdom, perhaps during the 700s BC.

HOW IS IT ORGANIZED?

- 1–12: God judges Judah, promises salvation, and calls Isaiah to be a prophet
- 13–23: The Lord judges the nations
- 24–27: More salvation promises
- 28–33: More judgments
- 34–35: More salvation promises
- 36–39: God rescues Jerusalem from an attack
- 40–48: God will deliver his captive people
- 49–57: The Suffering Servant as Savior
- 58–66: Everlasting judgment and salvation

FEATURE HIGHLIGHTS

+ *What Is the Purpose of Prophets?* (823)
+ *"Here I am. Send Me": Embracing Our Call* (830)
+ *Isaiah's Wife: Bearing Pain to Bear Hope* (833)
+ *Isaiah in the New Testament* (845)
+ *Woe? Promises* (850)

Words to Remember are highlighted throughout this book

HOW LONG DOES IT TAKE TO READ?

3:00

:30 | 1:00 | 1:30 | 2:00 | 2:30 | 3:00 | 3:30

Timeline (BC)

BC	Event
760	AMOS BECOMES A PROPHET
753	HOSEA BECOMES A PROPHET
742	MICAH BECOMES A PROPHET
740	ISAIAH BECOMES A PROPHET
735	AHAZ BECOMES KING OF JUDAH
732	HOSHEA BECOMES KING OF ISRAEL
722	ISRAEL FALLS TO THE ASSYRIANS
715	HEZEKIAH, SON OF ABIJAH AND AHAZ, BECOMES KING OF JUDAH
701	SENNACHERIB LAYS SIEGE TO JERUSALEM
697	MANASSEH BECOMES KING OF JUDAH
681	ISAIAH'S MINISTRY ENDS
640	JOSIAH, SON OF JEDIDAH AND AMON, BECOMES KING OF JUDAH
621	JOSIAH CONSULTS HULDAH THE PROPHET
586	JUDAH FALLS TO BABYLON; TEMPLE DESTROYED

ISAIAH 1

1 These are the visions that Isaiah son of Amoz saw concerning Judah and Jerusalem. He saw these visions during the years when Uzziah, Jotham, Ahaz, and Hezekiah were kings of Judah.*

A Message for Rebellious Judah

2 Listen, O heavens! Pay attention, earth!
   This is what the LORD says:
"The children I raised and cared for
   have rebelled against me.
3 Even an ox knows its owner,
   and a donkey recognizes its master's care—
but Israel doesn't know its master.
   My people don't recognize my care for them."
4 Oh, what a sinful nation they are—
   loaded down with a burden of guilt.
They are evil people,
   corrupt children who have rejected the LORD.
They have despised the Holy One of Israel
   and turned their backs on him.

5 Why do you continue to invite punishment?
   Must you rebel forever?
Your head is injured,
   and your heart is sick.
6 You are battered from head to foot—
   covered with bruises, welts, and infected wounds—
without any soothing ointments or bandages.
7 Your country lies in ruins,
   and your towns are burned.
Foreigners plunder your fields before your eyes
   and destroy everything they see.
8 Beautiful Jerusalem* stands abandoned
   like a watchman's shelter in a vineyard,
   like a lean-to in a cucumber field after the harvest,
   like a helpless city under siege.
9 If the LORD of Heaven's Armies
   had not spared a few of us,*
we would have been wiped out like Sodom,
   destroyed like Gomorrah.

10 Listen to the LORD, you leaders of "Sodom."
    Listen to the law of our God, people of "Gomorrah."
11 "What makes you think I want all your sacrifices?"
    says the LORD.
"I am sick of your burnt offerings of rams
    and the fat of fattened cattle.
I get no pleasure from the blood
    of bulls and lambs and goats.
12 When you come to worship me,
    who asked you to parade through my courts
       with all your ceremony?
13 Stop bringing me your meaningless gifts;
    the incense of your offerings disgusts me!
As for your celebrations of the new moon and the Sabbath
    and your special days for fasting—
they are all sinful and false.
    I want no more of your pious meetings.

1:1 These kings reigned from 792 to 686 B.C.   **1:8** Hebrew *The daughter of Zion.*   **1:9** Greek version reads *a few of our children.* Compare Rom 9:29.

1:1–3:26 Isaiah uses a courtroom metaphor in these first three chapters to describe the conflict between the Lord and his people. The people of Judah have broken the covenant and are on trial. Heaven and earth bear witness (1:2). One of the areas of blame is that the people of Judah have failed to act justly; 1:17 reveals God's core values: "Learn to do good. Seek justice. Help the oppressed. Defend the cause of orphans. Fight for the rights of widows." These are good reminders for us today: seeking justice for those who need help reveals God's heart and character as well as our own.

1:4–12:6 One of the central themes in the book of Isaiah is that God is "the Holy One of Israel." In this section, Isaiah opens with this reference to Yahweh (God's personal name, see Exodus 3:13-15) and closes with it, referring both times to God as the "Holy One of Israel." This section also opens with "Beautiful Jerusalem" (Isaiah 1:8, literally "the daughter of Zion") and closes with "people of Jerusalem" (12:6, literally "people of Zion"). This literary device is called an *inclusio*, where biblical images or specific words are found at the beginning and end of sections, like bookends on a shelf. Recognizing these literary devices helps us discover the important themes in these passages. Here, Yahweh as the "Holy One of Israel" and Yahweh's "people" as the "people of Jerusalem" are the main focus of this section.

1:8 In Hebrew, the phrase translated here as "beautiful Jerusalem" can also be translated literally "the daughter of Zion." The term *Zion* is used throughout the Old Testament in literal and metaphorical ways. As a place, Zion is a hill or mount in Jerusalem. It became the location of the Temple, where Solomon brought the Ark of the Covenant. After this, the Temple Mount area is often called Zion in the Psalms and the Prophets. Metaphorically, along with the Temple Mount, Zion also can refer to Jerusalem and the people living in Jerusalem. Zion carried with it the notion of God's presence (Psalm 46).

1:16 Isaiah is full of poetry. In Hebrew, *parallelism* is a literary device used to communicate a message in poetic form. For example, "wash yourselves and be clean" can seem redundant, but this repetitive language echoes and extends the idea of purity. Parallelism has many functions, and one is to take an idea and amplify it. Here, Yahweh asks the people to turn back and repent. They are worshiping through their outward activities only. God sees their unjust ways and calls them to worship with their lips *and* their actions, to reflect the character of the God they serve, by living righteous, just, and compassionate lives.

1:21-22 Marriage and faithfulness are metaphors used throughout Isaiah and the other prophets, such as Jeremiah (Jeremiah 3:6-14), for Israel's relationship to the Lord. Family metaphors are used to express intimacy and pain. Here, Jerusalem is described as a "prostitute" because of unfaithfulness. Some of the ways the people were unfaithful included worshiping other gods. Keeping our lives lovingly devoted to God first equates to faithfulness. Yet even when we are unfaithful, God is seeking us and desiring us to return to our first love (Revelation 2:4).

¹⁴ I hate your new moon celebrations and your
     annual festivals.
   They are a burden to me. I cannot stand them!
¹⁵ When you lift up your hands in prayer, I will not
     look.
   Though you offer many prayers, I will not
     listen,
   for your hands are covered with the blood of
     innocent victims.
¹⁶ Wash yourselves and be clean!
   Get your sins out of my sight.
   Give up your evil ways.
¹⁷ Learn to do good.
   Seek justice.
   Help the oppressed.
   Defend the cause of orphans.
   Fight for the rights of widows.

¹⁸ "Come now, let's settle this,"
     says the Lord.
   "Though your sins are like scarlet,
     I will make them as white as snow.
   Though they are red like crimson,
     I will make them as white as wool.
¹⁹ If you will only obey me,
     you will have plenty to eat.
²⁰ But if you turn away and refuse to listen,
     you will be devoured by the sword of your
       enemies.
   I, the Lord, have spoken!"

Unfaithful Jerusalem

²¹ See how Jerusalem, once so faithful,
     has become a prostitute.
   Once the home of justice and righteousness,
     she is now filled with murderers.
²² Once like pure silver,
     you have become like worthless slag.
   Once so pure,
     you are now like watered-down wine.
²³ Your leaders are rebels,
     the companions of thieves.
   All of them love bribes
     and demand payoffs,
   but they refuse to defend the cause of orphans
     or fight for the rights of widows.
²⁴ Therefore, the Lord, the Lord of Heaven's
     Armies,
     the Mighty One of Israel, says,
   "I will take revenge on my enemies
     and pay back my foes!
²⁵ I will raise my fist against you.
   I will melt you down and skim off your slag.
   I will remove all your impurities.
²⁶ Then I will give you good judges again
     and wise counselors like you used to have.
   Then Jerusalem will again be called the Home
     of Justice
     and the Faithful City."

Perspective

What is the purpose of prophets?

SCRIPTURE CONNECTION: ISAIAH 1:1

The Old Testament is full of words from people called *prophets*. But what does that even mean?

The very first verse of the first chapter relays Isaiah's vision concerning Judah and Jerusalem. The words he shares are difficult, predicting future and current condemnation, but also encouraging, promising God's salvation and restoration.

Theologian Walter Brueggemann says that prophets typically "nurture, nourish, and evoke a consciousness and perception alternative to the consciousness and perception of the dominant culture around us." Most often, prophets address people who are not doing justice or righteousness.

A prophet's words give people the opportunity to do what is right, to return to the heart of God, and to look and act like God's people.

VIEWPOINTS

HIS: *How do you think Isaiah felt about the people's reaction?*
MINE: *"Like Isaiah's audience, I can find it hard to hear that I am a part of the problem. Reframing words from a call-out to an invitation has helped me respond."*
YOURS: *Have you had someone act as a prophet in your life, calling you to repentance and moving closer to God? How?*

ALEXIANA FRY, MDiv, PhD, is a devoted academic in the Hebrew Bible. She is a professor, wife, and pug mom who is working on her first book post-dissertation.

²⁷ Zion will be restored by justice;
     those who repent will be revived by
       righteousness.
²⁸ But rebels and sinners will be completely
     destroyed,
     and those who desert the Lord will be consumed.
²⁹ You will be ashamed of your idol worship
     in groves of sacred oaks.

You will blush because you worshiped
  in gardens dedicated to idols.
30 You will be like a great tree with withered leaves,
  like a garden without water.
31 The strongest among you will disappear like straw;
  their evil deeds will be the spark that sets it on fire.
  They and their evil works will burn up together,
  and no one will be able to put out the fire.

The Lord's Future Reign

2 This is a vision that Isaiah son of Amoz saw concerning Judah and Jerusalem:

2 In the last days, the mountain of the Lord's house
  will be the highest of all—
  the most important place on earth.
It will be raised above the other hills,
  and people from all over the world will
  stream there to worship.
3 People from many nations will come and say,
  "Come, let us go up to the mountain of the Lord,
  to the house of Jacob's God.
There he will teach us his ways,
  and we will walk in his paths."
For the Lord's teaching will go out from Zion;
  his word will go out from Jerusalem.
4 The Lord will mediate between nations
  and will settle international disputes.
They will hammer their swords into plowshares
  and their spears into pruning hooks.
Nation will no longer fight against nation,
  nor train for war anymore.

A Warning of Judgment

5 Come, descendants of Jacob,
  let us walk in the light of the Lord!

2:16 Hebrew *every ship of Tarshish.*

6 For the Lord has rejected his people,
  the descendants of Jacob,
because they have filled their land with
  practices from the East
  and with sorcerers, as the Philistines do.
  They have made alliances with pagans.
7 Israel is full of silver and gold;
  there is no end to its treasures.
Their land is full of warhorses;
  there is no end to its chariots.
8 Their land is full of idols;
  the people worship things they have made
  with their own hands.
9 So now they will be humbled,
  and all will be brought low—
  do not forgive them.
10 Crawl into caves in the rocks.
  Hide in the dust
  from the terror of the Lord
  and the glory of his majesty.
11 Human pride will be brought down,
  and human arrogance will be humbled.
Only the Lord will be exalted
  on that day of judgment.
12 For the Lord of Heaven's Armies
  has a day of reckoning.
He will punish the proud and mighty
  and bring down everything that is exalted.
13 He will cut down the tall cedars of Lebanon
  and all the mighty oaks of Bashan.
14 He will level all the high mountains
  and all the lofty hills.
15 He will break down every high tower
  and every fortified wall.
16 He will destroy all the great trading ships*
  and every magnificent vessel.

2:1-3 In this vision, Isaiah reveals that Yahweh is Lord over every nation and that "people from many nations" will come to his house. The nations will seek the Lord, to learn the ways of truth and to "walk in his paths" (2:3). Every person will know and acknowledge God's transformative power!

2:2 In the Old Testament, the expression "the last days" is a general reference to the future era when God will judge all nations (see Jeremiah 49:39; Ezekiel 38:16; Hosea 3:5). In the New Testament, it is used to refer to the period that began with the coming of the Lord Jesus (Hebrews 1:2) and more specifically to the period immediately preceding the end of the present age (2 Peter 3:3). "The mountain of the Lord's house" referred to the Temple Mount. This location symbolized God's glorious enthronement (see Isaiah 6:1) and his kingdom on earth. Isaiah's focus on God's exalted and supreme kingship flows out of his famous vision of God (6:1-13). Far from being a dream only for Israel, Isaiah's prophetic hope extends beyond Judah and Jerusalem to include "people from all over the world."

2:5 Walking in God's "light" (his revelation) will lead to our glorious participation in his Kingdom (see 60:1; 1 John 1:7). God is the only light that overcomes the darkness of sin and evil (Isaiah 9:2). People cannot generate such light in and of themselves (59:9); they must walk in the light God provides, as they trust him and live in obedience to his will (50:10). The phrase "descendants of Jacob" alludes to Israel's special historic relationship with the Lord as well as their history of sinfulness and rebellion (see 14:1; 48:1).

2:11-12 A key theme in Isaiah is that the Lord will be "exalted," and humble people will be restored (57:15), while proud and mighty people are humbled (26:5). The "day of judgment" and the "day of reckoning" are also called the "day of the Lord" and "that day." There are seven such references in Isaiah 2–4 (2:11, 17, 20; 3:6, 18; 4:1, 2).

2:15-17 Building high towers and walls provides a sense of security against enemy threats. Great trading ships (literally, "every ship of Tarshish") reveal incredible economic human achievement and advancement. These human accomplishments can result in pride. In this judgment and warning against Judah and Jerusalem, Isaiah reminds them that everything they take pride in will be judged. None of these human achievements will last. The Lord is the only one worthy of our trust!

¹⁷ Human pride will be humbled,
    and human arrogance will be brought down.
Only the LORD will be exalted
    on that day of judgment.

¹⁸ Idols will completely disappear.
¹⁹ When the LORD rises to shake the earth,
    his enemies will crawl into holes in the ground.
They will hide in caves in the rocks
    from the terror of the LORD
    and the glory of his majesty.
²⁰ On that day of judgment they will abandon the gold and silver idols
    they made for themselves to worship.
They will leave their gods to the rodents and bats,
²¹   while they crawl away into caverns
    and hide among the jagged rocks in the cliffs.
They will try to escape the terror of the LORD
    and the glory of his majesty
    as he rises to shake the earth.
²² Don't put your trust in mere humans.
    They are as frail as breath.
    What good are they?

Judgment against Judah

3 The Lord, the LORD of Heaven's Armies,
    will take away from Jerusalem and Judah
    everything they depend on:
        every bit of bread
        and every drop of water,
² all their heroes and soldiers,
    judges and prophets,
    fortune-tellers and elders,
³ army officers and high officials,
    advisers, skilled sorcerers, and astrologers.
⁴ I will make boys their leaders,
    and toddlers their rulers.
⁵ People will oppress each other—
    man against man,
    neighbor against neighbor.
Young people will insult their elders,
    and vulgar people will sneer at the honorable.

⁶ In those days a man will say to his brother,
"Since you have a coat, you be our leader!
    Take charge of this heap of ruins!"
⁷ But he will reply,
    "No! I can't help.
    I don't have any extra food or clothes.
    Don't put me in charge!"

⁸ For Jerusalem will stumble,
    and Judah will fall,
because they speak out against the LORD and refuse to obey him.
    They provoke him to his face.
⁹ The very look on their faces gives them away.
    They display their sin like the people of Sodom
    and don't even try to hide it.
They are doomed!
    They have brought destruction upon themselves.

¹⁰ Tell the godly that all will be well for them.
    They will enjoy the rich reward they have earned!
¹¹ But the wicked are doomed,
    for they will get exactly what they deserve.

¹² Childish leaders oppress my people,
    and women rule over them.
O my people, your leaders mislead you;
    they send you down the wrong road.

¹³ The LORD takes his place in court
    and presents his case against his people.*
¹⁴ The LORD comes forward to pronounce judgment
    on the elders and rulers of his people:
"You have ruined Israel, my vineyard.
    Your houses are filled with things stolen from the poor.
¹⁵ How dare you crush my people,
    grinding the faces of the poor into the dust?"
    demands the Lord, the LORD of Heaven's Armies.

A Warning to Jerusalem

¹⁶ The LORD says, "Beautiful Zion* is haughty:
    craning her elegant neck,
    flirting with her eyes,
    walking with dainty steps,
    tinkling her ankle bracelets.
¹⁷ So the Lord will send scabs on her head;
    the LORD will make beautiful Zion bald."

¹⁸ On that day of judgment
    the Lord will strip away everything that makes her beautiful:
    ornaments, headbands, crescent necklaces,
¹⁹   earrings, bracelets, and veils;

3:13 As in Greek and Syriac versions; Hebrew reads *against the peoples.* **3:16** Or *The women of Zion* (with corresponding changes to plural forms through verse 24); Hebrew reads *The daughters of Zion;* also in 3:17.

3:10-11 Isaiah uses the language of the wisdom writers ("the godly" and "the wicked") in this judgment oracle. For example, Psalms 1 and 2 introduce these two paths. The themes of "the godly" (often those that are oppressed, poor, and needy) and "the wicked" (those that are greedy, violent, rejecting the Lord) weave all throughout the Psalms. Choosing the path of righteousness, the path of "the godly," leads to life (Psalms 1:1-6; 73:1, 26). The path of the godly involves recognizing our need for God.

3:12 In this passage, youth and women ruling are being viewed as an indictment of social disorder in a patriarchal society. This does not mean that women do not make good rulers (for example, Deborah in Judges 4–5).

²⁰ scarves, ankle bracelets, sashes,
   perfumes, and charms;
²¹ rings, jewels,
²² party clothes, gowns, capes, and purses;
²³ mirrors, fine linen garments,
   head ornaments, and shawls.

²⁴ Instead of smelling of sweet perfume, she will
      stink.
   She will wear a rope for a sash,
      and her elegant hair will fall out.
   She will wear rough burlap instead of rich robes.
      Shame will replace her beauty.*
²⁵ The men of the city will be killed with the sword,
      and her warriors will die in battle.
²⁶ The gates of Zion will weep and mourn.
      The city will be like a ravaged woman,
         huddled on the ground.

4 In that day so few men will be left that seven women will fight for each man, saying, "Let us all marry you! We will provide our own food and clothing. Only let us take your name so we won't be mocked as old maids."

A Promise of Restoration

² But in that day, the branch* of the LORD
      will be beautiful and glorious;
   the fruit of the land will be the pride and glory
      of all who survive in Israel.
³ All who remain in Zion
      will be a holy people—
   those who survive the destruction of Jerusalem
      and are recorded among the living.
⁴ The Lord will wash the filth from beautiful Zion*
      and cleanse Jerusalem of its bloodstains
      with the hot breath of fiery judgment.
⁵ Then the LORD will provide shade for Mount
      Zion
      and all who assemble there.
   He will provide a canopy of cloud during the day
      and smoke and flaming fire at night,
         covering the glorious land.
⁶ It will be a shelter from daytime heat
      and a hiding place from storms and rain.

A Song about the LORD's Vineyard

5 Now I will sing for the one I love
      a song about his vineyard:
   My beloved had a vineyard
      on a rich and fertile hill.
² He plowed the land, cleared its stones,
      and planted it with the best vines.
   In the middle he built a watchtower
      and carved a winepress in the nearby rocks.
   Then he waited for a harvest of sweet grapes,
      but the grapes that grew were bitter.

³ Now, you people of Jerusalem and Judah,
      you judge between me and my vineyard.
⁴ What more could I have done for my vineyard
      that I have not already done?
   When I expected sweet grapes,
      why did my vineyard give me bitter
         grapes?

⁵ Now let me tell you
      what I will do to my vineyard:
   I will tear down its hedges
      and let it be destroyed.
   I will break down its walls
      and let the animals trample it.
⁶ I will make it a wild place
      where the vines are not pruned and the
         ground is not hoed,
      a place overgrown with briers and thorns.
   I will command the clouds
      to drop no rain on it.

⁷ The nation of Israel is the vineyard of the LORD
      of Heaven's Armies.
   The people of Judah are his pleasant garden.
   He expected a crop of justice,
      but instead he found oppression.
   He expected to find righteousness,
      but instead he heard cries of violence.

Judah's Guilt and Judgment

⁸ What sorrow for you who buy up house after
      house and field after field,
   until everyone is evicted and you live alone
      in the land.

3:24 As in Dead Sea Scrolls; Masoretic Text reads *robes / because instead of beauty.* 4:2 Or *the Branch.* 4:4 Or *from the women of Zion;* Hebrew reads *from the daughters of Zion.*

4:2 "The branch" (or "the Branch") in this context probably refers to the remnant that would constitute Israel's new beginning after the Exile (see 6:13). Some also understand this as a reference to the ideal descendant of David, the Messiah (see 11:1; Jeremiah 23:5; 33:15-16; Zechariah 3:8; 6:12). God promises a "beautiful and glorious" transformation for his people from shame and disgrace (Isaiah 3:17-25) to fertility and beauty that would display God's presence and blessing for Israel's survivors (4:6). "The fruit of the land," nature itself, would also be transformed from desolation to glory. Elsewhere, Isaiah described the future circumstances as resembling the Garden of Eden (see 51:3; 65:22). The message of renewal finds its ultimate fulfillment in the new creation (see Romans 8:19-27; 2 Corinthians 5:17; Galatians 6:15; Ephesians 2:15; 4:24; Revelation 21:22-27). Those "who survive in Israel"—the remnant—would be the true citizens of Zion.

5:1-30 The prophets often represented the people of Israel as a vineyard, the Lord's vineyard. Isaiah describes how Yahweh has planted this vineyard and hopes to find good fruit but finds only bitter fruit (5:1-4). This bitter fruit is their oppression and violence (5:7). These acts will result in judgment, as the Lord warns that he will remove their protection (5:13; 26-30).

9 But I have heard the Lord of Heaven's Armies
  swear a solemn oath:
  "Many houses will stand deserted;
  even beautiful mansions will be empty.
10 Ten acres* of vineyard will not produce even six
  gallons* of wine.
  Ten baskets of seed will yield only one basket*
  of grain."

11 What sorrow for those who get up early in the
  morning
  looking for a drink of alcohol
  and spend long evenings drinking wine
  to make themselves flaming drunk.
12 They furnish wine and lovely music at their
  grand parties—
  lyre and harp, tambourine and flute—
  but they never think about the Lord
  or notice what he is doing.
13 So my people will go into exile far away
  because they do not know me.
  Those who are great and honored will starve,
  and the common people will die of thirst.
14 The grave* is licking its lips in anticipation,
  opening its mouth wide.
  The great and the lowly
  and all the drunken mob will be swallowed up.
15 Humanity will be destroyed, and people brought
  down;
  even the arrogant will lower their eyes in
  humiliation.
16 But the Lord of Heaven's Armies will be exalted
  by his justice.
  The holiness of God will be displayed by his
  righteousness.
17 In that day lambs will find good pastures,
  and fattened sheep and young goats* will feed
  among the ruins.

18 What sorrow for those who drag their sins
  behind them
  with ropes made of lies,
  who drag wickedness behind them like a cart!
19 They even mock God and say,
  "Hurry up and do something!
  We want to see what you can do.
  Let the Holy One of Israel carry out his plan,
  for we want to know what it is."

20 What sorrow for those who say
  that evil is good and good is evil,
  that dark is light and light is dark,
  that bitter is sweet and sweet is bitter.
21 What sorrow for those who are wise in their
  own eyes
  and think themselves so clever.
22 What sorrow for those who are heroes at
  drinking wine
  and boast about all the alcohol they can hold.
23 They take bribes to let the wicked go free,
  and they punish the innocent.

24 Therefore, just as fire licks up stubble
  and dry grass shrivels in the flame,
  so their roots will rot
  and their flowers wither.
  For they have rejected the law of the Lord of
  Heaven's Armies;
  they have despised the word of the Holy One
  of Israel.
25 That is why the Lord's anger burns against his
  people,
  and why he has raised his fist to crush them.
  The mountains tremble,
  and the corpses of his people litter the streets
  like garbage.
  But even then the Lord's anger is not satisfied.
  His fist is still poised to strike!

26 He will send a signal to distant nations far away
  and whistle to those at the ends of the earth.
  They will come racing toward Jerusalem.
27 They will not get tired or stumble.
  They will not stop for rest or sleep.
  Not a belt will be loose,
  not a sandal strap broken.
28 Their arrows will be sharp
  and their bows ready for battle.
  Sparks will fly from their horses' hooves,
  and the wheels of their chariots will spin like
  a whirlwind.
29 They will roar like lions,
  like the strongest of lions.
  Growling, they will pounce on their victims and
  carry them off,
  and no one will be there to rescue them.
30 They will roar over their victims on that day of
  destruction
  like the roaring of the sea.
  If someone looks across the land,
  only darkness and distress will be seen;
  even the light will be darkened by clouds.

5:10a Hebrew *A ten yoke*, that is, the area of land plowed by ten teams of oxen in one day.   **5:10b** Hebrew *a bath* [21 liters].
5:10c Hebrew *A homer* [5 bushels or 220 liters] *of seed will yield only an ephah* [20 quarts or 22 liters].   **5:14** Hebrew *Sheol*.
5:17 As in Greek version; Hebrew reads *and strangers*.

5:13 Israel and Judah would "go into exile" to Assyria (722 BC) and Babylon (586 BC). The people did not respond to the Lord because they did not "know" him or recognize how he cared for them (see 1:3). They likely knew about him, technically, but their behavior showed that they did not know him in any intimate way.

5:14 Sheol, translated here as "the grave," represented the place of the dead in ancient Israelite thinking.

Isaiah's Cleansing and Call

6 It was in the year King Uzziah died* that I saw the Lord. He was sitting on a lofty throne, and the train of his robe filled the Temple. ²Attending him were mighty seraphim, each having six wings. With two wings they covered their faces, with two they covered their feet, and with two they flew. ³They were calling out to each other,

> "Holy, holy, holy is the LORD of Heaven's Armies!
> The whole earth is filled with his glory!"

⁴Their voices shook the Temple to its foundations, and the entire building was filled with smoke.

⁵Then I said, "It's all over! I am doomed, for I am a sinful man. I have filthy lips, and I live among a people with filthy lips. Yet I have seen the King, the LORD of Heaven's Armies."

⁶Then one of the seraphim flew to me with a burning coal he had taken from the altar with a pair of tongs. ⁷He touched my lips with it and said, "See, this coal has touched your lips. Now your guilt is removed, and your sins are forgiven."

⁸Then I heard the Lord asking, "Whom should I send as a messenger to this people? Who will go for us?"

I said, "Here I am. Send me."

⁹And he said, "Yes, go, and say to this people,

> 'Listen carefully, but do not understand.
> Watch closely, but learn nothing.'

> ¹⁰ Harden the hearts of these people.
> Plug their ears and shut their eyes.
> That way, they will not see with their eyes,
> nor hear with their ears,
> nor understand with their hearts
> and turn to me for healing."*

¹¹Then I said, "Lord, how long will this go on?" And he replied,

> "Until their towns are empty,
> their houses are deserted,
> and the whole country is a wasteland;
> ¹² until the LORD has sent everyone away,
> and the entire land of Israel lies deserted.
> ¹³ If even a tenth—a remnant—survive,
> it will be invaded again and burned.
> But as a terebinth or oak tree leaves a stump
> when it is cut down,
> so Israel's stump will be a holy seed."

A Message for Ahaz

7 When Ahaz, son of Jotham and grandson of Uzziah, was king of Judah, King Rezin of Syria* and Pekah son of Remaliah, the king of Israel, set out to attack Jerusalem. However, they were unable to carry out their plan.

6:1 King Uzziah died in 740 B.C. **6:9-10** Greek version reads *And he said, "Go and say to this people, /'When you hear what I say, you will not understand. / When you see what I do, you will not comprehend.' / For the hearts of these people are hardened, / and their ears cannot hear, and they have closed their eyes—/ so their eyes cannot see, / and their ears cannot hear, / and their hearts cannot understand, / and they cannot turn to me and let me heal them."* Compare Matt 13:14-15; Mark 4:12; Luke 8:10; Acts 28:26-27. **7:1** Hebrew *Aram;* also in 7:2, 4, 5, 8.

6:1-13 This chapter depicts God's call of Isaiah as his prophet. This is one of the few places where there is a description of a direct encounter with the Lord. These encounters are called *theophanies*. Other theophanies you may be familiar with are Moses and the Lord at the burning bush (Exodus 3:1-2) and the Lord's visit to Abraham and Sarah to tell them that their son Isaac would be born (Genesis 18:1-15).

6:1-13 Isaiah's marvelous vision of God as King on his throne served as a pivotal event in the life of the prophet. The historical circumstances surrounding this event can be interpreted in two ways: (1) Some see Isaiah 6 as Isaiah's original call to ministry, meaning that Isaiah 1–5 and Isaiah 7–12 fit into the reign of Ahaz, who came to rule after the death of Uzziah (6:1). If this were so, why was Isaiah's call not at the beginning of the book? Perhaps his call was put in Isaiah 6 for literary reasons, serving as a conclusion to Isaiah 1–5 and an introduction to Isaiah 7–12. The prophet's own transformation and commissioning symbolizes the entire nation's need for repentance and change if it wants to fulfill its mandate to be God's light to the world. (2) Others understand Isaiah 1–12 as chronological; Isaiah's call in Isaiah 6 would then serve as a recommissioning of the prophet to minister in a new way in a different period (the time of Ahaz) when his words would be rejected. Those who hold this interpretation point to 2:7-9; 3:16-24; and 5:8-14, contending that these passages reflect a time of prosperity, military strength, pride, and splendor. These conditions existed during Uzziah's reign but not during Ahaz's reign.

6:2-6 The seraphim appear and play an important role in Isaiah's call. The seraphim (plural of *seraph*, which literally means "burning ones") are creatures that have six wings. These heavenly creatures gather near the Lord's throne.

6:3-8 The seraphim call out three times that the Lord is holy. This is a Hebrew literary device that emphasizes a superlative, which in English could sound like, "The holiest!" Not just holy (one time), or holier (two times), but the holiest (three times). In the overwhelming, unveiled awareness of God's holiness, Isaiah felt sinful and unclean. When one of the seraphim touched a burning coal to Isaiah's lips, this symbolic act revealed that Isaiah was forgiven by God. The connection of the coal touching Isaiah's tongue also seems to suggest that God's forgiveness prepares and propels Isaiah to go tell the people God's message (6:9-13). It was not the coal but the Lord who cleanses from sin. Even though Isaiah was afraid to do what the Lord called him to do, he said yes, "Here I am. Send me." Sometimes, we are called by the Lord to do something difficult. The Lord will give us the strength to carry it out, just like he did with Isaiah.

7:1–9:7 These chapters share the famous theme about expecting a child, "Immanuel" (7:14; 8:8). The name of the child, Immanuel, means "God is with us" (7:14). We see this ultimately fulfilled in Matthew 1:23 with the birth of Jesus, who is our Immanuel, "God is with us." This name is a reminder that you are never alone because Jesus is always with you.

²The news had come to the royal court of Judah: "Syria is allied with Israel* against us!" So the hearts of the king and his people trembled with fear, like trees shaking in a storm.

³Then the LORD said to Isaiah, "Take your son Shear-jashub* and go out to meet King Ahaz. You will find him at the end of the aqueduct that feeds water into the upper pool, near the road leading to the field where cloth is washed.* ⁴Tell him to stop worrying. Tell him he doesn't need to fear the fierce anger of those two burned-out embers, King Rezin of Syria and Pekah son of Remaliah. ⁵Yes, the kings of Syria and Israel are plotting against him, saying, ⁶'We will attack Judah and capture it for ourselves. Then we will install the son of Tabeel as Judah's king.' ⁷But this is what the Sovereign LORD says:

> "This invasion will never happen;
>   it will never take place;
> ⁸ for Syria is no stronger than its capital, Damascus,
>   and Damascus is no stronger than its king,
>   Rezin.
> As for Israel, within sixty-five years
>   it will be crushed and completely destroyed.
> ⁹ Israel is no stronger than its capital, Samaria,
>   and Samaria is no stronger than its king,
>   Pekah son of Remaliah.
> Unless your faith is firm,
>   I cannot make you stand firm."

The Sign of Immanuel

¹⁰Later, the LORD sent this message to King Ahaz: ¹¹"Ask the LORD your God for a sign of confirmation, Ahaz. Make it as difficult as you want—as high as heaven or as deep as the place of the dead.*"

¹²But the king refused. "No," he said, "I will not test the LORD like that."

> "Oh, God, here's my Bible! Here's my money! Here's me! Use me, God!"
>
> **GLADYS AYLWARD**
> (1902–1970) British missionary to China

¹³Then Isaiah said, "Listen well, you royal family of David! Isn't it enough to exhaust human patience? Must you exhaust the patience of my God as well? ¹⁴All right then, the Lord himself will give you the sign. Look! The virgin* will conceive a child! She will give birth to a son and will call him Immanuel (which means 'God is with us'). ¹⁵By the time this child is old enough to choose what is right and reject what is wrong, he will be eating yogurt* and honey. ¹⁶For before the child is that old, the lands of the two kings you fear so much will both be deserted.

¹⁷"Then the LORD will bring things on you, your nation, and your family unlike anything since Israel broke away from Judah. He will bring the king of Assyria upon you!"

¹⁸In that day the LORD will whistle for the army of southern Egypt and for the army of Assyria. They

---

7:2 Hebrew *Ephraim*, referring to the northern kingdom of Israel; also in 7:5, 8, 9, 17. **7:3a** *Shear-jashub* means "A remnant will return." **7:3b** Or *bleached*. **7:11** Hebrew *as deep as Sheol*. **7:14** Or *young woman*. **7:15** Or *curds*; also in 7:22.

7:1-2 Rezin was king of Syria (Hebrew *Aram*; also in 7:2, 4, 5, 8). Damascus was Syria's capital city. Pekah was king of Israel (740–732 BC). He was a renowned warrior (2 Chronicles 28:5-8). Pekah and Rezin began to "attack Jerusalem" while Jotham was king (750–732 BC), and they intensified their efforts during the early years of young King Ahaz (2 Kings 15:37; 16:5). When the people of Judah (the southern kingdom) heard this news about Israel (literally, "Ephraim," which was the northern kingdom), they "trembled with fear." In contrast, Ahaz's son King Hezekiah faced the Assyrians some thirty years later with great faith (701 BC; see Isaiah 37:6-7, 14-20).

7:3 The aqueduct was a place where political negotiations took place later during Hezekiah's reign (see 36:2).

7:4 This was a "fear not" prophecy (common in Isaiah) in which the Lord assured his people of his presence and purpose. If Ahaz had had God's perspective, he would have seen that Rezin and Pekah were minor threats who were about to be extinguished.

7:6 The "son of Tabeel," who is otherwise unknown, was obviously sympathetic to Israel's and Syria's resistance against Assyria.

7:14 The Hebrew translated here as "virgin" (*almah*) could also be translated "young woman." This prophecy received its ultimate fulfillment in the birth of Jesus Christ (Matthew 1:18-24). Yet it is likely that it also had a partial fulfillment in Isaiah's day, either with the birth of the godly king Hezekiah, Ahaz's son, or with the birth of one of Isaiah's children. The similar sequence of the verbs in Isaiah 7:14 and 8:3 (conceive . . . give birth . . . call) and the link between Immanuel and Maher-shalal-hash-baz in 8:5-10 suggest that Immanuel and Maher-shalal-hash-baz were the same person (see note on 8:5-10). The name "Immanuel (which means 'God is with us')" symbolized God's presence and protection. God was with Judah during the attack by the alliance of Syria and Israel (734 BC), in the Assyrian crisis (701 BC), and throughout their prolonged existence until their fall in 586 BC. The kingdom of Israel fell during the time of Isaiah (722 BC). The assurance "I am with you" remained significant during the Exile and in the postexilic period (41:10; 43:2, 5). The greatest assurance ultimately came in Jesus Christ, the incarnate Son of God (Matthew 1:23; see also Revelation 12:5).

will swarm around you like flies and bees. ¹⁹They will come in vast hordes and settle in the fertile areas and also in the desolate valleys, caves, and thorny places. ²⁰In that day the Lord will hire a "razor" from beyond the Euphrates River*—the king of Assyria—and use it to shave off everything: your land, your crops, and your people.*

²¹In that day a farmer will be fortunate to have a cow and two sheep or goats left. ²²Nevertheless, there will be enough milk for everyone because so

7:20a Hebrew *the river.* 7:20b Hebrew *shave off the head, the hair of the legs, and the beard.*

7:20 The metaphorical phrase "shave off everything: your land, your crops, and your people" could be rendered literally as "shave off the head, the hair of the legs, and the beard." In the ancient Near East, forced shaving was an act of disgrace (see 2 Samuel 10:4-5). Here it was a metaphor for the despoiling of the country.

IMAGE — MY STORY OF MY UNIQUE INFLUENCE

Embracing Our Call

SCRIPTURE CONNECTION: ISAIAH 6:1-8

Isaiah receives a vision that prompts his acknowledgment of unworthiness before God. As he glimpses God on his heavenly throne, Isaiah responds, "I am doomed" (6:5). He remembers his shortcomings—and others' too. An angelic being lays coal upon his mouth, saying, your guilt is gone, and your sins forgiven.

Major life events can cause us to look inward at ourselves and outward toward others. God's holiness shows us how we fall short, and that vision can paralyze us. When God cleanses, he calls us to embrace his direction.

When I think about my past, I can relate to Isaiah's feelings of inadequacy. When I was around people who seemed to have it all together, my insecurities heightened. My words often hurt intentionally, bringing pain. I needed to take three steps:

- See God with fresh eyes. Isaiah's God-encounter made him no longer see things the same way.
- Let God heal painful words spoken over my life. Words shape us, and some words spoken over me were not life-giving. I had to hear God's new words so I could do greater works.
- Remain Godward despite what others say. Like Isaiah, we hear others who speak with "filthy lips." We can respond to God: "Here I am. Send me."

> As we receive God's new words, we can do greater works.

IMAGINE

What may the Lord be inviting you into that you resist because of your past?

Are you ready to leave behind those things that God has cleansed?

"When God cleanses, he calls."

VIRGINIA WARD, MA, DMin, serves as the Dean of the Boston Campus for Gordon-Conwell Theological Seminary. She is a wife, a mother, and an associate pastor at Abundant Life Church in Cambridge, MA.

few people will be left in the land. They will eat their fill of yogurt and honey. ²³In that day the lush vineyards, now worth 1,000 pieces of silver,* will become patches of briers and thorns. ²⁴The entire land will become a vast expanse of briers and thorns, a hunting ground overrun by wildlife. ²⁵No one will go to the fertile hillsides where the gardens once grew, for briers and thorns will cover them. Cattle, sheep, and goats will graze there.

The Coming Assyrian Invasion

8 Then the LORD said to me, "Make a large signboard and clearly write this name on it: Maher-shalal-hash-baz.*" ²I asked Uriah the priest and Zechariah son of Jeberekiah, both known as honest men, to witness my doing this.

³Then I slept with my wife, and she became pregnant and gave birth to a son. And the LORD said, "Call him Maher-shalal-hash-baz. ⁴For before this child is old enough to say 'Papa' or 'Mama,' the king of Assyria will carry away both the abundance of Damascus and the riches of Samaria."

⁵Then the LORD spoke to me again and said, ⁶"My care for the people of Judah is like the gently flowing waters of Shiloah, but they have rejected it. They are rejoicing over what will happen to* King Rezin and King Pekah.* ⁷Therefore, the Lord will overwhelm them with a mighty flood from the Euphrates River*—the king of Assyria and all his glory. This flood will overflow all its channels ⁸and sweep into Judah until it is chin deep. It will spread its wings, submerging your land from one end to the other, O Immanuel.

⁹ "Huddle together, you nations, and be terrified.
  Listen, all you distant lands.
  Prepare for battle, but you will be crushed!
  Yes, prepare for battle, but you will be crushed!
¹⁰ Call your councils of war, but they will be worthless.
  Develop your strategies, but they will not succeed.
  For God is with us!*"

A Call to Trust the LORD

¹¹The LORD has given me a strong warning not to think like everyone else does. He said,

¹² "Don't call everything a conspiracy, like they do,
  and don't live in dread of what frightens them.
¹³ Make the LORD of Heaven's Armies holy in your life.
  He is the one you should fear.
  He is the one who should make you tremble.
¹⁴ He will keep you safe.
  But to Israel and Judah
  he will be a stone that makes people stumble,
  a rock that makes them fall.
  And for the people of Jerusalem
  he will be a trap and a snare.
¹⁵ Many will stumble and fall,
  never to rise again.
  They will be snared and captured."

¹⁶ Preserve the teaching of God;
  entrust his instructions to those who follow me.
¹⁷ I will wait for the LORD,
  who has turned away from the descendants of Jacob.
  I will put my hope in him.

¹⁸I and the children the LORD has given me serve as signs and warnings to Israel from the LORD of Heaven's Armies who dwells in his Temple on Mount Zion.

¹⁹Someone may say to you, "Let's ask the mediums and those who consult the spirits of the dead. With their whisperings and mutterings, they will

---

7:23 Hebrew *1,000 [shekels] of silver*, about 25 pounds or 11.4 kilograms in weight.   **8:1** *Maher-shalal-hash-baz* means "Swift to plunder and quick to carry away."   **8:6a** Or *They are rejoicing because of*.   **8:6b** Hebrew *and the son of Remaliah*.   **8:7** Hebrew *the river*.   **8:10** Hebrew *Immanuel!*

8:1 *Maher-shalal-hash-baz* means "swift to plunder and quick to carry away," and the words apply both to Judah's enemies (8:4) and to Judah itself (8:7-8). They had trusted Assyria in place of God, and now Assyria would turn on them and all but destroy them. God was with them (Immanuel; see 7:14), but his presence would be destructive if they refused to trust in him (see 8:14).

8:3 The Hebrew translated here as "my wife" is the word for "prophetess" (*nebiah*). This term tells us that she was Isaiah the prophet's wife, and it may also indicate that she, too, had her own prophetic calling and role. Although we don't have any additional information about her or her ministry, she played a role in this particular prophetic sign act by bearing a son, Maher-shalal-hash-baz.

8:5-10 This prophecy connects the sign of Maher-shalal-hash-baz with the sign of Immanuel (8:8, 10; see note on 7:14).

8:10 The translation here, "For God is with us," is the name *Immanuel* in Hebrew. When the Lord called someone, often the comfort given was that the Lord would be with them. The Lord did not promise an easy journey, but he promised that they would never be alone. For other instances of this reassurance, see Moses (Exodus 3:12), Joshua (Joshua 1:5), and Jeremiah (Jeremiah 1:8).

8:11-15 This text reveals the heart of Isaiah's message. The issue was fear of the Lord versus fear of people (see 7:9; 8:6). When an individual fears people, the Lord becomes a trap and destruction is certain (see Proverbs 29:25). For those who fear the Lord, he becomes a sanctuary; their salvation is assured.

8:16 The Hebrew word for teaching is *torah*. Torah comes from the verb *yarah* meaning "to teach" or "to instruct." Torah can also refer to the Bible's first five books, known as the Pentateuch (Genesis, Exodus, Leviticus, Numbers, Deuteronomy). Within the Bible itself, the word refers to God's instructions, often given through priests, prophets, and others with special God-given authority.

tell us what to do." But shouldn't people ask God for guidance? Should the living seek guidance from the dead? ²⁰Look to God's instructions and teachings! People who contradict his word are completely in the dark. ²¹They will go from one place to another, weary and hungry. And because they are hungry, they will rage and curse their king and their God. They will look up to heaven ²²and down at the earth, but wherever they look, there will be trouble and anguish and dark despair. They will be thrown out into the darkness.

Hope in the Messiah

9 ¹*Nevertheless, that time of darkness and despair will not go on forever. The land of Zebulun and Naphtali will be humbled, but there will be a time in the future when Galilee of the Gentiles, which lies along the road that runs between the Jordan and the sea, will be filled with glory.

²*The people who walk in darkness
  will see a great light.
For those who live in a land of deep darkness,*
  a light will shine.
³ You will enlarge the nation of Israel,
  and its people will rejoice.
They will rejoice before you
  as people rejoice at the harvest
  and like warriors dividing the plunder.
⁴ For you will break the yoke of their slavery
  and lift the heavy burden from their shoulders.
You will break the oppressor's rod,
  just as you did when you destroyed the army of Midian.
⁵ The boots of the warrior
  and the uniforms bloodstained by war
will all be burned.
  They will be fuel for the fire.

⁶ For a child is born to us,
  a son is given to us.
The government will rest on his shoulders.
  And he will be called:
Wonderful Counselor,* Mighty God,
  Everlasting Father, Prince of Peace.
⁷ His government and its peace
  will never end.
He will rule with fairness and justice from the
  throne of his ancestor David
  for all eternity.
The passionate commitment of the LORD of
  Heaven's Armies
  will make this happen!

The LORD's Anger against Israel

⁸ The Lord has spoken out against Jacob;
  his judgment has fallen upon Israel.
⁹ And the people of Israel* and Samaria,
  who spoke with such pride and arrogance,
  will soon know it.
¹⁰ They said, "We will replace the broken bricks of
  our ruins with finished stone,
  and replant the felled sycamore-fig trees with
  cedars."

¹¹ But the LORD will bring Rezin's enemies against
  Israel
  and stir up all their foes.
¹² The Syrians* from the east and the Philistines
  from the west
  will bare their fangs and devour Israel.
But even then the LORD's anger will not be satisfied.
  His fist is still poised to strike.

¹³ For after all this punishment, the people will still
  not repent.
  They will not seek the LORD of Heaven's Armies.

9:1 Verse 9:1 is numbered 8:23 in Hebrew text. **9:2a** Verses 9:2-21 are numbered 9:1-20 in Hebrew text. **9:2b** Greek version reads *a land where death casts its shadow*. Compare Matt 4:16. **9:6** Or *Wonderful, Counselor*. **9:9** Hebrew *of Ephraim*, referring to the northern kingdom of Israel. **9:12** Hebrew *Arameans*.

9:1-7 God promises a light to deliver the people from darkness. This light will take the form of a person, a child. This child will be called "Wonderful Counselor, Mighty God, Everlasting Father, Prince of Peace" (9:6). The child will be from the family of David and rule with justice forever (9:7). This promise would ultimately be fulfilled through Jesus who is called the "light of the world" (John 8:12). This passage in Isaiah is quoted in Matthew 4:14-16 to describe Jesus' role and ministry, to seek and save the lost. This gift of salvation is for everyone!

9:6 This child, the Messiah, would be David's descendant (11:1). His names ("he will be called") can be read as four royal titles, describing the nature of the child's rule: First, the Wonderful Counselor conforms to God's wisdom (11:1; 25:1; 28:29; 40:13), unlike the counselors of Judah (1:26; 3:3). Second, Mighty God is an affirmation of the Messiah's divine nature. Third, he cares for his children as the Everlasting Father, the father whose care continues forever (see also 22:21; 63:16). Finally, the Prince of Peace is a leader who brings peace. Alternatively, the four names could be collapsed into two: "A Wonderful Counselor [who is] the Mighty God"; and "the Everlasting Father [who is] a Prince of Peace" (on his nature, see 11:1-9). Jesus Christ, the Son of David (Matthew 1:1; Luke 1:32; see also Isaiah 7:14; 8:3, 18), will bring in the kingdom of his peace (Revelation 19).

9:8–10:34 The theme of the Lord's anger is repeated in 9:12, 17, 21; 10:4: "But even then the LORD's anger will not be satisfied." What is key to remember is that the Lord is concerned for the social injustices against the needy. The needy include the widows, the poor, the oppressed, and the orphans. In ancient society, these were the groups with little or no power, who were most vulnerable to being crushed by the world. Who do you think would be in these groups today? How can we act justly in our society?

9:8-12 This prophecy of judgment was against the northern kingdom of Israel. Despite God's message that the Assyrians would crush them (7:1–8:22), the people of Samaria were foolishly confident that they could withstand the siege.

Isaiah's Wife

IDENTITY | Bearing Pain to Bear Hope

She remembers...

O Lord, what are you doing? My husband is making a public spectacle of me! He's told everyone I will bear a son, and he will call him "Maher-shalal-hash-baz" (8:3). *And* he is writing it on a signboard for the whole world to see—and I am not even pregnant!

This child's name—"swift to plunder and quick to carry away"—is a prediction of disaster. Assyria will overwhelm Israel, Damascus, and then us, Judah, like a mighty flood. God cares for us, his people, but we reject him continually. So God has prepared this judgment for us. But do I have to bear the burden of this message of doom? Does my son? O Lord, this weighs heavy on my heart.

O God, I surrender to your will, for I see a glimmer of hope in the promise of Immanuel, a savior to come from you (7:14; 8:8, 10). Give me strength to bear the pain.

> We all experience pain in life, but God brings unexpected hope and fulfillment when we learn to trust him.

THE STORY OF ISAIAH'S WIFE BEARING THIS SON IS TOLD IN ISAIAH 8:1–10.

IDENTIFY

When have you found yourself in a situation that seemed too painful to bear and there was no way out?

If you had to go through it, where did God meet you with his gentle presence?

> "During menopause, I grieved the loss of childbearing. But the fruit of my labor has since become worldwide. I returned to school and have taught students from many nations for twenty years. My daughter's goddaughters from Asia all call me 'Gramma.' I am blessed beyond measure."

ELIZABETH GLANVILLE, PhD, is retired faculty from Fuller Theological Seminary, School of Mission and Theology. She is an international teacher on missions and leadership and chaplain for a local police department and her retirement community.

¹⁴ Therefore, in a single day the Lord will destroy
both the head and the tail,
the noble palm branch and the lowly reed.
¹⁵ The leaders of Israel are the head,
and the lying prophets are the tail.
¹⁶ For the leaders of the people have misled them.
They have led them down the path of
destruction.
¹⁷ That is why the Lord takes no pleasure in the
young men
and shows no mercy even to the widows and
orphans.
For they are all wicked hypocrites,
and they all speak foolishness.
But even then the Lord's anger will not be
satisfied.
His fist is still poised to strike.
¹⁸ This wickedness is like a brushfire.
It burns not only briers and thorns
but also sets the forests ablaze.
Its burning sends up clouds of smoke.
¹⁹ The land will be blackened
by the fury of the Lord of Heaven's Armies.
The people will be fuel for the fire,
and no one will spare even his own brother.
²⁰ They will attack their neighbor on the right
but will still be hungry.
They will devour their neighbor on the left
but will not be satisfied.
In the end they will even eat their own children.*
²¹ Manasseh will feed on Ephraim,
Ephraim will feed on Manasseh,
and both will devour Judah.
But even then the Lord's anger will not be
satisfied.
His fist is still poised to strike.

10 What sorrow awaits the unjust judges
and those who issue unfair laws.
² They deprive the poor of justice
and deny the rights of the needy among my
people.
They prey on widows
and take advantage of orphans.
³ What will you do when I punish you,
when I send disaster upon you from a distant
land?
To whom will you turn for help?
Where will your treasures be safe?

9:20 Or *eat their own arms.*

⁴ You will stumble along as prisoners
or lie among the dead.
But even then the Lord's anger will not be
satisfied.
His fist is still poised to strike.

Judgment against Assyria

⁵ "What sorrow awaits Assyria, the rod of my
anger.
I use it as a club to express my anger.
⁶ I am sending Assyria against a godless nation,
against a people with whom I am angry.
Assyria will plunder them,
trampling them like dirt beneath its feet.
⁷ But the king of Assyria will not understand that
he is my tool;
his mind does not work that way.
His plan is simply to destroy,
to cut down nation after nation.
⁸ He will say,
'Each of my princes will soon be a king.
⁹ We destroyed Calno just as we did Carchemish.
Hamath fell before us as Arpad did.
And we destroyed Samaria just as we did
Damascus.
¹⁰ Yes, we have finished off many a kingdom
whose gods were greater than those in
Jerusalem and Samaria.
¹¹ So we will defeat Jerusalem and her gods,
just as we destroyed Samaria with hers.'"

¹²After the Lord has used the king of Assyria to accomplish his purposes on Mount Zion and in Jerusalem, he will turn against the king of Assyria and punish him—for he is proud and arrogant. ¹³He boasts,

"By my own powerful arm I have done this.
With my own shrewd wisdom I planned it.
I have broken down the defenses of nations
and carried off their treasures.
I have knocked down their kings like a bull.
¹⁴ I have robbed their nests of riches
and gathered up kingdoms as a farmer
gathers eggs.
No one can even flap a wing against me
or utter a peep of protest."

¹⁵ But can the ax boast greater power than the
person who uses it?
Is the saw greater than the person who saws?

9:21 Manasseh and Ephraim represented the northern kingdom as its largest tribes. The two largest tribes of Israel and Judah fought among themselves. This is probably a reference to the war between Judah and the alliance of Syria and Israel, which is commonly called the Syro-Ephraimite War (7:1-12). In that conflict, brothers savagely fought against brothers (2 Chronicles 28).

10:13 "By my own powerful arm I have done this" is a metaphor of strength usually referring to the Lord's strength. References to God's "powerful arm" or hand appear throughout Scripture. For example, in Exodus 6:6, it describes God intervening to bring Israel out of oppression in Egypt. But here in Isaiah, this metaphor is used to describe God bringing judgment on Assyria because of its pride and arrogance (10:12).

Can a rod strike unless a hand moves it?
  Can a wooden cane walk by itself?
¹⁶ Therefore, the Lord, the LORD of Heaven's Armies,
  will send a plague among Assyria's proud troops,
  and a flaming fire will consume its glory.
¹⁷ The LORD, the Light of Israel, will be a fire;
  the Holy One will be a flame.
He will devour the thorns and briers with fire,
  burning up the enemy in a single night.
¹⁸ The LORD will consume Assyria's glory
  like a fire consumes a forest in a fruitful land;
  it will waste away like sick people in a plague.
¹⁹ Of all that glorious forest, only a few trees will survive—
  so few that a child could count them!

Hope for the LORD's People

²⁰ In that day the remnant left in Israel,
  the survivors in the house of Jacob,
will no longer depend on allies
  who seek to destroy them.
But they will faithfully trust the LORD,
  the Holy One of Israel.
²¹ A remnant will return;*
  yes, the remnant of Jacob will return to the Mighty God.
²² But though the people of Israel are as numerous as the sand of the seashore,
  only a remnant of them will return.
The LORD has rightly decided to destroy his people.
²³ Yes, the Lord, the LORD of Heaven's Armies,
  has already decided to destroy the entire land.*

²⁴So this is what the Lord, the LORD of Heaven's Armies, says: "O my people in Zion, do not be afraid of the Assyrians when they oppress you with rod and club as the Egyptians did long ago. ²⁵In a little while my anger against you will end, and then my anger will rise up to destroy them." ²⁶The LORD of Heaven's Armies will lash them with his whip, as he did when Gideon triumphed over the Midianites at the rock of Oreb, or when the LORD's staff was raised to drown the Egyptian army in the sea.

²⁷ In that day the LORD will end the bondage of his people.
He will break the yoke of slavery
  and lift it from their shoulders.*
²⁸ Look, the Assyrians are now at Aiath.
  They are passing through Migron
  and are storing their equipment at Micmash.
²⁹ They are crossing the pass
  and are camping at Geba.
Fear strikes the town of Ramah.
  All the people of Gibeah, the hometown of Saul,
  are running for their lives.
³⁰ Scream in terror,
  you people of Gallim!
Shout out a warning to Laishah.
  Oh, poor Anathoth!
³¹ There go the people of Madmenah, all fleeing.
  The citizens of Gebim are trying to hide.
³² The enemy stops at Nob for the rest of that day.
  He shakes his fist at beautiful Mount Zion, the mountain of Jerusalem.
³³ But look! The Lord, the LORD of Heaven's Armies,
  will chop down the mighty tree of Assyria with great power!
He will cut down the proud.
  That lofty tree will be brought down.
³⁴ He will cut down the forest trees with an ax.
  Lebanon will fall to the Mighty One.*

A Branch from David's Line

11 Out of the stump of David's family* will grow a shoot—
  yes, a new Branch bearing fruit from the old root.
² And the Spirit of the LORD will rest on him—
  the Spirit of wisdom and understanding,
the Spirit of counsel and might,
  the Spirit of knowledge and the fear of the LORD.
³ He will delight in obeying the LORD.
  He will not judge by appearance
  nor make a decision based on hearsay.
⁴ He will give justice to the poor
  and make fair decisions for the exploited.
The earth will shake at the force of his word,
  and one breath from his mouth will destroy the wicked.

10:21 Hebrew *Shear-jashub;* see 7:3; 8:18. **10:22-23** Greek version reads *only a remnant of them will be saved. / For he will carry out his sentence quickly and with finality and righteousness; / for God will carry out his sentence upon all the world with finality.* Compare Rom 9:27-28. **10:27** As in Greek version; Hebrew reads *The yoke will be broken, / for you have grown so fat.* **10:34** Or *with an ax / as even the mighty trees of Lebanon fall.* **11:1** Hebrew *the stump of the line of Jesse.* Jesse was King David's father.

11:2 "The Spirit of the LORD will rest on" the Messiah. The succession of David's line is guaranteed by the Spirit. The Messiah's coming would bring justice and righteousness (11:4-5), peace (11:8), and the extension of God's Kingdom to the nations (11:10). The promised Messiah would have great "wisdom and understanding," like Solomon, as well as "knowledge and the fear of the LORD" (1 Kings 3:28; 4:29; Proverbs 1:1-7; 2:6-7). "The Spirit of counsel and might" alludes to Isaiah 9:6. The Messiah will be full of wisdom and will have the power to execute his righteous rule. **11:3-4** The king judges fairly and justly. "He will give justice to the poor and make fair decisions for the exploited" (11:4). This theme of justice for the lowly reveals that a righteous king will obey the Lord by enacting just laws and having proper concern for the needy. Caring for others is one way we reveal obedience to God today.

⁵ He will wear righteousness like a belt
 and truth like an undergarment.

⁶ In that day the wolf and the lamb will live together;
 the leopard will lie down with the baby goat.
 The calf and the yearling will be safe with the lion,
 and a little child will lead them all.
⁷ The cow will graze near the bear.
 The cub and the calf will lie down together.
 The lion will eat hay like a cow.
⁸ The baby will play safely near the hole of a cobra.
 Yes, a little child will put its hand in a nest of deadly snakes without harm.
⁹ Nothing will hurt or destroy in all my holy mountain,
 for as the waters fill the sea,
 so the earth will be filled with people who know the LORD.

¹⁰ In that day the heir to David's throne*
 will be a banner of salvation to all the world.
 The nations will rally to him,
 and the land where he lives will be a glorious place.*
¹¹ In that day the Lord will reach out his hand a second time
 to bring back the remnant of his people—
 those who remain in Assyria and northern Egypt;
 in southern Egypt, Ethiopia,* and Elam;
 in Babylonia,* Hamath, and all the distant coastlands.
¹² He will raise a flag among the nations
 and assemble the exiles of Israel.
 He will gather the scattered people of Judah
 from the ends of the earth.
¹³ Then at last the jealousy between Israel* and Judah will end.
 They will not be rivals anymore.
¹⁴ They will join forces to swoop down on Philistia to the west.
 Together they will attack and plunder the nations to the east.
 They will occupy the lands of Edom and Moab,
 and Ammon will obey them.
¹⁵ The LORD will make a dry path through the gulf of the Red Sea.*
 He will wave his hand over the Euphrates River,*
 sending a mighty wind to divide it into seven streams
 so it can easily be crossed on foot.
¹⁶ He will make a highway for the remnant of his people,
 the remnant coming from Assyria,
 just as he did for Israel long ago
 when they returned from Egypt.

Songs of Praise for Salvation

12 In that day you will sing:
 "I will praise you, O LORD!
 You were angry with me, but not anymore.
 Now you comfort me.
² See, God has come to save me.
 I will trust in him and not be afraid.
 The LORD GOD is my strength and my song;
 he has given me victory."

³ With joy you will drink deeply
 from the fountain of salvation!
⁴ In that wonderful day you will sing:
 "Thank the LORD! Praise his name!
 Tell the nations what he has done.
 Let them know how mighty he is!
⁵ Sing to the LORD, for he has done wonderful things.
 Make known his praise around the world.
⁶ Let all the people of Jerusalem* shout his praise with joy!
 For great is the Holy One of Israel who lives among you."

11:10a Hebrew *the root of Jesse*. **11:10b** Greek version reads *In that day the heir to David's throne* [literally *the root of Jesse*] *will come, / and he will rule over the Gentiles. / They will place their hopes on him.* Compare Rom 15:12. **11:11a** Hebrew *in Pathros, Cush*. **11:11b** Hebrew *in Shinar*. **11:13** Hebrew *Ephraim*, referring to the northern kingdom of Israel. **11:15a** Hebrew *will destroy the tongue of the sea of Egypt*. **11:15b** Hebrew *the river*. **12:6** Hebrew *Zion*.

11:10-16 The events and imagery from the Exodus appear throughout the Prophets. Here in Isaiah, it is reimagined as a New Exodus. In the first act of deliverance, the Lord led the people through the Red Sea (or, in Hebrew, the reed sea) to freedom, through Moses (Exodus 14:15-31). In the New Exodus (Isaiah 11:15; 19:5; 43:2), the group includes peoples from every nation and all four corners of the earth.

11:10 The phrase "the heir to David's throne" can be translated literally as "the root of Jesse" (11:1; Revelation 5:5; 22:16). The Messiah will bring "salvation to all the world" (Isaiah 2:1-5). Members of other nations will even serve as priests and Levites (66:20-21), but only if they repent and believe in the true God.

12:2 In the final section of Isaiah 10:33–12:6, there is judgment, promise, salvation, and hope. The Lord proves to be the strength, not only in this final song, but in the memories and the hopes for what is to come. This final song is similar to a thanksgiving or praise psalm, proclaiming the mighty deeds of the Lord.

12:4 Sharing what the Lord has done is one way to give praise and honor to God. The testimonies of how the Lord has saved Israel do not end with the biblical story. The Lord is at work through our lives today. Has the Lord done good things in your life? Is there someone you can share this with? This can be encouraging for you and for them!

A Message about Babylon

13 Isaiah son of Amoz received this message concerning the destruction of Babylon:

2 "Raise a signal flag on a bare hilltop.
  Call up an army against Babylon.
Wave your hand to encourage them
  as they march into the palaces of the high and mighty.
3 I, the Lord, have dedicated these soldiers for this task.
  Yes, I have called mighty warriors to express my anger,
  and they will rejoice when I am exalted."

4 Hear the noise on the mountains!
  Listen, as the vast armies march!
It is the noise and shouting of many nations.
  The Lord of Heaven's Armies has called this army together.
5 They come from distant countries,
  from beyond the farthest horizons.
They are the Lord's weapons to carry out his anger.
  With them he will destroy the whole land.

6 Scream in terror, for the day of the Lord has arrived—
  the time for the Almighty to destroy.
7 Every arm is paralyzed with fear.
  Every heart melts,
8 and people are terrified.
Pangs of anguish grip them,
  like those of a woman in labor.
They look helplessly at one another,
  their faces aflame with fear.

9 For see, the day of the Lord is coming—
  the terrible day of his fury and fierce anger.
The land will be made desolate,
  and all the sinners destroyed with it.
10 The heavens will be black above them;
  the stars will give no light.
The sun will be dark when it rises,
  and the moon will provide no light.

11 "I, the Lord, will punish the world for its evil
  and the wicked for their sin.
I will crush the arrogance of the proud
  and humble the pride of the mighty.
12 I will make people scarcer than gold—
  more rare than the fine gold of Ophir.
13 For I will shake the heavens.
  The earth will move from its place
when the Lord of Heaven's Armies displays his wrath
  in the day of his fierce anger."

14 Everyone in Babylon will run about like a hunted gazelle,
  like sheep without a shepherd.
They will try to find their own people
  and flee to their own land.
15 Anyone who is captured will be cut down—
  run through with a sword.
16 Their little children will be dashed to death before their eyes.
  Their homes will be sacked, and their wives will be raped.

17 "Look, I will stir up the Medes against Babylon.
  They cannot be tempted by silver
  or bribed with gold.
18 The attacking armies will shoot down the young men with arrows.
  They will have no mercy on helpless babies
  and will show no compassion for children."

19 Babylon, the most glorious of kingdoms,
  the flower of Chaldean pride,
will be devastated like Sodom and Gomorrah
  when God destroyed them.
20 Babylon will never be inhabited again.
  It will remain empty for generation after generation.
Nomads will refuse to camp there,
  and shepherds will not bed down their sheep.
21 Desert animals will move into the ruined city,
  and the houses will be haunted by howling creatures.
Owls will live among the ruins,
  and wild goats will go there to dance.
22 Hyenas will howl in its fortresses,
  and jackals will make dens in its luxurious palaces.
Babylon's days are numbered;
  its time of destruction will soon arrive.

A Taunt for Babylon's King

14 But the Lord will have mercy on the descendants of Jacob. He will choose Israel as his special people once again. He will bring them back to settle once again in their own land. And people from many different nations will come and join them there and unite with the people of Israel.* 2 The nations of the world will help the people of Israel to return, and those who come to live in the Lord's

---

14:1 Hebrew *the house of Jacob*. The names "Jacob" and "Israel" are often interchanged throughout the Old Testament, referring sometimes to the individual patriarch and sometimes to the nation.

13:1-22 This chapter details the destruction of Babylon and describes the horrors of war. Often in war, the most vulnerable become the heartbreaking victims (13:16-17). One of the themes in this section of judgment is that even the strongest empires can fall.

WHAT THE BIBLE SAYS ABOUT Husbands

Husbands and Wives Share Responsibilities toward Each Other

"A newly married man must not be drafted into the army or be given any other official responsibilities. He must be free to spend one year at home, bringing happiness to the wife he has married."
DEUTERONOMY 24:5

The husband should fulfill his wife's sexual needs, and the wife should fulfill her husband's needs.
1 CORINTHIANS 7:3

Isaac brought Rebekah into his mother Sarah's tent, and she became his wife. He loved her deeply, and she was a special comfort to him. **GENESIS 24:67**

...and she became his wife.

A Faithful Husband Advances God's Mission

Joseph, to whom she was engaged, was a righteous man and did not want to disgrace her publicly, so he decided to break the engagement quietly.... When Joseph woke up, he did as the angel of the Lord commanded and took Mary as his wife. But he did not have sexual relations with her until her son was born. And Joseph named him Jesus. **MATTHEW 1:19, 24-25**

He loved her deeply, and she was a special comfort to him.

God Restores His People by Becoming Like Our Husband

'For your Creator will be your husband;
    the LORD of Heaven's Armies is his name!
He is your Redeemer, the Holy One of Israel,
    the God of all the earth.
For the LORD has called you back from your grief—
    as though you were a young wife abandoned
        by her husband,"
    says your God.
'For a brief moment I abandoned you,
    but with great compassion I will take you back.'
ISAIAH 54:5-7

'I will make you my wife forever,
    showing you righteousness and justice,
    unfailing love and compassion.
I will be faithful to you and make you mine,
    and you will finally know me as the LORD."
HOSEA 2:19-20

I saw a new heaven and a new earth, for the old heaven and the old earth had disappeared. And the sea was also gone. And I saw the holy city, the new Jerusalem, coming down from God out of heaven like a bride beautifully dressed for her husband. I heard a loud shout from the throne, saying, "Look, God's home is now among his people! He will live with them, and they will be his people. God himself will be with them." **REVELATION 21:1-3**

Marriage Is Designed by God

"Should a man be allowed to divorce his wife for just any reason?" "Haven't you read the Scriptures?" Jesus replied. "They record that from the beginning 'God made them male and female.'" And he said, "'This explains why a man leaves his father and mother and is joined to his wife, and the two are united into one.' Since they are no longer two but one, let no one split apart what God has joined together." **MATTHEW 19:3-6**

land will serve them. Those who captured Israel will themselves be captured, and Israel will rule over its enemies.

³In that wonderful day when the LORD gives his people rest from sorrow and fear, from slavery and chains, ⁴you will taunt the king of Babylon. You will say,

"The mighty man has been destroyed.
  Yes, your insolence* is ended.
⁵ For the LORD has crushed your wicked power
  and broken your evil rule.
⁶ You struck the people with endless blows of rage
  and held the nations in your angry grip
  with unrelenting tyranny.
⁷ But finally the earth is at rest and quiet.
  Now it can sing again!
⁸ Even the trees of the forest—
  the cypress trees and the cedars of Lebanon—
  sing out this joyous song:
'Since you have been cut down,
  no one will come now to cut us down!'

⁹ "In the place of the dead* there is excitement
  over your arrival.
The spirits of world leaders and mighty kings
    long dead
  stand up to see you.
¹⁰ With one voice they all cry out,
  'Now you are as weak as we are!
¹¹ Your might and power were buried with you.*
  The sound of the harp in your palace has ceased.
Now maggots are your sheet,
  and worms your blanket.'

¹² "How you are fallen from heaven,
  O shining star, son of the morning!
You have been thrown down to the earth,
  you who destroyed the nations of the world.
¹³ For you said to yourself,
  'I will ascend to heaven and set my throne
    above God's stars.
I will preside on the mountain of the gods
  far away in the north.*
¹⁴ I will climb to the highest heavens
  and be like the Most High.'
¹⁵ Instead, you will be brought down to the place of
    the dead,
  down to its lowest depths.
¹⁶ Everyone there will stare at you and ask,
  'Can this be the one who shook the earth
    and made the kingdoms of the world tremble?
¹⁷ Is this the one who destroyed the world
    and made it into a wasteland?

Is this the king who demolished the world's
    greatest cities
  and had no mercy on his prisoners?'

¹⁸ "The kings of the nations lie in stately glory,
  each in his own tomb,
¹⁹ but you will be thrown out of your grave
  like a worthless branch.
Like a corpse trampled underfoot,
  you will be dumped into a mass grave
  with those killed in battle.
You will descend to the pit.
²⁰ You will not be given a proper burial,
  for you have destroyed your nation
  and slaughtered your people.
The descendants of such an evil person
  will never again receive honor.
²¹ Kill this man's children!
  Let them die because of their father's sins!
They must not rise and conquer the earth,
  filling the world with their cities."

²² This is what the LORD of Heaven's Armies says:
  "I, myself, have risen against Babylon!
I will destroy its children and its children's
    children,"
  says the LORD.
²³ "I will make Babylon a desolate place of owls,
  filled with swamps and marshes.
I will sweep the land with the broom of destruction.
  I, the LORD of Heaven's Armies, have spoken!"

A Message about Assyria

²⁴The LORD of Heaven's Armies has sworn this oath:

"It will all happen as I have planned.
  It will be as I have decided.
²⁵ I will break the Assyrians when they are in Israel;
  I will trample them on my mountains.
My people will no longer be their slaves
  nor bow down under their heavy loads.
²⁶ I have a plan for the whole earth,
  a hand of judgment upon all the nations.
²⁷ The LORD of Heaven's Armies has spoken—
  who can change his plans?
When his hand is raised,
  who can stop him?"

A Message about Philistia

²⁸This message came to me the year King Ahaz died:*

²⁹ Do not rejoice, you Philistines,
  that the rod that struck you is broken—
  that the king who attacked you is dead.

14:4 As in Dead Sea Scrolls; the meaning of the Masoretic Text is uncertain. **14:9** Hebrew *Sheol;* also in 14:15. **14:11** Hebrew *were brought down to Sheol.* **14:13** Or *on the heights of Zaphon.* **14:28** King Ahaz died in 715 B.C.

14:12 Other translations, such as the Latin Vulgate and the King James Version, have translated "O shining star" as "Lucifer." These translations spurred on speculation that the "shining star" described Satan and how Satan "fell" from heaven. This is a faulty view, rejected by Old Testament scholars, because this section describes judgment on Babylon, not Satan.

For from that snake a more poisonous snake
    will be born,
    a fiery serpent to destroy you!
³⁰ I will feed the poor in my pasture;
    the needy will lie down in peace.
But as for you, I will wipe you out with famine
    and destroy the few who remain.
³¹ Wail at the gates! Weep in the cities!
    Melt with fear, you Philistines!
A powerful army comes like smoke from the north.
    Each soldier rushes forward eager to fight.

³² What should we tell the Philistine messengers?
Tell them,

"The LORD has built Jerusalem*;
    its walls will give refuge to his oppressed
        people."

A Message about Moab

15 This message came to me concerning Moab:

In one night the town of Ar will be leveled,
    and the city of Kir will be destroyed.
² Your people will go to their temple in Dibon to
        mourn.
    They will go to their sacred shrines to weep.
They will wail for the fate of Nebo and Medeba,
    shaving their heads in sorrow and cutting off
        their beards.
³ They will wear burlap as they wander the streets.
    From every home and public square will
        come the sound of wailing.
⁴ The people of Heshbon and Elealeh will cry out;
    their voices will be heard as far away as Jahaz!
The bravest warriors of Moab will cry out in
        utter terror.
    They will be helpless with fear.
⁵ My heart weeps for Moab.
    Its people flee to Zoar and Eglath-shelishiyah.
Weeping, they climb the road to Luhith.
    Their cries of distress can be heard all along
        the road to Horonaim.
⁶ Even the waters of Nimrim are dried up!
    The grassy banks are scorched.
The tender plants are gone;
    nothing green remains.
⁷ The people grab their possessions
    and carry them across the Ravine of Willows.
⁸ A cry of distress echoes through the land of Moab
    from one end to the other—
    from Eglaim to Beer-elim.
⁹ The stream near Dibon* runs red with blood,
    but I am still not finished with Dibon!
Lions will hunt down the survivors—
    both those who try to escape
    and those who remain behind.

16 Send lambs from Sela as tribute
    to the ruler of the land.
Send them through the desert
    to the mountain of beautiful Zion.
² The women of Moab are left like homeless birds
    at the shallow crossings of the Arnon River.
³ "Help us," they cry.
    "Defend us against our enemies.
Protect us from their relentless attack.
    Do not betray us now that we have escaped.
⁴ Let our refugees stay among you.
    Hide them from our enemies until the terror
        is past."

When oppression and destruction have ended
    and enemy raiders have disappeared,
⁵ then God will establish one of David's
        descendants as king.
    He will rule with mercy and truth.
He will always do what is just
    and be eager to do what is right.

⁶ We have heard about proud Moab—
    about its pride and arrogance and rage.
    But all that boasting has disappeared.
⁷ The entire land of Moab weeps.
    Yes, everyone in Moab mourns
for the cakes of raisins from Kir-hareseth.
    They are all gone now.
⁸ The farms of Heshbon are abandoned;
    the vineyards at Sibmah are deserted.
The rulers of the nations have broken down
        Moab—
    that beautiful grapevine.
Its tendrils spread north as far as the town of
        Jazer
    and trailed eastward into the wilderness.
Its shoots reached so far west
    that they crossed over the Dead Sea.*
⁹ So now I weep for Jazer and the vineyards of
        Sibmah;
    my tears will flow for Heshbon and Elealeh.
There are no more shouts of joy
    over your summer fruits and harvest.
¹⁰ Gone now is the gladness,
    gone the joy of harvest.
There will be no singing in the vineyards,
    no more happy shouts,
no treading of grapes in the winepresses.
    I have ended all their harvest joys.
¹¹ My heart's cry for Moab is like a lament on a harp.
    I am filled with anguish for Kir-hareseth.*
¹² The people of Moab will worship at their pagan
        shrines,
    but it will do them no good.
They will cry to the gods in their temples,
    but no one will be able to save them.

14:32 Hebrew *Zion.*   **15:9** As in Dead Sea Scrolls, some Greek manuscripts, and Latin Vulgate; Masoretic Text reads *Dimon;* also in 15:9b.   **16:8** Hebrew *the sea.*   **16:11** Hebrew *Kir-heres,* a variant spelling of Kir-hareseth.

¹³The Lord has already said these things about Moab in the past. ¹⁴But now the Lord says, "Within three years, counting each day,* the glory of Moab will be ended. From its great population, only a feeble few will be left alive."

A Message about Damascus and Israel

17 This message came to me concerning Damascus:

"Look, the city of Damascus will disappear!
 It will become a heap of ruins.
² The towns of Aroer will be deserted.
 Flocks will graze in the streets and lie down undisturbed,
 with no one to chase them away.
³ The fortified towns of Israel* will also be destroyed,
 and the royal power of Damascus will end.
All that remains of Syria*
 will share the fate of Israel's departed glory,"
 declares the Lord of Heaven's Armies.

⁴ "In that day Israel's* glory will grow dim;
 its robust body will waste away.
⁵ The whole land will look like a grainfield
 after the harvesters have gathered the grain.
It will be desolate,
 like the fields in the valley of Rephaim after the harvest.
⁶ Only a few of its people will be left,
 like stray olives left on a tree after the harvest.
Only two or three remain in the highest branches,
 four or five scattered here and there on the limbs,"
 declares the Lord, the God of Israel.

⁷ Then at last the people will look to their Creator
 and turn their eyes to the Holy One of Israel.
⁸ They will no longer look to their idols for help
 or worship what their own hands have made.
They will never again bow down to their Asherah poles
 or worship at the pagan shrines they have built.
⁹ Their largest cities will be like a deserted forest,
 like the land the Hivites and Amorites abandoned*
when the Israelites came here so long ago.
 It will be utterly desolate.

¹⁰ Why? Because you have turned from the God who can save you.
 You have forgotten the Rock who can hide you.
So you may plant the finest grapevines
 and import the most expensive seedlings.
¹¹ They may sprout on the day you set them out;
 yes, they may blossom on the very morning you plant them,
but you will never pick any grapes from them.
 Your only harvest will be a load of grief and unrelieved pain.

¹² Listen! The armies of many nations
 roar like the roaring of the sea.
Hear the thunder of the mighty forces
 as they rush forward like thundering waves.
¹³ But though they thunder like breakers on a beach,
 God will silence them, and they will run away.
They will flee like chaff scattered by the wind,
 like a tumbleweed whirling before a storm.
¹⁴ In the evening Israel waits in terror,
 but by dawn its enemies are dead.
This is the just reward of those who plunder us,
 a fitting end for those who destroy us.

A Message about Ethiopia

18 Listen, Ethiopia*—land of fluttering sails*
 that lies at the headwaters of the Nile,
² that sends ambassadors
 in swift boats down the river.

Go, swift messengers!
Take a message to a tall, smooth-skinned people,
 who are feared far and wide
for their conquests and destruction,
 and whose land is divided by rivers.

³ All you people of the world,
 everyone who lives on the earth—
when I raise my battle flag on the mountain, look!
 When I blow the ram's horn, listen!
⁴ For the Lord has told me this:
"I will watch quietly from my dwelling place—
 as quietly as the heat rises on a summer day,
 or as the morning dew forms during the harvest."
⁵ Even before you begin your attack,
 while your plans are ripening like grapes,
the Lord will cut off your new growth with pruning shears.
 He will snip off and discard your spreading branches.
⁶ Your mighty army will be left dead in the fields
 for the mountain vultures and wild animals.
The vultures will tear at the corpses all summer.
 The wild animals will gnaw at the bones all winter.

⁷ At that time the Lord of Heaven's Armies will receive gifts
 from this land divided by rivers,
from this tall, smooth-skinned people,
 who are feared far and wide for their conquests and destruction.
They will bring the gifts to Jerusalem,*
 where the Lord of Heaven's Armies dwells.

16:14 Hebrew *Within three years, as a servant bound by contract would count them.* **17:3a** Hebrew *of Ephraim,* referring to the northern kingdom of Israel. **17:3b** Hebrew *Aram.* **17:4** Hebrew *Jacob's.* See note on 14:1. **17:9** As in Greek version; Hebrew reads *like places of the wood and the highest bough.* **18:1a** Hebrew *Cush.* **18:1b** Or *land of many locusts;* Hebrew reads *land of whirring wings.* **18:7** Hebrew *to Mount Zion.*

A Message about Egypt

19 This message came to me concerning Egypt:

Look! The LORD is advancing against Egypt,
  riding on a swift cloud.
The idols of Egypt tremble.
  The hearts of the Egyptians melt with fear.

² "I will make Egyptian fight against Egyptian—
  brother against brother,
  neighbor against neighbor,
  city against city,
  province against province.
³ The Egyptians will lose heart,
  and I will confuse their plans.
They will plead with their idols for wisdom
  and call on spirits, mediums, and those who
    consult the spirits of the dead.
⁴ I will hand Egypt over
  to a hard, cruel master.
A fierce king will rule them,"
  says the Lord, the LORD of Heaven's Armies.

⁵ The waters of the Nile will fail to rise and flood
    the fields.
  The riverbed will be parched and dry.
⁶ The canals of the Nile will dry up,
  and the streams of Egypt will stink
    with rotting reeds and rushes.
⁷ All the greenery along the riverbank
  and all the crops along the river
    will dry up and blow away.
⁸ The fishermen will lament for lack of work.
  Those who cast hooks into the Nile will groan,
    and those who use nets will lose heart.
⁹ There will be no flax for the harvesters,
    no thread for the weavers.
¹⁰ They will be in despair,
    and all the workers will be sick at heart.

¹¹ What fools are the officials of Zoan!
  Their best counsel to the king of Egypt is
    stupid and wrong.
Will they still boast to Pharaoh of their wisdom?
  Will they dare brag about all their wise
    ancestors?
¹² Where are your wise counselors, Pharaoh?
  Let them tell you what God plans,
    what the LORD of Heaven's Armies is going to
      do to Egypt.
¹³ The officials of Zoan are fools,
    and the officials of Memphis* are deluded.
  The leaders of the people
    have led Egypt astray.
¹⁴ The LORD has sent a spirit of foolishness on them,
    so all their suggestions are wrong.
  They cause Egypt to stagger
    like a drunk in his vomit.

¹⁵ There is nothing Egypt can do.
  All are helpless—
    the head and the tail,
    the noble palm branch and the lowly reed.

¹⁶In that day the Egyptians will be as weak as women. They will cower in fear beneath the upraised fist of the LORD of Heaven's Armies. ¹⁷Just to speak the name of Israel will terrorize them, for the LORD of Heaven's Armies has laid out his plans against them.

¹⁸In that day five of Egypt's cities will follow the LORD of Heaven's Armies. They will even begin to speak Hebrew, the language of Canaan. One of these cities will be Heliopolis, the City of the Sun.*

¹⁹In that day there will be an altar to the LORD in the heart of Egypt, and there will be a monument to the LORD at its border. ²⁰It will be a sign and a witness that the LORD of Heaven's Armies is worshiped in the land of Egypt. When the people cry to the LORD for help against those who oppress them, he will send them a savior who will rescue them. ²¹The LORD will make himself known to the Egyptians. Yes, they will know the LORD and will give their sacrifices and offerings to him. They will make a vow to the LORD and will keep it. ²²The LORD will strike Egypt, and then he will bring healing. For the Egyptians will turn to the LORD, and he will listen to their pleas and heal them.

²³In that day Egypt and Assyria will be connected by a highway. The Egyptians and Assyrians will move freely between their lands, and they will both worship God. ²⁴In that day Israel will be the third, along with Egypt and Assyria, a blessing in the midst of the earth. ²⁵For the LORD of Heaven's Armies will say, "Blessed be Egypt, my people. Blessed be Assyria, the land I have made. Blessed be Israel, my special possession!"

A Message about Egypt and Ethiopia

20 In the year when King Sargon of Assyria sent his commander in chief to capture the Philistine city of Ashdod,* ²the LORD told Isaiah son of Amoz, "Take off the burlap you have been wearing, and remove your sandals." Isaiah did as he was told and walked around naked and barefoot.

³Then the LORD said, "My servant Isaiah has been walking around naked and barefoot for the last three years. This is a sign—a symbol of the terrible troubles I will bring upon Egypt and Ethiopia.* ⁴For the king of Assyria will take away the Egyptians and Ethiopians* as prisoners. He will make them walk naked and barefoot, both young and old, their buttocks bared, to the shame of Egypt. ⁵Then the Philistines will be thrown into panic, for they counted on the power of Ethiopia and boasted of their allies in Egypt! ⁶They will say, 'If this can happen to Egypt, what chance do we have? We were counting on Egypt to protect us from the king of Assyria.'"

19:13 Hebrew *Noph.* 19:18 Or *will be the City of Destruction.* 20:1 Ashdod was captured by Assyria in 711 B.C. 20:3 Hebrew *Cush;* also in 20:5. 20:4 Hebrew *Cushites.*

A Message about Babylon

21 This message came to me concerning Babylon—the desert by the sea*:

Disaster is roaring down on you from
   the desert,
like a whirlwind sweeping in from the Negev.
² I see a terrifying vision:
   I see the betrayer betraying,
   the destroyer destroying.
Go ahead, you Elamites and Medes,
   attack and lay siege.
I will make an end
   to all the groaning Babylon caused.
³ My stomach aches and burns with pain.
   Sharp pangs of anguish are upon me,
   like those of a woman in labor.
I grow faint when I hear what God is planning;
   I am too afraid to look.
⁴ My mind reels and my heart races.
   I longed for evening to come,
   but now I am terrified of the dark.
⁵ Look! They are preparing a great feast.
   They are spreading rugs for people to sit on.
   Everyone is eating and drinking.
But quick! Grab your shields and prepare for
   battle.
   You are being attacked!

⁶ Meanwhile, the Lord said to me,
"Put a watchman on the city wall.
   Let him shout out what he sees.
⁷ He should look for chariots
   drawn by pairs of horses,
and for riders on donkeys and camels.
   Let the watchman be fully alert."

⁸ Then the watchman* called out,
"Day after day I have stood on the watchtower,
   my lord.
Night after night I have remained at my post.
⁹ Now at last—look!
Here comes a man in a chariot
   with a pair of horses!"
Then the watchman said,
   "Babylon is fallen, fallen!
All the idols of Babylon
   lie broken on the ground!"
¹⁰ O my people, threshed and winnowed,
   I have told you everything the Lord of
      Heaven's Armies has said,
   everything the God of Israel has told me.

A Message about Edom

¹¹This message came to me concerning Edom*:

Someone from Edom* keeps calling to me,
"Watchman, how much longer until morning?
   When will the night be over?"
¹² The watchman replies,
"Morning is coming, but night will soon return.
   If you wish to ask again, then come back and
      ask."

A Message about Arabia

¹³This message came to me concerning Arabia:

O caravans from Dedan,
   hide in the deserts of Arabia.
¹⁴ O people of Tema,
   bring water to these thirsty people,
   food to these weary refugees.
¹⁵ They have fled from the sword,
   from the drawn sword,
from the bent bow
   and the terrors of battle.

¹⁶The Lord said to me, "Within a year, counting each day,* all the glory of Kedar will come to an end. ¹⁷Only a few of its courageous archers will survive. I, the Lord, the God of Israel, have spoken!"

A Message about Jerusalem

22 This message came to me concerning Jerusalem—the Valley of Vision*:

What is happening?
   Why is everyone running to the rooftops?
² The whole city is in a terrible uproar.
   What do I see in this reveling city?
Bodies are lying everywhere,
   killed not in battle but by famine and disease.
³ All your leaders have fled.
   They surrendered without resistance.
The people tried to slip away,
   but they were captured, too.
⁴ That's why I said, "Leave me alone to weep;
   do not try to comfort me.
Let me cry for my people
   as I watch them being destroyed."

⁵ Oh, what a day of crushing defeat!
   What a day of confusion and terror
brought by the Lord, the Lord of Heaven's
   Armies,
   upon the Valley of Vision!
The walls of Jerusalem have been broken,
   and cries of death echo from the
      mountainsides.
⁶ Elamites are the archers,
   with their chariots and charioteers.
The men of Kir hold up the shields.

21:1 Hebrew *concerning the desert by the sea.* 21:8 As in Dead Sea Scrolls and Syriac version; Masoretic Text reads *a lion.* 21:11a Hebrew *Dumah,* which means "silence" or "stillness." It is a wordplay on the word *Edom.* 21:11b Hebrew *Seir,* another name for Edom. 21:16 Hebrew *Within a year, as a servant bound by contract would count it.* Some ancient manuscripts read *Within three years,* as in 16:14. 22:1 Hebrew *concerning the Valley of Vision.*

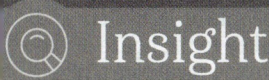

Insight: ISAIAH'S PROPHECIES IN THE NEW TESTAMENT

When the New Testament writers wanted to explain who Jesus was, their go-to source was Isaiah. Isaiah's prophecies are unique in their number and precision, connecting expectations for the future Messiah, or Savior, with who Jesus was and what he did. These charts detail where and how often the New Testament quotes Isaiah in comparison to other Old Testament books. They show how the Old Testament helps us understand Jesus and how the Bible weaves together.

Isaiah is quoted in these New Testament verses:

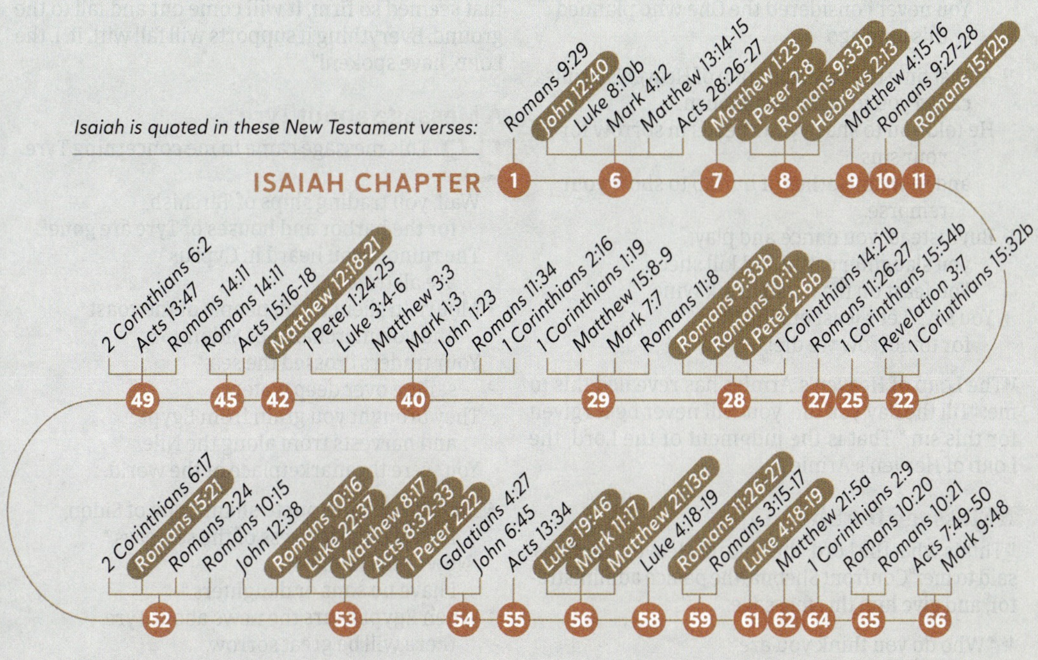

ISAIAH CHAPTER

Chapter	New Testament verses
1	Romans 9:29
6	John 12:40; Luke 8:10b; Mark 4:12
7	Matthew 1:23
8	Acts 28:26-27; Matthew 13:14-15
9	1 Peter 2:8
10	Romans 9:33b; Hebrews 2:13
11	Matthew 4:15-16; Romans 9:27-28; Romans 15:12b
22	1 Corinthians 15:32b
25	1 Corinthians 15:54b; Revelation 3:7
27	1 Corinthians 14:21b; Romans 11:26-27
28	Romans 9:33b; Romans 10:11; 1 Peter 2:6b
29	Romans 11:34; 1 Corinthians 2:16; 1 Corinthians 1:19; Matthew 15:8-9; Mark 7:7; Romans 11:8
40	Matthew 3:3; Mark 1:3; John 1:23
42	Matthew 12:18-21; 1 Peter 1:24-25; Luke 3:4-6
45	Romans 14:11; Acts 15:16-18
49	2 Corinthians 6:2; Acts 13:47
52	2 Corinthians 6:17; Romans 15:21; Romans 2:24; Romans 10:15; John 12:38
53	Romans 10:16; Luke 22:37; Matthew 8:17; Acts 8:32-33; 1 Peter 2:22
54	Galatians 4:27
55	John 6:45
56	Acts 13:34; Luke 19:46; Mark 11:17; Matthew 21:13a
58	Luke 4:18-19
59	Romans 11:26-27; Romans 3:15-17
61	Luke 4:18-19
62	Matthew 21:5a
64	1 Corinthians 2:9
65	Romans 10:20
66	Romans 10:21; Acts 7:49-50; Mark 9:48

● Verses highlighted in gold are prophecies Jesus fulfilled.

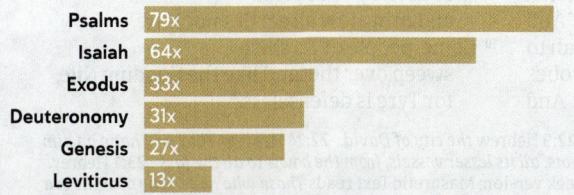

Most quoted Old Testament books

The number of times these Old Testament books are quoted in the New Testament:

- Psalms — 79x
- Isaiah — 64x
- Exodus — 33x
- Deuteronomy — 31x
- Genesis — 27x
- Leviticus — 13x

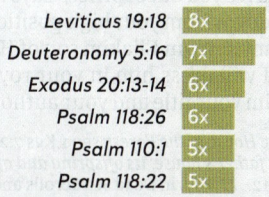

Most quoted Old Testament verses

The Old Testament verses that are quoted most often in the New Testament:

- Leviticus 19:18 — 8x
- Deuteronomy 5:16 — 7x
- Exodus 20:13-14 — 6x
- Psalm 118:26 — 6x
- Psalm 110:1 — 5x
- Psalm 118:22 — 5x

⁷ Chariots fill your beautiful valleys,
   and charioteers storm your gates.
⁸ Judah's defenses have been stripped away.
   You run to the armory* for your weapons.
⁹ You inspect the breaks in the walls of Jerusalem.*
   You store up water in the lower pool.
¹⁰ You survey the houses and tear some down
   for stone to strengthen the walls.
¹¹ Between the city walls, you build a reservoir
   for water from the old pool.
   But you never ask for help from the One who did all this.
   You never considered the One who planned this long ago.
¹² At that time the Lord, the LORD of Heaven's Armies,
   called you to weep and mourn.
   He told you to shave your heads in sorrow for your sins
   and to wear clothes of burlap to show your remorse.
¹³ But instead, you dance and play;
   you slaughter cattle and kill sheep.
   You feast on meat and drink wine.
   You say, "Let's feast and drink,
   for tomorrow we die!"

¹⁴The LORD of Heaven's Armies has revealed this to me: "Till the day you die, you will never be forgiven for this sin." That is the judgment of the Lord, the LORD of Heaven's Armies.

A Message for Shebna

¹⁵This is what the Lord, the LORD of Heaven's Armies, said to me: "Confront Shebna, the palace administrator, and give him this message:

¹⁶ "Who do you think you are,
   and what are you doing here,
   building a beautiful tomb for yourself—
   a monument high up in the rock?
¹⁷ For the LORD is about to hurl you away, mighty man.
   He is going to grab you,
¹⁸ crumple you into a ball,
   and toss you away into a distant, barren land.
   There you will die,
   and your glorious chariots will be broken and useless.
   You are a disgrace to your master!"

¹⁹"Yes, I will drive you out of office," says the LORD. "I will pull you down from your high position. ²⁰And then I will call my servant Eliakim son of Hilkiah to replace you. ²¹I will dress him in your royal robes and will give him your title and your authority. And he will be a father to the people of Jerusalem and Judah. ²²I will give him the key to the house of David—the highest position in the royal court. When he opens doors, no one will be able to close them; when he closes doors, no one will be able to open them. ²³He will bring honor to his family name, for I will drive him firmly in place like a nail in the wall. ²⁴They will give him great responsibility, and he will bring honor to even the lowliest members of his family.*"

²⁵But the LORD of Heaven's Armies also says: "The time will come when I will pull out the nail that seemed so firm. It will come out and fall to the ground. Everything it supports will fall with it. I, the LORD, have spoken!"

A Message about Tyre

23 This message came to me concerning Tyre:

Wail, you trading ships of Tarshish,
   for the harbor and houses of Tyre are gone!
The rumors you heard in Cyprus*
   are all true.
² Mourn in silence, you people of the coast
   and you merchants of Sidon.
Your traders crossed the sea,*
³   sailing over deep waters.
They brought you grain from Egypt*
   and harvests from along the Nile.
You were the marketplace of the world.

⁴ But now you are put to shame, city of Sidon,
   for Tyre, the fortress of the sea, says,*
"Now I am childless;
   I have no sons or daughters."
⁵ When Egypt hears the news about Tyre,
   there will be great sorrow.
⁶ Send word now to Tarshish!
   Wail, you people who live in distant lands!
⁷ Is this silent ruin all that is left of your once joyous city?
   What a long history was yours!
   Think of all the colonists you sent to distant places.
⁸ Who has brought this disaster on Tyre,
   that great creator of kingdoms?
   Her traders were all princes,
   her merchants were nobles.
⁹ The LORD of Heaven's Armies has done it
   to destroy your pride
   and bring low all earth's nobility.
¹⁰ Come, people of Tarshish,
   sweep over the land like the flooding Nile,
   for Tyre is defenseless.*

22:8 Hebrew *to the House of the Forest;* see 1 Kgs 7:2-5. **22:9** Hebrew *the city of David.* **22:24** Hebrew *They will hang on him all the glory of his father's house: its offspring and offshoots, all its lesser vessels, from the bowls to all the jars.* **23:1** Hebrew *Kittim;* also in 23:12. **23:2** As in Dead Sea Scrolls and Greek version; Masoretic Text reads *Those who have gone over the sea have filled you.* **23:3** Hebrew *from Shihor,* a branch of the Nile River. **23:4** Or *for the god of the sea says;* Hebrew reads *for the sea, the fortress of the sea, says.* **23:10** The meaning of the Hebrew in this verse is uncertain.

¹¹ The LORD held out his hand over the sea
 and shook the kingdoms of the earth.
He has spoken out against Phoenicia,*
 ordering that her fortresses be destroyed.
¹² He says, "Never again will you rejoice,
 O daughter of Sidon, for you have been crushed.
Even if you flee to Cyprus,
 you will find no rest."

¹³ Look at the land of Babylonia*—
 the people of that land are gone!
The Assyrians have handed Babylon over
 to the wild animals of the desert.
They have built siege ramps against its walls,
 torn down its palaces,
 and turned it to a heap of rubble.

¹⁴ Wail, you ships of Tarshish,
 for your harbor is destroyed!

¹⁵ For seventy years, the length of a king's life, Tyre will be forgotten. But then the city will come back to life as in the song about the prostitute:

¹⁶ Take a harp and walk the streets,
 you forgotten harlot.
Make sweet melody and sing your songs
 so you will be remembered again.

¹⁷ Yes, after seventy years the LORD will revive Tyre. But she will be no different than she was before. She will again be a prostitute to all kingdoms around the world. ¹⁸ But in the end her profits will be given to the LORD. Her wealth will not be hoarded but will provide good food and fine clothing for the LORD's priests.

Destruction of the Earth

24 Look! The LORD is about to destroy the earth
 and make it a vast wasteland.
He devastates the surface of the earth
 and scatters the people.
² Priests and laypeople,
 servants and masters,
 maids and mistresses,
 buyers and sellers,
 lenders and borrowers,
 bankers and debtors—none will be spared.
³ The earth will be completely emptied and looted.
 The LORD has spoken!

23:11 Hebrew *Canaan.*   23:13 Or *Chaldea.*

⁴ The earth mourns and dries up,
 and the land wastes away and withers.
Even the greatest people on earth waste away.
⁵ The earth suffers for the sins of its people,
 for they have twisted God's instructions,
violated his laws,
 and broken his everlasting covenant.
⁶ Therefore, a curse consumes the earth.
 Its people must pay the price for their sin.
They are destroyed by fire,
 and only a few are left alive.
⁷ The grapevines waste away,
 and there is no new wine.
All the merrymakers sigh and mourn.
⁸ The cheerful sound of tambourines is stilled;
 the happy cries of celebration are heard no
  more.
The melodious chords of the harp are silent.
⁹ Gone are the joys of wine and song;
 alcoholic drink turns bitter in the mouth.
¹⁰ The city writhes in chaos;
 every home is locked to keep out intruders.
¹¹ Mobs gather in the streets, crying out for wine.
 Joy has turned to gloom.
 Gladness has been banished from the land.
¹² The city is left in ruins,
 its gates battered down.
¹³ Throughout the earth the story is the same—
 only a remnant is left,
like the stray olives left on the tree
 or the few grapes left on the vine after harvest.

¹⁴ But all who are left shout and sing for joy.
 Those in the west praise the LORD's majesty.
¹⁵ In eastern lands, give glory to the LORD.
 In the lands beyond the sea, praise the name
  of the LORD, the God of Israel.
¹⁶ We hear songs of praise from the ends of
  the earth,
 songs that give glory to the Righteous One!

But my heart is heavy with grief.
 Weep for me, for I wither away.
Deceit still prevails,
 and treachery is everywhere.
¹⁷ Terror and traps and snares will be your lot,
 you people of the earth.

24:1–27:13 This section is often referred to as the "Little Apocalypse" because of its similarities to the book of Revelation. *Apocalypse* means "revelation," and apocalyptic writings and stories reveal visionary information from God. In these chapters Isaiah takes readers out of the present into a vision of God's plans for the world. The universal imagery of the Little Apocalypse makes it difficult to assign the events described to any precise historical situation—apocalypse is different from prophecy. That means that these chapters cannot be used to outline a sequence of events or create a historical blueprint for the future. Instead, the imagery is intended to create an impressionistic drama of an unfolding world that is both like and unlike the present. The combination of aspects of the old era with aspects of the new era (for instance, people of Zion will all be righteous [new era], but still long for their redemption [old era]) is consistent with the New Testament concept of the future age breaking into and overlapping with the present evil age (2 Corinthians 4:4; Galatians 1:4). Peter, for example, wrote of believers as living in the last days (1 Peter 1:20; 2 Peter 3:3) even though that last day remains yet future (2 Peter 3:10).

¹⁸ Those who flee in terror will fall into a trap,
and those who escape the trap will be caught
in a snare.

Destruction falls like rain from the heavens;
the foundations of the earth shake.
¹⁹ The earth has broken up.
It has utterly collapsed;
it is violently shaken.
²⁰ The earth staggers like a drunk.
It trembles like a tent in a storm.
It falls and will not rise again,
for the guilt of its rebellion is very heavy.

²¹ In that day the Lord will punish the gods in the
heavens
and the proud rulers of the nations on earth.
²² They will be rounded up and put in prison.
They will be shut up in prison
and will finally be punished.
²³ Then the glory of the moon will wane,
and the brightness of the sun will fade,
for the Lord of Heaven's Armies will rule on
Mount Zion.
He will rule in great glory in Jerusalem,
in the sight of all the leaders of his people.

Praise for Judgment and Salvation

25 O Lord, I will honor and praise your name,
for you are my God.
You do such wonderful things!
You planned them long ago,
and now you have accomplished them.
² You turn mighty cities into heaps of ruins.
Cities with strong walls are turned to rubble.
Beautiful palaces in distant lands disappear
and will never be rebuilt.
³ Therefore, strong nations will declare your glory;
ruthless nations will fear you.

⁴ But you are a tower of refuge to the poor, O Lord,
a tower of refuge to the needy in distress.
You are a refuge from the storm
and a shelter from the heat.
For the oppressive acts of ruthless people
are like a storm beating against a wall,
⁵ or like the relentless heat of the desert.
But you silence the roar of foreign nations.
As the shade of a cloud cools relentless heat,
so the boastful songs of ruthless people are
stilled.

⁶ In Jerusalem,* the Lord of Heaven's Armies
will spread a wonderful feast
for all the people of the world.
It will be a delicious banquet
with clear, well-aged wine and choice meat.
⁷ There he will remove the cloud of gloom,
the shadow of death that hangs over the earth.
⁸ He will swallow up death forever!
The Sovereign Lord will wipe away all tears.
He will remove forever all insults and mockery
against his land and people.
The Lord has spoken!

⁹ In that day the people will proclaim,
"This is our God!
We trusted in him, and he saved us!
This is the Lord, in whom we trusted.
Let us rejoice in the salvation he brings!"

¹⁰ For the Lord's hand of blessing will rest on
Jerusalem.
But Moab will be crushed.
It will be like straw trampled down and left
to rot.
¹¹ God will push down Moab's people
as a swimmer pushes down water with his
hands.
He will end their pride
and all their evil works.
¹² The high walls of Moab will be demolished.
They will be brought down to the ground,
down into the dust.

A Song of Praise to the Lord

26 In that day, everyone in the land of Judah will
sing this song:

Our city is strong!
We are surrounded by the walls of God's
salvation.
² Open the gates to all who are righteous;
allow the faithful to enter.
³ **You will keep in perfect peace
all who trust in you,
all whose thoughts are fixed on you!**
⁴ Trust in the Lord always,
for the Lord God is the eternal Rock.
⁵ He humbles the proud
and brings down the arrogant city.
He brings it down to the dust.
⁶ The poor and oppressed trample it underfoot,
and the needy walk all over it.

25:6 Hebrew *On this mountain*; also in 25:10.

25:8 Isaiah's hope was God's power over sin and sin's devastating results, that he would "swallow up death forever." In the New Testament this promise is realized in Jesus Christ (1 Corinthians 15:54). The Lord's presence will be a source of eternal comfort; he will "wipe every tear from their eyes" (Revelation 21:4).

26:1 "Our city" refers to Zion, the eternal city of God, where the Lord is present to protect and bless his people (see 1:8, 27; see also Psalm 46). Zion stands in direct contrast to the "mighty cities" of the nations, which are helpless and are brought down to "ruins" (Isaiah 25:2; 26:5). The "walls of God's salvation" protectively enclose his people; no one can hurt them again.

⁷ But for those who are righteous,
    the way is not steep and rough.
  You are a God who does what is right,
    and you smooth out the path ahead of them.
⁸ LORD, we show our trust in you by obeying your laws;
    our heart's desire is to glorify your name.
⁹ In the night I search for you;
    in the morning* I earnestly seek you.
  For only when you come to judge the earth
    will people learn what is right.
¹⁰ Your kindness to the wicked
    does not make them do good.
  Although others do right, the wicked keep doing wrong
    and take no notice of the LORD's majesty.
¹¹ O LORD, they pay no attention to your upraised fist.
  Show them your eagerness to defend your people.
  Then they will be ashamed.
    Let your fire consume your enemies.
¹² LORD, you will grant us peace;
    all we have accomplished is really from you.
¹³ O LORD our God, others have ruled us,
    but you alone are the one we worship.
¹⁴ Those we served before are dead and gone.
    Their departed spirits will never return!
  You attacked them and destroyed them,
    and they are long forgotten.
¹⁵ O LORD, you have made our nation great;
    yes, you have made us great.
  You have extended our borders,
    and we give you the glory!
¹⁶ LORD, in distress we searched for you.
    We prayed beneath the burden of your discipline.
¹⁷ Just as a pregnant woman
    writhes and cries out in pain as she gives birth,
  so were we in your presence, LORD.
¹⁸ We, too, writhe in agony,
    but nothing comes of our suffering.
  We have not given salvation to the earth,
    nor brought life into the world.
¹⁹ But those who die in the LORD will live;
    their bodies will rise again!
  Those who sleep in the earth
    will rise up and sing for joy!
  For your life-giving light will fall like dew
    on your people in the place of the dead!

Restoration for Israel

²⁰ Go home, my people,
    and lock your doors!
  Hide yourselves for a little while
    until the LORD's anger has passed.
²¹ Look! The LORD is coming from heaven
    to punish the people of the earth for their sins.
  The earth will no longer hide those who have been killed.
    They will be brought out for all to see.

27 In that day the LORD will take his terrible, swift sword and punish Leviathan,* the swiftly moving serpent, the coiling, writhing serpent. He will kill the dragon of the sea.

² "In that day,
    sing about the fruitful vineyard.
³ I, the LORD, will watch over it,
    watering it carefully.
  Day and night I will watch so no one can harm it.
⁴ My anger will be gone.
  If I find briers and thorns growing,
    I will attack them;
  I will burn them up—
⁵ unless they turn to me for help.
  Let them make peace with me;
    yes, let them make peace with me."
⁶ The time is coming when Jacob's descendants will take root.
  Israel will bud and blossom
    and fill the whole earth with fruit!
⁷ Has the LORD struck Israel
    as he struck her enemies?
  Has he punished her
    as he punished them?
⁸ No, but he exiled Israel to call her to account.
  She was exiled from her land
    as though blown away in a storm from the east.
⁹ The LORD did this to purge Israel's* wickedness,
    to take away all her sin.
  As a result, all the pagan altars will be crushed to dust.
    No Asherah pole or pagan shrine will be left standing.
¹⁰ The fortified towns will be silent and empty,
    the houses abandoned, the streets overgrown with weeds.
  Calves will graze there,
    chewing on twigs and branches.
¹¹ The people are like the dead branches of a tree,
    broken off and used for kindling beneath the cooking pots.
  Israel is a foolish and stupid nation,
    for its people have turned away from God.
  Therefore, the one who made them
    will show them no pity or mercy.

26:9 Hebrew *within me.* **27:1** The identification of Leviathan is disputed, ranging from an earthly creature to a mythical sea monster in ancient literature. **27:9** Hebrew *Jacob's.* See note on 14:1.

ISAIAH 28

¹²Yet the time will come when the LORD will gather them together like handpicked grain. One by one he will gather them—from the Euphrates River* in the east to the Brook of Egypt in the west. ¹³In that day the great trumpet will sound. Many who were dying in exile in Assyria and Egypt will return to Jerusalem to worship the LORD on his holy mountain.

A Message about Samaria

28 What sorrow awaits the proud city of Samaria—
the glorious crown of the drunks of Israel.*
It sits at the head of a fertile valley,
but its glorious beauty will fade like a flower.
It is the pride of a people
brought down by wine.
² For the Lord will send a mighty army against it.
Like a mighty hailstorm and a torrential rain,
they will burst upon it like a surging flood
and smash it to the ground.
³ The proud city of Samaria—
the glorious crown of the drunks of Israel*—
will be trampled beneath its enemies' feet.
⁴ It sits at the head of a fertile valley,
but its glorious beauty will fade like a flower.

27:12 Hebrew *the river.* 28:1 Hebrew *What sorrow awaits the crowning glory of the drunks of Ephraim,* referring to Samaria, capital of the northern kingdom of Israel. 28:3 Hebrew *The crowning glory of the drunks of Ephraim;* see note on 28:1.

Come Close — WOE? PROMISES

SCRIPTURE CONNECTION: ISAIAH 27:1-12

Sometimes—more often than I would like to acknowledge—I feel incapable of facing this world myself.

There are things I cannot change, like raising my income when my parents need more of me. Like getting healthier just by generating the positive power of my mind. Or like gaining a life where I prosper, with minimal effort and suffering.

But I am saved from myself by unconditional love. God shows me he is no more than a step away. No matter what, he is always by my side.

And that is why, even as I struggle most times, even when hardship blocks my perspective of his work in me, I choose to trust in his promises.

The Lord is my safeguard (Isaiah 27:3). It is good to know who is with me in this crazy world, where I fear violence, crises, and diseases, and where others' intentions against me could cause harm.

In him, my roots produce good fruit (Isaiah 27:6). My life, friends, coworkers, family, and even those I exchange a word or two with in the rush can be nourished by the fruitful vineyard that God has planted in me.

My trust in him removes my sin (Isaiah 27:9). All these promises come from this powerful God who has given me a beautiful relationship with him. He releases me from shame, fear, and the scars of my sin. I am forgiven.

REFLECT "In that day, sing about the fruitful vineyard. I, the LORD, will watch over it, watering it carefully. Day and night I will watch so no one can harm it." ISAIAH 27:2-3

Bad days perish. There is hope today, as we choose his love over choosing fear.

CONSIDER "Our lives are full of supposes. Suppose this should happen, or suppose that should happen; what could we do; how could we bear it? But, if we are living in the high tower of the dwelling place of God, all these supposes will drop out of our lives. We shall be quiet from the fear of evil, for no threatenings of evil can penetrate into the high tower of God."
HANNAH WHITALL SMITH

> God is no more than a step away. No matter what, he is always by your side.

DEBORA DA SILVA is from Brazil and found release from poverty through Compassion International. She works with Facebook in Colombia and lives to serve as she tries to be a channel—not only a recipient—of God's goodness.

Whoever sees it will snatch it up,
 as an early fig is quickly picked and eaten.

⁵ Then at last the LORD of Heaven's Armies
  will himself be Israel's glorious crown.
 He will be the pride and joy
  of the remnant of his people.
⁶ He will give a longing for justice
  to their judges.
 He will give great courage
  to their warriors who stand at the gates.

⁷ Now, however, Israel is led by drunks
  who reel with wine and stagger with alcohol.
 The priests and prophets stagger with alcohol
  and lose themselves in wine.
 They reel when they see visions
  and stagger as they render decisions.
⁸ Their tables are covered with vomit;
  filth is everywhere.

⁹ "Who does the LORD think we are?" they ask.
 "Why does he speak to us like this?
 Are we little children,
  just recently weaned?
¹⁰ He tells us everything over and over—
 one line at a time,
  one line at a time,
 a little here,
  and a little there!"

¹¹ So now God will have to speak to his people
  through foreign oppressors who speak a
   strange language!
¹² God has told his people,
 "Here is a place of rest;
  let the weary rest here.
 This is a place of quiet rest."
  But they would not listen.
¹³ So the LORD will spell out his message for them
   again,
 one line at a time,
  one line at a time,
 a little here,
  and a little there,
 so that they will stumble and fall.
  They will be injured, trapped, and captured.

¹⁴ Therefore, listen to this message from the LORD,
  you scoffing rulers in Jerusalem.
¹⁵ You boast, "We have struck a bargain to cheat death
  and have made a deal to dodge the grave.*
 The coming destruction can never touch us,
  for we have built a strong refuge made of lies
   and deception."

¹⁶ Therefore, this is what the Sovereign LORD says:
 "Look! I am placing a foundation stone in
   Jerusalem,*
 a firm and tested stone.

It is a precious cornerstone that is safe to build on.
 Whoever believes need never be shaken.*
¹⁷ I will test you with the measuring line of justice
  and the plumb line of righteousness.
 Since your refuge is made of lies,
  a hailstorm will knock it down.
 Since it is made of deception,
  a flood will sweep it away.
¹⁸ I will cancel the bargain you made to cheat
   death,
  and I will overturn your deal to dodge the
   grave.
 When the terrible enemy sweeps through,
  you will be trampled into the ground.
¹⁹ Again and again that flood will come,
  morning after morning,
 day and night,
  until you are carried away."

This message will bring terror to your people.
²⁰ The bed you have made is too short to lie on.
  The blankets are too narrow to cover you.
²¹ The LORD will come as he did against the
   Philistines at Mount Perazim
  and against the Amorites at Gibeon.
 He will come to do a strange thing;
  he will come to do an unusual deed:
²² For the Lord, the LORD of Heaven's Armies,
  has plainly said that he is determined to crush
   the whole land.
 So scoff no more,
  or your punishment will be even greater.

²³ Listen to me;
  listen, and pay close attention.
²⁴ Does a farmer always plow and never sow?
  Is he forever cultivating the soil and never
   planting?
²⁵ Does he not finally plant his seeds—
  black cumin, cumin, wheat, barley, and
   emmer wheat—
 each in its proper way,
  and each in its proper place?
²⁶ The farmer knows just what to do,
  for God has given him understanding.
²⁷ A heavy sledge is never used to thresh black
   cumin;
  rather, it is beaten with a light stick.
 A threshing wheel is never rolled on cumin;
  instead, it is beaten lightly with a flail.
²⁸ Grain for bread is easily crushed,
  so he doesn't keep on pounding it.
 He threshes it under the wheels of a cart,
  but he doesn't pulverize it.
²⁹ The LORD of Heaven's Armies is a wonderful
   teacher,
  and he gives the farmer great wisdom.

28:15 Hebrew *Sheol;* also in 28:18. **28:16a** Hebrew *in Zion.* **28:16b** Greek version reads *Look! I am placing a stone in the foundation of Jerusalem* [literally *Zion*], */ a precious cornerstone for its foundation, chosen for great honor. / Anyone who trusts in him will never be disgraced.* Compare Rom 9:33; 1 Pet 2:6.

ISAIAH 29

A Message about Jerusalem

29 "What sorrow awaits Ariel,* the City of David.
Year after year you celebrate your feasts.
² Yet I will bring disaster upon you,
and there will be much weeping and sorrow.
For Jerusalem will become what her name Ariel means—
an altar covered with blood.
³ I will be your enemy,
surrounding Jerusalem and attacking its walls.
I will build siege towers
and destroy it.
⁴ Then deep from the earth you will speak;
from low in the dust your words will come.
Your voice will whisper from the ground
like a ghost conjured up from the grave.

⁵ "But suddenly, your ruthless enemies will be crushed
like the finest of dust.
Your many attackers will be driven away
like chaff before the wind.
Suddenly, in an instant,
⁶ I, the Lord of Heaven's Armies, will act for you
with thunder and earthquake and great noise,
with whirlwind and storm and consuming fire.
⁷ All the nations fighting against Jerusalem*
will vanish like a dream!
Those who are attacking her walls
will vanish like a vision in the night.
⁸ A hungry person dreams of eating
but wakes up still hungry.
A thirsty person dreams of drinking
but is still faint from thirst when morning comes.
So it will be with your enemies,
with those who attack Mount Zion."

⁹ Are you amazed and incredulous?
Don't you believe it?
Then go ahead and be blind.
You are stupid, but not from wine!
You stagger, but not from liquor!
¹⁰ For the Lord has poured out on you a spirit of deep sleep.
He has closed the eyes of your prophets and visionaries.

¹¹ All the future events in this vision are like a sealed book to them. When you give it to those who can read, they will say, "We can't read it because it is sealed." ¹² When you give it to those who cannot read, they will say, "We don't know how to read."

¹³ And so the Lord says,

"These people say they are mine.
They honor me with their lips,
but their hearts are far from me.
And their worship of me
is nothing but man-made rules learned by rote.*
¹⁴ Because of this, I will once again astound these hypocrites
with amazing wonders.
The wisdom of the wise will pass away,
and the intelligence of the intelligent will disappear."

¹⁵ What sorrow awaits those who try to hide their plans from the Lord,
who do their evil deeds in the dark!
"The Lord can't see us," they say.
"He doesn't know what's going on!"
¹⁶ How foolish can you be?
He is the Potter, and he is certainly greater than you, the clay!
Should the created thing say of the one who made it,
"He didn't make me"?
Does a jar ever say,
"The potter who made me is stupid"?

¹⁷ Soon—and it will not be very long—
the forests of Lebanon will become a fertile field,
and the fertile field will yield bountiful crops.
¹⁸ In that day the deaf will hear words read from a book,
and the blind will see through the gloom and darkness.
¹⁹ The humble will be filled with fresh joy from the Lord.
The poor will rejoice in the Holy One of Israel.
²⁰ The scoffer will be gone,
the arrogant will disappear,
and those who plot evil will be killed.
²¹ Those who convict the innocent
by their false testimony will disappear.
A similar fate awaits those who use trickery to pervert justice
and who tell lies to destroy the innocent.

²² That is why the Lord, who redeemed Abraham, says to the people of Israel,*

"My people will no longer be ashamed
or turn pale with fear.
²³ For when they see their many children
and all the blessings I have given them,
they will recognize the holiness of the Holy One of Jacob.
They will stand in awe of the God of Israel.
²⁴ Then the wayward will gain understanding,
and complainers will accept instruction.

29:1 *Ariel* sounds like a Hebrew term that means "hearth" or "altar." **29:7** Hebrew *Ariel*. **29:13** Greek version reads *Their worship is a farce, / for they teach man-made ideas as commands from God.* Compare Mark 7:7. **29:22** Hebrew *of Jacob*. See note on 14:1.

Judah's Worthless Treaty with Egypt

30 "What sorrow awaits my rebellious children,"
    says the LORD.
"You make plans that are contrary to mine.
    You make alliances not directed by my Spirit,
        thus piling up your sins.
² For without consulting me,
    you have gone down to Egypt for help.
You have put your trust in Pharaoh's protection.
    You have tried to hide in his shade.
³ But by trusting Pharaoh, you will be humiliated,
    and by depending on him, you will be disgraced.
⁴ For though his power extends to Zoan
    and his officials have arrived in Hanes,
⁵ all who trust in him will be ashamed.
    He will not help you.
    Instead, he will disgrace you."

⁶ This message came to me concerning the animals in the Negev:

The caravan moves slowly
    across the terrible desert to Egypt—
    donkeys weighed down with riches
    and camels loaded with treasure—
    all to pay for Egypt's protection.
They travel through the wilderness,
    a place of lionesses and lions,
    a place where vipers and poisonous snakes live.
All this, and Egypt will give you nothing in return.
⁷ Egypt's promises are worthless!
    Therefore, I call her Rahab—
        the Harmless Dragon.*

A Warning for Rebellious Judah

⁸ Now go and write down these words.
    Write them in a book.
They will stand until the end of time
    as a witness
⁹ that these people are stubborn rebels
    who refuse to pay attention to the LORD's instructions.
¹⁰ They tell the seers,
    "Stop seeing visions!"
They tell the prophets,
    "Don't tell us what is right.
    Tell us nice things.
    Tell us lies.
¹¹ Forget all this gloom.
    Get off your narrow path.
    Stop telling us about your
        'Holy One of Israel.'"

¹² This is the reply of the Holy One of Israel:

"Because you despise what I tell you
    and trust instead in oppression and lies,
¹³ calamity will come upon you suddenly—
    like a bulging wall that bursts and falls.
In an instant it will collapse
    and come crashing down.
¹⁴ You will be smashed like a piece of pottery—
    shattered so completely that
there won't be a piece big enough
    to carry coals from a fireplace
    or a little water from the well."

¹⁵ This is what the Sovereign LORD,
    the Holy One of Israel, says:

"Only in returning to me
    and resting in me will you be saved.
In quietness and confidence is your strength.
    But you would have none of it.
¹⁶ You said, 'No, we will get our help from Egypt.
    They will give us swift horses for riding into battle.'
But the only swiftness you are going to see
    is the swiftness of your enemies chasing you!
¹⁷ One of them will chase a thousand of you.
    Five of them will make all of you flee.
You will be left like a lonely flagpole on a hill
    or a tattered banner on a distant mountaintop."

Blessings for the LORD's People

¹⁸ So the LORD must wait for you to come to him
    so he can show you his love and compassion.
For the LORD is a faithful God.
    Blessed are those who wait for his help.

¹⁹ O people of Zion, who live in Jerusalem,
    you will weep no more.
He will be gracious if you ask for help.
    He will surely respond to the sound of your cries.
²⁰ Though the Lord gave you adversity for food
    and suffering for drink,
he will still be with you to teach you.
    You will see your teacher with your own eyes.
²¹ Your own ears will hear him.
    Right behind you a voice will say,
"This is the way you should go,"
    whether to the right or to the left.
²² Then you will destroy all your silver idols
    and your precious gold images.
You will throw them out like filthy rags,
    saying to them, "Good riddance!"

²³ Then the LORD will bless you with rain at planting time. There will be wonderful harvests and plenty of pastureland for your livestock. ²⁴ The oxen and donkeys that till the ground will eat good grain,

---

30:7 Hebrew *Rahab who sits still*. Rahab is the name of a mythical sea monster that represents chaos in ancient literature. The name is used here as a poetic name for Egypt.

ISAIAH 31

its chaff blown away by the wind. ²⁵In that day, when your enemies are slaughtered and the towers fall, there will be streams of water flowing down every mountain and hill. ²⁶The moon will be as bright as the sun, and the sun will be seven times brighter— like the light of seven days in one! So it will be when the LORD begins to heal his people and cure the wounds he gave them.

²⁷ Look! The LORD is coming from far away,
    burning with anger,
    surrounded by thick, rising smoke.
His lips are filled with fury;
    his words consume like fire.
²⁸ His hot breath pours out like a flood
    up to the neck of his enemies.
He will sift out the proud nations for destruction.
    He will bridle them and lead them away to ruin.

²⁹ But the people of God will sing a song of joy,
    like the songs at the holy festivals.
You will be filled with joy,
    as when a flutist leads a group of pilgrims
    to Jerusalem, the mountain of the LORD—
    to the Rock of Israel.
³⁰ And the LORD will make his majestic voice heard.
    He will display the strength of his mighty arm.
It will descend with devouring flames,
    with cloudbursts, thunderstorms, and huge hailstones.
³¹ At the LORD's command, the Assyrians will be shattered.
    He will strike them down with his royal scepter.
³² And as the LORD strikes them with his rod of punishment,*
    his people will celebrate with tambourines and harps.
Lifting his mighty arm, he will fight the Assyrians.
³³ Topheth—the place of burning—
    has long been ready for the Assyrian king;
    the pyre is piled high with wood.
The breath of the LORD, like fire from a volcano,
    will set it ablaze.

The Futility of Relying on Egypt

31 What sorrow awaits those who look to Egypt for help,
    trusting their horses, chariots, and charioteers
and depending on the strength of human armies
    instead of looking to the LORD,
    the Holy One of Israel.
² In his wisdom, the LORD will send great disaster;
    he will not change his mind.
He will rise against the wicked
    and against their helpers.
³ For these Egyptians are mere humans, not God!
    Their horses are puny flesh, not mighty spirits!
When the LORD raises his fist against them,
    those who help will stumble,
    and those being helped will fall.
They will all fall down and die together.

⁴But this is what the LORD has told me:

"When a strong young lion
    stands growling over a sheep it has killed,
it is not frightened by the shouts and noise
    of a whole crowd of shepherds.
In the same way, the LORD of Heaven's Armies
    will come down and fight on Mount Zion.
⁵ The LORD of Heaven's Armies will hover over Jerusalem
    and protect it like a bird protecting its nest.
He will defend and save the city;
    he will pass over it and rescue it."

⁶Though you are such wicked rebels, my people, come and return to the LORD. ⁷I know the glorious day will come when each of you will throw away the gold idols and silver images your sinful hands have made.

⁸ "The Assyrians will be destroyed,
    but not by the swords of men.
The sword of God will strike them,
    and they will panic and flee.
The strong young Assyrians
    will be taken away as captives.
⁹ Even the strongest will quake with terror,
    and princes will flee when they see your battle flags,"
says the LORD, whose fire burns in Zion,
    whose flame blazes from Jerusalem.

Israel's Ultimate Deliverance

32 Look, a righteous king is coming!
    And honest princes will rule under him.
² Each one will be like a shelter from the wind
    and a refuge from the storm,
like streams of water in the desert
    and the shadow of a great rock in a parched land.

³ Then everyone who has eyes will be able to see the truth,
    and everyone who has ears will be able to hear it.
⁴ Even the hotheads will be full of sense and understanding.
    Those who stammer will speak out plainly.
⁵ In that day ungodly fools will not be heroes.
    Scoundrels will not be respected.
⁶ For fools speak foolishness
    and make evil plans.

30:32 As in some Hebrew manuscripts and Syriac version; Masoretic Text reads *with the founded rod.*

They practice ungodliness
and spread false teachings about the LORD.
They deprive the hungry of food
and give no water to the thirsty.
⁷ The smooth tricks of scoundrels are evil.
They plot crooked schemes.
They lie to convict the poor,
even when the cause of the poor is just.
⁸ But generous people plan to do what is generous,
and they stand firm in their generosity.

⁹ Listen, you women who lie around in ease.
Listen to me, you who are so smug.
¹⁰ In a short time—just a little more than a year—
you careless ones will suddenly begin to care.
For your fruit crops will fail,
and the harvest will never take place.
¹¹ Tremble, you women of ease;
throw off your complacency.
Strip off your pretty clothes,
and put on burlap to show your grief.
¹² Beat your breasts in sorrow for your bountiful farms
and your fruitful grapevines.
¹³ For your land will be overgrown with thorns and briers.
Your joyful homes and happy towns will be gone.
¹⁴ The palace and the city will be deserted,
and busy towns will be empty.
Wild donkeys will frolic and flocks will graze
in the empty forts* and watchtowers
¹⁵ until at last the Spirit is poured out
on us from heaven.
Then the wilderness will become a fertile field,
and the fertile field will yield bountiful crops.
¹⁶ Justice will rule in the wilderness
and righteousness in the fertile field.
¹⁷ And this righteousness will bring peace.
Yes, it will bring quietness and confidence forever.
¹⁸ My people will live in safety, quietly at home.
They will be at rest.
¹⁹ Even if the forest should be destroyed
and the city torn down,
²⁰ the LORD will greatly bless his people.
Wherever they plant seed, bountiful crops will spring up.
Their cattle and donkeys will graze freely.

A Message about Assyria

33

What sorrow awaits you Assyrians, who have destroyed others*
but have never been destroyed yourselves.
You betray others,
but you have never been betrayed.
When you are done destroying,
you will be destroyed.
When you are done betraying,
you will be betrayed.
² But LORD, be merciful to us,
for we have waited for you.
Be our strong arm each day
and our salvation in times of trouble.
³ The enemy runs at the sound of your voice.
When you stand up, the nations flee!
⁴ Just as caterpillars and locusts strip the fields and vines,
so the fallen army of Assyria will be stripped!

⁵ Though the LORD is very great and lives in heaven,
he will make Jerusalem* his home of justice and righteousness.
⁶ In that day he will be your sure foundation,
providing a rich store of salvation, wisdom, and knowledge.
The fear of the LORD will be your treasure.

⁷ But now your brave warriors weep in public.
Your ambassadors of peace cry in bitter disappointment.
⁸ Your roads are deserted;
no one travels them anymore.
The Assyrians have broken their peace treaty
and care nothing for the promises they made before witnesses.*
They have no respect for anyone.
⁹ The land of Israel wilts in mourning.
Lebanon withers with shame.
The plain of Sharon is now a wilderness.
Bashan and Carmel have been plundered.

¹⁰ But the LORD says: "Now I will stand up.
Now I will show my power and might.
¹¹ You Assyrians produce nothing but dry grass and stubble.
Your own breath will turn to fire and consume you.
¹² Your people will be burned up completely,
like thornbushes cut down and tossed in a fire.
¹³ Listen to what I have done, you nations far away!
And you that are near, acknowledge my might!"

¹⁴ The sinners in Jerusalem shake with fear.
Terror seizes the godless.
"Who can live with this devouring fire?" they cry.
"Who can survive this all-consuming fire?"
¹⁵ Those who are honest and fair,
who refuse to profit by fraud,
who stay far away from bribes,

32:14 Hebrew *the Ophel.* **33:1** Hebrew *What sorrow awaits you, O destroyer.* The Hebrew text does not specifically name Assyria as the object of the prophecy in this chapter. **33:5** Hebrew *Zion;* also in 33:14. **33:8** As in Dead Sea Scrolls; Masoretic Text reads *care nothing for the cities.*

who refuse to listen to those who plot murder,
　　who shut their eyes to all enticement to do
　　　wrong—
¹⁶ these are the ones who will dwell on high.
　　The rocks of the mountains will be their fortress.
　　Food will be supplied to them,
　　　and they will have water in abundance.

¹⁷ Your eyes will see the king in all his splendor,
　　and you will see a land that stretches into the
　　　distance.
¹⁸ You will think back to this time of terror, asking,
　　"Where are the Assyrian officers
　　　who counted our towers?
　　Where are the bookkeepers
　　　who recorded the plunder taken from our
　　　　fallen city?"
¹⁹ You will no longer see these fierce, violent people
　　with their strange, unknown language.

²⁰ Instead, you will see Zion as a place of holy
　　　festivals.
　　You will see Jerusalem, a city quiet and secure.
　　It will be like a tent whose ropes are taut
　　　and whose stakes are firmly fixed.
²¹ The LORD will be our Mighty One.
　　He will be like a wide river of protection
　　that no enemy can cross,
　　　that no enemy ship can sail upon.
²² For the LORD is our judge,
　　　our lawgiver, and our king.
　　He will care for us and save us.
²³ The enemies' sails hang loose
　　　on broken masts with useless tackle.
　　Their treasure will be divided by the people of God.
　　　Even the lame will take their share!
²⁴ The people of Israel will no longer say,
　　　"We are sick and helpless,"
　　for the LORD will forgive their sins.

A Message for the Nations

34 Come here and listen, O nations of the earth.
　　　Let the world and everything in it hear
　　　　my words.
² For the LORD is enraged against the nations.
　　His fury is against all their armies.
　　He will completely destroy* them,
　　　dooming them to slaughter.
³ Their dead will be left unburied,
　　and the stench of rotting bodies will fill the land.
　　The mountains will flow with their blood.
⁴ The heavens above will melt away
　　　and disappear like a rolled-up scroll.
　　The stars will fall from the sky
　　　like withered leaves from a grapevine,
　　　or shriveled figs from a fig tree.

⁵ And when my sword has finished its work in the
　　　heavens,
　　it will fall upon Edom,
　　　the nation I have marked for destruction.
⁶ The sword of the LORD is drenched with blood
　　　and covered with fat—
　　with the blood of lambs and goats,
　　　with the fat of rams prepared for sacrifice.
　　Yes, the LORD will offer a sacrifice in the city of
　　　Bozrah.
　　He will make a mighty slaughter in Edom.
⁷ Even men as strong as wild oxen will die—
　　　the young men alongside the veterans.
　　The land will be soaked with blood
　　　and the soil enriched with fat.

⁸ For it is the day of the LORD's revenge,
　　the year when Edom will be paid back for all
　　　it did to Israel.*
⁹ The streams of Edom will be filled with burning
　　　pitch,
　　and the ground will be covered with fire.
¹⁰ This judgment on Edom will never end;
　　　the smoke of its burning will rise forever.
　　The land will lie deserted from generation to
　　　generation.
　　No one will live there anymore.
¹¹ It will be haunted by the desert owl and the
　　　screech owl,
　　　the great owl and the raven.*
　　For God will measure that land carefully;
　　　he will measure it for chaos and destruction.
¹² It will be called the Land of Nothing,
　　　and all its nobles will soon be gone.*
¹³ Thorns will overrun its palaces;
　　　nettles and thistles will grow in its forts.
　　The ruins will become a haunt for jackals
　　　and a home for owls.
¹⁴ Desert animals will mingle there with hyenas,
　　　their howls filling the night.
　　Wild goats will bleat at one another among the
　　　ruins,
　　　and night creatures* will come there to rest.
¹⁵ There the owl will make her nest and lay her eggs.
　　　She will hatch her young and cover them with
　　　　her wings.
　　And the buzzards will come,
　　　each one with its mate.

¹⁶ Search the book of the LORD,
　　　and see what he will do.
　　Not one of these birds and animals will be
　　　missing,
　　　and none will lack a mate,
　　for the LORD has promised this.
　　　His Spirit will make it all come true.

34:2 The Hebrew term used here refers to the complete consecration of things or people to the LORD, either by destroying them or by giving them as an offering; similarly in 34:5. **34:8** Hebrew *to Zion.* **34:11** The identification of some of these birds is uncertain. **34:12** The meaning of the Hebrew is uncertain. **34:14** Hebrew *Lilith,* possibly a reference to a mythical demon of the night.

¹⁷ He has surveyed and divided the land
and deeded it over to those creatures.
They will possess it forever,
from generation to generation.

Hope for Restoration

35 Even the wilderness and desert will be glad in those days.
The wasteland will rejoice and blossom with spring crocuses.
² Yes, there will be an abundance of flowers and singing and joy!
The deserts will become as green as the mountains of Lebanon,
as lovely as Mount Carmel or the plain of Sharon.
There the LORD will display his glory,
the splendor of our God.
³ With this news, strengthen those who have tired hands,
and encourage those who have weak knees.
⁴ Say to those with fearful hearts,
"Be strong, and do not fear,
for your God is coming to destroy your enemies.
He is coming to save you."

⁵ And when he comes, he will open the eyes of the blind
and unplug the ears of the deaf.
⁶ The lame will leap like a deer,
and those who cannot speak will sing for joy!
Springs will gush forth in the wilderness,
and streams will water the wasteland.
⁷ The parched ground will become a pool,
and springs of water will satisfy the thirsty land.
Marsh grass and reeds and rushes will flourish
where desert jackals once lived.

⁸ And a great road will go through that once deserted land.
It will be named the Highway of Holiness.
Evil-minded people will never travel on it.
It will be only for those who walk in God's ways;
fools will never walk there.
⁹ Lions will not lurk along its course,
nor any other ferocious beasts.
There will be no other dangers.
Only the redeemed will walk on it.
¹⁰ Those who have been ransomed by the LORD will return.
They will enter Jerusalem* singing,
crowned with everlasting joy.
Sorrow and mourning will disappear,
and they will be filled with joy and gladness.

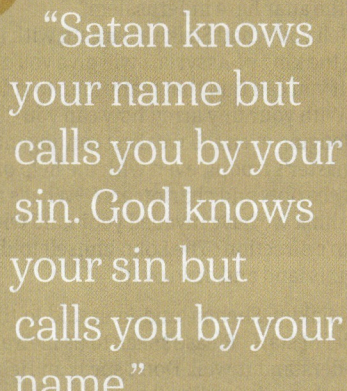

> "Satan knows your name but calls you by your sin. God knows your sin but calls you by your name."
>
> **BIANCA OLTHOFF**
> writer and Bible teacher

Assyria Invades Judah

36 In the fourteenth year of King Hezekiah's reign,* King Sennacherib of Assyria came to attack the fortified towns of Judah and conquered them. ²Then the king of Assyria sent his chief of staff* from Lachish with a huge army to confront King Hezekiah in Jerusalem. The Assyrians took up a position beside the aqueduct that feeds water into the upper pool, near the road leading to the field where cloth is washed.* ³These are the officials who went out to meet with them: Eliakim son of Hilkiah, the palace administrator; Shebna the court secretary; and Joah son of Asaph, the royal historian.

Sennacherib Threatens Jerusalem

⁴Then the Assyrian king's chief of staff told them to give this message to Hezekiah:

"This is what the great king of Assyria says: What are you trusting in that makes you so confident? ⁵Do you think* that mere words can substitute for military skill and strength? Who are you counting on, that you have rebelled against me? ⁶On Egypt? If you lean on Egypt, it will be like a reed that splinters beneath your weight and pierces your hand. Pharaoh, the king of Egypt, is completely unreliable! ⁷"But perhaps you will say to me, 'We are trusting in the LORD our God!' But isn't he the one who was insulted by Hezekiah? Didn't

---

35:10 Hebrew *Zion.* **36:1** The fourteenth year of Hezekiah's reign was 701 B.C. **36:2a** Or *the rabshakeh;* also in 36:4, 11, 12, 22. **36:2b** Or *bleached.* **36:5** As in Dead Sea Scrolls (see also 2 Kgs 18:20); Masoretic Text reads *Do I think.*

Hezekiah tear down his shrines and altars and make everyone in Judah and Jerusalem worship only at the altar here in Jerusalem?

⁸"I'll tell you what! Strike a bargain with my master, the king of Assyria. I will give you 2,000 horses if you can find that many men to ride on them! ⁹With your tiny army, how can you think of challenging even the weakest contingent of my master's troops, even with the help of Egypt's chariots and charioteers? ¹⁰What's more, do you think we have invaded your land without the LORD's direction? The LORD himself told us, 'Attack this land and destroy it!'"

¹¹Then Eliakim, Shebna, and Joah said to the Assyrian chief of staff, "Please speak to us in Aramaic, for we understand it well. Don't speak in Hebrew,* for the people on the wall will hear."

¹²But Sennacherib's chief of staff replied, "Do you think my master sent this message only to you and your master? He wants all the people to hear it, for when we put this city under siege, they will suffer along with you. They will be so hungry and thirsty that they will eat their own dung and drink their own urine."

¹³Then the chief of staff stood and shouted in Hebrew to the people on the wall, "Listen to this message from the great king of Assyria! ¹⁴This is what the king says: Don't let Hezekiah deceive you. He will never be able to rescue you. ¹⁵Don't let him fool you into trusting in the LORD by saying, 'The LORD will surely rescue us. This city will never fall into the hands of the Assyrian king!'

¹⁶"Don't listen to Hezekiah! These are the terms the king of Assyria is offering: Make peace with me—open the gates and come out. Then each of you can continue eating from your own grapevine and fig tree and drinking from your own well. ¹⁷Then I will arrange to take you to another land like this one—a land of grain and new wine, bread and vineyards.

¹⁸"Don't let Hezekiah mislead you by saying, 'The LORD will rescue us!' Have the gods of any other nations ever saved their people from the king of Assyria? ¹⁹What happened to the gods of Hamath and Arpad? And what about the gods of Sepharvaim? Did any god rescue Samaria from my power? ²⁰What god of any nation has ever been able to save its people from my power? So what makes you think that the LORD can rescue Jerusalem from me?"

²¹But the people were silent and did not utter a word because Hezekiah had commanded them, "Do not answer him."

²²Then Eliakim son of Hilkiah, the palace administrator; Shebna the court secretary; and Joah son of Asaph, the royal historian, went back to Hezekiah. They tore their clothes in despair, and they went in to see the king and told him what the Assyrian chief of staff had said.

Hezekiah Seeks the LORD's Help

37 When King Hezekiah heard their report, he tore his clothes and put on burlap and went into the Temple of the LORD. ²And he sent Eliakim the palace administrator, Shebna the court secretary, and the leading priests, all dressed in burlap, to the prophet Isaiah son of Amoz. ³They told him, "This is what King Hezekiah says: Today is a day of trouble, insults, and disgrace. It is like when a child is ready to be born, but the mother has no strength to deliver the baby. ⁴But perhaps the LORD your God has heard the Assyrian chief of staff,* sent by the king to defy the living God, and will punish him for his words. Oh, pray for those of us who are left!"

⁵After King Hezekiah's officials delivered the king's message to Isaiah, ⁶the prophet replied, "Say to your master, 'This is what the LORD says: Do not be disturbed by this blasphemous speech against me from the Assyrian king's messengers. ⁷Listen! I myself will move against him,* and the king will receive a message that he is needed at home. So he will return to his land, where I will have him killed with a sword.'"

⁸Meanwhile, the Assyrian chief of staff left Jerusalem and went to consult the king of Assyria, who had left Lachish and was attacking Libnah.

⁹Soon afterward King Sennacherib received word that King Tirhakah of Ethiopia* was leading an army to fight against him. Before leaving to meet the attack, he sent messengers back to Hezekiah in Jerusalem with this message:

¹⁰"This message is for King Hezekiah of Judah. Don't let your God, in whom you trust, deceive you with promises that Jerusalem will not be captured by the king of Assyria. ¹¹You know perfectly well what the kings of Assyria have done wherever they have gone. They have completely destroyed everyone who stood in their way! Why should you be any different? ¹²Have the gods of other nations rescued them—such nations as Gozan, Haran, Rezeph, and the people of Eden who were in Tel-assar? My predecessors destroyed them all! ¹³What happened to the king of Hamath and the king of Arpad? What happened to the kings of Sepharvaim, Hena, and Ivvah?"

¹⁴After Hezekiah received the letter from the messengers and read it, he went up to the LORD's Temple and spread it out before the LORD. ¹⁵And Hezekiah prayed this prayer before the LORD: ¹⁶"O LORD of Heaven's Armies, God of Israel, you are enthroned between the mighty cherubim! You alone are God of all the kingdoms of the earth. You alone created the heavens and the earth. ¹⁷Bend down, O LORD, and listen! Open your eyes, O LORD,

---

36:11 Hebrew *in the dialect of Judah;* also in 36:13. **37:4** Or *the rabshakeh;* also in 37:8. **37:7** Hebrew *I will put a spirit in him.* **37:9** Hebrew *of Cush.*

and see! Listen to Sennacherib's words of defiance against the living God.

¹⁸"It is true, LORD, that the kings of Assyria have destroyed all these nations. ¹⁹And they have thrown the gods of these nations into the fire and burned them. But of course the Assyrians could destroy them! They were not gods at all—only idols of wood and stone shaped by human hands. ²⁰Now, O LORD our God, rescue us from his power; then all the kingdoms of the earth will know that you alone, O LORD, are God.*"

Isaiah Predicts Judah's Deliverance

²¹Then Isaiah son of Amoz sent this message to Hezekiah: "This is what the LORD, the God of Israel, says: Because you prayed about King Sennacherib of Assyria, ²²the LORD has spoken this word against him:

"The virgin daughter of Zion
    despises you and laughs at you.
The daughter of Jerusalem
    shakes her head in derision as you flee.

²³ "Whom have you been defying and ridiculing?
    Against whom did you raise your voice?
At whom did you look with such haughty eyes?
    It was the Holy One of Israel!
²⁴ By your messengers you have defied the Lord.
    You have said, 'With my many chariots
I have conquered the highest mountains—
    yes, the remotest peaks of Lebanon.
I have cut down its tallest cedars
    and its finest cypress trees.
I have reached its farthest heights
    and explored its deepest forests.
²⁵ I have dug wells in many foreign lands*
    and refreshed myself with their water.
With the sole of my foot,
    I stopped up all the rivers of Egypt!'

²⁶ "But have you not heard?
    I decided this long ago.
Long ago I planned it,
    and now I am making it happen.
I planned for you to crush fortified cities
    into heaps of rubble.
²⁷ That is why their people have so little power
    and are so frightened and confused.
They are as weak as grass,
    as easily trampled as tender green shoots.
They are like grass sprouting on a housetop,
    scorched* before it can grow lush and tall.

²⁸ "But I know you well—
    where you stay
and when you come and go.
    I know the way you have raged against me.
²⁹ And because of your raging against me
    and your arrogance, which I have heard for myself,
I will put my hook in your nose
    and my bit in your mouth.
I will make you return
    by the same road on which you came."

³⁰Then Isaiah said to Hezekiah, "Here is the proof that what I say is true:

"This year you will eat only what grows up by itself,
    and next year you will eat what springs up from that.
But in the third year you will plant crops and harvest them;
    you will tend vineyards and eat their fruit.
³¹ And you who are left in Judah,
    who have escaped the ravages of the siege,
will put roots down in your own soil
    and grow up and flourish.
³² For a remnant of my people will spread out from Jerusalem,
    a group of survivors from Mount Zion.
The passionate commitment of the LORD of Heaven's Armies
    will make this happen!

³³"And this is what the LORD says about the king of Assyria:

"'His armies will not enter Jerusalem.
    They will not even shoot an arrow at it.
They will not march outside its gates with their shields
    nor build banks of earth against its walls.
³⁴ The king will return to his own country
    by the same road on which he came.
He will not enter this city,'
    says the LORD.
³⁵ 'For my own honor and for the sake of my servant David,
    I will defend this city and protect it.'"

³⁶That night the angel of the LORD went out to the Assyrian camp and killed 185,000 Assyrian soldiers. When the surviving Assyrians* woke up the next morning, they found corpses everywhere. ³⁷Then King Sennacherib of Assyria broke camp and returned to his own land. He went home to his capital of Nineveh and stayed there.

³⁸One day while he was worshiping in the temple of his god Nisroch, his sons Adrammelech and Sharezer killed him with their swords. They then escaped to the land of Ararat, and another son, Esarhaddon, became the next king of Assyria.

37:20 As in Dead Sea Scrolls (see also 2 Kgs 19:19); Masoretic Text reads *you alone are the LORD*. 37:25 As in Dead Sea Scrolls (see also 2 Kgs 19:24); Masoretic Text lacks *in many foreign lands*. 37:27 As in Dead Sea Scrolls and some Greek manuscripts (see also 2 Kgs 19:26); most Hebrew manuscripts read *like a terraced field*. 37:36 Hebrew *When they*.

Hezekiah's Sickness and Recovery

38 About that time Hezekiah became deathly ill, and the prophet Isaiah son of Amoz went to visit him. He gave the king this message: "This is what the Lord says: 'Set your affairs in order, for you are going to die. You will not recover from this illness.'"

² When Hezekiah heard this, he turned his face to the wall and prayed to the Lord, ³ "Remember, O Lord, how I have always been faithful to you and have served you single-mindedly, always doing what pleases you." Then he broke down and wept bitterly.

⁴ Then this message came to Isaiah from the Lord: ⁵ "Go back to Hezekiah and tell him, 'This is what the Lord, the God of your ancestor David, says: I have heard your prayer and seen your tears. I will add fifteen years to your life, ⁶ and I will rescue you and this city from the king of Assyria. Yes, I will defend this city.

⁷ "'And this is the sign from the Lord to prove that he will do as he promised: ⁸ I will cause the sun's shadow to move ten steps backward on the sundial* of Ahaz!'" So the shadow on the sundial moved backward ten steps.

Hezekiah's Poem of Praise

⁹ When King Hezekiah was well again, he wrote this poem:

¹⁰ I said, "In the prime of my life,
   must I now enter the place of the dead?*
   Am I to be robbed of the rest of my years?"
¹¹ I said, "Never again will I see the Lord God
      while still in the land of the living.
   Never again will I see my friends
      or be with those who live in this world.
¹² My life has been blown away
      like a shepherd's tent in a storm.
   It has been cut short,
      as when a weaver cuts cloth from a loom.
   Suddenly, my life was over.
¹³ I waited patiently all night,
      but I was torn apart as though by lions.
   Suddenly, my life was over.
¹⁴ Delirious, I chattered like a swallow or a crane,
      and then I moaned like a mourning dove.
   My eyes grew tired of looking to heaven for help.
      I am in trouble, Lord. Help me!"

¹⁵ But what could I say?
      For he himself sent this sickness.
   Now I will walk humbly throughout my years
      because of this anguish I have felt.
¹⁶ Lord, your discipline is good,
      for it leads to life and health.
   You restore my health
      and allow me to live!
¹⁷ Yes, this anguish was good for me,
      for you have rescued me from death
      and forgiven all my sins.

¹⁸ For the dead* cannot praise you;
      they cannot raise their voices in praise.
   Those who go down to the grave
      can no longer hope in your faithfulness.
¹⁹ Only the living can praise you as I do today.
      Each generation tells of your faithfulness to
         the next.
²⁰ Think of it—the Lord is ready to heal me!
      I will sing his praises with instruments
   every day of my life
      in the Temple of the Lord.

²¹ Isaiah had said to Hezekiah's servants, "Make an ointment from figs and spread it over the boil, and Hezekiah will recover."

²² And Hezekiah had asked, "What sign will prove that I will go to the Temple of the Lord?"

Envoys from Babylon

39 Soon after this, Merodach-baladan son of Baladan, king of Babylon, sent Hezekiah his best wishes and a gift. He had heard that Hezekiah had been very sick and that he had recovered. ² Hezekiah was delighted with the Babylonian envoys and showed them everything in his treasure-houses—the silver, the gold, the spices, and the aromatic oils. He also took them to see his armory and showed them everything in his royal treasuries! There was nothing in his palace or kingdom that Hezekiah did not show them.

³ Then Isaiah the prophet went to King Hezekiah and asked him, "What did those men want? Where were they from?"

Hezekiah replied, "They came from the distant land of Babylon."

⁴ "What did they see in your palace?" asked Isaiah.

"They saw everything," Hezekiah replied. "I showed them everything I own—all my royal treasuries."

⁵ Then Isaiah said to Hezekiah, "Listen to this message from the Lord of Heaven's Armies: ⁶ 'The time is coming when everything in your palace—all the treasures stored up by your ancestors until now—will be carried off to Babylon. Nothing will be left,' says the Lord. ⁷ 'Some of your very own sons will be taken away into exile. They will become eunuchs who will serve in the palace of Babylon's king.'"

⁸ Then Hezekiah said to Isaiah, "This message you have given me from the Lord is good." For the king was thinking, "At least there will be peace and security during my lifetime."

Comfort for God's People

40 "Comfort, comfort my people,"
      says your God.
² "Speak tenderly to Jerusalem.
   Tell her that her sad days are gone
      and her sins are pardoned.
   Yes, the Lord has punished her twice over
      for all her sins."

38:8 Hebrew *the steps.*   **38:10** Hebrew *enter the gates of Sheol?*   **38:18** Hebrew *Sheol.*

³ Listen! It's the voice of someone shouting,
  "Clear the way through the wilderness
      for the Lord!
  Make a straight highway through the wasteland
      for our God!
⁴ Fill in the valleys,
      and level the mountains and hills.
  Straighten the curves,
      and smooth out the rough places.
⁵ Then the glory of the Lord will be revealed,
      and all people will see it together.
  The Lord has spoken!"*

⁶ A voice said, "Shout!"
      I asked, "What should I shout?"

  "Shout that people are like the grass.
      Their beauty fades as quickly
      as the flowers in a field.
⁷ The grass withers and the flowers fade
      beneath the breath of the Lord.
      And so it is with people.
⁸ The grass withers and the flowers fade,
      but the word of our God stands forever."

⁹ O Zion, messenger of good news,
      shout from the mountaintops!
  Shout it louder, O Jerusalem.*
      Shout, and do not be afraid.
  Tell the towns of Judah,
      "Your God is coming!"
¹⁰ Yes, the Sovereign Lord is coming in power.
      He will rule with a powerful arm.
      See, he brings his reward with him as he
          comes.
¹¹ He will feed his flock like a shepherd.
      He will carry the lambs in his arms,
      holding them close to his heart.
      He will gently lead the mother sheep with
          their young.

The Lord Has No Equal

¹² Who else has held the oceans in his hand?
      Who has measured off the heavens with his
          fingers?
  Who else knows the weight of the earth
      or has weighed the mountains and hills on a
          scale?
¹³ Who is able to advise the Spirit of the Lord?*
      Who knows enough to give him advice or
          teach him?
¹⁴ Has the Lord ever needed anyone's advice?
      Does he need instruction about what is good?
      Did someone teach him what is right
      or show him the path of justice?

¹⁵ No, for all the nations of the world
      are but a drop in the bucket.
  They are nothing more
      than dust on the scales.
  He picks up the whole earth
      as though it were a grain of sand.
¹⁶ All the wood in Lebanon's forests
      and all Lebanon's animals would not be
          enough
      to make a burnt offering worthy of our God.
¹⁷ The nations of the world are worth nothing to
      him.
  In his eyes they count for less than nothing—
      mere emptiness and froth.

¹⁸ To whom can you compare God?
      What image can you find to resemble him?
¹⁹ Can he be compared to an idol formed in a mold,
      overlaid with gold, and decorated with silver
          chains?
²⁰ Or if people are too poor for that,
      they might at least choose wood that won't
          decay
  and a skilled craftsman
      to carve an image that won't fall down!

²¹ Haven't you heard? Don't you understand?
      Are you deaf to the words of God—
  the words he gave before the world began?
      Are you so ignorant?
²² God sits above the circle of the earth.
      The people below seem like grasshoppers to
          him!
  He spreads out the heavens like a curtain
      and makes his tent from them.
²³ He judges the great people of the world
      and brings them all to nothing.
²⁴ They hardly get started, barely taking root,
      when he blows on them and they wither.
      The wind carries them off like chaff.

²⁵ "To whom will you compare me?
      Who is my equal?" asks the Holy One.

²⁶ Look up into the heavens.
      Who created all the stars?
  He brings them out like an army, one after
      another,
      calling each by its name.
  Because of his great power and incomparable
      strength,
      not a single one is missing.

²⁷ O Jacob, how can you say the Lord does not see
      your troubles?
  O Israel, how can you say God ignores your
      rights?

40:3-5 Greek version reads *He is a voice shouting in the wilderness, / "Prepare the way for the Lord's coming! / Clear a road for our God! / Fill in the valleys, / and level the mountains and hills. / And then the glory of the Lord will be revealed, / and all people will see the salvation sent from God. / The Lord has spoken!"* Compare Matt 3:3; Mark 1:3; Luke 3:4-6. **40:9** Or *O messenger of good news, shout to Zion from the mountaintops! Shout it louder to Jerusalem.* **40:13** Greek version reads *Who can know the Lord's thoughts?* Compare Rom 11:34; 1 Cor 2:16.

He gives power to the weak and strength to the powerless.

ISAIAH 40:29

²⁸ Have you never heard?
　　Have you never understood?
　The Lord is the everlasting God,
　　the Creator of all the earth.
　He never grows weak or weary.
　　No one can measure the depths of his
　　　understanding.
²⁹ He gives power to the weak
　　and strength to the powerless.
³⁰ Even youths will become weak and tired,
　　and young men will fall in exhaustion.
³¹ But those who trust in the Lord will find new
　　　strength.
　They will soar high on wings like eagles.
　They will run and not grow weary.
　They will walk and not faint.

God's Help for Israel

41 "Listen in silence before me, you lands
　　　　beyond the sea.
　Bring your strongest arguments.
　Come now and speak.
　　The court is ready for your case.

² "Who has stirred up this king from the east,
　　rightly calling him to God's service?
　Who gives this man victory over many nations
　　and permits him to trample their kings
　　　underfoot?
　With his sword, he reduces armies to dust.
　　With his bow, he scatters them like chaff
　　　before the wind.
³ He chases them away and goes on safely,
　　though he is walking over unfamiliar ground.
⁴ Who has done such mighty deeds,
　　summoning each new generation from the
　　　beginning of time?
　It is I, the Lord, the First and the Last.
　　I alone am he."

⁵ The lands beyond the sea watch in fear.
　　Remote lands tremble and mobilize for war.
⁶ The idol makers encourage one another,
　　saying to each other, "Be strong!"
⁷ The carver encourages the goldsmith,
　　and the molder helps at the anvil.
　"Good," they say. "It's coming along fine."
　Carefully they join the parts together,
　　then fasten the thing in place so it won't fall
　　　over.

⁸ "But as for you, Israel my servant,
　　Jacob my chosen one,
　　descended from Abraham my friend,
⁹ I have called you back from the ends of the
　　　earth,
　　saying, 'You are my servant.'
　For I have chosen you
　　and will not throw you away.

¹⁰ Don't be afraid, for I am with you.
　　Don't be discouraged, for I am your God.
　I will strengthen you and help you.
　　I will hold you up with my victorious right
　　　hand.

¹¹ "See, all your angry enemies lie there,
　　confused and humiliated.
　Anyone who opposes you will die
　　and come to nothing.
¹² You will look in vain
　　for those who tried to conquer you.
　Those who attack you
　　will come to nothing.
¹³ For I hold you by your right hand—
　　I, the Lord your God.
　And I say to you,
　　'Don't be afraid. I am here to help you.
¹⁴ Though you are a lowly worm, O Jacob,
　　don't be afraid, people of Israel, for I will
　　　help you.
　I am the Lord, your Redeemer.
　　I am the Holy One of Israel.'

¹⁵ You will be a new threshing instrument
　　with many sharp teeth.
　You will tear your enemies apart,
　　making chaff of mountains.
¹⁶ You will toss them into the air,
　　and the wind will blow them all away;
　　a whirlwind will scatter them.
　Then you will rejoice in the Lord.
　　You will glory in the Holy One of Israel.

¹⁷ "When the poor and needy search for water and
　　　there is none,
　　and their tongues are parched from thirst,
　then I, the Lord, will answer them.
　　I, the God of Israel, will never abandon them.
¹⁸ I will open up rivers for them on the high plateaus.
　　I will give them fountains of water in the valleys.
　I will fill the desert with pools of water.
　　Rivers fed by springs will flow across the
　　　parched ground.
¹⁹ I will plant trees in the barren desert—
　　cedar, acacia, myrtle, olive, cypress, fir, and
　　　pine.
²⁰ I am doing this so all who see this miracle
　　will understand what it means—
　that it is the Lord who has done this,
　　the Holy One of Israel who created it.

²¹ "Present the case for your idols,"
　　says the Lord.
　"Let them show what they can do,"
　　says the King of Israel.*
²² "Let them try to tell us what happened long ago
　　so that we may consider the evidence.
　Or let them tell us what the future holds,
　　so we can know what's going to happen.

41:21 Hebrew *the King of Jacob.* See note on 14:1.

²³ Yes, tell us what will occur in the days ahead.
Then we will know you are gods.
In fact, do anything—good or bad!
Do something that will amaze and frighten us.
²⁴ But no! You are less than nothing and can do nothing at all.
Those who choose you pollute themselves.

²⁵ "But I have stirred up a leader who will approach from the north.
From the east he will call on my name.
I will give him victory over kings and princes.
He will trample them as a potter treads on clay.
²⁶ "Who told you from the beginning
that this would happen?
Who predicted this,
making you admit that he was right?
No one said a word!
²⁷ I was the first to tell Zion,
'Look! Help is on the way!'*
I will send Jerusalem a messenger with good news.
²⁸ Not one of your idols told you this.
Not one gave any answer when I asked.
²⁹ See, they are all foolish, worthless things.
All your idols are as empty as the wind.

The Lord's Chosen Servant

42 "Look at my servant, whom I strengthen.
He is my chosen one, who pleases me.
I have put my Spirit upon him.
He will bring justice to the nations.
² He will not shout
or raise his voice in public.
³ He will not crush the weakest reed
or put out a flickering candle.
He will bring justice to all who have been wronged.
⁴ He will not falter or lose heart
until justice prevails throughout the earth.
Even distant lands beyond the sea will wait for his instruction.*
⁵ God, the Lord, created the heavens and stretched them out.
He created the earth and everything in it.
He gives breath to everyone,
life to everyone who walks the earth.
And it is he who says,

⁶ "I, the Lord, have called you to demonstrate my righteousness.
I will take you by the hand and guard you,
and I will give you to my people, Israel,
as a symbol of my covenant with them.
And you will be a light to guide the nations.
⁷ You will open the eyes of the blind.
You will free the captives from prison,
releasing those who sit in dark dungeons.

⁸ "I am the Lord; that is my name!
I will not give my glory to anyone else,
nor share my praise with carved idols.
⁹ Everything I prophesied has come true,
and now I will prophesy again.
I will tell you the future before it happens."

A Song of Praise to the Lord

¹⁰ Sing a new song to the Lord!
Sing his praises from the ends of the earth!
Sing, all you who sail the seas,
all you who live in distant coastlands.
¹¹ Join in the chorus, you desert towns;
let the villages of Kedar rejoice!
Let the people of Sela sing for joy;
shout praises from the mountaintops!
¹² Let the whole world glorify the Lord;
let it sing his praise.
¹³ The Lord will march forth like a mighty hero;
he will come out like a warrior, full of fury.
He will shout his battle cry
and crush all his enemies.

¹⁴ He will say, "I have long been silent;
yes, I have restrained myself.
But now, like a woman in labor,
I will cry and groan and pant.
¹⁵ I will level the mountains and hills
and blight all their greenery.
I will turn the rivers into dry land
and will dry up all the pools.
¹⁶ I will lead blind Israel down a new path,
guiding them along an unfamiliar way.
I will brighten the darkness before them
and smooth out the road ahead of them.
Yes, I will indeed do these things;
I will not forsake them.
¹⁷ But those who trust in idols,
who say, 'You are our gods,'
will be turned away in shame.

41:27 Or *'Look! They are coming home.'* **42:4** Greek version reads *And his name will be the hope of all the world.* Compare Matt 12:21.

42:10-15 Biblical images of God show the diverse range of how he relates to us. Here, God is described as a warrior and a birthing mother. Both reveal portraits of strength, intensity, and commitment. These images can powerfully expand our thinking: God is not only strong but also intimate and tender.

42:14 God's silence is often described as God's absence. During the Exile, Israel wrestled, sang, and cried out to God. This is evidenced through Psalms and Lamentations. Even though the exiles felt like God was absent, they also had confidence that he was faithful and present (Lamentations 3:19-26). Here in Isaiah, we see both experiences within this song.

Israel's Failure to Listen and See

[18] "Listen, you who are deaf!
  Look and see, you blind!
[19] Who is as blind as my own people, my servant?
  Who is as deaf as my messenger?
Who is as blind as my chosen people,
  the servant of the Lord?
[20] You see and recognize what is right
  but refuse to act on it.
You hear with your ears,
  but you don't really listen."

[21] Because he is righteous,
  the Lord has exalted his glorious law.
[22] But his own people have been robbed and plundered,
  enslaved, imprisoned, and trapped.
They are fair game for anyone
  and have no one to protect them,
  no one to take them back home.

[23] Who will hear these lessons from the past
  and see the ruin that awaits you in the future?
[24] Who allowed Israel to be robbed and hurt?
  It was the Lord, against whom we sinned,
for the people would not walk in his path,
  nor would they obey his law.
[25] Therefore, he poured out his fury on them
  and destroyed them in battle.
They were enveloped in flames,
  but they still refused to understand.
They were consumed by fire,
  but they did not learn their lesson.

The Savior of Israel

43 But now, O Jacob, listen to the Lord who created you.
  O Israel, the one who formed you says,
"Do not be afraid, for I have ransomed you.
  I have called you by name; you are mine.
[2] When you go through deep waters,
  I will be with you.
When you go through rivers of difficulty,
  you will not drown.
When you walk through the fire of oppression,
  you will not be burned up;
  the flames will not consume you.
[3] For I am the Lord, your God,
  the Holy One of Israel, your Savior.
I gave Egypt as a ransom for your freedom;
  I gave Ethiopia* and Seba in your place.
[4] Others were given in exchange for you.
  I traded their lives for yours
because you are precious to me.
  You are honored, and I love you.

[5] "Do not be afraid, for I am with you.
  I will gather you and your children from east
    and west.
[6] I will say to the north and south,
  'Bring my sons and daughters back to Israel
  from the distant corners of the earth.
[7] Bring all who claim me as their God,
  for I have made them for my glory.
  It was I who created them.'"

[8] Bring out the people who have eyes but are blind,
  who have ears but are deaf.
[9] Gather the nations together!
  Assemble the peoples of the world!
Which of their idols has ever foretold such things?
  Which can predict what will happen tomorrow?
Where are the witnesses of such predictions?
  Who can verify that they spoke the truth?

[10] "But you are my witnesses, O Israel!" says the Lord.
  "You are my servant.
You have been chosen to know me, believe in me,
  and understand that I alone am God.
There is no other God—
  there never has been, and there never will be.
[11] I, yes I, am the Lord,
  and there is no other Savior.
[12] First I predicted your rescue,
  then I saved you and proclaimed it to the world.
No foreign god has ever done this.
  You are witnesses that I am the only God,"
  says the Lord.
[13] "From eternity to eternity I am God.
  No one can snatch anyone out of my hand.
  No one can undo what I have done."

The Lord's Promise of Victory

[14] This is what the Lord says—your Redeemer, the Holy One of Israel:

"For your sakes I will send an army against Babylon,
  forcing the Babylonians* to flee in those ships they are so proud of.
[15] I am the Lord, your Holy One,
  Israel's Creator and King.
[16] I am the Lord, who opened a way through the waters,
  making a dry path through the sea.
[17] I called forth the mighty army of Egypt
  with all its chariots and horses.
I drew them beneath the waves, and they drowned,
  their lives snuffed out like a smoldering candlewick.

[18] "But forget all that—
  it is nothing compared to what I am going to do.

43:3 Hebrew *Cush*. 43:14 Or *Chaldeans*.

¹⁹ For I am about to do something new.
　　See, I have already begun! Do you not see it?
　I will make a pathway through the wilderness.
　　I will create rivers in the dry wasteland.
²⁰ The wild animals in the fields will thank me,
　　the jackals and owls, too,
　　for giving them water in the desert.
　Yes, I will make rivers in the dry wasteland
　　so my chosen people can be refreshed.
²¹ I have made Israel for myself,
　　and they will someday honor me before the whole world.
²² "But, dear family of Jacob, you refuse to ask for my help.
　　You have grown tired of me, O Israel!
²³ You have not brought me sheep or goats for burnt offerings.
　　You have not honored me with sacrifices,
　though I have not burdened and wearied you
　　with requests for grain offerings and frankincense.
²⁴ You have not brought me fragrant calamus
　　or pleased me with the fat from sacrifices.
　Instead, you have burdened me with your sins
　　and wearied me with your faults.
²⁵ "I—yes, I alone—will blot out your sins for my own sake
　　and will never think of them again.
²⁶ Let us review the situation together,
　　and you can present your case to prove your innocence.
²⁷ From the very beginning, your first ancestor sinned against me;
　　all your leaders broke my laws.
²⁸ That is why I have disgraced your priests;
　　I have decreed complete destruction* for Jacob
　　and shame for Israel.

44

"But now, listen to me, Jacob my servant,
　　Israel my chosen one.
² The LORD who made you and helps you says:
　Do not be afraid, O Jacob, my servant,
　　O dear Israel,* my chosen one.
³ For I will pour out water to quench your thirst
　　and to irrigate your parched fields.
　And I will pour out my Spirit on your descendants,
　　and my blessing on your children.
⁴ They will thrive like watered grass,
　　like willows on a riverbank.
⁵ Some will proudly claim, 'I belong to the LORD.'
　Others will say, 'I am a descendant of Jacob.'
　Some will write the LORD's name on their hands
　　and will take the name of Israel as their own."

The Foolishness of Idols

⁶ This is what the LORD says—Israel's King and Redeemer, the LORD of Heaven's Armies:

"I am the First and the Last;
　　there is no other God.
⁷ Who is like me?
　　Let him step forward and prove to you his power.
　Let him do as I have done since ancient times
　　when I established a people and explained its future.
⁸ Do not tremble; do not be afraid.
　　Did I not proclaim my purposes for you long ago?
　You are my witnesses—is there any other God?
　　No! There is no other Rock—not one!"

⁹ How foolish are those who manufacture idols.
　　These prized objects are really worthless.
　The people who worship idols don't know this,
　　so they are all put to shame.
¹⁰ Who but a fool would make his own god—
　　an idol that cannot help him one bit?
¹¹ All who worship idols will be disgraced
　　along with all these craftsmen—mere humans—
　　who claim they can make a god.
　They may all stand together,
　　but they will stand in terror and shame.

¹² The blacksmith stands at his forge to make a sharp tool,
　　pounding and shaping it with all his might.
　His work makes him hungry and weak.
　　It makes him thirsty and faint.
¹³ Then the wood-carver measures a block of wood
　　and draws a pattern on it.
　He works with chisel and plane
　　and carves it into a human figure.
　He gives it human beauty
　　and puts it in a little shrine.
¹⁴ He cuts down cedars;
　　he selects the cypress and the oak;
　he plants the pine in the forest
　　to be nourished by the rain.

43:28 The Hebrew term used here refers to the complete consecration of things or people to the LORD, either by destroying them or by giving them as an offering.　44:2 Hebrew *Jeshurun,* a term of endearment for Israel.

44:3 The restoration theme is connected with God's promise to pour out his Spirit (see also 32:15-17; Joel 2:28-32; Acts 2:16-18). God's Spirit and blessings would be lavished on the next generation of Israelites, offering hope for the future.　44:15-19 This description of the process of making an idol drips with sarcasm and ridicule at the stupidity of the foolish idol worshipers. Idol worshipers cannot see the irony in using one part of a log to warm themselves and another part of the same log to be their god.

15 Then he uses part of the wood to make a fire.
   With it he warms himself and bakes his bread.
   Then—yes, it's true—he takes the rest of it
   and makes himself a god to worship!
   He makes an idol
   and bows down in front of it!
16 He burns part of the tree to roast his meat
   and to keep himself warm.
   He says, "Ah, that fire feels good."
17 Then he takes what's left
   and makes his god: a carved idol!
   He falls down in front of it,
   worshiping and praying to it.
   "Rescue me!" he says.
   "You are my god!"
18 Such stupidity and ignorance!
   Their eyes are closed, and they cannot see.
   Their minds are shut, and they cannot think.
19 The person who made the idol never stops to reflect,
   "Why, it's just a block of wood!
   I burned half of it for heat
   and used it to bake my bread and roast my meat.
   How can the rest of it be a god?
   Should I bow down to worship a piece of wood?"
20 The poor, deluded fool feeds on ashes.
   He trusts something that can't help him at all.
   Yet he cannot bring himself to ask,
   "Is this idol that I'm holding in my hand a lie?"

Come Close

THIRSTY? COME

SCRIPTURE CONNECTION: ISAIAH 44:1-5

I usually start looking for spiritual water when I'm restless, frustrated, bored, or lonely. My soul is shriveled like chapped lips. I'm peeling in places, and it's obvious my spiritual health is flagging. I'm short-tempered, craving carbohydrates (not the healthy kind), and mindlessly scrolling whatever social media is closest to my pointer finger.

> The thirst will come, and the world will offer. I will choose living water from the Source who satisfies.

And that's where trouble starts. So many shiny things are in my digital reach, and, at first, they satisfy. The number of likes makes me try the routine, subscribe to the app, sign up for the six-week transformation.

Meanwhile, my soul dehydrates. The results from that post, article, product, app don't come, or they do, but at a price I didn't expect. I go from chapped to parched to shriveled, spiritually speaking. My thirst gets desperate.

When it does, I don't want to ignore it. Or offer it something else. There is only one spring that satisfies me: God's Word. The Word seeps into the dry places. The more I drink, the more my soul is saturated.

REFLECT "For I will pour out water to quench your thirst and to irrigate your parched fields. And I will pour out my Spirit on your descendants, and my blessing on your children." ISAIAH 44:3

Lord, help me not waste my time, money, or strength on solutions that do not satisfy.

CONSIDER "Movie and television producers, authors, and marketing gurus have economic, personal, political, and social agendas. When I am told by a famous food chain that 'I deserve a break today,' it is intended to lead to more sales for the food chain, not a more healthy and nutritious meal for my benefit. God, on the other hand, is benevolent and needs nothing from us. ... He seeks my good. I need the input, the truths, and the beliefs that come from God." DONNA LAMOTHE

CARA DAY is a writer and illustrator. She has served with Stonecroft Ministries helping women live "extraordinary."

Restoration for Jerusalem

21 "Pay attention, O Jacob,
for you are my servant, O Israel.
I, the LORD, made you,
and I will not forget you.
22 I have swept away your sins like a cloud.
I have scattered your offenses like the morning mist.
Oh, return to me,
for I have paid the price to set you free."

23 Sing, O heavens, for the LORD has done this wondrous thing.
Shout for joy, O depths of the earth!
Break into song,
O mountains and forests and every tree!
For the LORD has redeemed Jacob
and is glorified in Israel.

24 This is what the LORD says—
your Redeemer and Creator:
"I am the LORD, who made all things.
I alone stretched out the heavens.
Who was with me
when I made the earth?
25 I expose the false prophets as liars
and make fools of fortune-tellers.
I cause the wise to give bad advice,
thus proving them to be fools.
26 But I carry out the predictions of my prophets!
By them I say to Jerusalem, 'People will live here again,'
and to the towns of Judah, 'You will be rebuilt;
I will restore all your ruins!'
27 When I speak to the rivers and say, 'Dry up!'
they will be dry.
28 When I say of Cyrus, 'He is my shepherd,'
he will certainly do as I say.
He will command, 'Rebuild Jerusalem';
he will say, 'Restore the Temple.'"

Cyrus, the LORD's Chosen One

45 This is what the LORD says to Cyrus, his anointed one,
whose right hand he will empower.
Before him, mighty kings will be paralyzed with fear.
Their fortress gates will be opened,
never to shut again.
2 This is what the LORD says:

"I will go before you, Cyrus,
and level the mountains.*
I will smash down gates of bronze
and cut through bars of iron.
3 And I will give you treasures hidden in the darkness—
secret riches.
I will do this so you may know that I am the LORD,
the God of Israel, the one who calls you by name.
4 "And why have I called you for this work?
Why did I call you by name when you did not know me?
It is for the sake of Jacob my servant,
Israel my chosen one.
5 I am the LORD;
there is no other God.
I have equipped you for battle,
though you don't even know me,
6 so all the world from east to west
will know there is no other God.
I am the LORD, and there is no other.
7 I create the light and make the darkness.
I send good times and bad times.
I, the LORD, am the one who does these things.

8 "Open up, O heavens,
and pour out your righteousness.
Let the earth open wide
so salvation and righteousness can sprout up together.
I, the LORD, created them.

45:2 As in Dead Sea Scrolls and Greek version; Masoretic Text reads *the swellings*.

44:21-23 The Lord promised to forgive Israel's sins, and all creation is called to celebrate God's redemption of Israel (compare to 1:2 where the heavens and earth are called to bear witness to Israel's rebellion against God).

44:24–45:8 The Lord alone is sovereign over history. Isaiah delivers the message here that God would eventually raise up Cyrus the Great to execute judgment on Babylon and restore Israel to the Promised Land. Isaiah's prophecy proved to be true. In 539 BC, Cyrus conquered Babylon and incorporated it into his empire. At that time, Cyrus decreed that conquered people living in Babylon could return to their homelands. He also commissioned the Jewish people to rebuild the Temple (2 Chronicles 36:22-23; Ezra 1:1-3).

44:28 Cyrus went beyond simply permitting the Jews to return to their homeland. He facilitated a major restoration project to "rebuild Jerusalem" and "restore the Temple" (see Isaiah 45:13; Ezra 1:2-4; 6:3-5).

45:1 The designation "anointed one," commonly reserved for David or the expected Messiah (Jesus), is here applied to Cyrus. Cyrus was anointed in the sense that he was selected by God to fulfill a special mission. This title was never used of any other foreign ruler (see also 1 Samuel 10:1; Romans 13:1). This anointing meant that the Lord would give Cyrus, "whose right hand he will empower," victory over Babylon (see Isaiah 43:14).

45:2-6 Cyrus's victories provided factual proof that the Lord has the power to fulfill his plans, whereas idols and false gods do not (see 41:21-29). Cyrus did not "know" the Lord, because Cyrus didn't worship him, but the Lord knew Cyrus. Isaiah predicted the rescuer Cyrus by name 150 years in advance of these actual events. This prophecy would prove to the exiles that the Lord is indeed God and that he knows the future.

⁹ "What sorrow awaits those who argue with
    their Creator.
  Does a clay pot argue with its maker?
  Does the clay dispute with the one who shapes
      it, saying,
    'Stop, you're doing it wrong!'
  Does the pot exclaim,
    'How clumsy can you be?'
¹⁰ How terrible it would be if a newborn baby said
      to its father,
    'Why was I born?'
  or if it said to its mother,
    'Why did you make me this way?'"

¹¹ This is what the LORD says—
    the Holy One of Israel and your Creator:
  "Do you question what I do for my children?
  Do you give me orders about the work of my
      hands?
¹² I am the one who made the earth
    and created people to live on it.
  With my hands I stretched out the heavens.
    All the stars are at my command.
¹³ I will raise up Cyrus to fulfill my righteous purpose,
    and I will guide his actions.
  He will restore my city and free my captive
      people—
    without seeking a reward!
  I, the LORD of Heaven's Armies, have spoken!"

Future Conversion of Gentiles

¹⁴ This is what the LORD says:

"You will rule the Egyptians,
  the Ethiopians,* and the Sabeans.
They will come to you with all their
    merchandise,
  and it will all be yours.
They will follow you as prisoners in chains.
  They will fall to their knees in front of you
      and say,
  'God is with you, and he is the only God.
    There is no other.'"

¹⁵ Truly, O God of Israel, our Savior,
    you work in mysterious ways.

¹⁶ All craftsmen who make idols will be
      humiliated.
    They will all be disgraced together.
¹⁷ But the LORD will save the people of Israel
      with eternal salvation.
  Throughout everlasting ages,
    they will never again be humiliated and
        disgraced.

¹⁸ For the LORD is God,
    and he created the heavens and earth
    and put everything in place.
  He made the world to be lived in,
    not to be a place of empty chaos.
  "I am the LORD," he says,
    "and there is no other.
¹⁹ I publicly proclaim bold promises.
    I do not whisper obscurities in some dark
        corner.
  I would not have told the people of Israel* to
      seek me
    if I could not be found.
  I, the LORD, speak only what is true
    and declare only what is right.

²⁰ "Gather together and come,
    you fugitives from surrounding nations.
  What fools they are who carry around their
      wooden idols
    and pray to gods that cannot save!
²¹ Consult together, argue your case.
    Get together and decide what to say.
  Who made these things known so long ago?
    What idol ever told you they would happen?
  Was it not I, the LORD?
    For there is no other God but me,
  a righteous God and Savior.
    There is none but me.
²² Let all the world look to me for salvation!
    For I am God; there is no other.
²³ I have sworn by my own name;
    I have spoken the truth,
    and I will never go back on my word:
  Every knee will bend to me,
    and every tongue will declare allegiance
        to me.*"

45:14 Hebrew *Cushites*. 45:19 Hebrew *of Jacob*. See note on 14:1. 45:23 Hebrew *will confess*; Greek version reads *will declare allegiance to God*. Compare Rom 14:11.

45:9-13 The Lord confronts those who question his right to use a pagan king to achieve his purposes. He, the Creator, is free and rules with authority in all he does. He promised to bring his people back to their land, and he would use anyone he chose to accomplish that purpose.

45:18-25 Salvation is from the Lord alone. God is the creator, the revealer, and the executor of his will in human history. God's purpose is to rescue the world from sin and reconcile all creation to a right relationship with himself. The Lord promised to establish a new era of salvation and righteousness (see 45:8). Every human being will submit to God, no matter what (45:23-24).

45:22 All humanity—each person—needs to seek the Lord, the true God who created all things, while he may be found (55:6). God provides salvation, the only hope for all humanity (45:8).

45:23 God's words are always true. God's swearing by his "own name" reinforces the certainty that he will "never go back on [his] word" (see also 14:24; 54:9; 62:8; Hebrews 6:13). At the end of time all nations will submit to God's authority because what God has declared will happen (see Romans 14:11; 1 Corinthians 15:25-27; Philippians 2:10-11).

Insight: THE SAVIOR IS COMING

Many of Isaiah's prophecies look into the future and see Israel as a restored and revived nation. God had promised to give David a dynasty that would last forever (2 Samuel 7:11-16). After Jerusalem's destruction and the end of Judah's kingdom, Israel never again had a

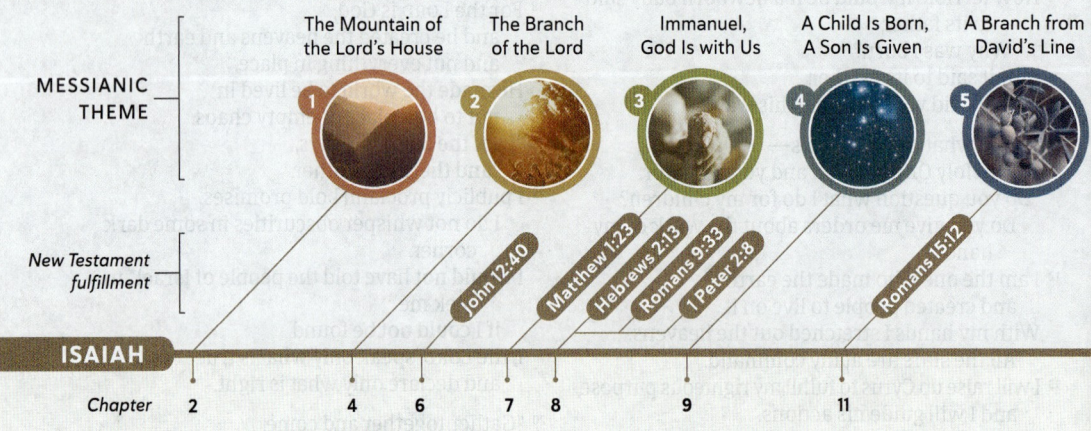

Messianic Theme	New Testament fulfillment	Isaiah Chapter
1. The Mountain of the Lord's House	John 12:40	2
2. The Branch of the Lord	Matthew 1:23	4
3. Immanuel, God Is with Us	Hebrews 2:13	6
4. A Child Is Born, A Son Is Given	Romans 9:33 / 1 Peter 2:8	7, 8
5. A Branch from David's Line	Romans 15:12	9, 11

24 The people will declare,
"The LORD is the source of all my righteousness and strength."
And all who were angry with him
will come to him and be ashamed.
25 In the LORD all the generations of Israel will be justified,
and in him they will boast.

Babylon's False Gods

46 Bel and Nebo, the gods of Babylon,
bow as they are lowered to the ground.
They are being hauled away on ox carts.
The poor beasts stagger under the weight.
2 Both the idols and their owners are bowed down.
The gods cannot protect the people,
and the people cannot protect the gods.
They go off into captivity together.

3 "Listen to me, descendants of Jacob,
all you who remain in Israel.
I have cared for you since you were born.
Yes, I carried you before you were born.
4 I will be your God throughout your lifetime—
until your hair is white with age.
I made you, and I will care for you.
I will carry you along and save you.

5 "To whom will you compare me?
Who is my equal?
6 Some people pour out their silver and gold
and hire a craftsman to make a god from it.
Then they bow down and worship it!
7 They carry it around on their shoulders,
and when they set it down, it stays there.
It can't even move!
And when someone prays to it, there is no answer.
It can't rescue anyone from trouble.

8 "Do not forget this! Keep it in mind!
Remember this, you guilty ones.
9 Remember the things I have done in the past.
For I alone am God!
I am God, and there is none like me.

46:1 Marduk was the chief god in the Babylonian pantheon. He was sometimes styled Marduk-bel, the title Bel (semantically similar to the Hebrew *Baal*) designating his lordship. Nabu (or Nebo, Nebu) was considered the son of Marduk and the patron of writing, and the inference that he wrote the fate of humanity made him a more popular deity than his father. Instead of being paraded in glory at a Babylonian festival, these gods would be "hauled away on ox carts" and disposed of, rejected by the Babylonian people.

46:3-4 Isaiah describes the motherly attributes of God in these verses—God as a mother bearing a child and caring for her infant. This image is one of protection and care. Here, the Lord reveals a commitment to "carry" them for a lifetime and "save" them (46:4). This beautiful image of the Lord as protector and provider, caregiver and savior, still rings true today.

46:3 Those "who remain in Israel" refers to the remnant that would be left alive after the destruction of Jerusalem in 586 BC. The Lord, the creator of humanity, cares for and carries his people (contrast the Babylonian idols that must be carried instead, 46:1). The Lord chose Israel even before they were a nation (see also 49:5).

descendant of David reigning over the nation. Isaiah's visions look toward a future when the Messiah, a king descended from David who would save Israel, would come. The New Testament announces that these hopes and promises are fulfilled in the person of Jesus Christ.

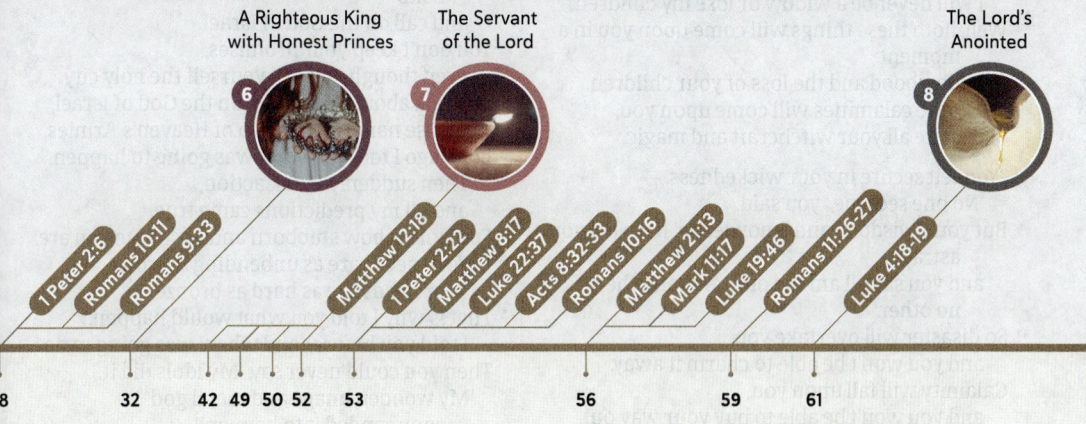

10 Only I can tell you the future
before it even happens.
Everything I plan will come to pass,
for I do whatever I wish.
11 I will call a swift bird of prey from the east—
a leader from a distant land to come and do my bidding.
I have said what I would do,
and I will do it.
12 "Listen to me, you stubborn people
who are so far from doing right.
13 For I am ready to set things right,
not in the distant future, but right now!
I am ready to save Jerusalem*
and show my glory to Israel.

Prediction of Babylon's Fall

47 "Come down, virgin daughter of Babylon,
and sit in the dust.
For your days of sitting on a throne have ended.

O daughter of Babylonia,* never again will you be
the lovely princess, tender and delicate.
2 Take heavy millstones and grind flour.
Remove your veil, and strip off your robe.
Expose yourself to public view.*
3 You will be naked and burdened with shame.
I will take vengeance against you
without pity."

4 Our Redeemer, whose name is the LORD of Heaven's Armies,
is the Holy One of Israel.

5 "O beautiful Babylon, sit now in darkness and silence.
Never again will you be known as the queen of kingdoms.
6 For I was angry with my chosen people
and punished them by letting them fall into your hands.

46:13 Hebrew *Zion.* 47:1 Or *Chaldea*; also in 47:5. 47:2 Hebrew *Bare your legs; pass through the rivers.*

46:10 God knows "the future before it even happens"; he has comprehensive control over all events, and all his acts match his words (41:4, 26). He is the First and the Last (44:6; 48:12).
46:11 The "swift bird of prey from the east" refers to Cyrus, the Persian king (see note on 44:24–45:8).
46:13 The good news for Israel was that God was coming to "set things right" (literally, "I will bring my righteousness near"; see 40:9; 51:5). Unlike a craftsman who bestows material splendor on an idol (44:13), the Lord bestows true dignity on his people.
47:1–51:23 In Scripture, cities are personified as daughters who speak for their inhabitants. In Lamentations, Daughter Zion (or Daughter Jerusalem) speaks often. In this section, Daughter Zion (or "Jerusalem") will voice her one speech, "The LORD has deserted us; the Lord has forgotten us" (49:14). She will receive comfort from the Lord to meet her fear: "For I will fight those who fight you, and I will save your children" (49:25).
47:1 To "sit in the dust" was a way of expressing humiliation.
47:5-11 Babylon's confidence and arrogance were well known (see 14:13-17; see Daniel 4:30). All of this nation's charms, magic, and wisdom were useless against the disaster decreed for it.

But you, Babylon, showed them no mercy.
  You oppressed even the elderly.
⁷ You said, 'I will reign forever as queen of the world!'
  You did not reflect on your actions
  or think about their consequences.

⁸ "Listen to this, you pleasure-loving kingdom,
  living at ease and feeling secure.
You say, 'I am the only one, and there is no other.
  I will never be a widow or lose my children.'
⁹ Well, both these things will come upon you in a moment:
  widowhood and the loss of your children.
Yes, these calamities will come upon you,
  despite all your witchcraft and magic.

¹⁰ "You felt secure in your wickedness.
  'No one sees me,' you said.
But your 'wisdom' and 'knowledge' have led you astray,
  and you said, 'I am the only one, and there is no other.'
¹¹ So disaster will overtake you,
  and you won't be able to charm it away.
Calamity will fall upon you,
  and you won't be able to buy your way out.
A catastrophe will strike you suddenly,
  one for which you are not prepared.

¹² "Now use your magical charms!
  Use the spells you have worked at all these years!
Maybe they will do you some good.
  Maybe they can make someone afraid of you.
¹³ All the advice you receive has made you tired.
  Where are all your astrologers,
  those stargazers who make predictions each month?
  Let them stand up and save you from what the future holds.

¹⁴ But they are like straw burning in a fire;
  they cannot save themselves from the flame.
You will get no help from them at all;
  their hearth is no place to sit for warmth.
¹⁵ And all your friends,
  those with whom you've done business since childhood,
will go their own ways,
  turning a deaf ear to your cries.

God's Stubborn People

48 "Listen to me, O family of Jacob,
  you who are called by the name of Israel
  and born into the family of Judah.
Listen, you who take oaths in the name of the LORD
  and call on the God of Israel.
You don't keep your promises,
² even though you call yourself the holy city
  and talk about depending on the God of Israel,
  whose name is the LORD of Heaven's Armies.
³ Long ago I told you what was going to happen.
  Then suddenly I took action,
  and all my predictions came true.
⁴ For I know how stubborn and obstinate you are.
  Your necks are as unbending as iron.
  Your heads are as hard as bronze.
⁵ That is why I told you what would happen;
  I told you beforehand what I was going to do.
Then you could never say, 'My idols did it.
  My wooden image and metal god commanded it to happen!'
⁶ You have heard my predictions and seen them fulfilled,
  but you refuse to admit it.
Now I will tell you new things,
  secrets you have not yet heard.
⁷ They are brand new, not things from the past.
  So you cannot say, 'We knew that all the time!'

⁸ "Yes, I will tell you of things that are entirely new,
  things you never heard of before.
For I know so well what traitors you are.
  You have been rebels from birth.
⁹ Yet for my own sake and for the honor of my name,
  I will hold back my anger and not wipe you out.
¹⁰ I have refined you, but not as silver is refined.
  Rather, I have refined you in the furnace of suffering.

47:10 In this context, "'wisdom'" and "'knowledge'" probably refer sarcastically to the pseudo-knowledge gained through occult practices, which actually led Babylon away from the truth and into disaster (47:11).

47:13 Babylon was advanced in astronomy, creating incredibly thorough and remarkably accurate astronomical records. Among the most famous of these texts is a collection of cuneiform tablets transcribing nightly observations for a period of five hundred years. But where modern astronomy examines the sky for scientific reasons, Babylonian stargazing was inseparably tied to divination. Since the gods were thought to send messages through the heavens, elite scholar-priests sought to find and interpret those messages by carefully observing, recording, and analyzing vast amounts of astronomical information.

48:1-22 The Lord here called on Israel to forsake its historic rebelliousness and listen to what he says. The Hebrew word translated "listen" (*shema*) is often synonymous with obeying or acting upon what is heard.

48:1 Although Isaiah's normal focus was on Judah, here he addressed all the tribes of Israel.

48:6-7 Even though Israel had repeatedly failed to believe God's past predictions, here he revealed "new things" that were "not yet heard." Specifically, God revealed that Babylon would fall, and Israel would be restored.

48:10 The Exile was a "furnace of suffering" (see also Deuteronomy 4:20) through which God "refined" Israel.

¹¹ I will rescue you for my sake—
    yes, for my own sake!
  I will not let my reputation be tarnished,
    and I will not share my glory with idols!

Freedom from Babylon

¹² "Listen to me, O family of Jacob,
    Israel my chosen one!
  I alone am God,
    the First and the Last.
¹³ It was my hand that laid the foundations of
    the earth,
  my right hand that spread out the heavens
    above.
  When I call out the stars,
    they all appear in order."

¹⁴ Have any of your idols ever told you this?
    Come, all of you, and listen:
  The LORD has chosen Cyrus as his ally.
    He will use him to put an end to the empire
      of Babylon
    and to destroy the Babylonian* armies.
¹⁵ "I have said it: I am calling Cyrus!
    I will send him on this errand and will help
      him succeed.
¹⁶ Come closer, and listen to this.
    From the beginning I have told you plainly
      what would happen."

  And now the Sovereign LORD and his Spirit
    have sent me with this message.

¹⁷ This is what the LORD says—
    your Redeemer, the Holy One of Israel:
  "I am the LORD your God,
    who teaches you what is good for you
    and leads you along the paths you should follow.
¹⁸ Oh, that you had listened to my commands!
    Then you would have had peace flowing like a
      gentle river
    and righteousness rolling over you like waves
      in the sea.

¹⁹ Your descendants would have been like the
    sands along the seashore—
    too many to count!
  There would have been no need for your
    destruction,
    or for cutting off your family name."

²⁰ Yet even now, be free from your captivity!
    Leave Babylon and the Babylonians.*
  Sing out this message!
    Shout it to the ends of the earth!
  The LORD has redeemed his servants,
    the people of Israel.*
²¹ They were not thirsty
    when he led them through the desert.
  He divided the rock,
    and water gushed out for them to drink.
²² "But there is no peace for the wicked,"
    says the LORD.

The LORD's Servant Commissioned

49 Listen to me, all you in distant lands!
    Pay attention, you who are far away!
  The LORD called me before my birth;
    from within the womb he called me by name.
² He made my words of judgment as sharp as a
    sword.
  He has hidden me in the shadow of his hand.
    I am like a sharp arrow in his quiver.

³ He said to me, "You are my servant, Israel,
    and you will bring me glory."

⁴ I replied, "But my work seems so useless!
    I have spent my strength for nothing and to
      no purpose.
  Yet I leave it all in the LORD's hand;
    I will trust God for my reward."

⁵ And now the LORD speaks—
    the one who formed me in my mother's womb
      to be his servant,
    who commissioned me to bring Israel back
      to him.

48:14 Or *Chaldean.* 48:20a Or *the Chaldeans.* 48:20b Hebrew *his servant, Jacob.* See note on 14:1.

48:11 Israel's exile raised questions among the nations about the Lord's character and reputation. The nations would not have perceived that Israel's wicked character had led to the Exile. Instead, they would have viewed it as a failure of Israel's God to protect his people and their land (see 36:19-20; 37:12; Ezekiel 36:19-26).
48:14 For more on God choosing Cyrus "as his ally" see 44:28; 45:1-2.
48:16 God's promises are clear, though not always specific as to manner and time. The identity of the one who is sent is unclear. Isaiah might be referring to himself as a Spirit-inspired prophet who spoke the very words of God to Israel. The connection with the Spirit suggests that it refers to the promised servant, the Messiah. The presence of the Spirit assures the servant's success.
48:18 Peace and righteousness will be established when the Kingdom of God comes in its fullness (see 66:12). An abundance of comforting peace and overflowing resources of righteousness (see Amos 5:24) could have been Israel's if its people had only listened to God.
48:19 The people having "descendants... like the sands" would fulfill God's covenant to Abraham (Genesis 22:17); by contrast, the Israelites were nearly wiped out in the Exile (see Isaiah 44:26).
49:1-26 God's servant is described as both a king and a prophet (42:1; 49:1). This servant is one who will be faithful. This servant's role is to be "a light to the Gentiles" (49:6): The servant comes for the entire world! Jesus became the ultimate fulfillment of a suffering servant (see note on 52:13–53:12). In this passage, Isaiah uses motherly images to describe the Lord's incredible love. Similar to a mother's love for her child, the Lord describes this love for us as even greater!

The Lord has honored me,
and my God has given me strength.
⁶ He says, "You will do more than restore the
people of Israel to me.
I will make you a light to the Gentiles,
and you will bring my salvation to the ends of
the earth."

⁷ The Lord, the Redeemer
and Holy One of Israel,
says to the one who is despised and rejected by
the nations,
to the one who is the servant of rulers:
"Kings will stand at attention when you pass by.
Princes will also bow low
because of the Lord, the faithful one,
the Holy One of Israel, who has chosen you."

Promises of Israel's Restoration

⁸ This is what the Lord says:

"At just the right time, I will respond to you.*
On the day of salvation I will help you.
I will protect you and give you to the people
as my covenant with them.
Through you I will reestablish the land of Israel
and assign it to its own people again.
⁹ I will say to the prisoners, 'Come out in freedom,'
and to those in darkness, 'Come into the light.'
They will be my sheep, grazing in green pastures
and on hills that were previously bare.
¹⁰ They will neither hunger nor thirst.
The searing sun will not reach them
anymore.
For the Lord in his mercy will lead them;
he will lead them beside cool waters.
¹¹ And I will make my mountains into level paths
for them.
The highways will be raised above the valleys.
¹² See, my people will return from far away,
from lands to the north and west,
and from as far south as Egypt.*"

¹³ Sing for joy, O heavens!
Rejoice, O earth!
Burst into song, O mountains!
For the Lord has comforted his people
and will have compassion on them in their
suffering.

¹⁴ Yet Jerusalem* says, "The Lord has deserted us;
the Lord has forgotten us."

¹⁵ "Never! Can a mother forget her nursing child?
Can she feel no love for the child she has
borne?
But even if that were possible,
I would not forget you!

¹⁶ See, I have written your name on the palms of
my hands.
Always in my mind is a picture of Jerusalem's
walls in ruins.
¹⁷ Soon your descendants will come back,
and all who are trying to destroy you will
go away.
¹⁸ Look around you and see,
for all your children will come back to you.
As surely as I live," says the Lord,
"they will be like jewels or bridal ornaments
for you to display.

¹⁹ "Even the most desolate parts of your
abandoned land
will soon be crowded with your people.
Your enemies who enslaved you
will be far away.
²⁰ The generations born in exile will return and say,
'We need more room! It's crowded here!'
²¹ Then you will think to yourself,
'Who has given me all these descendants?
For most of my children were killed,
and the rest were carried away into exile.
I was left here all alone.
Where did all these people come from?
Who bore these children?
Who raised them for me?'"

²² This is what the Sovereign Lord says:
"See, I will give a signal to the godless nations.
They will carry your little sons back to you in
their arms;
they will bring your daughters on their
shoulders.
²³ Kings and queens will serve you
and care for all your needs.
They will bow to the earth before you
and lick the dust from your feet.
Then you will know that I am the Lord.
Those who trust in me will never be put to
shame."

²⁴ Who can snatch the plunder of war from the
hands of a warrior?
Who can demand that a tyrant* let his
captives go?
²⁵ But the Lord says,
"The captives of warriors will be released,
and the plunder of tyrants will be retrieved.
For I will fight those who fight you,
and I will save your children.
²⁶ I will feed your enemies with their own flesh.
They will be drunk with rivers of their own
blood.
All the world will know that I, the Lord,
am your Savior and your Redeemer,
the Mighty One of Israel.*"

49:8 Greek version reads *I heard you.* Compare 2 Cor 6:2. 49:12 As in Dead Sea Scrolls, which read *from the region of Aswan,* which is in southern Egypt. Masoretic Text reads *from the region of Sinim.* 49:14 Hebrew *Zion.* 49:24 As in Dead Sea Scrolls, Syriac version, and Latin Vulgate (also see 49:25); Masoretic Text reads *a righteous person.* 49:26 Hebrew *of Jacob.* See note on 14:1.

50 This is what the LORD says:

"Was your mother sent away because I divorced her?
Did I sell you as slaves to my creditors?
No, you were sold because of your sins.
And your mother, too, was taken because of your sins.
² Why was no one there when I came?
Why didn't anyone answer when I called?
Is it because I have no power to rescue?
No, that is not the reason!
For I can speak to the sea and make it dry up!
I can turn rivers into deserts covered with dying fish.
³ I dress the skies in darkness,
covering them with clothes of mourning."

The LORD's Obedient Servant

⁴ The Sovereign LORD has given me his words of wisdom,
so that I know how to comfort the weary.
Morning by morning he wakens me
and opens my understanding to his will.
⁵ The Sovereign LORD has spoken to me,
and I have listened.
I have not rebelled or turned away.
⁶ I offered my back to those who beat me
and my cheeks to those who pulled out my beard.
I did not hide my face
from mockery and spitting.
⁷ Because the Sovereign LORD helps me,
I will not be disgraced.
Therefore, I have set my face like a stone,
determined to do his will.
And I know that I will not be put to shame.
⁸ He who gives me justice is near.
Who will dare to bring charges against me now?
Where are my accusers?
Let them appear!
⁹ See, the Sovereign LORD is on my side!
Who will declare me guilty?
All my enemies will be destroyed
like old clothes that have been eaten by moths!

¹⁰ Who among you fears the LORD
and obeys his servant?
If you are walking in darkness,
without a ray of light,
trust in the LORD
and rely on your God.
¹¹ But watch out, you who live in your own light
and warm yourselves by your own fires.
This is the reward you will receive from me:
You will soon fall down in great torment.

A Call to Trust the LORD

51 "Listen to me, all who hope for deliverance—
all who seek the LORD!
Consider the rock from which you were cut,
the quarry from which you were mined.
² Yes, think about Abraham, your ancestor,
and Sarah, who gave birth to your nation.
Abraham was only one man when I called him.
But when I blessed him, he became a great nation."

³ The LORD will comfort Israel* again
and have pity on her ruins.
Her desert will blossom like Eden,
her barren wilderness like the garden of the LORD.
Joy and gladness will be found there.
Songs of thanksgiving will fill the air.

⁴ "Listen to me, my people.
Hear me, Israel,
for my law will be proclaimed,
and my justice will become a light to the nations.
⁵ My mercy and justice are coming soon.
My salvation is on the way.
My strong arm will bring justice to the nations.
All distant lands will look to me
and wait in hope for my powerful arm.
⁶ Look up to the skies above,
and gaze down on the earth below.
For the skies will disappear like smoke,
and the earth will wear out like a piece of clothing.
The people of the earth will die like flies,
but my salvation lasts forever.
My righteous rule will never end!

51:3 Hebrew *Zion;* also in 51:16.

50:2 The Lord came and called the people through the prophets (see also Isaiah 65:1-3). The people had not responded to God's repeated call to trust in him and repent of their sins. They were deaf and stubborn (see 6:9-10; 29:18; 35:5; 42:18-19). God was fully able to rescue Israel and Judah from the Assyrians and Babylonians, but he first had to deal justly with his people's sinfulness (see 59:1). That the Lord can "speak to the sea and make it dry up" is an allusion to the parting of the Red Sea during the exodus from Egypt (Exodus 14:21-22).

50:4-11 This is the third of four servant songs. The faithful and suffering servant portrays an ideal Israel; the image was realized in Jesus Christ (read more about how to interpret prophecy on page 879).

50:8 God vindicates those who suffer for doing his will. Vindication is an act of God where he exalts those who have been wrongly disgraced and strikes down the wicked, self-exalted, and arrogant (see also 2 Thessalonians 1:6-9). Confidence in God's vindication removes our fears and bolsters our faith (see Romans 8:31-34).

⁷ "Listen to me, you who know right from wrong,
  you who cherish my law in your hearts.
Do not be afraid of people's scorn,
  nor fear their insults.
⁸ For the moth will devour them as it devours clothing.
  The worm will eat at them as it eats wool.
But my righteousness will last forever.
  My salvation will continue from generation to generation."

⁹ Wake up, wake up, O Lord! Clothe yourself with strength!
  Flex your mighty right arm!
Rouse yourself as in the days of old
  when you slew Egypt, the dragon of the Nile.*
¹⁰ Are you not the same today,
  the one who dried up the sea,
  making a path of escape through the depths
  so that your people could cross over?
¹¹ Those who have been ransomed by the Lord will return.
  They will enter Jerusalem* singing,
  crowned with everlasting joy.
Sorrow and mourning will disappear,
  and they will be filled with joy and gladness.

¹² "I, yes I, am the one who comforts you.
  So why are you afraid of mere humans,
  who wither like the grass and disappear?
¹³ Yet you have forgotten the Lord, your Creator,
  the one who stretched out the sky like a canopy
  and laid the foundations of the earth.
Will you remain in constant dread of human oppressors?
  Will you continue to fear the anger of your enemies?
Where is their fury and anger now?
  It is gone!
¹⁴ Soon all you captives will be released!
  Imprisonment, starvation, and death will not be your fate!
¹⁵ For I am the Lord your God,
  who stirs up the sea, causing its waves to roar.
  My name is the Lord of Heaven's Armies.
¹⁶ And I have put my words in your mouth
  and hidden you safely in my hand.
I stretched out* the sky like a canopy
  and laid the foundations of the earth.
I am the one who says to Israel,
  'You are my people!'"

¹⁷ Wake up, wake up, O Jerusalem!
  You have drunk the cup of the Lord's fury.
You have drunk the cup of terror,
  tipping out its last drops.
¹⁸ Not one of your children is left alive
  to take your hand and guide you.
¹⁹ These two calamities have fallen on you:
  desolation and destruction, famine and war.
And who is left to sympathize with you?
  Who is left to comfort you?*
²⁰ For your children have fainted and lie in the streets,
  helpless as antelopes caught in a net.
The Lord has poured out his fury;
  God has rebuked them.

²¹ But now listen to this, you afflicted ones
  who sit in a drunken stupor,
  though not from drinking wine.
²² This is what the Sovereign Lord,
  your God and Defender, says:
"See, I have taken the terrible cup from your hands.
  You will drink no more of my fury.
²³ Instead, I will hand that cup to your tormentors,
  those who said, 'We will trample you into the dust
  and walk on your backs.'"

Deliverance for Jerusalem

52 Wake up, wake up, O Zion!
    Clothe yourself with strength.
Put on your beautiful clothes, O holy city of Jerusalem,
  for unclean and godless people will enter your gates no longer.
² Rise from the dust, O Jerusalem.
  Sit in a place of honor.
Remove the chains of slavery from your neck,
  O captive daughter of Zion.
³ For this is what the Lord says:
"When I sold you into exile,
  I received no payment.
Now I can redeem you
  without having to pay for you."

51:9 Hebrew *You slew Rahab; you pierced the dragon.* Rahab is the name of a mythical sea monster that represents chaos in ancient literature. The name is used here as a poetic name for Egypt.   **51:11** Hebrew *Zion.*   **51:16** As in Syriac version (see also 51:13); Hebrew reads *planted.*   **51:19** As in Dead Sea Scrolls and Greek, Latin, and Syriac versions; Masoretic Text reads *How can I comfort you?*

51:17-23 The imagery here of Jerusalem, Daughter Zion, as a suffering woman, continues. One of the metaphors used to create this complete portrait of suffering is the emphasis on the loss of children. This imagery creates a painful portrait of loss that connects with anyone whose child has died. But in Isaiah 52, hope returns with shouts of joy. Here, all creation experiences the victory of God's return and protection (52:4-12). Even in some of our darkest moments of loss, we can be comforted that God is with us, *Immanuel.*

51:17 Israel used these same words in a prayer to the Lord, "Wake up, wake up" (see 51:9). Israel's problems were not the result of God's slowness to act; rather the people were slow to believe God's promises. The Lord will appropriately measure out his judgment, "the cup of the Lord's fury"; those who fall under his judgment must figuratively drink from his wrath (see also Matthew 26:39).

Savior

IDENTITY

Qualities of Our Restorer

When choosing a life partner, we want that person to possess certain qualities. Here in Isaiah, we see that our Savior met certain specifications for his role, too.

Isaiah 49–57 describes the Savior's physical, mental, and emotional characteristics. In addition, it shows the Savior's purpose: to bridge the gap between heaven and earth and rescue us from our wrongs. As Romans 6:23 puts it: "For the wages of sin is death, but the free gift of God is eternal life through Christ Jesus our Lord." The Savior reflects our heavenly Father's love, restoring our past, present, and future.

Like the Savior, God gives us certain qualities that can bring life to others as we receive the gift of life God offers. This intersection of purpose, calling, and obedience often surprises us. We wonder how we can have peace in the middle of our storms. We pray for those who purposely plot our undoing. We find joy in dark places and spread it like butter on a hot croissant!

I thank God for the characteristics of Jesus, our Savior. I also thank him for how he uniquely created me to represent and restore. When God looks at me, he sees all the beautiful, wonderful qualities Jesus possesses that he's molding me to have, too (2 Corinthians 3:18).

THE STORY OF THE SAVIOR IS TOLD IN ISAIAH 49–57.

> I have certain qualities, but they do not totally define who I am. It is Jesus in me that makes all the difference.

IDENTIFY

What does restoration look like in your life, and how has it shaped your identity?

What qualities has God given you that could help you bring restoration to others?

> "Although I have certain qualities, I have to remember that they do not totally define who I am. It is Jesus in me that makes all the difference."

QUANTRILLA ARD, PhD, is a faith-based personal and spiritual development author, speaker, Bible teacher, and literary agent who believes in the power of collective strength, community, and fellowship.

⁴This is what the Sovereign LORD says: "Long ago my people chose to live in Egypt. Now they are oppressed by Assyria. ⁵What is this?" asks the LORD. "Why are my people enslaved again? Those who rule them shout in exultation.* My name is blasphemed all day long.* ⁶But I will reveal my name to my people, and they will come to know its power. Then at last they will recognize that I am the one who speaks to them."

⁷ How beautiful on the mountains
    are the feet of the messenger who brings
        good news,
    the good news of peace and salvation,
    the news that the God of Israel* reigns!
⁸ The watchmen shout and sing with joy,
    for before their very eyes
    they see the LORD returning to
        Jerusalem.*
⁹ Let the ruins of Jerusalem break into
        joyful song,
    for the LORD has comforted his people.
    He has redeemed Jerusalem.
¹⁰ The LORD has demonstrated his holy power
    before the eyes of all the nations.
  All the ends of the earth will see
    the victory of our God.

¹¹ Get out! Get out and leave your captivity,
    where everything you touch is unclean.
  Get out of there and purify yourselves,
    you who carry home the sacred objects
        of the LORD.
¹² You will not leave in a hurry,
    running for your lives.
  For the LORD will go ahead of you;
    yes, the God of Israel will protect you from
        behind.

The LORD's Suffering Servant

¹³ See, my servant will prosper;
    he will be highly exalted.
¹⁴ But many were amazed when they saw him.*
    His face was so disfigured he seemed hardly
        human,
    and from his appearance, one would scarcely
        know he was a man.
¹⁵ And he will startle* many nations.
    Kings will stand speechless in his presence.
  For they will see what they had not been told;
    they will understand what they had not
        heard about.*

53 Who has believed our message?
    To whom has the LORD revealed his
        powerful arm?
² My servant grew up in the LORD's presence like a
        tender green shoot,
    like a root in dry ground.
  There was nothing beautiful or majestic about
        his appearance,
    nothing to attract us to him.
³ He was despised and rejected—
    a man of sorrows, acquainted with
        deepest grief.
  We turned our backs on him and looked the
        other way.
  He was despised, and we did not care.

⁴ Yet it was our weaknesses he carried;
    it was our sorrows* that weighed
        him down.
  And we thought his troubles were a punishment
        from God,
    a punishment for his own sins!
⁵ But he was pierced for our rebellion,
    crushed for our sins.
  He was beaten so we could be whole.
    He was whipped so we could be healed.
⁶ All of us, like sheep, have strayed away.
    We have left God's paths to follow our own.
  Yet the LORD laid on him
    the sins of us all.

52:5a As in Dead Sea Scrolls; Masoretic Text reads *Those who rule them wail*. **52:5b** Greek version reads *The Gentiles continually blaspheme my name because of you*. Compare Rom 2:24. **52:7** Hebrew *of Zion*. **52:8** Hebrew *to Zion*. **52:14** As in Syriac version; Hebrew reads *you*. **52:15a** Or *cleanse*. **52:15b** Greek version reads *Those who have never been told about him will see, / and those who have never heard of him will understand*. Compare Rom 15:21. **53:4** Or *Yet it was our sicknesses he carried; / it was our diseases*.

52:13–53:12 This is the fourth and final servant song in Isaiah. It is well known as the suffering servant song. Identifying the servant of Yahweh through the book of Isaiah could be difficult to pin down. Isaiah calls the people of Israel the servant of Yahweh (for example, 41:8; 44:1; 49:3), but Israel was not able to ultimately carry out God's plan. Jesus was more than able, acting as the ideal representative of Israel. The New Testament identifies this servant of Yahweh as Jesus (Acts 8:31-35).
53:4 The callous world would assume that the servant somehow brought his suffering on himself, never realizing that he was suffering for them. This description of the servant's humiliation contrasts with the descriptions of his exaltation (53:12).
53:5 Being "crushed . . . beaten . . . [and] whipped" were typically punishments for crimes. The servant was punished because of our sin, which is a crime against God (see also Zechariah 12:10). The Hebrew word *shalom*, usually translated "peace," is translated here "be whole." *Shalom* means to experience wholeness in body, in mind, and in relationships with others. The servant would be injured so that humanity can be whole and healthy in all aspects of life (see also 57:18). We do not need to suffer divine condemnation for our sins because the servant has already done so (see Galatians 1:4).
53:6 Straying sheep and "leaving God's path" are metaphors for sin (see also Romans 3:10-18).

⁷ He was oppressed and treated harshly,
  yet he never said a word.
 He was led like a lamb to the slaughter.
   And as a sheep is silent before the shearers,
   he did not open his mouth.
⁸ Unjustly condemned,
   he was led away.*
 No one cared that he died without descendants,
   that his life was cut short in midstream.*
 But he was struck down
   for the rebellion of my people.
⁹ He had done no wrong
   and had never deceived anyone.
 But he was buried like a criminal;
   he was put in a rich man's grave.

¹⁰ But it was the LORD's good plan to crush him
   and cause him grief.
 Yet when his life is made an offering for sin,
   he will have many descendants.
 He will enjoy a long life,
   and the LORD's good plan will prosper in his hands.
¹¹ When he sees all that is accomplished by his anguish,
   he will be satisfied.
 And because of his experience,
   my righteous servant will make it possible
   for many to be counted righteous,
   for he will bear all their sins.
¹² I will give him the honors of a victorious soldier,
   because he exposed himself to death.
 He was counted among the rebels.
   He bore the sins of many and interceded
   for rebels.

53:8a Greek version reads *He was humiliated and received no justice.* Compare Acts 8:33. 53:8b Or *As for his contemporaries, / who cared that his life was cut short in midstream?* Greek version reads *Who can speak of his descendants? / For his life was taken from the earth.* Compare Acts 8:33.

53:7-8 The treasurer of Ethiopia was reading this passage when Philip met him (Acts 8:32-33). Philip used this passage to explain the Good News about Jesus, his death and resurrection, to the man, who promptly wanted to be baptized.
53:7 This passage is alluded to in 1 Peter 2:21-25, connecting Isaiah's prophecy with the fulfillment in Jesus Christ.
53:9 The NLT translates the Hebrew wording here as "in a rich man's grave," but the Hebrew could also be more literally rendered "he was with the rich in his death." Many interpreters associate Jesus' burial in Joseph of Arimathea's family tomb with Isaiah's words here (see Matthew 27:57-61). Although the Bible often considers riches as a blessing from God, it regularly condemns the rich who are crooked and oppressive. The point here might be ironic: This good man would be buried with oppressors.
53:10-12 The final stanza of the poem first explains why the servant suffered and was treated unjustly in the place of others; it then explains what the result of that obedience would be.

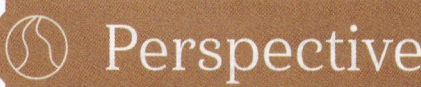

Perspective

How do we understand prophecies?

SCRIPTURE CONNECTION: ISAIAH 52:13–53:12

Prophets were chosen and gifted by God to see through spiritual vision rather than only physical eyesight. Sometimes they saw truth about themselves (6:5-8), or something that would happen soon (19:1-25). And sometimes, prophets saw what God would do in the future, such as providing a savior (7:14; Matthew 1:22-23).

Those hearing Isaiah's prophecies, originally, might have heard Isaiah 53 as describing Israel's suffering, personified as one suffering servant. Yet later readers understood those exact words as describing Jesus the Messiah.

Interpreters call this a "double-lens perspective" on Scripture. Just as you can focus a lens near or far, you can read Isaiah focused on the near-events of Israel or the far-events of Jesus Christ.

When I lived in Virginia, I would drive along the Blue Ridge Parkway. When viewed from the road, a mountain range looked like a cluster of peaks all about the same distance away. But when I hiked to one peak's summit, I could see that the next mountain was far off.

Biblical prophecy is like that. From one perspective, it looks close—like the way Isaiah's audience heard him and saw Israel's history. From the perspective of Jesus' death and resurrection, we read Isaiah and see Christ. Reading Scripture invites being both near- and far-sighted, at once.

VIEWPOINTS

HIS: *What did God inspire Isaiah to describe in the near-view and the distant-view in Isaiah 53 (Romans 5:6-8; Matthew 27:1-66)?*
MINE: *"I see God close-up in the day's details. And I see him at work in my future, too."*
YOURS: *What is God doing in your life now? What do you believe God is preparing for your future?*

SUSAN I. BUBBERS, MDiv, DMin, PhD, is the Dean of the Center for Anglican Theology in Orlando, FL. She is a professor, Anglican priest, spiritual director, and a Fellow of the Oxford Centre for Animal Ethics.

Future Glory for Jerusalem

54 "Sing, O childless woman,
you who have never given birth!
Break into loud and joyful song, O Jerusalem,
you who have never been in labor.
For the desolate woman now has more
children
than the woman who lives with her husband,"
says the LORD.
² "Enlarge your house; build an addition.
Spread out your home, and spare no expense!
³ For you will soon be bursting at the seams.
Your descendants will occupy other nations
and resettle the ruined cities.

⁴ "Fear not; you will no longer live in shame.
Don't be afraid; there is no more disgrace
for you.
You will no longer remember the shame of your
youth
and the sorrows of widowhood.
⁵ For your Creator will be your husband;
the LORD of Heaven's Armies is his name!
He is your Redeemer, the Holy One of Israel,
the God of all the earth.
⁶ For the LORD has called you back from your
grief—
as though you were a young wife abandoned
by her husband,"
says your God.
⁷ "For a brief moment I abandoned you,
but with great compassion I will take you
back.
⁸ In a burst of anger I turned my face away for a
little while.
But with everlasting love I will have
compassion on you,"
says the LORD, your Redeemer.

⁹ "Just as I swore in the time of Noah
that I would never again let a flood cover the
earth,
so now I swear
that I will never again be angry and punish
you.
¹⁰ For the mountains may move
and the hills disappear,
but even then my faithful love for you will
remain.
My covenant of blessing will never be
broken,"
says the LORD, who has mercy on you.

¹¹ "O storm-battered city,
troubled and desolate!
I will rebuild you with precious jewels
and make your foundations from lapis
lazuli.
¹² I will make your towers of sparkling rubies,
your gates of shining gems,
and your walls of precious stones.
¹³ I will teach all your children,
and they will enjoy great peace.
¹⁴ You will be secure under a government that is
just and fair.
Your enemies will stay far away.
You will live in peace,
and terror will not come near.
¹⁵ If any nation comes to fight you,
it is not because I sent them.
Whoever attacks you will go down in
defeat.

¹⁶ "I have created the blacksmith
who fans the coals beneath the forge
and makes the weapons of destruction.
And I have created the armies that
destroy.
¹⁷ But in that coming day
no weapon turned against you
will succeed.
You will silence every voice
raised up to accuse you.
These benefits are enjoyed by the servants
of the LORD;
their vindication will come from me.
I, the LORD, have spoken!

Invitation to the LORD's Salvation

55 "Is anyone thirsty?
Come and drink—
even if you have no money!
Come, take your choice of wine or milk—
it's all free!

54:10 God's "faithful love" for his people endures despite their unfaithfulness. God's "covenant of blessing" was the assurance of his presence, resulting in wholeness, blessing, and protection. It replaces the shame and disgrace of the Exile (see Ezekiel 34:25; 37:26).

54:11-17 This is a vision of the renewed Jerusalem as a city under God's protection, a place of peace and righteousness (see 59:21—60:22). This section forms the background of John's vision of the new Jerusalem (Revelation 21:10-21).

54:13 Jesus alluded to this verse in John 6:45. The benefits of God's presence and protection is the enjoyment of "great peace" (Isaiah 53:5; see 48:17-18; 54:10).

54:15 God gives assurance that no nation can defeat his people. The Lord has promised to protect them, just as he had promised Abraham (Genesis 12:3; see Isaiah 49:25).

54:17 God will protect his people in war and in the courtroom. Only the true children of God—redeemed people who come out of Israel and the nations—will enjoy the promised blessings of the age to come that God establishes.

55:1-13 This final chapter of the prophecies of comfort (Isaiah 40–55) summarizes the section's prominent themes: blessing, covenant, witness, word, nations, glory, forgiveness, and joy.

ISAIAH 55

² Why spend your money on food that does not give you strength?
Why pay for food that does you no good?
Listen to me, and you will eat what is good.
You will enjoy the finest food.

³ "Come to me with your ears wide open.
Listen, and you will find life.
I will make an everlasting covenant with you.
I will give you all the unfailing love I promised to David.

⁴ See how I used him to display my power among the peoples.
I made him a leader among the nations.

⁵ You also will command nations you do not know,
and peoples unknown to you will come running to obey,
because I, the LORD your God,
the Holy One of Israel, have made you glorious."

55:2 Responding positively to God satisfies one's spiritual, social, and physical being (see 1:19; 58:13-14; Proverbs 4:10).
55:3 Those who respond obediently to God's word find eternal life (see also 55:11). King David received a special covenant from God, a promise to preserve his royal line (see 2 Samuel 7:15-16). David's dynasty was eternally confirmed in the kingship of the Messiah, Jesus Christ (see Isaiah 9:6-7; 11:1-16; Acts 2:22-36; 13:34).

Come Close — DRY? MELT

SCRIPTURE CONNECTION: ISAIAH 55:8-13

Just as snow blankets the earth and rain waters our lands, giving a bountiful feast for our people, God also quenches our spiritual thirst. This image prompts me to ask, "Will I be dry land or a snowmelt of blessing?"

Is my soul a dry land? My sister or brother is thirsty or hungry, and I am too busy to offer drink or food. I pay lip service when I say I need God but ignore others' needs. When I say, "His ways and thoughts are higher than my thoughts" (see 55:8-9) but I don't imitate his visible compassion.

Or am I like snowmelt? I honor God when I go beyond lip service, when I melt from my ways to bless others.

Our great Creator God invites us to care for our Native families, as he:

- gives rain and snow that produces water and food for our tribes (55:10),
- places nature around us that displays his design (55:12-13), and
- sends his word that has fruits of joy and peace (55:11-12).

For me, this means caring for my Ojibwe family, who desperately need showers of blessings. God inspires me as he provides for my people in our sovereign nations. He pours down refreshing *nibi* (Ojibwe for "water") so my people can thrive in their *waginogan* (Ojibwe for "homes").

How can we refresh others? When I consider others better than myself, when I melt from my ways so others might drink from a snowmelt of God's blessings, only then am I satisfied.

REFLECT "The rain and snow come down from the heavens and stay on the ground to water the earth. They cause the grain to grow, producing seed for the farmer and bread for the hungry." ISAIAH 55:10

Just as the Lord gave us rain and snow that gives refreshing life, how will we serve others today?

CONSIDER "The decisions you're making today will impact your tomorrows."
PRISCILLA SHIRER

> When I consider others as better than myself, when I melt from my ways so others might drink from a snowmelt of God's blessings, only then am I satisfied.

LYNN LONG has studied at National Louis University and is completing her doctorate at Wheaton College. Lynn is a Native American writer and speaker with Stonecroft Ministries.

⁶ Seek the LORD while you can find him.
  Call on him now while he is near.
⁷ Let the wicked change their ways
    and banish the very thought of doing wrong.
  Let them turn to the LORD that he may have mercy on them.
  Yes, turn to our God, for he will forgive generously.

⁸ "My thoughts are nothing like your thoughts," says the LORD.
  "And my ways are far beyond anything you could imagine.
⁹ For just as the heavens are higher than the earth,
    so my ways are higher than your ways
    and my thoughts higher than your thoughts.

¹⁰ "The rain and snow come down from the heavens
    and stay on the ground to water the earth.
  They cause the grain to grow,
    producing seed for the farmer
    and bread for the hungry.
¹¹ It is the same with my word.
  I send it out, and it always produces fruit.
  It will accomplish all I want it to,
    and it will prosper everywhere I send it.
¹² You will live in joy and peace.
  The mountains and hills will burst into song,
    and the trees of the field will clap their hands!
¹³ Where once there were thorns, cypress trees will grow.
  Where nettles grew, myrtles will sprout up.
  These events will bring great honor to the LORD's name;
    they will be an everlasting sign of his power and love."

Blessings for All Nations

56 This is what the LORD says:

"Be just and fair to all.
  Do what is right and good,
    for I am coming soon to rescue you
    and to display my righteousness among you.
² Blessed are all those
    who are careful to do this.
  Blessed are those who honor my Sabbath days of rest
    and keep themselves from doing wrong.

³ "Don't let foreigners who commit themselves to the LORD say,
    'The LORD will never let me be part of his people.'
  And don't let the eunuchs say,
    'I'm a dried-up tree with no children and no future.'
⁴ For this is what the LORD says:
  I will bless those eunuchs
    who keep my Sabbath days holy
    and who choose to do what pleases me
    and commit their lives to me.
⁵ I will give them—within the walls of my house—
    a memorial and a name
    far greater than sons and daughters could give.
  For the name I give them is an everlasting one.
    It will never disappear!

⁶ "I will also bless the foreigners who commit themselves to the LORD,
    who serve him and love his name,
  who worship him and do not desecrate the Sabbath day of rest,
    and who hold fast to my covenant.
⁷ I will bring them to my holy mountain of Jerusalem

55:8-9 God's plans are marvelous (Psalm 92:5; compare Psalm 94:11). God's creatures, including humans, can never fully understand the Creator's thoughts, but his revelation through his messengers gives great insight and knowledge of some of the things he will do.

55:10-11 The Creator not only sends rain and snow but also his word. In this context, the Hebrew *dabar* means his will or plan (14:24; see 40:8). God's written word, as an expression of God's plan, accomplishes his purposes. God is effective in whatever he does (see 14:26-27; 46:10).

56:1–66:24 The final chapters of the book bring together themes from Isaiah 1–39 (sin, justice and righteousness, responsibility, vengeance, and vindication) and Isaiah 40–55 (blessing, covenant, words, nations, glory, forgiveness, and joy). The overarching themes here are salvation and the age to come.

56:1 A key aspect of the message of Isaiah 1–39 is the call for justice in relationship with others and God. True godliness comes only through having character that is shaped by the character of God, which only happens by understanding and consistently applying God's Word. The Lord's declaration, "I am coming soon," summarizes the message of Isaiah 40–55: The Lord is creating a world of harmony, peace, restoration, vindication, and the removal of enemies (46:13).

56:2-8 The Sabbath, as a sign of the covenant (Exodus 31:13-17), is God's gift to his people; it belongs to this age as well as to the age to come (Isaiah 56:4, 6; 58:13-14; see Hebrews 4:1-13). The essential ingredient for covenant fellowship is love for God (Deuteronomy 6:5; 30:20; Matthew 22:34-38).

56:7 God had previously rejected sinful Israel's expressions of piety, their "burnt offerings and sacrifices" (1:11-13), but would welcome offerings from righteous Gentiles or foreigners. Having the "right" lineage is worth little to God without true piety. The Lord would open the doors of the Temple to all nations (see 2:2-4). Later, Jesus rebuked the people for desecrating the Temple and for preventing it from functioning as the house of prayer (Matthew 21:13; Mark 11:17).

and will fill them with joy in my house of
    prayer.
I will accept their burnt offerings and
        sacrifices,
    because my Temple will be called a house of
        prayer for all nations.
⁸ For the Sovereign LORD,
    who brings back the outcasts of Israel, says:
I will bring others, too,
    besides my people Israel."

Sinful Leaders Condemned

⁹ Come, wild animals of the field!
    Come, wild animals of the forest!
    Come and devour my people!
¹⁰ For the leaders of my people—
    the LORD's watchmen, his shepherds—
    are blind and ignorant.
They are like silent watchdogs
    that give no warning when danger comes.
They love to lie around, sleeping and dreaming.
¹¹ Like greedy dogs, they are never satisfied.
They are ignorant shepherds,
    all following their own path
    and intent on personal gain.
¹² "Come," they say, "let's get some wine and have a
        party.
    Let's all get drunk.
Then tomorrow we'll do it again
    and have an even bigger party!"

57

Good people pass away;
    the godly often die before their time.
But no one seems to care or wonder why.
No one seems to understand
    that God is protecting them from the evil to
        come.
² For those who follow godly paths
    will rest in peace when they die.

Idolatrous Worship Condemned

³ "But you—come here, you witches' children,
    you offspring of adulterers and prostitutes!
⁴ Whom do you mock,
    making faces and sticking out your tongues?
    You children of sinners and liars!
⁵ You worship your idols with great passion
    beneath the oaks and under every
        green tree.
You sacrifice your children down in the valleys,
    among the jagged rocks in the cliffs.

⁶ Your gods are the smooth stones in the valleys.
    You worship them with liquid offerings and
        grain offerings.
They, not I, are your inheritance.
    Do you think all this makes me happy?
⁷ You have committed adultery on every high
        mountain.
    There you have worshiped idols
    and have been unfaithful to me.
⁸ You have put pagan symbols
    on your doorposts and behind your doors.
You have left me
    and climbed into bed with these detestable
        gods.
You have committed yourselves to them.
    You love to look at their naked bodies.
⁹ You have gone to Molech*
    with olive oil and many perfumes,
sending your agents far and wide,
    even to the world of the dead.*
¹⁰ You grew weary in your search,
    but you never gave up.
Desire gave you renewed strength,
    and you did not grow weary.
¹¹ "Are you afraid of these idols?
    Do they terrify you?
Is that why you have lied to me
    and forgotten me and my words?
Is it because of my long silence
    that you no longer fear me?
¹² Now I will expose your so-called good deeds.
    None of them will help you.
¹³ Let's see if your idols can save you
    when you cry to them for help.
Why, a puff of wind can knock them down!
    If you just breathe on them, they fall over!
But whoever trusts in me will inherit the land
    and possess my holy mountain."

God Forgives the Repentant

¹⁴ God says, "Rebuild the road!
    Clear away the rocks and stones
    so my people can return from captivity."
¹⁵ The high and lofty one who lives in eternity,
    the Holy One, says this:
"I live in the high and holy place
    with those whose spirits are contrite and
        humble.
I restore the crushed spirit of the humble
    and revive the courage of those with
        repentant hearts.

57:9a Or *to the king.* **57:9b** Hebrew *to Sheol.*

57:3-13 In this section, idolatry is condemned. The accusations are of a dark and sexual nature, equating idolatry with marital unfaithfulness. The metaphors of unfaithfulness used are sometimes those of "adulterers and prostitutes" (57:3). Actions of unfaithfulness might include sacrificing children and fertility rituals. Although there are not any examples of women ritually sacrificing children in the Bible, there are a few accounts of men partaking in these detestable rites (see Judges 11:39; 2 Kings 3:27; 21:6). These practices were condemned by God through the prophets (Jeremiah 7:30-31).

ISAIAH 58

¹⁶ For I will not fight against you forever;
   I will not always be angry.
If I were, all people would pass away—
   all the souls I have made.
¹⁷ I was angry,
   so I punished these greedy people.
I withdrew from them,
   but they kept going on their own stubborn way.
¹⁸ I have seen what they do,
   but I will heal them anyway!
I will lead them.
I will comfort those who mourn,
¹⁹   bringing words of praise to their lips.
May they have abundant peace, both near and far,"
   says the LORD, who heals them.
²⁰ "But those who still reject me are like the restless sea,
   which is never still
   but continually churns up mud and dirt.
²¹ There is no peace for the wicked,"
   says my God.

True and False Worship

58 "Shout with the voice of a trumpet blast.
   Shout aloud! Don't be timid.
Tell my people Israel* of their sins!
² Yet they act so pious!
They come to the Temple every day
   and seem delighted to learn all about me.
They act like a righteous nation
   that would never abandon the laws of its God.
They ask me to take action on their behalf,
   pretending they want to be near me.
³ 'We have fasted before you!' they say.
   'Why aren't you impressed?
We have been very hard on ourselves,
   and you don't even notice it!'

"I will tell you why!" I respond.
   "It's because you are fasting to please yourselves.
Even while you fast,
   you keep oppressing your workers.
⁴ What good is fasting
   when you keep on fighting and quarreling?
This kind of fasting
   will never get you anywhere with me.
⁵ You humble yourselves
   by going through the motions of penance,
bowing your heads
   like reeds bending in the wind.
You dress in burlap
   and cover yourselves with ashes.
Is this what you call fasting?
   Do you really think this will please the LORD?

⁶ "No, this is the kind of fasting I want:
Free those who are wrongly imprisoned;
   lighten the burden of those who work for you.
Let the oppressed go free,
   and remove the chains that bind people.
⁷ Share your food with the hungry,
   and give shelter to the homeless.
Give clothes to those who need them,
   and do not hide from relatives who need your help.

⁸ "Then your salvation will come like the dawn,
   and your wounds will quickly heal.
Your godliness will lead you forward,
   and the glory of the LORD will protect you from behind.
⁹ Then when you call, the LORD will answer.
   'Yes, I am here,' he will quickly reply.

"Remove the heavy yoke of oppression.
   Stop pointing your finger and spreading vicious rumors!
¹⁰ Feed the hungry,
   and help those in trouble.
Then your light will shine out from the darkness,
   and the darkness around you will be as bright as noon.
¹¹ The LORD will guide you continually,
   giving you water when you are dry
   and restoring your strength.
You will be like a well-watered garden,
   like an ever-flowing spring.
¹² Some of you will rebuild the deserted ruins of your cities.
   Then you will be known as a rebuilder of walls
   and a restorer of homes.

¹³ "Keep the Sabbath day holy.
   Don't pursue your own interests on that day,
but enjoy the Sabbath
   and speak of it with delight as the LORD's holy day.
Honor the Sabbath in everything you do on that day,
   and don't follow your own desires or talk idly.
¹⁴ Then the LORD will be your delight.
   I will give you great honor
and satisfy you with the inheritance I promised to your ancestor Jacob.
   I, the LORD, have spoken!"

Warnings against Sin

59 Listen! The LORD's arm is not too weak to save you,
   nor is his ear too deaf to hear you call.
² It's your sins that have cut you off from God.
   Because of your sins, he has turned away
   and will not listen anymore.

58:1 Hebrew *Jacob*. See note on 14:1.

³ Your hands are the hands of murderers,
  and your fingers are filthy with sin.
 Your lips are full of lies,
  and your mouth spews corruption.

⁴ No one cares about being fair and honest.
  The people's lawsuits are based on lies.
 They conceive evil deeds
  and then give birth to sin.
⁵ They hatch deadly snakes
  and weave spiders' webs.
 Whoever eats their eggs will die;
  whoever cracks them will hatch a viper.
⁶ Their webs can't be made into clothing,
  and nothing they do is productive.
 All their activity is filled with sin,
  and violence is their trademark.
⁷ Their feet run to do evil,
  and they rush to commit murder.
 They think only about sinning.
  Misery and destruction always follow them.
⁸ They don't know where to find peace
  or what it means to be just and good.
 They have mapped out crooked roads,
  and no one who follows them knows a
   moment's peace.

⁹ So there is no justice among us,
  and we know nothing about right living.
 We look for light but find only darkness.
  We look for bright skies but walk in gloom.
¹⁰ We grope like the blind along a wall,
  feeling our way like people without eyes.
 Even at brightest noontime,
  we stumble as though it were dark.
 Among the living,
  we are like the dead.
¹¹ We growl like hungry bears;
  we moan like mournful doves.
 We look for justice, but it never comes.
  We look for rescue, but it is far away
   from us.
¹² For our sins are piled up before God
  and testify against us.
 Yes, we know what sinners we are.
¹³ We know we have rebelled and have denied the
   LORD.
 We have turned our backs on our God.
 We know how unfair and oppressive we have
   been,
  carefully planning our deceitful lies.
¹⁴ Our courts oppose the righteous,
  and justice is nowhere to be found.
 Truth stumbles in the streets,
  and honesty has been outlawed.
¹⁵ Yes, truth is gone,
  and anyone who renounces evil is attacked.

 The LORD looked and was displeased
  to find there was no justice.
¹⁶ He was amazed to see that no one intervened
  to help the oppressed.
 So he himself stepped in to save them with his
   strong arm,
  and his justice sustained him.
¹⁷ He put on righteousness as his body armor
  and placed the helmet of salvation on his head.
 He clothed himself with a robe of vengeance
  and wrapped himself in a cloak of divine
   passion.
¹⁸ He will repay his enemies for their evil deeds.
  His fury will fall on his foes.
 He will pay them back even to the ends of the
   earth.
¹⁹ In the west, people will respect the name of the
   LORD;
  in the east, they will glorify him.
 For he will come like a raging flood tide
  driven by the breath of the LORD.*
²⁰ "The Redeemer will come to Jerusalem
  to buy back those in Israel
 who have turned from their sins,"*
  says the LORD.

²¹ "And this is my covenant with them," says the LORD. "My Spirit will not leave them, and neither will these words I have given you. They will be on your lips and on the lips of your children and your children's children forever. I, the LORD, have spoken!

Future Glory for Jerusalem

60 "Arise, Jerusalem! Let your light shine for all to see.
  For the glory of the LORD rises to shine on you.
² Darkness as black as night covers all the nations
   of the earth,
  but the glory of the LORD rises and appears
   over you.
³ All nations will come to your light;
  mighty kings will come to see your radiance.

⁴ "Look and see, for everyone is coming home!
  Your sons are coming from distant lands;
  your little daughters will be carried home.
⁵ Your eyes will shine,
  and your heart will thrill with joy,
 for merchants from around the world will come
   to you.
  They will bring you the wealth of many lands.
⁶ Vast caravans of camels will converge on you,
  the camels of Midian and Ephah.
 The people of Sheba will bring gold and
   frankincense
  and will come worshiping the LORD.

59:19 Or *When the enemy comes like a raging flood tide, / the Spirit of the LORD will drive him back.* **59:20** Hebrew *The Redeemer will come to Zion / to buy back those in Jacob / who have turned from their sins.* Greek version reads *The one who rescues will come on behalf of Zion, / and he will turn Jacob away from ungodliness.* Compare Rom 11:26.

ISAIAH 61

⁷ The flocks of Kedar will be given to you,
  and the rams of Nebaioth will be brought for my altars.
 I will accept their offerings,
  and I will make my Temple glorious.

⁸ "And what do I see flying like clouds to Israel,
  like doves to their nests?
⁹ They are ships from the ends of the earth,
  from lands that trust in me,
  led by the great ships of Tarshish.
 They are bringing the people of Israel home from far away,
  carrying their silver and gold.
 They will honor the LORD your God,
  the Holy One of Israel,
  for he has filled you with splendor.

¹⁰ "Foreigners will come to rebuild your towns,
  and their kings will serve you.
 For though I have destroyed you in my anger,
  I will now have mercy on you through my grace.
¹¹ Your gates will stay open day and night
  to receive the wealth of many lands.
 The kings of the world will be led as captives
  in a victory procession.
¹² For the nations that refuse to serve you
  will be destroyed.

¹³ "The glory of Lebanon will be yours—
  the forests of cypress, fir, and pine—
  to beautify my sanctuary.
 My Temple will be glorious!
¹⁴ The descendants of your tormentors
  will come and bow before you.
 Those who despised you
  will kiss your feet.
 They will call you the City of the LORD,
  and Zion of the Holy One of Israel.

¹⁵ "Though you were once despised and hated,
  with no one traveling through you,
 I will make you beautiful forever,
  a joy to all generations.
¹⁶ Powerful kings and mighty nations
  will satisfy your every need,
  as though you were a child
  nursing at the breast of a queen.
 You will know at last that I, the LORD,
  am your Savior and your Redeemer,
  the Mighty One of Israel.*

¹⁷ I will exchange your bronze for gold,
  your iron for silver,
 your wood for bronze,
  and your stones for iron.
 I will make peace your leader
  and righteousness your ruler.
¹⁸ Violence will disappear from your land;
  the desolation and destruction of war will end.
 Salvation will surround you like city walls,
  and praise will be on the lips of all who enter there.

¹⁹ "No longer will you need the sun to shine by day,
  nor the moon to give its light by night,
 for the LORD your God will be your everlasting light,
  and your God will be your glory.
²⁰ Your sun will never set;
  your moon will not go down.
 For the LORD will be your everlasting light.
 Your days of mourning will come to an end.
²¹ All your people will be righteous.
 They will possess their land forever,
  for I will plant them there with my own hands
  in order to bring myself glory.
²² The smallest family will become a thousand people,
  and the tiniest group will become a mighty nation.
 At the right time, I, the LORD, will make it happen."

Good News for the Oppressed

61 The Spirit of the Sovereign LORD is upon me,
  for the LORD has anointed me
 to bring good news to the poor.
 He has sent me to comfort the brokenhearted
  and to proclaim that captives will be released
  and prisoners will be freed.*
² He has sent me to tell those who mourn
  that the time of the LORD's favor has come,*
  and with it, the day of God's anger against their enemies.

60:16 Hebrew *of Jacob.* See note on 14:1. 61:1 Greek version reads *and the blind will see.* Compare Luke 4:18. 61:2 Or *to proclaim the acceptable year of the LORD.*

60:21 The citizens of Zion will be righteous, enjoying a right relationship with God and with others (Revelation 21:27).
60:22 The Lord identifies himself here as the covenant God of Israel. His identity ensures that he "will make it happen" (see 27:3-4).
61:1-3 The servant here proclaims the good news that his ministry will restore Zion. The Lord Jesus applied these words to his own mission (Luke 4:18-19).

61:1 The presence of God's Spirit ensures the success of the servant's mission (see 11:1-5; 42:1). The servant will restore and heal the marginalized poor and the brokenhearted (see 25:4).
61:2 The phrase "the time of the LORD's favor has come" could also be translated "to proclaim the acceptable year of the LORD," which is the day of God's salvation (see 49:8). God now turns his wrath against the enemies of his people on "the day of God's anger." It will be a day of righteous vengeance (see 34:8; 63:3-4).

³ To all who mourn in Israel,*
 he will give a crown of beauty for ashes,
 a joyous blessing instead of mourning,
  festive praise instead of despair.
In their righteousness, they will be like great oaks
 that the LORD has planted for his own glory.

⁴ They will rebuild the ancient ruins,
 repairing cities destroyed long ago.
They will revive them,
 though they have been deserted for many generations.
⁵ Foreigners will be your servants.
 They will feed your flocks
 and plow your fields
 and tend your vineyards.
⁶ You will be called priests of the LORD,
 ministers of our God.
You will feed on the treasures of the nations
 and boast in their riches.
⁷ Instead of shame and dishonor,
 you will enjoy a double share of honor.
You will possess a double portion of prosperity in your land,
 and everlasting joy will be yours.

⁸ "For I, the LORD, love justice.
 I hate robbery and wrongdoing.
I will faithfully reward my people for their suffering
 and make an everlasting covenant with them.
⁹ Their descendants will be recognized
 and honored among the nations.
Everyone will realize that they are a people
 the LORD has blessed."

¹⁰ I am overwhelmed with joy in the LORD my God!
 For he has dressed me with the clothing of salvation
 and draped me in a robe of righteousness.
I am like a bridegroom dressed for his wedding
 or a bride with her jewels.
¹¹ The Sovereign LORD will show his justice to the nations of the world.
 Everyone will praise him!
His righteousness will be like a garden in early spring,
 with plants springing up everywhere.

Isaiah's Prayer for Jerusalem

62 Because I love Zion,
 I will not keep still.
Because my heart yearns for Jerusalem,
 I cannot remain silent.
I will not stop praying for her
 until her righteousness shines like the dawn,
 and her salvation blazes like a burning torch.
² The nations will see your righteousness.
 World leaders will be blinded by your glory.
And you will be given a new name
 by the LORD's own mouth.
³ The LORD will hold you in his hand for all to see—
 a splendid crown in the hand of God.
⁴ Never again will you be called "The Forsaken City"*
 or "The Desolate Land."*
Your new name will be "The City of God's Delight"*
 and "The Bride of God,"*
for the LORD delights in you
 and will claim you as his bride.
⁵ Your children will commit themselves to you,
 O Jerusalem,
 just as a young man commits himself to his bride.
Then God will rejoice over you
 as a bridegroom rejoices over his bride.

⁶ O Jerusalem, I have posted watchmen on your walls;
 they will pray day and night, continually.
Take no rest, all you who pray to the LORD.
⁷ Give the LORD no rest until he completes his work,
 until he makes Jerusalem the pride of the earth.
⁸ The LORD has sworn to Jerusalem by his own strength:
 "I will never again hand you over to your enemies.
Never again will foreign warriors come
 and take away your grain and new wine.
⁹ You raised the grain, and you will eat it,
 praising the LORD.
Within the courtyards of the Temple,
 you yourselves will drink the wine you have pressed."

61:3 Hebrew *in Zion.* **62:4a** Hebrew *Azubah,* which means "forsaken." **62:4b** Hebrew *Shemamah,* which means "desolate." **62:4c** Hebrew *Hephzibah,* which means "my delight is in her." **62:4d** Hebrew *Beulah,* which means "married."

61:3 Putting ashes on one's head was a sign of mourning (note the reversal of the judgment stated in 3:16-25). Mourning would be replaced by joy. A face covered with oil was a sign of blessing and well-being (see Psalm 45:8; 133:2). The remnant would start out as small offshoots but would grow into great oaks (see Isaiah 60:21).

61:6 The nation would fulfill its original calling to be priests and ministers of the Lord to all people (Exodus 19:6).

61:8 Suffering can happen because you are doing the right thing. Here, Isaiah demonstrates that God is a God who loves justice and hates wrongdoing. These words are found through many of the prophets who call people back to God (Micah 6:8), to glorify God through loving their neighbor (Leviticus 19:18; Mark 12:30-31). If you find that you are suffering injustice, know that God is aware and is at work through every difficult situation (Zephaniah 3:5).

ISAIAH 63

¹⁰ Go out through the gates!
    Prepare the highway for my people
        to return!
Smooth out the road; pull out the boulders;
    raise a flag for all the nations to see.
¹¹ The LORD has sent this message to every land:
    "Tell the people of Israel,*
'Look, your Savior is coming.
    See, he brings his reward with him as he
        comes.'"
¹² They will be called "The Holy People"
    and "The People Redeemed by the LORD."
And Jerusalem will be known as "The Desirable
        Place"
    and "The City No Longer Forsaken."

Judgment against the LORD's Enemies

63 Who is this who comes from Edom,
        from the city of Bozrah,
    with his clothing stained red?
Who is this in royal robes,
    marching in his great strength?

"It is I, the LORD, announcing your salvation!
    It is I, the LORD, who has the power
        to save!"

² Why are your clothes so red,
    as if you have been treading out grapes?

³ "I have been treading the winepress alone;
    no one was there to help me.
In my anger I have trampled my enemies
    as if they were grapes.
In my fury I have trampled my foes.
    Their blood has stained my clothes.
⁴ For the time has come for me to avenge my
        people,
    to ransom them from their oppressors.
⁵ I was amazed to see that no one intervened
    to help the oppressed.
So I myself stepped in to save them with my
        strong arm,
    and my wrath sustained me.
⁶ I crushed the nations in my anger
    and made them stagger and fall to
        the ground,
    spilling their blood upon the earth."

Praise for Deliverance

⁷ I will tell of the LORD's unfailing love.
    I will praise the LORD for all he has done.
I will rejoice in his great goodness to Israel,
    which he has granted according to his mercy
        and love.
⁸ He said, "They are my very own people.
    Surely they will not betray me again."
    And he became their Savior.
⁹ In all their suffering he also suffered,
    and he personally* rescued them.
In his love and mercy he redeemed them.
    He lifted them up and carried them
        through all the years.
¹⁰ But they rebelled against him
    and grieved his Holy Spirit.
So he became their enemy
    and fought against them.
¹¹ Then they remembered those days of old
    when Moses led his people out of Egypt.
They cried out, "Where is the one who brought
        Israel through the sea,
    with Moses as their shepherd?
Where is the one who sent his Holy Spirit
    to be among his people?
¹² Where is the one whose power was displayed
    when Moses lifted up his hand—
the one who divided the sea before them,
    making himself famous forever?
¹³ Where is the one who led them through the
        bottom of the sea?
They were like fine stallions
    racing through the desert, never
        stumbling.
¹⁴ As with cattle going down into a peaceful
        valley,
    the Spirit of the LORD gave them rest.
You led your people, LORD,
    and gained a magnificent reputation."

Prayer for Mercy and Pardon

¹⁵ LORD, look down from heaven;
    look from your holy, glorious home,
        and see us.
Where is the passion and the might
    you used to show on our behalf?
Where are your mercy and compassion now?
¹⁶ Surely you are still our Father!
    Even if Abraham and Jacob* would
        disown us,
LORD, you would still be our Father.
    You are our Redeemer from ages past.
¹⁷ LORD, why have you allowed us to turn from
        your path?
    Why have you given us stubborn hearts so we
        no longer fear you?
Return and help us, for we are your servants,
    the tribes that are your special possession.
¹⁸ How briefly your holy people possessed your
        holy place,
    and now our enemies have destroyed it.
¹⁹ Sometimes it seems as though we never
        belonged to you,
    as though we had never been known as your
        people.

62:11 Hebrew *Tell the daughter of Zion.* **63:9** Hebrew *and the angel of his presence.* **63:16** Hebrew *Israel.* See note on 14:1.

64

¹*Oh, that you would burst from the heavens and come down!
　How the mountains would quake in your presence!
²*As fire causes wood to burn
　　and water to boil,
　your coming would make the nations tremble.
　　Then your enemies would learn the reason for your fame!
³ When you came down long ago,
　　you did awesome deeds beyond our highest expectations.
　And oh, how the mountains quaked!
⁴ For since the world began,
　　no ear has heard
　and no eye has seen a God like you,
　　who works for those who wait for him!
⁵ You welcome those who gladly do good,
　　who follow godly ways.
　But you have been very angry with us,
　　for we are not godly.
　We are constant sinners;
　　how can people like us be saved?
⁶ We are all infected and impure with sin.
　　When we display our righteous deeds,
　　they are nothing but filthy rags.
　Like autumn leaves, we wither and fall,
　　and our sins sweep us away like the wind.
⁷ Yet no one calls on your name
　　or pleads with you for mercy.
　Therefore, you have turned away from us
　　and turned us over* to our sins.
⁸ And yet, O Lord, you are our Father.
　　We are the clay, and you are the potter.
　　We all are formed by your hand.
⁹ Don't be so angry with us, Lord.
　　Please don't remember our sins forever.
　Look at us, we pray,
　　and see that we are all your people.
¹⁰ Your holy cities are destroyed.
　　Zion is a wilderness;
　　yes, Jerusalem is a desolate ruin.
¹¹ The holy and beautiful Temple
　　where our ancestors praised you
　　has been burned down,
　　and all the things of beauty are destroyed.
¹² After all this, Lord, must you still refuse to help us?
　　Will you continue to be silent and punish us?

Judgment and Final Salvation

65

The Lord says,

"I was ready to respond, but no one asked for help.
　I was ready to be found, but no one was looking for me.
　I said, 'Here I am, here I am!'
　　to a nation that did not call on my name.*
² All day long I opened my arms to a rebellious people.*
　　But they follow their own evil paths
　　and their own crooked schemes.
³ All day long they insult me to my face
　　by worshiping idols in their sacred gardens.
　They burn incense on pagan altars.
⁴ At night they go out among the graves,
　　worshiping the dead.
　They eat the flesh of pigs
　　and make stews with other forbidden foods.
⁵ Yet they say to each other,
　　'Don't come too close or you will defile me!
　　I am holier than you!'
　These people are a stench in my nostrils,
　　an acrid smell that never goes away.
⁶ "Look, my decree is written out* in front of me:
　　I will not stand silent;
　　I will repay them in full!
　　Yes, I will repay them—
⁷ both for their own sins
　　and for those of their ancestors,"
　　says the Lord.
"For they also burned incense on the mountains
　　and insulted me on the hills.
　I will pay them back in full!
⁸ "But I will not destroy them all,"
　　says the Lord.
"For just as good grapes are found among a cluster of bad ones
　　(and someone will say, 'Don't throw them all away—
　　some of those grapes are good!'),
　so I will not destroy all Israel.
　　For I still have true servants there.
⁹ I will preserve a remnant of the people of Israel*
　　and of Judah to possess my land.
　Those I choose will inherit it,
　　and my servants will live there.

64:1 In the Hebrew text this verse is included in 63:19. **64:2** Verses 64:2-12 are numbered 64:1-11 in Hebrew text. **64:7** As in Greek, Syriac, and Aramaic versions; Hebrew reads *melted us*. **65:1** Or *to a nation that did not bear my name*. **65:1-2** Greek version reads *I was found by people who were not looking for me. / I showed myself to those who were not asking for me. / All day long I opened my arms to them, / but they were disobedient and rebellious*. Compare Rom 10:20-21. **65:6** Or *their sins are written out*; Hebrew reads *it stands written*. **65:9** Hebrew *remnant of Jacob*. See note on 14:1.

65:1-2 The Lord opened up every opportunity for the people of Israel to seek him (Isaiah 55:6; 58:2), but they did not.
65:8-9 A remnant of Israel will remain. Even when all hope seems lost, there are always faithful ones who remain loyal to God. Even Elijah thought at one point he was the only loyal prophet left, but God revealed to him that there were seven thousand others who remained faithful to God (1 Kings 19:10-18).

Koinonia
IMAGE
MY STORY WITH COMMUNITY, WORKPLACE & CHURCH

Work *Works* When We Know Who's the Maker

SCRIPTURE CONNECTION: ISAIAH 64:1-12

Like the people of Israel, I can easily get turned around and think I am the potter. I try to make beautiful things with my own hands, in my strength and giftedness. I forget who made me and what I am made for—in my home, in my circles of friends and family, and in my organizational leadership. Isaiah reminds us that our only real hope is in the Father's unchanging, persistent, grace-filled love.

We hear echoes of our prayers in Isaiah's prayers for his people. "God, . . .

- "Please, do 'awesome deeds,' make your enemies learn your name. Don't lose patience, and abandon us, and lay to waste our pleasant things."
- "We acknowledge that we have become 'infected and impure with sin' and all 'our righteous deeds . . . are nothing but filthy rags' (64:6). We cannot survive without your loving mercy."
- "We know 'we are the clay, and you are the potter'" (64:8).

> We are the work of his hands, molded and refined for his purposes.

What a relief to let God give us a unique shape for his plans and purposes. We are the work of his hands, molded and refined for his purposes.

IMAGINE

God is the potter, and you are the clay. So how is he molding and shaping you today?

What purpose is he molding and shaping you for?

"Every little aspect of our work matters. Through his work in us, may he be glorified (Isaiah 60:21)."

KATHERINE LEARY ALSDORF founded and directed Redeemer Church's Center for Faith & Work. She co-authored *Every Good Endeavor: Connecting Your Work to God's Work* with Timothy Keller.

¹⁰ The plain of Sharon will again be filled with flocks
   for my people who have searched for me,
   and the valley of Achor will be a place to pasture herds.
¹¹ "But because the rest of you have forsaken the LORD
   and have forgotten his Temple,
   and because you have prepared feasts to honor the god of Fate
   and have offered mixed wine to the god of Destiny,
¹² now I will 'destine' you for the sword.
   All of you will bow down before the executioner.
   For when I called, you did not answer.
   When I spoke, you did not listen.
   You deliberately sinned—before my very eyes—
   and chose to do what you know I despise."
¹³ Therefore, this is what the Sovereign LORD says:
   "My servants will eat,
   but you will starve.
   My servants will drink,
   but you will be thirsty.
   My servants will rejoice,
   but you will be sad and ashamed.
¹⁴ My servants will sing for joy,
   but you will cry in sorrow and despair.
¹⁵ Your name will be a curse word among my people,
   for the Sovereign LORD will destroy you
   and will call his true servants by another name.
¹⁶ All who invoke a blessing or take an oath
   will do so by the God of truth.
   For I will put aside my anger
   and forget the evil of earlier days.

==**¹⁷ "Look! I am creating new heavens and a new earth,
   and no one will even think about the old ones anymore.**==
¹⁸ Be glad; rejoice forever in my creation!
   And look! I will create Jerusalem as a place of happiness.
   Her people will be a source of joy.
¹⁹ I will rejoice over Jerusalem
   and delight in my people.
   And the sound of weeping and crying
   will be heard in it no more.
²⁰ "No longer will babies die when only a few days old.
   No longer will adults die before they have lived a full life.
   No longer will people be considered old at one hundred!
   Only the cursed will die that young!
²¹ In those days people will live in the houses they build
   and eat the fruit of their own vineyards.
²² Unlike the past, invaders will not take their houses
   and confiscate their vineyards.
   For my people will live as long as trees,
   and my chosen ones will have time to enjoy their hard-won gains.
²³ They will not work in vain,
   and their children will not be doomed to misfortune.
   For they are people blessed by the LORD,
   and their children, too, will be blessed.
²⁴ I will answer them before they even call to me.
   While they are still talking about their needs,
   I will go ahead and answer their prayers!
²⁵ The wolf and the lamb will feed together.
   The lion will eat hay like a cow.
   But the snakes will eat dust.
   In those days no one will be hurt or destroyed on my holy mountain.
   I, the LORD, have spoken!"

66

This is what the LORD says:

"Heaven is my throne,
   and the earth is my footstool.
Could you build me a temple as good as that?
   Could you build me such a resting place?
² My hands have made both heaven and earth;
   they and everything in them are mine.*
   I, the LORD, have spoken!

"I will bless those who have humble and contrite hearts,
   who tremble at my word.
³ But those who choose their own ways—
   delighting in their detestable sins—
   will not have their offerings accepted.
When such people sacrifice a bull,
   it is no more acceptable than a human sacrifice.
When they sacrifice a lamb,
   it's as though they had sacrificed a dog!
When they bring an offering of grain,
   they might as well offer the blood of a pig.
When they burn frankincense,
   it's as if they had blessed an idol.
⁴ I will send them great trouble—
   all the things they feared.

66:2 As in Greek, Latin, and Syriac versions; Hebrew reads *these things are*.

66:2 God is pleased to dwell with "those who have humble and contrite hearts" (57:15; Psalm 51:17). The humble and contrite submit themselves to God's will, whereas the arrogant resist it.

For when I called, they did not answer.
When I spoke, they did not listen.
They deliberately sinned before my very eyes
and chose to do what they know I despise."

⁵ Hear this message from the LORD,
all you who tremble at his words:
"Your own people hate you
and throw you out for being loyal to my name.
'Let the LORD be honored!' they scoff.
'Be joyful in him!'
But they will be put to shame.
⁶ What is all the commotion in the city?
What is that terrible noise from the Temple?
It is the voice of the LORD
taking vengeance against his enemies.

⁷ "Before the birth pains even begin,
Jerusalem gives birth to a son.
⁸ Who has ever seen anything as strange as this?
Who ever heard of such a thing?
Has a nation ever been born in a single day?
Has a country ever come forth in a mere moment?
But by the time Jerusalem's* birth pains begin,
her children will be born.
⁹ Would I ever bring this nation to the point of birth
and then not deliver it?" asks the LORD.
"No! I would never keep this nation from being born,"
says your God.

¹⁰ "Rejoice with Jerusalem!
Be glad with her, all you who love her
and all you who mourn for her.
¹¹ Drink deeply of her glory
even as an infant drinks at its mother's comforting breasts."

¹² This is what the LORD says:
"I will give Jerusalem a river of peace and prosperity.
The wealth of the nations will flow to her.
Her children will be nursed at her breasts,
carried in her arms, and held on her lap.
¹³ I will comfort you there in Jerusalem
as a mother comforts her child.
¹⁴ When you see these things, your heart will rejoice.
You will flourish like the grass!

Everyone will see the LORD's hand of blessing on his servants—
and his anger against his enemies.
¹⁵ See, the LORD is coming with fire,
and his swift chariots roar like a whirlwind.
He will bring punishment with the fury of his anger
and the flaming fire of his hot rebuke.
¹⁶ The LORD will punish the world by fire
and by his sword.
He will judge the earth,
and many will be killed by him.

¹⁷ "Those who 'consecrate' and 'purify' themselves in a sacred garden with its idol in the center—feasting on pork and rats and other detestable meats—will come to a terrible end," says the LORD.

¹⁸ "I can see what they are doing, and I know what they are thinking. So I will gather all nations and peoples together, and they will see my glory. ¹⁹ I will perform a sign among them. And I will send those who survive to be messengers to the nations—to Tarshish, to the Libyans* and Lydians* (who are famous as archers), to Tubal and Greece,* and to all the lands beyond the sea that have not heard of my fame or seen my glory. There they will declare my glory to the nations. ²⁰ They will bring the remnant of your people back from every nation. They will bring them to my holy mountain in Jerusalem as an offering to the LORD. They will ride on horses, in chariots and wagons, and on mules and camels," says the LORD. ²¹ "And I will appoint some of them to be my priests and Levites. I, the LORD, have spoken!

²² "As surely as my new heavens and earth will remain,
so will you always be my people,
with a name that will never disappear,"
says the LORD.
²³ "All humanity will come to worship me
from week to week
and from month to month.
²⁴ And as they go out, they will see
the dead bodies of those who have rebelled against me.
For the worms that devour them will never die,
and the fire that burns them will never go out.
All who pass by
will view them with utter horror."

66:8 Hebrew *Zion's.* 66:19a As in some Greek manuscripts, which read *Put* [that is, *Libya*]; Hebrew reads *Pul.* 66:19b Hebrew *Lud.* 66:19c Hebrew *Javan.*

66:7-13 Isaiah uses the image of Yahweh as a midwife. This feminine image beautifully depicts God as being part of the birth process, from start to end. In 66:9, the image shifts from midwife to mother. Isaiah tells them, "I will comfort you there in Jerusalem as a mother comforts her child" (66:13). The Old Testament reveals both feminine and masculine images of Yahweh. The tender and comforting metaphors that Isaiah uses here help paint a complete portrait of who Yahweh is for Israel, and for us!

66:7-11 The book of Isaiah closes with maternal imagery that begins with Jerusalem (Daughter Zion) and transitions to God. A painless childbirth is described. Comfort from God is described as the comfort of a mother's breast milk. These intimate portraits of God as a nurturing parent bring hope and comfort.
66:22 God's promise to Abraham was secure (Genesis 17:7; see also Galatians 3:8, 14). The identity of this new people will last forever (see Isaiah 59:21).

Jeremiah

WHAT DO WE LEARN ABOUT GOD'S MISSION AND OURS?
When nothing goes right, keep doing right.

WHO WROTE IT? Jeremiah, son of Hilkiah, as identified by the book, assisted by Baruch.

WHEN DID IT HAPPEN? Jeremiah lived in the end of Israel's divided kingdom period, beginning his ministry in 626 BC. The book was complete by 580 BC.

HOW IS IT ORGANIZED?

- **1:** Jeremiah's call
- **2–29:** God's accusations against Israel
- **30–33:** Future salvation and a new covenant
- **34–45:** Judah captured by Babylon
- **46–51:** Judgments against Judah's neighbors
- **52:** The last days of Jerusalem

FEATURE HIGHLIGHTS

- *The Call of a Broken Heart* (902)
- *Renew? Re-Old!* (905)
- *Spinning? Rest* (919)
- *Bless Where You Are* (931)
- *Forgiveness and Freedom Are the Same* (939)
- *Time* (948)

Words to Remember are highlighted throughout this book

HOW LONG DOES IT TAKE TO READ?

3:15

| :30 | 1:00 | 1:30 | 2:00 | 2:30 | 3:00 | 3:30 |

Timeline (BC)

BC	Event
640	ZEPHANIAH BECOMES A PROPHET
627	JEREMIAH BECOMES A PROPHET
612	HABAKKUK BECOMES A PROPHET
609	KING JOSIAH, JEDIDAH AND AMON'S SON, KILLED IN BATTLE
605	DANIEL TAKEN CAPTIVE DURING BABYLON'S FIRST INVASION
597	EZEKIEL TAKEN CAPTIVE
593	EZEKIEL BEGINS TO PROPHESY IN BABYLON
586	JUDAH FALLS; JERUSALEM DESTROYED; JEREMIAH'S MINISTRY IN JERUSALEM ENDS
585	JUDAH'S REMAINING PEOPLE FLEE TO EGYPT, TAKING JEREMIAH WITH THEM
561	KING JEHOIACHIN (NEHUSHTA AND JEHOIAKIM'S SON) RELEASED FROM BABYLONIAN PRISON
538	FIRST EXILES RETURN TO JUDAH

JEREMIAH 1

1 These are the words of Jeremiah son of Hilkiah, one of the priests from the town of Anathoth in the land of Benjamin. ²The LORD first gave messages to Jeremiah during the thirteenth year of the reign of Josiah son of Amon, king of Judah.* ³The LORD's messages continued throughout the reign of King Jehoiakim, Josiah's son, until the eleventh year of the reign of King Zedekiah, another of Josiah's sons. In August* of that eleventh year the people of Jerusalem were taken away as captives.

Jeremiah's Call and First Visions

⁴The LORD gave me this message:

⁵ "I knew you before I formed you in your
    mother's womb.
Before you were born I set you apart
    and appointed you as my prophet to the
    nations."

⁶"O Sovereign LORD," I said, "I can't speak for you! I'm too young!"

⁷The LORD replied, "Don't say, 'I'm too young,' for you must go wherever I send you and say whatever I tell you. ⁸And don't be afraid of the people, for I will be with you and will protect you. I, the LORD, have spoken!" ⁹Then the LORD reached out and touched my mouth and said,

"Look, I have put my words in your mouth!
¹⁰ Today I appoint you to stand up
    against nations and kingdoms.
Some you must uproot and tear down,
    destroy and overthrow.
Others you must build up
    and plant."

¹¹Then the LORD said to me, "Look, Jeremiah! What do you see?"

And I replied, "I see a branch from an almond tree."

¹²And the LORD said, "That's right, and it means that I am watching,* and I will certainly carry out all my plans."

¹³Then the LORD spoke to me again and asked, "What do you see now?"

And I replied, "I see a pot of boiling water, spilling from the north."

¹⁴"Yes," the LORD said, "for terror from the north will boil out on the people of this land. ¹⁵Listen! I am calling the armies of the kingdoms of the north to come to Jerusalem. I, the LORD, have spoken!

"They will set their thrones
    at the gates of the city.
They will attack its walls
    and all the other towns of Judah.
¹⁶ I will pronounce judgment
    on my people for all their evil—
for deserting me and burning incense to other
    gods.
Yes, they worship idols made with their own
    hands!

1:2 The thirteenth year of Josiah's reign was 627 B.C. **1:3** Hebrew *In the fifth month,* of the ancient Hebrew lunar calendar. A number of events in Jeremiah can be cross-checked with dates in surviving Babylonian records and related accurately to our modern calendar. The fifth month in the eleventh year of Zedekiah's reign occurred within the months of August and September 586 B.C. Also see 52:12 and the note there. **1:12** The Hebrew word for "watching" *(shoqed)* sounds like the word for "almond tree" *(shaqed).*

1:1-19 This beginning section includes three main movements: an introduction (1:1-3), Jeremiah's calling (1:4-16), and Jeremiah's charges and promises from God (1:17-19).

1:2-3 Jeremiah was called by God in 627 BC, while Josiah was king of Judah (2 Kings 23:1-30). Jehoahaz and Jehoiachin are both missing from this list of kings. Neither of them reigned for longer than three months, and only a limited number of events are mentioned after the fall of Jerusalem. Jehoahaz was King Josiah's son, but he was captured and exiled to Egypt (2 Kings 23:31-33). Jehoiachin was captured and imprisoned in Babylon in 581 BC.

1:4-10 In the story of his calling, Jeremiah receives visions and a charge to become a prophet for God. Jeremiah feels too young and inadequate (1:6). Others that God has called, such as Moses, also voiced hesitation and fear (Exodus 3:11-13). God responds to Jeremiah with words of comfort, "And don't be afraid of the people, for I will be with you and will protect you. I, the LORD, have spoken!" (Jeremiah 1:8). Knowing this can comfort us today when we feel afraid of what is ahead or what God has called us to do. The idea that God is with us carries forward to Jesus, who is called *Immanuel,* "God is with us" (Isaiah 7:14; Matthew 1:23). We are never alone.

1:10 God calls Jeremiah to prophesy to the nations and uses six metaphors to illustrate this call. The first four have to do with judgment on the nations: "uproot and tear down, destroy and overthrow." The next two images have a restorative purpose: "build up and plant." Speaking truth can be harsh at times, similar to uprooting. However, God purposes to restore and reconcile ultimately.

1:11-12 God gives Jeremiah a vision with two distinct images regarding the task he is to do. The two images picture an almond tree and a boiling pot, common objects in Jeremiah's everyday life. The first vision, the almond tree, plays on the sound of the Hebrew words "watching" *(shoqed)* with "almond tree" *(shaqed).* This wordplay is called *paronomasia.* The almond tree is the first plant of the season to flower, usually in late January or early February. You can imagine Jeremiah watching for the first almond tree to blossom, remembering this vision each year!

1:13 The boiling pot, Jeremiah's second vision, is another everyday object. This pot was most likely one used for boiling water and cooking food. This pot tips away from the north, pouring into the south, meaning catastrophe would come to Jerusalem from the north. Because of the desert region to the east of Israel, invading countries like Babylon often advanced from the north into Judah. Babylon was technically east of Judah, but the desert east of Judah forced those coming from the east to travel up and arrive from the north. The idea of enemies coming from the north was a common way to describe impending disasters by conquering nations.

¹⁷ "Get up and prepare for action.
  Go out and tell them everything I tell you to say.
  Do not be afraid of them,
  or I will make you look foolish in front of them.
¹⁸ For see, today I have made you strong
  like a fortified city that cannot be captured,
  like an iron pillar or a bronze wall.
  You will stand against the whole land—
  the kings, officials, priests, and people of Judah.
¹⁹ They will fight you, but they will fail.
  For I am with you, and I will take care of you.
  I, the LORD, have spoken!"

The LORD's Case against His People

2 The LORD gave me another message. He said, ²"Go and shout this message to Jerusalem. This is what the LORD says:

"I remember how eager you were to please me
  as a young bride long ago,
how you loved me and followed me
  even through the barren wilderness.
³ In those days Israel was holy to the LORD,
  the first of his children.*
All who harmed his people were declared guilty,
  and disaster fell on them.
  I, the LORD, have spoken!"

⁴Listen to the word of the LORD, people of Jacob—all you families of Israel! ⁵This is what the LORD says:

"What did your ancestors find wrong with me
  that led them to stray so far from me?
They worshiped worthless idols,
  only to become worthless themselves.
⁶ They did not ask, 'Where is the LORD
  who brought us safely out of Egypt
and led us through the barren wilderness—
  a land of deserts and pits,
a land of drought and death,
  where no one lives or even travels?'
⁷ "And when I brought you into a fruitful land
  to enjoy its bounty and goodness,
you defiled my land
  and corrupted the possession I had
    promised you.

> ## "Lord, to the degree I don't want to do this, bless me."
>
> **LUCI SWINDOLL**
> (1932–2020) devotional author and speaker

⁸ The priests did not ask,
  'Where is the LORD?'
Those who taught my word ignored me,
  the rulers turned against me,
and the prophets spoke in the name of Baal,
  wasting their time on worthless idols.
⁹ Therefore, I will bring my case against you,"
  says the LORD.
"I will even bring charges against your
    children's children
  in the years to come.

¹⁰ "Go west and look in the land of Cyprus*;
  go east and search through the land
    of Kedar.
Has anyone ever heard of anything
  as strange as this?
¹¹ Has any nation ever traded its gods for new
    ones,
  even though they are not gods at all?
Yet my people have exchanged their glorious
    God*
  for worthless idols!
¹² The heavens are shocked at such a thing
  and shrink back in horror and dismay,"
  says the LORD.

2:3 Hebrew *the firstfruits of his harvest.* **2:10** Hebrew *Kittim.* **2:11** Hebrew *their glory.*

1:18 What irony! As a prophet, God is saying that he has made Jeremiah like a fortified city, an iron pillar, and a bronze wall. With an impending disaster, Jerusalem will be captured. Yet the prophet, Jeremiah, will stand firm as a mouthpiece for God.
2:1-8 God speaks through Jeremiah using the metaphor of Israel as a new bride, faithful to her husband, God. Israel is then described as unfaithful, forgetting all God has done for her (1:6). Even the priests and prophets taught Israel to worship the Canaanite god Baal.
2:3 "Israel was holy" because the Lord had separated her from other nations to be his special people and reflect his character (Exodus 19:5-6; Leviticus 19:1-37; 22:31-33), as the "first of his children" or "the firstfruits of his harvest." Mosaic law required the people to offer the first portion of every harvest to the Lord (Exodus 23:16, 19; 34:22, 26; Leviticus 2:12, 14; 23:10, 17, 20; Numbers 18:12; 28:26; Deuteronomy 18:4; 26:10; Zechariah 14:20). The people who made the covenant with God at Mount Sinai pledged their full commitment to the one true God. In return, the Lord protected them and punished their enemies during their journey to Canaan.
2:12 The heavens and the earth are often portrayed in the Bible as witnesses to events among humans (see Jeremiah 51:48; Deuteronomy 32:1, 43; 1 Chronicles 16:31; Psalm 96:11; Isaiah 1:2; 44:23; 49:13).

¹³ "For my people have done two evil things:
 They have abandoned me—
  the fountain of living water.
 And they have dug for themselves cracked cisterns
  that can hold no water at all!

The Results of Israel's Sin

¹⁴ "Why has Israel become a slave?
  Why has he been carried away as plunder?
¹⁵ Strong lions have roared against him,
  and the land has been destroyed.
 The towns are now in ruins,
  and no one lives in them anymore.
¹⁶ Egyptians, marching from their cities of Memphis* and Tahpanhes,
  have destroyed Israel's glory and power.
¹⁷ And you have brought this upon yourselves
  by rebelling against the LORD your God,
  even though he was leading you on the way!

¹⁸ "What have you gained by your alliances with Egypt
  and your covenants with Assyria?
 What good to you are the streams of the Nile*
  or the waters of the Euphrates River?*
¹⁹ Your wickedness will bring its own punishment.
  Your turning from me will shame you.
 You will see what an evil, bitter thing it is
  to abandon the LORD your God and not to fear him.
 I, the Lord, the LORD of Heaven's Armies, have spoken!

²⁰ "Long ago I broke the yoke that oppressed you
  and tore away the chains of your slavery,
 but still you said,
  'I will not serve you.'
 On every hill and under every green tree,
  you have prostituted yourselves by bowing down to idols.
²¹ But I was the one who planted you,
  choosing a vine of the purest stock—the very best.
 How did you grow into this corrupt wild vine?
²² No amount of soap or lye can make you clean.
  I still see the stain of your guilt.
 I, the Sovereign LORD, have spoken!

Israel, an Unfaithful Wife

²³ "You say, 'That's not true!
  I haven't worshiped the images of Baal!'
 But how can you say that?
  Go and look in any valley in the land!
 Face the awful sins you have done.
  You are like a restless female camel
  desperately searching for a mate.
²⁴ You are like a wild donkey,
  sniffing the wind at mating time.
 Who can restrain her lust?
  Those who desire her don't need to search,
  for she goes running to them!
²⁵ When will you stop running?
  When will you stop panting after other gods?
 But you say, 'Save your breath.
  I'm in love with these foreign gods,
  and I can't stop loving them now!'

²⁶ "Israel is like a thief
  who feels shame only when he gets caught.
 They, their kings, officials, priests, and prophets—
  all are alike in this.
²⁷ To an image carved from a piece of wood they say,
  'You are my father.'
 To an idol chiseled from a block of stone they say,
  'You are my mother.'
 They turn their backs on me,
  but in times of trouble they cry out to me,
  'Come and save us!'
²⁸ But why not call on these gods you have made?
  When trouble comes, let them save you if they can!
 For you have as many gods
  as there are towns in Judah.
²⁹ Why do you accuse me of doing wrong?
  You are the ones who have rebelled,"
  says the LORD.
³⁰ "I have punished your children,
  but they did not respond to my discipline.
 You yourselves have killed your prophets
  as a lion kills its prey.

³¹ "O my people, listen to the words of the LORD!
  Have I been like a desert to Israel?
  Have I been to them a land of darkness?
 Why then do my people say, 'At last we are free from God!
  We don't need him anymore!'

2:16 Hebrew *Noph*. **2:18a** Hebrew *of Shihor*, a branch of the Nile River. **2:18b** Hebrew *the river*.

2:23–3:5 The metaphor of Israel as a wife continues and shifts as the passage accuses Israel of acting like a restless female camel, a senseless donkey in heat, a thief, and a prostitute. All forget God. The faithless bride cannot even remember her jewelry or wedding attire (2:32)! The marriage metaphor appears throughout this section. The main point of such a potent metaphor is to reveal Israel's unfaithfulness, which provokes an emotional response in the hearers. The imagery communicates the intimate nature of God's relationship with his covenant people. These words were meant to communicate to mostly male listeners a metaphor they would feel deeply. The choice to depict the unfaithful ones as female is not designed to say that women are any less faithful than men. The point here is that Israel was like God's bride, and she had chosen to worship things aside from her Lover and Husband, the Lord.

32 Does a young woman forget her jewelry,
　　or a bride her wedding dress?
　Yet for years on end
　　my people have forgotten me.

33 "How you plot and scheme to win your lovers.
　　Even an experienced prostitute could learn
　　　from you!
34 Your clothing is stained with the blood of the
　　　innocent and the poor,
　　though you didn't catch them breaking into
　　　your houses!
35 And yet you say,
　　'I have done nothing wrong.
　　Surely God isn't angry with me!'
　But now I will punish you severely
　　because you claim you have not sinned.
36 First here, then there—
　　you flit from one ally to another asking for help.
　But your new friends in Egypt will let you down,
　　just as Assyria did before.
37 In despair, you will be led into exile
　　with your hands on your heads,
　for the LORD has rejected the nations you trust.
　　They will not help you at all.

3

"If a man divorces a woman
　　and she goes and marries someone else,
　he will not take her back again,
　　for that would surely corrupt the land.
　But you have prostituted yourself with many
　　　lovers,
　　so why are you trying to come back to me?"
　　says the LORD.
2 "Look at the shrines on every hilltop.
　　Is there any place you have not been defiled
　　　by your adultery with other gods?
　You sit like a prostitute beside the road waiting
　　　for a customer.
　　You sit alone like a nomad in the desert.
　You have polluted the land with your prostitution
　　　and your wickedness.
3 That's why even the spring rains have failed.
　　For you are a brazen prostitute and
　　　completely shameless.

4 Yet you say to me,
　　'Father, you have been my guide since my youth.
5 Surely you won't be angry forever!
　　Surely you can forget about it!'
　So you talk,
　　but you keep on doing all the evil you can."

Judah Follows Israel's Example

⁶During the reign of King Josiah, the LORD said to me, "Have you seen what fickle Israel has done? Like a wife who commits adultery, Israel has worshiped other gods on every hill and under every green tree. ⁷I thought, 'After she has done all this, she will return to me.' But she did not return, and her faithless sister Judah saw this. ⁸She saw* that I divorced faithless Israel because of her adultery. But that treacherous sister Judah had no fear, and now she, too, has left me and given herself to prostitution. ⁹Israel treated it all so lightly—she thought nothing of committing adultery by worshiping idols made of wood and stone. So now the land has been polluted. ¹⁰But despite all this, her faithless sister Judah has never sincerely returned to me. She has only pretended to be sorry. I, the LORD, have spoken!"

Hope for Wayward Israel

¹¹Then the LORD said to me, "Even faithless Israel is less guilty than treacherous Judah! ¹²Therefore, go and give this message to Israel.* This is what the LORD says:

"O Israel, my faithless people,
　　come home to me again,
　for I am merciful.
　　I will not be angry with you forever.
13 Only acknowledge your guilt.
　　Admit that you rebelled against the LORD
　　　your God
　and committed adultery against him
　　by worshiping idols under every green tree.
　Confess that you refused to listen to my voice.
　　I, the LORD, have spoken!

14 "Return home, you wayward children,"
　　says the LORD,
　"for I am your master.

3:8 As in Dead Sea Scrolls, one Greek manuscript, and Syriac version; Masoretic Text reads *I saw*. **3:12** Hebrew *toward the north*.

3:1–4:4 Jeremiah repeats the word "return" (*shuv*) many times throughout the book. The Lord wants his people to "Return! Return! Return!" In this section, Jeremiah says "return" or "repent" eleven times (3:1, 7, 10, 12, 14, 19, 22; 4:1). This word can also be translated "to turn to," "to turn back," "repent," and "to turn away or aside." Context determines if this word means repentance or turning away from God (8:4-5).
3:6-13 Israel and Judah are compared to adulterous wives, seeking out other gods (see also 2:13, 17, 19; 7:5-7). The passage names Israel and Judah's unfaithfulness to God, along with their unjust ways that have hurt the poor and the oppressed. Jeremiah 3 compares Israel and Judah to two sisters. Surely Judah saw her sister Israel being conquered and deported by Assyria and would respond differently! Over and over, it becomes clear that Judah will refuse to see and to hear, to heed warnings, and will be without shame or remorse (7:9-11). Judah's story will echo what happened with Israel and Assyria.
3:14–4:4 Carrying on the family metaphor, God now invites the "wayward children" to come home. What awaits the returning children is a renewed home and shepherds who love God's ways and will watch over them (3:15). The images shift to remind Israel that God has loved them, but they have been faithless and wayward. Beautifully, the next section details the children returning with words of repentance and praise (3:22-25).

I will bring you back to the land of Israel*—
  one from this town and two from that family—
  from wherever you are scattered.
¹⁵ And I will give you shepherds after my own heart,
  who will guide you with knowledge and
    understanding.

¹⁶ "And when your land is once more filled with people," says the LORD, "you will no longer wish for 'the good old days' when you possessed the Ark of the LORD's Covenant. You will not miss those days or even remember them, and there will be no need to rebuild the Ark. ¹⁷In that day Jerusalem will be known as 'The Throne of the LORD.' All nations will come there to honor the LORD. They will no longer stubbornly follow their own evil desires. ¹⁸In those days the people of Judah and Israel will return together from exile in the north. They will return to the land I gave your ancestors as an inheritance forever.

¹⁹ "I thought to myself,
    'I would love to treat you as my own children!'
  I wanted nothing more than to give you this
      beautiful land—
    the finest possession in the world.
  I looked forward to your calling me 'Father,'
    and I wanted you never to turn from me.
²⁰ But you have been unfaithful to me, you people
      of Israel!
  You have been like a faithless wife who leaves
      her husband.
  I, the LORD, have spoken."

²¹ Voices are heard high on the windswept
      mountains,
    the weeping and pleading of Israel's people.
  For they have chosen crooked paths
    and have forgotten the LORD their God.

²² "My wayward children," says the LORD,
  "come back to me, and I will heal your
      wayward hearts."

"Yes, we're coming," the people reply,
  "for you are the LORD our God.
²³ Our worship of idols on the hills
    and our religious orgies on the mountains
    are a delusion.
  Only in the LORD our God
    will Israel ever find salvation.
²⁴ From childhood we have watched
    as everything our ancestors worked for—
  their flocks and herds, their sons and
      daughters—
    was squandered on a delusion.
²⁵ Let us now lie down in shame
    and cover ourselves with dishonor,
  for we and our ancestors have sinned
    against the LORD our God.

From our childhood to this day
  we have never obeyed him."

4 "O Israel," says the LORD,
  "if you wanted to return to me, you could.
  You could throw away your detestable idols
    and stray away no more.
² Then when you swear by my name, saying,
    'As surely as the LORD lives,'
  you could do so
    with truth, justice, and righteousness.
  Then you would be a blessing to the nations of
      the world,
    and all people would come and praise
      my name."

Coming Judgment against Judah

³This is what the LORD says to the people of Judah and Jerusalem:

"Plow up the hard ground of your hearts!
  Do not waste your good seed among thorns.
⁴ O people of Judah and Jerusalem,
    surrender your pride and power.
  Change your hearts before the LORD,*
    or my anger will burn like an unquenchable
      fire
    because of all your sins.

⁵ "Shout to Judah, and broadcast to Jerusalem!
    Tell them to sound the alarm throughout
      the land:
  'Run for your lives!
    Flee to the fortified cities!'
⁶ Raise a signal flag as a warning for Jerusalem*:
    'Flee now! Do not delay!'
  For I am bringing terrible destruction
    upon you
    from the north."

⁷ A lion stalks from its den,
    a destroyer of nations.
  It has left its lair and is headed your way.
    It's going to devastate your land!
  Your towns will lie in ruins,
    with no one living in them anymore.
⁸ So put on clothes of mourning
    and weep with broken hearts,
  for the fierce anger of the LORD
    is still upon us.

⁹ "In that day," says the LORD,
  "the king and the officials will tremble in fear.
  The priests will be struck with horror,
    and the prophets will be appalled."

¹⁰ Then I said, "O Sovereign LORD,
    the people have been deceived by what you said,
  for you promised peace for Jerusalem.
    But the sword is held at their throats!"

3:14 Hebrew *to Zion.* **4:4** Hebrew *Circumcise yourselves to the LORD, and take away the foreskins of your heart.* **4:6** Hebrew *Zion.*

¹¹ The time is coming when the LORD will say
    to the people of Jerusalem,
"My dear people, a burning wind is blowing in
    from the desert,
and it's not a gentle breeze useful for
    winnowing grain.
¹² It is a roaring blast sent by me!
    Now I will pronounce your destruction!"

¹³ Our enemy rushes down on us like storm clouds!
    His chariots are like whirlwinds.
His horses are swifter than eagles.
    How terrible it will be, for we are doomed!
¹⁴ O Jerusalem, cleanse your heart
    that you may be saved.
How long will you harbor
    your evil thoughts?
¹⁵ Your destruction has been announced
    from Dan and the hill country of Ephraim.

¹⁶ "Warn the surrounding nations
    and announce this to Jerusalem:
The enemy is coming from a distant land,
    raising a battle cry against the towns of Judah.
¹⁷ They surround Jerusalem like watchmen around
        a field,
    for my people have rebelled against me,"
    says the LORD.
¹⁸ "Your own actions have brought this upon you.
    This punishment is bitter, piercing you to the
        heart!"

Jeremiah Weeps for His People

¹⁹ My heart, my heart—I writhe in pain!
    My heart pounds within me! I cannot be still.
For I have heard the blast of enemy trumpets
    and the roar of their battle cries.
²⁰ Waves of destruction roll over the land,
    until it lies in complete desolation.
Suddenly my tents are destroyed;
    in a moment my shelters are crushed.
²¹ How long must I see the battle flags
    and hear the trumpets of war?

²² "My people are foolish
    and do not know me," says the LORD.
"They are stupid children
    who have no understanding.
They are clever enough at doing wrong,
    but they have no idea how to do right!"

Jeremiah's Vision of Coming Disaster

²³ I looked at the earth, and it was empty and formless.
    I looked at the heavens, and there was no light.

²⁴ I looked at the mountains and hills,
    and they trembled and shook.
²⁵ I looked, and all the people were gone.
    All the birds of the sky had flown away.
²⁶ I looked, and the fertile fields had become a
        wilderness.
    The towns lay in ruins,
    crushed by the LORD's fierce anger.

²⁷ This is what the LORD says:
"The whole land will be ruined,
    but I will not destroy it completely.
²⁸ The earth will mourn
    and the heavens will be draped in black
because of my decree against my people.
    I have made up my mind and will not change it."

²⁹ At the noise of charioteers and archers,
    the people flee in terror.
They hide in the bushes
    and run for the mountains.
All the towns have been abandoned—
    not a person remains!
³⁰ What are you doing,
    you who have been plundered?
Why do you dress up in beautiful clothing
    and put on gold jewelry?
Why do you brighten your eyes with mascara?
    Your primping will do you no good!
The allies who were your lovers
    despise you and seek to kill you.

³¹ I hear a cry, like that of a woman in labor,
    the groans of a woman giving birth to her
        first child.
It is beautiful Jerusalem*
    gasping for breath and crying out,
    "Help! I'm being murdered!"

The Sins of Judah

5 "Run up and down every street in Jerusalem,"
    says the LORD.
"Look high and low; search throughout
    the city!
If you can find even one just and honest person,
    I will not destroy the city.
² But even when they are under oath,
    saying, 'As surely as the LORD lives,'
    they are still telling lies!"

³ LORD, you are searching for honesty.
You struck your people,
    but they paid no attention.
You crushed them,
    but they refused to be corrected.

4:31 Hebrew *the daughter of Zion.*

4:23-31 Creation is unraveling in this poem. The language reminds the audience of Genesis. Here, the scene depicts formlessness, and darkness, and even the birds have flown away. This traumatic depiction shocks the hearer with a sobering image of exile and sin's effects on all creation.

Theos IMAGE — MY STORY WITH GOD

The Call of a Broken Heart

SCRIPTURE CONNECTION: JEREMIAH 4:19-21; 8:18–9:2

"Lord, I weep. You love your people, but they are far from you. My soul breaks, hurts, cries in pain." Although not a direct quote, Jeremiah could have said these words, just as many women might have, too. How many of us, as friends, sisters, and mothers, have wept for loved ones who stray from the God who loves them?

Jeremiah knew God had called him to the people in Judah. He was committed to being faithful even when they turned against God. He came to be known for his broken, weeping heart that was behind his hard words.

Jeremiah probably found himself thinking, "I give them your message and call them to come back to you, but they put me in prison. They want to kill me because I speak for you. I come from your priestly family in Anathoth, but they have rejected us."

Jeremiah's only comfort was in the Lord's promises: "This I know: The steadfast love of the Lord never fails, his mercies never come to an end, they are new every morning. Great is his faithfulness" (Lamentations 3:21-23, author's paraphrase). Through his years of weeping, Jeremiah remained faithful to God's call on his life.

God calls us, even when the results don't look like what we want or expect. Even when our hearts break, God can help us remain faithful to what he has called us to be and do.

> Even when our hearts break, God can help us stay faithful to what he has called us to be and do.

IMAGINE

How can you tell God your feelings about the people you love who keep ignoring him?

How might you give God your feelings—your anger, your disappointment, your sadness—and ask him to renew you in his love?

> "I have prayed for family, friends, and acquaintances over the years. I don't know if some ever responded to God's love for them and may never know this side of heaven. But I know God loves them more than I do and hears my prayers."

ELIZABETH GLANVILLE, PhD, is retired faculty from Fuller Theological Seminary, School of Mission and Theology. She is an international teacher on missions and leadership and chaplain for a local police department and her retirement community.

They are determined, with faces set like stone;
  they have refused to repent.

⁴ Then I said, "But what can we expect from
    the poor?
  They are ignorant.
  They don't know the ways of the LORD.
    They don't understand God's laws.
⁵ So I will go and speak to their leaders.
    Surely they know the ways of the LORD
    and understand God's laws."
  But the leaders, too, as one man,
    had thrown off God's yoke
    and broken his chains.
⁶ So now a lion from the forest will attack them;
    a wolf from the desert will pounce on them.
  A leopard will lurk near their towns,
    tearing apart any who dare to venture out.
  For their rebellion is great,
    and their sins are many.

⁷ "How can I pardon you?
    For even your children have turned from me.
  They have sworn by gods that are not gods at all!
    I fed my people until they were full.
  But they thanked me by committing adultery
    and lining up at the brothels.
⁸ They are well-fed, lusty stallions,
    each neighing for his neighbor's wife.
⁹ Should I not punish them for this?" says the LORD.
  "Should I not avenge myself against such a
    nation?

¹⁰ "Go down the rows of the vineyards and destroy
    the grapevines,
    leaving a scattered few alive.
  Strip the branches from the vines,
    for these people do not belong to the LORD.
¹¹ The people of Israel and Judah
    are full of treachery against me,"
    says the LORD.
¹² "They have lied about the LORD
    and said, 'He won't bother us!
  No disasters will come upon us.
    There will be no war or famine.
¹³ God's prophets are all windbags
    who don't really speak for him.
  Let their predictions of disaster fall on
    themselves!'"

¹⁴Therefore, this is what the LORD God of Heaven's Armies says:

  "Because the people are talking like this,
    my messages will flame out of your mouth
    and burn the people like kindling wood.
¹⁵ O Israel, I will bring a distant nation against you,"
    says the LORD.
  "It is a mighty nation,
    an ancient nation,
  a people whose language you do not know,
    whose speech you cannot understand.
¹⁶ Their weapons are deadly;
    their warriors are mighty.
¹⁷ They will devour the food of your harvest;
    they will devour your sons and daughters.
  They will devour your flocks and herds;
    they will devour your grapes and figs.
  And they will destroy your fortified towns,
    which you think are so safe.

¹⁸"Yet even in those days I will not blot you out completely," says the LORD. ¹⁹"And when your people ask, 'Why did the LORD our God do all this to us?' you must reply, 'You rejected him and gave yourselves to foreign gods in your own land. Now you will serve foreigners in a land that is not your own.'

A Warning for God's People

²⁰ "Make this announcement to Israel,*
    and say this to Judah:
²¹ Listen, you foolish and senseless people,
    with eyes that do not see
    and ears that do not hear.
²² Have you no respect for me?
    Why don't you tremble in my presence?
  I, the LORD, define the ocean's sandy shoreline
    as an everlasting boundary that the waters
    cannot cross.
  The waves may toss and roar,
    but they can never pass the boundaries I set.
²³ But my people have stubborn and rebellious
    hearts.
  They have turned away and abandoned me.
²⁴ They do not say from the heart,
    'Let us live in awe of the LORD our God,
  for he gives us rain each spring and fall,
    assuring us of a harvest when the time is
    right.'
²⁵ Your wickedness has deprived you of these
    wonderful blessings.
  Your sin has robbed you of all these good
    things.

5:20 Hebrew *to the house of Jacob*. The names "Jacob" and "Israel" are often interchanged throughout the Old Testament, referring sometimes to the individual patriarch and sometimes to the nation.

5:11-13 Here, the words of the false prophets are like "wind" (*ruakh*). Jeremiah has the true spirit/wind of God in him, unlike these "windbags" who speak false prophecies and lies. False prophets said what the people wanted to hear, even though the words were untrue. Jeremiah called this out and suffered for it. Even so, God was with Jeremiah and protected him.

5:23 Stubbornness is a theme throughout Jeremiah (3:17; 7:24; 9:14; 11:8; 13:10; 16:12; 18:12; 23:17). God tirelessly worked to call Israel back to repentance. Though Israel was stubborn even while going into exile, God never gave up on them, nor us today. There is hope, even for the most stubborn!

26 "Among my people are wicked men
     who lie in wait for victims like a hunter hiding
        in a blind.
   They continually set traps
     to catch people.
27 Like a cage filled with birds,
     their homes are filled with evil plots.
   And now they are great and rich.
28 They are fat and sleek,
     and there is no limit to their wicked deeds.
   They refuse to provide justice to orphans
     and deny the rights of the poor.
29 Should I not punish them for this?" says the
        LORD.
   "Should I not avenge myself against such a
        nation?"
30 A horrible and shocking thing
     has happened in this land—
31 the prophets give false prophecies,
     and the priests rule with an iron hand.
   Worse yet, my people like it that way!
   But what will you do when the end comes?

Jerusalem's Last Warning

6 "Run for your lives, you people of Benjamin!
     Get out of Jerusalem!
   Sound the alarm in Tekoa!
     Send up a signal at Beth-hakkerem!
   A powerful army is coming from the north,
     coming with disaster and destruction.
2 O Jerusalem,* you are my beautiful and delicate
        daughter—
     but I will destroy you!
3 Enemies will surround you, like shepherds
        camped around the city.
   Each chooses a place for his troops
     to devour.
4 They shout, 'Prepare for battle!
     Attack at noon!'
   'No, it's too late; the day is fading,
     and the evening shadows are falling.'
5 'Well then, let's attack at night
     and destroy her palaces!'"
6 This is what the LORD of Heaven's Armies says:
   "Cut down the trees for battering rams.
     Build siege ramps against the walls of
        Jerusalem.
   This is the city to be punished,
     for she is wicked through and through.

6:2 Hebrew *Daughter of Zion.*

7 She spouts evil like a fountain.
     Her streets echo with the sounds of violence
        and destruction.
   I always see her sickness and sores.
8 Listen to this warning, Jerusalem,
     or I will turn from you in disgust.
   Listen, or I will turn you into a heap of ruins,
     a land where no one lives."

9 This is what the LORD of Heaven's Armies says:
   "Even the few who remain in Israel
     will be picked over again,
   as when a harvester checks each vine a second
        time
     to pick the grapes that were missed."

Judah's Constant Rebellion

10 To whom can I give warning?
     Who will listen when I speak?
   Their ears are closed,
     and they cannot hear.
   They scorn the word of the LORD.
     They don't want to listen at all.
11 So now I am filled with the LORD's fury.
     Yes, I am tired of holding it in!

   "I will pour out my fury on children playing in
        the streets
     and on gatherings of young men,
   on husbands and wives
     and on those who are old and gray.
12 Their homes will be turned over to their enemies,
     as will their fields and their wives.
   For I will raise my powerful fist
     against the people of this land,"
        says the LORD.
13 "From the least to the greatest,
     their lives are ruled by greed.
   From prophets to priests,
     they are all frauds.
14 They offer superficial treatments
     for my people's mortal wound.
   They give assurances of peace
     when there is no peace.
15 Are they ashamed of their disgusting actions?
     Not at all—they don't even know how to blush!
   Therefore, they will lie among the slaughtered.
     They will be brought down when I punish
        them,"
        says the LORD.

6:2-5 In the Hebrew, "Jerusalem" is Daughter Zion. Daughter Zion is a metaphor depicting Jerusalem in several places throughout the Old Testament. This metaphor relates the city in a feminine and familial way. Metaphors of relationship are powerful and convey intimacy, hurt, hope, and wounding in terms that evoke strong emotions and connections.

6:11 God encourages Jeremiah to express strong emotion, even rage, in this chapter. Strong emotions can help us identify our core values and the things and the people we love. The rage expressed in this chapter reveals two areas that both Jeremiah and God care about deeply: unfaithfulness to God and injustice toward the people around us. Jeremiah provides a helpful example of the importance of expressing our emotions.

Judah Rejects the LORD's Way

16 This is what the LORD says:
"Stop at the crossroads and look around.
  Ask for the old, godly way, and walk in it.
Travel its path, and you will find rest for your
    souls.
  But you reply, 'No, that's not the road we
    want!'
17 I posted watchmen over you who said,
  'Listen for the sound of the alarm.'
But you replied,
  'No! We won't pay attention!'
18 "Therefore, listen to this, all you nations.
  Take note of my people's situation.
19 Listen, all the earth!
  I will bring disaster on my people.
It is the fruit of their own schemes,
  because they refuse to listen to me.
  They have rejected my word.
20 There's no use offering me sweet frankincense
    from Sheba.
  Keep your fragrant calamus imported from
    distant lands!
I will not accept your burnt offerings.
  Your sacrifices have no pleasing aroma
    for me."

21 Therefore, this is what the LORD says:
"I will put obstacles in my people's
    path.
Fathers and sons will both fall over them.
  Neighbors and friends will die
    together."

Come Close — RENEW? RE-OLD!

SCRIPTURE CONNECTION: JEREMIAH 6:10-16

All of us have different personalities, but mine loves to deal with anxiety by seeking *more*.

Perhaps if I read one more blog post, try one more program, and hear from one more expert, I might bring renewal not just to myself but also to those in my care. I think, "If I learn more, try more, do more, surely I can help more."

But that's not what God's Word says. Jeremiah denounces those who promise wholeness—or *shalom*—where there is no wholeness. Bible commentator, Alexander Varughese puts it this way: "The attitude of deceit and falsehood has become a national characteristic . . . (6:13-15; see also 5:30-31). This is clearly evident in the preaching and teaching [that was] popular in the land. . . . These leaders proclaim šālôm to those who have no šālôm. They are not concerned with the spiritual and physical health (šālôm) of the nation. The leaders are therefore under Yahweh's judgment" (*Asbury Bible Commentary*).

But what renews us is old—God's way. Rather than searching someone else's latest recipe for success, we can return to God, whose ancient covenant offers restoration. Varughese continues, "The law given . . . is an expression of grace . . . which offers rest to the weary souls by pointing them to the right way (**the ancient paths, the good way**)." (Emphasis in original.)

We can ask God to help us run to the old way, through his Word, to find our new way, this day.

REFLECT "Ask for the old, godly way, and walk in it. Travel its path, and you will find rest for your souls." JEREMIAH 6:16

Lord, help me stop striving after new ideas. Help me spin around and single-heartedly seek you. Amen.

CONSIDER "Let your life reflect the faith you have in God. Fear nothing and pray about everything. Be strong, trust God's Word, and trust the process."
GERMANY KENT, journalist and author of *The Hope Handbook*

> God's promise is the old way worth pursuing as my new way, this day.

NAOMI CRAMER OVERTON, MBA, DIS, lives to realize beauty-filled visions that lift us to flourishing, with our families and beyond. Naomi has been CEO for Stonecroft and MOPS, director with Compassion International and World Vision, and General Editor for this Bible.

An Invasion from the North

²² This is what the LORD says:

"Look! A great army coming from the north!
 A great nation is rising against you from
  far-off lands.
²³ They are armed with bows and spears.
 They are cruel and show no mercy.
 They sound like a roaring sea
  as they ride forward on horses.
 They are coming in battle formation,
  planning to destroy you, beautiful Jerusalem.*
²⁴ We have heard reports about the enemy,
  and we wring our hands in fright.
 Pangs of anguish have gripped us,
  like those of a woman in labor.
²⁵ Don't go out to the fields!
  Don't travel on the roads!
 The enemy's sword is everywhere
  and terrorizes us at every turn!
²⁶ Oh, my people, dress yourselves in burlap
  and sit among the ashes.
 Mourn and weep bitterly, as for the loss of an
  only son.
 For suddenly the destroying armies will be
  upon you!

²⁷ "Jeremiah, I have made you a tester of metals,*
  that you may determine the quality of my people.
²⁸ They are the worst kind of rebel,
  full of slander.
 They are as hard as bronze and iron,
  and they lead others into corruption.
²⁹ The bellows fiercely fan the flames
  to burn out the corruption.
 But it does not purify them,
  for the wickedness remains.
³⁰ I will label them 'Rejected Silver,'
  for I, the LORD, am discarding them."

Jeremiah Speaks at the Temple

7 The LORD gave another message to Jeremiah. He said, ² "Go to the entrance of the LORD's Temple, and give this message to the people: 'O Judah, listen to this message from the LORD! Listen to it, all of you who worship here! ³ This is what the LORD of Heaven's Armies, the God of Israel, says:

"'Even now, if you quit your evil ways, I will let you stay in your own land. ⁴ But don't be fooled by those who promise you safety simply because the LORD's Temple is here. They chant, "The LORD's Temple is here! The LORD's Temple is here!" ⁵ But I will be merciful only if you stop your evil thoughts and deeds and start treating each other with justice; ⁶ only if you stop exploiting foreigners, orphans, and widows; only if you stop your murdering; and only if you stop harming yourselves by worshiping idols. ⁷ Then I will let you stay in this land that I gave to your ancestors to keep forever.

⁸ "'Don't be fooled into thinking that you will never suffer because the Temple is here. It's a lie! ⁹ Do you really think you can steal, murder, commit adultery, lie, and burn incense to Baal and all those other new gods of yours, ¹⁰ and then come here and stand before me in my Temple and chant, "We are safe!"—only to go right back to all those evils again? ¹¹ Don't you yourselves admit that this Temple, which bears my name, has become a den of thieves? Surely I see all the evil going on there. I, the LORD, have spoken!

¹² "'Go now to the place at Shiloh where I once put the Tabernacle that bore my name. See what I did there because of all the wickedness of my people, the Israelites. ¹³ While you were doing these wicked things, says the LORD, I spoke to you about it repeatedly, but you would not listen. I called out to you, but you refused to answer. ¹⁴ So just as I destroyed Shiloh, I will now destroy this Temple that bears my name, this Temple that you trust in for help, this place that I gave to you and your ancestors. ¹⁵ And I will send you out of my sight into exile, just as I did your relatives, the people of Israel.*

Judah's Persistent Idolatry

¹⁶ "Pray no more for these people, Jeremiah. Do not weep or pray for them, and don't beg me to help them, for I will not listen to you. ¹⁷ Don't you see what they are doing throughout the towns of Judah and in the streets of Jerusalem? ¹⁸ No wonder I am so angry! Watch how the children gather wood and

---

6:23 Hebrew *daughter of Zion.* 6:27 As in Greek version; Hebrew reads *a tester of my people a fortress.* 7:15 Hebrew *of Ephraim,* referring to the northern kingdom of Israel.

7:5-7 God's divine pleas are intended to restore. The warnings and metaphors offered throughout this book are designed to remind Judah of their covenant relationship with God. They invite Judah to be faithful to that covenant with God and one another.

7:12 Shiloh was a hill located halfway between Shechem and Jerusalem. The Tabernacle had been set up there after the conquest of Canaan led by Joshua (Joshua 18:1, 6-10; Judges 18:31). It remained the center of worship for the tribes of Israel until Shiloh was destroyed about 1045 BC by the Philistine army (see Psalm 78:60; Jeremiah 26:6).

7:18 "Queen of Heaven" appears in many ancient Near Eastern writings. This description referred to Astarte (the Canaanite goddess of sex and war), Asherah (the Canaanite mother goddess), or Ishtar (a Mesopotamian goddess of sex and war) and Inanna (the Sumerian counterpart to Ishtar). Women ritually baked and offered cakes in worship to these goddesses, sometimes in the shape of a multi-pointed star. Although they originated in other nations' pantheons, King Manasseh instructed the Israelite people to worship these goddesses (2 Kings 21:1-9), and Jeremiah brings up this goddess figure again in Jeremiah 44:15-30 in a message of judgment. These prophetic judgments were meant to call Israel back to God, the only one who deserved their worship.

the fathers build sacrificial fires. See how the women knead dough and make cakes to offer to the Queen of Heaven. And they pour out liquid offerings to their other idol gods! ¹⁹Am I the one they are hurting?" asks the LORD. "Most of all, they hurt themselves, to their own shame."

²⁰So this is what the Sovereign LORD says: "I will pour out my terrible fury on this place. Its people, animals, trees, and crops will be consumed by the unquenchable fire of my anger."

²¹This is what the LORD of Heaven's Armies, the God of Israel, says: "Take your burnt offerings and your other sacrifices and eat them yourselves! ²²When I led your ancestors out of Egypt, it was not burnt offerings and sacrifices I wanted from them. ²³This is what I told them: 'Obey me, and I will be your God, and you will be my people. Do everything as I say, and all will be well!'

²⁴"But my people would not listen to me. They kept doing whatever they wanted, following the stubborn desires of their evil hearts. They went backward instead of forward. ²⁵From the day your ancestors left Egypt until now, I have continued to send my servants, the prophets—day in and day out. ²⁶But my people have not listened to me or even tried to hear. They have been stubborn and sinful—even worse than their ancestors.

²⁷"Tell them all this, but do not expect them to listen. Shout out your warnings, but do not expect them to respond. ²⁸Say to them, 'This is the nation whose people will not obey the LORD their God and who refuse to be taught. Truth has vanished from among them; it is no longer heard on their lips. ²⁹Shave your head in mourning, and weep alone on the mountains. For the LORD has rejected and forsaken this generation that has provoked his fury.'

The Valley of Slaughter

³⁰"The people of Judah have sinned before my very eyes," says the LORD. "They have set up their abominable idols right in the Temple that bears my name, defiling it. ³¹They have built pagan shrines at Topheth, the garbage dump in the valley of Ben-Hinnom, and there they burn their sons and daughters in the fire. I have never commanded such a horrible deed; it never even crossed my mind to command such a thing! ³²So beware, for the time is coming," says the LORD, "when that garbage dump will no longer be called Topheth or the valley of Ben-Hinnom, but the Valley of Slaughter. They will bury the bodies in Topheth until there is no more room for them. ³³The bodies of my people will be food for the vultures and wild animals, and no one will be left to scare them away. ³⁴I will put an end to the happy singing and laughter in the streets of Jerusalem. The joyful voices of bridegrooms and brides will no longer be heard in the towns of Judah. The land will lie in complete desolation.

8 "In that day," says the LORD, "the enemy will break open the graves of the kings and officials of Judah, and the graves of the priests, prophets, and common people of Jerusalem. ²They will spread out their bones on the ground before the sun, moon, and stars—the gods my people have loved, served, and worshiped. Their bones will not be gathered up again or buried but will be scattered on the ground like manure. ³And the people of this evil nation who survive will wish to die rather than live where I will send them. I, the LORD of Heaven's Armies, have spoken!

Deception by False Prophets

⁴"Jeremiah, say to the people, 'This is what the LORD says:

"'When people fall down, don't they get
up again?
When they discover they're on the wrong
road, don't they turn back?
⁵ Then why do these people stay on their self-
destructive path?
Why do the people of Jerusalem refuse to turn
back?
They cling tightly to their lies
and will not turn around.
⁶ I listen to their conversations
and don't hear a word of truth.

7:21-23 God is asking Israel to obey: "Obey me, and I will be your God, and you will be my people. Do everything as I say, and all will be well!" (7:23). Obedience in the eyes of God is more than proper ritual performance and sacrifice. Obedience involves the whole person; it is a real relationship. God wanted them to worship with their hands, their hearts, and their minds! It can be easy for us, too, to slip into the external motions of worship while neglecting our relationship with God. God wants all of you; he loves you that much!

7:30-34 The valley of Ben-Hinnom began on the west side of Jerusalem and continued around the south side. This narrow, steep-sided valley opened into the Kidron Valley and was the city's combined garbage dump and graveyard. The bodies of the poor who had been murdered or had died of disease were dumped there, and child sacrifice (a practice abhorrent to the Lord; see 2 Chronicles 28:3; 33:6) was performed there. The place of sacrifice was also known as Topheth (2 Kings 23:10; Isaiah 30:33), perhaps referring to the ritual drums (Hebrew *top*) or to the sacrificial fires (Hebrew *tap*) that were used there. In the New Testament it is called Gehenna, and Jesus compared hell to the fire that burned continuously in that valley. In Jeremiah's day, it would come to be known as the Valley of Slaughter, because the siege and destruction of Jerusalem (588–586 BC) would fill the valley to overflowing with the bodies of the slain.

8:1-2 Scattering the bones of the dead was the ultimate act of contempt for a defeated nation. Jerusalem's favorite deities—the sun, moon, and stars—would be unable to prevent that from happening.

Is anyone sorry for doing wrong?
    Does anyone say, "What a terrible thing I
        have done"?
No! All are running down the path of sin
    as swiftly as a horse galloping into battle!
⁷ Even the stork that flies across the sky
    knows the time of her migration,
as do the turtledove, the swallow, and the crane.*
    They all return at the proper time each year.
But not my people!
    They do not know the LORD's laws.

⁸ "'How can you say, "We are wise because we
        have the word of the LORD,"
    when your teachers have twisted it by writing
        lies?
⁹ These wise teachers will fall
    into the trap of their own foolishness,
for they have rejected the word of the LORD.
    Are they so wise after all?
¹⁰ I will give their wives to others
    and their farms to strangers.
From the least to the greatest,
    their lives are ruled by greed.
Yes, even my prophets and priests are like that.
    They are all frauds.
¹¹ They offer superficial treatments
    for my people's mortal wound.
They give assurances of peace
    when there is no peace.
¹² Are they ashamed of these disgusting actions?
    Not at all—they don't even know how to blush!
Therefore, they will lie among the slaughtered.
    They will be brought down when I punish them,
        says the LORD.
¹³ I will surely consume them.
    There will be no more harvests of figs and
        grapes.
    Their fruit trees will all die.
Whatever I gave them will soon be gone.
    I, the LORD, have spoken!'

¹⁴ "Then the people will say,
    'Why should we wait here to die?
Come, let's go to the fortified towns and die there.
    For the LORD our God has decreed our destruction
and has given us a cup of poison to drink

because we sinned against the LORD.
¹⁵ We hoped for peace, but no peace came.
    We hoped for a time of healing, but found only
        terror.'

¹⁶ "The snorting of the enemies' warhorses can be
        heard
    all the way from the land of Dan in the north!
The neighing of their stallions makes the whole
        land tremble.
    They are coming to devour the land and
        everything in it—
    cities and people alike.
¹⁷ I will send these enemy troops among you
    like poisonous snakes you cannot charm.
They will bite you, and you will die.
    I, the LORD, have spoken!"

Jeremiah Weeps for Sinful Judah

¹⁸ My grief is beyond healing;
    my heart is broken.
¹⁹ Listen to the weeping of my people;
    it can be heard all across the land.
"Has the LORD abandoned Jerusalem?*" the
        people ask.
    "Is her King no longer there?"

"Oh, why have they provoked my anger with
        their carved idols
    and their worthless foreign gods?" says the LORD.

²⁰ "The harvest is finished,
    and the summer is gone," the people cry,
    "yet we are not saved!"

²¹ I hurt with the hurt of my people.
    I mourn and am overcome with grief.
²² Is there no medicine in Gilead?
    Is there no physician there?
Why is there no healing
    for the wounds of my people?

9 ¹*If only my head were a pool of water
    and my eyes a fountain of tears,
I would weep day and night
    for all my people who have been slaughtered.
²*Oh, that I could go away and forget my people
    and live in a travelers' shack in the desert.

8:7 The identification of some of these birds is uncertain.   **8:19** Hebrew *Zion?*   **9:1** Verse 9:1 is numbered 8:23 in Hebrew text.
9:2 Verses 9:2-26 are numbered 9:1-25 in Hebrew text.

8:9-10 The phrase "wise teachers" is sarcastic—the Lord calls their teachings foolishness and exposes their motivation as greed (compare to Job 28:28). This sin ruled the lives of the "prophets and priests," marking them as frauds.
8:13 Having presented the evidence, the Lord now decrees the punishment of the elite. They would be consumed along with the land's produce. The Lord even places his authority behind his decree
8:21-22 Jeremiah empathizes with the suffering of his people. The closeness between the Lord and his prophet means that sometimes the first-person pronouns refer to the Lord as

well—the Lord also hurts with the hurt of his people (compare to Matthew 23:37).
9:1-26 This lament alternates between the voice of God and the voice of Jeremiah. The people's injustice has become overwhelming (9:3). In this lament, we hear Jeremiah's desire to flee, "Oh, that I could go away and forget my people and live in a travelers' shack in the desert" (9:2). In this passage, anger at injustice and grief intertwine. This language is intense, but the intensity reveals God's deep love for Israel. Their actions matter, and—even in exile—God will continue to call them back to relationship with him.

For they are all adulterers—
  a pack of treacherous liars.

Judgment for Disobedience

³ "My people bend their tongues like bows
    to shoot out lies.
They refuse to stand up for the truth.
    They only go from bad to worse.
They do not know me,"
    says the LORD.
⁴ "Beware of your neighbor!
    Don't even trust your brother!
For brother takes advantage of brother,
    and friend slanders friend.
⁵ They all fool and defraud each other;
    no one tells the truth.
With practiced tongues they tell lies;
    they wear themselves out with all their sinning.
⁶ They pile lie upon lie
    and utterly refuse to acknowledge me,"
    says the LORD.
⁷ Therefore, this is what the LORD of Heaven's Armies says:
"See, I will melt them down in a crucible
    and test them like metal.
What else can I do with my people?*
⁸   For their tongues shoot lies like poisoned arrows.
They speak friendly words to their neighbors
    while scheming in their heart to kill them.
⁹ Should I not punish them for this?" says the LORD.
    "Should I not avenge myself against such a nation?"
¹⁰ I will weep for the mountains
    and wail for the wilderness pastures.
For they are desolate and empty of life;
    the lowing of cattle is heard no more;
    the birds and wild animals have all fled.
¹¹ "I will make Jerusalem into a heap of ruins," says the LORD.
    "It will be a place haunted by jackals.
The towns of Judah will be ghost towns,
    with no one living in them."

¹²Who is wise enough to understand all this? Who has been instructed by the LORD and can explain it to others? Why has the land been so ruined that no one dares to travel through it?

¹³The LORD replies, "This has happened because my people have abandoned my instructions; they have refused to obey what I said. ¹⁴Instead, they have stubbornly followed their own desires and worshiped the images of Baal, as their ancestors taught them. ¹⁵So now, this is what the LORD of Heaven's Armies, the God of Israel, says: Look! I will feed them with bitterness and give them poison to drink. ¹⁶I will scatter them around the world, in places they and their ancestors never heard of, and even there I will chase them with the sword until I have destroyed them completely."

Weeping in Jerusalem

¹⁷ This is what the LORD of Heaven's Armies says:
"Consider all this, and call for the mourners.
    Send for the women who mourn at funerals.
¹⁸ Quick! Begin your weeping!
    Let the tears flow from your eyes.
¹⁹ Hear the people of Jerusalem* crying in despair,
    'We are ruined! We are completely humiliated!
We must leave our land,
    because our homes have been torn down.'"

²⁰ Listen, you women, to the words of the LORD;
    open your ears to what he has to say.
Teach your daughters to wail;
    teach one another how to lament.
²¹ For death has crept in through our windows
    and has entered our mansions.
It has killed off the flower of our youth:
    Children no longer play in the streets,
    and young men no longer gather in the squares.
²² This is what the LORD says:
"Bodies will be scattered across the fields like clumps of manure,
    like bundles of grain after the harvest.
No one will be left to bury them."

> "Finding greater pleasure in God will not result from pursuing more experiences of him, but from knowing him better."
>
> **JEN WILKIN**
> author and Bible teacher

9:7 Hebrew *with the daughter of my people?* Greek version reads *with the evil daughter of my people?* 9:19 Hebrew *Zion.*

²³ This is what the Lord says:
"Don't let the wise boast in their wisdom,
 or the powerful boast in their power,
 or the rich boast in their riches.
²⁴ But those who wish to boast
 should boast in this alone:
that they truly know me and understand that I
  am the Lord
 who demonstrates unfailing love
 and who brings justice and righteousness to
  the earth,
and that I delight in these things.
 I, the Lord, have spoken!

²⁵"A time is coming," says the Lord, "when I will punish all those who are circumcised in body but not in spirit—²⁶the Egyptians, Edomites, Ammonites, Moabites, the people who live in the desert in remote places,* and yes, even the people of Judah. And like all these pagan nations, the people of Israel also have uncircumcised hearts."

Idolatry Brings Destruction

10 Hear the word that the Lord speaks to you, O Israel! ²This is what the Lord says:

"Do not act like the other nations,
 who try to read their future in the stars.
Do not be afraid of their predictions,
 even though other nations are terrified by
  them.
³ Their ways are futile and foolish.
 They cut down a tree, and a craftsman carves
  an idol.
⁴ They decorate it with gold and silver
 and then fasten it securely with hammer and
  nails
 so it won't fall over.
⁵ Their gods are like
 helpless scarecrows in a cucumber field!
They cannot speak,
 and they need to be carried because they
  cannot walk.
Do not be afraid of such gods,
 for they can neither harm you nor do you any
  good."

⁶ Lord, there is no one like you!
 For you are great, and your name is full of
  power.

⁷ Who would not fear you, O King of nations?
 That title belongs to you alone!
Among all the wise people of the earth
 and in all the kingdoms of the world,
 there is no one like you.

⁸ People who worship idols are stupid and
  foolish.
 The things they worship are made of wood!
⁹ They bring beaten sheets of silver from
  Tarshish
 and gold from Uphaz,
and they give these materials to skillful
  craftsmen
 who make their idols.
Then they dress these gods in royal blue and
  purple robes
 made by expert tailors.
¹⁰ But the Lord is the only true God.
 He is the living God and the everlasting King!
The whole earth trembles at his anger.
 The nations cannot stand up to his wrath.

¹¹Say this to those who worship other gods: "Your so-called gods, who did not make the heavens and earth, will vanish from the earth and from under the heavens."*

¹² But the Lord made the earth by his power,
 and he preserves it by his wisdom.
With his own understanding
 he stretched out the heavens.
¹³ When he speaks in the thunder,
 the heavens roar with rain.
He causes the clouds to rise over the earth.
 He sends the lightning with the rain
 and releases the wind from his storehouses.
¹⁴ The whole human race is foolish and has no
  knowledge!
 The craftsmen are disgraced by the idols they
  make,
for their carefully shaped works are a fraud.
 These idols have no breath or power.
¹⁵ Idols are worthless; they are ridiculous lies!
 On the day of reckoning they will all be
  destroyed.
¹⁶ But the God of Israel* is no idol!
 He is the Creator of everything that exists,
including Israel, his own special possession.
 The Lord of Heaven's Armies is his name!

9:26 Or *in the desert and clip the corners of their hair.*   10:11 The original text of this verse is in Aramaic.   10:16 Hebrew *the Portion of Jacob.* See note on 5:20.

10:11-16 God is revealed as different from idols, who are powerless, mute, and blind. Here, God as the creator of all things is shown through wisdom, understanding, speech, and knowledge. God created the earth and Israel, his "special possession" (10:16; Exodus 19:5).

10:16 The Hebrew idiom, translated here as "the God of Israel" can be more literally rendered "the Portion of Jacob." It suggests that God himself is everything the people need. The God of Israel is not to be compared to pagan deities. As "the Creator," God selected the people of Israel, rescued them from Egypt, and brought them into Canaan; the Lord redeemed them from slavery to make them his chosen people.

The Coming Destruction

17 Pack your bags and prepare to leave;
   the siege is about to begin.
18 For this is what the LORD says:
   "Suddenly, I will fling out
      all you who live in this land.
   I will pour great troubles upon you,
      and at last you will feel my anger."

19 My wound is severe,
      and my grief is great.
   My sickness is incurable,
      but I must bear it.
20 My home is gone,
      and no one is left to help me rebuild it.
   My children have been taken away,
      and I will never see them again.
21 The shepherds of my people have lost their senses.
      They no longer seek wisdom from the LORD.
   Therefore, they fail completely,
      and their flocks are scattered.
22 Listen! Hear the terrifying roar of great armies
      as they roll down from the north.
   The towns of Judah will be destroyed
      and become a haunt for jackals.

Jeremiah's Prayer

23 I know, LORD, that our lives are not our own.
      We are not able to plan our own course.
24 So correct me, LORD, but please be gentle.
      Do not correct me in anger, for I would die.
25 Pour out your wrath on the nations that refuse
      to acknowledge you—
      on the peoples that do not call upon your name.
   For they have devoured your people Israel*;
      they have devoured and consumed them,
      making the land a desolate wilderness.

Judah's Broken Covenant

11 The LORD gave another message to Jeremiah. He said, ²"Remind the people of Judah and Jerusalem about the terms of my covenant with them. ³Say to them, 'This is what the LORD, the God of Israel, says: Cursed is anyone who does not obey the terms of my covenant! ⁴For I said to your ancestors when I brought them out of the iron-smelting furnace of Egypt, "If you obey me and do whatever I command you, then you will be my people, and I will be your God." ⁵I said this so I could keep my promise to your ancestors to give you a land flowing with milk and honey—the land you live in today.'"

Then I replied, "Amen, LORD! May it be so."

⁶Then the LORD said, "Broadcast this message in the streets of Jerusalem. Go from town to town throughout the land and say, 'Remember the ancient covenant, and do everything it requires. ⁷For I solemnly warned your ancestors when I brought them out of Egypt, "Obey me!" I have repeated this warning over and over to this day, ⁸but your ancestors did not listen or even pay attention. Instead, they stubbornly followed their own evil desires. And because they refused to obey, I brought upon them all the curses described in this covenant.'"

⁹Again the LORD spoke to me and said, "I have discovered a conspiracy against me among the people of Judah and Jerusalem. ¹⁰They have returned to the sins of their ancestors. They have refused to listen to me and are worshiping other gods. Israel and Judah have both broken the covenant I made with their ancestors. ¹¹Therefore, this is what the LORD says: I am going to bring calamity upon them, and they will not escape. Though they beg for mercy, I will not listen to their cries. ¹²Then the people of Judah and Jerusalem will pray to their idols and burn incense before them. But the idols will not save them when disaster strikes! ¹³Look now, people of Judah; you have as many gods as you have towns. You have as many altars of shame—altars for burning incense to your god Baal—as there are streets in Jerusalem.

¹⁴"Pray no more for these people, Jeremiah. Do not weep or pray for them, for I will not listen to them when they cry out to me in distress.

10:25 Hebrew *devoured Jacob*. See note on 5:20.

10:17-22 An announcement of judgment (10:17-18) is followed by a lament over what that judgment would mean (10:19-22).
10:19 Jeremiah suffered personal loss along with his people; he speaks for the nation at large as well as for himself.
10:20 Jeremiah's beloved home community of Anathoth was destroyed; even the town's children were taken into exile.
10:21 The "shepherds" (that is, the priests and prophets; see 5:29-31) had turned their backs on the "wisdom from the LORD" that had been preserved in priestly memory and in the prophetic messages, both verbal and written. The divine decree predicted the utter failure of these leaders and the resultant scattering of the people.
11:1-17 The indictment against Israel expresses the people's failure to keep the covenant God made with them on Mount Sinai (Exodus 19–24). Many scholars connect this section to Deuteronomy 28 and King Josiah's reforms in 2 Kings 23:1-3. *Shema*—the Hebrew word meaning "to hear," "listen," or "obey,"—is used repeatedly throughout this section to express Israel's failure. The people did not hear and obey (Jeremiah 11:2, 3, 4, 6, 7, 8, 10), and God responded that he would not listen to their pleas for rescue (11:11, 14). The violation of the Mosaic covenant sets up the need for what is coming, a new covenant (31:31-34).
11:4 In Jeremiah's day, the Egyptians had begun to smelt iron, but the "iron-smelting furnace of Egypt" is a metaphor for the Israelites' slavery in that land from which the Lord had rescued them. God had promised to be uniquely theirs if they would be uniquely his (Exodus 6:7).

JEREMIAH 12

¹⁵ "What right do my beloved people have to come to my Temple,
   when they have done so many immoral things?
Can their vows and sacrifices prevent their destruction?
   They actually rejoice in doing evil!
¹⁶ I, the LORD, once called them a thriving olive tree,
   beautiful to see and full of good fruit.
But now I have sent the fury of their enemies
   to burn them with fire,
   leaving them charred and broken.

¹⁷ "I, the LORD of Heaven's Armies, who planted this olive tree, have ordered it destroyed. For the people of Israel and Judah have done evil, arousing my anger by burning incense to Baal."

A Plot against Jeremiah

¹⁸ Then the LORD told me about the plots my enemies were making against me. ¹⁹ I was like a lamb being led to the slaughter. I had no idea that they were planning to kill me! "Let's destroy this man and all his words," they said. "Let's cut him down, so his name will be forgotten forever."

²⁰ O LORD of Heaven's Armies,
   you make righteous judgments,
   and you examine the deepest thoughts and secrets.
Let me see your vengeance against them,
   for I have committed my cause to you.

²¹ This is what the LORD says about the men of Anathoth who wanted me dead. They had said, "We will kill you if you do not stop prophesying in the LORD's name." ²² So this is what the LORD of Heaven's Armies says about them: "I will punish them! Their young men will die in battle, and their boys and girls will starve to death. ²³ Not one of these plotters from Anathoth will survive, for I will bring disaster upon them when their time of punishment comes."

Jeremiah Questions the LORD's Justice

12 LORD, you always give me justice
   when I bring a case before you.
So let me bring you this complaint:
   Why are the wicked so prosperous?
   Why are evil people so happy?
² You have planted them,
   and they have taken root and prospered.
Your name is on their lips,
   but you are far from their hearts.
³ But as for me, LORD, you know my heart.
   You see me and test my thoughts.
Drag these people away like sheep to be butchered!
   Set them aside to be slaughtered!

⁴ How long must this land mourn?
   Even the grass in the fields has withered.
The wild animals and birds have disappeared
   because of the evil in the land.
For the people have said,
   "The LORD doesn't see what's ahead for us!"

The LORD's Reply to Jeremiah

⁵ "If racing against mere men makes you tired,
   how will you race against horses?
If you stumble and fall on open ground,
   what will you do in the thickets near the Jordan?
⁶ Even your brothers, members of your own family,
   have turned against you.
They plot and raise complaints against you.
Do not trust them,
   no matter how pleasantly they speak.

⁷ "I have abandoned my people, my special possession.
   I have surrendered my dearest ones to their enemies.
⁸ My chosen people have roared at me like a lion of the forest,
   so I have treated them with contempt.
⁹ My chosen people act like speckled vultures,*
   but they themselves are surrounded by vultures.
Bring on the wild animals to pick their corpses clean!

¹⁰ "Many rulers have ravaged my vineyard,
   trampling down the vines
   and turning all its beauty into a barren wilderness.
¹¹ They have made it an empty wasteland;
   I hear its mournful cry.
The whole land is desolate,
   and no one even cares.

12:9 Or *speckled hyenas.*

11:18-19 The Lord had warned Jeremiah at the time of his commissioning (1:19) that opposition would threaten his life. Jeremiah sees himself as "a lamb being led to the slaughter," with no power to resist (Psalm 23:1). This opposition occurred before Jeremiah's trial in the Temple courtyard, early in the reign of Jehoiakim (between 608 and 605 BC; see Jeremiah 26:1-17). Some scholars believe that 11:19 prefigures the death of Christ, as does the suffering servant of Isaiah 53:7.

12:7-13 Israel is called out here in this passage as God's "special possession" (*nakhalah*). Exodus 19:5 mirrors this description, which uses a related term "special treasure" (*segullah*). Israel's role was to mediate God's blessings to other nations, to be a kingdom of priests, a holy community. Here in Jeremiah, we see God's frustration that they have rejected their role and covenant promise (Exodus 19:8).

¹² On all the bare hilltops,
   destroying armies can be seen.
The sword of the Lord devours people
   from one end of the nation to the other.
   No one will escape!
¹³ My people have planted wheat
   but are harvesting thorns.
They have worn themselves out,
   but it has done them no good.
They will harvest a crop of shame
   because of the fierce anger of the Lord."

A Message for Israel's Neighbors

¹⁴Now this is what the Lord says: "I will uproot from their land all the evil nations reaching out for the possession I gave my people Israel. And I will uproot Judah from among them. ¹⁵But afterward I will return and have compassion on all of them. I will bring them home to their own lands again, each nation to its own possession. ¹⁶And if these nations truly learn the ways of my people, and if they learn to swear by my name, saying, 'As surely as the Lord lives' (just as they taught my people to swear by the name of Baal), then they will be given a place among my people. ¹⁷But any nation who refuses to obey me will be uprooted and destroyed. I, the Lord, have spoken!"

Jeremiah's Linen Loincloth

13 This is what the Lord said to me: "Go and buy a linen loincloth and put it on, but do not wash it." ²So I bought the loincloth as the Lord directed me, and I put it on.

³Then the Lord gave me another message: ⁴"Take the linen loincloth you are wearing, and go to the Euphrates River.* Hide it there in a hole in the rocks." ⁵So I went and hid it by the Euphrates as the Lord had instructed me.

⁶A long time afterward the Lord said to me, "Go back to the Euphrates and get the loincloth I told you to hide there." ⁷So I went to the Euphrates and dug it out of the hole where I had hidden it. But now it was rotting and falling apart. The loincloth was good for nothing.

⁸Then I received this message from the Lord: ⁹"This is what the Lord says: This shows how I will rot away the pride of Judah and Jerusalem. ¹⁰These wicked people refuse to listen to me. They stubbornly follow their own desires and worship other gods. Therefore, they will become like this loincloth—good for nothing! ¹¹As a loincloth clings to a man's waist, so I created Judah and Israel to cling to me, says the Lord. They were to be my people, my pride, my glory—an honor to my name. But they would not listen to me.

¹²"So tell them, 'This is what the Lord, the God of Israel, says: May all your jars be filled with wine.' And they will reply, 'Of course! Jars are made to be filled with wine!'

¹³"Then tell them, 'No, this is what the Lord means: I will fill everyone in this land with drunkenness—from the king sitting on David's throne to the priests and the prophets, right down to the common people of Jerusalem. ¹⁴I will smash them against each other, even parents against children, says the Lord. I will not let my pity or mercy or compassion keep me from destroying them.'"

A Warning against Pride

¹⁵ Listen and pay attention!
   Do not be arrogant, for the Lord has spoken.
¹⁶ Give glory to the Lord your God
   before it is too late.
Acknowledge him before he brings darkness
   upon you,
   causing you to stumble and fall on the
   darkening mountains.
For then, when you look for light,
   you will find only terrible darkness and gloom.
¹⁷ And if you still refuse to listen,
   I will weep alone because of your pride.
My eyes will overflow with tears,
   because the Lord's flock will be led away into
   exile.

¹⁸ Say to the king and his mother,
   "Come down from your thrones
   and sit in the dust,
for your glorious crowns
   will soon be snatched from your heads."
¹⁹ The towns of the Negev will close their gates,
   and no one will be able to open them.
The people of Judah will be taken away as
   captives.
   All will be carried into exile.

²⁰ Open up your eyes and see
   the armies marching down from the north!
Where is your flock—
   your beautiful flock—
   that he gave you to care for?
²¹ What will you say when the Lord takes the allies
   you have cultivated
   and appoints them as your rulers?

13:4 Hebrew *Perath;* also in 13:5, 6, 7.

13:1-11 In prophetic literature, prophets often perform dramatic symbolic actions. Here, Jeremiah is instructed to buy a linen loincloth and bury it. After many days, Jeremiah retrieves this loincloth, which has now rotted, as a visual representation of the people's refusal to obey God. Like the deteriorating and now useless loincloth, Israel's pride and stubbornness have deteriorated them, rendering Israel useless for their ultimate purpose as God's special possession. Similarly, when we persist in disobeying God, we can miss out on fulfilling our purpose.

Pangs of anguish will grip you,
    like those of a woman in labor!
²² You may ask yourself,
    "Why is all this happening to me?"
        It is because of your many sins!
That is why you have been stripped
    and raped by invading armies.
²³ Can an Ethiopian* change the color of his skin?
    Can a leopard take away its spots?
Neither can you start doing good,
    for you have always done evil.
²⁴ "I will scatter you like chaff
    that is blown away by the desert winds.
²⁵ This is your allotment,
    the portion I have assigned to you,"
        says the LORD,
"for you have forgotten me,
    putting your trust in false gods.
²⁶ I myself will strip you
    and expose you to shame.
²⁷ I have seen your adultery and lust,
    and your disgusting idol worship out in the fields and on the hills.
What sorrow awaits you, Jerusalem!
    How long before you are pure?"

Judah's Terrible Drought

14 This message came to Jeremiah from the LORD, explaining why he was holding back the rain:

² "Judah wilts;
    commerce at the city gates grinds to a halt.
All the people sit on the ground in mourning,
    and a great cry rises from Jerusalem.
³ The nobles send servants to get water,
    but all the wells are dry.
The servants return with empty pitchers,
    confused and desperate,
    covering their heads in grief.
⁴ The ground is parched
    and cracked for lack of rain.
The farmers are deeply troubled;
    they, too, cover their heads.
⁵ Even the doe abandons her newborn fawn
    because there is no grass in the field.
⁶ The wild donkeys stand on the bare hills
    panting like thirsty jackals.
They strain their eyes looking for grass,
    but there is none to be found."

⁷ The people say, "Our wickedness has caught up with us, LORD,
    but help us for the sake of your own reputation.
We have turned away from you
    and sinned against you again and again.
⁸ O Hope of Israel, our Savior in times of trouble,
    why are you like a stranger to us?
Why are you like a traveler passing through the land,
    stopping only for the night?
⁹ Are you also confused?
    Is our champion helpless to save us?
You are right here among us, LORD.
    We are known as your people.
    Please don't abandon us now!"

¹⁰ So this is what the LORD says to his people:
"You love to wander far from me
    and do not restrain yourselves.
Therefore, I will no longer accept you as my people.
Now I will remember all your wickedness
    and will punish you for your sins."

The LORD Forbids Jeremiah to Intercede

¹¹Then the LORD said to me, "Do not pray for these people anymore. ¹²When they fast, I will pay no attention. When they present their burnt offerings and grain offerings to me, I will not accept them. Instead, I will devour them with war, famine, and disease."

¹³Then I said, "O Sovereign LORD, their prophets are telling them, 'All is well—no war or famine will come. The LORD will surely send you peace.'"

¹⁴Then the LORD said, "These prophets are telling lies in my name. I did not send them or tell them to speak. I did not give them any messages. They prophesy of visions and revelations they have never seen or heard. They speak foolishness made up in their own lying hearts. ¹⁵Therefore, this is what the LORD says: I will punish these lying prophets, for they have spoken in my name even though I never sent them. They say that no war or famine will come, but they themselves will die by war and famine! ¹⁶As for the people to whom they prophesy—their bodies will be thrown out into the streets of Jerusalem, victims of famine and war. There will be no one left to bury them. Husbands, wives, sons, and daughters—all will be gone. For I will pour out their own wickedness on them. ¹⁷Now, Jeremiah, say this to them:

"Night and day my eyes overflow with tears.
    I cannot stop weeping,
for my virgin daughter—my precious people—
    has been struck down
    and lies mortally wounded.
¹⁸ If I go out into the fields,
    I see the bodies of people slaughtered by the enemy.

13:23 Hebrew *a Cushite.*

14:13-16 The government of Judah supported a corps of prophets who promoted the religious views of the king and his advisers. The Lord often condemned them, along with the officials and the priests. Here, the Lord exposed them as impostors and described what would happen to them and to the people to whom they prophesied.

If I walk the city streets,
> I see people who have died of starvation.
> The prophets and priests continue with their work,
> but they don't know what they're doing."

A Prayer for Healing

¹⁹ Lord, have you completely rejected Judah?
> Do you really hate Jerusalem?*
> Why have you wounded us past all hope of healing?
> We hoped for peace, but no peace came.
> We hoped for a time of healing, but found only terror.

²⁰ Lord, we confess our wickedness
> and that of our ancestors, too.
> We all have sinned against you.

²¹ For the sake of your reputation, Lord, do not abandon us.
> Do not disgrace your own glorious throne.
> Please remember us,
> and do not break your covenant with us.

²² Can any of the worthless foreign gods send us rain?
> Does it fall from the sky by itself?
> No, you are the one, O Lord our God!
> Only you can do such things.
> So we will wait for you to help us.

Judah's Inevitable Doom

15 Then the Lord said to me, "Even if Moses and Samuel stood before me pleading for these people, I wouldn't help them. Away with them! Get them out of my sight! ²And if they say to you, 'But where can we go?' tell them, 'This is what the Lord says:

> "'Those who are destined for death, to death;
> those who are destined for war, to war;
> those who are destined for famine, to famine;
> those who are destined for captivity, to captivity.'

³"I will send four kinds of destroyers against them," says the Lord. "I will send the sword to kill, the dogs to drag away, the vultures to devour, and the wild animals to finish up what is left. ⁴Because of the wicked things Manasseh son of Hezekiah, king of Judah, did in Jerusalem, I will make my people an object of horror to all the kingdoms of the earth.

⁵ "Who will feel sorry for you, Jerusalem?
> Who will weep for you?
> Who will even bother to ask how you are?

⁶ You have abandoned me
> and turned your back on me,"
> says the Lord.
> "Therefore, I will raise my fist to destroy you.
> I am tired of always giving you another chance.

⁷ I will winnow you like grain at the gates of your cities
> and take away the children you hold dear.
> I will destroy my own people,
> because they refuse to change their evil ways.

⁸ There will be more widows
> than the grains of sand on the seashore.
> At noontime I will bring a destroyer
> against the mothers of young men.
> I will cause anguish and terror
> to come upon them suddenly.

⁹ The mother of seven grows faint and gasps for breath;
> her sun has gone down while it is still day.
> She sits childless now,
> disgraced and humiliated.
> And I will hand over those who are left
> to be killed by the enemy.
> I, the Lord, have spoken!"

Jeremiah's Complaint

¹⁰ Then I said,

> "What sorrow is mine, my mother.
> Oh, that I had died at birth!
> I am hated everywhere I go.
> I am neither a lender who threatens to foreclose
> nor a borrower who refuses to pay—
> yet they all curse me."

¹¹ The Lord replied,

> "I will take care of you, Jeremiah.
> Your enemies will ask you to plead on their behalf
> in times of trouble and distress.

¹² Can a man break a bar of iron from the north,
> or a bar of bronze?

¹³ At no cost to them,
> I will hand over your wealth and treasures
> as plunder to your enemies,
> for sin runs rampant in your land.

¹⁴ I will tell your enemies to take you
> as captives to a foreign land.
> For my anger blazes like a fire
> that will burn forever.*"

14:19 Hebrew *Zion*?   **15:14** As in some Hebrew manuscripts (see also 17:4); most Hebrew manuscripts read *will burn against you*.

15:5 These three questions are rhetorical—the answer is, "No one!"

15:10-21 Jeremiah bares his heart to God over the unjust treatment he is receiving because he is delivering the Lord's message. In response, the Lord promises to protect and care for his prophet.

15:11-14 The Lord replied to Jeremiah's lament with reassurance and then explained what would be happening soon.

¹⁵Then I said,

"LORD, you know what's happening to me.
    Please step in and help me. Punish my
        persecutors!
Please give me time; don't let me die young.
    It's for your sake that I am suffering.
¹⁶ When I discovered your words, I devoured them.
    They are my joy and my heart's delight,
for I bear your name,
    O LORD God of Heaven's Armies.
¹⁷ I never joined the people in their merry feasts.
    I sat alone because your hand was on me.
    I was filled with indignation at their sins.
¹⁸ Why then does my suffering continue?
    Why is my wound so incurable?
Your help seems as uncertain as a seasonal brook,
    like a spring that has gone dry."

¹⁹This is how the LORD responds:

"If you return to me, I will restore you
    so you can continue to serve me.
If you speak good words rather than worthless
    ones,
    you will be my spokesman.
You must influence them;
    do not let them influence you!
²⁰ They will fight against you like an attacking
        army,
    but I will make you as secure as a fortified
        wall of bronze.
They will not conquer you,
    for I am with you to protect and rescue you.
    I, the LORD, have spoken!
²¹ Yes, I will certainly keep you safe from these
        wicked men.
    I will rescue you from their cruel hands."

Jeremiah Forbidden to Marry

16 The LORD gave me another message. He said, ²"Do not get married or have children in this place. ³For this is what the LORD says about the children born here in this city and about their mothers and fathers: ⁴They will die from terrible diseases. No one will mourn for them or bury them, and they will lie scattered on the ground like manure. They will die from war and famine, and their bodies will be food for the vultures and wild animals."

Judah's Coming Punishment

⁵This is what the LORD says: "Do not go to funerals to mourn and show sympathy for these people, for I have removed my protection and peace from them. I have taken away my unfailing love and my mercy. ⁶Both the great and the lowly will die in this land. No one will bury them or mourn for them. Their friends will not cut themselves in sorrow or shave their heads in sadness. ⁷No one will offer a meal to comfort those who mourn for the dead—not even at the death of a mother or father. No one will send a cup of wine to console them.

⁸"And do not go to their feasts and parties. Do not eat and drink with them at all. ⁹For this is what the LORD of Heaven's Armies, the God of Israel, says: In your own lifetime, before your very eyes, I will put an end to the happy singing and laughter in this land. The joyful voices of bridegrooms and brides will no longer be heard.

¹⁰"When you tell the people all these things, they will ask, 'Why has the LORD decreed such terrible things against us? What have we done to deserve such treatment? What is our sin against the LORD our God?'

¹¹"Then you will give them the LORD's reply: 'It is because your ancestors were unfaithful to me. They worshiped other gods and served them. They abandoned me and did not obey my word. ¹²And you are even worse than your ancestors! You stubbornly follow your own evil desires and refuse to listen to me. ¹³So I will throw you out of this land and send you into a foreign land where you and your ancestors have never been. There you can worship idols day and night—and I will grant you no favors!'

Hope despite the Disaster

¹⁴"But the time is coming," says the LORD, "when people who are taking an oath will no longer say, 'As surely as the LORD lives, who rescued the people of Israel from the land of Egypt.' ¹⁵Instead, they will say, 'As surely as the LORD lives, who brought the people of Israel back to their own land from the land of the north and from all the countries to which he had exiled them.' For I will bring them back to this land that I gave their ancestors.

¹⁶"But now I am sending for many fishermen who will catch them," says the LORD. "I am sending for hunters who will hunt them down in the mountains, hills, and caves. ¹⁷I am watching them closely, and I see every sin. They cannot hope to hide from me. ¹⁸I will double their punishment for all their sins, because they have defiled my land with lifeless images of their detestable gods and have filled my territory with their evil deeds."

Jeremiah's Prayer of Confidence

¹⁹ LORD, you are my strength and fortress,
    my refuge in the day of trouble!
Nations from around the world
    will come to you and say,
"Our ancestors left us a foolish heritage,
    for they worshiped worthless idols.
²⁰ Can people make their own gods?
    These are not real gods at all!"

²¹ The LORD says,
"Now I will show them my power;
    now I will show them my might.
At last they will know and understand
    that I am the LORD.

Judah's Sin and Punishment

17 "The sin of Judah
is inscribed with an iron chisel—
engraved with a diamond point on their stony
hearts
and on the corners of their altars.
² Even their children go to worship
at their pagan altars and Asherah poles,
beneath every green tree
and on every high hill.
³ So I will hand over my holy mountain—
along with all your wealth and treasures
and your pagan shrines—
as plunder to your enemies,
for sin runs rampant in your land.
⁴ The wonderful possession I have reserved
for you
will slip from your hands.
I will tell your enemies to take you
as captives to a foreign land.
For my anger blazes like a fire
that will burn forever."

Wisdom from the LORD

⁵ This is what the LORD says:
"Cursed are those who put their trust in mere
humans,
who rely on human strength
and turn their hearts away from the LORD.
⁶ They are like stunted shrubs in the desert,
with no hope for the future.
They will live in the barren wilderness,
in an uninhabited salty land.

⁷ "But blessed are those who trust in the LORD
and have made the LORD their hope and
confidence.
⁸ They are like trees planted along a riverbank,
with roots that reach deep into the water.
Such trees are not bothered by the heat
or worried by long months of drought.
Their leaves stay green,
and they never stop producing fruit.

⁹ "The human heart is the most deceitful of all
things,
and desperately wicked.
Who really knows how bad it is?
¹⁰ But I, the LORD, search all hearts
and examine secret motives.
I give all people their due rewards,
according to what their actions deserve."

Jeremiah's Trust in the LORD

¹¹ Like a partridge that hatches eggs she has not
laid,
so are those who get their wealth by unjust
means.
At midlife they will lose their riches;
in the end, they will become poor old fools.
¹² But we worship at your throne—
eternal, high, and glorious!
¹³ O LORD, the hope of Israel,
all who turn away from you will be disgraced.
They will be buried in the dust of the earth,
for they have abandoned the LORD, the
fountain of living water.

¹⁴ O LORD, if you heal me, I will be truly healed;
if you save me, I will be truly saved.
My praises are for you alone!
¹⁵ People scoff at me and say,
"What is this 'message from the LORD' you talk
about?
Why don't your predictions come true?"

¹⁶ LORD, I have not abandoned my job
as a shepherd for your people.
I have not urged you to send disaster.
You have heard everything I've said.
¹⁷ LORD, don't terrorize me!
You alone are my hope in the day of disaster.
¹⁸ Bring shame and dismay on all who persecute
me,
but don't let me experience shame and
dismay.
Bring a day of terror on them.
Yes, bring double destruction upon them!

Observing the Sabbath

¹⁹This is what the LORD said to me: "Go and stand in the gates of Jerusalem, first in the gate where the king goes in and out, and then in each of the other gates. ²⁰Say to all the people, 'Listen to this message from the LORD, you kings of Judah and all you people of Judah and everyone living in Jerusalem. ²¹This is what the LORD says: Listen to my warning! Stop carrying on your trade at Jerusalem's gates on the Sabbath day. ²²Do not do your work on the Sabbath, but make it a holy day. I gave this command to your ancestors, ²³but they did not listen or obey. They stubbornly refused to pay attention or accept my discipline.

²⁴"But if you obey me, says the LORD, and do not carry on your trade at the gates or work on the

---

17:2 Asherah poles were cut from trees and erected near altars dedicated to Baal, the Canaanite storm god. Asherah was the Canaanite goddess who symbolized the fertility of moist ground that could produce crops. Worshiping her was believed to cause rain to fall, seeds to sprout, and plants to grow. A tree growing near an altar could also represent this fertility goddess. The people of Judah were so depraved that parents encouraged their children to join them in these rituals.
17:7-8 "Those who trust in the LORD," like "trees planted along a riverbank," will have abundant resources and be well prepared to meet the changing nature of life. Water represents the law of the Lord (see also Psalm 1; Ezekiel 47:1-12; Revelation 22:1-2).

Sabbath day, and if you keep it holy, ²⁵then kings and their officials will go in and out of these gates forever. There will always be a descendant of David sitting on the throne here in Jerusalem. Kings and their officials will always ride in and out among the people of Judah in chariots and on horses, and this city will remain forever. ²⁶And from all around Jerusalem, from the towns of Judah and Benjamin, from the western foothills* and the hill country and the Negev, the people will come with their burnt offerings and sacrifices. They will bring their grain offerings, frankincense, and thanksgiving offerings to the Lord's Temple.

²⁷"'But if you do not listen to me and refuse to keep the Sabbath holy, and if on the Sabbath day you bring loads of merchandise through the gates of Jerusalem just as on other days, then I will set fire to these gates. The fire will spread to the palaces, and no one will be able to put out the roaring flames.'"

The Potter and the Clay

18 The Lord gave another message to Jeremiah. He said, ²"Go down to the potter's shop, and I will speak to you there." ³So I did as he told me and found the potter working at his wheel. ⁴But the jar he was making did not turn out as he had hoped, so he crushed it into a lump of clay again and started over.

⁵Then the Lord gave me this message: ⁶"O Israel, can I not do to you as this potter has done to his clay? As the clay is in the potter's hand, so are you in my hand. ⁷If I announce that a certain nation or kingdom is to be uprooted, torn down, and destroyed, ⁸but then that nation renounces its evil ways, I will not destroy it as I had planned. ⁹And if I announce that I will plant and build up a certain nation or kingdom, ¹⁰but then that nation turns to evil and refuses to obey me, I will not bless it as I said I would.

¹¹"Therefore, Jeremiah, go and warn all Judah and Jerusalem. Say to them, 'This is what the Lord says: I am planning disaster for you instead of good. So turn from your evil ways, each of you, and do what is right.'"

¹²But the people replied, "Don't waste your breath. We will continue to live as we want to, stubbornly following our own evil desires."

¹³So this is what the Lord says:

"Has anyone ever heard of such a thing,
    even among the pagan nations?
My virgin daughter Israel
    has done something terrible!
¹⁴ Does the snow ever disappear from the
    mountaintops of Lebanon?
Do the cold streams flowing from those
    distant mountains ever run dry?
¹⁵ But my people are not so reliable, for they have
    deserted me;
they burn incense to worthless idols.
They have stumbled off the ancient highways
    and walk in muddy paths.
¹⁶ Therefore, their land will become desolate,
    a monument to their stupidity.
All who pass by will be astonished
    and will shake their heads in amazement.
¹⁷ I will scatter my people before their enemies
    as the east wind scatters dust.
And in all their trouble I will turn my back on
    them
and refuse to notice their distress."

A Plot against Jeremiah

¹⁸Then the people said, "Come on, let's plot a way to stop Jeremiah. We have plenty of priests and wise men and prophets. We don't need him to teach the word and give us advice and prophecies. Let's spread rumors about him and ignore what he says."

¹⁹ Lord, hear me and help me!
    Listen to what my enemies are saying.
²⁰ Should they repay evil for good?
    They have dug a pit to kill me,
though I pleaded for them
    and tried to protect them from your anger.
²¹ So let their children starve!
    Let them die by the sword!
Let their wives become childless widows.
    Let their old men die in a plague,
and let their young men be killed in
    battle!
²² Let screaming be heard from their homes
    as warriors come suddenly upon them.
For they have dug a pit for me
    and have hidden traps along my path.
²³ Lord, you know all about their murderous plots
    against me.
Don't forgive their crimes and blot out their
    sins.
Let them die before you.
    Deal with them in your anger.

17:26 Hebrew *the Shephelah*.

18:1-11 The Lord has Jeremiah take part in an object lesson. What Jeremiah observes at the potter's shop becomes a picture of what the Lord is about to do with Judah.
18:1-4 Jeremiah watches as the potter forms an earthen jar, then crushes it and starts over.
18:5-6 The Lord likens himself to this potter. He could set standards of perfection and choose to destroy or reshape his work.
18:11 The Lord plans to deal with Judah and Jerusalem as the potter dealt with the clay (18:4). However, the people could still escape disaster if they would reject their evil ways and do what is right.

Jeremiah's Shattered Jar

19 This is what the LORD said to me: "Go and buy a clay jar. Then ask some of the leaders of the people and of the priests to follow you. ²Go out through the Gate of Broken Pots to the garbage dump in the valley of Ben-Hinnom, and give them this message. ³Say to them, 'Listen to this message from the LORD, you kings of Judah and citizens of Jerusalem! This is what the LORD of Heaven's Armies, the God of Israel, says: I will bring a terrible disaster on this place, and the ears of those who hear about it will ring!

⁴"'For Israel has forsaken me and turned this valley into a place of wickedness. The people burn incense to foreign gods—idols never before acknowledged by this generation, by their ancestors, or by the kings of Judah. And they have filled this place with the blood of innocent children. ⁵They have built pagan shrines to Baal, and there they burn their sons as sacrifices to Baal. I have never commanded such a horrible deed; it never even crossed my mind to command such a thing! ⁶So beware, for the time is coming, says the LORD, when this garbage dump will no longer be called Topheth or the valley of Ben-Hinnom, but the Valley of Slaughter.

19:4-5 Offering incense while worshiping the Lord was to be an act of the priests (Exodus 30:8), and offering this sacred incense to idols was an affront to the Lord. Scripture also mentions child sacrifice in relation to Baal worship, though scholars are divided on the specifics, and two kings of Judah are described as having participated in the practice as well (2 Kings 16:3; 21:6).

Come Close — SPINNING? REST

SCRIPTURE CONNECTION: JEREMIAH 19:1-15

Do you ever feel like you're spinning a lot of plates all at once? Between work, relationships, life administration, and more, spinning can feel a bit overwhelming. Yet, the temptation to keep pushing through the stress is real.

But Jeremiah shows us the risks are real, too: "For Israel has forsaken me and turned this valley into a place of wickedness" (19:4). In our attempts to keep everything spinning, we risk our tasks and relationships becoming idols. We forget that God is the potter, not us—we're the clay in his hands (18:6; Isaiah 29:16; 64:8).

When we make idols, we end up doing things that are not good for anyone nor pleasing to God. The Lord tells us, "I have never commanded such a horrible deed; it never even crossed my mind to command such a thing!" (Jeremiah 19:5). And the outcomes are disastrous (19:7-15).

What steps can we take to trust God's purposes rather than our self-sufficiency? How can we choose rest over restlessness? We begin by making space to listen to God's voice over our to-do list: "Listen to this message from the LORD" (19:3). "This is what the LORD ... says" (19:15). When we surrender to his rest, he'll direct us.

Resting in God by leaning into his Word realigns our motives with his. After all, he is the potter, and we are the clay.

REFLECT "For Israel has forsaken me and ... the people burn incense to foreign gods." JEREMIAH 19:4

Jesus, help me surrender my desires and concerns to you. Help me create space to center my perspective on you and to hear your voice. Amen.

CONSIDER "Rest time is not waste time. It is economy to gather fresh strength.... It is wisdom to take occasional furlough. In the long run, we shall do more by sometimes doing less."
CHARLES SPURGEON

> Resting in God by leaning into his Word realigns our motives with his.

SARAH OVERTON, MA, is a researcher specializing in refugee and asylum policy. She has worked in the UK Parliament, public-policy think tanks, and at Lambeth Palace.

⁷"'For I will upset the careful plans of Judah and Jerusalem. I will allow the people to be slaughtered by invading armies, and I will leave their dead bodies as food for the vultures and wild animals. ⁸I will reduce Jerusalem to ruins, making it a monument to their stupidity. All who pass by will be astonished and will gasp at the destruction they see there. ⁹I will see to it that your enemies lay siege to the city until all the food is gone. Then those trapped inside will eat their own sons and daughters and friends. They will be driven to utter despair.'

¹⁰"As these men watch you, Jeremiah, smash the jar you brought. ¹¹Then say to them, 'This is what the Lord of Heaven's Armies says: As this jar lies shattered, so I will shatter the people of Judah and Jerusalem beyond all hope of repair. They will bury the bodies here in Topheth, the garbage dump, until there is no more room for them. ¹²This is what I will do to this place and its people, says the Lord. I will cause this city to become defiled like Topheth. ¹³Yes, all the houses in Jerusalem, including the palace of Judah's kings, will become like Topheth—all the houses where you burned incense on the rooftops to your star gods, and where liquid offerings were poured out to your idols.'"

¹⁴Then Jeremiah returned from Topheth, the garbage dump where he had delivered this message, and he stopped in front of the Temple of the Lord. He said to the people there, ¹⁵"This is what the Lord of Heaven's Armies, the God of Israel, says: 'I will bring disaster upon this city and its surrounding towns as I promised, because you have stubbornly refused to listen to me.'"

Jeremiah and Pashhur

20 Now Pashhur son of Immer, the priest in charge of the Temple of the Lord, heard what Jeremiah was prophesying. ²So he arrested Jeremiah the prophet and had him whipped and put in stocks at the Benjamin Gate of the Lord's Temple.

³The next day, when Pashhur finally released him, Jeremiah said, "Pashhur, the Lord has changed your name. From now on you are to be called 'The Man Who Lives in Terror.'* ⁴For this is what the Lord says: 'I will send terror upon you and all your friends, and you will watch as they are slaughtered by the swords of the enemy. I will hand the people of Judah over to the king of Babylon. He will take them captive to Babylon or run them through with the sword. ⁵And I will let your enemies plunder Jerusalem. All the famed treasures of the city—the precious jewels and gold and silver of your kings—will be carried off to Babylon. ⁶As for you, Pashhur, you and all your household will go as captives to Babylon. There you will die and be buried, you and all your friends to whom you prophesied that everything would be all right.'"

Jeremiah's Complaint

⁷ O Lord, you misled me,
and I allowed myself to be misled.
You are stronger than I am,
and you overpowered me.
Now I am mocked every day;
everyone laughs at me.
⁸ When I speak, the words burst out.
"Violence and destruction!" I shout.
So these messages from the Lord
have made me a household joke.
⁹ But if I say I'll never mention the Lord
or speak in his name,
his word burns in my heart like a fire.
It's like a fire in my bones!
I am worn out trying to hold it in!
I can't do it!
¹⁰ I have heard the many rumors about me.
They call me "The Man Who Lives in Terror."
They threaten, "If you say anything, we will report it."
Even my old friends are watching me,
waiting for a fatal slip.
"He will trap himself," they say,
"and then we will get our revenge on him."
¹¹ But the Lord stands beside me like a great warrior.
Before him my persecutors will stumble.
They cannot defeat me.
They will fail and be thoroughly humiliated.
Their dishonor will never be forgotten.
¹² O Lord of Heaven's Armies,
you test those who are righteous,
and you examine the deepest thoughts and secrets.
Let me see your vengeance against them,
for I have committed my cause to you.
¹³ Sing to the Lord!
Praise the Lord!
For though I was poor and needy,
he rescued me from my oppressors.

¹⁴ Yet I curse the day I was born!
May no one celebrate the day of my birth.
¹⁵ I curse the messenger who told my father,
"Good news—you have a son!"

20:3 Hebrew *Magor-missabib*, which means "surrounded by terror"; also in 20:10.

19:14-15 Jeremiah concluded his message at the Temple of the Lord, where the common people could hear him.
20:1-6 As God's prophet, Jeremiah suffered both physically and emotionally. Pashhur the Temple priest arrested Jeremiah and had him beaten, an undeniably traumatic experience for Jeremiah. This priest, who held a position of privilege, was someone Jeremiah should have been able to trust, but was instead committing terrible acts of injustice. God sees when people use their authority to abuse others, especially when they hold positions of spiritual leadership. God will judge these acts of injustice and cruelty.

¹⁶ Let him be destroyed like the cities of old
  that the LORD overthrew without mercy.
  Terrify him all day long with battle shouts,
¹⁷ because he did not kill me at birth.
  Oh, that I had died in my mother's womb,
  that her body had been my grave!
¹⁸ Why was I ever born?
  My entire life has been filled
  with trouble, sorrow, and shame.

No Deliverance from Babylon

21 The LORD spoke through Jeremiah when King Zedekiah sent Pashhur son of Malkijah and Zephaniah son of Maaseiah, the priest, to speak with him. They begged Jeremiah, ²"Please speak to the LORD for us and ask him to help us. King Nebuchadnezzar* of Babylon is attacking Judah. Perhaps the LORD will be gracious and do a mighty miracle as he has done in the past. Perhaps he will force Nebuchadnezzar to withdraw his armies."

³Jeremiah replied, "Go back to King Zedekiah and tell him, ⁴'This is what the LORD, the God of Israel, says: I will make your weapons useless against the king of Babylon and the Babylonians* who are outside your walls attacking you. In fact, I will bring your enemies right into the heart of this city. ⁵I myself will fight against you with a strong hand and a powerful arm, for I am very angry. You have made me furious! ⁶I will send a terrible plague upon this city, and both people and animals will die. ⁷And after all that, says the LORD, I will hand over King Zedekiah, his staff, and everyone else in the city who survives the disease, war, and famine. I will hand them over to King Nebuchadnezzar of Babylon and to their other enemies. He will slaughter them and show them no mercy, pity, or compassion.'

⁸"Tell all the people, 'This is what the LORD says: Take your choice of life or death! ⁹Everyone who stays in Jerusalem will die from war, famine, or disease, but those who go out and surrender to the Babylonians will live. Their reward will be life! ¹⁰For I have decided to bring disaster and not good upon this city, says the LORD. It will be handed over to the king of Babylon, and he will reduce it to ashes.'

Judgment on Judah's Kings

¹¹"Say to the royal family of Judah, 'Listen to this message from the LORD! ¹²This is what the LORD says to the dynasty of David:

> "I felt as if aided from above. My tongue was cut loose, the stammerer spoke freely; the love of God, and of his service, burned with a vehement flame within me—his name was glorified among the people."
>
> **JARENA LEE**
> (1783–1849) first female preacher of the African Methodist Episcopal Church of America

"'Give justice each morning to the people you judge!
  Help those who have been robbed;
  rescue them from their oppressors.
Otherwise, my anger will burn like an unquenchable fire
because of all your sins.
¹³ I will personally fight against the people in Jerusalem,
  that mighty fortress—

21:2 Hebrew *Nebuchadrezzar*, a variant spelling of Nebuchadnezzar; also in 21:7. **21:4** Or *Chaldeans*; also in 21:9.

21:2 This event probably occurred around the beginning of the siege of Jerusalem in 588 BC (2 Kings 25:1). Zedekiah did not pray to the Lord as his ancestor Hezekiah had done (2 Kings 19:14-20, 29-37; 2 Chronicles 32:20-22; Isaiah 37:1-7, 14-20). However, the king expected Jeremiah to perform the miracle of turning away the Lord's anger.
21:3-7 The Lord answers King Zedekiah's messengers with a judicial decree. Resisting the Babylonians would be useless because the Lord was fighting against Jerusalem.
21:13-14 The people in Jerusalem had put their complete faith in the "mighty fortress" of the city, believing it could not be conquered (see 2 Kings 18:35-37; 2 Chronicles 32:20-23; Isaiah 37:36-38). The Lord had protected the city in the past, but now the Lord was fighting against it.

the people who boast, "No one can touch us here. No one can break in here." ¹⁴ And I myself will punish you for your sinfulness, says the LORD.
I will light a fire in your forests
  that will burn up everything around you.'"

A Message for Judah's Kings

22 This is what the LORD said to me: "Go over and speak directly to the king of Judah. Say to him, ²'Listen to this message from the LORD, you king of Judah, sitting on David's throne. Let your attendants and your people listen, too. ³This is what the LORD says: Be fair-minded and just. Do what is right! Help those who have been robbed; rescue them from their oppressors. Quit your evil deeds! Do not mistreat foreigners, orphans, and widows. Stop murdering the innocent! ⁴If you obey me, there will always be a descendant of David sitting on the throne here in Jerusalem. The king will ride through the palace gates in chariots and on horses, with his parade of attendants and subjects. ⁵But if you refuse to pay attention to this warning, I swear by my own name, says the LORD, that this palace will become a pile of rubble.'"

A Message about the Palace

⁶Now this is what the LORD says concerning Judah's royal palace:

"I love you as much as fruitful Gilead
  and the green forests of Lebanon.
But I will turn you into a desert,
  with no one living within your walls.
⁷ I will call for wreckers,
  who will bring out their tools to dismantle you.
They will tear out all your fine cedar beams
  and throw them on the fire.

⁸"People from many nations will pass by the ruins of this city and say to one another, 'Why did the LORD destroy such a great city?' ⁹And the answer will be, 'Because they violated their covenant with the LORD their God by worshiping other gods.'"

A Message about Jehoahaz

¹⁰ Do not weep for the dead king or mourn his loss.
  Instead, weep for the captive king being led away!
  For he will never return to see his native land again.

¹¹For this is what the LORD says about Jehoahaz,* who succeeded his father, King Josiah, and was taken away as a captive: "He will never return. ¹²He will die in a distant land and will never again see his own country."

A Message about Jehoiakim

¹³ And the LORD says, "What sorrow awaits Jehoiakim,*
  who builds his palace with forced labor.*
He builds injustice into its walls,
  for he makes his neighbors work for nothing.
  He does not pay them for their labor.
¹⁴ He says, 'I will build a magnificent palace
  with huge rooms and many windows.
I will panel it throughout with fragrant cedar
  and paint it a lovely red.'
¹⁵ But a beautiful cedar palace does not make a great king!
Your father, Josiah, also had plenty to eat and drink.
  But he was just and right in all his dealings.
  That is why God blessed him.
¹⁶ He gave justice and help to the poor and needy,
  and everything went well for him.
Isn't that what it means to know me?"
  says the LORD.
¹⁷ "But you! You have eyes only for greed and dishonesty!
You murder the innocent,
  oppress the poor, and reign ruthlessly."

22:11 Hebrew *Shallum*, another name for Jehoahaz.   22:13a The brother and successor of the exiled Jehoahaz. See 22:18.
22:13b Hebrew *by unrighteousness*.

22:1–23:8 This collection of messages to the last Davidic kings of Judah culminates in the promise that God would one day place a righteous descendant of David over his people.
22:1-5 Jeremiah delivers a statement, drawn from the covenant God had made with his people on Mount Sinai (Exodus 19–24), that summarized the duties of a king of Judah. Fulfillment of these duties would ensure the continuation of the dynasty of David in Jerusalem; refusal would bring the unimaginable disappearance of the palace and the kingdom.
22:10-12 The dead king was Josiah, who was killed by the Egyptians at the Battle of Megiddo in 609 BC. The people of Judah were not to weep or mourn his death. Their sorrow should center on Josiah's son, whom they had chosen as the new king. After three months, King Jehoahaz (Hebrew *Shallum*, another name for Jehoahaz) was taken into exile in Egypt, where he spent the rest of his life (2 Kings 23:1-33; 2 Chronicles 36:1-8).
22:13-23 Egypt placed another of Josiah's sons, Eliakim, on the throne in Jerusalem. His name was changed to Jehoiakim. Most of the material in Jeremiah 7:1–20:18 was probably written during Jehoiakim's reign (609–598 BC). The Lord indicted him because of his faithlessness and greed, brought him to trial, declared him guilty, and pronounced the death penalty against him.
22:13 Jehoiakim took advantage of people who were poor. Because he forced poor men to work as enslaved people without pay, his building projects had injustice built into their walls.
22:17 Unlike his father, Josiah, Jehoiakim practiced "greed and dishonesty" and ignored the requirements of the covenant.

¹⁸Therefore, this is what the LORD says about Jehoiakim, son of King Josiah:

"The people will not mourn for him, crying to one another,
'Alas, my brother! Alas, my sister!'
His subjects will not mourn for him, crying,
'Alas, our master is dead! Alas, his splendor is gone!'
¹⁹ He will be buried like a dead donkey—
dragged out of Jerusalem and dumped outside the gates!
²⁰ Weep for your allies in Lebanon.
Shout for them in Bashan.
Search for them in the regions east of the river.*
See, they are all destroyed.
Not one is left to help you.
²¹ I warned you when you were prosperous,
but you replied, 'Don't bother me.'
You have been that way since childhood—
you simply will not obey me!
²² And now the wind will blow away your allies.
All your friends will be taken away as captives.
Surely then you will see your wickedness and be ashamed.
²³ It may be nice to live in a beautiful palace paneled with wood from the cedars of Lebanon,
but soon you will groan with pangs of anguish—
anguish like that of a woman in labor.

A Message for Jehoiachin

²⁴"As surely as I live," says the LORD, "I will abandon you, Jehoiachin* son of Jehoiakim, king of Judah. Even if you were the signet ring on my right hand, I would pull you off. ²⁵I will hand you over to those who seek to kill you, those you so desperately fear—to King Nebuchadnezzar* of Babylon and the mighty Babylonian* army. ²⁶I will expel you and your mother from this land, and you will die in a foreign country, not in your native land. ²⁷You will never again return to the land you yearn for.

²⁸ "Why is this man Jehoiachin like a discarded, broken jar?
Why are he and his children to be exiled to a foreign land?
²⁹ O earth, earth, earth!
Listen to this message from the LORD!
³⁰ This is what the LORD says:
'Let the record show that this man Jehoiachin was childless.
He is a failure,
for none of his children will succeed him on the throne of David
to rule over Judah.'

The Righteous Descendant

23 "What sorrow awaits the leaders of my people—the shepherds of my sheep—for they have destroyed and scattered the very ones they were expected to care for," says the LORD. ²Therefore, this is what the LORD, the God of Israel, says to these shepherds: "Instead of caring for my flock and leading them to safety, you have deserted them and driven them to destruction. Now I will pour out judgment on you for the evil you have done to them. ³But I will gather together the remnant of my flock from the countries where I have driven them. I will bring them back to their own sheepfold, and they will be fruitful and increase in number. ⁴Then I will appoint responsible shepherds who will care for them, and they will never be afraid again. Not a single one will be lost or missing. I, the LORD, have spoken!

⁵ "For the time is coming,"
says the LORD,
"when I will raise up a righteous descendant*
from King David's line.
He will be a King who rules with wisdom.
He will do what is just and right throughout the land.
⁶ And this will be his name:
'The LORD Is Our Righteousness.'*
In that day Judah will be saved,
and Israel will live in safety.

⁷"In that day," says the LORD, "when people are taking an oath, they will no longer say, 'As surely as the LORD lives, who rescued the people of Israel from the land of Egypt.' ⁸Instead, they will say, 'As surely as the LORD lives, who brought the people of Israel back to their own land from the land of the north and from all the countries to which he had exiled them.' Then they will live in their own land."

22:20 Or *in Abarim*. **22:24** Hebrew *Coniah*, a variant spelling of Jehoiachin; also in 22:28. **22:25a** Hebrew *Nebuchadrezzar*, a variant spelling of Nebuchadnezzar. **22:25b** Or *Chaldean*. **23:5** Hebrew *a righteous branch*. **23:6** Hebrew *Yahweh Tsidqenu*.

22:19 Jehoiakim died in disgrace.
22:22 The days of prosperity were gone, and chaos enveloped Judah. Like a wind sweeping through the land, the Babylonians would defeat Judah's allies and take many captives. Royal self-delusions would be swept aside, and the consequences of wickedness would cause the king to be ashamed.
22:24-30 Jehoiachin (Hebrew *Coniah*, a variant spelling of Jehoiachin; also in 22:28), the son of Jehoiakim, came to the throne at the age of eighteen in 597 BC. The Babylonians attacked Jerusalem because of his father's rebellion against Nebuchadnezzar. After only three months on the throne, Jehoiachin had sense enough to surrender, and he was taken captive to Babylon along with most of the royal family (2 Kings 24:8-16).

Judgment on False Prophets

9 My heart is broken because of the false
 prophets,
 and my bones tremble.
I stagger like a drunkard,
 like someone overcome by wine,
because of the holy words
 the Lord has spoken against them.
10 For the land is full of adultery,
 and it lies under a curse.
The land itself is in mourning—
 its wilderness pastures are dried up.
For they all do evil
 and abuse what power they have.

11 "Even the priests and prophets
 are ungodly, wicked men.
I have seen their despicable acts
 right here in my own Temple,"
 says the Lord.
12 "Therefore, the paths they take
 will become slippery.
They will be chased through the dark,
 and there they will fall.
For I will bring disaster upon them
 at the time fixed for their punishment.
I, the Lord, have spoken!

13 "I saw that the prophets of Samaria were terribly
 evil,
 for they prophesied in the name of Baal
 and led my people of Israel into sin.
14 But now I see that the prophets of Jerusalem are
 even worse!
They commit adultery and love
 dishonesty.
They encourage those who are doing evil
 so that no one turns away from their sins.
These prophets are as wicked
 as the people of Sodom and Gomorrah once
 were."

15 Therefore, this is what the Lord of Heaven's Armies says concerning the prophets:

"I will feed them with bitterness
 and give them poison to drink.
For it is because of Jerusalem's prophets
 that wickedness has filled this land."

16 This is what the Lord of Heaven's Armies says to his people:

"Do not listen to these prophets when they
 prophesy to you,
 filling you with futile hopes.
They are making up everything they say.
 They do not speak for the Lord!
17 They keep saying to those who despise my word,
 'Don't worry! The Lord says you will have
 peace!'
And to those who stubbornly follow their own
 desires,
 they say, 'No harm will come your way!'

18 "Have any of these prophets been in the Lord's
 presence
 to hear what he is really saying?
Has even one of them cared enough to listen?
19 Look! The Lord's anger bursts out like a storm,
 a whirlwind that swirls down on the heads of
 the wicked.
20 The anger of the Lord will not diminish
 until it has finished all he has planned.
In the days to come
 you will understand all this very clearly.

21 "I have not sent these prophets,
 yet they run around claiming to speak for me.
I have given them no message,
 yet they go on prophesying.
22 If they had stood before me and listened to me,
 they would have spoken my words,
 and they would have turned my people
 from their evil ways and deeds.
23 Am I a God who is only close at hand?" says the
 Lord.
"No, I am far away at the same time.
24 Can anyone hide from me in a secret place?
 Am I not everywhere in all the heavens and
 earth?"
 says the Lord.

25 "I have heard these prophets say, 'Listen to the dream I had from God last night.' And then they proceed to tell lies in my name. 26 How long will this go on? If they are prophets, they are prophets of deceit, inventing everything they say. 27 By telling these false dreams, they are trying to get my people to forget me, just as their ancestors did by worshiping the idols of Baal.

28 "Let these false prophets tell their dreams,
 but let my true messengers faithfully
 proclaim my every word.
There is a difference between straw and
 grain!
29 Does not my word burn like fire?"
 says the Lord.
"Is it not like a mighty hammer
 that smashes a rock to pieces?

23:13-14 Samaria, the capital of the northern kingdom of Israel, had been dominated by Baal worship supported by the government prophets (1 Kings 18:19). The religious leaders of Judah were "even worse" (see also Jeremiah 16:12).
23:16 The false prophets gave the people futile hopes. Since they had not been commissioned to "speak for the Lord," their ideas came from their own imaginations.

"I have loved you... with an everlasting love."

JEREMIAH 31:3

³⁰"Therefore," says the LORD, "I am against these prophets who steal messages from each other and claim they are from me. ³¹I am against these smooth-tongued prophets who say, 'This prophecy is from the LORD!' ³²I am against these false prophets. Their imaginary dreams are flagrant lies that lead my people into sin. I did not send or appoint them, and they have no message at all for my people. I, the LORD, have spoken!

False Prophecies and False Prophets

³³"Suppose one of the people or one of the prophets or priests asks you, 'What prophecy has the LORD burdened you with now?' You must reply, 'You are the burden!* The LORD says he will abandon you!'

³⁴"If any prophet, priest, or anyone else says, 'I have a prophecy from the LORD,' I will punish that person along with his entire family. ³⁵You should keep asking each other, 'What is the LORD's answer?' or 'What is the LORD saying?' ³⁶But stop using this phrase, 'prophecy from the LORD.' For people are using it to give authority to their own ideas, turning upside down the words of our God, the living God, the LORD of Heaven's Armies.

³⁷"This is what you should say to the prophets: 'What is the LORD's answer?' or 'What is the LORD saying?' ³⁸But suppose they respond, 'This is a prophecy from the LORD!' Then you should say, 'This is what the LORD says: Because you have used this phrase, "prophecy from the LORD," even though I warned you not to use it, ³⁹I will forget you completely.* I will expel you from my presence, along with this city that I gave to you and your ancestors. ⁴⁰And I will make you an object of ridicule, and your name will be infamous throughout the ages.'"

Good and Bad Figs

24 After King Nebuchadnezzar* of Babylon exiled Jehoiachin* son of Jehoiakim, king of Judah, to Babylon along with the officials of Judah and all the craftsmen and artisans, the LORD gave me this vision. I saw two baskets of figs placed in front of the LORD's Temple in Jerusalem. ²One basket was filled with fresh, ripe figs, while the other was filled with bad figs that were too rotten to eat.

³Then the LORD said to me, "What do you see, Jeremiah?"

I replied, "Figs, some very good and some very bad, too rotten to eat."

⁴Then the LORD gave me this message: ⁵"This is what the LORD, the God of Israel, says: The good figs represent the exiles I sent from Judah to the land of the Babylonians.* ⁶I will watch over and care for them, and I will bring them back here again. I will build them up and not tear them down. I will plant them and not uproot them. ⁷I will give them hearts that recognize me as the LORD. They will be my people, and I will be their God, for they will return to me wholeheartedly.

⁸"But the bad figs," the LORD said, "represent King Zedekiah of Judah, his officials, all the people left in Jerusalem, and those who live in Egypt. I will treat them like bad figs, too rotten to eat. ⁹I will make them an object of horror and a symbol of evil to every nation on earth. They will be disgraced and mocked, taunted and cursed, wherever I scatter them. ¹⁰And I will send war, famine, and disease until they have vanished from the land of Israel, which I gave to them and their ancestors."

Seventy Years of Captivity

25 This message for all the people of Judah came to Jeremiah from the LORD during the fourth year of Jehoiakim's reign over Judah.* This was the year when King Nebuchadnezzar* of Babylon began his reign.

²Jeremiah the prophet said to all the people in Judah and Jerusalem, ³"For the past twenty-three years—from the thirteenth year of the reign of Josiah

---

23:33 As in Greek version and Latin Vulgate; Hebrew reads *What burden?* **23:39** Some Hebrew manuscripts and Greek version read *I will surely lift you up.* **24:1a** Hebrew *Nebuchadrezzar,* a variant spelling of Nebuchadnezzar. **24:1b** Hebrew *Jeconiah,* a variant spelling of Jehoiachin. **24:5** Or *Chaldeans.* **25:1a** The fourth year of Jehoiakim's reign and the accession year of Nebuchadnezzar's reign was 605 B.C. **25:1b** Hebrew *Nebuchadrezzar,* a variant spelling of Nebuchadnezzar; also in 25:9.

23:33 These false prophets might taunt Jeremiah by asking for the latest message the Lord had "burdened" him with. This is a wordplay—it was common for a prophetic message to be called "a burden." The false prophets themselves were a heavy load that the Lord would throw off and abandon.
24:1-10 This section is a discussion of the meaning of the exile of 597 BC. Some were saying that it had been God's way of getting the rotten figs out of the barrel (Jerusalem) so that the good figs would survive. Jeremiah said that the opposite was the case. The good figs had been taken out of the barrel (into exile) so that the rotten figs would not destroy them.
24:1 King Nebuchadnezzar II of Babylon had taken Jehoiachin into captivity to Babylon in 597 BC. Jehoiachin's surrender had spared Jerusalem, but its treasures and ten thousand elite citizens were taken into exile (2 Kings 24:8-16). Typically, baskets of figs would be displayed in a market rather than in the Temple area.
24:7 The Lord would do a marvelous work in the hearts of the exiles, helping them to recognize (literally "know") the Lord as a personal God (1 Chronicles 28:9; Psalms 9:10; 36:10; Isaiah 19:21; 52:6; Daniel 11:32; Hosea 2:20; Titus 1:16; 1 John 4:6-8). God's covenant with Israel would become a personal reality to them (Exodus 6:7; 19:5; Deuteronomy 29:13; Revelation 21:7). The exiles would not mix religious loyalties; they would be completely committed to the one true God.
24:8-10 The bad figs were those left in Jerusalem, and the Lord would scatter them because of their rottenness. Those included in this group ranged from the remainder of the royal family to the common people. In 586 BC, Zedekiah's reign ended exactly as predicted here.

son of Amon,* king of Judah, until now—the LORD has been giving me his messages. I have faithfully passed them on to you, but you have not listened.

⁴"Again and again the LORD has sent you his servants, the prophets, but you have not listened or even paid attention. ⁵Each time the message was this: 'Turn from the evil road you are traveling and from the evil things you are doing. Only then will I let you live in this land that the LORD gave to you and your ancestors forever. ⁶Do not provoke my anger by worshiping idols you made with your own hands. Then I will not harm you.'

⁷"But you would not listen to me," says the LORD. "You made me furious by worshiping idols you made with your own hands, bringing on yourselves all the disasters you now suffer. ⁸And now the LORD of Heaven's Armies says: Because you have not listened to me, ⁹I will gather together all the armies of the north under King Nebuchadnezzar of Babylon, whom I have appointed as my deputy. I will bring them all against this land and its people and against the surrounding nations. I will completely destroy* you and make you an object of horror and contempt and a ruin forever. ¹⁰I will take away your happy singing and laughter. The joyful voices of bridegrooms and brides will no longer be heard. Your millstones will fall silent, and the lights in your homes will go out. ¹¹This entire land will become a desolate wasteland. Israel and her neighboring lands will serve the king of Babylon for seventy years.

¹²"Then, after the seventy years of captivity are over, I will punish the king of Babylon and his people for their sins," says the LORD. "I will make the country of the Babylonians* a wasteland forever. ¹³I will bring upon them all the terrors I have promised in this book—all the penalties announced by Jeremiah against the nations. ¹⁴Many nations and great kings will enslave the Babylonians, just as they enslaved my people. I will punish them in proportion to the suffering they cause my people."

The Cup of the LORD's Anger

¹⁵This is what the LORD, the God of Israel, said to me: "Take from my hand this cup filled to the brim with my anger, and make all the nations to whom I send you drink from it. ¹⁶When they drink from it, they will stagger, crazed by the warfare I will send against them."

¹⁷So I took the cup of anger from the LORD and made all the nations drink from it—every nation to which the LORD sent me. ¹⁸I went to Jerusalem and the other towns of Judah, and their kings and officials drank from the cup. From that day until this, they have been a desolate ruin, an object of horror, contempt, and cursing. ¹⁹I gave the cup to Pharaoh, king of Egypt, his attendants, his officials, and all his people, ²⁰along with all the foreigners living in that land. I also gave it to all the kings of the land of Uz and the kings of the Philistine cities of Ashkelon, Gaza, Ekron, and what remains of Ashdod. ²¹Then I gave the cup to the nations of Edom, Moab, and Ammon, ²²and the kings of Tyre and Sidon, and the kings of the regions across the sea. ²³I gave it to Dedan, Tema, and Buz, and to the people who live in distant places.* ²⁴I gave it to the kings of Arabia, the kings of the nomadic tribes of the desert, ²⁵and to the kings of Zimri, Elam, and Media. ²⁶And I gave it to the kings of the northern countries, far and near, one after the other—all the kingdoms of the world. And finally, the king of Babylon* himself drank from the cup of the LORD's anger.

²⁷Then the LORD said to me, "Now tell them, 'This is what the LORD of Heaven's Armies, the God of Israel, says: Drink from this cup of my anger. Get drunk and vomit; fall to rise no more, for I am sending terrible wars against you.' ²⁸And if they refuse to accept the cup, tell them, 'The LORD of Heaven's Armies says: You have no choice but to drink from it. ²⁹I have begun to punish Jerusalem, the city that bears my name. Now should I let you go unpunished? No, you will not escape disaster. I will call for war against all the nations of the earth. I, the LORD of Heaven's Armies, have spoken!'

³⁰"Now prophesy all these things, and say to them,

"'The LORD will roar against his own land
    from his holy dwelling in heaven.
He will shout like those who tread grapes;
    he will shout against everyone on earth.
³¹ His cry of judgment will reach the ends of the earth,
    for the LORD will bring his case against all the nations.
He will judge all the people of the earth,
    slaughtering the wicked with the sword.
I, the LORD, have spoken!'"

³² This is what the LORD of Heaven's Armies says:
"Look! Disaster will fall upon nation after nation!
A great whirlwind of fury is rising
    from the most distant corners of the earth!"

25:3 The thirteenth year of Josiah's reign was 627 B.C. **25:9** The Hebrew term used here refers to the complete consecration of things or people to the LORD, either by destroying them or by giving them as an offering. **25:12** Or *Chaldeans*. **25:23** Or *who clip the corners of their hair*. **25:26** Hebrew *of Sheshach*, a code name for Babylon.

25:11 This is the first instance of a specific length of time being assigned for the Exile. The prediction was fulfilled either from 605 BC (the first exile to Babylon) to around 538 BC (when Cyrus the Great allowed the exiles to return to Judea), or from 586 BC (the destruction of the Temple) to 515 BC (the dedication of the second Temple). Or the number can be seen as symbolic: God's judgment on Jerusalem would last approximately one lifetime.

³³In that day those the Lord has slaughtered will fill the earth from one end to the other. No one will mourn for them or gather up their bodies to bury them. They will be scattered on the ground like manure.

³⁴ Weep and moan, you evil shepherds!
 Roll in the dust, you leaders of the flock!
 The time of your slaughter has arrived;
 you will fall and shatter like a fragile vase.
³⁵ You will find no place to hide;
 there will be no way to escape.
³⁶ Listen to the frantic cries of the shepherds.
 The leaders of the flock are wailing in despair,
 for the Lord is ruining their pastures.
³⁷ Peaceful meadows will be turned into a wasteland
 by the Lord's fierce anger.
³⁸ He has left his den like a strong lion seeking its prey,
 and their land will be made desolate
 by the sword* of the enemy
 and the Lord's fierce anger.

Jeremiah's Escape from Death

26 This message came to Jeremiah from the Lord early in the reign of Jehoiakim son of Josiah,* king of Judah. ²"This is what the Lord says: Stand in the courtyard in front of the Temple of the Lord, and make an announcement to the people who have come there to worship from all over Judah. Give them my entire message; include every word. ³Perhaps they will listen and turn from their evil ways. Then I will change my mind about the disaster I am ready to pour out on them because of their sins.

⁴"Say to them, 'This is what the Lord says: If you will not listen to me and obey my word I have given you, ⁵and if you will not listen to my servants, the prophets—for I sent them again and again to warn you, but you would not listen to them—⁶then I will destroy this Temple as I destroyed Shiloh, the place where the Tabernacle was located. And I will make Jerusalem an object of cursing in every nation on earth.'"

⁷The priests, the prophets, and all the people listened to Jeremiah as he spoke in front of the Lord's Temple. ⁸But when Jeremiah had finished his message, saying everything the Lord had told him to say, the priests and prophets and all the people at the Temple mobbed him. "Kill him!" they shouted. ⁹"What right do you have to prophesy in the Lord's name that this Temple will be destroyed like Shiloh? What do you mean, saying that Jerusalem will be destroyed and left with no inhabitants?" And all the people threatened him as he stood in front of the Temple.

¹⁰When the officials of Judah heard what was happening, they rushed over from the palace and sat down at the New Gate of the Temple to hold court. ¹¹The priests and prophets presented their accusations to the officials and the people. "This man should die!" they said. "You have heard with your own ears what a traitor he is, for he has prophesied against this city."

¹²Then Jeremiah spoke to the officials and the people in his own defense. "The Lord sent me to prophesy against this Temple and this city," he said. "The Lord gave me every word that I have spoken. ¹³But if you stop your sinning and begin to obey the Lord your God, he will change his mind about this disaster that he has announced against you. ¹⁴As for me, I am in your hands—do with me as you think best. ¹⁵But if you kill me, rest assured that you will be killing an innocent man! The responsibility for such a deed will lie on you, on this city, and on every person living in it. For it is absolutely true that the Lord sent me to speak every word you have heard."

¹⁶Then the officials and the people said to the priests and prophets, "This man does not deserve the death sentence, for he has spoken to us in the name of the Lord our God."

¹⁷Then some of the wise old men stood and spoke to all the people assembled there. ¹⁸They said, "Remember when Micah of Moresheth prophesied during the reign of King Hezekiah of Judah. He told the people of Judah,

'This is what the Lord of Heaven's Armies says:
Mount Zion will be plowed like an open field;
 Jerusalem will be reduced to ruins!
A thicket will grow on the heights
 where the Temple now stands.'*

¹⁹But did King Hezekiah and the people kill him for saying this? No, they turned from their sins and worshiped the Lord. They begged him for mercy. Then the Lord changed his mind about the terrible disaster he had pronounced against them. So we are about to do ourselves great harm."

25:38 As in some Hebrew manuscripts and Greek version; Masoretic Text reads *by the anger.* 26:1 The first year of Jehoiakim's reign was 608 B.C. 26:18 Mic 3:12.

26:10-15 In ancient Israel, trials and other public matters took place at a gateway to the city. City gateways at this time were covered and multi-chambered. In this location, the entry and exit point for commerce, the elders of the city would congregate where they could be called upon to apply their wisdom to legal conflicts. In the case of Jeremiah, the officials were fair; they gave each party an opportunity to present its side of the quarrel.

26:12-13 Jeremiah argued that the Lord had sent him to speak against the city and the Temple; he added that the impending disaster would not occur if the people of Jerusalem chose to obey the Lord.

[20] At this time Uriah son of Shemaiah from Kiriath-jearim was also prophesying for the Lord. And he predicted the same terrible disaster against the city and nation as Jeremiah did. [21] When King Jehoiakim and the army officers and officials heard what he was saying, the king sent someone to kill him. But Uriah heard about the plan and escaped in fear to Egypt. [22] Then King Jehoiakim sent Elnathan son of Acbor to Egypt along with several other men to capture Uriah. [23] They took him prisoner and brought him back to King Jehoiakim. The king then killed Uriah with a sword and had him buried in an unmarked grave.

[24] Nevertheless, Ahikam son of Shaphan stood up for Jeremiah and persuaded the court not to turn him over to the mob to be killed.

Jeremiah Wears an Ox Yoke

27 This message came to Jeremiah from the Lord early in the reign of Zedekiah* son of Josiah, king of Judah.

[2] This is what the Lord said to me: "Make a yoke, and fasten it on your neck with leather straps. [3] Then send messages to the kings of Edom, Moab, Ammon, Tyre, and Sidon through their ambassadors who have come to see King Zedekiah in Jerusalem. [4] Give them this message for their masters: 'This is what the Lord of Heaven's Armies, the God of Israel, says: [5] With my great strength and powerful arm I made the earth and all its people and every animal. I can give these things of mine to anyone I choose. [6] Now I will give your countries to King Nebuchadnezzar of Babylon, who is my servant. I have put everything, even the wild animals, under his control. [7] All the nations will serve him, his son, and his grandson until his time is up. Then many nations and great kings will conquer and rule over Babylon. [8] So you must submit to Babylon's king and serve him; put your neck under Babylon's yoke! I will punish any nation that refuses to be his slave, says the Lord. I will send war, famine, and disease upon that nation until Babylon has conquered it.

[9] "'Do not listen to your false prophets, fortune-tellers, interpreters of dreams, mediums, and sorcerers who say, "The king of Babylon will not conquer you." [10] They are all liars, and their lies will lead to your being driven out of your land. I will drive you out and send you far away to die. [11] But the people of any nation that submits to the king of Babylon will be allowed to stay in their own country to farm the land as usual. I, the Lord, have spoken!'"

[12] Then I repeated this same message to King Zedekiah of Judah. "If you want to live, submit to the yoke of the king of Babylon and his people. [13] Why do you insist on dying—you and your people? Why should you choose war, famine, and disease, which the Lord will bring against every nation that refuses to submit to Babylon's king? [14] Do not listen to the false prophets who keep telling you, 'The king of Babylon will not conquer you.' They are liars. [15] This is what the Lord says: 'I have not sent these prophets! They are telling you lies in my name, so I will drive you from this land. You will all die—you and all these prophets, too.'"

[16] Then I spoke to the priests and the people and said, "This is what the Lord says: 'Do not listen to your prophets who claim that soon the gold articles taken from my Temple will be returned from Babylon. It is all a lie! [17] Do not listen to them. Surrender to the king of Babylon, and you will live. Why should this whole city be destroyed? [18] If they really are prophets and speak the Lord's messages, let them pray to the Lord of Heaven's Armies. Let them pray that the articles remaining in the Lord's Temple and in the king's palace and in the palaces of Jerusalem will not be carried away to Babylon!'

[19] "For the Lord of Heaven's Armies has spoken about the pillars in front of the Temple, the great bronze basin called the Sea, the water carts, and all the other ceremonial articles. [20] King Nebuchadnezzar of Babylon left them here when he exiled Jehoiachin* son of Jehoiakim, king of Judah, to Babylon, along with all the other nobles of Judah and Jerusalem. [21] Yes, this is what the Lord of Heaven's Armies, the God of Israel, says about the precious things still in the Temple, in the palace of Judah's king, and in Jerusalem: [22] 'They will all be carried away to Babylon and will stay there until I send for them,' says the Lord. 'Then I will bring them back to Jerusalem again.'"

Jeremiah Condemns Hananiah

28 One day in late summer* of that same year—the fourth year of the reign of Zedekiah, king of Judah—Hananiah son of Azzur, a prophet from Gibeon, addressed me publicly in the Temple while

---

27:1 As in some Hebrew manuscripts and Syriac version (see also 27:3, 12); most Hebrew manuscripts read *Jehoiakim*. **27:20** Hebrew *Jeconiah*, a variant spelling of Jehoiachin. **28:1** Hebrew *In the fifth month*, of the ancient Hebrew lunar calendar. The fifth month in the fourth year of Zedekiah's reign occurred within the months of August and September 593 b.c. Also see note on 1:3.

27:9-18 Jeremiah warned the people not to listen to false prophets or spiritualists who dabbled in occult practices that had been forbidden by the law (Deuteronomy 18:9-22). He spoke the truth, even when it was very difficult. Sometimes, people claim to speak for God, but they speak falsely. It can take wisdom to discern the true voice of God. James 1:5-6 tells us that if we lack wisdom, all we need to do is ask.

28:1 The people were in the Temple, so it was probably the occasion of one of the annual fall festivals, either the Day of Atonement (Leviticus 23:26-32) or the Festival of Shelters (Leviticus 23:33-36).

all the priests and people listened. He said, ²"This is what the Lord of Heaven's Armies, the God of Israel, says: 'I will remove the yoke of the king of Babylon from your necks. ³Within two years I will bring back all the Temple treasures that King Nebuchadnezzar carried off to Babylon. ⁴And I will bring back Jehoiachin* son of Jehoiakim, king of Judah, and all the other captives that were taken to Babylon. I will surely break the yoke that the king of Babylon has put on your necks. I, the Lord, have spoken!'"

⁵Jeremiah responded to Hananiah as they stood in front of all the priests and people at the Temple. ⁶He said, "Amen! May your prophecies come true! I hope the Lord does everything you say. I hope he does bring back from Babylon the treasures of this Temple and all the captives. ⁷But listen now to the solemn words I speak to you in the presence of all these people. ⁸The ancient prophets who preceded you and me spoke against many nations, always warning of war, disaster, and disease. ⁹So a prophet who predicts peace must show he is right. Only when his predictions come true can we know that he is really from the Lord."

¹⁰Then Hananiah the prophet took the yoke off Jeremiah's neck and broke it in pieces. ¹¹And Hananiah said again to the crowd that had gathered, "This is what the Lord says: 'Just as this yoke has been broken, within two years I will break the yoke of oppression from all the nations now subject to King Nebuchadnezzar of Babylon.'" With that, Jeremiah left the Temple area.

¹²Soon after this confrontation with Hananiah, the Lord gave this message to Jeremiah: ¹³"Go and tell Hananiah, 'This is what the Lord says: You have broken a wooden yoke, but you have replaced it with a yoke of iron. ¹⁴The Lord of Heaven's Armies, the God of Israel, says: I have put a yoke of iron on the necks of all these nations, forcing them into slavery under King Nebuchadnezzar of Babylon. I have put everything, even the wild animals, under his control.'"

¹⁵Then Jeremiah the prophet said to Hananiah, "Listen, Hananiah! The Lord has not sent you, but the people believe your lies. ¹⁶Therefore, this is what the Lord says: 'You must die. Your life will end this very year because you have rebelled against the Lord.'"

¹⁷Two months later* the prophet Hananiah died.

A Letter to the Exiles

29 Jeremiah wrote a letter from Jerusalem to the elders, priests, prophets, and all the people who had been exiled to Babylon by King Nebuchadnezzar. ²This was after King Jehoiachin,* the queen mother, the court officials, the other officials of Judah, and all the craftsmen and artisans had been deported from Jerusalem. ³He sent the letter with Elasah son of Shaphan and Gemariah son of Hilkiah when they went to Babylon as King Zedekiah's ambassadors to Nebuchadnezzar. This is what Jeremiah's letter said:

⁴This is what the Lord of Heaven's Armies, the God of Israel, says to all the captives he has exiled to Babylon from Jerusalem: ⁵"Build homes, and plan to stay. Plant gardens, and eat the food they produce. ⁶Marry and have children. Then find spouses for them so that you may have many grandchildren. Multiply! Do not dwindle away! ⁷And work for the peace and prosperity of the city where I sent you into exile. Pray to the Lord for it, for its welfare will determine your welfare."

⁸This is what the Lord of Heaven's Armies, the God of Israel, says: "Do not let your prophets and fortune-tellers who are with you in the land of Babylon trick you. Do not listen to their dreams, ⁹because they are telling you lies in my name. I have not sent them," says the Lord.

¹⁰This is what the Lord says: "You will be in Babylon for seventy years. But then I will come and do for you all the good things I have

---

28:4 Hebrew *Jeconiah*, a variant spelling of Jehoiachin. **28:17** Hebrew *In the seventh month of that same year*. See 28:1 and the note there. **29:2** Hebrew *Jeconiah*, a variant spelling of Jehoiachin.

28:2-3 Hananiah's message was the approved propaganda, but he used strong terms to claim the Lord's authority. Judah had been under the "yoke of the king of Babylon" since 597 BC.
28:4 Jeremiah and Hananiah were in sharp disagreement over King Jehoiachin's future. Jeremiah prophesied he would not return, and Hananiah prophesied he would return, giving false hope and implying that Zedekiah's reign would soon end. Hananiah closed with the same appeal to divine authority that Jeremiah often used: "I, the Lord, have spoken."
28:10-11 The false prophet Hananiah took the yoke from around Jeremiah's neck and broke it, symbolizing that he thought the Lord would soon break the yoke of Nebuchadnezzar's oppressive rule. Jeremiah left the confrontation without replying, probably because he had not yet received the Lord's response.
28:12-14 Jeremiah received and delivered the Lord's response to the false prophecy. The wooden yoke that Hananiah broke was replaced by a metaphorical yoke of iron. Subjection to Babylon was an absolute certainty, for the Lord had decreed it.
28:15-17 The Lord's decree for Hananiah was the lawful penalty for false prophets (Deuteronomy 13:1-5). Jeremiah's prophecy was validated when the Lord carried out the decree that very year. In contrast, Hananiah's prediction that the Temple treasures would be returned in two years was not fulfilled. The Lord demonstrated that he was still in control.
29:5-7 Jeremiah urged the exiled people to plan to stay in Babylon for a long time. God wanted them to become productive citizens, concerned and praying to the Lord for the welfare of the Babylonian communities in which they lived, so their population could grow. They should not listen to false prophecies such as Hananiah's, promising that they would be coming home shortly.

Koinonia
IMAGE
MY STORY WITH COMMUNITY, WORKPLACE & CHURCH

Bless Where You Are
SCRIPTURE CONNECTION: JEREMIAH 29:1-14

"I will never leave my country; I will never marry someone who lives far away!" Little did I know that God had different plans, and one day I would live as an alien—just like the exiles living in Babylon.

The most famous verse in Jeremiah is 29:11. We all seek hope and a better future, especially when we feel like strangers in a strange land. But sometimes, we miss the "fine print" of what Jeremiah says if we do not look at nearby verses. When living in a place we didn't plan on, God wants us to:

1. Settle down, produce, and multiply (29:5-6)
2. Seek peace, bless the "city" we're in, and pray for its prosperity (29:7)
3. Seek the Lord; listen to and obey his words only (29:8, 13, 20)

> We all live in exile until we return to our ultimate home, God's Kingdom.

Moving wasn't easy for me. In Guatemala, I had a job, a church community, close friends, and relatives. When I moved to the United States, I had to build a support system from scratch. I had to wait for the permits to "do life" as a new resident. I felt lonely at times; I didn't have connections and felt like I wasn't productive at all (this was my captivity). Still, I decided to seek God and his Word. Attending a Bible study group allowed me to start learning about the culture and develop relationships.

When we follow God's wisdom for how to live, wherever we are, we can find his blessing and be a blessing to others. In some ways, we are all exiles. Yet, one day, he will take us all back home to his eternal Kingdom and free us from our earthly captivity (29:14).

IMAGINE

Are you living in a place that feels like exile or captivity? How can you be a blessing where you are living now?

How has God shaped you and made you prosper while in exile?

"After seven years of living in exile, I now have a family, church community, close friends, and two jobs! God has restored my fortunes."

BRENDA GARCIA de BRIZENDINE is the former communications manager for Compassion International's Guatemala office. She works with Iron Rose Sister Ministries and also interprets Spanish for CPCD-Head Start in Colorado Springs, CO.

promised, and I will bring you home again. ¹¹For I know the plans I have for you," says the Lord. "They are plans for good and not for disaster, to give you a future and a hope. ¹²In those days when you pray, I will listen. ¹³If you look for me wholeheartedly, you will find me. ¹⁴I will be found by you," says the Lord. "I will end your captivity and restore your fortunes. I will gather you out of the nations where I sent you and will bring you home again to your own land."

¹⁵You claim that the Lord has raised up prophets for you in Babylon. ¹⁶But this is what the Lord says about the king who sits on David's throne and all those still living here in Jerusalem—your relatives who were not exiled to Babylon. ¹⁷This is what the Lord of Heaven's Armies says: "I will send war, famine, and disease upon them and make them like bad figs, too rotten to eat. ¹⁸Yes, I will pursue them with war, famine, and disease, and I will scatter them around the world. In every nation where I send them, I will make them an object of damnation, horror, contempt, and mockery. ¹⁹For they refuse to listen to me, though I have spoken to them repeatedly through the prophets I sent. And you who are in exile have not listened either," says the Lord.

²⁰Therefore, listen to this message from the Lord, all you captives there in Babylon. ²¹This is what the Lord of Heaven's Armies, the God of Israel, says about your prophets—Ahab son of Kolaiah and Zedekiah son of Maaseiah—who are telling you lies in my name: "I will turn them over to Nebuchadnezzar* for execution before your eyes. ²²Their terrible fate will become proverbial, so that the Judean exiles will curse someone by saying, 'May the Lord make you like Zedekiah and Ahab, whom the king of Babylon burned alive!' ²³For these men have done terrible things among my people. They have committed adultery with their neighbors' wives and have lied in my name, saying things I did not command. I am a witness to this. I, the Lord, have spoken."

A Message for Shemaiah

²⁴The Lord sent this message to Shemaiah the Nehelamite in Babylon: ²⁵"This is what the Lord of Heaven's Armies, the God of Israel, says: You wrote a letter on your own authority to Zephaniah son of Maaseiah, the priest, and you sent copies to the other priests and people in Jerusalem. You wrote to Zephaniah,

²⁶"The Lord has appointed you to replace Jehoiada as the priest in charge of the house of the Lord. You are responsible to put into stocks and neck irons any crazy man who claims to be a prophet. ²⁷So why have you done nothing to stop Jeremiah from Anathoth, who pretends to be a prophet among you? ²⁸Jeremiah sent a letter here to Babylon, predicting that our captivity will be a long one. He said, 'Build homes, and plan to stay. Plant gardens, and eat the food they produce.'"

²⁹But when Zephaniah the priest received Shemaiah's letter, he took it to Jeremiah and read it to him. ³⁰Then the Lord gave this message to Jeremiah: ³¹"Send an open letter to all the exiles in Babylon. Tell them, 'This is what the Lord says concerning Shemaiah the Nehelamite: Since he has prophesied to you when I did not send him and has tricked you into believing his lies, ³²I will punish him and his family. None of his descendants will see the good things I will do for my people, for he has incited you to rebel against me. I, the Lord, have spoken!'"

Promises of Deliverance

30 The Lord gave another message to Jeremiah. He said, ²"This is what the Lord, the God of Israel, says: Write down for the record everything I have said to you, Jeremiah. ³For the time is coming when I will restore the fortunes of my people of Israel and Judah. I will bring them home to this land that I gave to their ancestors, and they will possess it again. I, the Lord, have spoken!"

⁴This is the message the Lord gave concerning Israel and Judah. ⁵This is what the Lord says:

29:21 Hebrew *Nebuchadrezzar*, a variant spelling of Nebuchadnezzar.

29:11 The Lord's "plans for good," to prosper the exiled people and to return them to the land of Judah, gave them "a future and a hope." This promise was specific to those exiles in Babylon, but it has given hope to millions of God's people in difficult circumstances.

29:24-32 Shemaiah, a prophet from Israel living in Babylon, took issue with Jeremiah's written advice that the exiles should expect a long exile (29:4-23). Shemaiah sent a letter to a leading priest in Jerusalem, urging him to take action against Jeremiah, who responded with a letter to the exiles that condemned Shemaiah.

30:1–33:26 These chapters are often called "The Book of Consolation." These messages proclaim hope and a future restoration for Israel.

30:3-24 The people of Israel would go into exile, but they would return home: "For the time is coming when I will restore the fortunes of my people of Israel and Judah." The people would face discipline for injustice and breaking the covenant but would also hear that God has not given up on them. Even today, when we make bad choices, God never gives up on us. Instead, God pursues us to bring us "home," extending grace and forgiveness (Ezekiel 34:11; Luke 19:10).

"I hear cries of fear;
  there is terror and no peace.
⁶ Now let me ask you a question:
  Do men give birth to babies?
Then why do they stand there, ashen-faced,
  hands pressed against their sides
  like a woman in labor?
⁷ In all history there has never been such a time
    of terror.
  It will be a time of trouble for my people
    Israel.*
  Yet in the end they will be saved!
⁸ For in that day,"
  says the LORD of Heaven's Armies,
"I will break the yoke from their necks
  and snap their chains.
Foreigners will no longer be their masters.
⁹ For my people will serve the LORD their God
  and their king descended from David—
    the king I will raise up for them.
¹⁰ "So do not be afraid, Jacob, my servant;
    do not be dismayed, Israel,"
  says the LORD.
"For I will bring you home again from distant
    lands,
  and your children will return from their exile.
Israel will return to a life of peace and quiet,
  and no one will terrorize them.
¹¹ For I am with you and will save you,"
  says the LORD.
"I will completely destroy the nations where I
    have scattered you,
  but I will not completely destroy you.
I will discipline you, but with justice;
  I cannot let you go unpunished."

¹² This is what the LORD says:
"Your injury is incurable—
  a terrible wound.
¹³ There is no one to help you
  or to bind up your injury.
  No medicine can heal you.
¹⁴ All your lovers—your allies—have left you
  and do not care about you anymore.
I have wounded you cruelly,
  as though I were your enemy.
For your sins are many,
  and your guilt is great.
¹⁵ Why do you protest your punishment—
  this wound that has no cure?
I have had to punish you
  because your sins are many
  and your guilt is great.
¹⁶ "But all who devour you will be devoured,
  and all your enemies will be sent into exile.
All who plunder you will be plundered,
  and all who attack you will be attacked.

¹⁷ I will give you back your health
  and heal your wounds," says the LORD.
"For you are called an outcast—
  'Jerusalem* for whom no one cares.'"

¹⁸ This is what the LORD says:
"When I bring Israel home again from
    captivity
  and restore their fortunes,
Jerusalem will be rebuilt on its ruins,
  and the palace reconstructed as before.
¹⁹ There will be joy and songs of thanksgiving,
  and I will multiply my people, not diminish
    them;
I will honor them, not despise them.
²⁰ Their children will prosper as they did long
    ago.
I will establish them as a nation before me,
  and I will punish anyone who hurts them.
²¹ They will have their own ruler again,
  and he will come from their own people.
I will invite him to approach me," says the LORD,
  "for who would dare to come unless
    invited?
²² You will be my people,
  and I will be your God."

²³ Look! The LORD's anger bursts out like a storm,
  a driving wind that swirls down on the heads
    of the wicked.
²⁴ The fierce anger of the LORD will not diminish
  until it has finished all he has planned.
In the days to come
  you will understand all this.

Hope for Restoration

31 "In that day," says the LORD, "I will be the God of all the families of Israel, and they will be my people. ²This is what the LORD says:

"Those who survive the coming destruction
  will find blessings even in the barren land,
  for I will give rest to the people of Israel."

³ Long ago the LORD said to Israel:
"I have loved you, my people, with an
    everlasting love.
  With unfailing love I have drawn you to
    myself.
⁴ I will rebuild you, my virgin Israel.
  You will again be happy
  and dance merrily with your tambourines.
⁵ Again you will plant your vineyards on the
    mountains of Samaria
  and eat from your own gardens there.
⁶ The day will come when watchmen will shout
    from the hill country of Ephraim,
'Come, let us go up to Jerusalem*
  to worship the LORD our God.'"

30:7 Hebrew *Jacob;* also in 30:10b, 18. See note on 5:20.   **30:17** Hebrew *Zion.*   **31:6** Hebrew *Zion;* also in 31:12.

⁷ Now this is what the LORD says:
"Sing with joy for Israel.*
  Shout for the greatest of nations!
Shout out with praise and joy:
'Save your people, O LORD,
  the remnant of Israel!'
⁸ For I will bring them from the north
  and from the distant corners of
    the earth.
I will not forget the blind and lame,
  the expectant mothers and women
    in labor.
  A great company will return!
⁹ Tears of joy will stream down their faces,
  and I will lead them home with great care.
They will walk beside quiet streams
  and on smooth paths where they will not
    stumble.
For I am Israel's father,
  and Ephraim is my oldest child.
¹⁰ "Listen to this message from the LORD,
  you nations of the world;
  proclaim it in distant coastlands:
The LORD, who scattered his people,
  will gather them and watch over them
  as a shepherd does his flock.
¹¹ For the LORD has redeemed Israel
  from those too strong for them.
¹² They will come home and sing songs of joy on
    the heights of Jerusalem.
  They will be radiant because of the LORD's
    good gifts—
the abundant crops of grain, new wine, and
    olive oil,
  and the healthy flocks and herds.
Their life will be like a watered garden,
  and all their sorrows will be gone.
¹³ The young women will dance for joy,
  and the men—old and young—will join in
    the celebration.
I will turn their mourning into joy.
  I will comfort them and exchange their
    sorrow for rejoicing.
¹⁴ The priests will enjoy abundance,
  and my people will feast on my good
    gifts.
  I, the LORD, have spoken!"

Rachel's Sadness Turns to Joy

¹⁵ This is what the LORD says:

"A cry is heard in Ramah—
  deep anguish and bitter weeping.
Rachel weeps for her children,
  refusing to be comforted—
  for her children are gone."

¹⁶ But now this is what the LORD says:
"Do not weep any longer,
  for I will reward you," says the LORD.
"Your children will come back to you
  from the distant land of the enemy.
¹⁷ There is hope for your future," says the LORD.
  "Your children will come again to their own
    land.
¹⁸ I have heard Israel* saying,
  'You disciplined me severely,
  like a calf that needs training for the yoke.
Turn me again to you and restore me,
  for you alone are the LORD my God.
¹⁹ I turned away from God,
  but then I was sorry.
I kicked myself for my stupidity!
  I was thoroughly ashamed of all I did in my
    younger days.'
²⁰ "Is not Israel still my son,
  my darling child?" says the LORD.
"I often have to punish him,
  but I still love him.
That's why I long for him
  and surely will have mercy on him.
²¹ Set up road signs;
  put up guideposts.
Mark well the path
  by which you came.
Come back again, my virgin Israel;
  return to your towns here.
²² How long will you wander,
  my wayward daughter?
For the LORD will cause something new to
  happen—
  Israel will embrace her God.*"

²³ This is what the LORD of Heaven's Armies, the God of Israel, says: "When I bring them back from captivity, the people of Judah and its towns will

---

31:7 Hebrew *Jacob*; also in 31:11. See note on 5:20. **31:18** Hebrew *Ephraim*, referring to the northern kingdom of Israel; also in 31:20. **31:22** Hebrew *a woman will surround a man.*

31:8 In this section on hope for the future, Jeremiah describes bringing home various vulnerable people such as people who have disabilities, pregnant women, and even women in labor. The remnant from the north, from Babylon, includes all people. This vision of a renewed future brings joy and celebration for every person.

31:15-18 Throughout history, this picture of Rachel weeping for her children has been very moving. Rachel was the favorite wife of Jacob and the mother of Joseph and Benjamin (Genesis 29:30; 30:22-24; 35:18). Matthew connects the fulfillment of this passage in Jeremiah with Herod's slaughter of Bethlehem's baby boys (Matthew 2:16-18). Here in Jeremiah, God invites Rachel to no longer weep because the Lord has promised to bring her exiled children out of captivity and back to their land.

again say, 'The LORD bless you, O righteous home, O holy mountain!' ²⁴Townspeople and farmers and shepherds alike will live together in peace and happiness. ²⁵For I have given rest to the weary and joy to the sorrowing."

²⁶At this, I woke up and looked around. My sleep had been very sweet.

²⁷"The day is coming," says the LORD, "when I will greatly increase the human population and the number of animals here in Israel and Judah. ²⁸In the past I deliberately uprooted and tore down this nation. I overthrew it, destroyed it, and brought disaster upon it. But in the future I will just as deliberately plant it and build it up. I, the LORD, have spoken!

²⁹"The people will no longer quote this proverb:

'The parents have eaten sour grapes,
but their children's mouths pucker at the taste.'

³⁰All people will die for their own sins—those who eat the sour grapes will be the ones whose mouths will pucker.

³¹"The day is coming," says the LORD, "when I will make a new covenant with the people of Israel and Judah. ³²This covenant will not be like the one I made with their ancestors when I took them by the hand and brought them out of the land of Egypt. They broke that covenant, though I loved them as a husband loves his wife," says the LORD.

³³"But this is the new covenant I will make with the people of Israel after those days," says the LORD. "I will put my instructions deep within them, and I will write them on their hearts. I will be their God, and they will be my people. ³⁴And they will not need to teach their neighbors, nor will they need to teach their relatives, saying, 'You should know the LORD.' For everyone, from the least to the greatest, will know me already," says the LORD. "And I will forgive their wickedness, and I will never again remember their sins."

³⁵ It is the LORD who provides the sun to light the day
and the moon and stars to light the night,
and who stirs the sea into roaring waves.
His name is the LORD of Heaven's Armies,
and this is what he says:
³⁶ "I am as likely to reject my people Israel
as I am to abolish the laws of nature!"

³⁷ This is what the LORD says:
"Just as the heavens cannot be measured
and the foundations of the earth cannot be explored,
so I will not consider casting them away
for the evil they have done.
I, the LORD, have spoken!

³⁸"The day is coming," says the LORD, "when all Jerusalem will be rebuilt for me, from the Tower of Hananel to the Corner Gate. ³⁹A measuring line will be stretched out over the hill of Gareb and across to Goah. ⁴⁰And the entire area—including the graveyard and ash dump in the valley, and all the fields out to the Kidron Valley on the east as far as the Horse Gate—will be holy to the LORD. The city will never again be captured or destroyed."

Jeremiah's Land Purchase

32 The following message came to Jeremiah from the LORD in the tenth year of the reign of Zedekiah,* king of Judah. This was also the eighteenth year of the reign of King Nebuchadnezzar.* ²Jerusalem was then under siege from the Babylonian army, and Jeremiah was imprisoned in the courtyard of the guard in the royal palace. ³King Zedekiah had put him there, asking why he kept giving this prophecy: "This is what the LORD says: 'I am about to hand this city over to the king of Babylon, and he will take it. ⁴King Zedekiah will be captured by the Babylonians* and taken to meet the king of Babylon face to face. ⁵He will take Zedekiah to Babylon, and I will deal with him there,' says the LORD. 'If you fight against the Babylonians, you will never succeed.'"

⁶At that time the LORD sent me a message. He said, ⁷"Your cousin Hanamel son of Shallum will come and say to you, 'Buy my field at Anathoth. By law you have the right to buy it before it is offered to anyone else.'"

⁸Then, just as the LORD had said he would, my cousin Hanamel came and visited me in the prison. He said, "Please buy my field at Anathoth in the land of Benjamin. By law you have the right to buy it before it is offered to anyone else, so buy it for yourself." Then I knew that the message I had heard was from the LORD.

⁹So I bought the field at Anathoth, paying Hanamel seventeen pieces* of silver for it. ¹⁰I signed and sealed the deed of purchase before witnesses,

---

32:1a The tenth year of Zedekiah's reign and the eighteenth year of Nebuchadnezzar's reign was 587 B.C. **32:1b** Hebrew *Nebuchadrezzar*, a variant spelling of Nebuchadnezzar; also in 32:28. **32:4** Or *Chaldeans*; also in 32:5, 24, 25, 28, 29, 43. **32:9** Hebrew *17 shekels*, about 7 ounces or 194 grams in weight.

31:31-34 The new covenant Jeremiah describes will not be completely different but more of a "renewed" covenant, fulfilling and yet expanding the older Mosaic covenant. With this new covenant, God's instruction will be internal, written on their hearts!

32:6-8 Anathoth was Jeremiah's hometown (1:1). The Lord directed Jeremiah to buy his cousin's field there. The timing of this purchase was during the siege when Babylon was taking control of the city. This seemingly untimely purchase was a symbolic act of faith and a physical sign that God would restore all things (32:37-41).

weighed out the silver, and paid him. ¹¹Then I took the sealed deed and an unsealed copy of the deed, which contained the terms and conditions of the purchase, ¹²and I handed them to Baruch son of Neriah and grandson of Mahseiah. I did all this in the presence of my cousin Hanamel, the witnesses who had signed the deed, and all the men of Judah who were there in the courtyard of the guardhouse.

¹³Then I said to Baruch as they all listened, ¹⁴"This is what the LORD of Heaven's Armies, the God of Israel, says: 'Take both this sealed deed and the unsealed copy, and put them into a pottery jar to preserve them for a long time.' ¹⁵For this is what the LORD of Heaven's Armies, the God of Israel, says: 'Someday people will again own property here in this land and will buy and sell houses and vineyards and fields.'"

Jeremiah's Prayer

¹⁶Then after I had given the papers to Baruch, I prayed to the LORD:

¹⁷"O Sovereign LORD! You made the heavens and earth by your strong hand and powerful arm. Nothing is too hard for you! ¹⁸You show unfailing love to thousands, but you also bring the consequences of one generation's sin upon the next. You are the great and powerful God, the LORD of Heaven's Armies. ¹⁹You have all wisdom and do great and mighty miracles. You see the conduct of all people, and you give them what they deserve. ²⁰You performed miraculous signs and wonders in the land of Egypt—things still remembered to this day! And you have continued to do great miracles in Israel and all around the world. You have made your name famous to this day.

²¹"You brought Israel out of Egypt with mighty signs and wonders, with a strong hand and powerful arm, and with overwhelming terror. ²²You gave the people of Israel this land that you had promised their ancestors long before—a land flowing with milk and honey. ²³Our ancestors came and conquered it and lived in it, but they refused to obey you or follow your word. They have not done anything you commanded. That is why you have sent this terrible disaster upon them.

²⁴"See how the siege ramps have been built against the city walls! Through war, famine, and disease, the city will be handed over to the Babylonians, who will conquer it. Everything has happened just as you said. ²⁵And yet, O Sovereign LORD, you have told me to buy the field—paying good money for it before these witnesses—even though the city will soon be handed over to the Babylonians."

A Prediction of Jerusalem's Fall

²⁶Then this message came to Jeremiah from the LORD: ²⁷"I am the LORD, the God of all the peoples of the world. Is anything too hard for me? ²⁸Therefore, this is what the LORD says: I will hand this city over to the Babylonians and to Nebuchadnezzar, king of Babylon, and he will capture it. ²⁹The Babylonians outside the walls will come in and set fire to the city. They will burn down all these houses where the people provoked my anger by burning incense to Baal on the rooftops and by pouring out liquid offerings to other gods. ³⁰Israel and Judah have done nothing but wrong since their earliest days. They have infuriated me with all their evil deeds," says the LORD. ³¹"From the time this city was built until now, it has done nothing but anger me, so I am determined to get rid of it.

³²"The sins of Israel and Judah—the sins of the people of Jerusalem, the kings, the officials, the priests, and the prophets—have stirred up my anger. ³³My people have turned their backs on me and have refused to return. Even though I diligently taught them, they would not receive instruction or obey. ³⁴They have set up their abominable idols right in my own Temple, defiling it. ³⁵They have built pagan shrines to Baal in the valley of Ben-Hinnom, and there they sacrifice their sons and daughters to Molech. I have never commanded such a horrible deed; it never even crossed my mind to command such a thing. What an incredible evil, causing Judah to sin so greatly!

A Promise of Restoration

³⁶"Now I want to say something more about this city. You have been saying, 'It will fall to the king of Babylon through war, famine, and disease.' But this is what the LORD, the God of Israel, says: ³⁷I will certainly bring my people back again from all the countries where I will scatter them in my fury. I will bring them back to this very city and let them live in peace and safety. ³⁸They will be my people, and I will be their God. ³⁹And I will give them one heart and one purpose: to worship me forever, for their own good and for the good of all their descendants.

32:15 Jeremiah explained the reason for his purchase: He was making an investment in the future that God had promised. Someday exiled survivors of the destruction of Judah would return, and worthless land would again become productive and valuable. Jeremiah had already predicted that the Exile would last for seventy years (25:11-12; 29:10), followed by restoration. His purchase was a declaration of faith in the Lord's plan.

32:18 The Lord showed his unfailing love, but he also carried over the consequences of sin from one generation to the next. Through his mercy and his judgment, the Lord demonstrated his unlimited power. Jeremiah was confident that the Lord would show his love to his people as he had promised.

⁴⁰And I will make an everlasting covenant with them: I will never stop doing good for them. I will put a desire in their hearts to worship me, and they will never leave me. ⁴¹I will find joy doing good for them and will faithfully and wholeheartedly replant them in this land.

⁴²"This is what the Lord says: Just as I have brought all these calamities on them, so I will do all the good I have promised them. ⁴³Fields will again be bought and sold in this land about which you now say, 'It has been ravaged by the Babylonians, a desolate land where people and animals have all disappeared.' ⁴⁴Yes, fields will once again be bought and sold—deeds signed and sealed and witnessed—in the land of Benjamin and here in Jerusalem, in the towns of Judah and in the hill country, in the foothills of Judah* and in the Negev, too. For someday I will restore prosperity to them. I, the Lord, have spoken!"

Promises of Peace and Prosperity

33 While Jeremiah was still confined in the courtyard of the guard, the Lord gave him this second message: ²"This is what the Lord says— the Lord who made the earth, who formed and established it, whose name is the Lord: ³Ask me and I will tell you remarkable secrets you do not know about things to come. ⁴For this is what the Lord, the God of Israel, says: You have torn down the houses of this city and even the king's palace to get materials to strengthen the walls against the siege ramps and swords of the enemy. ⁵You expect to fight the Babylonians,* but the men of this city are already as good as dead, for I have determined to destroy them in my terrible anger. I have abandoned them because of all their wickedness.

⁶"Nevertheless, the time will come when I will heal Jerusalem's wounds and give it prosperity and true peace. ⁷I will restore the fortunes of Judah and Israel and rebuild their towns. ⁸I will cleanse them of their sins against me and forgive all their sins of rebellion. ⁹Then this city will bring me joy, glory, and honor before all the nations of the earth! The people of the world will see all the good I do for my people, and they will tremble with awe at the peace and prosperity I provide for them.

¹⁰"This is what the Lord says: You have said, 'This is a desolate land where people and animals have all disappeared.' Yet in the empty streets of Jerusalem and Judah's other towns, there will be heard once more ¹¹the sounds of joy and laughter. The joyful voices of bridegrooms and brides will be heard again, along with the joyous songs of people bringing thanksgiving offerings to the Lord. They will sing,

> "If we can ever get the hang of life as God intended, then it becomes an adventure to be lived instead of an unknown to be feared."
>
> **ANGELA THOMAS**
> Bible teacher, speaker, and author

'Give thanks to the Lord of Heaven's Armies,
  for the Lord is good.
His faithful love endures forever!'

For I will restore the prosperity of this land to what it was in the past, says the Lord.

¹²"This is what the Lord of Heaven's Armies says: This land—though it is now desolate and has no people and animals—will once more have pastures where shepherds can lead their flocks. ¹³Once again shepherds will count their flocks in the towns of the hill country, the foothills of Judah,* the Negev, the land of Benjamin, the vicinity of Jerusalem, and all the towns of Judah. I, the Lord, have spoken!

¹⁴"The day will come, says the Lord, when I will do for Israel and Judah all the good things I have promised them.

¹⁵ "In those days and at that time
  I will raise up a righteous descendant* from
    King David's line.
  He will do what is just and right throughout
    the land.
¹⁶ In that day Judah will be saved,
  and Jerusalem will live in safety.
And this will be its name:
  'The Lord Is Our Righteousness.'*

32:44 Hebrew *the Shephelah.* **33:5** Or *Chaldeans.* **33:13** Hebrew *the Shephelah.* **33:15** Hebrew *a righteous branch.* **33:16** Hebrew *Yahweh Tsidqenu.*

32:38-40 The new covenant (31:31-34) would take root deep within the hearts of the people, both individually and as a community. A deep relationship between God and his people would finally be realized, as had been the intent of the covenant all along (7:23; Leviticus 26:12; Ezekiel 11:20; 37:23; Zechariah 8:8).

¹⁷For this is what the LORD says: David will have a descendant sitting on the throne of Israel forever. ¹⁸And there will always be Levitical priests to offer burnt offerings and grain offerings and sacrifices to me."

¹⁹Then this message came to Jeremiah from the LORD: ²⁰"This is what the LORD says: If you can break my covenant with the day and the night so that one does not follow the other, ²¹only then will my covenant with my servant David be broken. Only then will he no longer have a descendant to reign on his throne. The same is true for my covenant with the Levitical priests who minister before me. ²²And as the stars of the sky cannot be counted and the sand on the seashore cannot be measured, so I will multiply the descendants of my servant David and the Levites who minister before me."

²³The LORD gave another message to Jeremiah. He said, ²⁴"Have you noticed what people are saying?—'The LORD chose Judah and Israel and then abandoned them!' They are sneering and saying that Israel is not worthy to be counted as a nation. ²⁵But this is what the LORD says: I would no more reject my people than I would change my laws that govern night and day, earth and sky. ²⁶I will never abandon the descendants of Jacob or David, my servant, or change the plan that David's descendants will rule the descendants of Abraham, Isaac, and Jacob. Instead, I will restore them to their land and have mercy on them."

A Warning for Zedekiah

34 King Nebuchadnezzar* of Babylon came with all the armies from the kingdoms he ruled, and he fought against Jerusalem and the towns of Judah. At that time this message came to Jeremiah from the LORD: ²"Go to King Zedekiah of Judah, and tell him, 'This is what the LORD, the God of Israel, says: I am about to hand this city over to the king of Babylon, and he will burn it down. ³You will not escape his grasp but will be captured and taken to meet the king of Babylon face to face. Then you will be exiled to Babylon.

⁴"'But listen to this promise from the LORD, O Zedekiah, king of Judah. This is what the LORD says: You will not be killed in war ⁵but will die peacefully. People will burn incense in your memory, just as they did for your ancestors, the kings who preceded you. They will mourn for you, crying, "Alas, our master is dead!" This I have decreed, says the LORD.'"

⁶So Jeremiah the prophet delivered the message to King Zedekiah of Judah. ⁷At this time the Babylonian army was besieging Jerusalem, Lachish, and Azekah—the only fortified cities of Judah not yet captured.

Freedom for Hebrew Slaves

⁸This message came to Jeremiah from the LORD after King Zedekiah made a covenant with the people, proclaiming freedom for the slaves. ⁹He had ordered all the people to free their Hebrew slaves—both men and women. No one was to keep a fellow Judean in bondage. ¹⁰The officials and all the people had obeyed the king's command, ¹¹but later they changed their minds. They took back the men and women they had freed, forcing them to be slaves again.

¹²So the LORD gave them this message through Jeremiah: ¹³"This is what the LORD, the God of Israel, says: I made a covenant with your ancestors long ago when I rescued them from their slavery in Egypt. ¹⁴I told them that every Hebrew slave must be freed after serving six years. But your ancestors paid no attention to me. ¹⁵Recently you repented and did what was right, following my command. You freed your slaves and made a solemn covenant with me in the Temple that bears my name. ¹⁶But now you have shrugged off your oath and defiled my name by taking back the men and women you had freed, forcing them to be slaves once again.

¹⁷"Therefore, this is what the LORD says: Since you have not obeyed me by setting your countrymen free, I will set you free to be destroyed by war, disease, and famine. You will be an object of horror to all the nations of the earth. ¹⁸Because you have broken the terms of our covenant, I will cut you apart just as you cut apart the calf when you walked between its halves to solemnize your vows. ¹⁹Yes, I will cut you apart, whether you are officials of Judah or Jerusalem, court officials, priests, or common people—for you have broken your oath. ²⁰I will give you to your enemies, and they will kill you. Your bodies will be food for the vultures and wild animals.

²¹"I will hand over King Zedekiah of Judah and his officials to the army of the king of Babylon. And although they have left Jerusalem for a while, ²²I will call the Babylonian armies back again. They will fight against this city and will capture it and burn it down. I will see to it that all the towns of Judah are destroyed, with no one living there."

The Faithful Recabites

35 This is the message the LORD gave Jeremiah when Jehoiakim son of Josiah was king of Judah: ²"Go to the settlement where the families of the Recabites live, and invite them to the LORD's Temple. Take them into one of the inner rooms, and offer them some wine."

³So I went to see Jaazaniah son of Jeremiah and grandson of Habazziniah and all his brothers and

---

34:1 Hebrew *Nebuchadrezzar*, a variant spelling of Nebuchadnezzar.

34:1-7 The Lord encouraged Zedekiah, even though he was a weak leader who lacked courage. The message contains judgment and a promise.

Koinonia
IMAGE
MY STORY WITH COMMUNITY, WORKPLACE & CHURCH

Forgiveness and Freedom Are the Same

SCRIPTURE CONNECTION: JEREMIAH 34:8-22

Brazilian philosopher Paulo Freire wrote that societies are shocked when they see the oppressed become the oppressor. Hopeful thinking tells us that she—the one who others mistreated—will choose differently. "When she gets her chance, she will help others," we think.

How does the *oppressed* become the *oppressor* instead of the *forgiven* becoming the *forgiver*? Both the Bible and life experience show us how those who could offer mercy perpetuate injustice instead. They do the same as was done to them because revenge and hate is the only language they know.

The injustice and oppression we have received can prevent us from seeing ourselves the way we are and as God meant us to be—as agents of peace, hope, love, and freedom (34:13-16). God will never hold us down. Instead of condemnation, God offers consolation. He forgives and strengthens us to forgive others. Centering our identity in forgiveness and forgiving those who wrong us is *a constant choice* that only God can empower us to make.

> I can only freely forgive as God forgives me and gives me freedom!

As a child stands up and runs again right after stumbling and falling, may we quickly appreciate the beauty in our pitfalls. Instead of filling our hearts with bad feelings, let's move toward God's new opportunity to start over. Let's walk lightly and freely and embrace forgiveness.

Every day we have the chance and choice to be someone's oppressor or forgiver. Which will you choose today?

IMAGINE

Who or what do you need to forgive today so you can be free to uplift others?

What could you do for others this day to make their lives better?

"Born and raised in Brazil, released from poverty in Jesus' name through the ministry of Compassion International, I want to serve everyone I have the chance to walk alongside. I try to be a channel—instead of only a recipient—of God's goodness."

DEBORA DA SILVA is from Brazil and found release from poverty through Compassion International. She works with Facebook in Colombia and lives to serve as she tries to be a channel—not only a recipient—of God's goodness.

sons—representing all the Recabite families. ⁴I took them to the Temple, and we went into the room assigned to the sons of Hanan son of Igdaliah, a man of God. This room was located next to the one used by the Temple officials, directly above the room of Maaseiah son of Shallum, the Temple gatekeeper.

⁵I set cups and jugs of wine before them and invited them to have a drink, ⁶but they refused. "No," they said, "we don't drink wine, because our ancestor Jehonadab* son of Recab gave us this command: 'You and your descendants must never drink wine. ⁷And do not build houses or plant crops or vineyards, but always live in tents. If you follow these commands, you will live long, good lives in the land.' ⁸So we have obeyed him in all these things. We have never had a drink of wine to this day, nor have our wives, our sons, or our daughters. ⁹We haven't built houses or owned vineyards or farms or planted crops. ¹⁰We have lived in tents and have fully obeyed all the commands of Jehonadab, our ancestor. ¹¹But when King Nebuchadnezzar* of Babylon attacked this country, we were afraid of the Babylonian and Syrian* armies. So we decided to move to Jerusalem. That is why we are here."

¹²Then the LORD gave this message to Jeremiah: ¹³"This is what the LORD of Heaven's Armies, the God of Israel, says: Go and say to the people in Judah and Jerusalem, 'Come and learn a lesson about how to obey me. ¹⁴The Recabites do not drink wine to this day because their ancestor Jehonadab told them not to. But I have spoken to you again and again, and you refuse to obey me. ¹⁵Time after time I sent you prophets, who told you, "Turn from your wicked ways, and start doing things right. Stop worshiping other gods so that you might live in peace here in the land I have given to you and your ancestors." But you would not listen to me or obey me. ¹⁶The descendants of Jehonadab son of Recab have obeyed their ancestor completely, but you have refused to listen to me.'

¹⁷"Therefore, this is what the LORD God of Heaven's Armies, the God of Israel, says: 'Because you refuse to listen or answer when I call, I will send upon Judah and Jerusalem all the disasters I have threatened.'"

¹⁸Then Jeremiah turned to the Recabites and said, "This is what the LORD of Heaven's Armies, the God of Israel, says: 'You have obeyed your ancestor Jehonadab in every respect, following all his instructions.'

¹⁹Therefore, this is what the LORD of Heaven's Armies, the God of Israel, says: 'Jehonadab son of Recab will always have descendants who serve me.'"

Baruch Reads the LORD's Messages

36 During the fourth year that Jehoiakim son of Josiah was king in Judah,* the LORD gave this message to Jeremiah: ²"Get a scroll, and write down all my messages against Israel, Judah, and the other nations. Begin with the first message back in the days of Josiah, and write down every message, right up to the present time. ³Perhaps the people of Judah will repent when they hear again all the terrible things I have planned for them. Then I will be able to forgive their sins and wrongdoings."

⁴So Jeremiah sent for Baruch son of Neriah, and as Jeremiah dictated all the prophecies that the LORD had given him, Baruch wrote them on a scroll. ⁵Then Jeremiah said to Baruch, "I am a prisoner here and unable to go to the Temple. ⁶So you go to the Temple on the next day of fasting, and read the messages from the LORD that I have had you write on this scroll. Read them so the people who are there from all over Judah will hear them. ⁷Perhaps even yet they will turn from their evil ways and ask the LORD's forgiveness before it is too late. For the LORD has threatened them with his terrible anger."

⁸Baruch did as Jeremiah told him and read these messages from the LORD to the people at the Temple. ⁹He did this on a day of sacred fasting held in late autumn,* during the fifth year of the reign of Jehoiakim son of Josiah. People from all over Judah had come to Jerusalem to attend the services at the Temple on that day. ¹⁰Baruch read Jeremiah's words on the scroll to all the people. He stood in front of the Temple room of Gemariah, son of Shaphan the secretary. This room was just off the upper courtyard of the Temple, near the New Gate entrance.

¹¹When Micaiah son of Gemariah and grandson of Shaphan heard the messages from the LORD, ¹²he went down to the secretary's room in the palace where the administrative officials were meeting. Elishama the secretary was there, along with Delaiah son of Shemaiah, Elnathan son of Acbor, Gemariah son of Shaphan, Zedekiah son of Hananiah, and all the other officials. ¹³When Micaiah told them about the messages Baruch was reading to the people, ¹⁴the officials sent Jehudi son of Nethaniah, grandson of Shelemiah and great-grandson of

---

35:6 Hebrew *Jonadab*, a variant spelling of Jehonadab; also in 35:10, 19. See 2 Kgs 10:15. **35:11a** Hebrew *Nebuchadrezzar*, a variant spelling of Nebuchadnezzar. **35:11b** Or *Chaldean and Aramean*. **36:1** The fourth year of Jehoiakim's reign was 605 B.C. **36:9** Hebrew *in the ninth month*, of the ancient Hebrew lunar calendar (also in 36:22). The ninth month in the fifth year of Jehoiakim's reign occurred within the months of November and December 604 B.C. Also see note on 1:3.

36:8-9 Baruch filled the columns of the scroll with Jeremiah's messages from the Lord. On a day of fasting toward the end of 604 BC, Baruch read the scroll in the Temple, where many people crowded the courtyard. Israel had no traditional recurring festival during the ninth month, so apparently another day of sacred fasting had been scheduled.

36:11-14 Micaiah realized the importance of the messages from the Lord that Baruch was reading, so he made sure that the administrative officials of the palace knew what was being said.

Cushi, to ask Baruch to come and read the messages to them, too. So Baruch took the scroll and went to them. ¹⁵"Sit down and read the scroll to us," the officials said, and Baruch did as they requested.

¹⁶When they heard all the messages, they looked at one another in alarm. "We must tell the king what we have heard," they said to Baruch. ¹⁷"But first, tell us how you got these messages. Did they come directly from Jeremiah?"

¹⁸So Baruch explained, "Jeremiah dictated them, and I wrote them down in ink, word for word, on this scroll."

¹⁹"You and Jeremiah should both hide," the officials told Baruch. "Don't tell anyone where you are!" ²⁰Then the officials left the scroll for safekeeping in the room of Elishama the secretary and went to tell the king what had happened.

King Jehoiakim Burns the Scroll

²¹The king sent Jehudi to get the scroll. Jehudi brought it from Elishama's room and read it to the king as all his officials stood by. ²²It was late autumn, and the king was in a winterized part of the palace, sitting in front of a fire to keep warm. ²³Each time Jehudi finished reading three or four columns, the king took a knife and cut off that section of the scroll. He then threw it into the fire, section by section, until the whole scroll was burned up. ²⁴Neither the king nor his attendants showed any signs of fear or repentance at what they heard. ²⁵Even when Elnathan, Delaiah, and Gemariah begged the king not to burn the scroll, he wouldn't listen.

²⁶Then the king commanded his son Jerahmeel, Seraiah son of Azriel, and Shelemiah son of Abdeel to arrest Baruch and Jeremiah. But the Lord had hidden them.

Jeremiah Rewrites the Scroll

²⁷After the king had burned the scroll on which Baruch had written Jeremiah's words, the Lord gave Jeremiah another message. He said, ²⁸"Get another scroll, and write everything again just as you did on the scroll King Jehoiakim burned. ²⁹Then say to the king, 'This is what the Lord says: You burned the scroll because it said the king of Babylon would destroy this land and empty it of people and animals. ³⁰Now this is what the Lord says about King Jehoiakim of Judah: He will have no heirs to sit on the throne of David. His dead body will be thrown out to lie unburied—exposed to the heat of the day and the frost of the night. ³¹I will punish him and his family and his attendants for their sins. I will pour out on them and on all the people of Jerusalem and Judah all the disasters I promised, for they would not listen to my warnings.'"

³²So Jeremiah took another scroll and dictated again to his secretary, Baruch. He wrote everything that had been on the scroll King Jehoiakim had burned in the fire. Only this time he added much more!

Zedekiah Calls for Jeremiah

37 Zedekiah son of Josiah succeeded Jehoiachin* son of Jehoiakim as the king of Judah. He was appointed by King Nebuchadnezzar* of Babylon. ²But neither King Zedekiah nor his attendants nor the people who were left in the land listened to what the Lord said through Jeremiah.

³Nevertheless, King Zedekiah sent Jehucal son of Shelemiah, and Zephaniah the priest, son of Maaseiah, to ask Jeremiah, "Please pray to the Lord our God for us." ⁴Jeremiah had not yet been imprisoned, so he could come and go among the people as he pleased.

⁵At this time the army of Pharaoh Hophra* of Egypt appeared at the southern border of Judah. When the Babylonian* army heard about it, they withdrew from their siege of Jerusalem.

⁶Then the Lord gave this message to Jeremiah: ⁷"This is what the Lord, the God of Israel, says: The king of Judah sent you to ask me what is going to happen. Tell him, 'Pharaoh's army is about to return to Egypt, though he came here to help you. ⁸Then the Babylonians* will come back and capture this city and burn it to the ground.'

⁹"This is what the Lord says: Do not fool yourselves into thinking that the Babylonians are gone for good. They aren't! ¹⁰Even if you were to destroy the entire Babylonian army, leaving only a handful of wounded survivors, they would still stagger from their tents and burn this city to the ground!"

Jeremiah Is Imprisoned

¹¹When the Babylonian army left Jerusalem because of Pharaoh's approaching army, ¹²Jeremiah started to leave the city on his way to the territory of Benjamin, to claim his share of the property among his relatives there.* ¹³But as he was walking through the Benjamin Gate, a sentry arrested him and said, "You are defecting to the Babylonians!" The sentry

---

37:1a Hebrew *Coniah*, a variant spelling of Jehoiachin.   **37:1b** Hebrew *Nebuchadrezzar*, a variant spelling of Nebuchadnezzar.
37:5a Hebrew *army of Pharaoh;* see 44:30.   **37:5b** Or *Chaldean;* also in 37:10, 11.   **37:8** Or *Chaldeans;* also in 37:9, 13.
37:12 Hebrew *to separate from there in the midst of the people.*

36:29-31 To die without heirs or a decent burial was an unimaginable fate in the ancient Near East because some cultures' understandings of the afterlife relied on the deceased being remembered by people who were still alive. Jehoiakim's son Jehoiachin ruled for just three months. Unlike his father, Jehoiachin took Jeremiah's warning seriously and surrendered to the Babylonians, who took him and others to Babylon as captives (22:24-30; 2 Kings 24:8-16).

making the arrest was Irijah son of Shelemiah, grandson of Hananiah.

[14] "That's not true!" Jeremiah protested. "I had no intention of doing any such thing." But Irijah wouldn't listen, and he took Jeremiah before the officials. [15] They were furious with Jeremiah and had him flogged and imprisoned in the house of Jonathan the secretary. Jonathan's house had been converted into a prison. [16] Jeremiah was put into a dungeon cell, where he remained for many days.

[17] Later King Zedekiah secretly requested that Jeremiah come to the palace, where the king asked him, "Do you have any messages from the Lord?"

"Yes, I do!" said Jeremiah. "You will be defeated by the king of Babylon."

[18] Then Jeremiah asked the king, "What crime have I committed? What have I done against you, your attendants, or the people that I should be imprisoned like this? [19] Where are your prophets now who told you the king of Babylon would not attack you or this land? [20] Listen, my lord the king, I beg you. Don't send me back to the dungeon in the house of Jonathan the secretary, for I will die there."

[21] So King Zedekiah commanded that Jeremiah not be returned to the dungeon. Instead, he was imprisoned in the courtyard of the guard in the royal palace. The king also commanded that Jeremiah be given a loaf of fresh bread every day as long as there was any left in the city. So Jeremiah was put in the palace prison.

Jeremiah in a Cistern

38 Now Shephatiah son of Mattan, Gedaliah son of Pashhur, Jehucal* son of Shelemiah, and Pashhur son of Malkijah heard what Jeremiah had been telling the people. He had been saying, [2] "This is what the Lord says: 'Everyone who stays in Jerusalem will die from war, famine, or disease, but those who surrender to the Babylonians* will live. Their reward will be life. They will live!' [3] The Lord also says: 'The city of Jerusalem will certainly be handed over to the army of the king of Babylon, who will capture it.'"

[4] So these officials went to the king and said, "Sir, this man must die! That kind of talk will undermine the morale of the few fighting men we have left, as well as that of all the people. This man is a traitor!"

[5] King Zedekiah agreed. "All right," he said. "Do as you like. I can't stop you."

[6] So the officials took Jeremiah from his cell and lowered him by ropes into an empty cistern in the prison yard. It belonged to Malkijah, a member of the royal family. There was no water in the cistern, but there was a thick layer of mud at the bottom, and Jeremiah sank down into it.

[7] But Ebed-melech the Ethiopian,* an important court official, heard that Jeremiah was in the cistern. At that time the king was holding court at the Benjamin Gate, [8] so Ebed-melech rushed from the palace to speak with him. [9] "My lord the king," he said, "these men have done a very evil thing in putting Jeremiah the prophet into the cistern. He will soon die of hunger, for almost all the bread in the city is gone."

[10] So the king told Ebed-melech, "Take thirty of my men with you, and pull Jeremiah out of the cistern before he dies."

[11] So Ebed-melech took the men with him and went to a room in the palace beneath the treasury, where he found some old rags and discarded clothing. He carried these to the cistern and lowered them to Jeremiah on a rope. [12] Ebed-melech called down to Jeremiah, "Put these rags under your armpits to protect you from the ropes." Then when Jeremiah was ready, [13] they pulled him out. So Jeremiah was returned to the courtyard of the guard—the palace prison—where he remained.

Zedekiah Questions Jeremiah

[14] One day King Zedekiah sent for Jeremiah and had him brought to the third entrance of the Lord's Temple. "I want to ask you something," the king said. "And don't try to hide the truth."

[15] Jeremiah said, "If I tell you the truth, you will kill me. And if I give you advice, you won't listen to me anyway."

[16] So King Zedekiah secretly promised him, "As surely as the Lord our Creator lives, I will not kill you or hand you over to the men who want you dead."

[17] Then Jeremiah said to Zedekiah, "This is what the Lord God of Heaven's Armies, the God of Israel, says: 'If you surrender to the Babylonian officers, you and your family will live, and the city will not be burned down. [18] But if you refuse to surrender, you will not escape! This city will be handed over to the Babylonians, and they will burn it to the ground.'"

[19] "But I am afraid to surrender," the king said, "for the Babylonians may hand me over to the Judeans who have defected to them. And who knows what they will do to me!"

[20] Jeremiah replied, "You won't be handed over to them if you choose to obey the Lord. Your life will be spared, and all will go well for you. [21] But if you refuse to surrender, this is what the Lord has revealed to me: [22] All the women left in your palace will be brought out and given to the officers of the Babylonian army. Then the women will taunt you, saying,

'What fine friends you have!
  They have betrayed and misled you.
When your feet sank in the mud,
  they left you to your fate!'

[23] All your wives and children will be led out to the Babylonians, and you will not escape. You will be

---

38:1 Hebrew *Jucal*, a variant spelling of Jehucal; see 37:3. **38:2** Or *Chaldeans*; also in 38:18, 19, 23. **38:7** Hebrew *the Cushite*.

seized by the king of Babylon, and this city will be burned down."

²⁴Then Zedekiah said to Jeremiah, "Don't tell anyone you told me this, or you will die! ²⁵My officials may hear that I spoke to you, and they may say, 'Tell us what you and the king were talking about. If you don't tell us, we will kill you.' ²⁶If this happens, just tell them you begged me not to send you back to Jonathan's dungeon, for fear you would die there."

²⁷Sure enough, it wasn't long before the king's officials came to Jeremiah and asked him why the king had called for him. But Jeremiah followed the king's instructions, and they left without finding out the truth. No one had overheard the conversation between Jeremiah and the king. ²⁸And Jeremiah remained a prisoner in the courtyard of the guard until the day Jerusalem was captured.

The Fall of Jerusalem

39 In January* of the ninth year of King Zedekiah's reign, King Nebuchadnezzar* of Babylon came with his entire army to besiege Jerusalem. ²Two and a half years later, on July 18* in the eleventh year of Zedekiah's reign, a section of the city wall was broken down. ³All the officers of the Babylonian army came in and sat in triumph at the Middle Gate: Nergal-sharezer of Samgar, and Nebo-sarsekim,* a chief officer, and Nergal-sharezer, the king's adviser, and all the other officers of the king of Babylon.

⁴When King Zedekiah of Judah and all the soldiers saw that the Babylonians had broken into the city, they fled. They waited for nightfall and then slipped through the gate between the two walls behind the king's garden and headed toward the Jordan Valley.*

⁵But the Babylonian* troops chased them and overtook Zedekiah on the plains of Jericho. They captured him and took him to King Nebuchadnezzar of Babylon, who was at Riblah in the land of Hamath. There the king of Babylon pronounced judgment upon Zedekiah. ⁶The king of Babylon made Zedekiah watch as he slaughtered his sons at Riblah. The king of Babylon also slaughtered all the nobles of Judah. ⁷Then he gouged out Zedekiah's eyes and bound him in bronze chains to lead him away to Babylon.

⁸Meanwhile, the Babylonians burned Jerusalem, including the royal palace and the houses of the people, and they tore down the walls of the city. ⁹Then Nebuzaradan, the captain of the guard, took as exiles to Babylon the rest of the people who remained in the city, those who had defected to him, and everyone else who remained. ¹⁰But Nebuzaradan allowed some of the poorest people to stay behind in the land of Judah, and he assigned them to care for the vineyards and fields.

Jeremiah Remains in Judah

¹¹King Nebuchadnezzar had told Nebuzaradan, the captain of the guard, to find Jeremiah. ¹²"See that he isn't hurt," he said. "Look after him well, and give him anything he wants." ¹³So Nebuzaradan, the captain of the guard; Nebushazban, a chief officer; Nergal-sharezer, the king's adviser; and the other officers of Babylon's king ¹⁴sent messengers to bring Jeremiah out of the prison. They put him under the care of Gedaliah son of Ahikam and grandson of Shaphan, who took him back to his home. So Jeremiah stayed in Judah among his own people.

¹⁵The LORD had given the following message to Jeremiah while he was still in prison: ¹⁶"Say to Ebed-melech the Ethiopian,* 'This is what the LORD of Heaven's Armies, the God of Israel, says: I will do to this city everything I have threatened. I will send disaster, not prosperity. You will see its destruction, ¹⁷but I will rescue you from those you fear so much. ¹⁸Because you trusted me, I will give you your life as a reward. I will rescue you and keep you safe. I, the LORD, have spoken!'"

40 The LORD gave a message to Jeremiah after Nebuzaradan, the captain of the guard, had released him at Ramah. He had found Jeremiah bound in chains among all the other captives of Jerusalem and Judah who were being sent to exile in Babylon.

²The captain of the guard called for Jeremiah and said, "The LORD your God has brought this disaster on this land, ³just as he said he would. For these people have sinned against the LORD and disobeyed him. That is why it happened. ⁴But I am going to take off your chains and let you go. If you want to come with me to Babylon, you are welcome. I will see that you are well cared for. But if you don't want to come, you may stay here. The whole land is before you—go wherever you like. ⁵If you decide to stay, then return to Gedaliah son of Ahikam and grandson of Shaphan. He has been appointed governor of Judah by the king of Babylon. Stay there with the people he rules. But it's up to you; go wherever you like."

Then Nebuzaradan, the captain of the guard, gave Jeremiah some food and money and let him go. ⁶So Jeremiah returned to Gedaliah son of Ahikam at Mizpah, and he lived in Judah with the few who were still left in the land.

Gedaliah Governs in Judah

⁷The leaders of the Judean military groups in the countryside heard that the king of Babylon had appointed Gedaliah son of Ahikam as governor over

---

39:1a Hebrew *In the tenth month,* of the ancient Hebrew lunar calendar. A number of events in Jeremiah can be cross-checked with dates in surviving Babylonian records and related accurately to our modern calendar. This event occurred on January 15, 588 B.C.; see 52:4a and the note there. **39:1b** Hebrew *Nebuchadrezzar,* a variant spelling of Nebuchadnezzar; also in 39:5, 11. **39:2** Hebrew *On the ninth day of the fourth month.* This day was July 18, 586 B.C.; also see note on 39:1a. **39:3** Or *Nergal-sharezer, Samgar-nebo, Sarsekim.* **39:4** Hebrew *the Arabah.* **39:5** Or *Chaldean;* similarly in 39:8. **39:16** Hebrew *the Cushite.*

the poor people who were left behind in Judah—the men, women, and children who hadn't been exiled to Babylon. ⁸So they went to see Gedaliah at Mizpah. These included: Ishmael son of Nethaniah, Johanan and Jonathan sons of Kareah, Seraiah son of Tanhumeth, the sons of Ephai the Netophathite, Jezaniah son of the Maacathite, and all their men.

⁹Gedaliah vowed to them that the Babylonians* meant them no harm. "Don't be afraid to serve them. Live in the land and serve the king of Babylon, and all will go well for you," he promised. ¹⁰"As for me, I will stay at Mizpah to represent you before the Babylonians who come to meet with us. Settle in the towns you have taken, and live off the land. Harvest the grapes and summer fruits and olives, and store them away."

¹¹When the Judeans in Moab, Ammon, Edom, and the other nearby countries heard that the king of Babylon had left a few people in Judah and that Gedaliah was the governor, ¹²they began to return to Judah from the places to which they had fled. They stopped at Mizpah to meet with Gedaliah and then went into the Judean countryside to gather a great harvest of grapes and other crops.

A Plot against Gedaliah

¹³Soon after this, Johanan son of Kareah and the other military leaders came to Gedaliah at Mizpah. ¹⁴They said to him, "Did you know that Baalis, king of Ammon, has sent Ishmael son of Nethaniah to assassinate you?" But Gedaliah refused to believe them.

¹⁵Later Johanan had a private conference with Gedaliah and volunteered to kill Ishmael secretly. "Why should we let him come and murder you?" Johanan asked. "What will happen then to the Judeans who have returned? Why should the few of us who are still left be scattered and lost?"

¹⁶But Gedaliah said to Johanan, "I forbid you to do any such thing, for you are lying about Ishmael."

The Murder of Gedaliah

41 But in midautumn of that year,* Ishmael son of Nethaniah and grandson of Elishama, who was a member of the royal family and had been one of the king's high officials, went to Mizpah with ten men to meet Gedaliah. While they were eating together, ²Ishmael and his ten men suddenly jumped up, drew their swords, and killed Gedaliah, whom the king of Babylon had appointed governor. ³Ishmael also killed all the Judeans and the Babylonian* soldiers who were with Gedaliah at Mizpah.

⁴The next day, before anyone had heard about Gedaliah's murder, ⁵eighty men arrived from Shechem, Shiloh, and Samaria to worship at the Temple of the Lord. They had shaved off their beards, torn their clothes, and cut themselves, and had brought along grain offerings and frankincense. ⁶Ishmael left Mizpah to meet them, weeping as he went. When he reached them, he said, "Oh, come and see what has happened to Gedaliah!"

⁷But as soon as they were all inside the town, Ishmael and his men killed all but ten of them and threw their bodies into a cistern. ⁸The other ten had talked Ishmael into letting them go by promising to bring him their stores of wheat, barley, olive oil, and honey that they had hidden away. ⁹The cistern where Ishmael dumped the bodies of the men he murdered was the large one* dug by King Asa when he fortified Mizpah to protect himself against King Baasha of Israel. Ishmael son of Nethaniah filled it with corpses.

¹⁰Then Ishmael made captives of the king's daughters and the other people who had been left under Gedaliah's care in Mizpah by Nebuzaradan, the captain of the guard. Taking them with him, he started back toward the land of Ammon.

¹¹But when Johanan son of Kareah and the other military leaders heard about Ishmael's crimes, ¹²they took all their men and set out to stop him. They caught up with him at the large pool near Gibeon. ¹³The people Ishmael had captured shouted for joy when they saw Johanan and the other military leaders. ¹⁴And all the captives from Mizpah escaped and began to help Johanan. ¹⁵Meanwhile, Ishmael and eight of his men escaped from Johanan into the land of Ammon.

¹⁶Then Johanan son of Kareah and the other military leaders took all the people they had rescued in Gibeon—the soldiers, women, children, and court officials* whom Ishmael had captured after he killed Gedaliah. ¹⁷They took them all to the village of Geruth-kimham near Bethlehem, where they prepared to leave for Egypt. ¹⁸They were afraid of what the Babylonians* would do when they heard that Ishmael had killed Gedaliah, the governor appointed by the Babylonian king.

Warning to Stay in Judah

42 Then all the military leaders, including Johanan son of Kareah and Jezaniah* son of Hoshaiah, and all the people, from the least to the greatest, approached ²Jeremiah the prophet. They said, "Please pray to the Lord your God for us. As you can see, we are only a tiny remnant compared to what we were before. ³Pray that the Lord your God will show us what to do and where to go."

⁴"All right," Jeremiah replied. "I will pray to the

40:9 Or *Chaldeans;* also in 40:10. **41:1** Hebrew *in the seventh month,* of the ancient Hebrew lunar calendar. This month occurred within the months of October and November 586 B.C.; also see note on 39:1a. **41:3** Or *Chaldean.* **41:9** As in Greek version; Hebrew reads *murdered because of Gedaliah was one.* **41:16** Or *eunuchs.* **41:18** Or *Chaldeans.* **42:1** Greek version reads *Azariah;* compare 43:2.

LORD your God, as you have asked, and I will tell you everything he says. I will hide nothing from you."

⁵Then they said to Jeremiah, "May the LORD your God be a faithful witness against us if we refuse to obey whatever he tells us to do! ⁶Whether we like it or not, we will obey the LORD our God to whom we are sending you with our plea. For if we obey him, everything will turn out well for us."

⁷Ten days later the LORD gave his reply to Jeremiah. ⁸So he called for Johanan son of Kareah and the other military leaders, and for all the people, from the least to the greatest. ⁹He said to them, "You sent me to the LORD, the God of Israel, with your request, and this is his reply: ¹⁰'Stay here in this land. If you do, I will build you up and not tear you down; I will plant you and not uproot you. For I am sorry about all the punishment I have had to bring upon you. ¹¹Do not fear the king of Babylon anymore,' says the LORD. 'For I am with you and will save you and rescue you from his power. ¹²I will be merciful to you by making him kind, so he will let you stay here in your land.'

¹³"But if you refuse to obey the LORD your God, and if you say, 'We will not stay here; ¹⁴instead, we will go to Egypt where we will be free from war, the call to arms, and hunger,' ¹⁵then hear the LORD's message to the remnant of Judah. This is what the LORD of Heaven's Armies, the God of Israel, says: 'If you are determined to go to Egypt and live there, ¹⁶the very war and famine you fear will catch up to you, and you will die there. ¹⁷That is the fate awaiting every one of you who insists on going to live in Egypt. Yes, you will die from war, famine, and disease. None of you will escape the disaster I will bring upon you there.'

¹⁸"This is what the LORD of Heaven's Armies, the God of Israel, says: 'Just as my anger and fury have been poured out on the people of Jerusalem, so they will be poured out on you when you enter Egypt. You will be an object of damnation, horror, cursing, and mockery. And you will never see your homeland again.'

¹⁹"Listen, you remnant of Judah. The LORD has told you: 'Do not go to Egypt!' Don't forget this warning I have given you today. ²⁰For you were not being honest when you sent me to pray to the LORD your God for you. You said, 'Just tell us what the LORD our God says, and we will do it!' ²¹And today I have told you exactly what he said, but you will not obey the LORD your God any better now than you have in the past. ²²So you can be sure that you will die from war, famine, and disease in Egypt, where you insist on going."

Jeremiah Taken to Egypt

43 When Jeremiah had finished giving this message from the LORD their God to all the people, ²Azariah son of Hoshaiah and Johanan son of Kareah and all the other proud men said to Jeremiah, "You lie! The LORD our God hasn't forbidden us to go to Egypt! ³Baruch son of Neriah has convinced you to say this, because he wants us to stay here and be killed by the Babylonians* or be carried off into exile."

⁴So Johanan and the other military leaders and all the people refused to obey the LORD's command to stay in Judah. ⁵Johanan and the other leaders took with them all the people who had returned from the nearby countries to which they had fled. ⁶In the crowd were men, women, and children, the king's daughters, and all those whom Nebuzaradan, the captain of the guard, had left with Gedaliah. The prophet Jeremiah and Baruch were also included. ⁷The people refused to obey the voice of the LORD and went to Egypt, going as far as the city of Tahpanhes.

⁸Then at Tahpanhes, the LORD gave another message to Jeremiah. He said, ⁹"While the people of Judah are watching, take some large rocks and bury them under the pavement stones at the entrance of Pharaoh's palace here in Tahpanhes. ¹⁰Then say to the people of Judah, 'This is what the LORD of Heaven's Armies, the God of Israel, says: I will certainly bring my servant Nebuchadnezzar,* king of Babylon, here to Egypt. I will set his throne over these stones that I have hidden. He will spread his royal canopy over them. ¹¹And when he comes, he will destroy the land of Egypt. He will bring death to those destined for death, captivity to those destined for captivity, and war to those destined for war. ¹²He will set fire to the temples of Egypt's gods; he will burn the temples and carry the idols away as plunder. He will pick clean the land of Egypt as a shepherd picks fleas from his cloak. And he himself will leave unharmed. ¹³He will break down the sacred pillars standing in the temple of the sun* in Egypt, and he will burn down the temples of Egypt's gods.'"

Judgment for Idolatry

44 This is the message Jeremiah received concerning the Judeans living in northern Egypt in the cities of Migdol, Tahpanhes, and Memphis,* and in southern Egypt* as well: ²"This is what the LORD of Heaven's Armies, the God of Israel, says: You saw the calamity I brought on Jerusalem and all the towns of Judah. They now lie deserted and in ruins.

43:3 Or *Chaldeans.* 43:10 Hebrew *Nebuchadrezzar,* a variant spelling of Nebuchadnezzar. 43:13 Or *in Heliopolis.* 44:1a Hebrew *Noph.* 44:1b Hebrew *in Pathros.*

43:6 Baruch, Jeremiah's scribe, stayed with him when they were taken to Egypt. Baruch's shortened name means "blessed" and his full name, Berechiah, means "Yahweh blesses." God provided faithful companions for Jeremiah throughout his difficult ministry. How have you seen God provide someone to walk alongside you just when you needed it?

³They provoked my anger with all their wickedness. They burned incense and worshiped other gods—gods that neither they nor you nor any of your ancestors had ever even known.

⁴"Again and again I sent my servants, the prophets, to plead with them, 'Don't do these horrible things that I hate so much.' ⁵But my people would not listen or turn back from their wicked ways. They kept on burning incense to these gods. ⁶And so my fury boiled over and fell like fire on the towns of Judah and into the streets of Jerusalem, and they are still a desolate ruin today.

⁷"And now the LORD God of Heaven's Armies, the God of Israel, asks you: Why are you destroying yourselves? For not one of you will survive—not a man, woman, or child among you who has come here from Judah, not even the babies in your arms. ⁸Why provoke my anger by burning incense to the idols you have made here in Egypt? You will only destroy yourselves and make yourselves an object of cursing and mockery for all the nations of the earth. ⁹Have you forgotten the sins of your ancestors, the sins of the kings and queens of Judah, and the sins you and your wives committed in Judah and Jerusalem? ¹⁰To this very hour you have shown no remorse or reverence. No one has chosen to follow my word and the decrees I gave to you and your ancestors before you.

¹¹"Therefore, this is what the LORD of Heaven's Armies, the God of Israel, says: I am determined to destroy every one of you! ¹²I will take this remnant of Judah—those who were determined to come here and live in Egypt—and I will consume them. They will fall here in Egypt, killed by war and famine. All will die, from the least to the greatest. They will be an object of damnation, horror, cursing, and mockery. ¹³I will punish them in Egypt just as I punished them in Jerusalem, by war, famine, and disease. ¹⁴Of that remnant who fled to Egypt, hoping someday to return to Judah, there will be no survivors. Even though they long to return home, only a handful will do so."

¹⁵Then all the women present and all the men who knew that their wives had burned incense to idols—a great crowd of all the Judeans living in northern Egypt and southern Egypt*—answered Jeremiah, ¹⁶"We will not listen to your messages from the LORD! ¹⁷We will do whatever we want. We will burn incense and pour out liquid offerings to the Queen of Heaven just as much as we like—just as we, and our ancestors, and our kings and officials have always done in the towns of Judah and in the streets of Jerusalem. For in those days we had plenty to eat, and we were well off and had no troubles! ¹⁸But ever since we quit burning incense to the Queen of Heaven and stopped worshiping her with liquid offerings, we have been in great trouble and have been dying from war and famine."

¹⁹"Besides," the women added, "do you suppose that we were burning incense and pouring out liquid offerings to the Queen of Heaven, and making cakes marked with her image, without our husbands knowing it and helping us? Of course not!"

²⁰Then Jeremiah said to all of them, men and women alike, who had given him that answer, ²¹"Do you think the LORD did not know that you and your ancestors, your kings and officials, and all the people were burning incense to idols in the towns of Judah and in the streets of Jerusalem? ²²It was because the LORD could no longer bear all the disgusting things you were doing that he made your land an object of cursing—a desolate ruin without inhabitants—as it is today. ²³All these terrible things happened to you because you have burned incense to idols and sinned against the LORD. You have refused to obey him and have not followed his instructions, his decrees, and his laws."

²⁴Then Jeremiah said to them all, including the women, "Listen to this message from the LORD, all you citizens of Judah who live in Egypt. ²⁵This is what the LORD of Heaven's Armies, the God of Israel, says: 'You and your wives have said, "We will keep our promises to burn incense and pour out liquid offerings to the Queen of Heaven," and you have proved by your actions that you meant it. So go ahead and carry out your promises and vows to her!'

²⁶"But listen to this message from the LORD, all you Judeans now living in Egypt: 'I have sworn by my great name,' says the LORD, 'that my name will no longer be spoken by any of the Judeans in the land of Egypt. None of you may invoke my name or use this oath: "As surely as the Sovereign LORD lives." ²⁷For I will watch over you to bring you disaster and not good. Everyone from Judah who is now living in Egypt will suffer war and famine until all of you are dead. ²⁸Only a small number will escape death and return to Judah from Egypt. Then all those who came to Egypt will find out whose words are true—mine or theirs!

²⁹"'And this is the proof I give you,' says the LORD, 'that all I have threatened will happen to you and that I will punish you here.' ³⁰This is what the LORD says: 'I will turn Pharaoh Hophra, king of Egypt, over to his enemies who want to kill him, just as I turned King Zedekiah of Judah over to King Nebuchadnezzar* of Babylon.'"

A Message for Baruch

45 The prophet Jeremiah gave a message to Baruch son of Neriah in the fourth year of the reign of Jehoiakim son of Josiah,* after Baruch had written down everything Jeremiah had

---

44:15 Hebrew *in Egypt, in Pathros.* 44:30 Hebrew *Nebuchadrezzar,* a variant spelling of Nebuchadnezzar. 45:1 The fourth year of Jehoiakim's reign was 605 B.C.

dictated to him. He said, ²"This is what the LORD, the God of Israel, says to you, Baruch: ³You have said, 'I am overwhelmed with trouble! Haven't I had enough pain already? And now the LORD has added more! I am worn out from sighing and can find no rest.'

⁴"Baruch, this is what the LORD says: 'I will destroy this nation that I built. I will uproot what I planted. ⁵Are you seeking great things for yourself? Don't do it! I will bring great disaster upon all these people; but I will give you your life as a reward wherever you go. I, the LORD, have spoken!'"

Messages for the Nations

46 The following messages were given to Jeremiah the prophet from the LORD concerning foreign nations.

Messages about Egypt

²This message concerning Egypt was given in the fourth year of the reign of Jehoiakim son of Josiah, the king of Judah, on the occasion of the battle of Carchemish* when Pharaoh Neco, king of Egypt, and his army were defeated beside the Euphrates River by King Nebuchadnezzar* of Babylon.

³ "Prepare your shields,
    and advance into battle!
⁴ Harness the horses,
    and mount the stallions.
Take your positions.
    Put on your helmets.
Sharpen your spears,
    and prepare your armor.
⁵ But what do I see?
    The Egyptian army flees in terror.
The bravest of its fighting men run
    without a backward glance.
They are terrorized at every turn,"
    says the LORD.
⁶ "The swiftest runners cannot flee;
    the mightiest warriors cannot escape.
By the Euphrates River to the north,
    they stumble and fall.
⁷ "Who is this, rising like the Nile at floodtime,
    overflowing all the land?
⁸ It is the Egyptian army,
    overflowing all the land,
boasting that it will cover the earth like a flood,
    destroying cities and their people.
⁹ Charge, you horses and chariots;
    attack, you mighty warriors of Egypt!
Come, all you allies from Ethiopia, Libya, and Lydia*
    who are skilled with the shield and bow!
¹⁰ For this is the day of the Lord, the LORD of Heaven's Armies,
    a day of vengeance on his enemies.
The sword will devour until it is satisfied,
    yes, until it is drunk with your blood!
The Lord, the LORD of Heaven's Armies, will receive a sacrifice today
    in the north country beside the Euphrates River.
¹¹ "Go up to Gilead to get medicine,
    O virgin daughter of Egypt!
But your many treatments
    will bring you no healing.
¹² The nations have heard of your shame.
    The earth is filled with your cries of despair.
Your mightiest warriors will run into each other
    and fall down together."

¹³Then the LORD gave the prophet Jeremiah this message about King Nebuchadnezzar's plans to attack Egypt.

¹⁴ "Shout it out in Egypt!
    Publish it in the cities of Migdol, Memphis,* and Tahpanhes!
Mobilize for battle,
    for the sword will devour everyone around you.
¹⁵ Why have your warriors fallen?
    They cannot stand, for the LORD has knocked them down.
¹⁶ They stumble and fall over each other
    and say among themselves,
'Come, let's go back to our people,
    to the land of our birth.
Let's get away from the sword of the enemy!'
¹⁷ There they will say,
    'Pharaoh, the king of Egypt, is a loudmouth who missed his opportunity!'
¹⁸ "As surely as I live," says the King,
    whose name is the LORD of Heaven's Armies,
"one is coming against Egypt
    who is as tall as Mount Tabor,
    or as Mount Carmel by the sea!
¹⁹ Pack up! Get ready to leave for exile,
    you citizens of Egypt!
The city of Memphis will be destroyed,
    without a single inhabitant.
²⁰ Egypt is as sleek as a beautiful heifer,
    but a horsefly from the north is on its way!
²¹ Egypt's mercenaries have become like fattened calves.
    They, too, will turn and run,
for it is a day of great disaster for Egypt,
    a time of great punishment.

46:2a This event occurred in 605 B.C., during the fourth year of Jehoiakim's reign (according to the calendar system in which the new year begins in the spring). **46:2b** Hebrew *Nebuchadrezzar*, a variant spelling of Nebuchadnezzar; also in 46:13, 26. **46:9** Hebrew *from Cush, Put, and Lud.* **46:14** Hebrew *Noph;* also in 46:19.

WHAT THE BIBLE SAYS ABOUT Time

God Created and Is Beyond Time

God said, "Let lights appear in the sky to separate the day from the night. Let them be signs to mark the seasons, days, and years." **GENESIS 1:14**

You must not forget this one thing, dear friends: A day is like a thousand years to the Lord, and a thousand years is like a day. **2 PETER 3:8**

I am with you always, even to the end of the age

God Chooses the Right Timing

"In those days and at that time
 I will raise up a righteous descendant
  from King David's line.
 He will do what is just and right
  throughout the land."
JEREMIAH 33:15

For everything there is a season,
 a time for every activity under heaven.
A time to be born and a time to die.
 A time to plant and a time to harvest.
 A time to kill and a time to heal.
 A time to tear down and a time to build up.
ECCLESIASTES 3:1-3

God Is with Us throughout Time

Lord, through all the generations
 you have been our home!
PSALM 90:1

[Jesus said,] "And be sure of this: I am with you always, even to the end of the age." **MATTHEW 28:20**

We Can Use Time Wisely

Teach us to realize the brevity of life,
 so that we may grow in wisdom.
PSALM 90:12

Be careful how you live. Don't live like fools, but like those who are wise. Make the most of every opportunity in these evil days. **EPHESIANS 5:15-16**

²² Egypt flees, silent as a serpent gliding away.
> The invading army marches in;
> they come against her with axes like woodsmen.

²³ They will cut down her people like trees," says the LORD,
> "for they are more numerous than locusts.

²⁴ Egypt will be humiliated;
> she will be handed over to people from the north."

²⁵The LORD of Heaven's Armies, the God of Israel, says: "I will punish Amon, the god of Thebes,* and all the other gods of Egypt. I will punish its rulers and Pharaoh, too, and all who trust in him. ²⁶I will hand them over to those who want them killed—to King Nebuchadnezzar of Babylon and his army. But afterward the land will recover from the ravages of war. I, the LORD, have spoken!

²⁷ "But do not be afraid, Jacob, my servant;
> do not be dismayed, Israel.
> For I will bring you home again from distant lands,
> and your children will return from their exile.
> Israel* will return to a life of peace and quiet,
> and no one will terrorize them.

²⁸ Do not be afraid, Jacob, my servant,
> for I am with you," says the LORD.
> "I will completely destroy the nations to which I have exiled you,
> but I will not completely destroy you.
> I will discipline you, but with justice;
> I cannot let you go unpunished."

A Message about Philistia

47 This is the LORD's message to the prophet Jeremiah concerning the Philistines of Gaza, before it was captured by the Egyptian army. ²This is what the LORD says:

> "A flood is coming from the north
> to overflow the land.
> It will destroy the land and everything in it—
> cities and people alike.
> People will scream in terror,
> and everyone in the land will wail.

³ Hear the clatter of stallions' hooves
> and the rumble of wheels as the chariots rush by.
> Terrified fathers run madly,
> without a backward glance at their helpless children.

⁴ "The time has come for the Philistines to be destroyed,
> along with their allies from Tyre and Sidon.
> Yes, the LORD is destroying the remnant of the Philistines,
> those colonists from the island of Crete.*

⁵ Gaza will be humiliated, its head shaved bald;
> Ashkelon will lie silent.
> You remnant from the Mediterranean coast,*
> how long will you cut yourselves in mourning?

⁶ "Now, O sword of the LORD,
> when will you be at rest again?
> Go back into your sheath;
> rest and be still.

⁷ "But how can it be still
> when the LORD has sent it on a mission?
> For the city of Ashkelon
> and the people living along the sea
> must be destroyed."

A Message about Moab

48 This message was given concerning Moab. This is what the LORD of Heaven's Armies, the God of Israel, says:

> "What sorrow awaits the city of Nebo;
> it will soon lie in ruins.
> The city of Kiriathaim will be humiliated and captured;
> the fortress will be humiliated and broken down.

² No one will ever brag about Moab again,
> for in Heshbon there is a plot to destroy her.
> 'Come,' they say, 'we will cut her off from being a nation.'
> The town of Madmen,* too, will be silenced;
> the sword will follow you there.

³ Listen to the cries from Horonaim,
> cries of devastation and great destruction.

⁴ All Moab is destroyed.
> Her little ones will cry out.*

⁵ Her refugees weep bitterly,
> climbing the slope to Luhith.
> They cry out in terror,
> descending the slope to Horonaim.

⁶ Flee for your lives!
> Hide* in the wilderness!

⁷ Because you have trusted in your wealth and skill,
> you will be taken captive.
> Your god Chemosh, with his priests and officials,
> will be hauled off to distant lands!

⁸ "All the towns will be destroyed,
> and no one will escape—

46:25 Hebrew *of No.* **46:27** Hebrew *Jacob.* See note on 5:20. **47:4** Hebrew *from Caphtor.* **47:5** Hebrew *the plain.* **48:2** *Madmen* sounds like the Hebrew word for "silence"; it should not be confused with the English word *madmen.* **48:4** Greek version reads *Her cries are heard as far away as Zoar.* **48:6** Or *Hide like a wild donkey;* or *Hide like a juniper shrub;* or *Be like* [the town of] *Aroer.* The meaning of the Hebrew is uncertain.

either on the plateaus or in the valleys,
for the LORD has spoken.
⁹ Oh, that Moab had wings
so she could fly away,*
for her towns will be left empty,
with no one living in them.
¹⁰ Cursed are those who refuse to do the LORD's work,
who hold back their swords from shedding blood!

¹¹ "From his earliest history, Moab has lived in peace,
never going into exile.
He is like wine that has been allowed to settle.
He has not been poured from flask to flask,
and he is now fragrant and smooth.
¹² But the time is coming soon," says the LORD,
"when I will send men to pour him from his jar.
They will pour him out,
then shatter the jar!
¹³ At last Moab will be ashamed of his idol Chemosh,
as the people of Israel were ashamed of their gold calf at Bethel.*

¹⁴ "You used to boast, 'We are heroes,
mighty men of war.'
¹⁵ But now Moab and his towns will be destroyed.
His most promising youth are doomed to slaughter,"
says the King, whose name is the LORD of Heaven's Armies.
¹⁶ "Destruction is coming fast for Moab;
calamity threatens ominously.
¹⁷ You friends of Moab,
weep for him and cry!
See how the strong scepter is broken,
how the beautiful staff is shattered!

¹⁸ "Come down from your glory
and sit in the dust, you people of Dibon,
for those who destroy Moab will shatter Dibon, too.
They will tear down all your towers.
¹⁹ You people of Aroer,
stand beside the road and watch.
Shout to those who flee from Moab,
'What has happened there?'
²⁰ "And the reply comes back,
'Moab lies in ruins, disgraced;
weep and wail!
Tell it by the banks of the Arnon River:
Moab has been destroyed!'

²¹ Judgment has been poured out on the towns of the plateau—
on Holon and Jahaz* and Mephaath,
²² on Dibon and Nebo and Beth-diblathaim,
²³ on Kiriathaim and Beth-gamul and Beth-meon,
²⁴ on Kerioth and Bozrah—
all the towns of Moab, far and near.

²⁵ "The strength of Moab has ended.
His arm has been broken," says the LORD.
²⁶ "Let him stagger and fall like a drunkard,
for he has rebelled against the LORD.
Moab will wallow in his own vomit,
ridiculed by all.
²⁷ Did you not ridicule the people of Israel?
Were they caught in the company of thieves
that you should despise them as you do?

²⁸ "You people of Moab,
flee from your towns and live in the caves.
Hide like doves that nest
in the clefts of the rocks.
²⁹ We have all heard of the pride of Moab,
for his pride is very great.
We know of his lofty pride,
his arrogance, and his haughty heart.
³⁰ I know about his insolence,"
says the LORD,
"but his boasts are empty—
as empty as his deeds.
³¹ So now I wail for Moab;
yes, I will mourn for Moab.
My heart is broken for the men of Kir-hareseth.*

³² "You people of Sibmah, rich in vineyards,
I will weep for you even more than I did for Jazer.
Your spreading vines once reached as far as the Dead Sea,*
but the destroyer has stripped you bare!
He has harvested your grapes and summer fruits.
³³ Joy and gladness are gone from fruitful Moab.
The presses yield no wine.
No one treads the grapes with shouts of joy.
There is shouting, yes, but not of joy.

³⁴"Instead, their awful cries of terror can be heard from Heshbon clear across to Elealeh and Jahaz; from Zoar all the way to Horonaim and Eglath-shelishiyah. Even the waters of Nimrim are dried up now.

³⁵"I will put an end to Moab," says the LORD, "for the people offer sacrifices at the pagan shrines and burn incense to their false gods. ³⁶My heart moans like a flute for Moab and Kir-hareseth, for all their

---

48:9 Or *Put salt on Moab, / for she will be laid waste.* **48:13** Hebrew *ashamed when they trusted in Bethel.* **48:21** Hebrew *Jahzah,* a variant spelling of Jahaz. **48:31** Hebrew *Kir-heres,* a variant spelling of Kir-hareseth; also in 48:36. **48:32** Hebrew *the sea of Jazer.*

wealth has disappeared. ³⁷The people shave their heads and beards in mourning. They slash their hands and put on clothes made of burlap. ³⁸There is crying and sorrow in every Moabite home and on every street. For I have smashed Moab like an old, unwanted jar. ³⁹How it is shattered! Hear the wailing! See the shame of Moab! It has become an object of ridicule, an example of ruin to all its neighbors."

⁴⁰This is what the LORD says:

"Look! The enemy swoops down like an eagle,
    spreading his wings over Moab.
⁴¹ Its cities will fall,
    and its strongholds will be seized.
Even the mightiest warriors will be in anguish
    like a woman in labor.
⁴² Moab will no longer be a nation,
    for it has boasted against the LORD.
⁴³ "Terror and traps and snares will be your lot,
    O Moab," says the LORD.
⁴⁴ "Those who flee in terror will fall into a trap,
    and those who escape the trap will step into a snare.
I will see to it that you do not get away,
    for the time of your judgment has come,"
    says the LORD.
⁴⁵ "The people flee as far as Heshbon
    but are unable to go on.
For a fire comes from Heshbon,
    King Sihon's ancient home,
to devour the entire land
    with all its rebellious people.
⁴⁶ "What sorrow awaits you, O people of Moab!
    The people of the god Chemosh are destroyed!
Your sons and your daughters
    have been taken away as captives.
⁴⁷ But I will restore the fortunes of Moab
    in days to come.
I, the LORD, have spoken!"

This is the end of Jeremiah's prophecy concerning Moab.

A Message about Ammon

49 This message was given concerning the Ammonites. This is what the LORD says:

"Are there no descendants of Israel
    to inherit the land of Gad?
Why are you, who worship Molech,*
    living in its towns?
² In the days to come," says the LORD,
    "I will sound the battle cry against your city of Rabbah.
It will become a desolate heap of ruins,
    and the neighboring towns will be burned.
Then Israel will take back the land
    you took from her," says the LORD.

³ "Cry out, O Heshbon,
    for the town of Ai is destroyed.
Weep, O people of Rabbah!
    Put on your clothes of mourning.
Weep and wail, hiding in the hedges,
    for your god Molech, with his priests and officials,
    will be hauled off to distant lands.
⁴ You are proud of your fertile valleys,
    but they will soon be ruined.
You trusted in your wealth,
    you rebellious daughter,
    and thought no one could ever harm you.
⁵ But look! I will bring terror upon you,"
    says the Lord, the LORD of Heaven's Armies.
"Your neighbors will chase you from your land,
    and no one will help your exiles as they flee.
⁶ But I will restore the fortunes of the Ammonites
    in days to come.
I, the LORD, have spoken."

Messages about Edom

⁷This message was given concerning Edom. This is what the LORD of Heaven's Armies says:

"Is there no wisdom in Teman?
    Is no one left to give wise counsel?
⁸ Turn and flee!
    Hide in deep caves, you people of Dedan!
For when I bring disaster on Edom,*
    I will punish you, too!
⁹ Those who harvest grapes
    always leave a few for the poor.
If thieves came at night,
    they would not take everything.
¹⁰ But I will strip bare the land of Edom,
    and there will be no place left to hide.
Its children, its brothers, and its neighbors
    will all be destroyed,
    and Edom itself will be no more.
¹¹ But I will protect the orphans who remain among you.
    Your widows, too, can depend on me for help."

¹²And this is what the LORD says: "If the innocent must suffer, how much more must you! You will not go unpunished! You must drink this cup of judgment! ¹³For I have sworn by my own name," says the LORD, "that Bozrah will become an object of horror and a heap of ruins; it will be mocked and cursed. All its towns and villages will be desolate forever."

¹⁴ I have heard a message from the LORD
    that an ambassador was sent to the nations
    to say,

49:1 Hebrew *Malcam*, a variant spelling of Molech; also in 49:3.   49:8 Hebrew *Esau*; also in 49:10.

"Form a coalition against Edom,
  and prepare for battle!"

15 The LORD says to Edom,
"I will cut you down to size among the nations.
  You will be despised by all.
16 You have been deceived
  by the fear you inspire in others
  and by your own pride.
You live in a rock fortress
  and control the mountain heights.
But even if you make your nest among the peaks
    with the eagles,
  I will bring you crashing down,"
    says the LORD.

17 "Edom will be an object of horror.
  All who pass by will be appalled
  and will gasp at the destruction they see
    there.
18 It will be like the destruction of Sodom and
    Gomorrah
  and their neighboring towns," says
    the LORD.
"No one will live there;
  no one will inhabit it.
19 I will come like a lion from the thickets of the
    Jordan,
  leaping on the sheep in the pasture.
I will chase Edom from its land,
  and I will appoint the leader of my choice.
For who is like me, and who can challenge me?
  What ruler can oppose my will?"

20 Listen to the LORD's plans against Edom
  and the people of Teman.
Even the little children will be dragged off like
    sheep,
  and their homes will be destroyed.
21 The earth will shake with the noise of Edom's
    fall,
  and its cry of despair will be heard all the way
    to the Red Sea.*
22 Look! The enemy swoops down like an eagle,
  spreading his wings over Bozrah.
Even the mightiest warriors will be in anguish
  like a woman in labor.

A Message about Damascus

23 This message was given concerning Damascus. This is what the LORD says:

"The towns of Hamath and Arpad are struck
    with fear,
  for they have heard the news of their
    destruction.
Their hearts are troubled
  like a wild sea in a raging storm.

24 Damascus has become feeble,
  and all her people turn to flee.
Fear, anguish, and pain have gripped her
  as they grip a woman in labor.
25 That famous city, a city of joy,
  will be forsaken!
26 Her young men will fall in the streets and die.
  Her soldiers will all be killed,"
    says the LORD of Heaven's Armies.
27 "And I will set fire to the walls of Damascus
  that will burn up the palaces of Ben-hadad."

A Message about Kedar and Hazor

28 This message was given concerning Kedar and the kingdoms of Hazor, which were attacked by King Nebuchadnezzar* of Babylon. This is what the LORD says:

"Advance against Kedar!
  Destroy the warriors from the East!
29 Their flocks and tents will be captured,
  and their household goods and camels will be
    taken away.
Everywhere shouts of panic will be heard:
  'We are terrorized at every turn!'
30 Run for your lives," says the LORD.
  "Hide yourselves in deep caves, you people of
    Hazor,
  for King Nebuchadnezzar of Babylon has plotted
    against you
  and is preparing to destroy you.

31 "Go up and attack that complacent nation,"
    says the LORD.
"Its people live alone in the desert
  without walls or gates.
32 Their camels and other livestock will all be
    yours.
I will scatter to the winds these people
  who live in remote places.*
I will bring calamity upon them
  from every direction," says the LORD.
33 "Hazor will be inhabited by jackals,
  and it will be desolate forever.
No one will live there;
  no one will inhabit it."

A Message about Elam

34 This message concerning Elam came to the prophet Jeremiah from the LORD at the beginning of the reign of King Zedekiah of Judah. 35 This is what the LORD of Heaven's Armies says:

"I will destroy the archers of Elam—
  the best of their forces.
36 I will bring enemies from all directions,
  and I will scatter the people of Elam to the
    four winds.

49:21 Hebrew *sea of reeds.* 49:28 Hebrew *Nebuchadrezzar,* a variant spelling of Nebuchadnezzar; also in 49:30. 49:32 Or *who clip the corners of their hair.*

They will be exiled to countries around the
world.
37 I myself will go with Elam's enemies to
shatter it.
In my fierce anger, I will bring great disaster
upon the people of Elam," says the LORD.
"Their enemies will chase them with
the sword
until I have destroyed them completely.
38 I will set my throne in Elam," says the LORD,
"and I will destroy its king and officials.
39 But I will restore the fortunes of Elam
in days to come.
I, the LORD, have spoken!"

A Message about Babylon

50 The LORD gave Jeremiah the prophet this message concerning Babylon and the land of the Babylonians.* ²This is what the LORD says:

"Tell the whole world,
and keep nothing back.
Raise a signal flag
to tell everyone that Babylon will fall!
Her images and idols* will be shattered.
Her gods Bel and Marduk will be utterly
disgraced.
3 For a nation will attack her from the north
and bring such destruction that no one will
live there again.
Everything will be gone;
both people and animals will flee.

Hope for Israel and Judah

4 "In those coming days,"
says the LORD,
"the people of Israel will return home
together with the people of Judah.
They will come weeping
and seeking the LORD their God.
5 They will ask the way to Jerusalem*
and will start back home again.
They will bind themselves to the LORD
with an eternal covenant that will never be
forgotten.

6 "My people have been lost sheep.
Their shepherds have led them astray
and turned them loose in the mountains.
They have lost their way
and can't remember how to get back to the
sheepfold.
7 All who found them devoured them.
Their enemies said,
'We did nothing wrong in attacking them,
for they sinned against the LORD,

their true place of rest,
and the hope of their ancestors.'

8 "But now, flee from Babylon!
Leave the land of the Babylonians.
Like male goats at the head of the flock,
lead my people home again.
9 For I am raising up an army
of great nations from the north.
They will join forces to attack Babylon,
and she will be captured.
The enemies' arrows will go straight to the mark;
they will not miss!
10 Babylonia* will be looted
until the attackers are glutted with loot.
I, the LORD, have spoken!

Babylon's Sure Fall

11 "You rejoice and are glad,
you who plundered my chosen people.
You frisk about like a calf in a meadow
and neigh like a stallion.
12 But your homeland* will be overwhelmed
with shame and disgrace.
You will become the least of nations—
a wilderness, a dry and desolate land.
13 Because of the LORD's anger,
Babylon will become a deserted wasteland.
All who pass by will be horrified
and will gasp at the destruction they see
there.
14 "Yes, prepare to attack Babylon,
all you surrounding nations.
Let your archers shoot at her; spare no arrows.
For she has sinned against the LORD.
15 Shout war cries against her from every side.
Look! She surrenders!
Her walls have fallen.
It is the LORD's vengeance,
so take vengeance on her.
Do to her as she has done to others!
16 Take from Babylon all those who plant crops;
send all the harvesters away.
Because of the sword of the enemy,
everyone will run away and rush back to their
own lands.

Hope for God's People

17 "The Israelites are like sheep
that have been scattered by lions.
First the king of Assyria ate them up.
Then King Nebuchadnezzar* of Babylon
cracked their bones."
18 Therefore, this is what the LORD of Heaven's
Armies,

50:1 Or *Chaldeans;* also in 50:8, 25, 35, 45.   50:2 The Hebrew term (literally *round things*) probably alludes to dung.
50:5 Hebrew *Zion;* also in 50:28.   50:10 Or *Chaldea.*   50:12 Hebrew *your mother.*   50:17 Hebrew *Nebuchadrezzar,* a variant spelling of Nebuchadnezzar.

the God of Israel, says:
"Now I will punish the king of Babylon and his land,
just as I punished the king of Assyria.
¹⁹ And I will bring Israel home again to its own land,
to feed in the fields of Carmel and Bashan,
and to be satisfied once more
in the hill country of Ephraim and Gilead.
²⁰ In those days," says the Lord,
"no sin will be found in Israel or in Judah,
for I will forgive the remnant I preserve.

The Lord's Judgment on Babylon

²¹ "Go up, my warriors, against the land of Merathaim
and against the people of Pekod.
Pursue, kill, and completely destroy* them,
as I have commanded you," says the Lord.
²² "Let the battle cry be heard in the land,
a shout of great destruction.
²³ Babylon, the mightiest hammer in all the earth,
lies broken and shattered.
Babylon is desolate among the nations!
²⁴ Listen, Babylon, for I have set a trap for you.
You are caught, for you have fought against the Lord.
²⁵ The Lord has opened his armory
and brought out weapons to vent his fury.
The terror that falls upon the Babylonians
will be the work of the Sovereign Lord of Heaven's Armies.
²⁶ Yes, come against her from distant lands.
Break open her granaries.
Crush her walls and houses into heaps of rubble.
Destroy her completely, and leave nothing!
²⁷ Destroy even her young bulls—
it will be terrible for them, too!
Slaughter them all!
For Babylon's day of reckoning has come.
²⁸ Listen to the people who have escaped from Babylon,
as they tell in Jerusalem
how the Lord our God has taken vengeance
against those who destroyed his Temple.

²⁹ "Send out a call for archers to come to Babylon.
Surround the city so none can escape.
Do to her as she has done to others,
for she has defied the Lord, the Holy One of Israel.
³⁰ Her young men will fall in the streets and die.
Her soldiers will all be killed,"
says the Lord.

³¹ "See, I am your enemy, you arrogant people,"
says the Lord, the Lord of Heaven's Armies.
"Your day of reckoning has arrived—
the day when I will punish you.
³² O land of arrogance, you will stumble and fall,
and no one will raise you up.
For I will light a fire in the cities of Babylon
that will burn up everything around them."

³³ This is what the Lord of Heaven's Armies says:
"The people of Israel and Judah have been wronged.
Their captors hold them and refuse to let them go.
³⁴ But the one who redeems them is strong.
His name is the Lord of Heaven's Armies.
He will defend them
and give them rest again in Israel.
But for the people of Babylon
there will be no rest!

³⁵ "The sword of destruction will strike the Babylonians,"
says the Lord.
"It will strike the people of Babylon—
her officials and wise men, too.
³⁶ The sword will strike her wise counselors,
and they will become fools.
The sword will strike her mightiest warriors,
and panic will seize them.
³⁷ The sword will strike her horses and chariots
and her allies from other lands,
and they will all become like women.
The sword will strike her treasures,
and they all will be plundered.
³⁸ A drought* will strike her water supply,
causing it to dry up.
And why? Because the whole land is filled with idols,
and the people are madly in love with them.

³⁹ "Soon Babylon will be inhabited by desert animals and hyenas.
It will be a home for owls.
Never again will people live there;
it will lie desolate forever.
⁴⁰ I will destroy it as I* destroyed Sodom and Gomorrah
and their neighboring towns," says the Lord.
"No one will live there;
no one will inhabit it.

⁴¹ "Look! A great army is coming from the north.
A great nation and many kings
are rising against you from far-off lands.
⁴² They are armed with bows and spears.
They are cruel and show no mercy.

50:21 The Hebrew term used here refers to the complete consecration of things or people to the Lord, either by destroying them or by giving them as an offering.   **50:38** Or *sword;* the Hebrew words for *drought* and *sword* are very similar.   **50:40** Hebrew *as God.*

As they ride forward on horses,
  they sound like a roaring sea.
They are coming in battle formation,
  planning to destroy you, Babylon.
⁴³ The king of Babylon has heard reports about the enemy,
  and he is weak with fright.
Pangs of anguish have gripped him,
  like those of a woman in labor.

⁴⁴ "I will come like a lion from the thickets of the Jordan,
  leaping on the sheep in the pasture.
I will chase Babylon from its land,
  and I will appoint the leader of my choice.
For who is like me, and who can challenge me?
  What ruler can oppose my will?"

⁴⁵ Listen to the LORD's plans against Babylon
  and the land of the Babylonians.
Even the little children will be dragged off like sheep,
  and their homes will be destroyed.
⁴⁶ The earth will shake with the shout, "Babylon has been taken!"
  and its cry of despair will be heard around the world.

51

This is what the LORD says:
"I will stir up a destroyer against Babylon
  and the people of Babylonia.*
² Foreigners will come and winnow her,
  blowing her away as chaff.
They will come from every side
  to rise against her in her day of trouble.
³ Don't let the archers put on their armor
  or draw their bows.
Don't spare even her best soldiers!
  Let her army be completely destroyed.*
⁴ They will fall dead in the land of the Babylonians,*
  slashed to death in her streets.
⁵ For the LORD of Heaven's Armies
  has not abandoned Israel and Judah.
He is still their God,
  even though their land was filled with sin
  against the Holy One of Israel."

⁶ Flee from Babylon! Save yourselves!
  Don't get trapped in her punishment!
It is the LORD's time for vengeance;
  he will repay her in full.
⁷ Babylon has been a gold cup in the LORD's hands,
  a cup that made the whole earth drunk.
The nations drank Babylon's wine,
  and it drove them all mad.

⁸ But suddenly Babylon, too, has fallen.
  Weep for her.
Give her medicine.
  Perhaps she can yet be healed.
⁹ We would have helped her if we could,
  but nothing can save her now.
Let her go; abandon her.
  Return now to your own land.
For her punishment reaches to the heavens;
  it is so great it cannot be measured.
¹⁰ The LORD has vindicated us.
  Come, let us announce in Jerusalem*
  everything the LORD our God has done.

¹¹ Sharpen the arrows!
  Lift up the shields!*
For the LORD has inspired the kings of the Medes
  to march against Babylon and destroy her.
This is his vengeance against those
  who desecrated his Temple.
¹² Raise the battle flag against Babylon!
  Reinforce the guard and station the watchmen.
Prepare an ambush,
  for the LORD will fulfill all his plans against Babylon.
¹³ You are a city by a great river,
  a great center of commerce,
but your end has come.
  The thread of your life is cut.
¹⁴ The LORD of Heaven's Armies has taken this vow
  and has sworn to it by his own name:
"Your cities will be filled with enemies,
  like fields swarming with locusts,
  and they will shout in triumph over you."

A Hymn of Praise to the LORD

¹⁵ The LORD made the earth by his power,
  and he preserves it by his wisdom.
With his own understanding
  he stretched out the heavens.
¹⁶ When he speaks in the thunder,
  the heavens roar with rain.
He causes the clouds to rise over the earth.
  He sends the lightning with the rain
  and releases the wind from his storehouses.
¹⁷ The whole human race is foolish and has no knowledge!
  The craftsmen are disgraced by the idols they make,
for their carefully shaped works are a fraud.
  These idols have no breath or power.
¹⁸ Idols are worthless; they are ridiculous lies!
  On the day of reckoning they will all be destroyed.

51:1 Hebrew *of Leb-kamai*, a code name for Babylonia. 51:3 The Hebrew term used here refers to the complete consecration of things or people to the LORD, either by destroying them or by giving them as an offering. 51:4 Or *Chaldeans*; also in 51:54. 51:10 Hebrew *Zion*; also in 51:24. 51:11 Greek version reads *Fill up the quivers*.

19 But the God of Israel* is no idol!
>He is the Creator of everything that exists,
>including his people, his own special possession.
>The LORD of Heaven's Armies is his name!

Babylon's Great Punishment

20 "You* are my battle-ax and sword,"
>says the LORD.
>"With you I will shatter nations
>and destroy many kingdoms.
21 With you I will shatter armies—
>destroying the horse and rider,
>the chariot and charioteer.
22 With you I will shatter men and women,
>old people and children,
>young men and young women.
23 With you I will shatter shepherds and flocks,
>farmers and oxen,
>captains and officers.

24 "I will repay Babylon
>and the people of Babylonia*
>for all the wrong they have done
>to my people in Jerusalem," says the LORD.

25 "Look, O mighty mountain, destroyer of the earth!
>I am your enemy," says the LORD.
>"I will raise my fist against you,
>to knock you down from the heights.
>When I am finished,
>you will be nothing but a heap of burnt rubble.
26 You will be desolate forever.
>Even your stones will never again be used for building.
>You will be completely wiped out,"
>says the LORD.

27 Raise a signal flag to the nations.
>Sound the battle cry!
>Mobilize them all against Babylon.
>Prepare them to fight against her!
>Bring out the armies of Ararat, Minni, and Ashkenaz.
>Appoint a commander,
>and bring a multitude of horses like swarming locusts!
28 Bring against her the armies of the nations—
>led by the kings of the Medes
>and all their captains and officers.

29 The earth trembles and writhes in pain,
>for everything the LORD has planned against Babylon stands unchanged.
>Babylon will be left desolate without a single inhabitant.
30 Her mightiest warriors no longer fight.
>They stay in their barracks, their courage gone.
>They have become like women.
>The invaders have burned the houses
>and broken down the city gates.
31 The news is passed from one runner to the next
>as the messengers hurry to tell the king
>that his city has been captured.
32 All the escape routes are blocked.
>The marshes have been set aflame,
>and the army is in a panic.

33 This is what the LORD of Heaven's Armies, the God of Israel, says:
>"Babylon is like wheat on a threshing floor,
>about to be trampled.
>In just a little while
>her harvest will begin."

34 "King Nebuchadnezzar* of Babylon has eaten and crushed us
>and drained us of strength.
>He has swallowed us like a great monster
>and filled his belly with our riches.
>He has thrown us out of our own country.
35 Make Babylon suffer as she made us suffer,"
>say the people of Zion.
>"Make the people of Babylonia pay for spilling our blood,"
>says Jerusalem.

The LORD's Vengeance on Babylon

36 This is what the LORD says to Jerusalem:

>"I will be your lawyer to plead your case,
>and I will avenge you.
>I will dry up her river,
>as well as her springs,
37 and Babylon will become a heap of ruins,
>haunted by jackals.
>She will be an object of horror and contempt,
>a place where no one lives.
38 Her people will roar together like strong lions.
>They will growl like lion cubs.
39 And while they lie inflamed with all their wine,
>I will prepare a different kind of feast for them.

51:19 Hebrew *the Portion of Jacob.* See note on 5:20. 51:20 Possibly Cyrus, whom God used to conquer Babylon. Compare Isa 44:28; 45:1. 51:24 Or *Chaldea;* also in 51:35. 51:34 Hebrew *Nebuchadrezzar,* a variant spelling of Nebuchadnezzar.

51:36 In response to the people's request (51:35), the Lord would prosecute Babylon for its brutal sins, acting as Jerusalem's lawyer.

I will make them drink until they fall asleep,
and they will never wake up again,"
says the LORD.

⁴⁰ "I will bring them down
like lambs to the slaughter,
like rams and goats to be sacrificed.

⁴¹ "How Babylon* is fallen—
great Babylon, praised throughout
the earth!
Now she has become an object of horror
among the nations.

⁴² The sea has risen over Babylon;
she is covered by its crashing waves.

⁴³ Her cities now lie in ruins;
she is a dry wasteland
where no one lives or even passes by.

⁴⁴ And I will punish Bel, the god of Babylon,
and make him vomit up all he has eaten.
The nations will no longer come and worship
him.
The wall of Babylon has fallen!

A Message for the Exiles

⁴⁵ "Come out, my people, flee from Babylon.
Save yourselves! Run from the LORD's fierce
anger.

⁴⁶ But do not panic; don't be afraid
when you hear the first rumor of
approaching forces.
For rumors will keep coming year by year.
Violence will erupt in the land
as the leaders fight against each other.

⁴⁷ For the time is surely coming
when I will punish this great city and all her
idols.
Her whole land will be disgraced,
and her dead will lie in the streets.

⁴⁸ Then the heavens and earth will rejoice,
for out of the north will come destroying
armies
against Babylon," says the LORD.

⁴⁹ "Just as Babylon killed the people of Israel
and others throughout the world,
so must her people be killed.

⁵⁰ Get out, all you who have escaped the sword!
Do not stand and watch—flee while you can!
Remember the LORD, though you are in
a far-off land,
and think about your home in Jerusalem."

⁵¹ "We are ashamed," the people say.
"We are insulted and disgraced
because the LORD's Temple
has been defiled by foreigners."

⁵² "Yes," says the LORD, "but the time is coming
when I will destroy Babylon's idols.
The groans of her wounded people
will be heard throughout the land.

⁵³ Though Babylon reaches as high as
the heavens
and makes her fortifications incredibly
strong,
I will still send enemies to plunder her.
I, the LORD, have spoken!

Babylon's Complete Destruction

⁵⁴ "Listen! Hear the cry of Babylon,
the sound of great destruction from the land
of the Babylonians.

⁵⁵ For the LORD is destroying Babylon.
He will silence her loud voice.
Waves of enemies pound against her;
the noise of battle rings through the city.

⁵⁶ Destroying armies come against Babylon.
Her mighty men are captured,
and their weapons break in their hands.
For the LORD is a God who gives just
punishment;
he always repays in full.

⁵⁷ I will make her officials and wise men drunk,
along with her captains, officers, and
warriors.
They will fall asleep
and never wake up again!"
says the King, whose name is
the LORD of Heaven's Armies.

⁵⁸ This is what the LORD of Heaven's Armies says:
"The thick walls of Babylon will be leveled to the
ground,
and her massive gates will be burned.
The builders from many lands have worked in
vain,
for their work will be destroyed by fire!"

Jeremiah's Message Sent to Babylon

⁵⁹The prophet Jeremiah gave this message to Seraiah son of Neriah and grandson of Mahseiah, a staff officer, when Seraiah went to Babylon with King Zedekiah of Judah. This was during the fourth year of Zedekiah's reign.* ⁶⁰Jeremiah had recorded on a scroll all the terrible disasters that would soon come upon Babylon—all the words written here. ⁶¹He said to Seraiah, "When you get to Babylon, read aloud everything on this scroll. ⁶²Then say, 'LORD, you have said that you will destroy Babylon so that neither people nor animals will remain here. She will lie empty and abandoned forever.' ⁶³When you have finished reading the scroll, tie it to a stone and throw it into the Euphrates River. ⁶⁴Then say, 'In this same way Babylon and her people will sink, never again to rise, because of the disasters I will bring upon her.'"

This is the end of Jeremiah's messages.

51:41 Hebrew *Sheshach*, a code name for Babylon.   51:59 The fourth year of Zedekiah's reign was 593 B.C.

The Fall of Jerusalem

52 Zedekiah was twenty-one years old when he became king, and he reigned in Jerusalem eleven years. His mother was Hamutal, the daughter of Jeremiah from Libnah. ²But Zedekiah did what was evil in the LORD's sight, just as Jehoiakim had done. ³These things happened because of the LORD's anger against the people of Jerusalem and Judah, until he finally banished them from his presence and sent them into exile.

Zedekiah rebelled against the king of Babylon. ⁴So on January 15,* during the ninth year of Zedekiah's reign, King Nebuchadnezzar* of Babylon led his entire army against Jerusalem. They surrounded the city and built siege ramps against its walls. ⁵Jerusalem was kept under siege until the eleventh year of King Zedekiah's reign.

⁶By July 18 in the eleventh year of Zedekiah's reign,* the famine in the city had become very severe, and the last of the food was entirely gone. ⁷Then a section of the city wall was broken down, and all the soldiers fled. Since the city was surrounded by the Babylonians,* they waited for nightfall. Then they slipped through the gate between the two walls behind the king's garden and headed toward the Jordan Valley.*

⁸But the Babylonian troops chased King Zedekiah and overtook him on the plains of Jericho, for his men had all deserted him and scattered. ⁹They captured the king and took him to the king of Babylon at Riblah in the land of Hamath. There the king of Babylon pronounced judgment upon Zedekiah. ¹⁰The king of Babylon made Zedekiah watch as he slaughtered his sons. He also slaughtered all the officials of Judah at Riblah. ¹¹Then he gouged out Zedekiah's eyes and bound him in bronze chains, and the king of Babylon led him away to Babylon. Zedekiah remained there in prison until the day of his death.

The Temple Destroyed

¹²On August 17 of that year,* which was the nineteenth year of King Nebuchadnezzar's reign, Nebuzaradan, the captain of the guard and an official of the Babylonian king, arrived in Jerusalem. ¹³He burned down the Temple of the LORD, the royal palace, and all the houses of Jerusalem. He destroyed all the important buildings* in the city. ¹⁴Then he supervised the entire Babylonian* army as they tore down the walls of Jerusalem on every side. ¹⁵Then Nebuzaradan, the captain of the guard, took as exiles some of the poorest of the people, the rest of the people who remained in the city, the defectors who had declared their allegiance to the king of Babylon, and the rest of the craftsmen. ¹⁶But Nebuzaradan allowed some of the poorest people to stay behind to care for the vineyards and fields.

¹⁷The Babylonians broke up the bronze pillars in front of the LORD's Temple, the bronze water carts, and the great bronze basin called the Sea, and they carried all the bronze away to Babylon. ¹⁸They also took all the ash buckets, shovels, lamp snuffers, basins, dishes, and all the other bronze articles used for making sacrifices at the Temple. ¹⁹The captain of the guard also took the small bowls, incense burners, basins, pots, lampstands, ladles, bowls used for liquid offerings, and all the other articles made of pure gold or silver.

²⁰The weight of the bronze from the two pillars, the Sea with the twelve bronze oxen beneath it, and the water carts was too great to be measured. These things had been made for the LORD's Temple in the days of King Solomon. ²¹Each of the pillars was 27 feet tall and 18 feet in circumference.* They were hollow, with walls 3 inches thick.* ²²The bronze capital on top of each pillar was 7½ feet* high and was decorated with a network of bronze pomegranates all the way around. ²³There were 96 pomegranates on the sides, and a total of 100 pomegranates on the network around the top.

²⁴Nebuzaradan, the captain of the guard, took with him as prisoners Seraiah the high priest, Zephaniah the priest of the second rank, and the three chief gatekeepers. ²⁵And from among the people still hiding in the city, he took an officer who had been in charge of the Judean army; seven of the king's personal advisers; the army commander's chief secretary, who was in charge of recruitment; and sixty other citizens. ²⁶Nebuzaradan, the captain of the guard, took them all to the king of Babylon at Riblah. ²⁷And there at Riblah, in the land of Hamath, the king of Babylon had them all put to death. So the people of Judah were sent into exile from their land.

²⁸The number of captives taken to Babylon in the seventh year of Nebuchadnezzar's reign* was 3,023. ²⁹Then in Nebuchadnezzar's eighteenth year* he took 832 more. ³⁰In Nebuchadnezzar's

---

52:4a Hebrew *on the tenth day of the tenth month,* of the ancient Hebrew lunar calendar. A number of events in Jeremiah can be cross-checked with dates in surviving Babylonian records and related accurately to our modern calendar. This day was January 15, 588 B.C. **52:4b** Hebrew *Nebuchadrezzar,* a variant spelling of Nebuchadnezzar; also in 52:12, 28, 29, 30. **52:6** Hebrew *By the ninth day of the fourth month* [in the eleventh year of Zedekiah's reign]. This day was July 18, 586 B.C.; also see note on 52:4a. **52:7a** Or *the Chaldeans;* similarly in 52:8, 17. **52:7b** Hebrew *the Arabah.* **52:12** Hebrew *On the tenth day of the fifth month,* of the ancient Hebrew lunar calendar. This day was August 17, 586 B.C.; also see note on 52:4a. **52:13** Or *destroyed the houses of all the important people.* **52:14** Or *Chaldean.* **52:21a** Hebrew *18 cubits* [8.3 meters] *tall and 12 cubits* [5.5 meters] *in circumference.* **52:21b** Hebrew *4 fingers thick* [8 centimeters]. **52:22** Hebrew *5 cubits* [2.3 meters]. **52:28** This exile in the seventh year of Nebuchadnezzar's reign occurred in 597 B.C. **52:29** This exile in the eighteenth year of Nebuchadnezzar's reign occurred in 586 B.C.

twenty-third year* he sent Nebuzaradan, the captain of the guard, who took 745 more—a total of 4,600 captives in all.

Hope for Israel's Royal Line

³¹In the thirty-seventh year of the exile of King Jehoiachin of Judah, Evil-merodach ascended to the Babylonian throne. He was kind to* Jehoiachin and released him from prison on March 31 of that year.* ³²He spoke kindly to Jehoiachin and gave him a higher place than all the other exiled kings in Babylon. ³³He supplied Jehoiachin with new clothes to replace his prison garb and allowed him to dine in the king's presence for the rest of his life. ³⁴So the Babylonian king gave him a regular food allowance as long as he lived. This continued until the day of his death.

52:30 This exile in the twenty-third year of Nebuchadnezzar's reign occurred in 581 B.C. **52:31a** Hebrew *He raised the head of.* **52:31b** Hebrew *on the twenty-fifth day of the twelfth month,* of the ancient Hebrew lunar calendar. This day was March 31, 561 B.C.; also see note on 52:4a.

52:31-34 This paragraph repeats 2 Kings 25:27-30 and supplies the fulfillment of Jeremiah's prediction of Jehoiachin's future (see Jeremiah 22:24-30). Evil-merodach reigned in Babylon from 561 to 560 BC. Several inscriptions found in a basement near Babylon's Ishtar Gate tell of rations of food provided to Jehoiachin and his family.

Lamentations

WHAT DO WE LEARN ABOUT GOD'S MISSION AND OURS? Loss can lead us to trust God. Even if not in this life, God ultimately makes all things right.

WHO WROTE IT? We know that Jeremiah wrote laments (2 Chronicles 35:25), and that he witnessed the destruction of Jerusalem described in the book of Lamentations. He may be the author, but we do not know for certain because no author is named.

WHEN DID IT HAPPEN? The author laments the destruction of Jerusalem in 586 BC by the Babylonians. These laments were likely composed around the same time.

HOW IS IT ORGANIZED?

1: Destruction of Judah and Jerusalem
2: God's anger at the people's sin
3: Trusting in God's love, despite chaos
4: Jerusalem's past glory and present desolation
5: A prayer for God's forgiveness and restoration

FEATURE HIGHLIGHTS

+ *Why Do Bad Things Happen to Innocent People?* (963)
+ *Dare to Hope* (966)
+ *Is God's Judgment Just?* (968)

Words to Remember are highlighted throughout this book

HOW LONG DOES IT TAKE TO READ?

:15 | :30 | 1:00 | 1:30 | 2:00 | 2:30 | 3:00 | 3:30

Timeline

BC	
627	JEREMIAH BECOMES A PROPHET TO JUDAH
605	DANIEL TAKEN CAPTIVE TO BABYLON
597	ZEDEKIAH, HAMUTAL'S SON, BECOMES KING OF JUDAH
593	EZEKIEL BECOMES A PROPHET TO THE EXILES
586	NEBUCHADNEZZAR CAPTURES JERUSALEM
539	PERSIA OVERTHROWS BABYLON
538	CYRUS DECREES THAT THE JEWS CAN RETURN TO JUDAH AND REBUILD THE TEMPLE

Sorrow in Jerusalem

1 *Jerusalem, once so full of people,
  is now deserted.
She who was once great among the nations
  now sits alone like a widow.
Once the queen of all the earth,
  she is now a slave.

2 She sobs through the night;
  tears stream down her cheeks.
Among all her lovers,
  there is no one left to comfort her.
All her friends have betrayed her
  and become her enemies.

3 Judah has been led away into captivity,
  oppressed with cruel slavery.
She lives among foreign nations
  and has no place of rest.
Her enemies have chased her down,
  and she has nowhere to turn.

4 The roads to Jerusalem* are in mourning,
  for crowds no longer come to celebrate the festivals.
The city gates are silent,
  her priests groan,
her young women are crying—
  how bitter is her fate!

5 Her oppressors have become her masters,
  and her enemies prosper,
for the LORD has punished Jerusalem
  for her many sins.
Her children have been captured
  and taken away to distant lands.

6 All the majesty of beautiful Jerusalem*
  has been stripped away.
Her princes are like starving deer
  searching for pasture.
They are too weak to run
  from the pursuing enemy.

7 In the midst of her sadness and wandering,
  Jerusalem remembers her ancient splendor.
But now she has fallen to her enemy,
  and there is no one to help her.
Her enemy struck her down
  and laughed as she fell.

8 Jerusalem has sinned greatly,
  so she has been tossed away like a filthy rag.
All who once honored her now despise her,
  for they have seen her stripped naked and humiliated.
All she can do is groan
  and hide her face.

9 She defiled herself with immorality
  and gave no thought to her future.
Now she lies in the gutter
  with no one to lift her out.
"LORD, see my misery," she cries.
  "The enemy has triumphed."

10 The enemy has plundered her completely,
  taking every precious thing she owns.
She has seen foreigners violate her sacred Temple,
  the place the LORD had forbidden them to enter.

11 Her people groan as they search for bread.
  They have sold their treasures for food to stay alive.
"O LORD, look," she mourns,
  "and see how I am despised.

12 "Does it mean nothing to you, all you who pass by?
  Look around and see if there is any suffering like mine,
which the LORD brought on me
  when he erupted in fierce anger.

13 "He has sent fire from heaven that burns in my bones.
  He has placed a trap in my path and turned me back.

---

1 Each of the first four chapters of this book is an acrostic, laid out in the order of the Hebrew alphabet. The first word of each verse begins with a successive Hebrew letter. Chapters 1, 2, and 4 have one verse for each of the 22 Hebrew letters. Chapter 3 contains 22 stanzas of three verses each. Though chapter 5 has 22 verses, it is not an acrostic. **1:4** Hebrew *Zion;* also in 1:17. **1:6** Hebrew *of the daughter of Zion.*

1:1-22 Anyone who heard the book of Lamentations read aloud in ancient Israel would have recognized its mournful cadence. Funeral songs (*qinah* in Hebrew) had special rhythm—three beats, followed by two beats—and most of Lamentations is written this way. This type of dirge would have been chanted by professional mourners in ancient Israel—who were women. This association may be why Lamentations employs female voices and female personification throughout the poems.
1:1 Fallen Jerusalem is pictured here as a woman who was destitute because her family had died. In ancient Israel, the loss of one's husband was not only a personal tragedy: Women who didn't have a male family member to provide for them economically would struggle to survive. Childlessness was a source of shame (Genesis 30:1; 1 Samuel 1:1-18; Luke 1:7, 25) and a cause for financial worry, and was also considered a curse (Hosea 9:11-14). We should not draw the same conclusion, however, about infertility today. When God allowed a woman to experience infertility, it was for a particular purpose, explained in the Bible. He acted to judge (Hosea 9:11-14), to bless (Luke 1:25), or to glorify himself through a miraculous conception, as in Sarah's case (Genesis 18:9-15). Women who experience infertility today deserve our care and compassion. We should not interpret their painful situation as God's judgment.

He has left me devastated,
    racked with sickness all day long.

¹⁴ "He wove my sins into ropes
    to hitch me to a yoke of captivity.
The Lord sapped my strength and turned me
    over to my enemies;
    I am helpless in their hands.

¹⁵ "The Lord has treated my mighty men
    with contempt.
At his command a great army has come
    to crush my young warriors.
The Lord has trampled his beloved city*
    like grapes are trampled in a winepress.

¹⁶ "For all these things I weep;
    tears flow down my cheeks.
No one is here to comfort me;
    any who might encourage me are far away.
My children have no future,
    for the enemy has conquered us."

¹⁷ Jerusalem reaches out for help,
    but no one comforts her.
Regarding his people Israel,*
    the Lord has said,
"Let their neighbors be their enemies!
    Let them be thrown away like a filthy rag!"

¹⁸ "The Lord is right," Jerusalem says,
    "for I rebelled against him.
Listen, people everywhere;
    look upon my anguish and despair,
for my sons and daughters
    have been taken captive to distant lands.

¹⁹ "I begged my allies for help,
    but they betrayed me.
My priests and leaders
    starved to death in the city,
even as they searched for food
    to save their lives.

1:15 Hebrew *the virgin daughter of Judah.* **1:17** Hebrew *Jacob.* The names "Jacob" and "Israel" are often interchanged throughout the Old Testament, referring sometimes to the individual patriarch and sometimes to the nation.

1:12-14 The description of the Lord in these verses may seem incongruous with his love. By this point, God had extended his grace to the people of Israel repeatedly for centuries. He had redeemed them from slavery and led them through the wilderness to the Promised Land. God had chosen them for a special relationship with him (Exodus 19:5-6) and promised to bless them if they obeyed. God had established them in their land and had sent prophets to call them back when they rebelled. Despite God's faithfulness, Israel was defiant in sin. The punishment was the just judgment of a holy God. Indeed, this is what all sin deserves (Romans 6:23). God's mercy, however, was not exhausted by Israel's infidelity. Through judgment, God would purify his people and restore them to their homeland and their relationship with him.

Perspective

Why do bad things happen to innocent people?

SCRIPTURE CONNECTION: LAMENTATIONS 2:1-22

Jerusalem suffered because of the Israelites' unfaithfulness to their God, Yahweh, and the covenant agreement he had made with them (Exodus 19:1–24:18). Reading through Israel's history, we can't avoid the recurring themes of rebellion and sin. However, many who suffered sin's consequences—for example, children and babies (Lamentations 2:11-12)—were not the perpetrators.

Why would God allow innocent people to suffer? It seems so unjust, but this is where we see sin's destructive nature. The effects of sin are not always isolated to the individuals and their choices. It tends to affect families and communities, too. For example, adultery is not a sin that affects just one marriage: It reverberates through the community that surrounds this covenant union. The brokenness and pain touch the lives of many, even though they weren't directly responsible for the breakup.

The same was true for the people of Jerusalem. The consequences of their unfaithfulness reverberated into the lives of everyone around them, young and old.

VIEWPOINTS

HERS: *The personified city of Jerusalem weeps because she sees the havoc that her sins (1:8) have wreaked upon her community. Nevertheless, she cries out, asking God to show compassion and relent.*
MINE: *"Like Jerusalem, I recognize that my sins affect more than my individual life. I am part of a larger community, and my choices affect those around me. However, because of Christ, I can pray for forgiveness and ask God to bring about peace."*
YOURS: *Are there sins in your life that need to be addressed? Sin is destructive, but Jesus died to provide a way of restoration.*

MAY YOUNG, MDiv, PhD, is an associate professor of biblical studies at Taylor University, with a passion for discipleship, teaching, and writing.

20 "LORD, see my anguish!
My heart is broken
and my soul despairs,
for I have rebelled against you.
In the streets the sword kills,
and at home there is only death.

21 "Others heard my groans,
but no one turned to comfort me.
When my enemies heard about my troubles,
they were happy to see what you had done.
Oh, bring the day you promised,
when they will suffer as I have suffered.

22 "Look at all their evil deeds, LORD.
Punish them,
as you have punished me
for all my sins.
My groans are many,
and I am sick at heart."

God's Anger at Sin

2 The Lord in his anger
has cast a dark shadow over beautiful Jerusalem.*
The fairest of Israel's cities lies in the dust,
thrown down from the heights of heaven.
In his day of great anger,
the Lord has shown no mercy even to his Temple.*

2 Without mercy the Lord has destroyed
every home in Israel.*
In his anger he has broken down
the fortress walls of beautiful Jerusalem.*
He has brought them to the ground,
dishonoring the kingdom and its rulers.

3 All the strength of Israel
vanishes beneath his fierce anger.
The Lord has withdrawn his protection
as the enemy attacks.
He consumes the whole land of Israel
like a raging fire.

4 He bends his bow against his people,
as though he were their enemy.
His strength is used against them
to kill their finest youth.
His fury is poured out like fire
on beautiful Jerusalem.*

5 Yes, the Lord has vanquished Israel
like an enemy.
He has destroyed her palaces
and demolished her fortresses.
He has brought unending sorrow and tears
upon beautiful Jerusalem.

6 He has broken down his Temple
as though it were merely a garden shelter.
The LORD has blotted out all memory
of the holy festivals and Sabbath days.
Kings and priests fall together
before his fierce anger.

7 The Lord has rejected his own altar;
he despises his own sanctuary.
He has given Jerusalem's palaces
to her enemies.
They shout in the LORD's Temple
as though it were a day of celebration.

8 The LORD was determined
to destroy the walls of beautiful Jerusalem.
He made careful plans for their destruction,
then did what he had planned.
Therefore, the ramparts and walls
have fallen down before him.

9 Jerusalem's gates have sunk into the ground.
He has smashed their locks and bars.
Her kings and princes have been exiled to distant lands;
her law has ceased to exist.
Her prophets receive
no more visions from the LORD.

10 The leaders of beautiful Jerusalem
sit on the ground in silence.
They are clothed in burlap
and throw dust on their heads.
The young women of Jerusalem
hang their heads in shame.

11 I have cried until the tears no longer come;
my heart is broken.
My spirit is poured out in agony
as I see the desperate plight of my people.
Little children and tiny babies
are fainting and dying in the streets.

12 They cry out to their mothers,
"We need food and drink!"
Their lives ebb away in the streets
like the life of a warrior wounded in battle.
They gasp for life
as they collapse in their mothers' arms.

2:1a Hebrew *the daughter of Zion;* also in 2:8, 10, 18. 2:1b Hebrew *his footstool.* 2:2a Hebrew *Jacob;* also in 2:3b. See note on 1:17. 2:2b Hebrew *the daughter of Judah;* also in 2:5. 2:4 Hebrew *on the tent of the daughter of Zion.*

2:11-12 The Babylonian siege of Jerusalem resulted in severe food shortages. The suffering and death of Jerusalem's children were horrifying consequences of Israel's rebellion against God.

¹³ What can I say about you?
   Who has ever seen such sorrow?
O daughter of Jerusalem,
   to what can I compare your anguish?
O virgin daughter of Zion,
   how can I comfort you?
For your wound is as deep as the sea.
   Who can heal you?

¹⁴ Your prophets have said
   so many foolish things, false to the core.
They did not save you from exile
   by pointing out your sins.
Instead, they painted false pictures,
   filling you with false hope.

¹⁵ All who pass by jeer at you.
   They scoff and insult beautiful Jerusalem,*
      saying,
"Is this the city called 'Most Beautiful in All the
      World'
   and 'Joy of All the Earth'?"

¹⁶ All your enemies mock you.
   They scoff and snarl and say,
"We have destroyed her at last!
   We have long waited for this day,
   and it is finally here!"

¹⁷ But it is the LORD who did just as he planned.
   He has fulfilled the promises of disaster
      he made long ago.
He has destroyed Jerusalem without mercy.
   He has caused her enemies to gloat over her
   and has given them power over her.

¹⁸ Cry aloud* before the Lord,
   O walls of beautiful Jerusalem!
Let your tears flow like a river
   day and night.
Give yourselves no rest;
   give your eyes no relief.

¹⁹ Rise during the night and cry out.
   Pour out your hearts like water to
      the Lord.
Lift up your hands to him in prayer,
   pleading for your children,
for in every street
   they are faint with hunger.

²⁰ "O LORD, think about this!
   Should you treat your own people this way?
Should mothers eat their own children,
   those they once bounced on their knees?
Should priests and prophets be killed
   within the Lord's Temple?

²¹ "See them lying in the streets—
   young and old,
   boys and girls,
   killed by the swords of the enemy.
You have killed them in your anger,
   slaughtering them without mercy.

²² "You have invited terrors from all around,
   as though you were calling them to a day of
      feasting.
In the day of the LORD's anger,
   no one has escaped or survived.
The enemy has killed all the children
   whom I carried and raised."

Hope in the LORD's Faithfulness

3 I am the one who has seen the afflictions
   that come from the rod of the LORD's anger.
² He has led me into darkness,
   shutting out all light.
³ He has turned his hand against me
   again and again, all day long.
⁴ He has made my skin and flesh grow old.
   He has broken my bones.
⁵ He has besieged and surrounded me
   with anguish and distress.
⁶ He has buried me in a dark place,
   like those long dead.
⁷ He has walled me in, and I cannot escape.
   He has bound me in heavy chains.
⁸ And though I cry and shout,
   he has shut out my prayers.
⁹ He has blocked my way with a high stone wall;
   he has made my road crooked.
¹⁰ He has hidden like a bear or a lion,
   waiting to attack me.
¹¹ He has dragged me off the path and torn me
      in pieces,
   leaving me helpless and devastated.
¹² He has drawn his bow
   and made me the target for his arrows.
¹³ He shot his arrows
   deep into my heart.

2:15 Hebrew *the daughter of Jerusalem.* 2:18 Hebrew *Their heart cried.*

2:17 God's word from "long ago" refers to the consequences for breaking the covenant listed in Leviticus 26:14-39 and Deuteronomy 28:15-68. Long before the people of Israel and Judah experienced God's judgment through the Assyrians and the Babylonians, they had been warned about what would happen if they broke their covenant with God (read more about God's just judgment on page 968).

2:20 "Should mothers eat their own children?" The answer to this shocking question is unequivocally *no.* With little to no access to food in Jerusalem during the Babylonian siege, people resorted to the unthinkable: cannibalism. See also Leviticus 26:26-29; Deuteronomy 28:53-57; Jeremiah 19:9; Ezekiel 5:10; Lamentations 4:10.

Dare to Hope

SCRIPTURE CONNECTION: LAMENTATIONS 3:21-23

At some point, we lose someone close to us—a parent, a spouse, a child, a dear friend. Whether it comes after an accident, a long illness, or a life well lived, we are left feeling overwhelmed. The same happens after natural disasters—fires, tornados, hurricanes, earthquakes—or personal hardship, like an unexpected job loss or financial downturn.

Maybe we feel guilt, injustice, or just plain emptiness. As daughters, sisters, wives, friends, or mothers, we are often caught in grief that weighs heavily on our hearts. Our initial response may be, "God, this isn't fair. What did I do to deserve this?"

You are not alone. Jeremiah laments Jerusalem's fall and judgment. After describing the pain, destruction, poverty, and brutality, he cries out to God, "How much longer? The burden is too heavy. We cannot bear it."

But his conclusion, where he draws comfort, is to acknowledge God's steadfast love, mercy, and faithfulness. "Yet I still dare to hope.... The faithful love of the LORD never ends! His mercies never cease. Great is his faithfulness" (3:21-23).

Like Jeremiah, when we face devastation, we can still dare to hope. We can call on God's faithful love, mercy, and faithfulness.

> We are not alone. We can call on the Lord's faithful love.

IMAGINE

When have you found yourself in that dark hole, crying out to God for justice and mercy?

Where did God meet you? How were you able to draw comfort from his great love?

"When I lost my husband, when I miscarried our second child, I found myself in dark places. It was a process to trust God and walk in his steadfast love. But God met me again and again until I found comfort."

ELIZABETH GLANVILLE, PhD, is retired faculty from Fuller Theological Seminary, School of Mission and Theology. She is an international teacher on missions and leadership and chaplain for a local police department and her retirement community.

¹⁴ My own people laugh at me.
    All day long they sing their mocking songs.
¹⁵ He has filled me with bitterness
    and given me a bitter cup of sorrow to drink.
¹⁶ He has made me chew on gravel.
    He has rolled me in the dust.
¹⁷ Peace has been stripped away,
    and I have forgotten what prosperity is.
¹⁸ I cry out, "My splendor is gone!
    Everything I had hoped for from the Lord
        is lost!"
¹⁹ The thought of my suffering and homelessness
    is bitter beyond words.*
²⁰ I will never forget this awful time,
    as I grieve over my loss.
²¹ Yet I still dare to hope
    when I remember this:
²² The faithful love of the Lord never ends!*
    His mercies never cease.
²³ Great is his faithfulness;
    his mercies begin afresh each morning.
²⁴ I say to myself, "The Lord is my inheritance;
    therefore, I will hope in him!"
²⁵ The Lord is good to those who depend on him,
    to those who search for him.
²⁶ So it is good to wait quietly
    for salvation from the Lord.
²⁷ And it is good for people to submit at an
        early age
    to the yoke of his discipline:
²⁸ Let them sit alone in silence
    beneath the Lord's demands.
²⁹ Let them lie face down in the dust,
    for there may be hope at last.
³⁰ Let them turn the other cheek to those who
        strike them
    and accept the insults of their enemies.
³¹ For no one is abandoned
    by the Lord forever.
³² Though he brings grief, he also shows
        compassion
    because of the greatness of his
        unfailing love.
³³ For he does not enjoy hurting people
    or causing them sorrow.
³⁴ If people crush underfoot
    all the prisoners of the land,
³⁵ if they deprive others of their rights
    in defiance of the Most High,
³⁶ if they twist justice in the courts—
    doesn't the Lord see all these things?
³⁷ Who can command things to happen
    without the Lord's permission?
³⁸ Does not the Most High
    send both calamity and good?
³⁹ Then why should we, mere humans, complain
    when we are punished for our sins?
⁴⁰ Instead, let us test and examine our ways.
    Let us turn back to the Lord.
⁴¹ Let us lift our hearts and hands
    to God in heaven and say,
⁴² "We have sinned and rebelled,
    and you have not forgiven us.
⁴³ "You have engulfed us with your anger, chased
        us down,
    and slaughtered us without mercy.
⁴⁴ You have hidden yourself in a cloud
    so our prayers cannot reach you.
⁴⁵ You have discarded us as refuse and garbage
    among the nations.
⁴⁶ "All our enemies
    have spoken out against us.
⁴⁷ We are filled with fear,
    for we are trapped, devastated, and ruined."
⁴⁸ Tears stream from my eyes
    because of the destruction of my people!
⁴⁹ My tears flow endlessly;
    they will not stop
⁵⁰ until the Lord looks down
    from heaven and sees.
⁵¹ My heart is breaking
    over the fate of all the women of Jerusalem.
⁵² My enemies, whom I have never harmed,
    hunted me down like a bird.
⁵³ They threw me into a pit
    and dropped stones on me.

3:19 Or *is wormwood and gall.* 3:22 As in Syriac version; Hebrew reads *of the Lord keeps us from destruction.*

3:22-33 Our circumstances do not determine God's character. Sometimes, God allows us to experience hardship in order to bring about repentance and to develop a deeper trust in him. Alternatively, our suffering may result from someone else's failure or simply because we live in a world tainted by sin. Whatever the reason, this profound proclamation of God's unchanging character is a source of tremendous comfort for us when we are in distress.

3:22 The word translated "faithful love" here is the Hebrew word *khesed*. It refers to God's special love for his people based on their covenant relationship (Exodus 19:3-6). The full meaning of the word encompasses kindness, permanence, consistency, mercy, faithfulness, and trustworthiness.

3:33 God rightly punished Israel's rebellion, but he took no delight in their suffering. God is not cruel, but he is holy. God cannot cohabitate with evil. Because God wants to be with his people, he purges them of sin so that they can be in a right relationship with him. God has now provided forgiveness from sin and freedom from death through his Son, Jesus Christ (Romans 3:21-26), for all who repent and believe (Mark 1:15; Acts 3:19).

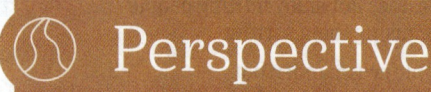

Perspective

Is God's judgment just?

SCRIPTURE CONNECTION: LAMENTATIONS 4:1-10

These events are difficult for most of us to imagine. However, Israel's repeated and flagrant rebellion against God required that he respond in judgment. The Lord is indeed gracious and merciful, but he is also *holy*. Sin is contrary to his nature and to God's intent for his people.

Neither Israel nor we were created for sin and rebellion against God—*it is an unnatural state*. Israel had been warned repeatedly of idolatry's consequences (Leviticus 26:14-39; Deuteronomy 28:15-68; compare Jeremiah 11:1-17). However, despite God's repeated efforts to woo his people, Israel served other gods—gods that could not save them. The people also formed alliances with foreign nations who would use and betray them. God's response is just (Romans 6:23). It only seems extreme to us, perhaps, because our understanding of God's holiness is far too small.

The good news, however, is that God is indeed merciful, and he is ready to show compassion (Lamentations 3:32). Through judgment, God would cleanse his people to restore their relationship with him (Jeremiah 31:31-34; Ezekiel 36:24-28). God would enable them, through his Spirit, to be holy (Luke 22:20; Hebrews 8:8-13; 12:24).

VIEWPOINTS

THEIRS: *Lamentations is a beautiful yet heart-wrenching example of confession and repentance. The author does not downplay Israel's guilt but confesses it in all its ugliness and asks God to forgive.*
MINE: *"God is serious about sin and he will judge against it. Yet he is full of mercy and grace. He is ready to forgive us if we turn from sin and follow him."*
OURS: *Forgiveness and restoration might have seemed far off to those in exile, but in Christ it is a reality. Regardless of our sin, God is ready and waiting to forgive us and restore us to himself.*

CATHERINE L. McDOWELL, PhD, is associate professor of Old Testament at Gordon-Conwell Theological Seminary. She has authored several books and articles on Bible backgrounds, Genesis, Isaiah, and Biblical Hebrew.

---

⁵⁴ The water rose over my head,
   and I cried out, "This is the end!"
⁵⁵ But I called on your name, LORD,
   from deep within the pit.
⁵⁶ You heard me when I cried, "Listen to my pleading!
   Hear my cry for help!"
⁵⁷ Yes, you came when I called;
   you told me, "Do not fear."

⁵⁸ Lord, you have come to my defense;
   you have redeemed my life.
⁵⁹ You have seen the wrong they have done to me, LORD.
   Be my judge, and prove me right.
⁶⁰ You have seen the vengeful plots
   my enemies have laid against me.

⁶¹ LORD, you have heard the vile names they call me.
   You know all about the plans they have made.
⁶² My enemies whisper and mutter
   as they plot against me all day long.
⁶³ Look at them! Whether they sit or stand,
   I am the object of their mocking songs.

⁶⁴ Pay them back, LORD,
   for all the evil they have done.
⁶⁵ Give them hard and stubborn hearts,
   and then let your curse fall on them!
⁶⁶ Chase them down in your anger,
   destroying them beneath the LORD's heavens.

God's Anger Satisfied

4 How the gold has lost its luster!
   Even the finest gold has become dull.
The sacred gemstones
   lie scattered in the streets!

² See how the precious children of Jerusalem,*
   worth their weight in fine gold,
are now treated like pots of clay
   made by a common potter.

³ Even the jackals feed their young,
   but not my people Israel.
They ignore their children's cries,
   like ostriches in the desert.

4:2 Hebrew *precious sons of Zion.*

3:64-66 Shouldn't the author forgive his enemies? Punishment for injustice is good and right. There is a time to forgive, but the Bible often links forgiveness with repentance. Israel's enemies showed only brute force and cruelty. There was no evidence of regret. Note that the author calls on *God* to avenge. He does not take it upon himself. God is the only one who can bring about true justice. We, too, can take our vengeful feelings to God in prayer. We can trust that ultimately, he will set injustice right. See also Psalm 137:8-9.

⁴ The parched tongues of their little ones
  stick to the roofs of their mouths in thirst.
The children cry for bread,
  but no one has any to give them.

⁵ The people who once ate the richest foods
  now beg in the streets for anything they
    can get.
Those who once wore the finest clothes
  now search the garbage dumps for food.

⁶ The guilt* of my people
  is greater than that of Sodom,
where utter disaster struck in a moment
  and no hand offered help.

⁷ Our princes once glowed with health—
  brighter than snow, whiter than milk.
Their faces were as ruddy as rubies,
  their appearance like fine jewels.*

⁸ But now their faces are blacker than soot.
  No one recognizes them in the streets.
Their skin sticks to their bones;
  it is as dry and hard as wood.

⁹ Those killed by the sword are better off
  than those who die of hunger.
Starving, they waste away
  for lack of food from the fields.

¹⁰ Tenderhearted women
  have cooked their own children.
They have eaten them
  to survive the siege.

¹¹ But now the anger of the LORD is satisfied.
  His fierce anger has been poured out.
He started a fire in Jerusalem*
  that burned the city to its foundations.

¹² Not a king in all the earth—
  no one in all the world—
would have believed that an enemy
  could march through the gates of Jerusalem.

¹³ Yet it happened because of the sins of her
    prophets
  and the sins of her priests,
who defiled the city
  by shedding innocent blood.

¹⁴ They wandered blindly
  through the streets,
so defiled by blood
  that no one dared touch them.

¹⁵ "Get away!" the people shouted at them.
  "You're defiled! Don't touch us!"
So they fled to distant lands
  and wandered among foreign nations,
  but none would let them stay.

¹⁶ The LORD himself has scattered them,
  and he no longer helps them.
People show no respect for the priests
  and no longer honor the leaders.

¹⁷ We looked in vain for our allies
  to come and save us,
but we were looking to nations
  that could not help us.

¹⁸ We couldn't go into the streets
  without danger to our lives.
Our end was near; our days were numbered.
  We were doomed!

¹⁹ Our enemies were swifter than eagles in flight.
  If we fled to the mountains, they found us.
If we hid in the wilderness,
  they were waiting for us there.

²⁰ Our king—the LORD's anointed, the very life of
    our nation—
  was caught in their snares.
We had thought that his shadow
  would protect us against any nation on earth!

²¹ Are you rejoicing in the land of Uz,
  O people of Edom?
But you, too, must drink from the cup of the
    LORD's anger.
  You, too, will be stripped naked in your
    drunkenness.

²² O beautiful Jerusalem,* your punishment
    will end;
  you will soon return from exile.
But Edom, your punishment is just beginning;
  soon your many sins will be exposed.

Prayer for Restoration

5 LORD, remember what has happened to us.
  See how we have been disgraced!
² Our inheritance has been turned over to strangers,
  our homes to foreigners.

4:6 Or *punishment.* 4:7 Hebrew *like lapis lazuli.* 4:11 Hebrew *in Zion.* 4:22 Hebrew *O daughter of Zion.*

4:7 Given that these men were Semitic, the description of their skin as bright and white refers to a healthy shine rather than to their skin tone. See Psalm 104:15 where "olive oil to soothe their skin" can also be translated more literally, "olive oil to make their face shine." A shining face was a sign of vitality and was considered a blessing from the Lord.
4:8 The princes who had once had a healthy glow (4:7) were now unrecognizable. The effects of starvation had darkened their skin (5:10; see also Job 30:28, 30). The author was not condemning dark skin tones, as some have misunderstood. We must interpret the statements within their original context. The change in their skin tone resulted from starvation, as the second half of the verse explains.
4:10 On women eating their children, see the note on 2:20.

The faithful love of the LORD never ends! ...His mercies begin afresh each morning.

LAMENTATIONS
3:22-23

³ We are orphaned and fatherless.
    Our mothers are widowed.
⁴ We have to pay for water to drink,
    and even firewood is expensive.
⁵ Those who pursue us are at our heels;
    we are exhausted but are given no rest.
⁶ We submitted to Egypt and Assyria
    to get enough food to survive.
⁷ Our ancestors sinned, but they have died—
    and we are suffering the punishment they deserved!
⁸ Slaves have now become our masters;
    there is no one left to rescue us.
⁹ We hunt for food at the risk of our lives,
    for violence rules the countryside.
¹⁰ The famine has blackened our skin
    as though baked in an oven.
¹¹ Our enemies rape the women in Jerusalem*
    and the young girls in all the towns of Judah.
¹² Our princes are being hanged by their thumbs,
    and our elders are treated with contempt.
¹³ Young men are led away to work at millstones,
    and boys stagger under heavy loads of wood.
¹⁴ The elders no longer sit in the city gates;
    the young men no longer dance and sing.
¹⁵ Joy has left our hearts;
    our dancing has turned to mourning.
¹⁶ The garlands have* fallen from our heads.
    Weep for us because we have sinned.
¹⁷ Our hearts are sick and weary,
    and our eyes grow dim with tears.
¹⁸ For Jerusalem* is empty and desolate,
    a place haunted by jackals.
¹⁹ But LORD, you remain the same forever!
    Your throne continues from generation to generation.
²⁰ Why do you continue to forget us?
    Why have you abandoned us for so long?
²¹ Restore us, O LORD, and bring us back to you again!
    Give us back the joys we once had!
²² Or have you utterly rejected us?
    Are you angry with us still?

5:11 Hebrew *in Zion.* **5:16** Or *The crown has.* **5:18** Hebrew *Mount Zion.*

5:10 On blackened skin, see the notes on 4:7; 4:8.
5:11 In antiquity, as is the case today, rape was a weapon of war used to humiliate and subjugate the victims. Rape is one of several horrors listed in 5:2-18, all of which the enemy committed to disgrace and degrade the people of Judah.

Ezekiel

WHAT DO WE LEARN ABOUT GOD'S MISSION AND OURS?
God loves single-heartedly and desires that we love him that way, too.

WHO WROTE IT? Ezekiel, who was a priest and prophet (1:3).

WHEN DID IT HAPPEN? Ezekiel ministered before and after the fall of Jerusalem in 586 BC and dates his visions and messages from 593 to 571 BC. The prophecies of Ezekiel fit during the period just before and during the Exile.

HOW IS IT ORGANIZED?

- 1–3: Ezekiel's call
- 4–24: Prophecies against Israel and Jerusalem
- 25–32: Prophecies against other nations
- 33–48: Israel's return and restoration

FEATURE HIGHLIGHTS

+ *The Prophet's Theater (977)*
+ *Jerusalem, Sodom, and Samaria: Unfaithful Wife and Her Sisters (989)*
+ *Faithfulness (994)*
+ *Tending and Thriving (1014)*
+ *Ezekiel's Important Dates (1022)*

Words to Remember are highlighted throughout this book

HOW LONG DOES IT TAKE TO READ?
3:00

| :30 | 1:00 | 1:30 | 2:00 | 2:30 | 3:00 | 3:30 |

BC Timeline

- **627** — JEREMIAH BECOMES A PROPHET TO JUDAH
- **605** — DANIEL TAKEN CAPTIVE TO BABYLON
- **597** — EZEKIEL TAKEN CAPTIVE TO BABYLON
- **593** — EZEKIEL BECOMES A PROPHET TO THE EXILES
- **586** — JUDAH FALLS; JERUSALEM DESTROYED
- **571** — EZEKIEL'S MINISTRY ENDS
- **539** — CYRUS THE GREAT OVERTHROWS BABYLON
- **538** — FIRST EXILES RETURN TO JUDAH

A Vision of Living Beings

1 On July 31* of my thirtieth year,* while I was with the Judean exiles beside the Kebar River in Babylon, the heavens were opened and I saw visions of God. ²This happened during the fifth year of King Jehoiachin's captivity. ³(The LORD gave this message to Ezekiel son of Buzi, a priest, beside the Kebar River in the land of the Babylonians,* and he felt the hand of the LORD take hold of him.)

⁴As I looked, I saw a great storm coming from the north, driving before it a huge cloud that flashed with lightning and shone with brilliant light. There was fire inside the cloud, and in the middle of the fire glowed something like gleaming amber.* ⁵From the center of the cloud came four living beings that looked human, ⁶except that each had four faces and four wings. ⁷Their legs were straight, and their feet had hooves like those of a calf and shone like burnished bronze. ⁸Under each of their four wings I could see human hands. So each of the four beings had four faces and four wings. ⁹The wings of each living being touched the wings of the beings beside it. Each one moved straight forward in any direction without turning around.

¹⁰Each had a human face in the front, the face of a lion on the right side, the face of an ox on the left side, and the face of an eagle at the back. ¹¹Each had two pairs of outstretched wings—one pair stretched out to touch the wings of the living beings on either side of it, and the other pair covered its body. ¹²They went in whatever direction the spirit chose, and they moved straight forward in any direction without turning around.

¹³The living beings looked like bright coals of fire or brilliant torches, and lightning seemed to flash back and forth among them. ¹⁴And the living beings darted to and fro like flashes of lightning.

¹⁵As I looked at these beings, I saw four wheels touching the ground beside them, one wheel belonging to each. ¹⁶The wheels sparkled as if made of beryl. All four wheels looked alike and were made the same; each wheel had a second wheel turning crosswise within it. ¹⁷The beings could move in any of the four directions they faced, without turning as they moved. ¹⁸The rims of the four wheels were tall and frightening, and they were covered with eyes all around.

¹⁹When the living beings moved, the wheels moved with them. When they flew upward, the wheels went up, too. ²⁰The spirit of the living beings was in the wheels. So wherever the spirit went, the wheels and the living beings also went. ²¹When the beings moved, the wheels moved. When the beings stopped, the wheels stopped. When the beings flew upward, the wheels rose up, for the spirit of the living beings was in the wheels.

²²Spread out above them was a surface like the sky, glittering like crystal. ²³Beneath this surface the wings of each living being stretched out to touch the others' wings, and each had two wings covering its body. ²⁴As they flew, their wings sounded to me like waves crashing against the shore or like the voice of the Almighty* or like the shouting of a mighty army. When they stopped, they let down their wings. ²⁵As they stood with wings lowered, a voice spoke from beyond the crystal surface above them.

²⁶Above this surface was something that looked like a throne made of blue lapis lazuli. And on this throne high above was a figure whose appearance resembled a man. ²⁷From what appeared to be his waist up, he looked like gleaming amber, flickering like a fire. And from his waist down, he looked like a burning flame, shining with splendor. ²⁸All around him was a glowing halo, like a rainbow shining in the clouds on a rainy day. This is what the glory of the LORD looked like to me. When I saw it, I fell face down on the ground, and I heard someone's voice speaking to me.

1:1a Hebrew *On the fifth day of the fourth month*, of the ancient Hebrew lunar calendar. A number of dates in Ezekiel can be cross-checked with dates in surviving Babylonian records and related accurately to our modern calendar. This event occurred on July 31, 593 B.C. **1:1b** Or *in the thirtieth year*. **1:3** Or *Chaldeans*. **1:4** Or *like burnished metal;* also in 1:27. **1:24** Hebrew *Shaddai*.

1:1–3:27 Ezekiel means "God strengthens" in Hebrew. Like Jeremiah (1:2) and Zechariah (1:1), God called Ezekiel, who had been serving as a priest, to be a prophet. The Jewish people admired priests but despised prophets. Ezekiel explained the reality of their situation to the exiles. He warned about their immoral conduct and false prophets' messages that the exiles would return home very soon. Ezekiel removed the exiles' false hope and declared God's word.
1:1-3 God called Ezekiel on July 31, 593 BC, through a vision. God's hand enabled Ezekiel to carry out God's calling to bring instruction to the people.
1:4-28 The language of this opening vision is that of *theophany*, a physical manifestation of God. It was difficult for Ezekiel to describe what he saw, as is evident from his frequent use of "looked like," "something like," and "seemed." Nonetheless, the overall effect of the vision is clear and menacing; verbs of motion are combined with symbols of judgment to warn that God's judgment will inevitably fall upon rebellious Jerusalem.
1:4 Storms often symbolize God's judgment in poetic writings (compare Proverbs 1:27; Isaiah 66:15). The windstorm's direction ("from the north") suggested Babylon's army would invade Jerusalem and destroy the city and its Temple. Light and fire sparked from the cloud, representing God's sacredness (Exodus 19:16, 18).
1:22-28 The surface above the cherubim, described by Ezekiel as "like the sky, glittering like crystal," delineated the heavens from the earth, God from humanity. The opening chapters of Genesis also mention the sky, cherubim, and a rainbow. Ezekiel was setting up to tell of destruction followed by re-creation. Just as God had destroyed the world he had made with a flood and then restored it through Noah, Ezekiel's world was being unmade but would be restored (Genesis 8:1–9:20).

Ezekiel's Call and Commission

2 "Stand up, son of man," said the voice. "I want to speak with you." ²The Spirit came into me as he spoke, and he set me on my feet. I listened carefully to his words. ³"Son of man," he said, "I am sending you to the nation of Israel, a rebellious nation that has rebelled against me. They and their ancestors have been rebelling against me to this very day. ⁴They are a stubborn and hard-hearted people. But I am sending you to say to them, 'This is what the Sovereign LORD says!' ⁵And whether they listen or refuse to listen—for remember, they are rebels—at least they will know they have had a prophet among them.

⁶"Son of man, do not fear them or their words. Don't be afraid even though their threats surround you like nettles and briers and stinging scorpions. Do not be dismayed by their dark scowls, even though they are rebels. ⁷You must give them my messages whether they listen or not. But they won't listen, for they are completely rebellious! ⁸Son of man, listen to what I say to you. Do not join them in their rebellion. Open your mouth, and eat what I give you."

⁹Then I looked and saw a hand reaching out to me. It held a scroll, ¹⁰which he unrolled. And I saw that both sides were covered with funeral songs, words of sorrow, and pronouncements of doom.

3 The voice said to me, "Son of man, eat what I am giving you—eat this scroll! Then go and give its message to the people of Israel." ²So I opened my mouth, and he fed me the scroll. ³"Fill your stomach with this," he said. And when I ate it, it tasted as sweet as honey in my mouth.

⁴Then he said, "Son of man, go to the people of Israel and give them my messages. ⁵I am not sending you to a foreign people whose language you cannot understand. ⁶No, I am not sending you to people with strange and difficult speech. If I did, they would listen! ⁷But the people of Israel won't listen to you any more than they listen to me! For the whole lot of them are hard-hearted and stubborn. ⁸But look, I have made you as obstinate and hard-hearted as they are. ⁹I have made your forehead as hard as the hardest rock! So don't be afraid of them or fear their angry looks, even though they are rebels."

¹⁰Then he added, "Son of man, let all my words sink deep into your own heart first. Listen to them carefully for yourself. ¹¹Then go to your people in exile and say to them, 'This is what the Sovereign LORD says!' Do this whether they listen to you or not."

¹²Then the Spirit lifted me up, and I heard a loud rumbling sound behind me. (May the glory of the LORD be praised in his place!)* ¹³It was the sound of the wings of the living beings as they brushed against each other and the rumbling of their wheels beneath them.

¹⁴The Spirit lifted me up and took me away. I went in bitterness and turmoil, but the LORD's hold on me was strong. ¹⁵Then I came to the colony of Judean exiles in Tel-abib, beside the Kebar River. I was overwhelmed and sat among them for seven days.

3:12 A possible reading for this verse is *Then the Spirit lifted me up, and as the glory of the LORD rose from its place, I heard a loud rumbling sound behind me.*

2:1-10 Being a prophet was not a career choice or an occupation passed down from father to son like the priesthood. God called prophets to their task, and the story of their call is often included in their writings (see, for example, Isaiah 6:1-13; Jeremiah 1:4-19; Jonah 1:1-2).
2:1-2 Ezekiel responded to the vision by falling to the ground (see 1:4-28). God astonished him with his glory and amazing acts. God's Spirit entered Ezekiel and brought him to his feet. When Ezekiel listened and obeyed, God's powerful Spirit empowered him throughout the book (2:2; 3:14; 8:3; 11:1, 24; 37:1; 43:5).
2:3 God calls Ezekiel "son of man" ninety-two times in the book, emphasizing Ezekiel's humanity (see Genesis 1:26; 3:19; Psalm 103:14). Ezekiel relied solely on God to carry out his prophetic duties. He needed God to tell him what to say and do. As prophets were known for predicting the future, Ezekiel's main task was to proclaim God's message of hope and forgiveness. However, first Ezekiel had to announce why God needed to forgive his people.
2:4-5 God had chosen Israel to be his people, and his blessing came with the responsibility of acting like God's holy people. Instead, the people's hearts toward God were rebellious and stubborn.
2:6-8 God told Ezekiel three times that fearing, dreading, or worrying about the people's response to his message was not an option. Ezekiel's responsibility was to deliver God's word to them. He could not control their response. God knew Ezekiel's fear could prevent him from boldly proclaiming God's word (see also Isaiah 51:12; Jeremiah 1:8; Matthew 10:26, 28, 31). God's command to eat what he gave Ezekiel meant Ezekiel must speak to the people sincerely from his heart (see also Jeremiah 15:16; Revelation 10:8-10).
2:9–3:3 Ezekiel ate the scroll filled with God's pronounced judgments and curses on the people. It tasted "as sweet as honey" (3:3; compare Psalms 19:10; 119:103). The vision of God and his glory motivated the prophet to stand even when things were tough (see also Isaiah 6:5-8; Habakkuk 3:16-19; Acts 7:55-60).
3:4-9 Ezekiel was sent to God's people, the people of Israel, who should have eagerly listened to the Lord. However, it would have been easier for the prophet if he had been sent to "people with strange and difficult speech" who could not understand him. This hard-hearted community refused to obey the Lord. God would make Ezekiel as thoroughly persistent in presenting God's message as the people were in rejecting it.
3:11 The Lord's message was not subject to debate or negotiation; things would happen as he had said.
3:14-15 Ezekiel was brought back from his visionary experience to the ordinary world of the exiles. Ezekiel regularly experienced the powerful impact of the Spirit's transporting him to another location (see also 8:3; 11:1, 24; 40:1-3; 43:5). Ezekiel experienced the conflicting emotions associated with his commission. As a prophet who was speaking for God, he began to feel the "bitterness and turmoil" of God's anger against the sins of his people.

A Watchman for Israel

¹⁶After seven days the LORD gave me a message. He said, ¹⁷"Son of man, I have appointed you as a watchman for Israel. Whenever you receive a message from me, warn people immediately. ¹⁸If I warn the wicked, saying, 'You are under the penalty of death,' but you fail to deliver the warning, they will die in their sins. And I will hold you responsible for their deaths. ¹⁹If you warn them and they refuse to repent and keep on sinning, they will die in their sins. But you will have saved yourself because you obeyed me.

²⁰"If righteous people turn away from their righteous behavior and ignore the obstacles I put in their way, they will die. And if you do not warn them, they will die in their sins. None of their righteous acts will be remembered, and I will hold you responsible for their deaths. ²¹But if you warn righteous people not to sin and they listen to you and do not sin, they will live, and you will have saved yourself, too."

²²Then the LORD took hold of me and said, "Get up and go out into the valley, and I will speak to you there." ²³So I got up and went, and there I saw the glory of the LORD, just as I had seen in my first vision by the Kebar River. And I fell face down on the ground.

²⁴Then the Spirit came into me and set me on my feet. He spoke to me and said, "Go to your house and shut yourself in. ²⁵There, son of man, you will be tied with ropes so you cannot go out among the people. ²⁶And I will make your tongue stick to the roof of your mouth so that you will be speechless and unable to rebuke them, for they are rebels. ²⁷But when I give you a message, I will loosen your tongue and let you speak. Then you will say to them, 'This is what the Sovereign LORD says!' Those who choose to listen will listen, but those who refuse will refuse, for they are rebels.

A Sign of the Coming Siege

4 "And now, son of man, take a large clay brick and set it down in front of you. Then draw a map of the city of Jerusalem on it. ²Show the city under siege. Build a wall around it so no one can escape. Set up the enemy camp, and surround the city with siege ramps and battering rams. ³Then take an iron griddle and place it between you and the city. Turn toward the city and demonstrate how harsh the siege will be against Jerusalem. This will be a warning to the people of Israel.

⁴"Now lie on your left side and place the sins of Israel on yourself. You are to bear their sins for the number of days you lie there on your side. ⁵I am requiring you to bear Israel's sins for 390 days—one day for each year of their sin. ⁶After that, turn over and lie on your right side for 40 days—one day for each year of Judah's sin.

3:16-19 Ezekiel was called to be a watchman, a familiar image for Old Testament prophets (see Isaiah 56:10; Jeremiah 6:17; Hosea 9:8). The watchman was a lookout for the community. He was responsible for warning of approaching enemies so that the people could take refuge in time. In this case, the enemy they had to fear was not a human invader but God. As difficult as his task was, the blood of those he failed to warn would be on his head if he remained silent.

3:20-21 The prophet spoke to two classes of people: the righteous and the wicked. Ezekiel was to address his message indiscriminately, for both the righteous and the wicked would be judged based on their response to his words (see also Matthew 13:3-9, 18-23). Those who heeded him would receive life; those who rejected his message would receive death, even if they had previously been righteous. Obedience to the Lord's word (through his prophet) was the sole criterion that divided those who would live from those who would die.

3:26-27 God instructed Ezekiel not to speak for seven years (593–586 BC), until the fall of Jerusalem. When people do not listen to God through conventional methods, God speaks through actions (see also Jeremiah 13; 16; 19). After Ezekiel's silence, the Jewish exiles learned that hearing God's word was both a privilege and a responsibility.

4:1–7:27 These chapters record four "sign acts," which are dramatic performances of God's messages for the people. Through them, Ezekiel communicated upsetting news about Jerusalem to the exiles. In words and mimed actions, he declared the certainty of impending judgment on Jerusalem. Having broken the terms of the Lord's covenant made with them at Mount Sinai, God's people now faced the curses of death and destruction that were attached to that covenant. Only after these curses had taken effect could there be any hope for the future.

4:1-2 Without using words, Ezekiel sketched a map of Jerusalem on a brick and set it on the ground. Then, he began marching toward it like a soldier charging into battle. He built a ramp and pretended to scale a wall and break down the city gates with a battering ram. The portrayed events later transpired in 588 BC when the Babylonian army besieged Jerusalem.

4:3 The priests used iron griddles to prepare offerings for sacrifice in the Temple (Leviticus 2:5; 6:21; 7:9). Ezekiel used the iron griddle to represent Jerusalem's wall. It symbolized the physical and spiritual separation between God and his people. The silence emphasized that God's judgment was final. Destruction was coming to Jerusalem.

4:4-8 Ezekiel's second sign act required him to lie on his side, facing the model of Jerusalem he had constructed. During specified times each day, he lay tied up with his arm exposed. He was required to eat the food described in 4:9-17. This sign act meant God's judgment would fall on Jerusalem, and the remaining Israelites would become exiles.

4:5-6 Each day of the sign act represented a year of Israel's history. After God had delivered his people from slavery in Egypt, they worked out their rebellious way in the wilderness for 40 years before entering the Promised Land. The number 390 signifies the time between King Rehoboam's reign in 930 BC to Zedekiah's (2 Kings 24:17-20). God had warned and disciplined Israel, but the nation continued to rebel. Israel did not provide an honest witness of God, so he followed through with his sworn consequences.

Insight — THE PROPHET'S THEATER

Ezekiel did a lot more than just talk. God frequently called him to behave in outrageous, attention-getting ways to make his point. Even from an ancient perspective, Ezekiel's prophetic tactics were odd. Ezekiel's displays are called "sign acts," and they provided dramatic visual aids to communicate the Lord's messages to his people. The goal was for the people to *feel* the message just as clearly as they *heard* the message. Consider reading each of these sign acts and then closing your eyes and picturing what it would have looked like to watch Ezekiel perform them. What do you feel?

REFERENCE	SIGN ACT	WHAT HAPPENED	WHAT IT MEANT
4:1-3	1	Ezekiel built a street diorama of a terrible siege on Jerusalem.	5:5-17 Because the people worshiped idols, Jerusalem would be besieged and one third of the people would die of famine and disease, one third would be killed, and one third would be scattered.
4:4-8	2	Ezekiel lay on his left side for 390 days and on his right side for 40 days while staring at the siege diorama.	
4:9-17	3	While lying on his side, Ezekiel baked bread to eat and rationed his water.	
5:1-4	4	Ezekiel cut off all his hair: One third he burned, one third he chopped up with a sword, and one third he scattered.	
12:1-7	5	Ezekiel packed a bag, left his home, dug a hole in the wall, and walked into the night.	12:8-20 King Zedekiah would escape Jerusalem through a hole in the city wall but be caught and exiled to Babylon.
21:6-7	6	Ezekiel groaned "with bitter anguish and a broken heart."	21:8-17 The people's enemies would massacre them.
21:18-23	7	For Babylon's king, Ezekiel placed a signpost marking the fork in the road.	21:24-27 Even though they shared a treaty, the Babylonian king would destroy them for breaking it.
24:15-18	8	Ezekiel's wife died, but he was not to mourn her death.	24:19-27 The Temple would be destroyed, and their daughters and sons would die, but the people would not mourn.
37:15-17	9	Ezekiel inscribed "Judah" on one stick and "Ephraim" (for Israel) on another and held them together as one.	37:18-28 One day, God would unify them, restore them, bring the people home, and give them a new king—it was an everlasting covenant of peace.

⁷"Meanwhile, keep staring at the siege of Jerusalem. Lie there with your arm bared and prophesy her destruction. ⁸I will tie you up with ropes so you won't be able to turn from side to side until the days of your siege have been completed.

⁹"Now go and get some wheat, barley, beans, lentils, millet, and emmer wheat, and mix them together in a storage jar. Use them to make bread for yourself during the 390 days you will be lying on your side. ¹⁰Ration this out to yourself, eight ounces* of food for each day, and eat it at set times. ¹¹Then measure out a jar* of water for each day, and drink it at set times. ¹²Prepare and eat this food as you would barley cakes. While all the people are watching, bake it over a fire using dried human dung as fuel and then eat the bread." ¹³Then the LORD said, "This is how Israel will eat defiled bread in the Gentile lands to which I will banish them!"

¹⁴Then I said, "O Sovereign LORD, must I be defiled by using human dung? For I have never been defiled before. From the time I was a child until now I have never eaten any animal that died of sickness or was killed by other animals. I have never eaten any meat forbidden by the law."

¹⁵"All right," the LORD said. "You may bake your bread with cow dung instead of human dung." ¹⁶Then he told me, "Son of man, I will make food very scarce in Jerusalem. It will be weighed out with great care and eaten fearfully. The water will be rationed out drop by drop, and the people will drink it with dismay. ¹⁷Lacking food and water, people will look at one another in terror, and they will waste away under their punishment.

A Sign of the Coming Judgment

5 "Son of man, take a sharp sword and use it as a razor to shave your head and beard. Use a scale to weigh the hair into three equal parts. ²Place a third of it at the center of your map of Jerusalem. After acting out the siege, burn it there. Scatter another third across your map and chop it with a sword. Scatter the last third to the wind, for I will scatter my people with the sword. ³Keep just a bit of the hair and tie it up in your robe. ⁴Then take some of these hairs out and throw them into the fire, burning them up. A fire will then spread from this remnant and destroy all of Israel.

⁵"This is what the Sovereign LORD says: This is an illustration of what will happen to Jerusalem. I placed her at the center of the nations, ⁶but she has rebelled against my regulations and decrees and has been even more wicked than the surrounding nations. She has refused to obey the regulations and decrees I gave her to follow.

⁷"Therefore, this is what the Sovereign LORD says: You people have behaved worse than your neighbors and have refused to obey my decrees and regulations. You have not even lived up to the standards of the nations around you. ⁸Therefore, I myself, the Sovereign LORD, am now your enemy. I will punish you publicly while all the nations watch. ⁹Because of your detestable idols, I will punish you like I have never punished anyone before or ever will again. ¹⁰Parents will eat their own children, and children will eat their parents. I will punish you and scatter to the winds the few who survive.

¹¹"As surely as I live, says the Sovereign LORD, I will cut you off completely. I will show you no pity at all because you have defiled my Temple with your vile images and detestable sins. ¹²A third of your people will die in the city from disease and famine. A third of them will be slaughtered by the enemy outside the city walls. And I will scatter a third to the winds, chasing them with my sword. ¹³Then at last my anger will be spent, and I will be satisfied. And when my fury against them has subsided, all Israel will know that I, the LORD, have spoken to them in my jealous anger.

¹⁴"So I will turn you into a ruin, a mockery in the eyes of the surrounding nations and to all who pass by. ¹⁵You will become an object of mockery and

---

4:10 Hebrew *20 shekels* [228 grams]. **4:11** Hebrew *⅙ of a hin* [about 1 pint or 0.6 liters].

4:9-17 The second set of sign acts emphasized the people's misery. God bestowed abundant blessings upon his people for their obedience. If they violated the covenant, they suffered curses (Leviticus 26:1-39; Deuteronomy 28:1–29:29). Ezekiel combined the grains and beans that produced the poorest quality of bread. He only consumed a small quantity each day. The Israelites understood a famine was imminent. Jerusalem would become barren, and the people would starve to death.
5:1 Ezekiel shaved his head and beard (see Isaiah 7:20). This sign act symbolized Israel's humiliation and grief over Jerusalem's coming destruction (see 2 Samuel 10:4-5). Using a sword instead of a razor to cut his hair implied the people would be cut down.
5:5-6 God did not desire for his people to suffer and to die shamefully by Babylonian hands. As his treasured possession, Israel was loved by God and had received his promises. However, God had purposed Israel to lead all other nations to him by living holy, responsible lives (Isaiah 42:6; 49:6). The people were accountable to God but did not follow through on their end of the agreement.
5:7-8 God is the ruler of all nations and he is holy (Deuteronomy 4:24; Hebrews 12:29). God punished Israel publicly to send a message to the other nations. Severe destruction fell on Israel, and only a few loyal people would remain to bring glory to God.
5:9-17 For God to live among creation, he established a law code and system of worship and sacrifice that would help his people remain holy. God told his people clearly and repeatedly what he expected from them—faithful obedience. Destruction comes to those living in sin and hostility toward God. A severe famine resulted in people eating their children (Leviticus 26:26-29; Deuteronomy 28:53-57; 2 Kings 6:28; Jeremiah 19:9; Lamentations 2:20; 4:10). God's actions perplex us because in our humanity we only see in part (1 Corinthians 13:12). Where understanding is lacking, faith is required.

taunting and horror. You will be a warning to all the nations around you. They will see what happens when the LORD punishes a nation in anger and rebukes it, says the LORD.

¹⁶"I will shower you with the deadly arrows of famine to destroy you. The famine will become more and more severe until every crumb of food is gone. ¹⁷And along with the famine, wild animals will attack you and rob you of your children. Disease and war will stalk your land, and I will bring the sword of the enemy against you. I, the LORD, have spoken!"

Judgment against Israel's Mountains

6 Again a message came to me from the LORD: ²"Son of man, turn and face the mountains of Israel and prophesy against them. ³Proclaim this message from the Sovereign LORD against the mountains of Israel. This is what the Sovereign LORD says to the mountains and hills and to the ravines and valleys: I am about to bring war upon you, and I will smash your pagan shrines. ⁴All your altars will be demolished, and your places of worship will be destroyed. I will kill your people in front of your idols.* ⁵I will lay your corpses in front of your idols and scatter your bones around your altars. ⁶Wherever you live there will be desolation, and I will destroy your pagan shrines. Your altars will be demolished, your idols will be smashed, your places of worship will be torn down, and all the religious objects you have made will be destroyed. ⁷The place will be littered with corpses, and you will know that I alone am the LORD.

⁸"But I will let a few of my people escape destruction, and they will be scattered among the nations of the world. ⁹Then when they are exiled among the nations, they will remember me. They will recognize how hurt I am by their unfaithful hearts and lustful eyes that long for their idols. Then at last they will hate themselves for all their detestable sins. ¹⁰They will know that I alone am the LORD and that I was serious when I said I would bring this calamity on them.

¹¹"This is what the Sovereign LORD says: Clap your hands in horror, and stamp your feet. Cry out because of all the detestable sins the people of Israel have committed. Now they are going to die from war and famine and disease. ¹²Disease will strike down those who are far away in exile. War will destroy those who are nearby. And anyone who survives will be killed by famine. So at last I will spend my fury on them. ¹³They will know that I am the LORD when their dead lie scattered among their idols and altars on every hill and mountain and under every green tree and every great shade tree—the places where they offered sacrifices to their idols. ¹⁴I will crush them and make their cities desolate from the wilderness in the south to Riblah* in the north. Then they will know that I am the LORD."

The Coming of the End

7 Then this message came to me from the LORD: ²"Son of man, this is what the Sovereign LORD says to Israel:

"The end is here!
　Wherever you look—
east, west, north, or south—
　your land is finished.
³ No hope remains,
　for I will unleash my anger against you.
I will call you to account
　for all your detestable sins.
⁴ I will turn my eyes away and show no pity.
　I will repay you for all your detestable sins.
Then you will know that I am the LORD.

6:4 The Hebrew term (literally *round things*) probably alludes to dung; also in 6:5, 6, 9, 13. 6:14 As in some Hebrew manuscripts; most Hebrew manuscripts read *Diblah*.

6:1-7 Ezekiel spoke to Jerusalem because the Israelites had ruined the land and discredited God. God used the Babylonian army to perform the covenant curses against Jerusalem (Leviticus 18:24-30; 26:14-39; Deuteronomy 28:25-42, 49-52).

6:1-3 The circle of judgment broadened from Jerusalem to include the mountains of Israel, which were Israel's political heartland. This territory had belonged to Israel continuously since the time of Joshua, and it had been infected by idolatry. The hill country had become home to many "pagan shrines" (literally "high places"). These were raised stone platforms that often housed idols or became the location for sacrifices and pagan festivities. Most predated Israel's entry into the land, and God had commanded Israel to destroy them (Deuteronomy 12:2-3). However, in many cases, the Israelites had permitted them to remain in place. The political and religious leaders had ignored or even encouraged those who worshiped there.

6:8-10 A remnant would be "scattered among the nations of the world" to bear witness to God's faithfulness to his covenant. They would recognize the reality of their "unfaithful hearts" and "hate themselves for all their detestable sins," and they would know that God's threat of calamity on covenant breakers was grave. Some of those who "know that I alone am the LORD" might even experience the other side of God's faithfulness: his swiftness to forgive those who repent. In the book of Exodus, Israel came to know that God is the Lord through his mighty acts of rescue (see Exodus 6:7). Unfortunately, their behavior showed that they had forgotten. They would come again to that knowledge through God's acts of judgment.

7:1-27 Israelites from the earliest generations who entered God's promised land—Abraham and Sarah, Isaac and Rebekah, Jacob and Leah and Rachel—stewarded it well and honored God. But the generation who lived in the land after Moses and Joshua led them out of Egypt began to desecrate the land and dishonor God. God disciplined them by allowing enemy nations to occupy and oppress them. When God's people would turn back to him, God would deliver them from enemy hands. Soon after, however, the people would return to their immoral lives—and this happened again and again. Choosing to live their own way required them to leave God's land.

⁵ "This is what the Sovereign LORD says:
Disaster after disaster
  is coming your way!
⁶ The end has come.
  It has finally arrived.
  Your final doom is waiting!
⁷ O people of Israel, the day of your destruction is
    dawning.
  The time has come; the day of trouble
    is near.
  Shouts of anguish will be heard on the
    mountains,
    not shouts of joy.
⁸ Soon I will pour out my fury on you
    and unleash my anger against you.
  I will call you to account
    for all your detestable sins.
⁹ I will turn my eyes away and show no pity.
  I will repay you for all your detestable sins.
  Then you will know that it is I, the LORD,
    who is striking the blow.

¹⁰ "The day of judgment is here;
    your destruction awaits!
  The people's wickedness and pride
    have blossomed to full flower.
¹¹ Their violence has grown into a rod
    that will beat them for their wickedness.
  None of these proud and wicked people will
    survive.
  All their wealth and prestige will be swept
    away.
¹² Yes, the time has come;
    the day is here!
  Buyers should not rejoice over bargains,
    nor sellers grieve over losses,
  for all of them will fall
    under my terrible anger.
¹³ Even if the merchants survive,
    they will never return to their business.
  For what God has said applies to everyone—
    it will not be changed!
  Not one person whose life is twisted by sin
    will ever recover.

The Desolation of Israel

¹⁴ "The trumpet calls Israel's army to mobilize,
    but no one listens,
  for my fury is against them all.
¹⁵ There is war outside the city
    and disease and famine within.
  Those outside the city walls
    will be killed by enemy swords.
  Those inside the city
    will die of famine and disease.
¹⁶ The survivors who escape to the mountains
    will moan like doves, weeping for their sins.
¹⁷ Their hands will hang limp,
    their knees will be weak as water.
¹⁸ They will dress themselves in burlap;
    horror and shame will cover them.
  They will shave their heads
    in sorrow and remorse.

¹⁹ "They will throw their money in the streets,
    tossing it out like worthless trash.
  Their silver and gold won't save them
    on that day of the LORD's anger.
  It will neither satisfy nor feed them,
    for their greed can only trip them up.
²⁰ They were proud of their beautiful jewelry
    and used it to make detestable idols and vile
      images.
  Therefore, I will make all their wealth
    disgusting to them.
²¹ I will give it as plunder to foreigners,
    to the most wicked of nations,
    and they will defile it.
²² I will turn my eyes from them
    as these robbers invade and defile my
      treasured land.

²³ "Prepare chains for my people,
    for the land is bloodied by terrible crimes.
  Jerusalem is filled with violence.
²⁴ I will bring the most ruthless of nations
    to occupy their homes.
  I will break down their proud fortresses
    and defile their sanctuaries.

7:12-27 The theme of this chapter is complete judgment. The parallel passages (7:12-18 and 7:19-27) describe the futility of wealth given the impending judgment. Then, judgment comes in the form of war. Each passage concludes with a word about widespread hopelessness, fear, and sorrow.

7:12-13 Every seven years, a sabbatical year came in Israel. All debts were to be canceled, and the land was to rest from agricultural production for one year (Deuteronomy 15:1-6). After seven cycles of seven years, the law of the Year of Jubilee instructed the Israelites to release those who had been enslaved. Any land purchased and sold was to revert to its original owners (Leviticus 25). Since the Israelites had not observed the laws, the laws flipped on them: God's people would go into captivity and lose their land.

7:14-15 During this time, watchmen sitting on the city walls would blow their trumpets to alert the soldiers to their post and protect the city if a threat emerged. However, with the Babylonian army waiting outside the city's wall, the watchmen and soldiers would not carry out their jobs. Soldiers were going to die by the sword outside the walls or from famine and disease inside. The hope for Jerusalem was lost.

7:16-18 Some of God's people escaped to the mountains, where they grieved their sin and apologized to God. Realizing their weak and powerless state, they sought God's mercy. Their actions fulfilled Ezekiel's sign act from 6:8-10.

7:19-22 In Jerusalem, the rich had oppressed the poor. Now the wealthy exiles threw their money, idols, and valuables into the street for the Babylonians to take because they were of no use to them. The gold and silver were too heavy for them to carry through the mountains.

²⁵ Terror and trembling will overcome
my people.
They will look for peace but not find it.
²⁶ Calamity will follow calamity;
rumor will follow rumor.
They will look in vain
for a vision from the prophets.
They will receive no teaching from the priests
and no counsel from the leaders.
²⁷ The king and the prince will stand helpless,
weeping in despair,
and the people's hands
will tremble with fear.
I will bring on them
the evil they have done to others,
and they will receive the punishment
they so richly deserve.
Then they will know that I am the Lord."

Idolatry in the Temple

8 Then on September 17,* during the sixth year of King Jehoiachin's captivity, while the leaders of Judah were in my home, the Sovereign Lord took hold of me. ²I saw a figure that appeared to be a man.* From what appeared to be his waist down, he looked like a burning flame. From the waist up he looked like gleaming amber.* ³He reached out what seemed to be a hand and took me by the hair. Then the Spirit lifted me up into the sky and transported me to Jerusalem in a vision from God. I was taken to the north gate of the inner courtyard of the Temple, where there is a large idol that has made the Lord very jealous. ⁴Suddenly, the glory of the God of Israel was there, just as I had seen it before in the valley.

⁵Then the Lord said to me, "Son of man, look toward the north." So I looked, and there to the north, beside the entrance to the gate near the altar, stood the idol that had made the Lord so jealous.

⁶"Son of man," he said, "do you see what they are doing? Do you see the detestable sins the people of Israel are committing to drive me from my Temple? But come, and you will see even more detestable sins than these!" ⁷Then he brought me to the door of the Temple courtyard, where I could see a hole in the wall. ⁸He said to me, "Now, son of man, dig into the wall." So I dug into the wall and found a hidden doorway.

⁹"Go in," he said, "and see the wicked and detestable sins they are committing in there!" ¹⁰So I went in and saw the walls covered with engravings of all kinds of crawling animals and detestable creatures. I also saw the various idols* worshiped by the people of Israel. ¹¹Seventy leaders of Israel were standing there with Jaazaniah son of Shaphan in the center. Each of them held an incense burner, from which a cloud of incense rose above their heads.

¹²Then the Lord said to me, "Son of man, have you seen what the leaders of Israel are doing with their idols in dark rooms? They are saying, 'The Lord doesn't see us; he has deserted our land!'" ¹³Then the Lord added, "Come, and I will show you even more detestable sins than these!"

¹⁴He brought me to the north gate of the Lord's Temple, and some women were sitting there, weeping for the god Tammuz. ¹⁵"Have you seen this?" he asked. "But I will show you even more detestable sins than these!"

¹⁶Then he brought me into the inner courtyard of the Lord's Temple. At the entrance to the sanctuary, between the entry room and the bronze altar, there were about twenty-five men with their backs to the sanctuary of the Lord. They were facing east, bowing low to the ground, worshiping the sun!

¹⁷"Have you seen this, son of man?" he asked. "Is it nothing to the people of Judah that they commit these detestable sins, leading the whole nation into violence, thumbing their noses at me, and provoking my anger? ¹⁸Therefore, I will respond in fury. I will neither pity nor spare them. And though they cry for mercy, I will not listen."

8:1 Hebrew *on the fifth [day] of the sixth month*, of the ancient Hebrew lunar calendar. This event occurred on September 17, 592 B.C.; also see note on 1:1. **8:2a** As in Greek version; Hebrew reads *appeared to be fire*. **8:2b** Or *like burnished metal*. **8:10** The Hebrew term (literally *round things*) probably alludes to dung.

8:1–11:25 Ezekiel recorded a vision God gave him to share with the Jewish exiles (11:25). The vision has four parts: the Temple's defilement (8:1-18); the people's misfortune (9:1-11); the Lord's glory departing (10:1-22); and the deceived leaders (11:1-25). Ezekiel's words corrected what the false prophets had predicted. However, the people did not understand why God would turn his holy Temple over to Babylon.

8:3-16 God showed Ezekiel four scenes of increasing abomination from the false worship that the people of Israel were performing in the Lord's Temple. The comprehensiveness of Jerusalem's defilement may be seen from the varied locations of their acts of idolatry, the kinds of people involved, the deities worshiped, and the varied cultures from which these deities had been imported. It was the ultimate eclectic worship service, with abomination piled upon abomination.

8:11 These seventy leaders are a shocking contrast to the seventy leaders of Moses' day. The latter were given the unique privilege of seeing God (Exodus 24:1-11) and were given the same Spirit as Moses (Numbers 11:16-30). Jaazaniah, the leader of the group in this verse, was, ironically, the son of Shaphan, a godly leader who had been prominently involved in King Josiah's reforms (2 Kings 22:3-14). The incense, intended to ward off dangers from demonic spirits, helped instead to bring God's judgment upon the land.

8:17-18 The abominations that the Israelites were committing in the Temple complex were tantamount to "thumbing" (literally "putting the twig [or branch] to") their noses at the Lord. This gesture was at best defiant, possibly even vulgar.

The Slaughter of Idolaters

9 Then the LORD thundered, "Bring on the men appointed to punish the city! Tell them to bring their weapons with them!" ²Six men soon appeared from the upper gate that faces north, each carrying a deadly weapon in his hand. With them was a man dressed in linen, who carried a writer's case at his side. They all went into the Temple courtyard and stood beside the bronze altar.

³Then the glory of the God of Israel rose up from between the cherubim, where it had rested, and moved to the entrance of the Temple. And the LORD called to the man dressed in linen who was carrying the writer's case. ⁴He said to him, "Walk through the streets of Jerusalem and put a mark on the foreheads of all who weep and sigh because of the detestable sins being committed in their city."

⁵Then I heard the LORD say to the other men, "Follow him through the city and kill everyone whose forehead is not marked. Show no mercy; have no pity! ⁶Kill them all—old and young, girls and women and little children. But do not touch anyone with the mark. Begin right here at the Temple." So they began by killing the seventy leaders.

⁷"Defile the Temple!" the LORD commanded. "Fill its courtyards with corpses. Go!" So they went and began killing throughout the city.

⁸While they were out killing, I was all alone. I fell face down on the ground and cried out, "O Sovereign LORD! Will your fury against Jerusalem wipe out everyone left in Israel?"

⁹Then he said to me, "The sins of the people of Israel and Judah are very, very great. The entire land is full of murder; the city is filled with injustice. They are saying, 'The LORD doesn't see it! The LORD has abandoned the land!' ¹⁰So I will not spare them or have any pity on them. I will fully repay them for all they have done."

¹¹Then the man in linen clothing, who carried the writer's case, reported back and said, "I have done as you commanded."

The LORD's Glory Leaves the Temple

10 In my vision I saw what appeared to be a throne of blue lapis lazuli above the crystal surface over the heads of the cherubim. ²Then the LORD spoke to the man in linen clothing and said, "Go between the whirling wheels beneath the cherubim, and take a handful of burning coals and scatter them over the city." He did this as I watched.

³The cherubim were standing at the south end of the Temple when the man went in, and the cloud of glory filled the inner courtyard. ⁴Then the glory of the LORD rose up from above the cherubim and went over to the entrance of the Temple. The Temple was filled with this cloud of glory, and the courtyard glowed brightly with the glory of the LORD. ⁵The moving wings of the cherubim sounded like the voice of God Almighty* and could be heard even in the outer courtyard.

⁶The LORD said to the man in linen clothing, "Go between the cherubim and take some burning coals from between the wheels." So the man went in and stood beside one of the wheels. ⁷Then one of the cherubim reached out his hand and took some live coals from the fire burning among them. He put the coals into the hands of the man in linen clothing, and the man took them and went out. ⁸(All the cherubim had what looked like human hands under their wings.)

⁹I looked, and each of the four cherubim had a wheel beside him, and the wheels sparkled like beryl. ¹⁰All four wheels looked alike and were made the same; each wheel had a second wheel turning crosswise within it. ¹¹The cherubim could move in any of the four directions they faced, without turning as they moved. They went straight in the direction they faced, never turning aside. ¹²Both the cherubim and the wheels were covered with eyes. The cherubim had eyes all over their bodies, including their hands, their backs, and their wings. ¹³I heard someone refer to the wheels as "the whirling wheels." ¹⁴Each of the four cherubim had four

---

10:5 Hebrew *El-Shaddai*.

9:1-2 The prophet did not have to wait long for judgment to come. The Lord summoned his angelic warriors to punish the city, and seven men appeared in response. Six men each carried a deadly weapon, while the seventh was dressed in linen and carried a writer's case. They stood ready for action in the Temple courtyard, next to the bronze altar where sacrifices were normally offered.

9:3 The glory of the God of Israel, the visible manifestation of his presence, now began to depart from the defiled Temple. First, it "rose up from between the cherubim," that is, from above the Ark in the Most Holy Place, where it normally rested. From there, it "moved to the entrance of the Temple," ready to leave its former throne.

9:4-7 The year was 592 BC, four years before Babylon would besiege the city (see 8:1 and text note). Already, people had died of famine and disease. Now God commanded the angels to execute everyone without a mark that distinguished those who mourned over the city's sins, including women and children. God's people were spreading decay and darkness instead of salt and light. Evil permeated society and consequences fell on the innocent (Genesis 12:10-20; 20:1-18). God's judgment starts with God's people (1 Peter 4:17).

10:1-22 The Temple provided an earthly residence where the Lord's glory could dwell among his people. This central blessing of the covenant could only be maintained if the people were holy. In the face of their defilement, the Lord abandoned his house, leaving it and the surrounding city vulnerable to the impending assault of the Babylonians.

10:8-22 Ezekiel retells his vision, this time adding that God's glory departed from the Temple and stood over the chariot throne. God's glory was leaving Israel (11:23). The people's willful disobedience required discipline. Living in the presence of God required more responsibility than the people of Israel had exhibited.

faces: the first was the face of an ox,* the second was a human face, the third was the face of a lion, and the fourth was the face of an eagle.

15Then the cherubim rose upward. These were the same living beings I had seen beside the Kebar River. 16When the cherubim moved, the wheels moved with them. When they lifted their wings to fly, the wheels stayed beside them. 17When the cherubim stopped, the wheels stopped. When they flew upward, the wheels rose up, for the spirit of the living beings was in the wheels.

18Then the glory of the LORD moved out from the entrance of the Temple and hovered above the cherubim. 19And as I watched, the cherubim flew with their wheels to the east gate of the LORD's Temple. And the glory of the God of Israel hovered above them.

20These were the same living beings I had seen beneath the God of Israel when I was by the Kebar River. I knew they were cherubim, 21for each had four faces and four wings and what looked like human hands under their wings. 22And their faces were just like the faces of the beings I had seen at the Kebar, and they traveled straight ahead, just as the others had.

Judgment on Israel's Leaders

11 Then the Spirit lifted me and brought me to the east gateway of the LORD's Temple, where I saw twenty-five prominent men of the city. Among them were Jaazaniah son of Azzur and Pelatiah son of Benaiah, who were leaders among the people.

2The Spirit said to me, "Son of man, these are the men who are planning evil and giving wicked counsel in this city. 3They say to the people, 'Is it not a good time to build houses? This city is like an iron pot. We are safe inside it like meat in a pot.'* 4Therefore, son of man, prophesy against them loudly and clearly."

5Then the Spirit of the LORD came upon me, and he told me to say, "This is what the LORD says to the people of Israel: I know what you are saying, for I know every thought that comes into your minds. 6You have murdered many in this city and filled its streets with the dead.

7"Therefore, this is what the Sovereign LORD says: This city is an iron pot all right, but the pieces of meat are the victims of your injustice. As for you, I will soon drag you from this pot. 8I will bring on you the sword of war you so greatly fear, says the Sovereign LORD. 9I will drive you out of Jerusalem and hand you over to foreigners, who will carry out my judgments against you. 10You will be slaughtered all the way to the borders of Israel. I will execute judgment on you, and you will know that I am the LORD. 11No, this city will not be an iron pot for you, and you will not be like meat safe inside it. I will judge you even to the borders of Israel, 12and you will know that I am the LORD. For you have refused to obey my decrees and regulations; instead, you have copied the standards of the nations around you."

13While I was still prophesying, Pelatiah son of Benaiah suddenly died. Then I fell face down on the ground and cried out, "O Sovereign LORD, are you going to kill everyone in Israel?"

Hope for Exiled Israel

14Then this message came to me from the LORD: 15"Son of man, the people still left in Jerusalem are talking about you and your relatives and all the people of Israel who are in exile. They are saying, 'Those people are far away from the LORD, so now he has given their land to us!'

16"Therefore, tell the exiles, 'This is what the Sovereign LORD says: Although I have scattered you in the countries of the world, I will be a sanctuary to you during your time in exile. 17I, the Sovereign LORD, will gather you back from the nations where you have been scattered, and I will give you the land of Israel once again.'

18"When the people return to their homeland, they will remove every trace of their vile images and detestable idols. 19And I will give them singleness of heart and put a new spirit within them. I will take away their stony, stubborn heart and give them a tender, responsive heart,* 20so they will obey my decrees and regulations. Then they will truly be my people, and I will be their God. 21But as for those who

---

10:14 Hebrew *the face of a cherub*; compare 1:10.   11:3 Hebrew *This city is the pot, and we are the meat.*   11:19 Hebrew *a heart of flesh.*

11:1-11 Having given Ezekiel a glimpse of the divine perspective on Jerusalem, the Spirit brought him back to overhear the words of the city's inhabitants. The wicked counselors asserted that though the assault by the Babylonians (the implied cooking fire) was troublesome, the defenses of the city (the iron pot) were sufficient to protect them (the meat). These counselors were telling people to build houses—on stolen land (see 11:15, 17)—in which they could live safely. God, however, was determined to judge the wicked.
11:7 The Babylonians were camped outside the city walls, but the leaders boasted they were like choice cuts of meat safely situated within the city. Ezekiel corrected their illusion by calling them butchers. They did not worship God alone. Instead, they brought idols into the Temple, which defiled it. Instead of conducting honest business deals, the leaders dealt exploitatively. They indirectly killed innocent people and stole others' possessions through their injustice and disloyalty to God.
11:13 As God's judgment fell on Pelatiah, Ezekiel dropped face-down to the ground and prayed that God would spare those left (9:8). He longed for the people of Israel to turn to and worship the Lord once again.
11:15-20 God's words here serve as an encouragement to those who have remained faithful to him. God made four promises to the exiles in Babylon. First, God would dwell among them in exile. Second, the exiles would return to the land and rebuild the Temple. Third, God would give them the determination to cleanse the land of idols. Finally, God promised a new covenant engraved on the hearts of the people that they would keep.

long for vile images and detestable idols, I will repay them fully for their sins. I, the Sovereign LORD, have spoken!"

The LORD's Glory Leaves Jerusalem

²²Then the cherubim lifted their wings and rose into the air with their wheels beside them, and the glory of the God of Israel hovered above them. ²³Then the glory of the LORD went up from the city and stopped above the mountain to the east.

²⁴Afterward the Spirit of God carried me back again to Babylonia,* to the people in exile there. And so ended the vision of my visit to Jerusalem. ²⁵And I told the exiles everything the LORD had shown me.

Signs of the Coming Exile

12 Again a message came to me from the LORD: ²"Son of man, you live among rebels who have eyes but refuse to see. They have ears but refuse to hear. For they are a rebellious people.

³"So now, son of man, pretend you are being sent into exile. Pack the few items an exile could carry, and leave your home to go somewhere else. Do this right in front of the people so they can see you. For perhaps they will pay attention to this, even though they are such rebels. ⁴Bring your baggage outside during the day so they can watch you. Then in the evening, as they are watching, leave your house as captives do when they begin a long march to distant lands. ⁵Dig a hole through the wall while they are watching and go out through it. ⁶As they watch, lift your pack to your shoulders and walk away into the night. Cover your face so you cannot see the land you are leaving. For I have made you a sign for the people of Israel."

⁷So I did as I was told. In broad daylight I brought my pack outside, filled with the things I might carry into exile. Then in the evening while the people looked on, I dug through the wall with my hands and went out into the night with my pack on my shoulder.

⁸The next morning this message came to me from the LORD: ⁹"Son of man, these rebels, the people of Israel, have asked you what all this means. ¹⁰Say to them, 'This is what the Sovereign LORD says: These actions contain a message for King Zedekiah in Jerusalem* and for all the people of Israel.' ¹¹Explain that your actions are a sign to show what will soon happen to them, for they will be driven into exile as captives.

¹²"Even Zedekiah will leave Jerusalem at night through a hole in the wall, taking only what he can carry with him. He will cover his face, and his eyes will not see the land he is leaving. ¹³Then I will throw my net over him and capture him in my snare. I will bring him to Babylon, the land of the Babylonians,* though he will never see it, and he will die there. ¹⁴I will scatter his servants and warriors to the four winds and send the sword after them. ¹⁵And when I scatter them among the nations, they will know that I am the LORD. ¹⁶But I will spare a few of them from death by war, famine, or disease, so they can confess all their detestable sins to their captors. Then they will know that I am the LORD."

¹⁷Then this message came to me from the LORD: ¹⁸"Son of man, tremble as you eat your food. Shake with fear as you drink your water. ¹⁹Tell the people, 'This is what the Sovereign LORD says concerning those living in Israel and Jerusalem: They will eat their food with trembling and sip their water in despair, for their land will be stripped bare because of their violence. ²⁰The cities will be destroyed and the farmland made desolate. Then you will know that I am the LORD.'"

A New Proverb for Israel

²¹Again a message came to me from the LORD: ²²"Son of man, you've heard that proverb they quote in Israel: 'Time passes, and prophecies come to nothing.' ²³Tell the people, 'This is what the Sovereign LORD says: I will put an end to this proverb, and you will soon stop quoting it.' Now give them this new proverb to replace the old one: 'The time has come for every prophecy to be fulfilled!'

²⁴"There will be no more false visions and flattering predictions in Israel. ²⁵For I am the LORD! If I say it, it will happen. There will be no more delays, you rebels of Israel. I will fulfill my threat of destruction in your own lifetime. I, the Sovereign LORD, have spoken!"

11:24 Or *Chaldea.* 12:10 Hebrew *the prince in Jerusalem;* similarly in 12:12. 12:13 Or *Chaldeans.*

12:1-28 When he called Ezekiel as a prophet, God told him the people would protest his words (2:1-10). God's people were spiritually disconnected and could not see or hear what God was doing and saying. Ezekiel performs two sign acts to get their attention.
12:12-13 King Zedekiah was unable to see the coming judgment, so he would be unable to see either "the land he is leaving" or "the land of the Babylonians" (or Chaldeans). This prophecy would be fulfilled when the Babylonians captured Zedekiah as he fled from besieged Jerusalem. After making him watch while his sons were killed, the Babylonians gouged out his eyes (2 Kings 25:1-7). This terrible fate for Judah's last king was not just a consequence of the Babylonians' putting down his revolt. The Lord would capture him in his snare.
12:17-20 For Ezekiel to tremble and shake while eating and drinking was a sign act that reflected the terrible anxiety of the inhabitants of Jerusalem and Judah as they saw their inevitable doom approaching. When the exiles learned that their former homeland had been destroyed, they would realize that they were not cast-offs from God's plan, but rather the fortunate ones who had escaped his comprehensive judgment (see Jeremiah 24:1-10).

²⁶Then this message came to me from the LORD: ²⁷"Son of man, the people of Israel are saying, 'He's talking about the distant future. His visions won't come true for a long, long time.' ²⁸Therefore, tell them, 'This is what the Sovereign LORD says: No more delay! I will now do everything I have threatened. I, the Sovereign LORD, have spoken!'"

Judgment against False Prophets

13 Then this message came to me from the LORD: ²"Son of man, prophesy against the false prophets of Israel who are inventing their own prophecies. Say to them, 'Listen to the word of the LORD. ³This is what the Sovereign LORD says: What sorrow awaits the false prophets who are following their own imaginations and have seen nothing at all!'

⁴"O people of Israel, these prophets of yours are like jackals digging in the ruins. ⁵They have done nothing to repair the breaks in the walls around the nation. They have not helped it to stand firm in battle on the day of the LORD. ⁶Instead, they have told lies and made false predictions. They say, 'This message is from the LORD,' even though the LORD never sent them. And yet they expect him to fulfill their prophecies! ⁷Can your visions be anything but false if you claim, 'This message is from the LORD,' when I have not even spoken to you?

⁸"Therefore, this is what the Sovereign LORD says: Because what you say is false and your visions are a lie, I will stand against you, says the Sovereign LORD. ⁹I will raise my fist against all the prophets who see false visions and make lying predictions, and they will be banished from the community of Israel. I will blot their names from Israel's record books, and they will never again set foot in their own land. Then you will know that I am the Sovereign LORD.

¹⁰"This will happen because these evil prophets deceive my people by saying, 'All is peaceful' when there is no peace at all! It's as if the people have built a flimsy wall, and these prophets are trying to reinforce it by covering it with whitewash! ¹¹Tell these whitewashers that their wall will soon fall down. A heavy rainstorm will undermine it; great hailstones and mighty winds will knock it down. ¹²And when the wall falls, the people will cry out, 'What happened to your whitewash?'

¹³"Therefore, this is what the Sovereign LORD says: I will sweep away your whitewashed wall with a storm of indignation, with a great flood of anger, and with hailstones of fury. ¹⁴I will break down your wall right to its foundation, and when it falls, it will crush you. Then you will know that I am the LORD. ¹⁵At last my anger against the wall and those who covered it with whitewash will be satisfied. Then I will say to you: 'The wall and those who whitewashed it are both gone. ¹⁶They were lying prophets who claimed peace would come to Jerusalem when there was no peace. I, the Sovereign LORD, have spoken!'

Judgment against False Women Prophets

¹⁷"Now, son of man, speak out against the women who prophesy from their own imaginations. ¹⁸This is what the Sovereign LORD says: What sorrow awaits you women who are ensnaring the souls of my people, young and old alike. You tie magic charms on their wrists and furnish them with magic veils. Do you think you can trap others without bringing destruction on yourselves? ¹⁹You bring shame on me among my people for a few handfuls of barley or a piece of bread. By lying to my people who love to listen to lies, you kill those who should not die, and you promise life to those who should not live.

²⁰"This is what the Sovereign LORD says: I am against all your magic charms, which you use to ensnare my people like birds. I will tear them from your arms, setting my people free like birds set free from a cage. ²¹I will tear off the magic veils and save my people from your grasp. They will no longer be your victims. Then you will know that I am the LORD. ²²You have discouraged the righteous with your lies, but I didn't want them to be sad. And you have encouraged the wicked by promising them life, even though they continue in their sins. ²³Because of all this, you will no longer talk of seeing visions that you never saw, nor will you make predictions. For I will rescue my people from your grasp. Then you will know that I am the LORD."

12:26-28 God's word never fails (Numbers 23:19; Joshua 21:45; Isaiah 40:8; Luke 1:37). Some of the exiles did not believe Ezekiel at all. Others distanced themselves from Ezekiel's message claiming it would not happen in their lifetime. God fulfilled Ezekiel's vision six years later.

13:1-23 Ezekiel spoke to the people's shallow faith in God by first addressing the false prophets' eagerness to speak in God's place. Next, Ezekiel spoke directly to the false female prophets. They had used magic and claimed their words came from God, which Ezekiel condemned.

13:1-3 While the false prophets were inventing their own prophecies, the true prophets spoke the word of the Lord. Now these false prophets would receive a word from the Lord about their own destruction. Sorrow awaited these deceived and deceiving messengers.

13:17-19 Like the false male prophets, some female prophets proclaimed words that came only from their own imaginations. The false male prophets had been using conventional forms of prophecy, but the women used magical techniques involving charms and veils. Motivated by personal gain ("a few handfuls of barley or a piece of bread"), they promised life and death (contrast with 3:17-21; 33:1-9), but to the wrong people.

13:20-23 The female false prophets did not define who qualified for life or death in the way that God did, so their ministry "discouraged the righteous" by making them feel that their obedience was in vain. It also "encouraged the wicked" to believe that they could continue in their sins without penalty. The result of this misdirection was to ensnare both the righteous and the wicked, giving both groups false ideas about God.

The Idolatry of Israel's Leaders

14 Then some of the leaders of Israel visited me, and while they were sitting with me, ²this message came to me from the LORD: ³"Son of man, these leaders have set up idols* in their hearts. They have embraced things that will make them fall into sin. Why should I listen to their requests? ⁴Tell them, 'This is what the Sovereign LORD says: The people of Israel have set up idols in their hearts and fallen into sin, and then they go to a prophet asking for a message. So I, the LORD, will give them the kind of answer their great idolatry deserves. ⁵I will do this to capture the minds and hearts of all my people who have turned from me to worship their detestable idols.'

⁶"Therefore, tell the people of Israel, 'This is what the Sovereign LORD says: Repent and turn away from your idols, and stop all your detestable sins. ⁷I, the LORD, will answer all those, both Israelites and foreigners, who reject me and set up idols in their hearts and so fall into sin, and who then come to a prophet asking for my advice. ⁸I will turn against such people and make a terrible example of them, eliminating them from among my people. Then you will know that I am the LORD.

⁹"'And if a prophet is deceived into giving a message, it is because I, the LORD, have deceived that prophet. I will lift my fist against such prophets and cut them off from the community of Israel. ¹⁰False prophets and those who seek their guidance will all be punished for their sins. ¹¹In this way, the people of Israel will learn not to stray from me, polluting themselves with sin. They will be my people, and I will be their God. I, the Sovereign LORD, have spoken!'"

The Certainty of the LORD's Judgment

¹²Then this message came to me from the LORD: ¹³"Son of man, suppose the people of a country were to sin against me, and I lifted my fist to crush them, cutting off their food supply and sending a famine to destroy both people and animals. ¹⁴Even if Noah, Daniel, and Job were there, their righteousness would save no one but themselves, says the Sovereign LORD.

¹⁵"Or suppose I were to send wild animals to invade the country, kill the people, and make the land too desolate and dangerous to pass through. ¹⁶As surely as I live, says the Sovereign LORD, even if those three men were there, they wouldn't be able to save their own sons or daughters. They alone would be saved, but the land would be made desolate.

¹⁷"Or suppose I were to bring war against the land, and I sent enemy armies to destroy both people and animals. ¹⁸As surely as I live, says the Sovereign LORD, even if those three men were there, they wouldn't be able to save their own sons or daughters. They alone would be saved.

¹⁹"Or suppose I were to pour out my fury by sending an epidemic into the land, and the disease killed people and animals alike. ²⁰As surely as I live, says the Sovereign LORD, even if Noah, Daniel, and Job were there, they wouldn't be able to save their own sons or daughters. They alone would be saved by their righteousness.

²¹"Now this is what the Sovereign LORD says: How terrible it will be when all four of these dreadful punishments fall upon Jerusalem—war, famine, wild animals, and disease—destroying all her people and animals. ²²Yet there will be survivors, and they will come here to join you as exiles in Babylon. You will see with your own eyes how wicked they are, and then you will feel better about what I have done to Jerusalem. ²³When you meet them and see their behavior, you will understand that these things are not being done to Israel without cause. I, the Sovereign LORD, have spoken!"

Jerusalem—a Useless Vine

15 Then this message came to me from the LORD: ²"Son of man, how does a grapevine compare to a tree? Is a vine's wood as useful as the wood of a tree? ³Can its wood be used for making things, like

---

14:3 The Hebrew term (literally *round things*) probably alludes to dung; also in 14:4, 5, 6, 7.

14:6-11 The exiles needed to turn to God and away from worshiping idols. God considers and judges each person individually. He made an example out of some to warn the others. Others he tested so that they would know the sinfulness of their hearts and embrace God with humility and reverence.

14:12-20 Israel had not been unjustly singled out for judgment. If any country were to sin against the Lord, the result would be the same. It is clear that Israel is in view here, however, because the language used to describe the people's sin is used elsewhere to describe a breach in Israel's covenant relationship with the Lord. The covenant was broken, so the nation would inevitably and justly experience the covenant curses that they had ratified at the time the covenant was first made (Leviticus 26). The covenant curses are itemized in four test cases. Each case envisions one of the curses listed in Leviticus 26: famine (Ezekiel 14:13-14; see Leviticus 26:26), wild animals (Ezekiel 14:15-16; see Leviticus 26:22), war (Ezekiel 14:17-18; see Leviticus 26:25), and disease (Ezekiel 14:19-20; see Leviticus 26:25).

14:22-23 Some survivors would emerge from the devastating judgment (14:21) and join those already in exile. They would not survive because of their righteousness or that of their relatives, but simply as an object lesson. Seeing the depravity of this remnant, those already in exile would feel better about what God had done to Jerusalem. They would know that God had not acted without cause but had acted with justice in his judgment upon Jerusalem.

15:1–24:14 This section contains a series of eight metaphors, each reiterating from a different angle the certainty of Jerusalem's forthcoming judgment. The images are of a useless vine (15:1-8), an unfaithful wife (16:1-63), a vine and two eagles (17:1-24), sour grapes (18:1-32), a lioness and her cubs (19:1-9), a sword (21:1-32), two degenerate sisters (23:1-49), and a cooking pot (24:1-14).

pegs to hang up pots and pans? ⁴No, it can only be used for fuel, and even as fuel, it burns too quickly. ⁵Vines are useless both before and after being put into the fire!

⁶"And this is what the Sovereign LORD says: The people of Jerusalem are like grapevines growing among the trees of the forest. Since they are useless, I have thrown them on the fire to be burned. ⁷And I will see to it that if they escape from one fire, they will fall into another. When I turn against them, you will know that I am the LORD. ⁸And I will make the land desolate because my people have been unfaithful to me. I, the Sovereign LORD, have spoken!"

Jerusalem—an Unfaithful Wife

16 Then another message came to me from the LORD: ²"Son of man, confront Jerusalem with her detestable sins. ³Give her this message from the Sovereign LORD: You are nothing but a Canaanite! Your father was an Amorite and your mother a Hittite. ⁴On the day you were born, no one cared about you. Your umbilical cord was not cut, and you were never washed, rubbed with salt, and wrapped in cloth. ⁵No one had the slightest interest in you; no one pitied you or cared for you. On the day you were born, you were unwanted, dumped in a field and left to die.

⁶"But I came by and saw you there, helplessly kicking about in your own blood. As you lay there, I said, 'Live!' ⁷And I helped you to thrive like a plant in the field. You grew up and became a beautiful jewel. Your breasts became full, and your body hair grew, but you were still naked. ⁸And when I passed by again, I saw that you were old enough for love. So I wrapped my cloak around you to cover your nakedness and declared my marriage vows. I made a covenant with you, says the Sovereign LORD, and you became mine.

⁹"Then I bathed you and washed off your blood, and I rubbed fragrant oils into your skin. ¹⁰I gave you expensive clothing of fine linen and silk, beautifully embroidered, and sandals made of fine goatskin leather. ¹¹I gave you lovely jewelry, bracelets, beautiful necklaces, ¹²a ring for your nose, earrings for your ears, and a lovely crown for your head. ¹³And so you were adorned with gold and silver. Your clothes were made of fine linen and costly fabric and were beautifully embroidered. You ate the finest foods—choice flour, honey, and olive oil—and became more beautiful than ever. You looked like a queen, and so you were! ¹⁴Your fame soon spread throughout the world because of your beauty. I dressed you in my splendor and perfected your beauty, says the Sovereign LORD.

¹⁵"But you thought your fame and beauty were your own. So you gave yourself as a prostitute to every man who came along. Your beauty was theirs for the asking. ¹⁶You used the lovely things I gave you to make shrines for idols, where you played the prostitute. Unbelievable! How could such a thing ever happen? ¹⁷You took the very jewels and gold and silver ornaments I had given you and made statues of men and worshiped them. This is adultery against me! ¹⁸You used the beautifully embroidered clothes I gave you to dress your idols. Then you used my special oil and my incense to worship them. ¹⁹Imagine it! You set before them as a sacrifice the choice flour, olive oil, and honey I had given you, says the Sovereign LORD.

15:1–17:24 Three parables explain the people's situation. God had rejected his people because they were unfaithful and broke God's covenant with them. But God planted Israel in the Promised Land as his chosen vine. It was not separation God sought but deeper intimacy in the relationship. Any judgment that would fall on God's people would confirm the covenant.

15:1-8 God compared the people to a grapevine. A grapevine becomes useless when it does not produce grapes. The Israelites' inability to honor God produced a fruitless life. So, God used the Babylonians to cut down and burn the dead vines in Jerusalem four times (605, 597, 588, and 586 BC). By contrast, one vine endures—Jesus, the true vine (John 15:1-8). Those who do not abide in him "are gathered into a pile to be burned" (John 15:6), but those who abide flourish (John 15:3-5).

16:1-63 This chapter graphically traces Israel's relationship with God from birth to adulthood. In ancient writings, cities were personified as women; Jerusalem is personified in this chapter and represents Israel. God created Jerusalem to be in a special relationship with him. He saved her at birth when her parents abandoned and left her to die. When she was of age, God took Jerusalem as his bride. However, Jerusalem dishonorably used all the gifts God gave her and engaged in spiritual prostitution. Here, God takes his "wife" to court and testifies to her unfaithfulness. Brokenhearted, God disciplines Jerusalem. God promises to forgive Jerusalem and pledges his devotion and love by remembering his covenant.

16:6-7 While Jerusalem was in a helpless and hopeless condition, the Lord intervened with his life-giving word. Without that, she certainly would have died. The Lord had no obligation to rescue this abandoned child, for she would simply have been one among many facing such a fate. Yet out of his grace and mercy, the Lord enabled her not merely to survive but to thrive. Instead of dying in the field, she grew up like a plant into maturity and beauty. The city of Jerusalem prospered before becoming an Israelite city, and it was the Lord's doing.

16:8 The Lord wrapped his cloak around Jerusalem, an act that represented a commitment to marriage (see Ruth 3:9). The Lord made a covenant with Jerusalem, and in the terms of the metaphor, he married her. When the Lord entered into a covenant with David and his descendants, he also chose Jerusalem as the place for his name to be honored (see 1 Kings 9:3-4; Psalm 132:1-18).

16:11-19 Jerusalem was adorned with jewelry and fed with the very finest foods. She was known throughout the world for her beauty and splendor—both being gifts from the Lord. Instead of appreciating the good things God had given her, Jerusalem prostituted her fame and beauty to false gods and offered to idols the clothes, jewels, food, and oil that the Lord had given her.

20"Then you took your sons and daughters—the children you had borne to me—and sacrificed them to your gods. Was your prostitution not enough? 21Must you also slaughter my children by sacrificing them to idols? 22In all your years of adultery and detestable sin, you have not once remembered the days long ago when you lay naked in a field, kicking about in your own blood.

23"What sorrow awaits you, says the Sovereign Lord. In addition to all your other wickedness, 24you built a pagan shrine and put altars to idols in every town square. 25On every street corner you defiled your beauty, offering your body to every passerby in an endless stream of prostitution. 26Then you added lustful Egypt to your lovers, provoking my anger with your increasing promiscuity. 27That is why I struck you with my fist and reduced your boundaries. I handed you over to your enemies, the Philistines, and even they were shocked by your lewd conduct. 28You have prostituted yourself with the Assyrians, too. It seems you can never find enough new lovers! And after your prostitution there, you still were not satisfied. 29You added to your lovers by embracing Babylonia,* the land of merchants, but you still weren't satisfied.

30"What a sick heart you have, says the Sovereign Lord, to do such things as these, acting like a shameless prostitute. 31You build your pagan shrines on every street corner and your altars to idols in every square. In fact, you have been worse than a prostitute, so eager for sin that you have not even demanded payment. 32Yes, you are an adulterous wife who takes in strangers instead of her own husband. 33Prostitutes charge for their services—but not you! You give gifts to your lovers, bribing them to come and have sex with you. 34So you are the opposite of other prostitutes. You pay your lovers instead of their paying you!

Judgment on Jerusalem's Prostitution

35"Therefore, you prostitute, listen to this message from the Lord! 36This is what the Sovereign Lord says: Because you have poured out your lust and exposed yourself in prostitution to all your lovers, and because you have worshiped detestable idols,* and because you have slaughtered your children as sacrifices to your gods, 37this is what I am going to do. I will gather together all your allies—the lovers with whom you have sinned, both those you loved and those you hated—and I will strip you naked in front of them so they can stare at you. 38I will punish you for your murder and adultery. I will cover you with blood in my jealous fury. 39Then I will give you to these many nations who are your lovers, and they will destroy you. They will knock down your pagan shrines and the altars to your idols. They will strip you and take your beautiful jewels, leaving you stark naked. 40They will band together in a mob to stone you and cut you up with swords. 41They will burn your homes and punish you in front of many women. I will stop your prostitution and end your payments to your many lovers.

42"Then at last my fury against you will be spent, and my jealous anger will subside. I will be calm and will not be angry with you anymore. 43But first, because you have not remembered your youth but have angered me by doing all these evil things, I will fully repay you for all of your sins, says the Sovereign Lord. For you have added lewd acts to all your detestable sins. 44Everyone who makes up proverbs will say of you, 'Like mother, like daughter.' 45For your mother loathed her husband and her children, and so do you. And you are exactly like your sisters, for they despised their husbands and their children. Truly your mother was a Hittite and your father an Amorite.

46"Your older sister was Samaria, who lived with her daughters in the north. Your younger sister was Sodom, who lived with her daughters in the south. 47But you have not merely sinned as they did. You quickly surpassed them in corruption. 48As surely as I live, says the Sovereign Lord, Sodom and her daughters were never as wicked as you and your daughters. 49Sodom's sins were pride, gluttony, and laziness, while the poor and needy suffered outside her door. 50She was proud and committed detestable sins, so I wiped her out, as you have seen.*

51"Even Samaria did not commit half your sins. You have done far more detestable things than your sisters ever did. They seem righteous compared to you. 52Shame on you! Your sins are so terrible that you make your sisters seem righteous, even virtuous.

16:29 Or *Chaldea.* **16:36** The Hebrew term (literally *round things*) probably alludes to dung. **16:50** As in a few Hebrew manuscripts and Greek version; Masoretic Text reads *as I have seen.*

16:35-38 Since Jerusalem had behaved like an adulteress, it was fitting that she should face the Levitical death sentence. God would strip her naked in a symbolic act of divorce, thus reversing the clothing metaphor of marriage (see 16:8; Hosea 2:2-3). Then the people would stone her (Leviticus 20:10; Deuteronomy 22:22). Since this would cover her naked body with blood, she would leave the world just as she came into it. This metaphor was fulfilled when the Babylonians destroyed the city in 586 BC. **16:38-47** After describing Israel's sin, God explained his just cause for punishment. Jerusalem had forgotten what God did for them and had become ungrateful. They took the glory for themselves. Further, they raised immoral and disloyal children, like Jerusalem's sister cities—Samaria and Sodom. More was expected from the people of Israel because God revealed more of himself to them through the law.

Jerusalem, Sodom, and Samaria

IDENTITY

Unfaithful Wife and Her Sisters

The people of Jerusalem denied Ezekiel's message: *Aren't we the people of Yahweh? He gave us this place—surely, he won't destroy it.*

Ezekiel depicts God's people as a wife who has prostituted herself, even paying others for sex. His story is meant to horrify, to show her sins' seriousness. She had relied on foreign kings to protect her. She had worshiped other gods—violating her vow (Exodus 20:1-6; 24:3). She owed her life to Yahweh—all her blessings had been a gift. But Jerusalem had been squandering that gift with gusto.

When her neighbors—Sodom and Samaria—were judged, Jerusalem assumed they deserved it. She didn't think she was that bad. But Yahweh declared her betrayal was worse.

Jerusalem lost everything—her land, her home, and the Temple. But God chose her once, and he'd chosen her forever. In exile, the Lord purified and restored her, and also Sodom and Samaria. By remaining faithful to his people, Yahweh displayed mercy for all.

This mercy came to fullness through God in the flesh, Jesus. Jesus purifies our unfaithfulness, returning us from exile. And—like Yahweh with Jerusalem, Sodom, and Samaria—he longs to restore all.

> By choosing Jerusalem, God displays the depths of his mercy for everyone.

THE STORY OF JERUSALEM, SODOM, AND SAMARIA IS TOLD IN EZEKIEL 16:1-63.

IDENTIFY

The people of Jerusalem chose to worship other gods instead of the one true God. How do we, in our sin, trust in something other than God for our provision and protection?

How would our lives change if we gave ourselves wholly to God and trusted him for what we need?

> "Yahweh's message to Jerusalem is hard to hear, but it reminds me that what we do matters to God. Keeping this in view helps us remain faithful."

ELLEN RICHARD VOSBURG, MA, is a Bible editor for Tyndale House Publishers. She studied Greek and Hebrew and lives to lead others into God's deep love by getting to know him through his Word.

⁵³"But someday I will restore the fortunes of Sodom and Samaria, and I will restore you, too. ⁵⁴Then you will be truly ashamed of everything you have done, for your sins make them feel good in comparison. ⁵⁵Yes, your sisters, Sodom and Samaria, and all their people will be restored, and at that time you also will be restored. ⁵⁶In your proud days you held Sodom in contempt. ⁵⁷But now your greater wickedness has been exposed to all the world, and you are the one who is scorned—by Edom* and all her neighbors and by Philistia. ⁵⁸This is your punishment for all your lewdness and detestable sins, says the LORD.

⁵⁹"Now this is what the Sovereign LORD says: I will give you what you deserve, for you have taken your solemn vows lightly by breaking your covenant. ⁶⁰Yet I will remember the covenant I made with you when you were young, and I will establish an everlasting covenant with you. ⁶¹Then you will remember with shame all the evil you have done. I will make your sisters, Samaria and Sodom, to be your daughters, even though they are not part of our covenant. ⁶²And I will reaffirm my covenant with you, and you will know that I am the LORD. ⁶³You will remember your sins and cover your mouth in silent shame when I forgive you of all that you have done. I, the Sovereign LORD, have spoken!"

A Story of Two Eagles

17 Then this message came to me from the LORD: ²"Son of man, give this riddle, and tell this story to the people of Israel. ³Give them this message from the Sovereign LORD:

"A great eagle with broad wings and long feathers,
  covered with many-colored plumage,
  came to Lebanon.
He seized the top of a cedar tree
⁴ and plucked off its highest branch.
He carried it away to a city filled with merchants.
  He planted it in a city of traders.
⁵ He also took a seedling from the land
  and planted it in fertile soil.
He placed it beside a broad river,
  where it could grow like a willow tree.
⁶ It took root there
  and grew into a low, spreading vine.
Its branches turned up toward the eagle,
  and its roots grew down into the ground.
It produced strong branches
  and put out shoots.
⁷ But then another great eagle came
  with broad wings and full plumage.
So the vine now sent its roots and branches
  toward him for water,
⁸ even though it was already planted in good soil
  and had plenty of water
so it could grow into a splendid vine
  and produce rich leaves and luscious fruit.

⁹ "So now the Sovereign LORD asks:
Will this vine grow and prosper?
  No! I will pull it up, roots and all!
I will cut off its fruit
  and let its leaves wither and die.
I will pull it up easily
  without a strong arm or a large army.
¹⁰ But when the vine is transplanted,
  will it thrive?
No, it will wither away
  when the east wind blows against it.
It will die in the same good soil
  where it had grown so well."

The Riddle Explained

¹¹Then this message came to me from the LORD: ¹²"Say to these rebels of Israel: Don't you understand the meaning of this riddle of the eagles? The king of Babylon came to Jerusalem, took away her king and princes, and brought them to Babylon. ¹³He made a treaty with a member of the royal family and forced him to take an oath of loyalty. He also exiled Israel's most influential leaders, ¹⁴so Israel would not become strong again and revolt. Only by keeping her treaty with Babylon could Israel survive.

¹⁵"Nevertheless, this man of Israel's royal family rebelled against Babylon, sending ambassadors to Egypt to request a great army and many horses. Can

---

16:57 As in many Hebrew manuscripts and Syriac version; Masoretic Text reads *Aram*.

16:59-63 Jerusalem's sins were serious and had to be judged, but judgment was not God's last word on Jerusalem. She had comprehensively broken God's covenant and deserved the consequence of death, but God would remember the covenant he had made with her in the beginning. God's purposes for his people cannot be derailed even by their sin, for his covenant commitment is everlasting (Psalm 136). God's forgiveness of her sins would finally bring Jerusalem to repentance.

17:3-24 Ezekiel spoke in a riddle. The imaginative context creates distance between the story and the reality and thus could disarm the hearers' defenses against an unpalatable message. Perhaps if the people of Israel would awaken their minds to comprehend the meaning of the riddle, they would find the truth.

17:11-18 The riddle involves a great tree, two eagles, and new shoots (17:3-8). The cedar tree represents King David's dynasty. God promised that a Savior would come from David (2 Samuel 7:16; Luke 1:32-33, 69). The shoots represent Israel's kings: Jehoiachin, Zedekiah, and the Messiah. The first eagle represents King Nebuchadnezzar II of Babylon, and the second symbolizes the Egyptian Pharaoh who was helping the Israelites fight Babylon.

Israel break her sworn treaties like that and get away with it? ¹⁶No! For as surely as I live, says the Sovereign LORD, the king of Israel will die in Babylon, the land of the king who put him in power and whose treaty he disregarded and broke. ¹⁷Pharaoh and all his mighty army will fail to help Israel when the king of Babylon lays siege to Jerusalem again and destroys many lives. ¹⁸For the king of Israel disregarded his treaty and broke it after swearing to obey; therefore, he will not escape.

¹⁹"So this is what the Sovereign LORD says: As surely as I live, I will punish him for breaking my covenant and disregarding the solemn oath he made in my name. ²⁰I will throw my net over him and capture him in my snare. I will bring him to Babylon and put him on trial for this treason against me. ²¹And all his best warriors* will be killed in battle, and those who survive will be scattered to the four winds. Then you will know that I, the LORD, have spoken.

²²"This is what the Sovereign LORD says: I will take a branch from the top of a tall cedar, and I will plant it on the top of Israel's highest mountain. ²³It will become a majestic cedar, sending forth its branches and producing seed. Birds of every sort will nest in it, finding shelter in the shade of its branches. ²⁴And all the trees will know that it is I, the LORD, who cuts the tall tree down and makes the short tree grow tall. It is I who makes the green tree wither and gives the dead tree new life. I, the LORD, have spoken, and I will do what I said!"

> "It's not about finding ways to avoid God's judgment and feeling like a failure if you don't do everything perfectly. It's about fully experiencing God's love and letting it perfect you. It's not about being somebody you are not. It's about becoming who you really are."
>
> **STORMIE OMARTIAN**
> speaker and bestselling author

The Justice of a Righteous God

18 Then another message came to me from the LORD: ²"Why do you quote this proverb concerning the land of Israel: 'The parents have eaten sour grapes, but their children's mouths pucker at the taste'? ³As surely as I live, says the Sovereign LORD, you will not quote this proverb anymore in Israel. ⁴For all people are mine to judge—both parents and children alike. And this is my rule: The person who sins is the one who will die.

⁵"Suppose a certain man is righteous and does what is just and right. ⁶He does not feast in the mountains before Israel's idols* or worship them. He does not commit adultery or have intercourse with a woman during her menstrual period. ⁷He is a merciful creditor, not keeping the items given as security by poor debtors. He does not rob the poor but instead gives food to the hungry and provides clothes for the needy. ⁸He grants loans without interest, stays away from injustice, is honest and fair when judging others, ⁹and faithfully obeys my decrees and regulations. Anyone who does these things is just and will surely live, says the Sovereign LORD.

17:21 As in many Hebrew manuscripts; Masoretic Text reads *his fleeing warriors*. The meaning is uncertain. **18:6** The Hebrew term (literally *round things*) probably alludes to dung; also in 18:12, 15.

17:19-24 Zedekiah broke his covenant with Nebuchadnezzar and with God (see 2 Kings 24:18–25:7). God disciplined Zedekiah through Nebuchadnezzar: Zedekiah's sons were killed in front of him before he was blinded and sent to Babylon, where he eventually died. As the last king of Israel, Zedekiah's death implied an end to King David's dynasty. However, God promised to take a branch from the cedar tree and plant it in Israel. That branch would grow and become the Messiah, Jesus (Isaiah 11:1-10; Jeremiah 23:5-6; 33:15-17).
18:1–21:32 The Israelites thought God was punishing them for their ancestors' sin because they assumed that they had done nothing wrong. Ezekiel explained that God was judging people individually, not for others' sins (18:1-32). The Israelite leaders caused their own demise with their own sin (19:1-14). Looking back into history, Ezekiel pointed out that Israel had been sinning for a long time (20:1-44). God models responsibility and holds himself and Israel accountable (21:1-17). God is just.
18:1-32 The generation Ezekiel was speaking to assumed they were innocent and that they were being punished for their ancestors' wrongdoing. Ezekiel explained that salvation came from an individual taking personal responsibility for their actions to correct their misunderstanding (18:20, 24, 26). The Lord is just and merciful, which means the righteous are rewarded and the wicked are punished, but he is always hoping that the wicked will repent and do what is right (18:20-24).
18:8 The law prohibited charging interest on a loan to someone in need. God did not condone exploitative lending practices (see Exodus 22:25-27).

¹⁰"But suppose that man has a son who grows up to be a robber or murderer and refuses to do what is right. ¹¹And that son does all the evil things his father would never do—he worships idols on the mountains, commits adultery, ¹²oppresses the poor and helpless, steals from debtors by refusing to let them redeem their security, worships idols, commits detestable sins, ¹³and lends money at excessive interest. Should such a sinful person live? No! He must die and must take full blame.

¹⁴"But suppose that sinful son, in turn, has a son who sees his father's wickedness and decides against that kind of life. ¹⁵This son refuses to worship idols on the mountains and does not commit adultery. ¹⁶He does not exploit the poor, but instead is fair to debtors and does not rob them. He gives food to the hungry and provides clothes for the needy. ¹⁷He helps the poor,* does not lend money at interest, and obeys all my regulations and decrees. Such a person will not die because of his father's sins; he will surely live. ¹⁸But the father will die for his many sins—for being cruel, robbing people, and doing what was clearly wrong among his people.

¹⁹"'What?' you ask. 'Doesn't the child pay for the parent's sins?' No! For if the child does what is just and right and keeps my decrees, that child will surely live. ²⁰The person who sins is the one who will die. The child will not be punished for the parent's sins, and the parent will not be punished for the child's sins. Righteous people will be rewarded for their own righteous behavior, and wicked people will be punished for their own wickedness. ²¹But if wicked people turn away from all their sins and begin to obey my decrees and do what is just and right, they will surely live and not die. ²²All their past sins will be forgotten, and they will live because of the righteous things they have done.

²³"Do you think that I like to see wicked people die? says the Sovereign LORD. Of course not! I want them to turn from their wicked ways and live. ²⁴However, if righteous people turn from their righteous behavior and start doing sinful things and act like other sinners, should they be allowed to live? No, of course not! All their righteous acts will be forgotten, and they will die for their sins.

18:17 Greek version reads *He refuses to do evil.*

²⁵"Yet you say, 'The Lord isn't doing what's right!' Listen to me, O people of Israel. Am I the one not doing what's right, or is it you? ²⁶When righteous people turn from their righteous behavior and start doing sinful things, they will die for it. Yes, they will die because of their sinful deeds. ²⁷And if wicked people turn from their wickedness, obey the law, and do what is just and right, they will save their lives. ²⁸They will live because they thought it over and decided to turn from their sins. Such people will not die. ²⁹And yet the people of Israel keep saying, 'The Lord isn't doing what's right!' O people of Israel, it is you who are not doing what's right, not I.

³⁰"Therefore, I will judge each of you, O people of Israel, according to your actions, says the Sovereign LORD. Repent, and turn from your sins. Don't let them destroy you! ³¹Put all your rebellion behind you, and find yourselves a new heart and a new spirit. For why should you die, O people of Israel? ³²I don't want you to die, says the Sovereign LORD. Turn back and live!

A Funeral Song for Israel's Kings

19 "Sing this funeral song for the princes of Israel:

² "What is your mother?
    A lioness among lions!
She lay down among the young lions
    and reared her cubs.
³ She raised one of her cubs
    to become a strong young lion.
He learned to hunt and devour prey,
    and he became a man-eater.
⁴ Then the nations heard about him,
    and he was trapped in their pit.
They led him away with hooks
    to the land of Egypt.
⁵ "When the lioness saw
    that her hopes for him were gone,
she took another of her cubs
    and taught him to be a strong young lion.
⁶ He prowled among the other lions
    and stood out among them in his strength.

18:21-24 Ezekiel introduces two more case studies. Wicked people who turn away from their sins can experience God's forgiveness, and righteous people who begin sinning will be judged. God does not "like to see wicked people die," so he appointed Ezekiel as a watchman. His role was to turn the wicked toward godly living while warning the righteous against falling away (see 3:16-19; 33:1-9).
18:30-32 This chapter concludes with a passionate appeal to the people of Israel to turn back and live. It was not too late for them to repent, turn from their sins, and be forgiven. God promised a new heart and a new spirit (11:19; 36:26) to all who would turn from their rebellion and humbly come to him.
19:1-14 Ancient Near Eastern funeral songs had a distinctive rhythm and style and usually extolled the virtues of the deceased, contrasting past glory with the current loss. In this case, those being lamented were not yet dead, and the dirge contained a catalogue of their faults. This dirge profoundly communicated the certainty of their fate and the reasons for it. The young lion (19:2-9) and the vine (19:10-14) were familiar images for the princes of Israel, the royal dynasty of Judah.
19:2-14 Israel's vine produced many rebellious kings. Had they honored God, Israel would have remained a commanding lion and fruitful vine that glorified God. Israel would have been a light to the nations, and more people would have known the one true God. Instead, the people followed their leaders in making the same rebellious choices. They would reap the consequences of living in exile without land, their Temple, or God's presence.

He learned to hunt and devour prey,
   and he, too, became a man-eater.
⁷ He demolished fortresses*
   and destroyed their towns and cities.
Their farms were desolated,
   and their crops were destroyed.
The land and its people trembled in fear
   when they heard him roar.
⁸ Then the armies of the nations attacked him,
   surrounding him from every direction.
They threw a net over him
   and captured him in their pit.
⁹ With hooks, they dragged him into a cage
   and brought him before the king of Babylon.
They held him in captivity,
   so his voice could never again be heard
   on the mountains of Israel.

¹⁰ "Your mother was like a vine
   planted by the water's edge.
It had lush, green foliage
   because of the abundant water.
¹¹ Its branches became strong—
   strong enough to be a ruler's scepter.
It grew very tall,
   towering above all others.
It stood out because of its height
   and its many lush branches.
¹² But the vine was uprooted in fury
   and thrown down to the ground.
The desert wind dried up its fruit
   and tore off its strong branches,
so that it withered
   and was destroyed by fire.
¹³ Now the vine is transplanted to the wilderness,
   where the ground is hard and dry.
¹⁴ A fire has burst out from its branches
   and devoured its fruit.
Its remaining limbs are not
   strong enough to be a ruler's scepter.

"This is a funeral song, and it will be used in a funeral."

The Rebellion of Israel

20 On August 14,* during the seventh year of King Jehoiachin's captivity, some of the leaders of Israel came to request a message from the LORD. They sat down in front of me to wait for his reply. ²Then this message came to me from the LORD: ³"Son of man, tell the leaders of Israel, 'This is what the Sovereign LORD says: How dare you come to ask me for a message? As surely as I live, says the Sovereign LORD, I will tell you nothing!'

⁴"Son of man, bring charges against them and condemn them. Make them realize how detestable the sins of their ancestors really were. ⁵Give them this message from the Sovereign LORD: When I chose Israel—when I revealed myself to the descendants of Jacob in Egypt—I took a solemn oath that I, the LORD, would be their God. ⁶I took a solemn oath that day that I would bring them out of Egypt to a land I had discovered and explored for them—a good land, a land flowing with milk and honey, the best of all lands anywhere. ⁷Then I said to them, 'Each of you, get rid of the vile images you are so obsessed with. Do not defile yourselves with the idols* of Egypt, for I am the LORD your God.'

⁸"But they rebelled against me and would not listen. They did not get rid of the vile images they were obsessed with, or forsake the idols of Egypt. Then I threatened to pour out my fury on them to satisfy my anger while they were still in Egypt. ⁹But I didn't do it, for I acted to protect the honor of my name. I would not allow shame to be brought on my name among the surrounding nations who saw me reveal myself by bringing the Israelites out of Egypt. ¹⁰So I brought them out of Egypt and led them into the wilderness. ¹¹There I gave them my decrees and regulations so they could find life by keeping them. ¹²And I gave them my Sabbath days of rest as a sign between them and me. It was to remind them that I am the LORD, who had set them apart to be holy.

¹³"But the people of Israel rebelled against me, and they refused to obey my decrees there in the wilderness. They wouldn't obey my regulations even though obedience would have given them life. They also violated my Sabbath days. So I threatened to pour out my fury on them, and I made plans to utterly consume them in the wilderness. ¹⁴But again I held back in order to protect the honor of my name before the nations who had seen my power in bringing Israel out of Egypt. ¹⁵But I took a solemn oath against them in the wilderness. I swore I would not bring them into

---

19:7 As in Greek version; Hebrew reads *He knew widows.*   20:1 Hebrew *In the fifth month, on the tenth day,* of the ancient Hebrew lunar calendar. This day was August 14, 591 B.C.; also see note on 1:1.   20:7 The Hebrew term (literally *round things*) probably alludes to dung; also in 20:8, 16, 18, 24, 31, 39.

20:1-3 Five more years would pass before the destruction of Jerusalem. The leaders of Israel—the leaders of the community in exile—came to Ezekiel once again, looking for a word from the Lord. Normally, seeking a message from the Lord is a good thing. But these leaders had already been condemned for their mixed motives (14:1-5), and the Lord would not receive their request. The question they asked Ezekiel is not recorded—perhaps they never had the opportunity to ask it.

20:8-21 Each generation of Israelites rebelled against the Lord and refused to obey the commandments he gave them (20:8, 13, 21). Each time, the Lord threatened to pour out his fury upon them (20:8, 13, 21), but he relented for the honor of his name, lest the nations around them think that the Lord's power was insufficient to bring his people into the Promised Land.

WHAT THE BIBLE SAYS ABOUT Grief

The Leaders of God's People Are Called to Grieve for Others Differently

Moses said to Aaron and his sons Eleazar and Ithamar, "Do not show grief by leaving your hair uncombed or by tearing your clothes." LEVITICUS 10:6

"Son of man,... I will take away your dearest treasure. Yet you must not show any sorrow at her death."...
    Then the people asked, "What does all this mean?"...
    "Ezekiel is an example for you; you will do just as he has done. And when that time comes, you will know that I am the Sovereign LORD." EZEKIEL 24:16, 19, 24

I [Jeremiah] hurt with the hurt of my people.
    I mourn and am overcome with grief.
JEREMIAH 8:21

My [Paul's] heart is filled with bitter sorrow and unending grief for my people. ROMANS 9:2-3

Have mercy on me, LORD, for I am in distress.... Tears blur my eyes.

Wrongdoing Invites Grief

Have mercy on me, LORD, for I am in distress.
  Tears blur my eyes.
  My body and soul are withering away.
I am dying from grief;
  my years are shortened by sadness.
Sin has drained my strength;
  I am wasting away from within.
PSALM 31:9-10

Humble yourselves before God.... Let there be tears for what you have done. Let there be sorrow and deep grief.... Humble yourselves before the Lord, and he will lift you up in honor.
JAMES 4:7, 9-10

My wounds fester and stink
  because of my foolish sins.
I am bent over and racked with pain.
  All day long I walk around filled with grief.
PSALM 38:5-6

Jesus and His Followers Grieve

He was despised and rejected—
  a man of sorrows, acquainted with deepest grief.
ISAIAH 53:3

"He [the Son of Man] will be killed, but on the third day he will be raised from the dead." And the disciples were filled with grief.
MATTHEW 17:23

He [Jesus] told them, "My soul is crushed with grief to the point of death. Stay here and keep watch with me." **MARK 14:34**

At last he [Jesus] stood up again and returned to the disciples, only to find them asleep, exhausted from grief. **LUKE 22:45**

[As Jesus approached the place where he would be executed:] A large crowd trailed behind, including many grief-stricken women.
LUKE 23:27

"I [Jesus] tell you the truth, you will weep and mourn over what is going to happen to me, but the world will rejoice. You will grieve, but your grief will suddenly turn to wonderful joy." **JOHN 16:20**

God Can Heal Our Grief

Though he [the LORD] brings
  grief, he also shows
  compassion
  because of the greatness
  of his unfailing love.
LAMENTATIONS 3:32

[The LORD says,] "Don't tear
  your clothing in your
  grief,
  but tear your hearts
  instead."
Return to the LORD your God,
  for he is merciful and
  compassionate,
  slow to get angry and filled
  with unfailing love.
JOEL 2:13

the land I had given them, a land flowing with milk and honey, the most beautiful place on earth. ¹⁶For they had rejected my regulations, refused to follow my decrees, and violated my Sabbath days. Their hearts were given to their idols. ¹⁷Nevertheless, I took pity on them and held back from destroying them in the wilderness.

¹⁸"Then I warned their children not to follow in their parents' footsteps, defiling themselves with their idols. ¹⁹'I am the Lord your God,' I told them. 'Follow my decrees, pay attention to my regulations, ²⁰and keep my Sabbath days holy, for they are a sign to remind you that I am the Lord your God.'

²¹"But their children, too, rebelled against me. They refused to keep my decrees and follow my regulations, even though obedience would have given them life. And they also violated my Sabbath days. So again I threatened to pour out my fury on them in the wilderness. ²²Nevertheless, I withdrew my judgment against them to protect the honor of my name before the nations that had seen my power in bringing them out of Egypt. ²³But I took a solemn oath against them in the wilderness. I swore I would scatter them among all the nations ²⁴because they did not obey my regulations. They scorned my decrees by violating my Sabbath days and longing for the idols of their ancestors. ²⁵I gave them over to worthless decrees and regulations that would not lead to life. ²⁶I let them pollute themselves* with the very gifts I had given them, and I allowed them to give their firstborn children as offerings to their gods—so I might devastate them and remind them that I alone am the Lord.

Judgment and Restoration

²⁷"Therefore, son of man, give the people of Israel this message from the Sovereign Lord: Your ancestors continued to blaspheme and betray me, ²⁸for when I brought them into the land I had promised them, they offered sacrifices on every high hill and under every green tree they saw! They roused my fury as they offered up sacrifices to their gods. They brought their perfumes and incense and poured out their liquid offerings to them. ²⁹I said to them, 'What is this high place where you are going?' (This kind of pagan shrine has been called Bamah—'high place'—ever since.)

³⁰"Therefore, give the people of Israel this message from the Sovereign Lord: Do you plan to pollute yourselves just as your ancestors did? Do you intend to keep prostituting yourselves by worshiping vile images? ³¹For when you offer gifts to them and give your little children to be burned as sacrifices,* you continue to pollute yourselves with idols to this day. Should I allow you to ask for a message from me, O people of Israel? As surely as I live, says the Sovereign Lord, I will tell you nothing.

³²"You say, 'We want to be like the nations all around us, who serve idols of wood and stone.' But what you have in mind will never happen. ³³As surely as I live, says the Sovereign Lord, I will rule over you with an iron fist in great anger and with awesome power. ³⁴And in anger I will reach out with my strong hand and powerful arm, and I will bring you back* from the lands where you are scattered. ³⁵I will bring you into the wilderness of the nations, and there I will judge you face to face. ³⁶I will judge you there just as I did your ancestors in the wilderness after bringing them out of Egypt, says the Sovereign Lord. ³⁷I will examine you carefully and hold you to the terms of the covenant. ³⁸I will purge you of all those who rebel and revolt against me. I will bring them out of the countries where they are in exile, but they will never enter the land of Israel. Then you will know that I am the Lord.

³⁹"As for you, O people of Israel, this is what the Sovereign Lord says: Go right ahead and worship your idols, but sooner or later you will obey me and will stop bringing shame on my holy name by worshiping idols. ⁴⁰For on my holy mountain, the great mountain of Israel, says the Sovereign Lord, the people of Israel will someday worship me, and I will accept them. There I will require that you bring me all your offerings and choice gifts and sacrifices. ⁴¹When I bring you home from exile, you will be like a pleasing sacrifice to me. And I will display my holiness through you as all the nations watch. ⁴²Then when I have brought you home to the land I promised with a solemn oath to give to your ancestors, you will know that I am the Lord. ⁴³You will look back on all the ways you defiled yourselves and will hate yourselves because of the evil you have done. ⁴⁴You will know that I am the Lord, O people of Israel, when I have honored my name by treating you mercifully in spite of your wickedness. I, the Sovereign Lord, have spoken!"

20:25-26 Or *I gave them worthless decrees and regulations. . . . I polluted them.* 20:31 Or *and make your little children pass through the fire.* 20:34 Greek version reads *I will welcome you.* Compare 2 Cor 6:17.

20:26 The Israelites even gave their firstborn children as offerings to the god Molech. This exactly reversed the Exodus, which freed Israel, the Lord's "firstborn son" (Exodus 4:22), to offer pure worship in the Promised Land.
20:27-31 Once in the Promised Land, the people of Israel continued to blaspheme and betray the Lord. Their idolatry and wickedness continued to Ezekiel's day. Such apostate people would receive no answer from the Lord.
20:33-44 Even though rebellion against God interlaces Israel's narrative, God is faithful as well as just. In his grace, he delivered a message of hope through Ezekiel. One day in the future, God would gather the people of Israel. As king, he would restore the natural order, which would bring peace and well-being. All the people would worship God and bear his holy name.

Judgment against the Negev

45*Then this message came to me from the LORD: 46"Son of man, turn and face the south* and speak out against it; prophesy against the brushlands of the Negev. 47Tell the southern wilderness, 'This is what the Sovereign LORD says: Hear the word of the LORD! I will set you on fire, and every tree, both green and dry, will be burned. The terrible flames will not be quenched and will scorch everything from south to north. 48And everyone in the world will see that I, the LORD, have set this fire. It will not be put out.'"

49Then I said, "O Sovereign LORD, they are saying of me, 'He only talks in riddles!'"

The LORD's Sword of Judgment

21 1*Then this message came to me from the LORD: 2"Son of man, turn and face Jerusalem and prophesy against Israel and her sanctuaries. 3Tell her, 'This is what the LORD says: I am your enemy, O Israel, and I am about to unsheath my sword to destroy your people—the righteous and the wicked alike. 4Yes, I will cut off both the righteous and the wicked! I will draw my sword against everyone in the land from south to north. 5Everyone in the world will know that I am the LORD. My sword is in my hand, and it will not return to its sheath until its work is finished.'

6"Son of man, groan before the people! Groan before them with bitter anguish and a broken heart. 7When they ask why you are groaning, tell them, 'I groan because of the terrifying news I have heard. When it comes true, the boldest heart will melt with fear; all strength will disappear. Every spirit will faint; strong knees will become as weak as water. And the Sovereign LORD says: It is coming! It's on its way!'"

8Then the LORD said to me, 9"Son of man, give the people this message from the Lord:

"A sword, a sword
 is being sharpened and polished.
10 It is sharpened for terrible slaughter
 and polished to flash like lightning!
 Now will you laugh?
 Those far stronger than you have fallen
  beneath its power!*

11 Yes, the sword is now being sharpened and
  polished;
 it is being prepared for the executioner.
12 "Son of man, cry out and wail;
 pound your thighs in anguish,
 for that sword will slaughter my people and
  their leaders—
  everyone will die!
13 It will put them all to the test.
 What chance do they have?*
 says the Sovereign LORD.

14 "Son of man, prophesy to them
 and clap your hands.
 Then take the sword and brandish it twice,
  even three times,
 to symbolize the great massacre,
  the great massacre facing them on every side.
15 Let their hearts melt with terror,
 for the sword glitters at every gate.
 It flashes like lightning
  and is polished for slaughter!
16 O sword, slash to the right,
  then slash to the left,
 wherever you will,
  wherever you want.
17 I, too, will clap my hands,
 and I will satisfy my fury.
 I, the LORD, have spoken!"

Omens for Babylon's King

18Then this message came to me from the LORD: 19"Son of man, make a map and trace two routes on it for the sword of Babylon's king to follow. Put a signpost on the road that comes out of Babylon where the road forks into two—20one road going to Ammon and its capital, Rabbah, and the other to Judah and fortified Jerusalem. 21The king of Babylon now stands at the fork, uncertain whether to attack Jerusalem or Rabbah. He calls his magicians to look for omens. They cast lots by shaking arrows from the quiver. They inspect the livers of animal sacrifices. 22The omen in his right hand says, 'Jerusalem!' With battering rams his soldiers will go against the gates, shouting for the kill. They will put up siege towers and build ramps against the walls. 23The people of

---

20:45 Verses 20:45-49 are numbered 21:1-5 in Hebrew text. 20:46 Hebrew *toward Teman.* 21:1 Verses 21:1-32 are numbered 21:6-37 in Hebrew text. 21:10 The meaning of the Hebrew is uncertain. 21:13 The meaning of the Hebrew is uncertain.

21:3-5 The Lord was the fundamental enemy Israel needed to fear, for he was about to unleash an all-encompassing judgment against them. One would expect the righteous to avoid judgment and the wicked to receive it. This pairing parallels the green tree and the dry tree of the previous parable (20:47-48), in which the judgment of sin would be like a very hot fire burning all it touched.
21:8-17 Ezekiel performed a series of actions representing the Babylonian massacre that would descend on Jerusalem. He cried and moaned, smacked his thigh, clapped his hands threateningly, and brandished a sword to represent the coming judgment and the people's response to it.
21:18-20 The sword of the Lord was not an abstract metaphor; it would take shape as "the sword of Babylon's king." Nebuchadnezzar's preparation for this campaign was depicted when Ezekiel drew a map showing Nebuchadnezzar's two possible campaign objectives—Rabbah, the capital of Ammon, and Jerusalem, the capital of Judah.

Jerusalem will think it is a false omen, because of their treaty with the Babylonians. But the king of Babylon will remind the people of their rebellion. Then he will attack and capture them.

24 "Therefore, this is what the Sovereign LORD says: Again and again you remind me of your sin and your guilt. You don't even try to hide it! In everything you do, your sins are obvious for all to see. So now the time of your punishment has come!

25 "O you corrupt and wicked prince of Israel, your final day of reckoning is here! 26 This is what the Sovereign LORD says:

> "Take off your jeweled crown,
>   for the old order changes.
> Now the lowly will be exalted,
>   and the mighty will be brought down.
> 27 Destruction! Destruction!
>   I will surely destroy the kingdom.
> And it will not be restored until the one
>   appears
>   who has the right to judge it.
> Then I will hand it over to him.

A Message for the Ammonites

28 "And now, son of man, prophesy concerning the Ammonites and their mockery. Give them this message from the Sovereign LORD:

> "A sword, a sword
>   is drawn for your slaughter.
> It is polished to destroy,
>   flashing like lightning!
> 29 Your prophets have given false visions,
>   and your fortune-tellers have told lies.
> The sword will fall on the necks of the wicked
>   for whom the day of final reckoning has
>   come.

30 "Now return the sword to its sheath,
  for in your own country,
  the land of your birth,
  I will pass judgment upon you.
31 I will pour out my fury on you
  and blow on you with the fire of my anger.
I will hand you over to cruel men
  who are skilled in destruction.
32 You will be fuel for the fire,
  and your blood will be spilled in your
    own land.
You will be utterly wiped out,
  your memory lost to history,
  for I, the LORD, have spoken!"

The Sins of Jerusalem

22 Now this message came to me from the LORD: 2 "Son of man, are you ready to judge Jerusalem? Are you ready to judge this city of murderers? Publicly denounce her detestable sins, 3 and give her this message from the Sovereign LORD: O city of murderers, doomed and damned—city of idols,* filthy and foul—4 you are guilty because of the blood you have shed. You are defiled because of the idols you have made. Your day of destruction has come! You have reached the end of your years. I will make you an object of mockery throughout the world. 5 O infamous city, filled with confusion, you will be mocked by people far and near.

6 "Every leader in Israel who lives within your walls is bent on murder. 7 Fathers and mothers are treated with contempt. Foreigners are forced to pay for protection. Orphans and widows are wronged and oppressed among you. 8 You despise my holy things and violate my Sabbath days of rest. 9 People accuse others falsely and send them to their death. You are filled with idol worshipers and people who

---

22:3 The Hebrew term (literally *round things*) probably alludes to dung; also in 22:4.

21:25-27 This judgment would extend against Zedekiah, the "corrupt and wicked prince of Israel," as well as against the people. Ezekiel identifies Zedekiah by title rather than by name, indicating that his office was also under judgment. He would be stripped of the emblems of royalty and brought low, while the Lord would exalt the lowly. The old order would experience destruction. This coming judge is often understood to be the Messiah (see Genesis 49:10). In this context, however, the Lord was handing Judah over to the Babylonians for judgment (see Ezekiel 23:24). Ezekiel was probably reshaping the traditional messianic oracle of Genesis 49:10 into a message of imminent judgment by the hand of Nebuchadnezzar, acting as an agent of God. God temporarily took away the scepter from Judah because Israel's rulers had sinned, but he would eventually give it back.

22:1-31 Jerusalem, the holy city where God had placed his name, was the spiritual heart of Judah. It had been corrupted and defiled; instead of being filled with God, Jerusalem was filled with bloodshed. As a result, God's wrath would certainly fall on the city.

22:1-5 God established Ezekiel as a prosecutor in a law court to bring two major charges against the people. They had worshiped other gods and shed innocent blood: The leaders had accepted bribes to condemn innocent people to death so others could claim their property (1 Kings 21:1-29; Amos 5:11-17). The people's unjust actions had dishonored God's name in the sight of the other nations. They were not living out their God-given purpose, to represent God to the other nations.

22:6-7 The people failed to maintain the law concerning parents, immigrants, orphans, and widows (Exodus 20:12; 22:21-24; 23:9-11; Leviticus 19:33-34; Jeremiah 5:28). God does not tolerate any abuse toward people, especially those who are particularly vulnerable. The Israelites were to love and honor all people as their own family. The consequence for oppressing afflicted people was that they themselves would become afflicted: The Israelite wives became widows and their children orphans (Ezekiel 22:25).

22:9-11 Ezekiel revealed that the Israelite men worshiped idols instead of the holy, living God. Idol worship led to immoral actions and vile crimes. Men were having sex with their own relatives, which had been expressly forbidden (see Leviticus 18:6-19; 20:10-21), and some were sexually abusing the women they were responsible to protect.

do obscene things. ¹⁰Men sleep with their fathers' wives and force themselves on women who are menstruating. ¹¹Within your walls live men who commit adultery with their neighbors' wives, who defile their daughters-in-law, or who rape their own sisters. ¹²There are hired murderers, loan racketeers, and extortioners everywhere. They never even think of me and my commands, says the Sovereign LORD.

¹³"But now I clap my hands in indignation over your dishonest gain and bloodshed. ¹⁴How strong and courageous will you be in my day of reckoning? I, the LORD, have spoken, and I will do what I said. ¹⁵I will scatter you among the nations and purge you of your wickedness. ¹⁶And when I have been dishonored among the nations because of you,* you will know that I am the LORD."

The LORD's Refining Furnace

¹⁷Then this message came to me from the LORD: ¹⁸"Son of man, the people of Israel are the worthless slag that remains after silver is smelted. They are the dross that is left over—a useless mixture of copper, tin, iron, and lead. ¹⁹So tell them, 'This is what the Sovereign LORD says: Because you are all worthless slag, I will bring you to my crucible in Jerusalem. ²⁰Just as silver, copper, iron, lead, and tin are melted down in a furnace, I will melt you down in the heat of my fury. ²¹I will gather you together and blow the fire of my anger upon you, ²²and you will melt like silver in fierce heat. Then you will know that I, the LORD, have poured out my fury on you.'"

The Sins of Israel's Leaders

²³Again a message came to me from the LORD: ²⁴"Son of man, give the people of Israel this message: In the day of my indignation, you will be like a polluted land, a land without rain. ²⁵Your princes* plot conspiracies just as lions stalk their prey. They devour innocent people, seizing treasures and extorting wealth. They make many widows in the land. ²⁶Your priests have violated my instructions and defiled my holy things. They make no distinction between what is holy and what is not. And they do not teach my people the difference between what is ceremonially clean and unclean. They disregard my Sabbath days so that I am dishonored among them. ²⁷Your leaders are like wolves who tear apart their victims. They actually destroy people's lives for money! ²⁸And your prophets cover up for them by announcing false visions and making lying predictions. They say, 'My message is from the Sovereign LORD,' when the LORD hasn't spoken a single word to them. ²⁹Even common people oppress the poor, rob the needy, and deprive foreigners of justice.

³⁰"I looked for someone who might rebuild the wall of righteousness that guards the land. I searched for someone to stand in the gap in the wall so I wouldn't have to destroy the land, but I found no one. ³¹So now I will pour out my fury on them, consuming them with the fire of my anger. I will heap on their heads the full penalty for all their sins. I, the Sovereign LORD, have spoken!"

The Adultery of Two Sisters

23 This message came to me from the LORD: ²"Son of man, once there were two sisters who were daughters of the same mother. ³They became prostitutes in Egypt. Even as young girls, they allowed men to fondle their breasts. ⁴The older girl was named Oholah, and her sister was Oholibah. I married them, and they bore me sons and daughters. I am speaking of Samaria and Jerusalem, for Oholah is Samaria and Oholibah is Jerusalem.

22:16 As in one Hebrew manuscript and Greek and Syriac versions; Masoretic Text reads *when you have been dishonored among the nations.* 22:25 As in Greek version; Hebrew reads *prophets.*

22:25-29 This list of Jerusalem's sins focuses on the sins of the leaders in Judah (compare Zephaniah 3:3-4). The princes and other leaders had abused their power by killing innocent people and seizing their wealth. The priests had sinned by not teaching people the law so that they could distinguish between holy and profane, clean and unclean. The prophets had announced false visions instead of a true word from God. As a result, the people had gone astray for lack of guidance.

22:30-31 In response to the sins of these former community leaders, the Lord sought someone who would rebuild the wall and stand in the gap as a true prophet, someone who would intercede for the people, as Moses did after the people sinned with the gold calf (Exodus 32:11-13). The Lord found no one to deflect his wrath, so his fury would now be poured out upon the people in full measure (see Ezekiel 11:21).

23:2-21 Israel divided into two kingdoms—Israel and Judah—after the reign of Solomon (1 Kings 12). In an extended metaphor, the capital cities of each kingdom are graphically depicted as two immoral sisters, emphasizing that the judgment was inevitable and well-deserved. Oholah (meaning "her tent") represents Samaria, and by extension all Israel. Her sister, Oholibah (meaning "my tent is in her"), represents Jerusalem, and all Judah. Israel abandoned God and established its own temple and priesthood, which was in direct disobedience to God. They worshiped idols and shrines while Judah remained faithful to God at first. God's presence remained with Judah, but eventually, they were also unfaithful and gave themselves to worship other gods. God wanted Judah to know he was just for disciplining them because they were even worse than Israel (Ezekiel 23:11-21). They disregarded God's warning when he judged Samaria.

23:4 Marriage is commonly used in the Bible as a symbol for the covenant relationship between God and his people (for example, Isaiah 54:1-8; Ephesians 5:22-33). Adultery symbolizes Israel's spiritual unfaithfulness (for example, Hosea 1:1–3:5). God makes his covenants in spite of, not because of, his people's character (Romans 5:6-11).

5 "Then Oholah lusted after other lovers instead of me, and she gave her love to the Assyrian officers. 6 They were all attractive young men, captains and commanders dressed in handsome blue, charioteers driving their horses. 7 And so she prostituted herself with the most desirable men of Assyria, worshiping their idols* and defiling herself. 8 For when she left Egypt, she did not leave her spirit of prostitution behind. She was still as lewd as in her youth, when the Egyptians slept with her, fondled her breasts, and used her as a prostitute.

9 "And so I handed her over to her Assyrian lovers, whom she desired so much. 10 They stripped her, took away her children as their slaves, and then killed her. After she received her punishment, her reputation was known to every woman in the land.

11 "Yet even though Oholibah saw what had happened to Oholah, her sister, she followed right in her footsteps. And she was even more depraved, abandoning herself to her lust and prostitution. 12 She fawned over all the Assyrian officers—those captains and commanders in handsome uniforms, those charioteers driving their horses—all of them attractive young men. 13 I saw the way she was going, defiling herself just like her older sister.

14 "Then she carried her prostitution even further. She fell in love with pictures that were painted on a wall—pictures of Babylonian* military officers, outfitted in striking red uniforms. 15 Handsome belts encircled their waists, and flowing turbans crowned their heads. They were dressed like chariot officers from the land of Babylonia.* 16 When she saw these paintings, she longed to give herself to them, so she sent messengers to Babylonia to invite them to come to her. 17 So they came and committed adultery with her, defiling her in the bed of love. After being defiled, however, she rejected them in disgust.

18 "In the same way, I became disgusted with Oholibah and rejected her, just as I had rejected her sister, because she flaunted herself before them and gave herself to satisfy their lusts. 19 Yet she turned to even greater prostitution, remembering her youth when she was a prostitute in Egypt. 20 She lusted after lovers with genitals as large as a donkey's and emissions like those of a horse. 21 And so, Oholibah, you relived your former days as a young girl in Egypt, when you first allowed your breasts to be fondled.

The LORD's Judgment of Oholibah

22 "Therefore, Oholibah, this is what the Sovereign LORD says: I will send your lovers against you from every direction—those very nations from which you turned away in disgust. 23 For the Babylonians will come with all the Chaldeans from Pekod and Shoa and Koa. And all the Assyrians will come with them—handsome young captains, commanders, chariot officers, and other high-ranking officers, all riding their horses. 24 They will all come against you from the north* with chariots, wagons, and a great army prepared for attack. They will take up positions on every side, surrounding you with men armed with shields and helmets. And I will hand you over to them for punishment so they can do with you as they please. 25 I will turn my jealous anger against you, and they will deal harshly with you. They will cut off your nose and ears, and any survivors will then be slaughtered by the sword. Your children will be taken away as captives, and everything that is left will be burned. 26 They will strip you of your beautiful clothes and jewels. 27 In this way, I will put a stop to the lewdness and prostitution you brought from Egypt. You will never again cast longing eyes on those things or fondly remember your time in Egypt.

28 "For this is what the Sovereign LORD says: I will surely hand you over to your enemies, to those you loathe, those you rejected. 29 They will treat you with hatred and rob you of all you own, leaving you stark naked. The shame of your prostitution will be exposed to all the world. 30 You brought all this on yourself by prostituting yourself to other nations, defiling yourself with all their idols. 31 Because you have followed in your sister's footsteps, I will force you to drink the same cup of terror she drank.

32 "Yes, this is what the Sovereign LORD says:

"You will drink from your sister's cup of terror,
  a cup that is large and deep.
It is filled to the brim
  with scorn and derision.

23:7 The Hebrew term (literally *round things*) probably alludes to dung; also in 23:30, 37, 39, 49. 23:14 Or *Chaldean*. 23:15 Or *Chaldea;* also in 23:16. 23:24 As in Greek version; the meaning of the Hebrew is uncertain.

23:5-13 The people of Samaria did not trust God to protect them, so they asked Assyria for help. Ezekiel graphically depicts Samaria as a prostitute seeking a lover to care for her. Because Samaria accepted Assyria's help and worshiped their gods, God used Assyria to discipline Samaria. Judah's complete lack of faith in God led them to follow in Samaria's footsteps.
23:14-35 Judah's rebellion extended past what Samaria had done. In addition to trusting Assyria, Judah put its faith in Babylon for protection. Judah witnessed God's judgment on Samaria. However, Judah did not change its attitude against God. Ezekiel delivered four messages to explain God's just punishment.

23:22-24 Jerusalem's depravity made God's judgment inevitable. The very nations that she had courted as her lovers would abuse her. Babylon would bring its allies, Pekod, Shoa, and Koa. The names of these obscure tribes sound like Hebrew words meaning "punishment," "war cry," and "shriek." Judah's sins were greater than her sister's, and her judgment would also be worse.
23:25-29 Stripping an adulterous wife naked—to expose in public what she had done in private—was a punishment for adultery (see note on 16:35-38). The Babylonians similarly stripped Jerusalem and Judah of everything valuable and exposed them to their own shame.

33 Drunkenness and anguish will fill you,
> for your cup is filled to the brim with distress and desolation,
> > the same cup your sister Samaria drank.
34 You will drain that cup of terror
> to the very bottom.
> Then you will smash it to pieces
> > and beat your breast in anguish.
> > > I, the Sovereign LORD, have spoken!

35 "And because you have forgotten me and turned your back on me, this is what the Sovereign LORD says: You must bear the consequences of all your lewdness and prostitution."

The LORD's Judgment on Both Sisters

36 The LORD said to me, "Son of man, you must accuse Oholah and Oholibah of all their detestable sins. 37 They have committed both adultery and murder—adultery by worshiping idols and murder by burning as sacrifices the children they bore to me. 38 Furthermore, they have defiled my Temple and violated my Sabbath day! 39 On the very day that they sacrificed their children to their idols, they boldly came into my Temple to worship! They came in and defiled my house.

40 "You sisters sent messengers to distant lands to get men. Then when they arrived, you bathed yourselves, painted your eyelids, and put on your finest jewels for them. 41 You sat with them on a beautifully embroidered couch and put my incense and my special oil on a table that was spread before you. 42 From your room came the sound of many men carousing. They were lustful men and drunkards* from the wilderness, who put bracelets on your wrists and beautiful crowns on your heads. 43 Then I said, 'If they really want to have sex with old worn-out prostitutes like these, let them!' 44 And that is what they did. They had sex with Oholah and Oholibah, these shameless prostitutes. 45 But righteous people will judge these sister cities for what they really are—adulterers and murderers.

46 "Now this is what the Sovereign LORD says: Bring an army against them and hand them over to be terrorized and plundered. 47 For their enemies will stone them and kill them with swords. They will butcher their sons and daughters and burn their homes. 48 In this way, I will put an end to lewdness and idolatry in the land, and my judgment will be a warning to all women not to follow your wicked example. 49 You will be fully repaid for all your prostitution—your worship of idols. Yes, you will suffer the full penalty. Then you will know that I am the Sovereign LORD."

The Sign of the Cooking Pot

24 On January 15,* during the ninth year of King Jehoiachin's captivity, this message came to me from the LORD: 2 "Son of man, write down today's date, because on this very day the king of Babylon is beginning his attack against Jerusalem. 3 Then give these rebels an illustration with this message from the Sovereign LORD:

> "Put a pot on the fire,
> > and pour in some water.
4 > Fill it with choice pieces of meat—
> > the rump and the shoulder
> > and all the most tender cuts.
5 > Use only the best sheep from the flock,
> > and heap fuel on the fire beneath the pot.
> Bring the pot to a boil,
> > and cook the bones along with the meat.

6 "Now this is what the Sovereign LORD says:
> What sorrow awaits Jerusalem,
> > the city of murderers!
> She is a cooking pot
> > whose corruption can't be cleaned out.
> Take the meat out in random order,
> > for no piece is better than another.
7 > For the blood of her murders
> > is splashed on the rocks.
> It isn't even spilled on the ground,
> > where the dust could cover it!
8 > So I will splash her blood on a rock
> > for all to see,
> an expression of my anger
> > and vengeance against her.

9 "This is what the Sovereign LORD says:
> What sorrow awaits Jerusalem,
> > the city of murderers!
> I myself will pile up the fuel beneath her.

23:42 Or *Sabeans.* **24:1** Hebrew *On the tenth day of the tenth month,* of the ancient Hebrew lunar calendar. This event occurred on January 15, 588 B.C.; also see note on 1:1.

23:36-43 The prophet again adopted the role of prosecuting attorney, whose task was to confront Jerusalem with her sins (described in detail in Ezekiel 22). Far from being holy cities, Jerusalem and Samaria had become worn-out prostitutes whose only attractiveness was in their availability.

23:44-49 The sisters' enemies would stone them like adulteresses and kill them with swords as an invading army would do. In the typical pattern of invasion, not only the prostitutes but also their sons and daughters would die, and the enemy would burn their homes. Those who rebelled against the Lord and pursued idolatry would suffer the full penalty, which is nothing short of death.

24:1-14 At first sight, the picture of a cooking pot seems positive, conjuring expectations of good food and fellowship. Various choice pieces of a sacrificial animal had been gathered, a fire was kindled underneath the pot, and the contents were brought to a simmer. However, as in many parables, there is a sting in the tail of the story. What ought to have been a tasty meal had became a foul, profane mess. The choice pieces of meat that had gone in were uniformly corrupt when they came out. The pot represented Jerusalem (24:9); the contents would be burned and destroyed.

10 Yes, heap on the wood!
    Let the fire roar to make the pot boil.
    Cook the meat with many spices,
        and afterward burn the bones.
11 Now set the empty pot on the coals.
        Heat it red hot!
        Burn away the filth and corruption.
12 But it's hopeless;
        the corruption can't be cleaned out.
    So throw it into the fire.
13 Your impurity is your lewdness
        and the corruption of your idolatry.
    I tried to cleanse you,
        but you refused.
    So now you will remain in your filth
        until my fury against you has been satisfied.

14 "I, the Lord, have spoken! The time has come, and I won't hold back. I will not change my mind, and I will have no pity on you. You will be judged on the basis of all your wicked actions, says the Sovereign Lord."

The Death of Ezekiel's Wife

15 Then this message came to me from the Lord: 16 "Son of man, with one blow I will take away your dearest treasure. Yet you must not show any sorrow at her death. Do not weep; let there be no tears. 17 Groan silently, but let there be no wailing at her grave. Do not uncover your head or take off your sandals. Do not perform the usual rituals of mourning or accept any food brought to you by consoling friends."

18 So I proclaimed this to the people the next morning, and in the evening my wife died. The next morning I did everything I had been told to do. 19 Then the people asked, "What does all this mean? What are you trying to tell us?"

20 So I said to them, "A message came to me from the Lord, 21 and I was told to give this message to the people of Israel. This is what the Sovereign Lord says: I will defile my Temple, the source of your security and pride, the place your heart delights in. Your sons and daughters whom you left behind in Judah will be slaughtered by the sword. 22 Then you will do as Ezekiel has done. You will not mourn in public or console yourselves by eating the food brought by friends. 23 Your heads will remain covered, and your sandals will not be taken off. You will not mourn or weep, but you will waste away because of your sins. You will groan among yourselves for all the evil you have done. 24 Ezekiel is an example for you; you will do just as he has done. And when that time comes, you will know that I am the Sovereign Lord."

25 Then the Lord said to me, "Son of man, on the day I take away their stronghold—their joy and glory, their heart's desire, their dearest treasure—I will also take away their sons and daughters. 26 And on that day a survivor from Jerusalem will come to you in Babylon and tell you what has happened. 27 And when he arrives, your voice will suddenly return so you can talk to him, and you will be a symbol for these people. Then they will know that I am the Lord."

A Message for Ammon

25 Then this message came to me from the Lord: 2 "Son of man, turn and face the land of Ammon and prophesy against its people. 3 Give the Ammonites this message from the Sovereign Lord: Hear the word of the Sovereign Lord! Because you cheered when my Temple was defiled, mocked Israel in her desolation, and laughed at Judah as she went away into exile, 4 I will allow nomads from the eastern deserts to overrun your country. They will set up their camps among you and pitch their tents on your land. They will harvest all your fruit and drink

---

24:15-17 Nowhere is a prophet's total involvement in his message demonstrated more vividly than when God took the life of Ezekiel's wife, and Ezekiel was not allowed to mourn his dearest treasure openly. Ezekiel was a priest (1:3), and all priests had restrictions placed on their mourning. The public rituals of torn clothes and an unkempt appearance would make one unclean, and priests were not permitted to make themselves unclean for any but the closest blood relatives (Leviticus 21:1-4). Ezekiel's lack of mourning was also a sign act that showed what was about to happen to Israel (Ezekiel 24:20-24).

24:18-19 Both Ezekiel and the people desired to know why God had taken Ezekiel's wife away. Ezekiel's wife did not die because of her own sin or Ezekiel's. While God did not reveal his reasons, Ezekiel remained God's faithful servant.

24:20-24 Ezekiel's lack of mourning (24:15-17) was a sign to the people of Israel of what lay ahead for them. The Lord was about to take away "the place your heart delights in"—the Temple of Jerusalem. God was going to desecrate it and destroy the sons and daughters they had left behind in Jerusalem. On that day, the people would behave as Ezekiel had done; they would not mourn in public or carry out the associated rituals. Though they would feel the loss deeply in their hearts, the scale of the devastation would be so overwhelming that there would be no opportunity for normal mourning rites. In the context of such terrible and complete desolation, only internal grief could be observed.

25:1–32:32 This section contains a series of oracles against surrounding nations. There are six shorter oracles against Judah's immediate neighbors, in clockwise geographical order, followed by a climactic seventh oracle against Egypt (30:1–32:32). Through their experience of God's judgment, the nations would recognize God's sovereignty over all things. The nations might be used to bring about God's judgment of his people, but that would not exempt them from judgment. One of the key purposes of these oracles against the nations was to affirm that the negative side of God's covenant with Abraham ("I will . . . curse those who treat you with contempt," Genesis 12:3) was in force. No one can assault God's people and escape unscathed, even when God's people are themselves under his judgment.

25:1-14 The people of Israel were related to the Ammonites, Moabites, and Edomites by blood through Lot's and Esau's descendants (Genesis 19:30-38; 36:1-43). Growing great hatred for the people of Israel, these nations plotted and protested against them.

the milk from your livestock. ⁵And I will turn the city of Rabbah into a pasture for camels, and all the land of the Ammonites into a resting place for sheep and goats. Then you will know that I am the LORD.

⁶"This is what the Sovereign LORD says: Because you clapped and danced and cheered with glee at the destruction of my people, ⁷I will raise my fist of judgment against you. I will give you as plunder to many nations. I will cut you off from being a nation and destroy you completely. Then you will know that I am the LORD.

A Message for Moab

⁸"This is what the Sovereign LORD says: Because the people of Moab* have said that Judah is just like all the other nations, ⁹I will open up their eastern flank and wipe out their glorious frontier towns—Beth-jeshimoth, Baal-meon, and Kiriathaim. ¹⁰And I will hand Moab over to nomads from the eastern deserts, just as I handed over Ammon. Yes, the Ammonites will no longer be counted among the nations. ¹¹In the same way, I will bring my judgment down on the Moabites. Then they will know that I am the LORD.

A Message for Edom

¹²"This is what the Sovereign LORD says: The people of Edom have sinned greatly by avenging themselves against the people of Judah. ¹³Therefore, says the Sovereign LORD, I will raise my fist of judgment against Edom. I will wipe out its people and animals with the sword. I will make a wasteland of everything from Teman to Dedan. ¹⁴I will accomplish this by the hand of my people of Israel. They will carry out my vengeance with anger, and Edom will know that this vengeance is from me. I, the Sovereign LORD, have spoken!

A Message for Philistia

¹⁵"This is what the Sovereign LORD says: The people of Philistia have acted against Judah out of bitter revenge and long-standing contempt. ¹⁶Therefore, this is what the Sovereign LORD says: I will raise my fist of judgment against the land of the Philistines. I will wipe out the Kerethites and utterly destroy the people who live by the sea. ¹⁷I will execute terrible vengeance against them to punish them for what they have done. And when I have inflicted my revenge, they will know that I am the LORD."

A Message for Tyre

26 On February 3, during the twelfth year of King Jehoiachin's captivity,* this message came to me from the LORD: ²"Son of man, Tyre has rejoiced over the fall of Jerusalem, saying, 'Ha! She who was the gateway to the rich trade routes to the east has been broken, and I am the heir! Because she has been made desolate, I will become wealthy!'

³"Therefore, this is what the Sovereign LORD says: I am your enemy, O Tyre, and I will bring many nations against you, like the waves of the sea crashing against your shoreline. ⁴They will destroy the walls of Tyre and tear down its towers. I will scrape away its soil and make it a bare rock! ⁵It will be just a rock in the sea, a place for fishermen to spread their nets, for I have spoken, says the Sovereign LORD. Tyre will become the prey of many nations, ⁶and its mainland villages will be destroyed by the sword. Then they will know that I am the LORD.

⁷"This is what the Sovereign LORD says: From the north I will bring King Nebuchadnezzar* of Babylon against Tyre. He is king of kings and brings his horses, chariots, charioteers, and great army. ⁸First he will destroy your mainland villages. Then he will attack you by building a siege wall, constructing a ramp, and raising a roof of shields against you. ⁹He will pound your walls with battering rams and demolish your towers with sledgehammers. ¹⁰The hooves of his horses will choke the city with dust, and the noise of the charioteers and chariot wheels will shake your walls as they storm through your broken gates. ¹¹His horsemen will trample through every street in the city. They will butcher your people, and your strong pillars will topple.

¹²"They will plunder all your riches and merchandise and break down your walls. They will destroy your lovely homes and dump your stones and timbers and even your dust into the sea. ¹³I will stop the music of your songs. No more will the sound of harps be heard among your people. ¹⁴I will make your island a bare rock, a place for fishermen to spread their nets. You will never be rebuilt, for I, the LORD, have spoken. Yes, the Sovereign LORD has spoken!

The Effect of Tyre's Destruction

¹⁵"This is what the Sovereign LORD says to Tyre: The whole coastline will tremble at the sound of your fall,

---

25:8 As in Greek version; Hebrew reads *Moab and Seir.* 26:1 Hebrew *In the eleventh year, on the first day of the month,* of the ancient Hebrew lunar calendar year. Since an element is missing in the date formula here, scholars have reconstructed this probable reading: *In the eleventh [month of the twelfth] year, on the first day of the month.* This reading would put this message on February 3, 585 B.C.; also see note on 1:1. 26:7 Hebrew *Nebuchadrezzar,* a variant spelling of Nebuchadnezzar.

25:15–28:19 After judging the nations related to Israel, Ezekiel pronounced judgment against Philistia (25:15-17) and Phoenicia. Ezekiel focused on Tyre, a prominent city in Phoenicia (26:1–28:19). The people of Tyre thought they were patriotic and just, but Ezekiel convicted them for their pride, hatred, and revenge. **26:15-21** The economic impact of Tyre's fall would spread out to her trading partners along the whole coastline, causing their rulers to abdicate. Tyre's trading practices were apparently based on conquest, subjugation, and exploitation (see 28:16, 18). God would demonstrate his sovereign power by destroying Tyre. It would be as though that great city had sunk into the depths of the chaotic sea, with its inhabitants condemned to the pit where the unrighteous dead reside, never to return.

as the screams of the wounded echo in the continuing slaughter. ¹⁶All the seaport rulers will step down from their thrones and take off their royal robes and beautiful clothing. They will sit on the ground trembling with horror at your destruction. ¹⁷Then they will wail for you, singing this funeral song:

"O famous island city,
  once ruler of the sea,
  how you have been destroyed!
Your people, with their naval power,
  once spread fear around the world.
¹⁸ Now the coastlands tremble at your fall.
  The islands are dismayed as you disappear.

¹⁹"This is what the Sovereign LORD says: I will make Tyre an uninhabited ruin, like many others. I will bury you beneath the terrible waves of enemy attack. Great seas will swallow you. ²⁰I will send you to the pit to join those who descended there long ago. Your city will lie in ruins, buried beneath the earth, like those in the pit who have entered the world of the dead. You will have no place of respect here in the land of the living. ²¹I will bring you to a terrible end, and you will exist no more. You will be looked for, but you will never again be found. I, the Sovereign LORD, have spoken!"

The End of Tyre's Glory

27 Then this message came to me from the LORD: ²"Son of man, sing a funeral song for Tyre, ³that mighty gateway to the sea, the trading center of the world. Give Tyre this message from the Sovereign LORD:

"You boasted, O Tyre,
  'My beauty is perfect!'
⁴ You extended your boundaries into the sea.
  Your builders made your beauty perfect.
⁵ You were like a great ship
  built of the finest cypress from Senir.*
They took a cedar from Lebanon
  to make a mast for you.
⁶ They carved your oars
  from the oaks of Bashan.
Your deck of pine from the coasts of Cyprus*
  was inlaid with ivory.
⁷ Your sails were made of Egypt's finest linen,
  and they flew as a banner above you.

You stood beneath blue and purple awnings
  made bright with dyes from the coasts of Elishah.
⁸ Your oarsmen came from Sidon and Arvad;
  your helmsmen were skilled men from Tyre itself.
⁹ Wise old craftsmen from Gebal did the caulking.
  Ships from every land came with goods to barter for your trade.

¹⁰"Men from distant Persia, Lydia, and Libya* served in your great army. They hung their shields and helmets on your walls, giving you great honor. ¹¹Men from Arvad and Helech stood on your walls. Your towers were manned by men from Gammad. Their shields hung on your walls, completing your beauty.

¹²"Tarshish sent merchants to buy your wares in exchange for silver, iron, tin, and lead. ¹³Merchants from Greece,* Tubal, and Meshech brought slaves and articles of bronze to trade with you.

¹⁴"From Beth-togarmah came riding horses, chariot horses, and mules, all in exchange for your goods. ¹⁵Merchants came to you from Dedan.* Numerous coastlands were your captive markets; they brought payment in ivory tusks and ebony wood.

¹⁶"Syria* sent merchants to buy your rich variety of goods. They traded turquoise, purple dyes, embroidery, fine linen, and jewelry of coral and rubies. ¹⁷Judah and Israel traded for your wares, offering wheat from Minnith, figs,* honey, olive oil, and balm.

¹⁸"Damascus sent merchants to buy your rich variety of goods, bringing wine from Helbon and white wool from Zahar. ¹⁹Greeks from Uzal* came to trade for your merchandise. Wrought iron, cassia, and fragrant calamus were bartered for your wares.

²⁰"Dedan sent merchants to trade their expensive saddle blankets with you. ²¹The Arabians and the princes of Kedar sent merchants to trade lambs and rams and male goats in exchange for your goods. ²²The merchants of Sheba and Raamah came with all kinds of spices, jewels, and gold in exchange for your wares.

²³"Haran, Canneh, Eden, Sheba, Asshur, and Kilmad came with their merchandise, too. ²⁴They brought choice fabrics to trade—blue cloth, embroidery, and multicolored carpets rolled up and bound with cords. ²⁵The ships of Tarshish were your ocean caravans. Your island warehouse was filled to the brim!

27:5 Or *Hermon.* 27:6 Hebrew *Kittim.* 27:10 Hebrew *Paras, Lud, and Put.* 27:13 Hebrew *Javan.* 27:15 Greek version reads *Rhodes.* 27:16 Hebrew *Aram;* some manuscripts read *Edom.* 27:17 The meaning of the Hebrew is uncertain. 27:19 Hebrew *Vedan and Javan from Uzal.* The meaning of the Hebrew is uncertain.

27:1-36 Ezekiel used a funeral song to mock Tyre and speak the truth about God. Tyre was a thriving seaport, which Ezekiel compared to a beautiful ship that eventually sank. The tragedy would bring grief to all its merchants, customers, and agents across the Mediterranean.

27:12-25 The vast system of transport was all at the service of Tyre's insatiable appetite for trade. The list of Tyre's trading partners goes on and on: Tyre was the source of a wide variety of commodities from enslaved people to horses, saddle blankets to silver, dyes to figs (compare Revelation 18:11-13). The cargo list for the ship is organized according to the different geographic regions with which she conducted trade, covering all points of the compass and including every trading center, major and minor. Virtually every precious object that could be bought or sold found a place somewhere on the list of Tyre's goods.

"I will give you a new heart, and I will put a new spirit in you."

EZEKIEL 36:26

The Destruction of Tyre

26 "But look! Your oarsmen
  have taken you into stormy seas!
A mighty eastern gale
  has wrecked you in the heart of the sea!
27 Everything is lost—
  your riches and wares,
  your sailors and pilots,
  your ship builders, merchants, and warriors.
On the day of your ruin,
  everyone on board sinks into the depths of
    the sea.
28 Your cities by the sea tremble
  as your pilots cry out in terror.
29 All the oarsmen abandon their ships;
  the sailors and pilots stand on the shore.
30 They cry aloud over you
  and weep bitterly.
They throw dust on their heads
  and roll in ashes.
31 They shave their heads in grief for you
  and dress themselves in burlap.
They weep for you with bitter anguish
  and deep mourning.
32 As they wail and mourn over you,
  they sing this sad funeral song:
'Was there ever such a city as Tyre,
  now silent at the bottom of the sea?
33 The merchandise you traded
  satisfied the desires of many nations.
Kings at the ends of the earth
  were enriched by your trade.
34 Now you are a wrecked ship,
  broken at the bottom of the sea.
All your merchandise and crew
  have gone down with you.
35 All who live along the coastlands
  are appalled at your terrible fate.
Their kings are filled with horror
  and look on with twisted faces.
36 The merchants among the nations
  shake their heads at the sight of you,*
for you have come to a horrible end
  and will exist no more.'"

A Message for Tyre's King

28 Then this message came to me from the Lord: 2"Son of man, give the prince of Tyre this message from the Sovereign Lord:

"In your great pride you claim, 'I am a god!
  I sit on a divine throne in the heart of
    the sea.'
But you are only a man and not a god,
  though you boast that you are a god.
3 You regard yourself as wiser than Daniel
  and think no secret is hidden from you.
4 With your wisdom and understanding you have
    amassed great wealth—
  gold and silver for your treasuries.
5 Yes, your wisdom has made you very rich,
  and your riches have made you very proud.

6 "Therefore, this is what the Sovereign Lord says:
Because you think you are as wise as a god,
7   I will now bring against you a foreign army,
  the terror of the nations.
They will draw their swords against your
    marvelous wisdom
  and defile your splendor!
8 They will bring you down to the pit,
  and you will die in the heart of the sea,
  pierced with many wounds.
9 Will you then boast, 'I am a god!'
  to those who kill you?
To them you will be no god
  but merely a man!
10 You will die like an outcast*
  at the hands of foreigners.
I, the Sovereign Lord, have spoken!"

11Then this further message came to me from the Lord: 12"Son of man, sing this funeral song for the king of Tyre. Give him this message from the Sovereign Lord:

"You were the model of perfection,
  full of wisdom and exquisite in beauty.
13 You were in Eden,
  the garden of God.
Your clothing was adorned with every precious
    stone*—
  red carnelian, pale-green peridot, white
    moonstone,
  blue-green beryl, onyx, green jasper,
  blue lapis lazuli, turquoise, and emerald—
all beautifully crafted for you
  and set in the finest gold.
They were given to you
  on the day you were created.

27:36 Hebrew *hiss at you.* 28:10 Hebrew *will die the death of the uncircumcised.* 28:13 The identification of some of these gemstones is uncertain.

28:1-19 These verses judge and lament the prince of Tyre (28:1-10) and the king of Tyre (28:11-19). The prince's and the king's wealth and wisdom made them arrogant. They abused their responsibilities. In claiming to be a god, the prince offended the one true God, who would use foreign invaders to destroy him but judge the king himself. This historical account also has a spiritual dimension. Satan's powers and principalities used these men as his agents in an attempt to battle God.
28:8 Being put to death by the Babylonians is the strongest indication that the prince of Tyre was a mortal man and not a divine being. His final resting place would not be in the heights with the gods, but in the pit, the residence of the dead. Like the city of Tyre, the prince of Tyre would die in the heart of the sea (see 27:26-27).

¹⁴ I ordained and anointed you
    as the mighty angelic guardian.*
You had access to the holy mountain of God
    and walked among the stones of fire.
¹⁵ "You were blameless in all you did
    from the day you were created
    until the day evil was found in you.
¹⁶ Your rich commerce led you to violence,
    and you sinned.
So I banished you in disgrace
    from the mountain of God.
I expelled you, O mighty guardian,
    from your place among the stones of fire.
¹⁷ Your heart was filled with pride
    because of all your beauty.
Your wisdom was corrupted
    by your love of splendor.
So I threw you to the ground
    and exposed you to the curious gaze of kings.
¹⁸ You defiled your sanctuaries
    with your many sins and your dishonest trade.
So I brought fire out from within you,
    and it consumed you.
I reduced you to ashes on the ground
    in the sight of all who were watching.
¹⁹ All who knew you are appalled at your fate.
    You have come to a terrible end,
    and you will exist no more."

A Message for Sidon

²⁰ Then another message came to me from the LORD: ²¹ "Son of man, turn and face the city of Sidon and prophesy against it. ²² Give the people of Sidon this message from the Sovereign LORD:

"I am your enemy, O Sidon,
    and I will reveal my glory by what I do to you.
When I bring judgment against you
    and reveal my holiness among you,
everyone watching will know
    that I am the LORD.
²³ I will send a plague against you,
    and blood will be spilled in your streets.
The attack will come from every direction,
    and your people will lie slaughtered within
        your walls.
Then everyone will know
    that I am the LORD.
²⁴ No longer will Israel's scornful neighbors
    prick and tear at her like briers and thorns.
For then they will know
    that I am the Sovereign LORD.

Restoration for Israel

²⁵ "This is what the Sovereign LORD says: The people of Israel will again live in their own land, the land I gave my servant Jacob. For I will gather them from the distant lands where I have scattered them. I will reveal to the nations of the world my holiness among my people. ²⁶ They will live safely in Israel and build homes and plant vineyards. And when I punish the neighboring nations that treated them with contempt, they will know that I am the LORD their God."

A Message for Egypt

29 On January 7,* during the tenth year of King Jehoiachin's captivity, this message came to me from the LORD: ² "Son of man, turn and face Egypt and prophesy against Pharaoh the king and all the

---

28:14 Hebrew *guardian cherub*; similarly in 28:16.   29:1 Hebrew *On the twelfth day of the tenth month,* of the ancient Hebrew lunar calendar. This event occurred on January 7, 587 B.C.; also see note on 1:1.

28:15-18 This sarcastic description of the king of Tyre's greatness and pride sets him up for his coming fall, which is cast in terms reminiscent of the fall of humanity (Genesis 3). As with Adam, the king of Tyre's supposedly blameless condition was not permanent but came to an abrupt end when evil was found in him. His rich commerce and dishonest trade led him to violence. One who claimed to be greater than Adam could experience a fall from favor similar to Adam's and be "banished . . . from the mountain of God," the place of God's favor. The king of Tyre's God-given beauty and wisdom were corrupted by his pride, which inevitably led to disaster and exposed his true nature.

28:25-26 The Lord would not reveal his holiness simply by judging the nations for their pride, arrogance, and enmity toward his chosen people. He would also gather his people back to the land of Israel. There they would live safely and be able to "build homes and plant vineyards," which were typical signs of covenantal blessing in the Old Testament (see Micah 4:4; Zechariah 3:10). After God acted to punish the neighboring nations and restore his people, they would be at rest. The nations would know that God is the sovereign Lord through his powerful acts of judgment, and Israel would know that he was "the LORD their

God," a title that speaks of God's covenant relationship of worship and fellowship with them.

29:1–32:32 The climactic seventh oracle against the nations is against Egypt, Israel's old enemy and ally. This is the longest of the oracles and, like the oracle against Tyre, it addresses both the land of Egypt and its ruler. Egypt played a central role through the centuries in tempting Israel and Judah away from their allegiance to the Lord. Israel had no sooner departed from Egypt than Egypt's idolatry became a snare for the people. Egypt caused Judah to trust in chariots and horses instead of in the Lord, but Egypt proved unreliable when the moment of truth arrived. The Lord judged Egypt because the people had tempted Judah away from loyalty to him (see also Luke 17:1-2).

29:1-16 This event occurred on January 7, 587 BC. It is a word of judgment against Pharaoh, who is addressed as a great sea monster. These creatures were a familiar part of ancient Near Eastern mythology as a manifestation of chaos that had to be tamed by the gods. Strikingly, these same sea monsters appear in demythologized form as part of God's good creation (Genesis 1:21). In this chapter, however, the mythical image blends with the image of Pharaoh as a great crocodile, resting comfortably in the streams that laced the delta of the Nile.

people of Egypt. ³Give them this message from the Sovereign LORD:

"I am your enemy, O Pharaoh, king of Egypt—
  you great monster, lurking in the streams of the Nile.
For you have said, 'The Nile River is mine;
  I made it for myself.'
⁴ I will put hooks in your jaws
  and drag you out on the land
  with fish sticking to your scales.
⁵ I will leave you and all your fish
  stranded in the wilderness to die.
You will lie unburied on the open ground,
  for I have given you as food to the wild animals and birds.
⁶ All the people of Egypt will know that I am the LORD,
  for to Israel you were just a staff made of reeds.
⁷ When Israel leaned on you,
  you splintered and broke
  and stabbed her in the armpit.
When she put her weight on you,
  you collapsed, and her legs gave way.

⁸"Therefore, this is what the Sovereign LORD says: I will bring an army against you, O Egypt, and destroy both people and animals. ⁹The land of Egypt will become a desolate wasteland, and the Egyptians will know that I am the LORD.

"Because you said, 'The Nile River is mine; I made it,' ¹⁰I am now the enemy of both you and your river. I will make the land of Egypt a totally desolate wasteland, from Migdol to Aswan, as far south as the border of Ethiopia.* ¹¹For forty years not a soul will pass that way, neither people nor animals. It will be completely uninhabited. ¹²I will make Egypt desolate, and it will be surrounded by other desolate nations. Its cities will be empty and desolate for forty years, surrounded by other ruined cities. I will scatter the Egyptians to distant lands.

¹³"But this is what the Sovereign LORD also says: At the end of the forty years I will bring the Egyptians home again from the nations to which they have been scattered. ¹⁴I will restore the prosperity of Egypt and bring its people back to the land of Pathros in southern Egypt from which they came. But Egypt will remain an unimportant, minor kingdom. ¹⁵It will be the lowliest of all the nations, never again great enough to rise above its neighbors.

¹⁶"Then Israel will no longer be tempted to trust in Egypt for help. Egypt's shattered condition will remind Israel of how sinful she was to trust Egypt in earlier days. Then Israel will know that I am the Sovereign LORD."

Nebuchadnezzar to Conquer Egypt

¹⁷On April 26, the first day of the new year,* during the twenty-seventh year of King Jehoiachin's captivity, this message came to me from the LORD: ¹⁸"Son of man, the army of King Nebuchadnezzar* of Babylon fought so hard against Tyre that the warriors' heads were rubbed bare and their shoulders were raw and blistered. Yet Nebuchadnezzar and his army won no plunder to compensate them for all their work. ¹⁹Therefore, this is what the Sovereign LORD says: I will give the land of Egypt to Nebuchadnezzar, king of Babylon. He will carry off its wealth, plundering everything it has so he can pay his army. ²⁰Yes, I have given him the land of Egypt as a reward for his work, says the Sovereign LORD, because he was working for me when he destroyed Tyre.

²¹"And the day will come when I will cause the ancient glory of Israel to revive,* and then, Ezekiel, your words will be respected. Then they will know that I am the LORD."

A Sad Day for Egypt

30 This is another message that came to me from the LORD: ²"Son of man, prophesy and give this message from the Sovereign LORD:

"Weep and wail
  for that day,
³ for the terrible day is almost here—
  the day of the LORD!
It is a day of clouds and gloom,
  a day of despair for the nations.
⁴ A sword will come against Egypt,
  and those who are slaughtered will cover the ground.

29:10 Hebrew *from Migdol to Syene as far as the border of Cush.* **29:17** Hebrew *On the first day of the first month,* of the ancient Hebrew lunar calendar. This event occurred on April 26, 571 B.C.; also see note on 1:1. **29:18** Hebrew *Nebuchadrezzar,* a variant spelling of Nebuchadnezzar; also in 29:19. **29:21** Hebrew *I will cause a horn to sprout for the house of Israel.*

29:14-16 Judah would ultimately be fully restored, but Egypt would "remain an unimportant . . . kingdom." Israel would never again be tempted to call on Egypt for help instead of calling on the Lord. Egypt's restored but reduced position would make it a constant reminder of Israel's past folly in trusting it.
29:17-21 This event occurred on April 26, 571 BC. Nebuchadnezzar had served God greatly through conquering Tyre. The spoils from the war did not provide adequate compensation for the time and effort expended. God determined Egypt would provide Babylon with its due wages. He allowed Nebuchadnezzar to invade Egypt. God also had a promise for Israel. He would fulfill Ezekiel's word, and Israel would return to the land.
30:1-19 Ezekiel delivered the third message against Egypt around the same time as his previous word (29:1-16). This time it was in the form of a lament. God had already disciplined Egypt for enslaving the Hebrew people. Now, God would use Babylon's ruthless army to devastate the nation. Judgment would come against Egypt. A great storm would blow in and destroy Egypt and all of its allies. Egypt would remember that God's sovereign power rules the entire earth.

Its wealth will be carried away
and its foundations destroyed.
The land of Ethiopia* will be ravished.
⁵ Ethiopia, Libya, Lydia, all Arabia,*
and all their other allies
will be destroyed in that war.

⁶ "For this is what the LORD says:
All of Egypt's allies will fall,
and the pride of her power will end.
From Migdol to Aswan*
they will be slaughtered by the sword,
says the Sovereign LORD.
⁷ Egypt will be desolate,
surrounded by desolate nations,
and its cities will be in ruins,
surrounded by other ruined cities.
⁸ And the people of Egypt will know that I am
the LORD
when I have set Egypt on fire
and destroyed all their allies.
⁹ At that time I will send swift messengers in
ships
to terrify the complacent Ethiopians.
Great panic will come upon them
on that day of Egypt's certain destruction.
Watch for it!
It is sure to come!

¹⁰ "For this is what the Sovereign LORD says:
By the power of King Nebuchadnezzar* of
Babylon,
I will destroy the hordes of Egypt.
¹¹ He and his armies—the most ruthless of all—
will be sent to demolish the land.
They will make war against Egypt
until slaughtered Egyptians cover the ground.
¹² I will dry up the Nile River
and sell the land to wicked men.
I will destroy the land of Egypt and everything
in it
by the hands of foreigners.
I, the LORD, have spoken!

¹³ "This is what the Sovereign LORD says:
I will smash the idols* of Egypt
and the images at Memphis.*
There will be no rulers left in Egypt;
terror will sweep the land.
¹⁴ I will destroy southern Egypt,*
set fire to Zoan,
and bring judgment against Thebes.*
¹⁵ I will pour out my fury on Pelusium,*
the strongest fortress of Egypt,
and I will stamp out
the hordes of Thebes.
¹⁶ Yes, I will set fire to all Egypt!
Pelusium will be racked with pain;
Thebes will be torn apart;
Memphis will live in constant terror.
¹⁷ The young men of Heliopolis and Bubastis* will
die in battle,
and the women* will be taken away as slaves.
¹⁸ When I come to break the proud strength of
Egypt,
it will be a dark day for Tahpanhes, too.
A dark cloud will cover Tahpanhes,
and its daughters will be led away as
captives.
¹⁹ And so I will greatly punish Egypt,
and they will know that I am the LORD."

The Broken Arms of Pharaoh

²⁰On April 29,* during the eleventh year of King Jehoiachin's captivity, this message came to me from the LORD: ²¹"Son of man, I have broken the arm of Pharaoh, the king of Egypt. His arm has not been put in a cast so that it may heal. Neither has it been bound up with a splint to make it strong enough to hold a sword. ²²Therefore, this is what the Sovereign LORD says: I am the enemy of Pharaoh, the king of Egypt! I will break both of his arms—the good arm along with the broken one—and I will make his sword clatter to the ground. ²³I will scatter the Egyptians to many lands throughout the world. ²⁴I will strengthen the arms of Babylon's king and put my sword in his hand. But I will break the arms of Pharaoh, king of Egypt, and he will lie there mortally wounded, groaning in pain. ²⁵I will strengthen the arms of the king of Babylon, while the arms of Pharaoh fall useless to his sides. And when I put my sword in the hand of Babylon's king and he brings it against the land of Egypt, Egypt will know that I am the LORD. ²⁶I will scatter the Egyptians among the nations, dispersing them throughout the earth. Then they will know that I am the LORD."

30:4 Hebrew *Cush;* similarly in 30:9. **30:5** Hebrew *Cush, Put, Lud, all Arabia, Cub. Cub* is otherwise unknown and may be another spelling for *Lub* (Libya). **30:6** Hebrew *to Syene.* **30:10** Hebrew *Nebuchadrezzar,* a variant spelling of Nebuchadnezzar. **30:13a** The Hebrew term (literally *round things*) probably alludes to dung. **30:13b** Hebrew *Noph;* also in 30:16. **30:14a** Hebrew *Pathros.* **30:14b** Hebrew *No;* also in 30:15, 16. **30:15** Hebrew *Sin;* also in 30:16. **30:17a** Hebrew *of Awen and Pi-beseth.* **30:17b** Or *and her cities.* **30:20** Hebrew *On the seventh day of the first month,* of the ancient Hebrew lunar calendar. This event occurred on April 29, 587 B.C.; also see note on 1:1.

30:20-26 This fourth message against Egypt shows that God had already begun to act against his old enemy. Ezekiel delivered this message on April 29, 587 BC. God ensured the Egyptians would remember that he is the sovereign Lord. The breaking of Pharaoh's arms symbolized that God would allow Babylon to take all of Egypt's power. Further, God would not allow Egypt to regain its power, so they could not defend Jerusalem against the Babylonians when the time came.

Egypt Compared to Fallen Assyria

31 On June 21,* during the eleventh year of King Jehoiachin's captivity, this message came to me from the LORD: ²"Son of man, give this message to Pharaoh, king of Egypt, and all his hordes:

"To whom would you compare your greatness?
³ You are like mighty Assyria,
  which was once like a cedar of Lebanon,
with beautiful branches that cast deep forest shade
  and with its top high among the clouds.
⁴ Deep springs watered it
  and helped it to grow tall and luxuriant.
The water flowed around it like a river,
  streaming to all the trees nearby.
⁵ This great tree towered high,
  higher than all the other trees around it.
It prospered and grew long thick branches
  because of all the water at its roots.
⁶ The birds nested in its branches,
  and in its shade all the wild animals gave birth.
All the great nations of the world
  lived in its shadow.
⁷ It was strong and beautiful,
  with wide-spreading branches,
for its roots went deep
  into abundant water.
⁸ No other cedar in the garden of God
  could rival it.
No cypress had branches to equal it;
  no plane tree had boughs to compare.
No tree in the garden of God
  came close to it in beauty.
⁹ Because I made this tree so beautiful,
  and gave it such magnificent foliage,
it was the envy of all the other trees of Eden,
  the garden of God.

¹⁰"Therefore, this is what the Sovereign LORD says: Because Egypt* became proud and arrogant, and because it set itself so high above the others, with its top reaching to the clouds, ¹¹I will hand it over to a mighty nation that will destroy it as its wickedness deserves. I have already discarded it. ¹²A foreign army—the terror of the nations—has cut it down and left it fallen on the ground. Its branches are scattered across the mountains and valleys and ravines of the land. All those who lived in its shadow have gone away and left it lying there.

¹³ "The birds roost on its fallen trunk,
  and the wild animals lie among its branches.
¹⁴ Let the tree of no other nation
  proudly exult in its own prosperity,
though it be higher than the clouds
  and it be watered from the depths.
For all are doomed to die,
  to go down to the depths of the earth.
They will land in the pit
  along with everyone else on earth.

¹⁵"This is what the Sovereign LORD says: When Assyria went down to the grave,* I made the deep springs mourn. I stopped its rivers and dried up its abundant water. I clothed Lebanon in black and caused the trees of the field to wilt. ¹⁶I made the nations shake with fear at the sound of its fall, for I sent it down to the grave with all the others who descend to the pit. And all the other proud trees of Eden, the most beautiful and the best of Lebanon, the ones whose roots went deep into the water, took comfort to find it there with them in the depths of the earth. ¹⁷Its allies, too, were all destroyed and had passed away. They had gone down to the grave—all those nations that had lived in its shade.

¹⁸"O Egypt, to which of the trees of Eden will you compare your strength and glory? You, too, will be brought down to the depths with all these other nations. You will lie there among the outcasts* who have died by the sword. This will be the fate of Pharaoh and all his hordes. I, the Sovereign LORD, have spoken!"

31:1 Hebrew *On the first day of the third month,* of the ancient Hebrew lunar calendar. This event occurred on June 21, 587 B.C.; also see note on 1:1.   **31:10** Hebrew *you.*   **31:15** Hebrew *to Sheol;* also in 31:16, 17.   **31:18** Hebrew *among the uncircumcised.*

31:1-18 On June 21, 587 BC, Ezekiel spoke to Egypt about its stature. Egypt believed they had the stature of Assyria, represented as a choice cedar tree in God's garden. Already, God had judged the weaker nations of Ammon, Moab, Edom, and Tyre. God would also cut down Assyria, the mighty nation, and it would fall to the depths of the underworld. Through this, God was sending Egypt a message. Those who exalt themselves will be lowered.

31:6 Assyria was once a great nation, like a great tree that provided shelter for all the birds and wild animals of the earth. This "tree" was more splendid than all the trees in the garden of God (that is, the Garden of Eden), with a God-given beauty and stature reminiscent of the king of Tyre (28:11-19). Assyria's power was once so great that "all the great nations of the world lived in its shadow." Egypt's power was comparable.

31:10-11 Egypt (literally "you" here; see text note on 31:10) forgot that God had created its beauty, and they had become proud and arrogant. As with Tyre, such pride would inevitably lead to a fall. The God who had once set Egypt in such an exalted position would send a divine lumberjack, a mighty nation that would destroy it as its wickedness deserved. The human agent would simply be carrying out God's decree.

31:16-17 The nations all shook with fear at the shock waves created by Assyria's fall. The great nations that had preceded it on the road to destruction and death were gratified to find it joining them in their disgrace, while its allies followed in its dangerous course.

A Warning for Pharaoh

32 On March 3,* during the twelfth year of King Jehoiachin's captivity, this message came to me from the Lord: ² "Son of man, mourn for Pharaoh, king of Egypt, and give him this message:

> "You think of yourself as a strong young lion
>   among the nations,
> but you are really just a sea monster,
> heaving around in your own rivers,
>   stirring up mud with your feet.
> ³ Therefore, this is what the Sovereign Lord says:
> I will send many people
>   to catch you in my net
>   and haul you out of the water.
> ⁴ I will leave you stranded on the land to die.
> All the birds of the heavens will land on you,
> and the wild animals of the whole earth
>   will gorge themselves on you.
> ⁵ I will scatter your flesh on the hills
>   and fill the valleys with your bones.
> ⁶ I will drench the earth with your gushing blood
>   all the way to the mountains,
>   filling the ravines to the brim.
> ⁷ When I blot you out,
>   I will veil the heavens and darken the stars.
> I will cover the sun with a cloud,
>   and the moon will not give you its light.
> ⁸ I will darken the bright stars overhead
>   and cover your land in darkness.
>   I, the Sovereign Lord, have spoken!

⁹ "I will disturb many hearts when I bring news of your downfall to distant nations you have never seen. ¹⁰ Yes, I will shock many lands, and their kings will be terrified at your fate. They will shudder in fear for their lives as I brandish my sword before them on the day of your fall. ¹¹ For this is what the Sovereign Lord says:

> "The sword of the king of Babylon
>   will come against you.
> ¹² I will destroy your hordes with the swords of
>   mighty warriors—
>   the terror of the nations.
> They will shatter the pride of Egypt,
>   and all its hordes will be destroyed.
> ¹³ I will destroy all your flocks and herds
>   that graze beside the streams.
> Never again will people or animals
>   muddy those waters with their feet.
> ¹⁴ Then I will let the waters of Egypt become calm again,
>   and they will flow as smoothly as olive oil,
>   says the Sovereign Lord.
> ¹⁵ And when I destroy Egypt
>   and strip you of everything you own
>   and strike down all your people,
>   then you will know that I am the Lord.
> ¹⁶ Yes, this is the funeral song
>   they will sing for Egypt.
> Let all the nations mourn.
> Let them mourn for Egypt and its hordes.
>   I, the Sovereign Lord, have spoken!"

Egypt Falls into the Pit

¹⁷ On March 17,* during the twelfth year, another message came to me from the Lord: ¹⁸ "Son of man, weep for the hordes of Egypt and for the other mighty nations.* For I will send them down to the world below in company with those who descend to the pit. ¹⁹ Say to them,

> 'O Egypt, are you lovelier than the other nations?
>   No! So go down to the pit and lie there among
>   the outcasts.*'

²⁰ The Egyptians will fall with the many who have died by the sword, for the sword is drawn against them. Egypt and its hordes will be dragged away to their judgment. ²¹ Down in the grave* mighty leaders will mockingly welcome Egypt and its allies, saying, 'They have come down; they lie among the outcasts, hordes slaughtered by the sword.'

²² "Assyria lies there surrounded by the graves of its army, those who were slaughtered by the sword. ²³ Their graves are in the depths of the pit, and they are surrounded by their allies. They struck terror in the hearts of people everywhere, but now they have been slaughtered by the sword.

²⁴ "Elam lies there surrounded by the graves of all its hordes, those who were slaughtered by the sword.

32:1 Hebrew *On the first day of the twelfth month,* of the ancient Hebrew lunar calendar. This event occurred on March 3, 585 B.C.; also see note on 1:1. **32:17** Hebrew *On the fifteenth day of the month,* presumably in the twelfth month of the ancient Hebrew lunar calendar (see 32:1). This would put this message at the end of King Jehoiachin's twelfth year of captivity, on March 17, 585 B.C.; also see note on 1:1. Greek version reads *On the fifteenth day of the first month,* which would put this message on April 27, 586 B.C., at the beginning of Jehoiachin's twelfth year. **32:18** The meaning of the Hebrew is uncertain. **32:19** Hebrew *the uncircumcised;* also in 32:21, 24, 25, 26, 28, 29, 30, 32. **32:21** Hebrew *in Sheol.*

32:1-16 Ezekiel delivered another monster-themed message on March 3, 585 BC. Two months earlier, the exiles found out Jerusalem had been destroyed (see 33:21). Pharaoh believed himself to be a great lion, but God saw him as a crocodile. Pharaoh was powerless and could only thrash around. God plucked him out of the water and left him on the land to die. Plague imagery from the time of the Exodus emphasized the totality of his judgment (see Exodus 7:20-24; 10:21-29).

32:17-32 Ezekiel's seventh message to Egypt took place on March 17, 585 BC. Ezekiel wept for the multitude of people who Babylon's sword would slay. Egypt would be humbled, lying in the underworld beside all those they once thought were inferior to them. Pharaoh would take comfort that he was not the only one judged and slain.

They struck terror in the hearts of people everywhere, but now they have descended as outcasts to the world below. Now they lie in the pit and share the shame of those who have gone before them. ²⁵They have a resting place among the slaughtered, surrounded by the graves of all their hordes. Yes, they terrorized the nations while they lived, but now they lie in shame with others in the pit, all of them outcasts, slaughtered by the sword.

²⁶"Meshech and Tubal are there, surrounded by the graves of all their hordes. They once struck terror in the hearts of people everywhere. But now they are outcasts, all slaughtered by the sword. ²⁷They are not buried in honor like their fallen heroes, who went down to the grave* with their weapons—their shields covering their bodies* and their swords beneath their heads. Their guilt rests upon them because they brought terror to everyone while they were still alive.

²⁸"You too, Egypt, will lie crushed and broken among the outcasts, all slaughtered by the sword.

²⁹"Edom is there with its kings and princes. Mighty as they were, they also lie among those slaughtered by the sword, with the outcasts who have gone down to the pit.

³⁰"All the princes of the north and the Sidonians are there with others who have died. Once a terror, they have been put to shame. They lie there as outcasts with others who were slaughtered by the sword. They share the shame of all who have descended to the pit.

³¹"When Pharaoh and his entire army arrive, he will take comfort that he is not alone in having his hordes killed, says the Sovereign LORD. ³²Although I have caused his terror to fall upon all the living, Pharaoh and his hordes will lie there among the outcasts who were slaughtered by the sword. I, the Sovereign LORD, have spoken!"

Ezekiel as Israel's Watchman

33 Once again a message came to me from the LORD: ²"Son of man, give your people this message: 'When I bring an army against a country, the people of that land choose one of their own to be a watchman. ³When the watchman sees the enemy coming, he sounds the alarm to warn the people. ⁴Then if those who hear the alarm refuse to take action, it is their own fault if they die. ⁵They heard the alarm but ignored it, so the responsibility is theirs. If they had listened to the warning, they could have saved their lives. ⁶But if the watchman sees the enemy coming and doesn't sound the alarm to warn the people, he is responsible for their captivity. They will die in their sins, but I will hold the watchman responsible for their deaths.'

⁷"Now, son of man, I am making you a watchman for the people of Israel. Therefore, listen to what I say and warn them for me. ⁸If I announce that some wicked people are sure to die and you fail to tell them to change their ways, then they will die in their sins, and I will hold you responsible for their deaths. ⁹But if you warn them to repent and they don't repent, they will die in their sins, but you will have saved yourself.

The Watchman's Message

¹⁰"Son of man, give the people of Israel this message: You are saying, 'Our sins are heavy upon us; we are wasting away! How can we survive?' ¹¹As surely as I live, says the Sovereign LORD, I take no pleasure in the death of wicked people. I only want them to turn from their wicked ways so they can live. Turn! Turn from your wickedness, O people of Israel! Why should you die?

¹²"Son of man, give your people this message: The righteous behavior of righteous people will not save them if they turn to sin, nor will the wicked behavior of wicked people destroy them if they repent and turn from their sins. ¹³When I tell righteous people that they will live, but then they sin, expecting their past righteousness to save them, then none of their righteous acts will be remembered. I will destroy them for their sins. ¹⁴And suppose I tell some wicked people that they will surely die,

32:27a Hebrew *to Sheol.* 32:27b The meaning of the Hebrew is uncertain.

33:1—35:15 God gives prophets the gift of foresight as well as hindsight and insight. Ezekiel exercises all three components of his prophetic gift as he addresses the sin of the Israelites, their leaders, and Edom.

33:5-9 Ezekiel's message encouraged the people of Israel even at this point to repent so that they might live and not die. The Lord had said that he would bring an army against their country, and this was evidently what was happening. Ezekiel had been faithful to his calling as a watchman; no one who had heard his prophecy thus far could say that he had not warned the people of the coming judgment. However, the people had not heeded the warning; without a change of heart, they would die in their sins.

33:10-11 Now that the people of Israel were finally taking the prophet's warnings seriously, there was danger of despair rather than a response of repentance and faith. Unlike deterministic fate, God's judgment leaves room for forgiveness. The sovereign Lord takes "no pleasure in the death of wicked people." Even the wicked "can live" if they repent and turn from their wickedness.

33:12-16 The principle stated in 33:10-11 is worked out in two case studies. The first involves righteous people who trust in their past righteousness to save them, even though they turn to sin. God will destroy these people in their sins, notwithstanding their earlier righteous behavior. The second case study involves wicked people who repent of wickedness. Complete forgiveness is available from the Lord. Whatever their past, those who "turn from their sins and do what is just and right" will live. As with the word concerning the watchman, what had been said earlier is revisited. In 18:1-32, the people said that they were being punished for their parents' sins. Here they were apparently saying that their parents' sins had put the nation under an endless curse, so repentance was useless.

but then they turn from their sins and do what is just and right. ¹⁵For instance, they might give back a debtor's security, return what they have stolen, and obey my life-giving laws, no longer doing what is evil. If they do this, then they will surely live and not die. ¹⁶None of their past sins will be brought up again, for they have done what is just and right, and they will surely live.

¹⁷"Your people are saying, 'The Lord isn't doing what's right,' but it is they who are not doing what's right. ¹⁸For again I say, when righteous people turn away from their righteous behavior and turn to evil, they will die. ¹⁹But if wicked people turn from their wickedness and do what is just and right, they will live. ²⁰O people of Israel, you are saying, 'The Lord isn't doing what's right.' But I judge each of you according to your deeds."

Explanation of Jerusalem's Fall

²¹On January 8,* during the twelfth year of our captivity, a survivor from Jerusalem came to me and said, "The city has fallen!" ²²The previous evening the Lord had taken hold of me and given me back my voice. So I was able to speak when this man arrived the next morning.

²³Then this message came to me from the Lord: ²⁴"Son of man, the scattered remnants of Israel living among the ruined cities keep saying, 'Abraham was only one man, yet he gained possession of the entire land. We are many; surely the land has been given to us as a possession.' ²⁵So tell these people, 'This is what the Sovereign Lord says: You eat meat with blood in it, you worship idols,* and you murder the innocent. Do you really think the land should be yours? ²⁶Murderers! Idolaters! Adulterers! Should the land belong to you?'

²⁷"Say to them, 'This is what the Sovereign Lord says: As surely as I live, those living in the ruins will die by the sword. And I will send wild animals to eat those living in the open fields. Those hiding in the forts and caves will die of disease.' ²⁸I will completely destroy the land and demolish her pride. Her arrogant power will come to an end. The mountains of Israel will be so desolate that no one will even travel through them. ²⁹When I have completely destroyed the land because of their detestable sins, then they will know that I am the Lord.'

³⁰"Son of man, your people talk about you in their houses and whisper about you at the doors. They say to each other, 'Come on, let's go hear the prophet tell us what the Lord is saying!' ³¹So my people come pretending to be sincere and sit before you. They listen to your words, but they have no intention of doing what you say. Their mouths are full of lustful words, and their hearts seek only after money. ³²You are very entertaining to them, like someone who sings love songs with a beautiful voice or plays fine music on an instrument. They hear what you say, but they don't act on it! ³³But when all these terrible things happen to them—as they certainly will—then they will know a prophet has been among them."

The Shepherds of Israel

34 Then this message came to me from the Lord: ²"Son of man, prophesy against the shepherds, the leaders of Israel. Give them this message from the Sovereign Lord: What sorrow awaits you shepherds who feed yourselves instead of your flocks. Shouldn't shepherds feed their sheep? ³You drink the milk, wear the wool, and butcher the best animals, but you let your flocks starve. ⁴You have not taken care of the weak. You have not tended the sick

---

33:21 Hebrew *On the fifth day of the tenth month,* of the ancient Hebrew lunar calendar. This event occurred on January 8, 585 B.C.; also see note on 1:1. **33:25** The Hebrew term (literally *round things*) probably alludes to dung.

33:30-33 The situation was not significantly better among the exiles in Babylon. Ezekiel's presentations were the topic of widespread discussion among the exiles, yet their hearts remained as untouched as the hearts of those in Judah. They sat before Ezekiel pretending to be sincere, but with no intention of doing what the Lord told them. They found his messages entertaining, but the Lord warned them that time would demonstrate the power behind the words of a true prophet.
34:1–37:28 These chapters show us the blessings that would flow from the Lord's return to his people. He would be their shepherd and provide them with better leadership (34:1-31). He would restore the fruitfulness of the land and thus vindicate his own honor (35:1–36:38). And he would restore his people to life and unity (37:1-28).
34:1-24 This chapter contains declarations of judgment and salvation. There would be judgment on the shepherds (the former kings of Judah) because they failed to care for their flocks (the people of Judah). The Lord would also judge the "fat" (selfish) sheep, but he would intervene as a good shepherd to feed the remainder of the flock. The image of the shepherd perfectly conveys the toughness and tenderness of God's dealings with his people. The shepherd was also a common metaphor for a king in the ancient Near East. The earthly king was understood to represent the divine shepherd who had set him over his people. Shepherds had to protect their flocks against beasts, including lions and bears, while also knowing their sheep by name and tenderly leading them to good pasture and quiet waters. They had to endure cold, heat, wind, rain, and snow out on the hills with their charges. Good kings who led their people strongly and wisely resembled shepherds. The same image is used in the New Testament to describe pastors and elders, who are to oversee the flock assigned to their care without lording it over them (1 Peter 5:2-4). Jesus perfectly combines toughness and tenderness as the "great Shepherd of the sheep" (Hebrews 13:20).
34:1-9 Kings and officers served as shepherds, a key metaphor for the way they were to lead God's people (2 Samuel 7:7-8; Psalm 78:70-71). They held the responsibility to protect and meet the needs of their people, but the selfish Judean leaders exploited and abused their people. As a result, the nation fell apart, and the sheep scattered.

or bound up the injured. You have not gone looking for those who have wandered away and are lost. Instead, you have ruled them with harshness and cruelty. ⁵So my sheep have been scattered without a shepherd, and they are easy prey for any wild animal. ⁶They have wandered through all the mountains and all the hills, across the face of the earth, yet no one has gone to search for them.

⁷"Therefore, you shepherds, hear the word of the LORD: ⁸As surely as I live, says the Sovereign LORD, you abandoned my flock and left them to be attacked by every wild animal. And though you were my shepherds, you didn't search for my sheep when they were lost. You took care of yourselves and left the sheep to starve. ⁹Therefore, you shepherds, hear the word of the LORD. ¹⁰This is what the Sovereign

Koinonia

IMAGE — MY STORY WITH COMMUNITY, WORKPLACE & CHURCH

Tending and Thriving

SCRIPTURE CONNECTION: EZEKIEL 34:1-31

Ezekiel 34 shows how Scripture can be viewed as a diamond. The facets of meaning reflect truth's light, illuminating the path to a life of thriving.

The terms *sheep*, *flock*, and *shepherd* can refer to animals and herd-tenders or to God's people and the ultimate Good Shepherd, Jesus Christ. Through this prism of shepherding language—like light through a diamond—shines a beautiful principle about righteous tending.

Humanity's first calling was to tend righteously, to steward, God's creation (Genesis 1:28-30). This timeless calling was established before humanity came under the power of sin and remains one of our fundamental assignments.

Ezekiel 34 illustrates this calling to tend righteously. Israel's flock-tenders (civic and religious leaders) were not fulfilling their calling to help their sheep (citizens) thrive. Their failure had consequences. But God promised to send a Savior, the perfect Good Shepherd (34:11-16), who we know as Jesus (John 10:11). This Good Shepherd would ultimately deliver all creation from sin (Romans 8:22-23; 2 Peter 3:13; Revelation 21:1). The Good Shepherd's tending will take us into a time of eternal thriving.

> The Good Shepherd's tending takes us into a time of eternal thriving.

IMAGINE

Why are people sometimes poor, or even, cruel flock-tenders?

When are you more likely, or less likely, to righteously tend your relationships?

How can you better tend your relationship with God?

"As a pastor and a woman, I am especially positioned to shepherd in ways that are both Christlike and nurturing. Jesus, the Good Shepherd, wanted to gather God's people together the way a hen gathers her chicks (Matthew 23:37). Shepherding is as much about gathering and helping, as it is about teaching and leading."

SUSAN I. BUBBERS, MDiv, DMin, PhD, is the Dean of the Center for Anglican Theology in Orlando, FL. She is a professor, Anglican priest, spiritual director, and a Fellow of the Oxford Centre for Animal Ethics.

Lord says: I now consider these shepherds my enemies, and I will hold them responsible for what has happened to my flock. I will take away their right to feed the flock, and I will stop them from feeding themselves. I will rescue my flock from their mouths; the sheep will no longer be their prey.

The Good Shepherd

¹¹"For this is what the Sovereign Lord says: I myself will search and find my sheep. ¹²I will be like a shepherd looking for his scattered flock. I will find my sheep and rescue them from all the places where they were scattered on that dark and cloudy day. ¹³I will bring them back home to their own land of Israel from among the peoples and nations. I will feed them on the mountains of Israel and by the rivers and in all the places where people live. ¹⁴Yes, I will give them good pastureland on the high hills of Israel. There they will lie down in pleasant places and feed in the lush pastures of the hills. ¹⁵I myself will tend my sheep and give them a place to lie down in peace, says the Sovereign Lord. ¹⁶I will search for my lost ones who strayed away, and I will bring them safely home again. I will bandage the injured and strengthen the weak. But I will destroy those who are fat and powerful. I will feed them, yes—feed them justice!

¹⁷"And as for you, my flock, this is what the Sovereign Lord says to his people: I will judge between one animal of the flock and another, separating the sheep from the goats. ¹⁸Isn't it enough for you to keep the best of the pastures for yourselves? Must you also trample down the rest? Isn't it enough for you to drink clear water for yourselves? Must you also muddy the rest with your feet? ¹⁹Why must my flock eat what you have trampled down and drink water you have fouled?

²⁰"Therefore, this is what the Sovereign Lord says: I will surely judge between the fat sheep and the scrawny sheep. ²¹For you fat sheep pushed and butted and crowded my sick and hungry flock until you scattered them to distant lands. ²²So I will rescue my flock, and they will no longer be abused. I will judge between one animal of the flock and another. ²³And I will set over them one shepherd, my servant David. He will feed them and be a shepherd to them. ²⁴And I, the Lord, will be their God, and my servant David will be a prince among my people. I, the Lord, have spoken!

The Lord's Covenant of Peace

²⁵"I will make a covenant of peace with my people and drive away the dangerous animals from the land. Then they will be able to camp safely in the wildest places and sleep in the woods without fear. ²⁶I will bless my people and their homes around my holy hill. And in the proper season I will send the showers they need. There will be showers of blessing. ²⁷The orchards and fields of my people will yield bumper crops, and everyone will live in safety. When I have broken their chains of slavery and rescued them from those who enslaved them, then they will know that I am the Lord. ²⁸They will no longer be prey for other nations, and wild animals will no longer devour them. They will live in safety, and no one will frighten them.

²⁹"And I will make their land famous for its crops, so my people will never again suffer from famines or the insults of foreign nations. ³⁰In this way, they will know that I, the Lord their God, am with them. And they will know that they, the people of Israel, are my people, says the Sovereign Lord. ³¹You are my flock, the sheep of my pasture. You are my people, and I am your God. I, the Sovereign Lord, have spoken!"

A Message for Edom

35 Again a message came to me from the Lord: ²"Son of man, turn and face Mount Seir, and prophesy against its people. ³Give them this message from the Sovereign Lord:

"I am your enemy, O Mount Seir,
  and I will raise my fist against you
    to destroy you completely.
⁴ I will demolish your cities
    and make you desolate.
Then you will know that I am the Lord.

34:10-16 The Lord vowed to hold the self-serving shepherds responsible for the consequences of their actions. He would remove them from their offices as shepherds and rescue his flock from their clutches so that they were no longer their prey. The Lord would go looking for his scattered flock and bring them home.

34:23-31 Ezekiel predicts future events here. When God regathers Israel back to the land, the Messiah would rule over them and be their Shepherd-King (2 Samuel 7:12-16). Ezekiel refers to "my servant David" as the "prince" in Ezekiel 37:24-25; 45:22; 46:4 to refer to the Messiah. Under the rule of this future king, God would also provide the conditions the people need to live safely and flourish in the land and would live among them.

34:27-31 In this covenant of peace, God's people would experience the blessings that flow from wholeness of relationship with God. This covenant would not be essentially different from the original covenant concluded at Sinai. It would offer the experience of genuine, lasting peace that the Sinai covenant offered but never delivered because of the sin of God's people. In place of the failed kings of the past, the people would receive a new and perfect king. In place of the relationship with God that had been repeatedly broken by sin, they would once again be God's people, the sheep of his pasture. Then they would achieve the goal of the covenant in that the sovereign Lord would be their God and once again dwell in their midst.

35:1-15 This oracle is addressed to Edom, Israel's neighbor to the southeast, here personified by its central mountain, Mount Seir. Edom was emblematic of all Israel's enemies (for example, in their rejoicing at Israel's fall, 36:2; see also 25:12-14). The demise of Judah at the hands of the Babylonians might have given Edom room to thrive, but the Lord declared that this prosperity would be short-lived (see the book of Obadiah).

⁵"Your eternal hatred for the people of Israel led you to butcher them when they were helpless, when I had already punished them for all their sins. ⁶As surely as I live, says the Sovereign LORD, since you show no distaste for blood, I will give you a bloodbath of your own. Your turn has come! ⁷I will make Mount Seir utterly desolate, killing off all who try to escape and any who return. ⁸I will fill your mountains with the dead. Your hills, your valleys, and your ravines will be filled with people slaughtered by the sword. ⁹I will make you desolate forever. Your cities will never be rebuilt. Then you will know that I am the LORD.

¹⁰"For you said, 'The lands of Israel and Judah will be ours. We will take possession of them. What do we care that the LORD is there!' ¹¹Therefore, as surely as I live, says the Sovereign LORD, I will pay back your angry deeds with my own. I will punish you for all your acts of anger, envy, and hatred. And I will make myself known to Israel* by what I do to you. ¹²Then you will know that I, the LORD, have heard every contemptuous word you spoke against the mountains of Israel. For you said, 'They are desolate; they have been given to us as food to eat!' ¹³In saying that, you boasted proudly against me, and I have heard it all!

¹⁴"This is what the Sovereign LORD says: The whole world will rejoice when I make you desolate. ¹⁵You rejoiced at the desolation of Israel's territory. Now I will rejoice at yours! You will be wiped out, you people of Mount Seir and all who live in Edom! Then you will know that I am the LORD.

Restoration for Israel

36 "Son of man, prophesy to Israel's mountains. Give them this message: O mountains of Israel, hear the word of the LORD! ²This is what the Sovereign LORD says: Your enemies have taunted you, saying, 'Aha! Now the ancient heights belong to us!' ³Therefore, son of man, give the mountains of Israel this message from the Sovereign LORD: Your enemies have attacked you from all directions, making you the property of many nations and the object of much mocking and slander. ⁴Therefore, O mountains of Israel, hear the word of the Sovereign LORD. He speaks to the hills and mountains, ravines and valleys, and to ruined wastes and long-deserted cities that have been destroyed and mocked by the surrounding nations. ⁵This is what the Sovereign LORD says: My jealous anger burns against these nations, especially Edom, because they have shown utter contempt for me by gleefully taking my land for themselves as plunder.

⁶"Therefore, prophesy to the hills and mountains, the ravines and valleys of Israel. This is what the Sovereign LORD says: I am furious that you have suffered shame before the surrounding nations. ⁷Therefore, this is what the Sovereign LORD says: I have taken a solemn oath that those nations will soon have their own shame to endure.

⁸"But the mountains of Israel will produce heavy crops of fruit for my people—for they will be coming home again soon! ⁹See, I care about you, and I will pay attention to you. Your ground will be plowed and your crops planted. ¹⁰I will greatly increase the population of Israel, and the ruined cities will be rebuilt and filled with people. ¹¹I will increase not only the people, but also your animals. O mountains of Israel, I will bring people to live on you once again. I will make you even more prosperous than you were before. Then you will know that I am the LORD. ¹²I will cause my people to walk on you once again, and you will be their territory. You will never again rob them of their children.

¹³"This is what the Sovereign LORD says: The other nations taunt you, saying, 'Israel is a land that devours its own people and robs them of their children!' ¹⁴But you will never again devour your people or rob them of their children, says the Sovereign LORD. ¹⁵I will not let you hear those other nations insult you, and you will no longer be mocked by them. You will not be a land that causes its nation to fall, says the Sovereign LORD."

¹⁶Then this further message came to me from the LORD: ¹⁷"Son of man, when the people of Israel were

---

35:11 Hebrew *to them*; Greek version reads *to you*.

35:5-10 The eternal (or ancient) hatred of Edom for Israel went all the way back to their respective ancestors, Esau and Jacob (see Genesis 25:19-34; 27:1-46; see also Numbers 20:14-21; 24:18; 2 Samuel 8:13-14; 1 Kings 11:14). Because of that enmity, the Edomites took advantage of the Babylonian destruction to butcher the Israelites when they were helpless. They wanted to wipe out the descendants of Jacob and seize the lands of Israel and Judah. The bloodbath they delighted to inflict on Israel would return on their own heads, as their people would be slaughtered by the sword. Their everlasting hatred would be punished: Their land would become desolate forever. This prophecy was fulfilled when the Edomites were displaced by a coalition of Arabian tribes sometime during the 400s BC.
35:13-15 The Edomites mistakenly assumed that God's judgment of his people and his abandonment of the Temple meant that his covenant with Israel was no longer in effect. The Edomites had boasted and elevated themselves against both Israel and the Lord. The God of Israel would not tolerate such boasting, for he is the sovereign Lord of all. His choice of Israel and his gift of the land would not be revoked.
36:1–37:28 Ezekiel's previous messages scolded the Israelites because of their wrongdoings. His messages in these chapters tell of hope for the future. Not only would the people of God return to a restored and cleansed land, but there would also be a new Temple, and God's glory would return to it.
36:1-15 God's jealous anger burned against the nations that devastated the Israelites' land and caused them shame. The Israelites would confidently dwell there in peace and rest from conflict.
36:16-20 God accused Israel of two serious wrongs. First, the Israelites polluted God's land (Leviticus 18:26-30). Second, the people dishonored God's name before the nations (Malachi 1:6-14). They did not live the life God laid out for them, representing God.

living in their own land, they defiled it by the evil way they lived. To me their conduct was as unclean as a woman's menstrual cloth. ¹⁸They polluted the land with murder and the worship of idols,* so I poured out my fury on them. ¹⁹I scattered them to many lands to punish them for the evil way they had lived. ²⁰But when they were scattered among the nations, they brought shame on my holy name. For the nations said, 'These are the people of the LORD, but he couldn't keep them safe in his own land!' ²¹Then I was concerned for my holy name, on which my people brought shame among the nations.

²²"Therefore, give the people of Israel this message from the Sovereign LORD: I am bringing you back, but not because you deserve it. I am doing it to protect my holy name, on which you brought shame while you were scattered among the nations. ²³I will show how holy my great name is—the name on which you brought shame among the nations. And when I reveal my holiness through you before their very eyes, says the Sovereign LORD, then the nations will know that I am the LORD. ²⁴For I will gather you up from all the nations and bring you home again to your land.

²⁵"Then I will sprinkle clean water on you, and you will be clean. Your filth will be washed away, and you will no longer worship idols. ²⁶And I will give you a new heart, and I will put a new spirit in you. I will take out your stony, stubborn heart and give you a tender, responsive heart.* ²⁷And I will put my Spirit in you so that you will follow my decrees and be careful to obey my regulations.

²⁸"And you will live in Israel, the land I gave your ancestors long ago. You will be my people, and I will be your God. ²⁹I will cleanse you of your filthy behavior. I will give you good crops of grain, and I will send no more famines on the land. ³⁰I will give you great harvests from your fruit trees and fields, and never again will the surrounding nations be able to scoff at your land for its famines. ³¹Then you will remember your past sins and despise yourselves for all the detestable things you did. ³²But remember, says the Sovereign LORD, I am not doing this because you deserve it. O my people of Israel, you should be utterly ashamed of all you have done!

³³"This is what the Sovereign LORD says: When I cleanse you from your sins, I will repopulate your cities, and the ruins will be rebuilt. ³⁴The fields that used to lie empty and desolate in plain view of

> "If you have a hole in your heart and you are seeking for other people to fill your neediness, it doesn't work that way."
>
> **PATSY CLAIRMONT**
> author and speaker

36:18 The Hebrew term (literally *round things*) probably alludes to dung; also in 36:25. 36:26 Hebrew *a heart of flesh.*

36:17 Covenant curses had come to Israel because God's people had defiled their own land with their sinful behavior. According to the law of Moses, a menstrual cloth was considered ritually unclean, in the same way that any contact with bodily fluids—blood, sweat, or semen—made people ceremonially unclean (see Leviticus 15:1-33).

36:21-24 Out of concern for his own holiness, God sent Israel into exile. Concern for the honor of his holy name would lead him to gather them again to the land. Israel did not deserve this return from exile; it was simply a manifestation of the Lord's holiness and power in the sight of the nations. Israel could not remain forever outside the land that God had sworn to give to Abraham and his descendants.

36:26 The Lord's renewal of his people would not be merely an outward cleansing; the Lord would give Israel a new heart and a new spirit (see 11:19; 18:31). The heart and spirit are the sources of the thoughts and will that underlie action. Their stony, stubborn heart would now become "a tender, responsive heart" (literally "a heart of flesh"), ready to serve the Lord. The spirit of rebellion would be replaced with a spirit of obedience.

36:27-28 The Spirit of God would create life and light out of darkness and chaos (compare Genesis 1:2-4), producing an entirely new ability to follow God's decrees and regulations. In the past, the Spirit of God had empowered people for specific tasks of service to the Lord (see Judges 3:10; 1 Samuel 16:13). In the future, a more widespread empowerment by God's Spirit would enable his people to lead holy lives (see Joel 2:28-29). This renewed people would again live in Israel and make it fit for God's presence to dwell among them once again.

36:29-32 This transformation would bring the blessings of the covenant made with Moses, not its curses, and a new glory among the surrounding nations. These blessings would cause God's people to be profoundly ashamed of their past and to appreciate both their lack of merit and God's overwhelming grace.

everyone will again be farmed. ³⁵And when I bring you back, people will say, 'This former wasteland is now like the Garden of Eden! The abandoned and ruined cities now have strong walls and are filled with people!' ³⁶Then the surrounding nations that survive will know that I, the Lord, have rebuilt the ruins and replanted the wasteland. For I, the Lord, have spoken, and I will do what I say.

³⁷"This is what the Sovereign Lord says: I am ready to hear Israel's prayers and to increase their numbers like a flock. ³⁸They will be as numerous as the sacred flocks that fill Jerusalem's streets at the time of her festivals. The ruined cities will be crowded with people once more, and everyone will know that I am the Lord."

A Valley of Dry Bones

37 The Lord took hold of me, and I was carried away by the Spirit of the Lord to a valley filled with bones. ²He led me all around among the bones that covered the valley floor. They were scattered everywhere across the ground and were completely dried out. ³Then he asked me, "Son of man, can these bones become living people again?"

"O Sovereign Lord," I replied, "you alone know the answer to that."

⁴Then he said to me, "Speak a prophetic message to these bones and say, 'Dry bones, listen to the word of the Lord! ⁵This is what the Sovereign Lord says: Look! I am going to put breath into you and make you live again! ⁶I will put flesh and muscles on you and cover you with skin. I will put breath into you, and you will come to life. Then you will know that I am the Lord.'"

⁷So I spoke this message, just as he told me. Suddenly as I spoke, there was a rattling noise all across the valley. The bones of each body came together and attached themselves as complete skeletons. ⁸Then as I watched, muscles and flesh formed over the bones. Then skin formed to cover their bodies, but they still had no breath in them.

⁹Then he said to me, "Speak a prophetic message to the winds, son of man. Speak a prophetic message and say, 'This is what the Sovereign Lord says: Come, O breath, from the four winds! Breathe into these dead bodies so they may live again.'"

¹⁰So I spoke the message as he commanded me, and breath came into their bodies. They all came to life and stood up on their feet—a great army.

¹¹Then he said to me, "Son of man, these bones represent the people of Israel. They are saying, 'We have become old, dry bones—all hope is gone. Our nation is finished.' ¹²Therefore, prophesy to them and say, 'This is what the Sovereign Lord says: O my people, I will open your graves of exile and cause you to rise again. Then I will bring you back to the land of Israel. ¹³When this happens, O my people, you will know that I am the Lord. ¹⁴I will put my Spirit in you, and you will live again and return home to your own land. Then you will know that I, the Lord, have spoken, and I have done what I said. Yes, the Lord has spoken!'"

Reunion of Israel and Judah

¹⁵Again a message came to me from the Lord: ¹⁶"Son of man, take a piece of wood and carve on it these words: 'This represents Judah and its allied tribes.' Then take another piece and carve these words on it: 'This represents Ephraim and the northern tribes of Israel.'* ¹⁷Now hold them together in your hand as if they were one piece of wood. ¹⁸When your people ask you what your actions mean, ¹⁹say to them, 'This is what the Sovereign Lord says: I will take Ephraim and the northern tribes and join them to Judah. I will make them one piece of wood in my hand.'

²⁰"Then hold out the pieces of wood you have inscribed, so the people can see them. ²¹And give them this message from the Sovereign Lord: I will gather the people of Israel from among the nations. I will bring them home to their own land from the places where they have been scattered. ²²I will unify them into one nation on the mountains of Israel. One king will rule them all; no longer will they be divided into two nations or into two kingdoms. ²³They will never again pollute themselves with their idols* and vile images and rebellion, for I will save them from their sinful apostasy.* I will

---

37:16 Hebrew *This is Ephraim's wood, representing Joseph and all the house of Israel;* similarly in 37:19. 37:23a The Hebrew term (literally *round things*) probably alludes to dung. 37:23b As in many Hebrew manuscripts and Greek version; Masoretic Text reads *from all their dwelling places where they sinned.*

36:35-38 The restored land would become "like the Garden of Eden," the ultimate symbol of fertility and fruitfulness. The original garden would be enhanced by restored cities, overflowing with renewed humanity like "Jerusalem's streets at the time of her festivals." The greatest blessing, however, would be God's willingness to "hear Israel's prayers" once more. He had once refused to listen to his rebellious people (14:3; 20:3), but now the Lord would turn his face toward them and hear their cries. The proof of this would be the number of people in the rebuilt cities who would acknowledge that the Lord is God.
37:1-14 Ezekiel had a vision of a valley filled with old, sun-bleached bones from human skeletons scattered everywhere. God covered the bones with flesh and muscles, and breathed life back into them. A great army rose to its feet. They represented the people of Israel. New life comes from God and God alone.
37:11-14 The message that follows explains this vision. The people in exile felt that they were as dead as old, dry bones. As a result, they felt that all hope was gone, but the Lord could and would restore them to life. God would once again call them "my people," and he promised that he would open their graves of exile and bring them back to the land of Israel.
37:15-28 For Ezekiel's last sign act, he took two pieces of wood to represent Israel's two kingdoms. Ezekiel put the two pieces together to symbolize that God would unite the nation under one king, worshiping one God. The people would no longer worship idols or ignore the law.

cleanse them. Then they will truly be my people, and I will be their God.

24 "My servant David will be their king, and they will have only one shepherd. They will obey my regulations and be careful to keep my decrees. 25 They will live in the land I gave my servant Jacob, the land where their ancestors lived. They and their children and their grandchildren after them will live there forever, generation after generation. And my servant David will be their prince forever. 26 And I will make a covenant of peace with them, an everlasting covenant. I will give them their land and increase their numbers,* and I will put my Temple among them forever. 27 I will make my home among them. I will be their God, and they will be my people. 28 And when my Temple is among them forever, the nations will know that I am the LORD, who makes Israel holy."

A Message for Gog

38 This is another message that came to me from the LORD: 2 "Son of man, turn and face Gog of the land of Magog, the prince who rules over the nations of Meshech and Tubal, and prophesy against him. 3 Give him this message from the Sovereign LORD: Gog, I am your enemy! 4 I will turn you around and put hooks in your jaws to lead you out with your whole army—your horses and charioteers in full armor and a great horde armed with shields and swords. 5 Persia, Ethiopia, and Libya* will join you, too, with all their weapons. 6 Gomer and all its armies will also join you, along with the armies of Beth-togarmah from the distant north, and many others.

7 "Get ready; be prepared! Keep all the armies around you mobilized, and take command of them. 8 A long time from now you will be called into action. In the distant future you will swoop down on the land of Israel, which will be enjoying peace after recovering from war and after its people have returned from many lands to the mountains of Israel. 9 You and all your allies—a vast and awesome army—will roll down on them like a storm and cover the land like a cloud.

10 "This is what the Sovereign LORD says: At that time evil thoughts will come to your mind, and you will devise a wicked scheme. 11 You will say, 'Israel is an unprotected land filled with unwalled villages! I will march against her and destroy these people who live in such confidence! 12 I will go to those formerly desolate cities that are now filled with people who have returned from exile in many nations. I will capture vast amounts of plunder, for the people are rich with livestock and other possessions now. They think the whole world revolves around them!' 13 But Sheba and Dedan and the merchants of Tarshish will ask, 'Do you really think the armies you have gathered can rob them of silver and gold? Do you think you can drive away their livestock and seize their goods and carry off plunder?'

14 "Therefore, son of man, prophesy against Gog. Give him this message from the Sovereign LORD: When my people are living in peace in their land, then you will rouse yourself.* 15 You will come from your homeland in the distant north with your vast cavalry and your mighty army, 16 and you will attack my people Israel, covering their land like a cloud. At that time in the distant future, I will bring you against my land as everyone watches, and my holiness will be displayed by what happens to you, Gog. Then all the nations will know that I am the LORD.

17 "This is what the Sovereign LORD asks: Are you the one I was talking about long ago, when I announced through Israel's prophets that in the future I would bring you against my people? 18 But this is what the Sovereign LORD says: When Gog invades the land of Israel, my fury will boil over! 19 In my jealousy and blazing anger, I promise a mighty shaking in the land of Israel on that day. 20 All living things—the fish in the sea, the birds of the sky, the animals of the field, the small animals that scurry along the ground, and all the people on earth—will quake in terror at my presence. Mountains will be thrown down; cliffs will crumble; walls will fall to the earth. 21 I will summon the sword against you on all the hills of Israel, says the Sovereign LORD. Your men will turn their swords against each other. 22 I will punish you and your armies with disease and bloodshed; I will send torrential rain, hailstones, fire, and burning sulfur!

37:26 Hebrew reads *I will give them and increase their numbers;* Greek version lacks the entire phrase.   38:5 Hebrew *Paras, Cush, and Put.*   38:14 As in Greek version; Hebrew reads *then you will know.*

37:25-28 The covenant of peace, which is the blessing of covenant obedience, would be everlasting. The people's earlier defilement had led to the Lord's destruction of the Temple; now, their new purity would be matched by a renewed sanctuary, a Temple in which God could dwell in their midst forever. This final Temple will be the culmination of the success of God's sanctifying program and demonstrate that the Lord is the one "who makes Israel holy."

38:1-13 God gives Ezekiel a message for Gog, the prince who rules Magog (meaning "my Gog" or "land of Gog"). He tells the prince to prepare to lead a coalition of nations that would mobilize in the distant future. At that time, Gog would devise a scheme to conquer Israel.

38:14-16 Israel would be rich, living in peace and experiencing the fruit of obedient trust in the Lord. However, such obedience does not eliminate the possibility of threatening circumstances (see John 16:33). The odds would seem stacked against Israel, but Gog would fail to reckon with the Lord. The Lord would use Gog and his allies as a tool for displaying his holiness in the sight of all the nations.

38:18-20 Instead of being the agent of divine wrath, Gog would be subject to it. The Lord would vent on Gog the jealousy and blazing anger he had earlier visited on Israel. The scene would be so frightening that even innocent bystanders would quake in terror. The earth would also tremble, destroying mountains, cliffs, and walls.

23In this way, I will show my greatness and holiness, and I will make myself known to all the nations of the world. Then they will know that I am the LORD.

The Slaughter of Gog's Hordes

39 "Son of man, prophesy against Gog. Give him this message from the Sovereign LORD: I am your enemy, O Gog, ruler of the nations of Meshech and Tubal. 2I will turn you around and drive you toward the mountains of Israel, bringing you from the distant north. 3I will knock the bow from your left hand and the arrows from your right hand, and I will leave you helpless. 4You and your army and your allies will all die on the mountains. I will feed you to the vultures and wild animals. 5You will fall in the open fields, for I have spoken, says the Sovereign LORD. 6And I will rain down fire on Magog and on all your allies who live safely on the coasts. Then they will know that I am the LORD.

7"In this way, I will make known my holy name among my people of Israel. I will not let anyone bring shame on it. And the nations, too, will know that I am the LORD, the Holy One of Israel. 8That day of judgment will come, says the Sovereign LORD. Everything will happen just as I have declared it.

9"Then the people in the towns of Israel will go out and pick up your small and large shields, bows and arrows, javelins and spears, and they will use them for fuel. There will be enough to last them seven years! 10They won't need to cut wood from the fields or forests, for these weapons will give them all the fuel they need. They will plunder those who planned to plunder them, and they will rob those who planned to rob them, says the Sovereign LORD.

11"And I will make a vast graveyard for Gog and his hordes in the Valley of the Travelers, east of the Dead Sea.* It will block the way of those who travel there, and they will change the name of the place to the Valley of Gog's Hordes. 12It will take seven months for the people of Israel to bury the bodies and cleanse the land. 13Everyone in Israel will help, for it will be a glorious victory for Israel when I demonstrate my glory on that day, says the Sovereign LORD.

14"After seven months, teams of men will be appointed to search the land for skeletons to bury, so the land will be made clean again. 15Whenever bones are found, a marker will be set up so the burial crews will take them to be buried in the Valley of Gog's Hordes. 16(There will be a town there named Hamonah, which means 'horde.') And so the land will finally be cleansed.

17"And now, son of man, this is what the Sovereign LORD says: Call all the birds and wild animals. Say to them: Gather together for my great sacrificial feast. Come from far and near to the mountains of Israel, and there eat flesh and drink blood! 18Eat the flesh of mighty men and drink the blood of princes as though they were rams, lambs, goats, and bulls—all fattened animals from Bashan! 19Gorge yourselves with flesh until you are glutted; drink blood until you are drunk. This is the sacrificial feast I have prepared for you. 20Feast at my banquet table—feast on horses and charioteers, on mighty men and all kinds of valiant warriors, says the Sovereign LORD.

21"In this way, I will demonstrate my glory to the nations. Everyone will see the punishment I have inflicted on them and the power of my fist when I strike. 22And from that time on the people of Israel will know that I am the LORD their God. 23The nations will then know why Israel was sent away to exile—it was punishment for sin, for they were unfaithful to their God. Therefore, I turned away from them and let their enemies destroy them. 24I turned my face away and punished them because of their defilement and their sins.

Restoration for God's People

25"So now, this is what the Sovereign LORD says: I will end the captivity of my people*; I will have mercy on all Israel, for I jealously guard my holy reputation! 26They will accept responsibility for* their past shame and unfaithfulness after they come home to live in peace in their own land, with no one to bother them. 27When I bring them home from the lands of their enemies, I will display my holiness among them for all the nations to see. 28Then my people will know that I

39:11 Hebrew *the sea*. **39:25** Hebrew *of Jacob*. **39:26** A few Hebrew manuscripts read *They will forget*.

39:1-8 God would bring Prince Gog to Israel's land. He would disarm the prince and his army, and in their helplessness, Gog's men would die. Further, God would bring judgment on Gog by devastating his land. God would restore his holy name through these activities, defend his redeemed people, and judge the wrongdoers.
39:9-10 Israel would be called upon to act only after Gog had been completely defeated and destroyed. As in some of their great battles in the past, Israel would be able to watch the Lord act and then pick up the spoils (for example, 2 Kings 6:1–7:20; 2 Chronicles 20). Ironically, the only items to survive the fire from heaven that destroyed Gog's army would be wooden weaponry that would now be fuel for Israel's fires for seven years, a number that often represents completeness in the Old Testament. Those who came to plunder would become plunder. Israel's weapons would be unnecessary now that Israel's last enemy had been destroyed.

39:12-20 The body count would be so large that everyone in Israel would be involved in the cleanup process for seven months. Even after that initial period, there would be a continuing need for teams of professional morticians to go through the land tagging remains so that they could be properly disposed of. God would also provide his own disposal team of birds and wild animals, which he would gather for his great sacrificial feast.
39:25-29 God would also demonstrate his glory through his people's return home from exile in "the lands of their enemies." Once God had exhausted his wrath upon them for their sins, he would bring them home again and leave none of them behind. He would pour out his Spirit upon the people of Israel, transforming them in order to prevent a recurrence of their former situation. He would never again turn his face from them. His future favor on his people was assured (see Romans 8:31-39).

am the LORD their God, because I sent them away to exile and brought them home again. I will leave none of my people behind. ²⁹And I will never again turn my face from them, for I will pour out my Spirit upon the people of Israel. I, the Sovereign LORD, have spoken!"

The New Temple Area

40 On April 28,* during the twenty-fifth year of our captivity—fourteen years after the fall of Jerusalem—the LORD took hold of me. ²In a vision from God he took me to the land of Israel and set me down on a very high mountain. From there I could see toward the south what appeared to be a city. ³As he brought me nearer, I saw a man whose face shone like bronze standing beside a gateway entrance. He was holding in his hand a linen measuring cord and a measuring rod.

⁴He said to me, "Son of man, watch and listen. Pay close attention to everything I show you. You have been brought here so I can show you many things. Then you will return to the people of Israel and tell them everything you have seen."

The East Gateway

⁵I could see a wall completely surrounding the Temple area. The man took a measuring rod that was 10½ feet* long and measured the wall, and the wall was 10½ feet* thick and 10½ feet high.

⁶Then he went over to the eastern gateway. He climbed the steps and measured the threshold of the gateway; it was 10½ feet front to back.* ⁷There were guard alcoves on each side built into the gateway passage. Each of these alcoves was 10½ feet square, with a distance between them of 8¾ feet* along the passage wall. The gateway's inner threshold, which led to the entry room at the inner end of the gateway passage, was 10½ feet front to back. ⁸He also measured the entry room of the gateway.* ⁹It was 14 feet* across, with supporting columns 3½ feet* thick. This entry room was at the inner end of the gateway structure, facing toward the Temple.

¹⁰There were three guard alcoves on each side of the gateway passage. Each had the same measurements, and the dividing walls separating them were also identical. ¹¹The man measured the gateway entrance, which was 17½ feet* wide at the opening and 22¾ feet* wide in the gateway passage. ¹²In front of each of the guard alcoves was a 21-inch* curb. The alcoves themselves were 10½ feet* on each side.

¹³Then he measured the entire width of the gateway, measuring the distance between the back walls of facing guard alcoves; this distance was 43¾ feet.* ¹⁴He measured the dividing walls all along the inside of the gateway up to the entry room of the gateway; this distance was 105 feet.* ¹⁵The full length of the gateway passage was 87½ feet* from one end to the other. ¹⁶There were recessed windows that narrowed inward through the walls of the guard alcoves and their dividing walls. There were also windows in the entry room. The surfaces of the dividing walls were decorated with carved palm trees.

The Outer Courtyard

¹⁷Then the man brought me through the gateway into the outer courtyard of the Temple. A stone pavement ran along the walls of the courtyard, and thirty rooms were built against the walls, opening onto the pavement. ¹⁸This pavement flanked the gates and extended out from the walls into the courtyard the same distance as the gateway entrance. This was the lower pavement. ¹⁹Then the man measured across the Temple's outer courtyard between the outer and inner gateways; the distance was 175 feet.*

The North Gateway

²⁰The man measured the gateway on the north just like the one on the east. ²¹Here, too, there were three guard alcoves on each side, with dividing walls and an entry room. All the measurements matched those of the east gateway. The gateway passage was 87½ feet long and 43¾ feet wide between the back walls of facing guard alcoves. ²²The windows, the entry room, and the palm tree decorations were identical to those in the east gateway. There were seven steps leading up to the gateway entrance, and the entry room was at the inner end of the gateway passage. ²³Here on the north side, just as on the east, there was another gateway leading to the Temple's inner

---

40:1 Hebrew *At the beginning of the year, on the tenth day of the month*, of the ancient Hebrew lunar calendar. This event occurred on April 28, 573 B.C.; also see note on 1:1. **40:5a** Hebrew *6 long cubits* [3.2 meters], *each being a cubit* [18 inches or 45 centimeters] *and a handbreadth* [3 inches or 8 centimeters] *in length*. **40:5b** Hebrew *1 rod* [3.2 meters]; also in 40:5c, 7. **40:6** As in Greek version, which reads *1 rod* [3.2 meters] *deep;* Hebrew reads *1 rod deep, and 1 threshold, 1 rod deep*. **40:7** Hebrew *5 cubits* [2.7 meters]; also in 40:48. **40:8** As in many Hebrew manuscripts and Syriac version; other Hebrew manuscripts add *which faced inward toward the Temple; it was 1 rod* [10.5 feet or 3.2 meters] *deep. ⁹Then he measured the entry room of the gateway*. **40:9a** Hebrew *8 cubits* [4.2 meters]. **40:9b** Hebrew *2 cubits* [1.1 meters]. **40:11a** Hebrew *10 cubits* [5.3 meters]. **40:11b** Hebrew *13 cubits* [6.9 meters]. **40:12a** Hebrew *1 cubit* [53 centimeters]. **40:12b** Hebrew *6 cubits* [3.2 meters]. **40:13** Hebrew *25 cubits* [13.3 meters]; also in 40:21, 25, 29, 30, 33, 36. **40:14** Hebrew *60 cubits* [31.8 meters]. Greek version reads *20 cubits* [35 feet or 10.6 meters]. The meaning of the Hebrew in this verse is uncertain. **40:15** Hebrew *50 cubits* [26.5 meters]; also in 40:21, 25, 29, 33, 36. **40:19** Hebrew *100 cubits* [53 meters]; also in 40:23, 27, 47.

40:1–48:35 On April 28, 573 BC, the first day of Passover, God gave Ezekiel a new vision. Situated on a high mountain, Ezekiel saw a flourishing land and a glorious new Temple. A bronzed man gave Ezekiel a tour of the Temple, which was the central symbol of God's restoration of the land and his people. In the man's hand was a linen cord and a rod used for taking measurements. The Temple details indicate God's plans for the future.

Insight: EZEKIEL'S IMPORTANT DATES

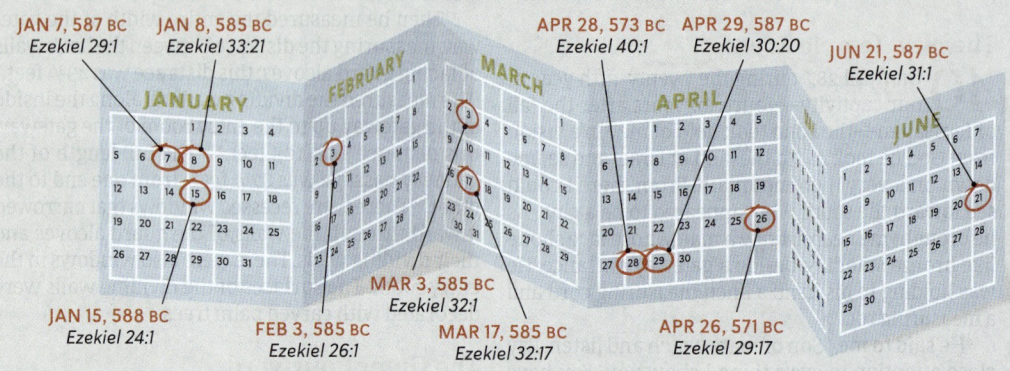

courtyard directly opposite this outer gateway. The distance between the two gateways was 175 feet.

The South Gateway

24 Then the man took me around to the south gateway and measured its various parts, and they were exactly the same as the others. 25 It had windows along the walls as the others did, and there was an entry room where the gateway passage opened into the outer courtyard. And like the others, the gateway passage was 87½ feet long and 43¾ feet wide between the back walls of facing guard alcoves. 26 This gateway also had a stairway of seven steps leading up to it, and an entry room at the inner end, and palm tree decorations along the dividing walls. 27 And here again, directly opposite the outer gateway, was another gateway that led into the inner courtyard. The distance between the two gateways was 175 feet.

Gateways to the Inner Courtyard

28 Then the man took me to the south gateway leading into the inner courtyard. He measured it, and it had the same measurements as the other gateways. 29 Its guard alcoves, dividing walls, and entry room were the same size as those in the others. It also had windows along its walls and in the entry room. And like the others, the gateway passage was 87½ feet long and 43¾ feet wide. 30 (The entry rooms of the gateways leading into the inner courtyard were 14 feet* across and 43¾ feet wide.) 31 The entry room to the south gateway faced into the outer courtyard. It had palm tree decorations on its columns, and there were eight steps leading to its entrance.

32 Then he took me to the east gateway leading to the inner courtyard. He measured it, and it had the same measurements as the other gateways. 33 Its guard alcoves, dividing walls, and entry room were the same size as those of the others, and there were windows along the walls and in the entry room. The gateway passage measured 87½ feet long and 43¾ feet wide. 34 Its entry room faced into the outer courtyard. It had palm tree decorations on its columns, and there were eight steps leading to its entrance.

35 Then he took me around to the north gateway leading to the inner courtyard. He measured it, and it had the same measurements as the other gateways. 36 The guard alcoves, dividing walls, and entry room of this gateway had the same measurements as in the others and the same window arrangements. The gateway passage measured 87½ feet long and 43¾ feet wide. 37 Its entry room* faced into the outer courtyard, and it had palm tree decorations on the columns. There were eight steps leading to its entrance.

Rooms for Preparing Sacrifices

38 A door led from the entry room of one of the inner gateways into a side room, where the meat for sacrifices was washed. 39 On each side of this entry room were two tables, where the sacrificial animals were slaughtered for the burnt offerings, sin offerings, and guilt offerings. 40 Outside the entry room, on each side of the stairs going up to the north entrance, were two more tables. 41 So there were eight tables in all—four inside and four outside—where the sacrifices were cut up and prepared. 42 There were also four tables of finished stone for preparation of the burnt offerings, each 31½ inches square and 21 inches high.* On these tables were placed the butchering knives and other implements

---

40:30 As in 40:9, which reads *8 cubits* [14 feet or 4.2 meters]; here the Hebrew reads *5 cubits* [8¾ feet or 2.7 meters]. Some Hebrew manuscripts and the Greek version lack this entire verse. **40:37** As in Greek version (compare parallels at 40:26, 31, 34); Hebrew reads *Its dividing wall.* **40:42** Hebrew *1½ cubits* [80 centimeters] *long and 1½ cubits wide and 1 cubit* [53 centimeters] *high.*

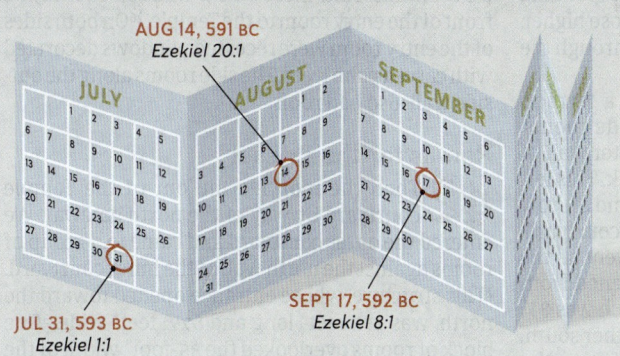

AUG 14, 591 BC
Ezekiel 20:1

JUL 31, 593 BC
Ezekiel 1:1

SEPT 17, 592 BC
Ezekiel 8:1

Ezekiel recorded specific dates for many of his messages, which allow us to locate the corresponding date on our modern-day calendar. Keeping track of when we "hear" from God can help us map out how we grow in our faith. Do you have a way to remember important moments in your walk with God?

for slaughtering the sacrificial animals. ⁴³There were hooks, each 3 inches* long, fastened all around the foyer walls. The sacrificial meat was laid on the tables.

Rooms for the Priests

⁴⁴Inside the inner courtyard were two rooms,* one beside the north gateway, facing south, and the other beside the south* gateway, facing north. ⁴⁵And the man said to me, "The room beside the north inner gate is for the priests who supervise the Temple maintenance. ⁴⁶The room beside the south inner gate is for the priests in charge of the altar—the descendants of Zadok—for they alone of all the Levites may approach the LORD to minister to him."

The Inner Courtyard and Temple

⁴⁷Then the man measured the inner courtyard, and it was a square, 175 feet wide and 175 feet across. The altar stood in the courtyard in front of the Temple. ⁴⁸Then he brought me to the entry room of the Temple. He measured the walls on either side of the opening to the entry room, and they were 8¾ feet thick. The entrance itself was 24½ feet wide, and the walls on each side of the entrance were an additional 5¼ feet long.* ⁴⁹The entry room was 35 feet* wide and 21 feet* deep. There were ten steps* leading up to it, with a column on each side.

41 After that, the man brought me into the sanctuary of the Temple. He measured the walls on either side of its doorway,* and they were 10½ feet* thick. ²The doorway was 17½ feet* wide, and the walls on each side of it were 8¾ feet* long. The sanctuary itself was 70 feet long and 35 feet wide.*

³Then he went beyond the sanctuary into the inner room. He measured the walls on either side of its entrance, and they were 3½ feet* thick. The entrance was 10½ feet wide, and the walls on each side of the entrance were 12¼ feet* long. ⁴The inner room of the sanctuary was 35 feet* long and 35 feet wide. "This," he told me, "is the Most Holy Place."

⁵Then he measured the wall of the Temple, and it was 10½ feet thick. There was a row of rooms along the outside wall; each room was 7 feet* wide. ⁶These

40:43 Hebrew *a handbreadth* [8 centimeters]. **40:44a** As in Greek version; Hebrew reads *rooms for singers.* **40:44b** As in Greek version; Hebrew reads *east.* **40:48** As in Greek version, which reads *The entrance was 14 cubits* [7.4 meters] *wide, and the walls of the entrance were 3 cubits* [1.6 meters] *on each side;* Hebrew lacks *14 cubits wide, and the walls of the entrance were.* **40:49a** Hebrew *20 cubits* [10.6 meters]. **40:49b** As in Greek version, which reads *12 cubits* [21 feet or 6.4 meters]; Hebrew reads *11 cubits* [19¼ feet or 5.8 meters]. **40:49c** As in Greek version; Hebrew reads *There were steps that were.* **41:1a** As in Greek version; the meaning of the Hebrew is uncertain. **41:1b** Hebrew *6 cubits* [3.2 meters]; also in 41:3, 5. **41:2a** Hebrew *10 cubits* [5.3 meters]. **41:2b** Hebrew *5 cubits* [2.7 meters]; also in 41:9, 11. **41:2c** Hebrew *40 cubits* [21.2 meters] *long and 20 cubits* [10.6 meters] *wide.* **41:3a** Hebrew *2 cubits* [1.1 meters]. **41:3b** Hebrew *7 cubits* [3.7 meters]. **41:4** Hebrew *20 cubits* [10.6 meters]; also in 41:4b, 10. **41:5** Hebrew *4 cubits* [2.1 meters].

40:48–43:12 The Temple's footprint was larger than that of the Tabernacle or Solomon's Temple because all people could come into the sanctuary, not just Israelite men without disabilities. The sanctuary did not have a curtain, the Ark of the Covenant, an atonement cover, or an incense altar. Instead, the Temple would be the Messiah's throne. His holy presence and glory would return and be available for all to experience.

41:5-26 Around the Temple building were ninety side rooms on three levels. To the rear was a large building of unspecified purpose that might have protected the back of the Temple from unauthorized access. No one was permitted to approach God's presence from behind. The side rooms might have been designed to store priestly clothing and equipment.

side rooms were built in three levels, one above the other, with thirty rooms on each level. The supports for these side rooms rested on exterior ledges on the Temple wall; they did not extend into the wall. ⁷Each level was wider than the one below it, corresponding to the narrowing of the Temple wall as it rose higher. A stairway led up from the bottom level through the middle level to the top level.

⁸I saw that the Temple was built on a terrace, which provided a foundation for the side rooms. This terrace was 10½ feet* high. ⁹The outer wall of the Temple's side rooms was 8¾ feet thick. This left an open area between these side rooms ¹⁰and the row of rooms along the outer wall of the inner courtyard. This open area was 35 feet wide, and it went all the way around the Temple. ¹¹Two doors opened from the side rooms into the terrace yard, which was 8¾ feet wide. One door faced north and the other south.

¹²A large building stood on the west, facing the Temple courtyard. It was 122½ feet wide and 157½ feet long, and its walls were 8¾ feet* thick. ¹³Then the man measured the Temple, and it was 175 feet* long. The courtyard around the building, including its walls, was an additional 175 feet in length. ¹⁴The inner courtyard to the east of the Temple was also 175 feet wide. ¹⁵The building to the west, including its two walls, was also 175 feet wide.

The sanctuary, the inner room, and the entry room of the Temple ¹⁶were all paneled with wood, as were the frames of the recessed windows. The inner walls of the Temple were paneled with wood above and below the windows. ¹⁷The space above the door leading into the inner room, and its walls inside and out, were also paneled. ¹⁸All the walls were decorated with carvings of cherubim, each with two faces, and there was a carving of a palm tree between each of the cherubim. ¹⁹One face—that of a man—looked toward the palm tree on one side. The other face—that of a young lion—looked toward the palm tree on the other side. The figures were carved all along the inside of the Temple, ²⁰from the floor to the top of the walls, including the outer wall of the sanctuary.

²¹There were square columns at the entrance to the sanctuary, and the ones at the entrance of the Most Holy Place were similar. ²²There was an altar made of wood, 5¼ feet high and 3½ feet across.* Its corners, base, and sides were all made of wood. "This," the man told me, "is the table that stands in the Lord's presence."

²³Both the sanctuary and the Most Holy Place had double doorways, ²⁴each with two swinging doors. ²⁵The doors leading into the sanctuary were decorated with carved cherubim and palm trees, just as on the walls. And there was a wooden roof at the front of the entry room to the Temple. ²⁶On both sides of the entry room were recessed windows decorated with carved palm trees. The side rooms along the outside wall also had roofs.

Rooms for the Priests

42 Then the man led me out of the Temple courtyard by way of the north gateway. We entered the outer courtyard and came to a group of rooms against the north wall of the inner courtyard. ²This structure, whose entrance opened toward the north, was 175 feet* long and 87½ feet* wide. ³One block of rooms overlooked the 35-foot* width of the inner courtyard. Another block of rooms looked out onto the pavement of the outer courtyard. The two blocks were built three levels high and stood across from each other. ⁴Between the two blocks of rooms ran a walkway 17½ feet* wide. It extended the entire 175 feet of the complex,* and all the doors faced north. ⁵Each of the two upper levels of rooms was narrower than the one beneath it because the upper levels had to allow space for walkways in front of them. ⁶Since there were three levels and they did not have supporting columns as in the courtyards, each of the upper levels was set back from the level beneath it. ⁷There was an outer wall that separated the rooms from the outer courtyard; it was 87½ feet long. ⁸This wall added length to the outer block of rooms, which extended for only 87½ feet, while the inner block—the rooms toward the Temple—extended for 175 feet. ⁹There was an eastern entrance from the outer courtyard to these rooms.

¹⁰On the south* side of the Temple there were two blocks of rooms just south of the inner courtyard between the Temple and the outer courtyard. These rooms were arranged just like the rooms on the north. ¹¹There was a walkway between the two blocks of rooms just like the complex on the north side of the Temple. This complex of rooms was the same length and width as the other one, and it had the same entrances and doors. The dimensions of each were identical. ¹²So there was an entrance in the wall facing the

---

41:8 Hebrew *1 rod, 6 cubits* [3.2 meters]. **41:12** Hebrew *70 cubits* [37.1 meters] *wide and 90 cubits* [47.7 meters] *long, and its walls were 5 cubits* [2.7 meters] *thick.* **41:13** Hebrew *100 cubits* [53 meters]; also in 41:13b, 14, 15. **41:22** Hebrew *3 cubits* [1.6 meters] *high and 2 cubits* [1.1 meters] *across.* **42:2a** Hebrew *100 cubits* [53 meters]; also in 42:8. **42:2b** Hebrew *50 cubits* [26.5 meters]; also in 42:7, 8. **42:3** Hebrew *20[-cubit]* [10.6-meter]. **42:4a** Hebrew *10 cubits* [5.3 meters]. **42:4b** As in Greek and Syriac versions, which read *Its length was 100 cubits* [53 meters]; Hebrew reads *and a passage 1 cubit* [21 inches or 53 centimeters] *wide.* **42:10** As in Greek version; Hebrew reads *east.*

41:15-20 The Temple building was "all paneled with wood" and decorated with palm trees and cherubim. The cherubim were similar to those described in Ezekiel's earlier visions of judgment (see 1:5-12; 10:2-14). But where those cherubim had four faces, the carved two-dimensional models were depicted with only two faces—one of a lion, the highest of the wild animals, and one of a human, the pinnacle of the created order. Cherubim also adorned Solomon's Temple (1 Kings 6:23-33); they were traditional symbols of judgment that complemented the palm trees, traditional symbols of blessing.

doors of the inner block of rooms, and another on the east at the end of the interior walkway.

¹³Then the man told me, "These rooms that overlook the Temple from the north and south are holy. Here the priests who offer sacrifices to the LORD will eat the most holy offerings. And because these rooms are holy, they will be used to store the sacred offerings—the grain offerings, sin offerings, and guilt offerings. ¹⁴When the priests leave the sanctuary, they must not go directly to the outer courtyard. They must first take off the clothes they wore while ministering, because these clothes are holy. They must put on other clothes before entering the parts of the building complex open to the public."

¹⁵When the man had finished measuring the inside of the Temple area, he led me out through the east gateway to measure the entire perimeter. ¹⁶He measured the east side with his measuring rod, and it was 875 feet long.* ¹⁷Then he measured the north side, and it was also 875 feet. ¹⁸The south side was also 875 feet, ¹⁹and the west side was also 875 feet. ²⁰So the area was 875 feet on each side with a wall all around it to separate what was holy from what was common.

The LORD's Glory Returns

43 After this, the man brought me back around to the east gateway. ²Suddenly, the glory of the God of Israel appeared from the east. The sound of his coming was like the roar of rushing waters, and the whole landscape shone with his glory. ³This vision was just like the others I had seen, first by the Kebar River and then when he came* to destroy Jerusalem. I fell face down on the ground. ⁴And the glory of the LORD came into the Temple through the east gateway. ⁵Then the Spirit took me up and brought me into the inner courtyard, and the glory of the LORD filled the Temple. ⁶And I heard someone speaking to me from within the Temple, while the man who had been measuring stood beside me. ⁷The LORD said to me, "Son of man, this is the place of my throne and the place where I will rest my feet. I will live here forever among the people of Israel. They and their kings will not defile my holy name any longer by their adulterous worship of other gods or by honoring the relics of their kings who have died.* ⁸They put their idol altars right next to mine with only a wall between them and me. They defiled my holy name by such detestable sin, so I consumed them in my anger. ⁹Now let them stop worshiping other gods and honoring the relics of their kings, and I will live among them forever.

¹⁰"Son of man, describe to the people of Israel the Temple I have shown you, so they will be ashamed of all their sins. Let them study its plan, ¹¹and they will be ashamed* of what they have done. Describe to them all the specifications of the Temple—including its entrances and exits—and everything else about it. Tell them about its decrees and laws. Write down all these specifications and decrees as they watch so they will be sure to remember and follow them. ¹²And this is the basic law of the Temple: absolute holiness! The entire top of the mountain where the Temple is built is holy. Yes, this is the basic law of the Temple.

The Altar

¹³"These are the measurements of the altar*: There is a gutter all around the altar 21 inches deep and 21 inches wide,* with a curb 9 inches* wide around its edge. And this is the height* of the altar: ¹⁴From the gutter the altar rises 3½ feet* to a lower ledge that surrounds the altar and is 21 inches* wide. From the lower ledge the altar rises 7 feet* to the upper ledge that is also 21 inches wide. ¹⁵The top of the altar, the hearth, rises another 7 feet higher, with a horn rising up from each of the four corners. ¹⁶The top of the altar is square, measuring 21 feet by 21 feet.* ¹⁷The upper ledge also forms a square, measuring 24½ feet by 24½ feet,* with a 21-inch gutter and a 10½-inch curb* all around the edge. There are steps going up the east side of the altar."

¹⁸Then he said to me, "Son of man, this is what the Sovereign LORD says: These will be the regulations for the burning of offerings and the sprinkling of blood when the altar is built. ¹⁹At that time, the Levitical priests of the family of Zadok, who minister before me, are to be given a young bull for a sin offering,

---

42:16 As in 45:2 and in Greek version at 42:17, which reads *500 cubits* [265 meters]; Hebrew reads *500 rods* [5,250 feet or 1,590 meters]; similarly in 42:17, 18, 19, 20. **43:3** As in some Hebrew manuscripts and Latin Vulgate; Masoretic Text reads *I came.* **43:7** Or *kings on their high places.* **43:11** As in Greek version; Hebrew reads *if they are ashamed.* **43:13a** Hebrew *measurements of the altar in long cubits, each being a cubit* [18 inches or 45 centimeters] *and a handbreadth* [3 inches or 8 centimeters] *in length.* **43:13b** Hebrew *a cubit* [53 centimeters] *deep and a cubit wide.* **43:13c** Hebrew *1 span* [23 centimeters]. **43:13d** As in Greek version; Hebrew reads *base.* **43:14a** Hebrew *2 cubits* [1.1 meters]. **43:14b** Hebrew *1 cubit* [53 centimeters]; also in 43:14d. **43:14c** Hebrew *4 cubits* [2.1 meters]; also in 43:15. **43:16** Hebrew *12 [cubits]* [6.4 meters] *long and 12 [cubits] wide.* **43:17a** Hebrew *14 [cubits]* [7.4 meters] *long and 14 [cubits] wide.* **43:17b** Hebrew *a gutter of 1 cubit* [53 centimeters] *and a curb of ½ a cubit* [27 centimeters].

43:10-11 At this point, the prophet was given the rationale for the whole Temple vision. He was not the first person to receive the blueprint for a sanctuary from God (see Exodus 25:1–40:38). This vision was not intended to spark a building project some time in the future when God would return his people to their land but to convey a message to the people of Ezekiel's generation. As they would study its plan, Ezekiel's hearers would be convicted of their sins and "be ashamed of what they have done." The conviction of sin would come upon them as they studied its entrances and exits, its decrees and laws, and the overall plan.

43:13-27; 45:13–46:24 The new Temple would observe the burnt, guilt, sin, peace, grain, and liquid offerings introduced with the Tabernacle. The sacrifices would continue to express love and devotion to God (Isaiah 56:5-7; 60:7). Also, they would bring the people together for fellowship and partaking in God's glory.

says the Sovereign LORD. ²⁰You will take some of its blood and smear it on the four horns of the altar, the four corners of the upper ledge, and the curb that runs around that ledge. This will cleanse and make atonement for the altar. ²¹Then take the young bull for the sin offering and burn it at the appointed place outside the Temple area.

²²"On the second day, sacrifice as a sin offering a young male goat that has no physical defects. Then cleanse and make atonement for the altar again, just as you did with the young bull. ²³When you have finished the cleansing ceremony, offer another young bull that has no defects and a perfect ram from the flock. ²⁴You are to present them to the LORD, and the priests are to sprinkle salt on them and offer them as a burnt offering to the LORD.

²⁵"Every day for seven days a male goat, a young bull, and a ram from the flock will be sacrificed as a sin offering. None of these animals may have physical defects of any kind. ²⁶Do this each day for seven days to cleanse and make atonement for the altar, thus setting it apart for holy use. ²⁷On the eighth day, and on each day afterward, the priests will sacrifice on the altar the burnt offerings and peace offerings of the people. Then I will accept you. I, the Sovereign LORD, have spoken!"

The Prince, Levites, and Priests

44 Then the man brought me back to the east gateway in the outer wall of the Temple area, but it was closed. ²And the LORD said to me, "This gate must remain closed; it will never again be opened. No one will ever open it and pass through, for the LORD, the God of Israel, has entered here. Therefore, it must always remain shut. ³Only the prince himself may sit inside this gateway to feast in the LORD's presence. But he may come and go only through the entry room of the gateway."

⁴Then the man brought me through the north gateway to the front of the Temple. I looked and saw that the glory of the LORD filled the Temple of the LORD, and I fell face down on the ground.

⁵And the LORD said to me, "Son of man, take careful notice. Use your eyes and ears, and listen to everything I tell you about the regulations concerning the LORD's Temple. Take careful note of the procedures for using the Temple's entrances and exits. ⁶And give these rebels, the people of Israel, this message from the Sovereign LORD: O people of Israel, enough of your detestable sins! ⁷You have brought uncircumcised foreigners into my sanctuary—people who have no heart for God. In this way, you defiled my Temple even as you offered me my food, the fat and blood of sacrifices. In addition to all your other detestable sins, you have broken my covenant. ⁸Instead of safeguarding my sacred rituals, you have hired foreigners to take charge of my sanctuary.

⁹"So this is what the Sovereign LORD says: No foreigners, including those who live among the people of Israel, will enter my sanctuary if they have not been circumcised and have not surrendered themselves to the LORD. ¹⁰And the men of the tribe of Levi who abandoned me when Israel strayed away from me to worship idols* must bear the consequences of their unfaithfulness. ¹¹They may still be Temple guards and gatekeepers, and they may slaughter the animals brought for burnt offerings and be present to help the people. ¹²But they encouraged my people to worship idols, causing Israel to fall into deep sin. So I have taken a solemn oath that they must bear the consequences for their sins, says the Sovereign LORD. ¹³They may not approach me to minister as priests. They may not touch any of my holy things or the holy offerings, for they must bear the shame of all the detestable sins they have committed. ¹⁴They are to serve as the Temple caretakers, taking charge of the maintenance work and performing general duties.

¹⁵"However, the Levitical priests of the family of Zadok continued to minister faithfully in the Temple when Israel abandoned me for idols. These men will serve as my ministers. They will stand in my presence and offer the fat and blood of the sacrifices, says the Sovereign LORD. ¹⁶They alone will enter my sanctuary and approach my table to serve me. They will fulfill all my requirements.

¹⁷"When they enter the gateway to the inner courtyard, they must wear only linen clothing. They must wear no wool while on duty in the inner courtyard or in the Temple itself. ¹⁸They must wear linen turbans and linen undergarments. They must not wear anything that would cause them to perspire. ¹⁹When they return to the outer courtyard where the people are, they must take off the clothes they wear while ministering to me. They must leave them in the sacred

---

44:10 The Hebrew term (literally *round things*) probably alludes to dung; also in 44:12.

44:12-14 The Levites had "encouraged . . . Israel to fall into deep sin" by abandoning the Lord and worshiping idols. One of the consequences of that sin was that they would no longer be allowed to enter the inner court of the Temple like the priests. However, by God's grace, they would still have a significant ministry in serving the people and slaughtering their sacrifices. The people as a whole would be placed at a greater distance from God because of their idolatry. Prior to the Exile they had slaughtered their own sacrifices (see Leviticus 1:5, 11); now they would have to hand them over to be slaughtered on their behalf.

44:15-16 In contrast to the Levites and the people who had abandoned the Lord for idols, the Levitical priests of the family of Zadok had remained faithful to the Lord. Zadok was the high priest of Solomon's day. His family's reward would be renewed access to the inner courtyard, where they would perform the crucial sacrificial rituals nearer to the presence of God. A repeated theme in these chapters is that those who had been faithful in the past would be rewarded with closer access to God and greater privilege in his presence, while those who had been unfaithful would be kept at a greater distance.

rooms and put on other clothes so they do not endanger anyone by transmitting holiness to them through this clothing.

[20]"They must neither shave their heads nor let their hair grow too long. Instead, they must trim it regularly. [21]The priests must not drink wine before entering the inner courtyard. [22]They may choose their wives only from among the virgins of Israel or the widows of the priests. They may not marry other widows or divorced women. [23]They will teach my people the difference between what is holy and what is common, what is ceremonially clean and unclean.

[24]"They will serve as judges to resolve any disagreements among my people. Their decisions must be based on my regulations. And the priests themselves must obey my instructions and decrees at all the sacred festivals, and see to it that the Sabbaths are set apart as holy days.

[25]"A priest must not defile himself by being in the presence of a dead person unless it is his father, mother, child, brother, or unmarried sister. In such cases it is permitted. [26]Even then, he can return to his Temple duties only after being ceremonially cleansed and then waiting for seven days. [27]The first day he returns to work and enters the inner courtyard and the sanctuary, he must offer a sin offering for himself, says the Sovereign LORD.

[28]"The priests will not have any property or possession of land, for I alone am their special possession. [29]Their food will come from the gifts and sacrifices brought to the Temple by the people—the grain offerings, the sin offerings, and the guilt offerings. Whatever anyone sets apart* for the LORD will belong to the priests. [30]The first of the ripe fruits and all the gifts brought to the LORD will go to the priests. The first batch of dough must also be given to the priests so the LORD will bless your homes. [31]The priests may not eat meat from any bird or animal that dies a natural death or that dies after being attacked by another animal.

Division of the Land

45 "When you divide the land among the tribes of Israel, you must set aside a section for the LORD as his holy portion. This piece of land will be 8¹⁄₃ miles long and 6²⁄₃ miles wide.* The entire area will be holy. [2]A section of this land, measuring 875 feet by 875 feet,* will be set aside for the Temple. An additional strip of land 87½ feet* wide is to be left empty all around it. [3]Within the larger sacred area, measure out a portion of land 8¹⁄₃ miles long and 3¹⁄₃ miles wide.* Within it the sanctuary of the Most Holy Place will be located. [4]This area will be holy, set aside for the priests who minister to the LORD in the sanctuary. They will use it for their homes, and my Temple will be located within it. [5]The strip of sacred land next to it, also 8¹⁄₃ miles long and 3¹⁄₃ miles wide, will be a living area for the Levites who work at the Temple. It will be their possession and a place for their towns.*

[6]"Adjacent to the larger sacred area will be a section of land 8¹⁄₃ miles long and 1²⁄₃ miles wide.* This will be set aside for a city where anyone in Israel can live.

[7]"Two special sections of land will be set apart for the prince. One section will share a border with the east side of the sacred lands and city, and the second section will share a border on the west side. Then the far eastern and western borders of the prince's lands will line up with the eastern and western boundaries of the tribal areas. [8]These sections of land will be the prince's allotment. Then my princes will no longer oppress and rob my people; they will assign the rest of the land to the people, giving an allotment to each tribe.

44:29 The Hebrew term used here refers to the complete consecration of things or people to the LORD, either by destroying them or by giving them as an offering. **45:1** As in Greek version, which reads *25,000 [cubits]* [13.3 kilometers] *long and 20,000 [cubits]* [10.6 kilometers] *wide;* Hebrew reads *25,000 [cubits] long and 10,000 [cubits]* [3¹⁄₃ miles or 5.3 kilometers] *wide.* Compare 45:3, 5; 48:9. **45:2a** Hebrew *500 [cubits]* [265 meters] *by 500 [cubits], a square.* **45:2b** Hebrew *50 cubits* [26.5 meters]. **45:3** Hebrew *25,000 [cubits]* [13.3 kilometers] *long and 10,000 [cubits]* [5.3 kilometers] *wide;* also in 45:5. **45:5** As in Greek version; Hebrew reads *They will have as their possession 20 rooms.* **45:6** Hebrew *25,000 [cubits]* [13.3 kilometers] *long and 5,000 [cubits]* [2.65 kilometers] *wide.*

44:20-27 The priests were to avoid contact with death, either from "being in the presence of a dead person" or from the ritual mourning practices in which they would shave their heads or let their hair grow completely free. They were not to drink wine before entering the inner courtyard to avoid the risk of potentially fatal alcohol-induced errors (see Leviticus 10:9). Since only the descendants of Zadok would serve as priests, there were additional marriage restrictions to ensure the continuing purity of the priestly line. In all of these ways, the priests would model for the people the radical distinction between holy and common and between the ceremonially clean and unclean.

44:28-30 Because the priests would belong to the Lord and would be provided for through a share of the sacrificial offerings of the Temple, they would "not have any property or possession of land." The Lord would be their inheritance, and their temporal needs would be supplied by the firstfruits of the people's harvests and the various offerings made at the Temple.

45:1–48:35 Ezekiel's vision reveals how God would divide the land in the future. The center portion would belong to God. The prince would receive a portion of land on the left and right sides of God's. Israel's twelve tribes would equally divide the rest of the land.

45:1-6; 48:8-9 God's portion of the land would be a fifty-five-square-mile area in and around the current city of Jerusalem and would include the new Temple. Although the priests would not be allowed to own land, they and other workers would live on the land to maintain the Temple's holiness and protect the grounds.

45:7–46:18; 48:21-22 The prince would be married with children. As the Temple's administrator, he would report to the Messiah and carry out the religious activities. God would give the prince the land on both sides of his holy area described in 45:1-6. The prince's sons would inherit the land.

Rules for the Princes

⁹"For this is what the Sovereign LORD says: Enough, you princes of Israel! Stop your violence and oppression and do what is just and right. Quit robbing and cheating my people out of their land. Stop expelling them from their homes, says the Sovereign LORD. ¹⁰Use only honest weights and scales and honest measures, both dry and liquid.* ¹¹The homer* will be your standard unit for measuring volume. The ephah and the bath* will each measure one-tenth of a homer. ¹²The standard unit for weight will be the silver shekel.* One shekel will consist of twenty gerahs, and sixty shekels will be equal to one mina.*

Special Offerings and Celebrations

¹³"You must give this tax to the prince: one bushel of wheat or barley for every 60* you harvest, ¹⁴one percent of your olive oil,* ¹⁵and one sheep or goat for every 200 in your flocks in Israel. These will be the grain offerings, burnt offerings, and peace offerings that will make atonement for the people who bring them, says the Sovereign LORD. ¹⁶All the people of Israel must join in bringing these offerings to the prince. ¹⁷The prince will be required to provide offerings that are given at the religious festivals, the new moon celebrations, the Sabbath days, and all other similar occasions. He will provide the sin offerings, burnt offerings, grain offerings, liquid offerings, and peace offerings to purify the people of Israel, making them right with the LORD.*

¹⁸"This is what the Sovereign LORD says: In early spring, on the first day of each new year,* sacrifice a young bull with no defects to purify the Temple. ¹⁹The priest will take blood from this sin offering and put it on the doorposts of the Temple, the four corners of the upper ledge of the altar, and the gateposts at the entrance to the inner courtyard. ²⁰Do this also on the seventh day of the new year for anyone who has sinned through error or ignorance. In this way, you will purify* the Temple.

²¹"On the fourteenth day of the first month,* you must celebrate the Passover. This festival will last for seven days. The bread you eat during that time must be made without yeast. ²²On the day of Passover the prince will provide a young bull as a sin offering for himself and the people of Israel. ²³On each of the seven days of the feast he will prepare a burnt offering to the LORD, consisting of seven young bulls and seven rams without defects. A male goat will also be given each day for a sin offering. ²⁴The prince will provide a basket of flour as a grain offering and a gallon of olive oil* with each young bull and ram.

²⁵"During the seven days of the Festival of Shelters, which occurs every year in early autumn,* the prince will provide these same sacrifices for the sin offering, the burnt offering, and the grain offering, along with the required olive oil.

46

"This is what the Sovereign LORD says: The east gateway of the inner courtyard will be closed during the six workdays each week, but it will be open on Sabbath days and the days of new moon celebrations. ²The prince will enter the entry room of the gateway from the outside. Then he will stand by the gatepost while the priest offers his burnt offering and peace offering. He will bow down in worship inside the gateway passage and then go back out the way he came. The gateway will not be closed until evening. ³The common people will bow down and worship the LORD in front of this gateway on Sabbath days and the days of new moon celebrations.

⁴"Each Sabbath day the prince will present to the LORD a burnt offering of six lambs and one ram, all with no defects. ⁵He will present a grain offering of a basket of choice flour to go with the ram and whatever amount of flour he chooses to go with each lamb, and he is to offer one gallon of olive oil* for each basket of flour. ⁶At the new moon celebrations, he will bring one young bull, six lambs, and one ram, all with no defects. ⁷With the young bull he must bring a basket of choice flour for a grain offering. With the ram he must bring another basket of flour. And with each lamb he is to bring whatever amount of flour he chooses to give. With each basket of flour he must offer one gallon of olive oil.

⁸"The prince must enter the gateway through the

45:10 Hebrew *Use honest scales, an honest ephah, and an honest bath.*   45:11a The *homer* measures about 50 gallons or 220 liters.   45:11b The *ephah* is a dry measure; the *bath* is a liquid measure.   45:12a The *shekel* weighs about 0.4 ounces or 11 grams.   45:12b Elsewhere the *mina* is equated to 50 shekels.   45:13 Hebrew ⅙ *of an ephah from each homer of wheat and* ⅙ *of an ephah from each homer of barley.*   45:14 Hebrew *the portion of oil, measured by the bath, is* ¹⁄₁₀ *of a bath from each cor, which consists of 10 baths or 1 homer, for 10 baths are equivalent to a homer.*   45:17 Or *to make atonement for the people of Israel.*   45:18 Hebrew *On the first day of the first month,* of the Hebrew calendar. This day in the ancient Hebrew lunar calendar occurred in March or April.   45:20 Or *will make atonement for.*   45:21 This day in the ancient Hebrew lunar calendar occurred in late March, April, or early May.   45:24 Hebrew *an ephah* [20 quarts or 22 liters] *of flour . . . and a hin* [3.8 liters] *of olive oil.*   45:25 Hebrew *the festival which begins on the fifteenth day of the seventh month* (see Lev 23:34). This day in the ancient Hebrew lunar calendar occurred in late September, October, or early November.   46:5 Hebrew *an ephah* [20 quarts or 22 liters] *of choice flour . . . a hin* [3.8 liters] *of olive oil;* similarly in 46:7, 11.

45:21-25 The annual festivals in the new Temple would have a similar purifying purpose. Instead of the three distinctive festivals of the Mosaic order (the Festivals of Passover, Harvest, and Shelters), there would now be only two virtually identical festivals, Passover and Shelters, spaced six months apart. The Passover feast would still take place on the fourteenth day of the first month and would resemble the earlier festival in many ways, though the number of sacrificial offerings would be significantly higher than those prescribed in Numbers 28. The Festival of Shelters, however, is not even explicitly named in the Hebrew text and has lost anything distinctive about its celebration except for the provision that the prince would provide the same sacrifices as for the Passover. It would still occur in the seventh month. The land's constant purification from sin emerges as a central theme.

entry room, and he must leave the same way. ⁹But when the people come in through the north gateway to worship the LORD during the religious festivals, they must leave by the south gateway. And those who entered through the south gateway must leave by the north gateway. They must never leave by the same gateway they came in, but must always use the opposite gateway. ¹⁰The prince will enter and leave with the people on these occasions.

¹¹"So at the special feasts and sacred festivals, the grain offering will be a basket of choice flour with each young bull, another basket of flour with each ram, and as much flour as the worshiper chooses to give with each lamb. Give one gallon of olive oil with each basket of flour. ¹²When the prince offers a voluntary burnt offering or peace offering to the LORD, the east gateway to the inner courtyard will be opened for him, and he will offer his sacrifices as he does on Sabbath days. Then he will leave, and the gateway will be shut behind him.

¹³"Each morning you must sacrifice a one-year-old lamb with no defects as a burnt offering to the LORD. ¹⁴With the lamb, a grain offering must also be given to the LORD—about three quarts of flour with a third of a gallon of olive oil* to moisten the choice flour. This will be a permanent law for you. ¹⁵The lamb, the grain offering, and the olive oil must be given as a daily sacrifice every morning without fail.

¹⁶"This is what the Sovereign LORD says: If the prince gives a gift of land to one of his sons as his inheritance, it will belong to him and his descendants forever. ¹⁷But if the prince gives a gift of land from his inheritance to one of his servants, the servant may keep it only until the Year of Jubilee, which comes every fiftieth year.* At that time the land will return to the prince. But when the prince gives gifts to his sons, those gifts will be permanent. ¹⁸And the prince may never take anyone's property by force. If he gives property to his sons, it must be from his own land, for I do not want any of my people unjustly evicted from their property."

The Temple Kitchens

¹⁹In my vision, the man brought me through the entrance beside the gateway and led me to the sacred rooms assigned to the priests, which faced toward the north. He showed me a place at the extreme west end of these rooms. ²⁰He explained, "This is where the priests will cook the meat from the guilt offerings and sin offerings and bake the flour from the grain offerings into bread. They will do it here to avoid carrying the sacrifices through the outer courtyard and endangering the people by transmitting holiness to them."

²¹Then he brought me back to the outer courtyard and led me to each of its four corners. In each corner I saw an enclosure. ²²Each of these enclosures was 70 feet long and 52½ feet wide,* surrounded by walls. ²³Along the inside of these walls was a ledge of stone with fireplaces under the ledge all the way around. ²⁴The man said to me, "These are the kitchens to be used by the Temple assistants to boil the sacrifices offered by the people."

The River of Healing

47 In my vision, the man brought me back to the entrance of the Temple. There I saw a stream flowing east from beneath the door of the Temple and passing to the right of the altar on its south side. ²The man brought me outside the wall through the north gateway and led me around to the eastern entrance. There I could see the water flowing out through the south side of the east gateway.

³Measuring as he went, he took me along the stream for 1,750 feet* and then led me across. The water was up to my ankles. ⁴He measured off another 1,750 feet and led me across again. This time the water was up to my knees. After another 1,750 feet, it was up to my waist. ⁵Then he measured another 1,750 feet, and the river was too deep to walk across. It was deep enough to swim in, but too deep to walk through.

⁶He asked me, "Have you been watching, son of man?" Then he led me back along the riverbank. ⁷When I returned, I was surprised by the sight of many trees growing on both sides of the river. ⁸Then he said to me, "This river flows east through the desert into the valley of the Dead Sea.* The waters of this stream will make the salty waters of the Dead Sea fresh and pure. ⁹There will be swarms of living things wherever the water of this river flows.* Fish will abound in the Dead Sea, for its waters will become fresh. Life will flourish wherever this water flows. ¹⁰Fishermen will stand along the shores of the Dead Sea. All the way from En-gedi to En-eglaim, the shores will be covered with nets drying in the sun. Fish of every kind will fill the Dead Sea, just as they fill the Mediterranean.* ¹¹But the marshes

---

46:14 Hebrew ⅙ of an ephah [3.7 liters] of flour with ⅓ of a hin [1.3 liters] of olive oil. **46:17** Hebrew until the Year of Release; see Lev 25:8-17. **46:22** Hebrew 40 [cubits] [21.2 meters] long and 30 [cubits] [15.9 meters] wide. **47:3** Hebrew 1,000 cubits [530 meters]; also in 47:4, 5. **47:8** Hebrew the sea. **47:9** As in Greek and Syriac versions; Hebrew reads of these two rivers flow. **47:10** Hebrew the Great Sea; also in 47:15, 17, 19, 20.

46:16-18 Because the land assigned to the prince was the Lord's gift to him and to his family, he could not give it permanently to one of his servants. Each Year of Jubilee, the fiftieth year when all land in Israel reverted to its original family owners, this land would revert to the crown. This provision was intended to remove the temptation for the prince to acquire more and more land with which to reward his faithful servants, resulting in less land for the ordinary people. The land belonged to the Lord, and he divided it among his people. No one, not even the prince, was permitted to tamper with the people's inheritance.

47:1-12 Once the Temple is restored to its central place among God's people, its beneficial influence, pictured here as a river, would spread outward, transforming death to life.

and swamps will not be purified; they will still be salty. ¹²Fruit trees of all kinds will grow along both sides of the river. The leaves of these trees will never turn brown and fall, and there will always be fruit on their branches. There will be a new crop every month, for they are watered by the river flowing from the Temple. The fruit will be for food and the leaves for healing."

Boundaries for the Land

¹³This is what the Sovereign LORD says: "Divide the land in this way for the twelve tribes of Israel: The descendants of Joseph will be given two shares of land.* ¹⁴Otherwise each tribe will receive an equal share. I took a solemn oath and swore that I would give this land to your ancestors, and it will now come to you as your possession.

¹⁵"These are the boundaries of the land: The northern border will run from the Mediterranean toward Hethlon, then on through Lebo-hamath to Zedad; ¹⁶then it will run to Berothah and Sibraim,* which are on the border between Damascus and Hamath, and finally to Hazer-hatticon, on the border of Hauran. ¹⁷So the northern border will run from the Mediterranean to Hazar-enan, on the border between Hamath to the north and Damascus to the south.

¹⁸"The eastern border starts at a point between Hauran and Damascus and runs south along the Jordan River between Israel and Gilead, past the Dead Sea* and as far south as Tamar.* This will be the eastern border.

¹⁹"The southern border will go west from Tamar to the waters of Meribah at Kadesh* and then follow the course of the Brook of Egypt to the Mediterranean. This will be the southern border.

²⁰"On the west side, the Mediterranean itself will be your border from the southern border to the point where the northern border begins, opposite Lebo-hamath.

²¹"Divide the land within these boundaries among the tribes of Israel. ²²Distribute the land as an allotment for yourselves and for the foreigners who have joined you and are raising their families among you. They will be like native-born Israelites to you and will receive an allotment among the tribes. ²³These foreigners are to be given land within the territory of the tribe with whom they now live. I, the Sovereign LORD, have spoken!

Division of the Land

48 "Here is the list of the tribes of Israel and the territory each is to receive. The territory of Dan is in the extreme north. Its boundary line follows the Hethlon road to Lebo-hamath and then runs on to Hazar-enan on the border of Damascus, with Hamath to the north. Dan's territory extends all the way across the land of Israel from east to west.

²"Asher's territory lies south of Dan's and also extends from east to west. ³Naphtali's land lies south of Asher's, also extending from east to west. ⁴Then comes Manasseh south of Naphtali, and its territory also extends from east to west. ⁵South of Manasseh is Ephraim, ⁶and then Reuben, ⁷and then Judah, all of whose boundaries extend from east to west.

⁸"South of Judah is the land set aside for a special purpose. It will be 8⅓ miles* wide and will extend as far east and west as the tribal territories, with the Temple at the center.

47:13 It was important to retain twelve portions of land. Since Levi had no portion, the descendants of Joseph's sons, Ephraim and Manasseh, received land as two tribes.   47:15-16 As in Greek version; Masoretic Text reads *then on through Lebo to Zedad; ¹⁶then it will run to Hamath, Berothah, and Sibraim.*   47:18a Hebrew *the eastern sea.*   47:18b As in Greek version; Hebrew reads *you will measure.*   47:19 Hebrew *waters of Meribath-kadesh.*   48:8 Hebrew *25,000 [cubits]* [13.3 kilometers].

47:15-20 The boundaries of the new Promised Land would be approximately those assigned in Numbers 34:1-12, from Lebo-hamath in the north to the Brook of Egypt in the south, and from the Mediterranean in the west to the Jordan River in the east. This promised land would be possessed by the people, something they had never before done. Absent from this land was Transjordan, the area east of the Jordan River, which was the historic home of Reuben, Gad, and half the tribe of Manasseh. It lay outside the boundaries promised to Moses and was therefore not part of the original promise, although historically many Israelites had lived there.

47:21-23 "The land within these boundaries" was to be divided "among the tribes of Israel." Instead of the divided preexilic kingdoms, the future would see a single kingdom formed from the diverse unity of the twelve tribes and incorporating even resident foreigners and their families, provided that they had joined Israel as converts. These people would receive an allotment, just like the native-born Israelites, and they could pass this inheritance on to their children. In view of the significance of the land to Ezekiel, this would be a high privilege.

48:1-8 The land assigned to the tribes would be arranged in strips running east to west through the land, rather than piecemeal as it was before the Exile. This would be more than simply a way of ensuring that each tribe received equal access to the various resources of the land. It would align the land with the sacred east–west axis that was so prominent in the Temple. As in the Temple, the size and shape of the central areas would be clearly defined, while those on the margins would be less closely determined. The four tribes most distant from the central sacred section (Dan, Asher, Naphtali, and Gad), and therefore in the least privileged position, were descended from the four sons of Jacob by Zilpah and Bilhah, the servants of his wives Leah and Rachel. The eight sons from Leah and Rachel would receive the strips immediately north and south of the holy portion that contained the Temple. Immediately next to the holy portion would be the tribes of Benjamin and Judah, which historically surrounded Jerusalem. Judah would receive the strip immediately to the north of the holy portion, as if to stress that whereas in the past the land had been divided into north and south—Israel and Judah—now Judah would be in the north.

⁹"The area set aside for the LORD's Temple will be 8⅓ miles long and 6⅔ miles wide.* ¹⁰For the priests there will be a strip of land measuring 8⅓ miles long by 3⅓ miles wide,* with the LORD's Temple at the center. ¹¹This area is set aside for the ordained priests, the descendants of Zadok who served me faithfully and did not go astray with the people of Israel and the rest of the Levites. ¹²It will be their special portion when the land is distributed, the most sacred land of all. Next to the priests' territory will lie the land where the other Levites will live.

¹³"The land allotted to the Levites will be the same size and shape as that belonging to the priests—8⅓ miles long and 3⅓ miles wide. Together these portions of land will measure 8⅓ miles long by 6⅔ miles wide.* ¹⁴None of this special land may ever be sold or traded or used by others, for it belongs to the LORD; it is set apart as holy.

¹⁵"An additional strip of land 8⅓ miles long by 1⅔ miles wide,* south of the sacred Temple area, will be allotted for public use—homes, pasturelands, and common lands, with a city at the center. ¹⁶The city will measure 1½ miles* on each side—north, south, east, and west. ¹⁷Open lands will surround the city for 150 yards* in every direction. ¹⁸Outside the city there will be a farming area that stretches 3⅓ miles to the east and 3⅓ miles to the west* along the border of the sacred area. This farmland will produce food for the people working in the city. ¹⁹Those who come from the various tribes to work in the city may farm it. ²⁰This entire area—including the sacred lands and the city—is a square that measures 8⅓ miles* on each side.

²¹"The areas that remain, to the east and to the west of the sacred lands and the city, will belong to the prince. Each of these areas will be 8⅓ miles wide, extending in opposite directions to the eastern and western borders of Israel, with the sacred lands and the sanctuary of the Temple in the center. ²²So the prince's land will include everything between the territories allotted to Judah and Benjamin, except for the areas set aside for the sacred lands and the city.

²³"These are the territories allotted to the rest of the tribes. Benjamin's territory lies just south of the prince's lands, and it extends across the entire land of Israel from east to west. ²⁴South of Benjamin's territory lies that of Simeon, also extending across the land from east to west. ²⁵Next is the territory of Issachar with the same eastern and western boundaries.

²⁶"Then comes the territory of Zebulun, which also extends across the land from east to west. ²⁷The territory of Gad is just south of Zebulun with the same borders to the east and west. ²⁸The southern border of Gad runs from Tamar to the waters of Meribah at Kadesh* and then follows the Brook of Egypt to the Mediterranean.*

²⁹"These are the allotments that will be set aside for each tribe's exclusive possession. I, the Sovereign LORD, have spoken!

The Gates of the City

³⁰"These will be the exits to the city: On the north wall, which is 1½ miles long, ³¹there will be three gates, each one named after a tribe of Israel. The first will be named for Reuben, the second for Judah, and the third for Levi. ³²On the east wall, also 1½ miles long, the gates will be named for Joseph, Benjamin, and Dan. ³³The south wall, also 1½ miles long, will have gates named for Simeon, Issachar, and Zebulun. ³⁴And on the west wall, also 1½ miles long, the gates will be named for Gad, Asher, and Naphtali.

³⁵"The distance around the entire city will be 6 miles.* And from that day the name of the city will be 'The LORD Is There.'*"

48:9 As in one Greek manuscript and the Greek reading in 45:1; *25,000 [cubits]* [13.3 kilometers] *long and 20,000 [cubits]* [10.6 kilometers] *wide;* Hebrew reads *25,000 [cubits] long and 10,000 [cubits]* [3⅓ miles or 5.3 kilometers] *wide.* Similarly in 48:13b. Compare 45:1-5; 48:10-13. **48:10** Hebrew *25,000 [cubits]* [13.3 kilometers] *long by 10,000 [cubits]* [5.3 kilometers] *wide;* also in 48:13a. **48:13** See note on 48:9. **48:15** Hebrew *25,000 [cubits]* [13.3 kilometers] *long by 5,000 [cubits]* [2.65 kilometers] *wide.* **48:16** Hebrew *4,500 [cubits]* [2.4 kilometers]; also in 48:30, 32, 33, 34. **48:17** Hebrew *250 [cubits]* [133 meters]. **48:18** Hebrew *10,000 [cubits]* [5.3 kilometers] *to the east and 10,000 [cubits] to the west.* **48:20** Hebrew *25,000 [cubits]* [13.3 kilometers]; also in 48:21. **48:28a** Hebrew *waters of Meribath-kadesh.* **48:28b** Hebrew *the Great Sea.* **48:35a** Hebrew *18,000 [cubits]* [9.6 kilometers]. **48:35b** Hebrew *Yahweh Shammah.*

48:30-31 At the end of the book, Ezekiel focuses attention on the "exits to the city," highlighting once again the theme of access that runs throughout 40:1–48:35. Like the Temple, the city would be a measured square with twelve gates, one for each of the tribes, which would establish a focus of tribal unity. Unusually, the three most important gates, named for Reuben (the oldest of the sons of Israel), Judah (the royal tribe), and Levi (the priestly tribe), would face north rather than east. This is because the most important direction was northward toward the Temple, the center of the renewed land. South was the second most important side because it would be on the axis that pointed toward the Temple.

48:35 To cap off the whole vision, the city was given a new name, "The LORD Is There" (Hebrew *Yahweh Shammah*). Although the Lord had once departed from Jerusalem and ordered its destruction because of the people's gross idolatry and bloodshed, the new city would be so much a part of the new order of things that it could receive that name. This also implies that the bloody city condemned in earlier chapters had now been replaced by a holy city, fit for God to dwell in among representatives of all twelve of Israel's tribes (compare Isaiah 4:2-6; Zechariah 14:20-21). Thus the prophecy of Ezekiel 37:26-27 would finally reach its conclusion and fulfillment, as God would establish his sanctuary among his people forever, just as he had promised.

Daniel

WHAT DO WE LEARN ABOUT GOD'S MISSION AND OURS? Even when we face pressure, God honors faithfulness and does more than we can imagine.

WHO WROTE IT? Daniel, though the narrative sections of the book are written in the third person.

WHEN DID IT HAPPEN? The action in Daniel took place between 605 and 536 BC, during the Exile. Daniel also received visions about future events.

HOW IS IT ORGANIZED?

1: Daniel and his friends are captured, tested, and promoted

2: Nebuchadnezzar's statue dream and Daniel's interpretation

3: Nebuchadnezzar demands statue worship; Daniel's friends refuse and are thrown in the blazing furnace

4: Nebuchadnezzar loses his sanity

5: Belshazzar's banquet and the writing on the wall

6: Daniel survives the den of lions

7–12: Amazing dreams and visions of the future

FEATURE HIGHLIGHTS

+ Fit to Flourish (1035)
+ Is God Color-Blind? (1046)

Words to Remember are highlighted throughout this book

HOW LONG DOES IT TAKE TO READ?

1:00						
:30	1:00	1:30	2:00	2:30	3:00	3:30

Timeline (BC)

BC	Event
612	HABAKKUK BECOMES A PROPHET TO JUDAH
609	JEHOIAKIM, SON OF ZEBIDAH AND JOSIAH, BECOMES KING OF JUDAH
605	DANIEL TAKEN CAPTIVE TO BABYLON
c. 600	DANIEL BECOMES A BABYLONIAN OFFICIAL; BLAZING FURNACE
597	NEBUCHADNEZZAR TAKES MORE CAPTIVES
593	EZEKIEL BECOMES A PROPHET TO THE EXILES
586	JUDAH FALLS; JERUSALEM IS DESTROYED
562	NEBUCHADNEZZAR DIES
553	DANIEL'S FIRST VISION
539	BABYLON OVERTHROWN BY THE PERSIANS
538	FIRST EXILES RETURN TO JUDAH
536	DANIEL'S MINISTRY ENDS

Daniel in Nebuchadnezzar's Court

1 During the third year of King Jehoiakim's reign in Judah,* King Nebuchadnezzar of Babylon came to Jerusalem and besieged it. ²The Lord gave him victory over King Jehoiakim of Judah and permitted him to take some of the sacred objects from the Temple of God. So Nebuchadnezzar took them back to the land of Babylonia* and placed them in the treasure-house of his god.

³Then the king ordered Ashpenaz, his chief of staff, to bring to the palace some of the young men of Judah's royal family and other noble families, who had been brought to Babylon as captives. ⁴"Select only strong, healthy, and good-looking young men," he said. "Make sure they are well versed in every branch of learning, are gifted with knowledge and good judgment, and are suited to serve in the royal palace. Train these young men in the language and literature of Babylon.*" ⁵The king assigned them a daily ration of food and wine from his own kitchens. They were to be trained for three years, and then they would enter the royal service.

⁶Daniel, Hananiah, Mishael, and Azariah were four of the young men chosen, all from the tribe of Judah. ⁷The chief of staff renamed them with these Babylonian names:

Daniel was called Belteshazzar.
Hananiah was called Shadrach.
Mishael was called Meshach.
Azariah was called Abednego.

⁸But Daniel was determined not to defile himself by eating the food and wine given to them by the king. He asked the chief of staff for permission not to eat these unacceptable foods. ⁹Now God had given the chief of staff both respect and affection for Daniel. ¹⁰But he responded, "I am afraid of my lord the king, who has ordered that you eat this food and wine. If you become pale and thin compared to the other youths your age, I am afraid the king will have me beheaded."

¹¹Daniel spoke with the attendant who had been appointed by the chief of staff to look after Daniel, Hananiah, Mishael, and Azariah. ¹²"Please test us for ten days on a diet of vegetables and water," Daniel said. ¹³"At the end of the ten days, see how we look compared to the other young men who are eating the king's food. Then make your decision in light of what you see." ¹⁴The attendant agreed to Daniel's suggestion and tested them for ten days.

¹⁵At the end of the ten days, Daniel and his three friends looked healthier and better nourished than the young men who had been eating the food assigned by the king. ¹⁶So after that, the attendant fed them only vegetables instead of the food and wine provided for the others.

¹⁷God gave these four young men an unusual aptitude for understanding every aspect of literature and wisdom. And God gave Daniel the special ability to interpret the meanings of visions and dreams.

¹⁸When the training period ordered by the king was completed, the chief of staff brought all the young men to King Nebuchadnezzar. ¹⁹The king

---

1:1 This event occurred in 605 B.C., during the third year of Jehoiakim's reign (according to the calendar system in which the new year begins in the spring). **1:2** Hebrew *the land of Shinar*. **1:4** Or *of the Chaldeans*.

1:1–6:28 The first half of Daniel establishes God as the ruler of the world. In the face of adversity, God's people can turn to his loving presence and power. He will help them overcome the fiercest challenges. Daniel and his three friends demonstrate how to live wisely and honor God, even when the society around them was encouraging them to turn away from God. But they resisted the temptation to become self-sufficient and proud.

1:1-21 God warned his people about their being unfaithful to him and worshiping created things. If they continued, enemies would invade and take the people captive (see Leviticus 26:14-39; Isaiah 39:1-8). Daniel and his three friends were among the first people taken by the Babylonians, under King Nebuchadnezzar II, from Jerusalem into exile in 605 BC. The Babylonians saw great promise in these teenagers and trained them to work in the royal court. Daniel and his friends resolved to remain faithful and serve the God of Israel as they were assimilated into the Babylonian culture.

1:1-2 The Lord, who is sovereign over history, gave Nebuchadnezzar the win; neither the king's might nor the power of Marduk, the chief god in the Babylonian pantheon, accomplished it. The real victory belonged to God. He remained loyal to his covenant agreement with Israel and fulfilled his promises through the Exile (Deuteronomy 27–30).

1:3-7 Nebuchadnezzar chose the best and the brightest to serve in his royal court, and God had already positioned people of integrity who would apply themselves and rise to influential places. Despite their circumstances and the formidable task they faced, Daniel and his three friends would excel in their Babylonian education yet remain faithful to God.

1:8-17 Daniel showed incredible grace under pressure. The king was providing lavish food and drink, which had likely been dedicated to Babylonian gods and would have been unclean according to Israel's dietary laws. But Daniel respectfully sought a compromise to consume only "vegetables and water," much like a fast mourning their exile and the destruction of their home. In his words and actions, Daniel demonstrated great tact and wisdom, and God blessed him and his friends with exceptional academic abilities and good health.

1:19-20 The king was deeply impressed by Daniel and his friends, whose intellects and wisdom outshone even the highly qualified advisers already in royal service. The word translated *magicians* appears earlier in the Old Testament to describe ancient Egyptian priests who could interpret dreams (Genesis 41:8) and perform mysterious acts (Exodus 7:11), and likely refers to a similar Babylonian profession. The term translated *enchanters*, found only in the book of Daniel, comes from an ancient Assyrian title for the physician-scholars who served at court diagnosing illnesses, performing rituals and incantations, and consulting on difficult decisions.

IMAGE — MY STORY OF MY UNIQUE INFLUENCE

Fit to Flourish

SCRIPTURE CONNECTION: DANIEL 1:8-21

Daniel knew that how he treated his body reflected how he worshiped God. The Israelites followed strict dietary laws that were tied to their relationship with God (see Leviticus 11:1-47). So how did Daniel's discipline and devotion in following God's laws prepare him to flourish in favor and faith while living in Babylon? What similar principles can we use in our lives?

For Daniel to decline the king's provisions would have put the chief of staff, who was responsible for his well-being, in a difficult position, facing serious consequences. However, Daniel embraced this opportunity and respectfully presented an alternative that honored God. The food he ate is just one example; Daniel lived his whole life this way. His discipline, courage, discretion, and devotion resulted in Daniel being appointed to a high position in the Babylonian court. He used that position to continually point people toward God.

What about our lives? Sometimes what God is asking us to do requires our discipline to accomplish something bigger than we can imagine, too. That might require us to change something about how we use our time, resources, and bodies so that we can be better equipped to serve God.

> Sometimes God requires our discipline to accomplish something bigger than we imagine.

IMAGINE

Is there a discipline you need to practice to be equipped for your assignment?

Is what you are allowing into your mind and body preparing you for increased influence as you serve the one true king?

"Every month I fast from social media for a week to focus on listening to God. It also helps break the habit of picking up my phone anytime I have a spare minute. Focusing on what God is saying, instead of what other people are saying, is one way I cultivate spiritual discipline."

MANDY ARIOTO is the president and CEO of MOPS International, influencing millions of moms around the world every year. She is a scholar of Greek, author, and speaker who believes in the transformational power of Scripture.

DANIEL 2

talked with them, and no one impressed him as much as Daniel, Hananiah, Mishael, and Azariah. So they entered the royal service. ²⁰Whenever the king consulted them in any matter requiring wisdom and balanced judgment, he found them ten times more capable than any of the magicians and enchanters in his entire kingdom.

²¹Daniel remained in the royal service until the first year of the reign of King Cyrus.*

Nebuchadnezzar's Dream

2 One night during the second year of his reign,* Nebuchadnezzar had such disturbing dreams that he couldn't sleep. ²He called in his magicians, enchanters, sorcerers, and astrologers,* and he demanded that they tell him what he had dreamed. As they stood before the king, ³he said, "I have had a dream that deeply troubles me, and I must know what it means."

1:21 Cyrus began his reign (over Babylon) in 539 B.C. 2:1 The second year of Nebuchadnezzar's reign was 603 B.C. 2:2 Or *Chaldeans;* also in 2:4, 5, 10.

1:21 Cyrus the Great of Persia overthrew the Median Empire (549 BC) before conquering the Lydian Empire (546 BC) and eventually the Babylonian Empire (539 BC). Thus, he created the largest empire of the ancient world—the Persian Empire (550–330 BC, see the notes on 5:1-30; 5:31; Isaiah 44:24–45:8). Despite the unexpected circumstances Daniel found himself in, God allowed him to rise to a highly influential role during the reigns of several powerful kings: Nebuchadnezzar, Darius, Belshazzar, and Cyrus.

2:1-49 God gave King Nebuchadnezzar a confusing dream predicting the future, and Daniel interpreted it. This chapter highlights two key themes of the book: God's Kingdom reigning on earth as history's greatest goal and unawareness of God's plans and activity (2:44-45; 7:9-14, 26-27).

2:1-15 Disturbed by a mysterious dream that he couldn't recall, the king demanded that his advisers tell him the dream and explain it, or he would kill them. Although these advisers were trained to interpret dreams, they needed the king to tell them the details so they could consult reference texts and provide an interpretation.

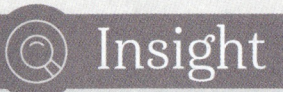

Insight — NEW NAMES

In the ancient Near East, a person's name could change with their social status. Assyrian and Babylonian kings sometimes took throne names when they ascended to power. Officials entering royal service, both native Babylonians and non-native professionals, could be given new names. Conquering kings might also change a captured official's name to express their authority. As part of their assimilation into Babylonian society, these four young men were also assigned new names, which they accepted while preserving their deep faith in God.

What significance does your name have? Were you given a family name or does your name have special meaning? God calls us his beloved children (1 John 3:1-2) and gives us new names (Revelation 2:17).

BIRTH NAME	HEBREW MEANING	CHANGED NAME	BABYLONIAN MEANING
Daniel	"God is my judge"	Belteshazzar	"Bel protect the king [or his life]" (Bel was the title of Marduk, the chief Babylonian god.)
Hananiah	"Yahweh has been gracious"	Shadrach	"I am fearful [of God]" or "Command of Aku" (another name for Sin, the Mesopotamian moon god)
Mishael	"Who is like God?"	Meshach	"I am of little account" or "Who is it that is Aku?"
Azariah	"Yahweh has helped"	Abednego	"Servant of the Shining One [Nabu]" or "Servant of Nabu" (the Babylonian god of wisdom)

⁴Then the astrologers answered the king in Aramaic,* "Long live the king! Tell us the dream, and we will tell you what it means."

⁵But the king said to the astrologers, "I am serious about this. If you don't tell me what my dream was and what it means, you will be torn limb from limb, and your houses will be turned into heaps of rubble! ⁶But if you tell me what I dreamed and what the dream means, I will give you many wonderful gifts and honors. Just tell me the dream and what it means!"

⁷They said again, "Please, Your Majesty. Tell us the dream, and we will tell you what it means."

⁸The king replied, "I know what you are doing! You're stalling for time because you know I am serious when I say, ⁹'If you don't tell me the dream, you are doomed.' So you have conspired to tell me lies, hoping I will change my mind. But tell me the dream, and then I'll know that you can tell me what it means."

¹⁰The astrologers replied to the king, "No one on earth can tell the king his dream! And no king, however great and powerful, has ever asked such a thing of any magician, enchanter, or astrologer! ¹¹The king's demand is impossible. No one except the gods can tell you your dream, and they do not live here among people."

¹²The king was furious when he heard this, and he ordered that all the wise men of Babylon be executed. ¹³And because of the king's decree, men were sent to find and kill Daniel and his friends.

¹⁴When Arioch, the commander of the king's guard, came to kill them, Daniel handled the situation with wisdom and discretion. ¹⁵He asked Arioch, "Why has the king issued such a harsh decree?" So Arioch told him all that had happened. ¹⁶Daniel went at once to see the king and requested more time to tell the king what the dream meant.

¹⁷Then Daniel went home and told his friends Hananiah, Mishael, and Azariah what had happened. ¹⁸He urged them to ask the God of heaven to show them his mercy by telling them the secret, so they would not be executed along with the other wise men of Babylon. ¹⁹That night the secret was revealed to Daniel in a vision. Then Daniel praised the God of heaven. ²⁰He said,

"Praise the name of God forever and ever,
  for he has all wisdom and power.
²¹ He controls the course of world events;
  he removes kings and sets up other kings.
He gives wisdom to the wise
  and knowledge to the scholars.
²² He reveals deep and mysterious things
  and knows what lies hidden in darkness,
  though he is surrounded by light.
²³ I thank and praise you, God of my ancestors,
  for you have given me wisdom and strength.
You have told me what we asked of you
  and revealed to us what the king
    demanded."

Daniel Interprets the Dream

²⁴Then Daniel went in to see Arioch, whom the king had ordered to execute the wise men of Babylon. Daniel said to him, "Don't kill the wise men. Take me to the king, and I will tell him the meaning of his dream."

²⁵Arioch quickly took Daniel to the king and said, "I have found one of the captives from Judah who will tell the king the meaning of his dream!"

²⁶The king said to Daniel (also known as Belteshazzar), "Is this true? Can you tell me what my dream was and what it means?"

²⁷Daniel replied, "There are no wise men, enchanters, magicians, or fortune-tellers who can reveal the king's secret. ²⁸But there is a God in heaven who reveals secrets, and he has shown King Nebuchadnezzar what will happen in the future. Now I will tell you your dream and the visions you saw as you lay on your bed.

²⁹"While Your Majesty was sleeping, you dreamed about coming events. He who reveals secrets has shown you what is going to happen. ³⁰And it is not because I am wiser than anyone else that I know the secret of your dream, but because God wants you to understand what was in your heart.

2:4 The original text from this point through chapter 7 is in Aramaic.

2:4 Aramaic was a common language used for international communication in the ancient Near East, originally accepted by the Assyrian Empire. At this point, the book of Daniel transitions into Aramaic (instead of Hebrew, the main language in which the Old Testament was written) until 7:28, where the book transitions back to Hebrew.

2:16 Daniel's ability to go "at once to see the king" speaks to his influence and reputation at court. To have earned direct access to the king, Daniel would have already demonstrated his diplomacy and trustworthiness, and even now with his life on the line, Daniel would show his wisdom and peaceable manner by using gentle words before the angry king (see Proverbs 15:1).

2:17-23 Daniel's faith and wisdom led him to pray that God would enter the situation (Philippians 4:6). Daniel asked God for his mercy (see Exodus 34:6-7) and gave thanks when God answered his prayer. By imparting the dream to Nebuchadnezzar and revealing its meaning to Daniel, God demonstrated his supremacy over Babylon's gods.

2:26-28 Nebuchadnezzar may have been surprised that a non-Babylonian could reveal the secrets of his dream, but Daniel deflected all credit to God, proclaiming the one true God who rules all things as the source of his wisdom (see 2:20-21).

³¹"In your vision, Your Majesty, you saw standing before you a huge, shining statue of a man. It was a frightening sight. ³²The head of the statue was made of fine gold. Its chest and arms were silver, its belly and thighs were bronze, ³³its legs were iron, and its feet were a combination of iron and baked clay. ³⁴As you watched, a rock was cut from a mountain,* but not by human hands. It struck the feet of iron and clay, smashing them to bits. ³⁵The whole statue was crushed into small pieces of iron, clay, bronze, silver, and gold. Then the wind blew them away without a trace, like chaff on a threshing floor. But the rock that knocked the statue down became a great mountain that covered the whole earth.

³⁶"That was the dream. Now we will tell the king what it means. ³⁷Your Majesty, you are the greatest of kings. The God of heaven has given you sovereignty, power, strength, and honor. ³⁸He has made you the ruler over all the inhabited world and has put even the wild animals and birds under your control. You are the head of gold.

³⁹"But after your kingdom comes to an end, another kingdom, inferior to yours, will rise to take your place. After that kingdom has fallen, yet a third kingdom, represented by bronze, will rise to rule the world. ⁴⁰Following that kingdom, there will be a fourth one, as strong as iron. That kingdom will smash and crush all previous empires, just as iron smashes and crushes everything it strikes. ⁴¹The feet and toes you saw were a combination of iron and baked clay, showing that this kingdom will be divided. Like iron mixed with clay, it will have some of the strength of iron. ⁴²But while some parts of it will be as strong as iron, other parts will be as weak as clay. ⁴³This mixture of iron and clay also shows that these kingdoms will try to strengthen themselves by forming alliances with each other through intermarriage. But they will not hold together, just as iron and clay do not mix.

⁴⁴"During the reigns of those kings, the God of heaven will set up a kingdom that will never be destroyed or conquered. It will crush all these kingdoms into nothingness, and it will stand forever. ⁴⁵That is the meaning of the rock cut from the mountain, though not by human hands, that crushed to pieces the statue of iron, bronze, clay, silver, and gold. The great God was showing the king what will happen in the future. The dream is true, and its meaning is certain."

Nebuchadnezzar Rewards Daniel

⁴⁶Then King Nebuchadnezzar threw himself down before Daniel and worshiped him, and he commanded his people to offer sacrifices and burn sweet incense before him. ⁴⁷The king said to Daniel, "Truly, your God is the greatest of gods, the Lord over kings, a revealer of mysteries, for you have been able to reveal this secret."

⁴⁸Then the king appointed Daniel to a high position and gave him many valuable gifts. He made Daniel ruler over the whole province of Babylon, as well as chief over all his wise men. ⁴⁹At Daniel's request, the king appointed Shadrach, Meshach, and Abednego to be in charge of all the affairs of the province of Babylon, while Daniel remained in the king's court.

Nebuchadnezzar's Gold Statue

3 King Nebuchadnezzar made a gold statue ninety feet tall and nine feet wide* and set it up on the plain of Dura in the province of Babylon. ²Then he sent messages to the high officers, officials, governors, advisers, treasurers, judges, magistrates, and all the provincial officials to come to the dedication of the statue he had set up. ³So all these officials* came and stood before the statue King Nebuchadnezzar had set up.

2:34 As in Greek version (see also 2:45); Hebrew lacks *from a mountain.* **3:1** Aramaic *60 cubits* [27 meters] *tall and 6 cubits* [2.7 meters] *wide.* **3:3** Aramaic *the high officers, officials, governors, advisers, treasurers, judges, magistrates, and all the provincial officials.*

2:31-45 The vision represented four future empires. The "head of gold" represented Nebuchadnezzar and the Babylonian Empire (625–539 BC; Jeremiah 51:7). The silver chest and arms represented Darius and the Persian Empire (539–330 BC). The bronze belly and thighs represented Alexander the Great and the Greek Empire (330–64 BC). The iron legs and iron-clay feet represented the Roman Empire (27 BC–AD 476).
2:44 Only a kingdom with authority and power from God could "stand forever" and "never be destroyed." *All* human kingdoms will crumble (see John 18:36). God's Kingdom is indestructible, ultimate, and supernatural. Jesus, who will reign forever and ever, is worthy of our faith and hope.
2:46-49 The king's "worship" of Daniel was a customary way of paying homage. He asked no further questions regarding his empire's future or Daniel's God. Recognizing God's power in Daniel, Nebuchadnezzar moved him into a higher position within the royal court and assigned important administrative duties to his three friends. In their new respective roles, Daniel and his friends diligently served Nebuchadnezzar's interests and worked for the prosperity of the empire where God had placed them (see Jeremiah 29:5-7).
3:1-30 Building off his vision (2:36-38), Nebuchadnezzar's megalomania inspired him to build a gilded statue and demand that everyone in his empire worship it. God tested Shadrach, Meshach, and Abednego, who proved their steadfast faith and glorified God. No human-made image could ever represent God. The three young men rightly refused to worship Nebuchadnezzar's golden image. The Lord recognized their obedience and rescued them from the king's rage.
3:1-7 The sheer size of Nebuchadnezzar's statue and the number of people required to worship it show his swelling pride and fear of rebellion. Everyone within earshot, regardless of rank, could hear the numerous musical instruments and see the "ninety feet tall and nine feet wide" statue. Whenever commanded, the people prostrated themselves or were burned to death.

⁴Then a herald shouted out, "People of all races and nations and languages, listen to the king's command! ⁵When you hear the sound of the horn, flute, zither, lyre, harp, pipes, and other musical instruments,* bow to the ground to worship King Nebuchadnezzar's gold statue. ⁶Anyone who refuses to obey will immediately be thrown into a blazing furnace."

⁷So at the sound of the musical instruments,* all the people, whatever their race or nation or language, bowed to the ground and worshiped the gold statue that King Nebuchadnezzar had set up.

⁸But some of the astrologers* went to the king and informed on the Jews. ⁹They said to King Nebuchadnezzar, "Long live the king! ¹⁰You issued a decree requiring all the people to bow down and worship the gold statue when they hear the sound of the horn, flute, zither, lyre, harp, pipes, and other musical instruments. ¹¹That decree also states that those who refuse to obey must be thrown into a blazing furnace. ¹²But there are some Jews—Shadrach, Meshach, and Abednego—whom you have put in charge of the province of Babylon. They pay no attention to you, Your Majesty. They refuse to serve your gods and do not worship the gold statue you have set up."

¹³Then Nebuchadnezzar flew into a rage and ordered that Shadrach, Meshach, and Abednego be brought before him. When they were brought in, ¹⁴Nebuchadnezzar said to them, "Is it true, Shadrach, Meshach, and Abednego, that you refuse to serve my gods or to worship the gold statue I have set up? ¹⁵I will give you one more chance to bow down and worship the statue I have made when you hear the sound of the musical instruments.* But if you refuse, you will be thrown immediately into the blazing furnace. And then what god will be able to rescue you from my power?"

¹⁶Shadrach, Meshach, and Abednego replied, "O Nebuchadnezzar, we do not need to defend ourselves before you. ¹⁷If we are thrown into the blazing furnace, the God whom we serve is able to save us. He will rescue us from your power, Your Majesty. ¹⁸But even if he doesn't, we want to make it clear to you, Your Majesty, that we will never serve your gods or worship the gold statue you have set up."

The Blazing Furnace

¹⁹Nebuchadnezzar was so furious with Shadrach, Meshach, and Abednego that his face became distorted with rage. He commanded that the furnace be heated seven times hotter than usual. ²⁰Then he ordered some of the strongest men of his army to bind Shadrach, Meshach, and Abednego and throw them into the blazing furnace. ²¹So they tied them up and threw them into the furnace, fully dressed in their pants, turbans, robes, and other garments. ²²And because the king, in his anger, had demanded such a hot fire in the furnace, the flames killed the soldiers as they threw the three men in. ²³So Shadrach, Meshach, and Abednego, securely tied, fell into the roaring flames.

²⁴But suddenly, Nebuchadnezzar jumped up in amazement and exclaimed to his advisers, "Didn't we tie up three men and throw them into the furnace?"

"Yes, Your Majesty, we certainly did," they replied.

²⁵"Look!" Nebuchadnezzar shouted. "I see four men, unbound, walking around in the fire unharmed! And the fourth looks like a god*!"

²⁶Then Nebuchadnezzar came as close as he could to the door of the flaming furnace and shouted: "Shadrach, Meshach, and Abednego, servants of the Most High God, come out! Come here!"

So Shadrach, Meshach, and Abednego stepped out of the fire. ²⁷Then the high officers, officials, governors, and advisers crowded around them and saw that the fire had not touched them. Not a hair on their heads was singed, and their clothing was not scorched. They didn't even smell of smoke!

3:5 The identification of some of these musical instruments is uncertain. **3:7** Aramaic *the horn, flute, zither, lyre, harp, and other musical instruments.* **3:8** Aramaic *Chaldeans.* **3:15** Aramaic *the horn, flute, zither, lyre, harp, pipes, and other musical instruments.* **3:25** Aramaic *like a son of the gods.*

3:11 All people live by faith of some sort. The difference is that a Christian puts their faith in God, while someone who is not a Christian might trust themselves, other people, or other things. Fear or scarcity can tempt us to trust in frail, false, or futile objects (compare John 14:6).

3:12 Shadrach, Meshach, and Abednego refused to worship the gold statue because respect for God filled their hearts (see Exodus 20:1-5). They trusted their lives to God's commands and promises (see Isaiah 43:1-2; compare Acts 4:19; 5:29; Romans 13:1-7). They did not fold to the king, to what everyone else was doing, or to superstition. They modeled faithfulness and obeyed God instead of letting their fear or circumstances direct their actions.

3:16-18 Note the three friends did not say, "We will serve your gods if our God does not defend us." They entrusted themselves wholly to God regardless of the king's threats, and they chose to follow the God who had the power to save them. But even in their refusal, Shadrach, Meshach, and Abednego remained polite and respectful.

3:16 God is more than capable of defending himself and protecting his people. Justifying ourselves through words or actions is unnecessary. We can trust and follow God, and rest in the confidence that he will act (Isaiah 12:2). Faith in God does not guarantee that he will perform extraordinary miracles for us when we ask, but he does provide the grace and strength needed to endure any situation.

3:19-30 The book of Daniel provides great encouragement to anyone facing hardship. It reminds us that the God who cared about the exiles also cares about our circumstances. He is the powerful and almighty, living God. He sustains the universe while showing loving compassion to those who have faith in him.

²⁸Then Nebuchadnezzar said, "Praise to the God of Shadrach, Meshach, and Abednego! He sent his angel to rescue his servants who trusted in him. They defied the king's command and were willing to die rather than serve or worship any god except their own God. ²⁹Therefore, I make this decree: If any people, whatever their race or nation or language, speak a word against the God of Shadrach, Meshach, and Abednego, they will be torn limb from limb, and their houses will be turned into heaps of rubble. There is no other god who can rescue like this!"

³⁰Then the king promoted Shadrach, Meshach, and Abednego to even higher positions in the province of Babylon.

Nebuchadnezzar's Dream about a Tree

4 ¹*King Nebuchadnezzar sent this message to the people of every race and nation and language throughout the world:

"Peace and prosperity to you!

²"I want you all to know about the miraculous signs and wonders the Most High God has performed for me.

³ How great are his signs,
 how powerful his wonders!
His kingdom will last forever,
 his rule through all generations.

⁴*"I, Nebuchadnezzar, was living in my palace in comfort and prosperity. ⁵But one night I had a dream that frightened me; I saw visions that terrified me as I lay in my bed. ⁶So I issued an order calling in all the wise men of Babylon, so they could tell me what my dream meant. ⁷When all the magicians, enchanters, astrologers,* and fortune-tellers came in, I told them the dream, but they could not tell me what it meant. ⁸At last Daniel came in before me, and I told him the dream. (He was named Belteshazzar after my god, and the spirit of the holy gods is in him.) ⁹"I said to him, 'Belteshazzar, chief of the magicians, I know that the spirit of the holy gods is in you and that no mystery is too great for you to solve. Now tell me what my dream means.

¹⁰"'While I was lying in my bed, this is what I dreamed. I saw a large tree in the middle of the earth. ¹¹The tree grew very tall and strong, reaching high into the heavens for all the world to see. ¹²It had fresh green leaves, and it was loaded with fruit for all to eat. Wild animals lived in its shade, and birds nested in its branches. All the world was fed from this tree.

¹³"'Then as I lay there dreaming, I saw a messenger,* a holy one, coming down from heaven. ¹⁴The messenger shouted,

"Cut down the tree and lop off its branches!
 Shake off its leaves and scatter its fruit!
Chase the wild animals from its shade
 and the birds from its branches.
¹⁵ But leave the stump and the roots in the ground,
 bound with a band of iron and bronze
 and surrounded by tender grass.
Now let him be drenched with the dew of heaven,
 and let him live with the wild animals
 among the plants of the field.
¹⁶ For seven periods of time,
 let him have the mind of a wild animal
 instead of the mind of a human.
¹⁷ For this has been decreed by the messengers*;
 it is commanded by the holy ones,
so that everyone may know
 that the Most High rules over the kingdoms of the world.
He gives them to anyone he chooses—
 even to the lowliest of people."

¹⁸"'Belteshazzar, that was the dream that I, King Nebuchadnezzar, had. Now tell me what it means, for none of the wise men of my kingdom can do so. But you can tell me because the spirit of the holy gods is in you.'

Daniel Explains the Dream

¹⁹"Upon hearing this, Daniel (also known as Belteshazzar) was overcome for a time, frightened by the meaning of the dream. Then the king said to him, 'Belteshazzar, don't be alarmed by the dream and what it means.'

"Belteshazzar replied, 'I wish the events foreshadowed in this dream would happen to

---

4:1 Verses 4:1-3 are numbered 3:31-33 in Aramaic text. **4:4** Verses 4:4-37 are numbered 4:1-34 in Aramaic text. **4:7** Or *Chaldeans.* **4:13** Aramaic *a watcher;* also in 4:23. **4:17** Aramaic *the watchers.*

3:30 The Hebrew verb translated here as *promoted* means "to make progress." God prospered the three men for their righteousness and their faithfulness to him. Daniel also made further progress (6:4, 28).

4:4-9 Through another dream, God disrupted the false peace the king was experiencing in his sheltered palace life. After the advisers failed to interpret the dream, Daniel arrived "at last" to help. This delay may have been due to Daniel's position as "chief over all his wise men" (2:48), his duties possibly having kept him from answering the king's summons as promptly as the others had. Or it may speak to his evidently elusive manner, frequently having to be sought out before he could be consulted. Either way, his reputation preceded him: The king acknowledged that "the spirit of the holy gods" was in Daniel and expressed complete faith in his abilities.

your enemies, my lord, and not to you! ²⁰The tree you saw was growing very tall and strong, reaching high into the heavens for all the world to see. ²¹It had fresh green leaves and was loaded with fruit for all to eat. Wild animals lived in its shade, and birds nested in its branches. ²²That tree, Your Majesty, is you. For you have grown strong and great; your greatness reaches up to heaven, and your rule to the ends of the earth.

²³"Then you saw a messenger, a holy one, coming down from heaven and saying, "Cut down the tree and destroy it. But leave the stump and the roots in the ground, bound with a band of iron and bronze and surrounded by tender grass. Let him be drenched with the dew of heaven. Let him live with the animals of the field for seven periods of time."

²⁴"This is what the dream means, Your Majesty, and what the Most High has declared will happen to my lord the king. ²⁵You will be driven from human society, and you will live in the fields with the wild animals. You will eat grass like a cow, and you will be drenched with the dew of heaven. Seven periods of time will pass while you live this way, until you learn that the Most High rules over the kingdoms of the world and gives them to anyone he chooses. ²⁶But the stump and roots of the tree were left in the ground. This means that you will receive your kingdom back again when you have learned that heaven rules.

²⁷"King Nebuchadnezzar, please accept my advice. Stop sinning and do what is right. Break from your wicked past and be merciful to the poor. Perhaps then you will continue to prosper.'

The Dream's Fulfillment

²⁸"But all these things did happen to King Nebuchadnezzar. ²⁹Twelve months later he was taking a walk on the flat roof of the royal palace in Babylon. ³⁰As he looked out across the city, he said, 'Look at this great city of Babylon! By my own mighty power, I have built this beautiful city as my royal residence to display my majestic splendor.'

³¹"While these words were still in his mouth, a voice called down from heaven, 'O King Nebuchadnezzar, this message is for you! You are no longer ruler of this kingdom. ³²You will be driven from human society. You will live in the fields with the wild animals, and you will eat grass like a cow. Seven periods of time will pass while you live this way, until you learn that the Most High rules over the kingdoms of the world and gives them to anyone he chooses.'

³³"That same hour the judgment was fulfilled, and Nebuchadnezzar was driven from human society. He ate grass like a cow, and he was drenched with the dew of heaven. He lived this way until his hair was as long as eagles' feathers and his nails were like birds' claws.

Nebuchadnezzar Praises God

³⁴"After this time had passed, I, Nebuchadnezzar, looked up to heaven. My sanity returned, and I praised and worshiped the Most High and honored the one who lives forever.

> His rule is everlasting,
> and his kingdom is eternal.
> ³⁵ All the people of the earth
> are nothing compared to him.
> He does as he pleases
> among the angels of heaven
> and among the people of the earth.
> No one can stop him or say to him,
> 'What do you mean by doing these things?'

³⁶"When my sanity returned to me, so did my honor and glory and kingdom. My advisers and nobles sought me out, and I was restored as head of my kingdom, with even greater honor than before.

³⁷"Now I, Nebuchadnezzar, praise and glorify and honor the King of heaven. All his acts are just and true, and he is able to humble the proud."

4:20-22 Trees were symbols of political authority (see Ezekiel 17:24; Hosea 14:5-8; Zechariah 11:1-2; Luke 23:31). God promised to build a vast empire under Nebuchadnezzar that sheltered many nations and people. The successful empire was God's doing, not Nebuchadnezzar's. God distributes leadership and power to whoever he will, "even to the lowliest" (Daniel 4:17).

4:23-26 Nebuchadnezzar's pride would require the tree to be cut down (4:27-33). The stump stood as a promise that Nebuchadnezzar would reign again after realizing it is *heaven that rules*. In a similar image, God allowed Israel's enemies to cut down the "tree" of Israel but promised the Messiah would come from the stump (Isaiah 6:13; 10:33–11:5).

4:27 Justice and righteousness exalt a nation and extend the ruler's reign (see Proverbs 29:14). Facing a king who tended to fly into a rage, Daniel still respectfully urged the king to stop sinning and humbly pled with him to show mercy to the poor. God's divine order and character require it (see Deuteronomy 15:10-15).

4:28-33 Daniel interjects into Nebuchadnezzar's official report to explain that Nebuchadnezzar chose not to heed Daniel's wisdom nor express remorse for his exploitative ways. God graciously gave the king an entire year to soften his heart and yield his pride (see Ecclesiastes 8:11; compare Proverbs 3:34; 6:16-19; 11:2; James 4:6). In an instant, God fulfilled his judgment by removing Nebuchadnezzar from both his kingdom and human society. God determined to glorify his name among the nations.

4:34-37 Nebuchadnezzar resumed his official report by praising the Lord. His words echo the prophet Isaiah: "The nations of the world are but a drop in the bucket. They are nothing more than dust on the scales" (Isaiah 40:15). Submitting to God's authority over all brought Nebuchadnezzar assurance, comfort, faith, and freedom.

The Writing on the Wall

5 Many years later King Belshazzar gave a great feast for 1,000 of his nobles, and he drank wine with them. ²While Belshazzar was drinking the wine, he gave orders to bring in the gold and silver cups that his predecessor,* Nebuchadnezzar, had taken from the Temple in Jerusalem. He wanted to drink from them with his nobles, his wives, and his concubines. ³So they brought these gold cups taken from the Temple, the house of God in Jerusalem, and the king and his nobles, his wives, and his concubines drank from them. ⁴While they drank from them they praised their idols made of gold, silver, bronze, iron, wood, and stone.

⁵Suddenly, they saw the fingers of a human hand writing on the plaster wall of the king's palace, near the lampstand. The king himself saw the hand as it wrote, ⁶and his face turned pale with fright. His knees knocked together in fear and his legs gave way beneath him.

⁷The king shouted for the enchanters, astrologers,* and fortune-tellers to be brought before him. He said to these wise men of Babylon, "Whoever can read this writing and tell me what it means will be dressed in purple robes of royal honor and will have a gold chain placed around his neck. He will become the third highest ruler in the kingdom!"

⁸But when all the king's wise men had come in, none of them could read the writing or tell him what it meant. ⁹So the king grew even more alarmed, and his face turned pale. His nobles, too, were shaken.

¹⁰But when the queen mother heard what was happening, she hurried to the banquet hall. She said to Belshazzar, "Long live the king! Don't be so pale and frightened. ¹¹There is a man in your kingdom who has within him the spirit of the holy gods. During Nebuchadnezzar's reign, this man was found to have insight, understanding, and wisdom like that of the gods. Your predecessor, the king—your predecessor King Nebuchadnezzar—made him chief over all the magicians, enchanters, astrologers, and fortune-tellers of Babylon. ¹²This man Daniel, whom the king named Belteshazzar, has exceptional ability and is filled with divine knowledge and understanding. He can interpret dreams, explain riddles, and solve difficult problems. Call for Daniel, and he will tell you what the writing means."

Daniel Explains the Writing

¹³So Daniel was brought in before the king. The king asked him, "Are you Daniel, one of the exiles brought from Judah by my predecessor, King Nebuchadnezzar? ¹⁴I have heard that you have the spirit of the gods within you and that you are filled with insight, understanding, and wisdom. ¹⁵My wise men and enchanters have tried to read the words on the wall and tell me their meaning, but they cannot do it. ¹⁶I am told that you can give interpretations and solve difficult problems. If you can read these words and tell me their meaning, you will be clothed in purple robes of royal honor, and you will have a gold chain placed around your neck. You will become the third highest ruler in the kingdom."

¹⁷Daniel answered the king, "Keep your gifts or give them to someone else, but I will tell you what the writing means. ¹⁸Your Majesty, the Most High God gave sovereignty, majesty, glory, and honor to your predecessor, Nebuchadnezzar. ¹⁹He made him so great that people of all races and nations and languages trembled before him in fear. He killed those he wanted to kill and spared those he wanted to spare. He honored those he wanted to honor and disgraced those he wanted to disgrace. ²⁰But when his heart and mind were puffed up with arrogance, he was brought down from his royal throne and stripped of his glory. ²¹He was driven from human society. He was given the mind of a wild animal, and he lived among the wild donkeys. He ate grass like a cow, and he was drenched with the dew of heaven, until he learned that the Most High God rules over

---

5:2 Aramaic *father;* also in 5:11, 13, 18. 5:7 Or *Chaldeans;* also in 5:11.

5:1-30 Civilizations rise and fall. Nebuchadnezzar's dream implied that the Babylonian Empire would fall, and a new empire would take its place (2:39). After Nebuchadnezzar died in 562 BC, corruption and debauchery increased in Babylon's palaces. During Belshazzar's feast in 539 BC, the vessels that had been in the Jewish Temple were polluted and defiled. God's judgment came with lightning swiftness that night (5:30), and the next empire rose (see 2:32, 39; 5:31).

5:1 This chapter opens in October 539 BC (see text note on 5:30; also see the note on 5:31). The name *Belshazzar* means "Bel protect the king." (Bel was the title of Marduk, the chief Babylonian god.) After a religious uprising, Belshazzar's father, Nabonidus, had appointed him coregent around 553 BC before exiling himself to northwest Arabia. Ten years later, Nabonidus returned to Babylon but fled when it fell to the Persians.

5:2-4 The Babylonians had taken all the precious items from the Israelite Temple when they conquered Jerusalem in 586 BC (1:2). The sacred vessels had been stored in a Babylonian temple, but Belshazzar chose to desecrate them by allowing his guests to drink from them while praising the Babylonian gods.

5:5-8 The supernatural hand shocked and terrified the carousers. However, like Nebuchadnezzar, Belshazzar remained unrepentant (5:22-23, 30; compare Jeremiah 38:19-24; Acts 24:25). Once again, the Babylonian advisers were unable to interpret the omen (see Daniel 2:4-11; 4:7; 5:15). God reveals his mind and will to those who revere him (see Proverbs 4–5).

5:10-17 Despite the panic in the banquet hall, the queen mother knew what to do. She stepped in and confidently pointed Belshazzar in the right direction: Find Daniel. Although he had been highly influential at court, Daniel didn't flaunt his position or seek to be the center of attention. Instead, he seems to have been reserved and, at times, difficult to locate as he unobtrusively carried out his responsibilities, never compromising his integrity before God or the quality of his work for the king.

the kingdoms of the world and appoints anyone he desires to rule over them.

²²"You are his successor,* O Belshazzar, and you knew all this, yet you have not humbled yourself. ²³For you have proudly defied the Lord of heaven and have had these cups from his Temple brought before you. You and your nobles and your wives and concubines have been drinking wine from them while praising gods of silver, gold, bronze, iron, wood, and stone—gods that neither see nor hear nor know anything at all. But you have not honored the God who gives you the breath of life and controls your destiny! ²⁴So God has sent this hand to write this message.

²⁵"This is the message that was written: MENE, MENE, TEKEL, and PARSIN. ²⁶This is what these words mean:

> *Mene* means 'numbered'—God has numbered the days of your reign and has brought it to an end.
> ²⁷ *Tekel* means 'weighed'—you have been weighed on the balances and have not measured up.
> ²⁸ *Parsin** means 'divided'—your kingdom has been divided and given to the Medes and Persians."

²⁹Then at Belshazzar's command, Daniel was dressed in purple robes, a gold chain was hung around his neck, and he was proclaimed the third highest ruler in the kingdom.

³⁰That very night Belshazzar, the Babylonian* king, was killed.*

³¹*And Darius the Mede took over the kingdom at the age of sixty-two.

Daniel in the Lions' Den

6 ¹*Darius the Mede decided to divide the kingdom into 120 provinces, and he appointed a high officer to rule over each province. ²The king also chose Daniel and two others as administrators to supervise the high officers and protect the king's interests. ³Daniel soon proved himself more capable than all the other administrators and high officers. Because of Daniel's great ability, the king made plans to place him over the entire empire.

> "Daily rituals, however small, add up to become largely impacting. For good or for bad."
>
> **RUTH CHOU SIMONS**
> author, artist, entrepreneur, and speaker

⁴Then the other administrators and high officers began searching for some fault in the way Daniel was handling government affairs, but they couldn't find anything to criticize or condemn. He was faithful, always responsible, and completely trustworthy. ⁵So they concluded, "Our only chance of finding grounds for accusing Daniel will be in connection with the rules of his religion."

⁶So the administrators and high officers went to the king and said, "Long live King Darius! ⁷We are all in agreement—we administrators, officials, high officers, advisers, and governors—that the king should make a law that will be strictly enforced. Give orders that for the next thirty days any person who prays to anyone, divine or human—except to you, Your Majesty—will be thrown into the den of lions. ⁸And now, Your Majesty, issue and sign this law so it cannot be changed, an official law of the Medes and Persians that cannot be revoked." ⁹So King Darius signed the law.

5:22 Aramaic *son*. 5:28 Aramaic *Peres*, the singular of *Parsin*. 5:30a Or *Chaldean*. 5:30b The Persians and Medes conquered Babylon in October 539 B.C. 5:31 Verse 5:31 is numbered 6:1 in Aramaic text. 6:1 Verses 6:1-28 are numbered 6:2-29 in Aramaic text.

5:31 Cyrus the Great conquered Babylon in 539 BC. Historical sources make no mention of someone named Darius the Mede. Darius and Cyrus were probably the same man with two different names—with the Medes referring to him by one name and the Persians by the other. Darius's portrayal in Daniel 6 suggests that he was Cyrus, the ruler of the Persian Empire.

6:1-28 This chapter is full of contrasts. First, Daniel's honesty and integrity challenged the other men serving the king, who were trying to find a flaw in him. Second, Daniel's faith in God ultimately protected him against the other administrators' scheming. Third, God's power usurps human authority.

6:4 No one could match Daniel's integrity or his abilities, and his handling of affairs left no room for criticism or legitimate accusations. Often people who live with such integrity aren't recognized in the same ways that God allowed Daniel to prosper, but having an extraordinary spirit and faith in God can make us stand out.

6:8 All human-made laws fade from existence, but God's word lasts forever (Psalms 93:5; 119:152). The inability to change Persian laws is mentioned elsewhere in Scripture (see Esther 1:19; 8:8).

¹⁰But when Daniel learned that the law had been signed, he went home and knelt down as usual in his upstairs room, with its windows open toward Jerusalem. He prayed three times a day, just as he had always done, giving thanks to his God. ¹¹Then the officials went together to Daniel's house and found him praying and asking for God's help. ¹²So they went straight to the king and reminded him about his law. "Did you not sign a law that for the next thirty days any person who prays to anyone, divine or human—except to you, Your Majesty—will be thrown into the den of lions?"

"Yes," the king replied, "that decision stands; it is an official law of the Medes and Persians that cannot be revoked."

¹³Then they told the king, "That man Daniel, one of the captives from Judah, is ignoring you and your law. He still prays to his God three times a day."

¹⁴Hearing this, the king was deeply troubled, and he tried to think of a way to save Daniel. He spent the rest of the day looking for a way to get Daniel out of this predicament.

¹⁵In the evening the men went together to the king and said, "Your Majesty, you know that according to the law of the Medes and the Persians, no law that the king signs can be changed."

¹⁶So at last the king gave orders for Daniel to be arrested and thrown into the den of lions. The king said to him, "May your God, whom you serve so faithfully, rescue you."

¹⁷A stone was brought and placed over the mouth of the den. The king sealed the stone with his own royal seal and the seals of his nobles, so that no one could rescue Daniel. ¹⁸Then the king returned to his palace and spent the night fasting. He refused his usual entertainment and couldn't sleep at all that night.

¹⁹Very early the next morning, the king got up and hurried out to the lions' den. ²⁰When he got there, he called out in anguish, "Daniel, servant of the living God! Was your God, whom you serve so faithfully, able to rescue you from the lions?"

²¹Daniel answered, "Long live the king! ²²My God sent his angel to shut the lions' mouths so that they would not hurt me, for I have been found innocent in his sight. And I have not wronged you, Your Majesty."

²³The king was overjoyed and ordered that Daniel be lifted from the den. Not a scratch was found on him, for he had trusted in his God.

²⁴Then the king gave orders to arrest the men who had maliciously accused Daniel. He had them thrown into the lions' den, along with their wives and children. The lions leaped on them and tore them apart before they even hit the floor of the den.

²⁵Then King Darius sent this message to the people of every race and nation and language throughout the world:

"Peace and prosperity to you!

²⁶"I decree that everyone throughout my kingdom should tremble with fear before the God of Daniel.

For he is the living God,
and he will endure forever.
His kingdom will never be destroyed,
and his rule will never end.
²⁷ He rescues and saves his people;
he performs miraculous signs and wonders
in the heavens and on earth.
He has rescued Daniel
from the power of the lions."

²⁸So Daniel prospered during the reign of Darius and the reign of Cyrus the Persian.*

Daniel's Vision of Four Beasts

7 Earlier, during the first year of King Belshazzar's reign in Babylon,* Daniel had a dream and saw visions as he lay in his bed. He wrote down the dream, and this is what he saw.

6:28 Or *of Darius, that is, the reign of Cyrus the Persian.* **7:1** The first year of Belshazzar's reign (who was co-regent with his father, Nabonidus) was 556 B.C. (or perhaps as late as 553 B.C.).

6:10-11 Daniel prayed three times a day facing Jerusalem, where the Temple had been. This was his regular and personal communication with God (compare Matthew 14:23; Philippians 4:6-7). He likely claimed the promises Solomon made when dedicating the Temple (1 Kings 8:28-30, 38-39, 46-51), asking God to keep his promise and deliver his people.

6:16-18 Darius offered a prayer to Daniel's God for his rescue. The king "spent the night fasting" and "couldn't sleep at all" because he mourned over what he had done. The king knew Daniel was an innocent and noble man.

6:23 God delivered Daniel from the lions' den because of his faithfulness. God is able to defend his people and his reputation. Daniel was justified in disobeying the Medes and Persians' law. Having integrity and being faithful to God's word is important regardless of human-made laws.

6:24 Persian kings were known to exact horrible revenge on a conspirator's family, sometimes slaughtering the person's sons or their entire family. Only trustworthy courtiers could surround the king and his family, and Darius likely did not want to risk any survivors rebelling or attempting to overthrow him.

6:25-27 As Nebuchadnezzar had done previously, King Darius sent out a message to his kingdom (see 3:28-29; 4:34-37). The mighty ruler testified that Daniel's God is the living God with real power and an everlasting kingdom.

7:1-28 Through a complex vision, Daniel foresaw the future beginning with the Babylonian Empire through to the ultimate reign of Christ on earth. The sequence of empires recalls Nebuchadnezzar's dream some forty-five years earlier (2:1-45). Daniel's vision occurred before the events in Daniel 5 and 6 (7:1).

²In my vision that night, I, Daniel, saw a great storm churning the surface of a great sea, with strong winds blowing from every direction. ³Then four huge beasts came up out of the water, each different from the others.

⁴The first beast was like a lion with eagles' wings. As I watched, its wings were pulled off, and it was left standing with its two hind feet on the ground, like a human being. And it was given a human mind. ⁵Then I saw a second beast, and it looked like a bear. It was rearing up on one side, and it had three ribs in its mouth between its teeth. And I heard a voice saying to it, "Get up! Devour the flesh of many people!"

⁶Then the third of these strange beasts appeared, and it looked like a leopard. It had four bird's wings on its back, and it had four heads. Great authority was given to this beast.

⁷Then in my vision that night, I saw a fourth beast—terrifying, dreadful, and very strong. It devoured and crushed its victims with huge iron teeth and trampled their remains beneath its feet. It was different from any of the other beasts, and it had ten horns.

⁸As I was looking at the horns, suddenly another small horn appeared among them. Three of the first horns were torn out by the roots to make room for it. This little horn had eyes like human eyes and a mouth that was boasting arrogantly.

⁹ I watched as thrones were put in place
and the Ancient One* sat down to judge.
His clothing was as white as snow,
his hair like purest wool.
He sat on a fiery throne
with wheels of blazing fire,
¹⁰ and a river of fire was pouring out,
flowing from his presence.
Millions of angels ministered to him;
many millions stood to attend him.
Then the court began its session,
and the books were opened.

¹¹I continued to watch because I could hear the little horn's boastful speech. I kept watching until the fourth beast was killed and its body was destroyed by fire. ¹²The other three beasts had their authority taken from them, but they were allowed to live a while longer.*

¹³As my vision continued that night, I saw someone like a son of man* coming with the clouds of heaven. He approached the Ancient One and was led into his presence. ¹⁴He was given authority, honor, and sovereignty over all the nations of the world, so that people of every race and nation and language would obey him. His rule is eternal—it will never end. His kingdom will never be destroyed.

The Vision Is Explained

¹⁵I, Daniel, was troubled by all I had seen, and my visions terrified me. ¹⁶So I approached one of those standing beside the throne and asked him what it all meant. He explained it to me like this: ¹⁷"These four huge beasts represent four kingdoms that will arise from the earth. ¹⁸But in the end, the holy people of the Most High will be given the kingdom, and they will rule forever and ever."

¹⁹Then I wanted to know the true meaning of the fourth beast, the one so different from the others and so terrifying. It had devoured and crushed its victims with iron teeth and bronze claws, trampling their remains beneath its feet. ²⁰I also asked about the ten horns on the fourth beast's head and the little horn that came up afterward and destroyed three of the other horns. This horn had seemed greater than the others, and it had human eyes and a mouth that was boasting arrogantly. ²¹As I watched, this horn was waging war against God's holy people and was defeating them, ²²until the Ancient One—the Most High—came and judged in favor of his holy people. Then the time arrived for the holy people to take over the kingdom.

²³Then he said to me, "This fourth beast is the fourth world power that will rule the earth. It will

---

7:9 Aramaic *an Ancient of Days*; also in 7:13, 22. 7:12 Aramaic *for a season and a time.* 7:13 Or *like a Son of Man.*

7:2 The sea is an image of evil or chaos in the Old Testament (see Psalm 89:10; Isaiah 5:30; 57:20), as it was throughout the ancient Near East. Jesus came proclaiming the Kingdom of God and exercised power to calm the sea (Mark 4:39-41).

7:3-5 The "four huge beasts" represent four empires (7:17; see also Revelation 13:1-2). Nebuchadnezzar and Babylon are represented by the lion with eagles' wings (compare Jeremiah 49:19, 22). The bear, known for its vicious attacks, probably characterizes Persia (see Daniel 2:39; 8:20; compare Proverbs 28:15). The three ribs may refer to Babylon, Media, and Lydia—smaller empires that Cyrus conquered and absorbed into the Persian Empire (Isaiah 41:2-3; 44:28; 45:1, 13; 46:11).

7:6-7 The leopard possessed great speed and agility (see also "cheetahs" in Habakkuk 1:8), and the leopard's four wings and four heads symbolized Alexander the Great's unprecedented military campaign to take over the known world. The fourth beast was different: impersonal, utterly violent, and merciless. Its iron teeth made for a perfect killing machine. Most commentators, both ancient and modern, find this fourth beast most closely embodied in the Roman Empire and its emperors.

7:8 Many interpreters believe Rome represented only part of the fourth kingdom. More brutal than Rome, a final little horn would emerge as a human being with great power and pride (see 8:9-12, 23-25; 9:25-27; 11:36-45; 12:1-7).

7:9-14 Fierce animals represented the world's empires, but the Ancient One (literally, "an Ancient of Days") describes the eternal, holy, and sovereign God. The "son of man" is God's chosen and anointed king—the Messiah, who would usher in God's Kingdom, which fills the earth. The river of fire speaks of God's purifying presence.

Perspective

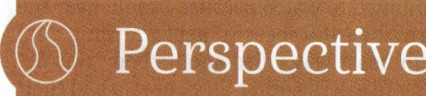

Is God color-blind?

SCRIPTURE CONNECTION: DANIEL 7:13-14

Talking about race may feel tricky, especially in our divided times. Some say that Christians shouldn't talk about race, citing that we are "all the same" in God's sight.

On the one hand, this is true: We are all equals before God—even if the world doesn't always act that way. But this does not mean that God doesn't see skin color. God created people in beautifully different hues, celebrating our unique attributes.

God has authority and sovereignty over the nations, not only that we would obey him (Daniel 7:14), but that we might show his beauty by our diversity, which we see illustrated in other visions of what worship in God's future kingdom will be like, too. God desires robust worship as well. Revelation 7:9 pictures what praising Jesus in his Kingdom will be like: we will all worship as a great multitude from every nation, tribe, people, and language.

VIEWPOINTS

HIS: *I had a dream that the Son of Man was given authority, honor, and sovereignty over all the nations of the world so that people of every race and nation and language would obey him!*
MINE: *"I'm not one to shy away from speaking about race, justice, and diversity. Growth happens in the tension of not knowing all the answers and learning from people who think differently. If Jesus were walking the earth today, I wonder where he'd march, who he'd engage with, and what he'd say. I imagine those conversations would sound nothing like the echo chambers where we find ourselves."*
OURS: *What do you think passages like Daniel 7:14 and Revelation 7:9 reveal about God's heart for people of all races?*

SUSIE GAMEZ, MA, is a teaching pastor at Midtown Covenant Church in Sacramento, CA, and preaches across the country, making the reconciling love of Jesus come alive through the Scriptures.

---

be different from all the others. It will devour the whole world, trampling and crushing everything in its path. [24] Its ten horns are ten kings who will rule that empire. Then another king will arise, different from the other ten, who will subdue three of them. [25] He will defy the Most High and oppress the holy people of the Most High. He will try to change their sacred festivals and laws, and they will be placed under his control for a time, times, and half a time.

[26] "But then the court will pass judgment, and all his power will be taken away and completely destroyed. [27] Then the sovereignty, power, and greatness of all the kingdoms under heaven will be given to the holy people of the Most High. His kingdom will last forever, and all rulers will serve and obey him."

[28] That was the end of the vision. I, Daniel, was terrified by my thoughts and my face was pale with fear, but I kept these things to myself.

Daniel's Vision of a Ram and Goat

8 [1]*During the third year of King Belshazzar's reign, I, Daniel, saw another vision, following the one that had already appeared to me. [2] In this vision I was at the fortress of Susa, in the province of Elam, standing beside the Ulai River.*

[3] As I looked up, I saw a ram with two long horns standing beside the river.* One of the horns was longer than the other, even though it had grown later than the other one. [4] The ram butted everything out of his way to the west, to the north, and to the south, and no one could stand against him or

---

8:1 The original text from this point through chapter 12 is in Hebrew. See note at 2:4. **8:2** Or *the Ulai Gate;* also in 8:16. **8:3** Or *the gate;* also in 8:6.

7:24-25 The number ten most likely symbolizes that the kingdom would last through many kings' reigns (see Revelation 13:1). Then another king, who is the "little horn" (Daniel 7:20-21), would challenge God and oppress the holy people by blaspheming the Lord and threatening them.
7:26-27 God's court would have the power and authority to pass judgment, remove, and destroy the arrogant king. God's Kingdom will rule forever over all the kingdoms under heaven (see Psalm 2:1-12; Isaiah 9:6-7). God's holy people would have authority in his Kingdom (see Luke 22:29-30; 1 Corinthians 6:2-3; Revelation 3:21; 20:4).
8:2 Persian kings traveled among four main residences, taking the royal court and support personnel with them, and the palace complexes and administrative centers of each constituted a "capital" of the Persian Empire. Located in the Zagros Mountain lowlands, Susa was one such capital (see Ezra 4:9; Nehemiah 1:1; Esther 1:2). Inscriptions found there mention fortification, and the excavated archives indicate Susa's administrative and financial significance. Although Daniel's vision took place around a decade before the rise of the Persian Empire, God transported Daniel to Susa in the vision since the Persians' victory over Babylon was imminent.

help his victims. He did as he pleased and became very great.

⁵While I was watching, suddenly a male goat appeared from the west, crossing the land so swiftly that he didn't even touch the ground. This goat, which had one very large horn between its eyes, ⁶headed toward the two-horned ram that I had seen standing beside the river, rushing at him in a rage. ⁷The goat charged furiously at the ram and struck him, breaking off both his horns. Now the ram was helpless, and the goat knocked him down and trampled him. No one could rescue the ram from the goat's power.

⁸The goat became very powerful. But at the height of his power, his large horn was broken off. In the large horn's place grew four prominent horns pointing in the four directions of the earth. ⁹Then from one of the prominent horns came a small horn whose power grew very great. It extended toward the south and the east and toward the glorious land of Israel. ¹⁰Its power reached to the heavens, where it attacked the heavenly army, throwing some of the heavenly beings and some of the stars to the ground and trampling them. ¹¹It even challenged the Commander of heaven's army by canceling the daily sacrifices offered to him and by destroying his Temple. ¹²The army of heaven was restrained from responding to this rebellion. So the daily sacrifice was halted, and truth was overthrown. The horn succeeded in everything it did.*

¹³Then I heard two holy ones talking to each other. One of them asked, "How long will the events of this vision last? How long will the rebellion that causes desecration stop the daily sacrifices? How long will the Temple and heaven's army be trampled on?"

¹⁴The other replied, "It will take 2,300 evenings and mornings; then the Temple will be made right again."

Gabriel Explains the Vision

¹⁵As I, Daniel, was trying to understand the meaning of this vision, someone who looked like a man stood in front of me. ¹⁶And I heard a human voice calling out from the Ulai River, "Gabriel, tell this man the meaning of his vision."

¹⁷As Gabriel approached the place where I was standing, I became so terrified that I fell with my face to the ground. "Son of man," he said, "you must understand that the events you have seen in your vision relate to the time of the end."

¹⁸While he was speaking, I fainted and lay there with my face to the ground. But Gabriel roused me with a touch and helped me to my feet.

¹⁹Then he said, "I am here to tell you what will happen later in the time of wrath. What you have seen pertains to the very end of time. ²⁰The two-horned ram represents the kings of Media and Persia. ²¹The shaggy male goat represents the king of Greece,* and the large horn between his eyes represents the first king of the Greek Empire. ²²The four prominent horns that replaced the one large horn show that the Greek Empire will break into four kingdoms, but none as great as the first.

²³"At the end of their rule, when their sin is at its height, a fierce king, a master of intrigue, will rise to power. ²⁴He will become very strong, but not by his own power. He will cause a shocking amount of destruction and succeed in everything he does. He will destroy powerful leaders and devastate the holy people. ²⁵He will be a master of deception and will become arrogant; he will destroy many without warning. He will even take on the Prince of princes in battle, but he will be broken, though not by human power.

²⁶"This vision about the 2,300 evenings and mornings* is true. But none of these things will happen for a long time, so keep this vision a secret."

8:11-12 The meaning of the Hebrew for these verses is uncertain. 8:21 Hebrew *of Javan*. 8:26 Hebrew *about the evenings and mornings;* compare 8:14.

8:3-4, 20 The lion and the eagle depict Babylon while the ram represents Persia. The two long horns symbolize the Medes and Persians, the Persians being the stronger of the two nations in this empire. God called Cyrus, the king of Persia, to defeat the Babylonians and permit the Jews to return to their land with their sacred vessels (Isaiah 44:28; see 2 Chronicles 36:22-23; Ezra 1:1-3, 5-11; 6:2-5). God used Israel and the other nations to accomplish his purposes.

8:5-8, 21-22 Daniel previously described Greece as a leopard with four heads (7:6). Here, a goat with one horn signifies Greece. The large horn represents the successful conqueror Alexander the Great, and the horn breaking signifies his death. The four sprouting horns symbolize the four successors who would divide Alexander's empire into four kingdoms after his death in 323 BC (see 7:4-6; 11:4). Despite the empire breaking apart, Alexander the Great uniquely unified the nations.

8:9-13, 23-25 The small horn whose power grew great depicts Antiochus IV (ruled 175–164 BC), who took the name "Epiphanes," meaning "the manifest presence [of God]." Because he ruled Syria as a cruel tyrant, many mockingly called him "Epimanes," meaning "madman." Antiochus persecuted the Jewish people and established laws preventing them from practicing their religion. He resolved to unify his kingdom under Greek culture, and some Jews adopted the Greek customs.

8:13-14 The phrase "the rebellion that causes desecration" describes Antiochus's utter disrespect for the Jewish Temple (see 9:27; 11:31; 12:11). Violation of the Temple disturbed Jesus greatly (Matthew 24:15; Mark 13:14). The two holy ones promised the Temple would be restored to its sacred function. However, this would not include physical rebuilding.

8:25 The "Prince of princes" is Jesus Christ, the King of Israel, the ruler of heaven and earth, "the God of gods" (11:36; see 7:9-10, 13-14). Antiochus, just before his death, exalted himself as a god and intended to destroy Jerusalem. Just as Antiochus came to power by supernatural means (8:24), so he would also be destroyed by a power greater than "human power."

²⁷Then I, Daniel, was overcome and lay sick for several days. Afterward I got up and performed my duties for the king, but I was greatly troubled by the vision and could not understand it.

Daniel's Prayer for His People

9 It was the first year of the reign of Darius the Mede, the son of Ahasuerus, who became king of the Babylonians.* ²During the first year of his reign, I, Daniel, learned from reading the word of the LORD, as revealed to Jeremiah the prophet, that Jerusalem must lie desolate for seventy years.* ³So I turned to the Lord God and pleaded with him in prayer and fasting. I also wore rough burlap and sprinkled myself with ashes.

⁴I prayed to the LORD my God and confessed:

"O Lord, you are a great and awesome God! You always fulfill your covenant and keep your promises of unfailing love to those who love you and obey your commands. ⁵But we have sinned and done wrong. We have rebelled against you and scorned your commands and regulations. ⁶We have refused to listen to your servants the prophets, who spoke on your authority to our kings and princes and ancestors and to all the people of the land.

⁷"Lord, you are in the right; but as you see, our faces are covered with shame. This is true of all of us, including the people of Judah and Jerusalem and all Israel, scattered near and far, wherever you have driven us because of our disloyalty to you. ⁸O LORD, we and our kings, princes, and ancestors are covered with shame because we have sinned against you. ⁹But the Lord our God is merciful and forgiving, even though we have rebelled against him. ¹⁰We have not obeyed the LORD our God, for we have not followed the instructions he gave us through his servants the prophets. ¹¹All Israel has disobeyed your instruction and turned away, refusing to listen to your voice.

"So now the solemn curses and judgments written in the Law of Moses, the servant of God, have been poured down on us because of our sin. ¹²You have kept your word and done to us and our rulers exactly as you warned. Never has there been such a disaster as happened in Jerusalem. ¹³Every curse written against us in the Law of Moses has come true. Yet we have refused to seek mercy from the LORD our God by turning from our sins and recognizing his truth. ¹⁴Therefore, the LORD has brought upon us the disaster he prepared. The LORD our God was right to do all of these things, for we did not obey him.

¹⁵"O Lord our God, you brought lasting honor to your name by rescuing your people from Egypt in a great display of power. But we have sinned and are full of wickedness. ¹⁶In view of all your faithful mercies, Lord, please turn your furious anger away from your city Jerusalem, your holy mountain. All the neighboring nations mock Jerusalem and your people because of our sins and the sins of our ancestors.

¹⁷"O our God, hear your servant's prayer! Listen as I plead. For your own sake, Lord, smile again on your desolate sanctuary. ¹⁸O my God, lean down and listen to me. Open your eyes and see our despair. See how your city—the city that bears your name—lies in ruins. We make this plea, not because we deserve help, but because of your mercy. ¹⁹O Lord, hear. O Lord, forgive. O Lord, listen and act! For your own sake, do not delay, O my God, for your people and your city bear your name."

Gabriel's Message about the Anointed One

²⁰I went on praying and confessing my sin and the sin of my people, pleading with the LORD my God for Jerusalem, his holy mountain. ²¹As I was praying,

---

9:1 Or *the Chaldeans.* 9:2 See Jer 25:11-12; 29:10.

8:27 Daniel's experience left him overwhelmed and physically ill, and he sought God for an understanding of the vision. Daniel carried a burden for God's people. Once he had recovered, Daniel returned to his royal service but did not disclose to anyone what God had revealed to him.

9:1-2 Daniel retained and read the Word of the Lord through Jeremiah over and over. Jeremiah had prophesied about the Exile Daniel was now living through. With each reading, God showed Daniel a vital part of his plan. God uses people—like Jeremiah, Daniel, and us—to fulfill his plan and purposes.

9:3-4 Daniel was not afraid to turn to God in repentance for how the Israelites had treated God. Compassionate, patient, and forgiving, God had saved and shown compassion to the Israelites, who had been enslaved in Egypt. Daniel trusted that God would show his unfailing love to them in Exile too (see Exodus 34:5-7; Leviticus 26:40-42; Deuteronomy 7:9; 27-28).

9:15-19 Daniel appealed to God's mercy for the restoration of God's reputation among the nations (9:18; see Deuteronomy 4:31; 13:17; 30:3). After Daniel prayed, Cyrus the Great issued a decree allowing the exiles to return to Judah (Ezra 1:1-4). In response to prayers—such as Daniel's here—God returned them from exile.

9:20-27 God sent his messenger, Gabriel, in response to Daniel's prayer. Gabriel described six specific purposes God would accomplish for the Jews. God's first three purposes would put an end to Israel's national wrongdoings against God and allow them to return to their land. The remaining three purposes focused on restoring God's perfect order and the future Messiah's just reign (Isaiah 4:2-6; Jeremiah 23:5-6; 31:31-34). God would accomplish this through Jesus' death on the cross and resurrection (Isaiah 53:8; John 1:29; 11:44-52; 1 John 2:2; Revelation 5:9; 7:9).

Gabriel, whom I had seen in the earlier vision, came swiftly to me at the time of the evening sacrifice. ²²He explained to me, "Daniel, I have come here to give you insight and understanding. ²³The moment you began praying, a command was given. And now I am here to tell you what it was, for you are very precious to God. Listen carefully so that you can understand the meaning of your vision.

²⁴"A period of seventy sets of seven* has been decreed for your people and your holy city to finish their rebellion, to put an end to their sin, to atone for their guilt, to bring in everlasting righteousness, to confirm the prophetic vision, and to anoint the Most Holy Place.* ²⁵Now listen and understand! Seven sets of seven plus sixty-two sets of seven* will pass from the time the command is given to rebuild Jerusalem until a ruler—the Anointed One*—comes. Jerusalem will be rebuilt with streets and strong defenses,* despite the perilous times.

²⁶"After this period of sixty-two sets of seven,* the Anointed One will be killed, appearing to have accomplished nothing, and a ruler will arise whose armies will destroy the city and the Temple. The end will come with a flood, and war and its miseries are decreed from that time to the very end. ²⁷The ruler will make a treaty with the people for a period of one set of seven,* but after half this time, he will put an end to the sacrifices and offerings. And as a climax to all his terrible deeds,* he will set up a sacrilegious object that causes desecration,* until the fate decreed for this defiler is finally poured out on him."

Daniel's Vision of a Messenger

10 In the third year of the reign of King Cyrus of Persia,* Daniel (also known as Belteshazzar) had another vision. He understood that the vision concerned events certain to happen in the future—times of war and great hardship.

²When this vision came to me, I, Daniel, had been in mourning for three whole weeks. ³All that time I had eaten no rich food. No meat or wine crossed my lips, and I used no fragrant lotions until those three weeks had passed.

⁴On April 23,* as I was standing on the bank of the great Tigris River, ⁵I looked up and saw a man dressed in linen clothing, with a belt of pure gold around his waist. ⁶His body looked like a precious gem. His face flashed like lightning, and his eyes flamed like torches. His arms and feet shone like polished bronze, and his voice roared like a vast multitude of people.

⁷Only I, Daniel, saw this vision. The men with me saw nothing, but they were suddenly terrified and ran away to hide. ⁸So I was left there all alone to see this amazing vision. My strength left me, my face grew deathly pale, and I felt very weak. ⁹Then I heard the man speak, and when I heard the sound of his voice, I fainted and lay there with my face to the ground.

¹⁰Just then a hand touched me and lifted me, still trembling, to my hands and knees. ¹¹And the man said to me, "Daniel, you are very precious to God, so listen carefully to what I have to say to you. Stand up, for I have been sent to you." When he said this to me, I stood up, still trembling.

9:24a Hebrew *seventy sevens.* **9:24b** Or *the Most Holy One.* **9:25a** Hebrew *Seven sevens plus sixty-two sevens.* **9:25b** Or *an anointed one;* similarly in 9:26. Hebrew reads *a messiah.* **9:25c** Or *and a moat,* or *and trenches.* **9:26** Hebrew *After sixty-two sevens.* **9:27a** Hebrew *for one seven.* **9:27b** Hebrew *And on the wing;* the meaning of the Hebrew is uncertain. **9:27c** Hebrew *an abomination of desolation.* **10:1** The third year of Cyrus's reign was 536 B.C. **10:4** Hebrew *On the twenty-fourth day of the first month,* of the ancient Hebrew lunar calendar. This date in the book of Daniel can be cross-checked with dates in surviving Persian records and can be related accurately to our modern calendar. This event occurred on April 23, 536 B.C.

9:24 The "period of seventy sets of seven" equates to 490 years. It generally refers to the time from the Jews' return to Jerusalem to rebuild the Temple until the time of "the Anointed One" (9:25).

9:25-26 Cyrus issued a decree in 538 BC allowing the Jews to return to Jerusalem to begin to rebuild the city. Daniel's vision included these events (9:24-27; see 5:31; 9:1; Ezra 1:2-4). The Jewish people completed the temple in 515 BC (Ezra 3:1–6:22), and in 445 BC, Nehemiah finished the wall around Jerusalem. Christians believe that Jesus is the Messiah—"the Anointed One"—that Daniel foresaw in this passage.

10:1-3 Daniel mourned for two reasons. First, he had probably heard that his Jewish brothers and sisters experienced hardship as they rebuilt the Temple. The Temple's slow rebuilding process served as a reminder that time belongs to God, who is never late in accomplishing his will. Second, Daniel's fast shows us that he was seeking a greater understanding of the visions God had given him.

10:4 One detail is certain from this passage: Daniel's visit with the angel occurred on April 23, 536 BC. Specific dating is unusual in the Bible and demonstrates importance. This visit follows a three-week mourning period, during which Daniel abstained from fine foods and comforts like fragrant lotions. The angel came in response to his prayers having been heard (10:12).

10:5-9 At least one supernatural being dressed in clothes similar to a priest's clothing came in dazzling brightness and awesome splendor. No wonder Daniel's friends were terrified and left and Daniel collapsed. Daniel's physical reaction to the angel was natural. Typically, when angels appear in the Bible, fear and dread come over people. An angel's first words were usually, "Don't be afraid" (see also Joshua 5:13-15; Isaiah 6:1-5; Luke 1:13, 30; 2:10; Acts 9:7-9; Revelation 1:17).

10:10-19 This was Daniel's third time being visited by an angel and the second time an angel had physically touched him (see 8:18; 9:21). The angel gave Daniel the strength to come to consciousness and helped him up so he could hear the angel's message.

DANIEL 11

¹²Then he said, "Don't be afraid, Daniel. Since the first day you began to pray for understanding and to humble yourself before your God, your request has been heard in heaven. I have come in answer to your prayer. ¹³But for twenty-one days the spirit prince* of the kingdom of Persia blocked my way. Then Michael, one of the archangels,* came to help me, and I left him there with the spirit prince of the kingdom of Persia.* ¹⁴Now I am here to explain what will happen to your people in the future, for this vision concerns a time yet to come."

¹⁵While he was speaking to me, I looked down at the ground, unable to say a word. ¹⁶Then the one who looked like a man* touched my lips, and I opened my mouth and began to speak. I said to the one standing in front of me, "I am filled with anguish because of the vision I have seen, my lord, and I am very weak. ¹⁷How can someone like me, your servant, talk to you, my lord? My strength is gone, and I can hardly breathe."

¹⁸Then the one who looked like a man touched me again, and I felt my strength returning. ¹⁹"Don't be afraid," he said, "for you are very precious to God. Peace! Be encouraged! Be strong!"

As he spoke these words to me, I suddenly felt stronger and said to him, "Please speak to me, my lord, for you have strengthened me."

²⁰He replied, "Do you know why I have come? Soon I must return to fight against the spirit prince of the kingdom of Persia, and after that the spirit prince of the kingdom of Greece* will come. ²¹Meanwhile, I will tell you what is written in the Book of Truth. (No one helps me against these spirit princes except Michael, your spirit prince.* ¹¹:¹I have been standing beside Michael* to support and strengthen him since the first year of the reign of Darius the Mede.)

Kings of the South and North

11 ²"Now then, I will reveal the truth to you. Three more Persian kings will reign, to be succeeded by a fourth, far richer than the others. He will use his wealth to stir up everyone to fight against the kingdom of Greece.*

³"Then a mighty king will rise to power who will rule with great authority and accomplish everything he sets out to do. ⁴But at the height of his power, his kingdom will be broken apart and divided into four parts. It will not be ruled by the king's descendants, nor will the kingdom hold the authority it once had. For his empire will be uprooted and given to others.

⁵"The king of the south will increase in power, but one of his own officials will become more powerful than he and will rule his kingdom with great strength.

⁶"Some years later an alliance will be formed between the king of the north and the king of the south. The daughter of the king of the south will be given in marriage to the king of the north to secure the alliance, but she will lose her influence over him, and so will her father. She will be abandoned along with her supporters. ⁷But when one of her relatives* becomes king of the south, he will raise an army and enter the fortress of the king of the north and defeat him. ⁸When he returns to Egypt, he will carry back their idols with him, along with priceless articles of gold and silver. For

---

10:13a Hebrew *the prince;* also in 10:13c, 20. **10:13b** Hebrew *the chief princes.* **10:13c** As in one Greek version; Hebrew reads *and I was left there with the kings of Persia.* The meaning of the Hebrew is uncertain. **10:16** As in most manuscripts of the Masoretic Text; one manuscript of the Masoretic Text and one Greek version read *Then something that looked like a human hand.* **10:20** Hebrew *of Javan.* **10:21** Hebrew *against these except Michael, your prince.* **11:1** Hebrew *him.* **11:2** Hebrew *of Javan.* **11:7** Hebrew *a branch from her roots.*

10:12-14 In his vision, Daniel heard about a spiritual war taking place between the evil forces and God. Some spiritual beings supported evil, while others assisted God.

11:2–12:7 Daniel's next vision describes various rulers who came to power, events that correspond to real people and their lives. God brought about these events that Daniel foretold. These rulers and their actions are now part of world history (11:1-35). Daniel's final vision addresses what would happen to Israel in the last days (11:36–12:13).

11:2 The four Persian kings who would rule in the future were Cambyses II (529–522 BC), Gaumāta (522 BC, a usurper), Darius the Great (522–486 BC), and Xerxes I (486–465 BC). Xerxes ruled an empire that reached from modern Ethiopia in the south to modern India in the east but failed to conquer Greece in the west.

11:3 Alexander the Great was the "mighty king." As part of God's sovereign plan, Alexander conquered much of the known world in thirteen years. The most far-flung reaches of the Persian Empire surrendered to him in 332 BC. When he died in 323 BC, Alexander's empire stretched as far north and west as Greece, modern India in the east, and Egypt in the south.

11:5-20 Daniel's vision concerned the battles that resulted between "the south" (Egypt) and "the north" (Syria). Their conflict impacted the small nation of Israel, which lay between the two superpowers. We know about these battles today from 1–3 Maccabees and the writings of Herodotus, Livy, Polybius, Porphyry, and Josephus who also recorded the historical events.

11:5-8 The first "king of the south" (Egypt) was Ptolemy I Soter, who was a former general of Alexander the Great and ruled from 323–285 BC. Following Alexander's death, Ptolemy and his dynasty controlled Palestine, including Judea. After a bitter war (259–255 BC), the Ptolemy family formed an alliance by Berenice marrying Antiochus II Theos of Syria. In the civil war following Antiochus's death, Berenice was murdered, prompting her brother to invade Syria and occupy Palestine.

some years afterward he will leave the king of the north alone.

⁹"Later the king of the north will invade the realm of the king of the south but will soon return to his own land. ¹⁰However, the sons of the king of the north will assemble a mighty army that will advance like a flood and carry the battle as far as the enemy's fortress.

¹¹"Then, in a rage, the king of the south will rally against the vast forces assembled by the king of the north and will defeat them. ¹²After the enemy army is swept away, the king of the south will be filled with pride and will execute many thousands of his enemies. But his success will be short lived.

¹³"A few years later the king of the north will return with a fully equipped army far greater than before. ¹⁴At that time there will be a general uprising against the king of the south. Violent men among your own people will join them in fulfillment of this vision, but they will not succeed. ¹⁵Then the king of the north will come and lay siege to a fortified city and capture it. The best troops of the south will not be able to stand in the face of the onslaught.

¹⁶"The king of the north will march onward unopposed; none will be able to stop him. He will pause in the glorious land of Israel,* intent on destroying it. ¹⁷He will make plans to come with the might of his entire kingdom and will form an alliance with the king of the south. He will give him a daughter in marriage in order to overthrow the kingdom from within, but his plan will fail.

¹⁸"After this, he will turn his attention to the coastland and conquer many cities. But a commander from another land will put an end to his insolence and cause him to retreat in shame. ¹⁹He will take refuge in his own fortresses but will stumble and fall and be seen no more.

²⁰"His successor will send out a tax collector to maintain the royal splendor. But after a very brief reign, he will die, though not from anger or in battle.

²¹"The next to come to power will be a despicable man who is not in line for royal succession. He will slip in when least expected and take over the kingdom by flattery and intrigue. ²²Before him great armies will be swept away, including a covenant prince. ²³With deceitful promises, he will make various alliances. He will become strong despite having only a handful of followers. ²⁴Without warning he will enter the richest areas of the land. Then he will distribute among his followers the plunder and wealth of the rich—something his predecessors had never done. He will plot the overthrow of strongholds, but this will last for only a short while.

²⁵"Then he will stir up his courage and raise a great army against the king of the south. The king of the south will go to battle with a mighty army, but to no avail, for there will be plots against him. ²⁶His own household will cause his downfall. His army will be swept away, and many will be killed. ²⁷Seeking nothing but each other's harm, these kings will plot against each other at the conference table, attempting to deceive each other. But it will make no difference, for the end will come at the appointed time.

²⁸"The king of the north will then return home with great riches. On the way he will set himself against the people of the holy covenant, doing much damage before continuing his journey.

²⁹"Then at the appointed time he will once again invade the south, but this time the result will be different. ³⁰For warships from western coastlands* will scare him off, and he will withdraw and return home. But he will vent his anger against the people of the holy covenant and reward those who forsake the covenant.

³¹"His army will take over the Temple fortress, pollute the sanctuary, put a stop to the daily sacrifices, and set up the sacrilegious object that causes desecration.* ³²He will flatter and win over those who have violated the covenant. But the people who know their God will be strong and will resist him.

³³"Wise leaders will give instruction to many, but these teachers will die by fire and sword, or they will be jailed and robbed. ³⁴During these persecutions, little help will arrive, and many who join them will not be sincere. ³⁵And some of the wise will fall victim to persecution. In this way, they will be refined and cleansed and made pure until the

---

11:16 Hebrew *the glorious land.* 11:30 Hebrew *from Kittim.* 11:31 Hebrew *the abomination of desolation.*

11:9-20 Eventually, Antiochus III attacked and defeated Ptolemy IV in 198 BC. Antiochus III had been conquering lands to the north and east, from which he raised "a fully equipped army far greater than before." The Ptolemy family of Egypt and the ruling family of Syria would continue to battle for power back and forth; at times, rebel groups, traitors, and allies would defeat one empire from the inside, and power would shift.

11:21-35 Antiochus IV Epiphanes (ruled 175–164 BC) came to power next (see 8:9-13, 23-25). He seized the throne after his brother, the king of the Syrian Empire, was murdered. Mid-December 167, Antiochus desecrated the Temple in Jerusalem. He would go on to install an altar to the Greek god Zeus and sacrifice a pig (an unclean animal according to the law of Moses). When he outlawed worshiping Yahweh, the Jewish people had a choice: Obey God and live by faith or follow Antiochus's policy and desert God. The Jewish people revolted, led by Judas Maccabeus. This revolt gained the Jewish people semi-autonomy for one hundred years, during which they were led by the descendants of the Maccabees.

time of the end, for the appointed time is still to come. ³⁶"The king will do as he pleases, exalting himself and claiming to be greater than every god, even blaspheming the God of gods. He will succeed, but only until the time of wrath is completed. For what has been determined will surely take place. ³⁷He will have no respect for the gods of his ancestors, or for the god loved by women, or for any other god, for he will boast that he is greater than them all. ³⁸Instead of these, he will worship the god of fortresses—a god his ancestors never knew—and lavish on him gold, silver, precious stones, and expensive gifts. ³⁹Claiming this foreign god's help, he will attack the strongest fortresses. He will honor those who submit to him, appointing them to positions of authority and dividing the land among them as their reward.*

⁴⁰"Then at the time of the end, the king of the south will attack the king of the north. The king of the north will storm out with chariots, charioteers, and a vast navy. He will invade various lands and sweep through them like a flood. ⁴¹He will enter the glorious land of Israel,* and many nations will fall, but Moab, Edom, and the best part of Ammon will escape. ⁴²He will conquer many countries, and even Egypt will not escape. ⁴³He will gain control over the gold, silver, and treasures of Egypt, and the Libyans and Ethiopians* will be his servants.

⁴⁴"But then news from the east and the north will alarm him, and he will set out in great anger to destroy and obliterate many. ⁴⁵He will stop between the glorious holy mountain and the sea and will pitch his royal tents. But while he is there, his time will suddenly run out, and no one will help him.

The Time of the End

12 "At that time Michael, the archangel* who stands guard over your nation, will arise. Then there will be a time of anguish greater than any since nations first came into existence. But at that time every one of your people whose name is written in the book will be rescued. ²Many of those whose bodies lie dead and buried will rise up, some to everlasting life and some to shame and everlasting disgrace. ³Those who are wise will shine as bright as the sky, and those who lead many to righteousness will shine like the stars forever. ⁴But you, Daniel, keep this prophecy a secret; seal up the book until the time of the end, when many will rush here and there, and knowledge will increase."

⁵Then I, Daniel, looked and saw two others standing on opposite banks of the river. ⁶One of them asked the man dressed in linen, who was now standing above the river, "How long will it be until these shocking events are over?"

⁷The man dressed in linen, who was standing above the river, raised both his hands toward heaven and took a solemn oath by the One who lives forever, saying, "It will go on for a time, times, and half a time. When the shattering of the holy people has finally come to an end, all these things will have happened."

⁸I heard what he said, but I did not understand what he meant. So I asked, "How will all this finally end, my lord?"

⁹But he said, "Go now, Daniel, for what I have said is kept secret and sealed until the time of the end. ¹⁰Many will be purified, cleansed, and refined by these trials. But the wicked will continue in their wickedness, and none of them will understand. Only those who are wise will know what it means.

¹¹"From the time the daily sacrifice is stopped

11:39 Or *at a price.*   **11:41** Hebrew *the glorious land.*   **11:43** Hebrew *Cushites.*   **12:1** Hebrew *the great prince.*

11:36–12:13 Daniel's vision shifts to a prediction about the last days. Daniel records an attack of an evil ruler (11:36-39), a battle (11:40-45), times of suffering (12:1), the dead rising (12:2), and the Kingdom of God coming into fullness (12:3).

11:36-39 The evil ruler would have no religious faith but would selfishly exalt himself as a god. He would replace "the gods of his ancestors" with "the god of fortresses" (see 11:31). The evil ruler would envision a world in which he had absolute power and control, and everyone would worship him alone.

11:40–12:1 At the end of time, the king of the north would move into the land of Israel. He would conquer many surrounding nations, but the Jewish people would be protected by Michael, an angel assigned by God. God will take all measures necessary to keep his covenant with Abraham and secure his blessed people in the land.

12:2 The image here is of dead bodies buried in the ground. Like planted seeds, they grow into thriving plants (see 1 Corinthians 15:35-57).

12:3 God will distinguish every person who models and teaches God's right living to others. They will shine as bright as the sky for all eternity. How we live and serve God will determine the rewards God gives us. God recognizes the cost to proclaim him in a world wrought with evil. He promises to share his glory with those who lead others in the right way. For them, eternity will be beyond compare.

12:4 To "seal up the book" did not mean to hide it away. The seal indicated that the world would not comprehend the whole meaning of what Daniel had written until the last days. There are parallel injunctions in some Akkadian literature and other apocalyptic stories to keep those stories secret, but the implication is that they should be kept safe and shared with wise people who would understand the meaning.

12:8-10 In the end times, trials will come to make believers wiser and more virtuous. At the same time, those inclined to evil will become more wicked (2 Timothy 3:13). God will allow those who do not believe in him to continue acting on improper thoughts (Romans 1:28). When times are dark, God's Word will illuminate our hearts and minds to his ways and set us back on the path of light.

and the sacrilegious object that causes desecration* is set up to be worshiped, there will be 1,290 days. ¹²And blessed are those who wait and remain until the end of the 1,335 days!

¹³"As for you, go your way until the end. You will rest, and then at the end of the days, you will rise again to receive the inheritance set aside for you."

12:11 Hebrew *the abomination of desolation.*

12:12-13 Daniel's question about how everything will end was not answered (12:8). God gave Daniel the wisdom he needed to carry out God's purposes during his lifetime. God knows precisely how much we need to know and how much truth we can understand. God tells his followers to hold on to his promises and be open to how he will fulfill them through our lives.

12:13 Daniel died before all the events of his visions came to pass, but he knew that he would rise again! Here, "the end of the days" refers to when the dead will rise and God will establish his everlasting Kingdom (12:1-3).

Insight — LIVING IN A PROPHETIC TIME

God's prophets brought his message to his people, urging them to turn from sin, honor God, and deal justly with one another—or else face exile from their land. Though exile eventually came, the prophets also foresaw hope for the future. God's people would return to their land, and one day, God would send an anointed messenger (the Messiah) to restore them. When reading the prophets, it can be confusing to follow. This chart shows when each prophet ministered in relation to the events they prophesied about. Understanding how each prophet fits into the timeline shows us how God works his plans over time.

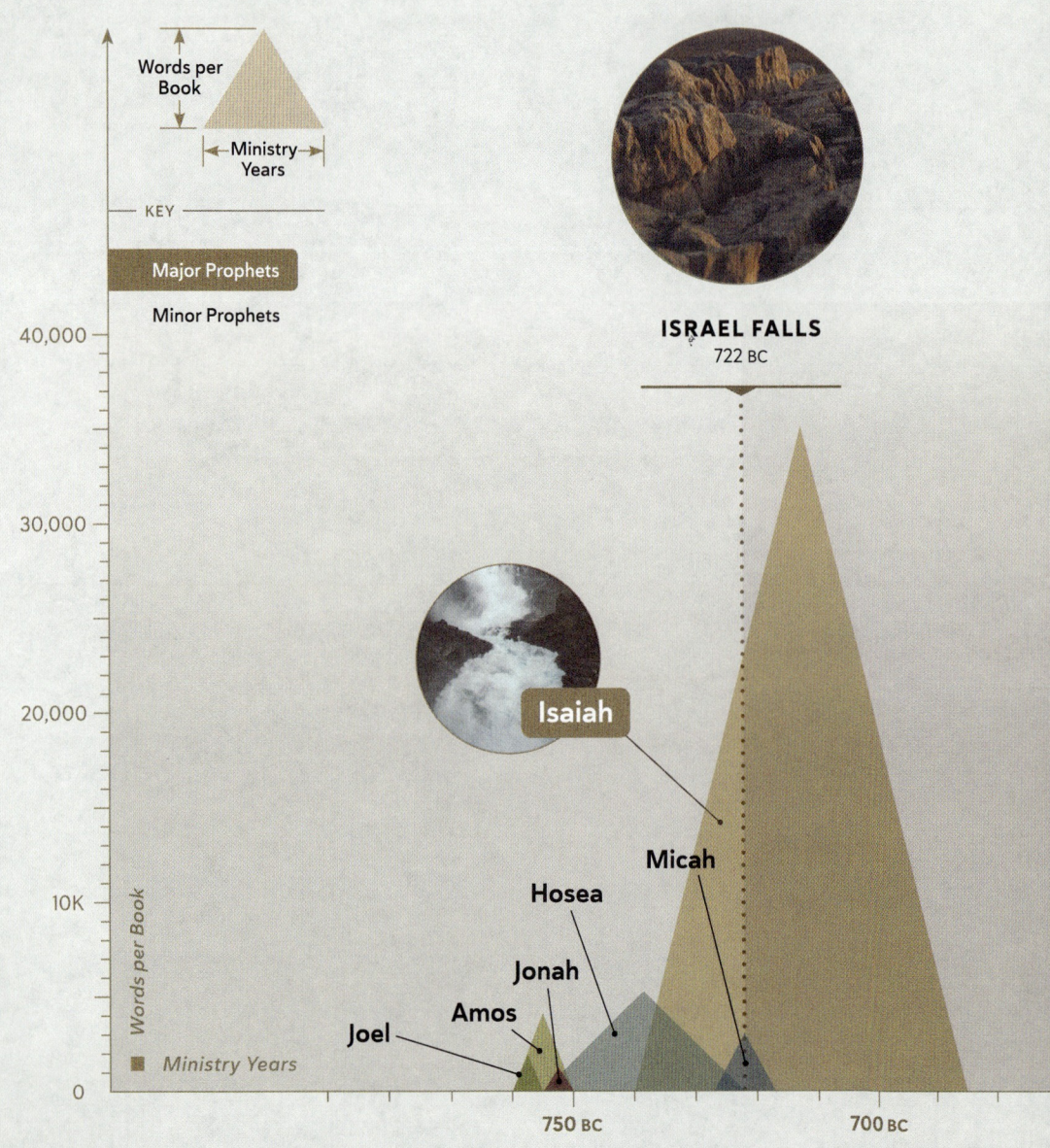

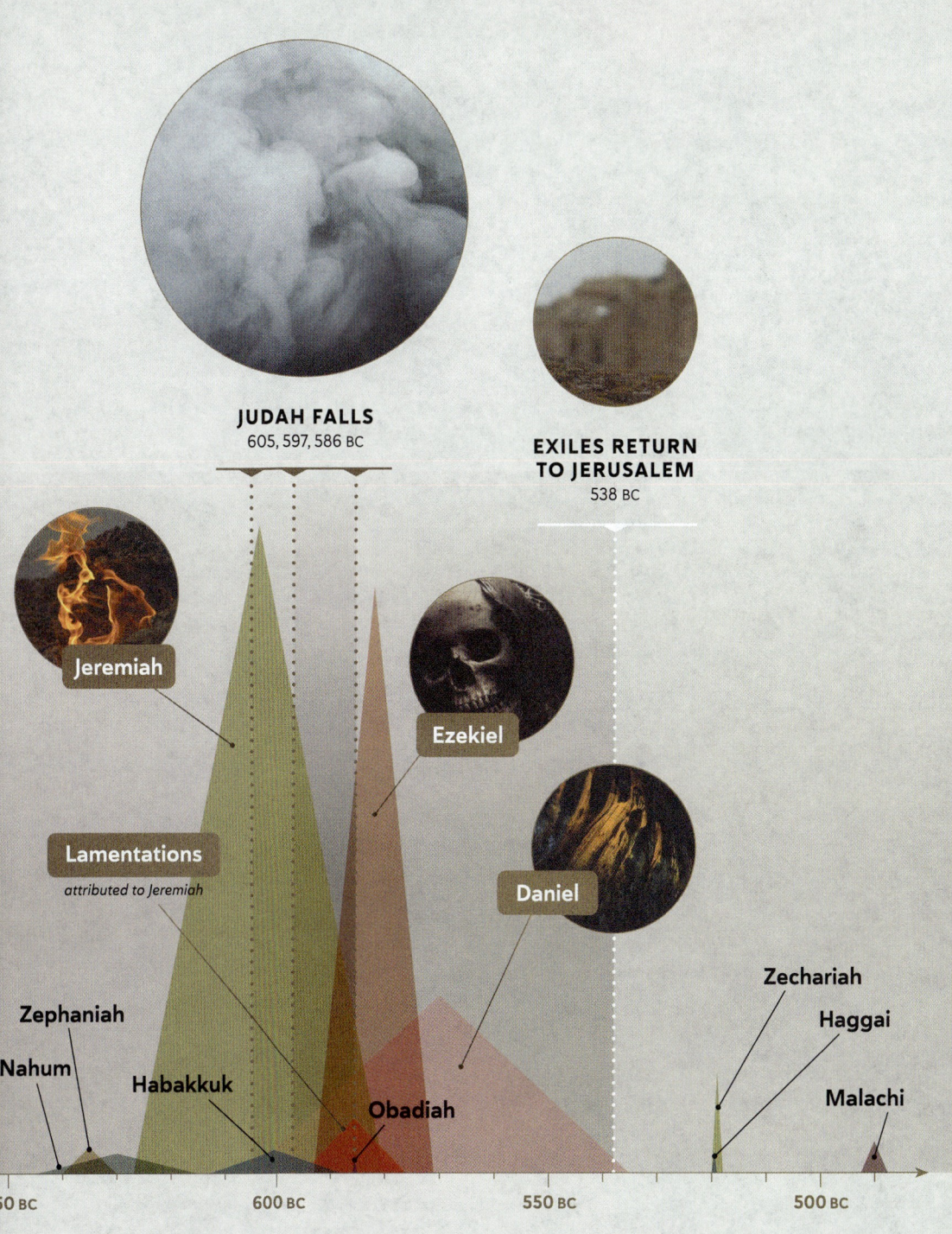

Hosea

WHAT DO WE LEARN ABOUT GOD'S MISSION AND OURS?
Motivated by faithful love, God pursues us and turns our hearts back to him.

WHO WROTE IT? Hosea.

WHEN DID IT HAPPEN? Hosea ministered in the northern kingdom from 753 to 715 BC, until its destruction by the Assyrians in 722 BC.

HOW IS IT ORGANIZED?

- **1–3:** God calls Hosea to marry Gomer, an unfaithful wife, perhaps even a prostitute, as a message about Israel's unfaithfulness
- **4–10:** God warns Israel about their future destruction at the hands of Assyria
- **11–14:** Because of God's faithful love, Israel will ultimately be restored

FEATURE HIGHLIGHTS

+ *Gomer: Wandering Yet Wanted* (1059)
+ *Unfaithful: Faithful* (1065)

Words to Remember are highlighted throughout this book

Timeline (BC)

BC	Event
793	JEROBOAM II BECOMES KING OF ISRAEL
760	AMOS BECOMES A PROPHET
753	HOSEA BECOMES A PROPHET; KING ZECHARIAH OF ISRAEL IS KILLED
752	KING SHALLUM OF ISRAEL IS KILLED
743	TIGLATH-PILESER III INVADES ISRAEL
742	MICAH BECOMES A PROPHET TO JUDAH
740	ISAIAH BECOMES A PROPHET TO JUDAH
722	ISRAEL (THE NORTHERN KINGDOM) FALLS
715	HOSEA'S MINISTRY ENDS

HOW LONG DOES IT TAKE TO READ?

| :30 | 1:00 | 1:30 | 2:00 | 2:30 | 3:00 | 3:30 |

¹ The LORD gave this message to Hosea son of Beeri during the years when Uzziah, Jotham, Ahaz, and Hezekiah were kings of Judah, and Jeroboam son of Jehoash* was king of Israel.

Hosea's Wife and Children

²When the LORD first began speaking to Israel through Hosea, he said to him, "Go and marry a prostitute,* so that some of her children will be conceived in prostitution. This will illustrate how Israel has acted like a prostitute by turning against the LORD and worshiping other gods."

³So Hosea married Gomer, the daughter of Diblaim, and she became pregnant and gave Hosea a son. ⁴And the LORD said, "Name the child Jezreel, for I am about to punish King Jehu's dynasty to avenge the murders he committed at Jezreel. In fact, I will bring an end to Israel's independence. ⁵I will break its military power in the Jezreel Valley."

⁶Soon Gomer became pregnant again and gave birth to a daughter. And the LORD said to Hosea, "Name your daughter Lo-ruhamah—'Not loved'— for I will no longer show love to the people of Israel or forgive them. ⁷But I will show love to the people of Judah. I will free them from their enemies—not with weapons and armies or horses and chariots, but by my power as the LORD their God."

⁸After Gomer had weaned Lo-ruhamah, she again became pregnant and gave birth to a second son. ⁹And the LORD said, "Name him Lo-ammi—'Not my people'—for Israel is not my people, and I am not their God.

¹⁰*"Yet the time will come when Israel's people will be like the sands of the seashore—too many to count! Then, at the place where they were told, 'You are not my people,' it will be said, 'You are children of the living God.' ¹¹Then the people of Judah and Israel will unite together. They will choose one leader for themselves, and they will return from exile together. What a day that will be—the day of Jezreel*—when God will again plant his people in his land.

²:¹*"In that day you will call your brothers Ammi—'My people.' And you will call your sisters Ruhamah—'The ones I love.'

Charges against an Unfaithful Wife

2 ²"But now bring charges against Israel—your mother—
for she is no longer my wife,
and I am no longer her husband.
Tell her to remove the prostitute's makeup from her face
and the clothing that exposes her breasts.
³ Otherwise, I will strip her as naked
as she was on the day she was born.
I will leave her to die of thirst,
as in a dry and barren wilderness.
⁴ And I will not love her children,
for they were conceived in prostitution.
⁵ Their mother is a shameless prostitute
and became pregnant in a shameful way.
She said, 'I'll run after other lovers
and sell myself to them for food and water,

1:1 Hebrew *Joash,* a variant spelling of Jehoash. 1:2 Or *a promiscuous woman.* 1:10 Verses 1:10-11 are numbered 2:1-2 in Hebrew text. 1:11 *Jezreel* means "God plants." 2:1 Verses 2:1-23 are numbered 2:3-25 in Hebrew text.

1:2-3 Some interpreters have found it impossible to believe that God would command a prophet to marry a prostitute. As a result, there is a long tradition of interpreting this passage symbolically. Many early church leaders believed this passage was an allegory where Hosea represented the Lord and Gomer represented Israel. Today, most interpreters regard the marriage as having been real, but they differ in their ideas about Gomer's occupation prior to the marriage. Some suggest that Gomer was truly a prostitute. Another possibility is that Gomer was "a promiscuous woman" (see text note on 1:2) in the sense of worshiping other gods, as most of Israel was guilty of prostituting themselves to idols.
1:6 In their rebellion against God, Israel's heart grew hard. To get their attention, God commanded his prophet to marry a prostitute and required that he give their children shocking names. Similar to other prophets who performed sign acts, Hosea's life enacted his message from God to Israel. We do not know what personal impact the name *Lo-ruhamah* ("Not loved") had on Hosea's daughter, but it was part of God's larger plan to expose the effects of Israel's idolatry in the hope the people would repent. In 2:1, God reversed the name. He will once again know his people as "Ruhamah—'The ones I love.'"
1:9 The name *Lo-ammi* carried the harshest judgment of all, because it seemed to announce the end of Israel's covenant relationship with the Lord. The cherished title "my people"— bestowed upon Israel when they lived obediently in covenant with the Lord their God (Leviticus 26:12; see also Exodus 6:7)— was now withdrawn due to their repeated unfaithfulness. The Hebrew behind "I am not their God" can be translated "I am not 'I AM' for you" (compare to Exodus 3:14). The third child's name prophetically announces that the Israelites stood outside the covenant and were no longer privileged to call upon the I AM.
1:10 The phrase, "You are children of the living God," does not appear anywhere else in the Old Testament. However, the parent-child relationship between God and his people is a prominent biblical theme (Exodus 4:23; Jeremiah 31:20; compare Isaiah 63:16-17; 64:8-9). The New Testament defines God's children as all who have faith in Jesus Christ (Galatians 3:16, 26-29; 1 John 3:1).
2:2-13 God's response may seem harsh, but the seriousness of Israel's offense required it. Israel had been consistently unfaithful to God, despite his abundant love and provision for them for centuries. They had also been warned about the consequences of their wayward behavior (Leviticus 26:14-45; Deuteronomy 28:15-68). The Lord was not an abusive husband seeking revenge. He put obstacles between the people of Israel and their "lovers," the "images of Baal," because idolatry is deadly. God's goal was the restoration of his beloved bride, Israel (see Hosea 2:14-16).

Gomer

IDENTITY — Wandering Yet Wanted

Gomer remembers...
I know deep down I'm not doing the right thing. I am fully aware of my actions and I feel guilty. I know I need to change, or there will be consequences: for me, personally—maybe something I'll have to live with forever—and for my family, as they share my disgrace and others judge *them* because of *me*.

What it comes down to is that I've been chasing fixes and happiness, chasing what feels good in the moment, chasing pleasure. I get it. I know what I'm doing.

I run into sin, forgetting the *only* one who can truly satisfy me. I pursue experiences and feelings only to find myself empty and wanting. Then, eventually, I want out, but I am afraid. Will God receive me this time? Will he punish me?

The crazy thing is, he *does* receive me. And not only receive, but he also *pursues* me and *welcomes* me. No matter what, he is there, ready to pick up our relationship right where I left him.

He removes the heart-stain of my distance and all that I've done. He holds me close and gives me peace, the peace I was looking for when I was chasing the world—only *better*.

He makes everything right and in its place again. And when I feel that rightness, all I can do is lean in and make him my heart's home.

GOMER'S STORY IS TOLD IN HOSEA 1; 3.

> God removes the heart-stain of my distance and all that I've done. He holds me.

IDENTIFY

Have you found yourself chasing empty, sinful fixes? If you are there now, would you pause and listen for the voice of the God who loves you and wants to bring you back to himself?

"More than once, I've found myself wandering after a poor choice, even when I knew there would be negative repercussions. Thankfully, God pursues and extravagantly loves me through it!"

EMILY SARMIENTO is a wife and mom of two school-aged children and serves as president and CEO of Tearfund USA, based in Denver, CO.

for clothing of wool and linen,
    and for olive oil and drinks.'

⁶ "For this reason I will fence her in with thornbushes.
    I will block her path with a wall
        to make her lose her way.
⁷ When she runs after her lovers,
    she won't be able to catch them.
She will search for them
    but not find them.
Then she will think,
'I might as well return to my husband,
    for I was better off with him than
        I am now.'
⁸ She doesn't realize it was I who gave her everything she has—
    the grain, the new wine, the olive oil;
I even gave her silver and gold.
But she gave all my gifts to Baal.

⁹ "But now I will take back the ripened grain and new wine
    I generously provided each harvest season.
I will take away the wool and linen clothing
    I gave her to cover her nakedness.
¹⁰ I will strip her naked in public,
    while all her lovers look on.
No one will be able
    to rescue her from my hands.
¹¹ I will put an end to her annual festivals,
    her new moon celebrations, and her Sabbath days—
    all her appointed festivals.
¹² I will destroy her grapevines and fig trees,
    things she claims her lovers gave her.
I will let them grow into tangled thickets,
    where only wild animals will eat the fruit.
¹³ I will punish her for all those times
    when she burned incense to her images of Baal,
when she put on her earrings and jewels
    and went out to look for her lovers
but forgot all about me,"
    says the LORD.

The LORD's Love for Unfaithful Israel

¹⁴ "But then I will win her back once again.
    I will lead her into the desert
        and speak tenderly to her there.
¹⁵ I will return her vineyards to her
    and transform the Valley of Trouble* into a gateway of hope.
She will give herself to me there,
    as she did long ago when she was young,
    when I freed her from her captivity
        in Egypt.
¹⁶ When that day comes," says the LORD,
    "you will call me 'my husband'
        instead of 'my master.'*
¹⁷ O Israel, I will wipe the many names of Baal from your lips,
    and you will never mention them again.
¹⁸ On that day I will make a covenant
    with all the wild animals and the birds of the sky
and the animals that scurry along the ground
    so they will not harm you.
I will remove all weapons of war from the land,
    all swords and bows,
so you can live unafraid
    in peace and safety.
¹⁹ I will make you my wife forever,
    showing you righteousness and justice,
    unfailing love and compassion.
²⁰ I will be faithful to you and make you mine,
    and you will finally know me as the LORD.

²¹ "In that day, I will answer,"
    says the LORD.
"I will answer the sky as it pleads for clouds.
    And the sky will answer the earth with rain.
²² Then the earth will answer the thirsty cries
    of the grain, the grapevines, and the olive trees.
And they in turn will answer,
    'Jezreel'—'God plants!'
²³ At that time I will plant a crop of Israelites
    and raise them for myself.
I will show love
    to those I called 'Not loved.'*
And to those I called 'Not my people,'*
    I will say, 'Now you are my people.'
And they will reply, 'You are our God!'"

Hosea's Wife Is Redeemed

3 Then the LORD said to me, "Go and love your wife again, even though she* commits adultery with another lover. This will illustrate that the LORD still loves Israel, even though the people have turned to other gods and love to worship them.*"

2:15 Hebrew *valley of Achor.*   **2:16** Hebrew *'my baal.'*   **2:23a** Hebrew *Lo-ruhamah;* see 1:6.   **2:23b** Hebrew *Lo-ammi;* see 1:9.
3:1a Or *Go and love a woman who.*   **3:1b** Hebrew *love their raisin cakes.*

2:18-20 After judgment comes restoration. God would provide a safe and peaceful environment for Israel, his wife. After generations of unfaithfulness, God's pledge to extend righteousness, justice, love, compassion, and fidelity to Israel is wholly remarkable.

²So I bought her back for fifteen pieces of silver* and five bushels of barley and a measure of wine.* ³Then I said to her, "You must live in my house for many days and stop your prostitution. During this time, you will not have sexual relations with anyone, not even with me.*"

⁴This shows that Israel will go a long time without a king or prince, and without sacrifices, sacred pillars, priests,* or even idols! ⁵But afterward the people will return and devote themselves to the LORD their God and to David's descendant, their king.* In the last days, they will tremble in awe of the LORD and of his goodness.

The LORD's Case against Israel

4 Hear the word of the LORD, O people of Israel!
The LORD has brought charges against you, saying:
"There is no faithfulness, no kindness,
no knowledge of God in your land.
² You make vows and break them;
you kill and steal and commit adultery.
There is violence everywhere—
one murder after another.
³ That is why your land is in mourning,
and everyone is wasting away.
Even the wild animals, the birds of the sky,
and the fish of the sea are disappearing.

⁴ "Don't point your finger at someone else
and try to pass the blame!
My complaint, you priests,
is with you.*
⁵ So you will stumble in broad daylight,
and your false prophets will fall with you in the night.
And I will destroy Israel, your mother.
⁶ My people are being destroyed
because they don't know me.
Since you priests refuse to know me,
I refuse to recognize you as my priests.
Since you have forgotten the laws of your God,
I will forget to bless your children.
⁷ The more priests there are,
the more they sin against me.

They have exchanged the glory of God
for the shame of idols.*

⁸ "When the people bring their sin offerings, the priests get fed.
So the priests are glad when the people sin!
⁹ 'And what the priests do, the people also do.'
So now I will punish both priests and people
for their wicked deeds.
¹⁰ They will eat and still be hungry.
They will play the prostitute and gain nothing from it,
for they have deserted the LORD
¹¹ to worship other gods.

"Wine has robbed my people
of their understanding.
¹² They ask a piece of wood for advice!
They think a stick can tell them the future!
Longing after idols
has made them foolish.
They have played the prostitute,
serving other gods and deserting their God.
¹³ They offer sacrifices to idols on the mountaintops.
They go up into the hills to burn incense
in the pleasant shade of oaks, poplars, and terebinth trees.

"That is why your daughters turn to prostitution,
and your daughters-in-law commit adultery.
¹⁴ But why should I punish them
for their prostitution and adultery?
For your men are doing the same thing,
sinning with whores and shrine prostitutes.
O foolish people! You refuse to understand,
so you will be destroyed.

¹⁵ "Though you, Israel, are a prostitute,
may Judah not be guilty of such things.
Do not join the false worship at Gilgal or Beth-aven,*
and do not take oaths there in the LORD's name.
¹⁶ Israel is stubborn,
like a stubborn heifer.
So should the LORD feed her
like a lamb in a lush pasture?

3:2a Hebrew *15 [shekels] of silver*, about 6 ounces or 171 grams in weight. **3:2b** As in Greek version, which reads *a homer of barley and a wineskin full of wine;* Hebrew reads *a homer* [5 bushels or 220 liters] *of barley and a lethek* [2.5 bushels or 110 liters] *of barley.* **3:3** Or *and I will live with you.* **3:4** Hebrew *ephod*, the vest worn by the priest. **3:5** Hebrew *to David their king.* **4:4** Hebrew *Your people are like those with a complaint against the priests.* **4:7** As in Syriac version and an ancient Hebrew tradition; Masoretic Text reads *I will turn their glory into shame.* **4:15** *Beth-aven* means "house of wickedness"; it is being used as another name for Bethel, which means "house of God."

3:2 Gomer was likely enslaved because of debt, which is why Hosea "bought her back." This suggests that Hosea had to pay off her debt to secure her freedom; the price he paid is relatively low and may signal her lack of usefulness as an enslaved woman. When read in context, this verse does not condone treating women as property but instead reflects the terrible reality of slavery in the ancient world. This is not what God intends for anyone. God created women and men equally in his image, and commissioned them together to rule wisely over his creation together (Genesis 1:26-28).

4:12 Craftsmen made idols using a solid wooden core that they overlaid with precious metal, like gold or silver. Hosea's reference to a "piece of wood" and "a stick" are likely derogatory terms for Israel's false gods.

¹⁷ Leave Israel* alone,
   because she is married to idolatry.
¹⁸ When the rulers of Israel finish their drinking,
   off they go to find some prostitutes.
   They love shame more than honor.*
¹⁹ So a mighty wind will sweep them away.
   Their sacrifices to idols will bring them shame.

The Failure of Israel's Leaders

5 "Hear this, you priests.
   Pay attention, you leaders of Israel.
Listen, you members of the royal family.
   Judgment has been handed down against you.
For you have led the people into a snare
   by worshiping the idols at Mizpah and Tabor.
² You have dug a deep pit to trap them at Acacia Grove.*
   But I will settle with you for what you have done.
³ I know what you are like, O Ephraim.
   You cannot hide yourself from me, O Israel.
You have left me as a prostitute leaves her husband;
   you are utterly defiled.
⁴ Your deeds won't let you return to your God.
   You are a prostitute through and through,
   and you do not know the LORD.

⁵ "The arrogance of Israel testifies against her;
   Israel and Ephraim will stumble under their load of guilt.
   Judah, too, will fall with them.
⁶ When they come with their flocks and herds
   to offer sacrifices to the LORD,
   they will not find him,
   because he has withdrawn from them.
⁷ They have betrayed the honor of the LORD,
   bearing children that are not his.
Now their false religion will devour them
   along with their wealth.*

⁸ "Sound the alarm in Gibeah!
   Blow the trumpet in Ramah!
   Raise the battle cry in Beth-aven*!
   Lead on into battle, O warriors of Benjamin!

⁹ One thing is certain, Israel*:
   On your day of punishment,
   you will become a heap of rubble.

¹⁰ "The leaders of Judah have become like thieves.*
   So I will pour my anger on them like a waterfall.
¹¹ The people of Israel will be crushed and broken by my judgment
   because they are determined to worship idols.*
¹² I will destroy Israel as a moth consumes wool.
   I will make Judah as weak as rotten wood.

¹³ "When Israel and Judah saw how sick they were,
   Israel turned to Assyria—
   to the great king there—
   but he could neither help nor cure them.
¹⁴ I will be like a lion to Israel,
   like a strong young lion to Judah.
   I will tear them to pieces!
I will carry them off,
   and no one will be left to rescue them.
¹⁵ Then I will return to my place
   until they admit their guilt and turn to me.
For as soon as trouble comes,
   they will earnestly search for me."

A Call to Repentance

6 "Come, let us return to the LORD.
   He has torn us to pieces;
   now he will heal us.
He has injured us;
   now he will bandage our wounds.
² In just a short time he will restore us,
   so that we may live in his presence.
³ Oh, that we might know the LORD!
   Let us press on to know him.
He will respond to us as surely as the arrival of dawn
   or the coming of rains in early spring."

⁴ "O Israel* and Judah,
   what should I do with you?" asks the LORD.
"For your love vanishes like the morning mist
   and disappears like dew in the sunlight.

4:17 Hebrew *Ephraim*, referring to the northern kingdom of Israel. 4:18 As in Greek version; the meaning of the Hebrew is uncertain. 5:2 Hebrew *at Shittim*. The meaning of the Hebrew for this sentence is uncertain. 5:7 The meaning of the Hebrew is uncertain. 5:8 *Beth-aven* means "house of wickedness"; it is being used as another name for Bethel, which means "house of God." 5:9 Hebrew *Ephraim*, referring to the northern kingdom of Israel; also in 5:11, 12, 13, 14. 5:10 Hebrew *like those who move a boundary marker*. 5:11 Or *determined to follow human commands*. The meaning of the Hebrew is uncertain. 6:4 Hebrew *Ephraim*, referring to the northern kingdom of Israel.

5:10-12 If God's response to Israel's idolatry seems extreme, it is because our view of sin and rebellion against God is far too small. As Paul tells us, "the wages of sin is death" (Romans 6:23). Judgment is what sin deserves. With God, however, judgment is never the end. He delights in restoring his people if they will only turn away from their sin (Hosea 2:14-20).
6:1 God allows his people to suffer the consequences of their sin, but his plans do not end there. When they repent, God promises to heal and restore his people so that they can know him and live in his holy presence.
6:3 The Hebrew verb translated here as "press on" means "to pursue, to follow," and even "to chase." Following the Lord requires *active* obedience on our part. That God will respond is as sure as the sunrise and rain in the spring!

⁵ I sent my prophets to cut you to pieces—
   to slaughter you with my words,
   with judgments as inescapable as light.
⁶ I want you to show love,*
   not offer sacrifices.
  I want you to know me*
   more than I want burnt offerings.
⁷ But like Adam,* you broke my covenant
   and betrayed my trust.
⁸ "Gilead is a city of sinners,
   tracked with footprints of blood.
⁹ Priests form bands of robbers,
   waiting in ambush for their victims.
  They murder travelers along the road to Shechem
   and practice every kind of sin.
¹⁰ Yes, I have seen something horrible in Ephraim
   and Israel:
  My people are defiled by prostituting
   themselves with other gods!
¹¹ "O Judah, a harvest of punishment is also
   waiting for you,
   though I wanted to restore the fortunes of
   my people.

Israel's Love for Wickedness

7 "I want to heal Israel, but its* sins are too great.
   Samaria is filled with liars.
  Thieves are on the inside
   and bandits on the outside!
² Its people don't realize
   that I am watching them.
  Their sinful deeds are all around them,
   and I see them all.
³ "The people entertain the king with their
   wickedness,
   and the princes laugh at their lies.
⁴ They are all adulterers,
   always aflame with lust.
  They are like an oven that is kept hot
   while the baker is kneading the dough.
⁵ On royal holidays, the princes get drunk with
   wine,
   carousing with those who mock them.
⁶ Their hearts are like an oven
   blazing with intrigue.

Their plot smolders* through the night,
   and in the morning it breaks out like a
   raging fire.
⁷ Burning like an oven,
   they consume their leaders.
  They kill their kings one after another,
   and no one cries to me for help.
⁸ "The people of Israel mingle with godless
   foreigners,
   making themselves as worthless as a half-
   baked cake!
⁹ Worshiping foreign gods has sapped their
   strength,
   but they don't even know it.
  Their hair is gray,
   but they don't realize they're old and weak.
¹⁰ Their arrogance testifies against them,
   yet they don't return to the LORD their God
   or even try to find him.
¹¹ "The people of Israel have become like silly,
   witless doves,
   first calling to Egypt, then flying to Assyria
   for help.
¹² But as they fly about,
   I will throw my net over them
   and bring them down like a bird from the sky.
   I will punish them for all the evil they do.*
¹³ "What sorrow awaits those who have
   deserted me!
  Let them die, for they have rebelled
   against me.
  I wanted to redeem them,
   but they have told lies about me.
¹⁴ They do not cry out to me with sincere hearts.
   Instead, they sit on their couches and wail.
  They cut themselves,* begging foreign gods for
   grain and new wine,
   and they turn away from me.
¹⁵ I trained them and made them strong,
   yet now they plot evil against me.
¹⁶ They look everywhere except to the Most High.
   They are as useless as a crooked bow.
  Their leaders will be killed by their enemies
   because of their insolence toward me.
  Then the people of Egypt
   will laugh at them.

6:6a Greek version translates this Hebrew term as *to show mercy.* Compare Matt 9:13; 12:7. **6:6b** Hebrew *to know God.* **6:7** Or *But at Adam.* **7:1** Hebrew *Ephraim's,* referring to the northern kingdom of Israel; similarly in 7:8, 11. **7:6** Hebrew *Their baker sleeps.* **7:12** Hebrew *I will punish them because of what was reported against them in the assembly.* **7:14** As in Greek version; Hebrew reads *They gather together.*

6:5 God is not spiteful nor are his actions unjust. His response to sin is harsh because it must be so—if we remain in sin, we are walking a deadly path which leads to separation from God. In God's economy, there is no place for evil. He necessarily must root out sin from his people so that we can enjoy life with him. Though painful, through God's judgment and our repentance, we become holy and are thus made able to dwell with God.

7:8-10 Idolatry can be subtle and difficult to detect despite its destructive power. It blinds the worshiper spiritually and desensitizes them to its deadly effects. The people of Israel were unaware that idolatry had stolen their youth and vigor. They were too deeply engaged in it to notice.

Israel Harvests the Whirlwind

8 "Sound the alarm!
The enemy descends like an eagle on the people of the Lord,
for they have broken my covenant
and revolted against my law.
² Now Israel pleads with me,
'Help us, for you are our God!'
³ But it is too late.
The people of Israel have rejected what is good,
and now their enemies will chase after them.
⁴ The people have appointed kings without my consent,
and princes without my approval.
By making idols for themselves from their silver and gold,
they have brought about their own destruction.
⁵ "O Samaria, I reject this calf—
this idol you have made.
My fury burns against you.
How long will you be incapable of innocence?
⁶ This calf you worship, O Israel,
was crafted by your own hands!
It is not God!
Therefore, it must be smashed to bits.
⁷ "They have planted the wind
and will harvest the whirlwind.
The stalks of grain wither
and produce nothing to eat.
And even if there is any grain,
foreigners will eat it.
⁸ The people of Israel have been swallowed up;
they lie among the nations like an old discarded pot.
⁹ Like a wild donkey looking for a mate,
they have gone up to Assyria.
The people of Israel* have sold themselves—
sold themselves to many lovers.
¹⁰ But though they have sold themselves to many allies,
I will now gather them together for judgment.
Then they will writhe
under the burden of the great king.
¹¹ "Israel has built many altars to take away sin,
but these very altars became places for sinning!
¹² Even though I gave them all my laws,
they act as if those laws don't apply to them.
¹³ The people love to offer sacrifices to me,
feasting on the meat,
but I do not accept their sacrifices.
I will hold my people accountable for their sins,
and I will punish them.
They will return to Egypt.
¹⁴ Israel has forgotten its Maker and built great palaces,
and Judah has fortified its cities.
Therefore, I will send down fire on their cities
and will burn up their fortresses."

Hosea Announces Israel's Punishment

9 O people of Israel,
do not rejoice as other nations do.
For you have been unfaithful to your God,
hiring yourselves out like prostitutes,
worshiping other gods on every threshing floor.
² So now your harvests will be too small to feed you.
There will be no grapes for making new wine.
³ You may no longer stay here in the Lord's land.
Instead, you will return to Egypt,
and in Assyria you will eat food
that is ceremonially unclean.
⁴ There you will make no offerings of wine to the Lord.
None of your sacrifices there will please him.
They will be unclean, like food touched by a person in mourning.
All who present such sacrifices will be defiled.
They may eat this food themselves,
but they may not offer it to the Lord.
⁵ What then will you do on festival days?
How will you observe the Lord's festivals?
⁶ Even if you escape destruction from Assyria,
Egypt will conquer you, and Memphis* will bury you.
Nettles will take over your treasures of silver;
thistles will invade your ruined homes.

8:9 Hebrew *Ephraim*, referring to the northern kingdom of Israel; also in 8:11. 9:6 Memphis was the capital of northern Egypt.

8:5-6 Jeroboam I was the first ruler of the northern kingdom of Israel, reigning from 931 to 910 BC. When he ascended the throne, he established places of worship in the cities of Dan and Bethel so that the people would not travel to the Temple in Jerusalem, the capital of the southern kingdom. At each site, he erected a gold calf for the people to worship (1 Kings 12:26-30).
8:13 The people needed to "return to Egypt," where they had been enslaved (Deuteronomy 26:6-8). God's dealing with Israel did not end with judgment. God would restore Israel to the status they had when they came out of Egypt so they could start anew (see Hosea 2:14-15). God would humble them so that they could be rebuilt into a faithful people.
9:1-6 Food shortages, unproductive land, rejection, and death were not the punishments of a merciless God. They were the consequences of Israel's rebellion against their covenant partner, who had lovingly provided them with everything they needed. (See the consequences of breaking the covenant in Leviticus 26:14-45; Deuteronomy 28:15-68.)

HOSEA 9

7 The time of Israel's punishment has come;
   the day of payment is here.
  Soon Israel will know this all too well.
  Because of your great sin and hostility,
   you say, "The prophets are crazy
   and the inspired men are fools!"
8 The prophet is a watchman over Israel* for my God,
   yet traps are laid for him wherever he goes.
  He faces hostility even in the house of God.
9 The things my people do are as depraved
   as what they did in Gibeah long ago.
  God will not forget.
  He will surely punish them for their sins.

10 The LORD says, "O Israel, when I first found you,
    it was like finding fresh grapes in the desert.
   When I saw your ancestors,
    it was like seeing the first ripe figs of the season.
   But then they deserted me for Baal-peor,
    giving themselves to that shameful idol.
   Soon they became vile,
    as vile as the god they worshiped.
11 The glory of Israel will fly away like a bird,
    for your children will not be born
    or grow in the womb
    or even be conceived.
12 Even if you do have children who grow up,
    I will take them from you.

9:8 Hebrew *Ephraim*, referring to the northern kingdom of Israel; also in 9:11, 13, 16.

9:7-8 Sin has a corrosive effect on our minds and our senses. It makes it difficult for us to distinguish right from wrong and good from evil.

9:11-13 Ancient covenant curses, including those in biblical covenants, included threats of infertility and children's deaths (Leviticus 26:22, 29; Deuteronomy 28:18, 41; compare Psalm 137:9). These curses were specific to nations that broke their covenant promises. Infertility is a deeply personal situation, and we should not make assumptions about it.

 Come Close **UNFAITHFUL: FAITHFUL**

SCRIPTURE CONNECTION: HOSEA 9:1-17

Once again, Israel was unfaithful. It might be easy for us to look at this passage and think, *Why don't those Israelites learn? How are they oblivious to how much their actions grieve God?*

And yet, I don't have to look far to realize that I, too, repeatedly grieve God. I sin. I inflict the sting of unfaithfulness. So often insipid, I slide into unfaithfulness with the justification that at least I am not like others. But when I harbor anger, gossip about someone else's sins, or value my appearance too much, I am unfaithful too.

> It can be easy to slide into unfaithfulness. God says, "Please don't. I love you and want you near."

What other gods get in the way of my pure worship of God, who is always faithful? How can I be more faithful, focused on God and not all the little temptations that turn me from him?

It takes intentionality. It takes vigilance not to slide slowly into unfaithfulness.

REFLECT "O people of Israel, do not rejoice as other nations do. For you have been unfaithful to your God." HOSEA 9:1

Father, please revive me each day with your pure love. Fill me and help me realize you are all I need, that I don't need to divert my focus to any other "gods." I just need you. Amen.

CONSIDER "He is no fool who gives what he cannot keep to gain what he cannot lose." JIM ELLIOT

ELISABETH SELZER ROGERS, MDiv, MA, PhD, is a passionate believer and follower of Christ, bringing his love to the secular world through mentoring, coaching, and modeling his unconditional love.

It will be a terrible day when I turn away
    and leave you alone.
[13] I have watched Israel become as beautiful as Tyre.
    But now Israel will bring out her children for
        slaughter."

[14] O LORD, what should I request for your people?
    I will ask for wombs that don't give birth
    and breasts that give no milk.
[15] The LORD says, "All their wickedness began at
        Gilgal;
    there I began to hate them.
I will drive them from my land
    because of their evil actions.
I will love them no more
    because all their leaders are rebels.
[16] The people of Israel are struck down.
    Their roots are dried up,
    and they will bear no more fruit.
And if they give birth,
    I will slaughter their beloved children."

[17] My God will reject the people of Israel
    because they will not listen or obey.
They will be wanderers,
    homeless among the nations.

The LORD's Judgment against Israel

10 How prosperous Israel is—
    a luxuriant vine loaded with fruit.
But the richer the people get,
    the more pagan altars they build.
The more bountiful their harvests,
    the more beautiful their sacred pillars.
[2] The hearts of the people are fickle;
    they are guilty and must be punished.
The LORD will break down their altars
    and smash their sacred pillars.
[3] Then they will say, "We have no king
    because we didn't fear the LORD.
But even if we had a king,
    what could he do for us anyway?"
[4] They spout empty words
    and make covenants they don't intend to keep.
So injustice springs up among them
    like poisonous weeds in a farmer's field.

[5] The people of Samaria tremble in fear
    for their calf idol at Beth-aven,*
    and they mourn for it.
Though its priests rejoice over it,
    its glory will be stripped away.*
[6] This idol will be carted away to Assyria,
    a gift to the great king there.
Ephraim will be ridiculed and Israel will be
        shamed,
    because its people have trusted in this idol.
[7] Samaria and its king will be cut off;
    they will float away like driftwood on an
        ocean wave.
[8] And the pagan shrines of Aven,* the place of
        Israel's sin, will crumble.
Thorns and thistles will grow up around their
        altars.
They will beg the mountains, "Bury us!"
    and plead with the hills, "Fall on us!"

[9] The LORD says, "O Israel, ever since Gibeah,
    there has been only sin and more sin!
You have made no progress whatsoever.
    Was it not right that the wicked men of
        Gibeah were attacked?
[10] Now whenever it fits my plan,
    I will attack you, too.
I will call out the armies of the nations
    to punish you for your multiplied sins.

[11] "Israel* is like a trained heifer treading out the
        grain—
    an easy job she loves.
But I will put a heavy yoke on her tender neck.
I will force Judah to pull the plow
    and Israel* to break up the hard ground.
[12] I said, 'Plant the good seeds of righteousness,
    and you will harvest a crop of love.
Plow up the hard ground of your hearts,
    for now is the time to seek the LORD,
that he may come
    and shower righteousness upon you.'

10:5a *Beth-aven* means "house of wickedness"; it is being used as another name for Bethel, which means "house of God."
10:5b Or *will be taken away into exile.*   **10:8** *Aven* is a reference to Beth-aven; see 10:5a and the note there.   **10:11a** Hebrew *Ephraim,* referring to the northern kingdom of Israel.   **10:11b** Hebrew *Jacob.* The names "Jacob" and "Israel" are often interchanged throughout the Old Testament, referring sometimes to the individual patriarch and sometimes to the nation.

9:16 In Leviticus 26:22, 29; Deuteronomy 28:18, 41, God tells Israel that covenant unfaithfulness would result in infertility—affecting the land, the animals, and the people. God would prevent conception, and children who survived birth would die. There was no greater curse in ancient Israel than for a family line to come to an end. However, God is not malicious, and he carried out the covenant curses because he is holy and just. He desired for his people to repent so that he could show them his great mercy. It is a dreadful picture, but this is what the Israelites' sin brought about. For the people to have any hope of restoration, God's response had to be severe. Here it is expressed in the most forceful of terms.
10:1 Although Israel was God's fruitful vine (see Isaiah 5:1-7; Jeremiah 2:21; Ezekiel 17:6), the people falsely attributed their prosperity to the Canaanite fertility gods rather than to the Lord, spending the riches God had given them to enhance their idol worship.
10:12 Using metaphors from agriculture, God set forth his requirements for his people and a promise of blessing if they did what he commanded. Even as Hosea announced God's judgment, he offered Israel the chance to repent and receive God's blessing.

13 "But you have cultivated wickedness
    and harvested a thriving crop of sins.
You have eaten the fruit of lies—
    trusting in your military might,
    believing that great armies
    could make your nation safe.
14 Now the terrors of war
    will rise among your people.
All your fortifications will fall,
    just as when Shalman destroyed Beth-arbel.
Even mothers and children
    were dashed to death there.
15 You will share that fate, Bethel,
    because of your great wickedness.
When the day of judgment dawns,
    the king of Israel will be completely
        destroyed.

The Lord's Love for Israel

11 "When Israel was a child, I loved him,
     and I called my son out of Egypt.
2 But the more I called to him,
    the farther he moved from me,*
offering sacrifices to the images of Baal
    and burning incense to idols.
3 I myself taught Israel* how to walk,
    leading him along by the hand.
But he doesn't know or even care
    that it was I who took care of him.
4 I led Israel along
    with my ropes of kindness and love.
I lifted the yoke from his neck,
    and I myself stooped to feed him.
5 "But since my people refuse to return to me,
    they will return to Egypt
    and will be forced to serve Assyria.
6 War will swirl through their cities;
    their enemies will crash through their gates.
They will destroy them,
    trapping them in their own evil plans.
7 For my people are determined to desert me.
They call me the Most High,
    but they don't truly honor me.
8 "Oh, how can I give you up, Israel?
    How can I let you go?
How can I destroy you like Admah
    or demolish you like Zeboiim?
My heart is torn within me,
    and my compassion overflows.
9 No, I will not unleash my fierce anger.
    I will not completely destroy Israel,
for I am God and not a mere mortal.
    I am the Holy One living among you,
    and I will not come to destroy.
10 For someday the people will follow me.
    I, the Lord, will roar like a lion.
And when I roar,
    my people will return trembling from
        the west.
11 Like a flock of birds, they will come from Egypt.
    Trembling like doves, they will return from
        Assyria.
And I will bring them home again,"
    says the Lord.

Charges against Israel and Judah

12 *Israel surrounds me with lies and deceit,
    but Judah still obeys God
    and is faithful to the Holy One.*

12 1*The people of Israel* feed on the wind;
     they chase after the east wind all day
        long.
They pile up lies and violence;
    they are making an alliance with Assyria
    while sending olive oil to buy support from
        Egypt.
2 Now the Lord is bringing charges against Judah.
    He is about to punish Jacob* for all his
        deceitful ways,
    and pay him back for all he has done.
3 Even in the womb,
    Jacob struggled with his brother;
when he became a man,
    he even fought with God.
4 Yes, he wrestled with the angel and won.
    He wept and pleaded for a blessing from him.
There at Bethel he met God face to face,
    and God spoke to him*—
5 the Lord God of Heaven's Armies,
    the Lord is his name!
6 So now, come back to your God.
    Act with love and justice,
    and always depend on him.

11:2 As in Greek version; Hebrew reads *the more they called to him, the farther he moved from them.*   11:3 Hebrew *Ephraim*, referring to the northern kingdom of Israel; also in 11:8, 9, 12.   11:12a Verse 11:12 is numbered 12:1 in Hebrew text.   11:12b Or *and Judah is unruly against God, the faithful Holy One.* The meaning of the Hebrew is uncertain.   12:1a Verses 12:1-14 are numbered 12:2-15 in Hebrew text.   12:1b Hebrew *Ephraim*, referring to the northern kingdom of Israel; also in 12:8, 14.   12:2 *Jacob* sounds like the Hebrew word for "deceiver."   12:4 As in Greek and Syriac versions; Hebrew reads *to us.*

11:1-4, 8-11 God's role as judge and executioner does not contradict his love and fatherly care for his beloved child, Israel. Holiness, justice, love, and compassion are not only compatible but are inextricably linked. Thinking otherwise misunderstands the character of God.

⁷ But no, the people are like crafty merchants
   selling from dishonest scales—
  they love to cheat.
⁸ Israel boasts, "I am rich!
   I've made a fortune all by myself!
  No one has caught me cheating!
   My record is spotless!"

⁹ "But I am the LORD your God,
   who rescued you from slavery in Egypt.
  And I will make you live in tents again,
   as you do each year at the Festival of Shelters.*
¹⁰ I sent my prophets to warn you
   with many visions and parables."

¹¹ But the people of Gilead are worthless
   because of their idol worship.
  And in Gilgal, too, they sacrifice bulls;
   their altars are lined up like the heaps of stone
   along the edges of a plowed field.
¹² Jacob fled to the land of Aram,
   and there he* earned a wife by tending sheep.
¹³ Then by a prophet
   the LORD brought Jacob's descendants* out of Egypt;
  and by that prophet
   they were protected.
¹⁴ But the people of Israel
   have bitterly provoked the LORD,
  so their Lord will now sentence them to death
   in payment for their sins.

The LORD's Anger against Israel

13 When the tribe of Ephraim spoke,
   the people shook with fear,
  for that tribe was important in Israel.
  But the people of Ephraim sinned by worshiping Baal
   and thus sealed their destruction.
² Now they continue to sin by making silver idols,
   images shaped skillfully with human hands.
  "Sacrifice to these," they cry,
   "and kiss the calf idols!"

³ Therefore, they will disappear like the morning mist,
   like dew in the morning sun,
  like chaff blown by the wind,
   like smoke from a chimney.

⁴ "I have been the LORD your God
   ever since I brought you out of Egypt.
  You must acknowledge no God but me,
   for there is no other savior.
⁵ I took care of you in the wilderness,
   in that dry and thirsty land.
⁶ But when you had eaten and were satisfied,
   you became proud and forgot me.
⁷ So now I will attack you like a lion,
   like a leopard that lurks along the road.
⁸ Like a bear whose cubs have been taken away,
   I will tear out your heart.
  I will devour you like a hungry lioness
   and mangle you like a wild animal.

⁹ "You are about to be destroyed, O Israel—
   yes, by me, your only helper.
¹⁰ Now where is* your king?
   Let him save you!
  Where are all the leaders of the land,
   the king and the officials you demanded of me?
¹¹ In my anger I gave you kings,
   and in my fury I took them away.

¹² "Ephraim's guilt has been collected,
   and his sin has been stored up for punishment.
¹³ Pain has come to the people
   like the pain of childbirth,
  but they are like a child
   who resists being born.
  The moment of birth has arrived,
   but they stay in the womb!

¹⁴ "Should I ransom them from the grave*?
   Should I redeem them from death?
  O death, bring on your terrors!
   O grave, bring on your plagues!*
  For I will not take pity on them.

12:9 Hebrew *as in the days of your appointed feast.* **12:12** Hebrew *Israel.* See note on 10:11b. **12:13** Hebrew *brought Israel.* See note on 10:11b. **13:10** As in Greek and Syriac versions and Latin Vulgate; Hebrew reads *I will be.* **13:14a** Hebrew *Sheol;* also in 13:14b. **13:14b** Greek version reads *O death, where is your punishment? / O grave* [Hades], *where is your sting?* Compare 1 Cor 15:55.

12:7-8 During the reign of Jeroboam II (793–753 BC), Israelite merchants became fabulously wealthy, often by using deceitful business practices like "dishonest scales" (see Amos 8:5-6). The Hebrew term translated "merchants" is *kenaan* (or "Canaan"). Canaanite traders were notorious in the ancient world for their crafty dealings. The Israelites had imitated their pagan neighbors not only in religion but also in commerce.
12:9 God's judgment on the wealthy Israelite merchants was for them to return to the humble tent dwellings of the Exodus.
There is also a word of hope here: God's plan of salvation for Israel would begin anew in the wilderness (see 2:14-15).
13:1 Although God brings the punishment, the blame for Israel's impending destruction is entirely their own.
13:8 Attacks by wild animals were referred to often in covenant curse language. Similar statements appear among the curses for disobedience to the covenant in Leviticus 26:22; Deuteronomy 28:26. Although shocking and graphic, this language was a *poetic* way of warning Israel that rebellion against God brings death. Not long after this prophecy, Assyria—where lions symbolized prowess and might—destroyed the entire northern kingdom of Israel.

¹⁵ Ephraim was the most fruitful of all his
    brothers,
  but the east wind—a blast from the Lord—
    will arise in the desert.
  All their flowing springs will run dry,
    and all their wells will disappear.
  Every precious thing they own
    will be plundered and carried away.
¹⁶ *The people of Samaria
    must bear the consequences of their guilt
    because they rebelled against their God.
  They will be killed by an invading army,
    their little ones dashed to death against the
      ground,
    their pregnant women ripped open by
      swords."

Healing for the Repentant

14 ¹ *Return, O Israel, to the Lord your God,
       for your sins have brought you down.
² Bring your confessions, and return to the Lord.
    Say to him,
  "Forgive all our sins and graciously receive us,
    so that we may offer you our praises.*
³ Assyria cannot save us,
    nor can our warhorses.
  Never again will we say to the idols we have
    made,
    'You are our gods.'
  No, in you alone
    do the orphans find mercy."

⁴ The Lord says,
  "Then I will heal you of your faithlessness;
    my love will know no bounds,
    for my anger will be gone forever.
⁵ I will be to Israel
    like a refreshing dew from heaven.
  Israel will blossom like the lily;
    it will send roots deep into the soil
    like the cedars in Lebanon.
⁶ Its branches will spread out like beautiful olive
    trees,
    as fragrant as the cedars of Lebanon.
⁷ My people will again live under my shade.
  They will flourish like grain and blossom like
    grapevines.
  They will be as fragrant as the wines of Lebanon.

⁸ "O Israel,* stay away from idols!
  I am the one who answers your prayers and
    cares for you.
  I am like a tree that is always green;
    all your fruit comes from me."

⁹ Let those who are wise understand these things.
    Let those with discernment listen carefully.
  The paths of the Lord are true and right,
    and righteous people live by walking in them.
  But in those paths sinners stumble and fall.

13:16 Verse 16 is numbered 14:1 in Hebrew text.   **14:1** Verses 14:1-9 are numbered 14:2-10 in Hebrew text.   **14:2** As in Greek and Syriac versions, which read *may repay the fruit of our lips;* Hebrew reads *may repay the bulls of our lips.*   **14:8** Hebrew *Ephraim,* referring to the northern kingdom of Israel.

13:16 In 722 BC, Assyria captured Samaria, the capital of the northern kingdom (2 Kings 17:5-6). Thousands died during the three-year siege, and thousands more were sent into exile. This happened "because they rebelled against their God." The horrible practice of killing pregnant women is also mentioned in 2 Kings 15:16; Amos 1:13.

14:1-9 The horrific curses mentioned in Hosea must be read in light of this final chapter and within the context of Leviticus 26; Deuteronomy 28. The prophet holds out hope for Israel, for a day when the people would confess their sin and repent. The Lord promised to respond with forgiveness, healing, and boundless love. He longed to bless Israel like the morning dew and see Israel grow and flourish, but it required their faithfulness.

Joel

WHAT DO WE LEARN ABOUT GOD'S MISSION AND OURS? Judgment for sin is real, but God stands ready to forgive. When we repent, God responds with grace, mercy, and blessing.

WHO WROTE IT? Joel.

WHEN DID IT HAPPEN? Joel does not provide a date for the events he records, but he prophesied sometime during the divided kingdom (930–722 BC). This may be the oldest prophetic book.

HOW IS IT ORGANIZED?

1:1–2:11: The plague of locusts

2:12-32: The Day of the Lord—judgment and restoration

3:1-21: Judgment on the nations and blessings for Judah

FEATURE HIGHLIGHTS

+ *Out of Brokenness Comes Blessing (1073)*

Words to Remember are highlighted throughout this book

HOW LONG DOES IT TAKE TO READ?

:15 | :30 | 1:00 | 1:30 | 2:00 | 2:30 | 3:00 | 3:30

Timeline (BC)

BC	Event
853	KING AHAB DIES IN BATTLE
848	ELISHA BECOMES A PROPHET
841	JEHU BECOMES KING OF ISRAEL; ATHALIAH SEIZES JUDAH'S THRONE
835	JOEL LIKELY BECOMES A PROPHET; JOASH BECOMES KING OF JUDAH
814	JEHOAHAZ, HAMUTAL'S SON, BECOMES KING OF ISRAEL
798	JEHOASH, HAMUTAL'S GRANDSON, BECOMES KING OF ISRAEL
c. 796	JOEL'S MINISTRY ENDS
793	JONAH BECOMES A PROPHET; JEROBOAM II BECOMES KING OF ISRAEL

JOEL 1

1
The LORD gave this message to Joel son of Pethuel.

Mourning over the Locust Plague

²Hear this, you leaders of the people.
  Listen, all who live in the land.
In all your history,
  has anything like this happened before?
³Tell your children about it in the years
      to come,
  and let your children tell their children.
  Pass the story down from generation to
    generation.
⁴After the cutting locusts finished eating the
    crops,
  the swarming locusts took what was left!
After them came the hopping locusts,
  and then the stripping locusts,* too!

⁵Wake up, you drunkards, and weep!
  Wail, all you wine-drinkers!
All the grapes are ruined,
  and all your sweet wine is gone.
⁶A vast army of locusts* has invaded my land,
  a terrible army too numerous to count.
Its teeth are like lions' teeth,
  its fangs like those of a lioness.
⁷It has destroyed my grapevines
  and ruined my fig trees,
stripping their bark and destroying it,
  leaving the branches white and bare.

⁸Weep like a bride dressed in black,
  mourning the death of her husband.
⁹For there is no grain or wine
  to offer at the Temple of the LORD.
So the priests are in mourning.
  The ministers of the LORD are weeping.
¹⁰The fields are ruined,
  the land is stripped bare.
The grain is destroyed,
  the grapes have shriveled,
  and the olive oil is gone.

¹¹Despair, all you farmers!
  Wail, all you vine growers!
Weep, because the wheat and barley—
  all the crops of the field—are ruined.
¹²The grapevines have dried up,
  and the fig trees have withered.
The pomegranate trees, palm trees, and apple
    trees—
  all the fruit trees—have dried up.
  And the people's joy has dried up with them.

¹³Dress yourselves in burlap and weep, you
      priests!
  Wail, you who serve before the altar!
Come, spend the night in burlap,
  you ministers of my God.
For there is no grain or wine
  to offer at the Temple of your God.
¹⁴Announce a time of fasting;
  call the people together for a solemn meeting.
Bring the leaders
  and all the people of the land
into the Temple of the LORD your God,
  and cry out to him there.

¹⁵The day of the LORD is near,
  the day when destruction comes from the
    Almighty.
  How terrible that day will be!
¹⁶Our food disappears before our very eyes.
  No joyful celebrations are held in the house of
    our God.
¹⁷The seeds die in the parched ground,
  and the grain crops fail.
The barns stand empty,
  and granaries are abandoned.
¹⁸How the animals moan with hunger!
  The herds of cattle wander about confused,
because they have no pasture.
  The flocks of sheep and goats bleat in
    misery.

¹⁹LORD, help us!
  The fire has consumed the wilderness pastures,
  and flames have burned up all the trees.
²⁰Even the wild animals cry out to you
  because the streams have dried up,
  and fire has consumed the wilderness
    pastures.

Locusts Invade like an Army

2
Sound the trumpet in Jerusalem*!
  Raise the alarm on my holy mountain!
Let everyone tremble in fear
  because the day of the LORD is upon us.

1:4 The precise identification of the four kinds of locusts mentioned here is uncertain. **1:6** Hebrew *A nation.* **2:1** Hebrew *Zion;* also in 2:15, 23.

1:3 Future generations need to know about God's past acts of judgment and redemption because, through them, God reveals himself and his great plan of redemption and salvation. Recounting these biblical stories is one of the primary ways we can form a biblical understanding of God, shaped by his Word rather than by our misconceptions or our culture.

1:10 God responded to Israel's unfaithfulness as described in the curses that accompany the covenant God had made with Israel on Mount Sinai (Exodus 19:1–24:18). Here God allowed the enemy to ravage the land and destroy the crops (see Leviticus 26:16, 26, 32; Deuteronomy 28:33, 38-40). Famine was sure to follow.

2:1-10 This section is a poetic description of an invading army portrayed as an unrelenting horde of locusts. The level of detail creates a vivid picture of an unstoppable, consuming force bent on destruction.

MY STORY WITH GOD

The Kindness of God's Correction

SCRIPTURE CONNECTION: JOEL 2:1-32

As a small child I learned the hard way what happens when you touch a hot stove—pain, a hospital visit, both hands bandaged and hurting.

As a mother, I kept my children from this lesson through warnings, explanations, and quick—even harsh—action when necessary. Correction doesn't feel good to a child, but we do what we must to protect our children.

Human caregivers reflect God's image, and like us, he provides discipline and correction to guide and protect his children. The story of God's people teaches us that God's discipline and judgment are acts of mercy, compassion, and love. When we fail to trust and obey, he knows we're headed for terrible danger.

In Joel 2:1-32, we read of impending judgment that God ordains as an act of mercy to lead his people to repent. And we see ahead to the fruit of repentance: abundant, marvelous, and overflowing blessing.

God will not bless our wrong living—living that can burn us. He will bring us to repentance because he loves us. His correction guides us to better plans than we would choose for ourselves.

> God corrects us because he loves us far more than we can understand.

IMAGINE

Joel says God is "eager to relent and not punish" (2:13). Does this affect how we see God? In what ways?

How can we promptly accept correction and repent when we do wrong? What would it take to feel the urgency for repentance as God sees it?

> "I often foolishly resist God's correction when I should be thanking him for graciously bringing me to repentance and renewed blessing."

AMY SIMPSON, MBA, is the Bible publisher at Tyndale House Publishers, and she can't think of a better job than making God's Word available and accessible around the world.

² It is a day of darkness and gloom,
  a day of thick clouds and deep blackness.
Suddenly, like dawn spreading across the mountains,
  a great and mighty army appears.
Nothing like it has been seen before
  or will ever be seen again.

³ Fire burns in front of them,
  and flames follow after them.
Ahead of them the land lies
  as beautiful as the Garden of Eden.
Behind them is nothing but desolation;
  not one thing escapes.
⁴ They look like horses;
  they charge forward like warhorses.*
⁵ Look at them as they leap along the mountaintops.
  Listen to the noise they make—like the rumbling of chariots,
like the roar of fire sweeping across a field of stubble,
  or like a mighty army moving into battle.

⁶ Fear grips all the people;
  every face grows pale with terror.
⁷ The attackers march like warriors
  and scale city walls like soldiers.
Straight forward they march,
  never breaking rank.
⁸ They never jostle each other;
  each moves in exactly the right position.
They break through defenses
  without missing a step.
⁹ They swarm over the city
  and run along its walls.
They enter all the houses,
  climbing like thieves through the windows.
¹⁰ The earth quakes as they advance,
  and the heavens tremble.
The sun and moon grow dark,
  and the stars no longer shine.

¹¹ The Lord is at the head of the column.
  He leads them with a shout.
This is his mighty army,
  and they follow his orders.
The day of the Lord is an awesome, terrible thing.
  Who can possibly survive?

A Call to Repentance

¹² That is why the Lord says,
  "Turn to me now, while there is time.
Give me your hearts.
  Come with fasting, weeping, and mourning.
¹³ Don't tear your clothing in your grief,
  but tear your hearts instead."
Return to the Lord your God,
  for he is merciful and compassionate,
slow to get angry and filled with unfailing love.
  He is eager to relent and not punish.
¹⁴ Who knows? Perhaps he will give you a reprieve,
  sending you a blessing instead of this curse.
Perhaps you will be able to offer grain and wine
  to the Lord your God as before.

¹⁵ Blow the ram's horn in Jerusalem!
  Announce a time of fasting;
call the people together
  for a solemn meeting.
¹⁶ Gather all the people—
  the elders, the children, and even the babies.
Call the bridegroom from his quarters
  and the bride from her private room.
¹⁷ Let the priests, who minister in the Lord's presence,
  stand and weep between the entry room to the Temple and the altar.
Let them pray, "Spare your people, Lord!
  Don't let your special possession become an object of mockery.
Don't let them become a joke for unbelieving foreigners who say,
  'Has the God of Israel left them?'"

The Lord's Promise of Restoration

¹⁸ Then the Lord will pity his people
  and jealously guard the honor of his land.
¹⁹ The Lord will reply,
  "Look! I am sending you grain and new wine and olive oil,
  enough to satisfy your needs.
You will no longer be an object of mockery
  among the surrounding nations.
²⁰ I will drive away these armies from the north.
  I will send them into the parched wastelands.
Those in the front will be driven into the Dead Sea,
  and those at the rear into the Mediterranean.*
The stench of their rotting bodies will rise over the land."

Surely the Lord has done great things!
²¹ Don't be afraid, O land.
Be glad now and rejoice,
  for the Lord has done great things.

2:4 Or *like charioteers.* 2:20 Hebrew *into the eastern sea, . . . into the western sea.*

2:11-14 The terrifying invaders belonged to the Lord! They were his instrument of judgment. But God's people could avert disaster if they would turn back to him. However, God was not interested in outward symbols of mourning. Instead, he required a genuine inner transformation. His army would bring utter destruction, but God stood ready to bless his people instead if they would repent.

"Everyone who calls on the name of The LORD will be saved."

JOEL 2:32

> "Most of the world around you doesn't read the Bible. So what does God do? ... He gives the world a living epistle—*you*."
>
> **KAY ARTHUR**
> Bible teacher and author

²² Don't be afraid, you animals of the field,
 for the wilderness pastures will soon be green.
The trees will again be filled with fruit;
 fig trees and grapevines will be loaded down once more.
²³ Rejoice, you people of Jerusalem!
 Rejoice in the LORD your God!
For the rain he sends demonstrates his faithfulness.
 Once more the autumn rains will come,
 as well as the rains of spring.
²⁴ The threshing floors will again be piled high with grain,
 and the presses will overflow with new wine and olive oil.
²⁵ The LORD says, "I will give you back what you lost to the swarming locusts, the hopping locusts, the stripping locusts, and the cutting locusts.*
 It was I who sent this great destroying army against you.

²⁶ Once again you will have all the food you want,
 and you will praise the LORD your God,
 who does these miracles for you.
 Never again will my people be disgraced.
²⁷ Then you will know that I am among my people Israel,
 that I am the LORD your God, and there is no other.
 Never again will my people be disgraced.

The LORD's Promise of His Spirit

²⁸*"Then, after doing all those things,
 I will pour out my Spirit upon all people.
Your sons and daughters will prophesy.
 Your old men will dream dreams,
 and your young men will see visions.
²⁹ In those days I will pour out my Spirit
 even on servants—men and women alike.
³⁰ And I will cause wonders in the heavens and on the earth—
 blood and fire and columns of smoke.
³¹ The sun will become dark,
 and the moon will turn blood red
 before that great and terrible* day of the LORD arrives.
³² But everyone who calls on the name of the LORD will be saved,
for some on Mount Zion in Jerusalem will escape,
 just as the LORD has said.
These will be among the survivors
 whom the LORD has called.

Judgment against Enemy Nations

3 ¹*"At the time of those events," says the LORD,
 "when I restore the prosperity of Judah and Jerusalem,
² I will gather the armies of the world
 into the valley of Jehoshaphat.*
There I will judge them
 for harming my people, my special possession,
for scattering my people among the nations,
 and for dividing up my land.
³ They threw dice* to decide which of my people would be their slaves.

2:25 The precise identification of the four kinds of locusts mentioned here is uncertain. **2:28** Verses 2:28-32 are numbered 3:1-5 in Hebrew text. **2:31** Greek version reads *glorious*. **3:1** Verses 3:1-21 are numbered 4:1-21 in Hebrew text. **3:2** *Jehoshaphat* means "the LORD judges." **3:3** Hebrew *They cast lots*.

2:28-29 In Israel, the empowering gift of God's Spirit had previously been given only to select individuals such as judges (Judges 3:10; 15:14), kings (1 Samuel 10:10), priests (2 Chronicles 24:20), and prophets (Isaiah 61:1). A time was coming when the Spirit would be given to every one of God's people, regardless of gender, age, or social position. This prophecy was fulfilled on the day of Pentecost, when the Holy Spirit descended on Jesus' followers (Acts 2:1-47). Peter declared that regardless of ethnicity, this prophecy included people from all over the world who were gathered in Jerusalem (Acts 2:39; see also Galatians 3:28).

3:3-8 The horrors of war included deportation, loss of land, and enslavement. Captors traded Judean children for sex and alcohol, and sold the others like animals. Such dehumanization is not God's design, and God promised to restore his people and punish those responsible.

They traded boys to obtain prostitutes
and sold girls for enough wine to get drunk.

⁴"What do you have against me, Tyre and Sidon and you cities of Philistia? Are you trying to take revenge on me? If you are, then watch out! I will strike swiftly and pay you back for everything you have done. ⁵You have taken my silver and gold and all my precious treasures, and have carried them off to your pagan temples. ⁶You have sold the people of Judah and Jerusalem to the Greeks,* so they could take them far from their homeland.

⁷"But I will bring them back from all the places to which you sold them, and I will pay you back for everything you have done. ⁸I will sell your sons and daughters to the people of Judah, and they will sell them to the people of Arabia,* a nation far away. I, the LORD, have spoken!"

⁹ Say to the nations far and wide:
"Get ready for war!
Call out your best warriors.
Let all your fighting men advance for the attack.
¹⁰ Hammer your plowshares into swords
and your pruning hooks into spears.
Train even your weaklings to be warriors.
¹¹ Come quickly, all you nations everywhere.
Gather together in the valley."

And now, O LORD, call out your warriors!

¹² "Let the nations be called to arms.
Let them march to the valley of Jehoshaphat.
There I, the LORD, will sit
to pronounce judgment on them all.
¹³ Swing the sickle,
for the harvest is ripe.*
Come, tread the grapes,
for the winepress is full.
The storage vats are overflowing
with the wickedness of these people."

¹⁴ Thousands upon thousands are waiting in the valley of decision.
There the day of the LORD will soon arrive.
¹⁵ The sun and moon will grow dark,
and the stars will no longer shine.
¹⁶ The LORD's voice will roar from Zion
and thunder from Jerusalem,
and the heavens and the earth will shake.
But the LORD will be a refuge for his people,
a strong fortress for the people of Israel.

Blessings for God's People

¹⁷ "Then you will know that I, the LORD your God, live in Zion, my holy mountain.
Jerusalem will be holy forever,
and foreign armies will never conquer her again.
¹⁸ In that day the mountains will drip with sweet wine,
and the hills will flow with milk.
Water will fill the streambeds of Judah,
and a fountain will burst forth from the LORD's Temple,
watering the arid valley of acacias.*
¹⁹ But Egypt will become a wasteland
and Edom will become a wilderness,
because they attacked the people of Judah
and killed innocent people in their land.
²⁰ "But Judah will be filled with people forever,
and Jerusalem will endure through all generations.
²¹ I will pardon my people's crimes,
which I have not yet pardoned;
and I, the LORD, will make my home
in Jerusalem* with my people."

3:6 Hebrew *to the peoples of Javan.* **3:8** Hebrew *to the Sabeans.* **3:13** Greek version reads *for the harvest time has come.* Compare Mark 4:29. **3:18** Hebrew *valley of Shittim.* **3:21** Hebrew *Zion.*

3:9-17 The purpose of God's judgment was twofold: to punish the guilty and to make himself known. Rarely do we consider the relationship between these two facets of God's character. Through judgment and the destruction of evil, God shows that he is good, sovereign, just, righteous, and holy.

Amos

WHAT DO WE LEARN ABOUT GOD'S MISSION AND OURS? Idolatry produces injustice of all kinds, but God will repair the brokenness, rebuild the ruins, and restore his people.

WHO WROTE IT? Although Amos may have used a scribe, the words are those of Amos, a shepherd from Tekoa in Judah.

WHEN DID IT HAPPEN? Around 760–750 BC, a few decades before the fall of Israel to the Assyrians.

HOW IS IT ORGANIZED?

- 1:1–2:5: God's judgment on the nations
- 2:6–5:17: God's judgment on Israel
- 5:18–6:14: Israel judged for pride and injustice
- 7:1–9:10: Visions about Israel's future
- 9:11-15: Israel will be restored

FEATURE HIGHLIGHTS

+ *No Exceptions* (1081)
+ *Wealthy Samaritan Wives: Comfort over Compassion* (1085)
+ *Return to Restoration* (1089)

Words to Remember are highlighted throughout this book

HOW LONG DOES IT TAKE TO READ?

:25						
:30	1:00	1:30	2:00	2:30	3:00	3:30

Timeline

BC	
793	JEROBOAM II BECOMES KING OF ISRAEL
760	AMOS BECOMES A PROPHET TO ISRAEL
753	HOSEA BECOMES A PROPHET TO ISRAEL
752	KING SHALLUM OF ISRAEL IS ASSASSINATED
750	AMOS'S MINISTRY ENDS
740	ISAIAH BECOMES A PROPHET TO JUDAH

¹ This message was given to Amos, a shepherd from the town of Tekoa in Judah. He received this message in visions two years before the earthquake, when Uzziah was king of Judah and Jeroboam II, the son of Jehoash,* was king of Israel.

² This is what he saw and heard:

"The LORD's voice will roar from Zion
  and thunder from Jerusalem!
The lush pastures of the shepherds will dry up;
  the grass on Mount Carmel will wither and die."

God's Judgment on Israel's Neighbors

³ This is what the LORD says:

"The people of Damascus have sinned again and again,*
  and I will not let them go unpunished!
They beat down my people in Gilead
  as grain is threshed with iron sledges.
⁴ So I will send down fire on King Hazael's palace,
  and the fortresses of King Ben-hadad will be destroyed.
⁵ I will break down the gates of Damascus
  and slaughter the people in the valley of Aven.
I will destroy the ruler in Beth-eden,
  and the people of Aram will go as captives to Kir,"
says the LORD.

⁶ This is what the LORD says:

"The people of Gaza have sinned again and again,
  and I will not let them go unpunished!
They sent whole villages into exile,
  selling them as slaves to Edom.
⁷ So I will send down fire on the walls of Gaza,
  and all its fortresses will be destroyed.
⁸ I will slaughter the people of Ashdod
  and destroy the king of Ashkelon.
Then I will turn to attack Ekron,
  and the few Philistines still left will be killed,"
says the Sovereign LORD.

⁹ This is what the LORD says:

"The people of Tyre have sinned again and again,
  and I will not let them go unpunished!
They broke their treaty of brotherhood with Israel,
  selling whole villages as slaves to Edom.
¹⁰ So I will send down fire on the walls of Tyre,
  and all its fortresses will be destroyed."

¹¹ This is what the LORD says:

"The people of Edom have sinned again and again,
  and I will not let them go unpunished!
They chased down their relatives, the Israelites, with swords,
  showing them no mercy.
In their rage, they slashed them continually
  and were unrelenting in their anger.
¹² So I will send down fire on Teman,
  and the fortresses of Bozrah will be destroyed."

¹³ This is what the LORD says:

1:1 Hebrew *Joash*, a variant spelling of Jehoash. 1:3 Hebrew *have committed three sins, even four*; also in 1:6, 9, 11, 13.

1:1 This introduction is a standard way of presenting a prophetic message (Jeremiah 1:1; see also Haggai 1:12) and emphasizes the book's form and content. The word translated "shepherd" (*noqed*) is used just one other time in the Old Testament, where it identifies the king of Moab as a "sheep breeder" (2 Kings 3:4). Amos describes himself as *boqer* or "herder" (Amos 7:14). In other words, Amos was not a professional prophet who served the royal court or the Temple. He received messages from God by divine revelation (see Isaiah 1:1). The earthquake is probably the one reported by Zechariah that occurred during the reign of Uzziah (Zechariah 14:5). Uzziah, also called Azariah (792–740 BC), was the most powerful king of Judah after the division of the kingdom. Jeroboam II (793–753 BC), a descendant of Jehu, took advantage of a power vacuum in the region and recovered territory lost earlier to the Arameans.
1:3–2:16 This prophecy's eight judgments proceed from the most obvious enemy, Damascus, to the least obvious, Israel itself. The sequence would have engaged Israel's attention as they heard God's judgment against their enemies. Still, Amos eventually confronted the people with God's judgment on them.
1:3 The expression "have sinned again and again" (or "have committed three sins, even four") is used for a repeated act of rebellion against the natural order established by God (also in 1:6, 9, 11, 13). The Hebrew phrase does not denote a strict count but a pattern of repeated violations. Threshing grain involved separating the heads of the grain from their hulls by pulling wooden sledges with sharp teeth over the cut grain (Isaiah 41:15; see Micah 4:13). This description provides a graphic picture of the brutality of the people of Damascus.
1:9 Tyre and Sidon were the principal seaports of Phoenicia. Tyre's crime, like Philistia's (1:6-8), was "selling whole villages" of Israelite captives to the Edomites, captivity made more bitter by a sense of betrayal (see 2 Samuel 5:11; 1 Kings 5:1, 11). Tyre's reputation was that anything could be had for money; Isaiah portrayed the city as a prostitute peddling her wares (Isaiah 23:15-17).
1:11 The Edomites, descendants of Jacob's brother Esau, were also betrayers (see 1:9; Genesis 25:23-30; 27:39-40; 36:1-43). The NLT adds "the Israelites" to make explicit what "relatives" (literally "brother") means (see Genesis 25:24-30). "Brothers" can also refer to parties to a treaty (see Amos 1:9). Apparently, Edom exerted constant pressure on the borders of Israel and Judah, raiding and plundering at moments of weakness (see Jeremiah 49:7-22; Obadiah 1:1-9).

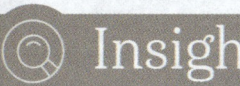

Insight — NO EXCEPTIONS

Amos prophesied in Israel (the northern kingdom) and began his message by declaring God's judgment on all Israel's neighbors (marked on the map). We can see how Amos went north and south and all around, getting closer and closer to his true audience. The people would have nodded at the judgment of their neighbors. Amos's delivery would have lulled them into thinking that Israel was the exception. But Amos had the strongest message against Israel. It's easy to see where everyone else is wrong and to ignore where we are wrong. How can we be more aware of our own sin instead of judging others?

"The people of Ammon have sinned again and again,
 and I will not let them go unpunished!
When they attacked Gilead to extend their borders,
 they ripped open pregnant women with their swords.
¹⁴ So I will send down fire on the walls of Rabbah,
 and all its fortresses will be destroyed.
The battle will come upon them with shouts,
 like a whirlwind in a mighty storm.
¹⁵ And their king* and his princes will go into exile together,"
 says the LORD.

2 This is what the LORD says:

"The people of Moab have sinned again and again,*
 and I will not let them go unpunished!
They desecrated the bones of Edom's king,
 burning them to ashes.
² So I will send down fire on the land of Moab,
 and all the fortresses in Kerioth will be destroyed.
The people will fall in the noise of battle,
 as the warriors shout and the ram's horn sounds.

1:15 Hebrew *malcam*, possibly referring to their god Molech. **2:1** Hebrew *have committed three sins, even four;* also in 2:4, 6.

1:13 Israel regarded the people of Ammon as kin who also betrayed them. The Ammonites (like the Moabites, 2:1) were descendants of Lot, Abraham's nephew (Genesis 19:37-38). Ammon had been a constant threat to Gilead (see Judges 10:7-9). In times of war, both ancient and modern, invading armies often perpetrate violence against women. Scripture does not gloss over these horrific acts and injustices (2 Kings 8:12; 15:16; Isaiah 13:16, 18; Lamentations 5:11; Hosea 10:14; 13:16; Nahum 3:10; Zechariah 14:2). In this series of judgments against Judah's enemies, the magnitude of human sin and evil is on full display.

2:2-3 Kerioth, a major town (Jeremiah 48:20-24), maintained as a shrine to Chemosh, Moab's national god. Perhaps the Moabites burned the remains of Edom's king or offered him as a human sacrifice at this site. Because of the desecration of the Edomite king's corpse, God would destroy the king of Moab and his officers. This fate probably came upon them through an invasion by Sargon II of Assyria (715/713 BC; see Isaiah 15–16). In his writings, the ancient historian Josephus implies further destruction in 582 BC (see also Jeremiah 48:1-47; Ezekiel 25:8-11; Zephaniah 2:8-11).

³ And I will destroy their king
　　and slaughter all their princes,"
　　　says the Lord.

God's Judgment on Judah and Israel

⁴ This is what the Lord says:

"The people of Judah have sinned again and again,
　　and I will not let them go unpunished!
They have rejected the instruction of the Lord,
　　refusing to obey his decrees.
They have been led astray by the same lies
　　that deceived their ancestors.
⁵ So I will send down fire on Judah,
　　and all the fortresses of Jerusalem will be destroyed."

⁶ This is what the Lord says:

"The people of Israel have sinned again and again,
　　and I will not let them go unpunished!
They sell honorable people for silver
　　and poor people for a pair of sandals.
⁷ They trample helpless people in the dust
　　and shove the oppressed out of the way.
Both father and son sleep with the same woman,
　　corrupting my holy name.
⁸ At their religious festivals,
　　they lounge in clothing their debtors put up as security.
In the house of their gods,*
　　they drink wine bought with unjust fines.

⁹ "But as my people watched,
　　I destroyed the Amorites,
though they were as tall as cedars
　　and as strong as oaks.
I destroyed the fruit on their branches
　　and dug out their roots.
¹⁰ It was I who rescued you from Egypt
　　and led you through the desert for forty years,
so you could possess the land of the Amorites.
¹¹ I chose some of your sons to be prophets
　　and others to be Nazirites.
Can you deny this, my people of Israel?"
　　asks the Lord.
¹² "But you caused the Nazirites to sin by making them drink wine,
　　and you commanded the prophets, 'Shut up!'

¹³ "So I will make you groan
　　like a wagon loaded down with sheaves of grain.
¹⁴ Your fastest runners will not get away.
　　The strongest among you will become weak.
Even mighty warriors will be unable to save themselves.
¹⁵ The archers will not stand their ground.
The swiftest runners won't be fast enough to escape.
　　Even those riding horses won't be able to save themselves.
¹⁶ On that day the most courageous of your fighting men
　　will drop their weapons and run for their lives,"
　　　says the Lord.

2:8 Or *their God*.

2:4 The pagan nations listed to this point had committed atrocities that violated a general sense of human decency, but Judah had gone further; they held the word of God and yet had rejected its teachings (see Hosea 4:6; 8:1). God holds people responsible in proportion to the privilege they have received (see Amos 3:2). Having discarded God's true instruction, Judah turned to a substitute found in pagan *syncretism* (combining elements from different belief systems) and idolatry (see 1 Kings 14:22-24).

2:6 "Honorable people" (literally, the "righteous") are those who enjoy a right relationship with God and others. The parallel with "poor people" creates the idea of the "righteous needy." The law of Moses urged those who lived comfortably to help those in need by being financially generous and lending freely (Deuteronomy 15:7-11). As a last resort, people who were unable to pay their debts could become indentured servants (Leviticus 25:39-43). These righteous needy were being enslaved for "a pair of sandals," a hyperbole for the pittance they owed (see Amos 8:6). The sandals were a pledge given for the debt or a token used to seal a bargain (see Ruth 4:7).

2:7 To "trample...people" means to treat them ruthlessly (see also 8:4). The helpless and oppressed were people exploited by a socioeconomic system that denied them the justice guaranteed by law (Exodus 23:6-8). That "father and son sleep with the same woman" demonstrated the moral destitution of the Israelites; the law of Moses prohibited this practice (Leviticus 18:7-8, 15; 20:11-12). In worshiping various fertility gods, Israel and surrounding nations engaged in "sacred prostitution" (see Hosea 4:10-14). Having sex with a shrine prostitute was thought to ensure plentiful crops and thriving herds of livestock. This verse suggests that these acts were performed in the name of the Lord. When performed as religious rituals, these corrupt actions treat God's name as worthless.

2:8 The irony is that the oppressors of the poor flaunted their sins at religious festivals. The law of Moses allowed a lender to take a poor man's cloak as security for a debt, but it was not to be kept overnight because the nights were cold (Exodus 22:26-27; Deuteronomy 24:12-13). A widow's clothing was never to be taken as security for a debt (Deuteronomy 24:17). The wealthy bribed judges and used their influence to keep the poor, who could not defend themselves, from obtaining a fair hearing (Amos 5:12).

2:11-12 In addition to priests, God provided prophets to speak his word and will (Deuteronomy 18:15-19) and holy men called *Nazirites*, who were dedicated to the Lord by vows that included abstaining from wine and other alcoholic drinks (Numbers 6:1-21). Israel showed its disregard for God by telling both the Nazirites and the prophets to ignore and violate God's calling (see Amos 7:12-13).

3 Listen to this message that the Lord has spoken against you, O people of Israel—against the entire family I rescued from Egypt:

² "From among all the families on the earth,
  I have been intimate with you alone.
That is why I must punish you
  for all your sins."

Witnesses against Guilty Israel

³ Can two people walk together
  without agreeing on the direction?
⁴ Does a lion ever roar in a thicket
  without first finding a victim?
Does a young lion growl in its den
  without first catching its prey?
⁵ Does a bird ever get caught in a trap
  that has no bait?
Does a trap spring shut
  when there's nothing to catch?
⁶ When the ram's horn blows a warning,
  shouldn't the people be alarmed?
Does disaster come to a city
  unless the Lord has planned it?

⁷ Indeed, the Sovereign Lord never does anything
  until he reveals his plans to his servants the prophets.

⁸ The lion has roared—
  so who isn't frightened?
The Sovereign Lord has spoken—
  so who can refuse to proclaim his message?

⁹ Announce this to the leaders of Philistia*
  and to the great ones of Egypt:
"Take your seats now on the hills around Samaria,
  and witness the chaos and oppression in Israel."

¹⁰ "My people have forgotten how to do right," says the Lord.
"Their fortresses are filled with wealth
  taken by theft and violence.
¹¹ Therefore," says the Sovereign Lord,
"an enemy is coming!
He will surround them and shatter their defenses.
Then he will plunder all their fortresses."

¹²This is what the Lord says:

"A shepherd who tries to rescue a sheep from a lion's mouth
  will recover only two legs or a piece of an ear.
So it will be for the Israelites in Samaria lying on luxurious beds,
  and for the people of Damascus reclining on couches.*

¹³"Now listen to this, and announce it throughout all Israel,*" says the Lord, the Lord God of Heaven's Armies.

¹⁴ "On the very day I punish Israel for its sins,
  I will destroy the pagan altars at Bethel.
The horns of the altar will be cut off
  and fall to the ground.

3:9 Hebrew *Ashdod*. 3:12 The meaning of the Hebrew in this sentence is uncertain. 3:13 Hebrew *the house of Jacob*. The names "Jacob" and "Israel" are often interchanged throughout the Old Testament, referring sometimes to the individual patriarch and sometimes to the nation.

3:2 The word translated "been intimate" indicates personal and experiential knowledge that often extends beyond mere intellectual awareness. It can indicate formal recognition and acknowledgment (Exodus 1:8; 5:2), personal experience (Genesis 2:17), or sexual experience (Genesis 4:1). This word is frequently used for God's relationship with Israel (Hosea 5:3) and Israel's ideal relationship with God (Hosea 2:20). Because of Israel's privileged status, God would hold them accountable for all their sins, not just some of them. God holds people accountable in terms of what has been given them (Luke 12:47-48).
3:9 The prophet here turns to two of Israel's enemies, Philistia (Hebrew *Ashdod*, one of the key cities of Philistia) and Egypt. He invites them to surround Samaria (the capital of the kingdom of Israel) to see its "chaos and oppression." Israel appeared strong from the outside, but it was rotten within, rife with class struggles. The enemies would take advantage of Israel's internal weakness (see 3:11).
3:12 The people of both Israel and Judah believed that God would never let them perish because of their chosen status and would intervene to rescue them. The prophet's words are ironic: their rescue would be like a shepherd who arrives too late to save the sheep and can pull "only two legs or a piece of an ear" from the mouth of the lion. The meaning of the Hebrew in the second half of this verse is uncertain. Some have interpreted this statement to mean that only the fabric of a few couches would survive the Assyrian siege of Samaria. Accordingly, the last two lines of this verse could be translated "So it will be when the Israelites in Samaria are rescued / with only a broken bed and a tattered pillow."
3:13 The Lord's message is to go to "all Israel" (literally "the house of Jacob"). The names Jacob and Israel are often interchanged in the Old Testament, sometimes referring to the individual patriarch and other times to the nation. Jacob was the ancestor of both Israel (the northern kingdom) and Judah (the southern kingdom). The witnesses who are told to listen could be the nations summoned in 3:9, the inhabitants of Samaria, or bands of prophets. The title "Lord God of Heaven's Armies" (traditionally "Lord God of Hosts") portrays God as commander of the heavenly armies. This is the true God of the universe, not a local deity (4:13; 5:14-16, 27; 6:8; see also Exodus 15:3).
3:14 The shrine at Bethel, built by Jeroboam I shortly after his inauguration (1 Kings 12:26-33), continued through the dynasty of Jehu (2 Kings 10:29), from whom Jeroboam II descended. This shrine merged worship of the Lord with the pagan symbol of a bull. When the altars were destroyed, the Bethel shrine, the king's official sanctuary (Amos 7:13), and the northern kingdom would also be ruined.

15 And I will destroy the beautiful homes of the wealthy—
their winter mansions and their summer houses, too—
all their palaces filled with ivory,"
says the LORD.

Israel's Failure to Learn

4 Listen to me, you fat cows*
living in Samaria,
you women who oppress the poor
and crush the needy,
and who are always calling to your husbands,
"Bring us another drink!"

2 The Sovereign LORD has sworn this by his holiness:
"The time will come when you will be led away
with hooks in your noses.
Every last one of you will be dragged away
like a fish on a hook!

3 You will be led out through the ruins of the wall;
you will be thrown from your fortresses,*"
says the LORD.

4 "Go ahead and offer sacrifices to the idols at Bethel.
Keep on disobeying at Gilgal.
Offer sacrifices each morning,
and bring your tithes every three days.

5 Present your bread made with yeast
as an offering of thanksgiving.
Then give your extra voluntary offerings
so you can brag about it everywhere!
This is the kind of thing you Israelites love to do,"
says the Sovereign LORD.

6 "I brought hunger to every city
and famine to every town.
But still you would not return to me,"
says the LORD.

7 "I kept the rain from falling
when your crops needed it the most.
I sent rain on one town
but withheld it from another.
Rain fell on one field,
while another field withered away.

8 People staggered from town to town looking for water,
but there was never enough.
But still you would not return to me,"
says the LORD.

9 "I struck your farms and vineyards with blight and mildew.
Locusts devoured all your fig and olive trees.
But still you would not return to me,"
says the LORD.

10 "I sent plagues on you
like the plagues I sent on Egypt long ago.
I killed your young men in war
and led all your horses away.*
The stench of death filled the air!
But still you would not return to me,"
says the LORD.

11 "I destroyed some of your cities,
as I destroyed* Sodom and Gomorrah.
Those of you who survived
were like charred sticks pulled from a fire.
But still you would not return to me,"
says the LORD.

12 "Therefore, I will bring upon you all the disasters I have announced.

4:1 Hebrew *you cows of Bashan.* 4:3 Or *thrown out toward Harmon,* possibly a reference to Mount Hermon. 4:10 Or *and slaughtered your captured horses.* 4:11 Hebrew *as when God destroyed.*

4:1 Bashan (see text note on this verse) was famous for its fierce, fat bulls, and Amos uses the feminine form ("cows") to paint a picture of Israel's wealthy wives, who did not care about people who were poor. Their only concern was to extract enough wealth from the needy to support their own indulgent lifestyles.

4:2 Holiness speaks of God as existing outside of and independent of creation; his nature is wholly other than what he has created. The oath is similar to those in 6:8; 8:7. The Assyrians were known for their brutal treatment of war captives (see 2 Chronicles 33:11; compare 2 Kings 19:28). A *stela* (stone pillar with an inscription) discovered in northern Syria shows the Assyrian king Esarhaddon holding cords that pass through the lips of two war captives. "Hooks" may refer to the rings inserted into the noses of cattle to manage them.

4:4 Amos lampoons the Israelites' worthless piety. Bethel, site of Jacob's famous vision of the ladder with angels descending and ascending (Genesis 28:11-22), was the southern seat of the religious system established by Jeroboam I (see Amos 3:14; 1 Kings 12:28-29). Gilgal, Israel's campsite after they crossed the Jordan (Joshua 4:19–5:9), had become a popular shrine by the time of Amos and Hosea (Hosea 4:15; 9:15; 12:11). Israelite males were to appear before the Lord at the sanctuary three times each year (Exodus 23:14-19; 34:23; Deuteronomy 16:16-17). Tithes were typically paid annually (Deuteronomy 14:22-29), with a special tithe paid every three years (see Deuteronomy 14:28; 26:12). Amos is making the point that the Israelites were religious to the point of absurdity, but they balked at being godly (Amos 5:15; Hosea 6:6; Micah 6:8; see Luke 11:42).

4:6-12 Although this punishment might seem cruel to a modern mindset, God's actions were just judgment for sin, and Israel had been repeatedly warned that covenant unfaithfulness would be catastrophic (Leviticus 26; Deuteronomy 28). However, God is not without compassion. He intended Israel's suffering to produce repentance and restoration. For those who follow him, judgment is never the final word.

4:10 God had used plagues to convince Egypt to let Israel go (Exodus 9:2-3; Psalm 91:6; Habakkuk 3:5). He promised to bring the plagues of Egypt on Israel if they continued to turn away from him to worship pagan gods (Deuteronomy 28:27, 60).

Wealthy Samaritan Wives

◎ IDENTITY Comfort over Compassion

They remember . . .

We wear the best clothes made from the finest linens in all the colors of the rainbow. We are adorned with gold jewelry that makes lovely tinkling sounds as we glide through the city. All see us and step aside.

We have more than enough to eat, and our wine goblets are never empty long. You might say we have too much money and too much spare time. We say we deserve every last crumb. We're entitled to our wealth.

If our husbands tell us not to buy that next treasure, we tell them to be more ruthless, squeeze every last bit out of the poor, cheat whoever gets in their way. We don't care if other people don't have enough to survive as long as we can sustain our lifestyles.

Amos thinks God can warn us, scare us, threaten us, call us names! We see nothing wrong with getting more, spending more, consuming more. How could our comfortable world come crashing down? That prophet Amos has no idea what he's talking about. Look at our full storerooms and storage chests full of goods! Look at our beautiful hair and clothes! Smell our oils and perfumes!

If there's a gold ring in our noses, we put it there as the latest fashion. They're not cattle hooks for leading to slaughter. "Fat cows"? Not us. Just see if Amos's God can ruin our perfect, comfortable lives.

THE WEALTHY SAMARITAN WIVES' STORY IS TOLD IN AMOS 4:1-12.

> Too much time and money can make us want more of comfort and less of God.

IDENTIFY

Do our comforts and wealth blind us to disobedience to God and the needs of others? God offers us something greater than comfort and wealth and requires that we repent and offer what we have to God.

> *"It's easy to want more instead of wanting God. The more comfortable I am, the less I see others' needs, and the more I value keeping my economic status. All this leads to poor decision-making."*

CARA DAY is a writer and illustrator. She has served with Stonecroft Ministries helping women live "extraordinary."

Prepare to meet your God in judgment, you people of Israel!"

¹³ For the Lord is the one who shaped the mountains,
stirs up the winds, and reveals his thoughts to mankind.
He turns the light of dawn into darkness
and treads on the heights of the earth.
The Lord God of Heaven's Armies is his name!

A Call to Repentance

5 Listen, you people of Israel! Listen to this funeral song I am singing:

² "The virgin Israel has fallen,
never to rise again!
She lies abandoned on the ground,
with no one to help her up."

³ The Sovereign Lord says:

"When a city sends a thousand men to battle,
only a hundred will return.
When a town sends a hundred,
only ten will come back alive."

⁴ Now this is what the Lord says to the family of Israel:

"Come back to me and live!
⁵ Don't worship at the pagan altars at Bethel;
don't go to the shrines at Gilgal or Beersheba.
For the people of Gilgal will be dragged off into exile,
and the people of Bethel will be reduced to nothing."

⁶ Come back to the Lord and live!
Otherwise, he will roar through Israel* like a fire,
devouring you completely.
Your gods in Bethel
won't be able to quench the flames.
⁷ You twist justice, making it a bitter pill for the oppressed.
You treat the righteous like dirt.

⁸ It is the Lord who created the stars,
the Pleiades and Orion.
He turns darkness into morning
and day into night.
He draws up water from the oceans
and pours it down as rain on the land.
The Lord is his name!
⁹ With blinding speed and power he destroys the strong,
crushing all their defenses.

¹⁰ How you hate honest judges!
How you despise people who tell the truth!
¹¹ You trample the poor,
stealing their grain through taxes and unfair rent.
Therefore, though you build beautiful stone houses,
you will never live in them.
Though you plant lush vineyards,
you will never drink wine from them.
¹² For I know the vast number of your sins
and the depth of your rebellions.
You oppress good people by taking bribes
and deprive the poor of justice in the courts.
¹³ So those who are smart keep their mouths shut,
for it is an evil time.

¹⁴ Do what is good and run from evil
so that you may live!
Then the Lord God of Heaven's Armies will be your helper,
just as you have claimed.
¹⁵ Hate evil and love what is good;
turn your courts into true halls of justice.
Perhaps even yet the Lord God of Heaven's Armies
will have mercy on the remnant of his people.*

¹⁶ Therefore, this is what the Lord, the Lord God of Heaven's Armies, says:

"There will be crying in all the public squares
and mourning in every street.
Call for the farmers to weep with you,
and summon professional mourners to wail.
¹⁷ There will be wailing in every vineyard,
for I will destroy them all,"
says the Lord.

5:6 Hebrew *the house of Joseph*. **5:15** Hebrew *the remnant of Joseph*.

4:13 Amos clearly states that God can sit in judgment over Israel because he is the creator of the universe and controls all things. See 5:8.
5:1 The Hebrew word for "funeral song" (*qinah*) describes a special rhythm (three beats, followed by two beats) used for funeral dirges (most of the book of Lamentations is written in this special rhythm). The ominous significance was clear: Israel had already died and now awaited burial.
5:2 When used to describe political powers, "virgin" referred to an independent state that had not been conquered by a foreign power. This terminology is used to describe Babylon in Isaiah 47:1, Jerusalem in Lamentations 2:13, and is reversed in Lamentations 1:1.
5:11 Again, Amos calls out the rich. The houses of peasants were built of mud brick. Cut stone, the result of laborious handwork, was costly.
5:13 Witnesses pleaded that they saw and heard nothing. Truthfulness had become a liability (5:10) and might endanger the one who spoke it.

Warning of Coming Judgment

18 What sorrow awaits you who say,
"If only the day of the LORD were here!"
You have no idea what you are wishing for.
That day will bring darkness, not light.
19 In that day you will be like a man who runs from a lion—
only to meet a bear.
Escaping from the bear, he leans his hand against a wall in his house—
and he's bitten by a snake.
20 Yes, the day of the LORD will be dark and hopeless,
without a ray of joy or hope.

21 "I hate all your show and pretense—
the hypocrisy of your religious festivals and solemn assemblies.
22 I will not accept your burnt offerings and grain offerings.
I won't even notice all your choice peace offerings.
23 Away with your noisy hymns of praise!
I will not listen to the music of your harps.
24 Instead, I want to see a mighty flood of justice,
an endless river of righteous living.

25 "Was it to me you were bringing sacrifices and offerings during the forty years in the wilderness, Israel? 26 No, you served your pagan gods—Sakkuth your king god and Kaiwan your star god—the images you made for yourselves. 27 So I will send you into exile, to a land east of Damascus,*" says the LORD, whose name is the God of Heaven's Armies.

6 What sorrow awaits you who lounge in luxury in Jerusalem,*
and you who feel secure in Samaria!
You are famous and popular in Israel,
and people go to you for help.
2 But go over to Calneh
and see what happened there.
Then go to the great city of Hamath
and down to the Philistine city of Gath.
You are no better than they were,
and look at how they were destroyed.
3 You push away every thought of coming disaster,
but your actions only bring the day of judgment closer.
4 How terrible for you who sprawl on ivory beds
and lounge on your couches,
eating the meat of tender lambs from the flock
and of choice calves fattened in the stall.
5 You sing trivial songs to the sound of the harp
and fancy yourselves to be great musicians like David.
6 You drink wine by the bowlful
and perfume yourselves with fragrant lotions.
You care nothing about the ruin of your nation.*

5:26-27 Greek version reads *No, you carried your pagan gods—the shrine of Molech, the star of your god Rephan, and the images you made for yourselves. So I will send you into exile, to a land east of Damascus.* Compare Acts 7:43. **6:1** Hebrew *in Zion.* **6:6** Hebrew *of Joseph.*

5:18–6:14 The pronouncements of sorrow in this section develop two themes: Israel's apostasy would make the "day of the LORD" (5:18) a day of judgment, not salvation; and Judah's spiritual complacency would also bring judgment.
5:18 Amos again confronts the Israelites' distorted view of their chosen status (see 3:2). The phrase "what sorrow awaits you" denotes despair brought on by a great tragedy. The "day of the LORD" in the Old Testament (see Isaiah 13:6, 9) was a time when God would intervene in the world to set right those things that had gone wrong. God's intervention would mean vindication for the righteous but judgment for the wicked (Amos 8:3, 9, 13; 9:11). Israel thought that God would save them on that day, but because the Israelites had been wicked, the Day of the Lord would "bring darkness, not light." Assyria conquered the northern kingdom in 722 BC (2 Kings 17:7-23), fulfilling this prophecy.
5:24 This is the second of the great thematic verses in Amos (see 4:12). The wadis (streams or gullies) in Israel's dry areas contained water only temporarily during rainy seasons. However, God wanted continual, not just seasonal, justice.
5:26-27 The names that appear in 5:26 have given rise to several conjectures. Still, many interpreters consider them to be names of unidentified pagan gods. The king god may well be Molech, god of the Ammonites (see text note on 1:15). The word translated "you served" may mean "you will lift up," in which case the prophet is making a contrast between Israel or Judah, who carried their idols, and God, who carries his people (see Isaiah 46:1-7).
6:1 A message including Jerusalem is unexpected, but it shows that God plays no favorites; whoever rebels against God would experience sorrow. The Hebrew text uses the terms "Zion . . . Mount Samaria," indicating the citadels of the two cities. The people of both Judah and Israel were smug and self-important, believing that the fortresses of the cities of Jerusalem and Samaria were impregnable (see also 4:3). Relying on physical power instead of on God is sin.
6:2 Calneh and Hamath were Aramean city-states under Israelite influence (see 2 Kings 14:28). Calneh fell to Assyria in 738 BC, and Hamath was forced to pay tribute shortly after. Uzziah had broken down the wall of Gath (2 Chronicles 26:6), but it also fell to Assyria in 711 BC. Israel itself fell in 722 BC (see note on Amos 5:18).
6:3 By the term "day of judgment," Amos either meant that Israel's behavior hastened the violence of the Assyrian conquest or that the people encouraged everyday violence against the poor by pushing the "thought of coming disaster" from their minds.
6:4 Meat was typically used to honor distinguished guests. The common food was bread, fruit, vegetables, and dairy products. The everyday use of meat shows the opulence of the wealthy classes.
6:6 The Hebrew word translated "bowl" (*mizraq*) is related to a verb meaning "sprinkle" or "splash" (*zaraq*; see Exodus 24:6). The same word identified the basins used for sprinkling blood or water in religious ceremonies (see 2 Kings 12:13; 25:15), adding a sense of sacrilege to this description of their drunkenness. The Hebrew text reads "of Joseph" (translated "of your nation"), referring to the northern kingdom of Israel; see text notes on Amos 5:6; 5:15.

⁷ Therefore, you will be the first to be led away as captives.
Suddenly, all your parties will end.

⁸The Sovereign LORD has sworn by his own name, and this is what he, the LORD God of Heaven's Armies, says:

"I despise the arrogance of Israel,*
and I hate their fortresses.
I will give this city
and everything in it to their enemies."

⁹(If there are ten men left in one house, they will all die. ¹⁰And when a relative who is responsible to dispose of the dead* goes into the house to carry out the bodies, he will ask the last survivor, "Is anyone else with you?" When the person begins to swear, "No, by . . . ," he will interrupt and say, "Stop! Don't even mention the name of the LORD.")

¹¹ When the LORD gives the command,
homes both great and small will be smashed to pieces.

¹² Can horses gallop over boulders?
Can oxen be used to plow them?
But that's how foolish you are when you turn justice into poison
and the sweet fruit of righteousness into bitterness.

¹³ And you brag about your conquest of Lo-debar.*
You boast, "Didn't we take Karnaim* by our own strength?"

¹⁴ "O people of Israel, I am about to bring an enemy nation against you,"
says the LORD God of Heaven's Armies.
"They will oppress you throughout your land— from Lebo-hamath in the north
to the Arabah Valley in the south."

A Vision of Locusts

7 The Sovereign LORD showed me a vision. I saw him preparing to send a vast swarm of locusts over the land. This was after the king's share had been harvested from the fields and as the main crop was coming up. ²In my vision the locusts ate every green plant in sight. Then I said, "O Sovereign LORD, please forgive us or we will not survive, for Israel* is so small."

³So the LORD relented from this plan. "I will not do it," he said.

A Vision of Fire

⁴Then the Sovereign LORD showed me another vision. I saw him preparing to punish his people with a great fire. The fire had burned up the depths of the sea and was devouring the entire land. ⁵Then I said, "O Sovereign LORD, please stop or we will not survive, for Israel is so small."

⁶Then the LORD relented from this plan, too. "I will not do that either," said the Sovereign LORD.

A Vision of a Plumb Line

⁷Then he showed me another vision. I saw the Lord standing beside a wall that had been built using a plumb line. He was using a plumb line to see if it was still straight. ⁸And the LORD said to me, "Amos, what do you see?"

I answered, "A plumb line."

And the Lord replied, "I will test my people with this plumb line. I will no longer ignore all their sins. ⁹The pagan shrines of your ancestors* will be ruined, and the temples of Israel will be destroyed; I will bring the dynasty of King Jeroboam to a sudden end."

6:8 Hebrew *Jacob*. See note on 3:13. **6:10** Or *to burn the dead*. The meaning of the Hebrew is uncertain. **6:13a** *Lo-debar* means "nothing." **6:13b** *Karnaim* means "horns," a term that symbolizes strength. **7:2** Hebrew *Jacob*; also in 7:5. See note on 3:13. **7:9** Hebrew *of Isaac*.

6:12 It would be foolish to run "horses . . . over boulders," because unshod horses cannot run on rocks without serious damage to their hooves. It is also evident that oxen cannot plow rocks. A slight adjustment to the word division of the Hebrew text yields "plow the sea with oxen," an equally absurd suggestion. The point of the comparisons now becomes obvious, as Israel's own absurdity in the moral realm surfaces. The people perverted what is just and right, turning it into something toxic and bitter (see also 5:7).

7:1 Locusts (see 4:9) were one of the plagues brought upon Egypt (Exodus 10:4). Great swarms of locusts periodically invaded these lands, typically in times of drought (see Joel 1–2). The first harvest went to the king as taxes, whereas the later harvest of the main crop fed the farmer and his family. However, if locusts devoured this crop, starvation would follow.

7:4 This fire symbolizes oppressive heat and drought. Although the Hebrew word indicates the sea, Amos probably did not expect the Mediterranean to disappear. More likely, this is a poetic reference to large freshwater bodies (such as the Kinnereth Sea or Sea of Galilee) which Israel used to irrigate its fields.

7:7-9 This vision begins like the previous two (7:2-3, 4-6), but the Lord allows no intercession this time. The abrupt shift in outcome contributed to the power of Amos's message.

7:8 The Hebrew word translated "plumb line" (*anak*) is similar to the word for groaning (*anakhah*, see Isaiah 35:10; Lamentations 1:22), alluding to great suffering when God would hold them accountable.

7:9 Every vestige of the apostate Israelite religion, from the common high places to the royal shrine at Bethel, would be destroyed. "Ancestors" (the Hebrew word used here is "Isaac") stands for the nation's fathers. Jeroboam II died of natural causes (2 Kings 14:29), but the murder of his son and successor, Zechariah, after a reign of less than a year (2 Kings 15:8-10; see 2 Kings 10:28-31), initiated instability in Israel's government that it never overcame (2 Kings 15:10-31).

Amos and Amaziah

¹⁰Then Amaziah, the priest of Bethel, sent a message to Jeroboam, king of Israel: "Amos is hatching a plot against you right here on your very doorstep! What he is saying is intolerable. ¹¹He is saying, 'Jeroboam will soon be killed, and the people of Israel will be sent away into exile.'"

¹²Then Amaziah sent orders to Amos: "Get out of here, you prophet! Go on back to the land of Judah, and earn your living by prophesying there! ¹³Don't bother us with your prophecies here in Bethel. This is the king's sanctuary and the national place of worship!"

¹⁴But Amos replied, "I'm not a professional prophet, and I was never trained to be one.* I'm just a shepherd, and I take care of sycamore-fig trees. ¹⁵But the LORD called me away from my flock and told me, 'Go and prophesy to my people in Israel.' ¹⁶Now then, listen to this message from the LORD:

7:14 Or *I'm not a prophet nor the son of a prophet.*

7:14 Amos was not a professional prophet or even a disciple in training (literally, "I'm not a prophet nor the son of a prophet"). He had no financial incentive to leave his livelihood to prophesy. The Hebrew word for "shepherd" here is not the same as in 1:1 and is not found elsewhere in the Old Testament. It is related to a word for cattle, suggesting that Amos may have raised cattle as a breeder or herder. The sycamore-fig was gathered for cattle feed.

Return to Restoration

MY STORY WITH GOD

SCRIPTURE CONNECTION: AMOS 9:1-15

I have done this—what Amos is confronting God's people for doing. I've succumbed to religiosity over the gritty work of loving and serving God by loving and serving *others*. I have distanced myself from God's goodness, however subtly or blatantly.

The Israelites chose a distancing path as well, away from God rather than toward him. Amos called out their betrayals and hypocrisy, warning that their rebellions would not go unanswered. But Amos also declared that God would preserve the faithful; not one true kernel would be lost.

According to Amos, God would not give up on his family. His rhythm may include rebuke in preparation to rebuild, repair, and restore all who belong to him.

So it is with us. We choose whether to align ourselves with God or not. As evidenced by Amos's prophecy—and basically all human history—we find that no number of miracles or blessings promised—and no number of warnings or threats issued—can force true faith into a person's heart. It is only God's unrelenting love, even when delivered through discipline, that inspires our devotion and completes us (Deuteronomy 8:5; Hebrews 12:5-7).

He offers restoration to Israel and to us. He has done it in my lifetime again and again. I trust him to do it in yours.

> Today I will practice the gritty work of loving and serving God by loving and serving *others*.

IMAGINE

In what areas of life might we receive correction, return to God, and ask him to rebuild, repair, and restore?

"It is God who does the restoring; my job is to return with willingness and follow his lead."

MISTY ARTERBURN is an author and speaker, contributing to Bible projects, devotionals, and recovery materials for over twenty years.

"You say,
  'Don't prophesy against Israel.
    Stop preaching against my people.*'
¹⁷ But this is what the LORD says:
  'Your wife will become a prostitute in this city,
    and your sons and daughters will be killed.
  Your land will be divided up,
    and you yourself will die in a foreign land.
  And the people of Israel will certainly become
      captives in exile,
    far from their homeland.'"

A Vision of Ripe Fruit

8 Then the Sovereign LORD showed me another vision. In it I saw a basket filled with ripe fruit. ²"What do you see, Amos?" he asked.

I replied, "A basket full of ripe fruit."

Then the LORD said, "Like this fruit, Israel is ripe for punishment! I will not delay their punishment again. ³In that day the singing in the temple will turn to wailing. Dead bodies will be scattered everywhere. They will be carried out of the city in silence. I, the Sovereign LORD, have spoken!"

⁴ Listen to this, you who rob the poor
    and trample down the needy!
⁵ You can't wait for the Sabbath day to be over
    and the religious festivals to end
  so you can get back to cheating the helpless.
  You measure out grain with dishonest measures
    and cheat the buyer with dishonest scales.*
⁶ And you mix the grain you sell
    with chaff swept from the floor.
  Then you enslave poor people
    for one piece of silver or a pair of sandals.

⁷ Now the LORD has sworn this oath
    by his own name, the Pride of Israel*:
  "I will never forget
    the wicked things you have done!

⁸ The earth will tremble for your deeds,
    and everyone will mourn.
  The ground will rise like the Nile River at floodtime;
    it will heave up, then sink again.

⁹ "In that day," says the Sovereign LORD,
  "I will make the sun go down at noon
    and darken the earth while it is still day.
¹⁰ I will turn your celebrations into times of mourning
    and your singing into weeping.
  You will wear funeral clothes
    and shave your heads to show your sorrow—
    as if your only son had died.
  How very bitter that day will be!

¹¹ "The time is surely coming," says the Sovereign LORD,
  "when I will send a famine on the land—
  not a famine of bread or water
    but of hearing the words of the LORD.
¹² People will stagger from sea to sea
    and wander from border to border*
  searching for the word of the LORD,
    but they will not find it.
¹³ Beautiful girls and strong young men
    will grow faint in that day,
    thirsting for the LORD's word.
¹⁴ And those who swear by the shameful idols of
      Samaria—
    who take oaths in the name of the god of Dan
    and make vows in the name of the god of
      Beersheba*—
  they will all fall down,
    never to rise again."

A Vision of God at the Altar

9 Then I saw a vision of the Lord standing beside the altar. He said,

  "Strike the tops of the Temple columns,
    so that the foundation will shake.

7:16 Hebrew *against the house of Isaac.* **8:5** Hebrew *You make the ephah* [a unit for measuring grain] *small and the shekel* [a unit of weight] *great, and you deal falsely by using deceitful balances.* **8:7** Hebrew *the pride of Jacob.* See note on 3:13. **8:12** Hebrew *from north to east.* **8:14** Hebrew *the way of Beersheba.*

8:2 Amos makes a play on the Hebrew words "ripe fruit" (*qayits*), and "the end has come" (*ba haqqets*). The end would come for God's people, Israel, because they were ripe fruit, ready to be harvested in judgment.
8:5 Work was explicitly forbidden on the Sabbath day (Exodus 20:8-11); Amos implies that shops were closed during pagan new moon religious festivals as well. The ephah was a unit for measuring grain, and the shekel was a unit of weight. Merchants cheated their customers by measuring grain with small ephahs, and they cheated their suppliers by using heavy shekels on the scales. This practice was forbidden by God's law (Leviticus 19:35-36; Deuteronomy 25:13-16; see Proverbs 11:1; 16:11; 20:10, 23).
8:9 The Day of the Lord would invert the cosmos. Jeremiah used similar imagery to describe the desecration of Judah as the Babylonian armies approached (Jeremiah 4:23; see also Isaiah 13:10; 34:4; 50:3; Ezekiel 32:7-8; Joel 2:10, 31; Micah 3:6).
8:11-14 God sent prophets to Israel to speak his words directly to them, but the people commanded the prophets not to prophesy (2:11-12). Now they had what they wanted, but it was a silence more terrible than God's roar and thunder: God became distant (see Ezekiel 7:26; 20:3; Micah 3:4, 7). The time for speaking was over; the time of judgment had come.
8:12 The natural boundaries of Israel were "from sea to sea"— the Mediterranean Sea on the west and the Dead Sea on the south. The other borders are simply called the north and the east.
8:14 The "god of Dan" refers to the northern shrine of the gold calf established by Jeroboam I (see 1 Kings 12:28-29; 2 Kings 10:29). Evidently, Beersheba had become a center of worship in the southern kingdom. Archaeologists have found the remains of a horned altar in the ruins of Beersheba.

Bring down the roof
   on the heads of the people below.
I will kill with the sword those who survive.
   No one will escape!

² "Even if they dig down to the place of the dead,*
   I will reach down and pull them up.
Even if they climb up into the heavens,
   I will bring them down.
³ Even if they hide at the very top of Mount Carmel,
   I will search them out and capture them.
Even if they hide at the bottom of the ocean,
   I will send the sea serpent after them to bite them.
⁴ Even if their enemies drive them into exile,
   I will command the sword to kill them there.
I am determined to bring disaster upon them
   and not to help them."

⁵ The Lord, the LORD of Heaven's Armies,
   touches the land and it melts,
   and all its people mourn.
The ground rises like the Nile River at floodtime,
   and then it sinks again.
⁶ The LORD's home reaches up to the heavens,
   while its foundation is on the earth.
He draws up water from the oceans
   and pours it down as rain on the land.
   The LORD is his name!

⁷ "Are you Israelites more important to me
   than the Ethiopians?*" asks the LORD.
"I brought Israel out of Egypt,
   but I also brought the Philistines from Crete*
   and led the Arameans out of Kir.

⁸ "I, the Sovereign LORD,
   am watching this sinful nation of Israel.
I will destroy it
   from the face of the earth.
But I will never completely destroy the family of Israel,*"
   says the LORD.
⁹ "For I will give the command
   and will shake Israel along with the other nations
as grain is shaken in a sieve,
   yet not one true kernel will be lost.
¹⁰ But all the sinners will die by the sword—
   all those who say, 'Nothing bad will happen to us.'

A Promise of Restoration

¹¹ "In that day I will restore the fallen house* of David.
   I will repair its damaged walls.
From the ruins I will rebuild it
   and restore its former glory.
¹² And Israel will possess what is left of Edom
   and all the nations I have called to be mine.*"
The LORD has spoken,
   and he will do these things.

¹³ "The time will come," says the LORD,
   "when the grain and grapes will grow faster
   than they can be harvested.
Then the terraced vineyards on the hills of Israel
   will drip with sweet wine!
¹⁴ I will bring my exiled people of Israel
   back from distant lands,
and they will rebuild their ruined cities
   and live in them again.
They will plant vineyards and gardens;
   they will eat their crops and drink their wine.
¹⁵ I will firmly plant them there
   in their own land.
They will never again be uprooted
   from the land I have given them,"
   says the LORD your God.

9:2 Hebrew *to Sheol.* **9:7a** Hebrew *the Cushites?* **9:7b** Hebrew *Caphtor.* **9:8** Hebrew *the house of Jacob.* See note on 3:13. **9:11a** Or *kingdom;* Hebrew reads *tent.* **9:11b-12** Greek version reads *and restore its former glory, / so that the rest of humanity, including the Gentiles— / all those I have called to be mine— / might seek me.* Compare Acts 15:16-17.

9:2-4 God is inescapable (compare Psalm 139:7-12). When people trust, believe, and obey God, his inescapability is a great blessing. But because Israel rejected God's revelation, his presence would mean judgment, not comfort.

9:3 Though Mount Carmel is not the highest mountain in the region, its lofty grandeur represented the beauty and richness of the land (see Song of Songs 7:5; Isaiah 35:2). In the ancient Near East, the sea symbolized chaos, often pitted against the national god (compare to Psalms 74:13-14; 89:9-10; 104:25-26). However, the biblical text does not grant divine status to the sea monster ("Leviathan," also called "Rahab"; see text note on Psalm 89:10) but sees it as subject to the Lord's command and judgment (Isaiah 27:1). Here, Amos portrays God's sovereign power to summon the sea serpent to his service.

9:7 Geographically equivalent to modern-day Ethiopia, Cush (see text note on 9:7a; also see Genesis 10:6-7) was south of the Second Cataract of the Nile (see Isaiah 18:1) and was often linked with Egypt, its neighbor to the north. Israel's exodus from Egypt is compared to two other ancient migrations: the Philistines from Crete (literally "from Caphtor"; see also Jeremiah 47:4) and the Arameans out of Kir (see Amos 1:5; 2 Kings 16:9).

9:11-15 As the prophets often did, Amos closes his litany of judgments with a message of hope and restoration. Though Jerusalem and its Temple would be destroyed, David's line of kings cut off (Psalm 89:38-51), and Israel's people taken into captivity, God would restore a remnant of Israel (see Isaiah 2:2-4; 4:2; 11:1-5).

9:11-12 Amos portrays true worship of God as built around the Jerusalem Temple, with a descendant of David ruling over a united kingdom, including Israel and Judah (see Isaiah 9:6-7; 11:1-5).

9:12 Edom (see 1:11) represented the enemies of God and Israel (see Isaiah 34:5-6, 11; 63:1). God's enemies would be subject to his people and to God himself in the time of restoration. God promised Abraham that he would be a blessing to all the people of the earth (Genesis 12:2-3). God's Kingdom would embrace the outcasts and foreigners previously excluded (Isaiah 56:1-8; see Acts 8:27-39).

9:13 Amos began (1:2) with a quote from Joel 3:16. He closes with an allusion to Joel 3:18, pointing poetically to a future time when people would once again live in harmony with God's creation.

Obadiah

WHAT DO WE LEARN ABOUT GOD'S MISSION AND OURS? God will punish arrogance and betrayal because he expects humility and faithfulness.

WHO WROTE IT? The book preserves Obadiah's vision from the Lord, but it does not tell us who recorded it.

WHEN DID IT HAPPEN? Obadiah's vision occurred after the Babylonian destruction of Jerusalem in 586 BC but before the fall of Edom in 553 BC.

HOW IS IT ORGANIZED?

1:1-16: Edom will be destroyed

1:17-21: Israel will be restored

Words to Remember are highlighted throughout this book

FEATURE HIGHLIGHTS

+ *Betrayal's Consequences* (1095)

HOW LONG DOES IT TAKE TO READ?

:05 | :30 | 1:00 | 1:30 | 2:00 | 2:30 | 3:00 | 3:30

This is the vision that the Sovereign LORD revealed to Obadiah concerning the land of Edom.

Edom's Judgment Announced

We have heard a message from the LORD
> that an ambassador was sent to the nations to say,
"Get ready, everyone!
> Let's assemble our armies and attack Edom!"

[2] The LORD says to Edom,
"I will cut you down to size among the nations;
> you will be greatly despised.
[3] You have been deceived by your own pride
> because you live in a rock fortress
> and make your home high in the mountains.
'Who can ever reach us way up here?'
> you ask boastfully.
[4] But even if you soar as high as eagles
> and build your nest among the stars,
I will bring you crashing down,"
> says the LORD.

[5] "If thieves came at night and robbed you
> (what a disaster awaits you!),
> they would not take everything.
Those who harvest grapes
> always leave a few for the poor.
But your enemies will wipe you out completely!
[6] Every nook and cranny of Edom*
> will be searched and looted.
> Every treasure will be found and taken.

[7] "All your allies will turn against you.
> They will help to chase you from your land.
They will promise you peace
> while plotting to deceive and destroy you.
Your trusted friends will set traps for you,
> and you won't even know about it.
[8] At that time not a single wise person
> will be left in the whole land of Edom,"
> says the LORD.
"For on the mountains of Edom
> I will destroy everyone who has understanding.
[9] The mightiest warriors of Teman
> will be terrified,
and everyone on the mountains of Edom
> will be cut down in the slaughter.

Reasons for Edom's Punishment

[10] "Because of the violence you did
> to your close relatives in Israel,*
you will be filled with shame
> and destroyed forever.
[11] When they were invaded,
> you stood aloof, refusing to help them.
Foreign invaders carried off their wealth
> and cast lots to divide up Jerusalem,
> but you acted like one of Israel's enemies.

[12] "You should not have gloated
> when they exiled your relatives to distant lands.
You should not have rejoiced
> when the people of Judah suffered such misfortune.
You should not have spoken arrogantly
> in that terrible time of trouble.
[13] You should not have plundered the land of Israel
> when they were suffering such calamity.
You should not have gloated over their destruction
> when they were suffering such calamity.
You should not have seized their wealth
> when they were suffering such calamity.
[14] You should not have stood at the crossroads,
> killing those who tried to escape.
You should not have captured the survivors
> and handed them over in their terrible time of trouble.

Edom Destroyed, Israel Restored

[15] "The day is near when I, the LORD,
> will judge all godless nations!
As you have done to Israel,
> so it will be done to you.
All your evil deeds
> will fall back on your own heads.
[16] Just as you swallowed up my people
> on my holy mountain,
so you and the surrounding nations
> will swallow the punishment I pour out on you.
Yes, all you nations will drink and stagger
> and disappear from history.

[17] "But Jerusalem* will become a refuge for those who escape;
> it will be a holy place.

---

6 Hebrew *Esau;* also in 8b, 9, 18, 19, 21. **10** Hebrew *your brother Jacob.* The names "Jacob" and "Israel" are often interchanged throughout the Old Testament, referring sometimes to the individual patriarch and sometimes to the nation. **17a** Hebrew *Mount Zion.*

1:3-4 The sandstone cliffs of Edom were, and still are, nesting grounds for both the imperial eagle and the griffon vulture (the Hebrew word here can mean either bird). Vultures nest in colonies and lay just one egg. Edom is described as this sort of powerful mother bird whose large nest is impregnable, whose offspring is beyond the reach of any who would harm it. Yet all this would be futile if Edom saw its security as a personal achievement, and its arrogance would be its ruin.

1:8 The "wise person" appears to be among the national treasures of Edom. Uz, where Job lived, was located in Edom (see Genesis 36:21, 28; 1 Chronicles 1:42; Lamentations 4:21). Job's friend Eliphaz was a Temanite, and Teman was the other name for Edom. A possible explanation for Edom's reputation for wisdom (see Jeremiah 49:7) is that the people had developed a sharp sense for trade and politics thanks to their geographical location along caravan routes that linked Asia with Egypt. Interestingly, the Bible's wise women were mediating in crisis (2 Samuel 14:2-20), negotiating peace in wartime (2 Samuel 20:14-22), arbitrating justice and leading people (Judges 4:1-16), and building families (Proverbs 14:1). In Scripture, wise women played vital roles in public and private spaces.

And the people of Israel* will come back
  to reclaim their inheritance.
¹⁸ The people of Israel will be a raging fire,
  and Edom a field of dry stubble.
The descendants of Joseph will be a flame
  roaring across the field, devouring everything.
There will be no survivors in Edom.
  I, the LORD, have spoken!

¹⁹ "Then my people living in the Negev
  will occupy the mountains of Edom.
Those living in the foothills of Judah*
  will possess the Philistine plains
and take over the fields of Ephraim and Samaria.
And the people of Benjamin
  will occupy the land of Gilead.
²⁰ The exiles of Israel will return to their land
  and occupy the Phoenician coast as far north as Zarephath.
The captives from Jerusalem exiled in the north*
  will return home and resettle the towns of the Negev.
²¹ Those who have been rescued* will go up to*
  Mount Zion in Jerusalem
to rule over the mountains of Edom.
And the LORD himself will be king!"

17b Hebrew *house of Jacob;* also in 18. See note on 10. 19 Hebrew *the Shephelah.* 20 Hebrew *in Sepharad.* 21a As in Greek and Syriac versions; Hebrew reads *Rescuers.* 21b Or *from.*

Koinonia

IMAGE — MY STORY WITH COMMUNITY, WORKPLACE & CHURCH

Betrayal's Consequences

SCRIPTURE CONNECTION: OBADIAH 1:1-21

Rather than come to their neighbor's aid, the Edomites took advantage of Judah's crisis. They looted Judah's cities, murdered Judean fugitives or turned them over to the enemy, and even gloated over their destruction.

As with all nations who oppose his people, God would judge Edom, leaving no survivors (1:10, 18). The book ends, however, on a hopeful note for God's people. After punishing the Israelites for their rebellion, God would restore his people, bringing them back from exile to inhabit the land once again, under his rule.

Obadiah stands toward the end of a long line of Old Testament prophets who, by the time of his vision, had been announcing God's judgment on evil and calling people back to the Lord for nearly two hundred years. However, Obadiah did not urge Edom to change their wicked ways. Instead, he simply exposed their evil and proclaimed their end.

Although difficult to accept, Scripture is clear that sin and rebellion against God are justly punishable by death (Romans 6:23). By betraying their neighbor, Edom violated all standards of human decency and brought God's judgment upon themselves. But judgment is never the final word. As Obadiah prophesied, God's people would again inhabit the land as part of a unified kingdom under the Lord's rule (Obadiah 1:19-21). This echoes the restoration promises so prominent in the Psalms and in the other Old Testament prophetic books and points forward to the culmination of God's Kingdom rule in the New Jerusalem (Revelation 21–22).

IMAGINE

What does this book show us about exalting ourselves?

Sometimes consequences teach best. What do we see here about what God judges and how God will restore?

"Although we grieve over the Edomites' rebellion against God, we can also find comfort in knowing that God will not permit evil to go unchecked forever."

CATHERINE L. McDOWELL, PhD, is associate professor of Old Testament at Gordon-Conwell Theological Seminary. She has authored several books and articles on Bible backgrounds, Genesis, Isaiah, and Biblical Hebrew.

Jonah

WHAT DO WE LEARN ABOUT GOD'S MISSION AND OURS?
It's not up to us to say which people God can draw close.

WHO WROTE IT? Tradition says it was Jonah himself, but it could have been written by someone in the group of prophets who also collected information about Elijah and Elisha.

WHEN DID IT HAPPEN? The events in Jonah probably took place in the 700s BC, during the time of the divided kingdom.

HOW IS IT ORGANIZED?

1: Jonah runs from God by sea and is swallowed by a fish

2: Jonah prays, and the fish spits him onto the beach

3: Jonah preaches to Nineveh, and the whole city repents

4: Jonah sulks because God forgave his enemies

FEATURE HIGHLIGHTS

+ *Jonah's Misdirection (1098)*
+ *Compassion: A Response to Humility (1101)*
+ *Diving in Despite Our Dislikes (1102)*

Words to Remember are highlighted throughout this book

Timeline

BC	
793	JONAH BECOMES A PROPHET; JEROBOAM II BECOMES KING OF ISRAEL
792	UZZIAH, WHOSE MOTHER WAS JECOLIAH, BECOMES KING OF JUDAH
c. 785	JONAH PREACHES TO NINEVEH
783	SHALMANESER IV BECOMES KING OF ASSYRIA
772	ASHUR-DAN III BECOMES KING OF ASSYRIA
760	AMOS BECOMES A PROPHET
754	ASHUR-NIRARI V BECOMES KING OF ASSYRIA
753	JONAH'S MINISTRY ENDS
722	ISRAEL FALLS TO ASSYRIA
612	NINEVEH IS CONQUERED BY THE BABYLONIANS

HOW LONG DOES IT TAKE TO READ?

:10 | :30 | 1:00 | 1:30 | 2:00 | 2:30 | 3:00 | 3:30

Insight: JONAH'S MISDIRECTION

After God's command to go to Nineveh, Jonah instead boarded a ship headed to Tarshish. But he couldn't hide from God! Eventually, God straightened Jonah out, and Jonah wound up where God had wanted him all along. Have you ever tried to run from God's plan for you? Even when we run away, God works creatively to bring us back to himself and his good plans.

Jonah Runs from the Lord

1 The Lord gave this message to Jonah son of Amittai: ²"Get up and go to the great city of Nineveh. Announce my judgment against it because I have seen how wicked its people are."

³But Jonah got up and went in the opposite direction to get away from the Lord. He went down to the port of Joppa, where he found a ship leaving for Tarshish. He bought a ticket and went on board, hoping to escape from the Lord by sailing to Tarshish.

⁴But the Lord hurled a powerful wind over the sea, causing a violent storm that threatened to break the ship apart. ⁵Fearing for their lives, the desperate sailors shouted to their gods for help and threw the cargo overboard to lighten the ship.

But all this time Jonah was sound asleep down in the hold. ⁶So the captain went down after him. "How can you sleep at a time like this?" he shouted. "Get up and pray to your god! Maybe he will pay attention to us and spare our lives."

⁷Then the crew cast lots to see which of them had offended the gods and caused the terrible storm. When they did this, the lots identified Jonah as the culprit. ⁸"Why has this awful storm come down on us?" they demanded. "Who are you? What is your line of work? What country are you from? What is your nationality?"

⁹Jonah answered, "I am a Hebrew, and I worship the Lord, the God of heaven, who made the sea and the land."

¹⁰The sailors were terrified when they heard this, for he had already told them he was running away from the Lord. "Oh, why did you do it?" they groaned. ¹¹And since the storm was getting worse all the time, they asked him, "What should we do to you to stop this storm?"

¹²"Throw me into the sea," Jonah said, "and it will become calm again. I know that this terrible storm is all my fault."

¹³Instead, the sailors rowed even harder to get the ship to the land. But the stormy sea was too violent for them, and they couldn't make it. ¹⁴Then they cried out to the Lord, Jonah's God. "O Lord," they pleaded, "don't make us die for this man's sin. And don't hold us responsible for his death. O Lord, you have sent this storm upon him for your own good reasons."

¹⁵Then the sailors picked Jonah up and threw him into the raging sea, and the storm stopped at once! ¹⁶The sailors were awestruck by the Lord's great power, and they offered him a sacrifice and vowed to serve him.

¹⁷*Now the Lord had arranged for a great fish to swallow Jonah. And Jonah was inside the fish for three days and three nights.

Jonah's Prayer

2 ¹*Then Jonah prayed to the Lord his God from inside the fish. ²He said,

"I cried out to the Lord in my great trouble,
    and he answered me.
I called to you from the land of the dead,*
    and Lord, you heard me!
³ You threw me into the ocean depths,
    and I sank down to the heart of the sea.
The mighty waters engulfed me;
    I was buried beneath your wild and stormy
    waves.

1:17 Verse 1:17 is numbered 2:1 in Hebrew text. **2:1** Verses 2:1-10 are numbered 2:2-11 in Hebrew text. **2:2** Hebrew *from Sheol.*

1:4 In ancient Phoenicia and Canaan, a storm at sea might be attributed to the displeasure of Yamm, the sea god, but from 1953 to 1978, weather forecasters in the West named Atlantic hurricanes after women. *The Washington Post* explained that men in these decades claimed that "people would not take storms seriously if names did not evoke images of female fury." Resistance to such sexism came in the seventies, with Roxcy Bolton recommending that the storms be called "him-icanes" since women "deeply resent being arbitrarily associated with disaster." Natural catastrophes can be caused by human excesses, or as in the story of Jonah, permitted by the Lord for particular purposes—here, not to destroy a ship and its terrified passengers but to save a great capital city and its people from punishment.

1:11-13 In Jonah's day, ships in the Mediterranean Sea navigated using a variety of methods, including using the stars or keeping land in sight. This latter method may explain why the sailors attempted to row the ship to land. What is impressive is that they were unwilling to follow Jonah's request, which was to sacrifice himself as a last resort. When the sailors asked, "What should we do to you?" they seem to have had in mind some ritual to shield him from the displeased deity's wrath or to neutralize his offense, not to sacrifice him. Remarkably, these non-Israelite sailors were willing to risk their lives to save Jonah. In contrast, the Israelite prophet was deeply reluctant to be the agent of salvation to Nineveh and its people. The sailors remind us of people throughout the Old Testament who protected others at risk to themselves, frequently women: Shiphrah and Puah (Exodus 1:15-21), Rahab (Joshua 2:1-24), Michal (1 Samuel 19:11-17), the woman whose name is not given (2 Samuel 17:18-20), Jehosheba (2 Kings 11:1-3), and Esther (Esther 4:10-16).

1:17 In the ancient world, three days was the length of time for a person to be considered clinically dead. Jonah spent three days in a grave-like situation, entombed in a fish which itself inhabited the great watery depths of the sea. Ironically, this "grave" is where Jonah's new life could begin. Jonah had the opportunity to emerge from this ordeal as a new person but he let it slip. He got a new lease on life but remained the same peevish prophet inside. Jesus would later refer to Jonah's stay in the fish's belly when he predicted how long he would remain in the grave (see Matthew 12:39-41).

⁴ Then I said, 'O LORD, you have driven me from your presence.
Yet I will look once more toward your holy Temple.'
⁵ "I sank beneath the waves,
and the waters closed over me.
Seaweed wrapped itself around my head.
⁶ I sank down to the very roots of the mountains.
I was imprisoned in the earth,
whose gates lock shut forever.
But you, O LORD my God,
snatched me from the jaws of death!
⁷ As my life was slipping away,
I remembered the LORD.
And my earnest prayer went out to you
in your holy Temple.
⁸ Those who worship false gods
turn their backs on all God's mercies.
⁹ But I will offer sacrifices to you with songs of praise,
and I will fulfill all my vows.
For my salvation comes from the LORD alone."

¹⁰Then the LORD ordered the fish to spit Jonah out onto the beach.

Jonah Goes to Nineveh

3 Then the LORD spoke to Jonah a second time: ²"Get up and go to the great city of Nineveh, and deliver the message I have given you."

³This time Jonah obeyed the LORD's command and went to Nineveh, a city so large that it took three days to see it all.* ⁴On the day Jonah entered the city, he shouted to the crowds: "Forty days from now Nineveh will be destroyed!" ⁵The people of Nineveh believed God's message, and from the greatest to the least, they declared a fast and put on burlap to show their sorrow.

⁶When the king of Nineveh heard what Jonah was saying, he stepped down from his throne and took off his royal robes. He dressed himself in burlap and sat on a heap of ashes. ⁷Then the king and his nobles sent this decree throughout the city:

"No one, not even the animals from your herds and flocks, may eat or drink anything at all. ⁸People and animals alike must wear garments of mourning, and everyone must pray earnestly to God. They must turn from their evil ways and stop all their violence. ⁹Who can tell? Perhaps even yet God will change his mind and hold back his fierce anger from destroying us."

¹⁰When God saw what they had done and how they had put a stop to their evil ways, he changed his mind and did not carry out the destruction he had threatened.

Jonah's Anger at the LORD's Mercy

4 This change of plans greatly upset Jonah, and he became very angry. ²So he complained to the LORD about it: "Didn't I say before I left home that you would do this, LORD? That is why I ran away to Tarshish! I knew that you are a merciful and compassionate God, slow to get angry and filled with unfailing love. You are eager to turn back from destroying people. ³Just kill me now, LORD! I'd rather be dead than alive if what I predicted will not happen."

⁴The LORD replied, "Is it right for you to be angry about this?"

⁵Then Jonah went out to the east side of the city and made a shelter to sit under as he waited to see what would happen to the city. ⁶And the LORD God arranged for a leafy plant to grow there, and soon it spread its broad leaves over Jonah's head, shading him from the sun. This eased his discomfort, and Jonah was very grateful for the plant.

⁷But God also arranged for a worm! The next

3:3 Hebrew *a great city to God, of three days' journey.*

2:4 On the brink of drowning, Jonah called out for help, for life, and for God's renewed presence. It is ironic that Jonah spoke of God as driving Jonah from his presence because that was Jonah's own aim in fleeing to Tarshish (1:3). Either Jonah was confident that he would be rescued and thus worship "once more" in the Temple in Jerusalem, or he was calling to the Lord in his Temple from the sea (as in 2:7).

3:5-6 For the second time in this short book, non-Israelites responded favorably to the Lord in contrast to Jonah the Israelite's response to God (see also 1:16). In ancient Israel, fasting would often accompany prayer and repentance in times of distress (2 Samuel 1:12; Nehemiah 1:4). Wearing burlap and sitting on a heap of ashes would often accompany mourning and sorrowful repentance (Genesis 37:34; Job 16:15; Lamentations 2:10). The Assyrians apparently had similar customs. These activities allowed the participants to express their grief in a tangible way for all, including God, to see. The repentance of the Ninevites was also an indictment against the hard-hearted in Jesus' day (Matthew 12:41).

3:5 What we wear changes according to the seasons, the current style, the occasion, or our age. People of the ancient Near East recorded their spiritual state of mind with their clothes. When they wished to express heartfelt repentance, they wore sackcloth—a rough, unattractive, and uncomfortable fabric.

4:2-3 Life and death dance circles around each other in this story. The sailors thought they would perish but didn't. God had a mind to destroy a city—its king, people, and livestock—but he didn't. However, a leafy plant that was coming along nicely was eaten up overnight. This is the only loss of life in the story. It happened to teach God's prophet—who himself thought he was going to die, but survived, and then wished he were dead—the lesson that God does not take pleasure in anyone's death (Ezekiel 18:32; 33:11).

Compassion

IDENTITY — A Response to Humility

Compassion is an attribute of God, a recurring theme for his actions throughout the Old Testament, and several Hebrew terms refer to it. In the book of Jonah, one of its facets is the word *rakhum*, often associated with a mother's love (4:2)—like a mother who protects her offspring, *rekhem* (a similar sounding word).

Another facet of compassion is the word *khus*, "to pity." This same word describes Jonah's feelings toward a plant and God's feelings toward Nineveh ("feel sorry," 4:10-11). God emphasized how it was right for him to respond compassionately to the people's humility and repentant actions (3:6-10).

Compassion is a part of God's character. He longs to show himself easily moved to love, even to those who forsake their evil ways to pursue God's truth.

Moreover, the compassion displayed through God's response to Nineveh was so much greater than Jonah's selfish concern about the plant. God's heart was for the lost, ruthless people of Nineveh who humbled themselves before him through fasting and repentance. God will always act in keeping with his character. We, too, will see God act with compassion when we respond in humility, even if our past is not something to be proud of.

> God's compassion never fails, even when we feel like we don't deserve it.

ONE STORY OF GOD'S COMPASSION IS TOLD IN THE BOOK OF JONAH.

IDENTIFY

Is God calling you to turn to him and receive his compassion? Is he calling you to show compassion toward someone who has hurt you?

> "God's compassion challenges me in two ways. First, I am never too far gone that I can't humbly repent. Second, I am not in God's place to judge who deserves God's compassion. I have received God's compassion, so I also need to show compassion for others, even those who have hurt me."

MAY YOUNG, MDiv, PhD, is an associate professor of biblical studies at Taylor University, with a passion for discipleship, teaching, and writing.

IMAGE — MY STORY OF MY UNIQUE INFLUENCE

Diving in Despite Our Dislikes

SCRIPTURE CONNECTION: JONAH 1–4

There she was, at the dinner table: hands crossed, pouting, her food untouched. Mealtimes were never a favorite for my four-year-old.

I said patiently, "Sweetheart, aren't you going to eat?"

"I'm not hungry," she responded.

"That's too bad," I said, which she agreed with, saying, "It's too bad for the food, Mommy!" Now, that made me smile. Too bad for the food and not for her!

Juxtaposing this with Jonah—who likely thought "too bad for those Ninevites"—we can draw some lessons:

1. Jonah was disarmingly honest. He did not like the Ninevites and he was not going to go to their country. He even confessed to the sailors that "he was running away from the LORD" (1:10).
2. Jonah knew God's character. The irony is that he used this as the reason for his disobedience: "I knew that you are a merciful and compassionate God" (4:2).
3. Jonah was deceived. Like a child covering his eyes in a game of peekaboo, believing others can't see him, Jonah forgot that he could not run from God: "Now the LORD had arranged for a great fish to swallow Jonah" (1:17).

> I am like Jonah, stuck on my dislikes and greatly in need of God!

Our dislikes can get in the way of doing what is good, as they did for Jonah and my daughter. But God never gives up on inviting us to what's best: overcoming our dislikes to follow God's call.

IMAGINE

Is there anything God is prompting us to do but we haven't obeyed?

How will we respond to his call today?

"Like Jonah, I have sometimes acted impulsively, yet I am so glad that God has not left me to my own devices!"

LILLIAN GITAU is a lifelong learner and an advocate for the marginalized. She finds satisfaction from seeing others realize their full potential. She is the author of *You Are Special* and *Pia Was Different*.

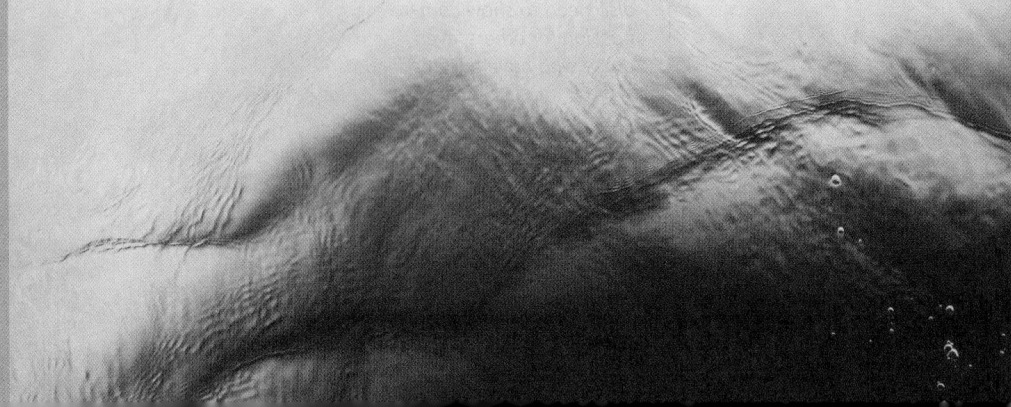

morning at dawn the worm ate through the stem of the plant so that it withered away. ⁸And as the sun grew hot, God arranged for a scorching east wind to blow on Jonah. The sun beat down on his head until he grew faint and wished to die. "Death is certainly better than living like this!" he exclaimed.

⁹Then God said to Jonah, "Is it right for you to be angry because the plant died?"

"Yes," Jonah retorted, "even angry enough to die!"

¹⁰Then the LORD said, "You feel sorry about the plant, though you did nothing to put it there. It came quickly and died quickly. ¹¹But Nineveh has more than 120,000 people living in spiritual darkness,* not to mention all the animals. Shouldn't I feel sorry for such a great city?"

4:11 Hebrew *people who don't know their right hand from their left.*

4:9 The literary genre of satire or parody existed in the ancient world, and the book of Jonah can be read as such. The parody is Jonah, the prophet. Everyone and everything in the book responded positively to God except his prophet: the stormy sea and its creatures; the pagan mariners; a non-Israelite king of the Assyrians, a people known for their cruelty; the citizens of a pagan capital, Nineveh; even a plant and a worm and the east wind! We know that we experience our greatest heartaches from those we're closest to, and this book encourages us not to give up on those nearest and dearest to us. God didn't give up on Jonah.

4:11 God graciously sent the light of his prophetic word into a wicked city. Not all who encounter God's light respond favorably (see John 3:19-21), but God is eager to save those who receive his word in genuine repentance and faith. The book closes abruptly, leaving the reader to ponder God's final question to Jonah. God would rather save than destroy. Those who have received and have truly recognized his mercy will be glad for that same mercy to be shown to others, even to their enemies.

Micah

WHAT DO WE LEARN ABOUT GOD'S MISSION AND OURS?
It's not people but God who builds lasting good.

WHO WROTE IT? Micah, a prophet from a rural area in southern Judah.

WHEN DID IT HAPPEN? During the years just before and after the fall of the northern kingdom in 722 BC.

HOW IS IT ORGANIZED?

- **1–2:** Predicted destruction of Israel and Judah
- **3:** Leaders are condemned
- **4–5:** Future hope for Israel and Judah
- **6:** God takes Israel to court
- **7:** Gloom turns to hope

FEATURE HIGHLIGHTS

+ Stripped, Then Gathered (1107)
+ A Ruler from Bethlehem: The Presence of the Peacemaker (1111)

Words to Remember are highlighted throughout this book

HOW LONG DOES IT TAKE TO READ?
:20 / :30 / 1:00 / 1:30 / 2:00 / 2:30 / 3:00 / 3:30

Timeline (BC)

BC	Event
753	HOSEA BECOMES A PROPHET
750	JOTHAM BECOMES KING OF JUDAH
743	TIGLATH-PILESER III INVADES ISRAEL
742	MICAH BECOMES A PROPHET; PEKAHIAH BECOMES KING OF ISRAEL
740	ISAIAH BECOMES A PROPHET
735	AHAZ BECOMES KING OF JUDAH
722	ISRAEL, THE NORTHERN KINGDOM, FALLS
715	HOSEA'S MINISTRY ENDS; HEZEKIAH BECOMES KING OF JUDAH
701	SENNACHERIB SURROUNDS JERUSALEM
687	MICAH'S MINISTRY ENDS

MICAH 1

¹ The LORD gave this message to Micah of Moresheth during the years when Jotham, Ahaz, and Hezekiah were kings of Judah. The visions he saw concerned both Samaria and Jerusalem.

Grief over Samaria and Jerusalem

² Attention! Let all the people of the world listen!
  Let the earth and everything in it hear.
The Sovereign LORD is making accusations against you;
  the Lord speaks from his holy Temple.
³ Look! The LORD is coming!
  He leaves his throne in heaven
  and tramples the heights of the earth.
⁴ The mountains melt beneath his feet
  and flow into the valleys
like wax in a fire,
  like water pouring down a hill.
⁵ And why is this happening?
  Because of the rebellion of Israel*—
  yes, the sins of the whole nation.
Who is to blame for Israel's rebellion?
  Samaria, its capital city!
Where is the center of idolatry in Judah?
  In Jerusalem, its capital!

⁶ "So I, the LORD, will make the city of Samaria
  a heap of ruins.
Her streets will be plowed up
  for planting vineyards.
I will roll the stones of her walls into the valley below,
  exposing her foundations.
⁷ All her carved images will be smashed.
  All her sacred treasures will be burned.
These things were bought with the money
  earned by her prostitution,
and they will now be carried away
  to pay prostitutes elsewhere."

⁸ Therefore, I will mourn and lament.
  I will walk around barefoot and naked.
I will howl like a jackal
  and moan like an owl.
⁹ For my people's wound
  is too deep to heal.
It has reached into Judah,
  even to the gates of Jerusalem.

¹⁰ Don't tell our enemies in Gath*;
  don't weep at all.
You people in Beth-leaphrah,*
  roll in the dust to show your despair.
¹¹ You people in Shaphir,*
  go as captives into exile—naked and ashamed.
The people of Zaanan*
  dare not come outside their walls.
The people of Beth-ezel* mourn,
  for their house has no support.
¹² The people of Maroth* anxiously wait
  for relief,
but only bitterness awaits them
  as the LORD's judgment reaches
  even to the gates of Jerusalem.

1:5 Hebrew *Jacob;* also in 1:5b. The names "Jacob" and "Israel" are often interchanged throughout the Old Testament, referring sometimes to the individual patriarch and sometimes to the nation.   **1:10a** *Gath* sounds like the Hebrew term for "tell."   **1:10b** *Beth-leaphrah* means "house of dust."   **1:11a** *Shaphir* means "pleasant."   **1:11b** *Zaanan* sounds like the Hebrew term for "come out."   **1:11c** *Beth-ezel* means "adjoining house."   **1:12** *Maroth* sounds like the Hebrew term for "bitter."

1:1–2:13 Micah—whose name means "Who is like the Lord?"—warned the Israelites that God's judgment would fall on them if they did not stop worshiping other gods. The people of Israel failed to be faithful. God fulfilled Micah's word when Assyria conquered Samaria in 722 BC and Judah fell to Babylon in 586 BC.
1:1-16 This scene employs the metaphor of a legal procedure with God standing as a witness and cosmic judge against the whole nation of Israel, represented by the two kingdoms' capital cities. Micah's role is to bring accusation and judgment against Samaria (northern kingdom) and Jerusalem (southern kingdom) for perpetually violating their covenant with the Lord.
1:1 Moresheth was a fortress city located a short distance southeast of Gath in the low-lying hills of southwestern Judah. The reigns of these three kings (Jotham, Ahaz, and Hezekiah) covered about sixty-five years total (about 750–686 BC). Samaria and Jerusalem were the capitals of northern Israel and Judah. Sometimes these city names refer to their entire countries.
1:2 The Hebrew word *shema* marks three divisions in the book of Micah, wherein the people of Israel are not only called to hear but also to respond and obey (1:2; 3:1; 6:1). It's usually translated "hear," "listen," or "attention." There is no separate word for obey in Hebrew. When the Lord tells Israel to *shema,* he is telling them to hear, respond, and obey.

1:3 The image of the Lord leaving "his throne in heaven" and coming down to earth portrays the Lord's sovereign and just intervention in human history (Genesis 11:5; Exodus 19:20; 34:5; Psalms 18:9; 96:13; 144:5).
1:7 Having children was a source of honor and pride in the world of the Old Testament. But foreign fertility gods posed a threat to Israel's following the first two commandments (to have only one God and not to worship idols, Exodus 20:3-6). As a part of their fertility rites, the people of Samaria offered gifts to the shrine prostitutes. This spiritual infidelity was rebellion. The Lord would judge Samaria for behaving unfaithfully by worshiping idols (Micah 1:6-7). Rather than trusting God completely, the people of Israel sought to ensure the blessing of fertility from additional gods. When people believe their worth and security originate apart from the Creator, idolatry is revealed.
1:8-9 Because of the Lord's coming judgment, Micah walked around barefoot and naked to show his grief (compare Isaiah 20:2; Lamentations 2:10; Ezekiel 24:17), while vividly depicting what would happen to Samaria (Israel) and Jerusalem (Judah). They would be stripped of their wealth, power, and population. Jackals and owls make mournful sounds and live in desolate wilderness areas (Isaiah 34:13; Jeremiah 50:39).

MICAH 2

¹³ Harness your chariot horses and flee,
  you people of Lachish.*
You were the first city in Judah
  to follow Israel in her rebellion,
  and you led Jerusalem* into sin.
¹⁴ Send farewell gifts to Moresheth-gath*;
  there is no hope of saving it.
The town of Aczib*
  has deceived the kings of Israel.
¹⁵ O people of Mareshah,*
  I will bring a conqueror to capture your town.
And the leaders* of Israel
  will go to Adullam.
¹⁶ Oh, people of Judah, shave your heads in sorrow,
  for the children you love will be snatched away.
Make yourselves as bald as a vulture,
  for your little ones will be exiled to distant lands.

Judgment against Wealthy Oppressors

2 What sorrow awaits you who lie awake at night,
  thinking up evil plans.
You rise at dawn and hurry to carry them out,
  simply because you have the power to do so.
² When you want a piece of land,
  you find a way to seize it.
When you want someone's house,
  you take it by fraud and violence.
You cheat a man of his property,
  stealing his family's inheritance.

1:13a *Lachish* sounds like the Hebrew term for "team of horses." 1:13b Hebrew *the daughter of Zion.* 1:14a *Moresheth* sounds like the Hebrew term for "gift" or "dowry." 1:14b *Aczib* means "deception." 1:15a *Mareshah* sounds like the Hebrew term for "conqueror." 1:15b Hebrew *the glory.*

2:1-11 The Lord's message is a judgment against those who exploited the poor by depriving them of land and security (see Numbers 36:7). As the Lord's representatives, every Israelite, especially the leaders, were called to imitate God's holiness. This included caring for the poor and following the Lord's commands (Leviticus 19:1-37).

Come Close — STRIPPED, THEN GATHERED

SCRIPTURE CONNECTION: MICAH 2:9-12

The year 2012 was very difficult. I felt so alone, stripped of my identity as a mom and a wife. It's not that I lost my faith or stopped believing. But things had been busy—high school activities for my youngest two children made five years a blur. My time with God became easy to push to the side—I had so much to do!

Then all at once, my world changed. The children I had spent so much focused time on were all out of the house. My marriage, kept on life support by the dizzying activity, was in shambles. Who was I? *Mother* and *wife* now seemed like empty labels. My foundation shaken, I cried out to God. I needed the one constant, the One who would always be there.

That is when God reached out to gather me back to him. To let me know that I matter to him. I had the one thing I really needed, my God, who loves me as he created me no matter what I do with my time. That is where my identity lies—as his child.

We are not simply the roles we play in life. We are treasures to our heavenly Father. And that will always be enough.

REFLECT "Someday, O Israel, I will gather you; I will gather the remnant who are left." MICAH 2:12

Dear God, thank you that your faithfulness doesn't depend on mine. Thank you for loving me, for being patient, for gathering me back to you. Amen.

CONSIDER "When you have nothing left but God, you become aware that God is enough." A. MAUDE ROYDEN

> We are not simply our roles.
> We are treasures to God.
> And that is enough.

ELISABETH SELZER ROGERS, MDiv, MA, PhD, is a passionate believer and follower of Christ, bringing his love to the secular world through mentoring, coaching, and modeling his unconditional love.

³ But this is what the LORD says:
"I will reward your evil with evil;
   you won't be able to pull your neck out of the noose.
You will no longer walk around proudly,
   for it will be a terrible time."

⁴ In that day your enemies will make fun of you
   by singing this song of despair about you:
"We are finished,
   completely ruined!
God has confiscated our land,
   taking it from us.
He has given our fields
   to those who betrayed us.*"

⁵ Others will set your boundaries then,
   and the LORD's people will have no say
   in how the land is divided.

True and False Prophets

⁶ "Don't say such things,"
   the people respond.*
"Don't prophesy like that.
   Such disasters will never come our way!"

⁷ Should you talk that way, O family of Israel?*
   Will the LORD's Spirit have patience with such behavior?
If you would do what is right,
   you would find my words comforting.
⁸ Yet to this very hour
   my people rise against me like an enemy!
You steal the shirts right off the backs
   of those who trusted you,
making them as ragged as men
   returning from battle.
⁹ You have evicted women from their pleasant homes
   and forever stripped their children of all that
   God would give them.
¹⁰ Up! Begone!
This is no longer your land and home,
   for you have filled it with sin
   and ruined it completely.

¹¹ Suppose a prophet full of lies would say to you,
   "I'll preach to you the joys of wine and alcohol!"
That's just the kind of prophet you would like!

Hope for Restoration

¹² "Someday, O Israel, I will gather you;
   I will gather the remnant who are left.
I will bring you together again like sheep in a pen,
   like a flock in its pasture.
Yes, your land will again
   be filled with noisy crowds!
¹³ Your leader will break out
   and lead you out of exile,
out through the gates of the enemy cities,
   back to your own land.
Your king will lead you;
   the LORD himself will guide you."

Judgment against Israel's Leaders

3 I said, "Listen, you leaders of Israel!
You are supposed to know right from wrong,
² but you are the very ones
   who hate good and love evil.
You skin my people alive
   and tear the flesh from their bones.
³ Yes, you eat my people's flesh,
   strip off their skin,
   and break their bones.
You chop them up
   like meat for the cooking pot.
⁴ Then you beg the LORD for help in times of trouble!
   Do you really expect him to answer?
After all the evil you have done,
   he won't even look at you!"

⁵ This is what the LORD says:
"You false prophets are leading my people astray!
You promise peace for those who give you food,
   but you declare war on those who refuse to feed you.
⁶ Now the night will close around you,
   cutting off all your visions.

2:4 Or *to those who took us captive*. **2:6** Or *the prophets respond;* Hebrew reads *they prophesy*. **2:7** Hebrew *O house of Jacob?* See note on 1:5a.

2:3-5 The Lord, the judge, reads out the sentence. He would pay back his people's evil hearts and actions with evil in kind. The prophet was engaging in wordplay here, with the Hebrew word translated "evil" having a range of meanings. It can denote moral evil, as in the first instance; it can also denote calamity or disaster as in the second instance. The Lord would bring calamity on them in response to their wickedness.

2:11 These evil people loved to hear deceptions from their favorite good-time prophets (see Jeremiah 28:8-9). False prophets spoke assurance that Israel and Judah could escape from judgment. But when judgment came, they had no comfort to give.

2:12-13 As Israel's shepherd, the Lord would gather his flock scattered in exile and bring them home. This refers to Israel's return to Jerusalem from Babylonian captivity in 538 BC (Ezra 1–2).

3:1–5:15 This message indicts the evil leaders who were destroying God's people. It contrasts them with a glorious vision of God's Kingdom and the reign of a righteous king. After suffering judgment and exile, a purified people of Israel would return and experience God's blessings.

3:1-3 There is perhaps no more precise picture of dehumanization than cannibalism. Micah strongly condemns Israel's leaders because they treat God's people as mere animals to be butchered and consumed, rather than caring for them and leading them to what is right.

Darkness will cover you,
  putting an end to your predictions.
The sun will set for you prophets,
  and your day will come to an end.
⁷ Then you seers will be put to shame,
  and you fortune-tellers will be disgraced.
And you will cover your faces
  because there is no answer from God."

⁸ But as for me, I am filled with power—
  with the Spirit of the LORD.
I am filled with justice and strength
  to boldly declare Israel's sin and rebellion.
⁹ Listen to me, you leaders of Israel!
  You hate justice and twist all that is right.
¹⁰ You are building Jerusalem
  on a foundation of murder and corruption.
¹¹ You rulers make decisions based on bribes;
  you priests teach God's laws only for a price;
  you prophets won't prophesy unless you are paid.
Yet all of you claim to depend on the LORD.
"No harm can come to us," you say,
  "for the LORD is here among us."
¹² Because of you, Mount Zion will be plowed like an open field;
  Jerusalem will be reduced to ruins!
A thicket will grow on the heights
  where the Temple now stands.

The LORD's Future Reign

4 In the last days, the mountain of the LORD's house
  will be the highest of all—
  the most important place on earth.
It will be raised above the other hills,

4:7 Hebrew *Mount Zion.*

and people from all over the world will
  stream there to worship.
² People from many nations will come and say,
"Come, let us go up to the mountain of the LORD,
  to the house of Jacob's God.
There he will teach us his ways,
  and we will walk in his paths."
For the LORD's teaching will go out from Zion;
  his word will go out from Jerusalem.
³ The LORD will mediate between peoples
  and will settle disputes between strong nations far away.
They will hammer their swords into plowshares
  and their spears into pruning hooks.
Nation will no longer fight against nation,
  nor train for war anymore.
⁴ Everyone will live in peace and prosperity,
  enjoying their own grapevines and fig trees,
  for there will be nothing to fear.
The LORD of Heaven's Armies
  has made this promise!
⁵ Though the nations around us follow their idols,
  we will follow the LORD our God forever and ever.

Israel's Return from Exile

⁶ "In that coming day," says the LORD,
"I will gather together those who are lame,
  those who have been exiles,
  and those whom I have filled with grief.
⁷ Those who are weak will survive as a remnant;
  those who were exiles will become a strong nation.
Then I, the LORD, will rule from Jerusalem*
  as their king forever."

3:8 Scripture draws a clear and distinct contrast between true and false prophets (Deuteronomy 18:15-22). The latter speak lies fueled by self-interest. Micah, however, is filled with the Spirit of the Lord. He is therefore enabled to address Israel's sin with power and boldness.
3:9-12 Micah addressed Israel's leaders, which included the rulers, priests, and prophets. Micah accused them of lying, treating people unjustly, taking bribes, and murdering innocent people—all while these leaders claimed to be serving God. They thought they were exempt, a protected class, and God's judgment would not fall on them. But they did not understand God's just character and his seriousness about upholding his covenant with his people. The leaders of Israel were building Jerusalem on a "foundation of murder and corruption" (3:10). Because of this, the city would be dismantled; it would be reduced to wilderness and ruins (3:12).
4:1-7 This section of Micah's prophecy concludes with a message of hope. Judgment would be followed by restoration. The people would turn their weapons of war into farming and gardening tools because there would be no more war. Grapevines and figs symbolize periods of extended peace and security because they take three to five years to produce fruit.

4:3 The *shalom* ("well-being" or "peace") of the Lord would cover the earth, and instruments of destruction would be used for peaceful pursuits. From its earliest records, ancient history is marred by accounts of war, of one people's subjugation of other peoples and nations. Warfare and violence reached a frenzied peak in the Assyrian and Babylonian kingdoms. Some scholars believe that to hammer swords into plowshares means reducing swords into metal shards, which would render them useless. Either way, Micah declares that war would come to an end.
4:4 The prophets frequently described God as "the LORD of Heaven's Armies." This military title expresses his control of the universe and his unlimited power, and the warrior kings of the ancient Near East were no match for him. The Lord's rule flips the usual intentions upside down: God planned to bring peace and end war forever.
4:6-7 In the ancient Near East, the people who were left alive after their cities were destroyed were either lost or assimilated into the conquering kingdoms. When Israel's remnant (the people who remained alive after being conquered) were rescued, it would be the foundation of the Lord's new people (Deuteronomy 4:26-31; 30:1-5; 2 Kings 19:31; Isaiah 10:21; Jeremiah 29:10-14; Ezra 9:8; Nehemiah 1:2).

MICAH 5

⁸ As for you, Jerusalem,
   the citadel of God's people,*
 your royal might and power
   will come back to you again.
 The kingship will be restored
   to my precious Jerusalem.

⁹ But why are you now screaming in terror?
   Have you no king to lead you?
 Have your wise people all died?
   Pain has gripped you like a woman in childbirth.

¹⁰ Writhe and groan like a woman in labor,
   you people of Jerusalem,*
 for now you must leave this city
   to live in the open country.
 You will soon be sent in exile
   to distant Babylon.
 But the LORD will rescue you there;
   he will redeem you from the grip of your enemies.

¹¹ Now many nations have gathered against you.
   "Let her be desecrated," they say.
 "Let us see the destruction of Jerusalem.*"
¹² But they do not know the LORD's thoughts
   or understand his plan.
 These nations don't know
   that he is gathering them together
 to be beaten and trampled
   like sheaves of grain on a threshing floor.
¹³ "Rise up and crush the nations, O Jerusalem!"*
   says the LORD.
 "For I will give you iron horns and bronze hooves,
   so you can trample many nations to pieces.
 You will present their stolen riches to the LORD,
   their wealth to the Lord of all the earth."

5 ¹*Mobilize! Marshal your troops!
   The enemy is laying siege to Jerusalem.
 They will strike Israel's leader
   in the face with a rod.

A Ruler from Bethlehem

² *But you, O Bethlehem Ephrathah,
   are only a small village among all the people of Judah.
 Yet a ruler of Israel,
   whose origins are in the distant past,
   will come from you on my behalf.
³ The people of Israel will be abandoned to their enemies
   until the woman in labor gives birth.
 Then at last his fellow countrymen
   will return from exile to their own land.
⁴ And he will stand to lead his flock with the LORD's strength,
   in the majesty of the name of the LORD his God.
 Then his people will live there undisturbed,
   for he will be highly honored around the world.
⁵ And he will be the source of peace.

When the Assyrians invade our land
   and break through our defenses,
 we will appoint seven rulers to watch over us,
   eight princes to lead us.
⁶ They will rule Assyria with drawn swords
   and enter the gates of the land of Nimrod.
 He will rescue us from the Assyrians
   when they pour over the borders to invade our land.

The Remnant Purified

⁷ Then the remnant left in Israel*
   will take their place among the nations.
 They will be like dew sent by the LORD
   or like rain falling on the grass,
 which no one can hold back
   and no one can restrain.
⁸ The remnant left in Israel
   will take their place among the nations.
 They will be like a lion among the animals of the forest,

4:8 Hebrew *As for you, Migdal-eder, / the Ophel of the daughter of Zion.* **4:10** Hebrew *O daughter of Zion.* **4:11** Hebrew *of Zion.* **4:13** Hebrew *"Rise up and thresh, O daughter of Zion."* **5:1** Verse 5:1 is numbered 4:14 in Hebrew text. **5:2** Verses 5:2-15 are numbered 5:1-14 in Hebrew text. **5:7** Hebrew *in Jacob;* also in 5:8. See note on 1:5a.

4:12 God reveals his plans to his servants (Daniel 2:19-23; Amos 3:7), but the "nations don't know." They are not privy to God's great plans or his behind-the-scenes activity on his people's behalf. The hopes and plans of the nations around Israel were in vain—the Lord's plans for his unique people would prevail, and he would rule the nations (Genesis 12:1-3; 15:12-21; Exodus 19:4-6; Isaiah 45:23; 66:23).
5:1-15 This section calls Israel to prepare for the vicious onslaught of Israel's enemy, Assyria (5:5-6). This siege of terror, death, and destruction would not annihilate Israel, for God would bring forth a ruler (5:2-5) to lead his people back from exile. God's preservation and purification of the remnant (5:7-14) would complete their restoration as God's victorious people.

5:1-5 Micah contrasts a future king of Israel with its current feeble leaders who are defeated by Israel's enemies. This future king would come from humble origins but would lead the people with "the LORD's strength." The future king would usher in an era of peace, *shalom*. Shalom means not only the absence of war but a state of security, prosperity, and overall well-being.
5:7-15 God's purpose was not to create another nation like all the other nations (Exodus 19:4-6; Numbers 23:9; Jeremiah 7:23) but to have his own people who would walk in his ways and be holy as he is holy (Leviticus 11:45). In that day (Micah 5:10), God would rule a redeemed and purified people, freed from idols and false prophets, healed of violence and the ravages of war.

A Ruler from Bethlehem

IDENTITY — The Presence of the Peacemaker

"Can you *please* stop pounding on the piano?" "Why are you so weird?" "Hey, take that off—that's *my* shirt."

All these phrases could be heard in a noisy family of nine on a school-day afternoon. That is until Dad got home. Dad, whose life word was *peace*.

"Daddy!" I'd squeal, running to the front door and encircling him in a bear hug. One of my brothers would bombard him next, "Hey, Dad, look at my race car. I think it can win the derby!"

And—really not that rarely—we "greeted" him with our conflicts. "Daddy, he tickled me until I couldn't breathe. Make him stop." "Dad, she won't stop singing, and I have a math test tomorrow."

"And he will be the source of peace" (5:5).

Some people yawn when they think of heaven—they think it will be boring. But far beyond floating on a cloud and playing harps lies a future where it's not the Peacemaker who comes home. We come home to the Peacemaker. And all is good.

> Peace begins by welcoming the Peacemaker.

ONE OF THE PEACEMAKER'S STORIES IS TOLD IN MICAH 5:1-6.

IDENTIFY

Until we go to the Peacemaker's house, how can we bring peace to our places? "Though the nations around us follow their idols, we will follow the LORD our God forever and ever" (Micah 4:5).

Since we are made in God's image (Genesis 1:26-27) and have God's peaceful Spirit within (Romans 14:17), what is our role in establishing peace?

"Sometimes my dad would say, 'I am setting the timer for fifteen minutes. I want you to keep your hands to yourselves and your voices on silent.' Quiet would come as I exchanged elbowing my siblings for honoring the one calling me to peace."

NAOMI CRAMER OVERTON, MBA, DIS, lives to realize beauty-filled visions that lift us to flourishing, with our families and beyond. Naomi has been CEO for Stonecroft and MOPS, director with Compassion International and World Vision, and General Editor for this Bible.

like a strong young lion among flocks of
  sheep and goats,
pouncing and tearing as they go
  with no rescuer in sight.
⁹ The people of Israel will stand up to
  their foes,
  and all their enemies will be wiped out.

¹⁰ "In that day," says the LORD,
"I will slaughter your horses
  and destroy your chariots.
¹¹ I will tear down your walls
  and demolish your defenses.
¹² I will put an end to all witchcraft,
  and there will be no more fortune-tellers.
¹³ I will destroy all your idols and sacred pillars,
  so you will never again worship the work of
  your own hands.
¹⁴ I will abolish your idol shrines with their
  Asherah poles
  and destroy your pagan cities.
¹⁵ I will pour out my vengeance
  on all the nations that refuse to obey me."

The LORD's Case against Israel

6 Listen to what the LORD is saying:

"Stand up and state your case against me.
  Let the mountains and hills be called to
  witness your complaints.
² And now, O mountains,
  listen to the LORD's complaint!
He has a case against his people.
He will bring charges against Israel.

³ "O my people, what have I done to you?
  What have I done to make you tired of me?
  Answer me!
⁴ For I brought you out of Egypt
  and redeemed you from slavery.
  I sent Moses, Aaron, and Miriam to help you.
⁵ Don't you remember, my people,
  how King Balak of Moab tried to have you
  cursed
  and how Balaam son of Beor blessed you
  instead?
And remember your journey from Acacia
  Grove* to Gilgal,
  when I, the LORD, did everything I could
  to teach you about my faithfulness."

⁶ What can we bring to the LORD?
  Should we bring him burnt offerings?
Should we bow before God Most High
  with offerings of yearling calves?
⁷ Should we offer him thousands of rams
  and ten thousand rivers of olive oil?
Should we sacrifice our firstborn children
  to pay for our sins?

⁸ No, O people, the LORD has told you what is good,
  and this is what he requires of you:
to do what is right, to love mercy,
  and to walk humbly with your God.

Israel's Guilt and Punishment

⁹ Fear the LORD if you are wise!
  His voice calls to everyone in Jerusalem:
"The armies of destruction are coming;
  the LORD is sending them.*

6:5 Hebrew *Shittim*.   6:9 Hebrew *"Listen to the rod. / Who appointed it?"*

5:13-14 Stones, or "sacred pillars," were set up as places or objects of worship; they could represent pagan deities. Asherah was thought to be the consort of Baal, the elder god of ancient Canaan, and her worship included fertility rites at sacred trees or poles.
6:1-16 The Lord presents, argues, and decides the case against his rebellious people, Israel. This section is formally presented as a legal court case (compare Isaiah 1:2-4; Jeremiah 2:4-9; Hosea 4:1-19). Using the setting of the courtroom, the Lord challenges his people to state their case against him, for he has a case against them (Micah 6:1-5)—they had not fulfilled his requirements (6:6-8), so they were guilty (6:9-12). The guilty verdict is followed by Israel's sentencing (6:13-16).
6:4-5 The Lord had brought the people of Israel out of Egypt, preserved them, and blessed them throughout their journey to the Promised Land. God encouraged and warned the Israelites always to remember what he had done for them from Sinai onward (Exodus 3:15-17; Deuteronomy 5:15; Psalms 77:11; 111:4; see Psalms 78:1-72; 136:1-26). Acacia Grove, located on the east bank of the Jordan River, was Israel's base camp before entering the Promised Land (see Numbers 25:1; Joshua 2:1; 3:1). The trip from there to Gilgal (west of the Jordan River) bears witness to God's covenant faithfulness. God's saving acts brought the Israelites into the Promised Land.
6:6-8 God is pleased not by empty ritual sacrifice but when his people act with justice, show steadfast love, and walk humbly with him. The Israelites wanted to rely on their usual practices for putting off the wrath of a deity, but while worshiping idols, they had forgotten that the Lord is not appeased like other gods. His mercy cannot be bought with empty sacrifices. Instead, God seeks faithful and repentant hearts (see 1 Samuel 15:22; 16:7).
6:8 "Good" means what is right in God's eyes; God is the source of all goodness (Genesis 1:1-31; Exodus 33:19; 34:6-7; Deuteronomy 12:28). God's order in the world (or "what is right") requires treatment of others in fair, non-manipulative, non-oppressive ways. This passionate, undeserved kindness ("mercy") is the defining quality in God's holy character (see Psalm 136). Those who know God should act in the same way toward others (see Genesis 21:22-24; Joshua 2:12-14; Matthew 5:43-48). Humility must characterize God's people. They must not live in a spirit of arrogance or special privilege. They must be humble and reverently fear God. Doing what is right and loving mercy are incompatible with human arrogance. God desires us to be in an ongoing intimate relationship with him (a "walk"; see Deuteronomy 28:9; Joshua 22:5) that transforms the way we relate to other people.

The LORD has told you what is good... to do what is right, To love mercy, and to walk humbly with your God.

MICAH
6:8

¹⁰ What shall I say about the homes of the wicked
 filled with treasures gained by cheating?
What about the disgusting practice
 of measuring out grain with dishonest
 measures?*
¹¹ How can I tolerate your merchants
 who use dishonest scales and weights?
¹² The rich among you have become wealthy
 through extortion and violence.
Your citizens are so used to lying
 that their tongues can no longer tell
 the truth.
¹³ "Therefore, I will wound you!
 I will bring you to ruin for all your sins.
¹⁴ You will eat but never have enough.
 Your hunger pangs and emptiness will
 remain.
And though you try to save your money,
 it will come to nothing in the end.
You will save a little,
 but I will give it to those who conquer you.
¹⁵ You will plant crops
 but not harvest them.
You will press your olives
 but not get enough oil to anoint yourselves.
You will trample the grapes
 but get no juice to make your wine.
¹⁶ You keep only the laws of evil King Omri;
 you follow only the example of wicked King
 Ahab!
Therefore, I will make an example of you,
 bringing you to complete ruin.
You will be treated with contempt,
 mocked by all who see you."

Misery Turned to Hope

7 How miserable I am!
 I feel like the fruit picker after the harvest
 who can find nothing to eat.
Not a cluster of grapes or a single early fig
 can be found to satisfy my hunger.
² The godly people have all disappeared;
 not one honest person is left on the earth.
They are all murderers,
 setting traps even for their own brothers.
³ Both their hands are equally skilled at doing
 evil!
Officials and judges alike demand bribes.
The people with influence get what they want,
 and together they scheme to twist justice.
⁴ Even the best of them is like a brier;
 the most honest is as dangerous as a hedge of
 thorns.
But your judgment day is coming swiftly now.
 Your time of punishment is here, a time of
 confusion.
⁵ Don't trust anyone—
 not your best friend or even your wife!
⁶ For the son despises his father.
 The daughter defies her mother.
The daughter-in-law defies her mother-in-law.
 Your enemies are right in your own
 household!

⁷ As for me, I look to the LORD for help.
 I wait confidently for God to save me,
 and my God will certainly hear me.
⁸ Do not gloat over me, my enemies!
 For though I fall, I will rise again.
Though I sit in darkness,
 the LORD will be my light.
⁹ I will be patient as the LORD punishes me,
 for I have sinned against him.
But after that, he will take up my case
 and give me justice for all I have suffered
 from my enemies.
The LORD will bring me into the light,
 and I will see his righteousness.
¹⁰ Then my enemies will see that the LORD is on my
 side.
They will be ashamed that they taunted me,
 saying,
"So where is the LORD—
 that God of yours?"
With my own eyes I will see their downfall;
 they will be trampled like mud in the
 streets.

6:10 Hebrew *of using the short ephah?* The ephah was a unit for measuring grain.

6:10-12 The Lord had specific accusations against his people. They had become a community of deceit that was ripe for rejection and destruction. Falsely acquired wealth, unethical business practices, threats, and violence characterized this supposed people of God (see Hosea 12:7-8; Amos 8:5-6). They could not change because lying was their way of life (compare Proverbs 6:16-19).
7:1-20 Hopeless deception and corruption permeated God's people (7:1-6); however, God's mercy would triumph, and Israel would be restored (7:11-13). God's mercy, compassion, and unfailing love would prevail (7:14-20). Micah mourned his people's condition and looked to the Lord for help (7:7-10).
7:4 The people of Israel would soon be conquered by the Assyrians, the people of Judah would soon face destruction at the hands of the Babylonians, and all the people of the earth would face God in judgment.
7:7-10 Amid despair, Micah prays a psalm of hope and confidence in the Lord (see Habakkuk 2:4; 3:16-18).
7:8 The prophet confidently trusts in God to be his light (see Psalm 27:1) even in deep difficulty, knowing that his enemies would not overcome him (see Psalm 23:4-5). God's Spirit gave him the power and confidence to perform his prophetic task (Micah 3:8).
7:9 The prophet and other godly people recognize their failure and guilt yet trust the Lord for redemption. The Lord's righteousness brings salvation and rescue for his people.

MICAH 7

[11] In that day, Israel, your cities will be rebuilt,
and your borders will be extended.
[12] People from many lands will come and honor you—
from Assyria all the way to the towns of Egypt,
from Egypt all the way to the Euphrates River,*
and from distant seas and mountains.
[13] But the land* will become empty and desolate
because of the wickedness of those who live there.

The LORD's Compassion on Israel

[14] O LORD, protect your people with your shepherd's staff;
lead your flock, your special possession.
Though they live alone in a thicket
on the heights of Mount Carmel,*
let them graze in the fertile pastures of Bashan and Gilead
as they did long ago.
[15] "Yes," says the LORD,
"I will do mighty miracles for you,
like those I did when I rescued you
from slavery in Egypt."
[16] All the nations of the world will stand amazed
at what the LORD will do for you.
They will be embarrassed
at their feeble power.
They will cover their mouths in silent awe,
deaf to everything around them.
[17] Like snakes crawling from their holes,
they will come out to meet the LORD our God.
They will fear him greatly,
trembling in terror at his presence.
[18] Where is another God like you,
who pardons the guilt of the remnant,
overlooking the sins of his special people?
You will not stay angry with your people forever,
because you delight in showing unfailing love.
[19] Once again you will have compassion on us.
You will trample our sins under your feet
and throw them into the depths of the ocean!
[20] You will show us your faithfulness and unfailing love
as you promised to our ancestors Abraham and Jacob long ago.

7:12 Hebrew *the river.* **7:13** Or *earth.* **7:14** Or *surrounded by a fruitful land.*

7:11-20 "That day" includes 538 BC, when Israel began to return from exile in Babylon (see Ezra 1–2), and the final restoration of God's people (see Amos 9:11-15). The Lord promised to renew Israel, his special possession, entirely (see Exodus 19:5; Malachi 3:17). Judgment would not mean the destruction of hope but a cleansing so that true hope could prevail. The restoration would be God's work alone as he restored the remnant of his special people and removed their guilt by his love, compassion, and faithfulness (see Exodus 32:12-14).

7:18-20 These verses provide a fine summary of how the Old Testament understands and portrays God. God is unique; there is no one and nothing else like him. Because of his "unfailing love" (Hebrew *khesed*), he does not destroy the people he judges but instead restores them (see Exodus 34:6-7). His faithfulness means that he can be trusted to do good regardless of the cost to himself (see Psalm 89:1-2). The question—"Where is another God like you?"—probably plays off of Micah's name ("Who is like the Lord?"). God's character is unequaled among the gods of the other nations. His actions and words spring from his character (Exodus 34:6-7). God pardons, shows compassion, triumphs over his peoples' sins, and seals those sins away. The Lord's unfailing love moved him to choose Israel from the beginning (Deuteronomy 7:8), consistent with his covenant faithfulness to Israel's ancestors (Deuteronomy 7:20; 9:1–10:22). By his unfailing love, God continues to offer hope to those who trust in him.

Nahum

WHAT DO WE LEARN ABOUT GOD'S MISSION AND OURS?
Nahum means "comfort," and we can take comfort in knowing God will bring justice.

WHO WROTE IT? The book preserves Nahum's vision from God. Whether or not he used a scribe, as was common practice, is unknown.

WHEN DID IT HAPPEN? Sometime in the seventh century, after the fall of the ancient Egyptian city of Thebes (663 BC) but before Nineveh's destruction (612 BC), approximately 150 years after Jonah's visit to Nineveh.

HOW IS IT ORGANIZED?

1: God is kind to those who trust him but judges those who rebel

2: Nineveh will be conquered

3: God will ensure Nineveh's destruction

FEATURE HIGHLIGHTS

+ *Mountain Messenger: Bringer of Peace (1119)*
+ *Is Nahum Denigrating Women? (1121)*

Words to Remember are highlighted throughout this book

Timeline

BC	
697	MANASSEH, HEPHZIBAH'S SON, BECOMES KING OF JUDAH
669	ASHURBANIPAL BECOMES KING OF ASSYRIA
663	NAHUM BECOMES A PROPHET; THE FALL OF THEBES
640	JOSIAH, SON OF JEDIDAH, BECOMES KING OF JUDAH; ZEPHANIAH BECOMES A PROPHET
627	JEREMIAH BECOMES A PROPHET
612	NINEVEH FALLS
609	ASSYRIA COMPLETELY CONQUERED
605	BABYLONIANS WIN BATTLE OF CARCHEMISH
586	JUDAH FALLS TO BABYLON

HOW LONG DOES IT TAKE TO READ?

:10 | :30 | 1:00 | 1:30 | 2:00 | 2:30 | 3:00 | 3:30

1 This message concerning Nineveh came as a vision to Nahum, who lived in Elkosh.

The Lord's Anger against Nineveh

² The Lord is a jealous God,
  filled with vengeance and rage.
He takes revenge on all who oppose him
  and continues to rage against his enemies!
³ The Lord is slow to get angry, but his power is great,
  and he never lets the guilty go unpunished.
He displays his power in the whirlwind and the storm.
  The billowing clouds are the dust beneath his feet.
⁴ At his command the oceans dry up,
  and the rivers disappear.
The lush pastures of Bashan and Carmel fade,
  and the green forests of Lebanon wither.
⁵ In his presence the mountains quake,
  and the hills melt away;
the earth trembles,
  and its people are destroyed.
⁶ Who can stand before his fierce anger?
  Who can survive his burning fury?
His rage blazes forth like fire,
  and the mountains crumble to dust in his presence.
⁷ The Lord is good,
  a strong refuge when trouble comes.
He is close to those who trust in him.
⁸ But he will sweep away his enemies*
  in an overwhelming flood.
He will pursue his foes
  into the darkness of night.
⁹ Why are you scheming against the Lord?
  He will destroy you with one blow;
  he won't need to strike twice!
¹⁰ His enemies, tangled like thornbushes
  and staggering like drunks,
  will be burned up like dry stubble in a field.
¹¹ Who is this wicked counselor of yours
  who plots evil against the Lord?
¹² This is what the Lord says:
"Though the Assyrians have many allies,
  they will be destroyed and disappear.
O my people, I have punished you before,
  but I will not punish you again.
¹³ Now I will break the yoke of bondage from your neck
  and tear off the chains of Assyrian oppression."

1:8 As in Greek version; Hebrew reads *sweep away her place*.

1:1 This book's opening, similar to that of other prophetic books (Obadiah 1:1; Habakkuk 1:1; Malachi 1:1), identifies Nahum as a prophet, one who uttered messages from God. Nineveh became the capital of the Assyrian empire shortly after 705 BC and remained so until its destruction in 612 BC. The name *Nahum* means "he [God] comforts." Although his description of Nineveh's destruction is graphic and shocking, Nahum's prophetic message was a great comfort to God's people. The Assyrians had brutalized them and many other nations for decades. By destroying them, God signaled his love, mercy, and faithfulness to Israel.

1:2 The Hebrew word translated "jealous" here could also be understood as "zealous." God zealously guards the welfare of his people and zealously desires their faithfulness (Exodus 20:4-5; Deuteronomy 4:23-24; 6:4; Jeremiah 2:1–3:5). God's "vengeance and rage" cannot be confused with the human attitude of getting even. God's actions emerge from his holiness (Jeremiah 50:28-29), justice (Isaiah 63:1-9), and faithfulness to the covenant with his people (Leviticus 26:23-25; Isaiah 1:24-26). His vengeance is never arbitrary or vindictive.

1:3 The phrase "slow to get angry" is a figure of speech that could be rendered literally as "long of nose." Behind this Hebrew idiom lies the idea that when someone is angry, the tip of their nose turns red. Hence, in the Old Testament, "short of nose" refers to one who angered easily. Proverbs 14:17 refers to this as "short-tempered." Conversely, the Old Testament describes God as "long of nose" (or "slow to anger": Exodus 34:6; Numbers 14:18; compare Psalm 86:15). Metaphorically speaking, it takes a long time for the tip of God's nose to turn red. English Bibles usually translate this idiom in several ways, such as "slow to anger," "longsuffering," or "patient."

1:4 Like clouds (1:3) and mountains (1:5), oceans and rivers are under God's sovereign control. The Old Testament prophets often recalled God's actions against the seas and rivers during the Exodus (Exodus 15:8-10; 2 Samuel 22:16; Psalms 66:6; 77:16; Habakkuk 3:15). God's power over the waters repudiated the mythology of the ancient Canaanites, in which oceans and the rivers were under the control of the sea god Yamm. Situated east of the Sea of Galilee, Bashan was known for its rich pastureland, ideal for raising cattle (see Micah 7:14). Carmel, on the Mediterranean coast in central Canaan, was noted for its beauty and fruitfulness (Song of Songs 7:5; Jeremiah 50:19). Lebanon was famed for its great cedars (1 Kings 5:6-18). Nahum lists these areas to demonstrate that even the most fertile and productive places on earth cannot withstand the power of God's judgment

1:6-8 The first few verses of Nahum affirm God's patience (1:3) and goodness (1:7). He provides security for those who trust in him (1:7). However, he does not hesitate to destroy his enemies. He directs his fierce anger at those who are evil, cruel, arrogant, and inhumane. At times we may be reluctant to consider aspects of God's character that seem cruel or unloving to us. But our view of God must conform to the full picture that Scripture provides. Even when described in violent terms that may make us uncomfortable, God's destruction of evil is an example of his holiness and justice on display. As sinful people, our tendency is to be lenient about sin, but God cannot be lenient when it comes to injustice and evil. He makes things right eventually, even if we don't see it.

Mountain Messenger

IDENTITY — Bringer of Peace

I'm a mountain messenger, a courier, bringing both good and bad news across the mountains. Today I bring something different.

Today, I bring peace, an ideal most people desire. Whether it's peace from war, peace in our families, or just a few minutes of peace and quiet, we all dream of the day peace will arrive.

My message of peace will be good news for Judah. One of their enemies will be destroyed.

A hundred years before me, the prophet Isaiah delivered a similar sentiment: "How beautiful on the mountains are the feet of the messenger who brings good news, the good news of peace" (Isaiah 52:7). Isaiah was looking toward the Babylonian captivity when Jerusalem would lie desolate. He wanted us to wake up and see God's salvation coming.

Just like the messenger Isaiah spoke of, today I'm a sure-footed messenger traveling across the Judean mountainside, carrying good news to a dejected society. I carry an important message—redemption is near! God will free us from our enemies. Rejoice and celebrate! Peace is on the way. As I think about the message, I travel even faster.

THE MOUNTAIN MESSENGER'S STORY IS TOLD IN NAHUM 1:15; ISAIAH 52:7.

> Where can you take the Good News today?

IDENTIFY

How swift are our feet to share God's Good News? There are people longing to hear. Let's be swift to share the message of Jesus' peace. Shout it from the mountaintops!

"The Medes destroyed Nineveh in 612 BC. Nahum's prophecy was indeed good news! Peace had come, at least for a while. Many years later, Paul used similar imagery: 'How beautiful are the feet of messengers who bring good news!' (Romans 10:15). Today we rejoice in our Good News—Jesus sets us free from sin's captivity!"

MELISSA HOUDMANN is the cofounder of GotQuestions Ministries, a website dedicated to answering Bible questions. She also wrote Stonecroft Ministries' *Why Believe* study.

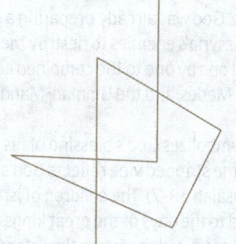

¹⁴ And this is what the LORD says concerning the Assyrians in Nineveh:
"You will have no more children to carry on your name.
I will destroy all the idols in the temples of your gods.
I am preparing a grave for you because you are despicable!"

¹⁵ *Look! A messenger is coming over the mountains with good news!
He is bringing a message of peace.
Celebrate your festivals, O people of Judah, and fulfill all your vows,
for your wicked enemies will never invade your land again.
They will be completely destroyed!

The Fall of Nineveh

2 ¹ *Your enemy is coming to crush you, Nineveh.
Man the ramparts! Watch the roads!
Prepare your defenses! Call out your forces!

² Even though the destroyer has destroyed Judah, the LORD will restore its honor.
Israel's vine has been stripped of branches, but he will restore its splendor.

³ Shields flash red in the sunlight!
See the scarlet uniforms of the valiant troops!
Watch as their glittering chariots move into position,
with a forest of spears waving above them.*

⁴ The chariots race recklessly along the streets and rush wildly through the squares.
They flash like firelight and move as swiftly as lightning.

⁵ The king shouts to his officers;
they stumble in their haste,
rushing to the walls to set up their defenses.

⁶ The river gates have been torn open!
The palace is about to collapse!

⁷ Nineveh's exile has been decreed,
and all the servant girls mourn its capture.
They moan like doves
and beat their breasts in sorrow.

⁸ Nineveh is like a leaking water reservoir!
The people are slipping away.
"Stop, stop!" someone shouts,
but no one even looks back.

⁹ Loot the silver!
Plunder the gold!
There's no end to Nineveh's treasures—
its vast, uncounted wealth.

¹⁰ Soon the city is plundered, empty, and ruined.
Hearts melt and knees shake.
The people stand aghast,
their faces pale and trembling.

¹¹ Where now is that great Nineveh,
that den filled with young lions?
It was a place where people—like lions and their cubs—
walked freely and without fear.

¹² The lion tore up meat for his cubs
and strangled prey for his mate.
He filled his den with prey,
his caverns with his plunder.

¹³ "I am your enemy!"
says the LORD of Heaven's Armies.
"Your chariots will soon go up in smoke.
Your young men* will be killed in battle.
Never again will you plunder conquered nations.
The voices of your proud messengers will be heard no more."

1:15 Verse 1:15 is numbered 2:1 in Hebrew text. **2:1** Verses 2:1-13 are numbered 2:2-14 in Hebrew text. **2:3** Greek and Syriac versions read *into position, / the horses whipped into a frenzy.* **2:13** Hebrew *young lions.*

1:14 Nineveh would be annihilated. Cutting off a person's name and leaving them without a descendant meant utterly destroying them (1 Samuel 24:21; Job 18:17; Isaiah 14:22). None of Assyria's venerated gods could deliver Nineveh from God's death sentence. God was already preparing a grave for Nineveh and directing Assyria's enemies to destroy the city. Assyria's proud cities fell one by one to the combined attacks of the Chaldeans, the Medes, and the Umman-Manda. Nineveh itself fell in 612 BC.
2:2 The vine symbolizes God's blessing of his people (Isaiah 27:2-6), while the stripped vine reflects God's previous discipline of them (Isaiah 5:1-7). The children of Israel were in a sad state compared to the days of the great kings David and Solomon, but God promised to restore the splendor of his people.
2:6 The rush to defend (2:5) would come too late because the defenses would already be breached. Nineveh was served by a reservoir formed by a double dam on the Khosr River, a tributary of the Tigris that flowed through the city. A series of flood gates augmented the reservoir. The Greek historian Diodorus reported that torrential rains had already swelled the city's river system during this time. By first closing, then opening the flood gates, Nineveh's attackers released the pent-up water as a battering ram against the city walls.
2:9 The "vast, uncounted wealth" of other nations poured into the Assyrian capital as trade, tribute, and spoils, but it would be gone in an instant. Ruthless aggression and wickedness may succeed temporarily, but ultimately they will be destroyed (Proverbs 13:22; Obadiah 1:15; Luke 12:16-20).
2:11-13 Following the description of Nineveh's fall (2:1-10), Nahum inserts the first of three taunt songs, a common genre in the ancient Near East (see also 3:8-13, 14-19). In biting satire, he compares Nineveh to a den of lions: "Your young men" in 2:13 is literally "your young lions" in Hebrew. In Assyrian stone reliefs, the lion was a symbol of strength and power. As a means of showing Assyrian sovereignty, their kings depicted themselves as successful lion hunters. Nahum adopts this image but turns it back on Assyria: The hunters would now be hunted, and they would not survive.

The Lord's Judgment against Nineveh

3 What sorrow awaits Nineveh,
 the city of murder and lies!
She is crammed with wealth
 and is never without victims.
[2] Hear the crack of whips,
 the rumble of wheels!
Horses' hooves pound,
 and chariots clatter wildly.
[3] See the flashing swords and glittering spears
 as the charioteers charge past!
There are countless casualties,
 heaps of bodies—
so many bodies that
 people stumble over them.
[4] All this because Nineveh,
 the beautiful and faithless city,
mistress of deadly charms,
 enticed the nations with her beauty.
She taught them all her magic,
 enchanting people everywhere.
[5] "I am your enemy!"
 says the Lord of Heaven's Armies.
"And now I will lift your skirts
 and show all the earth your nakedness and shame.
[6] I will cover you with filth
 and show the world how vile you really are.
[7] All who see you will shrink back and say,
 'Nineveh lies in ruins.
Where are the mourners?'
 Does anyone regret your destruction?"

3:1 The Assyrians' savage cruelty is well documented. Their practices included cutting off external body parts—such as noses, ears, hands, and feet—and execution by impalement on stakes. They heaped up severed heads before the gates of besieged cities. Victims' eyes were sometimes pulled out, and their skin flayed from their bodies while they were still alive.
3:3 When archaeologists excavated ancient Nineveh, they discovered the destruction from this battle. Excavations at one of the city's fifteen gates have revealed that at least twelve people died there, possibly trying to flee or defend Nineveh, and were buried by falling debris.
3:5 The Assyrians had charmed other nations with wealth and luxury (3:4) but then victimized them through military might and economic exploitation, so the punishment befits their crimes. God will humiliate and expose this once mighty city by stripping Nineveh bare and allowing the nations to see it in ruins (see also Jeremiah 13:22; Ezekiel 16:37-41), like the Assyrians did to other nations. Isaiah applies the same metaphor to Babylon (Isaiah 47:1-3).
3:5 Twice God tells Nineveh, "I am your enemy" (also 2:13). Nineveh's judgment stands as a historical reminder that the Lord hates sin and will deal with people and nations according to their deeds (Psalms 9:7-8; 62:12; Jeremiah 46:28; Acts 17:31). One day, God's justice will fall worldwide on those who have rebelled against him (Revelation 17–19).

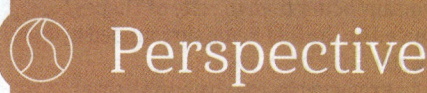

Perspective

Is Nahum denigrating women?

SCRIPTURE CONNECTION: NAHUM 3:13

At first, it might seem like Nahum 3:13 demeans or underestimates women. However, we must understand the historical and cultural contexts, and what the Bible overall says about women.

With few exceptions (like Deborah in Judges 4:1–5:31 and Jael in Judges 4:17-22; 5:24-27), women were not part of ancient Israel's military. They were busy in the fields (Ruth 2), marketplaces (Proverbs 31), and at home. Their work was not considered demeaning, and they would not have been insulted by Nahum's comments. Comparing fearful troops to women was common both in the Bible (see Isaiah 19:16; Jeremiah 49:22; 50:37; 51:30) and in other ancient writings.

When we look at the whole Bible, we see women are God's image-bearers (Genesis 1:26-27) and are commanded by God to reign along with men (Genesis 1:26). They are integral to God's salvation plan (see Sarah, Rahab, Ruth, Esther, Mary, Elizabeth, Priscilla, Phoebe), beloved by God (see Hagar, Hannah, Leah, the woman caught in adultery), and equal heirs of God's Kingdom (Galatians 3:26-28). The first people to see the resurrected Jesus were women (Mary Magdalene, Mary the mother of James, Salome, and Joanna)! Concluding that the Bible denigrates women is to misunderstand the original context and ignore the entirety of Scripture.

VIEWPOINTS

THEIRS: *The Lord gave unusual influence to some of the women who followed him.*
MINE: *"Rather than take other people's word for what women can do, I have learned to dive straight into the Bible for myself. There, I find that God calls his daughters to make a unique impact."*
YOURS: *What woman in the Bible would you like to learn more about to see how God values us?*

CATHERINE L. McDOWELL, PhD, is associate professor of Old Testament at Gordon-Conwell Theological Seminary. She has authored several books and articles on Bible backgrounds, Genesis, Isaiah, and Biblical Hebrew.

8 Are you any better than the city of Thebes,*
    situated on the Nile River, surrounded by
        water?
  She was protected by the river on all sides,
    walled in by water.
9 Ethiopia* and the land of Egypt
    gave unlimited assistance.
  The nations of Put and Libya
    were among her allies.
10 Yet Thebes fell,
    and her people were led away as captives.
  Her babies were dashed to death
    against the stones of the streets.
  Soldiers threw dice* to get Egyptian officers as
        servants.
  All their leaders were bound in chains.

11 And you, Nineveh, will also stagger like a
        drunkard.
  You will hide for fear of the attacking enemy.
12 All your fortresses will fall.
  They will be devoured like the ripe figs
    that fall into the mouths
      of those who shake the trees.
13 Your troops will be as weak
    and helpless as women.
  The gates of your land will be opened wide to
        the enemy
    and set on fire and burned.
14 Get ready for the siege!
    Store up water!
    Strengthen the defenses!
  Go into the pits to trample clay,
    and pack it into molds,
  making bricks to repair the walls.
15 But the fire will devour you;
    the sword will cut you down.
  The enemy will consume you like locusts,
    devouring everything they see.
  There will be no escape,
    even if you multiply like swarming locusts.
16 Your merchants have multiplied
    until they outnumber the stars.
  But like a swarm of locusts,
    they strip the land and fly away.
17 Your guards* and officials are also like
        swarming locusts
    that crowd together in the hedges on a cold
        day.
  But like locusts that fly away when the sun
        comes up,
    all of them will fly away and disappear.

18 Your shepherds are asleep, O Assyrian king;
    your princes lie dead in the dust.
  Your people are scattered across the mountains
    with no one to gather them together.
19 There is no healing for your wound;
    your injury is fatal.
  All who hear of your destruction
    will clap their hands for joy.
  Where can anyone be found
    who has not suffered from your continual
        cruelty?

3:8 Hebrew *No-amon*; also in 3:10. 3:9 Hebrew *Cush*. 3:10 Hebrew *They cast lots.* 3:17 Or *princes*.

3:13 Nahum is not the only prophet to compare weak and helpless troops to women (see Isaiah 19:16; Jeremiah 50:37; 51:30). Although it seems insulting to us, the seventh century BC was a different era. With rare exceptions, women in the ancient Near East did not engage in warfare because of the grotesque and brutal nature of ancient warfare and the expectations for women in those societies. Instead of being able to fight, women were victimized and taken as captives of war. Nahum's language here reflects the realities of ancient warfare and is not a commentary about women.

3:19 Nineveh deserved destruction rather than healing. Although God had been patient with Nineveh in Jonah's day when they repented for a time (Jonah 3:10), the Assyrians had returned to cruelty and would reap the harvest of their continued evil (see Proverbs 11:16-19; Isaiah 66:5-6; Hosea 8:7). Those who had suffered under Assyria's cruelty would welcome this message with joy.

Habakkuk

WHAT DO WE LEARN ABOUT GOD'S MISSION AND OURS?
We may never fully understand God's justice, but we can know God is good.

WHO WROTE IT? Habakkuk.

WHEN DID IT HAPPEN? Between 612 and 589 BC, around the time Babylon became the major world power.

HOW IS IT ORGANIZED?

1: Habakkuk asks God to punish Judah; God says he plans to do so, using the Babylonians

2: Habakkuk objects to God's use of such a wicked nation to carry out his justice; God says Babylon will also be punished

3: Habakkuk answers with a prayer of worship and trust

FEATURE HIGHLIGHTS

+ Called: Climbing (1128)

Words to Remember are highlighted throughout this book

HOW LONG DOES IT TAKE TO READ?
:10 | :30 | 1:00 | 1:30 | 2:00 | 2:30 | 3:00 | 3:30

Timeline (BC)

BC	Event
627	JEREMIAH BECOMES A PROPHET
612	HABAKKUK BECOMES A PROPHET
609	KING JOSIAH, SON OF JEDIDAH, DIES IN BATTLE
605	DANIEL TAKEN CAPTIVE TO BABYLON
597	EZEKIEL TAKEN CAPTIVE TO BABYLON; ZEDEKIAH BECOMES KING OF JUDAH
589	HABAKKUK'S MINISTRY ENDS
586	FALL OF JUDAH; JERUSALEM DESTROYED

HABAKKUK 1

1 This is the message that the prophet Habakkuk received in a vision.

Habakkuk's Complaint

² How long, O Lord, must I call for help?
  But you do not listen!
"Violence is everywhere!" I cry,
  but you do not come to save.
³ Must I forever see these evil deeds?
  Why must I watch all this misery?
Wherever I look,
  I see destruction and violence.
I am surrounded by people
  who love to argue and fight.
⁴ The law has become paralyzed,
  and there is no justice in the courts.
The wicked far outnumber the righteous,
  so that justice has become perverted.

The Lord's Reply

⁵ The Lord replied,

"Look around at the nations;
  look and be amazed!*
For I am doing something in your own day,
  something you wouldn't believe
  even if someone told you about it.
⁶ I am raising up the Babylonians,*
  a cruel and violent people.
They will march across the world
  and conquer other lands.
⁷ They are notorious for their cruelty
  and do whatever they like.
⁸ Their horses are swifter than cheetahs*
  and fiercer than wolves at dusk.
Their charioteers charge from far away.
  Like eagles, they swoop down to devour
  their prey.
⁹ "On they come, all bent on violence.
  Their hordes advance like a desert wind,
  sweeping captives ahead of them like sand.
¹⁰ They scoff at kings and princes
  and scorn all their fortresses.
They simply pile ramps of earth
  against their walls and capture them!
¹¹ They sweep past like the wind
  and are gone.
But they are deeply guilty,
  for their own strength is their god."

Habakkuk's Second Complaint

¹² O Lord my God, my Holy One, you who are eternal—
  surely you do not plan to wipe us out?
O Lord, our Rock, you have sent these
  Babylonians to correct us,
  to punish us for our many sins.
¹³ But you are pure and cannot stand the sight of evil.
  Will you wink at their treachery?
Should you be silent while the wicked
  swallow up people more righteous than
  they?
¹⁴ Are we only fish to be caught and killed?
  Are we only sea creatures that have no leader?
¹⁵ Must we be strung up on their hooks
  and caught in their nets while they rejoice
  and celebrate?
¹⁶ Then they will worship their nets
  and burn incense in front of them.
"These nets are the gods who have made us
  rich!"
  they will claim.
¹⁷ Will you let them get away with this forever?
  Will they succeed forever in their heartless
  conquests?

2 I will climb up to my watchtower
  and stand at my guardpost.
There I will wait to see what the Lord says
  and how he* will answer my complaint.

1:5 Greek version reads *Look, you mockers; / look and be amazed and die.* Compare Acts 13:41. **1:6** Or *Chaldeans.* **1:8** Or *leopards.* **2:1** As in Syriac version; Hebrew reads *I.*

1:1-2 Habakkuk served as the Lord's prophet in the second half of the seventh century BC. This was a time of significant moral, ethical, and spiritual decline in Judah. Rather than speaking directly to the people, as was typical of Israel's prophets, Habakkuk took his grief and frustration directly to God. Habakkuk's messages are framed as a dialogue with God.

1:2-4 Habakkuk's perspective on the people's circumstances suggests that God had abandoned his people. Judah was full of violence and destruction, and the people practiced all kinds of wickedness. Although Habakkuk's outcry is understandable, he would soon learn that God's character is not defined by the level of evil and injustice in the world nor by Habakkuk's understanding of events. God's plans are far greater than anything Habakkuk could possibly imagine. Habakkuk's current situation, although difficult, would not be the final word.

1:5-11 The Lord acknowledged that the Babylonians were cruel, violent, and arrogant. He did not choose them as an instrument of judgment against his people because they were righteous. In fact, God does not explain his choice at all. However, we know that God controls all rulers and nations (Proverbs 21:1), and he uses them to accomplish his greater purposes. God was fully aware of Babylon's evil, and their own judgment would be coming (Habakkuk 2:6-8, 16-17).

1:12-17 Habakkuk struggles to understand the justice of God. Why would he judge Judah with a people far more wicked? God does not answer Habakkuk's question directly. Instead, he assures him of what he truly needs to know: God would indeed punish Babylon for their evil, but the righteous would need to live by faithfulness to God (2:4; Hebrews 10:38), not according to their circumstances.

The Lord's Second Reply

²Then the Lord said to me,

"Write my answer plainly on tablets,
so that a runner can carry the correct message to others.
³ This vision is for a future time.
It describes the end, and it will be fulfilled.
If it seems slow in coming, wait patiently,
for it will surely take place.
It will not be delayed.

⁴ "Look at the proud!
They trust in themselves, and their lives are crooked.
But the righteous will live by their faithfulness to God.*
⁵ Wealth* is treacherous,
and the arrogant are never at rest.
They open their mouths as wide as the grave,*
and like death, they are never satisfied.
In their greed they have gathered up many nations
and swallowed many peoples.

⁶ "But soon their captives will taunt them.
They will mock them, saying,
'What sorrow awaits you thieves!
Now you will get what you deserve!
You've become rich by extortion,
but how much longer can this go on?'
⁷ Suddenly, your debtors will take action.
They will turn on you and take all you have,
while you stand trembling and helpless.
⁸ Because you have plundered many nations,
now all the survivors will plunder you.
You committed murder throughout the countryside
and filled the towns with violence.

⁹ "What sorrow awaits you who build big houses
with money gained dishonestly!
You believe your wealth will buy security,
putting your family's nest beyond the reach of danger.
¹⁰ But by the murders you committed,
you have shamed your name and forfeited your lives.
¹¹ The very stones in the walls cry out against you,
and the beams in the ceilings echo the complaint.

¹² "What sorrow awaits you who build cities
with money gained through murder and corruption!
¹³ Has not the Lord of Heaven's Armies promised
that the wealth of nations will turn to ashes?
They work so hard,
but all in vain!
¹⁴ For as the waters fill the sea,
the earth will be filled with an awareness of the glory of the Lord.

¹⁵ "What sorrow awaits you who make your neighbors drunk!
You force your cup on them
so you can gloat over their shameful nakedness.
¹⁶ But soon it will be your turn to be disgraced.
Come, drink and be exposed!*
Drink from the cup of the Lord's judgment,
and all your glory will be turned to shame.
¹⁷ You cut down the forests of Lebanon.
Now you will be cut down.
You destroyed the wild animals,
so now their terror will be yours.
You committed murder throughout the countryside
and filled the towns with violence.

¹⁸ "What good is an idol carved by man,
or a cast image that deceives you?
How foolish to trust in your own creation—
a god that can't even talk!
¹⁹ What sorrow awaits you who say to wooden idols,
'Wake up and save us!'
To speechless stone images you say,
'Rise up and teach us!'
Can an idol tell you what to do?
They may be overlaid with gold and silver,
but they are lifeless inside.
²⁰ But the Lord is in his holy Temple.
Let all the earth be silent before him."

2:3b-4 Greek version reads *If the vision is delayed, wait patiently, / for it will surely come and not delay. / ⁴I will take no pleasure in anyone who turns away. / But the righteous person will live by my faith.* Compare Rom 1:17; Gal 3:11; Heb 10:37-38. 2:5a As in Dead Sea Scroll 1QpHab; other Hebrew manuscripts read *Wine*. 2:5b Hebrew *as Sheol*. 2:16 Dead Sea Scrolls and Greek and Syriac versions read *and stagger!*

2:2 In some cases, prophets recorded their visions and oracles on wooden or stone tablets. The tablets would serve in the future as a testimony of God's word (see also Isaiah 30:8). Later audiences would read it and know that God's word is true, and he keeps his promises. Despite his frightening circumstances and unanswered questions, Habakkuk responded to God with praise and worship. Remembering God's mighty acts of redemption and recalling his character comforted Habakkuk. Although he lived in terrifying times, Habakkuk rejoiced in the Lord. He knew for certain that the Lord was his strength and security (Habakkuk 3:17-19).

Habakkuk's Prayer

3 This prayer was sung by the prophet Habakkuk*:

² I have heard all about you, LORD.
  I am filled with awe by your amazing works.
In this time of our deep need,
  help us again as you did in years gone by.
And in your anger,
  remember your mercy.

³ I see God moving across the deserts from Edom,*
  the Holy One coming from Mount Paran.*
His brilliant splendor fills the heavens,
  and the earth is filled with his praise.
⁴ His coming is as brilliant as the sunrise.
  Rays of light flash from his hands,
  where his awesome power is hidden.
⁵ Pestilence marches before him;
  plague follows close behind.

3:1 Hebrew adds *according to shigionoth,* probably indicating the musical setting for the prayer. **3:3a** Hebrew *Teman.* **3:3b** Hebrew adds *selah;* also in 3:9, 13. The meaning of this Hebrew term is uncertain; it is probably a musical or literary term.

---

⑧ Come Close — THOUGH: YET I WILL

SCRIPTURE CONNECTION: HABAKKUK 3:17-19

How odd it looks—an ultrasound image when you're not expecting a baby. Recently, because of some unexplained bleeding long after I was done having children, I found myself saddled in the exam table's stirrups. Once again, I felt warm goo on my belly and turned to view the screen.

For half a moment I instinctively expected to see what I saw years ago—twins! But I saw nothing. Or at least I hoped to see nothing—nothing cancerous, nothing malignant.

When we pass our years of childbearing and raising, we, too, may feel like nothing. Where we once saw fullness and growth that nurtured thriving, vocal life, now we see a small space the size of a fist, not a watermelon.

For so long, hormones and others' needs swooshed us through each day. But now, we're done raising people, and we see all the "thoughs": Though we could have done better, will our children still love us? Though we are glad they are independent, will we end life alone? Though we now have more energy for our careers, will our workplaces still want us?

Yet between childbearing and pallbearing, God is not done with us. He re-creates us as we conceive again who he is—our sovereign Lord. And new life comes as we take each "though" and find that God promises new life, impregnating our limits with his "yet I will" promises.

Though empty like fig trees without blossoms, yet I will believe God has much ahead for me.

Though alone with no sheep (little or big) in our home, yet I will know God is always here.

Though spent like the riches of crops and livestock, yet I will trust God for enough ahead.

We can't go back to full womb or full home. But we can conceive and bring to fruition what God has for us in full or less-full seasons, all as we meet each "though" with a "Yet, God, I will . . ."

> **REFLECT** "The LORD alone guided them; they followed no foreign gods. He let them ride over the highlands and feast on the crops of the fields." DEUTERONOMY 32:12-13
>
> *God, though I feel empty, alone, and spent, yet I will be joyful and strong in you. Amen.*
>
> **CONSIDER** "But those who, when they were full, *enjoyed God in all,* when they are emptied and impoverished, can *enjoy all in God.*" MATTHEW HENRY

Our nots are God's not yets.

NAOMI CRAMER OVERTON, MBA, DIS, lives to realize beauty-filled visions that lift us to flourishing, with our families and beyond. Naomi has been CEO for Stonecroft and MOPS, director with Compassion International and World Vision, and General Editor for this Bible.

⁶ When he stops, the earth shakes.
  When he looks, the nations tremble.
  He shatters the everlasting mountains
    and levels the eternal hills.
  He is the Eternal One!*
⁷ I see the people of Cushan in distress,
    and the nation of Midian trembling in terror.

⁸ Was it in anger, Lord, that you struck the rivers
    and parted the sea?
  Were you displeased with them?
    No, you were sending your chariots of
      salvation!
⁹ You brandished your bow
    and your quiver of arrows.
  You split open the earth with flowing rivers.
¹⁰ The mountains watched and trembled.
    Onward swept the raging waters.
  The mighty deep cried out,
    lifting its hands in submission.
¹¹ The sun and moon stood still in the sky
    as your brilliant arrows flew
    and your glittering spear flashed.

¹² You marched across the land in anger
    and trampled the nations in your fury.
¹³ You went out to rescue your chosen people,
    to save your anointed ones.
  You crushed the heads of the wicked
    and stripped their bones from head to toe.
¹⁴ With his own weapons,
    you destroyed the chief of those
  who rushed out like a whirlwind,
    thinking Israel would be easy prey.
¹⁵ You trampled the sea with your horses,
    and the mighty waters piled high.

¹⁶ I trembled inside when I heard this;
    my lips quivered with fear.
  My legs gave way beneath me,*
    and I shook in terror.
  I will wait quietly for the coming day
    when disaster will strike the people who
      invade us.
¹⁷ Even though the fig trees have no blossoms,
    and there are no grapes on the vines;
  even though the olive crop fails,
    and the fields lie empty and barren;
  even though the flocks die in the fields,
    and the cattle barns are empty,
¹⁸ yet I will rejoice in the Lord!
    I will be joyful in the God of my salvation!
¹⁹ The Sovereign Lord is my strength!
    He makes me as surefooted as a deer,*
    able to tread upon the heights.

(For the choir director: This prayer is to be accompanied by stringed instruments.)

3:6 Or *The ancient paths belong to him.*   **3:16** Hebrew *Decay entered my bones.*   **3:19** Or *He gives me the speed of a deer.*

3:8-15 The Lord is a Divine Warrior for his people, moving in redemptive power on their behalf. The motif of God as Divine Warrior spans the Old and New Testaments. We can observe it in Israel's exodus from Egypt, their movement to Mount Sinai (Exodus 15:1-18), their approach to the Promised Land from the south, and their triumphs in the early conquest period (for example, Judges 5:4-5; Psalms 18:8-16; 77:16-20; a key New Testament example is Revelation 19:11-21).

3:17-19 After recounting God's mighty acts of redemption (3:2-15) and pausing to consider them (3:16), Habakkuk now reaffirms his trust in God as he closes his prayer. Even if God never pours out material blessings on his people again, he is still worthy of all the trust and praise they can give. Come what may, the prophet could rejoice, knowing that the Lord is not only Israel's redeemer, but also the source of his own salvation.

Zephaniah

WHAT DO WE LEARN ABOUT GOD'S MISSION AND OURS?
Actions have consequences, but God will restore his people in the end.

WHO WROTE IT? Zephaniah.

WHEN DID IT HAPPEN? Probably between 640 and 630 BC, near the end of the divided kingdom.

HOW IS IT ORGANIZED?

1: The Day of the Lord is coming

2: Judgment on the nations

3: Judah will be judged, then restored

FEATURE HIGHLIGHTS

+ *Daughters of Jerusalem* (1135)

Words to Remember are highlighted throughout this book

HOW LONG DOES IT TAKE TO READ?

:10 | :30 | 1:00 | 1:30 | 2:00 | 2:30 | 3:00 | 3:30

Timeline

BC	
640	ZEPHANIAH BECOMES A PROPHET; JOSIAH BECOMES KING OF JUDAH
627	JEREMIAH BECOMES A PROPHET
622	BOOK OF THE LAW FOUND IN THE TEMPLE; HULDAH INSTRUCTS THE KING ON THE LAW
621	ZEPHANIAH'S MINISTRY ENDS
609	JOSIAH DIES IN BATTLE
605	FIRST CAPTIVES ARE TAKEN TO BABYLON
597	BABYLON'S SECOND ATTACK ON JUDAH
586	JUDAH, THE SOUTHERN KINGDOM, FALLS

ZEPHANIAH 1

1 The Lord gave this message to Zephaniah when Josiah son of Amon was king of Judah. Zephaniah was the son of Cushi, son of Gedaliah, son of Amariah, son of Hezekiah.

Coming Judgment against Judah

2 "I will sweep away everything
  from the face of the earth," says the Lord.
3 "I will sweep away people and animals alike.
  I will sweep away the birds of the sky and the fish in the sea.
 I will reduce the wicked to heaps of rubble,*
  and I will wipe humanity from the face of the earth," says the Lord.
4 "I will crush Judah and Jerusalem with my fist
  and destroy every last trace of their Baal worship.
 I will put an end to all the idolatrous priests,
  so that even the memory of them will disappear.
5 For they go up to their roofs
  and bow down to the sun, moon, and stars.
 They claim to follow the Lord,
  but then they worship Molech,* too.
6 And I will destroy those who used to worship me
  but now no longer do.
 They no longer ask for the Lord's guidance
  or seek my blessings."

7 Stand in silence in the presence of the Sovereign Lord,
  for the awesome day of the Lord's judgment is near.
 The Lord has prepared his people for a great slaughter
  and has chosen their executioners.*
8 "On that day of judgment,"
  says the Lord,
 "I will punish the leaders and princes of Judah
  and all those following pagan customs.
9 Yes, I will punish those who participate in pagan worship ceremonies,
  and those who fill their masters' houses with violence and deceit.

10 "On that day," says the Lord,
  "a cry of alarm will come from the Fish Gate
 and echo throughout the New Quarter of the city.*
 And a great crash will sound from the hills.
11 Wail in sorrow, all you who live in the market area,*
  for all the merchants and traders will be destroyed.

12 "I will search with lanterns in Jerusalem's darkest corners
  to punish those who sit complacent in their sins.
 They think the Lord will do nothing to them, either good or bad.
13 So their property will be plundered,
  their homes will be ransacked.
 They will build new homes
  but never live in them.
 They will plant vineyards
  but never drink wine from them.

14 "That terrible day of the Lord is near.
  Swiftly it comes—
 a day of bitter tears,
  a day when even strong men will cry out.
15 It will be a day when the Lord's anger is poured out—
  a day of terrible distress and anguish,
  a day of ruin and desolation,
  a day of darkness and gloom,
  a day of clouds and blackness,
16 a day of trumpet calls and battle cries.
 Down go the walled cities
  and the strongest battlements!

1:3 The meaning of the Hebrew is uncertain. **1:5** Hebrew *Malcam*, a variant spelling of Molech; or it could possibly mean *their king*. **1:7** Hebrew *has prepared a sacrifice and sanctified his guests*. **1:10** Or *the Second Quarter*, a newer section of Jerusalem. Hebrew reads *the Mishneh*. **1:11** Or *in the valley*, a lower section of Jerusalem. Hebrew reads *the Maktesh*.

1:1–2:3 Zephaniah's message from the Lord warns about worldwide judgment (1:1-6) and exhorts his readers to repent (1:7-13) before the devastation overtakes them (1:14-18) and to seek the Lord and live righteously and humbly before him in the hope that they may be spared his judgment (2:1-3).

1:8 The Hebrew phrase translated here as "all those following pagan customs" could also be rendered "all those dressed in foreign clothing." Clothes are an expression of identity. This message was delivered during the period after the northern kingdom of Israel had been razed by Assyria. Now, Assyria was in decline, and the rising world power was Babylon. While these superpowers sparred, the little kingdom of Judah was attempting to throw off the yoke of the Assyrian Empire and secure their future by allying themselves with Babylon (2 Kings 20:12-13). The foreign clothes, or possibly customs, mentioned here may be the Babylonian styles adopted by those in the king's court. More probable—and more offensive to God—is that these refer to those who worshiped deities of the surrounding nations and dressed themselves as their priests (Zephaniah 1:4-5). The people of Judah had transferred their loyalty to other gods, and their clothes reflected it.

1:12 Houses in ancient Israel had courtyards and flat rooftops for activities such as cooking and treatment of farm produce. The rooms themselves were usually small and may not always have had windows, so they would have been dark. Anything lost would need searching for with a lamp (Luke 15:8). Here, the Lord warns unrepentant Judah that none can hide from him when he brings judgment on them. It is an image designed to strike terror into their hearts. And the hope is that they will be terrified enough to repent.

> With his love,
> he will calm
> all your fears.
> He will rejoice
> over you with
> joyful songs.
>
> ZEPHANIAH 3:17

17 "Because you have sinned against the LORD,
   I will make you grope around like the blind.
Your blood will be poured into the dust,
   and your bodies will lie rotting on the ground."

18 Your silver and gold will not save you
      on that day of the LORD's anger.
   For the whole land will be devoured
      by the fire of his jealousy.
   He will make a terrifying end
      of all the people on earth.*

A Call to Repentance

2 Gather together—yes, gather together,
   you shameless nation.
2 Gather before judgment begins,
   before your time to repent is blown away like chaff.
Act now, before the fierce fury of the LORD falls
   and the terrible day of the LORD's anger begins.
3 Seek the LORD, all who are humble,
   and follow his commands.
Seek to do what is right
   and to live humbly.
Perhaps even yet the LORD will protect you—
   protect you from his anger on that day of destruction.

Judgment against Philistia

4 Gaza and Ashkelon will be abandoned,
   Ashdod and Ekron torn down.
5 And what sorrow awaits you Philistines*
   who live along the coast and in the land of Canaan,
for this judgment is against you, too!
The LORD will destroy you
   until not one of you is left.
6 The Philistine coast will become a wilderness pasture,
   a place of shepherd camps
   and enclosures for sheep and goats.
7 The remnant of the tribe of Judah will pasture there.
   They will rest at night in the abandoned houses in Ashkelon.
For the LORD their God will visit his people in kindness
   and restore their prosperity again.

Judgment against Moab and Ammon

8 "I have heard the taunts of the Moabites
      and the insults of the Ammonites,
   mocking my people
      and invading their borders.
9 Now, as surely as I live,"
      says the LORD of Heaven's Armies, the God of Israel,
"Moab and Ammon will be destroyed—
      destroyed as completely as Sodom and Gomorrah.
Their land will become a place of stinging nettles,
      salt pits, and eternal desolation.
The remnant of my people will plunder them
      and take their land."

10 They will receive the wages of their pride,
      for they have scoffed at the people of the LORD of Heaven's Armies.
11 The LORD will terrify them
      as he destroys all the gods in the land.
Then nations around the world will worship the LORD,
      each in their own land.

Judgment against Ethiopia and Assyria

12 "You Ethiopians* will also be slaughtered
      by my sword," says the LORD.

13 And the LORD will strike the lands of the north with his fist,
      destroying the land of Assyria.
He will make its great capital, Nineveh, a desolate wasteland,
      parched like a desert.
14 The proud city will become a pasture for flocks and herds,
      and all sorts of wild animals will settle there.
The desert owl and screech owl will roost on its ruined columns,
      their calls echoing through the gaping windows.
Rubble will block all the doorways,
      and the cedar paneling will be exposed to the weather.
15 This is the boisterous city,
      once so secure.

1:18 Or *the people living in the land.* 2:5 Hebrew *Kerethites.* 2:12 Hebrew *Cushites.*

2:8-10 God took offense at Judah's neighbors, somewhat like a mother would at someone threatening her child. Here are Moab and Ammon, who insulted and taunted Judah (Obadiah 1:12-13). They issued threats against God's people. God declared that he would act against them in ways that would neutralize their behavior. It is a comforting thought that God cares not only for our safety but also for our dignity and honor.
2:15 In ancient times, cities were referred to as feminine, and here the Hebrew pronouns referring to the city are feminine. Nineveh is personified as an arrogant woman while Jerusalem is spoken of as a woman who has heard good news and should be rejoicing (see 3:14). Such personifications can result in unfortunate stereotypes, but not all instances are negative. Woman Folly is balanced by Woman Wisdom (Proverbs 9); and the personification of God's city as an adulteress can be offset by one possible reading of Song of Songs, where the young woman is representative of faithful Israel.

Daughters of Jerusalem

IDENTITY — Restored and Rejoicing

They remember...

The journey has been difficult, painful, and almost hopeless for us in this great city—Jerusalem, the Holy City—the place God lovingly called "daughter." We refused to obey God, so he allowed oppressors to surround us and bring us hardships. We were blessed to be a blessing, but instead we allowed the opposite to happen.

Our leaders—kings, priests, judges, princes—did not obey the Lord, or take correction from his prophets. So we suffered shame before our neighbors. God called us to be a light to the nations, but we failed. We were warned about punishment, but we ignored the wisdom and pursued our own ways.

How could we forget what happened to our brothers and sisters in the northern kingdom only a century ago? Israel had forgotten the covenant and worshiped other gods. For their arrogance, God brought the Assyrians to oppress them and remove them from their land.

In his mercy, God raised up King Josiah who reformed our worship. He demolished the altars and shrines to Baal and Asherah and stopped idolatry in Jerusalem and Judah. The light began to shine again among us, in this city chosen by God to shine on a hill.

Now, once again, we sing aloud and shout in triumph because the Lord has delivered his daughter, Jerusalem, from the enemy and restored us to himself.

> Sometimes life is difficult, but God delights in restoring us to rejoicing.

THE DAUGHTERS OF JERUSALEM'S STORY IS TOLD IN ZEPHANIAH 3:14-17.

IDENTIFY

Do we see ourselves as beloved daughters of God? How could seeing ourselves this way change us?

What has God done that inspires us to sing and rejoice?

> "When I lived in Jerusalem, the city called 'daughter of Zion,' I knew it was special. Zephaniah's words, 'Sing, O daughter of Zion; shout aloud, O Israel!' still echo in this great city, thousands of years after he spoke. God always takes good care of his daughters."

HÉLÈNE M. DALLAIRE, PhD, serves as Earl S. Kalland Professor of Old Testament and Semitic Languages at Denver Seminary. She is deeply involved in the Messianic movement, serving in worship, prayer, teaching, and preaching.

"I am the greatest!" it boasted.
"No other city can compare with me!"
But now, look how it has become an utter ruin,
a haven for wild animals.
Everyone passing by will laugh in derision
and shake a defiant fist.

Jerusalem's Rebellion and Redemption

3 What sorrow awaits rebellious, polluted Jerusalem,
the city of violence and crime!
² No one can tell it anything;
it refuses all correction.
It does not trust in the LORD
or draw near to its God.
³ Its leaders are like roaring lions
hunting for their victims.
Its judges are like ravenous wolves at evening time,
who by dawn have left no trace of their prey.
⁴ Its prophets are arrogant liars seeking their own gain.
Its priests defile the Temple by disobeying God's instructions.
⁵ But the LORD is still there in the city,
and he does no wrong.
Day by day he hands down justice,
and he does not fail.
But the wicked know no shame.

⁶ "I have wiped out many nations,
devastating their fortress walls and towers.
Their streets are now deserted;
their cities lie in silent ruin.
There are no survivors—
none at all.
⁷ I thought, 'Surely they will have reverence for me now!
Surely they will listen to my warnings.
Then I won't need to strike again,
destroying their homes.'
But no, they get up early
to continue their evil deeds.
⁸ Therefore, be patient," says the LORD.
"Soon I will stand and accuse these evil nations.
For I have decided to gather the kingdoms of the earth
and pour out my fiercest anger and fury on them.
All the earth will be devoured
by the fire of my jealousy.

⁹ "Then I will purify the speech of all people,
so that everyone can worship the LORD together.
¹⁰ My scattered people who live beyond the rivers of Ethiopia*
will come to present their offerings.
¹¹ On that day you will no longer need to be ashamed,
for you will no longer be rebels against me.
I will remove all proud and arrogant people
from among you.
There will be no more haughtiness on my holy mountain.
¹² Those who are left will be the lowly and humble,
for it is they who trust in the name of the LORD.
¹³ The remnant of Israel will do no wrong;
they will never tell lies or deceive one another.
They will eat and sleep in safety,
and no one will make them afraid."

¹⁴ Sing, O daughter of Zion;
shout aloud, O Israel!
Be glad and rejoice with all your heart,
O daughter of Jerusalem!
¹⁵ For the LORD will remove his hand of judgment
and will disperse the armies of your enemy.
And the LORD himself, the King of Israel,
will live among you!
At last your troubles will be over,
and you will never again fear disaster.
¹⁶ On that day the announcement to Jerusalem will be,
"Cheer up, Zion! Don't be afraid!
¹⁷ For the LORD your God is living among you.
He is a mighty savior.
He will take delight in you with gladness.
With his love, he will calm all your fears.*
He will rejoice over you with joyful songs."
¹⁸ "I will gather you who mourn for the appointed festivals;
you will be disgraced no more.*

3:10 Hebrew *Cush.* 3:17 Or *He will be silent in his love.* Greek and Syriac versions read *He will renew you with his love.*
3:18 The meaning of the Hebrew for this verse is uncertain.

3:9 God intends for the blessings promised to the faithful remnant of 3:9-13 to reach people from every nation of the world. Not just Israel, but "all people" would be transformed, call on the Lord (see Isaiah 55:5), and serve him (see Isaiah 59:19-21; Zechariah 14:16). The spread of the Good News to all nations has furthered the fulfillment of this vision (Matthew 28:19-20; Romans 10:9-13).

3:17 God rejoices over Jerusalem with singing. Those of us who have cared for babies and little children know that singing is part of that care, whether or not we can sing. Crooning lullabies to a sleepy baby or humming to calm an uneasy one is not the picture here but more like an enthusiastic birthday song. God's song over Jerusalem is a rousing one. What a touching image of God's love for us!

¹⁹ And I will deal severely with all who have
    oppressed you.
  I will save the weak and helpless ones;
  I will bring together
    those who were chased away.
  I will give glory and fame to my former exiles,
    wherever they have been mocked and
    shamed.

²⁰ On that day I will gather you together
    and bring you home again.
  I will give you a good name, a name of
    distinction,
    among all the nations of the earth,
  as I restore your fortunes before their
    very eyes.
      I, the Lord, have spoken!"

Haggai

WHAT DO WE LEARN ABOUT GOD'S MISSION AND OURS?
When we take initiative to act on God's word, we spark others to follow.

WHO WROTE IT? Haggai.

WHEN DID IT HAPPEN? In 520 BC, after King Cyrus of Persia allowed the Jewish exiles to return home.

HOW IS IT ORGANIZED?

- 1:1-15: Message 1—Get busy and rebuild the Lord's Temple
- 2:1-9: Message 2—God's glory will fill the Temple
- 2:10-19: Message 3—God's wayward people will be blessed
- 2:20-23: Message 4—God is sovereign over the nations

FEATURE HIGHLIGHTS

+ God's House First (1141)

Words to Remember are highlighted throughout this book

HOW LONG DOES IT TAKE TO READ?

:10 | :30 | 1:00 | 1:30 | 2:00 | 2:30 | 3:00 | 3:30

Timeline (BC)

BC	Event
605	DANIEL TAKEN TO BABYLON
597	EZEKIEL TAKEN TO BABYLON
586	JERUSALEM FALLS
539	BABYLON OVERTHROWN BY CYRUS
538	CYRUS'S DECREE; EXILES RETURN TO JERUSALEM
536	TEMPLE RECONSTRUCTION BEGINS
530	TEMPLE WORK HALTED
520	HAGGAI AND ZECHARIAH BECOMES PROPHETS; TEMPLE WORK RESUMED
515	TEMPLE COMPLETED
479	ESTHER BECOMES QUEEN OF PERSIA
458	EZRA COMES TO JERUSALEM
445	NEHEMIAH COMES TO JERUSALEM

HAGGAI 1

A Call to Rebuild the Temple

1 On August 29* of the second year of King Darius's reign, the LORD gave a message through the prophet Haggai to Zerubbabel son of Shealtiel, governor of Judah, and to Jeshua* son of Jehozadak, the high priest.

²"This is what the LORD of Heaven's Armies says: The people are saying, 'The time has not yet come to rebuild the house of the LORD.'"

³Then the LORD sent this message through the prophet Haggai: ⁴"Why are you living in luxurious houses while my house lies in ruins? ⁵This is what the LORD of Heaven's Armies says: Look at what's happening to you! ⁶You have planted much but harvest little. You eat but are not satisfied. You drink but are still thirsty. You put on clothes but cannot keep warm. Your wages disappear as though you were putting them in pockets filled with holes!

⁷"This is what the LORD of Heaven's Armies says: Look at what's happening to you! ⁸Now go up into the hills, bring down timber, and rebuild my house. Then I will take pleasure in it and be honored, says the LORD. ⁹You hoped for rich harvests, but they were poor. And when you brought your harvest home, I blew it away. Why? Because my house lies in ruins, says the LORD of Heaven's Armies, while all of you are busy building your own fine houses. ¹⁰It's because of you that the heavens withhold the dew and the earth produces no crops. ¹¹I have called for a drought on your fields and hills—a drought to wither the grain and grapes and olive trees and all your other crops, a drought to starve you and your livestock and to ruin everything you have worked so hard to get."

Obedience to God's Call

¹²Then Zerubbabel son of Shealtiel, and Jeshua son of Jehozadak, the high priest, and the whole remnant of God's people began to obey the message from the LORD their God. When they heard the words of the prophet Haggai, whom the LORD their God had sent, the people feared the LORD. ¹³Then Haggai, the LORD's messenger, gave the people this message from the LORD: "I am with you, says the LORD!"

¹⁴So the LORD sparked the enthusiasm of Zerubbabel son of Shealtiel, governor of Judah, and the enthusiasm of Jeshua son of Jehozadak, the high priest, and the enthusiasm of the whole remnant of God's people. They began to work on the house of their God, the LORD of Heaven's Armies, ¹⁵on September 21* of the second year of King Darius's reign.

The New Temple's Diminished Splendor

2 Then on October 17 of that same year,* the LORD sent another message through the prophet Haggai. ²"Say this to Zerubbabel son of Shealtiel, governor of Judah, and to Jeshua* son of Jehozadak, the high priest, and to the remnant of God's people there in the land: ³'Does anyone remember this house—this Temple—in its former splendor? How, in comparison, does it look to you now? It must seem like nothing at all! ⁴But now the LORD says: Be strong, Zerubbabel. Be strong, Jeshua son of Jehozadak, the high priest. Be strong, all you people still left in the land. And now get to work, for I am with you, says the LORD of Heaven's Armies. ⁵My Spirit remains among you, just as I promised when you came out of Egypt. So do not be afraid.'

⁶"For this is what the LORD of Heaven's Armies says: In just a little while I will again shake the heavens and the earth, the oceans and the dry land. ⁷I will shake all the nations, and the treasures of all the nations will be brought to this Temple. I will fill this place with glory, says the LORD of Heaven's Armies. ⁸The silver is mine, and the gold is mine, says the LORD of Heaven's Armies. ⁹The future glory of this Temple will be greater than its past glory, says the LORD of Heaven's Armies. And in this place I will bring peace. I, the LORD of Heaven's Armies, have spoken!"

1:1a Hebrew *On the first day of the sixth month,* of the ancient Hebrew lunar calendar. A number of dates in Haggai can be cross-checked with dates in surviving Persian records and related accurately to our modern calendar. This event occurred on August 29, 520 B.C. **1:1b** Hebrew *Joshua,* a variant spelling of Jeshua; also in 1:12, 14. **1:15** Hebrew *on the twenty-fourth day of the sixth month,* of the ancient Hebrew lunar calendar. This event occurred on September 21, 520 B.C.; also see note on 1:1a. **2:1** Hebrew *on the twenty-first day of the seventh month,* of the ancient Hebrew lunar calendar. This event (in the second year of Darius's reign) occurred on October 17, 520 B.C.; also see note on 1:1a. **2:2** Hebrew *Joshua,* a variant spelling of Jeshua; also in 2:4.

1:4 The word translated as "luxurious" in this verse suggests the people were adding additional paneling or covering to their homes. Even today, interior paneling would be a luxury, but was especially expensive then, since ancient Israel would have had to import wood. Even more extravagant would have been ivory inlays in furniture such as bedsteads (Amos 6:4), couches, and in-wall panels. The Lord did not begrudge the people their home decoration, but he did condemn their priorities. In an age when a nation's patron deity was housed in the grandest architectural structure in their cities, God's Temple standing in ruins was in stark contrast to the lavish residences of the rich. God expects that we honor him in ways appropriate to our financial situation and to the times (Isaiah 29:13; Malachi 1:6).

2:3-4 While the Temple was being rebuilt, the older people who had seen Solomon's Temple couldn't help being disappointed at how poorly the new Temple compared with the grandeur of its predecessor. Even as its foundations were being re-laid, they wept to see how reduced their present circumstances were (Ezra 3:12). God's promise to glorify the rebuilt Temple beyond that of Solomon's must have been a mind-boggling promise. But that is the promise we have, too—that our physical bodies will be rendered glorious beyond our imagination one day (1 Corinthians 15:35-55).

Koinonia IMAGE — MY STORY WITH COMMUNITY, WORKPLACE & CHURCH

God's House First

SCRIPTURE CONNECTION: HAGGAI 1:2-11

How do you know what to do first? The Jewish people moved back from Babylon, began constructing God's Temple, then abandoned that work. They threw themselves into building their own houses and for their homes, they spared no expense. They added extravagant, ornate wood panels and décor. Whether from apathy, burnout, discouragement, or intentional disregard, the Jews began replacing God's priorities with their own.

God noticed. He noticed that his Temple sat half-built while his people busied themselves with their dwellings. The neglected and unfinished Temple represented their spiritual state, showing they put God in second place. There's a cost for that: In 1:9-11, God revealed that their neglect kept them from flourishing in the land, and he reminded them that what mattered now was to finish his house.

So, what is our top priority now? It is good to buy and build homes, keep them in repair, and provide for our families. But doing what God asks—first—puts all our priorities in order. Obeying God puts us on a path where we, our families, and our communities flourish.

> Doing what God asks—first—puts all our priorities in order.

IMAGINE

Take a moment and ask God to remind us of work he has asked us to do—perhaps work that we have set aside.

Ask, "God, what is your priority for me, now?"

> "I am reminded of a deeply personal writing project that I have put off for years. I need to consider God's priorities."

NANCY CHAMBERLIN SPROWLS is a devotional writer, mother, and grandmother. She encourages women to have a passion for God's Word and to leave a spiritual legacy for their families.

Blessings Promised for Obedience

[10] On December 18* of the second year of King Darius's reign, the LORD sent this message to the prophet Haggai: [11] "This is what the LORD of Heaven's Armies says. Ask the priests this question about the law: [12] 'If one of you is carrying some meat from a holy sacrifice in his robes and his robe happens to brush against some bread or stew, wine or olive oil, or any other kind of food, will it also become holy?'"

The priests replied, "No."

[13] Then Haggai asked, "If someone becomes ceremonially unclean by touching a dead person and then touches any of these foods, will the food be defiled?"

And the priests answered, "Yes."

[14] Then Haggai responded, "That is how it is with this people and this nation, says the LORD. Everything they do and everything they offer is defiled by their sin. [15] Look at what was happening to you before you began to lay the foundation of the LORD's Temple. [16] When you hoped for a twenty-bushel crop, you harvested only ten. When you expected to draw fifty gallons from the winepress, you found only twenty. [17] I sent blight and mildew and hail to destroy everything you worked so hard to produce. Even so, you refused to return to me, says the LORD.

[18] "Think about this eighteenth day of December, the day* when the foundation of the LORD's Temple was laid. Think carefully. [19] I am giving you a promise now while the seed is still in the barn.* You have not yet harvested your grain, and your grapevines, fig trees, pomegranates, and olive trees have not yet produced their crops. But from this day onward I will bless you."

Promises for Zerubbabel

[20] On that same day, December 18,* the LORD sent this second message to Haggai: [21] "Tell Zerubbabel, the governor of Judah, that I am about to shake the heavens and the earth. [22] I will overthrow royal thrones and destroy the power of foreign kingdoms. I will overturn their chariots and riders. The horses will fall, and their riders will kill each other.

[23] "But when this happens, says the LORD of Heaven's Armies, I will honor you, Zerubbabel son of Shealtiel, my servant. I will make you like a signet ring on my finger, says the LORD, for I have chosen you. I, the LORD of Heaven's Armies, have spoken!"

2:10 Hebrew *On the twenty-fourth day of the ninth month*, of the ancient Hebrew lunar calendar (similarly in 2:18). This event occurred on December 18, 520 B.C.; also see note on 1:1a. **2:18** Or *On this eighteenth day of December, think about the day.* **2:19** Hebrew *Is the seed yet in the barn?* **2:20** Hebrew *On the twenty-fourth day of the [ninth] month;* see note on 2:10.

2:14 Simply returning from exile to the land that God had promised Israel did not make the people of Judah holy. They were still unclean, "defiled by their sin," since they were not obeying the instructions of God's covenant with them. Their work and even their worship were contaminated by impurity; the ruins of the Lord's Temple symbolized the people's disobedience. The rebuilding of the Temple was a tangible sign of changed hearts and renewed obedience to God's covenant.

2:20-23 Haggai's final message is perhaps the most important; it reestablishes the prominence of David's descendant in Israel's religious and political life. The dynasty of David was key to restoring the Israelite people after the Babylonian exile (see Jeremiah 23:5; Ezekiel 37:24). God had cursed David's descendant, King Jehoiachin, at the time of the Exile (Jeremiah 22:24-30), but Haggai's last message overturns that curse and reinstates the covenant with David (see 2 Samuel 7:4-17) as the means by which God would carry out his promises to bless and restore Israel.

2:23 That God wears Zerubbabel as his signet ring is intriguing imagery. A signet ring was engraved, the pattern on it being unique to the owner. It was stamped onto seals of legal documents and served as the person's signature. We might treasure pieces of jewelry because they tell a story, because they belonged once to someone dear, because they were bought for a price, or because someone we love gifted it to us. None of them come close to the value God places on his people.

Zechariah

WHAT DO WE LEARN ABOUT GOD'S MISSION AND OURS? Like Zechariah, Jeshua, and Zerubbabel, we can point to the hope God has given us in the Messiah, Jesus.

WHO WROTE IT? Zechariah, a priest who was also a prophet.

WHEN DID IT HAPPEN? The writing in this book covers about forty years, beginning around 520 BC. This is the time period immediately following the Exile, after King Cyrus of Persia allowed the Jewish exiles to return home.

HOW IS IT ORGANIZED?

1:1–6: The Lord calls his people to return

1:7–6:15: God gives Zechariah visions

    7–8: God calls for repentance and promises blessing

    9–11: The Messiah will come and be rejected

    12–14: The Messiah will come and reign

FEATURE HIGHLIGHTS

+ *Wickedness: A Woman in a Basket* (1151)
+ LORD *of Heaven's Armies: Deliverance Ahead* (1153)

Words to Remember are highlighted throughout this book

HOW LONG DOES IT TAKE TO READ?

:30						
:30	1:00	1:30	2:00	2:30	3:00	3:30

Timeline

BC	
538	CYRUS'S DECREE; EXILES RETURN TO JERUSALEM
536	TEMPLE RECONSTRUCTION BEGINS
530	TEMPLE WORK HALTED
520	HAGGAI AND ZECHARIAH BECOME PROPHETS; TEMPLE WORK RESUMED
515	TEMPLE COMPLETED
479	ESTHER BECOMES QUEEN OF PERSIA
458	EZRA COMES TO JERUSALEM
445	NEHEMIAH COMES TO JERUSALEM

A Call to Return to the LORD

1 In November* of the second year of King Darius's reign, the LORD gave this message to the prophet Zechariah son of Berekiah and grandson of Iddo:

²"I, the LORD, was very angry with your ancestors. ³Therefore, say to the people, 'This is what the LORD of Heaven's Armies says: Return to me, and I will return to you, says the LORD of Heaven's Armies.' ⁴Don't be like your ancestors who would not listen or pay attention when the earlier prophets said to them, 'This is what the LORD of Heaven's Armies says: Turn from your evil ways, and stop all your evil practices.'

⁵"Where are your ancestors now? They and the prophets are long dead. ⁶But everything I said through my servants the prophets happened to your ancestors, just as I said. As a result, they repented and said, 'We have received what we deserved from the LORD of Heaven's Armies. He has done what he said he would do.'"

A Man among the Myrtle Trees

⁷Three months later, on February 15,* the LORD sent another message to the prophet Zechariah son of Berekiah and grandson of Iddo.

⁸In a vision during the night, I saw a man sitting on a red horse that was standing among some myrtle trees in a small valley. Behind him were riders on red, brown, and white horses. ⁹I asked the angel who was talking with me, "My lord, what do these horses mean?"

"I will show you," the angel replied.

¹⁰The rider standing among the myrtle trees then explained, "They are the ones the LORD has sent out to patrol the earth."

¹¹Then the other riders reported to the angel of the LORD, who was standing among the myrtle trees, "We have been patrolling the earth, and the whole earth is at peace."

¹²Upon hearing this, the angel of the LORD prayed this prayer: "O LORD of Heaven's Armies, for seventy years now you have been angry with Jerusalem and the towns of Judah. How long until you again show mercy to them?" ¹³And the LORD spoke kind and comforting words to the angel who talked with me.

¹⁴Then the angel said to me, "Shout this message for all to hear: 'This is what the LORD of Heaven's Armies says: My love for Jerusalem and Mount Zion is passionate and strong. ¹⁵But I am very angry with the other nations that are now enjoying peace and security. I was only a little angry with my people, but the nations inflicted harm on them far beyond my intentions.

¹⁶"'Therefore, this is what the LORD says: I have returned to show mercy to Jerusalem. My Temple will be rebuilt, says the LORD of Heaven's Armies, and measurements will be taken for the reconstruction of Jerusalem.*'

¹⁷"Say this also: 'This is what the LORD of Heaven's Armies says: The towns of Israel will again overflow with prosperity, and the LORD will again comfort Zion and choose Jerusalem as his own.'"

1:1 Hebrew *In the eighth month.* A number of dates in Zechariah can be cross-checked with dates in surviving Persian records and related accurately to our modern calendar. This month of the ancient Hebrew lunar calendar occurred within the months of October and November 520 B.C. **1:7** Hebrew *On the twenty-fourth day of the eleventh month, the month of Shebat, in the second year of Darius.* This event occurred on February 15, 519 B.C.; also see note on 1:1. **1:16** Hebrew *and the measuring line will be stretched out over Jerusalem.*

1:1 The prophet keeps a calendar of milestones over the years of his ministry to the community just returned from the Exile (1:1; 1:7; 7:1). With his last dated message in 518 BC (see text note on 7:1), we understand that his addresses to the people of Jerusalem were delivered over a span of more than two years. He marked this part of his life with the messages that God gave to him. Generally, women are more likely to be the keepers of milestones in a family, creating scrapbooks and albums of memories. What is important is to honor God at each milestone. These come from the hand of God and are meant for good, just as the messages came to Zechariah from the mouth of God.

1:8 In the ancient world, it was common for prophets to receive dreams and visions at night, as they slept. It was thought that sleep was when a deity chose to speak to people. The Neo-Sumerian Empire kept archives of dream oracles from the ancient world, and their scribes were professionally dedicated to the interpretation of prophetic dreams (approximately 2100–2000 BC). As in Zechariah, these night visions usually had political significance. On a much lesser scale, women, perhaps more than men, tend to wake up at odd hours of the night for reasons that may be related to our biology. If we find ourselves awake, how consoling it is to know that God keeps us company with words of comfort (1:13, 16-17).

1:12-13 As Jerusalem reeled under a continued economic depression, even the angel in Zechariah's vision cried out on their behalf: "How long . . . ?" Seventy years of exile were being followed by decades of poor crop harvests and repeated droughts. God replied, but we are not told exactly what he said. But what encourages us is that he spoke "kind and comforting words." When we comfort our loved ones, the words don't matter. They can even be nonsense words, just sounds and syllables. What matters is that they are kind and comforting—and that is what God is to us in the times when we cry out, "How long . . . ?"

1:15 God used the empires of the time to punish Judah for their lack of obedience. Much like an unruly child being sent off to time out, Israel had been sent into exile. But God was longing to see Jerusalem restored (1:16-17). "I was only a little angry with my people," he says. These are words that should have comforted the people of Judah. Certainly, they comfort us. Whether we are a little or a lot angry at our young ones who behave badly, the end goal of discipline should always be their restoration.

Four Horns and Four Blacksmiths

¹⁸*Then I looked up and saw four animal horns. ¹⁹"What are these?" I asked the angel who was talking with me.

He replied, "These horns represent the nations that scattered Judah, Israel, and Jerusalem." ²⁰Then the LORD showed me four blacksmiths. ²¹"What are these men coming to do?" I asked.

The angel replied, "These four horns—these nations—scattered and humbled Judah. Now these blacksmiths have come to terrify those nations and throw them down and destroy them."

Future Prosperity of Jerusalem

2 ¹*When I looked again, I saw a man with a measuring line in his hand. ²"Where are you going?" I asked.

He replied, "I am going to measure Jerusalem, to see how wide and how long it is."

³Then the angel who was with me went to meet a second angel who was coming toward him. ⁴The other angel said, "Hurry, and say to that young man, 'Jerusalem will someday be so full of people and livestock that there won't be room enough for everyone! Many will live outside the city walls. ⁵Then I, myself, will be a protective wall of fire around Jerusalem, says the LORD. And I will be the glory inside the city!'"

The Exiles Are Called Home

⁶The LORD says, "Come away! Flee from Babylon in the land of the north, for I have scattered you to the four winds. ⁷Come away, people of Zion, you who are exiled in Babylon!"

⁸After a period of glory, the LORD of Heaven's Armies sent me* against the nations who plundered you. For he said, "Anyone who harms you harms my most precious possession.* ⁹I will raise my fist to crush them, and their own slaves will plunder them." Then you will know that the LORD of Heaven's Armies has sent me.

¹⁰The LORD says, "Shout and rejoice, O beautiful Jerusalem,* for I am coming to live among you. ¹¹Many nations will join themselves to the LORD on that day, and they, too, will be my people. I will live among you, and you will know that the LORD of Heaven's Armies sent me to you. ¹²The land of Judah will be the LORD's special possession in the holy land, and he will once again choose Jerusalem to be his own city. ¹³Be silent before the LORD, all humanity, for he is springing into action from his holy dwelling."

Cleansing for the High Priest

3 Then the angel showed me Jeshua* the high priest standing before the angel of the LORD. The Accuser, Satan,* was there at the angel's right hand, making accusations against Jeshua. ²And the LORD said to Satan, "I, the LORD, reject your accusations, Satan. Yes, the LORD, who has chosen Jerusalem, rebukes you. This man is like a burning stick that has been snatched from the fire."

³Jeshua's clothing was filthy as he stood there before the angel. ⁴So the angel said to the others standing there, "Take off his filthy clothes." And

---

1:18 Verses 1:18-21 are numbered 2:1-4 in Hebrew text. **2:1** Verses 2:1-13 are numbered 2:5-17 in Hebrew text. **2:8a** The meaning of the Hebrew is uncertain. **2:8b** Hebrew *Anyone who touches you touches the pupil of his eye.* **2:10** Hebrew *O daughter of Zion.* **3:1a** Hebrew *Joshua,* a variant spelling of Jeshua; also in 3:3, 4, 6, 8, 9. **3:1b** Hebrew *The satan;* similarly in 3:2.

2:2 Temple building in the ancient world was far more complex than any architectural endeavor today. This was largely because the project was considered to be a joint one, involving both the divine and human parties. If a temple is being rebuilt on a pre-existing one, it was necessary to carefully identify the limits of the original before building on it. Sacred space was taken seriously. In a modification of this practice, God's representative comes to measure out the whole city, which is under reconstruction (1:16). The entire city is to become sacred space, where God dwells. We too have spaces that are more significant than others. This might be a nook in a room or garden, our kitchen or bedroom, or simply a place on the sofa. How much more significant this space becomes if we think of it as sacred, as being shared with God.

2:4-5 In ancient times, a city without walls would be defenseless. A capital city, especially, would invariably be secured with fortress-like walls, sometimes broad enough to accommodate a house (see, for example, Joshua 2:15). Jerusalem was one such city before its walls were razed by the Babylonians (2 Kings 25:10). Here, the news that Jerusalem would not need walls is good news. The current sparse and struggling population (Nehemiah 11:1) would multiply so rapidly that the city's usual limits would be exceeded. As for safety, God himself would be their defense, a "wall of fire."

2:9 It would take a major upheaval of existing social structures for enslaved people to have the ability to engage in plundering. We would call it a revolution, such as the French or Russian sociopolitical events when the peasant classes overthrew the nobility. In the ancient world, such a situation was unimaginable and represented chaos at its worst. This is the kind of punishment God says he will bring on those who have cruelly mistreated his people (1:15).

3:4 The matter of cleansing the high priest from sin is described with the imagery of clothing, a metaphor that readily resonates with us. His soiled clothes, stained with sin, are removed. Then, he is arrayed in fresh and fine garments. Now, no one can point an accusing finger at him, questioning his suitability for his post. One day, when we are raised from the dead—or if while still living we are caught up to meet Jesus (1 Thessalonians 4:13-18)—our very bodies will be that clothing. Our bodies won't be replaced, but they will be transformed gloriously "in the blink of an eye" (1 Corinthians 15:52).

turning to Jeshua he said, "See, I have taken away your sins, and now I am giving you these fine new clothes."

⁵Then I said, "They should also place a clean turban on his head." So they put a clean priestly turban on his head and dressed him in new clothes while the angel of the LORD stood by.

⁶Then the angel of the LORD spoke very solemnly to Jeshua and said, ⁷"This is what the LORD of Heaven's Armies says: If you follow my ways and carefully serve me, then you will be given authority over my Temple and its courtyards. I will let you walk among these others standing here.

⁸"Listen to me, O Jeshua the high priest, and all you other priests. You are symbols of things to come. Soon I am going to bring my servant, the Branch. ⁹Now look at the jewel I have set before Jeshua, a single stone with seven facets.* I will engrave an inscription on it, says the LORD of Heaven's Armies, and I will remove the sins of this land in a single day.

¹⁰"And on that day, says the LORD of Heaven's Armies, each of you will invite your neighbor to sit with you peacefully under your own grapevine and fig tree."

A Lampstand and Two Olive Trees

4 Then the angel who had been talking with me returned and woke me, as though I had been asleep. ²"What do you see now?" he asked.

I answered, "I see a solid gold lampstand with a bowl of oil on top of it. Around the bowl are seven lamps, each having seven spouts with wicks. ³And I see two olive trees, one on each side of the bowl." ⁴Then I asked the angel, "What are these, my lord? What do they mean?"

⁵"Don't you know?" the angel asked.

"No, my lord," I replied.

⁶Then he said to me, "This is what the LORD says to Zerubbabel: It is not by force nor by strength, but by my Spirit, says the LORD of Heaven's Armies. ⁷Nothing, not even a mighty mountain, will stand in Zerubbabel's way; it will become a level plain before him! And when Zerubbabel sets the final stone of the Temple in place, the people will shout: 'May God bless it! May God bless it!'*"

⁸Then another message came to me from the LORD: ⁹"Zerubbabel is the one who laid the foundation of this Temple, and he will complete it. Then you will know that the LORD of Heaven's Armies has sent me. ¹⁰Do not despise these small beginnings, for the LORD rejoices to see the work begin, to see the plumb line in Zerubbabel's hand."

(The seven lamps* represent the eyes of the LORD that search all around the world.)

¹¹Then I asked the angel, "What are these two olive trees on each side of the lampstand, ¹²and what are the two olive branches that pour out golden oil through two gold tubes?"

¹³"Don't you know?" he asked.

"No, my lord," I replied.

¹⁴Then he said to me, "They represent the two anointed ones* who stand in the court of the Lord of all the earth."

3:9 Hebrew *seven eyes*. **4:7** Hebrew *'Grace, grace to it.'* **4:10** Or *The seven facets* (see 3:9); Hebrew reads *These seven*. **4:14** Or *two heavenly beings*; Hebrew reads *two sons of fresh oil*.

3:9 The stone described here is possibly the first (and therefore, ceremonial) foundation stone, since the context is that of rebuilding the Temple and installing its rituals and personnel, starting with the high priest (3:7; 4:7). In Mesopotamia, gemstones might be part of the foundation deposit of a temple. The stone God presents to Jeshua the high priest appears to have seven precious stones inlaid. These were cut in the shape of eyes, a popular gem-cutting practice in the ancient world. God's promise of restoration spares no cost and is beautiful.

3:10 In the largely agrarian communities of Mesopotamia, to sit under one's own fruit-bearing trees was a metaphor for contentment (1 Kings 4:25). Young fruit trees usually took at least three years to bear fruit, and the first harvest was the reward for patient and sustained care of the trees. To invite a neighbor to come and sit under your tree was to invite them to celebrate your joy. It is a metaphor that resonates with anyone who enjoys or has experience gardening, whether it be for fruit or flowers. At many levels, we labor, and sometimes we get to see the reward with the yield (1 Corinthians 3:8).

4:7, 10 The capstone being brought out with much ceremony and public rejoicing appears to be the foundation stone of the Temple to be built. In Mesopotamia, if a temple was being rebuilt, a foundation stone from the previous temple would be used as the ceremonial first stone of the new temple's foundation. Before the debris of the old temple was removed and the site was leveled, a stone would be identified for this purpose, removed, and then brought back at the time of laying the new foundation. This practice achieved the desired purpose of keeping the new in continuity with the old. Perhaps it is from this nearly universal human desire to keep continuity that brides often wear jewelry passed down in the family or why the same names are given in a family from generation to generation.

4:10 Solomon's Temple had been the pinnacle of achievement in the golden age of Israel's history. Organized task forces gave dedicated time; a treasury flush with funds supported the project; its timber and gold were imported (1 Kings 5–7, 10). The new Temple was being built with limited funds, by a population struggling to make ends meet (Haggai 1:6). It was a much-diminished project compared to its predecessor. But God receives with respect the small contributions just as much as he receives greater offerings. Later, Jesus makes an example of the two small coins given by the widow, which received more praise than the bags of money that the rich were throwing into the collection box (Mark 12:41-44).

A Flying Scroll

5 I looked up again and saw a scroll flying through the air.

²"What do you see?" the angel asked.

"I see a flying scroll," I replied. "It appears to be about 30 feet long and 15 feet wide.*"

³Then he said to me, "This scroll contains the curse that is going out over the entire land. One side of the scroll says that those who steal will be banished from the land; the other side says that those who swear falsely will be banished from the land. ⁴And this is what the Lord of Heaven's Armies says: I am sending this curse into the house of every thief and into the house of everyone who swears falsely using my name. And my curse will remain in that house and completely destroy it—even its timbers and stones."

A Woman in a Basket

⁵Then the angel who was talking with me came forward and said, "Look up and see what's coming."

⁶"What is it?" I asked.

He replied, "It is a basket for measuring grain,* and it's filled with the sins* of everyone throughout the land."

⁷Then the heavy lead cover was lifted off the basket, and there was a woman sitting inside it. ⁸The angel said, "The woman's name is Wickedness," and he pushed her back into the basket and closed the heavy lid again.

⁹Then I looked up and saw two women flying toward us, gliding on the wind. They had wings like a stork, and they picked up the basket and flew into the sky.

¹⁰"Where are they taking the basket?" I asked the angel.

¹¹He replied, "To the land of Babylonia,* where they will build a temple for the basket. And when the temple is ready, they will set the basket there on its pedestal."

> "God doesn't need us to muster up strength. He needs us to step out in faith when he calls, and then to stand back and let him do his work."
>
> **DARLENE SCHACHT**
> writer and teacher

Four Chariots

6 Then I looked up again and saw four chariots coming from between two bronze mountains. ²The first chariot was pulled by red horses, the second by black horses, ³the third by white horses, and the fourth by powerful dappled-gray horses. ⁴"And what are these, my lord?" I asked the angel who was talking with me.

⁵The angel replied, "These are the four spirits* of heaven who stand before the Lord of all the earth. They are going out to do his work. ⁶The chariot with

---

5:2 Hebrew *20 cubits* [9.2 meters] *long and 10 cubits* [4.6 meters] *wide.* 5:6a Hebrew *an ephah* [20 quarts or 22 liters]; also in 5:7, 8, 9, 10, 11. 5:6b As in Greek version; Hebrew reads *the appearance.* 5:11 Hebrew *the land of Shinar.* 6:5 Or *the four winds.*

5:1 This is the sixth of eight visions that Zechariah had in the same night. The precursor to books or letters, scrolls were sheets of papyrus (plant-based writing surface) or parchment (animal-based writing surface) glued together to form a continuous roll. This scroll was flying, unfurled like a banner for all to see.

5:8 Evil generally, whether moral or ceremonial, is termed *wickedness.* It is opposed to righteousness (see Proverbs 13:6; Ezekiel 33:12). The Hebrew word *rishah,* translated "wickedness," is similar in Hebrew to the name Asherah, a fertility goddess in the ancient Near East (see Deuteronomy 7:5; 16:21; Jeremiah 44:17-25).

5:9 The depiction of divine or angelic winged creatures as women is unusual in the Old Testament. If the two women are the Lord's servants, they are unique angels. If they are the attendants of Wickedness (a foreign goddess), their submission to God's command demonstrates his power over false gods.

5:11 Idolatry was potently and aggressively evil; it could not be confined but needed to be shipped back to its source (Babylonia) by God's decree. This symbolism indicates that God is able to purge his people of all the various forms of wickedness that separated them from him. "The land of Babylonia" was the land of captivity for the Judeans (Micah 4:10). The prophets condemned it as wicked and idolatrous (Isaiah 46–47; Jeremiah 50–51). In the New Testament, Babylon represents the evil Roman Empire (Revelation 17:5; 18:2; compare 1 Peter 5:13); the people considered living under the rule of the Romans to be oppressive.

black horses is going north, the chariot with white horses is going west,* and the chariot with dappled-gray horses is going south."

⁷The powerful horses were eager to set out to patrol the earth. And the LORD said, "Go and patrol the earth!" So they left at once on their patrol.

⁸Then the LORD summoned me and said, "Look, those who went north have vented the anger of my Spirit* there in the land of the north."

The Crowning of Jeshua

⁹Then I received another message from the LORD: ¹⁰"Heldai, Tobijah, and Jedaiah will bring gifts of silver and gold from the Jews exiled in Babylon. As soon as they arrive, meet them at the home of Josiah son of Zephaniah. ¹¹Accept their gifts, and make a crown from the silver and gold. Then put the crown on the head of Jeshua* son of Jehozadak, the high priest. ¹²Tell him, 'This is what the LORD of Heaven's Armies says: Here is the man called the Branch. He will branch out from where he is and build the Temple of the LORD. ¹³Yes, he will build the Temple of the LORD. Then he will receive royal honor and will rule as king from his throne. He will also serve as priest from his throne,* and there will be perfect harmony between his two roles.'

¹⁴"The crown will be a memorial in the Temple of the LORD to honor those who gave it—Heldai,* Tobijah, Jedaiah, and Josiah* son of Zephaniah."

¹⁵People will come from distant lands to rebuild the Temple of the LORD. And when this happens, you will know that my messages have been from the LORD of Heaven's Armies. All this will happen if you carefully obey what the LORD your God says.

A Call to Justice and Mercy

7 On December 7* of the fourth year of King Darius's reign, another message came to Zechariah from the LORD. ²The people of Bethel had sent Sharezer and Regemmelech,* along with their attendants, to seek the LORD's favor. ³They were to ask this question of the prophets and the priests at the Temple of the LORD of Heaven's Armies: "Should we continue to mourn and fast each summer on the anniversary of the Temple's destruction,* as we have done for so many years?"

⁴The LORD of Heaven's Armies sent me this message in reply: ⁵"Say to all your people and your priests, 'During these seventy years of exile, when you fasted and mourned in the summer and in early autumn,* was it really for me that you were fasting? ⁶And even now in your holy festivals, aren't you eating and drinking just to please yourselves? ⁷Isn't this the same message the LORD proclaimed through the prophets in years past when Jerusalem and the towns of Judah were bustling with people, and the Negev and the foothills of Judah* were well populated?'"

⁸Then this message came to Zechariah from the LORD: ⁹"This is what the LORD of Heaven's Armies

---

6:6 Hebrew *is going after them*. **6:8** Hebrew *have given my Spirit rest*. **6:11** Hebrew *Joshua*, a variant spelling of Jeshua. **6:13** Or *There will be a priest by his throne*. **6:14a** As in Syriac version (compare 6:10); Hebrew reads *Helem*. **6:14b** As in Syriac version (compare 6:10); Hebrew reads *Hen*. **7:1** Hebrew *On the fourth day of the ninth month, the month of Kislev,* of the ancient Hebrew lunar calendar. This event occurred on December 7, 518 B.C.; also see note on 1:1. **7:2** Or *Bethel-sharezer had sent Regemmelech*. **7:3** Hebrew *mourn and fast in the fifth month*. The Temple had been destroyed in the fifth month of the ancient Hebrew lunar calendar (August 586 B.C.); see 2 Kgs 25:8. **7:5** Hebrew *fasted and mourned in the fifth and seventh months*. The fifth month of the ancient Hebrew lunar calendar usually occurs within the months of July and August. The seventh month usually occurs within the months of September and October; both the Day of Atonement and the Festival of Shelters were celebrated in the seventh month. **7:7** Hebrew *the Shephelah*.

6:9-15 This authoritative message accompanies Zechariah's eighth vision (6:1-8). Jeshua's symbolic coronation as both king and priest was not an actual political arrangement for Judah; it probably symbolizes the coming of the Messiah, "the Branch" (6:12; see also 3:8).

6:12-13 "The Branch" is a title for the Messiah (see 3:8), whom Jeshua represents. Just as Jeshua the high priest helped to rebuild the Temple in Jerusalem (Ezra 3:1-2, 8-9; 5:2), Jesus the Messiah would build the eternal heavenly Temple through his death, burial, and resurrection (John 2:19-22; 4:23-24; Ephesians 2:19-22; Hebrews 8:1-2). The Messiah would "rule as king," a role associated with David and the tribe of Judah (2 Samuel 7:12-16). The Messiah's priestly role is also associated with Aaron and the tribe of Levi (Exodus 29:44). Jeshua's crown, likely made with one silver band and one gold band, represents his "two roles." Melchizedek also fulfilled the double functions of priest and king (Genesis 14:17-20), as does the Messiah (Psalm 110:1-4; Hebrews 7:1-3, 15-17).

7:1-14 Zechariah's messages were prompted by delegates from Bethel who posed a practical question (7:2-3). Although Zechariah answered the question later (8:18-19), he responded first with rhetorical questions that focused on the people's self-centered motives (7:5-6). Zechariah then outlined God's expectations for Israel (7:8-10; see Jeremiah 22:3) and recounted what had happened to those who disobeyed previously (Zechariah 7:11-14).

7:4-7 Rather than answering the question right away, Zechariah first confronted his hearers with their selfish motives and hypocrisy. The most important issue was whether their hearts' desire was really to please God and to do his will; if not, it made no difference whether or not they kept a fast.

7:9 Alongside justice, God required that the people practice "mercy and kindness." The Hebrew translated here as "kindness" derives from the word for womb. Kindness is, then, something that moves a person from their most inward parts, and is a powerfully compelling emotion that cannot be ignored. Jesus' actions and words on many occasions were motivated by this same kind of kindness, or "compassion," indicated by an equivalent Greek word that is also related to emotions arising from the gut (Mark 6:34).

Wickedness

IDENTITY — A Woman in a Basket

Wickedness remembers . . .

I was hoping to remain in Judah to influence the people returning from exile. I once exercised power over the people and led them astray, but I am no longer welcome there. My power is diminished, and I am an outcast.

The holy God calls the Jewish people to worship him. This God calls them to love him with all their heart, soul, and strength (Deuteronomy 6:5), and to love their neighbors as themselves (Leviticus 19:18). The prophet Zechariah challenges the people to commit themselves fully to serving their one true God.

There is no room left for me and my evil schemes. I used to entice people into the vilest sins—debauchery, lust, drunkenness, orgies, carousing, magic arts, sexual immorality, murder, falsehood, covetousness, greed, slander, idolatry, and sacrificing children to Molech. But the people have turned their backs on me, just as they have done on Asherah, Astarte, and other colleagues of mine.

So I, Wickedness, was thrown into a basket, along with my powers. I am banished from the land given to Israel. A heavy lead cover prevents me from escaping. I sit humiliated in a basket, expelled to a land of idol worshipers. At least there I will find a home.

Two women with wings take me away to Babylon. They are honored for removing Wickedness from the land. With me out of the way, revival can take place and the worship of the true God can be restored—all as the second Temple is being built in Jerusalem by the returning exiles.

> Spiritual powers compete for our lives, but it is possible for us to remain close to Woman Wisdom.

THE WOMAN IN A BASKET'S STORY IS TOLD IN ZECHARIAH 5:5-11.

IDENTIFY

How might we embrace the ways of Wisdom instead of Wickedness? (Read more about Wisdom on page 763.)

"Wisdom and Wickedness compete for souls, but Wickedness is already defeated. Scripture introduces us to Wisdom, and she leads us into paths of righteousness and life. We have the power to influence others toward good or evil with our words, our actions, and our character. May we follow the example of Wisdom."

HÉLÈNE M. DALLAIRE, PhD, serves as Earl S. Kalland Professor of Old Testament and Semitic Languages at Denver Seminary. She is deeply involved in the Messianic movement, serving in worship, prayer, teaching, and preaching.

says: Judge fairly, and show mercy and kindness to one another. ¹⁰Do not oppress widows, orphans, foreigners, and the poor. And do not scheme against each other.

¹¹"Your ancestors refused to listen to this message. They stubbornly turned away and put their fingers in their ears to keep from hearing. ¹²They made their hearts as hard as stone, so they could not hear the instructions or the messages that the LORD of Heaven's Armies had sent them by his Spirit through the earlier prophets. That is why the LORD of Heaven's Armies was so angry with them.

¹³"Since they refused to listen when I called to them, I would not listen when they called to me, says the LORD of Heaven's Armies. ¹⁴As with a whirlwind, I scattered them among the distant nations, where they lived as strangers. Their land became so desolate that no one even traveled through it. They turned their pleasant land into a desert."

Promised Blessings for Jerusalem

8 Then another message came to me from the LORD of Heaven's Armies: ²"This is what the LORD of Heaven's Armies says: My love for Mount Zion is passionate and strong; I am consumed with passion for Jerusalem!

³"And now the LORD says: I am returning to Mount Zion, and I will live in Jerusalem. Then Jerusalem will be called the Faithful City; the mountain of the LORD of Heaven's Armies will be called the Holy Mountain.

⁴"This is what the LORD of Heaven's Armies says: Once again old men and women will walk Jerusalem's streets with their canes and will sit together in the city squares. ⁵And the streets of the city will be filled with boys and girls at play.

⁶"This is what the LORD of Heaven's Armies says: All this may seem impossible to you now, a small remnant of God's people. But is it impossible for me? says the LORD of Heaven's Armies.

⁷"This is what the LORD of Heaven's Armies says: You can be sure that I will rescue my people from the east and from the west. ⁸I will bring them home again to live safely in Jerusalem. They will be my people, and I will be faithful and just toward them as their God.

⁹"This is what the LORD of Heaven's Armies says: Be strong and finish the task! Ever since the laying of the foundation of the Temple of the LORD of Heaven's Armies, you have heard what the prophets have been saying about completing the building. ¹⁰Before the work on the Temple began, there were no jobs and no money to hire people or animals. No traveler was safe from the enemy, for there were enemies on all sides. I had turned everyone against each other.

¹¹"But now I will not treat the remnant of my people as I treated them before, says the LORD of Heaven's Armies. ¹²For I am planting seeds of peace and prosperity among you. The grapevines will be heavy with fruit. The earth will produce its crops, and the heavens will release the dew. Once more I will cause the remnant in Judah and Israel to inherit these blessings. ¹³Among the other nations, Judah and Israel became symbols of a cursed nation. But no longer! Now I will rescue you and make you both a symbol and a source of blessing. So don't be afraid. Be strong, and get on with rebuilding the Temple!

¹⁴"For this is what the LORD of Heaven's Armies says: I was determined to punish you when your ancestors angered me, and I did not change my mind, says the LORD of Heaven's Armies. ¹⁵But now I am determined to bless Jerusalem and the people of Judah. So don't be afraid. ¹⁶But this is what you must do: Tell the truth to each other. Render verdicts

---

7:11-12 The stubbornness of God's people is described in imagery that can be applied to both children and adults. Like particularly obstinate children, they turned their backs and covered their ears! This picture is almost comical, but the next one is not. The phrase "hearts as hard as stone" can also be translated more specifically as "hard as flint." Flint is a rock known for its hardness and durability, and it was historically used to make tools and to build stone walls. To make one's heart like flint is to render it impenetrable—much worse than the childish actions described.

8:2 Here God describes his love as "passionate," the Hebrew word denoting jealousy. We often think of jealousy as a negative emotion, but it has its proper place in marriage, a relationship built on mutual, exclusive love. The Old Testament uses the metaphor of marriage to describe the relationship between the Lord and his people, Israel. In the New Testament this metaphor is extended to Jesus and his people, the church. God's complete commitment to his people demands that they reciprocate his love (8:3). To tolerate a violation of that demand would be like being indifferent to the unfaithfulness of a spouse because one does not care about the relationship.

8:4-5 Here is a picture of a Jerusalem whose streets are filled with the shouts of children playing, while their aged grandparents or perhaps great-grandparents sit at the entrances of their homes, looking on with contentment. How different this is from Jerusalem in the aftermath of war, deserted but for people who roam the streets looking for places where they can buy bread by bartering family heirlooms (Lamentations 1:1, 11). In a famine following war, the most vulnerable age groups would have been the elderly and children. Thus, God's vision of a prosperous Jerusalem is conveyed through a picture of happy groups of young and old.

8:12 Gratitude for crop harvests takes many forms around the world, and most of these harvest festivals are set in a season of agricultural bounty. Even though many societies are moving toward becoming more urban—with farming sometimes going no further than a couple of potted plants—we recognize that the food on the table is provided by God's grace.

LORD of Heaven's Armies

IDENTITY

Deliverance Ahead

God is often simply called "the LORD" (in Hebrew, this sounds like "Yahweh"). But he also has names that highlight aspects of his relationship with his people. This is why he is referred to as "the LORD" (Yahweh) of Heaven's Armies eighteen times in Zechariah 8. In the Old Testament, he is prominently portrayed as a warrior, and this particular name refers to his role as Israel's deliverer.

After the exile to Babylon, the Jewish people felt discouraged because they had faced the Lord's wrath and experienced great oppression from their enemies. But in Zechariah's time, the people had come back to Jerusalem and were beginning to pick up the pieces.

This name repeats often to remind the people that, even though they were only beginning their restoration journey, the "LORD of Heaven's Armies" would fight on their behalf. He would see to it that they are fully restored and freed from their enemies, reminding them not to lose hope but to look forward to the day he will return and do all he has promised.

> When we are discouraged, God will fight for us and bring restoration.

THE LORD OF HEAVEN'S ARMIES'S STORY IS TOLD IN ZECHARIAH 8:1-23.

IDENTIFY

Have you ever felt discouraged and needed someone to fight on your behalf? How does this aspect of God encourage you?

"Sometimes life is hard, and I can become discouraged. Who will take up my cause? Who will fight for me? When I remember that the LORD of Heaven's Armies will fight on my behalf, I know he makes all things right. I can live with hope and confidence."

MAY YOUNG, MDiv, PhD, is an associate professor of biblical studies at Taylor University, with a passion for discipleship, teaching, and writing.

in your courts that are just and that lead to peace. ¹⁷Don't scheme against each other. Stop your love of telling lies that you swear are the truth. I hate all these things, says the LORD."

¹⁸Here is another message that came to me from the LORD of Heaven's Armies. ¹⁹"This is what the LORD of Heaven's Armies says: The traditional fasts and times of mourning you have kept in early summer, midsummer, autumn, and winter* are now ended. They will become festivals of joy and celebration for the people of Judah. So love truth and peace.

²⁰"This is what the LORD of Heaven's Armies says: People from nations and cities around the world will travel to Jerusalem. ²¹The people of one city will say to the people of another, 'Come with us to Jerusalem to ask the LORD to bless us. Let's worship the LORD of Heaven's Armies. I'm determined to go.' ²²Many peoples and powerful nations will come to Jerusalem to seek the LORD of Heaven's Armies and to ask for his blessing.

²³"This is what the LORD of Heaven's Armies says: In those days ten men from different nations and languages of the world will clutch at the sleeve of one Jew. And they will say, 'Please let us walk with you, for we have heard that God is with you.'"

Judgment against Israel's Enemies

9 This is the message* from the LORD against the land of Aram* and the city of Damascus, for the eyes of humanity, including all the tribes of Israel, are on the LORD.

² Doom is certain for Hamath,
    near Damascus,
  and for the cities of Tyre and Sidon,
    though they are so clever.
³ Tyre has built a strong fortress
  and has made silver and gold
    as plentiful as dust in the streets!
⁴ But now the Lord will strip away Tyre's
    possessions
  and hurl its fortifications into the sea,
    and it will be burned to the ground.
⁵ The city of Ashkelon will see Tyre fall
    and will be filled with fear.
  Gaza will shake with terror,
    as will Ekron, for their hopes will be dashed.
  Gaza's king will be killed,
    and Ashkelon will be deserted.
⁶ Foreigners will occupy the city of Ashdod.
    I will destroy the pride of the Philistines.
⁷ I will grab the bloody meat from their mouths
    and snatch the detestable sacrifices from
      their teeth.
  Then the surviving Philistines will worship
      our God
    and become like a clan in Judah.*
  The Philistines of Ekron will join my people,
    as the ancient Jebusites once did.
⁸ I will guard my Temple
    and protect it from invading armies.
  I am watching closely to ensure
    that no more foreign oppressors overrun my
      people's land.

Zion's Coming King

⁹ Rejoice, O people of Zion!*
    Shout in triumph, O people of Jerusalem!
  Look, your king is coming to you.
    He is righteous and victorious,*
  yet he is humble, riding on a donkey—
    riding on a donkey's colt.
¹⁰ I will remove the battle chariots from Israel*
    and the warhorses from Jerusalem.
  I will destroy all the weapons used in battle,
    and your king will bring peace to the nations.
  His realm will stretch from sea to sea
    and from the Euphrates River* to the ends of
      the earth.*

8:19 Hebrew *in the fourth, fifth, seventh, and tenth months.* The fourth month of the ancient Hebrew lunar calendar usually occurs within the months of June and July. The fifth month usually occurs within the months of July and August. The seventh month usually occurs within the months of September and October. The tenth month usually occurs within the months of December and January. **9:1a** Hebrew *An Oracle: The message.* **9:1b** Hebrew *land of Hadrach.* **9:7** Hebrew *like a leader in Judah.* **9:9a** Hebrew *O daughter of Zion!* **9:9b** Hebrew *and is being vindicated.* **9:10a** Hebrew *Ephraim,* referring to the northern kingdom of Israel; also in 9:13. **9:10b** Hebrew *the river.* **9:10c** Or *the end of the land.*

8:23 The phrase "clutch at the sleeve of one Jew" could also refer to clinging to the hem of someone's robe. In the ancient Near East, robes were long, and for someone to hold on to the hem of someone else's robe would mean that this person was on their knees, making their entreaty. The image is one of begging. This is the sort of desire that grips people who do not yet know the Lord. It turns even powerful people into desperate petitioners (8:20-22). The image of eagerly seeking after God, brought alive through the use of clothing, puts us who know the Lord to shame.

9:1-8 This encouraging message told the Judeans that they had nothing to fear from their three most prominent neighbors—Syria (Aram), the Phoenicians (Tyre and Sidon), and the Philistines. All three were rivals of Judah; they were always trying to take commercial and territorial advantage. God said that their efforts would be in vain.

9:9-17 The second portion of Zechariah's first message (9:1–11:17) presents the juxtaposition of warfare and peace that has defined human history. Judah's coming deliverer-king would be victorious in battle, yet righteous and humble (9:9), and would bring peace to the nations in his universal reign (9:10).

9:9 "Your king" refers to a future king from David's line, described earlier as the Branch (3:8; 6:12-13). The donkey was a humble animal, and "riding on a donkey" signaled that its rider would come in peace (see Matthew 21:5; John 12:15).

¹¹ Because of the covenant I made with you,
    sealed with blood,
I will free your prisoners
    from death in a waterless dungeon.
¹² Come back to the place of safety,
    all you prisoners who still have hope!
I promise this very day
    that I will repay two blessings for each of
        your troubles.
¹³ Judah is my bow,
    and Israel is my arrow.
Jerusalem* is my sword,
    and like a warrior, I will brandish it against
        the Greeks.*
¹⁴ The LORD will appear above his people;
    his arrows will fly like lightning!
The Sovereign LORD will sound the ram's
        horn
    and attack like a whirlwind from the
        southern desert.
¹⁵ The LORD of Heaven's Armies will protect his
        people,
    and they will defeat their enemies by hurling
        great stones.
They will shout in battle as though drunk with
        wine.
    They will be filled with blood like a bowl,
    drenched with blood like the corners of the
        altar.
¹⁶ On that day the LORD their God will rescue his
        people,
    just as a shepherd rescues his sheep.
They will sparkle in his land
    like jewels in a crown.
¹⁷ How wonderful and beautiful they will be!
The young men will thrive on abundant
        grain,
    and the young women will flourish on new
        wine.

The LORD Will Restore His People

10 Ask the LORD for rain in the spring,
    for he makes the storm clouds.
And he will send showers of rain
    so every field becomes a lush pasture.
² Household gods give worthless advice,
    fortune-tellers predict only lies,
and interpreters of dreams pronounce
    falsehoods that give no comfort.
So my people are wandering like lost sheep;
    they are attacked because they have no
        shepherd.

³ "My anger burns against your shepherds,
    and I will punish these leaders.*
For the LORD of Heaven's Armies has arrived
    to look after Judah, his flock.
He will make them strong and glorious,
    like a proud warhorse in battle.
⁴ From Judah will come the cornerstone,
    the tent peg,
the bow for battle,
    and all the rulers.
⁵ They will be like mighty warriors in battle,
    trampling their enemies in the mud under
        their feet.
Since the LORD is with them as they fight,
    they will overthrow even the enemy's
        horsemen.

⁶ "I will strengthen Judah and save Israel*;
    I will restore them because of my compassion.
It will be as though I had never rejected them,
    for I am the LORD their God, who will hear
        their cries.
⁷ The people of Israel* will become like mighty
        warriors,
    and their hearts will be made happy as if by
        wine.
Their children, too, will see it and be glad;
    their hearts will rejoice in the LORD.
⁸ When I whistle to them, they will come
        running,
    for I have redeemed them.
From the few who are left,
    they will grow as numerous as they were
        before.
⁹ Though I have scattered them like seeds among
        the nations,
    they will still remember me in distant lands.
They and their children will survive
    and return again to Israel.
¹⁰ I will bring them back from Egypt
    and gather them from Assyria.
I will resettle them in Gilead and Lebanon
    until there is no more room for them all.

9:13a Hebrew *Zion.*   9:13b Hebrew *the sons of Javan.*   10:3 Or *these male goats.*   10:6 Hebrew *save the house of Joseph.*
10:7 Hebrew *of Ephraim.*

10:4 A cornerstone is the first-laid foundation stone upon which a building's superstructure rests (see Job 38:6; Psalm 118:22; Isaiah 28:16; Ephesians 2:20). Just as a tent peg anchors a tent to the ground, so Judah would provide the future leaders needed to stabilize the Hebrew nation. Many understand cornerstone, tent peg, and bow for battle as titles for the Messiah (see Zechariah 9:13; Isaiah 22:20-23).

10:8 Shepherds in biblical times herded their flocks by whistling or piping to them (see Judges 5:16). "Redeemed" can also mean being ransomed—buying enslaved people out of their servitude or indentured status (see Deuteronomy 15:15; 24:18). The great increase of the Hebrew people was one of God's covenant promises to Abraham (Genesis 12:1-3; 22:17; 32:12).

¹¹ They will pass safely through the sea of
    distress,*
  for the waves of the sea will be held back,
    and the waters of the Nile will dry up.
  The pride of Assyria will be crushed,
    and the rule of Egypt will end.
¹² By my power* I will make my people strong,
    and by my authority they will go wherever
      they wish.
    I, the LORD, have spoken!"

11

Open your doors, Lebanon,
  so that fire may devour your cedar
    forests.
² Weep, you cypress trees, for all the ruined
    cedars;
  the most majestic ones have fallen.
  Weep, you oaks of Bashan,
    for the thick forests have been cut down.
³ Listen to the wailing of the shepherds,
    for their rich pastures are destroyed.
  Hear the young lions roaring,
    for their thickets in the Jordan Valley are
      ruined.

The Good and Evil Shepherds

⁴This is what the LORD my God says: "Go and care for the flock that is intended for slaughter. ⁵The buyers slaughter their sheep without remorse. The sellers say, 'Praise the LORD! Now I'm rich!' Even the shepherds have no compassion for them. ⁶Likewise, I will no longer have pity on the people of the land," says the LORD. "I will let them fall into each other's hands and into the hands of their king. They will turn the land into a wilderness, and I will not rescue them."

⁷So I cared for the flock intended for slaughter—the flock that was oppressed. Then I took two shepherd's staffs and named one Favor and the other Union. ⁸I got rid of their three evil shepherds in a single month.

But I became impatient with these sheep, and they hated me, too. ⁹So I told them, "I won't be your shepherd any longer. If you die, you die. If you are killed, you are killed. And let those who remain devour each other!"

¹⁰Then I took my staff called Favor and cut it in two, showing that I had revoked the covenant I had made with all the nations. ¹¹That was the end of my covenant with them. The suffering flock was watching me, and they knew that the LORD was speaking through my actions.

¹²And I said to them, "If you like, give me my wages, whatever I am worth; but only if you want to." So they counted out for my wages thirty pieces of silver.

¹³And the LORD said to me, "Throw it to the potter*"—this magnificent sum at which they valued me! So I took the thirty coins and threw them to the potter in the Temple of the LORD.

¹⁴Then I took my other staff, Union, and cut it in two, showing that the bond of unity between Judah and Israel was broken.

¹⁵Then the LORD said to me, "Go again and play the part of a worthless shepherd. ¹⁶This illustrates how I will give this nation a shepherd who will not care for those who are dying, nor look after the young, nor heal the injured, nor feed the healthy. Instead, this shepherd will eat the meat of the fattest sheep and tear off their hooves.

¹⁷ "What sorrow awaits this worthless
      shepherd
    who abandons the flock!
  The sword will cut his arm
    and pierce his right eye.
  His arm will become useless,
    and his right eye completely
      blind."

10:11 Or *the sea of Egypt,* referring to the Red Sea.   **10:12** Hebrew *In the LORD.*   **11:13** Syriac version reads *into the treasury;* also in 11:13b. Compare Matt 27:6-10.

11:4-17 The metaphor of the Judean leaders as shepherds binds together the last three portions (9:9–11:17) of Zechariah's first message (9:1–11:17). This message combines allegory with symbolic action on Zechariah's part to dramatize the wickedness of Israel's shepherds. The prophet acts out a parable in which a good shepherd is called by God to lead and unite his people but the people reject this shepherd along with the promise of protection from the nations (11:10) and unity between Judah and Israel (11:14). Zechariah's symbolic actions foreshadow the ministry of Jesus the Messiah as the Good Shepherd (see John 10:1-21).
11:4 The people of Israel are God's flock (Isaiah 40:11; Micah 5:4). The relative helplessness of sheep places a premium on their careful shepherding. Like sheep fattened for butchering, the people are being treated as disposable goods in a corrupt economy.
11:5 The sheep (the people of Judah) were being sold to buyers—occupying foreign powers, foreign allies, or domestic slave traders (see Amos 2:6). The sellers were the shepherds, leaders of the people who were more concerned with getting rich than with the well-being of the sheep.
11:10 Unlike Ezekiel, who dramatized the reunification of the northern and southern kingdoms (Ezekiel 37:15-19), Zechariah dramatized the division by cutting the staffs in two (see also Zechariah 11:14). The cutting of the staffs indicated the broken covenant bond between God and his people (11:11) and the broken bond of unity between the kingdoms of Judah and Israel (11:14). A covenant between the Lord and all the nations is otherwise unknown. Zechariah might actually have been proclaiming the dissolution of the covenant binding Israel to God as his people (see Hosea 1:6-9).

Future Deliverance for Jerusalem

12 This* message concerning the fate of Israel came from the LORD: "This message is from the LORD, who stretched out the heavens, laid the foundations of the earth, and formed the human spirit. ²I will make Jerusalem like an intoxicating drink that makes the nearby nations stagger when they send their armies to besiege Jerusalem and Judah. ³On that day I will make Jerusalem an immovable rock. All the nations will gather against it to try to move it, but they will only hurt themselves.

⁴"On that day," says the LORD, "I will cause every horse to panic and every rider to lose his nerve. I will watch over the people of Judah, but I will blind all the horses of their enemies. ⁵And the clans of Judah will say to themselves, 'The people of Jerusalem have found strength in the LORD of Heaven's Armies, their God.'

⁶"On that day I will make the clans of Judah like a flame that sets a woodpile ablaze or like a burning torch among sheaves of grain. They will burn up all the neighboring nations right and left, while the people living in Jerusalem remain secure.

⁷"The LORD will give victory to the rest of Judah first, before Jerusalem, so that the people of Jerusalem and the royal line of David will not have greater honor than the rest of Judah. ⁸On that day the LORD will defend the people of Jerusalem; the weakest among them will be as mighty as King David! And the royal descendants will be like God, like the angel of the LORD who goes before them! ⁹For on that day I will begin to destroy all the nations that come against Jerusalem.

¹⁰"Then I will pour out a spirit* of grace and prayer on the family of David and on the people of Jerusalem. They will look on me whom they have pierced and mourn for him as for an only son. They will grieve bitterly for him as for a firstborn son who has died. ¹¹The sorrow and mourning in Jerusalem on that day will be like the great mourning for Hadad-rimmon in the valley of Megiddo.

¹²"All Israel will mourn, each clan by itself, and with the husbands separate from their wives. The clan of David will mourn alone, as will the clan of Nathan, ¹³the clan of Levi, and the clan of Shimei. ¹⁴Each of the surviving clans from Judah will mourn separately, and with the husbands separate from their wives.

A Fountain of Cleansing

13 "On that day a fountain will be opened for the dynasty of David and for the people of Jerusalem, a fountain to cleanse them from all their sins and impurity.

²"And on that day," says the LORD of Heaven's Armies, "I will erase idol worship throughout the land, so that even the names of the idols will be forgotten. I will remove from the land both the false prophets and the spirit of impurity that came with them. ³If anyone continues to prophesy, his own father and mother will tell him, 'You must die, for you have prophesied lies in the name of the LORD.' And as he prophesies, his own father and mother will stab him.

12:1 Hebrew *An Oracle: This.* 12:10 Or *the Spirit.*

12:4 Madness, blindness, and panic were among the curses threatened against Israel for covenant disobedience (Deuteronomy 28:28). The Day of the Lord would witness a reversal as these curses would be turned against Israel's enemies (see 2 Kings 7:6-7). God would "watch over the people of Judah" (literally, "upon the house of Judah I will open my eyes"), a promise representing divine provision for those in desperate need (see Genesis 16:13-14; 21:19-21).

12:5 The title "the LORD of Heaven's Armies" emphasizes God's irrepressible power. The frequent repetition of this title in Zechariah's second message (12:1–14:21) assured his audience that the divine promises concerning Judah's victory would certainly be fulfilled (12:7).

12:10 One way God's people showed their repentance was though communal weeping (for example, Judges 2:4). Here, the Judeans understood how deeply they had wounded God, and they wept so bitterly at their actions that it was like weeping at the death of an only child. This would have been loud lamentation, wracking sobs. These dramatic emotions show the people's regret and desire to behave differently in the future. In male-dominated cultures where emotions—especially weeping—are disparagingly associated with women, we may also belittle our tears. Perhaps we need to give ourselves permission to see the value of tears for everyone, regardless of gender, and allow ourselves to weep in repentance.

13:1 A fountain is a spring of pure, flowing water for cleansing and purification (see 14:8; John 4:14; Revelation 22:1-2). God's cleansing of Israel would include leaders (represented by the "dynasty of David") and all the people of Judah and Israel (signified by "the people of Jerusalem," the spiritual center of the nation). This cleansing, symbolized in the ritual washings of Old Testament worship (see Exodus 30:17-21), was provided in the new covenant as promised by Jeremiah (Jeremiah 31:31-34) and Ezekiel (Ezekiel 36:25; see Hebrews 10:1-22). The people would experience a complete moral and spiritual cleansing following their sorrow over their sin (Zechariah 12:10-14).

13:3 It is hard to imagine a circumstance under which parents might stab their children to death. Here is one. Against all compulsions of maternal love, the mother here participates in dealing death to her grown child because they have dishonored God by making false prophecies in his name. This extreme situation pictures the drastic reversal that Judah would embrace. Shedding their long habit of going after false prophets (Jeremiah 14:13-16), they would practice utter devotion to God.

⁴"On that day people will be ashamed to claim the prophetic gift. No one will pretend to be a prophet by wearing prophet's clothes. ⁵He will say, 'I'm no prophet; I'm a farmer. I began working for a farmer as a boy.' ⁶And if someone asks, 'Then what about those wounds on your chest?*' he will say, 'I was wounded at my friends' house!'

The Scattering of the Sheep

⁷ "Awake, O sword, against my shepherd,
    the man who is my partner,"
    says the LORD of Heaven's Armies.
"Strike down the shepherd,
    and the sheep will be scattered,
    and I will turn against the lambs.
⁸ Two-thirds of the people in the land
    will be cut off and die," says the LORD.
"But one-third will be left in the land.
⁹ I will bring that group through the fire
    and make them pure.
I will refine them like silver
    and purify them like gold.
They will call on my name,
    and I will answer them.
I will say, 'These are my people,'
    and they will say, 'The LORD is our God.'"

The LORD Will Rule the Earth

14 Watch, for the day of the LORD is coming when your possessions will be plundered right in front of you! ²I will gather all the nations to fight against Jerusalem. The city will be taken, the houses looted, and the women raped. Half the population will be taken into captivity, and the rest will be left among the ruins of the city.

³Then the LORD will go out to fight against those nations, as he has fought in times past. ⁴On that day his feet will stand on the Mount of Olives, east of Jerusalem. And the Mount of Olives will split apart, making a wide valley running from east to west. Half the mountain will move toward the north and half toward the south. ⁵You will flee through this valley, for it will reach across to Azal.* Yes, you will flee as you did from the earthquake in the days of King Uzziah of Judah. Then the LORD my God will come, and all his holy ones with him.*

⁶On that day the sources of light will no longer shine,* ⁷yet there will be continuous day! Only the LORD knows how this could happen. There will be no normal day and night, for at evening time it will still be light.

⁸On that day life-giving waters will flow out from Jerusalem, half toward the Dead Sea and half toward the Mediterranean,* flowing continuously in both summer and winter.

⁹And the LORD will be king over all the earth. On that day there will be one LORD—his name alone will be worshiped.

¹⁰All the land from Geba, north of Judah, to Rimmon, south of Jerusalem, will become one vast plain. But Jerusalem will be raised up in its original place and will be inhabited all the way from the Benjamin Gate over to the site of the old gate, then to the Corner Gate, and from the Tower of Hananel to the king's winepresses. ¹¹And Jerusalem will be filled, safe at last, never again to be cursed and destroyed.

¹²And the LORD will send a plague on all the nations that fought against Jerusalem. Their people will become like walking corpses, their flesh rotting away. Their eyes will rot in their sockets, and their tongues will rot in their mouths. ¹³On that day they will be terrified, stricken by the LORD with great panic. They will fight their neighbors hand to hand. ¹⁴Judah, too, will be fighting at Jerusalem. The wealth of all the neighboring nations will be captured—great quantities of gold and silver and fine clothing. ¹⁵This same plague will strike the horses, mules, camels, donkeys, and all the other animals in the enemy camps.

¹⁶In the end, the enemies of Jerusalem who survive the plague will go up to Jerusalem each year

---

13:6 Hebrew *wounds between your hands?* **14:5a** The meaning of the Hebrew is uncertain. **14:5b** As in Greek version; Hebrew reads *with you.* **14:6** Hebrew *the precious ones shall diminish;* or *the precious ones and frost.* The meaning of the Hebrew is uncertain. **14:8** Hebrew *half toward the eastern sea and half toward the western sea.*

14:1-21 Zechariah closes with visions of judgment, salvation, and God's universal Kingdom. In the future, Israel would be besieged, teetering on the verge of total destruction, at which point the Lord himself would intervene and rescue his people (14:3-4) and punish their enemies with a terrible plague (14:12). Israel would be restored as God's people, and Jerusalem would be exalted as the center of civilization (14:16-17). God's rule would be established over all the earth (14:9), and the created order would be transformed (14:6-10). Fittingly, God's holiness would be the pervasive characteristic of his rule over all the earth (14:20-21). Zechariah's message stimulates the people to hope in God, the sovereign king of Israel, who would bring justice and restoration.

14:16 Another reversal would occur on the Day of the Lord when even Israel's enemies would worship God in Jerusalem (see Philippians 2:8-11). The annual Festival of Shelters marked the beginning of the fall harvest season and commemorated Israel's wilderness experience after the exodus from Egypt (see Exodus 23:14-19; Leviticus 23:33-43; Numbers 29:12-40; Deuteronomy 16:13-17). The festival gave the worshiping community an opportunity to thank God for his provision. It encouraged social concern for the disadvantaged and reliance on God as pilgrims in this world. Thanksgiving will characterize worship in the messianic era (see Isaiah 51:3; Jeremiah 33:11).

to worship the King, the LORD of Heaven's Armies, and to celebrate the Festival of Shelters. ¹⁷Any nation in the world that refuses to come to Jerusalem to worship the King, the LORD of Heaven's Armies, will have no rain. ¹⁸If the people of Egypt refuse to attend the festival, the LORD will punish* them with the same plague that he sends on the other nations who refuse to go. ¹⁹Egypt and the other nations will all be punished if they don't go to celebrate the Festival of Shelters.

²⁰On that day even the harness bells of the horses will be inscribed with these words: HOLY TO THE LORD. And the cooking pots in the Temple of the LORD will be as sacred as the basins used beside the altar. ²¹In fact, every cooking pot in Jerusalem and Judah will be holy to the LORD of Heaven's Armies. All who come to worship will be free to use any of these pots to boil their sacrifices. And on that day there will no longer be traders* in the Temple of the LORD of Heaven's Armies.

14:18 As in some Hebrew manuscripts and Greek and Syriac versions; Masoretic Text reads *will not punish*. 14:21 Hebrew *Canaanites*.

14:20-21 The phrase *holy to the Lord* was used to describe those things that were set apart for use within the sacred space, that is, the Tabernacle or Temple. For example, the golden medallion worn by the high priest had these words engraved on it (Exodus 28:36-38). In the age to come (Zechariah 14:9), both cooking pots, at the lowest rung of sacred items in the Temple, and sacred basins, at the top end, would be equally consecrated. Likewise, every cooking pot in the country would be made holy, fit for cooking sacrifices made in the Temple. Even the bells on a horse (usually metal discs that jangled against each other) would be sanctified. This is a picture of the complete removal of sin (13:1), the age that we eagerly anticipate with the second coming of Jesus. How charming that its glories are depicted using such everyday items as kitchenware!

Malachi

WHAT DO WE LEARN ABOUT GOD'S MISSION AND OURS?
God keeps his promises. Will we keep ours?

WHO WROTE IT? Malachi.

WHEN DID IT HAPPEN? Around the time of Nehemiah, sometime in the 400s BC, after King Cyrus of Persia allowed the exiles to return home.

HOW IS IT ORGANIZED?

1–2: God is faithful to his people, but they are unfaithful to him

3: God will purify his people

4: The "day of the LORD" is coming

FEATURE HIGHLIGHTS

+ *Divorce: Provision to Protect* (1163)
+ *Divorce* (1165)
+ *Children of God's Father-Heart* (1168)

Words to Remember are highlighted throughout this book

HOW LONG DOES IT TAKE TO READ?

:15 | :30 | 1:00 | 1:30 | 2:00 | 2:30 | 3:00 | 3:30

Timeline

BC	
586	JERUSALEM IS DESTROYED
538	CYRUS'S DECREE; EXILES RETURN TO JERUSALEM
536	TEMPLE RECONSTRUCTION BEGINS
520	HAGGAI AND ZECHARIAH BECOME PROPHETS
515	TEMPLE COMPLETED
479	ESTHER BECOMES QUEEN OF PERSIA
465	ARTAXERXES I BECOMES KING OF PERSIA
458	EZRA COMES TO JERUSALEM
445	NEHEMIAH COMES TO JERUSALEM
430	MALACHI BECOMES A PROPHET

MALACHI 1

1 This is the message* that the LORD gave to Israel through the prophet Malachi.*

The LORD's Love for Israel

²"I have always loved you," says the LORD.

But you retort, "Really? How have you loved us?"

And the LORD replies, "This is how I showed my love for you: I loved your ancestor Jacob, ³but I rejected his brother, Esau, and devastated his hill country. I turned Esau's inheritance into a desert for jackals."

⁴Esau's descendants in Edom may say, "We have been shattered, but we will rebuild the ruins."

But the LORD of Heaven's Armies replies, "They may try to rebuild, but I will demolish them again. Their country will be known as 'The Land of Wickedness,' and their people will be called 'The People with Whom the LORD Is Forever Angry.' ⁵When you see the destruction for yourselves, you will say, 'Truly, the LORD's greatness reaches far beyond Israel's borders!'"

Unworthy Sacrifices

⁶The LORD of Heaven's Armies says to the priests: "A son honors his father, and a servant respects his master. If I am your father and master, where are the honor and respect I deserve? You have shown contempt for my name!

"But you ask, 'How have we ever shown contempt for your name?'

⁷"You have shown contempt by offering defiled sacrifices on my altar.

"Then you ask, 'How have we defiled the sacrifices?*'

"You defile them by saying the altar of the LORD deserves no respect. ⁸When you give blind animals as sacrifices, isn't that wrong? And isn't it wrong to offer animals that are crippled and diseased? Try giving gifts like that to your governor, and see how pleased he is!" says the LORD of Heaven's Armies.

⁹"Go ahead, beg God to be merciful to you! But when you bring that kind of offering, why should he show you any favor at all?" asks the LORD of Heaven's Armies.

¹⁰"How I wish one of you would shut the Temple doors so that these worthless sacrifices could not be offered! I am not pleased with you," says the LORD of Heaven's Armies, "and I will not accept your offerings. ¹¹But my name is honored* by people of other nations from morning till night. All around the world they offer* sweet incense and pure offerings in honor of my name. For my name is great among the nations," says the LORD of Heaven's Armies.

¹²"But you dishonor my name with your actions. By bringing contemptible food, you are saying it's all right to defile the Lord's table. ¹³You say, 'It's

---

1:1a Hebrew *An Oracle: The message.* **1:1b** *Malachi* means "my messenger." **1:7** As in Greek version; Hebrew reads *defiled you?* **1:11a** Or *will be honored.* **1:11b** Or *will offer.*

1:1 This introduction classifies the book of Malachi as an authoritative message from God and identifies the author and audience, though not the date or reason for the message. The Hebrew text of Malachi begins with the word *massa*, which is often translated "oracle" and fills Malachi's message with authority and urgency. His audience was expected to pay attention and respond. Even the prophet's name, which means "my messenger," emphasizes his important role in proclaiming God's word.
1:2 In portraying a relationship between the Lord and Israel, love has implications related to the covenant agreement God made with the nation. The term *love* may be equated with God's choice, or election, of Israel as his people. Malachi's first message indicates that the other dimensions of God's unconditional covenant love for Israel (such as his patient mercy; see 3:6, 17) are also still operative, even after the Exile and Israel's breaking of the covenant.
1:2 We know from experience that a child's expectations of a parent can often be unreasonable. A child's perspective is mostly limited to the present and, at most, to the immediate future. A child might look in the wrong places for demonstrations of parental love and conclude that the parent doesn't really love them. This appeared to be Judah's situation as well. Malachi's post-exilic community was impoverished, living from hand to mouth. Their crops were pest-infested, and their vineyards were prematurely dropping the grapes (3:11). They demanded to know: Did God love them at all?
1:3 The word translated "rejected" means the opposite of *love*, so another possible translation is "hate." Love and hate form a polar word pair in both the Old Testament law and the prophets' writings (see Deuteronomy 7:9-10; Amos 5:15), and they are often used together to describe the alienation of a broken covenant relationship. Here, God says that he rejected Esau (and his descendants). Esau was the ancestor of the Edomite nation; his inheritance, the territory of Edom, was located on the southeastern rim of the Dead Sea. The mention of Jacob and Esau calls to mind the twin brothers' rivalry (Genesis 25:23-26) and the fallout between them. Esau had despised and rejected his covenant relationship with the Lord (see Genesis 25:34; 26:34-35).
1:4 "The LORD of Heaven's Armies" is a prominent name for God in the writings of the Old Testament prophets. "Heaven's Armies" are the angelic armies at God's command; the phrase emphasizes the invincible power of God. Esau was selfish and contemptuous of the tokens of the Lord's covenant (see note on 1:3). The nation of Edom came to personify the pride of self-centered existence (see Jeremiah 49:16). The Edomites were also allies of Babylon in the destruction of Jerusalem (see Psalm 137:7-9; Obadiah 1:10, 12).
1:13 At this time, the Temple had been rebuilt and the system of sacrifices had been reinstated. However, now that Judah was a province of the Persian Empire, the people were saddled with heavy taxes. This is probably one reason the tithes and offerings took a hit (3:8). Another is that the people faced economic depression with repeated droughts and blight (3:11; Haggai 1:6-10, 11; compare Zechariah 8:12). But the circumstances do not mitigate the people's bringing substandard offerings to God.

MY STORY WITH FAMILY & FRIENDS

Divorce: Provision to Protect

SCRIPTURE CONNECTION: MALACHI 2:14-16

God hates divorce. These three words get interpreted as God showing blanket disgust toward divorce. Stripped from their context in Scripture, they are quoted by people who perceive the end of any marriage as a shameful failure.

I, too, grew up viewing divorce as a scarlet letter of shame. And the ministry where I served perpetuated this belief. So, when my husband repeatedly betrayed me sexually, I donned the letter *D* and felt crushed by my so-called failure and shame.

But what is the Bible really talking about in Malachi 2:16? Let's look at two forms of divorce mentioned in Scripture: One is a marriage's legal end, setting a woman free to remarry (Deuteronomy 24:1-2). The other is abandonment—a man sends his wife away without a legal release, leaving her destitute. The husbands of Judah were abandoning their wives for other women (Malachi 2:14). *This* is the kind of divorce 2:16 references—the kind God hates.

Marriage is a God-designed holy institution that requires fidelity. But a legal divorce is also God's provision—to protect a person from a spouse unwilling to repent.

> How can I support people who need protection from toxic marriages?

IMAGINE

Do you perceive divorce as "all bad," a failure of the worst kind? Or do you value it as a potential protective measure for a person in a chronically toxic or unsafe marriage?

Tune into the protective heart of God. Then ask, "How can I support people in abusive or adulterous marriages, regardless of their decision to stay or to divorce?"

> "My divorce allowed me to smash idols: I released concerns I had about what others think and looked to God alone for approval. He lifted my head, validated me, and filled me with courage to turn divorce's pain into ministry to other betrayed women."

KRISTIN CARY, CPSAS, cofounded Living Truth with her husband. She guides women toward hope and healing after the devastating impact of sexual betrayal in their marriage.

too hard to serve the LORD,' and you turn up your noses at my commands," says the LORD of Heaven's Armies. "Think of it! Animals that are stolen and crippled and sick are being presented as offerings! Should I accept from you such offerings as these?" asks the LORD.

¹⁴"Cursed is the cheat who promises to give a fine ram from his flock but then sacrifices a defective one to the Lord. For I am a great king," says the LORD of Heaven's Armies, "and my name is feared among the nations!

A Warning to the Priests

2 "Listen, you priests—this command is for you! ²Listen to me and make up your minds to honor my name," says the LORD of Heaven's Armies, "or I will bring a terrible curse against you. I will curse even the blessings you receive. Indeed, I have already cursed them, because you have not taken my warning to heart. ³I will punish your descendants and splatter your faces with the manure from your festival sacrifices, and I will throw you on the manure pile. ⁴Then at last you will know it was I who sent you this warning so that my covenant with the Levites can continue," says the LORD of Heaven's Armies.

⁵"The purpose of my covenant with the Levites was to bring life and peace, and that is what I gave them. This required reverence from them, and they greatly revered me and stood in awe of my name. ⁶They passed on to the people the truth of the instructions they received from me. They did not lie or cheat; they walked with me, living good and righteous lives, and they turned many from lives of sin.

⁷"The words of a priest's lips should preserve knowledge of God, and people should go to him for instruction, for the priest is the messenger of the LORD of Heaven's Armies. ⁸But you priests have left God's paths. Your instructions have caused many to stumble into sin. You have corrupted the covenant I made with the Levites," says the LORD of Heaven's Armies. ⁹"So I have made you despised and humiliated in the eyes of all the people. For you have not obeyed me but have shown favoritism in the way you carry out my instructions."

A Call to Faithfulness

¹⁰Are we not all children of the same Father? Are we not all created by the same God? Then why do we betray each other, violating the covenant of our ancestors?

¹¹Judah has been unfaithful, and a detestable thing has been done in Israel and in Jerusalem. The men of Judah have defiled the LORD's beloved sanctuary by marrying women who worship idols. ¹²May the LORD cut off from the nation of Israel* every last man who has done this and yet brings an offering to the LORD of Heaven's Armies.

¹³Here is another thing you do. You cover the LORD's altar with tears, weeping and groaning because he pays no attention to your offerings and doesn't accept them with pleasure. ¹⁴You cry out, "Why doesn't the LORD accept my worship?" I'll tell you why! Because the LORD witnessed the vows you and your wife made when you were young. But you have been unfaithful to her, though she remained your faithful partner, the wife of your marriage vows.

¹⁵Didn't the LORD make you one with your wife? In body and spirit you are his.* And what does he want? Godly children from your union. So guard

---

2:12 Hebrew *from the tents of Jacob*. The names "Jacob" and "Israel" are often interchanged throughout the Old Testament, referring sometimes to the individual patriarch and sometimes to the nation. 2:15 Or *Didn't the one LORD make us and preserve our life and breath?* or *Didn't the one LORD make her, both flesh and spirit?* The meaning of the Hebrew is uncertain.

2:7 The priests had been entrusted with special "knowledge of God" as revealed in the law of Moses. Through their role as teachers, they were guardians of God's covenant agreement with Israel (Deuteronomy 33:9-10). The use of the word "messenger" (Hebrew *malak*) may be a wordplay on the name Malachi (*malaki*). Usually, this title was reserved for Hebrew prophets in the Old Testament. Still, Malachi ascribes prophetic duties to the priest since the priests were to interpret God's word.
2:11 Jewish men were likely divorcing their wives for the economic advantage of intermarriage with non-Jewish women who worshiped idols. Through these marriages, Jewish men could gain access to the merchant groups and trading monopolies already in place when the people returned from Babylonia. Malachi equates this betrayal with idolatry. Israelite history had shown that intermarriage with non-Israelite women went hand in hand with worshiping foreign gods. Loyalty was to be the hallmark of Israel's covenant relationships, whether with God or with a marriage partner. The circumstances and the selfish reasons these men had for divorcing their wives show contempt for the oneness of the marriage covenant (2:15; see Genesis 2:24).

2:12 The intent of "cut off" here was to blot out or destroy evildoers, in contrast to social banishment or religious excommunication.
2:14 The expression "faithful partner" identifies a marriage companion. The Hebrew word *khaveret*, related to the Hebrew verb *chavar* (meaning "to unite") used for a seam or a joint in construction (for example, Exodus 26:6-11), suggests a permanent bond. Marriage is a solemn covenant to which God is witness (see Proverbs 2:17).
2:15 In the ancient world, having children was of the utmost importance because they were the way to ensure a person's name and family line was carried on. For the Jewish people who had children, God's expectation was that they had "godly children"—that is, children who worshiped God and were raised in ways that honored him (Deuteronomy 6:6-7). The expectation of children in no way diminishes those married couples who have no children. Elsewhere, God promises to those who are faithful to him an "everlasting" name that is "far greater than sons and daughters could give" (Isaiah 56:3-5).

WHAT THE BIBLE SAYS ABOUT Divorce

Divorce Wasn't God's Original Plan

You cry out, "Why doesn't the LORD accept my worship?" I'll tell you why! Because the LORD witnessed the vows you and your wife made when you were young. But you have been unfaithful to her, though she remained your faithful partner, the wife of your marriage vows....

"For I hate divorce!" says the LORD, the God of Israel. "To divorce your wife is to overwhelm her with cruelty," says the LORD of Heaven's Armies. "So guard your heart; do not be unfaithful to your wife." **MALACHI 2:14, 16**

A Concession

Jesus replied, "Moses permitted divorce only as a concession to your hard hearts, but it was not what God had originally intended. ... whoever divorces his wife and marries someone else commits adultery—unless his wife has been unfaithful." **MATTHEW 19:8-9**

Loving an Unbelieving Spouse

Now, I will speak to the rest of you, though I do not have a direct command from the Lord. If a fellow believer has a wife who is not a believer and she is willing to continue living with him, he must not leave her. And if a believing woman has a husband who is not a believer and he is willing to continue living with her, she must not leave him. For the believing wife brings holiness to her marriage, and the believing husband brings holiness to his marriage. Otherwise, your children would not be holy, but now they are holy. **1 CORINTHIANS 7:12-14**

your heart; remain loyal to the wife of your youth. ¹⁶"For I hate divorce!"* says the LORD, the God of Israel. "To divorce your wife is to overwhelm her with cruelty,*" says the LORD of Heaven's Armies. "So guard your heart; do not be unfaithful to your wife."

¹⁷You have wearied the LORD with your words.

"How have we wearied him?" you ask.

You have wearied him by saying that all who do evil are good in the LORD's sight, and he is pleased with them. You have wearied him by asking, "Where is the God of justice?"

The Coming Day of Judgment

3 "Look! I am sending my messenger, and he will prepare the way before me. Then the Lord you are seeking will suddenly come to his Temple. The messenger of the covenant, whom you look for so eagerly, is surely coming," says the LORD of Heaven's Armies.

²"But who will be able to endure it when he comes? Who will be able to stand and face him when he appears? For he will be like a blazing fire that refines metal, or like a strong soap that bleaches clothes. ³He will sit like a refiner of silver, burning away the dross. He will purify the Levites, refining them like gold and silver, so that they may once again offer acceptable sacrifices to the LORD. ⁴Then once more the LORD will accept the offerings brought to him by the people of Judah and Jerusalem, as he did in the past.

⁵"At that time I will put you on trial. I am eager to witness against all sorcerers and adulterers and liars. I will speak against those who cheat employees of their wages, who oppress widows and orphans, or who deprive the foreigners living among you of justice, for these people do not fear me," says the LORD of Heaven's Armies.

A Call to Repentance

⁶"I am the LORD, and I do not change. That is why you descendants of Jacob are not already destroyed. ⁷Ever since the days of your ancestors, you have scorned my decrees and failed to obey them. Now return to me, and I will return to you," says the LORD of Heaven's Armies.

"But you ask, 'How can we return when we have never gone away?'

2:16a Hebrew *For he hates divorcing.* 2:16b Hebrew *to cover one's garment with violence.*

2:16 Levitical law permitted a man to divorce his wife only if he found something "wrong with her" (Deuteronomy 24:1). This is an ambiguous phrase, but considering that adultery with evidence was one of the few offenses which carried the death penalty in the law (Leviticus 20:10; Matthew 19:7-9), we may infer that divorce was allowed for cases of unproven adultery or something close to adultery. In contrast, in Malachi's day, the marriage contract (which covered all legal and economic contingencies such as bride price, dowry, property rights, and inheritance) allowed that either party, husband or wife, could initiate a divorce without even having to state a reason. However, a wife initiating a divorce at this time was rare.

2:16 The Hebrew text of this verse is challenging to understand, even for Old Testament scholars. Some translations, like the NLT, read, "'I hate divorce!' says the LORD," meaning that God hates the practice of divorce. This is appropriate because God's relationship with people is characterized by faithfulness, and he expected no less from Israel (Exodus 34:6; Deuteronomy 7:9). Alternatively, the Hebrew may mean, "The man who hates his wife and divorces her." In this case, God directs his hatred at the man's lack of love, or hatred, for his wife (see note on 1:3 about love and hate). In the Old Testament, God did not permit divorce due to loss of affection, only for sexual infidelity or neglect (Exodus 21:10-11; Deuteronomy 24:1-4). "To overwhelm her with cruelty" (literally "to cover one's garment with violence") is an expression that entails acts of violence or wrongdoing.

3:1 This instance of "my messenger" is also a wordplay on Malachi's name (see 2:7). The messenger may be either an angel or a human being functioning as a divine go-between. Jesus identified John the Baptist by pointing to this passage (see Matthew 11:10; Mark 1:2; Luke 7:27). Malachi's audience would probably have understood "the messenger of the covenant" to be a divine being (see Exodus 23:20-23). Christian interpreters have understood Jesus Christ to be the messenger of the new covenant.

3:2 The people's wickedness must be burned away by the fires of divine testing and judgment (Isaiah 1:25; Jeremiah 6:29; Ezekiel 22:22). The strong soap was made from plants (see Jeremiah 2:22). The "blazing fire" and "strong soap" signify the testing (by refining) and cleansing (by laundering) that would restore Israel's faithfulness to their covenant with the Lord.

3:5 Oppressing widows was a serious offense under the law of Moses (Exodus 22:22-24). Without a man to provide them security, widows without sons would have been among the most vulnerable in ancient Israelite society. Since they had no means of income, they had no way to repay debts that the deceased husband may have incurred. In such cases the creditor could seize their children to sell them into slavery (2 Kings 4:1). To categorize their oppression as being as serious as adultery and perjury shows how deeply God cares for this group.

3:7 In the context of their covenant relationship, "return" expresses a change of loyalty on the part of Israel or God. Typically, the term is understood as repentance, a complete change of direction back to God. The verb here conveys urgency and demands an immediate response from the audience. The accusation of insincere worship builds on similar charges in Malachi's second message (see 1:6-14), just as God's promise to "open the windows of heaven" (3:10) affirms his power as "a great king" (see 1:14).

⁸"Should people cheat God? Yet you have cheated me!

"But you ask, 'What do you mean? When did we ever cheat you?'

"You have cheated me of the tithes and offerings due to me. ⁹You are under a curse, for your whole nation has been cheating me. ¹⁰Bring all the tithes into the storehouse so there will be enough food in my Temple. If you do," says the Lord of Heaven's Armies, "I will open the windows of heaven for you. I will pour out a blessing so great you won't have enough room to take it in! Try it! Put me to the test! ¹¹Your crops will be abundant, for I will guard them from insects and disease.* Your grapes will not fall from the vine before they are ripe," says the Lord of Heaven's Armies. ¹²"Then all nations will call you blessed, for your land will be such a delight," says the Lord of Heaven's Armies.

¹³"You have said terrible things about me," says the Lord.

"But you say, 'What do you mean? What have we said against you?'

¹⁴"You have said, 'What's the use of serving God? What have we gained by obeying his commands or by trying to show the Lord of Heaven's Armies that we are sorry for our sins? ¹⁵From now on we will call the arrogant blessed. For those who do evil get rich, and those who dare God to punish them suffer no harm.'"

The Lord's Promise of Mercy

¹⁶Then those who feared the Lord spoke with each other, and the Lord listened to what they said. In his presence, a scroll of remembrance was written to record the names of those who feared him and always thought about the honor of his name.

¹⁷"They will be my people," says the Lord of Heaven's Armies. "On the day when I act in judgment, they will be my own special treasure. I will spare them as a father spares an obedient child. ¹⁸Then you will again see the difference between the righteous and the wicked, between those who serve God and those who do not."

3:11 Hebrew *from the devourer.*

> "When we let our children fly as arrows, we understand that we have been chosen by God to be the bow in their lives and point them in the right direction as we lead them to Jesus."
>
> **CRYSTAL MCDOWELL**
> writer, speaker, teacher, and mother of five

3:8-9 Malachi appeals to the people of Judah for a comprehensive renewal of their practice of giving to the Lord. Tithes, a tenth of the produce of the land, were required by the law of Moses (see Deuteronomy 12:6, 11, 17). Offerings were additional gifts or contributions made to the Lord or his sanctuary, including produce, material goods (such as construction materials or garments), or personal valuables (such as gold, silver, or precious stones). Judah's recent experience resulted from God's curse because they did not keep their part of the agreement (see Deuteronomy 28:20, 27). Malachi thus urgently called the community to repent, turn to the Lord, and do what the covenant required.

3:13–4:3 Malachi's final message contains two distinct but related speeches, the first emphasizing service to the Lord (3:13-18) and the second contrasting the fate of the wicked with that of the righteous (4:1-3). Each speech concludes with the messenger formula: "says the Lord of Heaven's Armies." The prophet revisits themes from the fourth message (see 3:1-5) as he reiterates that God desires honest and faithful worship in light of coming judgment on the Day of the Lord. While wickedness seems to triumph over righteousness and God seems delinquent in judging sin in the community, the coming Day of the Lord will vindicate God's justice as the wicked are separated from the righteous by the fire of God's judgment.

3:16-18 The prophet here serves as a recorder, reporting the audience's reaction to his final message and God's response to the discussion among "those who feared the Lord." Although God listened to their deliberations (see 3:16), there is no evidence that Malachi's message effected any real change in most of his listeners.

MALACHI 4

The Coming Day of Judgment

4 ¹*The LORD of Heaven's Armies says, "The day of judgment is coming, burning like a furnace. On that day the arrogant and the wicked will be burned up like straw. They will be consumed—roots, branches, and all.

²"But for you who fear my name, the Sun of Righteousness will rise with healing in his wings.* And you will go free, leaping with joy like calves let out to pasture. ³On the day when I act, you will tread upon the wicked as if they were dust under your feet," says the LORD of Heaven's Armies.

4:1 Verses 4:1-6 are numbered 3:19-24 in Hebrew text.   4:2 Or *the sun of righteousness will rise with healing in its wings.*

4:1 The furnace here refers to a fixed or portable cooking device equivalent to our stoves or ovens and used especially for baking bread. This would have made the metaphor particularly meaningful to women, who were primarily responsible for food production. Evildoers would meet their end—an end as final as that experienced by the stubble or wood fueling a furnace.

4:2 The source for the title "Sun of Righteousness" might have been the winged sun commonly seen in ancient Near Eastern imagery. Here it might be a title for the Messiah or a figurative description of a new era of righteousness in which God would overturn the curse of sin. Outstretched wings are a symbol of God's protection and rescue (see Exodus 19:4; Deuteronomy 32:10-11; Psalms 17:8; 18:10). Israel's spiritual restoration, or healing, would be based on God's cleansing the people and forgiving their sins (see Jeremiah 33:6-8; compare Jeremiah 8:14-15). It would result from a collective confession of sin and turning back to God (Malachi 3:7; see Jeremiah 14:19-20).

Come Close — CHILDREN OF GOD'S FATHER-HEART

SCRIPTURE CONNECTION: MALACHI 4:6

Every day we hear sad stories of children separated from their parents for many reasons.

"My Papa died young, so our Mama went to work in another country and left us to the care of our aunt and uncle who were mean to us. We were so afraid to let Mama know we were sad and hurting."

"When my dad was young, he was beaten up by his alcoholic father for no reason. He hated his dad. I cry myself to bed each night, wondering why he is doing the same thing to us today."

"I am not an orphan. But why do I feel like one? I have a mom and dad. But they are either at work or busy with their friends. I feel so alone at home."

In the last book of the Old Testament, God makes a promise to his people. In Malachi 4:6, we read about God's plans to send a prophet whose preaching will turn alienated fathers and children back to one another. God's biggest priority is to be a Father to his people. From his loving father-heart, we learn about his deep concern that fathers and mothers must care for their children and not neglect them. Because God has the heart of a loving father, he will help us be good parents to our children, and in turn, he will help our children turn their hearts to us, their parents.

REFLECT "His preaching will turn the hearts of fathers to their children, and the hearts of children to their fathers. Otherwise I will come and strike the land with a curse." MALACHI 4:16

We may have different experiences with our earthly parents, but we have a heavenly Father who knows our needs, who hears our prayers, who wipes away our tears, and who will never turn his heart away from us.

CONSIDER "Remember who you are and whose you are." THEA BOWMAN

The heart of our Father in heaven can lead our hearts as parents.

MENCHIT WONG, MBA, is a Gallup-certified Strengths Coach and leadership consultant. She also serves on the leadership of global mission movements that enable children to be disciples of Jesus.

MALACHI 4

⁴"Remember to obey the Law of Moses, my servant—all the decrees and regulations that I gave him on Mount Sinai* for all Israel.

⁵"Look, I am sending you the prophet Elijah before the great and dreadful day of the LORD arrives. ⁶His preaching will turn the hearts of fathers to their children, and the hearts of children to their fathers. Otherwise I will come and strike the land with a curse."

4:4 Hebrew *Horeb,* another name for Sinai.

4:4-6 The book concludes with appeals to heed Moses and Elijah, two ideal models of faith in God and obedience to the law (see Matthew 17:1-4). The two are upheld as examples for Malachi's audience to follow. In ancient Hebrew tradition, the two appeals may have served as postscripts for the scroll that contained the twelve Minor (shorter) Prophets. If so, the first postscript (Malachi 4:4) connects the scroll to the law of Moses. The second (4:5-6) ties the scroll of the Minor Prophets to the Major (longer) Prophets—Isaiah, Jeremiah, and Ezekiel.

4:4 The first postscript reminds Judah "to obey the Law of Moses." Israel's identity was rooted in the Exodus and defined by the Sinai covenant mediated by Moses (see Deuteronomy 34:10-12).

4:5-6 The second postscript warns that God's judgment of the wicked is indeed approaching and promises God's deliverance and restoration of the righteous. Elijah is a supreme example of a prophet of God who preached repentance with messages proven by signs and wonders (see Luke 1:17; James 5:17-18). Elijah would be a forerunner of the "day of the LORD" (see Malachi 3:1). The New Testament identifies John the Baptist as the prophet who prepared the way for Jesus the Messiah (see Matthew 11:11-15; Luke 1:17).

4:6 Two key themes prominent in Malachi and the Old Testament prophets, in general, are the turning of hearts and the ministry of reconciliation. *Turn* is the Old Testament term for repentance and indicates a complete change of loyalties. Turning toward God results in reconciliation between generations (see 2 Corinthians 5:18-20). The word *curse* implies total destruction (see Deuteronomy 7:26; 1 Samuel 15:18; Zechariah 14:11). The people who did not respond to God's prophet would face utter oblivion, as had been the fate of their Canaanite predecessors (for example, Joshua 6:17).

WHAT IS MY PURPOSE?
THREE PROVEN PRACTICES TO LIVE OUR STORY IN GOD'S STORY

Dear sister, you have a purpose and a story. And I want to help you discover how God enlivens your story and embraces you in his rescue story, his restoration purpose.

This section focuses on discovering your purpose and your role in living out God's story in this world. If your main question right now is, How do I explore a close relationship with God? then turn to page A14 to learn more.

Your story begins with God's story. Your purpose begins with God's creative purposes. And we can read about God's purpose for restoring us to himself, each other, and all creation through the whole Bible. From Genesis to Revelation, we see the story of God's desire to restore wholeness and relationship.

God's purpose invites you, as a main character with a critical role, to the greatest story of all time. God's purpose embraces everyone, especially those who are hurting and broken and know they're in need. And it's a story that culminates in healing, wholeness, and hope.

God has already designed you for your part in this story. And six of the questions you may be asking about your part in God's purpose are already answered in the Bible!

1. WHO? You, called as a child of God, image-bearer, ambassador, disciple-maker.

2. WHY? God is love and created all existence from his love, for love. Human wrongdoing broke what God created, and the world continues to suffer in brokenness. God wants to fix this problem and says that you, as his image bearer (Genesis 1:26-27) led by the Holy Spirit (Romans 8:9-17), can join him in this work, doing even greater works than his Son (John 14:12).

3. WHEN? Now.

4. WHERE? Your place and every place. God's mission is for everyone, everywhere.

5. WHAT? You are called to love God and love others (Mark 12:29-31), make disciples (Matthew 28:19), show and tell the Good News (Mark 16:15), and model goodness (Genesis 12:1-3).

6. HOW? This, *this*, is where your unique story comes in!

How you do your part in God's mission is unique to you. This *how* invites you to reaffirm that God has called you, now, where you are and where he is active, to restore and make things right. You know your part. Now your question is, "What am I to do?"

To answer this, we'll walk along a proven pathway, following Bible heroes and nowadays people, that winds from living "ho-hum" human stories to "holy moly!" godly adventures. I found this path by listening to the stories of those who believed God, acted upon what God told them, and were transformed into living their God-given purpose.

I searched from the Bible's first to its last pages, conducted nationwide focus groups and surveys, and interviewed more than three thousand women to uncover the path to living out God's purpose and story. It turns out we can't merely think or study our way into our unique story. Instead, we *practice* our way to purpose.

> In the following pages, you will learn three key practices to discover your purpose in God's purpose, your story in God's story. You'll read Bible and contemporary stories and clarify your own story through twelve experiences.

> You'll believe, belong, and become as you practice this path to purpose.

MY BELIEVE–BELONG–BECOME STORY

I'll let you in on a fear of mine—one I've actually shared with thirty-two thousand other people!

When I was CEO of MOPS International (Mothers of Preschoolers, a ministry that reaches a vast number of moms), I stood on a stage before tens of thousands. Leading up to the event, I'd participated in a nationwide, Bible-based "Courage Challenge" to embolden us moms to live out our God-given purposes. Trying to be a good leader modeling the way, I stood in front of these mostly strangers and on a sheet of cardboard wrote my greatest fear: *humiliation*.

But not long after opening my soul to thirty-two thousand strangers, I found the courage to make a career decision that could have seemed like public humiliation—leaving my role as CEO. I sensed God calling me to believe Romans 8:28-39, that God causes everything to work together for the good of those who love him and who are called according to his purpose, and that we have overwhelming victory through Christ who loved us.

As I sensed a call to leave my role, I had to accept a holy invitation to believe God's promise. I had to step forward in my weakness, not because of my strength. I chose to become who I sensed God calling me to grow into being. But I knew I wouldn't—and couldn't—do it alone. I reached out to my trusted people—my husband, a longtime MOPS staff member with keen insight, and my brother who happens to be a pastor. As I prayed and listened with my community for God's leading, I sensed God asking me to lay it all down—to give up this treasured role and the paycheck it provided too.

When I saw that I had given all that I could and that I needed to make space for a future leader and trust God for my next calling, God gave me courage. So God overcame what could have looked like my worst fear—humiliation—by giving me my greatest hope—that I would faithfully live my part in God's story.

The day I resigned was also my twenty-fifth wedding anniversary, and I said, "God has been faithful in my marriage and my time leading here. He's going to be faithful again." At my farewell party, I had already welcomed a new assignment with another organization, and the work I was about to do was the perfect fit for that season. Later God led me to be a CEO again (this time for Stonecroft Ministries). As I believe, belong, and become again and again through my life, I come to trust God more, and I sense his pleasure in my obedience. I am not perfect, but as I keep practicing, I am living an extraordinary purpose I never dreamed I would.

BY DR. NAOMI CRAMER OVERTON

PRACTICE 1 # Believe

We come to trust God and feel we can, and must, bless others

How will we live if we believe God's love is enough? This part of the journey sounds like this:

"God has a good purpose for me."

"I must do something."

"I can make a difference."

People filled with extraordinary purpose believe God's love is enough and then act on this belief.

A BELIEVE-BELONG-BECOME STORY FROM THE BIBLE

Hagar didn't receive a lot of love from the family she was part of in the Bible, but she did find her purpose in God's purpose (read more in Genesis 16:1-16; 21:8-21). She was Sarah's slave and ended up being the mom of Abraham's first son, Ishmael. And Hagar wasn't perfect. When she got pregnant, she taunted Sarah for being childless. Sarah started mistreating her so badly that Hagar ran away. And the story would have ended there, except that Hagar believed God's word to her.

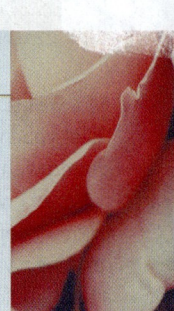

The angel of the Lord said to her, . . . "I will give you more descendants than you can count."

And the angel also said, "You are now pregnant and will give birth to a son. You are to name him Ishmael (which means 'God hears'), for the Lord has heard your cry of distress. . . ."

Thereafter, Hagar used another name to refer to the Lord, who had spoken to her. She said, "You are the God who sees me." **GENESIS 16:9-11, 13**

As you think about how God has come through for you, as God did for Hagar, and how you can trust and believe him, you might want to remember how God has come through for others.

EXPERIENCE 1 | GAIN STRENGTH AND LEARN FROM OTHERS' STORIES

Turn to page 1675 for the full list of Identity stories to explore. Most of these tell the story of a person who either found their purpose in God's mission or chose not to.

What do you see in common among the stories of those who God used greatly?

What did those who did evil or who shrunk back do differently?

Which of these stories feel like they resonate with your own? From these stories, what do you sense God could be saying about your story and your next steps?

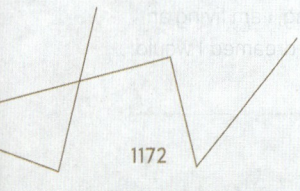

PRACTICE 2 — Belong

We invest in four core relationships to grow in and live out our faith

In this second practice of moving into God's story, we:

Discover a vision for living our God-given purpose.

Get closer to others who share this purpose.

Get to know and serve one person in need.

Again, this practice centers on action:

We commit ourselves to the purpose of loving God by connecting with others and loving the person or people group we feel called to. We begin to invest ongoing time and money.

It's tempting to believe in a "lone-ranger story," that it's just God and me changing the world together. But that's not how it works! We must find partners so that we can work together in God's purpose. And we also must find people we can serve, but we need to know people as people, not as projects.

This isn't a mystery either. Lots of people have discovered what really helps if we're seeking to invest in others. This happens as we:

1	Befriend people and serve their practical needs.
2	Ask questions about their spiritual story and listen and share our own.
3	Introduce them to Jesus by sharing the Good News. (We might study the Bible together or invite them to church. Or see page A14 for a way to introduce a friend to Jesus.)
4	Help them grow in God by introducing them to a faith community and showing them how to develop habits of reading God's Word, praying, and serving others.

As we look at the Bible, we see that God formed us for relationship. Made in God's image (Genesis 1:26-27), we are created to have a relationship with God and others. Made in family (Genesis 2:23-24; Psalm 68:5-6; John 19:25-27), we can lift each other up. Made to work together to bring wholeness to the world (Genesis 1:26; 12:3), we can link arms to advance what's good. And made with unique gifts and places to use them (1 Corinthians 12:4-11), we are responsible to influence as we uniquely are, from where we are.

A BELIEVE-BELONG-BECOME STORY FROM THE BIBLE

God gave a unique calling to Elizabeth, and an angel of God visited Mary to deliver her unique calling (read more in Luke 1:5–2:7). Each of these women believed that God had given them a huge privilege of bearing a special child. But they chose not to carry their callings alone, and both were better for it. We can see their relationship when Mary visited Elizabeth after accepting the call to bear God's Son:

Mary responded [to the angel], "I am the Lord's servant. May everything you have said about me come true." And then the angel left her.

A few days later Mary hurried to the hill country of Judea, to the town where Zechariah lived. She entered the house and greeted Elizabeth. At the sound of Mary's greeting, Elizabeth's child leaped within her, and Elizabeth was filled with the Holy Spirit.

Elizabeth gave a glad cry and exclaimed to Mary, "God has blessed you above all women, and your child is blessed. Why am I so honored, that the mother of my Lord should visit me? When I heard your greeting, the baby in my womb jumped for joy. You are blessed because you believed that the Lord would do what he said."

Mary responded,
"Oh, how my soul praises the Lord.
 How my spirit rejoices in God my Savior!
For he took notice of his lowly servant girl,
 and from now on all generations will call me blessed." LUKE 1:38-48

Do you see it? Mary didn't have to seek out Elizabeth, but she wanted to. I bet she knew that Elizabeth—who was also mysteriously pregnant after a visitation by God—would "get" her. And what joy that gave Elizabeth! Do you see the impact on Mary, too? A younger woman in the care of an older woman standing in similar shoes, with a similar call. Likewise, we see in the pathways of those who are fully alive in God's purposes that they do so alongside a trusted friend. Before they give birth to the fullness of their calling, they befriend each other and grow stronger together in God. We need companions on this path.

EXPERIENCE 2 — GOD'S DESIGN FOR OUR FOUR CORE RELATIONSHIPS

In our story, we will find we can bless and serve in four core relationships. Read more about that in the Image articles:

What is my story with God? Turn to page 1672 to find a list of the articles about our relationship with God: *Theos: My Story with God.*

Who are my family and friends, and how do I live my God story with them? Turn to page 1672 to find the *Oikos: My Story with Family & Friends* articles.

Who is in my community—at my workplace, church, neighborhood, school, or children's school—where I also want to bless others? Turn to page 1673 to find articles on relating to our communities: *Koinonia: My Story with Community, Workplace & Church.*

What is my unique way of bringing more wholeness to this world? Turn to page 1674 to find the articles about our unique callings: *Shalom: My Story of My Unique Influence.*

EXPERIENCE 3 | WHAT DO YOU LONG TO BE KNOWN FOR?

As you read the Image stories from Experience 2, you'll notice something each person was known for. What's your "known for"—a quality or Scripture verse you hope people might say about you?

At my dad's funeral, when his seven kids told of his legacy, there was no doubt about what he was *known for*: peace (you can also read about my father's *known for* on page 1111). When we think of people in the Bible, it's easy to think of one-word summaries, too. Here's a chart exploring some important people in the Bible and their *known for* qualities:

NAME	KNOWN FOR	REFERENCES
MARY	Embracing *(God's call, her Son)*	"I am the Lord's servant. May everything you have said about me come true." LUKE 1:38; SEE ALSO LUKE 1:26-56; 2:19; JOHN 19:25-27
RAHAB	Rescuing	"It was by faith that Rahab the prostitute was not destroyed with the people in her city who refused to obey God. For she had given a friendly welcome to the spies." HEBREWS 11:31; SEE ALSO JOSHUA 2:1-24; 6:22-23
SARAH	Doubting	"[Sarah] laughed.... Then the LORD said to Abraham, 'Why did Sarah laugh? Why did she say, "Can an old woman like me have a baby?" Is anything too hard for the LORD?'" GENESIS 18:12-14; SEE GENESIS 18:1-15
ESTHER	Daring	"Though it is against the law, I will go in to see the king. If I must die, I must die." ESTHER 4:16; SEE ESTHER 1:1–10:3
DEBORAH	Wisdom	"Deborah, the wife of Lappidoth, was a prophet who was judging Israel at that time. She would sit under the Palm of Deborah..., and the Israelites would go to her for judgment." JUDGES 4:4-5; SEE JUDGES 4:1–5:31

BIBLE PEOPLE & VERSES THAT INSPIRE ME	QUALITIES NOTED IN THESE VERSES	QUALITIES PEOPLE TELL ME I HAVE	WHICH OF THESE GIVE ME THE MOST HOPE?

| EXPERIENCE 4 | FOCUS OUR PURPOSE BY PICTURING OUR RELATIONSHIPS |

If you're unsure where to begin in discovering who God has positioned you to befriend, serve, and love, what do you do? A simple tool like this one helped me figure that out. Now I feel more intentional about investing where I feel most called rather than trying (and failing!) to be everything to everyone.

First, using the interlocking circles diagram below, write in the name (or for fun, doodle the face of) the main thirty or so people you interact with monthly. Maybe they're friends and family or colleagues, neighbors, fellow Christians, or other community members. Now add any others from places where you feel drawn and uniquely called—even if you're not involved there yet.

Following these three steps, fill in this diagram or draw a similar diagram in a journal or on a piece of paper.

1 First, write in the center circle (*Theos: My Story with God*) the weekly practices you engage in to invest in your relationship with God. Maybe that's praying daily, reading the Bible, or going on nature walks to meditate on God's creation. Write down whatever you do to draw close to God personally.

2 Using the names of the people you listed in the interlocking circles, place their names in the corresponding circles based on their relationship to you. Who belongs in the family and friends circle? Who do you meet in your community, workplace, and church? Who fits in the circle of your unique influence?

3 Now look at which circle is the fullest. Is that the way you want it to be, or are you overfocusing there and under-focusing on a circle where you know there's more you want to invest?

SHALOM MY STORY OF MY UNIQUE INFLUENCE
KOINONIA MY STORY WITH COMMUNITY, WORKPLACE & CHURCH
OIKOS MY STORY WITH FAMILY & FRIENDS
THEOS MY STORY WITH GOD

After you've filled out your relational circles, ask yourself a few questions:

1. **"WHAT PATTERNS DO I SEE?"** When I completed this exercise, I noticed the people I am closest to live in another state. This pointed me to find a way to spend more time near them.

2. **"HOW ARE THEY DOING?"** As I came back to that neighborhood, I arranged get-togethers with those people. I asked people, "How are you doing? How are you *really* doing?" And then I listened.

3. **"HOW WILL I PRAY AND PERSIST?"** I have to admit: What I learned when I asked and listened hurt my heart. Too many people were suffering. But now I knew how to pray, serve, listen, and invite them toward Jesus' restoration.

Our ordinary, daily relationships are usually where God appoints his extraordinary purpose.

So fill out your relational diagrams and notice who's already within reach. Pray over it and notice the hope-hungry people. Ask how they're really doing. And pray more and persist. As you love others as yourself, you'll find connection, and often friendship, and bring a smile to God's face, serving up hope where you find welcome.

PRACTICE 3 — Become
We step into our purpose and help others do the same

We've reached the third practice. Here, we:

Accept a task or a challenge.

Learn more about how to make an impact.

Make acting on our God-given purpose part of our regular life.

And this phase finishes with a big finale:

We begin to not only add our own good to the world but also multiply that good by coming alongside others to help them believe, belong, and become!

A BELIEVE–BELONG–BECOME STORY FROM THE BIBLE

Who would blame Esther for saying no when someone asked her to risk her life? I might have, before I understood Esther's backstory. Exiled, orphaned, and endangered if she accepted her calling, it makes sense she would say no. But I am so glad she became who God (and an important person in her life) invited her to be.

When Esther's cousin, Mordecai, told her (see Esther 4:1-17) that her husband, King Xerxes, had signed a decree to kill her people (the Jews in the empire), Esther didn't jump at the opportunity to *become* who God may have been inviting her to be. We know she already believed God. And she had found belonging with her cousin and guardian, Mordecai, who had cared for her and helped guide her as she gained influence as queen. But now, Mordecai called her to *become* what she may have been placed to be—the rescuer of her people. And Esther has a moment of hesitation. If she appeared before the king without being summoned, she could be killed (Esther 4:11).

A good friend doesn't tell you what to do; they remind you of who you are. And Mordecai reminded Esther that she may have been placed "for just such a time as this" to ask her husband, the king, to protect her people. Not only did Esther surrender, saying, "If I must die, I must die," she joined with others (belonging), asking those near and far to fast and pray with her. And then she *became*, as she stepped into the king's presence unbidden. She demonstrated the believe–belong–become pattern in its fullness! But like others who have walked this path, she didn't stop at just one act of courage. She pressed on. She kept talking with the king until her people were spared and those who wanted to destroy them were punished (Esther 5:1–9:19). She kept using her voice, becoming who God made her to be. Not only did she likely become more fully alive, but she multiplied her impact—allowing the Jews of Persia to live and thrive.

| EXPERIENCE 5 | SURFACE YOUR "YES, BUT" HESITATION STORY |

There's a lengthy list of people in the Bible who believed God and lived out his purposes. But sometimes we tell ourselves, "That's for Bible heroes, not me." Not true! You are also a hero in God's story, for God's purpose. We have met each of these women listed below in the believe–belong–become stories from the Bible. You can read more about them here (Hagar, page 25; Mary, page 1275; Esther, page 597). Then use their examples to reflect on your own story.

	BELIEVE *God is enough*	**BELONG** *Serve in community*	**BECOME** *Step into a daring calling*	**BUT** *I wouldn't, because*
Hagar	Hagar believed God cared about her, even though she was mistreated by Abraham and Sarah: "You are the God who sees me." **GENESIS 16:13**	Hagar returned to Abraham and Sarah's household and might have stayed if Sarah had not begged to send her away. She and Ishmael wandered into the desert, expecting to die. But God showed Hagar she still belonged. **GENESIS 21:17**	Hagar became the mother of a nation through her son, Ishmael. God blessed her faithfulness too. **GENESIS 21:18**	I'm not a person enslaved and forced to have my enslaver's child.
Mary	Mary believed that the terrifying announcement that she'd be the mother of the Messiah was actually good news. **LUKE 1:38**	Mary sought out Elizabeth, her relative who was in a similar situation. Together, the women found joy in their callings. **LUKE 1:43, 46**	Mary treasured God's gift and role for her and shared the news with Elizabeth. **LUKE 1:48**	I'm not God's mom, or even "good enough" to be God's mom (just ask my kids).
Esther	Esther believed that God would save the Jewish people with or without her. **ESTHER 4:14**	Esther listened to her cousin, Mordecai, as he guided her. She listened to the eunuch who also advised her. She showed a pattern of gaining strength in relationships. **ESTHER 4:15-16**	Esther risked her life by going before King Xerxes, but God used her obedience to stop the slaughter of her people. **ESTHER 4:16**	I'm not as beautiful or desirable as Esther must have been, much less a queen!
You	How did you come to believe God?	What was the crucial moment when you knew you needed to live out your faith? Who did you lean on? Who did you serve?	What action did you take? (Perhaps draw how this made you feel.)	What reason do you tell yourself that you could never, ever do something as significant as these Bible women did? How did telling yourself that make you feel?

| EXPERIENCE 6 | HOW DO YOU FIND COURAGE TO BECOME? |

Take a moment to reflect: Identify one feeling or need that you hold on to, some way you think you are not enough or that God is not enough as you face your next step. I struggle with God's love being enough. Your question might be one of these: Is his forgiveness enough? Is his provision enough? Is his protection enough? You may wonder if you are enough to conquer your need or satisfy that feeling. The Bible is pretty clear on the answer to that: You're not. But God is. God is enough.

But for right now, I want you to imagine holding that fear in your hand. Hold it tight, just like it holds you (in the next experience we'll bring that feeling, need, or question to God).

Get inspired by others who moved from doubt to daring. Take a look at the list of the Come Close articles (see page 1678) and read a few that might resonate with you. Each provides a Bible-based account of a person moving from where they started to God's better place.

| EXPERIENCE 7 | BRING YOUR FEELINGS TO GOD AND BECOME |

Only some emotions move us to action. Other emotions make us stuck. Emotion involves movement—the two even share the same Latin root word movere, *which means "to move" or "to stir." Action slows when we believe stories that evoke inertia, fear, self-doubt, isolation, and apathy. Action springs from stories of urgency, hope, solidarity, and anger. Stories that remind us "God can help me make a difference" mobilize us to do just that.*

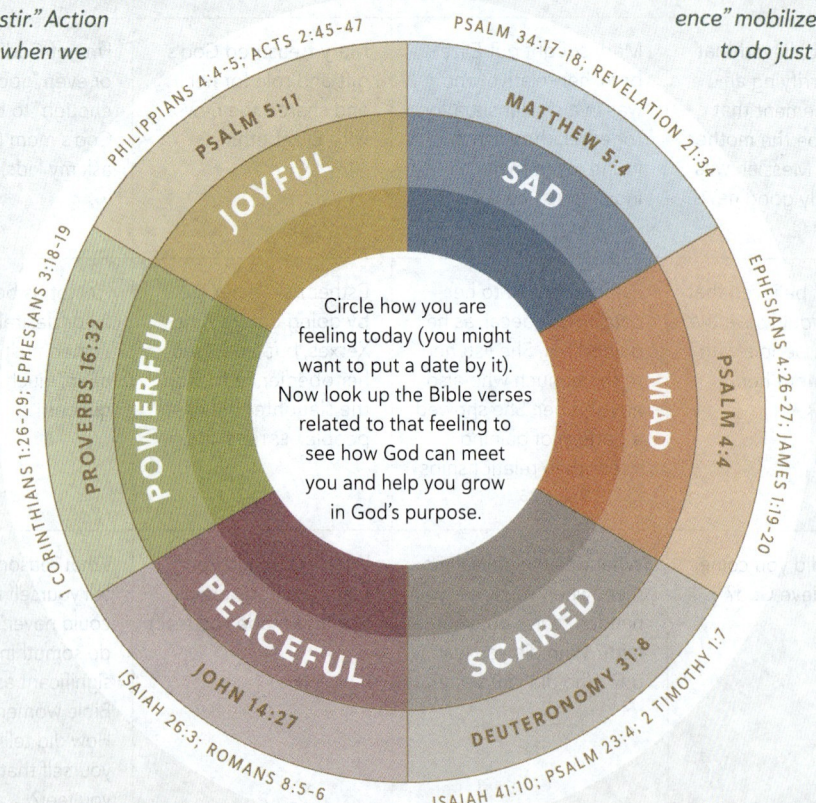

EXPERIENCE 8 | WHAT INSIGHTS DO YOU NEED IN ORDER TO BECOME?

What is one question you haven't wanted to ask aloud about the Bible or God? Sometimes, especially as women in faith communities, we feel unsure about who to go to with our questions. We want to honor God, and we know we're made to glorify God, but many of us lack role models or women who are a little further ahead on this journey. Or we don't have men in our lives who can resonate with the questions we have.

If you think about following God into his purpose for you and then feel a "yeah, but..." coming on, you know what I mean. Sometimes we hide our questions, wrongly thinking that asking them shows a lack of faith. But God gave us brains that form questions. We are to love him with all our minds (Matthew 22:36-38). The Perspective articles (turn to page 1680 for a full list) address top questions women have about the Bible.

Go ahead and write your questions in the space provided here or in a journal or on a piece of paper. Consider using different colored pens for each question or topic that represents certain feelings these questions evoke.

When we created the Perspective articles in this Bible, we were thinking of exactly this predicament. The Bible is a complex story written in cultures most of us have not studied. So we asked biblical scholars and experts to illuminate passages that some are quick to write off with pat answers. We wanted to focus on questions women readers might want to ask.

Glance at the questions you wrote, and then turn to page 1680 to see which of the Perspective articles may answer them. You'll surely have more questions when you're done, but we chose these passages after researching which parts of the Bible many women struggle with. We hope they help you on your road to greater understanding and love of God's Word.

EXPERIENCE 9 | REFRAMING NEGATIVE THOUGHTS WITH GOD'S WORD

Our thoughts drive our feelings, and our feelings drive action. So living our God-given purpose means asking God to refine how we think. Some call this exercise reframing, and we see it aplenty in the Bible.

You learned a bit about Hagar's, Mary's, and Esther's stories in Experience 5. Now let's see how Hagar, Mary, and Esther left behind their own negative thoughts to embrace God's positive ones. And how that led them to action that produced good for others. Then consider how you can do the same.

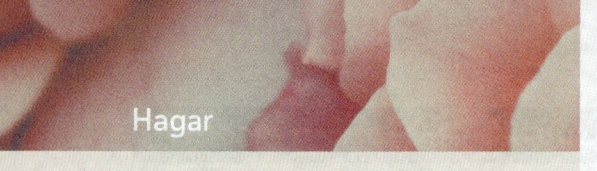

Hagar

SITUATION: GENESIS 21:8-21 Hagar is sent away after she makes the mistake of ridiculing Sarah's son, Isaac. Her son almost dies but is rescued by God.

POSSIBLE THOUGHT *My son and I are still roaming the desert—his life is saved, but where will we go now? We are doomed!*

GOD'S PROMISE God sees Hagar in her distress **GENESIS 16:7-14** and hears her son's cries **GENESIS 21:17** God promises Hagar that she would have many descendants **GENESIS 16:10; 21:18**

REFINED & REFRAMED Hagar is comforted. She may have reminded herself, *He knows our situation.*

ACTION Hagar takes heart, possibly thinking something like, *I will press on, believing that God sees even me, a servant, and hears my son, the less wanted one. He will care for us when others do not.*

Mary

SITUATION: LUKE 1:26-38 Mary is visited by an angel and told she will conceive and give birth to the Son of God.

POSSIBLE THOUGHT *Everyone is going to judge me, and I might be killed. At the very least, the man I was supposed to marry will reject me, and I will be single and poor forever.*

GOD'S PROMISE The angel reassures Mary that she has found favor with God and that her son will reign forever **LUKE 1:30-33**

REFINED & REFRAMED Mary may have comforted herself with this reminder: *The Lord has shown me his favor.* **SEE LUKE 1:30**

ACTION "I am the Lord's servant. May everything you have said about me come true." **LUKE 1:38**

Esther

SITUATION: ESTHER 4:1-9 Esther is told that her people are going to be destroyed and that she should speak up to stop it.

POSSIBLE THOUGHT *The king hasn't asked for me for thirty days (and has likely been sleeping with other wives). He could kill someone who goes to speak to him without invitation.*

GOD'S PROMISE God will deliver his people. "Perhaps you were made queen for just such a time as this." **ESTHER 4:14**

REFINED & REFRAMED Esther said, "Though it is against the law, I will go in to see the king. If I must die, I must die." **ESTHER 4:16**

ACTION Esther asked people to fast with her **ESTHER 4:16** She prepared banquets for the king and spoke up. **ESTHER 5:1-8; 7:1-6**

You

WHAT IS A SITUATION YOU'RE FACING?

POSSIBLE THOUGHT What is the negative thought you're having?

GOD'S PROMISE What has God promised you? Or what are some verses about God's promises you can meditate on? (If you need some help getting started, check out verses associated with the Come Close articles, page 1678.)

REFINED & REFRAMED What's a reframed, or more helpful, thought you can think instead?

ACTION What do you need to do now?

START WHERE YOU ARE: Enter Your Purpose-Story

While finding my purpose in God's purpose, my story in God's story, I've learned this:

It's about *believing* God is enough by learning his Word, praying and trusting him enough that I can act. It's about *belonging* by leaning on and serving others. These practices of believing and belonging lead to *becoming* what God invites us each, uniquely, to be and do in his amazing purposes of making everyone and everything new.

Where are you right now with God in living your story?

These final experiences will help you identify your next steps on the path of your purpose-story.

EXPERIENCE 10 — FIND YOUR CONFIDENCE AND YOUR NEXT STEP

Probably the biggest surprise to me about this process is that we do not think our way to purpose. We act our way to purpose. So, sister, as you identify your own believe–belong–become story, that means taking one next step. It's okay if it's a teeny-tiny step. Mine was. And Hagar, Mary, and Esther literally took one physical step at a time as they moved into God's story. Hagar stepped homeward. Mary stepped toward Elizabeth's house. Esther stepped toward her maids, to go pray and fast together. What is your next step?

	BELIEVE	BELONG	BECOME	BABY STEP
Me	God's presence is with me, no matter what. I recalled how good God had been in other areas of my life.	I prayed over my sense of calling with my community.	I resigned from an important job but found God blessed me and cares for me in every season.	I started praying and fasting each Friday until pizza and movie night at 5 p.m. I took the next step confident I was under God's care. ROMANS 8:28-39
You	What leads you to believe God is enough? (You might look back at the Believe section again.)	Who do you need to draw close to who can help you serve God? Who can you serve now?	What is one next step you sense Scripture, wise counsel, and God's Spirit calling you to take?	What is that initial step you need to take? What Bible verse or story gives you confidence to act?

EXPERIENCE 11 | IDENTIFY YOUR NEXT STEP

See the chart below that shows stages of growth in your story. Circle where you feel you are now, and then ask these questions.

What is one action you long to take?

Who is one person you can ask to pray for you as you begin to live out your purpose?

How will you celebrate when you take this step?

Believe

We come to trust God and feel we can, and must, bless others.

"God has a good purpose for me."

"I can make a difference."

"I must do something."

Step: I will believe God's love is enough, and then act on this belief.

Belong

We invest in four core relationships to grow in and live out our faith.

Discover a vision for living our God-given purpose.

Get closer to others who share this purpose.

Get to know and serve one person in need.

Step: I will commit to give my time and money for these people.

Become

We step into our purpose and help others do the same.

Accept a task or a challenge.

Learn more about how to make an impact.

Make acting on our God-given purpose part of our regular life.

Step: I will ask God to show me who I can help to discover their purpose and invite them to live it.

Living the spectacular story that God has for us is a process. Sometimes we take a step forward, and sometimes we take a step back. Saying yes to God, though, creates lasting good. It allows us to live out our part in God's rescue and restoration mission, our unique *how*. Through these practices God dwells in our ordinary moments, coloring them extraordinary.

EXPERIENCE 12 | BRING TO LIFE YOUR STORY'S COVER!

Whether you decided to follow God's call just now, years ago, or one day you don't remember, that decision began your extraordinary God-story. You have now walked through three practices to discover your purpose in God's purpose. And now you can create a story cover to celebrate!

In the thumbnail spaces below, draw some ideas for a cover design. Consider using colors that mean vibrant life to you, images that symbolize your next step, and then consider sharing your story with someone you trust who can walk alongside you as you follow Jesus.

COME WITH US

YOU ARE NEVER ALONE IN LIVING YOUR PURPOSE

Dear sister, it can be lonely and scary to discern and live out your unique purpose in God's story. Remember that in God, we are never alone.

As I invite you to pray this prayer and take your next step, I also want to encourage you to reach out to a trusted friend or advisor to talk about your story and your next steps with God. Help another person live their part in God's purpose by allowing them to pray with you for your next step. And encourage someone else with what God is showing you! Let's close by praying together.

DEAR GOD,

We know that you cause everything to work together for the good of those who love you, who have been called according to your purpose. If you are for us, who can be against us?

Strengthen us by your Holy Spirit to put on our purpose in your purpose, to write the lines of our story in your story, knowing nothing can ever separate us from your love.

Help us believe your heart of love. Replace our doubts and our lists of how we aren't good enough with your truth. Show us who can help us belong to you and live out our faith. And set our feet to take those baby steps of faith, to become part of your restoring-all-things mission.

IN JESUS' NAME WE PRAY, AMEN.

Matthew

WHAT DO WE LEARN ABOUT GOD'S MISSION AND OURS?
Jesus has the power to save us because he is the everlasting King.

WHO WROTE IT? Matthew (also known as Levi), a former tax collector and one of Jesus' twelve disciples.

WHEN DID IT HAPPEN? Matthew likely wrote this book between AD 65 and 80. Jesus' birth and the events of his life described by Matthew took place during the first three decades of the first century AD.

HOW IS IT ORGANIZED?

- **1–4:** Jesus born to Mary, baptized by John, and prepares for ministry
- **5–7:** Jesus preaches the Sermon on the Mount in Galilee
- **8–12:** Jesus preaches and heals throughout Galilee
- **13:** Jesus teaches about God's Kingdom using parables
- **14–18:** Jesus performs miracles, reveals he is the Messiah, and teaches on community
- **19–20:** Jesus preaches as he travels to Jerusalem
- **21–27:** Jesus teaches during his final week on earth, goes on trial, and dies
- **28:** Jesus rises from the dead and gives parting instructions to his disciples

Words to Remember are highlighted throughout this book

HOW LONG DOES IT TAKE TO READ?

2:00
:30 1:00 1:30 2:00 2:30 3:00 3:30

Timeline

BC

- **37** — HEROD THE GREAT BEGINS TO RULE AS KING OVER PALESTINE
- **7/6** — ELIZABETH AND ZECHARIAH CONCEIVE JOHN THE BAPTIST; MARY CONCEIVES JESUS BY GOD'S SPIRIT
- **6/5** — JESUS, MARY'S CHILD AND THE SON OF GOD, IS BORN
- **5/4** — MARY, JOSEPH, AND JESUS ESCAPE TO EGYPT
- **4** — HEROD THE GREAT DIES
- **4/3** — JESUS' FAMILY RETURNS TO NAZARETH

AD

- **6** — JUDEA BECOMES A ROMAN PROVINCE
- **6/7** — YOUNG JESUS VISITS THE TEMPLE
- **14** — TIBERIUS CAESAR BECOMES EMPEROR OF ROME
- **26** — PONTIUS PILATE APPOINTED GOVERNOR IN JUDEA; JOHN THE BAPTIST'S MINISTRY BEGINS
- **27** — JESUS BEGINS HIS PUBLIC MINISTRY
- **28** — JOHN BAPTIZES JESUS; JESUS CHOOSES TWELVE DISCIPLES
- **29** — JESUS FEEDS OVER 5,000 PEOPLE, INCLUDING WOMEN AND CHILDREN
- **30** — JESUS CRUCIFIED, RISES FROM THE DEAD, AND ASCENDS TO HEAVEN

MATTHEW 1

The Ancestors of Jesus the Messiah

1 This is a record of the ancestors of Jesus the Messiah, a descendant of David and of Abraham*:

2 Abraham was the father of Isaac.
Isaac was the father of Jacob.
Jacob was the father of Judah and his brothers.
3 Judah was the father of Perez and Zerah (whose mother was Tamar).
Perez was the father of Hezron.
Hezron was the father of Ram.*
4 Ram was the father of Amminadab.
Amminadab was the father of Nahshon.
Nahshon was the father of Salmon.
5 Salmon was the father of Boaz (whose mother was Rahab).
Boaz was the father of Obed (whose mother was Ruth).
Obed was the father of Jesse.
6 Jesse was the father of King David.
David was the father of Solomon (whose mother was Bathsheba, the widow of Uriah).
7 Solomon was the father of Rehoboam.
Rehoboam was the father of Abijah.
Abijah was the father of Asa.*
8 Asa was the father of Jehoshaphat.
Jehoshaphat was the father of Jehoram.*
Jehoram was the father* of Uzziah.
9 Uzziah was the father of Jotham.
Jotham was the father of Ahaz.
Ahaz was the father of Hezekiah.
10 Hezekiah was the father of Manasseh.
Manasseh was the father of Amon.*
Amon was the father of Josiah.
11 Josiah was the father of Jehoiachin* and his brothers (born at the time of the exile to Babylon).
12 After the Babylonian exile:
Jehoiachin was the father of Shealtiel.
Shealtiel was the father of Zerubbabel.
13 Zerubbabel was the father of Abiud.
Abiud was the father of Eliakim.
Eliakim was the father of Azor.
14 Azor was the father of Zadok.
Zadok was the father of Akim.
Akim was the father of Eliud.
15 Eliud was the father of Eleazar.
Eleazar was the father of Matthan.
Matthan was the father of Jacob.
16 Jacob was the father of Joseph, the husband of Mary.
Mary gave birth to Jesus, who is called the Messiah.

17 All those listed above include fourteen generations from Abraham to David, fourteen from David to the Babylonian exile, and fourteen from the Babylonian exile to the Messiah.

The Birth of Jesus the Messiah

18 This is how Jesus the Messiah was born. His mother, Mary, was engaged to be married to Joseph. But before the marriage took place, while she was still a virgin, she became pregnant through the power of the Holy Spirit. 19 Joseph, to whom she was engaged, was a righteous man and did not want to disgrace her publicly, so he decided to break the engagement* quietly.

20 As he considered this, an angel of the Lord appeared to him in a dream. "Joseph, son of David," the angel said, "do not be afraid to take Mary as your wife. For the child within her was conceived by the Holy Spirit. 21 And she will have a son, and you are to name him Jesus,* for he will save his people from their sins."

22 All of this occurred to fulfill the Lord's message through his prophet:

1:1 Greek *Jesus the Messiah, Son of David and son of Abraham.* **1:3** Greek *Aram,* a variant spelling of Ram; also in 1:4. See 1 Chr 2:9-10. **1:7** Greek *Asaph,* a variant spelling of Asa; also in 1:8. See 1 Chr 3:10. **1:8a** Greek *Joram,* a variant spelling of Jehoram; also in 1:8b. See 1 Kgs 22:50 and note at 1 Chr 3:11. **1:8b** Or *ancestor;* also in 1:11. **1:10** Greek *Amos,* a variant spelling of Amon; also in 1:10b. See 1 Chr 3:14. **1:11** Greek *Jeconiah,* a variant spelling of Jehoiachin; also in 1:12. See 2 Kgs 24:6 and note at 1 Chr 3:16. **1:19** Greek *to divorce her.* **1:21** *Jesus* means "The LORD saves."

1:2-6 Jesus' genealogy mentions four women from the Old Testament: Tamar (Genesis 38:6-30), Rahab (Joshua 2:1-21; 6:22-25), Ruth (Ruth 1:1–4:22), and Bathsheba (2 Samuel 11:1-27; 1 Kings 1:11-22). They were once associated with sex scandals, voluntarily or involuntarily, but now are remembered and honored as the Messiah's ancestral mothers. These four women are also Gentiles or closely associated with Gentiles, and so they signal that God's mission in Jesus is expanding beyond Israel to include all nations (see Matthew 28:19). These women's inclusion in the Messiah's genealogy should provide hope for women who feel ashamed of their past or are outcast because of their origins. In Christ, God cleanses all our shame and brings us into his family.
1:5 Rahab was the Gentile prostitute who risked her life to hide Joshua's two spies in Jericho (Joshua 2:1-21). Her inclusion in Jesus' genealogy emphasizes God's plan to bring the nations into his family. Elsewhere in the New Testament she is commended for her faith and her right actions (Hebrews 11:31; James 2:25).
1:18 "Jesus the Messiah" could also be translated "Jesus Christ." *Christ* is the English transliteration of the Greek word *christos,* which means "anointed one" or "Messiah." Using *Messiah* in the translation accurately communicates that it is a title rather than a personal name.
1:18 In Judaism, engagement (sometimes called betrothal) meant a permanent relationship that could be broken only by legal process; thus, Mary and Joseph were considered husband and wife (see 1:20; Deuteronomy 22:23-24), even though they were not living together yet and had not had sex. Mary's virginal conception of Jesus "through the power of the Holy Spirit" helps verify Jesus' divine origin as God's Son.

JESUS' UNNAMED Grandmothers

IDENTITY — Releasing to Rejoice

Jesus' grandmothers remember...

Plans. Looking back, we had such lovely plans for our children's lives. We would be grandmothers someday.

But first Mary and Joseph would have a happy engagement, and blessing would flow from our families and the community. Household gifts, fabrics from our looms, cherished recipes, marriage secrets—how we looked forward to celebrating!

We could picture their beautiful children sitting on our knees and cuddling, holding our hands as we walked to the synagogue. We would teach our grandchildren how to pray to the God of their mother and father, grandmothers and grandfathers.

Our plans were wonderful. But then came the threat: Mary was pregnant but not married. Joseph was not the father. We hadn't planned for shame.

We also hadn't planned for God to save the world through our grandchild Jesus. To us, he was the baby we sang lullabies to, the toddler we carried, the young boy who amazed us with his teaching.

Yes, God changed things. But he gave us so much more than our wonderful but predictable plans.

He gave us Jesus. He gave us salvation. Our grandson Jesus was God's gift to our world. He was the fulfillment of prophecy—a plan God put in place centuries ago. And, once we released our plans, we rejoiced. We were part of this amazing act of God.

> God's plans are more perfect than our predictable ones.

JESUS' GRANDMOTHERS' STORY IS DRAWN FROM THE HISTORICAL CONTEXT OF MATTHEW 1:18-25.

IDENTIFY

What plans have you made that fell through? How did God fill that gap?

What did you need to do to release that plan so you could rejoice in God's better one?

"When life gets messy, when we are dealing with disappointment, when doors slam in our faces, when our plans fail—God acts on our behalf to make amazing things happen."

VALERIE BELL is an author of several books on children, including *RESILIENT: Child Discipleship and the Fearless Future of the Church*. Valerie serves as Awana's CEO emerita and 2050 vision caster.

Insight: JESUS' FAMILY TREE

Jesus' genealogies appear in Matthew 1:1-17 and Luke 3:23-38 and make the case that Jesus was a likely candidate for the Messiah based on his lineage. The Bible's genealogies are selective, not exhaustive, and were included to prove a particular point. By tracing Jesus' genealogy through David and back to Abraham, Matthew was proving that Jesus is a legitimate heir to David's throne. Luke traces Jesus' genealogy back to Adam to emphasize that Jesus is the Savior of the world.

While these genealogies focus on fathers and sons, Matthew names several important women, and we can identify other mothers from the Old Testament.

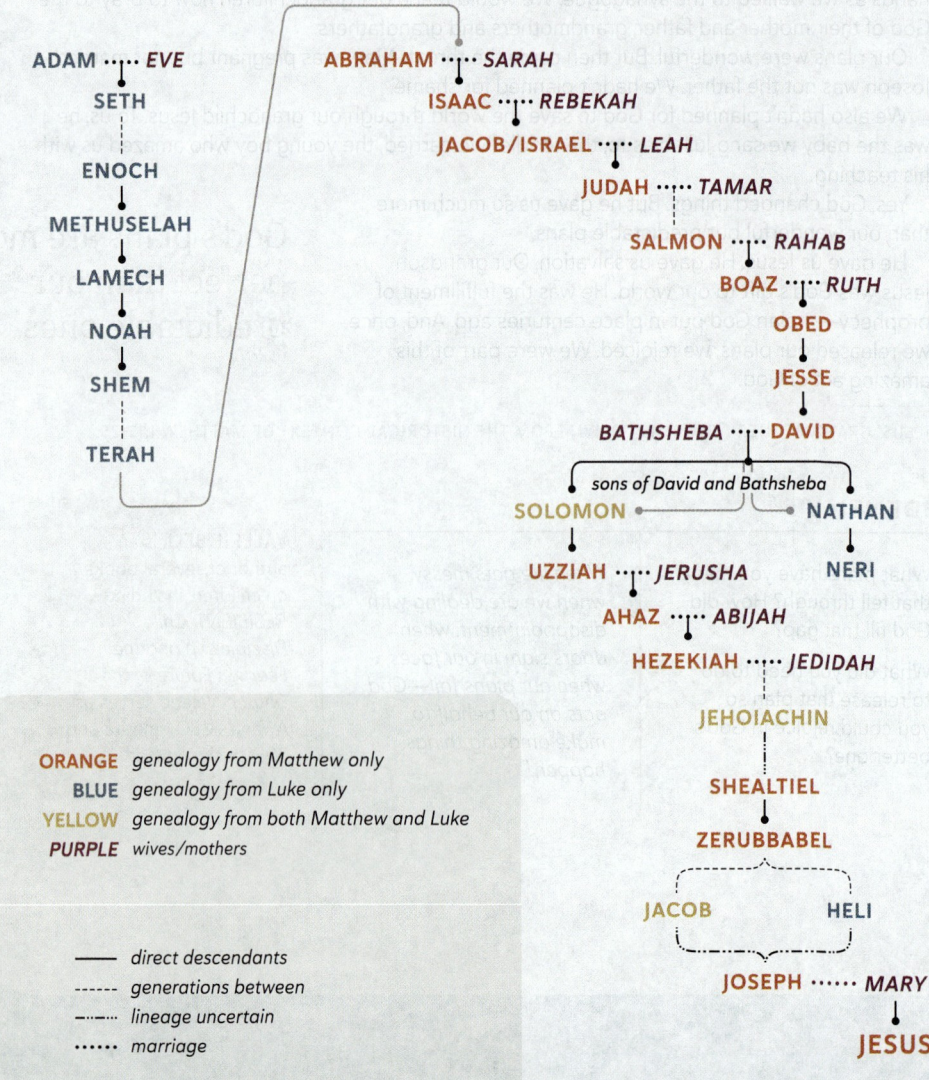

ORANGE genealogy from Matthew only
BLUE genealogy from Luke only
YELLOW genealogy from both Matthew and Luke
PURPLE wives/mothers

—— direct descendants
- - - generations between
-··- lineage uncertain
····· marriage

²³ "Look! The virgin will conceive a child!
She will give birth to a son,
and they will call him Immanuel,*
which means 'God is with us.'"

²⁴When Joseph woke up, he did as the angel of the Lord commanded and took Mary as his wife. ²⁵But he did not have sexual relations with her until her son was born. And Joseph named him Jesus.

Visitors from the East

2 Jesus was born in Bethlehem in Judea, during the reign of King Herod. About that time some wise men* from eastern lands arrived in Jerusalem, asking, ²"Where is the newborn king of the Jews? We saw his star as it rose,* and we have come to worship him."

³King Herod was deeply disturbed when he heard this, as was everyone in Jerusalem. ⁴He called a meeting of the leading priests and teachers of religious law and asked, "Where is the Messiah supposed to be born?"

⁵"In Bethlehem in Judea," they said, "for this is what the prophet wrote:

⁶ 'And you, O Bethlehem in the land of Judah,
are not least among the ruling cities* of Judah,
for a ruler will come from you
who will be the shepherd for my people Israel.'*"

⁷Then Herod called for a private meeting with the wise men, and he learned from them the time when the star first appeared. ⁸Then he told them, "Go to Bethlehem and search carefully for the child. And when you find him, come back and tell me so that I can go and worship him, too!"

⁹After this interview the wise men went their way. And the star they had seen in the east guided them to Bethlehem. It went ahead of them and stopped over the place where the child was. ¹⁰When they saw the star, they were filled with joy! ¹¹They entered the house and saw the child with his mother, Mary, and they bowed down and worshiped him. Then they opened their treasure chests and gave him gifts of gold, frankincense, and myrrh.

¹²When it was time to leave, they returned to their own country by another route, for God had warned them in a dream not to return to Herod.

The Escape to Egypt

¹³After the wise men were gone, an angel of the Lord appeared to Joseph in a dream. "Get up! Flee to Egypt with the child and his mother," the angel said. "Stay there until I tell you to return, because Herod is going to search for the child to kill him."

¹⁴That night Joseph left for Egypt with the child and Mary, his mother, ¹⁵and they stayed there until Herod's death. This fulfilled what the Lord had spoken through the prophet: "I called my Son out of Egypt."*

¹⁶Herod was furious when he realized that the wise men had outwitted him. He sent soldiers to kill all the boys in and around Bethlehem who were two years old and under, based on the wise men's report of the star's first appearance. ¹⁷Herod's brutal action fulfilled what God had spoken through the prophet Jeremiah:

¹⁸ "A cry was heard in Ramah—
weeping and great mourning.
Rachel weeps for her children,
refusing to be comforted,
for they are dead."*

The Return to Nazareth

¹⁹When Herod died, an angel of the Lord appeared in a dream to Joseph in Egypt. ²⁰"Get up!" the angel said. "Take the child and his mother back to the land of Israel, because those who were trying to kill the child are dead."

²¹So Joseph got up and returned to the land of Israel with Jesus and his mother. ²²But when he learned that the new ruler of Judea was Herod's son Archelaus, he was afraid to go there. Then, after being warned in a dream, he left for the region of Galilee. ²³So the family went and lived in a town called Nazareth. This fulfilled what the prophets had said: "He will be called a Nazarene."

John the Baptist Prepares the Way

3 In those days John the Baptist came to the Judean wilderness and began preaching. His message was, ²"Repent of your sins and turn to God, for the Kingdom of Heaven is near.*" ³The prophet Isaiah was speaking about John when he said,

"He is a voice shouting in the wilderness,
'Prepare the way for the LORD's coming!
Clear the road for him!'"*

1:23 Isa 7:14; 8:8, 10 (Greek version). 2:1 Or *royal astrologers;* Greek reads *magi;* also in 2:7, 16. 2:2 Or *star in the east.* 2:6a Greek *the rulers.* 2:6b Mic 5:2; 2 Sam 5:2. 2:15 Hos 11:1. 2:18 Jer 31:15. 3:2 Or *has come,* or *is coming soon.* 3:3 Isa 40:3 (Greek version).

2:16-18 Matthew links Herod's massacre of Bethlehem's baby boys to Israel's exile by quoting Jeremiah 31:15 and invites his readers to find hope in God's future despite human tragedy. In Jeremiah's context, Nebuchadnezzar's army had gathered the Judean captives at Ramah before taking them away to Babylon. Jeremiah imagined that Rachel (one of the people of Israel's ancestral mothers, whose burial place was Ramah) wept from her grave at this tragedy. Jeremiah also prophesied that hope would return in the future when the exiles' children returned to their land (Jeremiah 31:16-17).

2:16 Herod the Great was notorious for his viciousness—for example, he killed his own son for fear of a coup, which led people to say, "It is safer to be Herod's swine [Greek *hus*] than his son [Greek *huios*]," (Herod would not have killed a pig because he kept the Jewish dietary laws). Herod calculated the probable age of the child (two years old and under) from the wise men's report.

⁴John's clothes were woven from coarse camel hair, and he wore a leather belt around his waist. For food he ate locusts and wild honey. ⁵People from Jerusalem and from all of Judea and all over the Jordan Valley went out to see and hear John. ⁶And when they confessed their sins, he baptized them in the Jordan River.

⁷But when he saw many Pharisees and Sadducees coming to watch him baptize,* he denounced them. "You brood of snakes!" he exclaimed. "Who warned you to flee the coming wrath? ⁸Prove by the way you live that you have repented of your sins and turned to God. ⁹Don't just say to each other, 'We're safe, for we are descendants of Abraham.' That means nothing,

3:7 Or *coming to be baptized.*

MY STORY WITH FAMILY & FRIENDS

We're All Blended Family

SCRIPTURE CONNECTION: MATTHEW 1:18–2:23

God created people to need other people. Family is his way of modeling the answer to this need. Sometimes family is born, and sometimes it is chosen.

I love that Joseph isn't Jesus' biological father. It doesn't diminish his role. It doesn't dismiss his responsibility. It doesn't deny his relationship.

Right there, with God in human flesh, we glimpse a blended family.

Yes, most often, family ties are established by birth. But do you know what delights God? God loves to see people choose people. I think God cheers when we embrace others, regardless of how they are related to us. Just as Joseph shared fully in all of his chosen fatherhood. He said yes to the anticipation, the risk, the revelation, the joy, the celebration, the challenge, the changes.

Love is like that. Whether by blood or blended, love is always our choice to make, and love inevitably brings both blessings and burdens. God offers us a place in his family and then asks us to make room for others, too.

> When we belong to God, we make room for others, too.

God's definition of family will challenge us. Jesus had family in those who traveled with him, and he also found his home at the Temple (Luke 2:49). Later in his ministry, he broadened the family's definition by saying, "Anyone who does the will of my Father in heaven is my brother and sister and mother!" (Matthew 12:50).

And what does God want us to do? Just a few chapters later, Jesus frames it in the simplest possible terms: Love God and love others (22:37-40). Those are the most important commandments for God's blended family.

IMAGINE

In what ways has love been both blessing and burden in your life?

How does God refresh you to love people like family when you feel "out of love"?

"As a mom and stepmom to nine, and founder of a ministry for single moms, I've seen many forms of family. Love is the key to God's big, blended, beautiful family."

SUZY SHEPHERD is the founder of SHINE, creator of Stonecroft's Where Love Lives outreach experience, and mom to a blended tribe of nine. She finds great joy in creating experiences for people to know God's love.

for I tell you, God can create children of Abraham from these very stones. ¹⁰Even now the ax of God's judgment is poised, ready to sever the roots of the trees. Yes, every tree that does not produce good fruit will be chopped down and thrown into the fire.

¹¹"I baptize with* water those who repent of their sins and turn to God. But someone is coming soon who is greater than I am—so much greater that I'm not worthy even to be his slave and carry his sandals. He will baptize you with the Holy Spirit and with fire.* ¹²He is ready to separate the chaff from the wheat with his winnowing fork. Then he will clean up the threshing area, gathering the wheat into his barn but burning the chaff with never-ending fire."

The Baptism of Jesus

¹³Then Jesus went from Galilee to the Jordan River to be baptized by John. ¹⁴But John tried to talk him out of it. "I am the one who needs to be baptized by you," he said, "so why are you coming to me?"

¹⁵But Jesus said, "It should be done, for we must carry out all that God requires.*" So John agreed to baptize him.

¹⁶After his baptism, as Jesus came up out of the water, the heavens were opened* and he saw the Spirit of God descending like a dove and settling on him. ¹⁷And a voice from heaven said, "This is my dearly loved Son, who brings me great joy."

The Temptation of Jesus

4 Then Jesus was led by the Spirit into the wilderness to be tempted there by the devil. ²For forty days and forty nights he fasted and became very hungry.

³During that time the devil* came and said to him, "If you are the Son of God, tell these stones to become loaves of bread."

⁴But Jesus told him, "No! The Scriptures say,

'People do not live by bread alone,
    but by every word that comes from the mouth of God.'*"

⁵Then the devil took him to the holy city, Jerusalem, to the highest point of the Temple, ⁶and said, "If you are the Son of God, jump off! For the Scriptures say,

'He will order his angels to protect you.
And they will hold you up with their hands
    so you won't even hurt your foot on a stone.'*"

⁷Jesus responded, "The Scriptures also say, 'You must not test the LORD your God.'*"

⁸Next the devil took him to the peak of a very high mountain and showed him all the kingdoms of the world and their glory. ⁹"I will give it all to you," he said, "if you will kneel down and worship me."

¹⁰"Get out of here, Satan," Jesus told him. "For the Scriptures say,

'You must worship the LORD your God
    and serve only him.'*"

¹¹Then the devil went away, and angels came and took care of Jesus.

The Ministry of Jesus Begins

¹²When Jesus heard that John had been arrested, he left Judea and returned to Galilee. ¹³He went first to Nazareth, then left there and moved to Capernaum, beside the Sea of Galilee, in the region of Zebulun and Naphtali. ¹⁴This fulfilled what God said through the prophet Isaiah:

¹⁵ "In the land of Zebulun and of Naphtali,
    beside the sea, beyond the Jordan River,
    in Galilee where so many Gentiles live,
¹⁶ the people who sat in darkness
    have seen a great light.
And for those who lived in the land where death casts its shadow,
    a light has shined."*

¹⁷From then on Jesus began to preach, "Repent of your sins and turn to God, for the Kingdom of Heaven is near.*"

The First Disciples

¹⁸One day as Jesus was walking along the shore of the Sea of Galilee, he saw two brothers—Simon, also called Peter, and Andrew—throwing a net into the water, for they fished for a living. ¹⁹Jesus called out to them, "Come, follow me, and I will show you how to fish for people!" ²⁰And they left their nets at once and followed him.

²¹A little farther up the shore he saw two other brothers, James and John, sitting in a boat with their father, Zebedee, repairing their nets. And he called them to come, too. ²²They immediately followed him, leaving the boat and their father behind.

Crowds Follow Jesus

²³Jesus traveled throughout the region of Galilee, teaching in the synagogues and announcing the Good News about the Kingdom. And he healed every kind of disease and illness. ²⁴News about him spread as far as Syria, and people soon began bringing to him all who were sick. And whatever their sickness or disease, or if they were demon possessed or epileptic or paralyzed—he healed them all. ²⁵Large crowds followed him wherever he went—people from Galilee, the Ten Towns,* Jerusalem, from all over Judea, and from east of the Jordan River.

3:11a Or *in.* **3:11b** Or *in the Holy Spirit and in fire.* **3:15** Or *for we must fulfill all righteousness.* **3:16** Some manuscripts read *opened to him.* **4:3** Greek *the tempter.* **4:4** Deut 8:3. **4:6** Ps 91:11-12. **4:7** Deut 6:16. **4:10** Deut 6:13. **4:15-16** Isa 9:1-2 (Greek version). **4:17** Or *has come,* or *is coming soon.* **4:25** Greek *Decapolis.*

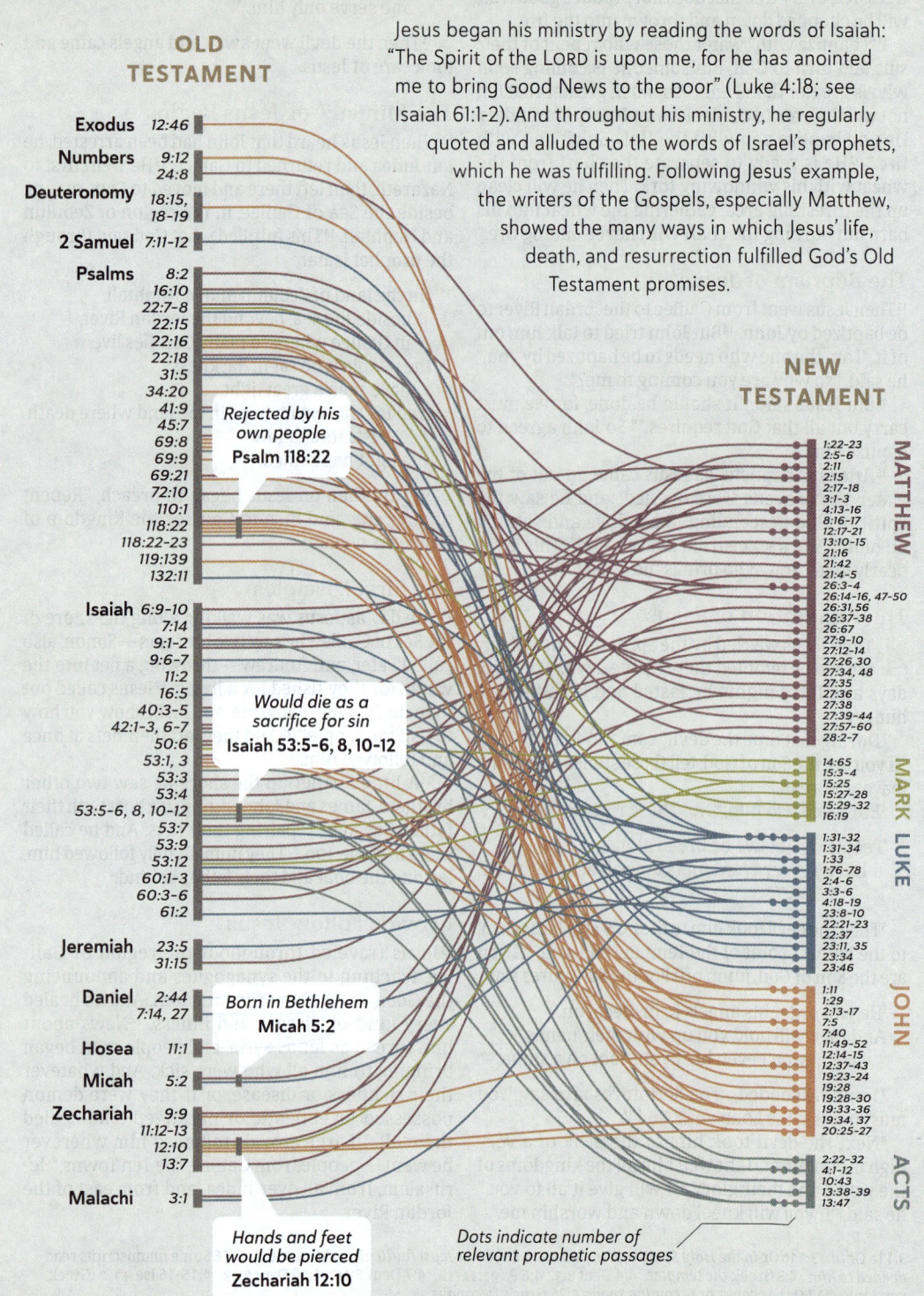

The Sermon on the Mount

5 One day as he saw the crowds gathering, Jesus went up on the mountainside and sat down. His disciples gathered around him, ²and he began to teach them.

The Beatitudes

³ "God blesses those who are poor and realize
 their need for him,*
 for the Kingdom of Heaven is theirs.
⁴ God blesses those who mourn,
 for they will be comforted.
⁵ God blesses those who are humble,
 for they will inherit the whole earth.
⁶ God blesses those who hunger and thirst for
 justice,*
 for they will be satisfied.
⁷ God blesses those who are merciful,
 for they will be shown mercy.
⁸ God blesses those whose hearts are pure,
 for they will see God.
⁹ God blesses those who work for peace,
 for they will be called the children of God.
¹⁰ God blesses those who are persecuted for doing
 right,
 for the Kingdom of Heaven is theirs.

¹¹"God blesses you when people mock you and persecute you and lie about you and say all sorts of evil things against you because you are my followers. ¹²Be happy about it! Be very glad! For a great reward awaits you in heaven. And remember, the ancient prophets were persecuted in the same way.

Teaching about Salt and Light

¹³"You are the salt of the earth. But what good is salt if it has lost its flavor? Can you make it salty again? It will be thrown out and trampled underfoot as worthless.

¹⁴"You are the light of the world—like a city on a hilltop that cannot be hidden. ¹⁵No one lights a lamp and then puts it under a basket. Instead, a lamp is placed on a stand, where it gives light to everyone in the house. ¹⁶In the same way, let your good deeds shine out for all to see, so that everyone will praise your heavenly Father.

Teaching about the Law

¹⁷"Don't misunderstand why I have come. I did not come to abolish the law of Moses or the writings of the prophets. No, I came to accomplish their purpose. ¹⁸I tell you the truth, until heaven and earth disappear, not even the smallest detail of God's law will disappear until its purpose is achieved. ¹⁹So if you ignore the least commandment and teach others to do the same, you will be called the least in the Kingdom of Heaven. But anyone who obeys God's laws and teaches them will be called great in the Kingdom of Heaven.

²⁰"But I warn you—unless your righteousness is better than the righteousness of the teachers of religious law and the Pharisees, you will never enter the Kingdom of Heaven!

Teaching about Anger

²¹"You have heard that our ancestors were told, 'You must not murder. If you commit murder, you are subject to judgment.'* ²²But I say, if you are even angry with someone,* you are subject to judgment! If you call someone an idiot,* you are in danger of being brought before the court. And if you curse someone,* you are in danger of the fires of hell.*

²³"So if you are presenting a sacrifice* at the altar in the Temple and you suddenly remember that someone has something against you, ²⁴leave your sacrifice there at the altar. Go and be reconciled to that person. Then come and offer your sacrifice to God.

²⁵"When you are on the way to court with your adversary, settle your differences quickly. Otherwise, your accuser may hand you over to the judge, who will hand you over to an officer, and you will be thrown into prison. ²⁶And if that happens, you surely won't be free again until you have paid the last penny.*

Teaching about Adultery

²⁷"You have heard the commandment that says, 'You must not commit adultery.'* ²⁸But I say, anyone who even looks at a woman with lust has already committed adultery with her in his heart. ²⁹So if your eye—even your good eye*—causes you to lust, gouge it out and throw it away. It is better for you to lose one part of your body than for your whole body to be thrown into hell. ³⁰And if your hand—even your stronger hand*—causes you to sin, cut it off and throw it away. It is better for you to lose one part of your body than for your whole body to be thrown into hell.

5:3 Greek *poor in spirit.* **5:6** Or *for righteousness.* **5:21** Exod 20:13; Deut 5:17. **5:22a** Some manuscripts add *without cause.* **5:22b** Greek uses an Aramaic term of contempt: *If you say to your brother, 'Raca.'* **5:22c** Greek *if you say, 'You fool.'* **5:22d** Greek *Gehenna;* also in 5:29, 30. **5:23** Greek *gift;* also in 5:24. **5:26** Greek *the last kodrantes* [i.e., quadrans]. **5:27** Exod 20:14; Deut 5:18. **5:29** Greek *your right eye.* **5:30** Greek *your right hand.*

5:27-30 Jesus explicitly gave men this call for radical separation from sexual immorality, thus acknowledging that sexual crimes are usually perpetrated by men against women. This language indicates clearly that God holds men accountable to guard their unhealthy sexual lust, rather than holding women accountable for how men may sin. However, Jesus' encouragement to guard against sexual sin also applies to everyone tempted to have sex with anyone other than their spouse at all times and in all places. No one is exempt from the consequences of their wrongdoing.

> "You who raise your voice with your kids. You who are addicted to social media. You who 'retail' your way out of depression.... You with your insecurity, your brokenness, your anxiety, your desperation. You. You are the light of the world."
>
> **REBEKAH LYONS**
> author and cofounder of Q Ideas

Teaching about Divorce

³¹"You have heard the law that says, 'A man can divorce his wife by merely giving her a written notice of divorce.'* ³²But I say that a man who divorces his wife, unless she has been unfaithful, causes her to commit adultery. And anyone who marries a divorced woman also commits adultery.

Teaching about Vows

³³"You have also heard that our ancestors were told, 'You must not break your vows; you must carry out the vows you make to the LORD.'* ³⁴But I say, do not make any vows! Do not say, 'By heaven!' because heaven is God's throne. ³⁵And do not say, 'By the earth!' because the earth is his footstool. And do not say, 'By Jerusalem!' for Jerusalem is the city of the great King. ³⁶Do not even say, 'By my head!' for you can't turn one hair white or black. ³⁷Just say a simple, 'Yes, I will,' or 'No, I won't.' Anything beyond this is from the evil one.

Teaching about Revenge

³⁸"You have heard the law that says the punishment must match the injury: 'An eye for an eye, and a tooth for a tooth.'* ³⁹But I say, do not resist an evil person! If someone slaps you on the right cheek, offer the other cheek also. ⁴⁰If you are sued in court and your shirt is taken from you, give your coat, too. ⁴¹If a soldier demands that you carry his gear for a mile,* carry it two miles. ⁴²Give to those who ask, and don't turn away from those who want to borrow.

Teaching about Love for Enemies

⁴³"You have heard the law that says, 'Love your neighbor'* and hate your enemy. ⁴⁴But I say, love your enemies!* Pray for those who persecute you! ⁴⁵In that way, you will be acting as true children of your Father in heaven. For he gives his sunlight to both the evil and the good, and he sends rain on the just and the unjust alike. ⁴⁶If you love only those who love you, what reward is there for that? Even corrupt tax collectors do that much. ⁴⁷If you are kind only to your friends,* how are you different from anyone else? Even pagans do that. ⁴⁸But you are to be perfect, even as your Father in heaven is perfect.

5:31 Deut 24:1. **5:33** Num 30:2. **5:38** Greek *the law that says: 'An eye for an eye and a tooth for a tooth.'* Exod 21:24; Lev 24:20; Deut 19:21. **5:41** Greek *milion* [4,854 feet or 1,478 meters]. **5:43** Lev 19:18. **5:44** Some manuscripts add *Bless those who curse you. Do good to those who hate you.* Compare Luke 6:27-28. **5:47** Greek *your brothers.*

5:31-32 This passage and Deuteronomy 24:1-4 assume a husband initiating and acquiring a divorce, even though both passages deal with the *aftermath* of a cultural practice rather than advocating it. But the implication is not that only men should initiate divorce. In a male-dominated society, Jesus' restriction protected women from being divorced casually due to their husbands' misapplication of Deuteronomy 24:1-4. We also shouldn't assume that these verses mean that women today cannot initiate a divorce, especially if they need one for cases of abandonment, neglect, adultery, or abuse. Anyone who abandons or abuses their spouse is also guilty of unfaithfulness. **5:31** A notice of divorce was a document stating the legality of a divorce. Evidence from other Jewish writings from this era suggests that such a document permitted women to remarry and may have specified what was financially owed to a woman when her husband divorced her, perhaps the equivalent of her dowry or any other assets she had brought into the marriage. **5:32** The exception stated here permitted but did not demand divorce when one partner "has been unfaithful" (see also 19:9). Notably, Jesus did not demand death for the guilty party (see Deuteronomy 22:21-22). The implication seems to be that by divorcing his wife for biblically illegitimate reasons, the man "causes her to commit adultery" by wrongly putting her in a situation where if she remarried, she would be breaking the law of Moses. But it is not clear whether Jesus was referring to any woman who was divorced, regardless of the reason, or only to a divorced woman who was divorced due to a reason deemed acceptable by Jewish law (for example, unfaithfulness). The underlying assumption in Jewish divorce law was simple: Legitimate divorces permitted remarriage.

Teaching about Giving to the Needy

6 "Watch out! Don't do your good deeds publicly, to be admired by others, for you will lose the reward from your Father in heaven. ²When you give to someone in need, don't do as the hypocrites do—blowing trumpets in the synagogues and streets to call attention to their acts of charity! I tell you the truth, they have received all the reward they will ever get. ³But when you give to someone in need, don't let your left hand know what your right hand is doing. ⁴Give your gifts in private, and your Father, who sees everything, will reward you.

Teaching about Prayer and Fasting

⁵"When you pray, don't be like the hypocrites who love to pray publicly on street corners and in the synagogues where everyone can see them. I tell you the truth, that is all the reward they will ever get. ⁶But when you pray, go away by yourself, shut the door behind you, and pray to your Father in private. Then your Father, who sees everything, will reward you.

⁷"When you pray, don't babble on and on as the Gentiles do. They think their prayers are answered merely by repeating their words again and again. ⁸Don't be like them, for your Father knows exactly what you need even before you ask him! ⁹Pray like this:

> Our Father in heaven,
> may your name be kept holy.
> ¹⁰ May your Kingdom come soon.
> May your will be done on earth,
> as it is in heaven.
> ¹¹ Give us today the food we need,*
> ¹² and forgive us our sins,
> as we have forgiven those who sin against us.
> ¹³ And don't let us yield to temptation,*
> but rescue us from the evil one.*

¹⁴"If you forgive those who sin against you, your heavenly Father will forgive you. ¹⁵But if you refuse to forgive others, your Father will not forgive your sins.

¹⁶"And when you fast, don't make it obvious, as the hypocrites do, for they try to look miserable and disheveled so people will admire them for their fasting. I tell you the truth, that is the only reward they will ever get. ¹⁷But when you fast, comb your hair* and wash your face. ¹⁸Then no one will notice that you are fasting, except your Father, who knows what you do in private. And your Father, who sees everything, will reward you.

Teaching about Money and Possessions

¹⁹"Don't store up treasures here on earth, where moths eat them and rust destroys them, and where thieves break in and steal. ²⁰Store your treasures in heaven, where moths and rust cannot destroy, and thieves do not break in and steal. ²¹Wherever your treasure is, there the desires of your heart will also be.

²²"Your eye is like a lamp that provides light for your body. When your eye is healthy, your whole body is filled with light. ²³But when your eye is unhealthy, your whole body is filled with darkness. And if the light you think you have is actually darkness, how deep that darkness is!

²⁴"No one can serve two masters. For you will hate one and love the other; you will be devoted to one and despise the other. You cannot serve God and be enslaved to money.

²⁵"That is why I tell you not to worry about everyday life—whether you have enough food and drink, or enough clothes to wear. Isn't life more than food, and your body more than clothing? ²⁶Look at the birds. They don't plant or harvest or store food in barns, for your heavenly Father feeds them. And aren't you far more valuable to him than they are? ²⁷Can all your worries add a single moment to your life?

²⁸"And why worry about your clothing? Look at the lilies of the field and how they grow. They don't work or make their clothing, ²⁹yet Solomon in all his glory was not dressed as beautifully as they are. ³⁰And if God cares so wonderfully for wildflowers that are here today and thrown into the fire tomorrow, he will certainly care for you. Why do you have so little faith?

³¹"So don't worry about these things, saying, 'What will we eat? What will we drink? What will we wear?' ³²These things dominate the thoughts of unbelievers, but your heavenly Father already knows all your needs. ³³Seek the Kingdom of God* above all else, and live righteously, and he will give you everything you need.

³⁴"So don't worry about tomorrow, for tomorrow will bring its own worries. Today's trouble is enough for today.

Do Not Judge Others

7 "Do not judge others, and you will not be judged. ²For you will be treated as you treat others.* The standard you use in judging is the standard by which you will be judged.*

6:11 Or *Give us today our food for the day;* or *Give us today our food for tomorrow.* **6:13a** Or *And keep us from being tested.* **6:13b** Or *from evil.* Some manuscripts add *For yours is the kingdom and the power and the glory forever. Amen.* **6:17** Greek *anoint your head.* **6:33** Some manuscripts do not include *of God.* **7:2a** Or *For God will judge you as you judge others.* **7:2b** Or *The measure you give will be the measure you get back.*

7:1 Jesus called for people to stop oppressively controlling others in the name of pastoral concern. Mercy is a dominant theme in Jesus' teaching and practice, but not at the expense of clear opposition to sin. The judgment Jesus prohibited often involves intense scrutiny of trivial matters (for example, 23:23-24). God alone has the right to judge (see James 4:11-12) and measures us by our treatment of others (see Matthew 18:21-35).

WHAT THE BIBLE SAYS ABOUT Forgiveness

Jesus Offers Everyone Forgiveness through His Sacrifice

God's will was for us to be made holy by the sacrifice of the body of Jesus Christ, once for all time.... Our High Priest offered himself to God as a single sacrifice for sins, good for all time.... And when sins have been forgiven, there is no need to offer any more sacrifices. **HEBREWS 10:10, 12, 18**

God presented Jesus as the sacrifice for sin. People are made right with God when they believe that Jesus sacrificed his life, shedding his blood. **ROMANS 3:25**

There is a great difference between Adam's sin and God's gracious gift. For the sin of this one man, Adam, brought death to many. But even greater is God's wonderful grace and his gift of forgiveness to many through this other man, Jesus Christ. **ROMANS 5:15**

"[Jesus] is the one all the prophets testified about, saying that everyone who believes in him will have their sins forgiven through his name." **ACTS 10:43**

For [God the Father] has rescued us from the kingdom of darkness and transferred us into the Kingdom of his dear Son, who purchased our freedom and forgave our sins.
COLOSSIANS 1:13-14

I am writing to you who are God's children because your sins have been forgiven through Jesus.
1 JOHN 2:12

Be kind to each other, tenderhearted ...

...forgiving one another...

God Expects Us to Forgive Because We Have Been Forgiven

"If you forgive those who sin against you, your heavenly Father will forgive you. But if you refuse to forgive others, your Father will not forgive your sins." **MATTHEW 6:14-15**

Be kind to each other, tenderhearted, forgiving one another, just as God through Christ has forgiven you. **EPHESIANS 4:32**

Make allowance for each other's faults, and forgive anyone who offends you. Remember, the Lord forgave you, so you must forgive others. **COLOSSIANS 3:13**

God Wants Us to Find Forgiveness

"'There is forgiveness of sins for all who repent.'" **LUKE 24:47**

"Each of you must repent of your sins and turn to God, and be baptized in the name of Jesus Christ for the forgiveness of your sins. Then you will receive the gift of the Holy Spirit." **ACTS 2:38**

If we confess our sins to him, he is faithful and just to forgive us our sins and to cleanse us from all wickedness. **1 JOHN 1:9**

God Forgave Israel through Sacrifices

Moses said to the people, "You have committed a terrible sin, but I will go back up to the Lord on the mountain. Perhaps I will be able to obtain forgiveness for your sin." **EXODUS 32:30**

"Through [a guilt offering], the priest will purify you before the Lord, making you right with him, and you will be forgiven for any of these sins you have committed." **LEVITICUS 6:7**

³"And why worry about a speck in your friend's eye* when you have a log in your own? ⁴How can you think of saying to your friend,* 'Let me help you get rid of that speck in your eye,' when you can't see past the log in your own eye? ⁵Hypocrite! First get rid of the log in your own eye; then you will see well enough to deal with the speck in your friend's eye.

⁶"Don't waste what is holy on people who are unholy.* Don't throw your pearls to pigs! They will trample the pearls, then turn and attack you.

Effective Prayer

⁷"Keep on asking, and you will receive what you ask for. Keep on seeking, and you will find. Keep on knocking, and the door will be opened to you. ⁸For everyone who asks, receives. Everyone who seeks, finds. And to everyone who knocks, the door will be opened.

⁹"You parents—if your children ask for a loaf of bread, do you give them a stone instead? ¹⁰Or if they ask for a fish, do you give them a snake? Of course not! ¹¹So if you sinful people know how to give good gifts to your children, how much more will your heavenly Father give good gifts to those who ask him.

The Golden Rule

¹²"Do to others whatever you would like them to do to you. This is the essence of all that is taught in the law and the prophets.

The Narrow Gate

¹³"You can enter God's Kingdom only through the narrow gate. The highway to hell* is broad, and its gate is wide for the many who choose that way. ¹⁴But the gateway to life is very narrow and the road is difficult, and only a few ever find it.

The Tree and Its Fruit

¹⁵"Beware of false prophets who come disguised as harmless sheep but are really vicious wolves. ¹⁶You can identify them by their fruit, that is, by the way they act. Can you pick grapes from thornbushes, or figs from thistles? ¹⁷A good tree produces good fruit, and a bad tree produces bad fruit. ¹⁸A good tree can't produce bad fruit, and a bad tree can't produce good fruit. ¹⁹So every tree that does not produce good fruit is chopped down and thrown into the fire. ²⁰Yes, just as you can identify a tree by its fruit, so you can identify people by their actions.

True Disciples

²¹"Not everyone who calls out to me, 'Lord! Lord!' will enter the Kingdom of Heaven. Only those who actually do the will of my Father in heaven will enter. ²²On judgment day many will say to me, 'Lord! Lord! We prophesied in your name and cast out demons in your name and performed many miracles in your name.' ²³But I will reply, 'I never knew you. Get away from me, you who break God's laws.'

Building on a Solid Foundation

²⁴"Anyone who listens to my teaching and follows it is wise, like a person who builds a house on solid rock. ²⁵Though the rain comes in torrents and the floodwaters rise and the winds beat against that house, it won't collapse because it is built on bedrock. ²⁶But anyone who hears my teaching and doesn't obey it is foolish, like a person who builds a house on sand. ²⁷When the rains and floods come and the winds beat against that house, it will collapse with a mighty crash."

²⁸When Jesus had finished saying these things, the crowds were amazed at his teaching, ²⁹for he taught with real authority—quite unlike their teachers of religious law.

Jesus Heals a Man with Leprosy

8 Large crowds followed Jesus as he came down the mountainside. ²Suddenly, a man with leprosy approached him and knelt before him. "Lord," the man said, "if you are willing, you can heal me and make me clean."

³Jesus reached out and touched him. "I am willing," he said. "Be healed!" And instantly the leprosy disappeared. ⁴Then Jesus said to him, "Don't tell anyone about this. Instead, go to the priest and let him examine you. Take along the offering required in the law of Moses for those who have been healed of leprosy.* This will be a public testimony that you have been cleansed."

The Faith of a Roman Officer

⁵When Jesus returned to Capernaum, a Roman officer* came and pleaded with him, ⁶"Lord, my young servant* lies in bed, paralyzed and in terrible pain."

7:3 Greek *your brother's eye;* also in 7:5. **7:4** Greek *your brother.* **7:6** Greek *Don't give the sacred to dogs.* **7:13** Greek *The road that leads to destruction.* **8:4** See Lev 14:2-32. **8:5** Greek *a centurion;* similarly in 8:8, 13. **8:6** Or *child;* also in 8:13.

8:1–9:34 Here, Jesus illustrated the nature of the Kingdom of God through his supernatural power (see also 4:23-25; 11:2-6). God's Kingdom was now reaching people previously excluded from the blessing of God: non-Jews, people who had physical illnesses or disabilities, people possessed by demons, tax collectors, those with chronic bleeding, and the dead. Jesus showed compassion, but the religious leaders were provoked to opposition. Jesus called his followers to faith and discipleship.

8:5-13 The centurion was a Roman soldier, and Jesus' ministry to him would have evoked strong resentment from members of Jewish society who especially hated Roman rule. Many Jewish people despised being ruled by non-Jewish people, and foreign rule inspired some to openly protest Roman authority. By healing the servant of a Roman officer, Jesus showed love for the Jewish people's primary enemy at this time (5:43-48).

⁷Jesus said, "I will come and heal him."
⁸But the officer said, "Lord, I am not worthy to have you come into my home. Just say the word from where you are, and my servant will be healed. ⁹I know this because I am under the authority of my superior officers, and I have authority over my soldiers. I only need to say, 'Go,' and they go, or 'Come,' and they come. And if I say to my slaves, 'Do this,' they do it."

¹⁰When Jesus heard this, he was amazed. Turning to those who were following him, he said, "I tell you the truth, I haven't seen faith like this in all Israel! ¹¹And I tell you this, that many Gentiles will come from all over the world—from east and west—and sit down with Abraham, Isaac, and Jacob at the feast in the Kingdom of Heaven. ¹²But many Israelites—those for whom the Kingdom was prepared—will be thrown into outer darkness, where there will be weeping and gnashing of teeth."

¹³Then Jesus said to the Roman officer, "Go back home. Because you believed, it has happened." And the young servant was healed that same hour.

Jesus Heals Many People

¹⁴When Jesus arrived at Peter's house, Peter's mother-in-law was sick in bed with a high fever. ¹⁵But when Jesus touched her hand, the fever left her. Then she got up and prepared a meal for him.

¹⁶That evening many demon-possessed people were brought to Jesus. He cast out the evil spirits with a simple command, and he healed all the sick. ¹⁷This fulfilled the word of the Lord through the prophet Isaiah, who said,

> "He took our sicknesses
>   and removed our diseases."*

The Cost of Following Jesus

¹⁸When Jesus saw the crowd around him, he instructed his disciples to cross to the other side of the lake.

¹⁹Then one of the teachers of religious law said to him, "Teacher, I will follow you wherever you go."

²⁰But Jesus replied, "Foxes have dens to live in, and birds have nests, but the Son of Man* has no place even to lay his head."

²¹Another of his disciples said, "Lord, first let me return home and bury my father."

²²But Jesus told him, "Follow me now. Let the spiritually dead bury their own dead.*"

Jesus Calms the Storm

²³Then Jesus got into the boat and started across the lake with his disciples. ²⁴Suddenly, a fierce storm struck the lake, with waves breaking into the boat. But Jesus was sleeping. ²⁵The disciples went and woke him up, shouting, "Lord, save us! We're going to drown!"

²⁶Jesus responded, "Why are you afraid? You have so little faith!" Then he got up and rebuked the wind and waves, and suddenly there was a great calm.

²⁷The disciples were amazed. "Who is this man?" they asked. "Even the winds and waves obey him!"

Jesus Heals Two Demon-Possessed Men

²⁸When Jesus arrived on the other side of the lake, in the region of the Gadarenes,* two men who were possessed by demons met him. They came out of the tombs and were so violent that no one could go through that area.

²⁹They began screaming at him, "Why are you interfering with us, Son of God? Have you come here to torture us before God's appointed time?"

³⁰There happened to be a large herd of pigs feeding in the distance. ³¹So the demons begged, "If you cast us out, send us into that herd of pigs."

³²"All right, go!" Jesus commanded them. So the demons came out of the men and entered the pigs, and the whole herd plunged down the steep hillside into the lake and drowned in the water.

³³The herdsmen fled to the nearby town, telling everyone what happened to the demon-possessed men. ³⁴Then the entire town came out to meet Jesus, but they begged him to go away and leave them alone.

Jesus Heals a Paralyzed Man

9 Jesus climbed into a boat and went back across the lake to his own town. ²Some people brought to him a paralyzed man on a mat. Seeing their faith, Jesus said to the paralyzed man, "Be encouraged, my child! Your sins are forgiven."

³But some of the teachers of religious law said to themselves, "That's blasphemy! Does he think he's God?"

⁴Jesus knew* what they were thinking, so he asked them, "Why do you have such evil thoughts in your hearts? ⁵Is it easier to say 'Your sins are forgiven,' or 'Stand up and walk'? ⁶So I will prove to you that the

---

8:17 Isa 53:4. **8:20** "Son of Man" is a title Jesus used for himself. **8:22** Greek *Let the dead bury their own dead.* **8:28** Other manuscripts read *Gerasenes*; still others read *Gergesenes.* Compare Mark 5:1; Luke 8:26. **9:4** Some manuscripts read *saw.*

8:11-12 Jesus' message here indicates the potential inclusion of Gentiles and exclusion of some Israelites in relation to the Kingdom of Heaven. Compared with the other synoptic Gospels, Mark and Luke (*synoptic* refers to these three books sharing significant overlap in content and wording), Matthew's Gospel is the most dependent on the context of Israel's history and worship to tell Jesus' story to his readers. Matthew likely sought to assure his non-Jewish readers that Jesus is the Messiah both of Israel and beyond Israel by including Jesus' teaching about this subject here.

MATTHEW 9

Son of Man* has the authority on earth to forgive sins." Then Jesus turned to the paralyzed man and said, "Stand up, pick up your mat, and go home!"

⁷And the man jumped up and went home! ⁸Fear swept through the crowd as they saw this happen. And they praised God for giving humans such authority.

Jesus Calls Matthew

⁹As Jesus was walking along, he saw a man named Matthew sitting at his tax collector's booth. "Follow me and be my disciple," Jesus said to him. So Matthew got up and followed him.

¹⁰Later, Matthew invited Jesus and his disciples to his home as dinner guests, along with many tax collectors and other disreputable sinners. ¹¹But when the Pharisees saw this, they asked his disciples, "Why does your teacher eat with such scum?*"

¹²When Jesus heard this, he said, "Healthy people don't need a doctor—sick people do." ¹³Then he added, "Now go and learn the meaning of this Scripture: 'I want you to show mercy, not offer sacrifices.'* For I have come to call not those who think they are righteous, but those who know they are sinners."

A Discussion about Fasting

¹⁴One day the disciples of John the Baptist came to Jesus and asked him, "Why don't your disciples fast* like we do and the Pharisees do?"

¹⁵Jesus replied, "Do wedding guests mourn while celebrating with the groom? Of course not. But someday the groom will be taken away from them, and then they will fast.

¹⁶"Besides, who would patch old clothing with new cloth? For the new patch would shrink and rip away from the old cloth, leaving an even bigger tear than before.

¹⁷"And no one puts new wine into old wineskins. For the old skins would burst from the pressure, spilling the wine and ruining the skins. New wine is stored in new wineskins so that both are preserved."

Jesus Heals in Response to Faith

¹⁸As Jesus was saying this, the leader of a synagogue came and knelt before him. "My daughter has just died," he said, "but you can bring her back to life again if you just come and lay your hand on her."

¹⁹So Jesus and his disciples got up and went with him. ²⁰Just then a woman who had suffered for twelve years with constant bleeding came up behind him. She touched the fringe of his robe, ²¹for she thought, "If I can just touch his robe, I will be healed."

²²Jesus turned around, and when he saw her he said, "Daughter, be encouraged! Your faith has made you well." And the woman was healed at that moment.

²³When Jesus arrived at the official's home, he saw the noisy crowd and heard the funeral music. ²⁴"Get out!" he told them. "The girl isn't dead; she's only asleep." But the crowd laughed at him. ²⁵After the crowd was put outside, however, Jesus went in and took the girl by the hand, and she stood up! ²⁶The report of this miracle swept through the entire countryside.

Jesus Heals the Blind

²⁷After Jesus left the girl's home, two blind men followed along behind him, shouting, "Son of David, have mercy on us!"

²⁸They went right into the house where he was staying, and Jesus asked them, "Do you believe I can make you see?"

"Yes, Lord," they told him, "we do."

²⁹Then he touched their eyes and said, "Because of your faith, it will happen." ³⁰Then their eyes were opened, and they could see! Jesus sternly warned them, "Don't tell anyone about this." ³¹But instead, they went out and spread his fame all over the region.

³²When they left, a demon-possessed man who couldn't speak was brought to Jesus. ³³So Jesus cast out the demon, and then the man began to speak. The crowds were amazed. "Nothing like this has ever happened in Israel!" they exclaimed.

9:6 "Son of Man" is a title Jesus used for himself.   9:11 Greek *with tax collectors and sinners?*   9:13 Hos 6:6 (Greek version).
9:14 Some manuscripts read *fast often*.

9:18-26 According to the law of Moses, anyone who touched a dead body or who experienced a bodily discharge would be considered ceremonially unclean for a certain period of time (Leviticus 15:1-33; Numbers 19:11-19). Touching anyone experiencing these types of impurity was taboo, especially for a rabbi (a Jewish teacher) like Jesus. Disregarding the taboo, Jesus responded to these requests for healing willingly and quickly, and he did not regard the encounter with the woman as inconvenient. We can trust that Jesus is also willing to meet us where we are today, regardless of whether we feel worthy. We don't have to fix ourselves before we come to Jesus; he heals us.
9:20 The woman's "constant bleeding" made her ceremonially unclean and made whoever she touched unclean as well (Leviticus 15:25-30). But instead of rendering Jesus unclean, her touching him made her clean, a stunning reversal that illustrates Jesus' power to purify and make all things new. The tassels at the bottom of a tunic, "the fringe of his robe" (see Numbers 15:37-41), reminded Jews to live in accordance with God's law.
9:22 This woman had likely lived with shame and helplessness for twelve years. Long-term isolation might have caused her to want a secret healing by touching just the fringe of Jesus' robe. Instead, Jesus *publicly* praised her faith and pronounced that she was made well. In doing so, Jesus healed not only her body but also her soul and social relationships. We can trust that Jesus' healing can reach all the broken parts of our lives, and that he offers the same kind of encouragement to us today.
9:24 Though she was physically dead the girl was just asleep from Jesus' perspective, and she would soon be raised back to life (see also John 11:11-14).

The Woman
JESUS HEALED OF BLEEDING

IDENTITY
Deep Care for Deep Wounds

She remembers . . .

Jesus was passing by, and I knew it was now or never.

Maybe in this large crowd, he wouldn't notice if I just touched his *tzitzit* (see Numbers 15:37-41). I had seen the power he has to bring wholeness to broken lives and broken bodies—could I be included in that too? I didn't want to draw attention to myself or risk being shamed, but I wondered—could this small contact heal me?

My fingers just barely brushed the dangling tassels, but something immediately felt different in my body.

And then, he turned and looked around. I felt terrified. Everyone was crowding around. How would this holy man respond to me touching his garment? Was I wrong to be so bold?

"Daughter, be encouraged!" he said to me, with tenderness in his voice. "Your faith has made you well" (9:22).

I hadn't realized I was holding my breath, but at the sound of his words, I finally exhaled. In front of the crowd and Jesus' closest followers, I was accepted and healed.

I will never forget that day, the day I learned that Jesus cares deeply about me and my imperfect body. He healed the brokenness in my body, and my faith in his power paved the way for new life.

> Jesus cares deeply about our bodies, our hurts, and our most profound pain and shame.

THIS WOMAN'S STORY IS TOLD IN MATTHEW 9:20-22; MARK 5:25-34; AND LUKE 8:43-48.

IDENTIFY

Where in your life are you desperate for healing? And how might God be calling you to trust him with those places even more?

How can you relate to this woman's boldness and faith in Jesus?

"Like this woman, I too dared to believe that encountering Jesus could change my life and heal my deepest wounds. In Jesus, I've found myself known and accepted, even with my brokenness and imperfections."

JENNIFER ROSNER, PhD, is a writer and Messianic Jewish theologian currently serving as Affiliate Assistant Professor at Fuller Theological Seminary. Much of her work focuses on the relationship between Judaism and Christianity.

34But the Pharisees said, "He can cast out demons because he is empowered by the prince of demons."

The Need for Workers

35Jesus traveled through all the towns and villages of that area, teaching in the synagogues and announcing the Good News about the Kingdom. And he healed every kind of disease and illness. 36When he saw the crowds, he had compassion on them because they were confused and helpless, like sheep without a shepherd. 37He said to his disciples, "The harvest is great, but the workers are few. 38So pray to the Lord who is in charge of the harvest; ask him to send more workers into his fields."

Jesus Sends Out the Twelve Apostles

10 Jesus called his twelve disciples together and gave them authority to cast out evil* spirits and to heal every kind of disease and illness. 2Here are the names of the twelve apostles:

first, Simon (also called Peter),
then Andrew (Peter's brother),
James (son of Zebedee),
John (James's brother),
3 Philip,
Bartholomew,
Thomas,
Matthew (the tax collector),
James (son of Alphaeus),
Thaddaeus,*
4 Simon (the zealot*),
Judas Iscariot (who later betrayed him).

5Jesus sent out the twelve apostles with these instructions: "Don't go to the Gentiles or the Samaritans, 6but only to the people of Israel—God's lost sheep. 7Go and announce to them that the Kingdom of Heaven is near.* 8Heal the sick, raise the dead, cure those with leprosy, and cast out demons. Give as freely as you have received!

9"Don't take any money in your money belts—no gold, silver, or even copper coins. 10Don't carry a traveler's bag with a change of clothes and sandals or even a walking stick. Don't hesitate to accept hospitality, because those who work deserve to be fed.

11"Whenever you enter a city or village, search for a worthy person and stay in his home until you leave town. 12When you enter the home, give it your blessing. 13If it turns out to be a worthy home, let your blessing stand; if it is not, take back the blessing. 14If any household or town refuses to welcome you or listen to your message, shake its dust from your feet as you leave. 15I tell you the truth, the wicked cities of Sodom and Gomorrah will be better off than such a town on the judgment day.

16"Look, I am sending you out as sheep among wolves. So be as shrewd as snakes and harmless as doves. 17But beware! For you will be handed over to the courts and will be flogged with whips in the synagogues. 18You will stand trial before governors and kings because you are my followers. But this will be your opportunity to tell the rulers and other unbelievers about me.* 19When you are arrested, don't worry about how to respond or what to say. God will give you the right words at the right time. 20For it is not you who will be speaking—it will be the Spirit of your Father speaking through you.

21"A brother will betray his brother to death, a father will betray his own child, and children will rebel against their parents and cause them to be killed. 22And all nations will hate you because you are my followers.* But everyone who endures to the end will be saved. 23When you are persecuted in one town, flee to the next. I tell you the truth, the Son of Man* will return before you have reached all the towns of Israel.

24"Students* are not greater than their teacher, and slaves are not greater than their master. 25Students are to be like their teacher, and slaves are to be like their master. And since I, the master of the household, have been called the prince of demons,* the members of my household will be called by even worse names!

26"But don't be afraid of those who threaten you. For the time is coming when everything that is covered will be revealed, and all that is secret will be made known to all. 27What I tell you now in the darkness, shout abroad when daybreak comes. What I whisper in your ear, shout from the housetops for all to hear!

28"Don't be afraid of those who want to kill your body; they cannot touch your soul. Fear only God, who can destroy both soul and body in hell.* 29What is the price of two sparrows—one copper coin*? But not a single sparrow can fall to the ground without your Father knowing it. 30And the very hairs on

---

10:1 Greek *unclean.* **10:3** Other manuscripts read *Lebbaeus;* still others read *Lebbaeus who is called Thaddaeus.* **10:4** Greek *the Cananean,* an Aramaic term for Jewish nationalists. **10:7** Or *has come,* or *is coming soon.* **10:18** Or *But this will be your testimony against the rulers and other unbelievers.* **10:22** Greek *on account of my name.* **10:23** "Son of Man" is a title Jesus used for himself. **10:24** Or *Disciples.* **10:25** Greek *Beelzeboul;* other manuscripts read *Beezeboul;* Latin version reads *Beelzebub.* **10:28** Greek *Gehenna.* **10:29** Greek *one assarion* [i.e., one "as," a Roman coin equal to 1/16 of a denarius].

10:21 Jews regularly associated family strife with the disintegration of social order that would characterize the last days (see Micah 7:6). Jesus experienced such conflicts as well (Matthew 12:46-50), which is evidence of the prophetic and controversial nature of his ministry.

10:22 "Everyone who endures to the end" refers to those who remain faithful to Jesus to the point of death or until his return. Though some have taken "will be saved" to mean deliverance from persecution (such as release from prison), the idea here is eternal salvation for those who remain faithful.

your head are all numbered. ³¹So don't be afraid; you are more valuable to God than a whole flock of sparrows.

³²"Everyone who acknowledges me publicly here on earth, I will also acknowledge before my Father in heaven. ³³But everyone who denies me here on earth, I will also deny before my Father in heaven.

³⁴"Don't imagine that I came to bring peace to the earth! I came not to bring peace, but a sword.

³⁵ 'I have come to set a man against his father,
    a daughter against her mother,
and a daughter-in-law against her
    mother-in-law.
³⁶   Your enemies will be right in your own
    household!'*

³⁷"If you love your father or mother more than you love me, you are not worthy of being mine; or if you love your son or daughter more than me, you are not worthy of being mine. ³⁸If you refuse to take up your cross and follow me, you are not worthy of being mine. ³⁹If you cling to your life, you will lose it; but if you give up your life for me, you will find it.

⁴⁰"Anyone who receives you receives me, and anyone who receives me receives the Father who sent me. ⁴¹If you receive a prophet as one who speaks for God,* you will be given the same reward as a prophet. And if you receive righteous people because of their righteousness, you will be given a reward like theirs. ⁴²And if you give even a cup of cold water to one of the least of my followers, you will surely be rewarded."

Jesus and John the Baptist

11 When Jesus had finished giving these instructions to his twelve disciples, he went out to teach and preach in towns throughout the region.

²John the Baptist, who was in prison, heard about all the things the Messiah was doing. So he sent his disciples to ask Jesus, ³"Are you the Messiah we've been expecting,* or should we keep looking for someone else?"

⁴Jesus told them, "Go back to John and tell him what you have heard and seen—⁵the blind see, the lame walk, those with leprosy are cured, the deaf hear, the dead are raised to life, and the Good News is being preached to the poor." ⁶And he added, "God blesses those who do not fall away because of me.*"

⁷As John's disciples were leaving, Jesus began talking about him to the crowds. "What kind of man did you go into the wilderness to see? Was he a weak reed, swayed by every breath of wind? ⁸Or were you expecting to see a man dressed in expensive clothes? No, people with expensive clothes live in palaces. ⁹Were you looking for a prophet? Yes, and he is more than a prophet. ¹⁰John is the man to whom the Scriptures refer when they say,

'Look, I am sending my messenger ahead of you,
    and he will prepare your way before you.'*

¹¹"I tell you the truth, of all who have ever lived, none is greater than John the Baptist. Yet even the least person in the Kingdom of Heaven is greater than he is! ¹²And from the time John the Baptist began preaching until now, the Kingdom of Heaven has been forcefully advancing,* and violent people are attacking it. ¹³For before John came, all the prophets and the law of Moses looked forward to this present time. ¹⁴And if you are willing to accept what I say, he is Elijah, the one the prophets said would come.* ¹⁵Anyone with ears to hear should listen and understand!

¹⁶"To what can I compare this generation? It is like children playing a game in the public square. They complain to their friends,

¹⁷ 'We played wedding songs,
    and you didn't dance,
so we played funeral songs,
    and you didn't mourn.'

¹⁸For John didn't spend his time eating and drinking, and you say, 'He's possessed by a demon.' ¹⁹The Son of Man,* on the other hand, feasts and drinks, and you say, 'He's a glutton and a drunkard, and a friend of tax collectors and other sinners!' But wisdom is shown to be right by its results."

10:35-36 Mic 7:6.   **10:41** Greek *receive a prophet in the name of a prophet.*   **11:3** Greek *Are you the one who is coming?*   **11:6** Or *who are not offended by me.*   **11:10** Mal 3:1.   **11:12** Or *the Kingdom of Heaven has suffered from violence.*   **11:14** See Mal 4:5.   **11:19** "Son of Man" is a title Jesus used for himself.

10:35-37 In other places, Jesus stressed the importance of honoring our parents and loving our neighbors (15:3-9; 19:18-19). Loving our family and neighbors is an essential virtue for Jesus' followers. But human love tends to be conditional and can be self-serving; it can be difficult to love those who feel like enemies in our own household, as Jesus said here. By contrast, if we learn to live as he has called us to, he can enable us to love our not-so-lovely family members more sacrificially.

10:34 Jesus did bring peace (John 14:27), but not of a social or political kind. Instead, Jesus called people to decide whether he is truly the Messiah, which brings a sword—meaning, division (see Matthew 8:21-22; 12:46-50; Luke 12:51).

10:37-38 Jesus' radical call to follow him leads us to prioritize Jesus over our family members and risk being alienated. Our family members' desires might conflict at times with what Jesus wants for us, or even what Jesus wants for our families. In some situations, family relationships may be dearer to women's hearts than to men's, and women also tend to bear the majority of child and elder care. So, it could be more painful for some women to follow Christ if their parents or children are opposed to their obedience to Jesus.

"Come to me, ...and I will give you rest."

MATTHEW 11:28

Judgment for the Unbelievers

²⁰Then Jesus began to denounce the towns where he had done so many of his miracles, because they hadn't repented of their sins and turned to God. ²¹"What sorrow awaits you, Korazin and Bethsaida! For if the miracles I did in you had been done in wicked Tyre and Sidon, their people would have repented of their sins long ago, clothing themselves in burlap and throwing ashes on their heads to show their remorse. ²²I tell you, Tyre and Sidon will be better off on judgment day than you.

²³"And you people of Capernaum, will you be honored in heaven? No, you will go down to the place of the dead.* For if the miracles I did for you had been done in wicked Sodom, it would still be here today. ²⁴I tell you, even Sodom will be better off on judgment day than you."

Jesus' Prayer of Thanksgiving

²⁵At that time Jesus prayed this prayer: "O Father, Lord of heaven and earth, thank you for hiding these things from those who think themselves wise and clever, and for revealing them to the childlike. ²⁶Yes, Father, it pleased you to do it this way!

²⁷"My Father has entrusted everything to me. No one truly knows the Son except the Father, and no one truly knows the Father except the Son and those to whom the Son chooses to reveal him."

²⁸Then Jesus said, "Come to me, all of you who are weary and carry heavy burdens, and I will give you rest. ²⁹Take my yoke upon you. Let me teach you, because I am humble and gentle at heart, and you will find rest for your souls. ³⁰For my yoke is easy to bear, and the burden I give you is light."

A Discussion about the Sabbath

12 At about that time Jesus was walking through some grainfields on the Sabbath. His disciples were hungry, so they began breaking off some heads of grain and eating them. ²But some Pharisees saw them do it and protested, "Look, your disciples are breaking the law by harvesting grain on the Sabbath."

³Jesus said to them, "Haven't you read in the Scriptures what David did when he and his companions were hungry? ⁴He went into the house of God, and he and his companions broke the law by eating the sacred loaves of bread that only the priests are allowed to eat. ⁵And haven't you read in the law of Moses that the priests on duty in the Temple may work on the Sabbath? ⁶I tell you, there is one here who is even greater than the Temple! ⁷But you would not have condemned my innocent friends if you knew the meaning of this Scripture: 'I want you to show mercy, not offer sacrifices.'* ⁸For the Son of Man* is Lord, even over the Sabbath!"

Jesus Heals on the Sabbath

⁹Then Jesus went over to their synagogue, ¹⁰where he noticed a man with a deformed hand. The Pharisees asked Jesus, "Does the law permit a person to work by healing on the Sabbath?" (They were hoping he would say yes, so they could bring charges against him.)

¹¹And he answered, "If you had a sheep that fell into a well on the Sabbath, wouldn't you work to pull it out? Of course you would. ¹²And how much more valuable is a person than a sheep! Yes, the law permits a person to do good on the Sabbath."

¹³Then he said to the man, "Hold out your hand." So the man held out his hand, and it was restored, just like the other one! ¹⁴Then the Pharisees called a meeting to plot how to kill Jesus.

Jesus, God's Chosen Servant

¹⁵But Jesus knew what they were planning. So he left that area, and many people followed him. He healed all the sick among them, ¹⁶but he warned them not to reveal who he was. ¹⁷This fulfilled the prophecy of Isaiah concerning him:

¹⁸ "Look at my Servant, whom I have chosen.
  He is my Beloved, who pleases me.
 I will put my Spirit upon him,
  and he will proclaim justice to the nations.
¹⁹ He will not fight or shout
  or raise his voice in public.
²⁰ He will not crush the weakest reed
  or put out a flickering candle.
 Finally he will cause justice to be victorious.
²¹ And his name will be the hope
  of all the world."*

Jesus and the Prince of Demons

²²Then a demon-possessed man, who was blind and couldn't speak, was brought to Jesus. He healed the man so that he could both speak and see. ²³The crowd was amazed and asked, "Could it be that Jesus is the Son of David, the Messiah?"

²⁴But when the Pharisees heard about the miracle, they said, "No wonder he can cast out demons. He gets his power from Satan,* the prince of demons."

²⁵Jesus knew their thoughts and replied, "Any kingdom divided by civil war is doomed. A town or family splintered by feuding will fall apart. ²⁶And if Satan is casting out Satan, he is divided and fighting against himself. His own kingdom will not survive. ²⁷And if I am empowered by Satan, what about your own exorcists? They cast out demons, too, so they will condemn you for what you have said. ²⁸But if I am casting out demons by the Spirit of God, then the Kingdom of God has arrived among you. ²⁹For who is powerful enough to enter the house of a strong man and plunder his goods? Only someone even

11:23 Greek *to Hades.* **12:7** Hos 6:6 (Greek version). **12:8** "Son of Man" is a title Jesus used for himself. **12:18-21** Isa 42:1-4 (Greek version for 42:4). **12:24** Greek *Beelzeboul;* also in 12:27. Other manuscripts read *Beezeboul;* Latin version reads *Beelzebub.*

stronger—someone who could tie him up and then plunder his house.

³⁰"Anyone who isn't with me opposes me, and anyone who isn't working with me is actually working against me.

³¹"So I tell you, every sin and blasphemy can be forgiven—except blasphemy against the Holy Spirit, which will never be forgiven. ³²Anyone who speaks against the Son of Man can be forgiven, but anyone who speaks against the Holy Spirit will never be forgiven, either in this world or in the world to come.

³³"A tree is identified by its fruit. If a tree is good, its fruit will be good. If a tree is bad, its fruit will be bad. ³⁴You brood of snakes! How could evil men like you speak what is good and right? For whatever is in your heart determines what you say. ³⁵A good person produces good things from the treasury of a good heart, and an evil person produces evil things from the treasury of an evil heart. ³⁶And I tell you this, you must give an account on judgment day for every idle word you speak. ³⁷The words you say will either acquit you or condemn you."

The Sign of Jonah

³⁸One day some teachers of religious law and Pharisees came to Jesus and said, "Teacher, we want you to show us a miraculous sign to prove your authority."

³⁹But Jesus replied, "Only an evil, adulterous generation would demand a miraculous sign; but the only sign I will give them is the sign of the prophet Jonah. ⁴⁰For as Jonah was in the belly of the great fish for three days and three nights, so will the Son of Man be in the heart of the earth for three days and three nights.

⁴¹"The people of Nineveh will stand up against this generation on judgment day and condemn it, for they repented of their sins at the preaching of Jonah. Now someone greater than Jonah is here—but you refuse to repent. ⁴²The queen of Sheba* will also stand up against this generation on judgment day and condemn it, for she came from a distant land to hear the wisdom of Solomon. Now someone greater than Solomon is here—but you refuse to listen.

⁴³"When an evil* spirit leaves a person, it goes into the desert, seeking rest but finding none. ⁴⁴Then it says, 'I will return to the person I came from.' So it returns and finds its former home empty, swept, and in order. ⁴⁵Then the spirit finds seven other spirits more evil than itself, and they all enter the person and live there. And so that person is worse off than before. That will be the experience of this evil generation."

The True Family of Jesus

⁴⁶As Jesus was speaking to the crowd, his mother and brothers stood outside, asking to speak to him. ⁴⁷Someone told Jesus, "Your mother and your brothers are standing outside, and they want to speak to you."*

⁴⁸Jesus asked, "Who is my mother? Who are my brothers?" ⁴⁹Then he pointed to his disciples and said, "Look, these are my mother and brothers. ⁵⁰Anyone who does the will of my Father in heaven is my brother and sister and mother!"

Parable of the Farmer Scattering Seed

13 Later that same day Jesus left the house and sat beside the lake. ²A large crowd soon gathered around him, so he got into a boat. Then he sat there and taught as the people stood on the shore. ³He told many stories in the form of parables, such as this one:

"Listen! A farmer went out to plant some seeds. ⁴As he scattered them across his field, some seeds fell on a footpath, and the birds came and ate them. ⁵Other seeds fell on shallow soil with underlying rock. The seeds sprouted quickly because the soil was shallow. ⁶But the plants soon wilted under the hot sun, and since they didn't have deep roots, they died. ⁷Other seeds fell among thorns that grew up and choked out the tender plants. ⁸Still other seeds fell on fertile soil, and they produced a crop that was thirty, sixty, and even a hundred times as much as had been planted! ⁹Anyone with ears to hear should listen and understand."

12:42 Greek *The queen of the south.* **12:43** Greek *unclean.* **12:47** Some manuscripts do not include verse 47. Compare Mark 3:32 and Luke 8:20.

12:41-42 Jesus cited two examples of non-Jewish people who praised the Lord when they saw his works: the queen of Sheba (1 Kings 10:1-13) and the people of Nineveh (Jonah 3:1-10). The queen of Sheba visited King Solomon, and once she understood the full scope of Solomon's wisdom and the immense prosperity with which God had blessed Solomon and Israel, she praised the Lord and gave Solomon fine gifts. When the people of Nineveh heard the Lord's judgment warning, they believed and showed sorrow for how they had offended God, and so God spared the city. Jesus used these examples to show how non-Jewish people in Israel's history properly responded to the Lord even with only a small amount of evidence. It's a warning for those who reject Jesus as the Messiah that the judgment against them will be more severe because they have seen even greater evidence of God's authority in Jesus.

12:46-50 Jesus' seeming indifference toward his mother and brothers instructs us about how the new community formed around Jesus is a family. Jesus used familial language for his disciples here, and throughout the New Testament Jesus' followers call one another brothers and sisters. But this doesn't mean that Jesus neglected his biological family (see Jesus' treatment of his mother in Luke 2:51 and John 19:25-27). Devotion to God and love for family are not incompatible, but we must learn to find the balance between serving God and caring for family. We must also learn to relate to our Christian community as our true family.

MATTHEW 13

¹⁰His disciples came and asked him, "Why do you use parables when you talk to the people?"

¹¹He replied, "You are permitted to understand the secrets* of the Kingdom of Heaven, but others are not. ¹²To those who listen to my teaching, more understanding will be given, and they will have an abundance of knowledge. But for those who are not listening, even what little understanding they have will be taken away from them. ¹³That is why I use these parables,

> For they look, but they don't really see.
> They hear, but they don't really listen or understand.

¹⁴This fulfills the prophecy of Isaiah that says,

> 'When you hear what I say,
> you will not understand.
> When you see what I do,
> you will not comprehend.
> ¹⁵ For the hearts of these people are hardened,
> and their ears cannot hear,
> and they have closed their eyes—
> so their eyes cannot see,
> and their ears cannot hear,
> and their hearts cannot understand,
> and they cannot turn to me
> and let me heal them.'*

¹⁶"But blessed are your eyes, because they see; and your ears, because they hear. ¹⁷I tell you the truth, many prophets and righteous people longed to see what you see, but they didn't see it. And they longed to hear what you hear, but they didn't hear it.

¹⁸"Now listen to the explanation of the parable about the farmer planting seeds: ¹⁹The seed that fell on the footpath represents those who hear the message about the Kingdom and don't understand it. Then the evil one comes and snatches away the seed that was planted in their hearts. ²⁰The seed on the rocky soil represents those who hear the message and immediately receive it with joy. ²¹But since they don't have deep roots, they don't last long. They fall away as soon as they have problems or are persecuted for believing God's word. ²²The seed that fell among the thorns represents those who hear God's word, but all too quickly the message is crowded out by the worries of this life and the lure of wealth, so no fruit is produced. ²³The seed that fell on good soil represents those who truly hear and understand God's word and produce a harvest of thirty, sixty, or even a hundred times as much as had been planted!"

Parable of the Wheat and Weeds

²⁴Here is another story Jesus told: "The Kingdom of Heaven is like a farmer who planted good seed in his field. ²⁵But that night as the workers slept, his enemy came and planted weeds among the wheat, then slipped away. ²⁶When the crop began to grow and produce grain, the weeds also grew.

²⁷"The farmer's workers went to him and said, 'Sir, the field where you planted that good seed is full of weeds! Where did they come from?'

²⁸"'An enemy has done this!' the farmer exclaimed.

"'Should we pull out the weeds?' they asked.

²⁹"'No,' he replied, 'you'll uproot the wheat if you do. ³⁰Let both grow together until the harvest. Then I will tell the harvesters to sort out the weeds, tie them into bundles, and burn them, and to put the wheat in the barn.'"

Parable of the Mustard Seed

³¹Here is another illustration Jesus used: "The Kingdom of Heaven is like a mustard seed planted in a field. ³²It is the smallest of all seeds, but it becomes the largest of garden plants; it grows into a tree, and birds come and make nests in its branches."

Parable of the Yeast

³³Jesus also used this illustration: "The Kingdom of Heaven is like the yeast a woman used in making bread. Even though she put only a little yeast in three measures of flour, it permeated every part of the dough."

³⁴Jesus always used stories and illustrations like these when speaking to the crowds. In fact, he never spoke to them without using such parables. ³⁵This fulfilled what God had spoken through the prophet:

> "I will speak to you in parables.
> I will explain things hidden since the creation of the world.*"

Parable of the Wheat and Weeds Explained

³⁶Then, leaving the crowds outside, Jesus went into the house. His disciples said, "Please explain to us the story of the weeds in the field."

³⁷Jesus replied, "The Son of Man* is the farmer who plants the good seed. ³⁸The field is the world, and the good seed represents the people of the Kingdom. The weeds are the people who belong to the evil one. ³⁹The enemy who planted the weeds among

---

13:11 Greek *the mysteries*. **13:14-15** Isa 6:9-10 (Greek version). **13:35** Some manuscripts do not include *of the world*. Ps 78:2.
13:37 "Son of Man" is a title Jesus used for himself.

13:33 Jesus' illustrations represent women primarily as concerned with or in charge of domestic life (see also 24:41). The book of Matthew also includes unexpected stories of women traveling with Jesus and resolutely accompanying him at the cross when most of his male disciples had abandoned him (27:55-56; see also Luke 8:1-3; John 19:25-27). For most women living in industrialized countries, our lives are not consumed entirely with domestic responsibilities. Most of us don't provide for our families from our farms, but balancing home, work, and community responsibilities is challenging and takes wisdom to do well.

Insight THE PARABLES OF JESUS

Jesus had a unique way of tantalizing audiences with parables. These stories frequently surprised his listeners and made them think. When we listen to these stories, we have insight into the unique nature of God's Kingdom. Here are more than thirty:

● number of gospels in which the parable is found

One Lost Sheep
Everyone counts to God.
MATTHEW 18:12-14; LUKE 15:3-7

The Lost Coin
Everyone counts to God.
LUKE 15:8-10

Two Houses, One Foundation
Don't just listen to Jesus; follow through.
MATTHEW 7:24-27; LUKE 6:47-49

The Lamp
God's Good News is for sharing.
MARK 4:21-23; LUKE 8:16-18

The True Vine
Apart from Jesus, we die.
JOHN 15:1-17

Patching Garments, Filling Wineskins
New truth requires new practices.
MATTHEW 9:14-17; MARK 2:18-22; LUKE 5:36-39

The Three Servants
Get to work with whatever God has given you.
MATTHEW 25:14-30

The Shrewd Manager
Believers are to use their resources for the benefit of others.
LUKE 16:1-18

The Good Samaritan
True neighbors love even their enemies.
LUKE 10:30-37

The Good Shepherd
Jesus cares for us.
JOHN 10:1-30

A Friend at Midnight
Don't hesitate to ask God for what you truly need.
LUKE 11:5-10

The Persistent Widow
We can count on God's justice.
LUKE 18:1-8

The Rich Fool
Material goods won't last.
LUKE 12:13-21

The Pharisee and Tax Collector
A genuine heart is more important to God than words or self-righteous actions.
LUKE 18:9-14

The Wedding Feast
Some people will miss God's invitation.
MATTHEW 22:1-14; LUKE 14:15-24

The Ten Servants
Get to work with whatever you've been given.
LUKE 19:11-27

The Generous Landowner
God's generosity goes beyond fairness.
MATTHEW 20:1-16

Four Kinds of Soil
People respond to the Good News differently.
MATTHEW 13:1-23;
MARK 4:1-20; LUKE 8:4-15

The Wheat and Weeds
Good and evil will get sorted out eventually.
MATTHEW 13:24-30, 37-43

The Mustard Seed
God's Kingdom may start out small—but just wait.
MATTHEW 13:31-32;
MARK 4:30-32; LUKE 13:18-19

Yeast in the Bread Dough
God's Kingdom can permeate everywhere.
MATTHEW 13:33; LUKE 13:20-21

The Unforgiving Debtor
We must forgive others because God has forgiven us.
MATTHEW 18:21-35

A Job for Two Sons
Talk is cheap; action is what counts.
MATTHEW 21:28-32

The Evil Tenants
Rejecting Jesus is not a smart idea.
MATTHEW 21:33-46;
MARK 12:1-12; LUKE 20:9-19

The Lost Son
God loves those who are lost and wants everyone to return to him.
LUKE 15:11-32

Hidden Treasure in a Field
Get the spiritual treasure, whatever it costs.
MATTHEW 13:44

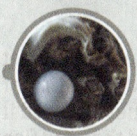
The Pearl of Great Value
Get the spiritual treasure, whatever it costs.
MATTHEW 13:45-46

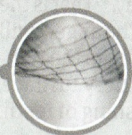
The Fishing Net
Good and evil will get sorted out eventually.
MATTHEW 13:47-52

The Growing Seed
God's Kingdom grows quietly and gradually.
MARK 4:26-29

Servants Whose Employer Is Away
We must be ready for Jesus' eventual return.
MATTHEW 24:42-51;
MARK 13:34-37; LUKE 12:42-48

The Ten Bridesmaids
We must be ready for Jesus' eventual return.
MATTHEW 25:1-13

The Barren Fig Tree
Obey Jesus or face judgment.
LUKE 13:6-9

the wheat is the devil. The harvest is the end of the world,* and the harvesters are the angels.

⁴⁰"Just as the weeds are sorted out and burned in the fire, so it will be at the end of the world. ⁴¹The Son of Man will send his angels, and they will remove from his Kingdom everything that causes sin and all who do evil. ⁴²And the angels will throw them into the fiery furnace, where there will be weeping and gnashing of teeth. ⁴³Then the righteous will shine like the sun in their Father's Kingdom. Anyone with ears to hear should listen and understand!

Parables of the Hidden Treasure and the Pearl

⁴⁴"The Kingdom of Heaven is like a treasure that a man discovered hidden in a field. In his excitement, he hid it again and sold everything he owned to get enough money to buy the field.

⁴⁵"Again, the Kingdom of Heaven is like a merchant on the lookout for choice pearls. ⁴⁶When he discovered a pearl of great value, he sold everything he owned and bought it!

Parable of the Fishing Net

⁴⁷"Again, the Kingdom of Heaven is like a fishing net that was thrown into the water and caught fish of every kind. ⁴⁸When the net was full, they dragged it up onto the shore, sat down, and sorted the good fish into crates, but threw the bad ones away. ⁴⁹That is the way it will be at the end of the world. The angels will come and separate the wicked people from the righteous, ⁵⁰throwing the wicked into the fiery furnace, where there will be weeping and gnashing of teeth. ⁵¹Do you understand all these things?"

"Yes," they said, "we do."

⁵²Then he added, "Every teacher of religious law who becomes a disciple in the Kingdom of Heaven is like a homeowner who brings from his storeroom new gems of truth as well as old."

Jesus Rejected at Nazareth

⁵³When Jesus had finished telling these stories and illustrations, he left that part of the country. ⁵⁴He returned to Nazareth, his hometown. When he taught there in the synagogue, everyone was amazed and said, "Where does he get this wisdom and the power to do miracles?" ⁵⁵Then they scoffed, "He's just the carpenter's son, and we know Mary, his mother, and his brothers—James, Joseph,* Simon, and Judas. ⁵⁶All his sisters live right here among us. Where did he learn all these things?" ⁵⁷And they were deeply offended and refused to believe in him.

Then Jesus told them, "A prophet is honored everywhere except in his own hometown and among his own family." ⁵⁸And so he did only a few miracles there because of their unbelief.

The Death of John the Baptist

14 When Herod Antipas, the ruler of Galilee,* heard about Jesus, ²he said to his advisers, "This must be John the Baptist raised from the dead! That is why he can do such miracles."

³For Herod had arrested and imprisoned John as a favor to his wife Herodias (the former wife of Herod's brother Philip). ⁴John had been telling Herod, "It is against God's law for you to marry her." ⁵Herod wanted to kill John, but he was afraid of a riot, because all the people believed John was a prophet.

⁶But at a birthday party for Herod, Herodias's daughter performed a dance that greatly pleased him, ⁷so he promised with a vow to give her anything she wanted. ⁸At her mother's urging, the girl said, "I want the head of John the Baptist on a tray!" ⁹Then the king regretted what he had said; but because of the vow he had made in front of his guests, he issued the necessary orders. ¹⁰So John was beheaded in the prison, ¹¹and his head was brought on a tray and given to the girl, who took it to her mother. ¹²Later, John's disciples came for his body and buried it. Then they went and told Jesus what had happened.

13:39 Or *the age;* also in 13:40, 49. **13:55** Other manuscripts read *Joses;* still others read *John.* **14:1** Greek *Herod the tetrarch.* Herod Antipas was a son of King Herod and was ruler over Galilee.

14:3-4 According to the first-century Jewish historian Josephus, Herodias was previously the wife of Herod Antipas's half-brother. Herodias and Antipas's marriage was unlawful to conservative Jews because they achieved it through two divorces rather than the deaths of their spouses. This union not only deepened the disaffection among the Jews for leaders appointed by Rome (which the Herods were) but also provoked a war with Antipas's former father-in-law, the Nabatean king of nearby Petra (*The Antiquities of the Jews,* book 18, chapter 5, paragraph 1). Although divorce or remarriage is not uncommon and even necessary in some situations today, we must calculate the ramifications of our decisions. The Herods exemplify how the personal morality of leaders can affect the people they lead; integrity and character matter, especially when vulnerable people are looking to you to make decisions.
14:5-9 These verses seem to show evidence of Herod's inconsistent attitude toward John the Baptist: Did Herod want to kill John or not? By contrast, Mark 6:17-29 provides a more coherent narrative in which Herodias manipulated Herod into killing John. Josephus described Herodias as a manipulative figure (*The Antiquities of the Jews,* book 18, chapter 7, paragraphs 1–2) and noted that Antipas saw John's ministry as a political threat. All writers' representations are biased, and Josephus's writings are not considered fully reliable. Still, we see here that anyone in authority, regardless of gender, is capable of abusing their power.
14:6 Herodias's unnamed daughter was probably Salome, from Herodias's previous marriage to Philip. Although the text does not describe her dance, interpreters have assumed it was provocative. It's possible that the dance was indeed erotic, and the women of Herod's family didn't show the typical discretion (members of the royal family would have been more likely to watch such a dance than to perform one). But it's also possible that the dance was not as sensual as has been implied.

Jesus Feeds Five Thousand

13 As soon as Jesus heard the news, he left in a boat to a remote area to be alone. But the crowds heard where he was headed and followed on foot from many towns. 14 Jesus saw the huge crowd as he stepped from the boat, and he had compassion on them and healed their sick.

15 That evening the disciples came to him and said, "This is a remote place, and it's already getting late. Send the crowds away so they can go to the villages and buy food for themselves."

16 But Jesus said, "That isn't necessary—you feed them."

17 "But we have only five loaves of bread and two fish!" they answered.

18 "Bring them here," he said. 19 Then he told the people to sit down on the grass. Jesus took the five loaves and two fish, looked up toward heaven, and blessed them. Then, breaking the loaves into pieces, he gave the bread to the disciples, who distributed it to the people. 20 They all ate as much as they wanted, and afterward, the disciples picked up twelve baskets

Koinonia IMAGE — MY STORY WITH COMMUNITY, WORKPLACE & CHURCH

Herodias and Hatred that Harms

SCRIPTURE CONNECTION: MATTHEW 14:1-12

If we could hear what Herodias was thinking, it might sound something like this:

I hate John the Baptist! By trying to convince Herod that our marriage is against God's law, he is going to ruin my life and my marriage. My husband may respect John, but I have to find a way to silence him. I want to destroy him before he destroys me.

Herod's birthday party—the perfect opportunity is here. After my daughter danced for him, he recklessly promised to give her anything she wanted. Now my daughter is asking me what she should say, and I intend to see John's head on a tray.

Indeed, Herodias did get John's head served up on a platter, but that did not please Herod. He regretted his promise to Herodias, probably because he couldn't take it back in front of his party guests. Herodias's desire for revenge manipulated her husband and led to the unjust execution of John.

Bitterness has a way of bringing destruction. The writer of the book of Hebrews warns us to watch "that no poisonous root of bitterness grows up to trouble you, corrupting many" (Hebrews 12:15). Herodias's hatred ate away at her to such a degree that she demanded a person's death to get what she wanted. Instead of listening to John, her anger and bitterness led her to reject and destroy God's messenger.

> Bitterness invites destruction, not justice.

IMAGINE

What leaves you feeling so angry that all you think about is revenge?

How have you handled anger well, and what did you do?

"When I fret over being hurt, replaying it in my mind, becoming more and more angry, I have learned to take that as a warning. I stop, pray, repent, and seek God's perspective. God can help now before bitterness destroys from the inside out."

ELIZABETH GLANVILLE, PhD, is retired faculty from Fuller Theological Seminary, School of Mission and Theology. She is an international teacher on missions and leadership and chaplain for a local police department and her retirement community.

of leftovers. ²¹About 5,000 men were fed that day, in addition to all the women and children!

Jesus Walks on Water

²²Immediately after this, Jesus insisted that his disciples get back into the boat and cross to the other side of the lake, while he sent the people home. ²³After sending them home, he went up into the hills by himself to pray. Night fell while he was there alone.

²⁴Meanwhile, the disciples were in trouble far away from land, for a strong wind had risen, and they were fighting heavy waves. ²⁵About three o'clock in the morning* Jesus came toward them, walking on the water. ²⁶When the disciples saw him walking on the water, they were terrified. In their fear, they cried out, "It's a ghost!"

²⁷But Jesus spoke to them at once. "Don't be afraid," he said. "Take courage. I am here!*"

²⁸Then Peter called to him, "Lord, if it's really you, tell me to come to you, walking on the water."

²⁹"Yes, come," Jesus said.

So Peter went over the side of the boat and walked on the water toward Jesus. ³⁰But when he saw the strong* wind and the waves, he was terrified and began to sink. "Save me, Lord!" he shouted.

³¹Jesus immediately reached out and grabbed him. "You have so little faith," Jesus said. "Why did you doubt me?"

³²When they climbed back into the boat, the wind stopped. ³³Then the disciples worshiped him. "You really are the Son of God!" they exclaimed.

³⁴After they had crossed the lake, they landed at Gennesaret. ³⁵When the people recognized Jesus, the news of his arrival spread quickly throughout the whole area, and soon people were bringing all their sick to be healed. ³⁶They begged him to let the sick touch at least the fringe of his robe, and all who touched him were healed.

Jesus Teaches about Inner Purity

15 Some Pharisees and teachers of religious law now arrived from Jerusalem to see Jesus. They asked him, ²"Why do your disciples disobey our age-old tradition? For they ignore our tradition of ceremonial hand washing before they eat."

³Jesus replied, "And why do you, by your traditions, violate the direct commandments of God? ⁴For instance, God says, 'Honor your father and mother,'* and 'Anyone who speaks disrespectfully of father or mother must be put to death.'* ⁵But you say it is all right for people to say to their parents, 'Sorry, I can't help you. For I have vowed to give to God what I would have given to you.' ⁶In this way, you say they don't need to honor their parents.* And so you cancel the word of God for the sake of your own tradition. ⁷You hypocrites! Isaiah was right when he prophesied about you, for he wrote,

⁸ 'These people honor me with their lips,
  but their hearts are far from me.
⁹ Their worship is a farce,
  for they teach man-made ideas as commands
    from God.'*"

¹⁰Then Jesus called to the crowd to come and hear. "Listen," he said, "and try to understand. ¹¹It's not what goes into your mouth that defiles you; you are defiled by the words that come out of your mouth."

¹²Then the disciples came to him and asked, "Do you realize you offended the Pharisees by what you just said?"

¹³Jesus replied, "Every plant not planted by my heavenly Father will be uprooted, ¹⁴so ignore them. They are blind guides leading the blind, and if one blind person guides another, they will both fall into a ditch."

¹⁵Then Peter said to Jesus, "Explain to us the parable that says people aren't defiled by what they eat."

¹⁶"Don't you understand yet?" Jesus asked. ¹⁷"Anything you eat passes through the stomach and then goes into the sewer. ¹⁸But the words you speak come from the heart—that's what defiles you. ¹⁹For from the heart come evil thoughts, murder, adultery, all sexual immorality, theft, lying, and slander. ²⁰These are what defile you. Eating with unwashed hands will never defile you."

The Faith of a Gentile Woman

²¹Then Jesus left Galilee and went north to the region of Tyre and Sidon. ²²A Gentile* woman who lived

---

14:25 Greek *In the fourth watch of the night.* **14:27** Or *The 'I AM' is here;* Greek reads *I am.* See Exod 3:14. **14:30** Some manuscripts do not include *strong.* **15:4a** Exod 20:12; Deut 5:16. **15:4b** Exod 21:17 (Greek version); Lev 20:9 (Greek version). **15:6** Greek *their father;* other manuscripts read *their father or their mother.* **15:8-9** Isa 29:13 (Greek version). **15:22** Greek *Canaanite.*

15:21-28 The encounter between Jesus and the Gentile woman highlights another controversial issue: Gentile participation in the Kingdom of the Messiah (see the note on 8:11-12). While Jesus' interaction with the Gentile woman feels rude to us, it follows a common trope in ancient literature meant to emphasize the virtue of both parties. In this form, a leader in an honor-based society was considered gracious when they acknowledged someone that custom would not have required them to acknowledge because of their social disparity. Here social custom wouldn't have required that Jesus, a Jewish teacher, submit to the request of a Gentile woman. But the woman knew that Jesus was always ready to heal regardless of societal expectations. When Jesus initially rebuffed her, she pushed him to prove his true character, which was to graciously heal her daughter. As the woman honored Jesus, so Jesus then honored the woman for her great faith (15:28).

there came to him, pleading, "Have mercy on me, O Lord, Son of David! For my daughter is possessed by a demon that torments her severely."

²³But Jesus gave her no reply, not even a word. Then his disciples urged him to send her away. "Tell her to go away," they said. "She is bothering us with all her begging."

²⁴Then Jesus said to the woman, "I was sent only to help God's lost sheep—the people of Israel."

²⁵But she came and worshiped him, pleading again, "Lord, help me!"

²⁶Jesus responded, "It isn't right to take food from the children and throw it to the dogs."

²⁷She replied, "That's true, Lord, but even dogs are allowed to eat the scraps that fall beneath their masters' table."

²⁸"Dear woman," Jesus said to her, "your faith is great. Your request is granted." And her daughter was instantly healed.

Jesus Heals Many People

²⁹Jesus returned to the Sea of Galilee and climbed a hill and sat down. ³⁰A vast crowd brought to him people who were lame, blind, crippled, those who couldn't speak, and many others. They laid them before Jesus, and he healed them all. ³¹The crowd was amazed! Those who hadn't been able to speak were talking, the crippled were made well, the lame were walking, and the blind could see again! And they praised the God of Israel.

Jesus Feeds Four Thousand

³²Then Jesus called his disciples and told them, "I feel sorry for these people. They have been here with me for three days, and they have nothing left to eat. I don't want to send them away hungry, or they will faint along the way."

³³The disciples replied, "Where would we get enough food here in the wilderness for such a huge crowd?"

³⁴Jesus asked, "How much bread do you have?"

They replied, "Seven loaves, and a few small fish."

³⁵So Jesus told all the people to sit down on the ground. ³⁶Then he took the seven loaves and the fish, thanked God for them, and broke them into pieces. He gave them to the disciples, who distributed the food to the crowd.

³⁷They all ate as much as they wanted. Afterward, the disciples picked up seven large baskets of leftover food. ³⁸There were 4,000 men who were fed that day, in addition to all the women and children. ³⁹Then Jesus sent the people home, and he got into a boat and crossed over to the region of Magadan.

Leaders Demand a Miraculous Sign

16 One day the Pharisees and Sadducees came to test Jesus, demanding that he show them a miraculous sign from heaven to prove his authority.

²He replied, "You know the saying, 'Red sky at night means fair weather tomorrow; ³red sky in the morning means foul weather all day.' You know how to interpret the weather signs in the sky, but you don't know how to interpret the signs of the times!* ⁴Only an evil, adulterous generation would demand a miraculous sign, but the only sign I will give them is the sign of the prophet Jonah.*" Then Jesus left them and went away.

Yeast of the Pharisees and Sadducees

⁵Later, after they crossed to the other side of the lake, the disciples discovered they had forgotten to bring any bread. ⁶"Watch out!" Jesus warned them. "Beware of the yeast of the Pharisees and Sadducees."

⁷At this they began to argue with each other because they hadn't brought any bread. ⁸Jesus knew what they were saying, so he said, "You have so little faith! Why are you arguing with each other about having no bread? ⁹Don't you understand even yet? Don't you remember the 5,000 I fed with five loaves, and the baskets of leftovers you picked up? ¹⁰Or the 4,000 I fed with seven loaves, and the large baskets of leftovers you picked up? ¹¹Why can't you understand that I'm not talking about bread? So again I say, 'Beware of the yeast of the Pharisees and Sadducees.'"

16:2-3 Several manuscripts do not include any of the words in 16:2-3 after *He replied.*   16:4 Greek *the sign of Jonah.*

15:22 The NLT calls her a "Gentile woman," but the Greek expression could also be translated "Canaanite woman." Matthew uses this archaic Old Testament expression to describe the woman as neither ethnically Jewish nor a worshiper of Yahweh. The woman apparently perceived that Jesus was the Messiah (see 1:1; 9:27; 17:15; 20:30). This is a common contrast throughout the book of Matthew where non-Jewish people recognized Jesus' true identity and many Jewish people were slower to see this or even reject him as Messiah.

15:26 Jews may have referred to non-Jews as "dogs" because they were ceremonially unclean under Jewish law (Leviticus 11:27). Jesus spoke to the woman of her spiritual condition as a Gentile—as unclean and separated from God (see also Matthew 7:6).

15:28 In a Gentile region, a dying child's mother sought Jesus out and interceded for her daughter courageously and humbly. To a Jewish teacher, she would have been considered an outsider. While she acknowledged the special status of Judaism among ancient religions, she refused to accept the traditional exclusion of non-Jews from the covenant, the focal point of Jesus' argument. This woman embodied trust: She humbly submitted to Christ, despite their cultural differences, and courageously pleaded with him to include her in his provision. Her faithfulness gave Jesus the chance to show just how far his Kingdom extends.

¹²Then at last they understood that he wasn't speaking about the yeast in bread, but about the deceptive teaching of the Pharisees and Sadducees.

Peter's Declaration about Jesus

¹³When Jesus came to the region of Caesarea Philippi, he asked his disciples, "Who do people say that the Son of Man is?"*

¹⁴"Well," they replied, "some say John the Baptist, some say Elijah, and others say Jeremiah or one of the other prophets."

¹⁵Then he asked them, "But who do you say I am?"

¹⁶Simon Peter answered, "You are the Messiah,* the Son of the living God."

¹⁷Jesus replied, "You are blessed, Simon son of John,* because my Father in heaven has revealed this to you. You did not learn this from any human being. ¹⁸Now I say to you that you are Peter (which means 'rock'),* and upon this rock I will build my church, and all the powers of hell* will not conquer it. ¹⁹And I will give you the keys of the Kingdom of Heaven. Whatever you forbid* on earth will be forbidden in heaven, and whatever you permit* on earth will be permitted in heaven."

²⁰Then he sternly warned the disciples not to tell anyone that he was the Messiah.

Jesus Predicts His Death

²¹From then on Jesus* began to tell his disciples plainly that it was necessary for him to go to Jerusalem, and that he would suffer many terrible things at the hands of the elders, the leading priests, and the teachers of religious law. He would be killed, but on the third day he would be raised from the dead.

²²But Peter took him aside and began to reprimand him* for saying such things. "Heaven forbid, Lord," he said. "This will never happen to you!"

²³Jesus turned to Peter and said, "Get away from me, Satan! You are a dangerous trap to me. You are seeing things merely from a human point of view, not from God's."

²⁴Then Jesus said to his disciples, "If any of you wants to be my follower, you must give up your own way, take up your cross, and follow me. ²⁵If you try to hang on to your life, you will lose it. But if you give up your life for my sake, you will save it. ²⁶And what do you benefit if you gain the whole world but lose your own soul?* Is anything worth more than your soul? ²⁷For the Son of Man will come with his angels in the glory of his Father and will judge all people according to their deeds. ²⁸And I tell you the truth, some standing here right now will not die before they see the Son of Man coming in his Kingdom."

The Transfiguration

17 Six days later Jesus took Peter and the two brothers, James and John, and led them up a high mountain to be alone. ²As the men watched, Jesus' appearance was transformed so that his face shone like the sun, and his clothes became as white as light. ³Suddenly, Moses and Elijah appeared and began talking with Jesus.

⁴Peter exclaimed, "Lord, it's wonderful for us to be here! If you want, I'll make three shelters as memorials*—one for you, one for Moses, and one for Elijah."

⁵But even as he spoke, a bright cloud overshadowed them, and a voice from the cloud said, "This is my dearly loved Son, who brings me great joy. Listen to him." ⁶The disciples were terrified and fell face down on the ground.

⁷Then Jesus came over and touched them. "Get up," he said. "Don't be afraid." ⁸And when they looked up, Moses and Elijah were gone, and they saw only Jesus.

⁹As they went back down the mountain, Jesus commanded them, "Don't tell anyone what you have seen until the Son of Man* has been raised from the dead."

¹⁰Then his disciples asked him, "Why do the teachers of religious law insist that Elijah must return before the Messiah comes?*"

¹¹Jesus replied, "Elijah is indeed coming first to get everything ready. ¹²But I tell you, Elijah has already come, but he wasn't recognized, and they chose to abuse him. And in the same way they will also make the Son of Man suffer." ¹³Then the disciples realized he was talking about John the Baptist.

Jesus Heals a Demon-Possessed Boy

¹⁴At the foot of the mountain, a large crowd was waiting for them. A man came and knelt before Jesus and said, ¹⁵"Lord, have mercy on my son. He has seizures and suffers terribly. He often falls into the fire or into the water. ¹⁶So I brought him to your disciples, but they couldn't heal him."

¹⁷Jesus said, "You faithless and corrupt people! How long must I be with you? How long must I put up with you? Bring the boy here to me." ¹⁸Then Jesus rebuked the demon in the boy, and it left him. From that moment the boy was well.

¹⁹Afterward the disciples asked Jesus privately, "Why couldn't we cast out that demon?"

²⁰"You don't have enough faith," Jesus told them. "I tell you the truth, if you had faith even as small as a mustard seed, you could say to this mountain, 'Move from here to there,' and it would move. Nothing would be impossible.*"

16:13 "Son of Man" is a title Jesus used for himself. **16:16** Or *the Christ. Messiah* (a Hebrew term) and *Christ* (a Greek term) both mean "anointed one." **16:17** Greek *Simon bar-Jonah;* see John 1:42; 21:15-17. **16:18a** Greek *that you are Peter.* **16:18b** Greek *and the gates of Hades.* **16:19a** Or *bind,* or *lock.* **16:19b** Or *loose,* or *open.* **16:21** Some manuscripts read *Jesus the Messiah.* **16:22** Or *began to correct him.* **16:26** Or *your self?* also in 16:26b. **17:4** Greek *three tabernacles.* **17:9** "Son of Man" is a title Jesus used for himself. **17:10** Greek *that Elijah must come first?* **17:20** Some manuscripts add verse 21, *But this kind of demon won't leave except by prayer and fasting.* Compare Mark 9:29.

THE FAITHFUL *Gentile Woman*

⊚ IDENTITY | Persistence Rewarded

She remembers...

I knew if I had the chance, I would ask him to heal my daughter. Did I have the right to ask? Maybe not. Maybe I assumed he would reject me. And at first, it seemed he did.

He did not answer me right away, but I was not deterred. Even when his disciples told him to dismiss me, I believed Jesus could heal her. Yes, he was a Jew and I a Gentile. We had nearly nothing in common.

But I persisted in my plea and knelt before him.

"Lord, help me!" I begged. My daughter was tormented by a demon. I knew he had delivered others from this affliction before.

When he said it wasn't right to throw the children's food to the dogs, I hesitated, but only for a moment. I trusted he had more to give, even to a Gentile.

So, I played his word game: "Even dogs are allowed to eat the scraps."

What I knew of him proved he had access to power beyond our understanding. He saw my faith in my persistence. I may be a Gentile, but the God of the Jews rewards persistent faith in us all.

My daughter was healed that very instant.

THE FAITHFUL GENTILE WOMAN'S STORY IS TOLD IN MATTHEW 15:21-28 AND MARK 7:24-30.

> Persistent faith is always rewarded by God.

IDENTIFY

If you were kneeling at Jesus' feet, what would you ask him for? What do you need from Jesus now?

How does this woman's persistent faith encourage you to courageously kneel at Jesus' feet and ask for what you need?

> "Sometimes I don't understand the Bible's traditions, written long ago to people different from me in many ways. But, even when I, like this Gentile woman, feel different, I know I can kneel before Jesus and make my requests. I have seen that Jesus welcomes my persistent asking."

CARA DAY is a writer and illustrator. She has served with Stonecroft Ministries helping women live "extraordinary."

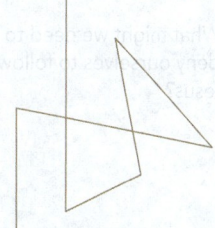

MATTHEW 17

Jesus Again Predicts His Death

[22] After they gathered again in Galilee, Jesus told them, "The Son of Man is going to be betrayed into the hands of his enemies. [23] He will be killed, but on the third day he will be raised from the dead." And the disciples were filled with grief.

Payment of the Temple Tax

[24] On their arrival in Capernaum, the collectors of the Temple tax* came to Peter and asked him, "Doesn't your teacher pay the Temple tax?"

[25] "Yes, he does," Peter replied. Then he went into the house.

17:24 Greek *the two-drachma [tax]*; also in 17:24b. See Exod 30:13-16; Neh 10:32-33.

Theos

IMAGE | MY STORY WITH GOD

Denying Ourselves to Find a Fulfilling Life

SCRIPTURE CONNECTION: MATTHEW 16:24-26

What does it mean to be Jesus' disciple? Why is Jesus' teaching here so relevant and so countercultural?

A significant piece of our Christian identity is found here. And, if we don't take time to understand its meaning, we miss out on the fullness of a life found only in Jesus.

It is unpopular to talk about denial, death, and suffering when the culture around us tells us to do everything we can not to suffer, not to age, not to deny ourselves. Isn't it normal to avoid pain and suffering? Don't we "deserve" to do whatever we want, whenever we want, and however we want? Shouldn't we pursue what our hearts desire above everything else?

> When we empty ourselves *of* ourselves, we make space for the fullness of life God promises us.

The world around us tells us that the answer to those questions is yes. So when Jesus invites us to a different way, we don't want it. We don't wish to deny ourselves, take up our cross, and follow him.

Yet, putting Jesus first—and letting him reshape what we want for our lives—lets us fully experience God's perfect ways. As odd as it may sound to our ears, by not pursuing happiness, but by pursuing Jesus instead, we find true happiness.

IMAGINE

What has first place in our hearts? Where have we not yet experienced God's fullness?

What might we need to deny ourselves to follow Jesus?

"When I was twenty years old, God asked me to work as a volunteer. Instead of earning a salary, I spent nine years volunteering full time, with no regular financial support. 'Give me this day my daily bread' was a true, daily prayer, and I learned what it means to deny myself to find life."

BELÉN PETERS is a mobilizer with Scatter Global. Since 2002, she has been mobilizing mission-minded Latinos to take their passion and profession to places where Christ is unknown.

But before he had a chance to speak, Jesus asked him, "What do you think, Peter?* Do kings tax their own people or the people they have conquered?*"

²⁶"They tax the people they have conquered," Peter replied.

"Well, then," Jesus said, "the citizens are free! ²⁷However, we don't want to offend them, so go down to the lake and throw in a line. Open the mouth of the first fish you catch, and you will find a large silver coin.* Take it and pay the tax for both of us."

The Greatest in the Kingdom

18 About that time the disciples came to Jesus and asked, "Who is greatest in the Kingdom of Heaven?"

²Jesus called a little child to him and put the child among them. ³Then he said, "I tell you the truth, unless you turn from your sins and become like little children, you will never get into the Kingdom of Heaven. ⁴So anyone who becomes as humble as this little child is the greatest in the Kingdom of Heaven.

⁵"And anyone who welcomes a little child like this on my behalf* is welcoming me. ⁶But if you cause one of these little ones who trusts in me to fall into sin, it would be better for you to have a large millstone tied around your neck and be drowned in the depths of the sea.

⁷"What sorrow awaits the world, because it tempts people to sin. Temptations are inevitable, but what sorrow awaits the person who does the tempting. ⁸So if your hand or foot causes you to sin, cut it off and throw it away. It's better to enter eternal life with only one hand or one foot than to be thrown into eternal fire with both of your hands and feet. ⁹And if your eye causes you to sin, gouge it out and throw it away. It's better to enter eternal life with only one eye than to have two eyes and be thrown into the fire of hell.*

¹⁰"Beware that you don't look down on any of these little ones. For I tell you that in heaven their angels are always in the presence of my heavenly Father.*

Parable of the Lost Sheep

¹²"If a man has a hundred sheep and one of them wanders away, what will he do? Won't he leave the ninety-nine others on the hills and go out to search for the one that is lost? ¹³And if he finds it, I tell you the truth, he will rejoice over it more than over the ninety-nine that didn't wander away! ¹⁴In the same way, it is not my heavenly Father's will that even one of these little ones should perish.

Correcting Another Believer

¹⁵"If another believer* sins against you,* go privately and point out the offense. If the other person listens and confesses it, you have won that person back. ¹⁶But if you are unsuccessful, take one or two others with you and go back again, so that everything you say may be confirmed by two or three witnesses. ¹⁷If the person still refuses to listen, take your case to the church. Then if he or she won't accept the church's decision, treat that person as a pagan or a corrupt tax collector.

¹⁸"I tell you the truth, whatever you forbid* on earth will be forbidden in heaven, and whatever you permit* on earth will be permitted in heaven.

¹⁹"I also tell you this: If two of you agree here on earth concerning anything you ask, my Father in heaven will do it for you. ²⁰For where two or three gather together as my followers,* I am there among them."

Parable of the Unforgiving Debtor

²¹Then Peter came to him and asked, "Lord, how often should I forgive someone* who sins against me? Seven times?"

²²"No, not seven times," Jesus replied, "but seventy times seven!*

²³"Therefore, the Kingdom of Heaven can be compared to a king who decided to bring his accounts up to date with servants who had borrowed money from him. ²⁴In the process, one of his debtors was brought in who owed him millions of dollars.* ²⁵He couldn't pay, so his master ordered that he be sold—along with his wife, his children, and everything he owned—to pay the debt.

²⁶"But the man fell down before his master and begged him, 'Please, be patient with me, and I will pay it all.' ²⁷Then his master was filled with pity for him, and he released him and forgave his debt.

²⁸"But when the man left the king, he went to a fellow servant who owed him a few thousand dollars.*

17:25a Greek *Simon*. **17:25b** Greek *their sons or others?* **17:27** Greek *a stater* [a Greek coin equivalent to four drachmas]. **18:5** Greek *in my name*. **18:9** Greek *the Gehenna of fire*. **18:10** Some manuscripts add verse 11, *And the Son of Man came to save those who are lost*. Compare Luke 19:10. **18:15a** Greek *If your brother*. **18:15b** Some manuscripts do not include *against you*. **18:18a** Or *bind*, or *lock*. **18:18b** Or *loose*, or *open*. **18:20** Greek *gather together in my name*. **18:21** Greek *my brother*. **18:22** Or *seventy-seven times*. **18:24** Greek *10,000 talents* [375 tons or 340 metric tons of silver]. **18:28** Greek *100 denarii*. A denarius was equivalent to a laborer's full day's wage.

18:1-35 In light of the growing polarization in responses to his being the Messiah, Jesus began to instruct his followers on the nature of community life. For a community to live according to Jesus' standards, people must live with humility, sensitivity, compassion, discipline, and forgiveness.

18:6-10 To "cause one . . . to fall into sin" is to lead believing children (or possibly believing adults who become "like little children"; see 18:3) to reject Christ and abandon the faith. The designation "little ones" emphasizes their humility (18:4; 19:13-15). Though the thought of being drowned with a large millstone around the neck is frightful, Jesus warned that causing another to fall away would bring far greater misery.

He grabbed him by the throat and demanded instant payment.

²⁹"His fellow servant fell down before him and begged for a little more time. 'Be patient with me, and I will pay it,' he pleaded. ³⁰But his creditor wouldn't wait. He had the man arrested and put in prison until the debt could be paid in full.

³¹"When some of the other servants saw this, they were very upset. They went to the king and told him everything that had happened. ³²Then the king called in the man he had forgiven and said, 'You evil servant! I forgave you that tremendous debt because you pleaded with me. ³³Shouldn't you have mercy on your fellow servant, just as I had mercy on you?' ³⁴Then the angry king sent the man to prison to be tortured until he had paid his entire debt.

³⁵"That's what my heavenly Father will do to you if you refuse to forgive your brothers and sisters* from your heart."

Discussion about Divorce and Marriage

19 When Jesus had finished saying these things, he left Galilee and went down to the region of Judea east of the Jordan River. ²Large crowds followed him there, and he healed their sick.

18:35 Greek *your brother.*

Come Close — FORGIVENESS IS A WAY OF LIFE

SCRIPTURE CONNECTION: MATTHEW 18:21-35

Does forgiveness seem elusive? Is it only the holiest of people who can forgive? Do we need to wait until we "feel" forgiving? In my own life, forgiving others has been a journey. But forgiveness is not a suggestion or a good idea: It's Jesus' command to all who follow him. And it can be challenging to follow this command, especially when we've been deeply hurt.

We forgive because we want to be like Jesus. And when we look at this passage, a few things jump out that confront our preconceived ideas about forgiveness:

1. When someone wrongs us, we are responsible for forgiving. It's not on them but on us! We forgive because we've been so generously forgiven by God.
2. Holding a grudge is a bit like slamming your hand in a car door and hoping it hurts the person who wronged you. When we refuse to forgive, *we* pay the price.
3. The number of times we should forgive refers to our attitude. We're not supposed to count—our forgiving others should be endless, like God's forgiveness of us.

Learning to forgive has been one of my life's greatest revelations. It's brought freedom, healing, and restoration to my relationship with God and people. It's not easy, but as I see the effects of forgiveness, I see the wisdom in God's command and example.

REFLECT "Shouldn't you have mercy on your fellow servant, just as I had mercy on you?" MATTHEW 18:33

Take a few minutes to pray and ask the Holy Spirit to reveal to you someone you could forgive or for what situations you need God to forgive you.

CONSIDER "Forgiveness is an act of the will, and the will can function regardless of the temperature of the heart."
CORRIE TEN BOOM

Forgiveness brings healing, restoration, and freedom. Are you ready?

BELÉN PETERS is a mobilizer with Scatter Global. Since 2002, she has been mobilizing mission-minded Latinos to take their passion and profession to places where Christ is unknown.

³Some Pharisees came and tried to trap him with this question: "Should a man be allowed to divorce his wife for just any reason?"

⁴"Haven't you read the Scriptures?" Jesus replied. "They record that from the beginning 'God made them male and female.'*" ⁵And he said, "'This explains why a man leaves his father and mother and is joined to his wife, and the two are united into one.'* ⁶Since they are no longer two but one, let no one split apart what God has joined together."

⁷"Then why did Moses say in the law that a man could give his wife a written notice of divorce and send her away?"* they asked.

⁸Jesus replied, "Moses permitted divorce only as a concession to your hard hearts, but it was not what God had originally intended. ⁹And I tell you this, whoever divorces his wife and marries someone else commits adultery—unless his wife has been unfaithful.*"

¹⁰Jesus' disciples then said to him, "If this is the case, it is better not to marry!"

¹¹"Not everyone can accept this statement," Jesus said. "Only those whom God helps. ¹²Some are born as eunuchs, some have been made eunuchs by others, and some choose not to marry* for the sake of the Kingdom of Heaven. Let anyone accept this who can."

Jesus Blesses the Children

¹³One day some parents brought their children to Jesus so he could lay his hands on them and pray for them. But the disciples scolded the parents for bothering him.

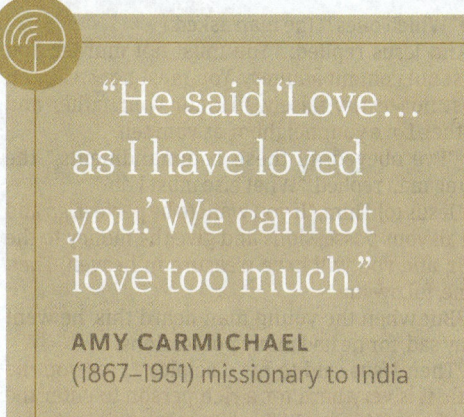

> "He said 'Love... as I have loved you.' We cannot love too much."
>
> AMY CARMICHAEL
> (1867–1951) missionary to India

¹⁴But Jesus said, "Let the children come to me. Don't stop them! For the Kingdom of Heaven belongs to those who are like these children." ¹⁵And he placed his hands on their heads and blessed them before he left.

The Rich Man

¹⁶Someone came to Jesus with this question: "Teacher,* what good deed must I do to have eternal life?"

¹⁷"Why ask me about what is good?" Jesus replied. "There is only One who is good. But to answer your question—if you want to receive eternal life, keep* the commandments."

19:4 Gen 1:27; 5:2. **19:5** Gen 2:24. **19:7** See Deut 24:1. **19:9** Some manuscripts add *And anyone who marries a divorced woman commits adultery.* Compare Matt 5:32. **19:12** Greek *and some make themselves eunuchs.* **19:16** Some manuscripts read *Good Teacher.* **19:17** Some manuscripts read *continue to keep.*

19:3-6 Jewish teachings on divorce assumed the legitimacy of divorce itself. Still, different rabbinical schools justified divorce differently according to their interpretations of Deuteronomy 24:1-4. The hard-line school considered a divorce legitimate only for sexual unfaithfulness, while the permissive school permitted a man to divorce his wife for trivial reasons. The Pharisees sought to trap Jesus in their debate between teachers. Instead, Jesus questioned their assumption and pointed them back to God's original purpose for marriage.

19:7-9 Both the Pharisees and Jesus assumed that men had the prerogative regarding divorce (see also 5:31-32), based on Jewish cultural practices of divorce and remarriage at the time. However, Jesus also put the blame and responsibility on men. First-century Greco-Roman society legislated divorce, and women, like men, in Rome and Greece could terminate their marriages. By emphasizing marriage's divine origin, Jesus raised marriage's ethical standard for all his followers, men and women.

19:9 Jesus permitted divorce only for unfaithfulness (see 5:32). Jesus' position on divorce favored women and protected them from the whims of unwise men (see the note on 19:3-6). In the face of those who thought divorce could be taken lightly, Jesus affirmed God's created order: Marriage was designed to be permanent (see Mark 10:11-12). This verse speaks only of the man who divorces his wife unlawfully. In such a case, his remarriage is adulterous. Jesus' motivation was to reestablish the permanency of marriage and protect women, who were especially vulnerable when they didn't have a close male relation to provide for them.

19:10-12 Celibacy is a sacrificial choice, and those who choose it experience freedom to follow God's calling in a unique way. Although the language used is masculine (Greek *eunuch*, see the note on 19:12), celibacy has been widespread among women missionaries throughout history. Chinese Christians still remember single women missionaries from the nineteenth- and early twentieth-centuries, such as Marie Monsen and Lottie Moon. These women chose not to marry to bring the gospel into China, focusing in particular on education and societal liberation for Chinese women. Today, women are still free to choose celibacy to fulfill a calling that God has placed on their lives.

19:12 Jesus uses the term *eunuchs* metaphorically for anyone—men or women—deciding to remain celibate to focus primarily on serving God's Kingdom (see Luke 14:26; 18:29-30; see also 1 Corinthians 7:7-8). Jesus was not denigrating marriage; he was simply indicating that those who choose to remain unmarried often have greater freedom for ministry (see 1 Corinthians 7:25-35).

¹⁸"Which ones?" the man asked.

And Jesus replied: "'You must not murder. You must not commit adultery. You must not steal. You must not testify falsely. ¹⁹Honor your father and mother. Love your neighbor as yourself.'*"

²⁰"I've obeyed all these commandments," the young man replied. "What else must I do?"

²¹Jesus told him, "If you want to be perfect, go and sell all your possessions and give the money to the poor, and you will have treasure in heaven. Then come, follow me."

²²But when the young man heard this, he went away sad, for he had many possessions.

²³Then Jesus said to his disciples, "I tell you the truth, it is very hard for a rich person to enter the Kingdom of Heaven. ²⁴I'll say it again—it is easier for a camel to go through the eye of a needle than for a rich person to enter the Kingdom of God!"

²⁵The disciples were astounded. "Then who in the world can be saved?" they asked.

²⁶Jesus looked at them intently and said, "Humanly speaking, it is impossible. But with God everything is possible."

²⁷Then Peter said to him, "We've given up everything to follow you. What will we get?"

²⁸Jesus replied, "I assure you that when the world is made new* and the Son of Man* sits upon his glorious throne, you who have been my followers will also sit on twelve thrones, judging the twelve tribes of Israel. ²⁹And everyone who has given up houses or brothers or sisters or father or mother or children or property, for my sake, will receive a hundred times as much in return and will inherit eternal life. ³⁰But many who are the greatest now will be least important then, and those who seem least important now will be the greatest then.*

Parable of the Vineyard Workers

20 "For the Kingdom of Heaven is like the landowner who went out early one morning to hire workers for his vineyard. ²He agreed to pay the normal daily wage* and sent them out to work.

³"At nine o'clock in the morning he was passing through the marketplace and saw some people standing around doing nothing. ⁴So he hired them, telling them he would pay them whatever was right at the end of the day. ⁵So they went to work in the vineyard. At noon and again at three o'clock he did the same thing.

⁶"At five o'clock that afternoon he was in town again and saw some more people standing around. He asked them, 'Why haven't you been working today?'

⁷"They replied, 'Because no one hired us.'

"The landowner told them, 'Then go out and join the others in my vineyard.'

⁸"That evening he told the foreman to call the workers in and pay them, beginning with the last workers first. ⁹When those hired at five o'clock were paid, each received a full day's wage. ¹⁰When those hired first came to get their pay, they assumed they would receive more. But they, too, were paid a day's wage. ¹¹When they received their pay, they protested to the owner, ¹²'Those people worked only one hour, and yet you've paid them just as much as you paid us who worked all day in the scorching heat.'

¹³"He answered one of them, 'Friend, I haven't been unfair! Didn't you agree to work all day for the usual wage? ¹⁴Take your money and go. I wanted to pay this last worker the same as you. ¹⁵Is it against the law for me to do what I want with my money? Should you be jealous because I am kind to others?'

¹⁶"So those who are last now will be first then, and those who are first will be last."

Jesus Again Predicts His Death

¹⁷As Jesus was going up to Jerusalem, he took the twelve disciples aside privately and told them what was going to happen to him. ¹⁸"Listen," he said, "we're going up to Jerusalem, where the Son of Man* will be betrayed to the leading priests and the teachers of religious law. They will sentence him to die. ¹⁹Then they will hand him over to the Romans* to be mocked, flogged with a whip, and crucified. But on the third day he will be raised from the dead."

Jesus Teaches about Serving Others

²⁰Then the mother of James and John, the sons of Zebedee, came to Jesus with her sons. She knelt respectfully to ask a favor. ²¹"What is your request?" he asked.

She replied, "In your Kingdom, please let my two sons sit in places of honor next to you, one on your right and the other on your left."

²²But Jesus answered by saying to them, "You don't know what you are asking! Are you able to drink from the bitter cup of suffering I am about to drink?"

"Oh yes," they replied, "we are able!"

19:18-19 Exod 20:12-16; Deut 5:16-20; Lev 19:18. **19:28a** Or *in the regeneration.* **19:28b** "Son of Man" is a title Jesus used for himself. **19:30** Greek *But many who are first will be last; and the last, first.* **20:2** Greek *a denarius,* the payment for a full day's labor; similarly in 20:9, 10, 13. **20:18** "Son of Man" is a title Jesus used for himself. **20:19** Greek *the Gentiles.*

20:20-21 This mother's request appears to have been inspired by her sons since Jesus responded to the sons rather than to the mother (compare to Mark 10:35-37).

20:20 A mother seeking her sons' advancement is not without biblical precedent, such as Bathsheba, who sought to secure the throne for her son Solomon (1 Kings 1:15-21). James and John's mother was one of Jesus' faithful disciples who followed him to the end (see Matthew 27:55-56). Although the request was problematic, it indicates that she valued her sons' positions in God's Kingdom. Caregivers and mothers are incredibly influential in pointing children to serve God's Kingdom.

²³Jesus told them, "You will indeed drink from my bitter cup. But I have no right to say who will sit on my right or my left. My Father has prepared those places for the ones he has chosen."

²⁴When the ten other disciples heard what James and John had asked, they were indignant. ²⁵But Jesus called them together and said, "You know that the rulers in this world lord it over their people, and officials flaunt their authority over those under them. ²⁶But among you it will be different. Whoever wants to be a leader among you must be your servant, ²⁷and whoever wants to be first among you must become your slave. ²⁸For even the Son of Man came not to be served but to serve others and to give his life as a ransom for many."

Jesus Heals Two Blind Men

²⁹As Jesus and the disciples left the town of Jericho, a large crowd followed behind. ³⁰Two blind men were sitting beside the road. When they heard that Jesus was coming that way, they began shouting, "Lord, Son of David, have mercy on us!"

³¹"Be quiet!" the crowd yelled at them.

But they only shouted louder, "Lord, Son of David, have mercy on us!"

³²When Jesus heard them, he stopped and called, "What do you want me to do for you?"

³³"Lord," they said, "we want to see!" ³⁴Jesus felt sorry for them and touched their eyes. Instantly they could see! Then they followed him.

Jesus' Triumphant Entry

21 As Jesus and the disciples approached Jerusalem, they came to the town of Bethphage on the Mount of Olives. Jesus sent two of them on ahead. ²"Go into the village over there," he said. "As soon as you enter it, you will see a donkey tied there, with its colt beside it. Untie them and bring them to me. ³If anyone asks what you are doing, just say, 'The Lord needs them,' and he will immediately let you take them."

⁴This took place to fulfill the prophecy that said,

⁵ "Tell the people of Jerusalem,*
   'Look, your King is coming to you.
He is humble, riding on a donkey—
   riding on a donkey's colt.'"*

⁶The two disciples did as Jesus commanded. ⁷They brought the donkey and the colt to him and threw their garments over the colt, and he sat on it.*

⁸Most of the crowd spread their garments on the road ahead of him, and others cut branches from the trees and spread them on the road. ⁹Jesus was in the center of the procession, and the people all around him were shouting,

"Praise God* for the Son of David!
   Blessings on the one who comes in the name
      of the Lord!
   Praise God in highest heaven!"*

¹⁰The entire city of Jerusalem was in an uproar as he entered. "Who is this?" they asked.

¹¹And the crowds replied, "It's Jesus, the prophet from Nazareth in Galilee."

Jesus Clears the Temple

¹²Jesus entered the Temple and began to drive out all the people buying and selling animals for sacrifice. He knocked over the tables of the money changers and the chairs of those selling doves. ¹³He said to them, "The Scriptures declare, 'My Temple will be called a house of prayer,' but you have turned it into a den of thieves!"*

¹⁴The blind and the lame came to him in the Temple, and he healed them. ¹⁵The leading priests and the teachers of religious law saw these wonderful miracles and heard even the children in the Temple shouting, "Praise God for the Son of David."

But the leaders were indignant. ¹⁶They asked Jesus, "Do you hear what these children are saying?"

"Yes," Jesus replied. "Haven't you ever read the Scriptures? For they say, 'You have taught children and infants to give you praise.'"* ¹⁷Then he returned to Bethany, where he stayed overnight.

Jesus Curses the Fig Tree

¹⁸In the morning, as Jesus was returning to Jerusalem, he was hungry, ¹⁹and he noticed a fig tree beside the road. He went over to see if there were any figs, but there were only leaves. Then he said to it, "May you never bear fruit again!" And immediately the fig tree withered up.

²⁰The disciples were amazed when they saw this and asked, "How did the fig tree wither so quickly?"

²¹Then Jesus told them, "I tell you the truth, if you have faith and don't doubt, you can do things like this and much more. You can even say to this mountain, 'May you be lifted up and thrown into the sea,' and it will happen. ²²You can pray for anything, and if you have faith, you will receive it."

21:5a Greek *Tell the daughter of Zion.* Isa 62:11. **21:5b** Zech 9:9. **21:7** Greek *over them, and he sat on them.* **21:9a** Greek *Hosanna,* an exclamation of praise that literally means "save now"; also in 21:9b, 15. **21:9b** Pss 118:25-26; 148:1. **21:13** Isa 56:7; Jer 7:11. **21:16** Ps 8:2 (Greek version).

20:25-28 The desire for power is characteristic of leaders in this world. It ought not be a trait of those who follow Jesus (18:1-5; 19:13-15; 23:1-12). Instead, Jesus calls his followers to a radical lifestyle of serving others.

The Authority of Jesus Challenged

²³When Jesus returned to the Temple and began teaching, the leading priests and elders came up to him. They demanded, "By what authority are you doing all these things? Who gave you the right?"

²⁴"I'll tell you by what authority I do these things if you answer one question," Jesus replied. ²⁵"Did John's authority to baptize come from heaven, or was it merely human?"

They talked it over among themselves. "If we say it was from heaven, he will ask us why we didn't believe John. ²⁶But if we say it was merely human, we'll be mobbed because the people believe John was a prophet." ²⁷So they finally replied, "We don't know."

And Jesus responded, "Then I won't tell you by what authority I do these things.

Parable of the Two Sons

²⁸"But what do you think about this? A man with two sons told the older boy, 'Son, go out and work in the vineyard today.' ²⁹The son answered, 'No, I won't go,' but later he changed his mind and went anyway. ³⁰Then the father told the other son, 'You go,' and he said, 'Yes, sir, I will.' But he didn't go.

³¹"Which of the two obeyed his father?"

They replied, "The first."*

Then Jesus explained his meaning: "I tell you the truth, corrupt tax collectors and prostitutes will get into the Kingdom of God before you do. ³²For John the Baptist came and showed you the right way to live, but you didn't believe him, while tax collectors and prostitutes did. And even when you saw this happening, you refused to believe him and repent of your sins.

Parable of the Evil Farmers

³³"Now listen to another story. A certain landowner planted a vineyard, built a wall around it, dug a pit for pressing out the grape juice, and built a lookout tower. Then he leased the vineyard to tenant farmers and moved to another country. ³⁴At the time of the grape harvest, he sent his servants to collect his share of the crop. ³⁵But the farmers grabbed his servants, beat one, killed one, and stoned another. ³⁶So the landowner sent a larger group of his servants to collect for him, but the results were the same.

³⁷"Finally, the owner sent his son, thinking, 'Surely they will respect my son.'

³⁸"But when the tenant farmers saw his son coming, they said to one another, 'Here comes the heir to this estate. Come on, let's kill him and get the estate for ourselves!' ³⁹So they grabbed him, dragged him out of the vineyard, and murdered him.

⁴⁰"When the owner of the vineyard returns," Jesus asked, "what do you think he will do to those farmers?"

⁴¹The religious leaders replied, "He will put the wicked men to a horrible death and lease the vineyard to others who will give him his share of the crop after each harvest."

⁴²Then Jesus asked them, "Didn't you ever read this in the Scriptures?

'The stone that the builders rejected
   has now become the cornerstone.
This is the LORD's doing,
   and it is wonderful to see.'*

⁴³I tell you, the Kingdom of God will be taken away from you and given to a nation that will produce the proper fruit. ⁴⁴Anyone who stumbles over that stone will be broken to pieces, and it will crush anyone it falls on.*"

⁴⁵When the leading priests and Pharisees heard this parable, they realized he was telling the story against them—they were the wicked farmers. ⁴⁶They wanted to arrest him, but they were afraid of the crowds, who considered Jesus to be a prophet.

Parable of the Great Feast

22 Jesus also told them other parables. He said, ²"The Kingdom of Heaven can be illustrated by the story of a king who prepared a great wedding feast for his son. ³When the banquet was ready, he sent his servants to notify those who were invited. But they all refused to come!

⁴"So he sent other servants to tell them, 'The feast has been prepared. The bulls and fattened cattle have been killed, and everything is ready. Come to the banquet!' ⁵But the guests he had invited ignored them and went their own way, one to his farm, another to his business. ⁶Others seized his messengers and insulted them and killed them.

⁷"The king was furious, and he sent out his army to destroy the murderers and burn their town. ⁸And he said to his servants, 'The wedding feast is ready, and the guests I invited aren't worthy of the honor. ⁹Now go out to the street corners and invite everyone you see.' ¹⁰So the servants brought in everyone they could find, good and bad alike, and the banquet hall was filled with guests.

21:29-31 Other manuscripts read *"The second."* In still other manuscripts the first son says "Yes" but does nothing, the second son says "No" but then repents and goes, and the answer to Jesus' question is that the second son obeyed his father. 21:42 Ps 118:22-23. 21:44 This verse is not included in some early manuscripts. Compare Luke 20:18.

21:31-32 Jesus told the leading priests and elders that tax collectors and prostitutes, whom they despised most, would go before them into the Kingdom of God. This announcement was another radical message of inclusion shocking to a male-dominated society (for more on Jesus' radically inclusive message, see 8:11-12). But to all women—of every background and stage of life—who feel ashamed, Jesus' message provides redemption and hope.

¹¹"But when the king came in to meet the guests, he noticed a man who wasn't wearing the proper clothes for a wedding. ¹²'Friend,' he asked, 'how is it that you are here without wedding clothes?' But the man had no reply. ¹³Then the king said to his aides, 'Bind his hands and feet and throw him into the outer darkness, where there will be weeping and gnashing of teeth.'

¹⁴"For many are called, but few are chosen."

Taxes for Caesar

¹⁵Then the Pharisees met together to plot how to trap Jesus into saying something for which he could be arrested. ¹⁶They sent some of their disciples, along with the supporters of Herod, to meet with him. "Teacher," they said, "we know how honest you are. You teach the way of God truthfully. You are impartial and don't play favorites. ¹⁷Now tell us what you think about this: Is it right to pay taxes to Caesar or not?"

¹⁸But Jesus knew their evil motives. "You hypocrites!" he said. "Why are you trying to trap me? ¹⁹Here, show me the coin used for the tax." When they handed him a Roman coin,* ²⁰he asked, "Whose picture and title are stamped on it?"

²¹"Caesar's," they replied.

"Well, then," he said, "give to Caesar what belongs to Caesar, and give to God what belongs to God."

²²His reply amazed them, and they went away.

Discussion about Resurrection

²³That same day Jesus was approached by some Sadducees—religious leaders who say there is no resurrection from the dead. They posed this question: ²⁴"Teacher, Moses said, 'If a man dies without children, his brother should marry the widow and have a child who will carry on the brother's name.'* ²⁵Well, suppose there were seven brothers. The oldest one married and then died without children, so his brother married the widow. ²⁶But the second brother also died, and the third brother married her. This continued with all seven of them. ²⁷Last of all, the woman also died. ²⁸So tell us, whose wife will she be in the resurrection? For all seven were married to her."

²⁹Jesus replied, "Your mistake is that you don't know the Scriptures, and you don't know the power

22:19 Greek *a denarius.* 22:24 Deut 25:5-6.

22:23-30 If we have enjoyed a married relationship and yearn to reunite with our loved one in heaven, we might feel stunned and maybe even discouraged by Jesus' words. While he said that marriage would not be present in heaven, he didn't say that love would fail. One thing is sure: Imagining heavenly life cannot be simply an extrapolation of our life on earth. The good things we experience now are only a small taste of the goodness God is preparing for his people in his Kingdom.

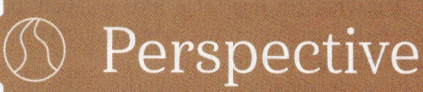

Perspective

Why does marriage matter?

SCRIPTURE CONNECTION: MATTHEW 22:23-33

The Sadducees' question about marriage in the afterlife was a setup. They believed that there was no bodily resurrection of the dead, and they were trying to expose Jesus' belief.

They created what they thought was a nonsensical scenario of a woman having seven husbands in the afterlife to prove their point. Jesus agreed it was nonsense but for a different reason.

The religious sacrament of marriage symbolizes God's loving faithfulness to us and Christ's loving, self-sacrificial oneness with his body, the church (Ephesians 5:21-33). By contrast, a civil marriage (in countries not governed by a religious legal system) is a government's way of recognizing and registering a marriage. Because of sin and evil in this world, many marriages do not experience a mutual and loving relationship.

Nevertheless, God establishes marriage to provide mutual companionship and (possibly) children (Genesis 1:26-28). God declares a man and a woman, united in marriage, to be good (Genesis 2:20-25).

People are made for intimacy without fear or shame. As one way we experience God's grace, marriage is a promise to our spouse of exclusive sexual, emotional, physical, and spiritual oneness before God and the wider community.

VIEWPOINTS

THEIRS: *Jesus showed the Sadducees the priority of marriage in relation to the resurrection.*
MINE: *"Jesus' promise to every believer of eternal life in a new, lasting body helps make sense of both the oneness of the husband-wife relationship and marriage's role in pointing us to our eternal relationship with God."*
OURS: *How can we better embrace the promise of marital companionship and faithfulness?*

LYNN H. COHICK, PhD, is Distinguished Professor of New Testament and Director of Houston Theological Seminary, where she leads the Doctor of Ministry program. She writes, speaks, and teaches internationally.

of God. ³⁰For when the dead rise, they will neither marry nor be given in marriage. In this respect they will be like the angels in heaven.

³¹"But now, as to whether there will be a resurrection of the dead—haven't you ever read about this in the Scriptures? Long after Abraham, Isaac, and Jacob had died, God said,* ³²'I am the God of Abraham, the God of Isaac, and the God of Jacob.'* So he is the God of the living, not the dead."

³³When the crowds heard him, they were astounded at his teaching.

The Most Important Commandment

³⁴But when the Pharisees heard that he had silenced the Sadducees with his reply, they met together to question him again. ³⁵One of them, an expert in religious law, tried to trap him with this question: ³⁶"Teacher, which is the most important commandment in the law of Moses?"

³⁷Jesus replied, "'You must love the LORD your God with all your heart, all your soul, and all your mind.'* ³⁸This is the first and greatest commandment. ³⁹A second is equally important: 'Love your neighbor as yourself.'* ⁴⁰The entire law and all the demands of the prophets are based on these two commandments."

Whose Son Is the Messiah?

⁴¹Then, surrounded by the Pharisees, Jesus asked them a question: ⁴²"What do you think about the Messiah? Whose son is he?"

They replied, "He is the son of David."

⁴³Jesus responded, "Then why does David, speaking under the inspiration of the Spirit, call the Messiah 'my Lord'? For David said,

⁴⁴ 'The LORD said to my Lord,
Sit in the place of honor at my right hand
   until I humble your enemies beneath your feet.'*

⁴⁵Since David called the Messiah 'my Lord,' how can the Messiah be his son?"

⁴⁶No one could answer him. And after that, no one dared to ask him any more questions.

Jesus Criticizes the Religious Leaders

23 Then Jesus said to the crowds and to his disciples, ²"The teachers of religious law and the Pharisees are the official interpreters of the law of Moses.* ³So practice and obey whatever they tell you, but don't follow their example. For they don't practice what they teach. ⁴They crush people with unbearable religious demands and never lift a finger to ease the burden.

⁵"Everything they do is for show. On their arms they wear extra wide prayer boxes with Scripture verses inside, and they wear robes with extra long tassels.* ⁶And they love to sit at the head table at banquets and in the seats of honor in the synagogues. ⁷They love to receive respectful greetings as they walk in the marketplaces, and to be called 'Rabbi.'*

⁸"Don't let anyone call you 'Rabbi,' for you have only one teacher, and all of you are equal as brothers and sisters.* ⁹And don't address anyone here on earth as 'Father,' for only God in heaven is your Father. ¹⁰And don't let anyone call you 'Teacher,' for you have only one teacher, the Messiah. ¹¹The greatest among you must be a servant. ¹²But those who exalt themselves will be humbled, and those who humble themselves will be exalted.

¹³"What sorrow awaits you teachers of religious law and you Pharisees. Hypocrites! For you shut the door of the Kingdom of Heaven in people's faces. You won't go in yourselves, and you don't let others enter either.*

¹⁵"What sorrow awaits you teachers of religious law and you Pharisees. Hypocrites! For you cross land and sea to make one convert, and then you turn that person into twice the child of hell* you yourselves are!

¹⁶"Blind guides! What sorrow awaits you! For you say that it means nothing to swear 'by God's Temple,' but that it is binding to swear 'by the gold in the Temple.' ¹⁷Blind fools! Which is more important—the gold or the Temple that makes the gold sacred? ¹⁸And you say that to swear 'by the altar' is not binding, but to swear 'by the gifts on the altar' is binding. ¹⁹How blind! For which is more important—the gift on the altar or the altar that makes the gift sacred? ²⁰When you swear 'by the altar,' you are swearing by it and by everything on it. ²¹And when you swear 'by the Temple,' you are swearing by it and by God, who lives in it. ²²And when you swear 'by heaven,' you are swearing by the throne of God and by God, who sits on the throne.

²³"What sorrow awaits you teachers of religious law and you Pharisees. Hypocrites! For you are careful to tithe even the tiniest income from your herb gardens,* but you ignore the more important aspects of the law—justice, mercy, and faith. You

---

22:31 Greek *read about this? God said.* **22:32** Exod 3:6. **22:37** Deut 6:5. **22:39** Lev 19:18. **22:44** Ps 110:1. **23:2** Greek *and the Pharisees sit in the seat of Moses.* **23:5** Greek *They enlarge their phylacteries and lengthen their tassels.* **23:7** *Rabbi,* from Aramaic, means "master" or "teacher." **23:8** Greek *brothers.* **23:13** Some manuscripts add verse 14, *What sorrow awaits you teachers of religious law and you Pharisees. Hypocrites! You shamelessly cheat widows out of their property and then pretend to be pious by making long prayers in public. Because of this, you will be severely punished.* Compare Mark 12:40 and Luke 20:47. **23:15** Greek *of Gehenna;* also in 23:33. **23:23** Greek *tithe the mint, the dill, and the cumin.*

22:30 Jesus was not teaching against gender differences nor disparaging the divine order of marriage and sexuality; rather, he was affirming that people will be transformed into a glorious new existence (see 1 Corinthians 15:35-49; 2 Corinthians 5:1-5) in which aspects of the present order, such as marriage, will not be present.

should tithe, yes, but do not neglect the more important things. ²⁴Blind guides! You strain your water so you won't accidentally swallow a gnat, but you swallow a camel!*

²⁵"What sorrow awaits you teachers of religious law and you Pharisees. Hypocrites! For you are so careful to clean the outside of the cup and the dish, but inside you are filthy—full of greed and self-indulgence! ²⁶You blind Pharisee! First wash the inside of the cup and the dish,* and then the outside will become clean, too.

²⁷"What sorrow awaits you teachers of religious law and you Pharisees. Hypocrites! For you are like whitewashed tombs—beautiful on the outside but filled on the inside with dead people's bones and all sorts of impurity. ²⁸Outwardly you look like righteous people, but inwardly your hearts are filled with hypocrisy and lawlessness.

²⁹"What sorrow awaits you teachers of religious law and you Pharisees. Hypocrites! For you build tombs for the prophets your ancestors killed, and you decorate the monuments of the godly people your ancestors destroyed. ³⁰Then you say, 'If we had lived in the days of our ancestors, we would never have joined them in killing the prophets.'

³¹"But in saying that, you testify against yourselves that you are indeed the descendants of those who murdered the prophets. ³²Go ahead and finish what your ancestors started. ³³Snakes! Sons of vipers! How will you escape the judgment of hell?

³⁴"Therefore, I am sending you prophets and wise men and teachers of religious law. But you will kill some by crucifixion, and you will flog others with whips in your synagogues, chasing them from city to city. ³⁵As a result, you will be held responsible for the murder of all godly people of all time—from the murder of righteous Abel to the murder of Zechariah son of Berekiah, whom you killed in the Temple between the sanctuary and the altar. ³⁶I tell you the truth, this judgment will fall on this very generation.

Jesus Grieves over Jerusalem

³⁷"O Jerusalem, Jerusalem, the city that kills the prophets and stones God's messengers! How often I have wanted to gather your children together as a hen protects her chicks beneath her wings, but you wouldn't let me. ³⁸And now, look, your house is abandoned and desolate.* ³⁹For I tell you this, you will never see me again until you say, 'Blessings on the one who comes in the name of the Lord!'*"

Jesus Speaks about the Future

24 As Jesus was leaving the Temple grounds, his disciples pointed out to him the various Temple buildings. ²But he responded, "Do you see all these buildings? I tell you the truth, they will be completely demolished. Not one stone will be left on top of another!"

³Later, Jesus sat on the Mount of Olives. His disciples came to him privately and said, "Tell us, when will all this happen? What sign will signal your return and the end of the world?*"

⁴Jesus told them, "Don't let anyone mislead you, ⁵for many will come in my name, claiming, 'I am the Messiah.' They will deceive many. ⁶And you will hear of wars and threats of wars, but don't panic. Yes, these things must take place, but the end won't follow immediately. ⁷Nation will go to war against nation, and kingdom against kingdom. There will be famines and earthquakes in many parts of the world. ⁸But all this is only the first of the birth pains, with more to come.

⁹"Then you will be arrested, persecuted, and killed. You will be hated all over the world because you are my followers.* ¹⁰And many will turn away from me and betray and hate each other. ¹¹And many false prophets will appear and will deceive many people. ¹²Sin will be rampant everywhere, and the love of many will grow cold. ¹³But the one who endures to the end will be saved. ¹⁴And the Good News about the Kingdom will be preached throughout the whole

---

23:24 See Lev 11:4, 23, where gnats and camels are both forbidden as food. **23:26** Some manuscripts do not include *and the dish*. **23:38** Some manuscripts do not include *and desolate*. **23:39** Ps 118:26. **24:3** Or *the age?* **24:9** Greek *on account of my name*.

23:37-39 Jesus used a feminine image to describe himself. He compared his mixed emotions for Jerusalem to a mother's *strong love* for her children. God yearns to provide protection and comfort for us, but rejecting his discipline has severe consequences. For Christians, living the way that God outlines in his Word means both protection and restriction. God's blessings come on his terms, not ours.

23:37 Despite the severe judgment Jesus had just leveled against Israel's teachers (23:29-36), he truly longed for the people of Jerusalem to repent and receive God's grace. The mother hen is an image of protective care (see also Deuteronomy 32:11; Ruth 2:12; Psalms 17:8; 61:4; 91:4).

24:3-8 Every generation asks whether the end comes in their age. Whether it's war, pandemic, economic depression, or any manner of strife, when we see bad things happening in the world, we may find it easy to wonder whether the end is near. It might be, but we don't know, and we still need to go on living. Despite our confusion and worries, we can choose to trust the Lord because he knows what we are experiencing.

24:9-14 Love for God and our neighbors is essential for following Jesus, but injustices and difficulties in life can cool our compassion. Why do we continue to follow Jesus to love *sacrificially* when many around us get away with living a sinful life? This question is a tough one, with which each of us needs to wrestle. But Jesus promises final salvation to the ones who endure and stay faithful to him.

24:13 The one who endures maintains faithful allegiance to Jesus despite persecution. Here, "the end" may refer to the end of one's own life, the judgment on Israel in AD 70 when the Temple was destroyed, or the end of history.

Shalom Image — My Story of My Unique Influence

Persisting in Our Purpose

SCRIPTURE CONNECTION: MATTHEW 24:1-51

Have you ever known your purpose but life felt ho-hum? Like the two women grinding flour, when we do the same things each day, it's easy to lose sight of God and our greater purpose.

Jesus commands us to "keep watch" and be ready for his return (24:42-44), remaining faithful to the responsibilities he has given us (24:45). But if we're not careful, we can let conflicting messages, urgent problems, or the world's chaos derail us from our God-given purpose.

Here are two ways we can stay attentive to our calling while we wait:

1. Focus on Jesus' words, which endure forever (24:35; see also 1 Peter 1:25). God promises that his words in the Bible will never fail. Instead, they will accomplish everything God sets out to do (Isaiah 55:11; Luke 1:37).
2. Keep watch for lies that break into our thoughts (2 Corinthians 10:5) and replace them with truths like these: As Jesus-followers, we are his chosen ones and God wants to protect us (Matthew 24:22, 24, 31). He considers us faithful, wise, dependable servants (24:45-47) and his friends (John 15:15).

> Jesus' words ground us in his peace and in our purpose.

As we focus on Jesus' words and partner with him in what he says, he grounds us in his peace and in our purpose.

IMAGINE

What helps you persist in your purpose when distractions hit or life feels mundane?

What words of truth can you focus on to remind you of your calling as you wait for God?

"When I persist in my purpose, I sense Jesus' pleasure and delight, my true reward."

GABRIELA MAGAÑA BANKS, PhD, is an author, teacher, and certified HeartSync inner healing prayer minister who facilitates freedom. Biblical principles and powerful moves of the Holy Spirit are her passion.

world, so that all nations* will hear it; and then the end will come.

¹⁵"The day is coming when you will see what Daniel the prophet spoke about—the sacrilegious object that causes desecration* standing in the Holy Place." (Reader, pay attention!) ¹⁶"Then those in Judea must flee to the hills. ¹⁷A person out on the deck of a roof must not go down into the house to pack. ¹⁸A person out in the field must not return even to get a coat. ¹⁹How terrible it will be for pregnant women and for nursing mothers in those days. ²⁰And pray that your flight will not be in winter or on the Sabbath. ²¹For there will be greater anguish than at any time since the world began. And it will never be so great again. ²²In fact, unless that time of calamity is shortened, not a single person will survive. But it will be shortened for the sake of God's chosen ones.

²³"Then if anyone tells you, 'Look, here is the Messiah,' or 'There he is,' don't believe it. ²⁴For false messiahs and false prophets will rise up and perform great signs and wonders so as to deceive, if possible, even God's chosen ones. ²⁵See, I have warned you about this ahead of time.

²⁶"So if someone tells you, 'Look, the Messiah is out in the desert,' don't bother to go and look. Or, 'Look, he is hiding here,' don't believe it! ²⁷For as the lightning flashes in the east and shines to the west, so it will be when the Son of Man* comes. ²⁸Just as the gathering of vultures shows there is a carcass nearby, so these signs indicate that the end is near.*

²⁹"Immediately after the anguish of those days,

> the sun will be darkened,
>   the moon will give no light,
> the stars will fall from the sky,
>   and the powers in the heavens will be shaken.*

³⁰And then at last, the sign that the Son of Man is coming will appear in the heavens, and there will be deep mourning among all the peoples of the earth. And they will see the Son of Man coming on the clouds of heaven with power and great glory.* ³¹And he will send out his angels with the mighty blast of a trumpet, and they will gather his chosen ones from all over the world*—from the farthest ends of the earth and heaven.

³²"Now learn a lesson from the fig tree. When its branches bud and its leaves begin to sprout, you know that summer is near. ³³In the same way, when you see all these things, you can know his return is very near, right at the door. ³⁴I tell you the truth, this generation* will not pass from the scene until all these things take place. ³⁵Heaven and earth will disappear, but my words will never disappear.

³⁶"However, no one knows the day or hour when these things will happen, not even the angels in heaven or the Son himself.* Only the Father knows.

³⁷"When the Son of Man returns, it will be like it was in Noah's day. ³⁸In those days before the flood, the people were enjoying banquets and parties and weddings right up to the time Noah entered his boat. ³⁹People didn't realize what was going to happen until the flood came and swept them all away. That is the way it will be when the Son of Man comes.

⁴⁰"Two men will be working together in the field; one will be taken, the other left. ⁴¹Two women will be grinding flour at the mill; one will be taken, the other left.

⁴²"So you, too, must keep watch! For you don't know what day your Lord is coming. ⁴³Understand this: If a homeowner knew exactly when a burglar was coming, he would keep watch and not permit his house to be broken into. ⁴⁴You also must be ready all the time, for the Son of Man will come when least expected.

⁴⁵"A faithful, sensible servant is one to whom the master can give the responsibility of managing his other household servants and feeding them. ⁴⁶If the master returns and finds that the servant has done a good job, there will be a reward. ⁴⁷I tell you the truth, the master will put that servant in charge of all he owns. ⁴⁸But what if the servant is evil and thinks, 'My master won't be back for a while,' ⁴⁹and he begins beating the other servants, partying, and getting drunk? ⁵⁰The master will return unannounced and unexpected, ⁵¹and he will cut the servant to pieces and assign him a place with the hypocrites. In that place there will be weeping and gnashing of teeth.

Parable of the Ten Bridesmaids

25 "Then the Kingdom of Heaven will be like ten bridesmaids* who took their lamps and went to meet the bridegroom. ²Five of them were foolish, and five were wise. ³The five who were foolish didn't take enough olive oil for their lamps, ⁴but the other five were wise enough to take along extra

---

24:14 Or *all peoples.* 24:15 Greek *the abomination of desolation.* See Dan 9:27; 11:31; 12:11. 24:27 "Son of Man" is a title Jesus used for himself. 24:28 Greek *Wherever the carcass is, the vultures gather.* 24:29 See Isa 13:10; 34:4; Joel 2:10. 24:30 See Dan 7:13. 24:31 Greek *from the four winds.* 24:34 Or *this age,* or *this nation.* 24:36 Some manuscripts do not include *or the Son himself.* 25:1 Or *virgins;* also in 25:7, 11.

25:1 "To meet the bridegroom" is an image for the coming of the Messiah (see Mark 2:19-20). Details of wedding customs during the period are not known. Some interpreters think that the bride was led to the home of the groom, who would stay away until the time appointed for the wedding feast. The bridesmaids (Greek *virgins;* also in Matthew 25:7, 11), who had already escorted the bride to the groom's home, would then wait for news of his arrival and escort him to the feast (25:10). Others think the groom may have come late in the night to the bride's home, where he was announced. Then, after celebrating with the bride's guests, the groom would take his bride under torches or lamps to his home.

> "Those who are wholly sanctified need not fear that God will hide his face, if they continue to walk in the light even as Christ is in the light."
>
> JULIA A. J. FOOTE
> (1823–1900) evangelist and deacon

oil. ⁵When the bridegroom was delayed, they all became drowsy and fell asleep.

⁶"At midnight they were roused by the shout, 'Look, the bridegroom is coming! Come out and meet him!'

⁷"All the bridesmaids got up and prepared their lamps. ⁸Then the five foolish ones asked the others, 'Please give us some of your oil because our lamps are going out.'

⁹"But the others replied, 'We don't have enough for all of us. Go to a shop and buy some for yourselves.'

¹⁰"But while they were gone to buy oil, the bridegroom came. Then those who were ready went in with him to the marriage feast, and the door was locked. ¹¹Later, when the other five bridesmaids returned, they stood outside, calling, 'Lord! Lord! Open the door for us!'

¹²"But he called back, 'Believe me, I don't know you!'

¹³"So you, too, must keep watch! For you do not know the day or hour of my return.

Parable of the Three Servants

¹⁴"Again, the Kingdom of Heaven can be illustrated by the story of a man going on a long trip. He called together his servants and entrusted his money to them while he was gone. ¹⁵He gave five bags of silver* to one, two bags of silver to another, and one bag of silver to the last—dividing it in proportion to their abilities. He then left on his trip.

¹⁶"The servant who received the five bags of silver began to invest the money and earned five more. ¹⁷The servant with two bags of silver also went to work and earned two more. ¹⁸But the servant who received the one bag of silver dug a hole in the ground and hid the master's money.

¹⁹"After a long time their master returned from his trip and called them to give an account of how they had used his money. ²⁰The servant to whom he had entrusted the five bags of silver came forward with five more and said, 'Master, you gave me five bags of silver to invest, and I have earned five more.'

²¹"The master was full of praise. 'Well done, my good and faithful servant. You have been faithful in handling this small amount, so now I will give you many more responsibilities. Let's celebrate together!*'

²²"The servant who had received the two bags of silver came forward and said, 'Master, you gave me two bags of silver to invest, and I have earned two more.'

²³"The master said, 'Well done, my good and faithful servant. You have been faithful in handling this small amount, so now I will give you many more responsibilities. Let's celebrate together!'

²⁴"Then the servant with the one bag of silver came and said, 'Master, I knew you were a harsh man, harvesting crops you didn't plant and gathering crops you didn't cultivate. ²⁵I was afraid I would lose your money, so I hid it in the earth. Look, here is your money back.'

²⁶"But the master replied, 'You wicked and lazy servant! If you knew I harvested crops I didn't plant and gathered crops I didn't cultivate, ²⁷why didn't you deposit my money in the bank? At least I could have gotten some interest on it.'

²⁸"Then he ordered, 'Take the money from this servant, and give it to the one with the ten bags of silver. ²⁹To those who use well what they are given, even more will be given, and they will have an abundance. But from those who do nothing, even what little they have will be taken away. ³⁰Now throw this useless servant into outer darkness, where there will be weeping and gnashing of teeth.'

The Final Judgment

³¹"But when the Son of Man* comes in his glory, and all the angels with him, then he will sit upon his glorious throne. ³²All the nations* will be gathered in his presence, and he will separate the people as a shepherd separates the sheep from the goats. ³³He will place the sheep at his right hand and the goats at his left.

³⁴"Then the King will say to those on his right, 'Come, you who are blessed by my Father, inherit the Kingdom prepared for you from the creation of

---

25:15 Greek *talents;* also throughout the story. A talent is equal to 75 pounds or 34 kilograms. **25:21** Greek *Enter into the joy of your master* [or *your Lord*]; also in 25:23. **25:31** "Son of Man" is a title Jesus used for himself. **25:32** Or *peoples.*

the world. ³⁵For I was hungry, and you fed me. I was thirsty, and you gave me a drink. I was a stranger, and you invited me into your home. ³⁶I was naked, and you gave me clothing. I was sick, and you cared for me. I was in prison, and you visited me.'

³⁷"Then these righteous ones will reply, 'Lord, when did we ever see you hungry and feed you? Or thirsty and give you something to drink? ³⁸Or a stranger and show you hospitality? Or naked and give you clothing? ³⁹When did we ever see you sick or in prison and visit you?'

⁴⁰"And the King will say, 'I tell you the truth, when you did it to one of the least of these my brothers and sisters,* you were doing it to me!'

⁴¹"Then the King will turn to those on the left and say, 'Away with you, you cursed ones, into the eternal fire prepared for the devil and his demons.* ⁴²For I was hungry, and you didn't feed me. I was thirsty, and you didn't give me a drink. ⁴³I was a stranger, and you didn't invite me into your home. I was naked, and you didn't give me clothing. I was sick and in prison, and you didn't visit me.'

⁴⁴"Then they will reply, 'Lord, when did we ever see you hungry or thirsty or a stranger or naked or sick or in prison, and not help you?'

⁴⁵"And he will answer, 'I tell you the truth, when you refused to help the least of these my brothers and sisters, you were refusing to help me.'

⁴⁶"And they will go away into eternal punishment, but the righteous will go into eternal life."

The Plot to Kill Jesus

26 When Jesus had finished saying all these things, he said to his disciples, ²"As you know, Passover begins in two days, and the Son of Man* will be handed over to be crucified."

³At that same time the leading priests and elders were meeting at the residence of Caiaphas, the high priest, ⁴plotting how to capture Jesus secretly and kill him. ⁵"But not during the Passover celebration," they agreed, "or the people may riot."

Jesus Anointed at Bethany

⁶Meanwhile, Jesus was in Bethany at the home of Simon, a man who had previously had leprosy. ⁷While he was eating,* a woman came in with a beautiful alabaster jar of expensive perfume and poured it over his head.

⁸The disciples were indignant when they saw this. "What a waste!" they said. ⁹"It could have been sold for a high price and the money given to the poor."

¹⁰But Jesus, aware of this, replied, "Why criticize this woman for doing such a good thing to me? ¹¹You will always have the poor among you, but you will not always have me. ¹²She has poured this perfume on me to prepare my body for burial. ¹³I tell you the truth, wherever the Good News is preached throughout the world, this woman's deed will be remembered and discussed."

Judas Agrees to Betray Jesus

¹⁴Then Judas Iscariot, one of the twelve disciples, went to the leading priests ¹⁵and asked, "How much will you pay me to betray Jesus to you?" And they gave him thirty pieces of silver. ¹⁶From that time on, Judas began looking for an opportunity to betray Jesus.

The Last Supper

¹⁷On the first day of the Festival of Unleavened Bread, the disciples came to Jesus and asked, "Where do you want us to prepare the Passover meal for you?"

¹⁸"As you go into the city," he told them, "you will see a certain man. Tell him, 'The Teacher says: My time has come, and I will eat the Passover meal with my disciples at your house.'" ¹⁹So the disciples did as Jesus told them and prepared the Passover meal there.

²⁰When it was evening, Jesus sat down at the table* with the Twelve. ²¹While they were eating, he said, "I tell you the truth, one of you will betray me."

²²Greatly distressed, each one asked in turn, "Am I the one, Lord?"

²³He replied, "One of you who has just eaten from this bowl with me will betray me. ²⁴For the Son of Man must die, as the Scriptures declared long ago. But how terrible it will be for the one who betrays him. It would be far better for that man if he had never been born!"

²⁵Judas, the one who would betray him, also asked, "Rabbi, am I the one?"

25:40 Greek *my brothers.*   25:41 Greek *his angels.*   26:2 "Son of Man" is a title Jesus used for himself.   26:7 Or *reclining.*   26:20 Or *Jesus reclined.*

26:6-13 Similar accounts of a woman anointing Jesus with expensive perfume are recorded in all four Gospel accounts (for accounts of the same event, see Mark 14:3-9; John 12:1-11; but Luke 7:36-50 records a different event). Whether or not the woman fully understood the full significance of her actions, she was honoring Jesus, which contrasts with the dishonor shown by those who would soon kill him. In addition to preparation for burial, the anointing also speaks of Jesus as King (1 Samuel 10:1; 2 Kings 9:6) and Priest (Exodus 29:7). Usually Israel's priests were responsible for anointing a king, but Jesus was rejected by the religious leaders. This woman served in that priestly role here instead, highlighting that in God's Kingdom "those who are last now will be first" (Matthew 20:16).

26:13 Jesus' command to remember her is remarkable given her anonymity in Matthew (and Mark 14:3-9). Whereas her identity is hidden, her act is remembered. It is also possible her namelessness here is another reflection of the male-dominated society where the early Christian movement arose. Nevertheless, despite the male disciples' complaint about her act, Jesus commended her and said that her deed would be remembered.

And Jesus told him, "You have said it."

²⁶As they were eating, Jesus took some bread and blessed it. Then he broke it in pieces and gave it to the disciples, saying, "Take this and eat it, for this is my body."

²⁷And he took a cup of wine and gave thanks to God for it. He gave it to them and said, "Each of you drink from it, ²⁸for this is my blood, which confirms the covenant* between God and his people. It is poured out as a sacrifice to forgive the sins of many. ²⁹Mark my words—I will not drink wine again until the day I drink it new with you in my Father's Kingdom."

³⁰Then they sang a hymn and went out to the Mount of Olives.

Jesus Predicts Peter's Denial

³¹On the way, Jesus told them, "Tonight all of you will desert me. For the Scriptures say,

'God will strike* the Shepherd,
 and the sheep of the flock will be scattered.'

³²But after I have been raised from the dead, I will go ahead of you to Galilee and meet you there."

³³Peter declared, "Even if everyone else deserts you, I will never desert you."

³⁴Jesus replied, "I tell you the truth, Peter—this very night, before the rooster crows, you will deny three times that you even know me."

³⁵"No!" Peter insisted. "Even if I have to die with you, I will never deny you!" And all the other disciples vowed the same.

Jesus Prays in Gethsemane

³⁶Then Jesus went with them to the olive grove called Gethsemane, and he said, "Sit here while I go over there to pray." ³⁷He took Peter and Zebedee's two sons, James and John, and he became anguished and distressed. ³⁸He told them, "My soul is crushed with grief to the point of death. Stay here and keep watch with me."

³⁹He went on a little farther and bowed with his face to the ground, praying, "My Father! If it is possible, let this cup of suffering be taken away from me. Yet I want your will to be done, not mine."

⁴⁰Then he returned to the disciples and found them asleep. He said to Peter, "Couldn't you watch with me even one hour? ⁴¹Keep watch and pray, so that you will not give in to temptation. For the spirit is willing, but the body is weak!"

⁴²Then Jesus left them a second time and prayed, "My Father! If this cup cannot be taken away* unless I drink it, your will be done." ⁴³When he returned to them again, he found them sleeping, for they couldn't keep their eyes open.

⁴⁴So he went to pray a third time, saying the same things again. ⁴⁵Then he came to the disciples and said, "Go ahead and sleep. Have your rest. But look—the time has come. The Son of Man is betrayed into the hands of sinners. ⁴⁶Up, let's be going. Look, my betrayer is here!"

Jesus Is Betrayed and Arrested

⁴⁷And even as Jesus said this, Judas, one of the twelve disciples, arrived with a crowd of men armed with swords and clubs. They had been sent by the leading priests and elders of the people. ⁴⁸The traitor, Judas, had given them a prearranged signal: "You will know which one to arrest when I greet him with a kiss." ⁴⁹So Judas came straight to Jesus. "Greetings, Rabbi!" he exclaimed and gave him the kiss.

⁵⁰Jesus said, "My friend, go ahead and do what you have come for."

Then the others grabbed Jesus and arrested him. ⁵¹But one of the men with Jesus pulled out his sword and struck the high priest's slave, slashing off his ear.

⁵²"Put away your sword," Jesus told him. "Those who use the sword will die by the sword. ⁵³Don't you realize that I could ask my Father for thousands* of angels to protect us, and he would send them instantly? ⁵⁴But if I did, how would the Scriptures be fulfilled that describe what must happen now?"

⁵⁵Then Jesus said to the crowd, "Am I some dangerous revolutionary, that you come with swords and clubs to arrest me? Why didn't you arrest me in the Temple? I was there teaching every day. ⁵⁶But this is all happening to fulfill the words of the prophets as recorded in the Scriptures." At that point, all the disciples deserted him and fled.

Jesus before the Council

⁵⁷Then the people who had arrested Jesus led him to the home of Caiaphas, the high priest, where the teachers of religious law and the elders had gathered. ⁵⁸Meanwhile, Peter followed him at a distance and came to the high priest's courtyard. He went in and sat with the guards and waited to see how it would all end.

⁵⁹Inside, the leading priests and the entire high council* were trying to find witnesses who would lie about Jesus, so they could put him to death. ⁶⁰But even though they found many who agreed to give false witness, they could not use anyone's testimony. Finally, two men came forward ⁶¹who declared, "This man said, 'I am able to destroy the Temple of God and rebuild it in three days.'"

⁶²Then the high priest stood up and said to Jesus, "Well, aren't you going to answer these charges? What do you have to say for yourself?" ⁶³But Jesus remained silent. Then the high priest said to him, "I demand in the name of the living God—tell us if you are the Messiah, the Son of God."

26:28 Some manuscripts read *the new covenant.* 26:31 Greek *I will strike.* Zech 13:7. 26:42 Greek *If this cannot pass.*
26:53 Greek *twelve legions.* 26:59 Greek *the Sanhedrin.*

⁶⁴Jesus replied, "You have said it. And in the future you will see the Son of Man seated in the place of power at God's right hand* and coming on the clouds of heaven."*

⁶⁵Then the high priest tore his clothing to show his horror and said, "Blasphemy! Why do we need other witnesses? You have all heard his blasphemy. ⁶⁶What is your verdict?"

"Guilty!" they shouted. "He deserves to die!"

⁶⁷Then they began to spit in Jesus' face and beat him with their fists. And some slapped him, ⁶⁸jeering, "Prophesy to us, you Messiah! Who hit you that time?"

Peter Denies Jesus

⁶⁹Meanwhile, Peter was sitting outside in the courtyard. A servant girl came over and said to him, "You were one of those with Jesus the Galilean."

⁷⁰But Peter denied it in front of everyone. "I don't know what you're talking about," he said.

⁷¹Later, out by the gate, another servant girl noticed him and said to those standing around, "This man was with Jesus of Nazareth."*

⁷²Again Peter denied it, this time with an oath. "I don't even know the man," he said.

⁷³A little later some of the other bystanders came over to Peter and said, "You must be one of them; we can tell by your Galilean accent."

⁷⁴Peter swore, "A curse on me if I'm lying—I don't know the man!" And immediately the rooster crowed.

⁷⁵Suddenly, Jesus' words flashed through Peter's mind: "Before the rooster crows, you will deny three times that you even know me." And he went away, weeping bitterly.

Judas Hangs Himself

27 Very early in the morning the leading priests and the elders of the people met again to lay plans for putting Jesus to death. ²Then they bound him, led him away, and took him to Pilate, the Roman governor.

³When Judas, who had betrayed him, realized that Jesus had been condemned to die, he was filled with remorse. So he took the thirty pieces of silver back to the leading priests and the elders. ⁴"I have sinned," he declared, "for I have betrayed an innocent man."

"What do we care?" they retorted. "That's your problem."

⁵Then Judas threw the silver coins down in the Temple and went out and hanged himself.

⁶The leading priests picked up the coins. "It wouldn't be right to put this money in the Temple treasury," they said, "since it was payment for murder."* ⁷After some discussion they finally decided to buy the potter's field, and they made it into a cemetery for foreigners. ⁸That is why the field is still called the Field of Blood. ⁹This fulfilled the prophecy of Jeremiah that says,

> "They took* the thirty pieces of silver—
> the price at which he was valued by the people of Israel,
> ¹⁰ and purchased the potter's field,
> as the LORD directed."*

Jesus' Trial before Pilate

¹¹Now Jesus was standing before Pilate, the Roman governor. "Are you the king of the Jews?" the governor asked him.

Jesus replied, "You have said it."

¹²But when the leading priests and the elders made their accusations against him, Jesus remained silent. ¹³"Don't you hear all these charges they are bringing against you?" Pilate demanded. ¹⁴But Jesus made no response to any of the charges, much to the governor's surprise.

¹⁵Now it was the governor's custom each year during the Passover celebration to release one prisoner to the crowd—anyone they wanted. ¹⁶This year there was a notorious prisoner, a man named Barabbas.* ¹⁷As the crowds gathered before Pilate's house that morning, he asked them, "Which one do you want me to release to you—Barabbas, or Jesus who is called the Messiah?" ¹⁸(He knew very well that the religious leaders had arrested Jesus out of envy.)

¹⁹Just then, as Pilate was sitting on the judgment seat, his wife sent him this message: "Leave that innocent man alone. I suffered through a terrible nightmare about him last night."

²⁰Meanwhile, the leading priests and the elders persuaded the crowd to ask for Barabbas to be released and for Jesus to be put to death. ²¹So the governor asked again, "Which of these two do you want me to release to you?"

The crowd shouted back, "Barabbas!"

²²Pilate responded, "Then what should I do with Jesus who is called the Messiah?"

They shouted back, "Crucify him!"

²³"Why?" Pilate demanded. "What crime has he committed?"

But the mob roared even louder, "Crucify him!"

26:64a Greek *seated at the right hand of the power.* See Ps 110:1. **26:64b** See Dan 7:13. **26:71** Or *Jesus the Nazarene.* **27:6** Greek *since it is the price for blood.* **27:9** Or *I took.* **27:9-10** Greek *as the LORD directed me.* Zech 11:12-13; Jer 32:6-9. **27:16** Some manuscripts read *Jesus Barabbas;* also in 27:17.

27:19 It is ironic that Pilate's wife, who we can assume was not a follower of Jesus, recognized and took a stand for Jesus' innocence, while the Jewish crowd did not.

²⁴Pilate saw that he wasn't getting anywhere and that a riot was developing. So he sent for a bowl of water and washed his hands before the crowd, saying, "I am innocent of this man's blood. The responsibility is yours!"

²⁵And all the people yelled back, "We will take responsibility for his death—we and our children!"*

²⁶So Pilate released Barabbas to them. He ordered Jesus flogged with a lead-tipped whip, then turned him over to the Roman soldiers to be crucified.

The Soldiers Mock Jesus

²⁷Some of the governor's soldiers took Jesus into their headquarters* and called out the entire regiment. ²⁸They stripped him and put a scarlet robe on him. ²⁹They wove thorn branches into a crown and put it on his head, and they placed a reed stick in his right hand as a scepter. Then they knelt before him in mockery and taunted, "Hail! King of the Jews!" ³⁰And they spit on him and grabbed the stick and struck him on the head with it. ³¹When they were finally tired of mocking him, they took off the robe and put his own clothes on him again. Then they led him away to be crucified.

The Crucifixion

³²Along the way, they came across a man named Simon, who was from Cyrene,* and the soldiers forced him to carry Jesus' cross. ³³And they went out to a place called Golgotha (which means "Place of the Skull"). ³⁴The soldiers gave Jesus wine mixed with bitter gall, but when he had tasted it, he refused to drink it.

³⁵After they had nailed him to the cross, the soldiers gambled for his clothes by throwing dice.* ³⁶Then they sat around and kept guard as he hung there. ³⁷A sign was fastened above Jesus' head, announcing the charge against him. It read: "This is Jesus, the King of the Jews." ³⁸Two revolutionaries* were crucified with him, one on his right and one on his left.

³⁹The people passing by shouted abuse, shaking their heads in mockery. ⁴⁰"Look at you now!" they yelled at him. "You said you were going to destroy the Temple and rebuild it in three days. Well then, if you are the Son of God, save yourself and come down from the cross!"

⁴¹The leading priests, the teachers of religious law, and the elders also mocked Jesus. ⁴²"He saved others," they scoffed, "but he can't save himself! So he is the King of Israel, is he? Let him come down from the cross right now, and we will believe in him! ⁴³He trusted God, so let God rescue him now if he wants him! For he said, 'I am the Son of God.'" ⁴⁴Even the revolutionaries who were crucified with him ridiculed him in the same way.

The Death of Jesus

⁴⁵At noon, darkness fell across the whole land until three o'clock. ⁴⁶At about three o'clock, Jesus called out with a loud voice, *"Eli, Eli,* lema sabachthani?"* which means *"My God, my God, why have you abandoned me?"**

⁴⁷Some of the bystanders misunderstood and thought he was calling for the prophet Elijah. ⁴⁸One of them ran and filled a sponge with sour wine, holding it up to him on a reed stick so he could drink. ⁴⁹But the rest said, "Wait! Let's see whether Elijah comes to save him."*

⁵⁰Then Jesus shouted out again, and he released his spirit. ⁵¹At that moment the curtain in the sanctuary of the Temple was torn in two, from top to bottom. The earth shook, rocks split apart, ⁵²and tombs opened. The bodies of many godly men and women who had died were raised from the dead. ⁵³They left the cemetery after Jesus' resurrection, went into the holy city of Jerusalem, and appeared to many people.

⁵⁴The Roman officer* and the other soldiers at the crucifixion were terrified by the earthquake and all that had happened. They said, "This man truly was the Son of God!"

⁵⁵And many women who had come from Galilee with Jesus to care for him were watching from a distance. ⁵⁶Among them were Mary Magdalene, Mary (the mother of James and Joseph), and the mother of James and John, the sons of Zebedee.

The Burial of Jesus

⁵⁷As evening approached, Joseph, a rich man from Arimathea who had become a follower of Jesus, ⁵⁸went to Pilate and asked for Jesus' body. And Pilate issued an order to release it to him. ⁵⁹Joseph took the body and wrapped it in a long sheet of clean linen cloth. ⁶⁰He placed it in his own new tomb, which had been carved out of the rock. Then he rolled a great stone across the entrance and left. ⁶¹Both Mary Magdalene and the other Mary were sitting across from the tomb and watching.

27:25 Greek *"His blood be on us and on our children."* **27:27** Or *into the Praetorium.* **27:32** *Cyrene* was a city in northern Africa. **27:35** Greek *by casting lots.* A few late manuscripts add *This fulfilled the word of the prophet: "They divided my garments among themselves and cast lots for my robe."* See Ps 22:18. **27:38** Or *criminals;* also in 27:44. **27:46a** Some manuscripts read *Eloi, Eloi.* **27:46b** Ps 22:1. **27:49** Some manuscripts add *And another took a spear and pierced his side, and out flowed water and blood.* Compare John 19:34. **27:54** Greek *The centurion.*

27:55-56 When Jesus explained the cost of being his disciple, he warned about the loss of family members (19:29). In spite of that, these women also chose to follow Jesus. While Jesus' male disciples abandoned him (26:56), these women overcame their fear and stayed with Jesus. They were also the first witnesses of Jesus' resurrection (28:1-10).

The Guard at the Tomb

⁶²The next day, on the Sabbath,* the leading priests and Pharisees went to see Pilate. ⁶³They told him, "Sir, we remember what that deceiver once said while he was still alive: 'After three days I will rise from the dead.' ⁶⁴So we request that you seal the tomb until the third day. This will prevent his disciples from coming and stealing his body and then telling everyone he was raised from the dead! If that happens, we'll be worse off than we were at first."

⁶⁵Pilate replied, "Take guards and secure it the best you can." ⁶⁶So they sealed the tomb and posted guards to protect it.

The Resurrection

28 Early on Sunday morning,* as the new day was dawning, Mary Magdalene and the other Mary went out to visit the tomb.

²Suddenly there was a great earthquake! For an angel of the Lord came down from heaven, rolled aside the stone, and sat on it. ³His face shone like lightning, and his clothing was as white as snow. ⁴The guards shook with fear when they saw him, and they fell into a dead faint.

⁵Then the angel spoke to the women. "Don't be afraid!" he said. "I know you are looking for Jesus, who was crucified. ⁶He isn't here! He is risen from the dead, just as he said would happen. Come, see where his body was lying. ⁷And now, go quickly and tell his disciples that he has risen from the dead, and he is going ahead of you to Galilee. You will see him there. Remember what I have told you."

⁸The women ran quickly from the tomb. They were very frightened but also filled with great joy, and they rushed to give the disciples the angel's message. ⁹And as they went, Jesus met them and greeted them. And they ran to him, grasped his feet, and worshiped him. ¹⁰Then Jesus said to them, "Don't be afraid! Go tell my brothers to leave for Galilee, and they will see me there."

The Report of the Guard

¹¹As the women were on their way, some of the guards went into the city and told the leading priests what had happened. ¹²A meeting with the elders was called, and they decided to give the soldiers a large bribe. ¹³They told the soldiers, "You must say, 'Jesus' disciples came during the night while we were sleeping, and they stole his body.' ¹⁴If the governor hears about it, we'll stand up for you so you won't get in trouble." ¹⁵So the guards accepted the bribe and said what they were told to say. Their story spread widely among the Jews, and they still tell it today.

The Great Commission

¹⁶Then the eleven disciples left for Galilee, going to the mountain where Jesus had told them to go. ¹⁷When they saw him, they worshiped him—but some of them doubted!

¹⁸Jesus came and told his disciples, "I have been given all authority in heaven and on earth. ¹⁹Therefore, go and make disciples of all the nations,* baptizing them in the name of the Father and the Son and the Holy Spirit. ²⁰Teach these new disciples to obey all the commands I have given you. And be sure of this: I am with you always, even to the end of the age."

27:62 Or *On the next day, which is after the Preparation.* 28:1 Greek *After the Sabbath, on the first day of the week.* 28:19 Or *all peoples.*

28:1 Mary Magdalene was one of the women who stayed with Jesus during his crucifixion (see 27:56). The mention of two women, Mary Magdalene and "the other Mary," as witnesses lends credibility to the historicity of the account. Under Jewish law, a woman's testimony was considered less reliable than a man's, so someone inventing a resurrection story would not have decided to use women as witnesses to such an important event. But in Matthew, women were the first to witness the empty tomb, and Jesus also met them in person on their way to tell the other disciples.

Mark

WHAT DO WE LEARN ABOUT GOD'S MISSION AND OURS?
Jesus did good deeds before he spoke good news.

WHO WROTE IT? John Mark, Barnabas's cousin and Paul's early traveling companion.

WHEN DID IT HAPPEN? Mark likely wrote this Gospel (using Peter's story and teachings) sometime between AD 55 and 65. The events took place early in the first century AD.

HOW IS IT ORGANIZED?

- **1:** Jesus begins his ministry with his baptism and calling his first followers
- **2–9:** Jesus heals and teaches in and around Galilee, his home region
- **10:** Jesus and his followers travel toward Judea, a region in the south
- **11–15:** Jesus spends his final week in Jerusalem, from a triumphant entry to his death
- **16:** Jesus rises from the dead

FEATURE HIGHLIGHTS

+ *Simon Peter's Mother-in-Law: Feverish to Fantastic, Fast (1241)*
+ *Healed Wholly (1242)*
+ *How Did Jesus Respond to Prejudice in His Society? (1252)*
+ *Calling? Called (1256)*

Words to Remember are highlighted throughout this book

HOW LONG DOES IT TAKE TO READ?

1:30

| :30 | 1:00 | 1:30 | 2:00 | 2:30 | 3:00 | 3:30 |

Timeline

BC

- **37** — HEROD THE GREAT BEGINS TO RULE AS KING OVER PALESTINE
- **6/5** — JESUS, MARY'S CHILD AND THE SON OF GOD, IS BORN
- **5/4** — MARY, JOSEPH, AND JESUS ESCAPE TO EGYPT
- **4** — HEROD THE GREAT DIES
- **4/3** — JESUS' FAMILY RETURNS TO NAZARETH

AD

- **6** — JUDEA BECOMES A ROMAN PROVINCE
- **6/7** — YOUNG JESUS VISITS THE TEMPLE
- **14** — TIBERIUS CAESAR BECOMES EMPEROR OF ROME
- **26** — JOHN THE BAPTIST'S MINISTRY BEGINS
- **27** — JESUS BEGINS HIS PUBLIC MINISTRY
- **28** — JOHN BAPTIZES JESUS; JESUS CHOOSES TWELVE DISCIPLES
- **29** — JESUS FEEDS 5,000+ INCLUDING WOMEN AND CHILDREN
- **30** — JESUS IS CRUCIFIED, RISES FROM THE DEAD, AND ASCENDS TO HEAVEN

John the Baptist Prepares the Way

1 This is the Good News about Jesus the Messiah, the Son of God.* It began ²just as the prophet Isaiah had written:

> "Look, I am sending my messenger ahead of you,
> and he will prepare your way.*
> ³ He is a voice shouting in the wilderness,
> 'Prepare the way for the Lord's coming!
> Clear the road for him!'*

⁴This messenger was John the Baptist. He was in the wilderness and preached that people should be baptized to show that they had repented of their sins and turned to God to be forgiven. ⁵All of Judea, including all the people of Jerusalem, went out to see and hear John. And when they confessed their sins, he baptized them in the Jordan River. ⁶His clothes were woven from coarse camel hair, and he wore a leather belt around his waist. For food he ate locusts and wild honey.

⁷John announced: "Someone is coming soon who is greater than I am—so much greater that I'm not even worthy to stoop down like a slave and untie the straps of his sandals. ⁸I baptize you with* water, but he will baptize you with the Holy Spirit!"

The Baptism and Temptation of Jesus

⁹One day Jesus came from Nazareth in Galilee, and John baptized him in the Jordan River. ¹⁰As Jesus came up out of the water, he saw the heavens splitting apart and the Holy Spirit descending on him* like a dove. ¹¹And a voice from heaven said, "You are my dearly loved Son, and you bring me great joy."

¹²The Spirit then compelled Jesus to go into the wilderness, ¹³where he was tempted by Satan for forty days. He was out among the wild animals, and angels took care of him.

¹⁴Later on, after John was arrested, Jesus went into Galilee, where he preached God's Good News.* ¹⁵**"The time promised by God has come at last!"** he announced. **"The Kingdom of God is near! Repent of your sins and believe the Good News!"**

The First Disciples

¹⁶One day as Jesus was walking along the shore of the Sea of Galilee, he saw Simon* and his brother Andrew throwing a net into the water, for they fished for a living. ¹⁷Jesus called out to them, **"Come, follow me, and I will show you how to fish for people!"** ¹⁸And they left their nets at once and followed him.

¹⁹A little farther up the shore Jesus saw Zebedee's sons, James and John, in a boat repairing their nets. ²⁰He called them at once, and they also followed him, leaving their father, Zebedee, in the boat with the hired men.

Jesus Casts Out an Evil Spirit

²¹Jesus and his companions went to the town of Capernaum. When the Sabbath day came, he went into the synagogue and began to teach. ²²The people were amazed at his teaching, for he taught with real authority—quite unlike the teachers of religious law.

²³Suddenly, a man in the synagogue who was possessed by an evil* spirit cried out, ²⁴"Why are you interfering with us, Jesus of Nazareth? Have you come to destroy us? I know who you are—the Holy One of God!"

²⁵But Jesus reprimanded him. **"Be quiet! Come out of the man,"** he ordered. ²⁶At that, the evil spirit screamed, threw the man into a convulsion, and then came out of him.

²⁷Amazement gripped the audience, and they began to discuss what had happened. "What sort of new teaching is this?" they asked excitedly. "It has such authority! Even evil spirits obey his orders!" ²⁸The news about Jesus spread quickly throughout the entire region of Galilee.

Jesus Heals Many People

²⁹After Jesus left the synagogue with James and John, they went to Simon and Andrew's home. ³⁰Now Simon's mother-in-law was sick in bed with a high fever. They told Jesus about her right away. ³¹So he went to her bedside, took her by the hand, and helped her sit up. Then the fever left her, and she prepared a meal for them.

³²That evening after sunset, many sick and demon-possessed people were brought to Jesus. ³³The whole town gathered at the door to watch. ³⁴So Jesus healed many people who were sick with various diseases, and he cast out many demons. But because the demons knew who he was, he did not allow them to speak.

Jesus Preaches in Galilee

³⁵Before daybreak the next morning, Jesus got up and went out to an isolated place to pray. ³⁶Later Simon and the others went out to find him. ³⁷When they found him, they said, "Everyone is looking for you."

1:1 Some manuscripts do not include *the Son of God.* **1:2** Mal 3:1. **1:3** Isa 40:3 (Greek version). **1:8** Or *in;* also in 1:8b. **1:10** Or *toward him,* or *into him.* **1:14** Some manuscripts read *the Good News of the Kingdom of God.* **1:16** *Simon* is called "Peter" in 3:16 and thereafter. **1:23** Greek *unclean;* also in 1:26, 27.

1:29-31 During the first century, Jewish women had restricted access to public affairs and so oversaw the home. Simon's mother-in-law began to host her guests immediately after Jesus healed her. Although women today are able to thrive beyond their domestic realms, women's influence in our household is still significant. We have great potential to bless those we share a home with and whoever enters our home.

SIMON PETER'S Mother-in-Law

IDENTITY

Feverish to Fantastic, Fast

She remembers...

The fever was intense. The heat was palpable. I couldn't remember ever feeling so immobilized.

I was sick—the kind of sick that kept me from my responsibilities. The kind of sick that worried my family. The kind of sick that put me in bed when I had so many things to do. It frustrated me, and then it scared me.

My son-in-law Simon, who would later be called Peter, had been following a new teacher. He was listening to him teach when he saw Jesus send demons out of a man. So, when they came to our house, Simon asked Jesus if he might heal me, too. Who would think that a man could do such things?

Jesus came to my bed; the fever was still strong. He stood beside me, grabbed my hand, and pulled me out of bed. I instantly felt better. If it hadn't happened to me, I wouldn't have believed it. I went from feverish to ready to tackle my to-do list. And now I had a house full of people with Jesus and his entourage there. I couldn't let them be hungry! So, I started doing what needed doing: preparing a meal for everyone to eat.

Suddenly my everyday tasks had new meaning. I was serving the healer, the one who put his hand on me and made the fever disappear. Simon was right; this is no ordinary teacher. This is someone who holds God's power in his touch.

> Jesus expects us to ask him for healing. It's what he does best.

SIMON PETER'S MOTHER-IN-LAW'S STORY IS TOLD IN MARK 1:29-31.

IDENTIFY

Have you ever asked God for healing for yourself or others?

Do you believe Jesus can heal you?

What do you think healing might look like for what ails you?

"I have had a few moments in my life when I've asked God to remove a barrier—a fear, a repetitive thought, a hardened heart—and he has, instantly. He works at both slow and fast paces, but I'm still surprised when it's fast."

ALEXANDRA KUYKENDALL is a cofounder of The Open Door Sisterhood and author of several books, including *Seeking Out Goodness: Finding the True and Beautiful All around You*.

³⁸But Jesus replied, "We must go on to other towns as well, and I will preach to them, too. That is why I came." ³⁹So he traveled throughout the region of Galilee, preaching in the synagogues and casting out demons.

Jesus Heals a Man with Leprosy

⁴⁰A man with leprosy came and knelt in front of Jesus, begging to be healed. "If you are willing, you can heal me and make me clean," he said. ⁴¹Moved with compassion,* Jesus reached out and touched him. "I am willing," he said. "Be healed!" ⁴²Instantly the leprosy disappeared, and the man was healed. ⁴³Then Jesus sent him on his way with a stern warning: ⁴⁴"Don't tell anyone about this. Instead, go to the priest and let him examine you. Take along the offering required in the law of Moses for those who have been healed of leprosy.* This will be a public testimony that you have been cleansed."

1:41 Some manuscripts read *Moved with anger.* 1:44 See Lev 14:2-32.

Healed Wholly

SCRIPTURE CONNECTION: MARK 1:40-45

This man should have been yelling for people to get away.

In Leviticus 13 and 14, we see how the Israelites dealt with disease and quarantine. None were more isolating than cases of leprosy. Anyone infected was required to cover their face when in public and call out to warn others that they were unclean, untouchable (Leviticus 13:45). The law also stated that they were to live outside the camp, alone (Leviticus 13:46). This sickness separated them completely.

Yet here, the man with leprosy boldly came close and knelt in front of Jesus with his request. Imagine the shock of the people when Jesus actually touched him (Mark 1:41)! In that moment, Jesus showed his power *and* great compassion by connecting with this man.

A while back, I received some very good news from a dear friend. By the time we hung up the phone, I had multiple missed messages of people sharing the same good news. Most people love sharing good news. Word travels fast!

Yet Jesus first wanted this man to follow the correct protocol and go to the priest so his healing would be officially recognized. He could then be invited back into his community. Jesus wanted not just the man's physical healing but his restoration from the pain of loneliness and isolation. For him to be welcomed home.

> When Jesus heals us, he heals completely. Body and soul and relationships—all wholly well.

IMAGINE

Where have you seen the healing power of Jesus in your community?

Where do you need Jesus to heal not just your body but also your soul?

"As I read this, I see more than healing. I see Jesus' invitation to heal and rebuild relationships. When Jesus heals, he heals completely. Body and soul and relationships—all wholly well."

ELIZA CORTÉS BAST, DEd candidate, is senior director of programs with Stonecroft. She is a pastor, professor, wife, mom, and mentor. She believes in passionately pursuing God and people by developing talent, asking strategic questions, and amplifying the good.

⁴⁵But the man went and spread the word, proclaiming to everyone what had happened. As a result, large crowds soon surrounded Jesus, and he couldn't publicly enter a town anywhere. He had to stay out in the secluded places, but people from everywhere kept coming to him.

Jesus Heals a Paralyzed Man

2 When Jesus returned to Capernaum several days later, the news spread quickly that he was back home. ²Soon the house where he was staying was so packed with visitors that there was no more room, even outside the door. While he was preaching God's word to them, ³four men arrived carrying a paralyzed man on a mat. ⁴They couldn't bring him to Jesus because of the crowd, so they dug a hole through the roof above his head. Then they lowered the man on his mat, right down in front of Jesus. ⁵Seeing their faith, Jesus said to the paralyzed man, "My child, your sins are forgiven."

⁶But some of the teachers of religious law who were sitting there thought to themselves, ⁷"What is he saying? This is blasphemy! Only God can forgive sins!"

⁸Jesus knew immediately what they were thinking, so he asked them, "Why do you question this in your hearts? ⁹Is it easier to say to the paralyzed man 'Your sins are forgiven,' or 'Stand up, pick up your mat, and walk'? ¹⁰So I will prove to you that the Son of Man* has the authority on earth to forgive sins." Then Jesus turned to the paralyzed man and said, ¹¹"Stand up, pick up your mat, and go home!"

¹²And the man jumped up, grabbed his mat, and walked out through the stunned onlookers. They were all amazed and praised God, exclaiming, "We've never seen anything like this before!"

Jesus Calls Levi (Matthew)

¹³Then Jesus went out to the lakeshore again and taught the crowds that were coming to him. ¹⁴As he walked along, he saw Levi son of Alphaeus sitting at his tax collector's booth. "Follow me and be my disciple," Jesus said to him. So Levi got up and followed him.

¹⁵Later, Levi invited Jesus and his disciples to his home as dinner guests, along with many tax collectors and other disreputable sinners. (There were many people of this kind among Jesus' followers.) ¹⁶But when the teachers of religious law who were Pharisees* saw him eating with tax collectors and other sinners, they asked his disciples, "Why does he eat with such scum?*"

¹⁷When Jesus heard this, he told them, "Healthy people don't need a doctor—sick people do. I have come to call not those who think they are righteous, but those who know they are sinners."

A Discussion about Fasting

¹⁸Once when John's disciples and the Pharisees were fasting, some people came to Jesus and asked, "Why don't your disciples fast like John's disciples and the Pharisees do?"

¹⁹Jesus replied, "Do wedding guests fast while celebrating with the groom? Of course not. They can't fast while the groom is with them. ²⁰But someday the groom will be taken away from them, and then they will fast.

²¹"Besides, who would patch old clothing with new cloth? For the new patch would shrink and rip away from the old cloth, leaving an even bigger tear than before.

²²"And no one puts new wine into old wineskins. For the wine would burst the wineskins, and the wine and the skins would both be lost. New wine calls for new wineskins."

A Discussion about the Sabbath

²³One Sabbath day as Jesus was walking through some grainfields, his disciples began breaking off heads of grain to eat. ²⁴But the Pharisees said to Jesus, "Look, why are they breaking the law by harvesting grain on the Sabbath?"

²⁵Jesus said to them, "Haven't you ever read in the Scriptures what David did when he and his companions were hungry? ²⁶He went into the house of God (during the days when Abiathar was high priest) and broke the law by eating the sacred loaves of bread that only the priests are allowed to eat. He also gave some to his companions."

²⁷Then Jesus said to them, "The Sabbath was made to meet the needs of people, and not people to meet the requirements of the Sabbath. ²⁸So the Son of Man is Lord, even over the Sabbath!"

Jesus Heals on the Sabbath

3 Jesus went into the synagogue again and noticed a man with a deformed hand. ²Since it was the Sabbath, Jesus' enemies watched him closely. If he healed the man's hand, they planned to accuse him of working on the Sabbath.

³Jesus said to the man with the deformed hand, "Come and stand in front of everyone." ⁴Then he turned to his critics and asked, "Does the law permit good deeds on the Sabbath, or is it a day for doing evil? Is this a day to save life or to destroy it?" But they wouldn't answer him.

⁵He looked around at them angrily and was deeply saddened by their hard hearts. Then he said to the man, "Hold out your hand." So the man held out his hand, and it was restored! ⁶At once the Pharisees went away and met with the supporters of Herod to plot how to kill Jesus.

2:10 "Son of Man" is a title Jesus used for himself. **2:16a** Greek *the scribes of the Pharisees.* **2:16b** Greek *with tax collectors and sinners.*

Insight: FIRST-CENTURY JEWISH HOME

Knowing more about the everyday lives of Bible people can help us understand the context of Jesus' teachings and help us know how to interpret what he had to say about our everyday lives, too. The lives of first-century Jewish people revolved around the home. The typical house in ancient Palestine had a flat roof and a central courtyard with three or four rooms surrounding it. Much like today, the size of the house reflected the wealth of the family. Women and men were responsible for the domestic and economic responsibilities of everyday life, including cooking, cleaning, farming, herding animals, and trading in the marketplace. But the way women earned esteem in the Hebrew worldview was through their virtues, especially by raising children and caring for their families and neighbors. Some wealthy women were able to pursue education, art, and politics outside their homes, but that was not the norm.

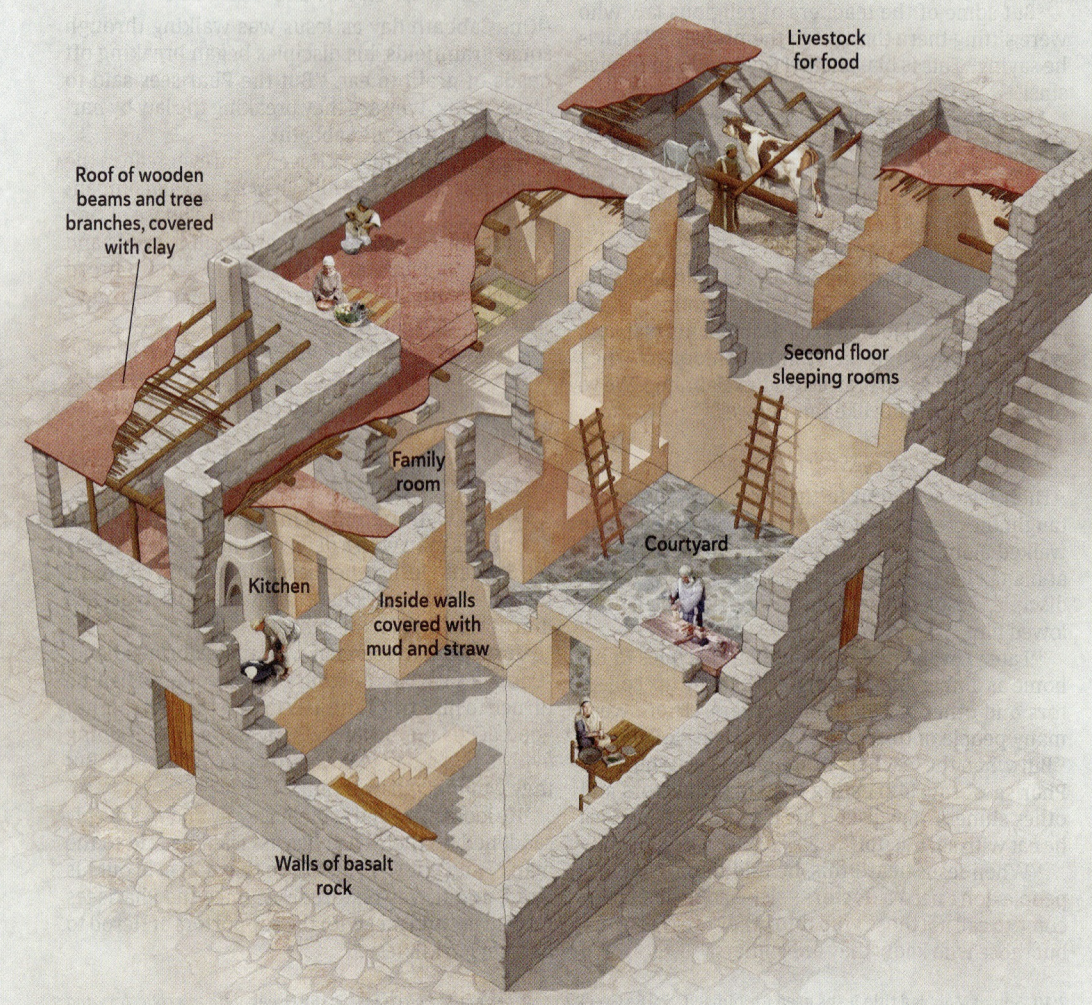

Crowds Follow Jesus

⁷Jesus went out to the lake with his disciples, and a large crowd followed him. They came from all over Galilee, Judea, ⁸Jerusalem, Idumea, from east of the Jordan River, and even from as far north as Tyre and Sidon. The news about his miracles had spread far and wide, and vast numbers of people came to see him.

⁹Jesus instructed his disciples to have a boat ready so the crowd would not crush him. ¹⁰He had healed many people that day, so all the sick people eagerly pushed forward to touch him. ¹¹And whenever those possessed by evil* spirits caught sight of him, the spirits would throw them to the ground in front of him shrieking, "You are the Son of God!" ¹²But Jesus sternly commanded the spirits not to reveal who he was.

Jesus Chooses the Twelve Apostles

¹³Afterward Jesus went up on a mountain and called out the ones he wanted to go with him. And they came to him. ¹⁴Then he appointed twelve of them and called them his apostles.* They were to accompany him, and he would send them out to preach, ¹⁵giving them authority to cast out demons. ¹⁶These are the twelve he chose:

Simon (whom he named Peter),
¹⁷ James and John (the sons of Zebedee, but Jesus nicknamed them "Sons of Thunder"*),
¹⁸ Andrew,
Philip,
Bartholomew,
Matthew,
Thomas,
James (son of Alphaeus),
Thaddaeus,
Simon (the zealot*),
¹⁹ Judas Iscariot (who later betrayed him).

Jesus and the Prince of Demons

²⁰One time Jesus entered a house, and the crowds began to gather again. Soon he and his disciples couldn't even find time to eat. ²¹When his family heard what was happening, they tried to take him away. "He's out of his mind," they said.

²²But the teachers of religious law who had arrived from Jerusalem said, "He's possessed by Satan,* the prince of demons. That's where he gets the power to cast out demons."

²³Jesus called them over and responded with an illustration. "How can Satan cast out Satan?" he asked. ²⁴"A kingdom divided by civil war will collapse. ²⁵Similarly, a family splintered by feuding will fall apart. ²⁶And if Satan is divided and fights against himself, how can he stand? He would never survive. ²⁷Let me illustrate this further. Who is powerful enough to enter the house of a strong man and plunder his goods? Only someone even stronger—someone who could tie him up and then plunder his house.

²⁸"I tell you the truth, all sin and blasphemy can be forgiven, ²⁹but anyone who blasphemes the Holy Spirit will never be forgiven. This is a sin with eternal consequences." ³⁰He told them this because they were saying, "He's possessed by an evil spirit."

The True Family of Jesus

³¹Then Jesus' mother and brothers came to see him. They stood outside and sent word for him to come out and talk with them. ³²There was a crowd sitting around Jesus, and someone said, "Your mother and your brothers* are outside asking for you."

³³Jesus replied, "Who is my mother? Who are my brothers?" ³⁴Then he looked at those around him and said, "Look, these are my mother and brothers. ³⁵Anyone who does God's will is my brother and sister and mother."

Parable of the Farmer Scattering Seed

4 Once again Jesus began teaching by the lakeshore. A very large crowd soon gathered around him, so he got into a boat. Then he sat in the boat while all the people remained on the shore. ²He taught them by telling many stories in the form of parables, such as this one:

³"Listen! A farmer went out to plant some seed. ⁴As he scattered it across his field, some of the seed fell on a footpath, and the birds came and ate it. ⁵Other seed fell on shallow soil with underlying rock. The

---

3:11 Greek *unclean;* also in 3:30. **3:14** Some manuscripts do not include *and called them his apostles.* **3:17** Greek *whom he named Boanerges, which means Sons of Thunder.* **3:18** Greek *the Cananean,* an Aramaic term for Jewish nationalists. **3:22** Greek *Beelzeboul;* other manuscripts read *Beezeboul;* Latin version reads *Beelzebub.* **3:32** Some manuscripts add *and sisters.*

3:20-35 Mark tends to place important teachings between two stories that are similar. Sometimes referred to as "Markan sandwiches," this feature of Mark's narrative indicates that the middle story should be read in light of the stories right before and right after. This story about Jesus and his family (3:20-21 and 3:31-35) brackets a controversy about Jesus' exorcisms (3:22-30); this arrangement identifies Jesus' family with the religious leaders in opposing him.

3:21 Mark does not explain whether the attempt by Jesus' family to seize him was motivated by sincere but misguided concern, or by hostility. Jesus' brothers and sisters were not among his followers until after his resurrection (3:31-35; John 7:3-5; 1 Corinthians 15:7 mentions James, the half brother of Jesus; Acts 15:13-21).

3:31-35 The Greek text describes the crowd as sitting in a *circle* around Jesus ("around him," 3:34), symbolizing an established bond between Jesus and his followers. The Greek also highlights that Jesus deliberately used inclusive language with the addition of "sister" in 3:35 (compare to 3:32-34, where only the words for "brothers" and "mother" are used). Women, just like men, were included within the Jesus circle. God's Kingdom is gender inclusive.

seed sprouted quickly because the soil was shallow. ⁶But the plant soon wilted under the hot sun, and since it didn't have deep roots, it died. ⁷Other seed fell among thorns that grew up and choked out the tender plants so they produced no grain. ⁸Still other seeds fell on fertile soil, and they sprouted, grew, and produced a crop that was thirty, sixty, and even a hundred times as much as had been planted!" ⁹Then he said, "Anyone with ears to hear should listen and understand."

¹⁰Later, when Jesus was alone with the twelve disciples and with the others who were gathered around, they asked him what the parables meant. ¹¹He replied, "You are permitted to understand the secret* of the Kingdom of God. But I use parables for everything I say to outsiders, ¹²so that the Scriptures might be fulfilled:

'When they see what I do,
  they will learn nothing.
When they hear what I say,
  they will not understand.
Otherwise, they will turn to me
  and be forgiven.'*

¹³Then Jesus said to them, "If you can't understand the meaning of this parable, how will you understand all the other parables? ¹⁴The farmer plants seed by taking God's word to others. ¹⁵The seed that fell on the footpath represents those who hear the message, only to have Satan come at once and take it away. ¹⁶The seed on the rocky soil represents those who hear the message and immediately receive it with joy. ¹⁷But since they don't have deep roots, they don't last long. They fall away as soon as they have problems or are persecuted for believing God's word. ¹⁸The seed that fell among the thorns represents others who hear God's word, ¹⁹but all too quickly the message is crowded out by the worries of this life, the lure of wealth, and the desire for other things, so no fruit is produced. ²⁰And the seed that fell on good soil represents those who hear and accept God's word and produce a harvest of thirty, sixty, or even a hundred times as much as had been planted!"

Parable of the Lamp

²¹Then Jesus asked them, "Would anyone light a lamp and then put it under a basket or under a bed? Of course not! A lamp is placed on a stand, where its light will shine. ²²For everything that is hidden will eventually be brought into the open, and every secret will be brought to light. ²³Anyone with ears to hear should listen and understand."

²⁴Then he added, "Pay close attention to what you hear. The closer you listen, the more understanding you will be given*—and you will receive even more. ²⁵To those who listen to my teaching, more understanding will be given. But for those who are not listening, even what little understanding they have will be taken away from them."

Parable of the Growing Seed

²⁶Jesus also said, "The Kingdom of God is like a farmer who scatters seed on the ground. ²⁷Night and day, while he's asleep or awake, the seed sprouts and grows, but he does not understand how it happens. ²⁸The earth produces the crops on its own. First a leaf blade pushes through, then the heads of wheat are formed, and finally the grain ripens. ²⁹And as soon as the grain is ready, the farmer comes and harvests it with a sickle, for the harvest time has come."

Parable of the Mustard Seed

³⁰Jesus said, "How can I describe the Kingdom of God? What story should I use to illustrate it? ³¹It is like a mustard seed planted in the ground. It is the smallest of all seeds, ³²but it becomes the largest of all garden plants; it grows long branches, and birds can make nests in its shade."

³³Jesus used many similar stories and illustrations to teach the people as much as they could understand. ³⁴In fact, in his public ministry he never taught without using parables; but afterward, when he was alone with his disciples, he explained everything to them.

Jesus Calms the Storm

³⁵As evening came, Jesus said to his disciples, "Let's cross to the other side of the lake." ³⁶So they took Jesus in the boat and started out, leaving the crowds behind (although other boats followed). ³⁷But soon a fierce storm came up. High waves were breaking into the boat, and it began to fill with water.

³⁸Jesus was sleeping at the back of the boat with his head on a cushion. The disciples woke him up, shouting, "Teacher, don't you care that we're going to drown?"

³⁹When Jesus woke up, he rebuked the wind and said to the waves, "Silence! Be still!" Suddenly the wind stopped, and there was a great calm. ⁴⁰Then he asked them, "Why are you afraid? Do you still have no faith?"

⁴¹The disciples were absolutely terrified. "Who is this man?" they asked each other. "Even the wind and waves obey him!"

Jesus Heals a Demon-Possessed Man

5 So they arrived at the other side of the lake, in the region of the Gerasenes.* ²When Jesus climbed out of the boat, a man possessed by an evil* spirit came out from the tombs to meet him. ³This man lived in the burial caves and could no longer be restrained, even with a chain. ⁴Whenever he was put

---

4:11 Greek *mystery.* **4:12** Isa 6:9-10 (Greek version). **4:24** Or *The measure you give will be the measure you get back.* **5:1** Other manuscripts read *Gadarenes;* still others read *Gergesenes.* See Matt 8:28; Luke 8:26. **5:2** Greek *unclean;* also in 5:8, 13.

into chains and shackles—as he often was—he snapped the chains from his wrists and smashed the shackles. No one was strong enough to subdue him. ⁵Day and night he wandered among the burial caves and in the hills, howling and cutting himself with sharp stones.

⁶When Jesus was still some distance away, the man saw him, ran to meet him, and bowed low before him. ⁷With a shriek, he screamed, "Why are you interfering with me, Jesus, Son of the Most High God? In the name of God, I beg you, don't torture me!" ⁸For Jesus had already said to the spirit, "Come out of the man, you evil spirit."

⁹Then Jesus demanded, "What is your name?"

And he replied, "My name is Legion, because there are many of us inside this man." ¹⁰Then the evil spirits begged him again and again not to send them to some distant place.

¹¹There happened to be a large herd of pigs feeding on the hillside nearby. ¹²"Send us into those pigs," the spirits begged. "Let us enter them."

¹³So Jesus gave them permission. The evil spirits came out of the man and entered the pigs, and the entire herd of about 2,000 pigs plunged down the steep hillside into the lake and drowned in the water.

¹⁴The herdsmen fled to the nearby town and the surrounding countryside, spreading the news as they ran. People rushed out to see what had happened. ¹⁵A crowd soon gathered around Jesus, and they saw the man who had been possessed by the legion of demons. He was sitting there fully clothed and perfectly sane, and they were all afraid. ¹⁶Then those who had seen what happened told the others about the demon-possessed man and the pigs. ¹⁷And the crowd began pleading with Jesus to go away and leave them alone.

¹⁸As Jesus was getting into the boat, the man who had been demon possessed begged to go with him. ¹⁹But Jesus said, "No, go home to your family, and tell them everything the Lord has done for you and how merciful he has been." ²⁰So the man started off to visit the Ten Towns* of that region and began to proclaim the great things Jesus had done for him; and everyone was amazed at what he told them.

Jesus Heals in Response to Faith

²¹Jesus got into the boat again and went back to the other side of the lake, where a large crowd gathered around him on the shore. ²²Then a leader of the local synagogue, whose name was Jairus, arrived. When he saw Jesus, he fell at his feet, ²³pleading fervently with him. "My little daughter is dying," he said. "Please come and lay your hands on her; heal her so she can live."

²⁴Jesus went with him, and all the people followed, crowding around him. ²⁵A woman in the crowd had suffered for twelve years with constant bleeding. ²⁶She had suffered a great deal from many doctors, and over the years she had spent everything she had to pay them, but she had gotten no better. In fact, she had gotten worse. ²⁷She had heard about Jesus, so she came up behind him through the crowd and touched his robe. ²⁸For she thought to herself, "If I can just touch his robe, I will be healed." ²⁹Immediately the bleeding stopped, and she could feel in her body that she had been healed of her terrible condition.

³⁰Jesus realized at once that healing power had gone out from him, so he turned around in the crowd and asked, "Who touched my robe?"

³¹His disciples said to him, "Look at this crowd pressing around you. How can you ask, 'Who touched me?'"

³²But he kept on looking around to see who had done it. ³³Then the frightened woman, trembling at the realization of what had happened to her, came and fell to her knees in front of him and told him what she had done. ³⁴And he said to her, "Daughter, your faith has made you well. Go in peace. Your suffering is over."

³⁵While he was still speaking to her, messengers arrived from the home of Jairus, the leader of the synagogue. They told him, "Your daughter is dead. There's no use troubling the Teacher now."

³⁶But Jesus overheard* them and said to Jairus, "Don't be afraid. Just have faith."

³⁷Then Jesus stopped the crowd and wouldn't let anyone go with him except Peter, James, and John (the brother of James). ³⁸When they came to the

---

5:20 Greek *Decapolis.* **5:36** Or *ignored.*

5:21-43 Jairus was a respected religious leader and a desperate father with a dying child. The woman with constant bleeding was an outcast deemed ritually unclean, without connection to the community or hope. They crossed paths with each other when seeking Jesus for help. Jesus cured the woman even on his way to fulfill Jairus's urgent request. Social status doesn't exempt us from disease or death. Neither can it stop us from receiving Jesus' blessing. Regardless of our social locations, we can reach out to Jesus and trust that he cares about our problems and concerns.

5:24-34 This woman's "constant bleeding" was most likely related to vaginal bleeding and made her ceremonially unclean. Thus she was unable to participate in the everyday life of the community (see Leviticus 15:25-27; "Holy, Clean, and Unclean"

on page 143). When Jesus touched the woman and healed her, he showed that his power encompasses healing and cleansing. Instead of Jesus being defiled by touching the woman, she was made clean. This prepares us to understand what happened next when Jesus came into contact with the dead little girl, too (Mark 5:35-43). Instead of being concerned about being defiled by a dead body, Jesus touched the girl and restored her life.

5:27-34 Mark's narrative of this story uses three different Greek words, one of which refers to being whole or healthy ("your suffering is over," 5:34). We might wonder why Jesus pronounced healing again after her bleeding already stopped. The different wordings might shed light on our confusion: Jesus' blessing in 5:34 refers to her whole wellness. Jesus cares about our whole well-being, soul and body, in a chaotic world.

home of the synagogue leader, Jesus saw much commotion and weeping and wailing. ³⁹He went inside and asked, "Why all this commotion and weeping? The child isn't dead; she's only asleep."

⁴⁰The crowd laughed at him. But he made them all leave, and he took the girl's father and mother and his three disciples into the room where the girl was lying. ⁴¹Holding her hand, he said to her, "*Talitha koum*," which means "Little girl, get up!" ⁴²And the girl, who was twelve years old, immediately stood up and walked around! They were overwhelmed and totally amazed. ⁴³Jesus gave them strict orders not to tell anyone what had happened, and then he told them to give her something to eat.

Intercede Until God Intervenes

SCRIPTURE CONNECTION: MARK 5:21-43

I was a young mom with a newborn son when, without warning, I suffered a massive brainstem stroke. I wouldn't remember even a moment of the following months. Still, I am told that many people, near and far, pleaded for my life through prayer.

Jairus's daughter had a similar experience. She might have told her story like this:

> I had my whole life ahead of me. Without warning, I became so ill that it seemed I would never wake up. Suddenly, there was nothing ahead of me, and I was suspended between life and death.
>
> I remember nothing of those dim days, but I'm told crowds gathered to mourn my impending death. My father, dissatisfied with the weight of grief and desperate to advocate for me, sought the last-resort help of Jesus, an itinerant teacher who had caused a stir with his miracles. As my father spoke to Jesus, some well-meaning messengers reported that I was dead. They said there was no sense in troubling the teacher.
>
> Undeterred, Jesus went to the house where I lay and curtailed the cries of my bereaved family. He declared, "The child isn't dead; she's only asleep" (5:39).
>
> He came inside, approached my deathbed, and uttered a single command: "Little girl, get up!" (5:41). Propelled into the land of the living, I sat up. I walked with Jesus into renewed physical and spiritual consciousness.

> When people intercede, Jesus intervenes.

Unlike this little girl, I did not actually die, but because of others' intercession and advocacy, I survived my ordeal, too. I'll never understand why some pleas are answered while others are not. But my life testifies to the power of intercession to prompt Jesus' intervention.

IMAGINE

Before we seek God's help, we might need to stop relying on ourselves. What do you need to release so you can intercede?

Who could use your prayers, right this moment?

"I now occupy the slimmest margin of medical statistics, albeit with significant physical disabilities. When people intercede, Jesus intervenes."

KATHERINE WOLF is a communicator, author, and advocate. She leverages her redemptive story to encourage those with broken bodies, broken brains, and broken hearts.

Jesus Rejected at Nazareth

6 Jesus left that part of the country and returned with his disciples to Nazareth, his hometown. ²The next Sabbath he began teaching in the synagogue, and many who heard him were amazed. They asked, "Where did he get all this wisdom and the power to perform such miracles?" ³Then they scoffed, "He's just a carpenter, the son of Mary* and the brother of James, Joseph,* Judas, and Simon. And his sisters live right here among us." They were deeply offended and refused to believe in him.

⁴Then Jesus told them, "A prophet is honored everywhere except in his own hometown and among his relatives and his own family." ⁵And because of their unbelief, he couldn't do any miracles among them except to place his hands on a few sick people and heal them. ⁶And he was amazed at their unbelief.

Jesus Sends Out the Twelve Disciples

Then Jesus went from village to village, teaching the people. ⁷And he called his twelve disciples together and began sending them out two by two, giving them authority to cast out evil* spirits. ⁸He told them to take nothing for their journey except a walking stick—no food, no traveler's bag, no money.* ⁹He allowed them to wear sandals but not to take a change of clothes.

¹⁰"Wherever you go," he said, "stay in the same house until you leave town. ¹¹But if any place refuses to welcome you or listen to you, shake its dust from your feet as you leave to show that you have abandoned those people to their fate."

¹²So the disciples went out, telling everyone they met to repent of their sins and turn to God. ¹³And they cast out many demons and healed many sick people, anointing them with olive oil.

The Death of John the Baptist

¹⁴Herod Antipas, the king, soon heard about Jesus, because everyone was talking about him. Some were saying,* "This must be John the Baptist raised from the dead. That is why he can do such miracles." ¹⁵Others said, "He's the prophet Elijah." Still others said, "He's a prophet like the other great prophets of the past."

¹⁶When Herod heard about Jesus, he said, "John, the man I beheaded, has come back from the dead."

¹⁷For Herod had sent soldiers to arrest and imprison John as a favor to Herodias. She had been his brother Philip's wife, but Herod had married her. ¹⁸John had been telling Herod, "It is against God's law for you to marry your brother's wife." ¹⁹So Herodias bore a grudge against John and wanted to kill him. But without Herod's approval she was powerless, ²⁰for Herod respected John; and knowing that he was a good and holy man, he protected him. Herod was greatly disturbed whenever he talked with John, but even so, he liked to listen to him.

²¹Herodias's chance finally came on Herod's birthday. He gave a party for his high government officials, army officers, and the leading citizens of Galilee. ²²Then his daughter, also named Herodias,* came in and performed a dance that greatly pleased Herod and his guests. "Ask me for anything you like," the king said to the girl, "and I will give it to you." ²³He even vowed, "I will give you whatever you ask, up to half my kingdom!"

²⁴She went out and asked her mother, "What should I ask for?"

Her mother told her, "Ask for the head of John the Baptist!"

²⁵So the girl hurried back to the king and told him, "I want the head of John the Baptist, right now, on a tray!"

6:3a Some manuscripts read *He's just the son of the carpenter and of Mary.* **6:3b** Most manuscripts read *Joses;* see Matt 13:55. **6:7** Greek *unclean.* **6:8** Greek *no copper coins in their money belts.* **6:14** Some manuscripts read *He was saying.* **6:22** Some manuscripts read *the daughter of Herodias herself.*

6:3-4 We would usually expect "son of Joseph" to follow Jesus' name instead of "son of Mary," as the usual construction for surnames among Jewish people during this period. This phrasing may hint at Jesus' remarkable birth or may indicate that Joseph had died by this time. The residents of Nazareth thought of Jesus only as a carpenter. Because of their familiarity, the people thought Jesus was claiming to be someone he could not possibly be. (On Jesus' brothers and sisters, see the note on 3:31-35.)

6:17-29 Different from Matthew's narrative of this scene (Matthew 14:1-12), Mark's describes Herodias as shrewdly using Herod's reckless vow against him and Herod as resignedly condemning John to death. Even if Herodias had sincerely wanted to protect the perception of her marriage, she did so at the expense of an innocent person's life. It's easy to become so focused on accomplishing a goal or acquiring something that we end up hurting other people, but Jesus calls us to help others, not hurt them.

6:17 The first-century Jewish historian Josephus says that John was imprisoned in the fortress of Machaerus in Perea. Josephus adds the detail that Herodias was the wife of Herod Antipas's half brother, Herod Philip, since Antipas and Philip had the same father and different mothers. (See *The Antiquities of the Jews,* book 18, chapter 5, paragraph 2 for more on Herod and John the Baptist.)

6:19-28 Herodias's role in the execution of John the Baptist echoes the story of Jezebel, an Israelite queen who sought to eliminate God's prophets for speaking the truth (1 Kings 18:1–19:2). Herod set himself up to fail and ultimately succumbed to Herodias's pressure to execute John—foreshadowing the later story of Pontius Pilate, who put Jesus to death against his better judgment (compare Mark 6:20, 25-28 with 15:6-15).

6:22 According to the first-century Jewish historian Josephus, Herodias's daughter was also named Salome (see *The Antiquities of the Jews,* book 18, chapter 5, paragraph 4).

²⁶Then the king deeply regretted what he had said; but because of the vows he had made in front of his guests, he couldn't refuse her. ²⁷So he immediately sent an executioner to the prison to cut off John's head and bring it to him. The soldier beheaded John in the prison, ²⁸brought his head on a tray, and gave it to the girl, who took it to her mother. ²⁹When John's disciples heard what had happened, they came to get his body and buried it in a tomb.

Jesus Feeds Five Thousand

³⁰The apostles returned to Jesus from their ministry tour and told him all they had done and taught. ³¹Then Jesus said, "Let's go off by ourselves to a quiet place and rest awhile." He said this because there were so many people coming and going that Jesus and his apostles didn't even have time to eat.

³²So they left by boat for a quiet place, where they could be alone. ³³But many people recognized them and saw them leaving, and people from many towns ran ahead along the shore and got there ahead of them. ³⁴Jesus saw the huge crowd as he stepped from the boat, and he had compassion on them because they were like sheep without a shepherd. So he began teaching them many things.

³⁵Late in the afternoon his disciples came to him and said, "This is a remote place, and it's already getting late. ³⁶Send the crowds away so they can go to the nearby farms and villages and buy something to eat."

³⁷But Jesus said, "You feed them."

"With what?" they asked. "We'd have to work for months to earn enough money* to buy food for all these people!"

³⁸"How much bread do you have?" he asked. "Go and find out."

They came back and reported, "We have five loaves of bread and two fish."

³⁹Then Jesus told the disciples to have the people sit down in groups on the green grass. ⁴⁰So they sat down in groups of fifty or a hundred.

⁴¹Jesus took the five loaves and two fish, looked up toward heaven, and blessed them. Then, breaking the loaves into pieces, he kept giving the bread to the disciples so they could distribute it to the people. He also divided the fish for everyone to share. ⁴²They all ate as much as they wanted, ⁴³and afterward, the disciples picked up twelve baskets of leftover bread and fish. ⁴⁴A total of 5,000 men and their families were fed.*

Jesus Walks on Water

⁴⁵Immediately after this, Jesus insisted that his disciples get back into the boat and head across the lake to Bethsaida, while he sent the people home. ⁴⁶After telling everyone good-bye, he went up into the hills by himself to pray.

⁴⁷Late that night, the disciples were in their boat in the middle of the lake, and Jesus was alone on land. ⁴⁸He saw that they were in serious trouble, rowing hard and struggling against the wind and waves. About three o'clock in the morning* Jesus came toward them, walking on the water. He intended to go past them, ⁴⁹but when they saw him walking on the water, they cried out in terror, thinking he was a ghost. ⁵⁰They were all terrified when they saw him.

But Jesus spoke to them at once. "Don't be afraid," he said. "Take courage! I am here!"* ⁵¹Then he climbed into the boat, and the wind stopped. They were totally amazed, ⁵²for they still didn't understand the significance of the miracle of the loaves. Their hearts were too hard to take it in.

⁵³After they had crossed the lake, they landed at Gennesaret. They brought the boat to shore ⁵⁴and climbed out. The people recognized Jesus at once, ⁵⁵and they ran throughout the whole area, carrying sick people on mats to wherever they heard he was. ⁵⁶Wherever he went—in villages, cities, or the countryside—they brought the sick out to the marketplaces. They begged him to let the sick touch at least the fringe of his robe, and all who touched him were healed.

Jesus Teaches about Inner Purity

7 One day some Pharisees and teachers of religious law arrived from Jerusalem to see Jesus. ²They noticed that some of his disciples failed to follow the Jewish ritual of hand washing before eating. ³(The Jews, especially the Pharisees, do not eat until they have poured water over their cupped hands,* as required by their ancient traditions. ⁴Similarly, they don't eat anything from the market until they immerse their hands* in water. This is but one of many traditions they have clung to—such as their ceremonial washing of cups, pitchers, and kettles.*)

⁵So the Pharisees and teachers of religious law asked him, "Why don't your disciples follow our age-old tradition? They eat without first performing the hand-washing ceremony."

⁶Jesus replied, "You hypocrites! Isaiah was right when he prophesied about you, for he wrote,

'These people honor me with their lips,
   but their hearts are far from me.
⁷ Their worship is a farce,
   for they teach man-made ideas as commands from God.'*

⁸For you ignore God's law and substitute your own tradition."

6:37 Greek *It would take 200 denarii.* A denarius was equivalent to a laborer's full day's wage. **6:44** Some manuscripts read *fed from the loaves.* **6:48** Greek *About the fourth watch of the night.* **6:50** Or *The 'I AM' is here;* Greek reads *I am.* See Exod 3:14. **7:3** Greek *have washed with the fist.* **7:4a** Some manuscripts read *sprinkle themselves.* **7:4b** Some manuscripts add *and dining couches.* **7:7** Isa 29:13 (Greek version).

⁹Then he said, "You skillfully sidestep God's law in order to hold on to your own tradition. ¹⁰For instance, Moses gave you this law from God: 'Honor your father and mother,'* and 'Anyone who speaks disrespectfully of father or mother must be put to death.'* ¹¹But you say it is all right for people to say to their parents, 'Sorry, I can't help you. For I have vowed to give to God what I would have given to you.'* ¹²In this way, you let them disregard their needy parents. ¹³And so you cancel the word of God in order to hand down your own tradition. And this is only one example among many others."

¹⁴Then Jesus called to the crowd to come and hear. "All of you listen," he said, "and try to understand. ¹⁵It's not what goes into your body that defiles you; you are defiled by what comes from your heart.*"

¹⁷Then Jesus went into a house to get away from the crowd, and his disciples asked him what he meant by the parable he had just used. ¹⁸"Don't you understand either?" he asked. "Can't you see that the food you put into your body cannot defile you? ¹⁹Food doesn't go into your heart, but only passes through the stomach and then goes into the sewer." (By saying this, he declared that every kind of food is acceptable in God's eyes.)

²⁰And then he added, "It is what comes from inside that defiles you. ²¹For from within, out of a person's heart, come evil thoughts, sexual immorality, theft, murder, ²²adultery, greed, wickedness, deceit, lustful desires, envy, slander, pride, and foolishness. ²³All these vile things come from within; they are what defile you."

The Faith of a Gentile Woman

²⁴Then Jesus left Galilee and went north to the region of Tyre.* He didn't want anyone to know which house he was staying in, but he couldn't keep it a secret. ²⁵Right away a woman who had heard about him came and fell at his feet. Her little girl was possessed by an evil* spirit, ²⁶and she begged him to cast out the demon from her daughter.

Since she was a Gentile, born in Syrian Phoenicia, ²⁷Jesus told her, "First I should feed the children—my own family, the Jews.* It isn't right to take food from the children and throw it to the dogs."

²⁸She replied, "That's true, Lord, but even the dogs under the table are allowed to eat the scraps from the children's plates."

²⁹"Good answer!" he said. "Now go home, for the demon has left your daughter." ³⁰And when she arrived home, she found her little girl lying quietly in bed, and the demon was gone.

Jesus Heals a Deaf Man

³¹Jesus left Tyre and went up to Sidon before going back to the Sea of Galilee and the region of the Ten Towns.* ³²A deaf man with a speech impediment was brought to him, and the people begged Jesus to lay his hands on the man to heal him.

³³Jesus led him away from the crowd so they could be alone. He put his fingers into the man's ears. Then, spitting on his own fingers, he touched the man's tongue. ³⁴Looking up to heaven, he sighed and said, "*Ephphatha*," which means, "Be opened!" ³⁵Instantly the man could hear perfectly, and his tongue was freed so he could speak plainly!

³⁶Jesus told the crowd not to tell anyone, but the more he told them not to, the more they spread the news. ³⁷They were completely amazed and said again and again, "Everything he does is wonderful. He even makes the deaf to hear and gives speech to those who cannot speak."

7:10a Exod 20:12; Deut 5:16. **7:10b** Exod 21:17 (Greek version); Lev 20:9 (Greek version). **7:11** Greek '*What I would have given to you is Corban*' (that is, a gift). **7:15** Some manuscripts add verse 16, *Anyone with ears to hear should listen and understand.* Compare 4:9, 23. **7:24** Some manuscripts add *and Sidon*. **7:25** Greek *unclean*. **7:27** Greek *Let the children eat first.* **7:31** Greek *Decapolis*.

7:11-12 The tradition referenced here said people could sidestep their obligation to support their parents by dedicating some of their resources to God, thus disregarding and dishonoring their needy parents. The contrast with God's law is glaring—their tradition repudiated God's command for people to honor their parents by providing for their needs (see text note on 7:11).

7:24-30 Mark places Jesus' encounter with the Gentile woman right after his interaction with the Pharisees and teachers of religious law (7:1-23). But the Jewish religious leaders and the woman sought Jesus out for opposite purposes. The leaders, who took pride in what society deemed worthiness, interrogated Jesus' ritual laxity. By contrast, the woman agreed to what society deemed unworthiness and begged Jesus for merciful inclusion. Who do we identify ourselves with more, the leaders or the woman? Jesus condemned the behavior of the religious leaders but applauded the woman's response after appearing to rebuff her to follow the prevailing social conventions.

7:25-26 The woman was from Syrian Phoenicia and, therefore, a Gentile. Historically, the territory belonged to the Canaanites, whom the Israelites reviled for their idolatry in the Old Testament. The urgency and intensity of the woman's petition are seen in her falling at Jesus' feet and begging. She recognized Jesus' true identity as the Messiah despite her people's idolatry and in contrast to Jesus' rejection by the Jewish religious leaders.

7:27-28 Jesus' reply to the woman seems like a harsh refusal. Still, their interaction indicates that he wanted to see her faith (see also Matthew 15:28). Jesus' use of "first" was indicating that his mission was chronologically first to the Jews, not excluding her as a Gentile (Acts 13:46; Romans 1:16). The woman responded to Jesus' words with humility and faith. She acknowledged the priority of the Jewish people but argued that there was more than enough food for the Gentiles as well. (In Jewish literature, Gentiles were frequently referred to as dogs, which were seen as filthy scavengers rather than as adorable pets.) The woman's persistence and acknowledgment of Jesus as Lord were rewarded.

Perspective

How did Jesus respond to prejudice in his society?

SCRIPTURE CONNECTION: MARK 7:24-30

Jesus' response to the woman in this story might feel confusing to us. We think of Jesus as always loving and welcoming to everyone. But here, Jesus appears to rebuke this woman for asking for help. Yet actions shout while words whisper. In action, we see Jesus tear down—not build up—ethnic divides.

First-century Jews maintained their distinct identity by guarding clear social boundaries between themselves and all non-Jewish people, called "Gentiles."

Traveling to Tyre, a non-Jewish territory, Jesus intended to remain incognito. But a Gentile woman desperate to have her demon-possessed daughter healed sought him out. We see profound faith and humility in this mother—and Jesus did, too (see also Matthew 15:21-28).

It seems like Jesus was reluctant to answer her request and offensive in his language because she was the "other." But Jesus engaged her, made her an example of faith, and taught his disciples that Jesus' healing is for everyone, regardless of differences.

Yes, this story may leave us feeling uncomfortable. But it was likely that the Jews present felt most provoked by Jesus' crossing their racial-ethnic boundary and extending *grace* to the "other." Jesus does not always fit our cultural expectations; he is our "Other." But Jesus also models how we can cross our social boundaries to include those who are different in God's Kingdom.

VIEWPOINTS

HERS: *How did the woman view Jesus? How did she see herself?*

MINE: *"Like the Gentile woman who sought Jesus, I was once the 'other,' as an atheist and communist. Thus, I'm mindful that it's through grace that I've become Jesus' follower and servant."*

YOURS: *What would motivate you to seek Jesus?*

ESTHER G. CEN, MDiv, PhD, is a follower of Christ and multilingual writer and teacher, currently serving as assistant professor of biblical studies at Seattle Pacific University and Seminary.

Jesus Feeds Four Thousand

8 About this time another large crowd had gathered, and the people ran out of food again. Jesus called his disciples and told them, ²"I feel sorry for these people. They have been here with me for three days, and they have nothing left to eat. ³If I send them home hungry, they will faint along the way. For some of them have come a long distance."

⁴His disciples replied, "How are we supposed to find enough food to feed them out here in the wilderness?"

⁵Jesus asked, "How much bread do you have?"

"Seven loaves," they replied.

⁶So Jesus told all the people to sit down on the ground. Then he took the seven loaves, thanked God for them, and broke them into pieces. He gave them to his disciples, who distributed the bread to the crowd. ⁷A few small fish were found, too, so Jesus also blessed these and told the disciples to distribute them.

⁸They ate as much as they wanted. Afterward, the disciples picked up seven large baskets of leftover food. ⁹There were about 4,000 men in the crowd that day, and Jesus sent them home after they had eaten. ¹⁰Immediately after this, he got into a boat with his disciples and crossed over to the region of Dalmanutha.

Pharisees Demand a Miraculous Sign

¹¹When the Pharisees heard that Jesus had arrived, they came and started to argue with him. Testing him, they demanded that he show them a miraculous sign from heaven to prove his authority. ¹²When he heard this, he sighed deeply in his spirit and said, "Why do these people keep demanding a miraculous sign? I tell you the truth, I will not give this generation any such sign." ¹³So he got back into the boat and left them, and he crossed to the other side of the lake.

Yeast of the Pharisees and Herod

¹⁴But the disciples had forgotten to bring any food. They had only one loaf of bread with them in the boat. ¹⁵As they were crossing the lake, Jesus warned them, "Watch out! Beware of the yeast of the Pharisees and of Herod."

¹⁶At this they began to argue with each other because they hadn't brought any bread. ¹⁷Jesus knew what they were saying, so he said, "Why are you arguing about having no bread? Don't you know or understand even yet? Are your hearts too hard to take it in? ¹⁸'You have eyes—can't you see? You have ears—can't you hear?'* Don't you remember anything at all? ¹⁹When I fed the 5,000 with five loaves of bread, how many baskets of leftovers did you pick up afterward?"

8:18 Jer 5:21.

"Twelve," they said.

[20] "And when I fed the 4,000 with seven loaves, how many large baskets of leftovers did you pick up?"

"Seven," they said.

[21] "Don't you understand yet?" he asked them.

Jesus Heals a Blind Man

[22] When they arrived at Bethsaida, some people brought a blind man to Jesus, and they begged him to touch the man and heal him. [23] Jesus took the blind man by the hand and led him out of the village. Then, spitting on the man's eyes, he laid his hands on him and asked, "Can you see anything now?"

[24] The man looked around. "Yes," he said, "I see people, but I can't see them very clearly. They look like trees walking around."

[25] Then Jesus placed his hands on the man's eyes again, and his eyes were opened. His sight was completely restored, and he could see everything clearly. [26] Jesus sent him away, saying, "Don't go back into the village on your way home."

Peter's Declaration about Jesus

[27] Jesus and his disciples left Galilee and went up to the villages near Caesarea Philippi. As they were walking along, he asked them, "Who do people say I am?"

[28] "Well," they replied, "some say John the Baptist, some say Elijah, and others say you are one of the other prophets."

[29] Then he asked them, "But who do you say I am?"

Peter replied, "You are the Messiah.*"

[30] But Jesus warned them not to tell anyone about him.

Jesus Predicts His Death

[31] Then Jesus began to tell them that the Son of Man* must suffer many terrible things and be rejected by the elders, the leading priests, and the teachers of religious law. He would be killed, but three days later he would rise from the dead. [32] As he talked about this openly with his disciples, Peter took him aside and began to reprimand him for saying such things.*

[33] Jesus turned around and looked at his disciples, then reprimanded Peter. "Get away from me, Satan!" he said. "You are seeing things merely from a human point of view, not from God's."

[34] Then, calling the crowd to join his disciples, he said, "If any of you wants to be my follower, you must give up your own way, take up your cross, and follow me. [35] If you try to hang on to your life, you will lose it. But if you give up your life for my sake and for the sake of the Good News, you will save it. [36] And what do you benefit if you gain the whole world but lose your own soul?* [37] Is anything worth more than your soul? [38] If anyone is ashamed of me and my message in these adulterous and sinful days, the Son of Man will be ashamed of that person when he returns in the glory of his Father with the holy angels."

9 Jesus went on to say, "I tell you the truth, some standing here right now will not die before they see the Kingdom of God arrive in great power!"

The Transfiguration

[2] Six days later Jesus took Peter, James, and John, and led them up a high mountain to be alone. As the men watched, Jesus' appearance was transformed, [3] and his clothes became dazzling white, far whiter than any earthly bleach could ever make them. [4] Then Elijah and Moses appeared and began talking with Jesus.

[5] Peter exclaimed, "Rabbi, it's wonderful for us to be here! Let's make three shelters as memorials*— one for you, one for Moses, and one for Elijah." [6] He said this because he didn't really know what else to say, for they were all terrified.

[7] Then a cloud overshadowed them, and a voice from the cloud said, "This is my dearly loved Son. Listen to him." [8] Suddenly, when they looked around, Moses and Elijah were gone, and they saw only Jesus with them.

[9] As they went back down the mountain, he told them not to tell anyone what they had seen until the

---

> "The Christian faith is the most exciting drama that ever staggered the imagination.... The plot pivots upon a single character, and the whole action is the answer to a single central problem: *What think ye of Christ?*"
>
> **DOROTHY L. SAYERS**
> (1893–1957) novelist, playwright, and Christian humanist

8:29 Or *the Christ. Messiah* (a Hebrew term) and *Christ* (a Greek term) both mean "anointed one." **8:31** "Son of Man" is a title Jesus used for himself. **8:32** Or *began to correct him.* **8:36** Or *your self?* also in 8:37. **9:5** Greek *three tabernacles.*

Son of Man* had risen from the dead. ¹⁰So they kept it to themselves, but they often asked each other what he meant by "rising from the dead."

¹¹Then they asked him, "Why do the teachers of religious law insist that Elijah must return before the Messiah comes?*"

¹²Jesus responded, "Elijah is indeed coming first to get everything ready. Yet why do the Scriptures say that the Son of Man must suffer greatly and be treated with utter contempt? ¹³But I tell you, Elijah has already come, and they chose to abuse him, just as the Scriptures predicted."

Jesus Heals a Demon-Possessed Boy

¹⁴When they returned to the other disciples, they saw a large crowd surrounding them, and some teachers of religious law were arguing with them. ¹⁵When the crowd saw Jesus, they were overwhelmed with awe, and they ran to greet him.

¹⁶"What is all this arguing about?" Jesus asked.

¹⁷One of the men in the crowd spoke up and said, "Teacher, I brought my son so you could heal him. He is possessed by an evil spirit that won't let him talk. ¹⁸And whenever this spirit seizes him, it throws him violently to the ground. Then he foams at the mouth and grinds his teeth and becomes rigid.* So I asked your disciples to cast out the evil spirit, but they couldn't do it."

¹⁹Jesus said to them,* "You faithless people! How long must I be with you? How long must I put up with you? Bring the boy to me."

²⁰So they brought the boy. But when the evil spirit saw Jesus, it threw the child into a violent convulsion, and he fell to the ground, writhing and foaming at the mouth.

²¹"How long has this been happening?" Jesus asked the boy's father.

He replied, "Since he was a little boy. ²²The spirit often throws him into the fire or into water, trying to kill him. Have mercy on us and help us, if you can."

²³"What do you mean, 'If I can'?" Jesus asked. "Anything is possible if a person believes."

²⁴The father instantly cried out, "I do believe, but help me overcome my unbelief!"

²⁵When Jesus saw that the crowd of onlookers was growing, he rebuked the evil* spirit. "Listen, you spirit that makes this boy unable to hear and speak," he said. "I command you to come out of this child and never enter him again!"

²⁶Then the spirit screamed and threw the boy into another violent convulsion and left him. The boy appeared to be dead. A murmur ran through the crowd as people said, "He's dead." ²⁷But Jesus took him by the hand and helped him to his feet, and he stood up.

²⁸Afterward, when Jesus was alone in the house with his disciples, they asked him, "Why couldn't we cast out that evil spirit?"

²⁹Jesus replied, "This kind can be cast out only by prayer.*"

Jesus Again Predicts His Death

³⁰Leaving that region, they traveled through Galilee. Jesus didn't want anyone to know he was there, ³¹for he wanted to spend more time with his disciples and teach them. He said to them, "The Son of Man is going to be betrayed into the hands of his enemies. He will be killed, but three days later he will rise from the dead." ³²They didn't understand what he was saying, however, and they were afraid to ask him what he meant.

The Greatest in the Kingdom

³³After they arrived at Capernaum and settled in a house, Jesus asked his disciples, "What were you discussing out on the road?" ³⁴But they didn't answer, because they had been arguing about which of them was the greatest. ³⁵He sat down, called the twelve disciples over to him, and said, "Whoever wants to be first must take last place and be the servant of everyone else."

³⁶Then he put a little child among them. Taking the child in his arms, he said to them, ³⁷"Anyone who welcomes a little child like this on my behalf* welcomes me, and anyone who welcomes me welcomes not only me but also my Father who sent me."

Using the Name of Jesus

³⁸John said to Jesus, "Teacher, we saw someone using your name to cast out demons, but we told him to stop because he wasn't in our group."

³⁹"Don't stop him!" Jesus said. "No one who

9:9 "Son of Man" is a title Jesus used for himself. 9:11 Greek *that Elijah must come first?* 9:18 Or *becomes weak.* 9:19 Or *said to his disciples.* 9:25 Greek *unclean.* 9:29 Some manuscripts read *by prayer and fasting.* 9:37 Greek *in my name.*

9:16-27 Mark records two other stories about parents' intercession on behalf of their sick children: Jairus for his daughter (5:21-23) and the Gentile woman for hers (7:24-30). In the ancient world, child mortality rates, especially of girls who were sometimes abandoned for economic reasons, were high due to natural and human causes. Today, parents' concerns for their children's health and well-being are still real. If you are worried about your children, Jesus invites you to go to him and intercede on your children's behalf. If you have doubts, repeat this father's words, "I do believe, but help me overcome my unbelief!" (9:24).

9:36-37 In Jesus' day, children were not romanticized as innocent and pure but were considered weak and inferior. Jesus told his followers that children were to be received "on my behalf." Welcoming a child is an example of humbly taking the last place and serving everyone else (9:35; see 10:13-16). Other teachings of Jesus about receiving or rejecting him also involve receiving or rejecting his followers (Matthew 10:40; 25:31-46; Luke 10:16; John 13:20).

performs a miracle in my name will soon be able to speak evil of me. ⁴⁰Anyone who is not against us is for us. ⁴¹If anyone gives you even a cup of water because you belong to the Messiah, I tell you the truth, that person will surely be rewarded.

⁴²"But if you cause one of these little ones who trusts in me to fall into sin, it would be better for you to be thrown into the sea with a large millstone hung around your neck. ⁴³If your hand causes you to sin, cut it off. It's better to enter eternal life with only one hand than to go into the unquenchable fires of hell* with two hands.* ⁴⁵If your foot causes you to sin, cut it off. It's better to enter eternal life with only one foot than to be thrown into hell with two feet.* ⁴⁷And if your eye causes you to sin, gouge it out. It's better to enter the Kingdom of God with only one eye than to have two eyes and be thrown into hell, ⁴⁸'where the maggots never die and the fire never goes out.'*

⁴⁹"For everyone will be tested with fire.* ⁵⁰Salt is good for seasoning. But if it loses its flavor, how do you make it salty again? You must have the qualities of salt among yourselves and live in peace with each other."

Discussion about Divorce and Marriage

10 Then Jesus left Capernaum and went down to the region of Judea and into the area east of the Jordan River. Once again crowds gathered around him, and as usual he was teaching them.

²Some Pharisees came and tried to trap him with this question: "Should a man be allowed to divorce his wife?"

³Jesus answered them with a question: "What did Moses say in the law about divorce?"

⁴"Well, he permitted it," they replied. "He said a man can give his wife a written notice of divorce and send her away."*

⁵But Jesus responded, "He wrote this commandment only as a concession to your hard hearts. ⁶But 'God made them male and female'* from the beginning of creation. ⁷'This explains why a man leaves his father and mother and is joined to his wife,* ⁸and the two are united into one.'* Since they are no longer two but one, ⁹let no one split apart what God has joined together."

¹⁰Later, when he was alone with his disciples in the house, they brought up the subject again. ¹¹He told them, "Whoever divorces his wife and marries someone else commits adultery against her. ¹²And if a woman divorces her husband and marries someone else, she commits adultery."

Jesus Blesses the Children

¹³One day some parents brought their children to Jesus so he could touch and bless them. But the disciples scolded the parents for bothering him.

¹⁴When Jesus saw what was happening, he was angry with his disciples. He said to them, "Let the children come to me. Don't stop them! For the Kingdom of God belongs to those who are like these children. ¹⁵I tell you the truth, anyone who doesn't receive the Kingdom of God like a child will never enter it." ¹⁶Then he took the children in his arms and placed his hands on their heads and blessed them.

9:43a Greek *Gehenna;* also in 9:45, 47. **9:43b** Some manuscripts add verse 44, 'where the maggots never die and the fire never goes out.' See 9:48. **9:45** Some manuscripts add verse 46, 'where the maggots never die and the fire never goes out.' See 9:48. **9:48** Isa 66:24. **9:49** Greek *salted with fire;* other manuscripts add *and every sacrifice will be salted with salt.* **10:4** See Deut 24:1. **10:6** Gen 1:27; 5:2. **10:7** Some manuscripts do not include *and is joined to his wife.* **10:7-8** Gen 2:24.

10:4 The Pharisees quoted what Moses "permitted," but simply because something is permissible does not make it the right or best thing to do. There was much debate among rabbis (Jewish teachers) contemporary with Jesus on what constituted the "something wrong" (Deuteronomy 24:1) that made divorce permissible. Rabbi Shammai allowed divorce only based on sexual immorality. Rabbi Hillel permitted divorce even if a woman burned her husband's dinner or was less attractive than someone else (*Mishnah Gittin* 9:10). Jesus took a position on this issue that recognized women's dignity and considered marriage as an important bond before God (see Mark 10:8-9).

10:5-9 God permitted divorce as a concession to the people's "hard hearts." But God's will is more aptly expressed in the passages that Jesus quotes from the law of Moses (Genesis 1:27; 2:23-24; see also Malachi 2:16). Jesus shows that God delights in marriage, which is the creation of a new union in which two become one.

10:11-12 The parallel passage in Luke 16:18 agrees with Mark and mentions no exceptions to this prohibition of divorce. Matthew's parallel account allows an exception in cases of infidelity (Matthew 19:9; see also Matthew 5:32). Paul also mentions an exception if an unbelieving partner deserts the marriage (1 Corinthians 7:15). Mark's account focuses on the core principles—divorce is not what God originally intended and marriage was meant to be for life.

10:12 Mark's remark about women is a *balancing* statement missing from Matthew 19:9 and Luke 16:18. "A woman" (simply "she" in Greek) likely referred to the wife of the man exemplified in the previous verse rather than *any* woman. Still, the agency implied by a woman taking action ("divorces," instead of "is divorced") is significant against the assumption that only men could initiate a divorce under Jewish law. Even though Mark's representation indicates more equality, we must keep in mind that Jesus' argument upheld God's original intent that marriage be a lifelong commitment.

10:14-15 Mark does not explain what characteristics of children make them fit for the Kingdom of God. But Matthew 18:4-5 suggests that the attributes include humility and the ability to receive things simply.

MARK 10 ❖ 1256

The Rich Man

17 As Jesus was starting out on his way to Jerusalem, a man came running up to him, knelt down, and asked, "Good Teacher, what must I do to inherit eternal life?"

18 "Why do you call me good?" Jesus asked. "Only God is truly good. 19 But to answer your question, you know the commandments: 'You must not murder. You must not commit adultery. You must not steal. You must not testify falsely. You must not cheat anyone. Honor your father and mother.'*"

20 "Teacher," the man replied, "I've obeyed all these commandments since I was young."

21 Looking at the man, Jesus felt genuine love for him. "There is still one thing you haven't done," he told him. "Go and sell all your possessions and give the money to the poor, and you will have treasure in heaven. Then come, follow me."

22 At this the man's face fell, and he went away sad, for he had many possessions.

23 Jesus looked around and said to his disciples, "How hard it is for the rich to enter the Kingdom of God!" 24 This amazed them. But Jesus said again, "Dear children, it is very hard* to enter the Kingdom of God. 25 In fact, it is easier for a camel to go through the eye of a needle than for a rich person to enter the Kingdom of God!"

10:19 Exod 20:12-16; Deut 5:16-20. 10:24 Some manuscripts read *very hard for those who trust in riches.*

Come Close — CALLING? CALLED

SCRIPTURE CONNECTION: MARK 10:46-52

What I admire most about Bartimaeus is how he kept calling out to Jesus.

Unlike Bartimaeus, I struggle with calling out to God. I cry or I may turn to something else. But I don't call out "Help me!" Then as I run away, I hear him: "Why are you looking there for love? I love you. I love you more than anyone who will ever love you."

I could ignore him. Or I could be like Bartimaeus and say, "Help me, God. I don't know how to get myself out of this desperate position."

"Come here," Jesus says (10:49).

When I go to Jesus, like Bartimaeus did, I hear Jesus say, "What are you doing seeking after other things and people that won't satisfy you? Come to me when you struggle, Katriel. I'm the source of life and love and everything else that's good."

"What do you want me to do for you?" Jesus asks (10:51).

I like that Jesus asks Bartimaeus to acknowledge what he wants. As a Christian living with autism, I have learned that when I trust God, it's not necessarily physical or mental health that's made well. But emotionally, I have peace. As long as I trust God, I have peace. I want to want God most and, even when I don't think I do that, I still feel this urging voice in my heart saying, "Trust me. I love you. I made you. I am good and have great plans for you."

REFLECT "Daughter," he said to her, "your faith has made you well. Go in peace." LUKE 8:48

Lord Jesus, when I struggle, when I need healing, help me to come to you because you call to me with love and everything that's good. Amen.

CONSIDER "In the 'secret of God's tabernacle' no enemy can find us, and no troubles can reach us. . . . I do not mean that no trials will come. They may come in abundance, but they cannot penetrate into the sanctuary of the soul, and we may dwell in perfect peace even in the midst of life's fiercest storms."
HANNAH WHITALL SMITH

> "Trust me. I love you. I made you. I am good and have great plans for you."

KATRIEL OVERTON is a Christian with autism who experiences and believes all people can feel and know God's love if they choose. She sees God helping her love people, including herself.

²⁶The disciples were astounded. "Then who in the world can be saved?" they asked.

²⁷Jesus looked at them intently and said, "Humanly speaking, it is impossible. But not with God. Everything is possible with God."

²⁸Then Peter began to speak up. "We've given up everything to follow you," he said.

²⁹"Yes," Jesus replied, "and I assure you that everyone who has given up house or brothers or sisters or mother or father or children or property, for my sake and for the Good News, ³⁰will receive now in return a hundred times as many houses, brothers, sisters, mothers, children, and property—along with persecution. And in the world to come that person will have eternal life. ³¹But many who are the greatest now will be least important then, and those who seem least important now will be the greatest then.*"

Jesus Again Predicts His Death

³²They were now on the way up to Jerusalem, and Jesus was walking ahead of them. The disciples were filled with awe, and the people following behind were overwhelmed with fear. Taking the twelve disciples aside, Jesus once more began to describe everything that was about to happen to him. ³³"Listen," he said, "we're going up to Jerusalem, where the Son of Man* will be betrayed to the leading priests and the teachers of religious law. They will sentence him to die and hand him over to the Romans.* ³⁴They will mock him, spit on him, flog him with a whip, and kill him, but after three days he will rise again."

Jesus Teaches about Serving Others

³⁵Then James and John, the sons of Zebedee, came over and spoke to him. "Teacher," they said, "we want you to do us a favor."

³⁶"What is your request?" he asked.

³⁷They replied, "When you sit on your glorious throne, we want to sit in places of honor next to you, one on your right and the other on your left."

³⁸But Jesus said to them, "You don't know what you are asking! Are you able to drink from the bitter cup of suffering I am about to drink? Are you able to be baptized with the baptism of suffering I must be baptized with?"

³⁹"Oh yes," they replied, "we are able!"

Then Jesus told them, "You will indeed drink from my bitter cup and be baptized with my baptism of suffering. ⁴⁰But I have no right to say who will sit on my right or my left. God has prepared those places for the ones he has chosen."

⁴¹When the ten other disciples heard what James and John had asked, they were indignant. ⁴²So Jesus called them together and said, "You know that the rulers in this world lord it over their people, and officials flaunt their authority over those under them. ⁴³But among you it will be different. Whoever wants to be a leader among you must be your servant, ⁴⁴and whoever wants to be first among you must be the slave of everyone else. ⁴⁵For even the Son of Man came not to be served but to serve others and to give his life as a ransom for many."

Jesus Heals Blind Bartimaeus

⁴⁶Then they reached Jericho, and as Jesus and his disciples left town, a large crowd followed him. A blind beggar named Bartimaeus (son of Timaeus) was sitting beside the road. ⁴⁷When Bartimaeus heard that Jesus of Nazareth was nearby, he began to shout, "Jesus, Son of David, have mercy on me!"

⁴⁸"Be quiet!" many of the people yelled at him.

But he only shouted louder, "Son of David, have mercy on me!"

⁴⁹When Jesus heard him, he stopped and said, "Tell him to come here."

So they called the blind man. "Cheer up," they said. "Come on, he's calling you!" ⁵⁰Bartimaeus threw aside his coat, jumped up, and came to Jesus.

⁵¹"What do you want me to do for you?" Jesus asked.

"My Rabbi,*" the blind man said, "I want to see!"

⁵²And Jesus said to him, "Go, for your faith has healed you." Instantly the man could see, and he followed Jesus down the road.*

Jesus' Triumphant Entry

11 As Jesus and his disciples approached Jerusalem, they came to the towns of Bethphage and Bethany on the Mount of Olives. Jesus sent two of them on ahead. ²"Go into that village over there," he told them. "As soon as you enter it, you will see a young donkey tied there that no one has ever ridden.

10:31 Greek *But many who are first will be last; and the last, first.* 10:33a "Son of Man" is a title Jesus used for himself. 10:33b Greek *the Gentiles.* 10:51 Greek uses the Hebrew term *Rabboni.* 10:52 Or *on the way.*

10:29-30 Jesus assured his disciples that they would receive whatever they had given up for him many times over, including a new family in Christ (brothers, sisters, mothers, children) and Christian hospitality (houses). What is gained in following Jesus far outweighs any loss. "And in the world to come" they will inherit the eternal life that the rich man desired but did not receive.

10:42-45 In a male-dominated society, Mark's male audience would have categories to internalize Jesus' lesson on servant leadership. But what about his female audience? As indicated by the Gospels, women were good and humble servants in the role their culture prescribed for them, but would they naturally consider themselves potential leaders? This may still feel true for women today. Even though our societies may strive for equality, men still hold the vast majority of leadership positions in cultural, social, and political spheres. Whereas serving others could be natural to some women, other women need *empowerment*, in general, to step into or remain in leadership roles.

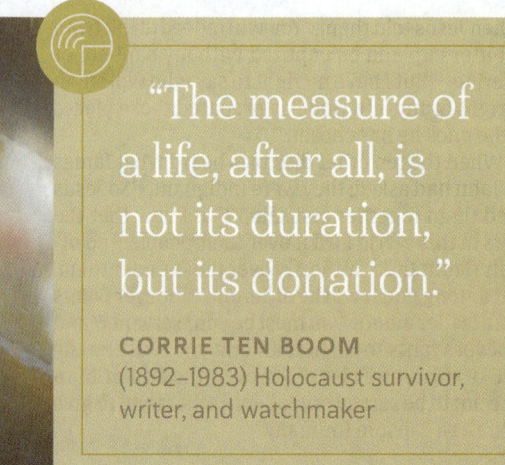

> "The measure of a life, after all, is not its duration, but its donation."
>
> **CORRIE TEN BOOM**
> (1892–1983) Holocaust survivor, writer, and watchmaker

Untie it and bring it here. ³If anyone asks, 'What are you doing?' just say, 'The Lord needs it and will return it soon.'"

⁴The two disciples left and found the colt standing in the street, tied outside the front door. ⁵As they were untying it, some bystanders demanded, "What are you doing, untying that colt?" ⁶They said what Jesus had told them to say, and they were permitted to take it. ⁷Then they brought the colt to Jesus and threw their garments over it, and he sat on it.

⁸Many in the crowd spread their garments on the road ahead of him, and others spread leafy branches they had cut in the fields. ⁹Jesus was in the center of the procession, and the people all around him were shouting,

"Praise God!*
   Blessings on the one who comes in the name
      of the Lord!
¹⁰ Blessings on the coming Kingdom of our
      ancestor David!
   Praise God in highest heaven!"*

¹¹So Jesus came to Jerusalem and went into the Temple. After looking around carefully at everything, he left because it was late in the afternoon. Then he returned to Bethany with the twelve disciples.

Jesus Curses the Fig Tree

¹²The next morning as they were leaving Bethany, Jesus was hungry. ¹³He noticed a fig tree in full leaf a little way off, so he went over to see if he could find any figs. But there were only leaves because it was too early in the season for fruit. ¹⁴Then Jesus said to the tree, "May no one ever eat your fruit again!" And the disciples heard him say it.

Jesus Clears the Temple

¹⁵When they arrived back in Jerusalem, Jesus entered the Temple and began to drive out the people buying and selling animals for sacrifices. He knocked over the tables of the money changers and the chairs of those selling doves, ¹⁶and he stopped everyone from using the Temple as a marketplace.* ¹⁷He said to them, "The Scriptures declare, 'My Temple will be called a house of prayer for all nations,' but you have turned it into a den of thieves."*

¹⁸When the leading priests and teachers of religious law heard what Jesus had done, they began planning how to kill him. But they were afraid of him because the people were so amazed at his teaching.

¹⁹That evening Jesus and the disciples left* the city. ²⁰The next morning as they passed by the fig tree he had cursed, the disciples noticed it had withered from the roots up. ²¹Peter remembered what Jesus had said to the tree on the previous day and exclaimed, "Look, Rabbi! The fig tree you cursed has withered and died!"

²²Then Jesus said to the disciples, "Have faith in God. ²³I tell you the truth, you can say to this mountain, 'May you be lifted up and thrown into the sea,' and it will happen. But you must really believe it will happen and have no doubt in your heart. ²⁴I tell you, you can pray for anything, and if you believe that you've received it, it will be yours. ²⁵But when you are praying, first forgive anyone you are holding a grudge against, so that your Father in heaven will forgive your sins, too.*"

The Authority of Jesus Challenged

²⁷Again they entered Jerusalem. As Jesus was walking through the Temple area, the leading priests, the teachers of religious law, and the elders came up to him. ²⁸They demanded, "By what authority are you doing all these things? Who gave you the right to do them?"

²⁹"I'll tell you by what authority I do these things if you answer one question," Jesus replied. ³⁰"Did John's authority to baptize come from heaven, or was it merely human? Answer me!"

³¹They talked it over among themselves. "If we say it was from heaven, he will ask why we didn't believe John. ³²But do we dare say it was merely human?" For they were afraid of what the people would do, because everyone believed that John was a prophet. ³³So they finally replied, "We don't know."

And Jesus responded, "Then I won't tell you by what authority I do these things."

11:9 Greek *Hosanna*, an exclamation of praise that literally means "save now"; also in 11:10. **11:9-10** Pss 118:25-26; 148:1. **11:16** Or *from carrying merchandise through the Temple.* **11:17** Isa 56:7; Jer 7:11. **11:19** Greek *they left;* other manuscripts read *he left.* **11:25** Some manuscripts add verse 26, *But if you refuse to forgive, your Father in heaven will not forgive your sins.* Compare Matt 6:15.

Parable of the Evil Farmers

12 Then Jesus began teaching them with stories: "A man planted a vineyard. He built a wall around it, dug a pit for pressing out the grape juice, and built a lookout tower. Then he leased the vineyard to tenant farmers and moved to another country. ²At the time of the grape harvest, he sent one of his servants to collect his share of the crop. ³But the farmers grabbed the servant, beat him up, and sent him back empty-handed. ⁴The owner then sent another servant, but they insulted him and beat him over the head. ⁵The next servant he sent was killed. Others he sent were either beaten or killed, ⁶until there was only one left—his son whom he loved dearly. The owner finally sent him, thinking, 'Surely they will respect my son.'

⁷"But the tenant farmers said to one another, 'Here comes the heir to this estate. Let's kill him and get the estate for ourselves!' ⁸So they grabbed him and murdered him and threw his body out of the vineyard.

⁹"What do you suppose the owner of the vineyard will do?" Jesus asked. "I'll tell you—he will come and kill those farmers and lease the vineyard to others. ¹⁰Didn't you ever read this in the Scriptures?

'The stone that the builders rejected
　has now become the cornerstone.
¹¹ This is the Lord's doing,
　and it is wonderful to see.'*"

¹²The religious leaders* wanted to arrest Jesus because they realized he was telling the story against them—they were the wicked farmers. But they were afraid of the crowd, so they left him and went away.

Taxes for Caesar

¹³Later the leaders sent some Pharisees and supporters of Herod to trap Jesus into saying something for which he could be arrested. ¹⁴"Teacher," they said, "we know how honest you are. You are impartial and don't play favorites. You teach the way of God truthfully. Now tell us—is it right to pay taxes to Caesar or not? ¹⁵Should we pay them, or shouldn't we?"

Jesus saw through their hypocrisy and said, "Why are you trying to trap me? Show me a Roman coin,* and I'll tell you." ¹⁶When they handed it to him, he asked, "Whose picture and title are stamped on it?"

"Caesar's," they replied.

¹⁷"Well, then," Jesus said, "give to Caesar what belongs to Caesar, and give to God what belongs to God."

His reply completely amazed them.

Discussion about Resurrection

¹⁸Then Jesus was approached by some Sadducees—religious leaders who say there is no resurrection from the dead. They posed this question: ¹⁹"Teacher, Moses gave us a law that if a man dies, leaving a wife without children, his brother should marry the widow and have a child who will carry on the brother's name.* ²⁰Well, suppose there were seven brothers. The oldest one married and then died without children. ²¹So the second brother married the widow, but he also died without children. Then the third brother married her. ²²This continued with all seven of them, and still there were no children. Last of all, the woman also died. ²³So tell us, whose wife will she be in the resurrection? For all seven were married to her."

²⁴Jesus replied, "Your mistake is that you don't know the Scriptures, and you don't know the power of God. ²⁵For when the dead rise, they will neither marry nor be given in marriage. In this respect they will be like the angels in heaven.

²⁶"But now, as to whether the dead will be raised—haven't you ever read about this in the writings of Moses, in the story of the burning bush? Long after Abraham, Isaac, and Jacob had died, God said to Moses,* 'I am the God of Abraham, the God of Isaac, and the God of Jacob.'* ²⁷So he is the God of the living, not the dead. You have made a serious error."

The Most Important Commandment

²⁸One of the teachers of religious law was standing there listening to the debate. He realized that Jesus had answered well, so he asked, "Of all the commandments, which is the most important?"

²⁹Jesus replied, "The most important commandment is this: 'Listen, O Israel! The Lord our God is the one and only Lord. ³⁰And you must love the Lord your God with all your heart, all your soul, all your mind, and all your strength.'* ³¹The second is equally important: 'Love your neighbor as yourself.'* No other commandment is greater than these."

³²The teacher of religious law replied, "Well said, Teacher. You have spoken the truth by saying that there is only one God and no other. ³³And I know it is important to love him with all my heart and all my understanding and all my strength, and to love my neighbor as myself. This is more important than to offer all of the burnt offerings and sacrifices required in the law."

³⁴Realizing how much the man understood, Jesus said to him, "You are not far from the Kingdom of God." And after that, no one dared to ask him any more questions.

12:10-11 Ps 118:22-23.　**12:12** Greek *They*.　**12:15** Greek *a denarius*.　**12:19** See Deut 25:5-6.　**12:26a** Greek *in the story of the bush? God said to him*.　**12:26b** Exod 3:6.　**12:29-30** Deut 6:4-5.　**12:31** Lev 19:18.

Whose Son Is the Messiah?

³⁵Later, as Jesus was teaching the people in the Temple, he asked, "Why do the teachers of religious law claim that the Messiah is the son of David? ³⁶For David himself, speaking under the inspiration of the Holy Spirit, said,

'The LORD said to my Lord,
Sit in the place of honor at my right hand
    until I humble your enemies beneath your
        feet.'*

³⁷Since David himself called the Messiah 'my Lord,' how can the Messiah be his son?" The large crowd listened to him with great delight.

³⁸Jesus also taught: "Beware of these teachers of religious law! For they like to parade around in flowing robes and receive respectful greetings as they walk in the marketplaces. ³⁹And how they love the seats of honor in the synagogues and the head table at banquets. ⁴⁰Yet they shamelessly cheat widows out of their property and then pretend to be pious by making long prayers in public. Because of this, they will be more severely punished."

The Widow's Offering

⁴¹Jesus sat down near the collection box in the Temple and watched as the crowds dropped in their money. Many rich people put in large amounts. ⁴²Then a poor widow came and dropped in two small coins.*

⁴³Jesus called his disciples to him and said, "I tell you the truth, this poor widow has given more than all the others who are making contributions. ⁴⁴For they gave a tiny part of their surplus, but she, poor as she is, has given everything she had to live on."

Jesus Speaks about the Future

13 As Jesus was leaving the Temple that day, one of his disciples said, "Teacher, look at these magnificent buildings! Look at the impressive stones in the walls."

²Jesus replied, "Yes, look at these great buildings. But they will be completely demolished. Not one stone will be left on top of another!"

³Later, Jesus sat on the Mount of Olives across the valley from the Temple. Peter, James, John, and Andrew came to him privately and asked him, ⁴"Tell us, when will all this happen? What sign will show us that these things are about to be fulfilled?"

⁵Jesus replied, "Don't let anyone mislead you, ⁶for many will come in my name, claiming, 'I am the Messiah.'* They will deceive many. ⁷And you will hear of wars and threats of wars, but don't panic. Yes, these things must take place, but the end won't follow immediately. ⁸Nation will go to war against nation, and kingdom against kingdom. There will be earthquakes in many parts of the world, as well as famines. But this is only the first of the birth pains, with more to come.

⁹"When these things begin to happen, watch out! You will be handed over to the local councils and beaten in the synagogues. You will stand trial before governors and kings because you are my followers. But this will be your opportunity to tell them about me.* ¹⁰For the Good News must first be preached to all nations.* ¹¹But when you are arrested and stand trial, don't worry in advance about what to say. Just say what God tells you at that time, for it is not you who will be speaking, but the Holy Spirit.

¹²"A brother will betray his brother to death, a father will betray his own child, and children will rebel against their parents and cause them to be killed. ¹³And everyone will hate you because you are my followers.* But the one who endures to the end will be saved.

¹⁴"The day is coming when you will see the sacrilegious object that causes desecration* standing where he* should not be." (Reader, pay attention!) "Then those in Judea must flee to the hills. ¹⁵A person out on the deck of a roof must not go down into the house to pack. ¹⁶A person out in the field must not return even to get a coat. ¹⁷How terrible it will

---

12:36 Ps 110:1. **12:42** Greek *two lepta, which is a kodrantes* [i.e., a quadrans]. **13:6** Greek *claiming, 'I am.'* **13:9** Or *But this will be your testimony against them.* **13:10** Or *all peoples.* **13:13** Greek *on account of my name.* **13:14a** Greek *the abomination of desolation.* See Dan 9:27; 11:31; 12:11. **13:14b** Or *it.*

12:41-44 Singling out the poor widow, Jesus again overturned his culture's conventional values. Similar to today, wealthy people were given special privilege, favor, and power, and the people who were poor and could not give as much were diminished and overlooked. By highlighting the example of the poor widow, Jesus was saying that neither how much one owns nor how much one gives matters to him. Instead, what matters is at what cost one gives because the cost likely indicates what motivates the giving.

12:43-44 Jesus called his disciples closer together to hear his teaching (see 3:23; 6:7; 8:1; 10:42; see also 7:14; 8:34). Jesus' pronouncement in 12:43 reveals a radical difference between his thinking and that of the world. No one would have named a building after the widow for her gift of two small coins, but God looks at a person's heart (1 Samuel 16:7). The widow was doing exactly what Jesus told the rich man to do (Mark 10:21) and what he taught his disciples (1:17-20; 8:34-37; 10:28-29). Like the woman of 14:3-9, the poor widow loved God with all her heart, soul, mind, and strength (12:30).

13:17 Jesus was not condemning motherhood. Practically, it was inconvenient for a pregnant woman or nursing mother to flee for her life. Paul recommended singleness to Jesus' followers because he perceived some similar impending crisis (1 Corinthians 7:26-28). In some cultures, women must marry or have children for their lives to be considered fulfilling. But both Jesus (Matthew 19:11-12) and Paul (1 Corinthians 7:32-35, 40) noted that being single can be a blessing and a means of devoting more time to the Kingdom.

be for pregnant women and for nursing mothers in those days. ¹⁸And pray that your flight will not be in winter. ¹⁹For there will be greater anguish in those days than at any time since God created the world. And it will never be so great again. ²⁰In fact, unless the Lord shortens that time of calamity, not a single person will survive. But for the sake of his chosen ones he has shortened those days.

²¹"Then if anyone tells you, 'Look, here is the Messiah,' or 'There he is,' don't believe it. ²²For false messiahs and false prophets will rise up and perform signs and wonders so as to deceive, if possible, even God's chosen ones. ²³Watch out! I have warned you about this ahead of time!

²⁴"At that time, after the anguish of those days,

the sun will be darkened,
the moon will give no light,
²⁵ the stars will fall from the sky,
and the powers in the heavens will be shaken.*

²⁶Then everyone will see the Son of Man* coming on the clouds with great power and glory.* ²⁷And he will send out his angels to gather his chosen ones from all over the world*—from the farthest ends of the earth and heaven.

²⁸"Now learn a lesson from the fig tree. When its branches bud and its leaves begin to sprout, you know that summer is near. ²⁹In the same way, when you see all these things taking place, you can know that his return is very near, right at the door. ³⁰I tell you the truth, this generation* will not pass from the scene before all these things take place. ³¹Heaven and earth will disappear, but my words will never disappear.

³²"However, no one knows the day or hour when these things will happen, not even the angels in heaven or the Son himself. Only the Father knows. ³³And since you don't know when that time will come, be on guard! Stay alert*!

³⁴"The coming of the Son of Man can be illustrated by the story of a man going on a long trip. When he left home, he gave each of his slaves instructions about the work they were to do, and he told the gatekeeper to watch for his return. ³⁵You, too, must keep watch! For you don't know when the master of the household will return—in the evening, at midnight, before dawn, or at daybreak. ³⁶Don't let him find you sleeping when he arrives without warning. ³⁷I say to you what I say to everyone: Watch for him!"

Jesus Anointed at Bethany

14 It was now two days before Passover and the Festival of Unleavened Bread. The leading priests and the teachers of religious law were still looking for an opportunity to capture Jesus secretly and kill him. ²"But not during the Passover celebration," they agreed, "or the people may riot."

³Meanwhile, Jesus was in Bethany at the home of Simon, a man who had previously had leprosy. While he was eating,* a woman came in with a beautiful alabaster jar of expensive perfume made from essence of nard. She broke open the jar and poured the perfume over his head.

⁴Some of those at the table were indignant. "Why waste such expensive perfume?" they asked. ⁵"It could have been sold for a year's wages* and the money given to the poor!" So they scolded her harshly.

⁶But Jesus replied, "Leave her alone. Why criticize her for doing such a good thing to me? ⁷You will always have the poor among you, and you can help them whenever you want to. But you will not always have me. ⁸She has done what she could and has anointed my body for burial ahead of time. ⁹I tell you the truth, wherever the Good News is preached throughout the world, this woman's deed will be remembered and discussed."

Judas Agrees to Betray Jesus

¹⁰Then Judas Iscariot, one of the twelve disciples, went to the leading priests to arrange to betray Jesus to them. ¹¹They were delighted when they heard why he had come, and they promised to give him money. So he began looking for an opportunity to betray Jesus.

The Last Supper

¹²On the first day of the Festival of Unleavened Bread, when the Passover lamb is sacrificed, Jesus' disciples

---

13:24-25 See Isa 13:10; 34:4; Joel 2:10. **13:26a** "Son of Man" is a title Jesus used for himself. **13:26b** See Dan 7:13. **13:27** Greek *from the four winds.* **13:30** Or *this age,* or *this nation.* **13:33** Some manuscripts add *and pray.* **14:3** Or *reclining.* **14:5** Greek *for 300 denarii.* A denarius was equivalent to a laborer's full day's wage.

14:3-9 The story of Jesus' being anointed by a woman in Bethany sets the scene for the events that follow. Luke's account (Luke 7:36-50) is significantly different and is probably a different event. The home belonged to Simon, a man who formerly had leprosy (those with leprosy were isolated from society; perhaps he had been healed by Jesus; see Mark 1:40-45). A woman (possibly Mary of Bethany, see John 12:3) broke the neck of a sealed, alabaster jar containing expensive perfume (essence of nard) and poured it all on Jesus' head). While Jesus credited her act with anointing his body for burial, her actions were also symbolic of Jesus' roles as prophet, priest, and king. In ancient Israel, priests and prophets were responsible for anointing Israel's kings (1 Samuel 10:1-8; 2 Kings 9:1-6) and priests (Exodus 29:4-7).
14:6-8 Jesus defended the woman's action. That the disciples would "always have the poor" among them did not minimize Jesus' concern for the poor. But the opportunity to minister directly to Jesus was limited. Only hours remained! She chose the best thing she could do with her resources.

asked him, "Where do you want us to go to prepare the Passover meal for you?"

¹³So Jesus sent two of them into Jerusalem with these instructions: "As you go into the city, a man carrying a pitcher of water will meet you. Follow him. ¹⁴At the house he enters, say to the owner, 'The Teacher asks: Where is the guest room where I can eat the Passover meal with my disciples?' ¹⁵He will take you upstairs to a large room that is already set up. That is where you should prepare our meal." ¹⁶So the two disciples went into the city and found everything just as Jesus had said, and they prepared the Passover meal there.

¹⁷In the evening Jesus arrived with the Twelve. ¹⁸As they were at the table* eating, Jesus said, "I tell you the truth, one of you eating with me here will betray me."

¹⁹Greatly distressed, each one asked in turn, "Am I the one?"

²⁰He replied, "It is one of you twelve who is eating from this bowl with me. ²¹For the Son of Man* must die, as the Scriptures declared long ago. But how terrible it will be for the one who betrays him. It would be far better for that man if he had never been born!"

²²As they were eating, Jesus took some bread and blessed it. Then he broke it in pieces and gave it to the disciples, saying, "Take it, for this is my body."

²³And he took a cup of wine and gave thanks to God for it. He gave it to them, and they all drank from it. ²⁴And he said to them, "This is my blood, which confirms the covenant* between God and his people. It is poured out as a sacrifice for many. ²⁵I tell you the truth, I will not drink wine again until the day I drink it new in the Kingdom of God."

²⁶Then they sang a hymn and went out to the Mount of Olives.

Jesus Predicts Peter's Denial

²⁷On the way, Jesus told them, "All of you will desert me. For the Scriptures say,

'God will strike* the Shepherd,
and the sheep will be scattered.'

²⁸But after I am raised from the dead, I will go ahead of you to Galilee and meet you there."

²⁹Peter said to him, "Even if everyone else deserts you, I never will."

³⁰Jesus replied, "I tell you the truth, Peter—this very night, before the rooster crows twice, you will deny three times that you even know me."

³¹"No!" Peter declared emphatically. "Even if I have to die with you, I will never deny you!" And all the others vowed the same.

Jesus Prays in Gethsemane

³²They went to the olive grove called Gethsemane, and Jesus said, "Sit here while I go and pray." ³³He took Peter, James, and John with him, and he became deeply troubled and distressed. ³⁴He told them, "My soul is crushed with grief to the point of death. Stay here and keep watch with me."

³⁵He went on a little farther and fell to the ground. He prayed that, if it were possible, the awful hour awaiting him might pass him by. ³⁶"Abba, Father,"* he cried out, "everything is possible for you. Please take this cup of suffering away from me. Yet I want your will to be done, not mine."

³⁷Then he returned and found the disciples asleep. He said to Peter, "Simon, are you asleep? Couldn't you watch with me even one hour? ³⁸Keep watch and pray, so that you will not give in to temptation. For the spirit is willing, but the body is weak."

³⁹Then Jesus left them again and prayed the same prayer as before. ⁴⁰When he returned to them again, he found them sleeping, for they couldn't keep their eyes open. And they didn't know what to say.

⁴¹When he returned to them the third time, he said, "Go ahead and sleep. Have your rest. But no—the time has come. The Son of Man is betrayed into the hands of sinners. ⁴²Up, let's be going. Look, my betrayer is here!"

Jesus Is Betrayed and Arrested

⁴³And immediately, even as Jesus said this, Judas, one of the twelve disciples, arrived with a crowd of men armed with swords and clubs. They had been sent by the leading priests, the teachers of religious law, and the elders. ⁴⁴The traitor, Judas, had given them a prearranged signal: "You will know which one to arrest when I greet him with a kiss. Then you can take him away under guard." ⁴⁵As soon as they arrived, Judas walked up to Jesus. "Rabbi!" he exclaimed, and gave him the kiss.

⁴⁶Then the others grabbed Jesus and arrested him. ⁴⁷But one of the men with Jesus pulled out his sword and struck the high priest's slave, slashing off his ear.

⁴⁸Jesus asked them, "Am I some dangerous revolutionary, that you come with swords and clubs to arrest me? ⁴⁹Why didn't you arrest me in the Temple? I was there among you teaching every day. But these things are happening to fulfill what the Scriptures say about me."

⁵⁰Then all his disciples deserted him and ran away. ⁵¹One young man following behind was clothed only in a long linen shirt. When the mob tried to grab him, ⁵²he slipped out of his shirt and ran away naked.

Jesus before the Council

⁵³They took Jesus to the high priest's home where the leading priests, the elders, and the teachers of religious law had gathered. ⁵⁴Meanwhile, Peter followed him at a distance and went right into the high

---

14:18 Or *As they reclined.* 14:21 "Son of Man" is a title Jesus used for himself. 14:24 Some manuscripts read *the new covenant.* 14:27 Greek *I will strike.* Zech 13:7. 14:36 *Abba* is an Aramaic term for "father."

The Woman WHO ANOINTED JESUS

IDENTITY: She Did What She Could

What if you did what you could today? Not *everything* you could do, but just what you, uniquely, could do. What difference might you make?

Just a few days before Jesus would enter Jerusalem to go to the cross, a woman came to Jesus and broke an alabaster jar and poured perfume on his head. Mark tells us the perfume was worth more than a year's wages and that some who were dining with Jesus objected harshly (14:4-5).

How did Jesus respond to this woman? He told his disciples to "leave her alone" because what she was doing was "such a good thing" (14:6). Another possible translation for Jesus' description of this woman's action is "She has done a beautiful thing to me." He also explained that this gesture prepared his body for burial.

> Instead of trying to do everything, she did what she could.

Notice this: Jesus didn't praise the woman because she did *everything* she could. He honored her because she did *what* she could. In that moment, yes, it was a lot. But it's the fact that she acted that Jesus highlighted.

This woman knew Jesus loved her—and the world—to the extent that he was headed to the cross to die. She showed her love for him in that moment by doing what she could, anointing his body before his upcoming death.

What if you did what you could today to make a difference for Jesus?

THIS WOMAN'S STORY IS TOLD IN MATTHEW 26:6-13; MARK 14:3-9; AND JOHN IDENTIFIES HER AS MARY OF BETHANY IN JOHN 12:1-11.

IDENTIFY

What do you imagine it felt like to be this woman? How do you think it felt for Jesus to honor her devotion to him?

What's one simple gesture you could try today to show your love for Jesus?

> "These five words—she did what she could—motivate me to put feet to my faith. I awake each day praying, how can I love Jesus today, by doing what I can?"

ELISA MORGAN, MDiv, speaks, writes, and cohosts podcasts for Our Daily Bread Ministries. For twenty years, she served as president of MOPS International, now as president emerita. Her motto is "Living really... Really living."

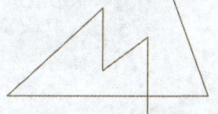

priest's courtyard. There he sat with the guards, warming himself by the fire.

⁵⁵Inside, the leading priests and the entire high council* were trying to find evidence against Jesus, so they could put him to death. But they couldn't find any. ⁵⁶Many false witnesses spoke against him, but they contradicted each other. ⁵⁷Finally, some men stood up and gave this false testimony: ⁵⁸"We heard him say, 'I will destroy this Temple made with human hands, and in three days I will build another, made without human hands.'" ⁵⁹But even then they didn't get their stories straight!

⁶⁰Then the high priest stood up before the others and asked Jesus, "Well, aren't you going to answer these charges? What do you have to say for yourself?" ⁶¹But Jesus was silent and made no reply. Then the high priest asked him, "Are you the Messiah, the Son of the Blessed One?"

⁶²Jesus said, "I Am.* And you will see the Son of Man seated in the place of power at God's right hand* and coming on the clouds of heaven.*"

⁶³Then the high priest tore his clothing to show his horror and said, "Why do we need other witnesses? ⁶⁴You have all heard his blasphemy. What is your verdict?"

"Guilty!" they all cried. "He deserves to die!"

⁶⁵Then some of them began to spit at him, and they blindfolded him and beat him with their fists. "Prophesy to us," they jeered. And the guards slapped him as they took him away.

Peter Denies Jesus

⁶⁶Meanwhile, Peter was in the courtyard below. One of the servant girls who worked for the high priest came by ⁶⁷and noticed Peter warming himself at the

14:55 Greek *the Sanhedrin.* 14:62a Or *The 'I Am' is here;* or *I am the Lord.* See Exod 3:14. 14:62b Greek *seated at the right hand of the power.* See Ps 110:1. 14:62c See Dan 7:13.

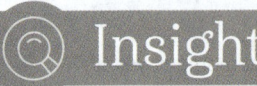

Insight — THE LAST SUPPER AND GETHSEMANE

Knowing the time for his death was drawing near, Jesus shared a final Passover meal with his disciples in an upper room in Jerusalem (14:12-25). After the meal, Jesus and his disciples went out to the garden of Gethsemane on the Mount of Olives, where Judas betrayed him (14:26-52).

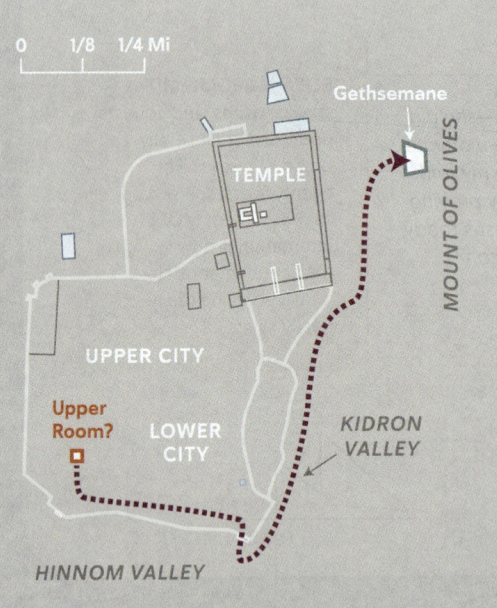

fire. She looked at him closely and said, "You were one of those with Jesus of Nazareth.*"

⁶⁸But Peter denied it. "I don't know what you're talking about," he said, and he went out into the entryway. Just then, a rooster crowed.*

⁶⁹When the servant girl saw him standing there, she began telling the others, "This man is definitely one of them!" ⁷⁰But Peter denied it again.

A little later some of the other bystanders confronted Peter and said, "You must be one of them, because you are a Galilean."

⁷¹Peter swore, "A curse on me if I'm lying—I don't know this man you're talking about!" ⁷²And immediately the rooster crowed the second time.

Suddenly, Jesus' words flashed through Peter's mind: "Before the rooster crows twice, you will deny three times that you even know me." And he broke down and wept.

Jesus' Trial before Pilate

15 Very early in the morning the leading priests, the elders, and the teachers of religious law—the entire high council*—met to discuss their next step. They bound Jesus, led him away, and took him to Pilate, the Roman governor.

²Pilate asked Jesus, "Are you the king of the Jews?" Jesus replied, "You have said it."

³Then the leading priests kept accusing him of many crimes, ⁴and Pilate asked him, "Aren't you going to answer them? What about all these charges they are bringing against you?" ⁵But Jesus said nothing, much to Pilate's surprise.

⁶Now it was the governor's custom each year during the Passover celebration to release one prisoner—anyone the people requested. ⁷One of the prisoners at that time was Barabbas, a revolutionary who had committed murder in an uprising. ⁸The crowd went to Pilate and asked him to release a prisoner as usual.

⁹"Would you like me to release to you this 'King of the Jews'?" Pilate asked. ¹⁰(For he realized by now that the leading priests had arrested Jesus out of envy.) ¹¹But at this point the leading priests stirred up the crowd to demand the release of Barabbas instead of Jesus. ¹²Pilate asked them, "Then what should I do with this man you call the king of the Jews?"

¹³They shouted back, "Crucify him!"

¹⁴"Why?" Pilate demanded. "What crime has he committed?"

But the mob roared even louder, "Crucify him!"

¹⁵So to pacify the crowd, Pilate released Barabbas to them. He ordered Jesus flogged with a lead-tipped whip, then turned him over to the Roman soldiers to be crucified.

The Soldiers Mock Jesus

¹⁶The soldiers took Jesus into the courtyard of the governor's headquarters (called the Praetorium) and called out the entire regiment. ¹⁷They dressed him in a purple robe, and they wove thorn branches into a crown and put it on his head. ¹⁸Then they saluted him and taunted, "Hail! King of the Jews!" ¹⁹And they struck him on the head with a reed stick, spit on him, and dropped to their knees in mock worship. ²⁰When they were finally tired of mocking him, they took off the purple robe and put his own clothes on him again. Then they led him away to be crucified.

The Crucifixion

²¹A passerby named Simon, who was from Cyrene,* was coming in from the countryside just then, and the soldiers forced him to carry Jesus' cross. (Simon was the father of Alexander and Rufus.) ²²And they brought Jesus to a place called Golgotha (which means "Place of the Skull"). ²³They offered him wine drugged with myrrh, but he refused it.

²⁴Then the soldiers nailed him to the cross. They divided his clothes and threw dice* to decide who would get each piece. ²⁵It was nine o'clock in the morning when they crucified him. ²⁶A sign announced the charge against him. It read, "The King of the Jews." ²⁷Two revolutionaries* were crucified with him, one on his right and one on his left.*

²⁹The people passing by shouted abuse, shaking their heads in mockery. "Ha! Look at you now!" they yelled at him. "You said you were going to destroy the Temple and rebuild it in three days. ³⁰Well then, save yourself and come down from the cross!"

³¹The leading priests and teachers of religious law also mocked Jesus. "He saved others," they scoffed, "but he can't save himself! ³²Let this Messiah, this King of Israel, come down from the cross so we can see it and believe him!" Even the men who were crucified with Jesus ridiculed him.

The Death of Jesus

³³At noon, darkness fell across the whole land until three o'clock. ³⁴Then at three o'clock Jesus called out with a loud voice, "Eloi, Eloi, lema sabachthani?" which means "My God, my God, why have you abandoned me?"*

³⁵Some of the bystanders misunderstood and thought he was calling for the prophet Elijah. ³⁶One of them ran and filled a sponge with sour wine, holding it up to him on a reed stick so he could drink. "Wait!" he said. "Let's see whether Elijah comes to take him down!"

14:67 Or *Jesus the Nazarene.* **14:68** Some manuscripts do not include *Just then, a rooster crowed.* **15:1** Greek *the Sanhedrin;* also in 15:43. **15:21** *Cyrene* was a city in northern Africa. **15:24** Greek *cast lots.* See Ps 22:18. **15:27a** Or *Two criminals.* **15:27b** Some manuscripts add verse 28, *And the Scripture was fulfilled that said, "He was counted among those who were rebels."* See Isa 53:12; also compare Luke 22:37. **15:34** Ps 22:1.

WHAT THE BIBLE SAYS ABOUT Serving

We Serve Because Jesus Served Us

We preach that Jesus Christ is Lord, and we ourselves are your servants for Jesus' sake.
2 CORINTHIANS 4:5

Jesus knew that the Father had given him authority over everything and that he had come from God and would return to God.... Then he began to wash the disciples' feet, drying them with the towel he had around him.... After washing their feet, he ... asked, "Do you understand what I was doing? You call me 'Teacher' and 'Lord,' and you are right, because that's what I am. And since I, your Lord and Teacher, have washed your feet, you ought to wash each other's feet. I have given you an example to follow. Do as I have done to you. I tell you the truth, slaves are not greater than their master. Nor is the messenger more important than the one who sends the message. Now that you know these things, God will bless you for doing them." **JOHN 13:3, 5, 12-17**

You know the generous grace of our Lord Jesus Christ. Though he was rich, yet for your sakes he became poor, so that by his poverty he could make you rich. **2 CORINTHIANS 8:9**

Don't be concerned for your own good...

Submit to one another out of reverence for Christ.

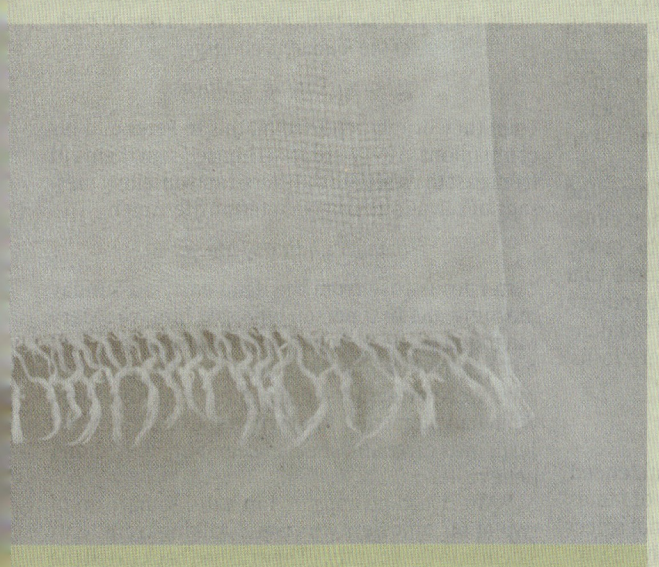

Service Starts with God

There are different kinds of service, but we serve the same Lord. God works in different ways, but it is the same God who does the work in all of us. A spiritual gift is given to each of us so we can help each other. **1 CORINTHIANS 12:5-7**

Submit to one another out of reverence for Christ.
EPHESIANS 5:21

Don't be selfish; don't try to impress others. Be humble, thinking of others as better than yourselves. Don't look out only for your own interests, but take an interest in others, too.
PHILIPPIANS 2:3-4

Godly Leaders Serve Others First

Jesus called them together and said, "You know that the rulers in this world lord it over their people, and officials flaunt their authority over those under them. But among you it will be different. Whoever wants to be a leader among you must be your servant, and whoever wants to be first among you must become your slave. For even the Son of Man came not to be served but to serve others and to give his life as a ransom for many." **MATTHEW 20:25-28**

He sat down, called the twelve disciples over to him, and said, "Whoever wants to be first must take last place and be the servant of everyone else." **MARK 9:35**

Don't be concerned for your own good but for the good of others. **1 CORINTHIANS 10:24**

³⁷Then Jesus uttered another loud cry and breathed his last. ³⁸And the curtain in the sanctuary of the Temple was torn in two, from top to bottom.

³⁹When the Roman officer* who stood facing him* saw how he had died, he exclaimed, "This man truly was the Son of God!"

⁴⁰Some women were there, watching from a distance, including Mary Magdalene, Mary (the mother of James the younger and of Joseph*), and Salome. ⁴¹They had been followers of Jesus and had cared for him while he was in Galilee. Many other women who had come with him to Jerusalem were also there.

The Burial of Jesus

⁴²This all happened on Friday, the day of preparation,* the day before the Sabbath. As evening approached, ⁴³Joseph of Arimathea took a risk and went to Pilate and asked for Jesus' body. (Joseph was an honored member of the high council, and he was waiting for the Kingdom of God to come.) ⁴⁴Pilate couldn't believe that Jesus was already dead, so he called for the Roman officer and asked if he had died yet. ⁴⁵The officer confirmed that Jesus was dead, so Pilate told Joseph he could have the body. ⁴⁶Joseph bought a long sheet of linen cloth. Then he took Jesus' body down from the cross, wrapped it in the cloth, and laid it in a tomb that had been carved out of the rock. Then he rolled a stone in front of the entrance. ⁴⁷Mary Magdalene and Mary the mother of Joseph saw where Jesus' body was laid.

The Resurrection

16 Saturday evening, when the Sabbath ended, Mary Magdalene, Mary the mother of James, and Salome went out and purchased burial spices so they could anoint Jesus' body. ²Very early on Sunday morning,* just at sunrise, they went to the tomb. ³On the way they were asking each other, "Who will roll away the stone for us from the entrance to the tomb?" ⁴But as they arrived, they looked up and saw that the stone, which was very large, had already been rolled aside.

⁵When they entered the tomb, they saw a young man clothed in a white robe sitting on the right side. The women were shocked, ⁶but the angel said, "Don't be alarmed. You are looking for Jesus of Nazareth,* who was crucified. He isn't here! He is risen from the dead! Look, this is where they laid his body. ⁷Now go and tell his disciples, including Peter, that Jesus is going ahead of you to Galilee. You will see him there, just as he told you before he died."

⁸The women fled from the tomb, trembling and bewildered, and they said nothing to anyone because they were too frightened.*

[The most ancient manuscripts of Mark conclude with verse 16:8. Later manuscripts add one or both of the following endings.]

[Shorter Ending of Mark]

Then they briefly reported all this to Peter and his companions. Afterward Jesus himself sent them out from east to west with the sacred and unfailing message of salvation that gives eternal life. Amen.

[Longer Ending of Mark]

⁹After Jesus rose from the dead early on Sunday morning, the first person who saw him was Mary Magdalene, the woman from whom he had cast out seven demons. ¹⁰She went to the disciples, who were grieving and weeping, and told them what had happened. ¹¹But when she told them that Jesus was alive and she had seen him, they didn't believe her.

¹²Afterward he appeared in a different form to two of his followers who were walking from Jerusalem into the country. ¹³They rushed back to tell the others, but no one believed them.

¹⁴Still later he appeared to the eleven disciples as they were eating together. He rebuked them for their stubborn unbelief because they refused to

---

15:39a Greek *the centurion;* similarly in 15:44, 45. **15:39b** Some manuscripts add *heard his cry and.* **15:40** Greek *Joses;* also in 15:47. See Matt 27:56. **15:42** Greek *It was the day of preparation.* **16:2** Greek *on the first day of the week;* also in 16:9. **16:6** Or *Jesus the Nazarene.* **16:8** The most reliable early manuscripts of the Gospel of Mark end at verse 8. Other manuscripts include various endings to the Gospel. A few include both the "shorter ending" and the "longer ending." The majority of manuscripts include the "longer ending" immediately after verse 8.

15:40-41 These women had supplied some of Jesus' economic needs (see Luke 8:2-3). They were also present at the burial (Mark 15:47) and the empty tomb (16:1-8) and would be the first witnesses of Jesus' resurrection. Mary Magdalene, from the village of Magdala near the shore of the Sea of Galilee, was a key figure in the resurrection accounts (16:1, 9; Matthew 28:1; Luke 24:10; John 20:1, 11-18). "Mary (the mother of James the younger)" might have been the mother of James the son of Alphaeus (Mark 3:18). Salome is mentioned only here and in 16:1.
16:1-8 Some of the most important ancient manuscripts that provide the text we use to translate the New Testament today bring Mark's narrative to a close at the end of 16:8, namely, "they were too frightened." With this shortest ending, Mark left his audience to conclude whether Jesus' disappearance from his tomb was the end of it all. There is a mysterious tension about what happens next. This ending sometimes reflects our Christian walk. We are often confused and afraid and not quite sure what comes next. We may often ask, "God, are you there? Do you care?" Despite our doubts, like the disciples, we can continue to trust and wait for the Holy Spirit's help.

believe those who had seen him after he had been raised from the dead.*

¹⁵And then he told them, "Go into all the world and preach the Good News to everyone. ¹⁶Anyone who believes and is baptized will be saved. But anyone who refuses to believe will be condemned. ¹⁷These miraculous signs will accompany those who believe: They will cast out demons in my name, and they will speak in new languages.* ¹⁸They will be able to handle snakes with safety, and if they drink anything poisonous, it won't hurt them. They will be able to place their hands on the sick, and they will be healed."

¹⁹When the Lord Jesus had finished talking with them, he was taken up into heaven and sat down in the place of honor at God's right hand. ²⁰And the disciples went everywhere and preached, and the Lord worked through them, confirming what they said by many miraculous signs.

16:14 Some early manuscripts add: *And they excused themselves, saying, "This age of lawlessness and unbelief is under Satan, who does not permit God's truth and power to conquer the evil [unclean] spirits. Therefore, reveal your justice now." This is what they said to Christ. And Christ replied to them, "The period of years of Satan's power has been fulfilled, but other dreadful things will happen soon. And I was handed over to death for those who have sinned, so that they may return to the truth and sin no more, and so they may inherit the spiritual, incorruptible, and righteous glory in heaven."* **16:17** Or *new tongues;* some manuscripts do not include *new.*

Luke

WHAT DO WE LEARN ABOUT GOD'S MISSION AND OURS? Jesus came to seek and save everyone, especially those whom society dismisses or excludes.

WHO WROTE IT? Luke, a physician who traveled with Paul.

WHEN DID IT HAPPEN? The book of Luke was likely written sometime between AD 60 and 90, describing events that happened early in the first century AD.

HOW IS IT ORGANIZED?

1: John the Baptist's birth; Jesus is conceived in Mary's womb

2: Jesus is born, prophesied over by Simeon and Anna, and grows

3–4: John baptizes Jesus; Jesus is tempted and begins his ministry

5–9: Jesus calls followers and teaches and heals in Galilee

10–19: Jesus ministers on his way to Jerusalem

20–23: Jesus spends his final week teaching in Jerusalem; he is arrested, tried, and put to death

24: Jesus rises from the dead and appears to his followers

Words to Remember are highlighted throughout this book

HOW LONG DOES IT TAKE TO READ? 2:15

| :30 | 1:00 | 1:30 | 2:00 | 2:30 | 3:00 | 3:30 |

Timeline

BC

- 37 — HEROD THE GREAT BEGINS TO RULE AS KING OVER PALESTINE
- 7/6 — ELIZABETH AND ZECHARIAH CONCEIVE JOHN THE BAPTIST; MARY CONCEIVES JESUS BY GOD'S SPIRIT
- 6/5 — JESUS, MARY'S CHILD AND THE SON OF GOD, IS BORN
- 5/4 — MARY, JOSEPH, AND JESUS ESCAPE TO EGYPT
- 4 — HEROD THE GREAT DIES
- 4/3 — JESUS' FAMILY RETURNS TO NAZARETH

AD

- 6 — JUDEA BECOMES A ROMAN PROVINCE
- 6/7 — YOUNG JESUS VISITS THE TEMPLE
- 14 — TIBERIUS CAESAR BECOMES EMPEROR OF ROME
- 26 — PONTIUS PILATE APPOINTED GOVERNOR IN JUDEA; JOHN THE BAPTIST'S MINISTRY BEGINS
- 26/27 — JESUS BEGINS HIS PUBLIC MINISTRY
- 28 — JOHN BAPTIZES JESUS; JESUS CHOOSES TWELVE DISCIPLES
- 29 — JESUS FEEDS 5,000+ INCLUDING WOMEN AND CHILDREN
- 30 — JESUS IS CRUCIFIED, RISES FROM THE DEAD, AND ASCENDS TO HEAVEN

LUKE 1

Introduction

1 Many people have set out to write accounts about the events that have been fulfilled among us. ²They used the eyewitness reports circulating among us from the early disciples.* ³Having carefully investigated everything from the beginning, I also have decided to write an accurate account for you, most honorable Theophilus, ⁴so you can be certain of the truth of everything you were taught.

The Birth of John the Baptist Foretold

⁵When Herod was king of Judea, there was a Jewish priest named Zechariah. He was a member of the priestly order of Abijah, and his wife, Elizabeth, was also from the priestly line of Aaron. ⁶Zechariah and Elizabeth were righteous in God's eyes, careful to obey all of the Lord's commandments and regulations. ⁷They had no children because Elizabeth was unable to conceive, and they were both very old.

⁸One day Zechariah was serving God in the Temple, for his order was on duty that week. ⁹As was the custom of the priests, he was chosen by lot to enter the sanctuary of the Lord and burn incense. ¹⁰While the incense was being burned, a great crowd stood outside, praying.

¹¹While Zechariah was in the sanctuary, an angel of the Lord appeared to him, standing to the right of the incense altar. ¹²Zechariah was shaken and overwhelmed with fear when he saw him. ¹³But the angel said, "Don't be afraid, Zechariah! God has heard your prayer. Your wife, Elizabeth, will give you a son, and you are to name him John. ¹⁴You will have great joy and gladness, and many will rejoice at his birth, ¹⁵for he will be great in the eyes of the Lord. He must never touch wine or other alcoholic drinks. He will be filled with the Holy Spirit, even before his birth.* ¹⁶And he will turn many Israelites to the Lord their God. ¹⁷He will be a man with the spirit and power of Elijah. He will prepare the people for the coming of the Lord. He will turn the hearts of the fathers to their children,* and he will cause those who are rebellious to accept the wisdom of the godly."

¹⁸Zechariah said to the angel, "How can I be sure this will happen? I'm an old man now, and my wife is also well along in years."

¹⁹Then the angel said, "I am Gabriel! I stand in the very presence of God. It was he who sent me to bring you this good news! ²⁰But now, since you didn't believe what I said, you will be silent and unable to speak until the child is born. For my words will certainly be fulfilled at the proper time."

²¹Meanwhile, the people were waiting for Zechariah to come out of the sanctuary, wondering why he was taking so long. ²²When he finally did come out, he couldn't speak to them. Then they realized from his gestures and his silence that he must have seen a vision in the sanctuary.

²³When Zechariah's week of service in the Temple was over, he returned home. ²⁴Soon afterward his wife, Elizabeth, became pregnant and went into seclusion for five months. ²⁵"How kind the Lord is!" she exclaimed. "He has taken away my disgrace of having no children."

The Birth of Jesus Foretold

²⁶In the sixth month of Elizabeth's pregnancy, God sent the angel Gabriel to Nazareth, a village in Galilee, ²⁷to a virgin named Mary. She was engaged to be married to a man named Joseph, a descendant of King David. ²⁸Gabriel appeared to her and said, "Greetings,* favored woman! The Lord is with you!*"

1:2 Greek *from those who from the beginning were servants of the word.* **1:15** Or *even from birth.* **1:17** See Mal 4:5-6. **1:28a** Or *Rejoice.* **1:28b** Some manuscripts add *Blessed are you among women.*

1:5 Luke pays careful attention throughout his narrative to establishing the historical context of Jesus' story by mentioning notable contemporaries, like Herod the Great. Herod was appointed by Rome as king of Judea at the time of Jesus' birth. Herod was known for his reconstruction of the Jerusalem Temple and for his ruthlessness and paranoia. Zechariah served as a priest in that Temple. Luke also connects Zechariah to the story's historical context by noting that he was a descendant of Abijah (1 Chronicles 24:10); Elizabeth, Zechariah's wife, was a descendant in the priestly line of Aaron. Marrying a woman from a priestly family was considered especially pious.

1:7 For women living in ancient Near Eastern cultures, having children was viewed as their highest calling, and infertility brought social stigma and shame to a family. Elizabeth and Zechariah's situation echoes their Israelite ancestors who had experienced long seasons of infertility, like Abraham and Sarah (Genesis 18:10-12). God's miraculous intervention in all their lives so they could have children is a common Old Testament theme (see Genesis 25:21; 30:22-23; Judges 13:1-25; 1 Samuel 1:1-28). So now, a new covenant, the new relationship or agreement that Jesus extends to all humanity, would begin with a miraculous fertility story, too.

1:18-38 We read about two responses to Gabriel's visits. Zechariah was a religious leader, a priest, serving for one week in Jerusalem, God's sacred city. Mary was an ordinary young woman living in Nazareth, a disreputable village in Galilee (see John 1:46). Gabriel's visits surprised both, but their responses were different. While Zechariah doubted, Mary showed incredible faith. Having low social status didn't keep God from working through her, and being a religious professional didn't necessarily make it easier to believe God.

1:24-38 Two women experience miraculous conceptions in Luke's birth narrative. Elizabeth was a woman experiencing infertility, well past her reproductive years; Mary was a virgin young woman, engaged but not yet married. Both pregnancies came about in circumstances that were embarrassing or shameful—instead, these pregnancies brought blessing in the end. Elizabeth praised God for his kindness, and Mary yielded to God despite the potential scandal. Following God involves risks, regardless of the outcome. Both women looked beyond their temporary troubles and waited for the Savior's coming.

Elizabeth

IDENTITY: Embracing God's Yes

Elizabeth remembers...

Before I had John, I struggled with my life. I wondered, *Does my life have meaning? What is out there for me?* With all my heart, I knew that overseeing my household mattered, but I couldn't help wondering—was there more to my future?

I prayed to God: "I want to glorify your name too, my Lord! What can I do for you? How can my desire for a child serve you?"

And then, one day, the Lord changed everything.

My husband, a priest, left for his week of service in the Temple far away in Jerusalem. But when he came back, he had lost the ability to hear and speak. I can still recall my bewildered reaction: "He cannot speak? Has he seen the Lord? God has promised us a baby? Yes! I knew God would keep his word! I knew it!"

I would become a mother, finally. I would give birth to a son! I promised the Lord right then to raise him in God's truth and in his Spirit. The angel told my husband that our son would be God's voice, preparing the people for the coming Messiah. Oh, how I rejoiced! My God had heard my cry and unveiled not only my future and calling but also the future all Israel waits for!

God has answered my prayers with a yes. And now I am a wife *and* a mother—what a joy and what a gift!

> We can trust God to use us whatever our roles.

ELIZABETH'S STORY IS TOLD IN LUKE 1:5-80.

IDENTIFY

What have you waited for that God eventually provided? How did you feel when God answered? How did you care for God's gift?

Is there something you are waiting to receive from the Lord right now? How can you offer that desire to God?

> "I remember when I gave birth to our first baby, a son. My lifestyle changed, and I couldn't be as active in my church and Bible school. At first, I was somewhat frustrated, but then the Holy Spirit spoke to me, saying, 'I've entrusted you with a life, a destiny, a son! Will you do your best to raise him?'"

ANGELA TKACHENKO is an evangelist, worshiper, and leader of Steiger Ukraine mission. She is passionate to see this generation love the Bible.

²⁹Confused and disturbed, Mary tried to think what the angel could mean. ³⁰"Don't be afraid, Mary," the angel told her, "for you have found favor with God! ³¹You will conceive and give birth to a son, and you will name him Jesus. ³²He will be very great and will be called the Son of the Most High. The Lord God will give him the throne of his ancestor David. ³³And he will reign over Israel* forever; his Kingdom will never end!"

³⁴Mary asked the angel, "But how can this happen? I am a virgin."

³⁵The angel replied, "The Holy Spirit will come upon you, and the power of the Most High will overshadow you. So the baby to be born will be holy, and he will be called the Son of God. ³⁶What's more, your relative Elizabeth has become pregnant in her old age! People used to say she was barren, but she has conceived a son and is now in her sixth month. ³⁷For the word of God will never fail.*"

³⁸Mary responded, "I am the Lord's servant. May everything you have said about me come true." And then the angel left her.

Mary Visits Elizabeth

³⁹A few days later Mary hurried to the hill country of Judea, to the town ⁴⁰where Zechariah lived. She entered the house and greeted Elizabeth. ⁴¹At the sound of Mary's greeting, Elizabeth's child leaped within her, and Elizabeth was filled with the Holy Spirit.

⁴²Elizabeth gave a glad cry and exclaimed to Mary, "God has blessed you above all women, and your child is blessed. ⁴³Why am I so honored, that the mother of my Lord should visit me? ⁴⁴When I heard your greeting, the baby in my womb jumped for joy. ⁴⁵You are blessed because you believed that the Lord would do what he said."

The Magnificat: Mary's Song of Praise

⁴⁶Mary responded,

"Oh, how my soul praises the Lord.
⁴⁷ How my spirit rejoices in God my Savior!
⁴⁸ For he took notice of his lowly servant girl,
 and from now on all generations will call me blessed.
⁴⁹ For the Mighty One is holy,
 and he has done great things for me.
⁵⁰ He shows mercy from generation to generation
 to all who fear him.
⁵¹ His mighty arm has done tremendous things!
 He has scattered the proud and haughty ones.
⁵² He has brought down princes from their thrones
 and exalted the humble.
⁵³ He has filled the hungry with good things
 and sent the rich away with empty hands.
⁵⁴ He has helped his servant Israel
 and remembered to be merciful.
⁵⁵ For he made this promise to our ancestors,
 to Abraham and his children forever."

⁵⁶Mary stayed with Elizabeth about three months and then went back to her own home.

The Birth of John the Baptist

⁵⁷When it was time for Elizabeth's baby to be born, she gave birth to a son. ⁵⁸And when her neighbors and relatives heard that the Lord had been very merciful to her, everyone rejoiced with her.

⁵⁹When the baby was eight days old, they all came for the circumcision ceremony. They wanted to name him Zechariah, after his father. ⁶⁰But Elizabeth said, "No! His name is John!"

⁶¹"What?" they exclaimed. "There is no one in all your family by that name." ⁶²So they used gestures to ask the baby's father what he wanted to name him. ⁶³He motioned for a writing tablet, and to everyone's surprise he wrote, "His name is John." ⁶⁴Instantly Zechariah could speak again, and he began praising God.

⁶⁵Awe fell upon the whole neighborhood, and the news of what had happened spread throughout the Judean hills. ⁶⁶Everyone who heard about it reflected on these events and asked, "What will this child turn out to be?" For the hand of the Lord was surely upon him in a special way.

1:33 Greek *over the house of Jacob.* 1:37 Some manuscripts read *For nothing is impossible with God.*

1:29, 38 Luke deliberately represents Mary as a reflective thinker and devout follower. She "thought out carefully" Gabriel's greeting, albeit feeling troubled (1:29, author's translation), but eventually surrendered despite confusion. Furthermore, she "remembered" the shepherd's words in her heart and kept "reflecting on" them (2:19, author's translation). When encountering unexpected events in life, Mary thought carefully and yet yielded wholeheartedly to God's will. Reason and trust aren't necessarily incompatible. Whether we tend to be people who think more or people who feel more, we can learn to find a balance as we discern God's way for us.

1:46-55 Mary's song is the first of three praise songs in the birth narrative. It is called the *Magnificat* (which means "magnifies"), from the first word in the Latin translation (here "praises," 1:46). The song has many parallels to Hannah's prayer in 1 Samuel 2:1-10. God caring for the oppressed and reversing their fortunes is a common theme throughout Luke's Gospel. The coming of God's Kingdom brings salvation to rejected and outcast people.

1:50-55 Mary's song conveys this message: The powerful God will empower those in underprivileged positions and judge the privileged who are arrogant and ruthless. This message is interwoven in Luke's narrative and remains an important message in today's society marked by hubris and overconfidence. If we find ourselves among the disadvantaged, let's seek God's mercy and justice. But if we are in privileged positions, let's fear God and share our resources with others in need.

Mary, Mother of Jesus

IDENTITY: Favored One

Mary remembers...

I listened to the angel Gabriel as he spoke to me: "Greetings! The Lord is with you! You've found favor with God! You will conceive and give birth to a son, and you will name him Jesus."

Are you talking to me? I questioned the future declared over my life and asked the angel, "How is this going to happen?" I wondered, *Why would God choose me to carry such a precious child?* But I said to the angel, "You can do this through me; I am your servant. Let your will be done in my life."

Gabriel also told me that my relative Elizabeth was pregnant, so I packed my bags and visited her and the rest of my family. It was so good to be with her. She told me that the baby leaped within her when she heard my voice, and she was filled with the Spirit of God as she confirmed what the angel had said to me.

My soul worships the Lord, for he has declared me a woman of favor! He has brought high the poor, rejected, and oppressed, and humbled the rich, proud, and esteemed. I accept the plans of the Lord with joyful, humble obedience.

> Favor turns my why me into a why not me!

MARY'S STORY IS TOLD IN LUKE 1:26–56; SHE ALSO APPEARS IN MATTHEW 1:16–2:23; 12:46-50; MARK 3:31-35; LUKE 8:19-21; JOHN 2:1-12; 19:25-27; ACTS 1:14.

IDENTIFY

Can you think of a time when the Lord gave you beyond what you expected? Did your "why me" turn into "why not me" with joy and obedience?

What helps you say yes to the Lord when he calls you to something that feels beyond you?

> "Over time I have learned that God's favor is often unexpected. It is our responsibility to agree with joy to God's plan."

VIRGINIA WARD, MA, DMin, serves as the Dean of the Boston Campus for Gordon-Conwell Theological Seminary. She is a wife, a mother, and an associate pastor at Abundant Life Church in Cambridge, MA.

Zechariah's Prophecy

⁶⁷Then his father, Zechariah, was filled with the Holy Spirit and gave this prophecy:

⁶⁸ "Praise the Lord, the God of Israel,
  because he has visited and redeemed his people.
⁶⁹ He has sent us a mighty Savior*
  from the royal line of his servant David,
⁷⁰ just as he promised
  through his holy prophets long ago.
⁷¹ Now we will be saved from our enemies
  and from all who hate us.
⁷² He has been merciful to our ancestors
  by remembering his sacred covenant—
⁷³ the covenant he swore with an oath
  to our ancestor Abraham.
⁷⁴ We have been rescued from our enemies
  so we can serve God without fear,
⁷⁵ in holiness and righteousness
  for as long as we live.

⁷⁶ "And you, my little son,
  will be called the prophet of the Most High,
  because you will prepare the way for the Lord.
⁷⁷ You will tell his people how to find salvation
  through forgiveness of their sins.
⁷⁸ Because of God's tender mercy,
  the morning light from heaven is about to break upon us,*
⁷⁹ to give light to those who sit in darkness and in the shadow of death,
  and to guide us to the path of peace."

⁸⁰John grew up and became strong in spirit. And he lived in the wilderness until he began his public ministry to Israel.

The Birth of Jesus

2 At that time the Roman emperor, Augustus, decreed that a census should be taken throughout the Roman Empire. ²(This was the first census taken when Quirinius was governor of Syria.) ³All returned to their own ancestral towns to register for this census. ⁴And because Joseph was a descendant of King David, he had to go to Bethlehem in Judea, David's ancient home. He traveled there from the village of Nazareth in Galilee. ⁵He took with him Mary, to whom he was engaged, who was now expecting a child. ⁶And while they were there, the time came for her baby to be born. ⁷She gave birth to her firstborn son. She wrapped him snugly in strips of cloth and laid him in a manger, because there was no lodging available for them.

The Shepherds and Angels

⁸That night there were shepherds staying in the fields nearby, guarding their flocks of sheep. ⁹Suddenly, an angel of the Lord appeared among them, and the radiance of the Lord's glory surrounded them. They were terrified, ¹⁰but the angel reassured them. "Don't be afraid!" he said. "I bring you good news that will bring great joy to all people. ¹¹The Savior—yes, the Messiah, the Lord—has been born today in Bethlehem, the city of David! ¹²And you will recognize him by this sign: You will find a baby wrapped snugly in strips of cloth, lying in a manger."

¹³Suddenly, the angel was joined by a vast host of others—the armies of heaven—praising God and saying,

¹⁴ "Glory to God in highest heaven,
  and peace on earth to those with whom God is pleased."

¹⁵When the angels had returned to heaven, the shepherds said to each other, "Let's go to Bethlehem! Let's see this thing that has happened, which the Lord has told us about."

¹⁶They hurried to the village and found Mary and Joseph. And there was the baby, lying in the manger. ¹⁷After seeing him, the shepherds told everyone what had happened and what the angel had said to them about this child. ¹⁸All who heard the shepherds' story were astonished, ¹⁹but Mary kept all these things in her heart and thought about them often. ²⁰The shepherds went back to their flocks, glorifying and praising God for all they had heard and seen. It was just as the angel had told them.

Jesus Is Presented in the Temple

²¹Eight days later, when the baby was circumcised, he was named Jesus, the name given him by the angel even before he was conceived.

²²Then it was time for their purification offering, as required by the law of Moses after the birth of a child; so his parents took him to Jerusalem to present him to the Lord. ²³The law of the Lord says, "If a woman's first child is a boy, he must be dedicated to the LORD."* ²⁴So they offered the sacrifice required in the law of the Lord—"either a pair of turtledoves or two young pigeons."*

The Prophecy of Simeon

²⁵At that time there was a man in Jerusalem named Simeon. He was righteous and devout and was eagerly waiting for the Messiah to come and rescue Israel. The Holy Spirit was upon him ²⁶and had revealed to him that he would not die until he had seen the Lord's Messiah. ²⁷That day the Spirit led him to the Temple. So when Mary and Joseph came to present the baby Jesus to the Lord as the law required, ²⁸Simeon was there. He took the child in his arms and praised God, saying,

---

1:69 Greek *has raised up a horn of salvation for us.* **1:78** Or *the Morning Light from Heaven is about to visit us.* **2:23** Exod 13:2. **2:24** Lev 12:8.

Anna, the Prophet

IDENTITY
Bereaved to Behold

According to the law of Moses, a widow would be given to her husband's brother or another close relative for care and protection (see Deuteronomy 25:5-10). If she were older, she would be supported by her grown children. But Anna had none of these options. She found protection in the Temple, where she was sustained by prayer and worship. God protected her and fulfilled her longing to see the promised Savior, Jesus. Luke refers to Anna as "a prophet," which likely reflects her knowledge of God and his will for his people, especially as she announces the presence of the child who would "rescue Jerusalem" (Luke 2:36, 38).

Can you imagine what it would have been like to serve God in his Temple your whole life, and then finally meet the Savior everyone was waiting for? Anna's prayers after that meeting might have sounded like this:

> I saw him this morning ... the one you, God, promised, our Savior. Oh, how his face glowed with your glory. You have heard my prayers. Hope rises in my heart. Now I can rest in peace in your presence. Take me home to be with you, for I am an old woman of eighty-four years.
>
> Oh, God, I thank you and praise your name. You have been like a husband to me these past sixty years, after losing my beloved after only seven years and having no children to support me. You have protected me, provided for me, and encouraged me. You gave me purpose when I was devastated and alone. Now I see the fruit of being committed to you. My heart fills to overflowing.

We can find peace and protection in God's presence.

ANNA'S STORY IS TOLD IN LUKE 2:36-38.

IDENTIFY

When have you experienced loss yet found strength and new direction from God?

How has the Lord been like a husband or family to you, calling you closer? If you are experiencing pain, call out to God, spend time in his presence, and let him love you.

"As a widow for almost ten years, I have experienced God's faithfulness. He has restored joy and given me mission and teaching opportunities beyond what I ever expected. While there have been times of pain and challenge, I have a deep, centering peace and joy that only comes from knowing God the Father and the Lord Jesus, much like Anna."

ELIZABETH GLANVILLE, PhD, is retired faculty from Fuller Theological Seminary, School of Mission and Theology. She is an international teacher on missions and leadership and chaplain for a local police department and her retirement community.

²⁹ "Sovereign Lord, now let your servant die in peace,
    as you have promised.
³⁰ I have seen your salvation,
³¹   which you have prepared for all people.
³² He is a light to reveal God to the nations,
    and he is the glory of your people Israel!"

³³Jesus' parents were amazed at what was being said about him. ³⁴Then Simeon blessed them, and he said to Mary, the baby's mother, "This child is destined to cause many in Israel to fall, and many others to rise. He has been sent as a sign from God, but many will oppose him. ³⁵As a result, the deepest thoughts of many hearts will be revealed. And a sword will pierce your very soul."

The Prophecy of Anna

³⁶Anna, a prophet, was also there in the Temple. She was the daughter of Phanuel from the tribe of Asher, and she was very old. Her husband died when they had been married only seven years. ³⁷Then she lived as a widow to the age of eighty-four.* She never left the Temple but stayed there day and night, worshiping God with fasting and prayer. ³⁸She came along just as Simeon was talking with Mary and Joseph, and she began praising God. She talked about the child to everyone who had been waiting expectantly for God to rescue Jerusalem.

³⁹When Jesus' parents had fulfilled all the requirements of the law of the Lord, they returned home to Nazareth in Galilee. ⁴⁰There the child grew up healthy and strong. He was filled with wisdom, and God's favor was on him.

Jesus Speaks with the Teachers

⁴¹Every year Jesus' parents went to Jerusalem for the Passover festival. ⁴²When Jesus was twelve years old, they attended the festival as usual. ⁴³After the celebration was over, they started home to Nazareth, but Jesus stayed behind in Jerusalem. His parents didn't miss him at first, ⁴⁴because they assumed he was among the other travelers. But when he didn't show up that evening, they started looking for him among their relatives and friends.

⁴⁵When they couldn't find him, they went back to Jerusalem to search for him there. ⁴⁶Three days later they finally discovered him in the Temple, sitting among the religious teachers, listening to them and asking questions. ⁴⁷All who heard him were amazed at his understanding and his answers.

⁴⁸His parents didn't know what to think. "Son," his mother said to him, "why have you done this to us? Your father and I have been frantic, searching for you everywhere."

⁴⁹"But why did you need to search?" he asked. "Didn't you know that I must be in my Father's house?"* ⁵⁰But they didn't understand what he meant.

⁵¹Then he returned to Nazareth with them and was obedient to them. And his mother stored all these things in her heart.

⁵²Jesus grew in wisdom and in stature and in favor with God and all the people.

John the Baptist Prepares the Way

3 It was now the fifteenth year of the reign of Tiberius, the Roman emperor. Pontius Pilate was governor over Judea; Herod Antipas was ruler* over Galilee; his brother Philip was ruler* over Iturea and Traconitis; Lysanias was ruler over Abilene. ²Annas and Caiaphas were the high priests. At this time a message from God came to John son of Zechariah, who was living in the wilderness. ³Then John went from place to place on both sides of the Jordan River, preaching that people should be baptized to show that they had repented of their sins and turned to God to be forgiven. ⁴Isaiah had spoken of John when he said,

"He is a voice shouting in the wilderness,
'Prepare the way for the LORD's coming!
    Clear the road for him!
⁵ The valleys will be filled,
    and the mountains and hills made level.
The curves will be straightened,
    and the rough places made smooth.
⁶ And then all people will see
    the salvation sent from God.'"*

⁷When the crowds came to John for baptism, he said, "You brood of snakes! Who warned you to flee the coming wrath? ⁸Prove by the way you live that you have repented of your sins and turned to God. Don't just say to each other, 'We're safe, for we are descendants of Abraham.' That means nothing, for I tell you, God can create children of Abraham from these very stones. ⁹Even now the ax of God's judgment is poised, ready to sever the roots of the trees. Yes, every tree that does not produce good fruit will be chopped down and thrown into the fire."

2:37 Or *She had been a widow for eighty-four years.* **2:49** Or *"Didn't you realize that I should be involved with my Father's affairs?"* **3:1a** Greek *Herod was tetrarch.* Herod Antipas was a son of King Herod. **3:1b** Greek *tetrarch;* also in 3:1c. **3:4-6** Isa 40:3-5 (Greek version).

2:36-38 *Anna* is the Greek equivalent of the Hebrew name Hannah, like Samuel's mother (1 Samuel 1–2; see the note on 1:46-55). Jewish tradition identifies seven Old Testament women as prophets: Sarah, Miriam, Deborah, Hannah, Abigail, Huldah, and Esther. Anna was another prophetic witness to Jesus' identity as the Messiah. She was from the tribe of Asher, one of the ten tribes that were lost when Assyria conquered and assimilated them, yet Anna was faithful, so God allowed her to meet the Messiah. **2:37** In the ancient world, older age was associated with wisdom and honor. The fact that Anna "never left the Temple" is probably hyperbole; we might say, "She was there all the time," reflecting her total dedication to God.

Koinonia

IMAGE — MY STORY WITH COMMUNITY, WORKPLACE & CHURCH

Gathering the Generations

SCRIPTURE CONNECTION: LUKE 2:41-47

On my dad's side of the family, I'm the oldest of fifteen cousins. Growing up, when we would gather for holidays or special meals, there were too many of us to fit around one table. So, my grandma and grandpa came up with a clever solution: They created the adults' table and the kids' table.

Our churches can feel like there are two tables. We have adult worship, fellowship, discipleship, and service—all of which stay separate from what we offer young people. We may separate these groups for practical reasons, like my grandparents with the holiday tables. Or maybe because it makes everyone happier with their church experience.

But this separation in churches is a long way from the intergenerational community that adolescent Jesus experienced in 2:41-47. When twelve-year-old Jesus was separated from his parents for three days, who likely took care of him? The adults nearby.

During those three days, Jesus didn't remain separate from older generations. Unlike meals at my grandparents' house, the generations interacted—so much so that Jesus was listening to the adult teachers and asking insightful questions (2:46-47). Sometimes adults can be worried about being "cool enough" for adolescents, but it's more important to foster intergenerational community where all ages are warmly welcomed.

How can your church become warmer by gathering everyone at the same table?

1. Intergenerational worship—for all of your worship services, or the first fifteen minutes, or once every month; just find a rhythm that works for your church
2. Intergenerational service—both local and global
3. Intergenerational mentoring—so that both old and young learn from each other

> When it comes to gathering generations in church, warm is the new cool.

IMAGINE

Who from an older generation would you like to make a closer friend?

Who from a younger generation would you like to grow closer to?

"As we've seen in Fuller Youth Institute's research on how to keep young people connected to their faith and involved in church, they are looking for authenticity and connection. In a word: warmth. When it comes to gathering the generations, 'Warm is the new cool.'"

KARA POWELL, PhD, is the executive director of the Fuller Youth Institute and chief of leadership formation at Fuller Theological Seminary. Kara speaks and has authored numerous books, including *3 Big Questions That Change Every Teenager.*

¹⁰The crowds asked, "What should we do?"

¹¹John replied, "If you have two shirts, give one to the poor. If you have food, share it with those who are hungry."

¹²Even corrupt tax collectors came to be baptized and asked, "Teacher, what should we do?"

¹³He replied, "Collect no more taxes than the government requires."

¹⁴"What should we do?" asked some soldiers.

John replied, "Don't extort money or make false accusations. And be content with your pay."

¹⁵Everyone was expecting the Messiah to come soon, and they were eager to know whether John might be the Messiah. ¹⁶John answered their questions by saying, "I baptize you with* water; but someone is coming soon who is greater than I am—so much greater that I'm not even worthy to be his slave and untie the straps of his sandals. He will baptize you with the Holy Spirit and with fire.* ¹⁷He is ready to separate the chaff from the wheat with his winnowing fork. Then he will clean up the threshing area, gathering the wheat into his barn but burning the chaff with never-ending fire." ¹⁸John used many such warnings as he announced the Good News to the people.

¹⁹John also publicly criticized Herod Antipas, the ruler of Galilee,* for marrying Herodias, his brother's wife, and for many other wrongs he had done. ²⁰So Herod put John in prison, adding this sin to his many others.

The Baptism of Jesus

²¹One day when the crowds were being baptized, Jesus himself was baptized. As he was praying, the heavens opened, ²²and the Holy Spirit, in bodily form, descended on him like a dove. And a voice from heaven said, "You are my dearly loved Son, and you bring me great joy.*"

The Ancestors of Jesus

²³Jesus was about thirty years old when he began his public ministry.

Jesus was known as the son of Joseph.
Joseph was the son of Heli.
²⁴ Heli was the son of Matthat.
Matthat was the son of Levi.
Levi was the son of Melki.
Melki was the son of Jannai.
Jannai was the son of Joseph.
²⁵ Joseph was the son of Mattathias.
Mattathias was the son of Amos.
Amos was the son of Nahum.
Nahum was the son of Esli.
Esli was the son of Naggai.
²⁶ Naggai was the son of Maath.
Maath was the son of Mattathias.
Mattathias was the son of Semein.
Semein was the son of Josech.
Josech was the son of Joda.
²⁷ Joda was the son of Joanan.
Joanan was the son of Rhesa.
Rhesa was the son of Zerubbabel.
Zerubbabel was the son of Shealtiel.
Shealtiel was the son of Neri.
²⁸ Neri was the son of Melki.
Melki was the son of Addi.
Addi was the son of Cosam.
Cosam was the son of Elmadam.
Elmadam was the son of Er.
²⁹ Er was the son of Joshua.
Joshua was the son of Eliezer.
Eliezer was the son of Jorim.
Jorim was the son of Matthat.
Matthat was the son of Levi.
³⁰ Levi was the son of Simeon.
Simeon was the son of Judah.
Judah was the son of Joseph.
Joseph was the son of Jonam.
Jonam was the son of Eliakim.
³¹ Eliakim was the son of Melea.
Melea was the son of Menna.
Menna was the son of Mattatha.
Mattatha was the son of Nathan.
Nathan was the son of David.
³² David was the son of Jesse.
Jesse was the son of Obed.
Obed was the son of Boaz.
Boaz was the son of Salmon.*
Salmon was the son of Nahshon.
³³ Nahshon was the son of Amminadab.
Amminadab was the son of Admin.
Admin was the son of Arni.*
Arni was the son of Hezron.
Hezron was the son of Perez.
Perez was the son of Judah.
³⁴ Judah was the son of Jacob.
Jacob was the son of Isaac.
Isaac was the son of Abraham.
Abraham was the son of Terah.
Terah was the son of Nahor.
³⁵ Nahor was the son of Serug.
Serug was the son of Reu.
Reu was the son of Peleg.

3:16a Or in. 3:16b Or in the Holy Spirit and in fire. 3:19 Greek Herod the tetrarch. 3:22 Some manuscripts read my Son, and today I have become your Father. 3:32 Greek Sala, a variant spelling of Salmon; also in 3:32b. See Ruth 4:20-21. 3:33 Some manuscripts read Amminadab was the son of Aram. Arni and Aram are alternate spellings of Ram. See 1 Chr 2:9-10.

3:19-20 Herod Antipas, the king of Galilee, had divorced his first wife and married Herodias, who had been the wife of his half brother Herod Philip. When John "publicly criticized" Herod for this, Herod imprisoned and later executed him (see 9:9; Mark 6:16-29). Herod's execution of John is also recorded by the Jewish historian Josephus.

Peleg was the son of Eber.
Eber was the son of Shelah.
³⁶ Shelah was the son of Cainan.
Cainan was the son of Arphaxad.
Arphaxad was the son of Shem.
Shem was the son of Noah.
Noah was the son of Lamech.
³⁷ Lamech was the son of Methuselah.
Methuselah was the son of Enoch.
Enoch was the son of Jared.
Jared was the son of Mahalalel.
Mahalalel was the son of Kenan.
³⁸ Kenan was the son of Enosh.*
Enosh was the son of Seth.
Seth was the son of Adam.
Adam was the son of God.

The Temptation of Jesus

4 Then Jesus, full of the Holy Spirit, returned from the Jordan River. He was led by the Spirit in the wilderness,* ²where he was tempted by the devil for forty days. Jesus ate nothing all that time and became very hungry.

³Then the devil said to him, "If you are the Son of God, tell this stone to become a loaf of bread."

⁴But Jesus told him, "No! The Scriptures say, 'People do not live by bread alone.'*"

⁵Then the devil took him up and revealed to him all the kingdoms of the world in a moment of time. ⁶"I will give you the glory of these kingdoms and authority over them," the devil said, "because they are mine to give to anyone I please. ⁷I will give it all to you if you will worship me."

⁸Jesus replied, "The Scriptures say,

'You must worship the Lord your God
 and serve only him.'*"

⁹Then the devil took him to Jerusalem, to the highest point of the Temple, and said, "If you are the Son of God, jump off! ¹⁰For the Scriptures say,

'He will order his angels to protect and guard you.
¹¹ And they will hold you up with their hands
 so you won't even hurt your foot on a stone.'*"

¹²Jesus responded, "The Scriptures also say, 'You must not test the Lord your God.'*"

¹³When the devil had finished tempting Jesus, he left him until the next opportunity came.

Jesus Rejected at Nazareth

¹⁴Then Jesus returned to Galilee, filled with the Holy Spirit's power. Reports about him spread quickly through the whole region. ¹⁵He taught regularly in their synagogues and was praised by everyone.

¹⁶When he came to the village of Nazareth, his boyhood home, he went as usual to the synagogue on the Sabbath and stood up to read the Scriptures. ¹⁷The scroll of Isaiah the prophet was handed to him. He unrolled the scroll and found the place where this was written:

¹⁸ "The Spirit of the Lord is upon me,
 for he has anointed me to bring Good News
  to the poor.
He has sent me to proclaim that captives will
  be released,
 that the blind will see,
that the oppressed will be set free,
¹⁹ and that the time of the Lord's favor has
  come.*"

²⁰He rolled up the scroll, handed it back to the attendant, and sat down. All eyes in the synagogue looked at him intently. ²¹Then he began to speak to them. "The Scripture you've just heard has been fulfilled this very day!"

²²Everyone spoke well of him and was amazed by the gracious words that came from his lips. "How can this be?" they asked. "Isn't this Joseph's son?"

²³Then he said, "You will undoubtedly quote me this proverb: 'Physician, heal yourself'—meaning, 'Do miracles here in your hometown like those you did in Capernaum.' ²⁴But I tell you the truth, no prophet is accepted in his own hometown.

²⁵"Certainly there were many needy widows in Israel in Elijah's time, when the heavens were closed for three and a half years, and a severe famine devastated the land. ²⁶Yet Elijah was not sent to any of them. He was sent instead to a foreigner—a widow of Zarephath in the land of Sidon. ²⁷And many in Israel had leprosy in the time of the prophet Elisha, but the only one healed was Naaman, a Syrian."

²⁸When they heard this, the people in the synagogue were furious. ²⁹Jumping up, they mobbed him and forced him to the edge of the hill on which the town was built. They intended to push him over the cliff, ³⁰but he passed right through the crowd and went on his way.

3:38 Greek *Enos*, a variant spelling of Enosh; also in 3:38b. See Gen 5:6. **4:1** Some manuscripts read *into the wilderness.* **4:4** Deut 8:3. **4:8** Deut 6:13. **4:10-11** Ps 91:11-12. **4:12** Deut 6:16. **4:18-19** Or *and to proclaim the acceptable year of the Lord.* Isa 61:1-2 (Greek version); 58:6.

4:18-19 In Jesus' world, "the poor" included people lacking status and honor because of their gender, economics, religious purity laws, ethnicity, or a combination of these. The "captives" could refer to those bound by sins or evil spirits, shunned from the community, or those physically imprisoned and politically persecuted. Jesus' Good News includes the marginalized and releases the captives. Notably, his message has significant spiritual and social ramifications. Today, Jesus invites those who are underprivileged to find hope in him, and the privileged to participate in his mission of freedom for all.

WHAT THE BIBLE SAYS ABOUT Questions

Jesus Values Questions

Three days later they finally discovered [Jesus] in the Temple, sitting among the religious teachers, listening to them and asking questions. **LUKE 2:46**

[Jesus'] disciples asked him what this parable meant. **LUKE 8:9**

"Teacher, what should I do to inherit eternal life?"

Jesus replied, "What does the law of Moses say? How do you read it?"

The man answered, "'You must love the LORD your God with all your heart, all your soul, all your strength, and all your mind.' And, 'Love your neighbor as yourself.'"

"Right!" Jesus told him. "Do this and you will live!" **LUKE 10:25-28**

We Can Ask Questions and Understand That God Is God and We Are Not

Abraham spoke again. "Since I have begun, let me speak further to my Lord, even though I am but dust and ashes. Suppose there are only forty-five righteous people rather than fifty? Will you destroy the whole city for lack of five?" **GENESIS 18:27-28**

You Don't Have to Answer Every Question—Just Keep Doing What's Right

The purpose of my instruction is that all believers would be filled with love that comes from a pure heart, a clear conscience, and genuine faith. But some people have missed this whole point. They have turned away from these things and spend their time in meaningless discussions. **1 TIMOTHY 1:5-6**

Timothy, guard what God has entrusted to you. Avoid godless, foolish discussions with those who oppose you with their so-called knowledge. **1 TIMOTHY 6:20**

Jesus Casts Out a Demon

³¹Then Jesus went to Capernaum, a town in Galilee, and taught there in the synagogue every Sabbath day. ³²There, too, the people were amazed at his teaching, for he spoke with authority.

³³Once when he was in the synagogue, a man possessed by a demon—an evil* spirit—cried out, shouting, ³⁴"Go away! Why are you interfering with us, Jesus of Nazareth? Have you come to destroy us? I know who you are—the Holy One of God!"

³⁵But Jesus reprimanded him. "Be quiet! Come out of the man," he ordered. At that, the demon threw the man to the floor as the crowd watched; then it came out of him without hurting him further.

³⁶Amazed, the people exclaimed, "What authority and power this man's words possess! Even evil spirits obey him, and they flee at his command!" ³⁷The news about Jesus spread through every village in the entire region.

Jesus Heals Many People

³⁸After leaving the synagogue that day, Jesus went to Simon's home, where he found Simon's mother-in-law very sick with a high fever. "Please heal her," everyone begged. ³⁹Standing at her bedside, he rebuked the fever, and it left her. And she got up at once and prepared a meal for them.

⁴⁰As the sun went down that evening, people throughout the village brought sick family members to Jesus. No matter what their diseases were, the touch of his hand healed every one. ⁴¹Many were possessed by demons; and the demons came out at his command, shouting, "You are the Son of God!" But because they knew he was the Messiah, he rebuked them and refused to let them speak.

Jesus Continues to Preach

⁴²Early the next morning Jesus went out to an isolated place. The crowds searched everywhere for him, and when they finally found him, they begged him not to leave them. ⁴³But he replied, "I must preach the Good News of the Kingdom of God in other towns, too, because that is why I was sent." ⁴⁴So he continued to travel around, preaching in synagogues throughout Judea.*

The First Disciples

5 One day as Jesus was preaching on the shore of the Sea of Galilee,* great crowds pressed in on him to listen to the word of God. ²He noticed two empty boats at the water's edge, for the fishermen had left them and were washing their nets. ³Stepping into one of the boats, Jesus asked Simon,* its owner, to push it out into the water. So he sat in the boat and taught the crowds from there.

⁴When he had finished speaking, he said to Simon, "Now go out where it is deeper, and let down your nets to catch some fish."

⁵"Master," Simon replied, "we worked hard all last night and didn't catch a thing. But if you say so, I'll let the nets down again." ⁶And this time their nets were so full of fish they began to tear! ⁷A shout for help brought their partners in the other boat, and soon both boats were filled with fish and on the verge of sinking.

⁸When Simon Peter realized what had happened, he fell to his knees before Jesus and said, "Oh, Lord, please leave me—I'm such a sinful man." ⁹For he was awestruck by the number of fish they had caught, as were the others with him. ¹⁰His partners, James and John, the sons of Zebedee, were also amazed.

Jesus replied to Simon, "Don't be afraid! From now on you'll be fishing for people!" ¹¹And as soon as they landed, they left everything and followed Jesus.

Jesus Heals a Man with Leprosy

¹²In one of the villages, Jesus met a man with an advanced case of leprosy. When the man saw Jesus, he bowed with his face to the ground, begging to be healed. "Lord," he said, "if you are willing, you can heal me and make me clean."

¹³Jesus reached out and touched him. "I am willing," he said. "Be healed!" And instantly the leprosy disappeared. ¹⁴Then Jesus instructed him not to tell anyone what had happened. He said, "Go to the priest and let him examine you. Take along the offering required in the law of Moses for those who have been healed of leprosy.* This will be a public testimony that you have been cleansed."

¹⁵But despite Jesus' instructions, the report of his power spread even faster, and vast crowds came to hear him preach and to be healed of their diseases. ¹⁶But Jesus often withdrew to the wilderness for prayer.

Jesus Heals a Paralyzed Man

¹⁷One day while Jesus was teaching, some Pharisees and teachers of religious law were sitting nearby. (It seemed that these men showed up from every village in all Galilee and Judea, as well as from Jerusalem.) And the Lord's healing power was strongly with Jesus. ¹⁸Some men came carrying a paralyzed man on a sleeping mat. They tried to take him inside to Jesus, ¹⁹but they couldn't reach him because of the crowd. So they went up to the roof and took off some tiles. Then they lowered the sick man on his mat down into the crowd, right in front of Jesus. ²⁰Seeing their faith, Jesus said to the man, "Young man, your sins are forgiven."

²¹But the Pharisees and teachers of religious law said to themselves, "Who does he think he is? That's blasphemy! Only God can forgive sins!"

4:33 Greek *unclean;* also in 4:36. **4:44** Some manuscripts read *Galilee.* **5:1** Greek *Lake Gennesaret,* another name for the Sea of Galilee. **5:3** *Simon* is called "Peter" in 6:14 and thereafter. **5:14** See Lev 14:2-32.

²²Jesus knew what they were thinking, so he asked them, "Why do you question this in your hearts? ²³Is it easier to say 'Your sins are forgiven,' or 'Stand up and walk'? ²⁴So I will prove to you that the Son of Man* has the authority on earth to forgive sins." Then Jesus turned to the paralyzed man and said, "Stand up, pick up your mat, and go home!"

²⁵And immediately, as everyone watched, the man jumped up, picked up his mat, and went home praising God. ²⁶Everyone was gripped with great wonder and awe, and they praised God, exclaiming, "We have seen amazing things today!"

Jesus Calls Levi (Matthew)

²⁷Later, as Jesus left the town, he saw a tax collector named Levi sitting at his tax collector's booth. "Follow me and be my disciple," Jesus said to him. ²⁸So Levi got up, left everything, and followed him.

²⁹Later, Levi held a banquet in his home with Jesus as the guest of honor. Many of Levi's fellow tax collectors and other guests also ate with them. ³⁰But the Pharisees and their teachers of religious law complained bitterly to Jesus' disciples, "Why do you eat and drink with such scum?*"

³¹Jesus answered them, "Healthy people don't need a doctor—sick people do. ³²I have come to call not those who think they are righteous, but those who know they are sinners and need to repent."

A Discussion about Fasting

³³One day some people said to Jesus, "John the Baptist's disciples fast and pray regularly, and so do the disciples of the Pharisees. Why are your disciples always eating and drinking?"

³⁴Jesus responded, "Do wedding guests fast while celebrating with the groom? Of course not. ³⁵But someday the groom will be taken away from them, and then they will fast."

³⁶Then Jesus gave them this illustration: "No one tears a piece of cloth from a new garment and uses it to patch an old garment. For then the new garment would be ruined, and the new patch wouldn't even match the old garment.

³⁷"And no one puts new wine into old wineskins. For the new wine would burst the wineskins, spilling the wine and ruining the skins. ³⁸New wine must be stored in new wineskins. ³⁹But no one who drinks the old wine seems to want the new wine. 'The old is just fine,' they say."

A Discussion about the Sabbath

6 One Sabbath day as Jesus was walking through some grainfields, his disciples broke off heads of grain, rubbed off the husks in their hands, and ate the grain. ²But some Pharisees said, "Why are you breaking the law by harvesting grain on the Sabbath?"

³Jesus replied, "Haven't you read in the Scriptures what David did when he and his companions were hungry? ⁴He went into the house of God and broke the law by eating the sacred loaves of bread that only the priests can eat. He also gave some to his companions." ⁵And Jesus added, "The Son of Man* is Lord, even over the Sabbath."

Jesus Heals on the Sabbath

⁶On another Sabbath day, a man with a deformed right hand was in the synagogue while Jesus was teaching. ⁷The teachers of religious law and the Pharisees watched Jesus closely. If he healed the man's hand, they planned to accuse him of working on the Sabbath.

⁸But Jesus knew their thoughts. He said to the man with the deformed hand, "Come and stand in front of everyone." So the man came forward. ⁹Then Jesus said to his critics, "I have a question for you. Does the law permit good deeds on the Sabbath, or is it a day for doing evil? Is this a day to save life or to destroy it?"

¹⁰He looked around at them one by one and then said to the man, "Hold out your hand." So the man held out his hand, and it was restored! ¹¹At this, the enemies of Jesus were wild with rage and began to discuss what to do with him.

Jesus Chooses the Twelve Apostles

¹²One day soon afterward Jesus went up on a mountain to pray, and he prayed to God all night. ¹³At daybreak he called together all of his disciples and chose twelve of them to be apostles. Here are their names:

¹⁴ Simon (whom he named Peter),
Andrew (Peter's brother),
James,
John,
Philip,
Bartholomew,
¹⁵ Matthew,
Thomas,
James (son of Alphaeus),
Simon (who was called the zealot),
¹⁶ Judas (son of James),
Judas Iscariot (who later betrayed him).

Crowds Follow Jesus

¹⁷When they came down from the mountain, the disciples stood with Jesus on a large, level area, surrounded by many of his followers and by the crowds. There were people from all over Judea and from Jerusalem and from as far north as the seacoasts of Tyre and Sidon. ¹⁸They had come to hear him and to be healed of their diseases; and those troubled by evil* spirits were healed. ¹⁹Everyone tried to touch him, because healing power went out from him, and he healed everyone.

5:24 "Son of Man" is a title Jesus used for himself.   **5:30** Greek *with tax collectors and sinners?*   **6:5** "Son of Man" is a title Jesus used for himself.   **6:18** Greek *unclean.*

The Beatitudes

²⁰Then Jesus turned to his disciples and said,

"God blesses you who are poor,
for the Kingdom of God is yours.
²¹ God blesses you who are hungry now,
for you will be satisfied.
God blesses you who weep now,
for in due time you will laugh.

²²What blessings await you when people hate you and exclude you and mock you and curse you as evil because you follow the Son of Man. ²³When that happens, be happy! Yes, leap for joy! For a great reward awaits you in heaven. And remember, their ancestors treated the ancient prophets that same way.

Sorrows Foretold

²⁴ "What sorrow awaits you who are rich,
for you have your only happiness now.
²⁵ What sorrow awaits you who are fat and prosperous now,
for a time of awful hunger awaits you.
What sorrow awaits you who laugh now,
for your laughing will turn to mourning and sorrow.
²⁶ What sorrow awaits you who are praised by the crowds,
for their ancestors also praised false prophets.

Love for Enemies

²⁷"But to you who are willing to listen, I say, love your enemies! Do good to those who hate you. ²⁸Bless those who curse you. Pray for those who hurt you. ²⁹If someone slaps you on one cheek, offer the other cheek also. If someone demands your coat, offer your shirt also. ³⁰Give to anyone who asks; and when things are taken away from you, don't try to get them back. ³¹Do to others as you would like them to do to you.

³²"If you love only those who love you, why should you get credit for that? Even sinners love those who love them! ³³And if you do good only to those who do good to you, why should you get credit? Even sinners do that much! ³⁴And if you lend money only to those who can repay you, why should you get credit? Even sinners will lend to other sinners for a full return.

³⁵"Love your enemies! Do good to them. Lend to them without expecting to be repaid. Then your reward from heaven will be very great, and you will truly be acting as children of the Most High, for he is kind to those who are unthankful and wicked. ³⁶You must be compassionate, just as your Father is compassionate.

> "When we die and it comes time for God to judge us, he will not ask, 'How many good things have you done in your life?' rather he will ask, 'How much love did you put into what you did?'"
>
> **MOTHER TERESA**
> (1910–1997) founder of the Missionaries of Charity

Do Not Judge Others

³⁷"Do not judge others, and you will not be judged. Do not condemn others, or it will all come back against you. Forgive others, and you will be forgiven. ³⁸Give, and you will receive. Your gift will return to you in full—pressed down, shaken together to make room for more, running over, and poured into your lap. The amount you give will determine the amount you get back.*"

³⁹Then Jesus gave the following illustration: "Can one blind person lead another? Won't they both fall into a ditch? ⁴⁰Students* are not greater than their teacher. But the student who is fully trained will become like the teacher.

⁴¹"And why worry about a speck in your friend's eye* when you have a log in your own? ⁴²How can you think of saying, 'Friend,* let me help you get rid of that speck in your eye,' when you can't see past the log in your own eye? Hypocrite! First get rid of the log in your own eye; then you will see well enough to deal with the speck in your friend's eye.

6:38 Or *The measure you give will be the measure you get back.* **6:40** Or *Disciples.* **6:41** Greek *your brother's eye;* also in 6:42. **6:42** Greek *Brother.*

The Tree and Its Fruit

⁴³"A good tree can't produce bad fruit, and a bad tree can't produce good fruit. ⁴⁴A tree is identified by its fruit. Figs are never gathered from thornbushes, and grapes are not picked from bramble bushes. ⁴⁵A good person produces good things from the treasury of a good heart, and an evil person produces evil things from the treasury of an evil heart. What you say flows from what is in your heart.

Building on a Solid Foundation

⁴⁶"So why do you keep calling me 'Lord, Lord!' when you don't do what I say? ⁴⁷I will show you what it's like when someone comes to me, listens to my teaching, and then follows it. ⁴⁸It is like a person building a house who digs deep and lays the foundation on solid rock. When the floodwaters rise and break against that house, it stands firm because it is well built. ⁴⁹But anyone who hears and doesn't obey is like a person who builds a house right on the ground, without a foundation. When the floods sweep down against that house, it will collapse into a heap of ruins."

The Faith of a Roman Officer

7 When Jesus had finished saying all this to the people, he returned to Capernaum. ²At that time the highly valued slave of a Roman officer* was sick and near death. ³When the officer heard about Jesus, he sent some respected Jewish elders to ask him to come and heal his slave. ⁴So they earnestly begged Jesus to help the man. "If anyone deserves your help, he does," they said, ⁵"for he loves the Jewish people and even built a synagogue for us."

⁶So Jesus went with them. But just before they arrived at the house, the officer sent some friends to say, "Lord, don't trouble yourself by coming to my home, for I am not worthy of such an honor. ⁷I am not even worthy to come and meet you. Just say the word from where you are, and my servant will be healed. ⁸I know this because I am under the authority of my superior officers, and I have authority over my soldiers. I only need to say, 'Go,' and they go, or 'Come,' and they come. And if I say to my slaves, 'Do this,' they do it."

⁹When Jesus heard this, he was amazed. Turning to the crowd that was following him, he said, "I tell you, I haven't seen faith like this in all Israel!" ¹⁰And when the officer's friends returned to his house, they found the slave completely healed.

Jesus Raises a Widow's Son

¹¹Soon afterward Jesus went with his disciples to the village of Nain, and a large crowd followed him. ¹²A funeral procession was coming out as he approached the village gate. The young man who had died was a widow's only son, and a large crowd from the village was with her. ¹³When the Lord saw her, his heart overflowed with compassion. "Don't cry!" he said. ¹⁴Then he walked over to the coffin and touched it, and the bearers stopped. "Young man," he said, "I tell you, get up." ¹⁵Then the dead boy sat up and began to talk! And Jesus gave him back to his mother.

¹⁶Great fear swept the crowd, and they praised God, saying, "A mighty prophet has risen among us," and "God has visited his people today." ¹⁷And the news about Jesus spread throughout Judea and the surrounding countryside.

Jesus and John the Baptist

¹⁸The disciples of John the Baptist told John about everything Jesus was doing. So John called for two of his disciples, ¹⁹and he sent them to the Lord to ask him, "Are you the Messiah we've been expecting,* or should we keep looking for someone else?"

²⁰John's two disciples found Jesus and said to him, "John the Baptist sent us to ask, 'Are you the Messiah we've been expecting, or should we keep looking for someone else?'"

²¹At that very time, Jesus cured many people of their diseases, illnesses, and evil spirits, and he restored sight to many who were blind. ²²Then he told John's disciples, "Go back to John and tell him what you have seen and heard—the blind see, the lame walk, those with leprosy are cured, the deaf hear, the dead are raised to life, and the Good News is being preached to the poor." ²³And he added, "God blesses those who do not fall away because of me.*"

²⁴After John's disciples left, Jesus began talking about him to the crowds. "What kind of man did you go into the wilderness to see? Was he a weak reed, swayed by every breath of wind? ²⁵Or were you expecting to see a man dressed in expensive clothes? No, people who wear beautiful clothes and live in luxury are found in palaces. ²⁶Were you looking for a

---

7:2 Greek *a centurion;* similarly in 7:6.   **7:19** Greek *Are you the one who is coming?* Also in 7:20.   **7:23** Or *who are not offended by me.*

7:11-17 This woman was husbandless, childless, and likely hopeless. She represents one of the poorest in society, in need of the Good News (4:18-19). Jesus saw her and had compassion for her. Among Jesus' healing stories, Jesus rarely acted without being asked. But this story is one exception. Sometimes, we don't even know how to pray amid suffering, but we can trust that the Lord sees us and will act with compassion.

7:12 In ancient Israel, a large crowd of mourners and their intense wailing signified great love for the deceased. In some cases, professional mourners were hired, and these were usually women. Widows were the most vulnerable members of society in the ancient world, and God shows a special concern for them, repeatedly (Exodus 22:22; Deuteronomy 10:18; 27:19). This widow's son was likely her only means of support and hope for the future; his death was a terrible loss (see Jeremiah 6:26; Amos 8:10; Zechariah 12:10).

prophet? Yes, and he is more than a prophet. ²⁷John is the man to whom the Scriptures refer when they say,

> 'Look, I am sending my messenger ahead of you,
>   and he will prepare your way before you.'*

²⁸I tell you, of all who have ever lived, none is greater than John. Yet even the least person in the Kingdom of God is greater than he is!"

²⁹When they heard this, all the people—even the tax collectors—agreed that God's way was right,* for they had been baptized by John. ³⁰But the Pharisees and experts in religious law rejected God's plan for them, for they had refused John's baptism.

³¹"To what can I compare the people of this generation?" Jesus asked. "How can I describe them? ³²They are like children playing a game in the public square. They complain to their friends,

> 'We played wedding songs,
>   and you didn't dance,
> so we played funeral songs,
>   and you didn't weep.'

³³For John the Baptist didn't spend his time eating bread or drinking wine, and you say, 'He's possessed by a demon.' ³⁴The Son of Man,* on the other hand, feasts and drinks, and you say, 'He's a glutton and a drunkard, and a friend of tax collectors and other sinners!' ³⁵But wisdom is shown to be right by the lives of those who follow it.*"

Jesus Anointed by a Sinful Woman

³⁶One of the Pharisees asked Jesus to have dinner with him, so Jesus went to his home and sat down to eat.* ³⁷When a certain immoral woman from that city heard he was eating there, she brought a beautiful alabaster jar filled with expensive perfume. ³⁸Then she knelt behind him at his feet, weeping. Her tears fell on his feet, and she wiped them off with her hair. Then she kept kissing his feet and putting perfume on them.

³⁹When the Pharisee who had invited him saw this, he said to himself, "If this man were a prophet, he would know what kind of woman is touching him. She's a sinner!"

⁴⁰Then Jesus answered his thoughts. "Simon," he said to the Pharisee, "I have something to say to you."

"Go ahead, Teacher," Simon replied.

⁴¹Then Jesus told him this story: "A man loaned money to two people—500 pieces of silver* to one and 50 pieces to the other. ⁴²But neither of them could repay him, so he kindly forgave them both, canceling their debts. Who do you suppose loved him more after that?"

⁴³Simon answered, "I suppose the one for whom he canceled the larger debt."

"That's right," Jesus said. ⁴⁴Then he turned to the woman and said to Simon, "Look at this woman kneeling here. When I entered your home, you didn't offer me water to wash the dust from my feet, but she has washed them with her tears and wiped them with her hair. ⁴⁵You didn't greet me with a kiss, but from the time I first came in, she has not stopped kissing my feet. ⁴⁶You neglected the courtesy of olive oil to anoint my head, but she has anointed my feet with rare perfume.

⁴⁷"I tell you, her sins—and they are many—have been forgiven, so she has shown me much love. But a person who is forgiven little shows only little love." ⁴⁸Then Jesus said to the woman, "Your sins are forgiven."

⁴⁹The men at the table said among themselves, "Who is this man, that he goes around forgiving sins?"

⁵⁰And Jesus said to the woman, "Your faith has saved you; go in peace."

7:27 Mal 3:1. 7:29 Or *praised God for his justice*. 7:34 "Son of Man" is a title Jesus used for himself. 7:35 Or *But wisdom is justified by all her children*. 7:36 Or *and reclined*. 7:41 Greek *500 denarii*. A denarius was equivalent to a laborer's full day's wage.

7:36-50 This is another story full of contrasts (similar to Mary and Zechariah in 1:1-38). Simon, the host, was a religious man, and the unwelcomed woman was associated with notorious sin. Simon didn't treat Jesus with hospitality, but this unnamed woman anointed Jesus with costly perfume from an alabaster jar. Jesus praised her action because it showed her knowledge of and gratefulness for Jesus' forgiveness. We, like Simon, might be tempted to merely welcome Jesus "into our house" without letting him come any further into our lives. Instead, we must *treasure* Jesus in our hearts.

7:37 We can't be certain what the woman's description as an "immoral woman" indicates about her. Some interpreters have speculated that she was a prostitute, but it's just as likely that she was guilty of adultery or simply married to a man known for being a notorious sinner. The nature of her being "immoral" does not matter; Jesus forgave her regardless (7:47-50).

7:38 At a first-century banquet, guests reclined on low couches around a low table with their feet extended outward. The unnamed woman would not have been able to reach Jesus' head to anoint him, so she poured the perfume on his feet. Since married women at this time wore their hair done up, some interpreters see this woman's letting down her hair in public as scandalous and believe this could have constituted grounds for her husband to divorce her. However, ancient evidence, both in literature and in funerary reliefs, show that women would unbind their hair when grieving in certain situations. Luke doesn't record whether the dinner guests were offended by this woman's action. Kissing his feet was a sign of reverence and was a notable act in a culture offended by feet (Luke mentions feet six times in this passage). Whether she was discarding propriety or expressing grief for sin, she showed her gratitude for Jesus' forgiveness.

7:47 This translation, "so she has shown me much love," conveys the meaning of Jesus' words here better than the traditional rendering, "because she loved much." It was not that the woman's great love for Jesus caused him to forgive her, but that the forgiveness she had already received from Jesus prompted her love.

Women Who Followed Jesus

8 Soon afterward Jesus began a tour of the nearby towns and villages, preaching and announcing the Good News about the Kingdom of God. He took his twelve disciples with him, ²along with some women who had been cured of evil spirits and diseases. Among them were Mary Magdalene, from whom he had cast out seven demons; ³Joanna, the wife of Chuza, Herod's business manager; Susanna; and many others who were contributing from their own resources to support Jesus and his disciples.

Parable of the Farmer Scattering Seed

⁴One day Jesus told a story in the form of a parable to a large crowd that had gathered from many towns to hear him: ⁵"A farmer went out to plant his seed. As he scattered it across his field, some seed fell on a footpath, where it was stepped on, and the birds ate it. ⁶Other seed fell among rocks. It began to grow, but the plant soon wilted and died for lack of moisture. ⁷Other seed fell among thorns that grew up with it and choked out the tender plants. ⁸Still other seed fell on fertile soil. This seed grew and produced a crop that was a hundred times as much as had been planted!" When he had said this, he called out, "Anyone with ears to hear should listen and understand."

⁹His disciples asked him what this parable meant. ¹⁰He replied, "You are permitted to understand the secrets* of the Kingdom of God. But I use parables to teach the others so that the Scriptures might be fulfilled:

'When they look, they won't really see.
When they hear, they won't understand.'*

¹¹"This is the meaning of the parable: The seed is God's word. ¹²The seeds that fell on the footpath represent those who hear the message, only to have the devil come and take it away from their hearts and prevent them from believing and being saved. ¹³The seeds on the rocky soil represent those who hear the message and receive it with joy. But since they don't have deep roots, they believe for a while, then they fall away when they face temptation. ¹⁴The seeds that fell among the thorns represent those who hear the message, but all too quickly the message is crowded out by the cares and riches and pleasures of this life. And so they never grow into maturity. ¹⁵And the seeds that fell on the good soil represent honest, good-hearted people who hear God's word, cling to it, and patiently produce a huge harvest.

Parable of the Lamp

¹⁶"No one lights a lamp and then covers it with a bowl or hides it under a bed. A lamp is placed on a stand, where its light can be seen by all who enter the house. ¹⁷For all that is secret will eventually be brought into the open, and everything that is concealed will be brought to light and made known to all.

¹⁸"So pay attention to how you hear. To those who listen to my teaching, more understanding will be given. But for those who are not listening, even what they think they understand will be taken away from them."

The True Family of Jesus

¹⁹Then Jesus' mother and brothers came to see him, but they couldn't get to him because of the crowd. ²⁰Someone told Jesus, "Your mother and your brothers are standing outside, and they want to see you."

²¹Jesus replied, "My mother and my brothers are all those who hear God's word and obey it."

Jesus Calms the Storm

²²One day Jesus said to his disciples, "Let's cross to the other side of the lake." So they got into a boat and started out. ²³As they sailed across, Jesus settled down for a nap. But soon a fierce storm came down on the lake. The boat was filling with water, and they were in real danger.

²⁴The disciples went and woke him up, shouting, "Master, Master, we're going to drown!"

When Jesus woke up, he rebuked the wind and the raging waves. Suddenly the storm stopped and all was calm. ²⁵Then he asked them, "Where is your faith?"

The disciples were terrified and amazed. "Who is this man?" they asked each other. "When he gives a command, even the wind and waves obey him!"

Jesus Heals a Demon-Possessed Man

²⁶So they arrived in the region of the Gerasenes,* across the lake from Galilee. ²⁷As Jesus was climbing out of the boat, a man who was possessed by demons came out to meet him. For a long time he had been homeless and naked, living in the tombs outside the town.

8:10a Greek *mysteries.* **8:10b** Isa 6:9 (Greek version). **8:26** Other manuscripts read *Gadarenes;* still others read *Gergesenes;* also in 8:37. See Matt 8:28; Mark 5:1.

8:2-3 Rabbis, or Jewish teachers, of Jesus' day did not have women disciples, so this was unusual. Some of these women, like Joanna, were from wealthy families and contributed financially to Jesus' ministry. Luke tells his readers that women were traveling with Jesus much earlier in his narrative than Mark and Matthew, who only mention it at the crucifixion (Matthew 27:55-56; Mark 15:40-41).

8:2 *Magdalene* means "from Magdala," a village on the northwestern side of the Sea of Galilee. Mary figures prominently in the burial and resurrection accounts (Luke 24:10; Mark 15:40, 47; John 19:25; 20:1, 18). Some interpreters have suggested that Mary Magdalene was the woman of Luke 7:36-50, leading to the belief that she had been a prostitute, but there is no basis for this speculation.

The Women WHO FINANCED JESUS' MINISTRY

IDENTITY

Giving Back Generously

Joanna: "Mary, you don't seem to mind a bit that everyone knows you were cured of not just one but seven demons. You're not ashamed or embarrassed at all."

Mary Magdalene: "I want everyone to know, Joanna! I wouldn't want anyone to miss out on being healed because their illness seemed shameful or was socially isolating, or because they had tried everything and thought it was impossible ever to get better, ever to be free! I want every person to have an encounter with Jesus."

Joanna: "I'm sure that people back home look down on me for following Jesus, but I hope it shows that Jesus' good news is for the rich and privileged just as much as it is for the downtrodden. I'm thankful that Chuza, my husband, has given me the freedom to join you and the other women in supporting and financing Jesus' ministry and learning from him. This man is constantly on the move. It's exciting to be a part of what he's doing!"

Susanna: "It really is! Joanna, your financial support goes a long way, and I have to say I admire your generosity. I see you quietly paying the bills and thanking vendors as they fill our baskets and sacks. You make sure to pay for our supplies before anyone else can. If I were writing a book about our adventures, your name would be in it! You're such a great example of humble, generous giving."

> Encounter Jesus.
> Experience change.
> Expand the Kingdom.

JOANNA, SUSANNA, AND THE OTHER WOMEN'S STORY IS TOLD IN LUKE 8:1-3. MARY MAGDALENE AND SOME OTHER WOMEN ARE ALSO MENTIONED IN MATTHEW 27:56, 61; 28:1; MARK 15:40, 47; 16:1, 9; LUKE 24:10; JOHN 19:25; 20:1, 11-18.

IDENTIFY

How can you serve, witness, and give to show how Jesus has impacted your life?

"Like Mary, I have been miraculously healed. My back was instantly made well—debilitating spasms disappeared and never returned. I, too, want the world to know the Jesus who saves, heals, and makes whole. It seems to have been that way for Joanna, Mary, Susanna, and others. Let's follow these women's examples in authentic witness, selfless service, and generous giving."

DONNA LEE LAMOTHE, MA, is executive director and founder of inSPIRE Channels at RSVP Ministries. She teaches and guides all to find wholeness through faith in Jesus.

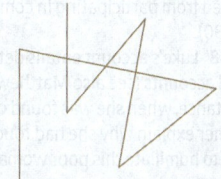

²⁸As soon as he saw Jesus, he shrieked and fell down in front of him. Then he screamed, "Why are you interfering with me, Jesus, Son of the Most High God? Please, I beg you, don't torture me!" ²⁹For Jesus had already commanded the evil* spirit to come out of him. This spirit had often taken control of the man. Even when he was placed under guard and put in chains and shackles, he simply broke them and rushed out into the wilderness, completely under the demon's power.

³⁰Jesus demanded, "What is your name?"

"Legion," he replied, for he was filled with many demons. ³¹The demons kept begging Jesus not to send them into the bottomless pit.*

³²There happened to be a large herd of pigs feeding on the hillside nearby, and the demons begged him to let them enter into the pigs.

So Jesus gave them permission. ³³Then the demons came out of the man and entered the pigs, and the entire herd plunged down the steep hillside into the lake and drowned.

³⁴When the herdsmen saw it, they fled to the nearby town and the surrounding countryside, spreading the news as they ran. ³⁵People rushed out to see what had happened. A crowd soon gathered around Jesus, and they saw the man who had been freed from the demons. He was sitting at Jesus' feet, fully clothed and perfectly sane, and they were all afraid. ³⁶Then those who had seen what happened told the others how the demon-possessed man had been healed. ³⁷And all the people in the region of the Gerasenes begged Jesus to go away and leave them alone, for a great wave of fear swept over them.

So Jesus returned to the boat and left, crossing back to the other side of the lake. ³⁸The man who had been freed from the demons begged to go with him. But Jesus sent him home, saying, ³⁹"No, go back to your family, and tell them everything God has done for you." So he went all through the town proclaiming the great things Jesus had done for him.

Jesus Heals in Response to Faith

⁴⁰On the other side of the lake the crowds welcomed Jesus, because they had been waiting for him. ⁴¹Then a man named Jairus, a leader of the local synagogue, came and fell at Jesus' feet, pleading with him to come home with him. ⁴²His only daughter,* who was about twelve years old, was dying.

As Jesus went with him, he was surrounded by the crowds. ⁴³A woman in the crowd had suffered for twelve years with constant bleeding,* and she could find no cure. ⁴⁴Coming up behind Jesus, she touched the fringe of his robe. Immediately, the bleeding stopped.

⁴⁵"Who touched me?" Jesus asked.

Everyone denied it, and Peter said, "Master, this whole crowd is pressing up against you."

⁴⁶But Jesus said, "Someone deliberately touched me, for I felt healing power go out from me." ⁴⁷When the woman realized that she could not stay hidden, she began to tremble and fell to her knees in front of him. The whole crowd heard her explain why she had touched him and that she had been immediately healed. ⁴⁸"Daughter," he said to her, "your faith has made you well. Go in peace."

⁴⁹While he was still speaking to her, a messenger arrived from the home of Jairus, the leader of the synagogue. He told him, "Your daughter is dead. There's no use troubling the Teacher now."

⁵⁰But when Jesus heard what had happened, he said to Jairus, "Don't be afraid. Just have faith, and she will be healed."

⁵¹When they arrived at the house, Jesus wouldn't let anyone go in with him except Peter, John, James, and the little girl's father and mother. ⁵²The house was filled with people weeping and wailing, but he said, "Stop the weeping! She isn't dead; she's only asleep."

⁵³But the crowd laughed at him because they all knew she had died. ⁵⁴Then Jesus took her by the hand and said in a loud voice, "My child, get up!" ⁵⁵And at that moment her life* returned, and she immediately stood up! Then Jesus told them to give her something to eat. ⁵⁶Her parents were overwhelmed, but Jesus insisted that they not tell anyone what had happened.

8:29 Greek *unclean*. **8:31** Or *the abyss,* or *the underworld*. **8:42** Or *His only child, a daughter*. **8:43** Some manuscripts add *having spent everything she had on doctors*. **8:55** Or *her spirit*.

8:43 This woman most likely was suffering from vaginal bleeding. This condition would have affected her both physically and spiritually, since this type of bleeding meant the woman was ceremonially unclean and therefore she would be excluded from participating in community worship (Leviticus 15:25-30).

8:47-48 Luke's account entails details not found in the other Gospel accounts (see also Matthew 9:18-26; Mark 5:21-34). For instance, when she was found out, "the whole crowd heard her explain why she had touched" Jesus. Did Jesus intend to humiliate this poor woman? Not likely. She had lived twelve years in isolation after being rendered ritually unclean by her bleeding (Leviticus 15:19-31). She would have remained excluded from the community until an authority pronounced her to be clean. Jesus called attention to the women so that he could proclaim her healing through her faith in his power and speak peace over her. Sometimes, healing requires reopening a wound.

8:48 Jesus said the same thing to the woman who had anointed his feet (7:50). The Greek word for "save" can indicate either spiritual or physical healing. "Peace," as is used here (compare to the Hebrew word *shalom*), means spiritual wholeness, not just lack of conflict (see 1:79; 2:14, 29; 7:50; 19:38, 42; 24:36).

Jairus's Daughter

IDENTITY

Dying to Live

She remembers...

When I was twelve, I became deathly ill. Though my father, Jairus, was a leader in our synagogue and faithfully followed God, my illness kept getting worse. Finally, after hearing stories about how the Teacher, Jesus, healed people, my father went to beg him for help.

I was surprised because the other synagogue leaders had said Jesus was a troublemaker. I knew going could cost my father his position and our social standing, but my parents were desperate.

The next thing I remember is waking up. Jesus was holding my hand and telling me to get up. To everyone's amazement, I stood up and walked.

Later, I learned that messengers had told my father that I was already dead. Jesus said not to be afraid but just to have faith. My father believed him and kept going, and then Jesus healed me.

At that moment, we all realized that Jesus could do anything. My father's persistence and trust in Jesus through what looked impossible saved my life.

JAIRUS'S DAUGHTER'S STORY IS TOLD IN LUKE 8:40-56; SHE ALSO APPEARS IN MATTHEW 9:18-26; MARK 5:21-43.

> Sometimes God uses our suffering and the prayers of others to deepen both our faith and theirs.

IDENTIFY

Have you had to rely on the help and prayers of others, knowing it required a sacrifice?

How did God use that in your life and theirs?

> "As an infant in India, I contracted polio, and my dad gave up his career to get better medical care for me. My sickness eventually brought me to faith, deepening my parents' trust in the Lord. They, too, saw God provide."

VANEETHA RENDALL RISNER is the author of *Walking Through Fire*. She and her family live in North Carolina, where she writes and speaks about how God meets us in suffering.

Insight: THE WOMEN DISCIPLES OF JESUS

When we picture Jesus traveling around Galilee, Judea, and Samaria, we likely picture him only with his twelve male disciples, but the Gospel writers tell us something different: Women traveled and ministered with Jesus, too. In fact, Jesus didn't travel with only twelve men and these eight named women, he traveled with a number of other women and men, as we can see evidence for in Luke 10:1-20, where Jesus sent out 72 disciples to preach and heal. Jesus may have traveled with up to 120 people, which is the number gathered awaiting the Holy Spirit in Acts 1:15.

Mary Magdalene
- Jesus healed her of seven demons
- Magdalene could be a reference to her hometown, possibly "Magdala," or a nickname meaning "strong tower"
- Traveled with Jesus
- Witness at the cross and the empty tomb
- Sent by Jesus to tell the apostles about the resurrection

Matthew 27:56, 61; 28:1-10
Mark 15:40, 47; 16:1-11
Luke 8:2; 23:49*, 55-56*; 24:1-10
John 19:25; 20:1-18
likely, Acts 1:14

Joanna
- Wife of Chuza, Herod's business manager
- High social standing and wealth
- Financially supported Jesus' ministry
- Probably at the cross
- Probably a witness of the empty tomb

Matthew 27:55*
Luke 8:3; 23:49*, 55-56*; 24:10
likely, Acts 1:14; 2:1

Susanna
- Only mentioned once, but we can assume she was among the women at the cross

Luke 8:3; likely, Acts 1:14

Mary
- Mother of James and Joseph
- Wife of Clopas (who could be Cleopas of Luke 24:18)

Matthew 27:55-56
Mark 15:40, 47; 16:1-11
Luke 24:10
John 19:25; likely, Acts 1:14

Mary
- Mother of James and John
- Wife of Zebedee

Matthew 20:20; 27:56

Martha
- Sister of Mary and Lazarus
- Probably the eldest sister
- Hospitality was a high value
- Calls Jesus "Messiah"

Luke 10:38-42; John 11:1–12:2

Mary of Bethany
- Sister of Martha and Lazarus
- Learned at Jesus' feet, like a male disciple would have
- Anointed Jesus' feet for burial

Luke 10:38-42; John 11:1–12:8

Salome
- Witness at the cross

Matthew 27:55*
Mark 15:40; 16:1-8
likely, Acts 1:14

Mary
- Mother of Jesus
- Based on her presence at the cross in John 19:25, we can assume she joined Jesus on his travels at some point
- Present in the upstairs room after Jesus' ascension and likely at Pentecost

Matthew 1:16–2:23; 27:55*
Luke 1:26-56; 2:1-52; 8:3*, 19-21; 11:27-28; 23:49*, 55-56*
John 19:25-27; Acts 1:14; 2:1*

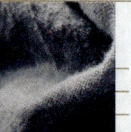

Other women
- Traveled with Jesus
- Witnesses at the cross and empty tomb
- Present in the upstairs room at Pentecost

Matthew 27:55; 27:61; 28:1-10
Mark 15:40; 16:1-8
Luke 8:2-3
likely, Acts 1:14; 2:1

*not mentioned by name

Jesus Sends Out the Twelve Disciples

9 One day Jesus called together his twelve disciples* and gave them power and authority to cast out all demons and to heal all diseases. ²Then he sent them out to tell everyone about the Kingdom of God and to heal the sick. ³"Take nothing for your journey," he instructed them. "Don't take a walking stick, a traveler's bag, food, money,* or even a change of clothes. ⁴Wherever you go, stay in the same house until you leave town. ⁵And if a town refuses to welcome you, shake its dust from your feet as you leave to show that you have abandoned those people to their fate."

⁶So they began their circuit of the villages, preaching the Good News and healing the sick.

Herod's Confusion

⁷When Herod Antipas, the ruler of Galilee,* heard about everything Jesus was doing, he was puzzled. Some were saying that John the Baptist had been raised from the dead. ⁸Others thought Jesus was Elijah or one of the other prophets risen from the dead.

⁹"I beheaded John," Herod said, "so who is this man about whom I hear such stories?" And he kept trying to see him.

Jesus Feeds Five Thousand

¹⁰When the apostles returned, they told Jesus everything they had done. Then he slipped quietly away with them toward the town of Bethsaida. ¹¹But the crowds found out where he was going, and they followed him. He welcomed them and taught them about the Kingdom of God, and he healed those who were sick.

¹²Late in the afternoon the twelve disciples came to him and said, "Send the crowds away to the nearby villages and farms, so they can find food and lodging for the night. There is nothing to eat here in this remote place."

¹³But Jesus said, "You feed them."

"But we have only five loaves of bread and two fish," they answered. "Or are you expecting us to go and buy enough food for this whole crowd?" ¹⁴For there were about 5,000 men there.

Jesus replied, "Tell them to sit down in groups of about fifty each." ¹⁵So the people all sat down. ¹⁶Jesus took the five loaves and two fish, looked up toward heaven, and blessed them. Then, breaking the loaves into pieces, he kept giving the bread and fish to the disciples so they could distribute it to the people. ¹⁷They all ate as much as they wanted, and afterward, the disciples picked up twelve baskets of leftovers!

Peter's Declaration about Jesus

¹⁸One day Jesus left the crowds to pray alone. Only his disciples were with him, and he asked them, "Who do people say I am?"

¹⁹"Well," they replied, "some say John the Baptist, some say Elijah, and others say you are one of the other ancient prophets risen from the dead."

²⁰Then he asked them, "But who do you say I am?"

Peter replied, "You are the Messiah* sent from God!"

Jesus Predicts His Death

²¹Jesus warned his disciples not to tell anyone who he was. ²²"The Son of Man* must suffer many terrible things," he said. "He will be rejected by the elders, the leading priests, and the teachers of religious law. He will be killed, but on the third day he will be raised from the dead."

²³Then he said to the crowd, "If any of you wants to be my follower, you must give up your own way, take up your cross daily, and follow me. ²⁴If you try to hang on to your life, you will lose it. But if you give up your life for my sake, you will save it. ²⁵And what do you benefit if you gain the whole world but are yourself lost or destroyed? ²⁶If anyone is ashamed of me and my message, the Son of Man will be ashamed of that person when he returns in his glory and in the glory of the Father and the holy angels. ²⁷I tell you the truth, some standing here right now will not die before they see the Kingdom of God."

The Transfiguration

²⁸About eight days later Jesus took Peter, John, and James up on a mountain to pray. ²⁹And as he was praying, the appearance of his face was transformed, and his clothes became dazzling white. ³⁰Suddenly, two men, Moses and Elijah, appeared and began talking with Jesus. ³¹They were glorious to see. And they were speaking about his exodus from this world, which was about to be fulfilled in Jerusalem.

³²Peter and the others had fallen asleep. When they woke up, they saw Jesus' glory and the two men standing with him. ³³As Moses and Elijah were starting to leave, Peter, not even knowing what he was saying, blurted out, "Master, it's wonderful for us to be here! Let's make three shelters as memorials*—one for you, one for Moses, and one for Elijah." ³⁴But even as he was saying this, a cloud overshadowed them, and terror gripped them as the cloud covered them.

³⁵Then a voice from the cloud said, "This is my Son, my Chosen One.* Listen to him." ³⁶When the voice finished, Jesus was there alone. They didn't tell anyone at that time what they had seen.

9:1 Greek *the Twelve;* other manuscripts read *the twelve apostles.* 9:3 Or *silver coins.* 9:7 Greek *Herod the tetrarch.* Herod Antipas was a son of King Herod and was ruler over Galilee. 9:20 Or *the Christ. Messiah* (a Hebrew term) and *Christ* (a Greek term) both mean "anointed one." 9:22 "Son of Man" is a title Jesus used for himself. 9:33 Greek *three tabernacles.* 9:35 Some manuscripts read *This is my dearly loved Son.*

Jesus Heals a Demon-Possessed Boy

³⁷The next day, after they had come down the mountain, a large crowd met Jesus. ³⁸A man in the crowd called out to him, "Teacher, I beg you to look at my son, my only child. ³⁹An evil spirit keeps seizing him, making him scream. It throws him into convulsions so that he foams at the mouth. It batters him and hardly ever leaves him alone. ⁴⁰I begged your disciples to cast out the spirit, but they couldn't do it."

⁴¹Jesus said, "You faithless and corrupt people! How long must I be with you and put up with you?" Then he said to the man, "Bring your son here."

⁴²As the boy came forward, the demon knocked him to the ground and threw him into a violent convulsion. But Jesus rebuked the evil* spirit and healed the boy. Then he gave him back to his father. ⁴³Awe gripped the people as they saw this majestic display of God's power.

Jesus Again Predicts His Death

While everyone was marveling at everything he was doing, Jesus said to his disciples, ⁴⁴"Listen to me and remember what I say. The Son of Man is going to be betrayed into the hands of his enemies." ⁴⁵But they didn't know what he meant. Its significance was hidden from them, so they couldn't understand it, and they were afraid to ask him about it.

The Greatest in the Kingdom

⁴⁶Then his disciples began arguing about which of them was the greatest. ⁴⁷But Jesus knew their thoughts, so he brought a little child to his side. ⁴⁸Then he said to them, "Anyone who welcomes a little child like this on my behalf* welcomes me, and anyone who welcomes me also welcomes my Father who sent me. Whoever is the least among you is the greatest."

Using the Name of Jesus

⁴⁹John said to Jesus, "Master, we saw someone using your name to cast out demons, but we told him to stop because he isn't in our group."

⁵⁰But Jesus said, "Don't stop him! Anyone who is not against you is for you."

Opposition from Samaritans

⁵¹As the time drew near for him to ascend to heaven, Jesus resolutely set out for Jerusalem. ⁵²He sent messengers ahead to a Samaritan village to prepare for his arrival. ⁵³But the people of the village did not welcome Jesus because he was on his way to Jerusalem. ⁵⁴When James and John saw this, they said to Jesus, "Lord, should we call down fire from heaven to burn them up*?" ⁵⁵But Jesus turned and rebuked them.* ⁵⁶So they went on to another village.

The Cost of Following Jesus

⁵⁷As they were walking along, someone said to Jesus, "I will follow you wherever you go."

⁵⁸But Jesus replied, "Foxes have dens to live in, and birds have nests, but the Son of Man has no place even to lay his head."

⁵⁹He said to another person, "Come, follow me."

The man agreed, but he said, "Lord, first let me return home and bury my father."

⁶⁰But Jesus told him, "Let the spiritually dead bury their own dead!* Your duty is to go and preach about the Kingdom of God."

⁶¹Another said, "Yes, Lord, I will follow you, but first let me say good-bye to my family."

⁶²But Jesus told him, "Anyone who puts a hand to the plow and then looks back is not fit for the Kingdom of God."

9:42 Greek *unclean*. **9:48** Greek *in my name*. **9:54** Some manuscripts add *as Elijah did*. **9:55** Some manuscripts add an expanded conclusion to verse 55 and an additional sentence in verse 56: *And he said, "You don't realize what your hearts are like. ⁵⁶For the Son of Man has not come to destroy people's lives, but to save them."* **9:60** Greek *Let the dead bury their own dead.*

9:38 Luke's stories about Jesus healing children share an interesting detail not found in Matthew and Mark—namely, that each was their parents' *only* child (see also 7:12; 8:42). Watching a child suffer is enough to break any parent's heart, not to mention if that child was their only child. Even in a society with better medical care, it's still consuming for any parent to care for a chronically sick child. As Jesus followers, we can provide supportive communities for families with sick children. If your child or a child you love is sick, you can find encouragement that Jesus may heal your child in this life. And if he doesn't, you can also take comfort from these stories that Jesus sees your pain, understands your grief, and offers you spiritual healing.

9:48 To welcome someone means to bestow honor and treat that person as a social equal. Jesus' statement here is shocking since children in Jesus' day had no social status in the community and were viewed as their parents' property. Jesus took the lowest, most vulnerable members of society and announced that welcoming them was equivalent to welcoming him. By placing great importance on including those who were not valued by their culture, Jesus showed his followers that true leadership in his Kingdom is achieved through sacrificial service, not the exercise of power (see also Mark 10:42-45).

9:57-62 Jesus was not undermining the command in the law of Moses to honor parents (Exodus 20:12; Deuteronomy 5:16). Instead, he stressed that work in his Kingdom presumes reprioritizing family relationships. This change of priority likely looks different for women and men, young and old. For some women, carrying out their callings could mean remaining single, delaying or forgoing parenthood, or moving far away from extended family. In our Christian communities, it's important for us to acknowledge and take care of those who sacrifice having close biological relations to follow and obey Christ. This could mean watching out for parents whose children are far away serving Christ or for those who remain single or without children. The people of God form a new kind of family that transcends biological family, but it requires a new way of relating to one another to truly call each other brother and sister.

Jesus Sends Out His Disciples

10 The Lord now chose seventy-two* other disciples and sent them ahead in pairs to all the towns and places he planned to visit. ²These were his instructions to them: "The harvest is great, but the workers are few. So pray to the Lord who is in charge of the harvest; ask him to send more workers into his fields. ³Now go, and remember that I am sending you out as lambs among wolves. ⁴Don't take any money with you, nor a traveler's bag, nor an extra pair of sandals. And don't stop to greet anyone on the road.

⁵"Whenever you enter someone's home, first say, 'May God's peace be on this house.' ⁶If those who live there are peaceful, the blessing will stand; if they are not, the blessing will return to you. ⁷Don't move around from home to home. Stay in one place, eating and drinking what they provide. Don't hesitate to accept hospitality, because those who work deserve their pay.

⁸"If you enter a town and it welcomes you, eat whatever is set before you. ⁹Heal the sick, and tell them, 'The Kingdom of God is near you now.' ¹⁰But if a town refuses to welcome you, go out into its streets and say, ¹¹'We wipe even the dust of your town from our feet to show that we have abandoned you to your fate. And know this—the Kingdom of God is near!' ¹²I assure you, even wicked Sodom will be better off than such a town on judgment day.

¹³"What sorrow awaits you, Korazin and Bethsaida! For if the miracles I did in you had been done in wicked Tyre and Sidon, their people would have repented of their sins long ago, clothing themselves in burlap and throwing ashes on their heads to show their remorse. ¹⁴Yes, Tyre and Sidon will be better off on judgment day than you. ¹⁵And you people of Capernaum, will you be honored in heaven? No, you will go down to the place of the dead.*"

¹⁶Then he said to the disciples, "Anyone who accepts your message is also accepting me. And anyone who rejects you is rejecting me. And anyone who rejects me is rejecting God, who sent me."

¹⁷When the seventy-two disciples returned, they joyfully reported to him, "Lord, even the demons obey us when we use your name!"

¹⁸"Yes," he told them, "I saw Satan fall from heaven like lightning! ¹⁹Look, I have given you authority over all the power of the enemy, and you can walk among snakes and scorpions and crush them. Nothing will injure you. ²⁰But don't rejoice because evil spirits obey you; rejoice because your names are registered in heaven."

> "For me, as a Christian, one of the most important of [Jesus'] teachings is ..., 'Who is my neighbour?' ... Everyone is our neighbour.... The need to look after a fellow human being is far more important than any cultural or religious differences."
>
> **QUEEN ELIZABETH II**
> (1926–2022) queen of England

Jesus' Prayer of Thanksgiving

²¹At that same time Jesus was filled with the joy of the Holy Spirit, and he said, "O Father, Lord of heaven and earth, thank you for hiding these things from those who think themselves wise and clever, and for revealing them to the childlike. Yes, Father, it pleased you to do it this way.

²²"My Father has entrusted everything to me. No one truly knows the Son except the Father, and no one truly knows the Father except the Son and those to whom the Son chooses to reveal him."

²³Then when they were alone, he turned to the disciples and said, "Blessed are the eyes that see what you have seen. ²⁴I tell you, many prophets and kings longed to see what you see, but they didn't see it. And they longed to hear what you hear, but they didn't hear it."

The Most Important Commandment

²⁵One day an expert in religious law stood up to test Jesus by asking him this question: "Teacher, what should I do to inherit eternal life?"

10:1 Some manuscripts read *seventy;* also in 10:17. **10:15** Greek *to Hades.*

10:25-37 In first-century Palestine, Jews regarded Samaritans as foes. The law expert talking to Jesus wanted a philosophical discussion: Let's *define* neighbor first. But Jesus called for action: *Love* those in need and then *become* their neighbor. It must have sounded shocking to first-century Palestinian Jews that Jesus used a Samaritan as a model. Jesus also invites us to "go and do the same."

²⁶Jesus replied, "What does the law of Moses say? How do you read it?"

²⁷The man answered, "'You must love the LORD your God with all your heart, all your soul, all your strength, and all your mind.' And, 'Love your neighbor as yourself.'"*

²⁸"Right!" Jesus told him. "Do this and you will live!"

²⁹The man wanted to justify his actions, so he asked Jesus, "And who is my neighbor?"

Parable of the Good Samaritan

³⁰Jesus replied with a story: "A Jewish man was traveling from Jerusalem down to Jericho, and he was attacked by bandits. They stripped him of his clothes, beat him up, and left him half dead beside the road.

³¹"By chance a priest came along. But when he saw the man lying there, he crossed to the other side of the road and passed him by. ³²A Temple assistant* walked over and looked at him lying there, but he also passed by on the other side.

³³"Then a despised Samaritan came along, and when he saw the man, he felt compassion for him. ³⁴Going over to him, the Samaritan soothed his wounds with olive oil and wine and bandaged them. Then he put the man on his own donkey and took him to an inn, where he took care of him. ³⁵The next day he handed the innkeeper two silver coins,* telling him, 'Take care of this man. If his bill runs higher than this, I'll pay you the next time I'm here.'

³⁶"Now which of these three would you say was a neighbor to the man who was attacked by bandits?" Jesus asked.

³⁷The man replied, "The one who showed him mercy."

Then Jesus said, "Yes, now go and do the same."

Jesus Visits Martha and Mary

³⁸As Jesus and the disciples continued on their way to Jerusalem, they came to a certain village where a woman named Martha welcomed him into her home. ³⁹Her sister, Mary, sat at the Lord's feet, listening to what he taught. ⁴⁰But Martha was distracted by the big dinner she was preparing. She came to Jesus and said, "Lord, doesn't it seem unfair to you that my sister just sits here while I do all the work? Tell her to come and help me."

⁴¹But the Lord said to her, "My dear Martha, you are worried and upset over all these details! ⁴²There is only one thing worth being concerned about. Mary has discovered it, and it will not be taken away from her."

Teaching about Prayer

11 Once Jesus was in a certain place praying. As he finished, one of his disciples came to him and said, "Lord, teach us to pray, just as John taught his disciples."

²Jesus said, "This is how you should pray:*

"Father, may your name be kept holy.
  May your Kingdom come soon.
³ Give us each day the food we need,*
⁴ and forgive us our sins,
  as we forgive those who sin against us.
  And don't let us yield to temptation.*"

⁵Then, teaching them more about prayer, he used this story: "Suppose you went to a friend's house at midnight, wanting to borrow three loaves of bread. You say to him, ⁶'A friend of mine has just arrived for a visit, and I have nothing for him to eat.' ⁷And suppose he calls out from his bedroom, 'Don't bother me. The door is locked for the night, and my family and I are all in bed. I can't help you.' ⁸But I tell you this—though he won't do it for friendship's sake, if you keep knocking long enough, he will get up and give you whatever you need because of your shameless persistence.*

⁹"And so I tell you, keep on asking, and you will receive what you ask for. Keep on seeking, and you will find. Keep on knocking, and the door will be opened to you. ¹⁰For everyone who asks, receives. Everyone who seeks, finds. And to everyone who knocks, the door will be opened.

10:27 Deut 6:5; Lev 19:18. 10:32 Greek *A Levite.* 10:35 Greek *two denarii.* A denarius was equivalent to a laborer's full day's wage. 11:2 Some manuscripts add additional phrases from the Lord's Prayer as it reads in Matt 6:9-13. 11:3 Or *Give us each day our food for the day;* or *Give us each day our food for tomorrow.* 11:4 Or *And keep us from being tested.* 11:8 Or *in order to avoid shame,* or *so his reputation won't be damaged.*

10:38-42 Martha, Mary, and their brother, Lazarus, were good friends of Jesus. They lived in Bethany, east of Jerusalem (see John 11:1).
10:39 When Mary "sat at the Lord's feet," she took up the position of a disciple (compare Acts 22:3). Rabbis, or Jewish teachers, did not usually have female disciples. Other women traveled with Jesus as his disciples too (Luke 8:2-3).
10:40 Hospitality was valued highly in this culture, and Martha was fulfilling the expected role of a woman. She was frustrated that Mary was not.
10:41 Jewish culture highly valued hospitality. Jesus didn't undermine Martha's hospitality but pointed out her worries.

When Martha tried her best to host her beloved guest, she neglected the guest himself. Today, it is common for working Christian women to juggle work, family, community, and church service. Perfect balance is likely impossible, so we must learn to prioritize and make peace with our choices. Jesus asks us to put him and what he's called us to do first, but what that will look like for each person depends on calling, purpose, and life stage.

10:42 Jesus' words about Mary were shocking. Women were expected to serve domestically and were forbidden to learn as disciples from a rabbi. Jesus validated Mary's desire to be his disciple.

Mary of Bethany

IDENTITY — Attending over Achieving

Mary of Bethany remembers...

People were hungry, and it was our task to feed them. Not just feed them but be hospitable to them. I knew what was expected of my sister—Martha—and me: prepare comforting food, set an inviting table, and make sure everyone felt welcomed and taken care of.

The trouble was that Jesus made *me* feel welcomed, and he was just so compelling. There he sat amid my sister's bustling hospitality, speaking of things that brought peace to my hungry heart. Torn between responsibility and awe, I couldn't bring myself to get up and help. I was enraptured by his every word, by his very presence.

At that moment, being with him mattered more than what my sister expected of me or what people thought I should be doing. When Martha asked Jesus if he cared that I wasn't helping, his answer set me free: "My dear Martha.... There is only one thing worth being concerned about. Mary has discovered it, and it will not be taken away from her" (Luke 10:41-42).

There I sat, accomplishing nothing, proving nothing, earning nothing, yet Jesus said that what I was doing was enough. Validation was found in his presence, not in my accomplishments, and it could not be taken from me.

> Jesus desires our attention more than our achievements.

MARY OF BETHANY'S STORY IS TOLD IN LUKE 10:38-42; SHE IS ALSO MENTIONED IN JOHN 11:1-44; 12:1-11.

IDENTIFY

How do you find yourself torn between what Jesus has for you and the hustle of everyday life?

What might Jesus say to you if you sat still before him right now?

How will it change our day if we trust that Jesus desires our attention more than our achievements?

> "It's easy to find our worth in what we do. However, Jesus' acceptance and love aren't contingent upon anything we do but on what he did for us."

MANDY ARIOTO is the president and CEO of MOPS International, influencing millions of moms around the world every year. She is a scholar of Greek, author, and speaker who believes in the transformational power of Scripture.

¹¹"You fathers—if your children ask* for a fish, do you give them a snake instead? ¹²Or if they ask for an egg, do you give them a scorpion? Of course not! ¹³So if you sinful people know how to give good gifts to your children, how much more will your heavenly Father give the Holy Spirit to those who ask him."

Jesus and the Prince of Demons

¹⁴One day Jesus cast out a demon from a man who couldn't speak, and when the demon was gone, the man began to speak. The crowds were amazed, ¹⁵but some of them said, "No wonder he can cast out demons. He gets his power from Satan,* the prince of demons." ¹⁶Others, trying to test Jesus, demanded that he show them a miraculous sign from heaven to prove his authority.

¹⁷He knew their thoughts, so he said, "Any kingdom divided by civil war is doomed. A family splintered by feuding will fall apart. ¹⁸You say I am empowered by Satan. But if Satan is divided and fighting against himself, how can his kingdom survive? ¹⁹And if I am empowered by Satan, what about your own exorcists? They cast out demons, too, so they will condemn you for what you have said. ²⁰But if I am casting out demons by the power of God,* then the Kingdom of God has arrived among you. ²¹For when a strong man is fully armed and guards his palace, his possessions are safe—²²until someone even stronger attacks and overpowers him, strips him of his weapons, and carries off his belongings.

²³"Anyone who isn't with me opposes me, and anyone who isn't working with me is actually working against me.

²⁴"When an evil* spirit leaves a person, it goes into the desert, searching for rest. But when it finds none, it says, 'I will return to the person I came from.' ²⁵So it returns and finds that its former home is all swept and in order. ²⁶Then the spirit finds seven other spirits more evil than itself, and they all enter the person and live there. And so that person is worse off than before."

²⁷As he was speaking, a woman in the crowd called out, "God bless your mother—the womb from which you came, and the breasts that nursed you!"

²⁸Jesus replied, "But even more blessed are all who hear the word of God and put it into practice."

The Sign of Jonah

²⁹As the crowd pressed in on Jesus, he said, "This evil generation keeps asking me to show them a miraculous sign. But the only sign I will give them is the sign of Jonah. ³⁰What happened to him was a sign to the people of Nineveh that God had sent him. What happens to the Son of Man* will be a sign to these people that he was sent by God.

³¹"The queen of Sheba* will stand up against this generation on judgment day and condemn it, for she came from a distant land to hear the wisdom of Solomon. Now someone greater than Solomon is here—but you refuse to listen. ³²The people of Nineveh will also stand up against this generation on judgment day and condemn it, for they repented of their sins at the preaching of Jonah. Now someone greater than Jonah is here—but you refuse to repent.

Receiving the Light

³³"No one lights a lamp and then hides it or puts it under a basket.* Instead, a lamp is placed on a stand, where its light can be seen by all who enter the house.

³⁴"Your eye is like a lamp that provides light for your body. When your eye is healthy, your whole body is filled with light. But when it is unhealthy, your body is filled with darkness. ³⁵Make sure that the light you think you have is not actually darkness. ³⁶If you are filled with light, with no dark corners, then your whole life will be radiant, as though a floodlight were filling you with light."

Jesus Criticizes the Religious Leaders

³⁷As Jesus was speaking, one of the Pharisees invited him home for a meal. So he went in and took his place at the table.* ³⁸His host was amazed to see that he sat down to eat without first performing the hand-washing ceremony required by Jewish custom. ³⁹Then the Lord said to him, "You Pharisees are so careful to clean the outside of the cup and the dish, but inside you are filthy—full of greed and wickedness! ⁴⁰Fools! Didn't God make the inside as well as the outside? ⁴¹So clean the inside by giving gifts to the poor, and you will be clean all over.

⁴²"What sorrow awaits you Pharisees! For you are careful to tithe even the tiniest income from your herb gardens,* but you ignore justice and the love of God. You should tithe, yes, but do not neglect the more important things.

⁴³"What sorrow awaits you Pharisees! For you love to sit in the seats of honor in the synagogues

---

11:11 Some manuscripts add *for bread, do you give them a stone? Or [if they ask]*. **11:15** Greek *Beelzeboul;* also in 11:18, 19. Other manuscripts read *Beezeboul;* Latin version reads *Beelzebub*. **11:20** Greek *by the finger of God*. **11:24** Greek *unclean*. **11:30** "Son of Man" is a title Jesus used for himself. **11:31** Greek *The queen of the south*. **11:33** Some manuscripts do not include *or puts it under a basket*. **11:37** Or *and reclined*. **11:42** Greek *tithe the mint, the rue, and every herb*.

11:31 Sheba was a kingdom in southern Arabia. The queen traveled a great distance to hear Solomon's wisdom (1 Kings 10:1-13; 2 Chronicles 9:1-12). (See "Queen of Sheba" on page 529; also see the note on Matthew 12:41-42.)

and receive respectful greetings as you walk in the marketplaces. ⁴⁴Yes, what sorrow awaits you! For you are like hidden graves in a field. People walk over them without knowing the corruption they are stepping on."

⁴⁵"Teacher," said an expert in religious law, "you have insulted us, too, in what you just said."

⁴⁶"Yes," said Jesus, "what sorrow also awaits you experts in religious law! For you crush people with unbearable religious demands, and you never lift a finger to ease the burden. ⁴⁷What sorrow awaits you! For you build monuments for the prophets your own ancestors killed long ago. ⁴⁸But in fact, you stand as witnesses who agree with what your ancestors did. They killed the prophets, and you join in their crime by building the monuments! ⁴⁹This is what God in his wisdom said about you:* 'I will send prophets and apostles to them, but they will kill some and persecute the others.'

⁵⁰"As a result, this generation will be held responsible for the murder of all God's prophets from the creation of the world—⁵¹from the murder of Abel to the murder of Zechariah, who was killed between the altar and the sanctuary. Yes, it will certainly be charged against this generation.

⁵²"What sorrow awaits you experts in religious law! For you remove the key to knowledge from the people. You don't enter the Kingdom yourselves, and you prevent others from entering."

⁵³As Jesus was leaving, the teachers of religious law and the Pharisees became hostile and tried to provoke him with many questions. ⁵⁴They wanted to trap him into saying something they could use against him.

A Warning against Hypocrisy

12 Meanwhile, the crowds grew until thousands were milling about and stepping on each other. Jesus turned first to his disciples and warned them, "Beware of the yeast of the Pharisees—their hypocrisy. ²The time is coming when everything that is covered up will be revealed, and all that is secret will be made known to all. ³Whatever you have said in the dark will be heard in the light, and what you have whispered behind closed doors will be shouted from the housetops for all to hear!

⁴"Dear friends, don't be afraid of those who want to kill your body; they cannot do any more to you after that. ⁵But I'll tell you whom to fear. Fear God, who has the power to kill you and then throw you into hell.* Yes, he's the one to fear.

⁶"What is the price of five sparrows—two copper coins*? Yet God does not forget a single one of them. ⁷And the very hairs on your head are all numbered. So don't be afraid; you are more valuable to God than a whole flock of sparrows.

⁸"I tell you the truth, everyone who acknowledges me publicly here on earth, the Son of Man* will also acknowledge in the presence of God's angels. ⁹But anyone who denies me here on earth will be denied before God's angels. ¹⁰Anyone who speaks against the Son of Man can be forgiven, but anyone who blasphemes the Holy Spirit will not be forgiven.

¹¹"And when you are brought to trial in the synagogues and before rulers and authorities, don't worry about how to defend yourself or what to say, ¹²for the Holy Spirit will teach you at that time what needs to be said."

Parable of the Rich Fool

¹³Then someone called from the crowd, "Teacher, please tell my brother to divide our father's estate with me."

¹⁴Jesus replied, "Friend, who made me a judge over you to decide such things as that?" ¹⁵Then he said, "Beware! Guard against every kind of greed. Life is not measured by how much you own."

¹⁶Then he told them a story: "A rich man had a fertile farm that produced fine crops. ¹⁷He said to himself, 'What should I do? I don't have room for all my crops.' ¹⁸Then he said, 'I know! I'll tear down my barns and build bigger ones. Then I'll have room enough to store all my wheat and other goods. ¹⁹And I'll sit back and say to myself, "My friend, you have enough stored away for years to come. Now take it easy! Eat, drink, and be merry!"'

²⁰"But God said to him, 'You fool! You will die this very night. Then who will get everything you worked for?'

²¹"Yes, a person is a fool to store up earthly wealth but not have a rich relationship with God."

Teaching about Money and Possessions

²²Then, turning to his disciples, Jesus said, "That is why I tell you not to worry about everyday life—whether you have enough food to eat or enough clothes to wear. ²³For life is more than food, and your body more than clothing. ²⁴Look at the ravens. They don't plant or harvest or store food in barns, for God feeds them. And you are far more valuable to him than any birds! ²⁵Can all your worries add a single moment to your life? ²⁶And if worry can't accomplish a little thing like that, what's the use of worrying over bigger things?

²⁷"Look at the lilies and how they grow. They don't work or make their clothing, yet Solomon in all his glory was not dressed as beautifully as they are. ²⁸And if God cares so wonderfully for flowers that are here today and thrown into the fire tomorrow, he will certainly care for you. Why do you have so little faith?

²⁹"And don't be concerned about what to eat and what to drink. Don't worry about such things. ³⁰These things dominate the thoughts of unbelievers

---

11:49 Greek *Therefore, the wisdom of God said.* **12:5** Greek *Gehenna.* **12:6** Greek *two assaria* [Roman coins equal to 1/16 of a denarius]. **12:8** "Son of Man" is a title Jesus used for himself.

all over the world, but your Father already knows your needs. ³¹Seek the Kingdom of God above all else, and he will give you everything you need.

³²"So don't be afraid, little flock. For it gives your Father great happiness to give you the Kingdom.

³³"Sell your possessions and give to those in need. This will store up treasure for you in heaven! And the purses of heaven never get old or develop holes. Your treasure will be safe; no thief can steal it and no moth can destroy it. ³⁴Wherever your treasure is, there the desires of your heart will also be.

Be Ready for the Lord's Coming

³⁵"Be dressed for service and keep your lamps burning, ³⁶as though you were waiting for your master to return from the wedding feast. Then you will be ready to open the door and let him in the moment he arrives and knocks. ³⁷The servants who are ready and waiting for his return will be rewarded. I tell you the truth, he himself will seat them, put on an apron, and serve them as they sit and eat! ³⁸He may come in the middle of the night or just before dawn.* But whenever he comes, he will reward the servants who are ready.

12:38 Greek *in the second or third watch.*

12:33 This is not a command to liquidate all personal possessions since elsewhere in the Bible it is assumed that believers will own property. It means recognizing that everything we have is God's and should be used to serve him and his people (see also Acts 2:44-45; 4:32-35). Believers are responsible for meeting the needs of the poor, especially in the church (Galatians 6:10). When God gives wealth, he also gives a ministry to help the unfortunate.

Come Close — SMALL: VALUED

SCRIPTURE CONNECTION: LUKE 12:1-34

People sometimes say they love us, but their actions show otherwise. This painful betrayal can leave us feeling insecure and devalued, hungering for so much more. Conversely, when someone genuinely loves us, that person speaks the truth, shows compassion, and warns of danger ahead. To feel the embrace of one who authenticates love with action is both comforting and delightful.

No one knows us more intimately than Jesus. He gave himself for us. His Spirit reveals to our hearts the truth about his love for us. Jesus waves red flags when there is danger: Resist hypocrisy, stop denying me, and steer clear of the deception that life consists of abundant possessions and achievements. These obstacles to faith prevent us from finding our riches in God. They draw us away from the God who came to save us and is coming again.

Whether we hear Jesus' words as a whisper or a shout, his commands—"don't be afraid" and "don't worry"—are unambiguous. Our Father faithfully provides what we need every day. In a culture of self-reliance, not worrying about what we will say, eat, or wear seems counterproductive. Yet, we who have "so little faith" can rest assured that our Father knows our needs and delights to give us his Kingdom.

When we peel back the layers of fear and insecurity encasing our hearts, we unearth the treasure of Jesus' ironclad guarantee: You are more valuable than a whole flock of sparrows. Trust the Savior who chose us and promises to feed us. We are more, so much more, in Jesus.

> **REFLECT** "Don't be afraid; you are more valuable to God than a whole flock of sparrows." LUKE 12:7
>
> *Lord Jesus, if I cannot do the least, please help me not worry about the rest. You nourish and satisfy. Help me remember that whoever comes to you, including me, shall never go hungry. Amen*
>
> **CONSIDER** "When we trust in God's goodness, we are fed by his faithfulness."
> JULIE ACKERMAN LINK

You'll never see a flock of sparrows grocery shopping, yet not one is forgotten.

IRENE PACE trusts the Lord Jesus Christ and believes his life-changing message of salvation. She writes about God's lessons learned through adversity; she speaks with gratitude and joy.

39 "Understand this: If a homeowner knew exactly when a burglar was coming, he would not permit his house to be broken into. 40 You also must be ready all the time, for the Son of Man will come when least expected."

41 Peter asked, "Lord, is that illustration just for us or for everyone?"

42 And the Lord replied, "A faithful, sensible servant is one to whom the master can give the responsibility of managing his other household servants and feeding them. 43 If the master returns and finds that the servant has done a good job, there will be a reward. 44 I tell you the truth, the master will put that servant in charge of all he owns. 45 But what if the servant thinks, 'My master won't be back for a while,' and he begins beating the other servants, partying, and getting drunk? 46 The master will return unannounced and unexpected, and he will cut the servant in pieces and banish him with the unfaithful.

47 "And a servant who knows what the master wants, but isn't prepared and doesn't carry out those instructions, will be severely punished. 48 But someone who does not know, and then does something wrong, will be punished only lightly. When someone has been given much, much will be required in return; and when someone has been entrusted with much, even more will be required.

Jesus Causes Division

49 "I have come to set the world on fire, and I wish it were already burning! 50 I have a terrible baptism of suffering ahead of me, and I am under a heavy burden until it is accomplished. 51 Do you think I have come to bring peace to the earth? No, I have come to divide people against each other! 52 From now on families will be split apart, three in favor of me, and two against—or two in favor and three against.

53 'Father will be divided against son
    and son against father;
mother against daughter
    and daughter against mother;
and mother-in-law against daughter-in-law
    and daughter-in-law against mother-in-law.'*"

54 Then Jesus turned to the crowd and said, "When you see clouds beginning to form in the west, you say, 'Here comes a shower.' And you are right. 55 When the south wind blows, you say, 'Today will be a scorcher.' And it is. 56 You fools! You know how to interpret the weather signs of the earth and sky, but you don't know how to interpret the present times.

57 "Why can't you decide for yourselves what is right? 58 When you are on the way to court with your accuser, try to settle the matter before you get there. Otherwise, your accuser may drag you before the judge, who will hand you over to an officer, who will throw you into prison. 59 And if that happens, you won't be free again until you have paid the very last penny.*"

A Call to Repentance

13 About this time Jesus was informed that Pilate had murdered some people from Galilee as they were offering sacrifices at the Temple. 2 "Do you think those Galileans were worse sinners than all the other people from Galilee?" Jesus asked. "Is that why they suffered? 3 Not at all! And you will perish, too, unless you repent of your sins and turn to God. 4 And what about the eighteen people who died when the tower in Siloam fell on them? Were they the worst sinners in Jerusalem? 5 No, and I tell you again that unless you repent, you will perish, too."

Parable of the Barren Fig Tree

6 Then Jesus told this story: "A man planted a fig tree in his garden and came again and again to see if there was any fruit on it, but he was always disappointed. 7 Finally, he said to his gardener, 'I've waited three years, and there hasn't been a single fig! Cut it down. It's just taking up space in the garden.'

8 "The gardener answered, 'Sir, give it one more chance. Leave it another year, and I'll give it special attention and plenty of fertilizer. 9 If we get figs next year, fine. If not, then you can cut it down.'"

Jesus Heals on the Sabbath

10 One Sabbath day as Jesus was teaching in a synagogue, 11 he saw a woman who had been crippled by an evil spirit. She had been bent double for eighteen years and was unable to stand up straight. 12 When Jesus saw her, he called her over and said, "Dear woman, you are healed of your sickness!" 13 Then he touched her, and instantly she could stand straight. How she praised God!

14 But the leader in charge of the synagogue was indignant that Jesus had healed her on the Sabbath day. "There are six days of the week for working," he said to the crowd. "Come on those days to be healed, not on the Sabbath."

12:53 Mic 7:6. 12:59 Greek *last lepton* [the smallest Jewish coin].

13:10-17 Satan had bound this woman with a physical illness, but Jesus set her free. The binding and releasing language Jesus uses here also echoes Jesus' messianic mission (4:18-19). Jesus' exorcisms and healings manifested the Kingdom of God and the defeat of Satan (see 11:20). As with the widow from Nain (7:11-17), Jesus initiated the healing in this story. He saw her and called her. This woman's body was literally bent with the oppression she was experiencing. The weight of life can bend us, physically or emotionally, and cause us to lose sight of the future. Jesus calls our names and wants to give us freedom, too.

¹⁵But the Lord replied, "You hypocrites! Each of you works on the Sabbath day! Don't you untie your ox or your donkey from its stall on the Sabbath and lead it out for water? ¹⁶This dear woman, a daughter of Abraham, has been held in bondage by Satan for eighteen years. Isn't it right that she be released, even on the Sabbath?"

¹⁷This shamed his enemies, but all the people rejoiced at the wonderful things he did.

Parable of the Mustard Seed

¹⁸Then Jesus said, "What is the Kingdom of God like? How can I illustrate it? ¹⁹It is like a tiny mustard seed that a man planted in a garden; it grows and becomes a tree, and the birds make nests in its branches."

Parable of the Yeast

²⁰He also asked, "What else is the Kingdom of God like? ²¹It is like the yeast a woman used in making bread. Even though she put only a little yeast in three measures of flour, it permeated every part of the dough."

The Narrow Door

²²Jesus went through the towns and villages, teaching as he went, always pressing on toward Jerusalem. ²³Someone asked him, "Lord, will only a few be saved?"

He replied, ²⁴"Work hard to enter the narrow door to God's Kingdom, for many will try to enter but will fail. ²⁵When the master of the house has locked the door, it will be too late. You will stand outside knocking and pleading, 'Lord, open the door for us!' But he will reply, 'I don't know you or where you come from.' ²⁶Then you will say, 'But we ate and drank with you, and you taught in our streets.' ²⁷And he will reply, 'I tell you, I don't know you or where you come from. Get away from me, all you who do evil.'

²⁸"There will be weeping and gnashing of teeth, for you will see Abraham, Isaac, Jacob, and all the prophets in the Kingdom of God, but you will be thrown out. ²⁹And people will come from all over the world—from east and west, north and south—to take their places in the Kingdom of God. ³⁰And note this: Some who seem least important now will be the greatest then, and some who are the greatest now will be least important then.*"

Jesus Grieves over Jerusalem

³¹At that time some Pharisees said to him, "Get away from here if you want to live! Herod Antipas wants to kill you!"

³²Jesus replied, "Go tell that fox that I will keep on casting out demons and healing people today and tomorrow; and the third day I will accomplish my purpose. ³³Yes, today, tomorrow, and the next day I must proceed on my way. For it wouldn't do for a prophet of God to be killed except in Jerusalem!

³⁴"O Jerusalem, Jerusalem, the city that kills the prophets and stones God's messengers! How often I have wanted to gather your children together as a hen protects her chicks beneath her wings, but you wouldn't let me. ³⁵And now, look, your house is abandoned. And you will never see me again until you say, 'Blessings on the one who comes in the name of the LORD!'*"

Jesus Heals on the Sabbath

14 One Sabbath day Jesus went to eat dinner in the home of a leader of the Pharisees, and the people were watching him closely. ²There was a man there whose arms and legs were swollen.* ³Jesus asked the Pharisees and experts in religious law, "Is it permitted in the law to heal people on the Sabbath day, or not?" ⁴When they refused to answer, Jesus touched the sick man and healed him and sent him away. ⁵Then he turned to them and said, "Which of you doesn't work on the Sabbath? If your son* or your cow falls into a pit, don't you rush to get him out?" ⁶Again they could not answer.

Jesus Teaches about Humility

⁷When Jesus noticed that all who had come to the dinner were trying to sit in the seats of honor near the head of the table, he gave them this advice: ⁸"When you are invited to a wedding feast, don't sit in the seat of honor. What if someone who is more distinguished than you has also been invited? ⁹The host will come and say, 'Give this person your seat.' Then you will be embarrassed, and you will have to take whatever seat is left at the foot of the table!

¹⁰"Instead, take the lowest place at the foot of the table. Then when your host sees you, he will come and say, 'Friend, we have a better place for you!' Then you will be honored in front of all the other guests. ¹¹For those who exalt themselves will be humbled, and those who humble themselves will be exalted."

¹²Then he turned to his host. "When you put on a luncheon or a banquet," he said, "don't invite your friends, brothers, relatives, and rich neighbors. For they will invite you back, and that will be your only reward. ¹³Instead, invite the poor, the crippled, the

---

13:30 Greek *Some are last who will be first, and some are first who will be last.* **13:35** Ps 118:26. **14:2** Or *who had dropsy.* **14:5** Some manuscripts read *donkey.*

13:15-16 Jesus accused the religious leaders of being hypocrites because they would take care of their own animals on the Sabbath but then refuse to meet the needs of a fellow human being. In an ironic wordplay, the same Greek word is translated "untie" (13:15) and "released" (13:16). The religious leaders would free their animals but not a "daughter of Abraham"—one of God's chosen people and a recipient of his favor.

lame, and the blind. ¹⁴Then at the resurrection of the righteous, God will reward you for inviting those who could not repay you."

Parable of the Great Feast

¹⁵Hearing this, a man sitting at the table with Jesus exclaimed, "What a blessing it will be to attend a banquet* in the Kingdom of God!"

¹⁶Jesus replied with this story: "A man prepared a great feast and sent out many invitations. ¹⁷When the banquet was ready, he sent his servant to tell the guests, 'Come, the banquet is ready.' ¹⁸But they all began making excuses. One said, 'I have just bought a field and must inspect it. Please excuse me.' ¹⁹Another said, 'I have just bought five pairs of oxen, and I want to try them out. Please excuse me.' ²⁰Another said, 'I just got married, so I can't come.'

²¹"The servant returned and told his master what they had said. His master was furious and said, 'Go quickly into the streets and alleys of the town and invite the poor, the crippled, the blind, and the lame.' ²²After the servant had done this, he reported, 'There is still room for more.' ²³So his master said, 'Go out into the country lanes and behind the hedges and urge anyone you find to come, so that the house will be full. ²⁴For none of those I first invited will get even the smallest taste of my banquet.'"

The Cost of Being a Disciple

²⁵A large crowd was following Jesus. He turned around and said to them, ²⁶"If you want to be my disciple, you must, by comparison, hate everyone else—your father and mother, wife and children, brothers and sisters—yes, even your own life. Otherwise, you cannot be my disciple. ²⁷And if you do not carry your own cross and follow me, you cannot be my disciple.

²⁸"But don't begin until you count the cost. For who would begin construction of a building without first calculating the cost to see if there is enough money to finish it? ²⁹Otherwise, you might complete only the foundation before running out of money, and then everyone would laugh at you. ³⁰They would say, 'There's the person who started that building and couldn't afford to finish it!'

³¹"Or what king would go to war against another king without first sitting down with his counselors to discuss whether his army of 10,000 could defeat the 20,000 soldiers marching against him? ³²And if he can't, he will send a delegation to discuss terms of peace while the enemy is still far away. ³³So you cannot become my disciple without giving up everything you own.

³⁴"Salt is good for seasoning. But if it loses its flavor, how do you make it salty again? ³⁵Flavorless salt is good neither for the soil nor for the manure pile. It is thrown away. Anyone with ears to hear should listen and understand!"

Parable of the Lost Sheep

15 Tax collectors and other notorious sinners often came to listen to Jesus teach. ²This made the Pharisees and teachers of religious law complain that he was associating with such sinful people—even eating with them!

³So Jesus told them this story: ⁴"If a man has a hundred sheep and one of them gets lost, what will he do? Won't he leave the ninety-nine others in the wilderness and go to search for the one that is lost until he finds it? ⁵And when he has found it, he will joyfully carry it home on his shoulders. ⁶When he arrives, he will call together his friends and neighbors, saying, 'Rejoice with me because I have found my lost sheep.' ⁷In the same way, there is more joy in heaven over one lost sinner who repents and returns to God than over ninety-nine others who are righteous and haven't strayed away!

Parable of the Lost Coin

⁸"Or suppose a woman has ten silver coins* and loses one. Won't she light a lamp and sweep the entire house and search carefully until she finds it? ⁹And when she finds it, she will call in her friends and neighbors and say, 'Rejoice with me because I have found my lost coin.' ¹⁰In the same way, there is joy in the presence of God's angels when even one sinner repents."

Parable of the Lost Son

¹¹To illustrate the point further, Jesus told them this story: "A man had two sons. ¹²The younger son told his father, 'I want my share of your estate now before you die.' So his father agreed to divide his wealth between his sons.

¹³"A few days later this younger son packed all his belongings and moved to a distant land, and there he wasted all his money in wild living. ¹⁴About the time his money ran out, a great famine swept over the land, and he began to starve. ¹⁵He persuaded a local farmer to hire him, and the man sent him into his fields to feed the pigs. ¹⁶The young man became so hungry that even the pods he was feeding the pigs looked good to him. But no one gave him anything.

14:15 Greek *to eat bread.* **15:8** Greek *ten drachmas.* A drachma was the equivalent of a full day's wage.

14:12-13 Jesus challenged the way people in his culture would use banquets to flaunt and elevate their status in the community. The host would invite friends of equal status and a few who were higher. These honored guests would then be expected to reciprocate, raising the first host's social position and reputation. Jesus turned this hierarchy upside down by instructing his followers to invite those who had no social status and could not reciprocate. God invites sinful human beings to dine at his banquet table of salvation.

¹⁷"When he finally came to his senses, he said to himself, 'At home even the hired servants have food enough to spare, and here I am dying of hunger! ¹⁸I will go home to my father and say, "Father, I have sinned against both heaven and you, ¹⁹and I am no longer worthy of being called your son. Please take me on as a hired servant."'

²⁰"So he returned home to his father. And while he was still a long way off, his father saw him coming. Filled with love and compassion, he ran to his

Pursuing God's Pursuit

SCRIPTURE CONNECTION: LUKE 15:1-32

The religious teachers seemed intrigued by Jesus' miracles and teachings but baffled by his association with the *others* in the crowd, those they called "sinners." Jesus' way of being with these people undermined the religious leaders' desire to avoid them.

Yet Jesus' intentional *way* of relating to those reviled by society reveals God's desire to restore all people. Being more like Jesus means developing a lifestyle of helping people know God—no matter where they come from or whether people will look down on us for associating with them. Jesus' parables in Luke 15 show us how:

1. *Notice them.* The man, vigilant about the sheep entrusted to his care, notices when just one goes missing. How might we stop and notice other people?
2. *Cultivate relentless pursuit.* The woman expends herself to find the lost coin. "Won't she light a lamp and sweep the entire house and search carefully until she finds it?" (15:8). What distractions might we need to set aside to notice who's missing?
3. *Remain close to the Father.* When the younger son leaves, no one pursues him. The older brother not only never searches for the younger, but he also takes offense at his father's pursuit when the younger son comes home. The older son's heart had grown too far removed from the father's heart. What do you need to do to stay close to the Father?
4. *Search together.* Each of these three parables closes with celebration. Friends and neighbors (and heaven!) gather to feast when the lost is found. Who are your friends that could join you in God's pursuit?

> God desperately longs for his children to come home, so let's help them find him.

God so desperately longs for his people to come home that loving God means pursuing others.

IMAGINE

What was surprising to the leaders about the way Jesus related to the people looked down on by society?

How can we invest in people God loves, whether or not they know his love yet?

"I've been gripped by the heart of the Father. Wherever I am—the park, a work meeting, our backyard—I'm forever looking for far-off brothers and sisters, ready to help them find their way home."

TRACI CROWDER is a joyful, energetic, Jesus-following wife, mom, and pastor. She serves with Stonecroft and deeply longs for every person to experience God's extraordinary in their ordinary, together in community.

son, embraced him, and kissed him. ²¹His son said to him, 'Father, I have sinned against both heaven and you, and I am no longer worthy of being called your son.*'

²²"But his father said to the servants, 'Quick! Bring the finest robe in the house and put it on him. Get a ring for his finger and sandals for his feet. ²³And kill the calf we have been fattening. We must celebrate with a feast, ²⁴for this son of mine was dead and has now returned to life. He was lost, but now he is found.' So the party began.

²⁵"Meanwhile, the older son was in the fields working. When he returned home, he heard music and dancing in the house, ²⁶and he asked one of the servants what was going on. ²⁷'Your brother is back,' he was told, 'and your father has killed the fattened calf. We are celebrating because of his safe return.'

²⁸"The older brother was angry and wouldn't go in. His father came out and begged him, ²⁹but he replied, 'All these years I've slaved for you and never once refused to do a single thing you told me to. And in all that time you never gave me even one young goat for a feast with my friends. ³⁰Yet when this son of yours comes back after squandering your money on prostitutes, you celebrate by killing the fattened calf!'

³¹"His father said to him, 'Look, dear son, you have always stayed by me, and everything I have is yours. ³²We had to celebrate this happy day. For your brother was dead and has come back to life! He was lost, but now he is found!'"

Parable of the Shrewd Manager

16 Jesus told this story to his disciples: "There was a certain rich man who had a manager handling his affairs. One day a report came that the manager was wasting his employer's money. ²So the employer called him in and said, 'What's this I hear about you? Get your report in order, because you are going to be fired.'

³"The manager thought to himself, 'Now what? My boss has fired me. I don't have the strength to dig ditches, and I'm too proud to beg. ⁴Ah, I know how to ensure that I'll have plenty of friends who will give me a home when I am fired.'

⁵"So he invited each person who owed money to his employer to come and discuss the situation. He asked the first one, 'How much do you owe him?' ⁶The man replied, 'I owe him 800 gallons of olive oil.' So the manager told him, 'Take the bill and quickly change it to 400 gallons.*'

⁷"'And how much do you owe my employer?' he asked the next man. 'I owe him 1,000 bushels of wheat,' was the reply. 'Here,' the manager said, 'take the bill and change it to 800 bushels.*'

⁸"The rich man had to admire the dishonest rascal for being so shrewd. And it is true that the children of this world are more shrewd in dealing with the world around them than are the children of the light. ⁹Here's the lesson: Use your worldly resources to benefit others and make friends. Then, when your possessions are gone, they will welcome you to an eternal home.*

¹⁰"If you are faithful in little things, you will be faithful in large ones. But if you are dishonest in little things, you won't be honest with greater responsibilities. ¹¹And if you are untrustworthy about worldly wealth, who will trust you with the true riches of heaven? ¹²And if you are not faithful with other people's things, why should you be trusted with things of your own?

¹³"No one can serve two masters. For you will hate one and love the other; you will be devoted to one and despise the other. You cannot serve God and be enslaved to money."

¹⁴The Pharisees, who dearly loved their money, heard all this and scoffed at him. ¹⁵Then he said to them, "You like to appear righteous in public, but God knows your hearts. What this world honors is detestable in the sight of God.

¹⁶"Until John the Baptist, the law of Moses and the messages of the prophets were your guides. But now the Good News of the Kingdom of God is preached, and everyone is eager to get in.* ¹⁷But that doesn't mean that the law has lost its force. It is easier for heaven and earth to disappear than for the smallest point of God's law to be overturned.

¹⁸"For example, a man who divorces his wife and marries someone else commits adultery. And anyone who marries a woman divorced from her husband commits adultery."

Parable of the Rich Man and Lazarus

¹⁹Jesus said, "There was a certain rich man who was splendidly clothed in purple and fine linen and who lived each day in luxury. ²⁰At his gate lay a poor man named Lazarus who was covered with sores. ²¹As Lazarus lay there longing for scraps from the rich man's table, the dogs would come and lick his open sores.

²²"Finally, the poor man died and was carried by the angels to sit beside Abraham at the heavenly banquet.* The rich man also died and was buried,

---

15:21 Some manuscripts add *Please take me on as a hired servant.* **16:6** Greek *100 baths . . . 50 [baths].* **16:7** Greek *100 korous . . . 80 [korous].* **16:9** Or *you will be welcomed into eternal homes.* **16:16** Or *everyone is urged to enter in.* **16:22** Greek *to Abraham's bosom.*

16:18 Set in a patriarchal society, this passage and Deuteronomy 24:1-4 assume a husband initiating and acquiring a divorce, even though both passages deal with the *aftermath* of a cultural practice rather than advocating for it. The rabbis of Jesus' day debated what grounds Jewish law considered legitimate. The hard-line school of thought allowed a man to divorce his wife only because of unfaithfulness, but the permissive school of thought allowed divorce for trivial reasons. Jesus' comments protected women from being divorced casually, and the underlying assumption in Jewish divorce law was simple: Legitimate divorces permitted remarriage.

[23] and he went to the place of the dead.* There, in torment, he saw Abraham in the far distance with Lazarus at his side.

[24] "The rich man shouted, 'Father Abraham, have some pity! Send Lazarus over here to dip the tip of his finger in water and cool my tongue. I am in anguish in these flames.'

[25] "But Abraham said to him, 'Son, remember that during your lifetime you had everything you wanted, and Lazarus had nothing. So now he is here being comforted, and you are in anguish. [26] And besides, there is a great chasm separating us. No one can cross over to you from here, and no one can cross over to us from there.'

[27] "Then the rich man said, 'Please, Father Abraham, at least send him to my father's home. [28] For I have five brothers, and I want him to warn them so they don't end up in this place of torment.'

[29] "But Abraham said, 'Moses and the prophets have warned them. Your brothers can read what they wrote.'

[30] "The rich man replied, 'No, Father Abraham! But if someone is sent to them from the dead, then they will repent of their sins and turn to God.'

[31] "But Abraham said, 'If they won't listen to Moses and the prophets, they won't be persuaded even if someone rises from the dead.'"

Teachings about Forgiveness and Faith

17 One day Jesus said to his disciples, "There will always be temptations to sin, but what sorrow awaits the person who does the tempting! [2] It would be better to be thrown into the sea with a millstone hung around your neck than to cause one of these little ones to fall into sin. [3] So watch yourselves!

"If another believer* sins, rebuke that person; then if there is repentance, forgive. [4] Even if that person wrongs you seven times a day and each time turns again and asks forgiveness, you must forgive."

[5] The apostles said to the Lord, "Show us how to increase our faith."

[6] The Lord answered, "If you had faith even as small as a mustard seed, you could say to this mulberry tree, 'May you be uprooted and be planted in the sea,' and it would obey you!

[7] "When a servant comes in from plowing or taking care of sheep, does his master say, 'Come in and eat with me'? [8] No, he says, 'Prepare my meal, put on your apron, and serve me while I eat. Then you can eat later.' [9] And does the master thank the servant for doing what he was told to do? Of course not. [10] In the same way, when you obey me you should say, 'We are unworthy servants who have simply done our duty.'"

Ten Healed of Leprosy

[11] As Jesus continued on toward Jerusalem, he reached the border between Galilee and Samaria. [12] As he entered a village there, ten men with leprosy stood at a distance, [13] crying out, "Jesus, Master, have mercy on us!"

[14] He looked at them and said, "Go show yourselves to the priests."* And as they went, they were cleansed of their leprosy.

[15] One of them, when he saw that he was healed, came back to Jesus, shouting, "Praise God!" [16] He fell to the ground at Jesus' feet, thanking him for what he had done. This man was a Samaritan.

[17] Jesus asked, "Didn't I heal ten men? Where are the other nine? [18] Has no one returned to give glory to God except this foreigner?" [19] And Jesus said to the man, "Stand up and go. Your faith has healed you.*"

The Coming of the Kingdom

[20] One day the Pharisees asked Jesus, "When will the Kingdom of God come?"

Jesus replied, "The Kingdom of God can't be detected by visible signs.* [21] You won't be able to say, 'Here it is!' or 'It's over there!' For the Kingdom of God is already among you.*"

[22] Then he said to his disciples, "The time is coming when you will long to see the day when the Son of Man returns,* but you won't see it. [23] People will tell you, 'Look, there is the Son of Man,' or 'Here he is,' but don't go out and follow them. [24] For as the lightning flashes and lights up the sky from one end to the other, so it will be on the day* when the Son of Man comes. [25] But first the Son of Man must suffer terribly* and be rejected by this generation.

[26] "When the Son of Man returns, it will be like it was in Noah's day. [27] In those days, the people enjoyed banquets and parties and weddings right up to the time Noah entered his boat and the flood came and destroyed them all.

[28] "And the world will be as it was in the days of Lot. People went about their daily business—eating and drinking, buying and selling, farming and building—[29] until the morning Lot left Sodom. Then fire and burning sulfur rained down from heaven and destroyed them all. [30] Yes, it will be 'business as usual' right up to the day when the Son of Man is revealed. [31] On that day a person out on the deck of a roof must not go

---

16:23 Greek *to Hades.* **17:3** Greek *If your brother.* **17:14** See Lev 14:2-32. **17:19** Or *Your faith has saved you.* **17:20** Or *by your speculations.* **17:21** Or *is within you,* or *is in your grasp.* **17:22** Or *long for even one day with the Son of Man.* "Son of Man" is a title Jesus used for himself. **17:24** Some manuscripts do not include *on the day.* **17:25** Or *suffer many things.*

17:11-19 In first-century Palestine, Jews avoided any contact with Samaritans. To Jews, Samaritans were the *foreigners* (17:18, literally "other race"). Similar suffering, however, had bonded these ten people with leprosy of different races together. But the "other," a Samaritan, was the only one who returned and thanked Jesus. All people, of all colors and nations, are welcome to come and taste the goodness of this Jewish Messiah, who is the Savior of the whole human race.

down into the house to pack. A person out in the field must not return home. ³²Remember what happened to Lot's wife! ³³If you cling to your life, you will lose it, and if you let your life go, you will save it. ³⁴That night two people will be asleep in one bed; one will be taken, the other left. ³⁵Two women will be grinding flour together at the mill; one will be taken, the other left.*"

³⁷"Where will this happen, Lord?"* the disciples asked.

Jesus replied, "Just as the gathering of vultures shows there is a carcass nearby, so these signs indicate that the end is near."*

Parable of the Persistent Widow

18 One day Jesus told his disciples a story to show that they should always pray and never give up. ²"There was a judge in a certain city," he said, "who neither feared God nor cared about

---

17:35 Some manuscripts add verse 36, *Two men will be working in the field; one will be taken, the other left.* Compare Matt 24:40. **17:37a** Greek *"Where, Lord?"* **17:37b** Greek *"Wherever the carcass is, the vultures gather."*

18:1-8 During this time period in Palestine, a Jewish woman could not serve as a witness in court, and a widow had no intrinsic social standing in her community. Therefore, a wronged widow who had no relative to bring her case to court was one of the most marginalized in society. When using this widow's petition for justice as an illustration, Jesus invites his followers, who live in an unjust world, to persevere in begging for God's just judgment. If even an unjust human judge eventually paid attention to persistence, then how much more will God, who is the all-powerful just judge, respond to our plea?

---

⑧ Come Close FORGIVING? FOREVER

SCRIPTURE CONNECTION: LUKE 17:3-10

The disciples wanted to know Jesus' response to the questions of everyday life.

Here, in Luke, Jesus astonished the disciples, saying to forgive even seven times a day. Knowing this is beyond them, they pleaded, "increase our faith." And Jesus taught how to grow our faith by obeying him (17:5-10).

In Matthew 18:15-35, while teaching about how to correct and forgive fellow believers, Jesus taught his disciples that they were to forgive others because they had been greatly forgiven by God. Jesus also gave another forgiveness-secret: the heart. Peter asked specifically about forgiveness, making it personal: "Lord, how often should I forgive someone who sins against me?"

Without stopping to hear Jesus' answer, Peter provided one: "Seven times?" (Matthew 18:21). This seems like a reasonable number. Jesus took Peter's number and multiplied it by seventy. Wow! How much can one person take?

Jesus followed with a parable about a servant who had been forgiven and chose not to forgive another who owed him money—and he was punished. The final judgment is God's: "That's what my heavenly Father will do to you if you refuse to forgive your brothers and sisters from your heart" (Matthew 18:35).

Jesus added, "forgive . . . from your heart." Peter and the disciples received a gift, God's teaching about the root of forgiveness: the heart.

A foundation stone of the Christian faith is forgiveness. God forgives us, so we forgive others—a never-ending cycle for all to experience freely. To forgive, we also need a growing faith and a growing heart.

> **REFLECT** "Even if that person wrongs you seven times a day and each time turns again and asks forgiveness, you must forgive." LUKE 17:4
>
> *Lord, please increase my faith so that I can forgive as you've forgiven me. Amen.*
>
> **CONSIDER** "We must develop and maintain the capacity to forgive. He who is devoid of the power to forgive is devoid of the power to love." DR. MARTIN LUTHER KING, JR.

Forever forgiveness takes a long time without faith and a heart of love.

VIRGINIA WARD, MA, DMin, serves as the Dean of the Boston Campus for Gordon-Conwell Theological Seminary. She is a wife, a mother, and an associate pastor at Abundant Life Church in Cambridge, MA.

people. ³A widow of that city came to him repeatedly, saying, 'Give me justice in this dispute with my enemy.' ⁴The judge ignored her for a while, but finally he said to himself, 'I don't fear God or care about people, ⁵but this woman is driving me crazy. I'm going to see that she gets justice, because she is wearing me out with her constant requests!'"

⁶Then the Lord said, "Learn a lesson from this unjust judge. ⁷Even he rendered a just decision in the end. So don't you think God will surely give justice to his chosen people who cry out to him day and night? Will he keep putting them off? ⁸I tell you, he will grant justice to them quickly! But when the Son of Man* returns, how many will he find on the earth who have faith?"

Parable of the Pharisee and Tax Collector

⁹Then Jesus told this story to some who had great confidence in their own righteousness and scorned everyone else: ¹⁰"Two men went to the Temple to pray. One was a Pharisee, and the other was a despised tax collector. ¹¹The Pharisee stood by himself and prayed this prayer*: 'I thank you, God, that I am not like other people—cheaters, sinners, adulterers. I'm certainly not like that tax collector! ¹²I fast twice a week, and I give you a tenth of my income.'

¹³"But the tax collector stood at a distance and dared not even lift his eyes to heaven as he prayed. Instead, he beat his chest in sorrow, saying, 'O God, be merciful to me, for I am a sinner.' ¹⁴I tell you, this sinner, not the Pharisee, returned home justified before God. For those who exalt themselves will be humbled, and those who humble themselves will be exalted."

Jesus Blesses the Children

¹⁵One day some parents brought their little children to Jesus so he could touch and bless them. But when the disciples saw this, they scolded the parents for bothering him.

¹⁶Then Jesus called for the children and said to the disciples, "Let the children come to me. Don't stop them! For the Kingdom of God belongs to those who are like these children. ¹⁷I tell you the truth, anyone who doesn't receive the Kingdom of God like a child will never enter it."

The Rich Man

¹⁸Once a religious leader asked Jesus this question: "Good Teacher, what should I do to inherit eternal life?"

¹⁹"Why do you call me good?" Jesus asked him. "Only God is truly good. ²⁰But to answer your question, you know the commandments: 'You must not commit adultery. You must not murder. You must not steal. You must not testify falsely. Honor your father and mother.'*"

²¹The man replied, "I've obeyed all these commandments since I was young."

²²When Jesus heard his answer, he said, "There is still one thing you haven't done. Sell all your possessions and give the money to the poor, and you will have treasure in heaven. Then come, follow me."

²³But when the man heard this he became very sad, for he was very rich.

²⁴When Jesus saw this,* he said, "How hard it is for the rich to enter the Kingdom of God! ²⁵In fact, it is easier for a camel to go through the eye of a needle than for a rich person to enter the Kingdom of God!"

²⁶Those who heard this said, "Then who in the world can be saved?"

²⁷He replied, "What is impossible for people is possible with God."

²⁸Peter said, "We've left our homes to follow you."

²⁹"Yes," Jesus replied, "and I assure you that everyone who has given up house or wife or brothers or parents or children, for the sake of the Kingdom of God, ³⁰will be repaid many times over in this life, and will have eternal life in the world to come."

Jesus Again Predicts His Death

³¹Taking the twelve disciples aside, Jesus said, "Listen, we're going up to Jerusalem, where all the predictions of the prophets concerning the Son of Man will come true. ³²He will be handed over to the Romans,* and he will be mocked, treated shamefully, and spit upon. ³³They will flog him with a whip and kill him, but on the third day he will rise again."

³⁴But they didn't understand any of this. The significance of his words was hidden from them, and they failed to grasp what he was talking about.

Jesus Heals a Blind Beggar

³⁵As Jesus approached Jericho, a blind beggar was sitting beside the road. ³⁶When he heard the noise of a crowd going past, he asked what was happening. ³⁷They told him that Jesus the Nazarene* was going by. ³⁸So he began shouting, "Jesus, Son of David, have mercy on me!"

³⁹"Be quiet!" the people in front yelled at him.

18:8 "Son of Man" is a title Jesus used for himself.   **18:11** Some manuscripts read *stood and prayed this prayer to himself.*   **18:20** Exod 20:12-16; Deut 5:16-20.   **18:24** Some manuscripts read *When Jesus saw how sad the man was.*   **18:32** Greek *the Gentiles.*   **18:37** Or *Jesus of Nazareth.*

18:3 God is especially concerned for the most vulnerable members of society—in this ancient context, the widows, orphans, foreigners, and those with limited resources or who had been cheated of fair wages—and he has promised judgment against those who oppress them (Deuteronomy 24:17; 27:19; Proverbs 14:31; Isaiah 10:1-2; Jeremiah 22:3; Amos 5:10-13; Malachi 3:5; James 5:4-6). The widow was in the right in this dispute—she was not asking for special favors.

But he only shouted louder, "Son of David, have mercy on me!"

⁴⁰When Jesus heard him, he stopped and ordered that the man be brought to him. As the man came near, Jesus asked him, ⁴¹"What do you want me to do for you?"

"Lord," he said, "I want to see!"

⁴²And Jesus said, "All right, receive your sight! Your faith has healed you." ⁴³Instantly the man could see, and he followed Jesus, praising God. And all who saw it praised God, too.

Jesus and Zacchaeus

19 Jesus entered Jericho and made his way through the town. ²There was a man there named Zacchaeus. He was the chief tax collector in the region, and he had become very rich. ³He tried to get a look at Jesus, but he was too short to see over the crowd. ⁴So he ran ahead and climbed a sycamore-fig tree beside the road, for Jesus was going to pass that way.

⁵When Jesus came by, he looked up at Zacchaeus and called him by name. "Zacchaeus!" he said. "Quick, come down! I must be a guest in your home today."

⁶Zacchaeus quickly climbed down and took Jesus to his house in great excitement and joy. ⁷But the people were displeased. "He has gone to be the guest of a notorious sinner," they grumbled.

⁸Meanwhile, Zacchaeus stood before the Lord and said, "I will give half my wealth to the poor, Lord, and if I have cheated people on their taxes, I will give them back four times as much!"

⁹Jesus responded, "Salvation has come to this home today, for this man has shown himself to be a true son of Abraham. ¹⁰For the Son of Man* came to seek and save those who are lost."

Parable of the Ten Servants

¹¹The crowd was listening to everything Jesus said. And because he was nearing Jerusalem, he told them a story to correct the impression that the Kingdom of God would begin right away. ¹²He said, "A nobleman was called away to a distant empire to be crowned king and then return. ¹³Before he left, he called together ten of his servants and divided among them ten pounds of silver,* saying, 'Invest this for me while I am gone.' ¹⁴But his people hated him and sent a delegation after him to say, 'We do not want him to be our king.'

¹⁵"After he was crowned king, he returned and called in the servants to whom he had given the money. He wanted to find out what their profits were. ¹⁶The first servant reported, 'Master, I invested your money and made ten times the original amount!'

¹⁷"'Well done!' the king exclaimed. 'You are a good servant. You have been faithful with the little I entrusted to you, so you will be governor of ten cities as your reward.'

¹⁸"The next servant reported, 'Master, I invested your money and made five times the original amount.'

¹⁹"'Well done!' the king said. 'You will be governor over five cities.'

²⁰"But the third servant brought back only the original amount of money and said, 'Master, I hid your money and kept it safe. ²¹I was afraid because you are a hard man to deal with, taking what isn't yours and harvesting crops you didn't plant.'

²²"'You wicked servant!' the king roared. 'Your own words condemn you. If you knew that I'm a hard man who takes what isn't mine and harvests crops I didn't plant, ²³why didn't you deposit my money in the bank? At least I could have gotten some interest on it.'

²⁴"Then, turning to the others standing nearby, the king ordered, 'Take the money from this servant, and give it to the one who has ten pounds.'

²⁵"'But, master,' they said, 'he already has ten pounds!'

²⁶"'Yes,' the king replied, 'and to those who use well what they are given, even more will be given. But from those who do nothing, even what little they have will be taken away. ²⁷And as for these enemies of mine who didn't want me to be their king—bring them in and execute them right here in front of me.'"

Jesus' Triumphant Entry

²⁸After telling this story, Jesus went on toward Jerusalem, walking ahead of his disciples. ²⁹As he came to the towns of Bethphage and Bethany on the Mount of Olives, he sent two disciples ahead. ³⁰"Go into that village over there," he told them. "As you enter it, you will see a young donkey tied there that no one has ever ridden. Untie it and bring it here. ³¹If anyone asks, 'Why are you untying that colt?' just say, 'The Lord needs it.'"

³²So they went and found the colt, just as Jesus had said. ³³And sure enough, as they were untying it, the owners asked them, "Why are you untying that colt?"

³⁴And the disciples simply replied, "The Lord needs it." ³⁵So they brought the colt to Jesus and threw their garments over it for him to ride on.

³⁶As he rode along, the crowds spread out their garments on the road ahead of him. ³⁷When he reached the place where the road started down the Mount of Olives, all of his followers began to shout and sing as they walked along, praising God for all the wonderful miracles they had seen.

³⁸ "Blessings on the King who comes in the name
    of the LORD!
  Peace in heaven, and glory in highest
    heaven!"*

19:10 "Son of Man" is a title Jesus used for himself.   **19:13** Greek *ten minas;* one mina was worth about three months' wages.   **19:38** Pss 118:26; 148:1.

⁶⁹But some of the Pharisees among the crowd said, "Teacher, rebuke your followers for saying things like that!"

⁴⁰He replied, "If they kept quiet, the stones along the road would burst into cheers!"

Jesus Weeps over Jerusalem

⁴¹But as he came closer to Jerusalem and saw the city ahead, he began to weep. ⁴²"How I wish today that you of all people would understand the way to peace. But now it is too late, and peace is hidden from your eyes. ⁴³Before long your enemies will build ramparts against your walls and encircle you and close in on you from every side. ⁴⁴They will crush you into the ground, and your children with you. Your enemies will not leave a single stone in place, because you did not recognize it when God visited you.*"

Jesus Clears the Temple

⁴⁵Then Jesus entered the Temple and began to drive out the people selling animals for sacrifices. ⁴⁶He said to them, "The Scriptures declare, 'My Temple will be a house of prayer,' but you have turned it into a den of thieves."*

⁴⁷After that, he taught daily in the Temple, but the leading priests, the teachers of religious law, and the other leaders of the people began planning how to kill him. ⁴⁸But they could think of nothing, because all the people hung on every word he said.

The Authority of Jesus Challenged

20 One day as Jesus was teaching the people and preaching the Good News in the Temple, the leading priests, the teachers of religious law, and the elders came up to him. ²They demanded, "By what authority are you doing all these things? Who gave you the right?"

³"Let me ask you a question first," he replied. ⁴"Did John's authority to baptize come from heaven, or was it merely human?"

⁵They talked it over among themselves. "If we say it was from heaven, he will ask why we didn't believe John. ⁶But if we say it was merely human, the people will stone us because they are convinced John was a prophet." ⁷So they finally replied that they didn't know.

⁸And Jesus responded, "Then I won't tell you by what authority I do these things."

Parable of the Evil Farmers

⁹Now Jesus turned to the people again and told them this story: "A man planted a vineyard, leased it to tenant farmers, and moved to another country to live for several years. ¹⁰At the time of the grape harvest, he sent one of his servants to collect his share of the crop. But the farmers attacked the servant, beat him up, and sent him back empty-handed. ¹¹So the owner sent another servant, but they also insulted him, beat him up, and sent him away empty-handed. ¹²A third man was sent, and they wounded him and chased him away.

¹³"'What will I do?' the owner asked himself. 'I know! I'll send my cherished son. Surely they will respect him.'

¹⁴"But when the tenant farmers saw his son, they said to each other, 'Here comes the heir to this estate. Let's kill him and get the estate for ourselves!' ¹⁵So they dragged him out of the vineyard and murdered him.

"What do you suppose the owner of the vineyard will do to them?" Jesus asked. ¹⁶"I'll tell you—he will come and kill those farmers and lease the vineyard to others."

"How terrible that such a thing should ever happen," his listeners protested.

¹⁷Jesus looked at them and said, "Then what does this Scripture mean?

'The stone that the builders rejected
has now become the cornerstone.'*

¹⁸Everyone who stumbles over that stone will be broken to pieces, and it will crush anyone it falls on."

¹⁹The teachers of religious law and the leading priests wanted to arrest Jesus immediately because they realized he was telling the story against them—they were the wicked farmers. But they were afraid of the people's reaction.

Taxes for Caesar

²⁰Watching for their opportunity, the leaders sent spies pretending to be honest men. They tried to get Jesus to say something that could be reported to the Roman governor so he would arrest Jesus. ²¹"Teacher," they said, "we know that you speak and teach what is right and are not influenced by what others think. You teach the way of God truthfully. ²²Now tell us—is it right for us to pay taxes to Caesar or not?"

²³He saw through their trickery and said, ²⁴"Show me a Roman coin.* Whose picture and title are stamped on it?"

"Caesar's," they replied.

²⁵"Well then," he said, "give to Caesar what belongs to Caesar, and give to God what belongs to God."

²⁶So they failed to trap him by what he said in front of the people. Instead, they were amazed by his answer, and they became silent.

Discussion about Resurrection

²⁷Then Jesus was approached by some Sadducees—religious leaders who say there is no resurrection from the dead. ²⁸They posed this question: "Teacher, Moses gave us a law that if a man dies, leaving a wife but no children, his brother should marry

---

19:44 Greek *did not recognize the time of your visitation*, a reference to the Messiah's coming.   **19:46** Isa 56:7; Jer 7:11.
20:17 Ps 118:22.   **20:24** Greek *a denarius.*

the widow and have a child who will carry on the brother's name.* ²⁹Well, suppose there were seven brothers. The oldest one married and then died without children. ³⁰So the second brother married the widow, but he also died. ³¹Then the third brother married her. This continued with all seven of them, who died without children. ³²Finally, the woman also died. ³³So tell us, whose wife will she be in the resurrection? For all seven were married to her!"

³⁴Jesus replied, "Marriage is for people here on earth. ³⁵But in the age to come, those worthy of being raised from the dead will neither marry nor be given in marriage. ³⁶And they will never die again. In this respect they will be like angels. They are children of God and children of the resurrection.

³⁷"But now, as to whether the dead will be raised—even Moses proved this when he wrote about the burning bush. Long after Abraham, Isaac, and Jacob had died, he referred to the Lord* as 'the God of Abraham, the God of Isaac, and the God of Jacob.'* ³⁸So he is the God of the living, not the dead, for they are all alive to him."

³⁹"Well said, Teacher!" remarked some of the teachers of religious law who were standing there. ⁴⁰And then no one dared to ask him any more questions.

Whose Son Is the Messiah?

⁴¹Then Jesus presented them with a question. "Why is it," he asked, "that the Messiah is said to be the son of David? ⁴²For David himself wrote in the book of Psalms:

'The LORD said to my Lord,
   Sit in the place of honor at my right hand
⁴³ until I humble your enemies,
   making them a footstool under your feet.'*

⁴⁴Since David called the Messiah 'Lord,' how can the Messiah be his son?"

⁴⁵Then, with the crowds listening, he turned to his disciples and said, ⁴⁶"Beware of these teachers of religious law! For they like to parade around in flowing robes and love to receive respectful greetings as they walk in the marketplaces. And how they love the seats of honor in the synagogues and the head table at banquets. ⁴⁷Yet they shamelessly cheat widows out of their property and then pretend to be pious by making long prayers in public. Because of this, they will be severely punished."

The Widow's Offering

21 While Jesus was in the Temple, he watched the rich people dropping their gifts in the collection box. ²Then a poor widow came by and dropped in two small coins.*

³"I tell you the truth," Jesus said, "this poor widow has given more than all the rest of them. ⁴For they have given a tiny part of their surplus, but she, poor as she is, has given everything she has."

Jesus Speaks about the Future

⁵Some of his disciples began talking about the majestic stonework of the Temple and the memorial decorations on the walls. But Jesus said, ⁶"The time is coming when all these things will be completely demolished. Not one stone will be left on top of another!"

⁷"Teacher," they asked, "when will all this happen? What sign will show us that these things are about to take place?"

⁸He replied, "Don't let anyone mislead you, for many will come in my name, claiming, 'I am the Messiah,'* and saying, 'The time has come!' But don't believe them. ⁹And when you hear of wars and insurrections, don't panic. Yes, these things must take place first, but the end won't follow immediately."

¹⁰Then he added, "Nation will go to war against nation, and kingdom against kingdom. ¹¹There will be great earthquakes, and there will be famines and plagues in many lands, and there will be terrifying things and great miraculous signs from heaven.

¹²"But before all this occurs, there will be a time of great persecution. You will be dragged into synagogues and prisons, and you will stand trial before kings and governors because you are my followers. ¹³But this will be your opportunity to tell them about me.* ¹⁴So don't worry in advance about how to answer the charges against you, ¹⁵for I will give you the right words and such wisdom that none of your opponents will be able to reply or refute you! ¹⁶Even those closest to you—your parents, brothers,

---

20:28 See Deut 25:5-6. **20:37a** Greek *when he wrote about the bush. He referred to the Lord.* **20:37b** Exod 3:6. **20:42-43** Ps 110:1. **21:2** Greek *two lepta* [the smallest of Jewish coins]. **21:8** Greek *claiming, 'I am.'* **21:13** Or *This will be your testimony against them.*

20:35 Jesus emphasized with this teaching that marriage is an institution while we live on earth, not for the resurrection. While we may feel sad thinking about how our relationships now won't be the same in the age to come, we can have peace knowing that our union now is only a shadow of the kind of union we will share with God and with one another in God for all eternity. **20:47** That the teachers of religious law would "shamelessly cheat widows out of their property" might mean exploiting widows' property over which they were appointed guardians. It could also mean coercing widows to give money beyond their means. Widows were the most vulnerable members of ancient society, and God had special concern for them. He would judge those who exploited them (Exodus 22:22; Deuteronomy 10:18; 27:19). **21:1-4** Jesus contrasted the sacrificial offering of the poor widow with the greed and hypocrisy of the rich people, including the teachers of religious law (20:45-47). Together, two small coins (two lepta) were worth only about 1/64 of a denarius, which was the standard day's wage for a laborer. The amount given by the widow, or any giver, counts for less than the intentions of the giver.

relatives, and friends—will betray you. They will even kill some of you. ¹⁷And everyone will hate you because you are my followers.* ¹⁸But not a hair of your head will perish! ¹⁹By standing firm, you will win your souls.

²⁰"And when you see Jerusalem surrounded by armies, then you will know that the time of its destruction has arrived. ²¹Then those in Judea must flee to the hills. Those in Jerusalem must get out, and those out in the country should not return to the city. ²²For those will be days of God's vengeance, and the prophetic words of the Scriptures will be fulfilled. ²³How terrible it will be for pregnant women and for nursing mothers in those days. For there will be disaster in the land and great anger against this people. ²⁴They will be killed by the sword or sent away as captives to all the nations of the world. And Jerusalem will be trampled down by the Gentiles until the period of the Gentiles comes to an end.

²⁵"And there will be strange signs in the sun, moon, and stars. And here on earth the nations will be in turmoil, perplexed by the roaring seas and strange tides. ²⁶People will be terrified at what they see coming upon the earth, for the powers in the heavens will be shaken. ²⁷Then everyone will see the Son of Man* coming on a cloud with power and great glory.* ²⁸So when all these things begin to happen, stand and look up, for your salvation is near!"

²⁹Then he gave them this illustration: "Notice the fig tree, or any other tree. ³⁰When the leaves come out, you know without being told that summer is near. ³¹In the same way, when you see all these things taking place, you can know that the Kingdom of God is near. ³²I tell you the truth, this generation will not pass from the scene until all these things have taken place. ³³Heaven and earth will disappear, but my words will never disappear.

³⁴"Watch out! Don't let your hearts be dulled by carousing and drunkenness, and by the worries of this life. Don't let that day catch you unaware, ³⁵like a trap. For that day will come upon everyone living on the earth. ³⁶Keep alert at all times. And pray that you might be strong enough to escape these coming horrors and stand before the Son of Man."

³⁷Every day Jesus went to the Temple to teach, and each evening he returned to spend the night on the Mount of Olives. ³⁸The crowds gathered at the Temple early each morning to hear him.

Judas Agrees to Betray Jesus

22 The Festival of Unleavened Bread, which is also called Passover, was approaching. ²The leading priests and teachers of religious law were plotting how to kill Jesus, but they were afraid of the people's reaction.

³Then Satan entered into Judas Iscariot, who was one of the twelve disciples, ⁴and he went to the leading priests and captains of the Temple guard to discuss the best way to betray Jesus to them. ⁵They were delighted, and they promised to give him money. ⁶So he agreed and began looking for an opportunity to betray Jesus so they could arrest him when the crowds weren't around.

The Last Supper

⁷Now the Festival of Unleavened Bread arrived, when the Passover lamb is sacrificed. ⁸Jesus sent Peter and John ahead and said, "Go and prepare the Passover meal, so we can eat it together."

⁹"Where do you want us to prepare it?" they asked him.

¹⁰He replied, "As soon as you enter Jerusalem, a man carrying a pitcher of water will meet you. Follow him. At the house he enters, ¹¹say to the owner, 'The Teacher asks: Where is the guest room where I can eat the Passover meal with my disciples?' ¹²He will take you upstairs to a large room that is already set up. That is where you should prepare our meal." ¹³They went off to the city and found everything just as Jesus had said, and they prepared the Passover meal there.

¹⁴When the time came, Jesus and the apostles sat down together at the table.* ¹⁵Jesus said, "I have been very eager to eat this Passover meal with you before my suffering begins. ¹⁶For I tell you now that I won't eat this meal again until its meaning is fulfilled in the Kingdom of God."

¹⁷Then he took a cup of wine and gave thanks to God for it. Then he said, "Take this and share it among yourselves. ¹⁸For I will not drink wine again until the Kingdom of God has come."

¹⁹He took some bread and gave thanks to God for it. Then he broke it in pieces and gave it to the disciples, saying, "This is my body, which is given for you. Do this in remembrance of me."

²⁰After supper he took another cup of wine and said, "This cup is the new covenant between God and his people—an agreement confirmed with my blood, which is poured out as a sacrifice for you.*

²¹"But here at this table, sitting among us as a friend, is the man who will betray me. ²²For it has been determined that the Son of Man* must die. But what sorrow awaits the one who betrays him." ²³The disciples began to ask each other which of them would ever do such a thing.

²⁴Then they began to argue among themselves about who would be the greatest among them. ²⁵Jesus told them, "In this world the kings and great men lord it over their people, yet they are called 'friends of the people.' ²⁶But among you it will be different. Those who are the greatest among you should

---

21:17 Greek *on account of my name.* 21:27a "Son of Man" is a title Jesus used for himself. 21:27b See Dan 7:13. 22:14 Or *reclined together.* 22:19-20 Some manuscripts do not include 22:19b-20, *which is given for you . . . which is poured out as a sacrifice for you.* 22:22 "Son of Man" is a title Jesus used for himself.

The Widow
WITH TWO SMALL COINS

◎ **IDENTITY**

Grieving to Giving

The widow remembers …

It wasn't a perfect marriage, but he made a good companion. But I wasn't sure my husband loved me because I never had children. I had so little; I'm not sure anyone loved me. Only my *Adonai*, my God. He stayed so near.

One morning, my husband went fishing. It was overcast, but only slightly. I went about kneading the bread for the evening meal. The storm rolled in and lasted a brief five minutes, but I heard the lightning crack. I said a quiet prayer.

"*Adonai*," whispering it over the waters, "Please, calm the storm. I can't survive without my husband."

One hour passed and then another. He didn't return. It wasn't until deep in the night that my husband's sister came running.

"He's dead," she cried. "The boat capsized."

Tears rolled down my cheeks as the bread hardened on the table. Flies swarmed, and grief set into my bones.

I stayed in bed for weeks, the bleakness consuming me. Yet, in my wailing, one, *Adonai*, stayed close.

One day, I rose. I changed my clothes and brushed my hair. God had been my closest friend, so I decided to give him all I had. And that, I did.

> God's faithfulness can turn our grieving to giving.

THE WIDOW'S STORY OF GIVING HER OFFERING IS TOLD IN LUKE 21:1-3.

IDENTIFY

Have you known profound loss? How did God meet you? Has that changed the way you follow him?

"My mom suffered a horrific disease. It stole her body starting at a young age, but cruelly left her mind intact to know the pain. I missed hearing her say, 'I love you' or 'I'm proud of you.' It was in that loss I crawled into God's arms. Because of God's faithfulness, I long to give him all I have."

WHITNEY PUTNAM is the senior director of women's events and marketing at New Life Ministries. She is an overall joy-chaser and is often found dancing in her kitchen.

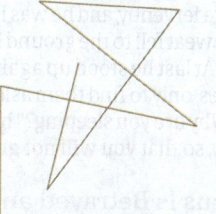

take the lowest rank, and the leader should be like a servant. ²⁷Who is more important, the one who sits at the table or the one who serves? The one who sits at the table, of course. But not here! For I am among you as one who serves.

²⁸"You have stayed with me in my time of trial. ²⁹And just as my Father has granted me a Kingdom, I now grant you the right ³⁰to eat and drink at my table in my Kingdom. And you will sit on thrones, judging the twelve tribes of Israel.

Jesus Predicts Peter's Denial

³¹"Simon, Simon, Satan has asked to sift each of you like wheat. ³²But I have pleaded in prayer for you, Simon, that your faith should not fail. So when you have repented and turned to me again, strengthen your brothers."

³³Peter said, "Lord, I am ready to go to prison with you, and even to die with you."

³⁴But Jesus said, "Peter, let me tell you something. Before the rooster crows tomorrow morning, you will deny three times that you even know me."

³⁵Then Jesus asked them, "When I sent you out to preach the Good News and you did not have money, a traveler's bag, or an extra pair of sandals, did you need anything?"

"No," they replied.

³⁶"But now," he said, "take your money and a traveler's bag. And if you don't have a sword, sell your cloak and buy one! ³⁷For the time has come for this prophecy about me to be fulfilled: 'He was counted among the rebels.'* Yes, everything written about me by the prophets will come true."

³⁸"Look, Lord," they replied, "we have two swords among us."

"That's enough," he said.

Jesus Prays on the Mount of Olives

³⁹Then, accompanied by the disciples, Jesus left the upstairs room and went as usual to the Mount of Olives. ⁴⁰There he told them, "Pray that you will not give in to temptation."

⁴¹He walked away, about a stone's throw, and knelt down and prayed, ⁴²"Father, if you are willing, please take this cup of suffering away from me. Yet I want your will to be done, not mine." ⁴³Then an angel from heaven appeared and strengthened him. ⁴⁴He prayed more fervently, and he was in such agony of spirit that his sweat fell to the ground like great drops of blood.*

⁴⁵At last he stood up again and returned to the disciples, only to find them asleep, exhausted from grief. ⁴⁶"Why are you sleeping?" he asked them. "Get up and pray, so that you will not give in to temptation."

Jesus Is Betrayed and Arrested

⁴⁷But even as Jesus said this, a crowd approached, led by Judas, one of the twelve disciples. Judas walked over to Jesus to greet him with a kiss. ⁴⁸But Jesus said, "Judas, would you betray the Son of Man with a kiss?"

⁴⁹When the other disciples saw what was about to happen, they exclaimed, "Lord, should we fight? We brought the swords!" ⁵⁰And one of them struck at the high priest's slave, slashing off his right ear.

⁵¹But Jesus said, "No more of this." And he touched the man's ear and healed him.

⁵²Then Jesus spoke to the leading priests, the captains of the Temple guard, and the elders who had come for him. "Am I some dangerous revolutionary," he asked, "that you come with swords and clubs to arrest me? ⁵³Why didn't you arrest me in the Temple? I was there every day. But this is your moment, the time when the power of darkness reigns."

Peter Denies Jesus

⁵⁴So they arrested him and led him to the high priest's home. And Peter followed at a distance. ⁵⁵The guards lit a fire in the middle of the courtyard and sat around it, and Peter joined them there. ⁵⁶A servant girl noticed him in the firelight and began staring at him. Finally she said, "This man was one of Jesus' followers!"

⁵⁷But Peter denied it. "Woman," he said, "I don't even know him!"

⁵⁸After a while someone else looked at him and said, "You must be one of them!"

"No, man, I'm not!" Peter retorted.

⁵⁹About an hour later someone else insisted, "This must be one of them, because he is a Galilean, too."

⁶⁰But Peter said, "Man, I don't know what you are talking about." And immediately, while he was still speaking, the rooster crowed.

⁶¹At that moment the Lord turned and looked at Peter. Suddenly, the Lord's words flashed through Peter's mind: "Before the rooster crows tomorrow morning, you will deny three times that you even know me." ⁶²And Peter left the courtyard, weeping bitterly.

⁶³The guards in charge of Jesus began mocking and beating him. ⁶⁴They blindfolded him and said, "Prophesy to us! Who hit you that time?" ⁶⁵And they hurled all sorts of terrible insults at him.

Jesus before the Council

⁶⁶At daybreak all the elders of the people assembled, including the leading priests and the teachers of religious law. Jesus was led before this high council,* ⁶⁷and they said, "Tell us, are you the Messiah?"

But he replied, "If I tell you, you won't believe me. ⁶⁸And if I ask you a question, you won't answer. ⁶⁹But from now on the Son of Man will be seated in the place of power at God's right hand.*"

⁷⁰They all shouted, "So, are you claiming to be the Son of God?"

22:37 Isa 53:12.   22:43-44 Verses 43 and 44 are not included in the most ancient manuscripts.   22:66 Greek *before their Sanhedrin.*   22:69 See Ps 110:1.

And he replied, "You say that I am." ⁷¹"Why do we need other witnesses?" they said. "We ourselves heard him say it."

Jesus' Trial before Pilate

23 Then the entire council took Jesus to Pilate, the Roman governor. ²They began to state their case: "This man has been leading our people astray by telling them not to pay their taxes to the Roman government and by claiming he is the Messiah, a king."

³So Pilate asked him, "Are you the king of the Jews?"

Jesus replied, "You have said it."

⁴Pilate turned to the leading priests and to the crowd and said, "I find nothing wrong with this man!"

⁵Then they became insistent. "But he is causing riots by his teaching wherever he goes—all over Judea, from Galilee to Jerusalem!"

⁶"Oh, is he a Galilean?" Pilate asked. ⁷When they said that he was, Pilate sent him to Herod Antipas, because Galilee was under Herod's jurisdiction, and Herod happened to be in Jerusalem at the time.

⁸Herod was delighted at the opportunity to see Jesus, because he had heard about him and had been hoping for a long time to see him perform a miracle. ⁹He asked Jesus question after question, but Jesus refused to answer. ¹⁰Meanwhile, the leading priests and the teachers of religious law stood there shouting their accusations. ¹¹Then Herod and his soldiers began mocking and ridiculing Jesus. Finally, they put a royal robe on him and sent him back to Pilate. ¹²(Herod and Pilate, who had been enemies before, became friends that day.)

¹³Then Pilate called together the leading priests and other religious leaders, along with the people, ¹⁴and he announced his verdict. "You brought this man to me, accusing him of leading a revolt. I have examined him thoroughly on this point in your presence and find him innocent. ¹⁵Herod came to the same conclusion and sent him back to us. Nothing this man has done calls for the death penalty. ¹⁶So I will have him flogged, and then I will release him."*

¹⁸Then a mighty roar rose from the crowd, and with one voice they shouted, "Kill him, and release Barabbas to us!" ¹⁹(Barabbas was in prison for taking part in an insurrection in Jerusalem against the government, and for murder.) ²⁰Pilate argued with them, because he wanted to release Jesus. ²¹But they kept shouting, "Crucify him! Crucify him!"

²²For the third time he demanded, "Why? What crime has he committed? I have found no reason to sentence him to death. So I will have him flogged, and then I will release him."

²³But the mob shouted louder and louder, demanding that Jesus be crucified, and their voices prevailed. ²⁴So Pilate sentenced Jesus to die as they demanded. ²⁵As they had requested, he released Barabbas, the man in prison for insurrection and murder. But he turned Jesus over to them to do as they wished.

The Crucifixion

²⁶As they led Jesus away, a man named Simon, who was from Cyrene,* happened to be coming in from the countryside. The soldiers seized him and put the cross on him and made him carry it behind Jesus. ²⁷A large crowd trailed behind, including many grief-stricken women. ²⁸But Jesus turned and said to them, "Daughters of Jerusalem, don't weep for me, but weep for yourselves and for your children. ²⁹For the days are coming when they will say, 'Fortunate indeed are the women who are childless, the wombs that have not borne a child and the breasts that have never nursed.' ³⁰People will beg the mountains, 'Fall on us,' and plead with the hills, 'Bury us.'* ³¹For if these things are done when the tree is green, what will happen when it is dry?"*

³²Two others, both criminals, were led out to be executed with him. ³³When they came to a place called The Skull,* they nailed him to the cross. And the criminals were also crucified—one on his right and one on his left.

³⁴Jesus said, "Father, forgive them, for they don't know what they are doing."* And the soldiers gambled for his clothes by throwing dice.*

³⁵The crowd watched and the leaders scoffed. "He saved others," they said, "let him save himself if he is really God's Messiah, the Chosen One." ³⁶The soldiers mocked him, too, by offering him a drink of sour

---

23:16 Some manuscripts add verse 17, *Now it was necessary for him to release one prisoner to them during the Passover celebration.* Compare Matt 27:15; Mark 15:6; John 18:39. **23:26** *Cyrene* was a city in northern Africa. **23:30** Hos 10:8. **23:31** Or *If these things are done to me, the living tree, what will happen to you, the dry tree?* **23:33** Sometimes rendered *Calvary*, which comes from the Latin word for "skull." **23:34a** This sentence is not included in many ancient manuscripts. **23:34b** Greek *by casting lots.* See Ps 22:18.

23:26-31 Although Jesus' words to the wailing women sound abrupt, they echo his prophecy about Jerusalem's destruction that he had delivered in the Temple earlier in the week (21:20-24). While these women were concerned with Jesus' situation, Jesus warned them of the worst yet to come. Nevertheless, Luke's story ends with Jesus' resurrection from the dead and ascension back to heaven to be with the Father, so there was hope for these women in the future. Every age has its disasters, but we can trust that the God who raised Jesus from the dead is coming again to rescue us and will renew all creation (Acts 1:11; 1 Thessalonians 4:13-18; Revelation 21:1-7).

23:29 Being childless was usually a cause of great shame (see the note on 1:7), but during this coming catastrophe, the fortunate ones would be those who didn't have to see their children starve to death.

wine. ³⁷They called out to him, "If you are the King of the Jews, save yourself!" ³⁸A sign was fastened above him with these words: "This is the King of the Jews."

³⁹One of the criminals hanging beside him scoffed, "So you're the Messiah, are you? Prove it by saving yourself—and us, too, while you're at it!"

⁴⁰But the other criminal protested, "Don't you fear God even when you have been sentenced to die? ⁴¹We deserve to die for our crimes, but this man hasn't done anything wrong." ⁴²Then he said, "Jesus, remember me when you come into your Kingdom."

⁴³And Jesus replied, "I assure you, today you will be with me in paradise."

The Death of Jesus

⁴⁴By this time it was about noon, and darkness fell across the whole land until three o'clock. ⁴⁵The light from the sun was gone. And suddenly, the curtain in the sanctuary of the Temple was torn down the middle. ⁴⁶Then Jesus shouted, "Father, I entrust my spirit into your hands!"* And with those words he breathed his last.

⁴⁷When the Roman officer* overseeing the execution saw what had happened, he worshiped God and said, "Surely this man was innocent."* ⁴⁸And when all the crowd that came to see the crucifixion saw what had happened, they went home in deep sorrow.* ⁴⁹But Jesus' friends, including the women who had followed him from Galilee, stood at a distance watching.

The Burial of Jesus

⁵⁰Now there was a good and righteous man named Joseph. He was a member of the Jewish high council, ⁵¹but he had not agreed with the decision and actions of the other religious leaders. He was from the town of Arimathea in Judea, and he was waiting for the Kingdom of God to come. ⁵²He went to Pilate and asked for Jesus' body. ⁵³Then he took the body down from the cross and wrapped it in a long sheet of linen cloth and laid it in a new tomb that had been carved out of rock. ⁵⁴This was done late on Friday afternoon, the day of preparation,* as the Sabbath was about to begin.

⁵⁵As his body was taken away, the women from Galilee followed and saw the tomb where his body was placed. ⁵⁶Then they went home and prepared spices and ointments to anoint his body. But by the time they were finished the Sabbath had begun, so they rested as required by the law.

The Resurrection

24 But very early on Sunday morning* the women went to the tomb, taking the spices they had prepared. ²They found that the stone had been rolled away from the entrance. ³So they went in, but they didn't find the body of the Lord Jesus. ⁴As they stood there puzzled, two men suddenly appeared to them, clothed in dazzling robes.

⁵The women were terrified and bowed with their faces to the ground. Then the men asked, "Why are you looking among the dead for someone who is alive? ⁶He isn't here! He is risen from the dead! Remember what he told you back in Galilee, ⁷that the Son of Man* must be betrayed into the hands of sinful men and be crucified, and that he would rise again on the third day."

⁸Then they remembered that he had said this. ⁹So they rushed back from the tomb to tell his eleven disciples—and everyone else—what had happened. ¹⁰It was Mary Magdalene, Joanna, Mary the mother of James, and several other women who told the apostles what had happened. ¹¹But the story sounded like nonsense to the men, so they didn't believe it. ¹²However, Peter jumped up and ran to the tomb to look. Stooping, he peered in and saw the empty linen wrappings; then he went home again, wondering what had happened.

The Walk to Emmaus

¹³That same day two of Jesus' followers were walking to the village of Emmaus, seven miles* from Jerusalem. ¹⁴As they walked along they were talking about

---

23:46 Ps 31:5. **23:47a** Greek *the centurion.* **23:47b** Or *righteous.* **23:48** Greek *went home beating their breasts.* **23:54** Greek *It was the day of preparation.* **24:1** Greek *But on the first day of the week, very early in the morning.* **24:7** "Son of Man" is a title Jesus used for himself. **24:13** Greek *60 stadia* [11.1 kilometers].

23:55–24:7 Luke pays special attention to Jesus' women followers, although they are supporting actors behind the scenes for most of the narrative. These women traveled with Jesus around Galilee and to Jerusalem, provided for their group (8:1-3), followed Jesus to "a place called The Skull" where he would be executed (23:27-33), stayed with him during his death (23:49), prepared spices and ointments, and came to his tomb to anoint him. Luke records none of their words, but their actions speak loudly. It can be easy to forget that a dedicated group of women traveled with Jesus and the twelve male apostles. But these women show us that Jesus' message didn't just inspire men to leave everything and follow him. These women testified in their faithful following that Jesus' message is good news for women, too. Similarly, we can show with our lives how compelling Jesus' message is for all people.

24:10, 22-24 In first-century Palestine, women were barred from being witnesses in Jewish courts. But regardless of social expectations, God chose a few women to be the first eyewitnesses of Jesus' resurrection and to carry that message back to Jesus' other disciples. Jesus' male followers at first refused to believe the women. Rejection doesn't make the resurrection message less real or significant. All we need to do is to *tell* others what we have experienced. And God will do the rest.

24:10 Mary Magdalene and Joanna are also named in 8:2-3. Mary the mother of James is not the mother of James and John (see Matthew 27:56), but might be the mother of James, the son of Alphaeus (Luke 6:15).

everything that had happened. ¹⁵As they talked and discussed these things, Jesus himself suddenly came and began walking with them. ¹⁶But God kept them from recognizing him.

¹⁷He asked them, "What are you discussing so intently as you walk along?"

They stopped short, sadness written across their faces. ¹⁸Then one of them, Cleopas, replied, "You must be the only person in Jerusalem who hasn't heard about all the things that have happened there the last few days."

¹⁹"What things?" Jesus asked.

"The things that happened to Jesus, the man from Nazareth," they said. "He was a prophet who did powerful miracles, and he was a mighty teacher in the eyes of God and all the people. ²⁰But our leading priests and other religious leaders handed him over to be condemned to death, and they crucified him. ²¹We had hoped he was the Messiah who had come to rescue Israel. This all happened three days ago.

²²"Then some women from our group of his followers were at his tomb early this morning, and they came back with an amazing report. ²³They said his body was missing, and they had seen angels who told them Jesus is alive! ²⁴Some of our men ran out to see, and sure enough, his body was gone, just as the women had said."

²⁵Then Jesus said to them, "You foolish people! You find it so hard to believe all that the prophets wrote in the Scriptures. ²⁶Wasn't it clearly predicted that the Messiah would have to suffer all these things before entering his glory?" ²⁷Then Jesus took them through the writings of Moses and all the prophets, explaining from all the Scriptures the things concerning himself.

²⁸By this time they were nearing Emmaus and the end of their journey. Jesus acted as if he were going on, ²⁹but they begged him, "Stay the night with us, since it is getting late." So he went home with them. ³⁰As they sat down to eat,* he took the bread and blessed it. Then he broke it and gave it to them. ³¹Suddenly, their eyes were opened, and they recognized him. And at that moment he disappeared!

³²They said to each other, "Didn't our hearts burn within us as he talked with us on the road and explained the Scriptures to us?" ³³And within the hour they were on their way back to Jerusalem. There they found the eleven disciples and the others who had gathered with them, ³⁴who said, "The Lord has really risen! He appeared to Peter.*"

Jesus Appears to the Disciples

³⁵Then the two from Emmaus told their story of how Jesus had appeared to them as they were walking along the road, and how they had recognized him as he was breaking the bread. ³⁶And just as they were telling about it, Jesus himself was suddenly standing there among them. "Peace be with you," he said. ³⁷But the whole group was startled and frightened, thinking they were seeing a ghost!

³⁸"Why are you frightened?" he asked. "Why are your hearts filled with doubt? ³⁹Look at my hands. Look at my feet. You can see that it's really me. Touch me and make sure that I am not a ghost, because ghosts don't have bodies, as you see that I do." ⁴⁰As he spoke, he showed them his hands and his feet.

⁴¹Still they stood there in disbelief, filled with joy and wonder. Then he asked them, "Do you have anything here to eat?" ⁴²They gave him a piece of broiled fish, ⁴³and he ate it as they watched.

⁴⁴Then he said, "When I was with you before, I told you that everything written about me in the law of Moses and the prophets and in the Psalms must be fulfilled." ⁴⁵Then he opened their minds to understand the Scriptures. ⁴⁶And he said, "Yes, it was written long ago that the Messiah would suffer and die and rise from the dead on the third day. ⁴⁷It was also written that this message would be proclaimed in the authority of his name to all the nations,* beginning in Jerusalem: 'There is forgiveness of sins for all who repent.' ⁴⁸You are witnesses of all these things.

⁴⁹"And now I will send the Holy Spirit, just as my Father promised. But stay here in the city until the Holy Spirit comes and fills you with power from heaven."

The Ascension

⁵⁰Then Jesus led them to Bethany, and lifting his hands to heaven, he blessed them. ⁵¹While he was blessing them, he left them and was taken up to heaven. ⁵²So they worshiped him and then returned to Jerusalem filled with great joy. ⁵³And they spent all of their time in the Temple, praising God.

24:30 Or *As they reclined.*   24:34 Greek *Simon.*   24:47 Or *all peoples.*

John

WHAT DO WE LEARN ABOUT GOD'S MISSION AND OURS?
Jesus gives life's true and best story.

WHO WROTE IT? John, the disciple Jesus loved.

WHEN DID IT HAPPEN? Tradition says John wrote later than the other three Gospel writers, after AD 85, describing events that occurred in the first three decades of the first century AD.

HOW IS IT ORGANIZED?

- **1:** God takes on human form as Jesus and begins ministry
- **2–6:** Jesus performs miracles and speaks with women and men who are insiders and outsiders
- **7–10:** Jesus teaches at Jewish festivals in Jerusalem
- **11–12:** Jesus raises his friend Lazarus from the dead, then goes to Jerusalem and announces his own death
- **13–17:** Jesus instructs his disciples at their last meal together
- **18–19:** Jesus is tried and executed
- **20–21:** Jesus rises from the dead and appears to his disciples

Words to Remember are highlighted throughout this book

HOW LONG DOES IT TAKE TO READ?

| :30 | 1:00 | 1:30 | 2:00 | 2:30 | 3:00 | 3:30 |

(marker at 1:30)

Timeline

BC

- **37** — HEROD THE GREAT BEGINS TO RULE AS KING OVER PALESTINE
- **7/6** — ELIZABETH AND ZECHARIAH CONCEIVE JOHN THE BAPTIST; MARY CONCEIVES JESUS BY GOD'S SPIRIT
- **6/5** — JESUS, MARY'S CHILD AND THE SON OF GOD, IS BORN
- **5/4** — MARY, JOSEPH, AND JESUS ESCAPE TO EGYPT
- **4** — HEROD THE GREAT DIES
- **4/3** — JESUS' FAMILY RETURNS TO NAZARETH

AD

- **6** — JUDEA BECOMES A ROMAN PROVINCE
- **6/7** — YOUNG JESUS VISITS THE TEMPLE
- **14** — TIBERIUS CAESAR BECOMES EMPEROR OF ROME
- **26** — PONTIUS PILATE APPOINTED GOVERNOR IN JUDEA; JOHN THE BAPTIST'S MINISTRY BEGINS
- **27** — JESUS BEGINS HIS PUBLIC MINISTRY; JESUS MEETS WITH NICODEMUS
- **28** — JOHN BAPTIZES JESUS; JESUS CHOOSES TWELVE DISCIPLES
- **29** — JESUS FEEDS 5,000+ INCLUDING WOMEN AND CHILDREN
- **30** — JESUS IS CRUCIFIED, RISES FROM THE DEAD, AND ASCENDS TO HEAVEN

Prologue: Christ, the Eternal Word

1 In the beginning the Word already existed.
  The Word was with God,
  and the Word was God.
² He existed in the beginning with God.
³ God created everything through him,
  and nothing was created except through him.
⁴ The Word gave life to everything that was created,*
  and his life brought light to everyone.
⁵ The light shines in the darkness,
  and the darkness can never extinguish it.*

⁶God sent a man, John the Baptist,* ⁷to tell about the light so that everyone might believe because of his testimony. ⁸John himself was not the light; he was simply a witness to tell about the light. ⁹The one who is the true light, who gives light to everyone, was coming into the world.

¹⁰He came into the very world he created, but the world didn't recognize him. ¹¹He came to his own people, and even they rejected him. ¹²But to all who believed him and accepted him, he gave the right to become children of God. ¹³They are reborn—not with a physical birth resulting from human passion or plan, but a birth that comes from God.

¹⁴So the Word became human* and made his home among us. He was full of unfailing love and faithfulness.* And we have seen his glory, the glory of the Father's one and only Son.

¹⁵John testified about him when he shouted to the crowds, "This is the one I was talking about when I said, 'Someone is coming after me who is far greater than I am, for he existed long before me.'"

¹⁶From his abundance we have all received one gracious blessing after another.* ¹⁷For the law was given through Moses, but God's unfailing love and faithfulness came through Jesus Christ. ¹⁸No one has ever seen God. But the unique One, who is himself God,* is near to the Father's heart. He has revealed God to us.

The Testimony of John the Baptist

¹⁹This was John's testimony when the Jewish leaders sent priests and Temple assistants* from Jerusalem to ask John, "Who are you?" ²⁰He came right out and said, "I am not the Messiah."

²¹"Well then, who are you?" they asked. "Are you Elijah?"

"No," he replied.

"Are you the Prophet we are expecting?"*

"No."

²²"Then who are you? We need an answer for those who sent us. What do you have to say about yourself?"

²³John replied in the words of the prophet Isaiah:

"I am a voice shouting in the wilderness,
  'Clear the way for the LORD's coming!'"*

²⁴Then the Pharisees who had been sent ²⁵asked him, "If you aren't the Messiah or Elijah or the Prophet, what right do you have to baptize?"

²⁶John told them, "I baptize with* water, but right here in the crowd is someone you do not recognize. ²⁷Though his ministry follows mine, I'm not even worthy to be his slave and untie the straps of his sandal." ²⁸This encounter took place in Bethany, an area east of the Jordan River, where John was baptizing.

Jesus, the Lamb of God

²⁹The next day John saw Jesus coming toward him and said, "Look! The Lamb of God who takes away the sin of the world! ³⁰He is the one I was talking about when I said, 'A man is coming after me who is far greater than I am, for he existed long before me.' ³¹I did not recognize him as the Messiah, but I have been baptizing with water so that he might be revealed to Israel."

³²Then John testified, "I saw the Holy Spirit descending like a dove from heaven and resting upon him. ³³I didn't know he was the one, but when God sent me to baptize with water, he told me, 'The one on whom you see the Spirit descend and rest is the one who will baptize with the Holy Spirit.' ³⁴I saw this happen to Jesus, so I testify that he is the Chosen One of God.*"

The First Disciples

³⁵The following day John was again standing with two of his disciples. ³⁶As Jesus walked by, John looked at him and declared, "Look! There is the Lamb of God!" ³⁷When John's two disciples heard this, they followed Jesus.

³⁸Jesus looked around and saw them following. "What do you want?" he asked them.

They replied, "Rabbi" (which means "Teacher"), "where are you staying?"

1:3-4 Or *and nothing that was created was created except through him. The Word gave life to everything.* **1:5** Or *and the darkness has not understood it.* **1:6** Greek *a man named John.* **1:14a** Greek *became flesh.* **1:14b** Or *grace and truth;* also in 1:17. **1:16** Or *received the grace of Christ rather than the grace of the law;* Greek reads *received grace upon grace.* **1:18** Some manuscripts read *But the one and only Son.* **1:19** Greek *and Levites.* **1:21** Greek *Are you the Prophet?* See Deut 18:15, 18; Mal 4:5-6. **1:23** Isa 40:3. **1:26** Or *in;* also in 1:31, 33. **1:34** Some manuscripts read *the Son of God.*

1:12-14 The book of John speaks of God as Father more than any other New Testament book. God's fatherhood in both testaments emphasizes God's authority and goodness, as well as his *relational* attribute. But, seeing God as Father is not the only way to understand our relationship with him. John also uses birth as the metaphor for how God brings us into his family (see also 3:3-8). Therefore, we can also connect with God as a mother who purposefully conceives us and gives birth to us. For women who have abusive or absent fathers, John invites us to believe that Jesus provides a way to join a new family, God's family (see 14:18).

"This is how God loved the world: He gave his one and only Son."

JOHN 3:16

³⁹"Come and see," he said. It was about four o'clock in the afternoon when they went with him to the place where he was staying, and they remained with him the rest of the day.

⁴⁰Andrew, Simon Peter's brother, was one of these men who heard what John said and then followed Jesus. ⁴¹Andrew went to find his brother, Simon, and told him, "We have found the Messiah" (which means "Christ"*).

⁴²Then Andrew brought Simon to meet Jesus. Looking intently at Simon, Jesus said, "Your name is Simon, son of John—but you will be called Cephas" (which means "Peter"*).

⁴³The next day Jesus decided to go to Galilee. He found Philip and said to him, "Come, follow me." ⁴⁴Philip was from Bethsaida, Andrew and Peter's hometown.

⁴⁵Philip went to look for Nathanael and told him, "We have found the very person Moses* and the prophets wrote about! His name is Jesus, the son of Joseph from Nazareth."

⁴⁶"Nazareth!" exclaimed Nathanael. "Can anything good come from Nazareth?"

"Come and see for yourself," Philip replied.

⁴⁷As they approached, Jesus said, "Now here is a genuine son of Israel—a man of complete integrity."

⁴⁸"How do you know about me?" Nathanael asked.

Jesus replied, "I could see you under the fig tree before Philip found you."

⁴⁹Then Nathanael exclaimed, "Rabbi, you are the Son of God—the King of Israel!"

⁵⁰Jesus asked him, "Do you believe this just because I told you I had seen you under the fig tree? You will see greater things than this." ⁵¹Then he said, "I tell you the truth, you will all see heaven open and the angels of God going up and down on the Son of Man, the one who is the stairway between heaven and earth.*"

The Wedding at Cana

2 The next day* there was a wedding celebration in the village of Cana in Galilee. Jesus' mother was there, ²and Jesus and his disciples were also invited to the celebration. ³The wine supply ran out during the festivities, so Jesus' mother told him, "They have no more wine."

⁴"Dear woman, that's not our problem," Jesus replied. "My time has not yet come."

⁵But his mother told the servants, "Do whatever he tells you."

⁶Standing nearby were six stone water jars, used for Jewish ceremonial washing. Each could hold twenty to thirty gallons.* ⁷Jesus told the servants, "Fill the jars with water." When the jars had been filled, ⁸he said, "Now dip some out, and take it to the master of ceremonies." So the servants followed his instructions.

⁹When the master of ceremonies tasted the water that was now wine, not knowing where it had come from (though, of course, the servants knew), he called the bridegroom over. ¹⁰"A host always serves the best wine first," he said. "Then, when everyone has had a lot to drink, he brings out the less expensive wine. But you have kept the best until now!"

¹¹This miraculous sign at Cana in Galilee was the first time Jesus revealed his glory. And his disciples believed in him.

¹²After the wedding he went to Capernaum for a few days with his mother, his brothers, and his disciples.

Jesus Clears the Temple

¹³It was nearly time for the Jewish Passover celebration, so Jesus went to Jerusalem. ¹⁴In the Temple area he saw merchants selling cattle, sheep, and doves for sacrifices; he also saw dealers at tables exchanging foreign money. ¹⁵Jesus made a whip from some ropes and chased them all out of the Temple. He drove out the sheep and cattle, scattered the money changers' coins over the floor, and turned over their tables. ¹⁶Then, going over to the people who sold doves, he told them, "Get these things out of here. Stop turning my Father's house into a marketplace!"

¹⁷Then his disciples remembered this prophecy from the Scriptures: "Passion for God's house will consume me."*

¹⁸But the Jewish leaders demanded, "What are you doing? If God gave you authority to do this, show us a miraculous sign to prove it."

¹⁹"All right," Jesus replied. "Destroy this temple, and in three days I will raise it up."

²⁰"What!" they exclaimed. "It has taken forty-six years to build this Temple, and you can rebuild it

---

1:41 *Messiah* (a Hebrew term) and *Christ* (a Greek term) both mean "anointed one." **1:42** The names *Cephas* (from Aramaic) and *Peter* (from Greek) both mean "rock." **1:45** Greek *Moses in the law.* **1:51** Greek *going up and down on the Son of Man;* see Gen 28:10-17. "Son of Man" is a title Jesus used for himself. **2:1** Greek *On the third day;* see 1:35, 43. **2:6** Greek *2 or 3 measures* [75 to 113 liters]. **2:17** Or *"Concern for God's house will be my undoing."* Ps 69:9.

2:3 An ancient Jewish wedding banquet was a week-long celebration, and if "the wine supply ran out," the host family would be embarrassed for not planning properly. Perhaps Jesus arrived unexpectedly (see also Matthew 25:1-13), accompanied by his disciples, which might explain why his mother brought the problem to him. This event also symbolized joy for the Messiah's arrival. **2:4** The NLT softens the original language's abruptness (literally "what [is it] to you and me, woman"). Though not rude, Jesus bluntly distanced himself from his mother and her request. One way we can understand this verse in context is through Jesus' earthly purpose: He came to fulfill his Father's will (5:30). Hence, even Jesus' mother couldn't dictate his schedule. From a human perspective, losing the prerogatives of motherhood could be challenging, but Mary submitted to Jesus' leadership. In fact, Jesus' submission to his Father's will was mirrored by Mary's own submission to God as Jesus' mother (Luke 1:38).

in three days?" ²¹But when Jesus said "this temple," he meant his own body. ²²After he was raised from the dead, his disciples remembered he had said this, and they believed both the Scriptures and what Jesus had said.

Jesus and Nicodemus

²³Because of the miraculous signs Jesus did in Jerusalem at the Passover celebration, many began to trust in him. ²⁴But Jesus didn't trust them, because he knew all about people. ²⁵No one needed to tell him about human nature, for he knew what was in each person's heart.

3 There was a man named Nicodemus, a Jewish religious leader who was a Pharisee. ²After dark one evening, he came to speak with Jesus. "Rabbi," he said, "we all know that God has sent you to teach us. Your miraculous signs are evidence that God is with you."

³Jesus replied, "I tell you the truth, unless you are born again,* you cannot see the Kingdom of God."

⁴"What do you mean?" exclaimed Nicodemus. "How can an old man go back into his mother's womb and be born again?"

⁵Jesus replied, "I assure you, no one can enter the Kingdom of God without being born of water and the Spirit.* ⁶Humans can reproduce only human life,

---

3:3 Or *born from above;* also in 3:7. **3:5** Or *and spirit.* The Greek word for *Spirit* can also be translated *wind;* see 3:8.

3:1-21 In Nicodemus's encounter with Jesus, Jesus used the new birth metaphor (literally "born from above [or again]"; see text note on 3:3) to talk about entering God's Kingdom. Nicodemus could only understand Jesus' metaphor in relation to physical birth. But Jesus explained that becoming part of God's Kingdom must be the Holy Spirit's work. Although it's not entirely clear how spiritual birth happens, it is evident when it happens (3:8).

Come Close — FREE TO FLOURISH

SCRIPTURE CONNECTION: JOHN 3:26-36

I've been reading and rereading about John the Baptist, the part about how his disciples came to him all frazzled by the fact that Jesus was *also* baptizing people and that those people were "flocking to Him," heaven forbid (John 3:26 AMP[C]). And isn't this how it is? When people start encroaching on our territory, gaining traction, we deploy our defenses because, well, do you see how many people are over there *flocking*?

For a while I was puzzled by John the Baptist's response to his followers [in John 3:27].... I pondered that phrase, wondering what in the world he meant by this. But then I realized he was merely setting his disciples free to flourish in the gifts and calling they'd been given. They no longer had to be threatened by what everyone else was doing, what kind of followers another person had. They didn't have to compete or circle the wagons to protect what was "theirs." Whatever God had given them to do, this would be their bread and oil, and it would never cease sufficing. It would forever flow from the great joy of accompanying the Savior. In other words, when Jesus is your portion, the author and finisher of your faith, comparisons gloriously melt into frivolousness.

REFLECT "No one can receive anything unless God gives it from heaven."
JOHN 3:27

Lord Jesus, when I feel threatened by others, please help me to be content with the gifts and calling you've given me. Amen.

CONSIDER "When you have the lover of your soul at your right hand and your lot is secure, you don't have to ask the questions 'What about him? Or her? Or the recognition? Or how come *she* made the cover?' Because you've already drunk your fill."

> Jesus sets his disciples free to flourish in their gifts and calling.

KELLY MINTER • *Wherever the River Runs*
© 2014 by Kelly Minter. Used by permission of David C Cook. May not be further reproduced. All rights reserved.

but the Holy Spirit gives birth to spiritual life.* ⁷So don't be surprised when I say, 'You* must be born again.' ⁸The wind blows wherever it wants. Just as you can hear the wind but can't tell where it comes from or where it is going, so you can't explain how people are born of the Spirit."

⁹"How are these things possible?" Nicodemus asked.

¹⁰Jesus replied, "You are a respected Jewish teacher, and yet you don't understand these things? ¹¹I assure you, we tell you what we know and have seen, and yet you won't believe our testimony. ¹²But if you don't believe me when I tell you about earthly things, how can you possibly believe if I tell you about heavenly things? ¹³No one has ever gone to heaven and returned. But the Son of Man* has come down from heaven. ¹⁴And as Moses lifted up the bronze snake on a pole in the wilderness, so the Son of Man must be lifted up, ¹⁵so that everyone who believes in him will have eternal life.*

¹⁶"For this is how God loved the world: He gave* his one and only Son, so that everyone who believes in him will not perish but have eternal life. ¹⁷God sent his Son into the world not to judge the world, but to save the world through him.

¹⁸"There is no judgment against anyone who believes in him. But anyone who does not believe in him has already been judged for not believing in God's one and only Son. ¹⁹And the judgment is based on this fact: God's light came into the world, but people loved the darkness more than the light, for their actions were evil. ²⁰All who do evil hate the light and refuse to go near it for fear their sins will be exposed. ²¹But those who do what is right come to the light so others can see that they are doing what God wants.*"

John the Baptist Exalts Jesus

²²Then Jesus and his disciples left Jerusalem and went into the Judean countryside. Jesus spent some time with them there, baptizing people.

²³At this time John the Baptist was baptizing at Aenon, near Salim, because there was plenty of water there; and people kept coming to him for baptism. ²⁴(This was before John was thrown into prison.) ²⁵A debate broke out between John's disciples and a certain Jew* over ceremonial cleansing. ²⁶So John's disciples came to him and said, "Rabbi, the man you met on the other side of the Jordan River, the one you identified as the Messiah, is also baptizing people. And everybody is going to him instead of coming to us."

²⁷John replied, "No one can receive anything unless God gives it from heaven. ²⁸You yourselves know how plainly I told you, 'I am not the Messiah. I am only here to prepare the way for him.' ²⁹It is the bridegroom who marries the bride, and the bridegroom's friend is simply glad to stand with him and hear his vows. Therefore, I am filled with joy at his success. ³⁰He must become greater and greater, and I must become less and less.

³¹"He has come from above and is greater than anyone else. We are of the earth, and we speak of earthly things, but he has come from heaven and is greater than anyone else.* ³²He testifies about what he has seen and heard, but how few believe what he tells them! ³³Anyone who accepts his testimony can affirm that God is true. ³⁴For he is sent by God. He speaks God's words, for God gives him the Spirit without limit. ³⁵The Father loves his Son and has put everything into his hands. ³⁶And anyone who believes in God's Son has eternal life. Anyone who doesn't obey the Son will never experience eternal life but remains under God's angry judgment."

Jesus and the Samaritan Woman

4 Jesus* knew the Pharisees had heard that he was baptizing and making more disciples than John ²(though Jesus himself didn't baptize them—his disciples did). ³So he left Judea and returned to Galilee.

⁴He had to go through Samaria on the way. ⁵Eventually he came to the Samaritan village of Sychar,

---

3:6 Greek *what is born of the Spirit is spirit.* **3:7** The Greek word for *you* is plural; also in 3:12. **3:13** Some manuscripts add *who lives in heaven.* "Son of Man" is a title Jesus used for himself. **3:15** Or *everyone who believes will have eternal life in him.* **3:16** Or *For God loved the world so much that he gave.* **3:21** Or *can see God at work in what he is doing.* **3:25** Some manuscripts read *some Jews.* **3:31** Some manuscripts do not include *and is greater than anyone else.* **4:1** Some manuscripts read *The Lord.*

3:29-30 In the Gospels' wedding metaphor, the bride is often absent. So who is the bride? Prophets in the Old Testament described the people of Israel as the bride of the Lord, and John the Baptist's illustration echoes this (see Isaiah 62:4-5; Jeremiah 2:2; Hosea 2:16-20). Although marriage represents Christ's relationship with the future global church, this idea of the church as his bride wasn't fully developed in Jesus' teachings. In this instance, "the bride" likely referred to Jesus' disciples collectively—men and women. John the Baptist clearly understood his role as a friend of the groom, even pointing his own disciples to Jesus (John 1:35-36). As Christ's followers, we are part of his bride, but individually, we are also Christ's friends who can rejoice in pointing others to him.

4:1-42 At the well Jacob may have dug while living in Shechem (Genesis 33:18-20), later Samaria, Jesus described himself to a Samaritan woman as living water. This interaction is typical of the way Jesus engaged and confronted people throughout his ministry, and they either followed or fell away. The Samaritan woman contrasted with Nicodemus at every turn: She was a woman, not a man; a Samaritan, not a Jew; and a religious outcast, not one of Israel's rabbis. While Nicodemus fell silent and didn't respond to Jesus' challenges (John 3:1-21), this unnamed woman acknowledged Jesus as Lord and was instrumental in her village's reception of him.

THE Samaritan Woman AT THE WELL

IDENTITY: Filled to Full

Why do we settle for empty when Jesus came to fill us to full?

On his way from Judea to Galilee, Jesus was tired and thirsty. The one who brought water into existence sat by a well and longed for a sip.

At the hour of noon, and all alone, a woman approached. Life had not treated this woman well—she may have experienced infertility, she had likely been sent away by more than one husband, and she wasn't married now.

When Jesus asked the woman for a drink, she reflexively pulled back. How bizarre! A Jewish man requesting a drink from a Samaritan woman? This violated a social taboo: Jewish teachers rarely spoke to women in public.

Jesus responded, "If you only knew the gift God has for you and who you are speaking to, you would ask me, and I would give you living water" (4:10). Jesus spoke straight to her emptiness: "Those who drink the water I give will never be thirsty again. It becomes a fresh, bubbling spring within them, giving them eternal life" (4:14). The sense here is not just a spring of water welling up but welling up and over.

Like the woman at the well, we can pull back from God's abundant filling, determining that we deserve only a sip. Looking at our past mistakes, current circumstances, or simply the disappointments of life, we conclude we're beyond God's love. When the unnamed woman in John 4 accepted Jesus' offer to the full, everything changed—for her and her whole town (4:39-42). Will you accept?

THE SAMARITAN WOMAN'S STORY IS TOLD IN JOHN 4:1-42.

> Why settle for empty when God came to fill us to full?

IDENTIFY

How is God offering you "living water" to fill you to full? How might you reflexively refuse his filling?

What do you need to accept the risk of letting God fill you with his love?

> "Perhaps the hardest step we can take in our life with God is to risk letting him fill us with his love. But what if when we let God fill us with his love, we are actually loving him back?"

ELISA MORGAN, MDiv, speaks, writes, and cohosts podcasts for Our Daily Bread Ministries. For twenty years, she served as president of MOPS International, now as president emerita. Her motto is "Living really . . . Really living."

near the field that Jacob gave to his son Joseph. ⁶Jacob's well was there; and Jesus, tired from the long walk, sat wearily beside the well about noontime. ⁷Soon a Samaritan woman came to draw water, and Jesus said to her, "Please give me a drink." ⁸He was alone at the time because his disciples had gone into the village to buy some food.

⁹The woman was surprised, for Jews refuse to have anything to do with Samaritans.* She said to Jesus, "You are a Jew, and I am a Samaritan woman. Why are you asking me for a drink?"

¹⁰Jesus replied, "If you only knew the gift God has for you and who you are speaking to, you would ask me, and I would give you living water."

¹¹"But sir, you don't have a rope or a bucket," she said, "and this well is very deep. Where would you get this living water? ¹²And besides, do you think you're greater than our ancestor Jacob, who gave us this well? How can you offer better water than he and his sons and his animals enjoyed?"

¹³Jesus replied, "Anyone who drinks this water will soon become thirsty again. ¹⁴But those who drink the water I give will never be thirsty again. It becomes a fresh, bubbling spring within them, giving them eternal life."

¹⁵"Please, sir," the woman said, "give me this water! Then I'll never be thirsty again, and I won't have to come here to get water."

¹⁶"Go and get your husband," Jesus told her.

¹⁷"I don't have a husband," the woman replied.

Jesus said, "You're right! You don't have a husband—¹⁸for you have had five husbands, and you aren't even married to the man you're living with now. You certainly spoke the truth!"

¹⁹"Sir," the woman said, "you must be a prophet. ²⁰So tell me, why is it that you Jews insist that Jerusalem is the only place of worship, while we Samaritans claim it is here at Mount Gerizim,* where our ancestors worshiped?"

²¹Jesus replied, "Believe me, dear woman, the time is coming when it will no longer matter whether you worship the Father on this mountain or in Jerusalem. ²²You Samaritans know very little about the one you worship, while we Jews know all about him, for salvation comes through the Jews. ²³But the time is coming—indeed it's here now—when true worshipers will worship the Father in spirit and in truth. The Father is looking for those who will worship him that way. ²⁴For God is Spirit, so those who worship him must worship in spirit and in truth."

²⁵The woman said, "I know the Messiah is coming—the one who is called Christ. When he comes, he will explain everything to us."

²⁶Then Jesus told her, "I Am the Messiah!"*

²⁷Just then his disciples came back. They were shocked to find him talking to a woman, but none of them had the nerve to ask, "What do you want with her?" or "Why are you talking to her?" ²⁸The woman left her water jar beside the well and ran back to the village, telling everyone, ²⁹"Come and see a man who told me everything I ever did! Could he possibly be the Messiah?" ³⁰So the people came streaming from the village to see him.

³¹Meanwhile, the disciples were urging Jesus, "Rabbi, eat something."

³²But Jesus replied, "I have a kind of food you know nothing about."

³³"Did someone bring him food while we were gone?" the disciples asked each other.

³⁴Then Jesus explained: "My nourishment comes from doing the will of God, who sent me, and from finishing his work. ³⁵You know the saying, 'Four months between planting and harvest.' But I say, wake up and look around. The fields are already ripe* for harvest. ³⁶The harvesters are paid good wages, and the fruit they harvest is people brought to eternal life. What joy awaits both the planter and the harvester alike! ³⁷You know the saying, 'One

---

4:9 Some manuscripts do not include this sentence. **4:20** Greek *on this mountain.* **4:26** Or *"The 'I Am' is here"*; or *"I am the Lord"*; Greek reads *"I am, the one speaking to you."* See Exod 3:14. **4:35** Greek *white.*

4:6-8 John sets the scene for the interaction between the Samaritan woman and Jesus. While John rarely portrays Jesus with weakness, here John makes a point of saying that it was midday ("about noontime") and that Jesus was "tired from the long walk." These details explain why Jesus would need to address the woman, who happened to come to the well for a divine appointment. Men were not usually responsible for drawing water, so Jesus wouldn't have had the tools necessary to get himself a drink. He needed the woman to help him. John also alerts the reader that Jesus' disciples had gone into the village, leaving Jesus alone. This also would have set up John's original audience to be surprised when Jesus addressed the woman.

4:9 When Jesus addressed her, "the woman was surprised" because social taboos prohibited a Jewish teacher like Jesus from speaking to a woman. However, Jesus did not let social taboos constrain him from ministering to someone in need.

4:19 The woman inferred that Jesus was a prophet because he knew things about her that a stranger could not have. As her understanding of Jesus unfolded, the way she addressed him became increasingly well informed. Initially, she recognized him as "a Jew" and called him "sir," later wondering if he might be "the Messiah" (4:9, 11, 25). In the end, the people of her village recognized him as "Savior of the world" (4:42).

4:28-42 The woman, despite being a non-Jew and an unlikely recipient of a divine meeting, eventually caught the theological implication of Jesus' initial talk about "living water" (4:10). Having recognized Jesus' messianic identity, she ran back to share her tentative discovery with her fellow villagers and led them to meet Jesus. Despite her humble position, she found her salvation and mission. God can meet you and me where we are and use us regardless of how much we know.

plants and another harvests.' And it's true. ³⁸I sent you to harvest where you didn't plant; others had already done the work, and now you will get to gather the harvest."

Many Samaritans Believe

³⁹Many Samaritans from the village believed in Jesus because the woman had said, "He told me everything I ever did!" ⁴⁰When they came out to see him, they begged him to stay in their village. So he stayed for two days, ⁴¹long enough for many more to hear his message and believe. ⁴²Then they said to the woman, "Now we believe, not just because of what you told us, but because we have heard him ourselves. Now we know that he is indeed the Savior of the world."

Jesus Heals an Official's Son

⁴³At the end of the two days, Jesus went on to Galilee. ⁴⁴He himself had said that a prophet is not honored in his own hometown. ⁴⁵Yet the Galileans welcomed him, for they had been in Jerusalem at the Passover celebration and had seen everything he did there.

⁴⁶As he traveled through Galilee, he came to Cana, where he had turned the water into wine. There was a government official in nearby Capernaum whose son was very sick. ⁴⁷When he heard that Jesus had come from Judea to Galilee, he went and begged Jesus to come to Capernaum to heal his son, who was about to die.

⁴⁸Jesus asked, "Will you never believe in me unless you see miraculous signs and wonders?"

⁴⁹The official pleaded, "Lord, please come now before my little boy dies."

⁵⁰Then Jesus told him, "Go back home. Your son will live!" And the man believed what Jesus said and started home.

⁵¹While the man was on his way, some of his servants met him with the news that his son was alive and well. ⁵²He asked them when the boy had begun to get better, and they replied, "Yesterday afternoon at one o'clock his fever suddenly disappeared!" ⁵³Then the father realized that that was the very time Jesus had told him, "Your son will live." And he and his entire household believed in Jesus. ⁵⁴This was the second miraculous sign Jesus did in Galilee after coming from Judea.

Jesus Heals a Lame Man

5 Afterward Jesus returned to Jerusalem for one of the Jewish holy days. ²Inside the city, near the Sheep Gate, was the pool of Bethesda,* with five covered porches. ³Crowds of sick people—blind, lame, or paralyzed—lay on the porches.* ⁵One of the men lying there had been sick for thirty-eight years.

> "The secret to 'doing it all' is not necessarily doing it all, but rather discovering which part of the 'all' He has given us to do and doing all of THAT."
>
> **JILL BRISCOE**
> teacher, pastor, editor, and writer

⁶When Jesus saw him and knew he had been ill for a long time, he asked him, "Would you like to get well?"

⁷"I can't, sir," the sick man said, "for I have no one to put me into the pool when the water bubbles up. Someone else always gets there ahead of me."

⁸Jesus told him, "Stand up, pick up your mat, and walk!"

⁹Instantly, the man was healed! He rolled up his sleeping mat and began walking! But this miracle happened on the Sabbath, ¹⁰so the Jewish leaders objected. They said to the man who was cured, "You can't work on the Sabbath! The law doesn't allow you to carry that sleeping mat!"

¹¹But he replied, "The man who healed me told me, 'Pick up your mat and walk.'"

¹²"Who said such a thing as that?" they demanded. ¹³The man didn't know, for Jesus had disappeared into the crowd. ¹⁴But afterward Jesus found him in the Temple and told him, "Now you are well; so stop sinning, or something even worse may happen to you." ¹⁵Then the man went and told the Jewish leaders that it was Jesus who had healed him.

Jesus Claims to Be the Son of God

¹⁶So the Jewish leaders began harassing* Jesus for breaking the Sabbath rules. ¹⁷But Jesus replied, "My

---

5:2 Other manuscripts read *Beth-zatha;* still others read *Bethsaida.* **5:3** Some manuscripts add an expanded conclusion to verse 3 and all of verse 4: *waiting for a certain movement of the water, ⁴for an angel of the Lord came from time to time and stirred up the water. And the first person to step in after the water was stirred was healed of whatever disease he had.* **5:16** Or *persecuting.*

God's Story Shows Us Our Own

MY STORY WITH GOD

SCRIPTURE CONNECTION: JOHN 5:31-47

The Bible is... a faithful declaration of the presence and holiness of God. We ask it to tell us about ourselves, and all the while it is telling us about "I AM."... We must read and study the Bible with our ears trained on hearing God's declaration of himself.

Does this mean that the Bible has nothing to say to us about who we are? Not at all.... The Bible does tell us who we are and what we should do, but it does so through the lens of who God is....

If I read the Bible looking for myself in the text before I look for God there, I may indeed learn that I should not be selfish. I may even try harder not to be selfish. But until I see my selfishness through the lens of the utter unselfishness of God, I have not properly understood its sinfulness. The Bible is a book about God....

In the New Testament, we find Jesus addressing the same problem with the Jewish leaders... ([see] John 5:39-40). The Jewish leaders searched the Scriptures asking the wrong question, looking for the wrong image to be revealed....

If our reading of the Bible focuses our eyes on anyone other than God, we have gotten backwards the transformation process.... We must turn around our habit of asking, "Who am I?" We must first ask, "What does this passage teach me about God?"

> We answer "Who am I?" by learning "Whose am I?"

IMAGINE

How might we read the Bible to know God better first?

So many books promise self-help, but the Bible says God is our help. How can this lighten our load to live as though it is not up to us but up to God?

"A vision of God high and lifted up reveals to me my sin and increases my love for him.... And I begin to be conformed to the image of the One I behold."

JEN WILKEN • Taken from *Women of the Word: How to Study the Bible with Both Our Hearts and Our Minds* by Jen Wilkin, © 2014 pp. 26-27. Used by permission of Crossway, a publishing ministry of Good News Publishers, Wheaton, IL 60187, www.crossway.org.

Father is always working, and so am I." ¹⁸So the Jewish leaders tried all the harder to find a way to kill him. For he not only broke the Sabbath, he called God his Father, thereby making himself equal with God.

¹⁹So Jesus explained, "I tell you the truth, the Son can do nothing by himself. He does only what he sees the Father doing. Whatever the Father does, the Son also does. ²⁰For the Father loves the Son and shows him everything he is doing. In fact, the Father will show him how to do even greater works than healing this man. Then you will truly be astonished. ²¹For just as the Father gives life to those he raises from the dead, so the Son gives life to anyone he wants. ²²In addition, the Father judges no one. Instead, he has given the Son absolute authority to judge, ²³so that everyone will honor the Son, just as they honor the Father. Anyone who does not honor the Son is certainly not honoring the Father who sent him.

²⁴"I tell you the truth, those who listen to my message and believe in God who sent me have eternal life. They will never be condemned for their sins, but they have already passed from death into life.

²⁵"And I assure you that the time is coming, indeed it's here now, when the dead will hear my voice—the voice of the Son of God. And those who listen will live. ²⁶The Father has life in himself, and he has granted that same life-giving power to his Son. ²⁷And he has given him authority to judge everyone because he is the Son of Man.* ²⁸Don't be so surprised! Indeed, the time is coming when all the dead in their graves will hear the voice of God's Son, ²⁹and they will rise again. Those who have done good will rise to experience eternal life, and those who have continued in evil will rise to experience judgment. ³⁰I can do nothing on my own. I judge as God tells me. Therefore, my judgment is just, because I carry out the will of the one who sent me, not my own will.

Witnesses to Jesus

³¹"If I were to testify on my own behalf, my testimony would not be valid. ³²But someone else is also testifying about me, and I assure you that everything he says about me is true. ³³In fact, you sent investigators to listen to John the Baptist, and his testimony about me was true. ³⁴Of course, I have no need of human witnesses, but I say these things so you might be saved. ³⁵John was like a burning and shining lamp, and you were excited for a while about his message. ³⁶But I have a greater witness than John—my teachings and my miracles. The Father gave me these works to accomplish, and they prove that he sent me. ³⁷And the Father who sent me has testified about me himself. You have never heard his voice or seen him face to face, ³⁸and you do not have his message in your hearts, because you do not believe me—the one he sent to you.

³⁹"You search the Scriptures because you think they give you eternal life. But the Scriptures point to me! ⁴⁰Yet you refuse to come to me to receive this life.

⁴¹"Your approval means nothing to me, ⁴²because I know you don't have God's love within you. ⁴³For I have come to you in my Father's name, and you have rejected me. Yet if others come in their own name, you gladly welcome them. ⁴⁴No wonder you can't believe! For you gladly honor each other, but you don't care about the honor that comes from the one who alone is God.*

⁴⁵"Yet it isn't I who will accuse you before the Father. Moses will accuse you! Yes, Moses, in whom you put your hopes. ⁴⁶If you really believed Moses, you would believe me, because he wrote about me. ⁴⁷But since you don't believe what he wrote, how will you believe what I say?"

Jesus Feeds Five Thousand

6 After this, Jesus crossed over to the far side of the Sea of Galilee, also known as the Sea of Tiberias. ²A huge crowd kept following him wherever he went, because they saw his miraculous signs as he healed the sick. ³Then Jesus climbed a hill and sat down with his disciples around him. ⁴(It was nearly time for the Jewish Passover celebration.) ⁵Jesus soon saw a huge crowd of people coming to look for him. Turning to Philip, he asked, "Where can we buy bread to feed all these people?" ⁶He was testing Philip, for he already knew what he was going to do.

⁷Philip replied, "Even if we worked for months, we wouldn't have enough money* to feed them!"

⁸Then Andrew, Simon Peter's brother, spoke up. ⁹"There's a young boy here with five barley loaves and two fish. But what good is that with this huge crowd?"

¹⁰"Tell everyone to sit down," Jesus said. So they all sat down on the grassy slopes. (The men alone numbered about 5,000.) ¹¹Then Jesus took the loaves, gave thanks to God, and distributed them to the people. Afterward he did the same with the fish. And they all ate as much as they wanted. ¹²After everyone was full, Jesus told his disciples, "Now gather the leftovers, so that nothing is wasted." ¹³So they picked up the pieces and filled twelve baskets with scraps left by the people who had eaten from the five barley loaves.

¹⁴When the people saw him* do this miraculous sign, they exclaimed, "Surely, he is the Prophet we have been expecting!"* ¹⁵When Jesus saw that they

---

5:27 "Son of Man" is a title Jesus used for himself. **5:44** Some manuscripts read *from the only One.* **6:7** Greek *Two hundred denarii would not be enough.* A denarius was equivalent to a laborer's full day's wage. **6:14a** Some manuscripts read *Jesus.* **6:14b** See Deut 18:15, 18; Mal 4:5-6.

were ready to force him to be their king, he slipped away into the hills by himself.

Jesus Walks on Water

[16] That evening Jesus' disciples went down to the shore to wait for him. [17] But as darkness fell and Jesus still hadn't come back, they got into the boat and headed across the lake toward Capernaum. [18] Soon a gale swept down upon them, and the sea grew very rough. [19] They had rowed three or four miles* when suddenly they saw Jesus walking on the water toward the boat. They were terrified, [20] but he called out to them, "Don't be afraid. I am here!*" [21] Then they were eager to let him in the boat, and immediately they arrived at their destination!

Jesus, the Bread of Life

[22] The next day the crowd that had stayed on the far shore saw that the disciples had taken the only boat, and they realized Jesus had not gone with them. [23] Several boats from Tiberias landed near the place where the Lord had blessed the bread and the people had eaten. [24] So when the crowd saw that neither Jesus nor his disciples were there, they got into the boats and went across to Capernaum to look for him. [25] They found him on the other side of the lake and asked, "Rabbi, when did you get here?"

[26] Jesus replied, "I tell you the truth, you want to be with me because I fed you, not because you understood the miraculous signs. [27] But don't be so concerned about perishable things like food. Spend your energy seeking the eternal life that the Son of Man* can give you. For God the Father has given me the seal of his approval."

[28] They replied, "We want to perform God's works, too. What should we do?"

[29] Jesus told them, "This is the only work God wants from you: Believe in the one he has sent."

[30] They answered, "Show us a miraculous sign if you want us to believe in you. What can you do? [31] After all, our ancestors ate manna while they journeyed through the wilderness! The Scriptures say, 'Moses gave them bread from heaven to eat.'*"

[32] Jesus said, "I tell you the truth, Moses didn't give you bread from heaven. My Father did. And now he offers you the true bread from heaven. [33] The true bread of God is the one who comes down from heaven and gives life to the world."

[34] "Sir," they said, "give us that bread every day."

[35] Jesus replied, "I am the bread of life. Whoever comes to me will never be hungry again. Whoever believes in me will never be thirsty. [36] But you haven't believed in me even though you have seen me. [37] However, those the Father has given me will come to me, and I will never reject them. [38] For I have come down from heaven to do the will of God who sent me, not to do my own will. [39] And this is the will of God, that I should not lose even one of all those he has given me, but that I should raise them up at the last day. [40] For it is my Father's will that all who see his Son and believe in him should have eternal life. I will raise them up at the last day."

[41] Then the people* began to murmur in disagreement because he had said, "I am the bread that came down from heaven." [42] They said, "Isn't this Jesus, the son of Joseph? We know his father and mother. How can he say, 'I came down from heaven'?"

[43] But Jesus replied, "Stop complaining about what I said. [44] For no one can come to me unless the Father who sent me draws them to me, and at the last day I will raise them up. [45] As it is written in the Scriptures,* 'They will all be taught by God.' Everyone who listens to the Father and learns from him comes to me. [46] (Not that anyone has ever seen the Father; only I, who was sent from God, have seen him.)

[47] "I tell you the truth, anyone who believes has eternal life. [48] Yes, I am the bread of life! [49] Your ancestors ate manna in the wilderness, but they all died. [50] Anyone who eats the bread from heaven, however, will never die. [51] I am the living bread that came down from heaven. Anyone who eats this bread will live forever; and this bread, which I will offer so the world may live, is my flesh."

[52] Then the people began arguing with each other about what he meant. "How can this man give us his flesh to eat?" they asked.

[53] So Jesus said again, "I tell you the truth, unless you eat the flesh of the Son of Man and drink his blood, you cannot have eternal life within you. [54] But anyone who eats my flesh and drinks my blood has eternal life, and I will raise that person at the last day. [55] For my flesh is true food, and my blood is true drink. [56] Anyone who eats my flesh and drinks my blood remains in me, and I in him. [57] I live because of the living Father who sent me; in the same way, anyone who feeds on me will live because of me. [58] I am the true bread that came down from heaven. Anyone who eats this bread will not die as your ancestors did (even though they ate the manna) but will live forever."

[59] He said these things while he was teaching in the synagogue in Capernaum.

Many Disciples Desert Jesus

[60] Many of his disciples said, "This is very hard to understand. How can anyone accept it?"

[61] Jesus was aware that his disciples were complaining, so he said to them, "Does this offend you? [62] Then what will you think if you see the Son of Man ascend to heaven again? [63] The Spirit alone gives eternal life.

6:19 Greek *25 or 30 stadia* [4.6 or 5.5 kilometers]. **6:20** Or *The 'I AM' is here;* Greek reads *I am.* See Exod 3:14. **6:27** "Son of Man" is a title Jesus used for himself. **6:31** Exod 16:4; Ps 78:24. **6:41** Greek *Jewish people;* also in 6:52. **6:45** Greek *in the prophets.* Isa 54:13.

Human effort accomplishes nothing. And the very words I have spoken to you are spirit and life. ⁶⁴But some of you do not believe me." (For Jesus knew from the beginning which ones didn't believe, and he knew who would betray him.) ⁶⁵Then he said, "That is why I said that people can't come to me unless the Father gives them to me."

⁶⁶At this point many of his disciples turned away and deserted him. ⁶⁷Then Jesus turned to the Twelve and asked, "Are you also going to leave?"

⁶⁸Simon Peter replied, "Lord, to whom would we go? You have the words that give eternal life. ⁶⁹We believe, and we know you are the Holy One of God.*"

⁷⁰Then Jesus said, "I chose the twelve of you, but one is a devil." ⁷¹He was speaking of Judas, son of Simon Iscariot, one of the Twelve, who would later betray him.

Jesus and His Brothers

7 After this, Jesus traveled around Galilee. He wanted to stay out of Judea, where the Jewish leaders were plotting his death. ²But soon it was time for the Jewish Festival of Shelters, ³and Jesus' brothers said to him, "Leave here and go to Judea, where your followers can see your miracles! ⁴You can't become famous if you hide like this! If you can do such wonderful things, show yourself to the world!" ⁵For even his brothers didn't believe in him.

⁶Jesus replied, "Now is not the right time for me to go, but you can go anytime. ⁷The world can't hate you, but it does hate me because I accuse it of doing evil. ⁸You go on. I'm not going* to this festival, because my time has not yet come." ⁹After saying these things, Jesus remained in Galilee.

Jesus Teaches Openly at the Temple

¹⁰But after his brothers left for the festival, Jesus also went, though secretly, staying out of public view. ¹¹The Jewish leaders tried to find him at the festival and kept asking if anyone had seen him. ¹²There was a lot of grumbling about him among the crowds. Some argued, "He's a good man," but others said, "He's nothing but a fraud who deceives the people." ¹³But no one had the courage to speak favorably about him in public, for they were afraid of getting in trouble with the Jewish leaders.

¹⁴Then, midway through the festival, Jesus went up to the Temple and began to teach. ¹⁵The people* were surprised when they heard him. "How does he know so much when he hasn't been trained?" they asked.

¹⁶So Jesus told them, "My message is not my own; it comes from God who sent me. ¹⁷Anyone who wants to do the will of God will know whether my teaching is from God or is merely my own. ¹⁸Those who speak for themselves want glory only for themselves, but a person who seeks to honor the one who sent him speaks truth, not lies. ¹⁹Moses gave you the law, but none of you obeys it! In fact, you are trying to kill me."

²⁰The crowd replied, "You're demon possessed! Who's trying to kill you?"

²¹Jesus replied, "I did one miracle on the Sabbath, and you were amazed. ²²But you work on the Sabbath, too, when you obey Moses' law of circumcision. (Actually, this tradition of circumcision began with the patriarchs, long before the law of Moses.) ²³For if the correct time for circumcising your son falls on the Sabbath, you go ahead and do it so as not to break the law of Moses. So why should you be angry with me for healing a man on the Sabbath? ²⁴Look beneath the surface so you can judge correctly."

Is Jesus the Messiah?

²⁵Some of the people who lived in Jerusalem started to ask each other, "Isn't this the man they are trying to kill? ²⁶But here he is, speaking in public, and they say nothing to him. Could our leaders possibly believe that he is the Messiah? ²⁷But how could he be? For we know where this man comes from. When the Messiah comes, he will simply appear; no one will know where he comes from."

²⁸While Jesus was teaching in the Temple, he called out, "Yes, you know me, and you know where I come from. But I'm not here on my own. The one who sent me is true, and you don't know him. ²⁹But I know him because I come from him, and he sent me to you." ³⁰Then the leaders tried to arrest him; but no one laid a hand on him, because his time* had not yet come.

³¹Many among the crowds at the Temple believed in him. "After all," they said, "would you expect the Messiah to do more miraculous signs than this man has done?"

³²When the Pharisees heard that the crowds were whispering such things, they and the leading priests sent Temple guards to arrest Jesus. ³³But Jesus told them, "I will be with you only a little longer. Then I will return to the one who sent me. ³⁴You will search for me but not find me. And you cannot go where I am going."

³⁵The Jewish leaders were puzzled by this statement. "Where is he planning to go?" they asked. "Is he thinking of leaving the country and going to the Jews in other lands?* Maybe he will even teach the Greeks! ³⁶What does he mean when he says, 'You will search for me but not find me,' and 'You cannot go where I am going'?"

6:69 Other manuscripts read *you are the Christ, the Holy One of God*; still others read *you are the Christ, the Son of God*; and still others read *you are the Christ, the Son of the living God*.   **7:8** Some manuscripts read *not yet going*.   **7:15** Greek *Jewish people*.   **7:30** Greek *his hour*.   **7:35** Or *the Jews who live among the Greeks?*

Jesus Promises Living Water

³⁷On the last day, the climax of the festival, Jesus stood and shouted to the crowds, "Anyone who is thirsty may come to me! ³⁸Anyone who believes in me may come and drink! For the Scriptures declare, 'Rivers of living water will flow from his heart.'"* ³⁹(When he said "living water," he was speaking of the Spirit, who would be given to everyone believing in him. But the Spirit had not yet been given,* because Jesus had not yet entered into his glory.)

Division and Unbelief

⁴⁰When the crowds heard him say this, some of them declared, "Surely this man is the Prophet we've been expecting."* ⁴¹Others said, "He is the Messiah." Still others said, "But he can't be! Will the Messiah come from Galilee? ⁴²For the Scriptures clearly state that the Messiah will be born of the royal line of David, in Bethlehem, the village where King David was born."* ⁴³So the crowd was divided about him. ⁴⁴Some even wanted him arrested, but no one laid a hand on him.

⁴⁵When the Temple guards returned without having arrested Jesus, the leading priests and Pharisees demanded, "Why didn't you bring him in?"

⁴⁶"We have never heard anyone speak like this!" the guards responded.

⁴⁷"Have you been led astray, too?" the Pharisees mocked. ⁴⁸"Is there a single one of us rulers or Pharisees who believes in him? ⁴⁹This foolish crowd follows him, but they are ignorant of the law. God's curse is on them!"

⁵⁰Then Nicodemus, the leader who had met with Jesus earlier, spoke up. ⁵¹"Is it legal to convict a man before he is given a hearing?" he asked.

⁵²They replied, "Are you from Galilee, too? Search the Scriptures and see for yourself—no prophet ever comes* from Galilee!"

[The most ancient Greek manuscripts do not include John 7:53–8:11.]

⁵³Then the meeting broke up, and everybody went home.

A Woman Caught in Adultery

8 Jesus returned to the Mount of Olives, ²but early the next morning he was back again at the Temple. A crowd soon gathered, and he sat down and taught them. ³As he was speaking, the teachers of religious law and the Pharisees brought a woman who had been caught in the act of adultery. They put her in front of the crowd.

⁴"Teacher," they said to Jesus, "this woman was caught in the act of adultery. ⁵The law of Moses says to stone her. What do you say?"

⁶They were trying to trap him into saying something they could use against him, but Jesus stooped down and wrote in the dust with his finger. ⁷They kept demanding an answer, so he stood up again and said, "All right, but let the one who has never sinned throw the first stone!" ⁸Then he stooped down again and wrote in the dust.

⁹When the accusers heard this, they slipped away one by one, beginning with the oldest, until only Jesus was left in the middle of the crowd with the woman. ¹⁰Then Jesus stood up again and said to the woman, "Where are your accusers? Didn't even one of them condemn you?"

¹¹"No, Lord," she said.

And Jesus said, "Neither do I. Go and sin no more."

Jesus, the Light of the World

¹²Jesus spoke to the people once more and said, "I am the light of the world. If you follow me, you won't have to walk in darkness, because you will have the light that leads to life."

¹³The Pharisees replied, "You are making those claims about yourself! Such testimony is not valid."

¹⁴Jesus told them, "These claims are valid even though I make them about myself. For I know where I came from and where I am going, but you don't know this about me. ¹⁵You judge me by human standards, but I do not judge anyone. ¹⁶And if I did, my judgment would be correct in every respect because I am not alone. The Father* who sent me is with me. ¹⁷Your own law says that if two people agree about

---

7:37-38 Or *"Let anyone who is thirsty come to me and drink. ³⁸For the Scriptures declare, 'Rivers of living water will flow from the heart of anyone who believes in me.'"* **7:39** Several early manuscripts read *But as yet there was no Spirit.* Still others read *But as yet there was no Holy Spirit.* **7:40** See Deut 18:15, 18; Mal 4:5-6. **7:42** See Mic 5:2. **7:52** Some manuscripts read *the prophet does not come.* **8:16** Some manuscripts read *The One.*

7:53–8:11 Jesus' conduct toward the woman caught in adultery sharply contrasts with the religious leaders' treatment. He didn't condemn the woman, but he didn't deny her sin or neglect her need for repentance. Although her adultery was wrong, Jesus was merciful toward a woman who was being exploited by the religious leaders.

8:5 Trying to trap Jesus, the woman's accusers stated that the law said she should be stoned, indicating that she was engaged or married (Leviticus 20:10; Deuteronomy 22:23-24). Unmarried women who were raped or who had sex were not executed. The law cited by these religious leaders also stated that the woman's lover should be killed with her, but they apparently ignored the man's participation and chose to blame only the woman. These men could have dealt with her privately and kept her from public shame, which is likely what they would have done under normal circumstances, but their goal was to trap Jesus.

The Woman CAUGHT IN ADULTERY

IDENTITY

Turned by Tenderness

She remembers...

I knew the possible consequences for infidelity, but I wasn't afraid. After all, the Temple police didn't even have the courage to arrest Jesus, the man claiming to be God. But when Jesus' accusers tested his commitment to the Torah, they used me as an object lesson.

Stripped of my dignity and completely shamed, I stood before the crowd while they questioned Jesus on my fate. Terror describes this near-death experience. Our law was clear—both my lover and I deserved death (Leviticus 20:10). But since the religious leaders chose not to follow the law and prosecute my lover, I was facing the repercussions all alone. I thought my only hope was Roman law—which forbade my execution without Roman approval.

But Jesus kept bending down and writing in the dust on the ground, deflecting attention away from me. My accusers had meant to trap Jesus by exposing me, but he exposed them: I may have been caught in the act of adultery, but these men were caught in the act of hypocrisy. One by one, they quietly walked away until just Jesus and I were left before the watching crowd. I had no idea he would pass the religious leaders' test and save my life.

Jesus didn't overlook my wrongdoing, but he did show me dignity. He forgave and corrected me, and the way he treated me changed my life's course. My faith story lives on in anyone who knows this tender kindness of Jesus.

> Jesus turns our hearts with tenderness.

THE WOMAN CAUGHT IN ADULTERY'S STORY IS TOLD IN JOHN 8:1-11.

IDENTIFY

How has the tender kindness of Jesus turned your life?

How has God's Word reminded you of your dignity when others' words or actions have not?

"My husband, Aaron, has at times stepped in front of me to buffer unwanted attention. The simple act of deflection is a tender kindness. On a deeper level, I feel similar protection from Jesus, my ultimate shame deflector. Jesus took time to welcome, rescue, heal, and commission women and dignify their existence and ministry."

KAT ARMSTRONG, MA, is a Bible teacher, preacher, coach, and ministry leader. She cofounded the Polished Network and authored *No More Holding Back*, *The In-Between Place*, and the Storyline Bible Studies series.

Insight — HEROD'S TEMPLE

The Temple in Jerusalem no longer exists, but artistic renderings can help us imagine what it would have looked like and what it would have been like to encounter Jesus there. Since Solomon's Temple had been destroyed in 586 BC, a smaller Second Temple was built during the time of the prophet Haggai, after the Jews returned from exile in Babylon (see Ezra 1–6) Several centuries later, Herod the Great, king of Judea at the time of Jesus' birth, reconstructed the structure, replacing and expanding it. Herod's massive project began in 20 BC, and while the core of the new structure was finished in a decade, the work was not fully completed until AD 64. This Temple was destroyed in AD 70, just six years after its completion. Many events of Jesus' life and ministry took place within the Temple compound.

- **Colonnade** — *Eastern side is Solomon's Colonnade* SEE JOHN 10:23; ACTS 3:11; 5:12
- **Gentiles' Court**
- **Israel Court**
- **Oil Storage**
- **Nazirites' Court**
- **Pharisee and tax collector** LUKE 18:10-14
- **Women's Court**
- **Widow's offering** MARK 12:41-44
- **Beautiful Gate**
- **Wood Storage**
- **Crippled beggar healed** ACTS 3:1-11

THE HOLY PLACE HEBREWS 9:1–10:25

The Temple in Jerusalem was God's sanctuary, the place where God met with his people through carefully prescribed rituals. The Holy Place was accessible only to priests, who daily conducted rituals within its walls (see Luke 1:5-25). Separated from the Holy Place by a thick curtain was the Most Holy Place, where only the high priest was allowed to enter, and only once a year on the Day of Atonement.

When Jesus died, the heavy curtain separating the Most Holy Place from the Holy Place was torn in two (Matthew 27:51-52). Jesus has gone as High Priest once for all time into the Most Holy Place in heaven to atone for sin (Hebrews 9:11-12, 24). Now God's holy presence is accessible to all (Hebrews 10:19-22).

Interior cutaway view

- Curtain
- The Holy Place
- The Most Holy Place

- The Holy Place
- Nicanor Gate — *Levite choirs performed on steps*
- Priests' Court
- Altar and Washbasin
- Priests' Living Quarters
- Lepers' Court
- Soreg Boundary — *No entry for non-Jews*
- Sacred Enclosure
- EAST

something, their witness is accepted as fact.* ¹⁸I am one witness, and my Father who sent me is the other."

¹⁹"Where is your father?" they asked.

Jesus answered, "Since you don't know who I am, you don't know who my Father is. If you knew me, you would also know my Father." ²⁰Jesus made these statements while he was teaching in the section of the Temple known as the Treasury. But he was not arrested, because his time* had not yet come.

The Unbelieving People Warned

²¹Later Jesus said to them again, "I am going away. You will search for me but will die in your sin. You cannot come where I am going."

²²The people* asked, "Is he planning to commit suicide? What does he mean, 'You cannot come where I am going'?"

²³Jesus continued, "You are from below; I am from above. You belong to this world; I do not. ²⁴That is why I said that you will die in your sins; for unless you believe that I AM who I claim to be,* you will die in your sins."

²⁵"Who are you?" they demanded.

Jesus replied, "The one I have always claimed to be.* ²⁶I have much to say about you and much to condemn, but I won't. For I say only what I have heard from the one who sent me, and he is completely truthful." ²⁷But they still didn't understand that he was talking about his Father.

²⁸So Jesus said, "When you have lifted up the Son of Man on the cross, then you will understand that I AM he.* I do nothing on my own but say only what the Father taught me. ²⁹And the one who sent me is with me—he has not deserted me. For I always do what pleases him." ³⁰Then many who heard him say these things believed in him.

Jesus and Abraham

³¹Jesus said to the people who believed in him, "You are truly my disciples if you remain faithful to my teachings. ³²And you will know the truth, and the truth will set you free."

³³"But we are descendants of Abraham," they said. "We have never been slaves to anyone. What do you mean, 'You will be set free'?"

³⁴Jesus replied, "I tell you the truth, everyone who sins is a slave of sin. ³⁵A slave is not a permanent member of the family, but a son is part of the family forever. ³⁶So if the Son sets you free, you are truly free. ³⁷Yes, I realize that you are descendants of Abraham. And yet some of you are trying to kill me because there's no room in your hearts for my message. ³⁸I am telling you what I saw when I was with my Father. But you are following the advice of your father."

³⁹"Our father is Abraham!" they declared.

"No," Jesus replied, "for if you were really the children of Abraham, you would follow his example.* ⁴⁰Instead, you are trying to kill me because I told you the truth, which I heard from God. Abraham never did such a thing. ⁴¹No, you are imitating your real father."

They replied, "We aren't illegitimate children! God himself is our true Father."

⁴²Jesus told them, "If God were your Father, you would love me, because I have come to you from God. I am not here on my own, but he sent me. ⁴³Why can't you understand what I am saying? It's because you can't even hear me! ⁴⁴For you are the children of your father the devil, and you love to do the evil things he does. He was a murderer from the beginning. He has always hated the truth, because there is no truth in him. When he lies, it is consistent with his character; for he is a liar and the father of lies. ⁴⁵So when I tell the truth, you just naturally don't believe me! ⁴⁶Which of you can truthfully accuse me of sin? And since I am telling you the truth, why don't you believe me? ⁴⁷Anyone who belongs to God listens gladly to the words of God. But you don't listen because you don't belong to God."

⁴⁸The people retorted, "You Samaritan devil! Didn't we say all along that you were possessed by a demon?"

⁴⁹"No," Jesus said, "I have no demon in me. For I honor my Father—and you dishonor me. ⁵⁰And though I have no wish to glorify myself, God is going to glorify me. He is the true judge. ⁵¹I tell you the truth, anyone who obeys my teaching will never die!"

⁵²The people said, "Now we know you are possessed by a demon. Even Abraham and the prophets died, but you say, 'Anyone who obeys my teaching will never die!' ⁵³Are you greater than our father Abraham? He died, and so did the prophets. Who do you think you are?"

⁵⁴Jesus answered, "If I want glory for myself, it doesn't count. But it is my Father who will glorify me. You say, 'He is our God,'* ⁵⁵but you don't even know him. I know him. If I said otherwise, I would be as great a liar as you! But I do know him and obey him. ⁵⁶Your father Abraham rejoiced as he looked forward to my coming. He saw it and was glad."

8:17 See Deut 19:15.   **8:20** Greek *his hour.*   **8:22** Greek *Jewish people;* also in 8:31, 48, 52, 57.   **8:24** Greek *unless you believe that I am.* See Exod 3:14.   **8:25** Or *Why do I speak to you at all?*   **8:28** Greek *When you have lifted up the Son of Man, then you will know that I am.* "Son of Man" is a title Jesus used for himself.   **8:39** Some manuscripts read *if you are really the children of Abraham, follow his example.*   **8:54** Some manuscripts read *You say he is your God.*

8:20 The Treasury was located in the section of the Temple called the Court of the Women. Jesus often taught there, allowing both men and women to hear him (see also Mark 12:41).

⁵⁷The people said, "You aren't even fifty years old. How can you say you have seen Abraham?*"

⁵⁸Jesus answered, "I tell you the truth, before Abraham was even born, I AM!*" ⁵⁹At that point they picked up stones to throw at him. But Jesus was hidden from them and left the Temple.

Jesus Heals a Man Born Blind

9 As Jesus was walking along, he saw a man who had been blind from birth. ²"Rabbi," his disciples asked him, "why was this man born blind? Was it because of his own sins or his parents' sins?"

³"It was not because of his sins or his parents' sins," Jesus answered. "This happened so the power of God could be seen in him. ⁴We must quickly carry out the tasks assigned us by the one who sent us.* The night is coming, and then no one can work. ⁵But while I am here in the world, I am the light of the world."

⁶Then he spit on the ground, made mud with the saliva, and spread the mud over the blind man's eyes. ⁷He told him, "Go wash yourself in the pool of Siloam" (Siloam means "sent"). So the man went and washed and came back seeing!

⁸His neighbors and others who knew him as a blind beggar asked each other, "Isn't this the man who used to sit and beg?" ⁹Some said he was, and others said, "No, he just looks like him!"

But the beggar kept saying, "Yes, I am the same one!"

¹⁰They asked, "Who healed you? What happened?"

¹¹He told them, "The man they call Jesus made mud and spread it over my eyes and told me, 'Go to the pool of Siloam and wash yourself.' So I went and washed, and now I can see!"

¹²"Where is he now?" they asked.

"I don't know," he replied.

¹³Then they took the man who had been blind to the Pharisees, ¹⁴because it was on the Sabbath that Jesus had made the mud and healed him. ¹⁵The Pharisees asked the man all about it. So he told them, "He put the mud over my eyes, and when I washed it away, I could see!"

¹⁶Some of the Pharisees said, "This man Jesus is not from God, for he is working on the Sabbath." Others said, "But how could an ordinary sinner do such miraculous signs?" So there was a deep division of opinion among them.

¹⁷Then the Pharisees again questioned the man who had been blind and demanded, "What's your opinion about this man who healed you?"

The man replied, "I think he must be a prophet."

¹⁸The Jewish leaders still refused to believe the man had been blind and could now see, so they called in his parents. ¹⁹They asked them, "Is this your son? Was he born blind? If so, how can he now see?"

²⁰His parents replied, "We know this is our son and that he was born blind, ²¹but we don't know how he can see or who healed him. Ask him. He is old enough to speak for himself." ²²His parents said this because they were afraid of the Jewish leaders, who had announced that anyone saying Jesus was the Messiah would be expelled from the synagogue. ²³That's why they said, "He is old enough. Ask him."

²⁴So for the second time they called in the man who had been blind and told him, "God should get the glory for this,* because we know this man Jesus is a sinner."

²⁵"I don't know whether he is a sinner," the man replied. "But I know this: I was blind, and now I can see!"

²⁶"But what did he do?" they asked. "How did he heal you?"

²⁷"Look!" the man exclaimed. "I told you once. Didn't you listen? Why do you want to hear it again? Do you want to become his disciples, too?"

²⁸Then they cursed him and said, "You are his disciple, but we are disciples of Moses! ²⁹We know God spoke to Moses, but we don't even know where this man comes from."

³⁰"Why, that's very strange!" the man replied. "He healed my eyes, and yet you don't know where he comes from? ³¹We know that God doesn't listen to sinners, but he is ready to hear those who worship him and do his will. ³²Ever since the world began, no one has been able to open the eyes of someone born

---

8:57 Some manuscripts read *How can you say Abraham has seen you?* **8:58** Or *before Abraham was even born, I have always been alive;* Greek reads *before Abraham was, I am.* See Exod 3:14. **9:4** Other manuscripts read *I must quickly carry out the tasks assigned me by the one who sent me;* still others read *We must quickly carry out the tasks assigned us by the one who sent me.* **9:24** Or *Give glory to God, not to Jesus;* Greek reads *Give glory to God.*

9:1-3 First-century Jews incorrectly assumed that physical disabilities and illnesses were caused by sin (see also 9:34). The disciples assumed that someone's sin—the man's or his parents'—had caused him to be born blind, but Jesus corrected this way of thinking.

9:7-38 Although the text uses this man's physical disability to describe him, his recorded actions give us the full picture of his character. This unnamed man demonstrated incredible faith, taking Jesus at his word and following his instructions without question. After he became able to see, the man bravely refused to lie about what had happened, even under great pressure from the religious leaders. When Jesus sought him out later, the man proclaimed his belief that Jesus was the Messiah and worshiped him.

9:20-22 Knowing what had happened to their son, the parents of the man born blind were fearful to testify to his healing. In the Gospels, we often read stories about parents begging Jesus on behalf of their children. But here, we read a story about parents distancing themselves from their child, whom Jesus had healed. In cultures where elders are highly respected, parents' support and blessing are essential to their children, even if they are old enough to speak for themselves.

blind. ³³If this man were not from God, he couldn't have done it."

³⁴"You were born a total sinner!" they answered. "Are you trying to teach us?" And they threw him out of the synagogue.

Spiritual Blindness

³⁵When Jesus heard what had happened, he found the man and asked, "Do you believe in the Son of Man?*"

³⁶The man answered, "Who is he, sir? I want to believe in him."

³⁷"You have seen him," Jesus said, "and he is speaking to you!"

³⁸"Yes, Lord, I believe!" the man said. And he worshiped Jesus.

³⁹Then Jesus told him,* "I entered this world to render judgment—to give sight to the blind and to show those who think they see* that they are blind."

⁴⁰Some Pharisees who were standing nearby heard him and asked, "Are you saying we're blind?"

⁴¹"If you were blind, you wouldn't be guilty," Jesus replied. "But you remain guilty because you claim you can see.

The Good Shepherd and His Sheep

10 "I tell you the truth, anyone who sneaks over the wall of a sheepfold, rather than going through the gate, must surely be a thief and a robber! ²But the one who enters through the gate is the shepherd of the sheep. ³The gatekeeper opens the gate for him, and the sheep recognize his voice and come to him. He calls his own sheep by name and leads them out. ⁴After he has gathered his own flock, he walks ahead of them, and they follow him because they know his voice. ⁵They won't follow a stranger; they will run from him because they don't know his voice."

9:35 Some manuscripts read *the Son of God?* "Son of Man" is a title Jesus used for himself.   9:38-39a Some manuscripts do not include "*Yes, Lord, I believe!" the man said. And he worshiped Jesus. Then Jesus told him.*   9:39b Greek *those who see.*

Come Close TO THE FULL

SCRIPTURE CONNECTION: JOHN 10:1-21

Jesus said, "The thief's purpose is to steal and kill and destroy. My purpose is to give them a rich and satisfying life" (10:10).

Sometimes we need reminding that life is meant to be lived to the full. That it is okay to enjoy ourselves, to let our hair down, to worry less. Because as far I can tell, this is exactly how God intended for us to live—fully and abundantly.

Are you living your life to the full? Are you waking up each day grateful, joyful, and hopeful?

Jesus says to us, "I am the good shepherd; I know my own sheep, and they know me" (10:14).

As we spend time with Jesus and learn his voice, we begin to know deep in our souls that we are protected and that he is for us. This allows us to relax and trust that God is working out everything for our good (Romans 8:28). He teaches us the way to go, when to run to him, and when it's safe to go out into the pasture. He has prepared the way for us, and we can trust him along the journey. We don't need to live as if it is all up to us, for we are led by the Good Shepherd who leads us toward green pastures and guards us as we rest.

REFLECT "I am the good shepherd. The good shepherd sacrifices his life for the sheep." JOHN 10:11

Lord Jesus, you are so good, kind, gentle, and trustworthy. Thank you for your tender care, your sacrificial love, and your protection. Increase my faith so that I may continue to follow you in confidence, walking in joy and full of hope. Allow your definition of full to define my life in every way. Amen.

CONSIDER "The world is waiting for who God has called you to be."
BISHOP VASHTI MURPHY MCKENZIE

This is exactly how God intended for us to live: fully and abundantly.

MANDY ARIOTO is the president and CEO of MOPS International, influencing millions of moms around the world every year. She is a scholar of Greek, author, and speaker who believes in the transformational power of Scripture.

⁶Those who heard Jesus use this illustration didn't understand what he meant, ⁷so he explained it to them: "I tell you the truth, I am the gate for the sheep. ⁸All who came before me* were thieves and robbers. But the true sheep did not listen to them. ⁹Yes, I am the gate. Those who come in through me will be saved.* They will come and go freely and will find good pastures. ¹⁰The thief's purpose is to steal and kill and destroy. My purpose is to give them a rich and satisfying life.

¹¹"I am the good shepherd. The good shepherd sacrifices his life for the sheep. ¹²A hired hand will run when he sees a wolf coming. He will abandon the sheep because they don't belong to him and he isn't their shepherd. And so the wolf attacks them and scatters the flock. ¹³The hired hand runs away because he's working only for the money and doesn't really care about the sheep.

¹⁴"I am the good shepherd; I know my own sheep, and they know me, ¹⁵just as my Father knows me and I know the Father. So I sacrifice my life for the sheep. ¹⁶I have other sheep, too, that are not in this sheepfold. I must bring them also. They will listen to my voice, and there will be one flock with one shepherd.

¹⁷"The Father loves me because I sacrifice my life so I may take it back again. ¹⁸No one can take my life from me. I sacrifice it voluntarily. For I have the authority to lay it down when I want to and also to take it up again. For this is what my Father has commanded."

¹⁹When he said these things, the people* were again divided in their opinions about him. ²⁰Some said, "He's demon possessed and out of his mind. Why listen to a man like that?" ²¹Others said, "This doesn't sound like a man possessed by a demon! Can a demon open the eyes of the blind?"

Jesus Claims to Be the Son of God

²²It was now winter, and Jesus was in Jerusalem at the time of Hanukkah, the Festival of Dedication. ²³He was in the Temple, walking through the section known as Solomon's Colonnade. ²⁴The people surrounded him and asked, "How long are you going to keep us in suspense? If you are the Messiah, tell us plainly."

²⁵Jesus replied, "I have already told you, and you don't believe me. The proof is the work I do in my Father's name. ²⁶But you don't believe me because you are not my sheep. ²⁷My sheep listen to my voice; I know them, and they follow me. ²⁸I give them eternal life, and they will never perish. No one can snatch them away from me, ²⁹for my Father has given them to me, and he is more powerful than anyone else.* No one can snatch them from the Father's hand. ³⁰The Father and I are one."

> "Women live in the knowledge that … because God is the God of life and Jesus has promised abundant life, the suffering of women cannot be the last word."
>
> **MERCY AMBA ODUYOYE**
> theologian and professor

³¹Once again the people picked up stones to kill him. ³²Jesus said, "At my Father's direction I have done many good works. For which one are you going to stone me?"

³³They replied, "We're stoning you not for any good work, but for blasphemy! You, a mere man, claim to be God."

³⁴Jesus replied, "It is written in your own Scriptures* that God said to certain leaders of the people, 'I say, you are gods!'* ³⁵And you know that the Scriptures cannot be altered. So if those people who received God's message were called 'gods,' ³⁶why do you call it blasphemy when I say, 'I am the Son of God'? After all, the Father set me apart and sent me into the world. ³⁷Don't believe me unless I carry out my Father's work. ³⁸But if I do his work, believe in the evidence of the miraculous works I have done, even if you don't believe me. Then you will know and understand that the Father is in me, and I am in the Father."

³⁹Once again they tried to arrest him, but he got away and left them. ⁴⁰He went beyond the Jordan River near the place where John was first baptizing and stayed there awhile. ⁴¹And many followed him. "John didn't perform miraculous signs," they

---

10:8 Some manuscripts do not include *before me*. **10:9** Or *will find safety*. **10:19** Greek *Jewish people*; also in 10:24, 31. **10:29** Other manuscripts read *for what my Father has given me is more powerful than anything*; still others read *for regarding that which my Father has given me, he is greater than all*. **10:34a** Greek *your own law*. **10:34b** Ps 82:6.

MY STORY WITH FAMILY & FRIENDS

Leading and Loved for It

SCRIPTURE CONNECTION: JOHN 11:20-28

My friend, who's a firstborn, says, "Martha gets a bad rap. She's the one who takes action!"

Although Martha does get lovingly redirected to what fulfills, Jesus never chides her for leading with strength. Martha shows us four things that can help us live our purpose with our families and friends:

1. *Martha was a doer!* And that isn't bad. She was the first one to run to Jesus instead of waiting for him to come to her: "When Martha got word that Jesus was coming, she went to meet him. But Mary stayed in the house" (11:20).
2. *She was a believer!* She trusted that Jesus had the power to change her situation: "Lord, if only you had been here, my brother would not have died. But even now I know that God will give you whatever you ask" (11:21).
3. *Martha was a perceiver!* She was one of the few who understood Jesus' real identity. "'Yes, Lord,' she told him. 'I have always believed you are the Messiah, the Son of God, the one who has come into the world from God'" (11:27).
4. *And Martha was a bringer!* After this powerful encounter with Jesus, she didn't keep his goodness to herself. No, she went to her sister Mary and pointed her to Jesus: "'The Teacher is here and wants to see you'" (11:28).

> Martha does get lovingly redirected to what fulfills. But she never gets chided for leading with strength.

Have you ever noticed that firstborn daughters tend to lead from childhood and never stop? I can see why my firstborn friend stands up for Martha—and I admire her understanding of who Jesus was too (11:27).

IMAGINE

What makes Martha effective in blessing others?

How has God fashioned you for leadership and influence?

"Like Martha, I've sometimes been told I'm 'too much.' When I recognize God affirmed Martha's 'much,' I celebrate!"

NAOMI CRAMER OVERTON, MBA, DIS, lives to realize beauty-filled visions that lift us to flourishing, with our families and beyond. Naomi has been CEO for Stonecroft and MOPS, director with Compassion International and World Vision, and General Editor for this Bible.

remarked to one another, "but everything he said about this man has come true." ⁴²And many who were there believed in Jesus.

The Raising of Lazarus

11 A man named Lazarus was sick. He lived in Bethany with his sisters, Mary and Martha. ²This is the Mary who later poured the expensive perfume on the Lord's feet and wiped them with her hair.* Her brother, Lazarus, was sick. ³So the two sisters sent a message to Jesus telling him, "Lord, your dear friend is very sick."

⁴But when Jesus heard about it he said, "Lazarus's sickness will not end in death. No, it happened for the glory of God so that the Son of God will receive glory from this." ⁵So although Jesus loved Martha, Mary, and Lazarus, ⁶he stayed where he was for the next two days. ⁷Finally, he said to his disciples, "Let's go back to Judea."

⁸But his disciples objected. "Rabbi," they said, "only a few days ago the people* in Judea were trying to stone you. Are you going there again?"

⁹Jesus replied, "There are twelve hours of daylight every day. During the day people can walk safely. They can see because they have the light of this world. ¹⁰But at night there is danger of stumbling because they have no light." ¹¹Then he said, "Our friend Lazarus has fallen asleep, but now I will go and wake him up."

¹²The disciples said, "Lord, if he is sleeping, he will soon get better!" ¹³They thought Jesus meant Lazarus was simply sleeping, but Jesus meant Lazarus had died.

¹⁴So he told them plainly, "Lazarus is dead. ¹⁵And for your sakes, I'm glad I wasn't there, for now you will really believe. Come, let's go see him."

¹⁶Thomas, nicknamed the Twin,* said to his fellow disciples, "Let's go, too—and die with Jesus."

¹⁷When Jesus arrived at Bethany, he was told that Lazarus had already been in his grave for four days. ¹⁸Bethany was only a few miles* down the road from Jerusalem, ¹⁹and many of the people had come to console Martha and Mary in their loss. ²⁰When Martha got word that Jesus was coming, she went to meet him. But Mary stayed in the house. ²¹Martha said to Jesus, "Lord, if only you had been here, my brother would not have died. ²²But even now I know that God will give you whatever you ask."

²³Jesus told her, "Your brother will rise again."

²⁴"Yes," Martha said, "he will rise when everyone else rises, at the last day."

²⁵Jesus told her, "I am the resurrection and the life.* Anyone who believes in me will live, even after dying. ²⁶Everyone who lives in me and believes in me will never ever die. Do you believe this, Martha?"

²⁷"Yes, Lord," she told him. "I have always believed you are the Messiah, the Son of God, the one who has come into the world from God." ²⁸Then she returned to Mary. She called Mary aside from the mourners and told her, "The Teacher is here and wants to see you." ²⁹So Mary immediately went to him.

³⁰Jesus had stayed outside the village, at the place where Martha met him. ³¹When the people who were at the house consoling Mary saw her leave so hastily, they assumed she was going to Lazarus's grave to weep. So they followed her there. ³²When Mary arrived and saw Jesus, she fell at his feet and said, "Lord, if only you had been here, my brother would not have died."

³³When Jesus saw her weeping and saw the other people wailing with her, a deep anger welled up within him,* and he was deeply troubled. ³⁴"Where have you put him?" he asked them.

11:2 This incident is recorded in chapter 12. **11:8** Greek *Jewish people;* also in 11:19, 31, 33, 36, 45, 54. **11:16** Greek *Thomas, who was called Didymus.* **11:18** Greek *was about 15 stadia* [about 2.8 kilometers]. **11:25** Some manuscripts do not include *and the life.* **11:33** Or *he was angry in his spirit.*

11:1-44 When invited to heal Lazarus, Jesus purposely delayed going. After he finally arrived, Martha and Mary expressed their trust in Jesus' healing power and their regret that he had arrived too late. Martha, the "thinker," entered into a theological discussion with Jesus, and Mary, the "feeler," merely knelt at his feet and wept. Like these sisters, we each connect with God in ways that are unique to our personalities, and we have the freedom and can feel empowered to love God with our minds and our hearts. Just as Jesus met each sister where she was, he meets us where we are.

11:1 Of the sisters, Martha was probably older: She represented the family here and acted as the host when Jesus had visited them earlier (Luke 10:38-42). In the next chapter, Mary showed herself to be incredibly perceptive, anointing Jesus with perfume shortly before he would die (John 12:1-8). The sisters lived in Bethany, a small village east of Jerusalem, and Jesus would have traveled through Bethany on his way to Jerusalem. The women lived with their brother, Lazarus, whose name is a shortened form of the name *Eleazar* ("God helps"). This was a common name among Jewish men in the first century.

11:20-27 Martha recognized Jesus' power and understood that he could still intervene in some way, but she misunderstood his words about her brother rising again. Jesus was asking Martha if she believed that life itself is linked to him. Even though she didn't quite grasp the full implications, she acknowledged that Jesus was indeed the Messiah.

11:28-32 Now that Martha had brought her to Jesus, Mary echoed her sister's earlier words (11:21). She fell at Jesus' feet, not in worship but in desperate grief. The Greek word used to describe Mary's "weeping" (11:33) indicates loud wailing and crying; in this culture, mourning was expressed publicly with strong displays of emotion.

11:33-36 In response to Mary's grief, Jesus was pained and "a deep anger welled up within him." Anger might strike us as a strange way to respond to someone's grief, but it's important to understand that Jesus wasn't angry with Mary or Martha. Jesus was angry about and troubled by the power of death. Before he moved to resurrect Lazarus, Jesus himself stopped to grieve.

They told him, "Lord, come and see." ³⁵Then Jesus wept. ³⁶The people who were standing nearby said, "See how much he loved him!" ³⁷But some said, "This man healed a blind man. Couldn't he have kept Lazarus from dying?"

³⁸Jesus was still angry as he arrived at the tomb, a cave with a stone rolled across its entrance. ³⁹"Roll the stone aside," Jesus told them.

But Martha, the dead man's sister, protested, "Lord, he has been dead for four days. The smell will be terrible."

⁴⁰Jesus responded, "Didn't I tell you that you would see God's glory if you believe?" ⁴¹So they rolled the stone aside. Then Jesus looked up to heaven and said, "Father, thank you for hearing me. ⁴²You always hear me, but I said it out loud for the sake of all these people standing here, so that they will believe you sent me." ⁴³Then Jesus shouted, "Lazarus, come out!" ⁴⁴And the dead man came out, his hands and feet bound in graveclothes, his face wrapped in a headcloth. Jesus told them, "Unwrap him and let him go!"

The Plot to Kill Jesus

⁴⁵Many of the people who were with Mary believed in Jesus when they saw this happen. ⁴⁶But some went to the Pharisees and told them what Jesus had done. ⁴⁷Then the leading priests and Pharisees called the high council* together. "What are we going to do?" they asked each other. "This man certainly performs many miraculous signs. ⁴⁸If we allow him to go on like this, soon everyone will believe in him. Then the Roman army will come and destroy both our Temple* and our nation."

⁴⁹Caiaphas, who was high priest at that time,* said, "You don't know what you're talking about! ⁵⁰You don't realize that it's better for you that one man should die for the people than for the whole nation to be destroyed."

⁵¹He did not say this on his own; as high priest at that time he was led to prophesy that Jesus would die for the entire nation. ⁵²And not only for that nation, but to bring together and unite all the children of God scattered around the world.

⁵³So from that time on, the Jewish leaders began to plot Jesus' death. ⁵⁴As a result, Jesus stopped his public ministry among the people and left Jerusalem. He went to a place near the wilderness, to the village of Ephraim, and stayed there with his disciples.

⁵⁵It was now almost time for the Jewish Passover celebration, and many people from all over the country arrived in Jerusalem several days early so they could go through the purification ceremony before Passover began. ⁵⁶They kept looking for Jesus, but as they stood around in the Temple, they said to each other, "What do you think? He won't come for Passover, will he?" ⁵⁷Meanwhile, the leading priests and Pharisees had publicly ordered that anyone seeing Jesus must report it immediately so they could arrest him.

Jesus Anointed at Bethany

12 Six days before the Passover celebration began, Jesus arrived in Bethany, the home of Lazarus—the man he had raised from the dead. ²A dinner was prepared in Jesus' honor. Martha served, and Lazarus was among those who ate* with him. ³Then Mary took a twelve-ounce jar* of expensive perfume made from essence of nard, and she anointed Jesus' feet with it, wiping his feet with her hair. The house was filled with the fragrance.

⁴But Judas Iscariot, the disciple who would soon betray him, said, ⁵"That perfume was worth a year's wages.* It should have been sold and the money given to the poor." ⁶Not that he cared for the poor—he was a thief, and since he was in charge of the disciples' money, he often stole some for himself.

⁷Jesus replied, "Leave her alone. She did this in preparation for my burial. ⁸You will always have the poor among you, but you will not always have me."

11:47 Greek *the Sanhedrin.* 11:48 Or *our position;* Greek reads *our place.* 11:49 Greek *that year;* also in 11:51. 12:2 Or *who reclined.* 12:3 Greek *took 1 litra* [327 grams]. 12:5 Greek *worth 300 denarii.* A denarius was equivalent to a laborer's full day's wage.

11:38-44 When he reached the tomb, Jesus was still angry. He was furious about the destruction brought about by death, and in this case it was even more personal because he knew the family. For John, Jesus' raising Lazarus from the dead, essentially in the direct middle of the story, foreshadows Jesus' ultimate defeat of death through his own death and resurrection (19:28–20:10).

11:51-52 The high priest predicted that Jesus would die not only for Jews but also for Gentiles (non-Jews). For Jewish people in Jesus' day, especially the religious leaders, including "other" nations into God's covenant was not a small deal. Many of us are Gentiles, but now Jesus' good news unites us into one family. John's account stresses oneness despite otherness (see 10:16; 17:21). Today we still live with the tension between diversity and unity, but Jesus invites us to embrace the tension we feel now to experience the rewards of full unity. We will see this unity fully in the Kingdom of God (Revelation 7:9-10).

12:1-8 In the first-century Jewish home, women often took charge. When hosting Jesus at their home, both Martha and Mary showed hospitality but in different ways. Martha prepared and served the meal, while Mary anointed Jesus' feet with her costly perfume. Today, women can serve Jesus in different ways according to their gifts. Find your gifts and use them to serve others.

12:3 Ancient Jews reclined on low couches at a formal meal like this, giving Mary access to Jesus' feet. Her dramatic gesture involved nard, a precious aromatic oil imported from the Himalayas of north India. Twelve ounces of nard cost a year's wages (12:5). The book of Mark records that Mary also anointed Jesus' head, and the perfume ran down and scented his body (Mark 14:3-8). Mary was acting with extravagant abandon and devotion.

⁹When all the people* heard of Jesus' arrival, they flocked to see him and also to see Lazarus, the man Jesus had raised from the dead. ¹⁰Then the leading priests decided to kill Lazarus, too, ¹¹for it was because of him that many of the people had deserted them* and believed in Jesus.

Jesus' Triumphant Entry

¹²The next day, the news that Jesus was on the way to Jerusalem swept through the city. A large crowd of Passover visitors ¹³took palm branches and went down the road to meet him. They shouted,

"Praise God!*
Blessings on the one who comes in the name of the LORD!
Hail to the King of Israel!"*

¹⁴Jesus found a young donkey and rode on it, fulfilling the prophecy that said:

¹⁵ "Don't be afraid, people of Jerusalem.*
Look, your King is coming,
riding on a donkey's colt."*

¹⁶His disciples didn't understand at the time that this was a fulfillment of prophecy. But after Jesus entered into his glory, they remembered what had happened and realized that these things had been written about him.

¹⁷Many in the crowd had seen Jesus call Lazarus from the tomb, raising him from the dead, and they were telling others* about it. ¹⁸That was the reason so many went out to meet him—because they had heard about this miraculous sign. ¹⁹Then the Pharisees said to each other, "There's nothing we can do. Look, everyone* has gone after him!"

Jesus Predicts His Death

²⁰Some Greeks who had come to Jerusalem for the Passover celebration ²¹paid a visit to Philip, who was from Bethsaida in Galilee. They said, "Sir, we want to meet Jesus." ²²Philip told Andrew about it, and they went together to ask Jesus.

²³Jesus replied, "Now the time has come for the Son of Man* to enter into his glory. ²⁴I tell you the truth, unless a kernel of wheat is planted in the soil and dies, it remains alone. But its death will produce many new kernels—a plentiful harvest of new lives. ²⁵Those who love their life in this world will lose it. Those who care nothing for their life in this world will keep it for eternity. ²⁶Anyone who wants to serve me must follow me, because my servants must be where I am. And the Father will honor anyone who serves me.

²⁷"Now my soul is deeply troubled. Should I pray, 'Father, save me from this hour'? But this is the very reason I came! ²⁸Father, bring glory to your name."

Then a voice spoke from heaven, saying, "I have already brought glory to my name, and I will do so again." ²⁹When the crowd heard the voice, some thought it was thunder, while others declared an angel had spoken to him.

³⁰Then Jesus told them, "The voice was for your benefit, not mine. ³¹The time for judging this world has come, when Satan, the ruler of this world, will be cast out. ³²And when I am lifted up from the earth, I will draw everyone to myself." ³³He said this to indicate how he was going to die.

³⁴The crowd responded, "We understood from Scripture* that the Messiah would live forever. How can you say the Son of Man will die? Just who is this Son of Man, anyway?"

³⁵Jesus replied, "My light will shine for you just a little longer. Walk in the light while you can, so the darkness will not overtake you. Those who walk in the darkness cannot see where they are going. ³⁶Put your trust in the light while there is still time; then you will become children of the light."

After saying these things, Jesus went away and was hidden from them.

The Unbelief of the People

³⁷But despite all the miraculous signs Jesus had done, most of the people still did not believe in him. ³⁸This is exactly what Isaiah the prophet had predicted:

"LORD, who has believed our message?
To whom has the LORD revealed his powerful arm?"*

³⁹But the people couldn't believe, for as Isaiah also said,

⁴⁰ "The Lord has blinded their eyes
and hardened their hearts—
so that their eyes cannot see,
and their hearts cannot understand,
and they cannot turn to me
and have me heal them."*

12:9 Greek *Jewish people;* also in 12:11. **12:11** Or *had deserted their traditions;* Greek reads *had deserted.* **12:13a** Greek *Hosanna,* an exclamation of praise adapted from a Hebrew expression that means "save now." **12:13b** Ps 118:25-26; Zeph 3:15. **12:15a** Greek *daughter of Zion.* **12:15b** Zech 9:9. **12:17** Greek *were testifying.* **12:19** Greek *the world.* **12:23** "Son of Man" is a title Jesus used for himself. **12:34** Greek *from the law.* **12:38** Isa 53:1. **12:40** Isa 6:10.

12:7 Of everyone in the room, even the male disciples who had been with Jesus for three years, Mary was the one who understood Jesus' coming death. Then she acted on her insight, symbolically preparing his body for burial.

12:8 Jesus was not saying that the poor should be neglected. Instead, he affirmed Mary's astute understanding that serving him in person was an unparalleled and brief opportunity. How we worship Jesus should inform how we serve everyone else. God specifically expresses his care for those in need (Luke 4:18-19), and what we do for them should enrich our praise to him.

⁴¹Isaiah was referring to Jesus when he said this, because he saw the future and spoke of the Messiah's glory. ⁴²Many people did believe in him, however, including some of the Jewish leaders. But they wouldn't admit it for fear that the Pharisees would expel them from the synagogue. ⁴³For they loved human praise more than the praise of God.

⁴⁴Jesus shouted to the crowds, "If you trust me, you are trusting not only me, but also God who sent me. ⁴⁵For when you see me, you are seeing the one who sent me. ⁴⁶I have come as a light to shine in this dark world, so that all who put their trust in me will no longer remain in the dark. ⁴⁷I will not judge those who hear me but don't obey me, for I have come to save the world and not to judge it. ⁴⁸But all who reject me and my message will be judged on the day of judgment by the truth I have spoken. ⁴⁹I don't speak on my own authority. The Father who sent me has commanded me what to say and how to say it. ⁵⁰And I know his commands lead to eternal life; so I say whatever the Father tells me to say."

Jesus Washes His Disciples' Feet

13 Before the Passover celebration, Jesus knew that his hour had come to leave this world and return to his Father. He had loved his disciples during his ministry on earth, and now he loved them to the very end.* ²It was time for supper, and the devil had already prompted Judas,* son of Simon Iscariot, to betray Jesus. ³Jesus knew that the Father had given him authority over everything and that he had come from God and would return to God. ⁴So he got up from the table, took off his robe, wrapped a towel around his waist, ⁵and poured water into a basin. Then he began to wash the disciples' feet, drying them with the towel he had around him.

⁶When Jesus came to Simon Peter, Peter said to him, "Lord, are you going to wash my feet?"

⁷Jesus replied, "You don't understand now what I am doing, but someday you will."

⁸"No," Peter protested, "you will never ever wash my feet!"

Jesus replied, "Unless I wash you, you won't belong to me."

⁹Simon Peter exclaimed, "Then wash my hands and head as well, Lord, not just my feet!"

¹⁰Jesus replied, "A person who has bathed all over does not need to wash, except for the feet,* to be entirely clean. And you disciples are clean, but not all of you." ¹¹For Jesus knew who would betray him. That is what he meant when he said, "Not all of you are clean."

¹²After washing their feet, he put on his robe again and sat down and asked, "Do you understand what I was doing? ¹³You call me 'Teacher' and 'Lord,' and you are right, because that's what I am. ¹⁴And since I, your Lord and Teacher, have washed your feet, you ought to wash each other's feet. ¹⁵I have given you an example to follow. Do as I have done to you. ¹⁶I tell you the truth, slaves are not greater than their master. Nor is the messenger more important than the one who sends the message. ¹⁷Now that you know these things, God will bless you for doing them.

Jesus Predicts His Betrayal

¹⁸"I am not saying these things to all of you; I know the ones I have chosen. But this fulfills the Scripture that says, 'The one who eats my food has turned against me.'* ¹⁹I tell you this beforehand, so that when it happens you will believe that I AM the Messiah.* ²⁰I tell you the truth, anyone who welcomes my messenger is welcoming me, and anyone who welcomes me is welcoming the Father who sent me."

²¹Now Jesus was deeply troubled,* and he exclaimed, "I tell you the truth, one of you will betray me!"

²²The disciples looked at each other, wondering whom he could mean. ²³The disciple Jesus loved was sitting next to Jesus at the table.* ²⁴Simon Peter motioned to him to ask, "Who's he talking about?" ²⁵So that disciple leaned over to Jesus and asked, "Lord, who is it?"

²⁶Jesus responded, "It is the one to whom I give the bread I dip in the bowl." And when he had dipped it, he gave it to Judas, son of Simon Iscariot. ²⁷When Judas had eaten the bread, Satan entered into him. Then Jesus told him, "Hurry and do what you're going to do." ²⁸None of the others at the table knew what Jesus meant. ²⁹Since Judas was their treasurer, some thought Jesus was telling him to go and pay for the food or to give some money to the poor. ³⁰So Judas left at once, going out into the night.

Jesus Predicts Peter's Denial

³¹As soon as Judas left the room, Jesus said, "The time has come for the Son of Man* to enter into his glory, and God will be glorified because of him. ³²And since God receives glory because of the Son,* he will give his own glory to the Son, and he will do so at once. ³³Dear children, I will be with you only a little longer. And as I told the Jewish leaders, you will search for me, but you can't come where I am going. ³⁴So now I am giving you a new commandment: Love each other. Just as I have loved you, you should love each other. ³⁵Your love for one another will prove to the world that you are my disciples."

13:1 Or *he showed them the full extent of his love.* **13:2** Or *the devil had already intended for Judas.* **13:10** Some manuscripts do not include *except for the feet.* **13:18** Ps 41:9. **13:19** Or *that the 'I AM' has come;* or *that I am the Lord;* Greek reads *that I am.* See Exod 3:14. **13:21** Greek *was troubled in his spirit.* **13:23** Greek *was reclining on Jesus' bosom.* The "disciple Jesus loved" was probably John. **13:31** "Son of Man" is a title Jesus used for himself. **13:32** Several early manuscripts do not include *And since God receives glory because of the Son.*

36 Simon Peter asked, "Lord, where are you going?" And Jesus replied, "You can't go with me now, but you will follow me later."

37 "But why can't I come now, Lord?" he asked. "I'm ready to die for you."

38 Jesus answered, "Die for me? I tell you the truth, Peter—before the rooster crows tomorrow morning, you will deny three times that you even know me.

Jesus, the Way to the Father

14 "Don't let your hearts be troubled. Trust in God, and trust also in me. 2 There is more than enough room in my Father's home.* If this were not so, would I have told you that I am going to prepare a place for you?* 3 When everything is ready, I will come and get you, so that you will always be with me where I am. 4 And you know the way to where I am going."

5 "No, we don't know, Lord," Thomas said. "We have no idea where you are going, so how can we know the way?"

6 Jesus told him, "I am the way, the truth, and the life. No one can come to the Father except through me. 7 If you had really known me, you would know who my Father is.* From now on, you do know him and have seen him!"

8 Philip said, "Lord, show us the Father, and we will be satisfied."

9 Jesus replied, "Have I been with you all this time, Philip, and yet you still don't know who I am? Anyone who has seen me has seen the Father! So why are you asking me to show him to you? 10 Don't you believe that I am in the Father and the Father is in me? The words I speak are not my own, but my Father who lives in me does his work through me. 11 Just believe that I am in the Father and the Father is in me. Or at least believe because of the work you have seen me do.

12 "I tell you the truth, anyone who believes in me will do the same works I have done, and even greater works, because I am going to be with the Father. 13 You can ask for anything in my name, and I will do it, so that the Son can bring glory to the Father. 14 Yes, ask me for anything in my name, and I will do it!

Jesus Promises the Holy Spirit

15 "If you love me, obey* my commandments. 16 And I will ask the Father, and he will give you another Advocate,* who will never leave you. 17 He is the Holy Spirit, who leads into all truth. The world cannot receive him, because it isn't looking for him and doesn't recognize him. But you know him, because he lives with you now and later will be in you.* 18 No, I will not abandon you as orphans—I will come to you. 19 Soon the world will no longer see me, but you will see me. Since I live, you also will live. 20 When I am raised to life again, you will know that I am in my Father, and you are in me, and I am in you. 21 Those who accept my commandments and obey them are the ones who love me. And because they love me, my Father will love them. And I will love them and reveal myself to each of them."

22 Judas (not Judas Iscariot, but the other disciple with that name) said to him, "Lord, why are you going to reveal yourself only to us and not to the world at large?"

23 Jesus replied, "All who love me will do what I say. My Father will love them, and we will come and make our home with each of them. 24 Anyone who doesn't love me will not obey me. And remember, my words are not my own. What I am telling you is from the Father who sent me. 25 I am telling you these things now while I am still with you. 26 But when the Father sends the Advocate as my representative—that is, the Holy Spirit—he will teach you everything and will remind you of everything I have told you.

27 "I am leaving you with a gift—peace of mind and heart. And the peace I give is a gift the world cannot give. So don't be troubled or afraid. 28 Remember what I told you: I am going away, but I will come back to you again. If you really loved me, you would be happy that I am going to the Father, who

---

> "What the law tried to do by a restraining power from without, the gospel does by an inspiring power from within."
>
> **CATHERINE BOOTH**
> (1829–1890) cofounder of The Salvation Army

14:2a Or *There are many rooms in my Father's house.* 14:2b Or *If this were not so, I would have told you that I am going to prepare a place for you.* Some manuscripts read *If this were not so, I would have told you. I am going to prepare a place for you.* 14:7 Some manuscripts read *If you have really known me, you will know who my Father is.* 14:15 Other manuscripts read *you will obey;* still others read *you should obey.* 14:16 Or *Comforter,* or *Encourager,* or *Counselor.* Greek reads *Paraclete;* also in 14:26. 14:17 Some manuscripts read *and is in you.*

is greater than I am. ²⁹I have told you these things before they happen so that when they do happen, you will believe.

³⁰"I don't have much more time to talk to you, because the ruler of this world approaches. He has no power over me, ³¹but I will do what the Father requires of me, so that the world will know that I love the Father. Come, let's be going.

Jesus, the True Vine

15 ¹"I am the true grapevine, and my Father is the gardener. ²He cuts off every branch of mine that doesn't produce fruit, and he prunes the branches that do bear fruit so they will produce even more. ³You have already been pruned and purified by the message I have given you. ⁴Remain in me, and I will remain in you. For a branch cannot produce fruit if it is severed from the vine, and you cannot be fruitful unless you remain in me.

⁵"Yes, I am the vine; you are the branches. Those who remain in me, and I in them, will produce much fruit. For apart from me you can do nothing. ⁶Anyone who does not remain in me is thrown away like a useless branch and withers. Such branches are gathered into a pile to be burned. ⁷But if you remain in me and my words remain in you, you may ask for anything you want, and it will be granted! ⁸When you produce much fruit, you are my true disciples. This brings great glory to my Father.

⁹"I have loved you even as the Father has loved me. Remain in my love. ¹⁰When you obey my commandments, you remain in my love, just as I obey my Father's commandments and remain in his love. ¹¹I have told you these things so that you will be filled with my joy. Yes, your joy will overflow! ¹²This is my commandment: Love each other in the same way I have loved you. ¹³There is no greater love than to lay down one's life for one's friends. ¹⁴You are my friends if you do what I command. ¹⁵I no longer call you slaves, because a master doesn't confide in his slaves. Now you are my friends, since I have told you everything the Father told me. ¹⁶You didn't choose me. I chose you. I appointed you to go and produce lasting fruit, so that the Father will give you whatever you ask for, using my name. ¹⁷This is my command: Love each other.

The World's Hatred

¹⁸"If the world hates you, remember that it hated me first. ¹⁹The world would love you as one of its own if you belonged to it, but you are no longer part of the world. I chose you to come out of the world, so it hates you. ²⁰Do you remember what I told you? 'A slave is not greater than the master.' Since they persecuted me, naturally they will persecute you. And if they had listened to me, they would listen to you. ²¹They will do all this to you because of me, for they have rejected the one who sent me. ²²They would not be guilty if I had not come and spoken to them. But now they have no excuse for their sin. ²³Anyone who hates me also hates my Father. ²⁴If I hadn't done such miraculous signs among them that no one else could do, they would not be guilty. But as it is, they have seen everything I did, yet they still hate me and my Father. ²⁵This fulfills what is written in their Scriptures*: 'They hated me without cause.'

²⁶"But I will send you the Advocate*—the Spirit of truth. He will come to you from the Father and will testify all about me. ²⁷And you must also testify about me because you have been with me from the beginning of my ministry.

16 ¹"I have told you these things so that you won't abandon your faith. ²For you will be expelled from the synagogues, and the time is coming when those who kill you will think they are doing a holy service for God. ³This is because they have never known the Father or me. ⁴Yes, I'm telling you these things now, so that when they happen, you will remember my warning. I didn't tell you earlier because I was going to be with you for a while longer.

The Work of the Holy Spirit

⁵"But now I am going away to the one who sent me, and not one of you is asking where I am going. ⁶Instead, you grieve because of what I've told you. ⁷But in fact, it is best for you that I go away, because if I don't, the Advocate* won't come. If I do go away, then I will send him to you. ⁸And when he comes, he will convict the world of its sin, and of God's righteousness, and of the coming judgment. ⁹The world's sin is that it refuses to believe in me. ¹⁰Righteousness is available because I go to the Father, and you will see me no more. ¹¹Judgment will come because the ruler of this world has already been judged.

¹²"There is so much more I want to tell you, but you can't bear it now. ¹³When the Spirit of truth comes, he will guide you into all truth. He will not speak on his own but will tell you what he has heard. He will tell you about the future. ¹⁴He will bring me glory by telling you whatever he receives from me. ¹⁵All that belongs to the Father is mine; this is why I said, 'The Spirit will tell you whatever he receives from me.'

15:25 Greek *in their law.* Pss 35:19; 69:4. **15:26** Or *Comforter,* or *Encourager,* or *Counselor.* Greek reads *Paraclete.* **16:7** Or *Comforter,* or *Encourager,* or *Counselor.* Greek reads *Paraclete.*

15:9-12 Jesus' command to "remain in my love" has two implications. First, staying in Jesus' love enables us to love each other. Second, we do that by obeying his commands, which means that love does not equate to indulging sins. For Christians, following Jesus and social responsibility go hand in hand.

Sadness Will Be Turned to Joy

¹⁶"In a little while you won't see me anymore. But a little while after that, you will see me again."

¹⁷Some of the disciples asked each other, "What does he mean when he says, 'In a little while you won't see me, but then you will see me,' and 'I am going to the Father'? ¹⁸And what does he mean by 'a little while'? We don't understand."

¹⁹Jesus realized they wanted to ask him about it, so he said, "Are you asking yourselves what I meant? I said in a little while you won't see me, but a little while after that you will see me again. ²⁰I tell you the truth, you will weep and mourn over what is going to happen to me, but the world will rejoice. You will grieve, but your grief will suddenly turn to wonderful joy. ²¹It will be like a woman suffering the pains of labor. When her child is born, her anguish gives way to joy because she has brought a new baby into the world. ²²So you have sorrow now, but I will see you again; then you will rejoice, and no one can rob you of that joy. ²³At that time you won't need to ask me for anything. I tell you the truth, you will ask the Father directly, and he will grant your request because you use my name. ²⁴You haven't done this before. Ask, using my name, and you will receive, and you will have abundant joy.

²⁵"I have spoken of these matters in figures of speech, but soon I will stop speaking figuratively and will tell you plainly all about the Father. ²⁶Then you will ask in my name. I'm not saying I will ask the Father on your behalf, ²⁷for the Father himself loves you dearly because you love me and believe that I came from God.* ²⁸Yes, I came from the Father into the world, and now I will leave the world and return to the Father."

²⁹Then his disciples said, "At last you are speaking plainly and not figuratively. ³⁰Now we understand that you know everything, and there's no need to question you. From this we believe that you came from God."

³¹Jesus asked, "Do you finally believe? ³²But the time is coming—indeed it's here now—when you will be scattered, each one going his own way, leaving me alone. Yet I am not alone because the Father is with me. ³³I have told you all this so that you may have peace in me. Here on earth you will have many trials and sorrows. But take heart, because I have overcome the world."

The Prayer of Jesus

17 After saying all these things, Jesus looked up to heaven and said, "Father, the hour has come. Glorify your Son so he can give glory back to you. ²For you have given him authority over everyone. He gives eternal life to each one you have given him. ³And this is the way to have eternal life—to know you, the only true God, and Jesus Christ, the one you sent to earth. ⁴I brought glory to you here on earth by completing the work you gave me to do. ⁵Now, Father, bring me into the glory we shared before the world began.

⁶"I have revealed you* to the ones you gave me from this world. They were always yours. You gave them to me, and they have kept your word. ⁷Now they know that everything I have is a gift from you, ⁸for I have passed on to them the message you gave me. They accepted it and know that I came from you, and they believe you sent me.

⁹"My prayer is not for the world, but for those you have given me, because they belong to you. ¹⁰All who are mine belong to you, and you have given them to me, so they bring me glory. ¹¹Now I am departing from the world; they are staying in this world, but I am coming to you. Holy Father, you have given me your name;* now protect them by the power of your name so that they will be united just as we are. ¹²During my time here, I protected them by the power of the name you gave me.* I guarded them so that not one was lost, except the one headed for destruction, as the Scriptures foretold.

¹³"Now I am coming to you. I told them many things while I was with them in this world so they would be filled with my joy. ¹⁴I have given them your word. And the world hates them because they do not belong to the world, just as I do not belong to the world. ¹⁵I'm not asking you to take them out of the world, but to keep them safe from the evil one. ¹⁶They do not belong to this world any more than I do. ¹⁷Make them holy by your truth; teach them your word, which is truth. ¹⁸Just as you sent me into the world, I am sending them into the world. ¹⁹And I give myself as a holy sacrifice for them so they can be made holy by your truth.

²⁰"I am praying not only for these disciples but also for all who will ever believe in me through their message. ²¹I pray that they will all be one, just as you and I are one—as you are in me, Father, and I am in you. And may they be in us so that the world will believe you sent me.

²²"I have given them the glory you gave me, so they may be one as we are one. ²³I am in them and you are in me. May they experience such perfect unity that the world will know that you sent me and that you love them as much as you love me. ²⁴Father, I want these whom you have given me to be with me where

---

16:27 Some manuscripts read *from the Father.*   **17:6** Greek *have revealed your name;* also in 17:26.   **17:11** Some manuscripts read *you have given me these [disciples].*   **17:12** Some manuscripts read *I protected those you gave me, by the power of your name.*

16:20-22 Jesus compared the disciples' future grief to intense labor pains. Against the background of high maternal and infant mortality rate, pain was accompanied by worry and fear of death. Jesus' last words assured his disciples that suffering—physical and emotional—was inevitable, but the joy yet to come would be greater. This metaphor is even more powerful to women, because we can fully understand the effort, pain, and risk involved in childbirth.

I am. Then they can see all the glory you gave me because you loved me even before the world began! ²⁵O righteous Father, the world doesn't know you, but I do; and these disciples know you sent me. ²⁶I have revealed you to them, and I will continue to do so. Then your love for me will be in them, and I will be in them."

Jesus Is Betrayed and Arrested

18 After saying these things, Jesus crossed the Kidron Valley with his disciples and entered a grove of olive trees. ²Judas, the betrayer, knew this place, because Jesus had often gone there with his disciples. ³The leading priests and Pharisees had given Judas a contingent of Roman soldiers and Temple guards to accompany him. Now with blazing torches, lanterns, and weapons, they arrived at the olive grove.

⁴Jesus fully realized all that was going to happen to him, so he stepped forward to meet them. "Who are you looking for?" he asked.

⁵"Jesus the Nazarene,"* they replied.

"I Am he,"* Jesus said. (Judas, who betrayed him, was standing with them.) ⁶As Jesus said "I Am he," they all drew back and fell to the ground! ⁷Once more he asked them, "Who are you looking for?"

And again they replied, "Jesus the Nazarene."

⁸"I told you that I Am he," Jesus said. "And since I am the one you want, let these others go." ⁹He did this to fulfill his own statement: "I did not lose a single one of those you have given me."*

¹⁰Then Simon Peter drew a sword and slashed off the right ear of Malchus, the high priest's slave. ¹¹But Jesus said to Peter, "Put your sword back into its sheath. Shall I not drink from the cup of suffering the Father has given me?"

Jesus at the High Priest's House

¹²So the soldiers, their commanding officer, and the Temple guards arrested Jesus and tied him up. ¹³First they took him to Annas, since he was the father-in-law of Caiaphas, the high priest at that time.* ¹⁴Caiaphas was the one who had told the other Jewish leaders, "It's better that one man should die for the people."

Peter's First Denial

¹⁵Simon Peter followed Jesus, as did another of the disciples. That other disciple was acquainted with the high priest, so he was allowed to enter the high priest's courtyard with Jesus. ¹⁶Peter had to stay outside the gate. Then the disciple who knew the high priest spoke to the woman watching at the gate, and she let Peter in. ¹⁷The woman asked Peter, "You're not one of that man's disciples, are you?"

"No," he said, "I am not."

¹⁸Because it was cold, the household servants and the guards had made a charcoal fire. They stood around it, warming themselves, and Peter stood with them, warming himself.

The High Priest Questions Jesus

¹⁹Inside, the high priest began asking Jesus about his followers and what he had been teaching them. ²⁰Jesus replied, "Everyone knows what I teach. I have preached regularly in the synagogues and the Temple, where the people* gather. I have not spoken in secret. ²¹Why are you asking me this question? Ask those who heard me. They know what I said."

²²Then one of the Temple guards standing nearby slapped Jesus across the face. "Is that the way to answer the high priest?" he demanded.

²³Jesus replied, "If I said anything wrong, you must prove it. But if I'm speaking the truth, why are you beating me?"

²⁴Then Annas bound Jesus and sent him to Caiaphas, the high priest.

Peter's Second and Third Denials

²⁵Meanwhile, as Simon Peter was standing by the fire warming himself, they asked him again, "You're not one of his disciples, are you?"

He denied it, saying, "No, I am not."

²⁶But one of the household slaves of the high priest, a relative of the man whose ear Peter had cut off, asked, "Didn't I see you out there in the olive grove with Jesus?" ²⁷Again Peter denied it. And immediately a rooster crowed.

Jesus' Trial before Pilate

²⁸Jesus' trial before Caiaphas ended in the early hours of the morning. Then he was taken to the headquarters of the Roman governor.* His accusers didn't go inside because it would defile them, and they wouldn't be allowed to celebrate the Passover. ²⁹So Pilate, the governor, went out to them and asked, "What is your charge against this man?"

³⁰"We wouldn't have handed him over to you if he weren't a criminal!" they retorted.

³¹"Then take him away and judge him by your own law," Pilate told them.

"Only the Romans are permitted to execute someone," the Jewish leaders replied. ³²(This fulfilled Jesus' prediction about the way he would die.*)

³³Then Pilate went back into his headquarters and called for Jesus to be brought to him. "Are you the king of the Jews?" he asked him.

³⁴Jesus replied, "Is this your own question, or did others tell you about me?"

³⁵"Am I a Jew?" Pilate retorted. "Your own people and their leading priests brought you to me for trial. Why? What have you done?"

18:5a Or *Jesus of Nazareth;* also in 18:7. **18:5b** Or *"The 'I Am' is here";* or *"I am the Lord";* Greek reads *I am;* also in 18:6, 8. See Exod 3:14. **18:9** See John 6:39 and 17:12. **18:13** Greek *that year.* **18:20** Greek *Jewish people;* also in 18:38. **18:28** Greek *to the Praetorium;* also in 18:33. **18:32** See John 12:32-33.

³⁶Jesus answered, "My Kingdom is not an earthly kingdom. If it were, my followers would fight to keep me from being handed over to the Jewish leaders. But my Kingdom is not of this world."

³⁷Pilate said, "So you are a king?"

Jesus responded, "You say I am a king. Actually, I was born and came into the world to testify to the truth. All who love the truth recognize that what I say is true."

³⁸"What is truth?" Pilate asked. Then he went out again to the people and told them, "He is not guilty of any crime. ³⁹But you have a custom of asking me to release one prisoner each year at Passover. Would you like me to release this 'King of the Jews'?"

⁴⁰But they shouted back, "No! Not this man. We want Barabbas!" (Barabbas was a revolutionary.)

Jesus Sentenced to Death

19 Then Pilate had Jesus flogged with a lead-tipped whip. ²The soldiers wove a crown of thorns and put it on his head, and they put a purple robe on him. ³"Hail! King of the Jews!" they mocked, as they slapped him across the face.

⁴Pilate went outside again and said to the people, "I am going to bring him out to you now, but understand clearly that I find him not guilty." ⁵Then Jesus came out wearing the crown of thorns and the purple robe. And Pilate said, "Look, here is the man!"

⁶When they saw him, the leading priests and Temple guards began shouting, "Crucify him! Crucify him!"

"Take him yourselves and crucify him," Pilate said. "I find him not guilty."

⁷The Jewish leaders replied, "By our law he ought to die because he called himself the Son of God."

⁸When Pilate heard this, he was more frightened than ever. ⁹He took Jesus back into the headquarters* again and asked him, "Where are you from?" But Jesus gave no answer. ¹⁰"Why don't you talk to me?" Pilate demanded. "Don't you realize that I have the power to release you or crucify you?"

¹¹Then Jesus said, "You would have no power over me at all unless it were given to you from above. So the one who handed me over to you has the greater sin."

¹²Then Pilate tried to release him, but the Jewish leaders shouted, "If you release this man, you are no 'friend of Caesar.'* Anyone who declares himself a king is a rebel against Caesar."

¹³When they said this, Pilate brought Jesus out to them again. Then Pilate sat down on the judgment seat on the platform that is called the Stone Pavement (in Hebrew, *Gabbatha*). ¹⁴It was now about noon on the day of preparation for the Passover. And Pilate said to the people,* "Look, here is your king!"

¹⁵"Away with him," they yelled. "Away with him! Crucify him!"

"What? Crucify your king?" Pilate asked.

"We have no king but Caesar," the leading priests shouted back.

¹⁶Then Pilate turned Jesus over to them to be crucified.

The Crucifixion

So they took Jesus away. ¹⁷Carrying the cross by himself, he went to the place called Place of the Skull (in Hebrew, *Golgotha*). ¹⁸There they nailed him to the cross. Two others were crucified with him, one on either side, with Jesus between them. ¹⁹And Pilate posted a sign on the cross that read, "Jesus of Nazareth,* the King of the Jews." ²⁰The place where Jesus was crucified was near the city, and the sign was written in Hebrew, Latin, and Greek, so that many people could read it.

²¹Then the leading priests objected and said to Pilate, "Change it from 'The King of the Jews' to 'He said, I am King of the Jews.'"

²²Pilate replied, "No, what I have written, I have written."

²³When the soldiers had crucified Jesus, they divided his clothes among the four of them. They also took his robe, but it was seamless, woven in one piece from top to bottom. ²⁴So they said, "Rather than tearing it apart, let's throw dice* for it." This fulfilled the Scripture that says, "They divided my garments among themselves and threw dice for my clothing."* So that is what they did.

²⁵Standing near the cross were Jesus' mother, and his mother's sister, Mary (the wife of Clopas),

---

19:9 Greek *the Praetorium*. **19:12** "Friend of Caesar" is a technical term that refers to an ally of the emperor. **19:14** Greek *Jewish people*; also in 19:20. **19:19** Or *Jesus the Nazarene*. **19:24a** Greek *cast lots*. **19:24b** Ps 22:18.

19:25-26 Four women stood near the cross during Jesus' execution. The sister of Jesus' mother might have been the wife of Zebedee and the mother of James and John (see Matthew 27:56), which would have made Jesus and John cousins. If so, being related by blood would help explain why Jesus assigned the "disciple he loved" (John) to care for Mary (John's aunt). Also mentioned only here, Mary (the wife of Clopas) might have been the mother of James and Joseph. This is the only place in Scripture to mention these two women. With them was Mary Magdalene, whom Jesus had healed and who went on to become one of his followers. She was the first person to see Jesus after he had risen from the dead. The fourth woman in this group was Jesus' mother.

19:25 John mentioned Jesus' mother twice, at the beginning of Jesus' ministry (2:1-12) and the end of Jesus' life. The implication is that Mary seemed to follow Jesus with all the other disciples. Imagine how Mary would have felt when watching her son bleeding and dying on the cross. This woman who bore and raised Jesus also had to obey the divine plan and let go of her son (Luke 1:38). Letting go of children is a challenging lesson for mothers in every age, but the importance of Jesus' mission and the strength of Mary's motherly love for him likely enabled her to stay by his side to the end.

and Mary Magdalene. ²⁶When Jesus saw his mother standing there beside the disciple he loved, he said to her, "Dear woman, here is your son." ²⁷And he said to this disciple, "Here is your mother." And from then on this disciple took her into his home.

The Death of Jesus

²⁸Jesus knew that his mission was now finished, and to fulfill Scripture he said, "I am thirsty."* ²⁹A jar of sour wine was sitting there, so they soaked a sponge in it, put it on a hyssop branch, and held it up to his lips. ³⁰When Jesus had tasted it, he said, "It is finished!" Then he bowed his head and gave up his spirit.

³¹It was the day of preparation, and the Jewish leaders didn't want the bodies hanging there the next day, which was the Sabbath (and a very special Sabbath, because it was Passover week). So they asked Pilate to hasten their deaths by ordering that their legs be broken. Then their bodies could be taken down. ³²So the soldiers came and broke the legs of the two men crucified with Jesus. ³³But when they came to Jesus, they saw that he was already dead, so they didn't break his legs. ³⁴One of the soldiers, however, pierced his side with a spear, and immediately blood and water flowed out. ³⁵(This report is from an eyewitness giving an accurate account. He speaks the truth so that you also may continue to believe.*) ³⁶These things happened in fulfillment of the Scriptures that say, "Not one of his bones will be broken,"* ³⁷and "They will look on the one they pierced."*

The Burial of Jesus

³⁸Afterward Joseph of Arimathea, who had been a secret disciple of Jesus (because he feared the Jewish leaders), asked Pilate for permission to take down Jesus' body. When Pilate gave permission, Joseph came and took the body away. ³⁹With him came Nicodemus, the man who had come to Jesus at night. He brought about seventy-five pounds* of perfumed ointment made from myrrh and aloes. ⁴⁰Following Jewish burial custom, they wrapped Jesus' body with the spices in long sheets of linen cloth. ⁴¹The place of crucifixion was near a garden, where there was a new tomb, never used before. ⁴²And so, because it was the day of preparation for the Jewish Passover* and since the tomb was close at hand, they laid Jesus there.

The Resurrection

20 Early on Sunday morning,* while it was still dark, Mary Magdalene came to the tomb and found that the stone had been rolled away from the entrance. ²She ran and found Simon Peter and the other disciple, the one whom Jesus loved. She said, "They have taken the Lord's body out of the tomb, and we don't know where they have put him!"

³Peter and the other disciple started out for the tomb. ⁴They were both running, but the other disciple outran Peter and reached the tomb first. ⁵He stooped and looked in and saw the linen wrappings lying there, but he didn't go in. ⁶Then Simon Peter arrived and went inside. He also noticed the linen wrappings lying there, ⁷while the cloth that had covered Jesus' head was folded up and lying apart from the other wrappings. ⁸Then the disciple who had reached the tomb first also went in, and he saw and believed—⁹for until then they still hadn't understood the Scriptures that said Jesus must rise from the dead. ¹⁰Then they went home.

Jesus Appears to Mary Magdalene

¹¹Mary was standing outside the tomb crying, and as she wept, she stooped and looked in. ¹²She saw two white-robed angels, one sitting at the head and the other at the foot of the place where the body of Jesus had been lying. ¹³"Dear woman, why are you crying?" the angels asked her.

19:28 See Pss 22:15; 69:21.   **19:35** Some manuscripts read *that you also may believe.*   **19:36** Exod 12:46; Num 9:12; Ps 34:20.   **19:37** Zech 12:10.   **19:39** Greek *100 litras* [32.7 kilograms].   **19:42** Greek *because of the Jewish day of preparation.*   **20:1** Greek *On the first day of the week.*

19:26-27 John depicts Jesus as controlling his death (10:18; 18:8, 36-37; 19:11, 28-30). On the cross, this control is displayed by Jesus calmly arranging for someone to care for his mother, indicating his love for her. This note about Jesus caring for his mother in his last moments can balance Scriptures that address the cost of following him, such as leaving behind someone's parents (like Matthew 19:27-30). Caring well for our families is in line with Jesus' calling for our lives, and we should try our best to do so. But it is important not to let our families keep us from following Jesus if they are opposed to him.

19:27 In leaving his mother to John's care, Jesus was employing a Jewish family law that assigned the care of one person to another. The scene had an additional significance: The people who were present represented the new community of the church that was born at the cross. Jesus wanted them to care for each other in obedience to his command to love one another (13:34; 15:12, 17).

20:1-2 John describes Mary Magdalene as venturing out at night to see Jesus' tomb (see also Matthew 28:1; Mark 16:1-2; Luke 24:1). Although the "we" in her words hints that she might not have been alone, traveling at night was unconventional and risky for a woman, even more so than it is today. This is one of the instances in which John shows women's individuality and their personalities, compared to the other Gospels.

20:11-18 Mary Magdalene became the first person to see the resurrected Jesus because, in her grief, she *stayed.* Although society emphasizes "getting back to normal" after loss, those of us experiencing grief know the necessity of slowing down and staying. Even when weeping is the only thing we know to do, we can hope that God will see our pain and tears.

Mary Magdalene

IDENTITY — When the Worst Happens

Mary Magdalene remembers…
What do you do when the worst happens, when everything you believe in, trust in, disappears?

That was the question ricocheting through my tortured mind as I approached his tomb. My tears increased as my steps slowed, delaying what I didn't want to face.

Suddenly I stopped. Something was wrong! The stone was gone from the entrance!

I approached hesitantly, leaned to look inside. No body, but two men who looked like angels. It made no sense.

"Why are you crying?" they asked.

"Because they have taken away my Lord," I sobbed, "and I don't know where they have put him" (John 20:13).

Turning to leave I saw another man, probably the gardener. He, too, asked why I was crying. How could they not know?

"Sir," I begged, "if you have taken him away, tell me where …"

"Mary!" (20:16).

The voice, so familiar, came from the gardener, but … I raised my eyes to his. Not the gardener. Jesus! Alive!

Despite the horror I'd witnessed three days ago—alive! I was overcome with joy, but he wasn't finished speaking yet: "Go find my brothers and tell them, 'I am ascending to my Father and your Father'" (20:17).

Only later did the questions come: Why me? Why did God honor me with the most momentous announcement of all time? Why not Peter or John who'd just been at the tomb?

I don't have the answer to that question, but I do to my other question: What do you do when the worst happens? You wait for Jesus. He always comes.

> Wait for Jesus. He always comes.

MARY MAGDALENE'S STORY IS TOLD IN JOHN 20:1-18; SHE ALSO APPEARS IN MATTHEW 27:55-61; 28:1-10; MARK 15:40, 47; 16:1-11; LUKE 8:2-3; 24:1-10; JOHN 19:25.

IDENTIFY

Can you think of a time when you'd lost all hope? When did Jesus show up then?

Are you waiting now for Jesus to show up? How does waiting affect how you relate to him?

"My family fractured, and my mom-heart spent endless time devising solutions. Terrified of making things worse, I did nothing, hoping God would step in. Months passed with holidays and birthdays celebrated separately. I resigned myself to a split family. Then a knock on the door. The person looked like family, but all I saw was Jesus."

JANICE MAYO MATHERS is author of multiple books and Bible studies, including *Every Season: Embracing a Forever Kind of Purpose* (Stonecroft) and *Mothers-in-Law vs. Daughters-in-Law: Let There Be Peace*. She helps women see adverse circumstances as godly challenges.

IMAGE — MY STORY OF MY UNIQUE INFLUENCE

Jesus Restores Us to Lead

SCRIPTURE CONNECTION: JOHN 21:15-19

Grieved and humbled by his threefold betrayal of Jesus, Peter was forgiven and given a threefold commission to seek, nourish, and shepherd Jesus' flock. This teaches us the good news that nothing from our past keeps us from a hopeful future of faithfully serving Jesus. We can see how Jesus restored and prepared Peter to lead:

1. *Brokenness revealed.* Early on, when Peter saw a miraculous catch of fish, he fell at Jesus' feet and said, "Oh, Lord, please leave me—I'm such a sinful man" (Luke 5:8). As Jesus predicted, Peter denied him three times before the rooster crowed, even though Peter had promised he would lay down his life for Jesus (John 13:37-38).
2. *Love declared.* Jesus asked three times if Peter truly loved him. Peter now understood that Jesus wanted to heal his shame-filled heart. He got that Jesus knew more about him than Peter knew about himself. He knew that there was no brokenness or sin that Jesus could not heal if Peter truly loved him. And Peter did love Jesus.
3. *Commissioned to follow Jesus and serve.* Like Jesus fed and cared for his own disciples, Peter was told three times to do the same for Jesus' followers. Even when serving meant suffering, his suffering would bring God recognition and praise.

> Nothing in our past keeps us from a hopeful future of serving Jesus.

Sometimes we need simple truths told to us more than once. As we embrace being forgiven sinners, as we love Jesus, and as we say yes to his purposes, you and I become fishers and shepherds of people. Nothing in our past keeps us from a future of serving the one who knows, loves, and commissions us.

IMAGINE

What brokenness in your life does Jesus want to heal?

How does Jesus know you love him and want to follow him?

> "My love for Jesus has opened the door for him to heal my brokenness. It qualifies me to follow him and to seek and shepherd his followers."

MARY SCHALLER, MDiv, is the former president of Q Place and coauthor of *The 9 Arts of Spiritual Conversations*. Her life mission is to build and nurture Christ-centered communities.

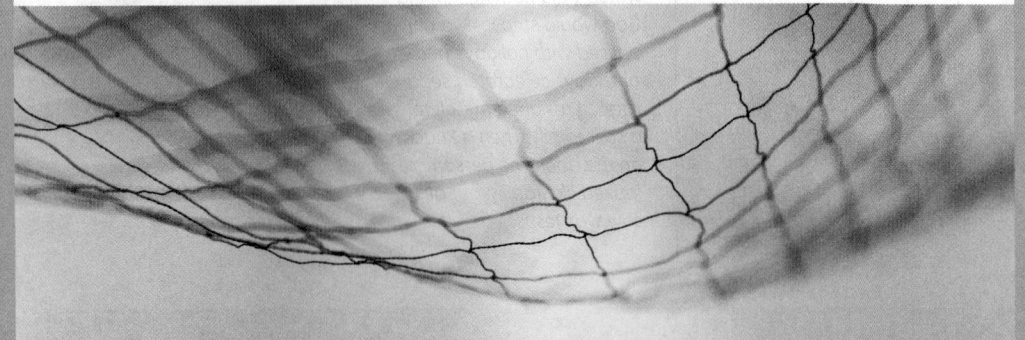

"Because they have taken away my Lord," she replied, "and I don't know where they have put him." ¹⁴She turned to leave and saw someone standing there. It was Jesus, but she didn't recognize him. ¹⁵"Dear woman, why are you crying?" Jesus asked her. "Who are you looking for?"

She thought he was the gardener. "Sir," she said, "if you have taken him away, tell me where you have put him, and I will go and get him."

¹⁶"Mary!" Jesus said.

She turned to him and cried out, "Rabboni!" (which is Hebrew for "Teacher").

¹⁷"Don't cling to me," Jesus said, "for I haven't yet ascended to the Father. But go find my brothers and tell them, 'I am ascending to my Father and your Father, to my God and your God.'"

¹⁸Mary Magdalene found the disciples and told them, "I have seen the Lord!" Then she gave them his message.

Jesus Appears to His Disciples

¹⁹That Sunday evening* the disciples were meeting behind locked doors because they were afraid of the Jewish leaders. Suddenly, Jesus was standing there among them! "Peace be with you," he said. ²⁰As he spoke, he showed them the wounds in his hands and his side. They were filled with joy when they saw the Lord! ²¹Again he said, "Peace be with you. As the Father has sent me, so I am sending you." ²²Then he breathed on them and said, "Receive the Holy Spirit. ²³If you forgive anyone's sins, they are forgiven. If you do not forgive them, they are not forgiven."

Jesus Appears to Thomas

²⁴One of the twelve disciples, Thomas (nicknamed the Twin),* was not with the others when Jesus came. ²⁵They told him, "We have seen the Lord!"

But he replied, "I won't believe it unless I see the nail wounds in his hands, put my fingers into them, and place my hand into the wound in his side."

²⁶Eight days later the disciples were together again, and this time Thomas was with them. The doors were locked; but suddenly, as before, Jesus was standing among them. "Peace be with you," he said. ²⁷Then he said to Thomas, "Put your finger here, and look at my hands. Put your hand into the wound in my side. Don't be faithless any longer. Believe!"

²⁸"My Lord and my God!" Thomas exclaimed.

²⁹Then Jesus told him, "You believe because you have seen me. Blessed are those who believe without seeing me."

Purpose of the Book

³⁰The disciples saw Jesus do many other miraculous signs in addition to the ones recorded in this book. ³¹But these are written so that you may continue to believe* that Jesus is the Messiah, the Son of God, and that by believing in him you will have life by the power of his name.

Epilogue: Jesus Appears to Seven Disciples

21 Later, Jesus appeared again to the disciples beside the Sea of Galilee.* This is how it happened. ²Several of the disciples were there—Simon Peter, Thomas (nicknamed the Twin),* Nathanael from Cana in Galilee, the sons of Zebedee, and two other disciples.

³Simon Peter said, "I'm going fishing."

"We'll come, too," they all said. So they went out in the boat, but they caught nothing all night.

⁴At dawn Jesus was standing on the beach, but the disciples couldn't see who he was. ⁵He called out, "Fellows,* have you caught any fish?"

"No," they replied.

⁶Then he said, "Throw out your net on the right-hand side of the boat, and you'll get some!" So they did, and they couldn't haul in the net because there were so many fish in it.

⁷Then the disciple Jesus loved said to Peter, "It's the Lord!" When Simon Peter heard that it was the

---

20:19 Greek *In the evening of that day, the first day of the week.* **20:24** Greek *Thomas, who was called Didymus.* **20:31** Some manuscripts read *that you may believe.* **21:1** Greek *Sea of Tiberias,* another name for the Sea of Galilee. **21:2** Greek *Thomas, who was called Didymus.* **21:5** Greek *Children.*

20:14-15 After Mary mistook him for the gardener, Jesus repeated the angel's question and added, "Who are you looking for?" Jesus' question was to provoke Mary's thinking: At this point Mary was looking for the body of Jesus, but she was about to meet the living Christ. Was she truly ready to meet her Lord?

20:17 Mary may have assumed that with the resurrection, things would go back to normal with Jesus and his disciples. She was trying to cling to the joy she discovered in her resurrected Lord, but he would relate to her in a new way (20:22). Jesus had not "yet ascended" to complete his return to the Father, but the process was underway (see Acts 1:6-11). Before his final departure, he would give the Holy Spirit (John 20:22; see also 14:15-21, 26; 15:26-27; 16:5-15).

20:18 Mary was the first eyewitness to see the Lord following his resurrection. She not only saw him, but she also heard him and touched him (see 1 John 1:1-4). This great privilege was given to a woman whose broken life had experienced healing (Luke 8:2). In Jewish culture this was astounding because a woman could not even be a witness in court. No Jew in this period would make up such a story because no one would be naturally inclined to believe it. God chose a woman to deliver his most important message, a choice that reinforces God's special preference for those marginalized by society. God's Kingdom does not abide by the rules and structures erected by humans for power and control over others.

Lord, he put on his tunic (for he had stripped for work), jumped into the water, and headed to shore. ⁸The others stayed with the boat and pulled the loaded net to the shore, for they were only about a hundred yards* from shore. ⁹When they got there, they found breakfast waiting for them—fish cooking over a charcoal fire, and some bread.

¹⁰"Bring some of the fish you've just caught," Jesus said. ¹¹So Simon Peter went aboard and dragged the net to the shore. There were 153 large fish, and yet the net hadn't torn.

¹²"Now come and have some breakfast!" Jesus said. None of the disciples dared to ask him, "Who are you?" They knew it was the Lord. ¹³Then Jesus served them the bread and the fish. ¹⁴This was the third time Jesus had appeared to his disciples since he had been raised from the dead.

¹⁵After breakfast Jesus asked Simon Peter, "Simon son of John, do you love me more than these?*"

"Yes, Lord," Peter replied, "you know I love you."

"Then feed my lambs," Jesus told him.

¹⁶Jesus repeated the question: "Simon son of John, do you love me?"

"Yes, Lord," Peter said, "you know I love you."

"Then take care of my sheep," Jesus said.

¹⁷A third time he asked him, "Simon son of John, do you love me?"

Peter was hurt that Jesus asked the question a third time. He said, "Lord, you know everything. You know that I love you."

Jesus said, "Then feed my sheep. ¹⁸I tell you the truth, when you were young, you were able to do as you liked; you dressed yourself and went wherever you wanted to go. But when you are old, you will stretch out your hands, and others* will dress you and take you where you don't want to go."

¹⁹Jesus said this to let him know by what kind of death he would glorify God. Then Jesus told him, "Follow me."

21:8 Greek *200 cubits* [90 meters].   21:15 Or *more than these others do?*   21:18 Some manuscripts read *and another one.*

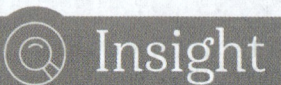

Insight — CAN WE TRUST THAT JESUS CONQUERED DEATH?

We may feel skeptical about the claim that Jesus rose from the dead because it defies what we know about death. At first, even Jesus' followers were stunned and skeptical about his resurrection. But Jesus appeared in person to many of his followers after he rose from the dead. Their eyewitness accounts help us have confidence in the truth of the Resurrection.

WHO	WHERE	REFERENCE
Mary Magdalene, Mary the mother of James, Joanna and Salome	At the tomb	Matthew 28:1-7; Mark 16:1-8; Luke 24:1-10
Mary Magdalene alone	At the tomb	Mark 16:9; John 20:11-17
Cleopas and his traveling companion	On the road to Emmaus	Mark 16:12-13; Luke 24:9-31
Eleven (or ten, according to John 20:24) disciples on Easter night	In a locked room	Mark 16:14; Luke 24:36-48; John 20:19-23
Eleven disciples a week later	Same room as before	John 20:26-29
Peter, Thomas, Nathanael, James, John, two others	Sea of Galilee	John 21:1-23
The eleven disciples	On a mountain in Galilee	Matthew 28:16-20
A large group (500+)	Unknown	1 Corinthians 15:6
James the Lord's brother; later "all the apostles"	Unknown	1 Corinthians 15:7
The eleven disciples	Near Bethany	Mark 16:19; Luke 24:50-52; Acts 1:3-9

²⁰Peter turned around and saw behind them the disciple Jesus loved—the one who had leaned over to Jesus during supper and asked, "Lord, who will betray you?" ²¹Peter asked Jesus, "What about him, Lord?"

²²Jesus replied, "If I want him to remain alive until I return, what is that to you? As for you, follow me." ²³So the rumor spread among the community of believers* that this disciple wouldn't die. But that isn't what Jesus said at all. He only said, "If I want him to remain alive until I return, what is that to you?"

²⁴This disciple is the one who testifies to these events and has recorded them here. And we know that his account of these things is accurate.

²⁵Jesus also did many other things. If they were all written down, I suppose the whole world could not contain the books that would be written.

21:23 Greek *the brothers.*

Acts OF THE APOSTLES

WHAT DO WE LEARN ABOUT GOD'S MISSION AND OURS? God's gift of new life through Jesus is for everyone and calls us together in community.

WHO WROTE IT? Luke, Paul's traveling companion. He addressed this book to Theophilus, as he did with the Gospel of Luke.

WHEN DID IT HAPPEN? The book covers a period of about thirty years, from Jesus being taken up into heaven to the early 60s AD, depicting the early church's growth.

HOW IS IT ORGANIZED?

- 1–5: The church begins in Jerusalem
- 6–12: The church grows from Jerusalem to Antioch
- 13–21: The Good News goes to the Gentiles
- 21–26: Paul arrested in Jerusalem and jailed in Caesarea
- 27–28: Paul takes the Good News to Rome

FEATURE HIGHLIGHTS

- Sapphira: Truth to Live By (1365)
- Why Should We Find Common Ground With Others? (1372)
- Working through Difficult Relationships (1380)
- Lessons from a First-Century Businesswoman-Believer (1383)
- Speaking to Be Heard (1387)

Words to Remember are highlighted throughout this book

HOW LONG DOES IT TAKE TO READ?

2:00

| :30 | 1:00 | 1:30 | 2:00 | 2:30 | 3:00 | 3:30 |

Timeline

AD	
30	THE HOLY SPIRIT COMES
35	STEPHEN KILLED FOR HIS FAITH IN JESUS; JESUS CALLS PAUL TO PREACH THE GOOD NEWS
44	JAMES THE APOSTLE KILLED; PETER ESCAPES PRISON AND RHODA ANNOUNCES A MIRACLE
46–48	PAUL GOES ON FIRST MISSIONARY JOURNEY, WITH BARNABAS AND JOHN MARK
50	JERUSALEM COUNCIL CONFIRMS GENTILE INCLUSION IN THE CHURCH
50–52	PAUL EMBARKS ON SECOND MISSIONARY JOURNEY, WITH SILAS; THEY SPEND 18 MONTHS IN CORINTH
50	PAUL MEETS PRISCILLA AND AQUILA IN CORINTH
	PAUL MEETS LYDIA IN PHILIPPI
53–57	PAUL TAKES A THIRD MISSIONARY JOURNEY
53–56	PAUL STAYS FOR AN EXTENDED TIME IN EPHESUS
57	PAUL ARRESTED IN JERUSALEM
59	PAUL VOYAGES TO ROME
64	PAUL KILLED FOR HIS FAITH IN ROME
70	ROME DESTROYS JERUSALEM AND THE TEMPLE

The Promise of the Holy Spirit

1 In my first book* I told you, Theophilus, about everything Jesus began to do and teach ²until the day he was taken up to heaven after giving his chosen apostles further instructions through the Holy Spirit. ³During the forty days after he suffered and died, he appeared to the apostles from time to time, and he proved to them in many ways that he was actually alive. And he talked to them about the Kingdom of God.

⁴Once when he was eating with them, he commanded them, "Do not leave Jerusalem until the Father sends you the gift he promised, as I told you before. ⁵John baptized with* water, but in just a few days you will be baptized with the Holy Spirit."

The Ascension of Jesus

⁶So when the apostles were with Jesus, they kept asking him, "Lord, has the time come for you to free Israel and restore our kingdom?"

⁷He replied, "The Father alone has the authority to set those dates and times, and they are not for you to know. ⁸But you will receive power when the Holy Spirit comes upon you. And you will be my witnesses, telling people about me everywhere—in Jerusalem, throughout Judea, in Samaria, and to the ends of the earth."

⁹After saying this, he was taken up into a cloud while they were watching, and they could no longer see him. ¹⁰As they strained to see him rising into heaven, two white-robed men suddenly stood among them. ¹¹"Men of Galilee," they said, "why are you standing here staring into heaven? Jesus has been taken from you into heaven, but someday he will return from heaven in the same way you saw him go!"

Matthias Replaces Judas

¹²Then the apostles returned to Jerusalem from the Mount of Olives, a distance of half a mile.* ¹³When they arrived, they went to the upstairs room of the house where they were staying.

Here are the names of those who were present: Peter, John, James, Andrew, Philip, Thomas, Bartholomew, Matthew, James (son of Alphaeus), Simon (the zealot), and Judas (son of James). ¹⁴They all met together and were constantly united in prayer, along with Mary the mother of Jesus, several other women, and the brothers of Jesus.

¹⁵During this time, when about 120 believers* were together in one place, Peter stood up and addressed them. ¹⁶"Brothers," he said, "the Scriptures had to be fulfilled concerning Judas, who guided those who arrested Jesus. This was predicted long ago by the Holy Spirit, speaking through King David. ¹⁷Judas was one of us and shared in the ministry with us."

¹⁸(Judas had bought a field with the money he received for his treachery. Falling headfirst there, his body split open, spilling out all his intestines. ¹⁹The news of his death spread to all the people of Jerusalem, and they gave the place the Aramaic name *Akeldama*, which means "Field of Blood.")

²⁰Peter continued, "This was written in the book of Psalms, where it says, 'Let his home become desolate, with no one living in it.' It also says, 'Let someone else take his position.'*

²¹"So now we must choose a replacement for Judas from among the men who were with us the entire time we were traveling with the Lord Jesus—²²from the time he was baptized by John until the day he was taken from us. Whoever is chosen will join us as a witness of Jesus' resurrection."

²³So they nominated two men: Joseph called Barsabbas (also known as Justus) and Matthias. ²⁴Then they all prayed, "O Lord, you know every heart. Show us which of these men you have chosen ²⁵as an apostle to replace Judas in this ministry, for he has deserted us and gone where he belongs." ²⁶Then

---

1:1 The reference is to the Gospel of Luke. **1:5** Or *in;* also in 1:5b. **1:12** Greek *a Sabbath day's journey.* **1:15** Greek *brothers.* **1:20** Pss 69:25; 109:8.

1:8 In Jesus' final instructions to his disciples, he outlined how the Good News would extend geographically from its Jewish starting point in Jerusalem and Judea (1:6–8:1), out to Samaria (8:4-25), Antioch in Syria (11:19-30), and eventually throughout the Mediterranean world to Rome (13:1–28:31). Luke's narrative uses Jesus' words as a road map for the story told in Acts. Christ later gave a similar call to carry his message to all people everywhere to Saul of Tarsus (9:15), who at one time had persecuted the Jewish Christians. Saul, later called Paul, would become the primary instrument for taking the Good News to the Gentiles. The Holy Spirit was the source of power for all this evangelistic and missionary effort, and the disciples were to wait for Jesus to send them the Holy Spirit before embarking on their work of witnessing (see Luke 24:49).

1:9 Jesus' ascension, when he was taken to heaven, shows us that Jesus lives now in his glorified, resurrected body with God the Father and the Holy Spirit. Jesus saves all people who come to him, and the bodies of all believers, both men and women, are made in God's image and will be raised to immortality (1 Corinthians 15:42-44). This means that our bodies are precious to God and should be respected and loved.

1:14 Jesus had many women followers, including his mother, who were also present at the cross when he died, at great risk to their own safety (Matthew 27:55-56). Acts highlights women's financial support of the Christian movement (Acts 16:15) and women's teaching and faithful witness to the gospel (9:36-42; 18:26). Women worked alongside men to spread the message of salvation and disciple new believers.

1:23-26 With prayer and humble dependence on God to reveal his will, the apostles "cast lots" to replace Judas. Casting lots was an established method of finding God's will at that time (see Leviticus 16:8; Numbers 27:21; Deuteronomy 33:8; Joshua 14:2; 18:3-10; Proverbs 16:33). Matthias was chosen to serve alongside the original eleven. After Pentecost, the Holy Spirit guided Jesus' followers through dreams, visions, and prophecies instead of through lots (see Acts 2:17-18; 13:2; 16:7-10).

they cast lots, and Matthias was selected to become an apostle with the other eleven.

The Holy Spirit Comes

2 On the day of Pentecost* all the believers were meeting together in one place. ²Suddenly, there was a sound from heaven like the roaring of a mighty windstorm, and it filled the house where they were sitting. ³Then, what looked like flames or tongues of fire appeared and settled on each of them. ⁴And everyone present was filled with the Holy Spirit and began speaking in other languages,* as the Holy Spirit gave them this ability.

⁵At that time there were devout Jews from every nation living in Jerusalem. ⁶When they heard the loud noise, everyone came running, and they were bewildered to hear their own languages being spoken by the believers.

⁷They were completely amazed. "How can this be?" they exclaimed. "These people are all from Galilee, ⁸and yet we hear them speaking in our own native languages! ⁹Here we are—Parthians, Medes, Elamites, people from Mesopotamia, Judea, Cappadocia, Pontus, the province of Asia, ¹⁰Phrygia, Pamphylia, Egypt, and the areas of Libya around Cyrene, visitors from Rome ¹¹(both Jews and converts to Judaism), Cretans, and Arabs. And we all hear these people speaking in our own languages about the wonderful things God has done!" ¹²They stood there amazed and perplexed. "What can this mean?" they asked each other.

¹³But others in the crowd ridiculed them, saying, "They're just drunk, that's all!"

Peter Preaches to the Crowd

¹⁴Then Peter stepped forward with the eleven other apostles and shouted to the crowd, "Listen carefully, all of you, fellow Jews and residents of Jerusalem! Make no mistake about this. ¹⁵These people are not drunk, as some of you are assuming. Nine o'clock in the morning is much too early for that. ¹⁶No, what you see was predicted long ago by the prophet Joel:

¹⁷ 'In the last days,' God says,
  'I will pour out my Spirit upon all people.
 Your sons and daughters will prophesy.
 Your young men will see visions,
  and your old men will dream dreams.
¹⁸ In those days I will pour out my Spirit
  even on my servants—men and women alike—
  and they will prophesy.
¹⁹ And I will cause wonders in the heavens above
  and signs on the earth below—
  blood and fire and clouds of smoke.
²⁰ The sun will become dark,
  and the moon will turn blood red
  before that great and glorious day of the Lord arrives.
²¹ But everyone who calls on the name of the Lord
  will be saved.'*

²²"People of Israel, listen! God publicly endorsed Jesus the Nazarene* by doing powerful miracles, wonders, and signs through him, as you well know. ²³But God knew what would happen, and his prearranged plan was carried out when Jesus was betrayed. With the help of lawless Gentiles, you nailed

---

2:1 The Festival of Pentecost came 50 days after Passover (when Jesus was crucified). 2:4 Or *in other tongues.* 2:17-21 Joel 2:28-32. 2:22 Or *Jesus of Nazareth.*

2:4 This event marks the coming of the Holy Spirit to fill Jesus' disciples, as he had promised, so that they could be powerful witnesses (1:4-5, 8). The Spirit's wisdom, energy, and power were the driving force behind the church's work and witness (for example, 2:14-41, 43; 4:31; 9:17, 20; 13:9-12; see also Ephesians 5:18). The Holy Spirit gave the disciples an extraordinary ability to communicate that made it possible for people from other countries to hear in their own languages about what God had done (Acts 2:6-11). This passage is one of several references to speaking in "other tongues" or "languages" (see also 10:44-48; 19:6; 1 Corinthians 14:2-28, 39). Here, this supernatural gift reveals the energizing presence of God's Spirit and marks the beginning of the proclamation of the Good News to people of every nation.

2:14-36 This is the first of about thirty speeches in Acts and one of the most important, standing as it does at the very inception of the church. It is a typical example of the preaching of the apostles, who proclaimed that the Old Testament promises had been fulfilled in the life, death, and resurrection of Jesus Christ. The apostles themselves were eyewitnesses of Jesus' entire public ministry and were his chosen representatives. In their speeches, the apostles called their audiences to repent of their sins and have faith in God through Christ, and they proclaimed that salvation and the presence of the Holy Spirit are promised to those who say yes to this message of Good News. This basic message is echoed in the sermons given in Acts 3, 4, 5, 8, 10, and 13. The same themes characterized Paul's preaching (see 1 Corinthians 15:3-9). This message was repeatedly preached to both Jews and Gentiles throughout the Mediterranean world; all people are called upon to repent of their sins and turn to God through faith in Jesus Christ.

2:17-21 Peter quoted from the Old Testament prophet Joel, whose prophecy was now fulfilled on the day of Pentecost. Women would prophesy, meaning that women were speaking and teaching and proclaiming God's truth about salvation and following Jesus, like the women who were present when the Holy Spirit fell on all Jesus' disciples (see 1:14). People of all social statuses—including those who were enslaved or who were servants, those who were male or female—would also prophesy. But despite the aforementioned inclusivity, Peter was only thinking of Jewish people here; later, with the conversion of the Roman army officer Cornelius, Peter would discover that the Holy Spirit also saves, fills, and empowers non-Jewish people (Gentiles). Class, ethnicity, social status, and gender would not be barriers to being given the gift of prophecy or proclamation of God's truth.

Insight — THE GOOD NEWS SPREADS

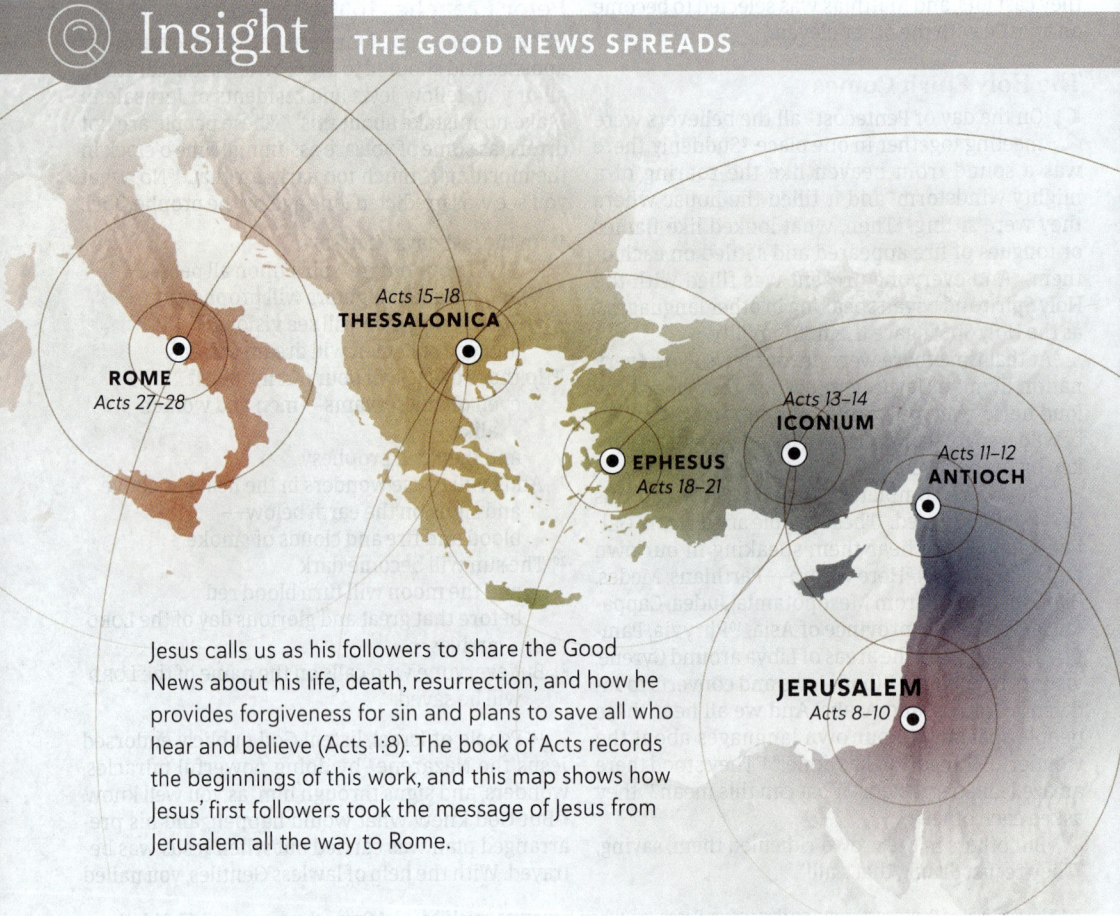

Jesus calls us as his followers to share the Good News about his life, death, resurrection, and how he provides forgiveness for sin and plans to save all who hear and believe (Acts 1:8). The book of Acts records the beginnings of this work, and this map shows how Jesus' first followers took the message of Jesus from Jerusalem all the way to Rome.

him to a cross and killed him. 24 But God released him from the horrors of death and raised him back to life, for death could not keep him in its grip. 25 King David said this about him:

'I see that the LORD is always with me.
  I will not be shaken, for he is right beside me.
26 No wonder my heart is glad,
  and my tongue shouts his praises!
  My body rests in hope.
27 For you will not leave my soul among the dead*
  or allow your Holy One to rot in the grave.
28 You have shown me the way of life,
  and you will fill me with the joy of your presence.'*

29 "Dear brothers, think about this! You can be sure that the patriarch David wasn't referring to himself, for he died and was buried, and his tomb is still here among us. 30 But he was a prophet, and he knew God had promised with an oath that one of David's own descendants would sit on his throne. 31 David was looking into the future and speaking of the Messiah's resurrection. He was saying that God would not leave him among the dead or allow his body to rot in the grave.

32 "God raised Jesus from the dead, and we are all witnesses of this. 33 Now he is exalted to the place of highest honor in heaven, at God's right hand. And the Father, as he had promised, gave him the Holy Spirit to pour out upon us, just as you see and hear today. 34 For David himself never ascended into heaven, yet he said,

'The LORD said to my Lord,
  "Sit in the place of honor at my right hand
35 until I humble your enemies,
  making them a footstool under your feet."'*

36 "So let everyone in Israel know for certain that God has made this Jesus, whom you crucified, to be both Lord and Messiah!"

37 Peter's words pierced their hearts, and they said to him and to the other apostles, "Brothers, what should we do?"

2:27 Greek *in Hades*; also in 2:31. 2:25-28 Ps 16:8-11 (Greek version). 2:34-35 Ps 110:1.

³⁸Peter replied, "Each of you must repent of your sins and turn to God, and be baptized in the name of Jesus Christ for the forgiveness of your sins. Then you will receive the gift of the Holy Spirit. ³⁹This promise is to you, to your children, and to those far away*—all who have been called by the Lord our God." ⁴⁰Then Peter continued preaching for a long time, strongly urging all his listeners, "Save yourselves from this crooked generation!"

⁴¹Those who believed what Peter said were baptized and added to the church that day—about 3,000 in all.

The Believers Form a Community

⁴²All the believers devoted themselves to the apostles' teaching, and to fellowship, and to sharing in meals (including the Lord's Supper*), and to prayer.

⁴³A deep sense of awe came over them all, and the apostles performed many miraculous signs and wonders. ⁴⁴And all the believers met together in one place and shared everything they had. ⁴⁵They sold their property and possessions and shared the money with those in need. ⁴⁶They worshiped together at the Temple each day, met in homes for the Lord's Supper, and shared their meals with great joy and generosity*—⁴⁷all the while praising God and enjoying the goodwill of all the people. And each day the Lord added to their fellowship those who were being saved.

Peter Heals a Crippled Beggar

3 Peter and John went to the Temple one afternoon to take part in the three o'clock prayer service. ²As they approached the Temple, a man lame from birth was being carried in. Each day he was put beside the Temple gate, the one called the Beautiful Gate, so he could beg from the people going into the Temple. ³When he saw Peter and John about to enter, he asked them for some money.

⁴Peter and John looked at him intently, and Peter said, "Look at us!" ⁵The lame man looked at them eagerly, expecting some money. ⁶But Peter said, "I don't have any silver or gold for you. But I'll give you what I have. In the name of Jesus Christ the Nazarene,* get up and* walk!"

⁷Then Peter took the lame man by the right hand and helped him up. And as he did, the man's feet and ankles were instantly healed and strengthened. ⁸He jumped up, stood on his feet, and began to walk! Then, walking, leaping, and praising God, he went into the Temple with them.

⁹All the people saw him walking and heard him praising God. ¹⁰When they realized he was the lame beggar they had seen so often at the Beautiful Gate, they were absolutely astounded! ¹¹They all rushed out in amazement to Solomon's Colonnade, where the man was holding tightly to Peter and John.

Peter Preaches in the Temple

¹²Peter saw his opportunity and addressed the crowd. "People of Israel," he said, "what is so surprising about this? And why stare at us as though we had made this man walk by our own power or godliness? ¹³For it is the God of Abraham, Isaac, and Jacob—the God of all our ancestors—who has brought glory to his servant Jesus by doing this. This is the same Jesus whom you handed over and rejected before Pilate, despite Pilate's decision to release him. ¹⁴You rejected this holy, righteous one and instead demanded the release of a murderer. ¹⁵You killed the author of life, but God raised him from the dead. And we are witnesses of this fact!

2:39 Or *and to people far in the future,* or *and to the Gentiles.* 2:42 Greek *the breaking of bread;* also in 2:46. 2:46 Or *and sincere hearts.* 3:6a Or *Jesus Christ of Nazareth.* 3:6b Some manuscripts do not include *get up and.*

2:42-47 Early Christians emphasized hospitality, and women's activities in preparing meals were highly valued and integral to their shared practice of eating together. Women also used their own money to support community needs (Luke 8:2-3; Acts 16:15; Romans 16:1-2). During this time period, they were free to sell their property and possessions, although certain legal documents, such as dowries, required a male guardian's signature. When we think about the early Christians, we may picture men primarily because we are most familiar with the men who were prominent early Christians, but the early church was diverse and full of women, men, girls, and boys from various places and circumstances.
3:1-11 Jesus' promise that his disciples would do even greater works than he had done (John 14:12) was fulfilled in the apostles' signs, wonders, and mighty works (Acts 2:43; 5:12; 8:4-8). Here, Peter clearly exercised power to heal "in the name of Jesus Christ the Nazarene" (3:6, 16). The cure was instant and undeniable (3:8), resulting in the man's "praising God" (3:8-9; see also Luke 17:15-18; 18:43; 19:37). This is the first of many demonstrations of divine power given to disciples in Acts (4:24-31; 5:12; 6:8; 8:6; 9:33-42; 28:8).

3:1 The Jerusalem Temple had a large "Gentiles' Court" that encircled the Temple building and was accessible to both Jews and Gentiles. The Temple building included a "Women's Court" in which both Jewish men and women worshiped. Women were not permitted to enter the place of sacrifice. Only priests entered the Holy Place beyond the sacrifice area, and only the high priest entered the Most Holy Place once each year on the Day of Atonement. Jesus' death and resurrection tore down the barrier between God and people, and allowed everyone—regardless of the previous societal restrictions—to meet God in the Most Holy Place (see Matthew 27:51; Mark 15:38).
3:10-11 What Luke calls the Beautiful Gate was probably officially named the Nicanor Gate, built of Corinthian bronze or brass, and located on the Temple's east side (see Josephus, *The Wars of the Jews,* book 5, chapter 5, paragraph 3). It was adorned more beautifully than the other gates. Solomon's Colonnade was a portico on the Temple's east side (see Josephus, *The Wars of the Jews,* book 5, chapter 5, paragraphs 1–3; *The Antiquities of the Jews,* book 20, chapter 9, paragraph 7).

> "I'm amazed to see how many of my own policies and beliefs trace back to my grandmother. The same thinking, the same ideas and approach. She taught them to my mother, and I was almost unconsciously reared upon these same precepts."
>
> **HENRIETTA MEARS**
> (1890–1963) pioneer of Christian education, evangelist, and author

God, so that your sins may be wiped away. ²⁰Then times of refreshment will come from the presence of the Lord, and he will again send you Jesus, your appointed Messiah. ²¹For he must remain in heaven until the time for the final restoration of all things, as God promised long ago through his holy prophets. ²²Moses said, 'The LORD your God will raise up for you a Prophet like me from among your own people. Listen carefully to everything he tells you.'* ²³Then Moses said, 'Anyone who will not listen to that Prophet will be completely cut off from God's people.'*

²⁴"Starting with Samuel, every prophet spoke about what is happening today. ²⁵You are the children of those prophets, and you are included in the covenant God promised to your ancestors. For God said to Abraham, 'Through your descendants* all the families on earth will be blessed.' ²⁶When God raised up his servant, Jesus, he sent him first to you people of Israel, to bless you by turning each of you back from your sinful ways."

Peter and John before the Council

4 While Peter and John were speaking to the people, they were confronted by the priests, the captain of the Temple guard, and some of the Sadducees. ²These leaders were very disturbed that Peter and John were teaching the people that through Jesus there is a resurrection of the dead. ³They arrested them and, since it was already evening, put them in jail until morning. ⁴But many of the people who heard their message believed it, so the number of men who believed now totaled about 5,000.

⁵The next day the council of all the rulers and elders and teachers of religious law met in Jerusalem. ⁶Annas the high priest was there, along with Caiaphas, John, Alexander, and other relatives of the high priest. ⁷They brought in the two disciples and

¹⁶"Through faith in the name of Jesus, this man was healed—and you know how crippled he was before. Faith in Jesus' name has healed him before your very eyes.

¹⁷"Friends,* I realize that what you and your leaders did to Jesus was done in ignorance. ¹⁸But God was fulfilling what all the prophets had foretold about the Messiah—that he must suffer these things. ¹⁹Now repent of your sins and turn to

---

3:17 Greek *Brothers.*   3:22 Deut 18:15.   3:23 Deut 18:19; Lev 23:29.   3:25 Greek *your seed;* see Gen 12:3; 22:18.

3:20-21 God's presence offers "refreshment" for his people (see Matthew 11:28-29). Peter teaches here that the second coming of Christ would be one of those "times of refreshment" from God when he would send Jesus to be present in body with his people.

3:25 God blessed Abraham and Sarah, his wife, with a son, Isaac, who the Jews today trace their lineage through (Genesis 21:2-3). Abraham had another son, named Ishmael, through Hagar, an enslaved Egyptian woman (Genesis 16:2-16). Muslims today trace their faith through Ishmael.

4:1-22 Persecution was a common experience of God's people throughout the Bible. God's servants often faced hostility and opposition (Deuteronomy 30:7; 1 Kings 18:13; Nehemiah 4:1-3; Jeremiah 37:1–38:28; Matthew 23:34-37; Luke 11:49-51; 1 Thessalonians 2:14-15). Jesus himself was persecuted (Luke 4:29; John 5:16), and he told his disciples to expect the same kind of treatment (Matthew 10:23; 24:9; Mark 13:9; Luke 21:12; John 16:2), but he promised that the Holy Spirit would provide strength and wisdom (Acts 1:8; Luke 12:11-12; 21:15). Acts records frequent times of persecution (Acts 4:3; 5:17-41; 7:54–8:3; 9:1-2; 11:19; 12:2; 13:50; 14:19; 16:19-24) but Acts also reiterates that the Holy Spirit empowers disciples to bear witness in such circumstances (4:8-13; 6:10; 7:55). The boldness of Peter and John before the hostile high council exemplifies facing persecution with courage and power (4:20).

4:4 It was standard practice in ancient documents to count only men in a group because they had legal standing in courts, while women under Roman law needed a legal guardian to help execute legal and financial matters. Additionally, women's opinions in public and religious matters were not valued. Acts mentions the high number of male followers to demonstrate the worthiness of the gospel message. The earliest readers would have inferred that alongside the men, there would be a large number of women who also chose to follow Jesus, and we can envision the same when we picture early Christians.

demanded, "By what power, or in whose name, have you done this?"

⁸Then Peter, filled with the Holy Spirit, said to them, "Rulers and elders of our people, ⁹are we being questioned today because we've done a good deed for a crippled man? Do you want to know how he was healed? ¹⁰Let me clearly state to all of you and to all the people of Israel that he was healed by the powerful name of Jesus Christ the Nazarene,* the man you crucified but whom God raised from the dead. ¹¹For Jesus is the one referred to in the Scriptures, where it says,

'The stone that you builders rejected
has now become the cornerstone.'*

¹²There is salvation in no one else! God has given no other name under heaven by which we must be saved."

¹³The members of the council were amazed when they saw the boldness of Peter and John, for they could see that they were ordinary men with no special training in the Scriptures. They also recognized them as men who had been with Jesus. ¹⁴But since they could see the man who had been healed standing right there among them, there was nothing the council could say. ¹⁵So they ordered Peter and John out of the council chamber* and conferred among themselves.

¹⁶"What should we do with these men?" they asked each other. "We can't deny that they have performed a miraculous sign, and everybody in Jerusalem knows about it. ¹⁷But to keep them from spreading their propaganda any further, we must warn them not to speak to anyone in Jesus' name again." ¹⁸So they called the apostles back in and commanded them never again to speak or teach in the name of Jesus.

¹⁹But Peter and John replied, "Do you think God wants us to obey you rather than him? ²⁰We cannot stop telling about everything we have seen and heard."

²¹The council then threatened them further, but they finally let them go because they didn't know how to punish them without starting a riot. For everyone was praising God ²²for this miraculous sign—the healing of a man who had been lame for more than forty years.

The Believers Pray for Courage

²³As soon as they were freed, Peter and John returned to the other believers and told them what the leading priests and elders had said. ²⁴When they heard the report, all the believers lifted their voices together in prayer to God: "O Sovereign Lord, Creator of heaven and earth, the sea, and everything in them—²⁵you spoke long ago by the Holy Spirit through our ancestor David, your servant, saying,

'Why were the nations so angry?
    Why did they waste their time with futile plans?
²⁶ The kings of the earth prepared for battle;
    the rulers gathered together
against the LORD
    and against his Messiah.'*

²⁷"In fact, this has happened here in this very city! For Herod Antipas, Pontius Pilate the governor, the Gentiles, and the people of Israel were all united against Jesus, your holy servant, whom you anointed. ²⁸But everything they did was determined beforehand according to your will. ²⁹And now, O Lord, hear their threats, and give us, your servants, great boldness in preaching your word. ³⁰Stretch out your hand with healing power; may miraculous signs and wonders be done through the name of your holy servant Jesus."

³¹After this prayer, the meeting place shook, and they were all filled with the Holy Spirit. Then they preached the word of God with boldness.

The Believers Share Their Possessions

³²All the believers were united in heart and mind. And they felt that what they owned was not their own, so they shared everything they had. ³³The apostles testified powerfully to the resurrection of the Lord Jesus, and God's great blessing was upon them all. ³⁴There were no needy people among them, because those who owned land or houses would sell them ³⁵and bring the money to the apostles to give to those in need.

³⁶For instance, there was Joseph, the one the apostles nicknamed Barnabas (which means "Son of Encouragement"). He was from the tribe of Levi and came from the island of Cyprus. ³⁷He sold a field he owned and brought the money to the apostles.

4:10 Or *Jesus Christ of Nazareth.* 4:11 Ps 118:22. 4:15 Greek *the Sanhedrin.* 4:25-26 Or *his anointed one;* or *his Christ.* Ps 2:1-2.

4:24-31 This group of believers included women, and all were filled with the Holy Spirit. These women and men preached the gospel with boldness despite the threat of persecution (see 4:21). Down through the centuries, women have been persecuted or martyred for the faith and have endured hardships as missionaries, doctors, evangelists, and Bible translators, among other professions used to advance the message of the Good News.
4:32-35 The sharing of early believers was remarkable (see also 2:44-45; contrast with 6:1). Being "united in heart and mind," they willingly offered anything they possessed to meet the needs of other believers. This sharing was voluntary and without coercion, meeting the pressing needs of the community and prompted by Christian love and concern for one another. As Christians, we can be encouraged to share what we have with those who are in need, especially our sisters and brothers in Christ, because everything we have belongs to God anyway (see Romans 11:36; 2 Corinthians 9:10-11).

Ananias and Sapphira

5 But there was a certain man named Ananias who, with his wife, Sapphira, sold some property. [2] He brought part of the money to the apostles, claiming it was the full amount. With his wife's consent, he kept the rest.

[3] Then Peter said, "Ananias, why have you let Satan fill your heart? You lied to the Holy Spirit, and you kept some of the money for yourself. [4] The property was yours to sell or not sell, as you wished. And after selling it, the money was also yours to give away. How could you do a thing like this? You weren't lying to us but to God!"

[5] As soon as Ananias heard these words, he fell to the floor and died. Everyone who heard about it was terrified. [6] Then some young men got up, wrapped him in a sheet, and took him out and buried him.

[7] About three hours later his wife came in, not knowing what had happened. [8] Peter asked her, "Was this the price you and your husband received for your land?"

"Yes," she replied, "that was the price."

[9] And Peter said, "How could the two of you even think of conspiring to test the Spirit of the Lord like this? The young men who buried your husband are just outside the door, and they will carry you out, too."

[10] Instantly, she fell to the floor and died. When the young men came in and saw that she was dead, they carried her out and buried her beside her husband. [11] Great fear gripped the entire church and everyone else who heard what had happened.

The Apostles Heal Many

[12] The apostles were performing many miraculous signs and wonders among the people. And all the believers were meeting regularly at the Temple in the area known as Solomon's Colonnade. [13] But no one else dared to join them, even though all the people had high regard for them. [14] Yet more and more people believed and were brought to the Lord—crowds of both men and women. [15] As a result of the apostles' work, sick people were brought out into the streets on beds and mats so that Peter's shadow might fall across some of them as he went by. [16] Crowds came from the villages around Jerusalem, bringing their sick and those possessed by evil* spirits, and they were all healed.

The Apostles Meet Opposition

[17] The high priest and his officials, who were Sadducees, were filled with jealousy. [18] They arrested the apostles and put them in the public jail. [19] But an angel of the Lord came at night, opened the gates of the jail, and brought them out. Then he told them, [20] "Go to the Temple and give the people this message of life!"

[21] So at daybreak the apostles entered the Temple, as they were told, and immediately began teaching.

When the high priest and his officials arrived, they convened the high council*—the full assembly of the elders of Israel. Then they sent for the apostles to be brought from the jail for trial. [22] But when the Temple guards went to the jail, the men were gone. So they returned to the council and reported, [23] "The jail was securely locked, with the guards standing outside, but when we opened the gates, no one was there!"

[24] When the captain of the Temple guard and the leading priests heard this, they were perplexed, wondering where it would all end. [25] Then someone arrived with startling news: "The men you put in jail are standing in the Temple, teaching the people!"

[26] The captain went with his Temple guards and arrested the apostles, but without violence, for they were afraid the people would stone them. [27] Then they brought the apostles before the high council, where the high priest confronted them. [28] "We gave you strict orders never again to teach in this man's name!" he said. "Instead, you have filled all

---

5:16 Greek *unclean*. **5:21** Greek *Sanhedrin*; also in 5:27, 41.

5:1-11 Luke is fond of balancing a positive example with a negative example. He had just recorded the remarkable story of Barnabas (4:36-37). Next Luke presented the opposite conduct of Ananias and Sapphira, who were tempted by the desire to be held in high regard. Ananias and Sapphira had not been forced to sell their property or give the proceeds away. The couple's sin was in their pretense and deception.

5:7-10 Sapphira conspired with her husband to deceive the apostles. During this time period, some women could own property under Roman law, buying and selling without male oversight. They could donate their money (Luke 8:2-3) and give gifts (Luke 21:1-4). Therefore, Sapphira was not bound by her husband's behavior alone and was held responsible for her sin of lying to God too. A similar event occurred at the beginning of Israel's entering the land God had promised them. But instead of keeping back money, Achan had stolen money and other goods that had been set aside for the Lord, and he and his family were put to death (Joshua 7:1-26).

5:17-40 The success of the apostles' ministry again aroused strong opposition (see 4:1-3). The wealthy and powerful Sadducees controlled the Temple establishment and had a Temple police force at their disposal. They opposed belief in the resurrection of the dead and were determined not to allow the apostles to proclaim their message about the resurrection of Jesus unchallenged. They also sensed that their hold on the Jewish people was loosening, so they attacked the apostles because they were jealous of the attention the apostles received.

5:28 While the Jewish religious leaders were the ones who sought to crucify Jesus, the Roman Empire ultimately carried out his execution. Many more Jews followed Jesus than persecuted him, but the religious leaders chose to preserve the status quo and their power instead of following him. We may want to judge the religious leaders for persecuting the early Christians when they were speaking the truth about God, but the same tendencies are found within the church today. People can desire power and control more than truth or love. The church also has a terrible history of persecuting Jews for the Jewish leaders' decision to call for Jesus' death, but the Jewish people are not responsible for Jesus' death.

Sapphira

IDENTITY — Truth to Live By

Let her life witness and her death proclaim truth. Sapphira was a warning to anyone who would listen.

It wasn't about the money or the property she and her husband had sold.

Perhaps it was about making themselves look good and thinking they could lie to God.

She and her husband joined this movement whose fellowship was strong, probably unlike anything they had known. They probably knew that Jesus had been hung from the cross and had heard the reports that his grave was empty. And when Peter stood so boldly and proclaimed who Jesus is, perhaps they believed. They knew that the Holy Spirit lived inside them and spoke to their community.

But maybe they lied to themselves, thinking God wasn't enough. So it was easy for Satan to insert that seed of doubt as they sold their property: *We can keep some of the money, just to be safe. How will they ever know?* That thought might have tickled their pride and greed.

But it was never about others knowing the truth. It was about lying to God and believing lies about God.

Let her life witness and her death proclaim truth. I hope Sapphira's story helps us live—in truth.

> We are known inside and out by the God who loves us.

SAPPHIRA'S STORY IS TOLD IN ACTS 5:1-11.

IDENTIFY

What might you want to hide from God or others?

How might believing that God knows everything about you and yet still loves you faithfully help you draw closer to him?

> "I remember my mother telling me I couldn't surprise God, that he knew all I would do. I would lie in bed and then shoot my arms into the air. 'Ha! How about that, God? Did you know I'd do that?' Indeed, I am known by him inside and out."

CARA DAY is a writer and illustrator. She has served with Stonecroft Ministries helping women live "extraordinary."

Jerusalem with your teaching about him, and you want to make us responsible for his death!"

²⁹But Peter and the apostles replied, "We must obey God rather than any human authority. ³⁰The God of our ancestors raised Jesus from the dead after you killed him by hanging him on a cross.* ³¹Then God put him in the place of honor at his right hand as Prince and Savior. He did this so the people of Israel would repent of their sins and be forgiven. ³²We are witnesses of these things and so is the Holy Spirit, who is given by God to those who obey him."

³³When they heard this, the high council was furious and decided to kill them. ³⁴But one member, a Pharisee named Gamaliel, who was an expert in religious law and respected by all the people, stood up and ordered that the men be sent outside the council chamber for a while. ³⁵Then he said to his colleagues, "Men of Israel, take care what you are planning to do to these men! ³⁶Some time ago there was that fellow Theudas, who pretended to be someone great. About 400 others joined him, but he was killed, and all his followers went their various ways. The whole movement came to nothing. ³⁷After him, at the time of the census, there was Judas of Galilee. He got people to follow him, but he was killed, too, and all his followers were scattered.

³⁸"So my advice is, leave these men alone. Let them go. If they are planning and doing these things merely on their own, it will soon be overthrown. ³⁹But if it is from God, you will not be able to overthrow them. You may even find yourselves fighting against God!"

⁴⁰The others accepted his advice. They called in the apostles and had them flogged. Then they ordered them never again to speak in the name of Jesus, and they let them go.

⁴¹The apostles left the high council rejoicing that God had counted them worthy to suffer disgrace for the name of Jesus.* ⁴²And every day, in the Temple and from house to house, they continued to teach and preach this message: "Jesus is the Messiah."

Seven Men Chosen to Serve

6 But as the believers* rapidly multiplied, there were rumblings of discontent. The Greek-speaking believers complained about the Hebrew-speaking believers, saying that their widows were being discriminated against in the daily distribution of food.

²So the Twelve called a meeting of all the believers. They said, "We apostles should spend our time teaching the word of God, not running a food program. ³And so, brothers, select seven men who are well respected and are full of the Spirit and wisdom. We will give them this responsibility. ⁴Then we apostles can spend our time in prayer and teaching the word."

⁵Everyone liked this idea, and they chose the following: Stephen (a man full of faith and the Holy Spirit), Philip, Procorus, Nicanor, Timon, Parmenas, and Nicolas of Antioch (an earlier convert to the Jewish faith). ⁶These seven were presented to the apostles, who prayed for them as they laid their hands on them.

⁷So God's message continued to spread. The number of believers greatly increased in Jerusalem, and many of the Jewish priests were converted, too.

Stephen Is Arrested

⁸Stephen, a man full of God's grace and power, performed amazing miracles and signs among the people. ⁹But one day some men from the Synagogue of Freed

5:30 Greek *on a tree.* 5:41 Greek *for the name.* 6:1 Greek *disciples;* also in 6:2, 7.

6:1-3 Languages barriers and cultural differences were the problems behind the lack of care for widows. The church in Jerusalem grew very quickly and included Jews from across the Roman Empire and perhaps also from Babylon in the Parthian Empire. Each group brought distinct perspectives, and the Jerusalem church (perhaps unwittingly) discriminated against those not from Judea. So too today, Christians must be vigilant to avoid discriminating against newcomers and immigrants in our churches and communities. When the church in Acts addressed the problem, their numbers began to grow again because they were living out Jesus' message of caring for their neighbors.
6:1 The category "widow" included women whose husbands had died, as well as divorced women or those who lacked family protection. The Greek-speaking widows were Jews who had moved to Jerusalem from elsewhere in the Roman Empire, similar to immigrants today. While some widows had wealth, many were poor. When their needs were brought to the apostles, the church acted quickly to provide for them. Caring for the needy and immigrants remains a critical role for the church today.
6:2-6 Wisely, the apostles "called a meeting of all the believers" to address the dispute. They recognized the seriousness of the problem, as well as their priority to pray and teach. The solution was to select wise and Spirit-filled men to oversee the food distribution. The community accepted the apostles' solution and chose good leaders from the ranks of the Greek-speaking believers (all of their names are Greek). These seven devoted themselves to this special ministry, allowing the apostles the freedom to focus on their ministry of prayer and teaching. However, we do see that Philip, one of these men, became an evangelist later (8:4-40). These seven men are sometimes called the first deacons because of the similarity of their role to the office of deacon (see 1 Timothy 3:8-13, where the Greek term translated "deacon" [Greek *diakonos,* "servant"] is used). In Acts 6:2, a related Greek word is translated "running a food program" (Greek *diakonein,* "to serve"). In Romans 16:1, Paul refers to Phoebe as "a deacon in the church in Cenchrea," which tells us women were also commissioned to this role in the early churches.
6:8-15 The Jewish leaders did to Stephen as they had done to Jesus (see Matthew 26:3-4, 59-66): They got some people to lie about him, accusing him of blasphemy. This accusation incited a riot, and they arrested him and posted false charges against him.

Slaves, as it was called, started to debate with him. They were Jews from Cyrene, Alexandria, Cilicia, and the province of Asia. ¹⁰None of them could stand against the wisdom and the Spirit with which Stephen spoke.

¹¹So they persuaded some men to lie about Stephen, saying, "We heard him blaspheme Moses, and even God." ¹²This roused the people, the elders, and the teachers of religious law. So they arrested Stephen and brought him before the high council.*

¹³The lying witnesses said, "This man is always speaking against the holy Temple and against the law of Moses. ¹⁴We have heard him say that this Jesus of Nazareth* will destroy the Temple and change the customs Moses handed down to us."

¹⁵At this point everyone in the high council stared at Stephen, because his face became as bright as an angel's.

Stephen Addresses the Council

7 Then the high priest asked Stephen, "Are these accusations true?"

²This was Stephen's reply: "Brothers and fathers, listen to me. Our glorious God appeared to our ancestor Abraham in Mesopotamia before he settled in Haran.* ³God told him, 'Leave your native land and your relatives, and come into the land that I will show you.'* ⁴So Abraham left the land of the Chaldeans and lived in Haran until his father died. Then God brought him here to the land where you now live.

⁵"But God gave him no inheritance here, not even one square foot of land. God did promise, however, that eventually the whole land would belong to Abraham and his descendants—even though he had no children yet. ⁶God also told him that his descendants would live in a foreign land, where they would be oppressed as slaves for 400 years. ⁷'But I will punish the nation that enslaves them,' God said, 'and in the end they will come out and worship me here in this place.'*

⁸"God also gave Abraham the covenant of circumcision at that time. So when Abraham became the father of Isaac, he circumcised him on the eighth day. And the practice was continued when Isaac became the father of Jacob, and when Jacob became the father of the twelve patriarchs of the Israelite nation.

⁹"These patriarchs were jealous of their brother Joseph, and they sold him to be a slave in Egypt. But God was with him ¹⁰and rescued him from all his troubles. And God gave him favor before Pharaoh, king of Egypt. God also gave Joseph unusual wisdom, so that Pharaoh appointed him governor over all of Egypt and put him in charge of the palace.

¹¹"But a famine came upon Egypt and Canaan. There was great misery, and our ancestors ran out of food. ¹²Jacob heard that there was still grain in Egypt, so he sent his sons—our ancestors—to buy some. ¹³The second time they went, Joseph revealed his identity to his brothers,* and they were introduced to Pharaoh. ¹⁴Then Joseph sent for his father, Jacob, and all his relatives to come to Egypt, seventy-five persons in all. ¹⁵So Jacob went to Egypt. He died there, as did our ancestors. ¹⁶Their bodies were taken to Shechem and buried in the tomb Abraham had bought for a certain price from Hamor's sons in Shechem.

¹⁷"As the time drew near when God would fulfill his promise to Abraham, the number of our people in Egypt greatly increased. ¹⁸But then a new king came to the throne of Egypt who knew nothing about Joseph. ¹⁹This king exploited our people and oppressed them, forcing parents to abandon their newborn babies so they would die.

²⁰"At that time Moses was born—a beautiful child in God's eyes. His parents cared for him at home for three months. ²¹When they had to abandon him, Pharaoh's daughter adopted him and raised him as her own son. ²²Moses was taught all the wisdom of the Egyptians, and he was powerful in both speech and action.

6:12 Greek *Sanhedrin*; also in 6:15. **6:14** Or *Jesus the Nazarene*. **7:2** *Mesopotamia* was the region now called Iraq. *Haran* was a city in what is now called Syria. **7:3** Gen 12:1. **7:5-7** Gen 12:7; 15:13-14; Exod 3:12. **7:13** Other manuscripts read *Joseph was recognized by his brothers*.

7:1-53 Stephen responded to the accusations by testifying about his Lord (see Luke 21:12-17). Instead of defending himself against their prosecution, he became a witness in God's prosecution of them, exposing their stubbornness and unfaithfulness to God. Stephen's recital of Israel's past reminded them of their repeated rejections of those whom God had sent. Stephen's review of Israel's history has three principal parts—the beginnings of God's covenant with their ancestors (Acts 7:2-16), the ministry of Moses (7:17-43), and the role of the Tabernacle and the Temple (7:44-50). Stephen followed up his historical survey with a clear attack on the hardheartedness of his own people. With a prophetic challenge, he urged them to stop rebelling against the Holy Spirit and turn to God with repentance and faith.

7:8 Jewish circumcision is performed on male babies, removing the foreskin of the penis. There is no Jewish ceremonial equivalent rite for girls. Female genital mutilation is not biblical and has no place in the church. Christians do not have a physical sign on our bodies to show our inclusion among God's people. Instead, the apostle Paul speaks of believers as "the ones who are truly circumcised" (Philippians 3:3), meaning that believers are baptized and the Holy Spirit fills them. Both men and women are given the gift of the Holy Spirit, or bear the spiritual mark of the Spirit (see Ephesians 1:13, especially the text note).

7:21 The story of Moses' mother and sister planning his rescue by Pharaoh's daughter demonstrates their bravery (Exodus 2:1-10). Stephen mentions them in his speech, recounting Israelite history, because these women played a vital role in God's salvation story. By rescuing and protecting Moses, they made it possible for him to grow and become God's chosen leader and mediator for his people. Women are empowered by God to act with the same bravery and resourcefulness today, advancing God's story and participating in his plan for saving everyone.

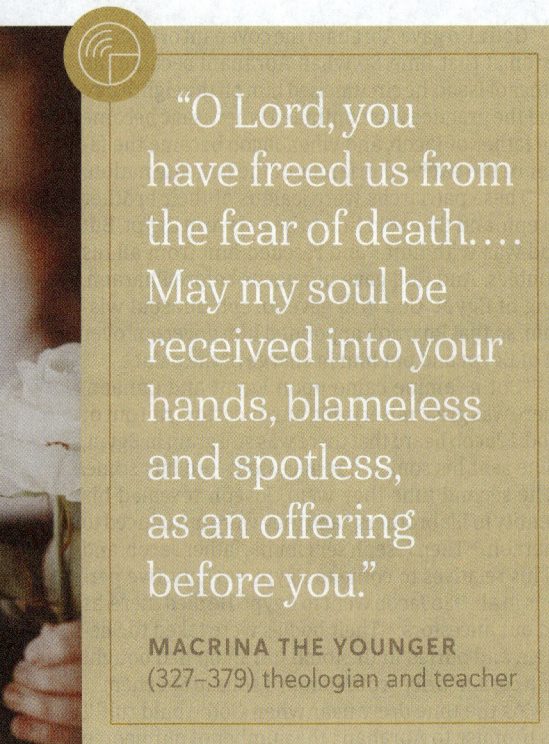

"O Lord, you have freed us from the fear of death.... May my soul be received into your hands, blameless and spotless, as an offering before you."

MACRINA THE YOUNGER
(327–379) theologian and teacher

²³"One day when Moses was forty years old, he decided to visit his relatives, the people of Israel. ²⁴He saw an Egyptian mistreating an Israelite. So Moses came to the man's defense and avenged him, killing the Egyptian. ²⁵Moses assumed his fellow Israelites would realize that God had sent him to rescue them, but they didn't.

²⁶"The next day he visited them again and saw two men of Israel fighting. He tried to be a peacemaker. 'Men,' he said, 'you are brothers. Why are you fighting each other?'

²⁷"But the man in the wrong pushed Moses aside. 'Who made you a ruler and judge over us?' he asked. ²⁸'Are you going to kill me as you killed that Egyptian yesterday?' ²⁹When Moses heard that, he fled the country and lived as a foreigner in the land of Midian. There his two sons were born.

³⁰"Forty years later, in the desert near Mount Sinai, an angel appeared to Moses in the flame of a burning bush. ³¹When Moses saw it, he was amazed at the sight. As he went to take a closer look, the voice of the LORD called out to him, ³²'I am the God of your ancestors—the God of Abraham, Isaac, and Jacob.' Moses shook with terror and did not dare to look.

³³"Then the LORD said to him, 'Take off your sandals, for you are standing on holy ground. ³⁴I have certainly seen the oppression of my people in Egypt. I have heard their groans and have come down to rescue them. Now go, for I am sending you back to Egypt.'*

³⁵"So God sent back the same man his people had previously rejected when they demanded, 'Who made you a ruler and judge over us?' Through the angel who appeared to him in the burning bush, God sent Moses to be their ruler and savior. ³⁶And by means of many wonders and miraculous signs, he led them out of Egypt, through the Red Sea, and through the wilderness for forty years.

³⁷"Moses himself told the people of Israel, 'God will raise up for you a Prophet like me from among your own people.'* ³⁸Moses was with our ancestors, the assembly of God's people in the wilderness, when the angel spoke to him at Mount Sinai. And there Moses received life-giving words to pass on to us.*

³⁹"But our ancestors refused to listen to Moses. They rejected him and wanted to return to Egypt. ⁴⁰They told Aaron, 'Make us some gods who can lead us, for we don't know what has become of this Moses, who brought us out of Egypt.' ⁴¹So they made an idol shaped like a calf, and they sacrificed to it and celebrated over this thing they had made. ⁴²Then God turned away from them and abandoned them to serve the stars of heaven as their gods! In the book of the prophets it is written,

'Was it to me you were bringing sacrifices and offerings
    during those forty years in the wilderness, Israel?
⁴³ No, you carried your pagan gods—
    the shrine of Molech,
    the star of your god Rephan,
    and the images you made to worship them.
So I will send you into exile
    as far away as Babylon.'*

⁴⁴"Our ancestors carried the Tabernacle* with them through the wilderness. It was constructed according to the plan God had shown to Moses. ⁴⁵Years later, when Joshua led our ancestors in battle against the nations that God drove out of this land, the Tabernacle was taken with them into their new territory. And it stayed there until the time of King David.

⁴⁶"David found favor with God and asked for the privilege of building a permanent Temple for the God of Jacob.* ⁴⁷But it was Solomon who actually built it. ⁴⁸However, the Most High doesn't live in temples made by human hands. As the prophet says,

⁴⁹ 'Heaven is my throne,
    and the earth is my footstool.
Could you build me a temple as good as that?'
    asks the LORD.
'Could you build me such a resting place?
⁵⁰ Didn't my hands make both heaven and earth?'*

7:31-34 Exod 3:5-10.   7:37 Deut 18:15.   7:38 Some manuscripts read *to you*.   7:42-43 Amos 5:25-27 (Greek version).   7:44 Greek *the tent of witness*.   7:46 Some manuscripts read *the house of Jacob*.   7:49-50 Isa 66:1-2.

⁵¹"You stubborn people! You are heathen* at heart and deaf to the truth. Must you forever resist the Holy Spirit? That's what your ancestors did, and so do you! ⁵²Name one prophet your ancestors didn't persecute! They even killed the ones who predicted the coming of the Righteous One—the Messiah whom you betrayed and murdered. ⁵³You deliberately disobeyed God's law, even though you received it from the hands of angels."

⁵⁴The Jewish leaders were infuriated by Stephen's accusation, and they shook their fists at him in rage.* ⁵⁵But Stephen, full of the Holy Spirit, gazed steadily into heaven and saw the glory of God, and he saw Jesus standing in the place of honor at God's right hand. ⁵⁶And he told them, "Look, I see the heavens opened and the Son of Man standing in the place of honor at God's right hand!"

⁵⁷Then they put their hands over their ears and began shouting. They rushed at him ⁵⁸and dragged him out of the city and began to stone him. His accusers took off their coats and laid them at the feet of a young man named Saul.*

⁵⁹As they stoned him, Stephen prayed, "Lord Jesus, receive my spirit." ⁶⁰He fell to his knees, shouting, "Lord, don't charge them with this sin!" And with that, he died.

8

Saul was one of the witnesses, and he agreed completely with the killing of Stephen.

Persecution Scatters the Believers

A great wave of persecution began that day, sweeping over the church in Jerusalem; and all the believers except the apostles were scattered through the regions of Judea and Samaria. ²(Some devout men came and buried Stephen with great mourning.) ³But Saul was going everywhere to destroy the church. He went from house to house, dragging out both men and women to throw them into prison.

Philip Preaches in Samaria

⁴But the believers who were scattered preached the Good News about Jesus wherever they went. ⁵Philip, for example, went to the city of Samaria and told the people there about the Messiah. ⁶Crowds listened intently to Philip because they were eager to hear his message and see the miraculous signs he did. ⁷Many evil* spirits were cast out, screaming as they left their victims. And many who had been paralyzed or lame were healed. ⁸So there was great joy in that city.

⁹A man named Simon had been a sorcerer there for many years, amazing the people of Samaria and claiming to be someone great. ¹⁰Everyone, from the least to the greatest, often spoke of him as "the Great One—the Power of God." ¹¹They listened closely to him because for a long time he had astounded them with his magic.

¹²But now the people believed Philip's message of Good News concerning the Kingdom of God and the name of Jesus Christ. As a result, many men and women were baptized. ¹³Then Simon himself believed and was baptized. He began following Philip wherever he went, and he was amazed by the signs and great miracles Philip performed.

¹⁴When the apostles in Jerusalem heard that the people of Samaria had accepted God's message, they sent Peter and John there. ¹⁵As soon as they arrived, they prayed for these new believers to receive the Holy Spirit. ¹⁶The Holy Spirit had not yet come upon any of them, for they had only been baptized in the name of the Lord Jesus. ¹⁷Then Peter and John laid their hands upon these believers, and they received the Holy Spirit.

¹⁸When Simon saw that the Spirit was given when the apostles laid their hands on people, he offered them money to buy this power. ¹⁹"Let me have this power, too," he exclaimed, "so that when I lay my hands on people, they will receive the Holy Spirit!"

²⁰But Peter replied, "May your money be destroyed with you for thinking God's gift can be bought! ²¹You can have no part in this, for your heart is not right with God. ²²Repent of your wickedness and pray to the Lord. Perhaps he will forgive your evil thoughts, ²³for I can see that you are full of bitter jealousy and are held captive by sin."

7:51 Greek *uncircumcised.* 7:54 Greek *they were grinding their teeth against him.* 7:58 *Saul* is later called *Paul;* see 13:9. 8:7 Greek *unclean.*

7:59-60 Stephen's prayer is strikingly similar to Jesus' prayer when he was dying on the cross (Luke 23:34). Jesus clearly taught his followers the importance of both forgiveness (Matthew 6:14-15; Mark 11:25; see Luke 11:4; 17:3-4) and prayer (Luke 11:5-10; 18:1-8; see also Acts 1:12-14; 4:23-31; 12:5; James 5:16-18). The Lord answered Stephen's prayer affirmatively in the case of Saul (Acts 9:1-31).
8:3 The mention of women here and in 8:12 signifies their importance in the early church. Both women and men were persecuted, arrested, and dragged into prison by Saul, the man who would become Paul, the apostle to the Gentiles (9:2, 15). Saul dragged women from their homes, the place where believers often met. The women must have been identified by those who knew of their testimony about Jesus as Messiah. Women, alongside men, faced persecution for their faithfulness.

8:9-24 Simon, a sorcerer, was a showman, dazzling the people of Samaria and making self-exalting claims. Simon's attempt to obtain spiritual power through payment gave the name *simony* to the later corrupt practice of buying and selling ordination to church leadership (see also 1 Timothy 6:9-10). Peter strongly rebuked Simon's wickedness.
8:12 As in 8:3, the mention of women here shows how important they were in the early church since, normally, they wouldn't have been mentioned in a mixed-gender setting. These women of the city of Samaria accepted Philip's message and received the Holy Spirit (8:17). In John 4, Jesus spoke with a Samaritan woman who embraced his message and shared it with those in her town, many of whom believed because of her testimony.

²⁴"Pray to the Lord for me," Simon exclaimed, "that these terrible things you've said won't happen to me!"

²⁵After testifying and preaching the word of the Lord in Samaria, Peter and John returned to Jerusalem. And they stopped in many Samaritan villages along the way to preach the Good News.

Philip and the Ethiopian Eunuch

²⁶As for Philip, an angel of the Lord said to him, "Go south* down the desert road that runs from Jerusalem to Gaza." ²⁷So he started out, and he met the treasurer of Ethiopia, a eunuch of great authority under the Kandake, the queen of Ethiopia. The eunuch had gone to Jerusalem to worship, ²⁸and he was now returning. Seated in his carriage, he was reading aloud from the book of the prophet Isaiah. ²⁹The Holy Spirit said to Philip, "Go over and walk along beside the carriage."

³⁰Philip ran over and heard the man reading from the prophet Isaiah. Philip asked, "Do you understand what you are reading?"

³¹The man replied, "How can I, unless someone instructs me?" And he urged Philip to come up into the carriage and sit with him.

³²The passage of Scripture he had been reading was this:

"He was led like a sheep to the slaughter.
 And as a lamb is silent before the shearers,
  he did not open his mouth.
³³ He was humiliated and received no justice.
 Who can speak of his descendants?
 For his life was taken from the earth."*

³⁴The eunuch asked Philip, "Tell me, was the prophet talking about himself or someone else?" ³⁵So beginning with this same Scripture, Philip told him the Good News about Jesus.

³⁶As they rode along, they came to some water, and the eunuch said, "Look! There's some water! Why can't I be baptized?"* ³⁸He ordered the carriage to stop, and they went down into the water, and Philip baptized him. ³⁹When they came up out of the water, the Spirit of the Lord snatched Philip away. The eunuch never saw him again but went on his way rejoicing. ⁴⁰Meanwhile, Philip found himself farther north at the town of Azotus. He preached the Good News there and in every town along the way until he came to Caesarea.

Saul's Conversion

9 Meanwhile, Saul was uttering threats with every breath and was eager to kill the Lord's followers.* So he went to the high priest. ²He requested letters addressed to the synagogues in Damascus, asking for their cooperation in the arrest of any followers of the Way he found there. He wanted to bring them—both men and women—back to Jerusalem in chains.

³As he was approaching Damascus on this mission, a light from heaven suddenly shone down around him. ⁴He fell to the ground and heard a voice saying to him, "Saul! Saul! Why are you persecuting me?"

⁵"Who are you, lord?" Saul asked.

And the voice replied, "I am Jesus, the one you are persecuting! ⁶Now get up and go into the city, and you will be told what you must do."

⁷The men with Saul stood speechless, for they heard the sound of someone's voice but saw no one! ⁸Saul picked himself up off the ground, but when he opened his eyes he was blind. So his companions led him by the hand to Damascus. ⁹He remained there blind for three days and did not eat or drink.

¹⁰Now there was a believer* in Damascus named Ananias. The Lord spoke to him in a vision, calling, "Ananias!"

"Yes, Lord!" he replied.

¹¹The Lord said, "Go over to Straight Street, to the house of Judas. When you get there, ask for a man from Tarsus named Saul. He is praying to me right now. ¹²I have shown him a vision of a man named Ananias coming in and laying hands on him so he can see again."

8:26 Or *Go at noon.*   **8:32-33** Isa 53:7-8 (Greek version).   **8:36** Some manuscripts add verse 37, *"You can," Philip answered, "if you believe with all your heart." And the eunuch replied, "I believe that Jesus Christ is the Son of God."*   **9:1** Greek *disciples.*   **9:10** Greek *disciple;* also in 9:26, 36.

8:27 In the ancient world, a eunuch was an official, typically castrated, who served in a royal court (see 2 Kings 9:30-32; Esther 1:10; 2:3, 14-15, 21; 4:4-5). Although respected for their political positions in other nations, eunuchs were often scorned by the Jews because they could not father children. The law of Moses excluded men who had damaged genitals from the assembly of Israel (Deuteronomy 23:1; see also Leviticus 21:17-23), but Isaiah spoke of God's acceptance of Gentiles and eunuchs (Isaiah 56:3-8; see also Matthew 19:12). In the new covenant, all who have genuine faith would have a place among the people of God. The eunuch in this story had traveled from Africa to Jerusalem to worship in the Temple, probably for one of the major Jewish festivals.

9:1-19 Saul's encounter with Jesus on the Damascus road is of central importance to the narrative of Acts—Luke recounts the story three times (also 22:1-21; 26:1-29). Paul alludes to this experience several times in his letters (1 Corinthians 15:8-10; Galatians 1:11-17; Philippians 3:4-11; see 1 Timothy 1:12-17). Jesus himself called Saul from persecuting Jesus and his followers to following Jesus , and he commissioned Saul as an apostle to make disciples (Acts 9:15; 22:15, 21; 26:15-18). No one is beyond the power of God, and nothing is impossible with God (see text note on Luke 1:37). He will reach, redeem, and use anyone for holy purposes. Saul was prepared through his training, upbringing, and experience to play a unique role in taking the gospel into the broader world as the "apostle to the Gentiles" (Romans 11:13; see 1 Corinthians 15:9; 2 Corinthians 12:11-12; Galatians 1:1; Ephesians 3:8).

¹³"But Lord," exclaimed Ananias, "I've heard many people talk about the terrible things this man has done to the believers* in Jerusalem! ¹⁴And he is authorized by the leading priests to arrest everyone who calls upon your name."

¹⁵But the Lord said, "Go, for Saul is my chosen instrument to take my message to the Gentiles and to kings, as well as to the people of Israel. ¹⁶And I will show him how much he must suffer for my name's sake."

¹⁷So Ananias went and found Saul. He laid his hands on him and said, "Brother Saul, the Lord Jesus, who appeared to you on the road, has sent me so that you might regain your sight and be filled with the Holy Spirit." ¹⁸Instantly something like scales fell from Saul's eyes, and he regained his sight. Then he got up and was baptized. ¹⁹Afterward he ate some food and regained his strength.

Saul in Damascus and Jerusalem

Saul stayed with the believers* in Damascus for a few days. ²⁰And immediately he began preaching about Jesus in the synagogues, saying, "He is indeed the Son of God!"

²¹All who heard him were amazed. "Isn't this the same man who caused such devastation among Jesus' followers in Jerusalem?" they asked. "And didn't he come here to arrest them and take them in chains to the leading priests?"

²²Saul's preaching became more and more powerful, and the Jews in Damascus couldn't refute his proofs that Jesus was indeed the Messiah. ²³After a while some of the Jews plotted together to kill him. ²⁴They were watching for him day and night at the city gate so they could murder him, but Saul was told about their plot. ²⁵So during the night, some of the other believers* lowered him in a large basket through an opening in the city wall.

²⁶When Saul arrived in Jerusalem, he tried to meet with the believers, but they were all afraid of him. They did not believe he had truly become a believer! ²⁷Then Barnabas brought him to the apostles and told them how Saul had seen the Lord on the way to Damascus and how the Lord had spoken to Saul. He also told them that Saul had preached boldly in the name of Jesus in Damascus.

²⁸So Saul stayed with the apostles and went all around Jerusalem with them, preaching boldly in the name of the Lord. ²⁹He debated with some Greek-speaking Jews, but they tried to murder him. ³⁰When the believers* heard about this, they took him down to Caesarea and sent him away to Tarsus, his hometown.

³¹The church then had peace throughout Judea, Galilee, and Samaria, and it became stronger as the believers lived in the fear of the Lord. And with the encouragement of the Holy Spirit, it also grew in numbers.

Peter Heals Aeneas and Raises Dorcas

³²Meanwhile, Peter traveled from place to place, and he came down to visit the believers in the town of Lydda. ³³There he met a man named Aeneas, who had been paralyzed and bedridden for eight years. ³⁴Peter said to him, "Aeneas, Jesus Christ heals you! Get up, and roll up your sleeping mat!" And he was healed instantly. ³⁵Then the whole population of Lydda and Sharon saw Aeneas walking around, and they turned to the Lord.

³⁶There was a believer in Joppa named Tabitha (which in Greek is Dorcas*). She was always doing kind things for others and helping the poor. ³⁷About this time she became ill and died. Her body was washed for burial and laid in an upstairs room. ³⁸But the believers had heard that Peter was nearby at Lydda, so they sent two men to beg him, "Please come as soon as possible!"

³⁹So Peter returned with them; and as soon as he arrived, they took him to the upstairs room. The room was filled with widows who were weeping and showing him the coats and other clothes Dorcas had made for them. ⁴⁰But Peter asked them all to leave the room; then he knelt and prayed. Turning to the body he said, "Get up, Tabitha." And she opened her eyes! When she saw Peter, she sat up! ⁴¹He gave her his hand and helped her up. Then he called in the widows and all the believers, and he presented her to them alive.

9:13 Greek *God's holy people;* also in 9:32, 41. **9:19** Greek *disciples;* also in 9:26, 38. **9:25** Greek *his disciples.* **9:30** Greek *brothers.* **9:36** The names *Tabitha* in Aramaic and *Dorcas* in Greek both mean "gazelle."

9:32-43 These verses describe Peter's itinerant ministry in Judea, particularly along the seacoast. Exercising spiritual powers given to him by God, Peter performed wonderful works, including the healing of Aeneas and the raising of Tabitha (Dorcas). Jesus had promised such signs and wonders to the disciples (John 14:12). Typical of Luke's writing, the healing of a man is matched by the healing of a woman (see Luke 13:10-17; 14:1-6). These miracles deeply moved the people in the area, and many were drawn to faith in Jesus (Acts 9:35, 42).

9:36 The name Tabitha (Dorcas) means "gazelle," and while this name was common among enslaved people, we cannot say with certainty whether she had been formerly enslaved. She is described as a "disciple," which the NLT renders as "believer." She likely studied and put into practice Jesus' teachings. She acted virtuously in giving to the poor (like Cornelius in 10:2), perhaps indicating that she had some wealth. However, she also made clothing, which indicates she supported herself. Her generosity was more remarkable given her status as one who needed to work for her living.

9:40-42 Peter raised Tabitha from the dead, and the believers celebrated. This news led many others to receive the Good News that Jesus is Lord. Like Lazarus (John 12:1-2), Tabitha would die again one day, but as with all believers, her eternal life was secure in Jesus Christ.

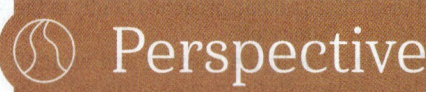

Perspective

Why should we find common ground with others?

SCRIPTURE CONNECTION: ACTS 10:9-43

The idea shocked Peter. Eat the food that Gentiles ate? Even visit them in their homes? Was God asking a man like him, who ate according to Jewish food laws, to meet and eat with "those people"?

Peter's story requires those who struggle looking beyond "good" religious practices, as we may see them, to the good God who wants everyone to know him.

Challenged by God and directed by the Holy Spirit, Peter went with the men sent by Cornelius. A great first step. Peter then went inside Cornelius's home, met the man's family and friends, and heard Cornelius's side of the story. Peter then confessed: "I see very clearly that God shows no favoritism" (10:34).

Peter didn't feel free to meet with Gentiles because he thought keeping the Jewish purity laws was more important. While we may not have such food laws, we can think of our tendencies that keep us separated from others. God showed Peter, through the Holy Spirit, that he wants to bring everyone into his family. Peter needed to gather with Gentiles—in their homes.

God's call today is the same for us: yes, we should go and be with those who are different from us, embracing them as our neighbors and potential family in Christ.

VIEWPOINTS

HIS: *God accepts all who fear him and do what is right, no matter who they are or where they come from.*
MINE: *"Like Peter, I'm willing to see Christ in all people because God wants me to treat everyone fairly."*
YOURS: *What bias do we have against others? When we see our bias, we can pray, "Lord, remove it."*

PATRICIA RAYBON is an award-winning Colorado author, essayist, and novelist who writes top-rated books and stories at the daring intersection of faith, race, and mystery—including the Annalee Spain mystery series.

---

⁴²The news spread through the whole town, and many believed in the Lord. ⁴³And Peter stayed a long time in Joppa, living with Simon, a tanner of hides.

Cornelius Calls for Peter

10 In Caesarea there lived a Roman army officer* named Cornelius, who was a captain of the Italian Regiment. ²He was a devout, God-fearing man, as was everyone in his household. He gave generously to the poor and prayed regularly to God. ³One afternoon about three o'clock, he had a vision in which he saw an angel of God coming toward him. "Cornelius!" the angel said.

⁴Cornelius stared at him in terror. "What is it, sir?" he asked the angel.

And the angel replied, "Your prayers and gifts to the poor have been received by God as an offering! ⁵Now send some men to Joppa, and summon a man named Simon Peter. ⁶He is staying with Simon, a tanner who lives near the seashore."

⁷As soon as the angel was gone, Cornelius called two of his household servants and a devout soldier, one of his personal attendants. ⁸He told them what had happened and sent them off to Joppa.

Peter Visits Cornelius

⁹The next day as Cornelius's messengers were nearing the town, Peter went up on the flat roof to pray. It was about noon, ¹⁰and he was hungry. But while a meal was being prepared, he fell into a trance. ¹¹He saw the sky open, and something like a large sheet was let down by its four corners. ¹²In the sheet were all sorts of animals, reptiles, and birds. ¹³Then a voice said to him, "Get up, Peter; kill and eat them."

¹⁴"No, Lord," Peter declared. "I have never eaten anything that our Jewish laws have declared impure and unclean.*"

10:1 Greek *a centurion;* similarly in 10:22. **10:14** Greek *anything common and unclean.*

10:2 Gentiles who are described as "God-fearing" were attracted to the high ethical standards of Judaism but were not prepared to accept the rite of circumcision or the full implications of the Jewish law by becoming full converts to Judaism. Christianity was an attractive option to Gentiles who worshiped God (18:7; see 13:48; 16:29-30; 17:4, 12, 17). These people would have been wide open to the gospel's message that announced that "there is peace with God through Jesus Christ" (10:36).
10:14-16 Peter declared that he had always followed Jewish dietary laws. Purity laws were closely followed in the first century, and Jesus often addressed questions about purity and cleanness (for example, Mark 7:14-23). Some purity laws were based on bodily conditions such as menstruation, childbirth, semen emissions, preparing dead bodies for burial, or rashes. Women and men were not viewed as sinful just because they were ritually unclean. Peter realized that he should not view Gentiles as inherently impure or unclean (Acts 10:28), for they were also invited to follow Jesus Christ.

¹⁵But the voice spoke again: "Do not call something unclean if God has made it clean." ¹⁶The same vision was repeated three times. Then the sheet was suddenly pulled up to heaven.

¹⁷Peter was very perplexed. What could the vision mean? Just then the men sent by Cornelius found Simon's house. Standing outside the gate, ¹⁸they asked if a man named Simon Peter was staying there.

¹⁹Meanwhile, as Peter was puzzling over the vision, the Holy Spirit said to him, "Three men have come looking for you. ²⁰Get up, go downstairs, and go with them without hesitation. Don't worry, for I have sent them."

²¹So Peter went down and said, "I'm the man you are looking for. Why have you come?"

²²They said, "We were sent by Cornelius, a Roman officer. He is a devout and God-fearing man, well respected by all the Jews. A holy angel instructed him to summon you to his house so that he can hear your message." ²³So Peter invited the men to stay for the night. The next day he went with them, accompanied by some of the brothers from Joppa.

²⁴They arrived in Caesarea the following day. Cornelius was waiting for them and had called together his relatives and close friends. ²⁵As Peter entered his home, Cornelius fell at his feet and worshiped him. ²⁶But Peter pulled him up and said, "Stand up! I'm a human being just like you!" ²⁷So they talked together and went inside, where many others were assembled.

²⁸Peter told them, "You know it is against our laws for a Jewish man to enter a Gentile home like this or to associate with you. But God has shown me that I should no longer think of anyone as impure or unclean. ²⁹So I came without objection as soon as I was sent for. Now tell me why you sent for me."

³⁰Cornelius replied, "Four days ago I was praying in my house about this same time, three o'clock in the afternoon. Suddenly, a man in dazzling clothes was standing in front of me. ³¹He told me, 'Cornelius, your prayer has been heard, and your gifts to the poor have been noticed by God! ³²Now send messengers to Joppa, and summon a man named Simon Peter. He is staying in the home of Simon, a tanner who lives near the seashore.' ³³So I sent for you at once, and it was good of you to come. Now we are all here, waiting before God to hear the message the Lord has given you."

The Gentiles Hear the Good News

³⁴Then Peter replied, "I see very clearly that God shows no favoritism. ³⁵In every nation he accepts those who fear him and do what is right. ³⁶This is the message of Good News for the people of Israel—that there is peace with God through Jesus Christ, who is Lord of all. ³⁷You know what happened throughout Judea, beginning in Galilee, after John began preaching his message of baptism. ³⁸And you know that God anointed Jesus of Nazareth with the Holy Spirit and with power. Then Jesus went around doing good and healing all who were oppressed by the devil, for God was with him.

³⁹"And we apostles are witnesses of all he did throughout Judea and in Jerusalem. They put him to death by hanging him on a cross,* ⁴⁰but God raised him to life on the third day. Then God allowed him to appear, ⁴¹not to the general public,* but to us whom God had chosen in advance to be his witnesses. We were those who ate and drank with him after he rose from the dead. ⁴²And he ordered us to preach everywhere and to testify that Jesus is the one appointed by God to be the judge of all—the living and the dead. ⁴³He is the one all the prophets testified about, saying that everyone who believes in him will have their sins forgiven through his name."

The Gentiles Receive the Holy Spirit

⁴⁴Even as Peter was saying these things, the Holy Spirit fell upon all who were listening to the message. ⁴⁵The Jewish believers* who came with Peter were amazed that the gift of the Holy Spirit had been poured out on the Gentiles, too. ⁴⁶For they heard them speaking in other tongues* and praising God.

Then Peter asked, ⁴⁷"Can anyone object to their being baptized, now that they have received the Holy Spirit just as we did?" ⁴⁸So he gave orders for them to be baptized in the name of Jesus Christ. Afterward Cornelius asked him to stay with them for several days.

10:39 Greek *on a tree.* 10:41 Greek *the people.* 10:45 Greek *The faithful ones of the circumcision.* 10:46 Or *in other languages.*

10:34-35 The application of this principle, "God shows no favoritism," is the meaning of Peter's vision (10:9-16). God welcomes the Gentiles into his family because of their faith in Jesus and their desire to live as his followers, so Jewish followers of Jesus shouldn't refuse to associate with Gentiles anymore. God's lack of favoritism is well-documented throughout the Bible: see Deuteronomy 10:17; 2 Chronicles 19:7; Job 34:19; Luke 20:21; Romans 2:11; Galatians 2:6; Colossians 3:25; 1 Peter 1:17.

10:45-48 Neither Peter nor the Jewish believers accompanying Peter had realized the full extent of Pentecost, for they assumed the fulfilled prophecy would be given only to Jews. Cornelius and those men and women with him, all Gentiles, received the *Holy* Spirit of God. Therefore, they were no longer "unclean." The Jewish believers heard them praise God and speak in tongues, just as those at Pentecost had done (2:4). Because of the confirmation of the Holy Spirit, the Gentiles were also baptized in Jesus' name (Matthew 28:19) and welcomed fully into the people of God.

Peter Explains His Actions

11 Soon the news reached the apostles and other believers* in Judea that the Gentiles had received the word of God. ²But when Peter arrived back in Jerusalem, the Jewish believers* criticized him. ³"You entered the home of Gentiles* and even ate with them!" they said.

⁴Then Peter told them exactly what had happened. ⁵"I was in the town of Joppa," he said, "and while I was praying, I went into a trance and saw a vision. Something like a large sheet was let down by its four corners from the sky. And it came right down to me. ⁶When I looked inside the sheet, I saw all sorts of tame and wild animals, reptiles, and birds. ⁷And I heard a voice say, 'Get up, Peter; kill and eat them.'

⁸"'No, Lord,' I replied. 'I have never eaten anything that our Jewish laws have declared impure or unclean.*'

⁹"But the voice from heaven spoke again: 'Do not call something unclean if God has made it clean.' ¹⁰This happened three times before the sheet and all it contained was pulled back up to heaven.

¹¹"Just then three men who had been sent from Caesarea arrived at the house where we were staying. ¹²The Holy Spirit told me to go with them and not to worry that they were Gentiles. These six brothers here accompanied me, and we soon entered the home of the man who had sent for us. ¹³He told us how an angel had appeared to him in his home and had told him, 'Send messengers to Joppa, and summon a man named Simon Peter. ¹⁴He will tell you how you and everyone in your household can be saved!'

¹⁵"As I began to speak," Peter continued, "the Holy Spirit fell on them, just as he fell on us at the beginning. ¹⁶Then I thought of the Lord's words when he said, 'John baptized with* water, but you will be baptized with the Holy Spirit.' ¹⁷And since God gave these Gentiles the same gift he gave us when we believed in the Lord Jesus Christ, who was I to stand in God's way?"

¹⁸When the others heard this, they stopped objecting and began praising God. They said, "We can see that God has also given the Gentiles the privilege of repenting of their sins and receiving eternal life."

The Church in Antioch of Syria

¹⁹Meanwhile, the believers who had been scattered during the persecution after Stephen's death traveled as far as Phoenicia, Cyprus, and Antioch of Syria. They preached the word of God, but only to Jews. ²⁰However, some of the believers who went to Antioch from Cyprus and Cyrene began preaching to the Gentiles* about the Lord Jesus. ²¹The power of the Lord was with them, and a large number of these Gentiles believed and turned to the Lord.

²²When the church at Jerusalem heard what had happened, they sent Barnabas to Antioch. ²³When he arrived and saw this evidence of God's blessing, he was filled with joy, and he encouraged the believers to stay true to the Lord. ²⁴Barnabas was a good man, full of the Holy Spirit and strong in faith. And many people were brought to the Lord.

²⁵Then Barnabas went on to Tarsus to look for Saul. ²⁶When he found him, he brought him back to Antioch. Both of them stayed there with the church for a full year, teaching large crowds of people. (It was at Antioch that the believers* were first called Christians.)

²⁷During this time some prophets traveled from Jerusalem to Antioch. ²⁸One of them named Agabus stood up in one of the meetings and predicted by the Spirit that a great famine was coming upon the entire Roman world. (This was fulfilled during

---

11:1 Greek *brothers*. **11:2** Greek *those of the circumcision*. **11:3** Greek *of uncircumcised men*. **11:8** Greek *anything common or unclean*. **11:16** Or *in;* also in 11:16b. **11:20** Greek *the Hellenists* (i.e., those who speak Greek); other manuscripts read *the Greeks*. **11:26** Greek *disciples;* also in 11:29.

11:1-17 After Peter's vision and the Gentiles' receiving the Holy Spirit, the news spread and Peter's fellow Jewish believers criticized him. Jews traditionally kept themselves separate and did not eat or associate with Gentiles as part of keeping their ritual purity according to the law of Moses. Peter addressed his skeptics and reviewed the sequence of events, explaining that the whole development resulted from God's initiative in the vision Peter received while praying (see 10:9-17; 11:12). Peter had eaten with Gentiles because God had made it clear that he should (11:4-12). Peter had then observed the Holy Spirit's definite action of coming upon Gentiles (see 10:44-48), and he realized that they were being accepted and blessed by God just as Jewish believers had been (11:15-17; see 1:5). Peter was submitting to God's will in admitting Gentiles to the church.

11:18 The recognition of Gentiles as full members of the church reshaped believers' views of what a holy community looked like. The church in Acts 2 was living in a single city and sharing, eating, and praying together. With the admittance of Gentiles, the community would look and feel very different, especially around the dining table (see note on 11:1-17). Believers today face similar challenges as new church members from other places, countries, and backgrounds gather together. At first, we may question or resist the practices of other Christians that are tied to their cultural roots simply because they are different from ours. But we should follow the lead of the ancient church and praise God that all people are given the privilege of repenting and receiving eternal life.

11:21-24 Once again, as had happened in the household of Cornelius, Gentiles believed the Good News about Jesus and "turned to the Lord" in considerable numbers. The explosion of Christian faith into the Gentile world had to remain in harmony with the church at Jerusalem, so the Jerusalem church sent Barnabas to Antioch to oversee developments there. He could see that God's blessing was on what was happening, so he endorsed it joyfully.

Rhoda

IDENTITY — Prayers Answered Miraculously

She remembers...

God answers my prayers! I believe that with all my heart.

Some would overlook me because I'm enslaved, but I prefer to see the blessing in my role. I'm working in a large home, the house of Mary, mother of John Mark. This home is where Jerusalem's believers sometimes meet. I may be enslaved, but I have a front-row seat to God's work.

Earlier today, the believers gathered here for urgent prayer. Our leader, Peter, was suffering in prison, and we fell to our knees, pleading with God for his release.

As we prayed, I heard a knock at the door, but I hesitated to answer. The persecution going on made me cautious that whoever was on the other side of that door might not have our best interests in mind.

Then I heard his voice. Peter's voice! I'd know it anywhere. Peter was here!

My soul filled with joy, and I ran to tell the others. "Peter is standing at the door!" Of course, I'm just a servant girl, so no one believed me. However, Peter kept knocking and I persisted in telling the others. Eventually, someone went and opened the door.

Who did they see? Peter!

I've often wondered why God's people are surprised when he answers prayer. We prayed for Peter's release, but people stood there amazed when God answered. As Peter shared his miraculous release, I quietly closed my eyes. I thanked God for answering my prayer—the humble prayer of a servant girl.

> God knows your situation, and he's ready to answer your prayers.

RHODA'S STORY IS TOLD IN ACTS 12:12-17.

IDENTIFY

Do people ever look down on you because of your status or situation? How can you show them God's love anyway?

Does it surprise you when God answers your prayers? How can you pray with humility and expectation, trusting that God will answer?

> "I desire to be like Rhoda and share my excitement with the world about God's answers to prayer! No matter my circumstances, I want God's joy to reign in my heart."

MELISSA HOUDMANN is the cofounder of GotQuestions Ministries, a website dedicated to answering Bible questions. She also wrote Stonecroft Ministries' *Why Believe* study.

the reign of Claudius.) ²⁹So the believers in Antioch decided to send relief to the brothers and sisters* in Judea, everyone giving as much as they could. ³⁰This they did, entrusting their gifts to Barnabas and Saul to take to the elders of the church in Jerusalem.

James Is Killed and Peter Is Imprisoned

12 About that time King Herod Agrippa* began to persecute some believers in the church. ²He had the apostle James (John's brother) killed with a sword. ³When Herod saw how much this pleased the Jewish people, he also arrested Peter. (This took place during the Passover celebration.*) ⁴Then he imprisoned him, placing him under the guard of four squads of four soldiers each. Herod intended to bring Peter out for public trial after the Passover. ⁵But while Peter was in prison, the church prayed very earnestly for him.

Peter's Miraculous Escape from Prison

⁶The night before Peter was to be placed on trial, he was asleep, fastened with two chains between two soldiers. Others stood guard at the prison gate. ⁷Suddenly, there was a bright light in the cell, and an angel of the Lord stood before Peter. The angel struck him on the side to awaken him and said, "Quick! Get up!" And the chains fell off his wrists. ⁸Then the angel told him, "Get dressed and put on your sandals." And he did. "Now put on your coat and follow me," the angel ordered.

⁹So Peter left the cell, following the angel. But all the time he thought it was a vision. He didn't realize it was actually happening. ¹⁰They passed the first and second guard posts and came to the iron gate leading to the city, and this opened for them all by itself. So they passed through and started walking down the street, and then the angel suddenly left him.

¹¹Peter finally came to his senses. "It's really true!" he said. "The Lord has sent his angel and saved me from Herod and from what the Jewish leaders* had planned to do to me!"

¹²When he realized this, he went to the home of Mary, the mother of John Mark, where many were gathered for prayer. ¹³He knocked at the door in the gate, and a servant girl named Rhoda came to open it. ¹⁴When she recognized Peter's voice, she was so overjoyed that, instead of opening the door, she ran back inside and told everyone, "Peter is standing at the door!"

¹⁵"You're out of your mind!" they said. When she insisted, they decided, "It must be his angel."

¹⁶Meanwhile, Peter continued knocking. When they finally opened the door and saw him, they were amazed. ¹⁷He motioned for them to quiet down and told them how the Lord had led him out of prison. "Tell James and the other brothers what happened," he said. And then he went to another place.

¹⁸At dawn there was a great commotion among the soldiers about what had happened to Peter. ¹⁹Herod Agrippa ordered a thorough search for him. When he couldn't be found, Herod interrogated the guards and sentenced them to death. Afterward Herod left Judea to stay in Caesarea for a while.

11:29 Greek *the brothers.* **12:1** Greek *Herod the king.* He was the nephew of Herod Antipas and a grandson of Herod the Great. **12:3** Greek *the days of unleavened bread.* **12:11** Or *the Jewish people.*

11:29 Healthy church gathering leads to giving. The Antioch church not only looked after their local neighbors but also sent gifts to aid fellow believers during the famine in Judea. This remarkable outpouring would have impressed non-believing Jews in Judea, for Gentiles did not typically offer aid to Jews. Everyone—Jews and Gentiles, women and men—were recipients of this aid.

12:1-5 Jesus had predicted persecution and hardship for his followers (Luke 11:49-51). King Herod Agrippa, nephew of Herod Antipas and a grandson of Herod the Great, attacked the church in a move that he found to be politically helpful with the Jewish people. For the first time since Jesus' death, Roman authorities, instigated by Herod, took direct violent action against the church. James, the brother of John, who had been among the first called to be disciples (Mark 1:16-20; Luke 5:1-11), would be one of the first Christians to be executed for his faith. The epistle of James, written by the half brother of Jesus (not this James), was probably written after this persecution to the scattered Christians (see Acts 8:1-4).

12:12 Mary, the mother of John Mark (see 13:5; 15:37-38; Colossians 4:10), hosted a church in her home. Her husband was either deceased or was not a believer because he was not mentioned. We know she had some wealth, because she had a servant, Rhoda, and the house was large enough to accommodate a number of other believers for prayer. She offered hospitality, a virtue highly valued in her culture and in many cultures today. She risked persecution by hosting other believers in her home.

12:13-15 Rhoda was a servant in Mary's home and may also have been a believer. She was overjoyed to hear that Peter had been freed from prison. But her message was not believed, even though the believers had been praying for precisely that, and she was even ridiculed as being out of her mind. This harsh judgment by her fellow believers reveals the society's low view of women's words and low trust in people who were servants or were enslaved. This narrative indicts the Christian leaders here because they fall into their wordly assumptions about social worth. However, Rhoda was vindicated when the group opened the door and saw Peter. This story can show us how we make assumptions about others, assumptions that make it hard for us to hear them.

12:18-23 When Peter couldn't be found after a careful search, Herod interrogated the guards and put them to death (compare 16:27). However, Herod met his painful end as a divine judgment on his conceit when he accepted the people's worship. The Jewish historian Josephus records the death of Herod in greater detail: He was beset by a violent stomachache after seeing an owl over his head, which he took as an omen of his imminent death (Josephus, *The Antiquities of the Jews,* book 19, chapter 8, paragraphs 1–2).

The Death of Herod Agrippa

[20] Now Herod was very angry with the people of Tyre and Sidon. So they sent a delegation to make peace with him because their cities were dependent upon Herod's country for food. The delegates won the support of Blastus, Herod's personal assistant, [21] and an appointment with Herod was granted. When the day arrived, Herod put on his royal robes, sat on his throne, and made a speech to them. [22] The people gave him a great ovation, shouting, "It's the voice of a god, not of a man!"

[23] Instantly, an angel of the Lord struck Herod with a sickness, because he accepted the people's worship instead of giving the glory to God. So he was consumed with worms and died.

[24] Meanwhile, the word of God continued to spread, and there were many new believers.

[25] When Barnabas and Saul had finished their mission to Jerusalem, they returned,* taking John Mark with them.

Barnabas and Saul Are Commissioned

13 Among the prophets and teachers of the church at Antioch of Syria were Barnabas, Simeon (called "the black man"*), Lucius (from Cyrene), Manaen (the childhood companion of King Herod Antipas*), and Saul. [2] One day as these men were worshiping the Lord and fasting, the Holy Spirit said, "Appoint Barnabas and Saul for the special work to which I have called them." [3] So after more fasting and prayer, the men laid their hands on them and sent them on their way.

Paul's First Missionary Journey

[4] So Barnabas and Saul were sent out by the Holy Spirit. They went down to the seaport of Seleucia and then sailed for the island of Cyprus. [5] There, in the town of Salamis, they went to the Jewish synagogues and preached the word of God. John Mark went with them as their assistant.

[6] Afterward they traveled from town to town across the entire island until finally they reached Paphos, where they met a Jewish sorcerer, a false prophet named Bar-Jesus. [7] He had attached himself to the governor, Sergius Paulus, who was an intelligent man. The governor invited Barnabas and Saul to visit him, for he wanted to hear the word of God. [8] But Elymas, the sorcerer (as his name means in Greek), interfered and urged the governor to pay no attention to what Barnabas and Saul said. He was trying to keep the governor from believing.

[9] Saul, also known as Paul, was filled with the Holy Spirit, and he looked the sorcerer in the eye. [10] Then he said, "You son of the devil, full of every sort of deceit and fraud, and enemy of all that is good! Will you never stop perverting the true ways of the Lord? [11] Watch now, for the Lord has laid his hand of punishment upon you, and you will be struck blind. You will not see the sunlight for some time." Instantly mist and darkness came over the man's eyes, and he began groping around begging for someone to take his hand and lead him.

[12] When the governor saw what had happened, he became a believer, for he was astonished at the teaching about the Lord.

Paul Preaches in Antioch of Pisidia

[13] Paul and his companions then left Paphos by ship for Pamphylia, landing at the port town of Perga. There John Mark left them and returned to Jerusalem. [14] But Paul and Barnabas traveled inland to Antioch of Pisidia.*

On the Sabbath they went to the synagogue for the services. [15] After the usual readings from the books of Moses* and the prophets, those in charge of the service sent them this message: "Brothers, if you have any word of encouragement for the people, come and give it."

[16] So Paul stood, lifted his hand to quiet them, and started speaking. "Men of Israel," he said, "and you God-fearing Gentiles, listen to me.

[17] "The God of this nation of Israel chose our ancestors and made them multiply and grow strong during their stay in Egypt. Then with a powerful arm he led them out of their slavery. [18] He put up with them* through forty years of wandering in the wilderness. [19] Then he destroyed seven nations in Canaan and gave their land to Israel as an inheritance. [20] All this took about 450 years.

"After that, God gave them judges to rule until the time of Samuel the prophet. [21] Then the people begged for a king, and God gave them Saul son of Kish, a man of the tribe of Benjamin, who reigned for forty years. [22] But God removed Saul and replaced him with David, a man about whom God

---

12:25 Or *mission, they returned to Jerusalem.* Other manuscripts read *mission, they returned from Jerusalem;* still others read *mission, they returned from Jerusalem to Antioch.* **13:1a** Greek *who was called Niger.* **13:1b** Greek *Herod the tetrarch.* **13:13-14** *Pamphylia* and *Pisidia* were districts in what is now Turkey. **13:15** Greek *from the law.* **13:18** Some manuscripts read *He cared for them;* compare Deut 1:31.

13:9 Luke makes the significant transition from the name *Saul* (a Hebrew name) to *Paul* (a Greco-Roman name), perhaps indicating that Paul was now on a predominantly Gentile mission. For the rest of the book of Acts, he is called Paul except when recounting his calling to follow Jesus (as in 22:7, 13; 26:14).
13:16 Paul addressed the crowd as "men of Israel," a form of respectful introduction in his context (see also 2:29; 13:26, 38), much as someone today would recognize heads of state or dignitaries present in an audience in their opening remarks. Women and men were present together in the ancient synagogue, so Paul was addressing both men and women in his sermon.

Insight: HOW FAR PAUL TRAVELED

Following Jesus can lead us on adventures we never expected to take. For Paul, his journeys to share the Good News, as recorded in Acts, took him across the Roman Empire several times, stretching from Jerusalem, through Asia Minor and Greece, to Rome, the capital city of the empire. This map shows the routes Paul took and how far those journeys reached.

PAUL'S MISSIONARY JOURNEYS

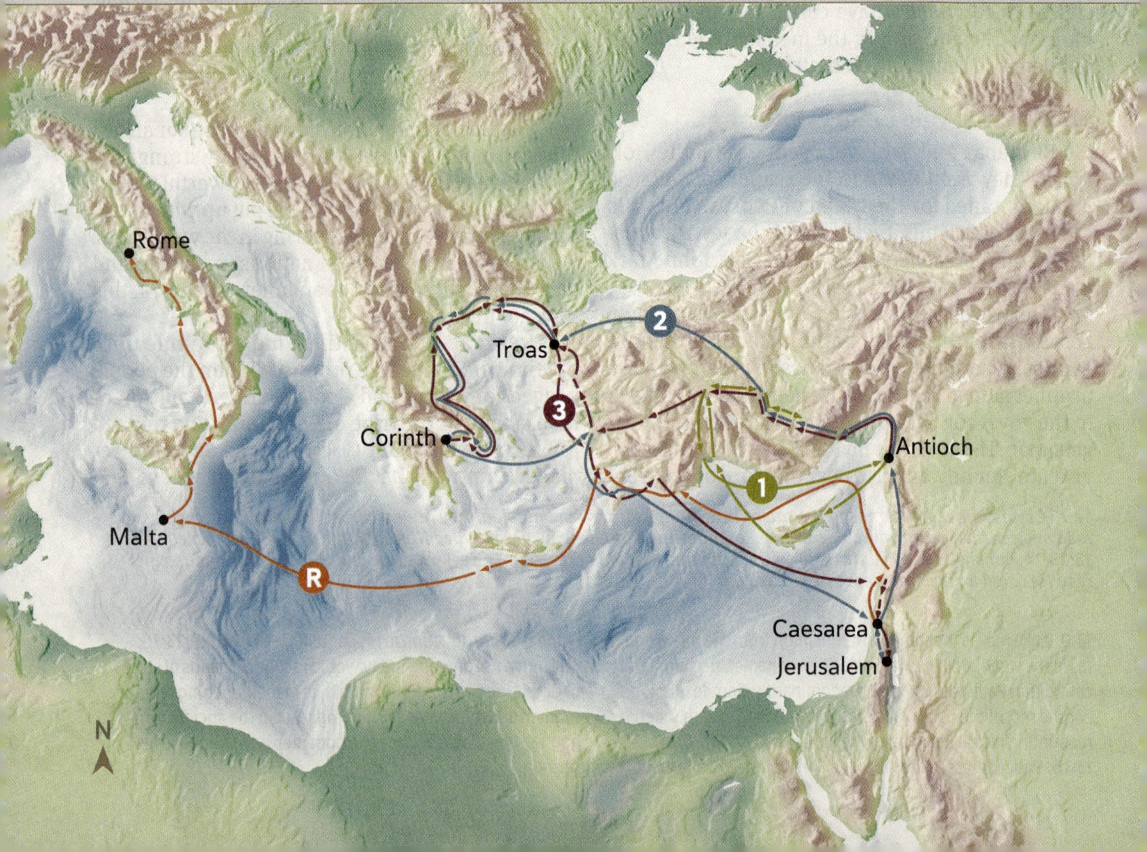

1	FIRST	Antioch—Antioch	Acts 13:1–14:28	1,190 miles
2	SECOND	Antioch—Antioch	Acts 15:36–18:22	2,685 miles
3	THIRD	Antioch—Jerusalem	Acts 18:23–21:16	2,802 miles
R	TO ROME	Caesarea—Rome	Acts 21:17–28:31	2,046 miles

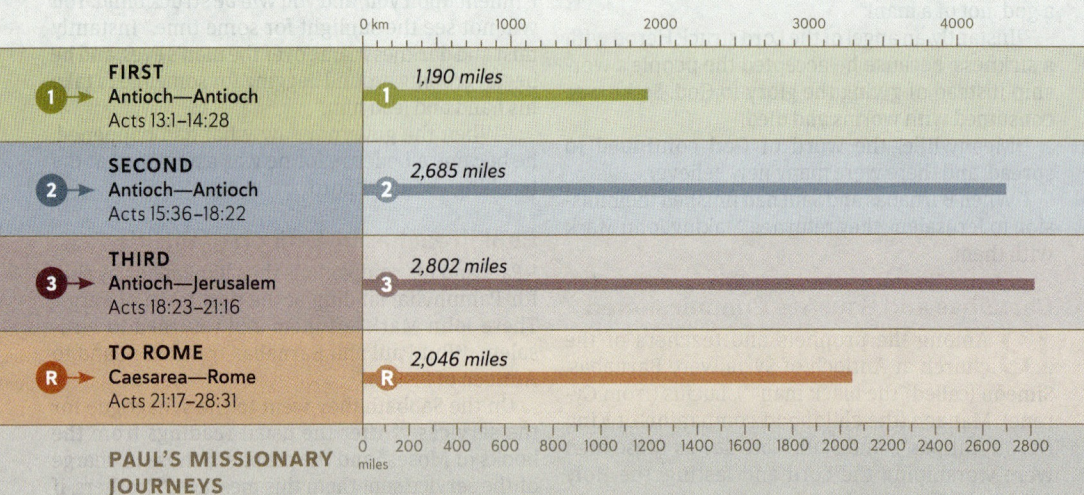

said, 'I have found David son of Jesse, a man after my own heart. He will do everything I want him to do.'*

²³"And it is one of King David's descendants, Jesus, who is God's promised Savior of Israel! ²⁴Before he came, John the Baptist preached that all the people of Israel needed to repent of their sins and turn to God and be baptized. ²⁵As John was finishing his ministry he asked, 'Do you think I am the Messiah? No, I am not! But he is coming soon—and I'm not even worthy to be his slave and untie the sandals on his feet.'

²⁶"Brothers—you sons of Abraham, and also you God-fearing Gentiles—this message of salvation has been sent to us! ²⁷The people in Jerusalem and their leaders did not recognize Jesus as the one the prophets had spoken about. Instead, they condemned him, and in doing this they fulfilled the prophets' words that are read every Sabbath. ²⁸They found no legal reason to execute him, but they asked Pilate to have him killed anyway.

²⁹"When they had done all that the prophecies said about him, they took him down from the cross* and placed him in a tomb. ³⁰But God raised him from the dead! ³¹And over a period of many days he appeared to those who had gone with him from Galilee to Jerusalem. They are now his witnesses to the people of Israel.

³²"And now we are here to bring you this Good News. The promise was made to our ancestors, ³³and God has now fulfilled it for us, their descendants, by raising Jesus. This is what the second psalm says about Jesus:

'You are my Son.
    Today I have become your Father.'*

³⁴For God had promised to raise him from the dead, not leaving him to rot in the grave. He said, 'I will give you the sacred blessings I promised to David.'* ³⁵Another psalm explains it more fully: 'You will not allow your Holy One to rot in the grave.'* ³⁶This is not a reference to David, for after David had done the will of God in his own generation, he died and was buried with his ancestors, and his body decayed. ³⁷No, it was a reference to someone else—someone whom God raised and whose body did not decay.

³⁸*"Brothers, listen! We are here to proclaim that through this man Jesus there is forgiveness for your sins. ³⁹Everyone who believes in him is made right in God's sight—something the law of Moses could never do. ⁴⁰Be careful! Don't let the prophets' words apply to you. For they said,

⁴¹ 'Look, you mockers,
    be amazed and die!
For I am doing something in your own day,
    something you wouldn't believe
    even if someone told you about it.'*"

⁴²As Paul and Barnabas left the synagogue that day, the people begged them to speak about these things again the next week. ⁴³Many Jews and devout converts to Judaism followed Paul and Barnabas, and the two men urged them to continue to rely on the grace of God.

Paul Turns to the Gentiles

⁴⁴The following week almost the entire city turned out to hear them preach the word of the Lord. ⁴⁵But when some of the Jews saw the crowds, they were jealous; so they slandered Paul and argued against whatever he said.

⁴⁶Then Paul and Barnabas spoke out boldly and declared, "It was necessary that we first preach the word of God to you Jews. But since you have rejected it and judged yourselves unworthy of eternal life, we will offer it to the Gentiles. ⁴⁷For the Lord gave us this command when he said,

'I have made you a light to the Gentiles,
    to bring salvation to the farthest corners of
      the earth.'*"

⁴⁸When the Gentiles heard this, they were very glad and thanked the Lord for his message; and all who were chosen for eternal life became believers. ⁴⁹So the Lord's message spread throughout that region.

⁵⁰Then the Jews stirred up the influential religious women and the leaders of the city, and they incited a mob against Paul and Barnabas and ran them out of town. ⁵¹So they shook the dust from their feet as a sign of rejection and went to the town of Iconium. ⁵²And the believers* were filled with joy and with the Holy Spirit.

13:22 1 Sam 13:14. **13:29** Greek *from the tree.* **13:33** Or *Today I reveal you as my Son.* Ps 2:7. **13:34** Isa 55:3. **13:35** Ps 16:10. **13:38** English translations divide verses 38 and 39 in various ways. **13:41** Hab 1:5 (Greek version). **13:47** Isa 49:6. **13:52** Greek *the disciples.*

13:26-41 Paul reviewed the shameful treatment Jesus had received, involving unjust condemnation and death. But God had raised Jesus from the dead, as attested by witnesses. This message is indeed good news, because through Jesus, anyone can experience forgiveness. But this message must be met with repentance and faith, or dire consequences will follow.

13:50 Despite their lack of decision-making power, women of wealth and high social status had a great deal of influence on religion, politics, and the marketplace in their cities and towns. Here the women are described as "religious," which could mean they were devout Gentiles like Cornelius (10:1-2). Lydia is also described this way (16:14).

Koinonia Image
MY STORY WITH COMMUNITY, WORKPLACE & CHURCH

Working through Difficult Relationships

SCRIPTURE CONNECTION: ACTS 13:1-13; 15:35-41

Working together does not always go the way we hope. What happens between Paul, Barnabas, and John Mark on their first and second missionary journeys illustrates the tough realities of co-laboring.

Paul (Saul) and Barnabas were commissioned for "the special work to which I have called them" (13:2). Both men were called as unique leaders and mentors for the mission, meaning extra responsibility. They chose John Mark as their assistant (13:5), possibly hoping to train him for future leadership.

No one is perfect—including Paul. We don't know why John Mark left (13:13). However, in my experience as a mentoring and diversity leader, people leave because of people more often than they leave because of the job. I wonder, *What must it have been like to work with Paul?* The man was relentless and brave, with very high standards. Working with him may have been high-pressure.

Paul didn't lower his standards or expectations, leading to discord. In fact, Paul's disagreement with Barnabas on whether to take John Mark on their next mission "was so sharp that they separated" (15:39). The Bible doesn't say who was right or wrong, but the conversation didn't go well.

But God's plan for John Mark continues with a different mentor. Barnabas, commissioned just like Paul, saw promise in John Mark, was willing to give him a second chance, and took over as mentor. John Mark willingly went with him—a better mentor-mentee match.

Reconciliation is possible, even after the breaking point. While we don't know if Barnabas and Paul ever worked together again, later, we see that Paul and John Mark repaired their relationship. They were working together while Paul was in prison (Colossians 4:10).

> Mentoring and working relationships are powerful when expectations are in sync.

IMAGINE

Have you ever been like Paul, having high expectations and then someone let you down? Or maybe you are like John Mark, the one who feels you cannot live up to another's expectations? Maybe you find yourself in Barnabas's position, caught between others and forced to choose a side?

What conversations could create realistic expectations in our relationships before things get to a breaking point?

"Like Paul, I have had people quit when the pace of work became difficult. I did not always have a Barnabas to come alongside and figure out the next steps. The pain of broken relationships is real. Agreeing quickly on expectations in a mentoring relationship, or any working relationship, is critical to success."

ELISABETH SELZER ROGERS, MDiv, MA, PhD, is a passionate believer and follower of Christ, bringing his love to the secular world through mentoring, coaching, and modeling his unconditional love.

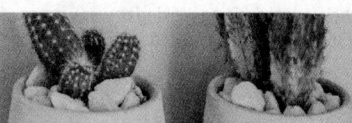

Paul and Barnabas in Iconium

14 The same thing happened in Iconium.* Paul and Barnabas went to the Jewish synagogue and preached with such power that a great number of both Jews and Greeks became believers. ²Some of the Jews, however, spurned God's message and poisoned the minds of the Gentiles against Paul and Barnabas. ³But the apostles stayed there a long time, preaching boldly about the grace of the Lord. And the Lord proved their message was true by giving them power to do miraculous signs and wonders. ⁴But the people of the town were divided in their opinion about them. Some sided with the Jews, and some with the apostles.

⁵Then a mob of Gentiles and Jews, along with their leaders, decided to attack and stone them. ⁶When the apostles learned of it, they fled to the region of Lycaonia—to the towns of Lystra and Derbe and the surrounding area. ⁷And there they preached the Good News.

Paul and Barnabas in Lystra and Derbe

⁸While they were at Lystra, Paul and Barnabas came upon a man with crippled feet. He had been that way from birth, so he had never walked. He was sitting ⁹and listening as Paul preached. Looking straight at him, Paul realized he had faith to be healed. ¹⁰So Paul called to him in a loud voice, "Stand up!" And the man jumped to his feet and started walking.

¹¹When the crowd saw what Paul had done, they shouted in their local dialect, "These men are gods in human form!" ¹²They decided that Barnabas was the Greek god Zeus and that Paul was Hermes, since he was the chief speaker. ¹³Now the temple of Zeus was located just outside the town. So the priest of the temple and the crowd brought bulls and wreaths of flowers to the town gates, and they prepared to offer sacrifices to the apostles.

¹⁴But when the apostles Barnabas and Paul heard what was happening, they tore their clothing in dismay and ran out among the people, shouting, ¹⁵"Friends,* why are you doing this? We are merely human beings—just like you! We have come to bring you the Good News that you should turn from these worthless things and turn to the living God, who made heaven and earth, the sea, and everything in them. ¹⁶In the past he permitted all the nations to go their own ways, ¹⁷but he never left them without evidence of himself and his goodness. For instance, he sends you rain and good crops and gives you food and joyful hearts." ¹⁸But even with these words, Paul and Barnabas could scarcely restrain the people from sacrificing to them.

¹⁹Then some Jews arrived from Antioch and Iconium and won the crowds to their side. They stoned Paul and dragged him out of town, thinking he was dead. ²⁰But as the believers* gathered around him, he got up and went back into the town. The next day he left with Barnabas for Derbe.

Paul and Barnabas Return to Antioch of Syria

²¹After preaching the Good News in Derbe and making many disciples, Paul and Barnabas returned to Lystra, Iconium, and Antioch of Pisidia, ²²where they strengthened the believers. They encouraged them to continue in the faith, reminding them that we must suffer many hardships to enter the Kingdom of God. ²³Paul and Barnabas also appointed elders in every church. With prayer and fasting, they turned the elders over to the care of the Lord, in whom they had put their trust. ²⁴Then they traveled back

---

14:1 *Iconium*, as well as *Lystra* and *Derbe* (14:6), were towns in what is now Turkey.   **14:15** Greek *Men*.   **14:20** Greek *disciples*; also in 14:22, 28.

14:1-22 Many women and men in Iconium and Lystra accepted the message brought by Paul and Barnabas of forgiveness of sins in Christ. These women and men heard the message in the local synagogue, a Jewish setting that included Gentiles interested in hearing the Scriptures read and praying to the one true God. The new disciples' faith would be tested very soon, as a mob of opponents stoned Paul and left him for dead (see 14:19). The new believers, women and men, gathered around Paul to take care of him, exposing themselves to possible hostility from their neighbors (14:20). Today Christian women around the world face strong opposition from neighbors and friends for their belief, but God will bless them as they enter the Kingdom of God (14:22).
14:3 The Spirit-inspired apostles were resilient to withstand the verbal attack against them, and they persisted in preaching the Good News that God's grace was available to Gentiles as well as to Jews. Spirit-inspired boldness is evident throughout Acts (see 2:14; 4:9-13; 7:2-53; 8:30-35; 9:27-28; 18:26; 19:8; 22:3-21; 23:1-6; 28:16-20, 23-31). In addition, the Holy Spirit confirmed the Christian message with "miraculous signs and wonders" (see 5:12-16; 15:12; 16:18; 19:11).

14:8-20 Paul's healing of a man with crippled feet recalls a similar incident in 3:1-12. In Acts, the work of Paul parallels the work of Peter, and the many miraculous signs and wonders performed among the Jews were also performed among the Gentiles.
14:23 Paul and Barnabas appointed "elders" here and in other churches. The Greek term translated "elders" is never used to describe a specific person in the New Testament, but rather groups of leaders or a role in the church. Earlier in Acts, we find the term used to describe Jewish men in Temple leadership (for example, 4:5, 8, 23). In Titus 1:5-9, the moral qualifications listed for an "elder" use the indefinite pronoun "whoever" or "anyone" (in 1:6, the NLT renders the Greek indefinite pronoun *ei tis* as "an elder," picking up "elder" from 1:5 and assuming masculine pronouns, subsequently), suggesting that Paul considered women and men as equally qualified for this responsibility within the congregation. In Titus 1:6; the phrase "faithful to his wife" (also in 1 Timothy 3:2) and "faithful to her husband" (1 Timothy 5:9) do not mandate that church leaders be married—or in the case of Titus 1:6-7, have adult children—but if they are married, they must be faithful to their spouse.

through Pisidia to Pamphylia. ²⁵They preached the word in Perga, then went down to Attalia.

²⁶Finally, they returned by ship to Antioch of Syria, where their journey had begun. The believers there had entrusted them to the grace of God to do the work they had now completed. ²⁷Upon arriving in Antioch, they called the church together and reported everything God had done through them and how he had opened the door of faith to the Gentiles, too. ²⁸And they stayed there with the believers for a long time.

The Council at Jerusalem

15 While Paul and Barnabas were at Antioch of Syria, some men from Judea arrived and began to teach the believers*: "Unless you are circumcised as required by the law of Moses, you cannot be saved." ²Paul and Barnabas disagreed with them, arguing vehemently. Finally, the church decided to send Paul and Barnabas to Jerusalem, accompanied by some local believers, to talk to the apostles and elders about this question. ³The church sent the delegates to Jerusalem, and they stopped along the way in Phoenicia and Samaria to visit the believers. They told them—much to everyone's joy—that the Gentiles, too, were being converted.

⁴When they arrived in Jerusalem, Barnabas and Paul were welcomed by the whole church, including the apostles and elders. They reported everything God had done through them. ⁵But then some of the believers who belonged to the sect of the Pharisees stood up and insisted, "The Gentile converts must be circumcised and required to follow the law of Moses."

⁶So the apostles and elders met together to resolve this issue. ⁷At the meeting, after a long discussion, Peter stood and addressed them as follows: "Brothers, you all know that God chose me from among you some time ago to preach to the Gentiles so that they could hear the Good News and believe. ⁸God knows people's hearts, and he confirmed that he accepts Gentiles by giving them the Holy Spirit, just as he did to us. ⁹He made no distinction between us and them, for he cleansed their hearts through faith. ¹⁰So why are you now challenging God by burdening the Gentile believers* with a yoke that neither we nor our ancestors were able to bear? ¹¹We believe that we are all saved the same way, by the undeserved grace of the Lord Jesus."

¹²Everyone listened quietly as Barnabas and Paul told about the miraculous signs and wonders God had done through them among the Gentiles.

¹³When they had finished, James stood and said, "Brothers, listen to me. ¹⁴Peter* has told you about the time God first visited the Gentiles to take from them a people for himself. ¹⁵And this conversion of Gentiles is exactly what the prophets predicted. As it is written:

¹⁶ 'Afterward I will return
   and restore the fallen house* of David.
   I will rebuild its ruins
   and restore it,
¹⁷ so that the rest of humanity might seek the
      LORD,
   including the Gentiles—
   all those I have called to be mine.
   The LORD has spoken—
¹⁸ he who made these things known so long ago.'*

¹⁹"And so my judgment is that we should not make it difficult for the Gentiles who are turning to God. ²⁰Instead, we should write and tell them to abstain from eating food offered to idols, from sexual immorality, from eating the meat of strangled animals, and from consuming blood. ²¹For these laws of Moses have been preached in Jewish synagogues in every city on every Sabbath for many generations."

15:1 Greek *brothers;* also in 15:3, 23, 32, 33, 36, 40. **15:10** Greek *disciples.* **15:14** Greek *Simeon.* **15:16** Or *kingdom;* Greek reads *tent.* **15:16-18** Amos 9:11-12 (Greek version); Isa 45:21.

15:1-29 This meeting in Jerusalem was the first church council, and the apostles, along with other leaders, resolved the dispute about whether Gentiles who became members of the church needed to be circumcised, following Jewish law. Peter, Paul, and Barnabas all gave testimony of the work of the Holy Spirit among Gentiles and advocated against circumcision. Essentially, they were arguing that Gentiles didn't need to convert to Judaism to follow Jesus. In the end, the apostles and elders asked the Gentile believers to follow a few guidelines. They asked that Gentiles refrain from eating food offered to idols, sexual immorality, eating the meat of strangled animals, and consuming blood. "Eating food offered to idols" is sinful if it involves knowingly partaking of an idolatrous sacrifice (see Exodus 20:4; Deuteronomy 5:8; 1 Corinthians 8:4-13; 10:14-31; Revelation 2:14, 20). Sexual immorality was common in the Greco-Roman world but is always sinful (Exodus 20:14; Deuteronomy 5:18; Galatians 5:19). The law of Moses prohibited eating meat that had blood in it (Leviticus 17:13-14) or consuming blood (17:10-12). This command was first given to Noah, the ancestor of Gentiles as well as Jews (Genesis 9:4).

15:1 Those who advocated circumcision of male Gentile converts to Christianity believed it was necessary to keep the church community pure and holy, in keeping with the law of Moses. God desires a holy people, but believers are made holy through being in Christ, filled with the Holy Spirit. When Christ saves us from our sins, we have eternal life, and the Holy Spirit helps us live a holy life.

15:21 James stated that the law of Moses, the Scriptures, were read each Sabbath in synagogues around the Roman Empire. This means that not only were men knowledgeable about the Scriptures, but Jewish and Gentile women who attended the synagogue were educated in the Word of God, too. Some women became teachers of the Word, including Priscilla (18:26). She likely learned the Scriptures while worshiping in a synagogue.

The Letter for Gentile Believers

²²Then the apostles and elders together with the whole church in Jerusalem chose delegates, and they sent them to Antioch of Syria with Paul and Barnabas to report on this decision. The men chosen were two of the church leaders*—Judas (also called Barsabbas) and Silas. ²³This is the letter they took with them:

15:22 Greek *were leaders among the brothers.*

"This letter is from the apostles and elders, your brothers in Jerusalem. It is written to the Gentile believers in Antioch, Syria, and Cilicia. Greetings!

²⁴"We understand that some men from here have troubled you and upset you with their teaching, but we did not send them! ²⁵So we decided, having come to complete agreement, to

---

Shalom IMAGE — MY STORY OF MY UNIQUE INFLUENCE

Lessons from a First-Century Businesswoman-Believer

SCRIPTURE CONNECTION: ACTS 16:13-15

Lydia is a model disciple worth imitating today by both women and men. Her story deserves our attention.

First, Lydia "worshiped God," which meant that she was a Gentile who followed some Jewish practices without converting. Typically, these Gentiles gathered for synagogue worship, worshiped the Jewish God, and gave donations.

Second, "the Lord opened" Lydia's heart. This is a unique phrase in Acts, but the same verb, "to open," is in Luke's story about the Lord opening the disciples' minds to understand Scripture (Luke 24:45). She chose to follow Jesus by obeying the Lord's prompting. Based on her example as the head of her home, the rest of her household was also baptized. The ancient world valued group identity, and the family leader's decision would be worth following.

Third, Lydia hosted Paul and Silas. Jews did not typically accept Gentiles' hospitality because of the differences in religion, including having small idols in their homes. Paul accepting her invitation made it clear that her conversion was full and complete. Her home was acceptable for Jewish followers of Jesus.

> Believe wholly, bring others along, and be bold.

Lydia was a dealer in purple cloth and likely a citizen from Thyatira, a city in Asia Minor (modern Turkey), whose business took her to Philippi. She employed workers who were considered part of her household, along with her relatives. She was not wealthy or elite but had sufficient funds to accommodate Paul and Silas in her home and to host a house church.

So what can we learn from a first-century businesswoman-believer? Believe wholly, bring others along, and offer boldly what we have.

IMAGINE

What can we take from Lydia unashamedly offering her home, knowing she might be rejected?

Following Lydia's example, who are people we influence, and how might we invite them to know God?

> "Lydia's passion for knowing God inspires me to reach beyond my comfort zone and embrace God's work around me."

LYNN H. COHICK, PhD, is Distinguished Professor of New Testament and Director of Houston Theological Seminary, where she leads the Doctor of Ministry program. She writes, speaks, and teaches internationally.

send you official representatives, along with our beloved Barnabas and Paul, [26]who have risked their lives for the name of our Lord Jesus Christ. [27]We are sending Judas and Silas to confirm what we have decided concerning your question.

[28]"For it seemed good to the Holy Spirit and to us to lay no greater burden on you than these few requirements: [29]You must abstain from eating food offered to idols, from consuming blood or the meat of strangled animals, and from sexual immorality. If you do this, you will do well. Farewell."

[30]The messengers went at once to Antioch, where they called a general meeting of the believers and delivered the letter. [31]And there was great joy throughout the church that day as they read this encouraging message.
[32]Then Judas and Silas, both being prophets, spoke at length to the believers, encouraging and strengthening their faith. [33]They stayed for a while, and then the believers sent them back to the church in Jerusalem with a blessing of peace.* [35]Paul and Barnabas stayed in Antioch. They and many others taught and preached the word of the Lord there.

Paul and Barnabas Separate

[36]After some time Paul said to Barnabas, "Let's go back and visit each city where we previously preached the word of the Lord, to see how the new believers are doing." [37]Barnabas agreed and wanted to take along John Mark. [38]But Paul disagreed strongly, since John Mark had deserted them in Pamphylia and had not continued with them in their work. [39]Their disagreement was so sharp that they separated. Barnabas took John Mark with him and sailed for Cyprus. [40]Paul chose Silas, and as he left, the believers entrusted him to the Lord's gracious care. [41]Then he traveled throughout Syria and Cilicia, strengthening the churches there.

Paul's Second Missionary Journey

16 Paul went first to Derbe and then to Lystra, where there was a young disciple named Timothy. His mother was a Jewish believer, but his father was a Greek. [2]Timothy was well thought of by the believers* in Lystra and Iconium, [3]so Paul wanted him to join them on their journey. In deference to the Jews of the area, he arranged for Timothy to be circumcised before they left, for everyone knew that his father was a Greek. [4]Then they went from town to town, instructing the believers to follow the decisions made by the apostles and elders in Jerusalem. [5]So the churches were strengthened in their faith and grew larger every day.

A Call from Macedonia

[6]Next Paul and Silas traveled through the area of Phrygia and Galatia, because the Holy Spirit had prevented them from preaching the word in the province of Asia at that time. [7]Then coming to the borders of Mysia, they headed north for the province of Bithynia,* but again the Spirit of Jesus did not allow them to go there. [8]So instead, they went on through Mysia to the seaport of Troas.

[9]That night Paul had a vision: A man from Macedonia in northern Greece was standing there, pleading with him, "Come over to Macedonia and help us!" [10]So we* decided to leave for Macedonia at once, having concluded that God was calling us to preach the Good News there.

15:33 Some manuscripts add verse 34, *But Silas decided to stay there.* **16:2** Greek *brothers;* also in 16:40. **16:6-7** *Phrygia, Galatia, Asia, Mysia,* and *Bithynia* were all districts in what is now Turkey. **16:10** Luke, the writer of this book, here joined Paul and accompanied him on his journey.

15:36-41 The Greek indicates a sharp but honest disagreement between Paul and Barnabas about whether John Mark (Barnabas's cousin, Colossians 4:10) should be given a second chance to accompany them on a mission journey after he had deserted them in Pamphylia during their first trip (see Acts 13:13). The rift between Paul and John Mark was eventually reconciled (2 Timothy 4:11).

16:1 Timothy's mother, Eunice, and his grandmother Lois are both praised elsewhere by Paul for their sincere faith, which they passed down to Timothy (2 Timothy 1:5). Although marrying a Gentile was not common at the time, Eunice still practiced her religion and communicated much of it to their son. However, Timothy was not circumcised, possibly because his father found the practice objectionable, as many Gentiles did. Later rabbinic tradition asserts that any child born of a Jewish woman is a Jew, regardless of the ethnic heritage of the father.

16:6-10 God directed the missionaries' travels: "The Holy Spirit had prevented them" from proceeding westward into the province of Asia, "the Spirit of Jesus did not allow them to go" north to Bithynia, and then "Paul had a vision" calling them to go northwest over the Aegean Sea to Macedonia. God's Spirit guided his servants in Acts in a variety of ways, including divine visions (see also 9:10; 10:9-16; 22:18), direct knowledge or apprehension (see 8:29, 39; 10:19; 20:22), counsel with other believers (see 15:29), guidance through prayer (13:2, 4), insight through Scripture (28:25-27), and prophecy (11:28). The power of the indwelling Holy Spirit helped them accomplish their mission to be Christ's witnesses (1:8; see also 4:8, 31; 11:24; 13:9).

16:10 The narrative switches from "they" to "we" here, which likely means that Luke, the writer, joined Paul and the others traveling with him and accompanied them on their journey. From the "we" passages in Acts, we can infer Luke's itinerary with Paul. Luke accompanied Paul from Troas to Philippi (16:10-17). Later Luke joined Paul again at Philippi and sailed with him to Troas, then to Miletus (20:5-15), then from Miletus to Jerusalem (21:1-18). After Paul's two-year imprisonment in Caesarea, Luke traveled with him to Rome (27:1–28:16).

Lydia

IDENTITY — From Struggle to Surrender

She remembers…

As a business owner and head of my household, I struggle, and being a woman in those spaces sometimes increases that struggle. Most days, I prove myself in the marketplace while providing faithfully for my family, but I can feel alone and lonely in those roles.

I guess that's how the Sabbath became the best day of the week for me.

Each week, I'd go outside the city gate to the riverbank. I went to pray, to worship, and to belong. In this gathering, I wasn't the one with the goods. I was simply still before God.

And I thought this pattern of prayer and pause and people was as good as life gets.

But one Sabbath morning, some visitors from out of town joined and told us a new story. Their story was all about a man named Jesus. And I couldn't help but be captivated.

According to them, Jesus is the fulfillment we'd been waiting for. He had fulfilled the requirement of the law. He had fulfilled the promise of the prophets. He filled the space between God and us.

My heart heard a whisper: *Lydia, he can fulfill you, too.*

I sensed that in my striving I had waited for this opportunity to surrender. I hadn't known what, or who, I was missing, but now I did.

I'd been missing Jesus.

That day, I led my household to choose Jesus. I released my identity as a misfit merchant/mom. In God's family, I belong. And I urged these messengers to come, come stay with me.

> God works more in our surrender than in our striving.

LYDIA'S STORY IS TOLD IN ACTS 16:13-15.

IDENTIFY

What areas of your life feel like they're missing something or someone?

How might you offer those areas to Jesus and ask how he alone can fill you and provide what you need to feel fulfilled?

"When I finally get still, God reminds me that Jesus alone fulfills my wants and needs. I've seen God work far more in my surrender than in my striving. He honors our resolve to rest in him."

SUZY SHEPHERD is the founder of SHINE, creator of Stonecroft's Where Love Lives outreach experience, and mom to a blended tribe of nine. She finds great joy in creating experiences for people to know God's love.

Lydia of Philippi Believes in Jesus

¹¹We boarded a boat at Troas and sailed straight across to the island of Samothrace, and the next day we landed at Neapolis. ¹²From there we reached Philippi, a major city of that district of Macedonia and a Roman colony. And we stayed there several days.

¹³On the Sabbath we went a little way outside the city to a riverbank, where we thought people would be meeting for prayer, and we sat down to speak with some women who had gathered there. ¹⁴One of them was Lydia from Thyatira, a merchant of expensive purple cloth, who worshiped God. As she listened to us, the Lord opened her heart, and she accepted what Paul was saying. ¹⁵She and her household were baptized, and she asked us to be her guests. "If you agree that I am a true believer in the Lord," she said, "come and stay at my home." And she urged us until we agreed.

Paul and Silas in Prison

¹⁶One day as we were going down to the place of prayer, we met a slave girl who had a spirit that enabled her to tell the future. She earned a lot of money for her masters by telling fortunes. ¹⁷She followed Paul and the rest of us, shouting, "These men are servants of the Most High God, and they have come to tell you how to be saved."

¹⁸This went on day after day until Paul got so exasperated that he turned and said to the demon within her, "I command you in the name of Jesus Christ to come out of her." And instantly it left her.

¹⁹Her masters' hopes of wealth were now shattered, so they grabbed Paul and Silas and dragged them before the authorities at the marketplace. ²⁰"The whole city is in an uproar because of these Jews!" they shouted to the city officials. ²¹"They are teaching customs that are illegal for us Romans to practice."

²²A mob quickly formed against Paul and Silas, and the city officials ordered them stripped and beaten with wooden rods. ²³They were severely beaten, and then they were thrown into prison. The jailer was ordered to make sure they didn't escape. ²⁴So the jailer put them into the inner dungeon and clamped their feet in the stocks.

²⁵Around midnight Paul and Silas were praying and singing hymns to God, and the other prisoners were listening. ²⁶Suddenly, there was a massive earthquake, and the prison was shaken to its foundations. All the doors immediately flew open, and the chains of every prisoner fell off! ²⁷The jailer woke up to see the prison doors wide open. He assumed the prisoners had escaped, so he drew his sword to kill himself. ²⁸But Paul shouted to him, "Stop! Don't kill yourself! We are all here!"

²⁹The jailer called for lights and ran to the dungeon and fell down trembling before Paul and Silas. ³⁰Then he brought them out and asked, "Sirs, what must I do to be saved?"

³¹They replied, "Believe in the Lord Jesus and you will be saved, along with everyone in your household." ³²And they shared the word of the Lord with him and with all who lived in his household. ³³Even at that hour of the night, the jailer cared for them and washed their wounds. Then he and everyone in his household were immediately baptized. ³⁴He brought them into his house and set a meal before them, and he and his entire household rejoiced because they all believed in God.

³⁵The next morning the city officials sent the police to tell the jailer, "Let those men go!" ³⁶So the jailer told Paul, "The city officials have said you and Silas are free to leave. Go in peace."

³⁷But Paul replied, "They have publicly beaten us without a trial and put us in prison—and we are Roman citizens. So now they want us to leave secretly? Certainly not! Let them come themselves to release us!"

³⁸When the police reported this, the city officials were alarmed to learn that Paul and Silas were Roman citizens. ³⁹So they came to the jail and apologized to them. Then they brought them out and begged them to leave the city. ⁴⁰When Paul and Silas

---

16:13-15 Lydia was a Gentile God-fearer who participated in Jewish worship at a place of prayer, a synonym for a synagogue (conceived as a gathering, not a building). She and other women had gathered on the Sabbath, and Lydia embraced the gospel message because "the Lord opened her heart." She invited Paul and Silas to accept her hospitality, even though she was a Gentile, because she was truly converted. She likely had some financial resources, because she managed a household that included those who worked for her in the lucrative purple cloth business.

16:16-18 The enslaved girl who told people's future was possessed by a "spirit that enabled her to tell the future" (literally "spirit of Python," related to the oracle at nearby Delphi). She was exploited by her enslavers, and her demons agitated against Paul's gospel message. Paul exorcised the demons, but we do not know her fate beyond that. With her healing, her enslavers would not be able to profit from her anymore. We can only hope that other believers in Philippi rescued her. Today many girls and women are caught in sex trafficking and other forms of human trafficking, and this enslaved girl's story should motivate believers to combat such horrific exploitation. Standing up to oppression can come at a cost—as with Paul and Silas, who were jailed because they had healed her.

16:37-39 Paul and Silas were Roman citizens, so the beating and imprisonment they suffered had been illegal. When the city officials learned of this, they were justifiably alarmed because their actions were considered criminal under Roman law. Paul made use of his rights as a Roman citizen to clear his name and ensure that no disrepute would attach to the Christian message or those who accepted it. Luke intended to show that Christianity should enjoy the same status as Judaism in the Roman Empire—to be classified as a permitted religion—since the Christian faith was compatible with the life of a Roman citizen. He was ready to use the privileges of Roman citizenship to advance the cause of Christ in a hostile world.

Speaking to Be Heard

SCRIPTURE CONNECTION: ACTS 17:16-34

Today, like the people of Athens in Paul's day, many search for God but have yet to be introduced to him. It is a huge task to make God known, but be encouraged. It's the Holy Spirit's work to draw people, and God loves partnering with us.

We can learn a lot about how to share with others from Paul's way of connecting with people. He observed his surroundings and matched his message to their context. When he arrived in Athens, he was "deeply troubled by all the idols he saw everywhere in the city" (17:16). Instead of speaking with anger or judgment, he piqued people's curiosity. He observed a truth about them—"I notice that you are very religious" (17:22)—but he also saw their deeper need as evidenced by the altar "To an Unknown God" (17:23). Then he made an even more intriguing statement, "This God, whom you worship without knowing, is the one I'm telling you about" (17:23). By then, he had their attention!

As Paul then spoke about Jesus, some sneered, and some wanted to hear more (17:32)—and the same will happen with us. Like Paul, may our hearts feel troubled enough to move to action yet compassionate enough to "speak the language" of the people so they can hear the Good News.

> God can help us survey our surroundings and match our message.

IMAGINE

How can we reimagine what it looks like to be on mission with God in our context?

How can those observations serve as a bridge to sharing the truth about who God is? What might encourage those you're engaging with to be open to what you say about God?

> "When I was a youth pastor, I often used lyrics from well-known, popular songs as a bridge to talk about Bible truths. Many people can remember the lyrics to their favorite songs but don't know what the Bible says about love, relationships, and the meaning of life. We can show people how God connects to what they already know."

SUSIE GAMEZ, MA, is a teaching pastor at Midtown Covenant Church in Sacramento, CA, and preaches across the country, making the reconciling love of Jesus come alive through the Scriptures.

left the prison, they returned to the home of Lydia. There they met with the believers and encouraged them once more. Then they left town.

Paul Preaches in Thessalonica

17 Paul and Silas then traveled through the towns of Amphipolis and Apollonia and came to Thessalonica, where there was a Jewish synagogue. ²As was Paul's custom, he went to the synagogue service, and for three Sabbaths in a row he used the Scriptures to reason with the people. ³He explained the prophecies and proved that the Messiah must suffer and rise from the dead. He said, "This Jesus I'm telling you about is the Messiah." ⁴Some of the Jews who listened were persuaded and joined Paul and Silas, along with many God-fearing Greek men and quite a few prominent women.*

⁵But some of the Jews were jealous, so they gathered some troublemakers from the marketplace to form a mob and start a riot. They attacked the home of Jason, searching for Paul and Silas so they could drag them out to the crowd.* ⁶Not finding them there, they dragged out Jason and some of the other believers* instead and took them before the city council. "Paul and Silas have caused trouble all over the world," they shouted, "and now they are here disturbing our city, too. ⁷And Jason has welcomed them into his home. They are all guilty of treason against Caesar, for they profess allegiance to another king, named Jesus."

⁸The people of the city, as well as the city council, were thrown into turmoil by these reports. ⁹So the officials forced Jason and the other believers to post bond, and then they released them.

Paul and Silas in Berea

¹⁰That very night the believers sent Paul and Silas to Berea. When they arrived there, they went to the Jewish synagogue. ¹¹And the people of Berea were more open-minded than those in Thessalonica, and they listened eagerly to Paul's message. They searched the Scriptures day after day to see if Paul and Silas were teaching the truth. ¹²As a result, many Jews believed, as did many of the prominent Greek women and men.

¹³But when some Jews in Thessalonica learned that Paul was preaching the word of God in Berea, they went there and stirred up trouble. ¹⁴The believers acted at once, sending Paul on to the coast, while Silas and Timothy remained behind. ¹⁵Those escorting Paul went with him all the way to Athens; then they returned to Berea with instructions for Silas and Timothy to hurry and join him.

Paul Preaches in Athens

¹⁶While Paul was waiting for them in Athens, he was deeply troubled by all the idols he saw everywhere in the city. ¹⁷He went to the synagogue to reason with the Jews and the God-fearing Gentiles, and he spoke daily in the public square to all who happened to be there.

¹⁸He also had a debate with some of the Epicurean and Stoic philosophers. When he told them about Jesus and his resurrection, they said, "What's this babbler trying to say with these strange ideas he's picked up?" Others said, "He seems to be preaching about some foreign gods."

¹⁹Then they took him to the high council of the city.* "Come and tell us about this new teaching," they said. ²⁰"You are saying some rather strange things, and we want to know what it's all about." ²¹(It should be explained that all the Athenians as well as the foreigners in Athens seemed to spend all their time discussing the latest ideas.)

²²So Paul, standing before the council,* addressed them as follows: "Men of Athens, I notice that you are very religious in every way, ²³for as I was walking

---

17:4 Some manuscripts read *quite a few of the wives of the leading men.* **17:5** Or *the city council.* **17:6** Greek *brothers;* also in 17:10, 14. **17:19** Or *the most learned society of philosophers in the city.* Greek reads *the Areopagus.* **17:22** Traditionally rendered *standing in the middle of Mars Hill;* Greek reads *standing in the middle of the Areopagus.*

17:4 Prominent women, those with some wealth and social status, accepted the gospel message. Their stature in the city afforded protection and aid to poorer believers, and their acceptance of the message would add respectability to the small group of Jesus followers.

17:10-12 In light of the strong opposition in Thessalonica, "the believers sent Paul and Silas to Berea," located about fifty miles southwest of Thessalonica. There the missionaries had a better reception than in Thessalonica. Many Jews came to faith, as did many of the prominent Greek women and men. The Bereans were exemplary in their attitude, for they were open-minded, eager to learn, good listeners, diligent Bible students, and thoughtful people. Their resulting faith had a strong foundation.

17:18 Epicureanism was a popular school of Greek philosophy, founded by Epicurus (341–270 BC). Epicureans believed that the principal aim of life was to secure happiness in the form of tranquility, freedom from fear, and freedom from physical pain. Their contemporaries often called them atheists because Epicureans believed there were no gods to fear and death simply marked the end of human existence. They sought security in organized communities where they could live in contentment apart from society. In contrast, Stoicism was founded by Zeno of Citium (335–263 BC) and it became a highly influential philosophy in the Greco-Roman world. Stoic philosophers viewed the universe as permeated by an eternal reason (sometimes referred to as God or Providence), and they believed that people could advance from ignorance (the source of vice) to true knowledge (the source of virtue). To that end, the Stoics developed extensive lists of virtues and vices, producing detailed household codes to guide family behavior. Paul's teaching resembles that of the Stoics in his use of household codes and lists of virtues and vices (Galatians 5:19-23; Ephesians 5:22-33; Colossians 3:18–4:1; 1 Timothy 3:1-13; 5:1–6:1). However, Paul's message of the Good News—focusing on the life, death, and resurrection of Jesus Christ—was strange and foreign to these Greek philosophers. The air of superiority with which they addressed Paul as "this babbler" indicates their arrogance.

along I saw your many shrines. And one of your altars had this inscription on it: 'To an Unknown God.' This God, whom you worship without knowing, is the one I'm telling you about.

24"He is the God who made the world and everything in it. Since he is Lord of heaven and earth, he doesn't live in man-made temples, 25and human hands can't serve his needs—for he has no needs. He himself gives life and breath to everything, and he satisfies every need. 26From one man* he created all the nations throughout the whole earth. He decided beforehand when they should rise and fall, and he determined their boundaries.

27"His purpose was for the nations to seek after God and perhaps feel their way toward him and find him—though he is not far from any one of us. 28For in him we live and move and exist. As some of your* own poets have said, 'We are his offspring.' 29And since this is true, we shouldn't think of God as an idol designed by craftsmen from gold or silver or stone.

30"God overlooked people's ignorance about these things in earlier times, but now he commands everyone everywhere to repent of their sins and turn to him. 31For he has set a day for judging the world with justice by the man he has appointed, and he proved to everyone who this is by raising him from the dead."

32When they heard Paul speak about the resurrection of the dead, some laughed in contempt, but others said, "We want to hear more about this later." 33That ended Paul's discussion with them, 34but some joined him and became believers. Among them were Dionysius, a member of the council,* a woman named Damaris, and others with them.

Paul Meets Priscilla and Aquila in Corinth

18 Then Paul left Athens and went to Corinth.* 2There he became acquainted with a Jew named Aquila, born in Pontus, who had recently arrived from Italy with his wife, Priscilla. They had left Italy when Claudius Caesar deported all Jews from Rome. 3Paul lived and worked with them, for they were tentmakers* just as he was.

4Each Sabbath found Paul at the synagogue, trying to convince the Jews and Greeks alike. 5And after Silas and Timothy came down from Macedonia, Paul spent all his time preaching the word. He testified to the Jews that Jesus was the Messiah. 6But when they opposed and insulted him, Paul shook the dust from his clothes and said, "Your blood is upon your own heads—I am innocent. From now on I will go preach to the Gentiles."

7Then he left and went to the home of Titius Justus, a Gentile who worshiped God and lived next door to the synagogue. 8Crispus, the leader of the synagogue, and everyone in his household believed in the Lord. Many others in Corinth also heard Paul, became believers, and were baptized.

9One night the Lord spoke to Paul in a vision and told him, "Don't be afraid! Speak out! Don't be silent! 10For I am with you, and no one will attack and harm you, for many people in this city belong to me." 11So Paul stayed there for the next year and a half, teaching the word of God.

12But when Gallio became governor of Achaia, some Jews rose up together against Paul and brought him before the governor for judgment. 13They accused Paul of "persuading people to worship God in ways that are contrary to our law."

14But just as Paul started to make his defense, Gallio turned to Paul's accusers and said, "Listen, you Jews, if this were a case involving some wrongdoing or a serious crime, I would have a reason to accept your case. 15But since it is merely a question of words and names and your Jewish law, take care of it yourselves. I refuse to judge such matters." 16And he threw them out of the courtroom.

17The crowd* then grabbed Sosthenes, the leader of the synagogue, and beat him right there in the courtroom. But Gallio paid no attention.

17:26 Greek *From one;* other manuscripts read *From one blood.* **17:28** Some manuscripts read *our.* **17:34** Greek *an Areopagite.* **18:1** *Athens* and *Corinth* were major cities in Achaia, the region in the southern portion of the Greek peninsula. **18:3** Or *leatherworkers.* **18:17** Greek *Everyone;* other manuscripts read *All the Greeks.*

17:34 Damaris is mentioned as one Athenian who accepted Paul's message, though her name is unattested in ancient sources outside of Acts. She may be Dionysius's wife, since the Greek term translated "woman" can mean "wife" or just "woman." She may have heard Paul speak in the public square, one of the few places in first-century Athens where women and men could freely interact. With some notable exceptions, Athenian women were largely absent in matters of philosophy, having not received an equal education to their male counterparts. **18:2-3** Priscilla was married to a Jew, Aquila. She is named six times in the New Testament, in four of those instances before her husband's name, perhaps signaling her higher social status, wealth, or activity in the church. They came to Corinth from Rome and established their business of working with leather, including tents. Priscilla worked alongside Aquila. When they moved to Ephesus, they supported a church in their home (1 Corinthians 16:19). Later they returned to Rome and established another house church (Romans 16:3-5). Paul speaks of Priscilla and her husband as coworkers and benefactors and as risking their lives for him. Her ministry included teaching men and women the full gospel message (for example, Apollos, Acts 18:26). **18:4-6** Once again, Paul followed his custom of preaching to the Jews first, and then reaching out to Gentiles after meeting with rejection and opposition (13:42-49; see 3:25-26; 26:20; Romans 1:16; 2:10; 3:29-30; 4:9-12). Paul probably wrote his letters to the Thessalonian Christians after Silas and Timothy arrived from Macedonia with a report of how things were going there (see 1 Thessalonians 3:6).

Paul Returns to Antioch of Syria

¹⁸Paul stayed in Corinth for some time after that, then said good-bye to the brothers and sisters* and went to nearby Cenchrea. There he shaved his head according to Jewish custom, marking the end of a vow. Then he set sail for Syria, taking Priscilla and Aquila with him.

¹⁹They stopped first at the port of Ephesus, where Paul left the others behind. While he was there, he went to the synagogue to reason with the Jews. ²⁰They asked him to stay longer, but he declined. ²¹As he left, however, he said, "I will come back later,* God willing." Then he set sail from Ephesus. ²²The next stop was at the port of Caesarea. From there he went up and visited the church at Jerusalem* and then went back to Antioch.

²³After spending some time in Antioch, Paul went back through Galatia and Phrygia, visiting and strengthening all the believers.*

Apollos Instructed at Ephesus

²⁴Meanwhile, a Jew named Apollos, an eloquent speaker who knew the Scriptures well, had arrived in Ephesus from Alexandria in Egypt. ²⁵He had been taught the way of the Lord, and he taught others about Jesus with an enthusiastic spirit* and with accuracy. However, he knew only about John's baptism. ²⁶When Priscilla and Aquila heard him preaching boldly in the synagogue, they took him aside and explained the way of God even more accurately.

²⁷Apollos had been thinking about going to Achaia, and the brothers and sisters in Ephesus encouraged him to go. They wrote to the believers in Achaia, asking them to welcome him. When he arrived there, he proved to be of great benefit to those who, by God's grace, had believed. ²⁸He refuted the Jews with powerful arguments in public debate. Using the Scriptures, he explained to them that Jesus was the Messiah.

Paul's Third Missionary Journey

19 While Apollos was in Corinth, Paul traveled through the interior regions until he reached Ephesus, on the coast, where he found several believers.* ²"Did you receive the Holy Spirit when you believed?" he asked them.

"No," they replied, "we haven't even heard that there is a Holy Spirit."

³"Then what baptism did you experience?" he asked.

And they replied, "The baptism of John."

⁴Paul said, "John's baptism called for repentance from sin. But John himself told the people to believe in the one who would come later, meaning Jesus."

⁵As soon as they heard this, they were baptized in the name of the Lord Jesus. ⁶Then when Paul laid his hands on them, the Holy Spirit came on them, and they spoke in other tongues* and prophesied. ⁷There were about twelve men in all.

Paul Ministers in Ephesus

⁸Then Paul went to the synagogue and preached boldly for the next three months, arguing persuasively about the Kingdom of God. ⁹But some became stubborn, rejecting his message and publicly speaking against the Way. So Paul left the synagogue and took the believers with him. Then he held daily discussions at the lecture hall of Tyrannus. ¹⁰This went on for the next two years, so that people throughout the province of Asia—both Jews and Greeks—heard the word of the Lord.

18:18 Greek *brothers;* also in 18:27. **18:21** Some manuscripts read *"I must by all means be at Jerusalem for the upcoming festival, but I will come back later."* **18:22** Greek *the church.* **18:23** Greek *disciples;* also in 18:27. **18:25** Or *with enthusiasm in the Spirit.* **19:1** Greek *disciples;* also in 19:9, 30. **19:6** Or *in other languages.*

18:19-23 Paul made a quick stop at Ephesus, the most important city in the Roman province of Asia. He left those traveling with him there, including Priscilla and Aquila (Acts 18:26). He sailed to Judea, landing at Caesarea, the headquarters of the Roman forces of occupation. After a visit to the church at Jerusalem, Paul returned to Antioch, the church that had initially commissioned him. This marked the end of his second missionary journey. In Antioch, he reported what God had done through him and his colleagues, sharing the excitement and challenges of their work with the home church. After his stay in Antioch, Paul began his third missionary journey. He went by land rather than by sea, traveling through Galatia and Phrygia and revisiting believers who he had led to faith in Christ on his previous trips. He wanted to equip these young believers so they would not be left to founder and shipwreck their faith (see Ephesians 6:10-20; 1 Timothy 1:18-20; 2 Timothy 1:15; 4:10).

18:26 Priscilla's ministry included teaching men and women the entire gospel message. When Priscilla and Aquila heard Apollos teaching an incomplete story of Jesus' Good News in the synagogue, they pulled him aside so as not to embarrass him publicly. Their teaching focused on understanding the baptism of Jesus, which includes the seal and presence of the Holy Spirit on the believer's life. Just like Priscilla, women throughout Christian history have preached and taught the gospel faithfully, equipping the church for further evangelism.

19:1-7 Paul traveled to Ephesus after Apollos had left. Subsequently, Apollos returned to Ephesus while Paul was still working there (1 Corinthians 16:12). The two men had different personalities, gifts, and roles, but God worked through both of them. Some believers in Ephesus still had an inadequate understanding of the Christian faith (for example, Acts 18:26) and did not receive the Holy Spirit when they believed. They had accepted John's baptism, which "called for repentance from sin" but had not received Jesus' baptism, which included the gift of the Holy Spirit. When Paul had instructed them further, they were baptized in Jesus' name and received the Holy Spirit (19:5-6; see also Matthew 28:19).

Priscilla and Aquila

IDENTITY — Collaborating in Ministry

Priscilla and Aquila, as well as Andronicus and Junia (Romans 16:7), demonstrate how the early church's women and men ministered together. Priscilla and Aquila show how leadership was based not on gender but on gifting.

Mentioned in the Bible six times, Priscilla and Aquila were a married couple who worked with Paul in a teaching ministry that extended from Corinth to Ephesus and back to Rome. Twice Aquila's name comes first, and four times Priscilla's name appears first. Naming a woman first was highly unusual and usually signified that the woman had a more prominent role or standing in the circumstance described.

When the Bible describes their tentmaking, Aquila is named first (Acts 18:2-7). Likewise, in 1 Corinthians 16:19, Aquila is probably named first because the Corinthians would have known the couple as tentmakers. In tentmaking, Aquila took the lead.

But when they were traveling with Paul and teaching Apollos about the Holy Spirit, Priscilla's name comes first, apparently because she was the primary teacher (Acts 18:18, 26). In Paul's letters, he greets them, commends "Priscilla and Aquila" for risking their lives, and greets the church that meets in their home (Romans 16:3-5; 2 Timothy 4:19).

In the early church, women and men collaborated in spreading the gospel, according to their gifts, not gender. Leadership based on gifting benefited all.

PRISCILLA AND AQUILA'S STORY IS TOLD IN ACTS 18:1-28; THEY ARE ALSO MENTIONED IN ROMANS 16:3-5; 1 CORINTHIANS 16:19; AND 2 TIMOTHY 4:19.

> Recognize, develop, and use your gifts for Christ, and encourage others to do the same.

IDENTIFY

How can women and men partner together in ministry for everyone's benefit?

If you are married, how can you and your spouse encourage each other to fully use your gifts?

If you are single, how can you maximize the gifts God has given you to serve Jesus? How can you encourage those you share work and ministry with to do so with theirs?

> "Over forty-six years of marriage, my husband and I jointly ministered. We learned to encourage our different giftings, realizing we could do more together."

ELIZABETH GLANVILLE, PhD, is retired faculty from Fuller Theological Seminary, School of Mission and Theology. She is an international teacher on missions and leadership and chaplain for a local police department and her retirement community.

¹¹God gave Paul the power to perform unusual miracles. ¹²When handkerchiefs or aprons that had merely touched his skin were placed on sick people, they were healed of their diseases, and evil spirits were expelled.

¹³A group of Jews was traveling from town to town casting out evil spirits. They tried to use the name of the Lord Jesus in their incantation, saying, "I command you in the name of Jesus, whom Paul preaches, to come out!" ¹⁴Seven sons of Sceva, a leading priest, were doing this. ¹⁵But one time when they tried it, the evil spirit replied, "I know Jesus, and I know Paul, but who are you?" ¹⁶Then the man with the evil spirit leaped on them, overpowered them, and attacked them with such violence that they fled from the house, naked and battered.

¹⁷The story of what happened spread quickly all through Ephesus, to Jews and Greeks alike. A solemn fear descended on the city, and the name of the Lord Jesus was greatly honored. ¹⁸Many who became believers confessed their sinful practices. ¹⁹A number of them who had been practicing sorcery brought their incantation books and burned them at a public bonfire. The value of the books was several million dollars.* ²⁰So the message about the Lord spread widely and had a powerful effect.

²¹Afterward Paul felt compelled by the Spirit* to go over to Macedonia and Achaia before going to Jerusalem. "And after that," he said, "I must go on to Rome!" ²²He sent his two assistants, Timothy and Erastus, ahead to Macedonia while he stayed awhile longer in the province of Asia.

The Riot in Ephesus

²³About that time, serious trouble developed in Ephesus concerning the Way. ²⁴It began with Demetrius, a silversmith who had a large business manufacturing silver shrines of the Greek goddess Artemis.* He kept many craftsmen busy. ²⁵He called them together, along with others employed in similar trades, and addressed them as follows:

"Gentlemen, you know that our wealth comes from this business. ²⁶But as you have seen and heard, this man Paul has persuaded many people that handmade gods aren't really gods at all. And he's done this not only here in Ephesus but throughout the entire province! ²⁷Of course, I'm not just talking about the loss of public respect for our business. I'm also concerned that the temple of the great goddess Artemis will lose its influence and that Artemis—this magnificent goddess worshiped throughout the province of Asia and all around the world—will be robbed of her great prestige!"

²⁸At this their anger boiled, and they began shouting, "Great is Artemis of the Ephesians!" ²⁹Soon the whole city was filled with confusion. Everyone rushed to the amphitheater, dragging along Gaius and Aristarchus, who were Paul's traveling companions from Macedonia. ³⁰Paul wanted to go in, too, but the believers wouldn't let him. ³¹Some of the officials of the province, friends of Paul, also sent a message to him, begging him not to risk his life by entering the amphitheater.

³²Inside, the people were all shouting, some one thing and some another. Everything was in confusion. In fact, most of them didn't even know why they were there. ³³The Jews in the crowd pushed Alexander forward and told him to explain the situation. He motioned for silence and tried to speak. ³⁴But when the crowd realized he was a Jew, they started shouting again and kept it up for about two hours: "Great is Artemis of the Ephesians! Great is Artemis of the Ephesians!"

³⁵At last the mayor was able to quiet them down enough to speak. "Citizens of Ephesus," he said. "Everyone knows that Ephesus is the official guardian of the temple of the great Artemis, whose image fell down to us from heaven. ³⁶Since this is an undeniable fact, you should stay calm and not do anything rash. ³⁷You have brought these men here, but they have stolen nothing from the temple and have not spoken against our goddess.

19:19 Greek *50,000 pieces of silver,* each of which was the equivalent of a day's wage. **19:21** Or *decided in his spirit.*
19:24 *Artemis* is otherwise known as Diana.

19:19 Both women and men in Ephesus used magic, including spells and incantations. Female prostitutes were charged with making clients fall in love with them, formally in the court of law and more generally by the general public's suspicions. Elite women were suspected of using magic to build political alliances or destroy political enemies. Throughout history, women in greater numbers than men have been accused of witchcraft and have been tortured and killed. This charge against women is often based on a society's misogynistic assumption of female moral weakness. But the Bible does not teach that women are morally or intellectually weaker than men. Women are included in the body of Christ on equal terms with men, receive the same baptism, and are expected to learn and grow in faith (see 2 Peter 1:3-11).
19:23-41 The patron deity of Ephesus was the Greek goddess Artemis (sometimes known by her Roman name, Diana). Although she had many attributes, the Ephesian manifestation of Artemis was worshiped as a mother goddess, much like the ancient Near Eastern goddess Ishtar. A large, ornate temple was located just outside the city of Ephesus and was crucial to the city's economy. Two annual festivals were associated with her—including a month-long celebration with athletics, music, theater, and a joyous parade from Ephesus to the great temple. It's possible that Paul's visit may have coincided with one of these festivals.
19:24 Ephesian artisans created small silver souvenir shrines to sell to tourists during the festival months. With Paul converting people in Ephesus, Demetrius the silversmith realized his livelihood was under threat. He valued profit more than the lives of his fellow Ephesians. Greed is strongly condemned in Scripture (for example, Ecclesiastes 5:10; 1 Timothy 6:10).

³⁸"If Demetrius and the craftsmen have a case against them, the courts are in session and the officials can hear the case at once. Let them make formal charges. ³⁹And if there are complaints about other matters, they can be settled in a legal assembly. ⁴⁰I am afraid we are in danger of being charged with rioting by the Roman government, since there is no cause for all this commotion. And if Rome demands an explanation, we won't know what to say." ⁴¹*Then he dismissed them, and they dispersed.

Paul Goes to Macedonia and Greece

20 When the uproar was over, Paul sent for the believers* and encouraged them. Then he said good-bye and left for Macedonia. ²While there, he encouraged the believers in all the towns he passed through. Then he traveled down to Greece, ³where he stayed for three months. He was preparing to sail back to Syria when he discovered a plot by some Jews against his life, so he decided to return through Macedonia.

⁴Several men were traveling with him. They were Sopater son of Pyrrhus from Berea; Aristarchus and Secundus from Thessalonica; Gaius from Derbe; Timothy; and Tychicus and Trophimus from the province of Asia. ⁵They went on ahead and waited for us at Troas. ⁶After the Passover* ended, we boarded a ship at Philippi in Macedonia and five days later joined them in Troas, where we stayed a week.

Paul's Final Visit to Troas

⁷On the first day of the week, we gathered with the local believers to share in the Lord's Supper.* Paul was preaching to them, and since he was leaving the next day, he kept talking until midnight. ⁸The upstairs room where we met was lighted with many flickering lamps. ⁹As Paul spoke on and on, a young man named Eutychus, sitting on the windowsill, became very drowsy. Finally, he fell sound asleep and dropped three stories to his death below. ¹⁰Paul went down, bent over him, and took him into his arms. "Don't worry," he said, "he's alive!" ¹¹Then they all went back upstairs, shared in the Lord's Supper,* and ate together. Paul continued talking to them until dawn, and then he left. ¹²Meanwhile, the young man was taken home alive and well, and everyone was greatly relieved.

> "I want to kick 'should' and 'ought' to the curb. I want to be operating from a moral core, and not just reacting to a cultural sense of obligation."
>
> **SARA GROVES**
> singer-songwriter

Paul Meets the Ephesian Elders

¹³Paul went by land to Assos, where he had arranged for us to join him, while we traveled by ship. ¹⁴He joined us there, and we sailed together to Mitylene. ¹⁵The next day we sailed past the island of Kios. The following day we crossed to the island of Samos, and* a day later we arrived at Miletus.

¹⁶Paul had decided to sail on past Ephesus, for he didn't want to spend any more time in the province of Asia. He was hurrying to get to Jerusalem, if possible, in time for the Festival of Pentecost. ¹⁷But when we landed at Miletus, he sent a message to the elders of the church at Ephesus, asking them to come and meet him.

19:41 Some translations include verse 41 as part of verse 40. **20:1** Greek *disciples.* **20:6** Greek *the days of unleavened bread.* **20:7** Greek *to break bread.* **20:11** Greek *broke the bread.* **20:15** Some manuscripts read *and having stayed at Trogyllium.*

20:7-12 On Sundays, the early church commemorated Jesus' resurrection (see Mark 16:9; see also John 20:19; Revelation 1:10). This was Paul's last visit to Troas, which included gathering "to share in the Lord's Supper" (literally "to break bread"). This meal probably included both communion and a common meal (see Acts 2:42, 46; Jude 1:12). The remarkable feature of this gathering was the understated miraculous restoration of Eutychus, the young man who fell asleep on a windowsill and dropped three stories to his death (see also Acts 9:36-41).
20:16 The Festival of Pentecost was one of three major Jewish festivals held in Jerusalem. Women and men traveled from across the Roman Empire to participate in renewing God's covenant with Israel and celebrating the first wheat harvest of the season. Acts 2 describes at least fifteen regions represented at the church's first Pentecost (2:5-11). Christians continue to celebrate the Festival of Pentecost to mark the arrival of the Holy Spirit and the birthday of the church.
20:17 Paul gathered the elders of the church for a final farewell message. Luke did not specify whether these elders included women, but nothing in the text itself precludes the group from being composed of both women and men (see note on 14:23). It is possible that Priscilla and Aquila, who led a church in their house in Ephesus, were considered elders; however, no specific person in the New Testament is identified as an elder.

¹⁸When they arrived he declared, "You know that from the day I set foot in the province of Asia until now ¹⁹I have done the Lord's work humbly and with many tears. I have endured the trials that came to me from the plots of the Jews. ²⁰I never shrank back from telling you what you needed to hear, either publicly or in your homes. ²¹I have had one message for Jews and Greeks alike—the necessity of repenting from sin and turning to God, and of having faith in our Lord Jesus.

²²"And now I am bound by the Spirit* to go to Jerusalem. I don't know what awaits me, ²³except that the Holy Spirit tells me in city after city that jail and suffering lie ahead. ²⁴But my life is worth nothing to me unless I use it for finishing the work assigned me by the Lord Jesus—the work of telling others the Good News about the wonderful grace of God.

²⁵"And now I know that none of you to whom I have preached the Kingdom will ever see me again. ²⁶I declare today that I have been faithful. If anyone suffers eternal death, it's not my fault,* ²⁷for I didn't shrink from declaring all that God wants you to know.

²⁸"So guard yourselves and God's people. Feed and shepherd God's flock—his church, purchased with his own blood*—over which the Holy Spirit has appointed you as leaders.* ²⁹I know that false teachers, like vicious wolves, will come in among you after I leave, not sparing the flock. ³⁰Even some men from your own group will rise up and distort the truth in order to draw a following. ³¹Watch out! Remember the three years I was with you—my constant watch and care over you night and day, and my many tears for you.

³²"And now I entrust you to God and the message of his grace that is able to build you up and give you an inheritance with all those he has set apart for himself.

³³"I have never coveted anyone's silver or gold or fine clothes. ³⁴You know that these hands of mine have worked to supply my own needs and even the needs of those who were with me. ³⁵And I have been a constant example of how you can help those in need by working hard. You should remember the words of the Lord Jesus: 'It is more blessed to give than to receive.'"

³⁶When he had finished speaking, he knelt and prayed with them. ³⁷They all cried as they embraced and kissed him good-bye. ³⁸They were sad most of all because he had said that they would never see him again. Then they escorted him down to the ship.

Paul's Journey to Jerusalem

21 After saying farewell to the Ephesian elders, we sailed straight to the island of Cos. The next day we reached Rhodes and then went to Patara. ²There we boarded a ship sailing for Phoenicia. ³We sighted the island of Cyprus, passed it on our left, and landed at the harbor of Tyre, in Syria, where the ship was to unload its cargo.

⁴We went ashore, found the local believers,* and stayed with them a week. These believers prophesied through the Holy Spirit that Paul should not go on to Jerusalem. ⁵When we returned to the ship at the end of the week, the entire congregation, including women* and children, left the city and came down to the shore with us. There we knelt, prayed, ⁶and said our farewells. Then we went aboard, and they returned home.

⁷The next stop after leaving Tyre was Ptolemais, where we greeted the brothers and sisters* and stayed for one day. ⁸The next day we went on to Caesarea and stayed at the home of Philip the Evangelist, one of the seven men who had been chosen to distribute food. ⁹He had four unmarried daughters who had the gift of prophecy.

¹⁰Several days later a man named Agabus, who also had the gift of prophecy, arrived from Judea. ¹¹He came over, took Paul's belt, and bound his own feet and hands with it. Then he said, "The Holy Spirit declares, 'So shall the owner of this belt be bound by the Jewish leaders in Jerusalem and turned over to the Gentiles.'" ¹²When we heard this, we and the local believers all begged Paul not to go on to Jerusalem.

20:22 Or *by my spirit*, or *by an inner compulsion*; Greek reads *by the spirit*. 20:26 Greek *I am innocent of the blood of all*. 20:28a Or *with the blood of his own [Son]*. 20:28b Or *overseers*, or *bishops*. 21:4 Greek *disciples*; also in 21:16. 21:5 Or *wives*. 21:7 Greek *brothers*; also in 21:17.

20:28 Paul refers to the church as "God's people" and "God's flock" (see also 1 Peter 2:25; 5:2, 4). Elsewhere the church is called the body of Christ (1 Corinthians 12:27; Ephesians 1:23; 4:12; Colossians 1:24); the bride of Christ (2 Corinthians 11:2; Revelation 19:7; see Ephesians 5:25-32); "the temple of God" (1 Corinthians 3:16) or "the temple of the living God" (2 Corinthians 6:16); "a chosen people, . . . royal priests, a holy nation, God's very own possession" (1 Peter 2:9); and "God's field," "God's building" (1 Corinthians 3:9). Paul expected the leaders to feed and shepherd the church "over which the Holy Spirit" had appointed them as leaders (Acts 20:28; see 1 Timothy 3:1-7; Titus 1:5-7; 1 Peter 5:1-4; see also Acts 6:2-4).

21:5 Women and children were typically present in church gatherings. They are mentioned here specifically because it would have been unusual for women and children to escort Paul to his ship. That the entire church saw him off indicates their great love for the apostle and their concern for his safety when he arrived at his destination, Jerusalem.

21:9 Prophecy primarily refers to explaining the will of God, not only telling the future. Philip's daughters would have taught as the Holy Spirit directed them, much as Agabus did (21:10-11). Anna is identified as a prophet (Luke 2:36), as is Miriam (Exodus 15:20), Deborah (Judges 4:4), and Huldah (2 Kings 22:14). Paul spoke of women praying and prophesying in the church (1 Corinthians 11:5).

¹³But he said, "Why all this weeping? You are breaking my heart! I am ready not only to be jailed at Jerusalem but even to die for the sake of the Lord Jesus." ¹⁴When it was clear that we couldn't persuade him, we gave up and said, "The Lord's will be done."

Paul Arrives at Jerusalem

¹⁵After this we packed our things and left for Jerusalem. ¹⁶Some believers from Caesarea accompanied us, and they took us to the home of Mnason, a man originally from Cyprus and one of the early believers. ¹⁷When we arrived, the brothers and sisters in Jerusalem welcomed us warmly.

¹⁸The next day Paul went with us to meet with James, and all the elders of the Jerusalem church were present. ¹⁹After greeting them, Paul gave a detailed account of the things God had accomplished among the Gentiles through his ministry.

²⁰After hearing this, they praised God. And then they said, "You know, dear brother, how many thousands of Jews have also believed, and they all follow the law of Moses very seriously. ²¹But the Jewish believers here in Jerusalem have been told that you are teaching all the Jews who live among the Gentiles to turn their backs on the laws of Moses. They've heard that you teach them not to circumcise their children or follow other Jewish customs. ²²What should we do? They will certainly hear that you have come.

²³"Here's what we want you to do. We have four men here who have completed their vow. ²⁴Go with them to the Temple and join them in the purification ceremony, paying for them to have their heads ritually shaved. Then everyone will know that the rumors are all false and that you yourself observe the Jewish laws.

²⁵"As for the Gentile believers, they should do what we already told them in a letter: They should abstain from eating food offered to idols, from consuming blood or the meat of strangled animals, and from sexual immorality."

Paul Is Arrested

²⁶So Paul went to the Temple the next day with the other men. They had already started the purification ritual, so he publicly announced the date when their vows would end and sacrifices would be offered for each of them.

²⁷The seven days were almost ended when some Jews from the province of Asia saw Paul in the Temple and roused a mob against him. They grabbed him, ²⁸yelling, "Men of Israel, help us! This is the man who preaches against our people everywhere and tells everybody to disobey the Jewish laws. He speaks against the Temple—and even defiles this holy place by bringing in Gentiles.*" ²⁹(For earlier that day they had seen him in the city with Trophimus, a Gentile from Ephesus,* and they assumed Paul had taken him into the Temple.)

³⁰The whole city was rocked by these accusations, and a great riot followed. Paul was grabbed and dragged out of the Temple, and immediately the gates were closed behind him. ³¹As they were trying to kill him, word reached the commander of the Roman regiment that all Jerusalem was in an uproar. ³²He immediately called out his soldiers and officers* and ran down among the crowd. When the mob saw the commander and the troops coming, they stopped beating Paul.

³³Then the commander arrested him and ordered him bound with two chains. He asked the crowd who he was and what he had done. ³⁴Some shouted one thing and some another. Since he couldn't find out the truth in all the uproar and confusion, he ordered that Paul be taken to the fortress. ³⁵As Paul reached the stairs, the mob grew so violent the soldiers had to lift him to their shoulders to protect him. ³⁶And the crowd followed behind, shouting, "Kill him, kill him!"

Paul Speaks to the Crowd

³⁷As Paul was about to be taken inside, he said to the commander, "May I have a word with you?"

"Do you know Greek?" the commander asked, surprised. ³⁸"Aren't you the Egyptian who led a rebellion some time ago and took 4,000 members of the Assassins out into the desert?"

³⁹"No," Paul replied, "I am a Jew and a citizen of Tarsus in Cilicia, which is an important city. Please, let me talk to these people." ⁴⁰The commander agreed, so Paul stood on the stairs and motioned to the people to be quiet. Soon a deep silence enveloped the crowd, and he addressed them in their own language, Aramaic.*

21:28 Greek *Greeks.* 21:29 Greek *Trophimus, the Ephesian.* 21:32 Greek *centurions.* 21:40 Or *Hebrew.*

21:20-25 The Jerusalem church leaders urged Paul to strengthen his credibility by demonstrating that he was not teaching Jews "to turn their backs on the laws of Moses." At the same time, no attempt was made to force Jewish rules on Gentile converts—those terms had been set previously (see 15:22-29) and were simply to be honored.

21:37-40 The commander had mistaken Paul for an Egyptian false messiah who had attempted to seize power from the Romans around AD 54 (roughly three years earlier; see Josephus, *The Wars of the Jews*, book 2, chapter 13, paragraph 5). Under oppressive Roman rule, during the first century and beyond, many false messiahs led uprisings against the empire that ended tragically. Paul corrected the mistake, gained permission to speak to the people, and addressed the crowd in Aramaic, the common language of Judea. He strongly stated his faith in Jesus as the Messiah (22:1-21).

22 "Brothers and esteemed fathers," Paul said, "listen to me as I offer my defense." ²When they heard him speaking in their own language,* the silence was even greater.

³Then Paul said, "I am a Jew, born in Tarsus, a city in Cilicia, and I was brought up and educated here in Jerusalem under Gamaliel. As his student, I was carefully trained in our Jewish laws and customs. I became very zealous to honor God in everything I did, just like all of you today. ⁴And I persecuted the followers of the Way, hounding some to death, arresting both men and women and throwing them in prison. ⁵The high priest and the whole council of elders can testify that this is so. For I received letters from them to our Jewish brothers in Damascus, authorizing me to bring the followers of the Way from there to Jerusalem, in chains, to be punished.

⁶"As I was on the road, approaching Damascus about noon, a very bright light from heaven suddenly shone down around me. ⁷I fell to the ground and heard a voice saying to me, 'Saul, Saul, why are you persecuting me?'

⁸"'Who are you, lord?' I asked.

"And the voice replied, 'I am Jesus the Nazarene,* the one you are persecuting.' ⁹The people with me saw the light but didn't understand the voice speaking to me.

¹⁰"I asked, 'What should I do, Lord?'

"And the Lord told me, 'Get up and go into Damascus, and there you will be told everything you are to do.'

¹¹"I was blinded by the intense light and had to be led by the hand to Damascus by my companions. ¹²A man named Ananias lived there. He was a godly man, deeply devoted to the law, and well regarded by all the Jews of Damascus. ¹³He came and stood beside me and said, 'Brother Saul, regain your sight.' And that very moment I could see him!

¹⁴"Then he told me, 'The God of our ancestors has chosen you to know his will and to see the Righteous One and hear him speak. ¹⁵For you are to be his witness, telling everyone what you have seen and heard. ¹⁶What are you waiting for? Get up and be baptized. Have your sins washed away by calling on the name of the Lord.'

¹⁷"After I returned to Jerusalem, I was praying in the Temple and fell into a trance. ¹⁸I saw a vision of Jesus* saying to me, 'Hurry! Leave Jerusalem, for the people here won't accept your testimony about me.'

¹⁹"'But Lord,' I argued, 'they certainly know that in every synagogue I imprisoned and beat those who believed in you. ²⁰And I was in complete agreement when your witness Stephen was killed. I stood by and kept the coats they took off when they stoned him.'

²¹"But the Lord said to me, 'Go, for I will send you far away to the Gentiles!'"

²²The crowd listened until Paul said that word. Then they all began to shout, "Away with such a fellow! He isn't fit to live!" ²³They yelled, threw off their coats, and tossed handfuls of dust into the air.

Paul Reveals His Roman Citizenship

²⁴The commander brought Paul inside and ordered him lashed with whips to make him confess his crime. He wanted to find out why the crowd had become so furious. ²⁵When they tied Paul down to lash him, Paul said to the officer* standing there, "Is it legal for you to whip a Roman citizen who hasn't even been tried?"

²⁶When the officer heard this, he went to the commander and asked, "What are you doing? This man is a Roman citizen!"

²⁷So the commander went over and asked Paul, "Tell me, are you a Roman citizen?"

"Yes, I certainly am," Paul replied.

²⁸"I am, too," the commander muttered, "and it cost me plenty!"

Paul answered, "But I am a citizen by birth!"

²⁹The soldiers who were about to interrogate Paul quickly withdrew when they heard he was a Roman citizen, and the commander was frightened because he had ordered him bound and whipped.

Paul before the High Council

³⁰The next day the commander ordered the leading priests into session with the Jewish high council.* He wanted to find out what the trouble was all about, so he released Paul to have him stand before them.

22:2 Greek *in Aramaic*, or *in Hebrew*. 22:8 Or *Jesus of Nazareth*. 22:18 Greek *him*. 22:25 Greek *the centurion*; also in 22:26. 22:30 Greek *Sanhedrin*.

22:1-21 Paul gave the premier defense of his life and faith before his own people in Jerusalem, illustrating his flexibility as a missionary, just as his speech to the Greek philosophers in Athens had done (17:22-31; see 1 Corinthians 9:20-23). Paul began by recognizing his kinship with his people, explaining his Jewish background and training under the noted rabbi Gamaliel the Elder, and describing his zealous desire "to honor God in everything," which they shared (Acts 22:1-3). Paul then described his persecution of Christians (22:4-5), the revelation of Jesus to him on the way to Damascus (22:6-10), and his conversion (22:11-16). Paul ended his speech by describing his conversation with the Lord in the Temple. The Lord had predicted the Jews' rejection of the message and was sending Paul to the Gentiles (22:17-21).
22:1 Paul addressed the crowd by honoring the leading men of the group. This typical protocol does not indicate that Paul was uninterested in speaking to the women in the crowd or that there were no women there.
22:23 There is no reason to doubt that women were part of the group that decried Paul's message. They would have been a part of the crowd interested in hearing Paul's message and as protective of traditional Jewish practices as were their male family members and friends.
22:25-29 Just as he was about to be tortured to force a confession, Paul claimed his status as a Roman citizen. Roman citizenship was a valuable asset, and claiming it falsely was a capital offense. Its principal benefits were immunity from scourging and the right to appeal to the emperor (25:11). The commander was frightened at having nearly violated Roman law (see also 16:35-39).

23 Gazing intently at the high council,* Paul began: "Brothers, I have always lived before God with a clear conscience!"

²Instantly Ananias the high priest commanded those close to Paul to slap him on the mouth. ³But Paul said to him, "God will slap you, you corrupt hypocrite!* What kind of judge are you to break the law yourself by ordering me struck like that?"

⁴Those standing near Paul said to him, "Do you dare to insult God's high priest?"

⁵"I'm sorry, brothers. I didn't realize he was the high priest," Paul replied, "for the Scriptures say, 'You must not speak evil of any of your rulers.'*"

⁶Paul realized that some members of the high council were Sadducees and some were Pharisees, so he shouted, "Brothers, I am a Pharisee, as were my ancestors! And I am on trial because my hope is in the resurrection of the dead!"

⁷This divided the council—the Pharisees against the Sadducees—⁸for the Sadducees say there is no resurrection or angels or spirits, but the Pharisees believe in all of these. ⁹So there was a great uproar. Some of the teachers of religious law who were Pharisees jumped up and began to argue forcefully. "We see nothing wrong with him," they shouted. "Perhaps a spirit or an angel spoke to him." ¹⁰As the conflict grew more violent, the commander was afraid they would tear Paul apart. So he ordered his soldiers to go and rescue him by force and take him back to the fortress.

¹¹That night the Lord appeared to Paul and said, "Be encouraged, Paul. Just as you have been a witness to me here in Jerusalem, you must preach the Good News in Rome as well."

The Plan to Kill Paul

¹²The next morning a group of Jews* got together and bound themselves with an oath not to eat or drink until they had killed Paul. ¹³There were more than forty of them in the conspiracy. ¹⁴They went to the leading priests and elders and told them, "We have bound ourselves with an oath to eat nothing until we have killed Paul. ¹⁵So you and the high council should ask the commander to bring Paul back to the council again. Pretend you want to examine his case more fully. We will kill him on the way."

¹⁶But Paul's nephew—his sister's son—heard of their plan and went to the fortress and told Paul. ¹⁷Paul called for one of the Roman officers* and said, "Take this young man to the commander. He has something important to tell him."

¹⁸So the officer did, explaining, "Paul, the prisoner, called me over and asked me to bring this young man to you because he has something to tell you."

¹⁹The commander took his hand, led him aside, and asked, "What is it you want to tell me?"

²⁰Paul's nephew told him, "Some Jews are going to ask you to bring Paul before the high council tomorrow, pretending they want to get some more information. ²¹But don't do it! There are more than forty men hiding along the way ready to ambush him. They have vowed not to eat or drink anything until they have killed him. They are ready now, just waiting for your consent."

²²"Don't let anyone know you told me this," the commander warned the young man.

Paul Is Sent to Caesarea

²³Then the commander called two of his officers and ordered, "Get 200 soldiers ready to leave for Caesarea at nine o'clock tonight. Also take 200 spearmen and 70 mounted troops. ²⁴Provide horses for Paul to ride, and get him safely to Governor Felix." ²⁵Then he wrote this letter to the governor:

²⁶"From Claudius Lysias, to his Excellency, Governor Felix: Greetings!

²⁷"This man was seized by some Jews, and they were about to kill him when I arrived with the troops. When I learned that he was a Roman citizen, I removed him to safety. ²⁸Then I took him to their high council to try to learn the basis of the accusations against him. ²⁹I soon discovered the charge was something regarding their religious law—certainly nothing worthy of imprisonment or death. ³⁰But when I was informed of a plot to kill him, I immediately sent him on to you. I have told his accusers to bring their charges before you."

³¹So that night, as ordered, the soldiers took Paul as far as Antipatris. ³²They returned to the fortress the next morning, while the mounted troops took

---

23:1 Greek *Sanhedrin;* also in 23:6, 15, 20, 28. 23:3 Greek *you whitewashed wall.* 23:5 Exod 22:28. 23:12 Greek *the Jews.* 23:17 Greek *centurions;* also in 23:23.

23:6 Paul focused on the vital issue in his trial, the hope of the resurrection of the dead. His preaching was simply the outworking of that hope and the fact of Jesus' resurrection. Still, the message was unacceptable to both groups of Jews because of its implications. Pharisees could not abide the inclusion of the Gentiles apart from circumcision and keeping the law of Moses (see 15:5), which was what the resurrection of Jesus and the outpouring of the Spirit had provided (2:39; 10:34-48). Sadducees could not stand the proclamation of the resurrection at all (see 4:1-2).
23:8 Women were known to have followed the Pharisaic teachings, based on later rabbinic texts (*Mishnah Sotah* 3:4; *Tosefta Niddah* 5:3). Reasons for choosing the Pharisaic sect might have included the women's concern for ritual purity, especially those who lived in Jerusalem, close to the Temple. Another possible reason is their agreement with specific teachings such as the resurrection of the dead.
23:16-22 Paul had a nephew, his sister's son. His sister may have lived in Jerusalem or sent her son to study there as Paul did in his youth (26:4). Perhaps the nephew or sister were believers, or the nephew may have acted out of familial love for his uncle.

WHAT THE BIBLE SAYS ABOUT

Needing Each Other

Jesus' Good News expands who can be included in God's chosen people from primarily the Jewish people to everyone who follows Jesus as Messiah. This new community is tied together by faith, not heritage. So what does God want us to know about why we need each other?

We Advance God's Good Together

You must live as citizens of heaven, conducting yourselves in a manner worthy of the Good News. Standing together with one spirit and one purpose, fighting together for the faith, which is the Good News. **PHILIPPIANS 1:27**

Let us not neglect our meeting together, as some people do, but encourage one another, especially now. **HEBREWS 10:25**

[Is there] any fellowship together in the Spirit? ... Then make me [Paul] truly happy by agreeing wholeheartedly with each other, loving one another, and working together with one mind and purpose. **PHILIPPIANS 2:1-2**

When you meet together, one will sing, another will teach, another will tell some special revelation God has given, one will speak in tongues, and another will interpret what is said. But everything that is done must strengthen all of you. **1 CORINTHIANS 14:26**

We are in this struggle together

Together We Flourish

[The believers] worshiped together at the Temple each day, met in homes for the Lord's Supper, and shared their meals with great joy and generosity. **ACTS 2:46**

I [Paul] long to see you again, for I remember your tears as we parted. And I will be filled with joy when we are together again. **2 TIMOTHY 1:4**

I [Paul] want them to be encouraged and knit together by strong ties of love. **COLOSSIANS 2:2**

[Christ] makes the whole body fit together perfectly. As each part does its own special work, it helps the other parts grow, so that the whole body is healthy and growing and full of love. **EPHESIANS 4:16**

We are in this struggle together. **PHILIPPIANS 1:30**

When we get together, I [Paul] want to encourage you in your faith, but I also want to be encouraged by yours. **ROMANS 1:12**

Faith Is Not a Solo Act

"For where two or three gather together as my followers, I [Jesus] am there among them." **MATTHEW 18:20**

Jesus would die . . . to bring together and unite all the children of God scattered around the world. **JOHN 11:51-52**

Together, we are his house, built on the foundation of the apostles and the prophets. And the cornerstone is Christ Jesus himself. We are carefully joined together in him, becoming a holy temple for the Lord. **EPHESIANS 2:20-21**

All of you together are Christ's body, and each of you is a part of it. **1 CORINTHIANS 12:27**

him on to Caesarea. ³³When they arrived in Caesarea, they presented Paul and the letter to Governor Felix. ³⁴He read it and then asked Paul what province he was from. "Cilicia," Paul answered.

³⁵"I will hear your case myself when your accusers arrive," the governor told him. Then the governor ordered him kept in the prison at Herod's headquarters.*

Paul Appears before Felix

24 Five days later Ananias, the high priest, arrived with some of the Jewish elders and the lawyer* Tertullus, to present their case against Paul to the governor. ²When Paul was called in, Tertullus presented the charges against Paul in the following address to the governor:

"You have provided a long period of peace for us Jews and with foresight have enacted reforms for us. ³For all of this, Your Excellency, we are very grateful to you. ⁴But I don't want to bore you, so please give me your attention for only a moment. ⁵We have found this man to be a troublemaker who is constantly stirring up riots among the Jews all over the world. He is a ringleader of the cult known as the Nazarenes. ⁶Furthermore, he was trying to desecrate the Temple when we arrested him.* ⁸You can find out the truth of our accusations by examining him yourself." ⁹Then the other Jews chimed in, declaring that everything Tertullus said was true.

¹⁰The governor then motioned for Paul to speak. Paul said, "I know, sir, that you have been a judge of Jewish affairs for many years, so I gladly present my defense before you. ¹¹You can quickly discover that I arrived in Jerusalem no more than twelve days ago to worship at the Temple. ¹²My accusers never found me arguing with anyone in the Temple, nor stirring up a riot in any synagogue or on the streets of the city. ¹³These men cannot prove the things they accuse me of doing. ¹⁴"But I admit that I follow the Way, which they call a cult. I worship the God of our ancestors, and I firmly believe the Jewish law and everything written in the prophets. ¹⁵I have the same hope in God that these men have, that he will raise both the righteous and the unrighteous. ¹⁶Because of this, I always try to maintain a clear conscience before God and all people.

¹⁷"After several years away, I returned to Jerusalem with money to aid my people and to offer sacrifices to God. ¹⁸My accusers saw me in the Temple as I was completing a purification ceremony. There was no crowd around me and no rioting. ¹⁹But some Jews from the province of Asia were there—and they ought to be here to bring charges if they have anything against me! ²⁰Ask these men here what crime the Jewish high council* found me guilty of, ²¹except for the one time I shouted out, 'I am on trial before you today because I believe in the resurrection of the dead!'"

²²At that point Felix, who was quite familiar with the Way, adjourned the hearing and said, "Wait until Lysias, the garrison commander, arrives. Then I will decide the case." ²³He ordered an officer* to keep Paul in custody but to give him some freedom and allow his friends to visit him and take care of his needs.

²⁴A few days later Felix came back with his wife, Drusilla, who was Jewish. Sending for Paul, they listened as he told them about faith in Christ Jesus. ²⁵As he reasoned with them about righteousness and self-control and the coming day of judgment, Felix became frightened. "Go away for now," he replied. "When it is more convenient, I'll call for you again." ²⁶He also hoped that Paul would bribe him, so he sent for him quite often and talked with him.

²⁷After two years went by in this way, Felix was succeeded by Porcius Festus. And because Felix wanted to gain favor with the Jewish people, he left Paul in prison.

23:35 Greek *Herod's Praetorium.* **24:1** Greek *some elders and an orator.* **24:6** Some manuscripts add an expanded conclusion to verse 6, all of verse 7, and an additional phrase in verse 8: *We would have judged him by our law, ⁷but Lysias, the commander of the garrison, came and violently took him away from us, ⁸commanding his accusers to come before you.* **24:20** Greek *Sanhedrin.* **24:23** Greek *a centurion.*

23:35 The governor followed the proper protocol and waited for Paul's accusers to arrive before granting an official hearing. Herod's headquarters was Herod the Great's palace at Caesarea; it subsequently became the residence of the Roman governors of Judea.
24:5 "Troublemaker" (or *agitator*) was a charge of political sedition. A Roman court would have taken this charge very seriously (see 16:21; 17:7; 18:13). Similar accusations came against Jesus before Pilate (Luke 23:2, 5, 14). The term "cult" (or *party*, or *sect*) is used here in a negative sense to put Paul's religion under suspicion or possibly pronounce it illegal (see also Acts 24:14).
24:10-21 Paul's gospel summary addresses the charges leveled against him. He did not bring a Gentile into the Jewish areas of the Temple; he did not start a riot; he faithfully worshiped the God of his people. The real issue at stake was the resurrection of the dead and who participated. Those Pharisees who rejected the gospel argued that only Jews had hope in the resurrection. The Sadducees did not believe in the resurrection of the dead for anyone. Paul believed that any person—male or female, Jew or Gentile, rich or poor—could become a believer through Christ's work on the cross and be resurrected.
24:24 Drusilla was Jewish, the daughter of Agrippa I, and the sister of Bernice and Agrippa II. She was the wife of Felix, the Gentile governor of Roman Palestine. She was known for her beauty (Josephus, *The Antiquities of the Jews*, book 20, chapter 7, paragraph 2). We do not know if Drusilla favored Paul or spoke on his behalf to Felix.
24:27–25:5 Felix's successor was Porcius Festus, appointed by Nero as governor of Judea, about AD 59–62. Josephus describes Festus as a conscientious administrator who took strong action against the party of the Assassins, the group led by the false Egyptian messiah (Josephus, *The Antiquities of the Jews*, book 20, chapter 8, paragraph 10; see Acts 21:38 and the study note on 21:37-40). But Festus could not stem in general the rising tide of Jewish unrest. Although he resisted the Jewish leaders' attempt to move Paul's trial to Jerusalem, he was not immune to their pressure (25:9).

Paul Appears before Festus

25 Three days after Festus arrived in Caesarea to take over his new responsibilities, he left for Jerusalem, ²where the leading priests and other Jewish leaders met with him and made their accusations against Paul. ³They asked Festus as a favor to transfer Paul to Jerusalem (planning to ambush and kill him on the way). ⁴But Festus replied that Paul was at Caesarea and he himself would be returning there soon. ⁵So he said, "Those of you in authority can return with me. If Paul has done anything wrong, you can make your accusations."

⁶About eight or ten days later Festus returned to Caesarea, and on the following day he took his seat in court and ordered that Paul be brought in. ⁷When Paul arrived, the Jewish leaders from Jerusalem gathered around and made many serious accusations they couldn't prove.

⁸Paul denied the charges. "I am not guilty of any crime against the Jewish laws or the Temple or the Roman government," he said.

⁹Then Festus, wanting to please the Jews, asked him, "Are you willing to go to Jerusalem and stand trial before me there?"

¹⁰But Paul replied, "No! This is the official Roman court, so I ought to be tried right here. You know very well I am not guilty of harming the Jews. ¹¹If I have done something worthy of death, I don't refuse to die. But if I am innocent, no one has a right to turn me over to these men to kill me. I appeal to Caesar!"

¹²Festus conferred with his advisers and then replied, "Very well! You have appealed to Caesar, and to Caesar you will go!"

¹³A few days later King Agrippa arrived with his sister, Bernice,* to pay their respects to Festus. ¹⁴During their stay of several days, Festus discussed Paul's case with the king. "There is a prisoner here," he told him, "whose case was left for me by Felix. ¹⁵When I was in Jerusalem, the leading priests and Jewish elders pressed charges against him and asked me to condemn him. ¹⁶I pointed out to them that Roman law does not convict people without a trial. They must be given an opportunity to confront their accusers and defend themselves.

¹⁷"When his accusers came here for the trial, I didn't delay. I called the case the very next day and ordered Paul brought in. ¹⁸But the accusations made against him weren't any of the crimes I expected. ¹⁹Instead, it was something about their religion and a dead man named Jesus, who Paul insists is alive. ²⁰I was at a loss to know how to investigate these things, so I asked him whether he would be willing to stand trial on these charges in Jerusalem. ²¹But Paul appealed to have his case decided by the emperor. So I ordered that he be held in custody until I could arrange to send him to Caesar."

²²"I'd like to hear the man myself," Agrippa said.

And Festus replied, "You will—tomorrow!"

Paul Speaks to Agrippa

²³So the next day Agrippa and Bernice arrived at the auditorium with great pomp, accompanied by military officers and prominent men of the city. Festus ordered that Paul be brought in. ²⁴Then Festus said, "King Agrippa and all who are here, this is the man whose death is demanded by all the Jews, both here and in Jerusalem. ²⁵But in my opinion he has done nothing deserving death. However, since he appealed his case to the emperor, I have decided to send him to Rome. ²⁶But what shall I write the emperor? For there is no clear charge against him. So I have brought him before all of you, and especially you, King Agrippa, so that after we examine him, I might have something to write. ²⁷For it makes no sense to send a prisoner to the emperor without specifying the charges against him!"

26 Then Agrippa said to Paul, "You may speak in your defense."

So Paul, gesturing with his hand, started his defense: ²"I am fortunate, King Agrippa, that you are the one hearing my defense today against all these

---

25:13 Greek *Agrippa the king and Bernice arrived.*

25:12 Festus granted Paul's appeal. This was in accordance with Paul's conviction that he must see Rome (19:21; see also 23:11; 27:24; Romans 1:13-15; 15:22-29).

25:13 Bernice is well known outside the pages of the New Testament. She was the sister of Drusilla and Agrippa II. At about age fifteen, she married a wealthy Jewish man from Alexandria. Widowed shortly after, Bernice married again and had two children, only for her second husband to die when she was twenty-two. She had the title "queen" as she ruled with her brother Agrippa II. Later in her life, she had a lengthy love affair in Rome with Titus, a general who would later become emperor. Few women experience Bernice's elite life, but many women shared her experience of widowhood.

25:23 Agrippa and Bernice arrived with the pomp due to a king and queen on an official royal visit. Rumors insinuated that Agrippa and Bernice had a sexual relationship, but other sources do not confirm this rumor (Josephus, *The Antiquities of the Jews*, book 20, chapter 7, paragraph 3).

26:1-23 In his eloquent defense before King Agrippa, Paul argued that his preaching was completely consistent with the Jewish faith. His defense began with a courteous acknowledgment of Agrippa's competence to hear the evidence (26:2-3), outlined the nature of his background, Jewish training, and membership in the Pharisees (26:4-5), and explained that the charges against him were merely for believing the fulfillment of Jewish hopes for the resurrection (26:6-8). Paul then told how he had once been a strong opponent of Christianity (26:9-11) and the story of his conversion through an encounter with Jesus on the way to Damascus (26:12-18; see 9:1-18). His preaching was nothing more than obeying this divine vision (26:19-20). Even though he encountered violent opposition from his fellow Jews (26:21), God protected him as he preached the Good News, which the Jews should have embraced (26:22-23). This defense is a model for Christians put on trial for their faith (see 9:15; Luke 21:12-15).

accusations made by the Jewish leaders, ³for I know you are an expert on all Jewish customs and controversies. Now please listen to me patiently!

⁴"As the Jewish leaders are well aware, I was given a thorough Jewish training from my earliest childhood among my own people and in Jerusalem. ⁵If they would admit it, they know that I have been a member of the Pharisees, the strictest sect of our religion. ⁶Now I am on trial because of my hope in the fulfillment of God's promise made to our ancestors. ⁷In fact, that is why the twelve tribes of Israel zealously worship God night and day, and they share the same hope I have. Yet, Your Majesty, they accuse me for having this hope! ⁸Why does it seem incredible to any of you that God can raise the dead?

⁹"I used to believe that I ought to do everything I could to oppose the very name of Jesus the Nazarene.* ¹⁰Indeed, I did just that in Jerusalem. Authorized by the leading priests, I caused many believers* there to be sent to prison. And I cast my vote against them when they were condemned to death. ¹¹Many times I had them punished in the synagogues to get them to curse Jesus.* I was so violently opposed to them that I even chased them down in foreign cities.

¹²"One day I was on such a mission to Damascus, armed with the authority and commission of the leading priests. ¹³About noon, Your Majesty, as I was on the road, a light from heaven brighter than the sun shone down on me and my companions. ¹⁴We all fell down, and I heard a voice saying to me in Aramaic,* 'Saul, Saul, why are you persecuting me? It is useless for you to fight against my will.'*

¹⁵"'Who are you, lord?' I asked.

"And the Lord replied, 'I am Jesus, the one you are persecuting. ¹⁶Now get to your feet! For I have appeared to you to appoint you as my servant and witness. Tell people that you have seen me, and tell them what I will show you in the future. ¹⁷And I will rescue you from both your own people and the Gentiles. Yes, I am sending you to the Gentiles ¹⁸to open their eyes, so they may turn from darkness to light and from the power of Satan to God. Then they will receive forgiveness for their sins and be given a place among God's people, who are set apart by faith in me.'

¹⁹"And so, King Agrippa, I obeyed that vision from heaven. ²⁰I preached first to those in Damascus, then in Jerusalem and throughout all Judea, and also to the Gentiles, that all must repent of their sins and turn to God—and prove they have changed by the good things they do. ²¹Some Jews arrested me in the Temple for preaching this, and they tried to kill me. ²²But God has protected me right up to this present time so I can testify to everyone, from the least to the greatest. I teach nothing except what the prophets and Moses said would happen—²³that the Messiah would suffer and be the first to rise from the dead, and in this way announce God's light to Jews and Gentiles alike."

²⁴Suddenly, Festus shouted, "Paul, you are insane. Too much study has made you crazy!"

²⁵But Paul replied, "I am not insane, Most Excellent Festus. What I am saying is the sober truth. ²⁶And King Agrippa knows about these things. I speak boldly, for I am sure these events are all familiar to him, for they were not done in a corner! ²⁷King Agrippa, do you believe the prophets? I know you do—"

²⁸Agrippa interrupted him. "Do you think you can persuade me to become a Christian so quickly?"*

²⁹Paul replied, "Whether quickly or not, I pray to God that both you and everyone here in this audience might become the same as I am, except for these chains."

³⁰Then the king, the governor, Bernice, and all the others stood and left. ³¹As they went out, they talked it over and agreed, "This man hasn't done anything to deserve death or imprisonment."

³²And Agrippa said to Festus, "He could have been set free if he hadn't appealed to Caesar."

Paul Sails for Rome

27 When the time came, we set sail for Italy. Paul and several other prisoners were placed in the custody of a Roman officer* named Julius, a captain of the Imperial Regiment. ²Aristarchus, a Macedonian from Thessalonica, was also with us. We left on a ship whose home port was Adramyttium on

---

26:9 Or *Jesus of Nazareth.* **26:10** Greek *many of God's holy people.* **26:11** Greek *to blaspheme.* **26:14a** Or *Hebrew.* **26:14b** Greek *It is hard for you to kick against the oxgoads.* **26:28** Or *"A little more, and your arguments would make me a Christian."* **27:1** Greek *centurion;* similarly in 27:6, 11, 31, 43.

26:10-11 Paul recounts that before he received his calling to follow Jesus, he pursued believers, both men and women, sending them to prison (8:3; 22:4-5). He punished them to get them to deny Jesus Christ and stop worshiping him. God calls women in every generation to stand fast in their confident faith, for they are saved from sin and rescued for eternal life in Christ.

26:27-28 Paul's question put Agrippa in a bind: If he said he believed the prophets, he knew Paul would press home the Christian message; if not, he would offend the devout Jews in his audience. Agrippa knew that Paul wasn't crazy and that Paul's testimony about Jesus was historically sound (26:26). So Agrippa evaded Paul's question and refused to face the claims of Christ.

26:30-32 Bernice was a part of the discussion of whether to acquit Paul or condemn him. Her role as queen explains her presence in such important conversations. There is no evidence that she accepted the gospel message, though she agreed with the others that Paul did not deserve death or imprisonment.

27:1–28:16 The vivid nautical language used throughout the account of Paul's journey to Rome yields one of the best available accounts of an ancient sea voyage. This is the last "we" section in Acts (see also 16:10-17; 20:5-15; 21:1-18; and the study note on 16:10). During the two years of Paul's imprisonment in Caesarea, Luke had probably done much research for his Gospel throughout Judea and Galilee. Here, as a member of Paul's sailing party, he was an eyewitness participant in the danger at sea.

Insight: PHYSICAL SIGNS OF GOD'S KINGDOM

Christians frequently ask God to heal their physical problems—and they should (see James 5:14-16). But in the days of the early church, healing often played an evangelistic role, getting the attention of unbelievers.

REFERENCE	PERSON(S)	AFFLICTION	FAITH?
Acts 3:1-10	Man Begging at the Beautiful Gate	Congenital paralysis	No
Acts 5:12, 15-16	Crowds of people	Various	No
Acts 6:8	"The people"	Various	No
Acts 8:5-7	Samaritans	Demons, paralysis, etc.	No
Acts 9:17-18	Saul of Tarsus	Sudden blindness	Not yet?
Acts 9:32-35	Aeneas	Paralysis	Yes
Acts 9:36-42	Tabitha (Dorcas)	Unknown, but fatal	Yes
Acts 14:1, 3	People at Iconium	Various	No
Acts 14:8-10	Man at Lystra	Paralysis	No
Acts 16:16-18	Enslaved fortune-telling girl	Demon possession	No
Acts 19:1, 11-12	People at Ephesus	Various, including demons	Unknown
Acts 20:7-12	Eutychus	Death from accident	Yes
Acts 28:3-6	Paul	Snakebite	Yes
Acts 28:7-8	Publius's father	Fever and dysentery	No
Acts 28:9	Other residents of Malta	Various	No
Philippians 2:25-30	Epaphroditus	Unknown, but serious	Yes

the northwest coast of the province of Asia;* it was scheduled to make several stops at ports along the coast of the province.

³The next day when we docked at Sidon, Julius was very kind to Paul and let him go ashore to visit with friends so they could provide for his needs. ⁴Putting out to sea from there, we encountered strong headwinds that made it difficult to keep the ship on course, so we sailed north of Cyprus between the island and the mainland. ⁵Keeping to the open sea, we passed along the coast of Cilicia and Pamphylia, landing at Myra, in the province of Lycia. ⁶There the commanding officer found an Egyptian ship from Alexandria that was bound for Italy, and he put us on board.

⁷We had several days of slow sailing, and after great difficulty we finally neared Cnidus. But the wind was against us, so we sailed across to Crete and along the sheltered coast of the island, past the cape of Salmone. ⁸We struggled along the coast with great difficulty and finally arrived at Fair Havens, near the town of Lasea. ⁹We had lost a lot of time. The weather was becoming dangerous for sea travel because it was so late in the fall,* and Paul spoke to the ship's officers about it.

¹⁰"Men," he said, "I believe there is trouble ahead if we go on—shipwreck, loss of cargo, and danger to our lives as well." ¹¹But the officer in charge of the prisoners listened more to the ship's captain and the owner than to Paul. ¹²And since Fair Havens was an exposed harbor—a poor place to spend the winter—most of the crew wanted to go on to Phoenix, farther up the coast of Crete, and spend the winter there. Phoenix was a good harbor with only a southwest and northwest exposure.

27:2 *Asia* was a Roman province in what is now western Turkey. 27:9 Greek *because the fast was now already gone by.* This fast was associated with the Day of Atonement (*Yom Kippur*), which occurred in late September or early October.

The Storm at Sea

[13] When a light wind began blowing from the south, the sailors thought they could make it. So they pulled up anchor and sailed close to the shore of Crete. [14] But the weather changed abruptly, and a wind of typhoon strength (called a "northeaster") burst across the island and blew us out to sea. [15] The sailors couldn't turn the ship into the wind, so they gave up and let it run before the gale.

[16] We sailed along the sheltered side of a small island named Cauda,* where with great difficulty we hoisted aboard the lifeboat being towed behind us. [17] Then the sailors bound ropes around the hull of the ship to strengthen it. They were afraid of being driven across to the sandbars of Syrtis off the African coast, so they lowered the sea anchor to slow the ship and were driven before the wind.

[18] The next day, as gale-force winds continued to batter the ship, the crew began throwing the cargo overboard. [19] The following day they even took some of the ship's gear and threw it overboard. [20] The terrible storm raged for many days, blotting out the sun and the stars, until at last all hope was gone.

[21] No one had eaten for a long time. Finally, Paul called the crew together and said, "Men, you should have listened to me in the first place and not left Crete. You would have avoided all this damage and loss. [22] But take courage! None of you will lose your lives, even though the ship will go down. [23] For last night an angel of the God to whom I belong and whom I serve stood beside me, [24] and he said, 'Don't be afraid, Paul, for you will surely stand trial before Caesar! What's more, God in his goodness has granted safety to everyone sailing with you.' [25] So take courage! For I believe God. It will be just as he said. [26] But we will be shipwrecked on an island."

The Shipwreck

[27] About midnight on the fourteenth night of the storm, as we were being driven across the Sea of Adria,* the sailors sensed land was near. [28] They dropped a weighted line and found that the water was 120 feet deep. But a little later they measured again and found it was only 90 feet deep.* [29] At this rate they were afraid we would soon be driven against the rocks along the shore, so they threw out four anchors from the back of the ship and prayed for daylight.

[30] Then the sailors tried to abandon the ship; they lowered the lifeboat as though they were going to put out anchors from the front of the ship. [31] But Paul said to the commanding officer and the soldiers, "You will all die unless the sailors stay aboard." [32] So the soldiers cut the ropes to the lifeboat and let it drift away.

[33] Just as day was dawning, Paul urged everyone to eat. "You have been so worried that you haven't touched food for two weeks," he said. [34] "Please eat something now for your own good. For not a hair of your heads will perish." [35] Then he took some bread, gave thanks to God before them all, and broke off a piece and ate it. [36] Then everyone was encouraged and began to eat—[37] all 276 of us who were on board. [38] After eating, the crew lightened the ship further by throwing the cargo of wheat overboard.

[39] When morning dawned, they didn't recognize the coastline, but they saw a bay with a beach and wondered if they could get to shore by running the ship aground. [40] So they cut off the anchors and left them in the sea. Then they lowered the rudders, raised the foresail, and headed toward shore. [41] But they hit a shoal and ran the ship aground too soon. The bow of the ship stuck fast, while the stern was repeatedly smashed by the force of the waves and began to break apart.

[42] The soldiers wanted to kill the prisoners to make sure they didn't swim ashore and escape. [43] But the commanding officer wanted to spare Paul, so he didn't let them carry out their plan. Then he ordered all who could swim to jump overboard first and make for land. [44] The others held on to planks or debris from the broken ship.* So everyone escaped safely to shore.

Paul on the Island of Malta

28 Once we were safe on shore, we learned that we were on the island of Malta. [2] The people of the island were very kind to us. It was cold and rainy, so they built a fire on the shore to welcome us.

[3] As Paul gathered an armful of sticks and was laying them on the fire, a poisonous snake, driven out by the heat, bit him on the hand. [4] The people of the island saw it hanging from his hand and said to each other, "A murderer, no doubt! Though he escaped the sea, justice will not permit him to live." [5] But Paul shook off the snake into the fire and was unharmed. [6] The people waited for him to swell up or suddenly drop dead. But when they had waited a long time

---

27:16 Some manuscripts read *Clauda*. **27:27** The *Sea of Adria* includes the central portion of the Mediterranean. **27:28** Greek *20 fathoms... 15 fathoms* [37 meters...27 meters]. **27:44** Or *or were helped by members of the ship's crew*.

27:33-35 Paul's words and actions were those of a true leader who personally assessed a dangerous situation, decided on an action, and led others in solving the problem (compare Nehemiah 1–3; contrast Jonah 1). Paul's positive example and strong faith in God (Acts 27:22-25) encouraged the others to eat and take heart.
27:36-37 Female passengers may have been among the 276 people on the grain ship. Women traveled around the Roman Empire for business, to visit family, and for religious pilgrimages. There were no female soldiers and probably no female sailors, given the taxing physical labor involved.
27:42-44 Even in a crisis, the prisoners remained the soldiers' responsibility (see 12:19; 16:27; 27:42). Fortunately, the commanding officer intervened on their behalf. It was a clear indication of God's protection and favor that all 276 people made it safely to shore, precisely fulfilling the angel's promise (see 27:24).

and saw that he wasn't harmed, they changed their minds and decided he was a god.

⁷Near the shore where we landed was an estate belonging to Publius, the chief official of the island. He welcomed us and treated us kindly for three days. ⁸As it happened, Publius's father was ill with fever and dysentery. Paul went in and prayed for him, and laying his hands on him, he healed him. ⁹Then all the other sick people on the island came and were healed. ¹⁰As a result we were showered with honors, and when the time came to sail, people supplied us with everything we would need for the trip.

Paul Arrives at Rome

¹¹It was three months after the shipwreck that we set sail on another ship that had wintered at the island—an Alexandrian ship with the twin gods* as its figurehead. ¹²Our first stop was Syracuse,* where we stayed three days. ¹³From there we sailed across to Rhegium.* A day later a south wind began blowing, so the following day we sailed up the coast to Puteoli. ¹⁴There we found some believers,* who invited us to spend a week with them. And so we came to Rome. ¹⁵The brothers and sisters* in Rome had heard we were coming, and they came to meet us at the Forum* on the Appian Way. Others joined us at The Three Taverns.* When Paul saw them, he was encouraged and thanked God.

¹⁶When we arrived in Rome, Paul was permitted to have his own private lodging, though he was guarded by a soldier.

Paul Preaches at Rome under Guard

¹⁷Three days after Paul's arrival, he called together the local Jewish leaders. He said to them, "Brothers, I was arrested in Jerusalem and handed over to the Roman government, even though I had done nothing against our people or the customs of our ancestors. ¹⁸The Romans tried me and wanted to release me, because they found no cause for the death sentence. ¹⁹But when the Jewish leaders protested the decision, I felt it necessary to appeal to Caesar, even though I had no desire to press charges against my own people. ²⁰I asked you to come here today so we could get acquainted and so I could explain to you that I am bound with this chain because I believe that the hope of Israel—the Messiah—has already come."

²¹They replied, "We have had no letters from Judea or reports against you from anyone who has come here. ²²But we want to hear what you believe, for the only thing we know about this movement is that it is denounced everywhere."

²³So a time was set, and on that day a large number of people came to Paul's lodging. He explained and testified about the Kingdom of God and tried to persuade them about Jesus from the Scriptures. Using the law of Moses and the books of the prophets, he spoke to them from morning until evening. ²⁴Some were persuaded by the things he said, but others did not believe. ²⁵And after they had argued back and forth among themselves, they left with this final word from Paul: "The Holy Spirit was right when he said to your ancestors through Isaiah the prophet,

²⁶ 'Go and say to this people:
When you hear what I say,
  you will not understand.
When you see what I do,
  you will not comprehend.
²⁷ For the hearts of these people are hardened,
  and their ears cannot hear,
  and they have closed their eyes—
so their eyes cannot see,
  and their ears cannot hear,
  and their hearts cannot understand,
and they cannot turn to me
  and let me heal them.'*

²⁸So I want you to know that this salvation from God has also been offered to the Gentiles, and they will accept it."*

³⁰For the next two years, Paul lived in Rome at his own expense.* He welcomed all who visited him, ³¹boldly proclaiming the Kingdom of God and teaching about the Lord Jesus Christ. And no one tried to stop him.

28:11 The *twin gods* were the Roman gods Castor and Pollux. **28:12** *Syracuse* was on the island of Sicily. **28:13** *Rhegium* was on the southern tip of Italy. **28:14** Greek *brothers.* **28:15a** Greek *brothers.* **28:15b** *The Forum* was about 43 miles (70 kilometers) from Rome. **28:15c** *The Three Taverns* was about 35 miles (57 kilometers) from Rome. **28:26-27** Isa 6:9-10 (Greek version). **28:28** Some manuscripts add verse 29, *And when he had said these words, the Jews departed, greatly disagreeing with each other.* **28:30** Or *in his own rented quarters.*

28:9 After the father of the island's chief official was healed (28:7-8), people brought others who were sick. In this number were certainly girls and women. The Gospels and Acts provide numerous examples of women being healed and raised from the dead (for example, 9:36-41; see also Luke 8:40-56; 13:10-13). This tangible expression of God's love and power is experienced today in God's churches around the globe.

28:14-15 News of Paul's arrival went before him, and believing women and men welcomed him warmly. Hospitality was held in high regard, for travelers were often in need, and food was not always in plentiful supply. Sharing one's goods was a significant gesture of kindness, one which the Bible praises (Psalm 112:5; Proverbs 11:24-25; Acts 20:35; Hebrews 13:16). Giving to those who might not be able to repay you is seen as giving to God, for God will reward such generosity (2 Corinthians 9:6-15).

Romans

WHAT DO WE LEARN ABOUT GOD'S MISSION AND OURS?
All of us fall short, but God brings us to victory.

WHO WROTE IT? Paul, the leader (apostle) sent to the Gentile people.

WHEN DID IT HAPPEN? Paul wrote this letter in AD 57 while he was staying in Corinth, likely toward the end of his third missionary journey, when he visited Christians throughout Asia Minor (modern-day Turkey) and Greece.

HOW IS IT ORGANIZED?

- **1–3:** All have sinned and fallen short of God's holiness
- **4–5:** God's grace, which we receive by faith and trust in Jesus, makes us right with him
- **6–8:** God's Spirit enables us to live a new life in Jesus
- **9–11:** Insights for community life
- **12–15:** Lessons for practical, faithful living
- **16:** Paul commends Phoebe and greets other Roman believers, including many women: Priscilla, Junia, Mary, Tryphena, Tryphosa, Persis, Rufus's mother, Julia, and Nereus's sister

Words to Remember are highlighted throughout this book

HOW LONG DOES IT TAKE TO READ?

1:00						
:30	1:00	1:30	2:00	2:30	3:00	3:30

Timeline

AD	
30	JESUS DIES, RISES FROM THE DEAD, ASCENDS TO REIGN IN HEAVEN, SENDS THE HOLY SPIRIT
35	JESUS CALLS PAUL TO PREACH THE GOOD NEWS
46–48	PAUL GOES ON FIRST MISSIONARY JOURNEY
50	JERUSALEM COUNCIL CONFIRMS GENTILE INCLUSION IN THE CHURCH
50–52	PAUL EMBARKS ON SECOND MISSIONARY JOURNEY, WITH SILAS; THEY SPEND 18 MONTHS IN CORINTH
50	PAUL MEETS PRISCILLA AND AQUILA IN CORINTH
	PAUL MEETS LYDIA IN PHILIPPI
53–57	PAUL TAKES A THIRD MISSIONARY JOURNEY
57	PAUL WRITES THE LETTER TO THE ROMANS FROM CORINTH AND SENDS IT WITH PHOEBE
57–59	PAUL IMPRISONED IN CAESAREA, WHERE HE IS QUESTIONED BY FESTUS, FELIX AND DRUSILLA, AND AGRIPPA AND BERNICE
60–62	PAUL LIVES UNDER HOUSE ARREST IN ROME
64	PAUL MARTYRED IN ROME
70	ROME DESTROYS JERUSALEM

Greetings from Paul

1 This letter is from Paul, a slave of Christ Jesus, chosen by God to be an apostle and sent out to preach his Good News. ²God promised this Good News long ago through his prophets in the holy Scriptures. ³The Good News is about his Son. In his earthly life he was born into King David's family line, ⁴and he was shown to be* the Son of God when he was raised from the dead by the power of the Holy Spirit.* He is Jesus Christ our Lord. ⁵Through Christ, God has given us the privilege* and authority as apostles to tell Gentiles everywhere what God has done for them, so that they will believe and obey him, bringing glory to his name.

⁶And you are included among those Gentiles who have been called to belong to Jesus Christ. ⁷I am writing to all of you in Rome who are loved by God and are called to be his own holy people.

May God our Father and the Lord Jesus Christ give you grace and peace.

God's Good News

⁸Let me say first that I thank my God through Jesus Christ for all of you, because your faith in him is being talked about all over the world. ⁹God knows how often I pray for you. Day and night I bring you and your needs in prayer to God, whom I serve with all my heart* by spreading the Good News about his Son.

¹⁰One of the things I always pray for is the opportunity, God willing, to come at last to see you. ¹¹For I long to visit you so I can bring you some spiritual gift that will help you grow strong in the Lord. ¹²When we get together, I want to encourage you in your faith, but I also want to be encouraged by yours.

¹³I want you to know, dear brothers and sisters,* that I planned many times to visit you, but I was prevented until now. I want to work among you and see spiritual fruit, just as I have seen among other Gentiles. ¹⁴For I have a great sense of obligation to people in both the civilized world and the rest of the world,* to the educated and uneducated alike. ¹⁵So I am eager to come to you in Rome, too, to preach the Good News.

¹⁶For I am not ashamed of this Good News about Christ. It is the power of God at work, saving everyone who believes—the Jew first and also the Gentile.* ¹⁷This Good News tells us how God makes us right in his sight. This is accomplished from start to finish by faith. As the Scriptures say, "It is through faith that a righteous person has life."*

God's Anger at Sin

¹⁸But God shows his anger from heaven against all sinful, wicked people who suppress the truth by their wickedness.* ¹⁹They know the truth about God because he has made it obvious to them. ²⁰For ever since the world was created, people have seen the earth and sky. Through everything God made, they can clearly see his invisible qualities—his eternal power and divine nature. So they have no excuse for not knowing God.

²¹Yes, they knew God, but they wouldn't worship him as God or even give him thanks. And they began to think up foolish ideas of what God was like. As a result, their minds became dark and confused. ²²Claiming to be wise, they instead became utter fools. ²³And instead of worshiping the glorious, ever-living God, they worshiped idols made to look like mere people and birds and animals and reptiles.

²⁴So God abandoned them to do whatever shameful things their hearts desired. As a result, they did

---

1:4a Or *and was designated.* **1:4b** Or *by the Spirit of holiness; or in the new realm of the Spirit.* **1:5** Or *the grace.* **1:9** Or *in my spirit.* **1:13** Greek *brothers.* **1:14** Greek *to Greeks and barbarians.* **1:16** Greek *also the Greek.* **1:17** Or *"The righteous will live by faith."* Hab 2:4. **1:18** Or *who, by their wickedness, prevent the truth from being known.*

1:13 The Greek word translated "brothers and sisters" describes people who are in a sibling relationship. Paul and other New Testament writers use this word to indicate that Christians are so intimately tied to one another in Christ that they are family. The word refers to both male and female Christians, so it is translated here and elsewhere as "brothers and sisters."

1:1-13 Paul wrote this letter to the house churches in Rome when he was in Corinth toward the end of his third missionary journey (see Acts 20:2-4; see also Romans 16:21-23). The need to plant and nourish churches in the eastern Mediterranean had occupied Paul up to this point. Before he could visit the Roman Christians, he first needed to return to Jerusalem to deliver a gift of money collected from the Gentile churches for the impoverished Jewish Christians who were suffering famines in Judea and persecution for their faith in Christ (15:23-29).

1:17 The key idea, "how God makes us right in his sight," appears in various iterations eight times in Romans (see also 3:5, 21, 22, 25, 26, 28; 10:3; the only other occurrence in Paul's writings is 2 Corinthians 5:21). The expression has Old Testament roots, where God's righteousness refers to his character (as holy or faithful) or to an act of declaring his people sinless and perfect in his eyes (see especially Isaiah 46:13; 51:5-8). Paul uses the second meaning in this verse. The Good News has the power to save because it is the fulfillment of God's promise to vindicate his people. The phrase "makes us right" comes from a court setting. It does not mean "makes us good people"; it means "puts us in right standing before God." At the end of this verse, Paul refers to the prophet Habakkuk ("The righteous will live by their faithfulness to God," Habakkuk 2:4). Habakkuk had struggled to understand how God could use pagan nations to judge his own people, Israel. God reminded Habakkuk that his true people—the righteous—need to live by faith. In Romans 1–4, Paul repeatedly insists that only through faith can human beings be made right in God's sight.

1:24-27 Paul makes clear that God allowed humanity's own sins to continue, with the consequence that idolatry grew. Paul condemned same-sex sexual activity as being outside of God's created order where men and women reflect his image (Genesis 1:27). Jewish writing at this time strongly spoke out against the common Greek and Roman practice of homosexuality, which typically manifested itself among men, and frequently involved teenage boys (now recognized as pederasty).

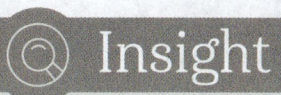

Insight: LETTERS FOR THE CHURCH

Letters were a valuable method for early church leaders to teach and disciple Christians. While New Testament letters were addressed to Christians in a certain city or region, and sometimes individuals, they circulated throughout early church communities, not just their first recipients.

New Testament letters are much longer and more complex than the average letters written at the time, and they were carefully and expensively crafted. In US currency today, Paul's letter to the Romans would have likely cost nearly $3,000 to write and send with Phoebe. Since the Roman postal system was only for government use and required a permit, civilians would send letters with trusted friends, colleagues, or traders, or they might send an enslaved person to deliver them.

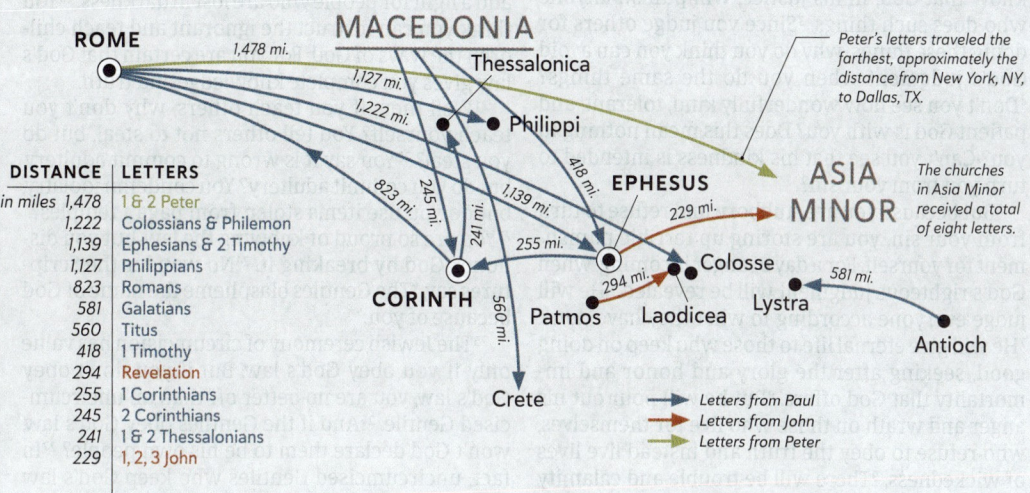

vile and degrading things with each other's bodies. 25They traded the truth about God for a lie. So they worshiped and served the things God created instead of the Creator himself, who is worthy of eternal praise! Amen. 26That is why God abandoned them to their shameful desires. Even the women turned against the natural way to have sex and instead indulged in sex with each other. 27And the men, instead of having normal sexual relations with women, burned with lust for each other. Men did shameful things with other men, and as a result of this sin, they suffered within themselves the penalty they deserved.

28Since they thought it foolish to acknowledge God, he abandoned them to their foolish thinking and let them do things that should never be done.

29Their lives became full of every kind of wickedness, sin, greed, hate, envy, murder, quarreling, deception, malicious behavior, and gossip. 30They are backstabbers, haters of God, insolent, proud, and boastful. They invent new ways of sinning, and they disobey their parents. 31They refuse to understand, break their promises, are heartless, and have no mercy. 32They know God's justice requires that those who do these things deserve to die, yet they do them anyway. Worse yet, they encourage others to do them, too.

God's Judgment of Sin

2 You may think you can condemn such people, but you are just as bad, and you have no excuse! When you say they are wicked and should be punished, you are condemning yourself, for you who

2:1-5 The "you" being addressed in these verses could refer to Gentiles who do not indulge their passions and vices but were moral and decent people. "You" could also refer to the implied Jewish audience explicitly mentioned in 2:17. In either case, Paul warns every reader of their own hypocrisy, failing to acknowledge the "log" in their own eye, while trying to remove the "speck" in their friend's eye (Matthew 7:5). Paul uses the rhetorical method of *diatribe*—asking questions to an imaginary opponent and providing answers—that structures his argument throughout this letter.

> "Faith is not faith which is not tried."
>
> KATHARINA ZELL
> (1497/8–1562) church reformer, theologian, and writer

judge others do these very same things. ²And we know that God, in his justice, will punish anyone who does such things. ³Since you judge others for doing these things, why do you think you can avoid God's judgment when you do the same things? ⁴Don't you see how wonderfully kind, tolerant, and patient God is with you? Does this mean nothing to you? Can't you see that his kindness is intended to turn you from your sin?

⁵But because you are stubborn and refuse to turn from your sin, you are storing up terrible punishment for yourself. For a day of anger is coming, when God's righteous judgment will be revealed. ⁶He will judge everyone according to what they have done. ⁷He will give eternal life to those who keep on doing good, seeking after the glory and honor and immortality that God offers. ⁸But he will pour out his anger and wrath on those who live for themselves, who refuse to obey the truth and instead live lives of wickedness. ⁹There will be trouble and calamity for everyone who keeps on doing what is evil—for the Jew first and also for the Gentile.* ¹⁰But there will be glory and honor and peace from God for all who do good—for the Jew first and also for the Gentile. ¹¹For God does not show favoritism.

¹²When the Gentiles sin, they will be destroyed, even though they never had God's written law. And the Jews, who do have God's law, will be judged by that law when they fail to obey it. ¹³For merely listening to the law doesn't make us right with God. It is obeying the law that makes us right in his sight. ¹⁴Even Gentiles, who do not have God's written law, show that they know his law when they instinctively obey it, even without having heard it. ¹⁵They demonstrate that God's law is written in their hearts, for their own conscience and thoughts either accuse them or tell them they are doing right. ¹⁶And this is the message I proclaim—that the day is coming when God, through Christ Jesus, will judge everyone's secret life.

The Jews and the Law

¹⁷You who call yourselves Jews are relying on God's law, and you boast about your special relationship with him. ¹⁸You know what he wants; you know what is right because you have been taught his law. ¹⁹You are convinced that you are a guide for the blind and a light for people who are lost in darkness. ²⁰You think you can instruct the ignorant and teach children the ways of God. For you are certain that God's law gives you complete knowledge and truth.

²¹Well then, if you teach others, why don't you teach yourself? You tell others not to steal, but do you steal? ²²You say it is wrong to commit adultery, but do you commit adultery? You condemn idolatry, but do you use items stolen from pagan temples?* ²³You are so proud of knowing the law, but you dishonor God by breaking it. ²⁴No wonder the Scriptures say, "The Gentiles blaspheme the name of God because of you."*

²⁵The Jewish ceremony of circumcision has value only if you obey God's law. But if you don't obey God's law, you are no better off than an uncircumcised Gentile. ²⁶And if the Gentiles obey God's law, won't God declare them to be his own people? ²⁷In fact, uncircumcised Gentiles who keep God's law will condemn you Jews who are circumcised and possess God's law but don't obey it.

²⁸For you are not a true Jew just because you were born of Jewish parents or because you have gone through the ceremony of circumcision. ²⁹No, a true Jew is one whose heart is right with God. And true circumcision is not merely obeying the letter of the law; rather, it is a change of heart produced by the Spirit. And a person with a changed heart seeks praise* from God, not from people.

2:9 Greek *also for the Greek;* also in 2:10.   **2:22** Greek *do you steal from temples?*   **2:24** Isa 52:5 (Greek version).   **2:29** Or *receives praise.*

2:7 Paul makes it clear elsewhere that no one can receive eternal life except as God's gift through faith (3:20, 28; 4:1-8). Here, Paul is either referring to Christians whose good deeds that result from faith will be taken into account in God's judgment; or he is reminding readers of the absolute standard that God's own holiness establishes, since only by perfection can sinners hope to find acceptance before God. As the argument of the letter unfolds, Paul will show that no one is capable of meeting that standard.

2:25 God instituted "the Jewish ceremony of circumcision" as a sign of his covenant with Abraham; it was to be performed on every male Israelite child (Genesis 17:9-13; see Romans 4:11). To the Jewish people, male circumcision therefore still represents God's covenant (special agreement and relationship) with his people Israel. The rite took on greater significance during the time period between the Old and New Testaments when the foreign king Antiochus IV Epiphanes tried to stamp out the Jewish faith by forbidding circumcision. The Jews resisted in the famous Maccabean Revolt (166–160 BC), from which the festival of Hanukkah emerged. After they restored the worship of the Lord in Israel, the Jews regarded circumcision as a highly prized mark of Jewish loyalty while living amid a pagan culture.

God Remains Faithful

3 Then what's the advantage of being a Jew? Is there any value in the ceremony of circumcision? ²Yes, there are great benefits! First of all, the Jews were entrusted with the whole revelation of God.*

³True, some of them were unfaithful; but just because they were unfaithful, does that mean God will be unfaithful? ⁴Of course not! Even if everyone else is a liar, God is true. As the Scriptures say about him,

"You will be proved right in what you say,
 and you will win your case in court."*

⁵"But," some might say, "our sinfulness serves a good purpose, for it helps people see how righteous God is. Isn't it unfair, then, for him to punish us?" (This is merely a human point of view.) ⁶Of course not! If God were not entirely fair, how would he be qualified to judge the world? ⁷"But," someone might still argue, "how can God condemn me as a sinner if my dishonesty highlights his truthfulness and brings him more glory?" ⁸And some people even slander us by claiming that we say, "The more we sin, the better it is!" Those who say such things deserve to be condemned.

All People Are Sinners

⁹Well then, should we conclude that we Jews are better than others? No, not at all, for we have already shown that all people, whether Jews or Gentiles,* are under the power of sin. ¹⁰As the Scriptures say,

"No one is righteous—
 not even one.
¹¹ No one is truly wise;
 no one is seeking God.
¹² All have turned away;
 all have become useless.
No one does good,
 not a single one."*
¹³ "Their talk is foul, like the stench from an open grave.
 Their tongues are filled with lies."
"Snake venom drips from their lips."*
¹⁴ "Their mouths are full of cursing and bitterness."*
¹⁵ "They rush to commit murder.
¹⁶ Destruction and misery always follow them.
¹⁷ They don't know where to find peace."*
¹⁸ "They have no fear of God at all."*

¹⁹Obviously, the law applies to those to whom it was given, for its purpose is to keep people from having excuses, and to show that the entire world is guilty before God. ²⁰For no one can ever be made right with God by doing what the law commands. The law simply shows us how sinful we are.

Christ Took Our Punishment

²¹But now God has shown us a way to be made right with him without keeping the requirements of the law, as was promised in the writings of Moses* and the prophets long ago. ²²We are made right with God by placing our faith in Jesus Christ. And this is true for everyone who believes, no matter who we are.

²³For everyone has sinned; we all fall short of God's glorious standard. ²⁴Yet God, in his grace, freely makes us right in his sight. He did this through Christ Jesus when he freed us from the penalty for our sins. ²⁵For God presented Jesus as the sacrifice for sin. People are made right with God when they believe that Jesus sacrificed his life, shedding his blood. This sacrifice shows that God was being fair when he held back and did not punish those who sinned in times past, ²⁶for he was looking ahead and including them in what he would do in this present time. God did this to demonstrate his righteousness, for he himself is fair and just, and he makes sinners right in his sight when they believe in Jesus.

²⁷Can we boast, then, that we have done anything to be accepted by God? No, because our acquittal is not based on obeying the law. It is based on faith. ²⁸So we are made right with God through faith and not by obeying the law.

²⁹After all, is God the God of the Jews only? Isn't he also the God of the Gentiles? Of course he is. ³⁰There is only one God, and he makes people right with himself only by faith, whether they are Jews or Gentiles.* ³¹Well then, if we emphasize faith, does this mean that we can forget about the law? Of course not! In fact, only when we have faith do we truly fulfill the law.

3:2 Greek *the oracles of God*. 3:4 Ps 51:4 (Greek version). 3:9 Greek *or Greeks*. 3:10-12 Pss 14:1-3; 53:1-3 (Greek version). 3:13 Pss 5:9 (Greek version); 140:3. 3:14 Ps 10:7 (Greek version). 3:15-17 Isa 59:7-8. 3:18 Ps 36:1. 3:21 Greek *in the law*. 3:30 Greek *whether they are circumcised or uncircumcised*.

3:1 Paul moves his argument along by raising questions. After preaching the Good News for over twenty years, he knew what questions people would ask when they heard a particular teaching. His emphasis on the equality of Jews and Gentiles before God (2:1-29) would inevitably lead people to ask whether he was eliminating all Jewish privileges. The question-and-answer style follows the pattern of the diatribe (see note on 2:1-5). **3:24** God "makes us right in his sight," not because he has to, but because he has freely chosen to give us his favor through Christ Jesus. Because we are helplessly enslaved to sin (3:9), our righteous status before God can never be earned (see 4:4-5). In Paul's day, *redemption* referred to the price paid to free an enslaved person. God paid our redemption price with the blood of his own Son to rescue us from our slavery to sin (see 3:9). This language was used in the Old Testament to refer to the Exodus, the first redemption of God's people from bondage (see 2 Samuel 7:23). God promised that he would again redeem his people (Isaiah 25:6-9; Micah 4:10).

Overwhelming victory is ours through Christ, who loved us.

ROMANS 8:37

The Faith of Abraham

4 Abraham was, humanly speaking, the founder of our Jewish nation. What did he discover about being made right with God? ²If his good deeds had made him acceptable to God, he would have had something to boast about. But that was not God's way. ³For the Scriptures tell us, "Abraham believed God, and God counted him as righteous because of his faith."*

⁴When people work, their wages are not a gift, but something they have earned. ⁵But people are counted as righteous, not because of their work, but because of their faith in God who forgives sinners. ⁶David also spoke of this when he described the happiness of those who are declared righteous without working for it:

⁷ "Oh, what joy for those
  whose disobedience is forgiven,
  whose sins are put out of sight.
⁸ Yes, what joy for those
  whose record the Lord has cleared of sin."*

⁹Now, is this blessing only for the Jews, or is it also for uncircumcised Gentiles?* Well, we have been saying that Abraham was counted as righteous by God because of his faith. ¹⁰But how did this happen? Was he counted as righteous only after he was circumcised, or was it before he was circumcised? Clearly, God accepted Abraham before he was circumcised!

¹¹Circumcision was a sign that Abraham already had faith and that God had already accepted him and declared him to be righteous—even before he was circumcised. So Abraham is the spiritual father of those who have faith but have not been circumcised. They are counted as righteous because of their faith. ¹²And Abraham is also the spiritual father of those who have been circumcised, but only if they have the same kind of faith Abraham had before he was circumcised.

¹³Clearly, God's promise to give the whole earth to Abraham and his descendants was based not on his obedience to God's law, but on a right relationship with God that comes by faith. ¹⁴If God's promise is only for those who obey the law, then faith is not necessary and the promise is pointless. ¹⁵For the law always brings punishment on those who try to obey it. (The only way to avoid breaking the law is to have no law to break!)

¹⁶So the promise is received by faith. It is given as a free gift. And we are all certain to receive it, whether or not we live according to the law of Moses, if we have faith like Abraham's. For Abraham is the father of all who believe. ¹⁷That is what the Scriptures mean when God told him, "I have made you the father of many nations."* This happened because Abraham believed in the God who brings the dead back to life and who creates new things out of nothing.

¹⁸Even when there was no reason for hope, Abraham kept hoping—believing that he would become the father of many nations. For God had said to him, "That's how many descendants you will have!"* ¹⁹And Abraham's faith did not weaken, even though, at about 100 years of age, he figured his body was as good as dead—and so was Sarah's womb. ²⁰Abraham never wavered in believing God's promise. In fact, his faith grew stronger, and in this he brought glory to God. ²¹He was fully convinced that God is able to do whatever he promises. ²²And because of Abraham's faith, God counted him as righteous. ²³And when God counted him as righteous, it wasn't just for Abraham's benefit. It was recorded ²⁴for our benefit, too, assuring us that God will also count us as righteous if we believe in him, the one who raised Jesus our Lord from the dead. ²⁵He was handed over to die because of our sins, and he was raised to life to make us right with God.

Faith Brings Joy

5 Therefore, since we have been made right in God's sight by faith, we have peace* with God because of what Jesus Christ our Lord has done for us. ²Because of our faith, Christ has brought us into this place of undeserved privilege where we now stand, and we confidently and joyfully look forward to sharing God's glory.

³We can rejoice, too, when we run into problems and trials, for we know that they help us develop endurance. ⁴And endurance develops strength of character, and character strengthens our confident hope of salvation. ⁵And this hope will not lead to disappointment. For we know how dearly God loves us, because he has given us the Holy Spirit to fill our hearts with his love.

⁶When we were utterly helpless, Christ came at just the right time and died for us sinners. ⁷Now, most people would not be willing to die for an upright

---

4:3 Gen 15:6.   **4:7-8** Ps 32:1-2 (Greek version).   **4:9** Greek *is this blessing only for the circumcised, or is it also for the uncircumcised?*   **4:17** Gen 17:5.   **4:18** Gen 15:5.   **5:1** Some manuscripts read *let us have peace.*

4:23-24 Abraham experienced the life-giving power of God in the birth of his son, Isaac. Christians witness it in the resurrection of Jesus. Throughout history, salvation has been available only through faith in God, who makes and keeps his promises.

5:2 God's grace (Greek *charis*) is the essential foundation of our faith, such that Paul can use this word to sum up our present situation as believers. "Where we now stand" indicates that God's grace is needed throughout the Christian life, not just at the beginning. "Sharing God's glory" describes the content of Christian hope, which Paul introduces here and expounds more fully in 8:18-30. Behind Paul's use of the word "glory" (Greek *doxa*) is the Hebrew word *kabod*, which depicts God's majesty and overwhelming presence. The prophets predicted a day when God's glory would return to dwell among his people (see, for example, Isaiah 60:1-2).

person, though someone might perhaps be willing to die for a person who is especially good. ⁸But God showed his great love for us by sending Christ to die for us while we were still sinners. ⁹And since we have been made right in God's sight by the blood of Christ, he will certainly save us from God's condemnation. ¹⁰For since our friendship with God was restored by the death of his Son while we were still his enemies, we will certainly be saved through the life of his Son. ¹¹So now we can rejoice in our wonderful new relationship with God because our Lord Jesus Christ has made us friends of God.

Adam and Christ Contrasted

¹²When Adam sinned, sin entered the world. Adam's sin brought death, so death spread to everyone, for everyone sinned. ¹³Yes, people sinned even before the law was given. But it was not counted as sin because

5:12 The Hebrew word *Adam* is both the word that means "human" and the name of the original man, Adam. Paul's use of this term here emphasizes the solidarity of Adam with the human race; Paul isn't neglecting to recognize Eve in his understanding of humanity but is using Adam as a type of literary foil for Jesus Christ. The significance that Paul ascribes to sin entering the world, and the parallel that he draws between Adam's sin and Christ's act of obedience on the cross make clear that Paul views Adam and his sin in the Garden of Eden as historical fact. Death and separation from God are universal because sin is universal. Paul's purpose here is not to explain when or how everyone sinned; he is simply attributing the condemnation of all people to the sin of Adam, their representative (5:18). Jewish tradition is divided on the relationship between Adam's sin and the sin and death of human beings generally. Some texts emphasize a solidarity between Adam and all other people, as in "when Adam sinned and death was decreed against those who were to be born" (*2 Baruch* 23:4). Other texts insist that people die because of their own sin: "Adam is, therefore, not the cause, except only for himself, but each of us has become our own Adam" (*2 Baruch* 54:19).

Come Close — FAILURE: GOD IS NOT MAD AT US

SCRIPTURE CONNECTION: ROMANS 5:1-11

I *know* the white-hot terror of failure. I know the high walls of the pit of defeat.

I thought God was rolling his eyes or shaking his head or flicking me off that pedestal every time I screwed up, every time I took on something beyond my capabilities, every time I made some mistake. I truly believed his anger burned toward me for every failure, big and small.

My heart was so severely fixed on my struggles that I couldn't see God there. But he stood ready to comfort me and strengthen me and ultimately free me from myself.

Do you have something you feel God is mad at you about? Maybe you feel he couldn't ever like you because of *that thing* you did.

God's Word tells us that while we were failing and miserable—*that* is when he loved us. He loved us with an everlasting love that brings grand perspective to our sins and mishaps. He is *not* looking down in condemnation at my shame. He is walking beside me with fond love.

God is not mad at us; God loves us. If you long to allow his love to sink into your heart, the way is clear.

While I was failing, he loved me.

While I was writhing in anxiety, he loved me.
While I was beating myself up endlessly, he loved me.
And loves me still.

REFLECT "God showed his great love for us by sending Christ to die for us while we were still sinners." ROMANS 5:8

God, thank you for showing your great love for me by sending Christ to die for me while I was messing it all up. Amen.

CONSIDER "Everything comes from love. All is ordained for the salvation of [humanity]. God does nothing without this goal in mind." CATHERINE OF SIENA

> Freedom from fearing failure comes when we fix our hearts on God's love.

CARA DAY is a writer and illustrator. She has served with Stonecroft Ministries helping women live "extraordinary."

there was not yet any law to break. ¹⁴Still, everyone died—from the time of Adam to the time of Moses—even those who did not disobey an explicit commandment of God, as Adam did. Now Adam is a symbol, a representation of Christ, who was yet to come. ¹⁵But there is a great difference between Adam's sin and God's gracious gift. For the sin of this one man, Adam, brought death to many. But even greater is God's wonderful grace and his gift of forgiveness to many through this other man, Jesus Christ. ¹⁶And the result of God's gracious gift is very different from the result of that one man's sin. For Adam's sin led to condemnation, but God's free gift leads to our being made right with God, even though we are guilty of many sins. ¹⁷For the sin of this one man, Adam, caused death to rule over many. But even greater is God's wonderful grace and his gift of righteousness, for all who receive it will live in triumph over sin and death through this one man, Jesus Christ.

¹⁸Yes, Adam's one sin brings condemnation for everyone, but Christ's one act of righteousness brings a right relationship with God and new life for everyone. ¹⁹Because one person disobeyed God, many became sinners. But because one other person obeyed God, many will be made righteous.

²⁰God's law was given so that all people could see how sinful they were. But as people sinned more and more, God's wonderful grace became more abundant. ²¹So just as sin ruled over all people and brought them to death, now God's wonderful grace rules instead, giving us right standing with God and resulting in eternal life through Jesus Christ our Lord.

Sin's Power Is Broken

6 Well then, should we keep on sinning so that God can show us more and more of his wonderful grace? ²Of course not! Since we have died to sin, how can we continue to live in it? ³Or have you forgotten that when we were joined with Christ Jesus in baptism, we joined him in his death? ⁴For we died and were buried with Christ by baptism. And just as Christ was raised from the dead by the glorious power of the Father, now we also may live new lives.

⁵Since we have been united with him in his death, we will also be raised to life as he was. ⁶We know that our old sinful selves were crucified with Christ so that sin might lose its power in our lives. We are no longer slaves to sin. ⁷For when we died with Christ we were set free from the power of sin. ⁸And since we died with Christ, we know we will also live with him. ⁹We are sure of this because Christ was raised from the dead, and he will never die again. Death no longer has any power over him. ¹⁰When he died, he died once to break the power of sin. But now that he lives, he lives for the glory of God. ¹¹So you also should consider yourselves to be dead to the power of sin and alive to God through Christ Jesus.

¹²Do not let sin control the way you live;* do not give in to sinful desires. ¹³Do not let any part of your body become an instrument of evil to serve sin. Instead, give yourselves completely to God, for you were dead, but now you have new life. So use your whole body as an instrument to do what is right for the glory of God. ¹⁴Sin is no longer your master, for you no longer live under the requirements of the law. Instead, you live under the freedom of God's grace.

¹⁵Well then, since God's grace has set us free from the law, does that mean we can go on sinning? Of course not! ¹⁶Don't you realize that you become the slave of whatever you choose to obey? You can

> "Joy begins with our convictions about spiritual truths we're willing to bet our lives on, truths that are lodged so deep within us that they produce a settled assurance about God."
>
> **KAY WARREN**
> author, speaker, mental health advocate, and pastor's wife

6:12 Or *Do not let sin reign in your body, which is subject to death.*

6:4 The believer's power over sin and the ability to lead a new life begins when we identify with Christ's death, burial, and resurrection (see 6:5, 8). From God's perspective, Jesus' death to sin (see 6:10) is ours as well. His rising to new life means that we also begin to lead a new life, and in the future our bodies will also be raised to eternal life.

6:14-22 Paul speaks of believers as once being "slaves" of sin and now, in Christ, being "slaves" of God. The Greek term *doulos* can be translated as "slave" or "servant." Paul draws on the Old Testament image of the faithful prophet as God's servant. The analogy of believers as being enslaved to righteousness is a limited one, for Paul does not condone the institution of slavery nor does he imagine God as a human enslaver, as one who dominates and threatens. Being "enslaved" to God is a choice we make and means we are free to live a life of flourishing in God.

be a slave to sin, which leads to death, or you can choose to obey God, which leads to righteous living. ¹⁷Thank God! Once you were slaves of sin, but now you wholeheartedly obey this teaching we have given you. ¹⁸Now you are free from your slavery to sin, and you have become slaves to righteous living.

¹⁹Because of the weakness of your human nature, I am using the illustration of slavery to help you understand all this. Previously, you let yourselves be slaves to impurity and lawlessness, which led ever deeper into sin. Now you must give yourselves to be slaves to righteous living so that you will become holy.

²⁰When you were slaves to sin, you were free from the obligation to do right. ²¹And what was the result? You are now ashamed of the things you used to do, things that end in eternal doom. ²²But now you are free from the power of sin and have become slaves of God. Now you do those things that lead to holiness and result in eternal life. ²³For the wages of sin is death, but the free gift of God is eternal life through Christ Jesus our Lord.

No Longer Bound to the Law

7 Now, dear brothers and sisters*—you who are familiar with the law—don't you know that the law applies only while a person is living? ²For example, when a woman marries, the law binds her to her husband as long as he is alive. But if he dies, the laws of marriage no longer apply to her. ³So while her husband is alive, she would be committing adultery if she married another man. But if her husband dies, she is free from that law and does not commit adultery when she remarries.

⁴So, my dear brothers and sisters, this is the point: You died to the power of the law when you died with Christ. And now you are united with the one who was raised from the dead. As a result, we can produce a harvest of good deeds for God. ⁵When we were controlled by our old nature,* sinful desires were at work within us, and the law aroused these evil desires that produced a harvest of sinful deeds, resulting in death. ⁶But now we have been released from the law, for we died to it and are no longer captive to its power. Now we can serve God, not in the old way of obeying the letter of the law, but in the new way of living in the Spirit.

God's Law Reveals Our Sin

⁷Well then, am I suggesting that the law of God is sinful? Of course not! In fact, it was the law that showed me my sin. I would never have known that coveting is wrong if the law had not said, "You must not covet."* ⁸But sin used this command to arouse all kinds of covetous desires within me! If there were no law, sin would not have that power. ⁹At one time I lived without understanding the law. But when I learned the command not to covet, for instance, the power of sin came to life, ¹⁰and I died. So I discovered that the law's commands, which were supposed to bring life, brought spiritual death instead. ¹¹Sin took advantage of those commands and deceived me; it used the commands to kill me. ¹²But still, the law itself is holy, and its commands are holy and right and good.

¹³But how can that be? Did the law, which is good, cause my death? Of course not! Sin used what was good to bring about my condemnation to death. So we can see how terrible sin really is. It uses God's good commands for its own evil purposes.

Struggling with Sin

¹⁴So the trouble is not with the law, for it is spiritual and good. The trouble is with me, for I am all too human, a slave to sin. ¹⁵I don't really understand myself, for I want to do what is right, but I don't do it. Instead, I do what I hate. ¹⁶But if I know that what I am doing is wrong, this shows that I agree that the law is good. ¹⁷So I am not the one doing wrong; it is sin living in me that does it.

¹⁸And I know that nothing good lives in me, that is, in my sinful nature.* I want to do what is right, but I can't. ¹⁹I want to do what is good, but I don't. I don't want to do what is wrong, but I do it anyway. ²⁰But if I do what I don't want to do, I am not really the one doing wrong; it is sin living in me that does it.

²¹I have discovered this principle of life—that when I want to do what is right, I inevitably do what is wrong. ²²I love God's law with all my heart. ²³But there is another power* within me that is at war with my mind. This power makes me a slave to the sin that is still within me. ²⁴Oh, what a miserable person I am! Who will free me from this life that is dominated by sin and death? ²⁵Thank God! The answer is in Jesus

---

7:1 Greek *brothers;* also in 7:4. **7:5** Greek *When we were in the flesh.* **7:7** Exod 20:17; Deut 5:21. **7:18** Greek *my flesh;* also in 7:25. **7:23** Greek *law;* also in 7:23b.

7:2-4 Paul uses a common example of a married woman's experience to explain the role and reach of the Jewish law. Because of the high death rates and age disparity in the first-century marriages, many women were widowed quite young. Jewish law (but not Roman law) allowed a husband to have more than one wife at the same time; however, cases of polygyny seem quite rare. Paul imagines the reader as both the dead husband and the living wife, concluding that believers have died and also can live again in Christ.
7:13-23 Paul uses "I" in a representational sense, not autobiographically. Either "I" represents an unregenerate Gentile or, more likely in this context, a Jew. Someone saying "I am all too human, a slave to sin" is unlikely to be the voice of a believer, for believers are to consider themselves "dead to the power of sin and alive to God" (6:11). "I love God's law with all my heart" is a phrase Jews would embrace, not Gentiles. Paul shows both the goodness of the law and its limitations, which are rooted in human frailty and sin. It is the new birth in Christ, and life in the Holy Spirit, that give full freedom from sin and death (8:1-2).

Christ our Lord. So you see how it is: In my mind I really want to obey God's law, but because of my sinful nature I am a slave to sin.

Life in the Spirit

8 So now there is no condemnation for those who belong to Christ Jesus. ²And because you belong to him, the power* of the life-giving Spirit has freed you* from the power of sin that leads to death. ³The law of Moses was unable to save us because of the weakness of our sinful nature.* So God did what the law could not do. He sent his own Son in a body like the bodies we sinners have. And in that body God declared an end to sin's control over us by giving his Son as a sacrifice for our sins. ⁴He did this so that the just requirement of the law would be fully satisfied for us, who no longer follow our sinful nature but instead follow the Spirit.

8:2a Greek *the law;* also in 8:2b.   8:2b Some manuscripts read *me.*   8:3 Greek *our flesh;* similarly in 8:4, 5, 6, 7, 8, 9, 12.

MY STORY WITH FAMILY & FRIENDS

Why We Need to Ask If Paul Valued Women

SCRIPTURE CONNECTION: ROMANS 8:14-25

Have you ever said, "I like Jesus but not Paul," and wondered if picking favorites really matters?

My friend Kate's mother-in-law, Gladys, said she could not get past what she described as the degrading way the apostle Paul wrote about women. Kate responded, "Let's forget Paul and look at how Jesus treated women." Gladys didn't mind Jesus' approach but knew Paul's letters were also part of the Bible.

Kate didn't know how to put Paul's letters in a better light. And when Gladys died, Kate wasn't sure what her mother-in-law believed about God.

> The Bible empowers and esteems every heir and heiress, man and woman, alike.

But after that, Kate discovered Paul's radical use of the Greek word *huiothesia,* which means "adopted as sons" (8:15, 23; 9:4; see also Galatians 4:5; Ephesians 1:5).

Huiothesia creates a male heir where there wasn't one biologically, and that heir enjoys all the legal privilege and power of a firstborn son. By including women equally as heirs and using this comparison to a male-only practice, Paul was radically esteeming women. Paul's use of this term uplifted women in a way that may have shocked people in his day. Going against cultural norms, Paul said that women, just like men, gain full inheritance in God's Kingdom (Romans 8:17).

Kate regrets not knowing how to show her mother-in-law this. She would have loved to explain in Paul's own words that God esteems every heir and heiress, man and woman, alike. And yes, Kate would now say that understanding how both Jesus and Paul value us really does matter.

IMAGINE

What have you been told about how the Bible views women?

How does knowing Paul wrote about you as an equal heir help you value his writings?

> "I grew up with five brothers and one sister. I always knew my parents esteemed us equally, as individuals, and not by our gender. So does God."

NAOMI CRAMER OVERTON, MBA, DIS, lives to realize beauty-filled visions that lift us to flourishing, with our families and beyond. Naomi has been CEO for Stonecroft and MOPS, director with Compassion International and World Vision, and General Editor for this Bible.

⁵Those who are dominated by the sinful nature think about sinful things, but those who are controlled by the Holy Spirit think about things that please the Spirit. ⁶So letting your sinful nature control your mind leads to death. But letting the Spirit control your mind leads to life and peace. ⁷For the sinful nature is always hostile to God. It never did obey God's laws, and it never will. ⁸That's why those who are still under the control of their sinful nature can never please God.

⁹But you are not controlled by your sinful nature. You are controlled by the Spirit if you have the Spirit of God living in you. (And remember that those who do not have the Spirit of Christ living in them do not belong to him at all.) ¹⁰And Christ lives within you, so even though your body will die because of sin, the Spirit gives you life* because you have been made right with God. ¹¹The Spirit of God, who raised Jesus from the dead, lives in you. And just as God raised Christ Jesus from the dead, he will give life to your mortal bodies by this same Spirit living within you.

¹²Therefore, dear brothers and sisters,* you have no obligation to do what your sinful nature urges you to do. ¹³For if you live by its dictates, you will die. But if through the power of the Spirit you put to death the deeds of your sinful nature,* you will live. ¹⁴For all who are led by the Spirit of God are children* of God.

¹⁵So you have not received a spirit that makes you fearful slaves. Instead, you received God's Spirit when he adopted you as his own children.* Now we call him, "Abba, Father."* ¹⁶For his Spirit joins with our spirit to affirm that we are God's children. ¹⁷And since we are his children, we are his heirs. In fact, together with Christ we are heirs of God's glory. But if we are to share his glory, we must also share his suffering.

The Future Glory

¹⁸Yet what we suffer now is nothing compared to the glory he will reveal to us later. ¹⁹For all creation is waiting eagerly for that future day when God will reveal who his children really are. ²⁰Against its will, all creation was subjected to God's curse. But with eager hope, ²¹the creation looks forward to the day when it will join God's children in glorious freedom from death and decay. ²²For we know that all creation has been groaning as in the pains of childbirth right up to the present time. ²³And we believers also groan, even though we have the Holy Spirit within us as a foretaste of future glory, for we long for our bodies to be released from sin and suffering. We, too, wait with eager hope for the day when God will give us our full rights as his adopted children,* including the new bodies he has promised us. ²⁴We were given this hope when we were saved. (If we already have something, we don't need to hope* for it. ²⁵But if we look forward to something we don't yet have, we must wait patiently and confidently.)

²⁶And the Holy Spirit helps us in our weakness. For example, we don't know what God wants us to pray for. But the Holy Spirit prays for us with groanings that cannot be expressed in words. ²⁷And the Father who knows all hearts knows what the Spirit is saying, for the Spirit pleads for us believers* in harmony with God's own will. ²⁸And we know that God causes everything to work together* for the good of those who love God and are called according to his purpose for them. ²⁹For God knew his people in advance, and he chose them to become like his Son, so that his Son would be the firstborn* among many brothers and sisters. ³⁰And having chosen them, he called them to come to him. And having called them, he gave them right standing with himself. And having given them right standing, he gave them his glory.

Nothing Can Separate Us from God's Love

³¹What shall we say about such wonderful things as these? If God is for us, who can ever be against us? ³²Since he did not spare even his own Son but gave him up for us all, won't he also give us everything else? ³³Who dares accuse us whom God has chosen for his own? No one—for God himself has given us right standing with himself. ³⁴Who then will

---

8:10 Or *your spirit is alive.* **8:12** Greek *brothers;* also in 8:29. **8:13** Greek *deeds of the body.* **8:14** Greek *sons;* also in 8:19. **8:15a** Greek *you received a spirit of sonship.* **8:15b** *Abba* is an Aramaic term for "father." **8:23** Greek *wait anxiously for sonship.* **8:24** Some manuscripts read *wait.* **8:27** Greek *for God's holy people.* **8:28** Some manuscripts read *And we know that everything works together.* **8:29** Or *would be supreme.*

8:9 In contrast to unbelievers, who continue to live under the domination of their sinful nature, the Holy Spirit directs the lives of believers. The Spirit does not take away human initiative or make it impossible for believers to sin. However, as the most powerful force in believers' lives, the Spirit makes it possible for them to resist the continuing power of sin.

8:22-23 Paul understands that Christ's redemptive work was not only for people's salvation, but also for the entire creation (Ephesians 1:10), which is why "all creation has been groaning as in the pains of childbirth." Just as a woman does not control the start of her labor but waits for it to begin, this expectant waiting serves as a model for all believers as we await Christ's return. Paul employs the metaphor of adoption to describe our inclusion in God's family and the inheritance we are waiting for in the new creation. Typically, in the ancient world, women were not adopted into a new family, but joined by marriage. Nor were enslaved people adopted, unless they were first freed. Israel became God's first adopted child, when he chose them to be his special people. The background of that relationship is likely in Paul's mind when he uses this term in his letters (see also Romans 9:4). Paul's adoption metaphor erases the cultural barriers of adoption by allowing every person—regardless of sex, race, social class, or ethnic heritage—to become members of God's family, through Christ.

Living on Purpose amid Pain

MY STORY WITH GOD

SCRIPTURE CONNECTION: ROMANS 8:26-39

In Romans 8, Paul reminds us that following our God-given purpose can lead to suffering. As followers of Jesus, we are bound to run into trials, heartache, and pain. So we may find ourselves asking many questions, like, *Where is God? Where am I?*

We may also wonder if we are suffering because we did something wrong. *Maybe God is mad at us or punishing us.* We may try to fix things or stop following our purpose because we feel afraid. We may even believe that our suffering happens because we have stepped too far from God. Or maybe he has stepped away from us. And suffering sometimes does result from unwise choices.

Paul answers all these questions by calling our attention to God's heart, which does not ignore or forget us in our pain (8:26-28). He works even the hard things out for our good. God calls and fiercely loves us, even amid our suffering (8:35-39). No matter suffering's source, God is still there, loving and forgiving us.

> God calls us and fiercely loves us, even when we suffer.

There have been times when I was sure the reason life hurt was that I had wandered too far from God. That the pain was punishment for my strong spirit (or hard head!), and that I had somehow outrun God's loving arms. Surely God was frustrated or mad at me!

But the Bible reminds us that following Jesus involves joy *and* pain. Because of Jesus, we always have an advocate for us, and absolutely nothing separates us from God's great love. This truth gives us hope that God is never far away, even when life hurts.

IMAGINE

Where has fearing pain stopped you from walking in your purpose?

What would you add to Paul's list of what can't separate us from God's love in 8:38-39?

> "When I have made choices that were not good, I felt the pain and ache of disconnection from God. God never leaves me, but sometimes pain is me closing the door to God. My whole being suffers when my unwise choices create distance."

ELIZA CORTÉS BAST, DEd candidate, is senior director of programs with Stonecroft. She is a pastor, professor, wife, mom, and mentor. She believes in passionately pursuing God and people by developing talent, asking strategic questions, and amplifying the good.

condemn us? No one—for Christ Jesus died for us and was raised to life for us, and he is sitting in the place of honor at God's right hand, pleading for us.

³⁵ Can anything ever separate us from Christ's love? Does it mean he no longer loves us if we have trouble or calamity, or are persecuted, or hungry, or destitute, or in danger, or threatened with death? ³⁶ (As the Scriptures say, "For your sake we are killed every day; we are being slaughtered like sheep."*) ³⁷ No, despite all these things, overwhelming victory is ours through Christ, who loved us.

³⁸ And I am convinced that nothing can ever separate us from God's love. Neither death nor life, neither angels nor demons,* neither our fears for today nor our worries about tomorrow—not even the powers of hell can separate us from God's love. ³⁹ No power in the sky above or in the earth below—indeed, nothing in all creation will ever be able to separate us from the love of God that is revealed in Christ Jesus our Lord.

God's Selection of Israel

9 With Christ as my witness, I speak with utter truthfulness. My conscience and the Holy Spirit confirm it. ² My heart is filled with bitter sorrow and unending grief ³ for my people, my Jewish brothers and sisters.* I would be willing to be forever cursed—cut off from Christ!—if that would save them. ⁴ They are the people of Israel, chosen to be God's adopted children.* God revealed his glory to them. He made covenants with them and gave them his law. He gave them the privilege of worshiping him and receiving his wonderful promises. ⁵ Abraham, Isaac, and Jacob are their ancestors, and Christ himself was an Israelite as far as his human nature is concerned. And he is God, the one who rules over everything and is worthy of eternal praise! Amen.*

⁶ Well then, has God failed to fulfill his promise to Israel? No, for not all who are born into the nation of Israel are truly members of God's people! ⁷ Being descendants of Abraham doesn't make them truly Abraham's children. For the Scriptures say, "Isaac is the son through whom your descendants will be counted,"* though Abraham had other children, too. ⁸ This means that Abraham's physical descendants are not necessarily children of God. Only the children of the promise are considered to be Abraham's children. ⁹ For God had promised, "I will return about this time next year, and Sarah will have a son."*

¹⁰ This son was our ancestor Isaac. When he married Rebekah, she gave birth to twins.* ¹¹ But before they were born, before they had done anything good or bad, she received a message from God. (This message shows that God chooses people according to his own purposes; ¹² he calls people, but not according to their good or bad works.) She was told, "Your older son will serve your younger son."* ¹³ In the words of the Scriptures, "I loved Jacob, but I rejected Esau."*

¹⁴ Are we saying, then, that God was unfair? Of course not! ¹⁵ For God said to Moses,

"I will show mercy to anyone I choose,
 and I will show compassion to anyone I choose."*

¹⁶ So it is God who decides to show mercy. We can neither choose it nor work for it.

¹⁷ For the Scriptures say that God told Pharaoh, "I have appointed you for the very purpose of displaying my power in you and to spread my fame throughout the earth."* ¹⁸ So you see, God chooses to show mercy to some, and he chooses to harden the hearts of others so they refuse to listen.

¹⁹ Well then, you might say, "Why does God blame people for not responding? Haven't they simply done what he makes them do?"

²⁰ No, don't say that. Who are you, a mere human being, to argue with God? Should the thing that was created say to the one who created it, "Why have you made me like this?" ²¹ When a potter makes jars out of clay, doesn't he have a right to use the same

---

8:36 Ps 44:22. **8:38** Greek *nor rulers.* **9:3** Greek *my brothers.* **9:4** Greek *chosen for sonship.* **9:5** Or *May God, the one who rules over everything, be praised forever. Amen.* **9:7** Gen 21:12. **9:9** Gen 18:10, 14. **9:10** Greek *she conceived children through this one man.* **9:12** Gen 25:23. **9:13** Mal 1:2-3. **9:15** Exod 33:19. **9:17** Exod 9:16 (Greek version).

9:4 Up to this point in Romans, Paul has called the Jewish people *Jews*. His shift to "the people of Israel," here and throughout most of Romans 9–11, is significant. *Jew* connotes national identity, but *Israel* emphasizes the covenant relationship of the people with God. The Old Testament called Israel God's "son" or "child" to emphasize that God had selected Israel to be his own people (for example, Exodus 4:22; Jeremiah 3:19; 31:9; Hosea 11:1). Israel's adopted status meant that they received God's blessing and promises, not that they were necessarily saved. The Old Testament includes several covenants between God and the people of Israel: one with Abraham (Genesis 17), one with the nation through Moses at Mount Sinai (Exodus 19–24), and one with David (2 Samuel 7:8-16; 23:5).
9:9-12 Paul draws on Genesis 18:10, 14—"Sarah will have a son"—to emphasize the importance of God's promise to Sarah that she would become pregnant by her husband, Abraham, and have a male heir, Isaac. Earlier, Abraham had used an enslaved Egyptian woman, Hagar, to have a son named Ishmael (Genesis 16:1-16; 21:8-21). The practice of using enslaved women as surrogate mothers was common in Abraham's day. God spoke with Hagar in the wilderness, and she called God "El-roi" ("the God who sees me," Genesis 16:13). Eventually, Sarah's son, Isaac, married Rebekah (Genesis 24:15-67). After years of waiting for a child, Rebekah became pregnant with twins. God spoke directly to her that her twins would be two nations and that the elder (Esau) would serve the younger brother (Jacob, Genesis 25:23). Sarah and Rebekah, along with Rachel and Leah (Jacob's wives), were considered the matriarchs of Judaism. Paul declares that God acts to accomplish his goals, showing great patience with his people.

Children of God

IDENTITY

Chosen through Adoption

I am a Native Alaskan, adopted by my Anglo-American family. My biological father and mother may have given me up, but God took me in as an adopted child in more than one way. He willed for me to grow up with adopted parents, just as he also wills to adopt us as his daughters and sons.

Israel's people were God's original adopted children, meant to inherit his promises (9:4-5). But Paul, with anguish of heart, realized that some had rejected Jesus, the one God sent to bring us into his family (9:2-3).

I am thankful that once we belong to Christ, our Father does not revoke our adoption. All who are led by the Spirit of God are children of God. And we have not received a spirit that makes us fearful children but one that affirms we are his own. Now we call him "Abba, Father," or Papa, because we are his children (8:15).

When God adopts us, we move from a familiar-feeling family to one that may feel different at first. But love turns the unfamiliar into family. Just as when I looked at my adopted family seated at a long table celebrating my mother's 104th birthday, I felt loved, accepted, and wanted.

I am not abandoned; I am chosen. I am not a stranger; I belong. I am not an outcast; I am wanted. By my earthly family, and by Papa God.

> We are loved so much that our Father has adopted us as his children.

GOD'S ADOPTED CHILDREN'S STORY IS TOLD IN ROMANS 8:14-17; 9:1-13;
PAUL ALSO TELLS THIS STORY IN GALATIANS 4:1-7; EPHESIANS 1:3-8.

IDENTIFY

Have you ever thought you did not belong? Have you ever felt unloved? How has God shown you that he wants to adopt you into his family?

"Three generations that had no bloodline connection to my mother gathered because of my adoption that had taken place years ago. Just so, God's choice to adopt us can bless generations."

SUSAN M. JONES is a US Army veteran, native Alaskan, wife, mother, and follower of Jesus Christ. She shares her testimony with Stonecroft Ministries. Sprinkling the love of Jesus is her joy.

lump of clay to make one jar for decoration and another to throw garbage into? ²²In the same way, even though God has the right to show his anger and his power, he is very patient with those on whom his anger falls, who are destined for destruction. ²³He does this to make the riches of his glory shine even brighter on those to whom he shows mercy, who were prepared in advance for glory. ²⁴And we are among those whom he selected, both from the Jews and from the Gentiles.

²⁵Concerning the Gentiles, God says in the prophecy of Hosea,

"Those who were not my people,
 I will now call my people.
And I will love those
 whom I did not love before."*

²⁶And,

"Then, at the place where they were told,
 'You are not my people,'
there they will be called
 'children of the living God.'"*

²⁷And concerning Israel, Isaiah the prophet cried out,

"Though the people of Israel are as numerous as
  the sand of the seashore,
 only a remnant will be saved.
²⁸ For the LORD will carry out his sentence upon
  the earth
 quickly and with finality."*

²⁹And Isaiah said the same thing in another place:

"If the LORD of Heaven's Armies
 had not spared a few of our children,
we would have been wiped out like Sodom,
 destroyed like Gomorrah."*

Israel's Unbelief

³⁰What does all this mean? Even though the Gentiles were not trying to follow God's standards, they were made right with God. And it was by faith that this took place. ³¹But the people of Israel, who tried so hard to get right with God by keeping the law, never succeeded. ³²Why not? Because they were trying to get right with God by keeping the law* instead of by trusting in him. They stumbled over the great rock in their path. ³³God warned them of this in the Scriptures when he said,

"I am placing a stone in Jerusalem* that makes
  people stumble,
 a rock that makes them fall.
But anyone who trusts in him
 will never be disgraced."*

10

Dear brothers and sisters,* the longing of my heart and my prayer to God is for the people of Israel to be saved. ²I know what enthusiasm they have for God, but it is misdirected zeal. ³For they don't understand God's way of making people right with himself. Refusing to accept God's way, they cling to their own way of getting right with God by trying to keep the law. ⁴For Christ has already accomplished the purpose for which the law was given.* As a result, all who believe in him are made right with God.

Salvation Is for Everyone

⁵For Moses writes that the law's way of making a person right with God requires obedience to all of its commands.* ⁶But faith's way of getting right with God says, "Don't say in your heart, 'Who will go up to heaven?' (to bring Christ down to earth). ⁷And don't say, 'Who will go down to the place of the dead?' (to bring Christ back to life again)." ⁸In fact, it says,

"The message is very close at hand;
 it is on your lips and in your heart."*

And that message is the very message about faith that we preach: ⁹If you openly declare that Jesus is Lord and believe in your heart that God raised him from the dead, you will be saved. ¹⁰For it is by believing in your heart that you are made right with God, and it is by openly declaring your faith that you are saved. ¹¹As the Scriptures tell us, "Anyone who trusts in him will never be disgraced."* ¹²Jew and Gentile* are the same in this respect. They have the same Lord, who gives generously to all who call on him. ¹³For "Everyone who calls on the name of the LORD will be saved."*

9:25 Hos 2:23.   9:26 Greek *sons of the living God.* Hos 1:10.   9:27-28 Isa 10:22-23 (Greek version).   9:29 Isa 1:9 (Greek version).   9:32 Greek *by works.*   9:33a Greek *in Zion.*   9:33b Isa 8:14; 28:16 (Greek version).   10:1 Greek *Brothers.*   10:4 Or *For Christ is the end of the law.*   10:5 See Lev 18:5.   10:6-8 Deut 30:12-14.   10:11 Isa 28:16 (Greek version).   10:12 Greek *and Greek.*   10:13 Joel 2:32.

9:24-26 God was free to select some people from the Jews who would have a true spiritual relationship with him; similarly, he was also free to choose some from the Gentiles to be saved as well. Paul used Hosea's prophecy to reinforce his point. Hosea predicted that God would renew his mercy to the ten northern tribes of Israel that had rebelled against God and were under his judgment. Paul saw a principle that applies to Gentiles as well.

10:6-8 Here Paul quotes three phrases from Deuteronomy 30:12-14 dealing with the law, and he applies them to the Good News about Christ. We do not need to "go up to heaven" to find Christ (and thus to be made right with God), because God has already brought him "down to earth" as a man. Nor do we need to "go down to the place of the dead" to find Christ, because God has already raised him from the dead. To find Christ, we must simply believe in the message that is "close at hand."

¹⁴But how can they call on him to save them unless they believe in him? And how can they believe in him if they have never heard about him? And how can they hear about him unless someone tells them? ¹⁵And how will anyone go and tell them without being sent? That is why the Scriptures say, "How beautiful are the feet of messengers who bring good news!"*

¹⁶But not everyone welcomes the Good News, for Isaiah the prophet said, "Lord, who has believed our message?"* ¹⁷So faith comes from hearing, that is, hearing the Good News about Christ. ¹⁸But I ask, have the people of Israel actually heard the message? Yes, they have:

> "The message has gone throughout the earth,
> and the words to all the world."*

¹⁹But I ask, did the people of Israel really understand? Yes, they did, for even in the time of Moses, God said,

> "I will rouse your jealousy through people who are not even a nation.
> I will provoke your anger through the foolish Gentiles."*

²⁰And later Isaiah spoke boldly for God, saying,

> "I was found by people who were not looking for me.
> I showed myself to those who were not asking for me."*

²¹But regarding Israel, God said,

> "All day long I opened my arms to them,
> but they were disobedient and rebellious."*

God's Mercy on Israel

11 I ask, then, has God rejected his own people, the nation of Israel? Of course not! I myself am an Israelite, a descendant of Abraham and a member of the tribe of Benjamin. ²No, God has not rejected his own people, whom he chose from the very beginning. Do you realize what the Scriptures say about this? Elijah the prophet complained to God about the people of Israel and said, ³"Lord, they have killed your prophets and torn down your altars. I am the only one left, and now they are trying to kill me, too."*

⁴And do you remember God's reply? He said, "No, I have 7,000 others who have never bowed down to Baal!"*

⁵It is the same today, for a few of the people of Israel* have remained faithful because of God's grace—his undeserved kindness in choosing them. ⁶And since it is through God's kindness, then it is not by their good works. For in that case, God's grace would not be what it really is—free and undeserved.

⁷So this is the situation: Most of the people of Israel have not found the favor of God they are looking for so earnestly. A few have—the ones God has chosen—but the hearts of the rest were hardened. ⁸As the Scriptures say,

> "God has put them into a deep sleep.
> To this day he has shut their eyes so they
> do not see,
> and closed their ears so they do not hear."*

⁹Likewise, David said,

> "Let their bountiful table become a snare,
> a trap that makes them think all is well.
> Let their blessings cause them to stumble,
> and let them get what they deserve.
> ¹⁰ Let their eyes go blind so they cannot see,
> and let their backs be bent forever."*

¹¹Did God's people stumble and fall beyond recovery? Of course not! They were disobedient, so God made salvation available to the Gentiles. But he wanted his own people to become jealous and claim it for themselves. ¹²Now if the Gentiles were enriched because the people of Israel turned down God's offer of salvation, think how much greater a blessing the world will share when they finally accept it.

¹³I am saying all this especially for you Gentiles. God has appointed me as the apostle to the Gentiles. I stress this, ¹⁴for I want somehow to make the people of Israel jealous of what you Gentiles have, so I might save some of them. ¹⁵For since their rejection meant that God offered salvation to the rest of the world, their acceptance will be even more

---

10:15 Isa 52:7. **10:16** Isa 53:1. **10:18** Ps 19:4. **10:19** Deut 32:21. **10:20** Isa 65:1 (Greek version). **10:21** Isa 65:2 (Greek version). **11:3** 1 Kgs 19:10, 14. **11:4** 1 Kgs 19:18. **11:5** Greek *for a remnant*. **11:8** Isa 29:10; Deut 29:4. **11:9-10** Ps 69:22-23 (Greek version).

10:14-15 "They" in this verse could refer to "everyone," in which case Paul challenges believers to spread the Good News of Jesus' saving grace to lands beyond their own. However, subsequent verses suggest that Paul's focus is on the response of his fellow Jews to God's message. Have the people of Israel actually heard the message? Yes, they have. Paul shows that God unfailingly reached out to Israel through his prophets but not all responded in obedience.

11:2-3 After the apostate King Ahab had already slaughtered many of the Lord's prophets, Queen Jezebel threatened Elijah with the same fate in 1 Kings 19:1-18. Elijah fled to the wilderness, where he bemoaned his lot in life. God responded with the assurance that many faithful people remained. Paul found the present situation to be somewhat parallel. While many Jews did not believe, and some were even hostile, God was (and is) still working to preserve a believing remnant from his people.

11:13-14 Paul addresses the Gentile Christians in Rome with the practical goal of correcting them for thinking too highly of themselves, especially in relation to their Jewish brothers and sisters. He shows that their enjoyment of salvation depends entirely on God's kindness, and that God's final goal is to stimulate repentance among the Jews. Paul devoted himself to the conversion of Gentiles because he knew that their salvation would ultimately lead to salvation for Jews as well.

> "Love well, laugh often, and find your life in Christ. Don't hide away or be a follower. Be the wonderful unique person God made you to be, and know that your purpose will always be best when defined by your faith in him."
>
> — KAREN KINGSBURY
> bestselling novelist

wonderful. It will be life for those who were dead! ¹⁶And since Abraham and the other patriarchs were holy, their descendants will also be holy—just as the entire batch of dough is holy because the portion given as an offering is holy. For if the roots of the tree are holy, the branches will be, too.

¹⁷But some of these branches from Abraham's tree—some of the people of Israel—have been broken off. And you Gentiles, who were branches from a wild olive tree, have been grafted in. So now you also receive the blessing God has promised Abraham and his children, sharing in the rich nourishment from the root of God's special olive tree. ¹⁸But you must not brag about being grafted in to replace the branches that were broken off. You are just a branch, not the root.

¹⁹"Well," you may say, "those branches were broken off to make room for me." ²⁰Yes, but remember— those branches were broken off because they didn't believe in Christ, and you are there because you do believe. So don't think highly of yourself, but fear what could happen. ²¹For if God did not spare the original branches, he won't* spare you either.

²²Notice how God is both kind and severe. He is severe toward those who disobeyed, but kind to you if you continue to trust in his kindness. But if you stop trusting, you also will be cut off. ²³And if the people of Israel turn from their unbelief, they will be grafted in again, for God has the power to graft them back into the tree. ²⁴You, by nature, were a branch cut from a wild olive tree. So if God was willing to do something contrary to nature by grafting you into his cultivated tree, he will be far more eager to graft the original branches back into the tree where they belong.

God's Mercy Is for Everyone

²⁵I want you to understand this mystery, dear brothers and sisters,* so that you will not feel proud about yourselves. Some of the people of Israel have hard hearts, but this will last only until the full number of Gentiles comes to Christ. ²⁶And so all Israel will be saved. As the Scriptures say,

> "The one who rescues will come from
>   Jerusalem,*
> and he will turn Israel* away from
>   ungodliness.
> ²⁷ And this is my covenant with them,
>   that I will take away their sins."*

²⁸Many of the people of Israel are now enemies of the Good News, and this benefits you Gentiles. Yet they are still the people he loves because he chose their ancestors Abraham, Isaac, and Jacob. ²⁹For God's gifts and his call can never be withdrawn. ³⁰Once, you Gentiles were rebels against God, but when the people of Israel rebelled against him, God was merciful to you instead. ³¹Now they are the rebels, and God's mercy has come to you so that they, too, will share* in God's mercy. ³²For God has imprisoned everyone in disobedience so he could have mercy on everyone.

³³Oh, how great are God's riches and wisdom and knowledge! How impossible it is for us to understand his decisions and his ways!

> ³⁴ For who can know the LORD's thoughts?
>   Who knows enough to give him advice?*
> ³⁵ And who has given him so much
>   that he needs to pay it back?*

³⁶For everything comes from him and exists by his power and is intended for his glory. All glory to him forever! Amen.

11:21 Some manuscripts read *perhaps he won't.* **11:25** Greek *brothers.* **11:26a** Greek *from Zion.* **11:26b** Greek *Jacob.* **11:26-27** Isa 59:20-21; 27:9 (Greek version). **11:31** Other manuscripts read *will now share;* still others read *will someday share.* **11:34** Isa 40:13 (Greek version). **11:35** See Job 41:11.

A Living Sacrifice to God

12 And so, dear brothers and sisters,* I plead with you to give your bodies to God because of all he has done for you. Let them be a living and holy sacrifice—the kind he will find acceptable. This is truly the way to worship him.* ²Don't copy the behavior and customs of this world, but let God transform you into a new person by changing the way you think. Then you will learn to know God's will for you, which is good and pleasing and perfect.

³Because of the privilege and authority* God has given me, I give each of you this warning: Don't think you are better than you really are. Be honest in your evaluation of yourselves, measuring yourselves by

12:1a Greek *brothers*. 12:1b Or *This is your spiritual worship;* or *This is your reasonable service.* 12:3a Or *Because of the grace;* compare 1:5.

Shalom IMAGE — MY STORY OF MY UNIQUE INFLUENCE

Losing Me or Using Me?

SCRIPTURE CONNECTION: ROMANS 12:1-8

True confession: I lost myself somewhere. Not like losing the back of an earring (although that's annoying) or my sunglasses in a murky lake (also frustrating). But like losing the inner part of what makes me *me*.

I might have lost myself in my 765,986th load of laundry or in too little sleep because of a newborn. Parts of me very well could have been scared away by comparing myself to a stranger on social media or watching too much Netflix because life is hard and furious.

Sadly, somewhere along the line I thought the world was better off with this version of me. I fooled myself into thinking this was humility (wasn't it?). Just fade into oblivion and show the world the smallest version of me.

However, Paul sees how we can approach the world much differently. He encourages us to present our bodies as living sacrifices. He leans in further, giving titles and descriptive actions to our giftings. Are you a giver? Give generously. Are you a teacher? Teach boldly. Are you a prophet? Prophesy passionately. This is your act of worship. Nowhere does he say "stuff," "squelch," or "lose" your gift. Instead, he says "use" your gift for the Kingdom of God.

> We don't need to lose ourselves—we need to use ourselves—for God's glory.

You might have lost yourself in your 765,986th load of laundry too, but let's not lose heart. Our gifting is still inside of us. We can take time to dust it off and use it to proclaim the goodness of God. The world needs God! And the world needs you and your gifts, too!

IMAGINE

What gifts has God given you?

How might you use them in your family, neighborhood, city, and beyond?

"I have often wanted to squelch my gifts, but God wants me to use my gifts for him and his glory!"

WHITNEY PUTNAM is the senior director of women's events and marketing at New Life Ministries. She is an overall joy-chaser and is often found dancing in her kitchen.

the faith God has given us.* ⁴Just as our bodies have many parts and each part has a special function, ⁵so it is with Christ's body. We are many parts of one body, and we all belong to each other.

⁶In his grace, God has given us different gifts for doing certain things well. So if God has given you the ability to prophesy, speak out with as much faith as God has given you. ⁷If your gift is serving others, serve them well. If you are a teacher, teach well. ⁸If your gift is to encourage others, be encouraging. If it is giving, give generously. If God has given you leadership ability, take the responsibility seriously. And if you have a gift for showing kindness to others, do it gladly.

⁹Don't just pretend to love others. Really love them. Hate what is wrong. Hold tightly to what is good. ¹⁰Love each other with genuine affection,* and take delight in honoring each other. ¹¹Never be lazy, but work hard and serve the Lord enthusiastically.* ¹²Rejoice in our confident hope. Be patient in trouble, and keep on praying. ¹³When God's people are in need, be ready to help them. Always be eager to practice hospitality.

¹⁴Bless those who persecute you. Don't curse them; pray that God will bless them. ¹⁵Be happy with those who are happy, and weep with those who weep. ¹⁶Live in harmony with each other. Don't be too proud to enjoy the company of ordinary people. And don't think you know it all!

¹⁷Never pay back evil with more evil. Do things in such a way that everyone can see you are honorable. ¹⁸Do all that you can to live in peace with everyone.

¹⁹Dear friends, never take revenge. Leave that to the righteous anger of God. For the Scriptures say,

"I will take revenge;
I will pay them back,"*
says the Lord.

²⁰Instead,

"If your enemies are hungry, feed them.
If they are thirsty, give them something to drink.
In doing this, you will heap
burning coals of shame on their heads."*

²¹Don't let evil conquer you, but conquer evil by doing good.

Respect for Authority

13 Everyone must submit to governing authorities. For all authority comes from God, and those in positions of authority have been placed there by God. ²So anyone who rebels against authority is rebelling against what God has instituted, and they will be punished. ³For the authorities do not strike fear in people who are doing right, but in those who are doing wrong. Would you like to live without fear of the authorities? Do what is right, and they will honor you. ⁴The authorities are God's servants, sent for your good. But if you are doing wrong, of course you should be afraid, for they have the power to punish you. They are God's servants, sent for the very purpose of punishing those who do what is wrong. ⁵So you must submit to them, not only to avoid punishment, but also to keep a clear conscience.

⁶Pay your taxes, too, for these same reasons. For government workers need to be paid. They are serving God in what they do. ⁷Give to everyone what you owe them: Pay your taxes and government fees to those who collect them, and give respect and honor to those who are in authority.

Love Fulfills God's Requirements

⁸Owe nothing to anyone—except for your obligation to love one another. If you love your neighbor, you will fulfill the requirements of God's law. ⁹For the commandments say, "You must not commit adultery. You must not murder. You must not steal. You must not covet."* These—and other such commandments—are summed up in this one commandment: "Love your neighbor as yourself."* ¹⁰Love does no wrong to others, so love fulfills the requirements of God's law.

¹¹This is all the more urgent, for you know how late it is; time is running out. Wake up, for our salvation is nearer now than when we first believed.

12:3b Or *by the faith God has given you;* or *by the standard of our God-given faith.* **12:10** Greek *with brotherly love.* **12:11** Or *but serve the Lord with a zealous spirit;* or *but let the Spirit excite you as you serve the Lord.* **12:19** Deut 32:35. **12:20** Prov 25:21-22. **13:9a** Exod 20:13-15, 17. **13:9b** Lev 19:18.

12:4-8 Paul stresses the diversity of God-given gifts by drawing on a common image, a body (see also 1 Corinthians 12:4-31). These gifts are given without regard to sex, race, ethnic heritage, or social status. These gifts are given by the Holy Spirit to help others in the body of Christ, the church. The ability to prophesy is a key gift, for its main purposes are to speak to the congregation on behalf of God and to strengthen, build up, and encourage (1 Corinthians 14:3). Paul affirms the women who prophesied in the Corinthian church (1 Corinthians 11:5). Paul also encourages women to lead, including his coworkers Euodia and Syntyche (Philippians 4:2-3), Nympha (Colossians 4:15), and three women named in Romans 16: Phoebe, Priscilla, and Junia.

12:16 All three exhortations in this verse use the Greek word *phroneō* (meaning "think"). Paul addresses the need for right Christian thinking when it comes to our relationships with other Christians. Paul encourages believers to be humble and not to assume we know everything.

13:1-2 The basic command of 13:1-7 is to "submit to governing authorities." In God's ordering of the world, we answer to "those in positions of authority." Our submission to them will usually take the form of obedience. However, because God stands over all governments, our obedience to governing authorities must always be in terms of our ultimate obedience to God (see Acts 4:19-20). The Roman Christians might have been resisting their government based on an incorrect understanding of the Good News, as if no longer copying "the behavior and customs of this world" (Romans 12:2) meant that they should ignore humanmade institutions.

¹²The night is almost gone; the day of salvation will soon be here. So remove your dark deeds like dirty clothes, and put on the shining armor of right living. ¹³Because we belong to the day, we must live decent lives for all to see. Don't participate in the darkness of wild parties and drunkenness, or in sexual promiscuity and immoral living, or in quarreling and jealousy. ¹⁴Instead, clothe yourself with the presence of the Lord Jesus Christ. And don't let yourself think about ways to indulge your evil desires.

The Danger of Criticism

14 Accept other believers who are weak in faith, and don't argue with them about what they think is right or wrong. ²For instance, one person believes it's all right to eat anything. But another believer with a sensitive conscience will eat only vegetables. ³Those who feel free to eat anything must not look down on those who don't. And those who don't eat certain foods must not condemn those who do, for God has accepted them. ⁴Who are you to condemn someone else's servants? Their own master will judge whether they stand or fall. And with the Lord's help, they will stand and receive his approval.

⁵In the same way, some think one day is more holy than another day, while others think every day is alike. You should each be fully convinced that whichever day you choose is acceptable. ⁶Those who worship the Lord on a special day do it to honor him. Those who eat any kind of food do so to honor the Lord, since they give thanks to God before eating. And those who refuse to eat certain foods also want to please the Lord and give thanks to God. ⁷For we don't live for ourselves or die for ourselves. ⁸If we live, it's to honor the Lord. And if we die, it's to honor the Lord. So whether we live or die, we belong to the Lord. ⁹Christ died and rose again for this very purpose—to be Lord both of the living and of the dead.

¹⁰So why do you condemn another believer*? Why do you look down on another believer? Remember, we will all stand before the judgment seat of God. ¹¹For the Scriptures say,

"'As surely as I live,' says the LORD,
'every knee will bend to me,
and every tongue will declare allegiance to God.*'"

¹²Yes, each of us will give a personal account to God. ¹³So let's stop condemning each other. Decide instead to live in such a way that you will not cause another believer to stumble and fall.

¹⁴I know and am convinced on the authority of the Lord Jesus that no food, in and of itself, is wrong to eat. But if someone believes it is wrong, then for that person it is wrong. ¹⁵And if another believer is distressed by what you eat, you are not acting in love if you eat it. Don't let your eating ruin someone for whom Christ died. ¹⁶Then you will not be criticized for doing something you believe is good. ¹⁷For the Kingdom of God is not a matter of what we eat or drink, but of living a life of goodness and peace and joy in the Holy Spirit. ¹⁸If you serve Christ with this attitude, you will please God, and others will approve of you, too. ¹⁹So then, let us aim for harmony in the church and try to build each other up.

²⁰Don't tear apart the work of God over what you eat. Remember, all foods are acceptable, but it is wrong to eat something if it makes another person stumble. ²¹It is better not to eat meat or drink wine or do anything else if it might cause another believer to stumble.* ²²You may believe there's nothing wrong with what you are doing, but keep it between yourself and God. Blessed are those who don't feel guilty for doing something they have decided is right. ²³But if you have doubts about whether or not you should eat something, you are sinning if you go ahead and do it. For you are not following your convictions. If you do anything you believe is not right, you are sinning.*

Living to Please Others

15 We who are strong must be considerate of those who are sensitive about things like this. We must not just please ourselves. ²We should help others do what is right and build them up in the Lord. ³For even Christ didn't live to please himself. As the Scriptures say, "The insults of those who insult you, O God, have fallen on me."* ⁴Such things were written in the Scriptures long ago to teach us. And the Scriptures give us hope and encouragement as we wait patiently for God's promises to be fulfilled.

⁵May God, who gives this patience and encouragement, help you live in complete harmony with each other, as is fitting for followers of Christ Jesus. ⁶Then all of you can join together with one voice, giving praise and glory to God, the Father of our Lord Jesus Christ.

⁷Therefore, accept each other just as Christ has accepted you so that God will be given glory. ⁸Remember that Christ came as a servant to the Jews* to show that God is true to the promises he made to their ancestors. ⁹He also came so that the Gentiles

---

14:10 Greek *your brother*; also in 14:10b, 13, 15, 21.   **14:11** Or *declare praise for God.* Isa 49:18; 45:23 (Greek version).
14:21 Some manuscripts read *to stumble or be offended or be weakened.*   **14:23** Some manuscripts place the text of 16:25-27 here.   **15:3** Greek *who insult you have fallen on me.* Ps 69:9.   **15:8** Greek *servant of circumcision.*

14:1–15:7 Paul moves to a specific issue that was causing conflict in the church at Rome. They were embroiled in a dispute between people who were "weak in faith" (14:1) and people who were "strong" (see 15:1) regarding certain practices. Throughout this section, Paul instructs believers to be tolerant toward others and their practices. He was convinced that people on both sides of the issue were genuine believers, and he didn't think the issues they were fighting over were essential to the faith. So he exhorted them to find a way to live together peaceably, even with their differences.

WHAT THE BIBLE SAYS ABOUT

Love and Obedience

Love Fulfills God's Requirements

"Teacher, which is the most important commandment in the law of Moses?"

Jesus replied, "'You must love the LORD your God with all your heart, all your soul, and all your mind.' This is the first and greatest commandment. A second is equally important: 'Love your neighbor as yourself.' The entire law and all the demands of the prophets are based on these two commandments." **MATTHEW 22:36-40**

Owe nothing to anyone—except for your obligation to love one another. If you love your neighbor, you will fulfill the requirements of God's law.... Love does no wrong to others, so love fulfills the requirements of God's law. **ROMANS 13:8, 10**

Jesus Models Love and Obedience

Live a life filled with love, following the example of Christ. He loved us and offered himself as a sacrifice for us, a pleasing aroma to God. **EPHESIANS 5:2**

For the law was given through Moses, but God's unfailing love and faithfulness came through Jesus Christ. **JOHN 1:17**

To all who are victorious, who obey me to the very end, ...

God Asks Us to Honor Everyone

Give to everyone what you owe them: Pay your taxes and government fees to those who collect them, and give respect and honor to those who are in authority. **ROMANS 13:7**

Respect everyone, and love the family of believers. Fear God, and respect the king. **1 PETER 2:17**

The whole law can be summed up in this one command: "Love your neighbor as yourself." **GALATIANS 5:14**

This is real love—not that we loved God, but that he loved us and sent his Son as a sacrifice to take away our sins. Dear friends, since God loved us that much, we surely ought to love each other. **1 JOHN 4:10-11**

God's Love Responds to Our Love and Obedience

"I lavish unfailing love for a thousand generations on those who love me and obey my commands." **EXODUS 20:6**

"Understand, therefore, that the LORD your God is indeed God. He is the faithful God who keeps his covenant for a thousand generations and lavishes his unfailing love on those who love him and obey his commands." **DEUTERONOMY 7:9**

We know that God causes everything to work together for the good of those who love God and are called according to his purpose for them. **ROMANS 8:28**

The LORD leads with unfailing love and faithfulness all who keep his covenant and obey his demands. **PSALM 25:10**

Those who obey God's word truly show how completely they love him. That is how we know we are living in him. **1 JOHN 2:5**

"To all who are victorious, who obey me to the very end, to them I will give authority over all the nations." **REVELATION 2:26**

... to them I will give authority over all the nations.

might give glory to God for his mercies to them. That is what the psalmist meant when he wrote:

> "For this, I will praise you among the Gentiles;
> I will sing praises to your name."*

[10] And in another place it is written,

> "Rejoice with his people,
> you Gentiles."*

[11] And yet again,

> "Praise the LORD, all you Gentiles.
> Praise him, all you people of the earth."*

[12] And in another place Isaiah said,

> "The heir to David's throne* will come,
> and he will rule over the Gentiles.
> They will place their hope on him."*

[13] I pray that God, the source of hope, will fill you completely with joy and peace because you trust in him. Then you will overflow with confident hope through the power of the Holy Spirit.

Paul's Reason for Writing

[14] I am fully convinced, my dear brothers and sisters,* that you are full of goodness. You know these things so well you can teach each other all about them. [15] Even so, I have been bold enough to write about some of these points, knowing that all you need is this reminder. For by God's grace, [16] I am a special messenger from Christ Jesus to you Gentiles. I bring you the Good News so that I might present you as an acceptable offering to God, made holy by the Holy Spirit. [17] So I have reason to be enthusiastic about all Christ Jesus has done through me in my service to God. [18] Yet I dare not boast about anything except what Christ has done through me, bringing the Gentiles to God by my message and by the way I worked among them. [19] They were convinced by the power of miraculous signs and wonders and by the power of God's Spirit.* In this way, I have fully presented the Good News of Christ from Jerusalem all the way to Illyricum.*

[20] My ambition has always been to preach the Good News where the name of Christ has never been heard, rather than where a church has already been started by someone else. [21] I have been following the plan spoken of in the Scriptures, where it says,

> "Those who have never been told about him will see,
> and those who have never heard of him will understand."*

[22] In fact, my visit to you has been delayed so long because I have been preaching in these places.

Paul's Travel Plans

[23] But now I have finished my work in these regions, and after all these long years of waiting, I am eager to visit you. [24] I am planning to go to Spain, and when I do, I will stop off in Rome. And after I have enjoyed your fellowship for a little while, you can provide for my journey.

[25] But before I come, I must go to Jerusalem to take a gift to the believers* there. [26] For you see, the believers in Macedonia and Achaia* have eagerly taken up an offering for the poor among the believers in Jerusalem. [27] They were glad to do this because they feel they owe a real debt to them. Since the Gentiles received the spiritual blessings of the Good News from the believers in Jerusalem, they feel the least they can do in return is to help them financially. [28] As soon as I have delivered this money and completed this good deed of theirs, I will come to see you on my way to Spain. [29] And I am sure that when I come, Christ will richly bless our time together.

[30] Dear brothers and sisters, I urge you in the name of our Lord Jesus Christ to join in my struggle by praying to God for me. Do this because of your love for me, given to you by the Holy Spirit. [31] Pray that I will be rescued from those in Judea who refuse to obey God. Pray also that the believers there will be willing to accept the donation* I am taking to Jerusalem. [32] Then, by the will of God, I will be able to come to you with a joyful heart, and we will be an encouragement to each other.

[33] And now may God, who gives us his peace, be with you all. Amen.*

15:9 Ps 18:49. **15:10** Deut 32:43. **15:11** Ps 117:1. **15:12a** Greek *The root of Jesse*. David was the son of Jesse. **15:12b** Isa 11:10 (Greek version). **15:14** Greek *brothers;* also in 15:30. **15:19a** Other manuscripts read *the Spirit;* still others read *the Holy Spirit*. **15:19b** *Illyricum* was a region northeast of Italy. **15:21** Isa 52:15 (Greek version). **15:25** Greek *God's holy people;* also in 15:26, 31. **15:26** *Macedonia* and *Achaia* were the northern and southern regions of Greece. **15:31** Greek *the ministry;* other manuscripts read *the gift*. **15:33** Some manuscripts do not include *Amen*. One very early manuscript places 16:25-27 here.

15:14–16:27 This final section contains elements common to the end of New Testament letters: the reason for writing (15:14-22), a discussion of travel plans (15:23-29), requests for prayer (15:30-33), references to ministry associates (16:1-2, 21-23), greetings (16:3-16), and a doxology or expression of praise to God (16:25-27). Only the warning about false teachers (16:17-19) is a unique feature in this conclusion.

15:24 In the first century, "Spain" included the entire Iberian Peninsula (modern Spain and Portugal). Parts of the peninsula had been occupied by the Romans since 200 BC, but only within Paul's lifetime had the area been organized into a Roman province. Spain was so far from Paul's previous sending church, Antioch in Syria, that he hoped the Roman church could serve as the logistical base for this future evangelistic effort. Paul saw Spain, at the far end of the Mediterranean, as his final target in fulfilling the promise of Isaiah 66:19-20.

Phoebe

IDENTITY — Paul's Gospel Partner

"You might know me as the woman Paul chose to send as his messenger, but I am also a trusted coworker and deacon serving the church in Cenchrea. Paul trusts me to read his letter and explain it to the Christians living in the capital…."

Paul describes Phoebe as a significant leader in her church in Cenchrea. He chose the same Greek word (*diakonos*, meaning "servant" or "deacon") to describe himself, Timothy, Epaphras, and Tychicus (1 Corinthians 3:5; Ephesians 6:21; Colossians 1:7; 1:25; 4:7). Phoebe was a deacon—minister or servant/person enslaved to the gospel—like other male church leaders.

Paul also trusted her with an important letter—to Christians in a most influential city. Paul engaged several letter carriers, including Timothy (Philippians 2:19) and Tychicus (Colossians 4:7). Carrying a letter meant that Phoebe likely had received instructions from Paul on how he wanted her to interpret the letter and answer recipients' questions. Once in Rome, Phoebe would have met with the various house churches, reading and explaining the letter to them.

Over the years, church leaders and Bible translators have downplayed the significance of Phoebe's title and responsibility. Yet she stands out as a prominent model for women in leadership. She was one of Paul's financial supporters or benefactors, and Paul trusted her to take one of his most important letters to Christians in the most influential city he reached, Rome.

PHOEBE'S STORY IS TOLD IN ROMANS 16:1-2.

> Leaders can support and encourage us. They can open doors for our ministry that we cannot open ourselves.

IDENTIFY

Who sees your God-given talents and calling? How do they open doors that you could not open?

"In my fifties, a professor saw my potential when I could not yet see it. He encouraged me to pursue a PhD, opened doors for a teaching position, and recommended me for a higher administrative position. All this led to a new, fulfilling career that I could never have imagined."

ELIZABETH GLANVILLE, PhD, is retired faculty from Fuller Theological Seminary, School of Mission and Theology. She is an international teacher on missions and leadership and chaplain for a local police department and her retirement community.

Paul Greets His Friends

16 I commend to you our sister Phoebe, who is a deacon in the church in Cenchrea. ²Welcome her in the Lord as one who is worthy of honor among God's people. Help her in whatever she needs, for she has been helpful to many, and especially to me.

³Give my greetings to Priscilla and Aquila, my co-workers in the ministry of Christ Jesus. ⁴In fact, they once risked their lives for me. I am thankful to them, and so are all the Gentile churches. ⁵Also give my greetings to the church that meets in their home.

Greet my dear friend Epenetus. He was the first person from the province of Asia to become a follower of Christ. ⁶Give my greetings to Mary, who has worked so hard for your benefit. ⁷Greet Andronicus and Junia,* my fellow Jews,* who were in prison with me. They are highly respected among the apostles and became followers of Christ before I did. ⁸Greet Ampliatus, my dear friend in the Lord. ⁹Greet Urbanus, our co-worker in Christ, and my dear friend Stachys.

¹⁰Greet Apelles, a good man whom Christ approves. And give my greetings to the believers from the household of Aristobulus. ¹¹Greet Herodion, my fellow Jew.* Greet the Lord's people from the household of Narcissus. ¹²Give my greetings to Tryphena and Tryphosa, the Lord's workers, and to dear Persis, who has worked so hard for the Lord. ¹³Greet Rufus, whom the Lord picked out to be his very own; and also his dear mother, who has been a mother to me.

¹⁴Give my greetings to Asyncritus, Phlegon, Hermes, Patrobas, Hermas, and the brothers and sisters* who meet with them. ¹⁵Give my greetings to Philologus, Julia, Nereus and his sister, and to Olympas and all the believers* who meet with them. ¹⁶Greet each other with a sacred kiss. All the churches of Christ send you their greetings.

Paul's Final Instructions

¹⁷And now I make one more appeal, my dear brothers and sisters. Watch out for people who cause divisions and upset people's faith by teaching things contrary to what you have been taught. Stay away from them. ¹⁸Such people are not serving Christ our Lord; they are serving their own personal interests. By smooth talk and glowing words they deceive innocent people. ¹⁹But everyone knows that you are obedient to the Lord. This makes me very happy. I want you to be wise in doing right and to stay innocent of any wrong. ²⁰The God of peace will soon crush Satan under your feet. May the grace of our Lord Jesus* be with you.

²¹Timothy, my fellow worker, sends you his greetings, as do Lucius, Jason, and Sosipater, my fellow Jews.

²²I, Tertius, the one writing this letter for Paul, send my greetings, too, as one of the Lord's followers.

²³Gaius says hello to you. He is my host and also serves as host to the whole church. Erastus, the city treasurer, sends you his greetings, and so does our brother Quartus.*

²⁵Now all glory to God, who is able to make you strong, just as my Good News says. This message about Jesus Christ has revealed his plan for you Gentiles, a plan kept secret from the beginning of time. ²⁶But now as the prophets* foretold and as the eternal God has commanded, this message is made known to all Gentiles everywhere, so that they too might believe and obey him. ²⁷All glory to the only wise God, through Jesus Christ, forever. Amen.*

16:7a *Junia* is a feminine name. Some late manuscripts accent the word so it reads *Junias*, a masculine name; still others read *Julia* (feminine). **16:7b** Or *compatriots;* also in 16:21. **16:11** Or *compatriot.* **16:14** Greek *brothers;* also in 16:17. **16:15** Greek *all of God's holy people.* **16:20** Some manuscripts read *Lord Jesus Christ.* **16:23** Some manuscripts add verse 24, *May the grace of our Lord Jesus Christ be with you all. Amen.* Still others add this sentence after verse 27. **16:26** Greek *the prophetic writings.* **16:25-27** Various manuscripts place the doxology (shown here as 16:25-27) after 14:23 or after 15:33 or after 16:23.

16:1-2 Phoebe served as a church leader in Cenchrea, the eastern port of Corinth. The word *deacon* is often translated as "minister" when referring to Epaphras, the leader in the church at Colosse (Colossians 1:7, NLT "servant"). Phoebe was Paul's patron (or benefactor), which is translated here too weakly as "has been helpful." A patron in the Greco-Roman world was a person of means who supported and promoted others in their community with their wealth and influence. Phoebe carried Paul's letter to the church, and would have read and interpreted it to them, as did all of Paul's letter carriers. Phoebe would have been the first interpreter of Romans.

16:3-5 Paul mentions the wife-husband team of Priscilla and Aquila also in 1 Corinthians 16:19, and we learn of their ministry in Acts 18:1-28. Like her husband and Paul, Priscilla was also a tentmaker: Women worked alongside men in shops—and they owned property and businesses (for example, see Lydia, Acts 16:14). Paul identifies Priscilla as his coworker, and as one who faced dangers on his behalf. Priscilla was very knowledgeable and taught Apollos, another of Paul's coworkers (Acts 18:26). As a house church leader, she would have also taught in her house church.

16:7 Paul commends Junia, most likely the wife of Andronicus (or, possibly, his sister). They endured prison for the sake of the gospel. In some older English translations, Junia's name was changed to a man's name, Junias. While there is no record of any such masculine name in the ancient world, feminine *Junia* is widely attested. Paul speaks of Junia as being connected in some way to the apostles. The most natural reading of this short Greek phrase is that Junia and Andronicus were themselves apostles and were well known among that group. Paul uses the definite article (the word *the*), indicating that he had a specific group in mind. The term *apostle* can mean a messenger (Philippians 2:25) and traveling missionary (perhaps 1 Thessalonians 2:7), or leader within the church. Junia fits the description of apostle as Paul describes it—as one who is least (1 Corinthians 4:9; 15:7-8; Ephesians 3:7) and who has this treasured ministry in "fragile clay jars" (2 Corinthians 4:1, 7).

Insight: PAUL'S WOMEN COWORKERS

Paul had many partners in ministry, including women. Several of those women are named in Romans 16, but they also appear in Acts and are mentioned in Paul's other letters. Although they have historically been minimized or overlooked, Paul's female coworkers in the New Testament testify otherwise. As we see among early Christians, women have always been active participants in ministry and important to God's mission.

Phoebe
Deacon from Cenchrea, patron, and letter carrier
Romans 16:1-2

Priscilla
Teacher, missionary, house church leader, and tentmaker; usually named with her husband, Aquila
Acts 18:1-3, 18-28
Romans 16:3
1 Corinthians 16:19
2 Timothy 4:19

Mary
A hard worker and a Christian known to the Roman Christians
Romans 16:6

Junia
Paul's prison mate, with her husband, Andronicus, and possibly an apostle, or well known to the apostles
Romans 16:7

Tryphena
With Tryphosa, who may have been her sister, "the Lord's workers"
Romans 16:12

Tryphosa
With Tryphena, who may have been her sister, "the Lord's workers"
Romans 16:12

Persis
A hard worker for the Lord
Romans 16:12

Rufus's mother
Cared for Paul, was like a mother to him
Romans 16:13

Julia
A house church leader, possibly Philologus's wife
Romans 16:15

Nereus's sister
Possibly Julia and Philologus's daughter, fellow house church member and leader
Romans 16:15

Chloe
Possible house church leader in Corinth
1 Corinthians 1:11

Euodia
Paul's coworker in telling others the Good News
Philippians 4:2

Syntyche
Paul's coworker in telling others the Good News
Philippians 4:2

1 Corinthians

WHAT DO WE LEARN ABOUT GOD'S MISSION AND OURS? God has guidance for all our practical concerns—including our relationships, our bodies, and our power.

WHO WROTE IT? Paul, the leader (apostle) sent to the Gentile people.

WHEN DID IT HAPPEN? Paul wrote 1 Corinthians near the end of his three-year stay in Ephesus during his third missionary journey, around AD 55.

HOW IS IT ORGANIZED?

- **1–4:** Divisions in the church
- **5–6:** Avoiding sexual immorality and lawsuits
- **7:** Questions about marriage, divorce, and singleness
- **8–10:** Freedom and community responsibility
- **11:** Instructions for worship and the Lord's Supper
- **12–14:** Gifts from the Holy Spirit and the priority of love
- **15:** Answering skepticism about the future resurrection of the dead
- **16:** Paul's final instructions and greetings

FEATURE HIGHLIGHTS

+ *Chloe: Courageous Voice for Unity (1437)*
+ *Women for Unity (1438)*
+ *Living Your Page in God's Story (1440)*

Words to Remember are highlighted throughout this book

HOW LONG DOES IT TAKE TO READ?

Timeline

AD	Event
30	JESUS DIES, RISES FROM THE DEAD, ASCENDS TO REIGN IN HEAVEN, SENDS THE HOLY SPIRIT
35	JESUS CALLS PAUL TO PREACH THE GOOD NEWS
46–48	PAUL GOES ON FIRST MISSIONARY JOURNEY, WITH BARNABAS AND JOHN MARK
50–52	PAUL EMBARKS ON SECOND MISSIONARY JOURNEY, WITH SILAS; THEY SPEND 18 MONTHS IN CORINTH
50	PAUL MEETS PRISCILLA AND AQUILA IN CORINTH
	PAUL MEETS LYDIA IN PHILIPPI
53–57	PAUL TAKES A THIRD MISSIONARY JOURNEY
53–56	PAUL STAYS FOR AN EXTENDED TIME IN EPHESUS, AND FOUNDS THE CHURCH IN COLOSSE
57	PAUL ARRESTED IN JERUSALEM
57–59	PAUL IMPRISONED IN CAESAREA, WHERE HE IS QUESTIONED BY FESTUS, FELIX AND DRUSILLA, AND AGRIPPA AND BERNICE
60–62	PAUL UNDER HOUSE ARREST IN ROME WRITES HIS LETTERS TO THE EPHESIANS, PHILIPPIANS, COLOSSIANS, AND PHILEMON
64	PAUL MARTYRED IN ROME
70	ROME DESTROYS JERUSALEM

1 CORINTHIANS 1

Greetings from Paul

1 This letter is from Paul, chosen by the will of God to be an apostle of Christ Jesus, and from our brother Sosthenes.

²I am writing to God's church in Corinth,* to you who have been called by God to be his own holy people. He made you holy by means of Christ Jesus,* just as he did for all people everywhere who call on the name of our Lord Jesus Christ, their Lord and ours.

³May God our Father and the Lord Jesus Christ give you grace and peace.

Paul Gives Thanks to God

⁴I always thank my God for you and for the gracious gifts he has given you, now that you belong to Christ Jesus. ⁵Through him, God has enriched your church in every way—with all of your eloquent words and all of your knowledge. ⁶This confirms that what I told you about Christ is true. ⁷Now you have every spiritual gift you need as you eagerly wait for the return of our Lord Jesus Christ. ⁸He will keep you strong to the end so that you will be free from all blame on the day when our Lord Jesus Christ returns. ⁹God will do this, for he is faithful to do what he says, and he has invited you into partnership with his Son, Jesus Christ our Lord.

Divisions in the Church

¹⁰I appeal to you, dear brothers and sisters,* by the authority of our Lord Jesus Christ, to live in harmony with each other. Let there be no divisions in the church. Rather, be of one mind, united in thought and purpose. ¹¹For some members of Chloe's household have told me about your quarrels, my dear brothers and sisters. ¹²Some of you are saying, "I am a follower of Paul." Others are saying, "I follow Apollos," or "I follow Peter,*" or "I follow only Christ."

¹³Has Christ been divided into factions? Was I, Paul, crucified for you? Were any of you baptized in the name of Paul? Of course not! ¹⁴I thank God that I did not baptize any of you except Crispus and Gaius, ¹⁵for now no one can say they were baptized in my name. ¹⁶(Oh yes, I also baptized the household of Stephanas, but I don't remember baptizing anyone else.) ¹⁷For Christ didn't send me to baptize, but to preach the Good News—and not with clever speech, for fear that the cross of Christ would lose its power.

The Wisdom of God

¹⁸The message of the cross is foolish to those who are headed for destruction! But we who are being saved know it is the very power of God. ¹⁹As the Scriptures say,

"I will destroy the wisdom of the wise
 and discard the intelligence of the
 intelligent."*

²⁰So where does this leave the philosophers, the scholars, and the world's brilliant debaters? God has made the wisdom of this world look foolish. ²¹Since God in his wisdom saw to it that the world would never know him through human wisdom, he has used our foolish preaching to save those who believe. ²²It is foolish to the Jews, who ask for signs from heaven. And it is foolish to the Greeks, who seek human wisdom. ²³So when we preach that Christ was crucified, the Jews are offended and the Gentiles say it's all nonsense. ²⁴But to those called by God to salvation, both Jews and Gentiles,* Christ is the power of God and the wisdom of God. ²⁵This foolish plan of God is wiser than the wisest of human plans, and God's weakness is stronger than the greatest of human strength.

²⁶Remember, dear brothers and sisters, that few of you were wise in the world's eyes or powerful or wealthy* when God called you. ²⁷Instead, God chose things the world considers foolish in order to shame those who think they are wise. And he chose things that are powerless to shame those who are powerful. ²⁸God chose things despised by the world,* things counted as nothing at all, and used them to bring to nothing what the world considers important. ²⁹As a result, no one can ever boast in the presence of God.

1:2a *Corinth* was the capital city of Achaia, the southern region of the Greek peninsula. **1:2b** Or *because you belong to Christ Jesus.* **1:10** Greek *brothers;* also in 1:11, 26. **1:12** Greek *Cephas.* **1:19** Isa 29:14. **1:24** Greek *and Greeks.* **1:26** Or *high born.* **1:28** Or *God chose those who are low born.*

1:5 Paul acknowledges that God had enriched the Corinthian church with abundant spiritual gifts, specifically "eloquent words" and "knowledge." This probably refers to the spiritual messages and understanding (see 1:7) on which the church prided itself. The terms *word* and *knowledge* occur frequently in this letter. Later, Paul corrects their distorted perspectives on these gifts (see 1:18–2:5; 3:18-20; 12:1–14:40).

1:11 Paul refers to a group of believers who live in Chloe's home. In the first-century Roman world, women managed the household, and widows might continue the family business. Households included women, children of any age, relatives, enslaved people, and freed persons. Lydia (Acts 16:14-15) is also an example in Scripture of a female head of house. It is not clear whether Chloe herself was a believer. She probably lived in Ephesus and traveled to Corinth for business, but it is possible that she lived in Corinth and had business in Ephesus.

1:17 The important thing for Paul is not baptism but the preaching of the Good News; baptism simply signifies a person's response to the message. The phrase "clever speech" also indicates eloquence or an appeal to human wisdom. Too much emphasis on the persuasiveness of eloquence and human reason can distract from the simple message that Christ died for people's sins so that they could be forgiven (2:1-5; 15:1-3).

Chloe

IDENTITY — Courageous Voice for Unity

Chloe was probably one of those women we would deeply admire. We don't know a lot about her, but considering how Paul refers to her, Chloe may have been the head of her household, a woman of some wealth and influence. She was no ordinary woman by any stretch.

She may have been leading a church that met in her home and, if she was, she was facing a problem. Unity was breaking down among the Christians in Corinth.

Unity can be a mighty force that overcomes barriers and damaging mindsets, such as racism, inequality, and sexism. Unified, we can build and include, transform and restore.

Unity is also as fragile as a meadow flower. When snatched and choked, it fades and dies. When the weed of disunity takes hold, we find dissonance and hostility, superiority and entitlement.

Then fear sets in. Fear is insidious. It warps our thinking, induces the right to dominate others, and jeers at those who disagree. Finally, in the worst cases, fear incites violence.

Knowing disunity's destructive power gives us courage to overcome our fears of speaking up. Knowing what is at stake, we can take our stand on the side of unity.

Chloe's household set an example by reaching out to Paul. When disunity threatens, raise the issue. Like Chloe, you are no ordinary woman. You have God to strengthen you.

> Like Chloe's household, we can confidently speak up for unity.

CHLOE'S AND HER CHURCH'S STORY IS TOLD IN 1 CORINTHIANS 1:10-17.

IDENTIFY

How often do we tolerate division and dysfunction, preferring to watch from the sidelines?

What holds us back from speaking up? Who or what might we fear?

"It takes courage, wisdom, and leadership to advocate for unity. So champion your inner Chloe. She's only a prayer away."

ANDREA GIBSON is a certified coach and trainer. She and her husband spent seventeen years church planting. Her deepest desire now is to mentor and train women in the art of wise, godly leadership.

³⁰God has united you with Christ Jesus. For our benefit God made him to be wisdom itself. Christ made us right with God; he made us pure and holy, and he freed us from sin. ³¹Therefore, as the Scriptures say, "If you want to boast, boast only about the LORD."*

Paul's Message of Wisdom

2 When I first came to you, dear brothers and sisters,* I didn't use lofty words and impressive wisdom to tell you God's secret plan.* ²For I decided that while I was with you I would forget everything except Jesus Christ, the one who was crucified. ³I

1:31 Jer 9:24. 2:1a Greek *brothers.* 2:1b Greek *God's mystery;* other manuscripts read *God's testimony.*

Koinonia
IMAGE
MY STORY WITH COMMUNITY, WORKPLACE & CHURCH

Women for Unity

SCRIPTURE CONNECTION: 1 CORINTHIANS 1:10-17

The year was 1976. The place, Northern Ireland. Amid violence tearing apart our nation grew the Women's Peace Movement. Every mother on both sides shouted, "Enough is enough."

That summer, fifty thousand women marched and prayed for peace between Protestants and Catholics. For a few short months, we thought, "This is it; women are on their feet. We can do something about this insanity!"

But once we hear the word *I*, unity starts to disintegrate. At eleven years old, I watched the Women's Peace Movement divide and fracture. Most of my friends were Catholic girls, and from that summer on our friendship was lost and gone. I never saw them again. That has stayed with me.

But so has the hope we see in Chloe's story: Women have also advanced unity that lasts. There was a division within the church that met in Chloe's household. She refused to ignore developing factions, and her household took the lead. They called on Paul for his advice and leadership.

As with Chloe's household, we must continually remind ourselves that we are one body, with one baptism (12:13). We are sealed with the same Holy Spirit, serving the same Lord, and bearing the same cross. We share the same hope and future.

> Like Chloe's people, women advancing unity can do great good.

IMAGINE

Striving for unity takes courage, strength, and wisdom. How might you ask God to revive these in you?

How might you gather women to address important conflicts in your community?

"Unity is more than a word, more than a belief, more than a wish, and seeking unity in itself does not bring the unity we strive for. But if I seek it in the light of God's word, there is strength, hope, courage and a confidence that cannot be shaken, for then our unity is built on solid ground."

ANDREA GIBSON is a certified coach and trainer. She and her husband spent seventeen years church planting. Her deepest desire now is to mentor and train women in the art of wise, godly leadership.

came to you in weakness—timid and trembling. ⁴And my message and my preaching were very plain. Rather than using clever and persuasive speeches, I relied only on the power of the Holy Spirit. ⁵I did this so you would trust not in human wisdom but in the power of God.

⁶Yet when I am among mature believers, I do speak with words of wisdom, but not the kind of wisdom that belongs to this world or to the rulers of this world, who are soon forgotten. ⁷No, the wisdom we speak of is the mystery of God*—his plan that was previously hidden, even though he made it for our ultimate glory before the world began. ⁸But the rulers of this world have not understood it; if they had, they would not have crucified our glorious Lord. ⁹That is what the Scriptures mean when they say,

"No eye has seen, no ear has heard,
　and no mind has imagined
what God has prepared
　for those who love him."*

¹⁰But* it was to us that God revealed these things by his Spirit. For his Spirit searches out everything and shows us God's deep secrets. ¹¹No one can know a person's thoughts except that person's own spirit, and no one can know God's thoughts except God's own Spirit. ¹²And we have received God's Spirit (not the world's spirit), so we can know the wonderful things God has freely given us.

¹³When we tell you these things, we do not use words that come from human wisdom. Instead, we speak words given to us by the Spirit, using the Spirit's words to explain spiritual truths.* ¹⁴But people who aren't spiritual* can't receive these truths from God's Spirit. It all sounds foolish to them and they can't understand it, for only those who are spiritual can understand what the Spirit means. ¹⁵Those who are spiritual can evaluate all things, but they themselves cannot be evaluated by others. ¹⁶For,

"Who can know the LORD's thoughts?
　Who knows enough to teach him?"*

But we understand these things, for we have the mind of Christ.

Paul and Apollos, Servants of Christ

3 Dear brothers and sisters,* when I was with you I couldn't talk to you as I would to spiritual people.* I had to talk as though you belonged to this world or as though you were infants in Christ. ²I had to feed you with milk, not with solid food, because you weren't ready for anything stronger. And you still aren't ready, ³for you are still controlled by your sinful nature. You are jealous of one another and quarrel with each other. Doesn't that prove you are controlled by your sinful nature? Aren't you living like people of the world? ⁴When one of you says, "I am a follower of Paul," and another says, "I follow Apollos," aren't you acting just like people of the world?

⁵After all, who is Apollos? Who is Paul? We are only God's servants through whom you believed the Good News. Each of us did the work the Lord gave us. ⁶I planted the seed in your hearts, and Apollos watered it, but it was God who made it grow. ⁷It's not important who does the planting, or who does the watering. What's important is that God makes the seed grow. ⁸The one who plants and the one who waters work together with the same purpose. And both will be rewarded for their own hard work. ⁹For we are both God's workers. And you are God's field. You are God's building.

¹⁰Because of God's grace to me, I have laid the foundation like an expert builder. Now others are building on it. But whoever is building on this foundation must be very careful. ¹¹For no one can lay any foundation other than the one we already have—Jesus Christ.

¹²Anyone who builds on that foundation may use a variety of materials—gold, silver, jewels, wood, hay, or straw. ¹³But on the judgment day, fire will reveal what kind of work each builder has done. The fire will show if a person's work has any value. ¹⁴If the work survives, that builder will receive a reward. ¹⁵But if the work is burned up, the builder will suffer great loss. The builder will be saved, but like someone barely escaping through a wall of flames.

¹⁶Don't you realize that all of you together are the temple of God and that the Spirit of God lives in* you? ¹⁷God will destroy anyone who destroys this temple. For God's temple is holy, and you are that temple.

2:7 Greek *But we speak God's wisdom in a mystery.* **2:9** Isa 64:4. **2:10** Some manuscripts read *For.* **2:13** Or *explaining spiritual truths in spiritual language,* or *explaining spiritual truths to spiritual people.* **2:14** Or *who don't have the Spirit;* or *who have only physical life.* **2:16** Isa 40:13 (Greek version). **3:1a** Greek *Brothers.* **3:1b** Or *to people who have the Spirit.* **3:16** Or *among.*

2:16 This quotation from Isaiah 40:13 (quoting the Greek version of the Old Testament) shows how divine wisdom transcends the limitations of human reasoning (compare Romans 11:34). Linked to Christ, believers have the Spirit of Christ to reveal Christ's thinking to them.

3:12-15 Some of the things that people build on the foundation of Christ will endure; other things will burn up in the fire of judgment (see Malachi 4:1). On judgment day, the work of "each builder" who instructs the church (preachers, teachers, and pastors) will be assessed (compare James 3:1; see also Romans 14:10-12; 2 Corinthians 5:10). Those whose teachings are faithful and true "will receive a reward"; the others "will suffer great loss," not of their salvation but of their reward. They themselves will be saved but just barely, like someone pulled to safety "through a wall of flames" (see Amos 4:11; Zechariah 3:2; Jude 1:23).

¹⁸Stop deceiving yourselves. If you think you are wise by this world's standards, you need to become a fool to be truly wise. ¹⁹For the wisdom of this world is foolishness to God. As the Scriptures say,

"He traps the wise
in the snare of their own cleverness."*

²⁰And again,

"The LORD knows the thoughts of the wise;
he knows they are worthless."*

²¹So don't boast about following a particular human leader. For everything belongs to you—²²whether Paul or Apollos or Peter,* or the world, or life and death, or the present and the future. Everything belongs to you, ²³and you belong to Christ, and Christ belongs to God.

3:19 Job 5:13. 3:20 Ps 94:11. 3:22 Greek *Cephas*.

MY STORY OF MY UNIQUE INFLUENCE

Living Your Page in God's Story

SCRIPTURE CONNECTION: 1 CORINTHIANS 3:5-9

It's easy to ruminate on what is lacking in our lives. But Paul gives us a better alternative: Instead of focusing on what we're missing, let's focus on our mission.

Two questions inspired by 1 Corinthians 3:5-9 can help us live out our mission.

First, whose story do you want to be part of? Your mission is contingent on whose story you make central in your life.

Paul cut his followers' ties to himself and another well-known leader, Apollos, because he knew God's story is what's most important. He wrote, "After all, who is Apollos? Who is Paul? We are only God's servants through whom you believed the Good News" (3:5).

Resisting the gravitational pull of human allegiance, Paul pointed to the God who set the universe in motion. God has been writing a story throughout human history. Would you like to make sure your page is part of it?

> **God has a big story. Live out your page.**

Second, who are the people you want to impact your story? It's said that we become the average of the five people we spend the most time with. So let's spend time with the right five people.

Even while Paul was encouraging the Corinthians to keep their focus on God as the one who "makes the seed grow" (3:7), he doesn't downplay the planting or watering done by others. The people who have influence over our lives shape our story too.

But above everyone else in your story, God is the central character. You're a supporting character. Who else can be supporting characters in your story?

IMAGINE

Whose story do you want to be part of?

Who are the people you want to impact your story?

"Like all of us, I find that the people I spend time with rub off on me. I want to make sure that I'm spending enough time with Jesus followers so that their passion and faith rub off on me!"

KARA POWELL, PhD, is the executive director of the Fuller Youth Institute and chief of leadership formation at Fuller Theological Seminary. Kara speaks and has authored numerous books, including *3 Big Questions That Change Every Teenager*.

Paul's Relationship with the Corinthians

4 So look at Apollos and me as mere servants of Christ who have been put in charge of explaining God's mysteries. [2]Now, a person who is put in charge as a manager must be faithful. [3]As for me, it matters very little how I might be evaluated by you or by any human authority. I don't even trust my own judgment on this point. [4]My conscience is clear, but that doesn't prove I'm right. It is the Lord himself who will examine me and decide.

[5]So don't make judgments about anyone ahead of time—before the Lord returns. For he will bring our darkest secrets to light and will reveal our private motives. Then God will give to each one whatever praise is due.

[6]Dear brothers and sisters,* I have used Apollos and myself to illustrate what I've been saying. If you pay attention to what I have quoted from the Scriptures,* you won't be proud of one of your leaders at the expense of another. [7]For what gives you the right to make such a judgment? What do you have that God hasn't given you? And if everything you have is from God, why boast as though it were not a gift?

[8]You think you already have everything you need. You think you are already rich. You have begun to reign in God's kingdom without us! I wish you really were reigning already, for then we would be reigning with you. [9]Instead, I sometimes think God has put us apostles on display, like prisoners of war at the end of a victor's parade, condemned to die. We have become a spectacle to the entire world—to people and angels alike.

[10]Our dedication to Christ makes us look like fools, but you claim to be so wise in Christ! We are weak, but you are so powerful! You are honored, but we are ridiculed. [11]Even now we go hungry and thirsty, and we don't have enough clothes to keep warm. We are often beaten and have no home. [12]We work wearily with our own hands to earn our living. We bless those who curse us. We are patient with those who abuse us. [13]We appeal gently when evil things are said about us. Yet we are treated like the world's garbage, like everybody's trash—right up to the present moment.

[14]I am not writing these things to shame you, but to warn you as my beloved children. [15]For even if you had ten thousand others to teach you about Christ, you have only one spiritual father. For I became your father in Christ Jesus when I preached the Good News to you. [16]So I urge you to imitate me.

[17]That's why I have sent Timothy, my beloved and faithful child in the Lord. He will remind you of how I follow Christ Jesus, just as I teach in all the churches wherever I go.

[18]Some of you have become arrogant, thinking I will not visit you again. [19]But I will come—and soon—if the Lord lets me, and then I'll find out whether these arrogant people just give pretentious speeches or whether they really have God's power. [20]For the Kingdom of God is not just a lot of talk; it is living by God's power. [21]Which do you choose? Should I come with a rod to punish you, or should I come with love and a gentle spirit?

Paul Condemns Spiritual Pride

5 I can hardly believe the report about the sexual immorality going on among you—something that even pagans don't do. I am told that a man in your church is living in sin with his stepmother.* [2]You are so proud of yourselves, but you should be mourning in sorrow and shame. And you should remove this man from your fellowship.

[3]Even though I am not with you in person, I am with you in the Spirit.* And as though I were there, I have already passed judgment on this man [4]in the name of the Lord Jesus. You must call a meeting of the church.* I will be present with you in spirit, and so will the power of our Lord Jesus. [5]Then you must throw this man out and hand him over to Satan so that his sinful nature will be destroyed* and he himself* will be saved on the day the Lord* returns.

[6]Your boasting about this is terrible. Don't you realize that this sin is like a little yeast that spreads

---

4:6a Greek *Brothers.* **4:6b** Or *If you learn not to go beyond "what is written."* **5:1** Greek *his father's wife.* **5:3** Or *in spirit.* **5:4** Or *In the name of the Lord Jesus, you must call a meeting of the church.* **5:5a** Or *so that his body will be destroyed;* Greek reads *for the destruction of the flesh.* **5:5b** Greek *and the spirit.* **5:5c** Other manuscripts read *the Lord Jesus;* still others read *our Lord Jesus Christ.*

4:8-13 Paul ironically highlights the difference between himself and the Corinthians Christians. Their attitudes reflected the wisdom of the society they lived in; his, the wisdom of God. In their pride, the Corinthians thought they had arrived, but they actually had a long way to go (compare Revelation 3:17-18; contrast Philippians 3:12-14). If they had truly arrived, they would be sharing more of the suffering that Paul experienced (1 Corinthians 4:11-13). In contrast to the Corinthians, who were so proud of their attainments and the respect they had from others, the apostles suffered scorn and contempt.

5:1-2 Paul focuses here on the man, perhaps because the woman was not a believer. Both Romans and Jews thought it was the height of arrogance for a son to have sex with his father's wife (see Leviticus 20:11; Deuteronomy 22:30). The woman was likely not the man's mother, but his father's wife from a different, later marriage. She could have been a freedwoman who the father married, in which case she may have been used sexually by both men before the father freed and married her. Paul does not condemn women for sexual sins done to them by men, but he does condemn the Corinthian church. They were "so proud" of themselves, perhaps because they wrongly believed that their new life in Christ canceled any previous familial relationship—so much so that the woman in question was no longer to be viewed as the father's wife. Alternatively, the Corinthians may have believed their spiritual life in Christ made any activity in the body irrelevant and were proud of the man for being so bold in living out that (false) belief of Christian freedom (see 1 Corinthians 6:12-20).

Koinonia IMAGE
MY STORY WITH COMMUNITY, WORKPLACE & CHURCH

People Power or Kingdom Power?

SCRIPTURE CONNECTION: 1 CORINTHIANS 4:1-21

How are we supposed to respond to powerful Christians who challenge our understanding of the gospel? I know I am tempted to put powerful people down out of anger or fear about their impact. But Paul did not. When the Corinthians challenged Paul, he urged them to evaluate his ministry by God's standards, not people's standards and to:

- *Be humble about our wisdom and how we present it.* Paul, one of the most influential Christian leaders, states, "My conscience is clear, but that doesn't prove I'm right. It is the Lord himself who will examine me and decide" (1 Corinthians 4:4). Doing my best to understand and speak the truth does not mean I am right. Only God's wisdom is true wisdom, and he will be our judge (4:5). The Corinthians thought that Paul lacked oratorical skills. Paul said that only God could judge his gospel presentation, which should portray Christ's humility.
- *Respond like Christ.* The Corinthians wielded power wrongly, wanting Paul to have worldly success so they would look successful too. (4:10). But like Jesus, Paul and the apostles chose to "bless those who curse us." He added, "We are patient with those who abuse us. We appeal gently when evil things are said about us" (4:12-13). Paul wanted the Corinthians to imitate him in accepting public putdowns.
- *Trust in the power of God.* Paul's reminder is that "the Kingdom of God is not just a lot of talk; it is living by God's power" (4:20). Rather than act from fear, I can choose to respond like Christ and have confidence that God's Word will prevail.

> We can choose to respond to people's power with Kingdom power.

Like the Corinthians, we sometimes use human standards to define power. But Kingdom power looks humble, non-retaliatory, and trusting. Leaders called by God may not look powerful to us, but they do look like Apollos and Paul. They look like servants.

IMAGINE

What might it look like for you to practice humility like Paul's?

Is there an issue where you need to trust Kingdom power rather than human influence?

"Instead of getting caught in fear or resentment, I'm learning to turn to God—trusting that God's righteousness and justice will be the last word—and then I can turn to others with gentleness and patience."

DELANEY OVERTON develops programs and business strategies for impact-oriented organizations in education, food access, environmentalism, and other sectors. She experiences God's love and glory through creation, especially the seemingly unending ocean.

through the whole batch of dough? ⁷Get rid of the old "yeast" by removing this wicked person from among you. Then you will be like a fresh batch of dough made without yeast, which is what you really are. Christ, our Passover Lamb, has been sacrificed for us.* ⁸So let us celebrate the festival, not with the old bread* of wickedness and evil, but with the new bread* of sincerity and truth.

⁹When I wrote to you before, I told you not to associate with people who indulge in sexual sin. ¹⁰But I wasn't talking about unbelievers who indulge in sexual sin, or are greedy, or cheat people, or worship idols. You would have to leave this world to avoid people like that. ¹¹I meant that you are not to associate with anyone who claims to be a believer* yet indulges in sexual sin, or is greedy, or worships idols, or is abusive, or is a drunkard, or cheats people. Don't even eat with such people.

¹²It isn't my responsibility to judge outsiders, but it certainly is your responsibility to judge those inside the church who are sinning. ¹³God will judge those on the outside; but as the Scriptures say, "You must remove the evil person from among you."*

Avoiding Lawsuits with Christians

6 When one of you has a dispute with another believer, how dare you file a lawsuit and ask a secular court to decide the matter instead of taking it to other believers*! ²Don't you realize that someday we believers will judge the world? And since you are going to judge the world, can't you decide even these little things among yourselves? ³Don't you realize that we will judge angels? So you should surely be able to resolve ordinary disputes in this life. ⁴If you have legal disputes about such matters, why go to outside judges who are not respected by the church? ⁵I am saying this to shame you. Isn't there anyone in all the church who is wise enough to decide these issues? ⁶But instead, one believer* sues another—right in front of unbelievers!

⁷Even to have such lawsuits with one another is a defeat for you. Why not just accept the injustice and leave it at that? Why not let yourselves be cheated? ⁸Instead, you yourselves are the ones who do wrong and cheat even your fellow believers.*

⁹Don't you realize that those who do wrong will not inherit the Kingdom of God? Don't fool yourselves. Those who indulge in sexual sin, or who worship idols, or commit adultery, or are male prostitutes, or practice homosexuality, ¹⁰or are thieves, or greedy people, or drunkards, or are abusive, or cheat people—none of these will inherit the Kingdom of God. ¹¹Some of you were once like that. But you were cleansed; you were made holy; you were made right with God by calling on the name of the Lord Jesus Christ and by the Spirit of our God.

Avoiding Sexual Sin

¹²You say, "I am allowed to do anything"—but not everything is good for you. And even though "I am allowed to do anything," I must not become a slave to anything. ¹³You say, "Food was made for the stomach, and the stomach for food." (This is true, though someday God will do away with both of them.) But you can't say that our bodies were made for sexual immorality. They were made for the Lord, and the Lord cares about our bodies. ¹⁴And God will raise us from the dead by his power, just as he raised our Lord from the dead.

¹⁵Don't you realize that your bodies are actually parts of Christ? Should a man take his body, which is part of Christ, and join it to a prostitute? Never! ¹⁶And don't you realize that if a man joins himself to a prostitute, he becomes one body with her? For the Scriptures say, "The two are united into one."* ¹⁷But the person who is joined to the Lord is one spirit with him.

¹⁸Run from sexual sin! No other sin so clearly affects the body as this one does. For sexual immorality is a sin against your own body. ¹⁹Don't you

---

5:7 Greek *has been sacrificed.* 5:8a Greek *not with old leaven.* 5:8b Greek *but with unleavened [bread].* 5:11 Greek *a brother.* 5:13 Deut 17:7. 6:1 Greek *God's holy people;* also in 6:2. 6:6 Greek *one brother.* 6:8 Greek *even the brothers.* 6:16 Gen 2:24.

5:11 Separation from a professing believer who was living in sin was intended to reinforce and maintain the high moral standards of the Christian community. The social pressure it exerted might also encourage repentance in an erring believer (see also 2 Thessalonians 3:6, 14).

6:11 Following the strong warning of 6:9-10, Paul reaffirms his confidence in the genuineness of his readers' conversion. Cleanliness is a metaphor for the righteousness that comes from forgiveness (compare Acts 22:16; see Titus 3:5). They "were made holy" by God himself (see 1 Corinthians 1:2). They were made right with God by their identification with Jesus and by the transforming work of the Holy Spirit. God had forgiven them and he viewed them as righteous (see Romans 1:17; 3:21-26), changing their lives for the better (see Titus 3:5-7).

6:15-20 Because their bodies were "temple[s] of the Holy Spirit," Paul rebuked the men who went to prostitutes. In Greco-Roman culture, a married man was not considered unfaithful to his wife if he had sex with a prostitute. The Corinthians believed that, because they had been baptized in Christ, the activities of their bodies, including sex, were of no spiritual importance. Paul strongly disagreed, stating that their baptism into Christ brought a call for holiness. But notice that Paul does not condemn the prostitute, who may have been an enslaved woman who had been forced into prostitution. Such women were used sexually by their male enslavers. Since up to 20 percent of the Roman population was enslaved, it's possible that this accounted for up to one fifth of the Corinthian congregation, and it is likely that among the enslaved believers, some were used sexually. Paul does not condemn them for what we would recognize today as rape (see Deuteronomy 22:25-29); instead, he reproves the men who violated them.

realize that your body is the temple of the Holy Spirit, who lives in you and was given to you by God? You do not belong to yourself, 20for God bought you with a high price. So you must honor God with your body.

Instruction on Marriage

7 Now regarding the questions you asked in your letter. Yes, it is good to abstain from sexual relations.* 2But because there is so much sexual

7:1 Or *to live a celibate life;* Greek reads *It is good for a man not to touch a woman.*

7:1-4 In principle, Paul accepts the Corinthians' claim that "it is good to abstain from sexual relations" because Paul valued celibacy. However, he also praises marriage and insists that sex is an important part of that relationship. In an astonishingly countercultural statement, Paul declares that "the husband gives authority over his body to his wife." This mutuality in marriage is rooted in the New Testament's vision of marriage wherein the husband loves his wife self-sacrificially and treats her as he does himself (see Ephesians 5:25-33).

MY STORY WITH GOD

Beautiful: Our Bodies as Temples

SCRIPTURE CONNECTION: 1 CORINTHIANS 6:19-20

For years, I trained as a dancer. In the ballet studio, all I knew were mirrors—my worth was attached to a black leotard and how my body looked within it. Slowly my heart filled with society's lies about my body.

Society told me that my worth is determined from a number on a scale, that acceptance is a "look" to be achieved, and that success is a strength to be fought for. With every day and every glance in the mirror, the lies accumulated. My heart grew heavy, and I carried it exhaustedly, choked by culture's whispers.

Women are not often taught to celebrate how we are created. Rather, our world creates unreasonable expectations and, if not achieved, we experience shame. But Paul reminds us of what our body really is—a home for the Holy Spirit.

This truth declares my body is a beautiful temple where God lives.

Learning to honor God in my body didn't happen overnight. It happened as I learned to speak the truth with every glance in the mirror. It happened as I remembered the Spirit's weight within me with every step on the scale. And it happened as I silenced every false musical ad with a song to the One who shaped me.

By cutting away one lie at a time, I began to make my body a roomier space for God. Sweeping away society's lies about our bodies and declaring the truth of the Holy Spirit within can free God's daughters to dance. Rather than look at mirrors, we can listen inwardly and discover we are already loved and lovely.

> Rather than look at mirrors, we can listen inwardly to discover we are already loved and lovely.

IMAGINE

What lie might you be carrying about your body? What truth can you begin to speak?

How can you say thank you for how God created you?

"Noticing the world's lies and making room for the truth of the female body honors God and honors women."

WHITNEY PUTNAM is the senior director of women's events and marketing at New Life Ministries. She is an overall joy-chaser and is often found dancing in her kitchen.

immorality, each man should have his own wife, and each woman should have her own husband.

³The husband should fulfill his wife's sexual needs, and the wife should fulfill her husband's needs. ⁴The wife gives authority over her body to her husband, and the husband gives authority over his body to his wife.

⁵Do not deprive each other of sexual relations, unless you both agree to refrain from sexual intimacy for a limited time so you can give yourselves more completely to prayer. Afterward, you should come together again so that Satan won't be able to tempt you because of your lack of self-control. ⁶I say this as a concession, not as a command. ⁷But I wish everyone were single, just as I am. Yet each person has a special gift from God, of one kind or another.

⁸So I say to those who aren't married and to widows—it's better to stay unmarried, just as I am. ⁹But if they can't control themselves, they should go ahead and marry. It's better to marry than to burn with lust.

¹⁰But for those who are married, I have a command that comes not from me, but from the Lord.* A wife must not leave her husband. ¹¹But if she does leave him, let her remain single or else be reconciled to him. And the husband must not leave his wife.

¹²Now, I will speak to the rest of you, though I do not have a direct command from the Lord. If a fellow believer* has a wife who is not a believer and she is willing to continue living with him, he must not leave her. ¹³And if a believing woman has a husband who is not a believer and he is willing to continue living with her, she must not leave him. ¹⁴For the believing wife brings holiness to her marriage, and the believing husband* brings holiness to his marriage. Otherwise, your children would not be holy, but now they are holy. ¹⁵(But if the husband or wife who isn't a believer insists on leaving, let them go. In such cases the believing husband or wife* is no longer bound to the other, for God has called you* to live in peace.) ¹⁶Don't you wives realize that your husbands might be saved because of you? And don't you husbands realize that your wives might be saved because of you?

¹⁷Each of you should continue to live in whatever situation the Lord has placed you, and remain as you were when God first called you. This is my rule for all the churches. ¹⁸For instance, a man who was circumcised before he became a believer should not try to reverse it. And the man who was uncircumcised when he became a believer should not be circumcised now. ¹⁹For it makes no difference whether or not a man has been circumcised. The important thing is to keep God's commandments.

²⁰Yes, each of you should remain as you were when God called you. ²¹Are you a slave? Don't let that worry you—but if you get a chance to be free, take it. ²²And remember, if you were a slave when the Lord called you, you are now free in the Lord. And if you were free when the Lord called you, you are now a slave of Christ. ²³God paid a high price for you, so don't be enslaved by the world.* ²⁴Each of you, dear brothers and sisters,* should remain as you were when God first called you.

²⁵Now regarding your question about the young women who are not yet married. I do not have a command from the Lord for them. But the Lord in his mercy has given me wisdom that can be trusted, and I will share it with you. ²⁶Because of the present crisis,* I think it is best to remain as you are. ²⁷If you have a wife, do not seek to end the marriage. If you do not have a wife, do not seek to get married. ²⁸But if you do get married, it is not a sin. And if a young woman gets married, it is not a sin. However, those who get married at this time will have troubles, and I am trying to spare you those problems.

²⁹But let me say this, dear brothers and sisters: The time that remains is very short. So from now on, those with wives should not focus only on their marriage. ³⁰Those who weep or who rejoice or who buy things should not be absorbed by their weeping or their joy or their possessions. ³¹Those who use the things of the world should not become attached to them. For this world as we know it will soon pass away.

³²I want you to be free from the concerns of this life. An unmarried man can spend his time doing the Lord's work and thinking how to please him. ³³But a married man has to think about his earthly responsibilities and how to please his wife. ³⁴His interests are divided. In the same way, a woman who is no longer married or has never been married can be devoted to the Lord and holy in body and in spirit. But a married woman has to think about her earthly responsibilities and how to please her husband. ³⁵I am saying this for your benefit, not to place restrictions on you. I want you to do whatever will help you serve the Lord best, with as few distractions as possible.

³⁶But if a man thinks that he's treating his fiancée improperly and will inevitably give in to his passion,

---

7:10 See Matt 5:32; 19:9; Mark 10:11-12; Luke 16:18. **7:12** Greek *a brother.* **7:14** Greek *the brother.* **7:15a** Greek *the brother or sister.* **7:15b** Some manuscripts read *us.* **7:23** Greek *don't become slaves of people.* **7:24** Greek *brothers;* also in 7:29. **7:26** Or *the pressures of life.*

7:25-40 Paul offered women the freedom to follow the Lord as they see best, whether that be as a married women or as a single, celibate women. Their first and final responsibility was to follow the Lord. Fathers and other family members were to give preference to women's choices. This was and still can be a revolutionary idea. Paul's encouragement that everyone can choose whether to wed or remain single in service to the Lord has allowed countless women over the centuries of the church to choose a life dedicated entirely to serving God. Women have used this freedom to do mission work, engage in traveling evangelism efforts, and teach and lead the people of God in creative ways.

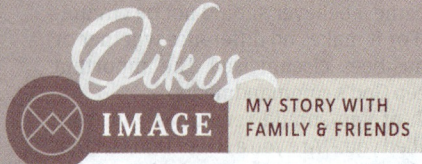

God's Design for Love

SCRIPTURE CONNECTION: 1 CORINTHIANS 7:1-11, 25-40

What did Paul mean when he said that it's good to abstain from having sex, but if you can't, then marry? What is marriage's purpose—just to fulfill a sexual need? If so, why would God give us sexual desires?

Paul, as a good pastor, answered his congregation's questions. Sometimes they were the wrong questions, so he redirected them to what was right. In 7:1, Paul responded to the Corinthians' claim that married couples should not be having sex. However, some men in the church were having sex with prostitutes, a common arrangement among Gentiles (but not Jews) in Paul's day (see 6:15-20).

Paul taught that having sex within marriage is good, for our bodies are made for intimacy (following Genesis 2:20-25). He said that the wife has authority over her husband's body (1 Corinthians 7:4). This was a revolutionary idea, for his culture said that a wife had to obey her husband in the bedroom. Paul also stressed mutuality and self-sacrificial love in marriage (see also Ephesians 5:25). Sexual desire and intimacy are rooted in love, but our culture objectifies and commercializes bodies.

> God created sexual desire to be fulfilled in marriage, but ultimately, God created humans to desire life with him.

Paul declared singleness as another path, one that allowed him to fulfill his life's calling (1 Corinthians 7:7; not all the apostles were single, 9:5). Women could choose whether to marry, which greatly empowered them.

God created sexual desire to be fulfilled in marriage, but ultimately, God created people to desire life with him. Paul wanted the Corinthians to desire what would last into eternity: a life of love (12:31–13:13), for the "greatest of these is love."

IMAGINE

What keeps you from undivided devotion to God?

What keeps you from embracing your body as God's gift to you to love others self-sacrificially, whether married or single?

"Our capacity for self-giving love starts with a proper love of our own body. I asked my wise Congolese friend what she thought of her body. She said that God had made her tall enough to reach the upper cupboard in the kitchen, healthy enough to do her tasks. God made her perfectly. How right she was!"

LYNN H. COHICK, PhD, is Distinguished Professor of New Testament and Director of Houston Theological Seminary, where she leads the Doctor of Ministry program. She writes, speaks, and teaches internationally.

let him marry her as he wishes. It is not a sin. ³⁷But if he has decided firmly not to marry and there is no urgency and he can control his passion, he does well not to marry. ³⁸So the person who marries his fiancée does well, and the person who doesn't marry does even better.

³⁹A wife is bound to her husband as long as he lives. If her husband dies, she is free to marry anyone she wishes, but only if he loves the Lord.* ⁴⁰But in my opinion it would be better for her to stay single, and I think I am giving you counsel from God's Spirit when I say this.

Food Sacrificed to Idols

8 Now regarding your question about food that has been offered to idols. Yes, we know that "we all have knowledge" about this issue. But while knowledge makes us feel important, it is love that strengthens the church. ²Anyone who claims to know all the answers doesn't really know very much. ³But the person who loves God is the one whom God recognizes.*

⁴So, what about eating meat that has been offered to idols? Well, we all know that an idol is not really a god and that there is only one God. ⁵There may be so-called gods both in heaven and on earth, and some people actually worship many gods and many lords. ⁶But for us,

There is one God, the Father,
   by whom all things were created,
   and for whom we live.
And there is one Lord, Jesus Christ,
   through whom all things were created,
   and through whom we live.

⁷However, not all believers know this. Some are accustomed to thinking of idols as being real, so when they eat food that has been offered to idols, they think of it as the worship of real gods, and their weak consciences are violated. ⁸It's true that we can't win God's approval by what we eat. We don't lose anything if we don't eat it, and we don't gain anything if we do.

⁹But you must be careful so that your freedom does not cause others with a weaker conscience to stumble. ¹⁰For if others see you—with your "superior knowledge"—eating in the temple of an idol, won't they be encouraged to violate their conscience by eating food that has been offered to an idol? ¹¹So because of your superior knowledge, a weak believer* for whom Christ died will be destroyed. ¹²And when you sin against other believers* by encouraging them to do something they believe is wrong, you are sinning against Christ. ¹³So if what I eat causes another believer to sin, I will never eat meat again as long as I live—for I don't want to cause another believer to stumble.

Paul Gives Up His Rights

9 Am I not as free as anyone else? Am I not an apostle? Haven't I seen Jesus our Lord with my own eyes? Isn't it because of my work that you belong to the Lord? ²Even if others think I am not an apostle, I certainly am to you. You yourselves are proof that I am the Lord's apostle.

³This is my answer to those who question my authority.* ⁴Don't we have the right to live in your homes and share your meals? ⁵Don't we have the right to bring a believing wife* with us as the other apostles and the Lord's brothers do, and as Peter* does? ⁶Or is it only Barnabas and I who have to work to support ourselves?

⁷What soldier has to pay his own expenses? What farmer plants a vineyard and doesn't have the right to eat some of its fruit? What shepherd cares for a flock of sheep and isn't allowed to drink some of the milk? ⁸Am I expressing merely a human opinion, or does the law say the same thing? ⁹For the law of Moses says, "You must not muzzle an ox to keep it from eating as it treads out the grain."* Was God thinking only about oxen when he said this? ¹⁰Wasn't he actually speaking to us? Yes, it was written for us,

7:39 Greek *but only in the Lord.* 8:3 Some manuscripts read *the person who loves has full knowledge.* 8:11 Greek *brother;* also in 8:13. 8:12 Greek *brothers.* 9:3 Greek *those who examine me.* 9:5a Greek *a sister a wife.* 9:5b Greek *Cephas.* 9:9 Deut 25:4.

8:1–11:1 Paul here addresses the Corinthians' "question about food that has been offered to idols." Throughout the Greco-Roman world, there were temples and shrines dedicated to pagan gods. It was common for worshipers of those gods to offer animal sacrifices, and the excess meat was then sold in the market by the priests. The question inevitably arose as to whether Christians were free to eat such meat. Was meat taken from an animal that has been sacrificed to a pagan god inherently defiled? Paul makes no mention here of the prohibition made by the Jewish Christian leaders in Acts 15:20, 29, but emphasizes that one's actions must be governed, above all, by loving consideration of others. After introducing the topic (1 Corinthians 8:1-13), he provides several illustrations of the principle of giving up one's rights for the sake of others (9:1-27), and then gives his advice on three specific situations in which believers faced this issue.

9:1-2 These four rhetorical questions each expect a positive answer. The first, following his discussion in 8:1-13, is an assertion of Paul's freedom from Jewish ritual obligations—though, as he later emphasizes (see 9:19-23), he freely accommodates himself to the practices of Jews in his desire to win them to Christ. The other three rhetorical questions are assertions of Paul's apostolic authority, which was apparently being questioned by some in Corinth. For those who seemed to be skeptical, the reality of Paul's apostolic calling was verified by his firsthand encounter with Jesus on the road to Damascus (see 15:8; Acts 9:3-6, 17). And the Corinthians themselves, who came to faith through Paul's evangelism (see Acts 18:1-11), were "proof" (literally "the seal") of his status as an apostle.

so that the one who plows and the one who threshes the grain might both expect a share of the harvest. ¹¹Since we have planted spiritual seed among you, aren't we entitled to a harvest of physical food and drink? ¹²If you support others who preach to you, shouldn't we have an even greater right to be supported? But we have never used this right. We would rather put up with anything than be an obstacle to the Good News about Christ.

¹³Don't you realize that those who work in the temple get their meals from the offerings brought to the temple? And those who serve at the altar get a share of the sacrificial offerings. ¹⁴In the same way, the Lord ordered that those who preach the Good News should be supported by those who benefit from it. ¹⁵Yet I have never used any of these rights. And I am not writing this to suggest that I want to start now. In fact, I would rather die than lose my right to boast about preaching without charge. ¹⁶Yet preaching the Good News is not something I can boast about. I am compelled by God to do it. How terrible for me if I didn't preach the Good News!

¹⁷If I were doing this on my own initiative, I would deserve payment. But I have no choice, for God has given me this sacred trust. ¹⁸What then is my pay? It is the opportunity to preach the Good News without

Prayer, an Act of Love

SCRIPTURE CONNECTION: 1 CORINTHIANS 7:1-40

Something amazing happens to our hearts when we pray for another person. The hardness melts. We become able to get beyond the hurts, and forgive. We even end up loving the person we are praying for. It's miraculous! It happens because when we pray we enter into the presence of God and He fills us with His Spirit of love. When you pray for your husband, the love of God will grow in your heart for him. Not only that, you'll find love growing in *his* heart for *you*, without him even knowing you are praying. That's because prayer is the ultimate love language. It communicates in ways we can't. I've seen women with no feelings of love for their husbands find that as they prayed, over time, those feelings came. Sometimes they felt differently even after the first heartfelt prayer.

> **Prayer is the ultimate love language.**

Talking to God about your husband is an act of love. Prayer gives rise to love, love begets more prayer, which in turn gives rise to more love. Even if your praying is not born out of completely selfless motives, your motives will become more unselfish as prayer continues. You'll find yourself more loving in your responses. You'll notice that issues which formerly caused strife between you will no longer do that. You'll be able to come to mutual agreements without a fight. This unity is vital.

We want to be on the same path together. We want to be deeply compatible, lifelong companions, and have the love that lasts a lifetime. Prayer, as the ultimate love language, can make that happen.

IMAGINE

Whether or not you are married, who can you pray for to love better?

What other words (such as criticisms or insults) might you need to stop saying—in your mind or aloud?

"As husband and wife we don't want to be taking separate roads."

STORMIE OMARTIAN
Taken from: *The Power of a Praying® Wife*, Copyright © 1997, 2014 by Stormie Omartian. Published by Harvest House Publishers, Eugene, Oregon 97408. www.harvesthousepublishers.com

charging anyone. That's why I never demand my rights when I preach the Good News.

¹⁹Even though I am a free man with no master, I have become a slave to all people to bring many to Christ. ²⁰When I was with the Jews, I lived like a Jew to bring the Jews to Christ. When I was with those who follow the Jewish law, I too lived under that law. Even though I am not subject to the law, I did this so I could bring to Christ those who are under the law. ²¹When I am with the Gentiles who do not follow the Jewish law,* I too live apart from that law so I can bring them to Christ. But I do not ignore the law of God; I obey the law of Christ.

²²When I am with those who are weak, I share their weakness, for I want to bring the weak to Christ. Yes, I try to find common ground with everyone, doing everything I can to save some. ²³I do everything to spread the Good News and share in its blessings.

²⁴Don't you realize that in a race everyone runs, but only one person gets the prize? So run to win! ²⁵All athletes are disciplined in their training. They do it to win a prize that will fade away, but we do it for an eternal prize. ²⁶So I run with purpose in every step. I am not just shadowboxing. ²⁷I discipline my body like an athlete, training it to do what it should. Otherwise, I fear that after preaching to others I myself might be disqualified.

Lessons from Israel's Idolatry

10 I don't want you to forget, dear brothers and sisters,* about our ancestors in the wilderness long ago. All of them were guided by a cloud that moved ahead of them, and all of them walked through the sea on dry ground. ²In the cloud and in the sea, all of them were baptized as followers of Moses. ³All of them ate the same spiritual food, ⁴and all of them drank the same spiritual water. For they drank from the spiritual rock that traveled with them, and that rock was Christ. ⁵Yet God was not pleased with most of them, and their bodies were scattered in the wilderness.

⁶These things happened as a warning to us, so that we would not crave evil things as they did, ⁷or worship idols as some of them did. As the Scriptures say, "The people celebrated with feasting and drinking, and they indulged in pagan revelry."* ⁸And we must not engage in sexual immorality as some of them did, causing 23,000 of them to die in one day.

⁹Nor should we put Christ* to the test, as some of them did and then died from snakebites. ¹⁰And don't grumble as some of them did, and then were destroyed by the angel of death. ¹¹These things happened to them as examples for us. They were written down to warn us who live at the end of the age.

¹²If you think you are standing strong, be careful not to fall. ¹³The temptations in your life are no different from what others experience. And God is faithful. He will not allow the temptation to be more than you can stand. When you are tempted, he will show you a way out so that you can endure.

¹⁴So, my dear friends, flee from the worship of idols. ¹⁵You are reasonable people. Decide for yourselves if what I am saying is true. ¹⁶When we bless the cup at the Lord's Table, aren't we sharing in the blood of Christ? And when we break the bread, aren't we sharing in the body of Christ? ¹⁷And though we are many, we all eat from one loaf of bread, showing that we are one body. ¹⁸Think about the people of Israel. Weren't they united by eating the sacrifices at the altar?

¹⁹What am I trying to say? Am I saying that food offered to idols has some significance, or that idols are real gods? ²⁰No, not at all. I am saying that these sacrifices are offered to demons, not to God. And I don't want you to participate with demons. ²¹You cannot drink from the cup of the Lord and from the cup of demons, too. You cannot eat at the Lord's Table and at the table of demons, too. ²²What? Do we dare to rouse the Lord's jealousy? Do you think we are stronger than he is?

²³You say, "I am allowed to do anything"*—but not everything is good for you. You say, "I am allowed to do anything"—but not everything is beneficial. ²⁴Don't be concerned for your own good but for the good of others.

²⁵So you may eat any meat that is sold in the marketplace without raising questions of conscience. ²⁶For "the earth is the LORD's, and everything in it."*

²⁷If someone who isn't a believer asks you home for dinner, accept the invitation if you want to. Eat whatever is offered to you without raising questions of conscience. ²⁸(But suppose someone tells you, "This meat was offered to an idol." Don't eat it, out of consideration for the conscience of the one who told you. ²⁹It might not be a matter of conscience for you, but it is for the other person.) For why should my freedom be limited by what someone else thinks? ³⁰If I can thank God for the food and enjoy it, why should I be condemned for eating it?

³¹So whether you eat or drink, or whatever you do, do it all for the glory of God. ³²Don't give offense to Jews or Gentiles* or the church of God. ³³I, too, try to please everyone in everything I do. I don't just do what is best for me; I do what is best for others so that many may be saved. ¹¹:¹And you should imitate me, just as I imitate Christ.

9:21 Greek *those without the law.* **10:1** Greek *brothers.* **10:7** Exod 32:6. **10:9** Some manuscripts read *the Lord.* **10:23** Greek *All things are lawful;* also in 10:23b. **10:26** Ps 24:1. **10:32** Greek *or Greeks.*

10:16-18 Paul affirms the spiritual meaning of sacred meals. In the Lord's Supper, believers share in the blood and body of Christ (see also 11:17-34; Matthew 26:26-28; Mark 14:22-24; Luke 22:19-20). Sharing one loaf unites believers as one body in Christ, just as the pagans' religious meals united them with the gods they worshiped (see 1 Corinthians 10:19-21).

WHAT THE BIBLE SAYS ABOUT Singleness

Advantages to Remaining Single

I want you to be free from the concerns of this life. An unmarried man can spend his time doing the Lord's work and thinking how to please him.... A woman who is no longer married or has never been married can be devoted to the Lord and holy in body and in spirit. But a married woman has to think about her earthly responsibilities and how to please her husband. I am saying this for your benefit, not to place restrictions on you. I want you to do whatever will help you serve the Lord best, with as few distractions as possible. **1 CORINTHIANS 7:32-35**

Singleness Is a Calling for Some

I say to those who aren't married and to widows—it's better to stay unmarried, just as I am. But if they can't control themselves, they should go ahead and marry. It's better to marry than to burn with lust. **1 CORINTHIANS 7:8-9**

"Not everyone can accept this statement," Jesus said. "Only those whom God helps. Some are born as eunuchs, some have been made eunuchs by others, and some choose not to marry for the sake of the Kingdom of Heaven. Let anyone accept this who can." **MATTHEW 19:11-12**

Singleness Is a Gift

I wish everyone were single, just as I am. Yet each person has a special gift from God, of one kind or another. **1 CORINTHIANS 7:7**

Instructions for Public Worship

11 ²I am so glad that you always keep me in your thoughts, and that you are following the teachings I passed on to you. ³But there is one thing I want you to know: The head of every man is Christ, the head of woman is man, and the head of Christ is God.* ⁴A man dishonors his head* if he covers his head while praying or prophesying. ⁵But a woman dishonors her head* if she prays or prophesies without a covering on her head, for this is the same as shaving her head. ⁶Yes, if she refuses to wear a head covering, she should cut off all her hair! But since it is shameful for a woman to have her hair cut or her head shaved, she should wear a covering.*

⁷A man should not wear anything on his head when worshiping, for man is made in God's image and reflects God's glory. And woman reflects man's glory. ⁸For the first man didn't come from woman, but the first woman came from man. ⁹And man was not made for woman, but woman was made for man. ¹⁰For this reason, and because the angels are watching, a woman should wear a covering on her head to show she is under authority.*

¹¹But among the Lord's people, women are not independent of men, and men are not independent of women. ¹²For although the first woman came from man, every other man was born from a woman, and everything comes from God.

¹³Judge for yourselves. Is it right for a woman to pray to God in public without covering her head? ¹⁴Isn't it obvious that it's disgraceful for a man to have long hair? ¹⁵And isn't long hair a woman's pride and joy? For it has been given to her as a covering. ¹⁶But if anyone wants to argue about this, I simply say that we have no other custom than this, and neither do God's other churches.

Order at the Lord's Supper

¹⁷But in the following instructions, I cannot praise you. For it sounds as if more harm than good is done when you meet together. ¹⁸First, I hear that there are divisions among you when you meet as a church, and to some extent I believe it. ¹⁹But, of course, there must be divisions among you so that you who have God's approval will be recognized!

²⁰When you meet together, you are not really interested in the Lord's Supper. ²¹For some of you hurry to eat your own meal without sharing with others. As a result, some go hungry while others get drunk. ²²What? Don't you have your own homes for eating and drinking? Or do you really want to disgrace God's church and shame the poor? What am

---

11:3 Or *to know: The source of every man is Christ, the source of woman is man, and the source of Christ is God.* Or *to know: Every man is responsible to Christ, a woman is responsible to her husband, and Christ is responsible to God.* **11:4** Or *dishonors Christ.* **11:5** Or *dishonors her husband.* **11:6** Or *should have long hair.* **11:10** Greek *should have an authority on her head.*

11:3 While this verse has been used to suppose a hierarchical relationship of men over women, there are many reasons to think that is not the correct interpretation of what Paul is saying. In ancient Greek, the word *head* rarely means a metaphorical leader, unlike in Hebrew and English. Instead, *head* can refer to a source (such as the *headwaters* of a river), denote prominence (such as a *head chef*), or be used as a figure of speech to represent a group (such as a *headcount*, meaning the number of people in attendance). Paul stresses that Christ is the source of every man, as the new Adam who redeems humanity (15:45-49; Romans 5:12-17). "The head of woman is man" refers to the source of the first woman, who was created from the first man's rib (1 Corinthians 11:12; Genesis 2:21-25). Had Paul wished to say that the husband or man has authority over the wife or woman, he could have used the common Greek term for authority (*exousia*); he uses this term in 1 Corinthians 7:4 to speak of each spouse having authority over the body of the other. Christ in his divine Person is not subordinate to God the Father but is equally God in substance and essence. Therefore, "head" in this passage does not teach that the Son is eternally subordinated to the Father. Instead, it shows the Father as the source of the Son's incarnation. The three phrases are not in hierarchical order, further confirming that "head" does not imply "leader" here.

11:5 Paul affirms the practice of women praying, speaking, and prophesying in the church service: Prophesying includes theologically astute encouragement, preaching, and teaching. The remarks might be prepared or spontaneous (14:3, 29-33). Paul's admonition here about head coverings pertains to the ancient Greco-Roman context, but there is uncertainty about exactly what was happening in the Corinthian church. It's possible that only married women were usually veiled, or that Paul was encouraging wealthy members of the congregation to abstain from showing off their wealth with elaborate hairstyles, which wealthy Roman woman often did. But it may be that men were denying enslaved women the honor of wearing a free woman's head covering and Paul was affirming that all women were free to wear a covering, thus minimizing class differences. It's also possible that the head-covering requirement was given by Corinthian men who misunderstand the Creation account, which states that men and women are both made in the image of God. In this case, Paul would have been citing their views, and then denouncing it later in 11:11-12.

11:7-12 This passage has confused interpreters because neither Genesis nor Paul elsewhere speaks of "glory" in this way; perhaps Paul was presenting the Corinthians' own false views in 11:7-9, establishing their argument before responding in 11:13-16. Alternatively, Paul could be stating that God bestowed his glory on man; then woman received glory as she was created out of man (she is also created in God's image, Genesis 1:26-27). Less likely is that a woman merely reflects man's glory. In 1 Corinthians 11:10 the Greek is literally that "a woman should have an authority on her head," and the plain meaning is her own authority. This meaning is supported by what Paul says in 11:11, which cautions that a woman's own authority over her person does not mean that women are independent of men (or vice versa).

Insight: THE GIFT REGISTRY

In several places Paul and Peter write about "spiritual gifts" and give examples. Here's an alphabetical list that combines all the gifts specifically tagged in the Greek text as *charismata* (literally, "grace-gifts") from God.

Is this list exhaustive? Not necessarily, say many Bible scholars. But even so, it forms a bountiful registry on its own.

SPIRITUAL GIFT	REFERENCE
Discernment of God's Spirit from other spirits	1 Corinthians 12:10
Encouragement	Romans 12:8
Great faith	1 Corinthians 12:9
Giving money	Romans 12:8
Healing the sick	1 Corinthians 12:9
Interpreting unknown languages	1 Corinthians 12:10
Kindness	Romans 12:8
Performing miracles	1 Corinthians 12:10
Prophecy	Romans 12:6; 1 Corinthians 12:10; 1 Peter 4:11
Serving	Romans 12:7; 1 Peter 4:10
Singleness	1 Corinthians 7:7
Speaking in unknown languages	1 Corinthians 12:10
Special knowledge	1 Corinthians 12:8
Teaching	Romans 12:7
Wise advice	1 Corinthians 12:8

I supposed to say? Do you want me to praise you? Well, I certainly will not praise you for this!

²³For I pass on to you what I received from the Lord himself. On the night when he was betrayed, the Lord Jesus took some bread ²⁴and gave thanks to God for it. Then he broke it in pieces and said, "This is my body, which is given for you.* Do this in remembrance of me." ²⁵In the same way, he took the cup of wine after supper, saying, "This cup is the new covenant between God and his people—an agreement confirmed with my blood. Do this in remembrance of me as often as you drink it." ²⁶For every time you eat this bread and drink this cup, you are announcing the Lord's death until he comes again.

²⁷So anyone who eats this bread or drinks this cup of the Lord unworthily is guilty of sinning against* the body and blood of the Lord. ²⁸That is why you should examine yourself before eating the bread and drinking the cup. ²⁹For if you eat the bread or drink the cup without honoring the body of Christ,* you are eating and drinking God's judgment upon yourself. ³⁰That is why many of you are weak and sick and some have even died.

³¹But if we would examine ourselves, we would not be judged by God in this way. ³²Yet when we are judged by the Lord, we are being disciplined so that we will not be condemned along with the world.

³³So, my dear brothers and sisters,* when you gather for the Lord's Supper, wait for each other. ³⁴If you are really hungry, eat at home so you won't bring judgment upon yourselves when you meet together. I'll give you instructions about the other matters after I arrive.

11:24 Greek *which is for you;* other manuscripts read *which is broken for you.* **11:27** Or *is responsible for.* **11:29** Greek *the body;* other manuscripts read *the Lord's body.* **11:33** Greek *brothers.*

Spiritual Gifts

12 Now, dear brothers and sisters,* regarding your question about the special abilities the Spirit gives us. I don't want you to misunderstand this. ²You know that when you were still pagans, you were led astray and swept along in worshiping speechless idols. ³So I want you to know that no one speaking by the Spirit of God will curse Jesus, and no one can say Jesus is Lord, except by the Holy Spirit.

⁴There are different kinds of spiritual gifts, but the same Spirit is the source of them all. ⁵There are different kinds of service, but we serve the same Lord. ⁶God works in different ways, but it is the same God who does the work in all of us.

⁷A spiritual gift is given to each of us so we can help each other. ⁸To one person the Spirit gives the ability to give wise advice*; to another the same Spirit gives a message of special knowledge.* ⁹The same Spirit gives great faith to another, and to someone else the one Spirit gives the gift of healing. ¹⁰He gives one person the power to perform miracles, and another the ability to prophesy. He gives someone else the ability to discern whether a message is from the Spirit of God or from another spirit. Still another person is given the ability to speak in unknown languages,* while another is given the ability to interpret what is being said. ¹¹It is the one and only Spirit who distributes all these gifts. He alone decides which gift each person should have.

One Body with Many Parts

¹²The human body has many parts, but the many parts make up one whole body. So it is with the body of Christ. ¹³Some of us are Jews, some are Gentiles,* some are slaves, and some are free. But we have all been baptized into one body by one Spirit, and we all share the same Spirit.*

¹⁴Yes, the body has many different parts, not just one part. ¹⁵If the foot says, "I am not a part of the body because I am not a hand," that does not make it any less a part of the body. ¹⁶And if the ear says, "I am not part of the body because I am not an eye," would that make it any less a part of the body? ¹⁷If the whole body were an eye, how would you hear? Or if your whole body were an ear, how would you smell anything?

¹⁸But our bodies have many parts, and God has put each part just where he wants it. ¹⁹How strange a body would be if it had only one part! ²⁰Yes, there are many parts, but only one body. ²¹The eye can never say to the hand, "I don't need you." The head can't say to the feet, "I don't need you."

²²In fact, some parts of the body that seem weakest and least important are actually the most necessary. ²³And the parts we regard as less honorable are those we clothe with the greatest care. So we carefully protect those parts that should not be seen, ²⁴while the more honorable parts do not require this special care. So God has put the body together such that extra honor and care are given to those parts that have less dignity. ²⁵This makes for harmony among the members, so that all the members care for each other. ²⁶If one part suffers, all the parts suffer with it, and if one part is honored, all the parts are glad.

²⁷All of you together are Christ's body, and each of you is a part of it. ²⁸Here are some of the parts God has appointed for the church:

first are apostles,
second are prophets,
third are teachers,
then those who do miracles,
those who have the gift of healing,
those who can help others,
those who have the gift of leadership,
those who speak in unknown languages.

²⁹Are we all apostles? Are we all prophets? Are we all teachers? Do we all have the power to do miracles? ³⁰Do we all have the gift of healing? Do we all have the ability to speak in unknown languages? Do we all have the ability to interpret unknown languages? Of course not! ³¹So you should earnestly desire the most helpful gifts.

But now let me show you a way of life that is best of all.

12:1 Greek *brothers.* **12:8a** Or *gives a word of wisdom.* **12:8b** Or *gives a word of knowledge.* **12:10** Or *in various tongues;* also in 12:28, 30. **12:13a** Greek *some are Greeks.* **12:13b** Greek *we were all given one Spirit to drink.*

12:10 The ability to prophesy here does not refer primarily to predicting the future, but to speaking a special message directly from God (see 11:4-5; 13:2, 8; 14:1-25, 29-33; 1 Thessalonians 5:20; compare Acts 13:1-2; 21:4, 10-11). Discerning between God's Spirit and other spirits is a necessary gift for any Christian community that is open to hearing a word directly from God (see 1 Corinthians 14:29; 1 Thessalonians 5:19-21; see also Acts 16:16-18; 1 John 4:1-3). For Paul, the ability to speak "in unknown languages" (or "in various tongues"; also in 1 Corinthians 12:28, 30) here refers to spiritual language that requires the spiritual gift of interpretation in order to be understood. By placing this gift near the bottom of the list (both here and in 12:28), Paul shows the lesser priority to be attached to the gift of tongues, with which the Corinthian church had become over-enamored (see 13:1, 8; 14:1-25, 27). "The ability to interpret" does not refer to natural intellectual ability to translate but to a spiritual ability to understand the meaning of the Spirit's message communicated through the gift of tongues (see 14:5, 13, 26-28).

12:28 Paul highlights gifts of the Spirit that build up the church. These gifts are given without regard to gender, race, class, or ethnicity. The gifts include roles that carry leadership responsibilities, such as apostle, prophet, and teacher. Women in the New Testament display these spiritual gifts. We see that women were praying and prophesying in Corinth (11:5), and Priscilla taught Apollos (Acts 18:26).

Love Is the Greatest

13 If I could speak all the languages of earth and of angels, but didn't love others, I would only be a noisy gong or a clanging cymbal. ²If I had the gift of prophecy, and if I understood all of God's secret plans and possessed all knowledge, and if I had such faith that I could move mountains, but didn't love others, I would be nothing. ³If I gave everything I have to the poor and even sacrificed my body, I could boast about it;* but if I didn't love others, I would have gained nothing.

⁴Love is patient and kind. Love is not jealous or boastful or proud ⁵or rude. It does not demand its own way. It is not irritable, and it keeps no record of being wronged. ⁶It does not rejoice about injustice but rejoices whenever the truth wins out. ⁷Love never gives up, never loses faith, is always hopeful, and endures through every circumstance.

⁸Prophecy and speaking in unknown languages* and special knowledge will become useless. But love will last forever! ⁹Now our knowledge is partial and incomplete, and even the gift of prophecy reveals only part of the whole picture! ¹⁰But when the time of perfection comes, these partial things will become useless.

¹¹When I was a child, I spoke and thought and reasoned as a child. But when I grew up, I put away childish things. ¹²Now we see things imperfectly, like puzzling reflections in a mirror, but then we will see everything with perfect clarity.* All that I know now is partial and incomplete, but then I will know everything completely, just as God now knows me completely.

¹³Three things will last forever—faith, hope, and love—and the greatest of these is love.

Tongues and Prophecy

14 Let love be your highest goal! But you should also desire the special abilities the Spirit gives—especially the ability to prophesy. ²For if you have the ability to speak in tongues,* you will be talking only to God, since people won't be able to understand you. You will be speaking by the power of the Spirit,* but it will all be mysterious. ³But one who prophesies strengthens others, encourages them, and comforts them. ⁴A person who speaks in tongues is strengthened personally, but one who speaks a word of prophecy strengthens the entire church.

⁵I wish you could all speak in tongues, but even more I wish you could all prophesy. For prophecy is greater than speaking in tongues, unless someone interprets what you are saying so that the whole church will be strengthened.

⁶Dear brothers and sisters,* if I should come to you speaking in an unknown language,* how would that help you? But if I bring you a revelation or some special knowledge or prophecy or teaching, that will be helpful. ⁷Even lifeless instruments like the flute or the harp must play the notes clearly, or no one will recognize the melody. ⁸And if the bugler doesn't sound a clear call, how will the soldiers know they are being called to battle?

⁹It's the same for you. If you speak to people in words they don't understand, how will they know what you are saying? You might as well be talking into empty space.

¹⁰There are many different languages in the world, and every language has meaning. ¹¹But if I don't understand a language, I will be a foreigner to someone who speaks it, and the one who speaks it will be a foreigner to me. ¹²And the same is true for you. Since you are so eager to have the special abilities the Spirit gives, seek those that will strengthen the whole church.

¹³So anyone who speaks in tongues should pray also for the ability to interpret what has been said. ¹⁴For if I pray in tongues, my spirit is praying, but I don't understand what I am saying.

¹⁵Well then, what shall I do? I will pray in the spirit,* and I will also pray in words I understand. I will sing in the spirit, and I will also sing in words I understand. ¹⁶For if you praise God only in the spirit, how can those who don't understand you praise God along with you? How can they join you in giving thanks when they don't understand what you are saying? ¹⁷You will be giving thanks very well, but it won't strengthen the people who hear you.

¹⁸I thank God that I speak in tongues more than any of you. ¹⁹But in a church meeting I would rather speak five understandable words to help others than ten thousand words in an unknown language.

²⁰Dear brothers and sisters, don't be childish in

13:3 Some manuscripts read *sacrificed my body to be burned.* **13:8** Or *in tongues.* **13:12** Greek *see face to face.* **14:2a** Or *in unknown languages;* also in 14:4, 5, 13, 14, 18, 22, 26, 27, 28, 39. **14:2b** Or *speaking in your spirit.* **14:6a** Greek *brothers;* also in 14:20, 26, 39. **14:6b** Or *in tongues;* also in 14:19, 23. **14:15** Or *in the Spirit;* also in 14:15b, 16.

13:12 The contrast between now and then is between this age and the coming age. In Paul's day, mirrors were usually made of polished bronze, so the view was imperfect. Our perception in this life is limited and our understanding is "partial and incomplete." When the end comes and Christ establishes his eternal Kingdom, "we will see everything with perfect clarity" (literally "[we will see] face to face"). Then the spiritual gifts that give knowledge will be unnecessary.

14:2-4 The problem with the gift of speaking "in tongues" (also in 14:4-5, 13-14, 18, 22, 26-28, 39; or "in unknown languages"; see 12:1, 10) is that hearers cannot readily understand the message. The gift of prophecy, however, is immediately intelligible and beneficial as a word from God that strengthens, encourages, and comforts those who hear.

Love

 IDENTITY   ## Our Origin and Canopy

Love comes from our source. The maker of the universe loved so abundantly that he said, at the pinnacle of creation, "Let us make human beings in our image" (Genesis 1:26). Our hearts seek love because of the genius who planted it into us. In Genesis, God pursues and re-creates unity despite our shame. The Gospels describe Jesus as the Way back to love, and here, Paul describes our longing for love, especially the priority of love in our relationships with one another.

Love branches out and includes at its truest core. When two friends asked me to officiate their wedding, I felt both honored and inadequate. I wracked my brain, wondering how to describe this couple planting themselves together, watering each other, becoming a unified tree, living 1 Corinthians 13.

Love opens our hearts to grow. Paul's teaching expands our understanding of love even further, to encompass the way we relate to each other in the body of Christ. God made us in love, made us to crave connection in love, and gave us our spiritual gifts so that we could love one another better. The Corinthians were creating disunity and hierarchy with their gifts, but love was what they needed to flourish.

The Divine Gardener knows what the seed needs in order to grow. The lover of our souls does not give according to our relationship status, our gender, our ethnicity. When we allow him to practice unity through us, he fulfills our affections entirely and gives us a whole, unified family.

> Our hearts seek love because of the genius who planted it into us.

PAUL TEACHES ON THE IMPORTANCE OF LOVE IN 1 CORINTHIANS 13:1-13; SEE ALSO MATTHEW 22:35-40; MARK 12:28-34; LUKE 10:27; ROMANS 13:8; 1 JOHN 4:7.

IDENTIFY

When have you needed to grow toward love?

How can you return to the original planter of love?

How could growing in love help you relate more deeply to your family in Christ?

"I'm rising toward my first love—God, the original planter of love that we crave."

AMANDA AZADIAN is a Christ follower on a mission to bridge traditional medicine and modern innovation. She is a doctoral student of acupuncture, a senior product manager in digital health strategy, and a lover of adventure.

> "You see, if Satan can get you to surrender your identity, then Satan will have won. Why is our identity so important? Because identity determines activity. What we do is determined by who we are."
>
> — PRATHIA HALL WYNN
> (1940–2002) minister and Civil Rights leader

your understanding of these things. Be innocent as babies when it comes to evil, but be mature in understanding matters of this kind. ²¹It is written in the Scriptures*:

"I will speak to my own people
through strange languages
and through the lips of foreigners.
But even then, they will not listen to me,"*
says the Lord.

²²So you see that speaking in tongues is a sign, not for believers, but for unbelievers. Prophecy, however, is for the benefit of believers, not unbelievers. ²³Even so, if unbelievers or people who don't understand these things come into your church meeting and hear everyone speaking in an unknown language, they will think you are crazy. ²⁴But if all of you are prophesying, and unbelievers or people who don't understand these things come into your meeting, they will be convicted of sin and judged by what you say. ²⁵As they listen, their secret thoughts will be exposed, and they will fall to their knees and worship God, declaring, "God is truly here among you."

A Call to Orderly Worship

²⁶Well, my brothers and sisters, let's summarize. When you meet together, one will sing, another will teach, another will tell some special revelation God has given, one will speak in tongues, and another will interpret what is said. But everything that is done must strengthen all of you.

²⁷No more than two or three should speak in tongues. They must speak one at a time, and someone must interpret what they say. ²⁸But if no one is present who can interpret, they must be silent in your church meeting and speak in tongues to God privately.

²⁹Let two or three people prophesy, and let the others evaluate what is said. ³⁰But if someone is prophesying and another person receives a revelation from the Lord, the one who is speaking must stop. ³¹In this way, all who prophesy will have a turn to speak, one after the other, so that everyone will learn and be encouraged. ³²Remember that people who prophesy are in control of their spirit and can take turns. ³³For God is not a God of disorder but of peace, as in all the meetings of God's holy people.*

³⁴Women should be silent during the church meetings. It is not proper for them to speak. They should be submissive, just as the law says. ³⁵If they have any questions, they should ask their husbands at home, for it is improper for women to speak in church meetings.*

³⁶Or do you think God's word originated with you Corinthians? Are you the only ones to whom it was given? ³⁷If you claim to be a prophet or think you are spiritual, you should recognize that what I am saying is a command from the Lord himself. ³⁸But if you do not recognize this, you yourself will not be recognized.*

14:21a Greek *in the law.* **14:21b** Isa 28:11-12. **14:33** The phrase *as in all the meetings of God's holy people* could instead be joined to the beginning of 14:34. **14:35** Some manuscripts place verses 34-35 after 14:40. **14:38** Some manuscripts read *If you are ignorant of this, stay in your ignorance.*

14:34-35 This passage seems to contradict Paul's statements earlier in the chapter and in 11:5, where women were clearly praying and prophesying to the church. Because these two verses are found at the end of the chapter in some ancient manuscripts, some scholars believe they are a later scribal notation that was inserted into the biblical text. More likely, Paul was citing the Corinthians' idea here and then refuting it in 14:36-37, and he encouraged both men and women to prophesy. Less likely, Paul was speaking here only regarding wives who talked to their husbands while the worship service was in process; Paul made clear that the entire community needed to allow each person to speak in turn (14:26-33).

³⁹So, my dear brothers and sisters, be eager to prophesy, and don't forbid speaking in tongues. ⁴⁰But be sure that everything is done properly and in order.

The Resurrection of Christ

15 Let me now remind you, dear brothers and sisters,* of the Good News I preached to you before. You welcomed it then, and you still stand firm in it. ²It is this Good News that saves you if you continue to believe the message I told you—unless, of course, you believed something that was never true in the first place.*

³I passed on to you what was most important and what had also been passed on to me. Christ died for our sins, just as the Scriptures said. ⁴He was buried, and he was raised from the dead on the third day, just as the Scriptures said. ⁵He was seen by Peter* and then by the Twelve. ⁶After that, he was seen by more than 500 of his followers* at one time, most of whom are still alive, though some have died. ⁷Then he was seen by James and later by all the apostles. ⁸Last of all, as though I had been born at the wrong time, I also saw him. ⁹For I am the least of all the apostles. In fact, I'm not even worthy to be called an apostle after the way I persecuted God's church.

¹⁰But whatever I am now, it is all because God poured out his special favor on me—and not without results. For I have worked harder than any of the other apostles; yet it was not I but God who was working through me by his grace. ¹¹So it makes no difference whether I preach or they preach, for we all preach the same message you have already believed.

The Resurrection of the Dead

¹²But tell me this—since we preach that Christ rose from the dead, why are some of you saying there will be no resurrection of the dead? ¹³For if there is no resurrection of the dead, then Christ has not been raised either. ¹⁴And if Christ has not been raised, then all our preaching is useless, and your faith is useless. ¹⁵And we apostles would all be lying about God—for we have said that God raised Christ from the grave. But that can't be true if there is no resurrection of the dead. ¹⁶And if there is no resurrection of the dead, then Christ has not been raised. ¹⁷And if Christ has not been raised, then your faith is useless and you are still guilty of your sins. ¹⁸In that case, all who have died believing in Christ are lost! ¹⁹And if our hope in Christ is only for this life, we are more to be pitied than anyone in the world.

²⁰But in fact, Christ has been raised from the dead. He is the first of a great harvest of all who have died.

²¹So you see, just as death came into the world through a man, now the resurrection from the dead has begun through another man. ²²Just as everyone dies because we all belong to Adam, everyone who belongs to Christ will be given new life. ²³But there is an order to this resurrection: Christ was raised as the first of the harvest; then all who belong to Christ will be raised when he comes back.

²⁴After that the end will come, when he will turn the Kingdom over to God the Father, having destroyed every ruler and authority and power. ²⁵For Christ must reign until he humbles all his enemies beneath his feet. ²⁶And the last enemy to be destroyed is death. ²⁷For the Scriptures say, "God has put all things under his authority."* (Of course, when it says "all things are under his authority," that does not include God himself, who gave Christ his authority.) ²⁸Then, when all things are under his authority, the Son will put himself under God's authority, so that God, who gave his Son authority over all things, will be utterly supreme over everything everywhere.

²⁹If the dead will not be raised, what point is there in people being baptized for those who are dead? Why do it unless the dead will someday rise again?

³⁰And why should we ourselves risk our lives hour by hour? ³¹For I swear, dear brothers and sisters, that I face death daily. This is as certain as my pride in what Christ Jesus our Lord has done in you. ³²And what value was there in fighting wild beasts—those people of Ephesus*—if there will be no resurrection from the dead? And if there is no resurrection, "Let's feast and drink, for tomorrow we die!"* ³³Don't be fooled by those who say such things, for "bad company corrupts good character." ³⁴Think carefully about what is right, and stop sinning. For to your shame I say that some of you don't know God at all.

The Resurrection Body

³⁵But someone may ask, "How will the dead be raised? What kind of bodies will they have?" ³⁶What a foolish question! When you put a seed into the ground, it doesn't grow into a plant unless it dies first. ³⁷And what you put in the ground is not the plant that will grow, but only a bare seed of wheat or whatever you are planting. ³⁸Then God gives it the new body he

---

15:1 Greek *brothers;* also in 15:31, 50, 58.   **15:2** Or *unless you never believed it in the first place.*   **15:5** Greek *Cephas.*   **15:6** Greek *the brothers.*   **15:27** Ps 8:6.   **15:32a** Greek *fighting wild beasts in Ephesus.*   **15:32b** Isa 22:13.

15:1-8 Paul summarizes the gospel: Christ died and was raised from the dead so that a person's sins would be forgiven. This salvation plan follows the Old Testament promises. Many trustworthy witnesses saw Jesus after his resurrection, including Paul himself (Acts 9:1-19).

15:12 Some believers in Corinth apparently had a difficult time accepting the Jewish notion of a bodily resurrection of the dead, preferring instead the Greek notion of the immortality of the soul alone (see Acts 17:18, 32).

wants it to have. A different plant grows from each kind of seed. ³⁹Similarly there are different kinds of flesh—one kind for humans, another for animals, another for birds, and another for fish.

⁴⁰There are also bodies in the heavens and bodies on the earth. The glory of the heavenly bodies is different from the glory of the earthly bodies. ⁴¹The sun has one kind of glory, while the moon and stars each have another kind. And even the stars differ from each other in their glory.

⁴²It is the same way with the resurrection of the dead. Our earthly bodies are planted in the ground when we die, but they will be raised to live forever. ⁴³Our bodies are buried in brokenness, but they will be raised in glory. They are buried in weakness, but they will be raised in strength. ⁴⁴They are buried as natural human bodies, but they will be raised as spiritual bodies. For just as there are natural bodies, there are also spiritual bodies.

⁴⁵The Scriptures tell us, "The first man, Adam, became a living person."* But the last Adam—that is, Christ—is a life-giving Spirit. ⁴⁶What comes first is the natural body, then the spiritual body comes later. ⁴⁷Adam, the first man, was made from the dust of the earth, while Christ, the second man, came from heaven. ⁴⁸Earthly people are like the earthly man, and heavenly people are like the heavenly man. ⁴⁹Just as we are now like the earthly man, we will someday be like* the heavenly man.

⁵⁰What I am saying, dear brothers and sisters, is that our physical bodies cannot inherit the Kingdom of God. These dying bodies cannot inherit what will last forever.

⁵¹But let me reveal to you a wonderful secret. We will not all die, but we will all be transformed! ⁵²It will happen in a moment, in the blink of an eye, when the last trumpet is blown. For when the trumpet sounds, those who have died will be raised to live forever. And we who are living will also be transformed. ⁵³For our dying bodies must be transformed into bodies that will never die; our mortal bodies must be transformed into immortal bodies.

⁵⁴Then, when our dying bodies have been transformed into bodies that will never die,* this Scripture will be fulfilled:

"Death is swallowed up in victory.*
⁵⁵ O death, where is your victory?
O death, where is your sting?*"

⁵⁶For sin is the sting that results in death, and the law gives sin its power. ⁵⁷But thank God! He gives us victory over sin and death through our Lord Jesus Christ.

⁵⁸So, my dear brothers and sisters, be strong and immovable. Always work enthusiastically for the Lord, for you know that nothing you do for the Lord is ever useless.

The Collection for Jerusalem

16 Now regarding your question about the money being collected for God's people in Jerusalem. You should follow the same procedure I gave to the churches in Galatia. ²On the first day of each week, you should each put aside a portion of the money you have earned. Don't wait until I get there and then try to collect it all at once. ³When I come, I will write letters of recommendation for the messengers you choose to deliver your gift to Jerusalem. ⁴And if it seems appropriate for me to go along, they can travel with me.

Paul's Final Instructions

⁵I am coming to visit you after I have been to Macedonia,* for I am planning to travel through Macedonia. ⁶Perhaps I will stay awhile with you, possibly all winter, and then you can send me on my way to my next destination. ⁷This time I don't want to make just a short visit and then go right on. I want to come and stay awhile, if the Lord will let me. ⁸In the meantime, I will be staying here at Ephesus until the Festival of Pentecost. ⁹There is a wide-open door for a great work here, although many oppose me.

¹⁰When Timothy comes, don't intimidate him. He is doing the Lord's work, just as I am. ¹¹Don't let anyone treat him with contempt. Send him on his way with your blessing when he returns to me. I expect him to come with the other believers.*

¹²Now about our brother Apollos—I urged him to visit you with the other believers, but he was not willing to go right now. He will see you later when he has the opportunity.

15:45 Gen 2:7. 15:49 Some manuscripts read *let us be like.* 15:54a Some manuscripts add *and our mortal bodies have been transformed into immortal bodies.* 15:54b Isa 25:8. 15:55 Hos 13:14 (Greek version). 16:5 *Macedonia* was in the northern region of Greece. 16:11 Greek *with the brothers;* also in 16:12.

15:45-49 Adam and Christ founded two distinct humanities: One is natural and earthly, enslaved to sin and death; the other is spiritual and heavenly, purified and destined for life. Adam represents the natural (physical) body and Christ the spiritual (resurrection) body. See also 15:21-22; Romans 5:12-21.
15:54 Resurrection defeats the ultimate enemy, death, just as the power of the Spirit enables believers to transcend sin here and now (see Romans 8:2, 11).
16:2 Christians met "on the first day of each week" (see Acts 20:7), the day of the Lord's resurrection, rather than the last day of the week, as in the Old Testament (Exodus 20:8; 34:21; Isaiah 58:13-14). The first day was the "Sunday," (Mark 16:9; in Luke 24:1 and John 20:19 the Greek says "on the first day of the week") or the "Lord's Day" (Revelation 1:10). On this day, the Corinthians were to begin collecting money to give to the believers in Jerusalem who were experiencing hardship. The amount of money they should set aside is not specified; Paul later encouraged them to give as generously as they could (2 Corinthians 8:1-4; 9:6-13; compare Luke 12:33-34; 21:1-4; 1 Timothy 6:18-19).

¹³Be on guard. Stand firm in the faith. Be courageous.* Be strong. ¹⁴And do everything with love.

¹⁵You know that Stephanas and his household were the first of the harvest of believers in Greece,* and they are spending their lives in service to God's people. I urge you, dear brothers and sisters,* ¹⁶to submit to them and others like them who serve with such devotion. ¹⁷I am very glad that Stephanas, Fortunatus, and Achaicus have come here. They have been providing the help you weren't here to give me. ¹⁸They have been a wonderful encouragement to me, as they have been to you. You must show your appreciation to all who serve so well.

Paul's Final Greetings

¹⁹The churches here in the province of Asia* send greetings in the Lord, as do Aquila and Priscilla* and all the others who gather in their home for church meetings. ²⁰All the brothers and sisters here send greetings to you. Greet each other with a sacred kiss.

²¹HERE IS MY GREETING IN MY OWN HANDWRITING—PAUL.

²²If anyone does not love the Lord, that person is cursed. Our Lord, come!*

²³May the grace of the Lord Jesus be with you.

²⁴My love to all of you in Christ Jesus.*

16:13 Greek *Be men.* **16:15a** Greek *in Achaia,* the southern region of the Greek peninsula. **16:15b** Greek *brothers;* also in 16:20. **16:19a** *Asia* was a Roman province in what is now western Turkey. **16:19b** Greek *Prisca.* **16:22** From Aramaic, *Marana tha.* Some manuscripts read *Maran atha,* "Our Lord has come." **16:24** Some manuscripts add *Amen.*

16:19 For more on Priscilla and Aquila, see Acts 18:1-3; Romans 16:3-5; and "Priscilla and Aquila: Collaborating in Ministry" on page 1391.

2 Corinthians

WHAT DO WE LEARN ABOUT GOD'S MISSION AND OURS?
God helps us keep going when the going gets tough.

WHO WROTE IT? Paul, an apostle, with Timothy (1:1).

WHEN DID IT HAPPEN? Paul wrote 2 Corinthians from Macedonia within a year of writing 1 Corinthians, around AD 56.

HOW IS IT ORGANIZED?

- 1–3: Paul's greetings, travel plans, and defense
- 4–6: Death, suffering, and ministry
- 7: Paul's relationship with the Corinthians and a good report from Titus
- 8–9: The joy of giving
- 10–13: Paul's defense of his authority as an apostle against false teachers

FEATURE HIGHLIGHTS

+ *Comforter: God Reaches to Restore (1463)*
+ *Suffering as God's Plan A (1465)*
+ *Christ's Ambassadors: Wherever He Assigns (1467)*
+ *Exercising Faith over Feelings (1473)*

Words to Remember are highlighted throughout this book

HOW LONG DOES IT TAKE TO READ?

| :30 | :40 | 1:00 | 1:30 | 2:00 | 2:30 | 3:00 | 3:30 |

Timeline

AD	Event
30	JESUS DIES, RISES FROM THE DEAD, ASCENDS TO REIGN IN HEAVEN, SENDS THE HOLY SPIRIT
35	JESUS CALLS PAUL TO PREACH THE GOOD NEWS
46–48	PAUL GOES ON FIRST MISSIONARY JOURNEY, WITH BARNABAS AND JOHN MARK
50	JERUSALEM COUNCIL CONFIRMS GENTILE INCLUSION IN THE CHURCH
50–52	PAUL EMBARKS ON SECOND MISSIONARY JOURNEY, WITH SILAS; THEY SPEND 18 MONTHS IN CORINTH
50	PAUL MEETS PRISCILLA AND AQUILA IN CORINTH
	PAUL MEETS LYDIA IN PHILIPPI
53–57	PAUL TAKES A THIRD MISSIONARY JOURNEY
55	PAUL WRITES 1 CORINTHIANS FROM EPHESUS
56	PAUL WRITES 2 CORINTHIANS FROM MACEDONIA
57	PAUL WRITES THE LETTER TO THE ROMANS FROM CORINTH AND SENDS IT WITH PHOEBE; PAUL ARRESTED IN JERUSALEM
60–62	PAUL LIVES UNDER HOUSE ARREST IN ROME
64	PAUL MARTYRED IN ROME
70	ROME DESTROYS JERUSALEM

Greetings from Paul

1 This letter is from Paul, chosen by the will of God to be an apostle of Christ Jesus, and from our brother Timothy.

I am writing to God's church in Corinth and to all of his holy people throughout Greece.*

²May God our Father and the Lord Jesus Christ give you grace and peace.

God Offers Comfort to All

³All praise to God, the Father of our Lord Jesus Christ. God is our merciful Father and the source of all comfort. ⁴He comforts us in all our troubles so that we can comfort others. When they are troubled, we will be able to give them the same comfort God has given us. ⁵For the more we suffer for Christ, the more God will shower us with his comfort through Christ. ⁶Even when we are weighed down with troubles, it is for your comfort and salvation! For when we ourselves are comforted, we will certainly comfort you. Then you can patiently endure the same things we suffer. ⁷We are confident that as you share in our sufferings, you will also share in the comfort God gives us.

⁸We think you ought to know, dear brothers and sisters,* about the trouble we went through in the province of Asia. We were crushed and overwhelmed beyond our ability to endure, and we thought we would never live through it. ⁹In fact, we expected to die. But as a result, we stopped relying on ourselves and learned to rely only on God, who raises the dead. ¹⁰And he did rescue us from mortal danger, and he will rescue us again. We have placed our confidence in him, and he will continue to rescue us. ¹¹And you are helping us by praying for us. Then many people will give thanks because God has graciously answered so many prayers for our safety.

Paul's Change of Plans

¹²We can say with confidence and a clear conscience that we have lived with a God-given holiness* and sincerity in all our dealings. We have depended on God's grace, not on our own human wisdom. That is how we have conducted ourselves before the world, and especially toward you. ¹³Our letters have been straightforward, and there is nothing written between the lines and nothing you can't understand. I hope someday you will fully understand us, ¹⁴even if you don't understand us now. Then on the day when the Lord Jesus* returns, you will be proud of us in the same way we are proud of you.

¹⁵Since I was so sure of your understanding and trust, I wanted to give you a double blessing by visiting you twice—¹⁶first on my way to Macedonia and again when I returned from Macedonia.* Then you could send me on my way to Judea.

¹⁷You may be asking why I changed my plan. Do you think I make my plans carelessly? Do you think I am like people of the world who say "Yes" when they really mean "No"? ¹⁸As surely as God is faithful, our word to you does not waver between "Yes" and "No." ¹⁹For Jesus Christ, the Son of God, does not waver between "Yes" and "No." He is the one whom Silas,* Timothy, and I preached to you, and as God's ultimate "Yes," he always does what he says. ²⁰For all of God's promises have been fulfilled in Christ with a resounding "Yes!" And through Christ, our "Amen" (which means "Yes") ascends to God for his glory.

²¹It is God who enables us, along with you, to stand firm for Christ. He has commissioned us, ²²and he has identified us as his own by placing the Holy Spirit in our hearts as the first installment that guarantees everything he has promised us.

²³Now I call upon God as my witness that I am telling the truth. The reason I didn't return to Corinth was to spare you from a severe rebuke. ²⁴But that does not mean we want to dominate you by telling you how to put your faith into practice. We want to work together with you so you will be full of joy, for it is by your own faith that you stand firm.

2 So I decided that I would not bring you grief with another painful visit. ²For if I cause you grief, who will make me glad? Certainly not someone I have grieved. ³That is why I wrote to you as I did, so that when I do come, I won't be grieved by the very ones who ought to give me the greatest joy. Surely you all know that my joy comes from your being joyful. ⁴I wrote that letter in great anguish, with a troubled heart and many tears. I didn't want to grieve you, but I wanted to let you know how much love I have for you.

1:1 Greek *Achaia*, the southern region of the Greek peninsula. 1:8 Greek *brothers*. 1:12 Some manuscripts read *honesty*. 1:14 Some manuscripts read *our Lord Jesus*. 1:16 *Macedonia* was in the northern region of Greece. 1:19 Greek *Silvanus*.

1:12-14 Paul's travel plans and his unfulfilled promise of a visit to Corinth were criticized; he was charged with being fickle like people "who say 'Yes' when they really mean 'No'" (1:17). Before responding to that charge, he clarified the motives in his ministry and in his letters.
1:18-22 It was bad enough that Paul's enemies at Corinth had attacked his character as unreliable and shifty (1:17). It was worse when they charged that his entire message was just as uncertain. In these verses Paul answers that allegation.

Comforter

IDENTITY — God Reaches to Restore

We often think of comfort as kind words and actions toward those who are suffering. Often, however, human comfort can't solve the problem or change the pain. Not so with God's comfort.

God's comfort is kindness and compassion in words and actions, *and* it is far more. God's comfort brings holistic restoration—healing to the deepest trauma, hope to the deepest despair, justice to the deepest wrongs, forgiveness to the deepest sin.

God has always offered comfort to his people when they suffered (Isaiah 40:1-2). At the beginning of the Babylonian captivity, God's people needed this comfort. Their entire world had been destroyed and many were forced into exile from their homes. During that time, the Judeans likely doubted every covenant promise that God had made. Where was God when they needed him most, when the Babylonians swept through, murdering, raping, and destroying?

Could God's comfort reach them? Isaiah's answer was a resounding yes. God's comfort can forgive the deepest rebellion and heal the greatest trauma.

The apostle Paul knew these truths in extremely personal ways, having endured danger and suffering in his own life (2 Corinthians 1:8-11; 12:8-10). He had experienced restoration after persecuting others (1 Corinthians 15:9; see also Acts 9:17-19). This is the deep comfort Paul seeks to share with the Corinthian Christians, challenging and assuring them that as they endure suffering, they will also know "the source of all comfort," God our Father (2 Corinthians 1:3).

> God's comfort brings holistic restoration—healing, hope, justice, forgiveness, and more.

THE COMFORTER'S STORY IS TOLD IN 2 CORINTHIANS 1:3-7; SEE ALSO ISAIAH 40:1-11; 51:3-23.

IDENTIFY

Have you ever felt too far from God to receive comfort?

How might you trust God to forgive your deepest rebellion and heal your deepest trauma?

"We all suffer. I suffer from my own sin and from those who sin against me. I have walked through trauma and met God there. Jesus knows trauma. He's already there in the darkness, ready to give us his life in the place of death."

MEGAN C. ROBERTS, PhD, teaches Old Testament at Prairie College in Three Hills, Alberta, Canada. She loves mountains, music, and the unending joy of discovering the depths of the gospel in Scripture and the church.

Forgiveness for the Sinner

⁵I am not overstating it when I say that the man who caused all the trouble hurt all of you more than he hurt me. ⁶Most of you opposed him, and that was punishment enough. ⁷Now, however, it is time to forgive and comfort him. Otherwise he may be overcome by discouragement. ⁸So I urge you now to reaffirm your love for him.

⁹I wrote to you as I did to test you and see if you would fully comply with my instructions. ¹⁰When you forgive this man, I forgive him, too. And when I forgive whatever needs to be forgiven, I do so with Christ's authority for your benefit, ¹¹so that Satan will not outsmart us. For we are familiar with his evil schemes.

¹²When I came to the city of Troas to preach the Good News of Christ, the Lord opened a door of opportunity for me. ¹³But I had no peace of mind because my dear brother Titus hadn't yet arrived with a report from you. So I said good-bye and went on to Macedonia to find him.

Ministers of the New Covenant

¹⁴But thank God! He has made us his captives and continues to lead us along in Christ's triumphal procession. Now he uses us to spread the knowledge of Christ everywhere, like a sweet perfume. ¹⁵Our lives are a Christ-like fragrance rising up to God. But this fragrance is perceived differently by those who are being saved and by those who are perishing. ¹⁶To those who are perishing, we are a dreadful smell of death and doom. But to those who are being saved, we are a life-giving perfume. And who is adequate for such a task as this?

¹⁷You see, we are not like the many hucksters* who preach for personal profit. We preach the word of God with sincerity and with Christ's authority, knowing that God is watching us.

3 Are we beginning to praise ourselves again? Are we like others, who need to bring you letters of recommendation, or who ask you to write such letters on their behalf? Surely not! ²The only letter of recommendation we need is you yourselves. Your lives are a letter written in our* hearts; everyone can read it and recognize our good work among you. ³Clearly, you are a letter from Christ showing the result of our ministry among you. This "letter" is written not with pen and ink, but with the Spirit of the living God. It is carved not on tablets of stone, but on human hearts.

⁴We are confident of all this because of our great trust in God through Christ. ⁵It is not that we think we are qualified to do anything on our own. Our qualification comes from God. ⁶He has enabled us to be ministers of his new covenant. This is a covenant not of written laws, but of the Spirit. The old written covenant ends in death; but under the new covenant, the Spirit gives life.

The Glory of the New Covenant

⁷The old way,* with laws etched in stone, led to death, though it began with such glory that the people of Israel could not bear to look at Moses' face. For his face shone with the glory of God, even though the brightness was already fading away. ⁸Shouldn't we expect far greater glory under the new way, now that the Holy Spirit is giving life? ⁹If the old way, which brings condemnation, was glorious, how much more glorious is the new way, which makes us right with God! ¹⁰In fact, that first glory was not glorious at all compared with the overwhelming glory of the new way. ¹¹So if the old way, which has been replaced, was glorious, how much more glorious is the new, which remains forever!

¹²Since this new way gives us such confidence, we can be very bold. ¹³We are not like Moses, who

---

2:17 Some manuscripts read *the rest of the hucksters*. 3:2 Some manuscripts read *your*. 3:7 Or *ministry*; also in 3:8, 9, 10, 11, 12.

2:5-11 Paul speaks of a past encounter with a man in the church at Corinth during a painful visit there, a visit not recorded in Acts, while his base of ministry at the time was Ephesus. Paul had rebuked those in the church who questioned his apostolic authority, and in response, one man insulted Paul. Paul requested that the church discipline him, which they did. The man repented, and Paul now desired that the church welcome him back so that bitterness and discouragement would not divide the community—for division is the very thing that Satan wishes to produce.
2:15-16 Burning incense was scattered along the parade route of a victorious Roman general, and it was received in one of two ways. For the captives, who were on their way to the arena and death, it was "a dreadful smell of death and doom." For the victors, it was "a life-giving perfume." So it is with the lives of those who proclaim the Good News: They are either a fragrance that leads a person to eternal life or a stench that seals the fate of the person who rejects it in death (see also 1 Corinthians 1:18).

3:1-3 Paul's ministry was validated by the lives of those who were changed by the Good News rather than by a recommendation letter (see Acts 18:27). Christ, the author of this transformation, used Paul to lead believers to him. The marks of genuineness are not in written letters with pen and ink on parchment but in the fruit of the Spirit (Galatians 5:22-23) in people's lives and carved on their hearts.
3:9-15 Paul recounts Exodus 34:27-35 and ties his ministry of the new covenant to the fading away of the old covenant. Paul points to the unbelieving generation of Israel who wandered in the wilderness and compares them with some Jews in Paul's day who expressed unbelief at God's work of redemption in Christ. Paul declares that the law points to Christ. Paul argues that his ministry holds one type of glory, while Moses' ministry held another glory, one which is fading away now that Christ has come. Paul does not disparage Moses or the old covenant, which is God's word, but points to the greater work of Christ and his fulfillment of the old covenant.

put a veil over his face so the people of Israel would not see the glory, even though it was destined to fade away. ¹⁴But the people's minds were hardened, and to this day whenever the old covenant is being read, the same veil covers their minds so they cannot understand the truth. And this veil can be removed only by believing in Christ. ¹⁵Yes, even today when they read Moses' writings, their hearts are covered with that veil, and they do not understand.

¹⁶But whenever someone turns to the Lord, the veil is taken away. ¹⁷For the Lord is the Spirit, and wherever the Spirit of the Lord is, there is freedom. ¹⁸So all of us who have had that veil removed can see and reflect the glory of the Lord. And the Lord—who is the Spirit—makes us more and more like him as we are changed into his glorious image.

Treasure in Fragile Clay Jars

4 Therefore, since God in his mercy has given us this new way,* we never give up. ²We reject all shameful deeds and underhanded methods. We don't try to trick anyone or distort the word of God. We tell the truth before God, and all who are honest know this.

4:1 Or *ministry.*

3:16-18 The person who turns to the Lord has freedom in the Spirit, and believers receive something that Moses didn't experience. We become more and more like Christ, who is the "exact likeness of God" (4:4; see John 1:1-14; Colossians 1:15; Hebrews 1:1-4), and we increasingly "reflect the glory of the Lord." Divine, unfading glory in this present life leads to our being like Christ in the next life (Romans 8:29; Galatians 4:19; Philippians 3:21; 1 John 3:2).

---

⑧ Come Close — SUFFERING AS GOD'S PLAN A

SCRIPTURE CONNECTION: 2 CORINTHIANS 4:7-10

Most of us have a fairly straightforward picture in our minds of how we want our lives to look. Those pretty, perfect, polished pictures don't often include suffering. But when hardship inevitably intrudes into the picture frame, we view it as a detour. We hope to get back on track as quickly as possible.

We who follow Jesus sometimes seem especially averse to reconciling suffering with the good plan we thought we were promised. But how could we believe that suffering and goodness don't walk together when we follow a Savior whose suffering—even to the point of death—made way for our salvation? In God's purpose, Jesus' suffering wasn't an accident, a detour, or a Plan B. It was Plan A.

My detour was a massive stroke that almost took my life when I was twenty-six, and I now live with significant physical disabilities. Just like mine, your life has probably twisted with big and small detours of its own. In fact, you have detours ahead of you this very day! You can decide if you'll approach those detours as reasons for disappointment or opportunities for trust.

Not all suffering is God's plan, but after nearly fifteen years, I'm convinced my "detour" was Plan A all along. If we can surrender our trust to the One who paved the roads and made the plans, perhaps we can see suffering doesn't have to be a detour. It might be the path, the picture, the Plan A.

REFLECT "Through suffering, our bodies continue to share in the death of Jesus so that the life of Jesus may also be seen in our bodies." 2 CORINTHIANS 4:10

Jesus, help me redefine my idea of suffering as an invitation to trust your perfect plan, rather than a detour to be avoided. Amen.

CONSIDER "All shall work together for good; everything is needful that He sends; nothing can be needful that He withholds." JOHN NEWTON

Suffering can be the path to God's good and perfect plan.

KATHERINE WOLF is a communicator, author, and advocate. She leverages her redemptive story to encourage those with broken bodies, broken brains, and broken hearts.

> "We should not move too quickly to a cheap reconciliation that forgets the past rather than honoring it as a clay vessel that contains a refined treasure bearing witness to the presence of Jesus at the margins."
>
> **LOVE L. SECHREST**
> professor and Bible scholar

³If the Good News we preach is hidden behind a veil, it is hidden only from people who are perishing. ⁴Satan, who is the god of this world, has blinded the minds of those who don't believe. They are unable to see the glorious light of the Good News. They don't understand this message about the glory of Christ, who is the exact likeness of God.

⁵You see, we don't go around preaching about ourselves. We preach that Jesus Christ is Lord, and we ourselves are your servants for Jesus' sake. ⁶For God, who said, "Let there be light in the darkness," has made this light shine in our hearts so we could know the glory of God that is seen in the face of Jesus Christ.

⁷We now have this light shining in our hearts, but we ourselves are like fragile clay jars containing this great treasure.* This makes it clear that our great power is from God, not from ourselves.

⁸We are pressed on every side by troubles, but we are not crushed. We are perplexed, but not driven to despair. ⁹We are hunted down, but never abandoned by God. We get knocked down, but we are not destroyed. ¹⁰Through suffering, our bodies continue to share in the death of Jesus so that the life of Jesus may also be seen in our bodies.

¹¹Yes, we live under constant danger of death because we serve Jesus, so that the life of Jesus will be evident in our dying bodies. ¹²So we live in the face of death, but this has resulted in eternal life for you.

¹³But we continue to preach because we have the same kind of faith the psalmist had when he said, "I believed in God, so I spoke."* ¹⁴We know that God, who raised the Lord Jesus,* will also raise us with Jesus and present us to himself together with you. ¹⁵All of this is for your benefit. And as God's grace reaches more and more people, there will be great thanksgiving, and God will receive more and more glory.

¹⁶That is why we never give up. Though our bodies are dying, our spirits are* being renewed every day. ¹⁷For our present troubles are small and won't last very long. Yet they produce for us a glory that vastly outweighs them and will last forever! ¹⁸So we don't look at the troubles we can see now; rather, we fix our gaze on things that cannot be seen. For the things we see now will soon be gone, but the things we cannot see will last forever.

New Bodies

5 For we know that when this earthly tent we live in is taken down (that is, when we die and leave this earthly body), we will have a house in heaven, an eternal body made for us by God himself and not

---

4:7 Greek *We now have this treasure in clay jars.* **4:13** Ps 116:10. **4:14** Some manuscripts read *who raised Jesus.* **4:16** Greek *our inner being is.*

4:7 The message of Good News is like "great treasure," but it is housed in "fragile clay jars"—our weak bodies. This insight gives purpose to suffering (4:8–5:10). We suffer now, but at the same time we are being renewed in spirit now. This spiritual renewal empowers us to endure suffering for the sake of Christ's glory and the advancement of the Good News. Eventually, our mortal bodies will be transformed into imperishable, immortal bodies. **4:18** Paul stresses the temporary nature of our current struggles and our existing frail and failing bodies. We are to look forward to the sure hope of our resurrection bodies (4:14) and our glorious life with God in the new heavens and the new earth, which will be eternal. **5:1-4** Gentiles in Paul's day desired immortality without a physical body, and some Corinthians falsely believed this too (1 Corinthians 15:12). Paul insists that believers will enjoy a glorified, immortal body (1 Corinthians 15:35-50; Philippians 3:20-21). Women's bodies will be raised as female, recognizable as the individuals we were while on this earth (Matthew 22:29-32).

Christ's Ambassadors

IDENTITY — Wherever He Assigns

Growing up as a British person in Asia, I never liked the question, "Where is home for you?" It felt limiting and unsettling. Yet, I have learned that my identity isn't defined by one place or nationality. I can be Christ's ambassador in whichever earthly home he puts me next.

I used to feel my weakness, failures, and mortality so acutely. Fear surrounded me. I was insecure, held grudges, and judged others all the time! But since coming to believe what God says about who I am, I can honestly say I have become a new person. I am so loved by Christ, and I want you to know you are too.

Paul teaches us that our worth is not defined by our earthly limitations; he says that we no longer need to evaluate ourselves or others from "a human point of view." In Christ, we are new people, and God has made a place for us in his Kingdom and with his people. I still sometimes feel burdened by my present and yearn for the fullness of that future with God. But Paul and the Holy Spirit himself remind me that we are on this earth for a reason: to serve as Christ's ambassadors.

> Confidence in our eternal home empowers us to be Christ's ambassadors.

We bear a responsibility to share the grace, freedom, reconciliation, and identity we have found in Christ. When I talk about Christ, some people might say I'm crazy, "Who is this lady, and why does she keep talking about God?!" But when that happens to me—or you—I can lean into who God tells me I am and share with confidence.

As my faith has deepened, I have come to appreciate the multiplicity of what "home" means to me. God has an eternal home for us, which makes us Christ's ambassadors no matter where we call our earthly home.

PAUL ENCOURAGES US AS CHRIST'S AMBASSADORS IN 2 CORINTHIANS 5:11-21.

IDENTIFY

Have you ever felt unsure about who and where you are in life?

How might God meet and make you his ambassador there?

> "Knowing I have a heavenly home is comforting and liberating; my identity isn't defined by one place or nationality but [by my identity] as Christ's ambassador."

SARAH OVERTON, MA, is a researcher specializing in refugee and asylum policy. She has worked in the UK Parliament, public-policy think tanks, and at Lambeth Palace.

by human hands. ²We grow weary in our present bodies, and we long to put on our heavenly bodies like new clothing. ³For we will put on heavenly bodies; we will not be spirits without bodies.* ⁴While we live in these earthly bodies, we groan and sigh, but it's not that we want to die and get rid of these bodies that clothe us. Rather, we want to put on our new bodies so that these dying bodies will be swallowed up by life. ⁵God himself has prepared us for this, and as a guarantee he has given us his Holy Spirit.

⁶So we are always confident, even though we know that as long as we live in these bodies we are not at home with the Lord. ⁷For we live by believing and not by seeing. ⁸Yes, we are fully confident, and we would rather be away from these earthly bodies, for then we will be at home with the Lord. ⁹So whether we are here in this body or away from this body, our goal is to please him. ¹⁰For we must all stand before Christ to be judged. We will each receive whatever we deserve for the good or evil we have done in this earthly body.

We Are God's Ambassadors

¹¹Because we understand our fearful responsibility to the Lord, we work hard to persuade others. God knows we are sincere, and I hope you know this, too. ¹²Are we commending ourselves to you again? No, we are giving you a reason to be proud of us,* so you can answer those who brag about having a spectacular ministry rather than having a sincere heart. ¹³If it seems we are crazy, it is to bring glory to God. And if we are in our right minds, it is for your benefit. ¹⁴Either way, Christ's love controls us.* Since we believe that Christ died for all, we also believe that we have all died to our old life.* ¹⁵He died for everyone so that those who receive his new life will no longer live for themselves. Instead, they will live for Christ, who died and was raised for them.

¹⁶So we have stopped evaluating others from a human point of view. At one time we thought of Christ merely from a human point of view. How differently we know him now! ¹⁷This means that anyone who belongs to Christ has become a new person. The old life is gone; a new life has begun!

¹⁸And all of this is a gift from God, who brought us back to himself through Christ. And God has given us this task of reconciling people to him. ¹⁹For God was in Christ, reconciling the world to himself, no longer counting people's sins against them. And he gave us this wonderful message of reconciliation. ²⁰So we are Christ's ambassadors; God is making his appeal through us. We speak for Christ when we plead, "Come back to God!" ²¹For God made Christ, who never sinned, to be the offering for our sin,* so that we could be made right with God through Christ.

6 As God's partners,* we beg you not to accept this marvelous gift of God's kindness and then ignore it. ²For God says,

"At just the right time, I heard you.
   On the day of salvation, I helped you."*

Indeed, the "right time" is now. Today is the day of salvation.

Paul's Hardships

³We live in such a way that no one will stumble because of us, and no one will find fault with our ministry. ⁴In everything we do, we show that we are true ministers of God. We patiently endure troubles and hardships and calamities of every kind. ⁵We have been beaten, been put in prison, faced angry mobs, worked to exhaustion, endured sleepless nights, and gone without food. ⁶We prove ourselves by our purity, our understanding, our patience, our kindness, by the Holy Spirit within us,* and by our sincere love. ⁷We faithfully preach the truth. God's power is working in us. We use the weapons of righteousness in the right hand for attack and the left hand for defense. ⁸We serve God whether people honor us or despise us, whether they slander us or praise us. We are honest, but they call us impostors. ⁹We are ignored, even though we are well known. We live close to death, but we are still alive. We have been beaten, but we have not been killed. ¹⁰Our hearts ache, but we always have joy. We are poor, but we give spiritual riches to others. We own nothing, and yet we have everything.

¹¹Oh, dear Corinthian friends! We have spoken honestly with you, and our hearts are open to you. ¹²There is no lack of love on our part, but you have withheld your love from us. ¹³I am asking you to

---

5:3 Greek *we will not be naked.* **5:12** Some manuscripts read *proud of yourselves.* **5:14a** Or *urges us on.* **5:14b** Greek *Since one died for all, then all died.* **5:21** Or *to become sin itself.* **6:1** Or *As we work together.* **6:2** Isa 49:8 (Greek version). **6:6** Or *by our holiness of spirit.*

5:9-10 The goal of the present life is to please the Lord (see also Romans 12:1-2; 14:18; Colossians 1:10; 1 Thessalonians 4:1). This ambition will be examined when we "stand before Christ to be judged." The judge is also our advocate, so we are confident of acquittal (Romans 8:1, 33-34). Even so, our actions now in this life will be assessed and called to account (Acts 17:31).

5:21 Christ became "the offering for our sin" (see Isaiah 53:10) on the cross when he took sin's penalty on himself and died a criminal's death. He did this, though he himself never sinned (John 8:46; 1 Peter 2:22; 1 John 3:5), so that we might be "made right with God"—which means set in right relationship with God and accepted by him (see Galatians 3:13).

respond as if you were my own children. Open your hearts to us!

The Temple of the Living God

¹⁴Don't team up with those who are unbelievers. How can righteousness be a partner with wickedness? How can light live with darkness? ¹⁵What harmony can there be between Christ and the devil*? How can a believer be a partner with an unbeliever? ¹⁶And what union can there be between God's temple and idols? For we are the temple of the living God. As God said:

> "I will live in them
>   and walk among them.
> I will be their God,
>   and they will be my people.*
> ¹⁷ Therefore, come out from among
>   unbelievers,
>   and separate yourselves from them,
>   says the LORD.
> Don't touch their filthy things,
>   and I will welcome you.*
> ¹⁸ And I will be your Father,
>   and you will be my sons and daughters,
>   says the LORD Almighty.*"

7 Because we have these promises, dear friends, let us cleanse ourselves from everything that can defile our body or spirit. And let us work toward complete holiness because we fear God.

²Please open your hearts to us. We have not done wrong to anyone, nor led anyone astray, nor taken advantage of anyone. ³I'm not saying this to condemn you. I said before that you are in our hearts, and we live or die together with you. ⁴I have the highest confidence in you, and I take great pride in you. You have greatly encouraged me and made me happy despite all our troubles.

Paul's Joy at the Church's Repentance

⁵When we arrived in Macedonia, there was no rest for us. We faced conflict from every direction, with battles on the outside and fear on the inside. ⁶But God, who encourages those who are discouraged, encouraged us by the arrival of Titus. ⁷His presence was a joy, but so was the news he brought of the encouragement he received from you. When he told us how much you long to see me, and how sorry you are for what happened, and how loyal you are to me, I was filled with joy!

⁸I am not sorry that I sent that severe letter to you, though I was sorry at first, for I know it was painful to you for a little while. ⁹Now I am glad I sent it, not because it hurt you, but because the pain caused you to repent and change your ways. It was the kind of sorrow God wants his people to have, so you were not harmed by us in any way. ¹⁰For the kind of sorrow God wants us to experience leads us away from sin and results in salvation. There's no regret for that kind of sorrow. But worldly sorrow, which lacks repentance, results in spiritual death.

¹¹Just see what this godly sorrow produced in you! Such earnestness, such concern to clear yourselves, such indignation, such alarm, such longing to see me, such zeal, and such a readiness to punish wrong. You showed that you have done everything necessary to make things right. ¹²My purpose, then, was not to write about who did the wrong or who was wronged. I wrote to you so that in the sight of God you could see for yourselves how loyal you are to us. ¹³We have been greatly encouraged by this.

In addition to our own encouragement, we were especially delighted to see how happy Titus was about the way all of you welcomed him and set his mind* at ease. ¹⁴I had told him how proud I was of you—and you didn't disappoint me. I have always told you the truth, and now my boasting to Titus has also proved true! ¹⁵Now he cares for you more than ever when he remembers the way all of you obeyed him and welcomed him with such fear and deep respect. ¹⁶I am very happy now because I have complete confidence in you.

6:15 Greek *Beliar;* various other manuscripts render this proper name of the devil as *Belian, Beliab,* or *Belial.* **6:16** Lev 26:12; Ezek 37:27. **6:17** Isa 52:11; Ezek 20:34 (Greek version). **6:18** 2 Sam 7:14. **7:13** Greek *his spirit.*

6:14 The instruction not to "team up with those who are unbelievers" alludes to the Jewish prohibition of certain mixtures (Leviticus 19:19; Deuteronomy 22:10). Paul was probably referring to how the Corinthians had been involving themselves in idolatrous practices (see 1 Corinthians 8–10, especially 10:14-22).

6:18 Paul references 2 Samuel 7:14, when he writes, "I will be your Father, and you will be my sons and daughters," with two important changes. Paul stresses the plural pronoun "you," rather than the singular "he," and adds "daughters." Paul makes it clear with this edit that women are empowered to live holy, virtuous lives, unlike the wider culture's portrayal of women as silly, fickle, and irrational.

7:5-7 Paul's joy leads him to tell about his recent meeting with Titus, whose "presence was a joy" when he joined Paul in Macedonia (Acts 20:1-2). Initially, Paul had only conflict, battles, and fear: "no rest." (The same Greek word for "rest" is also used in 2 Corinthians 2:13, where it is rendered "peace of mind.") Paul was deeply discouraged, but he received encouragement from "God, who encourages those who are discouraged" (compare Psalm 42:5-6). Then Titus arrived from Corinth with the news that Paul's letter (see 2 Corinthians 2:3-4) had done its work (7:8-16). This was the chief cause of Paul's joy.

Anyone who belongs to Christ has become a new person.

2 CORINTHIANS 5:17

A Call to Generous Giving

8 Now I want you to know, dear brothers and sisters,* what God in his kindness has done through the churches in Macedonia. ²They are being tested by many troubles, and they are very poor. But they are also filled with abundant joy, which has overflowed in rich generosity.

³For I can testify that they gave not only what they could afford, but far more. And they did it of their own free will. ⁴They begged us again and again for the privilege of sharing in the gift for the believers in Jerusalem.* ⁵They even did more than we had hoped, for their first action was to give themselves to the Lord and to us, just as God wanted them to do.

⁶So we have urged Titus, who encouraged your giving in the first place, to return to you and encourage you to finish this ministry of giving. ⁷Since you excel in so many ways—in your faith, your gifted speakers, your knowledge, your enthusiasm, and your love from us*—I want you to excel also in this gracious act of giving.

⁸I am not commanding you to do this. But I am testing how genuine your love is by comparing it with the eagerness of the other churches.

⁹You know the generous grace of our Lord Jesus Christ. Though he was rich, yet for your sakes he became poor, so that by his poverty he could make you rich.

¹⁰Here is my advice: It would be good for you to finish what you started a year ago. Last year you were the first who wanted to give, and you were the first to begin doing it. ¹¹Now you should finish what you started. Let the eagerness you showed in the beginning be matched now by your giving. Give in proportion to what you have. ¹²Whatever you give is acceptable if you give it eagerly. And give according to what you have, not what you don't have. ¹³Of course, I don't mean your giving should make life easy for others and hard for yourselves. I only mean that there should be some equality. ¹⁴Right now you have plenty and can help those who are in need. Later, they will have plenty and can share with you when you need it. In this way, things will be equal. ¹⁵As the Scriptures say,

> "Those who gathered a lot had nothing left over,
> and those who gathered only a little had enough."*

Titus and His Companions

¹⁶But thank God! He has given Titus the same enthusiasm for you that I have. ¹⁷Titus welcomed our request that he visit you again. In fact, he himself was very eager to go and see you. ¹⁸We are also sending another brother with Titus. All the churches praise him as a preacher of the Good News. ¹⁹He was appointed by the churches to accompany us as we take the offering to Jerusalem*—a service that glorifies the Lord and shows our eagerness to help.

²⁰We are traveling together to guard against any criticism for the way we are handling this generous gift. ²¹We are careful to be honorable before the Lord, but we also want everyone else to see that we are honorable.

²²We are also sending with them another of our brothers who has proven himself many times and has shown on many occasions how eager he is. He is now even more enthusiastic because of his great confidence in you. ²³If anyone asks about Titus, say that he is my partner who works with me to help you. And the brothers with him have been sent by the churches,* and they bring honor to Christ. ²⁴So show them your love, and prove to all the churches that our boasting about you is justified.

The Collection for Christians in Jerusalem

9 I really don't need to write to you about this ministry of giving for the believers in Jerusalem.* ²For I know how eager you are to help, and I have been boasting to the churches in Macedonia

---

8:1 Greek *brothers.* 8:4 Greek *for God's holy people.* 8:7 Some manuscripts read *your love for us.* 8:15 Exod 16:18. 8:19 See 1 Cor 16:3-4. 8:23 Greek *are apostles of the churches.* 9:1 Greek *about the offering for God's holy people.*

8:1–9:15 Paul here turns his attention to the collection for the Jerusalem church (8:4; 9:1). This relief fund was intended to aid the poverty-stricken Christians in the holy city (Acts 11:27-30; Romans 15:25-27, 31; Galatians 2:10). Paul had earlier given instructions about this matter (1 Corinthians 16:1-2); now it was time to collect the funds (2 Corinthians 8:6). Paul hoped this gift from Gentile congregations to the Jewish church would cement relations between the two groups in the early Christian community.

8:1-5 The churches in Macedonia included those in Philippi, Thessalonica, and Berea (Acts 16:11–17:15). They modeled Christian generosity, which is not limited by one's finances but is multiplied through joy in serving God's people. Wealthy or prominent Gentile women like Lydia (Acts 16:14-15) may have been among these generous believers; it's possible that women from the house churches, like Euodia and Syntyche (Philippians 4:1-3), were too. Women controlled their own wealth, even if they were married; their husbands only had use of dowry funds.

8:14-15 As he made the case for the Corinthians to generously give what they had, Paul pointed to the daily gift of manna from heaven that the Israelites received in the wilderness (Exodus 16:13-33). Their daily needs were met, whether they gathered much or little. No one could hoard the manna, for it would not keep overnight, except on Sabbath. Paul desired that all believers would have their physical needs met and assumed that every person would have times of plenty and times of want (Philippians 4:11-12). Paul asked the Corinthians, who were financially better off than the Judean churches, to give money, recognizing that the time might come when other churches would give support to the needy Corinthians.

that you in Greece* were ready to send an offering a year ago. In fact, it was your enthusiasm that stirred up many of the Macedonian believers to begin giving.

³But I am sending these brothers to be sure you really are ready, as I have been telling them, and that your money is all collected. I don't want to be wrong in my boasting about you. ⁴We would be embarrassed—not to mention your own embarrassment—if some Macedonian believers came with me and found that you weren't ready after all I had told them! ⁵So I thought I should send these brothers ahead of me to make sure the gift you promised is ready. But I want it to be a willing gift, not one given grudgingly.

⁶Remember this—a farmer who plants only a few seeds will get a small crop. But the one who plants generously will get a generous crop. ⁷You must each decide in your heart how much to give. And don't give reluctantly or in response to pressure. "For God loves a person who gives cheerfully."* ⁸And God will generously provide all you need. Then you will always have everything you need and plenty left over to share with others. ⁹As the Scriptures say,

> "They share freely and give generously
> to the poor.
> Their good deeds will be remembered
> forever."*

¹⁰For God is the one who provides seed for the farmer and then bread to eat. In the same way, he will provide and increase your resources and then produce a great harvest of generosity* in you.

¹¹Yes, you will be enriched in every way so that you can always be generous. And when we take your gifts to those who need them, they will thank God. ¹²So two good things will result from this ministry of giving—the needs of the believers in Jerusalem* will be met, and they will joyfully express their thanks to God.

¹³As a result of your ministry, they will give glory to God. For your generosity to them and to all believers will prove that you are obedient to the Good News of Christ. ¹⁴And they will pray for you with deep affection because of the overflowing grace God has given to you. ¹⁵Thank God for this gift* too wonderful for words!

Paul Defends His Authority

10 Now I, Paul, appeal to you with the gentleness and kindness of Christ—though I realize you think I am timid in person and bold only when I write from far away. ²Well, I am begging you now so that when I come I won't have to be bold with those who think we act from human motives.

³We are human, but we don't wage war as humans do. ⁴*We use God's mighty weapons, not worldly weapons, to knock down the strongholds of human reasoning and to destroy false arguments. ⁵We destroy every proud obstacle that keeps people from knowing God. We capture their rebellious thoughts and teach them to obey Christ. ⁶And after you have become fully obedient, we will punish everyone who remains disobedient.

⁷Look at the obvious facts.* Those who say they belong to Christ must recognize that we belong to Christ as much as they do. ⁸I may seem to be boasting too much about the authority given to us by the Lord. But our authority builds you up; it doesn't tear you down. So I will not be ashamed of using my authority.

9:2 Greek *in Achaia,* the southern region of the Greek peninsula. *Macedonia* was in the northern region of Greece. 9:7 See footnote on Prov 22:8. 9:9 Ps 112:9. 9:10 Greek *righteousness.* 9:12 Greek *of God's holy people.* 9:15 Greek *his gift.* 10:4 English translations divide verses 4 and 5 in various ways. 10:7 Or *You look at things only on the basis of appearance.*

9:10-14 The Corinthians' generosity (the same Greek word can be translated "righteousness") would be matched by God's generosity (9:10-11). It would also meet the needs of Jewish Christians (9:12), honor God (9:13), show believers in Jerusalem that their Gentile brothers and sisters were genuine believers (9:13), and result in the Jewish believers' intercessory prayer and affection for the Gentile believers (9:14). Paul envisioned a united, worldwide Christian church, composed of believing Jews and Gentiles who were all one in Christ Jesus (Galatians 3:28; Ephesians 2:11-22), which would become a powerful witness to the Lord's work of reconciliation.

10:1–13:10 In this section, Paul defends his ministry as an apostle, but the distinct change of tone and style from previous chapters poses several problems. The first section is full of joy stemming from the reconciliation of sinners with God and of the Corinthians with Paul. Yet from this point on, Paul is on the defensive. These chapters are full of harsh words, bitter recriminations, passionate irony, and rebuke. The remarkable break at 10:1 has inspired a number of explanations: First, these chapters might be a separate letter, perhaps the "severe letter" sent earlier to Corinth (2:3-4; 7:8-9). Another is that, while the majority of the church members were obedient to the appeal for reconciliation, there was still a rebellious minority to whom Paul addressed these four chapters. More likely, a new situation had arisen since Titus first brought back his glowing report of restored harmony (7:5-16). In this third scenario, some anti-Paul missionaries had arrived in Corinth and launched a virulent campaign against the apostolic message of the Good News (see 11:4, 13-15). They claimed that Paul was no real apostle or even a true Christian (10:7) and that he had no right to come to Corinth with the gospel message since it was territory that belonged to them (10:15-16). They brought an alien message (11:4) and exercised a domineering spirit. In short, they were doing Satan's work (11:13-15). Paul, concerned upon hearing of this new situation, reasserts his apostolic authority and engages in a form of writing that is distasteful to him (11:1, 16-17; 12:1) by boasting of his weaknesses and trials. Paul's apostolic authority is real and powerful, yet it is conditioned and controlled by the love exhibited by the crucified Jesus (10:1; 13:4-10).

Exercising Faith over Feelings

SCRIPTURE CONNECTION: 2 CORINTHIANS 10:3-5

Our feelings originate in our minds and live in our hearts. This is why Paul makes it clear in 2 Corinthians 10 that to combat opposition from the inside and the outside (which he himself faced when he wrote this letter), we must take on our feelings and "capture [our] rebellious thoughts" (10:5).

Exercising faith over feelings does not suppress or deny our emotions. It gives Jesus authority over them. Our feelings operate best when they are guided by truth and wisdom rather than allowed to be in charge. In this right positioning, these important facets of who we are come under the Holy Spirit's perfectly calibrated guidance.

Opposition that tries to disrupt our thoughts and feelings doesn't always look like what we assume. It might look like outside negativity or other people's opinions, but it also might look like an inner critic who constantly plays in our mind and consumes our thoughts.

Satan will use whatever he can to keep us from mental, physical, and spiritual wellness. We hear from him that we aren't going to be okay; we must take things into our own control; God doesn't love us; and our pain is in vain. The world serves up these damaging narratives, and many of our friends, neighbors, and loved ones readily believe them. Without engaging the strategy of a strong mind, we won't have victory over negative, dominating feelings.

The strategy for having a strong mind is to keep Jesus' power at the forefront of our thoughts. As we model correct responses to difficulty and pain, we influence those around us rather than being negatively influenced. As our mind renews, we grow in our faith, and our trust in the Lord increases.

IMAGINE

What occupies your thoughts most of the time: your faith or your feelings?

Name your current emotions by writing them down. Put a star by the ones you want or need to give to the Lord.

> Exercising faith over feelings does not suppress or deny our emotions. It gives Jesus the final say.

> "Exercising faith over feelings does not suppress or deny our emotions. It gives Jesus authority over them. Our feelings operate best when they are guided by truth and wisdom rather than allowed to be in charge."

LISA WHITTLE is a sought-out Bible teacher, podcast host, and bestselling author whose works include *Jesus Over Everything*. She is the founder of the online communities Ministry Strong and Called Creatives. She's a wife, mom, and a self-professed feisty work in progress.

⁹I'm not trying to frighten you by my letters. ¹⁰For some say, "Paul's letters are demanding and forceful, but in person he is weak, and his speeches are worthless!" ¹¹Those people should realize that our actions when we arrive in person will be as forceful as what we say in our letters from far away.

¹²Oh, don't worry; we wouldn't dare say that we are as wonderful as these other men who tell you how important they are! But they are only comparing themselves with each other, using themselves as the standard of measurement. How ignorant!

¹³We will not boast about things done outside our area of authority. We will boast only about what has happened within the boundaries of the work God has given us, which includes our working with you. ¹⁴We are not reaching beyond these boundaries when we claim authority over you, as if we had never visited you. For we were the first to travel all the way to Corinth with the Good News of Christ.

¹⁵Nor do we boast and claim credit for the work someone else has done. Instead, we hope that your faith will grow so that the boundaries of our work among you will be extended. ¹⁶Then we will be able to go and preach the Good News in other places far beyond you, where no one else is working. Then there will be no question of our boasting about work done in someone else's territory. ¹⁷As the Scriptures say, "If you want to boast, boast only about the Lord."*

¹⁸When people commend themselves, it doesn't count for much. The important thing is for the Lord to commend them.

Paul and the False Apostles

11 I hope you will put up with a little more of my foolishness. Please bear with me. ²For I am jealous for you with the jealousy of God himself. I promised you as a pure bride* to one husband—Christ. ³But I fear that somehow your pure and undivided devotion to Christ will be corrupted, just as Eve was deceived by the cunning ways of the serpent. ⁴You happily put up with whatever anyone tells you, even if they preach a different Jesus than the one we preach, or a different kind of Spirit than the one you received, or a different kind of gospel than the one you believed.

⁵But I don't consider myself inferior in any way to these "super apostles" who teach such things. ⁶I may be unskilled as a speaker, but I'm not lacking in knowledge. We have made this clear to you in every possible way.

⁷Was I wrong when I humbled myself and honored you by preaching God's Good News to you without expecting anything in return? ⁸I "robbed" other churches by accepting their contributions so I could serve you at no cost. ⁹And when I was with you and didn't have enough to live on, I did not become a financial burden to anyone. For the brothers who came from Macedonia brought me all that I needed. I have never been a burden to you, and I never will be. ¹⁰As surely as the truth of Christ is in me, no one in all of Greece* will ever stop me from boasting about this. ¹¹Why? Because I don't love you? God knows that I do.

¹²But I will continue doing what I have always done. This will undercut those who are looking for an opportunity to boast that their work is just like ours. ¹³These people are false apostles. They

---

10:17 Jer 9:24. **11:2** Greek *a virgin*. **11:10** Greek *Achaia*, the southern region of the Greek peninsula.

10:10 Paul's letters are sometimes difficult and demanding, as other Christians had also found (see also 2 Peter 3:16). But Paul did not have a domineering presence, bulldozing people into submission (see 2 Corinthians 1:24; 1 Corinthians 2:1-5). The earliest descriptions of Paul's personal appearance depict him as "a man of small height, almost bald, with crooked legs, but with a good body and eyebrows meeting. His nose was hooked, full of grace, for sometimes he appeared like a man and sometimes had the face of an angel" (see *Acts of Paul and Thecla*, around AD 200). Unlike Apollos (Acts 18:24), Paul was not an eloquent preacher or a captivating orator when he came to Corinth (2 Corinthians 11:6; 1 Corinthians 2:3-4). His message, however, was charged with a power no human rhetoric could command, as it was given by the Holy Spirit.

11:2 Paul speaks of the church as a bride, drawing on Old Testament images of Israel as the bride of God (for example, Isaiah 54:5; 62:5; Ezekiel 16:8). Paul puts himself in the role of the bride's parent arranging the marriage. Paul stresses that the bride is pure, a quality that all believers should espouse (Philippians 4:8). Paul uses a uniquely female experience—bride—as an example for all believers to emulate (see also Ephesians 5:25-27; Revelation 21:9).

11:3 Paul uses another female example to represent all believers, but here it is negative. Paul warns that the Corinthians could fail in the way same way Eve did, being deceived by Satan. Paul is clear that both men and women can be deceived. Paul emphasized Eve's deception and her resulting sin (1 Timothy 2:14) most likely to combat false teachings that wrongly interpreted the Genesis creation narrative and may have mixed it with myths related to Artemis, whose large temple shaped religion in Ephesus.

11:4 The false missionaries in Corinth evidently preached a "different Jesus," "a different kind of Spirit," and "a different kind of gospel" than those the Corinthians had believed. It is difficult to know exactly what these false teachers preached; based on Paul's response, they most likely promoted a powerful, dominant Christ and sidelined the suffering of the cross. Likewise, they probably saw themselves as powerful preachers, exempt from hardship and trial. Paul's message, by contrast, centered on Christ crucified (13:4), and Paul's own sufferings were a mark of true apostleship (12:1-12). The nature of this difference is the heart of Paul's defense of his apostleship in 10:1–13:10.

Paul's Final Greetings

¹¹Dear brothers and sisters,* I close my letter with these last words: Be joyful. Grow to maturity. Encourage each other. Live in harmony and peace. Then the God of love and peace will be with you. ¹²Greet each other with a sacred kiss. ¹³All of God's people here send you their greetings.

¹⁴*May the grace of the Lord Jesus Christ, the love of God, and the fellowship of the Holy Spirit be with you all.

13:11 Greek *Brothers*. **13:14** Some English translations include verse 13 as part of verse 12, and then verse 14 becomes verse 13.

13:14 Paul closes his letter with a prayer and blessing. He invokes the three persons of the Trinity, with "the grace of the Lord Jesus Christ" (see 8:9) coming first. As Christians, we rely on Christ's sacrificial love, which reconciles us to God the Father (5:18-21) and unites us through the "fellowship of the Holy Spirit" with all our fellow believers (Ephesians 4:3; Philippians 2:1). The "love of God" provides for our needs and graciously restores us to his family.

Galatians

WHAT DO WE LEARN ABOUT GOD'S MISSION AND OURS?
Faith alone saves us.

WHO WROTE IT? Paul, an apostle.

WHEN DID IT HAPPEN? Paul wrote Galatians around AD 48–49, fairly early in his ministry, not long after he preached for the first time in Galatia.

HOW IS IT ORGANIZED?

1–2: Paul's testimony about the role and the mission Christ gave him

3–4: Paul argues the issues of law and grace

5–6: Freedom Christ gives

FEATURE HIGHLIGHTS

+ *How Does Our Identity in Jesus Shape Our Other Identities?* (1482)
+ *How Living by Faith Helps Us Relate* (1485)
+ *Work Hard Where We Are* (1486)

Words to Remember are highlighted throughout this book

HOW LONG DOES IT TAKE TO READ?

| :20 | :30 | 1:00 | 1:30 | 2:00 | 2:30 | 3:00 | 3:30 |

Timeline

AD	
30	JESUS DIES, RISES FROM THE DEAD, ASCENDS TO REIGN IN HEAVEN, SENDS THE HOLY SPIRIT
35	JESUS CALLS PAUL TO PREACH THE GOOD NEWS
46–48	PAUL GOES ON FIRST MISSIONARY JOURNEY, WITH BARNABAS AND JOHN MARK
48–49	PAUL WRITES THE LETTER TO THE GALATIANS FROM ANTIOCH
50	JERUSALEM COUNCIL CONFIRMS GENTILE INCLUSION IN THE CHURCH
50–52	PAUL EMBARKS ON SECOND MISSIONARY JOURNEY, WITH SILAS; THEY SPEND 18 MONTHS IN CORINTH
50	PAUL MEETS PRISCILLA AND AQUILA IN CORINTH
	PAUL MEETS LYDIA IN PHILIPPI
53–57	PAUL TAKES A THIRD MISSIONARY JOURNEY
57	PAUL ARRESTED IN JERUSALEM
57–59	PAUL IMPRISONED IN CAESAREA, WHERE HE IS QUESTIONED BY FESTUS, FELIX AND DRUSILLA, AND AGRIPPA AND BERNICE
60–62	PAUL LIVES UNDER HOUSE ARREST IN ROME
64	PAUL MARTYRED IN ROME
70	ROME DESTROYS JERUSALEM

Greetings from Paul

1 This letter is from Paul, an apostle. I was not appointed by any group of people or any human authority, but by Jesus Christ himself and by God the Father, who raised Jesus from the dead. ²All the brothers and sisters* here join me in sending this letter to the churches of Galatia.

³May God the Father and our Lord Jesus Christ* give you grace and peace. ⁴Jesus gave his life for our sins, just as God our Father planned, in order to rescue us from this evil world in which we live. ⁵All glory to God forever and ever! Amen.

There Is Only One Good News

⁶I am shocked that you are turning away so soon from God, who called you to himself through the loving mercy of Christ.* You are following a different way that pretends to be the Good News ⁷but is not the Good News at all. You are being fooled by those who deliberately twist the truth concerning Christ.

⁸Let God's curse fall on anyone, including us or even an angel from heaven, who preaches a different kind of Good News than the one we preached to you. ⁹I say again what we have said before: If anyone preaches any other Good News than the one you welcomed, let that person be cursed.

¹⁰Obviously, I'm not trying to win the approval of people, but of God. If pleasing people were my goal, I would not be Christ's servant.

Paul's Message Comes from Christ

¹¹Dear brothers and sisters, I want you to understand that the gospel message I preach is not based on mere human reasoning. ¹²I received my message from no human source, and no one taught me. Instead, I received it by direct revelation from Jesus Christ.*

¹³You know what I was like when I followed the Jewish religion—how I violently persecuted God's church. I did my best to destroy it. ¹⁴I was far ahead of my fellow Jews in my zeal for the traditions of my ancestors.

¹⁵But even before I was born, God chose me and called me by his marvelous grace. Then it pleased him ¹⁶to reveal his Son to me* so that I would proclaim the Good News about Jesus to the Gentiles. When this happened, I did not rush out to consult with any human being.* ¹⁷Nor did I go up to Jerusalem to consult with those who were apostles before I was. Instead, I went away into Arabia, and later I returned to the city of Damascus.

¹⁸Then three years later I went to Jerusalem to get to know Peter,* and I stayed with him for fifteen days. ¹⁹The only other apostle I met at that time was James, the Lord's brother. ²⁰I declare before God that what I am writing to you is not a lie.

²¹After that visit I went north into the provinces of Syria and Cilicia. ²²And still the churches in Christ that are in Judea didn't know me personally. ²³All they knew was that people were saying, "The one who used to persecute us is now preaching the very faith he tried to destroy!" ²⁴And they praised God because of me.

The Apostles Accept Paul

2 Then fourteen years later I went back to Jerusalem again, this time with Barnabas; and Titus came along, too. ²I went there because God revealed to me that I should go. While I was there I met privately with those considered to be leaders of the church and shared with them the message I had been preaching to the Gentiles. I wanted to make sure that we were in agreement, for fear that all my efforts had been wasted and I was running the race for nothing. ³And they supported me and did not even demand that my companion Titus be circumcised, though he was a Gentile.*

⁴Even that question came up only because of some so-called believers there—false ones, really*—who were secretly brought in. They sneaked in to spy on us and take away the freedom we have in Christ Jesus. They wanted to enslave us and force us to follow their Jewish regulations. ⁵But we refused to give in to them for a single moment. We wanted to preserve the truth of the gospel message for you.

⁶And the leaders of the church had nothing to add to what I was preaching. (By the way, their reputation as great leaders made no difference to me, for God has no favorites.) ⁷Instead, they saw that God had given me the responsibility of preaching the gospel to the Gentiles, just as he had given Peter the responsibility of preaching to the Jews. ⁸For the same God

---

1:2 Greek *brothers;* also in 1:11. **1:3** Some manuscripts read *God our Father and the Lord Jesus Christ.* **1:6** Some manuscripts read *through loving mercy.* **1:12** Or *by the revelation of Jesus Christ.* **1:16a** Or *in me.* **1:16b** Greek *with flesh and blood.* **1:18** Greek *Cephas.* **2:3** Greek *a Greek.* **2:4** Greek *some false brothers.*

1:6 The Galatians were "turning away . . . from God" by rejecting the Good News Paul had proclaimed and looking instead to the law. God called them to himself "through the loving mercy of Christ," not through obeying the law (2:16). Some were teaching that Gentile Christians had to be circumcised to be considered members of God's family. Paul rejected any requirement besides faith in Jesus (see 5:2-4).

1:15-16 For the account of Paul's conversion, see Acts 9:1-19; 22:1-21; 26:9-23. Paul's calling was specifically to "proclaim the Good News about Jesus to the Gentiles" (see Galatians 2:7), and he even educated other apostles in what that means (for example, 2:11-21). The phrase "to reveal his Son to me" might refer to Paul's encounter with Christ on his way to Damascus (Acts 9:1-19; compare 1 Corinthians 9:1; 15:8). Another translation in the first text note on Galatians 1:16 renders the phrase "to reveal his Son *in me.*" "*In me*" [emphasis added] might also suggest an internal revelation (compare Galatians 2:20; 4:6-7), implying that Paul's changed heart revealed Christ to others.

who worked through Peter as the apostle to the Jews also worked through me as the apostle to the Gentiles. ⁹In fact, James, Peter,* and John, who were known as pillars of the church, recognized the gift God had given me, and they accepted Barnabas and me as their co-workers. They encouraged us to keep preaching to the Gentiles, while they continued their work with the Jews. ¹⁰Their only suggestion was that we keep on helping the poor, which I have always been eager to do.

Paul Confronts Peter

¹¹But when Peter came to Antioch, I had to oppose him to his face, for what he did was very wrong. ¹²When he first arrived, he ate with the Gentile believers, who were not circumcised. But afterward, when some friends of James came, Peter wouldn't eat with the Gentiles anymore. He was afraid of criticism from these people who insisted on the necessity of circumcision. ¹³As a result, other Jewish believers followed Peter's hypocrisy, and even Barnabas was led astray by their hypocrisy.

¹⁴When I saw that they were not following the truth of the gospel message, I said to Peter in front of all the others, "Since you, a Jew by birth, have discarded the Jewish laws and are living like a Gentile, why are you now trying to make these Gentiles follow the Jewish traditions?

¹⁵"You and I are Jews by birth, not 'sinners' like the Gentiles. ¹⁶Yet we know that a person is made right with God by faith in Jesus Christ, not by obeying the law. And we have believed in Christ Jesus, so that we might be made right with God because of our faith in Christ, not because we have obeyed the law. For no one will ever be made right with God by obeying the law."*

¹⁷But suppose we seek to be made right with God through faith in Christ and then we are found guilty because we have abandoned the law. Would that mean Christ has led us into sin? Absolutely not! ¹⁸Rather, I am a sinner if I rebuild the old system of law I already tore down. ¹⁹For when I tried to keep the law, it condemned me. So I died to the law—I stopped trying to meet all its requirements—so that I might live for God. ²⁰My old self has been crucified with Christ.* It is no longer I who live, but Christ lives in me. So I live in this earthly body by trusting in the Son of God, who loved me and gave himself for me. ²¹I do not treat the grace of God as meaningless. For if keeping the law could make us right with God, then there was no need for Christ to die.

> "No one tribe or group of people can adequately display the fullness of God. The truth is that it takes every tribe, tongue, and nation to reflect the image of God in his fullness."
>
> LATASHA MORRISON
> speaker, author, and advocate for racial reconciliation

The Law and Faith in Christ

3 Oh, foolish Galatians! Who has cast an evil spell on you? For the meaning of Jesus Christ's death was made as clear to you as if you had seen a picture of his death on the cross. ²Let me ask you this one question: Did you receive the Holy Spirit by obeying the law of Moses? Of course not! You received the Spirit because you believed the message you heard about Christ. ³How foolish can you be? After starting your new lives in the Spirit, why are you now trying to become perfect by your own human effort? ⁴Have you experienced* so much for nothing? Surely it was not in vain, was it?

⁵I ask you again, does God give you the Holy Spirit and work miracles among you because you obey the law? Of course not! It is because you believe the message you heard about Christ.

⁶In the same way, "Abraham believed God, and God counted him as righteous because of his faith."*

2:9 Greek *Cephas;* also in 2:11, 14. **2:16** Some translators hold that the quotation extends through verse 14; others through verse 16; and still others through verse 21. **2:20** Some English translations put this sentence in verse 19. **3:4** Or *Have you suffered.* **3:6** Gen 15:6.

2:17-21 The false teachers probably claimed that Paul's law-free Good News would lead to lawlessness, that people would flaunt their sinfulness, and that Christ would thus be seen as leading people into sin (2:17). Paul shows that this is false because those who place their faith in Christ are empowered by the Holy Spirit to live holy, God-honoring lives (see 5:13-26).

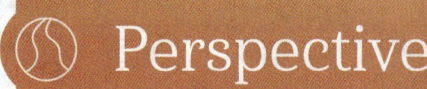

Perspective

How does our identity in Jesus shape our other identities?

SCRIPTURE CONNECTION: GALATIANS 3:26-28

In society, a "shared identity" (like political or religious beliefs) unites some but excludes others. In God's church, while differences are inevitable, divisions are not.

Some people interpret Galatians 3:26-28 as referring to Eve and Adam's equality before the Fall (Genesis 3:1-19). Others interpret it as a promise of emancipation. Nevertheless, all interpreters of this passage agree that our baptism in Christ is meant to repair divisions caused by differences of ethnicity, economic status, and gender in our world. Against the Greco-Roman cultural belief in women's inferiority, Paul provided a countercultural view: Women have equal standing in the church *through their shared identity in Christ*. Would this new spiritual identity nullify all social differences related to gender? Likely not, according to Paul's other writings, where he still had to address people and situations as they arose.

Even if cultures still condition women to feel or be treated as inferior, Jesus-followers are to believe and behave differently. We are called to live according to who we are in Jesus. Where different social identities can divide, a shared spiritual identity can and should unite.

VIEWPOINTS

HERS: *What might have changed about how the Galatian women viewed themselves when they clothed themselves with Christ?*

MINE: *"I am a Chinese-Canadian female Bible teacher. My social identity provides me a perspective when I read and interpret the Bible, but that doesn't make me inferior or superior in God's family."*

YOURS: *What motivates you to clothe yourself with Jesus? What hinders you from doing so?*

ESTHER G. CEN, MDiv, PhD, is a follower of Christ and multilingual writer and teacher, currently serving as assistant professor of biblical studies at Seattle Pacific University and Seminary.

---

⁷The real children of Abraham, then, are those who put their faith in God. ⁸What's more, the Scriptures looked forward to this time when God would make the Gentiles right in his sight because of their faith. God proclaimed this good news to Abraham long ago when he said, "All nations will be blessed through you."* ⁹So all who put their faith in Christ share the same blessing Abraham received because of his faith.

¹⁰But those who depend on the law to make them right with God are under his curse, for the Scriptures say, "Cursed is everyone who does not observe and obey all the commands that are written in God's Book of the Law."* ¹¹So it is clear that no one can be made right with God by trying to keep the law. For the Scriptures say, "It is through faith that a righteous person has life."* ¹²This way of faith is very different from the way of law, which says, "It is through obeying the law that a person has life."*

¹³But Christ has rescued us from the curse pronounced by the law. When he was hung on the cross, he took upon himself the curse for our wrongdoing. For it is written in the Scriptures, "Cursed is everyone who is hung on a tree."* ¹⁴Through Christ Jesus, God has blessed the Gentiles with the same blessing he promised to Abraham, so that we who are believers might receive the promised* Holy Spirit through faith.

The Law and God's Promise

¹⁵Dear brothers and sisters,* here's an example from everyday life. Just as no one can set aside or amend an irrevocable agreement, so it is in this case. ¹⁶God gave the promises to Abraham and his child.* And notice that the Scripture doesn't say "to his children,*" as if it meant many descendants. Rather, it says "to his child"—and that, of course, means Christ. ¹⁷This is what I am trying to say: The agreement God made with Abraham could not be canceled 430 years later when God gave the law to Moses. God would be breaking his promise. ¹⁸For if the inheritance could be received by keeping the law, then it would not be the result of accepting God's promise. But God graciously gave it to Abraham as a promise.

¹⁹Why, then, was the law given? It was given alongside the promise to show people their sins. But the law was designed to last only until the coming of the child who was promised. God gave his law through

---

3:8 Gen 12:3; 18:18; 22:18. **3:10** Deut 27:26. **3:11** Hab 2:4. **3:12** Lev 18:5. **3:13** Deut 21:23 (Greek version). **3:14** Some manuscripts read *the blessing of the*. **3:15** Greek *Brothers*. **3:16a** Greek *seed;* also in 3:16c, 19. See notes on Gen 12:7 and 13:15. **3:16b** Greek *seeds*.

3:12 The law itself is not opposed to faith (see 3:19-25; Romans 7:7-13) but trying to be righteous by keeping the law opposes righteousness by faith in Christ. Paul quotes Leviticus 18:5 to show that life under the law comes by obeying rather than believing. Right standing with God is impossible on that basis alone (Galatians 3:10-11).

angels to Moses, who was the mediator between God and the people. ²⁰Now a mediator is helpful if more than one party must reach an agreement. But God, who is one, did not use a mediator when he gave his promise to Abraham.

²¹Is there a conflict, then, between God's law and God's promises?* Absolutely not! If the law could give us new life, we could be made right with God by obeying it. ²²But the Scriptures declare that we are all prisoners of sin, so we receive God's promise of freedom only by believing in Jesus Christ.

God's Children through Faith

²³Before the way of faith in Christ was available to us, we were placed under guard by the law. We were kept in protective custody, so to speak, until the way of faith was revealed.

²⁴Let me put it another way. The law was our guardian until Christ came; it protected us until we could be made right with God through faith. ²⁵And now that the way of faith has come, we no longer need the law as our guardian.

²⁶For you are all children* of God through faith in Christ Jesus. ²⁷And all who have been united with Christ in baptism have put on Christ, like putting on new clothes.* ²⁸There is no longer Jew or Gentile,* slave or free, male and female. For you are all one in Christ Jesus. ²⁹And now that you belong to Christ, you are the true children* of Abraham. You are his heirs, and God's promise to Abraham belongs to you.

4 Think of it this way. If a father dies and leaves an inheritance for his young children, those children are not much better off than slaves until they grow up, even though they actually own everything their father had. ²They have to obey their guardians until they reach whatever age their father set. ³And that's the way it was with us before Christ came. We were like children; we were slaves to the basic spiritual principles* of this world.

⁴But when the right time came, God sent his Son, born of a woman, subject to the law. ⁵God sent him to buy freedom for us who were slaves to the law, so that he could adopt us as his very own children.* ⁶And because we* are his children, God has sent the Spirit of his Son into our hearts, prompting us to call out, "Abba, Father."* ⁷Now you are no longer a slave but God's own child.* And since you are his child, God has made you his heir.

Paul's Concern for the Galatians

⁸Before you Gentiles knew God, you were slaves to so-called gods that do not even exist. ⁹So now that you know God (or should I say, now that God knows you), why do you want to go back again and become slaves once more to the weak and useless spiritual principles of this world? ¹⁰You are trying to earn favor with God by observing certain days or months or seasons or years. ¹¹I fear for you. Perhaps all my hard work with you was for nothing. ¹²Dear brothers and sisters,* I plead with you to live as I do in freedom from these things, for I have become like you Gentiles—free from those laws.

You did not mistreat me when I first preached to you. ¹³Surely you remember that I was sick when I first brought you the Good News. ¹⁴But even though my condition tempted you to reject me, you did not despise me or turn me away. No, you took me in and cared for me as though I were an angel from God or even Christ Jesus himself. ¹⁵Where is that joyful and grateful spirit you felt then? I am sure you would have taken out your own eyes and given them to me if it had been possible. ¹⁶Have I now become your enemy because I am telling you the truth?

¹⁷Those false teachers are so eager to win your favor, but their intentions are not good. They are

---

3:21 Some manuscripts read *and the promises?* **3:26** Greek *sons.* **3:27** Greek *have put on Christ.* **3:28** Greek *Jew or Greek.* **3:29** Greek *seed.* **4:3** Or *powers;* also in 4:9. **4:5** Greek *sons;* also in 4:6. **4:6a** Greek *you.* **4:6b** *Abba* is an Aramaic term for "father." **4:7** Greek *son;* also in 4:7b. **4:12** Greek *brothers;* also in 4:28, 31.

3:21 No conflict of purpose exists between law and promise, or between law and faith. Law partners with the promise in bringing people to faith in Christ. Law has its proper roles of declaring people prisoners of sin (3:19, 22) and of restraining sin (3:23-25). In Galatia, the false teachers (referred to as "the Judaizers" by some scholars) tried to convince Gentile Christians that the law could do something it was never intended to do—give them new life and make people right with God. God does these things on the basis of faith in his promise, which was fulfilled in Jesus Christ (see 3:22).

3:28 Paul offers these three pairs ("Jew or Gentile, slave or free, male and female") as representative of the social and cultural divisions that prevent unity. Jews considered Gentiles to be idol worshipers (and most were) but in Christ, both Jew and Gentile now worship the one true God. Enslaved people were considered of no social worth, but in obeying the will of the Father, Christ himself took up the form of an enslaved person (Philippians 2:6-7). Therefore, both people who had been enslaved and people who were free are of equal worth in God's eyes (Ephesians 6:9). Paul borrowed his language from Genesis 1:27, rather than using the typical Greek terms for man and woman, likely drawing on the creation narrative that both men and women are made in God's image. The gospel denies any hierarchical structure of human worth and declares that believers "are all one in Christ Jesus."

4:4 Paul summarizes the Christmas story in one short phrase: "born of a woman." He also emphasizes the full humanity of Jesus in his incarnation by reminding the Galatians of how Jesus came into the world. Earlier he spoke of the promises to Abraham and his "child" (literally, "seed") who is Christ (3:16). Mary is that woman who gave birth to Christ, and in her song of praise, she thanked God for his mercy, for remembering Israel, and for his promise "to Abraham and his children forever" (Luke 1:46-55).

trying to shut you off from me so that you will pay attention only to them. ¹⁸If someone is eager to do good things for you, that's all right; but let them do it all the time, not just when I'm with you.

¹⁹Oh, my dear children! I feel as if I'm going through labor pains for you again, and they will continue until Christ is fully developed in your lives. ²⁰I wish I were with you right now so I could change my tone. But at this distance I don't know how else to help you.

Abraham's Two Children

²¹Tell me, you who want to live under the law, do you know what the law actually says? ²²The Scriptures say that Abraham had two sons, one from his slave wife and one from his freeborn wife.* ²³The son of the slave wife was born in a human attempt to bring about the fulfillment of God's promise. But the son of the freeborn wife was born as God's own fulfillment of his promise.

²⁴These two women serve as an illustration of God's two covenants. The first woman, Hagar, represents Mount Sinai where people received the law that enslaved them. ²⁵And now Jerusalem is just like Mount Sinai in Arabia,* because she and her children live in slavery to the law. ²⁶But the other woman, Sarah, represents the heavenly Jerusalem. She is the free woman, and she is our mother. ²⁷As Isaiah said,

> "Rejoice, O childless woman,
>   you who have never given birth!
> Break into a joyful shout,
>   you who have never been in labor!
> For the desolate woman now has more children
>   than the woman who lives with her husband!"*

²⁸And you, dear brothers and sisters, are children of the promise, just like Isaac. ²⁹But you are now being persecuted by those who want you to keep the law, just as Ishmael, the child born by human effort, persecuted Isaac, the child born by the power of the Spirit.

³⁰But what do the Scriptures say about that? "Get rid of the slave and her son, for the son of the slave woman will not share the inheritance with the free woman's son."* ³¹So, dear brothers and sisters, we are not children of the slave woman; we are children of the free woman.

Freedom in Christ

5 So Christ has truly set us free. Now make sure that you stay free, and don't get tied up again in slavery to the law.

²Listen! I, Paul, tell you this: If you are counting on circumcision to make you right with God, then Christ will be of no benefit to you. ³I'll say it again. If you are trying to find favor with God by being circumcised, you must obey every regulation in the whole law of Moses. ⁴For if you are trying to make yourselves right with God by keeping the law, you have been cut off from Christ! You have fallen away from God's grace.

⁵But we who live by the Spirit eagerly wait to receive by faith the righteousness God has promised to us. ⁶For when we place our faith in Christ Jesus, there is no benefit in being circumcised or being uncircumcised. What is important is faith expressing itself in love.

⁷You were running the race so well. Who has held you back from following the truth? ⁸It certainly isn't God, for he is the one who called you to freedom.

4:22 See Gen 16:15; 21:2-3. **4:25** Greek *And Hagar, which is Mount Sinai in Arabia, is now like Jerusalem;* other manuscripts read *And Mount Sinai in Arabia is now like Jerusalem.* **4:27** Isa 54:1. **4:30** Gen 21:10.

4:19 The Galatians were Paul's spiritual children (see also 1 Corinthians 4:14-15; Philemon 1:10). The process of bringing them to Christ had been like "going through labor pains," a hard labor with a definite and joyful conclusion. Now Paul felt that it wasn't finished after all. Paul uses wordplay, "until Christ is fully developed in your lives," switching the metaphor so that the Galatians would give birth to Christ's image if they continued in the faith that Paul had delivered to them. However, if they took up the law, they would produce a stillbirth. Paul would need to continue his hard work as a midwife in order to prevent this from happening.

4:21-31 Paul does not use an allegory like this anywhere else in his letters. This likely means that his Galatian opponents were making an argument that uncircumcised believers were like Ishmael, who was Abraham's son but was not part of Israel. Paul insisted that it is not Abraham who matters but God's promise. Isaac was Abraham's promised son, and Sarah was his mother. Paul emphasized the two sons' mothers to prove his point that Christ alone is the fulfillment of the promise. With the promise comes life in the Spirit, which brings freedom.

4:24 Hagar was an enslaved Gentile (Egyptian) woman who bore Abraham a son, Ishmael (Genesis 16:7-13; 21:17). In the story, an angel of the Lord visited her twice, and she suffered at the hand of her enslavers. But the Lord protected her and her son, and promised that Ishmael would be the father of a nation. She gave God the name "the God who sees me." Her story and Abraham's story share common plot features around slavery and freedom (see Genesis 15:13).

4:26 Sarah was the wife of Abraham, and she gave birth to a son named Isaac, the son promised to ensure future descendants and through whom the Lord would continue his covenant (Genesis 21:1-7). Abraham and Sarah were visited by God in the form of three messengers to tell them that Isaac would be born, even though their advanced ages made it seem impossible (Genesis 18:1-15). Sarah was not enslaved and, in Paul's allegory, represents "the free woman" and the children of faith in the Spirit.

5:5 The alternative to remaining faithful to the law is to live by complete reliance on the Spirit to make us pleasing to God. We receive God's righteousness upon our salvation (Romans 5:9-11; 10:10), in an ongoing way through the Spirit's sanctification (Romans 8:1-14), and fully at the resurrection when Christ returns (Romans 8:18-30). God's sole power provides righteousness and fulfills his promise (Galatians 3:14, 22).

⁹This false teaching is like a little yeast that spreads through the whole batch of dough! ¹⁰I am trusting the Lord to keep you from believing false teachings. God will judge that person, whoever he is, who has been confusing you.

¹¹Dear brothers and sisters,* if I were still preaching that you must be circumcised—as some say I do—why am I still being persecuted? If I were no longer preaching salvation through the cross of Christ, no one would be offended. ¹²I just wish that those troublemakers who want to mutilate you by circumcision would mutilate themselves.*

¹³For you have been called to live in freedom, my brothers and sisters. But don't use your freedom to satisfy your sinful nature. Instead, use your freedom to serve one another in love. ¹⁴For the whole law can be summed up in this one command: "Love your neighbor as yourself."* ¹⁵But if you are always biting and devouring one another, watch out! Beware of destroying one another.

5:11 Greek *Brothers;* similarly in 5:13. **5:12** Or *castrate themselves,* or *cut themselves off from you;* Greek reads *cut themselves off.*
5:14 Lev 19:18.

How Living by Faith Helps Us Relate

SCRIPTURE CONNECTION: GALATIANS 3:1-22; 5:13-26

When I'm living by faith in Christ through the Holy Spirit, my focus is on deepening my love relationship and unity with Jesus. I become more like him as I surrender: Love, peace, patience, and gentleness just flow through me. In contrast, when I live by rules or guidelines imposed by others (and sometimes I still do), I focus on being in control and getting it right.

Initially, my own effort gives me a familiar sense of calm or satisfaction. But in the end, it leads to misery. I mostly do "good" things and follow the rules, but I am not pleasant. Instead of the fruit of the Spirit flowing from my heart, I sputter out irritability, pride, perfectionism, and judgment.

God gave the law to show how much we need Jesus. As Christians, we can end up creating our own law and get hung up on religious rule-following and playing God, judging those who don't do what we think they should. When we do, our relationships with God, ourselves, and others suffer.

> The way of faith is not easy, but it is quite simple.

Fortunately, we can break the trying-to-do-better bond, as often as we notice it happening! As soon as we find ourselves controlling, pursuing perfection, or judging, we can ask God to show us what we're really feeling and what we really need. We can cry out to Jesus to live in and through our relationships.

IMAGINE

What leads you to live by rules instead of faith?

What steps can you take today to let the Holy Spirit guide your life (Galatians 5:16)?

"It is easy to slip into the driver's seat of my own life when I'm afraid. The way of faith is not easy, but it is quite simple."

KRISTIN CARY, CPSAS, cofounded Living Truth with her husband. She guides women toward hope and healing after the devastating impact of sexual betrayal in their marriage.

GALATIANS 5

Living by the Spirit's Power

¹⁶So I say, let the Holy Spirit guide your lives. Then you won't be doing what your sinful nature craves. ¹⁷The sinful nature wants to do evil, which is just the opposite of what the Spirit wants. And the Spirit gives us desires that are the opposite of what the sinful nature desires. These two forces are constantly fighting each other, so you are not free to carry out your good intentions. ¹⁸But when you are directed by the Spirit, you are not under obligation to the law of Moses.

¹⁹When you follow the desires of your sinful nature, the results are very clear: sexual immorality, impurity, lustful pleasures, ²⁰idolatry, sorcery, hostility, quarreling, jealousy, outbursts of anger, selfish ambition, dissension, division, ²¹envy, drunkenness, wild parties, and other sins like these. Let me tell you again, as I have before, that anyone living that sort of life will not inherit the Kingdom of God.

²²But the Holy Spirit produces this kind of fruit in our lives: love, joy, peace, patience, kindness,

---

Koinonia

IMAGE — MY STORY WITH COMMUNITY, WORKPLACE & CHURCH

Work Hard Where We Are

SCRIPTURE CONNECTION: GALATIANS 6:4-5

When we look at what others are doing, it's tempting to think their work is more fun, more happy, more fulfilling, more holy, or just plain *more* than ours.

Our online lives don't help. We scroll through each other's highlights without considering how edited and filtered they are. But wishing others' circumstances were our own is not unique to today. God speaks directly to our temptation to compare assignments and says flat out: "Stop."

In Galatians 6:4-5, Paul encourages us to be satisfied with the work we've been given and focus on our own behavior. Throughout his letters, Paul shows us that instead of comparing ourselves, we can:

- Know what we're good at and how we're wired. This may take some investigating, but God has designed us on purpose (Ephesians 2:10).
- Do what is in front of us with enthusiasm (Ephesians 6:7). It does not matter the job. If it is ours to do, God values it.
- Stay humble. Sometimes we are called to do the thing that is impressive by the world's standards. But we live by God's standards, and no part of the body of Christ is better than another (1 Corinthians 12:14-26).
- Avoid becoming distracted by others' work. Sometimes we may envy someone else's assignment. Remember that our part is an important one (1 Corinthians 12:4-6). God has not forgotten about us.
- Serve him through our work (Colossians 3:23). If God has placed you somewhere, it is a place to serve him and others (1 Corinthians 7:17). Give it your best go!

> Comparison steals the joy of the work God has given you today.

IMAGINE

What work have you been given?

How can you minimize the distractions of comparison?

How can you give the assignment in front of you your best effort?

> "When I focus on the assignment God has given me, I'm less likely to get distracted by what others are doing. It's freeing to say yes to him without worrying about what anyone else gets to do."

ALEXANDRA KUYKENDALL is a cofounder of The Open Door Sisterhood and author of several books, including *Seeking Out Goodness: Finding the True and Beautiful All around You.*

goodness, faithfulness, ²³gentleness, and self-control. There is no law against these things!

²⁴Those who belong to Christ Jesus have nailed the passions and desires of their sinful nature to his cross and crucified them there. ²⁵Since we are living by the Spirit, let us follow the Spirit's leading in every part of our lives. ²⁶Let us not become conceited, or provoke one another, or be jealous of one another.

We Harvest What We Plant

6 Dear brothers and sisters, if another believer* is overcome by some sin, you who are godly* should gently and humbly help that person back onto the right path. And be careful not to fall into the same temptation yourself. ²Share each other's burdens, and in this way obey the law of Christ. ³If you think you are too important to help someone, you are only fooling yourself. You are not that important. ⁴Pay careful attention to your own work, for then you will get the satisfaction of a job well done, and you won't need to compare yourself to anyone else. ⁵For we are each responsible for our own conduct.

⁶Those who are taught the word of God should provide for their teachers, sharing all good things with them.

⁷Don't be misled—you cannot mock the justice of God. You will always harvest what you plant. ⁸Those who live only to satisfy their own sinful nature will harvest decay and death from that sinful nature. But those who live to please the Spirit will harvest everlasting life from the Spirit. ⁹So let's not get tired of doing what is good. At just the right time we will reap a harvest of blessing if we don't give up. ¹⁰Therefore, whenever we have the opportunity, we should do good to everyone—especially to those in the family of faith.

Paul's Final Advice

¹¹NOTICE WHAT LARGE LETTERS I USE AS I WRITE THESE CLOSING WORDS IN MY OWN HANDWRITING.

¹²Those who are trying to force you to be circumcised want to look good to others. They don't want to be persecuted for teaching that the cross of Christ alone can save. ¹³And even those who advocate circumcision don't keep the whole law themselves. They only want you to be circumcised so they can boast about it and claim you as their disciples.

¹⁴As for me, may I never boast about anything except the cross of our Lord Jesus Christ. Because of that cross,* my interest in this world has been crucified, and the world's interest in me has also died. ¹⁵It doesn't matter whether we have been circumcised or not. What counts is whether we have been transformed into a new creation. ¹⁶May God's peace and mercy be upon all who live by this principle; they are the new people of God.*

¹⁷From now on, don't let anyone trouble me with these things. For I bear on my body the scars that show I belong to Jesus.

¹⁸Dear brothers and sisters,* may the grace of our Lord Jesus Christ be with your spirit. Amen.

6:1a Greek *Brothers, if a man.* 6:1b Greek *spiritual.* 6:14 Or *Because of him.* 6:16 Greek *this principle, and upon the Israel of God.* 6:18 Greek *Brothers.*

5:22 Unlike following our sinful nature (5:19-21), letting the Holy Spirit guide us (5:16) produces a life pleasing to God, which human effort and the law cannot do (see John 15:1-8). These virtues directly address the factions in the church of Galatia. The greatest Christian virtue, love, encompasses all the others (1 Corinthians 13:4-7). Only the Spirit of God can produce in us love for those who hate us (Matthew 5:43-48; Luke 6:35-36). Joy produced by the Spirit does not depend on circumstances (Romans 15:13; 2 Corinthians 6:10; 8:2; 1 Thessalonians 1:6). Peace with God creates internal well-being (Romans 5:1; Philippians 4:6-7) that spills into our relationships with others so that we become peacemakers (Matthew 5:9; Romans 8:6; 12:18; 14:17-19; 2 Corinthians 13:11; Ephesians 4:3; 6:15). Patience (or "tolerance," or "long-suffering") gives us forbearance toward other people and endurance under unfavorable circumstances (Ephesians 4:2; 2 Timothy 4:2; James 5:10-11). God is patient with us (Exodus 34:6; Psalm 103:8; Romans 2:4; 9:22; 1 Timothy 1:16; 2 Peter 3:15) and promises his presence with those who are patient with others (Isaiah 57:15). Kindness connotes generosity, a giving spirit that reflects how God treats us (Romans 2:4; 11:22; Titus 3:4-6). For more on goodness in Paul's letters, see Romans 15:14; Ephesians 5:9; 2 Thessalonians 1:11. Faithfulness (or "faith") means exercising good faith and fidelity in our relationships, just as God does with us (1 Corinthians 1:9; 10:13; 2 Thessalonians 3:3).

5:23 The fruit of gentleness is antithetical to the vices of 5:20 and requires strength (see Proverbs 15:1, 4; Matthew 11:28-29; Ephesians 4:2). The Holy Spirit does not give moral license but empowers people to avoid sin with the fruit of self-control (see Galatians 5:13; Romans 6:14-18; 1 Thessalonians 4:3-7; 1 Peter 2:16; see also Acts 24:25; Titus 1:8). Paul was stating the obvious when he said, "There is no law against these things," but he was also making the point that those who are virtuous by the Spirit do not need law to govern them.

6:16 "This principle" refers to putting trust in Christ for salvation (see 6:14-15). In the phrase, "they are the new people of God" (literally "and [or 'even'] upon the Israel of God"), the Greek word translated "and" can often mean "even." If it means "and," then the "Israel of God" is a separate group from "all who live by this principle"; if it means "even," then they are the same group. The Jewish people still have an identity before God (Romans 9:1-5; 10:1-4; 11:1-32). Gentiles who believe have been grafted in, and Jews who disbelieve have been pruned out of the spiritual Israel (Romans 11:17-24; compare Philippians 3:2-3; Colossians 2:11-12). Paul thus considers all Christians to be the true Israel (see Romans 2:28-29; 9:6-8; compare Galatians 4:21-31). The literal phrase "the Israel of God" does not appear elsewhere in the New Testament or in other literature; perhaps the false teachers promised this identification to Gentiles who would accept circumcision. If so, then Paul turned their argument on its head: The Gentiles in Galatia didn't need circumcision, for they were already God's Israel—his true people—through faith in Christ.

Ephesians

WHAT DO WE LEARN ABOUT GOD'S MISSION AND OURS?
God empowers us to live out our calling.

WHO WROTE IT? Paul, an apostle.

WHEN DID IT HAPPEN? Paul possibly wrote this book while imprisoned in Rome, around AD 60.

HOW IS IT ORGANIZED?

1:1-2: Greetings from Paul

1:3–3:21: God's amazing grace

4:1–6:20: Living like Christ

6:21-24: Final greetings

FEATURE HIGHLIGHTS

+ *Divided Yet Brought Closer (1491)*
+ *Generational Blessings (1492)*
+ *Brave Enough to Be the Light (1494)*
+ *Wives, Husbands, and Submission to Christ (1496)*
+ *Lies and God's Truth (1498)*

Words to Remember are highlighted throughout this book

HOW LONG DOES IT TAKE TO READ?

| :20 | :30 | 1:00 | 1:30 | 2:00 | 2:30 | 3:00 | 3:30 |

Timeline

AD	Event
30	JESUS DIES, RISES FROM THE DEAD, ASCENDS TO REIGN IN HEAVEN, SENDS THE HOLY SPIRIT
35	JESUS CALLS PAUL TO PREACH THE GOOD NEWS
46–48	PAUL GOES ON FIRST MISSIONARY JOURNEY, WITH BARNABAS AND JOHN MARK
50	JERUSALEM COUNCIL CONFIRMS GENTILE INCLUSION IN THE CHURCH
50–52	PAUL EMBARKS ON SECOND MISSIONARY JOURNEY, WITH SILAS; THEY SPEND 18 MONTHS IN CORINTH
50	PAUL MEETS PRISCILLA AND AQUILA IN CORINTH
	PAUL MEETS LYDIA IN PHILIPPI
53–56	PAUL STAYS FOR AN EXTENDED TIME IN EPHESUS WHERE HE WRITES 1 CORINTHIANS
57	PAUL ARRESTED IN JERUSALEM
57–59	PAUL IMPRISONED IN CAESAREA, WHERE HE IS QUESTIONED BY FESTUS, FELIX AND DRUSILLA, AND AGRIPPA AND BERNICE
60–62	PAUL UNDER HOUSE ARREST IN ROME WRITES HIS LETTERS TO THE EPHESIANS, PHILIPPIANS, COLOSSIANS, AND PHILEMON
64	PAUL MARTYRED IN ROME
70	ROME DESTROYS JERUSALEM

Greetings from Paul

1 This letter is from Paul, chosen by the will of God to be an apostle of Christ Jesus.

I am writing to God's holy people in Ephesus,* who are faithful followers of Christ Jesus.

²May God our Father and the Lord Jesus Christ give you grace and peace.

Spiritual Blessings

³All praise to God, the Father of our Lord Jesus Christ, who has blessed us with every spiritual blessing in the heavenly realms because we are united with Christ. ⁴Even before he made the world, God loved us and chose us in Christ to be holy and without fault in his eyes. ⁵God decided in advance to adopt us into his own family by bringing us to himself through Jesus Christ. This is what he wanted to do, and it gave him great pleasure. ⁶So we praise God for the glorious grace he has poured out on us who belong to his dear Son.* ⁷He is so rich in kindness and grace that he purchased our freedom with the blood of his Son and forgave our sins. ⁸He has showered his kindness on us, along with all wisdom and understanding.

⁹God has now revealed to us his mysterious will regarding Christ—which is to fulfill his own good plan. ¹⁰And this is the plan: At the right time he will bring everything together under the authority of Christ—everything in heaven and on earth. ¹¹Furthermore, because we are united with Christ, we have received an inheritance from God,* for he chose us in advance, and he makes everything work out according to his plan.

¹²God's purpose was that we Jews who were the first to trust in Christ would bring praise and glory to God. ¹³And now you Gentiles have also heard the truth, the Good News that God saves you. And when you believed in Christ, he identified you as his own* by giving you the Holy Spirit, whom he promised long ago. ¹⁴The Spirit is God's guarantee that he will give us the inheritance he promised and that he has purchased us to be his own people. He did this so we would praise and glorify him.

Paul's Prayer for Spiritual Wisdom

¹⁵Ever since I first heard of your strong faith in the Lord Jesus and your love for God's people everywhere,* ¹⁶I have not stopped thanking God for you. I pray for you constantly, ¹⁷asking God, the glorious Father of our Lord Jesus Christ, to give you spiritual wisdom* and insight so that you might grow in your knowledge of God. ¹⁸I pray that your hearts will be flooded with light so that you can understand the confident hope he has given to those he called—his holy people who are his rich and glorious inheritance.*

¹⁹I also pray that you will understand the incredible greatness of God's power for us who believe him. This is the same mighty power ²⁰that raised Christ from the dead and seated him in the place of honor at God's right hand in the heavenly realms. ²¹Now he is far above any ruler or authority or power or leader or anything else—not only in this world but also in the world to come. ²²God has put all things under the authority of Christ and has made him head over all things for the benefit of the church. ²³And the church is his body; it is made full and complete by Christ, who fills all things everywhere with himself.

Made Alive with Christ

2 Once you were dead because of your disobedience and your many sins. ²You used to live in sin, just like the rest of the world, obeying the devil—the commander of the powers in the unseen world.* He is the spirit at work in the hearts of those who refuse to obey God. ³All of us used to live that way, following the passionate desires and inclinations of our sinful nature. By our very nature we were subject to God's anger, just like everyone else.

⁴But God is so rich in mercy, and he loved us so much, ⁵that even though we were dead because of our sins, he gave us life when he raised Christ from the dead. (It is only by God's grace that you have been saved!) ⁶For he raised us from the dead along with Christ and seated us with him in the heavenly realms because we are united with Christ Jesus. ⁷So God can point to us in all future ages as examples of the incredible wealth of his grace and kindness toward us, as shown in all he has done for us who are united with Christ Jesus.

⁸God saved you by his grace when you believed. And you can't take credit for this; it is a gift from God. ⁹Salvation is not a reward for the good things

---

1:1 The most ancient manuscripts do not include *in Ephesus*. **1:6** Greek *to us in the beloved*. **1:11** Or *we have become God's inheritance*. **1:13** Or *he put his seal on you*. **1:15** Some manuscripts read *your faithfulness to the Lord Jesus and to God's people everywhere*. **1:17** Or *to give you the Spirit of wisdom*. **1:18** Or *called, and the rich and glorious inheritance he has given to his holy people*. **2:2** Greek *obeying the commander of the power of the air*.

1:5 By his sovereign initiative, God embraces and blesses as his children those who trust in Christ. They become heirs to all the promises God has made to his people (see 1:11, 14; 2:19; Romans 8:15-17, 29-30; Galatians 4:5).

2:1-10 Paul describes how Gentiles were under "the devil—the commander of the powers in the unseen world." He adds that even Jews (who were supposed to know God) followed their passions. Christ has ascended and is at God's right hand (1:20; 2:6). God's mercy rescued both believing Jews and Gentiles through Christ. We who believe, regardless of ethnicity, participate in his life, raised and seated with him in the heavenly realms. Paul insists that no one is saved but by faith in Christ, for salvation is God's gift. It is not our works or our worthiness as society might estimate, for we are of infinite value to God, his masterpiece.

we have done, so none of us can boast about it. ¹⁰For we are God's masterpiece. He has created us anew in Christ Jesus, so we can do the good things he planned for us long ago.

Oneness and Peace in Christ

¹¹Don't forget that you Gentiles used to be outsiders. You were called "uncircumcised heathens" by the Jews, who were proud of their circumcision, even though it affected only their bodies and not their hearts. ¹²In those days you were living apart from Christ. You were excluded from citizenship among the people of Israel, and you did not know the covenant promises God had made to them. You lived in this world without God and without hope. ¹³But now you have been united with Christ Jesus. Once you were far away from God, but now you have been brought near to him through the blood of Christ.

¹⁴For Christ himself has brought peace to us. He united Jews and Gentiles into one people when, in his own body on the cross, he broke down the wall

2:14 The peace that Christ brought to us is peace with God (2:16-17; Romans 5:1, 10-11, 18-21; Colossians 1:20-22) and between Jews and Gentiles (see Ephesians 2:15-16; 4:3). Social and religious practices traditionally divided Jews from Gentiles and at times, created an adversarial relationship between them. A low wall around the Temple in Jerusalem marked the boundary beyond which Gentiles were not allowed to step (see "Herod's Temple" on page 1334). It symbolized the distinction Jews drew between themselves and Gentiles.

⑧ Come Close — DIVIDED YET BROUGHT CLOSER

SCRIPTURE CONNECTION: EPHESIANS 2:11-18

She's a White woman whose politics are different. I'm a Black woman who questions her views. But here we are, stirring sugar into our teacups, seated in a restaurant willing to connect across our divides. But why does the breach feel so wide?

Problem: You want to make a connection with someone whose background differs from yours.

Solution: Draw close to Christ first.

Hint: Seeking the Lord's Spirit instead of just human solutions inspires the peace we seek: "For Christ himself has brought peace to us.... He broke down the wall of hostility that separated us" (2:14).

The apostle Paul understood this truth firsthand. So, his letter to the Ephesians reminds us:

- Jesus is our peace. He melts our barriers and brings down our walls.
- Jesus' way is unity. His purpose is to make "peace ... by creating in himself one new people from the two groups" (2:15).
- Jesus' blood heals. "Once you were far away from God, but now you have been brought near"—to him and each other—"through the blood of Christ" (2:13).

When divisions separate you from others, God's Spirit calls you to his "one body" (2:16, 18).

REFLECT "He brought this Good News of peace to you Gentiles who were far away from him, and peace to the Jews who were near" EPHESIANS 2:17

No matter who I am—or when or how I met Christ—he invites me to draw near to others in peace.

CONSIDER "God cannot give us a happiness and peace apart from Himself, because it is not there. There is no such thing." C. S. LEWIS

When you're torn from others, let Jesus heal the break.

PATRICIA RAYBON is an award-winning Colorado author, essayist, and novelist who writes top-rated books and stories at the daring intersection of faith, race, and mystery—including the Annalee Spain mystery series.

Generational Blessings

SCRIPTURE CONNECTION: EPHESIANS 3:14-21

My feet dangled above the floor as I sat on the wood bench at our family's dining table. Staring at the magazine picture of a child with a distended stomach, I asked, "Mommy, why is her tummy so big?"

My mother paused. "There are children who don't have enough food."

I pushed my plate of liver and onions her way, and said, "Can I send mine?"

Maybe ditching my least favorite meal motivated me at first, but my parents, like Paul, taught me to love "the other," people who are different from me. And, in so doing, they authored generational blessings.

A 2012 study from Baylor University has identified the most potent way families grow in faith: *they serve together*. My doctoral research showed the same. Jewish Paul, as he served the Gentiles, lived research-validated discipleship: Serving those who differ (3:14-15) helps us grow spiritually (3:16-19) and shapes generations to glorify Jesus (3:20-21).

My mom didn't let me donate my dinner, but she did invite me to load food and clothes into our blue station wagon and head to a nearby orphanage. As we unpacked, she asked me to do more than give handouts—she introduced me to new friends.

> We bless generations as we serve in Jesus' name.

Little did my mom and dad know that when they packed five-year-old me into the blue station wagon, they were writing blessings for my faith and my children's. Just as Paul prayed that all generations would know the Father from whom every family in heaven and on earth takes its name, so can we.

IMAGINE

Who are some people that differ from you, and how might you get to know and love them?

How can we engage different generations in serving?

> "My parents taught me the language spoken in that orphanage. Now my own children speak it too. Loving others in Jesus' name keeps on giving."

NAOMI CRAMER OVERTON, MBA, DIS, lives to realize beauty-filled visions that lift us to flourishing, with our families and beyond. Naomi has been CEO for Stonecroft and MOPS, director with Compassion International and World Vision, and General Editor for this Bible.

of hostility that separated us. ¹⁵He did this by ending the system of law with its commandments and regulations. He made peace between Jews and Gentiles by creating in himself one new people from the two groups. ¹⁶Together as one body, Christ reconciled both groups to God by means of his death on the cross, and our hostility toward each other was put to death.

¹⁷He brought this Good News of peace to you Gentiles who were far away from him, and peace to the Jews who were near. ¹⁸Now all of us can come to the Father through the same Holy Spirit because of what Christ has done for us.

A Temple for the Lord

¹⁹So now you Gentiles are no longer strangers and foreigners. You are citizens along with all of God's holy people. You are members of God's family. ²⁰Together, we are his house, built on the foundation of the apostles and the prophets. And the cornerstone is Christ Jesus himself. ²¹We are carefully joined together in him, becoming a holy temple for the Lord. ²²Through him you Gentiles are also being made part of this dwelling where God lives by his Spirit.

God's Mysterious Plan Revealed

3 When I think of all this, I, Paul, a prisoner of Christ Jesus for the benefit of you Gentiles* ... ²assuming, by the way, that you know God gave me the special responsibility of extending his grace to you Gentiles. ³As I briefly wrote earlier, God himself revealed his mysterious plan to me. ⁴As you read what I have written, you will understand my insight into this plan regarding Christ. ⁵God did not reveal it to previous generations, but now by his Spirit he has revealed it to his holy apostles and prophets.

⁶And this is God's plan: Both Gentiles and Jews who believe the Good News share equally in the riches inherited by God's children. Both are part of the same body, and both enjoy the promise of blessings because they belong to Christ Jesus.* ⁷By God's grace and mighty power, I have been given the privilege of serving him by spreading this Good News.

⁸Though I am the least deserving of all God's people, he graciously gave me the privilege of telling the Gentiles about the endless treasures available to them in Christ. ⁹I was chosen to explain to everyone* this mysterious plan that God, the Creator of all things, had kept secret from the beginning.

¹⁰God's purpose in all this was to use the church to display his wisdom in its rich variety to all the unseen rulers and authorities in the heavenly places. ¹¹This was his eternal plan, which he carried out through Christ Jesus our Lord.

¹²Because of Christ and our faith in him,* we can now come boldly and confidently into God's presence. ¹³So please don't lose heart because of my trials here. I am suffering for you, so you should feel honored.

Paul's Prayer for Spiritual Growth

¹⁴When I think of all this, I fall to my knees and pray to the Father,* ¹⁵the Creator of everything in heaven and on earth.* ¹⁶I pray that from his glorious, unlimited resources he will empower you with inner strength through his Spirit. ¹⁷Then Christ will make his home in your hearts as you trust in him. Your roots will grow down into God's love and keep you strong. ¹⁸And may you have the power to understand, as all God's people should, how wide, how long, how high, and how deep his love is. ¹⁹May you experience the love of Christ, though it is too great to understand fully. Then you will be made complete with all the fullness of life and power that comes from God.

²⁰Now all glory to God, who is able, through his mighty power at work within us, to accomplish infinitely more than we might ask or think. ²¹Glory to him in the church and in Christ Jesus through all generations forever and ever! Amen.

Unity in the Body

4 Therefore I, a prisoner for serving the Lord, beg you to lead a life worthy of your calling, for you have been called by God. ²Always be humble and gentle. Be patient with each other, making allowance for each other's faults because of your love. ³Make every effort to keep yourselves united in the Spirit, binding yourselves together with peace. ⁴For there is one body and one Spirit, just as you have been called to one glorious hope for the future.

3:1 Paul resumes this thought in verse 14: "When I think of all this, I fall to my knees and pray to the Father." 3:6 Or *because they are united with Christ Jesus.* 3:9 Some manuscripts do not include *to everyone.* 3:12 Or *Because of Christ's faithfulness.* 3:14 Some manuscripts read *the Father of our Lord Jesus Christ.* 3:15 Or *from whom every family in heaven and on earth takes its name.*

3:19 The whole Christian life is based on the experience and personal knowledge of God's grace and love in Jesus Christ (see Romans 12:1). Christ's love is much greater than ordinary human love (see Romans 5:6-8). The believer's life is "made complete" when it is filled "with all the fullness of life and power" by the presence of Christ within (see Ephesians 1:23; Galatians 2:20; Colossians 1:27). The believer then is conformed to Christ's image and reflects God (see Ephesians 4:14, 24; 5:1-2; Romans 8:29; 2 Corinthians 3:16-18).

4:4-6 These three verses might have been taken from a creedal statement, based on their formulaic structure. Whatever their ethnic differences, Jewish and Gentile Christians share one Lord and one faith, so they should live together in unity. Christ's one body is the church (see 1:23; 2:16). In Christ and through the Holy Spirit, God is especially present in believers' lives (see 1 Corinthians 6:19; 2 Corinthians 13:5; Galatians 2:20; Colossians 1:27; compare John 14:16-17, 23; 15:4-5).

Koinonia
IMAGE — MY STORY WITH COMMUNITY, WORKPLACE & CHURCH

Brave Enough to Be the Light

SCRIPTURE CONNECTION: EPHESIANS 5:8-9

Ever thought about what life would be like if darkness didn't exist? What if divorce wasn't a thing, abuse and heartache vanished, and wars and natural disasters were no longer a part of our stories?

The thought of a world like this, without pain and darkness, would reveal what God intended for us all along—paradise, goodness, and God's deep peace and flourishing, or *shalom*—before humanity did what was wrong. And while we cannot fully escape our broken world and our own brokenness right now, God has given us access to light in the middle of darkness, even from darkness that we may have caused.

In Ephesians 5:8, Paul writes that we were full of darkness, and his wording even indicates that we were darkness itself. *Don't be alarmed*. Paul also says that we now have light from the Lord and that we are light itself. Because of Jesus and the Holy Spirit in us and our identity as people of the light, we can illuminate a world full of darkness.

Just imagine: What if God doesn't want you to just face your demons but to quash the illusion of your brokenness so you can live the most colorful, light-filled life possible?

Maybe that seems too big for you right now, or maybe you just need to be the light in your own world of darkness right now. That's okay. God wants to do more in and through us than Jesus did while he was in the world (see John 14:12).

So take account of the darkness in your life, be brave enough to stop hiding what's been broken, and embrace the light you were always meant to be. God didn't promise us a life without darkness, but he did promise to be with us in it.

> God promises to be with us and give us light in our darkness.

IMAGINE

Which areas of your life could use the light of Jesus right now?

Who in your community could be safety nets who pull you back to the light when darkness comes in?

"I help women process through brokenness and get to healing and hope so that they can live in, and as, Jesus' light. My work teaches people all over the globe that we can be broken and worthy and unqualified and still called to do great things."

TONI J. COLLIER is a speaker, the founder of Broken Crayons Still Color, the host of the *Still Coloring* podcast, and the author of *Brave Enough to Be Broken: How to Embrace Your Pain and Discover Hope and Healing*.

⁵ There is one Lord, one faith, one baptism, ⁶ one God and Father of all,
 who is over all, in all, and living through all.

⁷However, he has given each one of us a special gift* through the generosity of Christ. ⁸That is why the Scriptures say,

"When he ascended to the heights,
 he led a crowd of captives
 and gave gifts to his people."*

⁹Notice that it says "he ascended." This clearly means that Christ also descended to our lowly world.* ¹⁰And the same one who descended is the one who ascended higher than all the heavens, so that he might fill the entire universe with himself.

¹¹Now these are the gifts Christ gave to the church: the apostles, the prophets, the evangelists, and the pastors and teachers. ¹²Their responsibility is to equip God's people to do his work and build up the church, the body of Christ. ¹³This will continue until we all come to such unity in our faith and knowledge of God's Son that we will be mature in the Lord, measuring up to the full and complete standard of Christ.

¹⁴Then we will no longer be immature like children. We won't be tossed and blown about by every wind of new teaching. We will not be influenced when people try to trick us with lies so clever they sound like the truth. ¹⁵Instead, we will speak the truth in love, growing in every way more and more like Christ, who is the head of his body, the church. ¹⁶He makes the whole body fit together perfectly. As each part does its own special work, it helps the other parts grow, so that the whole body is healthy and growing and full of love.

Living as Children of Light

¹⁷With the Lord's authority I say this: Live no longer as the Gentiles do, for they are hopelessly confused. ¹⁸Their minds are full of darkness; they wander far from the life God gives because they have closed their minds and hardened their hearts against him. ¹⁹They have no sense of shame. They live for lustful pleasure and eagerly practice every kind of impurity.

²⁰But that isn't what you learned about Christ. ²¹Since you have heard about Jesus and have learned the truth that comes from him, ²²throw off your old sinful nature and your former way of life, which is corrupted by lust and deception. ²³Instead, let the Spirit renew your thoughts and attitudes. ²⁴Put on your new nature, created to be like God—truly righteous and holy.

²⁵So stop telling lies. Let us tell our neighbors the truth, for we are all parts of the same body. ²⁶And "don't sin by letting anger control you."* Don't let the sun go down while you are still angry, ²⁷for anger gives a foothold to the devil.

²⁸If you are a thief, quit stealing. Instead, use your hands for good hard work, and then give generously to others in need. ²⁹Don't use foul or abusive language. Let everything you say be good and helpful, so that your words will be an encouragement to those who hear them.

³⁰And do not bring sorrow to God's Holy Spirit by the way you live. Remember, he has identified you as his own,* guaranteeing that you will be saved on the day of redemption.

³¹Get rid of all bitterness, rage, anger, harsh words, and slander, as well as all types of evil behavior. ³²Instead, be kind to each other, tenderhearted, forgiving one another, just as God through Christ has forgiven you.

Living in the Light

5 Imitate God, therefore, in everything you do, because you are his dear children. ²Live a life filled with love, following the example of Christ. He loved us* and offered himself as a sacrifice for us, a pleasing aroma to God.

³Let there be no sexual immorality, impurity, or greed among you. Such sins have no place among God's people. ⁴Obscene stories, foolish talk, and coarse jokes—these are not for you. Instead, let there be thankfulness to God. ⁵You can be sure that no immoral, impure, or greedy person will inherit the Kingdom of Christ and of God. For a greedy person is an idolater, worshiping the things of this world.

⁶Don't be fooled by those who try to excuse these sins, for the anger of God will fall on all who disobey him. ⁷Don't participate in the things these people do. ⁸For once you were full of darkness, but now you have light from the Lord. So live as people of light! ⁹For this light within you produces only what is good and right and true.

4:7 Greek *a grace*. **4:8** Ps 68:18. **4:9** Some manuscripts read *to the lower parts of the earth*. **4:26** Ps 4:4. **4:30** Or *has put his seal on you*. **5:2** Some manuscripts read *loved you*.

4:16 Each part of the body plays an important role and "helps the other parts grow." Christ, the head of the body, works through the individual parts, makes them fit together, and is the ultimate source of growth (see Colossians 2:19). When all believers are ministering effectively, the whole body will be "healthy and growing and full of love" (see 1 Corinthians 8:1). Love is the most important factor in Christian growth (1 Corinthians 13:1-13).

5:2 Christ's love is shown especially in his offering himself "as a sacrifice for us" (see 5:25; John 15:13; Romans 5:8). Christian love is motivated by and modeled after Christ's sacrificial love (see Philippians 2:5-8). Paul draws on Old Testament imagery, where the smell of a burning sacrifice was "a pleasing aroma to God" (see Leviticus 1:9; 2:2; see Romans 12:1).

Wives, Husbands, and Submission to Christ

SCRIPTURE CONNECTION: EPHESIANS 5:21-33

Paul *commands* husbands to love their wives. It is not a suggestion or an option, but a command issued three times (5:25, 28, 33), yet our English translations often mute the force of the original Greek. The love commanded is Christ's self-sacrificial, self-giving love (5:25-26).

Paul *does not command* wives to submit. In fact, the Greek text for 5:22 does not contain a verb, a practice common among ancient Greek writers in places where their audience could infer the verb from context. But because English doesn't work this way, translators borrow a word ("submit") from the previous verse and use it as a verb here. Just as every believer submits to others out of reverence for Christ, so too wives submit to their husbands. This submission presupposed that such actions would be in keeping with holy living, as Paul explains, "as to the Lord" (5:22).

Why doesn't Paul ask husbands to submit? Because men had the legal, social, and political power over their wives in his culture, they would not have grasped what Paul meant. But they knew Christ's story, how he humbled himself to be obedient to death on a cross (see Philippians 2:6-8). They could imagine this sort of love.

The word *head* in English and Hebrew is a common metaphor for a leader, but rarely so in Greek (Ephesians 5:23). Using the image of body and head in this passage, Paul stresses unity and oneness. Christ is "head," or Savior, of his body, the church. Christ certainly leads his church, but that is not the point of this body-and-head metaphor.

The revolutionary, countercultural teaching in this passage is directed toward husbands: They are to love as Christ loved—self-sacrificially.

> **Submission is for every believer.**

IMAGINE

How might the gospel give women a definition of love that surpasses our cultures' definitions?

How does it change your view to think that Paul's teaching on submission (5:21) applies to everyone—men and women, single and married?

"Churches often focus on wives submitting, but this misses the real, countercultural impact of the passage—husbands loving their wives with a self-sacrificial love like Christ, who embraced submission to the Father all the way to the cross."

LYNN H. COHICK, PhD, is Distinguished Professor of New Testament and Director of Houston Theological Seminary, where she leads the Doctor of Ministry program. She writes, speaks, and teaches internationally.

¹⁰Carefully determine what pleases the Lord. ¹¹Take no part in the worthless deeds of evil and darkness; instead, expose them. ¹²It is shameful even to talk about the things that ungodly people do in secret. ¹³But their evil intentions will be exposed when the light shines on them, ¹⁴for the light makes everything visible. This is why it is said,

"Awake, O sleeper,
 rise up from the dead,
 and Christ will give you light."

Living by the Spirit's Power

¹⁵So be careful how you live. Don't live like fools, but like those who are wise. ¹⁶Make the most of every opportunity in these evil days. ¹⁷Don't act thoughtlessly, but understand what the Lord wants you to do. ¹⁸Don't be drunk with wine, because that will ruin your life. Instead, be filled with the Holy Spirit, ¹⁹singing psalms and hymns and spiritual songs among yourselves, and making music to the Lord in your hearts. ²⁰And give thanks for everything to God the Father in the name of our Lord Jesus Christ.

Spirit-Guided Relationships: Wives and Husbands

²¹And further, submit to one another out of reverence for Christ.

²²For wives, this means submit to your husbands as to the Lord. ²³For a husband is the head of his wife as Christ is the head of the church. He is the Savior of his body, the church. ²⁴As the church submits to Christ, so you wives should submit to your husbands in everything.

²⁵For husbands, this means love your wives, just as Christ loved the church. He gave up his life for her ²⁶to make her holy and clean, washed by the cleansing of God's word.* ²⁷He did this to present her to himself as a glorious church without a spot or wrinkle or any other blemish. Instead, she will be holy and without fault. ²⁸In the same way, husbands ought to love their wives as they love their own bodies. For a man who loves his wife actually shows love for himself. ²⁹No one hates his own body but feeds and cares for it, just as Christ cares for the church. ³⁰And we are members of his body.

³¹As the Scriptures say, "A man leaves his father and mother and is joined to his wife, and the two are united into one."* ³²This is a great mystery, but it is an illustration of the way Christ and the church are one. ³³So again I say, each man must love his wife as he loves himself, and the wife must respect her husband.

Children and Parents

6 Children, obey your parents because you belong to the Lord,* for this is the right thing to do. ²"Honor your father and mother." This is the first commandment with a promise: ³If you honor your father and mother, "things will go well for you, and you will have a long life on the earth."*

⁴Fathers,* do not provoke your children to anger by the way you treat them. Rather, bring them up with the discipline and instruction that comes from the Lord.

Slaves and Masters

⁵Slaves, obey your earthly masters with deep respect and fear. Serve them sincerely as you would serve

---

5:26 Greek *washed by water with the word.* **5:31** Gen 2:24. **6:1** Or *Children, obey your parents who belong to the Lord;* some manuscripts read simply *Children, obey your parents.* **6:2-3** Exod 20:12; Deut 5:16. **6:4** Or *Parents.*

5:21–6:9 This section is an example of household codes (see note on Acts 17:18), but Paul actually begins talking about this subject in Ephesians 5:18 with his command to be filled with the Holy Spirit. He describes how a house church should worship, concluding that all should submit to one another out of reverence for Christ (5:21). The three pairs (wife and husband; child and parent; enslaved person and enslaver) reflect ancient society's configuration of the household. Although Paul does not condone the patriarchy or the legally-permissible slavery of his day, he addresses each person in the pair who held the position of power, challenging them to release their privilege. Paul presents this challenge because Christ's love is self-sacrificial and God shows no favoritism (see Acts 10:34; Romans 2:11; Galatians 2:6; Colossians 3:25). In God's household, an enslaved girl has an inheritance, and a female enslaver has no special standing or privilege with God.

5:21-33 The verb *submit* occurs in 5:21 and is assumed but not repeated in the Greek in 5:22, thereby closely linking a wife's submission to the submission that members of the church should extend to each other. In the honor-shame culture of the Greco-Roman world, submitting to another person demonstrated honor and was based on social standing. It wasn't simply a gender-based hierarchy that favored men. For example, men submitted to their female benefactors, and younger men submitted to older women who had higher social status. Paul further qualifies the wife's submission "as to the Lord," to protect the wife from possible abusive behavior. Almost without exception, the wider culture spoke of wives "obeying" their husbands (a different Greek word), but Paul does not impose this on Christian wives. In Greek, the metaphorical use of *head* rarely if ever means "leader." It typically indicates a source, beginning, or prominence. Christ as head of the church is its Savior, the source of its life (1:22; 4:15; Colossians 1:18, 2:19).

5:25-33 Paul commands husbands three times to love their wives (5:25, 28, 33), but he does not use a grammatical command when asking wives to submit. Paul commands husbands to love their wives in the self-sacrificial way that Christ loved his church. This demand is found nowhere else in ancient literature—it is clearly rooted in the countercultural claims of the gospel. Husbands are to love their wives "as they love their own bodies," which implies wives can also treat their husbands as their own bodies (see 1 Corinthians 7:4).

Christ. ⁶Try to please them all the time, not just when they are watching you. As slaves of Christ, do the will of God with all your heart. ⁷Work with enthusiasm, as though you were working for the Lord rather than for people. ⁸Remember that the Lord will reward each one of us for the good we do, whether we are slaves or free.

⁹Masters, treat your slaves in the same way. Don't threaten them; remember, you both have the same Master in heaven, and he has no favorites.

6:12 Some manuscripts read *you*.

The Whole Armor of God

¹⁰A final word: Be strong in the Lord and in his mighty power. ¹¹Put on all of God's armor so that you will be able to stand firm against all strategies of the devil. ¹²For we* are not fighting against flesh-and-blood enemies, but against evil rulers and authorities of the unseen world, against mighty powers in this dark world, and against evil spirits in the heavenly places.

6:11 Paul uses the metaphor of God's armor and weapons throughout his letters (see Romans 13:12; 2 Corinthians 10:4-5). It is only by the Lord's protection that a believer can "stand firm against all strategies of the devil" (see also 1 Peter 5:8-9).

Come Close — LIES AND GOD'S TRUTH

SCRIPTURE CONNECTION: EPHESIANS 6:10-17

So many soundbites, memes, and snippets aim to frame who we are. We put our trust in our labels—the letters after our names that certify we've earned degrees. The job descriptions or roles, like lawyer, teacher, CEO, or daughter, mother, sister. But any of those can drive us into the darkness of lives too small, too striving, to be called life at all. Instead of believing these lies, we can put on God's armor and live by faith.

The world tells us lies: that it knows who I am, that I'm only my labels, and that it can fix my problems. I wish I had known God's truth much earlier because I struggled for an unattainable acceptance from the world for years. When we are in distress, the world advises, "Put on your big-girl pants." But God empowers us and gives us armor. God says, "Put on every piece of God's armor so you will be able to resist the enemy" (Ephesians 6:13).

God replaces the world's lies with truth: God knows everything about me and you. He took delight in creating us. Each of us is an awesome, wonderful work of God (see Psalm 139:1-24). God is the only one we must please, and we do that by faith. "Hold up the shield of faith to stop the fiery arrows of the devil" (Ephesians 6:16). Our creator has good things for us, and he's given us the armor we need.

REFLECT "Be strong in the Lord and in his mighty power. Put on all of God's armor so that you will be able to stand firm against all strategies of the devil." EPHESIANS 6:10-11

Lord, thank you for the salvation you give me from the world's lies. Help me to live empowered by faith in your Son, Jesus. Amen.

CONSIDER "I will not allow my life's light to be determined by the darkness around me." SOJOURNER TRUTH

Put down the world's lies and put on God's truth.

ALICE PATTERSON, JD, is an associate court attorney in New York who has a fondness for teaching the Old Testament. She encourages everyone to put down the world's lies and put on God's truth.

¹³Therefore, put on every piece of God's armor so you will be able to resist the enemy in the time of evil. Then after the battle you will still be standing firm. ¹⁴Stand your ground, putting on the belt of truth and the body armor of God's righteousness. ¹⁵For shoes, put on the peace that comes from the Good News so that you will be fully prepared.* ¹⁶In addition to all of these, hold up the shield of faith to stop the fiery arrows of the devil.* ¹⁷Put on salvation as your helmet, and take the sword of the Spirit, which is the word of God.

¹⁸Pray in the Spirit at all times and on every occasion. Stay alert and be persistent in your prayers for all believers everywhere.*

¹⁹And pray for me, too. Ask God to give me the right words so I can boldly explain God's mysterious plan that the Good News is for Jews and Gentiles alike.* ²⁰I am in chains now, still preaching this message as God's ambassador. So pray that I will keep on speaking boldly for him, as I should.

Final Greetings

²¹To bring you up to date, Tychicus will give you a full report about what I am doing and how I am getting along. He is a beloved brother and faithful helper in the Lord's work. ²²I have sent him to you for this very purpose—to let you know how we are doing and to encourage you.

²³Peace be with you, dear brothers and sisters,* and may God the Father and the Lord Jesus Christ give you love with faithfulness. ²⁴May God's grace be eternally upon all who love our Lord Jesus Christ.

6:15 Or *For shoes, put on the readiness to preach the Good News of peace with God.* **6:16** Greek *the evil one.* **6:18** Greek *all of God's holy people.* **6:19** Greek *explain the mystery of the Good News;* some manuscripts read simply *explain the mystery.* **6:23** Greek *brothers.*

6:14-17 Paul uses the physical armor worn by Roman soldiers as imagery for spiritual armor used by believers. Most of this equipment is to defend, not to attack. Paul's focus is not on the precise functions of each piece but on the fact that God expects us to use them. Grounding in Christ and in Scripture provides protection and ability to "stand your ground" (see also James 4:7; 1 Peter 5:8-9).

Philippians

WHAT DO WE LEARN ABOUT GOD'S MISSION AND OURS?
Even when we suffer, God helps us stay true and gives us joy.

WHO WROTE IT? Paul, an apostle, with Timothy (1:1).

WHEN DID IT HAPPEN? Around AD 61.

HOW IS IT ORGANIZED?

1: Paul rejoices despite his suffering

2: Serving as Jesus served

3: Warning against wrong teaching

4: Urging unity with coworkers Euodia and Syntyche, personal notes

FEATURE HIGHLIGHTS

+ Disunity's Destruction and Our Creator's Repair (1503)
+ Euodia and Syntyche: Disharmony in the Church (1505)
+ Full or Empty? Same (1506)

Words to Remember are highlighted throughout this book

HOW LONG DOES IT TAKE TO READ?

| :15 | :30 | 1:00 | 1:30 | 2:00 | 2:30 | 3:00 | 3:30 |

Timeline

AD	Event
30	JESUS DIES, RISES FROM THE DEAD, ASCENDS TO REIGN IN HEAVEN, SENDS THE HOLY SPIRIT
35	JESUS CALLS PAUL TO PREACH THE GOOD NEWS
46–48	PAUL GOES ON FIRST MISSIONARY JOURNEY, WITH BARNABAS AND JOHN MARK
50	JERUSALEM COUNCIL CONFIRMS GENTILE INCLUSION IN THE CHURCH
50–52	PAUL EMBARKS ON SECOND MISSIONARY JOURNEY, WITH SILAS; THEY SPEND 18 MONTHS IN CORINTH
50	PAUL MEETS PRISCILLA AND AQUILA IN CORINTH
	PAUL MEETS LYDIA IN PHILIPPI
53–57	PAUL TAKES A THIRD MISSIONARY JOURNEY
57	PAUL ARRESTED IN JERUSALEM
57–59	PAUL IMPRISONED IN CAESAREA, WHERE HE IS QUESTIONED BY FELIX AND DRUSILLA, FESTUS, AND AGRIPPA AND BERNICE
60–62	PAUL UNDER HOUSE ARREST IN ROME WRITES HIS LETTERS TO THE EPHESIANS, PHILIPPIANS, COLOSSIANS, AND PHILEMON
64	PAUL MARTYRED IN ROME
70	ROME DESTROYS JERUSALEM

Greetings from Paul

1 This letter is from Paul and Timothy, slaves of Christ Jesus.

I am writing to all of God's holy people in Philippi who belong to Christ Jesus, including the church leaders* and deacons.

²May God our Father and the Lord Jesus Christ give you grace and peace.

Paul's Thanksgiving and Prayer

³Every time I think of you, I give thanks to my God. ⁴Whenever I pray, I make my requests for all of you with joy, ⁵for you have been my partners in spreading the Good News about Christ from the time you first heard it until now. ⁶And I am certain that God, who began the good work within you, will continue his work until it is finally finished on the day when Christ Jesus returns.

⁷So it is right that I should feel as I do about all of you, for you have a special place in my heart. You share with me the special favor of God, both in my imprisonment and in defending and confirming the truth of the Good News. ⁸God knows how much I love you and long for you with the tender compassion of Christ Jesus.

⁹I pray that your love will overflow more and more, and that you will keep on growing in knowledge and understanding. ¹⁰For I want you to understand what really matters, so that you may live pure and blameless lives until the day of Christ's return. ¹¹May you always be filled with the fruit of your salvation—the righteous character produced in your life by Jesus Christ*—for this will bring much glory and praise to God.

Paul's Joy That Christ Is Preached

¹²And I want you to know, my dear brothers and sisters,* that everything that has happened to me here has helped to spread the Good News. ¹³For everyone here, including the whole palace guard,* knows that I am in chains because of Christ. ¹⁴And because of my imprisonment, most of the believers* here have gained confidence and boldly speak God's message* without fear.

¹⁵It's true that some are preaching out of jealousy and rivalry. But others preach about Christ with pure motives. ¹⁶They preach because they love me, for they know I have been appointed to defend the Good News. ¹⁷Those others do not have pure motives as they preach about Christ. They preach with selfish ambition, not sincerely, intending to make my chains more painful to me. ¹⁸But that doesn't matter. Whether their motives are false or genuine, the message about Christ is being preached either way, so I rejoice. And I will continue to rejoice. ¹⁹For I know that as you pray for me and the Spirit of Jesus Christ helps me, this will lead to my deliverance.

Paul's Life for Christ

²⁰For I fully expect and hope that I will never be ashamed, but that I will continue to be bold for Christ, as I have been in the past. And I trust that my life will bring honor to Christ, whether I live or die. ²¹For to me, living means living for Christ, and dying is even better. ²²But if I live, I can do more fruitful work for Christ. So I really don't know which is better. ²³I'm torn between two desires: I long to go and be with Christ, which would be far better for me. ²⁴But for your sakes, it is better that I continue to live.

²⁵Knowing this, I am convinced that I will remain alive so I can continue to help all of you grow and experience the joy of your faith. ²⁶And when I come to you again, you will have even more reason to take pride in Christ Jesus because of what he is doing through me.

Live as Citizens of Heaven

²⁷Above all, you must live as citizens of heaven, conducting yourselves in a manner worthy of the Good News about Christ. Then, whether I come and see you again or only hear about you, I will know that you are standing together with one spirit and one purpose, fighting together for the faith, which is the Good News. ²⁸Don't be intimidated in any way by

---

1:1 Or *overseers*, or *bishops*.   **1:11** Greek *with the fruit of righteousness through Jesus Christ*.   **1:12** Greek *brothers*.   **1:13** Greek *including all the Praetorium*.   **1:14a** Greek *brothers in the Lord*.   **1:14b** Some manuscripts read *speak the message*.

1:1 Timothy was one of Paul's most trusted coworkers and was co-sender of this letter (also 2 Corinthians, Colossians, 1 Thessalonians, 2 Thessalonians, and Philemon). This letter is full of ideas about partnership. Paul and Timothy refer to themselves as "slaves of Christ Jesus," which means they were people belonging entirely to Christ and were devoted to his service (see Philippians 2:20-21). They address the recipients as "God's holy people," which acknowledges that they were made holy in God's sight by Christ's redeeming work (see Ephesians 1:4, 7; 5:25-27; Colossians 1:22). A city in the Roman province of Macedonia, Philippi saw some women leading in civic life and participating in the army. Lydia was the first convert from Europe in the early church (see Acts 16:14). Paul stresses working partnerships again when he specifically addresses the "church leaders and deacons." Unlike today, the early church had no professional preachers (see 1 Corinthians 14:26-31). It seems likely that the women Euodia and Syntyche (Philippians 4:2) were leaders in the church and may have been part of the original group of women gathering for prayer with Lydia (see Acts 16:13).

1:12-19 Paul wrote this letter from prison, possibly in Rome. While this was a difficult place to be, he used this as an opportunity to spread the Good News of Jesus Christ to the palace guards. He indirectly challenged the Philippians to set aside any personal motives (jealousy, rivalry, and selfish ambition) to focus on Christ. Paul looks for God's Spirit to bring him deliverance and encourages the church members to do likewise.

Oikos IMAGE — MY STORY WITH FAMILY & FRIENDS

Disunity's Destruction and Our Creator's Repair

SCRIPTURE CONNECTION: PHILIPPIANS 4:2-3

I view Paul's words through Native American eyes that have seen disunity's destruction: "To Euodia and Syntyche, do not let our sun go down in the western sky, but ask our Great Creator God to help you when your two thoughts disagree. You two worked alongside Clement and our tribal workers, whose names are carved in our Creator's Storybook of Life."

I experienced disunity's destruction when my husband of eleven years abandoned me. The security of our four-bedroom home, van, and retirement plan washed away overnight. I see disunity's impact on our villages, as paychecks and commodities aren't always enough, and fish and venison are not always plentiful.

When I sit by the *waawiyezi-dibik-giizis* (Ojibwa, "full moon") and the constellation *Mooz* (Ojibwa, "moose") and reflect on the Great Book (the Bible), my thoughts run fast. I am reminded to think about things that are true, honorable, right, pure, lovely, and admirable (4:8). My *ode* (Ojibwa, "heart") is satisfied, and I do all I can to mend disagreements. I find contentment even in my new title of "divorced single mom," as I stand in food pantry lines. For our villages, I see water still gives *bimaadiziwin* (Ojibwa, "life") and Creator God still sends meat packages to our door.

Despite disunity's destruction, my *minawaanigozi ode* (Ojibwa, "joyous heart") returns. After seeking the Elders' wisdom for my future and enrolling in school, my all-knowing Provider, God himself, strengthens my relationships.

> God satisfies my heart, and I can seek unity.

IMAGINE

How has disunity harmed or threatened to harm you? How are you healing?

Have you ever been discontent with what Creator God has given you? How did he provide?

"I still worry when disease and suicide threaten our people. I pray to Creator God and thank him for providing healthcare workers and anama'ewigamigoon (Ojibwa, 'churches') and for how they bring unity to our communities. God healed my COVID-19 pneumonia, and he healed my broken heart after great family and money loss."

LYNN LONG has studied at National Louis University and is completing her doctorate at Wheaton College. Lynn is a Native American writer and speaker with Stonecroft Ministries.

your enemies. This will be a sign to them that they are going to be destroyed, but that you are going to be saved, even by God himself. ²⁹For you have been given not only the privilege of trusting in Christ but also the privilege of suffering for him. ³⁰We are in this struggle together. You have seen my struggle in the past, and you know that I am still in the midst of it.

Have the Attitude of Christ

2 Is there any encouragement from belonging to Christ? Any comfort from his love? Any fellowship together in the Spirit? Are your hearts tender and compassionate? ²Then make me truly happy by agreeing wholeheartedly with each other, loving one another, and working together with one mind and purpose.

³Don't be selfish; don't try to impress others. Be humble, thinking of others as better than yourselves. ⁴Don't look out only for your own interests, but take an interest in others, too.

⁵You must have the same attitude that Christ Jesus had.

⁶ Though he was God,*
 he did not think of equality with God
 as something to cling to.
⁷ Instead, he gave up his divine privileges*;
 he took the humble position of a slave*
 and was born as a human being.
 When he appeared in human form,*
⁸ he humbled himself in obedience to God
 and died a criminal's death on a cross.

⁹ Therefore, God elevated him to the place of highest honor
 and gave him the name above all other names,
¹⁰ that at the name of Jesus every knee should bow,
 in heaven and on earth and under the earth,
¹¹ and every tongue declare that Jesus Christ is Lord,
 to the glory of God the Father.

Shine Brightly for Christ

¹²Dear friends, you always followed my instructions when I was with you. And now that I am away, it is even more important. Work hard to show the results of your salvation, obeying God with deep reverence and fear. ¹³For God is working in you, giving you the desire and the power to do what pleases him.

¹⁴Do everything without complaining and arguing, ¹⁵so that no one can criticize you. Live clean, innocent lives as children of God, shining like bright lights in a world full of crooked and perverse people. ¹⁶Hold firmly to the word of life; then, on the day of Christ's return, I will be proud that I did not run the race in vain and that my work was not useless. ¹⁷But I will rejoice even if I lose my life, pouring it out like a liquid offering to God,* just like your faithful service is an offering to God. And I want all of you to share that joy. ¹⁸Yes, you should rejoice, and I will share your joy.

Paul Commends Timothy

¹⁹If the Lord Jesus is willing, I hope to send Timothy to you soon for a visit. Then he can cheer me up by telling me how you are getting along. ²⁰I have no one else like Timothy, who genuinely cares about your welfare. ²¹All the others care only for themselves and not for what matters to Jesus Christ. ²²But you know how Timothy has proved himself. Like a son with his father, he has served with me in preaching the Good News. ²³I hope to send him to you just as soon as I find out what is going to happen to me here. ²⁴And I have confidence from the Lord that I myself will come to see you soon.

Paul Commends Epaphroditus

²⁵Meanwhile, I thought I should send Epaphroditus back to you. He is a true brother, co-worker, and fellow soldier. And he was your messenger to help me in my need. ²⁶I am sending him because he has been longing to see you, and he was very distressed that you heard he was ill. ²⁷And he certainly was ill; in fact, he almost died. But God had mercy on him—and also on me, so that I would not have one sorrow after another.

²⁸So I am all the more anxious to send him back to you, for I know you will be glad to see him, and then I will not be so worried about you. ²⁹Welcome him in the Lord's love* and with great joy, and give him the

---

2:6 Or *Being in the form of God.* **2:7a** Greek *he emptied himself.* **2:7b** Or *the form of a slave.* **2:7c** Some English translations put this phrase in verse 8. **2:17** Greek *I will rejoice even if I am to be poured out as a liquid offering.* **2:29** Greek *in the Lord.*

2:1-11 Paul encouraged the Philippians to be unified with each other and Christ (2:2, 5) by showing humility. The perfect example of humility is Christ, who gave up everything in heaven (his power, home, and rights) to come to earth as a human ("the humble position of a slave" [2:7], or literally "in the form of a slave"). Jesus' death on the cross showed his deep love for humanity, and God exalted him by raising him from the dead. One day everyone will bow before Jesus Christ as Lord and bring glory to God the Father.

2:16-18 Believers should maintain their faith in Christ's life-giving Good News. God is faithful, but we, too, must remain faithful (1:6; 2:12-13). Paul uses athletic language as a metaphor for continuing the Christian life (see 3:12-14; 1 Corinthians 9:24, 26; Galatians 2:2; 5:7; 2 Timothy 4:7). Paul rejoices that his life is being "pour[ed]...out like a liquid offering to God." Both Jews and Gentiles often poured out a drink offering of wine either on a sacrifice or at the base of the altar to honor their deity. Paul considered his entire life to be a joyful offering to God (see Romans 12:1; 15:16), which he likens to the Philippians' godly service, too. Their "faithful service" was a cause for rejoicing because even death could not render their work for God useless (see 1 Corinthians 15:58).

Euodia & Syntyche

IDENTITY — Disharmony in the Church

Euodia remembers...
I should have let it go.

Syntyche and I were friends. We'd devoted untold hours working together with Paul and Clement and the others, helping spread the gospel. We are sisters in Christ.

But then she said something, and I disagreed. I couldn't very well sit back and say nothing. So I responded. Then she retaliated. Before I knew it, others got involved and started taking sides. It got so bad that Paul heard about it in prison. He called us out in his letter to the church.

Paul asked the church leaders to help us resolve our differences. How embarrassing that was! At least he reassured everyone that our names were listed in the Book of Life. I was thankful for that. He told us all to rejoice in the Lord, to let our gentleness be known to others, and to guard our hearts and minds through Christ.

I hate that our disagreement got out of hand, but, oh, how thankful I am for the wisdom of Paul and the support from the rest of the church to help us work this out.

EUODIA AND SYNTYCHE'S STORY IS TOLD IN PHILIPPIANS 4:2-3.

> We need to stand with our sisters for good. Only then do we find peace.

IDENTIFY

What do you do when you disagree with a sister or brother in Christ?

Is there someone in your life who was once dear to you but now you're at odds with? If so, have you humbled yourself, asking God if the problem lies with you?

"We've all been there, haven't we? Just because we're Christians doesn't mean we're not going to have disagreements. In these days of so much conflict, we need to stand together with our sisters in Christ and work together. Then we can find the peace that we're seeking."

SHARON WILHARM is the host of the All God's Women podcast and internationally syndicated radio show. She loves bringing to life stories of Bible women and providing takeaways for modern women.

honor that people like him deserve. ³⁰For he risked his life for the work of Christ, and he was at the point of death while doing for me what you couldn't do from far away.

The Priceless Value of Knowing Christ

3 Whatever happens, my dear brothers and sisters,* rejoice in the Lord. I never get tired of telling you these things, and I do it to safeguard your faith. ²Watch out for those dogs, those people who do evil, those mutilators who say you must be circumcised to be saved. ³For we who worship by the Spirit of God* are the ones who are truly circumcised. We rely on what Christ Jesus has done for us. We put no confidence in human effort, ⁴though I could have confidence in my own effort if anyone could. Indeed, if others have reason for confidence in their own efforts, I have even more!

3:1 Greek *brothers*; also in 3:13, 17. 3:3 Some manuscripts read *worship God in spirit*; one early manuscript reads *worship in spirit*.

3:2-11 Paul warns the believers against being influenced by Jewish Christians who argued that circumcision is necessary for salvation. He then talks about his Jewish pedigree and credentials, which he gained prior to being called to serve Christ on his way to Damascus (Acts 9:1-19). He considered "these things" (Philippians 3:7) to be worthless compared to knowing Jesus. Paul reverses the traditional Jewish practice of referring to Gentiles as *dogs* by referring to Jewish Christians who were encouraging Gentile circumcision this way (compare Mark 7:27-28). Paul's strongest insults were directed against Jews who preached that Gentiles must be circumcised in order to be saved (see 2 Corinthians 11:13-15; Galatians 1:6-9; 5:1-6, 12).

⑧ Come Close — FULL OR EMPTY? SAME

SCRIPTURE CONNECTION: PHILIPPIANS 4:10-13

I've looked at my checking account balance and felt the doubt. Will we cover our bills this month? I've also looked at the balance and felt comfort. We've got a nice cushion to support us. God has been present in both. My job is to trust him no matter what the numbers say.

We all go through phases when things go well. We are healthy, our relationships are enjoyable, and our prayers seem to be answered. We also experience phases when life unravels. Nothing is going the way we'd hoped.

Do you trust God only when he is giving you what you want? Do you praise him only when the bank account is full? The diagnosis is good? The marriage is strong?

Or, no matter how bad life gets, do you say, "Lord, you are all I need"?

We will certainly be disappointed if we depend on our circumstances to determine our satisfaction. It turns out life is unpredictable and undependable. God, however, does not change, and we can always depend on him.

We can confidently say, "God, whether my hands are empty or full, you are the same. My contentment is in you."

REFLECT "I know how to live on almost nothing or with everything." PHILIPPIANS 4:12

No matter my situation, Lord, I trust you. Amen.

CONSIDER "The circumstances or details are not as I would wish or design if I were in charge. But that's part of the exercise, right? The loving within what is, rather than what I wish would be. So I look at them honestly, these parts that make up my every day, and I am grateful for the good. And I even work to be grateful for the difficult because I know, though painful, it can shape me for the better. So in all things, I give thanks."
ALEXANDRA KUYKENDALL, *Loving My Actual Life*

> God does not change with our circumstances, so we can relax knowing he is not afraid.

ALEXANDRA KUYKENDALL is a cofounder of The Open Door Sisterhood and author of several books, including *Seeking Out Goodness: Finding the True and Beautiful All around You*.

⁵I was circumcised when I was eight days old. I am a pure-blooded citizen of Israel and a member of the tribe of Benjamin—a real Hebrew if there ever was one! I was a member of the Pharisees, who demand the strictest obedience to the Jewish law. ⁶I was so zealous that I harshly persecuted the church. And as for righteousness, I obeyed the law without fault.

⁷I once thought these things were valuable, but now I consider them worthless because of what Christ has done. ⁸Yes, everything else is worthless when compared with the infinite value of knowing Christ Jesus my Lord. For his sake I have discarded everything else, counting it all as garbage, so that I could gain Christ ⁹and become one with him. I no longer count on my own righteousness through obeying the law; rather, I become righteous through faith in Christ.* For God's way of making us right with himself depends on faith. ¹⁰I want to know Christ and experience the mighty power that raised him from the dead. I want to suffer with him, sharing in his death, ¹¹so that one way or another I will experience the resurrection from the dead!

Pressing toward the Goal

¹²I don't mean to say that I have already achieved these things or that I have already reached perfection. But I press on to possess that perfection for which Christ Jesus first possessed me. ¹³No, dear brothers and sisters, I have not achieved it,* but I focus on this one thing: Forgetting the past and looking forward to what lies ahead, ¹⁴I press on to reach the end of the race and receive the heavenly prize for which God, through Christ Jesus, is calling us.

¹⁵Let all who are spiritually mature agree on these things. If you disagree on some point, I believe God will make it plain to you. ¹⁶But we must hold on to the progress we have already made.

¹⁷Dear brothers and sisters, pattern your lives after mine, and learn from those who follow our example. ¹⁸For I have told you often before, and I say it again with tears in my eyes, that there are many whose conduct shows they are really enemies of the cross of Christ. ¹⁹They are headed for destruction. Their god is their appetite, they brag about shameful things, and they think only about this life here on earth. ²⁰But we are citizens of heaven, where the Lord Jesus Christ lives. And we are eagerly waiting for him to return as our Savior. ²¹He will take our weak mortal bodies and change them into glorious bodies like his own, using the same power with which he will bring everything under his control.

4 Therefore, my dear brothers and sisters,* stay true to the Lord. I love you and long to see you, dear friends, for you are my joy and the crown I receive for my work.

Words of Encouragement

²Now I appeal to Euodia and Syntyche. Please, because you belong to the Lord, settle your disagreement. ³And I ask you, my true partner,* to help these two women, for they worked hard with me in telling others the Good News. They worked along with Clement and the rest of my co-workers, whose names are written in the Book of Life.

⁴Always be full of joy in the Lord. I say it again—rejoice! ⁵Let everyone see that you are considerate in all you do. Remember, the Lord is coming soon.*

⁶Don't worry about anything; instead, pray about everything. Tell God what you need, and thank him for all he has done. ⁷Then you will experience God's peace, which exceeds anything we can understand. His peace will guard your hearts and minds as you live in Christ Jesus.

⁸And now, dear brothers and sisters, one final thing. Fix your thoughts on what is true, and honorable, and right, and pure, and lovely, and admirable.

3:9 Or *through the faithfulness of Christ.* 3:13 Some manuscripts read *not yet achieved it.* 4:1 Greek *brothers;* also in 4:8. 4:3 Or *loyal Syzygus.* 4:5 Greek *the Lord is near.*

3:12-21 Paul keeps on moving forward no matter the difficulty, remembering that Jesus persevered through the cross (compare 2:16). And Paul calls his readers to imitate him as an earthly example to follow (3:17). By keeping the cross of Christ primary, they will avoid becoming "enemies of the cross," or people controlled by their sinful appetites. Instead, Paul encourages the believers to keep heaven and its rewards in mind as they live on earth. Paul refers to the Philippian Christians as "citizens of heaven" because of the significance of their Roman citizenship to their status in society. Citizenship was a prized possession in the New Testament world, and it had many benefits, like the right to property, entering contracts, a fair trial, and appeal to Caesar (see Acts 22:24-29; 25:11). Citizenship in heaven would be even greater than what they experienced in the Roman Empire.

4:2-3 Paul names Euodia and Syntyche, which shows their importance as leaders in this community. Paul wanted these women to reconcile their differences and come to agreement and unity in the Lord (2:2, 5; 4:2). Paul considered these women to be important coworkers who struggled beside him in the work of sharing the Good News. Paul's other important coworkers named in the New Testament include Priscilla, Aquila, Luke, Epaphroditus, Clement, Titus, Mark, and Timothy.

4:4 Paul emphasizes being joyful by repeating it. Paul wanted all the Philippians (including those who were experiencing disagreement, like Euodia and Syntyche) to find their joy in God.

4:8-9 Paul urges the Philippians to focus on God's good gifts so that, even during suffering and persecution, their lives will be exemplary, and their minds and hearts will be filled with peace (4:7, 9). The virtues Paul lists reflect God's nature and were cardinal virtues that Plato and other Greek philosophers also recognized and discussed in their writings and teachings. Paul encouraged his readers to keep following his example in their words and actions.

I can do everything through Christ, who gives me strength.

PHILIPPIANS 4:13

Think about things that are excellent and worthy of praise. ⁹Keep putting into practice all you learned and received from me—everything you heard from me and saw me doing. Then the God of peace will be with you.

Paul's Thanks for Their Gifts

¹⁰How I praise the Lord that you are concerned about me again. I know you have always been concerned for me, but you didn't have the chance to help me. ¹¹Not that I was ever in need, for I have learned how to be content with whatever I have. ¹²I know how to live on almost nothing or with everything. I have learned the secret of living in every situation, whether it is with a full stomach or empty, with plenty or little. ¹³For I can do everything through Christ,* who gives me strength. ¹⁴Even so, you have done well to share with me in my present difficulty.

¹⁵As you know, you Philippians were the only ones who gave me financial help when I first brought you the Good News and then traveled on from Macedonia. No other church did this. ¹⁶Even when I was in Thessalonica you sent help more than once. ¹⁷I don't say this because I want a gift from you. Rather, I want you to receive a reward for your kindness.

¹⁸At the moment I have all I need—and more! I am generously supplied with the gifts you sent me with Epaphroditus. They are a sweet-smelling sacrifice that is acceptable and pleasing to God. ¹⁹And this same God who takes care of me will supply all your needs from his glorious riches, which have been given to us in Christ Jesus.

²⁰Now all glory to God our Father forever and ever! Amen.

Paul's Final Greetings

²¹Give my greetings to each of God's holy people—all who belong to Christ Jesus. The brothers who are with me send you their greetings. ²²And all the rest of God's people send you greetings, too, especially those in Caesar's household.

²³May the grace of the Lord Jesus Christ be with your spirit.*

4:13 Greek *through the one.* 4:23 Some manuscripts add *Amen.*

4:11-13 Paul discusses contentment in life with "plenty or little." Writing from prison, he could still say: "I can do everything through Christ, who gives me strength." This confidence reflects Paul's ability to keep following Jesus through life's difficulties. "Everything" does not mean "anything," but we can keep moving forward because Jesus is Lord of all the world.

Colossians

WHAT DO WE LEARN ABOUT GOD'S MISSION AND OURS?
We are called to put Christ first in everything.

WHO WROTE IT? Paul, an apostle.

WHEN DID IT HAPPEN? Around AD 60.

HOW IS IT ORGANIZED?

1: Christ is supreme

2: Countering false teachings

3: Living the new life in Christ

4: Paul's encouragement to pray and final greetings

FEATURE HIGHLIGHTS

+ We Can Press On (1513)
+ What Does Paul Say about Women's Worth and Roles? (1515)

Words to Remember are highlighted throughout this book

HOW LONG DOES IT TAKE TO READ?

:15						
:30	1:00	1:30	2:00	2:30	3:00	3:30

Timeline

BC	
30	JESUS DIES, RISES FROM THE DEAD, ASCENDS TO REIGN IN HEAVEN, SENDS THE HOLY SPIRIT
35	JESUS CALLS PAUL TO PREACH THE GOOD NEWS
46–48	PAUL GOES ON FIRST MISSIONARY JOURNEY WITH BARNABAS AND JOHN MARK
50–52	PAUL EMBARKS ON SECOND MISSIONARY JOURNEY WITH SILAS; THEY SPEND 18 MONTHS IN CORINTH
50	PAUL MEETS PRISCILLA AND AQUILA IN CORINTH
	PAUL MEETS LYDIA IN PHILIPPI
53–57	PAUL TAKES A THIRD MISSIONARY JOURNEY
53–56	PAUL STAYS FOR AN EXTENDED TIME IN EPHESUS, FOUNDING THE CHURCH IN COLOSSE
57	PAUL ARRESTED IN JERUSALEM
57–59	PAUL IMPRISONED IN CAESAREA, WHERE HE IS QUESTIONED BY FELIX AND DRUSILLA, FESTUS, AND AGRIPPA AND BERNICE
60–62	PAUL UNDER HOUSE ARREST IN ROME WRITES HIS LETTERS TO THE EPHESIANS, PHILIPPIANS, COLOSSIANS, AND PHILEMON
64	PAUL MARTYRED IN ROME
70	ROME DESTROYS JERUSALEM

Greetings from Paul

1 This letter is from Paul, chosen by the will of God to be an apostle of Christ Jesus, and from our brother Timothy.

² We are writing to God's holy people in the city of Colosse, who are faithful brothers and sisters* in Christ.

May God our Father give you grace and peace.

Paul's Thanksgiving and Prayer

³ We always pray for you, and we give thanks to God, the Father of our Lord Jesus Christ. ⁴ For we have heard of your faith in Christ Jesus and your love for all of God's people, ⁵ which come from your confident hope of what God has reserved for you in heaven. You have had this expectation ever since you first heard the truth of the Good News.

⁶ This same Good News that came to you is going out all over the world. It is bearing fruit everywhere by changing lives, just as it changed your lives from the day you first heard and understood the truth about God's wonderful grace.

⁷ You learned about the Good News from Epaphras, our beloved co-worker. He is Christ's faithful servant, and he is helping us on your behalf.* ⁸ He has told us about the love for others that the Holy Spirit has given you.

⁹ So we have not stopped praying for you since we first heard about you. We ask God to give you complete knowledge of his will and to give you spiritual wisdom and understanding. ¹⁰ Then the way you live will always honor and please the Lord, and your lives will produce every kind of good fruit. All the while, you will grow as you learn to know God better and better.

¹¹ We also pray that you will be strengthened with all his glorious power so you will have all the endurance and patience you need. May you be filled with joy,* ¹² always thanking the Father. He has enabled you to share in the inheritance that belongs to his people, who live in the light. ¹³ For he has rescued us from the kingdom of darkness and transferred us into the Kingdom of his dear Son, ¹⁴ who purchased our freedom* and forgave our sins.

Christ Is Supreme

¹⁵ Christ is the visible image of the invisible God.
 He existed before anything was created and is supreme over all creation,*
¹⁶ for through him God created everything
 in the heavenly realms and on earth.
He made the things we can see
 and the things we can't see—
such as thrones, kingdoms, rulers, and
 authorities in the unseen world.
Everything was created through him and
 for him.
¹⁷ He existed before anything else,
 and he holds all creation together.
¹⁸ Christ is also the head of the church,
 which is his body.
He is the beginning,
 supreme over all who rise from the dead.*
So he is first in everything.
¹⁹ For God in all his fullness
 was pleased to live in Christ,
²⁰ and through him God reconciled
 everything to himself.
He made peace with everything in heaven
 and on earth
by means of Christ's blood on the cross.

²¹ This includes you who were once far away from God. You were his enemies, separated from him by your evil thoughts and actions. ²² Yet now he has reconciled you to himself through the death of Christ in his physical body. As a result, he has brought you into his own presence, and you are holy and blameless as you stand before him without a single fault.

²³ But you must continue to believe this truth and stand firmly in it. Don't drift away from the assurance you received when you heard the Good News. The Good News has been preached all over the world, and I, Paul, have been appointed as God's servant to proclaim it.

1:2 Greek *faithful brothers.* **1:7** Or *he is ministering on your behalf;* some manuscripts read *he is ministering on our behalf.* **1:11** Or *all the patience and endurance you need with joy.* **1:14** Some manuscripts add *with his blood.* **1:15** Or *He is the firstborn of all creation.* **1:18** Or *the firstborn from the dead.*

1:3-14 Paul prays for the Colossians who show faith in Christ and love for the saints because of the hope kept for them in heaven (see also 1 Corinthians 13:13). The Good News bears much fruit (in the form of good deeds or virtues) in the believers because they are being transformed by the powerful grace of God given in Jesus. Paul also prays that they will be given "spiritual wisdom and understanding" (Colossians 1:9). Wisdom is found in God rather than the world or its philosophies (see Proverbs 9:10).

1:15 In the Greek translation of the Old Testament, the term *eikōn* ("image," "representation") is used to refer to people as having been made in the image of God (Genesis 1:26-27) and also to the wisdom figure described in other Jewish writings as being an image of God (see *Wisdom of Solomon* 7:25-26). The New Testament writers speak about Christ as God's wisdom to help explain his significance (for example, 1 Corinthians 1:24, 30). The phrase "he existed before anything was created and is supreme over all creation" figured prominently in early Christian debates about the nature of Christ. The word *firstborn* does not mean he was created; it is a title, drawn from the Old Testament, indicating supremacy of rank and priority in time (see, for example, Psalm 89:27).

Koinonia
IMAGE
MY STORY WITH COMMUNITY, WORKPLACE & CHURCH

We Can Press On
SCRIPTURE CONNECTION: COLOSSIANS 2:6-23

There is no straight path to Christian maturity. I used to think I could plot it on a graph, a nice steady upward trend to the right. Instead, my graph ended up looking like a toddler got ahold of a red marker and scribbled.

I'm an avid goal-setter, so Paul's words speak deeply to my need for trajectory. Paul had learned—quite abruptly and supernaturally—that his pursuits needed to be surrendered toward following Christ (see Acts 9:1-19). By contrast, my learnings were not abrupt but the hard-fought truth of chasing goals that looked shiny but proved hollow.

Over time, I've learned to make my goal the daily pursuit of growing in Christ, letting my roots sink deeper into him. This growth takes time, patience, and dedication. You cannot wake up one day and produce specific, measurable, achievable, relevant, and time-bound methods to increase your faith. We have today one ever-present and achievable goal: knowing Christ Jesus as our Lord.

This is where our pressing on originates: from a Person, not a plan.

I got the upward part right, for he calls me out from the world that draws me to it. He beckons me to forget my past and any other hindrance so that I can press on, not to achievement or guidelines laid out by others but to him.

> May the only goal I set today be getting to know you, Jesus.

IMAGINE

What do you need to forget so you can press on toward Jesus?

How can you treat your walk with Jesus less like a project and more like knowing a person?

> "I am daily tempted to make my faith a thing to be managed and molded. I want to be molded by Christ Jesus in love and allow that to be fuel to press on."

CARA DAY is a writer and illustrator. She has served with Stonecroft Ministries helping women live "extraordinary."

Paul's Work for the Church

²⁴I am glad when I suffer for you in my body, for I am participating in the sufferings of Christ that continue for his body, the church. ²⁵God has given me the responsibility of serving his church by proclaiming his entire message to you. ²⁶This message was kept secret for centuries and generations past, but now it has been revealed to God's people. ²⁷For God wanted them to know that the riches and glory of Christ are for you Gentiles, too. And this is the secret: Christ lives in you. This gives you assurance of sharing his glory.

²⁸So we tell others about Christ, warning everyone and teaching everyone with all the wisdom God has given us. We want to present them to God, perfect* in their relationship to Christ. ²⁹That's why I work and struggle so hard, depending on Christ's mighty power that works within me.

2 I want you to know how much I have agonized for you and for the church at Laodicea, and for many other believers who have never met me personally. ²I want them to be encouraged and knit together by strong ties of love. I want them to have complete confidence that they understand God's mysterious plan, which is Christ himself. ³In him lie hidden all the treasures of wisdom and knowledge.

⁴I am telling you this so no one will deceive you with well-crafted arguments. ⁵For though I am far away from you, my heart is with you. And I rejoice that you are living as you should and that your faith in Christ is strong.

Freedom from Rules and New Life in Christ

⁶And now, just as you accepted Christ Jesus as your Lord, you must continue to follow him. ⁷Let your roots grow down into him, and let your lives be built on him. Then your faith will grow strong in the truth you were taught, and you will overflow with thankfulness.

⁸Don't let anyone capture you with empty philosophies and high-sounding nonsense that come from human thinking and from the spiritual powers* of this world, rather than from Christ. ⁹For in Christ lives all the fullness of God in a human body.* ¹⁰So you also are complete through your union with Christ, who is the head over every ruler and authority.

¹¹When you came to Christ, you were "circumcised," but not by a physical procedure. Christ performed a spiritual circumcision—the cutting away of your sinful nature.* ¹²For you were buried with Christ when you were baptized. And with him you were raised to new life because you trusted the mighty power of God, who raised Christ from the dead.

¹³You were dead because of your sins and because your sinful nature was not yet cut away. Then God made you alive with Christ, for he forgave all our sins. ¹⁴He canceled the record of the charges against us and took it away by nailing it to the cross. ¹⁵In this way, he disarmed* the spiritual rulers and authorities. He shamed them publicly by his victory over them on the cross.

¹⁶So don't let anyone condemn you for what you eat or drink, or for not celebrating certain holy days or new moon ceremonies or Sabbaths. ¹⁷For these rules are only shadows of the reality yet to come. And Christ himself is that reality. ¹⁸Don't let anyone condemn you by insisting on pious self-denial or the worship of angels,* saying they have had visions about these things. Their sinful minds have made them proud, ¹⁹and they are not connected to Christ, the head of the body. For he holds the whole body together with its joints and ligaments, and it grows as God nourishes it.

²⁰You have died with Christ, and he has set you free from the spiritual powers of this world. So why do you keep on following the rules of the world, such as, ²¹"Don't handle! Don't taste! Don't touch!"? ²²Such rules are mere human teachings about things that deteriorate as we use them. ²³These rules may seem wise because they require strong devotion,

---

1:28 Or *mature*. 2:8 Or *the spiritual principles*; also in 2:20. 2:9 Or *in him dwells all the completeness of the Godhead bodily*. 2:11 Greek *the cutting away of the body of the flesh*. 2:15 Or *he stripped off*. 2:18 Or *or worshiping with angels*.

2:8 There were many Greek philosophers who taught about how the world worked, what was important in life, and how to live. Paul does not condemn philosophy, but only "empty" philosophical speculation that stands opposed to God. "Spiritual powers of this world" describes teaching that rejects Jesus or spiritual beings who people thought controlled human events (see also 2:15, 20; Galatians 4:3).

2:16 Many religious teachings across the ancient world prohibited certain types of food and drink. The Old Testament does not condemn drinking alcohol, though some chose to abstain for various reasons (for example, Numbers 6:1-4; Daniel 1:8-16). Jesus is often seen eating and drinking (Matthew 11:18-19; Luke 5:29; 14:1; 15:1-2), and his followers look forward to a banquet in heaven where there will be "clear, well-aged wine and choice meat" (Isaiah 25:6). The Jews and other groups also had regular practices of celebration (see Numbers 10:10; Psalm 81:3; Isaiah 1:13). Jews followed the law of Moses concerning Sabbath rest, and Christians followed this practice on the Lord's Day or Sunday (Acts 20:7; Revelation 1:10); Paul notes that there is freedom for when to observe the Sabbath (Romans 14:5).

2:18 People in the first century were fascinated with spiritual beings. Some Jews believed that angels were present during their times of worship, and some might even have worshiped them. The false teachers were evidently saying they had had visions that established certain rituals as requirements for the community.

pious self-denial, and severe bodily discipline. But they provide no help in conquering a person's evil desires.

Living the New Life

3 Since you have been raised to new life with Christ, set your sights on the realities of heaven, where Christ sits in the place of honor at God's right hand. ²Think about the things of heaven, not the things of earth. ³For you died to this life, and your real life is hidden with Christ in God. ⁴And when Christ, who is your* life, is revealed to the whole world, you will share in all his glory.

⁵So put to death the sinful, earthly things lurking within you. Have nothing to do with sexual immorality, impurity, lust, and evil desires. Don't be greedy, for a greedy person is an idolater, worshiping the things of this world. ⁶Because of these sins, the anger of God is coming.* ⁷You used to do these things when your life was still part of this world. ⁸But now is the time to get rid of anger, rage, malicious behavior, slander, and dirty language. ⁹Don't lie to each other, for you have stripped off your old sinful nature and all its wicked deeds. ¹⁰Put on your new nature, and be renewed as you learn to know your Creator and become like him. ¹¹In this new life, it doesn't matter if you are a Jew or a Gentile,* circumcised or uncircumcised, barbaric, uncivilized,* slave, or free. Christ is all that matters, and he lives in all of us.

¹²Since God chose you to be the holy people he loves, you must clothe yourselves with tenderhearted mercy, kindness, humility, gentleness, and patience. ¹³Make allowance for each other's faults, and forgive anyone who offends you. Remember, the Lord forgave you, so you must forgive others. ¹⁴Above all, clothe yourselves with love, which binds us all together in perfect harmony. ¹⁵And let the peace that comes from Christ rule in your hearts. For as members of one body you are called to live in peace. And always be thankful.

¹⁶Let the message about Christ, in all its richness, fill your lives. Teach and counsel each other with all the wisdom he gives. Sing psalms and hymns and spiritual songs to God with thankful hearts. ¹⁷And whatever you do or say, do it as a representative of

3:4 Some manuscripts read *our*. 3:6 Some manuscripts read *is coming on all who disobey him.* 3:11a Greek *a Greek.*
3:11b Greek *Barbarian, Scythian.*

3:1-5 For Christians, our spiritual position is "raised . . . with Christ," and we are to focus on the realities of heaven, where he is seated at the right hand of God. Therefore, our thoughts and hopes are focused on Jesus' reign over all, not preoccupied with the worries of daily life here. Since we are alive in Christ, Paul says to "put to death" sinful behavior (like sexual immorality, unhealthy passions, evil desire, greed, or idol worship). We are now to look like Jesus, who is the "image" of God (1:15; see also Genesis 1:26-27).

Perspective

What does Paul say about women's worth and roles?

SCRIPTURE CONNECTION: COLOSSIANS 3:18–4:1

Some say that the Bible prescribes certain roles to women and others to men, but Jesus' message breaks the social status quo that puts people's worth on a sliding scale. Some wrongly claim that Paul's instructions here indicate that enslaved people and enslavers were of equal *spiritual* value to God but should have differing roles, responsibilities, and authority. This incorrect view misconstrues Paul's instructions by ignoring the background that the roles of enslaved people were created by free people (not God), and enslaved people were viewed as property over which the enslaver could show domination.

Paul did not reinforce the social structure's lines of authority between enslaved person and enslaver nor between wife and husband. These structures were based on fallen human beliefs. No person in their essence is less valuable or less rational than another person. No one is superior in worth and value to anyone else. Women, men, enslaved people, and enslavers have equal spiritual *and social* worth and authority, for the gospel upends social convention.

VIEWPOINTS

HERS: *She may have viewed instructions about submitting to husbands and being quiet in church as part of the culture of her day.*
MINE: *"Women have equal spiritual and social worth and authority, for the gospel upends social convention."*
YOURS: *Where do you need to claim your freedom in the Lord from fallen human social structures? Who can you encourage to embrace their full worth as beloved children of God, unrestrained by human cords of bondage?*

LYNN H. COHICK, PhD, is Distinguished Professor of New Testament and Director of Houston Theological Seminary, where she leads the Doctor of Ministry program. She writes, speaks, and teaches internationally.

> "It's time that Christians were judged more by their likeness to Christ than their notions of Christ."
>
> **LUCRETIA MOTT**
> (1793–1880) minister, abolitionist, and suffragist

the Lord Jesus, giving thanks through him to God the Father.

Instructions for Christian Households

¹⁸Wives, submit to your husbands, as is fitting for those who belong to the Lord.

¹⁹Husbands, love your wives and never treat them harshly.

²⁰Children, always obey your parents, for this pleases the Lord. ²¹Fathers, do not aggravate your children, or they will become discouraged.

²²Slaves, obey your earthly masters in everything you do. Try to please them all the time, not just when they are watching you. Serve them sincerely because of your reverent fear of the Lord. ²³Work willingly at whatever you do, as though you were working for the Lord rather than for people. ²⁴Remember that the Lord will give you an inheritance as your reward, and that the Master you are serving is Christ.* ²⁵But if you do what is wrong, you will be paid back for the wrong you have done. For God has no favorites.

4 Masters, be just and fair to your slaves. Remember that you also have a Master—in heaven.

An Encouragement for Prayer

²Devote yourselves to prayer with an alert mind and a thankful heart. ³Pray for us, too, that God will give us many opportunities to speak about his mysterious plan concerning Christ. That is why I am here in chains. ⁴Pray that I will proclaim this message as clearly as I should.

⁵Live wisely among those who are not believers, and make the most of every opportunity. ⁶Let your conversation be gracious and attractive* so that you will have the right response for everyone.

Paul's Final Instructions and Greetings

⁷Tychicus will give you a full report about how I am getting along. He is a beloved brother and faithful helper who serves with me in the Lord's work. ⁸I have sent him to you for this very purpose—to let you know how we are doing and to encourage you. ⁹I am also sending Onesimus, a faithful and beloved brother, one of your own people. He and Tychicus will tell you everything that's happening here.

¹⁰Aristarchus, who is in prison with me, sends you his greetings, and so does Mark, Barnabas's cousin. As you were instructed before, make Mark welcome if he comes your way. ¹¹Jesus (the one we call Justus) also sends his greetings. These are the only Jewish believers among my co-workers; they are working with me here for the Kingdom of God. And what a comfort they have been!

¹²Epaphras, a member of your own fellowship and a servant of Christ Jesus, sends you his greetings. He always prays earnestly for you, asking God to make you strong and perfect, fully confident that you are following the whole will

---

3:24 Or *and serve Christ as your Master.* 4:6 Greek *and seasoned with salt.*

3:18–4:1 This series of exhortations is called a *household code*. Such codes appear in Greco-Roman writings and elsewhere in the New Testament (see Ephesians 5:22–6:9; 1 Peter 2:18–3:7). This household code focuses on submission, on recognizing one's place within a social order. Here Paul gave instructions to specific people groups within the Colossian church—wives, husbands, children, fathers, enslaved people, and enslavers. Since the recipients of this letter were believers, their submission always implied that God is the head of all things and that his will is paramount (see Acts 4:19-20; 5:29). The exhortation to wives to submit to their husbands is immediately followed by a command to the husbands to love their wives (see also Ephesians 5:25-30; 1 Peter 3:7). Love and submission, or respect, are like two sides of one coin; men and women flourish together when they are both shown love and respect by their spouse.

4:3 The phrase that Paul uses here, "that God will give us many opportunities" can also be translated "that God might open for us a door." An open door is a metaphor for an opportunity to proclaim the Good News (see also Acts 14:27; 1 Corinthians 16:9; 2 Corinthians 2:12). Paul's dedication to preaching the Good News had led to his imprisonment, but it didn't stop him from seeking more opportunities to share Christ with others.

of God. ¹³I can assure you that he prays hard for you and also for the believers in Laodicea and Hierapolis.

¹⁴Luke, the beloved doctor, sends his greetings, and so does Demas. ¹⁵Please give my greetings to our brothers and sisters* at Laodicea, and to Nympha and the church that meets in her house.

¹⁶After you have read this letter, pass it on to the church at Laodicea so they can read it, too. And you should read the letter I wrote to them.

¹⁷And say to Archippus, "Be sure to carry out the ministry the Lord gave you."

¹⁸HERE IS MY GREETING IN MY OWN HANDWRITING—PAUL.

Remember my chains.

May God's grace be with you.

4:15 Greek *brothers*.

4:15 Nympha was a woman of importance in the Christian community in Laodicea. In the ancient world when a church met at someone's home, they played an authoritative role in the group. That is unlike today's home groups where the person may only be a social host.

1 Thessalonians

WHAT DO WE LEARN ABOUT GOD'S MISSION AND OURS?
We can press on by focusing on Jesus.

WHO WROTE IT? Paul, an apostle, with Silas and Timothy (1:1).

WHEN DID IT HAPPEN? Around AD 51.

HOW IS IT ORGANIZED?

1: Paul thanks God for the Thessalonians

2: Paul defends his, Silas's, and Timothy's ministry and explains their absence

3: Timothy's encouraging report

4–5: Some instructions for living and final greetings

FEATURE HIGHLIGHTS

+ *Working to Please the Lord* (1521)
+ *Satisfaction and Surrender* (1523)

Words to Remember are highlighted throughout this book

HOW LONG DOES IT TAKE TO READ?

| :15 | :30 | 1:00 | 1:30 | 2:00 | 2:30 | 3:00 | 3:30 |

AD | Timeline

- **30** — JESUS DIES, RISES FROM THE DEAD, ASCENDS TO REIGN IN HEAVEN, SENDS THE HOLY SPIRIT
- **35** — JESUS CALLS PAUL TO PREACH THE GOOD NEWS
- **46–48** — PAUL GOES ON FIRST MISSIONARY JOURNEY, WITH BARNABAS AND JOHN MARK
- **50** — JERUSALEM COUNCIL CONFIRMS GENTILE INCLUSION IN THE CHURCH
- **50–52** — PAUL EMBARKS ON SECOND MISSIONARY JOURNEY, WITH SILAS; THEY SPEND 18 MONTHS IN CORINTH
- **50** — PAUL MEETS PRISCILLA AND AQUILA IN CORINTH
- PAUL MEETS LYDIA IN PHILIPPI
- **50** — PAUL AND SILAS ESTABLISH THE CHURCH IN THESSALONICA
- **53–57** — PAUL TAKES A THIRD MISSIONARY JOURNEY
- **57** — PAUL ARRESTED IN JERUSALEM
- **57–59** — PAUL IMPRISONED IN CAESAREA, WHERE HE IS QUESTIONED BY FELIX AND DRUSILLA, FESTUS, AND AGRIPPA AND BERNICE
- **60–62** — PAUL UNDER HOUSE ARREST IN ROME WRITES HIS LETTERS TO THE EPHESIANS, PHILIPPIANS, COLOSSIANS, AND PHILEMON
- **64** — PAUL MARTYRED IN ROME
- **70** — ROME DESTROYS JERUSALEM

Greetings from Paul

1 This letter is from Paul, Silas,* and Timothy.

We are writing to the church in Thessalonica, to you who belong to God the Father and the Lord Jesus Christ.

May God give you grace and peace.

The Faith of the Thessalonian Believers

²We always thank God for all of you and pray for you constantly. ³As we pray to our God and Father about you, we think of your faithful work, your loving deeds, and the enduring hope you have because of our Lord Jesus Christ.

⁴We know, dear brothers and sisters,* that God loves you and has chosen you to be his own people. ⁵For when we brought you the Good News, it was not only with words but also with power, for the Holy Spirit gave you full assurance* that what we said was true. And you know of our concern for you from the way we lived when we were with you. ⁶So you received the message with joy from the Holy Spirit in spite of the severe suffering it brought you. In this way, you imitated both us and the Lord. ⁷As a result, you have become an example to all the believers in Greece—throughout both Macedonia and Achaia.*

⁸And now the word of the Lord is ringing out from you to people everywhere, even beyond Macedonia and Achaia, for wherever we go we find people telling us about your faith in God. We don't need to tell them about it, ⁹for they keep talking about the wonderful welcome you gave us and how you turned away from idols to serve the living and true God. ¹⁰And they speak of how you are looking forward to the coming of God's Son from heaven—Jesus, whom God raised from the dead. He is the one who has rescued us from the terrors of the coming judgment.

Paul Remembers His Visit

2 You yourselves know, dear brothers and sisters,* that our visit to you was not a failure. ²You know how badly we had been treated at Philippi just before we came to you and how much we suffered there. Yet our God gave us the courage to declare his Good News to you boldly, in spite of great opposition. ³So you can see we were not preaching with any deceit or impure motives or trickery.

⁴For we speak as messengers approved by God to be entrusted with the Good News. Our purpose is to please God, not people. He alone examines the motives of our hearts. ⁵Never once did we try to win you with flattery, as you well know. And God is our witness that we were not pretending to be your friends just to get your money! ⁶As for human praise, we have never sought it from you or anyone else.

⁷As apostles of Christ we certainly had a right to make some demands of you, but instead we were like children* among you. Or we were like a mother feeding and caring for her own children. ⁸We loved you so much that we shared with you not only God's Good News but our own lives, too.

⁹Don't you remember, dear brothers and sisters, how hard we worked among you? Night and day we toiled to earn a living so that we would not be a burden to any of you as we preached God's Good News to you. ¹⁰You yourselves are our witnesses—and so is God—that we were devout and honest and faultless toward all of you believers. ¹¹And you know that we treated each of you as a father treats his own children. ¹²We pleaded with you, encouraged you, and urged you to live your lives in a way that God would consider worthy. For he called you to share in his Kingdom and glory.

¹³Therefore, we never stop thanking God that when you received his message from us, you didn't think of our words as mere human ideas. You accepted what we said as the very word of God—which, of course, it is. And this word continues to work in you who believe.

¹⁴And then, dear brothers and sisters, you suffered persecution from your own countrymen. In this way, you imitated the believers in God's churches in Judea who, because of their belief in Christ Jesus, suffered from their own people, the Jews. ¹⁵For some of the

---

1:1 Greek *Silvanus*, the Greek form of the name. 1:4 Greek *brothers*. 1:5 Or *with the power of the Holy Spirit, so you can have full assurance*. 1:7 *Macedonia* and *Achaia* were the northern and southern regions of Greece. 2:1 Greek *brothers*; also in 2:9, 14, 17. 2:7 Some manuscripts read *we were gentle*.

1:4 Paul writes in familial terms to his "dear brothers and sisters," showing how precious the believers are to him. God loving them and having chosen them recalls God's care for Israel (Deuteronomy 7:7-8). God's election, or his choosing, is for all people: men and women, Jew and Gentile, poor and rich.

1:8-10 The believers' faith is demonstrated through their welcoming hospitality and their witness about God to others where the "word of the Lord" now rings out clearly like a bell (1:8). Rejecting pagan idols meant the believers didn't attend social events where gods were worshiped, thus risking rejection and suspicion in their community. Instead, they served "the living and true God" (1:9) and looked forward to Jesus' second coming (1:10).

2:7 Apostles could have expected financial support (2:9) and authority and dignity from the believers, but Paul, Silas, and Timothy (1:1) came to the Thessalonians as children. Children in the ancient world had no rights or social status but were instead accountable to their parents. This metaphor is positive, for children have pure motives and are without guile. Paul also likens their pastoral ministry to motherhood, using the feminine imagery of "feeding and caring for her own children." Since most women had limited public influence, Paul's imagery elevates them and makes marginalized people visible and valued.

2:11 In the ancient world, the moral instruction of children was a fundamental obligation of fathers. Roman fathers could be harsh, but the ancient philosopher Plutarch advised Greek fathers to use praise, reason, exhortations, and good counsel when teaching children to avoid vice and embrace virtue. Paul describes himself, Silas, and Timothy as this kind of father to the Thessalonians.

Jews killed the prophets, and some even killed the Lord Jesus. Now they have persecuted us, too. They fail to please God and work against all humanity ¹⁶as they try to keep us from preaching the Good News of salvation to the Gentiles. By doing this, they continue to pile up their sins. But the anger of God has caught up with them at last.

Timothy's Good Report about the Church

¹⁷Dear brothers and sisters, after we were separated from you for a little while (though our hearts never left you), we tried very hard to come back because of our intense longing to see you again. ¹⁸We wanted very much to come to you, and I, Paul, tried again and again, but Satan prevented us. ¹⁹After all, what gives us hope and joy, and what will be our proud reward and crown as we stand before our Lord Jesus when he returns? It is you! ²⁰Yes, you are our pride and joy.

3 Finally, when we could stand it no longer, we decided to stay alone in Athens, ²and we sent Timothy to visit you. He is our brother and God's

IMAGE — MY STORY OF MY UNIQUE INFLUENCE

Working to Please the Lord

SCRIPTURE CONNECTION: 1 THESSALONIANS 2:4-6

Do you ever feel you have to perform for love?

As a professional athlete, it's my job to perform. Every time I step to the starting line, I am watched not only by a stadium of people but also by millions of anonymous people on the internet. There are expectations for how I will race, what times I will run, what place I will finish. For a long time, those expectations caused me anxiety that kept me from performing my best.

People pleasing is an addictive trap.

Your every move may not be scrutinized—like Paul's, Timothy's, and Silas's seem to have been—but we all feel the need to perform to meet expectations. Perhaps it's frantically cleaning the house and cooking to perfection for your mother-in-law. Or trying to be upbeat with a friend when you're struggling on the inside.

We perform to get the love we deeply need.

So, it's easy to feel like we must also perform for God's love. Whether it's serving in the church, tithing, or doing daily Bible study, very good spiritual activities can become the works that Paul warned against in his other letters: "Salvation is not a reward for the good things we have done" (Ephesians 2:9). Colossians 3:23 reminds us that we "work willingly" as though all our work is done for the Lord, not for people.

The beautiful thing is, God loves us unconditionally.

So, we get to craft our craft and run our race with our whole hearts, not from trying to earn love, but from being already loved. And our work becomes true worship.

> We run our best race from being already loved.

IMAGINE

What are your "races," and who's watching?

How can knowing that God loves you free you to work willingly?

"Unlike harsh critics judging my races, there is nothing that makes God love us more. There is also nothing we do to make God love us less."

SARA HALL is a professional marathon runner and cofounder of the Hall Steps Foundation. She has been competing professionally for seventeen years in various distances and using her platform to bring aid to orphaned children in Ethiopia.

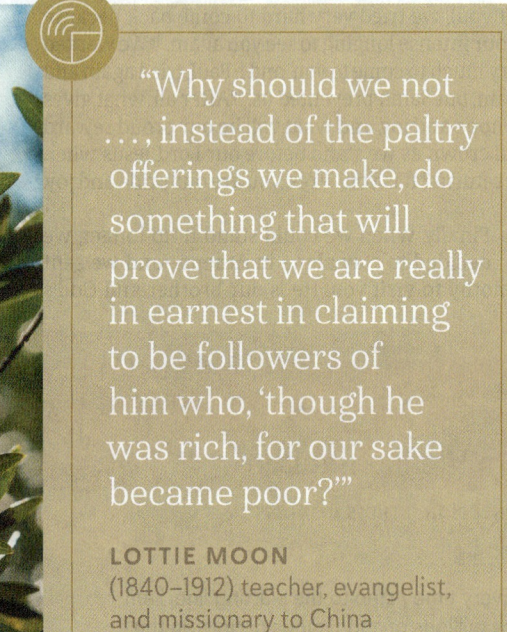

"Why should we not ..., instead of the paltry offerings we make, do something that will prove that we are really in earnest in claiming to be followers of him who, 'though he was rich, for our sake became poor?'"

LOTTIE MOON
(1840–1912) teacher, evangelist, and missionary to China

co-worker* in proclaiming the Good News of Christ. We sent him to strengthen you, to encourage you in your faith, ³and to keep you from being shaken by the troubles you were going through. But you know that we are destined for such troubles. ⁴Even while we were with you, we warned you that troubles would soon come—and they did, as you well know. ⁵That is why, when I could bear it no longer, I sent Timothy to find out whether your faith was still strong. I was afraid that the tempter had gotten the best of you and that our work had been useless.

⁶But now Timothy has just returned, bringing us good news about your faith and love. He reports that you always remember our visit with joy and that you want to see us as much as we want to see you. ⁷So we have been greatly encouraged in the midst of our troubles and suffering, dear brothers and sisters,* because you have remained strong in your faith. ⁸It gives us new life to know that you are standing firm in the Lord.

⁹How we thank God for you! Because of you we have great joy as we enter God's presence. ¹⁰Night and day we pray earnestly for you, asking God to let us see you again to fill the gaps in your faith.

¹¹May God our Father and our Lord Jesus bring us to you very soon. ¹²And may the Lord make your love for one another and for all people grow and overflow, just as our love for you overflows. ¹³May he, as a result, make your hearts strong, blameless, and holy as you stand before God our Father when our Lord Jesus comes again with all his holy people. Amen.

Live to Please God

4 Finally, dear brothers and sisters,* we urge you in the name of the Lord Jesus to live in a way that pleases God, as we have taught you. You live this way already, and we encourage you to do so even more. ²For you remember what we taught you by the authority of the Lord Jesus.

³God's will is for you to be holy, so stay away from all sexual sin. ⁴Then each of you will control his own body* and live in holiness and honor—⁵not in lustful passion like the pagans who do not know God and his ways. ⁶Never harm or cheat a fellow believer in this matter by violating his wife,* for the Lord avenges all such sins, as we have solemnly warned you before. ⁷God has called us to live holy lives, not impure lives. ⁸Therefore, anyone who refuses to live by these rules is not disobeying human teaching but is rejecting God, who gives his Holy Spirit to you.

⁹But we don't need to write to you about the importance of loving each other,* for God himself has taught you to love one another. ¹⁰Indeed, you already show your love for all the believers* throughout Macedonia. Even so, dear brothers and sisters, we urge you to love them even more.

3:2 Other manuscripts read *and God's servant;* still others read *and a co-worker,* or *and a servant and co-worker for God,* or *and God's servant and our co-worker.* **3:7** Greek *brothers.* **4:1** Greek *brothers;* also in 4:10, 13. **4:4** Or *will know how to take a wife for himself;* or *will learn to live with his own wife;* Greek reads *will know how to possess his own vessel.* **4:6** Greek *Never harm or cheat a brother in this matter.* **4:9** Greek *about brotherly love.* **4:10** Greek *the brothers.*

3:9 Paul's joy in God's presence is because of the Thessalonian believers, and his desire is to see them again so that he can help them grow strong in their faith. Paul trusted God to open this door to visit, ultimately. He had "tried again and again" to visit but was supernaturally prevented up to that point (2:18).
3:11-13 Paul prays to God the Father and the Lord Jesus to bring about the opportunity to visit (3:11) and for the believers' love to grow for one another and extend to all people (3:12). He desires that their hearts would be strong, without blame, and holy (or set apart for the Father) when "our Lord Jesus comes again with all his holy people" (those who have died with faith in Christ, 3:13). The theme of holiness will be developed further in this letter (4:3-4, 7). In Greek and Roman society, "blameless" described people of outstanding merit and exceptional civic consciousness, but the Judeo-Christian idea of "strong, blameless, and holy" (3:13) hearts raises the bar.
4:3-8 When we seek God's will for our lives, he transforms us into holy people (Romans 12:1-2; Hebrews 10:36; 13:20-21) and enables us to avoid sexual sin. Holiness for the Thessalonians meant separation from the Greco-Roman world where it was considered acceptable for men to have sex with prostitutes and enslaved people, but women were expected to remain faithful to their husbands. By contrast, Jewish and Christian authors alike prohibited all sexual involvement outside of marriage (Acts 15:20; 1 Corinthians 6:12-20; Colossians 3:5-6).

Satisfaction and Surrender

MY STORY WITH FAMILY & FRIENDS

SCRIPTURE CONNECTION: 1 THESSALONIANS 4:3-8

I want chocolate pretty much all the time. It can be a problem. But when I hold certain boundaries, chocolate can be a lovely part of my life.

Left to my own will, my urges and my wants become supreme; I make the rules and set the standards. Outside voices concur with what I already want: My way can make me happy (yum) and solve a problem (lifting my mood, until I feel regret).

Many of us have treated our sexual desires similarly. When we had an urge, we served it, letting our own wills reign supreme. Others may have encouraged us that what we wanted was not bad; it made us happy, felt good, and "solved" a problem. All while denying that, as we seized control, we paradoxically lost *self*-control. In reaching for what we *thought* we needed, we lost the wholeness we *really* needed.

Whether tricked or tempted, we reached for external pleasures to sate internal longings. But God knows the source of our longings, and his provisions begin on the inside. Filled with his Spirit and empowered to choose wisely, we can surrender our will to his. By listening to God rather than others or ourselves, real answers will come.

Our hungers can feed our connection with God. And when we surrender our will and live into God's will, we are made whole.

> To live satisfied, I can surrender my solutions and reach for God's.

IMAGINE

Beneath the surface, what feeling or situation are we left to face without solutions on our own terms?

What support would we need to face our circumstance with God's solutions instead?

"Though cultural standards and practices continue to change, it remains that only God will guide and empower us toward wholeness. I can ask God to show me how I've tried to replace him."

MISTY ARTERBURN is an author and speaker, contributing to Bible projects, devotionals, and recovery materials for over twenty years. Wife and mom to five, Misty is the founder of Recovery Girls and the general editor of *The One Year Bible for Women*.

¹¹Make it your goal to live a quiet life, minding your own business and working with your hands, just as we instructed you before. ¹²Then people who are not believers will respect the way you live, and you will not need to depend on others.

The Hope of the Resurrection

¹³And now, dear brothers and sisters, we want you to know what will happen to the believers who have died* so you will not grieve like people who have no hope. ¹⁴For since we believe that Jesus died and was raised to life again, we also believe that when Jesus returns, God will bring back with him the believers who have died.

¹⁵We tell you this directly from the Lord: We who are still living when the Lord returns will not meet him ahead of those who have died.* ¹⁶For the Lord himself will come down from heaven with a commanding shout, with the voice of the archangel, and with the trumpet call of God. First, the believers who have died* will rise from their graves. ¹⁷Then, together with them, we who are still alive and remain on the earth will be caught up in the clouds to meet the Lord in the air. Then we will be with the Lord forever. ¹⁸So encourage each other with these words.

5 Now concerning how and when all this will happen, dear brothers and sisters,* we don't really need to write you. ²For you know quite well that the day of the Lord's return will come unexpectedly, like a thief in the night. ³When people are saying, "Everything is peaceful and secure," then disaster will fall on them as suddenly as a pregnant woman's labor pains begin. And there will be no escape.

⁴But you aren't in the dark about these things, dear brothers and sisters, and you won't be surprised when the day of the Lord comes like a thief.* ⁵For you are all children of the light and of the day; we don't belong to darkness and night. ⁶So be on your guard, not asleep like the others. Stay alert and be clearheaded. ⁷Night is the time when people sleep and drinkers get drunk. ⁸But let us who live in the light be clearheaded, protected by the armor of faith and love, and wearing as our helmet the confidence of our salvation.

⁹For God chose to save us through our Lord Jesus Christ, not to pour out his anger on us. ¹⁰Christ died for us so that, whether we are dead or alive when he returns, we can live with him forever. ¹¹So encourage each other and build each other up, just as you are already doing.

Paul's Final Advice

¹²Dear brothers and sisters, honor those who are your leaders in the Lord's work. They work hard among you and give you spiritual guidance. ¹³Show them great respect and wholehearted love because of their work. And live peacefully with each other.

¹⁴Brothers and sisters, we urge you to warn those who are lazy. Encourage those who are timid. Take tender care of those who are weak. Be patient with everyone.

¹⁵See that no one pays back evil for evil, but always try to do good to each other and to all people.

¹⁶Always be joyful. ¹⁷Never stop praying. ¹⁸Be thankful in all circumstances, for this is God's will for you who belong to Christ Jesus.

¹⁹Do not stifle the Holy Spirit. ²⁰Do not scoff at prophecies, ²¹but test everything that is said. Hold on to what is good. ²²Stay away from every kind of evil.

Paul's Final Greetings

²³Now may the God of peace make you holy in every way, and may your whole spirit and soul and body be kept blameless until our Lord Jesus Christ comes again. ²⁴God will make this happen, for he who calls you is faithful.

²⁵Dear brothers and sisters, pray for us.

²⁶Greet all the brothers and sisters with a sacred kiss.

²⁷I command you in the name of the Lord to read this letter to all the brothers and sisters.

²⁸May the grace of our Lord Jesus Christ be with you.

4:13 Greek *those who have fallen asleep;* also in 4:14. **4:15** Greek *those who have fallen asleep.* **4:16** Greek *the dead in Christ.* **5:1** Greek *brothers;* also in 5:4, 12, 14, 25, 26, 27. **5:4** Some manuscripts read *comes upon you as if you were thieves.*

4:13-14 Paul introduces new information about believers "who have died," a phrase that can be literally translated as "fallen asleep" (sleep was a euphemism for death in this culture); however, this expression does not suggest *soul sleep,* which is a theory that our souls are dormant in death while we await the second coming of Jesus. Their grieving suggests their hope is not centered on the resurrection of the dead when Jesus returns. Paul clarifies that even though some believers have died, they will certainly be resurrected in the pattern of Jesus' resurrection. Grieving is not wrong if it is accompanied by Christian hope.
4:16-17 People of the ancient world believed the gods lived in the heavens (that is, above the clouds), and so Jesus is said to "come down from heaven." His arrival will be announced by shouting and a trumpet that will be heard by all people. Then the resurrection of the believers who have died will take place, and all Christians will then be united with Jesus. Being "caught up [snatched up] in the clouds" does not imply a "rapture" event but refutes pagan ideas of fate snatching life away.
5:1-2 Questions about the end of time have occupied the thoughts of both Jewish and Christian people (Daniel 12:6; Matthew 24:3; Luke 17:20; Acts 1:6; 1 Peter 1:10-11), but the details about how and when will not be known. Various New Testament authors compared Jesus' return to "a thief in the night" (see Matthew 24:43-44; Luke 12:39-40; 2 Peter 3:10; Revelation 3:3; 16:15.
5:9-10 God saved the believers though the Lord Jesus Christ, not their own effort, so they did not need to fear the time when God will judge the wicked. Christians will "live with him forever," for this is the gift of salvation.

Always be joyful.
Never stop praying.
Be thankful
in all
circumstances.

1 THESSALONIANS
5:16-18

2 Thessalonians

WHAT DO WE LEARN ABOUT GOD'S MISSION AND OURS?
We have important work to do while we wait for Jesus' return.

WHO WROTE IT? Paul, an apostle, with Silas and Timothy (1:1).

WHEN DID IT HAPPEN? Around AD 51–52.

HOW IS IT ORGANIZED?

1: Paul thanks God and prays for this church

2: Paul gives more instruction on Christ's return

3: Paul urges the people to pray and work hard

FEATURE HIGHLIGHTS
+ *Jesus' Return and Reign (1530)*

Words to Remember are highlighted throughout this book

HOW LONG DOES IT TAKE TO READ?
:10 | :30 | 1:00 | 1:30 | 2:00 | 2:30 | 3:00 | 3:30

Timeline

AD	Event
30	JESUS DIES, RISES FROM THE DEAD, ASCENDS TO REIGN IN HEAVEN, SENDS THE HOLY SPIRIT
35	JESUS CALLS PAUL TO PREACH THE GOOD NEWS
46–48	PAUL GOES ON FIRST MISSIONARY JOURNEY, WITH BARNABAS AND JOHN MARK
50	JERUSALEM COUNCIL CONFIRMS GENTILE INCLUSION IN THE CHURCH
50–52	PAUL EMBARKS ON SECOND MISSIONARY JOURNEY, WITH SILAS; THEY SPEND 18 MONTHS IN CORINTH
50	PAUL MEETS PRISCILLA AND AQUILA IN CORINTH
	PAUL MEETS LYDIA IN PHILIPPI
50	PAUL AND SILAS ESTABLISH THE CHURCH IN THESSALONICA
51–52	PAUL WRITES TWO LETTERS TO THE THESSALONIAN CHURCH
53–57	PAUL TAKES A THIRD MISSIONARY JOURNEY
57	PAUL ARRESTED IN JERUSALEM
57–59	PAUL IMPRISONED IN CAESAREA, WHERE HE IS QUESTIONED BY FELIX AND DRUSILLA, FESTUS, AND AGRIPPA AND BERNICE
64	PAUL MARTYRED IN ROME
70	ROME DESTROYS JERUSALEM

Greetings from Paul

1 This letter is from Paul, Silas,* and Timothy.

We are writing to the church in Thessalonica, to you who belong to God our Father and the Lord Jesus Christ.

²May God our Father* and the Lord Jesus Christ give you grace and peace.

Encouragement during Persecution

³Dear brothers and sisters,* we can't help but thank God for you, because your faith is flourishing and your love for one another is growing. ⁴We proudly tell God's other churches about your endurance and faithfulness in all the persecutions and hardships you are suffering. ⁵And God will use this persecution to show his justice and to make you worthy of his Kingdom, for which you are suffering. ⁶In his justice he will pay back those who persecute you.

⁷And God will provide rest for you who are being persecuted and also for us when the Lord Jesus appears from heaven. He will come with his mighty angels, ⁸in flaming fire, bringing judgment on those who don't know God and on those who refuse to obey the Good News of our Lord Jesus. ⁹They will be punished with eternal destruction, forever separated from the Lord and from his glorious power. ¹⁰When he comes on that day, he will receive glory from his holy people—praise from all who believe. And this includes you, for you believed what we told you about him.

¹¹So we keep on praying for you, asking our God to enable you to live a life worthy of his call. May he give you the power to accomplish all the good things your faith prompts you to do. ¹²Then the name of our Lord Jesus will be honored because of the way you live, and you will be honored along with him. This is all made possible because of the grace of our God and Lord, Jesus Christ.*

Events prior to the Lord's Second Coming

2 Now, dear brothers and sisters,* let us clarify some things about the coming of our Lord Jesus Christ and how we will be gathered to meet him. ²Don't be so easily shaken or alarmed by those who say that the day of the Lord has already begun. Don't believe them, even if they claim to have had a spiritual vision, a revelation, or a letter supposedly from us. ³Don't be fooled by what they say. For that day will not come until there is a great rebellion against God and the man of lawlessness* is revealed—the one who brings destruction.* ⁴He will exalt himself and defy everything that people call god and every object of worship. He will even sit in the temple of God, claiming that he himself is God.

⁵Don't you remember that I told you about all this when I was with you? ⁶And you know what is holding him back, for he can be revealed only when his time comes. ⁷For this lawlessness is already at work secretly, and it will remain secret until the one who is holding it back steps out of the way. ⁸Then the man of lawlessness will be revealed, but the Lord Jesus will slay him with the breath of his mouth and destroy him by the splendor of his coming.

⁹This man will come to do the work of Satan with counterfeit power and signs and miracles. ¹⁰He will use every kind of evil deception to fool those on their way to destruction, because they refuse to love and accept the truth that would save them. ¹¹So God will cause them to be greatly deceived, and they will believe these lies. ¹²Then they will be condemned for enjoying evil rather than believing the truth.

Believers Should Stand Firm

¹³As for us, we can't help but thank God for you, dear brothers and sisters loved by the Lord. We are always thankful that God chose you to be among the first* to experience salvation—a salvation that

---

1:1 Greek *Silvanus*, the Greek form of the name. **1:2** Some manuscripts read *God the Father*. **1:3** Greek *Brothers*. **1:12** Or *of our God and our Lord Jesus Christ*. **2:1** Greek *brothers;* also in 2:13, 15. **2:3a** Some manuscripts read *the man of sin*. **2:3b** Greek *the son of destruction*. **2:13** Some manuscripts read *chose you from the very beginning*.

1:4-6 Paul shows his pastoral concern for the Thessalonian Christians by encouraging them to embrace what Paul sees as the outcome of their pain. Their experience of suffering and persecution was building in them "endurance and faithfulness," making them "worthy of his Kingdom" and a faithful example for other Christians. Paul promises that God, who brings justice, would "pay back" (this language indicates God's judgment) those who are inflicting the suffering.

1:11-12 Paul had already commended their faithfulness and endurance (1:4) and had instructed them about Christian conduct in a previous letter (1 Thessalonians 2:12; 4:1-12). A life worthy of God brings honor to the Lord Jesus and will result in their honor. God fulfills their good choices through his gift of grace.

2:1-12 False teaching about the Day of the Lord had disturbed the Thessalonian church. Paul reminds them that two events will precede that day: a great rebellion and the unveiling of the man of lawlessness. Christ will destroy this man when he returns, and those who have been deceived will also be judged. The "man of lawlessness" is not Satan but is a servant of Satan whom John calls the "Antichrist" (1 John 2:18; 4:3). Jesus refers to this kind of figure in the plural as "false messiahs" (see Matthew 24:5, 23-24; Mark 13:21-22; compare Luke 21:8).

2:9-10 Paul warns of counterfeit demonstrations of "miracles" that the man of lawlessness may use to show his power. Paul encourages his readers not to be distracted by this "evil deception," for it would not lead to love and truth but to destruction. The source for this deception is Satan, while the Lord Jesus is the source of love and truth.

2:13 The Thessalonians were loved by God (the Father and the Son) and "the Spirit who makes you holy" (see also 2:16). The Holy Spirit resides within the repentant believer whose heart knows the truth of God. God "chose you" to be saved, which means he initiated the call to the believer, and the believer responded with trust and faith.

came through the Spirit who makes you holy and through your belief in the truth. ¹⁴He called you to salvation when we told you the Good News; now you can share in the glory of our Lord Jesus Christ.

¹⁵With all these things in mind, dear brothers and sisters, stand firm and keep a strong grip on the teaching we passed on to you both in person and by letter.

¹⁶Now may our Lord Jesus Christ himself and God our Father, who loved us and by his grace gave us eternal comfort and a wonderful hope, ¹⁷comfort you and strengthen you in every good thing you do and say.

Paul's Request for Prayer

3 Finally, dear brothers and sisters,* we ask you to pray for us. Pray that the Lord's message will spread rapidly and be honored wherever it goes, just as when it came to you. ²Pray, too, that we will be rescued from wicked and evil people, for not everyone is a believer. ³But the Lord is faithful; he will strengthen you and guard you from the evil one.* ⁴And we are confident in the Lord that you are doing and will continue to do the things we commanded you. ⁵May the Lord lead your hearts into a full understanding and expression of the love of God and the patient endurance that comes from Christ.

An Exhortation to Proper Living

⁶And now, dear brothers and sisters, we give you this command in the name of our Lord Jesus Christ: Stay away from all believers* who live idle lives and don't follow the tradition they received* from us. ⁷For you know that you ought to imitate us. We were not idle when we were with you. ⁸We never accepted food from anyone without paying for it. We worked hard day and night so we would not be a burden to any of you. ⁹We certainly had the right to ask you to feed us, but we wanted to give you an example to follow. ¹⁰Even while we were with you, we gave you this command: "Those unwilling to work will not get to eat."

¹¹Yet we hear that some of you are living idle lives, refusing to work and meddling in other people's business. ¹²We command such people and urge them in the name of the Lord Jesus Christ to settle down and work to earn their own living. ¹³As for the rest of you, dear brothers and sisters, never get tired of doing good.

¹⁴Take note of those who refuse to obey what we say in this letter. Stay away from them so they will be ashamed. ¹⁵Don't think of them as enemies, but warn them as you would a brother or sister.*

Paul's Final Greetings

¹⁶Now may the Lord of peace himself give you his peace at all times and in every situation. The Lord be with you all.

¹⁷HERE IS MY GREETING IN MY OWN HANDWRITING—PAUL. I DO THIS IN ALL MY LETTERS TO PROVE THEY ARE FROM ME.

¹⁸May the grace of our Lord Jesus Christ be with you all.

> "The gospel frees us from demanding our own way, because nothing we desire to obtain is worth sinning against such love and kindness."
>
> — ELYSE FITZPATRICK
> author and counselor

3:1 Greek *brothers;* also in 3:6, 13. **3:3** Or *from evil.* **3:6a** Greek *from every brother.* **3:6b** Some manuscripts read *you received.* **3:15** Greek *as a brother.*

3:7-10 Imitation was highly regarded in the ancient world, and Paul gave himself as a pattern to follow (see 3:9; 1 Corinthians 4:16; 11:1; Philippians 3:17; 1 Thessalonians 1:6; 2:14). Paul's instruction is similar to the instructions of Seneca, Epictetus, and other ancient philosophers who described moral exemplars in their writings. Paul called for the Thessalonians to imitate him and the other apostles as they looked to the Lord Jesus Christ as their exemplar (Philippians 2:6-8). Unlike those who could have worked but were relying only on others to support them, Paul worked to pay for his food and living costs.

3:13 The Greek term translated "doing good" is in the present tense, anticipating that good works are an ongoing Christian practice. These good works include supporting their households, providing material support for the church, and carrying out ongoing acts of charity. All of these are to be commonplace for believers. Christians most often supported one another through their own production of goods, and the use of those goods for others in need.

WHAT THE BIBLE SAYS ABOUT

Jesus' Return and Reign

Jesus' Return Brings Hope

We look forward with hope to that wonderful day when the glory of our great God and Savior, Jesus Christ, will be revealed. **TITUS 2:13**

"Don't let your hearts be troubled. Trust in God.... There is more than enough room in my Father's home.... When everything is ready, I will come and get you, so that you will always be with me where I am." **JOHN 14:1-3**

"Look, God's home is now among his people! He will live with them, and they will be his people.... He will wipe every tear from their eyes, and there will be no more death or sorrow or crying or pain. All these things are gone forever." **REVELATION 21:3-4**

We want you to know what will happen to the believers who have died so you will not grieve like people who have no hope.... When Jesus returns, God will bring back with him the believers who have died.... Then, together with them, we who are still alive and remain on the earth will be caught up in the clouds to meet the Lord in the air. Then we will be with the Lord forever. So encourage each other with these words. **1 THESSALONIANS 4:13-14, 17-18**

... He will wipe every tear from their eyes, and there will be no more death ...

Jesus Will Return Suddenly

You know quite well that the day of the Lord's return will come unexpectedly, like a thief in the night.... And you won't be surprised when the day of the Lord comes like a thief.... So be on your guard, not asleep like the others. Stay alert and be clearheaded. **1 THESSALONIANS 5:2, 4, 6**

"No one knows the day or hour when these things will happen.... Only the Father knows.... You also must be ready all the time, for the Son of Man will come when least expected." **MATTHEW 24:36, 44**

We Will Receive the Results of How We Lived

God will provide rest for you... when the Lord Jesus appears from heaven. He will come... bringing judgment on those who don't know God and on those who refuse to obey the Good News of our Lord Jesus. **2 THESSALONIANS 1:7-8**

After all, what gives us hope and joy, and what will be our proud reward and crown as we stand before our Lord Jesus when he returns? It is you! **1 THESSALONIANS 2:19**

I saw the souls of those who had been beheaded for their testimony about Jesus and for proclaiming the word of God. They had not worshiped the beast or his statue, nor accepted his mark on their foreheads or their hands. They all came to life again, and they reigned with Christ for a thousand years. **REVELATION 20:4**

1 Timothy

WHAT DO WE LEARN ABOUT GOD'S MISSION AND OURS?
Character matters in how we relate to God, his church, and each other.

WHO WROTE IT? Paul, an apostle.

WHEN DID IT HAPPEN? Around AD 63.

HOW IS IT ORGANIZED?
1: Focusing on sound teaching
2: Guiding community prayer and worship
3: Choosing qualified church leaders
4: Confronting false teachers and encouragement for leading
5: Relating to each other in God's household
6: Dealing with how we relate to wealth and find contentment

FEATURE HIGHLIGHTS
+ *Women Teaching and Holding Authority* (1535)
+ *Leading and Following Above Reproach* (1537)

Words to Remember are highlighted throughout this book

HOW LONG DOES IT TAKE TO READ?

:15							
	:30	1:00	1:30	2:00	2:30	3:00	3:30

Timeline

AD	
30	JESUS DIES, RISES FROM THE DEAD, ASCENDS TO REIGN IN HEAVEN, SENDS THE HOLY SPIRIT
35	JESUS CALLS PAUL TO PREACH THE GOOD NEWS
46–48	PAUL GOES ON FIRST MISSIONARY JOURNEY, WITH BARNABAS AND JOHN MARK
50	JERUSALEM COUNCIL CONFIRMS GENTILE INCLUSION IN THE CHURCH
50–52	PAUL EMBARKS ON SECOND MISSIONARY JOURNEY, WITH SILAS; THEY SPEND 18 MONTHS IN CORINTH
50	PAUL MEETS PRISCILLA AND AQUILA IN CORINTH
	PAUL MEETS LYDIA IN PHILIPPI
53–57	PAUL TAKES A THIRD MISSIONARY JOURNEY
53–56	PAUL STAYS FOR AN EXTENDED TIME IN EPHESUS
57	PAUL ARRESTED IN JERUSALEM
57–59	PAUL IMPRISONED IN CAESAREA, WHERE HE IS QUESTIONED BY FELIX AND DRUSILLA, FESTUS, AND AGRIPPA AND BERNICE
60–62	PAUL IMPRISONED IN ROME
63	PAUL WRITES LETTERS TO TIMOTHY AND TITUS FROM MACEDONIA
64	PAUL MARTYRED IN ROME
70	ROME DESTROYS JERUSALEM

Greetings from Paul

1 This letter is from Paul, an apostle of Christ Jesus, appointed by the command of God our Savior and Christ Jesus, who gives us hope.

²I am writing to Timothy, my true son in the faith.

May God the Father and Christ Jesus our Lord give you grace, mercy, and peace.

Warnings against False Teachings

³When I left for Macedonia, I urged you to stay there in Ephesus and stop those whose teaching is contrary to the truth. ⁴Don't let them waste their time in endless discussion of myths and spiritual pedigrees. These things only lead to meaningless speculations,* which don't help people live a life of faith in God.*

⁵The purpose of my instruction is that all believers would be filled with love that comes from a pure heart, a clear conscience, and genuine faith. ⁶But some people have missed this whole point. They have turned away from these things and spend their time in meaningless discussions. ⁷They want to be known as teachers of the law of Moses, but they don't know what they are talking about, even though they speak so confidently.

⁸We know that the law is good when used correctly. ⁹For the law was not intended for people who do what is right. It is for people who are lawless and rebellious, who are ungodly and sinful, who consider nothing sacred and defile what is holy, who kill their father or mother or commit other murders. ¹⁰The law is for people who are sexually immoral, or who practice homosexuality, or are slave traders,* liars, promise breakers, or who do anything else that contradicts the wholesome teaching ¹¹that comes from the glorious Good News entrusted to me by our blessed God.

Paul's Gratitude for God's Mercy

¹²I thank Christ Jesus our Lord, who has given me strength to do his work. He considered me trustworthy and appointed me to serve him, ¹³even though I used to blaspheme the name of Christ. In my insolence, I persecuted his people. But God had mercy on me because I did it in ignorance and unbelief. ¹⁴Oh, how generous and gracious our Lord was! He filled me with the faith and love that come from Christ Jesus.

¹⁵This is a trustworthy saying, and everyone should accept it: "Christ Jesus came into the world to save sinners"—and I am the worst of them all. ¹⁶But God had mercy on me so that Christ Jesus could use me as a prime example of his great patience with even the worst sinners. Then others will realize that they, too, can believe in him and receive eternal life. ¹⁷All honor and glory to God forever and ever! He is the eternal King, the unseen one who never dies; he alone is God. Amen.

Timothy's Responsibility

¹⁸Timothy, my son, here are my instructions for you, based on the prophetic words spoken about you earlier. May they help you fight well in the Lord's battles. ¹⁹Cling to your faith in Christ, and keep your conscience clear. For some people have deliberately violated their consciences; as a result, their faith has been shipwrecked. ²⁰Hymenaeus and Alexander are two examples. I threw them out and handed them over to Satan so they might learn not to blaspheme God.

Instructions about Worship

2 I urge you, first of all, to pray for all people. Ask God to help them; intercede on their behalf, and give thanks for them. ²Pray this way for kings and all who are in authority so that we can live peaceful and quiet lives marked by godliness and dignity. ³This is good and pleases God our Savior, ⁴who wants everyone to be saved and to understand the truth. ⁵For,

> There is one God and one Mediator who can reconcile God and humanity—the man Christ Jesus. ⁶He gave his life to purchase freedom for everyone.

1:4a Greek *in myths and endless genealogies, which cause speculation.* **1:4b** Greek *a stewardship of God in faith.* **1:10** Or *kidnappers.*

1:4 Paul might be dismissing their teaching as trivial, or he might be rejecting the fanciful nature of their interpretations (1:7; see also 2 Timothy 4:3-4; Titus 1:14; 3:9; 2 Peter 1:16) and their justification of immoral behavior (1 Timothy 1:8-11; 4:1-2, 7; see also Titus 1:15-16). In Judaism, one's genealogy established one's spiritual pedigree, so the false teachers might have been preoccupied with this. They were probably also exploiting Old Testament genealogies (Genesis 5:1-32) in fanciful interpretations of the law. Where the NLT reads, "which don't help people live a life of faith in God," the original Greek wording reflects household management (see 1 Timothy 3:15). This phrase can be translated in a number of ways, such as faithfulness to God's household management or faithfulness in managing God's household.

1:20 Hymenaeus and Alexander might have been elders in Ephesus (see 2 Timothy 2:17; 4:14; see also Acts 19:33; 20:29-31). Paul "handed them over to Satan" by removing them from the church, the realm of the Spirit's oversight (see also Job 2:6; Matthew 18:17-20; 1 Corinthians 5:2-5; 2 Corinthians 2:5-11; 2 Timothy 2:25-26). Blaspheming God means that they attacked and defamed the true Good News, and thus God (see 1 Timothy 1:13; see also 6:1; Titus 2:5; 2 Peter 2:2).

2:5 There is "one God" and therefore one mission involving all people (Romans 3:29-30; Galatians 3:26-29). Using the phrase "one God" suggests a fundamental declaration of Christian faith, analogous to the basics of the Jewish faith (Deuteronomy 6:4). There is one Mediator of God's covenant, Christ Jesus. He is fully human and fully God, and thus able to reconcile God and humanity (see 1 Corinthians 8:6; Ephesians 4:5-6).

Women Teaching and Holding Authority

SCRIPTURE CONNECTION: 1 TIMOTHY 2:11-15

While some interpret Paul's instructions as prohibiting women from leading in the church, we need to look deeply into this passage's often-misunderstood language and context.

It begins with a command that women must be educated. Religious education happened in synagogues but there was nothing comparable in the Greco-Roman culture. So Timothy needed to create learning environments for the (mostly Gentile) women believers in the Ephesian church.

The key verse in this passage is 2:12. The verb "do not let" looks like a command in English. But the original Greek can be translated, "I am not permitting," thus carrying an implicit timeline: When conditions change, permission will be granted. As women learn more about Scripture, they will be equipped to teach.

The infinitive "to teach" is not connected with the noun "men," so Paul states here simply that women were not to teach. Yet we know his coworker Priscilla taught a man, Apollos (Acts 18:26). So Paul had a specific situation in mind: He speaks about it in 1 Timothy 1:3, commanding Timothy to stop certain men from teaching because their content was false.

> When women learn, they will be equipped to teach.

The verb "to have authority over" is not used elsewhere in the New Testament, and it refers to abusive power. Men and women were expected to learn in submission to their teachers; men would also be condemned if they used such power over others.

False ideas that reinterpreted the Genesis creation story might have emerged, too (2:13-14). Hence the command for women to learn in 2:11. In Greek, Paul uses a singular subject in 2:15 (*she* "will be saved"), which could refer to Mary bearing Jesus, who all may receive redemption and forgiveness through. Encouraging holy living for all believers, not just women, echoes earlier calls for holiness (2:2).

IMAGINE

How can I learn deeply and faithfully about God's Word?

Am I swayed by false teachings because I do not put the time into deep study of the Bible?

"As a New Testament professor, I must always be learning, so I can faithfully teach God's Word."

LYNN H. COHICK, PhD, is Distinguished Professor of New Testament and Director of Houston Theological Seminary, where she leads the Doctor of Ministry program. She writes, speaks, and teaches internationally.

This is the message God gave to the world at just the right time. ⁷And I have been chosen as a preacher and apostle to teach the Gentiles this message about faith and truth. I'm not exaggerating—just telling the truth.

⁸In every place of worship, I want men to pray with holy hands lifted up to God, free from anger and controversy.

⁹And I want women to be modest in their appearance.* They should wear decent and appropriate clothing and not draw attention to themselves by the way they fix their hair or by wearing gold or pearls or expensive clothes. ¹⁰For women who claim to be devoted to God should make themselves attractive by the good things they do.

¹¹Women should learn quietly and submissively. ¹²I do not let women teach men or have authority over them.* Let them listen quietly. ¹³For God made Adam first, and afterward he made Eve. ¹⁴And it was not Adam who was deceived by Satan. The woman was deceived, and sin was the result. ¹⁵But women will be saved through childbearing,* assuming they continue to live in faith, love, holiness, and modesty.

Leaders in the Church

3 This is a trustworthy saying: "If someone aspires to be a church leader,* he desires an honorable position." ²So a church leader must be a man whose life is above reproach. He must be faithful to his wife.* He must exercise self-control, live wisely, and have a good reputation. He must enjoy having guests in his home, and he must be able to teach. ³He must not be a heavy drinker* or be violent. He must be gentle, not quarrelsome, and not love money. ⁴He must manage his own family well, having children who respect and obey him. ⁵For if a man cannot manage his own household, how can he take care of God's church?

⁶A church leader must not be a new believer, because he might become proud, and the devil would cause him to fall.* ⁷Also, people outside the church must speak well of him so that he will not be disgraced and fall into the devil's trap.

⁸In the same way, deacons must be well respected and have integrity. They must not be heavy drinkers or dishonest with money. ⁹They must be committed to the mystery of the faith now revealed and must live with a clear conscience. ¹⁰Before they are appointed as deacons, let them be closely examined. If they pass the test, then let them serve as deacons.

¹¹In the same way, their wives* must be respected and must not slander others. They must exercise self-control and be faithful in everything they do.

¹²A deacon must be faithful to his wife, and he must manage his children and household well. ¹³Those who do well as deacons will be rewarded with respect from others and will have increased confidence in their faith in Christ Jesus.

2:9 Or *to pray in modest apparel*. **2:12** Or *teach men or usurp their authority*. **2:15** Or *will be saved by accepting their role as mothers*, or *will be saved by the birth of the Child*. **3:1** Or *an overseer*, or *a bishop*; also in 3:2, 6. **3:2** Or *must have only one wife*, or *must be married only once*; Greek reads *must be the husband of one wife*; also in 3:12. **3:3** Greek *must not drink too much wine*; similarly in 3:8. **3:6** Or *he might fall into the same judgment as the devil*. **3:11** Or *the women deacons*. The Greek word can be translated *women* or *wives*.

2:9-10 The subject of Paul's teaching for men and women in this section (2:1-15) is community prayer. Paul wanted to correct the distracting or misleading ways the Ephesians had been conducting themselves when they gathered so that they could pray together well. Paul confronted the issue of modesty directly. While some have assumed that Paul's comments about "modesty" meant the women were dressing seductively, the primary concern was how Ephesian believers were dressing to display their wealth. Wealthy women spent long hours having their hair braided and they dressed in fine clothes. Flaunting wealth was strongly discouraged (6:6-10, 17-19; see also Luke 12:13-34; James 5:1-6) and harms the church body. Paul instructed the women in this community that they were to do good deeds for others, and not focus on enhancing their appearance. The women were to praise God rather than seek to be praised by others (see also 1 Peter 3:3-5).

2:12 The relationship between teaching and authority depends on how both are understood. Women did teach (Acts 18:26; Romans 16:1-2; Titus 2:3-5), but this passage says that women could not teach the men in Ephesus. Because women married early (usually in their teen years), their education stopped at a young age. Paul noted that women were being led astray by false teachers (2 Timothy 3:6), and so Paul's instructions were intended to stop them from teaching at this time, presumably until they had further education in the Scriptures. Women also prophesied (Luke 2:36-38; Acts 2:17-18; 21:9; 1 Corinthians 11:5), and some types of prophecy may have been understood as authoritative teaching (Acts 11:28; 21:10-11; 1 Corinthians 14:29). The verb "have authority" can denote a domineering attitude or could be the exercise of authority.

3:2 Living above reproach is the most general prerequisite for a community leader and public representative (see 3:7, 10; 5:7; 6:14; Titus 1:6-7; 2:8). The requirement of marital faithfulness (or literally, "a one-woman man"; that is, monogamous as opposed to polygamous) assumes but does not require the leader to be married. It mainly addresses purity and faithfulness in the marriage relationship, which could not be taken for granted in the surrounding culture. It probably does not prohibit remarriage after the death of a spouse (see 1 Timothy 5:11). Hospitality was likely a requirement because it was a valued part of both the ancient Near Eastern and Greco-Roman cultures. Any traveling Christian would seek out and probably stay with fellow believers (see 2 John 1:10-11; 3 John 1:1-15). In addition, first-century churches often met in private homes (for example, Colossians 4:15; Philemon 1:2).

3:8 Deacons (or ministers or servants) are leaders in the church. In Romans 16:1 the woman Phoebe is described as a deacon of the church at Cenchrea. Like all church leaders (1 Timothy 3:3), deacons must be sober and trustworthy with money. Greed is disreputable and improper (6:6-10, 17-19; Ephesians 5:3; Colossians 3:5), especially for those who lead in the church (1 Timothy 3:9; see Titus 1:7).

The Truths of Our Faith

¹⁴I am writing these things to you now, even though I hope to be with you soon, ¹⁵so that if I am delayed, you will know how people must conduct themselves in the household of God. This is the church of the living God, which is the pillar and foundation of the truth.

¹⁶Without question, this is the great mystery of our faith*:

Christ* was revealed in a human body
and vindicated by the Spirit.*
He was seen by angels
and announced to the nations.
He was believed in throughout the world
and taken to heaven in glory.

Warnings against False Teachers

4 Now the Holy Spirit tells us clearly that in the last times some will turn away from the true faith; they will follow deceptive spirits and teachings that come from demons. ²These people are hypocrites and liars, and their consciences are dead.*

3:16a Or *of godliness.* 3:16b Greek *He who*; other manuscripts read *God.* 3:16c Or *in his spirit.* 4:2 Greek *are seared.*

Koinonia IMAGE — MY STORY WITH COMMUNITY, WORKPLACE & CHURCH

Leading and Following Above Reproach

SCRIPTURE CONNECTION: 1 TIMOTHY 3:1-13

We're saddened by the downfall of so many church leaders. It seems the larger the following, the more devastating the fall.

Yet leadership of God's church deserves even greater guardianship than other leadership for two important reasons: The church is God's household, the pillar of his truth, and Christian witness to non-believers is either marred or won based on our leaders' integrity.

Paul recognized this danger in his warnings to the church in Ephesus, saying a church leader must live "above reproach" (3:2). This doesn't mean living without sin, or everyone would be disqualified! However, Paul describes leadership-worthy living next: Be gentle, not violent or quarrelsome; don't love money or power; be faithful to your spouse and manage your household well. He also warns against elevating new believers into leadership, to guard against immaturity.

But it is not just leaders who matter. The church's people also are susceptible to false teaching. Followers elevate entertaining preachers to celebrity status and underestimate the influence of pride, power, and money.

Of course, leaders are primarily responsible for their behavior and hearts. But followers also bear some responsibility for the kind of leaders we follow. Whether leader or follower, how can we cultivate heart awareness of the temptation of grandeur? The church needs leaders—and followers—living above reproach.

> The church needs leaders—and followers—living above reproach.

IMAGINE

How have you seen an excellent ministry leader remain humble by seeking correction?

How can followers give churches healthy feedback so they are led well?

"I know I'm not immune to the lure of praise and influence. May we humbly recognize our susceptibility and guard one another."

KATHERINE LEARY ALSDORF founded and directed Redeemer Church's Center for Faith & Work. She co-authored *Every Good Endeavor: Connecting Your Work to God's Work* with Timothy Keller.

³They will say it is wrong to be married and wrong to eat certain foods. But God created those foods to be eaten with thanks by faithful people who know the truth. ⁴Since everything God created is good, we should not reject any of it but receive it with thanks. ⁵For we know it is made acceptable* by the word of God and prayer.

A Good Servant of Christ Jesus

⁶If you explain these things to the brothers and sisters,* Timothy, you will be a worthy servant of Christ Jesus, one who is nourished by the message of faith and the good teaching you have followed. ⁷Do not waste time arguing over godless ideas and old wives' tales. Instead, train yourself to be godly. ⁸"Physical training is good, but training for godliness is much better, promising benefits in this life and in the life to come." ⁹This is a trustworthy saying, and everyone should accept it. ¹⁰This is why we work hard and continue to struggle,* for our hope is in the living God, who is the Savior of all people and particularly of all believers.

¹¹Teach these things and insist that everyone learn them. ¹²Don't let anyone think less of you because you are young. Be an example to all believers in what you say, in the way you live, in your love, your faith, and your purity. ¹³Until I get there, focus on reading the Scriptures to the church, encouraging the believers, and teaching them.

¹⁴Do not neglect the spiritual gift you received through the prophecy spoken over you when the elders of the church laid their hands on you. ¹⁵Give your complete attention to these matters. Throw yourself into your tasks so that everyone will see your progress. ¹⁶Keep a close watch on how you live and on your teaching. Stay true to what is right for the sake of your own salvation and the salvation of those who hear you.

Advice about Widows, Elders, and Slaves

5 Never speak harshly to an older man,* but appeal to him respectfully as you would to your own father. Talk to younger men as you would to your own brothers. ²Treat older women as you would your mother, and treat younger women with all purity as you would your own sisters.

³Take care of* any widow who has no one else to care for her. ⁴But if she has children or grandchildren, their first responsibility is to show godliness at home and repay their parents by taking care of them. This is something that pleases God.

⁵Now a true widow, a woman who is truly alone in this world, has placed her hope in God. She prays night and day, asking God for his help. ⁶But the widow who lives only for pleasure is spiritually dead even while she lives. ⁷Give these instructions to the church so that no one will be open to criticism.

⁸But those who won't care for their relatives, especially those in their own household, have denied the true faith. Such people are worse than unbelievers.

⁹A widow who is put on the list for support must be a woman who is at least sixty years old and was faithful to her husband.* ¹⁰She must be well respected by everyone because of the good she has done. Has she brought up her children well? Has she been kind to strangers and served other believers humbly?* Has she helped those who are in trouble? Has she always been ready to do good?

¹¹The younger widows should not be on the list, because their physical desires will overpower their devotion to Christ and they will want to remarry. ¹²Then they would be guilty of breaking their previous pledge. ¹³And if they are on the list, they will learn to be lazy and will spend their time gossiping from house to house, meddling in other people's business and talking about things they shouldn't. ¹⁴So I advise these younger widows to marry again, have children, and take care of their own homes. Then the enemy will not be able to say anything against them. ¹⁵For I am afraid that some of them have already gone astray and now follow Satan.

¹⁶If a woman who is a believer has relatives who are widows, she must take care of them and not put the responsibility on the church. Then the church can care for the widows who are truly alone.

¹⁷Elders who do their work well should be respected and paid well,* especially those who work

---

4:5 Or *made holy.* **4:6** Greek *brothers.* **4:10** Some manuscripts read *continue to suffer.* **5:1** Or *an elder.* **5:3** Or *Honor.* **5:9** Greek *was the wife of one husband.* **5:10** Greek *and washed the feet of God's holy people?* **5:17** Greek *should be worthy of double honor.*

4:4 "Everything God created is good" means that all food could be eaten and there were no restrictions, for God is the source of all things. Paul may be referring to some Jewish Christians who did not eat meat but ate only vegetables (see Romans 14:2). Meat was butchered in the temples and offered to idols as a sacrifice, and so some still believed it remained spiritually or ritually tainted.
4:14 Spiritual gifts are also mentioned in 1 Corinthians 12:27-31; Romans 12:6-8. Gifts are given to both men and women by God's Spirit and are to be used for the building up, encouragement, and consolation of the church (1 Corinthians 12:7; 14:3).
5:3-16 A widow without wealth or family was vulnerable in a world where marriage provided for economic needs. The Christian community was expected to care for such widows among its members (see Deuteronomy 10:17-19; Isaiah 1:17; see also Acts 6:1-6; James 1:27). There is some evidence of a religious order of widows in the first-century church that gathered widows to make and share goods (see Acts 9:36-37).
5:4 Widows who had children and grandchildren were to be taken care of by their own family, not by the church. In 5:11 younger widows were encouraged to marry again so that they could have provision. God is honored by our care for our own families. In the ancient world it was vital that everyone led productive lives and contributed to the work of the household; ninety percent of people lived hand to mouth to provide for their housing, clothing, and food.

hard at both preaching and teaching. ¹⁸For the Scripture says, "You must not muzzle an ox to keep it from eating as it treads out the grain." And in another place, "Those who work deserve their pay!"*

¹⁹Do not listen to an accusation against an elder unless it is confirmed by two or three witnesses. ²⁰Those who sin should be reprimanded in front of the whole church; this will serve as a strong warning to others.

²¹I solemnly command you in the presence of God and Christ Jesus and the highest angels to obey these instructions without taking sides or showing favoritism to anyone.

²²Never be in a hurry about appointing a church leader.* Do not share in the sins of others. Keep yourself pure.

²³Don't drink only water. You ought to drink a little wine for the sake of your stomach because you are sick so often.

²⁴Remember, the sins of some people are obvious, leading them to certain judgment. But there are others whose sins will not be revealed until later. ²⁵In the same way, the good deeds of some people are obvious. And the good deeds done in secret will someday come to light.

6

All slaves should show full respect for their masters so they will not bring shame on the name of God and his teaching. ²If the masters are believers, that is no excuse for being disrespectful. Those slaves should work all the harder because their efforts are helping other believers* who are well loved.

False Teaching and True Riches

Teach these things, Timothy, and encourage everyone to obey them. ³Some people may contradict our teaching, but these are the wholesome teachings of the Lord Jesus Christ. These teachings promote a godly life. ⁴Anyone who teaches something different is arrogant and lacks understanding. Such a person has an unhealthy desire to quibble over the meaning of words. This stirs up arguments ending in jealousy, division, slander, and evil suspicions. ⁵These people always cause trouble. Their minds are corrupt, and they have turned their backs on the truth. To them, a show of godliness is just a way to become wealthy.

⁶Yet true godliness with contentment is itself great wealth. ⁷After all, we brought nothing with us when we came into the world, and we can't take anything with us when we leave it. ⁸So if we have enough food and clothing, let us be content.

⁹But people who long to be rich fall into temptation and are trapped by many foolish and harmful desires that plunge them into ruin and destruction. ¹⁰For the love of money is the root of all kinds of evil. And some people, craving money, have wandered from the true faith and pierced themselves with many sorrows.

Paul's Final Instructions

¹¹But you, Timothy, are a man of God; so run from all these evil things. Pursue righteousness and a godly life, along with faith, love, perseverance, and gentleness. ¹²Fight the good fight for the true faith. Hold tightly to the eternal life to which God has called you, which you have declared so well before many witnesses. ¹³And I charge you before God, who gives life to all, and before Christ Jesus, who gave a good testimony before Pontius Pilate, ¹⁴that you obey this command without wavering. Then no one can find fault with you from now until our Lord Jesus Christ comes again. ¹⁵For,

> At just the right time Christ will be revealed from heaven by the blessed and only almighty God, the King of all kings and Lord of all lords.
> ¹⁶He alone can never die, and he lives in light so brilliant that no human can approach him. No human eye has ever seen him, nor ever will. All honor and power to him forever! Amen.

¹⁷Teach those who are rich in this world not to be proud and not to trust in their money, which is so unreliable. Their trust should be in God, who richly gives us all we need for our enjoyment. ¹⁸Tell them to use their money to do good. They should be rich in good works and generous to those in need, always being ready to share with others. ¹⁹By doing this they will be storing up their treasure as a good foundation for the future so that they may experience true life.

²⁰Timothy, guard what God has entrusted to you. Avoid godless, foolish discussions with those who oppose you with their so-called knowledge. ²¹Some people have wandered from the faith by following such foolishness.

May God's grace be with you all.

5:18 Deut 25:4; Luke 10:7. **5:22** Greek *about the laying on of hands*. **6:2** Greek *brothers*.

6:1-2 Paul addresses how enslaved Christians should relate to their enslavers. Enslaved people were vulnerable to abuse in the ancient world as they had no legal rights. Paul called them to "show full respect for" their enslavers, even though this would have been difficult. Paul connects their respect to their Christian witness. Some enslavers were believers, and Paul encouraged the enslaved people who served them to show love for their fellow believers. Paul's instructions ultimately subverted the status quo of how enslavers and the enslaved related because they acknowledged the agency and dignity of every person, regardless of social status.

6:17-19 Paul discusses what Timothy should teach Christians about money and wealth. Much like today, in the ancient world it was the few who held the bulk of the wealth while many had very little. Those who are wealthy should be generous and proactive in doing good works. Paul warns all believers that money cannot provide the stability and rich life that God alone can bring.

2 Timothy

WHAT DO WE LEARN ABOUT GOD'S MISSION AND OURS? Run a strong race, encouraging others to keep going after you're gone, and finish well.

WHO WROTE IT? Paul, an apostle.

WHEN DID IT HAPPEN? Around AD 64.

HOW IS IT ORGANIZED?

1: Paul encourages Timothy to be faithful to his calling

2: Paul urges Timothy to be strong in the Lord and endure suffering

3: Paul warns about the last days

4: Paul gives his final advice and asks Timothy to visit him in prison

FEATURE HIGHLIGHTS

+ *Fear Not* (1542)
+ *Lois and Eunice: Loving to Legacy* (1543)
+ *Mentoring for Success* (1545)

Words to Remember are highlighted throughout this book

HOW LONG DOES IT TAKE TO READ?

| :10 | :30 | 1:00 | 1:30 | 2:00 | 2:30 | 3:00 | 3:30 |

Timeline

AD	Event
30	JESUS DIES, RISES FROM THE DEAD, ASCENDS TO REIGN IN HEAVEN, SENDS THE HOLY SPIRIT
35	JESUS CALLS PAUL TO PREACH THE GOOD NEWS
46-48	PAUL GOES ON FIRST MISSIONARY JOURNEY, WITH BARNABAS AND JOHN MARK
50	JERUSALEM COUNCIL CONFIRMS GENTILE INCLUSION IN THE CHURCH
50-52	PAUL EMBARKS ON SECOND MISSIONARY JOURNEY, WITH SILAS
50	PAUL MEETS PRISCILLA AND AQUILA IN CORINTH
	PAUL MEETS LYDIA IN PHILIPPI
53-57	PAUL TAKES A THIRD MISSIONARY JOURNEY
53-56	PAUL STAYS FOR AN EXTENDED TIME IN EPHESUS
57-59	PAUL IMPRISONED IN CAESAREA, WHERE HE IS QUESTIONED BY FELIX AND DRUSILLA, FESTUS, AND AGRIPPA AND BERNICE
60-62	PAUL IMPRISONED IN ROME
63	PAUL WRITES LETTERS TO TIMOTHY AND TITUS FROM MACEDONIA
64	PAUL WRITES SECOND LETTER TO TIMOTHY WHILE IMPRISONED IN ROME
64	PAUL MARTYRED IN ROME
70	ROME DESTROYS JERUSALEM

Greetings from Paul

1 This letter is from Paul, chosen by the will of God to be an apostle of Christ Jesus. I have been sent out to tell others about the life he has promised through faith in Christ Jesus.

²I am writing to Timothy, my dear son.

May God the Father and Christ Jesus our Lord give you grace, mercy, and peace.

Encouragement to Be Faithful

³Timothy, I thank God for you—the God I serve with a clear conscience, just as my ancestors did. Night and day I constantly remember you in my prayers. ⁴I long to see you again, for I remember your tears as we parted. And I will be filled with joy when we are together again.

⁵I remember your genuine faith, for you share the faith that first filled your grandmother Lois and your mother, Eunice. And I know that same faith continues strong in you. ⁶This is why I remind you to fan into flames the spiritual gift God gave you when I laid my hands on you. ⁷For God has not given us a spirit of fear and timidity, but of power, love, and self-discipline.

1:5 When Paul first met Timothy, Timothy was already a believer. He had learned about Jesus from his mother, Eunice, as well as his grandmother Lois. Lois and Eunice had become believers in Jesus as the Messiah at Lystra (Acts 16:1). These two women are good examples of how mothers and grandmothers pass their faith in and knowledge of God on to their children and how this shapes a new generation of believers to spread the gospel widely.

1:6 The Spirit's work is not automatic—it must be cultivated (see Ephesians 5:18-21; 1 Thessalonians 5:19-20; see also Acts 4:31; 7:55; 13:9). The "spiritual gift" is the Holy Spirit's enabling for ministry, and all gifts are available to both men and women (see 1 Corinthians 12:1–14:40; see also Acts 6:3, 5; 11:24). Paul and the elders (1 Timothy 4:14) had ordained Timothy for ministry with the ceremonial laying on of hands.

Come Close — FEAR NOT

SCRIPTURE CONNECTION: 2 TIMOTHY 1:7

Another sleepless night. Anxious thoughts take over my mind. Out-of-control feelings seize with unexpected force. Why can't I turn these off?

Even Timothy probably grew anxious seeing Paul struggle. How relieved he must have been when he received Paul's letter encouraging him to embrace God's spirit of power, love, and self-discipline. An aha moment.

These thoughts and feelings that keep me awake are not from God. God does not give a spirit of fear or foreboding, invading terror. If not from God, then from where or whom? Perhaps they are an inborn tendency or are brought on by the evil one.

A time in my life of being nearly crazy with fear was resolved when my husband spoke this verse in prayer. The Spirit of God gives us:

- Power: His incomparably great power for all believers. His mighty strength raised Christ from the dead (1 Corinthians 6:14).
- Love: God's love is patient, kind, humble, self-sacrificing, gentle, truthful, hopeful, and persistent (1 Corinthians 13:4-7).
- Self-discipline (or a sound mind): Our minds can focus in peace because we trust in God (Isaiah 26:3).

That God is not the author of fear is a powerful declaration. Understanding that God gives us power, love, and self-discipline provides us with tools that keep us from giving in when fear comes. The next time you feel you lack strength or your mind begins to race, you can remind yourself of God's gifts.

REFLECT "God has not given us a spirit of fear and timidity, but of power, love, and self-discipline." 2 TIMOTHY 1:7

Lord, when I get caught up in fear that overwhelms, remind me to declare your spirit of power, love, and sound mind. Amen.

CONSIDER "Your anxiety decreases as your understanding of your father [God] increases." MAX LUCADO

When I am overwhelmed, God says, "Fear not."

NANCY CHAMBERLIN SPROWLS is a devotional writer, mother, and grandmother. She encourages women to have a passion for God's Word and to leave a spiritual legacy for their families.

Lois and Eunice

IDENTITY | Loving to Legacy

They remember...

As a grandmother and a mother, we had always hoped to raise Timothy in the nurturing and knowledge of God. We were a team—Eunice and I.

Eunice mothered him, singing spiritual songs as he nursed. She soothed his crying with the love of a mother whose hope is in the Lord. My special joy as a grandma was to pray with Timothy and tell him stories of how God has cared for his people.

As Abraham, Sarah, Moses, and David came to life through my stories, I always made sure Timothy knew these were God stories. I told him God was still writing his story through all our lives.

We started young with Timothy. Before he could lisp his first word, before the Temple said he was "of age" to begin spiritual training, we pointed his heart toward God.

We were a team, Eunice and I. Timothy, and all those who followed biologically and spiritually, are our legacy.

May our children and our children's children receive our most precious legacy. May they know from earliest days their mother's God, their grandmother's heavenly Father.

LOIS AND EUNICE'S STORY IS TOLD IN 1 TIMOTHY 1:5.

> May our lives leave a legacy of young people who know God.

IDENTIFY

What child might you love toward God?

What young leader can you encourage in their calling?

"My grandson wrote me a list, '10 Things I Love About Lovie' (my grandma name), including one thing no one had ever said about me. He wrote, 'I love you because you are godly.' While I know I'm not always godly—ask my husband—it motivated me to be a grandmother like Lois."

VALERIE BELL is an author of several books on children, including *RESILIENT: Child Discipleship and the Fearless Future of the Church.* Valerie serves as Awana's CEO emerita and 2050 vision caster.

⁸So never be ashamed to tell others about our Lord. And don't be ashamed of me, either, even though I'm in prison for him. With the strength God gives you, be ready to suffer with me for the sake of the Good News. ⁹For God saved us and called us to live a holy life. He did this, not because we deserved it, but because that was his plan from before the beginning of time—to show us his grace through Christ Jesus. ¹⁰And now he has made all of this plain to us by the appearing of Christ Jesus, our Savior. He broke the power of death and illuminated the way to life and immortality through the Good News. ¹¹And God chose me to be a preacher, an apostle, and a teacher of this Good News.

¹²That is why I am suffering here in prison. But I am not ashamed of it, for I know the one in whom I trust, and I am sure that he is able to guard what I have entrusted to him* until the day of his return. ¹³Hold on to the pattern of wholesome teaching you learned from me—a pattern shaped by the faith and love that you have in Christ Jesus. ¹⁴Through the power of the Holy Spirit who lives within us, carefully guard the precious truth that has been entrusted to you.

¹⁵As you know, everyone from the province of Asia has deserted me—even Phygelus and Hermogenes.

¹⁶May the Lord show special kindness to Onesiphorus and all his family because he often visited and encouraged me. He was never ashamed of me because I was in chains. ¹⁷When he came to Rome, he searched everywhere until he found me. ¹⁸May the Lord show him special kindness on the day of Christ's return. And you know very well how helpful he was in Ephesus.

A Good Soldier of Christ Jesus

2 Timothy, my dear son, be strong through the grace that God gives you in Christ Jesus. ²You have heard me teach things that have been confirmed by many reliable witnesses. Now teach these truths to other trustworthy people who will be able to pass them on to others.

³Endure suffering along with me, as a good soldier of Christ Jesus. ⁴Soldiers don't get tied up in the affairs of civilian life, for then they cannot please the officer who enlisted them. ⁵And athletes cannot win the prize unless they follow the rules. ⁶And hardworking farmers should be the first to enjoy the fruit of their labor. ⁷Think about what I am saying. The Lord will help you understand all these things.

⁸Always remember that Jesus Christ, a descendant of King David, was raised from the dead. This is the Good News I preach. ⁹And because I preach this Good News, I am suffering and have been chained like a criminal. But the word of God cannot be chained. ¹⁰So I am willing to endure anything if it will bring salvation and eternal glory in Christ Jesus to those God has chosen.

¹¹This is a trustworthy saying:

If we die with him,
  we will also live with him.
¹² If we endure hardship,
  we will reign with him.
If we deny him,
  he will deny us.
¹³ If we are unfaithful,
  he remains faithful,
  for he cannot deny who he is.

¹⁴Remind everyone about these things, and command them in God's presence to stop fighting over words. Such arguments are useless, and they can ruin those who hear them.

An Approved Worker

¹⁵Work hard so you can present yourself to God and receive his approval. Be a good worker, one who does not need to be ashamed and who correctly explains the word of truth. ¹⁶Avoid worthless, foolish talk that only leads to more godless behavior. ¹⁷This kind of talk spreads like cancer,* as in the case of Hymenaeus and Philetus. ¹⁸They have left the path of truth, claiming that the resurrection of the dead has already occurred; in this way, they have turned some people away from the faith.

1:12 Or *what has been entrusted to me.* **2:17** Greek *gangrene.*

2:18 These false teachers might have twisted Paul's own teaching on the resurrection of the dead (Romans 6:5; Galatians 2:20; Ephesians 1:3; 2:6; 5:14; Colossians 2:12; 3:1-4) by teaching that they were already fully participating in the heavenly life, and perhaps that physical resurrection would not occur. We can't be completely certain about what they were teaching, but they could have concluded that our bodily conduct now (that is, our morality) was irrelevant, since mortal bodies could have no impact on eternal spirits. Or, they could have gone the other way, toward world-denying asceticism (1 Timothy 4:3; see Colossians 2:8, 16-23), with the idea that enjoyment of material things is inappropriate for resurrected, spiritual persons. They might have understood from Jesus' teachings (see Matthew 19:10-12; 22:30) that marriage should be prohibited (1 Timothy 4:3). Their teachings on the Old Testament law (1 Timothy 1:7-11) might have led to the promotion of certain taboos. It's also possible that their teachings might have involved an overly aggressive promotion of liberty (see 2 Timothy 3:6; compare Galatians 3:28; 1 Timothy 2:11-15) in the belief that the age to come was already here. They might have focused exclusively on resurrection power, which would contradict Paul's message of suffering and the cross (see 2 Timothy 1:8, 12; 2:8-13; compare 1 Corinthians 4:8-13; 2 Corinthians 12:8-10). Whatever its exact form, Paul describes their teaching as "worthless, foolish talk" (2 Timothy 2:16).

Mentoring for Success

SCRIPTURE CONNECTION: 2 TIMOTHY 2:1-26

Mentoring is a powerful way to encourage growth and empower people. These verses compose a loving letter to a young man Paul believed in. They convey good mentoring principles:

- *Paul was the role model.* "You have heard me teach things . . ."(2:2). Paul went first so Timothy could see and follow.
- *Paul was an encourager.* Paul encouraged Timothy to "pursue righteous living, faithfulness, love, and peace" (2:22). Paul pointed to where the joy of knowing the living God resides.
- *Paul was a cautioner.* Paul cautioned Timothy to avoid worthless talk, because "this kind of talk spreads like cancer" (2:17).
- *Paul believed the best.* Throughout this passage Paul showed he knew the impact Timothy could have.

The mentoring relationship powerfully helps people push forward to success. I have seen it in my own life as strong women and men have mentored me into leadership.

Sometimes I needed a role model, sometimes an encourager, sometimes a cautioner, and sometimes I just needed someone to believe in me.

The Bible's mentors are many, encouraging us to tap into God-ordained guiding relationships. How can you find, and be, a mentor where you are today?

> The Bible's mentors are many, encouraging us to tap into God-ordained guiding relationships.

IMAGINE

Who has been a mentor to you? How have they contributed to your success and servanthood?

How could you come alongside and encourage another to become all they can be in Christ?

"Without selfless mentors, I would not be where I am on the path God especially chose for me."

ELISABETH SELZER ROGERS, MDiv, MA, PhD, is a passionate believer and follower of Christ, bringing his love to the secular world through mentoring, coaching, and modeling his unconditional love.

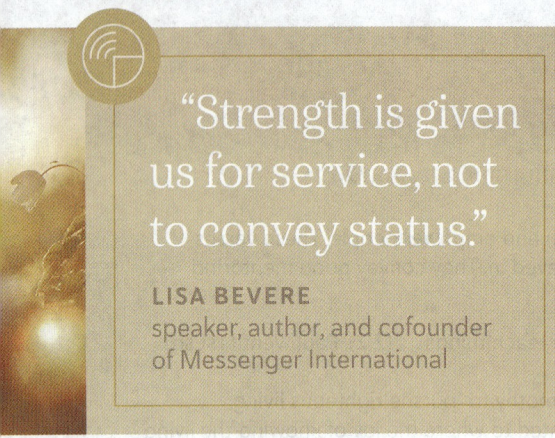

> "Strength is given us for service, not to convey status."
>
> LISA BEVERE
> speaker, author, and cofounder of Messenger International

The Dangers of the Last Days

3 You should know this, Timothy, that in the last days there will be very difficult times. ²For people will love only themselves and their money. They will be boastful and proud, scoffing at God, disobedient to their parents, and ungrateful. They will consider nothing sacred. ³They will be unloving and unforgiving; they will slander others and have no self-control. They will be cruel and hate what is good. ⁴They will betray their friends, be reckless, be puffed up with pride, and love pleasure rather than God. ⁵They will act religious, but they will reject the power that could make them godly. Stay away from people like that!

⁶They are the kind who work their way into people's homes and win the confidence of* vulnerable women who are burdened with the guilt of sin and controlled by various desires. ⁷(Such women are forever following new teachings, but they are never able to understand the truth.) ⁸These teachers oppose the truth just as Jannes and Jambres opposed Moses. They have depraved minds and a counterfeit faith. ⁹But they won't get away with this for long. Someday everyone will recognize what fools they are, just as with Jannes and Jambres.

Paul's Charge to Timothy

¹⁰But you, Timothy, certainly know what I teach, and how I live, and what my purpose in life is. You know my faith, my patience, my love, and my endurance. ¹¹You know how much persecution and suffering I have endured. You know all about how I was persecuted in Antioch, Iconium, and Lystra—but the Lord rescued me from all of it. ¹²Yes, and everyone who wants to live a godly life in Christ Jesus will suffer persecution. ¹³But evil people and impostors will flourish. They will deceive others and will themselves be deceived.

¹⁴But you must remain faithful to the things you have been taught. You know they are true, for you know you can trust those who taught you. ¹⁵You have been taught the holy Scriptures from childhood, and they have given you the wisdom to receive the salvation that comes by trusting in Christ Jesus. ¹⁶All Scripture

¹⁹But God's truth stands firm like a foundation stone with this inscription: "The Lord knows those who are his,"* and "All who belong to the Lord must turn away from evil."*

²⁰In a wealthy home some utensils are made of gold and silver, and some are made of wood and clay. The expensive utensils are used for special occasions, and the cheap ones are for everyday use. ²¹If you keep yourself pure, you will be a special utensil for honorable use. Your life will be clean, and you will be ready for the Master to use you for every good work.

²²Run from anything that stimulates youthful lusts. Instead, pursue righteous living, faithfulness, love, and peace. Enjoy the companionship of those who call on the Lord with pure hearts.

²³Again I say, don't get involved in foolish, ignorant arguments that only start fights. ²⁴A servant of the Lord must not quarrel but must be kind to everyone, be able to teach, and be patient with difficult people. ²⁵Gently instruct those who oppose the truth. Perhaps God will change those people's hearts, and they will learn the truth. ²⁶Then they will come to their senses and escape from the devil's trap. For they have been held captive by him to do whatever he wants.

2:19a Num 16:5.   2:19b See Isa 52:11.   3:6 Greek *and take captive.*

2:19-21 Paul reinforces the importance of resisting evil and remaining pure and available to the Lord because believers belong to God. Paul uses imagery about the utensils in a wealthy home to illustrate this idea (see Romans 9:21). Within God's household, Christians are to be like a utensil that is worthy of God's use at any time. Paul is saying we must live holy lives of service to God.
3:6-7 As women's education was limited due to how early they usually married, women were particularly vulnerable to false teaching. As Paul says these women were "following new teachings, but they [were] never able to understand the truth." When education stops at a young age, people's ability to discern truth in complex ideas can be limited. Paul's command is that women are to learn in the church so that they can know the truth (1 Timothy 2:12).
3:16 The fact that "Scripture is inspired by God" (literally "God-breathed," breathed out by God's own speech; see also Hebrews 4:12-13; 2 Peter 1:20-21) does not negate the active involvement of the human authors. But it does affirm that God is fully responsible for his word. Scripture is true, reliable, permanent, and powerful because it comes from God. Its message is coherent, and it is consistent in its testimony about Jesus Christ (see Luke 24:25-27, 44; John 5:39-40; Acts 3:24; 1 Corinthians 15:3-4). Scripture has the power to bring salvation and elicit faith. It must not be abused, as the false teachers had been doing (2 Timothy 4:2-4; 1 Timothy 1:4-7; see also 2 Peter 3:16), and must be taught properly by qualified people (2 Timothy 2:2, 15). Because it is inspired, all Scripture is useful. Both the Old Testament and the New Testament together are our guide and teacher in life.

is inspired by God and is useful to teach us what is true and to make us realize what is wrong in our lives. It corrects us when we are wrong and teaches us to do what is right. ¹⁷God uses it to prepare and equip his people to do every good work.

4 I solemnly urge you in the presence of God and Christ Jesus, who will someday judge the living and the dead when he comes to set up his Kingdom: ²Preach the word of God. Be prepared, whether the time is favorable or not. Patiently correct, rebuke, and encourage your people with good teaching.

³For a time is coming when people will no longer listen to sound and wholesome teaching. They will follow their own desires and will look for teachers who will tell them whatever their itching ears want to hear. ⁴They will reject the truth and chase after myths.

⁵But you should keep a clear mind in every situation. Don't be afraid of suffering for the Lord. Work at telling others the Good News, and fully carry out the ministry God has given you.

⁶As for me, my life has already been poured out as an offering to God. The time of my death is near. ⁷I have fought the good fight, I have finished the race, and I have remained faithful. ⁸And now the prize awaits me—the crown of righteousness, which the Lord, the righteous Judge, will give me on the day of his return. And the prize is not just for me but for all who eagerly look forward to his appearing.

Paul's Final Words

⁹Timothy, please come as soon as you can. ¹⁰Demas has deserted me because he loves the things of this life and has gone to Thessalonica. Crescens has gone to Galatia, and Titus has gone to Dalmatia. ¹¹Only Luke is with me. Bring Mark with you when you come, for he will be helpful to me in my ministry. ¹²I sent Tychicus to Ephesus. ¹³When you come, be sure to bring the coat I left with Carpus at Troas. Also bring my books, and especially my papers.*

¹⁴Alexander the coppersmith did me much harm, but the Lord will judge him for what he has done. ¹⁵Be careful of him, for he fought against everything we said.

¹⁶The first time I was brought before the judge, no one came with me. Everyone abandoned me. May it not be counted against them. ¹⁷But the Lord stood with me and gave me strength so that I might preach the Good News in its entirety for all the Gentiles to hear. And he rescued me from certain death.* ¹⁸Yes, and the Lord will deliver me from every evil attack and will bring me safely into his heavenly Kingdom. All glory to God forever and ever! Amen.

Paul's Final Greetings

¹⁹Give my greetings to Priscilla and Aquila and those living in the household of Onesiphorus. ²⁰Erastus stayed at Corinth, and I left Trophimus sick at Miletus.

²¹Do your best to get here before winter. Eubulus sends you greetings, and so do Pudens, Linus, Claudia, and all the brothers and sisters.*

²²May the Lord be with your spirit. And may his grace be with all of you.

4:13 Greek *especially the parchments.* **4:17** Greek *from the mouth of a lion.* **4:21** Greek *brothers.*

4:5 The Good News of Jesus does mean an escape from suffering, but Paul knew God's presence with him in difficulty. Paul was persecuted for proclaiming his faith in Jesus and suffered rejection and many beatings and imprisonments. His suffering was "for the Lord" and so purposeful. He calls for Timothy (and all Christians who read this letter) to endure their suffering and so finish their race well (4:7) and receive a crown of righteousness (4:8) when Jesus returns.

4:7 Paul had remained faithful to the trust that was committed to him (see 1:12; see also Acts 20:24). He had preserved the integrity of the Christian faith and wanted Timothy to follow his example (see 2 Timothy 2:3-7; 1 Timothy 1:18; 6:12; see also Romans 15:30-31; 1 Corinthians 9:25-27; Hebrews 12:1; Jude 1:3).

Titus

WHAT DO WE LEARN ABOUT GOD'S MISSION AND OURS?
We can live to show God's grace to others and so give God glory.

WHO WROTE IT? Paul, an apostle.

WHEN DID IT HAPPEN? Around AD 63.

HOW IS IT ORGANIZED?

1: Choosing good church leaders and correcting false teachers

2: Relating to each other in God's household

3: Living as a Jesus follower in the world

FEATURE HIGHLIGHTS

+ *Mentors: Giving for Mutual Good* (1551)

Words to Remember are highlighted throughout this book

HOW LONG DOES IT TAKE TO READ?

:10 :30 1:00 1:30 2:00 2:30 3:00 3:30

Timeline

AD	
30	JESUS DIES, RISES FROM THE DEAD, ASCENDS TO REIGN IN HEAVEN, SENDS THE HOLY SPIRIT
35	JESUS CALLS PAUL TO PREACH THE GOOD NEWS
46–48	PAUL GOES ON FIRST MISSIONARY JOURNEY, WITH BARNABAS AND JOHN MARK
50	JERUSALEM COUNCIL CONFIRMS GENTILE INCLUSION IN THE CHURCH
50–52	PAUL EMBARKS ON SECOND MISSIONARY JOURNEY, WITH SILAS; THEY SPEND 18 MONTHS IN CORINTH
50	PAUL MEETS PRISCILLA AND AQUILA IN CORINTH
	PAUL MEETS LYDIA IN PHILIPPI
53–57	PAUL TAKES A THIRD MISSIONARY JOURNEY
53–56	PAUL STAYS FOR AN EXTENDED TIME IN EPHESUS
57	PAUL ARRESTED IN JERUSALEM
57–59	PAUL IMPRISONED IN CAESAREA, WHERE HE IS QUESTIONED BY FELIX AND DRUSILLA, FESTUS, AND AGRIPPA AND BERNICE
60–62	PAUL IMPRISONED IN ROME
63	PAUL WRITES LETTERS TO TIMOTHY AND TITUS FROM MACEDONIA
64	PAUL MARTYRED IN ROME
70	ROME DESTROYS JERUSALEM

Greetings from Paul

1 This letter is from Paul, a slave of God and an apostle of Jesus Christ. I have been sent to proclaim faith to* those God has chosen and to teach them to know the truth that shows them how to live godly lives. ²This truth gives them confidence that they have eternal life, which God—who does not lie—promised them before the world began. ³And now at just the right time he has revealed this message, which we announce to everyone. It is by the command of God our Savior that I have been entrusted with this work for him.

⁴I am writing to Titus, my true son in the faith that we share.

May God the Father and Christ Jesus our Savior give you grace and peace.

Titus's Work in Crete

⁵I left you on the island of Crete so you could complete our work there and appoint elders in each town as I instructed you. ⁶An elder must live a blameless life. He must be faithful to his wife,* and his children must be believers who don't have a reputation for being wild or rebellious. ⁷A church leader* is a manager of God's household, so he must live a blameless life. He must not be arrogant or quick-tempered; he must not be a heavy drinker,* violent, or dishonest with money.

⁸Rather, he must enjoy having guests in his home, and he must love what is good. He must live wisely and be just. He must live a devout and disciplined life. ⁹He must have a strong belief in the trustworthy message he was taught; then he will be able to encourage others with wholesome teaching and show those who oppose it where they are wrong.

¹⁰For there are many rebellious people who engage in useless talk and deceive others. This is especially true of those who insist on circumcision for salvation. ¹¹They must be silenced, because they are turning whole families away from the truth by their false teaching. And they do it only for money. ¹²Even one of their own men, a prophet from Crete, has said about them, "The people of Crete are all liars, cruel animals, and lazy gluttons."* ¹³This is true. So reprimand them sternly to make them strong in the faith. ¹⁴They must stop listening to Jewish myths and the commands of people who have turned away from the truth.

¹⁵Everything is pure to those whose hearts are pure. But nothing is pure to those who are corrupt and unbelieving, because their minds and consciences are corrupted. ¹⁶Such people claim they know God, but they deny him by the way they live. They are detestable and disobedient, worthless for doing anything good.

Promote Right Teaching

2 As for you, Titus, promote the kind of living that reflects wholesome teaching. ²Teach the older men to exercise self-control, to be worthy of respect, and to live wisely. They must have sound faith and be filled with love and patience.

³Similarly, teach the older women to live in a way that honors God. They must not slander others or be heavy drinkers.* Instead, they should teach others what is good. ⁴These older women must train the younger women to love their husbands and their children, ⁵to live wisely and be pure, to work in their homes,* to do good, and to be submissive to their husbands. Then they will not bring shame on the word of God.

⁶In the same way, encourage the young men to live wisely. ⁷And you yourself must be an example to them by doing good works of every kind. Let everything you do reflect the integrity and seriousness of your teaching. ⁸Teach the truth so that your teaching can't be criticized. Then those who oppose us will be ashamed and have nothing bad to say about us.

⁹Slaves must always obey their masters and do their best to please them. They must not talk back ¹⁰or steal, but must show themselves to be entirely trustworthy and good. Then they will make the teaching about God our Savior attractive in every way.

1:1 Or *to strengthen the faith of.* **1:6** Or *must have only one wife, or must be married only once;* Greek reads *must be the husband of one wife.* **1:7a** Or *An overseer,* or *A bishop.* **1:7b** Greek *must not drink too much wine.* **1:12** This quotation is from Epimenides of Knossos. **2:3** Greek *be enslaved to much wine.* **2:5** Some manuscripts read *to care for their homes.*

1:2 The "confidence that they have eternal life" enables God's people to live in the present in light of the future (see 2:11-14; 3:7-8). The true God, "who does not lie," contrasts with popular Cretan ideas about the god Zeus. (The Cretans were accused of lying about the legend of Zeus by claiming that he had once been a human who died on Crete but whose bestowal of gifts to humans gave him god-like status.) This idea also underlines God's plan of salvation as unchanging: God can be trusted to fulfill his promises (see Numbers 23:19; 1 Samuel 15:29; Romans 3:3-4).
1:5-7 During that time, Crete was a province of the Roman Empire, and its people were considered wild and rebellious. Paul called for elders to be appointed who would decide questions about correct belief. Paul also lists the moral qualities of an elder (compare to 1 Timothy 3:2-7). There were no restrictions on the social status or ethnicity of an elder, but it's likely that many were men.
2:2-5 Paul speaks to male and female elders ("older men" and "older women"; the Greek uses male and female forms of the same noun here) about personal qualities which honor God and the importance of teaching the younger men and women. Older people who honor God can be wise guides for life. Women are encouraged to love their husbands and children and work in the home, which was expected for Greek women during this time. Most marriages were arranged and learning to love one's spouse was important for a healthy home.

Mentors

Giving for Mutual Good

I remember the first time someone asked if I would mentor them. I thought, *Who, me? What can I offer?* But God quieted my nervousness with a blanket of peace and an encouraging whisper, "You can do this because I am by your side."

Mentors can offer others a God-ordained relationship for growing together. We hunger for people who will build us up, encourage us to grow, and show us how to live well. Sometimes we find mentors easily in relationships that come naturally. But sometimes, they are difficult to find, requiring us to pray about how we might identify those who can speak to where God desires us to go.

As God's people, we are also called to *be mentors*, to "promote the kind of living that reflects wholesome teaching" (2:1). But how do we find the courage? How do we own what God has given us so that we might give it away? We do this by identifying and sharpening our God-given strengths to share with others, and by owning our challenges and sharing how we have overcome them.

We are all potential mentors and can encourage others to do good (2:12, 15). As mentors, a great charge has been given us—to model excellence and to help people to be accountable to the path God desires them to walk.

PAUL WRITES ABOUT MENTORING IN TITUS 2:1-8.

> Mentors encourage God's people to move toward his vision for their lives.

IDENTIFY

What can you offer others so that you can join the long line of godly mentors who have gone before you?

How can you come alongside another to encourage them on God's path for them?

"I have now mentored many people, and I have learned more from them than they have probably learned from me. I see each relationship as a blessing as I join God in the mentoring work he has laid out for us all."

ELISABETH SELZER ROGERS, MDiv, MA, PhD, is a passionate believer and follower of Christ, bringing his love to the secular world through mentoring, coaching, and modeling his unconditional love.

> "Truly, the best thing any of us have to bring leadership is our own transforming selves."
>
> **RUTH HALEY BARTON**
> author, spiritual director, and founder of Transforming Center

¹¹For the grace of God has been revealed, bringing salvation to all people. ¹²And we are instructed to turn from godless living and sinful pleasures. We should live in this evil world with wisdom, righteousness, and devotion to God, ¹³while we look forward with hope to that wonderful day when the glory of our great God and Savior, Jesus Christ, will be revealed. ¹⁴He gave his life to free us from every kind of sin, to cleanse us, and to make us his very own people, totally committed to doing good deeds.

¹⁵You must teach these things and encourage the believers to do them. You have the authority to correct them when necessary, so don't let anyone disregard what you say.

Do What Is Good

3 Remind the believers to submit to the government and its officers. They should be obedient, always ready to do what is good. ²They must not slander anyone and must avoid quarreling. Instead, they should be gentle and show true humility to everyone.

³Once we, too, were foolish and disobedient. We were misled and became slaves to many lusts and pleasures. Our lives were full of evil and envy, and we hated each other. ⁴But—

> When God our Savior revealed his kindness and love, ⁵he saved us, not because of the righteous things we had done, but because of his mercy. He washed away our sins, giving us a new birth and new life through the Holy Spirit.* ⁶He generously poured out the Spirit upon us through Jesus Christ our Savior. ⁷Because of his grace he made us right in his sight and gave us confidence that we will inherit eternal life.

⁸This is a trustworthy saying, and I want you to insist on these teachings so that all who trust in God will devote themselves to doing good. These teachings are good and beneficial for everyone.

⁹Do not get involved in foolish discussions about spiritual pedigrees* or in quarrels and fights about obedience to Jewish laws. These things are useless and a waste of time. ¹⁰If people are causing divisions among you, give a first and second warning. After that, have nothing more to do with them. ¹¹For people like that have turned away from the truth, and their own sins condemn them.

Paul's Final Remarks and Greetings

¹²I am planning to send either Artemas or Tychicus to you. As soon as one of them arrives, do your best to meet me at Nicopolis, for I have decided to stay there for the winter. ¹³Do everything you can to help Zenas the lawyer and Apollos with their trip. See that they are given everything they need. ¹⁴Our people must learn to do good by meeting the urgent needs of others; then they will not be unproductive.

¹⁵Everybody here sends greetings. Please give my greetings to the believers—all who love us.

May God's grace be with you all.

3:5 Greek *He saved us through the washing of regeneration and renewing of the Holy Spirit.* **3:9** Or *spiritual genealogies.*

2:14 Salvation produces a people who have the desire and capacity for the good deeds outlined in 2:2-10 (see also Ephesians 2:10). The phrase "his very own people" recalls the formation of Israel as a nation (see Exodus 19:5; Deuteronomy 7:6; 14:2). Those who follow Christ are now God's people—his nation—and the Spirit leads them to keep God's covenant.
3:1-2 In Crete, there was much civic hostility, and Paul reminds Titus that the Christians of Crete should be peaceable people who live within the laws of the government. This will make a clear distinction between them and those who are not Jesus' followers. Another possible application is that the troublemakers (1:10-16; 3:10) might have adopted unruly behaviors stemming from their erroneous teachings (as is likely the case in 1 Timothy 2:1-7). (See Paul elsewhere on relating to government officials, Romans 13:1-7; 1 Timothy 2:2.)
3:5 The contrast is between human actions that might be thought to merit salvation and God's grace (see Galatians 2:16). Salvation is through faith in God's mercy alone (Ephesians 2:8). Our new lives through the Holy Spirit signify a complete departure from the life of sin and death and a transfer into the realm of life and purity (see also Romans 12:2; 2 Corinthians 5:17; Colossians 3:10).

Philemon

WHAT DO WE LEARN ABOUT GOD'S MISSION AND OURS?
God wants us to forgive each other.

WHO WROTE IT? Paul, an apostle.

WHEN DID IT HAPPEN? About AD 60, the same time as Paul's letter to the Colossians.

HOW IS IT ORGANIZED?

- **1:1-7:** Paul greets Philemon, Apphia, Archippus, and their house church and gives thanks for Philemon
- **1:8-21:** Paul advocates for Philemon to take Onesimus back
- **1:22-25:** Paul ends with personal notes

Words to Remember are highlighted throughout this book

HOW LONG DOES IT TAKE TO READ? :05

| :30 | 1:00 | 1:30 | 2:00 | 2:30 | 3:00 | 3:30 |

Timeline

AD	Event
30	JESUS DIES, RISES FROM THE DEAD, ASCENDS TO REIGN IN HEAVEN, SENDS THE HOLY SPIRIT
35	JESUS CALLS PAUL TO PREACH THE GOOD NEWS
46-48	PAUL GOES ON FIRST MISSIONARY JOURNEY, WITH BARNABAS AND JOHN MARK
50	JERUSALEM COUNCIL CONFIRMS GENTILE INCLUSION IN THE CHURCH
50-52	PAUL EMBARKS ON SECOND MISSIONARY JOURNEY, WITH SILAS; THEY SPEND 18 MONTHS IN CORINTH
50	PAUL MEETS PRISCILLA AND AQUILA IN CORINTH
	PAUL MEETS LYDIA IN PHILIPPI
53-57	PAUL TAKES A THIRD MISSIONARY JOURNEY
53-56	PAUL STAYS FOR AN EXTENDED TIME IN EPHESUS, AND FOUNDS THE CHURCH IN COLOSSE
57	PAUL ARRESTED IN JERUSALEM
57-59	PAUL IMPRISONED IN CAESAREA, WHERE HE IS QUESTIONED BY FELIX AND DRUSILLA, FESTUS, AND AGRIPPA AND BERNICE
60-62	PAUL UNDER HOUSE ARREST IN ROME WRITES HIS LETTERS TO THE EPHESIANS, PHILIPPIANS, COLOSSIANS, AND PHILEMON
64	PAUL MARTYRED IN ROME
70	ROME DESTROYS JERUSALEM

PHILEMON

Greetings from Paul

This letter is from Paul, a prisoner for preaching the Good News about Christ Jesus, and from our brother Timothy.

I am writing to Philemon, our beloved co-worker, ²and to our sister Apphia, and to our fellow soldier Archippus, and to the church that meets in your* house.

³May God our Father and the Lord Jesus Christ give you grace and peace.

Paul's Thanksgiving and Prayer

⁴I always thank my God when I pray for you, Philemon, ⁵because I keep hearing about your faith in the Lord Jesus and your love for all of God's people. ⁶And I am praying that you will put into action the generosity that comes from your faith as you understand and experience all the good things we have in Christ. ⁷Your love has given me much joy and comfort, my brother, for your kindness has often refreshed the hearts of God's people.

Paul's Appeal for Onesimus

⁸That is why I am boldly asking a favor of you. I could demand it in the name of Christ because it is the right thing for you to do. ⁹But because of our love, I prefer simply to ask you. Consider this as a request from me—Paul, an old man and now also a prisoner for the sake of Christ Jesus.*

¹⁰I appeal to you to show kindness to my child, Onesimus. I became his father in the faith while here in prison. ¹¹Onesimus* hasn't been of much use to you in the past, but now he is very useful to both of us. ¹²I am sending him back to you, and with him comes my own heart.

¹³I wanted to keep him here with me while I am in these chains for preaching the Good News, and he would have helped me on your behalf. ¹⁴But I didn't want to do anything without your consent. I wanted you to help because you were willing, not because you were forced. ¹⁵It seems you lost Onesimus for a little while so that you could have him back forever. ¹⁶He is no longer like a slave to you. He is more than a slave, for he is a beloved brother, especially to me. Now he will mean much more to you, both as a man and as a brother in the Lord.

¹⁷So if you consider me your partner, welcome him as you would welcome me. ¹⁸If he has wronged you in any way or owes you anything, charge it to me. ¹⁹I, PAUL, WRITE THIS WITH MY OWN HAND: I WILL REPAY IT. AND I WON'T MENTION THAT YOU OWE ME YOUR VERY SOUL!

²⁰Yes, my brother, please do me this favor* for the Lord's sake. Give me this encouragement in Christ.

²¹I am confident as I write this letter that you will do what I ask and even more! ²²One more thing—please prepare a guest room for me, for I am hoping that God will answer your prayers and let me return to you soon.

Paul's Final Greetings

²³Epaphras, my fellow prisoner in Christ Jesus, sends you his greetings. ²⁴So do Mark, Aristarchus, Demas, and Luke, my co-workers.

²⁵May the grace of the Lord Jesus Christ be with your spirit.

---

2 Throughout this letter, *you* and *your* are singular except in verses 3, 22, and 25. 9 Or *a prisoner of Christ Jesus.* 11 *Onesimus* means "useful." 20 Greek *onaimen*, a play on the name Onesimus.

1:2 This is not a private letter to Philemon alone but is addressed also to his family and the church that met in their home. Apphia was probably Philemon's wife, and Archippus was probably their son (also mentioned in Colossians 4:17). Paul refers to him as a "fellow soldier" because the servant of Christ is involved in a spiritual war and must be prepared to stand firm in the face of opposition (Ephesians 6:10-17). The early Christians met together in private homes (see also Romans 16:5; 1 Corinthians 16:19; Colossians 4:15). Throughout this letter, *you* and *your* are singular except in Philemon 1:3, 22, 25.

1:8-9 Paul was "asking a favor" because Philemon had a reputation as a gracious, loving person (1:5-7). Paul could demand it by his authority as Christ's apostle, but love led Paul to request rather than demand. Paul appeals to the respect due to older people as well as to his status as "a prisoner for the sake of Christ Jesus," which would only increase a fellow Christian's respect.

1:16 An enslaved person was considered to be the property of their enslaver and had no legal rights over their own life. They could be required to perform any physical or sexual service. Paul identifies Onesimus as part of God's family and a "brother in the Lord" to Philemon. Paul called for Philemon to show Onesimus care and protection as a brother, which made them equal in status in God's family.

Hebrews

WHAT DO WE LEARN ABOUT GOD'S MISSION AND OURS?
Jesus deserves our highest trust because he is God's Son.

WHO WROTE IT? Unknown, but it was someone who knew Jewish religious practices and the Old Testament well. Probably not Paul, as the style differs. Some scholars speculate that the author could have been Priscilla.

WHEN DID IT HAPPEN? Likely written sometime between AD 60 and 70, before the Jerusalem Temple was destroyed.

HOW IS IT ORGANIZED?

- **1–2:** Jesus is God's perfect representative and is greater than the angels
- **3–4:** Jesus is greater than Moses, so we should follow him into God's promised rest for his people
- **5–7:** Jesus is a priest like Melchizedek and greater than the Old Testament priesthood
- **8–10:** Jesus is our High Priest and the sacrifice that brings us to God, once for all
- **11–12:** Old Testament examples of faithful perseverance
- **13:** Instructions for living as God's people

Words to Remember are highlighted throughout this book

FEATURE HIGHLIGHTS

+ *Hungry? Growing (1564)*
+ *Jesus Is Greater (1566)*
+ *Why Gathering Still Matters (1569)*
+ *Learning from the Great Go-Between (1570)*
+ *Rewarder: From Pressure to Pursuit (1573)*
+ *Champion: The One Who Initiates and Perfects (1577)*

HOW LONG DOES IT TAKE TO READ? :45

:30 | 1:00 | 1:30 | 2:00 | 2:30 | 3:00 | 3:30

Jesus Christ Is God's Son

1 Long ago God spoke many times and in many ways to our ancestors through the prophets. ²And now in these final days, he has spoken to us through his Son. God promised everything to the Son as an inheritance, and through the Son he created the universe. ³The Son radiates God's own glory and expresses the very character of God, and he sustains everything by the mighty power of his command. When he had cleansed us from our sins, he sat down in the place of honor at the right hand of the majestic God in heaven. ⁴This shows that the Son is far greater than the angels, just as the name God gave him is greater than their names.

The Son Is Greater Than the Angels

⁵For God never said to any angel what he said to Jesus:

"You are my Son.
  Today I have become your Father.*"

God also said,

"I will be his Father,
  and he will be my Son."*

⁶And when he brought his supreme* Son into the world, God said,*

"Let all of God's angels worship him."*

⁷Regarding the angels, he says,

"He sends his angels like the winds,
  his servants like flames of fire."*

⁸But to the Son he says,

"Your throne, O God, endures forever and ever.
  You rule with a scepter of justice.
⁹ You love justice and hate evil.
  Therefore, O God, your God has anointed you,
    pouring out the oil of joy on you more than on anyone else."*

¹⁰He also says to the Son,

"In the beginning, Lord, you laid the foundation of the earth
  and made the heavens with your hands.
¹¹ They will perish, but you remain forever.
  They will wear out like old clothing.
¹² You will fold them up like a cloak
  and discard them like old clothing.
But you are always the same;
  you will live forever."*

¹³And God never said to any of the angels,

"Sit in the place of honor at my right hand
  until I humble your enemies,
    making them a footstool under your feet."*

¹⁴Therefore, angels are only servants—spirits sent to care for people who will inherit salvation.

A Warning against Drifting Away

2 So we must listen very carefully to the truth we have heard, or we may drift away from it. ²For the message God delivered through angels has always stood firm, and every violation of the law and every act of disobedience was punished. ³So what makes us think we can escape if we ignore this great salvation that was first announced by the Lord Jesus himself and then delivered to us by those who heard him speak? ⁴And God confirmed the message by giving signs and wonders and various miracles and gifts of the Holy Spirit whenever he chose.

Jesus, the Man

⁵And furthermore, it is not angels who will control the future world we are talking about. ⁶For in one place the Scriptures say,

---

1:5a Or *Today I reveal you as my Son.* Ps 2:7. **1:5b** 2 Sam 7:14. **1:6a** Or *firstborn.* **1:6b** Or *when he again brings his supreme Son [or firstborn Son] into the world, God will say.* **1:6c** Deut 32:43. **1:7** Ps 104:4 (Greek version). **1:8-9** Ps 45:6-7. **1:10-12** Ps 102:25-27. **1:13** Ps 110:1.

1:1 "Long ago" refers to the Old Testament era, before the Messiah's coming. Throughout that past era, "God spoke many times and in many ways"—through dreams, visions, mighty acts, stories, commands, exhortations, angelic appearances, and appearances by God himself. The prophets were all those through whom God gave his revelation (see 2 Peter 1:19-21).
1:6 The supreme (or *firstborn*) son of a family in the ancient world shared the authority of the father, inherited most of his property, and was especially favored. In the New Testament, "firstborn" most frequently refers to Christ's supremacy both in the church and in the created order; his resurrection is often given as the evidence for this status (Acts 13:33; Romans 1:4; 8:29; Colossians 1:15, 18; Revelation 1:5; see Hebrews 12:23, where believers are called "firstborn children"). The quotation from Deuteronomy 32:43 demonstrates the lower status of the angels because they worship the Son.

2:3 Here the author presses the full force of the danger of turning away from Christ and his salvation. There is no escape from punishment for those who walk away, and the punishment will be of the greatest severity (see 6:4-12; 10:26-31; 12:29; Romans 2:5; 1 Thessalonians 2:16). *Salvation* refers to God's acts on behalf of his people. For example, God saved his people through the exodus from Egypt (Deuteronomy 26:5-9). In the New Testament, salvation primarily refers to Christ's work of rescuing people from the penalty of sin and giving them new life by his sacrificial death on the cross (Hebrews 5:9-10). This salvation was "first announced by the Lord Jesus himself" (for example, Matthew 4:17; 9:35; Mark 1:15; Luke 13:1-5). Jesus' message of salvation was then delivered through "those who heard him speak" to all who heard the message and put their trust in Christ (for example, Mark 6:12; Acts 2:38; 3:19-20).

God exists and... he rewards those who sincerely seek him.

HEBREWS 11:6

"What are mere mortals that you should think about them,
or a son of man* that you should care for him?
⁷ Yet for a little while you made them a little lower than the angels
and crowned them with glory and honor.*
⁸ You gave them authority over all things."*

Now when it says "all things," it means nothing is left out. But we have not yet seen all things put under their authority. ⁹What we do see is Jesus, who for a little while was given a position "a little lower than the angels"; and because he suffered death for us, he is now "crowned with glory and honor." Yes, by God's grace, Jesus tasted death for everyone. ¹⁰God, for whom and through whom everything was made, chose to bring many children into glory. And it was only right that he should make Jesus, through his suffering, a perfect leader, fit to bring them into their salvation.

¹¹So now Jesus and the ones he makes holy have the same Father. That is why Jesus is not ashamed to call them his brothers and sisters.* ¹²For he said to God,

"I will proclaim your name to my brothers and sisters.
I will praise you among your assembled people."*

¹³He also said,

"I will put my trust in him,"
that is, "I and the children God has given me."*

¹⁴Because God's children are human beings—made of flesh and blood—the Son also became flesh and blood. For only as a human being could he die, and only by dying could he break the power of the devil, who had* the power of death. ¹⁵Only in this way could he set free all who have lived their lives as slaves to the fear of dying.

¹⁶We also know that the Son did not come to help angels; he came to help the descendants of Abraham. ¹⁷Therefore, it was necessary for him to be made in every respect like us, his brothers and sisters,* so that he could be our merciful and faithful High Priest before God. Then he could offer a sacrifice that would take away the sins of the people. ¹⁸Since he himself has gone through suffering and testing, he is able to help us when we are being tested.

Jesus Is Greater Than Moses

3 And so, dear brothers and sisters who belong to God and* are partners with those called to heaven, think carefully about this Jesus whom we declare to be God's messenger* and High Priest. ²For he was faithful to God, who appointed him, just as Moses served faithfully when he was entrusted with God's entire* house.

³But Jesus deserves far more glory than Moses, just as a person who builds a house deserves more praise than the house itself. ⁴For every house has a builder, but the one who built everything is God. ⁵Moses was certainly faithful in God's house as a servant. His work was an illustration of the truths God would reveal later. ⁶But Christ, as the Son, is in charge of God's entire house. And we are God's house, if we keep our courage and remain confident in our hope in Christ.*

⁷That is why the Holy Spirit says,

"Today when you hear his voice,
⁸ don't harden your hearts
as Israel did when they rebelled,
when they tested me in the wilderness.
⁹ There your ancestors tested and tried my patience,
even though they saw my miracles for forty years.
¹⁰ So I was angry with them, and I said,
'Their hearts always turn away from me.
They refuse to do what I tell them.'
¹¹ So in my anger I took an oath:
'They will never enter my place of rest.'"*

¹²Be careful then, dear brothers and sisters.* Make sure that your own hearts are not evil and unbelieving, turning you away from the living God. ¹³You must warn each other every day, while it is still "today," so that none of you will be deceived by sin and hardened against God. ¹⁴For if we are faithful to the end, trusting God just as

---

2:6 Or *the Son of Man.* **2:7** Some manuscripts add *You gave them charge of everything you made.* **2:6-8** Ps 8:4-6 (Greek version). **2:11** Greek *brothers;* also in 2:12. **2:12** Ps 22:22. **2:13** Isa 8:17-18. **2:14** Or *has.* **2:17** Greek *like the brothers.* **3:1a** Greek *And so, holy brothers who.* **3:1b** Greek *God's apostle.* **3:2** Some manuscripts do not include *entire.* **3:6** Some manuscripts add *faithful to the end.* **3:7-11** Ps 95:7-11. **3:12** Greek *brothers.*

2:10 The author plays off the use of the identity of Jesus as "son of man" or "son," throughout 2:5-18, here referring to the "children" of God. By using *children,* the NLT makes it clear that this term refers to all God's people, male and female. The term translated "leader" had a wide range of meanings in the ancient world: *pioneer, founder, hero, champion, prince, captain, leader,* or *scout.* Jesus is a leader in that he blazed a trail for those who are saved, leading them to glory. Jesus' life as fully human equipped him as humanity's "faithful High Priest" (2:17).
3:1 Christians are holy because they belong to God and share in the fullness of all believers (both those who are alive and those who have died in faith). Focusing on Jesus is a primary means of persevering in the faith (2:9; 12:1-2). The description of Jesus as "God's messenger" might be highlighting the Son's role in bearing the proclamation of God's name and message (2:12; Matthew 10:40; Mark 9:37; Luke 10:16).
3:12-19 The author of Hebrews discusses the terms *heart, day, today, hear, enter, rest, unbelief,* and *oath,* all drawn from Psalm 95. Bible teachers of the ancient world would cite and then explain an Old Testament passage, often highlighting significant words from the text, just as teachers do today. This form of exposition is called *midrash.*
3:12 An evil heart stubbornly sets its will against the Lord due to unbelief, causing a person to turn "away from the living God."

firmly as when we first believed, we will share in all that belongs to Christ. ¹⁵Remember what it says:

> "Today when you hear his voice,
> don't harden your hearts
> as Israel did when they rebelled."*

¹⁶And who was it who rebelled against God, even though they heard his voice? Wasn't it the people Moses led out of Egypt? ¹⁷And who made God angry for forty years? Wasn't it the people who sinned, whose corpses lay in the wilderness? ¹⁸And to whom was God speaking when he took an oath that they would never enter his rest? Wasn't it the people who disobeyed him? ¹⁹So we see that because of their unbelief they were not able to enter his rest.

Promised Rest for God's People

4 God's promise of entering his rest still stands, so we ought to tremble with fear that some of you might fail to experience it. ²For this good news—that God has prepared this rest—has been announced to us just as it was to them. But it did them no good because they didn't share the faith of those who listened to God.* ³For only we who believe can enter his rest. As for the others, God said,

> "In my anger I took an oath:
> 'They will never enter my place of rest,'"*

even though this rest has been ready since he made the world. ⁴We know it is ready because of the place in the Scriptures where it mentions the seventh day: "On the seventh day God rested from all his work."* ⁵But in the other passage God said, "They will never enter my place of rest."*

⁶So God's rest is there for people to enter, but those who first heard this good news failed to enter because they disobeyed God. ⁷So God set another time for entering his rest, and that time is today. God announced this through David much later in the words already quoted:

> "Today when you hear his voice,
> don't harden your hearts."*

⁸Now if Joshua had succeeded in giving them this rest, God would not have spoken about another day of rest still to come. ⁹So there is a special rest* still waiting for the people of God. ¹⁰For all who have entered into God's rest have rested from their labors, just as God did after creating the world. ¹¹So let us do our best to enter that rest. But if we disobey God, as the people of Israel did, we will fall.

¹²For the word of God is alive and powerful. It is sharper than the sharpest two-edged sword, cutting between soul and spirit, between joint and marrow. It exposes our innermost thoughts and desires. ¹³Nothing in all creation is hidden from God. Everything is naked and exposed before his eyes, and he is the one to whom we are accountable.

Christ Is Our High Priest

¹⁴So then, since we have a great High Priest who has entered heaven, Jesus the Son of God, let us hold firmly to what we believe. ¹⁵This High Priest of ours understands our weaknesses, for he faced all of the

> "I indeed am a servant of the living God.... He alone is the end of salvation, and the basis of immortal life; for he is a refuge to the tempest-tossed, a solace to the afflicted, a shelter to the despairing."
>
> **THECLA**
> (mid-first century AD) noblewoman, death-defier, and reported follower of Paul

---

3:15 Ps 95:7-8. **4:2** Some manuscripts read *they didn't combine what they heard with faith.* **4:3** Ps 95:11. **4:4** Gen 2:2. **4:5** Ps 95:11. **4:7** Ps 95:7-8. **4:9** Or *a Sabbath rest.*

3:19 The terms *unbelief* and *disobedience* are closely associated in Hebrews and in the Old Testament (see Numbers 14:11; Deuteronomy 9:23; Psalm 78:22, 32). As a consequence of disobedience, the Israelites "were not able to enter his rest" by entering the land of Canaan (Deuteronomy 12:10; Joshua 1:13).

4:1-2 The author transitions to the promise that the faithful will enter God's rest and exhorts his listeners to take this promise seriously. Hearing is not enough: It must be combined with faith. To fear God means to have an appropriate reverence, even awe, for God and his will. It would be the worst of tragedies to "fail to experience" what God has promised. "This good news" is the message of salvation (2:3-4), but the original hearers were deficient in faith, distrusting God's word of promise, so they were unable to enter God's rest.

4:15 Our High Priest "understands our weaknesses," our human pull toward sin, because "he faced all of the same testings we do." He was tempted with all the essential aspects of sin, such as lust, greed, unforgiveness, and dishonesty. This makes him compassionate as our High Priest (5:2). Jesus is unlike the earthly high priests, who had to make offerings for their own sins before they could make offerings for the people, because he is without sin (5:3; 7:26-28; see also 1 Peter 2:22-23).

same testings we do, yet he did not sin. ¹⁶So let us come boldly to the throne of our gracious God. There we will receive his mercy, and we will find grace to help us when we need it most.

5 Every high priest is a man chosen to represent other people in their dealings with God. He presents their gifts to God and offers sacrifices for their sins. ²And he is able to deal gently with ignorant and wayward people because he himself is subject to the same weaknesses. ³That is why he must offer sacrifices for his own sins as well as theirs. ⁴And no one can become a high priest simply because he wants such an honor. He must be called by God for this work, just as Aaron was. ⁵That is why Christ did not honor himself by assuming he could become High Priest. No, he was chosen by God, who said to him,

"You are my Son.
  Today I have become your Father."*

⁶And in another passage God said to him,

"You are a priest forever in the order of
  Melchizedek."*

5:5 Or *Today I reveal you as my Son.* Ps 2:7.   **5:6** Ps 110:4.

5:2 A high priest was able to deal gently with those who sin because he was "subject to the same weaknesses," that is, he also sinned (5:3; contrast Jesus' high priesthood, 4:15). Jesus, as our High Priest, died in our place and is praying for us right now (Romans 8:34). We can trust him to be our true friend; he is gentle with his own, so we can turn to him in our frailties (Hebrews 4:15-16).

Come Close — HUNGRY? GROWING

SCRIPTURE CONNECTION: HEBREWS 5:11–6:3

Adults require a variety of foods for survival, whereas milk can satisfy babies, for a while. Little ones let us know when they're ready for solid food by being insatiably hungry, fussy, and crying out for more.

So it's no wonder a good parent wants their child to progress from solely drinking milk to eating solid foods. Parents want to see their children grow and develop, and eating solid food is one sign that's happening. In the same vein, God desires that we progress from a basic understanding to a deeper comprehension of biblical truths.

In Hebrews 5 and 6, we see Christians who should be mature still requiring milk. Just like newborns do not crave solid food, immature believers cannot desire heartier teaching overnight. But we must begin to cultivate a taste for it by consistently feeding our hunger with God's Word.

It's so easy to get comfortable with what we already know. Perhaps we so savor peace in our busy lives that we lose the desire to attain maturity in Christ. Yet, as we grow, we can also teach others and help them know God.

Strive for growth and maturity in Christ, as God's truths are satisfyingly rich. We will never lack when we seek him because he feeds us the insight we need, freely. Let's move beyond baby food to savor God's solid truths.

REFLECT "Let us stop going over the basic teachings about Christ again and again. Let us go on instead and become mature in our understanding." HEBREWS 6:1

Lord, help me resist the lure to stay comfortable with what I know but instead to desire and grow in your word and go on to maturity. Amen.

CONSIDER "Each stage of the believer's walk possesses its particular hazard. The new life within us wages a constant war against all which opposes its growth." WATCHMAN NEE

Let's move beyond baby food to savor God's solid truths.

STEPHANIE THOMAS is a follower of Jesus Christ. She is the coordinator and a contributing author at Pruned Life. She is also a gospel singer.

⁷While Jesus was here on earth, he offered prayers and pleadings, with a loud cry and tears, to the one who could rescue him from death. And God heard his prayers because of his deep reverence for God. ⁸Even though Jesus was God's Son, he learned obedience from the things he suffered. ⁹In this way, God qualified him as a perfect High Priest, and he became the source of eternal salvation for all those who obey him. ¹⁰And God designated him to be a High Priest in the order of Melchizedek.

A Call to Spiritual Growth

¹¹There is much more we would like to say about this, but it is difficult to explain, especially since you are spiritually dull and don't seem to listen. ¹²You have been believers so long now that you ought to be teaching others. Instead, you need someone to teach you again the basic things about God's word.* You are like babies who need milk and cannot eat solid food. ¹³For someone who lives on milk is still an infant and doesn't know how to do what is right. ¹⁴Solid food is for those who are mature, who through training have the skill to recognize the difference between right and wrong.

6 So let us stop going over the basic teachings about Christ again and again. Let us go on instead and become mature in our understanding. Surely we don't need to start again with the fundamental importance of repenting from evil deeds* and placing our faith in God. ²You don't need further instruction about baptisms, the laying on of hands, the resurrection of the dead, and eternal judgment. ³And so, God willing, we will move forward to further understanding.

⁴For it is impossible to bring back to repentance those who were once enlightened—those who have experienced the good things of heaven and shared in the Holy Spirit, ⁵who have tasted the goodness of the word of God and the power of the age to come—⁶and who then turn away from God. It is impossible to bring such people back to repentance; by rejecting the Son of God, they themselves are nailing him to the cross once again and holding him up to public shame.

⁷When the ground soaks up the falling rain and bears a good crop for the farmer, it has God's blessing. ⁸But if a field bears thorns and thistles, it is useless. The farmer will soon condemn that field and burn it.

⁹Dear friends, even though we are talking this way, we really don't believe it applies to you. We are confident that you are meant for better things, things that come with salvation. ¹⁰For God is not unjust. He will not forget how hard you have worked for him and how you have shown your love to him by caring for other believers,* as you still do. ¹¹Our great desire is that you will keep on loving others as long as life lasts, in order to make certain that what you hope for will come true. ¹²Then you will not become spiritually dull and indifferent. Instead, you will follow the example of those who are going to inherit God's promises because of their faith and endurance.

God's Promises Bring Hope

¹³For example, there was God's promise to Abraham. Since there was no one greater to swear by, God took an oath in his own name, saying:

¹⁴ "I will certainly bless you,
    and I will multiply your descendants beyond number."*

¹⁵Then Abraham waited patiently, and he received what God had promised.

¹⁶Now when people take an oath, they call on someone greater than themselves to hold them to it. And without any question that oath is binding. ¹⁷God also bound himself with an oath, so that those who received the promise could be perfectly sure that he would never change his mind. ¹⁸So God has given both his promise and his oath. These two things are unchangeable because it is impossible for God to lie. Therefore, we who have fled to him for refuge can have great confidence as we hold to the hope that lies before us. ¹⁹This hope is a strong and trustworthy anchor for our souls. It leads us through the curtain into God's inner sanctuary. ²⁰Jesus has already gone in there for us. He has become our eternal High Priest in the order of Melchizedek.

5:12 Or *about the oracles of God.*   6:1 Greek *from dead works.*   6:10 Greek *for God's holy people.*   6:14 Gen 22:17.

5:12 The believers' lack of spiritual vitality was especially shocking since they had been believers for a long time: They ought to have been spiritual leaders who were teaching others from their wealth of knowledge and Christian experience. The "basic things" are the most rudimentary aspects of the Christian faith (see 6:1-3). The imagery of milk and solid food was used to distinguish basic from advanced education and immature from mature students. We are to move to solid food, which represents maturity (see 5:14).
6:2 The term *baptisms* is plural, so it must mean more than just Christian baptism. Instruction about various washings was prevalent in first-century Judaism (see Matthew 15:2; Mark 7:3). The author might also have in mind the cleansing rituals of the Old Testament (see Hebrews 9:13; 10:22). The laying on of hands was associated with healing (Mark 5:22-23; Luke 13:13), ritual blessing (Matthew 19:13, 15), the reception of the Holy Spirit (Acts 8:17; 9:17; 19:6), and acknowledgement of a person's ministry (Acts 6:6; 13:2-3).
6:10 In showing that they love God and his people, their works bear witness to their true relationship with God (Romans 2:6-7; 1 Corinthians 3:13-15; James 2:14-20). God remembers (Exodus 2:24; 1 Chronicles 16:15; Psalm 106:45) and acknowledges those who are truly his.

Insight: Jesus Is Greater

Hebrews emphasizes that Jesus is the final and greatest revelation of God's plan and purpose for everything. The author of Hebrews makes the case for this by highlighting important people and practices of the old covenant and showing how Jesus has fulfilled and surpassed each one. Because of his exceeding greatness, Jesus deserves our worship and commitment.

JESUS IS GREATER THAN

PROPHETS Hebrews 1:1-2	**ANGELS** Hebrews 1:4, 5-14	**MOSES** Hebrews 3:3	**JOSHUA'S "REST"** Hebrews 4:8	**HIGH PRIESTS** Hebrews 7:23-28	**TABERNACLE** Hebrews 9:24	**SACRIFICE** Hebrews 10:11-12
Jesus clarifies the messages of the prophets.	Jesus surpasses the angels.	Jesus fulfills Moses' role between God and humans.	Jesus provides the final rest for God's people.	Jesus serves permanently as High Priest.	Jesus completes the Tabernacle's function.	Jesus is the perfect sacrifice for all time.

Melchizedek Is Greater Than Abraham

7 This Melchizedek was king of the city of Salem and also a priest of God Most High. When Abraham was returning home after winning a great battle against the kings, Melchizedek met him and blessed him. ²Then Abraham took a tenth of all he had captured in battle and gave it to Melchizedek. The name Melchizedek means "king of justice," and king of Salem means "king of peace." ³There is no record of his father or mother or any of his ancestors—no beginning or end to his life. He remains a priest forever, resembling the Son of God.

⁴Consider then how great this Melchizedek was. Even Abraham, the great patriarch of Israel, recognized this by giving him a tenth of what he had taken in battle. ⁵Now the law of Moses required that the priests, who are descendants of Levi, must collect a tithe from the rest of the people of Israel,* who are also descendants of Abraham. ⁶But Melchizedek, who was not a descendant of Levi, collected a tenth from Abraham. And Melchizedek placed a blessing upon Abraham, the one who had already received the promises of God. ⁷And without question, the person who has the power to give a blessing is greater than the one who is blessed.

7:5 Greek *from their brothers.*

7:2 Abraham was giving a tenth to the Lord by giving it to Melchizedek, the Lord's priest. This act anticipates the giving of tithes under the law (Leviticus 27:30, 32) and becomes a key point in the author's argument (Hebrews 7:4). *Melchi-* (Hebrew *melek*) means "king"; *-zedek* (Hebrew *tsedeq*) means "justice" or "righteousness." *Salem* (Hebrew *shalom*) means "peace." It was common for rabbis to bring out the theological significance of a biblical figure's name by making associations between the name and other Hebrew terms.

7:6-7 Although Melchizedek wasn't a descendant of Levi, he "collected a tenth from Abraham," the ancestor of the Levites. This demonstrates Melchizedek's eminence over both Abraham and his descendants, including the priests (7:8-10). Melchizedek's blessing (Genesis 14:19-20) is an example of the kind of blessing that a superior would give a subordinate—for example, a father would bless his children, and a priest would bless his people (Numbers 6:22-27). The power to give a blessing demonstrates that Melchizedek is greater than Abraham.

⁸The priests who collect tithes are men who die, so Melchizedek is greater than they are, because we are told that he lives on. ⁹In addition, we might even say that these Levites—the ones who collect the tithe—paid a tithe to Melchizedek when their ancestor Abraham paid a tithe to him. ¹⁰For although Levi wasn't born yet, the seed from which he came was in Abraham's body when Melchizedek collected the tithe from him.

¹¹So if the priesthood of Levi, on which the law was based, could have achieved the perfection God intended, why did God need to establish a different priesthood, with a priest in the order of Melchizedek instead of the order of Levi and Aaron?*

¹²And if the priesthood is changed, the law must also be changed to permit it. ¹³For the priest we are talking about belongs to a different tribe, whose members have never served at the altar as priests. ¹⁴What I mean is, our Lord came from the tribe of Judah, and Moses never mentioned priests coming from that tribe.

Jesus Is like Melchizedek

¹⁵This change has been made very clear since a different priest, who is like Melchizedek, has appeared. ¹⁶Jesus became a priest, not by meeting the physical requirement of belonging to the tribe of Levi, but by the power of a life that cannot be destroyed. ¹⁷And the psalmist pointed this out when he prophesied,

"You are a priest forever in the order of Melchizedek."*

¹⁸Yes, the old requirement about the priesthood was set aside because it was weak and useless. ¹⁹For the law never made anything perfect. But now we have confidence in a better hope, through which we draw near to God.

²⁰This new system was established with a solemn oath. Aaron's descendants became priests without such an oath, ²¹but there was an oath regarding Jesus. For God said to him,

"The LORD has taken an oath and will not break his vow:
'You are a priest forever.'"*

²²Because of this oath, Jesus is the one who guarantees this better covenant with God.

²³There were many priests under the old system, for death prevented them from remaining in office. ²⁴But because Jesus lives forever, his priesthood lasts forever. ²⁵Therefore he is able, once and forever, to save* those who come to God through him. He lives forever to intercede with God on their behalf.

²⁶He is the kind of high priest we need because he is holy and blameless, unstained by sin. He has been set apart from sinners and has been given the highest place of honor in heaven.* ²⁷Unlike those other high priests, he does not need to offer sacrifices every day. They did this for their own sins first and then for the sins of the people. But Jesus did this once for all when he offered himself as the sacrifice for the people's sins. ²⁸The law appointed high priests who were limited by human weakness. But after the law was given, God appointed his Son with an oath, and his Son has been made the perfect High Priest forever.

Christ Is Our High Priest

8 Here is the main point: We have a High Priest who sat down in the place of honor beside the throne of the majestic God in heaven. ²There he ministers in the heavenly Tabernacle,* the true place of worship that was built by the Lord and not by human hands.

³And since every high priest is required to offer gifts and sacrifices, our High Priest must make an offering, too. ⁴If he were here on earth, he would not even be a priest, since there already are priests who offer the gifts required by the law. ⁵They serve in a system of worship that is only a copy, a shadow of the real one in heaven. For when Moses was getting ready to build the Tabernacle, God gave him this warning: "Be sure that you make everything according to the pattern I have shown you here on the mountain."*

7:11 Greek *the order of Aaron?* **7:17** Ps 110:4. **7:21** Ps 110:4. **7:25** Or *is able to save completely.* **7:26** Or *has been exalted higher than the heavens.* **8:2** Or *tent;* also in 8:5. **8:5** Exod 25:40; 26:30.

7:26-27 Jesus is "unstained by sin" and "set apart from sinners" (see 4:15), which makes him superior to the priests of the old covenant, who had to deal with their own sins as well as those of the people (see also 5:1-3). Being "given the highest place of honor in heaven" is an affirmation of his uniqueness as High Priest (see 2:9; 5:9; Philippians 2:5-11). "Once for all" does not mean *once for all people* but rather *once, never to be repeated.*
8:1-3 The first two verses of this chapter transition from the discussion just completed and anticipate the discussion to come. The author is referring to the main purpose of Jesus' appointment as a superior High Priest (5:1-10; 7:1-28). Jesus' ministry in the "heavenly Tabernacle" anticipates the theme of his superior offering that is covered in the rest of this section (8:3–10:18). Unlike the Levitical priests who served in an earthly tent or building, Jesus' sacrifice is superior because he serves in "the true place of worship," the very presence of God in heaven (8:5; 9:11, 24; 10:12). Making offerings is a general requirement of priests, so Jesus also had to offer a sacrifice. Hebrews 8:3 reiterates what is stated in the first verse of the previous discussion (5:1), indicating another major movement in the book.
8:5 The earthly place of worship was an imitation that pointed to "the real one in heaven." That is why God warned Moses to make it "according to the pattern" that God gave him (see Exodus 25:40; 26:30; compare Acts 7:44). Judaism and early Christianity both spoke of a heavenly Temple within a heavenly Jerusalem, which would come down to earth at the end of the age (see Revelation 11:19; 21:2). Hebrews suggests that this heavenly place of worship was shown to Moses so he would know how to build the earthly Tabernacle. It is the heavenly Temple, however, in which Jesus ministers as High Priest.

⁶But now Jesus, our High Priest, has been given a ministry that is far superior to the old priesthood, for he is the one who mediates for us a far better covenant with God, based on better promises.

⁷If the first covenant had been faultless, there would have been no need for a second covenant to replace it. ⁸But when God found fault with the people, he said:

"The day is coming, says the LORD,
when I will make a new covenant
with the people of Israel and Judah.
⁹ This covenant will not be like the one
I made with their ancestors
when I took them by the hand
and led them out of the land of Egypt.
They did not remain faithful to my covenant,
so I turned my back on them, says the LORD.
¹⁰ But this is the new covenant I will make
with the people of Israel on that day,*
says the LORD:
I will put my laws in their minds,
and I will write them on their hearts.
I will be their God,
and they will be my people.
¹¹ And they will not need to teach their neighbors,
nor will they need to teach their relatives,*
saying, 'You should know the LORD.'
For everyone, from the least to the greatest,
will know me already.
¹² And I will forgive their wickedness,
and I will never again remember their sins."*

¹³When God speaks of a "new" covenant, it means he has made the first one obsolete. It is now out of date and will soon disappear.

Old Rules about Worship

9 That first covenant between God and Israel had regulations for worship and a place of worship here on earth. ²There were two rooms in that Tabernacle.* In the first room were a lampstand, a table, and sacred loaves of bread on the table. This room was called the Holy Place. ³Then there was a curtain, and behind the curtain was the second room* called the Most Holy Place. ⁴In that room were a gold incense altar and a wooden chest called the Ark of the Covenant, which was covered with gold on all sides. Inside the Ark were a gold jar containing manna, Aaron's staff that sprouted leaves, and the stone tablets of the covenant. ⁵Above the Ark were the cherubim of divine glory, whose wings stretched out over the Ark's cover, the place of atonement. But we cannot explain these things in detail now.

⁶When these things were all in place, the priests regularly entered the first room* as they performed their religious duties. ⁷But only the high priest ever entered the Most Holy Place, and only once a year. And he always offered blood for his own sins and for the sins the people had committed in ignorance. ⁸By these regulations the Holy Spirit revealed that the entrance to the Most Holy Place was not freely open as long as the Tabernacle* and the system it represented were still in use.

⁹This is an illustration pointing to the present time. For the gifts and sacrifices that the priests offer are not able to cleanse the consciences of the people who bring them. ¹⁰For that old system deals only with food and drink and various cleansing ceremonies—physical regulations that were in effect only until a better system could be established.

Christ Is the Perfect Sacrifice

¹¹So Christ has now become the High Priest over all the good things that have come.* He has entered that greater, more perfect Tabernacle in heaven, which was not made by human hands and is not part of this created world. ¹²With his own blood—not the blood of goats and calves—he entered the Most Holy Place once for all time and secured our redemption forever.

¹³Under the old system, the blood of goats and bulls and the ashes of a heifer could cleanse people's bodies from ceremonial impurity. ¹⁴Just think how much more the blood of Christ will purify our consciences from sinful deeds* so that we can worship the living God. For by

---

8:10 Greek *after those days.* 8:11 Greek *their brother.* 8:8-12 Jer 31:31-34. 9:2 Or *tent;* also in 9:11, 21. 9:3 Greek *second tent.* 9:6 Greek *first tent.* 9:8 Or *the first room;* Greek reads *the first tent.* 9:11 Some manuscripts read *that are about to come.* 9:14 Greek *from dead works.*

9:2-3 Israel's Tabernacle (or *tent;* also in 9:11, 21) was a tent with two rooms (see Exodus 25:1–31:11; 35:4–40:38). In the first room, the Holy Place, stood a lampstand (Exodus 25:31-40; 26:35) and a table for the sacred loaves of bread (Exodus 25:23-30). The priests went into the Holy Place daily in their ritual duties (Hebrews 9:6; see Exodus 28:43; Numbers 28:3-8). At the back of the first room of the Tabernacle was a curtain that separated the first room from the second room (literally *second tent*) called the Most Holy Place (Exodus 26:31-33). This curtain was a sacred barrier: Only the high priest could go behind it into the Most Holy Place, and only once a year on the Day of Atonement (Hebrews 9:7; see Exodus 30:6, 10; Leviticus 16:2-34; 23:26-32). **9:8** Free entrance into the presence of God was not available to all the people under the old covenant system. The outer room of the Tabernacle (or "the first room"; literally *the first tent;* see 9:2), which served as a sacred barrier keeping the people from the presence of God in the Most Holy Place, was symbolic of the whole system. Under that system, people were kept out of God's presence rather than led into it.
9:12 Christ's offering is superior because it was made "with his own blood" rather than "the blood of goats and calves" (for example, compare Leviticus 16:3-5). Christ's offering is superior because "he entered the Most Holy Place once for all time." Unlike the sacrifices in the old covenant, which had to be made year after year (Hebrews 10:1), Jesus' sacrificial death only had to be made once and was decisive in securing "our redemption forever."

Koinonia

IMAGE — MY STORY WITH COMMUNITY, WORKPLACE & CHURCH

Why Gathering Still Matters

SCRIPTURE CONNECTION: HEBREWS 9:11-28

As a mother of young children, I equated getting through the church doors with completing a triathlon race! When you cross the threshold, you, too, may find yourself exhausted.

Between finding shoes and outfits, making breakfast, dealing with a tantrum or two... going to a church gathering may feel like a hassle. At times, our individualistic societies challenge gathering. And we may find ourselves asking, *Is it worth it?*

Here in Hebrews 9:11-28, we see gathering in its ancient context; the Tabernacle and the functions of the high priest brought God's divine presence to the people. In this passage, we notice that all the Tabernacle activities now point to Christ. He became the final sacrifice for our sins, ushering in the new covenant. Jesus is our *Immanuel*, God with us!

Gathering roots us in whose we are and who we are. We remember our story as the people of God, now belonging to Jesus. Gathering also connects us, encouraging and enabling us to encourage others. In ancient times, such as we read in the book of Psalms, people from every life sphere and season gathered to sing, give thanks, lament, and praise.

Hebrews 10:24-25 specifically tells us to keep encouraging one another and not neglect meeting. Even when it's hard or we're tired, gathering is worth it because we need to be reminded who we are and whose we are. We need to encourage and be encouraged. Even when it is difficult, gathering together refreshes us in who and what we are made for.

> To worship and encourage one another, we gather as the church through all seasons of our lives.

IMAGINE

Have you ever been encouraged by the community when you went to worship?

How has God created you to encourage others?

"Even if it feels challenging when life is crazy to gather, I am always amazed at how the Christian community reorients our identity back as ones loved by Jesus!"

JENNIFER M. MATHENY, PhD, is associate professor of Old Testament at Nazarene Theological Seminary, Missouri, and director of the Wynkoop Center for Women in Leadership. She enjoys speaking engagements and research.

the power of the eternal Spirit, Christ offered himself to God as a perfect sacrifice for our sins. ¹⁵That is why he is the one who mediates a new covenant between God and people, so that all who are called can receive the eternal inheritance God has promised them. For Christ died to set them free from the penalty of the sins they had committed under that first covenant.

¹⁶Now when someone leaves a will,* it is necessary to prove that the person who made it is dead.* ¹⁷The will goes into effect only after the person's death. While the person who made it is still alive, the will cannot be put into effect.

¹⁸That is why even the first covenant was put into effect with the blood of an animal. ¹⁹For after Moses had read each of God's commandments to all the people, he took the blood of calves and goats,* along with water, and sprinkled both the book of God's law and all the people, using hyssop branches and scarlet wool. ²⁰Then he said, "This blood confirms the covenant God has made with you."* ²¹And in the same way, he sprinkled

9:16a Or *covenant*; also in 9:17. 9:16b Or *Now when someone makes a covenant, it is necessary to ratify it with the death of a sacrifice*. 9:19 Some manuscripts do not include *and goats*. 9:20 Exod 24:8.

Learning from the Great Go-Between

SCRIPTURE CONNECTION: HEBREWS 9:13-15

When my husband wanted to ask for my hand in marriage twenty years ago, he could not just approach my father, directly. Rather, a "go-between" used flowery, persuasive language and great negotiation skills to win the approval of my father and the clan elders.

I come from Uganda, an East African country with a population of about forty-six million people from fifty-six different tribes. One commonality in our cultures is how a "go-between" facilitates a marriage.

Although these days we no longer have as many arranged marriages, a young man still needs his family's blessing and that of the woman he is interested in marrying. That is where the go-between comes in. The groom's family will select someone either known to the bride's family or someone who understands the bride's culture (often both), so their request for her hand in marriage will be looked upon favorably.

> We can serve others as a go-between, just like Jesus does for us.

In this passage and elsewhere, we see Jesus is the go-between, setting up a new agreement for us, the bride of Christ, to enter into a covenant with God (see also 1 Timothy 2:5; Hebrews 8:6; 12:24; 1 John 2:1-2). We, also, are called go-betweens, introducing God and his wonderful gift of salvation through Jesus Christ to those who do not know him.

To present this Good News in a way that can be accepted, as Jesus did, we can learn from Ugandan go-betweens. We can learn to understand the others' situations and minister to them in their space and language. Ultimately, it is important for us to serve others as Jesus did.

IMAGINE

How do you respond to the idea of God pursuing you and sending Jesus to start a new relationship?

What kind of bridge are you between Christ and those who do not know him?

"I am thankful for the dear go-between who launched my marriage and advised my husband and [me] ever since. Just so, I am thankful for Jesus, my go-between to God and ever-present help."

DAISY ASIIMWE BYARUGABA is a learning and development professional passionate about empowering people to become the most productive version of themselves that God intended. She and her husband minister at Church of the Resurrection, Bugolobi, in Kampala, Uganda.

blood on the Tabernacle and on everything used for worship. ²²In fact, according to the law of Moses, nearly everything was purified with blood. For without the shedding of blood, there is no forgiveness.

²³That is why the Tabernacle and everything in it, which were copies of things in heaven, had to be purified by the blood of animals. But the real things in heaven had to be purified with far better sacrifices than the blood of animals.

²⁴For Christ did not enter into a holy place made with human hands, which was only a copy of the true one in heaven. He entered into heaven itself to appear now before God on our behalf. ²⁵And he did not enter heaven to offer himself again and again, like the high priest here on earth who enters the Most Holy Place year after year with the blood of an animal. ²⁶If that had been necessary, Christ would have had to die again and again, ever since the world began. But now, once for all time, he has appeared at the end of the age* to remove sin by his own death as a sacrifice.

²⁷And just as each person is destined to die once and after that comes judgment, ²⁸so also Christ was offered once for all time as a sacrifice to take away the sins of many people. He will come again, not to deal with our sins, but to bring salvation to all who are eagerly waiting for him.

Christ's Sacrifice Once for All

10 The old system under the law of Moses was only a shadow, a dim preview of the good things to come, not the good things themselves. The sacrifices under that system were repeated again and again, year after year, but they were never able to provide perfect cleansing for those who came to worship. ²If they could have provided perfect cleansing, the sacrifices would have stopped, for the worshipers would have been purified once for all time, and their feelings of guilt would have disappeared.

³But instead, those sacrifices actually reminded them of their sins year after year. ⁴For it is not possible for the blood of bulls and goats to take away sins. ⁵That is why, when Christ* came into the world, he said to God,

"You did not want animal sacrifices or sin offerings.
But you have given me a body to offer.
⁶ You were not pleased with burnt offerings
or other offerings for sin.
⁷ Then I said, 'Look, I have come to do your will,
O God—
as is written about me in the Scriptures.'"*

⁸First, Christ said, "You did not want animal sacrifices or sin offerings or burnt offerings or other offerings for sin, nor were you pleased with them" (though they are required by the law of Moses). ⁹Then he said, "Look, I have come to do your will." He cancels the first covenant in order to put the second into effect. ¹⁰For God's will was for us to be made holy by the sacrifice of the body of Jesus Christ, once for all time.

¹¹Under the old covenant, the priest stands and ministers before the altar day after day, offering the same sacrifices again and again, which can never take away sins. ¹²But our High Priest offered himself to God as a single sacrifice for sins, good for all time. Then he sat down in the place of honor at God's right hand. ¹³There he waits until his enemies are humbled and made a footstool under his feet. ¹⁴For by that one offering he forever made perfect those who are being made holy.

¹⁵And the Holy Spirit also testifies that this is so. For he says,

¹⁶ "This is the new covenant I will make
    with my people on that day,* says the LORD:
I will put my laws in their hearts,
    and I will write them on their minds."*

¹⁷Then he says,

"I will never again remember
    their sins and lawless deeds."*

¹⁸And when sins have been forgiven, there is no need to offer any more sacrifices.

A Call to Persevere

¹⁹And so, dear brothers and sisters,* we can boldly enter heaven's Most Holy Place because of the blood of Jesus. ²⁰By his death,* Jesus opened a new and life-giving way through the curtain into the Most Holy Place. ²¹And since we have a great High Priest who rules over God's house, ²²let us go right into the presence of God with sincere hearts fully trusting him. For our guilty consciences have been sprinkled with Christ's blood to make us clean, and our bodies have been washed with pure water.

²³Let us hold tightly without wavering to the hope we affirm, for God can be trusted to keep his promise. ²⁴Let us think of ways to motivate one another to acts of love and good works. ²⁵And let us not neglect our meeting together, as some people do, but encourage one another, especially now that the day of his return is drawing near.

9:26 Greek *the ages.* **10:5** Greek *he;* also in 10:8. **10:5-7** Ps 40:6-8 (Greek version). **10:16a** Greek *after those days.* **10:16b** Jer 31:33a. **10:17** Jer 31:34b. **10:19** Greek *brothers.* **10:20** Greek *Through his flesh.*

10:19-25 The author of Hebrews repeats words and concepts from 4:14-16 to mark off and summarize the central section of the book (4:14–10:18) and to introduce the exhortations that follow, offering a concise statement of the message of Hebrews: The new covenant, established by Jesus' superior ministry, gives us a superior basis for drawing near to God and for persevering in the Christian life. We can "boldly enter" the presence of God (10:19) when we have "sincere [or true] hearts" (10:22). A true heart points to genuineness and loyalty and is a fulfilment of Jeremiah 31:33; Ezekiel 36:26-27.

²⁶Dear friends, if we deliberately continue sinning after we have received knowledge of the truth, there is no longer any sacrifice that will cover these sins. ²⁷There is only the terrible expectation of God's judgment and the raging fire that will consume his enemies. ²⁸For anyone who refused to obey the law of Moses was put to death without mercy on the testimony of two or three witnesses. ²⁹Just think how much worse the punishment will be for those who have trampled on the Son of God, and have treated the blood of the covenant, which made us holy, as if it were common and unholy, and have insulted and disdained the Holy Spirit who brings God's mercy to us. ³⁰For we know the one who said,

"I will take revenge.
I will pay them back."*

He also said,

"The LORD will judge his own people."*

³¹It is a terrible thing to fall into the hands of the living God.

³²Think back on those early days when you first learned about Christ.* Remember how you remained faithful even though it meant terrible suffering. ³³Sometimes you were exposed to public ridicule and were beaten, and sometimes you helped others who were suffering the same things. ³⁴You suffered along with those who were thrown into jail, and when all you owned was taken from you, you accepted it with joy. You knew there were better things waiting for you that will last forever.

³⁵So do not throw away this confident trust in the Lord. Remember the great reward it brings you! ³⁶Patient endurance is what you need now, so that you will continue to do God's will. Then you will receive all that he has promised.

³⁷ "For in just a little while,
the Coming One will come and not delay.
³⁸ And my righteous ones will live by faith.*
But I will take no pleasure in anyone who turns away."*

³⁹But we are not like those who turn away from God to their own destruction. We are the faithful ones, whose souls will be saved.

Great Examples of Faith

11 Faith shows the reality of what we hope for; it is the evidence of things we cannot see. ²Through their faith, the people in days of old earned a good reputation.

³By faith we understand that the entire universe was formed at God's command, that what we now see did not come from anything that can be seen.

⁴It was by faith that Abel brought a more acceptable offering to God than Cain did. Abel's offering gave evidence that he was a righteous man, and God showed his approval of his gifts. Although Abel is long dead, he still speaks to us by his example of faith.

⁵It was by faith that Enoch was taken up to heaven without dying—"he disappeared, because God took him."* For before he was taken up, he was known as a person who pleased God. ⁶And it is impossible to please God without faith. Anyone who wants to come to him must believe that God exists and that he rewards those who sincerely seek him.

⁷It was by faith that Noah built a large boat to save his family from the flood. He obeyed God, who warned him about things that had never happened before. By his faith Noah condemned the rest of the world, and he received the righteousness that comes by faith.

⁸It was by faith that Abraham obeyed when God called him to leave home and go to another land that God would give him as his inheritance. He went without knowing where he was going. ⁹And even when he reached the land God promised him, he lived there by faith—for he was like a foreigner, living in tents. And so did Isaac and Jacob, who inherited the same promise. ¹⁰Abraham was confidently looking forward to a city with eternal foundations, a city designed and built by God.

¹¹It was by faith that even Sarah was able to have a child, though she was barren and was too old. She believed* that God would keep his promise. ¹²And so a whole nation came from this one man who was as

---

10:30a Deut 32:35. **10:30b** Deut 32:36. **10:32** Greek *when you were first enlightened.* **10:38** Or *my righteous ones will live by their faithfulness;* Greek reads *my righteous one will live by faith.* **10:37-38** Hab 2:3-4. **11:5** Gen 5:24. **11:11** Or *It was by faith that he [Abraham] was able to have a child, even though Sarah was barren and he was too old. He believed.*

10:26-27 The use of "deliberately" in this warning passage stresses the need to move away from sinful actions (see 6:4-8). The phrase "no longer any sacrifice" stresses the complete nature of Christ's sacrifice which covers all of humanity's sin, but Hebrews warns there will be judgment for anyone who repeatedly chooses to reject Christ. There is nowhere else to go for forgiveness except Jesus, and we have a constant need of Christ's redemptive work in our lives. A person who rejects Christ can only expect judgment as one of God's enemies (see Isaiah 26:10-11).
11:1-40 The long catalog of faith-filled heroes builds up overwhelming evidence that the life of faith is the only real way to live for God. The writer repeats the phrase "by faith" to drive this main message into the minds and hearts of hearers. The examples follow a pattern: the phrase "by faith," the name of the person, the event or action which demonstrated faith, and the outcome.
11:11 Many early manuscripts of Hebrews focus on Sarah while some highlight Abraham (see text note on 11:11). They had no children, and Sarah was past the normal age for childbearing (see Genesis 15:2-6; 18:10-15; 21:1-7), but Abraham's and Sarah's faith in God meant the nation of Israel was established. The Scriptures are clear that both of them were important in God's saving action (see Isaiah 51:2); God uses both men and women as partners together in his work in the world.

Rewarder

IDENTITY

From Pressure to Pursuit

Hebrews 11:6 hangs on my wall in my wedding vows, scripted in my hand lettering. I wrote these when I was straight out of college and preparing to wed.

But before I got married, I feared I'd lose my voice. As the youngest of seven, I know voiceless. You see, there was this dinner conversation my parents recorded—remembered as, "Please, pass the milk." Five times in that recording, little me asked, "May I, please, have the milk?" "Could you, please, pass the milk?" Those who hear the audio wonder, "Did Naomi ever get the milk?"

Just so, I feared being silenced. What if marriage meant submerging my identity, just as I was uncovering the me God made?

But Hebrews 11:6 made the promise clear: God isn't hiding or playing games. God rewards.

Later, when I became a mom, I again sensed pressures telling me, selling me on, how to parent. By then, I knew to mine the Rewarder's words. I looked up every passage in the Bible about child, mother, father, parent. I wrote my credo on childrearing. Not from what "others" said, but from the words of one who rewards sincere efforts to honor him.

God's words, God's promise to reward, unlocks my fears. The Rewarder doesn't depend on me seeking him perfectly—only sincerely.

> God rewards those who seek him—sincerely, not perfectly.

THE REWARDER'S STORY IS TOLD THROUGH THE LIVES OF FAITHFUL PEOPLE IN HEBREWS 11:1-40.

IDENTIFY

What is a decision you would tackle head-on if you believed God is the Rewarder?

How can you get to know your Rewarder's voice so that you can follow him sincerely?

> "Seeking the Rewarder's promises has come in handy not only in getting me to the altar but getting me to the big job interview, through the tough diagnosis, and now to the daily job of believing God not only calls me but blesses me, as a leader."

NAOMI CRAMER OVERTON, MBA, DIS, lives to realize beauty-filled visions that lift us to flourishing, with our families and beyond. Naomi has been CEO for Stonecroft and MOPS, director with Compassion International and World Vision, and General Editor for this Bible.

good as dead—a nation with so many people that, like the stars in the sky and the sand on the seashore, there is no way to count them.

¹³All these people died still believing what God had promised them. They did not receive what was promised, but they saw it all from a distance and welcomed it. They agreed that they were foreigners and nomads here on earth. ¹⁴Obviously people who say such things are looking forward to a country they can call their own. ¹⁵If they had longed for the country they came from, they could have gone back. ¹⁶But they were looking for a better place, a heavenly homeland. That is why God is not ashamed to be called their God, for he has prepared a city for them.

¹⁷It was by faith that Abraham offered Isaac as a sacrifice when God was testing him. Abraham, who had received God's promises, was ready to sacrifice his only son, Isaac, ¹⁸even though God had told him, "Isaac is the son through whom your descendants will be counted."* ¹⁹Abraham reasoned that if Isaac died, God was able to bring him back to life again. And in a sense, Abraham did receive his son back from the dead.

²⁰It was by faith that Isaac promised blessings for the future to his sons, Jacob and Esau.

²¹It was by faith that Jacob, when he was old and dying, blessed each of Joseph's sons and bowed in worship as he leaned on his staff.

²²It was by faith that Joseph, when he was about to die, said confidently that the people of Israel would leave Egypt. He even commanded them to take his bones with them when they left.

²³It was by faith that Moses' parents hid him for three months when he was born. They saw that God had given them an unusual child, and they were not afraid to disobey the king's command.

²⁴It was by faith that Moses, when he grew up, refused to be called the son of Pharaoh's daughter. ²⁵He chose to share the oppression of God's people instead of enjoying the fleeting pleasures of sin. ²⁶He thought it was better to suffer for the sake of Christ than to own the treasures of Egypt, for he was looking ahead to his great reward. ²⁷It was by faith that Moses left the land of Egypt, not fearing the king's anger. He kept right on going because he kept his eyes on the one who is invisible. ²⁸It was by faith that Moses commanded the people of Israel to keep the Passover and to sprinkle blood on the doorposts so that the angel of death would not kill their firstborn sons.

²⁹It was by faith that the people of Israel went right through the Red Sea as though they were on dry ground. But when the Egyptians tried to follow, they were all drowned.

³⁰It was by faith that the people of Israel marched around Jericho for seven days, and the walls came crashing down.

³¹It was by faith that Rahab the prostitute was not destroyed with the people in her city who refused to obey God. For she had given a friendly welcome to the spies.

³²How much more do I need to say? It would take too long to recount the stories of the faith of Gideon, Barak, Samson, Jephthah, David, Samuel, and all the prophets. ³³By faith these people overthrew kingdoms, ruled with justice, and received what God had promised them. They shut the mouths of lions, ³⁴quenched the flames of fire, and escaped death by the edge of the sword. Their weakness was turned to strength. They became strong in battle and put whole armies to flight. ³⁵Women received their loved ones back again from death.

But others were tortured, refusing to turn from God in order to be set free. They placed their hope in a better life after the resurrection. ³⁶Some were jeered at, and their backs were cut open with whips. Others were chained in prisons. ³⁷Some died by stoning, some were sawed in half,* and others were killed with the sword. Some went about wearing skins of sheep and goats, destitute and oppressed and mistreated. ³⁸They were too good for this world, wandering over deserts and mountains, hiding in caves and holes in the ground.

³⁹All these people earned a good reputation because of their faith, yet none of them received all that God had promised. ⁴⁰For God had something better in mind for us, so that they would not reach perfection without us.

God's Discipline Proves His Love

12 Therefore, since we are surrounded by such a huge crowd of witnesses to the life of faith, let us strip off every weight that slows us down, especially the sin that so easily trips us up. And let us run with endurance the race God has set before us. ²We do this by keeping our eyes on Jesus, the champion

---

11:18 Gen 21:12. **11:37** Some manuscripts add *some were tested*.

11:31 God used Rahab as protector of the Israelite spies after they crossed into the Promised Land (Joshua 2:1-24; 6:25). As a result, she and her family were not destroyed but joined the community of Israel. God uses all people, no matter their situation in life, if they are available for him. It is almost certain that she discontinued that profession once she settled in with the Israelite community. In fact, Rahab was an ancestor of Jesus (Matthew 1:5) and should be remembered as a woman of faith rather than for her past life as a prostitute.
12:2 Jesus is the supreme example of faithful endurance (3:1). Our endurance in the Christian life will depend on our "keeping our eyes on Jesus"—staying focused on him and his work on our behalf. Jesus has accomplished everything necessary for faith under the new covenant to be a reality. Crucifixion was the most shameful form of execution, meant to humiliate and torture the person crucified. It was used only for enslaved people and criminals who were not Roman citizens. Christ treated that shame as if it were nothing. Jesus now sits "in the place of honor"; the author again alludes to Psalm 110:1 (see also Hebrews 1:3, 13; 8:1; 10:12). Through endurance, Jesus reached the place of ultimate honor at the right hand of God.

who initiates and perfects our faith.* Because of the joy* awaiting him, he endured the cross, disregarding its shame. Now he is seated in the place of honor beside God's throne. ³Think of all the hostility he endured from sinful people;* then you won't become weary and give up. ⁴After all, you have not yet given your lives in your struggle against sin.

⁵And have you forgotten the encouraging words God spoke to you as his children?* He said,

> "My child,* don't make light of the Lord's discipline,
> and don't give up when he corrects you.
> ⁶ For the Lord disciplines those he loves,
> and he punishes each one he accepts as his child."*

⁷As you endure this divine discipline, remember that God is treating you as his own children. Who ever heard of a child who is never disciplined by its father? ⁸If God doesn't discipline you as he does all of his children, it means that you are illegitimate and are not really his children at all. ⁹Since we respected our earthly fathers who disciplined us, shouldn't we submit even more to the discipline of the Father of our spirits, and live forever?*

¹⁰For our earthly fathers disciplined us for a few years, doing the best they knew how. But God's discipline is always good for us, so that we might share in his holiness. ¹¹No discipline is enjoyable while it is happening—it's painful! But afterward there will be a peaceful harvest of right living for those who are trained in this way.

¹²So take a new grip with your tired hands and strengthen your weak knees. ¹³Mark out a straight path for your feet so that those who are weak and lame will not fall but become strong.

A Call to Listen to God

¹⁴Work at living in peace with everyone, and work at living a holy life, for those who are not holy will not see the Lord. ¹⁵Look after each other so that none of you fails to receive the grace of God. Watch out that no poisonous root of bitterness grows up to trouble you, corrupting many. ¹⁶Make sure that no one is immoral or godless like Esau, who traded his birthright as the firstborn son for a single meal. ¹⁷You know that afterward, when he wanted his father's blessing, he was rejected. It was too late for repentance, even though he begged with bitter tears.

> "Turn your soul's vision to Jesus, and look and look at Him, and a strange dimness will come over all that is apart from Him."
>
> **LILIAS TROTTER**
> (1853–1928) British artist and missionary to Algeria

¹⁸You have not come to a physical mountain,* to a place of flaming fire, darkness, gloom, and whirlwind, as the Israelites did at Mount Sinai. ¹⁹For they heard an awesome trumpet blast and a voice so terrible that they begged God to stop speaking. ²⁰They staggered back under God's command: "If even an animal touches the mountain, it must be stoned to death."* ²¹Moses himself was so frightened at the sight that he said, "I am terrified and trembling."*

²²No, you have come to Mount Zion, to the city of the living God, the heavenly Jerusalem, and to countless thousands of angels in a joyful gathering. ²³You have come to the assembly of God's firstborn children, whose names are written in heaven. You have come to God himself, who is the judge over all things. You have come to the spirits of the righteous ones in heaven who have now been made perfect. ²⁴You have come to Jesus, the one who mediates the new covenant between God and people, and to the sprinkled blood, which speaks of forgiveness instead of crying out for vengeance like the blood of Abel.

²⁵Be careful that you do not refuse to listen to the One who is speaking. For if the people of Israel did not escape when they refused to listen to Moses, the earthly messenger, we will certainly not escape if

12:2a Or *Jesus, the originator and perfecter of our faith.* 12:2b Or *Instead of the joy.* 12:3 Some manuscripts read *Think of how people hurt themselves by opposing him.* 12:5a Greek *sons;* also in 12:7, 8. 12:5b Greek *son;* also in 12:6, 7. 12:5-6 Prov 3:11-12 (Greek version). 12:9 Or *and really live?* 12:18 Greek *to something that can be touched.* 12:20 Exod 19:13. 12:21 Deut 9:19.

12:25 God speaks to his children, and it is wise to listen to everything he says for this is the path of peace (12:14), faith (11:1-40), and shows our worship (12:28). God has spoken through his Son (1:2), and when we listen to him, we will not "become weary" or "give up" (12:3). God spoke through Moses at Sinai (Deuteronomy 9:7-27), but the people grew weary waiting for him and didn't want to listen. We now listen to him through his Son and find eternal life and grace for our daily needs.

we reject the One who speaks to us from heaven! ²⁶When God spoke from Mount Sinai his voice shook the earth, but now he makes another promise: "Once again I will shake not only the earth but the heavens also."* ²⁷This means that all of creation will be shaken and removed, so that only unshakable things will remain.

²⁸Since we are receiving a Kingdom that is unshakable, let us be thankful and please God by worshiping him with holy fear and awe. ²⁹For our God is a devouring fire.

Concluding Words

13 Keep on loving each other as brothers and sisters.* ²Don't forget to show hospitality to strangers, for some who have done this have entertained angels without realizing it! ³Remember those in prison, as if you were there yourself. Remember also those being mistreated, as if you felt their pain in your own bodies.

⁴Give honor to marriage, and remain faithful to one another in marriage. God will surely judge people who are immoral and those who commit adultery.

⁵Don't love money; be satisfied with what you have. For God has said,

"I will never fail you.
  I will never abandon you."*

⁶So we can say with confidence,

"The LORD is my helper,
  so I will have no fear.
What can mere people do to me?"*

⁷Remember your leaders who taught you the word of God. Think of all the good that has come from their lives, and follow the example of their faith.

⁸Jesus Christ is the same yesterday, today, and forever. ⁹So do not be attracted by strange, new ideas. Your strength comes from God's grace, not from rules about food, which don't help those who follow them.

¹⁰We have an altar from which the priests in the Tabernacle* have no right to eat. ¹¹Under the old system, the high priest brought the blood of animals into the Holy Place as a sacrifice for sin, and the bodies of the animals were burned outside the camp. ¹²So also Jesus suffered and died outside the city gates to make his people holy by means of his own blood. ¹³So let us go out to him, outside the camp, and bear the disgrace he bore. ¹⁴For this world is not our permanent home; we are looking forward to a home yet to come.

¹⁵Therefore, let us offer through Jesus a continual sacrifice of praise to God, proclaiming our allegiance to his name. ¹⁶And don't forget to do good and to share with those in need. These are the sacrifices that please God.

¹⁷Obey your spiritual leaders, and do what they say. Their work is to watch over your souls, and they are accountable to God. Give them reason to do this with joy and not with sorrow. That would certainly not be for your benefit.

¹⁸Pray for us, for our conscience is clear and we want to live honorably in everything we do. ¹⁹And especially pray that I will be able to come back to you soon.

²⁰ Now may the God of peace—
  who brought up from the dead our Lord Jesus,
  the great Shepherd of the sheep,
    and ratified an eternal covenant with his
      blood—
²¹ may he equip you with all you need
  for doing his will.
May he produce in you,*
  through the power of Jesus Christ,
  every good thing that is pleasing to him.
    All glory to him forever and ever! Amen.

²²I urge you, dear brothers and sisters,* to pay attention to what I have written in this brief exhortation.

²³I want you to know that our brother Timothy has been released from jail. If he comes here soon, I will bring him with me to see you.

²⁴Greet all your leaders and all the believers there.* The believers from Italy send you their greetings.

²⁵May God's grace be with you all.

12:26 Hag 2:6. **13:1** Greek *Continue in brotherly love.* **13:5** Deut 31:6, 8. **13:6** Ps 118:6. **13:10** Or *tent.* **13:21** Some manuscripts read *in us.* **13:22** Greek *brothers.* **13:24** Greek *all of God's holy people.*

13:2 Hospitality was an important part of ancient Near Eastern culture and a foundational idea in Judaism and Christianity (1 Peter 4:9; see also Genesis 18:2-8, 16; Matthew 10:11; Acts 16:15; Titus 3:13; Philemon 1:22; 3 John 1:5-8). When people traveled, they relied on local people to host them (Luke 10:1-8); they did not stay at inns. Jesus taught the disciples to give hospitality when people could not return the favor (Matthew 25:31-46; Luke 14:12-14).

13:11-12 The author describes the sacrifice on the Day of Atonement (Leviticus 16:1-28), in which "animals were burned outside the camp" (Hebrews 13:11; see Leviticus 16:27). By analogy, "Jesus suffered and died outside the city gates" of Jerusalem (Hebrews 13:12). He was the supreme Day of Atonement sacrifice (Hebrews 9:11-14, 24-28; 10:1-4). This is the foundation upon which we find forgiveness and eternal life.

Champion

IDENTITY | The Initiator and Perfector

In heaven, I enjoyed my Father's comfort and love. Everything was perfect! But one day, my Father shared his passion for the perishing on earth. When he looked into my eyes, I whispered, "What is in my Father's heart?"

I shared the Father's will. I understood, there must be a sacrifice. Who else could go except me? No one.

I accepted my Father's mission and came to earth but was rejected. I suffered shame and evil from wicked ones. I never fought back because my heart broke for them.

With those sufferings, I endured. For the joy awaiting me, I conquered death. I was raised to life and returned to my Father, where I sit on the right side of his throne and live forevermore.

Now, those who trust me have hope to live eternally. This saving faith was my gift, and I sustain you as you struggle. I will shake and purify your faith to prove its stability, but my Kingdom stands and never shakes. Only those who look upon me—the Champion who initiates and perfects your faith—will continue in faith. You can trust me when you're sinking.

> You can trust Christ, our Champion, when you're sinking.

THE CHAMPION'S STORY IS TOLD IN HEBREWS 12:1-4.

IDENTIFY

Have you ever realized how much you need a sure and solid faith?

How could you go deeper with Jesus as your faith-champion and -perfecter?

> "When I began believing in Christ, I knew nothing about Jesus' sacrifice. I never knew I could hear God's voice. I experienced persecution—even my own family rejected me. I cannot understand my joy and I keep the faith for I know whom I believe—Jesus. He started a good work, and he will finish it. No turning back."

LORINA AVENIDO, BEEd with CAR, has served for thirty-seven years as a full-time pastor/missionary of Philippine Good News International Inc. She is a licensed minister of Worldwide Impact Group, preaching the gospel and empowering women leaders.

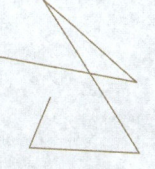

James

WHAT DO WE LEARN ABOUT GOD'S MISSION AND OURS?
We are called to do what we say we believe.

WHO WROTE IT? James, Jesus' half brother.

WHEN DID IT HAPPEN? In the mid-to-late 40s AD, early in the church's development.

HOW IS IT ORGANIZED?

1: Growing in endurance when faith is tested

2: Living out our faith in action

3: Talk that pleases God

4: Challenges for believers and unbelievers

5: Instructions for the rich, the impatient, and the sick

Words to Remember are highlighted throughout this book

FEATURE HIGHLIGHTS
+ *Just Love* (1581)
+ *Not Why But How* (1582)
+ *Prayer-Fueled Passion* (1585)

HOW LONG DOES IT TAKE TO READ?

:15 | :30 | 1:00 | 1:30 | 2:00 | 2:30 | 3:00 | 3:30

Greetings from James

1 This letter is from James, a slave of God and of the Lord Jesus Christ.

I am writing to the "twelve tribes"—Jewish believers scattered abroad.

Greetings!

Faith and Endurance

²Dear brothers and sisters,* when troubles of any kind come your way, consider it an opportunity for great joy. ³For you know that when your faith is tested, your endurance has a chance to grow. ⁴So let it grow, for when your endurance is fully developed, you will be perfect and complete, needing nothing.

⁵If you need wisdom, ask our generous God, and he will give it to you. He will not rebuke you for asking. ⁶But when you ask him, be sure that your faith is in God alone. Do not waver, for a person with divided loyalty is as unsettled as a wave of the sea that is blown and tossed by the wind. ⁷Such people should not expect to receive anything from the Lord. ⁸Their loyalty is divided between God and the world, and they are unstable in everything they do.

⁹Believers who are* poor have something to boast about, for God has honored them. ¹⁰And those who are rich should boast that God has humbled them. They will fade away like a little flower in the field. ¹¹The hot sun rises and the grass withers; the little flower droops and falls, and its beauty fades away. In the same way, the rich will fade away with all of their achievements.

¹²God blesses those who patiently endure testing and temptation. Afterward they will receive the crown of life that God has promised to those who love him. ¹³And remember, when you are being tempted, do not say, "God is tempting me." God is never tempted to do wrong,* and he never tempts anyone else. ¹⁴Temptation comes from our own desires, which entice us and drag us away. ¹⁵These desires give birth to sinful actions. And when sin is allowed to grow, it gives birth to death.

¹⁶So don't be misled, my dear brothers and sisters. ¹⁷Whatever is good and perfect is a gift coming down to us from God our Father, who created all the lights in the heavens.* He never changes or casts a shifting shadow.* ¹⁸He chose to give birth to us by giving us his true word. And we, out of all creation, became his prized possession.*

Listening and Doing

¹⁹Understand this, my dear brothers and sisters: You must all be quick to listen, slow to speak, and slow to get angry. ²⁰Human anger* does not produce the righteousness* God desires. ²¹So get rid of all the filth and evil in your lives, and humbly accept the word God has planted in your hearts, for it has the power to save your souls.

²²But don't just listen to God's word. You must do what it says. Otherwise, you are only fooling yourselves. ²³For if you listen to the word and don't obey, it is like glancing at your face in a mirror. ²⁴You see yourself, walk away, and forget what you look like. ²⁵But if you look carefully into the perfect law that sets you free, and if you do what it says and don't forget what you heard, then God will bless you for doing it.

²⁶If you claim to be religious but don't control your tongue, you are fooling yourself, and your religion is worthless. ²⁷Pure and genuine religion in the sight of God the Father means caring for orphans and widows in their distress and refusing to let the world corrupt you.

A Warning against Prejudice

2 My dear brothers and sisters,* how can you claim to have faith in our glorious Lord Jesus Christ if you favor some people over others?

²For example, suppose someone comes into your meeting* dressed in fancy clothes and expensive jewelry, and another comes in who is poor and dressed in dirty clothes. ³If you give special attention and a good seat to the rich person, but you say to the poor one, "You can stand over there, or else sit on the

---

1:2 Greek *brothers;* also in 1:16, 19.   **1:9** Greek *The brother who is.*   **1:13** Or *God should not be put to a test by evil people.*
1:17a Greek *from above, from the Father of lights.*   **1:17b** Some manuscripts read *He never changes, as a shifting shadow does.*
1:18 Greek *we became a kind of firstfruit of his creatures.*   **1:20a** Greek *A man's anger.*   **1:20b** Or *the justice.*   **2:1** Greek *brothers;* also in 2:5, 14.   **2:2** Greek *your synagogue.*

1:1 James was the half brother of Jesus and an important leader of the church in Jerusalem (Acts 15:13-21). By identifying his readers as the "twelve tribes," James affirms the church's continuity with Israel's heritage. The Exile had dispersed the twelve tribes, but Jewish interpreters looked forward to God reuniting them (see *Psalms of Solomon* 17:26-28; see also Ezekiel 37:15-28; Matthew 19:28). Christ has spiritually brought an end to Israel's exile and reunited the tribes symbolically by calling twelve Jewish men as his first disciples. Jews "scattered abroad" were those living outside Palestine (John 7:35; Acts 2:5; 8:1; 11:19). "Greetings!" is a typical opening in first-century Greek letters (Acts 15:23; 23:26) and interpersonally (Matthew 26:49; Luke 1:28).

1:12-13 There is the reward of God's blessings for those who endure testing and temptation: "the crown of life." The Jews often used a blessing formula in writing and speech (Psalm 1:1; see also Matthew 5:3-12), and here James reminds the people of God's ongoing blessing of his people in the difficulties of life. God tests his people but never pushes them toward sin. Any inner enticement to sin should be resisted; instead, we can endure temptation by asking for God's help.

2:3-4 It can be natural to "give special attention" to wealthy people because of their social status, political power, and potential generosity as patrons. The church might gain whatever economic or social benefits the wealthy wished to give. James warns that discrimination reflects "evil motives," a division between loyalty to God (1:6) and a desire for the benefits of worldly wealth and influence (4:4).

floor"—well, ⁴doesn't this discrimination show that your judgments are guided by evil motives?

⁵Listen to me, dear brothers and sisters. Hasn't God chosen the poor in this world to be rich in faith? Aren't they the ones who will inherit the Kingdom he promised to those who love him? ⁶But you dishonor the poor! Isn't it the rich who oppress you and drag you into court? ⁷Aren't they the ones who slander Jesus Christ, whose noble name* you bear?

⁸Yes indeed, it is good when you obey the royal law as found in the Scriptures: "Love your neighbor as yourself."* ⁹But if you favor some people over others, you are committing a sin. You are guilty of breaking the law.

¹⁰For the person who keeps all of the laws except one is as guilty as a person who has broken all of God's laws. ¹¹For the same God who said, "You must not commit adultery," also said, "You must not murder."* So if you murder someone but do not commit adultery, you have still broken the law.

2:7 Greek *slander the noble name.* 2:8 Lev 19:18. 2:11 Exod 20:13-14; Deut 5:17-18.

Just Love

SCRIPTURE CONNECTION: JAMES 1:19-27

I believe that being "quick to listen, slow to speak, and slow to get angry" (1:19) does not necessarily mean staying silent. There is a way to communicate in love and allow God's righteousness to shine, even when something needs to be addressed. It all begins with listening.

Are we willing to listen to learn? Do we want to have a conversation rather than a debate? Are we listening with compassion and empathy—the highest level of listening?

Our environment and culture cultivate our communication style, and not necessarily in the way God wants us to represent him. Where I live, we've been shaped as opinion bearers and not listeners. Many times, our goal is to get others to agree with us rather than to understand them. When we do this, we may hinder God's righteousness (or justice) from being done. God's justice gives everyone a fair hearing and changes what's broken out of love for others. Instead of clinging to our preferred perspective, we would do well to ask, "Do I listen for understanding, or am I trying to serve up my opinion?"

Conversing and asking questions as Jesus did is the key to connecting to people and drawing them closer. If we can get beyond our own perspective and approach people with a great level of curiosity, we can begin to understand what people have experienced and how it has shaped them. Listening goes a long way in building relationships and respect. Such justice-oriented love can say the right thing and understand how to be heard.

> Justice-oriented love listens before speaking.

IMAGINE

How has your environment and culture influenced your ability to be "quick to listen, slow to speak, and slow to get angry"?

Does our approach to communication allow others to see Jesus' justice-oriented love in action?

"I'm challenged daily—almost hourly—to listen with the patience and love of Jesus, and I pray my intentional effort honors him *with every opportunity presented."*

CATHY SCRIVNER has twenty-five years of experience as a diversity, equity, and inclusion consultant. She is a devoted Christian who believes in loving people to Christ.

JAMES 2

¹²So whatever you say or whatever you do, remember that you will be judged by the law that sets you free. ¹³There will be no mercy for those who have not shown mercy to others. But if you have been merciful, God will be merciful when he judges you.

Faith without Good Deeds Is Dead

¹⁴What good is it, dear brothers and sisters, if you say you have faith but don't show it by your actions? Can that kind of faith save anyone? ¹⁵Suppose you see a brother or sister who has no food or clothing, ¹⁶and you say, "Good-bye and have a good day; stay warm and eat well"—but then you don't give that person any food or clothing. What good does that do?

¹⁷So you see, faith by itself isn't enough. Unless it produces good deeds, it is dead and useless.

¹⁸Now someone may argue, "Some people have faith; others have good deeds." But I say, "How can you show me your faith if you don't have good deeds? I will show you my faith by my good deeds."

¹⁹You say you have faith, for you believe that there is one God.* Good for you! Even the demons believe this, and they tremble in terror. ²⁰How foolish! Can't you see that faith without good deeds is useless?

²¹Don't you remember that our ancestor Abraham was shown to be right with God by his actions when he offered his son Isaac on the altar? ²²You see, his faith and his actions worked together. His actions made his faith complete. ²³And so it happened just as the Scriptures say: "Abraham believed God, and God counted him as righteous because of his faith."* He was even called the friend of God.* ²⁴So you see,

2:19 Some manuscripts read *that God is one;* see Deut 6:4. 2:23a Gen 15:6. 2:23b See Isa 41:8.

2:14 Faith and action are two sides of one coin; that is, they cannot be separated. Having faith in Jesus Christ compels us to action (see 2 Corinthians 5:14). Likewise, this action demonstrates that we have faith, and that faith shines a light to reveal God to others.

 Come Close NOT WHY BUT HOW

SCRIPTURE CONNECTION: JAMES 1:2-5

I learned to stop asking God why a long time ago. But I frequently ask Him how. How can I go forward? How can I endure this? . . .

How can we care about others when we carry such a heavy load ourselves? How can we be kind and civil when we are racked with pain so much of the time?

My friend Dr. Michael Easley, who suffers constant pain from degenerative disk disease, will often say, "Just do the next thing." It's what I tell myself when pain intrudes, elbowing and clawing its way into my day. I will say, "Joni, just do the next thing." It's overwhelming at times, and I tire of the journey, but God remains faithful and kind to us in the midst of our suffering. . . .

So, friend, if you are dealing with pain today, or depression or grief or paralyzing anxiety, I encourage you to "just do the next thing." It may mean simply getting out of bed or up off the couch. Or getting out of the house. Or doing the laundry or washing those dishes that have been sitting in the sink. And as you do it, ask Him to give you joy in some small but noticeable way.

REFLECT "When troubles of any kind come your way, consider it an opportunity for great joy. For you know that when your faith is tested, your endurance has a chance to grow." JAMES 1:2-3

What is the "next thing" in your life today? Ask the Lord for the grace and courage to step into it, whatever it is.

CONSIDER "Take heart. One of these days you will hear those wonderful words from your Savior, 'Well done, good and faithful servant,' all because you got up and did the next thing."

> "Just do the next thing." It's what I tell myself when pain intrudes.

JONI EARECKSON TADA • Content taken from *Beside Bethseda* by Joni Eareckson Tada. Copyright © 2014 by Joni Eareckson Tada. Used by permission of NavPress, represented by Tyndale House Publishers. All rights reserved.

we are shown to be right with God by what we do, not by faith alone.

²⁵Rahab the prostitute is another example. She was shown to be right with God by her actions when she hid those messengers and sent them safely away by a different road. ²⁶Just as the body is dead without breath,* so also faith is dead without good works.

Controlling the Tongue

3 Dear brothers and sisters,* not many of you should become teachers in the church, for we who teach will be judged more strictly. ²Indeed, we all make many mistakes. For if we could control our tongues, we would be perfect and could also control ourselves in every other way.

³We can make a large horse go wherever we want by means of a small bit in its mouth. ⁴And a small rudder makes a huge ship turn wherever the pilot chooses to go, even though the winds are strong. ⁵In the same way, the tongue is a small thing that makes grand speeches.

But a tiny spark can set a great forest on fire. ⁶And among all the parts of the body, the tongue is a flame of fire. It is a whole world of wickedness, corrupting your entire body. It can set your whole life on fire, for it is set on fire by hell itself.*

⁷People can tame all kinds of animals, birds, reptiles, and fish, ⁸but no one can tame the tongue. It is restless and evil, full of deadly poison. ⁹Sometimes it praises our Lord and Father, and sometimes it curses those who have been made in the image of God. ¹⁰And so blessing and cursing come pouring out of the same mouth. Surely, my brothers and sisters, this is not right! ¹¹Does a spring of water bubble out with both fresh water and bitter water? ¹²Does a fig tree produce olives, or a grapevine produce figs? No, and you can't draw fresh water from a salty spring.*

True Wisdom Comes from God

¹³If you are wise and understand God's ways, prove it by living an honorable life, doing good works with the humility that comes from wisdom. ¹⁴But if you are bitterly jealous and there is selfish ambition in your heart, don't cover up the truth with boasting and lying. ¹⁵For jealousy and selfishness are not God's kind of wisdom. Such things are earthly, unspiritual, and demonic. ¹⁶For wherever there is jealousy and selfish ambition, there you will find disorder and evil of every kind.

¹⁷But the wisdom from above is first of all pure. It is also peace loving, gentle at all times, and willing to yield to others. It is full of mercy and the fruit of good deeds. It shows no favoritism and is always sincere. ¹⁸And those who are peacemakers will plant seeds of peace and reap a harvest of righteousness.*

Drawing Close to God

4 What is causing the quarrels and fights among you? Don't they come from the evil desires at war within you? ²You want what you don't have, so you scheme and kill to get it. You are jealous of what others have, but you can't get it, so you fight and wage war to take it away from them. Yet you don't have what you want because you don't ask God for it. ³And even when you ask, you don't get it because your motives are all wrong—you want only what will give you pleasure.

⁴You adulterers!* Don't you realize that friendship with the world makes you an enemy of God? I say it

> "You can pray until you faint, but if you don't get up and try to do something, God is not going to put it in your lap."
>
> **FANNIE LOU HAMER**
> (1917–1977) community organizer and Civil Rights activist

2:26 Or *without spirit.* **3:1** Greek *brothers;* also in 3:10. **3:6** Or *for it will burn in hell* (Greek *Gehenna*). **3:12** Greek *from salt.* **3:18** Or *of good things,* or *of justice.* **4:4** Greek *You adulteresses!*

3:1-12 The tongue (or *words,* or *speech*) can produce good and evil. Our speech is very powerful and can be "full of deadly poison" (3:8). This might allude to the serpent in the Garden of Eden (Genesis 3:1), who is identified in the New Testament with the devil (2 Corinthians 11:3; Revelation 20:2). The best action for the tongue is to praise God. This produces good fruit and brings health (as opposed to corruption) to the entire body.

3:13 The wisdom that comes from God (1:5) is not mere intellectual skill or the collection of information. It is practical insight and spiritual understanding, which expresses itself in moral uprightness, as described in 3:17-18 (see also Job 28:28; Proverbs 1:2-4; 2:10-15).

4:4 James uses opposing ideas of *friend* and *enemy* to make the point that God's ways for living and the world's ways will compete for your attention. The "world" here refers to the world system, the forces that oppose God and work against the intent of God's Kingdom. God's creation is good, but the ways of sin and our finite, human perspective may lead us away from God. James wants his hearers to choose God's way, which brings life.

again: If you want to be a friend of the world, you make yourself an enemy of God. ⁵Do you think the Scriptures have no meaning? They say that God is passionate that the spirit he has placed within us should be faithful to him.* ⁶And he gives grace generously. As the Scriptures say,

> "God opposes the proud
> but gives grace to the humble."*

⁷So humble yourselves before God. Resist the devil, and he will flee from you. ⁸Come close to God, and God will come close to you. Wash your hands, you sinners; purify your hearts, for your loyalty is divided between God and the world. ⁹Let there be tears for what you have done. Let there be sorrow and deep grief. Let there be sadness instead of laughter, and gloom instead of joy. ¹⁰Humble yourselves before the Lord, and he will lift you up in honor.

Warning against Judging Others

¹¹Don't speak evil against each other, dear brothers and sisters.* If you criticize and judge each other, then you are criticizing and judging God's law. But your job is to obey the law, not to judge whether it applies to you. ¹²God alone, who gave the law, is the Judge. He alone has the power to save or to destroy. So what right do you have to judge your neighbor?

Warning about Self-Confidence

¹³Look here, you who say, "Today or tomorrow we are going to a certain town and will stay there a year. We will do business there and make a profit." ¹⁴How do you know what your life will be like tomorrow? Your life is like the morning fog—it's here a little while, then it's gone. ¹⁵What you ought to say is, "If the Lord wants us to, we will live and do this or that." ¹⁶Otherwise you are boasting about your own pretentious plans, and all such boasting is evil.

¹⁷Remember, it is sin to know what you ought to do and then not do it.

Warning to the Rich

5 Look here, you rich people: Weep and groan with anguish because of all the terrible troubles ahead of you. ²Your wealth is rotting away, and your fine clothes are moth-eaten rags. ³Your gold and silver are corroded. The very wealth you were counting on will eat away your flesh like fire. This corroded treasure you have hoarded will testify against you on the day of judgment. ⁴For listen! Hear the cries of the field workers whom you have cheated of their pay. The cries of those who harvest your fields have reached the ears of the Lord of Heaven's Armies.

⁵You have spent your years on earth in luxury, satisfying your every desire. You have fattened yourselves for the day of slaughter. ⁶You have condemned and killed innocent people,* who do not resist you.*

Patience and Endurance

⁷Dear brothers and sisters,* be patient as you wait for the Lord's return. Consider the farmers who patiently wait for the rains in the fall and in the spring. They eagerly look for the valuable harvest to ripen. ⁸You, too, must be patient. Take courage, for the coming of the Lord is near.

⁹Don't grumble about each other, brothers and sisters, or you will be judged. For look—the Judge is standing at the door!

¹⁰For examples of patience in suffering, dear brothers and sisters, look at the prophets who spoke in the name of the Lord. ¹¹We give great honor to those who endure under suffering. For instance, you know about Job, a man of great endurance. You can see how the Lord was kind to him at the end, for the Lord is full of tenderness and mercy.

¹²But most of all, my brothers and sisters, never take an oath, by heaven or earth or anything else. Just say a simple yes or no, so that you will not sin and be condemned.

The Power of Prayer

¹³Are any of you suffering hardships? You should pray. Are any of you happy? You should sing praises. ¹⁴Are any of you sick? You should call for the elders of the church to come and pray over you, anointing you with oil in the name of the Lord. ¹⁵Such a prayer offered in faith will heal the sick, and the Lord will make you well. And if you have committed any sins, you will be forgiven.

¹⁶Confess your sins to each other and pray for

4:5 Or *They say that the spirit God has placed within us is filled with envy;* or *They say that the Holy Spirit, whom God has placed within us, opposes our envy.* 4:6 Prov 3:34 (Greek version). 4:11 Greek *brothers.* 5:6a Or *killed the Righteous One.* 5:6b Or *Don't they resist you?* or *Doesn't God oppose you?* or *Aren't they now accusing you before God?* 5:7 Greek *brothers;* also in 5:9, 10, 12, 19.

4:7-10 To those who humble themselves before him, God gives honor in place of the shame of their persecution and oppression (2:6-7). God is such a wise, loving, and gracious God that humility is the correct posture to have toward him. Humility toward our God also brings great joy, peace, and thankfulness to us. The devil can bring no good thing, and so we must resist him. If we live in humility before God, we will stand firmly against the enemy.
5:1-4 These "rich people" were exploitative employers. To increase their own wealth, these landowners were taking advantage of their employees and underpaying the day laborers who worked in their fields. But God is not pleased by exploitative business practices, and he is decidedly on the side of the oppressed and hates the exploitation of poor and marginalized people (see Deuteronomy 24:14-15; Ezekiel 22:1-31; 29:1-21). Believers who are also employers are called to do business honorably and pay workers fairly.
5:7-8 The ultimate resolution to injustice on earth is the Lord's return, and James urged the early believers to be patient in waiting for this to happen. Oppression and marginalization are still common in the world today, and while believers patiently wait for the Lord's return, we can take action to seek justice and live generously.

each other so that you may be healed. The earnest prayer of a righteous person has great power and produces wonderful results. [17]Elijah was as human as we are, and yet when he prayed earnestly that no rain would fall, none fell for three and a half years! [18]Then, when he prayed again, the sky sent down rain and the earth began to yield its crops.

Restore Wandering Believers

[19]My dear brothers and sisters, if someone among you wanders away from the truth and is brought back, [20]you can be sure that whoever brings the sinner back from wandering will save that person from death and bring about the forgiveness of many sins.

MY STORY WITH GOD

Prayer-Fueled Passion

SCRIPTURE CONNECTION: JAMES 5:13-18

Fervent prayer is fueled by passion.

By faith. By fire.

When everything else inside you is pulling you in twenty million different directions—off to the next busy thing in your busy day, if not off to bed and off the clock—passion is what plasters your knees to that floor. And digs in for dear life. It's your oomph. Your hutzpah. Your cutting edge.

Passion is what pushes the athlete to run one more lap, to crunch through one more set of reps. It's what silences those screaming thigh and stomach muscles, making them do what their owner demands of them, no matter how loudly they complain. *Passion* is what keeps a piano player anchored to the practice bench when no one else is around to notice the effort or give a pat on the back for approval. *Passion* is what inspires the eager young employee to out-perform expectations, instead of just punching the clock to earn a paycheck like everybody else. *Passion* is what burns up the road between a child in danger and a parent in pursuit. It glows red-hot. And goes on driving. And grows even larger, the larger the obstacles become.

> Passion is the fuel in the engine of your purpose.

Passion is the fuel in the engine of your purpose. It's your "want-to." It's what keeps you going when mundane tasks bore you or difficult ones dissuade you. Passion is what keeps you moving in the direction your best intentions want you to go.

Because praying—reaching outward and upward to Him—is the way His passion comes down. Even prayers that begin with the blunt edge of willpower, dragging your heart along kicking and screaming, can soon begin to shine with the cutting edge of hope, faith, and passionate confidence in Christ.

IMAGINE

When was a time your passion allowed you to go beyond?

What new passion would you like to pray about and ask God for right now?

"I see every aspect of my life as an opportunity to glorify God and draw attention to Jesus.... I'm always asking the Holy Spirit to show me how I can turn that encounter into a sacred opportunity to make Jesus' name great."

PRISCILLA SHIRER
Fervent: A Woman's Battle Plan to Serious, Specific and Strategic Prayer by Priscilla Shirer, © 2015 B&H Publishing Group, Nashville, Tennessee. Used by permission. All rights reserved.

1 Peter

WHAT DO WE LEARN ABOUT GOD'S MISSION AND OURS?
Jesus' followers won't always be popular, and that's okay.

WHO WROTE IT? Peter, an apostle, missionary, and teacher, with the help of Silas (see 5:12).

WHEN DID IT HAPPEN? Between AD 60 and 65.

HOW IS IT ORGANIZED?

- **1:1–2:3:** A call to holy living
- **2:4-12:** Our identity as believers
- **2:13–3:12:** Mutual respect in relationships
- **3:13–4:19:** Suffering as part of our faith in Jesus and living for God
- **5:1-14:** Service is the key to living in community

Words to Remember are highlighted throughout this book

FEATURE HIGHLIGHTS
- *Devoted Daughter: Learning from the Son* (1589)
- *Why Is the Bible So Concerned about What We Wear?* (1591)
- *Identity* (1592)

HOW LONG DOES IT TAKE TO READ?

Greetings from Peter

1 This letter is from Peter, an apostle of Jesus Christ.

I am writing to God's chosen people who are living as foreigners in the provinces of Pontus, Galatia, Cappadocia, Asia, and Bithynia.* ²God the Father knew you and chose you long ago, and his Spirit has made you holy. As a result, you have obeyed him and have been cleansed by the blood of Jesus Christ.

May God give you more and more grace and peace.

The Hope of Eternal Life

³All praise to God, the Father of our Lord Jesus Christ. It is by his great mercy that we have been born again, because God raised Jesus Christ from the dead. Now we live with great expectation, ⁴and we have a priceless inheritance—an inheritance that is kept in heaven for you, pure and undefiled, beyond the reach of change and decay. ⁵And through your faith, God is protecting you by his power until you receive this salvation, which is ready to be revealed on the last day for all to see.

⁶So be truly glad.* There is wonderful joy ahead, even though you must endure many trials for a little while. ⁷These trials will show that your faith is genuine. It is being tested as fire tests and purifies gold—though your faith is far more precious than mere gold. So when your faith remains strong through many trials, it will bring you much praise and glory and honor on the day when Jesus Christ is revealed to the whole world.

⁸You love him even though you have never seen him. Though you do not see him now, you trust him; and you rejoice with a glorious, inexpressible joy. ⁹The reward for trusting him will be the salvation of your souls.

¹⁰This salvation was something even the prophets wanted to know more about when they prophesied about this gracious salvation prepared for you. ¹¹They wondered what time or situation the Spirit of Christ within them was talking about when he told them in advance about Christ's suffering and his great glory afterward.

¹²They were told that their messages were not for themselves, but for you. And now this Good News has been announced to you by those who preached in the power of the Holy Spirit sent from heaven. It is all so wonderful that even the angels are eagerly watching these things happen.

A Call to Holy Living

¹³So prepare your minds for action and exercise self-control. Put all your hope in the gracious salvation that will come to you when Jesus Christ is revealed to the world. ¹⁴So you must live as God's obedient children. Don't slip back into your old ways of living to satisfy your own desires. You didn't know any better then. ¹⁵But now you must be holy in everything you do, just as God who chose you is holy. ¹⁶For the Scriptures say, "You must be holy because I am holy."*

¹⁷And remember that the heavenly Father to whom you pray has no favorites. He will judge or reward you according to what you do. So you must live in reverent fear of him during your time here as "temporary residents." ¹⁸For you know that God paid a ransom to save you from the empty life you inherited from your ancestors. And it was not paid with mere gold or silver, which lose their value. ¹⁹It was the precious blood of Christ, the sinless, spotless Lamb of God. ²⁰God chose him as your ransom long before the world began, but now in these last days he has been revealed for your sake.

²¹Through Christ you have come to trust in God. And you have placed your faith and hope in God because he raised Christ from the dead and gave him great glory.

²²You were cleansed from your sins when you obeyed the truth, so now you must show sincere love to each other as brothers and sisters.* Love each other deeply with all your heart.*

²³For you have been born again, but not to a life that will quickly end. Your new life will last forever because it comes from the eternal, living word of God. ²⁴As the Scriptures say,

> "People are like grass;
>   their beauty is like a flower in the field.
> The grass withers and the flower fades.
> ²⁵ But the word of the Lord remains forever."*

And that word is the Good News that was preached to you.

1:1 *Pontus, Galatia, Cappadocia, Asia,* and *Bithynia* were Roman provinces in what is now Turkey. **1:6** Or *So you are truly glad.* **1:16** Lev 11:44-45; 19:2; 20:7. **1:22a** Greek *must have brotherly love.* **1:22b** Some manuscripts read *with a pure heart.* **1:24-25** Isa 40:6-8.

1:13–5:14 Living a holy life as a faithful Christian is often countercultural and can result in opposition (4:4). We may be tempted to slip back into previous ways of life (4:3) to relieve such pressures or to satisfy our own desires (1:14; 2:11). Nonetheless, enduring such trials will refine our faith and God will honor such faith (1:7; 3:9). Such honorable lives will bring glory to God (2:12) and also witness against those who falsely accuse Christians (2:12; 3:16). Others may even be attracted to Christ as a result (2:12; 3:1-2).

1:13-21 New birth and the hope of salvation require that Christians live as God's people, separating themselves from the values of the world and emulating the holiness of God, who redeemed them.

1:22–2:3 Following his call to holiness (1:13-21), Peter specifies how believers must live in a loving way with fellow Christians. Holy living is a result of our love for God, and loving others, especially our fellow Christians, is the fruit of living a life that pleases God.

Devoted Daughter

IDENTITY — Learning from the Son

If I want to know how I'm doing, living as God's child, I watch my response when my faith is tested. My reaction reveals what I actually believe, and God's Spirit reminds me that being a devoted daughter means following Jesus' example of a devoted son.

Unlike us, Jesus had every right to live like he owned this world, but he chose humility. He did not cling to being God's equal; he humbled himself by becoming human and by dying so we could be made God's children (Philippians 2:6-11).

Like us, Jesus was tested. His moments of testing revealed his obedience. While Jesus was being crucified, the people watching tried to tempt him by telling him to save himself (Mark 15:29-32). Instead, he obeyed the Father. Jesus prayed, "Father, forgive them, for they don't know what they are doing" (Luke 23:34). Jesus obediently chose to stay in this moment of testing, the cross, out of devotion to his Father.

When my faith is tested, and I want to be a devoted daughter, I remember Jesus, the devoted Son. Jesus who said, "Let me teach you, because I am humble and gentle at heart, and you will find rest for your souls" (Matthew 11:29).

> Jesus' humility and obedience shows us how to live as God's devoted daughters.

PETER TEACHES US ABOUT BEING GOD'S DEVOTED DAUGHTERS IN 1 PETER 1:13-25.

IDENTIFY

How do you respond when your faith in God is tested?

What does your response to testing tell you about your heart's condition?

"Trials and adversities are part of our pilgrimage with Christ; no one is exempt. But Jesus shows us how devoted daughters can respond."

MILLIE SERRANO is a faithful follower of Jesus Christ devoted to supporting women in their pursuit of growing a biblical, strong, and fruitful relationship with God through his Son, Jesus.

> "Run to God and cling to Him. God understands every verbal barb, every covert injustice, every emotional shard, every leering look, every jeering smirk. He also keeps the books, and one day He will make everything right."
>
> **ANNE GRAHAM LOTZ**
> evangelist, author, and founder/president of AnGeL Ministries

⁵And you are living stones that God is building into his spiritual temple. What's more, you are his holy priests.* Through the mediation of Jesus Christ, you offer spiritual sacrifices that please God. ⁶As the Scriptures say,

"I am placing a cornerstone in Jerusalem,*
    chosen for great honor,
and anyone who trusts in him
    will never be disgraced."*

⁷Yes, you who trust him recognize the honor God has given him.* But for those who reject him,

"The stone that the builders rejected
    has now become the cornerstone."*

⁸And,

"He is the stone that makes people stumble,
    the rock that makes them fall."*

They stumble because they do not obey God's word, and so they meet the fate that was planned for them. ⁹But you are not like that, for you are a chosen people. You are royal priests,* a holy nation, God's very own possession. As a result, you can show others the goodness of God, for he called you out of the darkness into his wonderful light.

¹⁰ "Once you had no identity as a people;
    now you are God's people.
Once you received no mercy;
    now you have received God's mercy."*

¹¹Dear friends, I warn you as "temporary residents and foreigners" to keep away from worldly desires that wage war against your very souls. ¹²Be careful to live properly among your unbelieving neighbors. Then even if they accuse you of doing wrong, they will see your honorable behavior, and they will give honor to God when he judges the world.*

2 So get rid of all evil behavior. Be done with all deceit, hypocrisy, jealousy, and all unkind speech. ²Like newborn babies, you must crave pure spiritual milk so that you will grow into a full experience of salvation. Cry out for this nourishment, ³now that you have had a taste of the Lord's kindness.

Living Stones for God's House

⁴You are coming to Christ, who is the living cornerstone of God's temple. He was rejected by people, but he was chosen by God for great honor.

Respecting People in Authority

¹³For the Lord's sake, submit to all human authority—whether the king as head of state, ¹⁴or the officials he has appointed. For the king has sent them to punish those who do wrong and to honor those who do right.

¹⁵It is God's will that your honorable lives should silence those ignorant people who make foolish accusations against you. ¹⁶For you are free, yet you are God's slaves, so don't use your freedom as an excuse

2:5 Greek *holy priesthood.* 2:6a Greek *in Zion.* 2:6b Isa 28:16 (Greek version). 2:7a Or *Yes, for you who believe, there is honor.* 2:7b Ps 118:22. 2:8 Isa 8:14. 2:9 Greek *a royal priesthood.* 2:10 Hos 1:6, 9; 2:23. 2:12 Or *on the day of visitation.*

2:13–3:7 This section revolves around the key phrase "submit to [or respect] all human authority," which Peter applies to several relationships: Christians should accept the authority of those in government (2:13-17), enslaved Christians should accept the authority of their enslavers (2:18-25), Christian wives should accept the authority of their husbands (3:1-6), and Christian husbands are to honor and respect their wives (3:7). Peter seems to be following an early Christian usage of the traditional household code, in which a series of instructions was given for different members of the household (see Ephesians 5:21–6:9; Colossians 3:18–4:1; 1 Timothy 5:1–6:2; Titus 2:1-10).

to do evil. ¹⁷Respect everyone, and love the family of believers.* Fear God, and respect the king.

Slaves

¹⁸You who are slaves must submit to your masters with all respect.* Do what they tell you—not only if they are kind and reasonable, but even if they are cruel. ¹⁹For God is pleased when, conscious of his will, you patiently endure unjust treatment. ²⁰Of course, you get no credit for being patient if you are beaten for doing wrong. But if you suffer for doing good and endure it patiently, God is pleased with you.

²¹For God called you to do good, even if it means suffering, just as Christ suffered* for you. He is your example, and you must follow in his steps.

²² He never sinned,
   nor ever deceived anyone.*
²³ He did not retaliate when he was insulted,
   nor threaten revenge when he suffered.
He left his case in the hands of God,
   who always judges fairly.
²⁴ He personally carried our sins
   in his body on the cross
so that we can be dead to sin
   and live for what is right.
By his wounds
   you are healed.
²⁵ Once you were like sheep
   who wandered away.
But now you have turned to your Shepherd,
   the Guardian of your souls.

Wives

3 In the same way, you wives must accept the authority of your husbands. Then, even if some refuse to obey the Good News, your godly lives will speak to them without any words. They will be won over ²by observing your pure and reverent lives.

³Don't be concerned about the outward beauty of fancy hairstyles, expensive jewelry, or beautiful clothes. ⁴You should clothe yourselves instead with

---

2:17 Greek *love the brotherhood*. 2:18 Or *because you fear God*; Greek reads *in all fear*. 2:21 Some manuscripts read *died*. 2:22 Isa 53:9.

3:1-7 The last of Peter's three exhortations about accepting authority (2:13–3:7) concerns wives and husbands (see also Ephesians 5:21-33; Colossians 3:18-19). In Peter's understanding, husband and wife show mutual respect when the wife accepts her husband's authority and when the husband honors his wife. As both are equal recipients of God's gift of life, being obedient does not necessarily imply a lower status for the wife. For women, whether married or not, inner beauty—good character that is precious in God's sight—matters more than external appearances as defined by contemporary conventions. Many women of the time used appearance to flaunt wealth and social status, and the writers of the New Testament encouraged Christians to deny that impulse (see also 1 Timothy 2:9-10).

Perspective

Why is the Bible so concerned about what we wear?

SCRIPTURE CONNECTION: 1 PETER 3:3-6

Women's clothing seems be an issue in cultures around the world, but the Bible does not support any notion that women are by nature more promiscuous or vain than men. The apostles urged women to forgo expensive jewelry, clothing, and elaborate hairstyles. Concerns about modesty as they relate to displays of wealth underpin these verses. At that time, modesty expressed a woman's self-control, a virtue also prized by men.

What counted as modest behavior depended upon the circumstances. For example, a woman could speak in public without being judged immodest, if she were showing loyalty to her family, another important virtue.

Displays of wealth such as fine clothing and jewelry signaled high social status and reinforced social hierarchies. Wealthy women had enslaved people braid their hair, interweaving it with gold thread. The apostles warned against embracing cultural values that devalued other believers and promoted conspicuous consumption. Expensive attire in a house church setting or in the marketplace would send the wrong message about the gospel of the crucified Lord, reinforcing social divides. A relationship with God through Jesus is offered freely to all, and what we wear can convey, or cloud, that message.

VIEWPOINTS

HERS: *What am I saying about the worth of my poorer sisters in Christ when I wear my jewels and fancy clothes?*
MINE: *"I must consider how my appearance uplifts the self-worth of my friends and sisters in Christ."*
YOURS: *How do I embrace my inner beauty that comes from God and reject social pressure to compete with others in expensive clothes and jewelry?*

LYNN H. COHICK, PhD, is Distinguished Professor of New Testament and Director of Houston Theological Seminary, where she leads the Doctor of Ministry program. She writes, speaks, and teaches internationally.

WHAT THE BIBLE SAYS ABOUT Identity

We Are Goodness-Bearers

"You are the salt of the earth." MATTHEW 5:13

"If you are filled with light, with no dark corners, then your whole life will be radiant, as though a floodlight were filling you with light." LUKE 11:36

"For you are to be his witness, telling everyone what you have seen and heard." ACTS 22:15

You are a chosen people. You are royal priests, a holy nation, God's very own possession. As a result, you can show others the goodness of God, for he called you out of the darkness into his wonderful light. 1 PETER 2:9

Above all, you must live as citizens of heaven, conducting yourselves in a manner worthy of the Good News about Christ ... standing together with one spirit and one purpose, fighting together for the faith, which is the Good News. PHILIPPIANS 1:27

> Now you are free from the power of sin ...

We Are Defined by Our Relationship to Jesus

In this new life, it doesn't matter if you are a Jew or a Gentile, circumcised or uncircumcised, barbaric, uncivilized, slave, or free. Christ is all that matters, and he lives in all of us. COLOSSIANS 3:11

Now he has reconciled you to himself through the death of Christ.... As a result ... you are holy and blameless as you stand before him without a single fault. COLOSSIANS 1:22

We Are Freed from Sin and Death

"I tell you the truth, everyone who sins is a slave of sin.... So if the Son sets you free, you are truly free." **JOHN 8:34, 36**

Now you are free from the power of sin.... Now you do those things that lead to holiness and result in eternal life. **ROMANS 6:22**

We Are Adopted into God's Household

"Once you had no identity as a people;
  now you are God's people."
1 PETER 2:10

You are living stones that God is building into his spiritual temple. ... You are his holy priests. Through the mediation of Jesus Christ, you offer spiritual sacrifices that please God. **1 PETER 2:5**

You are all children of God through faith in Christ Jesus.... There is no longer Jew or Gentile, slave or free, male and female. For you are all one in Christ Jesus. And now that you belong to Christ, you are the true children of Abraham. You are his heirs, and God's promise to Abraham belongs to you.
GALATIANS 3:26, 28-29

You are citizens along with all of God's holy people. You are members of God's family. **EPHESIANS 2:19**

We Are Unpopular

"God blesses you when people ... say all sorts of evil things against you because you are my followers." **MATTHEW 5:11**

"All nations will hate you because you are my followers. But everyone who endures to the end will be saved." **MATTHEW 10:22**

the beauty that comes from within, the unfading beauty of a gentle and quiet spirit, which is so precious to God. ⁵This is how the holy women of old made themselves beautiful. They put their trust in God and accepted the authority of their husbands. ⁶For instance, Sarah obeyed her husband, Abraham, and called him her master. You are her daughters when you do what is right without fear of what your husbands might do.

Husbands

⁷In the same way, you husbands must give honor to your wives. Treat your wife with understanding as you live together. She may be weaker than you are, but she is your equal partner in God's gift of new life. Treat her as you should so your prayers will not be hindered.

All Christians

⁸Finally, all of you should be of one mind. Sympathize with each other. Love each other as brothers and sisters.* Be tenderhearted, and keep a humble attitude. ⁹Don't repay evil for evil. Don't retaliate with insults when people insult you. Instead, pay them back with a blessing. That is what God has called you to do, and he will grant you his blessing. ¹⁰For the Scriptures say,

"If you want to enjoy life
    and see many happy days,
keep your tongue from speaking evil
    and your lips from telling lies.
¹¹ Turn away from evil and do good.
    Search for peace, and work to maintain it.
¹² The eyes of the LORD watch over those who do right,
    and his ears are open to their prayers.
But the LORD turns his face
    against those who do evil."*

Suffering for Doing Good

¹³Now, who will want to harm you if you are eager to do good? ¹⁴But even if you suffer for doing what is right, God will reward you for it. So don't worry or be afraid of their threats. ¹⁵Instead, you must worship Christ as Lord of your life. And if someone asks about your hope as a believer, always be ready to explain it. ¹⁶But do this in a gentle and respectful way.* Keep your conscience clear. Then if people speak against you, they will be ashamed when they see what a good life you live because you belong to Christ. ¹⁷Remember, it is better to suffer for doing good, if that is what God wants, than to suffer for doing wrong!

¹⁸Christ suffered* for our sins once for all time. He never sinned, but he died for sinners to bring you safely home to God. He suffered physical death, but he was raised to life in the Spirit.*

¹⁹So he went and preached to the spirits in prison—²⁰those who disobeyed God long ago when God waited patiently while Noah was building his boat. Only eight people were saved from drowning in that terrible flood.* ²¹And that water is a picture of baptism, which now saves you, not by removing dirt from your body, but as a response to God from* a clean conscience. It is effective because of the resurrection of Jesus Christ.

²²Now Christ has gone to heaven. He is seated in the place of honor next to God, and all the angels and authorities and powers accept his authority.

Living for God

4 So then, since Christ suffered physical pain, you must arm yourselves with the same attitude he had, and be ready to suffer, too. For if you have suffered physically for Christ, you have finished with sin.* ²You won't spend the rest of your lives chasing your own desires, but you will be anxious to do the will of God. ³You have had enough in the past of the evil things that godless people enjoy—their immorality and lust, their feasting and drunkenness and wild parties, and their terrible worship of idols.

⁴Of course, your former friends are surprised when you no longer plunge into the flood of wild and destructive things they do. So they slander you. ⁵But remember that they will have to face God, who stands ready to judge everyone, both the living and the dead. ⁶That is why the Good News was preached to those who are now dead*—so although they were destined to die like all people,* they now live forever with God in the Spirit.*

⁷The end of the world is coming soon. Therefore, be earnest and disciplined in your prayers. ⁸Most important of all, continue to show deep love for each other, for love covers a multitude of sins. ⁹Cheerfully share your home with those who need a meal or a place to stay.

¹⁰God has given each of you a gift from his great variety of spiritual gifts. Use them well to serve one another. ¹¹Do you have the gift of speaking? Then speak as though God himself were speaking through you. Do you have the gift of helping others? Do it with all the strength and energy that God supplies. Then everything you do will bring glory to God through Jesus Christ. All glory and power to him forever and ever! Amen.

Suffering for Being a Christian

¹²Dear friends, don't be surprised at the fiery trials you are going through, as if something strange were happening to you. ¹³Instead, be very glad—for these

---

3:8 Greek *Show brotherly love.* 3:10-12 Ps 34:12-16. 3:16 Some English translations put this sentence in verse 15. 3:18a Some manuscripts read *died.* 3:18b Or *in spirit.* 3:20 Greek *saved through water.* 3:21 Or *as an appeal to God for.* 4:1 Or *For the one [or One] who has suffered physically has finished with sin.* 4:6a Greek *preached even to the dead.* 4:6b Or *so although people had judged them worthy of death.* 4:6c Or *in spirit.*

trials make you partners with Christ in his suffering, so that you will have the wonderful joy of seeing his glory when it is revealed to all the world.

¹⁴If you are insulted because you bear the name of Christ, you will be blessed, for the glorious Spirit of God* rests upon you.* ¹⁵If you suffer, however, it must not be for murder, stealing, making trouble, or prying into other people's affairs. ¹⁶But it is no shame to suffer for being a Christian. Praise God for the privilege of being called by his name! ¹⁷For the time has come for judgment, and it must begin with God's household. And if judgment begins with us, what terrible fate awaits those who have never obeyed God's Good News? ¹⁸And also,

"If the righteous are barely saved,
what will happen to godless sinners?"*

¹⁹So if you are suffering in a manner that pleases God, keep on doing what is right, and trust your lives to the God who created you, for he will never fail you.

Advice for Elders and Young Men

5 And now, a word to you who are elders in the churches. I, too, am an elder and a witness to the sufferings of Christ. And I, too, will share in his glory when he is revealed to the whole world. As a fellow elder, I appeal to you: ²Care for the flock that God has entrusted to you. Watch over it willingly, not grudgingly—not for what you will get out of it, but because you are eager to serve God. ³Don't lord it over the people assigned to your care, but lead them by your own good example. ⁴And when the Great Shepherd appears, you will receive a crown of never-ending glory and honor.

⁵In the same way, you who are younger must accept the authority of the elders. And all of you, dress yourselves in humility as you relate to one another, for

"God opposes the proud
but gives grace to the humble."*

⁶So humble yourselves under the mighty power of God, and at the right time he will lift you up in honor. ⁷Give all your worries and cares to God, for he cares about you.

⁸Stay alert! Watch out for your great enemy, the devil. He prowls around like a roaring lion, looking for someone to devour. ⁹Stand firm against him, and be strong in your faith. Remember that your family of believers* all over the world is going through the same kind of suffering you are.

¹⁰In his kindness God called you to share in his eternal glory by means of Christ Jesus. So after you have suffered a little while, he will restore, support, and strengthen you, and he will place you on a firm foundation. ¹¹All power to him forever! Amen.

Peter's Final Greetings

¹²I have written and sent this short letter to you with the help of Silas,* whom I commend to you as a faithful brother. My purpose in writing is to encourage you and assure you that what you are experiencing is truly part of God's grace for you. Stand firm in this grace.

¹³Your sister church here in Babylon* sends you greetings, and so does my son Mark. ¹⁴Greet each other with a kiss of love.

Peace be with all of you who are in Christ.

4:14a Or *for the glory of God, which is his Spirit.* **4:14b** Some manuscripts add *On their part he is blasphemed, but on your part he is glorified.* **4:18** Prov 11:31 (Greek version). **5:5** Prov 3:34 (Greek version). **5:9** Greek *your brotherhood.* **5:12** Greek *Silvanus.* **5:13** Greek *The elect one in Babylon.* Babylon was probably symbolic for Rome.

5:9-10 It is such an encouragement to faithful Christians to know these truths: There is a sense of solidarity because other members of God's family are also going through similar trials; and we are not only exhorted to endure suffering for doing right, but God promises to strengthen and support us to do so. **5:9** Persecution was not confined to the churches of Asia Minor. In various forms and with varying intensity, Christians were persecuted almost everywhere the Good News about Jesus Christ was preached. Peter reminded his readers of this to console them and encourage them to emulate those who had successfully endured the test of suffering.

2 Peter

WHAT DO WE LEARN ABOUT GOD'S MISSION AND OURS?
We choose Christ over critics and con artists.

WHO WROTE IT? Peter, an apostle and the disciple Jesus built his church on (Matthew 16:18).

WHEN DID IT HAPPEN? Around AD 65 to 67.

HOW IS IT ORGANIZED?

1: Standing firm in the truth

2: Guarding against false teachers

3: Correcting mistaken ideas about Jesus' return

Words to Remember are highlighted throughout this book

FEATURE HIGHLIGHTS
+ *Shame and Honor (1600)*

HOW LONG DOES IT TAKE TO READ?

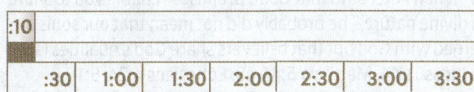

> "I said to the Lord, I'm going to hold steady on to you, and I know you will see me through."
>
> HARRIET TUBMAN
> (1820–1913) abolitionist and political activist

Greetings from Peter

1 This letter is from Simon* Peter, a slave and apostle of Jesus Christ.

I am writing to you who share the same precious faith we have. This faith was given to you because of the justice and fairness* of Jesus Christ, our God and Savior.

² May God give you more and more grace and peace as you grow in your knowledge of God and Jesus our Lord.

Growing in Faith

³ By his divine power, God has given us everything we need for living a godly life. We have received all of this by coming to know him, the one who called us to himself by means of his marvelous glory and excellence. ⁴ And because of his glory and excellence, he has given us great and precious promises. These are the promises that enable you to share his divine nature and escape the world's corruption caused by human desires.

⁵ In view of all this, make every effort to respond to God's promises. Supplement your faith with a generous provision of moral excellence, and moral excellence with knowledge, ⁶ and knowledge with self-control, and self-control with patient endurance, and patient endurance with godliness, ⁷ and godliness with brotherly affection, and brotherly affection with love for everyone.

⁸ The more you grow like this, the more productive and useful you will be in your knowledge of our Lord Jesus Christ. ⁹ But those who fail to develop in this way are shortsighted or blind, forgetting that they have been cleansed from their old sins.

¹⁰ So, dear brothers and sisters,* work hard to prove that you really are among those God has called and chosen. Do these things, and you will never fall away. ¹¹ Then God will give you a grand entrance into the eternal Kingdom of our Lord and Savior Jesus Christ.

Paying Attention to Scripture

¹² Therefore, I will always remind you about these things—even though you already know them and are standing firm in the truth you have been taught. ¹³ And it is only right that I should keep on reminding you as long as I live.* ¹⁴ For our Lord Jesus Christ has shown me that I must soon leave this earthly life,* ¹⁵ so I will work hard to make sure you always remember these things after I am gone.

¹⁶ For we were not making up clever stories when we told you about the powerful coming of our Lord Jesus Christ. We saw his majestic splendor with our own eyes ¹⁷ when he received honor and glory from God the Father. The voice from the majestic glory of God said to him, "This is my dearly loved Son, who brings me great joy."* ¹⁸ We ourselves heard that voice from heaven when we were with him on the holy mountain.

¹⁹ Because of that experience, we have even greater confidence in the message proclaimed by the prophets. You must pay close attention to what they wrote, for their words are like a lamp shining in a dark place—until the Day dawns, and Christ the Morning Star shines* in your hearts. ²⁰ Above all, you must realize that no prophecy in Scripture ever came from the prophet's own understanding,* ²¹ or from human initiative. No, those prophets were moved by the Holy Spirit, and they spoke from God.

The Danger of False Teachers

2 But there were also false prophets in Israel, just as there will be false teachers among you. They will cleverly teach destructive heresies and

---

1:1a Greek *Simeon.* **1:1b** Or *to you in the righteousness.* **1:10** Greek *brothers.* **1:13** Greek *as long as I am in this tent* [or *tabernacle*]. **1:14** Greek *I must soon put off my tent* [or *tabernacle*]. **1:17** Matt 17:5; Mark 9:7; Luke 9:35. **1:19** Or *rises.* **1:20** Or *is a matter of one's own interpretation.*

1:3-4 God's people are able to live godly lives not by our own strength but by divine empowerment. God's divine power and his promises are the means by which we are able to "escape the world's corruption caused by human desires."
1:3 In this verse, the name of God does not occur in the Greek text; Peter could be referring to the divine power of "Jesus our Lord" (1:2).
1:4 When Peter says that God's promises "enable you to share his divine nature," he probably did not mean that our souls are merged with God but that believers share God's qualities (see Leviticus 11:44; Matthew 5:43-48; Ephesians 4:24; 5:1).

even deny the Master who bought them. In this way, they will bring sudden destruction on themselves. ²Many will follow their evil teaching and shameful immorality. And because of these teachers, the way of truth will be slandered. ³In their greed they will make up clever lies to get hold of your money. But God condemned them long ago, and their destruction will not be delayed.

⁴For God did not spare even the angels who sinned. He threw them into hell,* in gloomy pits of darkness,* where they are being held until the day of judgment. ⁵And God did not spare the ancient world—except for Noah and the seven others in his family. Noah warned the world of God's righteous judgment. So God protected Noah when he destroyed the world of ungodly people with a vast flood. ⁶Later, God condemned the cities of Sodom and Gomorrah and turned them into heaps of ashes. He made them an example of what will happen to ungodly people. ⁷But God also rescued Lot out of Sodom because he was a righteous man who was sick of the shameful immorality of the wicked people around him. ⁸Yes, Lot was a righteous man who was tormented in his soul by the wickedness he saw and heard day after day. ⁹So you see, the Lord knows how to rescue godly people from their trials, even while keeping the wicked under punishment until the day of final judgment. ¹⁰He is especially hard on those who follow their own twisted sexual desire, and who despise authority.

These people are proud and arrogant, daring even to scoff at supernatural beings* without so much as trembling. ¹¹But the angels, who are far greater in power and strength, do not dare to bring from the Lord* a charge of blasphemy against those supernatural beings.

¹²These false teachers are like unthinking animals, creatures of instinct, born to be caught and destroyed. They scoff at things they do not understand, and like animals, they will be destroyed. ¹³Their destruction is their reward for the harm they have done. They love to indulge in evil pleasures in broad daylight. They are a disgrace and a stain among you. They delight in deception* even as they eat with you in your fellowship meals. ¹⁴They commit adultery with their eyes, and their desire for sin is never satisfied. They lure unstable people into sin, and they are well trained in greed. They live under God's curse. ¹⁵They have wandered off the right road and followed the footsteps of Balaam son of Beor,* who loved to earn money by doing wrong. ¹⁶But Balaam was stopped from his mad course when his donkey rebuked him with a human voice.

¹⁷These people are as useless as dried-up springs or as mist blown away by the wind. They are doomed to blackest darkness. ¹⁸They brag about themselves with empty, foolish boasting. With an appeal to twisted sexual desires, they lure back into sin those who have barely escaped from a lifestyle of deception. ¹⁹They promise freedom, but they themselves are slaves of sin and corruption. For you are a slave to whatever controls you. ²⁰And when people escape from the wickedness of the world by knowing our Lord and Savior Jesus Christ and then get tangled up and enslaved by sin again, they are worse off than before. ²¹It would be better if they had never known the way to righteousness than to know it and then reject the command they were given to live a holy life. ²²They prove the truth of this proverb: "A dog returns to its vomit."* And another says, "A washed pig returns to the mud."

The Day of the Lord Is Coming

3 This is my second letter to you, dear friends, and in both of them I have tried to stimulate your wholesome thinking and refresh your memory. ²I want you to remember what the holy prophets said long ago and what our Lord and Savior commanded through your apostles.

2:4a Greek *Tartarus.* 2:4b Some manuscripts read *in chains of gloom.* 2:10 Greek *at glorious ones,* which are probably evil angels. 2:11 Other manuscripts read *to the Lord;* still others do not include this phrase at all. 2:13 Some manuscripts read *in fellowship meals.* 2:15 Some manuscripts read *Bosor.* 2:22 Prov 26:11.

2:10-18 These false teachers lure into sin those who are new or not firm in their faith by appealing to "twisted sexual desires" (2:18). The problem is not with sexual desires in themselves but with twisted ones (for example, Leviticus 18:1-30; 20:10-24). Song of Songs celebrates love and sexual desire within marriage (see the notes in Song of Songs, especially on 4:1–5:1). God is "hard on those who follow [that is, act on] their own twisted sexual desire" (2 Peter 2:10; see also 1 Corinthians 6:9-20), because these acts can not only lead to disease and broken relationships but also be harmful and destructive to life.
2:10 The reference here is to illicit sexual desire generally and probably to same-sex relationships in particular (compare reference to Sodom and Gomorrah, 2:6). The false teachers were so arrogant that they refused to listen to any authority but their own.

2:17-22 Peter continues his description of the false teachers by explaining their effect on other people.
2:18 The false teachers cleverly targeted new converts, people who had only recently committed themselves to Christ. New Christians might be particularly vulnerable to sins, not because they are less committed to Christ, but because they have less practice living a holy life and might feel pressure from nonbelieving family or friends to continue in their previous lifestyle.
3:1-13 Peter shifts from denouncing false teachers to encouraging believers. The false teachers' skepticism about Christ's return required clear teaching. Christians need to hold onto the apostolic message about the day of judgment and live godly lives in anticipation of that day.

WHAT THE BIBLE SAYS ABOUT Shame & Honor

Where Shame Began

The LORD God warned him, "You may freely eat the fruit of every tree in the garden—except the tree of the knowledge of good and evil. If you eat its fruit, you are sure to die." **GENESIS 2:16-17**

The woman was convinced [by the serpent]. She saw that the tree was beautiful and its fruit looked delicious, and she wanted the wisdom it would give her. So she took some of the fruit and ate it. Then she gave some to her husband, who was with her, and he ate it, too. At that moment their eyes were opened, and they suddenly felt shame at their nakedness. **GENESIS 3:6-7**

Sometimes Shame Makes Sense

I can hardly believe the report about the sexual immorality going on among you—something that even pagans don't do. I am told that a man in your church is living in sin with his stepmother. You are so proud of yourselves, but you should be mourning in sorrow and shame. And you should remove this man from your fellowship. **1 CORINTHIANS 5:1-2**

God Replaces Shame with Honor...

Those who look to him for help will be radiant with joy;
no shadow of shame will darken their faces.
PSALM 34:5

Dear children, remain in fellowship with Christ so that when he returns, you will be full of courage and not shrink back from him in shame. **1 JOHN 2:28**

Be careful to live properly among your unbelieving neighbors. Then even if they accuse you of doing wrong, they will see your honorable behavior, and they will give honor to God when he judges the world. **1 PETER 2:12**

I fully expect and hope that I will never be ashamed, but that I will continue to be bold for Christ, as I have been in the past. And I trust that my life will bring honor to Christ, whether I live or die.
PHILIPPIANS 1:20

...So We Can Honor Jesus

I am not ashamed of this Good News about Christ. It is the power of God at work, saving everyone who believes—the Jew first and also the Gentile. **ROMANS 1:16**

Never be ashamed to tell others about our Lord. And don't be ashamed of me, either, even though I'm in prison for him. With the strength God gives you, be ready to suffer with me for the sake of the Good News. **2 TIMOTHY 1:8**

"If anyone is ashamed of me [Jesus] and my message, the Son of Man will be ashamed of that person when he returns in his glory and in the glory of the Father and the holy angels." **LUKE 9:26**

...At that moment their eyes were opened...

³Most importantly, I want to remind you that in the last days scoffers will come, mocking the truth and following their own desires. ⁴They will say, "What happened to the promise that Jesus is coming again? From before the times of our ancestors, everything has remained the same since the world was first created."

⁵They deliberately forget that God made the heavens long ago by the word of his command, and he brought the earth out from the water and surrounded it with water. ⁶Then he used the water to destroy the ancient world with a mighty flood. ⁷And by the same word, the present heavens and earth have been stored up for fire. They are being kept for the day of judgment, when ungodly people will be destroyed.

⁸But you must not forget this one thing, dear friends: A day is like a thousand years to the Lord, and a thousand years is like a day. ⁹The Lord isn't really being slow about his promise, as some people think. No, he is being patient for your sake. He does not want anyone to be destroyed, but wants everyone to repent. ¹⁰But the day of the Lord will come as unexpectedly as a thief. Then the heavens will pass away with a terrible noise, and the very elements themselves will disappear in fire, and the earth and everything on it will be found to deserve judgment.*

¹¹Since everything around us is going to be destroyed like this, what holy and godly lives you should live, ¹²looking forward to the day of God and hurrying it along. On that day, he will set the heavens on fire, and the elements will melt away in the flames. ¹³But we are looking forward to the new heavens and new earth he has promised, a world filled with God's righteousness.

¹⁴And so, dear friends, while you are waiting for these things to happen, make every effort to be found living peaceful lives that are pure and blameless in his sight.

¹⁵And remember, our Lord's patience gives people time to be saved. This is what our beloved brother Paul also wrote to you with the wisdom God gave him—¹⁶speaking of these things in all of his letters. Some of his comments are hard to understand, and those who are ignorant and unstable have twisted his letters to mean something quite different, just as they do with other parts of Scripture. And this will result in their destruction.

Peter's Final Words

¹⁷You already know these things, dear friends. So be on guard; then you will not be carried away by the errors of these wicked people and lose your own secure footing. ¹⁸Rather, you must grow in the grace and knowledge of our Lord and Savior Jesus Christ.

All glory to him, both now and forever! Amen.

3:10 Other manuscripts read *will be burned up;* one early manuscript reads *will be found destroyed.*

3:3 Peter was not merely predicting an event in the future; he was speaking about his reader's situation. In the New Testament, "the last days" refers to the period from Jesus' first coming to his second coming (see Acts 2:17; Hebrews 1:2). It is the time when God's promises are fulfilled. According to Peter, there will be scoffers who are skeptical that Jesus will return to judge (Proverbs 1:22; 9:7-8; 13:1). Rather than using evidence and logic to argue, scoffers belittle and make fun of the truth.

1 John

WHAT DO WE LEARN ABOUT GOD'S MISSION AND OURS?
Because God's love through Jesus has brought us close, let's love him first and best.

WHO WROTE IT? John, an apostle and the disciple Jesus loved (John 13:23).

WHEN DID IT HAPPEN? Around AD 85 to 90.

HOW IS IT ORGANIZED?

1–2: We enjoy closeness with God and each other

3: We are God's children and so we love one another

4: Watch out for false teachers and God is love

5: Love is the evidence of our relationship with God, the source of our life, and how we can resist sin

Words to Remember are highlighted throughout this book

FEATURE HIGHLIGHTS
+ *Confidence (1608)*
+ *Great Love, Great Pain (1610)*

HOW LONG DOES IT TAKE TO READ?

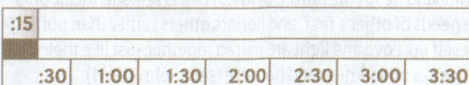

1 JOHN 1

Introduction

1 We proclaim to you the one who existed from the beginning,* whom we have heard and seen. We saw him with our own eyes and touched him with our own hands. He is the Word of life. ²This one who is life itself was revealed to us, and we have seen him. And now we testify and proclaim to you that he is the one who is eternal life. He was with the Father, and then he was revealed to us. ³We proclaim to you what we ourselves have actually seen and heard so that you may have fellowship with us. And our fellowship is with the Father and with his Son, Jesus Christ. ⁴We are writing these things so that you may fully share our joy.*

Living in the Light

⁵This is the message we heard from Jesus* and now declare to you: God is light, and there is no darkness in him at all. ⁶So we are lying if we say we have fellowship with God but go on living in spiritual darkness; we are not practicing the truth. ⁷But if we are living in the light, as God is in the light, then we have fellowship with each other, and the blood of Jesus, his Son, cleanses us from all sin.

⁸If we claim we have no sin, we are only fooling ourselves and not living in the truth. ⁹But if we confess our sins to him, he is faithful and just to forgive us our sins and to cleanse us from all wickedness. ¹⁰If we claim we have not sinned, we are calling God a liar and showing that his word has no place in our hearts.

2 My dear children, I am writing this to you so that you will not sin. But if anyone does sin, we have an advocate who pleads our case before the Father. He is Jesus Christ, the one who is truly righteous. ²He himself is the sacrifice that atones for our sins—and not only our sins but the sins of all the world.

³And we can be sure that we know him if we obey his commandments. ⁴If someone claims, "I know God," but doesn't obey God's commandments, that person is a liar and is not living in the truth. ⁵But those who obey God's word truly show how completely they love him. That is how we know we are living in him. ⁶Those who say they live in God should live their lives as Jesus did.

A New Commandment

⁷Dear friends, I am not writing a new commandment for you; rather it is an old one you have had from the very beginning. This old commandment—to love one another—is the same message you heard before. ⁸Yet it is also new. Jesus lived the truth of this commandment, and you also are living it. For the darkness is disappearing, and the true light is already shining.

⁹If anyone claims, "I am living in the light," but hates a fellow believer,* that person is still living in darkness. ¹⁰Anyone who loves a fellow believer* is living in the light and does not cause others to stumble. ¹¹But anyone who hates a fellow believer is still living and walking in darkness. Such a person does not know the way to go, having been blinded by the darkness.

¹² I am writing to you who are God's children
   because your sins have been forgiven through Jesus.*
¹³ I am writing to you who are mature in the faith*
   because you know Christ, who existed from the beginning.
I am writing to you who are young in the faith
   because you have won your battle with the evil one.
¹⁴ I have written to you who are God's children
   because you know the Father.

1:1 Greek *What was from the beginning.* **1:4** Or *so that our joy may be complete;* some manuscripts read *your joy.* **1:5** Greek *from him.* **2:9** Greek *hates his brother;* also in 2:11. **2:10** Greek *loves his brother.* **2:12** Greek *through his name.* **2:13** Or *to you fathers;* also in 2:14.

1:1-4 This poetic prologue is similar to the one in John's Gospel (John 1:1-18). The *we* that occurs throughout the prologue refers to John and the other apostles, which likely includes other Christians who had seen and touched Jesus Christ. While we may think the only apostles were the Twelve appointed by Jesus, plus Paul, Romans 16:7 points to the woman Junia and her husband (or possibly brother) Andronicus as apostles, too. The apostles were the first eyewitnesses of Jesus and had personal fellowship with God through him. John, representing the apostles, now invites readers to join in that fellowship.

1:5 This light shone through Jesus Christ to all he met, to expose their sin and to illumine the moral nature and character of God (see John 1:4-5, 9; 3:19-21; 8:12; 9:5; 12:35-36, 46). In John's Gospel, *light* represents God's holiness and revelation. It is the opposite of false teaching and undisciplined living, which is "darkness" (1 John 1:6).

2:1 If we are to live in the light (1:5-7), we must confess our sin (1:9) and stop sinning. John emphasized sin in 1 John to encourage believers to despise their sin and avoid it. Believers should repudiate sin, but they should not fear confessing sins to God because God is gracious and ready to forgive. Christ is named here as our advocate (Greek *paraklētos*, "one who is called to our side" as comforter or advocate). He acts as our defense attorney, representing us before the Father in heaven (see Romans 8:26-34; compare John 14:16). Because Christ fulfilled the law and paid sin's penalty for us, he can plead for us on the basis of justice as well as mercy. When God raised Christ from the dead, he accepted once for all Christ's plea for our acquittal (see Romans 4:23-25).

2:7-8 This commandment came from the earliest times in Israel (Leviticus 19:18, 33-34), while Jesus called it a "new commandment" (John 13:34-35). John repeats what Jesus' disciples already know—the message of love—Jesus has shown through his life and death the nature of love. Love is self-sacrificial, puts the needs of other's first, and honors others rather than puffing oneself up. Love and light are paired together, just like their opposites of darkness and hate are (see 1 John 2:9-11).

I have written to you who are mature in the faith
  because you know Christ, who existed from
    the beginning.
I have written to you who are young
    in the faith
  because you are strong.
God's word lives in your hearts,
  and you have won your battle with the evil
    one.

Do Not Love This World

¹⁵Do not love this world nor the things it offers you, for when you love the world, you do not have the love of the Father in you. ¹⁶For the world offers only a craving for physical pleasure, a craving for everything we see, and pride in our achievements and possessions. These are not from the Father, but are from this world. ¹⁷And this world is fading away, along with everything that people crave. But anyone who does what pleases God will live forever.

Warning about Antichrists

¹⁸Dear children, the last hour is here. You have heard that the Antichrist is coming, and already many such antichrists have appeared. From this we know that the last hour has come. ¹⁹These people left our churches, but they never really belonged with us; otherwise they would have stayed with us. When they left, it proved that they did not belong with us.

²⁰But you are not like that, for the Holy One has given you his Spirit,* and all of you know the truth. ²¹So I am writing to you not because you don't know the truth but because you know the difference between truth and lies. ²²And who is a liar? Anyone who says that Jesus is not the Christ.* Anyone who denies the Father and the Son is an antichrist.* ²³Anyone who denies the Son doesn't have the Father, either. But anyone who acknowledges the Son has the Father also.

²⁴So you must remain faithful to what you have been taught from the beginning. If you do, you will remain in fellowship with the Son and with the Father. ²⁵And in this fellowship we enjoy the eternal life he promised us.

²⁶I am writing these things to warn you about those who want to lead you astray. ²⁷But you have received the Holy Spirit,* and he lives within you, so you don't need anyone to teach you what is true. For the Spirit* teaches you everything you need to know, and what he teaches is true—it is not a lie. So just as he has taught you, remain in fellowship with Christ.

Living as Children of God

²⁸And now, dear children, remain in fellowship with Christ so that when he returns, you will be full of courage and not shrink back from him in shame.

²⁹Since we know that Christ is righteous, we also know that all who do what is right are God's children.

3 See how very much our Father loves us, for he calls us his children, and that is what we are! But the people who belong to this world don't recognize that we are God's children because they don't know him. ²Dear friends, we are already God's children, but he has not yet shown us what we will be like when Christ appears. But we do know that we will be like him, for we will see him as he really is. ³And all who have this eager expectation will keep themselves pure, just as he is pure.

⁴Everyone who sins is breaking God's law, for all sin is contrary to the law of God. ⁵And you know that Jesus came to take away our sins, and there is no sin in him. ⁶Anyone who continues to live in him will not sin. But anyone who keeps on sinning does not know him or understand who he is.

⁷Dear children, don't let anyone deceive you about this: When people do what is right, it shows that they are righteous, even as Christ is righteous. ⁸But when people keep on sinning, it shows that they belong to the devil, who has been sinning since the beginning. But the Son of God came to destroy the works of the devil. ⁹Those who have been born into God's family do not make a practice of sinning, because God's life* is in them. So they can't keep on sinning, because they are children of God. ¹⁰So now we can tell who are children of God and who are children of the devil. Anyone who does not live righteously and does not love other believers* does not belong to God.

Love One Another

¹¹This is the message you have heard from the beginning: We should love one another. ¹²We must not be like Cain, who belonged to the evil one and killed his brother. And why did he kill him? Because Cain had been doing what was evil, and his brother had been

---

2:20 Greek *But you have an anointing from the Holy One.*   **2:22a** Or *not the Messiah.*   **2:22b** Or *the antichrist.*   **2:27a** Greek *the anointing from him.*   **2:27b** Greek *the anointing.*   **3:9** Greek *because his seed.*   **3:10** Greek *does not love his brother.*

3:2 As believers we are part of the family of God. The family is designed for stability, kindness, discipline, and for our needs to be met. God is the source of all we need. In heaven we will be completely transformed as Christ-like people, who bring honor, praise, and glory to God in all things. At that time, we "will see him as he really is," meaning we will finally see the fullness of Jesus Christ.

3:9-10 We "live righteously" when we live in a right relationship with God. This is in contrast to the false teachers, who held that life in the spirit could not be contaminated by any behavior in a physical body. This does not mean that we act perfectly (1:8), but that we keep ourselves in a good relationship with God (1:9).

 WHAT THE BIBLE SAYS ABOUT

Confidence

God Gives Us Confidence That We Will Live with Him Forever

As for me, I look to the LORD for help.
   I wait confidently for God to save me,
   and my God will certainly hear me.
MICAH 7:7

Because of our faith, Christ has brought us into this place of undeserved privilege where we now stand, and we confidently and joyfully look forward to sharing God's glory. **ROMANS 5:2**

Let us who live in the light be clearheaded, protected by the armor of faith and love, and wearing as our helmet the confidence of our salvation. **1 THESSALONIANS 5:8**

Following God Gives Us Confidence

Because of my imprisonment, most of the believers here have gained confidence and boldly speak God's message without fear. **PHILIPPIANS 1:14**

Those who do well as deacons . . . will have increased confidence in their faith in Christ Jesus. **1 TIMOTHY 3:13**

As we live in God, our love grows more perfect. So we will not be afraid on the day of judgment, but we can face him with confidence because we live like Jesus here in this world. **1 JOHN 4:17**

Rejoice in our confident hope. Be patient in trouble, and keep on praying. **ROMANS 12:12**

Because of Christ and our faith in him, we can now come boldly and confidently into God's presence. **EPHESIANS 3:12**

We have placed our confidence in him...

Trusting God Gives Us Confidence

"Blessed are those who trust in the LORD and have made the LORD their hope and confidence."
JEREMIAH 17:7

This is what the Sovereign LORD, the Holy One of Israel, says: "Only in returning to me and resting in me will you be saved. In quietness and confidence is your strength." **ISAIAH 30:15**

My heart is confident in you, O God; no wonder I can sing your praises with all my heart!
PSALM 108:1

We have placed our confidence in him, and he will continue to rescue us. **2 CORINTHIANS 1:10**

It is impossible for God to lie. Therefore, we who have fled to him for refuge can have great confidence.
HEBREWS 6:18

We are confident that [the Son of God] hears us whenever we ask for anything that pleases him.
1 JOHN 5:14

Some Things Don't Deserve Our Confidence

Oh, the joys of those who trust the LORD, who have no confidence in the proud or in those who worship idols.
PSALM 40:4

Don't put your confidence in powerful people; there is no help for you there.
PSALM 146:3

Fools plunge ahead with reckless confidence.
PROVERBS 14:16

Putting confidence in an unreliable person in times of trouble is like chewing with a broken tooth or walking on a lame foot.
PROVERBS 25:19

We put no confidence in human effort.
PHILIPPIANS 3:3

MY STORY WITH GOD

Great Love, Great Pain

SCRIPTURE CONNECTION: 1 JOHN 4:7-21

How can pain be good? Why would God allow pain?

My doctor tells me that the presence of pain is the body's indicator that something is wrong. Nowhere is that felt more than when a person experiences the pain of sudden loss, like death.

I remember hearing my mother-in-law say, "Lisa, your daughter is in heaven, but Jesus still loves you." How could that be? This was pain, and pain means something is wrong!

I'm sure you've said the same thing when divorce, job loss, betrayal, financial ruin, the storm, or the diagnosis came your way. "God, but this hurts!"

How can God be in the pain? And how can pain turn into love?

God lost his firstborn to a horrible death, and he did it voluntarily. It was only through betrayal, pain, separation, death, and loss that Jesus could show the world how dearly God loves each person. Jesus' pain brought us to God.

Don't let your pain drive you from him because Jesus relates to your pain. The stretching, the pulling, the tearing, and the breaking all help to build you, me—us—up in love.

> The stretching, the pulling, the tearing, and the breaking are all to build us up in love.

IMAGINE

How do you see God allowing pain to bring life, like he did with the cross?

What might God be calling you to sacrifice so that great love will result?

"After losing a child, I realized God, too, knew the pain and separation one feels when losing a child. It took great pain to bring unmatched love."

LISA D. EDMONDS is mother of two daughters, a Stonecroft Ministries speaker and speaker trainer, worship leader, and constituent care director for The Dr. James Dobson Family Institute.

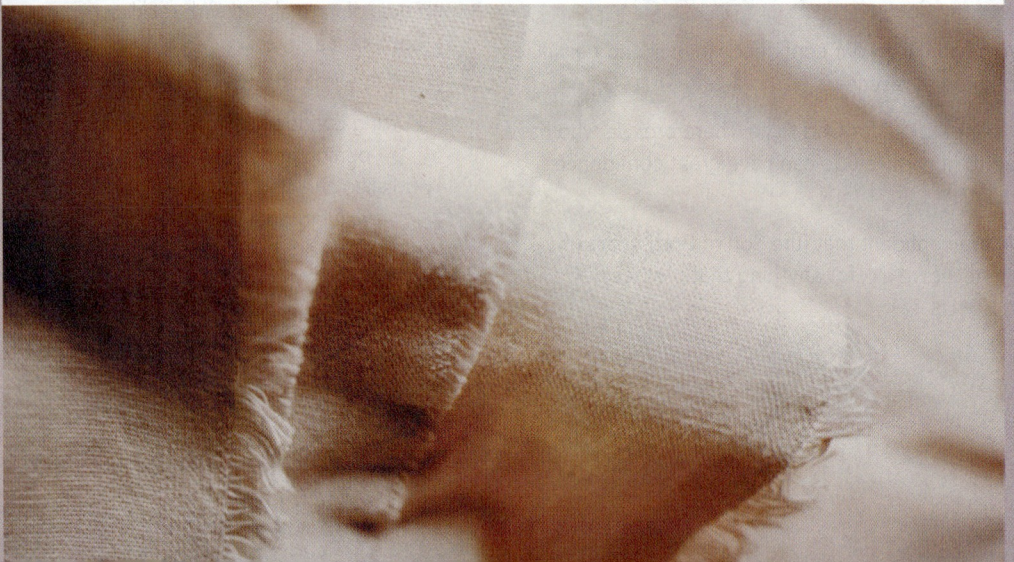

doing what was righteous. ¹³So don't be surprised, dear brothers and sisters,* if the world hates you.

¹⁴If we love our brothers and sisters who are believers,* it proves that we have passed from death to life. But a person who has no love is still dead. ¹⁵Anyone who hates another brother or sister* is really a murderer at heart. And you know that murderers don't have eternal life within them.

¹⁶We know what real love is because Jesus gave up his life for us. So we also ought to give up our lives for our brothers and sisters. ¹⁷If someone has enough money to live well and sees a brother or sister* in need but shows no compassion—how can God's love be in that person?

¹⁸Dear children, let's not merely say that we love each other; let us show the truth by our actions. ¹⁹Our actions will show that we belong to the truth, so we will be confident when we stand before God. ²⁰Even if we feel guilty, God is greater than our feelings, and he knows everything.

²¹Dear friends, if we don't feel guilty, we can come to God with bold confidence. ²²And we will receive from him whatever we ask because we obey him and do the things that please him.

²³And this is his commandment: We must believe in the name of his Son, Jesus Christ, and love one another, just as he commanded us. ²⁴Those who obey God's commandments remain in fellowship with him, and he with them. And we know he lives in us because the Spirit he gave us lives in us.

Discerning False Prophets

4 Dear friends, do not believe everyone who claims to speak by the Spirit. You must test them to see if the spirit they have comes from God. For there are many false prophets in the world. ²This is how we know if they have the Spirit of God: If a person claiming to be a prophet* acknowledges that Jesus Christ came in a real body, that person has the Spirit of God. ³But if someone claims to be a prophet and does not acknowledge the truth about Jesus, that person is not from God. Such a person has the spirit of the Antichrist, which you heard is coming into the world and indeed is already here.

⁴But you belong to God, my dear children. You have already won a victory over those people, because the Spirit who lives in you is greater than the spirit who lives in the world. ⁵Those people belong to this world, so they speak from the world's viewpoint, and the world listens to them. ⁶But we belong to God, and those who know God listen to us. If they do not belong to God, they do not listen to us. That is how we know if someone has the Spirit of truth or the spirit of deception.

Loving One Another

⁷Dear friends, let us continue to love one another, for love comes from God. Anyone who loves is a child of God and knows God. ⁸But anyone who does not love does not know God, for God is love.

⁹God showed how much he loved us by sending his one and only Son into the world so that we might have eternal life through him. ¹⁰This is real love—not that we loved God, but that he loved us and sent his Son as a sacrifice to take away our sins.

¹¹Dear friends, since God loved us that much, we surely ought to love each other. ¹²No one has ever seen God. But if we love each other, God lives in us, and his love is brought to full expression in us.

¹³And God has given us his Spirit as proof that we live in him and he in us. ¹⁴Furthermore, we have seen with our own eyes and now testify that the Father sent his Son to be the Savior of the world. ¹⁵All who declare that Jesus is the Son of God have God living in them, and they live in God. ¹⁶We know how much God loves us, and we have put our trust in his love.

God is love, and all who live in love live in God, and God lives in them. ¹⁷And as we live in God, our love grows more perfect. So we will not be afraid on the day of judgment, but we can face him with confidence because we live like Jesus here in this world.

¹⁸Such love has no fear, because perfect love expels all fear. If we are afraid, it is for fear of punishment, and this shows that we have not fully experienced his perfect love. ¹⁹We love each other* because he loved us first.

²⁰If someone says, "I love God," but hates a fellow believer,* that person is a liar; for if we don't love people we can see, how can we love God, whom we cannot see? ²¹And he has given us this command: Those who love God must also love their fellow believers.*

3:13 Greek *brothers*. 3:14 Greek *the brothers*; similarly in 3:16. 3:15 Greek *hates his brother*. 3:17 Greek *sees his brother*.
4:2 Greek *If a spirit*; similarly in 4:3. 4:19 Greek *We love*. Other manuscripts read *We love God*; still others read *We love him*.
4:20 Greek *hates his brother*. 4:21 Greek *The one who loves God must also love his brother*.

4:1-6 Those who "belong to God" (4:4) can distinguish spiritual truth from error because the Spirit's presence (3:23-24) teaches them (see 2:20, 27; John 14:15-26; 16:5-15). Yet John provides concrete tests for the believers to apply so that there will be no confusion. These tests are a starting point for true teachers, not an exhaustive set; they were designed to address the false teachings that were being promoted in the churches of John's readers.

4:17 The Greek idea of perfection does not mean flawless, but mature and complete. We mature as our relationship with God grows, and God's love makes our love complete. Experiencing and expressing God's love and doing what it requires does not make us acceptable to God, but it does give us the assurance that we have been accepted, and our fears of the final judgment can melt away.

> "God's love is not confusing. It's not something you have to wonder about. It's not something you have to worry about losing, because he is love. His love is from the beginning to the end."
>
> SADIE ROBERTSON HUFF
> actress, businesswoman, and author

world? Only those who believe that Jesus is the Son of God.

⁶And Jesus Christ was revealed as God's Son by his baptism in water and by shedding his blood on the cross*—not by water only, but by water and blood. And the Spirit, who is truth, confirms it with his testimony. ⁷So we have these three witnesses*—⁸the Spirit, the water, and the blood—and all three agree. ⁹Since we believe human testimony, surely we can believe the greater testimony that comes from God. And God has testified about his Son. ¹⁰All who believe in the Son of God know in their hearts that this testimony is true. Those who don't believe this are actually calling God a liar because they don't believe what God has testified about his Son.

¹¹And this is what God has testified: He has given us eternal life, and this life is in his Son. ¹²Whoever has the Son has life; whoever does not have God's Son does not have life.

Conclusion

¹³I have written this to you who believe in the name of the Son of God, so that you may know you have eternal life. ¹⁴And we are confident that he hears us whenever we ask for anything that pleases him. ¹⁵And since we know he hears us when we make our requests, we also know that he will give us what we ask for.

¹⁶If you see a fellow believer* sinning in a way that does not lead to death, you should pray, and God will give that person life. But there is a sin that leads to death, and I am not saying you should pray for those who commit it. ¹⁷All wicked actions are sin, but not every sin leads to death.

¹⁸We know that God's children do not make a practice of sinning, for God's Son holds them securely, and the evil one cannot touch them. ¹⁹We know that we are children of God and that the world around us is under the control of the evil one.

²⁰And we know that the Son of God has come, and he has given us understanding so that we can know the true God.* And now we live in fellowship with the true God because we live in fellowship with his Son, Jesus Christ. He is the only true God, and he is eternal life.

²¹Dear children, keep away from anything that might take God's place in your hearts.*

Faith in the Son of God

5 Everyone who believes that Jesus is the Christ* has become a child of God. And everyone who loves the Father loves his children, too. ²We know we love God's children if we love God and obey his commandments. ³Loving God means keeping his commandments, and his commandments are not burdensome. ⁴For every child of God defeats this evil world, and we achieve this victory through our faith. ⁵And who can win this battle against the

---

5:1 Or *the Messiah.* **5:6** Greek *This is he who came by water and blood.* **5:7** A few very late manuscripts add *in heaven—the Father, the Word, and the Holy Spirit, and these three are one. And we have three witnesses on earth.* **5:16** Greek *a brother.* **5:20** Greek *the one who is true.* **5:21** Greek *keep yourselves from idols.*

5:3 Following the ways of God shows our commitment to God and our faith in him. And because we have faith (which is a gracious gift) we are surrounded by the love of God. Therefore, we can say that God's commands bring us into even more of his grace, and so they are not a burden to us; they result in more revelation of his love for us and his world.

5:13 John is clear that Christians can be certain of God's gift of eternal life for they have placed their faith (belief) in Jesus Christ. The implication for believers is that we may live stable and joyous lives today with the true and certain hope of our future resurrection from the dead.

2 John

WHAT DO WE LEARN ABOUT GOD'S MISSION AND OURS?
Examine messages, and messengers, carefully.

WHO WROTE IT? John, the elder, referring to his role as a church leader (1:1).

WHEN DID IT HAPPEN? About AD 85 to 90.

HOW IS IT ORGANIZED?

1:1-3: Greeting

1:4-6: Love each other

1:7-11: Beware of false teachers

1:12-13: Closing remarks

Words to Remember are highlighted throughout this book

FEATURE HIGHLIGHTS
- *Never Alone (1616)*
- *The Chosen Lady: Love in Truth (1617)*

HOW LONG DOES IT TAKE TO READ?

:05 | :30 | 1:00 | 1:30 | 2:00 | 2:30 | 3:00 | 3:30

2 JOHN

Greetings

This letter is from John, the elder.*

I am writing to the chosen lady and to her children,* whom I love in the truth—as does everyone else who knows the truth—²because the truth lives in us and will be with us forever.

³Grace, mercy, and peace, which come from God the Father and from Jesus Christ—the Son of the Father—will continue to be with us who live in truth and love.

Live in the Truth

⁴How happy I was to meet some of your children and find them living according to the truth, just as the Father commanded.

⁵I am writing to remind you, dear friends,* that we should love one another. This is not a new commandment, but one we have had from the beginning. ⁶Love means doing what God has commanded us, and he has commanded us to love one another, just as you heard from the beginning.

⁷I say this because many deceivers have gone out into the world. They deny that Jesus Christ came* in a real body. Such a person is a deceiver and an antichrist. ⁸Watch out that you do not lose what we* have worked so hard to achieve. Be diligent so that you receive your full reward. ⁹Anyone who wanders away from this teaching has no relationship with God. But anyone who remains in the teaching of Christ has a relationship with both the Father and the Son.

¹⁰If anyone comes to your meeting and does not teach the truth about Christ, don't invite that person into your home or give any kind of encouragement. ¹¹Anyone who encourages such people becomes a partner in their evil work.

Conclusion

¹²I have much more to say to you, but I don't want to do it with paper and ink. For I hope to visit you soon and talk with you face to face. Then our joy will be complete.

¹³Greetings from the children of your sister,* chosen by God.

1a Greek *From the elder.* 1b Or *the church God has chosen and its members.* 5 Greek *I urge you, lady.* 7 Or *will come.* 8 Some manuscripts read *you.* 13 Or *from the members of your sister church.*

Come Close — NEVER ALONE

SCRIPTURE CONNECTION: 2 JOHN 1:3

Have you ever had a health crisis or known someone who has? What thoughts raced through your mind when it happened?

One day, while I was still in my twenties, I passed out on my way to work. Once I received medical attention, I learned I had a brain tumor. Because it had gone undiagnosed, it was already advanced to Stage III. I wondered, "Will I be alone in this?"

Can you imagine the problem that was thrust upon me? I had a job, had always been healthy, and—suddenly—I didn't know what to do.

But the Bible tells us the solution to this problem: Pray and rest in God's grace, mercy, and peace. He is with you at all times.

When we find ourselves in unexpected trouble or suffering, our first reaction may be to doubt the truth of God's Word. But we can trust what he says: Even in a crisis, even one as unpredictable as my own, Jesus stays close.

Later, I came through the surgery. And the recovery. Though the aftermath still affects me, God's answer to my questions is always, "No, you are never alone."

We are never alone. Thank you, Jesus!

REFLECT "Grace, mercy, and peace, which come from God the Father and from Jesus Christ—the Son of the Father—will continue to be with us who live in truth and love." 2 JOHN 1:3

It is truly a blessing that we experience grace, mercy, and peace from God the Father.

CONSIDER "Snuggle in God's arms. When you are hurting, when you feel lonely, left out. Let him cradle you, comfort you, reassure you of his all-sufficient power and love." KAY ARTHUR

God's grace, mercy, and peace will stay with you.

RACHEL LINDSAY McCANTS is an author, speaker, and founder of R. Lindsay Unlimited, which encourages, inspires, and challenges ladies to raise their self-worth and standards and to walk in God's will, in Jesus' name.

The Chosen Lady

 **IDENTITY** — Love in Truth

She remembers...

I just received a letter from John, who I highly respect and honor, encouraging me but also issuing a warning. His instruction on walking in truth and love—and avoiding those who do not—brings peace to my troubled soul after what our community went through. I have made some mistakes.

The first time I was told to love, I did it indiscriminately, opening my house to everyone. Then I let in a false teacher who lied to us. But it took time for us to realize he was teaching wrong things about who Jesus is. So he also took advantage of my kindness and hospitality as an opportunity to expand his teaching.

Feeling deceived and ashamed, I retreated, did not want to host anymore, and felt unusable to the church. But now, I am beginning to understand why John is reminding me that God is both truth and love. Love cannot be love if it steps outside of truth and discernment. And believing the truth about Jesus is the most important thing.

It's humbling to see that John and those who walk in truth still love and commend me. I have received a second invitation to love, but this time within the boundaries of truth. Truly Jesus has turned his face toward me and given me grace, mercy, and peace.

> God is truth and God is love. Let's love in truth, like him.

THE CHOSEN LADY AND HER CHILDREN'S STORY IS TOLD IN 2 JOHN 1:1-13.

IDENTIFY

Have you ever made a mistake and felt ashamed or unusable?

How does it feel to know that God's love can help us walk in truth?

> "Even when we make mistakes and feel like we don't want to try again or that God doesn't want to use us anymore, he extends us a hand. For now, let's arise and not give up. God can restore us."

LOIS NANGUDI, MA, studied spiritual formation and discipleship at Moody Seminary. She served as an advocate with Compassion International, founded Awaken To Follow, and is currently serving in the Pastors Discipleship Network.

1:1 According to some early commentators (including some ancient interpreters, like Athanasius and Clement of Alexandria), John's address to "the chosen [or elect] lady" refers to a specific woman and her actual, physical children. However, many modern commentators read this as most likely a metaphor referring to a local church of God, rather than to a particular woman. Referring to this church as "chosen" recalls Israel's election (Deuteronomy 7:7). The phrase translated "whom I love in the truth" either means "truly love" (see 2 John 1:5-6) or, more likely, it refers to love between those who profess the same truth about Christ in contrast to the lies of the false teachers (1:7; see 1 John 2:21-23). John emphasizes the pronoun *I* to contrast sharply with the lovelessness of the false teachers, who reject the true church.

1:4 Believers who follow the truths of God bring joy to John, to God, and to our own church leaders today. The use of "some" suggests others were not doing this and falling prey to deception (1:7-9). When we follow godly leaders grounded in the Scriptures, we are on a stable path which will bring us again and again to the centrality of the cross and the ways of God.

3 John

WHAT DO WE LEARN ABOUT GOD'S MISSION AND OURS?
Be a gracious yet discerning host.

WHO WROTE IT? John, the elder, referring to his role as a church leader (1:1).

WHEN DID IT HAPPEN? Around AD 85 to 90.

HOW IS IT ORGANIZED?

1:1-4: Greeting

1:5-8: Praise for Gaius' hospitality

1:9-10: Warning against Diotrephes

1:11-12: Praise for Demetrius' actions

1:13-15: Closing remarks

Words to Remember are highlighted throughout this book

HOW LONG DOES IT TAKE TO READ?

:05 | :30 | 1:00 | 1:30 | 2:00 | 2:30 | 3:00 | 3:30

Greetings

This letter is from John, the elder.*

I am writing to Gaius, my dear friend, whom I love in the truth.

²Dear friend, I hope all is well with you and that you are as healthy in body as you are strong in spirit. ³Some of the traveling teachers* recently returned and made me very happy by telling me about your faithfulness and that you are living according to the truth. ⁴I could have no greater joy than to hear that my children are following the truth.

Caring for the Lord's Workers

⁵Dear friend, you are being faithful to God when you care for the traveling teachers who pass through, even though they are strangers to you. ⁶They have told the church here of your loving friendship. Please continue providing for such teachers in a manner that pleases God. ⁷For they are traveling for the Lord,* and they accept nothing from people who are not believers.* ⁸So we ourselves should support them so that we can be their partners as they teach the truth.

⁹I wrote to the church about this, but Diotrephes, who loves to be the leader, refuses to have anything to do with us. ¹⁰When I come, I will report some of the things he is doing and the evil accusations he is making against us. Not only does he refuse to welcome the traveling teachers, he also tells others not to help them. And when they do help, he puts them out of the church.

¹¹Dear friend, don't let this bad example influence you. Follow only what is good. Remember that those who do good prove that they are God's children, and those who do evil prove that they do not know God.*

¹²Everyone speaks highly of Demetrius, as does the truth itself. We ourselves can say the same for him, and you know we speak the truth.

Conclusion

¹³I have much more to say to you, but I don't want to write it with pen and ink. ¹⁴For I hope to see you soon, and then we will talk face to face.

¹⁵*Peace be with you.

Your friends here send you their greetings. Please give my personal greetings to each of our friends there.

---

1 Greek *From the elder.* **3** Greek *the brothers;* also in verses 5 and 10. **7a** Greek *They went out on behalf of the Name.* **7b** Greek *from Gentiles.* **11** Greek *they have not seen God.* **15** Some English translations combine verses 14 and 15 into verse 14.

1:1 The author of this letter calls himself "the elder" (the translation provides "John" out of tradition; see also 2 John 1:1). Some scholars argue that this is not same person as John the apostle, but another John known in Church history. Gaius may have been Paul's traveling companion (Acts 19:29), Gaius from Derbe (Acts 20:4), Gaius from Corinth (1 Corinthians 1:14), or Paul's host in Corinth (Romans 16:23). These references suggest there are at least two different people with the same name, and John the elder's Gaius, "my dear friend" (or "Gaius, whom I truly love"), may be yet another person.

1:7-8 A literal rendering of the Greek "for the Lord" could say, "for the Name," but the NLT explains the meaning for contemporary readers. The writer did not need to identify whose name this was because all the early Christians knew that *the Name* represented Jesus Christ (see Acts 5:41). The traveling teachers had chosen to "accept nothing" offered to them "from people who are not believers" (literally "from Gentiles"), but to rely fully on the churches for their support. Christians who support legitimate traveling teachers become "their partners as they teach the truth" (see Matthew 10:41-42; Philippians 4:15-19).

Jude

WHAT DO WE LEARN ABOUT GOD'S MISSION AND OURS?
We are called to build each other up with faithful instruction.

WHO WROTE IT? Jude, a brother of James and therefore Jesus' brother.

WHEN DID IT HAPPEN? Around AD 65.

HOW IS IT ORGANIZED?

1:1-4: Why Jude is writing

1:5-16: The dangers of false teachers, in Israel's history and Jude's day

1:17-23: A call to remain faithful

1:24-25: Concluding praise to God

Words to Remember are highlighted throughout this book

HOW LONG DOES IT TAKE TO READ?

:05

| :30 | 1:00 | 1:30 | 2:00 | 2:30 | 3:00 | 3:30 |

JUDE

Greetings from Jude

This letter is from Jude, a slave of Jesus Christ and a brother of James.

I am writing to all who have been called by God the Father, who loves you and keeps you safe in the care of Jesus Christ.*

²May God give you more and more mercy, peace, and love.

The Danger of False Teachers

³Dear friends, I had been eagerly planning to write to you about the salvation we all share. But now I find that I must write about something else, urging you to defend the faith that God has entrusted once for all time to his holy people. ⁴I say this because some ungodly people have wormed their way into your churches, saying that God's marvelous grace allows us to live immoral lives. The condemnation of such people was recorded long ago, for they have denied our only Master and Lord, Jesus Christ.

⁵So I want to remind you, though you already know these things, that Jesus* first rescued the nation of Israel from Egypt, but later he destroyed those who did not remain faithful. ⁶And I remind you of the angels who did not stay within the limits of authority God gave them but left the place where they belonged. God has kept them securely chained in prisons of darkness, waiting for the great day of judgment. ⁷And don't forget Sodom and Gomorrah and their neighboring towns, which were filled with immorality and every kind of sexual perversion. Those cities were destroyed by fire and serve as a warning of the eternal fire of God's judgment.

⁸In the same way, these people—who claim authority from their dreams—live immoral lives, defy authority, and scoff at supernatural beings.* ⁹But even Michael, one of the mightiest of the angels,* did not dare accuse the devil of blasphemy, but simply said, "The Lord rebuke you!" (This took place when Michael was arguing with the devil about Moses' body.) ¹⁰But these people scoff at things they do not understand. Like unthinking animals, they do whatever their instincts tell them, and so they bring about their own destruction. ¹¹What sorrow awaits them! For they follow in the footsteps of Cain, who killed his brother. Like Balaam, they deceive people for money. And like Korah, they perish in their rebellion.

¹²When these people eat with you in your fellowship meals commemorating the Lord's love, they are like dangerous reefs that can shipwreck you.* They are like shameless shepherds who care only for themselves. They are like clouds blowing over the land without giving any rain. They are like trees in autumn that are doubly dead, for they bear no fruit and have been pulled up by the roots. ¹³They are like wild waves of the sea, churning up the foam of their shameful deeds. They are like wandering stars, doomed forever to blackest darkness.

¹⁴Enoch, who lived in the seventh generation after Adam, prophesied about these people. He said, "Listen! The Lord is coming with countless thousands of his holy ones ¹⁵to execute judgment on the people of the world. He will convict every person of all the ungodly things they have done and for all the insults that ungodly sinners have spoken against him."*

¹⁶These people are grumblers and complainers, living only to satisfy their desires. They brag loudly about themselves, and they flatter others to get what they want.

A Call to Remain Faithful

¹⁷But you, my dear friends, must remember what the apostles of our Lord Jesus Christ predicted. ¹⁸They told you that in the last times there would be scoffers whose purpose in life is to satisfy their ungodly desires. ¹⁹These people are the ones who are creating divisions among you. They follow their natural instincts because they do not have God's Spirit in them.

²⁰But you, dear friends, must build each other up in your most holy faith, pray in the power of the

---

1 Or *keeps you for Jesus Christ.* **5** Other manuscripts read *[the] Lord,* or *God,* or *God Christ.* **8** Greek *at glorious ones,* which are probably evil angels. **9** Greek *Michael, the archangel.* **12** Or *they are contaminants among you;* or *they are stains.* **14-15** The quotation comes from intertestamental literature: 1 Enoch 1:9.

1:1-23 Jude wrote this letter to combat false teachers in the early church. Jude focuses less on what these people were teaching than on the way they were living; at the heart of Jude's critique is the charge that they were libertines—they assumed that God's grace revealed in Christ gave them the freedom to do whatever they pleased (1:4). They had no respect for authority (see 1:8-9). They engaged in many sinful behaviors (1:16, 19). These profligates, who claimed to be Christians (1:4), were effectively denying the Lord and were therefore destined for the condemnation of all who rebel against God.
1:3-4 In place of the thanksgiving that usually comes at this point in a New Testament letter (for example, Romans 1:8-14; 1 Corinthians 1:4-9), Jude explains his central purpose. False teaching was a potent danger to the faith of his readers (see Jude 1:22-23).
1:4-7 The problem with false teachings lies in not only the content of such teachings but more so the immoral lifestyle that results from such beliefs (see the note on 1:1-23). Even more problematic is distorting the teaching of God's grace as an excuse to justify and indulge in immoral lifestyles. Thus, with three examples, Jude reminds his letter recipients that those who live immorally will not escape from God's judgment.
1:5-16 This section elaborates on the "condemnation ... recorded long ago" (1:4) by applying to the false teachers Old Testament examples of God's judgment.
1:17-23 After condemning the false teachers, Jude again encourages his readers directly (see 1:3-4). They had been warned by the apostles about false teaching (1:17-19). They should encourage each other in the faith (1:20-21) and reach out to those who might be going astray through the false teachers' influence (1:22-23).

Holy Spirit,* ²¹and await the mercy of our Lord Jesus Christ, who will bring you eternal life. In this way, you will keep yourselves safe in God's love.

²²And you must show mercy to* those whose faith is wavering. ²³Rescue others by snatching them from the flames of judgment. Show mercy to still others,* but do so with great caution, hating the sins that contaminate their lives.*

A Prayer of Praise

²⁴Now all glory to God, who is able to keep you from falling away and will bring you with great joy into his glorious presence without a single fault. ²⁵All glory to him who alone is God, our Savior through Jesus Christ our Lord. All glory, majesty, power, and authority are his before all time, and in the present, and beyond all time! Amen.

20 Greek *pray in the Holy Spirit.* 22 Some manuscripts read *must reprove.* 22-23a Some manuscripts have only two categories of people: (1) those whose faith is wavering and therefore need to be snatched from the flames of judgment, and (2) those who need to be shown mercy. 23b Greek *with fear, hating even the clothing stained by the flesh.*

1:20-21 Believers are to "keep [themselves] safe in God's love" by: building each other up in their most holy faith, praying in the power of the Holy Spirit, and awaiting the mercy of our Lord Jesus Christ. It is also comforting that God will keep believers safe from falling away (1:1, 24). There are still false teachers, like those of Jude's context, who have infiltrated the church in our day. Thus, it is important for us to beware so that we may also guard against becoming co-perpetrators or victims of the false teachers' greed and exploitation.

Revelation

WHAT DO WE LEARN ABOUT GOD'S MISSION AND OURS?
We can live victoriously, knowing God triumphs in the end.

WHO WROTE IT? John, an apostle, and the disciple Jesus loved (John 13:23).

WHEN DID IT HAPPEN? Around AD 95, while John was exiled on the island of Patmos because of his faith.

FEATURE HIGHLIGHTS

- A Gentleman: Waiting to Cherish (1629)
- How to Make Work and Worship Wonderful (1631)
- Ancient Churches, Anytime Challenges (1632)
- The Worthy Lamb: God's Idea of Best (1635)
- What the Numbers Mean (1641)
- If Sex Is a Good Thing, Then Why Are Virgins Being Rewarded? (1642)
- The Great Prostitute: Come Away (1645)
- Eve and the Bride of Christ: Better Than Before (1651)
- Revelation's Old Testament Imagery (1652)

Words to Remember are highlighted throughout this book

HOW IS IT ORGANIZED?

- **1:** John has a vision of Jesus
- **2–3:** Letters to the seven churches in the province of Asia
- **4:** John visits the throne room in heaven and sees angels and elders worshiping God
- **5–6:** The worthy Lamb opens the scroll with seven seals, bringing judgment
- **7:** God preserves his faithful people, and they worship the Lamb
- **8–9:** Breaking the final seal; angels blow six of the seven trumpets, bringing judgment
- **10–11:** John eats a scroll, two prophets warn, and the final trumpet is blown
- **12:** The pregnant woman, the dragon, and the war in heaven
- **13–14:** A beast slanders God, a second beast rules, and God's judgment is coming
- **15–16:** Angels pour out the seven bowls of God's wrath
- **17–18:** The fall of Babylon, the great prostitute
- **19–20:** Christ returns in victory, defeats Satan, and judges the dead
- **21:** A new heaven and a new earth; the new Jerusalem
- **22:** Jesus promises to return soon

HOW LONG DOES IT TAKE TO READ?

| :30 | 1:00 | 1:30 | 2:00 | 2:30 | 3:00 | 3:30 |

> "Where your heart, relationships, dreams and life have been broken, God's hands are strong for the mending."
>
> — AMENA BROWN
> poet, speaker, author

⁷ Look! He comes with the clouds of heaven.
And everyone will see him—
even those who pierced him.
And all the nations of the world will mourn for him.
Yes! Amen!

⁸"I am the Alpha and the Omega—the beginning and the end,"* says the Lord God. "I am the one who is, who always was, and who is still to come—the Almighty One."

Vision of the Son of Man

⁹I, John, am your brother and your partner in suffering and in God's Kingdom and in the patient endurance to which Jesus calls us. I was exiled to the island of Patmos for preaching the word of God and for my testimony about Jesus. ¹⁰It was the Lord's Day, and I was worshiping in the Spirit.* Suddenly, I heard behind me a loud voice like a trumpet blast. ¹¹It said, "Write in a book* everything you see, and send it to the seven churches in the cities of Ephesus, Smyrna, Pergamum, Thyatira, Sardis, Philadelphia, and Laodicea."

¹²When I turned to see who was speaking to me, I saw seven gold lampstands. ¹³And standing in the middle of the lampstands was someone like the Son of Man.* He was wearing a long robe with a gold sash across his chest. ¹⁴His head and his hair were white like wool, as white as snow. And his eyes were like flames of fire. ¹⁵His feet were like polished bronze refined in a furnace, and his voice thundered like mighty ocean waves. ¹⁶He held seven stars in his right hand, and a sharp two-edged sword came from his mouth. And his face was like the sun in all its brilliance.

¹⁷When I saw him, I fell at his feet as if I were dead. But he laid his right hand on me and said, "Don't be afraid! I am the First and the Last. ¹⁸I am the living one. I died, but look—I am alive forever and ever! And I hold the keys of death and the grave.*

¹⁹"Write down what you have seen—both the things that are now happening and the things that will happen.* ²⁰This is the meaning of the mystery of the seven stars you saw in my right hand and the seven gold lampstands: The seven stars are the angels* of the seven churches, and the seven lampstands are the seven churches.

Prologue

1 This is a revelation from* Jesus Christ, which God gave him to show his servants the events that must soon* take place. He sent an angel to present this revelation to his servant John, ²who faithfully reported everything he saw. This is his report of the word of God and the testimony of Jesus Christ.

³God blesses the one who reads the words of this prophecy to the church, and he blesses all who listen to its message and obey what it says, for the time is near.

John's Greeting to the Seven Churches

⁴This letter is from John to the seven churches in the province of Asia.*

Grace and peace to you from the one who is, who always was, and who is still to come; from the sevenfold Spirit* before his throne; ⁵and from Jesus Christ. He is the faithful witness to these things, the first to rise from the dead, and the ruler of all the kings of the world.

All glory to him who loves us and has freed us from our sins by shedding his blood for us. ⁶He has made us a Kingdom of priests for God his Father. All glory and power to him forever and ever! Amen.

1:1a Or *of.* **1:1b** Or *suddenly,* or *quickly.* **1:4a** *Asia* was a Roman province in what is now western Turkey. **1:4b** Greek *the seven spirits.* **1:8** Greek *I am the Alpha and the Omega,* referring to the first and last letters of the Greek alphabet. **1:10** Or *in spirit.* **1:11** Or *on a scroll.* **1:13** Or *like a son of man.* See Dan 7:13. "Son of Man" is a title Jesus used for himself. **1:18** Greek *and Hades.* **1:19** Or *what you have seen and what they mean—the things that have already begun to happen.* **1:20** Or *the messengers.*

1:1-11 The word *revelation* introduces this book's visionary nature as apocalyptic writing. Apocalyptic writing is a genre of ancient Jewish literature that shows God communicating his inspired message through mysterious symbols, numbers, and word pictures. It's a style particularly associated with living under oppression. Revelation opens with a three-part introduction, including a prologue (1:1-3), a letter introduction (1:4-8), and a historical introduction (1:9-11).

A Gentleman

IDENTITY — Waiting to Cherish

I am a gentleman. Though I have the power of a thousand suns and the authority to destroy and to judge, I hold back.

In days of old, I sent prophets, my personal representatives, each with a mission and message that was true to my character. You did not listen, but still, I held back.

A new covenant was born, and my only Son came to bring my Kingdom to its rightful place. You killed him. Still, I did not retaliate.

For generations, I have placed my ambassadors all over the earth, proclaiming my offer of love and peace. You tear at them and one another and pervert all that was meant for good.

I am a gentleman. My judgment is in check, but only for so long.

So, I send these final missives and have not yet released my wrath because you are so especially important to me. I have done all I can to open your eyes and ears. See and hear.

My mercy soon will end, and I must raise my hand of justice. Then it would be a mercy that I end your suffering early.

I never have and never will force myself upon you. But my hand is open. I am holding the door for you. I offer to lift you over the threshold to safety and love and rest.

THE GENTLEMAN'S STORY IS TOLD IN REVELATION 3:20.

> God is a gentleman. Allow him to cherish you.

IDENTIFY

Why do you think God has delayed his judgment?

How do you think we can respond while God waits for us?

"Father, Son, and Holy Spirit are the truest gentlemen I have ever known. God will always wait for me to step, reach, and accept. And meanwhile, I am fiercely guarded and lavishly provisioned. Longing to be cared for is not a weakness. It is an acknowledgment of our desire to be cherished. And that is what God will do for us."

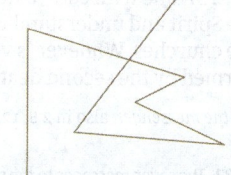

CARA DAY is a writer and illustrator. She has served with Stonecroft Ministries helping women live "extraordinary."

The Message to the Church in Ephesus

2 "Write this letter to the angel* of the church in Ephesus. This is the message from the one who holds the seven stars in his right hand, the one who walks among the seven gold lampstands:

² "I know all the things you do. I have seen your hard work and your patient endurance. I know you don't tolerate evil people. You have examined the claims of those who say they are apostles but are not. You have discovered they are liars. ³ You have patiently suffered for me without quitting.

⁴ "But I have this complaint against you. You don't love me or each other as you did at first!* ⁵ Look how far you have fallen! Turn back to me and do the works you did at first. If you don't repent, I will come and remove your lampstand from its place among the churches. ⁶ But this is in your favor: You hate the evil deeds of the Nicolaitans, just as I do.

⁷ "Anyone with ears to hear must listen to the Spirit and understand what he is saying to the churches. To everyone who is victorious I will give fruit from the tree of life in the paradise of God.

The Message to the Church in Smyrna

⁸ "Write this letter to the angel of the church in Smyrna. This is the message from the one who is the First and the Last, who was dead but is now alive:

⁹ "I know about your suffering and your poverty—but you are rich! I know the blasphemy of those opposing you. They say they are Jews, but they are not, because their synagogue belongs to Satan. ¹⁰ Don't be afraid of what you are about to suffer. The devil will throw some of you into prison to test you. You will suffer for ten days. But if you remain faithful even when facing death, I will give you the crown of life.

¹¹ "Anyone with ears to hear must listen to the Spirit and understand what he is saying to the churches. Whoever is victorious will not be harmed by the second death.

The Message to the Church in Pergamum

¹² "Write this letter to the angel of the church in Pergamum. This is the message from the one with the sharp two-edged sword:

¹³ "I know that you live in the city where Satan has his throne, yet you have remained loyal to me. You refused to deny me even when Antipas, my faithful witness, was martyred among you there in Satan's city.

¹⁴ "But I have a few complaints against you. You tolerate some among you whose teaching is like that of Balaam, who showed Balak how to trip up the people of Israel. He taught them to sin by eating food offered to idols and by committing sexual sin. ¹⁵ In a similar way, you have some Nicolaitans among you who follow the same teaching. ¹⁶ Repent of your sin, or I will come to you suddenly and fight against them with the sword of my mouth.

¹⁷ "Anyone with ears to hear must listen to the Spirit and understand what he is saying to the churches. To everyone who is victorious I will give some of the manna that has been hidden away in heaven. And I will give to each one a white stone, and on the stone will be engraved a new name that no one understands except the one who receives it.

The Message to the Church in Thyatira

¹⁸ "Write this letter to the angel of the church in Thyatira. This is the message from the Son of God, whose eyes are like flames of fire, whose feet are like polished bronze:

¹⁹ "I know all the things you do. I have seen your love, your faith, your service, and your patient endurance. And I can see your constant improvement in all these things.

²⁰ "But I have this complaint against you. You are permitting that woman—that Jezebel who calls herself a prophet—to lead my servants astray. She teaches them to commit sexual sin and to eat food offered to idols. ²¹ I gave her time to repent, but she does not want to turn away from her immorality.

2:1 Or *the messenger;* also in 2:8, 12, 18. 2:4 Greek *You have lost your first love.*

2:1–3:22 The seven messages to the seven churches reflect the state of Christ's church when Revelation was written, and it is similar today. God still calls Christians to faithfulness and integrity. Those who heed Christ's message will reap God's promised rewards; those who fail to do so will be judged.

2:18-29 Giving sinners "time to repent" (3:21) before punishing them shows how merciful Christ is towards those who err. Willful unrepentance will only result in deserved punishment. Going along with bad influence is not inevitable, for there were those who did not follow Jezebel's teaching.

2:20-21 The mention of Jezebel, who led Israel into pagan idolatry and immorality (1 Kings 16:31-33; 21:5-26), indicates a serious problem. Like the Old Testament queen who protected and promoted the pagan cult of Baal (see 1 Kings 16:31; 18:4; 19:1-3), this unknown Jezebel called herself a prophet but was leading God's people into various forms of immorality, including sexual misconduct and straying from God into idolatrous alliances and actions (Exodus 34:15-16; Psalm 106:39; Isaiah 57:7-8). Idol worship and sexual immorality are regularly connected in the Old Testament, and Revelation highlights this connection, too (see the note on Revelation 17:1-2).

Koinonia IMAGE
MY STORY WITH COMMUNITY, WORKPLACE & CHURCH

How to Make Work and Worship Wonderful

SCRIPTURE CONNECTION: REVELATION 3:1-22

Do we believe that Jesus sees our work? Revelation 3 reveals that he saw the work of the first-century churches and pleaded for change. Just so today, out of his love, he sees our condition, rebukes in judgment, and offers a way of reform.

His heart breaks to see us (and our churches):

1. *Appear to be busy and alive when we are actually dead!* Despite our many programs, have we so embraced the things of this world (wealth, comfort, and immorality) that our faith is dead (like Sardis, 3:1-6)?
2. *Worn out!* Are we weakened by the instability and hostility of our current culture? If so, Jesus says, "Hold on." In our poverty of spirit, we will come to know God's strength (like Philadelphia, 3:7-13).
3. *Rich and self-sufficient!* When things are going well for us, we lose sight of our need for God. Our lukewarm faith makes us blind to our brokenness and that of the world. Jesus wants us to see that, in fact, we are "wretched and miserable and poor and blind and naked," in need of a savior (like Laodicea, 3:14-22).

> God sees our work and invites us into greater dependency, for our good.

Through these words, God invites us to depend on his strength and truth. To envision our work joined to God's work as part of his redemptive plan for this broken world. To look forward to a new heaven and a new earth where all our work is fruitful and God-glorifying.

IMAGINE

Which of these three churches can you relate to most? What about their situation seems similar to yours?

What do you hear God telling us today about how we can depend on him more?

"My work can be fruitless for all these reasons. Yet, things are not hopeless; I can change. I can turn from the ways of the world to God's truth, repent of lukewarmness, and let God apply his salve to my blind eyes and see as he sees. I can return to God as I rely on the Lord's strength."

KATHERINE LEARY ALSDORF founded and directed Redeemer Church's Center for Faith & Work. She co-authored *Every Good Endeavor: Connecting Your Work to God's Work* with Timothy Keller.

Insight: ANCIENT CHURCHES, ANYTIME CHALLENGES

All seven of the churches addressed by John were within 120 miles of each other. This area is part of southwestern Turkey today. While these churches struggled with typical problems that we still struggle with today, Christ identified each local congregation and challenged each to follow him faithfully. These letters also call us to examine ourselves and our communities too.

²²"Therefore, I will throw her on a bed of suffering,* and those who commit adultery with her will suffer greatly unless they repent and turn away from her evil deeds. ²³I will strike her children dead. Then all the churches will know that I am the one who searches out the thoughts and intentions of every person. And I will give to each of you whatever you deserve.

²⁴"But I also have a message for the rest of you in Thyatira who have not followed this false teaching ('deeper truths,' as they call them—depths of Satan, actually). I will ask nothing more of you ²⁵except that you hold tightly to what you have until I come. ²⁶To all who are victorious, who obey me to the very end,

To them I will give authority over all the nations.
²⁷ They will rule the nations with an iron rod and smash them like clay pots.*

²⁸They will have the same authority I received from my Father, and I will also give them the morning star!

²⁹"Anyone with ears to hear must listen to the Spirit and understand what he is saying to the churches.

The Message to the Church in Sardis

3 "Write this letter to the angel* of the church in Sardis. This is the message from the one who has the sevenfold Spirit* of God and the seven stars:

"I know all the things you do, and that you have a reputation for being alive—but you are dead. ²Wake up! Strengthen what little remains, for even what is left is almost dead. I find that your actions do not meet the requirements of my God. ³Go back to what you heard and believed at first; hold to it firmly. Repent and turn to me again. If you don't wake up, I will come to you suddenly, as unexpected as a thief.

⁴"Yet there are some in the church in Sardis who have not soiled their clothes with evil. They will walk with me in white, for they are worthy. ⁵All who are victorious will be clothed in white. I will never erase their names from the Book of

2:22 Greek *a bed.* 2:26-27 Ps 2:8-9 (Greek version). 3:1a Or *the messenger;* also in 3:7, 14. 3:1b Greek *the seven spirits.*

Life, but I will announce before my Father and his angels that they are mine.

⁶"Anyone with ears to hear must listen to the Spirit and understand what he is saying to the churches.

The Message to the Church in Philadelphia

⁷"Write this letter to the angel of the church in Philadelphia.

This is the message from the one who is holy
 and true,
the one who has the key of David.
What he opens, no one can close;
 and what he closes, no one can open:*

⁸"I know all the things you do, and I have opened a door for you that no one can close. You have little strength, yet you obeyed my word and did not deny me. ⁹Look, I will force those who belong to Satan's synagogue—those liars who say they are Jews but are not—to come and bow down at your feet. They will acknowledge that you are the ones I love.

¹⁰"Because you have obeyed my command to persevere, I will protect you from the great time of testing that will come upon the whole world to test those who belong to this world. ¹¹I am coming soon.* Hold on to what you have, so that no one will take away your crown. ¹²All who are victorious will become pillars in the Temple of my God, and they will never have to leave it. And I will write on them the name of my God, and they will be citizens in the city of my God—the new Jerusalem that comes down from heaven from my God. And I will also write on them my new name.

¹³"Anyone with ears to hear must listen to the Spirit and understand what he is saying to the churches.

The Message to the Church in Laodicea

¹⁴"Write this letter to the angel of the church in Laodicea. This is the message from the one who is the Amen—the faithful and true witness, the beginning* of God's new creation:

¹⁵"I know all the things you do, that you are neither hot nor cold. I wish that you were one or the other! ¹⁶But since you are like lukewarm water, neither hot nor cold, I will spit you out of my mouth! ¹⁷You say, 'I am rich. I have everything I want. I don't need a thing!' And you don't realize that you are wretched and miserable and poor and blind and naked. ¹⁸So I advise you to buy gold from me—gold that has been purified by fire. Then you will be rich. Also buy white garments from me so you will not be shamed by your nakedness, and ointment for your eyes so you will be able to see. ¹⁹I correct and discipline everyone I love. So be diligent and turn from your indifference.

²⁰"Look! I stand at the door and knock. If you hear my voice and open the door, I will come in, and we will share a meal together as friends. ²¹Those who are victorious will sit with me on my throne, just as I was victorious and sat with my Father on his throne.

²²"Anyone with ears to hear must listen to the Spirit and understand what he is saying to the churches."

Worship in Heaven

4 Then as I looked, I saw a door standing open in heaven, and the same voice I had heard before spoke to me like a trumpet blast. The voice said, "Come up here, and I will show you what must happen after this." ²And instantly I was in the Spirit,* and I saw a throne in heaven and someone sitting on it. ³The one sitting on the throne was as brilliant as gemstones—like jasper and carnelian. And the glow of an emerald circled his throne like a rainbow. ⁴Twenty-four thrones surrounded him, and twenty-four elders sat on them. They were all clothed in white and had gold crowns on their heads. ⁵From the throne came flashes of lightning and the rumble of thunder. And in front of the throne were seven torches with burning flames. This is the sevenfold Spirit* of God. ⁶In front of the throne was a shiny sea of glass, sparkling like crystal.

In the center and around the throne were four living beings, each covered with eyes, front and back. ⁷The first of these living beings was like a lion; the second was like an ox; the third had a human face; and the fourth was like an eagle in flight. ⁸Each of these living beings had six wings, and their wings were covered all over with eyes, inside and out. Day after day and night after night they keep on saying,

"Holy, holy, holy is the Lord God, the Almighty—
 the one who always was, who is, and who is
  still to come."

⁹Whenever the living beings give glory and honor and thanks to the one sitting on the throne (the one who lives forever and ever), ¹⁰the twenty-four elders fall down and worship the one sitting on the throne (the one who lives forever and ever). And they lay their crowns before the throne and say,

¹¹ "You are worthy, O Lord our God,
 to receive glory and honor and power.
For you created all things,
 and they exist because you created what you
  pleased."

3:7 Isa 22:22.   3:11 Or *suddenly*, or *quickly*.   3:14 Or *the ruler*, or *the source*.   4:2 Or *in spirit*.   4:5 Greek *They are the seven spirits*.

The Lamb Opens the Scroll

5 Then I saw a scroll* in the right hand of the one who was sitting on the throne. There was writing on the inside and the outside of the scroll, and it was sealed with seven seals. ²And I saw a strong angel, who shouted with a loud voice: "Who is worthy to break the seals on this scroll and open it?" ³But no one in heaven or on earth or under the earth was able to open the scroll and read it.

⁴Then I began to weep bitterly because no one was found worthy to open the scroll and read it. ⁵But one of the twenty-four elders said to me, "Stop weeping! Look, the Lion of the tribe of Judah, the heir to David's throne,* has won the victory. He is worthy to open the scroll and its seven seals."

⁶Then I saw a Lamb that looked as if it had been slaughtered, but it was now standing between the throne and the four living beings and among the twenty-four elders. He had seven horns and seven eyes, which represent the sevenfold Spirit* of God that is sent out into every part of the earth. ⁷He stepped forward and took the scroll from the right hand of the one sitting on the throne. ⁸And when he took the scroll, the four living beings and the twenty-four elders fell down before the Lamb. Each one had a harp, and they held gold bowls filled with incense, which are the prayers of God's people. ⁹And they sang a new song with these words:

> "You are worthy to take the scroll
> and break its seals and open it.
> For you were slaughtered, and your blood has
> ransomed people for God
> from every tribe and language and people
> and nation.
> ¹⁰ And you have caused them to become
> a Kingdom of priests for our God.
> And they will reign* on the earth."

¹¹Then I looked again, and I heard the voices of thousands and millions of angels around the throne and of the living beings and the elders. ¹²And they sang in a mighty chorus:

> "Worthy is the Lamb who was slaughtered—
> to receive power and riches
> and wisdom and strength
> and honor and glory and blessing."

¹³And then I heard every creature in heaven and on earth and under the earth and in the sea. They sang:

> "Blessing and honor and glory and power
> belong to the one sitting on the throne
> and to the Lamb forever and ever."

¹⁴And the four living beings said, "Amen!" And the twenty-four elders fell down and worshiped the Lamb.

The Lamb Breaks the First Six Seals

6 As I watched, the Lamb broke the first of the seven seals on the scroll.* Then I heard one of the four living beings say with a voice like thunder, "Come!" ²I looked up and saw a white horse standing there. Its rider carried a bow, and a crown was placed on his head. He rode out to win many battles and gain the victory.

³When the Lamb broke the second seal, I heard the second living being say, "Come!" ⁴Then another horse appeared, a red one. Its rider was given a mighty sword and the authority to take peace from the earth. And there was war and slaughter everywhere.

⁵When the Lamb broke the third seal, I heard the third living being say, "Come!" I looked up and saw a black horse, and its rider was holding a pair of scales in his hand. ⁶And I heard a voice from among the four living beings say, "A loaf of wheat bread or three loaves of barley will cost a day's pay.* And don't waste* the olive oil and wine."

⁷When the Lamb broke the fourth seal, I heard the fourth living being say, "Come!" ⁸I looked up and saw a horse whose color was pale green. Its rider was named Death, and his companion was the Grave.* These two were given authority over one-fourth of the earth, to kill with the sword and famine and disease* and wild animals.

⁹When the Lamb broke the fifth seal, I saw under the altar the souls of all who had been martyred for the word of God and for being faithful in their testimony. ¹⁰They shouted to the Lord and said, "O Sovereign Lord, holy and true, how long before you judge the people who belong to this world and avenge our blood for what they have done to us?" ¹¹Then a white robe was given to each of them. And they were told to rest a little longer until the full number of their brothers and sisters*—their fellow servants of Jesus who were to be martyred—had joined them.

¹²I watched as the Lamb broke the sixth seal, and there was a great earthquake. The sun became as dark as black cloth, and the moon became as red as blood. ¹³Then the stars of the sky fell to the earth like green figs falling from a tree shaken by a strong wind. ¹⁴The sky was rolled up like a scroll, and all of the mountains and islands were moved from their places.

¹⁵Then everyone—the kings of the earth, the rulers, the generals, the wealthy, the powerful, and every slave and free person—all hid themselves in the caves and among the rocks of the mountains.

5:1 Or *book;* also in 5:2, 3, 4, 5, 7, 8, 9. **5:5** Greek *the root of David.* See Isa 11:10. **5:6** Greek *which are the seven spirits.* **5:10** Some manuscripts read *they are reigning.* **6:1** Or *book.* **6:6a** Greek *A choinix* [1 quart or 1 liter] *of wheat for a denarius, and 3 choinix of barley for a denarius.* A denarius was equivalent to a laborer's full day's wage. **6:6b** Or *harm.* **6:8a** Greek *was Hades.* **6:8b** Greek *death.* **6:11** Greek *their brothers.*

The Worthy Lamb

 IDENTITY

God's Idea of Best

"When God is asking for a sheep without blemish or deformity, he's . . . asking for our best," Lynne [a shepherd] said. . . .

"But what's the best?" I asked.

"When you list God's standards for a sacrificial sheep, you're describing the best of the flock—the one with the finest fleece that will produce the strongest offspring—and that takes years to produce." . . .

I knew that the spotless sheep was representative of the flawless sacrifice—the Son of God. . . . But when God asked for the sheep without blemish, spot, or defect, he was asking the people not just to hand over their best, but also to sacrifice something they had worked years to develop. . . .

And God didn't just ask for the perfect sheep; he also wanted its wool. Deuteronomy 18:4 instructs shepherds to give the first shearing of the sheep as an offering to God. . . .

"Is a first shearing a once-in-a-lifetime offering?" I asked [Lynne].

"Yes, everybody wants the first shearing, especially if it's from one of your best lambs. . . . First fleece is . . . the wool everyone wants next to their skin. It's also the smallest shearing, because of the size of the sheep. To ask for that is a real sacrifice!" . . .

Lynne handed me the . . . wool from [one sheep's] first shearing. I . . . felt the delicate, velvety texture. . . .

For the first time . . . I had felt with my own hands what God desired from sacrifice. It was nothing like what I expected.

> God doesn't want more—he wants the best.

THE WORTHY LAMB'S STORY IS TOLD IN REVELATION 5:1-14.

IDENTIFY

What ideas about giving to God do you want to set aside so you can give your best?

How might you thank him for giving you his best?

"All too often when I think about giving my best to God, I think about giving big. But in asking for the first fleece, God isn't asking for the biggest. He wants the smallest and softest. He doesn't want more—he wants the best."

MARGARET FEINBERG
Excerpt taken from *Scouting the Divine* by Margaret Feinberg. Copyright © 2009 by Margaret Feinberg. Used by permission of Zondervan. www.zondervan.com

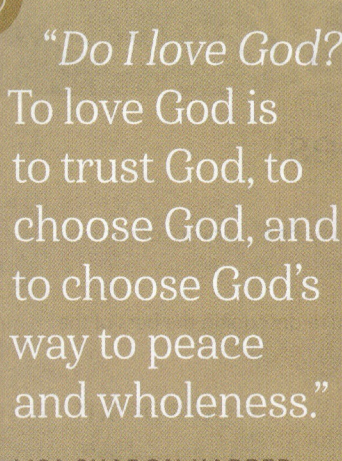

> "Do I love God?
> To love God is
> to trust God, to
> choose God, and
> to choose God's
> way to peace
> and wholeness."
>
> LISA SHARON HARPER
> speaker, writer, activist, and artist

God's People Will Be Preserved

7 Then I saw four angels standing at the four corners of the earth, holding back the four winds so they did not blow on the earth or the sea, or even on any tree. ²And I saw another angel coming up from the east, carrying the seal of the living God. And he shouted to those four angels, who had been given power to harm land and sea, ³"Wait! Don't harm the land or the sea or the trees until we have placed the seal of God on the foreheads of his servants."

⁴And I heard how many were marked with the seal of God—144,000 were sealed from all the tribes of Israel:

⁵ from Judah	12,000
from Reuben	12,000
from Gad	12,000
⁶ from Asher	12,000
from Naphtali	12,000
from Manasseh	12,000
⁷ from Simeon	12,000
from Levi	12,000
from Issachar	12,000
⁸ from Zebulun	12,000
from Joseph	12,000
from Benjamin	12,000

Praise from the Great Crowd

⁹After this I saw a vast crowd, too great to count, from every nation and tribe and people and language, standing in front of the throne and before the Lamb. They were clothed in white robes and held palm branches in their hands. ¹⁰And they were shouting with a great roar,

> "Salvation comes from our God who sits on the throne
> and from the Lamb!"

¹¹And all the angels were standing around the throne and around the elders and the four living beings. And they fell before the throne with their faces to the ground and worshiped God. ¹²They sang,

> "Amen! Blessing and glory and wisdom
> and thanksgiving and honor
> and power and strength belong to our God
> forever and ever! Amen."

¹³Then one of the twenty-four elders asked me, "Who are these who are clothed in white? Where did they come from?"

¹⁴And I said to him, "Sir, you are the one who knows."

Then he said to me, "These are the ones who died in* the great tribulation.* They have washed their robes in the blood of the Lamb and made them white.

> ¹⁵ "That is why they stand in front of God's throne
> and serve him day and night in his Temple.
> And he who sits on the throne
> will give them shelter.
> ¹⁶ They will never again be hungry or thirsty;
> they will never be scorched by the heat of the sun.
> ¹⁷ For the Lamb on the throne*
> will be their Shepherd.
> He will lead them to springs of life-giving water.
> And God will wipe every tear from their eyes."

¹⁶And they cried to the mountains and the rocks, "Fall on us and hide us from the face of the one who sits on the throne and from the wrath of the Lamb. ¹⁷For the great day of their wrath has come, and who is able to survive?"

7:14a Greek *who came out of.* **7:14b** Or *the great suffering.* **7:17** Greek *on the center of the throne.*

7:1–14:20 Within 6:1–16:21, three interludes occur amid God's release of his judgment and wrath (7:1-17; 10:1–11:13; 12:1–14:20) to define the place of God's holy people and to provide perspective on the previous scenes. In this first interlude before the seventh seal is broken, two visions communicate how God protects his people and assures them of his calling. **7:1-17** Amid suffering from the effects of corrupt power structures, faithful Christians may feel overwhelmed by frustration, pain, and death, wondering whether God will ever intervene to deal with injustice. This interlude provides the answer: God will protect his faithful people with his seal on their foreheads (7:1-8; see also 14:1-5); and God's redeemed people will eventually emerge triumphant from their suffering (7:9-17, especially 7:14).

The Lamb Breaks the Seventh Seal

8 When the Lamb broke the seventh seal on the scroll,* there was silence throughout heaven for about half an hour. ²I saw the seven angels who stand before God, and they were given seven trumpets.

³Then another angel with a gold incense burner came and stood at the altar. And a great amount of incense was given to him to mix with the prayers of God's people as an offering on the gold altar before the throne. ⁴The smoke of the incense, mixed with the prayers of God's holy people, ascended up to God from the altar where the angel had poured them out. ⁵Then the angel filled the incense burner with fire from the altar and threw it down upon the earth; and thunder crashed, lightning flashed, and there was a terrible earthquake.

The First Four Trumpets

⁶Then the seven angels with the seven trumpets prepared to blow their mighty blasts.

⁷The first angel blew his trumpet, and hail and fire mixed with blood were thrown down on the earth. One-third of the earth was set on fire, one-third of the trees were burned, and all the green grass was burned.

⁸Then the second angel blew his trumpet, and a great mountain of fire was thrown into the sea. One-third of the water in the sea became blood, ⁹one-third of all things living in the sea died, and one-third of all the ships on the sea were destroyed.

¹⁰Then the third angel blew his trumpet, and a great star fell from the sky, burning like a torch. It fell on one-third of the rivers and on the springs of water. ¹¹The name of the star was Bitterness.* It made one-third of the water bitter, and many people died from drinking the bitter water.

¹²Then the fourth angel blew his trumpet, and one-third of the sun was struck, and one-third of the moon, and one-third of the stars, and they became dark. And one-third of the day was dark, and also one-third of the night.

¹³Then I looked, and I heard a single eagle crying loudly as it flew through the air, "Terror, terror, terror to all who belong to this world because of what will happen when the last three angels blow their trumpets."

The Fifth Trumpet Brings the First Terror

9 Then the fifth angel blew his trumpet, and I saw a star that had fallen to earth from the sky, and he was given the key to the shaft of the bottomless pit.* ²When he opened it, smoke poured out as though from a huge furnace, and the sunlight and air turned dark from the smoke. ³Then locusts came from the smoke and descended on the earth, and they were given power to sting like scorpions. ⁴They were told not to harm the grass or plants or trees, but only the people who did not have the seal of God on their foreheads. ⁵They were told not to kill them but to torture them for five months with pain like the pain of a scorpion sting. ⁶In those days people will seek death but will not find it. They will long to die, but death will flee from them!

⁷The locusts looked like horses prepared for battle. They had what looked like gold crowns on their heads, and their faces looked like human faces. ⁸They had hair like women's hair and teeth like the teeth of a lion. ⁹They wore armor made of iron, and their wings roared like an army of chariots rushing into battle. ¹⁰They had tails that stung like scorpions, and for five months they had the power to torment people. ¹¹Their king is the angel from the bottomless pit; his name in Hebrew is *Abaddon,* and in Greek, *Apollyon*—the Destroyer.

¹²The first terror is past, but look, two more terrors are coming!

The Sixth Trumpet Brings the Second Terror

¹³Then the sixth angel blew his trumpet, and I heard a voice speaking from the four horns of the gold altar that stands in the presence of God. ¹⁴And the voice said to the sixth angel who held the trumpet, "Release the four angels who are bound at the great Euphrates River." ¹⁵Then the four angels who had been prepared for this hour and day and month and year were turned loose to kill one-third of all the people on earth. ¹⁶I heard the size of their army, which was 200 million mounted troops.

¹⁷And in my vision, I saw the horses and the riders sitting on them. The riders wore armor that was fiery red and dark blue and yellow. The horses had heads like lions, and fire and smoke and burning sulfur billowed from their mouths. ¹⁸One-third of all the people on earth were killed by these three plagues—by the fire and smoke and burning sulfur that came from the mouths of the horses. ¹⁹Their power was in their mouths and in their tails. For their tails had heads like snakes, with the power to injure people.

²⁰But the people who did not die in these plagues still refused to repent of their evil deeds and turn to God. They continued to worship demons and idols made of gold, silver, bronze, stone, and wood—idols that can neither see nor hear nor walk! ²¹And they did not repent of their murders or their witchcraft or their sexual immorality or their thefts.

8:1 Or *book.* **8:11** Greek *Wormwood.* **9:1** Or *the abyss,* or *the underworld;* also in 9:11.

He...says,
"Yes, I am
coming soon!"
Amen!
Come, Lord Jesus!

REVELATION
22:20

The Angel and the Small Scroll

10 Then I saw another mighty angel coming down from heaven, surrounded by a cloud, with a rainbow over his head. His face shone like the sun, and his feet were like pillars of fire. ²And in his hand was a small scroll* that had been opened. He stood with his right foot on the sea and his left foot on the land. ³And he gave a great shout like the roar of a lion. And when he shouted, the seven thunders answered.

⁴When the seven thunders spoke, I was about to write. But I heard a voice from heaven saying, "Keep secret* what the seven thunders said, and do not write it down."

⁵Then the angel I saw standing on the sea and on the land raised his right hand toward heaven. ⁶He swore an oath in the name of the one who lives forever and ever, who created the heavens and everything in them, the earth and everything in it, and the sea and everything in it. He said, "There will be no more delay. ⁷When the seventh angel blows his trumpet, God's mysterious plan will be fulfilled. It will happen just as he announced it to his servants the prophets."

⁸Then the voice from heaven spoke to me again: "Go and take the open scroll from the hand of the angel who is standing on the sea and on the land."

⁹So I went to the angel and told him to give me the small scroll. "Yes, take it and eat it," he said. "It will be sweet as honey in your mouth, but it will turn sour in your stomach!" ¹⁰So I took the small scroll from the hand of the angel, and I ate it! It was sweet in my mouth, but when I swallowed it, it turned sour in my stomach.

¹¹Then I was told, "You must prophesy again about many peoples, nations, languages, and kings."

The Two Witnesses

11 Then I was given a measuring stick, and I was told, "Go and measure the Temple of God and the altar, and count the number of worshipers. ²But do not measure the outer courtyard, for it has been turned over to the nations. They will trample the holy city for 42 months. ³And I will give power to my two witnesses, and they will be clothed in burlap and will prophesy during those 1,260 days."

⁴These two prophets are the two olive trees and the two lampstands that stand before the Lord of all the earth. ⁵If anyone tries to harm them, fire flashes from their mouths and consumes their enemies. This is how anyone who tries to harm them must die. ⁶They have power to shut the sky so that no rain will fall for as long as they prophesy. And they have the power to turn the rivers and oceans into blood, and to strike the earth with every kind of plague as often as they wish.

⁷When they complete their testimony, the beast that comes up out of the bottomless pit* will declare war against them, and he will conquer them and kill them. ⁸And their bodies will lie in the main street of Jerusalem,* the city that is figuratively called "Sodom" and "Egypt," the city where their Lord was crucified. ⁹And for three and a half days, all peoples, tribes, languages, and nations will stare at their bodies. No one will be allowed to bury them. ¹⁰All the people who belong to this world will gloat over them and give presents to each other to celebrate the death of the two prophets who had tormented them.

¹¹But after three and a half days, God breathed life into them, and they stood up! Terror struck all who were staring at them. ¹²Then a loud voice from heaven called to the two prophets, "Come up here!" And they rose to heaven in a cloud as their enemies watched.

¹³At the same time there was a terrible earthquake that destroyed a tenth of the city. Seven thousand people died in that earthquake, and everyone else was terrified and gave glory to the God of heaven.

¹⁴The second terror is past, but look, the third terror is coming quickly.

The Seventh Trumpet Brings the Third Terror

¹⁵Then the seventh angel blew his trumpet, and there were loud voices shouting in heaven:

"The world has now become the Kingdom of our
    Lord and of his Christ,*
and he will reign forever and ever."

¹⁶The twenty-four elders sitting on their thrones before God fell with their faces to the ground and worshiped him. ¹⁷And they said,

"We give thanks to you, Lord God, the Almighty,
    the one who is and who always was,
for now you have assumed your great power
    and have begun to reign.
¹⁸ The nations were filled with wrath,
    but now the time of your wrath has come.
It is time to judge the dead
    and reward your servants the prophets,
    as well as your holy people,
and all who fear your name,
    from the least to the greatest.
It is time to destroy
    all who have caused destruction on the earth."

10:2 Or *book;* also in 10:8, 9, 10.   **10:4** Greek *Seal up.*   **11:7** Or *the abyss,* or *the underworld.*   **11:8** Greek *the great city.*
11:15 Or *his Messiah.*

10:1–11:13 This interlude describes the responsibility of God's people among the unrepentant world—they are to continue to testify for him faithfully, as represented by John and the two witnesses. While suffering the effects of judgment may not bring forth repentance (9:20-21), there is sometimes a short-lived acknowledgement of God (11:7, 13).

¹⁹Then, in heaven, the Temple of God was opened and the Ark of his covenant could be seen inside the Temple. Lightning flashed, thunder crashed and roared, and there was an earthquake and a terrible hailstorm.

The Woman and the Dragon

12 Then I witnessed in heaven an event of great significance. I saw a woman clothed with the sun, with the moon beneath her feet, and a crown of twelve stars on her head. ²She was pregnant, and she cried out because of her labor pains and the agony of giving birth.

³Then I witnessed in heaven another significant event. I saw a large red dragon with seven heads and ten horns, with seven crowns on his heads. ⁴His tail swept away one-third of the stars in the sky, and he threw them to the earth. He stood in front of the woman as she was about to give birth, ready to devour her baby as soon as it was born.

⁵She gave birth to a son who was to rule all nations with an iron rod. And her child was snatched away from the dragon and was caught up to God and to his throne. ⁶And the woman fled into the wilderness, where God had prepared a place to care for her for 1,260 days.

⁷Then there was war in heaven. Michael and his angels fought against the dragon and his angels. ⁸And the dragon lost the battle, and he and his angels were forced out of heaven. ⁹This great dragon—the ancient serpent called the devil, or Satan, the one deceiving the whole world—was thrown down to the earth with all his angels.

¹⁰Then I heard a loud voice shouting across the heavens,

"It has come at last—
salvation and power
and the Kingdom of our God,
and the authority of his Christ.*
For the accuser of our brothers and sisters*
has been thrown down to earth—
the one who accuses them
before our God day and night.
¹¹ And they have defeated him by the blood of the Lamb
and by their testimony.
And they did not love their lives so much
that they were afraid to die.
¹² Therefore, rejoice, O heavens!
And you who live in the heavens, rejoice!
But terror will come on the earth and the sea,
for the devil has come down to you in great anger,
knowing that he has little time."

¹³When the dragon realized that he had been thrown down to the earth, he pursued the woman who had given birth to the male child. ¹⁴But she was given two wings like those of a great eagle so she could fly to the place prepared for her in the wilderness. There she would be cared for and protected from the dragon* for a time, times, and half a time.

¹⁵Then the dragon tried to drown the woman with a flood of water that flowed from his mouth. ¹⁶But the earth helped her by opening its mouth and swallowing the river that gushed out from the mouth of the dragon. ¹⁷And the dragon was angry at the woman and declared war against the rest of her children—all who keep God's commandments and maintain their testimony for Jesus.

¹⁸Then the dragon took his stand* on the shore beside the sea.

12:10a Or *his Messiah.* **12:10b** Greek *brothers.* **12:14** Greek *the serpent;* also in 12:15. See 12:9. **12:18** Greek *Then he took his stand;* some manuscripts read *Then I took my stand.* Some translations put this entire sentence into 13:1.

12:1–14:20 This interlude justifies God's execution of these three cycles of judgments (seals, trumpets, and bowls). It explains the evil spiritual causes behind the persecution of God's people (12:1-18) and how such evil manifests in the world (13:1-18). It also provides a preview of the ultimate victory of the Lamb's faithful followers (compare 14:1-5; 15:2-4) and God's vengeance on those who collude with evil (14:6-20).

12:1-18 Both the Old Testament (for example, Lamentations 2:13; Zephaniah 3:14) and the Greco-Roman culture of the first century use the image of "a woman" to symbolize the people of a nation or a city. In Revelation, there are three such instances: the woman crowned with twelve stars (Revelation 12:1-18); the great prostitute (17:1–19:3); and the bride (19:7-8; 21:1–22:17). Modern women might feel uncomfortable with the use of such female imagery. Nonetheless, it is noteworthy that Revelation uses both female and male imagery (see the note on 14:4-5) to depict God's faithful people. Furthermore, female imagery is used both positively and negatively. Thus, the focus of these images in Revelation is not on gender, but rather on behavior.

12:1-17 Satan (pictured as a dragon) plots to challenge God's purposes but is thwarted. Having failed in direct confrontation with God and Christ, he attempts to attack God's people. Three brief scenes present an overview of the story (12:1-6), followed by elaborations of the war in heaven (12:7-9) and the war on earth (12:13-17).

12:1 The number twelve suggests that the woman represents God's people Israel (compare 12:15-17), who the Messiah came from. This woman is marked by God's glory in contrast with the prostitute (see 17:1-6), who is destined for destruction.

12:2 The symbolic woman going through the agony of labor portrays Mary giving birth to Christ, reflecting the biblical theme of Israel's trauma while waiting to be delivered (see Isaiah 26:16-18; Jeremiah 4:31; Micah 4:9-10; John 16:21).

12:11-17 Although Satan (pictured here as a dragon) wages war against God's people again and again throughout the ages, the way to defeat him is not by violent retaliation, but rather "by the blood of the Lamb and by [the angels'] testimony." Christ has already conquered sin and Satan by his redeeming death. By keeping God's commandments and maintaining our testimony for Jesus, God's people (here, the woman's children) can claim Christ's victory over sin and Satan.

Insight: WHAT THE NUMBERS MEAN

The numbers used in Revelation (and elsewhere in Scripture) have often inspired wild predictions for the future. But numbers throughout Scripture have commonly had symbolic meanings. The chart below describes their biblical meaning.

Number	Meaning	References
1	God's oneness	DEUTERONOMY 6:4; GALATIANS 3:20; JAMES 2:19
2	The minimum number required to give a legitimate witness	DEUTERONOMY 17:6; REVELATION 11:3
3	The representation of the divine	GENESIS 18:1-2; 2 CORINTHIANS 13:14; REVELATION 1:4-5
4	The known world, represented in Genesis by four rivers and in Revelation by living creatures, horse riders, winds, and angels	GENESIS 2:10-14; REVELATION 4:6-8; 6:1-8; 7:1
5	Human completeness (for example, *five* fingers per hand)	REVELATION 9:5, 10
6	An implication of evil, being neither humanly complete (*five*) nor divinely complete (*seven*)	
7 (=3+4)	Perfection or divine completeness or fulfillment, indicating that God and the world are in harmony	
10	A symbolic way to indicate *many*	
12 (=3x4)	God's people	GENESIS 35:22-26; EXODUS 24:4; 28:21; NUMBERS 17:2; JOSHUA 4:3-8; 1 KINGS 18:31; MATTHEW 10:1-4; 19:28; JAMES 1:1; REVELATION 12:1; 21:12–22:2
666	Supreme evil (three *sixes*)	REVELATION 13:18
1,000	A huge time period with an indefinite ending point	REVELATION 20:1-10
10,000	A huge number rather than a precise count	LEVITICUS 26:8; DEUTERONOMY 32:30; 1 SAMUEL 18:7; PSALM 3:6; 1 CORINTHIANS 14:19
12,000	A large number of God's people	REVELATION 7:5-8; 21:16 (SEE TEXT NOTE)
144,000	The complete people of God	REVELATION 7:4; 14:1

The Beast out of the Sea

13 Then I saw a beast rising up out of the sea. It had seven heads and ten horns, with ten crowns on its horns. And written on each head were names that blasphemed God. ²This beast looked like a leopard, but it had the feet of a bear and the mouth of a lion! And the dragon gave the beast his own power and throne and great authority.

³I saw that one of the heads of the beast seemed wounded beyond recovery—but the fatal wound was healed! The whole world marveled at this miracle and gave allegiance to the beast. ⁴They worshiped the dragon for giving the beast such power, and they also worshiped the beast. "Who is as great as the beast?" they exclaimed. "Who is able to fight against him?"

⁵Then the beast was allowed to speak great blasphemies against God. And he was given authority to do whatever he wanted for forty-two months. ⁶And he spoke terrible words of blasphemy against God, slandering his name and his dwelling—that is, those who dwell in heaven.* ⁷And the beast was allowed to wage war against God's holy people and to conquer them. And he was given authority to rule over every tribe and people and language and nation. ⁸And all the people who belong to this world worshiped the beast. They are the ones whose names were not written in the Book of Life that belongs to the Lamb who was slaughtered before the world was made.*

⁹ Anyone with ears to hear
　should listen and understand.
¹⁰ Anyone who is destined for prison
　will be taken to prison.
Anyone destined to die by the sword
　will die by the sword.

This means that God's holy people must endure persecution patiently and remain faithful.

13:6 Some manuscripts read *and his dwelling and all who dwell in heaven.* **13:8** Or *not written in the Book of Life before the world was made—the Book that belongs to the Lamb who was slaughtered.*

The Beast out of the Earth

[11] Then I saw another beast come up out of the earth. He had two horns like those of a lamb, but he spoke with the voice of a dragon. [12] He exercised all the authority of the first beast. And he required all the earth and its people to worship the first beast, whose fatal wound had been healed. [13] He did astounding miracles, even making fire flash down to earth from the sky while everyone was watching. [14] And with all the miracles he was allowed to perform on behalf of the first beast, he deceived all the people who belong to this world. He ordered the people to make a great statue of the first beast, who was fatally wounded and then came back to life. [15] He was then permitted to give life to this statue so that it could speak. Then the statue of the beast commanded that anyone refusing to worship it must die.

[16] He required everyone—small and great, rich and poor, free and slave—to be given a mark on the right hand or on the forehead. [17] And no one could buy or sell anything without that mark, which was either the name of the beast or the number representing his name. [18] Wisdom is needed here. Let the one with understanding solve the meaning of the number of the beast, for it is the number of a man.* His number is 666.*

The Lamb and the 144,000

14 Then I saw the Lamb standing on Mount Zion, and with him were 144,000 who had his name and his Father's name written on their foreheads. [2] And I heard a sound from heaven like the roar of mighty ocean waves or the rolling of loud thunder. It was like the sound of many harpists playing together.

[3] This great choir sang a wonderful new song in front of the throne of God and before the four living beings and the twenty-four elders. No one could learn this song except the 144,000 who had been redeemed from the earth. [4] They have kept themselves as pure as virgins,* following the Lamb wherever he

13:18a Or *of humanity*. 13:18b Some manuscripts read *616*.
14:4a Greek *They are virgins who have not defiled themselves with women.*

14:1-14 These faithful followers of the Lamb have withstood the temptation of compromising their faith, even when they suffered economic losses (13:17) and then their lives (13:15). The beast's followers (13:16-17; 14:9, 11) will have no relief (rest) from the punishment of eternal torment, but the Lamb's followers (see 7:3-4) are blessed and will find eternal rest (relief) from their hard work of persevering in their faith. This contrast calls for a response: Is it more worthwhile to compromise our faith for temporary relief or to persevere toward eternal rest and victory?

14:1-5 The true Lamb and his followers starkly contrast with the evil trinity of the dragon, the beast of the sea, and the beast of the earth (12:1–13:18).

Perspective

If sex is a good thing, then why are virgins being rewarded?

SCRIPTURE CONNECTION: REVELATION 14:4

At first, it might seem jarring to read that Revelation 14:4 could be translated "They are virgins who have not defiled themselves with women" (see first text note on 14:4). After all, in Genesis 2:18 and elsewhere, God called "good" his creation of male and female companionship and sex (Genesis 1:28, 31; 2:23-25).

To understand why John portrays virgins, specifically, gaining rewards, we need to understand something about the Old Testament ritual purity system and something about angelic existence.

In the law of Moses, ritual impurity stems broadly from three sources: corpses, genital discharges, and skin abnormalities (see Leviticus 12:1–15:33; Numbers 19:11-16). It was a normal part of everyday life to experience ritual impurity. But entering sacred spaces (the Tabernacle and later the Temple) required a certain kind of purification.

Another possible reason the 144,000 may have devoted themselves to being virgins was to aspire to a kind of angelic existence (see Matthew 22:30). This resulted in special access to God's presence.

Furthermore, John envisions those who worship God faithfully as a virginal bride (Revelation 19:7-9). The 144,000 are characterized as virgins to symbolize their faithfulness to God and their preparation to worship him in his holy Kingdom.

VIEWPOINTS

HERS: *How does keeping ourselves faithfully devoted to God reach all aspects of our lives, perhaps even our choices to marry or have sex?*
MINE: *"Like the 144,000 virgins, I have learned that intimacy with God often comes through sacrifice and obedience."*
YOURS: *How is God calling you into deeper relationship, and what might this look like in your life?*

JENNIFER ROSNER, PhD, is a writer and Messianic Jewish theologian currently serving as Affiliate Assistant Professor at Fuller Theological Seminary. Much of her work focuses on the relationship between Judaism and Christianity.

goes. They have been purchased from among the people on the earth as a special offering* to God and to the Lamb. ⁵They have told no lies; they are without blame.

The Three Angels

⁶And I saw another angel flying through the sky, carrying the eternal Good News to proclaim to the people who belong to this world—to every nation, tribe, language, and people. ⁷"Fear God," he shouted. "Give glory to him. For the time has come when he will sit as judge. Worship him who made the heavens, the earth, the sea, and all the springs of water."

⁸Then another angel followed him through the sky, shouting, "Babylon is fallen—that great city is fallen—because she made all the nations of the world drink the wine of her passionate immorality."

⁹Then a third angel followed them, shouting, "Anyone who worships the beast and his statue or who accepts his mark on the forehead or on the hand ¹⁰must drink the wine of God's anger. It has been poured full strength into God's cup of wrath. And they will be tormented with fire and burning sulfur in the presence of the holy angels and the Lamb. ¹¹The smoke of their torment will rise forever and ever, and they will have no relief day or night, for they have worshiped the beast and his statue and have accepted the mark of his name."

¹²This means that God's holy people must endure persecution patiently, obeying his commands and maintaining their faith in Jesus.

¹³And I heard a voice from heaven saying, "Write this down: Blessed are those who die in the Lord from now on. Yes, says the Spirit, they are blessed indeed, for they will rest from their hard work; for their good deeds follow them!"

The Harvest of the Earth

¹⁴Then I saw a white cloud, and seated on the cloud was someone like the Son of Man.* He had a gold crown on his head and a sharp sickle in his hand.

¹⁵Then another angel came from the Temple and shouted to the one sitting on the cloud, "Swing the sickle, for the time of harvest has come; the crop on earth is ripe." ¹⁶So the one sitting on the cloud swung his sickle over the earth, and the whole earth was harvested.

¹⁷After that, another angel came from the Temple in heaven, and he also had a sharp sickle. ¹⁸Then another angel, who had power to destroy with fire, came from the altar. He shouted to the angel with the sharp sickle, "Swing your sickle now to gather the clusters of grapes from the vines of the earth, for they are ripe for judgment." ¹⁹So the angel swung his sickle over the earth and loaded the grapes into the great winepress of God's wrath. ²⁰The grapes were trampled in the winepress outside the city, and blood flowed from the winepress in a stream about 180 miles* long and as high as a horse's bridle.

The Song of Moses and of the Lamb

15 Then I saw in heaven another marvelous event of great significance. Seven angels were holding the seven last plagues, which would bring God's wrath to completion. ²I saw before me what seemed to be a glass sea mixed with fire. And on it stood all the people who had been victorious over the beast and his statue and the number representing his name. They were all holding harps that God had given them. ³And they were singing the song of Moses, the servant of God, and the song of the Lamb:

> "Great and marvelous are your works,
>   O Lord God, the Almighty.
> Just and true are your ways,
>   O King of the nations.*
> ⁴ Who will not fear you, Lord,
>   and glorify your name?
> For you alone are holy.
> All nations will come and worship before you,
>   for your righteous deeds have been revealed."

The Seven Bowls of the Seven Plagues

⁵Then I looked and saw that the Temple in heaven, God's Tabernacle, was thrown wide open. ⁶The seven angels who were holding the seven plagues came out of the Temple. They were clothed in spotless white linen* with gold sashes across their chests. ⁷Then one of the four living beings handed each of the seven angels a gold bowl filled with the wrath of God, who lives forever and ever. ⁸The Temple was filled with smoke from God's glory and power. No one could enter the Temple until the seven angels had completed pouring out the seven plagues.

14:4b Greek *as firstfruits.* **14:14** Or *like a son of man.* See Dan 7:13. "Son of Man" is a title Jesus used for himself. **14:20** Greek *1,600 stadia* [300 kilometers]. **15:3** Some manuscripts read *King of the ages.* **15:6** Other manuscripts read *white stone;* still others read *white [garments] made of linen.*

14:4-5 These warriors are ritually pure (unpolluted) and morally without blame. They have kept themselves as pure as virgins (literally, "They are virgins who have not defiled themselves with women"). Referring to men as virgins is a metaphor for the faithfulness of God's people. The image might refer to the church as the virgin bride of Christ (see 2 Corinthians 11:2; Ephesians 5:25-27); it also suggests that the church constitutes soldiers in a holy war, where they are required to keep themselves chaste (see Deuteronomy 23:9-10; 1 Samuel 21:5). These faithful people are a special offering (literally "firstfruits"; see Exodus 13:14-16; 23:19; Leviticus 23:9-14; Numbers 3:40-51; 18:15-20; Luke 2:22-24) who have been purchased for God. John teaches that liars will never enter heaven (Revelation 21:8, 27; 22:15; see also John 8:44). The followers of Jesus speak and live the truth (see also John 8:32; 14:6).

16 Then I heard a mighty voice from the Temple say to the seven angels, "Go your ways and pour out on the earth the seven bowls containing God's wrath."

²So the first angel left the Temple and poured out his bowl on the earth, and horrible, malignant sores broke out on everyone who had the mark of the beast and who worshiped his statue.

³Then the second angel poured out his bowl on the sea, and it became like the blood of a corpse. And everything in the sea died.

⁴Then the third angel poured out his bowl on the rivers and springs, and they became blood. ⁵And I heard the angel who had authority over all water saying,

> "You are just, O Holy One, who is and who always was,
> because you have sent these judgments.
> ⁶ Since they shed the blood
> of your holy people and your prophets,
> you have given them blood to drink.
> It is their just reward."

⁷And I heard a voice from the altar,* saying,

> "Yes, O Lord God, the Almighty,
> your judgments are true and just."

⁸Then the fourth angel poured out his bowl on the sun, causing it to scorch everyone with its fire. ⁹Everyone was burned by this blast of heat, and they cursed the name of God, who had control over all these plagues. They did not repent of their sins and turn to God and give him glory.

¹⁰Then the fifth angel poured out his bowl on the throne of the beast, and his kingdom was plunged into darkness. His subjects ground their teeth* in anguish, ¹¹and they cursed the God of heaven for their pains and sores. But they did not repent of their evil deeds and turn to God.

¹²Then the sixth angel poured out his bowl on the great Euphrates River, and it dried up so that the kings from the east could march their armies toward the west without hindrance. ¹³And I saw three evil* spirits that looked like frogs leap from the mouths of the dragon, the beast, and the false prophet. ¹⁴They are demonic spirits who work miracles and go out to all the rulers of the world to gather them for battle against the Lord on that great judgment day of God the Almighty.

> ¹⁵"Look, I will come as unexpectedly as a thief! Blessed are all who are watching for me, who keep their clothing ready so they will not have to walk around naked and ashamed."

¹⁶And the demonic spirits gathered all the rulers and their armies to a place with the Hebrew name *Armageddon.*

¹⁷Then the seventh angel poured out his bowl into the air. And a mighty shout came from the throne in the Temple, saying, "It is finished!" ¹⁸Then the thunder crashed and rolled, and lightning flashed. And a great earthquake struck—the worst since people were placed on the earth. ¹⁹The great city of Babylon split into three sections, and the cities of many nations fell into heaps of rubble. So God remembered all of Babylon's sins, and he made her drink the cup that was filled with the wine of his fierce wrath. ²⁰And every island disappeared, and all the mountains were leveled. ²¹There was a terrible hailstorm, and hailstones weighing as much as seventy-five pounds* fell from the sky onto the people below. They cursed God because of the terrible plague of the hailstorm.

The Great Prostitute

17 One of the seven angels who had poured out the seven bowls came over and spoke to me. "Come with me," he said, "and I will show you the judgment that is going to come on the great prostitute, who rules over many waters. ²The kings of the world have committed adultery with her, and the

---

16:7 Greek *I heard the altar.* **16:10** Greek *gnawed their tongues.* **16:13** Greek *unclean.* **16:16** Or *Harmagedon.* **16:21** Greek *1 talent* [34 kilograms].

16:15 In the New Testament, "clothing" is a metaphor for a person's way of life in terms of disposition and deeds (compare Ephesians 4:21-24; Colossians 3:10, 12, 14). "Nakedness" therefore denotes lack of a pure and righteous way of life. Thus, it is important for us to be prepared for Christ's coming by putting on our proper "clothing."

17:1–19:10 The great drama in this section focuses on the powers that are hostile to God and responsible for the persecution and suffering of God's people. Rome's power was captivating to many (17:6); John purposely defines Rome's sins and provides God's assessment (17:3-18) before outlining its fall (18:1-24) and heaven's response (19:1-10).

17:1-2 The Old Testament uses adultery and sexual immorality as metaphors for being unfaithful to God by serving other gods (see Ezekiel 16:1-63; Hosea 4:1-19; see also the notes on Revelation 14:4-5; 17:2). This unfaithfulness is also often accompanied by other immoral behaviors such as exploitation of the poor, injustice, and killing of the innocent (for example, Isaiah 1:21-31). Similarly, Revelation takes on this imagery of sexual immorality as a metaphor, and in its first-century context depicts unfaithfulness to God by idol and emperor worship. Such unfaithful behavior is also accompanied by other immoral behaviors that are similar to those in the Old Testament times (see Revelation 9:21; 18:13, 23-24; 19:2), including literal immoral sexual conduct. The teaching in both the Old Testament and Revelation is clear—such immoral behaviors will incur God's righteous punishment, whether in the past, present, or future.

17:2 "Adultery with her" is a biblical image for serving other gods (see, for example, Exodus 34:12-16; Judges 2:17; Hosea 2:1-23). Drunkenness in Scripture often depicts nations that indulge in wanton and immoral behavior (see Revelation 18:3, 9; Jeremiah 25:27; 51:7; Lamentations 4:21; Ezekiel 23:33).

The Great Prostitute

IDENTITY — Come Away

She remembers ...

"Look!" they exclaim from afar, "Look at her devastation! Didn't she boast that she is queen on her throne and would never need to mourn?"

Yes, kings, merchants, and sea captains are all grieving because they can no longer benefit from the wealth I used to give them. Trade flourished thanks to my extravagant and luxurious lifestyle, and they grew rich! My power extended over rulers and peoples of the world. I even made them use unscrupulous means to gain power and wealth. Who could resist me?

But I soon discovered a group of people who stood by their so-called true God and their Lord Jesus Christ. They claimed that joining with me was immoral and unfaithful. They even persuaded some not to follow me. How dare they resist me? I was so angry that I slaughtered many of them.

The choking smoke is coming from me! How could this complete devastation have happened to me? I am the great city that rules over the world's kings! I symbolize the society whose ideologies and actions bring wealth! I mock this so-called true God's holiness. But I never thought that this God could wipe me out in just a day! God had warned, but I had not heeded.

THE GREAT PROSTITUTE'S STORY IS TOLD IN REVELATION 17:1–19:10; SEE SPECIFICALLY THE NOTES ON 17:9; 18:4; 19:2-9.

> Being faithful to God may lead to temporal losses but eternal glory.

IDENTIFY

How can you heed the call to "come away" from sin (18:4)?

What lure of gain tempts you? How can you ask God to satisfy you instead?

> "The lure of immoral sensuality and unjust gains can be strong. Compromising may give us temporal gains but eternal losses. Being faithful to God may lead to temporal losses and suffering but eternal glory. God is just; he will avenge and reward his people."

CHEE-CHIEW LEE, PhD, is associate professor in New Testament at Singapore Bible College, and her passion is studying the Word of God and sharing its life-transforming message with people.

people who belong to this world have been made drunk by the wine of her immorality."

³So the angel took me in the Spirit* into the wilderness. There I saw a woman sitting on a scarlet beast that had seven heads and ten horns, and blasphemies against God were written all over it. ⁴The woman wore purple and scarlet clothing and beautiful jewelry made of gold and precious gems and pearls. In her hand she held a gold goblet full of obscenities and the impurities of her immorality. ⁵A mysterious name was written on her forehead: "Babylon the Great, Mother of All Prostitutes and Obscenities in the World." ⁶I could see that she was drunk—drunk with the blood of God's holy people who were witnesses for Jesus. I stared at her in complete amazement.

⁷"Why are you so amazed?" the angel asked. "I will tell you the mystery of this woman and of the beast with seven heads and ten horns on which she sits. ⁸The beast you saw was once alive but isn't now. And yet he will soon come up out of the bottomless pit* and go to eternal destruction. And the people who belong to this world, whose names were not written in the Book of Life before the world was made, will be amazed at the reappearance of this beast who had died.

⁹"This calls for a mind with understanding: The seven heads of the beast represent the seven hills where the woman rules. They also represent seven kings. ¹⁰Five kings have already fallen, the sixth now reigns, and the seventh is yet to come, but his reign will be brief.

¹¹"The scarlet beast that was, but is no longer, is the eighth king. He is like the other seven, and he, too, is headed for destruction. ¹²The ten horns of the beast are ten kings who have not yet risen to power. They will be appointed to their kingdoms for one brief moment to reign with the beast. ¹³They will all agree to give him their power and authority. ¹⁴Together they will go to war against the Lamb, but the Lamb will defeat them because he is Lord of all lords and King of all kings. And his called and chosen and faithful ones will be with him."

¹⁵Then the angel said to me, "The waters where the prostitute is ruling represent masses of people of every nation and language. ¹⁶The scarlet beast and his ten horns all hate the prostitute. They will strip her naked, eat her flesh, and burn her remains with fire. ¹⁷For God has put a plan into their minds, a plan that will carry out his purposes. They will agree to give their authority to the scarlet beast, and so the words of God will be fulfilled. ¹⁸And this woman you saw in your vision represents the great city that rules over the kings of the world."

The Fall of Babylon

18 After all this I saw another angel come down from heaven with great authority, and the earth grew bright with his splendor. ²He gave a mighty shout:

"Babylon is fallen—that great city is fallen!
    She has become a home for demons.
She is a hideout for every foul* spirit,
    a hideout for every foul vulture
    and every foul and dreadful animal.*
³ For all the nations have fallen*
    because of the wine of her passionate immorality.
The kings of the world
    have committed adultery with her.
Because of her desires for extravagant luxury,
    the merchants of the world have grown rich."

⁴Then I heard another voice calling from heaven,

"Come away from her, my people.
    Do not take part in her sins,
    or you will be punished with her.
⁵ For her sins are piled as high as heaven,
    and God remembers her evil deeds.
⁶ Do to her as she has done to others.
    Double her penalty* for all her evil deeds.
She brewed a cup of terror for others,
    so brew twice as much* for her.
⁷ She glorified herself and lived in luxury,
    so match it now with torment and sorrow.

17:3 Or *in spirit.* **17:8** Or *the abyss,* or *the underworld.* **18:2a** Greek *unclean;* also in each of the two following phrases. **18:2b** Some manuscripts condense the last two lines to read *a hideout for every foul [unclean] and dreadful vulture.* **18:3** Some manuscripts read *have drunk.* **18:6a** Or *Give her an equal penalty.* **18:6b** Or *brew just as much.*

17:5 Using code language (compare the note on 12:1-18), John was probably referring to Rome (see 17:9) as "Babylon the Great, Mother of All Prostitutes." Babylon was a symbol of the idolatries and demonic obscenities of the world. As a mother-like figure, she had produced offspring who copied her character. Rome, like Babylon, prostituted herself to false gods and led other nations into adultery and idolatry.
17:9 "This calls for a mind with understanding" is similar to the wording in 13:18. God's holy people need wisdom to discern the circumstances that may tempt us to collude with the great prostitute and the beast for economic benefits (see 18:3-4, 9, 11, 15) or to avoid persecution (see 13:15-18).

17:15-16 While the prostitute rules over the masses, her rule does not bring her victory. Instead, the beast hates and kills the great prostitute. Satan strikes even those he uses for his evil purposes.
18:1-24 This chapter contains seven poetic responses to the fall of Babylon (or Rome; see the note on 17:5).
18:4 The voice from heaven calls God's holy people to dissociate with the great prostitute and not take part in her sins or they will be punished together with her. Such collusion can take the form of unethical business practices like exploitation of workers, corruption, and bribery. The seduction of ill-gotten wealth can easily tempt us to become unfaithful to him.

She boasted in her heart,
'I am queen on my throne.
I am no helpless widow,
and I have no reason to mourn.'
⁸ Therefore, these plagues will overtake her in a single day—
death and mourning and famine.
She will be completely consumed by fire,
for the Lord God who judges her is mighty."

⁹And the kings of the world who committed adultery with her and enjoyed her great luxury will mourn for her as they see the smoke rising from her charred remains. ¹⁰They will stand at a distance, terrified by her great torment. They will cry out,

"How terrible, how terrible for you,
O Babylon, you great city!
In a single moment
God's judgment came on you."

¹¹The merchants of the world will weep and mourn for her, for there is no one left to buy their goods. ¹²She bought great quantities of gold, silver, jewels, and pearls; fine linen, purple, silk, and scarlet cloth; things made of fragrant thyine wood, ivory goods, and objects made of expensive wood; and bronze, iron, and marble. ¹³She also bought cinnamon, spice, incense, myrrh, frankincense, wine, olive oil, fine flour, wheat, cattle, sheep, horses, wagons, and bodies—that is, human slaves.

¹⁴ "The fancy things you loved so much
are gone," they cry.
"All your luxuries and splendor
are gone forever,
never to be yours again."

¹⁵The merchants who became wealthy by selling her these things will stand at a distance, terrified by her great torment. They will weep and cry out,

¹⁶ "How terrible, how terrible for that great city!
She was clothed in finest purple and scarlet linens,
decked out with gold and precious stones and pearls!
¹⁷ In a single moment
all the wealth of the city is gone!"

And all the captains of the merchant ships and their passengers and sailors and crews will stand at a distance. ¹⁸They will cry out as they watch the smoke ascend, and they will say, "Where is there another city as great as this?" ¹⁹And they will weep and throw dust on their heads to show their grief. And they will cry out,

"How terrible, how terrible for that great city!
The shipowners became wealthy
by transporting her great wealth on the seas.
In a single moment it is all gone."

²⁰ Rejoice over her fate, O heaven
and people of God and apostles and prophets!
For at last God has judged her
for your sakes.

²¹Then a mighty angel picked up a boulder the size of a huge millstone. He threw it into the ocean and shouted,

"Just like this, the great city Babylon
will be thrown down with violence
and will never be found again.
²² The sound of harps, singers, flutes, and trumpets
will never be heard in you again.
No craftsmen and no trades
will ever be found in you again.
The sound of the mill
will never be heard in you again.
²³ The light of a lamp
will never shine in you again.
The happy voices of brides and grooms
will never be heard in you again.
For your merchants were the greatest in the world,
and you deceived the nations with your sorceries.
²⁴ In your* streets flowed the blood of the prophets
and of God's holy people
and the blood of people slaughtered all over the world."

Songs of Victory in Heaven

19 After this, I heard what sounded like a vast crowd in heaven shouting,

"Praise the LORD!*
Salvation and glory and power belong to our God.
² His judgments are true and just.
He has punished the great prostitute
who corrupted the earth with her immorality.
He has avenged the murder of his servants."

18:24 Greek *her*. 19:1 Greek *Hallelujah*; also in 19:3, 4, 6. *Hallelujah* is the transliteration of a Hebrew term that means "Praise the LORD."

18:13 Buying and selling enslaved people was a huge market in ancient Rome, and historians currently estimate that enslaved people comprised 20 percent of the population.
19:2-9 God's "judgments are true and just." He avenges his servants who have suffered faithfully by punishing the great prostitute with permanent destruction. The good deeds of God's holy people in resisting evil are depicted as the pure white linen that the bride wears. God's justice is a great encouragement to his faithful people because their suffering and good deeds are not in vain.
19:2 In his righteous justice, God kept his promise of judging the great prostitute, who represents moral and spiritual corruption and persecution of God's people (see 15:3; 16:7).

> "All shall be well, and all shall be well, and all manner of things shall be well."
>
> **JULIAN OF NORWICH**
> (1342–1416) theologian who lived in voluntary seclusion to pray

[3] And again their voices rang out:

"Praise the Lord!
 The smoke from that city ascends forever and ever!"

[4] Then the twenty-four elders and the four living beings fell down and worshiped God, who was sitting on the throne. They cried out, "Amen! Praise the Lord!"

[5] And from the throne came a voice that said,

"Praise our God,
 all his servants,
all who fear him,
 from the least to the greatest."

[6] Then I heard again what sounded like the shout of a vast crowd or the roar of mighty ocean waves or the crash of loud thunder:

"Praise the Lord!
 For the Lord our God,* the Almighty, reigns.
[7] Let us be glad and rejoice,
 and let us give honor to him.
For the time has come for the wedding feast of the Lamb,
 and his bride has prepared herself.
[8] She has been given the finest of pure white linen to wear."

For the fine linen represents the good deeds of God's holy people.

[9] And the angel said to me, "Write this: Blessed are those who are invited to the wedding feast of the Lamb." And he added, "These are true words that come from God."

[10] Then I fell down at his feet to worship him, but he said, "No, don't worship me. I am a servant of God, just like you and your brothers and sisters* who testify about their faith in Jesus. Worship only God. For the essence of prophecy is to give a clear witness for Jesus.*"

The Rider on the White Horse

[11] Then I saw heaven opened, and a white horse was standing there. Its rider was named Faithful and True, for he judges fairly and wages a righteous war. [12] His eyes were like flames of fire, and on his head were many crowns. A name was written on him that no one understood except himself. [13] He wore a robe dipped in blood, and his title was the Word of God. [14] The armies of heaven, dressed in the finest of pure white linen, followed him on white horses. [15] From his mouth came a sharp sword to strike down the nations. He will rule them with an iron rod. He will release the fierce wrath of God, the Almighty, like juice flowing from a winepress. [16] On his robe at his thigh* was written this title:

King of all kings and Lord of all lords.

[17] Then I saw an angel standing in the sun, shouting to the vultures flying high in the sky: "Come! Gather together for the great banquet God has prepared. [18] Come and eat the flesh of kings, generals, and strong warriors; of horses and their riders; and of all humanity, both free and slave, small and great."

[19] Then I saw the beast and the kings of the world and their armies gathered together to fight against the one sitting on the horse and his army. [20] And the beast was captured, and with him the false prophet who did mighty miracles on behalf of the beast—miracles that deceived all who had accepted the mark of the beast and who worshiped his statue. Both the beast and his false prophet were thrown alive into the fiery lake of burning sulfur. [21] Their entire army was killed by the sharp sword that came from the mouth of the one riding the white horse. And the vultures all gorged themselves on the dead bodies.

The Thousand Years

20 Then I saw an angel coming down from heaven with the key to the bottomless pit* and a heavy chain in his hand. [2] He seized the dragon—that old serpent, who is the devil, Satan—and bound him in chains for a thousand years. [3] The

---

19:6 Some manuscripts read *the Lord God.* **19:10a** Greek *brothers.* **19:10b** Or *is the message confirmed by Jesus.* **19:16** Or *On his robe and thigh.* **20:1** Or *the abyss,* or *the underworld;* also in 20:3.

19:7 This event—the wedding of the Messiah with his bride, the church (see Isaiah 54:5; 61:10; Jeremiah 31:32; Ezekiel 16:7-14; Hosea 2:16-20; Mark 2:19-20; 2 Corinthians 11:2)—symbolizes complete victory and eternal fellowship.

angel threw him into the bottomless pit, which he then shut and locked so Satan could not deceive the nations anymore until the thousand years were finished. Afterward he must be released for a little while.

⁴Then I saw thrones, and the people sitting on them had been given the authority to judge. And I saw the souls of those who had been beheaded for their testimony about Jesus and for proclaiming the word of God. They had not worshiped the beast or his statue, nor accepted his mark on their foreheads or their hands. They all came to life again, and they reigned with Christ for a thousand years.

⁵This is the first resurrection. (The rest of the dead did not come back to life until the thousand years had ended.) ⁶Blessed and holy are those who share in the first resurrection. For them the second death holds no power, but they will be priests of God and of Christ and will reign with him a thousand years.

The Defeat of Satan

⁷When the thousand years come to an end, Satan will be let out of his prison. ⁸He will go out to deceive the nations—called Gog and Magog—in every corner of the earth. He will gather them together for battle—a mighty army, as numberless as sand along the seashore. ⁹And I saw them as they went up on the broad plain of the earth and surrounded God's people and the beloved city. But fire from heaven came down on the attacking armies and consumed them.

¹⁰Then the devil, who had deceived them, was thrown into the fiery lake of burning sulfur, joining the beast and the false prophet. There they will be tormented day and night forever and ever.

The Final Judgment

¹¹And I saw a great white throne and the one sitting on it. The earth and sky fled from his presence, but they found no place to hide. ¹²I saw the dead, both great and small, standing before God's throne. And the books were opened, including the Book of Life. And the dead were judged according to what they had done, as recorded in the books. ¹³The sea gave up its dead, and death and the grave* gave up their dead. And all were judged according to their deeds. ¹⁴Then death and the grave were thrown into the lake of fire. This lake of fire is the second death. ¹⁵And anyone whose name was not found recorded in the Book of Life was thrown into the lake of fire.

The New Jerusalem

21 Then I saw a new heaven and a new earth, for the old heaven and the old earth had disappeared. And the sea was also gone. ²And I saw the holy city, the new Jerusalem, coming down from God out of heaven like a bride beautifully dressed for her husband.

³I heard a loud shout from the throne, saying, "Look, God's home is now among his people! He will live with them, and they will be his people. God himself will be with them.* ⁴He will wipe every tear from their eyes, and there will be no more death or sorrow or crying or pain. All these things are gone forever."

⁵And the one sitting on the throne said, "Look, I am making everything new!" And then he said to me, "Write this down, for what I tell you is trustworthy and true." ⁶And he also said, "It is finished! I am the Alpha and the Omega—the Beginning and the End. To all who are thirsty I will give freely from the springs of the water of life. ⁷All who are victorious will inherit all these blessings, and I will be their God, and they will be my children.

⁸"But cowards, unbelievers, the corrupt, murderers, the immoral, those who practice witchcraft, idol worshipers, and all liars—their fate is in the fiery lake of burning sulfur. This is the second death."

⁹Then one of the seven angels who held the seven bowls containing the seven last plagues came and said to me, "Come with me! I will show you the bride, the wife of the Lamb."

20:13 Greek *and Hades;* also in 20:14.   **21:3** Some manuscripts read *God himself will be with them, their God.*

20:1-10 There are three parts to this passage: the binding of Satan (20:1-3), the reign of God's holy people (20:4-6), and the release of Satan for his final attempt at a battle (20:7-10). Four themes emerge: Satan's war is futile—he cannot withstand even an angel; God's holy people will be vindicated and glorified; God will have the final victory; and even when sinful and depraved human beings experience Christ's good purposes in the world, they still flock after Satan when he gains even a small amount of freedom to act.

21:9–22:9 This symbolic vision of the new Jerusalem uses vivid word pictures to describe the bride, the wife of the Lamb—all those who respond to Christ's message of salvation (see 21:2; 22:17; Ephesians 5:22-32).

21:9-21 Although both are adorned with gold, precious gems, and pearls, the purity and glory of the bride—the new Jerusalem—far outweighs and contrasts with the foul nature and seemingly luxurious clothing of the great prostitute—the great Babylon (17:4-5; 18:3). This contrast helps us to understand the true nature of what these two women represent (see the notes on 12:1-18; 21:9-10) so that we may make the right choice to persevere and stand firm in our faith.

21:9-10 Like other Jewish literature, Revelation repeats identical phrases in the narrative as a signal for the audience or readers to compare and contrast two sections of the narrative. The identical phrases "come with me" in 17:1 and 21:9 mark the beginning of the section on the great prostitute (Babylon) and the bride (New Jerusalem), while those in 19:10 and 22:9 mark the ending ("No, don't worship me. I am a servant of God. . . . Worship only God"). The contrast is stark. Those who collude with the great prostitute seem to enjoy many political and economic benefits at that time, but they will eventually meet with destruction, like the great prostitute. Those who choose to remain faithful seem to suffer unjustly at the time, but they will eventually emerge victorious and glorious, like the bride of Christ. This calls for a response: Which woman do we want to identify ourselves with?

¹⁰So he took me in the Spirit* to a great, high mountain, and he showed me the holy city, Jerusalem, descending out of heaven from God. ¹¹It shone with the glory of God and sparkled like a precious stone—like jasper as clear as crystal. ¹²The city wall was broad and high, with twelve gates guarded by twelve angels. And the names of the twelve tribes of Israel were written on the gates. ¹³There were three gates on each side—east, north, south, and west. ¹⁴The wall of the city had twelve foundation stones, and on them were written the names of the twelve apostles of the Lamb.

¹⁵The angel who talked to me held in his hand a gold measuring stick to measure the city, its gates, and its wall. ¹⁶When he measured it, he found it was a square, as wide as it was long. In fact, its length and width and height were each 1,400 miles.* ¹⁷Then he measured the walls and found them to be 216 feet thick* (according to the human standard used by the angel).

¹⁸The wall was made of jasper, and the city was pure gold, as clear as glass. ¹⁹The wall of the city was built on foundation stones inlaid with twelve precious stones:* the first was jasper, the second sapphire, the third agate, the fourth emerald, ²⁰the fifth onyx, the sixth carnelian, the seventh chrysolite, the eighth beryl, the ninth topaz, the tenth chrysoprase, the eleventh jacinth, the twelfth amethyst.

²¹The twelve gates were made of pearls—each gate from a single pearl! And the main street was pure gold, as clear as glass.

²²I saw no temple in the city, for the Lord God Almighty and the Lamb are its temple. ²³And the city has no need of sun or moon, for the glory of God illuminates the city, and the Lamb is its light. ²⁴The nations will walk in its light, and the kings of the world will enter the city in all their glory. ²⁵Its gates will never be closed at the end of day because there is no night there. ²⁶And all the nations will bring their glory and honor into the city. ²⁷Nothing evil* will be allowed to enter, nor anyone who practices shameful idolatry and dishonesty—but only those whose names are written in the Lamb's Book of Life.

22

Then the angel showed me a river with the water of life, clear as crystal, flowing from the throne of God and of the Lamb. ²It flowed down the center of the main street. On each side of the river grew a tree of life, bearing twelve crops of fruit,* with a fresh crop each month. The leaves were used for medicine to heal the nations.

³No longer will there be a curse upon anything. For the throne of God and of the Lamb will be there, and his servants will worship him. ⁴And they will see his face, and his name will be written on their foreheads. ⁵And there will be no night there—no need for lamps or sun—for the Lord God will shine on them. And they will reign forever and ever.

⁶Then the angel said to me, "Everything you have heard and seen is trustworthy and true. The Lord God, who inspires his prophets,* has sent his angel to tell his servants what will happen soon.*"

Jesus Is Coming

⁷"Look, I am coming soon! Blessed are those who obey the words of prophecy written in this book.*"

⁸I, John, am the one who heard and saw all these things. And when I heard and saw them, I fell down to worship at the feet of the angel who showed them to me. ⁹But he said, "No, don't worship me. I am a servant of God, just like you and your brothers the prophets, as well as all who obey what is written in this book. Worship only God!"

¹⁰Then he instructed me, "Do not seal up the prophetic words in this book, for the time is near. ¹¹Let the one who is doing harm continue to do harm; let the one who is vile continue to be vile; let the one who is righteous continue to live righteously; let the one who is holy continue to be holy."

¹²"Look, I am coming soon, bringing my reward with me to repay all people according to their deeds. ¹³I am the Alpha and the Omega, the First and the Last, the Beginning and the End."

¹⁴Blessed are those who wash their robes. They will be permitted to enter through the gates of the city and eat the fruit from the tree of life. ¹⁵Outside the city are the dogs—the sorcerers, the sexually immoral, the murderers, the idol worshipers, and all who love to live a lie.

¹⁶"I, Jesus, have sent my angel to give you this message for the churches. I am both the source of David and the heir to his throne.* I am the bright morning star."

21:10 Or *in spirit*. 21:16 Greek *12,000 stadia* [2,220 kilometers]. 21:17 Greek *144 cubits* [65 meters]. 21:19 The identification of some of these gemstones is uncertain. 21:27 Or *ceremonially unclean*. 22:2 Or *twelve kinds of fruit*. 22:6a Or *The Lord, the God of the spirits of the prophets*. 22:6b Or *suddenly*, or *quickly*; also in 22:7, 12, 20. 22:7 Or *scroll*; also in 22:9, 10, 18, 19. 22:16 Greek *I am the root and offspring of David*.

21:10 In Scripture, experiences with God frequently take place on mountains (compare Ezekiel 40:2; see also Exodus 3:1; 19:10-25; Deuteronomy 34:1-4; 1 Kings 18:20-40; 19:8-18; Matthew 5:1; 15:29; 17:1; 24:3; 28:16). God's presence and eternal life cannot be reached by human effort but are received as a gift (Ephesians 2:8-9; see also 2 Corinthians 5:1).

22:6-7 Like the Old Testament prophets who call God's people to repent from their disobedience and unfaithfulness to God, the prophecy in Revelation does the same. The warnings of punishment and promises of reward in the future are not merely a prediction, but "trustworthy and true" words meant to spur repentance and obedience. Thus, blessed are those who obey (see also 1:3).

Eve and the Bride of Christ

IDENTITY — Better Than Before

Eve remembers...

It's been millennia since I messed up in the Garden of Eden. I thought I knew better than God what would be good. I saw what I wanted and took it. My husband went along with that tragic choice and, as they say, "the rest is history."

But here, at the end of the Bible's story, the angel reveals a vision that takes away my breath! The garden of God's presence merges with the holy city where God dwells, and the result stuns me. Darkness flees. Sorrow is silenced. Thirst is quenched. God's benevolent rule brings healing and safety—and blessing.

Nothing I did, and nothing you have done, can undermine God's glorious plan: He will make all things new. And not just new but beyond our wildest dreams. Imagine, together we are his bride, reigning with Christ! We must simply wash our robes, allowing Christ to cleanse us from our wrongs.

His forgiveness restores our access to God, the kind I had once when I walked with God in the Garden. Though Adam and I brought sin and death into the world, sin and death do not get the final word. What God intended from the beginning will be realized more than we thought possible. Once again, we will be intimate with God. But for more than our lifetimes. At last, we can live forever and eat from the tree of life!

> With Jesus, the best is yet to come!

EVE AND THE BRIDE OF CHRIST'S STORY IS TOLD IN REVELATION 21:1–22:21; THE BEGINNING OF EVE'S STORY IS TOLD IN GENESIS 1:1–3:24.

IDENTIFY

What do you imagine it will be like to live forever in God's presence?

How can focusing on our future with God change the way we live today?

> "The weight of this world can be crushing. Now, more than ever, I need to fix my eyes on the grand finale of God's work on the stage of human history. John's vision gives me hope that the brokenness in myself and all around me is not the final word. Even now, we can live within this future hope."

CARMEN JOY IMES, PhD, is an author, speaker, blogger, YouTuber, and serves as associate professor of Old Testament at Biola University in California.

Insight: REVELATION'S OLD TESTAMENT IMAGERY

We tend to describe things using language and images we know. As Jesus conveyed a vision to John, John's descriptions reflect how he understood the world—through pictures and events of the Old Testament. Understanding how these images appear in the Old Testament can help us better interpret Revelation.

THE SON OF MAN — Revelation 1; 13; 14 ← → Daniel 7

FOUR LIVING BEINGS — Revelation 4 ← → Ezekiel 1; 10

FOUR RIDERS — Revelation 6 ← → Zechariah 6

THE SEAL OR THE MARK — Revelation 7; 13 ← → Ezekiel 9

TRUMPET & BOWL PLAGUES — Revelation 8; 16 ← → Exodus 7–10

GOD REIGNS IN THE NEW JERUSALEM — Revelation 21 ← → Isaiah 60; Ezekiel 28; 36; Zechariah 14

TREE OF LIFE AND RIVER OF LIFE — Revelation 22 ← → Genesis 2–3; Ezekiel 47

¹⁷The Spirit and the bride say, "Come." Let anyone who hears this say, "Come." Let anyone who is thirsty come. Let anyone who desires drink freely from the water of life. ¹⁸And I solemnly declare to everyone who hears the words of prophecy written in this book: If anyone adds anything to what is written here, God will add to that person the plagues described in this book. ¹⁹And if anyone removes any of the words from this book of prophecy, God will remove that person's share in the tree of life and in the holy city that are described in this book.

²⁰He who is the faithful witness to all these things says, "Yes, I am coming soon!"

Amen! Come, Lord Jesus!

²¹May the grace of the Lord Jesus be with God's holy people.*

22:21 Other manuscripts read *be with all*; still others read *be with all of God's holy people*. Some manuscripts add *Amen*.

22:17 "Come" is a repeated invitation and a confession (see 22:20). The Lamb's wife (see 21:9) is the church, the people of God. The thirsty can drink freely from God's provision (see 21:6; 22:1; Psalm 42:1; Isaiah 55:1; John 4:10-14).

THE ONE YEAR BIBLE READING PLAN

JANUARY 1
Genesis 1:1–2:25
Matthew 1:1–2:12
Psalm 1:1-6
Proverbs 1:1-6

JANUARY 2
Genesis 3:1–4:26
Matthew 2:13–3:6
Psalm 2:1-12
Proverbs 1:7-9

JANUARY 3
Genesis 5:1–7:24
Matthew 3:7–4:11
Psalm 3:1-8
Proverbs 1:10-19

JANUARY 4
Genesis 8:1–10:32
Matthew 4:12-25
Psalm 4:1-8
Proverbs 1:20-23

JANUARY 5
Genesis 11:1–13:4
Matthew 5:1-26
Psalm 5:1-12
Proverbs 1:24-28

JANUARY 6
Genesis 13:5–15:21
Matthew 5:27-48
Psalm 6:1-10
Proverbs 1:29-33

JANUARY 7
Genesis 16:1–18:15
Matthew 6:1-24
Psalm 7:1-17
Proverbs 2:1-5

JANUARY 8
Genesis 18:16–19:38
Matthew 6:25–7:14
Psalm 8:1-9
Proverbs 2:6-15

JANUARY 9
Genesis 20:1–22:24
Matthew 7:15-29
Psalm 9:1-12
Proverbs 2:16-22

JANUARY 10
Genesis 23:1–24:51
Matthew 8:1-17
Psalm 9:13-20
Proverbs 3:1-6

JANUARY 11
Genesis 24:52–26:16
Matthew 8:18-34
Psalm 10:1-15
Proverbs 3:7-8

JANUARY 12
Genesis 26:17–27:46
Matthew 9:1-17
Psalm 10:16-18
Proverbs 3:9-10

JANUARY 13
Genesis 28:1–29:35
Matthew 9:18-38
Psalm 11:1-7
Proverbs 3:11-12

JANUARY 14
Genesis 30:1–31:16
Matthew 10:1-23
Psalm 12:1-8
Proverbs 3:13-15

JANUARY 15
Genesis 31:17–32:12
Matthew 10:24–11:6
Psalm 13:1-6
Proverbs 3:16-18

JANUARY 16
Genesis 32:13–34:31
Matthew 11:7-30
Psalm 14:1-7
Proverbs 3:19-20

JANUARY 17
Genesis 35:1–36:43
Matthew 12:1-21
Psalm 15:1-5
Proverbs 3:21-26

JANUARY 18
Genesis 37:1–38:30
Matthew 12:22-45
Psalm 16:1-11
Proverbs 3:27-32

JANUARY 19
Genesis 39:1–41:16
Matthew 12:46–13:23
Psalm 17:1-15
Proverbs 3:33-35

JANUARY 20
Genesis 41:17–42:17
Matthew 13:24-46
Psalm 18:1-15
Proverbs 4:1-6

JANUARY 21
Genesis 42:18–43:34
Matthew 13:47–14:12
Psalm 18:16-36
Proverbs 4:7-10

JANUARY 22
Genesis 44:1–45:28
Matthew 14:13-36
Psalm 18:37-50
Proverbs 4:11-13

JANUARY 23
Genesis 46:1–47:31
Matthew 15:1-28
Psalm 19:1-14
Proverbs 4:14-19

JANUARY 24
Genesis 48:1–49:33
Matthew 15:29–16:12
Psalm 20:1-9
Proverbs 4:20-27

JANUARY 25
Genesis 50:1—Exodus 2:10
Matthew 16:13–17:9
Psalm 21:1-13
Proverbs 5:1-6

JANUARY 26
Exodus 2:11–3:22
Matthew 17:10-27
Psalm 22:1-18
Proverbs 5:7-14

JANUARY 27
Exodus 4:1–5:21
Matthew 18:1-20
Psalm 22:19-31
Proverbs 5:15-21

JANUARY 28
Exodus 5:22–7:25
Matthew 18:21–19:12
Psalm 23:1-6
Proverbs 5:22-23

JANUARY 29
Exodus 8:1–9:35
Matthew 19:13-30
Psalm 24:1-10
Proverbs 6:1-5

JANUARY 30
Exodus 10:1–12:13
Matthew 20:1-28
Psalm 25:1-15
Proverbs 6:6-11

JANUARY 31
Exodus 12:14–13:16
Matthew 20:29–21:22
Psalm 25:16-22
Proverbs 6:12-15

FEBRUARY 1
Exodus 13:17–15:18
Matthew 21:23-46
Psalm 26:1-12
Proverbs 6:16-19

FEBRUARY 2
Exodus 15:19–17:7
Matthew 22:1-33
Psalm 27:1-6
Proverbs 6:20-26

FEBRUARY 3
Exodus 17:8–19:15
Matthew 22:34–23:12
Psalm 27:7-14
Proverbs 6:27-35

FEBRUARY 4
Exodus 19:16–21:21
Matthew 23:13-39
Psalm 28:1-9
Proverbs 7:1-5

FEBRUARY 5
Exodus 21:22–23:13
Matthew 24:1-28
Psalm 29:1-11
Proverbs 7:6-23

FEBRUARY 6
Exodus 23:14–25:40
Matthew 24:29-51
Psalm 30:1-12
Proverbs 7:24-27

FEBRUARY 7
Exodus 26:1–27:21
Matthew 25:1-30
Psalm 31:1-8
Proverbs 8:1-11

FEBRUARY 8
Exodus 28:1-43
Matthew 25:31–26:13
Psalm 31:9-18
Proverbs 8:12-13

FEBRUARY 9
Exodus 29:1–30:10
Matthew 26:14-46
Psalm 31:19-24
Proverbs 8:14-26

FEBRUARY 10
Exodus 30:11–31:18
Matthew 26:47-68
Psalm 32:1-11
Proverbs 8:27-32

FEBRUARY 11
Exodus 32:1–33:23
Matthew 26:69–27:14
Psalm 33:1-11
Proverbs 8:33-36

FEBRUARY 12
Exodus 34:1–35:9
Matthew 27:15-31
Psalm 33:12-22
Proverbs 9:1-6

FEBRUARY 13
Exodus 35:10–36:38
Matthew 27:32-66
Psalm 34:1-10
Proverbs 9:7-8

FEBRUARY 14
Exodus 37:1–38:31
Matthew 28:1-20
Psalm 34:11-22
Proverbs 9:9-10

FEBRUARY 15
Exodus 39:1–40:38
Mark 1:1-28
Psalm 35:1-16
Proverbs 9:11-12

FEBRUARY 16
Leviticus 1:1–3:17
Mark 1:29–2:12
Psalm 35:17-28
Proverbs 9:13-18

FEBRUARY 17
Leviticus 4:1–5:19
Mark 2:13–3:6
Psalm 36:1-12
Proverbs 10:1-2

FEBRUARY 18
Leviticus 6:1–7:27
Mark 3:7-30
Psalm 37:1-11
Proverbs 10:3-4

FEBRUARY 19
Leviticus 7:28–9:6
Mark 3:31–4:25
Psalm 37:12-29
Proverbs 10:5

FEBRUARY 20
Leviticus 9:7–10:20
Mark 4:26–5:20
Psalm 37:30-40
Proverbs 10:6-7

FEBRUARY 21
Leviticus 11:1–12:8
Mark 5:21-43
Psalm 38:1-22
Proverbs 10:8-9

FEBRUARY 22
Leviticus 13:1-59
Mark 6:1-29
Psalm 39:1-13
Proverbs 10:10

FEBRUARY 23
Leviticus 14:1-57
Mark 6:30-56
Psalm 40:1-10
Proverbs 10:11-12

FEBRUARY 24
- Leviticus 15:1–16:28
- Mark 7:1-23
- Psalm 40:11-17
- Proverbs 10:13-14

FEBRUARY 25
- Leviticus 16:29–18:30
- Mark 7:24–8:10
- Psalm 41:1-13
- Proverbs 10:15-16

FEBRUARY 26
- Leviticus 19:1–20:21
- Mark 8:11-38
- Psalm 42:1-11
- Proverbs 10:17

FEBRUARY 27
- Leviticus 20:22–22:16
- Mark 9:1-29
- Psalm 43:1-5
- Proverbs 10:18

FEBRUARY 28
- Leviticus 22:17–23:44
- Mark 9:30–10:12
- Psalm 44:1-8
- Proverbs 10:19

MARCH 1
- Leviticus 24:1–25:46
- Mark 10:13-31
- Psalm 44:9-26
- Proverbs 10:20-21

MARCH 2
- Leviticus 25:47–27:13
- Mark 10:32-52
- Psalm 45:1-17
- Proverbs 10:22

MARCH 3
- Leviticus 27:14—Numbers 1:54
- Mark 11:1-26
- Psalm 46:1-11
- Proverbs 10:23

MARCH 4
- Numbers 2:1–3:51
- Mark 11:27–12:17
- Psalm 47:1-9
- Proverbs 10:24-25

MARCH 5
- Numbers 4:1–5:31
- Mark 12:18-37
- Psalm 48:1-14
- Proverbs 10:26

MARCH 6
- Numbers 6:1–7:89
- Mark 12:38–13:13
- Psalm 49:1-20
- Proverbs 10:27-28

MARCH 7
- Numbers 8:1–9:23
- Mark 13:14-37
- Psalm 50:1-23
- Proverbs 10:29-30

MARCH 8
- Numbers 10:1–11:23
- Mark 14:1-21
- Psalm 51:1-19
- Proverbs 10:31-32

MARCH 9
- Numbers 11:24–13:33
- Mark 14:22-52
- Psalm 52:1-9
- Proverbs 11:1-3

MARCH 10
- Numbers 14:1–15:16
- Mark 14:53-72
- Psalm 53:1-6
- Proverbs 11:4

MARCH 11
- Numbers 15:17–16:40
- Mark 15:1-47
- Psalm 54:1-7
- Proverbs 11:5-6

MARCH 12
- Numbers 16:41–18:32
- Mark 16:1-20
- Psalm 55:1-23
- Proverbs 11:7

MARCH 13
- Numbers 19:1–20:29
- Luke 1:1-25
- Psalm 56:1-13
- Proverbs 11:8

MARCH 14
- Numbers 21:1–22:20
- Luke 1:26-56
- Psalm 57:1-11
- Proverbs 11:9-11

MARCH 15
- Numbers 22:21–23:30
- Luke 1:57-80
- Psalm 58:1-11
- Proverbs 11:12-13

MARCH 16
- Numbers 24:1–25:18
- Luke 2:1-35
- Psalm 59:1-17
- Proverbs 11:14

MARCH 17
- Numbers 26:1-51
- Luke 2:36-52
- Psalm 60:1-12
- Proverbs 11:15

MARCH 18
- Numbers 26:52–28:15
- Luke 3:1-22
- Psalm 61:1-8
- Proverbs 11:16-17

MARCH 19
- Numbers 28:16–29:40
- Luke 3:23-38
- Psalm 62:1-12
- Proverbs 11:18-19

MARCH 20
- Numbers 30:1–31:54
- Luke 4:1-30
- Psalm 63:1-11
- Proverbs 11:20-21

MARCH 21
- Numbers 32:1–33:39
- Luke 4:31–5:11
- Psalm 64:1-10
- Proverbs 11:22

MARCH 22
- Numbers 33:40–35:34
- Luke 5:12-28
- Psalm 65:1-13
- Proverbs 11:23

MARCH 23
- Numbers 36:1—Deuteronomy 1:46
- Luke 5:29–6:11
- Psalm 66:1-20
- Proverbs 11:24-26

MARCH 24
- Deuteronomy 2:1–3:29
- Luke 6:12-38
- Psalm 67:1-7
- Proverbs 11:27

MARCH 25
- Deuteronomy 4:1-49
- Luke 6:39–7:10
- Psalm 68:1-18
- Proverbs 11:28

MARCH 26
Deuteronomy 5:1–6:25
Luke 7:11-35
Psalm 68:19-35
Proverbs 11:29-31

MARCH 27
Deuteronomy 7:1–8:20
Luke 7:36–8:3
Psalm 69:1-18
Proverbs 12:1

MARCH 28
Deuteronomy 9:1–10:22
Luke 8:4-21
Psalm 69:19-36
Proverbs 12:2-3

MARCH 29
Deuteronomy 11:1–12:32
Luke 8:22-39
Psalm 70:1-5
Proverbs 12:4

MARCH 30
Deuteronomy 13:1–15:23
Luke 8:40–9:6
Psalm 71:1-24
Proverbs 12:5-7

MARCH 31
Deuteronomy 16:1–17:20
Luke 9:7-27
Psalm 72:1-20
Proverbs 12:8-9

APRIL 1
Deuteronomy 18:1–20:20
Luke 9:28-50
Psalm 73:1-28
Proverbs 12:10

APRIL 2
Deuteronomy 21:1–22:30
Luke 9:51–10:12
Psalm 74:1-23
Proverbs 12:11

APRIL 3
Deuteronomy 23:1–25:19
Luke 10:13-37
Psalm 75:1-10
Proverbs 12:12-14

APRIL 4
Deuteronomy 26:1–27:26
Luke 10:38–11:13
Psalm 76:1-12
Proverbs 12:15-17

APRIL 5
Deuteronomy 28:1-68
Luke 11:14-36
Psalm 77:1-20
Proverbs 12:18

APRIL 6
Deuteronomy 29:1–30:20
Luke 11:37–12:7
Psalm 78:1-31
Proverbs 12:19-20

APRIL 7
Deuteronomy 31:1–32:27
Luke 12:8-34
Psalm 78:32-55
Proverbs 12:21-23

APRIL 8
Deuteronomy 32:28-52
Luke 12:35-59
Psalm 78:56-64
Proverbs 12:24

APRIL 9
Deuteronomy 33:1-29
Luke 13:1-21
Psalm 78:65-72
Proverbs 12:25

APRIL 10
Deuteronomy 34:1—
 Joshua 2:24
Luke 13:22–14:6
Psalm 79:1-13
Proverbs 12:26

APRIL 11
Joshua 3:1–4:24
Luke 14:7-35
Psalm 80:1-19
Proverbs 12:27-28

APRIL 12
Joshua 5:1–7:15
Luke 15:1-32
Psalm 81:1-16
Proverbs 13:1

APRIL 13
Joshua 7:16–9:2
Luke 16:1-18
Psalm 82:1-8
Proverbs 13:2-3

APRIL 14
Joshua 9:3–10:43
Luke 16:19–17:10
Psalm 83:1-18
Proverbs 13:4

APRIL 15
Joshua 11:1–12:24
Luke 17:11-37
Psalm 84:1-12
Proverbs 13:5-6

APRIL 16
Joshua 13:1–14:15
Luke 18:1-17
Psalm 85:1-13
Proverbs 13:7-8

APRIL 17
Joshua 15:1-63
Luke 18:18-43
Psalm 86:1-17
Proverbs 13:9-10

APRIL 18
Joshua 16:1–18:28
Luke 19:1-27
Psalm 87:1-7
Proverbs 13:11

APRIL 19
Joshua 19:1–20:9
Luke 19:28-48
Psalm 88:1-18
Proverbs 13:12-14

APRIL 20
Joshua 21:1–22:20
Luke 20:1-26
Psalm 89:1-13
Proverbs 13:15-16

APRIL 21
Joshua 22:21–23:16
Luke 20:27-47
Psalm 89:14-37
Proverbs 13:17-19

APRIL 22
Joshua 24:1-33
Luke 21:1-28
Psalm 89:38-52
Proverbs 13:20-23

APRIL 23
Judges 1:1–2:9
Luke 21:29–22:13
Psalms 90:1–91:16
Proverbs 13:24-25

APRIL 24
Judges 2:10–3:31
Luke 22:14-34
Psalms 92:1–93:5
Proverbs 14:1-2

☐ **APRIL 25**
Judges 4:1–5:31
Luke 22:35-53
Psalm 94:1-23
Proverbs 14:3-4

☐ **APRIL 26**
Judges 6:1-40
Luke 22:54–23:12
Psalms 95:1–96:13
Proverbs 14:5-6

☐ **APRIL 27**
Judges 7:1–8:17
Luke 23:13-43
Psalms 97:1–98:9
Proverbs 14:7-8

☐ **APRIL 28**
Judges 8:18–9:21
Luke 23:44–24:12
Psalm 99:1-9
Proverbs 14:9-10

☐ **APRIL 29**
Judges 9:22–10:18
Luke 24:13-53
Psalm 100:1-5
Proverbs 14:11-12

☐ **APRIL 30**
Judges 11:1–12:15
John 1:1-28
Psalm 101:1-8
Proverbs 14:13-14

☐ **MAY 1**
Judges 13:1–14:20
John 1:29-51
Psalm 102:1-28
Proverbs 14:15-16

☐ **MAY 2**
Judges 15:1–16:31
John 2:1-25
Psalm 103:1-22
Proverbs 14:17-19

☐ **MAY 3**
Judges 17:1–18:31
John 3:1-21
Psalm 104:1-23
Proverbs 14:20-21

☐ **MAY 4**
Judges 19:1–20:48
John 3:22–4:3
Psalm 104:24-35
Proverbs 14:22-24

☐ **MAY 5**
Judges 21:1 Ruth 1:22
John 4:4-42
Psalm 105: 1-15
Proverbs 14:25

☐ **MAY 6**
Ruth 2:1–4:22
John 4:43-54
Psalm 105:16-36
Proverbs 14:26-27

☐ **MAY 7**
1 Samuel 1:1–2:21
John 5:1-23
Psalm 105:37-45
Proverbs 14:28-29

☐ **MAY 8**
1 Samuel 2:22–4:22
John 5:24-47
Psalm 106:1-12
Proverbs 14:30-31

☐ **MAY 9**
1 Samuel 5:1–7:17
John 6:1-21
Psalm 106:13-31
Proverbs 14:32-33

☐ **MAY 10**
1 Samuel 8:1–9:27
John 6:22-42
Psalm 106:32-48
Proverbs 14:34-35

☐ **MAY 11**
1 Samuel 10:1–11:15
John 6:43-71
Psalm 107:1-43
Proverbs 15:1-3

☐ **MAY 12**
1 Samuel 12:1–13:23
John 7:1-30
Psalm 108:1-13
Proverbs 15:4

☐ **MAY 13**
1 Samuel 14:1-52
John 7:31-53
Psalm 109:1-31
Proverbs 15:5-7

☐ **MAY 14**
1 Samuel 15:1–16:23
John 8:1-20
Psalm 110:1-7
Proverbs 15:8-10

☐ **MAY 15**
1 Samuel 17:1–18:4
John 8:21-30
Psalm 111:1-10
Proverbs 15:11

☐ **MAY 16**
1 Samuel 18:5–19:24
John 8:31-59
Psalm 112:1-10
Proverbs 15:12-14

☐ **MAY 17**
1 Samuel 20:1–21:15
John 9:1-41
Psalms 113:1–114:8
Proverbs 15:15-17

☐ **MAY 18**
1 Samuel 22:1–23:29
John 10:1-21
Psalm 115:1-18
Proverbs 15:18-19

☐ **MAY 19**
1 Samuel 24:1–25:44
John 10:22-42
Psalm 116:1-19
Proverbs 15:20-21

☐ **MAY 20**
1 Samuel 26:1–28:25
John 11:1-54
Psalm 117:1-2
Proverbs 15:22-23

☐ **MAY 21**
1 Samuel 29:1–31:13
John 11:55–12:19
Psalm 118:1-18
Proverbs 15:24-26

☐ **MAY 22**
2 Samuel 1:1–2:11
John 12:20-50
Psalm 118:19-29
Proverbs 15:27-28

☐ **MAY 23**
2 Samuel 2:12–3:39
John 13:1-30
Psalm 119:1-16
Proverbs 15:29-30

☐ **MAY 24**
2 Samuel 4:1–6:23
John 13:31–14:14
Psalm 119:17-32
Proverbs 15:31-32

MAY 25
2 Samuel 7:1–8:18
John 14:15-31
Psalm 119:33-48
Proverbs 15:33

MAY 26
2 Samuel 9:1–11:27
John 15:1-27
Psalm 119:49-64
Proverbs 16:1-3

MAY 27
2 Samuel 12:1-31
John 16:1-33
Psalm 119:65-80
Proverbs 16:4-5

MAY 28
2 Samuel 13:1-39
John 17:1-26
Psalm 119:81-96
Proverbs 16:6-7

MAY 29
2 Samuel 14:1–15:22
John 18:1-24
Psalm 119:97-112
Proverbs 16:8-9

MAY 30
2 Samuel 15:23–16:23
John 18:25–19:22
Psalm 119:113-128
Proverbs 16:10-11

MAY 31
2 Samuel 17:1-29
John 19:23-42
Psalm 119:129-152
Proverbs 16:12-13

JUNE 1
2 Samuel 18:1–19:10
John 20:1-31
Psalm 119:153-176
Proverbs 16:14-15

JUNE 2
2 Samuel 19:11–20:13
John 21:1-25
Psalm 120:1-7
Proverbs 16:16-17

JUNE 3
2 Samuel 20:14–21:22
Acts 1:1-26
Psalm 121:1-8
Proverbs 16:18

JUNE 4
2 Samuel 22:1–23:23
Acts 2:1-47
Psalm 122:1-9
Proverbs 16:19-20

JUNE 5
2 Samuel 23:24–24:25
Acts 3:1-26
Psalm 123:1-4
Proverbs 16:21-23

JUNE 6
1 Kings 1:1-53
Acts 4:1-37
Psalm 124:1-8
Proverbs 16:24

JUNE 7
1 Kings 2:1–3:2
Acts 5:1-42
Psalm 125:1-5
Proverbs 16:25

JUNE 8
1 Kings 3:3–4:34
Acts 6:1-15
Psalm 126:1-6
Proverbs 16:26-27

JUNE 9
1 Kings 5:1–6:38
Acts 7:1-29
Psalm 127:1-5
Proverbs 16:28-30

JUNE 10
1 Kings 7:1-51
Acts 7:30-50
Psalm 128:1-6
Proverbs 16:31-33

JUNE 11
1 Kings 8:1-66
Acts 7:51–8:13
Psalm 129:1-8
Proverbs 17:1

JUNE 12
1 Kings 9:1–10:29
Acts 8:14-40
Psalm 130:1-8
Proverbs 17:2-3

JUNE 13
1 Kings 11:1–12:19
Acts 9:1-25
Psalm 131:1-3
Proverbs 17:4-5

JUNE 14
1 Kings 12:20–13:34
Acts 9:26-43
Psalm 132:1-18
Proverbs 17:6

JUNE 15
1 Kings 14:1–15:24
Acts 10:1-23
Psalm 133:1-3
Proverbs 17:7-8

JUNE 16
1 Kings 15:25–17:24
Acts 10:24-48
Psalm 134:1-3
Proverbs 17:9-11

JUNE 17
1 Kings 18:1-46
Acts 11:1-30
Psalm 135:1-21
Proverbs 17:12-13

JUNE 18
1 Kings 19:1-21
Acts 12:1-23
Psalm 136:1-26
Proverbs 17:14-15

JUNE 19
1 Kings 20:1–21:29
Acts 12:24–13:15
Psalm 137:1-9
Proverbs 17:16

JUNE 20
1 Kings 22:1-53
Acts 13:16-41
Psalm 138:1-8
Proverbs 17:17-18

JUNE 21
2 Kings 1:1–2:25
Acts 13:42–14:7
Psalm 139:1-24
Proverbs 17:19-21

JUNE 22
2 Kings 3:1–4:17
Acts 14:8-28
Psalm 140:1-13
Proverbs 17:22

JUNE 23
2 Kings 4:18–5:27
Acts 15:1-35
Psalm 141:1-10
Proverbs 17:23

JUNE 24
2 Kings 6:1–7:20
Acts 15:36–16:15
Psalm 142:1-7
Proverbs 17:24-25

JUNE 25
2 Kings 8:1–9:13
Acts 16:16-40
Psalm 143:1-12
Proverbs 17:26

JUNE 26
2 Kings 9:14–10:31
Acts 17:1-34
Psalm 144:1-15
Proverbs 17:27-28

JUNE 27
2 Kings 10:32–12:21
Acts 18:1-22
Psalm 145:1-21
Proverbs 18:1

JUNE 28
2 Kings 13:1–14:29
Acts 18:23–19:12
Psalm 146:1-10
Proverbs 18:2-3

JUNE 29
2 Kings 15:1–16:20
Acts 19:13-41
Psalm 147:1-20
Proverbs 18:4-5

JUNE 30
2 Kings 17:1–18:12
Acts 20:1-38
Psalm 148:1-14
Proverbs 18:6-7

JULY 1
2 Kings 18:13–19:37
Acts 21:1-17
Psalm 149:1-9
Proverbs 18:8

JULY 2
2 Kings 20:1–22:2
Acts 21:18-36
Psalm 150:1-6
Proverbs 18:9-10

JULY 3
2 Kings 22:3–23:30
Acts 21:37–22:16
Psalm 1:1-6
Proverbs 18:11-12

JULY 4
2 Kings 23:31–25:30
Acts 22:17–23:10
Psalm 2:1-12
Proverbs 18:13

JULY 5
1 Chronicles 1:1–2:17
Acts 23:11-35
Psalm 3:1-8
Proverbs 18:14-15

JULY 6
1 Chronicles 2:18–4:4
Acts 24:1-27
Psalm 4:1-8
Proverbs 18:16-18

JULY 7
1 Chronicles 4:5–5:17
Acts 25:1-27
Psalm 5:1-12
Proverbs 18:19

JULY 8
1 Chronicles 5:18–6:81
Acts 26:1-32
Psalm 6:1-10
Proverbs 18:20-21

JULY 9
1 Chronicles 7:1–8:40
Acts 27:1-20
Psalm 7:1-17
Proverbs 18:22

JULY 10
1 Chronicles 9:1–10:14
Acts 27:21-44
Psalm 8:1-9
Proverbs 18:23-24

JULY 11
1 Chronicles 11:1–12:18
Acts 28:1-31
Psalm 9:1-12
Proverbs 19:1-3

JULY 12
1 Chronicles 12:19–14:17
Romans 1:1-17
Psalm 9:13-20
Proverbs 19:4-5

JULY 13
1 Chronicles 15:1–16:36
Romans 1:18-32
Psalm 10:1-15
Proverbs 19:6-7

JULY 14
1 Chronicles 16:37–18:17
Romans 2:1-24
Psalm 10:16-18
Proverbs 19:8-9

JULY 15
1 Chronicles 19:1–21:30
Romans 2:25–3:8
Psalm 11:1-7
Proverbs 19:10-12

JULY 16
1 Chronicles 22:1–23:32
Romans 3:9-31
Psalm 12:1-8
Proverbs 19:13-14

JULY 17
1 Chronicles 24:1–26:11
Romans 4:1-12
Psalm 13:1-6
Proverbs 19:15-16

JULY 18
1 Chronicles 26:12–27:34
Romans 4:13–5:5
Psalm 14:1-7
Proverbs 19:17

JULY 19
1 Chronicles 28:1–29:30
Romans 5:6-21
Psalm 15:1-5
Proverbs 19:18-19

JULY 20
2 Chronicles 1:1–3:17
Romans 6:1-23
Psalm 16:1-11
Proverbs 19:20-21

JULY 21
2 Chronicles 4:1–6:11
Romans 7:1-13
Psalm 17:1-15
Proverbs 19:22-23

JULY 22
2 Chronicles 6:12–8:10
Romans 7:14–8:8
Psalm 18:1-15
Proverbs 19:24-25

JULY 23
2 Chronicles 8:11–10:19
Romans 8:9-25
Psalm 18:16-36
Proverbs 19:26

JULY 24
2 Chronicles 11:1–13:22
Romans 8:26-39
Psalm 18:37-50
Proverbs 19:27-29

JULY 25
2 Chronicles 14:1–16:14
Romans 9:1-24
Psalm 19:1-14
Proverbs 20:1

JULY 26
2 Chronicles 17:1–18:34
Romans 9:25–10:13
Psalm 20:1-9
Proverbs 20:2-3

JULY 27
2 Chronicles 19:1–20:37
Romans 10:14–11:12
Psalm 21:1-13
Proverbs 20:4-6

JULY 28
2 Chronicles 21:1–23:21
Romans 11:13-36
Psalm 22:1-18
Proverbs 20:7

JULY 29
2 Chronicles 24:1–25:28
Romans 12:1-21
Psalm 22:19-31
Proverbs 20:8-10

JULY 30
2 Chronicles 26:1–28:27
Romans 13:1-14
Psalm 23:1-6
Proverbs 20:11

JULY 31
2 Chronicles 29:1-36
Romans 14:1-23
Psalm 24:1-10
Proverbs 20:12

AUGUST 1
2 Chronicles 30:1–31:21
Romans 15:1-22
Psalm 25:1-15
Proverbs 20:13-15

AUGUST 2
2 Chronicles 32:1–33:13
Romans 15:23–16:9
Psalm 25:16-22
Proverbs 20:16-18

AUGUST 3
2 Chronicles 33:14–34:33
Romans 16:10-27
Psalm 26:1-12
Proverbs 20:19

AUGUST 4
2 Chronicles 35:1–36:23
1 Corinthians 1:1-17
Psalm 27:1-6
Proverbs 20:20-21

AUGUST 5
Ezra 1:1–2:70
1 Corinthians 1:18–2:5
Psalm 27:7-14
Proverbs 20:22-23

AUGUST 6
Ezra 3:1–4:23
1 Corinthians 2:6–3:4
Psalm 28:1-9
Proverbs 20:24-25

AUGUST 7
Ezra 4:24–6:22
1 Corinthians 3:5-23
Psalm 29:1-11
Proverbs 20:26-27

AUGUST 8
Ezra 7:1–8:20
1 Corinthians 4:1-21
Psalm 30:1-12
Proverbs 20:28-30

AUGUST 9
Ezra 8:21–9:15
1 Corinthians 5:1-13
Psalm 31:1-8
Proverbs 21:1-2

AUGUST 10
Ezra 10:1-44
1 Corinthians 6:1-20
Psalm 31:9-18
Proverbs 21:3

AUGUST 11
Nehemiah 1:1–3:14
1 Corinthians 7:1-24
Psalm 31:19-24
Proverbs 21:4

AUGUST 12
Nehemiah 3:15–5:13
1 Corinthians 7:25-40
Psalm 32:1-11
Proverbs 21:5-7

AUGUST 13
Nehemiah 5:14–7:73a
1 Corinthians 8:1-13
Psalm 33:1-11
Proverbs 21:8-10

AUGUST 14
Nehemiah 7:73b–9:21
1 Corinthians 9:1-18
Psalm 33:12-22
Proverbs 21:11-12

AUGUST 15
Nehemiah 9:22–10:39
1 Corinthians 9:19–10:13
Psalm 34:1-10
Proverbs 21:13

AUGUST 16
Nehemiah 11:1–12:26
1 Corinthians 10:14-33
Psalm 34:11-22
Proverbs 21:14-16

AUGUST 17
Nehemiah 12:27–13:31
1 Corinthians 11:1-16
Psalm 35:1-16
Proverbs 21:17-18

AUGUST 18
Esther 1:1–3:15
1 Corinthians 11:17-34
Psalm 35:17-28
Proverbs 21:19-20

AUGUST 19
Esther 4:1–7:10
1 Corinthians 12:1-26
Psalm 36:1-12
Proverbs 21:21-22

AUGUST 20
Esther 8:1–10:3
1 Corinthians 12:27–13:13
Psalm 37:1-11
Proverbs 21:23-24

AUGUST 21
Job 1:1–3:26
1 Corinthians 14:1-17
Psalm 37:12-29
Proverbs 21:25-26

AUGUST 22
Job 4:1–7:21
1 Corinthians 14:18-40
Psalm 37:30-40
Proverbs 21:27

AUGUST 23
Job 8:1–11:20
1 Corinthians 15:1-28
Psalm 38:1-22
Proverbs 21:28-29

AUGUST 24
Job 12:1–15:35
1 Corinthians 15:29-58
Psalm 39:1-13
Proverbs 21:30-31

AUGUST 25
Job 16:1–19:29
1 Corinthians 16:1-24
Psalm 40:1-10
Proverbs 22:1

AUGUST 26
Job 20:1–22:30
2 Corinthians 1:1-11
Psalm 40:11-17
Proverbs 22:2-4

AUGUST 27
Job 23:1–27:23
2 Corinthians 1:12–2:11
Psalm 41:1-13
Proverbs 22:5-6

AUGUST 28
Job 28:1–30:31
2 Corinthians 2:12-17
Psalm 42:1-11
Proverbs 22:7

AUGUST 29
Job 31:1–33:33
2 Corinthians 3:1-18
Psalm 43:1-5
Proverbs 22:8-9

AUGUST 30
Job 34:1–36:33
2 Corinthians 4:1-12
Psalm 44:1-8
Proverbs 22:10-12

AUGUST 31
Job 37:1–39:30
2 Corinthians 4:13–5:10
Psalm 44:9-26
Proverbs 22:13

SEPTEMBER 1
Job 40:1–42:17
2 Corinthians 5:11-21
Psalm 45:1-17
Proverbs 22:14

SEPTEMBER 2
Ecclesiastes 1:1–3:22
2 Corinthians 6:1-13
Psalm 46:1-11
Proverbs 22:15

SEPTEMBER 3
Ecclesiastes 4:1–6:12
2 Corinthians 6:14–7:7
Psalm 47:1-9
Proverbs 22:16

SEPTEMBER 4
Ecclesiastes 7:1–9:18
2 Corinthians 7:8-16
Psalm 48:1-14
Proverbs 22:17-19

SEPTEMBER 5
Ecclesiastes 10:1–12:14
2 Corinthians 8:1-15
Psalm 49:1-20
Proverbs 22:20-21

SEPTEMBER 6
Song of Songs 1:1–4:16
2 Corinthians 8:16-24
Psalm 50:1-23
Proverbs 22:22-23

SEPTEMBER 7
Song of Songs 5:1–8:14
2 Corinthians 9:1-15
Psalm 51:1-19
Proverbs 22:24-25

SEPTEMBER 8
Isaiah 1:1–2:22
2 Corinthians 10:1-18
Psalm 52:1-9
Proverbs 22:26-27

SEPTEMBER 9
Isaiah 3:1–5:30
2 Corinthians 11:1-15
Psalm 53:1-6
Proverbs 22:28-29

SEPTEMBER 10
Isaiah 6:1–7:25
2 Corinthians 11:16-33
Psalm 54:1-7
Proverbs 23:1-3

SEPTEMBER 11
Isaiah 8:1–9:21
2 Corinthians 12:1-10
Psalm 55:1-23
Proverbs 23:4-5

SEPTEMBER 12
Isaiah 10:1–11:16
2 Corinthians 12:11-21
Psalm 56:1-13
Proverbs 23:6-8

SEPTEMBER 13
Isaiah 12:1–14:32
2 Corinthians 13:1-14
Psalm 57:1-11
Proverbs 23:9-11

SEPTEMBER 14
Isaiah 15:1–18:7
Galatians 1:1-24
Psalm 58:1-11
Proverbs 23:12

SEPTEMBER 15
Isaiah 19:1–21:17
Galatians 2:1-16
Psalm 59:1-17
Proverbs 23:13-14

SEPTEMBER 16
Isaiah 22:1–24:23
Galatians 2:17–3:9
Psalm 60:1-12
Proverbs 23:15-16

SEPTEMBER 17
Isaiah 25:1–28:13
Galatians 3:10-22
Psalm 61:1-8
Proverbs 23:17-18

SEPTEMBER 18
Isaiah 28:14–30:11
Galatians 3:23–4:31
Psalm 62:1-12
Proverbs 23:19-21

SEPTEMBER 19
Isaiah 30:12–33:9
Galatians 5:1-12
Psalm 63:1-11
Proverbs 23:22

SEPTEMBER 20
Isaiah 33:10–36:22
Galatians 5:13-26
Psalm 64:1-10
Proverbs 23:23

SEPTEMBER 21
Isaiah 37:1–38:22
Galatians 6:1-18
Psalm 65:1-13
Proverbs 23:24

SEPTEMBER 22
Isaiah 39:1–41:16
Ephesians 1:1-23
Psalm 66:1-20
Proverbs 23:25-28

SEPTEMBER 23
Isaiah 41:17–43:13
Ephesians 2:1-22
Psalm 67:1-7
Proverbs 23:29-35

SEPTEMBER 24
Isaiah 43:14–45:10
Ephesians 3:1-21
Psalm 68:1-18
Proverbs 24:1-2

SEPTEMBER 25
Isaiah 45:11–48:11
Ephesians 4:1-16
Psalm 68:19-35
Proverbs 24:3-4

SEPTEMBER 26
Isaiah 48:12–50:11
Ephesians 4:17-32
Psalm 69:1-18
Proverbs 24:5-6

SEPTEMBER 27
Isaiah 51:1–53:12
Ephesians 5:1-33
Psalm 69:19-36
Proverbs 24:7

SEPTEMBER 28
Isaiah 54:1–57:14
Ephesians 6:1-24
Psalm 70:1-5
Proverbs 24:8

SEPTEMBER 29
Isaiah 57:15–59:21
Philippians 1:1-26
Psalm 71:1-24
Proverbs 24:9-10

SEPTEMBER 30
Isaiah 60:1–62:5
Philippians 1:27–2:18
Psalm 72:1-20
Proverbs 24:11-12

OCTOBER 1
Isaiah 62:6–65:25
Philippians 2:19–3:3
Psalm 73:1-28
Proverbs 24:13-14

OCTOBER 2
Isaiah 66:1-24
Philippians 3:4-21
Psalm 74:1-23
Proverbs 24:15-16

OCTOBER 3
Jeremiah 1:1–2:30
Philippians 4:1-23
Psalm 75:1-10
Proverbs 24:17-20

OCTOBER 4
Jeremiah 2:31–4:18
Colossians 1:1-17
Psalm 76:1-12
Proverbs 24:21-22

OCTOBER 5
Jeremiah 4:19–6:15
Colossians 1:18–2:7
Psalm 77:1-20
Proverbs 24:23-25

OCTOBER 6
Jeremiah 6:16–8:7
Colossians 2:8-23
Psalm 78:1-31
Proverbs 24:26

OCTOBER 7
Jeremiah 8:8–9:26
Colossians 3:1-17
Psalm 78:32-55
Proverbs 24:27

OCTOBER 8
Jeremiah 10:1–11:23
Colossians 3:18–4:18
Psalm 78:56-72
Proverbs 24:28-29

OCTOBER 9
Jeremiah 12:1–14:10
1 Thessalonians 1:1–2:8
Psalm 79:1-13
Proverbs 24:30-34

OCTOBER 10
Jeremiah 14:11–16:15
1 Thessalonians 2:9–3:13
Psalm 80:1-19
Proverbs 25:1-5

OCTOBER 11
Jeremiah 16:16–18:23
1 Thessalonians 4:1–5:3
Psalm 81:1-16
Proverbs 25:6-8

OCTOBER 12
Jeremiah 19:1–21:14
1 Thessalonians 5:4-28
Psalm 82:1-8
Proverbs 25:9-10

OCTOBER 13
Jeremiah 22:1–23:20
2 Thessalonians 1:1-12
Psalm 83:1-18
Proverbs 25:11-14

OCTOBER 14
Jeremiah 23:21–25:38
2 Thessalonians 2:1-17
Psalm 84:1-12
Proverbs 25:15

OCTOBER 15
Jeremiah 26:1–27:22
2 Thessalonians 3:1-18
Psalm 85:1-13
Proverbs 25:16

OCTOBER 16
Jeremiah 28:1–29:32
1 Timothy 1:1-20
Psalm 86:1-17
Proverbs 25:17

OCTOBER 17
Jeremiah 30:1–31:26
1 Timothy 2:1-15
Psalm 87:1-7
Proverbs 25:18-19

OCTOBER 18
Jeremiah 31:27–32:44
1 Timothy 3:1-16
Psalm 88:1-18
Proverbs 25:20-22

OCTOBER 19
Jeremiah 33:1–34:22
1 Timothy 4:1-16
Psalm 89:1-13
Proverbs 25:23-24

OCTOBER 20
Jeremiah 35:1–36:32
1 Timothy 5:1-25
Psalm 89:14-37
Proverbs 25:25-27

OCTOBER 21
Jeremiah 37:1–38:28
1 Timothy 6:1-21
Psalm 89:38-52
Proverbs 25:28

OCTOBER 22
Jeremiah 39:1–41:18
2 Timothy 1:1-18
Psalms 90:1–91:16
Proverbs 26:1-2

OCTOBER 23
Jeremiah 42:1–44:23
2 Timothy 2:1-21
Psalms 92:1–93:5
Proverbs 26:3-5

OCTOBER 24
Jeremiah 44:24–47:7
2 Timothy 2:22–3:17
Psalm 94:1-23
Proverbs 26:6-8

OCTOBER 25
Jeremiah 48:1–49:22
2 Timothy 4:1-22
Psalms 95:1–96:13
Proverbs 26:9-12

OCTOBER 26
Jeremiah 49:23–50:46
Titus 1:1-16
Psalms 97:1–98:9
Proverbs 26:13-16

OCTOBER 27
Jeremiah 51:1-53
Titus 2:1-15
Psalm 99:1-9
Proverbs 26:17

OCTOBER 28
Jeremiah 51:54–52:34
Titus 3:1-15
Psalm 100:1-5
Proverbs 26:18-19

OCTOBER 29
Lamentations 1:1–2:22
Philemon 1-25
Psalm 101:1-8
Proverbs 26:20

OCTOBER 30
Lamentations 3:1-66
Hebrews 1:1-14
Psalm 102:1-28
Proverbs 26:21-22

OCTOBER 31
Lamentations 4:1–5:22
Hebrews 2:1-18
Psalm 103:1-22
Proverbs 26:23

NOVEMBER 1
Ezekiel 1:1–3:15
Hebrews 3:1-19
Psalm 104:1-23
Proverbs 26:24-26

NOVEMBER 2
Ezekiel 3:16–6:14
Hebrews 4:1-16
Psalm 104:24-35
Proverbs 26:27

NOVEMBER 3
Ezekiel 7:1–9:11
Hebrews 5:1-14
Psalm 105:1-15
Proverbs 26:28

NOVEMBER 4
Ezekiel 10:1–11:25
Hebrews 6:1-20
Psalm 105:16-36
Proverbs 27:1-2

NOVEMBER 5
Ezekiel 12:1–14:11
Hebrews 7:1-17
Psalm 105:37-45
Proverbs 27:3

NOVEMBER 6
Ezekiel 14:12–16:41
Hebrews 7:18-28
Psalm 106:1-12
Proverbs 27:4-6

NOVEMBER 7
Ezekiel 16:42–17:24
Hebrews 8:1-13
Psalm 106:13-31
Proverbs 27:7-9

NOVEMBER 8
Ezekiel 18:1–19:14
Hebrews 9:1-10
Psalm 106:32-48
Proverbs 27:10

NOVEMBER 9
Ezekiel 20:1-49
Hebrews 9:11-28
Psalm 107:1-43
Proverbs 27:11

NOVEMBER 10
Ezekiel 21:1–22:31
Hebrews 10:1-17
Psalm 108:1-13
Proverbs 27:12

NOVEMBER 11
Ezekiel 23:1-49
Hebrews 10:18-39
Psalm 109:1-31
Proverbs 27:13

NOVEMBER 12
Ezekiel 24:1–26:21
Hebrews 11:1-16
Psalm 110:1-7
Proverbs 27:14

NOVEMBER 13
Ezekiel 27:1–28:26
Hebrews 11:17-31
Psalm 111:1-10
Proverbs 27:15-16

NOVEMBER 14
Ezekiel 29:1–30:26
Hebrews 11:32–12:13
Psalm 112:1-10
Proverbs 27:17

NOVEMBER 15
Ezekiel 31:1–32:32
Hebrews 12:14-29
Psalms 113:1–114:8
Proverbs 27:18-20

NOVEMBER 16
Ezekiel 33:1–34:31
Hebrews 13:1-25
Psalm 115:1-18
Proverbs 27:21-22

NOVEMBER 17
Ezekiel 35:1–36:38
James 1:1-18
Psalm 116:1-19
Proverbs 27:23-27

NOVEMBER 18
Ezekiel 37:1–38:23
James 1:19–2:17
Psalm 117:1-2
Proverbs 28:1

NOVEMBER 19
Ezekiel 39:1–40:27
James 2:18–3:18
Psalm 118:1-18
Proverbs 28:2

NOVEMBER 20
Ezekiel 40:28–41:26
James 4:1-17
Psalm 118:19-29
Proverbs 28:3-5

NOVEMBER 21
Ezekiel 42:1–43:27
James 5:1-20
Psalm 119:1-16
Proverbs 28:6-7

NOVEMBER 22
Ezekiel 44:1–45:12
1 Peter 1:1-12
Psalm 119:17-32
Proverbs 28:8-10

NOVEMBER 23
Ezekiel 45:13–46:24
1 Peter 1:13–2:10
Psalm 119:33-48
Proverbs 28:11

NOVEMBER 24
Ezekiel 47:1–48:35
1 Peter 2:11–3:7
Psalm 119:49-64
Proverbs 28:12-13

NOVEMBER 25
Daniel 1:1–2:23
1 Peter 3:8–4:6
Psalm 119:65-80
Proverbs 28:14

NOVEMBER 26
Daniel 2:24–3:30
1 Peter 4:7–5:14
Psalm 119:81-96
Proverbs 28:15-16

NOVEMBER 27
Daniel 4:1-37
2 Peter 1:1-21
Psalm 119:97-112
Proverbs 28:17-18

NOVEMBER 28
Daniel 5:1-31
2 Peter 2:1-22
Psalm 119:113-128
Proverbs 28:19-20

NOVEMBER 29
Daniel 6:1-28
2 Peter 3:1-18
Psalm 119:129-152
Proverbs 28:21-22

NOVEMBER 30
Daniel 7:1-28
1 John 1:1-10
Psalm 119:153-176
Proverbs 28:23-24

DECEMBER 1
Daniel 8:1-27
1 John 2:1-17
Psalm 120:1-7
Proverbs 28:25-26

DECEMBER 2
Daniel 9:1–11:1
1 John 2:18–3:6
Psalm 121:1-8
Proverbs 28:27-28

DECEMBER 3
Daniel 11:2-35
1 John 3:7-24
Psalm 122:1-9
Proverbs 29:1

DECEMBER 4
Daniel 11:36–12:13
1 John 4:1-21
Psalm 123:1-4
Proverbs 29:2-4

DECEMBER 5
Hosea 1:1–3:5
1 John 5:1-21
Psalm 124:1-8
Proverbs 29:5-8

DECEMBER 6
Hosea 4:1–5:15
2 John 1-13
Psalm 125:1-5
Proverbs 29:9-11

DECEMBER 7
Hosea 6:1–9:17
3 John 1-15
Psalm 126:1-6
Proverbs 29:12-14

DECEMBER 8
Hosea 10:1–14:9
Jude 1:1-25
Psalm 127:1-5
Proverbs 29:15-17

DECEMBER 9
Joel 1:1–3:21
Revelation 1:1-20
Psalm 128:1-6
Proverbs 29:18

DECEMBER 10
Amos 1:1–3:15
Revelation 2:1-17
Psalm 129:1-8
Proverbs 29:19-20

DECEMBER 11
Amos 4:1–6:14
Revelation 2:18–3:6
Psalm 130:1-8
Proverbs 29:21-22

DECEMBER 12
Amos 7:1–9:15
Revelation 3:7-22
Psalm 131:1-3
Proverbs 29:23

DECEMBER 13
Obadiah 1-21
Revelation 4:1-11
Psalm 132:1-18
Proverbs 29:24-25

DECEMBER 14
Jonah 1:1–4:11
Revelation 5:1-14
Psalm 133:1-3
Proverbs 29:26-27

DECEMBER 15
Micah 1:1–4:13
Revelation 6:1-17
Psalm 134:1-3
Proverbs 30:1-4

DECEMBER 16
Micah 5:1–7:20
Revelation 7:1-17
Psalm 135:1-21
Proverbs 30:5-6

DECEMBER 17
Nahum 1:1–3:19
Revelation 8:1-13
Psalm 136:1-26
Proverbs 30:7-9

DECEMBER 18
Habakkuk 1:1–3:19
Revelation 9:1-21
Psalm 137:1-9
Proverbs 30:10

DECEMBER 19
Zephaniah 1:1–3:20
Revelation 10:1-11
Psalm 138:1-8
Proverbs 30:11-14

DECEMBER 20
Haggai 1:1–2:23
Revelation 11:1-19
Psalm 139:1-24
Proverbs 30:15-16

DECEMBER 21
Zechariah 1:1-21
Revelation 12:1-17
Psalm 140:1-13
Proverbs 30:17

DECEMBER 22
Zechariah 2:1–3:10
Revelation 12:18–13:18
Psalm 141:1-10
Proverbs 30:18-20

DECEMBER 23
Zechariah 4:1–5:11
Revelation 14:1-20
Psalm 142:1-7
Proverbs 30:21-23

DECEMBER 24
Zechariah 6:1–7:14
Revelation 15:1-8
Psalm 143:1-12
Proverbs 30:24-28

DECEMBER 25
Zechariah 8:1-23
Revelation 16:1-21
Psalm 144:1-15
Proverbs 30:29-31

DECEMBER 26
Zechariah 9:1-17
Revelation 17:1-18
Psalm 145:1-21
Proverbs 30:32

DECEMBER 27
Zechariah 10:1–11:17
Revelation 18:1-24
Psalm 146:1-10
Proverbs 30:33

DECEMBER 28
Zechariah 12:1–13:9
Revelation 19:1-21
Psalm 147:1-20
Proverbs 31:1-7

DECEMBER 29
Zechariah 14:1-21
Revelation 20:1-15
Psalm 148:1-4
Proverbs 31:8-9

DECEMBER 30
Malachi 1:1–2:17
Revelation 21:1-27
Psalm 149:1-9
Proverbs 31:10-24

DECEMBER 31
Malachi 3:1–4:6
Revelation 22:1-21
Psalm 150:1-6
Proverbs 31:25-31

WHAT DO WE LEARN ABOUT GOD'S MISSION AND OURS?

GENESIS 3
God made women and men in God's image, to be like God, and reign over creation.

1 SAMUEL 333
God wants us to love him wholeheartedly.

ESTHER 593
God can use our obedience, right where we are, for great impact.

EXODUS 79
God's laws and presence enable the people of Israel to fulfill God's mission.

2 SAMUEL 371
Only God is our perfect leader.

JOB 607
When life falls apart, we can trust God's wisdom and know he stays with us.

LEVITICUS 131
God gives instructions about how to pursue our holiness so that we can be close to him.

1 KINGS 407
If we don't listen to God, we'll wish we had.

PSALMS 649
God desires and deserves our true selves and our full range of emotions.

NUMBERS 167
The road to God's best for us may not be short.

2 KINGS 441
We become like what we worship.

PROVERBS 753
We need—and can find—God's wisdom for life.

DEUTERONOMY 217
On your way to a great future, don't forget the past.

1 CHRONICLES 477
A godly person has great impact.

ECCLESIASTES 793
Following God alone is our purpose, and nothing and no one else will satisfy our desires.

JOSHUA 257
God is with us, so let's be brave.

2 CHRONICLES 515
Relying on the Lord makes us a good influence.

SONG OF SONGS 809
God created us to long for and enjoy intimacy with another.

JUDGES 289
God forgives us as we return to his ways.

EZRA 557
Time reading and studying God's Word and praying is time well spent.

ISAIAH 821
God won't overlook our wrongs, but he longs to forgive and restore.

RUTH 323
Our faithful God honors our faithfulness.

NEHEMIAH 573
God rebuilds when our hearts belong to him.

JEREMIAH 895
When nothing goes right, keep doing right.

LAMENTATIONS 961
Loss can lead us to trust God. Even if not in this life, God ultimately makes all things right.

 JONAH 1097
It's not up to us to say who God can draw close.

 MALACHI 1161
God keeps his promises. Will we keep ours?

 EZEKIEL 973
God loves singleheartedly and desires that we love him that way, too.

 MICAH 1105
It's not people but God who builds lasting good.

 MATTHEW 1189
Jesus has the power to save us because he is the everlasting King.

 DANIEL 1033
Even when we face pressure, God honors faithfulness and does more than we imagine.

 NAHUM 1117
Nahum means "comfort," and we can take comfort in knowing God will bring justice.

 MARK 1239
Jesus did good deeds before he spoke good news.

 HOSEA 1057
Motivated by faithful love, God pursues us and turns our hearts back to him.

 HABAKKUK 1125
We may never fully understand God's justice, but we can know God is good.

 LUKE 1271
Jesus came to seek and save everyone, especially those who society dismisses or excludes.

 JOEL 1071
Judgment for sin is real, but God stands ready to forgive. When we repent, God responds with grace, mercy, and blessing.

 ZEPHANIAH 1131
Actions have consequences, but God will restore his people in the end.

 JOHN 1319
Jesus gives life's true and best story.

 AMOS 1079
Idolatry produces injustice of all kinds, but God will repair the brokenness, rebuild the ruins, and restore his people.

 HAGGAI 1139
When we take initiative to act on God's word, we spark others to follow.

 ACTS 1357
God's gift of new life through Jesus is for everyone and calls us together in community.

 OBADIAH 1093
God will punish arrogance and betrayal because he expects humility and faithfulness.

 ZECHARIAH 1145
Like Zechariah, Jeshua, and Zerubbabel, we can point to the hope God has given us in the Messiah, Jesus.

 ROMANS 1407
All of us fall short, but God brings us to victory.

1 CORINTHIANS 1435
God has guidance for all our practical concerns—including our relationships, our bodies, and our power.

 2 THESSALONIANS 1527
We have important work to do while we wait for Jesus' return.

 1 PETER 1587
Jesus' followers won't always be popular, and that's okay.

 2 CORINTHIANS 1461
God helps us keep going when the going gets tough.

 1 TIMOTHY 1533
Character matters in how we relate to God, his church, and each other.

 2 PETER 1597
We choose Christ over critics and con artists.

 GALATIANS 1479
Faith alone saves us.

 2 TIMOTHY 1541
Run a strong race, encouraging others to keep going after you're gone, and finish well.

 1 JOHN 1605
Because God's love through Jesus has brought us close, let's love him first and best.

 EPHESIANS 1489
God empowers us to live out our calling.

 TITUS 1549
We can live to show God's grace to others and so give God glory.

 2 JOHN 1615
Examine messages and messengers, carefully.

 PHILIPPIANS 1501
Even when we suffer, God helps us stay true and gives us joy.

 PHILEMON 1555
God wants us to forgive each other.

 3 JOHN 1619
Be a gracious yet discerning host.

 COLOSSIANS 1511
We are called to put Christ first in everything.

 HEBREWS 1559
Jesus deserves our highest trust because he is God's Son.

 JUDE 1623
We are called to build each other up with faithful instruction.

 1 THESSALONIANS 1519
We can press on by focusing on Jesus.

 JAMES 1579
We are called to do what we say we believe.

 REVELATION 1627
We can live victoriously knowing God triumphs in the end.

IMAGE INDEX

THEOS: MY STORY WITH GOD

Being God's Image—Finding Our Human Identity and Vocation	5
A Good Name: Name Changes Reveal Purpose	40
God's Glory: An Invitation to Awe	141
Persisting in Prayer	334
The Praise Factor	499
Pray-paring for Our Purpose	575
Esther: Victor or Victim?	598
How to Grieve with Others	623
The Discipline of Delight	651
God Declares Our Purpose	660
Women of the Word	734
The Fear We Need	806
The Call of a Broken Heart	902
Dare to Hope	966
The Kindness of God's Correction	1073
Return to Restoration	1089
Denying Ourselves to Find a Fulfilling Life	1220
God's Story Shows Us Our Own	1328
Living on Purpose amid Pain	1419
Beautiful: Our Bodies As Temples	1444
Prayer, an Act of Love	1448
Exercising Faith over Feelings	1473
Working to Please the Lord	1521
Prayer-Fueled Passion	1585
Great Love, Great Pain	1610

OIKOS: MY STORY WITH FAMILY & FRIENDS

Seeing Our Families Shine	11
No Perfect Family	59
Family Flourishing: I Want You to Love Jesus for the Rest of Your Life	249
Presence As Love	326
A Wise Wife	363
A Family Blessing	470

Reflecting God's Love in Relationships	635
Tell Me a Story	704
Watching Our Words	772
Divorce: Provision to Protect	1163
We're All Blended Family	1194
Leading and Loved for It	1340
Why We Need to Ask If Paul Valued Women	1417
God's Design for Love	1446
How Living by Faith Helps Us Relate	1485
Generational Blessings	1492
Wives, Husbands, and Submission to Christ	1496
Disunity's Destruction and Our Creator's Repair	1503
Satisfaction and Surrender	1523

KOINONIA: MY STORY WITH COMMUNITY, WORKPLACE & CHURCH

Work Is More Than a Four-Letter Word	77
The Lord Himself Leads Us	99
Celebrating toward Our Destiny	159
Asking the Real Question	184
Purity Is Public	202
Our Call to the Vulnerable	446
Succession: Everyone Is an Interim	505
Surprising Influence	567
Desperate Words but Solid Identity	626
Sisters Who Help You Wait	812
Work *Works* When We Know Who's the Maker	890
Bless Where You Are	931
Forgiveness and Freedom Are the Same	939
Tending and Thriving	1014
Betrayal's Consequences	1095
God's House First	1141
Herodias and Hatred That Harms	1215
Healed Wholly	1242
Intercede until God Intervenes	1248

Gathering the Generations	1279
Pursuing God's Pursuit	1304
Working through Difficult Relationships	1380
Women for Unity	1438
People Power or Kingdom Power?	1442
Work Hard Where We Are	1486
Brave Enough to Be the Light	1494
We Can Press On	1513
Women Teaching and Holding Authority	1535
Leading and Following Above Reproach	1537
Why Gathering Still Matters	1569
How to Make Work and Worship Wonderful	1631

SHALOM: MY STORY OF MY UNIQUE INFLUENCE

God's Call and Mine	20
Promises and Our Purpose: Our Covenant-Keeping God	225
Influence Where (and from Who) You Are	259
Companioned for Courage	261
Leading by Words and Deeds	294
Pursuing God's Justice	676
God's Word Invites Women to Use Our Voices	696
The Right Kind of Busy: Monkey or Monk?	768
Our Footprint, Our Legacy	787
Embracing Our Call	830
Fit to Flourish	1035
Diving in Despite Our Dislikes	1102
Persisting in Our Purpose	1230
Jesus Restores Us to Lead	1352
Lessons from a First-Century Businesswoman-Believer	1383
Speaking to Be Heard	1387
Losing Me or Using Me?	1425
Living Your Page in God's Story	1440
Mentoring for Success	1545
Learning from the Great Go-Between	1570
Just Love	1581

IDENTITY INDEX

These articles showcase Bible people's stories and stories of God's character. Many of these explore stories through imaginative, first-person narrative based on what the Bible suggests the woman might tell us herself if she could. The writers based these narratives on what the Bible tells us and what we can know about the ancient context.

Anna, the Prophet: Bereaved to Behold	1277
Champion: The Initiator and Perfector	1577
Children of God: Chosen through Adoption	1421
Chloe: Courageous Voice for Unity	1437
The Chosen Lady: Love in Truth	1617
Christ's Ambassadors: Wherever He Assigns	1467
Comforter: God Reaches to Restore	1463
Compassion: A Response to Humility	1101
Daughters of Jerusalem: Restored and Rejoicing	1135
Daughters of Zelophehad: Be Bold to Behold	207
Deborah: Leading by Singing	297
Devoted Daughter: Learning from the Son	1589
Elizabeth: Embracing God's Yes	1273
Esther: Opportunity through Others	597
Euodia & Syntyche: Disharmony in the Church	1505
Eve and the Bride of Christ: Better Than Before	1651
Eve: Ruined to Redeemed	9
An Excellent Woman: Qualities to Guide	789
The Faithful Gentile Woman: Persistence Rewarded	1219
Faithful Lover: Finding Strength to Overcome	743
Five Women Who Made a Difference: Delivering and Raising Moses	81
A Gentleman: Waiting to Cherish	1629
Gomer: Wandering Yet Wanted	1059
A Good Companion: Ruth and Naomi, Paired for Life	799
The Good Shepherd: Assurance of Light	667
The Great Prostitute: Come Away	1645
Hagar: Honored by Names	25
Hannah: Empty to Overflow	337
Huldah: A Prophet of Courage and Boldness	553

Isaiah's Wife: Bearing Pain to Bear Hope 833
Jairus's Daughter: Dying to Live 1291
Jerusalem, Sodom, and Samaria: Unfaithful Wife and Her Sisters 989
Jesus' Unnamed Grandmothers: Releasing to Rejoice 1191
Job's Daughters: What's in a Name 645
Job's Wife: Grieving to Perceiving 611
Leah & Rachel: Love Triangle Tragedy 49
Lois and Eunice: Loving to Legacy 1543
Lord of Heaven's Armies: Deliverance Ahead 1153
Love: Our Origin and Canopy 1455
Lydia: From Struggle to Surrender 1385
Mary of Bethany: Attending over Achieving 1297
Mary Magdalene: When the Worst Happens 1351
Mary, Mother of Jesus: Favored One 1275
Mentors: Giving for Mutual Good 1551
Michal: A Pawn to Play 375
Miriam: Your Pain Is Building You 183
Mountain Messenger: Bringer of Peace 1119
Phoebe: Paul's Gospel Partner 1431
Priscilla and Aquila: Collaborating in Ministry 1391
Queen of Sheba: A Foreign Queen Who Worshiped God 529
Rahab: All I Can 265
Rebekah: More Than Her Circumstances 37
Rewarder: From Pressure to Pursuit 1573
Rhoda: Prayers Answered Miraculously 1375
A Ruler from Bethlehem: The Presence of the Peacemaker 1111
Ruth: Nothing to Everything 329
The Samaritan Woman at the Well: Filled to Full 1325
Sapphira: Truth to Live By 1365
Sarah: Lies and Laughter 31
Savior: Qualities of Our Restorer 877
Simon Peter's Mother-in-Law: Feverish to Fantastic, Fast 1241
The Enslaved Girl in Naaman's Household: Small Acts Change Everything 449
Tamar: Reliving or Living? 393

Tamar: Rewarded Anyway 61
Vulnerable Women: Redefining Strong 239
Wealthy Samaritan Wives: Comfort over Compassion 1085
Wickedness: A Woman in a Basket 1151
The Widow with Two Small Coins: Grieving to Giving 1313
The Widow at Zarephath: When It's Hard to Trust 431
Wife of Manoah: An Unnamed Wise Woman 311
The Woman from Shunem: Dare to Desire 453
The Woman Jesus Healed of Bleeding: Deep Care for Deep Wounds 1205
Women Wanderers: Where to Find Help 737
Woman Wisdom: Call and I Will Answer 763
The Woman Caught in Adultery: Turned by Tenderness 1333
The Woman Who Anointed Jesus: She Did What She Could 1263
The Women Who Financed Jesus' Ministry: Giving Back Generously 1289
The Worthy Lamb: God's Idea of Best 1635
Young Woman: Chosen and Cherished 817
Zipporah: A Surprising Marriage 103

COME CLOSE INDEX

Needing Favor: Finding God's Gift	13
Fearful: God Is Stronger Still	32
Violated: The Real "Fix"	54
Lust: Notice When You Notice	62
Failure: Not Enough or Not Willing?	85
Oppressed: Confronting Fear	97
Distant: Called Close	133
Remembering: My Family Tassel	188
Trust: Just Go!	219
Our Role: Courage to Serve	286
Hiding: Step Away from the Small	300
Used or User: Find Freedom to Choose	314
Grief: Finding Blessing in Community	324
Competing: Celebrating Our Team	355
Unfairness: Finding God Near	390
Satisfaction: One Turn Away	423
Face Off	432
My Plans: God's Perfect One	501
Wholehearted: Covered	546
Disrepair: Persist	590
Dissatisfied: Open-Handed	612
Pained? Pursue	643
Cruddy Mood? Cry Out	669
Caught: Come Clean	686
Wondering? Release	728
False Image: True Worth	744
Wisdom Where? Here, Now	755
Stressed? Savor	800
Woe? Promises	850
Thirsty? Come	867
Dry? Melt	881
Renew? Re-Old!	905
Spinning? Rest	919
Unfaithful: Faithful	1065

Stripped, Then Gathered	1107
Though: Yet I Will	1128
Children of God's Father-Heart	1168
Forgiveness Is a Way of Life	1222
Calling? Called	1256
Small: Valued	1300
Forgiving? Forever	1307
Free to Flourish	1323
To the Full	1338
Failure: God Is Not Mad at Us	1414
Suffering As God's Plan A	1465
Divided Yet Brought Closer	1491
Lies and God's Truth	1498
Full or Empty? Same	1506
Fear Not	1542
Hungry? Growing	1564
Not Why but How	1582
Never Alone	1616

PERSPECTIVE INDEX

Why would God punish Eve like that? Genesis 3:1-19 8
Does God okay the "forcible taking" of women? Genesis 6:1-8 12
Where are the women? Genesis 10:1-32 17
God's ideal or our real? Genesis 14:11-16 23
Are concubines God's plan? Genesis 16:1-10 26
How could Lot do that? Genesis 19:1-8 29
Where are the role models? Genesis 22:1-19 34
Is the bride free to choose? Genesis 24:1-58 36
Why so long? Exodus 2:23-25 82
Are women property or partners? Exodus 20:17 105
Does God condone slavery? Exodus 21:1-11 107
What's up with all these sacrifices? Leviticus 1:1–7:38 134
Why did having a baby make her unclean? Leviticus 12:1-8 144
How do we follow God when the rules seem wrong? Deuteronomy 22:13-20 240
How can a woman's faithfulness lead to victory? Judges 4:9, 17-22; 5:24-27 296
How should we respond to violence against women? Judges 19:1–21:25 318
How does God show he values immigrants? Ruth 2:5-12; 3:7-13; 4:1-22 327
What leads us down the path toward harm? 2 Samuel 13:1-22 389
Have I allowed evil to influence my choices? 1 Kings 21:1-29 436
What makes one woman choose evil and another good? 2 Kings 11:1-3 457
How do I live my faith at work? Ezra 1:1-6 559
What's the cost of ignoring God? Ezra 9–10 570
How do we lead when we lack power? Nehemiah 2:1-8; Esther 5:1-8 580
What is a woman's worth? Esther 1:10-22 595
What can God see that we can't? Job 1:6-12; 2:1-7 610
Did anyone get it right? Job 32–37 637
Do we get what we deserve? Job 32–37 640
How can I be more comfortable in my own skin? Psalm 139 746
Why the warning about an "immoral woman"? Proverbs 5:1-23; 6:20–7:27 760
Does Proverbs say men are wiser than women? Proverbs 8–9 764
Should we try everything to know what's true? Ecclesiastes 1:2-18 795
What is God's design for sex? Song of Songs 8:6-7 818
What is the purpose of prophets? Isaiah 1:1 823
How do we understand prophecies? Isaiah 52:13–53:12 879

Why do bad things happen to innocent people? Lamentations 2:1-22	963
Is God's judgment just? Lamentations 4:1-10	968
Is God color-blind? Daniel 7:13-14	1046
Is Nahum denigrating women? Nahum 3:13	1121
Why does marriage matter? Matthew 22:23-33	1227
How did Jesus respond to prejudice in his society? Mark 7:24-30	1252
Why should we find common ground with others? Acts 10:9-43	1372
How does our identity in Jesus shape our other identities? Galatians 3:26-28	1482
What does Paul say about women's worth and roles? Colossians 3:18–4:1	1515
Why is the Bible so concerned about what we wear? 1 Peter 3:3-6	1591
If sex is a good thing, then why are virgins being rewarded? Revelation 14:4	1642

WHAT THE BIBLE SAYS ABOUT... INDEX

Image	43
Work	66
Extended Family	122
Nourishing Our Bodies and Spirits	152
Living Wholeheartedly	194
Courage	276
A Guilty or Clean Conscience	306
Prayer	346
Influence and Leadership	382
Bitterness and Healing	394
Our Bodies	480
Giving	518
Faithfulness	562
Falling Short and Favor	584
Our Feelings	690
Anger	721
Wisdom	784
Enjoyment	802
Sex	814
Husbands	838
Time	948
Grief	994
Divorce	1165
Forgiveness	1200
Serving	1266
Questions	1282
Needing Each Other	1398
Love and Obedience	1428
Singleness	1450
Jesus' Return and Reign	1530
Identity	1592
Shame and Honor	1600
Confidence	1608

INSIGHT INDEX

Days of Creation	6
Noah's Ark	14
Nations of the Ancient World	18
Sarai and Abram's Travels	22
Could You Lift That?	38
Israel's Family Tree	47
Family Travels through Canaan	53
Mothers and Fathers of Faith	72
The Reluctant Leader	83
Ten Plagues against Ten False Gods	89
Israel's Calendar of Festivals	93
If You Could Bring Just One Food on a Trip	100
The Tabernacle	113
Israel's Sacrifices	136
Holy, Clean, and Unclean	143
Israel's Camp	169
Opinion Poll	185
Israel in the Wilderness	191
The Cities of Refuge	237
Conquest of Canaan	268
The Cycle of Judges	292
The Ark of the Covenant	339
David on the Run	359
Saul's Journey away from God	366
David's Wives and Their Children	376
Jerusalem: The City of David	378
God Has a Better Plan	387
Solomon's Wealth	420
Twice the Power	444
The Power of Owning Our Place and Part	472
Jerusalem through Time	496
Solomon's Temple	522
Strong Headwinds	578

Numbering Job's Losses	615
Relying on God's Wisdom	620
Jesus in the Psalms	652
Kinds of Psalms	656
Mountains and God	680
The Music of the Psalms	709
Themes in Proverbs	775
Isaiah's Prophecies in the New Testament	845
The Savior Is Coming	870
The Prophet's Theater	977
Ezekiel's Important Dates	1022
New Names	1036
Living in a Prophetic Time	1054
No Exceptions	1081
Jonah's Misdirection	1098
Jesus' Family Tree	1192
Prophecies about the Messiah	1196
The Parables of Jesus	1212
First-Century Jewish Home	1244
The Last Supper and Gethsemane	1264
The Women Disciples of Jesus	1292
Herod's Temple	1334
Can We Trust That Jesus Conquered Death?	1354
The Good News Spreads	1360
How Far Paul Traveled	1378
Physical Signs of God's Kingdom	1403
Letters for the Church	1409
Paul's Women Coworkers	1433
The Gift Registry	1452
Jesus Is Greater	1566
Ancient Churches, Anytime Challenges	1632
What the Numbers Mean	1641
Revelation's Old Testament Imagery	1652

SHE SAYS INDEX

Aimee Semple McPherson 693
  Divine Healing Sermons (New Kensington, PA: Whitaker House, 1923, 2014).

Amena Brown 1628
  Breaking Old Rhythms: Answering the Call of a Creative God (Downers Grove, IL: IVP Books, 2013), 63.

Amy Carmichael 1223

Angela Thomas 937
  Do You Think I'm Beautiful?: The Question Every Woman Asks (Nashville: Thomas Nelson, 2003), chap. 4.

Anne Graham Lotz 1590
  Wounded by God's People (Grand Rapids, MI: Zondervan, 2013), preface.

Argula von Grumbach 215
  Kristen Padilla, "No Woman's Chit-Chat: Argula von Grumbach as Prophetess, Writer, and Defender of the Reformation," Credo Magazine, vol. 7, no. 3 (May 7, 2018), https://credomag.com/article/no-womans-chit-chat/.

Beth Moore 750
  Praying God's Word: Breaking Free from Spiritual Strongholds (Nashville: B&H Publishing, 2009), 44.

Bianca Olthoff 857
  As quoted in "Fight for Your Field," a sermon delivered at James River Church, July 16, 2017, https://jamesriver.online/sermon/fight-for-your-field/ (14:30).

Catherine Booth 1345
  "Sayings of Catherine Booth," Christianity Today (website), accessed August 2, 2022, https://www.christianitytoday.com/history/issues/issue-26/sayings-of-catherine-booth.html.

Catherine of Siena 155
  Dialog of Catherine of Siena, Christian Classics Ethereal Library, accessed August 2, 2022, https://www.ccel.org/ccel/catherine/dialog.iv.ii.vi.html.

Christy Nockels 771
  @christynockels, Twitter, August 25, 2020, https://twitter.com/christynockels/status/1298374938177544192.

Clara Barton 576
  Robert C. Plumb, The Better Angels: Five Women Who Changed Civil War America (Lincoln, NE: Potomac Books, 2020), 212.

Corrie Ten Boom 1258
  Clippings from My Notebook (Nashville: Thomas Nelson, 1982), 23.

Crispina 231
  "The Martyrdom of Crispina," In Her Words: Women's Writings in the History of Christian Thought, ed. Amy Oden (Nashville: Abingdon, 1994), 45.

Crystal McDowell 1167
  "Let Those Arrows Fly," Daughters of the Creator (blog), accessed August 2, 2022, https://daughtersofthecreator.com/let-those-arrows-fly/.

Darlene Schacht 1149

Dorothy Day 683

Dorothy L. Sayers 1253
  Letters to a Diminished Church: Passionate Arguments for the Relevance of Christian Doctrine (Nashville: Thomas Nelson, 2004), 1.

Elisabeth Elliot 158
  Secure in the Everlasting Arms: Trusting the God Who Never Leaves Your Side (Grand Rapids: Revell, 2002), chap. 5.

Ellen G. White 790
  Malcolm Bull and Keith Lockhart, Seeking a Sanctuary: Seventh-day Adventism and the American Dream (Bloomington: Indiana University Press, 2007), 91.

Elyse Fitzpatrick 1529
  Because He Loves Me: How Christ Transforms Our Daily Life (Wheaton: Crossway Books, 2008), 134.

Evangeline Cory Booth 35
Fannie Lou Hamer 1583
"We're on Our Way," Speech Delivered at a Mass Meeting in Indianola, Mississippi, September 1964, in The Speeches of Fannie Lou Hamer: To Tell It Like It Is, eds. Maegan Parker Brooks and Davis W. Houck (University of Mississippi Press, 2011), 53.

Fanny Crosby 474
Flannery O'Connor 58
Mystery and Manners: Occasional Prose (New York: Farrar, Straus & Giroux, 1969), 84.

Florence Nightingale 70
Sir Edward Cook, The Life of Florence Nightingale, vol. 2 (London: Macmillan, 1914), 434.

Francine Rivers 654
A Lineage of Grace (Carol Stream, IL: Tyndale House Publishers, 2012), 391.

Gladys Aylward 829
Andrew T. Kaiser, The Rushing on of the Purposes of God (Eugene, OR: Pickwick, 2016), 203.

Grace Ji-Sun Kim 741
"Why I Wrote about Hope in Disarray," Baptist News Global, February 19, 2021, accessed August 2, 2022, https://baptistnews.com/article/why-i-wrote-about-hope-in-disarray/#.YuInDXbMJjV.

Harriet Tubman 1598
Sarah H. Bradford, Scenes in the Life of Harriet Tubman (Auburn, NY: W. J. Moses, 1869), 20.

Henrietta Mears 1362
Earl O. Roe, ed., Dream Big: The Henrietta Mears Story (Carol Stream, IL: Tyndale House Publishers, 1990), 57.

Hildegard of Bingen 128
Isobel Miller Kuhn 396
Vinita Hampton and Carol Plueddemann, World Shapers: A Treasury of Quotes from Great Missionaries (Wheaton: Harold Shaw, 1991), 14.

Jackie Hill Perry 412
Gay Girl, Good God: The Story of Who I Was and Who God Has Always Been (Nashville: B&H Publishing, 2018).

Jarena Lee 921
The Life and Religious Experience of Jarena Lee (Cincinnati, printed and published for the author, 2nd ed., 1839), 24.

Jen Wilkin 909
Women of the Word: How to Study the Bible with Both Our Hearts and Our Minds (Wheaton: Crossway Books, 2014), 31.

Jill Briscoe 1327
Christin Ditchfield, What Women Should Know about Letting It Go (Abilene, TX: Leafwood Publishers, 2015).

Joan of Arc 281
Julia A. J. Foote 1232
"A Word to My Christians Sisters," in Preaching with Sacred Fire: An Anthology of African American Sermons, 1750 to the Present, ed. Martha Simmons and Frank A. Thomas (New York: Norton, 2010), 176.

Julian of Norwich 1648
Revelations of Divine Love, Barry Windeatt, trans. (New York: Oxford University Press, 2015), 74.

Karen Kingsbury 1424
Unlocked (Grand Rapids: Zondervan, 2010), 317.

Katharina Zell 1410
Rudolph W. Heinze, Reform and Conflict: From the Medieval World to the Wars of Religion, A.D. 1350–1648 (Oxford: Monarch Books, 2005, 2006), 293.

Katherine Johnson 536
"Katherine Johnson: A Lifetime of STEM," NASA (website), February 24, 2020, accessed August 2, 2022, https://www.nasa.gov/audience/foreducators/a-lifetime-of-stem.html.

Kay Arthur 1076
As Silver Refined: Learning to Embrace Life's Disappointments (Colorado Springs: WaterBrook, 1997), 46.

Kay Warren 1415
Choose Joy: Because Happiness Isn't Enough (Grand Rapids: Revell, 2012), 100.

Latasha Morrison 1481
Be the Bridge: Pursuing God's Heart for Racial Reconciliation (Colorado Springs: WaterBrook, 2019), 22.

Lilias Trotter 1575
Miriam Huffman Rockness, *A Passion for the Impossible* (Wheaton: Harold Shaw, 1999), 289.

Lisa Bevere 1546
Lioness Arising: Wake Up and Change Your World (Colorado Springs: WaterBrook, 2010), 86.

Lisa Sharon Harper 1636
The Very Good Gospel: How Everything Wrong Can Be Made Right (Colorado Springs: WaterBrook, 2016), 46.

Lottie Moon 1522
Letter from Tungchow, September 15, 1887, first published in the Foreign Mission Journal, December 1887, in *Send the Light: Lottie Moon's Letters and Other Writings*, ed. Keith Harper (Macon, GA: Mercer University Press, 2002), 223.

Love L. Sechrest 1466
"Race Relations in the Church in the Age of Obama," Fuller Studio, accessed August 2, 2022, https://fullerstudio.fuller.edu/race-relations-in-the-church-in-the-age-of-obama/.

Luci Swindoll 897

Lucretia Mott 1516
"Likeness to Christ," in *In Her Words: Women's Writings in the History of Christian Thought*, ed. Amy Oden (Nashville: Abingdon, 1994), 293.

Macrina the Younger 1368
"Saint Macrina: Feast Day July 19," Loyola Press (website), accessed August 2, 2022, https://www.loyolapress.com/catholic-resources/saints/saints-stories-for-all-ages/saint-macrina/.

Madeleine L'Engle 328
Walking on Water: Reflections on Faith and Art (Crown Publishing, 2016), 12.

Margaret Feinberg 713
Wonderstruck: Awaken to the Nearness of God (Brentwood, TN: Worthy Publishing, 2012).

Mary Beth Chapman 631
Choosing to SEE: A Journey of Struggle and Hope (Grand Rapids: Baker Books, 2010).

Mercy Amba Oduyoye 1339
Introducing African Women's Theology (Sheffield: Sheffield Academic Press, 2001), 119.

Mother Teresa 1285
Arun Anand, *Indian Nobel Laureates* (New Dehli: Ocean Books, 2013), 83.

Pandita Ramabai 251
Rev. H. Ingham, "'The House of a Thousand Widows': A Day with Pandita Ramabai at Mukti," The Christian Advocate, October 19, 1916, https://www.google.com/books/edition/The_Christian_Advocate/1LQ6AQAAMAAJ?hl=en&gbpv=0.

Patsy Clairmont 1017
You Are More than You Know: Face Your Fears, Grow Stronger (Brentwood, TN: Worthy Publishing, 2015).

Phoebe Palmer 463
Richard Wheatley, *The Life and Letters of Mrs. Phoebe Palmer* (New York: W. C. Palmer, Jr., 1876), 30.

Prathia Hall Wynn 1456
"Between the Wilderness and a Cliff (June 1992)," in *Preaching with Sacred Fire: An Anthology of African American Sermons, 1750 to the Present*, eds. Martha Simmons and Frank A. Thomas (New York: Norton, 2010), 691.

Priscilla Shirer 180
One in a Million: Journey to Your Promised Land (Nashville: B&H Publishing, 2010), 115.

Queen Elizabeth II 1295
"Christmas Broadcast 2004," published December 25, 2004, accessed August 2, 2022, https://www.royal.uk/christmas-broadcast-2004.

Rachel Gilson 759
Born Again This Way: Coming Out, Coming to Faith, and What Comes Next (Epsom, England: The Good Book Company, 2020), 93.

Rebekah Lyons 1198
You Are Free: Be Who You Already Are (Grand Rapids: Zondervan, 2017), 64.

Rosa Parks 365
"A Life of Global Impact," Library (website), Library of Congress, accessed August 2, 2022, https://www.loc.gov/exhibitions/rosa-parks-in-her-own-words/about-this-exhibition/a-life-of-global-impact/.

Ruth Chou Simons 1043
"The Macro-Effect of Micro-Rituals," gracelaced.com (website by Ruth Chou Simons), July 1, 2013, accessed August 2, 2022, https://gracelaced.com/blogs/blog/the-macro-effect-of-micro-rituals.

Ruth Haley Barton 1552
Strengthening the Soul of Your Leadership (Downers Grove, IL: InterVarsity Press, 2018), 19.

Ruth Padilla DeBorst 409
"Songs of Hope Out of a Crying Land: An Overview of Contemporary Latin American Theology" in Global Theology in Evangelical Perspective, ed. by Jeffrey P. Greenman and Gene L. Green (Downers Grove, IL: IVP Academic, 2012), 101.

Sadie Robertson Huff 1612
"Does God Love Me?," simplysheblog.com (website), accessed August 2, 2022, https://simplysheblog.com/podcasts/does-god-love-me-ft-sadie-robertson.

Sara Groves 1393
"On Making Music and Home: Jill Phillips Interviews Sara Groves," Art House America Blog, accessed August 2, 2022, https://www.arthouseamerica.com/blog/on-making-music-and-home-jill-phillips-interviews-sara-grove.html.

Shauna Niequist 644
Bittersweet: Thoughts on Change, Grace, and Learning the Hard Way (Grand Rapids: Zondervan, 2010), 13.

Sojourner Truth 94
Harriet Beecher Stowe, "Sojourner Truth, The Libyan Sibyl," The Atlantic (April 1863), https://www.theatlantic.com/magazine/archive/1863/04/sojourner-truth-the-libyan-sibyl/308775/.

Stasi Eldredge 302
with John Eldredge, Captivating: Unveiling the Mystery of a Woman's Soul (Nashville: Thomas Nelson, 2005, 2010), 11.

Stormie Omartian 991
The Power of a Praying Woman (Eugene, OR: Harvest House, 2002), 36.

Susanna Wesley 565
Susanna Wesley: The Complete Writings, ed. Charles Wallace Jr. (New York: Oxford University Press, 1997), 341.

Syncletica of Alexandria 1475
V. K. McCarty, "Encouragement from the Desert Mothers in Troubling Times," Public Orthodoxy: Bridging the Ecclesial, the Academic, and the Political, https://publicorthodoxy.org/2020/12/04/encouragement-from-the-desert-mothers-in-troubling-times/.

Thecla 1563
"Acts of Paul and Thecla," in In Her Words: Women's Writings in the History of Christian Thought, ed. Amy Oden (Nashville: Abingdon, 1994), 25.

Theodora of Alexandria 603
V. K. McCarty, "Encouragement from the Desert Mothers in Troubling Times," Public Orthodoxy: Bridging the Ecclesial, the Academic, and the Political, https://publicorthodoxy.org/2020/12/04/encouragement-from-the-desert-mothers-in-troubling-times/.

Thérèse of Lisieux 664

SCRIPTURE PAUSE INDEX

Exodus 14:14	117
Numbers 6:24	174
Deuteronomy 6:4	244
Joshua 1:9	272
Ruth 1:16	331
1 Samuel 12:20	342
2 Samuel 22:31	402
1 Chronicles 4:10	488
Esther 4:14	601
Psalm 27:13	673
Psalm 100:5	718
Proverbs 3:6	757
Proverbs 24:3-4	780
Ecclesiastes 3:11	796
Isaiah 40:29	862
Jeremiah 31:3	925
Lamentations 3:22-23	970
Ezekiel 36:26	1005
Joel 2:32	1075
Micah 6:8	1113
Zephaniah 3:17	1133
Matthew 11:28	1208
John 3:16	1321
Romans 8:37	1412
2 Corinthians 5:17	1470
Philippians 4:13	1508
1 Thessalonians 5:16-18	1525
Hebrews 11:6	1561
Revelation 22:20	1638

CONTRIBUTORS INDEX

This is a list of everyone who contributed to the features of this Bible. For the contributors who wrote study notes, the first page of each book is listed.

ALLEN, ESTHER FLEECE
623

ALSDORF, KATHERINE LEARY
99, 890, 1537, 1631

ARD, QUANTRILLA
13, 144, 314, 595, 877

ARIOTO, MANDY
1035, 1297, 1338

ARMSTRONG, KAT
26, 1333

ARTERBURN, MISTY
29, 36, 202, 240, 296, 389, 423, 436, 457, 760, 818, 1089, 1523

AVENIDO, LORINA
1577

AZADIAN, AMANDA
1455

BANKS, GABRIELA MAGAÑA
651, 1230

BAST, ELIZA CORTÉS
1242, 1419

BELL, VALERIE
249, 326, 470, 1191, 1543

BUBBERS, SUSAN I.
768, 879, 1014

BYARUGABA, DAISY ASIIMWE
1570

CALIGUIRE, MINDY
141, 219

CARY, KRISTIN
1163, 1485

CEN, ESTHER G.
1190, 1240, 1252, 1272, 1320, 1482

COHICK, LYNN H.
1227, 1358, 1383, 1408, 1436, 1446, 1462, 1480, 1490, 1496, 1515, 1535, 1591

COLLIER, TONI J.
1494

CROWDER, TRACI
1304

DA SILVA, DEBORA
850, 939

DALLAIRE, HÉLÈNE M.
696, 1135, 1151

DAY, CARA
31, 61, 62, 85, 265, 297, 329, 337, 393, 559, 611, 686, 763, 800, 867, 1085, 1219, 1365, 1414, 1513, 1629

DHARAMRAJ, HAVILAH
290, 311, 1094, 1099, 1132, 1140, 1146, 1162

DILLOW, LINDA
286

EDMONDS, LISA D.
183, 239, 1610

FEINBERG, MARGARET
1635

FITZWATER, MARGARET
432

FRY, ALEXIANA
318, 324, 334, 372, 546, 795, 823

FULLER, CHERI
772

GAMEZ, SUSIE
1046, 1387

GARCIA de BRIZENDINE, BRENDA
931

GIBSON, ANDREA
1437, 1438

GITAU, LILLIAN
1102

GLANVILLE, ELIZABETH
9, 40, 103, 225, 449, 529, 553, 575, 580, 597, 645, 789, 833, 902, 966, 1215, 1277, 1391, 1431

HALL, SARA
1521

HARRIS, SARAH
1502, 1512, 1520, 1528, 1534, 1542, 1550, 1556, 1560, 1580, 1606, 1616, 1620

HEIM, TAMI
77, 501

HO, SHIRLEY SIONG SHU
258

HOUDMANN, MELISSA
375, 567, 570, 1119, 1375

IMES, CARMEN JOY
4, 5, 17, 23, 34, 80, 82, 105, 107, 610, 637, 746, 764, 806, 1651

JAMES, AVA
787

JONES, JENNIFER BROWN
132, 134, 168, 184, 218, 608, 650, 754

JONES, SUSAN M.
1421

KELLER, JENNIFER
590

KUYKENDALL, ALEXANDRA
37, 59, 431, 1241, 1486, 1506

LAMOTHE, DONNA LEE
363, 499, 755, 1289

LEE, CHEE-CHIEW
1588, 1598, 1624, 1628, 1645

LONG, LYNN
881, 1503

MABUNI, VIVIAN
25

MATHENY, JENNIFER M.
324, 327, 408, 442, 478, 516, 558, 574, 594, 794, 810, 822, 896, 1569

MATHERS, JANICE MAYO
453, 734, 1351

McCANTS, RACHEL LINDSAY
612, 799, 812, 1616

McDOWELL, CATHERINE L.
962, 968, 1058, 1072, 1080, 1095, 1118, 1121, 1126, 1162

MINTER, KELLY
1323

MORGAN, ELISA
81, 334, 1263, 1325

MORRISON, LATASHA
1481

MUCHETU, ADELAIDE MANYARA
188

NANGUDI, LOIS
1617

OMARTIAN, STORMIE
1448

OVERTON, DELANEY
1442

OVERTON, KATRIEL
1256

OVERTON, NAOMI CRAMER
20, 159, 261, 300, 598, 643, 667, 669, 905, 1111, 1128, 1340, 1417, 1492, 1573

OVERTON, SARAH
676, 919, 1467

PACE, IRENE
1300

PATTERSON, ALICE
744, 1498

PETERS, BELÉN
737, 1220, 1222

POLSLEY, EVIE
133

POWELL, KARA
1279, 1440

PUTNAM, WHITNEY
32, 49, 355, 1313, 1425, 1444

RAYBON, PATRICIA
1372, 1491

REESE, ROBIN
446

RISNER, VANEETHA RENDALL
626, 1291

ROBERTS, MEGAN C.
1463

ROGERS, ELISABETH SELZER
54, 390, 1065, 1107, 1380, 1545, 1551

ROSNER, JENNIFER
1205, 1642

SARMIENTO, EMILY
1059

SCHALLER, MARY
1352

SCRIVNER, CATHY
1581

SERRANO, MILLIE
635, 1589

SHEPHERD, SUZY
11, 259, 1194, 1385

SHIRER, PRISCILLA
1585

SIMONS, RUTH CHOU
660

SIMPSON, AMY
1073

SPROWLS, NANCY CHAMBERLIN
704, 1141, 1542

STRICKLAND, DANIELLE
97

TADA, JONI EARECKSON
1582

THOMAS, STEPHANIE
1564

TKACHENKO, ANGELA
743, 1273

VOSBURG, ELLEN RICHARD
989

WALKER, CHRISTINE
974, 1034, 1106

WARD, VIRGINIA
294, 505, 830, 1275, 1307

WHITTLE, LISA
1473

WILHARM, SHARON
1505

WILKIN, JEN
1328

WOLF, KATHERINE
1248, 1465

WONG, MENCHIT
1168

WRIGHT, JULIE
207, 817

YODER, BRENDA L.
728

YOUNG, MAY
640, 963, 1101, 1153

NLT DICTIONARY/CONCORDANCE

A

AARON First high priest of Israel; elder brother and spokesman of Moses (Exod 4:14-31; 7:1-2); confronted Pharaoh with Moses (Exod 5–12); held up Moses' hands during battle (Exod 17:8-15); led Israel while Moses was absent (Exod 24:14); priestly clothing and accessories (Exod 28); his ordination (Exod 29; Lev 8); his failure with the gold calf (Exod 32; Acts 7:40); spoke against Moses, then interceded on behalf of sister, Miriam (Num 12:1-16); helped stop the plague (Num 16:45-48); priesthood confirmed (Num 17; Heb 5:1-4); failed at Meribah and was denied entry to Promised Land (Num 20:1-13); died (Num 20:22-29; 33:38-39).

ABANDON, ABANDONED, ABANDONS (v) *to desert or forsake*
Josh 1:5 ... will not fail you or *a* you.
Josh 24:16 ... We would never *a* the LORD
Ezra 9:9 ... God did not *a* us in our slavery.
Neh 9:31 ... completely or *a* them forever.
Ps 22:1 ... why have you *a-ed* me?
Ps 37:25 ... never seen the godly *a-ed*
Ps 37:28 ... he will never *a* the godly.
Prov 15:10 ... Whoever *a-s* the right path
Matt 27:46 ... why have you *a-ed* me?
John 16:1 ... you won't *a* your faith.
Rom 1:24 ... So God *a-ed* them to do
Rom 1:28 ... *a-ed* them to their foolish
2 Cor 4:9 ... down, but never *a-ed* by God.
Heb 13:5 ... I will never *a* you.

ABASED (KJV)
Ezek 21:26 ... mighty will be *brought down*.
Matt 23:12 ... themselves will be *humbled*
Phil 4:12 ... how to *live on almost nothing*

ABIDE(TH), ABIDING (KJV)
Luke 2:8 ... shepherds *staying* in the fields
John 12:46 ... no longer *remain* in the dark
John 15:4 ... be fruitful unless you *remain*

ABOUND(ED) (KJV)
Prov 28:20 ... person will *get a rich reward*
Matt 24:12 ... Sin will *be rampant everywhere*
Rom 5:15 ... *even greater* is God's wonderful grace
Rom 5:20 ... grace *became more abundant*
2 Cor 8:7 ... *excel* also in this gracious act

ABRAHAM (ABRAM) Father of the nation of Israel (Isa 51:2; John 8:37-59); friend of God (Isa 41:8); father of all people of faith (Gen 12–25; Rom 4; Heb 11); made covenant with the Lord (Gen 12:1-3; 13:14-17; 15:12-21; 22:15-18; 50:24; Exod 2:24; 32:13; Lev 26:42; 2 Kgs 13:23; 1 Chr 16:16; Neh 9:8; Ps 105:9; Luke 1:73; Acts 3:25; Gal 3:17-20; Heb 6:13); descendant of Terah from Ur (Gen 11:27-31); husband of Sarah (Sarai) (Gen 11:29); called to leave home (Gen 12:1-9; Acts 7:2-4; Heb 11:8-10); went to Egypt and deceived the Pharaoh (Gen 12:10-20); chose Canaan over the Jordan Plain (Gen 13); rescued Lot from enemies (Gen 14:11-16); blessed by Melchizedek (Gen 14:18-24; Heb 7:1); covenant restated by God (Gen 15); faith counted as righteousness (Gen 15:6; Rom 4:3; Gal 3:6-9; Jas 2:21-23); given son (Ishmael) by Hagar (Gen 16); circumcision commanded (Gen 17; Rom 4:9-12); name changed to "Abraham" (Gen 17:5; Neh 9:7); son promised to Sarah (Gen 17:16; 18:10); welcomed heavenly visitor (Gen 18:1-15); bargained to save Sodom and Gomorrah (Gen 18:16-33); deceived Abimelech (Gen 20); named as a prophet (Gen 20:7); given son (Isaac) by Sarah (Gen 21:1-7; Heb 11:11-12); sent Hagar and Ishmael away (Gen 21:9-14; Gal 4:21-31); offered Isaac as test (Gen 22:1-19; Heb 11:17-19; Jas 2:21); secured burial ground for Sarah (Gen 23); found a wife for Isaac (Gen 24); descendants through wife Keturah (Gen 25:1-6); died (Gen 25:7-11).

ABUNDANCE (n) *great quantity, affluence; more than ample*
Job 36:31 ... giving them food in *a.*
Ps 66:12 ... a place of great *a.*
Jer 31:14 ... The priests will enjoy *a,*
Matt 13:12 ... have an *a* of knowledge.
Matt 25:29 ... they will have an *a.*
John 1:16 ... From his *a* we have all

ABUNDANT (adj) *marked by great plenty, abounding*
Deut 28:11 ... livestock, and *a* crops.
Ps 68:9 ... You sent *a* rain, O God
Jer 31:12 ... good gifts—the *a* crops
John 16:24 ... you will have *a* joy.
2 Cor 8:2 ... are also filled with *a* joy,

ABUSIVE (adj) *using harsh, insulting language; characterized by wrong or improper use or action*
1 Cor 5:11 ... worships idols, or is *a,*
1 Cor 6:10 ... drunkards, or are *a,* or
Eph 4:29 ... use foul or *a* language.

ABYSS (KJV)
Luke 8:31 ... send them into the *bottomless pit*
Rev 9:1 ... the shaft of the *bottomless pit*
Rev 9:11 ... the angel from the *bottomless pit*

ACCEPT, ACCEPTED, ACCEPTS (v) *to receive willingly*
Gen 4:4 ... The LORD *a-ed* Abel
Gen 4:7 ... be *a-ed* if you do what is right.
Deut 16:19 ... Never *a* a bribe, for bribes
Job 42:8 ... I will *a* his prayer
Job 42:9 ... the LORD *a-ed* Job's prayer.
Eccl 5:18 ... to *a* their lot in life.
Luke 4:24 ... no prophet is *a-ed* in his
Luke 10:16 ... who *a-s* your message
John 1:12 ... believed him and *a-ed* him,
John 17:8 ... They *a-ed* it and know that
Rom 11:12 ... when they finally *a* it.
Gal 2:9 ... they *a-ed* Barnabas and me
Col 2:6 ... just as you *a-ed* Christ Jesus
1 Tim 1:15 ... everyone should *a* it:
1 Tim 4:9 ... everyone should *a* it.
Jas 1:21 ... *a* the word God has planted

ACCEPTABLE (adj) *capable or worthy of being accepted; welcome, pleasing, favorable*
Mark 7:19 ... every kind of food is *a*
Rom 4:2 ... had made him *a* to God,
Rom 12:1 ... the kind he will find *a.*
Rom 14:20 ... all foods are *a,* but it is
2 Cor 8:12 ... is *a* if you give it eagerly.
1 Tim 4:5 ... made *a* by the word of God

ACCURSED (KJV)
Deut 21:23 ... anyone who is hung is *cursed*
Josh 6:18 ... things *set apart for destruction*
1 Cor 12:3 ... will *curse* Jesus, and no one
Gal 1:9 ... let that person be *cursed*

ACCUSE, ACCUSED, ACCUSES, ACCUSING (v) *to charge with fault or offense; to blame*
Job 22:4 ... *a-s* you and brings judgment
Ps 27:12 ... For they *a* me of things
Dan 6:5 ... grounds for *a-ing* Daniel
Luke 23:14 ... *a-ing* him of leading a revolt.
John 5:45 ... it isn't I who will *a*
John 7:7 ... because I *a* it of doing evil.
John 8:46 ... can truthfully *a* me of sin?
Acts 18:13 ... *a-d* Paul of "persuading
Rom 2:15 ... and thoughts either *a* them
Rom 8:33 ... Who dares *a* us whom God
Rev 12:10 ... who *a-s* them before our God

ACKNOWLEDGE, ACKNOWLEDGES (v) *to express a gratitude of debt; to recognize as valid; to confess (wrongdoing)*
Jer 3:13 ... Only *a* your guilt. Admit
Matt 10:32 ... Everyone who *a-s* me
Luke 12:8 ... Son of Man will also *a*
Rom 1:28 ... thought it foolish to *a* God,
1 Jn 2:23 ... anyone who *a-s* the Son
1 Jn 4:3 ... and does not *a* the truth

ADAM First man (Gen 1:26–2:25; Rom 5:14; 1 Tim 2:13-14); son of God (Luke 3:38); sinned (Gen 3:1-19; Hos 6:7; Rom 5:12-21); descendants of (Gen 5); died (Gen 5:5; 1 Cor 15:22-49).

1693

ADD, ADDED (v) *to make or serve as an addition*
Deut 4:2 … Do not *a* to or subtract from
Deut 12:32 … You must not *a* anything to
Prov 30:6 … Do not *a* to his words,
Eccl 3:14 … Nothing can be *a-ed* to it
Matt 6:27 … worries *a* a single moment
Luke 12:25 … worries *a* a single moment
Acts 2:47 … each day the Lord *a-ed* to their
Rev 22:18 … God will *a* to that person

ADMONISH(ED) (KJV)
Eccl 12:12 … give you *some further advice*
Jer 42:19 … Don't forget this *warning* I
2 Thes 3:15 … *warn* them as you would
Heb 8:5 … God gave him this *warning*

ADMONITION (KJV)
1 Cor 10:11 … written down *to warn us*
Eph 6:4 … *instruction* that comes from the Lord
Titus 3:10 … a first and second *warning*

ADOPT, ADOPTED (v) *to take another's child into one's own family*
Rom 8:15 … when he *a-ed* you as his own
Rom 8:23 … rights as his *a-ed* children,
Rom 9:4 … to be God's *a-ed* children.
Gal 4:5 … so that he could *a* us as
Eph 1:5 … decided in advance to *a* us

ADULTERY (n) *unlawful sexual relations between a married person and someone other than their spouse; symbolic of idolatry*
Exod 20:14 … You must not commit *a*.
Deut 5:18 … You must not commit *a*.
Prov 6:32 … who commits *a* is an utter fool,
Matt 5:27 … You must not commit *a*.
Matt 19:18 … You must not commit *a*.
Mark 10:11 … someone else commits *a*
Luke 18:20 … You must not commit *a*.
John 8:4 … caught in the act of *a*.
1 Cor 6:9 … *a*, or are male prostitutes,

ADVICE (n) *recommendation regarding a decision or course of conduct; counsel*
1 Kgs 12:8 … rejected the *a* of
2 Chr 10:8 … rejected the *a* of
Prov 12:5 … *a* of the wicked is
Prov 12:26 … godly give good *a* to their
Prov 15:22 … Plans go wrong for lack of *a*;
Isa 44:25 … I cause the wise to give bad *a*,
Rom 11:34 … enough to give him *a*?

ADVISE (v) *to give advice; counsel*
Ps 32:8 … I will *a* you and watch over
1 Tim 5:14 … I *a* these younger widows
Rev 3:18 … I *a* you to buy gold from me—

ADVISERS (n) *one who gives advice; counselor*
1 Sam 28:23 … his *a* joined the woman in
1 Kgs 12:14 … counsel of his younger *a*.
Esth 1:13 … consulted with his wise *a*,
Prov 11:14 … safety in having many *a*.
Prov 29:12 … all his *a* will be wicked.

ADVOCATE (n) *one who pleads the cause of another; defender*
see also HOLY SPIRIT, COUNSELOR
Job 16:19 … My *a* is there on high.
John 14:16 … he will give you another *A*,
John 14:26 … the Father sends the *A*
John 15:26 … I will send you the *A*—
John 16:7 … if I don't, the *A* won't come.
1 Jn 2:1 … an *a* who pleads our case

AFRAID (adj) *fearful or apprehensive about an unwanted or uncertain situation*
Gen 3:10 … I was *a* because I was naked.
Gen 26:24 … Do not be *a*, for I am
Exod 3:6 … he was *a* to look at God.
Deut 1:21 … Don't be *a*!
Deut 20:1 … your own, do not be *a*.
Ps 23:4 … I will not be *a*, for you are
Isa 10:24 … do not be *a* of the Assyrians
Isa 41:10 … Don't be *a*, for I am
Isa 43:1 … Do not be *a*, for I have
Matt 8:26 … Why are you *a*?
Matt 10:31 … So don't be *a*;
Mark 5:36 … Don't be *a*.
John 14:27 … don't be troubled or *a*.
2 Tim 4:5 … Don't be *a* of suffering
1 Pet 3:14 … don't worry or be *a*

AGREE, AGREED, AGREEING (v) *to admit, concede*
Matt 18:19 … If two of you *a* here on
Luke 7:29 … *a-d* that God's way was right,
Rom 7:16 … that I *a* that the law is good.
Phil 2:2 … make me truly happy by *a-ing*

ALCOHOL (n) *drink (as wine or beer) containing ethanol*
Prov 20:1 … *a* leads to brawls.
Isa 5:22 … boast about all the *a* they

ALCOHOLIC (adj) *containing alcohol*
Num 6:3 … give up wine and other *a*

ALIEN (KJV)
Exod 18:3 … a *foreigner* in a foreign
Job 19:15 … I am like a *foreigner* to them
Eph 2:12 … were *excluded from citizenship*

ALIENATED (KJV)
Ezek 48:14 … traded or *used by others*
Eph 4:18 … *wander far from* the life God
Col 1:21 … were once *far away from* God

ALIVE (adj) *animate, having life; active; aware*
Gen 45:7 … keep you and your families *a*
Ps 41:2 … them and keeps them *a*.
Luke 24:23 … Jesus is *a*!
Acts 1:3 … ways that he was actually *a*.
Rom 6:11 … the power of sin and *a* to God
Rev 2:8 … who was dead but is now *a*:

ALLELUIA (KJV)
Rev 19:1 … shouting, "*Praise the Lord!*
Rev 19:3 … rang out: "*Praise the Lord!*
Rev 19:4 … "Amen! *Praise the Lord!*"
Rev 19:6 … "*Praise the Lord!* For the Lord

ALMIGHTY (adj) *having absolute power over all; God*
see also (HEAVEN'S) ARMIES
Gen 17:1 … I am El-Shaddai—'God *A*.'
Exod 6:3 … as El-Shaddai—'God *A*'—
Ruth 1:20 … *A* has made life very bitter
Job 6:14 … without any fear of the *A*.
Job 33:4 … breath of the *A* gives me life.
Ps 91:1 … rest in the shadow of the *A*.
Rev 4:8 … the *A*—the one who always was,
Rev 15:3 … O Lord God, the *A*.
Rev 19:6 … our God, the *A*, reigns.

ALTAR, ALTARS (n) *high places of worship on which sacrifices are offered or incense is burned*
Gen 8:20 … Noah built an *a* to the LORD.
Gen 12:7 … Abram built an *a* there
Gen 22:9 … Abraham built an *a* and

Gen 26:25 … Isaac built an *a* there
Exod 30:1 … make another *a* of acacia
Exod 37:25 … incense *a* of acacia wood.
Josh 8:30 … Joshua built an *a* to the LORD,
Josh 22:10 … a large and imposing *a*.
1 Sam 7:17 … Samuel built an *a* to the
2 Chr 4:1 … made a bronze *a* 30 feet long,
2 Chr 4:19 … Temple of God: the gold *a*;
2 Chr 32:12 … only at the *a* at the Temple
2 Chr 33:16 … restored the *a* of the LORD
Ezra 3:2 … rebuilding the *a* of the God
Isa 6:6 … coal he had taken from the *a*
Matt 5:23 … presenting a sacrifice at the *a*
Acts 17:23 … your *a-s* had this inscription
Heb 13:10 … an *a* from which the priests
Rev 6:9 … I saw under the *a* the souls

ALWAYS (adv) *at all times; forever, perpetually*
1 Kgs 2:4 … will *a* sit on the throne
Ps 16:8 … the LORD is *a* with me.
Ps 52:8 … will *a* trust in God's unfailing
Ps 102:27 … But you are *a* the same;
Ps 106:3 … and *a* do what is right.
Prov 23:7 … They are *a* thinking about
Isa 16:5 … He will *a* do what is just
Matt 28:20 … I am with you *a*, even to
Mark 14:7 … You will *a* have the poor
John 12:8 … you will not *a* have me.
1 Pet 3:15 … *a* be ready to explain it.

AMAZED (v) *to fill with wonder, astound*
Matt 7:28 … were *a* at his teaching
Mark 7:37 … They were completely *a* and
Mark 10:24 … This *a* them. But Jesus
Luke 2:33 … Jesus' parents were *a* at
Acts 2:7 … They were completely *a*.

AMAZING (adj) *causing amazement, great wonder, or surprise*
1 Chr 16:24 … about the *a* things he does.
Ps 96:3 … about the *a* things he does.
Ps 126:2 … What *a* things the LORD has

AMBASSADOR, AMBASSADORS (n) *an authorized representative or messenger*
2 Cor 5:20 … So we are Christ's *a-s*;
Eph 6:20 … this message as God's *a*.

AMBITION (n) *aspiration to achieve a particular goal, good or bad*
Gal 5:20 … anger, selfish *a*, dissension,
Phil 1:17 … They preach with selfish *a*,
Jas 3:14 … there is selfish *a* in your heart,

ANCESTOR, ANCESTORS (n) *one from whom a person is descended; forefather*
Exod 3:15 … God of your *a-s*—the God of
Deut 19:14 … markers your *a-s* set up
Isa 9:7 … throne of his *a* David for all
Isa 43:27 … your first *a* sinned against me;
Mark 11:10 … Kingdom of our *a* David!
Luke 1:32 … the throne of his *a* David.
Rom 9:5 … Abraham, Isaac, and Jacob are their *a-s*,
Gal 1:14 … for the traditions of my *a-s*.
Heb 1:1 … to our *a-s* through the prophets.

ANGEL, ANGELS (n) *human or superhuman agent or messenger of God*
Exod 23:20 … I am sending an *a*
2 Sam 24:16 … and said to the death *a*,
Ps 91:11 … will order his *a-s* to protect
Matt 4:6 … will order his *a-s* to protect
Matt 28:2 … an *a* of the Lord came down
Luke 1:26 … God sent the *a* Gabriel
Luke 2:9 … an *a* of the Lord appeared
Luke 20:36 … they will be like *a-s*.

Acts 12:7 ... The *a* struck him on the side
1 Cor 6:3 ... we will judge *a-s?*
2 Cor 11:14 ... disguises himself as an *a*
Gal 1:8 ... or even an *a* from heaven,
Heb 1:6 ... all of God's *a-s* worship him.
Heb 2:7 ... a little lower than the *a-s*
Heb 13:2 ... entertained *a-s* without
1 Pet 1:12 ... the *a-s* are eagerly watching
2 Pet 2:4 ... even the *a-s* who sinned.
Jude 1:6 ... I remind you of the *a-s*

ANGER (n) *a strong feeling of displeasure*
Exod 34:6 ... slow to *a* and filled with
Num 14:18 ... slow to *a* and filled with
Deut 9:19 ... furious *a* of the LORD,
Deut 29:28 ... In great *a* and fury
2 Kgs 22:13 ... LORD's great *a* is burning
Ps 30:5 ... his *a* lasts only a moment,
Ps 78:38 ... Many times he held back his *a*
Rom 1:18 ... God shows his *a* from heaven
Rom 2:5 ... a day of *a* is coming,
Eph 4:26 ... by letting *a* control you.
1 Thes 5:9 ... pour out his *a* on us.
Jas 1:20 ... Human *a* does not produce
Rev 14:10 ... the wine of God's *a*.

ANGRY (adj) *feeling or showing anger; wrathful*
Exod 32:11 ... so *a* with your own people
Neh 9:17 ... merciful, slow to become *a*,
Ps 103:8 ... merciful, slow to get *a*
Prov 22:24 ... Don't befriend *a* people
Jon 4:2 ... slow to get *a* and filled
Matt 5:22 ... if you are even *a* with
Mark 10:14 ... he was *a* with his disciples.
John 3:36 ... under God's *a* judgment.
Acts 4:25 ... Why were the nations so *a*?
Jas 1:19 ... to speak, and slow to get *a*.

ANGUISH (n) *extreme pain, distress, or anxiety*
Isa 53:11 ... by his *a*, he will be satisfied.
Zeph 1:15 ... of terrible distress and *a*,
Matt 24:21 ... greater *a* than at any time
Luke 16:24 ... I am in *a* in these flames.
Rev 16:10 ... ground their teeth in *a*,

ANOINT, ANOINTED, ANOINTING (v) *to smear or rub with oil; used for healing or consecration to sacred duty; used for grooming or burial; figurative for divine appointment*
see also ANOINTED ONE
Exod 30:26 ... oil to *a* the Tabernacle,
Exod 30:30 ... *A* Aaron and his sons
Lev 8:12 ... *a-ing* him and making him holy
1 Sam 15:1 ... told me to *a* you as king
2 Sam 2:4 ... David and *a-ed* him king over
2 Sam 23:1 ... man *a-ed* by the God of Jacob,
Ps 23:5 ... honor me by *a-ing* my head
Ps 92:10 ... You have *a-ed* me with
Isa 61:1 ... the LORD has *a-ed* me
Dan 9:24 ... and to *a* the Most Holy Place.
Acts 10:38 ... you know that God *a-ed* Jesus
Heb 1:9 ... your God has *a-ed* you,
Jas 5:14 ... over you, *a-ing* you with oil

ANOINTED ONE (n) *one chosen by divine election*
see also MESSIAH
1 Sam 2:10 ... the strength of his *a*."
1 Sam 26:9 ... attacking the LORD's *a*?
Ps 132:17 ... my *a* will be a light for
Isa 45:1 ... the LORD says to Cyrus, his *a*
Dan 9:25 ... a ruler—the *A*—comes.

ANTICHRIST, ANTICHRISTS (n) *opponent of Christ; the personification of evil*
1 Jn 2:18 ... heard that the *A* is coming,
1 Jn 2:18 ... many such *a-s* have appeared.
1 Jn 4:3 ... has the spirit of the *A*,
2 Jn 1:7 ... deceiver and an *a*.

ANXIETY, CARE(S) (KJV)
Ps 139:23 ... know my anxious thoughts
Phil 4:6 ... Don't worry about anything
1 Pet 5:7 ... your worries and cares to God,

APPEAR, APPEARED, APPEARING, APPEARS (v) *to come out of hiding and show up in public view; to make one's presence known*
Gen 1:9 ... so dry ground may *a*.
Num 14:10 ... presence of the LORD *a-ed*
Deut 33:16 ... *a-ed* in the burning bush.
Mal 3:2 ... and face him when he *a-s?*
Matt 1:20 ... angel of the Lord *a-ed* to him
Matt 24:30 ... will *a* in the heavens,
Luke 2:9 ... angel of the Lord *a-ed* among
Luke 16:15 ... You like to *a* righteous
Phil 2:7 ... When he *a-ed* in human form,
2 Thes 1:7 ... the Lord Jesus *a-s* from
2 Tim 1:10 ... by the *a-ing* of Christ Jesus,
Heb 9:24 ... *a* now before God on our
Heb 9:26 ... *a-ed* at the end of the age
1 Pet 5:4 ... when the Great Shepherd *a-s*,
1 Jn 3:2 ... will be like when Christ *a-s*.

APPROVAL (n) *an act or instance of approving*
Ps 90:17 ... LORD our God show us his *a*
John 6:27 ... the seal of his *a*.
Rom 14:4 ... stand and receive his *a*.
1 Cor 11:19 ... you who have God's *a*
2 Tim 2:15 ... and receive his *a*.
Heb 11:4 ... God showed his *a* of his gifts.

APPROVE, APPROVED, APPROVES (v) *to have or express a favorable opinion of; to attest*
Gen 7:2 ... animal I have *a-ed* for eating
Prov 12:2 ... LORD *a-s* of those who
Rom 14:18 ... and others will *a* of you,
Rom 16:10 ... a good man whom Christ *a-s*.
1 Thes 2:4 ... speak as messengers *a-ed*

ARARAT (n) *a mountain on the far east border of modern Turkey; the mountain Noah's ark rested on after the Flood*
Gen 8:4 ... to rest on the mountains of *A*.

ARCHANGEL, ARCHANGELS (n) *a leader and chief angel; the Bible identifies Michael as one*
Dan 10:13 ... one of the *a-s*, came to help
Dan 12:1 ... At that time Michael, the *a*
1 Thes 4:16 ... with the voice of the *a*,

ARGUE, ARGUING (v) *to contend or disagree in words; to dispute*
Job 13:8 ... Will you *a* God's case
Job 40:2 ... to *a* with the Almighty?
Prov 25:9 ... *a-ing* with your neighbor,
Isa 45:9 ... those who *a* with their Creator.
Rom 14:1 ... and don't *a* with them
1 Cor 11:16 ... anyone wants to *a*

ARM, ARMS (n) *upper limb of the body; extension or projection of; lineage; figurative of power or might*
Num 11:23 ... Has my *a* lost its power?
Deut 4:34 ... a powerful *a*, and terrifying
Deut 7:19 ... strong hand and powerful *a*
Deut 33:27 ... everlasting *a-s* are under

Ps 44:3 ... it was not their own strong *a*
Ps 98:1 ... his holy *a* has shown
Isa 40:11 ... carry the lambs in his *a-s*,
Isa 65:2 ... opened my *a-s* to a rebellious
Jer 27:5 ... powerful *a* I made the earth
Mark 10:16 ... took the children in his *a-s*

ARMAGEDDON (n) *the gathering place for the final battle between God's forces and Satan's forces associated with Christ's second coming*
Rev 16:16 ... with the Hebrew name *A*.

ARMOR (n) *weapons of war or self-defense; figurative of spiritual resources*
Ps 91:4 ... are your *a* and protection.
Isa 59:17 ... righteousness as his body *a*
Jer 46:4 ... and prepare your *a*.
Rom 13:12 ... put on the shining *a*
Eph 6:11 ... Put on all of God's *a*
Eph 6:13 ... put on every piece of God's *a*
1 Thes 5:8 ... protected by the *a* of faith

ARMY, ARMIES (n) *large band of men organized and armed for war; any large multitude devoted to a cause*
Ps 33:16 ... best-equipped *a* cannot save
Ps 84:12 ... LORD of Heaven's *A-ies*,
Isa 6:3 ... LORD of Heaven's *A-ies!*
Isa 45:13 ... LORD of Heaven's *A-ies*,
Isa 51:15 ... the LORD of Heaven's *A-ies*.
Joel 2:2 ... great and mighty *a* appears.
Joel 2:5 ... like a mighty *a* moving into
Joel 2:11 ... This is his mighty *a*,
Hag 1:5 ... LORD of Heaven's *A-ies* says:
Zech 8:6 ... LORD of Heaven's *A-ies* says:
Rev 19:14 ... The *a-ies* of heaven,
Rev 19:19 ... the horse and his *a*.

ARROGANCE (n) *a feeling or an impression of superiority manifested in an overbearing manner or presumptuous claims*
1 Sam 2:3 ... Don't speak with such *a*!
Prov 8:13 ... I hate pride and *a*,
Isa 16:6 ... its pride and *a* and rage.
2 Cor 12:20 ... slander, gossip, *a*,

ARROGANT (adj) *exaggerating or disposed to exaggerate one's own worth or importance in an overbearing manner*
Ps 31:23 ... harshly punishes the *a*.
Ps 119:78 ... upon the *a* people who lied
1 Tim 6:4 ... is *a* and lacks understanding.
Titus 1:7 ... not be *a* or quick-tempered;

ASHAMED (adj) *feeling shame, guilt, or disgrace*
Ps 69:6 ... be *a* because of me,
Jer 31:19 ... I was thoroughly *a* of all I did
Jer 48:13 ... were *a* of their gold calf
Mark 8:38 ... If anyone is *a* of me
Luke 9:26 ... If anyone is *a* of me
Rom 1:16 ... I am not *a* of this Good News
2 Tim 1:8 ... So never be *a* to tell others
2 Tim 2:15 ... who does not need to be *a*

ASLEEP (adj) *state of bodily rest; figurative for physical death or spiritual dullness*
see also DIE, SLEEP
Judg 4:21 ... Sisera fell *a* from exhaustion,
1 Kgs 18:27 ... away on a trip, or is *a* and
Matt 9:24 ... isn't dead; she's only *a*."
Matt 26:40 ... disciples and found them *a*.
John 11:11 ... Lazarus has fallen *a*, but
1 Thes 5:6 ... be on your guard, not *a* like

1695

ASTRAY (adv) *off the right path or route; in error, away from what is desirable or proper*
Prov 20:1 ... Those led *a* by drink
Isa 47:10 ... 'knowledge' have led you *a*,
Jer 50:6 ... shepherds have led them *a*
1 Jn 2:26 ... who want to lead you *a*.

ASTROLOGERS (n) *one who studies the stars and planets to foresee or foretell future events by their positions and aspects*
Isa 47:13 ... all your *a*, those stargazers
Dan 2:2 ... enchanters, sorcerers, and *a*,

ATE (v) *to partake of food*
see also EAT
Gen 3:6 ... some of the fruit and *a* it.
Ezek 3:3 ... And when I *a* it, it tasted as
Matt 15:37 ... *a* as much as they wanted.
Rev 10:10 ... I *a* it! It was sweet

ATHLETE, ATHLETES (n) *a person who is trained or skilled in exercises, sports, or games requiring physical strength, agility, or stamina*
Ps 19:5 ... like a great *a* eager to run
1 Cor 9:25 ... All *a-s* are disciplined
1 Cor 9:27 ... body like an *a*, training it
2 Tim 2:5 ... *a-s* cannot win the prize unless

ATONE, ATONES (v) *to supply satisfaction for; to make amends; to reconcile*
see also FORGIVE
Dan 9:24 ... their sin, to *a* for their guilt,
1 Jn 2:2 ... sacrifice that *a-s* for our sins—

ATONEMENT (n) *reconciliation; reparation for an offense or injury; cleansing*
see also FORGIVENESS
Exod 25:17 ... cover—the place of *a*—
Lev 23:27 ... Day of *A* on the tenth day
2 Chr 29:24 ... to make *a* for the sins
Prov 16:6 ... faithfulness make *a* for sin.

ATTITUDE, ATTITUDES (n) *a mental position with regard to a fact or state; a feeling or emotion toward a fact or state*
Eph 4:23 ... your thoughts and *a-s*.
Phil 2:5 ... have the same *a* that Christ
1 Pet 3:8 ... keep a humble *a*.
1 Pet 4:1 ... with the same *a* he had,

AUTHORITY, AUTHORITIES (n) *the right to govern; the freedom or ability to act; one entrusted with the right to govern*
Matt 28:18 ... been given all *a* in heaven
Luke 10:19 ... have given you *a* over
John 5:22 ... absolute *a* to judge,
Acts 1:7 ... *a* to set those dates and times,
Rom 13:1 ... submit to governing *a-ies*.
Rom 13:1 ... For all *a* comes from God,
Rom 13:2 ... anyone who rebels against *a*
Rom 13:3 ... without fear of the *a-ies*?
1 Cor 4:3 ... by any human *a*.
1 Cor 15:24 ... ruler and *a* and power.
Eph 1:22 ... things under the *a* of Christ
Eph 3:10 ... all the unseen rulers and *a-ies*
Eph 6:12 ... against evil rulers and *a-ies*
Col 2:10 ... every ruler and *a*.
Col 2:15 ... the spiritual rulers and *a-ies*.
1 Tim 2:2 ... all who are in *a* so that
Titus 2:15 ... You have the *a* to correct
1 Pet 3:1 ... accept the *a* of your husbands.

1 Pet 3:22 ... the angels and *a-ies* and
1 Pet 5:5 ... accept the *a* of the elders.
Jude 1:6 ... the limits of *a* God gave them

AVOID, AVOIDING (v) *to keep away from; to depart or withdraw from*
Prov 4:24 ... *A* all perverse talk;
Prov 14:16 ... are cautious and *a* danger;
Prov 16:6 ... By fearing the LORD, people *a*
Prov 20:3 ... *A-ing* a fight is a mark
Eccl 7:18 ... fears God will *a* both
Rom 2:3 ... think you can *a* God's

AWE (n) *an emotion variously combining dread, respect, and wonder that is inspired by authority or the sacred*
see also FEAR, REVERENCE
1 Kgs 3:28 ... people were in *a* of the king,
Ps 119:120 ... I stand in *a* of your
Luke 5:26 ... with great wonder and *a*,
Acts 2:43 ... sense of *a* came over them
Heb 12:28 ... holy fear and *a*.

AWESOME (adj) *characterized by reverential fear; expressive of or inspiring awe*
see also WONDERFUL
Exod 34:10 ... the *a* power I will display
Deut 7:21 ... a great and *a* God.
2 Sam 7:23 ... You performed *a* miracles
Neh 1:5 ... the great and *a* God
Job 10:16 ... display your *a* power
Ps 47:2 ... Most High is *a*.
Ps 65:5 ... answer our prayers with *a*
Ps 99:3 ... your great and *a* name.
Ps 106:22 ... such *a* deeds at the Red Sea.
Ps 131:1 ... too *a* for me to grasp.
Dan 9:4 ... a great and *a* God!

B

BABY, BABIES (n) *infant child; youngest of a group; figurative of new or immature Christians*
Exod 2:7 ... women to nurse the *b* for you?
Luke 1:44 ... *b* in my womb jumped for
Luke 2:12 ... find a *b* wrapped snugly
Luke 2:16 ... the *b*, lying in the manger.
Acts 7:19 ... abandon their newborn *b-ies*
1 Cor 14:20 ... Be innocent as *b-ies* when
1 Pet 2:2 ... Like newborn *b-ies*, you must

BABYLON (n) *capital city of the Babylonian Empire; a city devoted to materialism and sensual pleasure; biblical writers used as model of paganism and idolatry*
Ps 137:1 ... Beside the rivers of *B*, we sat
Jer 29:10 ... will be in *B* for seventy years.
Jer 51:37 ... *B* will become a heap of ruins,
Rev 14:8 ... shouting, "*B* is fallen—

BAPTISM, BAPTISMS (n) *a Christian ordinance; a washing with water to demonstrate cleansing from sin, linked with repentance and admission into the community of faith; figurative of an ordeal or initiation*
Matt 3:16 ... After his *b*, as Jesus came up
Luke 3:7 ... crowds came to John for *b*,
Acts 19:3 ... what *b* did you experience?
Rom 6:3 ... joined with Christ Jesus in *b*,
Gal 3:27 ... united with Christ in *b*
Eph 4:5 ... one Lord, one faith, one *b*,
Heb 6:2 ... further instruction about *b-s*,
1 Pet 3:21 ... that water is a picture of *b*,

BAPTIZE, BAPTIZED, BAPTIZING (v) *to engage in the ordinance of baptism (see above)*
see also WASH
Matt 3:13 ... River to be *b-d* by John.
Matt 28:19 ... of all the nations, *b-ing*
Mark 1:4 ... that people should be *b-d*
Mark 1:8 ... will *b* you with the Holy Spirit!
Mark 10:38 ... suffering I must be *b-d* with?
Luke 3:3 ... that people should be *b-d*
Luke 3:16 ... I *b* you with water;
Luke 3:21 ... Jesus himself was *b-d*.
John 1:28 ... where John was *b-ing*.
John 1:31 ... I have been *b-ing* with water
John 1:33 ... is the one who will *b* with
John 3:22 ... with them there, *b-ing* people.
John 3:26 ... is also *b-ing* people.
John 4:1 ... was *b-ing* and making more
John 4:2 ... Jesus himself didn't *b* them—
John 10:40 ... where John was first *b-ing*
Acts 1:5 ... be *b-d* with the Holy Spirit.
Acts 1:22 ... time he was *b-d* by John
Acts 2:41 ... *b-d* and added to the church
Acts 8:12 ... and women were *b-d*.
Acts 8:38 ... water, and Philip *b-d* him.
Acts 11:16 ... will be *b-d* with the Holy
Acts 16:15 ... She and her household were *b-d*,
Acts 16:33 ... were immediately *b-d*.
Acts 19:5 ... *b-d* in the name of the Lord
1 Cor 1:13 ... you *b-d* in the name of Paul?
1 Cor 1:14 ... I did not *b* any of you
1 Cor 1:16 ... *b-d* the household of
1 Cor 10:2 ... were *b-d* as followers
1 Cor 15:29 ... *b-d* for those who are dead?
Col 2:12 ... when you were *b-d*.

BEAST, BEASTS (n) *devilish creature(s) ravishing the earth during the Tribulation; animals, as distinguished from plants or humans; a contemptible person*
Dan 7:3 ... Then four huge *b-s* came up
Dan 7:6 ... authority was given to this *b*.
1 Cor 15:32 ... fighting wild *b-s*—those
Rev 13:18 ... number of the *b*, for it is
Rev 16:2 ... had the mark of the *b*
Rev 19:20 ... accepted the mark of the *b*

BEAUTIFUL (adj) *lovely, handsome, or pleasing to the eye; excellent*
Gen 2:9 ... trees that were *b*
Gen 6:2 ... sons of God saw the *b*
Prov 11:22 ... A *b* woman who lacks
Eccl 3:11 ... everything *b* for its own time.
Isa 53:2 ... was nothing *b* or majestic
Lam 2:15 ... the city called 'Most *B*
Acts 3:2 ... the one called the *B* Gate,
Rom 10:15 ... How *b* are the feet of

BEAUTY (n) *a particularly graceful, ornamental, or excellent quality; the quality in a person or thing that gives pleasure to the senses*
2 Sam 11:2 ... a woman of unusual *b*
Ps 50:2 ... the perfection of *b*, God shines
Prov 31:30 ... and *b* does not last;
Isa 28:1 ... but its glorious *b* will fade
Jas 1:11 ... and its *b* fades away.
1 Pet 1:24 ... their *b* is like a flower
1 Pet 3:4 ... *b* of a gentle and quiet spirit,

BEGINNING (n) *the point at which something starts; the first part; the origin, source*
Gen 1:1 ... In the *b* God created
John 1:1 ... In the *b* the Word already

Rom 16:25 … secret from the **b** of time.
1 Jn 1:1 … one who existed from the **b,**
Rev 21:6 … the **B** and the End.
Rev 22:13 … the **B** and the End.

BELIEVE, BELIEVED, BELIEVES, BELIEVING (v) *to trust in; to hold a firm conviction about; to accept as true, genuine, or real*
see also FAITH, TRUST
Gen 15:6 … Abram **b-d** the LORD,
Prov 14:15 … simpletons **b** everything
Isa 53:1 … Who has **b-d** our message?
Matt 27:42 … we will **b** in him!
Mark 9:23 … is possible if a person **b-s.**
Mark 9:24 … I do **b,** but help me
Mark 15:32 … we can see it and **b** him!
Luke 8:12 … prevent them from **b-ing**
Luke 24:25 … You find it so hard to **b**
John 1:7 … so that everyone might **b**
John 1:12 … all who **b-d** him and accepted
John 3:16 … everyone who **b-s** in him
John 4:41 … hear his message and **b.**
John 5:38 … because you do not **b** me—
John 6:69 … We **b,** and we know you are
John 7:5 … his brothers didn't **b** in him.
John 7:39 … to everyone **b-ing** in him.
John 9:35 … asked, "Do you **b** in the Son
John 9:38 … Yes, Lord, I **b!**
John 10:37 … Don't **b** me unless
John 11:25 … Anyone who **b-s** in me
John 11:27 … **b-d** you are the Messiah,
John 11:40 … see God's glory if you **b?**
John 12:37 … did not **b** in him.
John 12:38 … who has **b-d** our message?
John 13:19 … you will **b** that I AM
John 14:11 … Or at least **b** because of the
John 14:12 … anyone who **b-s** in me
John 16:30 … **b** that you came from God.
John 17:21 … world will **b** you sent me.
John 19:35 … you also may continue to **b.**
John 20:8 … and he saw and **b-d**—
John 20:29 … **b** because you have seen
John 20:31 … and that by **b-ing** in him
Acts 10:43 … that everyone who **b-s** in him
Acts 13:8 … keep the governor from **b-ing.**
Acts 16:31 … **B** in the Lord Jesus and
Acts 19:4 … **b** in the one who would come
Acts 26:27 … do you **b** the prophets?
Acts 27:25 … For I **b** God. I will be just
Rom 1:16 … saving everyone who **b-s.**
Rom 3:22 … for everyone who **b-s,** no
Rom 3:25 … **b** that Jesus sacrificed his life,
Rom 4:3 … tell us, "Abraham **b-d** God,
Rom 4:20 … never wavered in **b-ing** God's
Rom 10:9 … **b** in your heart that God
Rom 10:10 … For it is by **b-ing** in your heart
Rom 10:14 … unless they **b** in him?
Rom 14:23 … anything you **b** is not right,
Rom 16:26 … they too might **b** and obey
1 Cor 1:21 … to save those who **b.**
1 Cor 15:2 … **b-d** something that was never
2 Cor 5:7 … by **b-ing** and not by seeing.
2 Cor 5:14 … Since we **b** that Christ
Gal 3:2 … because you **b-d** the message
Gal 3:6 … same way, "Abraham **b-d** God,
Eph 2:8 … his grace when you **b-d.**
Col 1:23 … continue to **b** this truth
1 Thes 4:14 … For since we **b** that Jesus
2 Thes 2:11 … and they will **b** these lies.
2 Thes 2:12 … enjoying evil rather than **b-ing**
1 Tim 3:16 … He was **b-d** in throughout the
Heb 3:14 … firmly as when we first **b-d,**
Heb 11:6 … must **b** that God exists
Heb 11:13 … still **b-ing** what God had
Jas 2:19 … you **b** that there is one God.

1 Jn 3:23 … We must **b** in the name
1 Jn 4:1 … friends, do not **b** everyone
1 Jn 5:1 … Everyone who **b-s** that Jesus is
1 Jn 5:10 … All who **b** in the Son

BELONG, BELONGED, BELONGS (v) *to be the property of a person or thing*
Lev 25:55 … people of Israel **b** to me.
Lev 27:30 … **b-s** to the LORD and
Ps 22:28 … royal power **b-s** to the LORD.
John 8:47 … Anyone who **b-s** to God
John 15:19 … if you **b-ed** to it, but you
Rom 1:6 … called to **b** to Jesus
Rom 12:5 … we all **b** to each other.
2 Cor 10:7 … who say they **b** to Christ
Gal 5:24 … Those who **b** to Christ
1 Thes 5:5 … we don't **b** to darkness
2 Tim 2:19 … All who **b** to the LORD
1 Pet 3:16 … because you **b** to Christ.
1 Jn 4:6 … If they do not **b** to God,

BENEFIT, BENEFITS (n) *advantages or blessings; something that promotes well-being*
Prov 12:14 … Wise words bring many **b-s.**
Acts 18:27 … he proved to be of great **b** to
2 Cor 4:15 … this is for your **b.**

BENEFIT, BENEFITS (v) *to be useful or profitable to; to favor (another) or gain (for oneself)*
Job 36:28 … and everyone **b-s.**
Prov 9:12 … you will be the one to **b.**
Luke 9:25 … what do you **b** if you gain
1 Cor 9:14 … by those who **b** from it.

BESTOWED (KJV)
Isa 63:7 … he has *granted* according

BETHLEHEM (n) *a city about five miles south of Jerusalem in the hill country of Judah; the ancestral home of King David and the birthplace of Jesus Christ*
Ruth 1:19 … When they came to **B,**
1 Sam 16:1 … go to **B.** Find a man named
2 Sam 23:15 … the well by the gate in **B.**
Mic 5:2 … **B** Ephrathah, are only a small
Matt 2:1 … Jesus was born in **B** in Judea,
Matt 2:6 … you, O **B** in the land of Judah,

BETRAY, BETRAYED (v) *to turn your back on a friend; to deliver to an enemy by treachery; to lead astray, seduce*
Num 5:6 … men or women—**b** the LORD
Deut 32:51 … both of you **b-ed** me
Jer 38:22 … They have **b-ed** and misled
Mal 2:10 … Then why do we **b** each other,
Matt 10:21 … A brother will **b** his brother
Matt 24:10 … and **b** and hate each other.
Matt 26:21 … one of you will **b** me.
Matt 27:4 … I have **b-ed** an innocent man.
Luke 6:16 … (who later **b-ed** him).
John 18:5 … Judas, who **b-ed** him,

BIRTH (n) *the emergence of a new individual from the body of its parent; beginning, start*
Gen 25:24 … the time came to give **b,**
Ps 58:3 … even from **b** they have lied
Matt 24:8 … only the first of the **b** pains.
John 3:6 … Spirit gives **b** to spiritual life.
Titus 3:5 … giving us a new **b** and new life
Jas 1:15 … it gives **b** to death.

BIRTHRIGHT (KJV)
Gen 25:31 … your *rights as the firstborn son*
1 Chr 5:1 … *birthright* was given to the
Heb 12:16 … *birthright as the firstborn son*

BITTERNESS (n) *an intense or severe expression or feeling of pain, grief, or regret; exhibiting intense animosity*
Prov 14:10 … Each heart knows its own **b,**
Prov 17:25 … **b** to the one who gave them
Rom 3:14 … full of cursing and **b.**
Eph 4:31 … Get rid of all **b,** rage,

BLAME (n) *an expression of disapproval or reproach; responsibility for something believed to deserve censure*
1 Cor 1:8 … free from all **b** on the day
Rev 14:5 … they are without **b.**

BLAMELESS (adj) *characterized by being free from sin and fault*
see also INTEGRITY, RIGHTEOUS
Gen 6:9 … only **b** person living on earth
Job 1:8 … **b**—a man of complete integrity.
Ps 18:23 … I am **b** before God;
Prov 13:6 … guards the path of the **b,**
Prov 29:10 … The bloodthirsty hate **b**
Phil 1:10 … live pure and **b** lives
Col 1:22 … and you are holy and **b**
1 Thes 5:23 … kept **b** until our Lord
Titus 1:6 … must live a **b** life.
2 Pet 3:14 … pure and **b** in his sight.

BLASPHEME, BLASPHEMED, BLASPHEMES, BLASPHEMING (v) *to dishonor or revile God; to speak of or address with irreverence*
Lev 24:11 … son of an Israelite woman **b-ed**
Lev 24:16 … Anyone who **b-s** the Name
Num 15:30 … have **b-ed** the LORD,
Isa 52:5 … My name is **b-ed** all day long.
Dan 11:36 … even **b-ing** the God of gods.
Mark 3:29 … who **b-s** the Holy Spirit
Luke 12:10 … who **b-s** the Holy Spirit
Acts 6:11 … We heard him **b** Moses,
Rom 2:24 … Gentiles **b** the name of God
1 Tim 1:13 … to **b** the name of Christ.
1 Tim 1:20 … learn not to **b** God.
Rev 13:1 … were names that **b-ed** God.

BLASPHEMY, BLASPHEMIES (n) *the words or actions that dishonor God; the act of insulting or showing contempt or lack of reverence for God*
Neh 9:18 … They committed terrible **b-ies.**
Mark 3:28 … all sin and **b** can be forgiven,
Mark 14:64 … You have all heard his **b.**
John 10:33 … for any good work, but for **b!**
2 Pet 2:11 … a charge of **b** against those
Rev 13:5 … speak great **b-ies** against God.
Rev 13:6 … words of **b** against God,
Rev 17:3 … and **b-ies** against God were

BLESS, BLESSED, BLESSES (v) *to confer prosperity or happiness upon; to honor in worship; to offer approval or encouragement; to bring pleasure or divine favor*
Gen 1:22 … Then God **b-ed** them,
Gen 12:3 … I will **b** those who **b** you
Gen 22:18 … of the earth will be **b-ed**—
Ps 16:7 … I will **b** the LORD who guides
Prov 31:28 … Her children stand and
Matt 5:3 … God **b-es** those who are poor
Matt 5:7 … **b-es** those who are merciful,
Matt 5:9 … God **b-es** those who work for
Matt 5:11 … God **b-es** you when people
Jas 1:12 … God **b-es** those who patiently
Rev 22:7 … **B-ed** are those who obey
Rev 22:14 … **B-ed** are those who wash

1697

BLESSING, BLESSINGS (n) *happiness; praise; divine favor or heavenly reward; the antidote to cursings*
Josh 8:34 … *b-s* and curses Moses
Prov 13:21 … *b-s* reward the righteous.
John 12:13 … *B-s* on the one who comes in
Acts 4:33 … God's great *b* was upon them
Acts 11:23 … evidence of God's *b*,
Rom 15:27 … spiritual *b-s* of the Good
Eph 3:6 … both enjoy the promise of *b-s*
Rev 7:12 … *B* and glory and wisdom

BLIND (adj) *sightless; lacking spiritual discernment*
Matt 11:5 … the *b* see, the lame walk,
Matt 15:14 … *b* guides leading the *b*,
Mark 10:46 … *b* beggar named
Luke 6:39 … Can one *b* person lead

BLINDED (v) *to withhold light from; to be without sight*
John 12:40 … The Lord has *b* their eyes
2 Cor 4:4 … god of this world, has *b* the

BLOOD (n) *fluid in the circulatory system; signifies human life; kinfolk; of animals, used in priestly sacrifices; of Christ, effective for the forgiveness of sins; on hands or head, symbolic of guilt*
Exod 12:13 … When I see the *b*, I will pass
Deut 12:23 … But never consume the *b*,
Isa 1:11 … no pleasure from the *b* of bulls
Mark 14:24 … my *b*, which confirms the
John 6:53 … and drink his *b*, you cannot
Acts 15:20 … and from consuming *b*.
1 Cor 11:25 … confirmed with my *b*.
Eph 1:7 … with the *b* of his Son
Eph 2:13 … through the *b* of Christ.
Heb 9:7 … offered *b* for his own sins
Heb 9:20 … This *b* confirms the covenant
1 Pet 1:2 … cleansed by the *b* of Jesus
1 Pet 1:19 … the precious *b* of Christ,
1 Jn 1:7 … the *b* of Jesus, his Son, cleanses
Rev 1:5 … by shedding his *b* for us.
Rev 5:9 … your *b* has ransomed people
Rev 7:14 … in the *b* of the Lamb
Rev 12:11 … by the *b* of the Lamb
Rev 19:13 … He wore a robe dipped in *b*,

BLOT (v) *to wipeout, destroy; to erase or cover up*
Ps 51:1 … *b* out the stain of my sins.
Isa 43:25 … I alone—will *b* out your sins

BOAST, BOASTED, BOASTING (v) *to puff oneself up in speech, brag*
Isa 20:5 … *b-ed* of their allies in Egypt!
Jer 9:23 … the wise *b* in their wisdom,
Rom 2:17 … *b* about your special
1 Cor 1:31 … *b*, *b* only about the LORD.
2 Cor 8:24 … our *b-ing* about you is justified.
2 Cor 10:13 … We will *b* only about
Gal 6:14 … *b* about anything except
Eph 2:9 … none of us can *b* about it.
Jas 1:9 … have something to *b* about,
Jas 4:16 … *b-ing* about your own pretentious

BODY, BODIES (n) *one's physical essence; a corpse; a group of people*
see also FLESH
Job 19:26 … in my *b* I will see God!
Ps 49:14 … Their *b-ies* will rot in the grave,
Isa 26:19 … their *b-ies* will rise again!
Matt 26:41 … willing, but the *b* is weak!
Mark 14:22 … Take it, for this is my *b*.
Rom 12:4 … our *b-ies* have many parts
1 Cor 6:15 … that your *b-ies* are actually

1 Cor 6:19 … that your *b* is the temple
1 Cor 6:20 … honor God with your *b*.
1 Cor 11:24 … my *b*, which is given for
1 Cor 12:13 … into one *b* by one Spirit,
1 Cor 15:44 … be raised as spiritual *b-ies*
2 Cor 5:1 … eternal *b* made for us by God
2 Cor 5:2 … to put on our heavenly *b-ies*
2 Cor 5:4 … so that these dying *b-ies* will
Eph 1:23 … the church is his *b*;
Eph 3:6 … Both are part of the same *b*,
Eph 5:28 … love their own *b-ies*.
Eph 5:30 … are members of his *b*.
Col 1:24 … for his *b*, the church.

BOLD (adj) *fearless before danger; self-assured, confident; prominent*
2 Sam 7:27 … been *b* enough to pray
1 Chr 17:25 … been *b* enough to pray
Phil 1:20 … continue to be *b* for Christ,

BOLDLY (adv) *showing a fearless, daring spirit*
Acts 26:26 … I speak *b*, for I am sure
Eph 3:12 … *b* and confidently into God's
Heb 4:16 … let us come *b* to the throne
Heb 10:19 … *b* enter heaven's Most Holy

BOLDNESS (n) *fearlessness before danger; self-assurance, confidence; prominence*
Acts 4:13 … they saw the *b* of Peter
Acts 4:29 … give us, your servants, great *b*

BONE, BONES (n) *one of the hard parts of the skeleton*
Gen 2:23 … This one is *b* from my *b*,
Ps 22:14 … all my *b-s* are out of joint.
Ps 22:17 … I can count all my *b-s*.
Ezek 37:1 … a valley filled with *b-s*.
John 19:36 … Not one of his *b-s* will be

BOOK, BOOKS (n) *a long written or printed literary composition; written records, register, or accounting*
Josh 1:8 … Study this *B* of Instruction
Ps 69:28 … names from the *B* of Life;
Ps 139:16 … recorded in your *b*.
Eccl 12:12 … for writing *b-s* is endless,
Dan 7:10 … and the *b-s* were opened.
Dan 12:1 … name is written in the *b*
John 21:25 … could not contain the *b-s*
Phil 4:3 … are written in the *B* of Life.
Rev 3:5 … names from the *B* of Life,
Rev 20:12 … including the *B* of Life.
Rev 20:12 … as recorded in the *b-s*.
Rev 21:27 … in the Lamb's *B* of Life.

BORN (v) *to give birth to or produce; to be productive; spiritually, to renew or confirm a commitment of faith*
Ps 51:5 … For I was *b* a sinner—
Eccl 3:2 … time to be *b* and a time to die.
Isa 9:6 … For a child is *b* to us,
Luke 2:11 … the Lord—has been *b* today
John 3:3 … unless you are *b* again,
John 3:7 … You must be *b* again.
1 Pet 1:3 … we have been *b* again,
1 Pet 1:23 … you have been *b* again,

BOTTOMLESS (adj) *unfathomable; boundless, unlimited*
Luke 8:31 … into the *b* pit.
Rev 9:1 … shaft of the *b* pit.
Rev 9:11 … the angel from the *b* pit;
Rev 11:7 … up out of the *b* pit
Rev 17:8 … up out of the *b* pit
Rev 20:1 … the key to the *b* pit
Rev 20:3 … into the *b* pit,

BRANCH, BRANCHES (n) *limb of a (family) tree; part of a complex body (of knowledge); figurative of offspring and of disciples (of Christ and his disciples)*
Isa 4:2 … the *b* of the LORD will be beautiful
Dan 4:21 … nested in its *b-es*.
Zech 3:8 … bring my servant, the *B*.
Matt 13:32 … make nests in its *b-es*."
John 15:2 … *b* of mine that doesn't
John 15:4 … a *b* cannot produce fruit if
John 15:5 … you are the *b-es*.
Rom 11:20 … those *b-es* were broken off
Rom 11:21 … not spare the original *b-es*,

BREAD (n) *basic staple in diet of ancient Israel, usually baked using flour or meal; signifies livelihood*
see also FOOD
Exod 23:15 … Festival of Unleavened *B*.
Prov 20:17 … Stolen *b* tastes sweet,
Mark 14:22 … Jesus took some *b* and
Luke 4:3 … stone to become a loaf of *b*.
Luke 9:13 … only five loaves of *b*
John 6:48 … Yes, I am the *b* of life!
John 6:51 … I am the living *b*
1 Cor 10:16 … when we break the *b*,
1 Cor 11:23 … the Lord Jesus took some *b*
1 Cor 11:26 … eat this *b* and drink

BREATH (n) *air inhaled and exhaled in breathing; a spoken sound, utterance; a slight indication, suggestion*
Gen 2:7 … He breathed the *b* of life
Exod 15:8 … At the blast of your *b*,
Ps 18:15 … at the blast of your *b*,
Ps 144:4 … we are like a *b* of air;

BREATHED (v) *to inhale and exhale freely; to blow softly*
Gen 2:7 … He *b* the breath of life
Mark 15:37 … and *b* his last.
John 20:22 … Then he *b* on them

BRIBE (n) *something that serves to induce or influence*
Deut 16:19 … Never accept a *b*,

BRIBERY (n) *the act or practice of giving or taking a bribe*
Job 15:34 … homes, enriched through *b*,

BRIDE (n) *a woman just married or about to be married*
2 Cor 11:2 … as a pure *b* to one husband—
Rev 19:7 … *b* has prepared herself.
Rev 21:2 … like a *b* beautifully dressed
Rev 21:9 … the *b*, the wife of the Lamb
Rev 22:17 … Spirit and the *b* say, "Come."

BRIDEGROOM (n) *a man just married or about to be married*
Ps 19:5 … like a radiant *b* after
Matt 25:1 … and went to meet the *b*.
Matt 25:5 … When the *b* was delayed,

BRIDESMAIDS (n) *women attendants of a bride*
Matt 25:1 … will be like ten *b* who

BROTHER, BROTHERS (n) *male family members with the same parents; kinsmen in the extended family, church, or nation; co-workers in ministry; fellow believers, followers, or friends in Christ*
Ps 133:1 … *b-s* live together in harmony!
Prov 18:24 … friend sticks closer than a *b*.
Prov 27:10 … to ask your *b* for assistance.
Mark 3:33 … Who are my *b-s*?

Mark 10:29 . . . given up house or **b-s** or
John 7:5 . . . even his **b-s** didn't believe
Heb 2:11 . . . ashamed to call them his **b-s**
Heb 13:1 . . . each other as **b-s** and sisters.
Jas 2:15 . . . you see a **b** or sister
Jas 4:11 . . . against each other, dear **b-s**
1 Pet 1:22 . . . each other as **b-s** and sisters.
1 Pet 3:8 . . . Love each other as **b-s** and
1 Jn 3:16 . . . for our **b-s** and sisters.
1 Jn 3:17 . . . sees a **b** or sister in need
Rev 12:10 . . . the accuser of our **b-s** and

BUILD, BUILDING, BUILDS, BUILT (v) *to erect or construct; to edify or encourage; to increase, enlarge*
Gen 6:14 . . . **B** a large boat from cypress
1 Kgs 6:14 . . . Solomon finished **b-ing** the
Neh 4:17 . . . who were **b-ing** the wall.
Ps 127:1 . . . Unless the LORD **b-s** a house,
Prov 14:1 . . . A wise woman **b-s** her home,
Prov 16:12 . . . his rule is **b-t** on justice.
Hag 1:9 . . . **b-ing** your own fine houses.
Matt 7:24 . . . who **b-s** a house on solid rock
Matt 16:18 . . . rock I will **b** my church,
Rom 14:19 . . . try to **b** each other up.
1 Cor 3:10 . . . Now others are **b-ing** on it.
1 Cor 3:12 . . . Anyone who **b-s** on that
2 Cor 10:8 . . . But our authority **b-s** you up;
Eph 2:20 . . . **b-t** on the foundation of the
Eph 4:12 . . . work and **b** up the church,
Col 2:7 . . . let your lives be **b-t** on him.
1 Thes 5:11 . . . and **b** each other up, just as
Heb 3:3 . . . as a person who **b-s** a house
1 Pet 2:5 . . . God is **b-ing** into his spiritual
Jude 1:20 . . . friends, must **b** each other up

BUILDER, BUILDERS (n) *one who builds*
Ps 118:22 . . . The stone that the **b-s** rejected
Mark 12:10 . . . stone that the **b-s** rejected
Acts 4:11 . . . The stone that you **b-s** rejected
1 Cor 3:10 . . . foundation like an expert **b**.
1 Cor 3:14 . . . that **b** will receive a reward.
Heb 3:4 . . . For every house has a **b**,
1 Pet 2:7 . . . The stone that the **b-s** rejected

BURDEN, BURDENS (n) *a (usually) heavy load to be borne—physically, emotionally, or spiritually*
Ps 38:4 . . . a **b** too heavy to bear.
Matt 11:28 . . . weary and carry heavy **b-s**,
Matt 11:30 . . . the **b** I give you is light.
Acts 15:28 . . . to lay no greater **b** on you
2 Cor 11:9 . . . a financial **b** to anyone.
2 Cor 11:28 . . . the daily **b** of my concern
2 Cor 12:14 . . . I will not be a **b** to you.
Gal 6:2 . . . Share each other's **b-s**,
1 Thes 2:9 . . . so that we would not be a **b**
2 Thes 3:8 . . . so we would not be a **b**

BURDENED (v) *to load; to oppress*
Isa 43:23 . . . I have not **b** and wearied you
Isa 43:24 . . . Instead, you have **b** me
2 Tim 3:6 . . . are **b** with the guilt of sin

BURN, BURNED, BURNING (v) *to consume by fire; to be emotionally excited or agitated; to produce or undergo discomfort or pain*
see also BURNING
Exod 27:20 . . . keep the lamps **b-ing**
Lev 6:9 . . . must be kept **b-ing** all night.
Deut 7:5 . . . Asherah poles and **b** their idols.
Ps 79:5 . . . will your jealousy **b** like fire?
Isa 30:27 . . . far away, **b-ing** with anger,
Jer 23:29 . . . Does not my word **b** like fire?
Luke 24:32 . . . "Didn't our hearts **b** within us
Rom 1:27 . . . **b-ed** with lust for each other.
1 Cor 7:9 . . . to marry than to **b** with lust.

BURNING (adj) *being on fire*
see also BURN
Prov 25:22 . . . heap **b** coals of shame
Rom 12:20 . . . heap **b** coals of shame
Rev 19:20 . . . fiery lake of **b** sulfur.

BURY, BURIED (v) *to deposit in the earth or in a tomb; figurative of denying oneself and submitting to Christ*
Deut 34:6 . . . The LORD **b-ied** him
Ruth 1:17 . . . and there I will be **b-ied**.
Mark 6:29 . . . get his body and **b-ied** it in
Luke 9:60 . . . dead **b** their own dead!
Luke 23:30 . . . plead with the hills, '**B** us.'
Rom 6:4 . . . and were **b-ied** with Christ
1 Cor 15:4 . . . **b-ied**, and he was raised
Col 2:12 . . . For you were **b-ied** with Christ

BUSH (n) *a low, densely branched shrub*
Exod 3:2 . . . fire from the middle of a **b**.
Mark 12:26 . . . story of the burning **b**?
Luke 20:37 . . . wrote about the burning **b**.
Acts 7:35 . . . him in the burning **b**,

C

CAESAR (n) *a title applied to several emperors of the Roman Empire*
Matt 22:21 . . . to **C** what belongs to **C**,

CALF (n) *the young of a domestic cow*
Exod 32:4 . . . it into the shape of a **c**.
Luke 15:23 . . . kill the **c** we have been
Acts 7:41 . . . made an idol shaped like a **c**,

CALL, CALLED, CALLING, CALLS (v) *to make a request or demand; to designate or name*
see also CHOSE, CHOSEN
Gen 2:23 . . . She will be **c-ed** 'woman,'
1 Kgs 18:24 . . . **c** on the name of your god,
2 Kgs 5:11 . . . leprosy and **c** on the name
2 Chr 7:14 . . . who are **c-ed** by my name
Ps 147:4 . . . stars and **c-s** them all by name.
Isa 40:26 . . . **c-ing** each by its name.
Isa 45:3 . . . the one who **c-s** you by name.
Isa 56:7 . . . Temple will be **c-ed** a house of
Hos 11:1 . . . I **c-ed** my son out of Egypt.
Joel 2:32 . . . everyone who **c-s** on the name
Matt 2:15 . . . I **c-ed** my Son out of Egypt.
Matt 9:13 . . . I have come to **c** not those
Matt 22:14 . . . many are **c-ed**, but few are
Matt 22:43 . . . **c** the Messiah 'my Lord'?
Mark 2:17 . . . I have come to **c** not those
Mark 10:49 . . . Come on, he's **c-ing** you!
Luke 1:32 . . . **c-ed** the Son of the Most High.
Luke 23:15 . . . this man has done **c-s**
Acts 2:21 . . . everyone who **c-s** on the name
Acts 2:39 . . . have been **c-ed** by the Lord
Acts 9:14 . . . arrest everyone who **c-s** upon
Acts 22:16 . . . sins washed away by **c-ing** on
Rom 1:6 . . . **c-ed** to belong to Jesus
Rom 8:28 . . . **c-ed** according to his purpose
Rom 10:12 . . . to all who **c** on him.
Rom 10:13 . . . Everyone who **c-s** on the
Rom 11:29 . . . **c** can never be withdrawn.
1 Cor 1:2 . . . who have been **c-ed** by God
1 Cor 1:2 . . . **c** on the name of our Lord
1 Cor 1:24 . . . **c-ed** by God to salvation,
1 Cor 7:17 . . . when God first **c-ed** you.
Gal 1:6 . . . so soon from God, who **c-ed**
Gal 5:13 . . . been **c-ed** to live in freedom,
Eph 1:18 . . . to those he **c-ed**—his holy
Col 3:15 . . . you are **c-ed** to live in peace.
1 Thes 2:12 . . . **c-ed** you to share in his
1 Thes 4:7 . . . God has **c-ed** us to live holy
1 Thes 5:24 . . . he who **c-s** you is faithful.

2 Tim 2:22 . . . those who **c** on the Lord
Heb 9:15 . . . all who are **c-ed** can receive
1 Pet 2:9 . . . he **c-ed** you out of the darkness
1 Pet 3:9 . . . what God has **c-ed** you to do,
1 Pet 5:10 . . . God **c-ed** you to share in his
2 Pet 1:10 . . . are among those God has **c-ed**

CALVARY (KJV)
Luke 23:33 . . . place called *The Skull*,

CAMEL (n) *either of two large ruminant mammals used as draft and saddle animals in desert regions especially of Africa and Asia*
Matt 19:24 . . . easier for a **c** to go through
Matt 23:24 . . . but you swallow a **c**!

CANDLE (n) *a usually molded or dipped mass of wax or tallow containing a wick that may be burned*
Isa 42:3 . . . or put out a flickering **c**.
Matt 12:20 . . . or put out a flickering **c**.

CANDLESTICK(S) (KJV)
Exod 25:31 . . . Make a *lampstand* of pure,
Dan 5:5 . . . palace, near the *lampstand*.
Matt 5:15 . . . a lamp is placed on a *stand*
Heb 9:2 . . . a *lampstand*, a table, and
Rev 1:12 . . . I saw seven gold *lampstands*

CAPSTONE, HEADSTONE (KJV)
Ps 118:22 . . . become the *cornerstone*
Zech 4:7 . . . the *final stone* of the Temple
Matt 21:42 . . . now become the *cornerstone*.
Luke 20:17 . . . now become the *cornerstone*.

CAPTIVE (adj) *(people) taken and held against their will*
Prov 5:22 . . . is held **c** by his own sins;
Acts 8:23 . . . and are held **c** by sin.
2 Tim 2:26 . . . they have been held **c**

CAPTIVES (n) *prisoners*
Ps 68:18 . . . you led a crowd of **c**.
Isa 60:11 . . . led as **c** in a victory
Isa 61:1 . . . that **c** will be released
Luke 4:18 . . . that **c** will be released,

CARE, CARED, CARES, CARING (v) *to feel interest or concern; to attend to or provide for the needs, operation, or treatment of*
Deut 1:31 . . . LORD your God **c-d** for you
Ps 8:4 . . . human beings that you should **c**
Ps 37:17 . . . LORD takes **c** of the godly.
Ps 65:9 . . . take **c** of the earth and
Ps 116:15 . . . **c-s** deeply when his loved
Ps 138:6 . . . is **c** for the humble,
Prov 12:10 . . . godly **c** for their animals,
Prov 27:23 . . . into **c-ing** for your herds,
Isa 53:7 . . . **c-d** that he died without
Jer 23:2 . . . Instead of **c-ing** for my flock
Matt 6:30 . . . if God **c-s** so wonderfully for
Matt 25:36 . . . sick, and you **c-d** for me.
Luke 10:34 . . . an inn, where he took **c** of
John 10:13 . . . really **c** about the sheep.
John 12:25 . . . who **c** nothing for their life
John 21:16 . . . Then take **c** of my sheep,
Eph 5:29 . . . just as Christ **c-s** for the church.
Phil 2:21 . . . others **c** only for themselves
1 Thes 2:7 . . . **c-ing** for her own children.
1 Tim 5:14 . . . take **c** of their own homes.
1 Tim 5:16 . . . she must take **c** of them and
Heb 2:6 . . . that you should **c** for him?
1 Pet 5:2 . . . **C** for the flock that God
1 Pet 5:7 . . . and cares to God, for he **c-s**

1699

CAREFUL (adj) *marked by wary caution; meticulous*
Exod 34:12 ... *c* never to make a treaty
Lev 18:4 ... and be *c* to obey my decrees,
Lev 22:2 ... be very *c* with the sacred gifts
Lev 26:3 ... are *c* to obey my commands,
Deut 4:9 ... But watch out! Be *c* never to
Deut 6:3 ... and be *c* to obey.
Deut 8:1 ... Be *c* to obey all the commands
Deut 12:1 ... *c* to obey when you live in
Deut 12:28 ... Be *c* to obey all my
Josh 1:7 ... and very courageous. Be *c*
Josh 23:11 ... be very *c* to love the LORD
2 Kgs 21:8 ... Israelites will be *c* to obey
1 Cor 8:9 ... be *c* so that your freedom
1 Cor 10:12 ... strong, be *c* not to fall.
Eph 5:15 ... So be *c* how you live.

CARNAL(LY) (KJV)
Rom 7:14 ... *all too human,* a slave to sin
Rom 8:6 ... letting your *sinful nature* control
1 Cor 3:3 ... still *controlled by your sinful nature*
2 Cor 10:4 ... not *worldly* weapons

CARPENTER (n) *a worker who builds or repairs wooden structures or their structural parts*
Matt 13:55 ... He's just the *c*'s son,
Mark 6:3 ... He's just a *c,* the son of Mary

CARRY, CARRIED, CARRIES (v) *to transport or convey; to sustain the weight of; to bring to a successful end*
Exod 19:4 ... how I *c-ied* you on eagles'
Lev 16:22 ... will *c* all the people's sins
Deut 32:11 ... to take them up and *c-ied*
Ps 68:19 ... For each day he *c-ies* us in his
Ps 103:20 ... ones who *c* out his plans,
Isa 40:11 ... *c* the lambs in his arms,
Isa 53:4 ... it was our weaknesses he *c-ied;*
Isa 63:9 ... He lifted them up and *c-ied*
Luke 14:27 ... do not *c* your own cross
Col 4:17 ... Be sure to *c* out the ministry
1 Pet 2:24 ... He personally *c-ied* our sins
2 Pet 3:17 ... not be *c-ied* away by the errors

CATTLE (n) *bovine animals on a farm or ranch*
Ps 50:10 ... I own the *c* on a thousand

CELEBRATE, CELEBRATED, CELEBRATING (v) *to perform (a sacrament or ceremony) publicly and with appropriate rites; to observe a notable occasion with festivities*
Exod 10:9 ... together in *c-ing* a festival
Exod 12:47 ... Israel must *c* this Passover
Exod 13:5 ... You must *c* this event in this
Exod 23:14 ... *c* three festivals in my
Exod 34:18 ... *c* the Festival of Unleavened
Exod 34:22 ... *c* the Festival of the Final
Num 9:2 ... *c* the Passover at the
Deut 16:1 ... your God, *c* the Passover
2 Sam 6:21 ... so I *c* before the LORD.
2 Kgs 23:21 ... *c* the Passover to the LORD
2 Chr 30:1 ... Jerusalem to *c* the Passover.
2 Chr 30:13 ... *c* the Festival of Unleavened
2 Chr 30:23 ... *c-d* joyfully for another
Neh 8:12 ... to *c* with great joy
Esth 8:15 ... people of Susa *c-d* the new
Esth 9:19 ... villages *c* an annual festival
Esth 9:21 ... to *c* an annual festival
Matt 25:21 ... Let's *c* together!"
Luke 15:23 ... We must *c* with a feast,
Luke 15:32 ... We had to *c* this happy day.

John 18:28 ... to *c* the Passover.
Col 2:16 ... for not *c-ing* certain holy days
Rev 11:10 ... to *c* the death of the two prophets

CELEBRATION, CELEBRATIONS (n) *a party or festival in honor of a religious ceremony or holiday; the observation of a notable occasion with festivities*
Num 9:3 ... regulations concerning this *c.*
2 Sam 6:12 ... City of David with a great *c.*
Esth 8:17 ... had a great *c* and declared
Jer 31:13 ... young—will join in the *c.*
Joel 1:16 ... No joyful *c-s* are held in the
Zech 8:19 ... *c* for the people of Judah.
John 11:55 ... for the Jewish Passover *c,*

CHAFF (n) *the seed coverings and other debris separated from the seed in threshing grain; something comparatively worthless*
Ps 1:4 ... *c,* scattered by the wind.
Ps 35:5 ... Blow them away like *c* in the
Dan 2:35 ... like *c* on a threshing floor.
Matt 3:12 ... separate the *c* from the

CHANGE, CHANGED, CHANGES (v) *to make different or transform; to shift, exchange, or transfer*
Exod 32:14 ... the LORD *c-d* his mind about
1 Sam 10:6 ... be *c-d* into a different person.
1 Sam 15:29 ... human that he should *c*
Ps 93:5 ... Your royal laws cannot be *c-d.*
Isa 14:27 ... who can *c* his plans?
Jer 33:25 ... than I would *c* my laws
Jon 3:9 ... even yet God will *c* his mind
Mal 3:6 ... I am the LORD, and I do not *c.*
2 Cor 3:18 ... we are *c-d* into his glorious
Heb 6:17 ... he would never *c* his mind.
Jas 1:17 ... never *c-s* or casts a shifting

CHARACTER (n) *moral excellence and firmness; main or essential nature*
Rom 5:4 ... develops strength of *c,*
1 Cor 15:33 ... corrupts good *c.*
Heb 1:3 ... expresses the very *c* of God,

CHARITY (KJV)
1 Cor 8:1 ... *love* that strengthens the church
1 Cor 13:1 ... but didn't *love* others, I would
Col 3:14 ... clothe yourselves with *love,*
1 Tim 4:12 ... in your *love,* your faith, and
2 Pet 1:7 ... with *love* for everyone

CHASTE (KJV)
2 Cor 11:2 ... a *pure* bride to one husband—
Titus 2:5 ... to live wisely and be *pure*
1 Pet 3:2 ... *pure* and reverent lives

CHASTEN(ED) (KJV)
Ps 6:1 ... or *discipline* me in your rage
Prov 19:18 ... *Discipline* your children
1 Cor 11:32 ... being *disciplined* so that we
Heb 12:11 ... No *discipline* is enjoyable
Rev 3:19 ... I correct and *discipline*

CHEAT, CHEATED, CHEATING, CHEATS (v) *to deprive of something valuable by deceit or fraud; to practice fraud or trickery*
Gen 31:7 ... he has *c-ed* me, changing my
1 Sam 12:3 ... Have I ever *c-ed* any of you?
1 Sam 12:4 ... have never *c-ed* or oppressed
Amos 8:5 ... get back to *c-ing* the helpless.
Mal 3:8 ... You have *c-ed* me of the tithes
Mark 10:19 ... You must not *c* anyone.
Mark 12:40 ... they shamelessly *c* widows
1 Cor 5:10 ... are greedy, or *c* people,
1 Cor 5:11 ... is a drunkard, or *c-s* people.

1 Cor 6:7 ... not let yourselves be *c-ed?*
1 Cor 6:8 ... who do wrong and *c* even
1 Cor 6:10 ... abusive, or *c* people—

CHEEK (n) *the fleshy side of the face below the eye and above and to the side of the mouth*
Matt 5:39 ... slaps you on the right *c,*
Luke 6:29 ... offer the other *c* also.

CHEERFUL (adj) *full of good spirits; merry, ungrudging*
Prov 15:30 ... A *c* look brings joy
Prov 17:22 ... A *c* heart is good medicine,

CHEERFULLY (adv) *marked by or suggestive of lighthearted ease of mind and spirit; cheerily, gladly*
2 Cor 9:7 ... loves a person who gives *c.*
1 Pet 4:9 ... *C* share your home with those

CHERUBIM (n) *winged angelic beings, often associated with worship and praise of God*
Gen 3:24 ... God stationed mighty *c* to the
Exod 25:19 ... Mold the *c* on each end
1 Sam 4:4 ... enthroned between the *c.*
1 Kgs 6:23 ... He made two *c* of wild olive
Isa 37:16 ... between the mighty *c!*
Ezek 10:1 ... over the heads of the *c.*

CHILD, CHILDREN (n) *an unborn or recently born person; a young person between infancy and youth, not yet of age; offspring or descendants*
see also SON(S)
Exod 20:5 ... family is affected—even *c-ren*
Deut 24:16 ... sins of their *c-ren,* nor *c-ren*
Deut 32:43 ... avenge the blood of his *c-ren;*
Deut 32:46 ... as a command to your *c-ren*
1 Kgs 3:26 ... Give her the *c*—please do
Job 1:5 ... Perhaps my *c-ren* have sinned
Ps 8:2 ... have taught *c-ren* and infants
Prov 20:7 ... blessed are their *c-ren* who
Prov 23:13 ... discipline your *c-ren.*
Prov 29:15 ... To discipline a *c* produces
Prov 31:28 ... Her *c-ren* stand and bless
Isa 7:14 ... The virgin will conceive a *c!*
Isa 9:6 ... For a *c* is born to us,
Isa 54:13 ... I will teach all your *c-ren,*
Mal 4:6 ... hearts of *c-ren* to their fathers.
Matt 1:23 ... The virgin will conceive a *c!*
Matt 5:9 ... will be called the *c-ren* of God.
Matt 18:3 ... and become like little *c-ren,*
Mark 9:37 ... welcomes a little *c* like this
Mark 10:14 ... Let the *c-ren* come to me.
Mark 10:16 ... took the *c-ren* in his arms
Luke 1:42 ... and your *c* is blessed.
Luke 6:35 ... as *c-ren* of the Most High,
Luke 18:15 ... their little *c-ren* to Jesus
John 1:12 ... to become *c-ren* of God.
John 12:36 ... become *c-ren* of the light.
Acts 2:39 ... to your *c-ren,* and to those far
Rom 9:26 ... called '*c-ren* of the living God.'
1 Cor 13:11 ... and reasoned as a *c.*
Gal 3:26 ... you are all *c-ren* of God
Eph 3:6 ... riches inherited by God's *c-ren.*
Eph 6:1 ... *C-ren,* obey your parents
Eph 6:4 ... not provoke your *c-ren* to anger
Col 3:21 ... do not aggravate your *c-ren,*
1 Tim 3:4 ... having *c-ren* who respect and
1 Tim 3:12 ... manage his *c-ren* and
1 Tim 5:10 ... brought up her *c-ren* well?
Heb 12:7 ... treating you as his own *c-ren.*
1 Jn 4:7 ... who loves is a *c* of God
1 Jn 5:4 ... every *c* of God defeats this evil
1 Jn 5:18 ... God's *c-ren* do not make a

1700

CHILDLESS (adj) *a person characterized by lack of children; barren*
Ps 113:9 ... He gives the *c* woman a family,
Isa 54:1 ... Sing, O *c* woman, you who
Gal 4:27 ... Rejoice, O *c* woman, you who

CHILDLIKE (adj) *resembling, suggesting, or appropriate to a child; marked by innocence, trust, and ingenuousness*
Ps 116:6 ... protects those of *c* faith;
Matt 11:25 ... revealing them to the *c*.

CHOOSE, CHOOSES (v) *to decide; to have a preference for; to select freely and after consideration*
see also CALL, CHOSE
Deut 30:19 ... Oh, that you would *c* life, so
Josh 24:15 ... *c* today whom you will serve.
Eccl 10:2 ... A wise person *c-s* the right road;
Jer 27:5 ... things of mine to anyone I *c*.
Dan 4:25 ... gives them to anyone he *c-s*.
John 15:16 ... You didn't *c* me. I chose you.
Rom 9:11 ... God *c-s* people according to
Rom 9:18 ... he *c-s* to harden the hearts of

CHOSE, CHOSEN (v) *to decide; to have a preference for*
see also CALL, CHOOSE, CHOSEN
Matt 22:14 ... called, but few are *c-n*.
John 15:16 ... You didn't choose me. I *c* you.
Rom 1:1 ... *c-n* by God to be an apostle
Rom 8:29 ... *c* them to become like his
1 Cor 1:1 ... Paul, *c-n* by the will of God
1 Cor 1:27 ... *c* things that are powerless
Eph 1:4 ... loved us and *c* us in Christ
Eph 1:11 ... God, for he *c* us in advance,
2 Thes 2:13 ... thankful that God *c* you
1 Pet 1:15 ... as God who *c* you is holy.
2 Pet 1:10 ... God has called and *c-n*.

CHOSEN (adj) *selected or marked for special favor or privilege*
see also CALLED
1 Chr 16:22 ... Do not touch my *c* people,
Isa 41:8 ... my *c* one, descended from Abraham
Mark 13:20 ... for the sake of his *c* ones
Luke 23:35 ... God's Messiah, the *C* One.
John 1:34 ... that he is the *C* One of God.
1 Pet 1:1 ... writing to God's *c* people
1 Pet 2:9 ... for you are a *c* people.

CHRIST (n) *Son of God, Messiah, Anointed One*
see also JESUS, MESSIAH
John 1:17 ... faithfulness came through Jesus *C*.
Rom 1:4 ... he is Jesus *C* our Lord.
Rom 3:22 ... by placing our faith in Jesus *C*.
Rom 5:1 ... Jesus *C* our Lord has done
Rom 5:6 ... *C* came at just the right time
Rom 5:11 ... *C* has made us friends of God.
Rom 6:4 ... as *C* was raised from the dead
Rom 6:23 ... eternal life through *C* Jesus
Rom 7:4 ... when you died with *C*.
Rom 8:1 ... who belong to *C* Jesus.
Rom 8:34 ... *C* Jesus died for us and
Rom 8:35 ... separate us from *C*'s love?
Rom 14:9 ... *C* died and rose again for this
Rom 15:5 ... fitting for followers of *C* Jesus.
Rom 15:20 ... where the name of *C* has never
1 Cor 1:2 ... the name of our Lord Jesus *C*,
1 Cor 1:13 ... Has *C* been divided into
1 Cor 1:17 ... cross of *C* would lose its power.
1 Cor 1:23 ... preach that *C* was crucified,
1 Cor 1:30 ... God has united you with *C*
1 Cor 5:7 ... *C*, our Passover Lamb,

1 Cor 6:15 ... his body, which is part of *C*,
1 Cor 8:12 ... you are sinning against *C*.
1 Cor 9:19 ... to bring many to *C*.
1 Cor 10:4 ... that rock was *C*.
1 Cor 10:9 ... Nor should we put *C* to the test,
1 Cor 11:3 ... and the head of *C* is God.
1 Cor 12:27 ... you together are *C*'s body,
1 Cor 15:3 ... *C* died for our sins,
2 Cor 1:5 ... the more we suffer for *C*, the
2 Cor 3:3 ... you are a letter from *C*
2 Cor 3:14 ... removed only by believing in *C*.
2 Cor 5:10 ... stand before *C* to be judged.
2 Cor 5:14 ... *C*'s love controls us.
2 Cor 5:20 ... we are *C*'s ambassadors;
Gal 1:7 ... twist the truth concerning *C*.
Gal 2:4 ... the freedom we have in *C* Jesus.
Gal 2:21 ... need for *C* to die.
Gal 3:13 ... But *C* has rescued us
Gal 4:19 ... continue until *C* is fully developed
Gal 5:4 ... you have been cut off from *C*!
Gal 5:24 ... Those who belong to *C* Jesus
Eph 1:3 ... because we are united with *C*.
Eph 1:10 ... under the authority of *C*—
Eph 1:20 ... that raised *C* from the dead
Eph 2:10 ... created us anew in *C* Jesus,
Eph 2:20 ... the cornerstone is *C* Jesus
Eph 4:7 ... through the generosity of *C*.
Eph 4:32 ... God through *C* has forgiven you.
Eph 5:21 ... out of reverence for *C*.
Eph 5:23 ... head of his wife as *C*
Eph 5:25 ... wives, just as *C* loved the
Phil 1:21 ... living means living for *C*,
Phil 1:23 ... with *C*, which would be far better
Phil 1:29 ... the privilege of trusting in *C*
Phil 2:5 ... same attitude that *C* Jesus had.
Phil 3:18 ... enemies of the cross of *C*.
Col 1:22 ... through the death of *C*
Col 2:2 ... mysterious plan, which is *C*
Col 2:6 ... accepted *C* Jesus as your Lord,
Col 2:13 ... God made you alive with *C*,
Col 3:1 ... raised to new life with *C*,
Col 3:3 ... life is hidden with *C* in God.
Col 3:15 ... peace that comes from *C*
1 Thes 5:9 ... through our Lord Jesus *C*,
1 Tim 1:15 ... *C* Jesus came into the world
1 Tim 2:5 ... humanity—the man *C* Jesus.
2 Tim 1:10 ... by the appearing of *C* Jesus,
2 Tim 2:3 ... as a good soldier of *C* Jesus.
2 Tim 2:10 ... eternal glory in *C* Jesus
2 Tim 3:12 ... a godly life in *C* Jesus will
2 Tim 3:15 ... by trusting in *C* Jesus.
2 Tim 4:1 ... of God and *C* Jesus, who will
Titus 2:13 ... and Savior, Jesus *C*, will be
Heb 3:14 ... share in all that belongs to *C*.
Heb 6:1 ... teachings about *C* again and
Heb 9:14 ... the blood of *C* will purify
Heb 9:28 ... *C* was offered once for all
Heb 10:10 ... body of Jesus *C*, once for all
Heb 13:8 ... Jesus *C* is the same yesterday,
1 Pet 1:11 ... the Spirit of *C* within them
1 Pet 1:19 ... blood of *C*, the sinless,
1 Pet 2:21 ... just as *C* suffered for you.
1 Pet 3:15 ... you must worship *C* as Lord
1 Pet 4:13 ... partners with *C* in his suffering,
2 Pet 1:16 ... coming of our Lord Jesus *C*.
1 Jn 2:1 ... He is Jesus *C*, the one who is
1 Jn 2:22 ... says that Jesus is not the *C*.
1 Jn 4:2 ... that Jesus *C* came in a real
1 Jn 5:1 ... Jesus is the *C* has become
1 Jn 5:20 ... fellowship with his Son, Jesus *C*.
Rev 1:1 ... from Jesus *C*, which God gave
Rev 1:5 ... his throne; and from Jesus *C*.
Rev 20:4 ... and they reigned with *C* for
Rev 20:6 ... God and of *C* and will reign

CHRISTIAN, CHRISTIANS (n) *one who professes belief in and follows the teachings of Jesus Christ; believer*
Acts 11:26 ... believers were first called *C-s*
Acts 26:28 ... persuade me to become a *C*
1 Pet 4:16 ... to suffer for being a *C*.

CHURCH, CHURCHES (n) *"assembly" or "called ones"; the body of believers gathered to worship Jesus (not the building in which they meet)*
Matt 16:18 ... this rock I will build my *c*,
Matt 18:17 ... take your case to the *c*.
Acts 16:5 ... the *c-es* were strengthened
Acts 20:28 ... shepherd God's flock—his *c*,
1 Cor 15:9 ... way I persecuted God's *c*.
Gal 1:13 ... I violently persecuted God's *c*.
Eph 5:23 ... Christ is the head of the *c*.
Col 1:18 ... head of the *c*, which is his
Col 1:24 ... continue for his body, the *c*.
2 Thes 1:4 ... tell God's other *c-es* about your
Rev 1:20 ... angels of the seven *c-es*,

CIRCUMCISE, CIRCUMCISED, CIRCUMCISING (v) *to cut off the foreskin of a male*
Gen 17:10 ... among you must be *c-d*.
Gen 17:12 ... *c-d* on the eighth day after his
Josh 5:3 ... made flint knives and *c*
John 7:23 ... correct time for *c-ing* your son
Acts 21:21 ... not to *c* their children
Rom 4:11 ... even before he was *c-d*.
1 Cor 7:19 ... or not a man has been *c-d*.

CIRCUMCISION (n) *the condition of being circumcised; the ceremony signifying Israel's covenant with God; act symbolic of cleansing*
Rom 2:25 ... *c* has value only if you obey
Rom 2:29 ... true *c* is not merely
Gal 5:2 ... If you are counting on *c* to make

CITIZEN, CITIZENS (n) *a person owing allegiance to and deriving protection from a sovereign state*
Acts 22:28 ... But I am a *c* by birth!
Eph 2:19 ... You are *c-s* along with
Phil 3:20 ... But we are *c-s* of heaven,

CLAY (n) *an earthy material that is pliable when moist but hard when fired and is used for brick, tile, and pottery*
Isa 45:9 ... Does the *c* dispute with the one
Isa 64:8 ... *c*, and you are the potter.
Lam 4:2 ... are now treated like pots of *c*
Dan 2:33 ... of iron and baked *c*.
Rom 9:21 ... to use the same lump of *c*
2 Cor 4:7 ... *c* jars containing this great
2 Tim 2:20 ... are made of wood and *c*.

CLEAN (adj) *unadulterated, pure; without guilt or moral corruption; without ceremonial defilement*
see also PURE
Lev 10:10 ... unclean and what is *c*.
Ps 51:2 ... Wash me *c* from my guilt.
Ps 51:7 ... and I will be *c*; wash me,
Ps 51:10 ... Create in me a *c* heart, O God.
John 13:10 ... you disciples are *c*, but not all
Acts 10:15 ... if God has made it *c*.
2 Tim 2:21 ... Your life will be *c*,

CLEANSE, CLEANSED, CLEANSES (v) *to make clean, pure, holy*
see also PURIFY, WASH
Ps 19:12 ... *C* me from these hidden
Prov 20:9 ... Who can say, "I have *c-d* my
Jer 4:14 ... O Jerusalem, *c* your heart

Acts 15:9 . . . he **c-d** their hearts through
1 Cor 6:11 . . . were **c-d**; you were made holy;
2 Cor 7:1 . . . let us **c** ourselves from
Titus 2:14 . . . **c** us, and to make us his
Heb 1:3 . . . he had **c-d** us from our sins,
Heb 9:13 . . . of a heifer could **c** people's
1 Pet 1:2 . . . and have been **c-d** by the blood
1 Pet 1:22 . . . You were **c-d** from your sins
2 Pet 1:9 . . . that they have been **c-d**
1 Jn 1:7 . . . blood of Jesus, his Son, **c-s**
1 Jn 1:9 . . . to **c** us from all wickedness.

CLING (v) *to adhere as if glued firmly; to hold or hold on tightly or tenaciously*
Deut 10:20 . . . worship him and **c** to him.
Deut 13:4 . . . listen to his voice, and **c** to
Matt 10:39 . . . If you **c** to your life,
Luke 8:15 . . . who hear God's word, **c** to it,
John 20:17 . . . "Don't **c** to me," Jesus
Phil 2:6 . . . as something to **c** to.

CLOSE, CLOSED, CLOSES (v) *to draw near; to contract, fold, swing, or slide so as to leave no opening*
Gen 19:10 . . . Then the LORD **c-d** the door
Prov 28:27 . . . who **c** their eyes to poverty
Isa 22:22 . . . no one will be able to **c** them;
Acts 28:27 . . . and they have **c-d** their eyes—
Rev 3:7 . . . what he **c-s**, no one can open:
Rev 21:25 . . . Its gates will never be **c-d**

CLOUD, CLOUDS (n) *a visible mass of particles of condensed vapor suspended in the atmosphere*
1 Kgs 18:44 . . . I saw a little **c** about the
Ps 68:4 . . . praises to him who rides the **c-s.**
Ps 108:4 . . . faithfulness reaches to the **c-s.**
Isa 19:1 . . . Egypt, riding on a swift **c.**
Dan 7:13 . . . coming with the **c-s** of heaven.
Mark 13:26 . . . coming on the **c-s** with great
Luke 21:27 . . . Son of Man coming on a **c**
1 Thes 4:17 . . . up in the **c-s** to meet the Lord
Rev 1:7 . . . comes with the **c-s** of heaven.
Rev 14:14 . . . I saw a white **c**, and seated on

COALS (n) *a piece of glowing carbon or charred wood; ember*
Prov 25:22 . . . heap burning **c** of shame
Rom 12:20 . . . heap burning **c** of shame

COAT (n) *an outer garment worn on the upper body*
Matt 5:40 . . . give your **c**, too.
Luke 6:29 . . . your **c**, offer your shirt

COIN, COINS (n) *a usually flat piece of metal issued by governmental authority as money*
Mark 12:15 . . . Show me a Roman **c**,
Mark 12:42 . . . dropped in two small **c-s.**
Luke 12:6 . . . sparrows—two copper **c-s?**
Luke 15:8 . . . woman has ten silver **c-s**

COMFORT (n) *consolation in time of trouble or worry; solace*
Gen 24:67 . . . she was a special **c** to him
Job 10:20 . . . I may have a moment of **c**
Ps 94:19 . . . your **c** gave me renewed hope
Zech 10:2 . . . falsehoods that give no **c.**
2 Cor 1:5 . . . shower us with his **c**
2 Cor 1:7 . . . share in the **c** God gives us.
Col 4:11 . . . And what a **c** they have been!

COMFORT, COMFORTED, COMFORTS (v) *to give strength and hope to; to console*
Gen 37:35 . . . he refused to be **c-ed.**
Ruth 2:13 . . . You have **c-ed** me by speaking
Job 2:11 . . . traveled from their homes to **c**
Job 42:11 . . . consoled him and **c-ed** him
Ps 69:20 . . . one would turn and **c** me.
Ps 86:17 . . . O LORD, help and **c** me.
Ps 119:50 . . . it **c-s** me in all my troubles.
Ps 119:52 . . . O LORD, they **c** me.
Isa 40:1 . . . **C, c** my people,
Isa 49:13 . . . the LORD has **c-ed** his people
Isa 51:3 . . . The LORD will **c** Israel again
Isa 51:12 . . . yes I, am the one who **c-s** you.
Isa 51:19 . . . Who is left to **c** you?
Isa 52:9 . . . the LORD has **c-ed** his people.
Isa 61:1 . . . to **c** the brokenhearted
Isa 66:13 . . . as a mother **c-s** her child.
Lam 1:2 . . . there is no one left to **c** her.
Lam 1:17 . . . but no one **c-s** her.
Zech 1:17 . . . the LORD will again **c** Zion
Matt 5:4 . . . mourn, for they will be **c-ed.**
1 Cor 14:3 . . . encourages them, and **c-s**
2 Cor 1:4 . . . He **c-s** us in all our troubles
2 Cor 1:4 . . . so that we can **c** others.
2 Cor 1:6 . . . when we ourselves are **c-ed,**
2 Cor 1:6 . . . we will certainly **c** you.
2 Cor 2:7 . . . forgive and **c** him.

COMFORTER (KJV)
John 14:16 . . . another *Advocate*, who will
John 14:26 . . . sends the *Advocate* as my
John 15:26 . . . the *Advocate*—the Spirit of
John 16:7 . . . if I don't, the *Advocate* won't

COMMAND, COMMANDS (n) *an order given; religious instruction*
see also COMMANDMENT
Exod 20:6 . . . who love me and obey my **c-s.**
Exod 24:12 . . . the instructions and **c-s**
Lev 22:31 . . . keep all my **c-s**
Num 15:39 . . . and obey all the **c-s**
Deut 4:2 . . . or subtract from these **c-s**
Deut 6:6 . . . wholeheartedly to these **c-s**
Deut 7:9 . . . who love him and obey his **c-s**
Deut 8:1 . . . Be careful to obey all the **c-s**
Deut 11:1 . . . decrees, regulations, and **c-s**
Deut 11:27 . . . if you obey the **c-s** of the
Deut 28:1 . . . keep all his **c-s** that I am giving
Deut 32:46 . . . as a **c** to your children
Josh 1:9 . . . my **c**—be strong and
1 Kgs 8:58 . . . obey all the **c-s**, decrees,
1 Kgs 8:61 . . . obey his decrees and **c-s**
1 Chr 28:7 . . . if he continues to obey my **c-s**
Neh 1:5 . . . who love him and obey his **c-s,**
Job 36:10 . . . **c-s** that they turn from evil.
Ps 33:9 . . . It appeared at his **c.**
Ps 78:7 . . . and obeying his **c-s.**
Ps 103:20 . . . listening for each of his **c-s**
Ps 112:1 . . . and delight in obeying his **c-s**
Ps 119:32 . . . I will pursue your **c-s,**
Ps 119:47 . . . How I delight in your **c-s!**
Ps 119:73 . . . the sense to follow your **c-s.**
Ps 119:96 . . . your **c-s** have no limit.
Ps 119:127 . . . I love your **c-s** more than
Ps 119:143 . . . I find joy in your **c-s.**
Ps 119:172 . . . all your **c-s** are right.
Ps 119:176 . . . I have not forgotten your **c-s.**
Prov 3:1 . . . Store my **c-s** in your heart.
Prov 6:23 . . . For their **c** is a lamp
Eccl 12:13 . . . Fear God and obey his **c-s,**
Isa 48:18 . . . you had listened to my **c-s!**
Dan 9:4 . . . who love and obey your **c-s.**
Matt 28:20 . . . disciples to obey all the **c-s**
John 15:17 . . . my **c:** Love each other.
Acts 17:30 . . . he **c-s** everyone everywhere to
Rom 7:8 . . . sin used this **c** to arouse
Rom 7:9 . . . I learned the **c** not to covet,
Rom 7:12 . . . law itself is holy, and its **c-s** are
1 Cor 14:37 . . . saying is a **c** from the Lord
Gal 5:14 . . . summed up in this one **c:**
2 Thes 3:6 . . . we give you this **c**
2 Pet 2:21 . . . reject the **c** they were given

COMMAND, COMMANDED, COMMANDING (v) *to issue a charge or directive*
Gen 7:5 . . . everything as the LORD **c-ed**
Exod 7:6 . . . did just as the LORD had **c-ed**
Exod 19:7 . . . everything the LORD had **c-ed**
Deut 6:1 . . . your God **c-ed** me to teach
Deut 6:24 . . . our God **c-ed** us to obey
Deut 15:11 . . . why I am **c-ing** you to share
John 15:14 . . . my friends if you do what I **c.**
2 Tim 2:14 . . . **c** them in God's presence
2 Pet 3:2 . . . Savior **c-ed** through your
1 Jn 3:23 . . . just as he **c-ed** us.
2 Jn 1:4 . . . just as the Father **c-ed.**

COMMANDMENT, COMMANDMENTS (n) *a gracious provision of God's law or covenant, obeyed as an act of love and devotion*
see also COMMAND
Exod 34:28 . . . Ten **C-s**—on the stone
Deut 4:13 . . . his covenant—the Ten **C-s**
Deut 10:4 . . . LORD wrote the Ten **C-s** on
Ps 103:18 . . . of those who obey his **c-s!**
Ps 111:7 . . . all his **c-s** are trustworthy.
Ps 111:10 . . . who obey his **c-s** will grow
Ps 119:93 . . . I will never forget your **c-s,**
Prov 19:16 . . . the **c-s** and keep your life;
Matt 5:19 . . . if you ignore the least **c**
Matt 19:17 . . . eternal life, keep the **c-s.**
Matt 22:36 . . . the most important **c**
Matt 22:38 . . . the first and greatest **c.**
Mark 10:19 . . . you know the **c-s:**
Mark 12:28 . . . **c-s**, which is the most
Luke 18:20 . . . you know the **c-s:**
John 13:34 . . . a new **c:** Love each other.
John 14:15 . . . If you love me, obey my **c-s.**
Rom 13:9 . . . in this one **c:** "Love your
1 Cor 7:19 . . . is to keep God's **c-s.**
Eph 2:15 . . . law with its **c-s** and regulations.
Eph 6:2 . . . the first **c** with a promise:
Heb 9:19 . . . had read each of God's **c-s**
1 Jn 2:3 . . . know him if we obey his **c-s.**
1 Jn 3:24 . . . Those who obey God's **c-s**
1 Jn 5:3 . . . God means keeping his **c-s.**
Rev 12:17 . . . who keep God's **c-s** and

COMMIT, COMMITS, COMMITTED, COMMITTING (v) *to carry into action deliberately, perpetrate; to obligate or pledge oneself*
Deut 30:20 . . . **c-ting** yourself firmly to him.
2 Chr 16:9 . . . hearts are fully **c-ted** to him.
2 Chr 17:6 . . . deeply **c-ted** to the ways
Prov 6:32 . . . the man who **c-s** adultery
Prov 29:22 . . . a hot-tempered person **c-s**
Matt 5:28 . . . has already **c-ted** adultery
Matt 5:32 . . . causes her to **c** adultery
Matt 19:9 . . . someone else **c-s** adultery—
Mark 10:11 . . . someone else **c-s** adultery
Mark 10:19 . . . You must not **c** adultery.
Luke 16:18 . . . her husband **c-s** adultery.
Rom 13:9 . . . You must not **c** adultery.
Titus 2:14 . . . totally **c-ted** to doing good
Jas 2:11 . . . You must not **c** adultery,
Rev 18:3 . . . world have **c-ted** adultery with
Rev 18:9 . . . the world who **c-ted** adultery

COMPANY (n) *association with another, fellowship; companions, associates*
Prov 21:16 . . . end up in the **c** of the dead.
Prov 24:1 . . . or desire their **c.**

Rom 12:16 ... to enjoy the *c* of ordinary
1 Cor 15:33 ... for "bad *c* corrupts good

COMPASSION (n) *sympathy, usually granted because of unusual or distressing circumstances*
Exod 34:6 ... The God of *c* and mercy!
Ps 51:1 ... Because of your great *c*,
Ps 86:15 ... a God of *c* and mercy, slow to
Ps 145:9 ... He showers *c* on all
Isa 49:13 ... and will have *c* on them
Isa 63:15 ... your mercy and *c* now?
Lam 3:32 ... brings grief, he also shows *c*
Hos 2:19 ... unfailing love and *c*,
Mic 7:19 ... you will have *c* on us.
Zech 10:6 ... because of my *c*.
Mark 1:41 ... Moved with *c*, Jesus reached
Mark 6:34 ... and he had *c* on them
Luke 15:20 ... with love and *c*, he ran to
Rom 9:15 ... show *c* to anyone I choose.

COMPASSIONATE (adj) *having or showing compassion; sympathetic*
Ps 103:13 ... tender and *c* to those who
Ps 112:4 ... They are generous, *c*,
Ps 145:8 ... is merciful and *c*, slow to
Joel 2:13 ... he is merciful and *c*, slow to
Luke 6:36 ... You must be *c*, just as your
Phil 2:1 ... Are your hearts tender and *c*?

COMPLAINED, COMPLAINING (v) *to express grief, pain, or discontent; to make a formal accusation or charge*
Exod 15:24 ... the people *c* and turned
Num 14:2 ... in the wilderness!" they *c*.
Num 14:29 ... Because you *c* against me,
John 6:43 ... Jesus replied, "Stop *c-ing*
Phil 2:14 ... Do everything without *c-ing*

CONCEIT (n) *excessive appreciation of one's own worth or virtue*
Ps 36:2 ... In their blind *c*, they cannot

CONCEITED (adj) *having or showing an excessively high opinion of oneself*
Gal 5:26 ... us not become *c*, or provoke

CONDEMN, CONDEMNED, CONDEMNING, CONDEMNS (v) *to declare guilty; to sentence or doom*
Job 15:6 ... Your own mouth *c-s* you, not I.
Job 40:8 ... my justice and *c* me just to
Ps 37:33 ... or let the godly be *c-ed*
Ps 102:20 ... to release those *c-ed* to die.
Prov 12:2 ... *c-s* those who plan wickedness.
Prov 17:15 ... guilty and *c-ing* the innocent—
Isa 53:8 ... Unjustly *c-ed*, he was led away.
Matt 12:7 ... not have *c-ed* my innocent
Matt 12:37 ... acquit you or *c* you.
Matt 12:41 ... on judgment day and *c* it,
Matt 27:3 ... Jesus had been *c-ed* to die,
Luke 11:31 ... on judgment day and *c* it,
John 8:10 ... even one of them *c* you?
Rom 2:1 ... think you can *c* such people,
Rom 2:1 ... you are *c-ing* yourself,
Rom 3:7 ... how can God *c* me as a sinner
Rom 3:8 ... deserve to be *c-ed*.
Rom 8:34 ... Who then will *c* us? No one—
Rom 14:3 ... foods must not *c* those who
Rom 14:13 ... So let's stop *c-ing* each other.
1 Cor 4:9 ... a victor's parade, *c-ed* to die.
2 Cor 7:3 ... saying this to *c* you.
Col 2:16 ... So don't let anyone *c* you
Jas 5:6 ... You have *c-ed* and killed
Jas 5:12 ... not sin and be *c-ed*.

CONDEMNATION (n) *conviction of guilt; censure or blame*

Rom 5:9 ... save us from God's *c*.
Rom 5:18 ... Adam's one sin brings *c*
Rom 7:13 ... bring about my *c* to death.
Rom 8:1 ... there is no *c* for those who
2 Cor 3:9 ... which brings *c*, was glorious,

CONFESS, CONFESSED, CONFESSES, CONFESSING (v) *to admit or acknowledge (sin or faith)*
1 Sam 7:6 ... *c-ed* that they had sinned
Ezra 10:11 ... So now *c* your sin to
Ps 32:3 ... I refused to *c* my sin,
Ps 32:5 ... Finally, I *c-ed* all my sins
Ps 38:18 ... But I *c* my sins;
Ps 66:18 ... If I had not *c-ed* the sin in my
Dan 9:4 ... to the LORD my God and *c-ed*:
Dan 9:20 ... praying and *c-ing* my sin
Matt 18:15 ... *c-es* it, you have won
Mark 1:5 ... And when they *c-ed* their sins
Jas 5:16 ... *C* your sins to each other
1 Jn 1:9 ... But if we *c* our sins to him,

CONFIDENCE (n) *faith or belief that one will act in a right, proper, or effective way; a feeling or consciousness of one's powers; a quality or state of being certain*
Ps 146:3 ... Don't put your *c* in powerful
Isa 30:15 ... In quietness and *c* is your
2 Cor 8:22 ... of his great *c* in you.
Phil 1:14 ... believers here have gained *c*
Phil 2:24 ... And I have *c* from the Lord
Phil 3:4 ... I could have *c* in my own
Col 2:2 ... want them to have complete *c*
1 Thes 5:8 ... as our helmet the *c* of our
Titus 1:2 ... This truth gives them *c*
2 Pet 1:19 ... we have even greater *c*
1 Jn 4:17 ... but we can face him with *c*

CONFIDENT (adj) *full of conviction, certain; trustful*
Ps 27:13 ... Yet I am *c* I will see the
Ps 57:7 ... My heart is *c* in you, O God;
2 Cor 3:4 ... We are *c* of all this
Eph 1:18 ... can understand the *c* hope
Col 1:5 ... *c* hope of what God has reserved
Col 4:12 ... fully *c* that you are following
2 Thes 3:4 ... And we are *c* in the Lord
Heb 3:6 ... keep our courage and remain *c*

CONFIDENTLY (adv) *acting with confidence*
Ps 112:7 ... they *c* trust the LORD
Rom 5:2 ... we *c* and joyfully look forward
Eph 3:12 ... boldly and *c* into God's

CONFLICT (n) *fight, battle, war*
Prov 13:10 ... Pride leads to *c*;
Prov 17:1 ... filled with feasting—and *c*.
Gal 3:21 ... Is there a *c*, then, between

CONQUEROR (n) *one who subdues, defeats, or vanquishes*
Mic 1:15 ... I will bring a *c* to capture

CONSCIENCE, CONSCIENCES (n) *one's moral sensitivity or scruples*
2 Sam 24:10 ... census, David's *c* began to
Acts 24:16 ... maintain a clear *c* before God
Rom 14:2 ... with a sensitive *c* will eat
1 Cor 8:7 ... their weak *c-s* are violated.
1 Cor 8:10 ... to violate their *c* by eating
1 Cor 10:25 ... raising questions of *c*.
1 Tim 1:5 ... a clear *c*, and genuine faith.
1 Tim 1:19 ... and keep your *c* clear.
Titus 1:15 ... minds and *c-s* are corrupted.
Heb 9:9 ... are not able to cleanse the *c-s*
Heb 9:14 ... will purify our *c-s* from sinful

Heb 10:22 ... guilty *c-s* have been sprinkled
Heb 13:18 ... for our *c* is clear
1 Pet 3:16 ... Keep your *c* clear.
1 Pet 3:21 ... to God from a clean *c*.

CONSECRATE, CONSECRATED (v) *to devote irrevocably to God by a solemn ceremony; to make or declare sacred*
see also DEDICATE, DEVOTE
Exod 40:9 ... all its furnishings to *c* them
Lev 19:24 ... the entire crop must be *c-d*
2 Chr 29:31 ... you have *c-d* yourselves

CONSIDERATE (adj) *thoughtful of the rights and feelings of others*
Phil 4:5 ... see that you are *c* in all you

CONSTANT (adj) *marked by steadfast faithfulness; continually occurring or recurring*
Ps 119:98 ... they are my *c* guide.
Prov 27:15 ... is as annoying as *c* dripping
Luke 18:5 ... with her *c* requests!

CONTAIN (v) *to keep within limits; to restrain or control*
1 Kgs 8:27 ... heavens cannot *c* you.
John 21:25 ... world could not *c* the books

CONTENT, CONTENTED (adj) *feeling or showing satisfaction with one's possessions, status, or situation; pleased*
Josh 7:7 ... If only we had been *c*
1 Kgs 4:20 ... They were very *c-ed*,
Prov 13:25 ... godly eat to their hearts' *c*,
Luke 3:14 ... And be *c* with your pay.
Phil 4:11 ... I have learned how to be *c*
1 Tim 6:8 ... food and clothing, let us be *c*.

CONTENTMENT (n) *the quality or state of being contented*
1 Tim 6:6 ... godliness with *c* is

CONTROL, CONTROLS (v) *to exercise restraining or directing influence over; to rule*
Job 37:15 ... know how God *c-s* the storm
Rom 6:12 ... Do not let sin *c*
Rom 8:6 ... letting the Spirit *c* your mind
Rom 8:8 ... still under the *c* of
1 Cor 7:9 ... they can't *c* themselves,
1 Cor 7:37 ... and he can *c* his passion,
2 Cor 5:14 ... Christ's love *c-s* us.
Jas 1:26 ... but don't *c* your tongue,
Jas 3:2 ... could also *c* ourselves
2 Pet 2:19 ... a slave to whatever *c-s* you.

CONVICT, CONVICTED (v) *to find or prove guilty of an offense*
Prov 24:25 ... for those who *c* the guilty;
John 7:51 ... Is it legal to *c* a man
John 16:8 ... he will *c* the world of
1 Cor 14:24 ... they will be *c-ed* of sin
Jude 1:15 ... He will *c* every person

CONVINCE, CONVINCED, CONVINCING (v) *to persuade to a belief, consent, or course of action*
Exod 4:31 ... people of Israel were *c-d*
Acts 18:4 ... to *c* the Jews and Greeks
Rom 2:19 ... are *c-d* that you are a guide
Rom 8:38 ... I am *c-d* that nothing
Rom 14:14 ... I know and am *c-d*
Rom 15:14 ... I am fully *c-d*,
Phil 1:25 ... I am *c-d* that I will

CORNERSTONE (n) *a stone forming a corner or angle in a wall; foundation*
Ps 118:22 ... now become the *c*.

1703

Mark 12:10 . . . now become the *c*.
Acts 4:11 . . . now become the *c*.
Eph 2:20 . . . And the *c* is Christ
1 Pet 2:7 . . . now become the *c*.

CORRECT, CORRECTED, CORRECTING, CORRECTS (v) *to set right with remedies, revisions, or reforms*
Job 5:17 . . . joy of those *c-ed* by God!
Ps 141:5 . . . If they *c* me,
Prov 3:12 . . . For the LORD *c-s* those
Prov 9:8 . . . don't bother *c-ing* mockers;
Prov 19:25 . . . if you *c* the wise,
Jer 5:3 . . . refused to be *c-ed*.
Jer 10:24 . . . Do not *c* me in anger,
2 Tim 3:16 . . . It *c-s* us when we
2 Tim 4:2 . . . Patiently *c*, rebuke,
Titus 2:15 . . . the authority to *c* them
Heb 12:5 . . . give up when he *c-s* you.

CORRECTION (n) *a rebuke or punishment; the action of making right*
Prov 10:17 . . . those who ignore *c*
Prov 12:1 . . . it is stupid to hate *c*.
Prov 15:5 . . . learns from *c* is wise.
Prov 15:10 . . . whoever hates *c* will die.
Prov 15:32 . . . if you listen to *c*,
Zeph 3:2 . . . it refuses all *c*.

CORRUPT (adj) *morally degenerate and perverted; depraved*
Gen 6:11 . . . the earth had become *c*
Ps 14:1 . . . They are *c*,
Ps 14:3 . . . all have become *c*.
Prov 19:28 . . . A *c* witness
Luke 9:41 . . . faithless and *c* people!

CORRUPT, CORRUPTED, CORRUPTS (v) *to change from good to bad, physically or morally*
Eccl 7:7 . . . and bribes *c* the heart.
1 Cor 15:33 . . . bad company *c-s* good
Titus 1:15 . . . and consciences are *c-ed*.
Jas 1:27 . . . let the world *c* you.

COST (n) *loss or penalty incurred especially in gaining something; price*
Num 16:38 . . . sinned at the *c* of their lives,
Luke 14:28 . . . calculating the *c*

COST (v) *to require effort, suffering, or loss*
Prov 7:23 . . . it would *c* him his life.
Rev 6:6 . . . barley will *c* a day's pay.

COUNSEL (n) *advice; policy, plan, or action*
Ps 37:30 . . . godly offer good *c*;
Ps 73:24 . . . guide me with your *c*,
Ps 107:11 . . . scorning the *c* of the
Prov 27:9 . . . The heartfelt *c* of a friend
1 Cor 7:40 . . . I am giving you *c*

COUNSEL (v) *to advise*
Col 3:16 . . . Teach and *c* each other

COUNSELOR (n) *one who gives advice or wisdom*
see also ADVOCATE, HOLY SPIRIT
Isa 9:6 . . . Wonderful *C*, Mighty God,

COUNT, COUNTED, COUNTING, COUNTS (v) *to number; to consider*
Gen 15:6 . . . and the LORD *c-ed* him as
Ps 22:17 . . . I can *c* all my bones.
Ps 130:5 . . . yes, I am *c-ing* on him.
Ps 147:4 . . . He *c-s* the stars
Prov 20:25 . . . and only later *c-ing* the cost.
Acts 5:41 . . . *c-ed* them worthy to suffer

Rom 4:9 . . . Abraham was *c-ed* as righteous
Rom 4:24 . . . that God will also *c* us
Rom 5:13 . . . it was not *c-ed* as sin
2 Cor 5:19 . . . no longer *c-ing* people's sins
Gal 3:6 . . . and God *c-ed* him as righteous
Jas 2:23 . . . and God *c-ed* him as righteous

COUNTENANCE (KJV)
Gen 4:6 . . . Why do you *look* so dejected
Num 6:26 . . . LORD *show you his favor*
1 Sam 16:7 . . . Don't judge by his *appearance*
Prov 15:13 . . . glad heart makes a happy *face*
Luke 9:29 . . . *appearance of his face* was transformed

COURAGE (n) *mental or moral strength*
Judg 5:21 . . . March on with *c*, my soul!
2 Chr 15:8 . . . he took *c* and removed
Dan 11:25 . . . stir up his *c* and raise a
Mark 6:50 . . . Take *c!* I am here!
Acts 27:22 . . . But take *c!*
Heb 3:6 . . . if we keep our *c*
Jas 5:8 . . . Take *c*, for the coming
1 Jn 2:28 . . . be full of *c* and not shrink

COURAGEOUS (adj) *having or characterized by courage; brave*
Deut 31:6 . . . So be strong and *c!*
Josh 1:6 . . . Be strong and *c*,
2 Sam 10:12 . . . Be *c!* Let us fight
2 Chr 32:7 . . . Be strong and *c!*
Ps 31:24 . . . be strong and *c*,
1 Cor 16:13 . . . Be *c*. Be strong.

COURT, COURTS (n) *a place for the administration of justice; an open space enclosed by buildings*
Ps 82:1 . . . presides over heaven's *c*;
Ps 84:10 . . . single day in your *c-s*
Ps 96:8 . . . come into his *c-s*.
Ps 100:4 . . . go into his *c-s*
Prov 22:22 . . . exploit the needy in *c*.
Prov 25:8 . . . to go to *c*.
Isa 3:13 . . . takes his place in *c*
Amos 5:15 . . . *c* into true halls of justice.
Zech 8:16 . . . verdicts in your *c-s*
Matt 5:25 . . . are on the way to *c*

COVENANT, COVENANTS (n) *a mutual agreement or contract (between persons, between nations, or between God and humanity) with conditions and consequences spelled out*
see also PROMISE, VOW
Gen 9:9 . . . hereby confirm my *c*
Gen 17:2 . . . I will make a *c* with you,
Exod 19:5 . . . and keep my *c*,
Deut 4:13 . . . He proclaimed his *c*—
Judg 2:1 . . . never break my *c*
1 Kgs 8:21 . . . which contains the *c*
2 Kgs 23:2 . . . Book of the *C* that had been
2 Chr 6:14 . . . You keep your *c*
Neh 1:5 . . . keeps his *c* of unfailing love
Ps 105:8 . . . stands by his *c*—
Prov 2:17 . . . and ignores the *c*
Isa 61:8 . . . an everlasting *c* with them.
Jer 31:31 . . . make a new *c* with the people
Hos 10:4 . . . make *c-s* they don't intend
Mal 3:1 . . . messenger of the *c*,
Mark 14:24 . . . confirms the *c* between God
Luke 22:20 . . . new *c* between God and his
Rom 9:4 . . . He made *c-s* with them
1 Cor 11:25 . . . new *c* between God and his
2 Cor 3:6 . . . under the new *c*,
Heb 8:6 . . . a far better *c* with God,

Heb 9:15 . . . mediates a new *c* between
Heb 12:24 . . . the new *c* between God and

COVER (n) *something that is placed over or about another thing; lid or top piece*
Exod 25:17 . . . make the Ark's *c*—
Exod 25:21 . . . put the atonement *c*
Lev 16:2 . . . the atonement *c*.

COVER, COVERED, COVERS (v) *to hide from sight or knowledge; to lay or spread something over; to lie over*
Gen 3:7 . . . to *c* themselves.
Exod 33:22 . . . and *c* you with my hand
Job 29:14 . . . Righteousness *c-ed* me
Ps 85:2 . . . you *c-ed* all their sins.
Ps 91:4 . . . He will *c* you with
Isa 6:2 . . . they *c-ed* their faces,
Matt 10:26 . . . everything that is *c-ed*
1 Cor 11:4 . . . if he *c-s* his head while
2 Cor 3:15 . . . their hearts are *c-ed*
Jas 3:14 . . . don't *c* up the truth
1 Pet 4:8 . . . love *c-s* a multitude of sins.

COVET, COVETED, COVETING (v) *to inordinately desire unjust gain or another's property*
see also DESIRE
Exod 20:17 . . . not *c* your neighbor's wife,
Exod 34:24 . . . so no one will *c* and conquer
Deut 7:25 . . . must not *c* the silver or gold
Acts 20:33 . . . *c-ed* anyone's silver or gold
Rom 7:7 . . . known that *c-ing* is wrong
Rom 13:9 . . . You must not *c*.

CREATE, CREATED, CREATING (v) *to bring into being; to form, make, or produce*
see also FORMED, MADE, MAKE
Gen 1:1 . . . God *c-d* the heavens
Gen 1:27 . . . male and female he *c-d* them;
Gen 6:7 . . . human race I have *c-d* from
Ps 51:10 . . . *C* in me a clean heart
Ps 104:30 . . . life is *c-d*, and you renew
Prov 8:22 . . . before he *c-d* anything else.
Isa 43:1 . . . the LORD who *c-d* you.
Isa 43:7 . . . I who *c-d* them.
Isa 45:8 . . . I, the LORD, *c-d* them.
Isa 54:16 . . . I have *c-d* the blacksmith
Isa 65:17 . . . I am *c-ing* new heavens and
John 1:3 . . . *c-d* everything through him,
Rom 1:20 . . . since the world was *c-d*,
Rom 1:25 . . . served the things God *c-d*
Rom 9:20 . . . the thing that was *c-d* say
Eph 2:10 . . . He has *c-d* us anew
Eph 2:15 . . . by *c-ing* in himself
Eph 4:24 . . . *c-d* to be like God—
Col 1:16 . . . Everything was *c-d* through
1 Tim 4:3 . . . But God *c-d* those foods
Heb 1:2 . . . through the Son he *c-d*
1 Pet 4:19 . . . to the God who *c-d* you,
Rev 4:11 . . . For you *c-d* all things,
Rev 10:6 . . . who *c-d* the heavens

CREATION (n) *something that is created; the world; the act of bringing the world into existence*
Gen 2:3 . . . from all his work of *c*.
Mark 10:6 . . . from the beginning of *c*.
Rom 8:19 . . . For all *c* is waiting
Rom 8:39 . . . nothing in all *c* will ever
Gal 6:15 . . . into a new *c*.
Col 1:17 . . . holds all *c* together.
Heb 12:27 . . . all of *c* will be shaken
Jas 1:18 . . . we, out of all *c*,
Rev 3:14 . . . of God's new *c*:

CREATOR (n) *maker; one who creates*
see also MAKER
Gen 14:19 ... God Most High, *C* of heaven
Job 40:19 ... only its *C* can threaten
Eccl 12:1 ... to forget your *C.*
Isa 40:28 ... the *C* of all the earth.
Isa 45:9 ... argue with their *C.*
Isa 51:13 ... the LORD, your *C,*
Jer 51:19 ... He is the *C* of everything
Rom 1:25 ... instead of the *C* himself,
Eph 3:9 ... the *C* of all things,
Eph 3:15 ... the *C* of everything

CRITICISM (n) *a critical observation or remark; critique*
Prov 15:31 ... listen to constructive *c,*
Prov 25:12 ... valid *c* is like a gold
Prov 28:23 ... people appreciate honest *c*
Prov 29:1 ... refuses to accept *c*
2 Cor 8:20 ... guard against any *c*

CRITICIZE, CRITICIZED, CRITICIZING (v) *to find fault with; to point out the faults of*
Job 34:29 ... who can *c* him?
Eccl 7:5 ... be *c-d* by a wise person
Rom 14:16 ... not be *c-d* for doing
Phil 2:15 ... no one can *c* you.
Titus 2:8 ... teaching can't be *c-d.*
Jas 4:11 ... *c-ing* and judging God's law.

CROOKED (adj) *not straight, twisted; dishonest, evil*
2 Sam 22:27 ... but to the *c* you show
Ps 18:26 ... but to the *c* you show
Ps 125:5 ... those who turn to *c* ways,
Prov 5:6 ... staggers down a *c* trail
Prov 8:8 ... nothing devious or *c* in it.
Prov 10:9 ... those who follow *c* paths
Prov 21:8 ... The guilty walk a *c* path;
Eccl 7:13 ... what he has made *c?*
Isa 59:8 ... have mapped out *c* roads,

CROSS (n) *an upright post used as an instrument of death in ancient times; the means by which atonement was made between God and humanity*
Mark 8:34 ... take up your *c,*
Luke 9:23 ... take up your *c* daily,
Acts 2:23 ... you nailed him to a *c*
Acts 5:30 ... hanging him on a *c.*
1 Cor 1:18 ... message of the *c* is
Gal 3:1 ... death on the *c.*
Gal 6:12 ... that the *c* of Christ alone
Phil 2:8 ... criminal's death on a *c.*
Col 1:20 ... Christ's blood on the *c.*
Heb 12:2 ... he endured the *c,*
1 Pet 2:24 ... his body on the *c*

CROWN, CROWNS (n) *top of the head; a cap or headdress worn by victors, priests, or royalty*
Prov 16:31 ... Gray hair is a *c* of glory;
Song 3:11 ... He wears the *c* his mother
Isa 61:3 ... will give a *c* of beauty
Isa 62:3 ... a splendid *c* in the hand
Zech 9:16 ... like jewels in a *c.*
Matt 27:29 ... thorn branches into a *c*
Mark 15:17 ... thorn branches into a *c*
John 19:2 ... wove a *c* of thorns
John 19:5 ... wearing the *c* of thorns
Phil 4:1 ... and the *c* I receive
1 Thes 2:19 ... our proud reward and *c*
Jas 1:12 ... will receive the *c* of life
Rev 2:10 ... will give you the *c* of life.
Rev 3:11 ... take away your *c.*
Rev 4:4 ... had gold *c-s* on their heads.
Rev 4:10 ... lay their *c-s* before the throne
Rev 12:3 ... with seven *c-s* on his heads.
Rev 14:14 ... He had a gold *c* on his head
Rev 19:12 ... on his head were many *c-s.*

CROWNED, CROWNS (v) *to place a crown on the head of; to bless or adorn*
Ps 8:5 ... and *c-ed* them with
Ps 149:4 ... he *c-s* the humble
Prov 14:18 ... are *c-ed* with knowledge.
Isa 51:11 ... *c-ed* with everlasting joy.
Heb 2:7 ... and *c-ed* them with
Heb 2:9 ... *c-ed* with glory and honor.

CRUCIFIXION (n) *the execution or death of a person on a cross*
Matt 23:34 ... you will kill some by *c,*
John 19:41 ... The place of *c* was near

CRUCIFY, CRUCIFIED (v) *to execute or nail to the cross; to put to death*
Matt 26:2 ... handed over to be *c-ied.*
Matt 27:22 ... "*C* him!"
Matt 27:44 ... who were *c-ied* with him
Mark 15:13 ... "*C* him!"
Mark 15:27 ... revolutionaries were *c-ied*
Mark 15:32 ... who were *c-ied* with Jesus
Mark 16:6 ... who was *c-ied.*
Luke 23:21 ... "*C* him! *C* him!"
Luke 23:23 ... that Jesus be *c-ied,*
Luke 23:33 ... criminals were also *c-ied*—
Luke 24:20 ... and they *c-ied* him.
John 19:6 ... "*C* him! *C* him!"
John 19:10 ... to release you or *c* you?
John 19:20 ... where Jesus was *c-ied*
John 19:32 ... the two men *c-ied* with Jesus.
Acts 4:10 ... the man you *c-ied*
Rom 6:6 ... were *c-ied* with Christ
1 Cor 1:13 ... Was I, Paul, *c-ied* for you?
1 Cor 1:23 ... preach that Christ was *c-ied,*
1 Cor 2:8 ... would not have *c-ied*
2 Cor 13:4 ... he was *c-ied* in weakness,
Gal 5:24 ... and *c-ied* them there.
Rev 11:8 ... where their Lord was *c-ied.*

CRY, CRIES (n) *entreaty, appeal; an inarticulate utterance of distress, rage, or pain*
Exod 2:23 ... their *c* rose up to God.
Ps 5:2 ... Listen to my *c* for help,
Ps 34:15 ... open to their *c-ies* for help.
Ps 40:1 ... and heard my *c.*
Ps 142:6 ... Hear my *c,* for I am
Prov 21:13 ... to the *c-ies* of the poor

CRY, CRIED (v) *to shout; to beg or beseech; to shed tears often noisily*
Exod 14:10 ... They *c-ied* out to the LORD,
Josh 24:7 ... When your ancestors *c-ied* out
Judg 3:9 ... people of Israel *c-ied* out
Judg 4:3 ... people of Israel *c-ied* out
Judg 6:6 ... Then the Israelites *c-ied* out
Judg 10:12 ... you *c-ied* out to me
Ps 18:6 ... in my distress I *c-ied* out
Eccl 3:4 ... A time to *c* and a time
Lam 2:18 ... *C* aloud before the Lord,
Hab 2:11 ... walls *c* out against you,

CUP (n) *a drinking vessel; figurative of human vessel; token of tangible consolation, salvation of Christ, wrath of God, drunkenness, or fate*
Ps 23:5 ... My *c* overflows
Matt 26:39 ... let this *c* of suffering
Matt 26:42 ... If this *c* cannot be
Mark 10:39 ... drink from my bitter *c*
Mark 14:23 ... And he took a *c* of wine
Mark 14:36 ... take this *c* of suffering
Luke 22:20 ... This *c* is the new covenant
John 18:11 ... from the *c* of suffering
1 Cor 10:16 ... When we bless the *c*
1 Cor 10:21 ... from the *c* of the Lord
1 Cor 11:25 ... took the *c* of wine after
1 Cor 11:25 ... This *c* is the new covenant

CURE (n) *recovery or relief from a disease; a complete or permanent solution*
Jer 30:15 ... wound that has no *c?*
Luke 8:43 ... she could find no *c.*

CURE, CURED (v) *to restore to health, soundness, or normality*
Isa 30:26 ... and *c* the wounds
Matt 11:5 ... those with leprosy are *c-d,*
John 5:10 ... said to the man who was *c-d,*

CURSE, CURSES, CURSING (n) *a condemnation or judgment*
Num 5:23 ... priest will write these *c-s*
Josh 8:34 ... blessings and *c-s* Moses had
Rom 3:14 ... full of *c-ing* and bitterness.
Rom 8:20 ... was subjected to God's *c.*
Gal 3:10 ... right with God are under his *c,*
Gal 3:13 ... the *c* for our wrongdoing.
Jas 3:10 ... and *c-ing* come pouring out
Rev 22:3 ... No longer will there be a *c*

CURSE, CURSES (v) *to pronounce a sentence; to afflict; to call upon a supernatural power to bring injury upon; to utter profane language against*
Gen 8:21 ... will never again *c* the ground
Gen 12:3 ... *c* those who treat you
Prov 3:33 ... *c-s* the house of the wicked.
Matt 5:22 ... And if you *c* someone,
Rom 12:14 ... Don't *c* them;
1 Cor 12:3 ... will *c* Jesus, and no one
Jas 3:9 ... and sometimes it *c-s* those who

CURSED (adj) *being under or deserving a curse*
Gen 3:17 ... the ground is *c* because
Deut 21:23 ... anyone who is hung is *c*
Deut 27:16 ... *C* is anyone who dishonors
Deut 27:18 ... *C* is anyone who leads
Deut 27:20 ... *C* is anyone who has sexual
Deut 27:24 ... *C* is anyone who attacks a
Deut 27:26 ... *C* is anyone who does not
Prov 28:27 ... poverty will be *c.*
Gal 3:10 ... *C* is everyone who does not
Gal 3:13 ... *C* is everyone who is hung

CURTAIN (n) *a hanging screen usually capable of being drawn back or up*
Isa 40:22 ... the heavens like a *c*
Mark 15:38 ... And the *c* in the sanctuary

D

DANCE, DANCING (n) *a series of rhythmic bodily movements usually performed to music*
Ps 30:11 ... into joyful *d-ing.*
Mark 6:22 ... a *d* that greatly pleased

DANCE, DANCED (v) *to move in a rhythmic manner, usually to music*
2 Sam 6:14 ... David *d-d* before the LORD
Eccl 3:4 ... and a time to *d.*
Matt 11:17 ... and you didn't *d,*

DANGER (n) *harm or damage*
Ps 57:1 ... until the *d* passes by.
Prov 22:3 ... prudent person foresees *d*
Matt 5:22 ... in *d* of being brought

1705

Rom 8:35 ... or in *d*, or threatened
2 Cor 1:10 ... did rescue us from mortal *d*,
2 Cor 11:26 ... I have faced *d* from rivers

DANGEROUS (adj) *able or likely to inflict injury or harm*
Prov 29:25 ... Fearing people is a *d* trap,

DARK, DARKEST (adj) *devoid or partially devoid of light; wholly or partially black*
Exod 20:21 ... approached the *d* cloud
Ps 23:4 ... walk through the *d-est* valley,
Song 1:6 ... because I am *d*—
Song 5:10 ... My lover is *d* and dazzling,
Joel 2:31 ... The sun will become *d*,
Acts 2:20 ... The sun will become *d*,
2 Pet 1:19 ... lamp shining in a *d* place—

DARKENED (v) *to make dark*
Matt 24:29 ... the sun will be *d*,

DARKNESS (n) *the state of being devoid of light; nightfall; in spiritual terms, secret, closed, blinded, or evil; place of punishment (hell)*
Gen 1:2 ... and *d* covered the deep waters.
Gen 1:4 ... the light from the *d*.
Ps 18:28 ... my God, lights up my *d*.
Matt 4:16 ... people who sat in *d*
Luke 23:44 ... it was about noon, and *d* fell
John 1:5 ... light shines in the *d*,
John 3:19 ... people loved the *d* more
John 12:35 ... the *d* will not overtake
2 Cor 4:6 ... Let there be light in the *d*,
2 Cor 6:14 ... can light live with *d*?
Eph 5:8 ... once you were full of *d*,
Eph 5:11 ... deeds of evil and *d*;
1 Pet 2:9 ... called you out of the *d*
1 Jn 1:5 ... there is no *d* in him at all.
1 Jn 2:9 ... is still living in *d*.
Jude 1:6 ... chained in prisons of *d*,

DAUGHTER, DAUGHTERS (n) *the female offspring or adopted child of parents*
Gen 19:36 ... Lot's *d-s* became pregnant
Num 36:10 ... The *d-s* of Zelophehad
Judg 11:40 ... the fate of Jephthah's *d*.
Esth 2:7 ... raised her as his own *d*.
Joel 2:28 ... sons and *d-s* will prophesy.
Mark 5:34 ... said to her, "*D*, your faith
Mark 7:29 ... the demon has left your *d*.

DAVID King of Israel (united kingdom); son of Jesse, in the family line of Jesus (Ruth 4:17-22; Matt 1:1; Luke 3:31); anointed king (1 Sam 16:1-13); skillful musician to Saul (1 Sam 16:14-23; 18:10); David and Goliath (1 Sam 17); faithful friendship with Jonathan (1 Sam 18:1-4); envied by Saul; loved by the people (1 Sam 18:5-16); married Michal (1 Sam 18:17-30); wives and children (2 Sam 3:2-5; 5:13-16; 1 Chr 3:1-9); fled from Saul (1 Sam 19–23); ate used "Bread of the Presence" (1 Sam 21:1-6; Matt 12:3-4); dealings with the Philistines (1 Sam 21:10-14; 27–30); spared Saul twice (1 Sam 22–24; 26); married widow Abigail (1 Sam 25:2-42); lamented death of Saul and Jonathan (2 Sam 1); contended with Saul's dynasty (2 Sam 2–4); anointed king of Judah (2 Sam 2:1-7); lamented Abner's death (2 Sam 3:31-39); made king over all Israel (2 Sam 5:1-5); victories over the Philistines (2 Sam 5:17-25; 21:15-22; 1 Chr 14:8-17; 20:4-8); made Jerusalem the royal city (2 Sam 5:6-16); moved Ark to Jerusalem (2 Sam 6); eternal covenant with God (2 Sam 7; 1 Chr 17); showed loyal love to Mephibosheth (2 Sam 9); committed adultery with Bathsheba (2 Sam 11–12; Pss 32; 51); plotted Uriah's death (2 Sam 11:14-25); rebuked by Nathan (2 Sam 12:1-12); repented of affair and intrigue (2 Sam 12:13); rebellion and death of Absalom (2 Sam 14–18); lamented Absalom's death (2 Sam 18:33–19:8); rebellion and death of Sheba (2 Sam 20); judged for taking census (2 Sam 24:1-25); made Solomon next king (1 Kgs 1:28–2:9); final words to Solomon (1 Kgs 2:1-9); died (1 Kgs 2:10-12); preparations for the Temple (1 Chr 22–29).

DAY, DAYS (n) *the time of light between one night and the next; a specified time or period; a 24-hour time period*
Gen 1:5 ... called the light "*d*" and the
Gen 2:2 ... On the seventh *d* God had
Exod 16:30 ... any food on the seventh *d*.
Lev 23:28 ... it is the *D* of Atonement,
Josh 1:8 ... Meditate on it *d* and night so
2 Kgs 7:9 ... This is a *d* of good news,
Ps 23:6 ... all the *d-s* of my life,
Ps 84:10 ... A single *d* in your
Ps 118:24 ... This is the *d* the LORD has
Isa 13:9 ... coming—the terrible *d* of his
Jer 46:10 ... this is the *d* of the Lord,
Jer 50:31 ... Your *d* of reckoning
Hos 3:5 ... In the last *d-s*, they will
Joel 1:15 ... How terrible that *d* will be!
Joel 2:31 ... great and terrible *d* of the
Amos 5:20 ... Yes, the *d* of the LORD
Zeph 1:14 ... That terrible *d* of the
Zech 14:1 ... Watch, for the *d* of the LORD
Zech 14:7 ... there will be continuous *d*!
Mal 4:5 ... great and dreadful *d* of the
Matt 24:38 ... In those *d-s* before the
Luke 11:3 ... Give us each *d* the food we
Acts 2:17 ... 'In the last *d-s*,' God says,
Rom 14:5 ... some think one *d* is more holy
1 Cor 5:5 ... be saved on the *d* the Lord
2 Cor 4:16 ... renewed every *d*.
1 Thes 5:2 ... the *d* of the Lord's return
1 Thes 5:4 ... surprised when the *d* of the
2 Thes 2:2 ... say that the *d* of the Lord
2 Tim 3:1 ... in the last *d-s* there will be
Heb 1:2 ... now in these final *d-s*, he has
2 Pet 3:3 ... in the last *d-s* scoffers will
2 Pet 3:10 ... But the *d* of the Lord
Rev 16:14 ... that great judgment *d* of God

DEAD (n) *Those who have died (physically or spiritually)*
Matt 8:22 ... the spiritually *d* bury their
Luke 24:46 ... rise from the *d* on the third
1 Cor 15:29 ... If the *d* will not be raised
Rev 20:12 ... I saw the *d*, both great and

DEAD (adj) *without (physical or spiritual) life; fatal; useless; unresponsive*
Rom 6:11 ... be *d* to the power of sin
Eph 2:1 ... Once you were *d* because of
Jas 2:17 ... good deeds, it is *d* and useless.
1 Pet 2:24 ... that we can be *d* to sin and
Rev 2:8 ... Last, who was *d* but is now

DEATH (n) *the cessation of (physical or spiritual) life; personification and consequence of evil*
Exod 21:12 ... must be put to *d*.
Ruth 1:17 ... anything but *d* to separate
Prov 11:19 ... evil people find *d*.
Prov 14:12 ... it ends in *d*.
Prov 23:14 ... save them from *d*.
Song 8:6 ... love is as strong as *d*,
Isa 38:17 ... have rescued me from *d*
Acts 2:24 ... for *d* could not keep him
Rom 5:12 ... brought *d*, so *d* spread to
Rom 6:23 ... the wages of sin is *d*,
Rom 7:24 ... dominated by sin and *d*?
1 Cor 15:21 ... see, just as *d* came into the
1 Cor 15:26 ... enemy to be destroyed is *d*.
2 Cor 3:6 ... written covenant ends in *d*;
Gal 3:1 ... the meaning of Jesus Christ's *d*
2 Tim 1:10 ... power of *d* and illuminated
Heb 2:14 ... who had the power of *d*.
Heb 9:17 ... after the person's *d*.
1 Jn 5:16 ... there is a sin that leads to *d*,
Rev 2:11 ... by the second *d*.
Rev 20:6 ... them the second *d* holds no
Rev 20:14 ... of fire is the second *d*.
Rev 21:4 ... be no more *d* or sorrow or
Rev 21:8 ... This is the second *d*.

DEBAUCHERY (KJV)
Rom 13:13 ... promiscuity and *immoral living*
2 Cor 12:21 ... eagerness for *lustful pleasure*
Gal 5:19 ... impurity, *lustful pleasures*
1 Pet 4:3 ... their *immorality* and lust, their

DEBT, DEBTS (n) *what is owed; sense of obligation*
Deut 15:1 ... cancel the *d-s* of everyone
Deut 15:3 ... This release from *d*, however,
Deut 15:9 ... year for canceling *d-s* is close
1 Sam 22:2 ... trouble or in *d* or who were
2 Kgs 4:7 ... pay your *d-s*, and
Neh 10:31 ... will cancel all *d-s* owed to us.
Prov 22:26 ... another person's *d* or put up
Matt 18:25 ... to pay the *d*.
Matt 18:27 ... and forgave his *d*.
Matt 18:30 ... in prison until the *d* could
Matt 18:32 ... you that tremendous *d*
Luke 7:42 ... canceling their *d-s*.
Luke 7:43 ... canceled the larger *d*.

DECEIT (n) *fraud; trickery; lying*
Mark 7:22 ... greed, wickedness, *d*, lustful
Acts 13:10 ... of every sort of *d* and fraud,
1 Pet 2:1 ... done with all *d*, hypocrisy,

DECEITFUL (adj) *not honest; misleading, deceptive*
Isa 59:13 ... planning our *d* lies.
2 Cor 11:13 ... They are *d* workers who

DECEIVE, DECEIVED, DECEIVES, DECEIVING (v) *to lead astray; to cause to accept as true what is false*
Gen 3:13 ... "The serpent *d-d* me," she
Prov 10:31 ... the tongue that *d-s* will be
Prov 14:8 ... but fools *d* themselves.
Prov 26:24 ... but they're *d-ing* you.
Matt 24:24 ... so as to *d*, if possible, even
Mark 13:6 ... They will *d* many.
Rom 7:11 ... those commands and *d-d* me;
Rom 16:18 ... they *d* innocent people.
1 Cor 3:18 ... Stop *d-ing* yourselves.
2 Cor 11:3 ... as Eve was *d-d* by the cunning
Col 2:4 ... so no one will *d* you with
1 Tim 2:14 ... The woman was *d-d*, and sin
2 Tim 3:13 ... They will *d* others and will
2 Tim 3:13 ... will themselves be *d-d*.
Heb 3:13 ... you will be *d-d* by sin
Rev 20:3 ... Satan could not *d* the nations
Rev 20:10 ... devil, who had *d-d* them, was

DECEPTION (n) *something that deceives; trick; the act of deceiving*
Isa 28:15 ... refuge made of lies and *d*.

Dan 8:25 ... He will be a master of *d*
Rom 1:29 ... quarreling, *d,* malicious
Eph 4:22 ... corrupted by lust and *d.*
2 Thes 2:10 ... kind of evil *d* to fool those
1 Jn 4:6 ... truth or spirit of *d.*

DECIDE, DECIDED, DECIDES (v) *to make a final choice or judgment about; to select as a course of action*
1 Sam 14:7 ... whatever you *d.*
Job 14:5 ... You have *d-d* the length of
Ps 75:7 ... he *d-s* who will rise and
Rom 14:13 ... *D* instead to live
Rom 14:22 ... they have *d-d* is right.
1 Cor 2:2 ... For I *d-d* that while I
1 Cor 6:2 ... can't you *d* even these
1 Cor 12:11 ... He alone *d-s* which gift
2 Cor 9:7 ... You must each *d* in your heart

DECISION, DECISIONS (n) *a determination arrived at after consideration; conclusion*
Joel 3:14 ... waiting in the valley of *d.*
Mic 3:11 ... You rulers make *d-s* based on
Rom 11:33 ... to understand his *d-s* and his

DEDICATE, DEDICATED (v) *to devote to the worship of a divine being; to set apart to a definite use*
see also CONSECRATE, DEVOTE
Exod 13:2 ... *D* to me every firstborn
Num 6:9 ... the hair they have *d-d* will be
Num 6:18 ... the hair that had been *d-d*
Num 18:6 ... a gift to you, *d-d* to the LORD
1 Kgs 8:63 ... Israel *d-d* the Temple
Neh 3:1 ... which they *d-d,* and the Tower
Luke 2:23 ... he must be *d-d* to the LORD.

DEED, DEEDS (n) *a signed instrument containing some legal transfer, bargain, or contract; a usually illustrious act or action; feat, exploit*
see also WORK(S)
Ps 45:4 ... perform awe-inspiring *d-s!*
Ps 66:3 ... awesome are your *d-s!*
Ps 71:24 ... your righteous *d-s* all day
Ps 88:12 ... your wonderful *d-s?*
Ps 96:3 ... his glorious *d-s* among the
Ps 105:2 ... his wonderful *d-s.*
Prov 31:31 ... Let her *d-s* publicly declare
Isa 64:6 ... our righteous *d-s,* they are
Jer 32:10 ... and sealed the *d* of purchase
Matt 5:16 ... let your good *d-s* shine out for
Rom 4:2 ... If his good *d-s* had made him
2 Cor 9:9 ... Their good *d-s* will be
Col 3:9 ... all its wicked *d-s.*
Jas 2:18 ... my faith by my good *d-s.*
Jas 2:20 ... without good *d-s* is useless?

DEFEND, DEFENDING, DEFENDS (v) *to maintain or support in the face of argument or hostile criticism; to drive danger or attack away from*
Deut 33:7 ... strength to *d* their cause;
Ps 10:14 ... You *d* the orphans.
Ps 34:7 ... he surrounds and *d-s* all who
Ps 72:4 ... Help him to *d* the poor,
Ps 106:8 ... saved them—to *d* the honor of
Phil 1:7 ... and in *d-ing* and confirming
Phil 1:16 ... been appointed to *d* the Good
Jude 1:3 ... urging you to *d* the faith

DEFENDER (n) *one who guards or protects*
Ps 68:5 ... the fatherless, *d* of widows—
Prov 22:23 ... the LORD is their *d.*
Isa 51:22 ... your God and *D,* says:

DEFILE, DEFILED, DEFILING (v) *to make unclean—either physically, sexually, ethically, or ceremonially*
Num 6:7 ... must not *d* themselves,
Num 15:39 ... desires and *d-ing* yourselves,
Ezek 23:7 ... idols and *d-ing* herself.
Ezek 44:7 ... In this way, you *d-d* my Temple
Matt 15:11 ... you are *d-d* by the words
Mark 7:23 ... they are what *d* you.
Acts 21:28 ... even *d-s* this holy place
2 Cor 7:1 ... that can *d* our body or

DELIGHT, DELIGHTS (n) *source of great pleasure; joy*
Ps 36:8 ... your river of *d-s.*
Ps 40:6 ... You take no *d* in sacrifices
Ps 119:111 ... they are my heart's *d.*
Prov 8:30 ... I was his constant *d,*
Isa 58:13 ... and speak of it with *d*
Jer 15:16 ... my joy and my heart's *d,*
Mal 3:12 ... your land will be such a *d,*
Mark 12:37 ... to him with great *d.*

DELIGHT, DELIGHTED, DELIGHTING, DELIGHTS (v) *to enjoy*
Exod 4:14 ... He will be *d-ed* to see you.
2 Sam 22:20 ... because he *d-s* in me.
Ps 1:2 ... But they *d* in the law of
Ps 18:19 ... he rescued me because he *d-s*
Ps 27:4 ... *d-ing* in the LORD's
Ps 37:4 ... Take *d* in the LORD,
Ps 119:70 ... I *d* in your instructions.
Prov 3:12 ... a child in whom he *d-s.*
Prov 11:1 ... he *d-s* in accurate weights.
Prov 11:20 ... he *d-s* in those with integrity.
Song 8:10 ... he is *d-ed* with what he sees.
Isa 11:3 ... He will *d* in obeying
Isa 65:19 ... and *d* in my people.
Isa 66:3 ... *d-ing* in their detestable sins—
Jer 9:24 ... I *d* in these things.

DEMON-POSSESSED (adj) *characterized by the possession or control of demons*
Matt 4:24 ... if they were *d* or epileptic
Matt 8:16 ... That evening many *d* people
Matt 8:33 ... happened to the *d* men.
Matt 9:32 ... When they left, a *d* man who
Matt 12:22 ... Then a *d* man, who was
Mark 1:32 ... many sick and *d* people were
Mark 5:16 ... about the *d* man and
Luke 8:36 ... others how the *d* man had

DEMON, DEMONS (n) *an agent of the Devil; an evil spirit*
Deut 32:17 ... They offered sacrifices to *d-s,*
Matt 8:31 ... So the begged, "If you cast
Matt 9:34 ... by the prince of *d-s.*
Matt 11:18 ... He's possessed by a *d.*
Matt 12:24 ... he can cast out *d-s.*
Matt 12:28 ... if I am casting out *d-s* by the
Matt 17:18 ... Jesus rebuked the *d,*
Mark 1:34 ... But because the *d-s* knew who
Mark 5:15 ... by the legion of *d-s.*
Mark 5:18 ... been *d* possessed begged
Mark 7:29 ... the *d* has left your daughter.
Mark 9:38 ... to cast out *d-s,* but we told
Mark 16:9 ... cast out seven *d-s.*
Mark 16:17 ... will cast out *d-s* in my name,
Luke 4:33 ... possessed by a *d*—an evil
Luke 7:33 ... He's possessed by a *d.*
Luke 8:2 ... he had cast out seven *d-s;*
Luke 8:30 ... with many *d-s.*
Luke 8:33 ... Then the *d-s* came out of the
Luke 8:38 ... freed from the *d-s* begged
Luke 9:49 ... to cast out *d-s,* but we told
Luke 10:17 ... Lord, even the *d-s* obey us

Luke 11:14 ... Jesus cast out a *d* from
Luke 11:19 ... They cast out *d-s,* too, so they
Luke 11:20 ... casting out *d-s* by the power
John 8:49 ... Jesus said, "I have no *d* in me.
John 10:21 ... possessed by a *d!*
Rom 8:38 ... neither angels nor *d-s,*
1 Cor 10:20 ... to participate with *d-s.*
1 Cor 10:21 ... the cup of *d-s,* too.
1 Cor 10:21 ... the table of *d-s,* too.
1 Tim 4:1 ... teachings that come from *d-s.*
Rev 9:20 ... to worship *d-s* and idols made
Rev 18:2 ... become a home for *d-s.*

DENY, DENIED, DENIES (v) *to disavow or refuse to accept as true; to refuse to grant*
Exod 23:6 ... you must not *d* justice to the
Deut 27:19 ... is anyone who *d-ies* justice
Prov 30:9 ... I may *d* you and say,
Matt 10:33 ... everyone who *d-ies* me
Matt 26:35 ... I will never *d* you!
Matt 26:70 ... But Peter *d-ied* it
Luke 12:9 ... anyone who *d-ies* me
Luke 22:34 ... you will *d* three times
John 18:25 ... He *d-ied* it, saying,
Acts 4:16 ... We can't *d* that they
1 Tim 5:8 ... have *d-ied* the true faith.
2 Tim 2:12 ... *d* him, he will *d* us.
Titus 1:16 ... *d* him by the way they live.
2 Pet 2:1 ... and even *d* the Master who
1 Jn 2:22 ... Anyone who *d-ies* the Father
1 Jn 2:23 ... Anyone who *d-ies* the Son
Jude 1:4 ... they have *d-ied* our only Master
Rev 3:8 ... and did not *d* me.

DEPEND (v) *to place reliance or trust*
Prov 3:5 ... do not *d* on your own
Jer 49:11 ... widows, too, can *d* on me
Gal 3:10 ... But those who *d* on the law

DEPRIVE (v) *to withhold something from; to remove*
Isa 10:2 ... They *d* the poor
1 Cor 7:5 ... Do not *d* each other of

DESERT, DESERTS (n) *arid land with usually sparse vegetation*
see also WILDERNESS
Prov 21:19 ... better to live alone in the *d*
Isa 32:2 ... like streams of water in the *d*
Isa 43:20 ... giving them water in the *d.*
2 Cor 11:26 ... cities, in the *d-s,* and on the

DESERVE, DESERVED, DESERVES (v) *to be worthy, fit, or suitable for some reward or requital; to merit*
Judg 9:16 ... the honor he *d-s* for all he
2 Sam 12:5 ... do such a thing *d-s* to die!
Neh 9:33 ... gave us only what we *d-d.*
Ps 103:10 ... with us, as we *d.*
Prov 14:14 ... Backsliders get what they *d;*
Dan 9:18 ... not because we *d* help,
Zech 1:6 ... received what we *d-d* from the
Luke 7:4 ... If anyone *d-s* your help,
Acts 26:31 ... done anything to *d* death or
Rom 3:8 ... why not say such things *d* to be
Rom 11:9 ... get what they *d.*
2 Cor 11:15 ... their wicked deeds *d.*
1 Tim 5:18 ... Those who work *d* their pay!
Heb 3:3 ... But Jesus *d-s* far more

DESIRABLE (adj) *attractive; worth seeking or doing*
Ps 19:10 ... They are more *d* than gold,

DESIRE, DESIRES (n) *conscious impulse toward something that promises enjoyment or satisfaction in its attainment; longing, craving*

Job 17:11 ... My heart's **d-s** are broken.
Ps 10:3 ... brag about their evil **d-s;**
Ps 37:4 ... give you your heart's **d-s.**
Ps 145:19 ... He grants the **d-s** of those who
Song 6:12 ... my strong **d-s** had taken me
Mark 4:19 ... wealth, and the **d** for other
Rom 1:26 ... to their shameful **d-s.**
Rom 6:12 ... not give in to sinful **d-s.**
Rom 7:5 ... sinful **d-s** were at work
Rom 13:14 ... indulge your evil **d-s.**
Gal 5:24 ... the passions and **d-s** of their
Phil 2:13 ... you the **d** and the power
Col 2:23 ... a person's evil **d-s.**
Col 3:5 ... lust, and evil **d-s.**
1 Tim 6:9 ... and harmful **d-s** that plunge
2 Tim 4:3 ... follow their own **d-s** and will
Jas 1:14 ... from our own **d-s,** which entice
Jas 4:1 ... from the evil **d-s** at war within
1 Pet 2:11 ... from worldly **d-s** that wage
1 Pet 4:2 ... chasing your own **d-s,**
2 Pet 2:10 ... their own twisted sexual **d,**
2 Pet 2:18 ... twisted sexual **d-s,** they lure
2 Pet 3:3 ... following their own **d-s.**
Jude 1:18 ... their ungodly **d-s.**

DESIRE, DESIRED, DESIRES (v) to long or hope for; to wish or request
see also COVET
Gen 3:16 ... And you will **d** to control
Ps 51:6 ... But you **d** honesty from
Ps 51:16 ... You do not **d** a sacrifice,
Prov 8:11 ... Nothing you **d** can compare
Prov 21:10 ... Evil people **d** evil;
Rom 1:24 ... things their hearts **d-d.**
1 Cor 12:31 ... earnestly **d** the most
1 Cor 14:1 ... you should also **d** the special
1 Tim 3:1 ... church leader, he **d-s** an honorable
Jas 1:20 ... righteousness God **d-s.**
Rev 22:17 ... Let anyone who **d-s** drink

DESPAIR (n) utter loss of hope
Ps 40:2 ... out of the pit of **d,**
Ps 79:8 ... on the brink of **d.**
Ps 130:1 ... the depths of **d,** O LORD,
Isa 61:3 ... praise instead of **d.**
2 Cor 4:8 ... but not driven to **d.**

DESPISE, DESPISED, DESPISES (n) to scorn or regard as unworthy, sometimes with malice or outrage
2 Sam 12:9 ... you **d-d** the word of the LORD
Job 5:17 ... Do not **d** the discipline
Job 9:21 ... to me—I **d** my life.
Ps 22:6 ... I am scorned and **d-d** by all!
Prov 1:7 ... but fools **d** wisdom and
Prov 12:8 ... a warped mind is **d-d.**
Prov 15:5 ... Only a fool **d-s** a parent's
Prov 15:20 ... foolish children **d** their
Prov 29:27 ... The righteous the unjust;
Prov 30:17 ... and **d-s** a mother's
Isa 53:3 ... He was **d-d,** and we did not
Mic 7:6 ... For the son **d-s** his father.
Luke 16:13 ... to one and **d** the other.
Gal 4:14 ... you did not **d** me or
2 Pet 2:10 ... and who **d** authority.

DESTINED (v) to decree beforehand; to predetermine
Luke 2:34 ... This child is **d** to cause
Heb 9:27 ... each person is **d** to die once

DESTITUTE (adj) lacking possessions and resources; suffering extreme poverty
Ps 82:3 ... of the oppressed and the **d.**
Ps 102:17 ... prayers of the **d.**

Rom 8:35 ... or hungry, or **d,** or in
Heb 11:37 ... **d** and oppressed

DESTROY, DESTROYED, DESTROYING, DESTROYS (v) to kill; to cause devastation or ruin
see also PERISH
Gen 6:17 ... that will **d** every living
Gen 9:11 ... will a flood **d** the earth.
Num 32:15 ... responsible for **d-ing** this
Deut 28:63 ... find pleasure in **d-ing** you.
Josh 10:40 ... He completely **d-ed** everyone
Prov 6:32 ... fool, for he **d-s** himself.
Prov 10:21 ... fools are **d-ed** by their lack
Prov 10:29 ... but it **d-s** the wicked.
Prov 11:3 ... dishonesty **d-s** treacherous
Prov 11:9 ... the godless **d** their friends,
Prov 18:9 ... as someone who **d** things.
Prov 18:24 ... "friends" who **d** each other,
Prov 29:1 ... will suddenly be **d-ed** beyond
Isa 11:4 ... his mouth will **d** the wicked.
Dan 2:44 ... never be **d-ed** or conquered.
Jon 3:9 ... fierce anger from **d-ing** us.
Jon 4:2 ... turn back from **d-ing** people.
Matt 10:28 ... God, who can **d** both soul
Luke 9:25 ... but are yourself lost or **d-ed?**
John 10:10 ... and kill and **d.**
Rom 2:12 ... they will be **d-ed,** even though
1 Cor 3:17 ... anyone who **d-s** this temple.
1 Cor 5:5 ... nature will be **d-ed** and he
1 Cor 8:11 ... died will be **d-ed.**
1 Cor 15:24 ... **d-ed** every ruler and
1 Cor 15:26 ... enemy to be **d-ed** is death.
2 Cor 4:9 ... are not **d-ed.**
Gal 5:15 ... Beware of **d-ing** one another.
Heb 7:16 ... that cannot be **d-ed.**
2 Pet 2:12 ... be caught and **d-ed.**
2 Pet 3:7 ... people will be **d-ed.**
Jude 1:5 ... but later he **d-ed** those who did
Rev 11:18 ... It is time to **d** all who have

DESTRUCTION (n) the state or fact of being destroyed, ruin; place of punishment (hell)
Ps 1:6 ... of the wicked leads to **d.**
Prov 16:18 ... Pride goes before **d,**
1 Cor 1:18 ... are headed for **d!**
2 Thes 1:9 ... punished with eternal **d,**
2 Thes 2:3 ... the one who brings **d.**
1 Tim 6:9 ... into ruin and **d.**
2 Pet 2:3 ... their **d** will not be delayed.
Rev 17:8 ... and go to eternal **d.**

DETERMINE, DETERMINED, DETERMINES (v) to decide; to resolve
Exod 28:30 ... objects used to **d** the LORD's
Ezra 7:10 ... because Ezra had **d-d** to study
Ps 17:3 ... I am **d-d** not to sin in
Ps 119:30 ... I have **d-d** to live by
Ps 119:112 ... I am **d-d** to keep your
Prov 4:23 ... it **d-s** the course of your life.
Prov 16:9 ... but the LORD **d-s** our steps.
Dan 1:8 ... But Daniel was **d-d** not to
Dan 11:36 ... what has been **d-d** will surely
Matt 12:34 ... heart **d-s** what you say.
Luke 22:22 ... it has been **d-d** that the Son
Acts 4:28 ... was **d-d** beforehand according

DETEST, DETESTS (v) to loathe; to denounce
Prov 8:7 ... the truth and **d** every kind of
Prov 12:22 ... The LORD **d-s** lying lips,
Prov 15:8 ... The LORD **d-s** the sacrifice
Prov 15:26 ... The LORD **d-s** evil plans,
Prov 16:5 ... The LORD **d-s** the proud;
Prov 20:10 ... the LORD **d-s** double
Prov 24:9 ... everyone **d-s** a mocker.

DETESTABLE (adj) arousing or meriting intense dislike; abominable
Lev 11:10 ... They are **d** to you.
Prov 3:32 ... wicked people are **d** to the
Prov 17:15 ... both are **d** to the LORD.
Prov 21:27 ... an evil person is **d,**
Luke 16:15 ... What this world honors is **d**

DEVIL (n) Satan; enemy of God and of everything good; destroyer, tempter, adversary
see also SATAN
Matt 4:1 ... tempted there by the **d.**
Matt 4:11 ... Then the **d** went away,
Matt 13:39 ... among the wheat is the **d.**
Matt 25:41 ... prepared for the **d** and his
Luke 4:2 ... tempted by the **d** for forty
Luke 4:13 ... When the **d** had finished
Luke 8:12 ... to have the **d** come and take
John 6:70 ... twelve of you, but one is a **d.**
John 13:2 ... **d** had already prompted
Eph 4:27 ... foothold to the **d.**
Eph 6:11 ... strategies of the **d.**
Eph 6:16 ... fiery arrows of the **d.**
2 Tim 2:26 ... escape from the **d's** trap.
Jas 4:7 ... Resist the **d,** and he
1 Jn 3:8 ... the works of the **d.**
1 Jn 3:10 ... children of the **d.**
Jude 1:9 ... accuse the **d** of blasphemy,
Rev 12:9 ... called the **d,** or Satan,

DEVOTE, DEVOTED (v) to commit by a solemn act
see also CONSECRATE, DEDICATE
2 Chr 31:4 ... could **d** themselves fully
Acts 2:42 ... the believers **d-d** themselves to
Col 4:2 ... **D** yourselves to prayer

DEVOTED (adj) characterized by loyalty and devotion
1 Kgs 18:3 ... (Obadiah was a **d** follower of
Ps 86:2 ... for I am **d** to you.
Matt 6:24 ... you will be **d** to one and
1 Tim 2:10 ... claim to be **d** to God should

DICE (n) small cubes marked on each face with numbers and used usually for games and gambling by being shaken and thrown
Ps 22:18 ... throw **d** for my clothing
Matt 27:35 ... his clothes by throwing **d.**

DIE, DIED, DIES (v) to pass from physical life; to cease from existence
see also PERISH
Gen 2:17 ... you are sure to **d.**
Gen 3:3 ... if you do, you will **d.**
Esth 4:16 ... If I must **d,** I must **d.**
Job 2:9 ... Curse God and **d.**
Prov 5:23 ... He will **d** for lack of
Prov 11:7 ... When the wicked **d,** their
Prov 11:10 ... when the wicked **d,**
Eccl 7:2 ... After all, everyone **d-s**—
Isa 22:13 ... drink, for tomorrow we **d!**
Isa 66:24 ... that devour them will never **d,**
Jer 31:30 ... All people will **d** for their
Matt 26:52 ... will **d** by the sword.
Mark 9:48 ... the maggots never **d** and the
Luke 16:22 ... The rich man also **d** and
John 13:37 ... I'm ready to **d** for you.
Rom 4:25 ... handed over to **d** because of
Rom 5:6 ... the right time and **d-d** for us
Rom 5:7 ... be willing to **d** for a person
Rom 5:8 ... by sending Christ to **d** for us
Rom 5:14 ... Still, everyone **d-d**—from the
Rom 6:7 ... when we **d-d** with Christ we
Rom 6:10 ... When he **d-d,** he **d-d** once

Rom 7:2 . . . But if he *d-s,* the laws of
Rom 7:6 . . . the law, for we *d-d* to it and
Rom 14:8 . . . whether we live or *d,* we
1 Cor 7:39 . . . If her husband *d-s,* she is free
1 Cor 9:15 . . . I would rather *d* than lose
1 Cor 15:6 . . . though some have *d-d.*
1 Cor 15:18 . . . all who have *d-d* believing in
1 Cor 15:22 . . . Just as everyone *d-s* because
1 Cor 15:32 . . . for tomorrow we *d!*
1 Cor 15:36 . . . plant unless it *d-s* first.
1 Cor 15:42 . . . in the ground when we *d,*
1 Cor 15:51 . . . will not all *d,* but we will
2 Cor 5:15 . . . for Christ, who *d-d* and was
Col 2:20 . . . You have *d-d* with Christ,
1 Thes 4:16 . . . who have *d-d* will rise from
1 Thes 5:10 . . . Christ *d-d* for us so
1 Tim 6:16 . . . He alone can never *d,*
2 Tim 2:11 . . . saying: If we *d* with him,
Heb 9:27 . . . is destined to *d* once and
1 Pet 3:18 . . . sinned, but he *d-d* for sinners

DIFFERENCE (n) *the quality or state of being different; a significant change in or effect on a situation*
2 Chr 12:8 . . . know the *d* between serving
Ezek 22:26 . . . teach my people the *d*
Gal 2:6 . . . leaders made no *d* to me,

DILIGENT (adj) *characterized by steady, earnest, and energetic effort; painstaking*
Ezra 4:22 . . . Be *d,* and don't
Prov 12:27 . . . but the *d* make use of

DISAPPEAR, DISAPPEARED, DISAPPEARING (v) *to pass from view; to cease to be*
1 Kgs 20:40 . . . the prisoner *d-ed!*
Job 17:11 . . . My hopes have *d-ed.*
Ps 37:20 . . . they will *d* like smoke.
Prov 26:20 . . . and quarrels *d* when gossip
Isa 29:14 . . . of the intelligent will *d.*
Isa 51:6 . . . the skies will *d* like smoke,
Matt 5:18 . . . until heaven and earth *d,*
Matt 24:35 . . . Heaven and earth will *d,*
Mark 13:31 . . . Heaven and earth will *d,*
Luke 16:17 . . . and earth to *d* than for the
John 5:13 . . . for Jesus had *d-ed* into the
Heb 8:13 . . . and will soon *d.*
1 Jn 2:8 . . . the darkness is *d-ing,* and the

DISASTER, DISASTERS (n) *a sudden calamitous event bringing great damage, loss, or destruction; a sudden or great misfortune or failure*
Exod 32:12 . . . this terrible *d* you have
Deut 31:17 . . . will say, 'These *d-s* have come
Deut 31:21 . . . when great *d-s* come down
Ps 91:6 . . . nor the *d* that strikes at
Prov 3:25 . . . not be afraid of sudden *d*
Prov 27:10 . . . When *d* strikes,
Jer 17:17 . . . my hope in the day of *d.*
Jer 29:11 . . . plans for good and not for *d,*
1 Thes 5:3 . . . then *d* will fall on them

DISCERNMENT (n) *the quality of being able to grasp and comprehend what is obscure*
Ps 119:125 . . . Give *d* to me,
Prov 1:4 . . . knowledge and *d* to the young.
Prov 5:2 . . . you will show *d,* and your
Prov 8:12 . . . knowledge and *d.*
Prov 28:11 . . . a poor person with *d* can see

DISCIPLE, DISCIPLES (n) *student or follower of some doctrine or teacher*
Matt 28:19 . . . go and make *d-s* of all the
Mark 16:20 . . . the *d-s* went everywhere and
Luke 6:13 . . . all of his *d-s* and chose twelve
Luke 14:26 . . . you cannot be my *d.*
Luke 14:33 . . . become my *d* without
John 6:66 . . . many of his *d-s* turned away
John 8:31 . . . are truly my *d-s* if you remain
John 13:5 . . . to wash the *d-s'* feet, drying
John 13:23 . . . The *d* Jesus loved
John 15:8 . . . fruit, you are my true *d-s.*
John 19:26 . . . there beside the *d* he loved,
John 21:7 . . . Then the *d* Jesus loved
John 21:20 . . . the *d* Jesus loved—

DISCIPLINE (n) *punishment; instruction*
Deut 11:2 . . . the *d* of the LORD
Prov 10:17 . . . People who accept *d* are on
Prov 13:1 . . . child accepts a parent's *d;*
Prov 13:24 . . . spare the rod of *d* hate their
Prov 15:32 . . . If you reject *d,* you only
Heb 12:5 . . . of the LORD's *d,* and don't
Heb 12:11 . . . No *d* is enjoyable

DISCIPLINE, DISCIPLINED, DISCIPLINES (v) *to punish or correct with love; to exercise self-control*
Deut 8:5 . . . as a parent *d-s* a child,
Deut 8:5 . . . your God *d-s* you for your
Ps 38:1 . . . in your anger or *d* me in your
Ps 39:11 . . . When you *d* us for our
Ps 119:67 . . . wander off until you *d-d* me;
Ps 119:75 . . . you *d-d* me because I needed
Prov 15:10 . . . right path will be severely *d-d;*
Jer 30:11 . . . I will *d* you, but with
Jer 31:18 . . . saying, 'You *d-d* me severely,
1 Cor 9:25 . . . All athletes are *d-d* in their
1 Cor 9:27 . . . I *d* my body like an athlete
1 Cor 11:32 . . . we are being *d-d* so that we
Heb 12:6 . . . For the LORD *d-s* those he
Heb 12:7 . . . who is never *d* by its father?
Heb 12:9 . . . fathers who *d-d* us, shouldn't
1 Pet 4:7 . . . be earnest and *d-d* in your

DISCOURAGED (v) *to dissuade or hinder; to deprive of courage or confidence*
Deut 31:8 . . . be afraid or *d,* for the LORD
2 Sam 11:25 . . . not to be *d,"* David said.
1 Chr 28:20 . . . afraid or *d,* for the LORD
Isa 41:10 . . . Don't be *d,* for I am
2 Cor 7:6 . . . who are *d,* encouraged us by
Col 3:21 . . . will become *d.*

DISCOURAGEMENT (n) *the state of being discouraged*
2 Cor 7:7 . . . may be overcome by *d.*

DISCRIMINATION (n) *prejudiced outlook, action, or treatment* see also FAVORITISM, PARTIALITY
Jas 2:4 . . . doesn't this *d* show that your

DISEASE, DISEASES (n) *sickness, malady*
Exod 4:6 . . . a severe skin *d.*
2 Chr 16:12 . . . a serious foot *d.*
Ps 91:6 . . . not dread the *d* that stalks
Ps 103:3 . . . heals all my *d-s.*
Matt 9:35 . . . every kind of *d* and illness.
Matt 10:1 . . . every kind of *d* and illness.
Luke 4:40 . . . matter what their *d-s* were,

DISGRACE (n) *loss of grace, favor, or honor; source of shame*
Prov 11:2 . . . Pride leads to *d,* but with
Prov 14:34 . . . but sin is a *d* to any people.
Acts 5:41 . . . worthy to suffer *d* for the
Heb 13:13 . . . and bear the *d* he bore.

DISGRACE, DISGRACED (v) *to cause to lose favor or standing; to be a source of shame to*
Ps 25:3 . . . trusts in you will ever be *d-d,*
Ps 37:19 . . . will not be *d-d* in hard times;
Prov 29:15 . . . but a mother is *d-d* by an
Matt 1:19 . . . did not want to *d* her
Rom 9:33 . . . in him will never be *d-d.*
Rom 10:11 . . . in him will never be *d-d.*
1 Tim 3:7 . . . will not be *d-d* and fall into

DISHONEST (adj) *characterized by lack of truth, honesty, or trustworthiness*
Lev 19:35 . . . Do not use *d* standards when
Prov 20:23 . . . not pleased by *d* scales.
Luke 16:8 . . . to admire the *d* rascal for
Luke 16:10 . . . But if you are *d* in little

DISHONESTY (n) *lack of honesty or integrity*
Jer 22:17 . . . eyes only for greed and *d!*
Jer 23:14 . . . commit adultery and love *d.*
Rom 3:7 . . . sinner if my *d* highlights his
Rev 21:27 . . . idolatry and *d*—but only

DISHONOR, DISHONORED, DISHONORING, DISHONORS (v) *to degrade or bring shame upon*
Exod 21:17 . . . Anyone who *d-s* father or
Exod 22:28 . . . You must not *d* God or
Lev 20:19 . . . This would *d* a close
Deut 27:16 . . . is anyone who *d-s* father or
Ezra 4:14 . . . see the king *d-ed* in this way,
Lam 2:2 . . . *d-ing* the kingdom and its
John 8:49 . . . my Father—and you *d* me.
Rom 2:23 . . . the law, but you *d* God by
1 Cor 11:4 . . . A man *d-s* his head if
1 Cor 11:5 . . . a woman *d-s* her head if
Jas 2:6 . . . But you *d* the poor!

DISOBEY, DISOBEYED, DISOBEYING (v) *to fail to obey*
Judg 2:2 . . . But you *d-ed* my command.
1 Kgs 13:26 . . . man of God who *d-ed* the
2 Chr 24:20 . . . says: Why do you *d*
Neh 9:29 . . . and obstinate and *d-ed* your
Esth 3:3 . . . Why are you *d-ing* the king's
Dan 9:11 . . . Israel has *d-ed* your instruction
Acts 7:53 . . . You deliberately *d-ed* God's
Rom 1:30 . . . and they *d* their parents.
Rom 5:19 . . . Because one person *d-ed* God,
Eph 5:6 . . . fall on all who *d* him.
Heb 3:18 . . . the people who *d-ed* him?
Heb 4:6 . . . enter because they *d-ed* God.
Heb 4:11 . . . But if we *d* God, as the
1 Pet 3:20 . . . those who *d-ed* God long ago

DISORDER (n) *lack of order; confusion*
1 Cor 14:33 . . . not a God of *d* but of peace,
Jas 3:16 . . . you will find *d* and evil of

DISORDERLY (adj) *in a manner that lacks order; turbulent*
2 Cor 12:20 . . . arrogance, and *d* behavior.

DISPUTE, DISPUTES (n) *verbal controversy; quarrel or debate*
Prov 18:18 . . . it settles *d-s* between
1 Cor 6:1 . . . you has a *d* with another

DISSENSION (n) *disagreement; discord*
Gal 5:20 . . . selfish ambition, *d,* division,

DISTRESS (n) *a troubling or painful situation; a state of danger or desperate need*
Exod 3:7 . . . their cries of *d* because of
Job 36:16 . . . to a place free from *d.*
Ps 18:6 . . . But in my *d* I cried out

Ps 118:5 ... In my *d* I prayed to
Ps 143:11 ... bring me out of this *d*.
Jas 1:27 ... and widows in their *d*

DIVIDE, DIVIDED (v) *to separate into parts; to distribute; to make distinctions*
Ps 22:18 ... They *d* my garments
Luke 12:51 ... have come to *d* people
1 Cor 1:13 ... Has Christ been *d-d* into
Jas 4:8 ... loyalty is *d-d* between God

DIVISION, DIVISIONS (n) *act or process of dividing, separating, distributing; a portion, part, grouping, or distinction*
1 Cor 1:10 ... there be no *d-s* in the church.
1 Cor 11:18 ... that there are *d-s* among
Gal 5:20 ... selfish ambition, dissension, *d*,
Titus 3:10 ... are causing *d-s* among you,

DIVORCE (n) *the action or an instance of legally dissolving a marriage*
Deut 24:1 ... a document of *d*, hands it to
Mal 2:16 ... "For I hate *d*!" says the
Matt 19:8 ... Moses permitted *d* only as a

DIVORCE, DIVORCED, DIVORCES (v) *to dissolve a marriage; to end a relationship*
Lev 21:7 ... a woman who is *d-d* from her
Lev 21:14 ... who is *d*, or a woman
Lev 22:13 ... a widow or is *d-d* and has no
Num 30:9 ... is a widow or is *d-d*, she must
Deut 22:19 ... and he may never *d* her.
1 Chr 8:8 ... After Shaharaim *d-d* his wives
Jer 3:1 ... If a man *d-s* a woman and
Jer 3:8 ... saw that I *d-d* faithless Israel
Matt 5:31 ... A man can *d* his wife by
Matt 5:32 ... a man who *d-s* his wife, unless
Matt 5:32 ... who marries a *d-d* woman also
Mark 10:2 ... be allowed to *d* his wife?
Mark 10:11 ... Whoever *d-s* his wife and
Mark 10:12 ... if a woman *d-s* her husband
Luke 16:18 ... a man who *d-s* his wife and
Luke 16:18 ... marries a woman *d-d* from

DOG, DOGS (n) *a carnivorous (usually domestic) mammal similar to wolves and coyotes*
Prov 26:11 ... As a *d* returns to its
Eccl 9:4 ... to be a live *d* than a dead
Matt 15:26 ... throw it to the *d-s*.
Phil 3:2 ... Watch out for those *d-s*,
2 Pet 2:22 ... this proverb: "A *d* returns to

DONKEY (n) *a domestic mammal smaller than the horse and having long ears*
Num 22:30 ... same *d* you have ridden
Matt 21:5 ... riding on a *d*—riding on a
2 Pet 2:16 ... when his *d* rebuked him

DOOR, DOORS (n) *a barrier by which an entry is closed and opened; a means of access or participation*
Ps 24:7 ... Open up, ancient *d-s*, and let
Matt 7:7 ... the *d* will be opened to you.
Luke 13:24 ... enter the narrow *d* to God's
Acts 14:27 ... had opened the *d* of faith to
1 Cor 16:9 ... is a wide-open *d* for a great
2 Cor 2:12 ... opened a *d* of opportunity
Rev 3:20 ... stand at the *d* and knock.

DOUBT, DOUBTS (n) *uncertainty of belief or opinion; lack of confidence; distrust*
Mark 11:23 ... have no *d* in your heart.
Luke 24:38 ... hearts filled with *d*?
Rom 14:23 ... if you have *d-s* about whether

DOUBT (v) *to distrust; to be uncertain*
Matt 14:31 ... Why did you *d* me?
Matt 21:21 ... faith and don't *d*, you

DRAGON (n) *a huge serpent*
Rev 12:7 ... fought against the *d* and his
Rev 20:2 ... He seized the *d*—that old

DREAM, DREAMS (n) *a strongly desired goal or purpose; a series of thoughts, images, or emotions occurring during sleep*
Prov 13:12 ... sick, but a *d* fulfilled is a
Prov 13:19 ... pleasant to see *d-s* come true,
Eccl 5:3 ... gives you restless *d-s*;

DREAM (v) *to have a dream*
Joel 2:28 ... old men will *d* dreams.
Acts 2:17 ... old men will *d* dreams.

DRINK, DRINKING, DRINKS (v) *to swallow; to partake of alcoholic beverages*
1 Sam 1:13 ... she had been *d-ing*.
Isa 5:22 ... who are heroes at *d-ing* wine
Isa 12:3 ... you will *d* deeply from
Matt 26:27 ... Each of you *d* from it,
Mark 16:18 ... *d* anything poisonous,
John 4:13 ... Anyone who *d-s* this water
John 6:54 ... my flesh and *d-s* my blood has
Rom 14:17 ... we eat or *d*, but of living a
1 Cor 11:27 ... this bread or *d-s* this cup of
Rev 14:10 ... *d* the wine of God's anger.
Rev 22:17 ... who desires *d* freely from

DRINKER, DRINKERS (n) *a person who drinks alcoholic beverages*
1 Tim 3:3 ... not be a heavy *d* or be violent.
1 Tim 3:8 ... not be heavy *d-s* or dishonest
Titus 2:3 ... or be heavy *d-s*.

DROWNED (v) *to suffocate by submersion especially in water*
Exod 15:4 ... officers are *d* in the Red
Matt 18:6 ... neck and be *d* in the depths
Heb 11:29 ... they were all *d*.

DRUNK (adj) *having the faculties impaired by alcohol; intoxicated*
Acts 2:15 ... These people are not *d*, as

DRUNKARD, DRUNKARDS (n) *one who is habitually drunk*
Prov 23:20 ... not carouse with *d-s* or feast
Matt 11:19 ... glutton and a *d*, and a friend
1 Cor 5:11 ... or is a *d*, or cheats people.
1 Cor 6:10 ... greedy people, or *d-s*, or are

DRY (adj) *free or relatively free from a liquid, especially water*
Gen 1:9 ... so *d* ground may appear.
Exod 14:16 ... of the sea on *d* ground.
Josh 3:17 ... Covenant stood on *d* ground
Isa 53:2 ... a root in *d* ground.

DUST (n) *specks or clumps of earthy matter; ground or earth*
Gen 2:7 ... man from the *d* of the ground.
Gen 3:19 ... were made from *d*, and to *d*
Ps 22:15 ... laid me in the *d* and left me
Eccl 3:20 ... they return to *d*.
Matt 10:14 ... shake its *d* from your feet
1 Cor 15:47 ... from the *d* of the earth,

E

EAGLE, EAGLES (n) *any of various large diurnal birds of prey noted for their strength, size, keenness of vision, and powers of flight*
Deut 32:11 ... Like an *e* that rouses her chicks
Isa 40:31 ... soar high on wings like *e-s*.
Rev 4:7 ... was like an *e* in flight.
Rev 12:14 ... wings like those of a great *e*

EARNEST (adj) *characterized by or proceeding from an intense and serious state of mind; ardent or fervent*
Jas 5:16 ... The *e* prayer of a righteous
1 Pet 4:7 ... be and disciplined

EARNESTLY (adv) *in a manner that is intense and serious; fervently*
2 Chr 15:15 ... they *e* sought after God,
Col 4:12 ... He always prays *e* for you,

EARS (n) *the external organ for hearing, expressing the entire faculty of understanding*
Prov 2:2 ... Tune your *e* to wisdom,
Eccl 5:1 ... *e* open and your mouth shut.
2 Tim 4:3 ... whatever their itching *e* want

EARTH (n) *The ground; the planet on which we live*
Gen 1:1 ... created the heavens and the *e*.
Gen 7:24 ... floodwaters covered the *e*
Gen 14:19 ... Creator of heaven and *e*,
Job 26:7 ... and hangs the *e* on nothing.
Job 38:4 ... I laid the foundations of the *e*?
Ps 24:1 ... The *e* is the Lord's, and
Ps 108:5 ... your glory shine over all the *e*.
Prov 8:23 ... first, before the *e* began.
Prov 8:26 ... had made the *e* and fields
Isa 6:3 ... whole *e* is filled with his glory!
Isa 40:22 ... God sits above the circle of the *e*.
Isa 44:23 ... O depths of the *e*!
Isa 55:9 ... higher than the *e*, so my ways
Isa 65:17 ... new heavens and a new *e*,
Isa 66:1 ... and the *e* is my footstool.
Jer 23:24 ... in all the heavens and *e*?
Hab 2:20 ... Let all the *e* be silent
Matt 5:18 ... until heaven and *e* disappear.
Matt 5:35 ... do not say, 'By the *e*!'
Matt 6:10 ... your will be done on *e*,
Matt 16:19 ... Whatever you forbid on *e*
Matt 28:18 ... in heaven and on *e*.
Luke 2:14 ... and peace on *e*
Acts 4:24 ... Creator of heaven and *e*,
Acts 7:49 ... the *e* is my footstool.
Rom 8:39 ... or in the *e* below—
1 Cor 10:26 ... the *e* is the Lord's,
Eph 3:15 ... in heaven and on *e*.
Phil 2:10 ... in heaven and on *e* and under
Col 3:2 ... not the things of *e*.
Heb 1:10 ... laid the foundation of the *e*
2 Pet 3:13 ... and new *e* he has promised,
Rev 20:11 ... the *e* and sky fled
Rev 21:1 ... a new heaven and a new *e*,
Rev 21:1 ... the old *e* had disappeared.

EAST (n) *the general direction of the sunrise*
Gen 2:8 ... a garden in Eden in the *e*,
Ps 103:12 ... far from us as the *e* is from

EAT, EATEN, EATING, EATS (v) *to ingest, chew, and swallow in turn*
see also ATE
Gen 2:16 ... You may freely *e* the fruit
Gen 3:11 ... Have you *e-en* from the tree
Deut 14:4 ... the animals you may *e*:
Isa 65:25 ... The lion will *e* hay
Jer 31:29 ... parents have *e-en* sour grapes,
Matt 26:26 ... Take this and *e* it,

Luke 15:2 ... sinful people—even *e-ing* with
John 6:52 ... give us his flesh to *e*?
John 6:54 ... anyone who *e-s* my flesh and
Acts 10:13 ... "Get up, Peter; kill and *e* them.
Acts 10:14 ... I have never *e-en* anything
Rom 14:15 ... Don't let your *e-ing* ruin
1 Cor 8:4 ... So, what about *e-ing* meat that
1 Cor 8:10 ... *e-ing* in the temple of an idol,
1 Cor 10:31 ... So whether you *e* or drink,
1 Cor 11:26 ... every time you *e* this bread
1 Cor 11:27 ... anyone who *e-s* this bread or

EDEN (n) *the garden where Adam and Eve first lived*
Gen 2:8 ... a garden in *E* in the east,
Ezek 28:13 ... in *E*, the garden of God.

EDIFY, EDIFYING (KJV)
1 Cor 10:23 ... but not everything is *beneficial*
1 Cor 14:5 ... will be *strengthened*
1 Cor 14:17 ... won't *strengthen* the people
Eph 4:12 ... work and *build up* the church,

ELECT (KJV)
Isa 42:1 ... *chosen one*, who pleases me
Matt 24:31 ... gather his *chosen ones* from all
Rom 8:33 ... us whom God has *chosen* for
Col 3:12 ... *chose* you to be the holy people
2 Tim 2:10 ... Jesus to *those God has chosen*

ELIJAH Powerful prophet in Israel (northern kingdom); proclaimed drought (1 Kgs 17:1; Jas 5:17); hid and was fed by ravens (1 Kgs 17:2-6); performed miracles for widow (1 Kgs 17:8-24; Luke 4:25); proclaimed truth to King Ahab (1 Kgs 18:1-15); defeated Baal and his prophets on Mount Carmel (1 Kgs 18:16-40); brought rain (1 Kgs 18:41-46; Jas 5:17); ran for his life (1 Kgs 19:3); served by angels (1 Kgs 19:1-9); given assurance by God (1 Kgs 19:9-18); put mantle on Elisha (1 Kgs 19:19-21); condemned by Ahab (1 Kgs 21:17-29); whirlwind and fire took him into heaven (2 Kgs 2:11); return prophesied and expected (Mal 4:5-6; Matt 11:14; Luke 1:17; John 1:25); compared to John the Baptist (Matt 17:9-13; Mark 9:9-13; Luke 1:17); appeared at Jesus' Transfiguration (Matt 17:1-8; Mark 9:1-8).

ELISHA Powerful prophet in Israel (northern kingdom) who replaced Elijah (1 Kgs 19:16-21); inherited Elijah's cloak (2 Kgs 2:1-18); asked for double measure of spirit (2 Kgs 2:9); witnessed Elijah's departure (2 Kgs 2:11-12); healed bad water (2 Kgs 2:19-22); cursed 42 mockers (2 Kgs 2:23-25); prophesied victory over Moab (2 Kgs 3:11-27); provided abundant oil for widow (2 Kgs 4:1-7); raised child to life (2 Kgs 4:32-37); made stew edible (2 Kgs 4:38-41); fed a multitude with few loaves (2 Kgs 4:42-44); healed Naaman's leprosy (2 Kgs 5:14-15); made an ax head float (2 Kgs 6:1-7); prophesied the availability of food (2 Kgs 7:1); prophesied death of Ben-hadad (2 Kgs 8:7-15); died (2 Kgs 13:20); bones produced miracle after death (2 Kgs 13:21).

EMPTY (adj) *containing nothing; having no purpose or result; destitute of effect or force*
Gen 1:2 ... formless and *e*, and darkness
Deut 32:47 ... not *e* words—they are your life!
Job 26:7 ... the northern sky over *e* space

Isa 45:18 ... not to be a place of *e* chaos.
Jer 4:23 ... and it was *e* and formless.
Luke 1:53 ... the rich away with *e* hands.
Luke 14:9 ... be talking into *e* space.
1 Pet 1:18 ... to save you from the *e* life
2 Pet 2:18 ... with *e*, foolish boasting.

ENCOURAGE, ENCOURAGED, ENCOURAGES, ENCOURAGING (v) *to inspire with courage or hope; to spur on*
Isa 41:7 ... The carver *e-s* the goldsmith,
Acts 11:23 ... and he *e-d* the believers
Acts 15:32 ... length to the believers, *e-ing*
Acts 20:1 ... sent for the believers and *e-d*
Acts 28:15 ... he was *e-d* and thanked God.
Rom 1:12 ... I also want to be *e-d* by yours.
Rom 12:8 ... your gift is to *e* others,
1 Cor 8:12 ... other believers by *e-ing*
1 Cor 14:3 ... strengthens others, *e-s* them,
2 Cor 7:6 ... who *e-s* those who are
2 Cor 7:6 ... *e-d* us by the arrival of Titus.
2 Cor 7:13 ... have been greatly *e-d* by this.
Eph 6:22 ... how we are doing and to *e*
Col 4:8 ... how we are doing and to *e* you.
1 Thes 2:12 ... pleaded with you, *e-d* you,
1 Thes 3:2 ... to strengthen you, to *e* you
1 Thes 3:7 ... we have been greatly *e-d* in
1 Thes 5:11 ... So *e* each other and build
1 Thes 5:14 ... *E* those who are timid.
Titus 1:9 ... he will be able to *e* others
Heb 12:5 ... you forgotten the *e-ing* words
1 Pet 5:12 ... purpose in writing is to *e* you
2 Jn 1:11 ... Anyone who *e-s* such people

ENCOURAGEMENT (n) *the act of encouraging; the state of being encouraged*
Rom 15:5 ... who gives this patience and *e*,
1 Cor 16:18 ... a wonderful *e* to me,
2 Cor 7:13 ... In addition to our own *e*,
Eph 4:29 ... an *e* to those who hear them.
Phil 2:1 ... any *e* from belonging to Christ?
Phlm 1:20 ... Give me this *e* in Christ.

END, ENDS (n) *the point where something ceases to exist; death and destruction; the goal or result toward which some action or agent is heading*
Ps 65:8 ... live at the *e-s* of the earth stand
Eccl 3:11 ... work from beginning to *e*.
Isa 30:8 ... stand until the *e* of time
Isa 49:6 ... bring my salvation to the *e-s*
Matt 24:13 ... the one who endures to the *e*
Matt 24:14 ... and then the *e* will come.
Matt 24:31 ... farthest *e-s* of the earth
1 Cor 15:24 ... After that the *e* will come,
Phil 3:14 ... press on to reach the *e*
Rev 21:6 ... the Beginning and the *E*.
Rev 22:13 ... the Beginning and the *E*.

END, ENDING, ENDS (v) *to come to an end; to die*
1 Sam 12:23 ... sin against the LORD by *e-ing*
Prov 14:12 ... but it *e-s* in death.
Prov 14:13 ... the laughter *e-s*, the grief
Prov 29:23 ... Pride *e-s* in humiliation,
Isa 9:7 ... its peace will never *e*.
Eph 2:15 ... by *e-ing* the system of law

ENDURANCE (n) *the ability to withstand hardship or adversity*
see also PERSEVERANCE
Rom 5:3 ... they help us develop *e*.
Col 1:11 ... have all the *e* and patience
2 Thes 1:4 ... your *e* and faithfulness
Heb 12:1 ... let us run with *e* the race
Jas 1:3 ... your faith is tested, your *e*

2 Pet 1:6 ... self-control with patient *e*,
Rev 1:9 ... in the patient *e* to which Jesus

ENDURE, ENDURED, ENDURES, ENDURING (v) *to withstand, suffer, or persevere*
see also PERSEVERE
Ps 89:2 ... Your faithfulness is as *e-ing* as
Ps 136:1 ... faithful love *e-s* forever.
Matt 10:22 ... everyone who *e-s* to the end
Mark 13:13 ... one who *e-s* to the end
1 Cor 13:7 ... *e-s* through every
2 Cor 1:6 ... Then you can patiently *e*
2 Cor 6:4 ... patiently *e* troubles and
2 Tim 2:3 ... *E* suffering along with me,
2 Tim 2:12 ... If we *e* hardship,
2 Tim 3:11 ... suffering I have *e-d*.
Heb 12:2 ... he *e-d* the cross,
Heb 12:3 ... hostility he *e-d* from sinful
Heb 12:7 ... As you *e* this divine discipline,
Jas 1:12 ... who patiently *e* testing and
Jas 5:11 ... those who *e* under suffering.
1 Pet 2:19 ... patiently *e* unjust treatment.
Rev 13:10 ... must *e* persecution patiently

ENEMY, ENEMIES (n) *foe—personal, national, or spiritual*
Ps 23:5 ... the presence of my *e-ies*.
Ps 62:7 ... rock where no *e* can reach me.
Prov 16:7 ... even their *e-ies* are at peace
Prov 24:17 ... rejoice when your *e-ies* fall;
Prov 25:21 ... If your *e-ies* are hungry,
Prov 27:6 ... than many kisses from an *e*.
Isa 51:13 ... fear the anger of your *e-ies*?
Isa 59:18 ... repay his *e-ies* for their evil
Matt 5:44 ... love your *e-ies*! Pray for those
Luke 6:35 ... Love your *e-ies*! Do good to
Luke 10:19 ... over all the power of the *e*,
Rom 5:10 ... while we were still his *e-ies*,
Rom 12:20 ... If your *e-ies* are hungry,
1 Cor 15:25 ... until he humbles all his *e-ies*
1 Cor 15:26 ... the last *e* to be destroyed
Phil 3:18 ... they are really *e-ies* of the cross
Jas 4:4 ... makes you an *e* of God?
1 Pet 5:8 ... Watch out for your great *e*,

ENTER, ENTERED, ENTERING, ENTERS (v) *to go or come in*
Ps 100:4 ... *E* his gates with thanksgiving
Matt 5:20 ... you will never *e* the Kingdom
Matt 7:13 ... *e* God's Kingdom only
Matt 19:23 ... rich person to *e* the
Mark 9:43 ... *e* eternal life with only
Mark 10:23 ... for the rich to *e* the
Luke 11:52 ... prevent others from *e-ing*.
Luke 13:24 ... Work hard to *e* the narrow
Luke 18:17 ... like a child will never *e* it.
John 3:5 ... no one can *e* the Kingdom
John 10:2 ... who *e-s* through the gate
Rom 5:12 ... When Adam sinned, sin *e-ed*
Heb 3:11 ... will never *e* my place of rest.
Heb 4:1 ... God's promise of *e-ing* his rest
Heb 4:11 ... do our best to *e* that rest.
Heb 9:12 ... of goats and calves—he *e-ed*

ENTHRONED (v) *to seat ceremonially on a throne or in a place associated with power and authority*
1 Sam 4:4 ... *e* between the cherubim.
2 Kgs 19:15 ... *e* between the mighty
1 Chr 13:6 ... *e* between the cherubim.
Ps 22:3 ... you are holy, *e* on the praises
Ps 113:5 ... God, who is *e* on high?
Isa 37:16 ... God of Israel, you are *e*

ENTHUSIASM (n) *strong excitement of feeling; zeal, fervor, passion*
Neh 4:6 ... the people had worked with **e.**
Prov 19:2 ... **E** without knowledge
Rom 10:2 ... I know what **e** they have
2 Cor 8:7 ... your **e,** and your love
2 Cor 8:16 ... Titus the same **e** for you
2 Cor 9:2 ... your **e** that stirred up
Eph 6:7 ... Work with **e,** as though

ENTHUSIASTIC (adj) *filled with or marked by zeal, fervor, or passion*
Ps 45:15 ... a joyful and **e** procession
Acts 18:25 ... about Jesus with an **e** spirit
Rom 15:17 ... I have reason to be **e** about

ENTRUST, ENTRUSTED (v) *to commit to another with confidence*
Ps 31:5 ... I **e** my spirit into your hand.
Luke 12:48 ... has been **e-ed** with much,
Luke 23:46 ... I **e** my spirit into your
Acts 15:40 ... left, the believers **e-ed** him
Acts 20:32 ... And now I **e** you to God
Rom 3:2 ... Jews were **e-ed** with the whole
1 Thes 2:4 ... to be **e-ed** with the Good News.
1 Tim 1:11 ... Good News **e-ed** to me
2 Tim 1:14 ... truth that has been **e-ed** to you.
1 Pet 5:2 ... flock that God has **e-ed** to you.

ENVY (n) *discontent or resentment because of another's success, advantages, or superiority*
see also JEALOUSY
Mark 7:22 ... lustful desires, **e,** slander,
Rom 1:29 ... sin, greed, hate, **e,** murder,
Gal 5:21 ... **e,** drunkenness, wild parties,
Titus 3:3 ... full of evil and **e,** and we hated
Jas 4:5 ... within us is filled with **e?**

ENVY (v) *to feel or show envy; to begrudge*
Prov 3:31 ... Don't **e** violent people
Prov 24:1 ... Don't **e** evil people

EPILEPTIC (adj) *relating to, affected with, or having characteristics of epilepsy*
Matt 4:24 ... were demon-possessed or **e** or

EQUIP (v) *to prepare; to furnish for service or action*
Eph 4:12 ... to **e** God's people to do
2 Tim 3:17 ... to prepare and **e** his people
Heb 13:21 ... **e** you with all you need

ESCAPE (n) *evasion of something undesirable*
1 Thes 5:3 ... there will be no **e.**

ESCAPE, ESCAPED, ESCAPING (v) *to avoid; to get free of or break away from*
Ps 89:48 ... can **e** the power of the grave.
Ps 139:7 ... I can never **e** from your Spirit!
Matt 23:33 ... will you **e** the judgment
1 Cor 3:15 ... barely **e-ing** through a wall of
Heb 2:3 ... think we can **e** if we ignore
Heb 12:25 ... we will certainly not **e** if we
2 Pet 2:18 ... those who have barely **e-d**
2 Pet 2:20 ... **e** from the wickedness

ETERNAL (adj) *having infinite duration; valid or existing at all times*
see also EVERLASTING, FOREVER
Gen 9:16 ... will remember the **e** covenant
Exod 3:15 ... my **e** name, my name to
Lev 24:8 ... expression of the **e** covenant
Num 18:19 ... an **e** and unbreakable
Ps 119:142 ... Your justice is **e,**
Jer 50:5 ... with an **e** covenant

Dan 4:34 ... and his kingdom is **e.**
Dan 7:14 ... His rule is **e**—
Matt 18:8 ... better to enter **e** life with
Matt 19:16 ... must I do to have **e** life?
Matt 25:41 ... into the **e** fire prepared
Matt 25:46 ... away into **e** punishment,
Mark 3:29 ... a sin with **e** consequences.
Luke 10:25 ... should I do to inherit **e** life?
Luke 18:18 ... should I do to inherit **e** life?
John 3:15 ... in him will have **e** life.
John 3:16 ... not perish but have **e** life.
John 3:36 ... believes in God's Son has **e**
John 5:29 ... will rise to experience **e** life,
John 5:39 ... you think they give you **e** life.
John 6:68 ... the words that give **e** life.
John 12:50 ... his commands lead to **e** life;
John 17:2 ... He gives **e** life prepared for
Rom 1:20 ... **e** power and divine nature
Rom 5:21 ... resulting in **e** life through
Rom 6:23 ... free gift of God is **e** life
Rom 9:5 ... is worthy of **e** praise! Amen.
Rom 16:26 ... the **e** God has commanded,
Eph 3:11 ... This was his **e** plan,
2 Thes 1:9 ... punished with **e** destruction,
1 Tim 6:12 ... Hold tightly to the **e** life
Titus 3:7 ... we will inherit **e** life.
Heb 5:9 ... source of **e** salvation
Heb 9:15 ... **e** inheritance God has
Heb 13:20 ... an **e** covenant with his blood—
1 Pet 1:23 ... from the **e,** living word
1 Pet 5:10 ... to share in his **e** glory
1 Jn 1:2 ... he is the one who is **e** life.
1 Jn 2:25 ... we enjoy the **e** life he
1 Jn 5:20 ... and he is **e** life.
Jude 1:7 ... the **e** fire of God's judgment.
Jude 1:21 ... who will bring you **e** life.

ETERNITY (n) *immortality; infinite time*
Eccl 3:11 ... has planted **e** in the human
Isa 57:15 ... who lives in **e,** the Holy One,
John 12:25 ... will keep it for **e.**

EVERLASTING (adj) *continuing indefinitely*
see also ETERNAL, FOREVER
Gen 17:7 ... This is the **e** covenant:
Gen 48:4 ... as an **e** possession.
2 Sam 23:5 ... made an **e** covenant with
Ps 139:24 ... lead me along the path of **e** life.
Isa 9:6 ... God, **E** Father, Prince of Peace.
Isa 35:10 ... crowned with **e** joy.
Isa 40:28 ... The LORD is the **e** God,
Isa 54:8 ... But with **e** love
Isa 55:3 ... an **e** covenant with you.
Isa 60:19 ... God will be your **e** light,
Isa 60:20 ... the LORD will be your **e** light.
Isa 61:7 ... and **e** joy will be yours.
Isa 61:8 ... an **e** covenant with them.
Jer 10:10 ... the living God and the **e** King!
Jer 31:3 ... with an **e** love.
Ezek 16:60 ... establish an **e** covenant with
Dan 4:34 ... His rule is **e,**
Dan 9:24 ... to bring in **e** righteousness,
Dan 12:2 ... to **e** life and some to shame
Gal 6:8 ... will harvest **e** life from the

EVIL (adj) *bad, sinful, or morally reprehensible; of the devil*
Gen 6:5 ... was consistently and totally **e.**
Exod 32:22 ... know how **e** these people
Ps 51:4 ... what is **e** in your sight.
Ps 140:8 ... not let **e** people have their way.
Prov 15:26 ... The LORD detests **e** plans,
Matt 6:13 ... rescue us from the **e** one.
Matt 12:45 ... spirits more **e** than itself,
Matt 15:19 ... from the heart come **e**
Mark 7:21 ... heart, come **e** thoughts,

Luke 11:24 ... When an **e** spirit leaves
John 17:15 ... them safe from the **e** one.
Acts 19:13 ... casting out **e** spirits.
Rom 2:9 ... keeps on doing what is **e**—
Rom 13:14 ... to indulge your **e** desires.
1 Cor 5:13 ... remove the **e** person from
Eph 5:16 ... in these **e** days.
Col 3:5 ... lust, and **e** desires.
2 Thes 3:3 ... guard you from the **e** one.
1 Tim 6:4 ... slander, and **e** suspicions.
2 Tim 3:13 ... **e** people and impostors
1 Jn 2:13 ... your battle with the **e** one.
1 Jn 3:12 ... who belonged to the **e** one
1 Jn 5:18 ... the **e** one cannot touch

EVIL (n) *something that brings sorrow, distress, or misfortune*
Gen 2:9 ... the knowledge of good and **e.**
Gen 3:5 ... knowing both good and **e.**
Judg 6:1 ... The Israelites did **e**
Ps 5:5 ... for you hate all who do **e.**
Ps 14:4 ... those who do **e** never learn?
Ps 34:13 ... tongue from speaking **e**
Ps 37:27 ... Turn from **e** and do good,
Ps 45:7 ... You love justice and hate **e.**
Ps 53:4 ... those who do **e** never learn?
Ps 92:15 ... There is no **e** in him!
Ps 101:4 ... and stay away from every **e.**
Ps 125:5 ... with those who do **e.**
Prov 6:18 ... a heart that plots **e,**
Prov 8:13 ... fear the LORD will hate **e.**
Prov 11:27 ... search for **e,** it will find you!
Prov 13:6 ... but the **e** are misled by sin.
Prov 17:13 ... repay good with **e,** **e** will
Prov 20:30 ... cleanses away **e;** such
Isa 5:20 ... those who say that **e** is good
Isa 13:11 ... punish the world for its **e**
Jer 23:14 ... who are doing **e** so that
Hab 1:13 ... cannot stand the sight of **e.**
Mal 3:15 ... those who do **e** get rich,
Matt 5:45 ... to both the **e** and the good,
Luke 13:27 ... all you who do **e.**
John 3:20 ... All who do **e** hate the light
Rom 12:21 ... Don't let **e** conquer you,
1 Cor 14:20 ... babies when it comes to **e,**
1 Thes 5:15 ... no one pays back **e** for **e,**
1 Thes 5:22 ... away from every kind of **e.**
1 Tim 6:10 ... the root of all kinds of **e.**
2 Tim 2:19 ... must turn away from **e.**
Heb 1:9 ... You love justice and hate **e.**
Jas 1:21 ... get rid of all the filth and **e**
Jas 3:8 ... It is restless and **e,**
1 Pet 2:16 ... as an excuse to do **e.**
1 Pet 3:9 ... Don't repay **e** for **e.**
1 Pet 3:11 ... Turn away from **e** and do
3 Jn 1:11 ... those who do **e** prove that they

EVILDOERS (n) *one who does evil*
Ps 92:7 ... like weeds and flourish,
Ps 92:9 ... perish; all **e** will be scattered.
Ps 94:16 ... will stand up for me against **e?**
Prov 21:15 ... it terrifies **e.**
Prov 24:19 ... Don't fret because of **e;**

EXALT, EXALTED, EXALTING, EXALTS (v) *to elevate; to glorify; to raise in rank or power*
see also GLORIFY, HONOR
Exod 15:2 ... and I will **e** him!
2 Sam 22:47 ... of my salvation, be **e-ed!**
Neh 9:5 ... be **e-ed** above all blessing
Job 36:7 ... kings and **e-s** them forever.
Ps 18:46 ... God of my salvation be **e-ed!**
Ps 30:1 ... I will **e** you, LORD,
Ps 92:8 ... O LORD, will be **e-ed** forever.
Ps 97:9 ... you are **e-ed** far above all gods.
Ps 107:32 ... Let them **e** him publicly

Ps 145:1 ... I will *e* you, my God and King,
Dan 11:36 ... as he pleases, *e-ing* himself
Luke 14:11 ... those who *e* themselves will
Acts 2:33 ... is *e-ed* to the place of highest
2 Thes 2:4 ... He will *e* himself

EXAMINE, EXAMINED, EXAMINES, EXAMINING (v) *to test the condition of; to inspect closely*
1 Chr 29:17 ... you *e* our hearts
Ps 11:4 ... *e-ing* every person on earth.
Ps 11:5 ... The LORD *e-s* both
Ps 17:3 ... *e-d* my heart in the night.
Ps 139:1 ... LORD, you have *e-d* my heart
Prov 5:21 ... *e-ing* every path he takes.
Prov 21:2 ... the LORD *e-s* their heart.
Jer 11:20 ... you *e* the deepest thoughts
Jer 17:10 ... and *e* secret motives.
Lam 3:40 ... let us test and *e* our ways.
1 Cor 4:4 ... Lord himself who will *e*
1 Cor 11:28 ... you should *e* yourself
2 Cor 13:5 ... *E* yourselves to see
1 Thes 2:4 ... He alone *e-s* the motives

EXAMPLE, EXAMPLES (n) *one that serves as a pattern to be or not to be imitated*
John 13:15 ... given you an *e* to
1 Cor 10:11 ... happened to them as *e-s* for
2 Thes 3:9 ... give you an *e* to follow.
Titus 2:7 ... *e* to them by doing good
Heb 13:7 ... and follow the *e* of their faith.
Jas 5:10 ... For *e-s* of patience in suffering,
1 Pet 2:21 ... He is your *e*, and you must

EXCUSE (n) *the apology or justification offered*
John 15:22 ... they have no *e* for their sin.
Rom 1:20 ... no *e* for not knowing God.
Rom 2:1 ... and you have no *e*!
1 Pet 2:16 ... your freedom as an *e*

EXCUSE (v) *to overlook, justify, or make an apology for*
Exod 34:7 ... But I do not *e* the guilty.
Eph 5:6 ... those who try to *e* these sins,

EXHORT(ATION) (KJV)
Rom 12:8 ... If your gift is to *encourage*
1 Thes 2:3 ... not *preaching* with any deceit
Heb 3:13 ... You must *warn* each other

EXORCISTS (n) *one who expels evil spirits*
Luke 11:19 ... what about your own *e*?

EXPLAIN, EXPLAINED, EXPLAINS (v) *to make plain or understandable; to give the reason or cause*
Gen 2:24 ... This *e-s* why a man leaves his
Neh 8:8 ... and clearly *e-ed* the meaning
Matt 19:5 ... This *e-s* why a man leaves his
Acts 17:3 ... He *e-ed* the prophecies
Acts 18:28 ... *e-ed* to them that Jesus was
Eph 6:19 ... *e* God's mysterious plan
2 Tim 2:15 ... correctly *e-s* the word of
1 Pet 3:15 ... always be ready to *e* it.

EXPLOIT (v) *to make use of meanly or unfairly for one's own advantage*
Exod 22:22 ... not *e* a widow or an orphan.
Prov 22:22 ... or *e* the needy in court.

EXPLOITED (n) *one unfairly used for another's advantage*
Isa 11:4 ... fair decisions for the *e*.

EXTOL(LED) (KJV)
Ps 30:1 ... will *exalt* you, LORD, for you

Ps 66:17 ... to him for help, *praising* him
Ps 68:4 ... *Sing loud praises* to him who
Isa 52:13 ... he will be *highly exalted*

EYE, EYES (n) *organ of (physical and spiritual) sight*
Exod 21:24 ... an *e* for an *e*,
Deut 16:19 ... bribes blind the *e-s* of
Job 36:7 ... never takes his *e-s* off the
Ps 119:18 ... Open my *e-s* to see
Ps 119:37 ... Turn my *e-s* from worthless
Ps 123:1 ... I lift my *e-s* to you,
Prov 4:25 ... and fix your *e-s* on what
Matt 5:29 ... *e*—causes you to lust,
Matt 5:38 ... An *e* for an *e*,
Matt 6:22 ... When your *e* is healthy,
1 Cor 2:9 ... when they say, "No *e* has seen,
Heb 12:2 ... by keeping our *e-s* on Jesus,
2 Pet 1:16 ... with our own *e-s*
Rev 21:4 ... wipe every tear from their *e-s*,

F

FACE (n) *in or into direct contact or confrontation (as in "face to face"); countenance; presence; the front part of the head*
Gen 32:30 ... I have seen God *f* to *f*,
Exod 33:11 ... speak to Moses *f* to *f*,
Exod 34:29 ... his *f* had become radiant
Num 12:8 ... I speak to him *f* to *f*,
Deut 31:17 ... hiding my *f* from them,
Judg 6:22 ... angel of the LORD *f* to *f*!
2 Chr 7:14 ... and seek my *f* and turn from
Ps 4:6 ... Let your *f* smile on us,
Ps 17:15 ... I will see you *f* to *f*
Ps 67:1 ... May his *f* smile with favor
Luke 9:29 ... appearance of his *f* was
2 Cor 3:7 ... For his *f* shone with the glory
Rev 1:16 ... And his *f* was like the sun
Rev 22:4 ... they will see his *f*,

FACE, FACED, FACING (v) *to confront; to be confronted by*
Ps 112:8 ... *f* their foes triumphantly.
Ps 116:6 ... I was *f-ing* death, and he saved
2 Cor 6:5 ... *f-d* angry mobs,

FADE, FADING (v) *to lose freshness, strength, or vitality*
Isa 40:7 ... and the flowers *f*
1 Cor 9:25 ... to win a prize that will *f*
2 Cor 3:7 ... brightness was already *f-ing*
2 Cor 3:13 ... it was destined to *f* away.
Jas 1:11 ... the rich will *f* away
1 Jn 2:17 ... this world is *f-ing* away,

FAIL, FAILED, FAILS (v) *to disappoint; to fall short; to weaken; to miss performing an expected service; to be unsuccessful*
Num 23:19 ... spoken and *f-ed* to act?
Deut 31:6 ... He will neither *f* you
Josh 23:14 ... Not a single one has *f-ed*!
1 Kgs 8:56 ... Not one word has *f-ed*
Ps 77:8 ... his promises permanently *f-ed*?
Luke 13:24 ... try to enter but will *f*.
Luke 22:32 ... faith should not *f*.
Rom 9:6 ... has God *f-ed* to fulfill his promise
2 Cor 13:5 ... if not, you have *f-ed* the test
2 Cor 13:6 ... we have not *f-ed* the test
Heb 12:15 ... none of you *f-s* to receive
Heb 13:5 ... I will never *f* you.
1 Pet 4:19 ... he will never *f* you.

FAINT (adj) *lacking strength or vigor*
Jon 4:8 ... grew *f* and wished to die.

FAINT (v) *to become weak or lose courage in body or spirit*
Isa 40:31 ... will walk and not *f*.

FAIR (adj) *free from self-interest, prejudice, or favoritism; beautiful*
Prov 1:3 ... do what is right, just, and *f*.
Song 2:13 ... away with me, my *f* one!
Isa 11:4 ... make *f* decisions for the
Rom 3:25 ... God was being *f* when he
Rom 3:26 ... he himself is *f* and just,
Col 4:1 ... be just and *f* to your slaves.

FAIRNESS (n) *the quality of being free from self-interest, prejudice, or favoritism*
Ps 9:8 ... rule the nations with *f*.
Ps 98:9 ... and the nations with *f*.
Ps 99:4 ... you have established *f*.
Isa 9:7 ... will rule with *f* and justice

FAITH (n) *reliance, loyalty, or complete trust in God; a system of religious beliefs* see also BELIEVE TRUST
Exod 14:31 ... They put their *f* in the LORD
Isa 7:9 ... Unless your *f* is firm,
Matt 9:2 ... Seeing their *f*, Jesus said
Matt 9:29 ... Because of your *f*, it will
Matt 15:28 ... your *f* is great.
Matt 17:20 ... *f* even as small as a mustard
Matt 21:22 ... if you have *f*, you will receive
Mark 10:52 ... for your *f* has healed you.
Luke 5:20 ... Seeing their *f*, Jesus said
Luke 7:50 ... Your *f* has saved you;
Luke 8:48 ... your *f* has made you well.
Luke 12:28 ... Why do you have so little *f*?
Luke 17:6 ... *f* even as small as a mustard
Luke 18:8 ... find on the earth who have *f*?
John 16:1 ... won't abandon your *f*.
Acts 6:5 ... full of *f* and the Holy Spirit
Acts 14:9 ... he had *f* to be healed.
Acts 14:27 ... opened the door of *f* to the
Acts 16:5 ... strengthened in their *f* and
Acts 24:24 ... told them about *f* in Christ
Rom 1:8 ... *f* in him is being talked about
Rom 1:12 ... to encourage you in your *f*,
Rom 1:17 ... from start to finish by *f*.
Rom 1:17 ... through *f* that a righteous
Rom 3:28 ... right with God through *f*
Rom 3:30 ... right with himself only by *f*,
Rom 3:31 ... only when we have *f*
Rom 4:5 ... because of their *f* in God
Rom 4:9 ... righteous because of his *f*.
Rom 4:12 ... same kind of *f* Abraham had
Rom 4:13 ... with God that comes by *f*.
Rom 4:14 ... then *f* is not necessary
Rom 4:16 ... the promise is received by *f*.
Rom 4:16 ... if we have *f* like Abraham's.
Rom 4:19 ... Abraham's *f* did not weaken,
Rom 4:20 ... In fact, his *f* grew stronger,
Rom 5:1 ... made right in God's sight by *f*,
Rom 5:2 ... Because of our *f*, Christ has
Rom 10:8 ... message about *f* that we preach:
Rom 10:17 ... So *f* comes from hearing,
Rom 12:6 ... speak out with as much *f* as
Rom 14:1 ... believers who are weak in *f*,
1 Cor 12:9 ... gives great *f* to another,
1 Cor 13:13 ... *f*, hope, and love—
1 Cor 15:14 ... and your *f* is useless.
1 Cor 16:13 ... Stand firm in the *f*.
2 Cor 1:24 ... put your *f* into practice.
2 Cor 13:5 ... failed the test of genuine *f*.
Gal 1:23 ... the very *f* he tried to destroy!
Gal 3:9 ... all who put their *f* in Christ
Gal 3:11 ... *f* that a righteous person
Gal 3:12 ... This way of *f* is very different

1713

Gal 3:14 ... Holy Spirit through *f*.
Gal 3:23 ... way of *f* in Christ was available
Gal 3:24 ... made right with God through *f*.
Gal 3:25 ... the way of *f* has come,
Gal 3:26 ... of God through *f* in Christ
Gal 5:5 ... eagerly wait to receive by *f*.
Eph 1:15 ... of your strong *f* in the Lord
Eph 4:5 ... one Lord, one *f*, one baptism,
Eph 6:16 ... hold up the shield of *f*
Phil 1:25 ... experience the joy of your *f*.
Phil 3:9 ... righteous through *f* in Christ.
Col 1:4 ... have heard of your *f* in Christ
1 Thes 1:8 ... telling us about your *f* in God.
1 Thes 3:5 ... your *f* was still strong.
1 Thes 3:10 ... fill the gaps in your *f*.
2 Thes 1:3 ... because your *f* is flourishing
1 Tim 1:4 ... live a life of *f* in God.
1 Tim 1:19 ... Cling to your *f* in Christ,
1 Tim 3:9 ... mystery of the *f* now
1 Tim 4:1 ... will turn away from the true *f*;
1 Tim 6:10 ... have wandered from the true *f*
1 Tim 6:12 ... good fight for the true *f*.
2 Tim 1:5 ... remember your genuine *f*,
2 Tim 2:18 ... away from the *f*.
2 Tim 3:10 ... You know my *f*, my patience,
Titus 1:1 ... have been sent to proclaim *f*
Titus 1:13 ... make them strong in the *f*.
Titus 2:2 ... must have sound *f* and be filled
Phlm 1:5 ... about your *f* in the Lord
Phlm 1:6 ... that comes from your *f*
Heb 4:2 ... they didn't share the *f*
Heb 6:1 ... and placing our *f* in God.
Heb 6:12 ... their *f* and endurance.
Heb 10:38 ... righteous ones will live by *f*.
Heb 11:5 ... It was by *f* that Enoch
Heb 11:7 ... It was by *f* that Noah
Heb 11:8 ... It was by *f* that Abraham
Heb 11:23 ... It was by *f* that Moses' parents
Heb 11:29 ... It was by *f* that the people
Heb 12:2 ... initiates and perfects our *f*.
Jas 1:3 ... when your *f* is tested,
Jas 2:5 ... this world to be rich in *f*?
Jas 2:14 ... Can that kind of *f* save anyone?
Jas 2:17 ... *f* by itself isn't enough.
Jas 2:18 ... Some people have *f*;
Jas 2:20 ... *f* without good deeds
Jas 2:22 ... made his *f* complete.
Jas 2:24 ... what we do, not by *f* alone.
Jas 2:26 ... so also *f* is dead without good
Jas 5:15 ... prayer offered in *f* will heal
1 Pet 1:21 ... have placed your *f* and hope
2 Pet 1:1 ... the same precious *f* we have.
Jude 1:3 ... defend the *f* that God
Jude 1:20 ... in your most holy *f*,

FAITHFUL (adj) *firm in adherence, utterly loyal*
see also LOYAL, TRUSTWORTHY
Deut 7:9 ... He is the *f* God who keeps his
1 Sam 2:9 ... will protect his *f* ones,
1 Sam 20:14 ... me with the *f* love of the
2 Sam 22:26 ... you show yourself *f*; to those
1 Kgs 8:61 ... you be completely *f* to the
1 Kgs 15:14 ... remained completely *f* to
2 Kgs 20:3 ... have always been *f* to you
Ps 18:25 ... you show yourself *f*.
Ps 71:22 ... because you are *f* to your
Ps 89:8 ... You are entirely *f*.
Ps 89:49 ... to David with a *f* pledge.
Ps 143:1 ... you are *f* and righteous.
Isa 38:3 ... have always been *f* to you and
Hos 11:12 ... God and is *f* to the Holy One.
Zech 8:3 ... be called the *f* City;
Zech 8:8 ... I will be *f* and just toward
Matt 24:45 ... A *f*, sensible servant is one
Matt 25:21 ... You have been *f* in handling

Matt 25:23 ... my good and *f* servant.
Luke 12:42 ... Lord replied, "A *f*, sensible
Luke 16:10 ... If you are *f* in little things,
1 Cor 4:17 ... my beloved and *f* child in the
2 Cor 1:18 ... as God is *f*, our word to you
Eph 1:1 ... who are *f* followers of Christ
Phil 2:17 ... just like your *f* service is
Col 4:7 ... brother and *f* helper who
Col 4:9 ... Onesimus, a *f* and beloved
1 Thes 1:3 ... we think of your *f* work,
1 Thes 5:24 ... for he who calls you is *f*.
2 Thes 3:3 ... But the Lord is *f*; he will
1 Tim 3:2 ... He must be *f* to his wife.
1 Tim 3:11 ... and be *f* in everything they
1 Tim 5:9 ... old and was *f* to her husband.
2 Tim 4:7 ... I have remained *f*.
Heb 2:17 ... merciful and *f* High Priest
Heb 3:2 ... For he was *f* to God, who
Heb 8:9 ... They did not remain *f* to my
Heb 13:4 ... marriage, and remain *f* to one
1 Jn 1:9 ... to him, he is *f* and just to
Rev 1:5 ... He is the *f* witness to these
Rev 2:10 ... But if you remain *f* even when
Rev 3:14 ... is the Amen—the *f* and true
Rev 17:14 ... chosen and *f* ones will be

FAITHFULNESS (n) *the quality of steadfast loyalty or firm adherence to promises*
Exod 34:6 ... unfailing love and *f*.
Ps 25:10 ... with unfailing love and *f*
Ps 36:5 ... your *f* reaches beyond
Ps 57:10 ... Your *f* reaches to the clouds.
Ps 92:2 ... your *f* in the evening,
Ps 100:5 ... *f* continues to each
Prov 14:22 ... unfailing love and *f*.
Prov 16:6 ... love and *f* make atonement
Prov 20:28 ... love and *f* protect the king;
Isa 38:18 ... no longer hope in your *f*.
Lam 3:23 ... Great is his *f*;
Gal 5:22 ... kindness, goodness, *f*,
Eph 6:23 ... give you love with *f*.
2 Thes 1:4 ... your endurance and *f*
2 Tim 2:22 ... pursue righteous living, *f*,

FALL, FALLEN, FALLING (v) *to collapse; to drop down (wounded or dead); to become lower in degree or level; to come by assignment or inheritance; to descend; to stumble or stray (morally)*
2 Sam 1:19 ... the mighty heroes have *f-en*!
Ps 37:24 ... they will never *f*,
Ps 69:9 ... who insult you have *f-en* on
Prov 10:8 ... babbling fools *f* flat on their
Prov 24:17 ... when your enemies *f*;
Isa 14:12 ... How you are *f-en* from heaven,
Matt 13:21 ... They *f* away as soon as
Luke 10:18 ... I saw Satan *f* from heaven
Rom 3:23 ... we all *f* short of God's glorious
Rom 14:13 ... believer to stumble and *f*.
Gal 5:4 ... *f-en* away from God's grace.
2 Pet 1:10 ... and you will never *f* away.
Jude 1:24 ... to keep you from *f-ing* away

FALSE (adj) *intentionally untrue; dishonest; misleading; unwise; faithless*
Prov 12:17 ... a *f* witness tells lies.
Isa 44:25 ... I expose the *f* prophets as
Matt 24:11 ... And many *f* prophets will
Mark 13:22 ... For *f* messiahs and *f* prophets
2 Cor 11:13 ... These people are *f* apostles.
Titus 1:11 ... by their *f* teaching.
2 Pet 2:1 ... were also *f* prophets in Israel,
1 Jn 4:1 ... many *f* prophets in the world.
Rev 16:13 ... and the *f* prophet.
Rev 19:20 ... beast and his *f* prophet were
Rev 20:10 ... the beast and the *f* prophet.

FAMILY, FAMILIES (n) *a household unit of related people, as in a clan*
see also HOUSEHOLD
Josh 24:15 ... my *f*, we will serve the LORD.
Ps 68:6 ... God places the lonely in *f-ies*;
Mark 3:25 ... a *f* splintered by feuding
Luke 9:61 ... let me say good-bye to my *f*.
Luke 12:52 ... *f-ies* will be split apart,
Gal 6:10 ... to those in the *f* of faith.
Eph 2:19 ... members of God's *f*.
1 Tim 3:4 ... manage his own *f* well,
Titus 1:11 ... whole *f-ies* away from the truth
1 Jn 3:9 ... have been born into God's *f*

FAST, FASTING (v) *to abstain from food*
Ps 35:13 ... denied myself by *f-ing* for
Matt 6:16 ... when you *f*, don't make it
Acts 13:2 ... worshiping the Lord and *f-ing*,

FATHER, FATHERS (n) *male parent; ancestor(s); characteristic of a mentor or provider relationship; name and role for God in relation to the children he adopts; originator or creator*
see also PARENT
Gen 2:24 ... a man leaves his *f* and mother
Gen 17:4 ... make you the *f* of a multitude
Exod 20:12 ... Honor your *f* and mother.
Exod 21:15 ... Anyone who strikes *f* or
Deut 32:6 ... he your **F** who created you?
2 Sam 7:14 ... I will be his *f*, and he
Ps 2:7 ... Today I have become your **F**.
Ps 89:26 ... You are my **F**, my God,
Prov 10:1 ... wise child brings joy to a *f*;
Prov 23:22 ... Listen to your *f*, who gave you
Isa 9:6 ... Everlasting **F**, Prince of Peace.
Isa 63:16 ... you would still be our **F**.
Jer 3:19 ... forward to your calling me '**F**,'
Ezek 22:10 ... sleep with their *f-s'* wives
Mal 2:10 ... children of the same **F**?
Mal 4:6 ... will turn the hearts of *f-s*
Matt 5:16 ... will praise your heavenly **F**.
Matt 6:9 ... Our **F** in heaven, may your
Matt 6:14 ... heavenly **F** will forgive
Matt 10:37 ... If you love your *f* or mother
Matt 11:27 ... no one truly knows the **F**
Matt 15:4 ... Honor your *f* and mother,
Matt 16:27 ... in the glory of his **F**
Matt 19:5 ... a man leaves his *f* and mother
Matt 19:29 ... or *f* or mother or children
Matt 23:9 ... God in heaven is your **F**.
Luke 1:17 ... hearts of the *f-s* to their
Luke 9:59 ... return home and bury my *f*."
John 4:21 ... you worship the **F** on this
John 5:17 ... My **F** is always working,
John 5:20 ... For the **F** loves the Son
John 6:44 ... come to me unless the **F**
John 6:65 ... unless the **F** gives them
John 8:19 ... you don't know who my **F** is.
John 8:41 ... God himself is our true **F**.
John 10:38 ... understand that the **F** is in me,
John 14:6 ... come to the **F** except through
John 14:21 ... love me, my **F** will love
John 15:8 ... brings great glory to my **F**.
John 15:23 ... also hates my **F**.
John 20:17 ... ascending to my **F** and
Acts 13:33 ... Today I have become your **F**.
Rom 4:11 ... Abraham is the spiritual *f*
Rom 4:16 ... Abraham is the *f* of all who
Rom 8:15 ... we call him, "Abba, **F**."
2 Cor 6:18 ... I will be your **F**, and you
Eph 5:31 ... man leaves his *f* and mother
Eph 6:2 ... Honor your *f* and mother.
Eph 6:4 ... **F-s**, do not provoke
Phil 2:11 ... to the glory of God the **F**.
Col 3:21 ... **F-s**, do not aggravate

Heb 12:7 ... is never disciplined by its *f*?
Heb 12:9 ... earthly *f-s* who disciplined
1 Jn 1:3 ... fellowship is with the *F* and
1 Jn 2:15 ... the love of the *F* in you.
1 Jn 2:22 ... who denies the *F* and the Son
1 Jn 3:1 ... See how very much our *F* loves
Rev 3:21 ... sat with my *F* on his throne.

FAVOR, FAVORS (n) *gracious kindness; approval from a superior; a special privilege or right granted or conceded*
see also GRACE
Gen 6:8 ... Noah found *f* with the LORD.
Exod 34:9 ... if it is true that I have found *f*
1 Sam 2:26 ... and grew in *f* with the LORD
Prov 3:4 ... you will find *f* with both God
Prov 18:22 ... receives *f* from the LORD.
Prov 19:6 ... Many seek *f-s* from a ruler;
Zech 11:7 ... named one *F* and the other
Luke 1:30 ... you have found *f* with God!
Luke 2:40 ... and God's *f* was on him.
Luke 2:52 ... and in *f* with God
Luke 4:19 ... the time of the LORD's *f*
Rom 11:7 ... have not found the *f* of God
Phil 1:7 ... with me the special *f* of God,

FAVOR, FAVORING (v) *to show partiality toward*
Lev 19:15 ... justice in legal matters by *f-ing*
Jas 2:9 ... But if you *f* some people over

FAVORITE (adj) *specially favored or liked*
Gen 27:4 ... Prepare my *f* dish,

FAVORITES (n) *persons specially loved, trusted, or provided with favors*
see also PARTIALITY
Job 32:21 ... I won't play *f*
Matt 22:16 ... and don't play *f*.
Gal 2:6 ... for God has no *f*.
Eph 6:9 ... he has no *f*.
Col 3:25 ... For God has no *f*.

FAVORITISM (n) *the showing of special favor; partiality*
see also DISCRIMINATION, PARTIALITY
Prov 24:23 ... *f* when passing judgment.
Mal 2:9 ... *f* in the way you carry out
Acts 10:34 ... that God shows no *f*.
Rom 2:11 ... God does not show *f*.
Jas 3:17 ... It shows no *f* and is always

FEAR, FEARS (n) *dread or alarm in facing danger; profound reverence and awe*
2 Sam 23:3 ... who rules in the *f* of God,
Ps 2:11 ... Serve the LORD with reverent *f*,
Ps 34:4 ... freed me from all my *f-s*.
Prov 1:33 ... untroubled by *f* of harm.
Heb 13:6 ... will have no *f*.

FEAR, FEARED, FEARING, FEARS (v) *to have reverential awe of God; to be afraid or apprehensive*
Deut 6:13 ... You must *f* the LORD your
Deut 8:6 ... walking in his ways and *f-ing*
Deut 13:4 ... your God and *f* him alone.
Deut 31:12 ... learn to *f* the LORD your God
Josh 4:24 ... might *f* the LORD your God
1 Sam 12:14 ... if you *f* and worship
2 Chr 26:5 ... taught him to *f* God.
Neh 5:15 ... But because I *f-ed* God,
Neh 7:2 ... a faithful man who *f-ed* God
Job 1:1 ... He *f-ed* God and stayed
Job 1:8 ... *f-s* God and stays away from
Ps 34:7 ... and defends all who *f* him.
Ps 46:2 ... not *f* when earthquakes come

Ps 61:5 ... for those who *f* your name.
Ps 76:7 ... you are greatly *f-ed*!
Ps 103:17 ... with those who *f* him.
Ps 128:1 ... joyful are those who *f* the
Prov 8:13 ... All who *f* the LORD will
Prov 28:14 ... those who *f* to do wrong,
Prov 31:30 ... a woman who *f-s* the LORD
Isa 25:3 ... nations will *f* you.
Jer 2:19 ... your God and not to *f* him.
Mal 3:16 ... those who *f-ed* the LORD spoke
Mal 4:2 ... for you who *f* my name,
2 Cor 7:1 ... because we *f* God.
Rev 11:18 ... and all who *f* your name,

FEAST (n) *an elaborate meal; banquet*
Ps 23:5 ... You prepare a *f* for me
Prov 15:15 ... life is a continual *f*.
Luke 15:29 ... goat for a *f* with my friends.

FEAST, FEASTING (v) *to enjoy a good meal*
Esth 9:17 ... a day of *f-ing* and gladness.
Prov 17:1 ... a house filled with *f-ing*—and
Prov 23:20 ... or *f* with gluttons,
Isa 22:13 ... You *f* on meat and drink wine.

FEED, FEEDS (v) *to give food to; to eat; to provide something essential to the development, sustenance, maintenance, or operation of*
Prov 15:14 ... while the fool *f-s* on trash.
Prov 22:9 ... because they *f* the poor.
Jer 50:19 ... own land, to *f* in the fields
Matt 6:26 ... your heavenly Father *f-s* them.
Matt 14:16 ... necessary—you *f* them."
Matt 25:42 ... and you didn't *f* me.
John 6:57 ... anyone who *f-s* on me will live
John 21:15 ... "Then *f* my lambs,"
John 21:17 ... "Then *f* my sheep."
Rom 12:20 ... enemies are hungry, *f* them.

FEET (n) see also FOOT
Ps 22:16 ... pierced my hands and *f*.
Ps 40:2 ... He set my *f* on solid ground
Ps 73:2 ... My *f* were slipping,
Ps 119:105 ... a lamp to guide my *f*
Isa 52:7 ... are the *f* of the messenger
Matt 10:14 ... shake its dust from your *f*
Luke 24:39 ... Look at my *f*.
John 13:5 ... began to wash the disciples' *f*,
John 13:14 ... wash each other's *f*.
Rom 10:15 ... beautiful are the *f* of
Rom 16:20 ... crush Satan under your *f*.
1 Cor 15:25 ... his enemies beneath his *f*.
Heb 1:13 ... a footstool under your *f*.
Heb 12:13 ... a straight path for your *f*

FELLOWSHIP (n) *friendship; association; company; partnership*
Gen 5:24 ... walking in close *f* with God.
1 Cor 5:2 ... remove this man from your *f*.
2 Cor 13:14 ... and the *f* of the Holy Spirit
1 Jn 1:3 ... you may have *f* with us.
1 Jn 1:3 ... our *f* is with the Father and
1 Jn 1:6 ... we say we have *f* with God but
1 Jn 2:27 ... remain in *f* with Christ.

FIELD, FIELDS (n) *an open land area free of woods and buildings; an area of cleared land used for cultivation*
Lev 19:9 ... along the edges of your *f-s*,
Ruth 2:2 ... into the harvest *f-s* to pick
Isa 40:6 ... the flowers in a *f*.
Matt 6:28 ... Look at the lilies of the *f*
Matt 13:44 ... discovered hidden in a *f*.
Luke 2:8 ... staying in the *f-s* nearby,
John 4:35 ... The *f-s* are already ripe

1 Cor 3:9 ... And you are God's *f*.
1 Pet 1:24 ... like a flower in the *f*.

FIGHT, FIGHTS (n) *a hostile encounter; a struggle for a goal or an objective*
Prov 15:18 ... hot-tempered person starts *f-s*;
Prov 20:3 ... Avoiding a *f* is a mark of
Prov 29:22 ... An angry person starts *f-s*;
2 Tim 4:7 ... fought the good *f*,
Jas 4:1 ... causing the quarrels and *f-s*

FIGHT, FIGHTING, FIGHTS (v) *to actively oppose or combat, as with weapons; to gain by struggle*
see also FOUGHT
Exod 14:14 ... LORD himself will *f* for you.
Josh 23:10 ... LORD your God *f-s* for you,
1 Sam 17:32 ... I'll go *f* him!
1 Sam 25:28 ... are *f-ing* the LORD's battles.
Neh 4:20 ... our God will *f* for us!
Ps 35:1 ... *F* those who *f* against me.
Prov 28:25 ... Greed causes *f-ing*;
Isa 49:25 ... I will *f* those who *f* you,
1 Cor 15:32 ... value was there in *f-ing* wild
Phil 1:27 ... one purpose, *f-ing* together for
1 Tim 6:12 ... *F* the good fight
Jas 4:2 ... so you *f* and wage war

FILL, FILLED, FILLS (v) *to occupy the whole of; to supply fully; to spread through*
Gen 1:28 ... *F* the earth and govern it.
Exod 34:6 ... *f-ed* with unfailing love
1 Kgs 8:11 ... presence of the LORD *f-ed*
Ps 81:10 ... and I will *f* it with good things.
Ps 107:9 ... the thirsty and *f-s* the hungry
Ps 119:64 ... unfailing love *f-s* the earth;
Ps 123:3 ... have had our *f* of contempt.
Isa 6:3 ... earth is *f-ed* with his glory!
Joel 2:13 ... and *f-ed* with unfailing love.
Jon 4:2 ... and *f-ed* with unfailing love.
Hag 2:7 ... I will *f* this place with glory,
Luke 1:15 ... be *f-ed* with the Holy Spirit,
Luke 1:41 ... was *f-ed* with the Holy Spirit.
Luke 1:67 ... *f-ed* with the Holy Spirit
Luke 2:40 ... He was *f-ed* with wisdom,
Luke 24:49 ... Holy Spirit comes and *f-s*
Acts 2:4 ... was *f-ed* with the Holy Spirit
Acts 2:28 ... you will *f* me with the joy
Acts 4:8 ... *f-ed* with the Holy Spirit.
Acts 4:31 ... all *f-ed* with the Holy Spirit.
Acts 9:17 ... be *f-ed* with the Holy Spirit.
Acts 13:9 ... was *f-ed* with the Holy Spirit,
Rom 5:5 ... Holy Spirit to *f* our hearts
Rom 15:13 ... *f* you completely with joy
Eph 1:23 ... by Christ, who *f-s* all things
Eph 5:18 ... be *f-ed* with the Holy Spirit,
Col 3:16 ... in all its richness, *f* your lives.

FIND, FINDS (v) *to attain or reach (a goal or conclusion); to discover by searching or effort; to experience*
1 Chr 28:9 ... seek him, you will *f* him.
Job 23:3 ... knew where to *f* God,
Prov 3:13 ... the person who *f-s* wisdom,
Prov 8:17 ... who search will surely *f* me.
Prov 8:35 ... For whoever *f-s* me *f-s* life
Prov 11:27 ... you will *f* favor;
Prov 31:10 ... Who can *f* a virtuous and
Isa 55:6 ... while you can *f* him.
Jer 6:16 ... will *f* rest for your souls.
Matt 7:7 ... seeking, and you will *f*.
Matt 7:8 ... Everyone who seeks, *f-s*.
Matt 10:39 ... your life for me, you will *f* it.
Luke 11:9 ... and you will *f*.
Luke 11:10 ... Everyone who seeks, *f-s*.

Luke 15:4 ... that is lost until he *f-s* it?
Luke 15:8 ... search carefully until she *f-s* it

FINGER, FINGERS (n) *any of the five terminating members of the hand; figurative for the power of God*
Exod 8:19 ... This is the *f* of God!
Exod 31:18 ... written by the *f* of God.
Deut 9:10 ... had written with his own *f*
Luke 16:24 ... dip the tip of his *f* in water
John 8:6 ... wrote in the dust with his *f*.
John 20:25 ... in his hands, put my *f-s* into

FIRE, FIRES (n) *hot flame and burning light; symbolic of hell; severe trial or ordeal*
Exod 3:2 ... *f* from the middle of a bush.
Exod 13:21 ... at night with a pillar of *f*.
Dan 3:25 ... walking around in the *f*
Matt 3:11 ... the Holy Spirit and with *f*.
Matt 5:22 ... are in danger of the *f-s* of hell.
Matt 18:8 ... be thrown into eternal *f*
Mark 9:43 ... the unquenchable *f-s* of hell
Mark 9:49 ... be tested with *f*.
Luke 3:16 ... with the Holy Spirit and with *f*.
Acts 2:3 ... tongues of *f* appeared and
1 Cor 3:13 ... The *f* will show
Heb 12:29 ... God is a devouring *f*.
Jas 3:6 ... it is set on *f* by hell itself.

FIRMAMENT (KJV)
Gen 1:7 ... *space* to separate the waters
Ps 19:1 ... *skies* display his craftsmanship
Ezek 1:22 ... surface like the *sky*, glittering
Dan 12:3 ... will shine as bright as the *sky*

FIRST (adj) *preceding all others in time, order, or importance*
Gen 1:5 ... came, marking the *f* day.
Isa 44:6 ... I am the *F* and the Last;
Isa 48:12 ... God, the *F* and the Last.
Matt 22:38 ... the *f* and greatest
Mark 9:35 ... wants to be *f* must take last
Mark 13:10 ... Good News must *f* be
Rom 1:16 ... Jew *f* and also the Gentile.
Rom 2:9 ... Jew *f* and also for the Gentile.
1 Cor 15:45 ... The *f* man, Adam,
Eph 6:2 ... the *f* commandment with a
1 Tim 2:13 ... God made Adam *f*,
Heb 10:9 ... He cancels the *f* covenant
1 Jn 4:19 ... because he loved us *f*.
Rev 1:17 ... I am the *F* and the Last.
Rev 22:13 ... and the Omega, the *F* and the

FIRSTBEGOTTEN (KJV)
Heb 1:6 ... his *supreme Son* into the world

FIRSTBORN (adj) *eldest; the most prominent; the rightful heir*
Exod 11:5 ... All the *f* sons will die
Exod 34:20 ... buy back every *f* son.
Ps 89:27 ... I will make him my *f* son,
Mic 6:7 ... sacrifice our *f* children to pay
Heb 12:23 ... assembly of God's *f* children

FIRSTBORN (n) *the eldest offspring; one possessing special rights of inheritance*
Gen 25:34 ... for his rights as the *f*.
Exod 13:2 ... every *f* among the Israelites.
Exod 34:19 ... The *f* of every animal

FIRSTFRUITS (KJV)
Exod 23:16 ... the *first crops* of your harvest
Exod 23:19 ... bring the *very best* of

Lev 2:14 ... *first portion* of your harvest
Lev 23:10 ... you harvest its *first crops*,
Num 28:26 ... the *first* of your new grain
Rev 14:4 ... as a *special offering* to God

FISH (n) *any of numerous cold-blooded aquatic vertebrates*
Jon 1:17 ... had arranged for a great *f*
Matt 12:40 ... in the belly of the great *f*
Luke 9:13 ... loaves of bread and two *f*,
John 6:9 ... five barley loaves and two *f*.

FISH, FISHED, FISHING (v) *to attempt to catch fish*
Mark 1:16 ... for they *f-ed* for a living.
Mark 1:17 ... how to *f* for people!
Luke 5:10 ... you'll be *f-ing* for people!

FISHERMEN (n) *those who engage in fishing as an occupation*
Ezek 26:5 ... a rock in the sea, a place for *f*

FISHERS (KJV)
Isa 19:8 ... *fishermen* will lament for lack of work
Jer 16:16 ... *fishermen* who will catch
Matt 4:19 ... *how to fish* for people

FLATTER (v) *to praise excessively out of self-interest*
Job 32:21 ... or try to *f* anyone.
Prov 29:5 ... To *f* friends is
Dan 11:32 ... He will *f* and win over those
Jude 1:16 ... *f* others to get what they want.

FLATTERING (adj) *characterized by excessive praise out of self-interest*
Ps 12:2 ... speaking with *f* lips
Ps 12:3 ... cut off their *f* lips
Prov 26:28 ... and *f* words cause ruin.

FLATTERY (n) *insincere or excessive praise*
Job 32:22 ... For if I tried *f*, my Creator
Ps 5:9 ... tongues are filled with *f*.
Prov 28:23 ... criticism far more than *f*.
1 Thes 2:5 ... try to win you with *f*,

FLESH (n) *the meaty part of animal and human bodies*
see also BODY, HUMAN
Gen 2:23 ... and *f* from my *f*!
John 6:51 ... so the world may live, is my *f*.
1 Cor 15:39 ... different kinds of *f*—

FLOCK, FLOCKS (n) *a group of animals assembled or herded together; a group under the guidance of a leader*
Isa 40:11 ... feed his *f* like a shepherd.
Jer 10:21 ... and their *f-s* are scattered.
Jer 31:10 ... as a shepherd does his *f*.
Zech 11:17 ... who abandons the *f*!
Matt 26:31 ... the *f* will be scattered.
Luke 2:8 ... guarding their *f-s* of sheep.
Luke 12:32 ... don't be afraid, little *f*.
John 10:16 ... one *f* with one shepherd.
Acts 20:28 ... shepherd God's *f*—

FLOOD, FLOODS (n) *a rising and overflowing of a body of water; the destruction of the world by water during the time of Noah*
Gen 7:7 ... the boat to escape the *f*—
Prov 27:4 ... cruel, and wrath is like a *f*.
Matt 24:38 ... In those days before the *f*,
Luke 6:49 ... the *f-s* sweep down against
2 Pet 2:5 ... ungodly people with a vast *f*.

FOLLOW, FOLLOWED, FOLLOWING, FOLLOWS (v) *to pursue or run after; to imitate; to obey*
Deut 1:36 ... because he has *f-ed* the LORD
Deut 5:32 ... *f-ing* his instructions
Josh 14:14 ... he wholeheartedly *f-ed* the
1 Kgs 3:3 ... loved the LORD and *f-ed*
2 Chr 10:14 ... and *f-ed* the counsel
Prov 4:27 ... feet from *f-ing* evil.
Prov 10:9 ... those who *f* crooked paths
Isa 57:2 ... For those who *f* godly paths
Isa 65:2 ... But they *f* their own evil paths
Matt 4:20 ... at once and *f-ed* him.
Matt 7:24 ... listens to my teaching and *f-s*
Matt 8:19 ... I will *f* you wherever you go.
Matt 8:22 ... *F* me now. Let the
Matt 9:9 ... got up and *f-ed* him.
Matt 16:24 ... take up your cross, and *f*
Matt 19:27 ... given up everything to *f* you.
Matt 26:58 ... Meanwhile, Peter *f-ed* him
Mark 1:17 ... Come, *f* me, and I will show
Luke 9:23 ... your cross daily, and *f* me.
Luke 17:23 ... go out and *f* them.
Luke 18:43 ... *f-ed* Jesus, praising God.
John 8:12 ... If you *f* me, you won't have to
John 10:4 ... they *f* him because they know
John 10:27 ... know them, and they *f* me.
John 12:26 ... wants to serve me must *f* me,
John 21:19 ... Jesus told him, "*F* me."
1 Cor 1:12 ... or "I *f* only Christ."
1 Cor 4:17 ... of how I *f* Christ Jesus,
Gal 5:7 ... you back from *f-ing* the truth?
Gal 5:25 ... *f* the Spirit's leading
Phil 2:12 ... always *f-ed* my instructions
Phil 3:17 ... those who *f* our example.
2 Thes 3:6 ... and don't *f* the tradition
1 Pet 2:21 ... must *f* in his steps.
Rev 14:4 ... as virgins, *f-ing* the Lamb

FOLLOWER, FOLLOWERS (n) *one who follows the teachings of another; a disciple*
1 Kgs 18:3 ... was a devoted *f* of the LORD.
Matt 10:42 ... one of the least of my *f-s*,
Matt 18:20 ... together as my *f-s*, I am there
Acts 9:21 ... Jesus' *f-s* in Jerusalem?

FOLLY (KJV)
Prov 14:18 ... clothed with *foolishness*
Prov 26:11 ... a fool repeats his *foolishness*
Eccl 2:13 ... is better than *foolishness*
Isa 9:17 ... they all speak *foolishness*
2 Tim 3:9 ... recognize what *fools* they are

FOOD (n) *something that nourishes, sustains, or supplies energy and vitality*
see also BREAD
Lev 11:2 ... the ones you may use for *f*.
Prov 25:21 ... hungry, give them *f* to eat.
Isa 58:7 ... Share your *f* with the hungry,
Dan 1:8 ... defile himself by eating the *f*
Matt 6:11 ... today the *f* we need,
Matt 6:25 ... Isn't life more than *f*,
Mark 7:19 ... every kind of *f* is acceptable
John 6:55 ... my flesh is true *f*, and my
John 13:18 ... eats my *f* has turned against
Acts 15:20 ... abstain from eating *f*
Rom 14:6 ... kind of *f* do so to honor
1 Tim 6:8 ... have enough *f* and clothing,
Jas 2:15 ... who has no *f* or clothing,

FOOL, FOOLS (n) *one deficient in intellectual, practical, or moral sense*
1 Sam 25:25 ... He is a *f*, just as his name
Ps 14:1 ... Only *f-s* say in their hearts,
Prov 6:32 ... commits adultery is an utter *f*,
Prov 10:8 ... babbling *f-s* fall flat on
Prov 10:23 ... wrong is fun for a *f*,

Prov 17:7 ... are not fitting for a *f*;
Prov 17:16 ... senseless to pay to educate a *f*,
Prov 26:1 ... associated with *f-s* than snow
Prov 26:7 ... A proverb in the mouth of a *f*
Prov 29:11 ... *F-s* vent their anger,
Prov 29:20 ... more hope for a *f* than for
Rom 1:22 ... became utter *f-s*.
1 Cor 3:18 ... need to become a *f* to be
2 Cor 11:21 ... I'm talking like a *f* again—
Eph 5:15 ... Don't live like *f-s*,
2 Tim 3:9 ... recognize what *f-s* they are,

FOOLISH (adj) *lacking in sense, judgment, or discretion; irreverent*
Prov 26:4 ... the *f* arguments of fools,
Prov 26:17 ... else's argument is as *f*
Rom 1:28 ... abandoned them to their *f*
1 Cor 1:18 ... the cross is *f* to those who
1 Cor 1:27 ... world considers *f* in order to
1 Cor 2:14 ... It all sounds *f* to them
Eph 5:4 ... Obscene stories, *f* talk,
1 Tim 6:20 ... Avoid godless, *f* discussions
Titus 3:9 ... not get involved in *f* discussions

FOOT (n) *the end of the leg upon which an individual stands*
see also FEET
Josh 1:3 ... Wherever you set *f*,
Matt 18:8 ... with only one hand or one *f*
Luke 4:11 ... won't even hurt your *f*
1 Cor 12:15 ... If the *f* says,
Rev 10:2 ... and his left *f* on the land.

FOOTSTOOL (n) *a low stool used to support the feet*
Ps 110:1 ... making them a *f* under
Isa 66:1 ... throne, and the earth is my *f*.
Matt 5:35 ... the earth is his *f*.
Acts 7:49 ... the earth is my *f*.
Heb 1:13 ... making them a *f* under
Heb 10:13 ... and made a *f* under

FORCE (n) *violence, compulsion, or constraint exerted upon or against a person or thing*
Zech 4:6 ... is not by *f* nor by strength,

FORCE, FORCED (v) *to compel by physical, moral, or intellectual means*
Matt 27:32 ... soldiers *f-d* him to carry
John 6:15 ... were ready to *f* him to be

(FORE)FATHERS (KJV)
Exod 10:6 ... ancestors seen a plague like
Num 11:12 ... swore to give their ancestors
Jer 11:10 ... the sins of their forefathers
Matt 23:32 ... what your ancestors started

FOREHEAD, FOREHEADS (n) *the part of the face above the eyes*
Exod 13:9 ... on your hand or your *f*.
Deut 6:8 ... wear them on your *f*
1 Sam 17:49 ... hit the Philistine in the *f*.
Rev 9:4 ... seal of God on their *f-s*.
Rev 13:16 ... right hand or on the *f*.
Rev 14:1 ... written on their *f-s*.

FOREIGNER, FOREIGNERS (n) *nonresident, alien, or sojourner*
see also STRANGER
Exod 22:21 ... not mistreat or oppress *f-s*
Exod 23:9 ... must not oppress *f-s*.
Lev 24:22 ... to the *f-s* living among you.
Neh 9:2 ... separated themselves from all *f-s*
Ps 119:19 ... I am only a *f* in the land
Hos 7:8 ... mingle with godless *f-s*,
Luke 17:18 ... glory to God except this *f*?
1 Cor 14:11 ... I will be a *f* to someone

Eph 2:19 ... no longer strangers and *f-s*.
1 Pet 1:1 ... living as *f-s* in the provinces
1 Pet 2:11 ... temporary residents and *f-s*

FOREKNOW, FOREKNEW, FOREKNOWLEDGE (KJV)
Acts 2:23 ... God knew what would happen
Rom 8:29 ... God knew his people *in advance*
Rom 11:2 ... whom he chose from the very beginning
1 Pet 1:2 ... Father knew you and chose you

FOREORDAINED (KJV)
1 Pet 1:20 ... chose him *as* your ransom

FOREVER (adv) *for a limitless time; continually*
see also ETERNAL, EVERLASTING
Gen 3:22 ... they will live *f*!
Gen 17:8 ... be their possession *f*,
2 Sam 7:26 ... name be honored *f*
1 Chr 17:24 ... be established and honored *f*
1 Chr 29:10 ... be praised *f* and ever!
Ezra 9:12 ... prosperity to your children *f*.
Ps 9:7 ... the LORD reigns *f*,
Ps 21:4 ... of his life stretch on *f*.
Ps 28:9 ... in your arms *f*.
Ps 37:28 ... keep them safe *f*,
Ps 61:8 ... sing praises to your name *f*
Ps 73:26 ... he is mine *f*.
Ps 79:13 ... will thank you *f* and ever,
Ps 86:12 ... glory to your name *f*,
Ps 92:8 ... will be exalted *f*.
Ps 100:5 ... unfailing love continues *f*,
Ps 103:7 ... the LORD remains *f* with
Ps 107:1 ... faithful love endures *f*.
Ps 110:4 ... are a priest *f*
Ps 111:8 ... They are *f* true,
Ps 112:6 ... be remembered *f*.
Ps 119:152 ... laws will last *f*,
Ps 146:6 ... every promise *f*.
Isa 32:17 ... and confidence *f*.
Isa 51:6 ... but my salvation lasts *f*.
Isa 60:15 ... make you beautiful *f*,
Isa 63:12 ... making himself famous *f*?
Jer 25:5 ... you and your ancestors *f*.
Dan 2:44 ... and it will stand *f*.
Dan 4:3 ... kingdom will last *f*, his rule
Dan 7:27 ... kingdom will last *f*,
John 6:51 ... eats this bread will live *f*;
1 Cor 13:8 ... But love will last *f*!
1 Cor 13:13 ... Three things will last *f*—
1 Cor 15:42 ... will be raised to live *f*.
1 Cor 15:50 ... inherit what will last *f*.
2 Cor 4:17 ... and will last *f*!
2 Cor 4:18 ... cannot see will last *f*.
1 Thes 4:17 ... will be with the Lord *f*.
2 Thes 1:9 ... destruction, *f* separated
Heb 5:6 ... a priest *f* in the order
Heb 7:17 ... a priest *f* in the order
Heb 7:24 ... Jesus lives *f*,
Heb 9:12 ... secured our redemption *f*.
Heb 13:8 ... yesterday, today, and *f*.
1 Pet 1:25 ... word of the Lord remains *f*.
1 Jn 2:17 ... will live *f*.
Rev 22:5 ... they will reign *f* and ever.

FORGAVE (v) *to pardon or acquit of guilt*
see also FORGIVE
Ps 78:38 ... was merciful and *f* their sins
Luke 7:42 ... so he kindly *f* them both,
Eph 1:7 ... his Son and *f* our sins.
Col 1:14 ... our freedom and *f* our sins.
Col 2:13 ... with Christ, for he *f* all our

FORGIVE, FORGIVEN, FORGIVES, FORGIVING (v) *to pardon or acquit of sins*
see also FORGAVE
Gen 50:17 ... Please *f* your brothers
Exod 23:21 ... he will not *f* your rebellion.
Exod 34:7 ... I *f* iniquity, rebellion,
Exod 34:9 ... but please *f* our iniquity and
Num 14:18 ... *f-ing* every kind of sin
Num 14:19 ... just as you have *f-n* them
1 Sam 3:14 ... never be *f-n* by sacrifices
1 Kgs 8:34 ... hear from heaven and *f*
Ps 65:3 ... by our sins, you *f* them all.
Ps 79:9 ... Save us and *f* our sins
Ps 86:5 ... so good, so ready to *f*,
Ps 103:3 ... He *f-s* all my sins
Prov 17:9 ... when a fault is *f-n*,
Isa 22:14 ... you will never be *f-n* for this
Isa 38:17 ... and *f-n* all my sins.
Isa 55:7 ... for he will *f* generously.
Jer 31:34 ... I will *f* their wickedness,
Dan 9:19 ... O Lord, hear. O Lord, *f*.
Hos 14:2 ... *F* all our sins and
Matt 6:12 ... and *f* us our sins,
Matt 6:14 ... If you *f* those who sin
Matt 6:15 ... if you refuse to *f* others,
Matt 9:6 ... authority on earth to *f* sins.
Matt 18:21 ... how often should I *f*
Matt 26:28 ... to *f* the sins of many.
Mark 2:7 ... Only God can *f* sins!
Mark 2:10 ... authority on earth to *f* sins.
Mark 3:29 ... will never be *f-n*.
Mark 11:25 ... first *f* anyone you are
Mark 11:25 ... will *f* your sins,
Luke 5:21 ... Only God can *f* sins!
Luke 5:24 ... authority on earth to *f* sins.
Luke 6:37 ... *F* others, and you will be
Luke 7:47 ... a person who is *f-n* little
Luke 7:49 ... he goes around *f-ing* sins?
Luke 11:4 ... *f* us our sins, as we
Luke 17:3 ... if there is repentance, *f*.
Luke 17:4 ... asks forgiveness, you must *f*.
Luke 23:34 ... Father, *f* them,
John 20:23 ... If you *f* anyone's sins,
Acts 5:31 ... repent of their sins and be *f-n*.
Acts 8:22 ... Perhaps he will *f* your evil
Rom 4:5 ... faith in God who *f-s* sinners.
Rom 4:7 ... whose disobedience is *f-n*,
2 Cor 2:7 ... time to *f* and comfort
2 Cor 2:10 ... When you *f* this man,
Col 3:13 ... so you must *f* others.
Heb 8:12 ... I will *f* their wickedness,
1 Jn 1:9 ... is faithful and just to *f* us

FORGIVENESS (n) *acquittal or pardon of sins*
see also ATONEMENT, MERCY
Neh 9:17 ... you are a God of *f*,
Luke 24:47 ... There is *f* of sins for all
Acts 13:38 ... this man Jesus there is *f*
Rom 5:15 ... his gift of *f* to many
Heb 9:22 ... of blood, there is no *f*.
Jas 5:20 ... bring about the *f* of many sins.

FORMED (v) *to create, fashion, or give shape to something*
see also CREATE(D), MADE, MAKE
Gen 2:7 ... the LORD God *f* the man
Gen 2:19 ... LORD God *f* from the ground
Ps 94:9 ... the one who *f* your eyes?
Isa 49:5 ... the one who *f* me
Jer 1:5 ... knew you before I *f* you
Heb 11:3 ... universe was *f* at God's

FORNICATION (KJV)
Isa 23:17 ... *be a prostitute* to all kingdoms
Matt 19:9 ... wife has been *unfaithful*

1717

1 Cor 5:1 . . . *sexual immorality* going on
1 Cor 6:18 . . . *sexual immorality* is a sin
Jude 1:7 . . . were filled with *immorality*

FORTRESS (n) *a fortified place; a place of security or survival*
see also REFUGE
2 Sam 22:2 . . . my *f*, and my savior;
Ps 27:1 . . . The LORD is my *f*,
Ps 71:3 . . . my rock and my *f*.
Ps 144:2 . . . and my *f*, my tower of safety,
Prov 18:10 . . . LORD is a strong *f*;
Zeph 3:6 . . . devastating their *f* walls and

FORTY (adj) *the number 40*
Gen 7:4 . . . for *f* days and *f* nights,
Exod 16:35 . . . Israel ate manna for *f* years
Exod 24:18 . . . *f* days and *f* nights.
Num 14:34 . . . wilderness for *f* years—
Matt 4:2 . . . For *f* days and *f* nights
Acts 1:3 . . . the *f* days after he suffered,
Acts 13:18 . . . *f* years of wandering

FOUGHT (v) see also FIGHT
Gen 32:28 . . . because you have *f* with God
Josh 10:14 . . . Surely the LORD *f* for Israel
2 Tim 4:7 . . . I have *f* the good fight,

FOUNDATION (n) *basis upon which something is built, supported, or added to; substructure*
Prov 1:7 . . . Fear of the LORD is the *f*
Prov 9:10 . . . the LORD is the *f* of wisdom.
Isa 28:16 . . . placing a *f* stone in Jerusalem,
Luke 6:49 . . . on the ground, without a *f*.
Eph 2:20 . . . built on the *f* of the apostles
1 Tim 3:15 . . . pillar and *f* of the truth.
2 Tim 2:19 . . . stands firm like a *f* stone
Heb 1:10 . . . you laid the *f* of the earth

FOUNTAIN (n) *source; spring of water*
Isa 12:3 . . . from the *f* of salvation!
Zech 13:1 . . . a *f* to cleanse them

FREE (adj) *not bound, confined, or detained by force; without restraint, inhibition, or cost; possessing the rights of citizenship*
John 8:32 . . . the truth will set you *f*.
John 8:36 . . . sets you *f*, you are truly *f*.
Rom 6:7 . . . we were set *f* from the power
Rom 6:18 . . . are *f* from your slavery
Gal 3:28 . . . slave or *f*, male and female.
Jas 1:25 . . . the perfect law that sets you *f*,
1 Pet 2:16 . . . For you are *f*, yet

FREED, FREES (v) *to relieve or rid of what restrains, confines, restricts, or embarrasses*
Ps 116:16 . . . *f-d* me from my chains.
Ps 146:7 . . . The LORD *f-s* the prisoners.
Isa 61:1 . . . prisoners will be *f-d*.
Rom 3:24 . . . he *f-d* us from the penalty
1 Cor 1:30 . . . and he *f-d* us from sin.
Rev 1:5 . . . and has *f-d* us from our sins

FREEDOM (n) *liberation from slavery, restraint, or the power of another*
Ps 119:45 . . . I will walk in *f*, for I have
2 Cor 3:17 . . . the Lord is, there is *f*.
Gal 2:4 . . . the *f* we have in Christ
Gal 4:5 . . . sent him to buy *f* for us
Gal 5:13 . . . don't use your *f* to satisfy
Eph 1:7 . . . purchased our *f* with the blood
1 Pet 2:16 . . . don't use your *f* as an excuse

FRIEND, FRIENDS (n) *intimate associate; a favored companion*
Prov 16:28 . . . separates the best of *f-s*.

Prov 17:9 . . . on it separates close *f-s*.
Prov 20:6 . . . will say they are loyal *f-s*,
Prov 27:6 . . . Wounds from a sincere *f* are
Prov 28:7 . . . with wild *f-s* bring shame
Prov 29:5 . . . To flatter *f-s* is to lay a trap
Isa 41:8 . . . from Abraham my *f*,
Zech 13:6 . . . was wounded at my *f-s'* house!
John 11:3 . . . Lord, your dear *f* is very sick.
John 15:13 . . . one's life for one's *f-s*.
John 15:14 . . . You are my *f-s* if you do
John 15:15 . . . Now you are my *f-s*,
John 19:12 . . . you are no '*f* of Caesar.'
Jas 2:23 . . . even called the *f* of God.
Jas 4:4 . . . want to be a *f* of the world,

FRIENDSHIP (n) *association of familiarity and companionship*
Prov 3:32 . . . he offers *f* to the godly.
Rom 5:10 . . . since our *f* with God was
Jas 4:4 . . . you realize that *f* with the world

FRUIT (n) *a product of plant growth; product or result*
Ps 1:3 . . . bearing *f* each season.
Isa 11:1 . . . new Branch bearing *f* from
Dan 4:12 . . . loaded with *f* for all to eat.
Matt 3:10 . . . not produce good *f* will be
Matt 7:20 . . . can identify a tree by its *f*,
Matt 12:33 . . . is bad, its *f* will be bad.
John 15:2 . . . that doesn't produce *f*
John 15:16 . . . go and produce lasting *f*,
Gal 5:22 . . . produces this kind of *f*
Phil 1:11 . . . the *f* of your salvation—
2 Tim 2:6 . . . first to enjoy the *f*
Rev 22:2 . . . bearing twelve crops of *f*,

FRUITFUL (adj) *bearing fruit (product of a tree or plant); abundant (at producing work or in bearing children)*
Gen 1:22 . . . Be *f* and multiply.
Gen 9:1 . . . Be *f* and multiply.
Gen 35:11 . . . Be *f* and multiply.
Ps 128:3 . . . will be like a *f* grapevine,
Jer 2:7 . . . brought you into a *f* land
Phil 1:22 . . . do more *f* work for Christ.

FULFILL, FULFILLED, FULFILLS (v) *to complete or perform as promised; to measure up or satisfy*
Ps 57:2 . . . to God who will *f* his purpose
Dan 9:4 . . . You always *f* your covenant
Matt 2:15 . . . This *f-ed* what the Lord had
Matt 2:23 . . . This *f-ed* what the prophets
Matt 13:35 . . . *f-ed* what God had spoken
Matt 27:9 . . . This *f-ed* the prophecy of
Luke 4:21 . . . has been *f-ed* this very day!
Luke 24:44 . . . Psalms must be *f-ed*.
John 18:9 . . . this to *f* his own statement:
John 19:28 . . . and to *f* Scripture he said,
Acts 1:16 . . . Scriptures had to be *f-ed*
Rom 3:31 . . . do we truly *f* the law.
Rom 13:8 . . . you will *f* the requirements
Rom 13:10 . . . love *f-s* the requirements
Eph 1:9 . . . to *f* his own good plan.

FULL (adj) *possessing or containing a great amount*
Deut 34:9 . . . was *f* of the spirit of wisdom,
Luke 4:1 . . . Then Jesus, *f* of the Holy Spirit,
Acts 6:3 . . . *f* of the Spirit and wisdom.
Acts 6:5 . . . Stephen (a man *f* of faith and
Acts 7:55 . . . Stephen, *f* of the Holy Spirit,
Acts 11:24 . . . man, *f* of the Holy Spirit

FULLNESS (n) *the quality or state of containing all that is wanted, needed, or possible*

Eph 3:19 . . . with all the *f* of life and
Col 1:19 . . . God in all his *f* was pleased
Col 2:9 . . . lives all the *f* of God

FURNACE (n) *an enclosed structure in which heat is produced*
Dan 3:6 . . . be thrown into a blazing *f*.
Matt 13:42 . . . throw them into the fiery *f*,

FURY (n) *wrath; fierceness; rage*
Exod 15:7 . . . You unleash your blazing *f*;
Deut 29:28 . . . In great anger and *f*
Ps 7:6 . . . against the *f* of my enemies!
Jer 32:37 . . . will scatter them in my *f*.
Zeph 2:2 . . . the fierce *f* of the Lord.

FUTURE (adj) *existing or occurring at a later time*
Deut 29:15 . . . also with the *f* generations
Rom 8:19 . . . waiting eagerly for that *f* day
Eph 2:7 . . . can point to us in all *f* ages
Heb 2:5 . . . will control the *f* world

FUTURE (n) *time that is to come; what is going to happen*
Num 24:14 . . . do to your people in the *f*.
Ps 31:15 . . . My *f* is in your hands.
Ps 37:37 . . . a wonderful *f* awaits those
Isa 42:9 . . . tell you the *f* before it happens.
Isa 46:10 . . . can tell you the *f* before it
Jer 29:11 . . . to give you a *f* and a hope.
Jer 31:17 . . . There is hope for your *f*,

G

GAIN (n) *winnings or profits*
Isa 56:11 . . . intent on personal *g*.

GAIN, GAINED, GAINS (v) *to acquire or win; to profit or increase*
Prov 3:13 . . . one who *g-s* understanding.
Prov 11:16 . . . gracious woman *g-s* respect,
Mark 8:36 . . . *g* the whole world but lose
Luke 9:25 . . . *g* the whole world but are
1 Cor 13:3 . . . I would have *g-ed* nothing.

GALILEE (n) *a Roman province of Palestine during the time of Jesus*
Isa 9:1 . . . a time in the future when *G*
Matt 4:15 . . . beyond the Jordan River, in *G*
Matt 26:32 . . . I will go ahead of you to *G*
Matt 28:10 . . . my brothers to leave for *G*,

GARDEN (n) *a planted area where fruits, vegetables, and flowers are cultivated*
Gen 2:8 . . . God planted a *g* in Eden
Gen 2:15 . . . God placed the man in the *G*
1 Kgs 4:25 . . . had its own home and *g*.
Song 4:12 . . . my private *g*, my treasure,
Isa 58:11 . . . will be like a well-watered *g*,
Jer 31:12 . . . life will be like a watered *g*,
Ezek 28:13 . . . in Eden, the *g* of God.

GARDENER (n) *one who takes care of a garden*
John 15:1 . . . my Father is the *g*.
John 20:15 . . . She thought he was the *g*.

GATE, GATES (n) *opening in a (city) wall or fence, consisting of a door and protected by defensive structures (as towers); the place of judicial decisions, town criers, and marketplace trade; entrance*
Esth 6:10 . . . sits at the *g* of the palace.
Ps 24:7 . . . Open up, ancient *g-s*!
Ps 100:4 . . . his *g-s* with thanksgiving;
Isa 62:10 . . . Go out through the *g-s*!

Matt 7:13 ... only through the narrow **g**.
John 10:1 ... going through the **g**,
John 10:2 ... who enters through the **g**
John 10:7 ... I am the **g** for the sheep.
Heb 13:12 ... died outside the city **g-s**
Rev 21:21 ... **g.s** were made of pearls—
Rev 21:21 ... each **g** from a single pearl!

GAVE (v) *to suffer the loss of*
see also GIVE
John 3:16 ... He **g** his one and only Son,
Rom 8:32 ... **g** him up for us all,
Gal 2:20 ... loved me and **g** himself for me.
1 Tim 2:6 ... He **g** his life to purchase

GENERATION, GENERATIONS (n) *the whole body of individuals born about the same time (nation or racial group); the period of time during which those individuals lived (also, age or era); offspring*
Gen 17:7 ... after you, from **g** to **g**.
Exod 20:6 ... love for a thousand **g-s**
Num 32:13 ... the entire **g** that sinned
Judg 2:10 ... After that **g** died,
1 Chr 16:15 ... to a thousand **g-s**.
Ps 71:18 ... your power to this new **g**,
Ps 100:5 ... continues to each **g**.
Ps 102:12 ... endure to every **g**.
Ps 102:18 ... recorded for future **g-s**,
Ps 105:8 ... to a thousand **g-s**.
Ps 119:90 ... extends to every **g**,
Ps 145:4 ... Let each **g** tell its children
Ps 146:10 ... throughout the **g-s**.
Prov 27:24 ... not be passed to the next **g**.
Isa 41:4 ... summoning each new **g**
Lam 5:19 ... continues from **g** to **g**.
Joel 1:3 ... the story down from **g** to **g**.
Matt 12:39 ... Only an evil, adulterous **g**
Mark 13:30 ... this **g** will not pass
Luke 1:48 ... all **g-s** will call me blessed.
Luke 11:29 ... This evil **g** keeps asking me
Acts 2:40 ... from this crooked **g**!
Eph 3:5 ... not reveal it to previous **g-s**,
Eph 3:21 ... all **g-s** forever and ever!

GENEROSITY (n) *the quality or fact of being magnanimous, kindly, or openhanded; abundance*
Acts 2:46 ... meals with great joy and **g**—
2 Cor 9:10 ... a great harvest of **g** in you.
Eph 4:7 ... through the **g** of Christ.
Phlm 1:6 ... put into action the **g** that

GENEROUS (adj) *magnanimous, kindly; liberal in giving; abundant*
Deut 15:8 ... Instead, be **g** and lend
Ps 37:26 ... godly always give **g** loans to
2 Cor 9:6 ... will get a **g** crop.
1 Tim 6:18 ... **g** to those in need,

GENTILE, GENTILES (n) *non-Jewish individuals or nations, often connoting heathens or pagans*
see also NATION(S)
Isa 49:6 ... make you a light to the **G-s**,
Luke 21:24 ... period of the **G-s** comes
Acts 10:45 ... out on the **G-s**, too.
Acts 14:27 ... faith to the **G-s**, too.
Acts 15:14 ... God first visited the **G-s**
Acts 21:25 ... As for the **G** believers,
Acts 28:28 ... also been offered to the **G-s**,
Rom 1:16 ... Jews first and also the **G**.
Rom 2:9 ... Jews first and also for the **G**.
Rom 3:9 ... people, whether Jews or **G-s**,
Rom 3:29 ... God of the **G-s**?
Rom 10:12 ... Jew and **G** are the same

Rom 11:11 ... available to the **G-s**.
Rom 15:9 ... the **G-s** might give glory
Rom 15:27 ... **G-s** received the spiritual
Gal 2:2 ... preaching to the **G-s**.
Gal 2:8 ... apostle to the **G-s**.
Gal 2:9 ... keep preaching to the **G-s**,
Gal 3:8 ... God would make the **G-s**
Gal 3:14 ... blessed the **G-s** with the same
Gal 3:28 ... no longer Jew or **G**, slave or
Eph 3:8 ... the privilege of telling the **G-s**
Col 3:11 ... a Jew or a **G**, circumcised or

GENTLE (adj) *kind; mild-mannered; soft*
1 Kgs 19:12 ... sound of a **g** whisper.
Prov 15:1 ... A **g** answer deflects anger,
Prov 15:4 ... **G** words are a tree of life;
Matt 11:29 ... am humble and **g** at heart,
1 Cor 4:21 ... love and a **g** spirit?
Eph 4:2 ... be humble and **g**. Be patient
1 Tim 3:3 ... must be **g**, not quarrelsome,
Titus 3:2 ... be **g** and show true humility
Jas 3:17 ... **g** at all times,

GENTLENESS (n) *mildness of manners or disposition*
Gal 5:23 ... **g**, and self-control.
Col 3:12 ... kindness, humility, **g**, and
1 Tim 6:11 ... perseverance, and **g**.

GENUINE (adj) *actual, true, authentic, sincere*
John 1:47 ... here is a **g** son of Israel—
2 Cor 8:8 ... I am testing how **g** your love
Phil 1:18 ... motives are false or **g**,
2 Tim 1:5 ... I remember your **g** faith,

GETHSEMANE (n) *the garden where Jesus often went for prayer, rest, or fellowship; the site where Judas betrayed Jesus before the crucifixion*
Matt 26:36 ... to the olive grove called **G**,
Mark 14:32 ... to the olive grove called **G**,

GIFT, GIFTS (n) *a present from people to people (often a bribe); a sacrifice from people to God; anything given voluntarily or at no cost; that which is given from God, enabling or empowering his people*
Prov 18:16 ... Giving a **g** can open doors;
Matt 2:11 ... and gave him **g-s** of gold,
Luke 11:13 ... how to give good **g-s** to your
Rom 4:16 ... given as a free **g**.
Rom 5:15 ... and God's gracious **g**.
Rom 6:23 ... free **g** of God is eternal
Rom 11:29 ... For God's **g-s** and his call
1 Cor 12:4 ... kinds of spiritual **g-s**,
1 Cor 12:7 ... A spiritual **g** is given
1 Cor 12:31 ... the most helpful **g-s**.
2 Cor 9:5 ... I want it to be a willing **g**,
2 Cor 9:15 ... Thank God for this **g**
Gal 2:9 ... recognized the **g** God had
Eph 2:8 ... it is a **g** from God.
Eph 4:8 ... and gave **g-s** to his people.
2 Tim 1:6 ... the spiritual **g** God gave you
Heb 2:4 ... **g-s** of the Holy Spirit
1 Pet 3:7 ... equal partner in God's **g**
1 Pet 4:10 ... of spiritual **g-s**.

GIVE, GIVEN, GIVES, GIVING (v) *to grant, bestow, convey, offer, provide, or designate; to yield or produce; to suffer the loss of (life)*
Exod 30:15 ... poor must not **g** less.
1 Sam 1:28 ... **g-ing** him to the LORD,
Ps 112:9 ... share freely and **g** generously
Ps 119:130 ... your word **g-s** light,
Prov 21:26 ... the godly love to **g**!

Prov 23:26 ... O my son, **g** me your heart.
Isa 9:6 ... a son is **g-n** to us.
Matt 7:11 ... heavenly Father **g** good gifts
Matt 16:19 ... And I will **g** you the keys
Matt 22:30 ... marry nor be **g-n** in marriage.
Mark 6:7 ... by two, **g-ing** them authority
Luke 11:13 ... know how to **g** good gifts to
Luke 14:33 ... my disciple without **g-ing** up
Luke 22:19 ... body, which is **g-n** for you.
John 1:17 ... the law was **g-n** through Moses,
John 5:21 ... so the Son **g-s** life to anyone
John 13:34 ... So now I am **g-ing** you a new
John 14:27 ... And the peace I **g** is a gift
Acts 5:32 ... Spirit, who is **g-n** by God
Acts 14:3 ... was true by **g-ing** them power
Acts 15:8 ... by **g-ing** them the Holy Spirit
Acts 20:35 ... is more blessed to **g** than to
Rom 2:7 ... He will **g** eternal life
Rom 5:5 ... because he has **g-n** us the Holy
Rom 8:32 ... won't he also **g** us everything
Rom 10:12 ... Lord, who **g-s** generously
Rom 12:8 ... is giving, **g** generously.
Rom 14:12 ... each of us will **g** a personal
1 Cor 9:17 ... God has **g-n** me this sacred
1 Cor 11:24 ... body, which is **g-n** for you.
1 Cor 15:57 ... thank God! He **g-s** us victory
2 Cor 3:6 ... the Spirit **g-s** life.
2 Cor 8:6 ... this ministry of **g-ing**.
2 Cor 9:7 ... how much to **g**.
Eph 4:7 ... he has **g-n** each one of us
Eph 4:28 ... and then **g** generously to
1 Thes 4:8 ... rejecting God, who **g-s**
1 Tim 6:17 ... God, who richly **g-s** us all we
1 Jn 4:13 ... And God has **g-n** us his Spirit

GLAD (adj) *joyful or happy, often with shouts*
Ps 16:9 ... my heart is **g**, and I rejoice.
Ps 32:11 ... LORD and be **g**, all you who
Ps 69:32 ... at work and be **g**.
Ps 97:1 ... coastlands be **g**.
Ps 104:15 ... wine to make them **g**,
Ps 118:24 ... will rejoice and be **g** in it.
Prov 10:8 ... The wise are **g** to be
Prov 27:11 ... make my heart **g**.
Isa 35:1 ... and desert will be **g**
Zeph 3:14 ... O Israel! Be **g** and rejoice
Matt 5:12 ... Be very **g**!
John 11:15 ... for your sakes, I'm **g** I wasn't
Acts 13:48 ... they were very **g**
1 Cor 12:26 ... the parts are **g**.
2 Cor 2:2 ... will make me **g**?
Rev 19:7 ... Let us be **g** and rejoice,

GLORIFY, GLORIFIED, GLORIFIES, GLORIFYING (v) *to bestow honor or praise (as in worship); to magnify*
see also EXALT, HONOR
Ps 147:12 ... **G** the LORD, O Jerusalem!
Isa 26:8 ... desire is to **g** your name.
Isa 42:12 ... the whole world **g** the LORD;
Dan 4:37 ... praise and **g** and honor the
Luke 2:20 ... flocks, **g-ing** and praising
John 8:50 ... no wish to **g** myself, God is
John 13:31 ... God will be **g-ied**
John 17:1 ... **G** your Son so
John 21:19 ... of death he would **g** God.
2 Cor 8:19 ... a service that **g-ies** the Lord
Eph 1:14 ... would praise and **g** him.
Rev 15:4 ... you, Lord, and **g** your name?

GLORIOUS (adj) *possessing or deserving special honor; splendid or magnificent*
Exod 15:6 ... O LORD, is **g** in power.
Exod 33:18 ... show me your **g** presence.
Deut 32:3 ... the LORD; how **g** is our God!

1719

1 Chr 16:28 ... the LORD is **g** and strong.
Neh 9:5 ... prayed: "May your **g** name be
Job 37:5 ... God's voice is **g** in the
Ps 45:3 ... You are so **g**, so majestic!
Ps 76:4 ... You are **g** and more majestic
Ps 96:3 ... Publish his **g** deeds among the
Ps 147:5 ... This is the **g** privilege of
Isa 55:5 ... of Israel, have made you **g**.
Isa 63:15 ... from your holy, **g** home,
Dan 8:9 ... east and toward the **g** land of
Dan 11:45 ... between the **g** holy mountain
Matt 19:28 ... sits upon his **g** throne,
Acts 2:20 ... that great and **g** day of the
Acts 7:2 ... Our **g** God appeared to
Rom 1:23 ... worshiping the **g**, ever-living
Rom 3:23 ... of God's **g** standard.
Rom 8:21 ... children in **g** freedom from
2 Cor 3:9 ... how much more **g** is the new
2 Cor 3:10 ... first glory was not **g** at all
2 Cor 3:18 ... into his **g** image.
Eph 1:6 ... God for the **g** grace he has
Eph 1:17 ... asking God, the **g** Father of
Eph 3:16 ... that from his **g**, unlimited
Eph 5:27 ... himself as a **g** church without
Phil 3:21 ... them into **g** bodies like his
Phil 4:19 ... from his **g** riches, which have
Col 1:11 ... with all his **g** power so you
Jas 2:1 ... faith in our **g** Lord Jesus
1 Pet 1:8 ... with a **g**, inexpressible joy.
1 Pet 4:14 ... for the **g** Spirit of God rests
Jude 1:24 ... into his **g** presence without a

GLORY (n) *honor bestowed; splendor or magnificence; a distinguishing quality, asset, or attribute*
Exod 16:10 ... awesome **g** of the LORD
Num 14:21 ... filled with the LORD's **g**,
Josh 7:19 ... My son, give **g** to the LORD,
1 Sam 4:21 ... said, "Israel's **g** is gone."
Ps 8:5 ... them with **g** and honor.
Ps 19:1 ... proclaim the **g** of God.
Ps 29:1 ... LORD for his **g** and strength.
Ps 44:8 ... O God, we give **g** to you
Ps 57:11 ... May your **g** shine over all the
Ps 71:8 ... I declare your **g** all day
Ps 86:12 ... I will give **g** to your name
Ps 108:5 ... May your **g** shine over all the
Ps 145:12 ... the majesty and **g** of your
Prov 16:31 ... is a crown of **g**; it is gained
Isa 6:3 ... earth is filled with his **g**!
Isa 24:16 ... songs that give **g** to the
Isa 35:2 ... display his **g**, the splendor
Isa 42:8 ... not give my **g** to anyone else,
Isa 48:11 ... not share my **g** with idols!
Isa 66:11 ... Drink deeply of her **g** even
Isa 66:19 ... they will declare my **g** to the
Ezek 44:4 ... saw that the **g** of the LORD
Matt 16:27 ... angels in the **g** of his Father
Matt 25:31 ... comes in his **g**, and all the
Mark 13:26 ... great power and **g**.
Luke 2:14 ... **G** to God in highest heaven,
Luke 9:26 ... and in the **g** of the Father
Luke 9:32 ... they saw Jesus' **g** and the two
Luke 21:27 ... power and great **g**.
John 1:14 ... have seen his **g**, the **g** of
John 7:39 ... not yet entered into his **g**.
John 11:40 ... you would see God's **g** if
John 12:23 ... enter into his **g**.
John 12:41 ... the Messiah's **g**.
John 14:13 ... the Son can bring **g** to the
John 16:14 ... will bring me **g** by telling
John 17:22 ... given them the **g** you gave
Acts 3:13 ... who has brought **g** to his
Rom 2:7 ... seeking after the **g** and honor
Rom 2:10 ... there will be **g** and honor and
Rom 3:7 ... and brings him more **g**?

Rom 4:20 ... in this he brought **g** to God.
Rom 8:17 ... heirs of God's **g**.
Rom 8:18 ... compared to the **g** he will
Rom 8:30 ... gave them his **g**.
Rom 9:4 ... God revealed his **g** to them.
Rom 9:23 ... riches of his **g** shine even
Rom 9:23 ... in advance for **g**.
Rom 15:6 ... giving praise and **g** to God,
Rom 15:9 ... Gentiles might give **g** to God
Rom 16:27 ... All **g** to the only wise God
1 Cor 2:7 ... for our ultimate **g** before the
1 Cor 10:31 ... all for the **g** of God.
1 Cor 15:43 ... will be raised in **g**.
2 Cor 1:20 ... to God for his **g**.
2 Cor 3:7 ... shone with the **g** of God, even
2 Cor 3:10 ... In fact, that first **g** was not
2 Cor 4:4 ... about the **g** of Christ, who is
2 Cor 4:17 ... for us a **g** that vastly
Eph 1:12 ... bring praise and **g** to God.
Phil 1:11 ... will bring much **g** and praise
Phil 2:11 ... is Lord, to the **g** of God the
Phil 4:20 ... Now all **g** to God our
1 Thes 2:12 ... Kingdom and **g**.
2 Thes 2:14 ... share in the **g** of our Lord
1 Tim 1:17 ... All honor and **g** to God
1 Tim 3:16 ... to heaven in **g**.
2 Tim 4:18 ... All **g** to God forever
Titus 2:13 ... when the **g** of our great God
Heb 1:3 ... God's own **g** and expresses the
Heb 2:9 ... crowned with **g** and honor.
Heb 3:3 ... far more **g** than Moses, just
1 Pet 1:7 ... much praise and **g** and honor
1 Pet 1:21 ... gave him great **g**.
1 Pet 5:4 ... of never-ending **g** and honor.
2 Pet 1:3 ... means of his marvelous **g** and
2 Pet 1:17 ... from the majestic of God
Jude 1:25 ... All **g**, majesty, power,
Rev 4:9 ... beings give **g** and honor and
Rev 4:11 ... God, to receive **g** and honor
Rev 5:12 ... honor and **g** and blessing.
Rev 5:13 ... and honor and **g** and power
Rev 11:13 ... terrified and gave **g** to the
Rev 16:9 ... God and give him **g**.
Rev 21:11 ... shone with the **g** of God and
Rev 21:23 ... for the **g** of God
Rev 21:26 ... will bring their **g** and honor

GNAT, GNATS (n) *any of various small usually biting dipteran flies*
Exod 8:16 ... swarms of **g-s** throughout the
Matt 23:24 ... swallow a **g**, but you swallow

GOD, GODS (n) *eternal, infinite Spirit; Creator, Redeemer, sovereign Lord; impotent pagan deity; image of pagan deity (made of wood, metal, or stone) see also* IDOL(S)
Gen 1:1 ... In the beginning **G** created
Gen 1:27 ... In the image of **G** he created
Gen 3:1 ... Did **G** really say you must not
Gen 6:2 ... The sons of **G** saw the
Gen 14:18 ... a priest of **G** Most High,
Gen 17:1 ... El-Shaddai—'**G** Almighty.'
Gen 22:12 ... I know that you truly fear **G**.
Gen 50:20 ... **G** intended it all for good.
Exod 20:5 ... am a jealous **G** who will not
Exod 22:28 ... must not dishonor **G** or curse
Exod 32:4 ... these are the **g-s** who brought
Exod 34:6 ... The **G** of compassion
Deut 6:4 ... LORD is our **G**, the LORD
Deut 23:5 ... LORD your **G** loves you.
Deut 32:16 ... by worshiping foreign **g-s**; they
Deut 32:39 ... There is no other **g** but me!
Deut 33:27 ... The eternal **G** is
Josh 24:19 ... a holy and jealous **G**.
1 Kgs 8:23 ... there is no **G** like you

1 Kgs 18:21 ... if Baal is **G**, then follow
2 Kgs 19:15 ... You alone are **G** of all
Ezra 9:9 ... unfailing love our **G** did not
Neh 1:5 ... awesome **G** who keeps
Ps 19:1 ... proclaim the glory of **G**.
Ps 22:1 ... My **G**, my **G**, why have
Ps 42:2 ... I thirst for **G**, the living **G**.
Ps 42:8 ... praying to **G** who gives
Ps 51:10 ... a clean heart, O **G**.
Ps 82:6 ... say, 'You are **g-s**; you are all
Ps 100:3 ... the LORD is **G**!
Ps 139:23 ... Search me, O **G**, and know
Prov 24:12 ... For **G** understands all
Eccl 12:13 ... conclusion: Fear **G** and obey
Isa 9:6 ... Mighty **G**, Everlasting Father,
Isa 43:10 ... I alone am **G**.
Dan 6:16 ... May your **G**, whom you
Jon 4:2 ... compassionate **G**, slow to
Mic 6:8 ... walk humbly with your **G**.
Mic 7:18 ... Where is another **G** like you,
Nah 1:2 ... a jealous **G**, filled with
Mark 2:7 ... Only **G** can forgive
Mark 3:35 ... Anyone who does **G**'s will is
Mark 15:34 ... My **G**, my **G**, why
Luke 2:14 ... Glory to **G** in highest
Luke 10:9 ... The Kingdom of **G** is near
Luke 16:13 ... cannot serve **G** and be enslaved
Luke 20:38 ... So he is the **G** of the living,
John 1:1 ... Word was with **G**
John 1:18 ... One, who is himself **G**, is near
John 1:29 ... The Lamb of **G** who
John 3:16 ... For this is how **G** loved the world:
John 10:34 ... I say, you are **g-s**!
John 14:1 ... Trust in **G**, and trust also
Acts 5:29 ... We must obey **G** rather than
Acts 12:24 ... word of **G** continued to
Acts 19:26 ... aren't really **g-s** at all.
Rom 1:16 ... the power of **G** at work,
Rom 3:23 ... short of **G**'s glorious
Rom 5:1 ... have peace with **G** because
Rom 5:5 ... know how dearly **G** loves us,
Rom 6:23 ... free gift of **G** is eternal
Rom 8:17 ... are heirs of **G**'s glory.
Rom 12:2 ... learn to know **G**'s will for you,
1 Cor 1:18 ... the very power of **G**.
1 Cor 1:25 ... foolish plan of **g** is wiser
1 Cor 6:20 ... you must honor **G** with your
1 Cor 14:33 ... not a **G** of disorder but
2 Cor 10:4 ... We use **G**'s mighty weapons,
Gal 3:6 ... believed **G**, and **G** counted him
Eph 2:10 ... For we are **G**'s masterpiece.
Eph 5:1 ... Imitate **G**, therefore, in
Phil 2:6 ... equality with **G** as something
Phil 4:7 ... you will experience **G**'s peace,
Col 2:9 ... the fullness of **G** in a human
1 Thes 5:18 ... for this is **G**'s will
1 Tim 2:5 ... There is one **G** and one
Titus 1:2 ... **G**—who does not lie—
Heb 6:18 ... is impossible for **G** to lie.
Heb 7:19 ... we draw near to **G**.
Heb 11:6 ... believe that **G** exists
Jas 2:19 ... there is one **G**.
Jas 2:23 ... Abraham believed **G**, and **G**
Jas 4:8 ... Come close to **G**, and **G**
1 Pet 2:15 ... It is **G**'s will that your
1 Pet 5:5 ... for "**G** opposes the proud
1 Jn 1:5 ... declare to you: **G** is light,
1 Jn 4:21 ... Those who love **G** must also
Rev 19:6 ... the Lord our **G**, the Almighty,
Rev 21:23 ... glory of **G** illuminates the

GOD-BREATHED (KJV)
2 Tim 3:16 ... Scripture is *inspired by God*

GODLINESS (n) *devotion to God; piety see also* RIGHTEOUSNESS

Prov 16:8 ... Better to have little, with *g*,
1 Tim 4:8 ... but training for *g* is much
1 Tim 5:4 ... to show *g* at home
1 Tim 6:6 ... Yet true *g* with contentment

GODLY (adj) *marked by or showing reverence for God and devotion to worship*
see also RIGHTEOUS, UPRIGHT
Ps 31:23 ... LORD, all you *g* ones!
Ps 34:9 ... LORD, you his *g* people,
Prov 16:31 ... by living a *g* life.
Prov 23:24 ... The father of *g* children has
Acts 22:12 ... He was a *g* man, deeply
Gal 6:1 ... you who are *g* should gently
1 Tim 6:3 ... promote a *g* life.
2 Tim 3:12 ... to live a *g* life in Christ
Titus 1:1 ... how to live *g* lives.
2 Pet 2:9 ... how to rescue *g* people from
2 Pet 3:11 ... what holy and *g* lives you

GODLY (n) *people who are righteous or devout*
Ps 1:5 ... no place among the *g*.
Ps 37:21 ... but the *g* are generous givers.
Ps 37:30 ... The *g* offer good counsel;
Ps 68:3 ... But let the *g* rejoice.
Ps 118:20 ... LORD, and the *g* enter there.
Prov 3:32 ... friendship to the *g*.
Prov 10:11 ... The words of the *g* are a
Prov 10:20 ... The words of the *g* are like
Prov 10:28 ... The hopes of the *g* result in
Prov 11:5 ... The *g* are directed by
Prov 11:28 ... But the *g* flourish like
Prov 13:9 ... The life of the *g* is full of
Prov 20:7 ... The *g* walk with
Prov 21:15 ... Justice is a joy to the *g*,
Prov 28:1 ... the *g* are as bold as lions.

GOLD (n) *a valuable yellow malleable metal especially used in coins and jewelry*
1 Kgs 20:3 ... Your silver and *g* are mine,
Ps 19:10 ... more desirable than *g*,
Ps 119:127 ... even the finest *g*.
Prov 3:14 ... are better than *g*.
Matt 2:11 ... gifts of *g*, frankincense,
Rev 3:18 ... advise you to buy *g* from me—

GOLGOTHA (n) *a hill just outside Jerusalem; the place where Jesus was crucified*
Matt 27:33 ... a place called *G*
Mark 15:22 ... a place called *G*
John 19:17 ... (in Hebrew, *G*).

GOOD (adj) *kind; profitable; excellent; fitting or appropriate; morally right*
Gen 1:4 ... that the light was *g*.
Gen 1:31 ... it was very *g*!
Gen 2:18 ... It is not *g* for the man to
2 Chr 7:3 ... He is *g*! His faithful
2 Chr 31:20 ... was pleasing and *g* in the
Ps 34:8 ... see that the LORD is *g*.
Ps 119:68 ... You are *g* and do only
Eccl 7:20 ... earth is always *g* and never
Isa 5:20 ... that evil is *g* and *g* is
Isa 45:1 ... I send *g* times and
Mic 6:8 ... told you what is *g*, and this is
Matt 5:29 ... eye—even your *g* eye—causes
Matt 19:17 ... is only One who is *g*.
Matt 22:10 ... they could find, *g* and bad
Matt 25:21 ... Well done, my *g* and
Mark 3:4 ... the law permit *g* deeds on the
Mark 10:18 ... God is truly *g*.
Luke 6:45 ... person produces *g* things from
Luke 6:45 ... treasury of a *g* heart,

Luke 8:15 ... seeds that fell on the *g* soil
Luke 14:34 ... Salt is *g* for seasoning.
Luke 18:19 ... God is truly *g*.
Luke 19:17 ... You are a *g* servant.
John 10:11 ... I am the *g* shepherd.
Rom 7:12 ... and right and *g*.
Rom 7:16 ... that the law is *g*.
Rom 7:18 ... know that nothing *g* lives in
Rom 7:19 ... do what is *g*, but I don't.
Rom 12:2 ... you, which is *g* and pleasing
Rom 12:9 ... Hold tightly to what is *g*,
1 Cor 6:12 ... not everything is *g* for you.
1 Cor 7:1 ... Yes, it is *g* to abstain
1 Cor 15:33 ... corrupts *g* character.
Gal 6:9 ... doing what is *g*,
Eph 2:10 ... so we can do the g things he
Phil 1:6 ... who began the *g* work within
1 Thes 5:21 ... Hold on to what is *g*.
1 Tim 4:4 ... everything God created is *g*,
1 Tim 6:12 ... Fight the *g* fight
2 Tim 3:17 ... people to do every *g* work.
2 Tim 4:7 ... I have fought the *g* fight,
Titus 3:8 ... These teachings are *g*
Heb 10:24 ... of love and *g* works.
Heb 12:10 ... is always *g* for us,
Jas 2:8 ... indeed, it is *g* when you obey

GOOD (n) *something that is excellent, profitable, or morally right; advancement of prosperity or well-being; something useful or beneficial*
Gen 2:9 ... the knowledge of *g* and evil.
Gen 3:22 ... knowing both *g* and evil.
Gen 50:20 ... God intended it all for *g*.
1 Sam 26:23 ... reward for doing *g* and for
Ps 14:1 ... not one of them does *g*!
Ps 53:3 ... No one does *g*, not a single
Prov 3:27 ... Do not withhold *g* from those
Prov 11:27 ... If you search for *g*, you will
Prov 31:12 ... She brings him *g*, not harm,
Isa 55:2 ... does you no *g*?
Jer 13:23 ... you start doing *g*, for you
Jer 32:39 ... for their own *g* and for the
Matt 5:45 ... evil and the *g*, and he sends
Rom 3:12 ... No one does *g*, not a single
Rom 8:28 ... together for the *g* of those
Rom 13:4 ... sent for your *g*.
1 Cor 10:24 ... but for the *g* of others.
Gal 6:10 ... we should do *g* to everyone—
Eph 6:8 ... each one of us for the *g* we do,
1 Tim 5:10 ... because of the *g* she has
Heb 13:16 ... forget to do *g* and to share
1 Pet 2:20 ... suffer for doing *g* and endure
1 Pet 3:17 ... suffer for doing *g*, if that

GOODNESS (n) *the beneficial quality of something; kindness*
Ps 145:7 ... the story of your wonderful *g*;
Isa 63:7 ... in his great *g* to Israel,
Rom 14:17 ... a life of *g* and peace and joy
Rom 15:14 ... that you are full of *g*.

GOSPEL (KJV)
Mark 1:1 ... the *Good News* about Jesus
Luke 4:18 ... anointed me to bring *Good News*
Rom 1:16 ... not ashamed of this *Good News*
Rom 10:15 ... feet of messengers who bring *good news*
Gal 3:8 ... proclaimed this *good news*

GOSSIP (n) *rumor or report revealing personal or sensational facts about others*
Prov 16:28 ... of strife; *g* separates the
Prov 26:20 ... disappear when *g* stops.
2 Cor 12:20 ... slander, *g*, arrogance,

GOSSIP, GOSSIPING (v) *to relate rumors or reports about others*
Ps 15:3 ... who refuse to *g* or harm their
1 Tim 5:13 ... spend their time *g-ing*

GOVERNMENT (n) *the organization or agency through which a political unit exercises authority*
Isa 9:6 ... The *g* will rest on his
Rom 13:6 ... For *g* workers need
Titus 3:1 ... to submit to the *g* and its

GRACE (n) *God's free and unmerited favor toward sinful humanity*
see also FAVOR
Acts 6:8 ... full of God's *g* and power,
Acts 14:3 ... about the *g* of the Lord.
Acts 15:11 ... by the undeserved *g* of the
Acts 20:32 ... message of his *g* that is able
Rom 5:15 ... is God's wonderful *g* and his
Rom 5:21 ... now God's wonderful *g* rules
Rom 6:1 ... of his wonderful *g*?
Rom 11:5 ... of God's *g*—his undeserved
Rom 12:6 ... In his *g*, God has given us
1 Cor 3:10 ... Because of God's *g* to me,
1 Cor 16:23 ... May the *g* of the Lord
2 Cor 4:15 ... And as God's *g* reaches more
2 Cor 9:14 ... of the overflowing *g* God has
Gal 1:15 ... by his marvelous *g*,
Gal 2:21 ... do not treat the *g* of God as
Gal 5:4 ... away from God's *g*.
Eph 1:7 ... in kindness and *g* that he
Eph 2:5 ... only by God's *g* that you have
Eph 2:7 ... wealth of his *g* and kindness
Eph 2:8 ... saved you by his *g* when you
Eph 3:2 ... of extending his *g* to you
Eph 3:7 ... By God's *g* and mighty
Phil 4:23 ... May the *g* of the Lord
2 Thes 1:12 ... because of the *g* of our God
2 Thes 2:16 ... and by his *g* gave us eternal
1 Tim 1:2 ... Lord give you *g*, mercy,
2 Tim 1:9 ... show us his *g* through Christ
2 Tim 2:1 ... strong through the *g* that God
2 Tim 4:22 ... And may his *g* be with all of
Titus 2:11 ... For the *g* of God has
Titus 3:7 ... Because of his *g* he made
Titus 3:15 ... May God's *g* be with you
Heb 4:16 ... and we will find *g* to help us
Heb 12:15 ... to receive the *g* of God.
Heb 13:9 ... comes from God's *g*, not from
Heb 13:25 ... May God's *g* be with you all.
Jas 4:6 ... And he gives *g* generously
1 Pet 5:12 ... Stand firm in this *g*.
2 Pet 3:18 ... grow in the *g* and knowledge
Rev 22:21 ... May the *g* of the Lord

GRACIOUS (adj) *abounding in grace and kindness; merciful, compassionate*
2 Kgs 13:23 ... The LORD was *g* and merciful
Ps 145:13 ... he is *g* in all he
Prov 11:16 ... A *g* woman gains
John 1:16 ... received one *g* blessing after
2 Cor 8:7 ... also in this *g* act of giving.
Col 4:6 ... your conversation be *g* and
1 Tim 1:14 ... generous and *g* our Lord was!
1 Pet 1:10 ... about this *g* salvation
1 Pet 1:13 ... in the *g* salvation that will

GRAPEVINE (n) *the vine on which grapes grow*
Ps 128:3 ... a fruitful *g*, flourishing
Isa 36:16 ... from your own *g* and fig tree
John 15:1 ... am the true *g*, and my Father

GRASS (n) *green plants that grow from the ground and are suitable for grazing animals*

1721

Isa 40:6 ... people are like the *g.*
1 Pet 1:24 ... The *g* withers and

GRAVE, GRAVES (n) *burial place; euphemism for Hades, hell, or Sheol*
Ps 5:9 ... from an open *g.*
Ps 49:15 ... power of the *g.*
John 5:28 ... dead in their *g-s* will hear the
Acts 2:27 ... rot in the *g.*
Rom 3:13 ... from an open *g.*
Rev 20:13 ... death and the *g* gave up their

GREED (n) *a selfish and excessive desire for more of something (as money) than is needed*
Prov 15:27 ... **G** brings grief
Rom 1:29 ... of wickedness, sin, *g*, hate,
2 Pet 2:3 ... In their *g* they will make up
2 Pet 2:14 ... well trained in *g.*

GREEDY (adj) *having or showing a selfish desire for wealth and possessions*
1 Sam 8:3 ... for they were *g* for money.
Prov 1:19 ... all who are *g* for money;
Prov 21:26 ... people are always *g*
1 Cor 6:10 ... are thieves, or *g* people,
Eph 5:5 ... For a *g* person is an
Col 3:5 ... Don't be *g*, for a *g*

GRIEF (n) *deep and poignant distress due to bereavement; a cause of suffering*
Job 16:5 ... take away your *g.*
Ps 10:14 ... the trouble and *g* they cause.
Prov 10:1 ... a foolish child brings *g* to a
Prov 15:27 ... Greed brings *g* to the
John 16:20 ... your *g* will suddenly turn
Rom 9:2 ... sorrow and unending *g*

GRIEVE, GRIEVED (v) *to feel, show, or cause distress, vexation, sorrow, or regret*
Eccl 3:4 ... A time to *g* and a time
Isa 63:10 ... rebelled against him and *g-d*
Lam 3:20 ... time, as I *g* over my loss.
1 Thes 4:13 ... so you will not *g* like people

GROAN, GROANING, GROANINGS (n) *a deep moan indicative of pain, grief, or annoyance*
Exod 2:24 ... God heard their *g-ing*, and he
Ps 90:9 ... ending our years with a *g.*
Rom 8:26 ... for us with *g-ings* that cannot

GROUND (n) *soil, earth, or territory*
Gen 1:10 ... called the dry *g* "land" and
Gen 3:17 ... the *g* is cursed because of you.
Gen 4:2 ... Cain cultivated the *g.*
Gen 4:10 ... cries out to me from the *g!*
Exod 3:5 ... standing on holy *g.*
Exod 15:19 ... sea on dry *g!*
Isa 53:2 ... like a root in dry *g.*
Matt 10:29 ... fall to the *g* without your

GROW, GROWING, GROWS (v) *to become; to spring up and develop to maturity*
Isa 40:31 ... run and not *g* weary.
1 Cor 3:6 ... God who made it *g.*
Eph 4:16 ... is healthy and *g-ing* and full of
Phil 1:25 ... all of you *g* and experience
Col 2:19 ... it *g-s* as God nourishes it.
2 Thes 1:3 ... one another is *g-ing.*
Jas 1:15 ... when sin is allowed to *g,*
2 Pet 3:18 ... Rather, you must *g* in the

GRUMBLE (v) *to mutter in discontent*
1 Cor 10:10 ... And don't *g* as some
Jas 5:9 ... Don't *g* about each other

GRUMBLERS (n) *those who mutter in discontent*
Jude 1:16 ... people are *g* and complainers,

GUARD (adj) *defensively watchful; alert*
2 Pet 3:17 ... Be on *g*; then you will

GUARD, GUARDING, GUARDS (v) *to protect by watchful attention; to watch over*
see also KEEP
Prov 4:23 ... **G** your heart
Prov 7:2 ... as you *g* your own eyes.
Prov 24:12 ... He who *g-s* your soul knows
Luke 2:8 ... fields nearby, *g-ing* their flocks
Phil 4:7 ... His peace will *g* your hearts
2 Thes 3:3 ... and *g* you from

GUARDIAN (n) *one caring for another person or the property of another*
Gen 4:9 ... Am I my brother's *g?*
Gal 3:25 ... the law as our *g.*
1 Pet 2:25 ... your Shepherd, the **G** of your

GUIDANCE (n) *direction or counsel provided by another person*
2 Chr 26:5 ... as the king sought *g* from
Prov 24:6 ... go to war without wise *g;*
Prov 29:18 ... do not accept divine *g,*

GUIDE, GUIDED, GUIDES, GUIDING (v) *to direct, supervise, or influence usually to a particular end*
Exod 13:21 ... He *g-d* them during the
Exod 15:13 ... In your might, you *g* them
Deut 1:33 ... *g-ing* you with a pillar of fire
Job 10:10 ... *g-d* my conception and formed
Ps 16:7 ... bless the LORD who *g-s* me;
Ps 23:3 ... He *g-s* me along
Ps 32:8 ... I will *g* you along
Ps 139:10 ... your hand will *g* me,
John 16:13 ... he will *g* you into all
Gal 5:16 ... let the Holy Spirit *g* your lives.
Jas 2:4 ... are *g-d* by evil motives?

GUILT (n) *the state or feeling of one who has committed an offense*
Job 6:29 ... Stop assuming my *g,* for I
Ps 32:2 ... the LORD has cleared of *g,*
Ps 38:4 ... My *g* overwhelms me—
Ps 51:2 ... Wash me clean from my *g.*
Isa 6:7 ... Now your *g* is removed,
Dan 9:24 ... atone for their *g,* to bring

GUILTY (adj) *justly chargeable with wrongdoing*
Lev 19:17 ... not be held *g* for their sin.
Rom 3:19 ... entire world is *g* before God.
1 Cor 11:27 ... *g* of sinning against
1 Jn 3:20 ... if we feel *g*, God is greater
1 Jn 3:21 ... we don't feel *g*, we can come

H

HAIR, HAIRS (n) *a slender threadlike outgrowth of the skin of an animal or human*
Lev 19:27 ... Do not trim off the *h* on your
2 Sam 18:9 ... his *h* got caught in the tree.
Matt 10:30 ... And the very *h-s* on your head
1 Cor 11:6 ... to have her *h* cut or her head
1 Cor 11:14 ... man to have long *h?*
1 Cor 11:15 ... And isn't long *h* a woman's
Rev 1:14 ... His head and his *h* were white

HALLELUJAH (KJV)
Rev 19:1 ... shouting, "Praise the Lord!
Rev 19:3 ... rang out: "Praise the Lord!
Rev 19:4 ... "Amen! *Praise the Lord!*"
Rev 19:6 ... "*Praise the Lord!* For the Lord

HALLOW(ED) (KJV)
Exod 20:11 ... Sabbath day and *set it apart as holy*
Lev 25:10 ... Set this year *apart as holy*
1 Kgs 9:3 ... set this Temple *apart to be holy*
Matt 6:9 ... may your name *be kept holy*

HAND, HANDS (n) *the end of the arm that serves as a grasping and handling tool for humans; symbolic of power*
Gen 47:29 ... Put your *h* under my
Exod 15:6 ... Your right *h,* O LORD,
Exod 29:10 ... will lay their *h-s* on its head.
Exod 33:22 ... cover you with my *h* until
1 Kgs 13:4 ... king's *h* became paralyzed
Ps 22:16 ... have pierced my *h-s* and feet.
Ps 24:4 ... those whose *h-s* and hearts
Ps 32:4 ... your *h* of discipline
Ps 44:3 ... It was your right *h* and
Ps 63:4 ... my *h-s* to you in prayer.
Ps 75:8 ... a cup in his *h* that is full
Ps 110:1 ... at my right *h* until I humble
Ps 137:5 ... let my right *h* forget how to
Ps 145:16 ... you open your *h,* you satisfy
Isa 40:12 ... the oceans in his *h?*
Isa 41:13 ... by your right *h*—I, the LORD
Isa 55:12 ... will clap their *h-s!*
Isa 64:8 ... formed by your *h.*
Dan 10:10 ... Just then a *h* touched me
Matt 5:30 ... And if your *h*—even your
Matt 6:3 ... don't let your left *h* know what
Matt 18:8 ... with only one *h* or one foot
Matt 26:64 ... at God's right *h* and coming
Mark 12:36 ... at my right *h* until I humble
Acts 6:6 ... they laid their *h-s* on them.
Acts 7:55 ... at God's right *h.*
Acts 8:18 ... laid their *h-s* on people,
Acts 13:3 ... men laid their *h-s* on them
Acts 19:6 ... Paul laid his *h-s* on them,
Acts 28:8 ... and laying his *h-s* on him,
1 Thes 4:11 ... working with your *h-s,*
1 Tim 2:8 ... pray with holy *h-s* lifted up
1 Tim 4:14 ... church laid their *h-s* on you.
2 Tim 1:6 ... when I laid my *h-s* on you.
Heb 1:13 ... at my right *h* until I humble
Rev 13:16 ... mark on the right *h* or on the

HAPPINESS (n) *a state of well-being and contentment; joy*
Deut 24:5 ... *h* to the wife he has married.
Job 7:7 ... never again feel *h.*
Job 9:25 ... a glimpse of *h.*
Ps 86:4 ... Give me *h,* O Lord,
Ps 119:35 ... that is where my *h* is found.
Eccl 8:15 ... *h* along with all the hard work
Isa 65:18 ... Jerusalem as a place of *h.*
Luke 6:24 ... you have your only *h* now.

HAPPY (adj) *expressing, reflecting, or suggestive of happiness*
see also BLESSED
Deut 16:14 ... festival will be a *h* time
Ps 113:9 ... making her a *h* mother.
Prov 15:13 ... A glad heart makes a *h* face;
Prov 15:15 ... for the *h* heart, life is
Prov 23:25 ... she who gave you birth be *h.*
Eccl 9:7 ... drink your wine with a *h* heart,
Zech 10:7 ... will be made *h* as if by wine.
Rom 12:15 ... Be *h* with those who are *h,*
Phil 2:2 ... make me truly *h* by agreeing
Jas 5:13 ... Are any of you *h?*

HARD (adj) *lacking in responsiveness, unfeeling; demanding the exertion of energy*
Rom 11:25 ... of Israel have *h* hearts,
Rev 2:2 ... I have seen your *h* work and

HARD, HARDER (adv) *with great or utmost effort or energy*
Prov 13:4 ... those who work *h*
Acts 20:35 ... in need by working *h.*
Rom 16:12 ... has worked so *h*
1 Cor 15:10 ... worked *h-er* than any of
2 Cor 11:23 ... worked *h-er,* been put in
1 Thes 5:12 ... They work *h* among you
2 Thes 3:8 ... We worked *h* day and night

HARDEN, HARDENED (v) *to make callous or unfeeling*
Exod 4:21 ... But I will *h* his heart
Exod 10:20 ... Lord *h-ed* Pharaoh's heart
Ps 95:8 ... Don't *h* your hearts as Israel did
Isa 6:10 ... *H* the hearts of these people.
Matt 13:15 ... hearts of these people are *h-ed,*
John 12:40 ... and *h-ed* their hearts
Eph 4:18 ... minds and *h-ed* their hearts
Heb 3:8 ... don't *h* your hearts as Israel did

HARLOT (KJV)
Gen 38:15 ... thought she was a *prostitute*
Josh 2:1 ... a *prostitute* named Rahab
Hos 4:15 ... you, Israel, are a *prostitute*
Matt 21:31 ... *prostitutes* will get into the Kingdom
Rev 17:5 ... Mother of All *Prostitutes* and

HARMONY (n) *tranquility; agreement; unity*
Zech 6:13 ... will be perfect *h* between his
Rom 12:16 ... Live in *h* with each other.
Rom 14:19 ... aim for *h* in the church
Rom 15:5 ... live in complete *h* with each
1 Cor 12:25 ... This makes for *h*
2 Cor 6:15 ... What *h* can there be
2 Cor 13:11 ... Live in *h* and peace.
Col 3:14 ... together in perfect *h.*

HARVEST, HARVESTS (n) *the time or fruit of reaping or gathering in a crop—physically or spiritually*
Deut 16:15 ... blesses you with bountiful *h-s*
Matt 9:37 ... The *h* is great, but
John 4:35 ... fields are already ripe for *h.*
1 Cor 15:23 ... raised as the first of the *h;*
2 Cor 9:10 ... great *h* of generosity
Gal 6:9 ... we will reap a *h* of blessing
Heb 12:11 ... peaceful *h* of right living
Jas 3:18 ... reap a *h* of righteousness.
Rev 14:15 ... the time of *h* has come;

HARVEST, HARVESTS (v) *to gather in (a crop); to reap*
Gen 8:22 ... there will be planting and *h,*
Job 4:8 ... and cultivate evil will *h*
Prov 10:5 ... wise youth *h-s* in the summer,
Gal 6:8 ... sinful nature will *h* decay and

HARVESTER, HARVESTERS (n) *one who gathers in (a crop)*
Ruth 2:3 ... to gather grain behind the *h-s.*
John 4:36 ... planter and the *h* alike!

HATE, HATED, HATES, HATING (v) *to feel extreme enmity toward; to have a strong aversion to*
Ps 45:7 ... love justice and *h* evil.
Prov 1:22 ... you fools *h* knowledge?
Prov 6:16 ... six things the Lord *h-s*—
Prov 13:5 ... The godly *h* lies;
Prov 15:27 ... those who *h* bribes will live.
Prov 26:28 ... A lying tongue *h-s* its victims,
Prov 28:16 ... but one who *h-s* corruption
Mal 2:16 ... "For I *h* divorce!"
Matt 5:43 ... and *h* your enemy.
Matt 24:9 ... be *h-d* all over the world
Luke 6:22 ... when people *h* you
John 3:20 ... All who do evil *h* the light
John 15:18 ... remember that it *h-d* me
2 Tim 3:3 ... be cruel and *h* what is good.
Heb 1:9 ... You love justice and *h* evil.
1 Jn 2:9 ... but *h-s* a fellow believer,
1 Jn 4:20 ... *h-s* a fellow believer, that person
Jude 1:23 ... *h-ing* the sins that contaminate

HATRED (n) *strong emotional aversion*
Lev 19:17 ... Do not nurse *h* in your heart
Prov 26:24 ... People may cover their *h*

HEAD, HEADS (n) *top part of the body that contains the brain; one in charge; person, individual*
Gen 3:15 ... He will strike your *h,* and
Lev 26:13 ... walk with your *h-s* held high.
Ps 22:7 ... shake their *h-s,* saying,
Ps 23:5 ... by anointing my *h* with oil.
Ps 133:2 ... over Aaron's *h,* that ran
Prov 25:22 ... coals of shame on their *h-s,*
Matt 27:39 ... shaking their *h-s* in mockery.
John 19:2 ... thorns and put it on his *h,*
Acts 18:6 ... your own *h-s*—I am innocent.
Rom 12:20 ... coals of shame on their *h-s.*
Eph 1:22 ... and has made him *h* over all
Eph 5:23 ... as Christ is the *h* of the
Rev 4:4 ... crowns on their *h-s.*
Rev 14:14 ... He had a gold crown on his *h*
Rev 19:12 ... on his *h* were many crowns.

HEAL, HEALED, HEALING, HEALS (v) *to mend, cure, make whole; to restore to health*
Gen 20:17 ... and God *h-ed* Abimelech,
Exod 15:26 ... I am the Lord who *h-s* you.
Num 12:13 ... I beg you, please *h* her!
Deut 32:39 ... one who wounds and *h-s;*
2 Chr 30:20 ... prayer and *h-ed* the people.
Job 5:18 ... his hands also *h.*
Ps 6:2 ... *H* me, Lord,
Ps 103:3 ... and *h-s* all my diseases.
Ps 107:20 ... his word and *h-ed* them,
Prov 3:8 ... will have *h-ing* for your body
Prov 13:17 ... messenger brings *h-ing.*
Isa 6:10 ... and turn to me for *h-ing.*
Isa 30:26 ... Lord begins to *h* his people
Isa 57:18 ... but I will *h* them anyway!
Isa 57:19 ... the Lord, who *h-s* them.
Jer 8:18 ... My grief is beyond *h-ing;*
Jer 17:14 ... O Lord, if you *h* me, I will
Jer 17:14 ... I will be truly *h-ed;*
Jer 30:13 ... No medicine can *h* you.
Hos 6:1 ... now he will *h* us.
Hos 7:1 ... I want to *h* Israel, but its
Hos 14:4 ... Then I will *h* you of your
Zech 11:16 ... nor *h* the injured,
Mal 4:2 ... with *h-ing* in his wings.
Matt 4:23 ... And he *h-ed* every kind
Matt 8:7 ... will come and *h* him.
Matt 8:16 ... and he *h-ed* all the sick.
Matt 9:35 ... he *h-ed* every kind of disease
Matt 10:8 ... *H* the sick, raise the
Matt 15:30 ... Jesus, and he *h-ed* them all.
Matt 17:16 ... they couldn't *h* him.
Mark 1:34 ... So Jesus *h-ed* many people
Mark 3:2 ... If he *h-ed* the man's
Mark 3:10 ... He had *h-ed* many people
Mark 5:28 ... touch his robe, I will be *h-ed.*
Mark 6:5 ... sick people and *h* them.
Mark 6:13 ... and *h-ed* many sick
Mark 6:56 ... who touched him were *h-ed.*
Mark 10:52 ... your faith has *h-ed* you.
Luke 4:23 ... Physician, *h* yourself
Luke 4:40 ... his hand *h-ed* every one.
Luke 6:7 ... If he *h-ed* the man's
Luke 8:50 ... faith, and she will be *h-ed.*
Luke 10:9 ... *H* the sick, and tell them
Luke 13:14 ... indignant that Jesus had *h-ed*
Luke 14:3 ... *h* people on the Sabbath
Luke 14:4 ... the sick man and *h-ed* him
Luke 17:19 ... Your faith has *h-ed* you.
Luke 18:42 ... Your faith has *h-ed* you.
Luke 22:51 ... man's ear and *h-ed* him.
John 4:47 ... to Capernaum to *h* his son,
John 7:23 ... angry with me for *h-ing* a man
John 12:40 ... and have me *h* them.
Acts 3:16 ... this man was *h-ed*—
Acts 4:9 ... to know how he was *h-ed?*
Acts 4:14 ... see the man who had been *h-ed*
Acts 4:22 ... sign—the *h-ing* of a man
Acts 8:7 ... or lame were *h-ed.*
Acts 9:34 ... Jesus Christ *h-s* you! Get up,
Acts 10:38 ... and *h-ing* all who were
Acts 28:8 ... his hands on him, he *h-ed*
Acts 28:27 ... turn to me and let me *h*
1 Cor 12:28 ... the gift of *h-ing,*
1 Cor 12:30 ... have the gift of *h-ing?*
Jas 5:16 ... so that you may be *h-ed.*
1 Pet 2:24 ... By his wounds you are *h-ed.*
Rev 13:3 ... fatal wound was *h-ed!*
Rev 13:12 ... wound had been *h-ed.*

HEALING (adj) *marked by restoring to original purity or integrity*
Luke 6:19 ... *h* power went out from him,
Acts 4:30 ... your hand with *h* power;

HEALTH (n) *the general condition of the body*
Ps 38:3 ... my *h* is broken because of
Ps 38:7 ... and my *h* is broken.
Prov 15:30 ... makes for good *h.*
Isa 38:16 ... You restore my *h*
Jer 30:17 ... I will give you back your *h*

HEALTHY, HEALTHIER (adj) *enjoying good health and vigor of body, mind, or spirit*
Ps 73:4 ... bodies are so *h* and strong.
Prov 16:24 ... the soul and *h* for the body.
Dan 1:15 ... friends looked *h-ier* and better
Zech 11:16 ... nor feed the *h.* Instead,
Matt 9:12 ... he said, "*H* people don't need
Mark 2:17 ... *H* people don't need
Luke 5:31 ... answered them, "*H* people
Eph 4:16 ... whole body is *h* and growing
3 Jn 1:2 ... that you are as *h* in body as

HEAR, HEARD, HEARING (v) *to perceive sound; to listen with attention; to be informed of; to take testimony from and make a legal decision*
see also LISTEN
Gen 3:8 ... and his wife *h-d* the Lord God
Exod 2:24 ... God *h-d* their groaning,
Deut 1:16 ... judges, 'You must *h* the cases
Josh 7:9 ... people living in the land *h*
1 Kgs 8:30 ... May you *h* the humble
2 Chr 7:14 ... I will *h* from heaven and will
Neh 1:11 ... O Lord, please *h* my prayer!
Ps 5:1 ... O Lord, *h* me as I pray;
Ps 89:1 ... Young and old will *h* of your
Isa 29:18 ... the deaf will *h* words read
Isa 30:21 ... own ears will *h* him.
Isa 40:28 ... Have you never *h-d?*

Isa 59:1 ... too deaf to *h* you call.
Dan 10:12 ... has been *h-d* in heaven.
Matt 5:21 ... have *h-d* that our ancestors
Matt 5:43 ... You have *h-d* the law
Matt 11:5 ... cured, the deaf *h,* the dead
Matt 13:14 ... When you *h* what I say,
Mark 4:12 ... When they *h* what I say,
Luke 7:22 ... cured, the deaf *h,* the dead
John 8:26 ... what I have *h-d* from the one
Acts 2:6 ... When they *h-d* the loud noise,
Acts 13:7 ... he wanted to *h* the word of
Rom 10:14 ... how can they *h* about him
Rom 10:17 ... faith comes from *h-ing,*
1 Cor 2:9 ... no ear has *h-d,* and no mind
1 Cor 12:17 ... how would you *h?*
Heb 3:7 ... Today when you *h* his voice,
2 Jn 1:6 ... just as you *h-d* from the
Rev 3:20 ... If you *h* my voice and
Rev 22:8 ... I, John, am the one who *h-d*

HEART, HEARTS (n) *figuratively, the seat of emotions, thoughts, and intentions; personality, disposition; courage; love, affection; central or most vital part of something*
Gen 6:6 ... It broke his *h.*
Exod 4:21 ... will harden his *h* so he
Exod 35:21 ... All whose *h-s* were stirred
Deut 6:5 ... LORD your God with all your *h,*
Deut 9:10 ... from the *h* of the fire
Deut 20:3 ... Do not lose *h* or panic
Deut 28:65 ... will cause your *h* to tremble,
Josh 22:5 ... with all your *h* and all your
Josh 23:14 ... Deep in your *h-s* you know
1 Sam 1:15 ... pouring out my *h*
1 Sam 10:9 ... God gave him a new *h,*
1 Sam 12:20 ... the LORD with all your *h,*
1 Sam 13:14 ... a man after his own *h.*
1 Sam 16:7 ... but the LORD looks at the *h.*
1 Kgs 8:48 ... with their whole *h* and soul
1 Kgs 11:2 ... turn your *h-s* to their gods.
1 Kgs 11:3 ... turn his *h* away from the LORD.
1 Kgs 14:8 ... followed me with all his *h*
2 Kgs 23:3 ... with all his *h* and soul.
1 Chr 22:19 ... God with all your *h* and soul.
2 Chr 6:38 ... with their whole *h* and soul
2 Chr 22:9 ... sought the LORD with all his *h.*
2 Chr 34:31 ... with all his *h* and soul.
Ezra 1:5 ... stirred the *h-s* of the priests
Job 4:5 ... trouble strikes, you lose *h.*
Ps 9:1 ... praise you, LORD, with all my *h;*
Ps 14:1 ... say in their *h-s,* "There is no
Ps 19:14 ... meditation of my *h*
Ps 24:4 ... whose hands and *h-s* are pure,
Ps 27:8 ... my *h* responds, "LORD,
Ps 36:1 ... within their *h-s.* They have no
Ps 42:11 ... Why is my *h* so sad?
Ps 45:1 ... Beautiful words stir my *h.*
Ps 51:10 ... Create in me a clean *h,* O God.
Ps 57:7 ... my *h* is confident.
Ps 73:7 ... everything their *h-s* could ever
Ps 73:26 ... the strength of my *h;*
Ps 108:1 ... with all my *h!*
Ps 111:1 ... thank the LORD with all my *h-s.*
Ps 119:2 ... with all their *h.*
Ps 119:11 ... hidden your word in my *h,*
Ps 119:58 ... With all my *h* I want your
Ps 119:145 ... I pray with all my *h;*
Ps 139:23 ... and know my *h;* test me and
Prov 3:3 ... deep within your *h.*
Prov 4:23 ... Guard your *h* above all else,
Prov 13:12 ... deferred makes the *h* sick,
Prov 14:30 ... A peaceful *h* leads to a
Prov 15:13 ... a broken *h* crushes the
Prov 15:30 ... look brings joy to the *h;*
Prov 17:22 ... A cheerful *h* is good
Prov 20:9 ... have cleansed my *h;* I am pure
Prov 23:15 ... wise, my own *h* will rejoice!
Prov 27:23 ... and put your *h* into caring
Song 4:9 ... captured my *h,* my treasure,
Song 5:2 ... I slept, but my *h* was awake,
Song 5:4 ... and my *h* thrilled within me.
Song 8:6 ... like a seal over your *h,*
Isa 1:5 ... and your *h* is sick.
Isa 6:10 ... Harden the *h-s* of these people.
Isa 42:4 ... or lose *h* until justice
Jer 3:15 ... shepherds after my own *h,*
Jer 3:22 ... your wayward *h-s.*
Jer 9:26 ... have uncircumcised *h-s.*
Jer 20:9 ... burns in my *h* like a fire.
Jer 32:39 ... will give them one *h* and one
Ezek 44:7 ... who have no *h* for God.
Joel 2:12 ... Give me your *h-s.* Come with
Matt 5:8 ... those whose *h-s* are pure,
Matt 5:28 ... adultery with her in his *h.*
Matt 11:29 ... I am humble and gentle at *h,*
Matt 12:34 ... whatever is in your *h*
Matt 15:19 ... For from the *h* come evil
Matt 18:35 ... and sisters from your *h.*
Matt 22:37 ... God with all your *h,* all your
Mark 11:23 ... have no doubt in your *h.*
Mark 12:30 ... God with all your *h,* all your
Mark 12:33 ... love him with all my *h* and
Luke 6:45 ... treasury of a good *h,*
Luke 10:27 ... God with all your *h,* all your
Luke 12:34 ... desires of your *h* will also
Luke 24:38 ... Why are your *h-s* filled with
John 5:38 ... your *h-s,* because you do not
Acts 1:24 ... you know every *h.* Show us
Acts 4:32 ... were united in *h* and mind.
Acts 8:21 ... this, for your *h* is not right
Acts 15:8 ... God knows people's *h-s,* and
Acts 16:14 ... Lord opened her *h,* and she
Acts 28:27 ... hear, and their *h-s* cannot
Rom 1:9 ... with all my *h* by serving
Rom 2:15 ... written in their *h-s,* for their
Rom 2:29 ... changed *h* seeks praise
Rom 10:9 ... believe in your *h* that God
2 Cor 2:4 ... with a troubled *h* and many
2 Cor 7:2 ... Please open your *h-s* to us.
2 Cor 9:7 ... decide in your *h* how much to
Eph 1:18 ... I pray that your *h-s* will be
Eph 3:13 ... don't lose *h* because of my
Eph 5:19 ... music to the Lord in your *h-s.*
Eph 6:6 ... of God with all your *h.*
Phil 1:7 ... place in my *h.* You share with
1 Tim 1:5 ... comes from a pure *h,* a clear

HEAVEN, HEAVENS (n) *sky and stars above; God's dwelling place; abode of eternal bliss*
Deut 30:12 ... is not kept in *h,* so distant
Job 41:11 ... Everything under *h* is mine.
Ps 18:16 ... down from *h* and rescued me;
Ps 71:19 ... to the highest *h-s.* You have
Ps 108:4 ... than the *h-s.* Your faithfulness
Matt 11:25 ... Father, Lord of *h* and earth,
Matt 24:30 ... appear in the *h-s,* and there
Rom 10:6 ... go up to *h?*' (to bring Christ
2 Cor 12:2 ... to the third *h* fourteen years
Heb 9:24 ... He entered into *h* itself to

HELL (n) *abode of the dead; place of punishment; personification of evil; lowest place one can go*
Matt 5:22 ... of the fires of *h.*
Matt 16:18 ... all the powers of *h* will not
Matt 23:33 ... judgment of *h?*
Mark 9:43 ... fires of *h* with two hands.
Luke 12:5 ... throw you into *h.*
Jas 3:6 ... on fire by *h* itself.
2 Pet 2:4 ... threw them into *h,* in gloomy

HELMET (n) *any of various protective head coverings usually made of hard metal*
Isa 59:17 ... and placed the *h* of salvation
Eph 6:17 ... salvation as your *h,* and take

HELP (n) *aid, assistance*
2 Sam 22:36 ... your *h* has made me great.
Ps 30:2 ... I cried to you for *h,* and you
Ps 33:20 ... He is our *h* and our shield.
Ps 108:12 ... for all human *h* is useless.
Isa 30:18 ... wait for his *h.*
Isa 38:14 ... looking to heaven for *h.* I am
Phil 4:16 ... you sent *h* more than once.

HELP, HELPED, HELPING, HELPS (v) *to give assistance or support; to rescue or save*
Exod 23:5 ... Instead, stop and *h.*
Deut 2:36 ... our God also *h-ed* us conquer
1 Sam 7:12 ... the LORD has *h-ed* us!
Ps 46:1 ... always ready to *h* in times of
Ps 72:12 ... he will *h* the oppressed,
Ps 145:14 ... The LORD *h-s* the fallen
Prov 11:4 ... Riches won't *h* on the
Prov 14:31 ... their Maker, but *h-ing* the poor
Prov 19:17 ... If you *h* the poor,
Isa 41:10 ... strengthen you and *h* you.
Isa 44:10 ... that cannot *h* him one bit?
Jer 51:9 ... We would have *h-ed* her if we
Lam 4:16 ... he no longer *h-s* them.
Mark 9:24 ... but *h* me overcome
Acts 9:36 ... for others and *h-ing* the poor.
Acts 16:9 ... to Macedonia and *h* us!
Rom 12:13 ... be ready to *h* them.
1 Cor 12:28 ... those who can *h* others,
2 Cor 6:2 ... salvation, I *h-ed* you.
Gal 6:1 ... and humbly *h* that person back
1 Tim 5:10 ... Has she *h-ed* those who
2 Tim 2:7 ... Lord will *h* you understand
Heb 10:33 ... you *h-ed* others who
1 Pet 4:11 ... the gift of *h-ing* others?

HELPER (n) *one who gives aid; co-worker*
Gen 2:18 ... I will make a *h* who is just
Ps 70:5 ... You are my *h* and my savior;
Ps 115:9 ... He is your *h* and your shield.
Heb 13:6 ... The LORD is my *h,* so I will

HELPLESS (adj) *without any aid, comfort, protection, or chance of success*
Ps 9:12 ... cares for the *h.* He does not
Ps 10:12 ... not ignore the *h!*
Ps 34:2 ... let all who are *h* take heart.
Ps 35:10 ... Who else protects the *h*
Amos 2:7 ... They trample *h* people in the
Matt 9:36 ... confused and *h,* like sheep
Rom 5:6 ... were utterly *h,* Christ came

HID, HIDDEN (v) *to remain out of sight; unrevealed*
see also HIDE
Ps 119:11 ... I have *h-den* your word
Matt 13:35 ... explain things *h-den* since the
Matt 13:44 ... discovered *h-den* in a field.
Matt 13:44 ... he *h* it again and
Matt 25:25 ... your money, so I *h* it in the
Mark 4:22 ... that is *h-den* will eventually be
1 Cor 2:7 ... was previously *h-den,* even
Col 3:3 ... real life is *h-den* with Christ in
Heb 11:23 ... that Moses' parents *h* him

HIDE, HIDING (v) *to shield; to seek protection; to put or remain out of sight*
see also HID
Deut 31:17 ... abandon them, *h-ing* my face

1 Sam 10:22 . . . "He is **h-ing** among the
Ps 27:5 . . . he will **h** me in his
Ps 57:1 . . . I will **h** beneath the shadow
Ps 143:9 . . . run to you to **h** me.
Jer 16:17 . . . cannot hope to **h** from me.
Matt 11:25 . . . thank you for **h-ing** these

HOLINESS (n) *sanctity or purity*
Exod 15:11 . . . glorious in **h**, awesome in
Deut 32:51 . . . to demonstrate my **h** to the
Ps 29:2 . . . the splendor of his **h**.
Luke 1:75 . . . in **h** and righteousness for
1 Cor 7:14 . . . wife brings **h** to her
2 Cor 1:12 . . . a God-given **h** and sincerity
1 Thes 4:4 . . . and live in **h** and honor—
1 Tim 2:15 . . . faith, love, **h**, and modesty.
Heb 12:10 . . . share in his **h**.

HOLY (adj) *consecrated or set aside for sacred use (as opposed to pagan or common use); standing apart from sin and evil; characteristic of God, especially the third person of the Trinity*
see also PURE
Gen 2:3 . . . and declared it **h**, because it
Exod 3:5 . . . are standing on **h** ground.
Exod 19:6 . . . priests, my **h** nation.
Exod 26:33 . . . separate the **H** Place
Exod 29:37 . . . be absolutely **h**,
Exod 30:10 . . . LORD's most **h** altar.
Exod 31:13 . . . the LORD, who makes you **h**.
Lev 11:45 . . . you must be **h** because I am
Lev 19:8 . . . for defiling what is **h** to the
Lev 20:7 . . . set yourselves apart to be **h**,
Lev 20:26 . . . You must be **h** because I,
Lev 21:12 . . . for he has been made **h** by the
Lev 22:32 . . . the LORD who makes you **h**.
Lev 27:9 . . . LORD will be considered **h**.
Deut 5:12 . . . by keeping it **h**, as the LORD
Josh 5:15 . . . where you are standing is **h**.
Josh 24:19 . . . he is a **h** and jealous God.
1 Chr 16:35 . . . we can thank your **h** name
Neh 11:1 . . . in Jerusalem, the **h** city.
Ps 22:3 . . . Yet you are **h**, enthroned on
Ps 30:4 . . . Praise his **h** name.
Ps 99:3 . . . Your name is **h**!
Ps 105:3 . . . Exult in his **h** name; rejoice,
Ps 111:9 . . . What a **h**, awe-inspiring name
Prov 9:10 . . . of the **H** One results in good
Isa 6:3 . . . to each other, "**H**, **h**, **h**
Isa 40:25 . . . my equal?" asks the **H** One.
Isa 54:5 . . . your Redeemer, the **H** One of
Isa 66:20 . . . them to my **h** mountain in
Dan 7:18 . . . But in the end, the **h** people
Dan 9:24 . . . anoint the Most **H** Place.
Zech 14:5 . . . and all his **h** ones with him.
Matt 24:15 . . . standing in the **H** Place.
Mark 1:24 . . . you are—the **H** One of God
Luke 1:35 . . . baby to be born will be **h**,
Luke 1:49 . . . Mighty One is **h**, and he has
Luke 4:34 . . . you are—the **H** One of God
Luke 11:2 . . . may your name be kept **h**.
John 6:69 . . . you are the **H** One of God!"
John 17:17 . . . Make them **h** by your
Acts 13:35 . . . not allow your **H** One to rot
Rom 7:12 . . . the law itself is **h**, and its
Rom 14:5 . . . day is more **h** than another
Rom 15:16 . . . made **h** by the **H** Spirit.
1 Cor 1:2 . . . be his own **h** people.
1 Cor 1:30 . . . made us pure and **h**,
1 Cor 3:17 . . . God's temple is **h**, and you
1 Cor 6:11 . . . you were made **h**; you were
1 Cor 7:14 . . . children would not be **h**, but
Eph 1:4 . . . in Christ to be **h** and without
Eph 2:21 . . . becoming a **h** temple for
Eph 4:24 . . . righteous and **h**.

Eph 5:26 . . . to make her **h** and clean,
Col 1:22 . . . and you are **h** and blameless
1 Thes 3:13 . . . blameless, and **h** as you
1 Thes 4:7 . . . called us to live **h** lives,
1 Thes 5:23 . . . make you **h** in every
2 Thes 1:10 . . . from his **h** people—praise
1 Tim 2:8 . . . to pray with **h** hands lifted
2 Tim 1:9 . . . called us to live a **h** life.
2 Tim 3:15 . . . taught the **h** Scriptures from
Heb 2:11 . . . ones he makes **h** have the same
Heb 10:14 . . . those who are being made **h**.
Heb 10:19 . . . heaven's Most **H** Place
Heb 10:29 . . . which made us **h**, as if it
Heb 13:12 . . . make his people **h** by means
1 Pet 1:16 . . . You must be **h** because I am
1 Pet 2:5 . . . you are his **h** priests.
1 Pet 2:9 . . . priests, a **h** nation, God's
1 Pet 3:5 . . . is how the **h** women of old
2 Pet 1:18 . . . on the **h** mountain.
2 Pet 2:21 . . . to live a **h** life.
2 Pet 3:11 . . . like this, what **h** and godly
Rev 3:7 . . . one who is **h** and true,
Rev 4:8 . . . on saying, "**H**, **h**, **h** is
Rev 15:4 . . . you alone are **h**. All nations
Rev 20:6 . . . Blessed and **h** are those who
Rev 22:11 . . . continue to be **h**.

HOLY GHOST (KJV)
Matt 1:18 . . . the power of the *Holy Spirit*
Matt 3:11 . . . baptize you with the *Holy Spirit*
Matt 28:19 . . . the Son and the *Holy Spirit*
Luke 3:22 . . . *Holy Spirit*, in bodily form,
1 Jn 5:7-8 . . . three witnesses—the *Spirit*

HOLY SPIRIT *the third person of the Holy Trinity*
see also ADVOCATE, COUNSELOR
Luke 11:13 . . . give the **H** to those
2 Cor 5:5 . . . he has given us his **H**.
Eph 1:13 . . . **H**, whom he promised
Eph 4:30 . . . sorrow to God's **H**
1 Thes 4:8 . . . gives his **H** to you

HOME (n) *one's place of residence; place of origin, destiny, or comfort; family-style social unit*
see also HOUSE
Deut 11:19 . . . when you are at **h** and
1 Chr 16:43 . . . turned and went **h** to bless
Ps 46:4 . . . God, the sacred **h** of the Most
Prov 3:33 . . . but he blesses the **h** of the
Prov 27:8 . . . person who strays from **h**
Matt 10:11 . . . stay in his **h** until you leave
Luke 10:7 . . . move around from **h**
Luke 19:9 . . . has come to this **h** today,
John 14:2 . . . in my Father's **h**. If this
John 14:23 . . . make our **h** with each
Acts 16:15 . . . come and stay at my **h**.
Rom 16:5 . . . meets in their **h**. Greet my
Eph 3:17 . . . will make his **h** in your
1 Tim 5:4 . . . show godliness at **h**
Heb 13:14 . . . not our permanent **h**; we are
1 Pet 4:9 . . . share your **h** with those who

HOMOSEXUALITY (n) *erotic activity with another of the same sex*
1 Cor 6:9 . . . prostitutes, or practice **h**,
1 Tim 1:10 . . . or who practice **h**, or are

HONEST (adj) *truthful; genuine; reputable; marked by integrity*
Exod 18:21 . . . some capable, **h** men
2 Kgs 12:15 . . . were **h** and trustworthy
Ps 37:37 . . . those who are **h** and good,
Prov 12:17 . . . An **h** witness tells
Prov 28:6 . . . Better to be poor and **h** than

Jer 5:1 . . . even one just and **h** person,
Matt 22:16 . . . we know how **h** you are.
1 Thes 2:10 . . . devout and **h** and faultless

HONESTY (n) *fairness and straight-forwardness of conduct; sincerity*
Ps 51:6 . . . But you desire **h** from the
Prov 11:5 . . . are directed by **h**; the wicked
Jer 5:3 . . . searching for **h**. You struck

HONEY (n) *a sweet liquid substance produced by bees; symbolic of abundance or delight in God's word*
Exod 3:8 . . . with milk and **h**—the land
1 Sam 14:26 . . . They didn't dare touch the **h**
Ps 19:10 . . . sweeter than **h**, even **h**
Ps 119:103 . . . they are sweeter than **h**.
Isa 7:15 . . . eating yogurt and **h**
Rev 10:9 . . . be sweet as **h** in your mouth,

HONEYCOMB (n) *a mass of hexagonal wax cells in a honeybee nest that stores honey*
Song 5:1 . . . and eat **h** with my honey.

HONOR, HONORS (n) *having a renowned reputation or social standing; physical or spiritual blessing (from God); a showing of merited respect*
Ps 8:5 . . . crowned them with glory and **h**.
Ps 104:1 . . . are robed with **h** and majesty.
Prov 3:35 . . . The wise inherit **h**, but fools
Prov 15:33 . . . humility precedes **h**.
Prov 25:27 . . . not good to seek **h-s**
Isa 53:12 . . . I will give him the **h-s** of a
Isa 55:13 . . . will bring great **h** to the
Luke 14:8 . . . don't sit in the seat of **h**.
Eph 1:20 . . . the place of **h** at God's right
Heb 13:4 . . . Give **h** to marriage,
1 Pet 2:6 . . . chosen for great **h**, and
1 Pet 2:12 . . . they will give **h** to God when
1 Pet 3:7 . . . husbands must give **h** to
2 Pet 1:17 . . . when he received **h** and glory
Rev 4:9 . . . give glory and **h** and thanks
Rev 19:7 . . . and let us give **h** to him.

HONOR, HONORED, HONORING, HONORS (v) *of God, to reverence his majesty; of man, to respect or esteem, to confer honor upon*
Exod 20:12 . . . **H** your father and mother.
1 Kgs 8:43 . . . Temple I have built **h-s**
Neh 1:11 . . . who delight in **h-ing** you.
Ps 29:1 . . . **H** the LORD, you
Ps 45:11 . . . **H** him, for he is your lord.
Ps 50:16 . . . I will be **h-ed** by every nation.
Ps 47:9 . . . He is highly **h-ed** everywhere.
Prov 14:31 . . . helping the poor **h-s** him.
Isa 66:5 . . . the LORD be **h-ed**!
Matt 15:4 . . . God says, '**H** your father and
Mark 6:4 . . . A prophet is **h-ed** everywhere
Luke 16:15 . . . What this world **h-s**
John 5:23 . . . that everyone will **h** the Son,
John 12:26 . . . the Father will **h** anyone who
Rom 12:10 . . . delight in **h-ing** each other.
Rom 13:3 . . . and they will **h** you.
1 Cor 6:20 . . . So you must **h** God with your
1 Cor 12:26 . . . if one part is **h-ed**, all the
Eph 6:2 . . . **H** your father and mother
Col 1:10 . . . the way you live will always **h**
1 Thes 5:12 . . . and sisters, **h** those who are
2 Thes 1:12 . . . be **h-ed** along with him.
Titus 2:3 . . . a way that **h-s** God.

HOPE, HOPES (n) *confident trust with the expectation of fulfillment*
1 Sam 9:20 . . . focus of all Israel's **h-s**.
Job 31:16 . . . crushed the **h-s** of widows?

1725

Ps 10:17 ... LORD, you know the *h-s* of the
Ps 42:5 ... I will put my *h* in God!
Ps 112:10 ... slink away, their *h-s* thwarted.
Ps 119:49 ... to me; it is my only *h*.
Ps 119:74 ... I have put my *h* in your word.
Prov 10:24 ... the *h-s* of the godly will be
Prov 13:12 ... *H* deferred makes the heart
Zech 9:12 ... prisoners who still have *h!*
Rom 5:4 ... our confident *h* of salvation.
Rom 8:20 ... curse. But with eager *h*,
Rom 12:12 ... Rejoice in our confident *h*.
Rom 15:4 ... give us *h* and encouragement
Rom 15:13 ... God, the source of *h*, will
1 Cor 13:13 ... faith, *h*, and love—
1 Cor 15:19 ... And if our *h* in Christ is
Eph 2:12 ... without God and without *h*.
1 Thes 1:3 ... and the enduring *h* you have
1 Tim 4:10 ... struggle, for our *h* is in the
Heb 10:23 ... wavering to the *h* we affirm,
1 Pet 3:15 ... about your *h* as a believer,

HORSE (n) *a large solid-hoofed herbivorous mammal often used for working or riding*
Ps 147:10 ... strength of a *h* or in human
Prov 26:3 ... Guide a *h* with a
Zech 1:8 ... on a red *h* that was standing
Rev 6:2 ... saw a white *h* standing there.
Rev 6:4 ... Then another *h* appeared,
Rev 6:5 ... saw a black *h*, and its rider
Rev 6:8 ... and saw a *h* whose color was
Rev 19:11 ... and a white *h* was standing

HOSANNA (KJV)
Matt 21:9 ... *Praise God* in highest heaven!
Matt 21:15 ... *Praise God* for the Son of David
Mark 11:9 ... *Praise God!* Blessings on the
Mark 11:10 ... *Praise God* in highest heaven
John 12:13 ... *Praise God!* Blessings on the

HOSPITALITY (n) *generous and cordial treatment, reception, or disposition*
Matt 25:38 ... and show you *h?*
Luke 10:7 ... Don't hesitate to accept *h*,
Rom 12:13 ... be eager to practice *h*.

HOSTILITY (n) *deep-seated ill will; enmity*
Gen 3:15 ... I will cause *h* between you
Lev 26:28 ... I will give full vent to my *h*.
Gal 5:20 ... sorcery, *h*, quarreling,
Eph 2:14 ... the wall of *h* that separated
Eph 2:16 ... our *h* toward each other was
Heb 12:3 ... of all the *h* he endured from

HOUSE, HOUSES (n) *living quarters; a family including ancestors, descendants, and kindred extended family unit, including ancestors and descendants*
see also HOME, TEMPLE
Exod 12:22 ... doorframes of your *h-s*.
Exod 12:27 ... he passed over the *h-s* of the
Exod 20:17 ... your neighbor's *h*.
2 Sam 7:11 ... he will make a *h* for you—
Ps 23:6 ... live in the *h* of the LORD
Ps 27:4 ... to live in the *h* of the LORD
Ps 69:9 ... for your *h* has consumed me,
Ps 127:1 ... Unless the LORD builds a *h*,
Isa 54:2 ... Enlarge your *h*; build an
Amos 5:11 ... beautiful stone *h-s*, you will
Matt 7:24 ... who builds a *h* on solid rock.
Matt 19:29 ... given up *h-s* or brothers or
Mark 11:17 ... be called a *h* of prayer for
John 2:17 ... for God's *h* will consume me.

HOUSEHOLD (n) *a social unit composed of those living together in the same dwelling; family*
see also FAMILY
Exod 12:3 ... one animal for each *h*.
Acts 16:31 ... everyone in your *h*.
1 Tim 3:5 ... manage his own *h*,
1 Tim 3:12 ... children and *h* well.
1 Tim 3:15 ... themselves in the *h* of God.
1 Pet 4:17 ... begin with God's *h*.

HUMAN (adj) *of, relating to, or characteristic of men and women collectively; mortal; finite*
see also FLESH
Gen 1:26 ... Let us make *h* beings in our
Gen 3:22 ... Look, the *h* beings have
Gen 9:6 ... If anyone takes a *h* life,
Ps 9:20 ... they are merely *h*.
Ps 33:13 ... sees the whole *h* race.
Ps 89:47 ... futile this *h* existence!
John 1:14 ... So the Word became *h*.
John 2:25 ... to tell him about *h* nature,
John 8:15 ... judge me by *h* standards,
Rom 6:19 ... weakness of your *h* nature,
1 Cor 2:5 ... trust not in *h* wisdom but in
1 Cor 2:13 ... come from *h* wisdom.
2 Cor 3:3 ... of stone, but on *h* hearts.
2 Cor 10:3 ... We are *h*, but we
Gal 3:3 ... by your own *h* effort?
Col 2:9 ... of God in a *h* body.
1 Thes 2:13 ... words as mere *h* ideas.
Heb 7:28 ... limited by *h* weakness.
2 Pet 1:21 ... or from *h* initiative.

HUMAN, HUMANS (n) *a homo sapien; mankind*
Gen 6:3 ... Spirit will not put up with *h-s*
Isa 2:22 ... trust in mere *h-s*. They are as
Jer 17:5 ... trust in mere *h-s*, who rely on

HUMBLE (adj) *not proud or haughty; can imply lower social or economic status; meek or gentle*
Num 12:3 ... Moses was very *h*—
Ps 138:6 ... cares for the *h*, but he keeps
Ps 149:4 ... he crowns the *h* with victory.
Zech 9:9 ... yet he is *h*, riding on a
Matt 5:5 ... those who are *h*,
Matt 11:29 ... I am *h* and gentle at
Matt 21:5 ... He is *h*, riding on a
Eph 4:2 ... Always be *h* and gentle.
Phil 2:3 ... Be *h*, thinking of
Jas 4:6 ... but gives grace to the *h*.
1 Pet 3:8 ... and keep a *h* attitude.

HUMBLE, HUMBLED, HUMBLES (v) *to not think too highly of oneself; to bring low or prostrate*
Isa 26:5 ... He *h-s* the proud and
Luke 14:11 ... themselves will be *h-d*,
Luke 18:14 ... will be *h-d*, and those who
2 Cor 11:7 ... wrong when I *h-d* myself
Phil 2:8 ... he *h-d* himself in obedience
Jas 1:10 ... that God has *h-d* them.
Jas 4:10 ... *H* yourselves before the Lord,
1 Pet 5:6 ... So *h* yourselves under

HUMILIATE, HUMILIATED (v) *to shame or mortify*
Deut 21:14 ... for you have *h-ed* her.
2 Sam 22:28 ... watch the proud and *h*
Ps 18:27 ... but you *h* the proud

HUMILITY (n) *show of meekness; quality of being humble*
Prov 11:2 ... but with *h* comes wisdom.
Prov 15:33 ... *h* precedes honor.

Prov 22:4 ... True *h* and fear
Col 3:12 ... kindness, *h*, gentleness,
Jas 3:13 ... works with the *h* that comes
1 Pet 5:5 ... dress yourselves in *h* as you

HUNGER (n) *a craving or urgent need for food*
Ps 145:16 ... you satisfy the *h* and thirst

HUNGRY (adj) *feeling a strong desire for food; a craving for anything*
Prov 25:21 ... If your enemies are *h*,
Matt 15:32 ... to send them away *h*,
Matt 25:35 ... For I was *h*, and you fed me.
Luke 1:53 ... He has filled the *h* with good
Luke 6:21 ... you who are *h* now, for you
John 6:35 ... never be *h* again.
Rom 8:35 ... or are persecuted, or *h*, or
Rom 12:20 ... enemies are *h*, feed them.
Rev 7:16 ... never again be *h* or thirsty;

HUSBAND, HUSBANDS (n) *male partner in a marriage; head of family; protector and provider; figurative of Christ*
Ruth 1:8 ... kindness to your *h-s* and to me.
Prov 12:4 ... is a crown for her *h*,
Prov 31:28 ... Her *h* praises her:
Jer 3:20 ... wife who leaves her *h*.
Rom 7:2 ... binds her to her *h* as long as
1 Cor 7:3 ... The *h* should fulfill
1 Cor 7:10 ... not leave her *h*.
1 Cor 7:39 ... is bound to her *h* as long as
2 Cor 11:2 ... bride to one *h*—Christ.
Gal 4:27 ... lives with her *h!*
Eph 5:22 ... submit to your *h-s* as to the
Eph 5:23 ... For a *h* is the head
Eph 5:25 ... For *h-s*, this means
Eph 5:28 ... same way, *h-s* ought to love
Col 3:18 ... submit to your *h-s*, as is
Col 3:19 ... *H-s*, love your
1 Tim 5:9 ... faithful to her *h*.
Titus 2:4 ... to love their *h-s* and their
1 Pet 3:1 ... the authority of your *h-s*.
1 Pet 3:7 ... same way, you *h-s* must give

HYMN, HYMNS (n) *a song of praise to God*
Ps 40:3 ... to sing, a *h* of praise to our
Matt 26:30 ... they sang a *h* and went out
Mark 14:26 ... they sang a *h* and went out
Acts 16:25 ... praying and singing *h-s*
Eph 5:19 ... psalms and *h-s* and spiritual
Col 3:16 ... psalms and *h-s* and spiritual

HYPOCRISY (n) *feigning to be what one is not; pretense of piety*
Matt 23:28 ... your hearts are filled with *h*
Mark 12:15 ... saw through their *h*
Gal 2:13 ... followed Peter's *h*, and even
Gal 2:13 ... led astray by their *h*.
1 Pet 2:1 ... all deceit, *h*, jealousy,

HYPOCRITE, HYPOCRITES (n) *a person who portrays a false appearance of religion; a pretender*
Matt 6:16 ... make it obvious, as the *h-s*
Matt 7:5 ... *H!* First get rid of the log
Matt 23:13 ... and you Pharisees. *H-s!*
Luke 6:42 ... the log in your own eye? *H!*
Luke 13:15 ... Lord replied, "You *h-s!*
1 Tim 4:2 ... These people are *h-s* and liars,

I

IDOL, IDOLS (n) *a representation or symbol of a false god*
Exod 20:4 ... make for yourself an *i*
Deut 27:15 ... who carves or casts an *i*

1 Sam 15:23 ... as bad as worshiping *i-s.*
Isa 40:19 ... Can he be compared to an *i*
Isa 44:9 ... who worship *i-s* don't know
Isa 44:15 ... makes an *i* and bows down
Isa 44:17 ... and makes his god: a carved *i!*
Isa 44:19 ... who made the *i* never stops to
Hab 2:18 ... What good is an *i* carved
Acts 15:20 ... eating food offered to *i-s,*
Rom 1:23 ... worshiped *i-s* made to look
1 Cor 6:9 ... or who worship *i-s,* or commit
1 Cor 8:1 ... has been offered to *i-s.*
1 Cor 8:4 ... an *i* is not really a god
Rev 2:14 ... sin by eating food offered to *i-s*

IDOLATRY (n) *the worship of a physical object as a god; immoderate attachment or devotion to something*
Gal 5:20 ... pleasures, *i,* sorcery,

IMAGE (n) *a God-given likeness or reflection; a tangible or visible representation*
Gen 1:26 ... make human beings in our *i,*
Gen 1:27 ... human beings in his own *i.*
Gen 9:6 ... made human beings in his own *i.*
Col 1:15 ... Christ is the visible *i* of the
Jas 3:9 ... made in the *i* of God.

IMITATE, IMITATED (v) *to follow as a pattern, model, or example; to resemble; to mimic*
1 Cor 4:16 ... I urge you to *i* me.
1 Cor 11:1 ... should *i* me, just as I *i*
1 Thes 1:6 ... you *i-d* both us and the Lord
1 Thes 2:14 ... you *i-d* the believers
2 Thes 3:7 ... that you ought to *i* us.

IMMANUEL *Hebrew name meaning "God is with us"*
Isa 7:14 ... to a son and will call him *I*
Isa 8:8 ... one end to the other, O *I.*
Matt 1:23 ... a son, and they will call him *I,*

IMMATURE (adj) *lacking complete growth, development, or maturity*
Eph 4:14 ... no longer be *i* like children.

IMMORAL (adj) *characterized by conflicting with traditionally (biblically) held moral principles; sinful or impure*
Prov 2:16 ... save you from the *i* woman,
Prov 6:24 ... keep you from the *i* woman,
Prov 22:14 ... an *i* woman is a dangerous
Luke 7:37 ... a certain *i* woman from
Rom 13:13 ... promiscuity and *i* living,
Eph 5:5 ... be sure that no *i,* impure,
1 Tim 1:10 ... people who are sexually *i,*
Jude 1:4 ... grace allows us to live *i* lives.
Rev 22:15 ... the sorcerers, the sexually *i,*

IMMORALITY (n) *the quality or state of being immoral; an immoral act or practice*
Matt 15:19 ... all sexual *i,* theft, lying,
Acts 15:29 ... animals, and from sexual *i.*
1 Cor 6:13 ... made for sexual *i.*
1 Cor 6:18 ... *i* is a sin against
1 Cor 7:2 ... there is so much sexual *i,*
Gal 5:19 ... very clear: sexual *i,* impurity,
2 Pet 2:7 ... who was sick of the shameful *i*
Jude 1:7 ... towns, which were filled with *i*

IMPARTIAL (adj) *not partial or biased; treating all equally*
Deut 1:17 ... and *i* in your judgments.
Matt 22:16 ... *i* and don't play favorites.

IMPOSSIBLE (adj) *incapable of being or occurring*

Zech 8:6 ... this may seem *i* to you now,
Heb 6:4 ... it is *i* to bring back
Heb 11:6 ... it is *i* to please God

INDULGE, INDULGED, INDULGES (v) *to take unrestrained pleasure in*
Rom 1:26 ... *i-d* in sex with each other.
Rom 13:14 ... ways to *i* your evil desires.
1 Cor 5:9 ... people who *i* in sexual sin.
1 Cor 5:11 ... claims to be a believer yet *i-s*

INFANTS (n) *a child in the first period of (physical or spiritual) life*
Ps 8:2 ... and *i* to tell of your strength,
Matt 21:16 ... and *i* to give you praise.
1 Cor 3:1 ... were *i* in the Christian life.

INHERIT, INHERITED (v) *to receive as a legacy or promise; to take possession as a rightful heir*
Matt 5:5 ... they will *i* the whole earth.
Matt 25:34 ... *i* the Kingdom prepared
Mark 10:17 ... I do to *i* eternal life?
1 Cor 6:9 ... will not *i* the Kingdom
Eph 3:6 ... share equally in the riches *i-ed*
Eph 5:5 ... impure, or greedy person will *i*
Rev 21:7 ... All who are victorious will *i*

INHERITANCE (n) *the acquisition of a possession, condition, or trait from past generations; something that is or may be inherited*
Ps 16:6 ... What a wonderful *i!*
Ps 33:12 ... people he has chosen as his *i.*
Ps 61:5 ... an *i* reserved for those who
Gal 4:30 ... will not share the *i*
Eph 1:14 ... give us the *i* he promised
Col 3:24 ... give you an *i* as your reward,
Heb 9:15 ... receive the eternal *i* God has

INIQUITY, INIQUITIES (KJV)
Ps 51:9 ... Remove the stain of my *guilt*
Isa 6:7 ... your *guilt* is removed,
Isa 53:6 ... laid on him the *sins* of us all.
1 Cor 13:6 ... not rejoice about *injustice*
Rev 18:5 ... God remembers her *evil deeds*

INNOCENCE (n) *freedom from guilt or sin through being unacquainted with evil; blamelessness*
Gen 20:5 ... I acted in complete *i!*
2 Sam 22:25 ... He has seen my *i.*
Hos 8:5 ... will you be incapable of *i?*

INNOCENT (adj) *regarded as righteous; free from guilt or sin; unaware or ignorant*
Job 13:18 ... I will be proved *i.*
Job 34:5 ... Job also said, 'I am *i,*
Ps 7:8 ... for I am *i,* O Most High!
Ps 26:1 ... Declare me *i,* O LORD, for I
Ps 143:2 ... no one is *i* before you.
Matt 27:4 ... I have betrayed an *i* man.
Matt 27:24 ... I am *i* of this man's blood.
Rom 16:18 ... they deceive *i* people.

INSIGHT (n) *the power or act of seeing into a situation; discernment*
Ps 19:8 ... are clear, giving *i* for living.
Prov 7:4 ... make *i* a beloved member
Eph 1:17 ... and *i* so that you might grow

INSPIRED (adj) *influenced, moved; guided or created by divine influence*
2 Tim 3:16 ... All Scripture is *i* by God

INSTRUCT, INSTRUCTED, INSTRUCTS (v) *to provide with authoritative*

information or advice; to teach, train, or direct
Exod 4:12 ... I will *i* you in what to say.
Deut 2:1 ... just as the LORD had *i-ed* me,
Deut 4:36 ... so he could *i* you.
Josh 11:9 ... chariots, as the LORD had *i-ed.*
Josh 11:23 ... as the LORD had *i-ed* Moses.
Ps 105:22 ... He could *i* the king's aides
Prov 9:9 ... *I* the wise, and they will be
Prov 10:8 ... The wise are glad to be *i-ed,*
Prov 21:11 ... if you *i* the wise,
Acts 8:31 ... unless someone *i-s* me?
2 Tim 2:25 ... Gently *i* those who oppose
Titus 2:12 ... *i-ed* to turn from godless living

INSTRUCTION, INSTRUCTIONS (n) *a command or principle intended especially as a general rule of action; an order; directions; the action, practice, or profession of teaching*
see also COMMANDMENT(S), LAW(S)
Exod 34:32 ... Moses gave them all the *i-s*
Deut 31:11 ... you must read this Book of *I*
Josh 1:7 ... Be careful to obey all the *i-s*
Josh 1:8 ... Study this Book of *I*
Ps 19:7 ... The *i-s* of the LORD are perfect,
Ps 40:8 ... *i-s* are written on my heart.
Ps 119:97 ... Oh, how I love your *i-s!*
Prov 4:13 ... Take hold of my *i-s;*
Prov 7:2 ... Guard my *i-s* as you guard
Prov 8:33 ... Listen to my *i* and be wise.
Prov 23:12 ... Commit yourself to *i;*
Isa 40:14 ... need *i* about what is good?
Jer 31:33 ... put my *i-s* deep within
Zech 7:12 ... they could not hear the *i-s*
1 Tim 1:5 ... purpose of my *i* is that all
1 Tim 1:18 ... here are my *i-s* for you,

INSULT, INSULTS (n) *a gross indignity*
Job 20:3 ... I've had to endure your *i-s,*
Ps 69:7 ... For I endure *i-s* for your sake;
Ps 69:9 ... the *i-s* of those who insult you
Ps 69:20 ... Their *i-s* have broken my heart,
Prov 9:7 ... will get an *i* in return.
Prov 22:10 ... and *i-s* will disappear.
Rom 15:3 ... The *i-s* of those who insult you,
2 Cor 12:10 ... and in the *i-s,* hardships,
Jude 1:15 ... all the *i-s* that ungodly sinners

INSULT, INSULTED (v) *to treat with insolence, indignity, or contempt*
Prov 12:16 ... stays calm when *i-ed.*
Prov 20:20 ... *i* your father or mother,
Prov 30:9 ... and thus *i* God's holy name.
Heb 10:29 ... have *i-ed* and disdained
1 Pet 2:23 ... not retaliate when he was *i-ed,*
1 Pet 3:9 ... insults when people *i* you.
1 Pet 4:14 ... If you are *i-ed* because you

INTEGRITY (n) *honesty; without compromise or corruption*
Job 2:3 ... a man of complete *i.*
Job 2:9 ... still trying to maintain your *i?*
Job 27:5 ... I will defend my *i* until I die.
Ps 25:21 ... May *i* and honesty protect me,
Ps 26:11 ... I live with *i.* So redeem
Ps 111:8 ... faithfully and with *i.*
Ps 119:1 ... Joyful are people of *i,*
Prov 2:7 ... shield to those who walk with *i.*
Prov 10:9 ... People with *i* walk safely,
Titus 2:7 ... you do reflect the *i*

INTERCEDE, INTERCEDED (v) *to mediate or plead another's case for justice or mercy*
Isa 53:12 ... of many and *i-d* for rebels.
1 Tim 2:1 ... *i* on their behalf, and
Heb 7:25 ... lives forever to *i* with God

1727

INTERPRET, INTERPRETS (v) *to explain; to translate*
Gen 41:15 ... a dream you can *i* it.
Matt 16:3 ... how to *i* the weather
1 Cor 12:30 ... to *i* unknown languages?
1 Cor 14:5 ... unless someone *i-s* what you
1 Cor 14:13 ... *i* what has been said.
1 Cor 14:26 ... another will *i* what is said.
1 Cor 14:27 ... must *i* what they say.
1 Cor 14:28 ... is present who can *i*,

INVISIBLE (adj) *hidden; imperceptible*
Rom 1:20 ... see his *i* qualities—
Col 1:15 ... visible image of the *i* God.
Heb 11:27 ... his eyes on the one who is *i*.

IRON (n) *metal used in instruments of war, farming, and building; symbolic of strength for both security and destruction*
Ps 2:9 ... break them with an *i* rod
Prov 27:17 ... As *i* sharpens *i*, so
Dan 2:33 ... its legs were *i*, and its feet
Rev 2:27 ... rule the nations with an *i* rod
Rev 12:5 ... nations with an *i* rod
Rev 19:15 ... rule them with an *i* rod.

ISAAC Patriarch, son of Abraham; promised by God (Gen 17:16-22; 18:14); born (Gen 21:1-7; 1 Chr 1:28; Acts 7:8); recipient of divine covenant (Gen 17:21; 26:2-5); offered to God by Abraham (Gen 22:1-19; Heb 11:17-19); took Rebekah as wife (Gen 24:67); inherited wealth (Gen 25:5); prayed for wife to have children (Gen 25:20-21); father of twins, Esau and Jacob (Gen 25:24; 1 Chr 1:34); preferred Esau (Gen 25:28); dealings with Abimelech (Gen 26:1-31); tricked into blessing Jacob (Gen 27:1-29); died (Gen 35:27-29); father of a nation (Deut 29:13; Rom 9:7, 10); often mentioned in NT (Luke 3:34; Gal 4:28; Heb 11:9, 17-20; Jas 2:21).

ISRAEL
1. Another name for Jacob (Gen 32:28)
2. The united kingdom of Israel, including all twelve tribes, as ruled by Saul, David, and Solomon.
3. The northern kingdom of Israel, including the ten northern tribes, in contrast to Judah (southern kingdom) (see 2 Sam 19:41-43).

Exod 3:9 ... cry of the people of *I* has
Exod 12:37 ... *I* left Rameses and started
Exod 16:1 ... *I* set out from Elim
Exod 28:29 ... *I* on the sacred chestpiece
Exod 31:16 ... *I* must keep the Sabbath day
Exod 39:42 ... *I* followed all of the LORD's
Lev 25:55 ... the people of *I* belong to me.
Num 6:23 ... *I* with this special blessing:
Num 9:17 ... *I* would break camp and follow
Num 20:22 ... community of *I* left Kadesh
Num 27:12 ... I have given the people of *I*.
Num 35:10 ... instructions to the people of *I*.
Deut 10:12 ... *I*, what does the LORD your
Josh 21:3 ... *I* gave the Levites the following
Judg 17:6 ... In those days *I* had no king;
1 Sam 3:20 ... And all *I*, from Dan
1 Sam 4:21 ... said, "*I*'s glory is gone."
1 Sam 15:26 ... rejected you as king of *I*.
1 Sam 18:16 ... all *I* and Judah loved David
2 Sam 14:25 ... handsome man in all *I*.
1 Kgs 1:35 ... him to be ruler over *I*
1 Kgs 12:1 ... I had gathered to make him king.
1 Kgs 19:18 ... preserve 7,000 others in *I*
2 Kgs 17:24 ... replacing the people of *I*.

1 Chr 11:4 ... and all *I* went to Jerusalem
1 Chr 21:1 ... Satan rose up against *I*
2 Chr 9:8 ... Because God loves *I*
Ps 73:1 ... Truly God is good to *I*,
Ps 98:3 ... to love and be faithful to *I*.
Isa 44:6 ... says—*I*'s King and Redeemer,
Isa 44:21 ... you are my servant, O *I*.
Jer 2:3 ... In those days *I* was holy
Jer 31:2 ... give rest to the people of *I*.
Jer 31:9 ... For I am *I*'s father,
Jer 31:31 ... covenant with the people of *I*
Ezek 3:17 ... as a watchman for *I*.
Hos 1:10 ... *I*'s people will be like the sands
Hos 3:1 ... LORD still loves *I*, even though
Amos 4:12 ... in judgment, you people of *I*!
Amos 8:2 ... Like this fruit, *I* is ripe
Mic 5:2 ... a ruler of *I*, whose origins are
Mal 1:5 ... far beyond *I*'s borders!
Matt 2:6 ... the shepherd for my people *I*.
Matt 10:6 ... people of *I*—God's lost sheep.
Matt 15:24 ... lost sheep—the people of *I*.
Mark 12:29 ... Listen, O *I*!
Acts 1:6 ... time come for you to free *I*
Acts 9:15 ... as well as to the people of *I*.
Rom 9:4 ... *I*, chosen to be God's adopted
Rom 9:6 ... *I* are truly members of God's
Rom 9:27 ... *I* are as numerous as the sand
Rom 9:31 ... *I*, who tried so hard to get
Rom 10:1 ... the people of *I* to be saved.
Rom 11:7 ... *I* have not found the favor
Rom 11:26 ... And so all *I* will be saved.
Eph 2:12 ... citizenship among the people of *I*,
Phil 3:5 ... a pure-blooded citizen of *I* and
Heb 8:8 ... covenant with the people of *I*
Rev 7:4 ... sealed from all the tribes of *I*:
Rev 21:12 ... *I* were written on the gates.

J

JACOB Patriarch, son of Isaac, grandson of Abraham; younger twin son of Isaac and Rebekah (Gen 25:23-35:26; 48-49); also known as "Israel" (Gen 32:28); favored by Rebekah (Gen 25:28); bought Esau's birthright for a meal (Gen 25:29-34); deceived Isaac to receive his blessing (Gen 27:1-29); fled from Esau (Gen 27:41-45); married inside of clan (Gen 28:1-5); Jacob's ladder (Gen 28:12); covenant extended to Jacob in a dream (Gen 28:13-15); wives and concubines, Rachel favored (Gen 29:1-30); children (Gen 29:31-30:24; 35:16-26); prospered at his uncle Laban's expense (Gen 30:25-43); fled from Laban (Gen 31); name changed to "Israel" (Gen 32:22-32); reconciled with Esau (Gen 33); favored Rachel's oldest son Joseph (Gen 37:3); overwhelmed by loss of Joseph (Gen 37:33-35); migrated to Egypt (Gen 46:5-7); blessed Joseph's sons (Gen 48); blessed his own sons (Gen 49:1-28); died (Gen 49:33); buried (Gen 50:1-14); often mentioned in NT (John 4:5-6, 12; Acts 7:8-15; Rom 9:13; Heb 11:20-21). see also ISRAEL

JEALOUS (adj) *intolerant of rivalry or unfaithfulness; hostile toward a rival*
Exod 20:5 ... am a *j* God who will not
Exod 34:14 ... whose very name is *J*,
Prov 6:34 ... *j* husband will be furious,
Nah 1:2 ... a *j* God, filled with vengeance
Rom 11:14 ... *j* of what you Gentiles have,
1 Cor 13:4 ... Love is not *j* or boastful
Gal 5:26 ... provoke one another, or be *j*
Jas 3:14 ... if you are bitterly *j* and there is

JEALOUSY (n) *a jealous feeling, disposition, or attitude*
Prov 27:4 ... but *j* is even more dangerous.
Rom 10:19 ... I will rouse your *j*
Rom 13:13 ... or in quarreling and *j*.
1 Cor 10:22 ... dare to rouse the Lord's *j*?
2 Cor 11:2 ... you with the *j* of God
Gal 5:20 ... *j*, outbursts of anger,
1 Tim 6:4 ... arguments ending in *j*,
1 Pet 2:1 ... with all deceit, hypocrisy, *j*,

JEHOVAH (KJV)
Exod 6:3 ... did not reveal my name, Yahweh, to them
Ps 83:18 ... you alone are called the LORD
Isa 12:2 ... The LORD GOD is my strength
Isa 26:4 ... the LORD GOD is the eternal

JERICHO (n) *a city in the plain of the Jordan Valley at the foot of the ascent to the Judean mountains*
Num 22:1 ... across from *J*.
Josh 3:16 ... near the town of *J*.
Josh 5:10 ... at Gilgal on the plains of *J*,
Luke 10:30 ... from Jerusalem down to *J*,
Heb 11:30 ... around *J* for seven days,

JERUSALEM (n) *sacred city and well-known capital of Israel since the reign of King David*
Josh 10:1 ... Adoni-zedek, king of *J*, heard
Josh 15:8 ... where the city of *J* is located.
Judg 1:8 ... attacked *J* and captured it,
2 Sam 5:5 ... *J* he reigned over all Israel
2 Sam 11:1 ... David stayed behind in *J*.
1 Kgs 9:15 ... terraces, the wall of *J*,
1 Kgs 10:26 ... and some near him in *J*.
1 Kgs 14:25 ... came up and attacked *J*.
2 Kgs 8:17 ... he reigned in *J* eight years.
2 Kgs 12:1 ... He reigned in *J* forty years.
2 Kgs 14:2 ... reigned in *J* twenty-nine years.
2 Kgs 15:2 ... he reigned in *J* fifty-two years.
2 Kgs 16:2 ... he reigned in *J* sixteen years.
2 Kgs 18:2 ... reigned in *J* twenty-nine years.
2 Kgs 19:31 ... will spread out from *J*,
2 Kgs 21:12 ... I will bring such disaster on *J*
2 Kgs 22:1 ... reigned in *J* thirty-one years.
2 Kgs 23:31 ... he reigned in *J* three months.
2 Kgs 24:8 ... he reigned in *J* three months.
2 Kgs 24:14 ... Nebuchadnezzar took all of *J*
2 Kgs 24:20 ... anger against the people of *J*
2 Kgs 25:9 ... and all the houses of *J*.
1 Chr 21:16 ... reaching out over *J*.
2 Chr 3:1 ... the Temple of the LORD in *J*
2 Chr 9:1 ... she came to *J* to test him
2 Chr 20:15 ... all you people of Judah and *J*!
2 Chr 29:8 ... has fallen upon Judah and *J*.
2 Chr 36:19 ... tore down the walls of *J*,
Ezra 2:1 ... but now they returned to *J*
Ezra 4:12 ... came here to *J* from Babylon
Ezra 6:12 ... who has chosen the city of *J*
Ezra 9:9 ... a protective wall in Judah and *J*.
Neh 1:3 ... The wall of *J* has been torn
Neh 3:8 ... They left out a section of *J*
Neh 11:1 ... of the people were living in *J*,
Neh 12:43 ... joy of the people of *J* could be
Ps 9:11 ... the LORD who reigns in *J*.
Ps 51:18 ... rebuild the walls of *J*.
Ps 74:2 ... remember *J*, your home here
Ps 79:1 ... made *J* a heap of ruins.
Ps 87:2 ... He loves the city of *J* more than
Ps 102:13 ... arise and have mercy on *J*—
Ps 122:2 ... standing inside your gates, O *J*.
Ps 122:6 ... Pray for peace in *J*.
Ps 125:2 ... *J*, so the LORD surrounds
Ps 128:5 ... May you see *J* prosper
Ps 137:3 ... Sing us one of those songs of *J*!

Ps 137:5 ... If I forget you, O *J*,
Ps 147:2 ... The LORD is rebuilding *J*
Ps 147:12 ... Glorify the LORD, O *J*!
Isa 1:1 ... saw concerning Judah and *J*.
Isa 3:1 ... take away from *J* and Judah
Isa 4:3 ... who survive the destruction of *J*
Isa 27:13 ... return to *J* to worship the LORD
Isa 31:5 ... will hover over *J* and protect it
Isa 40:2 ... Speak tenderly to *J*.
Isa 51:11 ... They will enter *J* singing,
Isa 52:1 ... clothes, O holy city of *J*,
Isa 52:8 ... see the LORD returning to *J*.
Isa 62:7 ... makes *J* the pride of the earth.
Jer 2:2 ... Go and shout this message to *J*.
Jer 4:5 ... to Judah, and broadcast to *J*!
Jer 6:6 ... ramps against the walls of *J*.
Jer 9:11 ... will make *J* into a heap of ruins,
Jer 23:14 ... prophets of *J* are even worse!
Jer 26:18 ... *J* will be reduced to ruins!
Jer 39:1 ... with his entire army to besiege *J*.
Jer 51:50 ... think about your home in *J*.
Lam 1:7 ... *J* remembers her ancient splendor.
Dan 6:10 ... windows open toward *J*.
Dan 9:2 ... *J* must lie desolate for seventy
Dan 9:12 ... a disaster as happened in *J*.
Dan 9:25 ... command is given to rebuild *J*
Joel 3:16 ... from Zion and thunder from *J*.
Amos 2:5 ... fortresses of *J* will be destroyed.
Obad 1:11 ... and cast lots to divide up *J*,
Mic 4:2 ... his word will go out from *J*.
Zeph 3:16 ... the announcement of *J* will be,
Zech 1:17 ... Zion and choose *J* as his own.
Zech 2:4 ... *J* will someday be so full
Zech 8:8 ... home again to live safely in *J*.
Zech 8:22 ... nations will come to *J* to seek
Zech 9:10 ... and the warhorses from *J*.
Zech 12:10 ... and on the people of *J*.
Zech 14:8 ... waters will flow out from *J*,
Matt 20:18 ... going up to *J*, where the Son
Matt 21:10 ... city of *J* was in an uproar
Matt 23:37 ... *J*, the city that kills the
Mark 10:33 ... going up to *J*, where the Son
Luke 2:22 ... parents took him to *J*
Luke 2:41 ... Jesus' parents went to *J*
Luke 4:9 ... Then the devil took him to *J*,
Luke 9:31 ... about to be fulfilled in *J*.
Luke 13:34 ... O *J*, *J*, the city that kills
Luke 18:31 ... to *J*, where all the predictions
Luke 21:20 ... you see *J* surrounded
Luke 24:47 ... nations, beginning in *J*:
Acts 1:8 ... about me everywhere—in *J*,
Acts 6:7 ... believers greatly increased in *J*,
Acts 20:22 ... bound by the Spirit to go to *J*.
Acts 23:11 ... a witness to me here in *J*,
Rom 9:33 ... I am placing a stone in *J*
Rom 11:26 ... rescues will come from *J*,
Rom 15:19 ... from *J* all the way to Illyricum.
Gal 4:25 ... *J* is just like Mount Sinai
Gal 4:26 ... represents the heavenly *J*.
Heb 12:22 ... living God, the heavenly *J*,
Rev 21:10 ... he showed me the holy city, *J*,

JESUS see also CHRIST, MESSIAH
Family line (Matt 1:1-17; Luke 3:23-38); birth announced (Matt 1:18-25; Luke 1:26-38); born in Bethlehem (Luke 2:1-20); circumcised, officially named, and presented at Temple (Luke 2:21-40); visited by Magi (Matt 2:1-12); escape to and return from Egypt (Matt 2:13-23); amazed the Temple scholars (Luke 2:41-50); summary of youth (Luke 2:51-52); baptized by John (Matt 3:13-17; Mark 1:9-11; Luke 3:21-22; John 1:32-34); tempted by Satan (Matt 4:1-11; Mark 1:12-13; Luke 4:1-13); ministered in Galilee (Matt 4:12–18:35; Mark 1:14–9:50); transfigured on a mountain (Matt 17:1-13; Mark 9:2-13; Luke 9:28-36; 2 Pet 1:16-18); triumphal entry (Matt 21:1-11; Mark 11:1-11; Luke 19:28-44; John 12:12-19); the Last Supper (Matt 26:17-35; Mark 14:12-31; Luke 22:7-38; John 13–17); betrayed and tried (Matt 26:36–27:31; Mark 14:32–15:20; Luke 22:39–23:25; John 18:1–19:16); crucified, died, and was buried (Matt 27:32-66; Mark 15:21-47; Luke 23:26-56; John 19:17-42); rose again and appeared to followers (Matt 28; Mark 16; Luke 24; John 20–21; Acts 1:1-11; 7:55-56; 9:3-6; 1 Cor 15:1-8; Rev 1:1-20); ascended to heaven (Mark 16:19; Luke 24:50-53; John 1:51; Acts 1:9; Eph 4:8).

JOHN
1. The Baptist, son of Zechariah and Elizabeth (Luke 1:5-25, 57-80); called to prepare the way for the Messiah (Isa 40:3-5; Luke 3:1-6; John 1:19-28); called to preach and baptize (Matt 3:1-12; Mark 1:1-8); preached repentance (Luke 3:7-20); baptized Jesus (Matt 3:13-17; Luke 3:21-22); confirmed Jesus' ministry (Matt 3:11-12; Mark 1:7-8; Luke 3:15-18; John 3:22-36; 5:33); ministry compared to Elijah (Mal 4:5; Matt 11:11-19; Mark 9:11-13; Luke 7:24-35); arrested and beheaded by Herod Antipas (Matt 14:1-12; Mark 6:14-29; Luke 9:7-9).
2. One of the 12 disciples, brother of James, son of Zebedee (Matt 10:2; Mark 3:17); witnessed the Transfiguration (Matt 17:1-9; Mark 9:2-8; Luke 9:28-36); inner circle of Jesus' followers (Matt 17:1; Mark 5:37; 9:2; 13:3; Luke 8:51; 9:28; Gal 2:9); with Peter, healed a man and was arrested (Acts 3–4); with Peter, rebuked sorcerer (Acts 8:14-25); wrote fourth Gospel (John 13:23-25; see also 20:2; 21:20-25), letters of John (the "elder," 2 Jn 1:1; 3 Jn 1:1), and Revelation (the "servant," Rev 1:1, 9; 22:8).
3. See MARK, also known as John Mark.

JOIN, JOINED, JOINS (v) *to put or bring into close association or relationship; to take part in a collective activity*
Ps 26:5 ... I refuse to *j* in with the wicked.
Dan 11:34 ... who *j* them will not be sincere.
Zech 2:11 ... will *j* themselves to the LORD
Matt 19:6 ... what God has *j-ed* together.
Mark 10:9 ... what God has *j-ed* together.
Rom 6:3 ... *j-ed* with Christ Jesus in baptism,
Rom 8:16 ... his Spirit *j-s* with our spirit
Rom 15:30 ... *j* in my struggle by praying
1 Cor 6:16 ... if a man *j-s* himself to
Eph 2:21 ... carefully *j-ed* together in him,

JOY, JOYS (n) *the emotion evoked by well-being, success, or good fortune*
Deut 16:15 ... be a time of great *j* for all.
1 Sam 18:6 ... danced for *j* with tambourines
1 Chr 16:27 ... and *j* fill his dwelling.
1 Chr 29:22 ... with great *j* that day.
Ezra 3:12 ... however, were shouting for *j*.
Neh 8:10 ... *j* of the LORD is your strength!
Neh 8:17 ... they were all filled with great *j*!
Esth 9:22 ... and their mourning into *j*.
Job 3:22 ... with *j* when they finally die,
Job 8:21 ... your lips with shouts of *j*.
Ps 1:1 ... *j-s* of those who do not follow
Ps 2:12 ... *j* for all who take refuge in him!
Ps 9:2 ... filled with *j* because of you.
Ps 19:8 ... bringing *j* to the heart.
Ps 21:1 ... He shouts with *j*
Ps 28:7 ... my heart is filled with *j*.
Ps 30:11 ... and clothed me with *j*,
Ps 32:2 ... what *j* for those whose record
Ps 33:12 ... *j* for the nation whose God
Ps 41:1 ... *j-s* of those who are kind
Ps 42:4 ... singing for *j* and giving thanks
Ps 45:7 ... pouring out the oil of *j* on you
Ps 46:4 ... A river brings *j* to the city
Ps 51:12 ... to me the *j* of your salvation,
Ps 65:8 ... you inspire shouts of *j*.
Ps 65:13 ... They all shout and sing for *j*!
Ps 71:23 ... I will shout for *j* and sing
Ps 92:4 ... I sing for *j* because of what
Ps 98:4 ... in praise and sing for *j*!
Ps 105:43 ... his people out of Egypt with *j*,
Ps 106:5 ... Let me rejoice in the *j*
Ps 119:92 ... hadn't sustained me with *j*,
Ps 126:2 ... laughter, and we sang for *j*.
Ps 132:9 ... loyal servants sing for *j*.
Ps 132:16 ... servants will sing for *j*.
Ps 145:7 ... *j* about your righteousness.
Prov 10:1 ... A wise child brings *j*
Prov 11:10 ... *j* when the wicked die.
Prov 14:10 ... no one else can fully share its *j*.
Prov 15:20 ... Sensible children bring *j* to
Prov 21:15 ... Justice is a *j* to the godly,
Prov 23:25 ... your father and mother *j*!
Prov 29:6 ... righteous escape, shouting for *j*.
Isa 12:6 ... shout his praise with *j*!
Isa 16:9 ... no more shouts of *j* over your
Isa 16:10 ... gone the *j* of harvest.
Isa 26:19 ... will rise up and sing for *j*!
Isa 35:10 ... crowned with everlasting *j*.
Isa 42:11 ... Let the people of Sela sing for *j*;
Isa 49:13 ... Sing for *j*, O heavens!
Isa 51:11 ... filled with *j* and gladness.
Isa 52:8 ... watchmen shout and sing with *j*,
Isa 56:7 ... fill them with *j* in my house
Isa 60:15 ... beautiful forever, a *j* to all
Isa 61:7 ... everlasting *j* will be yours.
Isa 65:14 ... My servants will sing for *j*, but
Jer 31:13 ... young women will dance for *j*,
Jer 31:13 ... turn their mourning into *j*.
Jer 33:11 ... the sounds of *j* and laughter.
Jer 48:33 ... treads the grapes with shouts of *j*.
Jer 49:25 ... a city of *j*, will be forsaken!
Joel 1:12 ... the people's *j* has dried up
Matt 2:10 ... they were filled with *j*!
Matt 28:8 ... but also filled with great *j*,
Mark 1:11 ... Son, and you bring me great *j*.
Mark 4:16 ... receive it with *j*.
Luke 1:14 ... have great *j* and gladness,
Luke 1:44 ... in my womb jumped for *j*.
Luke 2:10 ... bring great *j* to all people.
Luke 6:23 ... be happy! Yes, leap for *j*!
Luke 10:21 ... with the *j* of the Holy Spirit,
Luke 24:41 ... filled with *j* and wonder.
John 15:11 ... you will be filled with my *j*.
John 16:20 ... turn to wonderful *j*.
John 16:24 ... and you will have abundant *j*.
John 20:20 ... *j* when they saw the Lord!
Acts 2:28 ... you will fill me with the *j*
Acts 2:46 ... their meals with great *j*
Acts 11:23 ... he was filled with *j*,
Acts 13:52 ... believers were filled with *j*
Acts 15:3 ... much to everyone's *j*—
Rom 14:17 ... and *j* in the Holy Spirit.
Rom 15:13 ... with *j* and peace because
2 Cor 1:24 ... so you will be full of *j*,
2 Cor 2:3 ... ought to give me the greatest *j*.
2 Cor 2:3 ... *j* comes from your being joyful.
2 Cor 6:10 ... but we always have *j*.
2 Cor 7:7 ... I was filled with *j*!
Gal 5:22 ... fruit in our lives: love, *j*, peace,
Phil 1:4 ... requests for all of you with *j*,
Phil 1:25 ... experience the *j* of your faith.

Phil 4:1 … you are my *j* and the crown
1 Thes 1:6 … received the message with *j*
1 Thes 2:19 … what gives us hope and *j*,
1 Thes 2:20 … Yes, you are our pride and *j*.
1 Thes 3:9 … we have great *j*
2 Tim 1:4 … with *j* when we are together
Heb 10:34 … you accepted it with *j*.
Heb 12:2 … Because of the *j* awaiting him,
Heb 13:17 … reason to do this with *j*
Jas 1:2 … it an opportunity for great *j*.
1 Pet 1:8 … a glorious, inexpressible *j*.
1 Pet 4:13 … the wonderful *j* of seeing his
1 Jn 1:4 … you may fully share our *j*.

JUDEA (n) *the Greco-Roman name for the land of Judah*
Matt 2:1 … was born in Bethlehem in *J*,
Matt 24:16 … in *J* must flee to the hills.
Luke 3:1 … Pilate was governor over *J*;
Acts 1:8 … throughout *J*, in Samaria,
Acts 9:31 … had peace throughout *J*,
1 Thes 2:14 … in God's churches in *J*

JUDGE, JUDGES (n) *a public official authorized to decide issues brought before a court; one of a cycle of charismatic deliverers of ancient Israel*
Deut 17:12 … to reject the verdict of the *j*
Judg 2:16 … LORD raised up *j-s* to rescue
Judg 2:18 … the LORD raised up a *j*
1 Sam 7:6 … Samuel became Israel's *j*.)
1 Sam 7:15 … continued as Israel's *j*
Ps 50:6 … God himself will be the *j*.
Isa 33:22 … the LORD is our *j*, our lawgiver,
Acts 7:35 … you a ruler and *j* over us?
Acts 10:42 … *j* of all—the living and
Rev 14:7 … he will sit as *j*.

JUDGE, JUDGED, JUDGES, JUDGING (v) *to form an evaluation of; to decide as a judge; to govern or rule; to punish or condemn; to form a negative opinion about*
1 Sam 16:7 … Don't *j* by his appearance or
1 Sam 24:12 … the LORD *j* between us.
2 Chr 19:7 … *j* with integrity, for the LORD
Ps 7:8 … The LORD *j-s* the nations.
Ps 9:4 … For you have *j-d* in my favor;
Ps 9:8 … He will *j* the world
Ps 82:8 … Rise up, O God, and *j* the earth,
Ps 96:10 … He will *j* all peoples fairly.
Ps 96:13 … will *j* the world with justice,
Prov 16:10 … he must never *j* unfairly.
Prov 29:14 … If a king *j-s* the poor fairly,
Isa 11:3 … He will not *j* by appearance
Isa 66:16 … He will *j* the earth,
Matt 7:1 … Do not *j* others, and you
Matt 16:27 … will *j* all people according
Matt 19:28 … thrones, *j-ing* the twelve
John 3:18 … been *j-d* for not believing
John 5:22 … the Father *j-s* no one.
John 5:22 … absolute authority to *j*,
John 5:27 … authority to *j* everyone
John 5:30 … I *j* as God tells me.
John 12:31 … time for *j-ing* this world
John 12:47 … not *j* those who hear me
Acts 17:31 … he has set a day for *j-ing*
Rom 2:16 … Jesus, will *j* everyone's secret
Rom 3:6 … be qualified to *j* the world?
1 Cor 6:2 … we believers will *j*
1 Cor 11:31 … we would not be *j-d*
2 Cor 5:10 … stand before Christ to be *j-d*.
2 Tim 4:1 … Jesus, who will someday *j*
Heb 10:30 … The LORD will *j* his own
Heb 13:4 … *j* people who are immoral
Jas 2:13 … will be merciful when he *j-s*
Jas 3:1 … we who teach will be *j-d* more

Jas 4:11 … criticizing and *j-ing* God's law.
Jas 4:12 … So what right do you have to *j*
1 Pet 1:17 … He will *j* or reward you
1 Pet 2:23 … God, who always *j-s* fairly.
Rev 19:11 … *j-s* fairly and wages a righteous
Rev 20:4 … given the authority to *j*.
Rev 20:12 … the dead were *j-d* according to

JUDGMENT, JUDGMENTS (n) *a ruling or decision by a ruler, a judge, or an individual; the process of forming an opinion or evaluation by discerning and comparing*
see also JUSTICE
Deut 1:17 … impartial in your *j-s*.
1 Sam 3:13 … warned him that *j* is coming
Ps 1:5 … be condemned at the time of *j*.
Ps 37:13 … he sees their day of *j* coming.
Ps 51:4 … your *j* against me is just.
Prov 4:1 … Pay attention and learn good *j*,
Prov 4:7 … else you do, develop good *j*.
Prov 9:10 … results in good *j*.
Isa 3:14 … comes forward to pronounce *j*
Jer 11:20 … you make righteous *j-s*,
Jer 25:31 … His cry of *j* will reach
Dan 9:11 … curses and *j-s* written in
Hos 6:5 … with *j-s* as inescapable as light.
Joel 3:12 … LORD, will sit to pronounce *j*
Matt 5:21 … murder, you are subject to *j*.
Matt 11:24 … will be better off on *j* day
Matt 12:36 … on *j* day for every idle word
Matt 12:41 … this generation on *j* day
John 5:30 … *j* is just, because I carry out
John 8:16 … if I did, my *j* would be correct
John 16:8 … and of the coming *j*.
Acts 24:25 … coming day of *j*,
1 Cor 4:3 … I don't even trust my own *j*
1 Cor 4:5 … don't make *j-s* about anyone
1 Cor 11:29 … eating and drinking God's *j*
2 Thes 1:8 … *j* on those who don't know
Heb 9:27 … and after that comes *j*,
1 Pet 4:17 … And if *j* begins with us,
2 Pet 2:9 … until the day of final *j*.
2 Pet 3:7 … being kept for the day of *j*,
Jude 1:6 … waiting for the great day of *j*.
Rev 16:7 … your *j-s* are true and just.

JUST (adj) *conforming to a standard of correctness; faithful to the original design; honest, fair, upright*
see also RIGHT, RIGHTEOUS
Gen 18:19 … by doing what is right and *j*.
Deut 32:4 … Everything he does is *j*
2 Sam 8:15 … did what was *j* and right
Neh 9:13 … and instructions that were *j*,
Job 37:23 … he is *j* and righteous,
Ps 33:5 … loves whatever is *j* and good;
Ps 92:15 … The LORD is *j*! He is
Ps 119:121 … I have done what is *j*
Prov 1:3 … do what is right, *j*, and fair.
Prov 2:9 … will understand what is right, *j*,
Prov 12:5 … The plans of the godly are *j*;
Isa 16:5 … He will always do what is *j*
Isa 59:8 … or what it means to be *j*
Jer 22:3 … Be fair-minded and *j*.
Ezek 18:5 … and does what is *j* and right.
Dan 4:37 … All his acts are *j* and true,
Matt 5:45 … rain on the *j* and the unjust
1 Jn 1:9 … he is faithful and *j* to forgive
Rev 15:3 … *J* and true are your ways,
Rev 16:5 … You are *j*, O Holy One,
Rev 16:7 … your judgments are true and *j*.
Rev 19:2 … His judgments are true and *j*.

JUSTICE (n) *the administration of law that determines what is right, based on principles of equity and correctness,*

and rewards accordingly; the quality of being just, impartial, or fair
see also JUDGMENT, RIGHTEOUS
Exod 23:2 … by the crowd to twist *j*.
Lev 19:15 … Do not twist *j* in legal matters
Deut 16:19 … never twist *j* or show partiality
Deut 32:36 … LORD will give *j* to his
1 Sam 8:3 … bribes and perverted *j*.
1 Kgs 3:11 … governing my people with *j*
1 Kgs 7:7 … Hall of *J*, where he sat to hear
2 Chr 9:8 … so you can rule with *j*
Job 8:3 … Does God twist *j*?
Job 19:7 … I protest, but there is no *j*.
Job 31:6 … weigh me on the scales of *j*,
Job 34:17 … God govern if he hated *j*?
Ps 9:8 … He will judge the world with *j*
Ps 10:18 … You will bring *j* to the orphans
Ps 36:6 … your *j* like the ocean depths.
Ps 45:4 … defending truth, humility, and *j*.
Ps 45:7 … You love *j* and hate evil.
Ps 72:1 … Give your love of *j* to the king,
Ps 82:3 … Give *j* to the poor
Ps 96:13 … He will judge the world with *j*,
Ps 98:9 … *j*, and the nations with fairness.
Ps 99:4 … You have acted with *j*
Ps 103:6 … *j* to all who are treated
Ps 146:7 … He gives *j* to the oppressed
Prov 16:12 … his rule is built on *j*.
Prov 19:28 … makes a mockery of *j*;
Prov 29:26 … but *j* comes from the LORD.
Prov 31:9 … and see that they get *j*.
Isa 1:17 … Seek *j*. Help the oppressed.
Isa 1:27 … Zion will be restored by *j*;
Isa 5:16 … will be exalted by his *j*.
Isa 10:2 … They deprive the poor of *j*
Isa 28:17 … with the measuring line of *j*
Isa 33:5 … make Jerusalem his home of *j*
Isa 42:1 … He will bring *j* to the nations.
Isa 51:4 … my *j* will become a light
Isa 59:9 … there is no *j* among us,
Isa 59:14 … *j* is nowhere to be found.
Isa 61:8 … I, the LORD, love *j*.
Jer 4:2 … you could do so with truth, *j*,
Jer 9:24 … who brings *j* and righteousness
Jer 21:12 … Give *j* each morning
Jer 30:11 … discipline you, but with *j*;
Lam 3:36 … if they twist *j* in the courts—
Hos 2:19 … righteousness and *j*,
Amos 5:7 … You twist *j*, making it a bitter
Amos 5:15 … courts into halls of *j*.
Amos 6:12 … when you turn *j* into poison
Mic 3:8 … I am filled with *j* and strength
Hab 1:4 … there is no *j* in the courts.
Zeph 3:5 … Day by day he hands down *j*,
Mal 2:17 … Where is the God of *j*?
Matt 5:6 … who hunger and thirst for *j*,
Matt 12:18 … proclaim *j* to the nations.
Matt 23:23 … aspects of the law—*j*,
Luke 11:42 … ignore *j* and the love of God.
Luke 18:3 … Give me *j* in this dispute
Acts 8:33 … humiliated and received no *j*.
Acts 17:31 … by the man he has appointed
Rom 2:2 … God, in his *j*, will punish
2 Thes 1:5 … persecution to show his *j*
2 Thes 1:6 … In his *j* he will pay back
Heb 1:8 … You rule with a scepter of *j*.
Heb 7:2 … Melchizedek means "king of *j*,"
Heb 11:33 … ruled with *j*, and received

JUSTIFY, JUSTIFIED (v) *to prove to be just, right, or reasonable; to acquit or absolve*
see also RIGHT, RIGHTEOUS
Luke 10:29 … wanted to *j* his actions,
Luke 18:14 … returned home *j-ied*.
2 Cor 8:24 … boasting about you is *j-ied*.

K

KEEP, KEEPING, KEEPS, KEPT (v) *to be faithful to; to have in control; to refrain from granting, giving, or allowing; to cause to remain in a given place, situation, or condition; to refrain from revealing; to maintain or preserve*
see also GUARD, OBEY, PROTECT
Exod 12:42 ... the LORD **k-pt** his promise
Exod 20:8 ... Sabbath day by **k-ing** it holy.
Exod 31:13 ... Be careful to **k** my Sabbath
Deut 5:12 ... Sabbath day by **k-ing** it holy,
Deut 7:8 ... **k-ing** the oath he had sworn
Deut 7:9 ... God who **k-s** his covenant for a
Deut 7:12 ... your God will **k** his covenant
2 Chr 6:14 ... You **k** your covenant
2 Chr 34:31 ... to obey the LORD by **k-ing**
Neh 1:5 ... God who **k-s** his covenant of
Ps 15:4 ... **k** their promises even when
Ps 116:14 ... I will **k** my promises to
Ps 119:100 ... **k-pt** your commandments.
Ps 121:7 ... The LORD **k-s** you from
Ps 130:3 ... LORD, if you **k-pt** a record of
Ps 146:6 ... He **k-s** every promise
Prov 10:19 ... and **k** your mouth shut
Prov 15:3 ... **k-ing** his eye on
Prov 21:23 ... your tongue and **k**
Eccl 3:6 ... A time to **k** and a time to
John 17:6 ... and they have **k-pt** your word.
Acts 2:24 ... death could not **k** him in its
Rom 10:3 ... by trying to **k** the law.
Rom 14:22 ... **k** it between yourself
1 Cor 1:8 ... He will **k** you strong
1 Cor 7:19 ... **k** God's commandments.
1 Cor 13:5 ... it **k-s** no record
Eph 4:3 ... effort to **k** yourselves united
1 Tim 5:22 ... **K** yourself pure.
2 Tim 4:5 ... But you should **k** a clear mind
Heb 11:27 ... going because he **k-pt** his eyes
Jas 2:10 ... the person who **k-s** all of the
1 Pet 1:4 ... **k-pt** in heaven for you, pure
1 Jn 5:3 ... **k-ing** his commandments,
Jude 1:21 ... **k** yourselves safe in God's love.
Rev 12:17 ... **k** God's commandments

KILL, KILLED, KILLING, KILLS (v) *to take or deprive of life*
Gen 4:8 ... Abel, and **k-ed** him.
Exod 2:12 ... Moses **k-ed** the Egyptian
Exod 21:12 ... assaults and **k-s** another
Lev 24:21 ... whoever **k-s** another person
2 Sam 2:26 ... always be **k-ing** each other?
Neh 9:26 ... they **k-ed** your prophets
Job 13:15 ... God might **k** me, but I
Ps 44:22 ... for your sake we are **k-ed**
Prov 6:17 ... hands that **k** the innocent,
Prov 23:13 ... punishment won't **k** them
Eccl 3:3 ... A time to **k** and a time to
Matt 10:28 ... who want to **k** your body;
Matt 16:21 ... He would be **k-ed,**
Mark 10:34 ... flog him with a whip, and **k**
Luke 11:48 ... They **k-ed** the prophets,
Acts 3:15 ... You **k-ed** the author
Rom 8:36 ... For your sake we are **k-ed**
1 Tim 1:9 ... who **k** their father or mother
1 Jn 3:12 ... evil one and **k-ed** his brother.

KIND (adj) *affectionate, loving; of a sympathetic or helping nature; gentle*
Luke 6:35 ... for he is **k** to those who are
1 Cor 13:4 ... is patient and **k**. Love is not
Eph 4:32 ... Instead, be **k** to each other,
2 Tim 2:24 ... but must be **k** to everyone,

KIND, KINDS (n) *nature, family, type, or category*
Gen 1:12 ... and trees of the same **k**.
1 Cor 12:4 ... different **k-s** of spiritual gifts,
1 Tim 6:10 ... root of all **k-s** of evil.

KINDNESS (n) *a kind deed; affection; the quality or state of being kind*
Ps 106:7 ... his many acts of **k** to them.
Rom 2:4 ... his **k** is intended to turn you
Rom 12:8 ... gift for showing **k** to others,
2 Cor 6:1 ... marvelous gift of God's **k**
2 Cor 8:1 ... God in his **k** has done through
2 Cor 10:1 ... gentleness and **k** of Christ—
Gal 5:22 ... peace, patience, **k**, goodness,
Eph 2:7 ... his grace and **k** toward us,
Col 3:12 ... mercy, **k**, humility,
Titus 3:4 ... revealed his **k** and love,
1 Pet 2:3 ... a taste of the Lord's **k**.

KINGDOM (n) *rule or realm; dominion of a king*
Exod 19:6 ... will be my **k** of priests,
1 Kgs 11:31 ... to tear the **k** from the hand
1 Chr 28:7 ... make his **k** last forever.
Ps 145:11 ... glory of your **k;**
Matt 3:2 ... for the **K** of Heaven is near.
Matt 4:23 ... Good News about the **K**.
Matt 5:10 ... right, for the **K** of Heaven is
Matt 5:19 ... great in the **K** of Heaven.
Matt 6:10 ... May your **K** come soon.
Matt 7:21 ... will enter the **K** of Heaven.
Matt 8:12 ... for whom the **K** was prepared—
Matt 10:7 ... them that the **K** of Heaven is
Matt 11:12 ... until now, the **K** of Heaven
Matt 12:26 ... His own **k** will not
Matt 13:11 ... secrets of the **K** of Heaven,
Matt 13:38 ... represents the people of the **K**.
Matt 13:43 ... their Father's **K**. Anyone with
Matt 13:45 ... Again, the **K** of Heaven is
Matt 13:52 ... a disciple in the **K** of Heaven
Matt 16:28 ... Son of Man coming in his **K**.
Matt 18:4 ... greatest in the **K** of Heaven.
Matt 19:12 ... sake of the **K** of Heaven.
Matt 19:23 ... to enter the **K** of Heaven.
Matt 20:1 ... For the **K** of Heaven is
Matt 21:43 ... I tell you, the **K** of God will
Matt 23:13 ... shut the door of the **K** of Heaven
Matt 24:14 ... Good News about the **K** will be
Matt 25:34 ... inherit the **K** prepared for
Mark 3:24 ... A **k** divided by
Mark 4:11 ... secret of the **K** of God.
Mark 4:30 ... I describe the **K** of God?
Mark 9:1 ... they see the **K** of God arrive
Mark 10:15 ... doesn't receive the **K** of God
Mark 10:24 ... to enter the **K** of God.
Mark 11:10 ... on the coming **K** of our
Mark 13:8 ... and **k** against **k**.
Mark 15:43 ... waiting for the **K** of God to
Luke 4:43 ... Good News of the **K** of God in
Luke 7:28 ... least person in the **K** of God
Luke 8:10 ... secrets of the **K** of God.
Luke 9:11 ... taught them about the **K** of God,
Luke 9:60 ... preach about the **K** of God.
Luke 10:9 ... tell them, 'The **K** of God is
Luke 10:11 ... know this—the **K** of God
Luke 11:17 ... he said, "Any **k** divided
Luke 11:20 ... the **K** of God has arrived
Luke 12:31 ... Seek the **K** of God
Luke 13:18 ... What is the **K** of God like?
Luke 14:15 ... a banquet in the **K** of God!
Luke 17:20 ... When will the **K** of God
Luke 17:21 ... For the **K** of God is
Luke 18:24 ... to enter the **K** of God!
Luke 18:29 ... for the sake of the **K** of God,
Luke 21:10 ... and **k** against **k**.
Luke 22:16 ... fulfilled in the **K** of God.
Luke 22:29 ... granted me a **K**, I now grant
Luke 23:42 ... come into your **K**.
John 3:3 ... you cannot see the **K** of God.
John 3:5 ... no one can enter the **K** of God
John 18:36 ... But my **K** is not of
Acts 1:3 ... talked to them about the **K** of God.
Acts 1:6 ... restore our **k?**
Acts 8:12 ... News concerning the **K** of God
Acts 19:8 ... about the **K** of God.
Acts 28:23 ... testified about the **K** of God
Rom 14:17 ... For the **K** of God is
1 Cor 4:20 ... For the **K** of God is
1 Cor 6:10 ... will inherit the **K** of God.
1 Cor 15:24 ... will turn the **K** over to God
1 Cor 15:50 ... cannot inherit the **K** of God.
Gal 5:21 ... will not inherit the **K** of God.
Eph 5:5 ... will inherit the **K** of Christ
Col 4:11 ... with me here for the **K** of God.
1 Thes 2:12 ... to share in his **K** and glory.
2 Thes 1:5 ... worthy of his **K**, for which
2 Tim 4:18 ... his heavenly **K**. All glory to
Heb 12:28 ... we are receiving a **K** that is
Jas 2:5 ... inherit the **K** he promised to
2 Pet 1:11 ... into the eternal **K** of our
Rev 1:6 ... made us a **K** of priests for
Rev 5:10 ... to become a **K** of priests for
Rev 11:15 ... now become the **K** of our Lord
Rev 12:10 ... power and the **K** of our God,
Rev 16:10 ... **k** was plunged into darkness.

KISS, KISSES (n) *a greeting or caress with the lips; an expression of affection*
Prov 27:6 ... better than many **k-es** from an
Song 7:9 ... May your **k-es** be as
Mark 14:45 ... and gave him the **k**.
Luke 22:48 ... the Son of Man with a **k?**

KISS, KISSING (v) *to caress with the lips*
Song 1:2 ... **K** me and **k** me again,
Song 8:1 ... Then I could **k** you no matter
Luke 7:38 ... Then she kept **k-ing** his feet

KNEE, KNEES (n) *the joint in the middle part of the leg; when bent, symbolic of submission or defeat*
Isa 35:3 ... those who have weak **k-s**.
Isa 45:23 ... Every **k** will bend to me,
Luke 5:8 ... he fell to his **k-s** before Jesus
Rom 14:11 ... every **k** will bend to me,
Eph 3:14 ... I fall to my **k-s** and pray to
Phil 2:10 ... at the name of Jesus every **k**
Heb 12:12 ... strengthen your weak **k-s**.

KNEEL, KNELT (v) *to bend the knee; to fall or rest on the knees; usually a gesture of submission, defeat, or reverence*
2 Chr 6:13 ... then he **k-lt** in front of
Ps 95:6 ... Let us **k** before the LORD
Dan 6:10 ... went home and **k-lt** down
Matt 8:2 ... approached him and **k-lt**
Matt 9:18 ... came and **k-lt** before him.
Matt 17:14 ... came and **k-lt** before Jesus
Matt 27:29 ... **k-lt** before him in mockery
Luke 22:41 ... stone's throw, and **k-lt** down
Acts 20:36 ... speaking, he **k-lt** and prayed
Acts 21:5 ... There we **k-lt**, prayed,

KNEW (v) *to be familiar with*
see also KNOW
Matt 7:23 ... reply, 'I never **k** you.

John 2:24 ... because he *k* all about people.
John 19:28 ... Jesus *k* that his mission
Acts 2:23 ... But God *k* what would
Rom 1:21 ... Yes, they *k* God,
Rom 8:29 ... God *k* his people in advance,
1 Pet 1:2 ... God the Father *k* you and

KNOCK, KNOCKING, KNOCKS (v) *to strike sharply*
Matt 7:7 ... Keep on *k-ing,* and the door
Matt 7:8 ... to everyone who *k-s,* the door
Luke 11:9 ... Keep on *k-ing,* and the door
Rev 3:20 ... I stand at the door and *k.*

KNOW, KNOWING, KNOWN, KNOWS (v) *to be intimately familiar with; to discern, recognize, regard, acknowledge, pay heed to, approve, learn*
see also KNEW
Gen 3:5 ... like God, *k-ing* both good and
Gen 3:22 ... like us, *k-ing* both good and
Gen 22:12 ... for now I *k* that you truly
Exod 6:7 ... Then you will *k* that I am the
Deut 18:21 ... How will we *k* whether or not
Deut 29:29 ... God has secrets *k-n* to no
Josh 23:14 ... Deep in your hearts you *k* that
Job 19:25 ... for me, I *k* that my Redeemer
Ps 9:10 ... Those who *k* your name trust
Ps 19:2 ... after night they make him *k-n.*
Ps 44:21 ... for he *k-s* the secrets of
Ps 46:10 ... Be still, and *k* that I am
Ps 94:10 ... doesn't he also *k* what you
Ps 94:11 ... The LORD *k-s* people's thoughts;
Ps 103:14 ... For he *k-s* how weak we are;
Ps 119:168 ... you *k* everything I do.
Ps 139:2 ... You *k* when I sit
Ps 139:23 ... O God, and *k* my heart;
Isa 12:4 ... Let them *k* how mighty
Jer 9:24 ... that they truly *k* me and
Jer 31:34 ... will *k* me already,
Dan 11:32 ... the people who *k* their God
Matt 6:3 ... don't let your left hand *k* what
Matt 10:29 ... without your Father *k-ing* it.
Matt 11:27 ... no one truly *k-s* the Father
Mark 12:24 ... you don't *k* the Scriptures,
Luke 11:13 ... if you sinful people *k* how to
Luke 13:25 ... will reply, 'I don't *k* you
Luke 16:15 ... but God *k-s* your hearts.
Luke 23:34 ... they don't *k* what they are
John 3:11 ... you what we *k* and have seen,
John 4:42 ... Now we *k* that he
John 6:69 ... we *k* you are the Holy One
John 7:28 ... Yes, you *k* me, and you
John 8:14 ... For I *k* where I came
John 8:32 ... And you will *k* the truth,
John 10:4 ... because they *k* his voice.
John 10:27 ... I *k* them, and they follow
John 13:17 ... Now that you *k* these things,
John 14:7 ... If you had really *k-n* me,
John 16:30 ... we understand that you *k*
John 17:23 ... the world will *k* that you sent
John 21:15 ... Peter replied, "you *k* I love
Acts 1:24 ... O Lord, you *k* every heart.
Rom 1:19 ... They *k* the truth
Rom 7:18 ... And I *k* that nothing good
Rom 8:26 ... we don't *k* what God wants us
Rom 8:27 ... the Father who *k-s* all hearts
Rom 11:34 ... For who can *k* the LORD's
Rom 12:16 ... And don't think you *k* it all!
Rom 16:26 ... message is made *k-n* to all
1 Cor 2:11 ... no one can *k* God's thoughts
1 Cor 13:12 ... All that I *k* now is partial
2 Cor 4:6 ... so we could *k* the glory of
Gal 4:9 ... now that you *k* God (or should
Phil 3:10 ... I want to *k* Christ and

Col 1:10 ... you learn to *k* God better and
1 Thes 3:3 ... But you *k* that we
1 Thes 5:2 ... For you *k* quite well
2 Thes 1:8 ... on those who don't *k* God
1 Tim 1:7 ... but they don't *k* what they
1 Tim 3:15 ... you will *k* how people must
2 Tim 1:12 ... I *k* the one in whom I trust,
2 Tim 2:19 ... The LORD *k-s* those who are
Heb 8:11 ... greatest, will *k* me already.
Heb 11:8 ... without *k-ing* where he
Jas 1:3 ... For you *k* that when your faith
Jas 4:14 ... How do you *k* what your life
Jas 4:17 ... it is sin to *k* what you ought
2 Pet 2:21 ... they had never *k-n* the way to
1 Jn 2:3 ... we can be sure that we *k* him
1 Jn 2:4 ... claims, "I *k* God," but
1 Jn 2:5 ... is how we *k* we are living in
1 Jn 2:11 ... person does not *k* the way to
1 Jn 2:29 ... Since we *k* that Christ
1 Jn 3:1 ... they don't *k* him.
1 Jn 3:2 ... But we do *k* that we will be
1 Jn 3:24 ... And we *k* he lives in us
1 Jn 4:6 ... is how we *k* if someone has
1 Jn 4:7 ... is a child of God and *k-s* God.
1 Jn 4:8 ... does not *k* God, for God
1 Jn 5:13 ... you may *k* you have eternal
1 Jn 5:15 ... And since we *k* he hears us
1 Jn 5:20 ... And we *k* that the Son of
Rev 3:15 ... I *k* all the things you do,

KNOWLEDGE (n) *the fact or condition of being aware of something, of having information, or of being learned; information, wisdom*
Gen 2:9 ... the tree of the *k* of good and
Gen 2:17 ... the tree of the *k* of good and
Prov 1:7 ... foundation of true *k,* but fools
Prov 2:6 ... From his mouth come *k* and
Prov 3:20 ... By his *k* the deep
Prov 8:10 ... *k* rather than pure gold.
Prov 14:6 ... *k* comes easily to those with
Prov 18:15 ... Their ears are open for *k.*
Isa 11:2 ... the Spirit of *k* and the fear
Luke 11:52 ... remove the key to *k* from
Rom 2:20 ... gives you complete *k*
1 Cor 12:8 ... gives a message of special *k.*
1 Cor 13:2 ... and possessed all *k,*
1 Cor 13:9 ... Now our *k* is partial
2 Cor 2:14 ... to spread the *k* of Christ
Eph 1:17 ... grow in your *k* of God.
Eph 4:13 ... our faith and *k* of God's Son
Phil 1:9 ... will keep on growing in *k*
Col 1:9 ... to give you complete *k* of his
Col 2:3 ... treasures of wisdom and *k.*
Heb 10:26 ... we have received *k* of the
2 Pet 1:5 ... and moral excellence with *k,*
2 Pet 1:8 ... *k* of our Lord Jesus Christ.
2 Pet 3:18 ... the grace and *k* of our Lord

L

LAID (v) *to place or set down*
see also LAY
Isa 53:6 ... Yet the LORD *l* on him the
Acts 6:6 ... as they *l* their hands on them.
Acts 8:18 ... the apostles *l* their hands on
1 Tim 4:14 ... elders of the church *l* their
2 Tim 1:6 ... when I *l* my hands on

LAKE (n) *a considerable inland body of standing water*
Matt 8:24 ... a fierce storm struck the *l,*
Luke 8:33 ... into the *l* and drowned.
John 6:25 ... on the other side of the *l*
Rev 19:20 ... into the fiery *l* of burning
Rev 20:14 ... This *l* of fire is

LAMB, LAMBS (n) *a young sheep that is less than one year old*
Exod 12:21 ... pick out a *l* or young goat
Isa 53:7 ... He was led like a *l* to the
Mark 14:12 ... the Passover *l* is sacrificed,
Luke 10:3 ... out as *l-s* among wolves.
John 1:29 ... and said, "Look! The *L* of God
John 21:15 ... "Then feed my *l-s,*" Jesus
Acts 8:32 ... And as a *l* is silent before
1 Pet 1:19 ... sinless, spotless *L* of God.
Rev 5:6 ... Then I saw a *L* that looked as
Rev 5:12 ... Worthy is the *L* who was
Rev 7:14 ... robes in the blood of the *L*
Rev 15:3 ... the song of the *L*:
Rev 17:14 ... to war against the *L,* but the
Rev 19:9 ... to the wedding feast of the *L.*
Rev 21:23 ... and the *L* is its light.

LAME (adj) *having a disabled body part as to impair freedom of movement*
Isa 33:23 ... Even the *l* will take
Isa 35:6 ... The *l* will leap like a
Matt 11:5 ... blind see, the *l* walk,
Matt 15:31 ... the *l* were walking,
Luke 14:21 ... the blind, and the *l.*
Heb 12:13 ... weak and *l* will not fall

LAMP, LAMPS (n) *a source of intellectual or spiritual illumination; any of various devices for producing light*
2 Sam 22:29 ... O LORD, you are my *l.*
Ps 18:28 ... You light a *l* for me.
Ps 119:105 ... Your word is a *l* to guide my
Prov 6:23 ... For their command is a *l*
Prov 31:18 ... her *l* burns late
Matt 6:22 ... Your eye is like a *l* that
Matt 25:1 ... who took their *l-s*
Matt 25:7 ... got up and prepared their *l-s.*
Luke 8:16 ... No one lights a *l* and then
Luke 12:35 ... and keep your *l-s* burning,
Rev 22:5 ... no need for *l-s* or sun—for the

LAMPSTAND, LAMPSTANDS (n) *a support that holds a lamp*
Exod 25:31 ... Make the entire *l* and its
2 Chr 4:7 ... cast ten gold *l-s* according to
Zech 4:2 ... a solid gold *l* with a bowl of
Zech 4:11 ... on each side of the *l,*
Heb 9:2 ... In the first room were a *l,*
Rev 1:12 ... I saw seven gold *l-s.*
Rev 1:20 ... the seven gold *l-s:*
Rev 2:5 ... and remove your *l* from its

LAND (n) *the solid part of the surface of the earth; a portion of the earth's solid surface distinguishable by boundaries or ownership*
Gen 1:10 ... the dry ground "*l*" and the
Gen 15:18 ... I have given this *l* to your
Exod 6:8 ... you into the *l* I swore to
Deut 8:7 ... you into a good *l* of flowing
Ps 37:11 ... will possess the *l* and will

LANGUAGE, LANGUAGES (n) *means of communication peculiar to a certain people; a special language gift given by the Holy Spirit*
see also TONGUE(S)
Gen 11:9 ... the people with different *l-s.*
Isa 28:11 ... speak a strange *l!*
Mark 16:17 ... they will speak in new *l-s.*
Acts 2:4 ... speaking in other *l-s,* as the
1 Cor 12:28 ... speak in unknown *l-s.*
1 Cor 12:30 ... to interpret unknown *l-s?*
1 Cor 13:8 ... in unknown *l-s* and special
1 Cor 14:19 ... in an unknown *l.*
Eph 4:29 ... or abusive *l.* Let everything

Col 3:8 ... slander, and dirty *l*.
Rev 5:9 ... every tribe and *l* and people
Rev 7:9 ... and tribe and people and *l*,
Rev 14:6 ... nation, tribe, *l*, and people.

LASCIVIOUSNESS (KJV)
Mark 7:22 ... deceit, *lustful desires*, envy,
2 Cor 12:21 ... and *eagerness for lustful pleasure*
Gal 5:19 ... impurity, *lustful pleasures*
Eph 4:19 ... They live for *lustful pleasure*
1 Pet 4:3 ... their *immorality* and lust,

LAST, LASTING (adj) *following all the rest; being the only remaining; belonging to the final stage; of or relating to being continuous in time; existing or continuing a long while*
Prov 10:25 ... have a *l-ing* foundation.
Matt 20:16 ... who are *l* now will be first
John 15:16 ... to go and produce *l-ing* fruit,
Acts 2:17 ... 'In the *l* days,' God says,
1 Cor 15:26 ... And the *l* enemy to be
1 Cor 15:52 ... *l* trumpet is blown.
2 Tim 3:1 ... that in the *l* days there will
2 Pet 3:3 ... that in the *l* days scoffers
Jude 1:18 ... you that in the *l* times there
Rev 1:17 ... I am the First and the *L*.
Rev 22:13 ... the Omega, the First and the *L*,

LAST (n) *the one who is at or endures to the end*
Isa 41:4 ... First and the *L*. I alone
Isa 44:6 ... First and the *L*; there is no
Isa 48:12 ... God, the First and the *L*.

LAST, LASTS (v) *to continue in time*
Ps 30:5 ... For his anger *l* only a moment,
1 Cor 13:13 ... *l* forever—faith, hope, and

LAUGH, LAUGHED, LAUGHS (v) *to show mirth or joy or to despise or mock something with a chuckle or explosive vocal sound*
Gen 17:17 ... *l-ed* to himself in disbelief.
Gen 18:12 ... So she *l-ed* silently to herself
Ps 2:4 ... one who rules in heaven *l-s*.
Ps 37:13 ... the LORD just *l-s*, for he sees
Ps 59:8 ... But LORD, you *l* at them.
Prov 31:25 ... and she *l-s* without fear of
Eccl 3:4 ... and a time to *l*. A time to
Luke 6:21 ... for in due time you will *l*.
Luke 6:25 ... awaits you who *l* now,

LAUGHTER (n) *a chuckle or explosive vocal sound; cause for merriment*
Gen 21:6 ... God has brought me *l*.
Ps 126:2 ... We were filled with *l*, and we
Eccl 2:2 ... So I said, "*L* is silly."
Jer 7:34 ... happy singing and *l* in the
Jas 4:9 ... instead of *l*, and gloom

LAW, LAWS (n) *words of Moses; a binding decree; a universal principle; governing authority*
see also COMMANDMENT(S), INSTRUCTION(S), REGULATIONS, TEACHING(S)
2 Chr 17:9 ... the Book of the *L*
Ps 1:2 ... delight in the *l* of the LORD.
Ps 93:5 ... Your royal *l-s* cannot be
Ps 119:14 ... rejoiced in your *l-s* as much as
Ps 119:36 ... for your *l-s* rather than a love
Ps 119:125 ... I will understand your *l-s*.
Ps 119:152 ... days that your *l-s* will last
Matt 5:17 ... to abolish the *l* of Moses or
Matt 5:19 ... who obeys God's *l-s*
Matt 22:40 ... The entire *l* and all the
Matt 23:23 ... of the *l*—justice, mercy,

Mark 7:8 ... ignore God's *l* and substitute
Luke 11:52 ... experts in religious *l*!
Luke 23:56 ... rested as required by the *l*.
Luke 24:44 ... written about me in the *l*
John 1:17 ... For the *l* was given
Rom 2:12 ... be judged by that *l* when they
Rom 2:15 ... that God's *l* is written in
Rom 2:20 ... that God's *l* gives you
Rom 2:25 ... if you don't obey God's *l*,
Rom 3:19 ... Obviously, the *l* applies to
Rom 3:21 ... requirements of the *l*, as was
Rom 3:28 ... not by obeying the *l*.
Rom 4:13 ... his obedience to God's *l*,
Rom 4:16 ... according to the *l* of Moses,
Rom 5:13 ... was not yet any *l* to break.
Rom 6:15 ... has set us free from the *l*,
Rom 7:4 ... power of the *l* when you died
Rom 7:5 ... the *l* aroused these evil desires
Rom 7:8 ... If there were no *l*, sin would
Rom 7:12 ... But still, the *l* itself is
Rom 7:22 ... I love God's *l* with all my
Rom 7:25 ... I really want to obey God's *l*,
Rom 8:3 ... did what the *l* could not do.
Rom 8:4 ... requirement of the *l* would be
Rom 8:7 ... did obey God's *l-s*, and it
Rom 9:4 ... gave them his *l*. He gave them
Rom 9:31 ... with God by keeping the *l*,
Rom 10:4 ... for which the *l* was given.
Rom 13:10 ... requirements of God's *l*.
1 Cor 9:9 ... For the *l* of Moses
1 Cor 9:21 ... I obey the *l* of Christ.
2 Cor 3:6 ... not of written *l-s*, but of the
Gal 2:16 ... by obeying the *l*. And we have
Gal 2:19 ... So I died to the *l*—I stopped
Gal 3:2 ... by obeying the *l* of Moses?
Gal 3:5 ... because you obey the *l*?
Gal 3:11 ... by trying to keep the *l*.
Gal 3:19 ... But the *l* was designed
Gal 3:21 ... If the *l* could give us
Gal 3:23 ... placed under guard by the *l*.
Gal 4:21 ... live under the *l*, do you know
Gal 5:3 ... in the whole *l* of Moses.
Gal 5:14 ... the whole *l* can be summed
Gal 6:2 ... this way obey the *l* of Christ.
Eph 2:15 ... the system of *l* with its
Phil 3:6 ... I obeyed the *l* without fault.
1 Tim 1:8 ... know that the *l* is good when
Heb 10:1 ... under the *l* of Moses
Jas 1:25 ... into the perfect *l* that sets
Jas 2:8 ... obey the royal *l* as found in
Jas 2:10 ... all of the *l-s* except one is as

LAWLESSNESS (n) *the quality or state of not being restrained or controlled by law*
2 Thes 2:3 ... the man of *l* is revealed—
2 Thes 2:7 ... For this *l* is already
2 Thes 2:8 ... Then the man of *l* will be

LAWSUITS (n) *an act or instance of suing*
1 Cor 6:7 ... Even to have such *l* with one

LAY, LAYING (v) *to put or set down*
see also LAID
Exod 29:10 ... his sons will *l* their hands
Lev 1:4 ... *L* your hand on
Lev 4:15 ... must then *l* their hands on
Num 8:10 ... of Israel must *l* their hands
Num 27:18 ... in him, and *l* your hands on
Acts 8:19 ... so that when I *l* my hands on
Heb 6:2 ... the *l-ing* on of hands,
Rev 4:10 ... And they *l* their crowns

LAZINESS (n) *a disinclination to activity or exertion*
Prov 31:27 ... suffers nothing from *l*.
Ezek 16:49 ... gluttony, and *l*, while the

LAZY (adj) *disinclined to activity or exertion; not energetic or vigorous*
Prov 12:27 ... *L* people don't
Prov 20:4 ... Those too *l* to plow in the
Rom 12:11 ... Never be *l*, but work
1 Tim 5:13 ... they will learn to be *l*
Titus 1:12 ... animals, and *l* gluttons.

LEAD, LEADING, LEADS (v) *to guide by direction or example; to go at the head of; to result in*
see also LED
Deut 27:18 ... anyone who *l-s* a blind
Deut 31:2 ... no longer able to *l* you.
Josh 1:6 ... one who will *l* these people
2 Chr 1:10 ... knowledge to *l* them
Ps 25:9 ... He *l-s* the humble in
Ps 73:24 ... with your counsel, *l-ing* me to a
Prov 6:22 ... counsel will *l* you.
Prov 14:30 ... A peaceful heart *l-s* to a
Prov 19:23 ... Fear of the LORD *l-s* to life,
Isa 11:6 ... little child will *l* them all.
Matt 15:14 ... blind guides *l-ing* the blind,
John 10:3 ... by name and *l-s* them out.
Rom 6:16 ... to sin, which *l-s* to death,
Rom 6:22 ... things that *l* to holiness and
1 Tim 5:24 ... *l-ing* them to certain judgment.
Rev 7:17 ... He will *l* them to

LEADER, LEADERS (n) *a person who has commanding authority or influence; chief among others*
1 Sam 13:14 ... to be the *l* of his people,
Prov 17:26 ... to flog *l-s* for being honest.
Jer 51:46 ... *l-s* fight against each other.
Matt 20:26 ... a *l* among you must be
Mark 10:43 ... a *l* among you must be
Luke 22:26 ... *l* should be like a servant.
Acts 13:27 ... Jerusalem and their *l-s* did not
1 Thes 5:12 ... who are your *l-s* in the Lord's
Heb 13:7 ... Remember your *l-s* who taught
Heb 13:17 ... Obey your spiritual *l-s*, and do
3 Jn 1:9 ... to be the *l*, refuses to have

LEADERSHIP (n) *the office or position of a leader; capacity to lead*
Num 33:1 ... under the *l* of Moses
1 Cor 12:28 ... those who have the gift of *l*,

LEARN, LEARNED, LEARNS (v) *to come to know or realize; to acquire knowledge, skill, or behavioral tendency*
Deut 4:10 ... Then they will *l* to fear me
Deut 5:1 ... so you may *l* them and obey
Prov 9:9 ... and they will *l* even more.
Prov 18:15 ... are always ready to *l*.
Isa 1:17 ... *L* to do good.
Isa 26:9 ... will people *l* what is right.
Isa 29:13 ... man-made rules *l-ed* by rote.
Matt 2:7 ... and he *l-ed* from them the time
John 6:45 ... listens to the Father and *l-s*
Phil 4:9 ... all you *l-ed* and received from
Phil 4:11 ... have *l-ed* how to be content
Col 1:10 ... grow as you *l* to know God
1 Tim 2:11 ... Women should *l* quietly and
2 Tim 1:13 ... teaching you *l-ed* from me—
Heb 5:8 ... he *l-ed* obedience from the

LEAVEN (KJV)
Exod 12:20 ... anything made with *yeast*
Exod 13:7 ... any *yeast* at all found within
Matt 13:33 ... of Heaven is like the *yeast*
Matt 16:6 ... the *yeast* of the Pharisees
1 Cor 5:6 ... this sin is like a little *yeast*

LED (v) *to guide by direction or example*
see also LEAD
Ps 68:18 ... the heights, you *l* a crowd of
Isa 53:7 ... He was *l* like a lamb
Jer 11:19 ... like a lamb being *l* to the
Luke 4:1 ... He was *l* by the Spirit
Acts 8:32 ... He was *l* like a sheep
Rom 8:14 ... all who are *l* by the Spirit
Eph 4:8 ... the heights, he *l* a crowd of

LEFT (adj) *of, relating to, situated on, or being the side of the body in which the heart is mostly located*
Matt 6:3 ... don't let your *l* hand know

LEFT (n) *the location or direction of the left side*
Josh 1:7 ... or to the *l*. Then you will be
Josh 23:6 ... either to the right or to the *l*.
Isa 30:21 ... to the right or to the *l*.
Matt 25:33 ... and the goats at his *l*.
Matt 25:41 ... those on the *l* and say, 'Away

LEGION (n) *a very large number; multitude*
Mark 5:9 ... My name is *L*, because there

LEND, LENDING (v) *to give for temporary use on condition that the same or its equivalent be returned*
Lev 25:37 ... interest on money you *l*
Deut 15:8 ... and *l* them whatever
Ps 15:5 ... They *l* money without
Prov 19:17 ... you are *l-ing* to the LORD—
Luke 6:34 ... Even sinners will *l* to other

LENDER, LENDERS (n) *one who loans to another*
Exod 22:25 ... as a money *l* would.
Prov 22:7 ... borrower is servant to the *l*.
Isa 24:2 ... and sellers, *l-s* and borrowers,

LEPROSY (n) *a chronic infectious disease affecting the skin and peripheral nerves which causes loss of sensation, paralysis, and deformities*
Num 12:10 ... as white as snow from *l*.
2 Kgs 5:1 ... he suffered from *l*.
2 Kgs 7:3 ... four men with *l* sitting at
2 Chr 26:21 ... King Uzziah had *l* until the
Matt 11:5 ... those with *l* are cured,
Luke 17:12 ... ten men with *l* stood

LIAR, LIARS (n) *a person who deceives by telling untruths or falsehoods*
Ps 63:11 ... while *l-s* will be silenced.
Ps 116:11 ... These people are all *l-s!*
Prov 17:4 ... *l-s* pay close attention to
Prov 29:12 ... pays attention to *l-s*, all his
Prov 30:6 ... expose you as a *l*.
Isa 57:4 ... of sinners and *l-s!*
John 8:44 ... a *l* and the father of lies.
Rom 3:4 ... else is a *l*, God is true.
1 Tim 1:10 ... are slave traders, *l-s*, promise
Titus 1:12 ... are all *l-s*, cruel animals,
1 Jn 1:10 ... calling God a *l* and showing
1 Jn 2:4 ... that person is a *l* and is not
1 Jn 4:20 ... that person is a *l*; for if we
1 Jn 5:10 ... calling God a *l* because they
Rev 3:9 ... synagogue—those *l-s* who say
Rev 21:8 ... and all *l-s*—their fate is in

LIE, LIES (n) *an untrue or inaccurate statement; something that misleads or deceives*
Ps 7:14 ... give birth to *l-s*.
Ps 24:4 ... and never tell *l-s*.
Ps 34:13 ... lips from telling *l-s!*
Prov 12:17 ... a false witness tells *l-s*.
Prov 30:8 ... never to tell a *l*.
John 8:44 ... the father of *l-s*.
Rom 1:25 ... about God for a *l*.
Rom 3:13 ... filled with *l-s*.
Eph 4:14 ... to trick us with *l-s* so clever
Eph 4:25 ... So stop telling *l-s*.
2 Thes 2:11 ... they will believe these *l-s*.
1 Pet 3:10 ... and your lips from telling *l-s*
2 Pet 2:3 ... make up clever *l-s* to get hold
1 Jn 2:21 ... between truth and *l-s*.
Rev 14:5 ... They have told no *l-s;*

LIE, LIED, LIES (v) *to make an untrue statement with intent to deceive; to create a false or misleading impression*
see also LYING
Lev 6:3 ... lost property and *l* about it,
Job 31:5 ... Have *l l-d* to anyone or
Ps 58:3 ... even from birth they have *l-d*
Ps 89:35 ... in my holiness I cannot *l:*
Prov 24:28 ... don't *l* about them.
Prov 26:19 ... who *l-s* to a friend
Jer 7:9 ... commit adultery, *l*, and burn
Matt 5:11 ... persecute you and *l*
Col 3:9 ... Don't *l* to each other,
Titus 1:2 ... God—who does not *l*

LIFE (n) *the quality that distinguishes a vital and functional being from a dead body; period from birth to death; a way or manner of living; spiritual existence transcending death; salvation*
see also LIVES
Gen 1:30 ... everything that has *l*.
Gen 2:7 ... He breathed the breath of *l*
Gen 2:9 ... the tree of *l* and the tree of
Gen 9:5 ... who takes another person's *l*.
Gen 9:6 ... a human *l*, that person's *l*
Exod 21:23 ... the injury: a *l* for a *l*,
Num 35:31 ... payment for the *l* of someone
Deut 19:21 ... be *l* for *l*, eye for eye,
Deut 30:19 ... choice between *l* and death,
Deut 32:39 ... kills and gives *l*; I am the
1 Sam 2:6 ... both death and *l*; he brings
Ps 23:6 ... the days of my *l*, and I will
Ps 69:28 ... the Book of *L*; don't let them
Ps 91:16 ... with a long *l* and give them
Ps 139:24 ... the path of everlasting *l*.
Prov 3:2 ... your *l* will be satisfying.
Prov 6:26 ... will cost you your *l*.
Prov 13:3 ... have a long *l*; opening your
Prov 15:4 ... Gentle words are a tree of *l*;
Prov 21:21 ... will find *l*, righteousness,
Prov 28:16 ... will have a long *l*.
Isa 53:8 ... that his *l* was cut short in
Isa 55:3 ... you will find *l*. I will make
Lam 3:58 ... you have redeemed my *l*.
Dan 12:2 ... to everlasting *l* and some to
Matt 7:14 ... But the gateway to *l* is very
Matt 18:8 ... to enter eternal *l* with only
Matt 20:28 ... and to give his *l* as a ransom
Mark 8:35 ... to hang on to your *l*,
Mark 10:45 ... and to give his *l* as a ransom
Luke 6:9 ... a day to save *l* or to destroy
Luke 9:24 ... give up your *l* for my sake,
Luke 12:25 ... single moment to your *l*?
John 1:4 ... The Word gave *l* to everything
John 3:15 ... will have eternal *l*.
John 4:14 ... giving them eternal *l*.
John 5:24 ... passed from death into *l*.
John 5:39 ... they give you eternal *l*.
John 6:27 ... the eternal *l* that the Son of
John 6:35 ... I am the bread of *l*.
John 6:47 ... who believes has eternal *l*.
John 6:53 ... have eternal *l* within you.
John 6:68 ... the words that give eternal *l*.
John 10:10 ... a rich and satisfying *l*.
John 10:15 ... So I sacrifice my *l* for the
John 10:28 ... give them eternal *l*, and they
John 12:25 ... nothing for their *l* in this
John 14:6 ... the truth, and the *l*.
John 17:2 ... He gives eternal *l* to each
John 20:31 ... you will have *l* by the power
Acts 3:15 ... You killed the author of *l*,
Rom 1:17 ... a righteous person has *l*.
Rom 2:7 ... will give eternal *l* to those
Rom 4:25 ... he was raised to *l* to make us
Rom 5:10 ... be saved through the *l* of his
Rom 5:18 ... God and new *l* for everyone.
Rom 5:21 ... in eternal *l* through Jesus
Rom 6:13 ... now you have new *l*.
Rom 6:22 ... result in eternal *l*.
Rom 6:23 ... is eternal *l* through Christ
Rom 8:6 ... mind leads to *l* and peace.
Rom 8:11 ... he will give *l* to your mortal
Rom 8:38 ... death nor *l*, neither angels
2 Cor 3:6 ... the Spirit gives *l*.
2 Cor 4:10 ... so that the *l* of Jesus may
Gal 3:11 ... a righteous person has *l*.
Gal 3:21 ... give us new *l*, we could be
Gal 6:8 ... harvest everlasting *l* from
Eph 2:5 ... he gave us *l* when he raised
Eph 4:1 ... to lead a *l* worthy of your
Phil 2:16 ... Hold firmly to the word of *l*;
Phil 4:3 ... written in the Book of *L*.
Col 3:3 ... and your real *l* is hidden
1 Tim 1:16 ... and receive eternal *l*.
1 Tim 4:8 ... and in the *l* to come.
1 Tim 6:19 ... may experience true *l*.
2 Tim 1:9 ... called us to live a holy *l*.
2 Tim 3:12 ... to live a godly *l* in Christ
Titus 3:5 ... new *l* through the Holy Spirit.
Heb 7:16 ... power of a *l* that cannot be
Jas 1:12 ... the crown of *l* that God has
1 Pet 3:7 ... God's gift of new *l*.
1 Pet 3:10 ... want to enjoy *l* and see many
1 Pet 3:16 ... see what a good *l* you live
2 Pet 1:3 ... for living a godly *l*.
1 Jn 1:1 ... He is the Word of *l*.
1 Jn 3:14 ... have passed from death to *l*.
1 Jn 3:16 ... gave up his *l* for us.
1 Jn 5:20 ... God, and he is eternal *l*.
Jude 1:21 ... bring you eternal *l*.
Rev 3:5 ... names from the Book of *L*,
Rev 13:8 ... in the Book of *L* that belongs
Rev 17:8 ... in the Book of *L* before the
Rev 20:12 ... the Book of *L*. And the dead
Rev 21:27 ... in the Lamb's Book of *L*.
Rev 22:1 ... with the water of *l*, clear as
Rev 22:2 ... a tree of *l*, bearing twelve
Rev 22:14 ... eat the fruit from the tree of *l*.
Rev 22:17 ... from the water of *l*.
Rev 22:19 ... in the tree of *l* and in the

LIFT, LIFTED, LIFTING, LIFTS (v) *to raise from a lower to a higher position; to raise in rank or condition*
Lev 23:11 ... the priest will *l* it up
1 Sam 2:7 ... some down and *l-s* others up.
Neh 8:6 ... as they *l-ed* their hands.
Ps 28:2 ... I *l* my hands toward your holy
Ps 63:4 ... *l-ing* up my hands to you in prayer.
Ps 89:13 ... Your right hand is *l-ed* high in
Ps 113:7 ... He *l-s* the poor from the dust
Ps 123:1 ... I *l* my eyes to you, O God
Ps 134:2 ... *L* your hands toward
Lam 1:9 ... no one to *l* her out.
Lam 3:41 ... Let us *l* our hearts and
John 3:14 ... Son of Man must be *l-ed* up,
John 8:28 ... When you have *l-ed* up the Son
John 12:32 ... And when I am *l-ed* up

1 Tim 2:8 … holy hands *l-ed* up to God,
Jas 4:10 … he will *l* you up in honor.
1 Pet 5:6 … he will *l* you up in honor.

LIGHT, LIGHTS (n) *daylight; brightness; illumination; celestial body; spiritual enlightenment; exposure to the truth and justice*
Gen 1:3 … "Let there be *l*," and there
Gen 1:14 … said, "Let *l-s* appear in the sky
Exod 13:21 … and he provided *l* at night
Job 38:19 … Where does *l* come from,
Ps 27:1 … The LORD is my *l* and my
Ps 56:13 … in your life-giving *l*.
Ps 119:105 … my feet and a *l* for my path.
Ps 132:17 … will be a *l* for my people.
Ps 139:12 … Darkness and *l* are the
Isa 2:5 … us walk in the *l* of the LORD!
Isa 42:6 … you will be a *l* to guide the
Isa 45:7 … I create the *l* and make the
Isa 49:6 … make you a *l* to the Gentiles,
Matt 5:14 … You are the *l* of the world—
Luke 2:32 … He is a *l* to reveal God to
Luke 11:33 … its *l* can be seen by all
John 1:4 … life brought *l* to everyone.
John 1:9 … who is the true *l*, who gives
John 3:20 … All who do evil hate the *l*
John 3:21 … come to the *l* so others can
John 8:12 … I am the *l* of the world.
John 9:5 … I am the *l* of the world.
John 12:46 … I have come as a *l* to shine
Acts 13:47 … made you a *l* to the Gentiles,
2 Cor 4:6 … said, "Let there be *l*" in the
2 Cor 6:14 … can *l* live with darkness?
2 Cor 11:14 … as an angel of *l*.
Eph 1:18 … be flooded with *l* so that you
Eph 5:8 … live as people of *l!*
Phil 2:15 … like bright *l-s* in a world
1 Thes 5:5 … children of the *l* and of the
1 Tim 6:16 … he lives in *l* so brilliant
1 Pet 2:9 … into his wonderful *l*.
1 Jn 1:5 … God is *l*, and there is
1 Jn 1:7 … living in the *l*, as God is in
1 Jn 2:9 … I am living in the *l*,
Rev 21:23 … city, and the Lamb is its *l*.

LIGHT, LIGHTS (v) *to brighten; to ignite something*
Ps 18:28 … The LORD, my God, *l-s* up my
Luke 8:16 … No one *l-s* a lamp and

LIGHTNING (n) *the flashing of light produced by a discharge of atmospheric electricity*
Exod 9:23 … *l* flashed toward the earth.
Exod 20:18 … saw the flashes of *l* and the
Dan 10:6 … face flashed like *l*, and his
Matt 24:27 … For as the *l* flashes in the
Matt 28:3 … face shone like *l*, and his
Luke 10:18 … from heaven like *l!*
Rev 4:5 … came flashes of *l* and the

LION, LIONS (n) *a wild beast with a threatening roar; symbolic of a strong and fierce enemy*
Isa 11:7 … The *l* will eat hay like a cow.
Isa 65:25 … The *l* will eat hay like a cow.
Dan 6:7 … thrown into the den of *l-s*.
Dan 7:4 … was like a *l* with eagles'
1 Pet 5:8 … like a roaring *l*, looking for
Rev 5:5 … Look, the *L* of the tribe of

LIPS (n) *the fleshy, muscular folds that surround the mouth; symbolic of speech*
Ps 140:3 … drips from their *l*.
Prov 12:22 … The LORD detests lying *l*,
Isa 6:5 … I have filthy *l*, and I live

Matt 15:8 … honor me with their *l*,
Rom 3:13 … venom drips from their *l*.
1 Pet 3:10 … evil and your *l* from telling

LISTEN, LISTENED, LISTENING (v) *to hear something with thoughtful attention*
see also HEAR
Deut 6:4 … *L*, O Israel! The LORD
Deut 18:15 … You must *l* to him.
1 Sam 3:9 … LORD, your servant is *l-ing*.
Neh 8:3 … All the people *l-ed* closely to
Ps 95:7 … If only you would *l* to his voice
Prov 12:15 … but the wise *l* to others.
Prov 18:13 … Spouting off before *l-ing* to
Isa 6:9 … to this people, '*L* carefully,
Dan 9:6 … We have refused to *l* to your
Mark 9:7 … dearly loved Son. *L* to him.
Luke 10:39 … the Lord's feet, *l-ing*
Luke 16:31 … If they won't *l* to Moses and
John 10:27 … My sheep *l* to my
John 15:20 … And if they had *l-ed* to me,
Rom 2:13 … For merely *l-ing* to the law
1 Tim 2:12 … Let them *l* quietly.
Jas 1:19 … be quick to *l*, slow to speak,
1 Jn 4:6 … they do not *l* to us.
Rev 1:3 … he blesses all who *l* to its
Rev 2:7 … to hear must *l* to the Spirit

LIVE, LIVED, LIVES, LIVING (v) *to be alive or come to life; to endure a period of time (a life span); to attain eternal life; to dwell; to subsist; to continue alive; to conduct or pass one's life*
Gen 3:22 … Then they will *l* forever!
Exod 20:12 … Then you will *l* a long, full
Lev 26:11 … I will *l* among you,
Deut 6:2 … as long as you *l*.
Deut 8:3 … that people do not *l* by bread
Job 14:14 … Can the dead *l* again?
Job 19:25 … that my Redeemer *l-s*, and he
Ps 23:6 … and I will *l* in the house of
Ps 37:3 … Then you will *l* safely in the
Ps 61:4 … Let me *l* forever in your
Ps 104:33 … as long as I *l*. I will praise
Prov 21:19 … It's better to *l* alone in the
Isa 33:14 … Who can *l* with this
Isa 45:18 … He made the world to be *l-d* in,
Amos 5:6 … to the LORD and *l!*
Hab 2:4 … the righteous will *l* by their
Zech 2:11 … I will *l* among you,
Matt 4:4 … People do not *l* by bread
John 14:19 … Since I *l*, you also will *l*.
Acts 17:28 … For in him we *l* and move
Rom 2:8 … on those who *l* for themselves,
Rom 6:10 … he *l-s*, he *l-s* for the glory
Rom 8:11 … same Spirit *l-ing* within you.
Rom 13:13 … we must *l* decent lives
Rom 14:7 … For we don't *l* for ourselves
1 Cor 3:16 … Spirit of God *l-s* in you?
2 Cor 5:7 … For we *l* by believing
2 Cor 6:16 … said: "I will *l* in them and
Gal 2:20 … no longer who *l*, but Christ
Gal 5:25 … Since we are *l-ing* by the Spirit,
Col 1:19 … was pleased to *l* in Christ,
Col 2:5 … you are *l-ing* as you should
1 Thes 4:11 … your goal to *l* a quiet life,
1 Thes 5:13 … And *l* peacefully with
1 Tim 2:2 … so that we can *l* peaceful and
1 Tim 4:16 … close watch on how you *l*
2 Tim 3:12 … who wants to *l* a godly life
Heb 10:38 … righteous ones will *l* by faith.
Heb 12:14 … and work at *l-ing* a holy life,
1 Pet 1:17 … So you must *l* in reverent
1 Jn 1:7 … But if we are *l-ing* in the light,
1 Jn 4:16 … God, and God *l-s* in them.

LIVES (n) *way or manner of living*
see also LIFE
Exod 23:26 … I will give you long, full *l*.
1 Thes 2:8 … but our own *l*, too.
1 Tim 2:2 … and quiet *l* marked by
1 Pet 3:2 … pure and reverent *l*.
1 Pet 4:2 … rest of your *l* chasing your

LOAN, LOANS (n) *money lent at interest*
Deut 15:2 … must cancel the *l-s* they have
Deut 15:9 … refuse someone a *l*
Deut 24:6 … as security for a *l*, for the
Ps 37:26 … give generous *l-s* to others,

LOANED (v) *to give for temporary use*
Luke 7:41 … A man *l* money to two

LOCUSTS (n) *a short-horned grasshopper*
Exod 10:4 … a swarm of *l* on your country.
Joel 2:25 … and the cutting *l*. It was I
Matt 3:4 … he ate *l* and wild honey.
Rev 9:3 … Then *l* came from

LOG (n) *a usually bulky piece or length of a tree*
Matt 7:3 … you have a *l* in your own?
Luke 6:41 … you have a *l* in your own?

LONGSUFFERING (KJV)
Exod 34:6 … I am *slow to anger* and filled
Num 14:18 … LORD is *slow to anger*
Ps 86:15 … mercy, *slow to get angry*
Gal 5:22 … love, joy, peace, *patience*,
Eph 4:2 … Be *patient* with each other

LOOK (n) *glance*
Prov 15:30 … A cheerful *l* brings joy to

LOOK, LOOKED, LOOKING, LOOKS (v) *to direct the eyes; to examine; to see; to make sure or take care (that something is done); to regard with contempt; to seem; to search*
Gen 19:17 … And don't *l* back or
Gen 19:26 … But Lot's wife *l-ed* back as she
Exod 3:6 … was afraid to *l* at God.
1 Sam 6:19 … they *l-ed* into the Ark
1 Sam 16:7 … LORD *l-s* at the heart.
Ps 34:5 … Those who *l* to him for
Ps 113:6 … He stoops to *l* down on heaven
Ps 123:2 … We keep *l-ing* to the LORD
Isa 65:1 … but no one was *l-ing* for me.
Dan 10:5 … I *l-ed* up and saw a man
Hab 3:6 … When he *l-s*, the nations
Zech 12:10 … They will *l* on me
Matt 5:28 … who even *l-s* at a woman
Mark 16:6 … You are *l-ing* for Jesus
Luke 9:62 … plow and then *l-s* back is not
Luke 22:61 … turned and *l-ed* at Peter.
John 4:23 … The Father is *l-ing* for those
John 17:1 … Jesus *l-ed* up to heaven
Rom 14:10 … Why do you *l* down
Phil 2:4 … Don't *l* out only
Heb 11:16 … they were *l-ing* for a better
Jas 1:25 … But if you *l* carefully into
2 Pet 3:12 … *l-ing* forward to the day
Rev 5:6 … I saw a Lamb that *l-ed* as if it

LORD (n) *traditionally rendered, Jehovah (Hebrew Yahweh); the sovereign God Almighty*
see also YAHWEH
Gen 2:4 … When the *L* God made
Gen 4:4 … The *L* accepted Abel
Gen 15:6 … Abram believed the *L*, and
Gen 22:14 … the *L* will provide
Gen 31:49 … May the *L* keep watch

1735

Exod 6:2 … I am Yahweh—'the *L*.'
Exod 15:26 … I am the *L* who heals you.
Exod 40:34 … the glory of the *L* filled
Lev 20:26 … because I, the *L*, am holy.
Lev 23:4 … these are the *L*'s appointed
Num 6:24 … May the *L* bless you and
Num 14:18 … The *L* is slow to anger
Num 14:21 … filled with the *L*'s glory,
Num 14:41 … disobeying the *L*'s orders
Deut 5:9 … I, the *L* your God, am a jealous
Deut 6:5 … love the *L* your God with all
Deut 6:18 … good in the *L*'s sight,
Deut 10:13 … obey the *L*'s commands
Deut 10:20 … must fear the *L* your God
Deut 11:1 … must love the *L* your God
Deut 29:29 … The *L* our God has secrets
Deut 30:20 … obey the *L*, you will live
Josh 23:11 … to love the *L* your God.
2 Sam 22:2 … sang: "The *L* is my rock,
2 Sam 22:31 … All the *L*'s promises prove
2 Kgs 22:2 … pleasing in the *L*'s sight
2 Kgs 22:8 … Law in the *L*'s Temple!
1 Chr 17:1 … Ark of the *L*'s Covenant is
2 Chr 16:9 … The eyes of the *L* search
Neh 9:6 … You alone are the *L*.
Job 38:1 … Then the *L* answered Job
Ps 1:6 … For the *L* watches over
Ps 12:6 … The *L*'s promises are pure,
Ps 18:30 … All the *L*'s promises prove
Ps 23:1 … The *L* is my shepherd;
Ps 24:1 … The earth is the *L*'s,
Ps 34:3 … tell of the *L*'s greatness;
Ps 34:8 … see that the *L* is good.
Ps 89:1 … sing of the *L*'s unfailing love
Ps 92:13 … to the *L*'s own house.
Ps 95:6 … kneel before the *L* our maker,
Ps 97:1 … The *L* is king!
Ps 99:5 … Exalt the *L* our God!
Ps 100:5 … For the *L* is good.
Ps 107:1 … thanks to the *L*, for he is
Ps 118:8 … better to take refuge in the *L*
Ps 118:23 … This is the *L*'s doing,
Ps 121:2 … help comes from the *L*, who
Ps 145:3 … Great is the *L*!
Ps 145:17 … The *L* is righteous
Ps 146:7 … The *L* frees the prisoners.
Ps 147:11 … No, the *L*'s delight is
Prov 3:5 … Trust in the *L* with all your
Prov 3:9 … Honor the *L* with your
Prov 3:11 … reject the *L*'s discipline,
Prov 12:22 … The *L* detests lying
Prov 15:33 … Fear of the *L*
Prov 19:21 … the *L*'s purpose will prevail.
Prov 21:2 … the *L* examines their heart.
Prov 31:30 … a woman who fears the *L* will
Isa 6:3 … holy is the *L* of Heaven's
Isa 24:14 … praise the *L*'s majesty.
Isa 30:9 … to the *L*'s instructions.
Isa 42:8 … I am the *L*; that is my name!
Isa 43:11 … I, am the *L*, and there is
Isa 49:4 … leave it all in the *L*'s hand;
Isa 53:6 … Yet the *L* laid on him
Isa 53:10 … was the *L*'s good plan
Isa 55:13 … honor to the *L*'s name;
Isa 61:2 … time of the *L*'s favor
Isa 66:15 … See, the *L* is coming
Jer 8:7 … do not know the *L*'s laws.
Jer 17:10 … But I, the *L*, search all
Jer 31:11 … For the *L* has redeemed
Jer 48:10 … to do the *L*'s work,
Jer 51:7 … cup in the *L*'s hands,
Ezek 7:19 … day of the *L*'s anger.
Ezek 44:4 … the glory of the *L* filled
Joel 1:15 … The day of the *L* is near,
Joel 3:18 … from the *L*'s Temple, watering
Jon 2:9 … salvation comes from the *L*

Mic 4:1 … mountain of the *L*'s house
Mic 6:2 … listen to the *L*'s complaint!
Nah 1:2 … The *L* is a jealous God,
Nah 1:7 … The *L* is good, a strong
Hab 2:16 … cup of the *L*'s judgment,
Zeph 2:3 … yet the *L* will protect
Matt 3:3 … way for the *L*'s coming!
Matt 4:7 … not test the *L* your God.
Matt 4:10 … must worship the *L* your God
Matt 22:37 … must love the *L* your God
Mark 1:3 … way for the *L*'s coming!
Mark 12:11 … This is the *L*'s doing,
John 1:23 … way for the *L*'s coming!
Acts 2:21 … name of the *L* will be saved.
Rom 10:13 … name of the *L* will be saved.
Rom 11:34 … can know the *L*'s thoughts?
1 Cor 10:26 … the earth is the *L*'s,
Heb 12:5 … of the *L*'s discipline,

LORD, LORDS (n) *honored one or a superior; master (to a slave); king or ruler; God or Jesus*
see also LORD
Deut 10:17 … of gods and *L* of *l-s*.
Neh 4:14 … Remember the *L*, who is
Isa 6:1 … I saw the *L*. He was sitting
Dan 9:19 … O *L*, listen and act!
Matt 12:8 … Son of Man is *L*, even
Luke 1:38 … I am the *L*'s servant.
Acts 10:36 … Christ, who is *L* of all.
Acts 16:31 … Believe in the *L* Jesus
Rom 10:9 … that Jesus is *L* and believe
1 Cor 8:6 … only one *L*, Jesus Christ,
1 Cor 11:26 … announcing the *L*'s death
1 Cor 12:3 … say Jesus is *L*, except
Eph 4:5 … There is one *L*, one faith,
Phil 2:11 … Jesus Christ is *L*,
Col 2:6 … Jesus as your *L*, you must
1 Thes 5:2 … day of the *L*'s return
1 Tim 6:15 … kings and *L* of all *l-s*.
Jas 5:8 … the coming of the *L* is near.
1 Pet 2:3 … taste of the *L*'s kindness.
1 Pet 3:15 … worship Christ as *L* of
Rev 4:8 … holy, holy is the *L* God,
Rev 4:11 … are worthy, O *L* our God,
Rev 19:16 … kings and *L* of all *l-s*.
Rev 22:20 … Amen! Come, *L* Jesus!

LOSE, LOSES (v) *to fail to keep, sustain, or maintain; to damn*
Matt 10:39 … cling to your life, you will *l*
Mark 8:36 … whole world but *l* your own
Luke 15:8 … silver coins and *l-s* one.
Luke 17:33 … cling to your life, you will *l*
John 6:39 … I should not *l* even one of
2 Jn 1:8 … you do not *l* what we have

LOST (adj) *no longer possessed or known; lacking assurance of eternal salvation*
Jer 50:6 … have been *l* sheep.
Ezek 34:16 … will search for my *l* ones
Luke 15:4 … and one of them gets *l*,
Luke 15:6 … I have found my *l* sheep.
Luke 15:9 … have found my *l* coin.
Luke 15:24 … He was *l*, but now he

LOVE (n) *the ultimate expression of God's loyalty, purity, and mercy extended toward his people—to be reflected in human relationships of brotherly concern, marital fidelity, and adoration of God; a beloved person*
Gen 24:12 … unfailing *l* to my master,
Gen 32:10 … unfailing *l* and faithfulness
Gen 34:3 … he fell in *l* with her, and he
Gen 39:21 … showed him his faithful *l*.

Exod 20:6 … unfailing *l* for a thousand
Exod 34:6 … filled with unfailing *l* and
Num 14:18 … with unfailing *l*, forgiving
Num 14:19 … unfailing *l*, please pardon
Deut 5:10 … unfailing *l* for a thousand
Deut 7:9 … his unfailing *l* on those who
Deut 10:15 … the objects of his *l*.
Deut 10:18 … He shows *l* to the
Deut 10:19 … must show *l* to foreigners,
Judg 16:4 … Samson fell in *l* with a woman
1 Sam 18:20 … had fallen in *l* with David,
1 Kgs 8:23 … and show unfailing *l* to all
1 Kgs 10:9 … LORD's eternal *l* for Israel,
1 Chr 16:41 … for "his faithful *l* endures
1 Chr 29:18 … See to it that their *l*
2 Chr 5:13 … His faithful *l* endures
2 Chr 20:21 … faithful *l* endures forever!
Ezra 3:11 … His faithful *l* for Israel
Job 37:13 … to show his unfailing *l*.
Ps 6:4 … because of your unfailing *l*.
Ps 13:5 … I trust in your unfailing *l*.
Ps 18:50 … you show unfailing *l* to your
Ps 21:7 … The unfailing *l* of the
Ps 23:6 … and unfailing *l* will pursue
Ps 25:6 … and unfailing *l*, which you
Ps 25:10 … leads with unfailing *l* and
Ps 26:3 … of your unfailing *l*, for you
Ps 31:7 … in your unfailing *l*, for you
Ps 31:16 … your unfailing *l*, rescue me.
Ps 32:10 … but unfailing *l* surrounds
Ps 33:5 … the unfailing *l* of the
Ps 33:18 … who rely on his unfailing *l*.
Ps 33:22 … your unfailing *l* surround us,
Ps 36:5 … Your unfailing *l*, O LORD, is
Ps 36:10 … Pour out your unfailing *l* on
Ps 40:10 … of your unfailing *l* and
Ps 40:11 … Let your unfailing *l* and
Ps 42:8 … his unfailing *l* upon me,
Ps 48:9 … on your unfailing *l* as we
Ps 51:1 … your unfailing *l*. Because of
Ps 57:3 … send forth his unfailing *l* and
Ps 57:10 … For your unfailing *l* is as
Ps 59:10 … In his unfailing *l*, my God
Ps 59:16 … your unfailing *l*. For you
Ps 59:17 … shows me unfailing *l*.
Ps 62:12 … unfailing *l*, O Lord, is yours.
Ps 66:20 … his unfailing *l* from me.
Ps 69:16 … LORD, for your unfailing *l* is
Ps 77:8 … his unfailing *l* gone forever?
Ps 85:7 … us your unfailing *l*, O LORD,
Ps 86:5 … full of unfailing *l* for all
Ps 86:15 … filled with unfailing *l* and
Ps 88:11 … your unfailing *l*?
Ps 89:1 … LORD's unfailing *l* forever!
Ps 89:14 … Unfailing *l* and truth
Ps 89:49 … is your unfailing *l*?
Ps 90:14 … with your unfailing *l*, so we
Ps 92:2 … your unfailing *l* in the
Ps 100:5 … His unfailing *l* continues
Ps 101:1 … sing of your *l* and justice,
Ps 103:4 … crowns me with *l* and tender
Ps 103:11 … his unfailing *l* toward those
Ps 103:17 … But the *l* of the LORD
Ps 106:1 … His faithful *l* endures
Ps 106:45 … because of his unfailing *l*.
Ps 107:31 … for his great *l* and for the
Ps 107:43 … the faithful *l* of the LORD.
Ps 108:4 … your unfailing *l* is higher
Ps 109:26 … because of your unfailing *l*.
Ps 115:1 … for your unfailing *l* and
Ps 118:1 … His faithful *l* endures
Ps 119:41 … give me your unfailing *l*,
Ps 119:76 … let your unfailing *l* comfort
Ps 119:124 … deal with me in unfailing *l*,
Ps 130:7 … LORD there is unfailing *l*.
Ps 138:2 … unfailing *l* and faithfulness;

Ps 143:12 … your unfailing *l*, silence all
Ps 147:11 … hope in his unfailing *l*.
Prov 5:19 … be captivated by her *l*.
Prov 14:22 … will receive unfailing *l* and
Prov 16:6 … Unfailing *l* and
Prov 20:28 … is made secure through *l*.
Prov 21:21 … and unfailing *l* will find
Prov 27:5 … better than hidden *l!*
Song 1:4 … We praise your *l* even more
Song 1:7 … Tell me, my *l*, where are you
Song 1:16 … so handsome, my *l*, pleasing
Song 2:7 … not to awaken *l* until the
Song 2:17 … to me, my *l*, like a gazelle
Song 3:4 … I found my *l!*
Song 4:10 … Your *l* delights me,
Song 4:16 … your garden, my *l*; taste its
Song 5:5 … door for my *l*, and my hands
Song 5:8 … tell him I am weak with *l*.
Song 7:6 … How pleasing, my *l*, how full
Song 7:12 … will give you my *l*.
Song 8:4 … not to awaken *l* until the
Song 8:6 … for *l* is as strong as death
Song 8:7 … cannot quench *l*, nor can
Song 8:14 … Come away, my *l!*
Isa 55:3 … the unfailing *l* I promised to
Isa 63:7 … LORD's unfailing *l*.
Isa 63:9 … In his *l* and mercy he
Jer 2:25 … I'm in *l* with these
Jer 9:24 … demonstrates unfailing *l* and
Jer 16:5 … taken away my unfailing *l*
Jer 31:3 … with an everlasting *l*.
Jer 33:11 … His faithful *l* endures
Lam 3:22 … The faithful *l* of the
Lam 3:32 … the greatness of his unfailing *l*.
Dan 9:4 … of unfailing *l* to those who
Hos 1:7 … I will show *l* to the people
Hos 2:19 … and justice, unfailing *l* and
Hos 2:23 … I will show *l* to those I
Hos 6:4 … For your *l* vanishes like the
Hos 6:6 … want you to show *l*, not offer
Hos 11:4 … my ropes of kindness and *l*.
Hos 12:6 … Act with *l* and justice,
Joel 2:13 … filled with unfailing *l*.
Jon 4:2 … filled with unfailing *l*.
Zeph 3:17 … With his *l*, he will
Zech 8:17 … Stop your *l* of telling
Mark 10:21 … Jesus felt genuine *l* for him.
John 5:42 … have God's *l* within you.
John 15:9 … Remain in my *l*.
John 15:10 … remain in his *l*.
John 15:13 … is no greater *l* than to lay
John 17:26 … Then your *l* for me will
Rom 5:5 … fill our hearts with his *l*.
Rom 5:8 … showed his great *l* for us by
Rom 8:35 … us from Christ's *l?*
Rom 8:39 … us from the *l* of God that is
Rom 13:10 … *L* does no wrong
Rom 13:10 … to others, so *l* fulfills the
Rom 14:15 … not acting in *l* if you eat
Rom 15:30 … because of your *l* for me,
1 Cor 4:21 … I come with *l* and a gentle
1 Cor 8:1 … it is *l* that strengthens the
1 Cor 13:13 … faith, hope, and *l*—and the
1 Cor 13:13 … the greatest of these is *l*.
2 Cor 2:4 … know how much I have for
2 Cor 2:8 … to reaffirm your *l* for him.
2 Cor 5:14 … Either way, Christ's *l* controls
2 Cor 8:7 … and your *l* from us—I want
2 Cor 8:24 … show them your *l*, and prove
Gal 5:22 … *l*, joy, peace, patience,
Eph 1:15 … Jesus and your *l* for God's
Eph 3:17 … down into God's *l* and keep
Eph 3:18 … how deep his *l* is.
Eph 4:15 … the truth in *l*, growing in
Eph 5:2 … filled with *l*, following the
Eph 6:23 … give you *l* with faithfulness.

Phil 1:9 … that your *l* will overflow
Col 1:4 … Jesus and your *l* for all of
Col 1:8 … told us about the *l* for others
Col 2:2 … strong ties of *l*.
1 Thes 3:6 … your faith and *l*.
1 Thes 3:12 … the Lord make your *l* for one
1 Thes 5:13 … and wholehearted *l* because of
2 Thes 3:5 … expression of the *l* of God
1 Tim 1:5 … be filled with *l* that comes
1 Tim 2:15 … in faith, *l*, holiness,
1 Tim 4:12 … live, in your *l*, your faith,
1 Tim 6:10 … For the *l* of money is the
1 Tim 6:11 … with faith, *l*, perseverance,
2 Tim 1:7 … but of power, *l*, and
2 Tim 1:13 … the faith and *l* that you have
2 Tim 2:22 … living, faithfulness, *l*, and
2 Tim 3:10 … my patience, my *l*, and my
Titus 2:2 … filled with *l* and patience.
Titus 3:4 … revealed his kindness and *l*,
Heb 10:24 … to acts of *l* and good works.
1 Pet 4:8 … for *l* covers a multitude
1 Pet 5:14 … with a kiss of *l*.
1 Jn 3:14 … who has no *l* is still dead.
1 Jn 3:16 … know what real *l* is because
1 Jn 4:7 … for *l* comes from God.
1 Jn 4:8 … for God is *l*.
1 Jn 4:10 … This is real *l*—not that we
1 Jn 4:16 … put our trust in his *l*.
1 Jn 4:16 … God is *l*, and all who
1 Jn 4:17 … live in God, our *l* grows more
1 Jn 4:18 … because perfect *l* expels all
Jude 1:12 … commemorating the Lord's *l*,
Jude 1:21 … safe in God's *l*.
Rev 2:19 … have seen your *l*, your faith,

LOVE, LOVED, LOVES, LOVING (v) to hold dear; to feel a lover's passion, devotion, or tenderness for; to feel affection or experience desire; to like or desire actively

Gen 22:2 … Isaac, whom you *l* so much—
Gen 29:32 … my husband will *l*
Exod 21:5 … may declare, 'I *l* my master,
Lev 19:34 … as you *l* yourself.
Deut 4:37 … Because he *l-d* your ancestors,
Deut 6:5 … And you must *l* the LORD your
Deut 7:8 … that the LORD *l-s* you, and he
Deut 7:13 … He will *l* you and
Deut 11:13 … and if you *l* the LORD your
Deut 13:3 … if you truly *l* him with all
Deut 15:16 … because he *l-s* you and
Deut 21:15 … son of the wife he does not *l*.
Deut 23:5 … LORD your God *l-s* you.
Deut 30:6 … that you will *l* him with all
Deut 30:16 … to *l* the LORD
Deut 30:20 … this choice by *l-ing* the LORD
Deut 30:20 … And if you *l* and obey the
Deut 33:3 … Indeed, he *l-s* his people;
Josh 23:11 … be very careful to *l* the LORD
Judg 14:16 … said, "You don't *l* me;
Judg 16:15 … tell me, 'I *l* you,' when you
1 Sam 18:1 … for Jonathan *l-d* David.
2 Sam 12:24 … The LORD *l-d* the child
2 Sam 19:6 … You seem to *l* those who hate
1 Kgs 3:3 … Solomon *l-d* the LORD and
1 Kgs 11:1 … Solomon *l-d* many foreign
2 Chr 2:11 … the LORD *l-s* his people
2 Chr 19:2 … the wicked and *l* those who
Neh 1:5 … with those who *l* him and obey
Neh 13:26 … *l-d* him and made him king
Ps 11:5 … those who *l* violence.
Ps 11:7 … righteous LORD *l-s* justice.
Ps 18:1 … I *l* you, LORD,
Ps 26:8 … I *l* your sanctuary,
Ps 36:10 … on those who *l* you;
Ps 40:16 … those who *l* your salvation

Ps 44:3 … helped them, for you *l-d* them.
Ps 45:7 … You *l* justice and
Ps 52:3 … You *l* evil more
Ps 52:4 … You *l* to destroy
Ps 70:4 … those who *l* your salvation
Ps 78:68 … Mount Zion, which he *l-d*.
Ps 89:28 … I will *l* him and be
Ps 89:33 … I will never stop *l-ing* him nor
Ps 91:14 … rescue those who *l* me.
Ps 97:10 … You who *l* the LORD,
Ps 98:3 … his promise to *l* and be
Ps 119:48 … I honor and *l* your commands.
Ps 119:97 … how I *l* your instructions!
Ps 119:113 … but I *l* your instructions.
Ps 119:119 … no wonder I I *l* to obey your
Ps 119:127 … I *l* your commands more
Ps 119:140 … that is why I *l* them so much.
Ps 122:6 … May all who *l* this city
Ps 145:20 … all those who *l* him, but he
Ps 146:8 … The LORD *l-s* the godly.
Prov 3:12 … corrects those he *l-s*, just as
Prov 8:17 … *I* all who *l* me.
Prov 8:21 … Those who *l* me inherit
Prov 8:36 … All who hate me *l* death.
Prov 9:8 … and they will *l* you.
Prov 12:1 … you must *l* discipline; it is
Prov 15:17 … with someone you *l* is better
Prov 17:19 … Anyone who *l-s* to quarrel
Prov 18:21 … those who *l* to talk
Prov 19:8 … wisdom is to *l* yourself;
Prov 21:17 … Those who *l* pleasure
Prov 22:11 … Whoever *l-s* a pure
Prov 30:19 … how a man *l-s* a woman.
Eccl 3:8 … A time to *l* and a time
Eccl 9:9 … the woman you *l* through all
Song 1:3 … the young women *l* you!
Song 3:2 … search for the one I *l*.
Song 3:3 … Have you seen the one I *l?*
Isa 1:23 … All of them *l* bribes and
Isa 56:6 … serve him and *l* his name, who
Isa 61:8 … I, the LORD, *l* justice.
Jer 2:2 … long ago, how you *l-d* me and
Jer 8:2 … my people have *l-d*, served,
Jer 31:20 … to punish him, but I still *l* him,
Hos 2:1 … Ruhamah—'The ones I *l*.'
Hos 2:4 … I will not *l* her children,
Hos 2:23 … to those I called 'Not *l-d*.'
Hos 9:15 … I will *l* them no
Hos 11:1 … was a child, I *l-d* him, and I
Hos 12:7 … scales—they *l* to cheat.
Amos 4:5 … you Israelites *l* to do," says
Amos 5:15 … Hate evil and *l* what is good;
Mic 6:8 … is right, to *l* mercy, and to
Mal 1:2 … "I have always *l-d* you," says
Matt 5:43 … that says, '*L* your neighbor'
Matt 5:44 … But I say, *l* your enemies!
Matt 5:46 … If you *l* only those
Matt 6:24 … hate one and *l* the other;
Matt 10:37 … If you *l* your father or
Matt 19:19 … *L* your neighbor
Matt 22:37 … You must *l* the LORD your
Mark 12:6 … his son whom he *l-d* dearly.
Mark 12:30 … you must *l* the LORD your
Mark 12:33 … it is important to *l* him with
Mark 12:33 … and to *l* my neighbor as
Luke 6:27 … I say, *l* your enemies!
Luke 6:32 … If you *l* only those who
Luke 6:35 … *L* your enemies!
Luke 10:27 … You must *l* the LORD your
Luke 10:27 … And, '*L* your neighbor
Luke 16:13 … hate one and *l* the other;
John 3:16 … For this is how God *l-d* the world:
John 3:35 … The Father *l-s* his Son
John 5:20 … For the Father *l-s* the Son and
John 8:42 … you would *l* me, because I

1737

John 10:17 . . . The Father *l-s* me because I
John 11:36 . . . See how much he *l-d* him!
John 12:25 . . . Those who *l* their life
John 12:43 . . . For they *l-d* human praise more
John 13:1 . . . He had *l-d* his disciples during
John 13:34 . . . ***L*** each other. Just as I have
John 13:34 . . . as I have *l-d* you, you should
John 14:21 . . . are the ones who *l* me.
John 14:28 . . . If you really *l-d* me, you
John 14:31 . . . know that I *l* the Father.
John 17:23 . . . and that you *l* them as much
John 17:24 . . . gave me because you *l-d* me
John 19:26 . . . beside the disciple he *l-d,*
John 20:2 . . . one whom Jesus *l-d.*
John 21:15 . . . do you *l* me more than
John 21:16 . . . son of John, do you *l* me?
John 21:20 . . . the disciple Jesus *l-d*—the one
Rom 8:28 . . . of those who *l* God and are
Rom 8:37 . . . through Christ, who *l-d* us.
Rom 9:13 . . . Scriptures, "I *l-d* Jacob, but I
Rom 9:25 . . . And I will *l* those whom I did
Rom 12:10 . . . ***L*** each other with genuine
1 Cor 2:9 . . . for those who *l* him.
1 Cor 13:2 . . . but didn't *l* others, I would
1 Cor 16:22 . . . anyone does not *l* the Lord,
2 Cor 9:7 . . . For God *l-s* a person
2 Cor 12:15 . . . the more I *l* you, the less
Gal 2:20 . . . of God, who *l-d* me and gave
Eph 1:4 . . . God *l-d* us and chose us
Eph 2:4 . . . mercy, and he *l-d* us so much,
Eph 5:25 . . . this means *l* your wives, just
Eph 5:25 . . . just as Christ *l-d* the church.
Eph 5:28 . . . their wives as they *l* their own
Eph 5:28 . . . a man who *l-s* his wife actually
Eph 5:33 . . . love his wife as he *l-s* himself,
Phil 1:16 . . . preach because they *l* me,
Phil 2:2 . . . each other, *l-ing* one another,
1 Thes 1:4 . . . God *l-s* you and has chosen
1 Thes 4:10 . . . urge you to *l* them even
2 Thes 2:10 . . . they refuse to *l* and accept
2 Thes 2:16 . . . our Father, who *l-d* us and
1 Tim 3:3 . . . and not *l* money.
1 Tim 6:2 . . . believers who are well *l-d.*
2 Tim 3:2 . . . people will *l* only themselves
Titus 1:8 . . . and he must *l* what is good.
Titus 2:4 . . . women to *l* their husbands
Titus 3:15 . . . believers—all who *l* us.
Heb 12:6 . . . disciplines those he *l-s,*
Heb 13:1 . . . Keep on *l-ing* each other as
Heb 13:5 . . . Don't *l* money;
Jas 2:5 . . . to those who *l* him?
1 Pet 1:8 . . . You *l* him even though
1 Pet 2:17 . . . Respect everyone, and *l*
1 Pet 3:8 . . . ***L*** each other as brothers
2 Pet 2:15 . . . *l-d* to earn money by doing
1 Jn 2:5 . . . how completely they *l* him.
1 Jn 2:10 . . . Anyone who *l-s* a fellow
1 Jn 3:1 . . . very much our Father *l-s* us,
1 Jn 3:14 . . . If we *l* our brothers and
1 Jn 4:9 . . . how much he *l-d* us by sending
1 Jn 4:10 . . . not that we *l-d* God, but that
1 Jn 4:11 . . . since God *l-d* us that much,
1 Jn 4:11 . . . surely ought to *l* each other.
1 Jn 4:19 . . . We *l* each other because he *l-d*
1 Jn 4:20 . . . someone says, "I *l* God," but
1 Jn 4:20 . . . how can we *l* God, whom we
1 Jn 5:1 . . . everyone who *l-s* the Father
Jude 1:1 . . . God the Father, who *l-s* you and
Rev 1:5 . . . glory to him who *l-s* us and has
Rev 2:4 . . . You don't *l* me or each other
Rev 3:9 . . . you are the ones I *l.*
Rev 3:19 . . . discipline everyone I *l.*
Rev 12:11 . . . they did not *l* their lives so
Rev 22:15 . . . and all who *l* to live a lie.

LOVE, LOVED, LOVING (adj) *of or relating to a strong affection for another; affectionate, painstaking*
Ps 88:18 . . . my companions and *l-d* ones.
Ps 127:2 . . . gives rest to his *l-d* ones.
Ezek 33:32 . . . who sings *l* songs with a
Mark 1:11 . . . are my dearly *l-d* Son, and you
Mark 9:7 . . . is my dearly *l-d* Son.
1 Thes 1:3 . . . work, your *l-ing* deeds, and the

LOVINGKINDNESS (KJV)
Ps 25:6 . . . *unfailing love,* which you have
Ps 40:11 . . . Let your *unfailing love* and
Ps 63:3 . . . *unfailing love* is better than life
Ps 143:8 . . . *unfailing love* each morning
Isa 63:7 . . . according to his *mercy and love*

LOYAL (adj) *unswerving in allegiance; faithful*
see also FAITHFUL, TRUSTWORTHY
1 Sam 26:23 . . . and for being *l,*
2 Sam 2:6 . . . May the LORD be *l* to you in
1 Chr 12:33 . . . and completely *l* to David.
Ps 31:23 . . . those who are *l* to him,
Ps 51:10 . . . Renew a *l* spirit within
Prov 17:17 . . . A friend is always *l,* and a
Prov 20:6 . . . say they are *l* friends,

LOYALTY, LOYALTIES (n) *the quality or state or an instance of being loyal*
Judg 8:35 . . . Nor did they show any *l* to
Ps 119:113 . . . I hate those with divided *l-ies,*
Prov 19:22 . . . ***L*** makes a person

LUST, LUSTS (n) *unbridled sexual desire; an intense longing*
1 Cor 7:9 . . . than to burn with *l.*
Eph 4:22 . . . corrupted by *l* and deception.
Col 3:5 . . . immorality, impurity, *l,* and
2 Tim 2:22 . . . stimulates youthful *l-s.*
Titus 3:3 . . . to many *l-s* and pleasures.

LUST, LUSTED (v) *to have an intense (sexual) desire*
Prov 6:25 . . . Don't *l* for her
Ezek 23:5 . . . Then Oholah *l-ed* after other

LUSTFUL (adj) *excited by lust; lecherous*
Mark 7:22 . . . deceit, *l* desires, envy,
Gal 5:19 . . . impurity, *l* pleasures,
Eph 4:19 . . . They live for *l* pleasure and

LYING (adj) *marked by or containing falsehoods; false*
Prov 6:17 . . . haughty eyes, a *l* tongue,
Prov 12:22 . . . The LORD detests *l* lips,
Prov 21:6 . . . Wealth created by a *l* tongue
Prov 26:28 . . . A *l* tongue hates

LYING (v) *to make an untrue statement with the intent to deceive*
see also LIE
Mic 6:12 . . . are so used to *l* that their
Matt 15:19 . . . immorality, theft, *l,* and
Acts 5:4 . . . You weren't *l* to us but
1 Cor 15:15 . . . would all be *l* about God—

M

MADE (v) *to create, prepare, or fashion; to bring about*
see also CREATE(D), FORMED, MAKE
Gen 1:7 . . . God *m* this space to separate
Gen 1:16 . . . He also *m* the stars.
Gen 1:25 . . . *m* all sorts of wild animals,
Gen 1:31 . . . God looked over all he had *m,*
Gen 2:4 . . . LORD God *m* the earth and
Gen 2:22 . . . LORD God *m* a woman
Gen 6:6 . . . LORD was sorry he had ever *m*
Gen 9:6 . . . God *m* human beings in his
Exod 20:11 . . . the LORD *m* the heavens,
Deut 32:6 . . . Has he not *m* you and
2 Chr 2:12 . . . *m* the heavens and
Job 10:9 . . . that you *m* me from dust—
Ps 95:5 . . . sea belongs to him, for he *m* it.
Ps 115:15 . . . who *m* heaven and earth.
Prov 22:2 . . . The LORD *m* them both.
Eccl 3:11 . . . God has *m* everything
Isa 27:11 . . . the one who *m* them will
Isa 43:7 . . . I have *m* them for my glory.
Isa 57:16 . . . all the souls I have *m.*
Jer 51:15 . . . The LORD *m* the earth
Jon 1:9 . . . God of heaven, who *m* the sea
Matt 19:4 . . . *m* them male and female.
Matt 19:28 . . . when the world is *m* new
1 Cor 11:9 . . . man was not *m* for woman,
2 Cor 5:1 . . . an eternal body *m* for us by
1 Tim 2:13 . . . For God *m* Adam first,
Heb 4:3 . . . since he *m* the world.
Rev 13:8 . . . before the world was *m.*
Rev 14:7 . . . him who *m* the heavens,

MAJESTIC (adj) *having or exhibiting majesty; grand, stately*
Ps 8:1 . . . your *m* name fills the earth!
Ps 29:4 . . . the voice of the LORD is *m.*
Ps 145:5 . . . I will meditate on your *m,*
Isa 53:2 . . . nothing beautiful or *m* about
Heb 1:3 . . . hand of the *m* God in heaven.
Heb 8:1 . . . the throne of the *m* God
2 Pet 1:16 . . . saw his *m* splendor with our
2 Pet 1:17 . . . from the *m* glory of God

MAKE, MAKES, MAKING (v) *to create, prepare, or fashion; to force; to bring about; to render*
see also CREATE(D), FORMED, MADE
Gen 1:26 . . . Let us *m* human beings in our
Gen 2:18 . . . will *m* a helper who is just
Exod 4:11 . . . Who *m-s* a person's mouth?
Exod 25:40 . . . you *m* everything
Lev 16:34 . . . *m-ing* them right with the
Ps 19:7 . . . *m-ing* wise the simple.
Ps 139:14 . . . *m-ing* me so wonderfully
Prov 13:12 . . . Hope deferred *m-s* the heart
Isa 8:14 . . . stone that *m-s* people stumble,
Isa 29:16 . . . "He didn't *m* me"?
Isa 44:10 . . . fool would *m* his own god—
Jer 18:4 . . . he was *m-ing* did not turn out
Jer 23:16 . . . *m-ing* up everything they say.
Jer 31:31 . . . when I will *m* a new covenant
Matt 28:19 . . . *m* disciples of all
John 5:18 . . . *m-ing* himself equal with God.
Rom 14:20 . . . it *m-s* another person stumble,
1 Cor 3:7 . . . that God *m-s* the seed grow.
Heb 8:5 . . . you *m* everything according to
1 Pet 2:8 . . . stone that *m-s* people stumble,

MAKER (n) *one who makes; God*
see also CREATOR
Ps 95:6 . . . before the LORD our *m,*
Ps 149:2 . . . Israel, rejoice in your ***M.***
Prov 17:5 . . . mock the poor insult their ***M;***
Isa 45:9 . . . clay pot argue with its *m?*
Hos 8:14 . . . Israel has forgotten its ***M***

MAMMON (KJV)
Matt 6:24 . . . serve God and be enslaved to *money*
Luke 16:9 . . . *worldly resources* to benefit
Luke 16:11 . . . untrustworthy about *worldly wealth,*

MAN (n) *an adult male human; individual, person*
Gen 2:7 ... the *m* from the dust
Gen 2:15 ... the *m* in the Garden
Gen 2:18 ... for the *m* to be alone.
Gen 2:23 ... she was taken from '*m.*'
Gen 2:25 ... *m* and his wife were both
Gen 3:9 ... God called to the *m*, "Where
Isa 53:3 ... rejected—a *m* of sorrows,
1 Cor 11:3 ... of every *m* is Christ,
1 Cor 11:3 ... the head of woman is *m*,
1 Cor 15:45 ... The first *m*, Adam,
Eph 5:31 ... A *m* leaves his father and
1 Tim 2:5 ... the *m* Christ Jesus.

MANAGE, MANAGING (v) *to handle or direct with a degree of skill*
Luke 12:42 ... of *m*-ing his other household
1 Tim 3:4 ... *m* his own family well,
1 Tim 3:12 ... he must *m* his children

MANAGER (n) *a person who conducts business or household affairs*
Luke 16:1 ... a *m* handling his affairs.
1 Cor 4:2 ... as a *m* must be faithful.
Titus 1:7 ... a *m* of God's household,

MANGER (n) *a trough or open box in a stable designed to hold feed for livestock*
Luke 2:7 ... cloth and laid him in a *m*,
Luke 2:12 ... strips of cloth, lying in a *m*.

MANNA (n) *miraculous supply of food given to Israel in the wilderness; symbolic of spiritual nourishment*
Exod 16:31 ... Israelites called the food *m*.
Deut 8:16 ... He fed you with *m* in the
John 6:49 ... Your ancestors ate *m* in the
Rev 2:17 ... some of the *m* that has been

MARRIAGE (adj) *of or relating to marriage*
Gen 49:4 ... you defiled my *m* couch.
Mal 2:14 ... the wife of your *m* vows.

MARRIAGE (n) *the state of being lawfully united to a person of the opposite sex as husband or wife; an act of marrying*
Matt 22:30 ... marry nor be given in *m*.
Rom 7:2 ... laws of *m* no longer apply
1 Cor 7:14 ... brings holiness to her *m*,
1 Cor 7:27 ... do not seek to end the *m*.
Heb 13:4 ... Give honor to *m*, and remain

MARRY, MARRIED, MARRIES, MARRYING (v) *to take a spouse according to law or custom*
Exod 21:10 ... who has *m*-ied a slave wife
Deut 24:4 ... first husband may not *m* her
Deut 24:5 ... newly *m*-ied man must not be
Deut 25:5 ... husband's brother should *m*
Ezra 10:10 ... By *m*-ing pagan women,
Hos 1:2 ... be *m* a prostitute, so that
Matt 1:18 ... to be *m*-ied to Joseph.
Matt 19:9 ... divorces his wife and *m*-ies
Matt 22:30 ... will neither *m* nor be given
Mark 12:23 ... all seven were *m*-ied to her.
Luke 16:18 ... his wife and *m*-ies someone
Rom 7:2 ... when a woman *m*-ies, the law
1 Cor 7:9 ... better to *m* than to burn
1 Cor 7:28 ... if you do get *m*-ied, it is not
1 Cor 7:33 ... a *m*-ied man has to think
1 Tim 5:14 ... these younger widows to *m*

MARY
1. Mother of Jesus, the foretold virgin (Matt 1:16-25; Luke 1:26-38); psalmist of the *Magnificat* (Luke 1:46-56); gave birth in Bethlehem (Luke 2:5-20); at first sign (miracle) of Jesus (John 2:1-5); at the cross (John 19:25-27); Jesus assigned her care to John (John 19:25-27); in upper room after the ascension (Acts 1:14).
2. Mary Magdalene, former demoniac, supporter of Jesus (Luke 8:1-3); at the cross and Jesus' burial (Matt 27:55-61; Mark 15:40-47; John 19:25); saw angel after resurrection (Matt 28:1-10; Mark 16:1-9; Luke 24:10); saw Jesus after resurrection (John 20:1-18).
3. Sister of Martha and Lazarus (Luke 10:38-42; John 11; 12:1-8).
4. Mother of James and Joseph (Matt 27:56; Mark 15:40, 47; 16:1).
5. Mother of John Mark (Acts 12:12).
6. A woman in Rome greeted by Paul (Rom 16:6).

MASTER, MASTERS (n) *one in authority or leadership; employer; teacher; lord or Lord*
Jer 3:14 ... the LORD, "for I am your *m*.
Matt 10:24 ... are not greater than their *m*.
Luke 16:13 ... No one can serve two *m*-s.
Rom 6:14 ... Sin is no longer your *m*,
Eph 6:5 ... obey your earthly *m*-s with
Col 3:22 ... Slaves, obey your earthly *m*-s
1 Tim 6:1 ... full respect for their *m*-s
1 Tim 6:2 ... If the *m*-s are believers,
2 Tim 2:21 ... ready for the *M* to use you
Titus 2:9 ... always obey their *m*-s and do
1 Pet 2:18 ... must submit to your *m*-s
2 Pet 2:1 ... deny the *M* who bought them.
Jude 1:4 ... denied our only *M* and Lord,

MATURE (adj) *of or relating to a condition of full development or to attaining a desired or final state*
1 Cor 2:6 ... I am among *m* believers,
1 Cor 14:20 ... but be *m* in understanding
2 Cor 13:9 ... that you will become *m*.
Eph 4:13 ... we will be *m* in the Lord,
Phil 3:15 ... all who are spiritually *m* agree
Heb 6:1 ... *m* in our understanding.
1 Jn 2:13 ... who are *m* in the faith

MATURITY (n) *the quality or state of being fully developed*
Luke 8:14 ... so they never grow into *m*.
2 Cor 13:11 ... Grow to *m*. Encourage each

MEASURE, MEASURED, MEASURING (v) *to gauge or regulate the specific dimensions of; to have a specified measurement; to regulate by a standard*
Ps 145:3 ... No one can *m* his greatness.
Isa 40:28 ... No one can *m* the depths
Jer 31:37 ... heavens cannot be *m*-d and
Ezek 45:3 ... area, *m* out a portion of land
Dan 5:27 ... balances and have not *m*-d up.
Zech 2:2 ... I am going to *m* Jerusalem,
Luke 12:15 ... Life is not *m*-d by how much
Eph 4:13 ... mature in the Lord, *m*-ing up
Rev 11:1 ... Go and *m* the Temple

MEDIATE, MEDIATES (v) *to act as an intermediary agent in bringing, effecting, or communicating; to interpose*
Job 16:21 ... to *m* between God and me,
Isa 2:4 ... LORD will *m* between nations
Heb 8:6 ... the one who *m*-s for us a far
Heb 9:15 ... who *m*-s a new covenant
Heb 12:24 ... Jesus, the one who *m*-s

MEDIATOR (n) *one who mediates*
Job 9:33 ... If only there were a *m* between
1 Tim 2:5 ... one God and one *M* who can

MEDICINE (n) *a substance or preparation used in treating disease; something that affects well-being*
Prov 17:22 ... A cheerful heart is good *m*,
Jer 8:22 ... Is there no *m* in Gilead?
Rev 22:2 ... The leaves were used for *m*

MEDITATE, MEDITATING (v) *to contemplate, reflect, or ponder*
see also THINK
Gen 24:63 ... *m*-ing in the fields,
Ps 1:2 ... *m*-ing on it day and night.
Ps 48:9 ... O God, we *m* on your unfailing
Ps 63:6 ... *m*-ing on you through the night.
Ps 119:23 ... but I will *m* on your decrees.
Ps 119:27 ... *m* on your wonderful deeds.
Ps 119:48 ... I *m* on your decrees.
Ps 145:5 ... I will *m* on your majestic,

MEDITATION (n) *the act or process of meditating*
Ps 19:14 ... words of my mouth and the *m*

MERCIFUL (adj) *compassionate; forgiving*
Deut 4:31 ... your God is a *m* God;
Ps 78:38 ... Yet he was *m* and forgave
Dan 4:27 ... and be *m* to the poor.
Dan 9:9 ... our God is *m* and forgiving,
Matt 5:7 ... God blesses those who are *m*,
Luke 1:54 ... and remembered to be *m*.
Heb 2:17 ... *m* and faithful High Priest
Jas 2:13 ... God will be *m* when he judges

MERCY, MERCIES (n) *a blessing that is an act of divine favor or compassion; withholding of the punishment or judgment our sins deserve*
see also COMPASSION, FORGIVENESS
Exod 34:6 ... God of compassion and *m*!
2 Sam 24:14 ... for his *m* is great.
Neh 9:27 ... In your great *m*, you sent
Job 41:3 ... beg you for *m* or implore
Ps 28:6 ... he has heard my cry for *m*.
Ps 103:4 ... me with love and tender *m*-ies.
Ps 119:77 ... with your tender *m*-ies so I
Ps 119:156 ... how great is your *m*;
Isa 14:1 ... LORD will have *m* on
Isa 49:10 ... LORD in his *m* will lead
Isa 60:10 ... I will now have *m* on you
Lam 3:22 ... His *m*-ies never cease.
Lam 3:23 ... *m*-ies begin afresh each morning.
Dan 9:18 ... because of your *m*.
Jon 2:8 ... their backs on all God's *m*-ies.
Mic 6:8 ... do what is right, to love *m*,
Matt 5:7 ... for they will be shown *m*.
Matt 9:13 ... I want you to show *m*,
Matt 18:33 ... just as I had *m* on you?
Matt 23:23 ... law—justice, *m*, and faith.
Rom 9:15 ... I will show *m* to anyone
Rom 9:18 ... God chooses to show *m*
Rom 11:32 ... have *m* on everyone.
2 Cor 4:1 ... God in his *m* has given us
Gal 1:6 ... through the loving *m* of Christ.
Eph 2:4 ... But God is so rich in *m*, and
1 Tim 1:13 ... But God had *m* on me
Titus 3:5 ... but because of his *m*.
Heb 4:16 ... we will receive his *m*,
Heb 10:29 ... who brings God's *m* to us.
Jas 2:13 ... will be no *m* for those
Jas 3:17 ... It is full of *m* and the fruit
1 Pet 1:3 ... by his great *m* that we
Jude 1:22 ... show *m* to those whose faith

MESSENGER, MESSENGERS (n) *one who bears a message or does an errand*
Prov 13:17 . . . a reliable *m* brings healing.
Prov 25:13 . . . Trustworthy *m-s* refresh like
Isa 52:7 . . . feet of the *m* who brings good
Isa 66:19 . . . who survive to be *m-s* to the
Mal 3:1 . . . my *m*, and he will prepare
Matt 11:10 . . . am sending my *m* ahead
Rom 10:15 . . . feet of *m-s* who bring good
Rom 15:16 . . . a special *m* from Christ
2 Cor 12:7 . . . *m* from Satan to torment
Phil 2:25 . . . he was your *m* to help me
1 Thes 2:4 . . . speak as *m-s* approved by God
Heb 3:1 . . . to be God's *m* and High Priest.

MESSIAH, MESSIAHS (n) *the one anointed by God to deliver His people and establish His kingdom*
see also CHRIST, JESUS
Matt 24:24 . . . false *m-s* and false
Mark 13:22 . . . false *m-s* and false
John 1:41 . . . him, "We have found the *M*"
John 4:25 . . . I know the *M* is coming—

MIGHTY, MIGHTIER, MIGHTIEST (adj) *powerful; great or imposing in size or extent*
Gen 49:24 . . . hands of the *M* One of Jacob,
Deut 10:17 . . . God, the *m* and awesome
Deut 34:12 . . . With *m* power, Moses
2 Sam 23:8 . . . David's *m-iest* warriors.
2 Chr 20:6 . . . You are powerful and *m*;
Neh 9:32 . . . and *m* and awesome God,
Job 9:4 . . . For God is so wise and so *m*.
Job 36:5 . . . He is *m* in both power and
Ps 24:8 . . . LORD, strong and *m*;
Ps 47:5 . . . ascended with a *m* shout.
Ps 50:1 . . . LORD, the *M* One, is God,
Ps 71:16 . . . I will praise your *m* deeds,
Ps 77:12 . . . thinking about your *m* works.
Ps 89:27 . . . son, the *m-iest* king on earth.
Ps 93:4 . . . *m-ier* than the violent raging
Ps 93:4 . . . LORD above is *m-ier* than these!
Ps 95:4 . . . and the *m-iest* mountains.
Ps 145:4 . . . children of your *m* acts;
Ps 145:12 . . . will tell about your *m* deeds
Ps 150:2 . . . Praise him for his *m* works;
Prov 24:5 . . . wise are *m-ier* than the strong,
Isa 9:6 . . . Wonderful Counselor, *M* God,
Isa 60:16 . . . your Redeemer, the *M* One of
Zeph 3:17 . . . He is a *m* savior.
Eph 1:19 . . . This is the same *m* power
Eph 6:10 . . . in the Lord and in his *m*
Heb 1:3 . . . sustains everything by the *m*
1 Pet 5:6 . . . yourselves under the *m*
Jude 1:9 . . . Michael, one of the *m-iest* of the angels,

MILK (n) *from goats, cows, or sheep, used for food and drink; figurative of abundant produce, prosperity, spiritual food, or salvation*
Exod 3:8 . . . flowing with *m* and honey—
1 Cor 3:2 . . . feed you with *m*, not with
1 Pet 2:2 . . . must crave pure spiritual *m*

MIND, MINDS (n) *the part of humans that engages in conscious thinking, feeling, and decision making; in the Bible, mind is akin to the heart, not the brain*
Num 23:19 . . . he does not change his *m*.
1 Sam 15:29 . . . nor will he change his *m*,
Mark 12:30 . . . all your soul, all your *m*,
Luke 24:45 . . . opened their *m-s*
Acts 4:32 . . . were united in heart and *m*.
Rom 8:6 . . . Spirit control your *m*

1 Cor 1:10 . . . be of one *m*, united in
1 Cor 2:9 . . . heard, and no *m* has imagined
2 Cor 4:4 . . . has blinded the *m-s* of those
Col 2:18 . . . sinful *m-s* have made them
2 Tim 4:5 . . . clear *m* in every situation.
Heb 8:10 . . . I will put my laws in their *m-s*,
Heb 10:16 . . . I will write them on their *m-s*.
1 Pet 1:13 . . . So prepare your *m-s* for action

MIRACLE, MIRACLES (n) *an extraordinary event manifesting divine intervention in human affairs*
Exod 3:20 . . . performing all kinds of *m-s*
Exod 7:9 . . . demand, 'Show me a *m*.'
Deut 13:1 . . . they promise you signs or *m-s*,
Job 9:10 . . . He performs countless *m-s*.
Ps 105:5 . . . he has performed, his *m-s*,
Ps 106:2 . . . the glorious *m-s* of the LORD?
Jer 32:19 . . . and do great and mighty *m-s*.
Matt 7:22 . . . and performed many *m-s*
Matt 13:54 . . . and the power to do *m-s?*
Mark 6:2 . . . power to perform such *m-s?*
Mark 9:39 . . . No one who performs a *m*
Luke 19:37 . . . wonderful *m-s* they had
Luke 23:8 . . . to see him perform a *m*.
John 7:21 . . . I did one *m* on the Sabbath,
Acts 2:22 . . . by doing powerful *m-s*,
Acts 8:13 . . . *m-s* Philip performed.
Acts 19:11 . . . to perform unusual *m-s*.
1 Cor 12:28 . . . those who do *m-s*, those
2 Cor 12:12 . . . and *m-s* among you.
Gal 3:5 . . . and work *m-s* among you
Heb 2:4 . . . and various *m-s* and gifts of

MIRROR (n) *a polished or smooth surface (as of glass) that forms images by reflection*
1 Cor 13:12 . . . puzzling reflections in a *m*,
Jas 1:23 . . . glancing at your face in a *m*.

MONEY (n) *officially coined currency*
see also POSSESSION(S), RICHES, TREASURE(S), WEALTH
2 Chr 24:10 . . . gladly brought their *m* and
Eccl 5:10 . . . who love *m* will never have
Matt 6:24 . . . serve God and be enslaved to *m*.
Luke 3:14 . . . Don't extort *m* or make false
1 Tim 3:3 . . . and not love *m*.
1 Tim 6:10 . . . love of *m* is the root of all
1 Tim 6:17 . . . and not to trust in their *m*,
1 Jn 3:17 . . . If someone has enough *m*

MOON (n) *a celestial body that orbits the earth*
Josh 10:13 . . . and the *m* stayed in place
Ps 121:6 . . . harm you by day, nor the *m* at
Ps 148:3 . . . Praise him, sun and *m!*
Joel 2:31 . . . the *m* will turn blood red
Hab 3:11 . . . The sun and *m* stood still
Matt 24:29 . . . the *m* will give no light,
Acts 2:20 . . . the *m* will turn blood red
Col 2:16 . . . or new *m* ceremonies
Rev 21:23 . . . city has no need of sun or *m*,

MORNING (n) *the time from sunrise to noon*
Gen 1:5 . . . evening passed and *m* came,
Ps 5:3 . . . Listen to my voice in the *m*,
Lam 3:23 . . . mercies begin afresh each *m*.

MORTAL (adj) *subject to death*
Gen 6:3 . . . for they are only *m* flesh.
Rom 8:11 . . . will give life to your *m* bodies
1 Cor 15:53 . . . our *m* bodies must be

MORTALS (n) *human beings*
Ps 8:4 . . . mere *m* that you should think
Ps 144:3 . . . mere *m* that you should think

MOSES Deliverer of Israel from Egypt, lawgiver, servant of God; "drawn out" of the Nile, raised in Pharaoh's house (Exod 2:1-10); killed an Egyptian and fled to Midian (Exod 2:11-15; Acts 7:24); married Zipporah and had a child (Exod 2:16-22); saw the Lord at the burning bush (Exod 3:1–4:17); returned to Egypt (Exod 4:18-31); conflict with Pharaoh and the 10 plagues (Exod 5–11); brother of Aaron and Miriam (1 Chr 6:3); Passover and the Exodus (Exod 12–14; 1 Cor 10:2); song of salvation and praise (Exod 15:1-21; Rev 15:3); heavenly provisions (Exod 15:22–17:7); raised arms to defeat enemies (Exod 17:8-16); delegated judgeships (Exod 18); received the law at Sinai (Exod 19–23; John 1:17; Heb 12:21); received Tabernacle plans (Exod 25–31); broke tablets at golden calf incident (Exod 32); received new tablets (Exod 33–34); face glowed with the Lord's glory (Exod 34:29-35; 2 Cor 3:13-15); directed the building of the Tabernacle (Exod 35–40); anointed Tabernacle and Aaronic priesthood (Lev 8–9); opposed by Aaron and Miriam, interceded for sister (Num 12); interceded for Israel when they refused to enter Canaan (Num 14:11-25); Korah's rebellion (Num 16); water at Meribah (Num 20:1-13); denied entrance to Promised Land (Num 20:12; Deut 1:37; 3:23-28); bronze snake healed (Num 21:4-9; John 3:14); succeeded by Joshua (Num 27:12-23; Deut 31:1-8); received additional laws (Num 28–30); gave concluding messages to Israel (Deut 1–33); gave final blessings to the tribes (Deut 33; see also Gen 49); died and was exalted (Deut 34; Heb 3:2); wrote a psalm (Ps 90); recorded book of the law (Ezra 3:2; Neh 13:1; Luke 24:44); appeared with Elijah at the Transfiguration (Luke 9:30).

MOTHER (n) *a female parent; a woman in authority*
see also PARENT
Gen 2:24 . . . a man leaves his father and *m*
Gen 3:20 . . . she would be the *m* of all who
Exod 20:12 . . . Honor your father and *m*.
Deut 21:18 . . . not obey his father or *m*,
Judg 5:7 . . . Deborah arose as a *m*
Prov 10:1 . . . brings grief to a *m*.
Prov 23:22 . . . don't despise your *m*
Isa 66:13 . . . as a *m* comforts her child.
Matt 10:35 . . . a daughter against her *m*,
Matt 10:37 . . . father or *m* more than you
Matt 12:48 . . . Who is my *m?*
Mark 10:19 . . . Honor your father and *m*.
John 19:27 . . . disciple, "Here is your *m*."
Eph 5:31 . . . A man leaves his father and *m*
Eph 6:2 . . . Honor your father and *m*,

MOTIVES (n) *something (as a need or desire) that causes a person to act*
1 Chr 29:17 . . . all this with good *m*,
Ps 26:2 . . . Test my *m* and my heart.
Prov 16:2 . . . LORD examines their *m*.
Jer 17:10 . . . hearts and examine secret *m*.
1 Cor 4:5 . . . will reveal our private *m*.
Phil 1:18 . . . Whether their *m* are false or
1 Thes 2:3 . . . with any deceit or impure *m*,
1 Thes 2:4 . . . He alone examines the *m* of
Jas 4:3 . . . your *m* are all wrong—

MOUNTAIN, MOUNTAINS (n) *a landmass that projects conspicuously above its surroundings and is higher than a hill*

Exod 24:18 ... on the *m* forty days
Deut 5:4 ... At the *m* the LORD
Ps 36:6 ... is like the mighty *m-s,*
Ps 121:1 ... I look up to the *m-s*—
Isa 14:13 ... preside on the *m* of the gods
Matt 17:20 ... say to this *m,* 'Move
Mark 9:2 ... led them up a high *m*
Mark 9:9 ... went back down the *m,*
Luke 23:30 ... beg the *m-s,* 'Fall on us,'
1 Cor 13:2 ... faith that I could move *m-s,*
2 Pet 1:18 ... with him on the holy *m.*
Rev 6:16 ... they cried to the *m-s* and

MOURN (v) *to feel or express grief or sorrow*
Gen 50:11 ... watched them *m*
Zech 12:10 ... have pierced and *m* for him
Matt 5:4 ... God blesses those who *m,*

MOURNING (n) *the act of sorrowing; a period of time during which signs of grief are shown*
Ps 30:11 ... my clothes of *m* and clothed
Isa 60:20 ... Your days of *m* will come to
Isa 61:3 ... instead of *m,* festive praise
Jer 31:13 ... I will turn their *m* into joy.
Zech 8:19 ... times of *m* you have kept

MOUTH, MOUTHS (n) *the natural opening through which food passes into the body of an animal; voice, speech*
Ps 10:7 ... Their *m-s* are full of cursing,
Ps 19:14 ... words of my *m* and
Prov 13:3 ... opening your *m* can ruin
Isa 51:16 ... have put my words in your *m*
Isa 53:7 ... he did not open his *m.*
Isa 59:3 ... and your *m* spews corruption.
Jer 31:29 ... their children's *m-s* pucker
Matt 4:4 ... word that comes from the *m*
Rom 3:14 ... Their *m-s* are full of cursing
Rev 2:16 ... with the sword of my *m.*

MOVE, MOVED, MOVES, MOVING (v) *to change the place or position of; to go from one place to another in continuous motion; to carry on one's life or activities in a specified environment; to stir the emotions or passions of; to prompt to the doing of something*
Exod 35:21 ... and whose spirits were *m-d*
Deut 19:14 ... steal anyone's land by *m-ing*
Deut 23:14 ... LORD your God *m-s* around
Prov 4:15 ... Turn away and keep *m-ing.*
Prov 23:10 ... cheat your neighbor by *m-ing*
Isa 54:10 ... For the mountains may *m*
Acts 17:28 ... For in him we live and *m*
1 Cor 13:2 ... faith that I could *m*
2 Pet 1:21 ... were *m-d* by the Holy Spirit,

MURDER (n) *the personal, intentional killing of another person*
Matt 5:21 ... If you commit *m,*
Rom 1:29 ... hate, envy, *m,* quarreling,

MURDER, MURDERED, MURDERS (v) *to kill (a human being) unlawfully and with premeditated malice*
Gen 9:5 ... *m-s* a fellow human must die.
Exod 20:13 ... You must not *m.*
Deut 5:17 ... You must not *m.*
Matt 23:31 ... who *m-ed* the prophets.
Acts 7:52 ... whom you betrayed and *m-ed.*
Rom 13:9 ... You must not *m.*
Jas 2:11 ... You must not *m.*

MURDERER, MURDERERS (n) *one who commits the crime of murder*
Num 35:16 ... *m* must be executed.
Ps 5:6 ... LORD detests *m-s* and deceivers.
Ps 26:9 ... condemn me along with *m-s.*
Ps 59:2 ... save me from these *m-s.*
Ezek 18:10 ... a robber or *m* and refuses
1 Jn 3:15 ... brother or sister is really a *m*
Rev 21:8 ... the corrupt, *m-s,* the immoral,
Rev 22:15 ... the sexually immoral, the *m-s,*

MUSIC (n) *vocal, instrumental, or mechanical sounds having rhythm, melody, or harmony*
Judg 5:3 ... I will make *m* to the LORD,
1 Chr 6:31 ... lead the *m* at the house of
Neh 12:27 ... and with the *m* of cymbals,
Ps 45:8 ... the *m* of strings entertains
Amos 5:23 ... to the *m* of your harps.
Eph 5:19 ... and making *m* to the Lord

MUSTARD (n) *a plant whose seeds are used as a condiment and for oil; in Jesus' time, the smallest seed known*
Matt 13:31 ... is like a *m* seed planted
Matt 17:20 ... as small as a *m* seed,
Mark 4:31 ... is like a *m* seed planted

MUZZLE (v) *to fit with a fastening or covering for the mouth of an animal to prevent eating or biting*
Deut 25:4 ... You must not *m* an ox
1 Tim 5:18 ... You must not *m* an ox

MYSTERIOUS (adj) *exciting wonder, curiosity, or surprise while baffling efforts to comprehend or identify; of, relating to, or constituting mystery*
1 Cor 14:2 ... Spirit, but it will all be *m.*
Eph 1:9 ... now revealed to us his *m* will
Eph 3:3 ... revealed his *m* plan to me.
Eph 6:19 ... explain God's *m* plan that the
Col 2:2 ... they understand God's *m* plan,
Col 4:3 ... about his *m* plan concerning
Rev 10:7 ... God's *m* plan will be fulfilled.

MYSTERY, MYSTERIES (n) *something not understood or beyond understanding; a religious truth that one can know only by revelation and cannot fully understand*
see also SECRET(S)
Dan 4:9 ... and that no *m* is too great
Rom 11:25 ... to understand this *m,*
1 Cor 2:7 ... speak of is the *m* of God—
1 Cor 4:1 ... explaining God's *m-ies.*
1 Tim 3:9 ... to the *m* of the faith
1 Tim 3:16 ... the great *m* of our faith:
Rev 1:20 ... the *m* of the seven stars
Rev 17:7 ... tell you the *m* of this woman

N

NAILED, NAILING (v) *to fasten with or as if with a nail*
Matt 27:35 ... had *n* him to the cross,
Mark 15:24 ... soldiers *n* him to the
Acts 2:23 ... you *n* him to a cross
Col 2:14 ... away by *n-ing* it to the cross.
Heb 6:6 ... are *n-ing* him to the cross

NAKED (adj) *not covered by clothing; nude*
Gen 2:25 ... man and his wife were both *n,*
Job 1:21 ... and I will be *n* when I leave.
Eccl 5:15 ... the end of our lives as *n*

NAME, NAMES (n) *a word or phrase that constitutes the distinctive designation of a person or thing; reputation*
see also REPUTATION
Gen 2:19 ... the man chose a *n* for each
Exod 3:15 ... my *n* to remember
Exod 28:9 ... on them the *n-s* of the tribes
Exod 34:14 ... whose very *n* is Jealous,
Lev 24:11 ... blasphemed the *N*
Deut 18:5 ... minister in the LORD's *n.*
Deut 28:58 ... awesome *n* of the LORD
1 Chr 17:8 ... will make your *n* as famous
2 Chr 7:14 ... called by my *n* will humble
Ps 8:1 ... your majesty *n* fills the earth!
Ps 23:3 ... paths, bringing honor to his *n.*
Ps 34:3 ... let us exalt his *n* together.
Ps 66:2 ... Sing about the glory of his *n!*
Ps 103:1 ... I will praise his holy *n.*
Ps 138:2 ... I praise your *n* for your
Ps 147:4 ... stars and calls them all by *n.*
Isa 40:26 ... calling each by its *n.*
Isa 42:8 ... I am the LORD; that is my *n!*
Jer 15:16 ... I bear your *n,* O LORD
Dan 12:1 ... people whose *n* is written in
Joel 2:32 ... calls on the *n* of the LORD
Mic 5:4 ... majesty of the *n* of the LORD
Zech 14:9 ... one LORD—his *n* alone
Mal 1:6 ... shown contempt for my *n!*
Matt 24:5 ... come in my *n,* claiming, 'I am
Matt 28:19 ... baptizing them in the *n* of
Luke 10:20 ... your *n-s* are registered
Luke 11:2 ... may your *n* be kept holy.
John 16:24 ... Ask, using my *n,* and you
Acts 2:21 ... calls on the *n* of the LORD
Acts 4:12 ... no other *n* under heaven
Rom 10:13 ... calls on the *n* of the LORD
Phil 2:9 ... gave him the *n* above all
Phil 2:10 ... that at the *n* of Jesus every
Phil 4:3 ... whose *n-s* are written in the Book of Life.
Heb 12:23 ... *n-s* are written in heaven.
Jas 5:14 ... with oil in the *n* of the Lord.
Rev 2:17 ... stone will be engraved a new *n*
Rev 3:5 ... erase their *n-s* from the Book
Rev 3:12 ... write on them the *n*
Rev 20:15 ... whose *n* was not found
Rev 21:27 ... *n-s* are written in the Lamb's

NARROW (adj) *of slender width*
Matt 7:13 ... only through the *n* gate.
Matt 7:14 ... the gateway to life is very *n*

NATION, NATIONS (n) *group of people defined by geography or ethnicity*
see also GENTILE(S), PEOPLE(S)
Gen 12:2 ... I will make you into a great *n.*
Gen 17:4 ... father of a multitude of *n-s!*
Gen 17:16 ... the mother of many *n-s.*
Gen 25:23 ... will become two *n-s.*
Gen 28:3 ... and become many *n-s!*
Exod 19:6 ... of priests, my holy *n.*
Deut 15:6 ... You will rule many *n-s,* but
Deut 28:10 ... the *n-s* of the world will see
Ps 2:8 ... you the *n-s* as your inheritance,
Ps 22:28 ... He rules all the *n-s.*
Ps 46:10 ... I will be honored by every *n.*
Ps 66:7 ... every movement of the *n-s;*
Ps 68:30 ... Scatter the *n-s* that delight in
Ps 87:6 ... the LORD registers the *n-s,*
Ps 99:2 ... exalted above all the *n-s.*
Ps 113:4 ... LORD is high above the *n-s;*
Prov 14:34 ... Godliness makes a *n* great,
Isa 11:10 ... The *n-s* will rally to him,
Isa 34:1 ... listen, O *n-s* of the earth.
Isa 40:15 ... for all the *n-s* of the world

1741

Isa 42:1 ... He will bring justice to the **n-s.**
Isa 52:15 ... And he will startle many **n-s.**
Isa 56:7 ... a house of prayer for all **n-s.**
Isa 60:12 ... the **n-s** that refuse to serve
Isa 66:8 ... Has a **n** ever been born in a
Ezek 37:22 ... divided into two **n-s** or into
Joel 3:2 ... my people among the **n-s,**
Amos 9:12 ... **n-s** I have called to be mine.
Mic 4:3 ... disputes between strong **n-s**
Mic 5:7 ... take their place among the **n-s.**
Zeph 3:8 ... stand and accuse these evil **n-s.**
Hag 2:7 ... I will shake all the **n-s,**
Zech 8:13 ... Among the other **n-s,** Judah
Zech 12:2 ... makes the nearby **n-s** stagger
Matt 12:18 ... proclaim justice to the **n-s.**
Matt 24:14 ... so that all **n-s** will hear it;
Matt 28:19 ... make disciples of all the **n-s,**
Mark 11:17 ... house of prayer for all **n-s,**
Acts 4:25 ... Why were the **n-s** so angry?
Gal 3:8 ... All **n-s** will be blessed through
1 Pet 2:9 ... royal priests, a holy **n,**
Rev 5:9 ... language and people and **n.**
Rev 14:6 ... to every **n,** tribe, language,
Rev 21:24 ... The **n-s** will walk in its light,
Rev 22:2 ... for medicine to heal the **n-s.**

NATURE (n) *inherent character or essence*
Rom 1:20 ... eternal power and divine **n.**
Rom 8:4 ... follow our sinful **n**
Rom 8:7 ... For the sinful **n** is always
Gal 5:19 ... the desires of your sinful **n,**
Gal 5:24 ... desires of their sinful **n** to
2 Pet 1:4 ... share his divine **n** and escape

NEED, NEEDS (n) *a condition requiring supply or relief; poverty; obligation; a lack of something requisite, desirable, or useful*
1 Kgs 8:59 ... according to each day's **n-s,**
Ps 79:8 ... quickly meet our **n-s,**
Ps 112:9 ... give generously to those in **n.**
Prov 11:26 ... who sells in time of **n.**
Prov 30:8 ... just enough to satisfy my **n-s.**
Matt 6:2 ... give to someone in **n.**
Acts 2:45 ... the money with those in **n.**
Acts 20:35 ... you can help those in **n** by
Rom 12:13 ... God's people are in **n,**
1 Cor 7:3 ... fulfill his wife's sexual **n-s.**
Eph 4:28 ... give generously to others in **n.**
Phil 4:19 ... supply all your **n-s** from his
Titus 3:14 ... by meeting the urgent **n-s**

NEED, NEEDED, NEEDING (v) *to require; to be necessary; to be in want*
Ps 34:9 ... fear him will have all they **n.**
Ps 119:75 ... disciplined me because I **n-ed**
Phil 4:6 ... Tell God what you **n,** and
Heb 4:16 ... grace to help us when we **n** it
Jas 1:4 ... complete, **n-ing** nothing.
Jas 1:5 ... If you **n** wisdom, ask our

NEEDY (adj) *poverty-stricken; marked by want of affection, attention, or emotional support*
1 Sam 2:8 ... **n** from the garbage dump.
Ps 9:18 ... the **n** will not be ignored
Ps 68:10 ... you provided for your **n**
Ps 69:33 ... LORD hears the cries of the **n;**
Prov 22:22 ... or exploit her **n** in court.
Prov 31:20 ... opens her arms to the **n.**

NEIGHBOR, NEIGHBORS (n) *one living or located near another; fellow human*
Lev 19:18 ... but love your **n** as yourself.
Ps 15:3 ... to gossip or harm their **n-s**
Prov 24:28 ... your **n-s** without cause;

Prov 27:10 ... better to go to a **n** than
Jer 31:34 ... not need to teach their **n-s,**
Mark 12:31 ... Love your **n** as yourself.
Luke 10:29 ... And who is my **n?**
Rom 13:8 ... If you love your **n,** you will
Gal 5:14 ... Love your **n** as yourself.
Eph 4:25 ... Let us tell our **n-s** the truth,
Heb 8:11 ... not need to teach their **n-s,**
Jas 2:8 ... Love your **n** as yourself.

NEW (adj) *fresh; original; different than before; unfamiliar*
Ps 98:1 ... Sing a **n** song to the LORD,
Jer 31:31 ... I will make a **n** covenant with
Ezek 36:26 ... I will give you a **n** heart,
Mark 16:17 ... will speak in **n** languages.
Luke 22:20 ... cup is the **n** covenant
Rom 6:4 ... we also may live **n** lives.
Rom 12:2 ... you into a **n** person
1 Cor 11:25 ... cup is the **n** covenant
2 Cor 3:6 ... but under the **n** covenant,
2 Cor 5:17 ... is gone; a **n** life has begun!
Gal 6:15 ... into a **n** creation.
Eph 4:24 ... Put on your **n** nature,
Col 3:10 ... Put on your **n** nature,
Heb 8:8 ... when I will make a **n** covenant
Heb 9:15 ... mediates a **n** covenant
Heb 12:24 ... the **n** covenant
2 Pet 3:13 ... **n** heavens and **n** earth he
Rev 2:17 ... a **n** name that no one
Rev 21:1 ... **n** heaven and a **n** earth,

NEWBORN (adj) *recently born*
1 Pet 2:2 ... Like **n** babies, you must crave

NEWS (n) *a report of recent events; "Good News": the gospel of Jesus Christ*
Isa 40:9 ... of good **n,** shout from the
Matt 4:23 ... the Good **N** about
Mark 1:15 ... sins and believe the Good **N!**
Luke 4:43 ... I must preach the Good **N**
Acts 13:32 ... to bring you this Good **N.**
Acts 14:21 ... preaching the Good **N**
Rom 1:16 ... not ashamed of this Good **N**
Rom 10:17 ... the Good **N** about Christ.
Rom 15:16 ... I bring you the Good **N**
Rom 16:25 ... just as my Good **N** says.
1 Cor 1:17 ... to preach the Good **N—**
1 Cor 9:12 ... an obstacle to the Good **N**
1 Cor 9:16 ... preach the Good **N!**
1 Cor 9:23 ... to spread the Good **N**
1 Cor 15:1 ... the Good **N** I preached
2 Cor 4:4 ... glorious light of the Good **N.**
2 Cor 9:13 ... obedient to the Good **N**
2 Cor 11:7 ... preaching God's Good **N**
Gal 1:7 ... is not the Good **N** at all.
Eph 6:15 ... comes from the Good **N**
Phil 1:27 ... worthy of the Good **N**
Col 1:5 ... heard the truth of the Good **N.**
Col 1:23 ... Good **N** has been preached
1 Thes 2:4 ... entrusted with the Good **N.**
2 Thes 1:8 ... obey the Good **N** of our Lord
2 Tim 1:10 ... through the Good **N.**
2 Tim 4:5 ... telling others the Good **N,**
Rev 14:6 ... the eternal Good **N**

NIGHT, NIGHTS (n) *period of darkness between sunset and sunrise; figurative of suffering and sorrow or the reign of sin and immorality*
Gen 1:16 ... smaller one to govern the **n.**
Exod 13:21 ... provided light at **n**
Job 35:10 ... who gives songs in the **n?**
Ps 1:2 ... meditating on it day and **n.**
Ps 19:2 ... **n** after **n** they make him
Ps 77:6 ... my **n-s** were filled with joyful
Jon 1:17 ... for three days and three **n-s.**

Matt 4:2 ... days and forty **n-s** he fasted
Matt 12:40 ... for three days and three **n-s.**
Luke 2:8 ... That **n** there were shepherds
2 Cor 6:5 ... endured sleepless **n-s,** and
1 Thes 5:2 ... like a thief in the **n.**
1 Thes 5:5 ... belong to darkness and **n.**
Rev 21:25 ... there is no **n** there.

NINETY-NINE (n) *the number 99*
Matt 18:13 ... than over the **n** that didn't
Luke 15:7 ... to God than over **n** others

NOAH Builder of great boat, survivor of the Flood (Gen 6–9; Matt 24:37-38; Luke 17:26-27; Heb 11:7; 1 Pet 3:20; 2 Pet 2:5); family line (Gen 5:25-32); found favor with God (Gen 6:8); enacted covenant between God and all creatures (Gen 9:1-17); made wine and became drunk (Gen 9:18-23); gave blessings and curse to descendants (Gen 9:24-27); considered righteous (Ezek 14:14, 20).

O

OATH (n) *an appeal to God to witness the truth of some statement*
Ps 95:11 ... in my anger I took an **o:**
Ps 110:4 ... LORD has taken an **o**
Ezek 20:42 ... I promised with a solemn **o**
Heb 6:16 ... people take an **o,** they call
Heb 7:20 ... established with a solemn **o.**
Heb 7:21 ... was an **o** regarding Jesus.
Jas 5:12 ... never take an **o,** by heaven

OBEDIENCE (n) *an act or instance of obeying; the quality or state of being obedient*
Judg 2:17 ... who had walked in **o** to the
1 Sam 15:22 ... **O** is better than sacrifice,
Phil 2:8 ... humbled himself in **o** to God
Heb 5:8 ... learned **o** from the things he

OBEDIENT (adj) *submissive to authority; willing to obey*
Luke 2:51 ... with them and was **o** to them.
Rom 16:19 ... that you are **o** to the Lord.
2 Cor 9:13 ... that you are **o** to the Good
2 Cor 10:6 ... you have become fully **o,**
1 Pet 1:14 ... as God's **o** children.

OBEY, OBEYED, OBEYING, OBEYS (v) *to follow the commands or guidance of; to conform to or comply with*
see also KEEP
Gen 22:18 ... because you have **o-ed** me.
Exod 20:6 ... love me and **o** my commands.
Lev 18:4 ... be careful to **o** my decrees,
Lev 25:18 ... decrees and **o** my regulations.
Deut 4:2 ... Just **o** the commands of the
Deut 5:27 ... we will listen and **o.**
Deut 6:17 ... diligently **o** the commands of
Deut 6:25 ... when we **o** all the commands
Deut 11:1 ... and always **o** his requirements,
Deut 11:22 ... be careful to **o** all these
Deut 13:4 ... **O** his commands, listen to his
Deut 26:16 ... to **o** them wholeheartedly.
Deut 28:1 ... If you fully **o** the LORD
Deut 30:2 ... if you **o** with all your heart
Deut 30:12 ... so we can hear it and **o?**
Deut 30:20 ... love and **o** the LORD,
Josh 1:7 ... to **o** all the instructions Moses
Josh 22:5 ... all his ways, **o** his commands,
1 Sam 7:3 ... to the LORD and **o** him alone;
1 Kgs 8:61 ... May you always **o** his decrees
2 Kgs 17:13 ... **O** my commands and
2 Kgs 18:6 ... **o-ed** all the commands

2 Kgs 23:3 ... pledged to *o* the LORD
Neh 1:5 ... love him and *o* his commands,
Job 36:11 ... they listen and *o* God,
Ps 111:10 ... All who *o* his commandments
Ps 119:17 ... I may live and *o* your word.
Ps 119:129 ... No wonder I *o* them!
Eccl 8:2 ... *O* the king since you vowed
Eccl 12:13 ... and *o* his commands,
Isa 11:3 ... delight in *o-ing* the LORD.
Jer 32:33 ... not receive instruction or *o*.
Jer 42:6 ... For if we *o* him, everything
Jer 43:4 ... refused to *o* the LORD's
Dan 9:4 ... love you and *o* your commands.
Dan 9:10 ... We have not *o-ed* the LORD
Jon 3:3 ... This time Jonah *o-ed* the LORD's
Mic 5:15 ... nations that refuse to *o* me.
Matt 5:19 ... anyone who *o-s* God's laws
Matt 8:27 ... the winds and waves *o* him!
Matt 19:20 ... *o-ed* all these commandments,
Matt 28:20 ... to *o* all the commands
Luke 8:21 ... hear God's word and *o* it.
John 3:36 ... who doesn't *o* the Son
John 8:51 ... anyone who *o-s* my teaching
John 14:15 ... *o* my commandments.
Acts 4:19 ... to *o* you rather than him?
Acts 5:29 ... We must *o* God rather than
Rom 1:5 ... believe and *o* him,
Rom 2:27 ... possess God's law but don't *o*
Rom 3:28 ... and not by *o-ing* the law.
Rom 6:16 ... of whatever you choose to *o*?
Rom 6:17 ... wholeheartedly *o* this
Rom 15:31 ... in Judea who refuse to *o* God.
2 Cor 10:5 ... teach them to *o* Christ.
Gal 2:16 ... Christ, not by *o-ing* the law.
Gal 3:2 ... by *o-ing* the law of Moses?
Gal 3:10 ... and *o* all the commands
Eph 2:2 ... who refuse to *o* God.
Eph 6:1 ... Children, *o* your parents
Eph 6:5 ... Slaves, *o* your earthly masters
2 Thes 3:14 ... who refuse to *o* what we
1 Tim 3:4 ... who respect and *o* him.
Titus 2:9 ... Slaves must always *o* their
Heb 11:8 ... that Abraham *o-ed* when God
Heb 11:31 ... who refused to *o* God.
Jas 2:8 ... good when you *o* the royal law
1 Pet 1:2 ... you have *o-ed* him and have
1 Pet 1:22 ... when you *o-ed* the truth,
1 Pet 2:8 ... they do not *o* God's word,
1 Jn 3:22 ... because we *o* him and do
Rev 22:7 ... Blessed are those who *o* the

OFFER, OFFERED, OFFERING (v) *to present for acceptance as an act of worship or devotion; to sacrifice*
Ps 4:5 ... *O* sacrifices in the right spirit,
Ps 116:12 ... What can I *o* the LORD
Mic 6:7 ... Should we *o* him thousands of
1 Cor 10:20 ... sacrifices are *o-ed* to demons,
Eph 5:2 ... He loved us and *o-ed* himself
Heb 7:27 ... when he *o-ed* himself
Heb 9:14 ... Christ *o-ed* himself to God
Heb 9:25 ... to *o* himself again and again,
Heb 10:11 ... *o-ing* the same sacrifices again
Heb 11:17 ... that Abraham *o-ed* Isaac
Heb 13:15 ... let us *o* through Jesus
Jas 5:15 ... a prayer *o-ed* in faith will heal

OFFERING, OFFERINGS (n) *a sacrifice ceremonially offered as a part of worship; a contribution to the support of a church*
Gen 22:8 ... a sheep for the burnt *o*,
1 Sam 13:9 ... Bring me the burnt *o*
1 Sam 15:22 ... burnt *o-s* and sacrifices
Ps 40:6 ... no delight in sacrifices or *o-s.*
Ps 141:2 ... hands as an evening *o.*
Isa 53:10 ... his life is made an *o* for sin,
Hos 6:6 ... more than I want burnt *o-s.*
Mal 3:8 ... of the tithes and *o-s*
Mark 12:33 ... all of the burnt *o-s*
Rom 15:26 ... taken up an *o* for the poor
Phil 2:17 ... faithful service is an *o*
Heb 10:5 ... animal sacrifices or sin *o-s.*
Heb 10:14 ... that one *o* he forever made
Heb 11:4 ... Abel's *o* gave evidence that he

OIL (n) *liquid produced from olives used in biblical times for lamp fuel, anointing, and dressing wounds; often symbolic of the Holy Spirit*
Exod 29:7 ... anointing *o* over his head.
Exod 30:25 ... to make a holy anointing *o.*
1 Sam 10:1 ... *o* and poured it over Saul's
1 Sam 16:13 ... *o* he had brought and
Ps 23:5 ... anointing my head with *o.*
Ps 133:2 ... as precious as the anointing *o*
Heb 1:9 ... pouring out the *o* of joy

OLIVE, OLIVES (n) *a Mediterranean evergreen tree with berries that ripen black; the berries of an olive tree*
Gen 8:11 ... evening with a fresh *o* leaf
Jer 11:16 ... a thriving *o* tree, beautiful
Zech 4:3 ... And I see two *o* trees,
Zech 14:4 ... the Mount of *O-s* will split
Matt 24:3 ... Jesus sat on the Mount of *O-s.*
Rom 11:17 ... of God's special *o* tree.
Rom 11:24 ... cut from a wild *o* tree.
Jas 3:12 ... Does a fig tree produce *o-s*, or
Rev 11:4 ... prophets are the two *o* trees

OPPOSE, OPPOSED, OPPOSES (v) *to set oneself against or opposite someone or something; to resist*
Exod 23:22 ... *o* those who *o* you.
Ps 8:2 ... enemies and all who *o* you.
Ps 35:1 ... *o* those who *o* me.
Acts 26:11 ... was so violently *o-d* to them
Gal 2:11 ... I had to *o* him to his face,
1 Tim 6:20 ... with those who *o*
2 Tim 2:25 ... instruct those who *o*
Titus 1:9 ... show those who *o* it
Titus 2:8 ... who *o* us will be ashamed
Jas 4:6 ... God *o-s* the proud but favors
1 Pet 5:5 ... God *o-s* the proud but gives

OPPRESS, OPPRESSES, OPPRESSING (v) *to crush or burden by abuse of power or authority*
Exod 22:21 ... not mistreat or *o* foreigners
Prov 22:16 ... gets ahead by *o-ing* the poor
Prov 28:16 ... no understanding will *o*
Isa 3:5 ... People will *o* each other—
Isa 58:3 ... you keep *o-ing* your workers.
Ezek 18:12 ... *o-es* the poor and helpless,
Dan 7:25 ... defy the Most High and *o* the
Amos 5:12 ... *o* good people by taking
Zech 7:10 ... Do not *o* widows, orphans,
Jas 2:6 ... the rich who *o* you and drag

OPPRESSED (n) *those subject to the abuse of another's power or authority*
Ps 9:9 ... a shelter for the *o*, a refuge
Ps 14:6 ... frustrate the plans of the *o*,
Ps 82:3 ... uphold the rights of the *o*
Ps 146:7 ... He gives justice to the *o*
Prov 31:5 ... not give justice to the *o.*
Isa 1:17 ... Seek justice. Help the *o.*
Amos 2:7 ... shove the *o* out of the way.
Luke 4:18 ... that the *o* will be set free,

OPPRESSION (n) *unjust or cruel exercise of power or authority*
Judg 2:18 ... burdened by *o* and suffering.
Ps 72:14 ... redeem them from *o* and
Ps 119:134 ... Ransom me from the *o* of
Isa 58:9 ... Remove the heavy yoke of *o.*
Heb 11:25 ... chose to share the *o* of God's

ORPHAN, ORPHANS (n) *a child deprived by death of one or usually both parents*
Exod 22:22 ... not exploit a widow or an *o.*
Deut 10:18 ... *o-s* and widows receive
Deut 24:17 ... among you and to *o-s,*
Deut 24:19 ... *o-s,* and widows.
Ps 10:14 ... in you. You defend the *o-s.*
Ps 82:3 ... justice to the poor and the *o;*
Prov 23:10 ... the land of defenseless *o-s.*
John 14:18 ... will not abandon you as *o-s*—
Jas 1:27 ... caring for *o-s* and widows in

OVERSEER(S) (KJV)
2 Chr 2:18 ... and 3,600 as *foremen*
Neh 11:22 ... *chief officer* of the Levites
Prov 6:7 ... or *governor* or ruler to make
Acts 20:28 ... appointed you as *leaders*

OWE (v) *to be under obligation to pay or repay in return for something received*
Rom 13:7 ... Give to everyone what you *o*
Phlm 1:19 ... that you *o* me your very soul!

OWN (adj) *belonging to oneself or itself*
Luke 18:9 ... in their *o* righteousness
1 Cor 13:5 ... does not demand its *o* way.
Titus 2:14 ... to make us his very *o* people,

OWN (v) *to have or hold as property*
Gen 28:4 ... May you *o* this land

OX, OXEN (n) *a domestic bovine mammal*
Deut 25:4 ... not muzzle an *o* to keep it
1 Kgs 7:25 ... base of twelve bronze *o-en,*
1 Kgs 19:20 ... Elisha left the *o-en*
Isa 1:3 ... *o* knows its owner, and a
Ezek 1:10 ... the face of an *o* on the left
1 Cor 9:9 ... not muzzle an *o* to keep it
1 Tim 5:18 ... not muzzle an *o* to keep it
Rev 4:7 ... the second was like an *o;*

P

PAGAN (adj) *of or relating to a pagan*
1 Sam 17:26 ... Who is this *p* Philistine

PAGAN, PAGANS (n) *a follower of a false god or religion; one who delights in sensual pleasures and material goods*
Ps 106:35 ... they mingled among the *p-s*
Isa 2:6 ... have made alliances with *p-s.*
Matt 5:47 ... Even *p-s* do that.
Matt 18:17 ... treat that person as a *p*
1 Cor 5:1 ... something that even *p-s* don't
1 Cor 12:2 ... when you were still *p-s,* you

PAID (v) *to render payment or due return* see also PAY
1 Cor 7:23 ... God *p* a high price for you,
Col 3:25 ... be *p* back for the wrong
1 Tim 5:17 ... should be respected and *p*

PAIN, PAINS (n) *physical, mental, or emotional suffering; the spasms of childbirth*
Job 6:10 ... Despite the *p,* I have not
Ps 73:14 ... every morning brings me *p.*
Jer 4:19 ... my heart—I writhe in *p!*

Matt 24:8 ... only the first of the birth **p-s,**
John 16:21 ... suffering the **p-s** of labor.
Rom 8:22 ... in the **p-s** of childbirth
Gal 4:19 ... going through labor **p-s** for
1 Thes 5:3 ... woman's labor **p-s** begin.
Heb 13:3 ... as if you felt their **p** in your
Rev 21:4 ... death or sorrow or crying or **p.**

PAINFUL (adj) *feeling or giving pain*
Gen 5:29 ... the **p** labor of farming
Prov 17:21 ... **p** to be the parent of a fool;
2 Cor 2:1 ... grief with another **p** visit.
Heb 12:11 ... while it is happening—it's **p!**

PANIC (n) *a sudden unreasoning terror often accompanied by mass flight*
1 Sam 14:15 ... Suddenly, **p** broke out
Zech 14:13 ... by the LORD with great **p.**

PANIC (v) *to be affected with panic*
Deut 20:3 ... Do not lose heart or **p**
Mark 13:7 ... threats of wars, but don't **p.**

PARABLE, PARABLES (n) *a brief narrative story told with earthly analogies to illustrate a spiritual truth*
Ps 78:2 ... I will speak to you in a **p.**
Matt 13:35 ... I will speak to you in **p-s.**
Luke 8:10 ... I use **p-s** to teach the

PARADISE (n) *an intermediate place where the souls of the righteous await resurrection and the final judgment*
Luke 23:43 ... you will be with me in **p.**
2 Cor 12:4 ... that I was caught up to **p**

PARALYZED (adj) *characterized by the inability to move*
Matt 9:2 ... Jesus said to the **p** man,
Mark 2:3 ... men arrived carrying a **p** man
John 5:3 ... blind, lame, or **p**—

PARDON, PARDONED (v) *to allow (an offense) to pass without punishment; to forgive*
Num 14:19 ... **p** the sins of this people,
Deut 29:20 ... LORD will never **p** such
2 Kgs 5:18 ... may the LORD **p** me
2 Chr 30:18 ... LORD, who is good, **p**
Isa 40:2 ... gone and her sins are **p-ed.**
Jer 5:7 ... How can I **p** you?
Joel 3:21 ... I will **p** my people's crimes,
Joel 3:21 ... which I have not yet **p-ed;**

PARENT, PARENTS (n) *one who produces and cares for offspring*
see also FATHER, MOTHER
Exod 20:5 ... I lay the sins of the **p-s** upon
Prov 13:1 ... child accepts a **p's** discipline;
Jer 31:29 ... **p-s** have eaten sour grapes,
Ezek 18:19 ... child pay for the **p's** sins?
Matt 10:21 ... will rebel against their **p-s**
Rom 1:30 ... and they disobey their **p-s.**
Eph 6:1 ... Children, obey your **p-s**
Col 3:20 ... always obey your **p-s,**

PARTIAL (adj) *inclined to favor one party more than the other; of or relating to a part rather than the whole*
Lev 19:15 ... or being **p** to the rich
1 Cor 13:10 ... **p** things will become

PARTIALITY (n) *the quality or state of being partial*
see also FAVORITES, FAVORITISM
Deut 10:17 ... God, who shows no **p** and
Deut 16:19 ... twist justice or show **p.**
2 Chr 19:7 ... perverted justice, **p,**

PARTNER, PARTNERS (n) *a person with whom one shares an intimate relationship; one associated with another, especially in action*
Mal 2:14 ... she remained your faithful **p,**
2 Cor 6:14 ... can righteousness be a **p**
Phil 1:5 ... **p-s** in spreading the Good
1 Pet 3:7 ... but she is your equal **p**
1 Pet 4:13 ... trials make you **p-s** with
3 Jn 1:8 ... be their **p-s** as they teach
Rev 1:9 ... your **p** in suffering and in God's Kingdom

PASSION, PASSIONS (n) *intense, driving, or overmastering feeling or conviction; ardent affection; sexual desire*
Isa 59:17 ... himself in a cloak of divine **p.**
Zech 8:2 ... with **p** for Jerusalem!
1 Cor 7:37 ... he can control his **p,** he does
Gal 5:24 ... Jesus have nailed the **p-s**
1 Thes 4:5 ... lustful **p** like the pagans

PASSIONATE (adj) *capable of, affected by, or expressing intense feeling*
2 Kgs 19:31 ... **p** commitment of the LORD
Isa 9:7 ... **p** commitment of the LORD
Isa 37:32 ... **p** commitment of the LORD
Zech 1:14 ... Mount Zion is **p** and strong.
Zech 8:2 ... Mount Zion is **p** and strong;

PASSOVER (n) *a festival that commemorated the Hebrew departure from Egypt in haste*
Num 9:2 ... celebrate the **P**
Deut 16:1 ... celebrate the **P** each year
Ezra 6:19 ... returned exiles celebrated **P.**
Mark 14:12 ... **P** lamb is sacrificed,
Heb 11:28 ... to keep the **P** and to sprinkle

PASTORS (n) *spiritual overseers*
Eph 4:11 ... and the **p** and teachers.

PATH, PATHS (n) *course, route; a way of life, conduct, or thought*
1 Kgs 8:36 ... follow the right **p,**
Ps 23:3 ... He guides me along right **p-s,**
Ps 27:11 ... Lead me along the right **p,**
Prov 2:13 ... to walk down dark **p-s.**
Prov 3:6 ... show you which **p** to take.
Prov 5:21 ... examining every **p** he takes.
Prov 8:20 ... in **p-s** of justice.
Prov 14:12 ... a **p** before each person that
Isa 48:17 ... leads you along the **p-s**
Hos 14:9 ... **p-s** of the LORD are true
2 Tim 2:18 ... have left the **p** of truth,
Heb 12:13 ... Mark out a straight **p**

PATIENCE (n) *the power or capacity to endure without complaint something difficult or disagreeable; forbearance, longsuffering*
Rom 15:5 ... May God, who gives this **p**
Gal 5:22 ... joy, peace, **p,** kindness,
Col 1:11 ... endurance and **p** you need.
Col 3:12 ... humility, gentleness, and **p.**
2 Tim 3:10 ... my faith, my **p,** my love,
Titus 2:2 ... and be filled with love and **p.**
Jas 5:10 ... examples of **p** in suffering,
2 Pet 3:15 ... Lord's **p** gives people time

PATIENT (adj) *bearing pains or trials calmly or without complaint; steadfast despite opposition, difficulty, or adversity; not hasty or impetuous*
Rom 2:4 ... and **p** God is with you?
Rom 12:12 ... Be **p** in trouble,
1 Cor 4:12 ... We are **p** with those who
1 Cor 13:4 ... Love is **p** and kind.
1 Thes 5:14 ... Be **p** with everyone.
Jas 5:8 ... You, too, must be **p.**

PATIENTLY (adv) *in a patient manner*
Ps 40:1 ... I waited **p** for the LORD
1 Pet 3:20 ... God waited **p** while Noah
Rev 14:12 ... endure persecution **p,**

PAUL Pharisee and Roman citizen (Acts 22:3); from city of Tarsus (Acts 9:11; Phil 3:5); became apostle (Gal 1) to the Gentiles (Rom 11:13); also known as "Saul" (Acts 7:58; 13:9); supported stoning of Stephen (Acts 8:1); attacked early Christians (Acts 8:1-3; 9:1-2; Gal 1:13); converted on road to Damascus (Acts 9:1-9; 22:6-16; 26:12-18); preached in Damascus (Acts 9:20-22); escaped over the wall in basket (Acts 9:23-25); escaped to Jerusalem, then on to Tarsus (Acts 9:26-30); saw visions in Arabia (Gal 1:17); with Barnabas in Antioch (Acts 11:22-26); sent to Jerusalem (Acts 11:27-30); first missionary journey: Cyprus and Galatia (Acts 13–14); advocate for Gentile believers (Acts 15:1-5); testified at Jerusalem Council (Acts 15:12); split with Barnabas over John Mark (Acts 15:36-41); second missionary journey with Silas: northern and southern Greece, western Asia (Acts 15:36–18:22); received call to Macedonia (Acts 16:6-10); Philippi, Thessalonica, Berea (Acts 16–17); Athens, Corinth (Acts 17–18); third missionary journey: returned to northern and southern Greece, western Asia (Acts 18:23–21:14); Corinth, Ephesus, Macedonia, Troas—to Jerusalem (Acts 18–21); farewell to Ephesian elders (Acts 20:13-38); journey to Rome (Acts 21–28); falsely arrested and in hands of mob (Acts 21:26–22:21); saved by Roman custody (Acts 22:22-29; 23:10); before the Jewish high council (Acts 23:1-11); relocated to Caesarea (Acts 23:12-35); trial before Felix (Acts 24); appealed to Caesar before Festus (Acts 25:1-12), before Herod Agrippa (Acts 25:13–26:32); sailed to Rome, was shipwrecked (Acts 27); arrived in Rome (Acts 28); pattern of self-denial (1 Cor 9); his gospel message (Rom 1–5; Gal 3–6); catalog of trials (2 Cor 11:22-33); his goal (Phil 3:7 15); last known written words (2 Tim 4); intervened for returning slave (Phlm 1:8-22); wrote letters: Romans through Philemon (see the first verse of each book).

PAY (n) *something paid for a purpose and especially as a salary or wage*
1 Tim 5:18 ... who work deserve their **p!**

PAY, PAYS (v) *to suffer the consequences of an act; to requite according to what is deserved; to make due return to for services or goods rendered*
see also PAID
Exod 22:3 ... A thief who is caught must **p**
Deut 32:35 ... I will **p** them back.
Ps 137:8 ... Happy is the one who **p-s** you
Matt 22:17 ... to **p** taxes to Caesar or not?
Rom 12:19 ... I will **p** them back,
1 Thes 5:15 ... no one **p-s** back evil
2 Thes 1:6 ... he will **p** back those who

PAYMENT (n) *the act of paying; something that is paid*
Deut 15:2 ... must not demand **p**
Deut 27:25 ... anyone who accepts **p**
Hos 9:7 ... the day of **p** is here.

PEACE (n) *a state of tranquility or quiet; a pact or agreement to end hostilities between those who have been at war or in a state of enmity; harmony in personal relations, especially with God; a state of security or order within a community; freedom from disquieting or oppressive thoughts or emotions*
Exod 20:24 … and *p* offerings, your sheep
Lev 26:6 … I will give you *p* in the land,
Num 6:26 … his favor and give you his *p*.
Deut 20:10 … offer its people terms for *p*.
1 Sam 7:14 … there was *p* between Israel
1 Kgs 5:4 … God has given me *p* on every
1 Chr 22:9 … a son who will be a man of *p*.
2 Chr 14:7 … has given us *p* on every side.
Job 3:26 … I have no *p*, no quietness.
Job 25:2 … He enforces *p* in the heavens.
Ps 34:14 … Search for *p*, and work to
Ps 37:37 … awaits those who love *p*.
Ps 120:7 … I search for *p*; but when I
Ps 147:14 … He sends *p* across your nation
Prov 12:20 … hearts that are planning *p*!
Eccl 3:8 … for war and a time for *p*.
Isa 9:6 … Everlasting Father, Prince of *P*.
Isa 32:17 … righteousness will bring *p*.
Isa 48:22 … there is no *p* for the wicked,
Isa 52:7 … good news of *p* and salvation,
Jer 6:14 … give assurances of *p* when
Jer 46:27 … return to a life of *p* and quiet,
Ezek 34:25 … I will make a covenant of *p*
Zech 8:19 … So love truth and *p*.
Matt 5:9 … blesses those who work for *p*,
Mark 9:50 … live in *p* with each other.
Luke 1:79 … guide us to the path of *p*.
John 16:33 … you may have *p* in me.
Rom 5:1 … by faith, we have *p* with God
Rom 8:6 … your mind leads to life and *p*.
1 Cor 14:33 … God of disorder but of *p*,
Gal 5:22 … love, joy, *p*, patience,
Eph 2:14 … Christ himself has brought *p*
Eph 2:15 … made *p* between Jews and
Eph 2:17 … Good News of *p* to you Gentiles
Eph 6:15 … put on the *p* that comes from
Phil 4:7 … experience God's *p*,
1 Thes 5:23 … God of *p* make you holy
2 Thes 3:16 … Lord of *p* himself give you
2 Tim 2:22 … faithfulness, love, and *p*,
Heb 13:20 … the God of *p*—who brought
Jas 3:17 … It is also *p* loving, gentle
1 Pet 3:11 … Search for *p*, and work to

PEACEFUL (adj) *quiet, tranquil; devoid of violence or force; of or relating to a state or time of peace*
Ps 23:2 … leads me beside *p* streams.
Prov 14:30 … A *p* heart leads to a healthy
1 Thes 5:3 … Everything is *p* and secure,
1 Tim 2:2 … we can live *p* and quiet lives
Heb 12:11 … a *p* harvest of right living
2 Pet 3:14 … effort to be found *p*

PEACEMAKER, PEACEMAKERS (n) *one who makes peace especially by reconciling parties at variance*
Acts 7:26 … He tried to be *p*
Jas 3:18 … *p-s* will plant seeds of peace

PEARL, PEARLS (n) *a white translucent jewel created within certain species of mollusks*
Matt 7:6 … throw your *p-s* to pigs!
Matt 13:45 … on the lookout for choice *p-s*.
1 Tim 2:9 … or by wearing gold or *p-s*
Rev 21:21 … were made of *p-s*—
Rev 21:21 … each gate from a single *p*!

PENNY (n) *the smallest monetary unit*
Matt 5:26 … you have paid the last *p*.
Luke 12:59 … paid the very last *p*.

PENTECOST (n) *a Jewish feast celebrated on the 50th day after the Feast of Unleavened Bread; the day God sent the Holy Spirit after Christ's resurrection*
Acts 2:1 … the day of *P* all the believers
Acts 20:16 … in time for the Festival of *P*.
1 Cor 16:8 … until the Festival of *P*.

PEOPLE, PEOPLES (n) *human beings making up a group or assembly or linked by a common interest; clan or nation; humanity*
see also NATION(S)
Exod 5:1 … says: Let my *p* go
Exod 8:23 … between my *p* and your *p*.
Exod 19:5 … among all the *p-s* on earth;
Exod 19:8 … all the *p* responded together,
Exod 33:13 … nation is your very own *p*.
Lev 26:12 … and you will be my *p*.
Num 14:11 … How long will these *p*
Deut 7:6 … you are a holy *p*, who belong
Deut 14:1 … are the *p* of the LORD
Deut 32:9 … For the *p* of Israel belong
Deut 33:29 … *p* saved by the LORD?
Ruth 1:16 … Your *p* will be my *p*,
2 Chr 7:20 … uproot the *p* from this land
Neh 1:10 … The *p* you rescued by your
Neh 8:1 … the *p* assembled with a unified
Ps 33:12 … whose *p* he has chosen
Ps 53:6 … When God restores his *p*,
Ps 94:14 … will not reject his *p*;
Ps 96:10 … He will judge all *p-s* fairly.
Ps 135:14 … will give justice to his *p*
Isa 2:2 … *p* from all over the world
Isa 6:10 … Harden the hearts of these *p*.
Isa 40:1 … Comfort, comfort my *p*,
Isa 49:13 … LORD has comforted his *p*
Isa 52:6 … I will reveal my name to my *p*,
Isa 53:8 … for the rebellion of my *p*.
Isa 55:4 … my power among the *p-s*.
Jer 2:11 … Yet my *p* have exchanged their
Jer 2:32 … my *p* have forgotten me.
Jer 7:16 … Pray no more for these *p*,
Jer 32:27 … of all the *p-s* of the world.
Dan 8:24 … and devastate the holy *p*.
Dan 9:24 … decreed for your *p*
Hos 1:10 … You are not my *p*,
Hos 2:23 … Now you are my *p*.
Mic 4:1 … *p* from all over the world
Mic 4:3 … LORD will mediate between *p-s*
Matt 4:19 … show you how to fish for *p*!
Mark 7:6 … *p* honor me with their lips,
Mark 8:27 … Who do *p* say I am?
Luke 1:68 … visited and redeemed his *p*.
John 11:50 … should die for the *p*
John 18:14 … should die for the *p*
Rom 9:25 … Those who were not my *p*,
Rom 11:1 … *p*, the nation of Israel?
2 Cor 6:16 … and they will be my *p*.
Gal 6:16 … they are the new *p* of God.
Eph 1:14 … purchased us to be his own *p*.
Eph 1:18 … he called—his holy *p*
Eph 2:15 … creating in himself one new *p*
Eph 4:8 … and gave gifts to his *p*.
2 Tim 2:2 … trustworthy *p* who will
2 Tim 3:17 … and equip his *p* to do every
Titus 2:11 … bringing salvation to all *p*.
Titus 2:14 … make us his very own *p*,
Heb 4:9 … waiting for the *p* of God.
1 Pet 2:9 … for you are a chosen *p*.
1 Pet 2:10 … now you are God's *p*.

Rev 5:8 … prayers of God's *p*.
Rev 10:11 … again about many *p-s*,
Rev 18:4 … from her, my *p*.
Rev 19:8 … of God's holy *p*.
Rev 21:3 … home is now among his *p*!

PERFECT (adj) *being entirely without fault or defect; corresponding to an ideal standard or abstract concept; mature, pure, complete*
Deut 32:4 … the Rock; his deeds are *p*.
Ps 19:7 … instructions of the LORD are *p*,
Ps 119:138 … laws are *p* and completely
Matt 5:48 … you are to be *p*, even as
John 17:23 … experience such *p* unity
Gal 3:3 … become *p* by your
Col 4:12 … God to make you strong and *p*,
Heb 2:10 … suffering, a *p* leader,
Heb 5:9 … as a *p* High Priest,
Heb 7:19 … law never made anything *p*.
Heb 9:11 … greater, more *p* Tabernacle
Heb 9:14 … as a *p* sacrifice for our sins.
Heb 10:14 … he forever made *p* those
Heb 12:23 … who have now been made *p*.
Jas 1:25 … look carefully into the *p* law
1 Jn 4:18 … because *p* love expels all fear.

PERFECT, PERFECTED, PERFECTS (v) *to bring to final form; to refine or improve*
Ezek 16:14 … splendor and *p-ed* your beauty,
Heb 12:2 … champion who initiates and *p-s*

PERFECTION (n) *flawlessness; maturity; an exemplification of supreme excellence*
Job 37:16 … with wonderful *p* and skill?
Ps 50:2 … Mount Zion, the *p* of beauty,
1 Cor 13:10 … when the time of *p* comes,
Phil 3:12 … I have already reached *p*.
Heb 7:11 … achieved the *p* God intended,
Heb 11:40 … not reach *p* without us.

PERFUME (n) *a substance that emits a pleasant odor*
Eccl 7:1 … more valuable than costly *p*.
Mark 14:3 … poured the *p* over his head.
2 Cor 2:14 … everywhere, like a sweet *p*.
2 Cor 2:16 … saved, we are a life-giving *p*.

PERISH, PERISHING (v) *to become destroyed or ruined physically or spiritually; to die*
see also DESTROY, DIE
Ps 102:26 … They will *p*, but you remain
John 3:16 … believes in him will not *p* but
John 10:28 … they will never *p*.
2 Cor 2:15 … by those who are *p-ing*.
2 Cor 4:3 … from people who are *p-ing*.
Jude 1:11 … they *p* in their rebellion.

PERSECUTE, PERSECUTED, PERSECUTING (v) *to harass or punish in a manner designed to injure, grieve, or afflict; to cause to suffer because of belief*
Ps 140:12 … help those they *p*;
Matt 5:10 … blesses those who are *p-d*
Matt 5:11 … when people mock you and *p*
Matt 5:12 … prophets were *p-d*
Matt 5:44 … Pray for those who *p* you!
Matt 13:21 … *p-d* for believing God's
John 15:20 … they *p-d* me, naturally they will *p* you.
Acts 9:4 … Why are you *p-ing* me?
Rom 8:35 … or are *p-d*, or hungry,
Rom 12:14 … Bless those who *p* you.
1 Cor 15:9 … the way I *p-d* God's church.
2 Thes 1:7 … for you who are being *p-d*

1745

PERSECUTION, PERSECUTIONS (n) *the condition of being persecuted, harassed, or annoyed*
Mark 10:30 … along with *p*.
2 Cor 12:10 … insults, hardships, *p-s,*
2 Thes 1:4 … all the *p-s* and hardships
2 Thes 1:5 … God will use this *p* to show
2 Tim 3:11 … You know how much *p* and
2 Tim 3:12 … in Christ Jesus will suffer *p*.
Rev 13:10 … must endure *p* patiently

PERSEVERANCE (n) *enduring hardships with patience; steadfastness*
see also Endurance
1 Tim 6:11 … along with faith, love, *p,* and

PERSEVERE (v) *to persist in a state, enterprise, or undertaking in spite of opposition or discouragement*
see also Endure
Rev 3:10 … obeyed my command to *p,*

PETER Leader of the twelve disciples, also known as "Simon son of John" (John 21:17) and "Cephas" (John 1:42); called to "fish for people" (Matt 4:18-20; Mark 1:16-20; Luke 5:1-11; see also John 21:3); mother-in-law healed (Matt 8:14-15; Mark 1:29-31; Luke 4:38-39); called to preach (Mark 1:36-39); brother of Andrew (Matt 10:2; Mark 3:16; Luke 6:14; Acts 1:13); present at raising of the dead (Mark 5:37; Luke 8:51); walked on water (Matt 14:22-33; Mark 6:45-52; John 6:15-21); identified Jesus as the Christ (Matt 16:13-20; Mark 8:27-30; Luke 9:18-20; see also John 6:68-69); rebuked by Jesus for lack of heavenly perspective (Matt 16:21-23; Mark 8:32-33; see also John 13:6-11); witnessed the Transfiguration (Matt 16:28–17:8; Mark 9:1-13; Luke 9:28-36; 2 Pet 1:16-20); noticed the withered fig tree (Mark 11:21; see also Matt 21:20); his denial predicted by Jesus (Matt 26:31-35; Mark 14:27-31; Luke 22:31-34; John 13:36-38); in Gethsemane (Matt 26:36-46; Mark 14:32-42; Luke 22:39-46); cut off ear of Malchus (Matt 26:51; Mark 14:47; Luke 22:50); denied Jesus—then wept (Matt 26:69-75; Mark 14:66-72; Luke 22:54-62; John 18:15-27); visited empty tomb (Luke 24:12; John 20:1-10; see also Matt 28:1-8); saw Jesus (Luke 24:34; 1 Cor 15:5); told by Jesus to shepherd his flock (John 21:15-19); in upper room before Pentecost (Acts 1:13); preached at Pentecost (Acts 2); performed miracles (Acts 3:1-10; 5:14-16; 9:32-43); preached at Temple (Acts 3:11-26); preached before Jewish high council (Acts 4:1-22); prophesied death of Ananias and Sapphira (Acts 5:1-11); preached again before Jewish high council (Acts 5:29-32); rebuked power seeker (Acts 8:14-25); healed sick (Acts 9:32-34); raised dead (Acts 9:36-43); introduced Gentiles to gospel (Acts 10–11); rescued by angel from prison (Acts 12:3-19); preached grace at Jerusalem Council (Acts 15); became pillar of the church (Gal 2:9); was correctable (Gal 2:14); wrote letters (1 Pet 1:1; 2 Pet 1:1); had believing wife (1 Cor 9:5).

PHARISEE, PHARISEES (n) *a religious and political party in Palestine in New Testament times known for strict observance of rites and ceremonies of the written law and for insistence on the validity of their own oral traditions concerning the law*
Matt 5:20 … *P-s,* you will never enter
Matt 16:6 … of the yeast of the *P-s*
Matt 23:13 … and you *P-s.* Hypocrites!
John 3:1 … religious leader who was a *P.*
Acts 23:6 … *P,* as were my ancestors!

PHYSICAL (adj) *having material existence; of or relating to the body*
John 1:13 … reborn—not with a *p* birth
Col 1:22 … of Christ in his *p* body.
1 Tim 4:8 … *P* training is good, but
1 Tim 5:11 … *p* desires will overpower
1 Jn 2:16 … a craving for *p* pleasure

PIERCE, PIERCED (v) *to make a hole through; to stab*
Exod 21:6 … and publicly *p* his ear
Ps 22:16 … have *p-d* my hands and feet.
Zech 12:10 … me whom they have *p-d*
Luke 2:35 … sword will *p* your very soul.
John 19:37 … look on the one they *p-d.*
Rev 1:7 … even those who *p-d* him.

PIG, PIGS (n) *a wild or domestic swine*
Matt 7:6 … Don't throw your pearls to *p-s!*
Mark 5:11 … a large herd of *p-s* feeding
Luke 15:15 … his fields to feed the *p-s.*
2 Pet 2:22 … washed *p* returns to the mud.

PILGRIMS (KJV)
Heb 11:13 … nomads here on earth
1 Pet 2:11 … as "temporary residents and foreigners"

PILLAR, PILLARS (n) *a column or shaft standing alone as a monument or supporting a superstructure; miraculous cloud by day and fire by night; memorial pile of stones; a supporting, integral, or upstanding member of a group*
Gen 19:26 … she turned into a *p* of salt.
Exod 13:21 … night with a *p* of fire.
Exod 24:4 … set up twelve *p-s,* one for
Deut 1:33 … by night and a *p* of cloud by
Judg 16:26 … my hands against the *p-s*
Gal 2:9 … known as *p-s* of the church,
1 Tim 3:15 … *p* and foundation of
Rev 3:12 … victorious will become *p-s*

PIOUS (adj) *marked by or showing reverence for God and devotion to worship; religious*
Isa 58:2 … Yet they act so *p!*
Col 2:18 … insisting on *p* self-denial,
Col 2:23 … strong devotion, *p* self-denial,

PITY (n) *sympathetic sorrow for one suffering, distressed, or unhappy*
Judg 2:18 … For the Lord took *p* on
Ps 17:10 … They are without *p.*
Ps 69:20 … would show some *p;*
Ps 72:13 … He feels *p* for the weak
Isa 27:11 … show them no *p* or mercy.
Hos 13:14 … I will not take *p* on them.

PLAGUE, PLAGUES (n) *a disastrous evil, affliction, or epidemic of infectious disease, issued by God in judgment*
2 Chr 6:28 … or a *p* or crop disease
Luke 21:11 … will be famines and *p-s*
Rev 21:9 … the seven last *p-s* came
Rev 22:18 … add to that person the *p-s*

PLAGUED (v) *to smite, infest, or afflict with disease, calamity, or natural evil*
Ps 73:5 … they're not *p* with problems

PLAN, PLANS (n) *a detailed formulation of a program of action; goal, aim*
see also Purpose
Ps 2:1 … waste their time with futile *p-s?*
Ps 33:10 … frustrates the *p-s* of the
Ps 40:5 … *p-s* for us are too numerous
Isa 30:1 … You make *p-s* that are contrary
Isa 32:6 … and make evil *p-s.*
Jer 29:11 … I know the *p-s* I have for you
Acts 2:23 … his prearranged *p* was carried
Acts 4:25 … waste their time with futile *p-s?*
Acts 7:44 … according to the *p* God had
Rom 16:25 … *p* kept secret from
Eph 3:9 … this mysterious *p* that God,
Eph 3:11 … This was his eternal *p,*
2 Tim 1:9 … *p* from before the beginning

PLANNED, PLANNING (v) *to devise or project the realization or achievement of*
Prov 12:20 … hearts that are *p-ning* peace!
Isa 25:1 … You *p-ed* them long ago,
Jer 23:20 … has finished all he has *p-ed.*
Eph 2:10 … do the good things he *p-ed*

PLANT (n) *a young tree, vine, shrub, or herb planted or suitable for planting*
Matt 15:13 … *p* not planted by
1 Cor 15:36 … it doesn't grow into a *p*

PLANT, PLANTED, PLANTING, PLANTS (v) *to put or set (seeds or plants) in the ground for growth; to establish or settle*
Gen 2:8 … the Lord God *p-ed* a garden
Gen 8:22 … there will be *p-ing* and harvest,
Ps 1:3 … like trees *p-ed* along the riverbank,
Ps 126:5 … who *p* in tears will harvest
Prov 22:8 … who *p* injustice will harvest
Prov 31:16 … earnings she *p-s* a vineyard.
Hos 10:12 … *P* the good seeds
Amos 9:15 … I will firmly *p* them there
Matt 6:26 … They don't *p* or harvest or
Matt 13:3 … A farmer went out to *p* some
Matt 13:18 … about the farmer *p-ing*
1 Cor 3:6 … *p-ed* the seed in your hearts,
1 Cor 3:7 … who does the *p-ing,*
1 Cor 9:7 … What farmer *p-s* a vineyard
1 Cor 15:42 … earthly bodies are *p-ed*
2 Cor 9:6 … a farmer who *p-s* only a few
Jas 1:21 … accept the word God has *p-ed,*
Jas 3:18 … will *p* seeds of peace

PLEASANT (adj) *having qualities that tend to give pleasure; agreeable*
Gen 49:15 … and how *p* the land,
Ps 16:6 … given me is a *p* land.
Prov 16:21 … and *p* words are persuasive.
Isa 5:7 … of Judah are his *p* garden.

PLEASE, PLEASED, PLEASES (v) *to make glad; to satisfy; to like or wish; to be the will or pleasure of*
Deut 12:25 … doing what *p-s* the Lord.
Ps 135:6 … The Lord does whatever *p-s*
Prov 16:7 … people's lives *p* the Lord,
Isa 42:1 … my chosen one, who *p-s* me.
Matt 12:18 … my Beloved, who *p-s* me.
Luke 2:14 … those with whom God is *p-d.*
Luke 10:21 … Yes, Father, it *p-d* you to do
John 8:29 … I always do what *p-s* him.
Rom 8:8 … sinful nature can never *p* God.
Rom 14:18 … this attitude, you will *p* God,
2 Cor 5:9 … our goal is to *p* him.
Gal 6:8 … live to *p* the Spirit will harvest
Eph 5:10 … determine what *p-s* the
Phil 2:13 … power to do what *p-s* him.
Col 1:10 … always honor and *p* the Lord,
Col 1:19 … God in all his fullness was *p-d*
1 Thes 2:4 … Our purpose is to *p* God,
1 Thes 2:15 … They fail to *p* God

1 Tim 2:3 ... is good and **p-s** God our
1 Tim 5:4 ... is something that **p-s** God.
Heb 10:6 ... not **p-d** with burnt offerings
Heb 11:6 ... to **p** God without faith.
Heb 13:16 ... sacrifices that **p** God.
1 Pet 2:19 ... God is **p-d** when, conscious of
1 Jn 2:17 ... does what **p-s** God will live
Rev 4:11 ... you created what you **p-d**.

PLEASURE, PLEASURES (n) *desire, inclination; a source of delight or joy; sensual gratification*
Ps 5:4 ... you take no **p** in wickedness;
Ps 16:3 ... I take **p** in them!
Ps 16:11 ... the **p-s** of living with you
Isa 1:11 ... I get no **p** from the blood of
Luke 8:14 ... cares and riches and **p-s**
1 Tim 5:6 ... widow who lives only for **p**
2 Tim 3:4 ... and love **p** rather than God.
Titus 2:12 ... living and sinful **p-s**.
Titus 3:3 ... slaves to many lusts and **p-s**.
Heb 11:25 ... the fleeting **p-s** of sin.
Jas 4:3 ... only what will give you **p**.

PLOWS (v) *to turn, break up, or work with a plow*
1 Cor 9:10 ... the one who **p** and the one

PLOWSHARES (n) *a part of a plow that cuts the furrow*
Isa 2:4 ... hammer their swords into **p**
Joel 3:10 ... Hammer your **p** into swords
Mic 4:3 ... hammer their swords into **p**

POISON (n) *a substance that usually kills, injures, or impairs an organism; something destructive or harmful*
2 Kgs 4:40 ... there's **p** in this stew!
Jas 3:8 ... and evil, full of deadly **p**.

POISONOUS (adj) *destructive, harmful; venomous*
Mark 16:18 ... **p**, it won't hurt them.

POOR (adj) *characterized by poverty or insufficient resources; humble*
Deut 15:4 ... should be no **p** among you,
Deut 15:11 ... some in the land who are **p**.
Deut 24:12 ... If your neighbor is **p**
1 Sam 2:7 ... The LORD makes some **p**
Prov 10:4 ... Lazy people are soon **p**;
Prov 13:7 ... Some who are **p** pretend
Mark 12:42 ... Then a **p** widow came and
2 Cor 8:9 ... for your sakes he became **p**,
Jas 2:2 ... another comes in who is **p**

POOR (n) *those characterized by poverty or insufficient resources*
Lev 19:10 ... Leave them for the **p**
Job 5:16 ... at last the **p** have hope,
Ps 35:10 ... protects the helpless and **p**
Ps 41:1 ... those who are kind to the **p**!
Ps 82:3 ... Give justice to the **p** and the
Prov 14:21 ... those who help the **p**.
Prov 17:5 ... mock the **p** insult
Prov 21:13 ... cries of the **p** will be ignored
Prov 22:2 ... rich and **p** have this
Prov 22:22 ... Don't rob the **p** just because
Prov 28:27 ... Whoever gives to the **p** will
Prov 31:20 ... helping hand to the **p**
Isa 3:14 ... things stolen from the **p**.
Isa 14:30 ... I will feed the **p** in my pasture;
Isa 32:7 ... They lie to convict the **p**,
Isa 61:1 ... to bring good news to the **p**.
Jer 22:16 ... help to the **p** and needy,
Amos 4:1 ... who oppress the **p** and crush
Amos 5:11 ... trample the **p**, stealing their
Zech 7:10 ... foreigners, and the **p**.

Matt 11:5 ... is being preached to the **p**."
Matt 19:21 ... and give the money to the **p**,
Mark 14:7 ... You will always have the **p**
Luke 4:18 ... to bring Good News to the **p**.
Luke 14:13 ... Instead, invite the **p**, the
John 12:8 ... You will always have the **p**
Rom 15:26 ... an offering for the **p** among
Jas 2:6 ... you dishonor the **p**!

POSSESS, POSSESSED (v) *to seize, gain, or take (control of); to own*
see also INHERIT
Ps 37:11 ... The lowly will **p** the land
Ps 37:29 ... The godly will **p** the land
John 7:20 ... You're demon **p-ed**!
John 8:48 ... you were **p-ed** by a demon?
John 8:52 ... you are **p-ed** by a demon.
John 10:20 ... He's demon **p-ed** and
John 10:21 ... like a man **p-ed** by a demon!
Phil 3:12 ... press on to **p** that perfection

POSSESSION, POSSESSIONS (n) *something owned, occupied, or controlled*
see also INHERITANCE, RICHES, TREASURE(S), WEALTH
Exod 6:8 ... as your very own **p**.
Deut 4:20 ... and his special **p**,
Deut 32:9 ... is his special **p**.
Zech 2:12 ... the LORD's special **p**
Matt 19:21 ... sell all your **p-s** and
Mark 10:22 ... for he had many **p-s**.
1 Pet 2:9 ... God's very own **p**.

POSSIBLE (adj) *being within the limits of ability, capacity, or realization*
Matt 19:26 ... with God everything is **p**.
Matt 26:39 ... **p**, let this cup of suffering
Mark 9:23 ... Anything is **p** if a person
Mark 10:27 ... Everything is **p** with God.
Mark 14:35 ... if it were **p**, the awful hour
Heb 10:4 ... it is not **p** for the blood

POTTER (n) *one who makes pottery*
Isa 29:16 ... **p** who made me is stupid"?
Isa 64:8 ... the clay, and you are the **p**.
Zech 11:13 ... threw them to the **p**
Matt 27:7 ... to buy the **p**'s field,
Rom 9:21 ... a **p** makes jars out of clay,

POUR, POURED, POURING, POURS (v) *to move or come continuously; to supply or produce freely*
Ps 42:8 ... LORD **p-s** his unfailing love
Ps 45:7 ... **p-ing** out the oil of joy on
Isa 32:15 ... Spirit is **p-ed** out on us
Isa 44:3 ... I will **p** out my Spirit
Ezek 39:29 ... I will **p** out my Spirit
Joel 2:28 ... I will **p** out my Spirit
Zech 12:10 ... I will **p** out a spirit of
Mal 3:10 ... I will **p** out a blessing
Luke 22:20 ... blood, which is **p-ed** out
Acts 2:17 ... I will **p** out my Spirit
Acts 2:33 ... the Holy Spirit to **p** out
Acts 10:45 ... Holy Spirit had been **p-ed**
Eph 1:6 ... grace he has **p-ed** out on us
Phil 2:17 ... **p-ing** it out like a liquid
Titus 3:6 ... generously **p-ed** out the Spirit

POVERTY (n) *the state of one who lacks money or material possessions*
Prov 6:11 ... **p** will pounce on you like
Prov 13:18 ... end in **p** and disgrace;
Prov 21:5 ... hasty shortcuts lead to **p**.
Prov 24:34 ... **p** will pounce on you like
Prov 31:7 ... drink to forget their **p**
2 Cor 8:9 ... by his **p** he could make you
Rev 2:9 ... your suffering and your **p**—

POWER, POWERS (n) *ability to act or produce an effect; possession of control, authority, or influence over others; physical might; mental or moral efficacy; a controlling group*
see also STRENGTH
Exod 15:6 ... LORD, is glorious in **p**.
Deut 8:18 ... one who gives you **p** to be
Ps 89:7 ... angelic **p-s** stand in awe
Isa 40:26 ... great **p** and incomparable
Jer 9:23 ... the powerful boast in their **p**,
Mic 3:8 ... I am filled with **p**—
Matt 16:18 ... all the **p-s** of hell will not
Matt 22:29 ... don't know the **p** of God.
Luke 1:35 ... the **p** of the Most High will
Luke 4:14 ... the Holy Spirit's **p**.
Luke 9:1 ... gave them **p** and authority
Luke 10:19 ... over all the **p** of the enemy,
Luke 11:20 ... demons by the **p** of God,
Acts 1:8 ... receive **p** when the Holy Spirit
Rom 1:16 ... the **p** of God at work,
Rom 1:20 ... his eternal **p** and divine
Rom 6:9 ... Death no longer has any **p** over
Rom 7:23 ... another **p** within me that is
Rom 8:38 ... not even the **p-s** of hell can
Rom 15:13 ... the **p** of the Holy Spirit.
1 Cor 1:18 ... is the very **p** of God.
1 Cor 6:14 ... from the dead by his **p**,
1 Cor 15:24 ... ruler and authority and **p**.
2 Cor 4:7 ... our great **p** is from God,
2 Cor 13:4 ... now lives by the **p** of God.
Eph 6:10 ... Lord and in his mighty **p**.
Phil 3:10 ... and experience the mighty **p**
Col 1:11 ... with all his glorious **p**.
Col 1:29 ... on Christ's mighty **p**
1 Thes 1:5 ... words but also with **p**,
2 Tim 1:7 ... but of **p**, love, and
2 Tim 3:5 ... reject the **p** that could make
Heb 2:14 ... break the **p** of the devil,
Jas 5:16 ... righteous person has great **p**
1 Pet 1:5 ... is protecting you by his **p**
1 Pet 3:22 ... **p-s** accept his authority.
1 Pet 4:11 ... All glory and **p** to him
2 Pet 1:3 ... **p**, God has given us everything
Jude 1:25 ... **p**, and authority are his
Rev 4:11 ... receive glory and honor and **p**.
Rev 5:12 ... receive **p** and riches and
Rev 19:1 ... glory and **p** belong to our God.
Rev 20:6 ... the second death holds no **p**,

POWERFUL (adj) *having great power, prestige, or influence*
Exod 6:6 ... will redeem you with a **p** arm
Deut 5:15 ... strong hand and **p** arm.
Job 25:2 ... God is **p** and dreadful.
Ps 29:4 ... the LORD is **p**;
Ps 136:12 ... strong hand and **p** arm.
Jer 9:23 ... the **p** boast in their power,
Jer 27:5 ... my great strength and **p** arm
Luke 24:19 ... who did **p** miracles,
1 Cor 1:27 ... to shame those who are **p**.

PRAISE, PRAISES (n) *worship; commendation; value, merit*
Deut 26:19 ... **p**, honor, and renown.
2 Sam 22:4 ... LORD, who is worthy of **p**,
2 Chr 29:30 ... So they offered joyous **p**
Ps 7:17 ... I will sing **p** to the name
Ps 18:49 ... I will sing **p-s** to your name.
Ps 34:1 ... will constantly speak his **p-s**.
Ps 65:1 ... What mighty **p**, O God,
Ps 81:1 ... Sing **p-s** to God,
Ps 100:4 ... into his courts with **p**.
Ps 108:1 ... your **p-s** with all my heart!
Ps 145:3 ... He is most worthy of **p**!
Ps 149:6 ... Let the **p-s** of God be in

1747

John 12:43 ... loved human *p* more than
Rom 2:29 ... heart seeks *p* from God,
Rom 15:9 ... will sing *p-s* to your name.
1 Thes 2:6 ... As for human *p,*
2 Thes 1:10 ... his holy people—*p* from all
Jas 5:13 ... You should sing *p-s.*

PRAISE, PRAISED, PRAISES, PRAISING
(v) *to worship, commend, or give honor to*
Exod 15:2 ... and I will *p* him—
1 Chr 16:35 ... name and rejoice and *p* you.
2 Chr 5:13 ... together in unison to *p* and
2 Chr 20:21 ... *p-ing* him for his holy
Neh 9:5 ... Stand up and *p* the LORD
Ps 9:1 ... I will *p* you, LORD,
Ps 12:8 ... evil is *p-d* throughout the land.
Ps 34:1 ... I will *p* the LORD
Ps 42:5 ... I will *p* him again—
Ps 45:17 ... nations will *p* you forever
Ps 51:15 ... my mouth may *p* you.
Ps 63:3 ... how I *p* you!
Ps 71:8 ... I can never stop *p-ing* you;
Ps 71:14 ... I will *p* you more and
Ps 74:21 ... and needy *p* your name.
Ps 89:5 ... angels will *p* you for your
Ps 96:2 ... LORD; *p* his name.
Ps 102:18 ... not yet born will *p* the
Ps 104:1 ... all that I am *p* the
Ps 115:18 ... But we can *p* the LORD
Ps 135:20 ... LORD, *p* the LORD!
Ps 144:1 ... *P* the LORD, who is
Ps 148:13 ... Let them all *p* the name
Ps 150:2 ... *p* his unequaled greatness!
Prov 27:2 ... Let someone else *p* you,
Prov 27:21 ... person is tested by being *p-d.*
Isa 63:7 ... I will *p* the LORD
Dan 2:19 ... Daniel *p-d* the God of heaven.
Dan 2:20 ... He said, "*P* the name
Dan 4:34 ... *p-d* and worshiped the Most
Matt 5:16 ... will *p* your heavenly Father.
Mark 11:9 ... were shouting, "*P* God!
Luke 1:46 ... how my soul *p-s* the Lord.
Luke 2:13 ... armies of heaven—*p-ing* God
Luke 2:20 ... glorifying and *p-ing* God for
Luke 18:43 ... all who saw it *p-d* God, too.
Luke 19:37 ... *p-ing* God for all the wonderful
Acts 2:47 ... all the while *p-ing* God
Acts 10:46 ... in other tongues and *p-ing* God
1 Cor 14:16 ... if you *p* God only in
Gal 1:24 ... they *p-d* God because of me.
Eph 1:6 ... we *p* God for the glorious
Jas 3:9 ... Sometimes it *p-s* our Lord
Rev 19:1 ... heaven shouting, "*P* the LORD!

PRAY, PRAYED, PRAYING, PRAYS (v) *to address God with adoration, confession, supplication, or thanksgiving; to intercede*
Gen 24:45 ... I had finished *p-ing* in my
1 Sam 1:12 ... she was *p-ing* to the LORD,
2 Chr 7:14 ... humble themselves and *p* and
2 Chr 30:18 ... King Hezekiah *p-ed* for
Neh 4:9 ... we *p-ed* to our God and
Job 42:8 ... servant Job will *p* for you,
Job 42:10 ... When Job *p-ed* for his friends,
Ps 5:2 ... I *p* to no one but you.
Ps 32:6 ... all the godly *p* to you
Ps 34:6 ... In my desperation I *p-ed,*
Dan 6:10 ... He *p-ed* three times a day,
Dan 9:4 ... I *p-ed* to the LORD
Jon 2:1 ... Jonah *p-ed* to the LORD
Matt 6:5 ... When you *p,* don't be like
Matt 6:9 ... *P* like this: Our Father in

Matt 26:39 ... face to the ground, *p-ing,*
Mark 11:24 ... you can *p* for anything,
Mark 11:25 ... when you are *p-ing,* first
Luke 3:21 ... *p-ing,* the heavens opened,
Luke 9:29 ... he was *p-ing,* the appearance
Luke 11:1 ... teach us to *p,* just as John
Luke 22:41 ... and knelt down and *p-ed,*
John 17:20 ... I am *p-ing* not only for these
Acts 6:6 ... apostles, who *p-ed* for them
Acts 9:11 ... He is *p-ing* to me right now.
Acts 16:25 ... Paul and Silas were *p-ing*
Rom 8:26 ... the Holy Spirit *p-s* for us
Rom 12:12 ... and keep on *p-ing.*
Rom 15:30 ... join in my struggle by *p-ing*
1 Cor 14:14 ... For if I *p* in tongues,
1 Cor 14:14 ... my spirit is *p-ing,*
2 Cor 13:9 ... We *p* that you will become
Eph 1:18 ... I *p* that your hearts will be
Eph 3:16 ... I *p* that from his glorious,
Phil 4:6 ... instead, *p* about everything.
1 Thes 1:3 ... As we *p* to our God and
1 Thes 5:17 ... Never stop *p-ing.*
2 Thes 1:11 ... we keep on *p-ing* for you,
1 Tim 2:8 ... to *p* with holy hands
Jas 5:13 ... You should *p.*
Jas 5:16 ... *p* for each other so that
Jude 1:20 ... *p* in the power of the Holy

PRAYER, PRAYERS (n) *conversation with God—in praise, thanksgiving, or intercession*
2 Chr 30:27 ... God heard their *p* from
Ps 4:1 ... mercy on me and hear my *p.*
Ps 17:1 ... Pay attention to my *p,*
Ps 20:5 ... LORD answer all your *p-s.*
Ps 86:6 ... Listen closely to my *p,*
Prov 15:8 ... in the *p-s* of the upright.
Isa 1:15 ... Though you offer many *p-s,*
Isa 56:7 ... will be called a house of *p*
Matt 11:25 ... Jesus prayed this *p:*
John 17:9 ... My *p* is not for the world,
Acts 1:14 ... were constantly united in *p,*
Acts 4:31 ... After this *p,* the meeting
Acts 6:4 ... can spend our time in *p*
Acts 10:31 ... your *p* has been heard,
Acts 13:3 ... So after more fasting and *p,*
Eph 6:18 ... persistent in your *p-s* for all
Col 4:2 ... Devote yourselves to *p* with an
1 Pet 3:7 ... your *p-s* will not be hindered.
1 Pet 3:12 ... ears are open to their *p-s.*
Rev 5:8 ... are the *p-s* of God's people.

PREACH, PREACHED, PREACHES, PREACHING (v) *to deliver a sermon; to exhort an idea or course of action*
see also PROCLAIM, TEACH
Luke 9:6 ... *p-ing* the Good News and
Luke 9:60 ... go and *p* about the Kingdom
Acts 5:42 ... teach and *p* this message:
Acts 9:20 ... he began *p-ing* about Jesus
Acts 16:10 ... to *p* the Good News
Acts 18:5 ... all his time *p-ing* the word.
Rom 1:15 ... to *p* the Good News.
1 Cor 2:4 ... my message and my *p-ing*
1 Cor 9:27 ... I fear that after *p-ing* to
1 Cor 15:1 ... Good News I *p-ed* to you
2 Cor 4:5 ... We *p* that Jesus Christ is Lord,
2 Cor 11:4 ... Jesus than the one we *p,*
Gal 1:8 ... *p-es* a different kind of Good
Gal 1:8 ... than the one we *p-ed* to you.
Gal 1:9 ... *p-es* any other Good News
Gal 5:11 ... no longer *p-ing* salvation
Phil 1:18 ... Christ is being *p-ed* either way,
Col 1:23 ... Good News has been *p-ed* all
1 Tim 5:17 ... work hard at both *p-ing* and
2 Tim 4:17 ... might *p* the Good News

1 Pet 1:25 ... Good News that was *p-ed* to
1 Pet 3:19 ... went and *p-ed* to the spirits

PREACHER (n) *one who delivers sermons or proclaims the gospel*
1 Tim 2:7 ... chosen as a *p* and apostle
2 Tim 1:11 ... God chose me to be a *p,*

PRECEPT(S) (KJV)
Ps 119:15 ... study your *commandments*
Ps 119:159 ... I love your *commandments,*
Mark 10:5 ... this *commandment* only as a
Heb 9:19 ... each of God's *commandments*

PREDICTED (v) *to declare or indicate in advance; to foretell*
Isa 43:12 ... First I *p* your rescue,
John 12:38 ... the prophet had *p:*
Acts 7:52 ... *p* the coming of

PREDICTIONS (n) *something that is predicted; forecast*
Isa 44:26 ... I carry out the *p* of my
Jer 28:9 ... Only when his *p* come true

PREGNANCY (n) *the condition of being pregnant*
Gen 3:16 ... sharpen the pain of your *p,*

PREGNANT (adj) *containing a developing unborn offspring within the body*
Gen 11:30 ... was unable to become *p*
Matt 24:19 ... How terrible it will be for *p*
1 Thes 5:3 ... as a *p* woman's labor

PREPARE, PREPARED (v) *to make ready beforehand for some purpose, use, or activity; to get ready*
Exod 23:20 ... to the place I have *p-d* for
Ps 23:5 ... You *p* a feast for me
Zeph 1:7 ... LORD has *p-d* his people
Mal 3:1 ... he will *p* the way before me.
Matt 3:3 ... '*P* the way for the Lord's
Matt 25:34 ... inherit the Kingdom *p-d*
John 14:2 ... I am going to *p* a place
1 Cor 2:9 ... has *p-d* for those who love
2 Cor 5:5 ... God himself has *p-d* us for
2 Tim 4:2 ... the word of God. Be *p-d,*
1 Pet 1:13 ... So *p* your minds for action

PRESBYTERY (KJV)
1 Tim 4:14 ... *elders of the church* laid their hands

PRESENT (adj) *being in view or at hand; now existing or in progress*
Lev 16:2 ... I myself am *p* in the cloud
1 Cor 7:26 ... Because of the *p* crisis,

PRESENT, PRESENTED, PRESENTING (v) *to give or bestow formally*
Gen 28:22 ... I will *p* to God a tenth
Matt 5:23 ... you are *p-ing* a sacrifice
Rom 3:25 ... *p-ed* Jesus as the sacrifice
Rom 15:19 ... fully *p-ed* the Good News
Eph 5:27 ... did this to *p* her to himself
2 Tim 2:15 ... Work hard so you can *p*

PRESERVE, PRESERVES (v) *to keep safe from injury, harm, or destruction*
see also SAVE
Gen 45:5 ... ahead of you to *p* your lives.
Deut 33:12 ... *p-s* them from every harm.
1 Kgs 19:18 ... I will *p* 7,000 others
Jer 10:12 ... he *p-s* it by his wisdom.

PRETEND, PRETENDED (v) *to give a false appearance of being, possessing, or performing*

1 Sam 21:13 . . . So he **p-ed** to be insane,
Zech 13:4 . . . No one will **p** to be a prophet
Rom 12:9 . . . Don't just **p** to love

PRICE (n) *the quantity of one thing that is exchanged or demanded in barter or sale for another*
Job 28:18 . . . **p** of wisdom is far above
1 Cor 6:20 . . . bought you with a high **p**.

PRIDE (n) *inordinate self-esteem or conceit; disdainful behavior or treatment of others*
Ps 101:5 . . . will not endure conceit and **p**.
Prov 6:3 . . . Now swallow your **p**;
Prov 8:13 . . . I hate **p** and arrogance,
Mark 7:22 . . . envy, slander, **p**, and
1 Jn 2:16 . . . **p** in our achievements and

PRIEST, PRIESTS (n) *one authorized to perform the sacred rites of sacrifice and worship; a mediator between God and humans*
Exod 19:6 . . . will be my kingdom of **p-s**,
Ps 110:4 . . . You are a **p** forever
Mal 1:6 . . . Armies says to the **p-s**:
Heb 4:14 . . . since we have a great High **P**
Heb 5:6 . . . You are a **p** forever
Heb 6:20 . . . our eternal High **P**
Heb 8:1 . . . a High **P** who sat down
1 Pet 2:5 . . . you are his holy **p-s**.
1 Pet 2:9 . . . You are royal **p-s**,
Rev 5:10 . . . Kingdom of **p-s** for our God.
Rev 20:6 . . . but they will be **p-s** of God

PRISON, PRISONS (n) *a state of confinement or captivity; jail*
Ps 142:7 . . . Bring me out of **p**
Isa 42:7 . . . will free the captives from **p**,
Matt 25:36 . . . I was in **p**, and you visited
2 Cor 11:23 . . . been put in **p** more often,
Heb 11:36 . . . were chained in **p-s**.
Heb 13:3 . . . Remember those in **p**,
1 Pet 3:19 . . . preached to the spirits in **p**—
Jude 1:6 . . . chained in **p-s** of darkness,
Rev 20:7 . . . Satan will be let out of his **p**.

PRISONER, PRISONERS (n) *a person deprived of liberty and kept under involuntary restraint, confinement, or custody*
Ps 79:11 . . . to the moaning of the **p-s**.
Ps 146:7 . . . The LORD frees the **p-s**.
Zech 9:12 . . . you **p-s** who still have hope!
Gal 3:22 . . . we are all **p-s** of sin,
Eph 3:1 . . . I, Paul, a **p** of Christ Jesus

PRIZE (n) *something offered or striven for in competitions or in contests*
1 Cor 9:24 . . . one person gets the **p**?
1 Cor 9:25 . . . we do it for an eternal **p**.
Phil 3:14 . . . heavenly **p** for which God,
2 Tim 2:5 . . . cannot win the **p** unless
2 Tim 4:8 . . . **p** awaits me—the crown

PROCLAIM, PROCLAIMING, PROCLAIMS (v) *to declare publicly*
see also PREACH
Lev 25:10 . . . a time to **p** freedom
Deut 32:3 . . . I will **p** the name of
1 Chr 16:8 . . . and **p** his greatness.
Ps 2:7 . . . king **p-s** the LORD's decree:
Ps 50:6 . . . heavens **p** his justice,
Ps 97:6 . . . heavens **p** his righteousness,
Ps 145:4 . . . let them **p** your power.
Isa 61:1 . . . to **p** that captives will be
Acts 28:31 . . . **p-ing** the Kingdom of God
Col 1:25 . . . **p-ing** his entire message to you.

1 Thes 3:2 . . . in **p-ing** the Good News
Titus 1:1 . . . I have been sent to **p** faith
1 Jn 1:1 . . . **p** to you the one who existed

PRODUCE, PRODUCES (v) *to yield, make, or manufacture*
Prov 3:9 . . . best part of everything you **p**.
Isa 55:11 . . . and it always **p-s** fruit.
Matt 7:18 . . . good tree can't **p** bad fruit,
Luke 3:9 . . . tree that does not **p** good fruit
John 15:8 . . . When you **p** much fruit,
John 15:16 . . . to go and **p** lasting fruit,
Rom 7:4 . . . **p** a harvest of good deeds
Eph 5:9 . . . light within you **p-s** only what
Col 1:10 . . . lives will **p** every kind of good
Jas 2:17 . . . Unless it **p-s** good deeds, it is

PROMISCUITY (n) *sexual excesses*
see also IMMORALITY
Rom 13:13 . . . **p** and immoral living,

PROMISCUOUS (adj) *not restricted to one sexual partner*
Prov 23:27 . . . a **p** woman is as dangerous

PROMISE, PROMISES (n) *a declaration that one will do or refrain from doing something specified*
see also COVENANT, VOW
2 Sam 7:25 . . . a **p** that will last forever.
Neh 5:13 . . . If you fail to keep your **p**,
Ps 91:4 . . . faithful **p-s** are your armor
Ps 116:14 . . . keep my **p-s** to the LORD
Ps 145:13 . . . LORD always keeps his **p-s**;
Ps 146:6 . . . He keeps every **p** forever.
Rom 4:20 . . . in believing God's **p**.
Rom 9:4 . . . receiving his wonderful **p-s**.
Rom 15:4 . . . patiently for God's **p-s** to be
2 Cor 1:20 . . . **p-s** have been fulfilled
2 Cor 7:1 . . . Because we have these **p-s**,
Eph 2:12 . . . covenant **p-s** God had made
Heb 6:13 . . . God's **p** to Abraham.
Heb 8:6 . . . based on better **p-s**.
Heb 10:23 . . . be trusted to keep his **p**.
Heb 11:11 . . . that God would keep his **p**.
2 Pet 3:4 . . . **p** that Jesus is coming again?
2 Pet 3:9 . . . being slow about his **p**,

PROMISED, PROMISES, PROMISING (v) *to pledge to do, bring about, or provide*
Exod 3:17 . . . I have **p-d** to rescue you
Deut 15:6 . . . bless you as he has **p-d**.
Josh 23:15 . . . the good things he **p-d**,
Luke 24:49 . . . as my Father **p-d**.
Acts 1:4 . . . sends you the gift he **p-d**,
Rom 4:21 . . . able to do whatever he **p-s**.
Gal 3:14 . . . blessing he **p-d** to Abraham,
1 Tim 4:8 . . . **p-ing** benefits in this life
Titus 1:2 . . . God—who does not lie—**p-d**
Heb 10:36 . . . receive all that he has **p-d**.
Jas 1:12 . . . of life that God has **p-d**
Jas 2:5 . . . inherit the Kingdom he **p-d**
2 Pet 3:13 . . . new earth he has **p-d**,
1 Jn 2:25 . . . eternal life he **p-d** us.

PROPHECY, PROPHECIES (n) *the spoken or written word from God; may forthtell (consoling or corrective) and/or foretell (predictive)*
Matt 13:14 . . . fulfills the **p** of Isaiah
Acts 13:29 . . . all that the **p-ies** said about
Acts 17:3 . . . **p-ies** and proved that the Messiah
Acts 21:9 . . . who had the gift of **p**.
Acts 21:10 . . . who also had the gift of **p**,
1 Cor 13:2 . . . If I had the gift of **p**,
1 Cor 13:9 . . . gift of **p** reveals only part

1 Cor 14:6 . . . knowledge or **p** or teaching,
Rev 22:18 . . . words of **p** written in

PROPHESY, PROPHESIED, PROPHESIES, PROPHESYING (v) *to issue a prophecy*
Num 11:25 . . . upon them, they **p-ied**.
1 Sam 19:24 . . . day and all night, **p-ing**
Isa 42:9 . . . Everything I **p-ied** has come true,
Joel 2:28 . . . sons and daughters will **p**.
Matt 7:22 . . . We **p-ied** in your name and
Acts 2:17 . . . sons and daughters will **p**.
Acts 19:6 . . . in other tongues and **p-ied**.
Rom 12:6 . . . the ability to **p**,
1 Cor 11:4 . . . head while praying or **p-ing**.
1 Cor 12:10 . . . the ability to **p**,
1 Cor 14:1 . . . the ability to **p**.
1 Cor 14:3 . . . one who **p-ies** strengthens
1 Cor 14:39 . . . be eager to **p**,

PROPHET, PROPHETS (n) *an interpreter of the times and people's hearts; one who issues divinely inspired revelations*
Exod 7:1 . . . Aaron, will be your **p**.
Exod 15:20 . . . Miriam the **p**, Aaron's
Deut 13:1 . . . there are **p-s** among you
Deut 18:18 . . . I will raise up a **p** like you
1 Sam 9:9 . . . **p-s** used to be called seers.
1 Kgs 18:36 . . . Elijah the **p** walked up to
2 Kgs 5:8 . . . a true **p** here in Israel.
2 Kgs 6:12 . . . Elisha, the **p** in Israel,
Isa 44:26 . . . the predictions of my **p-s**!
Hos 9:7 . . . you say, "The **p-s** are crazy
Amos 7:14 . . . I'm not a professional **p**,
Hab 1:1 . . . that the **p** Habakkuk received
Zech 7:12 . . . through the earlier **p-s**.
Mal 4:5 . . . the **p** Elijah before the great
Matt 5:17 . . . or the writings of the **p-s**.
Matt 7:12 . . . in the law and the **p-s**.
Matt 10:41 . . . the same reward as a **p**.
Matt 11:9 . . . Yes, and he is more than a **p**.
Matt 12:39 . . . sign of the **p** Jonah.
Matt 23:37 . . . the city that kills the **p-s**
Matt 26:56 . . . fulfill the words of the **p-s**
Luke 4:24 . . . no **p** is accepted in his own
Luke 7:16 . . . A mighty **p** has risen
Luke 11:49 . . . will send **p-s** and apostles
Luke 24:19 . . . **p** who did powerful
Luke 24:25 . . . all that the **p-s** wrote in
Luke 24:44 . . . law of Moses and the **p-s**.
John 1:21 . . . you the **P** we are expecting?
Acts 7:37 . . . a **P** like me from among your
Acts 10:43 . . . all the **p-s** testified about,
Acts 13:1 . . . Among the **p-s** and teachers
Rom 1:2 . . . long ago through his **p-s**
Rom 3:21 . . . Moses and the **p-s** long ago.
Rom 11:3 . . . they have killed your **p-s**
1 Cor 12:28 . . . second are **p-s**, third are
1 Cor 14:37 . . . If you claim to be a **p** or
Eph 2:20 . . . of the apostles and the **p-s**.
Eph 3:5 . . . to his holy apostles and **p-s**.
Eph 4:11 . . . the apostles, the **p-s**, the
1 Pet 1:10 . . . the **p-s** wanted to know
1 Pet 1:19 . . . proclaimed by the **p-s**.
2 Pet 1:21 . . . those **p-s** were moved by
2 Pet 3:2 . . . what the holy **p-s** said long
Rev 11:10 . . . death of the two **p-s** who
Rev 18:20 . . . God and apostles and **p-s**!

PROPITIATION (KJV)
Rom 3:25 . . . Jesus as the *sacrifice* for sin
1 Jn 2:2 . . . the *sacrifice that atones*
1 Jn 4:10 . . . *sacrifice to take away* our sins

PROSPER, PROSPERS (v) *to achieve economic success; to become strong and flourishing*

1749

Deut 28:63 ... pleasure in causing you to *p*
Ps 37:3 ... safely in the land and *p.*
Ps 73:3 ... *p* despite their wickedness.
Prov 16:20 ... listen to instruction will *p;*
Prov 17:9 ... Love *p-s* when a fault is forgiven,
Prov 19:8 ... cherish understanding will *p.*
Isa 53:10 ... LORD's good plan will *p.*
Isa 55:11 ... it will *p* everywhere I send it.
Dan 4:27 ... then you will continue to *p.*

PROSPERITY (n) *the condition of being successful or thriving*
Gen 41:29 ... will be a period of great *p*
Deut 28:11 ... LORD will give you *p*
Deut 30:15 ... life and death, between *p*
1 Sam 25:6 ... Peace and *p* to you,
Ps 41:2 ... He gives them *p* in the land
Prov 21:5 ... and hard work lead to *p,*
Prov 28:25 ... trusting the LORD leads to *p.*
Jer 33:6 ... give it *p* and true peace.
Mic 4:4 ... will live in peace and *p,*

PROSPEROUS (adj) *marked by success or economic well-being; flourishing*
Deut 5:33 ... live long and *p* lives
Ps 30:6 ... When I was *p,* I said,
Ps 34:12 ... a life that is long and *p?*
Ps 128:2 ... How joyful and *p* you will be!
Ps 132:15 ... bless this city and make it *p;*
Jer 12:1 ... Why are the wicked so *p?*

PROSTITUTE, PROSTITUTES (n) *a person who engages in promiscuous sexual relations, especially for money*
Josh 6:17 ... Rahab the *p* and
Prov 6:26 ... a *p* will bring you to poverty,
Prov 29:3 ... hangs around with *p-s,*
Ezek 16:15 ... as a *p* to every man
Ezek 23:3 ... They became *p-s* in Egypt.
Matt 21:31 ... *p-s* will get into the
Luke 15:30 ... your money on *p-s,*
1 Cor 6:16 ... if a man joins himself to a *p,*
Rev 17:1 ... going to come on the great *p,*

PROSTITUTION (n) *the act or practice of engaging in promiscuous sexual relations especially for money*
Lev 20:6 ... who commit spiritual *p* by
Hos 3:3 ... days and stop your *p.*

PROTECT, PROTECTED, PROTECTING, PROTECTS (v) *to cover or shield from exposure, injury, destruction; to defend*
see also KEEP
Gen 15:1 ... for I will *p* you,
Num 6:24 ... bless you and *p* you.
Josh 6:17 ... for she *p-ed* our spies.
1 Sam 2:9 ... He will *p* his faithful ones,
Ps 23:4 ... your staff *p* and comfort me.
Ps 27:1 ... fortress, *p-ing* me from danger,
Ps 41:2 ... LORD *p-s* them and keeps
Ps 116:6 ... LORD *p-s* those of childlike
Ps 127:1 ... Unless the LORD *p-s* a city,
Ps 145:20 ... LORD *p-s* all those who love
Ps 146:9 ... LORD *p-s* the foreigners
Prov 2:8 ... *p-s* those who are faithful
Isa 31:5 ... like a bird *p-ing* its nest.
Isa 57:1 ... God is *p-ing* them from the
John 17:11 ... now *p* them by the power of
Acts 26:22 ... But God has *p-ed* me
Gal 3:24 ... *p-ed* us until we could be
1 Pet 1:5 ... God is *p-ing* you by his power
Rev 3:10 ... I will *p* you from the great

PROTECTION (n) *the act of protecting; the state of being protected*
see also REFUGE

2 Sam 22:3 ... my rock, in whom I find *p.*
2 Sam 22:31 ... look to him for *p.*
Ps 5:11 ... Spread your *p* over them,
Ps 31:2 ... Be my rock of *p,*
Ps 71:1 ... I have come to you for *p;*
Ps 91:4 ... promises are your armor and *p.*
Prov 19:23 ... security and *p* from harm.

PROUD (adj) *having or displaying excessive self-esteem*
Ps 5:5 ... *p* may not stand in your
Prov 21:4 ... Haughty eyes, a *p* heart,
Rom 1:30 ... haters of God, insolent, *p,*
1 Cor 13:4 ... not jealous or boastful or *p*
1 Tim 3:6 ... he might become *p,*
1 Tim 6:17 ... rich in this world not to be *p*
2 Tim 3:2 ... They will be boastful and *p,*

PROUD (n) *those having or displaying excessive self-esteem*
Prov 16:5 ... LORD detests the *p;*
Dan 4:37 ... he is able to humble the *p.*
Jas 4:6 ... God opposes the *p* but gives
1 Pet 5:5 ... God opposes the *p* but gives

PROVIDE, PROVIDED, PROVIDES (v) *to furnish or supply, implying foresight in making provision for the future*
Gen 22:8 ... God will *p* a sheep
Gen 22:14 ... means "the LORD will *p"*
Ps 68:10 ... O God, you *p-d* for your needy
Isa 4:5 ... the LORD will *p* shade
Jer 5:28 ... refuse to *p* justice to orphans
Ezek 18:7 ... and *p-s* clothes for the needy.
2 Cor 9:8 ... God will generously *p* all you
2 Cor 9:10 ... he will *p* and increase your

PRUDENT (adj) *marked by wisdom or judiciousness; discreet*
Prov 14:8 ... *p* understand where they are
Prov 14:18 ... the *p* are crowned with
Prov 22:3 ... A *p* person foresees danger

PUBLICAN(S) (KJV)
Matt 5:46 ... Even corrupt *tax collectors*
Matt 9:10 ... with many *tax collectors*
Matt 10:3 ... Matthew (the *tax collector*),
Luke 5:30 ... and drink with *such scum?*
Luke 18:11 ... not like that *tax collector*

PUNISH, PUNISHED, PUNISHES, PUNISHING (v) *to impose a penalty to fit the crime: from corrective measures (fines or scolding) and corporal punishment (spanking or whipping) to capital punishment and eternal damnation*
Gen 15:14 ... But I will *p* the nation
1 Kgs 8:32 ... *P* the guilty as they deserve.
Prov 11:21 ... people will surely be *p-ed,*
Jer 25:14 ... I will *p* them in proportion
Lam 3:39 ... when we are *p-ed* for our sins?
Mark 12:40 ... will be more severely *p-ed.*
Acts 7:7 ... But I will *p* the nation
Rom 2:2 ... God, in his justice, will *p*
Rom 13:4 ... they have the power to *p* you.
Rom 13:4 ... the very purpose of *p-ing*
2 Thes 1:9 ... *p-ed* with eternal destruction,
Heb 2:2 ... act of disobedience was *p-ed.*
Heb 12:6 ... he *p-es* each one he accepts
1 Pet 2:14 ... sent them to *p* those who
Rev 19:2 ... has *p-ed* the great prostitute

PUNISHMENT (n) *suffering, pain, or loss that serves as retribution*
Prov 23:13 ... The rod of *p* won't kill
Isa 53:4 ... troubles were a *p* from God,
Jer 2:19 ... will bring its own *p.*

Jer 4:18 ... This *p* is bitter, piercing
Hos 5:9 ... On your day of *p,* you will
Matt 25:46 ... will go away into eternal *p,*
Rom 13:5 ... not only to avoid *p,* but also
2 Pet 2:9 ... keeping the wicked under *p*

PURCHASE, PURCHASED (v) *to gain or acquire; to buy*
see also REDEEM
Acts 20:28 ... *p-d* with his own blood—
Eph 1:7 ... *p-d* our freedom with the
Eph 1:14 ... *p-d* us to be his own people.
Col 1:14 ... who *p-d* our freedom
1 Tim 2:6 ... gave his life to *p* freedom
Rev 14:4 ... have been *p-d* from among

PURE (adj) *free of contamination or impurities; ritually clean; guileless; faultless; guiltless; chaste*
see also CLEAN, HOLY
Ps 19:9 ... Reverence for the LORD is *p,*
Prov 20:9 ... I am *p* and free
Matt 5:8 ... those whose hearts are *p,*
1 Cor 1:30 ... he made us *p* and holy,
Phil 4:8 ... right, and *p,* and lovely,
1 Tim 5:22 ... Keep yourself *p.*
2 Tim 2:21 ... If you keep yourself *p,*
Titus 1:15 ... Everything is *p* to those
Titus 2:5 ... to live wisely and be *p,*
Jas 1:27 ... *P* and genuine religion
1 Pet 3:2 ... your *p* and reverent
2 Pet 3:14 ... are *p* and blameless
1 Jn 3:3 ... will keep themselves *p,* just as

PURIFY, PURIFIED (v) *to make pure or remove (physical or moral) blemishes; to make ritually clean*
see also CLEANSE
Exod 30:10 ... offering made to *p* the people
Exod 30:15 ... given to the LORD to *p*
Num 25:13 ... *p-ied* the people of Israel,
1 Chr 15:12 ... You must *p* yourselves and
2 Chr 30:17 ... had not *p-ied* themselves,
Neh 12:30 ... Levites first *p-ied* themselves;
Isa 52:11 ... and *p* yourselves,
John 15:3 ... pruned and *p-ied* by the
Heb 9:14 ... Christ will *p* our consciences
Heb 9:22 ... was *p-ied* with blood.
Jas 4:8 ... you sinners; *p* your hearts,

PURITY (n) *the quality or state of being pure*
Job 14:4 ... Who can bring *p* out of an
Ps 86:11 ... Grant me *p* of heart,
2 Cor 6:6 ... by our *p,* our understanding,
1 Tim 4:12 ... love, your faith, and your *p.*
1 Tim 5:2 ... younger women with all *p*

PURPOSE, PURPOSES (n) *something set up as an object or end to be attained; resolution, determination*
see also PLAN
Exod 9:16 ... I have spared you for a *p—*
Prov 19:21 ... the LORD's *p* will prevail.
Rom 8:28 ... according to his *p* for them.
Rom 9:11 ... according to his own *p-s;*
Rom 9:17 ... for the very *p* of displaying
1 Cor 3:8 ... with the same *p.*
1 Cor 9:26 ... I run with *p* in every step.
Phil 2:2 ... together with one mind and *p.*

PURSUE, PURSUES (v) *to follow in order to overtake, capture, kill, or defeat; to seek*
Ps 23:6 ... unfailing love will *p* me
Ps 119:32 ... I will *p* your commands,
Prov 15:9 ... those who *p* godliness.
Prov 21:21 ... Whoever *p-s* righteousness

1 Tim 6:11 ... **P** righteousness and a godly
2 Tim 2:22 ... Instead, **p** righteous living,

Q

QUARREL, QUARRELS (n) *a usually verbal conflict between antagonists*
Prov 10:12 ... Hatred stirs up **q-s**.
Prov 17:14 ... Starting a **q** is like opening
Prov 26:20 ... **q-s** disappear when gossip
Prov 30:33 ... anger causes **q-s**.
Titus 3:9 ... **q-s** and fights about
Jas 4:1 ... causing the **q-s** and fights

QUARREL, QUARRELING (v) *to find fault; to contend or dispute actively*
Exod 21:18 ... "Now suppose two men **q**,
Prov 17:19 ... Anyone who loves to **q** loves
Prov 20:3 ... fools insist on **q-ing**.
Isa 58:4 ... keep on fighting and **q-ing**?
Rom 13:13 ... or in **q-ing** and jealousy.
1 Cor 3:3 ... and **q** with each other.
2 Cor 12:20 ... will find **q-ing**, jealousy,

QUARRELSOME (adj) *apt or disposed to quarrel in an often petty manner; contentious*
Prov 19:13 ... **q** wife is as annoying as
Prov 21:9 ... than with a **q** wife in a lovely
Prov 26:21 ... A **q** person starts fights
1 Tim 3:3 ... He must be gentle, not **q**,

QUIET (adj) *calm; gentle; peaceful, still; free from noise*
Prov 11:12 ... a sensible person keeps **q**.
Eccl 3:7 ... A time to be **q** and a time
Eccl 9:17 ... to hear the **q** words of a wise
Luke 19:40 ... If they kept **q**, the stones
1 Thes 4:11 ... to live a **q** life,
1 Tim 2:2 ... peaceful and **q** lives marked

QUIETNESS (n) *the state of being quiet; calmness; stillness*
Eccl 4:6 ... one handful with **q** than two
Isa 30:15 ... **q** and confidence is
Isa 32:17 ... it will bring **q** and confidence

R

RABBI (n) *a title of honor and respect given by the Jews to a teacher of the Law*
Matt 23:8 ... anyone call you '**R**,'
John 3:2 ... "**R**," he said, "we all know

RACE (n) *an athletic contest; an ethnic classification*
Ps 19:5 ... athlete eager to run the **r**.
Eccl 9:11 ... doesn't always win the **r**,
Dan 7:14 ... people of every **r** and nation
1 Cor 9:24 ... that in a **r** everyone runs,
Gal 2:2 ... running the **r** for nothing.
Gal 5:7 ... were running the **r** so well.
2 Tim 4:7 ... I have finished the **r**,
Heb 12:1 ... run with endurance the **r** God

RACE (v) *to go, move, or function at top speed or out of control*
Prov 6:18 ... feet that **r** to do wrong,

RADIANCE (n) *the quality or state of being radiant*
Isa 60:3 ... will come to see your **r**.
Luke 2:9 ... and the **r** of the Lord's

RADIANT (adj) *vividly bright and shining; marked by or expressive of love, confidence, or happiness*
Exod 34:29 ... face had become **r** because

Ps 34:5 ... help will be **r** with joy;
Ps 80:1 ... display your **r** glory

RAIN, RAINS (n) *water falling in drops from the sky*
Deut 11:14 ... will send the **r-s** in their
1 Kgs 17:1 ... no dew or **r** during the next
1 Kgs 18:1 ... that I will soon send **r**!
Prov 16:15 ... refreshes like a spring **r**.
Matt 5:45 ... and he sends **r** on the just
Jas 5:17 ... earnestly that no **r** would fall,
Jude 1:12 ... land without giving any **r**.

RAINBOW (n) *an arch of colors in the sky caused by light passing through moisture in the air*
Gen 9:13 ... I have placed my **r** in the

RAISE, RAISED (v) *to recall from death*
see also RESURRECTION
Judg 2:16 ... the Lord **r-d** up judges
Luke 7:22 ... the dead are **r-d** to life,
John 6:39 ... that I should **r** them up
Acts 2:32 ... God **r-d** Jesus from the dead,
Acts 24:15 ... that he will **r** both the
Rom 1:4 ... he was **r-d** from the dead
Rom 6:5 ... we will also be **r-d** to life
Rom 10:9 ... God **r-d** him from the dead,
1 Cor 15:4 ... he was **r-d** from the dead
Phil 3:10 ... mighty power that **r-d** him
1 Thes 4:14 ... died and was **r-d** to life
1 Pet 1:3 ... because God **r-d** Jesus Christ

RAM, RAMS (n) *a male sheep*
Gen 22:13 ... he took the **r** and sacrificed
1 Sam 15:22 ... offering the fat of **r-s**.
Dan 8:3 ... I saw a **r** with two long
Mic 6:7 ... him thousands of **r-s** and ten

RANSOM (n) *price paid or demanded to release someone or something from captivity*
Matt 20:28 ... his life as a **r** for many.
Mark 10:45 ... his life as a **r** for many.
1 Pet 1:18 ... that God paid a **r** to save

RANSOM, RANSOMED (v) *to deliver especially from sin or its penalty; to free from captivity or punishment by paying a price*
see also REDEEM(ED)
Ps 44:26 ... Help us! **R** us because of
Ps 71:23 ... for you have **r-ed** me.
Isa 35:10 ... have been **r-ed** by the LORD
Hos 13:14 ... Should I **r** them from
Rev 5:9 ... your blood has **r-ed** people

READ, READING, READS (v) *to receive and interpret letters or symbols by sight*
Deut 17:19 ... with him and **r** it daily
Josh 8:34 ... Joshua then **r** to them
2 Kgs 23:2 ... There the king **r** to them
Acts 8:28 ... carriage, he was **r-ing** aloud
2 Cor 3:2 ... everyone can **r** it and
1 Tim 4:13 ... focus on **r-ing** the Scriptures
Rev 1:3 ... the one who **r-s** the words of

REAP (v) *to harvest or gather; to obtain*
see also HARVEST
Gal 6:9 ... will **r** a harvest of blessing
Jas 3:18 ... **r** a harvest of righteousness.

REAPERS (KJV)
Ruth 2:3 ... grain behind the *harvesters*
2 Kgs 4:18 ... working with the *harvesters*
Matt 13:30 ... the *harvesters* to sort out
Matt 13:39 ... the *harvesters* are the angels

REBEL, REBELLED, REBELLING, REBELS (v) *to oppose or disobey one in authority or control*
Num 14:9 ... Do not **r** against the
Num 27:14 ... of Israel **r-led**, you failed to
1 Sam 12:14 ... if you do not **r** against the
Ps 78:56 ... testing and **r-ling** against God
Isa 63:10 ... But they **r-led** against him
Matt 10:21 ... children will **r** against their
Rom 13:2 ... So anyone who **r-s** against

REBELLION (n) *opposition to one in authority or dominance; defiance*
Exod 34:7 ... forgive iniquity, **r**, and sin.
Ps 32:5 ... I will confess my **r** to the
Ps 39:8 ... Rescue me from my **r**.
Ps 51:3 ... I recognize my **r**; it haunts
Isa 53:5 ... was pierced for our **r**,
Isa 53:8 ... for the **r** of my people.
Dan 9:24 ... to finish their **r**, to put an
2 Thes 2:3 ... is a great **r** against God

REBELLIOUS (adj) *given to or engaged in rebellion*
Isa 65:2 ... opened my arms to a **r** people.
Luke 1:17 ... those who are **r** to accept
Rom 10:21 ... were disobedient and **r**.
1 Tim 1:9 ... people who are lawless and **r**,
Titus 1:6 ... reputation for being wild or **r**.

REBELS (n) *those who rebel or participate in a rebellion*
Ps 51:13 ... will teach your ways to **r**,
Isa 53:12 ... He was counted among the **r**.
Luke 22:37 ... was counted among the **r**.
Rom 11:30 ... Gentiles were **r** against God,
Rom 11:31 ... they are the **r**, and God's

REBUKE (n) *an expression of strong disapproval; reprimand*
see also CORRECT, DISCIPLINE
Prov 17:10 ... A single **r** does more for
Prov 27:5 ... An open **r** is better than

REBUKE, REBUKED (v) *to criticize sharply; to reprimand*
Prov 30:6 ... or he may **r** you and expose
Mark 16:14 ... He **r-d** them for their
Luke 17:3 ... believer sins, **r** that person;
2 Tim 4:2 ... Patiently correct, **r**, and
Jas 1:5 ... He will not **r** you for asking.

RECEIVE, RECEIVED, RECEIVES (v) *to acquire or take possession of; to welcome*
Matt 7:8 ... For everyone who asks, **r-s**.
Matt 19:17 ... you want to **r** eternal life,
John 20:22 ... said, "**R** the Holy Spirit.
Acts 1:8 ... But you will **r** power when the
Acts 2:38 ... Then you will **r** the gift of
Acts 8:17 ... they **r-d** the Holy Spirit.
Acts 10:47 ... they have **r-d** the Holy
Acts 19:2 ... Did you **r** the Holy Spirit
Rom 8:15 ... Instead, you **r-d** God's Spirit
1 Tim 1:16 ... in him and **r** eternal life.
Rev 4:11 ... our God, to **r** glory and honor

RECONCILED, RECONCILING (v) *to restore to friendship or harmony, especially between God and human beings*
2 Cor 5:18 ... task of **r-ing** people to him.
Eph 2:16 ... Christ **r-d** both groups to God
Col 1:20 ... God **r-d** everything to himself.
Col 1:22 ... now he has **r-d** you to himself

RECONCILIATION (n) *the action of reconciling; the state of being reconciled*
Prov 14:9 … acknowledge it and seek *r.*
2 Cor 5:19 … this wonderful message of *r.*

RED (adj) *of the color red*
Exod 15:4 … are drowned in the **R** Sea.
Ps 106:9 … He commanded the **R** Sea to
Prov 23:31 … wine, seeing how *r* it is,
Isa 1:18 … they are *r* like crimson,
Isa 63:1 … with his clothing stained *r?*

REDEEM, REDEEMED, REDEEMS (v) *to buy back; to save by payment of a ransom; to free from the consequences of sin*
see also PURCHASE, RANSOM, RESCUE
Exod 6:6 … I will *r* you with a powerful
2 Sam 7:23 … have you *r-ed* from slavery
Ps 34:22 … the LORD will *r* those
Ps 49:15 … God will *r* my life.
Ps 74:2 … the tribe you *r-ed* as your own
Ps 103:4 … He *r-s* me from death and
Ps 107:2 … Has the LORD *r-ed* you?
Ps 130:8 … He himself will *r* Israel from
Isa 35:9 … Only the *r-ed* will walk
Isa 63:9 … love and mercy he *r-ed* them.
Hos 7:13 … I wanted to *r* them, but they

REDEEMER (n) *one who frees or delivers another from difficulty, danger, or bondage, usually by the payment of a ransom price*
Ruth 3:9 … for you are my family *r.*
Ruth 4:14 … has now provided a *r* for
Job 19:25 … I know that my **R** lives,
Ps 19:14 … LORD, my rock and my *r.*
Prov 23:11 … For their **R** is strong;
Isa 44:6 … Israel's King and **R**, the LORD
Isa 48:17 … your **R**, the Holy One of Israel:
Isa 59:20 … The **R** will come to Jerusalem

REDEMPTION (n) *the act, process, or an instance of redeeming*
Ps 130:7 … love. His *r* overflows.
Eph 4:30 … be saved on the day of *r.*
Heb 9:12 … and secured our *r* forever.

REFUGE (n) *shelter or protection from danger or distress*
see also FORTRESS, PROTECTION, SHELTER
Deut 33:27 … eternal God is your *r,*
2 Sam 22:3 … He is my *r,* my savior,
Ps 2:12 … for all who take *r* in him!
Ps 5:11 … But let all who take *r* in you
Ps 17:7 … those who seek *r* from their
Ps 34:8 … those who take *r* in him!
Ps 46:1 … God is our *r* and strength,
Ps 91:2 … He alone is my *r,* my place

REGENERATION (KJV)
Matt 19:28 … world is *made new* and the
Titus 3:5 … giving us a *new birth* and new

REGULATIONS (n) *authoritative rules dealing with details or procedure*
see also LAW(S)
Exod 21:1 … These are the *r* you must
Deut 33:10 … They teach your *r* to Jacob;
Ps 119:30 … determined to live by your *r.*
Ps 119:43 … for your *r* are my only hope.
Ps 119:120 … I stand in awe of your *r.*
Ps 119:164 … because all your *r* are just.
Ps 119:175 … and may your *r* help me.

REIGN, REIGNED, REIGNING, REIGNS (v) *to possess or exercise sovereign power; to rule*
Exod 15:18 … The LORD will *r* forever
Ps 9:7 … But the LORD *r-s* forever,
Ps 29:10 … LORD *r-s* as king forever.
Ps 96:10 … The LORD *r-s!*
Ps 146:10 … The LORD will *r* forever.
Isa 52:7 … that the God of Israel *r-s!*
1 Cor 4:8 … we would be *r-ing* with you.
1 Cor 15:25 … For Christ must *r* until he
Rev 5:10 … And they will *r* on the earth.
Rev 11:15 … and he will *r* forever
Rev 19:6 … our God, the Almighty, *r-s.*
Rev 20:4 … and they *r-ed* with Christ
Rev 22:5 … And they will *r* forever

REIGNS (n) *the time during which one (as a sovereign) rules*
Dan 2:44 … During the *r* of those kings,

REJECT, REJECTED, REJECTING, REJECTS (v) *to refuse to accept, consider, submit to, or take for some purpose, or use; to refuse to hear, receive, or admit*
1 Sam 8:7 … they are *r-ing* me, not you.
Ps 51:17 … not *r* a broken and repentant
Ps 118:22 … stone that the builders *r-ed*
Prov 3:11 … My child, don't *r* the LORD's
Mal 1:3 … but I *r-ed* his brother,
Matt 21:42 … stone that the builders *r-ed*
Luke 10:16 … who *r-s* me is *r-ing* God,
John 6:37 … I will never *r* them.
John 12:48 … But all who *r* me and my
Rom 9:13 … loved Jacob, but I *r-ed* Esau.
1 Thes 4:8 … teaching but is *r-ing* God,
1 Tim 4:4 … we should not *r* any of it
2 Tim 3:5 … but they will *r* the power
Heb 6:6 … by *r-ing* the Son of God, they
1 Pet 2:4 … He was *r-ed* by people,
1 Pet 2:7 … stone that the builders *r-ed*

REJOICE, REJOICED, REJOICES, REJOICING (v) *to feel joy or great delight; to gladden*
1 Chr 16:31 … glad, and the earth *r!*
1 Chr 29:17 … *r* when you find integrity
Esth 8:17 … decree arrived, the Jews *r-d*
Ps 5:11 … who take refuge in you *r;*
Ps 13:5 … I will *r* because you
Ps 35:9 … I will *r* in the LORD.
Ps 48:2 … the whole earth *r-s* to see it!
Ps 58:10 … The godly will *r* when they
Ps 66:6 … There we *r-d* in him.
Ps 68:4 … LORD—*r* in his presence!
Ps 119:14 … I have *r-d* in your laws
Ps 119:162 … I *r* in your word like one
Prov 8:31 … I *r-d* with the human family!
Prov 17:5 … who *r* at the misfortune
Prov 29:2 … in authority, the people *r.*
Isa 9:3 … and its people will *r.*
Isa 35:1 … wasteland will *r* and blossom
Isa 62:5 … *r* over you as a bridegroom *r-s*
Jer 51:48 … the heavens and earth will *r,*
Lam 4:21 … Are you *r-ing* in the land
Hab 1:15 … while they *r* and celebrate?
Zeph 3:17 … He will *r* over you
Zech 2:10 … Shout and *r,* O beautiful
Luke 1:14 … and many will *r* at his birth,
Luke 1:47 … How my spirit *r-s* in God my
Luke 1:58 … everyone *r-d* with her.
Luke 10:20 … But don't *r* because evil
Luke 13:17 … but all the people *r-d* at the
Acts 5:41 … high council *r-ing* that God
Acts 16:34 … his entire household *r-d*
1 Cor 13:6 … *r* about injustice but *r-s*
Phil 2:18 … you should *r,* and I will

Phil 3:1 … and sisters, *r* in the Lord.
Phil 4:4 … I say it again—*r!*
Col 2:5 … I *r* that you are living as
Rev 19:7 … Let us be glad and *r,* and

RELIABLE (adj) *dependable*
1 Chr 9:22 … they were *r* men.
Prov 13:17 … but a *r* messenger brings
Prov 20:6 … find one who is truly *r?*
2 Tim 2:2 … by many *r* witnesses.

RELIGION, RELIGIONS (n) *a personal set or institutionalized system of religious attitudes, beliefs, and practices; the service and worship of God or the supernatural*
Acts 25:19 … something about their *r* and
Acts 26:5 … the strictest sect of our *r.*
Gal 1:13 … I followed the Jewish *r—*
Jas 1:26 … and your *r* is worthless.

RELIGIOUS (adj) *relating to or manifesting faithful devotion to God or a god*
Luke 11:46 … with unbearable *r* demands,
Acts 13:50 … the influential *r* women and
Jas 1:26 … you claim to be *r* but don't

REMAIN, REMAINED, REMAINS (v) *to stay in the same place or with the same person or group; to continue unchanged*
2 Kgs 18:6 … He *r-ed* faithful to the LORD
John 15:7 … But if you *r* in me and my
John 15:9 … loved me. **R** in my love.
Rom 11:5 … of Israel have *r-ed* faithful
2 Tim 2:13 … unfaithful, he *r-s* faithful,
2 Tim 3:14 … But you must *r* faithful
2 Tim 4:7 … and I have *r-ed* faithful.
Heb 7:3 … He *r-s* a priest forever,
Heb 10:32 … how you *r-ed* faithful even
Heb 13:4 … and *r* faithful to one another
1 Pet 1:25 … word of the Lord *r-s*
1 Jn 2:27 … *r* in fellowship with Christ.

REMEMBER, REMEMBERED, REMEMBERING, REMEMBERS (v) *to bring to mind or think of again; to keep in mind for attention or consideration; to retain in the memory*
Gen 9:15 … I will *r* my covenant with
Exod 2:24 … *r-ed* his covenant promise
1 Chr 16:12 … **R** the wonders he has
Ps 49:13 … though they are *r-ed* as being
Ps 103:14 … he *r-s* we are only dust.
Ps 106:45 … *r-ed* his covenant with them
Ps 111:5 … he always *r-s* his covenant.
Ps 136:23 … He *r-ed* us in our weakness.
Jer 31:34 … never again *r* their sins.
Jer 32:20 … things still *r-ed* to this day!
Hab 3:2 … in your anger, *r* your mercy.
Matt 26:13 … will be *r-ed* and discussed.
Luke 1:72 … *r-ing* his sacred covenant—
2 Tim 2:8 … Always *r* that Jesus
Heb 8:12 … never again *r* their sins.
2 Pet 1:15 … you always *r* these things

REMISSION (KJV)
Matt 26:28 … as a sacrifice *to forgive*
Acts 10:43 … sins *forgiven* through his
Rom 3:25 … he held back and did not *punish*
Heb 9:22 … blood, there is no *forgiveness*

REMNANT (n) *a usually small part, member, or trace remaining; the few people left who gathered together after God scattered them into exile*

Ezra 9:8 ... few of us to survive as a *r.*
Isa 6:13 ... a tenth—a *r*—survive,
Isa 11:11 ... to bring back the *r* of his
Jer 23:3 ... gather together the *r* of my
Zech 8:12 ... will cause the *r* in Judah

RENEW, RENEWED, RENEWS (v) *to restore to freshness, vigor, or perfection; to make new spiritually*
Ps 23:3 ... He *r-s* my strength.
Ps 51:10 ... *R* a loyal spirit within me.
Isa 57:10 ... Desire gave you *r-ed* strength,
Eph 4:23 ... let the Spirit *r* your thoughts
Col 3:10 ... be *r-ed* as you learn to know

RENOWN (KJV)
Gen 6:4 ... the *heroes* and famous warriors
Isa 14:20 ... will never again receive *honor*
Ezek 16:14 ... *fame* soon spread
Ezek 39:13 ... a *glorious victory* for Israel

REPAY, REPAYS (v) *to give or inflict in return or requital; to pay back (money)*
Ps 62:12 ... Surely you *r* all people
Prov 17:13 ... If you *r* good with evil,
Prov 19:17 ... and he will *r* you!
Jer 51:6 ... he will *r* her in full.
Jer 51:56 ... he always *r-s* in full.
Luke 6:34 ... to those who can *r* you,
Luke 7:42 ... neither of them could *r* him,
1 Tim 5:4 ... *r* their parents by taking
1 Pet 3:9 ... Don't *r* evil for evil.

REPENT, REPENTED, REPENTING, REPENTS (v) *to turn from sin and change one's heart and behavior; to feel regret and contrition*
Matt 3:2 ... *R* of your sins and turn
Matt 3:8 ... that you have *r-ed* of your sins
Matt 4:17 ... began to preach, "*R* of your
Matt 11:21 ... people would have *r-ed* of
Luke 3:8 ... that you have *r-ed* of your sins
Luke 15:7 ... sinner who *r-s* and returns
Luke 15:10 ... when even one sinner *r-s.*
Acts 2:38 ... you must *r* of your sins
Acts 17:30 ... everywhere to *r* of their sins
Acts 20:21 ... necessity of *r-ing* from sin
Heb 6:1 ... importance of *r-ing* from evil
2 Pet 3:9 ... but wants everyone to *r.*
Rev 2:5 ... If you don't *r,* I will come

REPENTANCE (n) *a turning away from sin, disobedience, or rebellion, and a turning back to God*
1 Kgs 8:47 ... to you in *r* and pray,
Job 42:6 ... dust and ashes to show my *r.*
Luke 17:3 ... if there is *r,* forgive.
2 Cor 7:10 ... sorrow, which lacks *r,*

REPUTATION (n) *overall quality or character as seen or judged by people in general*
see also NAME
Ps 109:21 ... the sake of your own *r!*
Prov 3:4 ... you will earn a good *r.*
Prov 22:1 ... Choose a good *r* over great
Eccl 7:1 ... A good *r* is more valuable
1 Tim 3:2 ... wisely, and have a good *r.*
Heb 11:39 ... good *r* because of their

RESCUE, RESCUED, RESCUES, RESCUING (v) *to save or deliver*
see also REDEEM, SAVE
2 Kgs 13:5 ... someone to *r* the Israelites
Ps 9:14 ... rejoice that you have *r-d* me.
Ps 17:7 ... mighty power you *r* those who
Ps 22:8 ... let the LORD *r* him!
Ps 31:2 ... listen to me; *r* me quickly.

Ps 37:39 ... The LORD *r-s* the godly;
Ps 37:40 ... LORD helps them, *r-ing* them
Ps 68:20 ... The Sovereign LORD *r-s* us
Ps 72:12 ... He will *r* the poor when
Ps 145:19 ... cries for help and *r-s* them.
Prov 11:8 ... godly are *r-d* from trouble,
Isa 56:1 ... coming soon to *r* you and
Dan 6:27 ... He *r-s* and saves his people;
Zech 8:7 ... that I will *r* my people from
Matt 6:13 ... but *r* us from the evil one.
Rom 11:26 ... The one who *r-s* will come
2 Cor 1:10 ... And he did *r* us from mortal
Gal 1:4 ... in order to *r* us from this
Gal 3:13 ... But Christ has *r-d* us from the
Col 1:13 ... For he has *r-d* us from the
1 Thes 1:10 ... the one who has *r-d* us
2 Pet 2:9 ... knows how to *r* godly people

RESIST (v) *to withstand the force or effect of; to counteract or defeat*
Dan 11:32 ... will be strong and will *r* him.
Matt 5:39 ... do not *r* an evil person!
Jas 4:7 ... *R* the devil, and he will flee

RESPECT (n) *a high or special regard; esteem*
see also AWE, REVERENCE
Prov 11:16 ... A gracious woman gains *r,*
Mal 1:6 ... the honor and *r* I deserve?
Titus 2:2 ... be worthy of *r,* and to live

RESPECT, RESPECTED (v) *to consider worthy of high regard; to esteem*
Eph 5:33 ... the wife must *r* her husband.
1 Tim 3:4 ... children who *r* and obey him.
1 Tim 3:8 ... deacons must be well *r-ed*
1 Tim 3:11 ... their wives must be *r-ed*
1 Tim 5:17 ... work well should be *r-ed*
1 Pet 2:17 ... Fear God, and *r* the king.

RESPONSIBLE (adj) *marked by or involving responsibility or accountability; liable to be called to account as the primary cause, motive, or agent*
Exod 32:34 ... hold them *r* for their sins.
Num 1:53 ... The Levites are *r* to stand
Ezek 33:6 ... he is *r* for their captivity.
Jon 1:14 ... And don't hold us *r* for his
Gal 6:5 ... For we are each *r* for our own

REST (n) *freedom from activity or labor; peace of mind or spirit; repose, sleep*
see also SABBATH
Exod 31:15 ... day of complete *r,* a holy
Exod 33:14 ... and I will give you *r*—
Ps 91:1 ... Most High will find *r* in the
Ps 127:2 ... for God gives *r* to his loved
Jer 6:16 ... you will find *r* for your
Matt 11:28 ... and I will give you *r.*
2 Thes 1:7 ... God will provide *r* for you
Heb 3:11 ... even though this *r* has been
Heb 4:9 ... a special *r* still waiting
Heb 4:10 ... who have entered into God's *r*

REST, RESTED, RESTING, RESTS (v) *to sit or lie on; to cease from action or motion; to take relief or respite*
Gen 2:2 ... of creation, so he *r-ed* from all
Ps 16:9 ... My body *r-s* in safety.
Ps 23:2 ... He lets me *r* in green
Isa 11:2 ... Spirit of the LORD will *r*
Isa 30:15 ... and *r-ing* in me will you
John 1:32 ... from heaven and *r-ing* upon
Heb 4:4 ... seventh day God *r-ed* from all
Rev 14:13 ... will *r* from their hard work;

RESTITUTION (n) *a making good of or giving an equivalent for some injury*

Lev 6:5 ... You must make *r* by paying
Num 5:8 ... relatives to whom *r* can be

RESTORE, RESTORED, RESTORES, RESTORING (v) *to give back, return; to renew*
Ps 14:7 ... When the LORD *r-s* his people,
Ps 30:2 ... and you *r-d* my health.
Isa 58:11 ... dry and *r-ing* your strength.
Jer 30:3 ... when I will *r* the fortunes of
Jer 30:18 ... from captivity and *r* their
Jer 31:18 ... Turn me again to you and *r*
Hos 6:2 ... a short time he will *r* us,
Nah 2:2 ... but he will *r* its splendor.
Rom 5:10 ... friendship with God was *r-d*
1 Pet 5:10 ... will *r,* support, and strengthen

RESURRECTION (n) *the state of one risen from the dead; the rising again to life of all the human dead before the final judgment*
see also RAISE, RISE
Matt 27:53 ... cemetery after Jesus' *r,*
Mark 12:23 ... will she be in the *r?*
Luke 20:36 ... children of the *r.*
John 11:25 ... I am the *r* and the life.
Acts 1:22 ... as a witness of Jesus' *r.*
Acts 2:31 ... speaking of the Messiah's *r.*
Acts 4:2 ... there is a *r* of the dead.
Acts 4:33 ... powerfully to the *r* of
Acts 17:32 ... Paul speak about the *r* of
1 Cor 15:13 ... if there is no *r* of the
1 Cor 15:42 ... way with the *r* of the dead.
Phil 3:11 ... experience the *r* from the
2 Tim 2:18 ... claiming that the *r* of the
Heb 6:2 ... of hands, the *r* of the dead,
Heb 11:35 ... a better life after the *r.*
1 Pet 3:21 ... because of the *r* of Jesus
Rev 20:5 ... This is the first *r.*

REVEAL, REVEALED (v) *to make known through divine inspiration; to make (something secret or hidden) publicly or generally known; to display*
Exod 6:3 ... did not *r* my name, Yahweh,
Deut 29:29 ... all that he has *r-ed* to us,
Isa 40:5 ... the LORD will be *r-ed,*
Isa 53:1 ... the LORD *r-ed* his powerful
Matt 10:26 ... is covered will be *r-ed,*
Matt 11:27 ... Son chooses to *r* him.
Luke 2:32 ... He is a light to *r* God
John 12:38 ... the LORD *r-ed* his powerful
John 14:21 ... love them and *r* myself
John 17:6 ... I have *r-ed* you to the
Rom 8:18 ... glory he will *r* to us
Rom 16:25 ... Christ has *r-ed* his plan
1 Cor 2:10 ... that God *r-ed* these things
Gal 1:16 ... to *r* his Son to me so that
Gal 2:2 ... because God *r-ed* to me
Eph 3:3 ... himself *r-ed* his mysterious
Col 1:26 ... it has been *r-ed* to God's
2 Thes 2:3 ... man of lawlessness is *r-ed*
Titus 2:13 ... Christ, will be *r-ed.*
Heb 9:8 ... the Holy Spirit *r-ed* that
1 Pet 1:7 ... when Jesus Christ is *r-ed*

REVELATION, REVELATIONS (n) *something that is revealed by God to humans; an act of revealing or communicating divine truth*
1 Cor 14:6 ... bring you a *r* or some
1 Cor 14:30 ... person receives a *r* from
2 Cor 12:1 ... visions and *r-s* from the
2 Cor 12:7 ... wonderful *r-s* from God.
Gal 1:12 ... by direct *r* from Jesus
Rev 1:1 ... This is a *r* from Jesus

REVELRY (n) *noisy partying or merrymaking*
Exod 32:6 … they indulged in pagan *r*.
1 Cor 10:7 … they indulged in pagan *r*.

REVENGE (n) *an act or instance of retaliating in order to get even*
Lev 19:18 … Do not seek *r* or bear
Num 31:3 … war of *r* against Midian.
Deut 32:35 … I will take *r*; I will
Josh 20:3 … relatives seeking *r* for
Judg 20:10 … will take *r* on Gibeah
Isa 34:8 … day of the LORD'S *r*,
Heb 10:30 … I will take *r*. I will

REVERENCE (n) *profound, adoring, awed respect*
see also AWE, FEAR, RESPECT
Lev 19:30 … of rest, and show *r* toward
Job 15:4 … fear of God, no *r* for him?
Job 37:24 … who are wise show him *r*.
Eph 5:21 … another out of *r* for Christ.
Heb 5:7 … of his deep *r* for God.

REVERENT (adj) *expressing or characterized by reverence; worshipful*
Col 3:22 … because of your *r* fear
1 Pet 1:17 … must live in *r* fear
1 Pet 3:2 … your pure and *r* lives.

REWARD, REWARDS (n) *something that is given in return for good or evil done or received or that is offered or given for some service or attainment*
Gen 15:1 … and your *r* will be
1 Sam 26:23 … gives his own *r* for doing
Prov 12:14 … and hard work brings *r-s*.
Isa 49:4 … I will trust God for my *r*.
Matt 5:12 … For a great *r* awaits you
Matt 6:5 … all the *r* they will ever
Luke 6:23 … For a great *r* awaits you
Luke 6:35 … your *r* from heaven will
Phil 4:17 … you to receive a *r* for your
1 Thes 2:19 … be our proud *r* and crown
Heb 10:35 … the great *r* it brings you!
1 Pet 1:9 … The *r* for trusting him

REWARD, REWARDED, REWARDS (v) *to give a reward to or for; to recompense*
2 Sam 22:21 … The LORD *r-ed* me for
Prov 13:21 … while blessings *r* the
Prov 25:22 … the LORD will *r* you.
Jer 31:16 … for I will *r* you," says
Matt 6:18 … sees everything, will *r* you.
Luke 12:37 … for his return will be *r-ed*.
Luke 14:14 … God will *r* you for
1 Cor 3:8 … both will be *r-ed* for their
Eph 6:8 … the Lord will *r* each one
1 Tim 3:13 … will be *r-ed* with respect
Heb 11:6 … that he *r-s* those who
Rev 11:18 … the dead and *r* your servants

RICH (adj) *having abundant possessions and especially material wealth*
Job 34:19 … no more attention to the *r*
Ps 49:16 … the wicked grow *r* and
Prov 10:4 … poor; hard workers get *r*.
Prov 11:18 … Evil people get *r* for
Prov 13:7 … are poor pretend to be *r*;
Prov 21:17 … and luxury will never be *r*.
Prov 22:2 … The *r* and poor have this
Prov 23:4 … yourself out trying to get *r*.
Prov 28:6 … than to be dishonest and *r*.
Prov 28:22 … Greedy people try to get *r*
Eccl 5:12 … But the *r* seldom get a
Isa 53:9 … put in a *r* man's grave.

Matt 19:23 … hard for a *r* person to enter
Luke 1:53 … and sent the *r* away with
Luke 6:24 … you who are *r*, for you have
Luke 16:1 … was a certain *r* man who had
Luke 21:1 … watched the *r* people
2 Cor 8:9 … Though he was *r*, yet for your
1 Tim 6:9 … who long to be *r* fall into
1 Tim 6:17 … who are *r* in this world
Jas 1:10 … those who are *r* should boast
Jas 2:3 … seat to the *r* person, but you
Jas 5:1 … Look here, you *r* people:

RICHES (n) *things that make one rich; wealth*
see also MONEY, POSSESSION(S), TREASURE(S), WEALTH
2 Chr 1:11 … ask for wealth, *r*, fame,
Ps 49:6 … wealth and boast of great *r*.
Prov 27:24 … for *r* don't last forever,
Eccl 5:13 … Hoarding *r* harms the
Jer 9:23 … rich boast in their *r*.
Luke 8:14 … cares and *r* and pleasures
Rom 11:33 … great are God's *r* and
2 Cor 6:10 … give spiritual *r* to others.
Col 1:27 … know that the *r* and glory

RIGHT (adj) *being in accordance with what is good, just, or proper; being in a correct or proper state; located opposite of left; acting or judging in accordance with truth or fact*
see also JUST, JUSTIFY, RIGHTEOUS, UPRIGHT
Gen 4:7 … do what is *r*, then watch out!
Gen 18:19 … by doing what is *r* and just.
Exod 15:26 … do what is *r* in his sight,
Num 25:13 … making them *r* with me.
Deut 6:18 … Do what is *r* and good
Deut 25:1 … that one is *r* and the other
Josh 1:7 … either to the *r* or to the
Judg 17:6 … whatever seemed *r* in their
1 Sam 12:23 … what is good and *r*.
1 Kgs 3:9 … difference between *r* and
2 Chr 12:6 … The LORD is *r* in doing
Ps 19:8 … LORD are *r*, bringing joy
Ps 24:5 … have a *r* relationship with
Ps 25:8 … does what is *r*; he shows the
Ps 37:30 … they teach *r* from wrong.
Ps 64:10 … do what is *r* will praise him.
Ps 71:2 … do what is *r*. Turn your ear
Ps 84:11 … from those who do what is *r*.
Ps 97:11 … on those whose hearts are *r*.
Ps 106:3 … and always do what is *r*.
Ps 119:144 … laws are always *r*; help me
Prov 1:3 … do what is *r*, just, and fair.
Prov 2:13 … men turn from the *r* way
Prov 14:2 … who follow the *r* path
Prov 14:12 … person that seems *r*, but
Prov 15:21 … stays on the *r* path.
Prov 15:23 … to say the *r* thing at the
Prov 18:17 … in court sounds *r*—until
Eccl 8:5 … and a way to do what is *r*,
Eccl 9:11 … being in the *r* place at the
Isa 7:15 … choose what is *r* and reject
Isa 16:5 … be eager to do what is *r*.
Isa 26:7 … who does what is *r*, and you
Jer 23:5 … is just and *r* throughout the
Ezek 18:5 … and does what is just and *r*.
Ezek 18:21 … and do what is just and *r*,
Hos 14:9 … are true and *r*, and righteous
Mic 3:1 … to know *r* from wrong,
Mic 6:8 … do what is *r*, to love mercy,
Zeph 2:3 … to do what is *r* and to live
Matt 6:3 … hand know what your *r* hand
Matt 22:44 … of honor at my *r* hand until
Acts 2:34 … the place of honor at my *r* hand
Acts 7:55 … honor at God's *r* hand.

Acts 13:39 … is made *r* in God's sight—
Rom 1:17 … God makes us *r* in his sight.
Rom 2:13 … doesn't make us *r* with God.
Rom 3:4 … will be proved *r* in what you
Rom 3:20 … ever be made *r* with God by
Rom 3:22 … We are made *r* with God by
Rom 3:28 … So we are made *r* with God
Rom 3:30 … makes people *r* with himself
Rom 4:13 … but on a *r* relationship with
Rom 4:25 … life to make us *r* with God.
Rom 5:1 … we have been made *r* in God's
Rom 5:16 … being made *r* with God,
Rom 6:13 … to do what is *r* for the glory
Rom 8:10 … have been made *r* with God.
Rom 8:30 … given them *r* standing,
Rom 9:30 … they were made *r* with God
Rom 10:3 … way of getting *r* with God by
Rom 10:10 … you are made *r* with God,
1 Cor 6:11 … you were made *r* with God,
2 Cor 3:9 … which makes us *r* with God!
2 Cor 5:21 … be made *r* with God
Gal 2:16 … person is made *r* with God by
Gal 2:17 … to be made *r* with God through
Gal 2:21 … law could make us *r* with God,
Gal 3:11 … can be made *r* with God by
Gal 3:21 … could be made *r* with God by
Gal 3:24 … could be made *r* with God
Gal 5:4 … to make yourselves *r* with God
Eph 5:9 … what is good and *r* and true.
Phil 4:8 … honorable, and, *r*, and pure,
2 Tim 3:16 … teaches us to do what is *r*,
Heb 2:10 … it was only *r* that he should
Heb 12:11 … harvest of *r* living for those
Jas 2:24 … are shown to be *r* with God by
1 Jn 2:29 … who do what is *r* are God's

RIGHT, RIGHTS (n) *correct or moral behavior; something to which one has a just claim*
Job 27:2 … has taken away my *r-s*, by
Ps 25:9 … in doing *r*, teaching them his
Ps 34:15 … those who do *r*; his ears are
Ps 82:3 … the *r-s* of the oppressed
Prov 29:7 … about the *r-s* of the poor;
Isa 1:17 … Fight for the *r-s* of widows.
Isa 10:2 … and deny the *r-s* of the needy
Lam 3:35 … others of their *r-s* in
Matt 5:10 … for doing *r*, for the Kingdom
John 1:12 … he gave the *r* to become
Rom 9:21 … he have a *r* to use the same
1 Cor 9:4 … have the *r* to live in your
1 Pet 3:12 … those who do *r*, and his ears

RIGHTEOUS (adj) *acting in accord with divine or moral law; free from guilt or sin; morally right or justifiable*
see also JUST, JUSTIFY, RIGHT, UPRIGHT
Gen 6:9 … Noah was a *r* man, the only
Gen 15:6 … counted him as *r* because of
Gen 18:23 … sweep away both the *r* and
Ps 7:8 … Declare me *r*, O LORD, for
Ps 17:15 … Because I am *r*, I will see
Ps 106:31 … regarded as a *r* man ever
Ps 119:7 … I learn your *r* regulations,
Ps 119:137 … O LORD, you are *r*,
Ps 145:17 … The LORD is *r* in everything
Prov 4:18 … The way of the *r* is like the
Prov 9:9 … Teach the *r*, and they
Prov 29:6 … but the *r* escape, shouting
Isa 26:2 … to all who are *r*; allow the
Isa 42:21 … Because he is *r*, the LORD
Isa 64:6 … we display our *r* deeds,
Jer 11:20 … you make *r* judgments, and
Jer 23:5 … raise up a *r* descendant from
Ezek 3:20 … None of their *r* acts will be
Amos 5:24 … river of *r* living.

Hab 2:4 ... But the *r* will live
Mal 3:18 ... between the *r* and the wicked,
Matt 9:13 ... think they are *r*, but those
Matt 13:43 ... Then the *r* will shine
Matt 25:37 ... Then these *r* ones will
Luke 1:6 ... and Elizabeth were *r* in God's
Luke 16:15 ... like to appear *r* in public,
Rom 1:17 ... faith that a *r* person has
Rom 3:5 ... people see how *r* God is.
Rom 3:10 ... No one is *r*—not even one.
Rom 4:3 ... counted him as *r* because of
Rom 4:6 ... who are declared *r* without
Rom 4:22 ... God counted him as *r*.
Rom 6:19 ... be slaves to *r* living so that
Gal 3:6 ... counted him as *r* because of
Eph 4:24 ... like God—truly *r* and holy.
Phil 1:11 ... salvation—the *r* character
2 Tim 2:22 ... Instead, pursue *r* living,
Jas 2:23 ... counted him as *r* because of
Jas 5:16 ... prayer of a *r* person has
1 Jn 2:1 ... the one who is truly *r*.
1 Jn 3:7 ... that they are *r*, even as

RIGHTEOUSNESS (n) *the state or quality of being righteous*
see also GODLINESS, JUSTICE
Ps 36:6 ... Your *r* is like the mighty
Ps 71:15 ... tell everyone about your *r*.
Ps 85:10 ... *R* and peace have kissed!
Ps 98:2 ... has revealed his *r* to every
Ps 111:3 ... His *r* never fails.
Prov 21:21 ... Whoever pursues *r* and
Isa 11:5 ... He will wear *r* like a belt
Isa 42:6 ... you to demonstrate my *r*.
Isa 45:8 ... so salvation and *r* can sprout
Isa 56:1 ... to display my *r* among you.
Isa 59:17 ... He put on *r* as his body
Jer 9:24 ... brings justice and *r* to the
Jer 23:6 ... LORD Is Our *R*.
Hos 10:12 ... come and shower *r* upon
Mic 7:9 ... and I will see his *r*.
Mal 4:2 ... the Sun of *R* will rise
Matt 5:20 ... unless your *r* is better
John 16:8 ... and of God's *r*, and of the
Acts 24:25 ... about *r* and self-control
Rom 3:26 ... to demonstrate his *r*, for he
Rom 5:18 ... one act of *r* brings a right
2 Cor 6:7 ... the weapons of *r* in the
Eph 6:14 ... the body armor of God's *r*.
Phil 3:6 ... And as for *r*, I obeyed the
2 Tim 4:8 ... the crown of *r*, which
Heb 11:7 ... he received the *r* that comes
Jas 3:18 ... and reap a harvest of *r*.
2 Pet 3:13 ... filled with God's *r*.

RISE, RISEN, RISES (v) *to ascend or extend above other objects; to return from death; to assume an upright position*
see also RESURRECTION
Num 24:17 ... A star will *r* from Jacob;
Isa 26:19 ... bodies will *r* again!
Mal 4:2 ... of Righteousness will *r* with
Matt 22:30 ... when the dead *r*, they will
Matt 27:63 ... I will *r* from the dead.
Matt 28:6 ... He is *r-n* from the dead,
Mark 8:31 ... later he would *r* from the
Mark 16:6 ... He is *r-n* from the dead!
Luke 18:33 ... day he will *r* again.
Luke 24:34 ... The Lord has really *r-n*!
John 5:29 ... and they will *r* again.
John 11:24 ... everyone else *r-s*, at
John 20:9 ... said Jesus must *r* from the
Acts 17:3 ... must suffer and *r* from the
1 Thes 4:16 ... have died will *r* from

ROCK (n) *a stone; a cliff; foundation, support; refuge*
Exod 17:6 ... Moses struck the *r* as he was
Num 20:8 ... speak to the *r* over there,
Deut 32:13 ... honey from the *r* and olive
2 Sam 22:2 ... LORD is my *r*, my
Ps 18:2 ... God is my *r*, in whom I
Ps 19:14 ... LORD, my *r* and my redeemer.
Ps 61:2 ... to the towering *r* of safety,
Ps 62:7 ... my refuge, a *r* where no enemy
Ps 92:15 ... He is my *r*!
Isa 26:4 ... GOD is the eternal *R*.
Matt 7:24 ... builds a house on solid *r*.
Matt 16:18 ... upon this *r* I will build
Rom 9:33 ... stumble, a *r* that makes them
1 Cor 10:4 ... and that *r* was Christ.
1 Pet 2:8 ... stumble, the *r* that makes

ROD, RODS (n) *a straight, slender stick used as a walking stick, a club or weapon, a shepherd's crook, a paddling stick, a royal scepter, or a measuring stick; figurative of divine authority*
see also STAFF
2 Sam 7:14 ... him with the *r*, like any
Ps 2:9 ... will break them with an iron *r*
Ps 23:4 ... Your *r* and your staff
Prov 13:24 ... spare the *r* of discipline
Prov 23:13 ... The *r* of punishment won't
2 Cor 11:25 ... times I was beaten with *r-s*.
Rev 2:27 ... the nations with an iron *r*
Rev 12:5 ... rule all nations with an iron *r*.
Rev 19:15 ... rule them with an iron *r*.

ROOSTER (n) *an adult male domestic chicken*
Matt 26:34 ... before the *r* crows, you will

ROOT, ROOTS (n) *the part of a plant usually found underground; something that is an origin or source (as of a condition or quality)*
Isa 11:1 ... bearing fruit from the old *r*.
Isa 53:2 ... green shoot, like a *r* in dry
Matt 3:10 ... to sever the *r-s* of the trees.
Matt 13:21 ... don't have deep *r-s*, they
Eph 3:17 ... Your *r-s* will grow down
1 Tim 6:10 ... money is the *r* of all kinds
Jude 1:12 ... have been pulled up by the *r-s*.

RUDDER (n) *an underwater blade that steers a boat or ship*
Jas 3:4 ... a small *r* makes a huge ship

RUIN (n) *physical, moral, economic, or social collapse*
Eccl 4:5 ... idle hands, leading them to *r*.
1 Tim 6:9 ... them into *r* and destruction.

RUIN, RUINED, RUINING, RUINS (v) *to damage irreparably; to subject to frustration, failure, or disaster*
Prov 19:3 ... People *r* their lives by
Prov 19:18 ... you will *r* their lives.
Prov 22:23 ... he will *r* anyone who *r-s*
Isa 3:14 ... You have *r-ed* Israel,
Matt 9:17 ... the wine and *r-ing* the skins.
2 Tim 2:14 ... they can *r* those who hear

RULE, RULES (n) *a prescribed guide for conduct or action*
Isa 29:13 ... but man-made *r-s* learned by
2 Tim 2:5 ... unless they follow the *r-s*.
Heb 13:9 ... not from *r-s* about food,

RULE, RULED, RULES (v) *to exert control, direction, or influence on; to exercise authority or power over*
Gen 3:16 ... but he will *r* over you.
Ps 2:4 ... But the one who *r-s* in heaven
Ps 11:4 ... LORD still *r-s* from heaven.
Ps 55:19 ... God, who has *r-d* forever,
Ps 66:7 ... great power he *r-s* forever.
Ps 89:9 ... You *r* the oceans.
Ps 103:19 ... there he *r-s* over everything.
Prov 17:2 ... wise servant will *r* over the
Isa 9:7 ... He will *r* with fairness
Isa 40:10 ... He will *r* with a powerful
Jer 23:5 ... a King who *r-s* with wisdom.
Zech 6:13 ... honor and will *r* as king
Rom 5:21 ... as sin *r-d* over all people
Rom 15:12 ... come, and he will *r* over
Col 3:15 ... comes from Christ *r* in your
Rev 19:15 ... He will *r* them with

RULER, RULERS (n) *person with authority; tribal chief; prince or king; city magistrate; powerful spiritual beings; God himself*
Judg 8:22 ... to Gideon, "Be our *r*!
1 Sam 10:1 ... to be the *r* over Israel,
Prov 19:6 ... favors from a *r*; everyone is
Prov 23:1 ... with a *r*, pay attention to
Jer 30:21 ... have their own *r* again,
Dan 7:27 ... all *r-s* will serve and obey him.
Dan 9:25 ... until a *r*—the Anointed One—
Mic 5:2 ... a *r* of Israel whose origins
Matt 2:6 ... for a *r* will come from
Matt 20:25 ... that the *r-s* in this world
John 12:31 ... when Satan, the *r* of this
1 Cor 2:6 ... or to the *r-s* of this world,
Eph 1:21 ... far above any *r* or authority
Eph 3:10 ... the unseen *r-s* and authorities
Eph 6:12 ... but against evil *r-s* and
Col 1:16 ... as thrones, kingdoms, *r-s*, and
Col 2:15 ... disarmed the spiritual *r-s* and
Rev 1:5 ... and the *r* of all the kings

RUMORS (n) *a statement or report without known authority for its truth*
Exod 23:1 ... must not pass along false *r*.
Prov 18:8 ... *R* are dainty morsels that
Jer 51:46 ... For *r* will keep coming year

RUN, RUNNING (v) *to go faster than a walk; to flee*
Ps 19:5 ... athlete eager to *r* the race.
Prov 4:12 ... when you *r*, you won't
Isa 40:31 ... will *r* and not grow weary.
1 Cor 9:26 ... So I *r* with purpose in
Gal 2:2 ... and I was *r-ning* the race for
Gal 5:7 ... You were *r-ning* the race so
Phil 2:16 ... that I did not *r* the race in
1 Tim 6:11 ... so *r* from all these evil
2 Tim 2:22 ... *R* from anything that
Heb 12:1 ... let us *r* with endurance

RUNNER (n) *a messenger*
Hab 2:2 ... so that a *r* can carry

RUST (n) *the reddish brittle coating formed on iron*
Matt 6:19 ... them and *r* destroys them,

S

SABAOTH (KJV)
Rom 9:29 ... the LORD of *Heaven's Armies*
Jas 5:4 ... the LORD of *Heaven's Armies*

SABBATH, SABBATHS (n) *cessation of activity; a holy day set aside to honor God through rest and worship*
see also REST
Exod 20:8 ... to observe the *S* day by
Exod 31:14 ... must keep the *S* day, for it

Lev 25:2 ... must observe a **S** rest before
Deut 5:12 ... Observe the **S** day by
2 Chr 2:4 ... and evening, on the **S-s**,
Isa 56:2 ... who honor my **S** days of rest
Isa 56:6 ... do not desecrate the **S** day
Isa 58:13 ... Honor the **S** in everything
Matt 12:1 ... some grainfields on the **S**.
Luke 13:10 ... One **S** day as Jesus was
Col 2:16 ... new moon ceremonies or **S-s**.

SACRIFICE, SACRIFICES (n) *worship or atonement offering; something given up or lost*
Exod 12:27 ... It is the Passover **s** to the
1 Sam 15:22 ... Obedience is better than **s**,
Ps 40:6 ... no delight in **s-s** or offerings.
Ps 51:16 ... do not desire a **s**, or I would
Ps 51:17 ... The **s** you desire is
Ps 107:22 ... offer **s-s** of thanksgiving
Prov 15:8 ... LORD detests the **s** of
Hos 6:6 ... to show love, not offer **s-s**.
Matt 9:13 ... to show mercy, not offer **s-s**.
Rom 3:25 ... Jesus as the **s** for sin.
Rom 8:3 ... Son as a **s** for our sins.
Rom 12:1 ... a living and holy **s**—the
Eph 5:2 ... himself as a **s** for us,
Heb 5:3 ... he must offer **s-s** for his own
Heb 7:27 ... need to offer **s-s** every day.
Heb 9:28 ... time as a **s** to take away
Heb 10:5 ... did not want animal **s-s** or sin
Heb 10:10 ... holy by the **s** of the body of
Heb 13:15 ... Jesus a continual **s** of praise
Heb 13:16 ... These are the **s-s** that please
1 Pet 2:5 ... offer spiritual **s-s** that please
1 Jn 2:2 ... himself is the **s** that atones
1 Jn 4:10 ... his Son as a **s** to take away

SACRIFICE, SACRIFICED, SACRIFICES (v) *to suffer loss of, give up, renounce, injure, kill, or destroy, especially for an ideal, belief, or end*
Gen 22:2 ... Go and **s** him as a
John 10:11 ... good shepherd **s-s** his life
John 10:15 ... I **s** my life for the sheep.
1 Cor 5:7 ... Lamb, has been **s-d** for us.
1 Cor 13:3 ... poor and even **s-d** my body,

SAFE (adj) *free from harm or risk; secure from threat of danger, harm, or loss*
Deut 29:19 ... I am **s**, even though I am
1 Sam 30:23 ... has kept us **s** and helped
Ps 4:8 ... O LORD, will keep me **s**.
Ps 28:8 ... He is a **s** fortress for his
Prov 2:11 ... will keep you **s**.
Prov 4:26 ... stay on the **s** path.
Prov 18:10 ... run to him and are **s**.
Prov 28:26 ... who walks in wisdom is **s**.
John 17:15 ... keep them **s** from the evil

SAFETY (n) *the condition of being safe from undergoing or causing hurt, injury, or loss*
Deut 33:12 ... and live in **s** beside him.
2 Sam 23:5 ... ensure my **s** and success.
Ps 16:9 ... My body rests in **s**.
Ps 59:16 ... my refuge, a place of **s**
Prov 11:14 ... is **s** in having many advisers.
Prov 29:25 ... trusting the LORD means **s**.
Hos 2:18 ... live unafraid in peace and **s**.

SAINTS (KJV)
Ps 34:9 ... you his *godly people*, for
Ps 97:10 ... the lives of his *godly people*
Dan 7:18 ... *holy people* of the Most High
Rom 8:27 ... Spirit pleads for *us believers*
1 Cor 6:2 ... *we believers* will judge the

SALT (n) *the mineral sodium chloride used mainly for seasoning and as a preservative*
Gen 19:26 ... she turned into a pillar of **s**.
Matt 5:13 ... You are the **s** of the earth.

SALVATION (n) *deliverance from the power and effects of sin, danger, or difficulty by God's intervention*
see also SAVE
2 Sam 22:47 ... Rock of my **s**, be exalted!
2 Chr 6:41 ... be clothed with **s**; may your
Ps 18:46 ... God of my **s** be exalted!
Ps 27:1 ... light and my **s**—so why should
Ps 40:16 ... love your **s** repeatedly shout,
Ps 51:12 ... joy of your **s**, and make me
Ps 62:2 ... rock and my **s**, my fortress
Ps 69:13 ... my prayer with your sure **s**.
Ps 74:12 ... ages past, bringing **s** to
Ps 85:4 ... us again, O God of our **s**.
Ps 89:26 ... and the Rock of my **s**.
Ps 91:16 ... long life and give them my **s**.
Ps 95:1 ... joyfully to the Rock of our **s**.
Isa 25:9 ... rejoice in the **s** he brings!
Isa 26:18 ... We have not given **s** to the
Isa 33:6 ... rich store of eternal **s**, wisdom,
Isa 45:8 ... wide so **s** and righteousness
Isa 45:22 ... the world look to me for **s**!
Isa 49:6 ... will bring my **s** to the ends
Isa 51:6 ... but my **s** lasts forever.
Isa 52:7 ... of peace and **s**, the news that
Isa 59:17 ... the helmet of **s** on his head.
Isa 62:1 ... dawn, and her **s** blazes like
Lam 3:26 ... wait quietly for **s** from the
Jon 2:9 ... For my **s** comes from the
Luke 1:77 ... to find **s** through forgiveness
Luke 2:30 ... I have seen your **s**,
Luke 3:6 ... will see the **s** sent from
Luke 21:28 ... up, for your **s** is near!
John 4:22 ... him, for **s** comes through the
Acts 13:26 ... this message of **s** has been
Acts 13:47 ... Gentiles, to bring **s** to the
Acts 28:28 ... know that this **s** from God
Rom 11:11 ... so God made **s** available to
Rom 13:11 ... for our **s** is nearer now
2 Cor 6:2 ... the day of **s**, I helped you.
2 Cor 7:10 ... from sin and results in **s**.
Eph 6:17 ... Put on **s** as your helmet,
Phil 2:12 ... show the results of your **s**,
2 Thes 2:13 ... to experience **s**—a **s**
Titus 2:11 ... bringing **s** to all people.
Heb 2:3 ... if we ignore this great **s** that
Heb 5:9 ... source of eternal **s** for all
Heb 9:28 ... but to bring **s** to all who
1 Pet 1:9 ... will be the **s** of your souls.
1 Pet 1:13 ... in the gracious **s** that will
1 Pet 2:2 ... into a full experience of **s**.
Rev 7:10 ... a great roar, "**S** comes from

SAMARITAN (n or adj) *a native or inhabitant of Samaria*
Luke 10:33 ... a despised **S** came along,
Luke 17:16 ... man was a **S**.
John 4:5 ... he came to the **S** village of
John 4:7 ... a **S** woman came to draw

SAMUEL Judge and prophet of Israel (Heb 11:32); prophet's birth and dedication (1 Sam 1); raised by Eli in the Temple (1 Sam 2:11, 18-21); called as a prophet (1 Sam 3); served as judge over Israel (1 Sam 7:15); warned Israel of the tyranny of kingship (1 Sam 8:10-18); anointed Saul (1 Sam 10:1); rejected Saul (1 Sam 15:23); anointed David (1 Sam 16:13); protected David from Saul (1 Sam 19:18-24); died (1 Sam 25:1); ghost of Samuel rebuked Saul (1 Sam 28:14-19).

SANCTIFY, SANCTIFIED (KJV)
Gen 2:3 ... and *declared it holy*
Exod 31:13 ... LORD, who *makes you holy*
Deut 5:12 ... Sabbath day by *keeping it holy*
John 17:19 ... myself as a *holy sacrifice*
Heb 10:10 ... for us to *be made holy* by

SANCTUARY (n) *a holy place set apart for worship of God or refuge from danger*
see also TABERNACLE, TEMPLE
Exod 25:8 ... build me a holy **s** so I can
Lev 19:30 ... show reverence toward my **s**.
Ps 27:5 ... he will hide me in his **s**.
Ps 63:2 ... you in your **s** and gazed upon
Ps 68:35 ... God is awesome in his **s**.
Ps 150:1 ... Praise God in his **s**; praise
Heb 6:19 ... curtain into God's inner **s**.

SAND (n) *fine grains of rock that are worn away by wind and rain*
Gen 22:17 ... in the sky and the **s** on
Matt 7:26 ... who builds a house on **s**.

SANDAL, SANDALS (n) *a shoe consisting of a sole strapped to the foot*
Exod 3:5 ... Take off your **s-s**, for you are
Exod 12:11 ... wear your **s-s**, and carry
Deut 25:9 ... elders, pull his **s** from his
Josh 5:15 ... Take off your **s-s**, for the
Ruth 4:7 ... to remove his **s** and hand it
Matt 3:11 ... his slave and carry his **s-s**.

SANG (v) *to produce musical tones by means of the voice*
see also SING(ING)
Exod 15:1 ... people of Israel **s** this
Exod 15:21 ... And Miriam **s** this song:
Num 21:17 ... the Israelites **s** this song:
Judg 5:1 ... son of Abinoam **s** this song:
2 Sam 22:1 ... David **s** this song to
Ezra 3:11 ... and thanks, they **s** this song
Job 38:7 ... morning stars **s** together and
Ps 106:12 ... Then they **s** his praise.
Matt 26:30 ... Then they **s** a hymn
Rev 5:9 ... And they **s** a new song
Rev 5:13 ... They **s**: "Blessing and
Rev 14:3 ... great choir **s** a wonderful

SARAH (SARAI) Wife of Abraham (Abram) (Gen 11:30-31); was infertile (Gen 11:30; Rom 4:19) and very beautiful (Gen 12:11); with Abraham, deceived Pharaoh (Gen 12:10-20); dealings with Hagar and Ishmael (Gen 16); name changed (Gen 17:15); Isaac promised (Gen 18:10-15; Rom 9:9); example of faith (Heb 11:11); with Abraham, deceived Abimelech (Gen 20); Isaac born (Gen 21:1-7); Hagar and Ishmael sent away (Gen 21:8-21); died and was buried (Gen 23); Paul's analogy using Sarah and Hagar (Gal 4:25-26).

SATAN (n) *"adversary" of God and man; the personal name of the devil*
see also DEVIL
Job 1:6 ... and the Accuser, **S**, came with
Zech 3:2 ... your accusations, **S**. Yes,
Matt 12:26 ... if **S** is casting out **S**, he
Matt 16:23 ... Get away from me, **S**!
Mark 4:15 ... only to have **S** come at once
Luke 10:18 ... told them, "I saw **S** fall from
Luke 22:3 ... Then **S** entered into Judas
Rom 16:20 ... soon crush **S** under your
1 Cor 5:5 ... him over to **S** so that his
2 Cor 11:14 ... Even **S** disguises himself as
2 Cor 12:7 ... from **S** to torment
1 Tim 1:20 ... them over to **S** so they might
Rev 12:9 ... the devil, or **S**, the one

Rev 20:2 … is the devil, **S**—and bound
Rev 20:7 … come to an end, **S** will be let

SAVE, SAVED, SAVES, SAVING (v) *to rescue or deliver from danger or harm; to deliver from sin; to preserve or guard from injury, destruction, or loss; to maintain or preserve*
see also PRESERVE, RESCUE, SALVATION
2 Sam 22:3 … the power that **s-s** me,
1 Chr 16:23 … good news that he **s-s**
Ps 7:10 … is my shield, **s-ing** those whose
Ps 18:48 … you **s** me from violent
Ps 22:8 … let the LORD **s** him!
Ps 25:5 … you are the God who **s-s** me.
Ps 33:16 … army cannot **s** a king, nor
Ps 34:6 … LORD listened; he **s-d** me
Ps 44:6 … not count on my sword to **s**
Ps 68:20 … Our God is a God who **s-s!**
Ps 109:31 … the needy, ready to **s** them
Ps 116:6 … death, and he **s-d** me.
Prov 2:16 … Wisdom will **s** you from
Prov 10:2 … right living can **s** your
Isa 25:9 … trusted in him, and he **s-d** us!
Isa 30:15 … resting in me will you be **s-d.**
Isa 35:4 … He is coming to **s** you.
Isa 59:1 … arm is not too weak to **s**
Isa 63:1 … who has the power to **s!**
Jer 4:14 … your heart that you may be **s-d.**
Jer 17:14 … if you **s** me, I will
Jer 51:9 … nothing can **s** her now.
Dan 3:17 … we serve is able to **s** us.
Joel 2:32 … name of the LORD will be **s-d,**
Mic 7:7 … wait confidently for God to **s**
Zeph 1:18 … gold will not **s** you
Matt 1:21 … he will **s** his people
Matt 16:25 … my sake, you will **s** it.
Matt 24:13 … to the end will be **s-d.**
Luke 17:33 … life go, you will **s** it.
Luke 19:10 … seek and **s** those who are
John 10:9 … in through me will be **s-d.**
John 12:47 … I have come to **s** the world
Acts 2:21 … name of the LORD will be **s-d.**
Acts 4:12 … by which we must be **s-d.**
Acts 15:11 … we are all **s-d** the same way,
Acts 16:30 … what must I do to be **s-d?**
Rom 1:16 … God at work, **s-ing** everyone
Rom 5:9 … he will certainly **s** us from
Rom 10:9 … the dead, you will be **s-d.**
Rom 10:13 … of the LORD will be **s-d.**
1 Cor 1:18 … we who are being **s-d** know
1 Cor 5:5 … himself will be **s-d** on the
1 Cor 7:16 … wives might be **s-d** because
1 Cor 10:33 … so that many may be **s-d.**
1 Cor 15:2 … this Good News that **s-s**
Eph 1:13 … Good News that God **s-s** you.
1 Thes 5:9 … God chose to **s** us through
1 Tim 1:15 … the world to **s** sinners
1 Tim 2:4 … wants everyone to be **s-d** and
1 Tim 2:15 … women will be **s-d** through
2 Tim 1:9 … For God **s-d** us and called
Titus 3:5 … he **s-d** us, not because of the
Heb 7:25 … and forever, to **s** those who
Jas 5:20 … will **s** that person from death
2 Pet 3:15 … gives people time to be **s-d.**

SAVING (adj) *of or relating to delivering or rescuing*
Ps 40:10 … faithfulness and **s** power.
Ps 67:2 … the earth, your **s** power
Ps 69:29 … God, by your **s** power.
Ps 71:15 … proclaim your **s** power,
Ps 98:1 … has shown his **s** power!

SAVIOR (n) *one who delivers from trouble, sin, or judgment*
2 Sam 22:2 … my fortress, and my **s;**

Ps 38:22 … help me, O Lord my **s.**
Ps 40:17 … You are my helper and my **s.**
Ps 106:21 … They forgot God, their **s,**
Isa 43:11 … and there is no other **S.**
Isa 45:21 … a righteous God and **S.**
Isa 49:26 … the LORD, am your **S** and
Isa 62:11 … Look, your **S** is coming.
Jer 14:8 … Hope of Israel, our **S**
Hos 13:4 … for there is no other **s.**
Zeph 3:17 … He is a mighty **s.**
Luke 1:47 … rejoices in God my **S!**
Luke 1:69 … He has sent us a mighty **S**
John 4:42 … he is indeed the **S** of the
Acts 5:31 … right hand as Prince and **S.**
Acts 13:23 … God's promised **S** of Israel!
Eph 5:23 … He is the **S** of his body,
1 Tim 2:3 … good and pleases God our **S,**
1 Tim 4:10 … who is the **S** of all people
Titus 2:10 … about God our **S** attractive
Titus 3:4 … When God our **S** revealed his
2 Pet 3:2 … Lord and **S** commanded
1 Jn 4:14 … Son to be the **S** of the world.

SCAPEGOAT (n) *a goat upon whose head the sins of the people are symbolically placed, after which he is sent into the wilderness on the Day of Atonement*
Lev 16:10 … other goat, the **s** chosen by

SCARLET (adj) *of the color of any various bright reds*
Josh 2:21 … leaving the **s** rope hanging
Isa 1:18 … sins are like **s,** I will make
Matt 27:28 … and put a **s** robe on him.

SCATTER, SCATTERED (v) *to separate and go in various directions; to disperse*
Deut 4:27 … the LORD will **s** you
Neh 1:8 … to me, I will **s** you among
Isa 11:12 … will gather the **s-ed** people
Jer 9:16 … I will **s** them around
Jer 30:11 … where I have **s-ed** you, but I
Jer 31:10 … LORD, who **s-ed** his people,
Ezek 34:21 … flock until you **s-ed** them to
Zech 2:6 … for I have **s-ed** you to the four
Zech 10:9 … Though I have **s-ed** them like
Zech 13:7 … sheep will be **s-ed,** and I will
Matt 26:31 … of the flock will be **s-ed.**
John 11:52 … children of God **s-ed** around
Acts 8:4 … were **s-ed** preached the Good
Jas 1:1 … Jewish believers **s-ed** abroad.

SCEPTER (n) *the official staff of a ruler, symbolizing his authority and power*
Gen 49:10 … The **s** will not depart from
Num 24:17 … a **s** will emerge from Israel.
Heb 1:8 … rule with a **s** of justice.

SCOFF (v) *to show contempt by derisive acts or language; to mock*
Lam 2:15 … They **s** and insult
1 Thes 5:20 … Do not **s** at prophecies,
2 Pet 2:12 … They **s** at things they do not
Jude 1:8 … defy authority, and **s** at

SCORN (n) *open dislike, disrespect, or derision often mixed with indignation*
Ps 109:25 … they shake their heads in **s.**
Isa 51:7 … not be afraid of people's **s,**

SCORN, SCORNED (v) *to reject or dismiss as contemptible or unworthy*
Ps 22:6 … I am **s-ed** and despised by all!
Ps 119:22 … Don't let them **s** and insult
Prov 9:12 … If you **s** wisdom, you will
Jer 6:10 … They **s** the word of the LORD.

SCRIPTURE, SCRIPTURES (n) *the law; the writings of Moses; the entire collection of sacred books*
Matt 21:16 … you ever read the **S-s?**
Matt 22:29 … you don't know the **S-s,**
Luke 24:27 … from all the **S-s** the things
Luke 24:45 … to understand the **S-s.**
John 2:22 … believed both the **S-s** and
John 5:39 … You search the **S-s** because
John 7:42 … the **S-s** clearly state that
John 10:35 … know that the **S-s** cannot
Acts 8:32 … The passage of **S** he had
1 Cor 4:6 … quoted from the **S-s,** you won't
1 Tim 4:13 … focus on reading the **S-s** to
2 Tim 3:16 … All **S** is inspired by God
Heb 10:7 … written about me in the **S-s.**
2 Pet 1:20 … no prophecy in **S** ever came
2 Pet 3:16 … do with other parts of **S.**

SCROLL (n) *a roll (as of papyrus, leather, or parchment) for writing a document*
Isa 34:4 … disappear like a rolled-up **s.**
Ezek 3:1 … giving you—eat this **s!**
Rev 6:14 … sky was rolled up like a **s,**
Rev 10:8 … take the open **s** from the hand

SEA, SEAS (n) *a great body of salt water that covers much of the earth; a large basin used in the Temple*
Exod 14:16 … middle of the **s** on dry
Deut 30:13 … not kept beyond the **s,**
1 Kgs 7:23 … rim to rim, called the **S.**
Job 11:9 … and wider than the **s.**
Ps 93:4 … violent raging of the **s-s,**
Ps 95:5 … The **s** belongs to him,
Eccl 11:1 … your grain across the **s-s,**
Isa 57:20 … like the restless **s,** which
Jon 1:4 … wind over the **s,** causing a
Hab 2:14 … waters fill the **s,** the earth
Matt 18:6 … in the depths of the **s.**
Jas 1:6 … wave of the **s** that is blown
Jude 1:13 … waves of the **s,** churning up
Rev 10:2 … right foot on the **s** and
Rev 13:1 … rising up out of the **s.**
Rev 20:13 … The **s** gave up its dead,
Rev 21:1 … And the **s** was also gone.

SEARCH, SEARCHES (v) *to investigate or examine thoroughly in an effort to find or verify something*
Ps 34:14 … **S** for peace, and work
Ps 139:23 … **S** me, O God, and know
Eccl 3:6 … A time to **s** and a time to
Jer 17:10 … I, the LORD, **s** all hearts
1 Cor 2:10 … Spirit **s-es** out everything
1 Pet 3:11 … **S** for peace, and work

SEAT, SEATS (n) *a chair, stool, or bench intended to be sat in or on*
Luke 11:43 … to sit in the **s** of honor
Luke 14:9 … to take whatever **s** is left

SEATED (v) *to put into a sitting position; to take one's seat or place*
Matt 26:64 … Son of Man **s** in the place
Luke 22:69 … of Man will be **s** in the place
Eph 1:20 … the dead and **s** him in the
Eph 2:6 … with Christ and **s** us with him
Heb 12:2 … Now he is **s** in the place of
Rev 14:14 … a white cloud, and **s** on the

SECRET (adj) *kept from knowledge or view; hidden*
Ps 90:8 … before you—our **s** sins—
Jer 23:24 … from me in a **s** place?
Matt 10:26 … all that is **s** will be
Rom 2:16 … judge everyone's **s** life.

Rom 16:25 ... a plan kept **s** from the
1 Cor 13:2 ... all of God's **s** plans
1 Cor 14:25 ... their **s** thoughts will be
Col 1:26 ... was kept **s** for centuries and

SECRET, SECRETS (n) *something kept hidden or unexplained; something kept from the knowledge of others or shared only confidentially with a few*
see also MYSTERY
Deut 29:29 ... God has **s-s** known to no
Judg 16:15 ... don't share your **s-s** with
Ps 44:21 ... he knows the **s-s** of every
Prov 11:13 ... goes around telling **s-s**,
Dan 2:28 ... heaven who reveals **s-s**, and
Dan 2:29 ... who reveals **s-s** has shown
Mark 4:11 ... to understand the **s**
Mark 4:22 ... and every **s** will be brought
Luke 8:10 ... to understand the **s-s** of
1 Cor 15:51 ... reveal to you a wonderful **s.**
Phil 4:12 ... have learned the **s** of living
Col 1:27 ... the **s:** Christ lives in you.

SEE, SEEING, SEES (v) *to perceive by the eye; to understand or recognize; to come to know*
Ps 34:8 ... Taste and **s** that the
Ps 36:2 ... they cannot **s** how wicked
Ps 90:8 ... sins—and you **s** them
Ps 119:82 ... straining to **s** your promises
Prov 5:21 ... For the LORD **s-s** clearly
Prov 13:19 ... pleasant to **s** dreams come
Eccl 3:11 ... people cannot **s** the whole
Matt 6:18 ... Father, who **s** everything,
John 12:45 ... you are **s-ing** the one who
Rom 1:20 ... can clearly **s** his invisible
Rom 7:13 ... So we can **s** how terrible sin
1 Cor 13:12 ... we will **s** everything with
2 Cor 4:18 ... things we cannot **s** will last
2 Cor 5:7 ... by believing and not by **s-ing.**
2 Cor 8:21 ... everyone else to **s** that we
Phil 4:5 ... Let everyone **s** that you are
Col 1:16 ... things we can't **s**—such as
Rev 1:7 ... everyone will **s** him—even

SEED, SEEDS (n) *the grains of plants used for sowing*
Gen 1:11 ... These **s-s** will then produce
Prov 11:30 ... The **s-s** of good deeds
Matt 13:3 ... went out to plant some **s-s.**
Matt 13:31 ... like a mustard **s** planted in
Matt 17:20 ... as a mustard **s**, you could say
Mark 4:15 ... The **s** that fell on
Luke 8:12 ... The **s-s** that fell on
1 Cor 3:6 ... I planted the **s** in your
2 Cor 9:6 ... few **s-s** will get a small
2 Cor 9:10 ... one who provides **s** for the

SEEK, SEEKING, SEEKS (v) *to go in search of; to try to acquire or gain*
2 Chr 7:14 ... pray and **s** my face and
2 Chr 15:2 ... Whenever you **s** him,
Prov 3:6 ... **S** his will in all you do,
Prov 25:27 ... not good to **s** honors
Prov 29:26 ... Many **s** the ruler's favor,
Isa 55:6 ... **S** the LORD while you can
Hos 10:12 ... time to **s** the LORD,
Zeph 2:3 ... **S** the LORD, all who are
Matt 6:33 ... **S** the Kingdom of God above
Matt 7:7 ... Keep on **s-ing,** and you
Matt 7:8 ... Everyone who **s-s**, finds.
Luke 12:31 ... **S** the Kingdom of God
Luke 19:10 ... Son of Man came to **s** and
Rom 3:11 ... no one is **s-ing** God.
1 Cor 7:27 ... have a wife, do not **s** to get
Heb 11:6 ... those who sincerely **s** him.

SELF-CONTROL (n) *restraint exercised over one's own impulses, emotions, or desires*
Prov 5:23 ... He will die for lack of **s;**
Prov 16:32 ... better to have **s** than to
Acts 24:25 ... righteousness and **s** and the
Gal 5:23 ... gentleness, and **s.** There is no
1 Tim 3:2 ... must exercise **s,** live wisely,
1 Tim 3:11 ... They must exercise **s** and be
Titus 2:2 ... older men to exercise **s,**
1 Pet 1:13 ... for action and exercise **s.**
2 Pet 1:6 ... and knowledge with **s,** and

SELF-DISCIPLINE (n) *correction or regulation of oneself for the sake of improvement*
2 Tim 1:7 ... but of power, love, and **s.**

SELFISH (adj) *seeking or concentrating on one's own advantage, pleasure, or well-being without regard for others*
Gal 5:20 ... of anger, **s** ambition,
Phil 1:17 ... They preach with **s** ambition,
Jas 3:14 ... and there is **s** ambition in
Jas 3:16 ... is jealousy and **s** ambition,

SELL, SELLING (v) *to give up (property) to another for something of value (as money)*
Prov 23:23 ... truth and never **s** it;
Prov 31:24 ... and sashes to **s** to the
Mark 10:21 ... and **s** all your possessions
Luke 17:28 ... buying and **s-ing,** farming and
Rev 13:17 ... could buy or **s** anything

SEND, SENDING (v) *to direct, order, or request to go*
see also SENT
Isa 6:8 ... Here I am. **S** me.
Isa 55:11 ... with my word. I **s** it out,
Mal 3:1 ... I am **s-ing** my messenger,
Matt 9:38 ... ask him to **s** more workers
Mark 1:2 ... I am **s-ing** my messenger
1 Cor 1:17 ... For Christ didn't **s** me to

SENSE (n) *sound and prudent judgment based on a simple perception of the situation or facts; intelligence*
Prov 3:21 ... common **s** and discernment.
Prov 8:14 ... Common **s** and success
Prov 12:11 ... chases fantasies has no **s.**
Prov 15:21 ... brings joy to those with no **s;**
Prov 18:1 ... they lash out at common **s.**
Prov 24:30 ... of one with no common **s.**

SENSIBLE (adj) *having, containing, or indicative of good sense or reason; rational, reasonable*
Prov 10:23 ... brings pleasure to the **s.**
Prov 11:12 ... a **s** person keeps quiet.
Prov 15:21 ... **s** person stays on the right
Matt 24:45 ... A faithful, **s** servant is one

SENT (v) *to direct, order, or request to go*
see also SEND
Exod 3:14 ... I AM has **s** me
Matt 10:40 ... the Father who **s** me.
Luke 10:16 ... God, who **s** me.
John 3:17 ... God **s** his Son into the
John 20:21 ... As the Father has **s** me, so
Rom 8:3 ... He **s** his own Son in a
Rom 10:15 ... them without being **s?**
Gal 4:4 ... time came, God **s** his Son,

SEPARATE, SEPARATED, SEPARATES (v) *to set or keep apart; to sort*
Prov 17:9 ... on it **s-s** close friends.
Matt 25:32 ... a shepherd **s-s** the sheep
Rom 8:35 ... Can anything ever **s** us

Eph 2:14 ... of hostility that **s-d** us.
Col 1:21 ... his enemies, **s-d** from him

SERAPHIM (n) *six-winged angels standing in God's presence*
Isa 6:2 ... were mighty **s,** each having
Isa 6:6 ... Then one of the **s** flew to me

SERPENT (n) *a snake or crawling reptile often associated with temptation, sin, and evil; Satan*
Gen 3:1 ... The **s** was the shrewdest of
Isa 27:1 ... **s,** the coiling, writhing **s.**
2 Cor 11:3 ... the cunning ways of the **s.**
Rev 12:9 ... the ancient **s** called the devil,
Rev 20:2 ... that old **s,** who is the devil,

SERVANT, SERVANTS (n) *one who performs tasks under the direction of another*
see also SLAVE(S)
Exod 14:31 ... LORD and in his **s** Moses.
Lev 25:55 ... They are my **s-s,** whom I
1 Sam 3:10 ... Speak, your **s** is listening.
2 Kgs 17:13 ... my **s-s** the prophets.
Job 1:8 ... Have you noticed my **s** Job?
Ps 19:13 ... Keep your **s** from deliberate
Ps 31:16 ... your favor shine on your **s.**
Ps 89:3 ... with David, my chosen **s.**
Ps 104:4 ... flames of fire are your **s-s.**
Prov 14:35 ... king rejoices in wise **s-s**
Prov 17:2 ... A wise **s** will rule
Prov 22:7 ... so the borrower is **s** to the
Prov 31:15 ... work for her **s** girls.
Eccl 7:21 ... may hear your **s** curse you.
Eccl 10:7 ... seen **s-s** riding horseback
Isa 53:11 ... my righteous **s** will make it
Isa 65:8 ... I still have true **s-s** there.
Zech 3:8 ... to bring my **s,** the Branch.
Mal 1:6 ... father, and a **s** respects his
Matt 20:26 ... among you must be your **s,**
Matt 24:45 ... faithful, sensible **s** is one
Luke 1:48 ... of his lowly **s** girl, and
Luke 17:10 ... We are unworthy **s-s** who
Luke 22:26 ... leader should be like a **s.**
John 12:26 ... because my **s-s** must be
Rom 13:4 ... authorities are God's **s-s,**
1 Cor 3:5 ... are only God's **s-s** through
Col 1:23 ... God's **s** to proclaim it.
1 Tim 4:6 ... be a worthy **s** of Christ
Heb 1:7 ... his **s-s** like flames of fire.
Heb 1:14 ... angels are only **s-s**—spirits

SERVE, SERVED, SERVES, SERVING (v) *to meet the needs of and subject one's will to that of another*
Deut 10:12 ... love him and **s** him with
Deut 11:13 ... your God and **s** him with
Deut 28:47 ... If you do not **s** the LORD
Deut 30:17 ... drawn away to **s** and
Josh 24:15 ... family, we will **s** the LORD.
2 Chr 12:8 ... between **s-ing** me and
Ps 34:22 ... redeem those who **s** him.
Ps 101:6 ... be allowed to **s** me.
Ps 103:21 ... of angels who **s** him and do
Isa 38:3 ... have **s-d** you single-mindedly
Dan 3:17 ... the God whom we **s** is able to
Matt 4:10 ... your God and **s** only him.
Matt 6:24 ... No one can **s** two masters.
Matt 20:28 ... not to be **s-d** but to **s**
Luke 22:27 ... among you as one who **s-s.**
John 12:2 ... Martha **s-d,** and Lazarus was
John 12:26 ... honor anyone who **s-s** me.
Acts 17:25 ... hands can't **s** his needs—
Rom 1:25 ... worshiped and **s-d** the things
Rom 12:7 ... your gift is **s-ing** others, **s**
Rom 12:11 ... work hard and **s** the Lord

Rom 13:6 ... They are *s-ing* God in what
Rom 14:18 ... If you *s* Christ with
Rom 16:18 ... people are not *s-ing* Christ
1 Cor 16:18 ... to all who *s* so well.
Gal 5:13 ... your freedom to *s* one another
Col 3:24 ... Master you are *s-ing* is Christ.
1 Tim 5:10 ... kind to strangers and *s-d* other

SEVEN (adj) *of or relating to the number 7*
Josh 6:4 ... around the town *s* times, with
Prov 6:16 ... LORD hates—no, *s* things
Prov 24:16 ... godly may trip *s* times,
Isa 4:1 ... so few men will be left that *s*
Luke 11:26 ... spirit finds *s* other spirits
Rev 1:4 ... John to the *s* churches in the
Rev 6:1 ... first of the *s* seals on the
Rev 8:2 ... were given *s* trumpets.
Rev 10:4 ... what the *s* thunders said,
Rev 15:7 ... handed each of the *s* angels

SEXUAL (adj) *of, relating to, or associated with sex or the sexes; having or involving sex*
Exod 22:19 ... who has *s* relations with
Lev 18:6 ... never have *s* relations with
Num 25:1 ... by having *s* relations with
Matt 1:25 ... did not have *s* relations with
Matt 15:19 ... adultery, all *s* immorality,
Acts 15:20 ... to idols, from *s* immorality,
1 Cor 5:1 ... about the *s* immorality going
1 Cor 5:11 ... yet indulges in *s* sin
1 Cor 6:9 ... who indulge in *s* sin, or who
1 Cor 6:18 ... Run from *s* sin! No other
1 Cor 7:1 ... to abstain from *s* relations.
1 Cor 10:8 ... not engage in *s* immorality
2 Cor 12:21 ... impurity, *s* immorality,
Eph 5:3 ... be no *s* immorality, impurity,
Col 3:5 ... to do with *s* immorality,
1 Thes 4:3 ... stay away from all *s* sin
2 Pet 2:10 ... own twisted *s* desire, and
2 Pet 2:18 ... to twisted *s* desires,
Rev 2:14 ... and by committing *s* sin.
Rev 2:20 ... teaches them to commit *s* sin

SHADOW, SHADOWS (n) *shelter from danger or observation; an imperfect and faint representation; partial darkness or obscurity within a part of space*
Ps 17:8 ... me in the *s* of your wings.
Ps 36:7 ... shelter in the *s* of your
Ps 39:6 ... are merely moving *s-s*, and
Ps 91:1 ... find rest in the *s* of the
Col 2:17 ... these rules are only *s-s* of
Heb 8:5 ... only a copy, a *s* of the real
Heb 10:1 ... was only a *s*, a dim preview

SHAME (n) *a condition or feeling of humiliating disgrace or disrepute; something that brings censure and reproach*
Lev 19:12 ... Do not bring *s* on the name
Ps 34:5 ... no shadow of *s* will darken
Prov 28:7 ... wild friends bring *s* to
Dan 12:2 ... some to *s* and everlasting
Titus 2:5 ... not bring *s* on the word
Heb 6:6 ... holding him up to public *s*.
1 Jn 2:28 ... shrink back from him in *s*.

SHAME (v) *to disgrace*
1 Cor 1:27 ... in order to *s* those who
1 Cor 11:22 ... church and *s* the poor?

SHAMEFUL (adj) *bringing shame*
Prov 18:13 ... facts is both *s* and foolish.
Hab 2:15 ... over their *s* nakedness.
Rom 1:24 ... do whatever *s* things their
Rom 1:27 ... Men did *s* things with
2 Cor 4:2 ... We reject all *s* deeds
2 Pet 2:2 ... teaching and *s* immorality.

SHARE (n) *a portion belonging to or due to*
Deut 10:9 ... Levites have no *s* of property
2 Kgs 2:9 ... inherit a double *s* of your
Matt 21:34 ... to collect his *s* of the crop.
Rev 22:19 ... remove that person's *s* in

SHARE, SHARED, SHARING (v) *to grant or give a share in; to partake of, use, experience, occupy, or enjoy with others; to have in common*
Gen 21:10 ... to *s* the inheritance
1 Sam 30:24 ... We *s* and *s* alike—
Ps 41:9 ... the one who *s-d* my food,
Luke 3:11 ... If you have food, *s* it with
Acts 2:42 ... fellowship, and to *s-ing* in
Acts 2:45 ... possessions and *s-d* the
Rom 8:17 ... we must also *s* his suffering.
Rom 11:31 ... they, too, will *s* in God's
1 Cor 10:16 ... aren't we *s-ing* in the blood
1 Cor 12:13 ... we all *s* the same Spirit.
2 Cor 1:7 ... as you *s* in our sufferings,
2 Cor 9:8 ... left over to *s* with others.
Gal 4:30 ... will not *s* the inheritance
Gal 6:6 ... teachers, *s-ing* all good things
Phil 3:10 ... suffer with him, *s-ing* in his
Col 1:12 ... has enabled you to *s* in the
1 Thes 2:8 ... much that we *s-d* with you
2 Thes 2:14 ... you can *s* in the glory
1 Tim 6:18 ... ready to *s* with others.
Heb 6:4 ... and *s-d* in the Holy Spirit,
Heb 12:10 ... we might *s* in his holiness.
Heb 13:16 ... to *s* with those in need.
Rev 3:20 ... and we will *s* a meal together

SHEARERS (n) *those who cut or clip (as hair or wool) from someone or something*
Isa 53:7 ... silent before the *s*, he did
Acts 8:32 ... silent before the *s*, he did

SHEEP (n) *a small domesticated animal, representing wealth and livelihood for many Israelites; figurative of God's people*
Gen 22:8 ... God will provide a *s* for
Num 27:17 ... not be like *s* without a
Deut 17:1 ... defective cattle, *s*, or
1 Sam 15:14 ... bleating of *s* and goats
Ps 44:22 ... being slaughtered like *s*.
Ps 78:52 ... people like a flock of *s*,
Ps 100:3 ... We are his people, the *s*
Ps 119:176 ... wandered away like a lost *s*;
Isa 53:7 ... as a *s* is silent before
Jer 50:6 ... people have been lost *s*.
Matt 7:15 ... disguised as harmless *s* but
Matt 9:36 ... like *s* without a shepherd.
Matt 10:16 ... you out as *s* among wolves.
Matt 12:11 ... a *s* that fell into a well
Matt 25:32 ... separates the *s* from the
John 10:3 ... calls his own *s* by name
John 10:7 ... I am the gate for the *s*.
John 10:15 ... sacrifice my life for the *s*.
John 21:17 ... Then feed my *s*.
1 Pet 2:25 ... were like *s* who wandered

SHELTER, SHELTERS (n) *something that covers or affords protection*
see also REFUGE
Lev 23:34 ... the Festival of *S-s* on the
Deut 16:16 ... the Festival of *S-s*.
Ps 9:9 ... LORD is a *s* for the
Ps 31:20 ... hide them in the *s* of your
Ps 36:7 ... All humanity finds *s* in the
Ps 61:4 ... safe beneath the *s* of your
Isa 4:6 ... will be a *s* from daytime heat
Isa 32:2 ... be like a *s* from the wind
Isa 58:7 ... give *s* to the homeless.
Zech 14:16 ... the Festival of *S-s*.

SHEPHERD, SHEPHERDS (n) *a person who tends sheep; figurative of political and religious leaders, especially those who care for God's people*
Gen 48:15 ... has been my *s* all my life,
Gen 49:24 ... by the *S*, the Rock of Israel.
Num 27:17 ... be like sheep without a *s*.
2 Sam 7:7 ... tribal leaders, the *s-s* of my
1 Kgs 22:17 ... like sheep without a *s*.
Ps 23:1 ... The LORD is my *s*;
Ps 28:9 ... Lead them like a *s*, and
Isa 40:11 ... feed his flock like a *s*.
Jer 23:1 ... my people—the *s-s* of my
Jer 31:10 ... as a *s* does his flock.
Ezek 34:5 ... scattered without a *s*, and
Ezek 34:8 ... you were my *s-s*, you didn't
Ezek 34:12 ... like a *s* looking for his
Zech 11:9 ... won't be your *s* any longer.
Zech 13:7 ... Strike down the *s*, and
Matt 2:6 ... will be the *s* for my people
Matt 9:36 ... like sheep without a *s*.
Matt 26:31 ... God will strike the *S*,
John 10:11 ... I am the good *s*.
Acts 20:28 ... Feed and God's flock—
Heb 13:20 ... Jesus, the great *S* of the
Jude 1:12 ... are like shameless *s-s* who care
Rev 7:17 ... on the throne will be their *S*.

SHIELD (n) *a broad piece of defensive armor carried on the arm; one who protects or defends*
2 Sam 22:3 ... He is my *s*, the power that
2 Sam 22:36 ... me your *s* of victory;
Ps 3:3 ... LORD, are a *s* around me;
Ps 5:12 ... them with your *s* of love.
Ps 7:10 ... God is my *s*, saving those
Ps 18:2 ... He is my *s*, the power that
Ps 28:7 ... LORD is my strength and *s*.
Ps 33:20 ... is our help and our *s*.
Ps 35:2 ... armor, and take up your *s*.
Ps 84:11 ... God is our sun and our *s*.
Ps 119:114 ... are my refuge and my *s*;
Ps 144:2 ... He is my *s*, and I take refuge
Prov 2:7 ... He is a *s* to those who walk
Eph 6:16 ... hold up the *s* of faith

SHINE, SHINES, SHINING (v) *to emit rays of light; to be eminent, conspicuous, or distinguished; to have a bright, glowing appearance*
Ps 37:6 ... of your cause will *s* like
Ps 50:2 ... God *s-s* in glorious radiance.
Ps 112:4 ... Light *s-s* in the darkness for
Ps 118:27 ... LORD is God, *s-ing* upon us.
Isa 60:1 ... Let your light *s* for all
Ezek 1:27 ... like a burning flame, *s-ing*
Dan 12:3 ... righteousness will *s* like
Matt 13:43 ... the righteous will *s* like
John 1:5 ... The light *s-s* in the darkness,
2 Cor 4:6 ... has made this light *s* in
Phil 2:15 ... of God, *s-ing* like bright lights

SHORT (adj) *brief; not coming up to a measure or requirement*
Ps 89:47 ... Remember how *s* my life is,
Rom 3:23 ... all fall *s* of God's glorious
1 Cor 7:29 ... time that remains is very *s*.

SHOULDERS (n) *the place on the human body where the arm is joined to the trunk*
Isa 9:6 ... government will rest on his *s*.
Luke 15:5 ... carry it home on his *s*.

SHOUT, SHOUTED, SHOUTING (v) *to utter a loud cry or call out in a loud voice*
Job 38:7 ... all the angels **s-ed** for joy?
Ps 95:1 ... Let us **s** joyfully to
Ps 100:1 ... **S** with joy to the LORD,
Isa 12:6 ... people of Jerusalem **s** his
Isa 40:3 ... someone **s-ing**, "Clear the way
Isa 40:9 ... **s** from the mountaintops!
Isa 42:2 ... He will not **s** or raise his
Zech 9:9 ... people of Zion! **S** in triumph,
Matt 3:3 ... a voice **s-ing** in the wilderness,
Matt 10:27 ... **s** from the housetops for

SHOW (n) *an impressive display*
Matt 23:5 ... Everything they do is for **s**.

SHOW, SHOWED, SHOWN, SHOWS (v) *to cause or permit to be seen; to point out; to reveal or demonstrate; to bestow*
Exod 33:18 ... Then **s** me your glorious
2 Sam 22:26 ... To the faithful you **s**
Neh 9:19 ... pillar of fire **s-ed** them the
Ps 4:6 ... Who will **s** us better times?
Ps 16:11 ... You will **s** me the way
Ps 119:132 ... Come and **s** me your
Prov 3:6 ... he will **s** you which path
Prov 24:23 ... wrong to **s** favoritism
Eccl 9:1 ... God will **s** them favor.
Isa 30:18 ... so he can **s** you his love
Hos 6:6 ... I want you to **s** love, not
Zech 7:9 ... Judge fairly, and **s** mercy
Luke 24:40 ... **s-ed** them his hands and his
Acts 2:28 ... You have **s-n** me the way
Acts 10:34 ... that God **s-s** no favoritism.
Rom 3:20 ... The law simply **s-s** us how
Rom 3:21 ... But now God has **s-n** us a way
Rom 5:8 ... God **s-ed** his great love for us
Rom 9:22 ... the right to **s** his anger
Eph 2:7 ... as **s-n** in all he has done
Jas 2:18 ... I will **s** you my faith
1 Jn 4:9 ... God **s-ed** how much he loved

SHUT (v) *to close*
Isa 6:10 ... their ears and **s** their eyes.
Dan 6:22 ... his angel to **s** the lions'
Amos 5:13 ... keep their mouths **s**, for it
Heb 11:33 ... They **s** the mouths of lions,

SICK (adj) *affected with disease or ill health; lacking vigor*
Ps 41:3 ... when they are **s** and restores
Prov 13:12 ... deferred makes the heart **s**,
Matt 9:12 ... need a doctor—**s** people do.
Matt 10:8 ... Heal the **s**, raise the dead,
Matt 25:36 ... I was **s**, and you cared for
Mark 3:10 ... all the **s** people eagerly
1 Cor 11:30 ... many of you are weak and **s**
Jas 5:14 ... Are any of you **s**?

SICKNESS, SICKNESSES (n) *a disordered, weakened, or unsound condition; illness*
Matt 4:24 ... whatever their **s** or disease,
Matt 8:17 ... He took our **s-es** and removed

SIGN, SIGNS (n) *something indicating the presence or existence of something else; something material or external that stands for or signifies something spiritual*
Gen 9:12 ... you a **s** of my covenant
Gen 17:11 ... your foreskin as a **s** of
Ps 105:27 ... performed miraculous **s-s**
Isa 55:13 ... be an everlasting **s** of
Dan 6:27 ... he performs miraculous **s-s**
Matt 12:38 ... a miraculous **s** to prove
Matt 24:3 ... What **s** will signal your

Matt 24:30 ... the **s** that the Son of Man
Mark 16:17 ... These miraculous **s-s** will
Luke 11:29 ... them is the **s** of Jonah.
John 3:2 ... Your miraculous **s-s** are
John 20:30 ... do many other miraculous **s-s**
1 Cor 14:22 ... in tongues is a **s**, not for
2 Cor 12:12 ... did many **s-s** and wonders
2 Thes 2:9 ... counterfeit power and **s-s**

SILENCE (n) *absence of speech, sound, or noise*
Ps 39:2 ... I stood there in **s**—not even
Rev 8:1 ... there was **s** throughout heaven

SILENCE, SILENCED, SILENCING (v) *to compel or reduce to silence; to cause to cease criticism*
Ps 8:2 ... strength, **s-ing** your enemies
Titus 1:11 ... They must be **s-d**, because they
1 Pet 2:15 ... honorable lives should **s**

SILENT (adj) *mute, speechless; still*
Ps 30:12 ... praises to you and not be **s**.
Isa 53:7 ... as a sheep is **s** before the
Isa 62:1 ... Jerusalem, I cannot remain **s**.
Hab 2:20 ... the earth be **s** before him.
Acts 8:32 ... And as a lamb is **s** before
Acts 18:9 ... Speak out! Don't be **s**!
1 Cor 14:34 ... Women should be **s** during

SILVER (adj) *made of silver*
Prov 25:11 ... apples in a **s** basket.
Dan 2:32 ... and arms were **s**, its belly

SILVER (n) *a shiny gray metal valued next to gold, capable of a high polish; coin made of silver*
Ps 66:10 ... have purified us like **s**.
Prov 3:14 ... is more profitable than **s**,
Prov 8:10 ... instruction rather than **s**,
Prov 22:1 ... is better than **s** or gold.
Isa 48:10 ... but not as **s** is refined.
Zech 11:12 ... wages thirty pieces of **s**.
Zech 13:9 ... refine them like **s** and
Matt 25:15 ... two bags of **s** to another,
Matt 26:15 ... gave him thirty pieces of **s**.
Luke 7:41 ... 500 pieces of **s** to one
Acts 3:6 ... don't have any **s** or gold
1 Cor 3:12 ... materials—gold, **s**, jewels,

SIMPLE (n) *a person lacking in knowledge or expertise*
Ps 19:7 ... trustworthy, making wise the **s**.

SIMPLEMINDED (adj) *foolish*
Prov 19:25 ... the **s** will learn a lesson;

SIN, SINS (n) *moral evil; transgression of or rebellion against God's laws*
Gen 4:7 ... **S** is crouching at the door,
Lev 5:5 ... ways, you must confess your **s**.
Num 32:23 ... be sure that your **s** will find
Deut 24:16 ... to death for the **s-s** of their
Ps 19:13 ... servant from deliberate **s-s**!
Ps 32:1 ... whose **s** is put out of sight!
Ps 38:18 ... I confess my **s-s**; I am deeply
Ps 51:1 ... blot out the stain of my **s-s**.
Ps 51:2 ... Purify me from my **s**.
Ps 65:3 ... are overwhelmed by our **s-s**,
Ps 79:9 ... Save us and forgive our **s-s**
Ps 103:12 ... removed our **s-s** as far from
Prov 5:22 ... held captive by his own **s-s**;
Prov 10:19 ... Too much talk leads to **s**.
Prov 14:21 ... **s** to belittle one's neighbor;
Prov 17:19 ... who loves to quarrel loves **s**;
Prov 28:13 ... who conceal their **s-s** will
Prov 29:22 ... commits all kinds of **s**.
Isa 1:18 ... your **s-s** are like scarlet,

Isa 53:6 ... laid on him the **s-s** of us all.
Isa 59:2 ... Because of your **s-s**, he has
Jer 31:30 ... die for their own **s-s**—
Jer 31:34 ... again remember their **s-s**.
Ezek 18:19 ... pay for the parent's **s-s**?
Matt 1:21 ... save his people from their **s-s**.
Matt 6:12 ... forgive us our **s-s**, as we
Matt 26:28 ... to forgive the **s-s** of many.
Mark 3:29 ... This is a **s** with eternal
Luke 5:24 ... on earth to forgive **s-s**.
John 1:29 ... takes away the **s** of the world!
John 20:23 ... forgive anyone's **s-s**, they
Acts 2:38 ... repent of your **s-s** and turn
Rom 4:25 ... because of our **s-s**, and he
Rom 6:2 ... we have died to **s**, how can
Rom 6:11 ... the power of **s** and alive to
Rom 6:23 ... the wages of **s** is death,
Rom 7:7 ... law that showed me my **s**.
Rom 7:25 ... nature I am a slave to **s**,
1 Cor 6:18 ... is a **s** against your own body.
1 Cor 15:3 ... died for our **s-s**, just as
1 Cor 15:56 ... the law gives **s** its power.
Gal 1:4 ... gave his life for our **s-s**, just
Gal 6:1 ... believer is overcome by some **s**,
Eph 2:5 ... were dead because of our **s-s**,
1 Tim 5:22 ... share in the **s-s** of others.
Heb 2:17 ... would take away the **s-s** of
Heb 9:28 ... to take away the **s-s** of many
Heb 10:12 ... sacrifice for **s-s**, good for
Heb 12:1 ... the **s** that so easily trips
Jas 1:15 ... when **s** is allowed to grow,
Jas 4:17 ... is **s** to know what you ought
Jas 5:16 ... Confess your **s-s** to each other
1 Pet 2:24 ... carried our **s-s** in his body
1 Pet 3:18 ... suffered for our **s-s** once for
1 Jn 1:8 ... claim we have no **s**, we are
1 Jn 1:9 ... to forgive us our **s-s** and to
1 Jn 2:1 ... if anyone does **s**, we have
1 Jn 3:5 ... take away our **s-s**, and
1 Jn 3:5 ... there is no **s** in him.
1 Jn 5:16 ... a **s** that leads to death,
Rev 1:5 ... from our **s-s** by shedding his

SIN, SINNED, SINNING, SINS (v) *to commit an offense or fault against God; to break God's law*
Exod 20:20 ... will keep you from **s-ning**
2 Sam 12:13 ... I have **s-ned** against the
2 Chr 6:37 ... We have **s-ned**, done evil,
Job 1:5 ... my children have **s-ned**
Ps 51:4 ... and you alone, have I **s-ned**;
Ps 119:11 ... I might not **s** against you.
Jer 14:20 ... all have **s-ned** against you.
Dan 9:5 ... have **s-ned** and done wrong.
Mark 9:43 ... causes you to **s**, cut it off.
Luke 15:18 ... I have **s-ned** against both
Luke 17:3 ... another believer **s-s**, rebuke
John 8:7 ... who has never **s-ned** throw
John 8:11 ... Go and **s** no more.
Rom 1:30 ... invent new ways of **s-ning**,
Rom 3:23 ... everyone has **s-ned**; we all
Rom 5:12 ... When Adam **s-ned**, sin entered
Rom 14:23 ... is not right, you are **s-ning**.
1 Cor 15:34 ... is right, and stop **s-ning**.
Heb 4:15 ... we do, yet he did not **s**.
Heb 10:26 ... deliberately continue **s-ning**
1 Pet 2:22 ... He never **s-ned**, nor ever
1 Jn 1:10 ... we have not **s-ned**, we are
1 Jn 3:6 ... who keeps on **s-ning** does not
1 Jn 5:18 ... not make a practice of **s-ning**,

SINFUL (adj) *tainted with, marked by, or full of sin; wicked*
Lev 5:1 ... is **s** to refuse to testify,
1 Sam 15:23 ... is as **s** as witchcraft,
Luke 11:13 ... So if you **s** people know

Rom 5:20 ... could see how *s* they were.
Rom 7:5 ... harvest of *s* deeds, resulting
Rom 7:18 ... is, in my *s* nature.
Rom 7:25 ... because of my *s* nature I am
Rom 8:4 ... follow our *s* nature but
Rom 8:13 ... deeds of your *s* nature,
Gal 5:13 ... to satisfy your *s* nature.
Col 2:11 ... away of your *s* nature.

SING, SINGING (v) *to produce musical tones by means of the voice*
Exod 15:1 ... I will *s* to the LORD,
Ps 5:11 ... let them *s* joyful praises
Ps 13:6 ... I will *s* to the LORD
Ps 47:6 ... to our King, *s* praises!
Ps 51:14 ... I will joyfully *s* of
Ps 63:7 ... my helper, I *s* for joy
Ps 69:30 ... praise God's name with *s-ing*,
Ps 89:1 ... I will *s* of the LORD's unfailing
Ps 95:1 ... let us *s* to the LORD!
Ps 96:1 ... *S* a new song to the LORD!
Ps 98:4 ... praise and *s* for joy!
Ps 100:2 ... Come before him, *s-ing* with
Ps 101:1 ... I will *s* of your love
Ps 108:1 ... can *s* your praises with all
Ps 147:1 ... How good to *s* praises to
Isa 35:10 ... enter Jerusalem *s-ing*
Jer 16:9 ... to the happy *s-ing* and laughter
Acts 16:25 ... praying and *s-ing* hymns
1 Cor 14:15 ... I will also *s* in words
1 Cor 14:26 ... one will *s*, another will
Col 3:16 ... *S* psalms and hymns and
Rev 15:3 ... And they were *s-ing* the song

SINNER, SINNERS (n) *those guilty of sin*
Ps 51:5 ... I was born a *s*—yes,
Prov 1:10 ... if *s-s* entice you, turn
Prov 23:17 ... Don't envy *s-s*, but
Eccl 9:18 ... one *s* can destroy much that
Isa 59:12 ... we know what *s-s* we are.
Isa 64:5 ... We are constant *s-s;* how
Matt 9:13 ... who know they are *s-s*.
Luke 15:7 ... over one lost *s* who repents
Luke 18:13 ... to me, for I am a *s*.
Rom 4:5 ... faith in God who forgives *s-s*.
Rom 5:6 ... time and died for us *s-s*.
1 Tim 1:15 ... into the world to save *s-s*
Jas 5:20 ... whoever brings the *s* back
1 Pet 3:18 ... he died for *s-s* to bring

SKY, SKIES (n) *the upper atmosphere appearing as a great vault or arch above the earth*
Gen 1:8 ... God called the space "*s*."
Deut 33:26 ... across the *s-ies* in majestic
Ps 19:1 ... *s-ies* display his craftsmanship.
Prov 30:19 ... eagle glides through the *s*,
Isa 34:4 ... fall from the *s* like withered
Jer 33:22 ... the stars of the *s* cannot
Matt 24:29 ... will fall from the *s*,
Rev 20:11 ... The earth and *s* fled from

SLANDER (n) *the utterance of false charges or misrepresentations that defame and damage another's reputation*
Matt 15:19 ... theft, lying, and *s*.
Mark 7:22 ... desires, envy, *s*, pride,
2 Cor 12:20 ... selfishness, *s*, gossip,
Eph 4:31 ... harsh words, and *s*, as
Col 3:8 ... malicious behavior, *s*,

SLANDER, SLANDERED, SLANDERING (v) *to utter slander; to malign or defame*
Prov 10:18 ... *s-ing* others makes you a
1 Tim 3:11 ... must not *s* others.
2 Tim 3:3 ... they will *s* others

Titus 2:3 ... They must not *s* others
Titus 3:2 ... They must not *s* anyone
2 Pet 2:2 ... way of truth will be *s-ed*.

SLAUGHTER (n) *the butchering of livestock for market or sacrifice*
Isa 53:7 ... led like a lamb to the *s*.
Jer 11:19 ... lamb being led to the *s*.
Acts 8:32 ... led like a sheep to the *s*.

SLAUGHTER, SLAUGHTERED (v) *to discredit, defeat, or demolish completely; to kill in a bloody or violent manner*
Hos 6:5 ... to *s* you with my words,
Rev 5:6 ... looked as if it had been *s-ed*,
Rev 5:12 ... is the Lamb who was *s-ed*

SLAVE, SLAVES (n) *a person bound in servitude; one who has lost his liberty and has no rights*
see also SERVANT(S)
Matt 20:27 ... must become your *s*.
John 8:34 ... who sins is a *s* of sin.
John 15:15 ... longer call you *s-s*, because
Rom 1:1 ... is from Paul, a *s* of Christ
Rom 6:6 ... are no longer *s-s* to sin.
Rom 6:16 ... you become the *s* of whatever
Rom 6:22 ... and have become *s-s* of God.
Rom 7:23 ... makes me a *s* to the sin
1 Cor 6:12 ... not become a *s* to anything.
1 Cor 9:19 ... have become a *s* to all
1 Cor 12:13 ... some are *s-s*, and some
Gal 3:28 ... Jew or Gentile, *s* or free,
Gal 4:7 ... no longer a *s* but God's own
Gal 4:8 ... you were *s-s* to so-called gods
Gal 4:30 ... rid of the *s* and her son,
Eph 6:5 ... *S-s*, obey your earthly masters
Phil 2:7 ... position of a *s* and was born
Col 3:11 ... barbaric, uncivilized, *s*, or
Col 4:1 ... be just and fair to your *s-s*.
1 Tim 1:10 ... or are *s* traders, liars,
Titus 3:3 ... became *s-s* to many lusts
Phlm 1:16 ... no longer like a *s* to you.
2 Pet 2:19 ... For you are a *s* to whatever

SLAVERY (n) *submission to a dominating influence; the practice of slaveholding*
Exod 2:23 ... under their burden of *s*.
Rom 6:19 ... the illustration of *s* to help

SLEEP (n) *natural or induced state of rest; a state of lazy inactivity*
Gen 2:21 ... man to fall into a deep *s*.
Gen 15:12 ... Abram fell into a deep *s*,
Prov 20:13 ... If you love *s*, you will
Prov 23:21 ... too much *s* clothes them
Rom 11:8 ... has put them into a deep *s*.

SLEEP, SLEEPING, SLEEPS (v) *to rest in a state of natural unconsciousness*
Gen 28:11 ... against and lay down to *s*.
Ps 4:8 ... peace I will lie down and *s*,
Ps 121:4 ... Israel never slumbers or *s-s*.
Prov 6:9 ... how long will you *s*?
Eccl 5:12 ... who work hard *s* well,
Mark 13:36 ... find you *s-ing* when he

SLOTHFUL(NESS) (KJV)
Prov 15:19 ... *lazy* person's way is blocked
Prov 21:25 ... the *lazy* will come to ruin,
Eccl 10:18 ... *Laziness* leads to a sagging roof
Rom 12:11 ... Never be *lazy*, but work hard
Heb 6:12 ... spiritually dull and indifferent

SLUGGARD (KJV)
Prov 6:6 ... a lesson from the ants, you *lazybones*

Prov 10:26 ... *Lazy people* irritate their employers
Prov 13:4 ... *Lazy people* want much but
Prov 20:4 ... *Those too lazy* to plow
Prov 26:16 ... *Lazy people* consider themselves smarter

SMILE (v) *to bestow approval*
Num 6:25 ... May the LORD *s* on you and
Ps 4:6 ... Let your face *s* on us, LORD.
Ps 67:1 ... May his face *s* with favor on

SMOKE (n) *the gaseous products of burning materials*
Exod 19:18 ... The *s* billowed into the sky
Isa 6:4 ... building was filled with *s*.
Joel 2:30 ... and fire and columns of *s*.
Acts 2:19 ... and fire and clouds of *s*.
Rev 9:2 ... air turned dark from the *s*.
Rev 15:8 ... filled with *s* from God's

SMOKE (v) *to emit smoke*
Ps 104:32 ... the mountains *s* at his touch.

SNAKE, SNAKES (n) *any of numerous limbless scaled reptiles*
Num 21:8 ... replica of a poisonous *s* and
Prov 23:32 ... it bites like a poisonous *s*;
Matt 10:16 ... shrewd as *s-s* and harmless
Luke 3:7 ... You brood of *s-s!* Who warned
John 3:14 ... lifted up the bronze *s* on a
Rom 3:13 ... *S* venom drips from their

SNOW (n) *precipitation in the form of small white ice crystals*
Prov 25:13 ... refresh like *s* in summer.
Isa 1:18 ... will make them as white as *s*.
Dan 7:9 ... clothing was as white as *s*,

SODOM (n) *a city at the southern end of the Dead Sea destroyed because of its wickedness*
Gen 13:12 ... to a place near *S* and settled
Gen 19:24 ... the sky on *S* and Gomorrah.
Isa 1:9 ... have been wiped out like *S*,
Luke 10:12 ... you, even wicked *S* will be
Rom 9:29 ... have been wiped out like *S*,
Rev 11:8 ... figuratively called "*S*"

SOLDIER (n) *one engaged in military service*
1 Cor 9:7 ... What *s* has to pay his own
2 Tim 2:3 ... a good *s* of Christ Jesus.

SOLOMON King of Israel (united kingdom), second son of David and Bathsheba (2 Sam 12:24-25); chosen as successor by David (1 Kgs 1:28-40); given final advice by David (1 Kgs 2:1-9); enemies of his rule removed (1 Kgs 2:13-46); prayed for wisdom (1 Kgs 3:3-15; 4:29-34); demonstrated wisdom (1 Kgs 3:16-28); built and dedicated the Temple (1 Kgs 5—8); the Lord's second appearance (1 Kgs 9:1-9); became famous and powerful (9:10–10:29); visited by the queen of Sheba (1 Kgs 10:1-13); practiced idolatry and warned by God (1 Kgs 11:1-13); troubled by enemies (1 Kgs 11:14-40); died (1 Kgs 11:41-43); wrote many things (1 Kgs 4:32; Ps 72; 127; Prov 1:1; 10:1; 25:1; Eccl 1:1; Song 1:1); often mentioned in NT (Matt 6:29; 12:42; Luke 11:31; 12:27; Acts 7:47).

SON, SONS (n) *a parent's male child or descendant further removed; spiritual heir; relationship of Jesus to the heavenly Father*
see also CHILD(REN)
Gen 17:19 ... birth to a *s* for you.

Gen 21:10 ... slave-woman and her **s**.
Gen 22:2 ... Take your **s**, your only
Ruth 4:15 ... better to you than seven **s-s**!
Ps 2:7 ... You are my **s**. Today I have
Isa 7:14 ... birth to a **s** and will call
Dan 7:13 ... someone like a **s** of man
Hos 11:1 ... I called my **s** out of Egypt.
Joel 2:28 ... **s-s** and daughters will
Matt 1:21 ... will have a **s**, and you are
Matt 2:15 ... I called my **S** out of Egypt.
Matt 3:17 ... my dearly loved **S**, who brings
Matt 4:3 ... you are the **S** of God, tell
Matt 11:27 ... truly knows the **S** except the
Matt 13:55 ... the carpenter's **s**, and we
Matt 14:33 ... really are the **S** of God!
Matt 16:16 ... are the Messiah, the **S**
Matt 17:5 ... my dearly loved **S**, who brings
Matt 21:9 ... God for the **S** of David!
Matt 27:54 ... truly was the **S** of God!
Matt 28:19 ... Father and the **S** and the
Mark 14:62 ... will see the **S** of Man seated
Luke 1:32 ... be called the **S** of the Most
Luke 2:7 ... her firstborn **s**. She wrapped
Luke 9:35 ... This is my **S**, my Chosen One.
Luke 12:8 ... on earth, the **S** of Man will
Luke 15:20 ... ran to his **s**, embraced him,
John 3:16 ... his one and only **S**, so that
John 3:36 ... doesn't obey the **S** will never
John 17:1 ... Glorify your **S** so he
Acts 13:33 ... You are my **S**. Today I have
Rom 1:4 ... shown to be the **S** of God
Rom 5:10 ... death of his **S** while we
Rom 8:3 ... He sent his own **S** in a body
Rom 8:29 ... to become like his **S**, so
Rom 8:32 ... even his own **S** but gave him
1 Cor 15:28 ... who gave his **S** authority
2 Cor 6:18 ... be my **s-s** and daughters,
Gal 4:4 ... God sent his **S**, born of a
Gal 4:30 ... slave and her **s**, for the **s**
Heb 1:2 ... and through the **S** he created
Heb 1:5 ... You are my **S**. Today I have
Heb 7:28 ... God appointed his **S** with an
Heb 10:29 ... trampled on the **S** of God,
1 Jn 2:23 ... acknowledges the **S** has the
1 Jn 4:9 ... one and only **S** into the world
1 Jn 5:5 ... Jesus is the **S** of God.
Rev 1:13 ... someone like the **S** of Man.

SONG, SONGS (n) *a short musical composition of words and music; the act of singing*
Exod 15:2 ... my strength and my **s**;
Job 35:10 ... who gives **s-s** in the night?
Ps 40:3 ... given me a new **s** to sing,
Ps 63:5 ... praise you with **s-s** of joy.
Ps 96:1 ... Sing a new **s** to the LORD!
Ps 119:54 ... theme of my **s-s** wherever
Ps 137:3 ... of those **s-s** of Jerusalem!
Ps 149:1 ... Sing to the LORD a new **s**.
Isa 49:13 ... Burst into **s**, O mountains!
Isa 55:12 ... and hills will burst into **s**,
Rev 5:9 ... they sang a new **s** with these
Rev 15:3 ... God, and the **s** of the Lamb:

SORCERER, SORCERERS (n) *a person who practices sorcery*
Exod 7:11 ... his own wise men and **s-s**,
Acts 8:9 ... a **s** there for many years,
Acts 13:6 ... a Jewish **s**, a false prophet
Rev 22:15 ... the dogs—the **s**, the sexually

SORCERY (n) *the use of power gained from the assistance or control of evil spirits, especially for divining*
Gal 5:20 ... idolatry, **s**, hostility, quarreling,

SORROW, SORROWS (n) *deep distress, sadness, or regret*
Ps 116:3 ... I saw only trouble and **s**.
Isa 65:14 ... will cry in **s** and despair.
Jer 31:12 ... all their **s-s** will be gone.
Ezek 34:2 ... What **s** awaits you
Amos 5:18 ... What **s** awaits you
Matt 18:7 ... What **s** awaits the
Matt 23:13 ... What **s** awaits you
Luke 11:46 ... what **s** also awaits
Rom 9:2 ... with bitter **s** and unending
2 Cor 7:10 ... the kind of **s** God wants
Eph 4:30 ... do not bring **s** to God's Holy
1 Tim 6:10 ... themselves with many **s-s**.
Heb 13:17 ... with joy and not with **s**.
Jude 1:11 ... What **s** awaits them!
Rev 21:4 ... more death or **s** or crying

SORRY (adj) *feeling sorrow, regret, or penitence; inspiring pity*
Gen 6:6 ... So the LORD was **s** he had
2 Chr 21:20 ... No one was **s** when he died.
Ps 38:18 ... I am deeply **s** for what I have
Mal 3:14 ... that we are **s** for our sins?
Matt 15:32 ... I feel **s** for these people.
Matt 20:34 ... Jesus felt **s** for them and
Mark 8:2 ... I feel **s** for these people.

SOUL, SOULS (n) *the inner life of a human being, the seat of emotions, and the center of human personality*
Deut 6:5 ... heart, all your **s**, and all
Deut 28:65 ... fail, and your **s** to despair.
Deut 30:6 ... your heart and **s** and so you
Josh 22:5 ... all your heart and all your **s**.
2 Kgs 23:25 ... heart and **s** and strength,
Prov 3:22 ... for they will refresh your **s**.
Prov 16:24 ... sweet to the **s** and healthy
Jer 6:16 ... you will find rest for your **s-s**.
Matt 10:28 ... can destroy both **s** and body
Matt 11:29 ... you will find rest for your **s-s**.
Matt 22:37 ... all your heart, all your **s**,
Mark 8:37 ... worth more than your **s**?
Mark 12:30 ... heart, all your **s**, all your
Luke 21:19 ... firm, you will win your **s-s**.
John 12:27 ... my **s** is deeply troubled.
Heb 4:12 ... cutting between **s** and spirit,

SOW(ED), SOWING (KJV)
Lev 25:3 ... you may *plant* your fields
Ps 126:5 ... Those who *plant* in tears
Matt 13:4 ... As he *scattered* them across
Luke 12:24 ... the ravens. They don't *plant*
Luke 19:21 ... crops you didn't *plant*

SOWER (KJV)
Isa 55:10 ... producing seed for the *farmer*
Jer 50:16 ... all *those who plant* crops
Matt 13:18 ... the *farmer planting seeds*
2 Cor 9:10 ... provides seed for the *farmer*

SPARE, SPARED, SPARES (v) *to hold back from destroying, punishing, or harming; to have left over or as margin; to rescue from the necessity of doing or undergoing something*
Esth 7:3 ... lives of my people will be **s-d**.
Prov 13:24 ... Those who **s** the rod of
Isa 54:2 ... your home, and **s** no expense!
Mal 3:17 ... as a father **s-s** an obedient
Rom 8:32 ... did not **s** even his own Son
Rom 11:21 ... if God did not **s** the original
2 Pet 2:4 ... God did not **s** even the angels
2 Pet 2:5 ... And God did not **s** the ancient

SPEAK, SPEAKING, SPEAKS (v) *to express thoughts, opinions, or feelings orally; to talk*
Deut 18:22 ... If the prophet **s-s** in the
Ps 15:3 ... or **s** evil of their friends.
Ps 78:2 ... will **s** to you in a parable.
Isa 3:8 ... because they **s** out against
Isa 32:4 ... stammer will **s** out plainly.
Matt 12:34 ... men like you **s** what is good
Matt 15:18 ... the words you **s** come from
Acts 2:11 ... hear these people **s-ing** in our
1 Cor 14:2 ... ability to **s** in tongues,
1 Cor 14:19 ... I would rather **s** five
1 Pet 3:16 ... if people **s** against you,

SPEECH (n) *the communication of thoughts in spoken words*
Prov 16:23 ... a wise mind comes wise **s**;
Prov 22:11 ... gracious **s** will have the king
Prov 25:15 ... soft **s** can break bones.
Zeph 3:9 ... I will purify the **s** of all
1 Cor 1:17 ... not with clever **s**, for

SPEND, SPENT (v) *to use up or pay out; to exhaust or wear out*
Prov 21:20 ... but fools **s** whatever they
Isa 55:2 ... Why **s** your money on food
Mark 5:26 ... she had **s-t** everything she had
2 Cor 12:15 ... I will gladly **s** myself

SPIRIT, SPIRITS (n) *"wind" or "breath"; a supernatural being; the third member of the Trinity, with God the Father and Jesus the Son; an attitude, mood, or disposition; an evil presence that can possess or influence a person; invisible, nonmaterial part of humans (as opposed to body or flesh)* see also ADVOCATE, HOLY SPIRIT
Gen 1:2 ... the **S** of God was hovering
Gen 6:3 ... My **S** will not put up with
Exod 31:3 ... filled him with the **S** of God,
Num 11:25 ... **S** rested upon them, they
Deut 34:9 ... full of the **s** of wisdom,
Judg 13:25 ... And the **S** of the LORD
1 Sam 16:13 ... And the **S** of the LORD
1 Sam 16:14 ... a tormenting **s** that filled
2 Kgs 2:9 ... double share of your **s** and
Job 33:4 ... the **S** of God has made me,
Ps 31:5 ... I entrust my **s** into your
Ps 34:18 ... those whose **s-s** are crushed.
Ps 51:10 ... Renew a loyal **s** within me.
Ps 51:17 ... you desire is a broken **s**.
Ps 139:7 ... can never escape from your **S**!
Isa 11:2 ... **S** of the LORD will rest
Isa 44:3 ... I will pour out my **S** on your
Isa 63:10 ... him and grieved his Holy **S**.
Ezek 11:19 ... put a new **s** within them.
Joel 2:28 ... I will pour out my **S** upon all
Zech 4:6 ... by my **S**, says the LORD
Matt 3:11 ... baptize you with the Holy **S**
Matt 3:16 ... and he saw the **S** of God
Matt 4:1 ... was led by the **S** into the
Matt 28:19 ... and the Son and the Holy **S**.
Mark 1:8 ... baptize you with the Holy **S**!
Mark 5:12 ... pigs," the **s-s** begged.
Luke 1:35 ... The Holy **S** will come upon
John 3:5 ... born of water and the **S**.
John 6:63 ... **S** alone gives eternal life.
John 14:26 ... the Holy **S**—he will teach
John 16:13 ... When the **S** of truth comes,
Acts 1:8 ... when the Holy **S** comes
Acts 2:4 ... as the Holy **S** gave them this
Acts 2:17 ... will pour out my **S** upon all
Acts 5:3 ... You lied to the Holy **S**, and
Acts 6:3 ... full of the **S** and wisdom.
Acts 8:15 ... to receive the Holy **S**.
Acts 9:17 ... and be filled with the Holy **S**.
Acts 11:16 ... be baptized with the Holy **S**.
Acts 19:2 ... receive the Holy **S** when you

Rom 8:5 ... controlled by the Holy **S** think
Rom 8:9 ... do not have the **S** of Christ
Rom 8:26 ... the Holy **S** prays for us
1 Cor 2:10 ... For his **S** searches out
1 Cor 12:1 ... abilities the **S** gives us.
1 Cor 12:13 ... one body by one **S,** and we
1 Cor 14:1 ... abilities the **S** gives—
2 Cor 3:6 ... covenant, the **S** gives life.
2 Cor 3:17 ... and wherever the **S** of the
2 Cor 5:3 ... not be **s-s** without bodies.
Gal 3:2 ... receive the Holy **S** by obeying
Gal 5:22 ... But the Holy **S** produces this
Eph 4:4 ... body and one **S,** just as you
Eph 4:30 ... to God's Holy **S** by the way
Eph 6:12 ... and against evil **s-s** in the
Eph 6:17 ... sword of the **S,** which is the
1 Thes 5:19 ... Do not stifle the Holy **S.**
1 Tim 3:16 ... vindicated by the **S.**
2 Tim 1:7 ... not given us a **s** of fear
1 Pet 3:4 ... gentle and quiet **s,** which
1 Jn 4:1 ... who claims to speak by the **S.**

SPIRITUAL (adj) *having to do with the spirit, usually God's Spirit*
Jon 4:11 ... living in **s** darkness, not
Rom 7:14 ... for it is **s** and good.
1 Cor 2:14 ... who are **s** can understand
1 Cor 14:37 ... think you are **s,** you should
1 Cor 15:44 ... there are also **s** bodies.
Eph 5:19 ... and hymns and **s** songs among
1 Pet 2:5 ... you offer **s** sacrifices that

SPLENDOR (n) *great brightness or luster; magnificence*
2 Chr 20:21 ... him for his holy **s.**
Ps 29:2 ... the LORD in the **s** of
Ps 145:5 ... majestic, glorious **s** and
Prov 20:29 ... experience is the **s** of
Isa 33:17 ... see the king in all his **s,**
Hab 3:3 ... brilliant **s** fills the heavens,

SPOT, SPOTS (n) *a small area visibly different (as in color, finish, or material) from the surrounding area; a taint on character or reputation*
Jer 13:23 ... leopard take away its **s-s?**
Eph 5:27 ... church without a **s** or wrinkle

SPOTLESS (adj) *free from impurity; unblemished*
1 Pet 1:19 ... the sinless, **s** Lamb of God.

STAFF (n) *a long stick used for walking or a weapon, often a symbol of authority and protection*
see also ROD
Gen 49:10 ... nor the ruler's **s** from his
Exod 7:12 ... then Aaron's **s** swallowed up
Num 17:6 ... Aaron, brought Moses a **s.**
2 Kgs 4:29 ... travel; take my **s** and go!
Ps 23:4 ... Your rod and your **s** protect

STAND, STANDING, STANDS (v) *to remain stationary; to remain erect; to maintain one's position; to endure successfully*
see also STOOD
Exod 3:5 ... you are **s-ing** on holy ground.
Josh 5:15 ... where you are **s-ing** is holy.
Josh 10:12 ... Let the sun **s** still
2 Chr 20:17 ... then **s** still and
Ps 24:3 ... Who may **s** in his holy
Ps 33:11 ... LORD's plans **s** firm
Ps 76:7 ... Who can **s** before you
Ps 119:89 ... word, O LORD, **s-s** firm
Prov 12:7 ... family of the godly **s-s** firm.
Isa 40:8 ... word of our God **s-s** forever.
Mal 3:2 ... be able to **s** and face him

Luke 6:48 ... that house, it **s-s** firm because
Rom 14:10 ... all **s** before the judgment
1 Cor 10:12 ... think you are **s-ing** strong,
1 Cor 10:13 ... to be more than you can **s.**
2 Cor 5:10 ... we must all **s** before Christ
Eph 6:14 ... **S** your ground, putting on the
Phil 1:27 ... you are **s-ing** together with
2 Tim 2:19 ... But God's truth **s-s** firm like
1 Pet 5:9 ... **S** firm against him, and
Rev 3:20 ... I **s** at the door and knock.

STANDING (n) *a position or condition*
Rom 8:33 ... us right **s** with himself.

STAR, STARS (n) *a natural luminous body visible in the sky especially at night; sometimes symbolic for angels*
Gen 1:16 ... He also made the **s-s.**
Num 24:17 ... A **s** will rise from Jacob;
Job 38:7 ... morning **s-s** sang together
Isa 14:12 ... O shining **s,** son of the
Dan 12:3 ... shine like the **s-s** forever.
Matt 2:2 ... We saw his **s** as it rose,
2 Pet 1:19 ... the Morning **S** shines in
Rev 2:28 ... also give them the morning **s!**
Rev 22:16 ... I am the bright morning **s.**

STATUTES (KJV)
Exod 15:26 ... keeping all his *decrees*
Deut 4:40 ... If you obey all the *decrees*
1 Kgs 3:14 ... *decrees* and my commands
Ps 19:8 ... *commandments* of the LORD
Ps 119:112 ... to keep your *decrees*

STEAL, STEALING, STEALS (v) *to take the property of another wrongfully*
Exod 20:15 ... You must not **s.**
Lev 19:11 ... Do not **s.**
Deut 5:19 ... You must not **s.**
Prov 28:24 ... who **s-s** from his father
Matt 19:18 ... You must not **s.**
Matt 27:64 ... coming and **s-ing** his body
Rom 13:9 ... You must not **s.**
Eph 4:28 ... If you are a thief, quit **s-ing.**
1 Pet 4:15 ... not be for murder, **s-ing,**

STEDFAST (KJV)
Ps 78:37 ... They did not *keep* his covenant
1 Cor 15:58 ... be *strong* and immovable.
Heb 3:14 ... if we are *faithful* to the end,
1 Pet 5:9 ... and be *strong* in your faith

STEPS (n) *course, way*
Ps 37:23 ... LORD directs the **s** of
Prov 20:24 ... LORD directs our **s,**
1 Pet 2:21 ... you must follow in his **s.**

STIFFHEARTED (KJV)
Ezek 2:4 ... *stubborn* and *hard-hearted*

STIFFNECKED (KJV)
Exod 32:9 ... how *stubborn and rebellious*
Exod 34:9 ... *stubborn and rebellious* people
Deut 10:16 ... stop being *stubborn*
2 Chr 30:8 ... not be *stubborn,* as they
Acts 7:51 ... You *stubborn* people! You are

STILL (adj) *devoid of or abstaining from motion; quiet, calm*
Ps 46:10 ... Be **s,** and know that I am
Isa 57:20 ... never **s** but continually
Mark 4:39 ... Silence! Be **s!**

STILL (adv) *without motion*
Exod 14:13 ... Just stand **s** and watch
Josh 10:13 ... sun stood **s** and the moon
2 Chr 20:17 ... then stand **s** and watch

STING (n) *a wound or pain caused by or as if by stinging*
1 Cor 15:55 ... where is your **s?**

STONE (adj) *of, relating to, or made of stone*
Deut 4:13 ... he wrote on two **s** tablets.

STONE, STONES (n) *hardened mineral or rock; figurative of Christ or of hardened hearts*
Exod 28:10 ... Six names will be on each **s,**
Josh 4:3 ... Take twelve **s-s** from the very
1 Sam 17:40 ... picked up five smooth **s-s**
Ps 91:12 ... even hurt your foot on a **s.**
Ps 118:22 ... **s** that the builders rejected
Isa 8:14 ... a **s** that makes people stumble,
Isa 28:16 ... a foundation **s** in Jerusalem,
Isa 50:7 ... face like a **s,** determined to
Jer 51:26 ... Even your **s-s** will never again
Matt 3:9 ... Abraham from these very **s-s.**
Matt 7:9 ... give them a **s** instead?
Matt 21:42 ... **s** that the builders rejected
Matt 24:2 ... Not one **s** will be left
Mark 16:3 ... roll away the **s** for us from
Luke 4:3 ... tell this **s** to become a loaf
John 8:7 ... sinned throw the first **s!**
1 Pet 2:5 ... you are living **s-s** that God

STONED, STONING (v) *to kill by pelting with stones*
2 Cor 11:25 ... with rods. Once I was **s-d.**
Heb 11:37 ... Some died by **s-ing,** some were

STONY (adj) *insensitive to pity or human feeling*
Ezek 11:19 ... away their **s,** stubborn heart

STOOD (v) *to maintain one's position*
see also STAND
Josh 10:13 ... So the sun **s** still and
2 Tim 4:17 ... But the Lord **s** with me

STOP, STOPS (v) *to cease activity or operation; to pause or hesitate; to restrain or prevent*
Job 37:14 ... **S** and consider the wonderful
Prov 15:18 ... cool-tempered person **s-s**
Jer 7:5 ... only if you **s** your evil
Jer 32:40 ... I will never **s** doing good
Lam 3:49 ... flow endlessly; they will not **s**
Dan 4:35 ... No one can **s** him or say to
Matt 19:14 ... come to me. Don't **s** them!
Eph 6:16 ... shield of faith to **s** the

STORE (n) *a large quantity, supply, or number*
Isa 33:6 ... a rich **s** of salvation,

STORE, STORED (v) *to lay away; to accumulate*
Matt 6:19 ... Don't **s** up treasures
Matt 6:26 ... plant or harvest or **s** food
Luke 2:51 ... And his mother **s-d** all these

STORM (n) *a heavy fall of rain, snow, or hail sometimes accompanied by thunder and lightning; a disturbed or agitated state*
see also WHIRLWIND
Ps 50:3 ... and a great **s** rages around
Ps 55:8 ... from this wild **s** of hatred.
Ps 107:29 ... He calmed the **s** to a whisper
Luke 8:24 ... **s** stopped and all was calm.

STRANGER, STRANGERS (n) *a person who is unknown or with whom one is unacquainted*
see also FOREIGNER(S)
Job 31:32 ... turned away a **s** but have
Matt 25:35 ... I was a **s,** and you invited
John 10:5 ... They won't follow a **s;**

1 Tim 5:10 ... been kind to **s-s** and served
Heb 13:2 ... to show hospitality to **s-s**, for

STRAYED (v) *to wander*
Isa 53:6 ... like sheep, have **s** away.
Ezek 34:16 ... lost ones who **s** away, and

STREAMS (n) *bodies of running water (as a river or brook)*
Ps 23:2 ... leads me beside peaceful **s**.
Jer 31:9 ... walk beside quiet **s** and

STRENGTH (n) *capacity for exertion or endurance; support; the power of a person or of God, measured variously in terms of wealth, wisdom, military might, or physical prowess*
Exod 15:2 ... LORD is my **s** and my
Deut 6:5 ... your soul, and all your **s**.
2 Kgs 23:25 ... his heart and soul and **s**,
1 Chr 16:11 ... LORD and for his **s**;
Neh 8:10 ... of the LORD is your **s**!
Ps 23:3 ... He renews my **s**. He guides me
Ps 28:7 ... LORD is my **s** and shield.
Ps 33:16 ... nor is great **s** enough to save
Ps 46:1 ... God is our refuge and **s**,
Ps 59:17 ... O my **S**, to you I sing
Ps 65:6 ... armed yourself with mighty **s**.
Ps 84:5 ... for those whose **s** comes from
Ps 139:10 ... your **s** will support me.
Isa 31:1 ... depending on the **s** of human
Isa 40:26 ... power and incomparable **s**,
Jer 27:5 ... With my great **s** and powerful
Mic 5:4 ... with the LORD's **s**, in
Hab 3:19 ... LORD is my **s**!
Zech 4:6 ... nor by **s**, but by my Spirit,
Mark 12:30 ... your mind, and all your **s**.
1 Cor 1:25 ... the greatest of human **s**.
Phil 4:13 ... Christ, who gives me **s**.
Heb 11:34 ... weakness was turned to **s**.
Heb 13:9 ... Your **s** comes from God's

STRENGTHEN, STRENGTHENED, STRENGTHENS (v) *to make or become stronger*
2 Chr 16:9 ... in order to **s** those whose
Isa 41:10 ... I will **s** you and help you.
1 Cor 8:1 ... is love that **s-s** the church.
1 Cor 14:4 ... in tongues is **s-ed** personally,
1 Cor 14:4 ... word of prophecy **s-s** the
1 Cor 14:5 ... whole church will be **s-ed**.
1 Cor 14:12 ... seek those that will **s** the
1 Cor 14:17 ... but it won't **s** the people
1 Cor 14:26 ... is done must **s** all of you.
2 Cor 13:10 ... has given me to **s** you, not
Heb 12:12 ... tired hands and **s** your weak
1 Pet 5:10 ... support, and **s** you, and he

STRONG, STRONGER, STRONGEST (adj) *having or marked by great physical power, moral or intellectual power, or great resources (as of wealth or talent); firm*
Exod 6:1 ... force of my **s** hand, he
Deut 5:15 ... you out with his **s** hand
Deut 7:8 ... with such a **s** hand from your
Deut 31:6 ... So be **s** and courageous!
Josh 1:6 ... Be **s** and courageous,
Judg 16:5 ... makes him so **s** and how he
2 Sam 22:33 ... God is my **s** fortress, and
1 Kgs 8:42 ... and your **s** hand and your
1 Chr 28:20 ... Be **s** and courageous, and
Ezra 10:4 ... so be **s** and take action.
Ps 24:8 ... The LORD, **s** and mighty;
Ps 96:7 ... LORD is glorious and **s**.
Prov 18:10 ... LORD is a **s** fortress;
Prov 24:5 ... wise are mightier than the **s**,

Prov 30:25 ... Ants—they aren't **s**, but
Prov 31:17 ... She is energetic and **s**, a
Eccl 9:11 ... **s-est** warrior doesn't always
Isa 35:4 ... Be **s**, and do not fear,
Jer 50:34 ... one who redeems them is **s**.
Zeph 1:14 ... when even **s** men will cry
Luke 1:80 ... and became **s** in spirit.
Luke 2:40 ... grew up healthy and **s**.
Luke 11:22 ... someone even **s-er** attacks
1 Cor 1:8 ... keep you **s** to the end
1 Cor 1:25 ... God's weakness is **s-er** than
1 Cor 16:13 ... Be courageous. Be **s**.
Eph 6:10 ... final word: Be **s** in the Lord
1 Thes 3:13 ... your hearts **s**, blameless,
2 Tim 2:1 ... dear son, be **s** through the

STRUGGLE (n) *strife; a violent effort or exertion*
Rom 15:30 ... to join in my **s** by praying
Heb 12:4 ... lives in your **s** against sin.

STRUGGLE (v) *to proceed with difficulty or with great effort; to make strenuous or violent efforts in the face of difficulties or opposition*
Gen 3:17 ... will **s** to scratch a living
Col 1:29 ... why I work and **s** so hard,
1 Tim 4:10 ... and continue to **s**, for our

STUBBORN (adj) *unreasonably or perversely unyielding*
Exod 33:5 ... You are a **s** and rebellious
Exod 34:9 ... this is a **s** and rebellious
Lev 26:41 ... at last their **s** hearts will
Deut 10:16 ... hearts and stop being **s**.
2 Chr 36:13 ... a hard and **s** man, refusing
Ps 78:8 ... ancestors—**s**, rebellious,
Prov 28:14 ... the **s** are headed for serious
Ezek 36:26 ... out your stony, **s** heart and
Rom 2:5 ... because you are **s** and refuse

STUDY (n) *application of the mental faculties to the acquisition of knowledge*
Eccl 12:12 ... and much **s** wears you

STUDY (v) *to read in detail, especially with the intention of learning*
Josh 1:8 ... **S** this Book of Instruction
Ezra 7:10 ... had determined to **s** and obey

STUMBLE, STUMBLES, STUMBLING (v) *to trip or walk unsteadily; to fall into sin or waywardness*
Lev 19:14 ... or cause the blind to **s**.
Ps 37:24 ... Though they **s**, they will
Ps 66:9 ... he keeps our feet from **s-ing**.
Ps 119:165 ... great peace and do not **s**.
Ps 121:3 ... He will not let you **s**;
Prov 3:23 ... and your feet will not **s**.
Prov 24:17 ... don't be happy when they **s**.
Isa 8:14 ... stone that makes people **s**,
Jer 13:16 ... causing you to **s** and fall
Hos 14:9 ... paths sinners **s** and fall.
Mal 2:8 ... caused many to **s** into sin.
Matt 21:44 ... Anyone who **s-s** over that
John 11:10 ... is in danger of **s-ing** because
Rom 9:33 ... that makes people **s**,
Rom 14:13 ... believer to **s** and fall.
Rom 14:20 ... makes another person **s**.
1 Cor 8:9 ... weaker conscience to **s**.
2 Cor 6:3 ... no one will **s** because of us,
1 Jn 2:10 ... does not cause others to **s**.

STUMP (n) *the part of a tree remaining attached to the root after the trunk is cut*
Isa 6:13 ... so Israel's **s** will be a
Isa 11:1 ... Out of the **s** of David's

STUPID (adj) *lacking intelligence or reason*
Ps 119:70 ... hearts are dull and **s**,
Prov 12:1 ... is **s** to hate correction.

SUBMISSIVE (adj) *submitting to others*
1 Cor 14:34 ... They should be **s**, just
Titus 2:5 ... be **s** to their husbands.

SUBMIT, SUBMITS (v) *to yield to authority or be accountable to another—God, society, or fellow believers*
Ps 2:12 ... **S** to God's royal son,
Rom 13:1 ... Everyone must **s** to governing
Rom 13:5 ... So you must **s** to them, not
Eph 5:21 ... **s** to one another out of
Eph 5:24 ... As the church **s-s** to Christ,
Col 3:18 ... Wives, **s** to your husbands,
Heb 12:9 ... shouldn't we **s** even more
1 Pet 2:18 ... must **s** to your masters

SUCCEED (v) *to turn out well; to attain a desired end*
Gen 39:23 ... everything he did to **s**.
Josh 1:8 ... prosper and **s** in all you
1 Sam 2:9 ... No one will **s** by strength
1 Sam 18:14 ... continued to **s** in
2 Chr 20:20 ... prophets, and you will **s**.
Ps 20:4 ... and make all your plans **s**.
Prov 11:10 ... celebrates when the godly **s**;
Prov 13:13 ... respect a command will **s**.
Prov 16:3 ... and your plans will **s**.
Prov 20:18 ... Plans **s** through good
Prov 28:12 ... When the godly **s**, everyone
Eccl 10:10 ... wisdom; it helps you **s**.

SUCCESS (n) *the attainment of wealth, favor, or eminence; favorable or desired outcome*
1 Chr 12:18 ... and **s** to all who help
2 Chr 26:5 ... LORD, God gave him **s**.
Prov 15:22 ... many advisers bring **s**.

SUCCESSFUL (adj) *resulting or terminating in success; gaining or having gained success*
Deut 8:18 ... gives you power to be **s**,
Deut 30:9 ... make you **s** in everything
1 Kgs 2:3 ... that you will be **s** in all
2 Kgs 18:7 ... Hezekiah was **s** in
1 Chr 22:13 ... For you will be **s** if you
2 Chr 31:21 ... result, he was very **s**.
Ps 90:17 ... and make our efforts **s**.
Prov 1:3 ... disciplined and **s** lives,
Eccl 9:11 ... don't always lead **s** lives.

SUES (v) *to seek justice or right from (a person) by legal process*
1 Cor 6:6 ... one believer **s** another—

SUFFER, SUFFERED, SUFFERING, SUFFERS (v) *to endure death, pain, distress, or loss*
Job 36:15 ... rescues those who **s**.
Mark 8:31 ... Son of Man must **s** many
Luke 24:26 ... would have to **s** all these
Luke 24:46 ... Messiah would **s** and die
Rom 8:18 ... Yet what we **s** now is nothing
1 Cor 12:26 ... If one part **s-s**, all the parts
2 Cor 1:5 ... the more we **s** for Christ,
2 Cor 12:10 ... troubles that I **s** for Christ.
Phil 3:10 ... I want to **s** with him, sharing
2 Thes 1:4 ... and hardships you are **s-ing**.
Heb 11:26 ... better to **s** for the sake
1 Pet 2:21 ... just as Christ **s-ed** for you.
1 Pet 4:1 ... since Christ **s-ed** physical pain,
1 Pet 4:16 ... is no shame to **s** for being

1 Pet 5:10 . . . So after you have **s-ed** a little
Rev 2:3 . . . You have patiently **s-ed** for me

SUFFERING, SUFFERINGS (n) *the state or experience of one that suffers; pain, distress*
Deut 16:3 . . . the bread of **s**—so that
Job 36:15 . . . means of their **s**, he rescues
Ps 119:71 . . . My **s** was good for me,
Isa 48:10 . . . you in the furnace of **s**.
Isa 49:13 . . . on them in their **s**.
Lam 1:12 . . . if there is any **s** like mine,
Luke 22:15 . . . you before my **s** begins.
2 Cor 1:7 . . . as you share in our **s-s**, you
Phil 1:29 . . . the privilege of **s** for him.
Col 1:24 . . . participating in the **s-s** of
2 Tim 2:3 . . . Endure **s** along with me,
2 Tim 4:5 . . . afraid of **s** for the Lord.
Heb 2:10 . . . through his **s**, a perfect
Heb 2:18 . . . gone through **s** and testing,
1 Pet 1:11 . . . about Christ's **s** and his
1 Pet 4:13 . . . Christ in his **s**, so that

SUN (n) *the star that sustains life on the earth, being the source of heat and light*
Josh 10:13 . . . So the **s** stood still and
Judg 5:31 . . . rise like the **s** in all its
Ps 84:11 . . . God is our **s** and our shield.
Ps 121:6 . . . The **s** will not harm you
Ps 136:8 . . . the **s** to rule the day,
Eccl 1:9 . . . Nothing under the **s** is truly
Isa 60:19 . . . you need the **s** to shine by
Mal 4:2 . . . name, the **S** of Righteousness
Matt 13:43 . . . shine like the **s** in their
Matt 17:2 . . . shone like the **s**, and his
Luke 23:45 . . . light from the **s** was gone.
Eph 4:26 . . . Don't let the **s** go down while
Rev 1:16 . . . was like the **s** in all its
Rev 21:23 . . . has no need of **s** or moon,

SUSTAINS (v) *to keep up or prolong*
Heb 1:3 . . . God, and he **s** everything by

SWADDLED, SWADDLING (KJV)
Ezek 16:4 . . . salt, and *wrapped in cloth*
Luke 2:7 . . . wrapped him *snugly in strips of cloth*
Luke 2:12 . . . baby *wrapped snugly in strips*

SWALLOW, SWALLOWED (v) *to take through the mouth and esophagus into the stomach; to envelop or absorb*
Isa 25:8 . . . He will **s** up death
Jon 1:17 . . . a great fish to **s** Jonah.
Hab 1:13 . . . while the wicked **s** up people
Matt 23:24 . . . a gnat, but you **s** a camel!
1 Cor 15:54 . . . fulfilled: "Death is **s-ed** up
2 Cor 5:4 . . . bodies will be **s-ed** up by life.

SWORD, SWORDS (n) *a handheld weapon with a long blade; figurative of war or persecution by government, also of God's word in spiritual warfare*
Gen 3:24 . . . a flaming **s** that flashed
Deut 32:41 . . . my flashing **s** and begin
1 Sam 17:45 . . . come to me with **s**, spear,
1 Sam 31:4 . . . Take your **s** and kill me
2 Sam 12:10 . . . live by the **s** because you
1 Kgs 20:11 . . . putting on his **s** for battle
Ps 44:6 . . . not count on my **s** to save me.
Ps 45:3 . . . Put on your **s**, O mighty
Ps 64:3 . . . their tongues like **s-s** and aim
Joel 3:10 . . . plowshares into **s-s** and your
Amos 9:4 . . . I will command the **s** to kill
Mic 4:3 . . . will hammer their **s-s** into
Matt 10:34 . . . not to bring peace, but a **s**.
Matt 26:52 . . . who use the **s** will die by

Luke 2:35 . . . a **s** will pierce your very
Eph 6:17 . . . take the **s** of the Spirit,
Heb 4:12 . . . sharpest two-edged **s**, cutting
Rev 1:16 . . . sharp two-edged **s** came
Rev 19:15 . . . came a sharp **s** to strike

SYNAGOGUE (n) *the house of worship and communal center of a Jewish congregation*
Luke 4:16 . . . to the **s** on the Sabbath
John 12:42 . . . expel them from the **s**.
Acts 17:2 . . . he went to the **s** service,
Rev 3:9 . . . who belong to Satan's **s**—

T

TABERNACLE (n) *portable shrine or tent designated for the worship of God; metaphor for God dwelling among his people*
see also SANCTUARY, TEMPLE
Exod 27:21 . . . stand in the **T**, in front of
Exod 40:2 . . . Set up the **T** on the first
Exod 40:34 . . . cloud covered the **T**, and
Exod 40:34 . . . of the LORD filled the **T**.
Num 3:29 . . . area south of the **T** for their
Heb 8:5 . . . to build the **T**, God gave him
Heb 9:11 . . . more perfect **T** in heaven,
Heb 9:21 . . . blood on the **T** and on
Rev 15:5 . . . heaven, God's **T**, was thrown

TABLETS (n) *flat slabs or plaques suited for or bearing an inscription*
Exod 31:18 . . . two stone **t** inscribed with
Deut 10:5 . . . and placed the **t** in the Ark
2 Cor 3:3 . . . carved not on **t** of stone,

TAME (v) *to domesticate; to harness*
Jas 3:7 . . . People can **t** all kinds of
Jas 3:8 . . . no one can **t** the tongue.

TASTE (n) *the act of tasting; a sample experience*
Prov 24:13 . . . honeycomb is sweet to the **t**.
1 Pet 2:3 . . . a **t** of the Lord's kindness.

TASTE, TASTED, TASTES (v) *to become acquainted with by experience; to ascertain the flavor of by taking a little into the mouth*
Ps 34:8 . . . **T** and see that the LORD
Prov 9:17 . . . eaten in secret **t-s** the best!
Song 2:3 . . . and **t** his delicious fruit.
Ezek 3:3 . . . I ate it, it **t-d** as sweet as
Col 2:21 . . . Don't handle! Don't **t**!

TAX, TAXES (n) *a charge usually of money imposed by authority on persons or property for public purposes*
Matt 17:24 . . . teacher pay the Temple **t**?
Matt 22:17 . . . right to pay **t-es** to Caesar
Rom 13:7 . . . Pay your **t-es** and

TEACH, TEACHES, TEACHING (v) *to cause to know something; to instruct by precept, example, or experience*
see also INSTRUCT, PREACH, TRAIN
Lev 10:11 . . . you must **t** the Israelites
Deut 6:1 . . . commanded me to **t** you.
2 Chr 17:9 . . . of Judah, **t**-ing the people.
Job 21:22 . . . who can **t** a lesson to God,
Ps 37:30 . . . they **t** right from wrong.
Ps 51:13 . . . Then I will **t** your ways
Prov 15:33 . . . the LORD **t-es** wisdom;
Isa 2:3 . . . he will **t** us his ways,
Matt 5:19 . . . obeys God's laws and **t-es**
Matt 11:29 . . . Let me **t** you, because
Matt 15:9 . . . they **t** man-made ideas

Matt 22:16 . . . You **t** the way of God
Matt 28:20 . . . **T** these new disciples to
Mark 10:1 . . . as usual he was **t**-ing them.
Luke 11:1 . . . Lord, **t** us to pray,
Luke 12:12 . . . Holy Spirit will **t** you
John 14:26 . . . he will **t** you everything
Acts 6:4 . . . in prayer and **t**-ing the word.
Rom 15:4 . . . Scriptures long ago to **t**
Rom 15:14 . . . you can **t** each other all
1 Cor 2:16 . . . knows enough to **t** him?
1 Cor 14:26 . . . another will **t**, another
1 Tim 2:12 . . . do not let women **t** men
1 Tim 3:2 . . . he must be able to **t**.
2 Tim 3:16 . . . is useful to **t** us what
2 Tim 3:16 . . . **t-es** us to do what is right.
Titus 2:15 . . . You must **t** these things
Heb 5:12 . . . you ought to be **t**-ing others.
1 Jn 2:27 . . . need anyone to **t** you what

TEACHER, TEACHERS (n) *one who teaches*
Job 36:22 . . . Who is a **t** like him?
Prov 5:13 . . . didn't I listen to my **t-s**?
Eccl 1:1 . . . words of the **T**, King David's
Matt 10:24 . . . not greater than their **t**,
Matt 23:10 . . . only one **t**, the Messiah.
Luke 6:40 . . . will become like the **t**.
Luke 20:46 . . . these **t-s** of religious law!
John 13:14 . . . Lord and **T**, have washed
Rom 12:7 . . . If you are a **t**, teach well.
1 Cor 12:28 . . . third are **t-s**, then those
Gal 6:6 . . . should provide for their **t-s**,
Eph 4:11 . . . and the pastors and **t-s**.
2 Tim 4:3 . . . look for **t-s** who will tell
Jas 3:1 . . . of you should become **t-s**
3 Jn 1:10 . . . the traveling **t-s**, he also

TEACHING, TEACHINGS (n) *something taught; doctrine*
see also INSTRUCTION(S), LAW(S)
Isa 8:20 . . . to God's instructions and **t-s**!
Luke 6:47 . . . listens to my **t**, and then
John 7:17 . . . whether my **t** is from God
John 8:31 . . . remain faithful to my **t-s**.
Acts 2:42 . . . themselves to the apostles' **t**,
Eph 4:14 . . . about by every wind of new **t**.
1 Thes 4:8 . . . not disobeying human **t** but
2 Thes 2:15 . . . grip on the **t** we passed on
1 Tim 1:3 . . . those whose **t** is contrary to
1 Tim 1:10 . . . contradicts the wholesome **t**
1 Tim 4:6 . . . and the good **t** you have
1 Tim 4:16 . . . how you live and on your **t**.
1 Tim 6:3 . . . people may contradict our **t**,
2 Tim 4:2 . . . your people with good **t**.
Titus 1:9 . . . with wholesome **t** and show
Titus 3:8 . . . insist on these **t-s** so that
Heb 6:1 . . . stop going over the basic **t-s**

TEAR, TEARS (n) *a drop of clear saline fluid secreted from the eye*
Job 16:20 . . . I pour out my **t-s** to God.
Isa 25:8 . . . will wipe away all **t-s**.
Rev 7:17 . . . will wipe every **t** from their
Rev 21:4 . . . will wipe every **t** from their

TEMPER (n) *disposition; characteristic state of mind or emotion; proneness to anger*
Ps 37:8 . . . Do not lose your **t**—it only
Prov 14:29 . . . **t** shows great foolishness.
Prov 19:11 . . . people control their **t**;
Eccl 7:9 . . . Control your **t**, for anger

TEMPLE, TEMPLES (n) *first built in Solomon's reign as a permanent worship center, which was destroyed then rebuilt under Herod's reign;*

1765

figurative of the human body and of Christ
see also HOUSE, SANCTUARY, TABERNACLE
1 Kgs 6:1 ... to construct the *T* of the
1 Kgs 8:10 ... cloud filled the *T* of the
1 Chr 29:16 ... to build a *T* to honor your
2 Chr 36:19 ... his army burned the *T*
Ps 27:4 ... meditating in his *T*.
Isa 6:1 ... train of his robe filled the *T*.
Jer 7:8 ... suffer because the *T* is here.
Joel 3:18 ... forth from the LORD's *T*,
Hab 2:20 ... LORD is in his holy *T*.
Hag 2:18 ... of the LORD's *T* was laid.
Matt 12:6 ... is even greater than the *T*!
Matt 26:61 ... able to destroy the *T* of God
Matt 27:51 ... sanctuary of the *T* was torn
Luke 21:5 ... stonework of the *T* and the
John 2:14 ... the *T* area he saw merchants
Acts 5:20 ... Go to the *T* and give the
Acts 17:24 ... live in man-made *t-s*.
1 Cor 3:16 ... together are the *t* of God
1 Cor 6:19 ... body is the *t* of the Holy
Eph 2:21 ... becoming a holy *t* for the
1 Pet 2:5 ... building into his spiritual *t*.
Rev 21:22 ... and the Lamb are its *t*.

TEMPT, TEMPTED, TEMPTING (v) *to entice to do wrong by promise of pleasure or gain; to test*
Isa 13:17 ... They cannot be *t-ed* by silver
Matt 4:1 ... wilderness to be *t-ed* there by
Luke 4:2 ... where he was *t-ed* by the devil
Luke 4:13 ... finished *t-ing* Jesus, he left
1 Cor 7:5 ... be able to *t* you because
1 Cor 10:13 ... When you are *t-ed*, he will
Jas 1:13 ... you are being *t-ed*, do not say,
Jas 1:13 ... God is never *t-ed* to do wrong,

TEMPTATION, TEMPTATIONS (n) *a cause or occasion of enticement*
Matt 6:13 ... don't let us yield to *t*,
Matt 18:7 ... *T-s* are inevitable, but what
Matt 26:41 ... will not give in to *t*.
Luke 8:13 ... fall away when they face *t*.
1 Cor 10:13 ... The *t-s* in your life are
1 Cor 10:13 ... not allow the *t* to be
Gal 6:1 ... fall into the same *t* yourself.
1 Tim 6:9 ... to be rich fall into *t* and
Jas 1:12 ... endure testing and *t*.

TEN (n) *the number 10*
Exod 34:28 ... the *T* Commandments—
Deut 10:4 ... wrote the *T* Commandments,
Luke 15:8 ... a woman has *t* silver coins
Rev 12:3 ... seven heads and *t* horns, with

TENDERHEARTED (adj) *easily moved to love, pity, or sorrow; compassionate*
Deut 28:54 ... The most *t* man among you
Eph 4:32 ... each other, *t*, forgiving one
Col 3:12 ... yourselves with *t* mercy,

TENDERNESS (n) *the quality or state of being gentle, fond, or loving*
Jas 5:11 ... is full of *t* and mercy.

TENTH (n) *one-tenth of any property or produce*
see also TITHE
Gen 14:20 ... gave Melchizedek a *t* of all
Heb 7:2 ... Abraham took a *t* of all he

TERRIBLE (adj) *extremely bad; terrifying*
Jer 8:6 ... What a *t* thing I have done
Zeph 1:15 ... a day of *t* distress and
Heb 10:31 ... It is a *t* thing to fall into

TERRIFY, TERRIFIED, TERRIFIES (v) *to scare, deter, or intimidate; to fill with terror*
Deut 2:25 ... the earth *t-ied* because of you.
Deut 28:67 ... you will be *t-ied* by the awful
1 Sam 12:18 ... were *t-ied* of the LORD
Prov 21:15 ... but it *t-ies* evildoers.
Isa 13:8 ... and people are *t-ied*. Pangs of
Zeph 2:11 ... The LORD will *t* them
Matt 14:26 ... on the water, they were *t-ied*.
Matt 17:6 ... disciples were *t-ied* and fell
Matt 27:54 ... the crucifixion were *t-ied*
Mark 4:41 ... disciples were absolutely *t-ied*.
Luke 21:26 ... will be *t-ied* at what they

TERRIFYING (adj) *causing terror or apprehension*
Deut 4:34 ... powerful arm, and *t* acts?
Deut 34:12 ... Moses performed *t* acts in the
Judg 13:6 ... of God's angels, *t* to see.

TERROR, TERRORS (n) *a state of intense fear; a frightening aspect*
Deut 7:19 ... Remember the great *t-s* the
Job 9:34 ... no longer live in *t* of his
Ps 53:5 ... will grip them, *t* like they
Ps 91:5 ... afraid of the *t-s* of the night,
Prov 22:8 ... their reign of *t* will come to
Isa 51:17 ... the cup of *t*, tipping out its
Mic 7:17 ... trembling in *t* at his
Luke 9:34 ... them, and *t* gripped them
Acts 7:32 ... Moses shook with *t* and did

TEST, TESTINGS, TESTS (n) *a critical examination, observation, or evaluation*
see also TRIAL(S), TROUBLE(S)
Deut 29:3 ... all the great *t-s* of strength,
1 Cor 10:9 ... should we put Christ to the *t*,
1 Tim 3:10 ... If they pass the *t*, then let
Heb 4:15 ... of the same *t-ings* we do, yet

TEST, TESTED, TESTING, TESTS (v) *to put to test or proof*
Gen 22:1 ... God *t-ed* Abraham's faith.
Deut 6:16 ... You must not *t* the LORD your
Judg 3:1 ... land to *t* those Israelites
1 Kgs 10:1 ... she came to *t* him with hard
Job 23:10 ... when he *t-s* me, I will come
Ps 17:3 ... You have *t-ed* my thoughts
Ps 66:10 ... You have *t-ed* us,
Ps 78:18 ... They stubbornly *t-ed* God in
Ps 106:14 ... ran wild, *t-ing* God's patience
Ps 139:23 ... *t* me and know my anxious
Prov 17:3 ... the LORD *t-s* the heart.
Luke 4:12 ... You must not *t* the LORD your
Acts 5:9 ... of conspiring to *t* the Spirit
1 Thes 5:21 ... but *t* everything that is said.
Heb 2:18 ... suffering and *t-ing*, he is able
Heb 2:18 ... us when we are being *t-ed*.
Heb 3:8 ... they *t-ed* me in the wilderness.
Heb 11:17 ... when God was *t-ing* him.
Jas 1:3 ... when your faith is *t-ed*, your
Jas 1:12 ... who patiently endure *t-ing* and
1 Pet 1:7 ... It is being *t-ed* as fire tests
1 Jn 4:1 ... You must *t* them to see if
Rev 2:10 ... you into prison to *t* you.
Rev 3:10 ... great time of *t-ing* that will

TESTIFY, TESTIFIED, TESTIFIES, TESTIFYING (v) *to make a statement based on personal knowledge or belief; to give evidence or proof*
Exod 20:16 ... must not *t* falsely against
Deut 5:20 ... must not *t* falsely against
Prov 24:28 ... Don't *t* against your
Luke 18:20 ... You must not *t* falsely.
John 1:34 ... Jesus, so I *t* that he is

John 5:32 ... else is also *t-ing* about me,
John 15:26 ... Father and will *t* all about
John 18:37 ... the world to *t* to the truth.
John 21:24 ... one who *t-ies* to these events
Acts 4:33 ... The apostles *t-ied* powerfully
Acts 10:43 ... the prophets *t-ied* about,
1 Jn 4:14 ... own eyes and now *t* that the

TESTIMONY (n) *the evidence given by a witness*
see also TESTIFY
Num 35:30 ... to death on the *t* of only
John 1:7 ... might believe because of his *t*.
1 Tim 6:13 ... gave a good *t* before Pontius
1 Jn 5:9 ... Since we believe human *t*,
Rev 12:11 ... of the Lamb and by their *t*.

THANK, THANKING (v) *to express gratitude to; to acknowledge God's goodness*
Ps 35:18 ... Then I will *t* you in front
Ps 79:13 ... pasture, will *t* you forever
Ps 145:10 ... works will *t* you, LORD,
Isa 12:4 ... sing: "*T* the LORD!
1 Cor 10:30 ... If I can *t* God for the food
Phil 4:6 ... and *t* him for all he has done.
1 Thes 2:13 ... we never stop *t-ing* God
1 Thes 3:9 ... How we *t* God for you!

THANKFUL (adj) *conscious of benefit received; expressive of thanks*
Col 3:15 ... And always be *t*.
Col 3:16 ... to God with *t* hearts.
1 Thes 5:18 ... Be *t* in all circumstances,
Heb 12:28 ... let us be *t* and please God by

THANKS (n) *kindly or grateful thoughts; gratitude*
1 Chr 16:4 ... to give *t*, and to praise
Ps 30:12 ... I will give you *t* forever!
Ps 107:1 ... Give *t* to the LORD,
Rom 1:21 ... as God or even give him *t*.
1 Cor 11:24 ... gave *t* to God for it.
Phil 1:3 ... of you, I give *t* to my God.
1 Tim 2:1 ... behalf, and give *t* for them.
1 Tim 4:3 ... be eaten with *t* by faithful
Rev 4:9 ... and honor and *t* to the one

THANKSGIVING (n) *a prayer expressing gratitude; a public acknowledgment or celebration of God's goodness*
Ps 26:7 ... singing a song of *t* and telling
Ps 28:7 ... I burst into songs of *t*.
Ps 100:4 ... Enter his gates with *t*; go
Isa 51:3 ... Songs of *t* will fill the air.

THIEF, THIEVES (n) *one who steals, especially stealthily or secretly*
Prov 6:30 ... might be found for a *t*
Prov 29:24 ... If you assist a *t*, you only
Jer 7:11 ... has become a den of *t-ves*?
Matt 6:19 ... where *t-ves* break in and steal.
Luke 19:46 ... turned it into a den of *t-ves*.
John 10:1 ... surely be a *t* and a robber!
John 10:8 ... me were *t-ves* and robbers.
1 Cor 6:10 ... or are *t-ves*, or greedy people,
1 Thes 5:2 ... unexpectedly, like a *t* in the
Rev 16:15 ... as unexpectedly as a *t*!

THINK, THINKING, THINKS (v) *to reflect, ponder, or remember; to subject to the processes of logical thought; to have an opinion; to conceive or reason*
see also MEDITATE
1 Sam 12:24 ... *T* of all the wonderful
2 Chr 19:6 ... Always *t* carefully before
Ps 8:4 ... you should *t* about them,
Ps 63:6 ... I lie awake *t-ing* of you,

Ps 77:12 . . . I cannot stop **t-ing** about your
Ps 119:97 . . . I **t** about them all day long.
Ps 119:148 . . . the night, **t-ing** about your
Prov 13:16 . . . Wise people **t** before they
Prov 15:28 . . . godly **t-s** carefully before
Prov 21:29 . . . the virtuous **t** before they
Prov 23:7 . . . are always **t-ing** about how
Prov 29:20 . . . who speaks without **t-ing.**
Isa 44:18 . . . are shut, and they cannot **t.**
Matt 22:42 . . . What do you **t** about the
Rom 11:20 . . . So don't **t** highly of
Phil 1:3 . . . Every time I **t** of you, I give
Phil 2:3 . . . Be humble, **t-ing** of others as
Phil 3:19 . . . they **t** only about this life
Heb 10:24 . . . Let us **t** of ways to motivate

THIRST (v) *to crave vehemently and urgently*
Ps 42:2 . . . I **t** for God, the living God.
Matt 5:6 . . . who hunger and **t** for justice,

THIRSTY (adj) *feeling a desire for liquids; having a strong desire*
Ps 107:9 . . . he satisfies the **t** and fills
Prov 25:21 . . . If they are **t,** give them
Isa 55:1 . . . Is anyone **t?** Come and drink—
Matt 25:35 . . . I was **t,** and you gave
John 4:14 . . . will never be **t** again.
John 19:28 . . . Scripture he said, "I am **t.**"
Rom 12:20 . . . If they are **t,** give them
2 Cor 11:27 . . . been hungry and **t** and
Rev 7:16 . . . never again be hungry or **t;**
Rev 22:17 . . . Let anyone who is **t** come.

THORN, THORNS (n) *a woody plant bearing sharp impeding prickles or spines; something that causes distress or irritation*
Gen 3:18 . . . It will grow **t-s** and thistles
Num 33:55 . . . in your eyes and **t-s** in your
Matt 13:7 . . . seeds fell among **t-s** that
Matt 27:29 . . . wove **t** branches into a
2 Cor 12:7 . . . I was given a **t** in my flesh,
Heb 6:8 . . . a field bears **t-s** and thistles,

THORNBUSHES (n) *any of various spiny or thorny shrubs or small trees*
Luke 6:44 . . . never gathered from **t,** nor

THOUGHT, THOUGHTS (n) *the action or process of thinking; a developed intention or plan; recollection, remembrance*
Ps 77:12 . . . They are constantly in my **t-s.**
Ps 92:5 . . . And how deep are your **t-s.**
Ps 94:11 . . . LORD knows people's **t-s;**
Ps 104:34 . . . May all my **t-s** be pleasing
Ps 139:23 . . . and know my anxious **t-s.**
Ps 142:4 . . . no one gives me a passing **t!**
Isa 26:3 . . . whose **t-s** are fixed on you!
Isa 55:8 . . . My **t-s** are nothing like your
Matt 9:4 . . . you have such evil **t-s** in your
Matt 15:19 . . . heart come evil **t-s,** murder,
1 Cor 14:25 . . . their secret **t-s** will be
Eph 4:23 . . . renew your **t-s** and attitudes.
Rev 2:23 . . . searches out the **t-s** and

THOUSAND (adj) *of the number 1,000*
Ps 90:4 . . . For you, a **t** years are as
Rev 20:7 . . . When the **t** years come to an

THOUSANDS (n) *a very large number*
Joel 3:14 . . . **T** upon **t** are waiting

THREE (adj) *the number 3*
Deut 19:15 . . . of two or **t** witnesses.
Jon 1:17 . . . **t** days and **t** nights.
Matt 12:40 . . . **t** days and **t** nights,
Matt 18:20 . . . where two or **t** gather

Matt 26:34 . . . you will deny **t** times that
Mark 8:31 . . . but **t** days later he would rise
1 Jn 5:7 . . . have these **t** witnesses—

THRONE, THRONES (n) *seat of power for a king or deity; symbolic of royal authority and the king's role as a judge*
Deut 17:18 . . . he sits on the **t** as king,
2 Sam 7:16 . . . and your **t** will be secure
1 Chr 17:12 . . . will secure his **t** forever.
Job 36:7 . . . sets them on **t-s** with kings
Ps 45:6 . . . Your **t,** O God, endures
Ps 47:8 . . . nations, sitting on his holy **t.**
Ps 89:14 . . . are the foundation of your **t.**
Ps 99:1 . . . He sits on his **t** between the
Ps 102:12 . . . sit on your **t** forever.
Ps 103:19 . . . has made the heavens his **t;**
Isa 6:1 . . . He was sitting on a lofty **t,**
Isa 66:1 . . . Heaven is my **t,** and the
Dan 7:9 . . . on a fiery **t** with wheels
Matt 19:28 . . . upon his glorious **t,** you who
Matt 19:28 . . . sit on twelve **t-s,** judging
Acts 7:49 . . . Heaven is my **t,** and the
Rom 15:12 . . . heir to David's **t** will come,
Col 1:16 . . . such as **t-s,** kingdoms, rulers,
Heb 12:2 . . . place of honor beside God's **t.**
Rev 3:21 . . . sat with my Father on his **t.**
Rev 4:2 . . . and I saw a **t** in heaven
Rev 4:4 . . . Twenty-four **t-s** surrounded
Rev 5:5 . . . heir to David's **t,** has won
Rev 20:11 . . . a great white **t** and the
Rev 22:3 . . . the **t** of God and of the Lamb

TIME, TIMES (n) *occasion; an opportune or suitable moment; an appointed, fixed, or customary moment or hour for something to happen, begin, or end; duration; conditions at present or at some specified period; added or accumulated quantities or instances*
Esth 4:14 . . . just such a **t** as this?"
Ps 9:9 . . . a refuge in **t-s** of trouble.
Ps 62:8 . . . trust in him at all **t-s.**
Eccl 3:1 . . . a **t** for every activity under
Eccl 7:14 . . . when hard **t-s** strike,
Eccl 8:5 . . . wise will find a **t** and a way
Dan 12:7 . . . for a **t, t-s,** and half a **t.**
Hos 10:12 . . . for now is the **t** to seek the
Amos 5:13 . . . shut, for it is an evil **t.**
Matt 16:3 . . . interpret the signs of the **t-s!**
Matt 18:21 . . . sins against me? Seven **t-s?**
Luke 12:40 . . . ready all the **t,** for the Son
John 4:53 . . . was the very **t** Jesus had told
John 12:23 . . . the **t** has come for the Son
Acts 1:7 . . . those dates and **t-s,** and they
Acts 18:5 . . . spent all his **t** preaching
1 Cor 7:29 . . . The **t** that remains is very
2 Cor 6:2 . . . the "right **t"** is now.
Gal 6:9 . . . just the right **t** we will reap
2 Tim 1:9 . . . the beginning of **t**—to show
Heb 9:28 . . . once for all **t** as a sacrifice
Heb 10:12 . . . for sins, good for all **t.**
1 Pet 4:17 . . . For the **t** has come for
Rev 12:14 . . . for a **t, t-s,** and half a **t.**

TITHE, TITHES (n) *one-tenth of any property or produce*
see also TENTH
Num 18:21 . . . give them the **t-s** from the

Deut 12:17 . . . neither the **t** of your grain
2 Chr 31:12 . . . brought all the gifts, **t-s,** and
Amos 4:4 . . . bring your **t-s** every three
Mal 3:8 . . . of the **t-s** and offerings due
Mal 3:10 . . . Bring all the **t-s** into the

TITHE (v) *to pay or give a tenth of as an offering to God*
Matt 23:23 . . . You should **t,** yes,
Luke 11:42 . . . you are careful to **t** even the

TODAY (adv) *on or for this day; at the present time*
Ps 2:7 . . . **T** I have become your Father.
Ps 95:7 . . . listen to his voice **t!**
Matt 6:11 . . . Give us **t** the food we
Luke 2:11 . . . born **t** in Bethlehem.
Luke 23:43 . . . I assure you, **t** you will be
Heb 1:5 . . . **T** I have become your Father.
Heb 3:7 . . . **T** when you hear his voice,
Heb 13:8 . . . is the same yesterday, **t,** and

TOMORROW (n) *the day after the present; the future*
Prov 27:1 . . . Don't brag about **t,** since you
Isa 22:13 . . . and drink, for **t** we die!
Rom 8:38 . . . our worries about **t**—not even
1 Cor 15:32 . . . and drink, for **t** we die!

TONGUE, TONGUES (n) *part of the mouth that enables speech; dialect or language of a people; a special gift of speech given by the Holy Spirit*
see also LANGUAGE(S)
Ps 5:9 . . . Their **t-s** are filled
Ps 34:13 . . . keep your **t** from speaking
Ps 39:1 . . . I will hold my **t** when
Ps 45:1 . . . king, for my **t** is like
Ps 78:36 . . . lied to him with their **t-s.**
Ps 119:172 . . . Let my **t** sing about
Ps 137:6 . . . May my **t** stick to the
Prov 13:3 . . . who control their **t** will have
Prov 15:4 . . . a deceitful **t** crushes the
Prov 17:20 . . . the lying **t** tumbles into
Prov 21:23 . . . Watch your **t** and keep
Luke 16:24 . . . in water and cool my **t.**
Acts 2:3 . . . like flames or **t-s** of fire
Acts 10:46 . . . speaking in other **t-s** and
Acts 19:6 . . . in other **t-s** and prophesied.
Rom 14:11 . . . me, and every **t** will declare
1 Cor 14:2 . . . to speak in **t-s,** you will
1 Cor 14:4 . . . speaks in **t-s** is strengthened
1 Cor 14:5 . . . speak in **t-s,** but even more
1 Cor 14:13 . . . speaks in **t-s** should pray
1 Cor 14:18 . . . I speak in **t-s** more than
1 Cor 14:27 . . . three should speak in **t-s.**
1 Cor 14:39 . . . forbid speaking in **t-s.**
Phil 2:11 . . . and every **t** declare that
Jas 3:2 . . . if we could control our **t-s,** we
Jas 3:5 . . . same way, the **t** is a small

TOOTH (n) *a bonelike structure in the mouth used for chewing*
Exod 21:24 . . . eye for an eye, a **t** for a **t,**
Matt 5:38 . . . eye for an eye, and a **t** for a **t.**

TORTURED (v) *to punish or coerce by inflicting excruciating pain*
Matt 18:34 . . . prison to be **t** until he
Heb 11:35 . . . others were **t,** refusing to

TOUCH, TOUCHED, TOUCHES (v) *to reach out or come in contact with; to lay hands upon; to have an influence upon*
Gen 3:3 . . . must not eat it or even **t** it;
Exod 19:12 . . . or even **t** its boundaries.
Exod 19:12 . . . Anyone who **t-es** the mountain
Isa 6:7 . . . this coal has **t-ed** your lips.

Matt 9:21 … If I can just *t* his robe,
Matt 14:36 … who *t-ed* him were healed.
Luke 8:45 … "Who *t-ed* me?" Jesus asked.
Luke 18:15 … so he could *t* and bless
Luke 24:39 … *T* me and make sure that
2 Cor 6:17 … Don't *t* their filthy things,
Col 2:21 … Don't taste! Don't *t!*"?
1 Jn 1:1 … *t-ed* him with our own hands.
1 Jn 5:18 … evil one cannot *t* them.

TRADE, TRADED (v) *to give one thing in exchange for another*
Gen 25:31 … Jacob replied, "but *t* me your
Ps 106:20 … They *t-d* their glorious God
Rom 1:25 … They *t-d* the truth about God

TRADITION, TRADITIONS (n) *an inherited, customary, or established pattern of thought, action, or behavior*
Matt 15:6 … for the sake of your own *t.*
Mark 7:5 … disciples follow our age-old *t?*
Mark 7:8 … law and substitute your own *t.*
Mark 7:13 … to hand down your own *t.*
Gal 1:14 … in my zeal for the *t-s* of my

TRAIN (n) *a part of a gown that trails behind the wearer*
Isa 6:1 … throne, and the *t* of his robe

TRAIN, TRAINED (v) *to form by or undergo instruction or discipline* see also TEACH
Isa 2:4 … against nation, nor *t* for war
Luke 6:40 … who is fully *t-ed* will become
John 7:15 … when he hasn't been *t-ed?*
Acts 22:3 … I was carefully *t-ed* in our
1 Tim 4:7 … *t* yourself to be godly.
Titus 2:4 … women must *t* the younger
Heb 12:11 … those who are *t-ed* in this way.

TRAITORS (n) *those who betray another's trust, are false to an obligation or duty, or commit treason*
Ps 59:5 … Show no mercy to wicked *t.*
Ps 119:158 … Seeing these *t* makes me

TRAMPLE, TRAMPLED (v) *to crush, injure, or destroy by or as if by treading*
Ps 60:12 … for he will *t* down our foes.
Ps 91:13 … You will *t* upon lions
Amos 5:11 … You *t* the poor,
Amos 8:4 … rob the poor and *t* down the
Mic 4:13 … so you can *t* many nations to
Mic 7:19 … You will *t* our sins under
Matt 7:6 … They will *t* the pearls,
Luke 21:24 … Jerusalem will be *t-d* down
Heb 10:29 … who have *t-d* on the Son
Rev 14:20 … The grapes were *t-d* in the

TRANSFIGURED (KJV)
Matt 17:2 … Jesus' appearance was transformed
Mark 9:2 … Jesus' appearance was transformed

TRANSFORM, TRANSFORMED (v) *to change the outward appearance of; to change in character or condition* see also CHANGE(D)
Matt 17:2 … appearance was *t-ed* so that
Rom 12:2 … let God *t* you into a new
1 Cor 15:51 … but we will all be *t-ed!*

TRANSGRESSED, TRANSGRESSION (KJV)
Josh 7:11 … and *broken* my covenant
1 Chr 5:25 … tribes were *unfaithful*
1 Chr 10:13 … because he was *unfaithful*
Rom 4:15 … to avoid *breaking* the law
1 Jn 3:4 … sin is *contrary* to the law

TRAP, TRAPS (n) *something by which one is caught or stopped unawares; a position or situation from which it is difficult or impossible to escape; a device for taking game or other animals*
Deut 7:25 … will become a *t* to you,
Deut 12:30 … fall into the *t* of following
Ps 91:3 … you from every *t* and protect
Prov 1:17 … a bird sees a *t* being set,
Prov 3:26 … foot from being caught in a *t.*
Prov 28:10 … into their own *t*, but the
Prov 29:5 … is to lay a *t* for their feet.
Prov 29:25 … a dangerous *t*, but trusting
Isa 8:14 … he will be a *t* and a snare.
Isa 24:17 … Terror and *t-s* and snares will
Matt 16:23 … are a dangerous *t* to me.
Rom 11:9 … a snare, a *t* that makes them
1 Tim 3:7 … into the devil's *t.*
2 Tim 2:26 … from the devil's *t.*

TRAP, TRAPPED, TRAPS (v) *to catch or take in or as if in a trap*
Ps 7:15 … a deep pit to *t* others, then
Ps 9:16 … wicked are *t-ped* by their own
Prov 6:2 … if you have *t-ped* yourself by
Prov 12:13 … wicked are *t-ped* by their
Prov 18:7 … they *t* themselves with
Matt 22:15 … to plot how to *t* Jesus into
1 Cor 3:19 … He *t-s* the wise in the snare
1 Tim 6:9 … temptation and are *t-ped* by

TREAD, TREADING, TREADS (v) *to beat or press with the feet*
Deut 25:4 … eating as it *t-s* out the grain.
Isa 63:2 … have been *t-ing* out grapes?
Joel 3:13 … Come, *t* the grapes,
1 Cor 9:9 … from eating as it *t-s* out
1 Tim 5:18 … from eating as it *t-s* out

TREASURE, TREASURES (n) *wealth or a collection of precious things; something of great value*
Exod 19:5 … my own special *t* from
Deut 7:6 … to be his own special *t.*
1 Chr 29:3 … my own private *t-s* of gold
Ps 119:111 … Your laws are my *t;*
Ps 135:4 … Israel for his own special *t.*
Prov 2:4 … seek them like hidden *t-s.*
Prov 18:22 … finds a wife finds a *t,*
Song 4:10 … delights me, my *t*, my bride.
Isa 10:3 … Where will your *t-s* be safe?
Hag 2:7 … the *t-s* of all the nations
Mal 3:17 … they will be my own special *t.*
Matt 6:19 … Don't store up *t-s* here on
Matt 6:21 … Wherever your *t* is, there the
Matt 13:44 … Heaven is like a *t* that a man
Luke 12:33 … will store up *t* for you in
2 Cor 4:7 … jars containing this great *t.*
Eph 3:8 … the endless *t-s* available to
Col 2:3 … hidden all the *t-s* of wisdom
1 Tim 6:19 … storing up their *t* as a good
Heb 11:26 … to own the *t-s* of Egypt, for

TREASURE, TREASURED (v) *to hold or keep as precious*
Job 23:12 … but have *t-d* his words more
Prov 2:1 … I say, and *t* my commands.
Prov 7:1 … always *t* my commands.
Prov 10:14 … Wise people *t* knowledge,

TREASURY (n) *a place in which stores of wealth are kept*
Deut 28:12 … time from his rich *t* in the
Luke 6:45 … things from the *t* of a good

TREE, TREES (n) *woody perennial plants, many of which produce crops; highly treasured natural resource; often*

linked with worship of pagan gods; symbolic of a growing believer
Gen 2:9 … he placed the *t* of life and
Deut 21:23 … from the *t* overnight.
Judg 9:8 … the *t-s* decided to choose
2 Sam 18:9 … got caught in the *t.*
1 Kgs 14:23 … and under every green *t.*
Ps 1:3 … They are like *t-s* planted along
Ps 52:8 … like an olive *t*, thriving in
Ps 92:12 … like palm *t-s* and grow
Ps 96:12 … Let the *t-s* of the forest
Prov 3:18 … Wisdom is a *t* of life to
Prov 11:30 … deeds become a *t* of life;
Isa 55:12 … and the *t-s* of the field
Isa 65:22 … people will live as long as *t-s,*
Jer 17:8 … They are like *t-s* planted along
Dan 4:10 … saw a large *t* in the middle
Mic 4:4 … and fig *t-s*, for there will be
Matt 3:10 … sever the roots of the *t-s.*
Matt 3:10 … every *t* that does not produce
Matt 12:33 … *t* is identified by its fruit.
Mark 8:24 … look like *t-s* walking
Luke 19:4 … a sycamore-fig *t* beside the
Rom 11:24 … cut from a wild olive *t.*
Gal 3:13 … everyone who is hung on a *t.*
Jas 3:12 … Does a fig *t* produce olives,
Jude 1:12 … They are like *t-s* in autumn
Rev 22:2 … the river grew a *t* of life,
Rev 22:14 … the fruit from the *t* of life.
Rev 22:19 … share in the *t* of life and

TREMBLE, TREMBLED, TREMBLES, TREMBLING (v) *to be affected with great fear or anxiety; to shake involuntarily*
Exod 15:14 … hear and *t;* anguish grips
Exod 19:16 … horn, and all the people *t-d.*
Exod 20:18 … a distance, *t-ing* with fear.
2 Sam 22:8 … the earth quaked and *t-d.*
1 Chr 16:30 … all the earth *t* before him.
Ps 2:11 … fear, and rejoice with *t-ing.*
Ps 97:4 … The earth sees and *t-s.*
Ps 102:15 … the earth will *t* before his
Ps 104:32 … The earth *t-s* at his glance;
Isa 66:2 … contrite hearts, who *t* at my
Jer 10:10 … whole earth *t-s* at his anger.
Dan 10:10 … and lifted me, still *t-ing,*
Joel 2:1 … Let everyone in fear
Nah 1:5 … hills melt away; the earth *t-s,*
Hab 3:6 … the nations *t.* He shatters
Heb 4:1 … we ought to *t* with fear that
Heb 12:21 … I am terrified and *t-ing.*

TRESPASS(ES) (KJV)
Lev 19:21 … a ram as a *guilt* offering
2 Chr 24:18 … Because of this *sin*, divine
Matt 6:15 … Father will not forgive your *sins*
Matt 18:15 … believer *sins* against you,
Eph 2:1 … because of your *disobedience*

TRIAL, TRIALS (n) *a legal proceeding based in court; a test of faith, patience, or stamina through subjection to suffering or temptation* see also TEMPTATION(S), TEST(S), TROUBLE(S)
Job 42:11 … all the *t-s* the LORD had
Ps 26:2 … Put me on *t,* LORD,
Ps 37:33 … when they are put on *t.*
Ps 143:2 … Don't put your servant on *t,*
Mark 13:11 … and stand *t*, don't worry in
Luke 22:28 … with me in my time of *t.*
John 16:33 … have many *t-s* and sorrows.
Rom 5:3 … into problems and *t-s*, for we
1 Pet 1:7 … through many *t-s*, it will
1 Pet 4:12 … the fiery *t-s* you are going
2 Pet 2:9 … from their *t-s*, even while

TRIBULATION (n) *a period of unparalleled suffering in the last days*
Rev 7:14 ... who died in the great *t*.

TRICK, TRICKED (v) *to deceive or cheat*
Gen 27:35 ... and he *t-ed* me
Gen 29:25 ... Why have you *t-ed* me
Jer 29:31 ... has *t-ed* you into believing
2 Cor 4:2 ... We don't try to *t* anyone
Eph 4:14 ... people try to *t* us with lies

TRICKERY (n) *deception*
Isa 29:21 ... those who use *t* to pervert
2 Cor 12:16 ... advantage of you by *t*.

TROUBLE, TROUBLES (n) *a state, condition, or cause of distress, annoyance, difficulty, or inconvenience*
see also TEST(S), TRIAL(S)
Gen 41:51 ... made me forget all my *t-s*
Josh 7:25 ... have you brought *t* on us?
2 Chr 15:4 ... they were in *t* and turned
Job 5:7 ... are born for *t* as readily as
Ps 7:14 ... they are pregnant with *t*
Ps 9:9 ... a refuge in times of *t*.
Ps 10:14 ... you see the *t* and grief
Ps 22:11 ... from me, for *t* is near,
Ps 27:5 ... me there when *t-s* come;
Ps 32:7 ... you protect me from *t*.
Ps 34:17 ... them from all their *t-s*.
Ps 37:39 ... their fortress in times of *t*.
Ps 40:12 ... For *t-s* surround me—
Ps 41:1 ... them when they are in *t*.
Ps 46:1 ... ready to help in times of *t*.
Ps 49:5 ... I fear when *t* comes, when
Ps 50:15 ... when you are in *t*, and I will
Ps 54:7 ... have rescued me from my *t-s*
Ps 55:3 ... They bring *t* on me
Ps 66:14 ... I was in deep *t*.
Ps 81:7 ... cried to me in *t*, and
Ps 86:7 ... whenever I'm in *t*, and
Ps 91:15 ... I will be with them in *t*.
Ps 107:6 ... they cried in their *t*,
Ps 107:41 ... rescues the poor from *t*
Ps 116:3 ... I saw only *t* and sorrow.
Ps 120:1 ... took my *t-s* to the LORD;
Ps 138:7 ... I am surrounded by *t-s*, you
Prov 6:14 ... they constantly stir up *t*.
Prov 10:10 ... who wink at wrong cause *t*,
Prov 11:8 ... godly are rescued from *t*,
Prov 11:29 ... Those who bring *t* on their
Prov 12:13 ... the godly escape such *t*.
Prov 12:21 ... wicked have their fill of *t*.
Prov 13:20 ... with fools and get in *t*.
Prov 25:19 ... in times of *t* is like chewing
Eccl 4:10 ... falls alone is in real *t*.
Isa 38:14 ... I am in *t*, Lord. Help me!
Isa 53:4 ... And we thought his *t-s* were
Isa 58:10 ... and help those in *t*,
Hos 5:15 ... as soon as *t* comes, they
Nah 1:7 ... strong refuge when *t* comes.
Matt 6:34 ... Today's *t* is enough
Rom 8:35 ... if we have *t* or calamity,
1 Cor 7:28 ... at this time will have *t-s*,
2 Cor 4:17 ... our present *t-s* are small
2 Cor 6:4 ... We patiently endure *t-s* and
2 Cor 7:4 ... me happy despite all our *t-s*.
2 Cor 8:2 ... being tested by many *t-s*,
1 Thes 3:3 ... shaken by the *t-s* you were
1 Tim 6:5 ... These people always cause *t*.
Jas 1:2 ... when *t-s* of any kind come
Jas 5:1 ... all the terrible *t-s* ahead

TROUBLE (v) *to worry or disturb*
Luke 7:6 ... Lord, don't *t* yourself by

TRUE (adj) *fully realized or fulfilled; accurate; properly so called; steadfast, loyal, honest, and just; ideal, essential; being in accordance with the actual state of affairs; legitimate, rightful*
Num 11:23 ... my word comes *t*!
Deut 18:22 ... does not happen or come *t*,
Josh 23:14 ... your God has come *t*.
1 Sam 9:6 ... everything he says comes *t*.
1 Kgs 10:6 ... and wisdom is *t*!
2 Chr 15:3 ... without the *t* God,
Ps 7:10 ... hearts are *t* and right.
Ps 19:9 ... laws of the LORD are *t*;
Ps 119:142 ... instructions are perfectly *t*.
Ps 119:151 ... your commands are *t*.
Isa 45:19 ... speak only what is *t* and
Jer 10:10 ... is the only *t* God.
Jer 26:15 ... it is absolutely *t* that
Jer 28:9 ... when his predictions come *t*
Luke 16:11 ... the *t* riches of heaven?
Luke 18:31 ... Son of Man will come *t*.
John 1:9 ... one who is the *t* light,
John 3:33 ... can affirm that God is *t*.
John 4:23 ... *t* worshipers will worship
John 6:32 ... offers you the *t* bread
John 6:55 ... my flesh is *t* food, and
John 7:28 ... one who sent me is *t*,
John 15:1 ... I am the *t* grapevine,
John 17:3 ... know you, the only *t* God,
Rom 3:4 ... else is a liar, God is *t*.
Rom 15:8 ... God is *t* to the promises
Eph 5:9 ... is good and right and *t*.
Phil 4:1 ... stay *t* to the Lord.
Phil 4:8 ... thoughts on what is *t*,
Jas 1:18 ... giving us his *t* word.
1 Jn 2:8 ... the *t* light is already
1 Jn 2:27 ... to teach you what is *t*.
1 Jn 5:20 ... He is the only *t* God,
Rev 19:9 ... These are *t* words that come
Rev 22:6 ... seen is trustworthy and *t*.

TRUMPET, TRUMPETS (n) *a wind instrument made of metal or an animal horn used to rally troops on the battlefield or by priests during sacrifices*
Isa 27:13 ... the great *t* will sound.
Matt 24:31 ... blast of a *t*, and they will
1 Cor 15:52 ... when the last *t* is blown.
1 Thes 4:16 ... with the *t* call of God.
Rev 8:2 ... they were given seven *t-s*.
Rev 8:7 ... angel blew his *t*, and hail
Rev 18:22 ... flutes, and *t-s* will never

TRUST (n) *assured reliance on the character, ability, strength, or truth of someone or something; hope*
see also BELIEVE, FAITH
Job 31:24 ... Have I put my *t* in money
Ps 40:3 ... put their *t* in the LORD.
Ps 56:3 ... I will put my *t* in you.
Isa 2:22 ... Don't put your *t* in mere
Jer 13:25 ... putting your *t* in false
Jer 17:5 ... who put their *t* in mere
John 12:46 ... who put their *t* in me
Heb 2:13 ... will put my *t* in him,
1 Jn 4:16 ... have put our *t* in his love.

TRUST, TRUSTED, TRUSTING, TRUSTS (v) *to place confidence or depend; to commit or place in one's care or keeping; to rely on the truthfulness or accuracy of*
see also BELIEVE, FAITH
Gen 39:8 ... master *t-s* me with everything
Deut 1:32 ... refused to *t* the LORD
Deut 28:52 ... walls you *t-ed* to protect
2 Kgs 18:5 ... Hezekiah *t-ed* in the

2 Kgs 18:19 ... What are you *t-ing* in that
1 Chr 5:20 ... because they *t-ed* in him.
2 Chr 13:18 ... they *t-ed* in the LORD,
Job 4:18 ... God does not *t* his own angels
Job 15:31 ... fool themselves by *t-ing* in
Ps 13:5 ... I *t* in your unfailing love.
Ps 21:7 ... the king *t-s* in the LORD.
Ps 25:2 ... I *t* in you, my God!
Ps 25:3 ... No one who *t-s* in you will
Ps 31:14 ... I am *t-ing* you, O LORD,
Ps 33:4 ... we can *t* everything he
Ps 37:3 ... *T* in the LORD and do
Ps 41:9 ... the one I *t-ed* completely,
Ps 44:6 ... I do not *t* in my bow;
Ps 55:23 ... but I am *t-ing* you to save
Ps 62:8 ... O my people, *t* in him at
Ps 71:5 ... I've *t-ed* you, O LORD,
Ps 84:12 ... for those who *t* in you.
Ps 86:2 ... serve you and *t* you.
Ps 112:7 ... confidently *t* the LORD
Ps 115:8 ... as are all who *t* in them.
Ps 118:8 ... LORD than to *t* in
Ps 119:42 ... for I *t* in your word.
Prov 3:5 ... *T* in the LORD with
Prov 21:22 ... fortress in which they *t*.
Prov 28:25 ... *t-ing* the LORD leads to
Prov 28:26 ... who *t* their own insight
Prov 29:25 ... *t-ing* the LORD means safety.
Prov 31:11 ... Her husband can *t* her,
Isa 12:2 ... I will *t* in him and
Isa 25:9 ... We *t-ed* in him, and he saved
Isa 26:3 ... peace all who *t* in you,
Isa 31:1 ... for help, *t-ing* their horses,
Isa 40:31 ... who *t* in the LORD
Jer 7:14 ... this Temple that you *t* in
Jer 12:6 ... Do not *t* them, no matter
Jer 48:7 ... Because you have *t-ed* in your
Dan 3:28 ... his servants who *t-ed* in him.
Dan 6:23 ... for he had *t-ed* in his God.
Nah 1:7 ... to those who *t* in him.
Hab 2:4 ... They *t* in themselves,
Hab 2:18 ... foolish to *t* in your own
Matt 18:6 ... little ones who *t-s* in me to
John 2:24 ... Jesus didn't *t* them,
John 12:44 ... you are *t-ing* not only me,
John 14:1 ... in God, and *t* also in me.
Rom 9:32 ... instead of by *t-ing* in him.
Rom 9:33 ... But anyone who *t-s* in him will
Rom 10:11 ... Anyone who *t-s* in him will
Rom 15:13 ... peace because you *t* in
1 Cor 2:5 ... so you would *t* not in
1 Cor 7:25 ... wisdom that can be *t-ed*,
Eph 3:17 ... hearts as you *t* in him.
Phil 1:29 ... the privilege of *t-ing* in Christ
Col 2:12 ... because you *t-ed* the mighty
1 Tim 6:17 ... not to *t* in their money,
2 Tim 1:12 ... the one in whom I *t*,
2 Tim 3:15 ... that comes by *t-ing* in Christ
Heb 10:22 ... hearts fully *t-ing* him.
Heb 10:23 ... God can be *t-ed* to keep his
1 Pet 1:9 ... reward for *t-ing* him will be
1 Pet 2:6 ... anyone who *t-s* in him will
1 Pet 2:7 ... you who *t* him recognize

TRUSTWORTHY (adj) *worthy of confidence; dependable*
see also FAITHFUL, LOYAL
2 Kgs 22:7 ... honest and *t* men.
Ps 19:7 ... of the LORD are *t*,
Ps 119:86 ... All your commands are *t*.
Ps 119:138 ... perfect and completely *t*.
Prov 11:13 ... those who are *t* can keep
Dan 6:4 ... responsible, and completely *t*.
Titus 2:10 ... to be entirely *t* and good.
Heb 6:19 ... a strong and *t* anchor

1769

TRUTH, TRUTHS (n) *the property (as of a statement) of being in accord with fact or reality (natural and spiritual); sincerity in action, character, and utterance*
Ps 15:2 … speaking the *t* from sincere
Ps 25:5 … Lead me by your *t* and teach
Ps 26:3 … lived according to your *t.*
Ps 43:3 … light and your *t*; let them
Ps 45:4 … defending *t*, humility, and
Ps 86:11 … live according to your *t!*
Ps 119:160 … essence of your words is *t*;
Prov 8:7 … for I speak the *t* and detest
Prov 12:17 … honest witness tells the *t*;
Prov 12:22 … in those who tell the *t.*
Prov 23:23 … Get the *t* and never sell
Isa 45:23 … I have spoken the *t,*
Isa 59:15 … Yes, *t* is gone,
Jer 4:2 … do so with *t*, justice,
Jer 9:3 … to stand up for the *t.*
Dan 10:21 … written in the Book of *T.*
Dan 11:2 … I will reveal the *t* to you.
Amos 5:10 … people who tell the *t!*
Zech 8:16 … Tell the *t* to each other.
Zech 8:19 … So love *t* and peace.
Luke 1:4 … can be certain of the *t*
John 4:23 … Father in spirit and in *t.*
John 7:18 … him speaks *t*, not lies.
John 8:32 … the *t* will set you free.
John 8:44 … there is no *t* in him.
John 14:6 … way, the *t*, and the life.
John 14:17 … who leads into all *t.*
John 15:26 … Advocate—the Spirit of *t.*
John 16:13 … the Spirit of *t* comes,
John 17:17 … your word, which is *t.*
John 18:37 … to testify to the *t.*
Acts 20:30 … distort the *t* in order
Acts 21:34 … find out the *t* in all
Acts 24:8 … can find out the *t* of our
Rom 1:18 … who suppress the *t* by their
Rom 1:25 … They traded the *t* about God
Rom 2:8 … to obey the *t* and instead
Rom 2:20 … complete knowledge and *t.*
1 Cor 2:13 … to explain spiritual *t-s.*
2 Cor 6:7 … We faithfully preach the *t.*
2 Cor 13:8 … always stand for the *t.*
Gal 2:5 … wanted to preserve the *t*
Gal 5:7 … back from following the *t?*
Eph 1:13 … also heard the *t*, the Good
Eph 4:15 … will speak the *t* in love,
Eph 6:14 … the belt of *t* and the body
2 Thes 2:10 … *t* that would save them.
2 Thes 2:12 … rather than believing the *t.*
1 Tim 2:4 … and to understand the *t.*
1 Tim 3:15 … and foundation of the *t.*
1 Tim 4:3 … people who know the *t.*
1 Tim 6:5 … their backs on the *t.*
2 Tim 2:15 … explains the word of *t.*
2 Tim 3:7 … able to understand the *t.*
Titus 1:14 … turned away from the *t.*
Heb 10:26 … received knowledge of the *t,*
Jas 3:14 … don't cover up the *t* with
Jas 5:19 … wanders away from the *t*
1 Pet 1:22 … you obeyed the *t*, so now
2 Pet 1:12 … standing firm in the *t*
2 Pet 2:2 … the way of *t* will be
1 Jn 1:8 … and not living in the *t.*
1 Jn 2:20 … all of you know the *t.*
1 Jn 3:19 … belong to the *t*, so we
1 Jn 4:6 … Spirit of *t* or the spirit
1 Jn 5:6 … Spirit, who is *t*, confirms
2 Jn 1:2 … because the *t* lives
2 Jn 1:3 … who live in *t* and love.
3 Jn 1:3 … living according to the *t.*
3 Jn 1:8 … partners as they teach the *t.*

TURN, TURNED, TURNING, TURNS (v) *to convert or change allegiance; to return or change direction; to face toward or away; to divert one's attention from; to become or transform; to shape or bend*
Deut 28:14 … You must not *t* away from
Deut 30:10 … if you *t* to the LORD
1 Kgs 11:4 … old age, they *t-ed* his heart
2 Chr 7:14 … seek my face and *t* from
2 Chr 34:33 … they did not *t* away from
Esth 9:22 … sorrow was *t-ed* into gladness
Ps 14:3 … no, all have *t-ed* away; all
Ps 30:11 … You have *t-ed* my mourning
Ps 40:1 … and he *t-ed* to me and
Ps 119:59 … I *t-ed* to follow your
Ps 119:102 … I haven't *t-ed* away from
Prov 3:7 … fear the LORD and *t* away
Prov 28:13 … confess and *t* from them,
Isa 17:7 … Creator and *t* their eyes to
Isa 54:8 … anger I *t-ed* my face away
Isa 55:7 … Let them *t* to the LORD
Isa 59:2 … he has *t-ed* away and will
Jer 14:7 … We have *t-ed* away from you
Jer 31:13 … I will *t* their mourning into
Jer 31:19 … I *t-ed* away from God,
Lam 3:40 … Let us *t* back to the LORD.
Mal 4:6 … preaching will *t* the hearts
Matt 3:8 … your sins and *t-ed* to God.
Matt 18:3 … truth, unless you *t* from your
Mark 4:12 … Otherwise, they will *t* to me
Luke 1:17 … He will *t* the hearts of
Luke 17:4 … *t-s* again and asks forgiveness
Luke 22:32 … you have repented and *t-ed*
John 12:40 … and they cannot *t* to me
John 16:20 … will suddenly *t* to wonderful
Acts 3:19 … of your sins and *t* to God,
Acts 7:42 … Then God *t-ed* away from
Acts 26:18 … so they may *t* from darkness
Rom 1:26 … Even the women *t-ed* against
Rom 2:4 … to *t* you from your sin?
Rom 3:12 … All have *t-ed* away;
Gal 1:6 … that you are *t-ing* away so
2 Tim 2:19 … LORD must *t* away from
Titus 2:12 … instructed to *t* from godless
Heb 10:38 … in anyone who *t-s* away.
1 Pet 2:25 … But now you have *t-ed* to

TWELVE (adj) *of or relating to the number 12*
Gen 35:22 … names of the *t* sons of Jacob:
Gen 49:28 … These are the *t* tribes of
Matt 10:1 … Jesus called his *t* disciples
Luke 9:17 … picked up *t* baskets of
Rev 21:12 … names of the *t* tribes of
Rev 21:14 … names of the *t* apostles of
Rev 21:21 … The *t* gates were made of

U

UNBELIEF (n) *incredulity or skepticism in matters of religious truth*
Matt 13:58 … there because of their *u.*
Mark 6:6 … he was amazed at their *u.*
Mark 9:24 … help me overcome my *u!*
Mark 16:14 … them for their stubborn *u*
Rom 11:23 … Israel turn from their *u,*
1 Tim 1:13 … it in ignorance and *u.*
Heb 3:19 … because of their *u* they

UNBELIEVER, UNBELIEVERS (n) *one who does not believe; a non-Christian*
Matt 6:32 … dominate the thoughts of *u-s,*
Luke 12:30 … the thoughts of *u-s* all over
1 Cor 6:6 … right in front of *u-s!*
1 Cor 14:22 … for believers, but for *u-s.*
2 Cor 6:15 … a partner with an *u?*
1 Tim 5:8 … people are worse than *u-s.*
Rev 21:8 … But cowards, *u-s,* the corrupt,

UNCLEAN (adj) *morally or spiritually impure; prohibited by ritual law for use or contact*
Lev 10:10 … is ceremonially *u* and what is
Lev 11:4 … it is ceremonially *u* for you.
Lev 17:15 … remain ceremonially *u* until
Lev 27:11 … vow involves an *u* animal—
Isa 52:11 … everything you touch is *u.*
Acts 10:14 … have declared impure and *u.*
Acts 10:15 … not call something *u* if God

UNDERSTAND (v) *to grasp the meaning or reasonableness of; to be thoroughly familiar with*
Job 5:9 … things too marvelous to *u.*
Job 36:26 … is greater than we can *u.*
Ps 73:16 … tried to *u* why the wicked
Ps 119:27 … Help me *u* the meaning of
Ps 119:125 … then I will *u* your laws.
Ps 119:130 … so even the simple can *u.*
Prov 2:5 … will *u* what it means to fear
Prov 2:9 … you will *u* what is right,
Prov 28:5 … the LORD *u* completely.
Prov 30:18 … things that I don't *u:*
Eccl 7:25 … no one can *u* the reason
Isa 6:9 … carefully, but do not *u.*
Isa 40:21 … you heard? Don't you *u?*
Jer 9:24 … truly know me and *u* that
Hos 14:9 … who are wise *u* these things.
Matt 13:11 … permitted to *u* the secrets
Matt 13:23 … truly hear and *u* God's
Luke 19:42 … people would *u* the way
Luke 24:45 … minds to *u* the Scriptures.
Acts 8:30 … Do you *u* what you are
Rom 7:15 … I don't really *u* myself,
Rom 15:21 … never heard of him will *u.*
1 Cor 2:14 … and they can't *u* it,
1 Cor 14:14 … but I don't *u* what I am
2 Cor 3:14 … they cannot *u* the truth.
Gal 1:11 … you to *u* that the gospel
Eph 1:18 … you can *u* the confident
Eph 5:17 … thoughtlessly, but *u* what
Phil 1:10 … want you to *u* what really
Phil 4:7 … exceeds anything we can *u.*
Col 2:2 … that they *u* God's mysterious
1 Tim 2:4 … saved and to *u* the truth.
2 Tim 2:7 … will help you *u* all these
Heb 11:3 … By faith we *u* that the entire
2 Pet 3:16 … are hard to *u,* and those

UNDERSTANDABLE (adj) *marked by being able to understand; comprehensible*
1 Cor 14:19 … rather speak five *u* words

UNITED (v) *to become one or as if one; in one accord or spirit*
Gen 2:24 … the two are *u* into one.
Mark 10:8 … the two are *u* into one.
Rom 6:5 … we have been *u* with him
Rom 7:4 … now you are *u* with the one
1 Cor 6:16 … The two are *u* into one.
Eph 4:3 … to keep yourselves *u* in the
Eph 5:31 … the two are *u* into one."

UNITY (n) *the quality or state of oneness or harmony*
John 17:23 … perfect *u* that the world
Eph 4:13 … come to such *u* in our faith

UNWORTHILY (adv) *in an undeserving manner*
1 Cor 11:27 … this cup of the Lord *u*

UPRIGHT (adj) *marked by strong moral integrity*
see also GODLY, RIGHT, RIGHTEOUS
Deut 32:4 . . . how just and *u* he is!
Prov 3:33 . . . blesses the home of the *u*.
Prov 15:8 . . . in the prayers of the *u*.

USEFUL (adj) *serviceable for an end or purpose*
2 Tim 3:16 . . . inspired by God and is *u* to
2 Pet 1:8 . . . productive and *u* you will be

USELESS (adj) *having or being of no use; ineffectual, inept*
John 15:6 . . . thrown away like a *u* branch
Acts 26:14 . . . It is *u* for you to fight
1 Cor 13:8 . . . knowledge will become *u*.
1 Cor 15:14 . . . *u*, and your faith is *u*.
1 Cor 15:58 . . . do for the Lord is ever *u*.
2 Tim 2:14 . . . Such arguments are *u*, and
Titus 1:10 . . . who engage in *u* talk and
Heb 7:18 . . . because it was weak and *u*.

V

VALLEY, VALLEYS (n) *a depression in the earth's surface between ranges of mountains, hills, or other uplands*
Ps 23:4 . . . through the darkest *v*, I will
Song 2:1 . . . lily of the *v*.
Isa 40:4 . . . Fill in the *v-s*, and level
Joel 3:14 . . . waiting in the *v* of decision.
Luke 3:5 . . . The *v-s* will be filled, and

VALUABLE (adj) *having desirable or esteemed characteristics or qualities; of great use or service*
Job 28:17 . . . Wisdom is more *v* than gold
Ps 119:72 . . . instructions are more *v*
Prov 8:11 . . . is far more *v* than rubies.
Prov 20:15 . . . words are more *v* than
Matt 10:31 . . . you are more *v* to God than
Luke 12:24 . . . are far more *v* to him than
Phil 3:7 . . . these things were *v*, but now

VALUE (n) *monetary worth of something; relative worth, utility, or importance*
Matt 13:46 . . . a pearl of great *v*, he sold
1 Cor 3:13 . . . a person's work has any *v*.
Phil 3:8 . . . the infinite *v* of knowing

VEIL (n) *a facial covering*
Exod 34:33 . . . covered his face with a *v*.
2 Cor 3:14 . . . same *v* covers their minds
2 Cor 3:18 . . . have had that *v* removed can

VENGEANCE (n) *punishment inflicted in retaliation for an injury or offense*
1 Sam 25:26 . . . taking *v* into your own
1 Sam 25:33 . . . carrying out *v* with my
Ps 94:1 . . . O LORD, the God of *v*,
Isa 66:6 . . . the LORD taking *v* against
Luke 21:22 . . . be days of God's *v*, and the

VICTORY, VICTORIES (n) *the overcoming of an enemy, antagonist, or struggle*
Exod 15:2 . . . he has given me *v*.
2 Sam 22:51 . . . You give great *v-ies* to your
Ps 18:50 . . . You give great *v-ies* to your
Ps 20:5 . . . we hear of your *v* and
Ps 21:1 . . . because you give him *v*.
Ps 35:3 . . . I will give you *v*!
Ps 44:4 . . . You command *v-ies* for Israel.
Ps 45:4 . . . majesty, ride out to *v*,
Ps 48:10 . . . right hand is filled with *v*.
Ps 62:1 . . . for my *v* comes from him.

Ps 98:3 . . . have seen the *v* of our God.
Ps 118:14 . . . he has given me *v*.
Ps 149:4 . . . crowns the humble with *v*.
Isa 12:2 . . . he has given me *v*.
Isa 52:10 . . . see the *v* of our God.
Rom 8:37 . . . overwhelming *v* is ours
1 Cor 15:54 . . . Death is swallowed up in *v*.
Col 2:15 . . . publicly by his *v* over them
Rev 5:5 . . . David's throne, has won the *v*.

VINEYARD (n) *a plantation of grapevines*
1 Kgs 21:1 . . . who owned a *v* in Jezreel
Prov 31:16 . . . earnings she plants a *v*.
Song 1:6 . . . for myself—my own *v*.
Isa 5:1 . . . beloved had a *v* on a rich
1 Cor 9:7 . . . farmer plants a *v* and

VIOLATE, VIOLATED, VIOLATES, VIOLATING (v) *to do harm to the person or especially the chastity of; to fail to show proper respect for; to break or disregard*
Lev 18:7 . . . Do not *v* your father
Lev 18:8 . . . for this would *v* your father.
Lev 18:10 . . . this would *v* yourself.
Lev 18:14 . . . Do not *v* your uncle,
Lev 18:16 . . . this would *v* your brother.
Lev 20:11 . . . If a man *v-s* his father by
Lev 20:20 . . . he has *v-d* his uncle.
Lev 20:21 . . . He has *v-d* his brother, and
Num 15:30 . . . who brazenly *v* the LORD's
Deut 22:30 . . . for this would *v* his father.
Deut 27:20 . . . for he has *v-d* his father.
Isa 24:5 . . . instructions, *v-d* his laws,
Mal 2:10 . . . each other, *v-ing* the covenant

VIOLENCE (n) *exertion of physical force so as to injure or abuse*
Gen 6:11 . . . and was filled with *v*.
Ps 12:5 . . . I have seen *v* done to the
Ps 72:14 . . . them from oppression and *v*,
Isa 60:18 . . . *V* will disappear from your
Jon 3:8 . . . and stop all their *v*.
Mic 2:2 . . . take it by fraud and *v*.

VIOLENT (adj) *emotionally agitated to the point of loss of self-control*
1 Tim 3:3 . . . a heavy drinker or be *v*.
Titus 1:7 . . . not be a heavy drinker, *v*,

VIRGIN (n) *an unmarried woman who has not had sexual intercourse*
Gen 24:16 . . . but she was still a *v*.
Isa 7:14 . . . The *v* will conceive a child!
Matt 1:18 . . . while she was still a *v*, she
Matt 1:23 . . . The *v* will conceive a child!
Luke 1:34 . . . this happen? I am a *v*.

VIRGINITY (n) *the quality or state of being virgin*
Deut 22:15 . . . proof of her *v* to the elders

VIRTUOUS (adj) *morally excellent; righteous*
Ruth 3:11 . . . you are a *v* woman.
Prov 31:10 . . . Who can find a *v* and
Prov 31:29 . . . There are many *v* and

VOICE (n) *verbal communication by human and divine means*
Isa 40:3 . . . the *v* of someone shouting,
Mark 1:3 . . . He is a *v* shouting in the
John 10:3 . . . sheep recognize his *v* and
John 12:28 . . . a *v* spoke from heaven,
Rev 3:20 . . . If you hear my *v* and open

VOMIT (n) *matter disgorged from the stomach*

Prov 26:11 . . . returns to its *v*, so a fool
2 Pet 2:22 . . . A dog returns to its *v*.

VOMIT (v) *to eject violently or abundantly*
Lev 18:28 . . . it will *v* out the people

VOW, VOWS (n) *a binding promise or pledge*
see also COVENANT, PROMISE
Num 6:2 . . . the special *v* of a Nazirite,
Judg 11:30 . . . Jephthah made a *v* to the
Ps 110:4 . . . and will not break his *v*:
Matt 5:34 . . . do not make any *v-s!*
Heb 7:21 . . . and will not break his *v*:

VOWED (v) *to promise solemnly*
Eccl 8:2 . . . since you *v* to God that
Mark 7:11 . . . For I have *v* to give to

W

WAGE, WAGES (n) *payment for labor or services; compensation*
Hag 1:6 . . . Your *w-s* disappear as though
Zech 11:12 . . . give me my *w-s*, whatever
Mal 3:5 . . . cheat employees of their *w-s*,
Matt 20:2 . . . the normal daily *w* and
Rom 4:4 . . . their *w-s* are not a gift,
Rom 6:23 . . . For the *w-s* of sin is death,

WAIT, WAITED, WAITING (v) *to look forward expectantly; to stay in place in expectation of*
Ps 40:1 . . . I *w-ed* patiently for the LORD
Ps 62:5 . . . that I am *w* quietly before
Ps 69:3 . . . *w-ing* for my God to help me.
Isa 30:18 . . . Blessed are those who *w* for
Mic 7:7 . . . I *w* confidently for God to
Hab 3:16 . . . I will *w* quietly for the
Luke 12:37 . . . who are ready and *w-ing*
Rom 8:19 . . . all creation is *w-ing* eagerly
Rom 8:23 . . . We, too, *w* with eager hope
Heb 9:28 . . . are eagerly *w-ing* for him.

WALK, WALKED, WALKING (v) *to roam, traverse, or advance by steps; to pursue a course of action or way of life*
Gen 3:8 . . . God *w-ing* about in the garden.
Lev 26:12 . . . I will *w* among you;
Deut 11:22 . . . God by *w-ing* in his ways,
Deut 26:17 . . . promised to *w* in his ways,
Josh 22:5 . . . God, *w* in all his ways,
Ps 23:4 . . . when I *w* through the
Ps 89:15 . . . they will *w* in the light
Prov 4:12 . . . When you *w*, you won't
Prov 6:22 . . . When you *w*, their counsel
Isa 2:3 . . . we will *w* in his paths.
Isa 40:31 . . . They will *w* and not
Isa 43:2 . . . When you *w* through the
Jer 6:16 . . . godly way, and *w* in it.
Dan 3:25 . . . *w-ing* around in the fire
Amos 3:3 . . . two people *w* together
Mic 6:8 . . . to *w* humbly with your God.
Mal 2:6 . . . they *w-ed* with me, living good
Matt 14:29 . . . boat and *w-ed* on the water
Mark 2:9 . . . pick up your mat, and *w*
John 8:12 . . . have to *w* in darkness,

WANDER, WANDERED, WANDERS (v) *to follow a winding course; to stray*
Num 32:13 . . . them *w* in the wilderness
Ps 119:10 . . . don't let me *w* from your
Ps 119:67 . . . I used to *w* off until you
Ps 119:176 . . . I have *w-ed* away like a
Matt 18:12 . . . one of them *w-s* away
Eph 4:18 . . . *w* far from the life God
1 Tim 6:10 . . . have *w-ed* from the true

Jas 5:19 ... someone among you **w-s**
1 Pet 2:25 ... like sheep who **w-ed** away.
2 Pet 2:15 ... They have **w-ed** off the

WAR, WARS (n) *armed conflict with an opposing military force; a state of hostility, conflict, or antagonism*
Josh 11:23 ... finally had rest from **w.**
Ps 46:9 ... He causes **w-s** to end
Ps 68:30 ... nations that delight in **w.**
Ps 120:7 ... peace, they want **w!**
Ps 144:1 ... He trains my hands for **w**
Isa 2:4 ... nor train for **w** anymore.
2 Cor 10:3 ... we don't wage **w** as humans
1 Pet 2:11 ... that wage **w** against your
Rev 12:7 ... Then there was **w** in heaven.
Rev 19:11 ... and wages a righteous **w.**

WARN, WARNED, WARNING (v) *to give notice to beforehand especially of danger or evil; to counsel*
Gen 2:16 ... God **w-ed** him, "You may
Gen 31:24 ... told him, "I'm **w-ing** you—
Gen 31:29 ... to me last night and **w-ed** me,
Exod 20:1 ... down and **w** the people
Num 16:40 ... This would **w** the Israelites
1 Sam 8:9 ... but solemnly **w** them about
1 Kgs 2:42 ... LORD and **w** you not to
2 Kgs 17:13 ... and seers to **w** both Israel
2 Chr 19:10 ... must **w** them not to sin
Ezek 3:18 ... If I **w** the wicked,
Ezek 33:3 ... the alarm to **w** the people.
Matt 16:6 ... "Watch out!" Jesus **w-ed** them.
Luke 16:28 ... I want him to **w** them so
Acts 4:17 ... must **w** them not to speak
1 Cor 4:14 ... to **w** you as my beloved
1 Cor 10:11 ... written down to **w** us who
Col 1:28 ... **w-ing** everyone and teaching
1 Thes 4:6 ... solemnly **w-ed** you before.
1 Thes 5:14 ... urge you to **w** those who
2 Thes 3:15 ... but **w** them as you would
Heb 3:13 ... You must **w** each other

WARNING, WARNINGS (n) *something that warns or serves to warn; the act of warning*
Ps 19:11 ... They are a **w** to your servant,
Ps 81:8 ... while I give you stern **w.**
Jer 6:8 ... Listen to this **w,** Jerusalem,
Jer 42:19 ... Don't forget this **w** I have
Zeph 3:7 ... they will listen to my **w-s.**
1 Cor 10:6 ... happened as a **w** to us,
1 Tim 5:20 ... as a strong **w** to others.
Titus 3:10 ... give a first and second **w.**

WARRIOR, WARRIORS (n) *a man engaged or experienced in warfare*
Gen 6:4 ... and famous **w-s** of ancient
Exod 15:3 ... LORD is a **w;** Yahweh
Josh 1:14 ... strong **w-s,** fully armed,
1 Chr 28:3 ... for you are a **w** and
Ps 45:3 ... your sword, O mighty **w!**
Jer 20:11 ... beside me like a great **w.**

WASH, WASHED (v) *to cleanse—of physical, ceremonial, or spiritual significance*
see also BAPTIZE(D), CLEANSE
Ps 51:7 ... **w** me, and I will be whiter
John 13:5 ... he began to **w** the disciples'
John 13:10 ... does not need to **w,** except
Acts 22:16 ... Have your sins **w-ed** away
Eph 5:26 ... holy and clean, **w-ed** by the
Titus 3:5 ... He **w-ed** away our sins,
Heb 10:22 ... bodies have been **w-ed**
Jas 4:8 ... **W** your hands, you sinners;
2 Pet 2:22 ... **w-ed** pig returns to the mud.

Rev 7:14 ... They have **w-ed** their robes in
Rev 22:14 ... those who **w** their robes.

WASTE, WASTED (v) *to spend or use carelessly or inefficiently*
Ps 127:1 ... work of the builders is **w-d.**
Prov 29:3 ... prostitutes, his wealth is **w-d.**
Prov 31:3 ... do not **w** your strength
Luke 15:13 ... there he **w-d** all his money
John 6:12 ... so that nothing is **w-d.**
Gal 2:2 ... all my efforts had been **w-d**

WATCH (n) *the act of keeping awake to guard, protect, or attend*
Matt 24:42 ... you, too, must keep **w!**
Acts 20:31 ... my constant **w** and care

WATCH, WATCHES, WATCHING (v) *to diligently wait or keep guard; to observe closely*
Judg 18:6 ... the LORD is **w-ing** over
Job 14:16 ... my steps, instead of **w-ing**
Job 34:21 ... God **w-es** how people live;
Ps 1:6 ... For the LORD **w-es** over the
Ps 17:11 ... and surround me, **w-ing** for
Ps 61:7 ... faithfulness **w** over him.
Ps 121:3 ... one who **w-es** over you will
Prov 2:11 ... Wise choices will **w** over
Prov 31:27 ... carefully **w-es** everything
Eccl 11:4 ... If they **w** every cloud,
Jer 24:6 ... I will **w** over and care for
Jer 31:10 ... gather them and **w** over
Acts 1:9 ... while they were **w-ing,** and
Eph 6:6 ... just when they are **w-ing** you.
Heb 13:17 ... is to **w** over your souls,
1 Pet 1:12 ... eagerly **w-ing** these things
1 Pet 3:12 ... eyes of the LORD **w** over

WATER, WATERS (n) *precious resource for drink and irrigation, usually associated with blessing; a body of water*
Exod 7:20 ... struck the **w** of the Nile.
Exod 17:1 ... there was no **w** there for
Num 20:2 ... was no **w** for the people
2 Sam 23:15 ... good **w** from the well
Ps 42:1 ... streams of **w,** so I long
Prov 25:21 ... give them **w** to drink.
Song 8:7 ... Many **w-s** cannot quench
Isa 11:9 ... for as the **w-s** fill the sea,
Isa 32:2 ... like streams of **w** in the
Isa 43:2 ... through deep **w-s,** I will be
Isa 49:10 ... lead them beside cool **w-s.**
Jer 17:8 ... reach deep into the **w.**
Jon 2:3 ... The mighty **w-s** engulfed me;
Hab 2:14 ... For as the **w-s** fill the sea,
Zech 14:8 ... life-giving **w-s** will flow
Matt 14:25 ... them, walking on the **w.**
John 3:5 ... born of **w** and the Spirit.
John 4:10 ... would give you living **w.**
John 7:38 ... Rivers of living **w** will
1 Jn 5:6 ... his baptism in **w** and by
Rev 7:17 ... springs of life-giving **w.**
Rev 21:6 ... springs of the **w** of life.

WAY, WAYS (n) *characteristic, regular, or habitual manner or mode of being, behaving, or happening; manner or method of doing or happening; a course of action; route*
Exod 33:13 ... let me know your **w-s,**
Deut 26:17 ... to walk in his **w-s,** and
Deut 30:16 ... by walking in his **w-s.**
Josh 22:5 ... walk in all his **w-s,** obey
2 Sam 22:31 ... God's **w** is perfect.
Ps 77:13 ... O God, your **w-s** are holy.
Ps 86:11 ... Teach me your **w-s,** O LORD,

Prov 2:9 ... find the right **w** to go.
Prov 4:11 ... teach you wisdom's **w-s**
Eccl 8:6 ... and a **w** for everything,
Isa 2:3 ... teach us his **w-s,** and we will
Isa 40:3 ... Clear the **w** through the
Jer 6:16 ... old, godly **w,** and walk in
Mic 4:2 ... teach us his **w-s,** and we will
Mal 3:1 ... prepare the **w** before me.
Matt 3:3 ... Prepare the **w** for the
Matt 3:8 ... Prove by the **w** you live
Luke 7:27 ... prepare your **w** before you.
John 14:6 ... I am the **w,** the truth,
Acts 9:2 ... followers of the **W** he
Acts 24:14 ... I follow the **W,** which
Rom 1:30 ... invent new **w-s** of sinning,
1 Cor 10:13 ... will show you a **w** out
1 Cor 12:31 ... show you a **w** of life
Col 1:10 ... Then the **w** you live will
Heb 10:20 ... and life-giving **w** through

WEAK, WEAKER, WEAKEST (adj) *lacking strength; not able to withstand temptation or persuasion*
Ps 72:13 ... pity for the **w** and the
Ps 103:14 ... he knows how **w** we are;
Isa 59:1 ... arm is not too **w** to save
Matt 12:20 ... will not crush the **w-est** reed
Matt 26:41 ... but the body is **w!**
Rom 14:1 ... who are **w** in faith,
1 Cor 8:9 ... others with a **w-er** conscience
1 Cor 9:22 ... bring the **w** to Christ.
1 Cor 11:30 ... many of you are **w** and
1 Cor 12:22 ... of the body that seem **w-est**
2 Cor 12:10 ... For when I am **w,** then
1 Thes 5:14 ... care of those who are **w.**

WEAKNESS, WEAKNESSES (n) *the quality or state of being weak*
Ps 136:23 ... He remembered us in our **w.**
Isa 53:4 ... it was our **w-es** he carried;
Rom 8:3 ... the **w** of our sinful nature.
Rom 8:26 ... Spirit helps us in our **w.**
1 Cor 1:25 ... God's **w** is stronger than
1 Cor 2:3 ... I came to you in **w**—timid
2 Cor 12:5 ... boast only about my **w-es.**
2 Cor 12:10 ... take pleasure in my **w-es,**
2 Cor 13:4 ... he was crucified in **w,**
Heb 5:2 ... is subject to the same **w-es.**

WEALTH (n) *abundance of valuable material possessions or resources*
see also MONEY, POSSESSION(S), RICHES, TREASURE(S)
2 Chr 1:11 ... not ask for **w,** riches,
Job 36:18 ... you may be seduced by **w.**
Ps 39:6 ... We heap up **w,** not knowing
Ps 62:10 ... if your **w** increases, don't
Prov 3:9 ... the LORD with your **w**
Prov 10:2 ... Tainted **w** has no lasting
Prov 13:11 ... from hard work grows
Prov 21:20 ... wise have **w** and luxury,
Prov 29:3 ... prostitutes, his **w** is wasted.
Eccl 4:8 ... gain as much **w** as he can.
Luke 19:8 ... give half my **w** to the poor,
Eph 2:7 ... of the incredible **w** of his
1 Tim 6:6 ... contentment is itself great **w.**
Jas 5:3 ... The very **w** you were counting

WEALTHY (adj) *characterized by abundance*
Prov 11:24 ... freely and become more **w;**
Eccl 2:26 ... sinner becomes **w,** God takes
1 Cor 1:26 ... or **w** when God called you.

WEAPON, WEAPONS (n) *something used to injure, defeat, or destroy*
Prov 26:18 ... shooting a deadly **w**

Eccl 9:18 … have wisdom than **w-s** of war,
2 Cor 6:7 … use the **w-s** of righteousness

WEARY (adj) *exhausted in strength, endurance, or vigor*
Isa 40:31 … They will run and not grow **w**.
Isa 50:4 … know how to comfort the **w**.
Matt 11:28 … you who are **w** and carry
2 Cor 5:2 … We grow **w** in our present
Heb 12:3 … won't become **w** and give up.

WEDDING, WEDDINGS (n) *a marriage ceremony usually with its accompanying festivities*
Matt 11:17 … We played **w** songs, and
Matt 22:11 … the proper clothes for a **w**.
Matt 24:38 … parties and **w-s** right up
Rev 19:7 … for the feast of the Lamb,

WEEP, WEEPING (v) *to cry aloud, often linked with prayer and repentance*
2 Sam 1:26 … How I **w** for you,
Ps 126:6 … They **w** as they go to
Jer 31:16 … Do not **w** any longer,
Jer 50:4 … will come **w-ing** and seeking
Matt 2:18 … heard in Ramah—**w-ing** and
Matt 8:12 … will be **w-ing** and gnashing
Luke 6:21 … blesses you who **w** now,
Luke 22:62 … the courtyard, **w-ing** bitterly.
Luke 23:28 … don't **w** for me, but **w**
Rom 12:15 … and **w** with those who **w**.

WEEPING (n) *shedding of tears out of grief or sadness*
Jer 31:15 … deep anguish and bitter **w**.
Matt 2:18 … heard in Ramah—**w** and
Matt 8:12 … will be **w** and gnashing

WEST (n) *the general direction of the sunset*
Ps 103:12 … as the east is from the **w**.
Ps 107:3 … from east and **w**, from north

WHEAT (n) *a cereal grain that yields a fine white flour*
Matt 3:12 … gathering the **w** into his barn
Matt 13:25 … among the **w**, then slipped
Mark 4:28 … the heads of **w** are formed,
Luke 22:31 … sift each of you like **w**.
John 12:24 … a kernel of **w** is planted in

WHIRLWIND (n) *a small rotating windstorm, sometimes violent and destructive*
see also STORM
2 Kgs 2:1 … to heaven in a **w**,
Job 38:1 … answered Job from the **w**:
Hos 8:7 … and will harvest the **w**.
Nah 1:3 … in the **w** and the storm.

WHISPER (n) *a minor or softer reflection of the original noise; hint, trace*
1 Kgs 19:12 … sound of a gentle **w**.
Job 26:14 … merely a **w** of his power.
Ps 107:29 … calmed the storm to a **w**

WHISPER (v) *to speak softly with little or no vibration of the vocal cords*
Matt 10:27 … What I **w** in your ear,

WHITE, WHITER (adj) *free from color; of the color white*
Ps 51:7 … I will be **w-r** than snow.
Isa 1:18 … make them as **w** as snow.
Dan 7:9 … clothing was as **w** as snow,
Matt 28:3 … clothing was as **w** as snow.
Rev 1:14 … like wool, as **w** as snow.

Rev 6:2 … saw a **w** horse standing
Rev 19:11 … a **w** horse was standing
Rev 20:11 … saw a great **w** throne

WHITE (n) *the absence of color; free from spot or blemish*
Rev 3:4 … will walk with me in **w**,
Rev 7:13 … who are clothed in **w**?

WHITEWASHED (adj) *glossed over with whitewash*
Matt 23:27 … are like **w** tombs—

WHOLE (adj) *entire; complete, unmodified; undivided*
1 Sam 1:28 … LORD his **w** life.
1 Sam 17:46 … the **w** world will know
1 Chr 28:9 … him with your **w** heart
Ps 72:19 … Let the **w** earth be filled
Ps 103:1 … with my **w** heart, I will
Prov 4:22 … healing to their **w** body.
Eccl 12:13 … That's the **w** story.
Isa 6:3 … The **w** earth is filled
Isa 14:26 … plan for the **w** earth,
Dan 2:35 … covered the **w** earth.
Zeph 1:18 … For the **w** land will be
Matt 6:22 … eye is healthy, your **w** body
Matt 16:26 … gain the **w** world but lose
Matt 24:14 … throughout the **w** world,
John 21:25 … I suppose the **w** world
Acts 17:26 … throughout the **w** earth.
1 Cor 12:17 … Or if your **w** body were
Gal 5:3 … regulation in the **w** law of

WHORE (KJV)
Lev 21:7 … woman *defiled by prostitution*
Deut 23:18 … the earnings of a *prostitute*
Prov 23:27 … *prostitute* is a dangerous trap
Hos 4:14 … sinning with *whores*
Rev 17:1 … *prostitute*, who rules over

WICKED (adj) *morally very bad*
Gen 13:13 … area were extremely **w** and
Ps 7:9 … those who are **w**, and defend
Prov 10:7 … name of a **w** person rots
Prov 26:23 … may hide a **w** heart, just
Jer 35:15 … Turn from your **w** ways,
Ezek 18:21 … But if **w** people turn away
Ezek 21:25 … you corrupt and **w** prince
Ezek 33:8 … that some **w** people are sure
Hos 10:9 … not right that the **w** men of
Jon 1:2 … I have seen how **w** its people
Luke 6:35 … who are unthankful and **w**.
1 Jn 5:17 … All **w** actions are sin,

WICKED (n) *those who practice evil*
Ps 1:1 … the advice of the **w**, or stand
Ps 10:13 … Why do the **w** get away with
Ps 12:8 … though the **w** strut about,
Ps 14:6 … The **w** frustrate the plans
Ps 37:1 … worry about the **w** or envy
Ps 82:2 … by favoring the **w**?
Ps 101:8 … ferret out the **w** and free
Ps 139:19 … you would destroy the **w**!
Ps 146:9 … the plans of the **w**.
Prov 4:14 … Don't do as the **w** do,
Prov 9:7 … who corrects the **w** will
Prov 10:28 … expectations of the **w** come
Prov 12:5 … of the **w** is treacherous.
Prov 29:7 … the **w** don't care at all.
Isa 5:23 … to let the **w** go free,
Isa 31:4 … mouth will destroy the **w**.
Isa 26:10 … the **w** keep doing wrong
Isa 48:22 … no peace for the **w**,
Mal 4:1 … arrogant and the **w** will be

WICKEDNESS (n) *the quality or state of being wicked; something wicked*

Lev 16:21 … it all the **w**, rebellion,
Lev 19:29 … with prostitution and **w**.
Deut 9:4 … because of the **w** of the other
Ps 73:3 … them prosper despite their **w**.
Jer 3:2 … your prostitution and your **w**.
Jer 14:16 … out their own **w** on them.
Jer 14:20 … we confess our **w** and that
Ezek 33:19 … turn from their **w** and do
Luke 11:39 … of greed and **w**!
Rom 1:18 … the truth by their **w**.
Rom 1:29 … every kind of **w**, sin, greed,
Rom 2:8 … and instead live lives of **w**.
2 Cor 6:14 … be a partner with **w**?
Heb 8:12 … I will forgive their **w**,

WIDOW, WIDOWS (n) *a woman whose husband has died*
Deut 10:18 … orphans and **w-s** receive
Ps 68:5 … defender of **w-s**—this is God,
Ps 146:9 … for the orphans and **w-s**, but
Isa 1:17 … Fight for the rights of **w-s**.
Luke 21:2 … Then a poor **w** came by and
Acts 6:1 … that their **w-s** were being
1 Cor 7:8 … aren't married and to **w-s**—
1 Tim 5:3 … Take care of any **w** who
1 Tim 5:16 … care for the **w-s** who are
Jas 1:27 … for orphans and **w-s** in their

WIFE (n) *the female partner in a marriage*
see also WIVES
Gen 2:24 … and is joined to his **w**,
Gen 19:26 … But Lot's **w** looked back
Exod 20:17 … covet your neighbor's **w**,
Lev 20:10 … his neighbor's **w**, both
Deut 5:21 … not covet your neighbor's **w**.
Deut 24:5 … happiness to the **w** he has
Prov 5:18 … Rejoice in the **w** of your
Prov 12:4 … A worthy **w** is a crown
Prov 18:22 … man who finds a **w**
Prov 19:13 … a quarrelsome **w** is as
Prov 21:9 … a quarrelsome **w** in a
Prov 31:10 … a virtuous and capable **w**?
Mal 2:14 … vows you and your **w** made
Matt 1:20 … to take Mary as your **w**.
Matt 19:3 … to divorce his **w** for just
Luke 17:32 … happened to Lot's **w**!
Luke 18:29 … up house or **w** or brothers
1 Cor 7:2 … should have his own **w**,
1 Cor 7:15 … the husband or **w** who isn't
1 Cor 7:33 … and how to please his **w**.
Eph 5:23 … head of his **w** as Christ
Eph 5:33 … love his **w** as he loves
1 Tim 3:12 … be faithful to his **w**,
Titus 1:6 … be faithful to his **w**,
1 Pet 3:7 … Treat your **w** with
Rev 21:9 … bride, the **w** of the Lamb,

WILDERNESS (n) *any desolate, barren, or unpopulated area, usually linked with danger*
see also DESERT
Num 16:13 … kill us here in this **w**,
Num 26:65 … all die in the **w**.
Num 32:13 … wander in the **w** for forty
Deut 8:16 … manna in the **w**, a food
Deut 29:5 … led you through the **w**,
Ps 78:19 … give us food in the **w**.
Ps 78:52 … safely through the **w**.
Isa 32:15 … **w** will become a fertile
Isa 35:6 … will gush forth in the **w**,
Matt 3:3 … the **w**, 'Prepare the way
Luke 5:16 … withdrew to the **w** for
Rev 12:6 … fled into the **w**, where God

WILDFLOWERS (n) *the flower of a wild or uncultivated plant*

1773

Ps 103:15 ... like grass; like *w*, we bloom
Matt 6:30 ... so wonderfully for *w* that are

WILL (n) *desire, wish*
Ps 40:8 ... in doing your *w*, my God,
Ps 143:10 ... me to do your *w*, for you
Prov 3:6 ... Seek his *w* in all you do,
Matt 6:10 ... May your *w* be done on
Matt 7:21 ... who actually do the *w*
Matt 12:50 ... does the *w* of my Father
Matt 18:14 ... heavenly Father's *w* that
Matt 26:39 ... want your *w* to be done,
Matt 26:42 ... I drink it, your *w* be done.
John 5:30 ... carry out the *w* of the one
John 6:38 ... heaven to do the *w* of God
Rom 12:2 ... learn to know God's *w*
1 Thes 5:18 ... this is God's *w* for you
Heb 10:7 ... come to do your *w*, O God—
Heb 13:21 ... need for doing his *w*.
1 Pet 4:2 ... to do the *w* of God.

WINE (n) *the fermented juice of grapes, linked positively with blessings and negatively with drunkenness*
Ps 104:15 ... *w* to make them glad,
Prov 31:6 ... and *w* for those in bitter
Song 1:2 ... love is sweeter than *w*.
Isa 28:7 ... who reel with *w* and stagger
Mark 15:36 ... with sour *w*, holding it
John 2:3 ... The *w* supply ran out
Rom 14:21 ... to eat meat or drink *w*
Eph 5:18 ... Don't be drunk with *w*,
1 Tim 5:23 ... drink a little *w* for
Rev 16:19 ... was filled with the *w*

WINEBIBBER(S) (KJV)
Prov 23:20 ... not carouse with *drunkards*
Matt 11:19 ... glutton and a *drunkard*, and
Luke 7:34 ... glutton and a *drunkard*, and

WINESKINS (n) *a bag used for holding wine, made from the skin of an animal*
Matt 9:17 ... stored in new *w* so that
Luke 5:37 ... new wine into old *w*.

WINGS (n) *feathered appendages of a bird, figurative of freedom, strength, and protection from God*
Exod 19:4 ... carried you on eagles' *w*
Ps 17:8 ... in the shadow of your *w*.
Ps 91:4 ... shelter you with his *w*.
Isa 6:2 ... each having six *w*.
Isa 40:31 ... high on *w* like eagles.
Mal 4:2 ... rise with healing in his *w*.
Luke 13:34 ... chicks beneath her *w*,
Rev 4:8 ... living beings had six *w*,

WISDOM (n) *knowledge, insight, judgment*
Gen 3:6 ... she wanted the *w* it would
1 Kgs 4:29 ... gave Solomon very great *w*
1 Kgs 10:24 ... to hear the *w* God had
2 Chr 1:10 ... Give me the *w* and
Job 11:6 ... *w*, for true *w* is not
Job 42:3 ... that questions my *w* with such
Ps 51:6 ... teaching me *w* even there.
Prov 2:6 ... the LORD grants *w*!
Prov 3:13 ... the person who finds *w*,
Prov 8:11 ... *w* is far more valuable
Prov 11:2 ... with humility comes *w*.
Prov 16:16 ... better to get *w* than gold,
Prov 23:23 ... also get *w*, discipline,
Prov 29:3 ... man who loves *w* brings joy
Eccl 10:10 ... the value of *w*; it helps
Isa 11:2 ... on him—the Spirit of *w*
Isa 50:4 ... me his words of *w*, so that
Luke 2:52 ... Jesus grew in *w* and in
Acts 6:3 ... full of the Spirit and *w*.

1 Cor 1:21 ... him through human *w*, he
Eph 1:17 ... you spiritual *w* and insight
Col 2:3 ... treasures of *w* and knowledge.
Col 3:16 ... with all the *w* he gives.
2 Tim 3:15 ... given you the *w* to receive
Titus 2:12 ... world with *w*, righteousness,
Jas 1:5 ... If you need *w*, ask our
Rev 5:12 ... riches and *w* and strength

WISE, WISER, WISEST (adj) *marked by deep understanding, keen discernment, and a capacity for sound judgment*
1 Kgs 3:12 ... you a *w* and understanding
Job 9:4 ... God is so *w* and so mighty.
Ps 14:2 ... anyone is truly *w*, if anyone
Ps 19:7 ... are trustworthy, making *w* the
Ps 119:100 ... I am even *w-r* than my
Prov 4:7 ... wisdom is the *w-st* thing
Prov 9:8 ... correct the *w*, and they
Prov 10:1 ... A *w* child brings joy to
Prov 11:30 ... a *w* person wins friends.
Prov 12:16 ... a *w* person stays calm
Prov 12:18 ... of the *w* bring healing.
Prov 13:1 ... A *w* child accepts a parent's
Prov 13:10 ... who take advice are *w*.
Prov 13:20 ... Walk with the *w* and
Prov 15:5 ... learns from correction is *w*.
Prov 16:23 ... From a *w* mind comes
Prov 18:4 ... wisdom flows from the *w*
Prov 19:25 ... they will be all the *w-r*.
Prov 24:5 ... *w* are mightier than the
Prov 28:7 ... who obey the law are *w*;
Eccl 8:5 ... who are *w* will find a time
Eccl 9:17 ... quiet words of a *w* person
Matt 2:1 ... some *w* men from eastern
Matt 11:25 ... who think themselves *w*
Matt 25:2 ... foolish, and five were *w*.
Rom 3:11 ... No one is truly *w*; no one
1 Cor 1:19 ... wisdom of the *w* and
1 Cor 1:25 ... plan of God is *w-r* than
1 Cor 12:8 ... ability to give *w* advice;
Jas 3:13 ... If you are *w* and understand

WITCHCRAFT (n) *the use of sorcery or magic*
Lev 19:26 ... practice fortune-telling or *w*.
Deut 18:10 ... omens, or engage in *w*,
Rev 21:8 ... those who practice *w*, idol

WITHER, WITHERS (v) *to shrivel and lose vitality, force, or freshness*
Job 14:2 ... like a flower and then *w*.
Ps 1:3 ... leaves never *w*, and they
Isa 40:7 ... grass *w-s* and the flowers
Isa 64:6 ... autumn leaves, we *w* and fall,
1 Pet 1:24 ... grass *w-s* and the flower

WITNESS, WITNESSES (n) *a person who gives testimony; one asked to be present at a transaction so as to be able to testify to its having taken place*
Deut 19:15 ... of two or three *w-es*.
Prov 19:5 ... A false *w* will not go
Prov 21:28 ... but a credible *w* will be
Matt 18:16 ... by two or three *w-es*.
John 1:8 ... simply a *w* to tell about
Acts 1:8 ... will be my *w-es*, telling people
1 Tim 5:19 ... by two or three *w-es*.
1 Jn 5:7 ... we have these three *w-es*—

WITNESSED (v) *to have personal or direct cognizance of*
Mal 2:14 ... the LORD *w* the vows

WIVES (n) *the female partner in marriage*
see also WIFE
Eph 5:22 ... For *w*, this means submit

Eph 5:25 ... this means love your *w*,
1 Pet 3:1 ... way, you *w* must accept

WOE (KJV)
Isa 6:5 ... *It's all over!* I am doomed
Matt 18:7 ... *What sorrow awaits* the world
Matt 23:13 ... *What sorrow awaits* you
1 Cor 9:16 ... *How terrible* for me if I didn't
Rev 8:13 ... *Terror, terror, terror* to all who

WOLVES (n) *any of several wild, predatory animals that resemble large dogs*
Matt 7:15 ... but are really vicious *w*.
Matt 10:16 ... you out as sheep among *w*.

WOMAN (n) *an adult female person*
see also WOMEN
Gen 2:22 ... God made a *w* from the rib,
Gen 3:6 ... The *w* was convinced.
Gen 3:12 ... It was the *w* you gave me
Gen 3:16 ... he said to the *w*, "I will
Exod 3:22 ... Every Israelite *w* will ask
Lev 12:2 ... If a *w* becomes pregnant
Lev 15:19 ... a *w* has her menstrual
Lev 15:25 ... a *w* has a flow of blood
Num 5:29 ... If a *w* goes astray and defiles
Judg 4:9 ... be at the hands of a *w*.
Judg 16:4 ... love with a *w* named Delilah,
Ruth 3:11 ... knows you are a virtuous *w*.
2 Sam 11:2 ... he noticed a *w* of unusual
2 Sam 20:16 ... But a wise *w* in the town
Prov 11:16 ... A gracious *w* gains respect,
Prov 11:22 ... A beautiful *w* who lacks
Prov 14:1 ... A wise *w* builds her
Prov 30:19 ... how a man loves a *w*.
Prov 30:23 ... a bitter *w* who finally gets
Prov 31:30 ... *w* who fears the LORD
Matt 5:28 ... looks at a *w* with lust
Matt 9:20 ... Just then a *w* who had
Matt 26:7 ... was eating, a *w* came in
Mark 7:25 ... Right away a *w* whose
Luke 7:39 ... what kind of *w* is touching
John 4:7 ... Soon a Samaritan *w* came to
John 8:3 ... Pharisees brought a *w* who
Rom 7:2 ... when a *w* marries, the law
1 Cor 7:2 ... and each *w* should have
1 Cor 7:34 ... a married *w* has to think
1 Cor 11:3 ... the head of *w* is man, and
1 Cor 11:6 ... shameful for a *w* to have
1 Cor 11:13 ... it right for a *w* to pray
Gal 4:4 ... born of a *w*, subject to the
Gal 4:31 ... are children of the free *w*.
Rev 12:1 ... I saw a *w* clothed with the
Rev 12:13 ... he pursued the *w* who had
Rev 17:3 ... There I saw a *w* sitting on a

WOMB (n) *uterus*
Ps 139:13 ... together in my mother's *w*.
Prov 31:2 ... O son of my *w*, O son
Jer 1:5 ... you in your mother's *w*.
Luke 1:44 ... baby in my *w* jumped for joy.
John 3:4 ... into his mother's *w* and be

WOMEN (n) *adult female persons*
see also WOMAN
Gen 6:2 ... saw the beautiful *w* and took
Song 1:3 ... all the young *w* love you!
Mark 15:41 ... Many other *w* who had
Luke 1:42 ... you above all *w*, and your
Luke 23:27 ... many grief-stricken *w*.
Rom 1:26 ... Even the *w* turned against
1 Cor 7:25 ... the young *w* who are not
1 Tim 2:9 ... I want *w* to be modest in
2 Tim 3:6 ... of vulnerable *w* who are
Titus 2:3 ... teach the older *w* to live in
Titus 2:4 ... train the younger *w* to love
1 Pet 3:5 ... how the holy *w* of old made

WONDERFUL (adj) *marked by a marvelous, amazing, or extraordinary quality*
1 Chr 16:9 ... about his **w** deeds.
Job 37:14 ... consider the **w** miracles
Ps 16:6 ... What a **w** inheritance!
Ps 17:7 ... unfailing love in **w** ways.
Ps 71:17 ... about the **w** things you
Ps 72:18 ... does such **w** things.
Ps 75:1 ... tell of your **w** deeds.
Ps 105:2 ... about his **w** deeds.
Ps 118:23 ... it is **w** to see.
Ps 119:18 ... to see the **w** truths in
Ps 119:27 ... meditate on your **w** deeds.
Ps 119:129 ... Your laws are **w**.
Ps 139:6 ... knowledge is too **w** for
Ps 145:5 ... and your **w** miracles.
Eccl 11:9 ... Young people, it's **w** to be
Isa 9:6 ... be called: **W** Counselor,
Isa 12:5 ... he has done **w** things.
Isa 25:1 ... You do such **w** things!
Matt 21:15 ... saw these **w** miracles
Matt 21:42 ... and it is **w** to see.
Luke 13:17 ... rejoiced at the **w** things
Acts 2:11 ... about the **w** things God has
Acts 20:24 ... News about the **w** grace of
2 Cor 10:12 ... we are as **w** as these
Titus 2:13 ... hope to that **w** day when

WONDERS (n) *mighty works, miracles*
1 Chr 16:12 ... Remember the **w** he has
Ps 26:7 ... and telling of all your **w**.
Ps 31:21 ... has shown me the **w** of his
Ps 77:14 ... are the God of great **w**!
Ps 89:5 ... your great **w**, LORD;
Mark 13:22 ... perform signs and **w** so
Acts 2:19 ... will cause **w** in the heavens
Acts 5:12 ... signs and **w** among the people.
2 Cor 12:12 ... signs and **w** and miracles
Heb 2:4 ... signs and **w** and various

WORD, WORDS (n) *something that is said; special revelation from God; commands*
Deut 8:3 ... live by every **w** that comes
Deut 11:18 ... to these **w-s** of mine. Tie
Job 38:2 ... with such ignorant **w-s**?
Ps 19:3 ... speak without a sound or **w**;
Ps 52:4 ... others with your **w-s**, you liar!
Ps 119:9 ... pure? By obeying your **w**.
Ps 119:11 ... hidden your **w** in my heart,
Ps 119:103 ... How sweet your **w** taste
Ps 119:160 ... essence of your **w-s** is
Ps 119:162 ... I rejoice in your **w** like
Prov 12:19 ... Truthful **w-s** stand the test
Prov 12:25 ... an encouraging **w** cheers
Prov 16:24 ... Kind **w-s** are like honey—
Prov 17:27 ... wise person uses few **w-s**;
Prov 26:23 ... Smooth **w-s** may hide a
Isa 40:21 ... deaf to the **w** of God—
Jer 15:16 ... your **w-s**, I devoured
Jer 23:29 ... Does not my **w** burn like
Amos 8:13 ... for the LORD's **w**.
Matt 4:4 ... but by every **w** that comes
Matt 15:6 ... you cancel the **w** of God
Matt 24:35 ... **w-s** will never disappear.
John 1:1 ... the beginning the **W** already
John 6:68 ... the **w-s** that give eternal life.
John 15:7 ... and my **w-s** remain in you,
John 17:17 ... teach them your **w**, which
Rom 10:18 ... the **w-s** to all the world.
1 Cor 2:1 ... use lofty **w-s** and impressive
1 Cor 2:13 ... do not use **w-s** that come
1 Cor 14:9 ... to people in **w-s** they don't
1 Cor 14:19 ... than ten thousand **w-s** in
2 Cor 2:17 ... We preach the **w** of God

2 Cor 4:2 ... or distort the **w** of God.
Eph 6:17 ... which is the **w** of God.
Phil 2:16 ... firmly to the **w** of life;
2 Tim 2:15 ... explains the **w** of truth.
Titus 2:5 ... shame on the **w** of God.
Heb 4:12 ... For the **w** of God is
Heb 5:12 ... things about God's **w**.
Jas 1:22 ... listen to God's **w**.
1 Pet 1:23 ... eternal, living **w** of God.
1 Pet 2:8 ... not obey God's **w**, and so
1 Pet 3:1 ... to them without any **w-s**.
2 Pet 3:5 ... long ago by the **w** of
Rev 19:13 ... title was the **W** of God.
Rev 22:19 ... of the **w-s** from this book

WORK, WORKS (n) *one's occupation; physical or creative effort; see also* DEED(s)
Gen 2:2 ... finished his **w** of creation,
Exod 20:9 ... week for your ordinary **w**,
Deut 5:13 ... week for your ordinary **w**,
Ps 77:12 ... about your mighty **w-s**.
Ps 107:24 ... impressive **w-s** on the
Ps 127:1 ... **w** of the builders is wasted.
Ps 150:2 ... Praise him for his mighty **w-s**;
Prov 21:5 ... planning and hard **w** lead
Eccl 2:19 ... my skill and hard **w** under
Eccl 5:19 ... To enjoy your **w** and accept
John 4:34 ... and from finishing his **w**.
John 5:36 ... Father gave me these **w-s** to
John 10:32 ... have done many good **w-s**.
Acts 13:2 ... for the special **w** to which
Acts 20:24 ... finishing the **w** assigned
Rom 4:5 ... not because of their **w**, but
1 Cor 3:5 ... the **w** the Lord gave us.
Gal 6:4 ... attention to your own **w**, for
Eph 4:12 ... people to do his **w** and build
Eph 4:16 ... part does its own special **w**,
Eph 4:28 ... your hands for good hard **w**,
Phil 1:6 ... began the good **w** within you,
1 Tim 6:18 ... rich in good **w-s** and
2 Tim 3:17 ... people to do every good **w**.
Heb 10:24 ... acts of love and good **w-s**.
Jas 2:26 ... faith is dead without good **w-s**.
Rev 15:3 ... marvelous are your **w-s**,

WORK, WORKED, WORKING (v) *to exert oneself physically or mentally*
Prov 13:4 ... but those who **w** hard will
Eccl 5:12 ... who **w** hard sleep well,
Matt 6:28 ... They don't **w** or make their
Matt 12:30 ... anyone who isn't **w-ing** with
Luke 10:7 ... who **w** deserve their pay.
Luke 13:24 ... **W** hard to enter the narrow
Rom 4:6 ... righteous without **w-ing** for
Rom 8:28 ... to **w** together for the good
Rom 12:11 ... Never be lazy, but **w** hard
1 Cor 15:10 ... I have **w-ed** harder than
1 Cor 15:58 ... Always **w** enthusiastically
2 Cor 11:27 ... I have **w-ed** hard and
Eph 6:7 ... you were **w-ing** for the Lord
1 Thes 4:11 ... and **w-ing** with your hands,
2 Thes 3:10 ... unwilling to **w** will not
1 Tim 5:18 ... Those who **w** deserve their
1 Tim 6:2 ... slaves should **w** all the harder
Heb 6:10 ... how hard you have **w-ed** for
2 Pet 1:10 ... **w** hard to prove that you

WORLD (n) *the earth and its inhabitants; the human race; the current age and its value system*
Ps 33:9 ... he spoke, the **w** began!
Ps 50:12 ... for all the **w** is mine
Ps 96:13 ... judge the **w** with justice,
Isa 13:11 ... will punish the **w** for its
Matt 16:26 ... you gain the whole **w** but
John 1:29 ... away the sin of the **w**!

John 3:16 ... how God loved the **w**:
John 8:12 ... I am the light of the **w**.
John 13:35 ... prove to the **w** that you
John 16:33 ... I have overcome the **w**.
John 17:5 ... shared before the **w** began.
John 17:14 ... And the **w** hates them
John 18:36 ... Kingdom is not of this **w**.
Rom 3:19 ... the entire **w** is guilty
1 Cor 1:27 ... things the **w** considers
1 Cor 2:7 ... glory before the **w** began.
1 Cor 3:1 ... you belonged to this **w** or
1 Cor 3:19 ... of this **w** is foolishness
1 Cor 6:2 ... to judge the **w**, can't you
2 Cor 5:19 ... reconciling the **w** to himself,
Eph 2:12 ... lived in this **w** without God
Eph 4:9 ... also descended to our lowly **w**.
Phil 2:15 ... lights in a **w** full of crooked
Titus 1:2 ... them before the **w** began.
Heb 9:26 ... ever since the **w** began.
Jas 2:5 ... poor in this **w** to be rich
Jas 4:4 ... a friend of the **w**, you make
1 Jn 2:2 ... the sins of all the **w**.
1 Jn 2:15 ... Do not love this **w** nor
1 Jn 5:4 ... defeats this evil **w**, and

WORRY, WORRIES (n) *mental distress or agitation resulting from concern; anxiety*
Prov 12:25 ... **W** weighs a person down;
Matt 6:27 ... Can all your **w-ies** add a single
Luke 21:34 ... and by the **w-ies** of this life.
1 Pet 5:7 ... Give all your **w-ies** and cares

WORRY, WORRIED, WORRYING (v) *to feel or experience concern or anxiety*
Deut 20:8 ... anyone here afraid or **w-ied**?
Ps 37:1 ... Don't **w** about the wicked
Isa 7:4 ... Tell him to stop **w-ing**.
Matt 6:25 ... I tell you not to **w** about
Matt 10:19 ... don't **w** about how to
Luke 6:41 ... And why **w** about a speck in
Acts 27:33 ... You have been so **w-ied** that
Phil 4:6 ... Don't **w** about anything;

WORSHIP (n) *reverent devotion and allegiance pledged to God or a god*
1 Cor 10:14 ... flee from the **w** of idols.

WORSHIP, WORSHIPED, WORSHIPING, WORSHIPS (v) *to regard with great respect, honor, or devotion*
Gen 12:8 ... and he **w-ed** the LORD.
Gen 13:4 ... and there he **w-ed** the LORD
Gen 21:33 ... and there he **w-ed** the LORD,
Gen 26:25 ... there and **w-ed** the LORD.
Deut 12:30 ... and **w-ing** their gods.
2 Kgs 17:36 ... But **w** only the LORD,
Ps 29:2 ... **W** the LORD in the splendor
Ps 95:6 ... Come, let us **w** and bow down.
Ps 105:3 ... rejoice, you who **w** the LORD.
Isa 44:19 ... bow down to a piece of
Jer 16:11 ... **w-ed** other gods and served
Dan 3:28 ... die rather than serve or **w** any
Hos 9:1 ... like prostitutes, **w-ing** other
Hos 9:10 ... as vile as the god they **w-ed**.
Hos 13:1 ... Ephraim sinned by **w-ing** Baal
Zeph 3:9 ... everyone can **w** the LORD
Zech 14:17 ... to Jerusalem to **w** the King,
Matt 2:2 ... we have come to **w** him.
Matt 4:9 ... kneel down and **w** me.
Matt 15:25 ... she came and **w-ed** him,
Matt 28:9 ... grasped his feet, and **w-ed**
Luke 23:47 ... he **w-ed** God and said,
John 4:24 ... **w** in spirit and in truth.
1 Cor 5:11 ... is greedy, or **w-s** idols,
Heb 9:14 ... we can **w** the living God.

WORTHLESS (adj) *valueless, useless, contemptible*
1 Sam 12:21 ... worshiping **w** idols that
Prov 6:12 ... **w** and wicked people
1 Cor 3:20 ... he knows they are **w**.
Eph 5:11 ... part in the **w** deeds of evil
Titus 1:16 ... **w** for doing anything good.

WORTHY (adj) *having sufficient merit or importance; estimable, honorable*
Gen 32:10 ... I am not **w** of all the
Prov 12:4 ... A **w** wife is a crown
Matt 8:8 ... Lord, I am not **w** to have
Matt 10:37 ... are not **w** of being mine;
Matt 22:8 ... I invited aren't **w** of the
Luke 15:19 ... I am no longer **w** of being
1 Cor 15:9 ... I'm not even **w** to be called
Eph 4:1 ... lead a life **w** of your calling,
Phil 1:27 ... a manner **w** of the Good News
Rev 5:5 ... He is **w** to open the scroll

WOUNDS (n) *injuries to the body*
Isa 30:26 ... and cure the **w** he gave them.
Zech 13:6 ... what about those **w** on your
John 20:20 ... he showed them the **w** in
1 Pet 2:24 ... By his **w** you are healed.

WRATH (n) *extreme displeasure, anger, or hostility; God's response to sin*
Isa 13:13 ... Armies displays his **w** in
Rev 6:16 ... and from the **w** of the Lamb.
Rev 16:19 ... the wine of his fierce **w**.

WRITE, WRITING (v) *to inscribe or engrave; to record*
see also WRITTEN
Deut 10:2 ... I will **w** on the tablets
Prov 3:3 ... **W** them deep within your
Prov 7:3 ... **W** them deep within your
Eccl 12:12 ... for **w**-ing books is endless,
Jer 31:33 ... I will **w** them on their hearts.
1 Tim 3:14 ... I am **w**-ing these things to
Heb 8:10 ... I will **w** them on their hearts.
Rev 3:12 ... I will **w** on them the name of

WRITTEN (v) *inscribed or engraved; recorded*
see also WRITE
Deut 28:58 ... that are **w** in this book,
Josh 1:8 ... to obey everything **w** in it.
Isa 49:16 ... See, I have **w** your name
Dan 12:1 ... whose name is **w** in the book
Mal 3:16 ... scroll of remembrance was **w**
Luke 24:44 ... everything **w** about me in
John 20:31 ... these are **w** so that you
John 21:25 ... the books that would be **w**.
Rom 2:15 ... law is **w** in their hearts,
1 Cor 10:11 ... They were **w** down to warn
Heb 12:23 ... names are **w** in heaven.
Rev 21:27 ... whose names are **w** in the

WRONG (adj) *incorrect, sinful, immoral, or improper*
Prov 14:2 ... who take the **w** path
Rom 7:19 ... don't want to do what is **w**,
Rom 12:9 ... Hate what is **w**. Hold tightly
Rom 14:14 ... of itself, is **w** to eat.
2 Tim 3:16 ... make us realize what is **w**

WRONG (adv) *in an unsuccessful or unfortunate way*
Prov 15:22 ... Plans go **w** for lack

WRONG (n) *an injurious, unfair, or unjust act; something wrong, immoral, or unethical*
Exod 23:2 ... the crowd in doing **w**.
Deut 32:4 ... faithful God who does no **w**;
Job 34:10 ... The Almighty can do no **w**.
Ps 141:9 ... snares of those who do **w**.
Isa 53:9 ... done no **w** and had never
Rom 13:10 ... Love does no **w** to others,
Rom 16:19 ... to stay innocent of any **w**.
1 Cor 6:9 ... those who do **w** will not
Jas 1:13 ... God is never tempted to do **w**,
1 Pet 3:17 ... to suffer for doing **w**!

WRONGED (v) *to injure or harm; to malign or discredit*
Num 5:7 ... to the person who was **w**.
Isa 42:3 ... to all who have been **w**.
1 Cor 13:5 ... keeps no record of being **w**.

X

XERXES Persian king (486–465 BC); mentioned in Ezra 4:6; made Esther queen (Esth 2:16-18); ordered the execution of Haman (Esth 7:9).

Y

YAHWEH (n) *"I Am Who I Am" or "I Will Be What I Will Be"; the personal name of God revealed to Moses in the burning bush*
see also LORD
Gen 22:14 ... named the place **Y**-Yireh
Exod 3:15 ... **Y**, the God of your ancestors
Exod 6:2 ... I am **Y**—'the LORD'
Exod 15:3 ... warrior; **Y** is his name!
Exod 17:15 ... there and named it **Y**-Nissi
Exod 33:19 ... I will call out my name, **Y**,
Exod 34:5 ... called out his own name, **Y**.
Judg 6:24 ... there and named it **Y**-Shalom

YEAR, YEARS (n) *the period of about 365 days; a period having special significance; a measure of age or duration*
Gen 1:14 ... the seasons, days, and **y-s**.
Exod 12:40 ... lived in Egypt for 430 **y-s**.
Exod 16:35 ... manna for forty **y-s** until
Exod 34:23 ... Three times each **y** every
Lev 16:34 ... the LORD once each **y**.
Lev 25:11 ... During that **y** you must
Job 36:26 ... His **y-s** cannot be counted.
Ps 90:4 ... a thousand **y-s** are as a
Luke 3:23 ... about thirty **y-s** old when
Heb 10:1 ... again and again, **y** after **y**,
Heb 10:3 ... of their sins **y** after **y**.
2 Pet 3:8 ... like a thousand **y-s** to the
Rev 20:2 ... in chains for a thousand **y-s**.

YEAST (n) *a fungus used for making alcohol and bread*
Exod 12:8 ... and bread made without **y**.
Exod 12:15 ... bread made with **y** during
Matt 16:6 ... Beware of the **y** of the
1 Cor 5:6 ... a little **y** that spreads

YOKE (n) *a wooden crossbar linking two load-pulling animals together; figurative of bondage or linkage between people*
Hos 11:4 ... lifted the **y** from his neck,
Matt 11:29 ... Take my **y** upon you.

YOUNG, YOUNGER (adj) *being in the first or an early stage of life, growth, or development*
2 Chr 10:14 ... counsel of his **y-er** advisers.
Ps 119:9 ... How can a **y** person stay pure?
Prov 20:29 ... The glory of the **y** is their
Joel 2:28 ... your **y** men will see visions.
Acts 2:17 ... Your **y** men will see visions,
Acts 7:58 ... feet of a **y** man named Saul.
1 Tim 5:1 ... Talk to **y-er** men as you
Titus 2:4 ... must train the **y-er** women to
Titus 2:6 ... encourage the **y** men to live
1 Pet 5:5 ... same way, you who are **y-er**
1 Jn 2:13 ... you who are **y** in the faith

Z

ZEAL (n) *eagerness and ardent interest in pursuit of something*
Num 25:13 ... in his **z** for me, his God,
Rom 10:2 ... but it is misdirected **z**.
Gal 1:14 ... **z** for the traditions of my ancestors

ZEALOT (n) *a Jewish revolutionary who sought liberation from Roman rule near and during the time of Christ*
Matt 10:4 ... Simon (the **z**), Judas Iscariot,
Mark 3:18 ... Thaddaeus, Simon (the **z**),
Acts 1:13 ... Simon (the **z**), and Judas

IMAGE CREDITS

Cover illustrations and photographs are the property of their respective copyright holders, and all rights are reserved. Abstract watercolor © Basia Stryjecka/Creative Market; grunge texture © PeterPencil/Getty Images. Unless otherwise noted, all interior photographs are courtesy of Unsplash.com and all maps and illustrations are copyright © Tyndale House Ministries. Presentation page dried flowers © Rachel Bellinsky/Stocksy.com.

FRONT MATTER
Open Bible © Timothy Eberly; coffee on Bible © Sixteen Miles Out

OLD TESTAMENT OPENER
Blossoms © J Lee

GENESIS
Peony © Alison Winterroth/Stocksy; Red leaves © Emre; Waves © Samara Doole; Sunrise © Jessica Ruscello; pink sky © Jakub Kriz; birds flying © Vincent Van Zalinge; oxen © DDP; clouds © Chuttersnap; Plants © Cloé Tourdot Fuentes; Ark Diagrams © Answers in Genesis, AnswersinGenesis.org; CreationMuseum.org; and ArkEncounter.com; Mountains © Gantas Vaičiulėnas; Rose © Alex Blăjan; Daisy © Farrinni; Window shadow © Henrique Hanemann; Plants © Kira Porotikova; Woman in hat © Roman Shilin; Light © Tobias; Flowers © Annie Spratt; Bokeh © Amjd Rdwan; Watercolor flower © Yaoqi; Agenda © Covene; Texture © Tim Mossholder; Eggs © Dessy Dimcheva; Moon © Martin Berrios; Blossom © J Lee; Sunset © Vivaan Trivedii; Oranges lifestyle © Vojtech Bartonicek

EXODUS
Palms © Charlotte Harrison; Brown wheat © Sam Kramer; Burning bush © Vlad Bagacian; Cloud © Daniel Gregoire; Sunset © Youhana Nassif; Mountains © Seif Amir; Flowers © Whoisbenjamin; Model of Tabernacle © ruk7, used under Creative Commons Attribution license; Hands © Liz Brenden; Tree and sky © Tina Xinia; Jar © Mhmd Sedky

LEVITICUS
Plant burning © Alfred Kenneally; Fire © Torbjorn Sandbakk; Wheat © Alekon pictures; Sheep © Adrian Infernus; Smoke © Viktor Talashuk; Lamb © Daniel Sandvik; Flowers © Ellie Ellien; Clouds © Asa Akmelia; Water © Samara Doole; Mold © Sandy Millar; Feeding sheep © Alexandra Fuller; Bread © NordWood Themes; Honey © Ian Dziuk; Window curtain © Mathias Reding; Sunlight © Oleg Solovjn; Sparkler © Oskars Sylwan

NUMBERS
Wilderness © Eddie & Carolina Stigson; Desert sand © Sam Mgrdichian; Raindrop on plant © Kira Porotikova; Tree © Gina X; Open book © Pierre Bamin; Basket of flowers © Sixteen Miles Out; Sheets © Mathilde Langevin; Flowers © Yan Liu; Landscape © Wesley Armstrong

DEUTERONOMY
Valley © Vlad Kiselov; Rainbow © Greg Nunes/Look Up Look Down Photography; Clouds © Jason Wong; Flowers © Illiya Vjestica; Cathedral © David Levêque; Bread © Vicky Ng

JOSHUA
Rocks © Nicole Herrero; Window © Jeff Ma; Mountain peaks © Brice Lan; Flowers © Ryunosuke Kikuno; Plant in sand © Jeremy Bishop; Wall © Gabriella Clare Marino; Greenhouse © Annie Spratt; Cave © Eric Muhr; Forest path © Patrik László; Treetops © Gryffyn M

JUDGES
Dark Clouds © Daoudi Aissa; Cocunut tree © Antony; Palm tree © Kellen Riggin; Sunlight through trees © Wonderlane; Linen © Maite Oñate; Window © Cecile Hournau; Water © Samara Doole; Daisies © George McVeigh; Sunset © Byron Breytenbach; Dandelions © Edgar Perez

RUTH
Wheat © Sixteen Miles Out; Coffee cup © Gaelle Marcel; Brown bottle © Abi Baurer; Wheat field © Lucas Santos

1 SAMUEL
Oil lamp © Gadiel Lazcano; Stones © Whoisbenjamin; Peony © Annie Spratt; Ark of the Covenant © George Dukinas/Dollar Photo Club; Woman outdoors © Levi Stute; Sunlight © Thamara Prada; Hand © Oliver Pacas; Curtain © Jonas Vandermeiren; Pottery cup © Jocelyn Morales; White clouds © Matt Palmer

2 SAMUEL
Crown © Thais Varela Spain/Stocksy.com; Bouquet © Annie Spratt; Woman by the sea © Philipp Cordts; Mountain range © Aryan Nikhil; Oil lamp © Sonika Agarwal; Puddle raindrops © Tomasz Sroka; Rocky path © John Salzarulo; Rose © Thoa Ngo; Woman behind curtain © Claudia Soraya; Morning sunshine © Xin Hui

1 KINGS
Hallway © Ryan Miglinczy; Oil lamp © Gadiel Lazcano; Rose © Jakob Owens; Flowers © Jeff W

2 KINGS
Smoke cloud © Christian Buehner; Smoke © Tim Mossholder; Pottery © Oshin Khandelwal; Plant © Albert Vincent Wu; Flower © Bianca Ackermann; Candle © Paolo Nicolello; Open book © Ben White; Dried flowers © Abi Baurer; Sunrise © Clay Banks

1 CHRONICLES
Mountain range © Benaja Germann; Window in mirror © Jackson David; Woman © Elia Pellegrini; Hand © Jesus Eca; Woman in sunlight © Julia Caesar; Wheat basket © Andrea Scully

2 CHRONICLES
Jerusalem wall © Levi Meir Clancy; Coins © Annie Spratt; Apple crate © Zoe; Basket of squash © Markus Spiske; Bokeh light © Luke Besley; Grass texture © Yaoqi; Floral cloth © Kirill Pershin; Purple flowers © Annie Spratt

EZRA
Torah scroll © tygrys74/Adobe Stock; People © Nsey Benajah; Clouds © Etienne Assenheimer; Seeds © Joshua Lanzarini; Sunset © Sasha Rubaniuk; Harvest © Katie Azi; Candles © Pascal Muller

NEHEMIAH
Wall © Valery Shanin/Adobe Stock; Book by candlelight © Huzeyfe Turan; Hand on window © Milada Vigerova; Crashing waves © Eberhard Grossgasteiger

ESTHER
Columns © Nathaniel Shuman; Flowers © Annie Spratt; Shadow © Tomasz Rynkiewicz

JOB
Clouds © Patrick Hendry; Dried plant © Markus Spiske; Torch © Paul Harrison/Wikimedia Commons; Fireball © Caseen Kyle Registos; King of Assyria © Carole Raddato/Wikimedia Commons; Tornado © Nikolas Noonan; Boils © Timothy Dykes; Rain on window © Atul Vinayak; Flower closeup © Kirill Pershin; Stairs © Jon Tyson; Grapes © Alexandra Kikot; Sunshine © Magnus Jonasson; Feather on rocks © Mikhail Tyrsyna

PSALMS
Tree roots © Anton Malanin; Plant © Munro Studio; Rolled paper © Ananya Mittal; Light through leaves © Avinash Kumar; Pathway © Eberhard Grossgasteiger; Books by window © Ioann-Mark Kuznietsov; Sheep © Kiwihug; Branch © Jeremy Perkins; Mt. Hermon/Wikimedia Commons, Public Domain; Steaming coffee © Erik Witsoe; Dark cloud © Simon Maisch; Broken glass © Egor Vikhrev; Firework © Anton Darius; Frost © Kelly Sikkema; Hand © Tatum Bergen; Desert plant © Amy Humphries; Open hands © McKenna Phillips; House © Tanya Pro; Guitar © Charlie Robert; Open Bible © Duncan Kidd; Woman holding head © ariyan Dv; Sky © José Ignacio Pompé; Mountain Landscape © Igor Lypnytskyi; Mountain plant © Jo Jo; Rock © Hans Isaacson; Flowers © Noelle; Window © Jace Afsoon

PROVERBS
Crystals © Kier in Sight Archives; Peach rose © Georgia de Lotz; Wildflowers © Christina Deravedisian; Metal plates © Ulises Ruiz; Train interior © Markus Spiske; Lemon © Jana Ladia; Olive blossoms © Jasmin Ne; Architecture © Mick Haupt; Church © Ehud Neuhaus; Tree shadow © Suhyeon Choi; Garden post © Annie Spratt; Tulips © Anthony Delanoix; Light stream © Jon Tyson

ECCLESIASTES
Smoke © Wolfgang Hasselmann; Roses © Anne Sack; Movement © Milo Weiler; Woman's shadow © Foad Roshan; Dancing © Emma

SONG OF SONGS
Calla lily © Tatjana Zlatkovic/Stocksy.com; Gowns © Filipp Romanovski; White textile © Mathias Reding; Pomegranate © Ben Mirzaei; Woman © Rae Angela; Flower © Kyaw Tun; Rose closeup © Jason Leung

ISAIAH
Rushing water © Meritt Thomas; Flowers on Bible © Anuja Mary Tilj; White plants © Evie S.; Wildflowers © Jatniel Tunon; House © Caseen Kyle Registos; Light © Jessica Delp; Bride © Peter Bucks; House plant © Robert Katzki; Mountain © Ramy Kabalan; Baby © Nathan Dumlao; Stars © Bryan Goff; Olive branch © Emre; Crown © Jared Subia; Pink flowers © Ameen Fahmy; Hands in sunlight © Elia Pellegrini; Waterfall © Mariola Grobelska

JEREMIAH
Forest fire © Cristofer Maximilian; Ladder © Nick Page; Wilted roses © Annie Spratt; Stained glass © David Clarke; Fire © Alfred Kenneally; Vases © Tamara Schipchinskaya; Streetlamp © Mikael Kristenson; Window

1777

© The Blowup; Woman © Andreas Dress; Open Bible © Jessica Mangano; Starry sky © Kristaps Ungurs

LAMENTATIONS
Wood table © Jordan Graff; Pew © Josh Applegate

EZEKIEL
Skull © Chelms Varthoumlien; Diorama © Stefan Cosma; Bedding © Hans Isaacson; Bread dough © Nathan Dumlao; Hair © Christian Buehner; Water © Nova; Signpost © Sara Kurfeß; Sackcloth © Urja Bhatt; Sticks © Lennart Hellwig; Plant © Finn Hechenberger; Mountain © Marek Piwnicki; Clouds © Artin Bakhan; Lily © Evie S.; Rain on window © Priscilla Du Preez; Ancient tree © Antoine Perier; Woman © Natalia Sobolivska; Glacial cave © Damien Schnorhk; Cave sunlight © Bruno van der Kraan

DANIEL
Cave © Ivana Cajina; Leafy greens © Monika Grabkowska; Garden shadow © Cecile Hournau; Desert landscape © Silvan Schuppisser; Waterfall © Wandering Echo; Smoke © Corina Rainer; Skull © Jon Butterworth; Cave © Bangkit Prayogi

HOSEA
Poppy © Annie Spratt; Clover © Серëй Гусев

JOEL
Fire clouds © Amir Esrafili; Window light © Matt Hanns Schroeter; Sunshine © Joaquin

AMOS
Red grapes © Eiliv Sonas Aceron; Flowers © Mak

OBADIAH
Mounain landscape © Aleks Dahlberg

JONAH
Crashing waves © Lucas Revilla Vacas; Underwater © Christina Spiliotopoulou; Branches © Thomas Marquize; Water surface © Matheus Farias

MICAH
Fig tree © Benigno Hoyuela; Olive branch © Emre

NAHUM
Dust tornado © Mariola Grobelska; Wildflowers © Melina Kiefer; Rocks © Hans Isaacson

HABAKKUK
Deer © John Royle

ZEPHANIAH
Dandelion © Saad Chaudhry; Dahlias © Irina Iriser

HAGGAI
Rock flowers © Eberhard Grossgasteiger; Mud wall © Johny Goerend; Yellow flowers © Javi Hoffens

ZECHARIAH
Horses © Isaac Ibbott; Mountain sunrise © Martin Jernberg; Lilacs in basket © Emma Dau; Flowering bush © Annie Spratt

MALACHI
Incense burning © Anup Ghag; Wedding rings © Zoriana Stakhniv; Green leaves © Micah Hallahan; Brown leaves © Kushagra Kevat; Forest © Simon Joseph; Archer © GVZ 42

BETWEEN THE TESTAMENTS
Yellow flower © Nanda Green

NEW TESTAMENT OPENER
Plant © Sergi Dolcet Escrig

MATTHEW
Desert sky © Shot by Cerqueira; Flowers © Annie Spratt; Rocks on cloth © Olesia Bahrii; Sunset © Gemma Evans; Thorns © Nikhil; Burlap © Johnstons of Elgin; Mountain © Sascha Bosshard; Lambs © Tim Marshall; Red leaves © Shyam; lost sheep © Bonnie Kittle; lost coin © Thomas Fatin; foundation © Hans Isaacson; lamp © Jeremy Bishop; blueberries © Valentin Balan; Grey textile © Hari AV; Sprout © Jeremy Bishop; Palms © Joshua Fuller; Textile © Maite Onate; Sheep © Julian Hochgesang; Moon © Jessica Wong; Woman © Pham Trọng Họ; beans © Mockupo; Raised hands © Jon Tyson; wedding table © Kasia Sikorska; grass © Arindam Mondal; landscape © Mark Harpur; pigs © Kenneth Schipper Vera; hands in soil © Greenforce Staffing; flower © Esteban Abalsa; wheat © Jussi Hellsten; pearl © Marin Tulard; net © Andres Canchon; flat bread © Jeff Siepman; seeds floating © Hasan Almasi; jail cell © Tuyen Vo; landscape © Collins Lesulie; Woman holding vase © Ella Arie; Vineyard © Martin Katler; fig tree © Kendal; Plant © Slava Pluzhnov/Shutterstock; Pottery © Tom Crew; Sunlight © Michael Jin; Flour © Duncan Kidd; Plants in window © Fabian Bachli

MARK
Blurry light © Isaac Quesada; Fabric © Urja Bhatt; White gauze © Kerri Shaver; First Century Jewish home © 5W Infographics, LLC; Green grime © Thom Milkovic; Mother carrying child © Matt Hoffman; Colorful light © Dyana Wing So; Perfume pitcher © Anne Nygård; Branches © Jorge Roman; Baskets © Mary Zighmi; Textiles © Debby Hudson; Rock wall © Annie Spratt

LUKE
Communion © Morgan Winston; Lifestyle © Gaelle Marcel; Pink flowers © Tamara Schipchinskaya; Window table © Oana Hodirnau; Forest fog © Thom Milkovic; Unfocused light © Anthony Delanoix; Green leaves © Marita Mones; Windowsill © Martin Templeman; Brown leaves © Amy Luo; Bouquet © Annie Spratt; Red rose © Michael Yuan; Woman in sunshine © Hatham; Cross © Alicia Quan; Woman silhouette © Freestocks; Fan © Dmitry Mashkin; Pitcher © Yana Hurskaya; Flower closeup © Roonz; Sheet © Kateryna Hliznitsova; Head scarf © Levi Meir Clancy; Red fruit © Carlos Lozano; Sheep © Danny Lines; Tree leaf © John Silliman

JOHN
Sheep in field © Kiwihug; Ceramic vases © Oshin Khandelwal; Clouds © Jayden Yoon ZK; Rocks © Rawad Semaan; Herod's Temple © 5W Infographics LLC; Birdhouse © Sixteen Miles Out; Burning Leaf © Ahmed Zayan

ACTS
Flame © Paul Bulai; Window © Jon Tyson; Flowers © Shlomi Platzman; Woman with rose © Annie Spratt; Dried leaves © Alexis Chloe; Cactus © Annie Spratt; Purple cloth © Sharon McCutcheon; Purple flowers © Christina Deravedisian; Ancient ruin © Alex Azabache; Drapery © Miguel Carraça; Pink glass © Kate Hliznitsova; People © Annie Williams; Grass © Gaelle Marcel; Church © Samuele Giglio; Teacups © Henny Kasa; Woman in water © Esther Ann

ROMANS
Colosseum © Jorgen Hendriksen; Straw © Kjartan Einarsson; Holding leaf © Anshu A; Escargot © Tolga Ahmetler; Flowers © Annie Spratt; Tulips © Priscilla Du Preez; Plant on windowsill © Eduard Militaru; Open Bible © Sixteen Miles Out; Hammer and nails © Fausto Marqués; Parchment © Anastasiya Leskova; Vaulted hallway © Hartmut Tobies; Clay pots © Pravin Suthar

1 CORINTHIANS
Plant at sunset © Shyam; Pink flowers © Munro Studio; Candles © Sixteen Miles Out; Fanned book © Olga Tutunaru; Cloud © Kristaps Ungurs; Blurry movement © Milo Weiler; Hands raised © Jon Tyson; Vase © Toby; Butterfly © Martin Vysoudil; Flame © Arman Khadangan; Balloons © Roland Deason; Bread © Ellie Ellien; City lights © Thong Vo; Rain on glass © Chris Barbalis; Sun through tree © Gina X

2 CORINTHIANS
Frayed fabric © Maresa Smith/Stocksy.com; Clay vases © Oshin Khandelwal; Birds flying © Jonas Vandermeiren; Monarch butterfly © Peter Lloyd; Fire © Benjamin DeYoung

GALATIANS
Fruit © Don Ricardo; Sunshine © Benn McGuinness; Plant shadow © Masha Kotliarenko

EPHESIANS
Building sunshine © Justin Bautista; Stool © Feliphe Schiarolli; Cloud reflection © Tobias Rademacher; Light stream © Gryffyn M

PHILIPPIANS
Cracked glass © Thomas Dumortier; Cherry blossoms © Melanie Karrer

COLOSSIANS
Ropes © Marc Mintel; Waterfall © Matej Pribanic; Flowers © Fachy Marin

1 THESSALONIANS
Trumpet © Kirill Bordon photography/Stocksy .com; Bush © Tyler Casey; Chocolate © Juliette G

2 THESSALONIANS
Clouds © Nabi Tang/Stocksy.com; Bokeh light © Bruno Nascimento; Mountain peak © Jo Jo; Sunrays © Chuttersnap; White grass © Sam Moghadam Khamseh; Textile roll © Taylor Wilcox

1 TIMOTHY
Palms © Jasmin Ne; Candles © Sixteen Miles Out

2 TIMOTHY
Rough road © Martino Pietropoli; White flower © Katarzyna Grabowska; Colorful bowls © Yan Lee; Sunlight © Ilja Tulit

TITUS
Seaside vase © Egor Myznik; Roses © Embla Munk Rynkebjerg; Wildflower © Basil Smith; Domed Building © Jose Llamas

PHILEMON
Chain © Aida L; Sunlight © Thomas Kinto

HEBREWS
Linen © Luca Laurence; Church window © Allan Rolim; Forks © Wolfgang Rottmann; Grass closeup © Annie Spratt; Forest sunshine © Lena Albers; Flower petals © Jason Leung

JAMES
Sprouts © Nik Shuliahin; Drapery © Jonas Vandermeiren; Piano © Paul Arky

1 PETER
Ocean wave © Karl Fredrickson; Yellow leaf © Nathan McGregor; Blurry light © Luiz Felipe; Shutters © Kadir Celep; Thorns © Julian Paolo Dayag; Light stream © Patrick Hendry; Rocky shore © Adam Kring; Frost on grass © Kajetan Sumila

2 PETER
Sailboat © Joel Bengs; Woman silhouette © Hassan Ouajbir; Pomegranate © Praveen Kumar Mathivanan; Frosted flower © Mario Verduzco; Snake © Adrien Stachowiak; Foggy field © Marina Reich; Field grass © Annie Spratt

1 JOHN
Brown plant © Aedrian; Headlight © Gontran Isnard; Open book © Sixteen Miles Out; Bedding © Kawe Rodrigues; Grass © Gebhartyler; Wheat field © Nadiia Ploshchenko

2 JOHN
Apple tree © Rhamely; Rose bush © Tommy Nguyen

3 JOHN
Sea sunset © Kunj Parekh; Gray sand © Harpal Singh

JUDE
Coral reef © Chris Reyem

REVELATION
Eclipse © Micah Williams; Open hand © Dyu Ha; treetops © Rishabh Dharmani; pears © Karolina Grabowska; sheep © Kiwihug; golden hour © Abe Mello; hydrangea © Annie Spratt; waves closeup © Dustin Humes; flowers © Kelly Sikkema; sunrays © Rajiv Bajaj

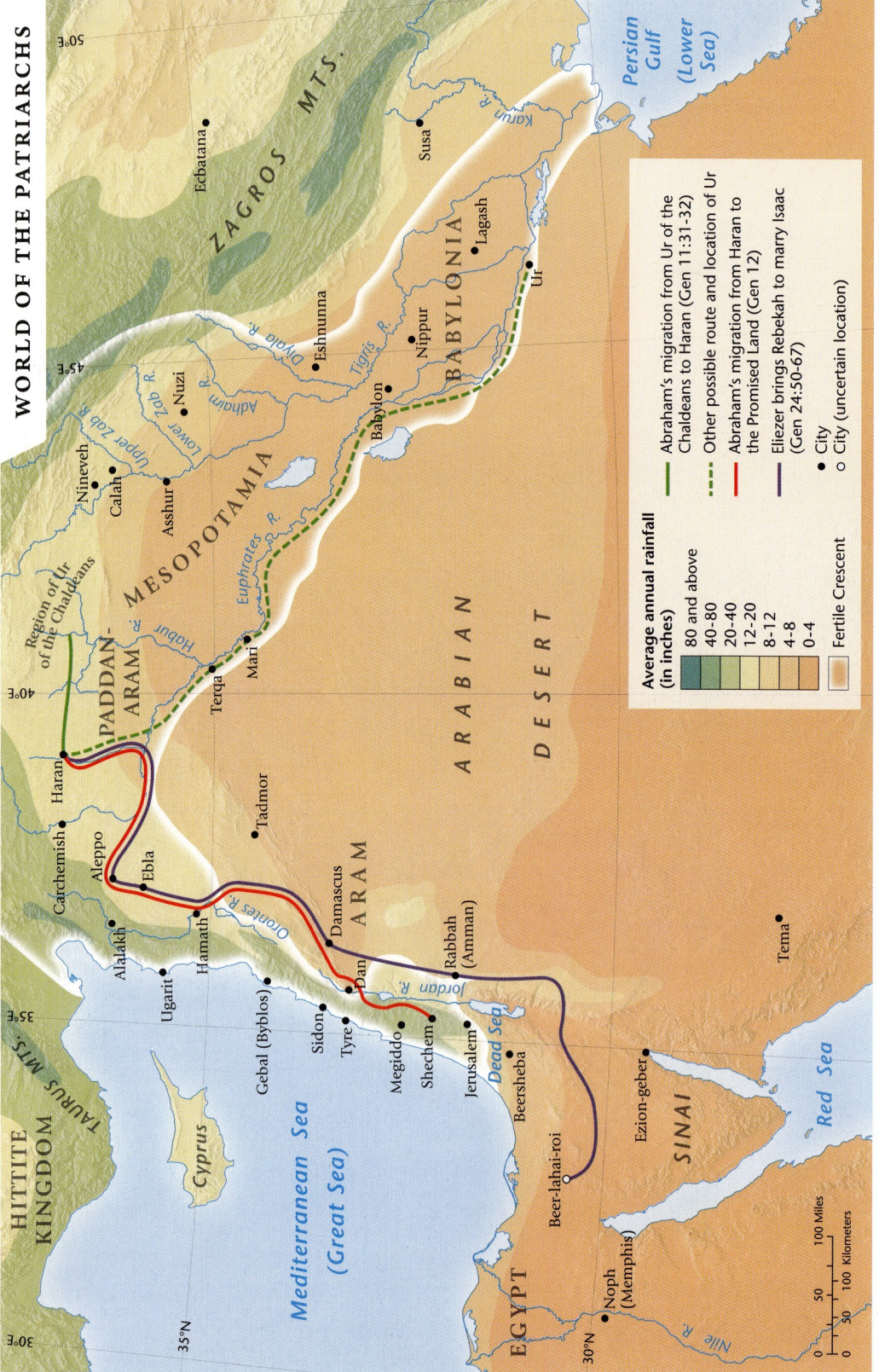

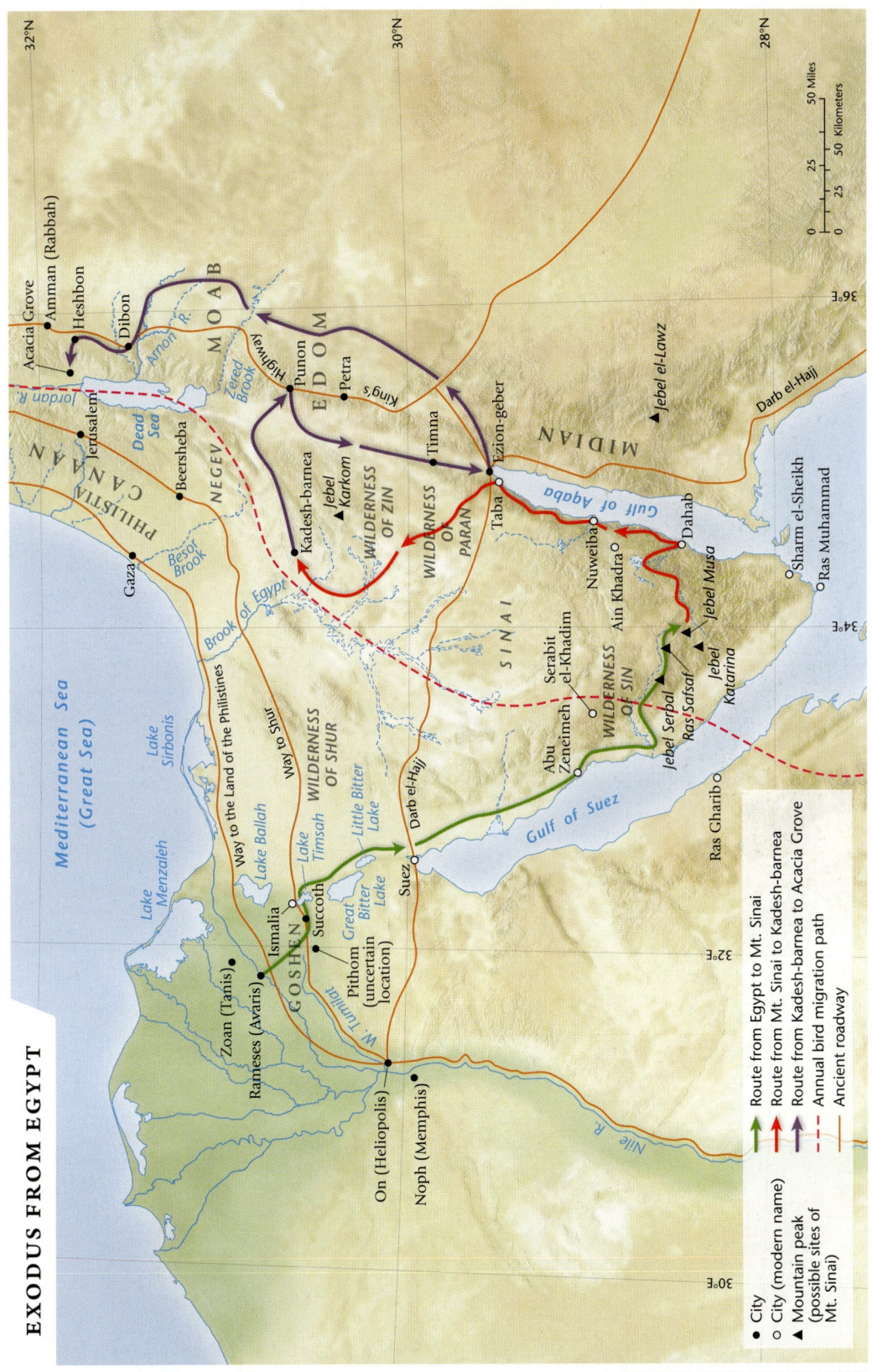

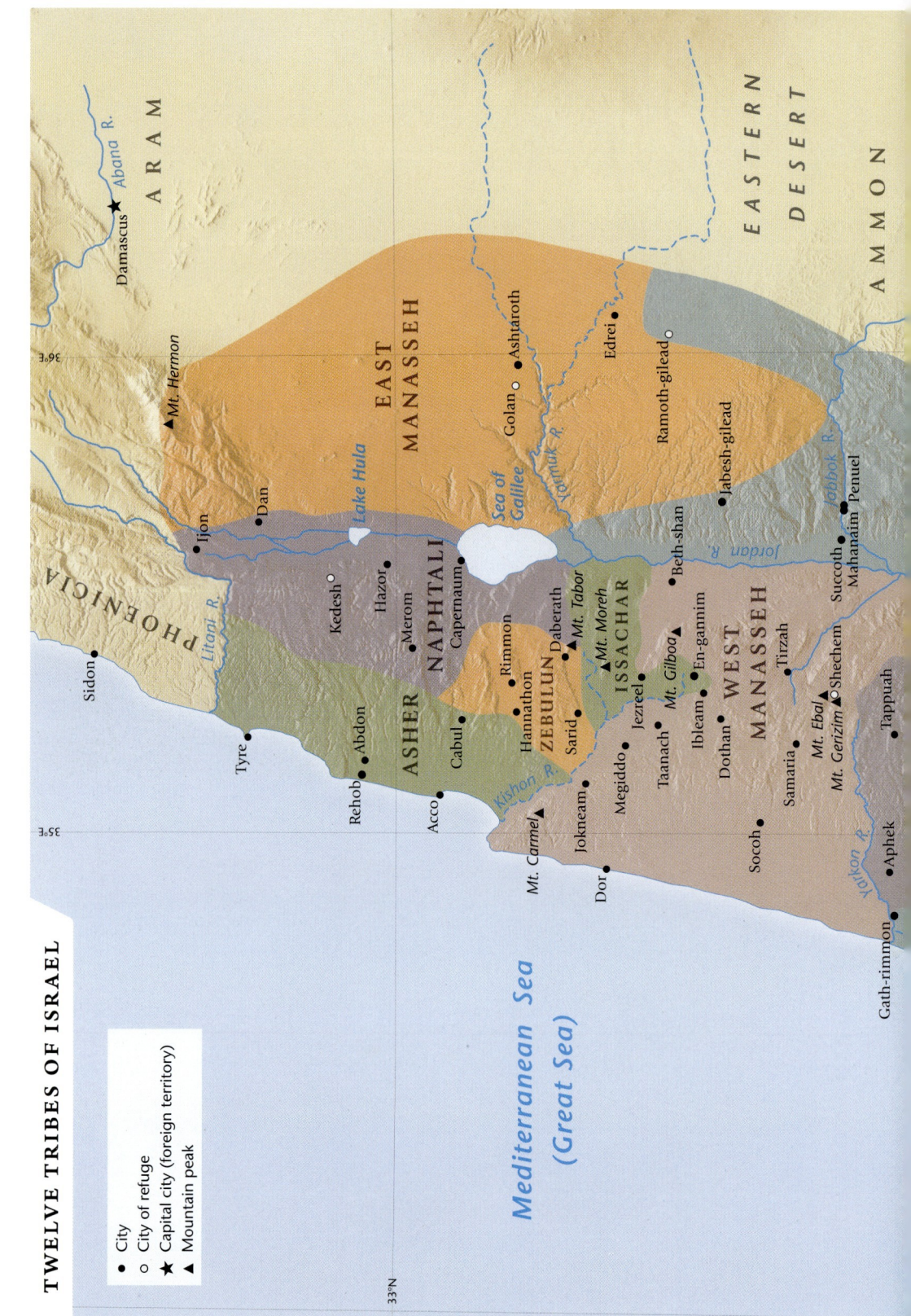

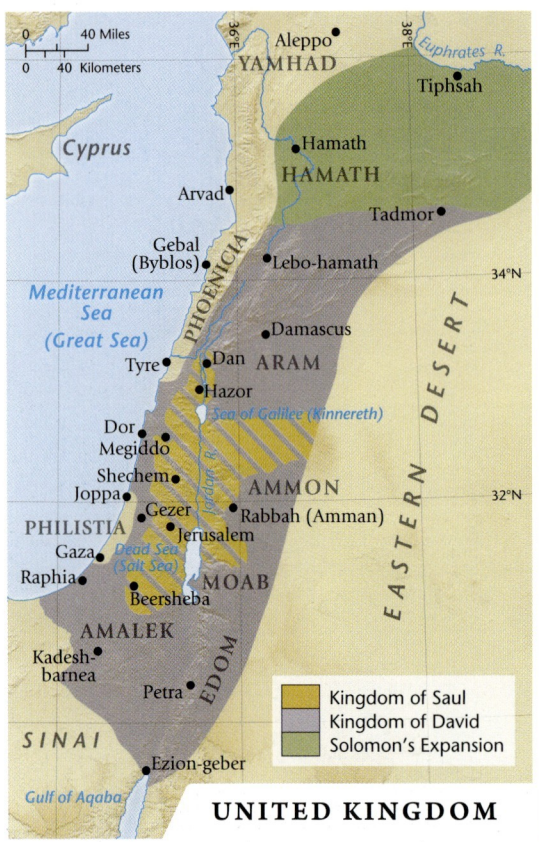

KINGDOMS OF ISRAEL

The United Kingdom of Israel came into being at the coronation of Saul, grew in size and influence under David, and reached its height during Solomon's reign. Solomon inherited a powerful kingdom from his father, David, covering the entire area inhabited by the 12 tribes of Israel. Throughout Solomon's reign, his power and influence increased as he also gained control over many of the surrounding nations.

After the death of Solomon, the kingdom of Israel divided. Solomon's son Rehoboam remained king of the southern kingdom of Judah, with Jerusalem as its capital. Jeroboam became the king of the northern kingdom of Israel and rebuilt Shechem as his capital. He also built new worship centers in Bethel and Dan, influencing his people to stay away from Jerusalem and its annual religious festivals. The division of the kingdom of Israel began a downward spiral into idolatry and godless leadership for both nations, eventually leading to the exile of the northern kingdom to Assyria and the southern kingdom to Babylon.

COPYRIGHT © 2018 TYNDALE HOUSE PUBLISHERS

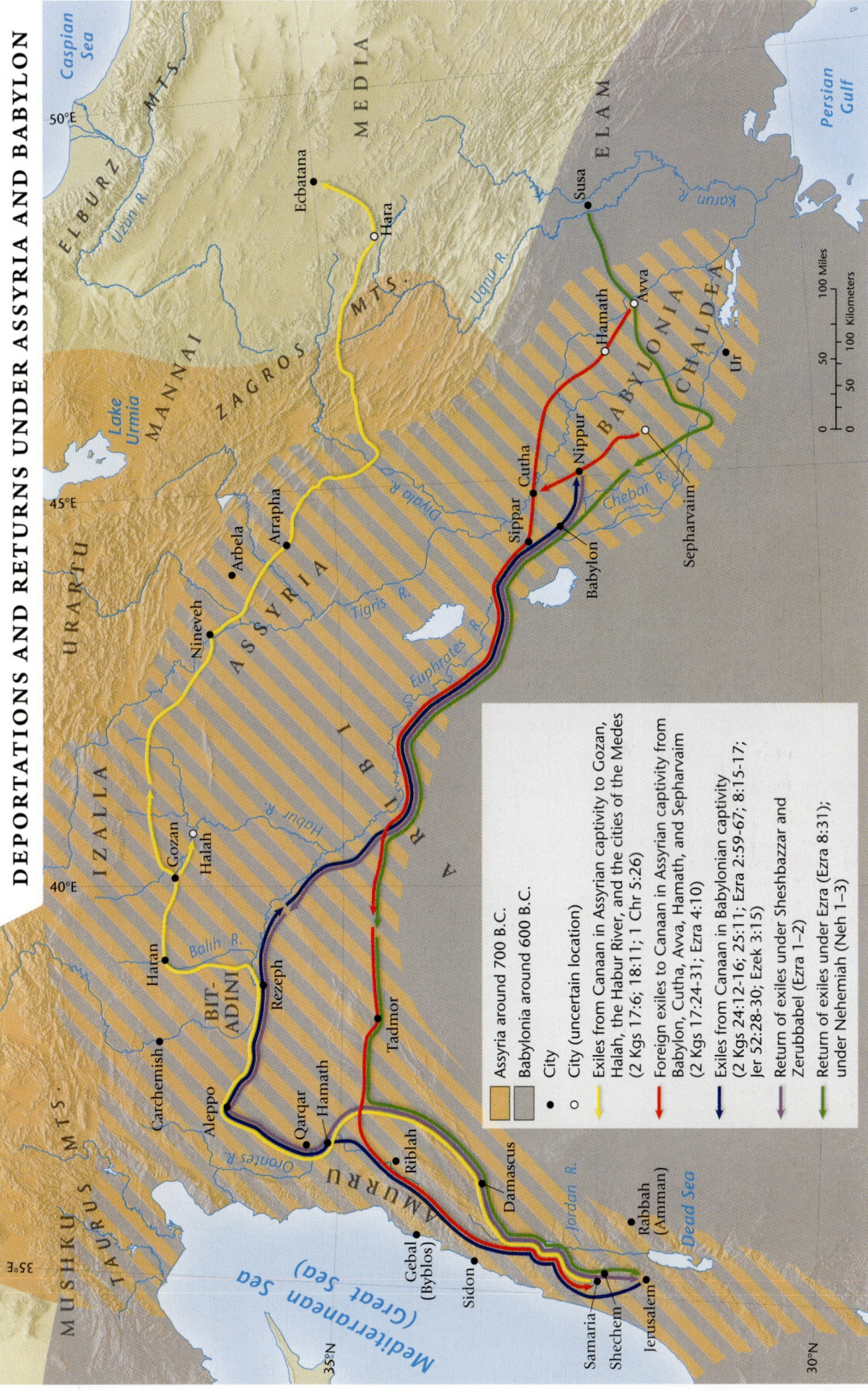

ASSYRIAN AND BABYLONIAN EMPIRES

- Assyria around 700 B.C.
- Babylonia around 600 B.C.

GREEK EMPIRE

- Extent of Alexandrian empire
- Ptolemaic realm
- Seleucid realm
- Antigonid realm
- Minor Hellenistic provinces

COPYRIGHT © 2018 TYNDALE HOUSE PUBLISHERS

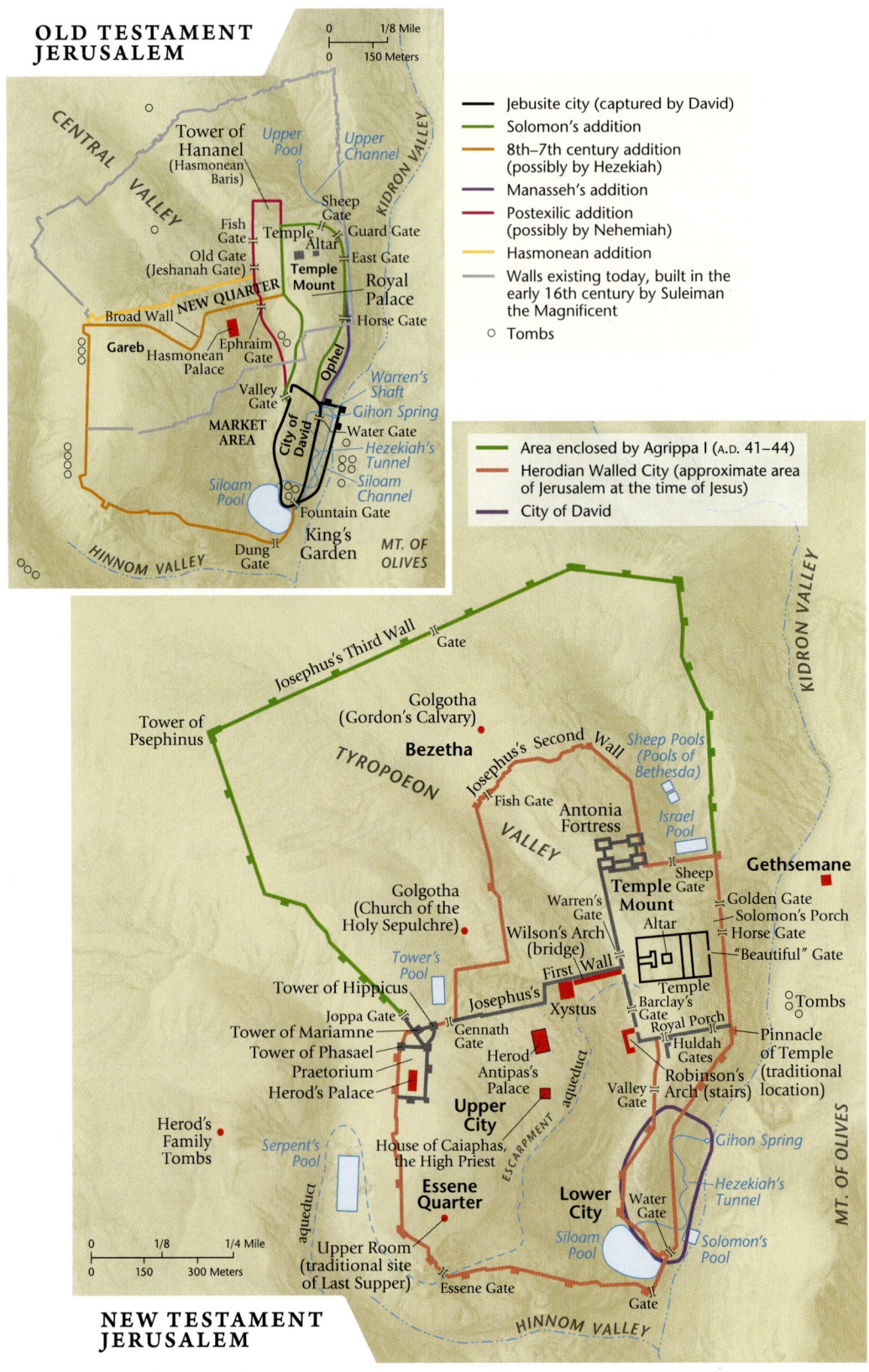

MINISTRY OF JESUS

Chronologically speaking, it is not possible to sequentially arrange the events in the life of Christ in any definitive way; none of the New Testament Gospels follows an overtly chronological pattern. Accordingly, the arrangement here follows a geographic order, basically proceeding from north to south on the map. Because the Gospel of Matthew most frequently contains information cited here, and because it is the most geographically particularistic Gospel, synoptic passages are keyed to the book of Matthew, except where they are unattested there or where more pertinent information about the event cited is available in another Gospel.

- **A** *Region of Phoenicia:* Gentile woman's daughter healed (Mt 15:21-28)
- **B** *Caesarea Philippi:* Peter's great declaration (Mt 16:13-20)
- **C** *Mt. Meron/Mt. Tabor/Mt. Hermon:* (1) possible location of Transfiguration (Mt 17:1-13); (2) demon-possessed boy healed nearby (Mt 17:14-21)
- **D** *Cana of Galilee:* (1) water changed to wine (Jn 2:1-11); (2) Capernaum official's son healed (Jn 4:46-54)
- **E** *Gennesaret:* (1) possible location of feeding of multitudes (Mt 14:13-21; 15:32-39); (2) many healings (Mk 6:53-56)
- **F** *Area of Korazin:* (1) judgment pronounced on the cities of Korazin, Bethsaida, and Capernaum (Mt 11:20-24); (2) possible area of Sermon on the Mount (Mt 5–7)
- **G** *Capernaum:* (1) catch of fish (Lk 5:1-11); (2) evil spirit cast out (Mk 1:21-28); (3) Sermon on the Mount (Mt 5–7); (4) Peter's mother-in-law healed (Mt 8:14-15); (5) Roman officer's servant healed (Mt 8:5-13); (6) paralyzed man healed (Mk 2:1-12); (7) woman with a hemorrhage healed (Mk 5:25-34); (8) Jairus's daughter raised (Lk 8:40-56); (9) two blind men healed (Mt 9:27-31); (10) a mute, demon-possessed man healed (Mt 9:32-34); (11) the twelve apostles sent out (Mt 10:1-15); (12) man with deformed hand healed (Mt 12:9-13); (13) another demon-possessed man healed (Mt 12:22-37); (14) Temple tax provided (Mt 17:24-27); (15) Bread of Life discourse (Jn 6:22-59)
- **H** *Bethsaida:* (1) possible location of feeding of multitudes (Mt 14:13-21; 15:32-39); (2) blind man healed (Mk 8:22-26)
- **I** *Sea of Galilee near Bethsaida:* walking on water (Mt 14:22-33)
- **J** *Sea of Galilee:* storm quieted (Mt 8:23-27)
- **K** *Gergesa/Gadara:* possible location of casting out demons, which enter pigs; the pigs then rush down a steep bank and drown (Lk 8:26-39)
- **L** *Nazareth:* (1) childhood home (Mt 2:19-23); (2) rejected by townspeople (Lk 4:16-30)
- **M** *Nain:* widow's son raised (Lk 7:11-17)
- **N** *Region of Galilee:* (1) leper cleansed (Mk 1:40-45); (2) post-resurrection appearances to the disciples (Mt 28:16-20)
- **O** *Decapolis (Region of Ten Towns):* many healings (Mt 15:29-31; Mk 7:31-37)
- **P** *Region between Galilee and Samaria:* (1) refused entry into village (Lk 9:51-56); (2) ten lepers healed (Lk 17:11-19)
- **Q** *Sychar:* woman at the well of Samaria (Jn 4:1-42)
- **R** *Ephraim:* enters into seclusion with the disciples (Jn 11:54)
- **S** *Region of Perea:* (1) teaching on marriage (Mt 19:1-12); (2) possible location of healing of woman with infirmity (Lk 13:10-13); (3) possible location of healing of man with swollen limbs (Lk 14:1-6); (4) possible location of the rich young ruler (Lk 18:18-30)
- **T** *Jericho:* (1) Bartimaeus healed (Mk 10:46-52); (2) Zacchaeus converted (Lk 19:1-10)

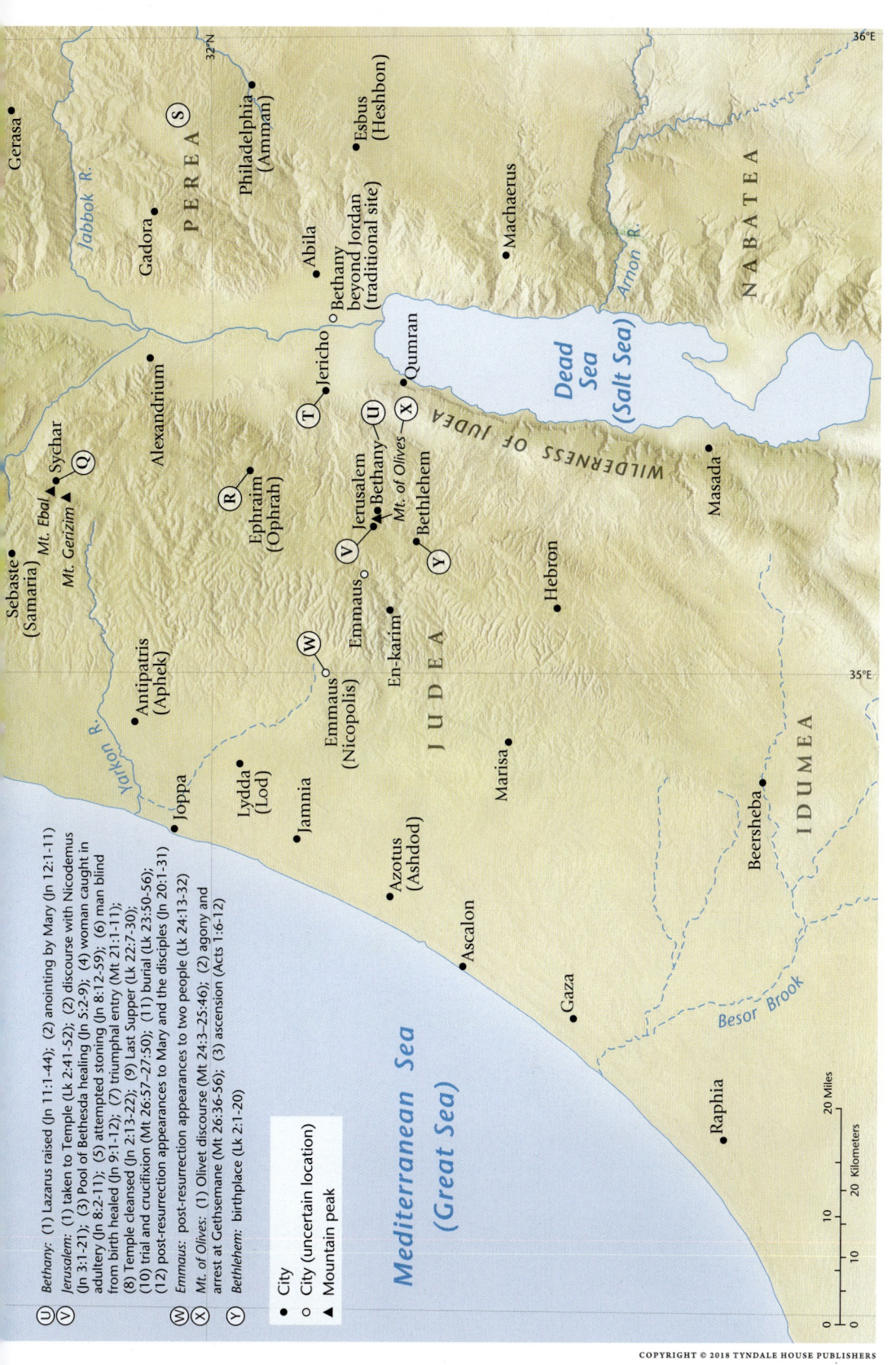